THE AUTHORITY SINCE 1868

# THE WORLD ALMANAC®

## AND BOOK OF FACTS

## 1997

WORLD ALMANAC BOOKS
AN IMPRINT OF K-III REFERENCE CORPORATION
A K-III Communications Company

# THE WORLD ALMANAC®
## AND BOOK OF FACTS
# 1997

**Editor:** Robert Famighetti
**Deputy Editor:** William A. McGeveran, Jr.
**Associate Editors:** Matthew Friedlander, Mark S. O'Malley, Lori P. Wiesenfeld
**Desktop Publishing Associate:** Melissa Janssens
**Chronology Editor:** Donald Young
**Index:** AEIOU Inc.
**Cover:** Bill Smith Studio

**K-III REFERENCE CORPORATION**
**Vice President & Editorial Director:** Leon L. Bram
**Vice President–Manufacturing:** Sally McCravey
**Director of Editorial Production:** Andrea J. Pitluk
**Manager of Promotion Production:** Edward A. Thomas
**Desktop Publishing Assistant:** Hana Shaki

**WORLD ALMANAC BOOKS**
**Vice President & Publisher:** Richard W. Eiger
**Vice President–Sales:** James R. Keenley
**Director of Marketing:** Joyce H. Stein
**Manager of Licensing:** Robert Rothman

The editors acknowledge with thanks the many letters of helpful comment and criticism from readers of THE WORLD ALMANAC. Because of the volume of mail directed to the editorial offices, it is not possible to reply to each letter writer. However, every communication is read by the editors and all comments and suggestions receive careful attention. THE WORLD ALMANAC's e-mail address is Walmanac@aol.com.

THE WORLD ALMANAC does not decide wagers.

The first edition of THE WORLD ALMANAC, a 120-page volume with 12 pages of advertising, was published by the New York World in 1868. Annual publication was suspended in 1876. Joseph Pulitzer, publisher of the New York World, revived THE WORLD ALMANAC in 1886 with the goal of making it a "compendium of universal knowledge." It has been published annually since then.

**THE WORLD ALMANAC and BOOK OF FACTS 1997**

Library of Congress Catalog Card Number 4-3781
International Standard Serial Number (ISSN) 0084-1382
ISBN (softcover) 0-88687-800-4
ISBN (hardcover) 0-88687-801-2
Microform Edition: University Microfilms Intl.
Printed in the United States of America
The softcover and hardcover editions are distributed to the book trade by St. Martin's Press; the paperback edition is distributed to the magazine trade by ICD/The Hearst Corporation.

**WORLD ALMANAC BOOKS**
An Imprint of K-III Reference Corporation
One International Boulevard, Suite 444
Mahwah, New Jersey 07495-0017

# CONTENTS


GENERAL INDEX .......... 4

THE TOP 10 NEWS STORIES .......... 33

FEATURE ARTICLES .......... 33

ELECTION '96 .......... 33
*BY DONALD YOUNG*

THE NEXT FOUR YEARS .......... 35
*BY GEOFFREY M. HORN*

THE FASCINATION OF DINOSAURS .......... 36
*BY STEPHEN JAY GOULD*

MAJOR ACTIONS OF THE 104TH CONGRESS .......... 38

NOTABLE SUPREME COURT DECISIONS, 1995-96 .......... 39

THE 1996 NOBEL PRIZES .......... 39

CHRONOLOGY OF THE YEAR'S EVENTS .......... 40

NOTABLE QUOTES IN 1996 .......... 70

OFFBEAT NEWS STORIES OF 1996 .......... 71

MISCELLANEOUS FACTS .......... 71

HISTORICAL ANNIVERSARIES .......... 72

OBITUARIES .......... 74

PRESIDENTIAL ELECTIONS. .......... 76

CONGRESS .......... 111

STATE AND LOCAL GOVERNMENT .......... 121

ECONOMICS .......... 129

AGRICULTURE .......... 156

EMPLOYMENT .......... 165

NATIONAL DEFENSE .......... 176

UNITED STATES GOVERNMENT .......... 185

1996 IN PICTURES .......... 193

CABINETS OF THE U.S. .......... 201

COMPUTERS .......... 207

SCIENCE AND TECHNOLOGY .......... 215

METEOROLOGY .......... 220

ENVIRONMENT .......... 228

ENERGY .......... 235

TRADE AND TRANSPORTATION .......... 240

EDUCATION .......... 251

ARTS AND MEDIA .......... 283

DISASTERS .......... 298

AEROSPACE .......... 309

AWARDS—MEDALS—PRIZES .......... 317

NOTED PERSONALITIES .......... 334

UNITED STATES POPULATION .......... 377

ASTRONOMY AND CALENDAR .......... 440

FLAGS AND MAPS .......... 481

UNITED STATES HISTORY .......... 497

BIOGRAPHIES OF U.S. PRESIDENTS .......... 530

UNITED STATES FACTS .......... 540

WORLD HISTORY .......... 551

HISTORICAL FIGURES .......... 577

WORLD EXPLORATION AND GEOGRAPHY .......... 586

WEIGHTS AND MEASURES. .......... 600

HEALTH .......... 608

ASSOCIATIONS AND SOCIETIES .......... 620

POSTAL INFORMATION .......... 632

LANGUAGE .......... 637

RELIGIOUS INFORMATION .......... 644

STATES AND OTHER AREAS OF THE U.S. .......... 655

CITIES OF THE U.S. .......... 686

BUILDINGS, BRIDGES, TUNNELS, & DAMS .......... 696

SOCIAL SECURITY .......... 708

CONSUMER INFORMATION .......... 713

TAXES .......... 730

NATIONS OF THE WORLD .......... 737

1996 IN PICTURES *(CONTINUED)* .......... 777

SPORTS .......... 849

CRIME .......... 957

VITAL STATISTICS .......... 962

QUICK REFERENCE INDEX .......... 976

# GENERAL INDEX

**Note:** Page numbers in *italics* indicate photos.


— A —

**Abbreviations** . . . 639
- Canada . . . postal, 634
- International organizations. . . . 842-43
- States, postal . . . 634
- UN agencies. . . . 845

**Abortion**
- Legalized (1973) . . . 506, 524
- "Partial-birth" procedure veto (1996) 38, 53
- Patients, by characteristics . . . 964

**Academy Awards** (Oscars) . . 330-32, *780*

**Accidents and disasters** . . . 298-308
- Assassinations . . . 307-8, 539
- Aviation . . . 299-300, 314, 968
  - Brown plane crash (1996) . . . 53, 65, 74, *197*, 300
  - Dubroff plane crash (1996). . . . 55
  - TWA Flight 800 crash (1996) . . 33, 61, 63-64, 66, *198*, 300
  - ValuJet crash (1996) . . . 55-56, 59, *198*, 300
- Blizzards . . . 46, *196*, 302
- Deaths (number, causes) . . 964, 967, 968
- Earthquakes (1989, 1994, 1995). . . 303-4, 508, 510
- Explosions . . . 305-6
  - Oklahoma City bombing (1995, 1996). . . . 49, 510
- Fires . . . 304-5
- Floods (1993) . . . 303, 509
- Home . . . 968
- Hurricanes . . . 302
- Kidnappings . . . 308
- Mining . . . 301
- Motor vehicle . . . 168, 964, 967
- Nuclear (1979) . . . 306, 507, 574
- Occupational. . . . 68
- Oil spills (1989) . . . 306, 508
- Railroad . . . 300-301
- Ship (1915, 1989) . . . 298-99, 502, 508
- Space exploration (1986) . . . 309, 310, 311, 508
- Storms. . . . 302
- Tidal waves . . . 303
- Tornadoes . . . 302
- Typhoons . . . 302
- Volcanic eruptions (1980) . . 507, 588-89
- *see also* Terrorism

**Acquired Immune Deficiency Syndrome**
- Cases worldwide (1996) . . . 62, 840
- Deaths, new cases. . . . 964, 975
- Epidemic magnitude (1986) . . . 508
- Help organizations . . . 617
- Research (1996) . . . 57

**Actors, actresses**
- Birthplaces, birth dates . . . 360-72
- Movies (1995-96). . . . 283, *780*
- Movie, theater, TV awards. . . 329-32, 333
- New York theater (1995-96). . . . 285, *781*
- Notable past . . . 372-75
- Original names . . . 375-76

**Adams, John** . . . 109, 110, 530, 539
- *see also* Presidents, U.S.

**Adams, John Quincy** . . . 109, 531
- *see also* Presidents, U.S.

**Address, forms of** . . . 641

**Addresses**
- Abbreviations, postal . . . 634
- Armed forces, U.S. . . . 182
- Associations and societies . . . 620-31
- Businesses, major U.S. . . . 714-19
- Colleges and universities . . . 258-82
- Internet sites . . . 210-11
  - Cities, U.S. . . . 686-95
  - Government, U.S. . . . 210, 378
  - Internal Revenue Service . . . 730
  - Presidential libraries . . . 539
  - Sports organizations . . . 903-4
  - States, U.S. . . . 655-81
  - Television, cable networks . . . 294
- Labor unions. . . . 174-75
- Religious groups, U.S. . . . 645-46
- Sports, organizations . . . 903-4
- Television, cable networks. . . . 294
- U.S. government departments, agencies . . . 185-88
- U.S. judiciary . . . 189-92
- ZIP codes. . . . 390-420, 439

**Admirals, USN** . . . 176
- Address, forms of . . . 641
- Personal salutes, honors. . . . 177

**Adventist churches** . . . 644, 646

**Advertising**. . . . 297

**Aerospace.** *See* Aviation; Space developments

**Afghanistan** . . . 575, 737, 846
- Flag, map. . . . 481, 492
- Refugees from . . . 840
- Taliban faction takeover (1996) . . . 67

**AFL.** *See* American Football League

**AFL-CIO.** *See* American Federation of Labor and Congress of Industrial Organizations

**Africa** . . . 838-39
- AIDS cases. . . . 840
- Commercial fishing . . . 164
- Gold production . . . 153
- Highest, lowest points . . . 597
- History . . . 554, 558, 560, 567, 572, 575, 576
- Lakes . . . 598
- Languages . . . 642-43
- Map . . . 494-95
- Mountain peaks . . . 590
- Religious adherents . . . 646
- Volcanoes. . . . 589
- Waterfalls . . . 599
- *see also specific countries*

**African Americans.** *See* Blacks

**Agriculture** . . . 156-64
- Acreage, number of farms . . . 156, 157
- Employment . . . 166, 167, 156
  - Minimum hourly rates. . . . 170
  - Social Security benefits . . . 710
- Exports, imports. . . . 159, 163, 241
- Foreign production . . . 163, 737-837
- Income. . . . 159
- Land grants (1862) . . . 500
- Legislation (1916, 1929) . . . 502, 503
- Occupational injuries. . . . 168
- Population. . . . 156, 377
- Prices received . . . 162
- Production . . . 157, 160-61, 163
- Real estate debt. . . . 160
- Subsidies (1996) . . . 38, 51, 158
- U.S. programs . . . 158
- *see also* Food; Grains

**Agriculture, Department of** . . . 186
- Employees, payroll . . . 169
- Expenditures . . . 129
- Internet address. . . . 210
- Secretaries . . . 185, 186, 204

**AIDS.** *See* Acquired Immune Deficiency Syndrome

**Air**
- Composition, temperature . . . 458
- Density. . . . 458, 605
- Pollution . . . 228
- Quality, by metropolitan area . . . 229

**Air conditioning**. . . . 237

**Aircraft.** *See* Aviation

**Air Force, Department of the**
- Employees, payroll . . . 169
- Secretary . . . 186

**Air Force, U.S.**
- Academy . . . 178, 268
- Address for information . . . 182
- Flights, notable . . . 316
- Generals, active duty . . . 176
- Insignia. . . . 178
- Military units . . . 177
- Personnel, active duty. . . . 179
- Training centers. . . . 177
- Women, active duty . . . 180

**Airlines, leading U.S.** . . . 314
- *see also* Aviation

**Air mail** . . . 315, 634, 635-36

**Airplane pilots**. . . . 315

**Airports, busiest** . . . 313

**Airships** . . . 299, 316

**Akron, OH.** *See* Cities U.S.

**Alabama** . . . 655
- Admission, area, capital. . . 542, 543, 655
- Agriculture . . . 156-61
- Altitudes (high, low) . . . 541
- Birth, death statistics. . . . 963
- Budget . . . 135
- Coastline . . . 541
- Congressional representation . . . 111, 112, 380
- Courts, U.S. . . . 190
- Crime, prisons, death penalty . . . 959, 960, 961
- Energy consumption . . . 237
- Federally owned land . . . 545
- Governor, state officials. . . . 124, 125
- Hazardous waste sites . . . 228
- Health insurance coverage. . . . 971
- Immigrants admitted (1995) . . . 383
- Indians, American. . . . 550
- Interest laws, rates . . . 721, 722
- Marriage, divorce laws . . . 728, 729
- Motor vehicles . . . 245, 248
- Name origin, nickname . . . 544, 655
- Population. . . . 380-81, 384
  - Cities, towns. . . . 390, 687, 691
  - Counties, county seats . . . 421
- Port traffic. . . . 242
- Poverty rates . . . 388
- Presidential elections. . . . 76, 77, 106
- Schools and libraries . . . 252-53, 257
- Taxes . . . 245, 735
- Temperature, precipitation . . . 222, 224
- Toxic chemical pollution . . . 228
- Unemployment benefits . . . 165
- Welfare assistance . . . 389

**Alaska** . . . 655-56
- Accession . . . 545
- Admission, area, capital . . . 542, 543, 655
- Agriculture. . . . 156-60
- Altitudes (high, low). . . . 541
- Birth, death statistics . . . 963
- Budget . . . 135
- Coastline. . . . 541
- Commercial fishing . . . 164
- Congressional representation . . 111, 112, 380
- Courts, U.S.. . . . 190
- Crime, prisons, death penalty . . . 959, 960
- Energy consumption . . . 237
- Federally owned land. . . . 545
- Governor, state officials . . . 124, 125
- Hazardous waste sites. . . . 228
- Health insurance coverage . . . 971
- Immigrants admitted (1995) . . . 383
- Indians, American. . . . 550
- Interest laws, rates . . . 721, 722
- Marriage, divorce laws. . . . 728, 729
- Motor vehicles . . . 245, 248
- Name origin, nickname . . . 544, 655
- Population . . . 380-81, 384
  - Census divisions . . . 421
  - Cities, towns . . . 390, 686
- Port traffic . . . 242
- Poverty rates . . . 388
- Presidential elections. . . . 76, 77-78, 106
- Schools and libraries . . . 252-53, 257
- Taxes . . . 245, 735
- Temperature, precipitation . . . 222, 224
- Time zones . . . 479
- Unemployment benefits . . . 165
- Welfare assistance . . . 389

**Albania** . . . 481, 571, 737-38, 846

**Albany, NY**. . . . 121, 696

**Albuquerque, NM** . . . 686

**Alcohol boiling point** . . . 605

**Alcoholic beverages.** *See* Liquor

**Alcohol, Tobacco, and Firearms, Bureau of** . . . 186, 188
- Waco (TX) standoff (1993, 1994) . . . 509

**Aleutian Islands** . . . 592

**Aleuts, U.S.** . . . 377, 378, 379, 550

**Alexander the Great** . . . 554

**Algeria** . . . 481, 738, 846
- Chronology (1995) . . . 40, 43

**Aliens**
- Admissions, exclusions, U.S. . . . 840-41
- Illegal, amnesty (1988). . . . 508
- Legislation (1952, 1990). . . . 504, 840-41
- Naturalization. . . . 841
- Visas . . . 840-41

**Allen, Ethan** (1775) . . . 343, 498

**Allentown, PA** . . . 121, 414

**Allergies** . . . 616, 617

**Alps** . . . 590-91

**Altitudes**
- Cities (U.S., world) . . . 593-95
- Highest, lowest
  - U.S.. . . . 541
  - World. . . . 597
- Mountains . . . 590-91

**Aluminum** . . . 151, 153

**Alzheimer's disease** . . . 615, 617

**Amazon River** . . . 596

**Ambassadors and envoys**. . . . 846-48
- Address, form of. . . . 641
- Salute to (artillery). . . . 177

**"America"** ("My Country 'Tis of Thee") . 528

**American College Testing (ACT) Program**. . . . 255

**American Federation of Labor and Congress of Industrial Organizations**
- Address, affiliates . . . 174-75
- AFL formed (1886) . . . 501
- CIO formed (1935) . . . 503
- Merger (1955) . . . 505
- Sweeney election (1995) . . . 40

**American Football League**
- Conference leaders (1960-69). . . . 873
- Division champions . . . 872
- Professional records . . . 878-79
- *see also* Football, pro

**American Kennel Club registrations**. . 234

**American Manual Alphabet** . . . 643

**American Revolution** (1775-83) . . . 564
- Articles of Confederation (1777) . 498, 514

Battlefields, monuments 547-48
Battles 498
Black troops 180
Casualties, numbers serving 184
Costs 181
Declaration of Independence (1776) 498, 512-13
Liberty Bell 528-29
Military leaders 343-44
**Americans, notable** 334-76
Actors, actresses 329-32, 333, 360-76
Architects 335-36
Artists 336-39
Athletes 925-27
Blacks 328-29, 339-40
Business leaders 340-41
Cartoonists 322-23, 328, 341
Composers 326-27, 355-57
Contemporary personalities 334-35
Country music artists 359
Dancers, choreographers 357-58
Economists 319, 342-43
Educators 350
Historians 324-25, 342-43
Humanitarians 350
Industrialists 340-41
Jazz, blues artists 358-59
Journalists 320-23
Lyricists 357
Military leaders 343-44
Obituaries (1995-96) 74-75
Opera singers 358
Philanthropists 340-41
Philosophers 344-45
Photographers 323, 336-39
Playwrights 324, 330, 350-51, 351-55
Poets 326
Political leaders 345-48
Religious figures 344-45
Rock & roll musicians 333, 359-60
Scientists 317-18, 348-49
Social reformers 350
Social scientists 342-43
Statesmen, stateswomen 319, 345-48
Writers 318, 324-26, 327-28, 350-51, 351-55
**American Samoa.** *See* Samoa, American
**American's Creed** 525
**American Stock Exchange**
Address 630
Volume, transactions 149
**America's Cup** (yachting) 936
**"America, the Beautiful"** 528
**Ames, Aldrich** (1994) 509
**Amnesty**
Confederate citizens (1872) 501
Illegal aliens (1988) 508
Vietnam draft evaders (1977) 507
**Anaheim, CA.** *See* Cities, U.S.
**Anchorage, AL.** *See* Cities, U.S.
**Ancient civilizations** 551-56
Historical figures 577
Measures 605
Seven Wonders 555
**Andaman Sea** 593
**Andorra** 134, 481, 738, 846
**Anesthesia** (1842) 500
**Anglicanism** 646, 829
**Angola** 575, 739
Ambassadors, envoys 846
Flag 481
Refugees from 840
Trade 240
**Anguilla** 831
**Animals**
American Kennel Club 234
Cat breeds 234
Classification 231
Collectives, names for 639
Dinosaurs 36-37, *199*
Endangered species 230
Farm (*see* Livestock)
Gestation, incubation, longevity 231
Speeds 231
Venomous 232
Westminster Kennel Club 936
Young, names for 638
Zoos, major 233
**Annapolis** (MD) (Naval Academy) 178, 268
**Anniversaries**
Historical events (1897, 1947, 1972) 72-73
Holidays 480
Wedding 727
**Antarctica** 838
Australian Territory 741
British Territory 831
Explorations 587-88
French 765
Highest, lowest points 597
Mountain peaks 591
Volcanoes 589
**Antigua and Barbuda** 243, 481, 592, 739, 846
**Antoinette Perry Awards** (Tonys) 330
**Apartheid** 576, 818
**APEC.** *See* Asia-Pacific Economic Cooperation Group
**Aphelion, perihelion** 443
**Apogee of moon** 457
**Apollo space missions** (1969) 309-10, 506
**Appliances, home** 237
**Appomattox Court House** (1865) 500, 546
**Apportionment, congressional** 380
**Arab-Israeli conflict**
Gunfire clashes (1996) 67
Lebanon (1996) 54, 56-57, 575, 576, 785, 792
October War (1973) 507, 575, 761, 785, 815
Palestine settlement expansion (1996) 65
Palestinian militancy, uprisings 575, 576, 785
Palestinian self-rule (1995-96) 45, 47-48, 55, 786
Six-Day War (1967) 574, 761, 785, 815
Suicide bombings (1996) 50, 52, 306, *778*
**Arab League** 573, 842
**Arafat, Yasir** (1996) 47-48, 67
**Archaeological finds** (1996) *199*
**Archer Daniels Midland Co.** 68
**Archery** 850
**Architects, notable** 329, 335-36
**Archives, National** 685
**Arctic explorations** 586-87
**Arctic Ocean** 593
Coast length, U.S. 541
Islands, areas 592
**Area codes, telephone** 390-420
**Areas** (geographical)
Continents 838
Earth 457
Islands 592
Lakes 598
Largest countries 838
National parks 546-47
National recreation 545, 549
Nations, world 737-837
Oceans, seas, gulfs 593
United States 382, 540
Counties, by state 421-39
States 542, 655-80
Territories 439, 545, 681-83
**Areas** (mathematical)
Formulas 607
Measures (units) 600-603
**Arenas, stadiums**
Baseball 954
Basketball 913
Football 879
**Argentina** 739-40
Ambassadors, envoys 846
Flag 481
Gross domestic product 134
History 573, 575
Motor vehicle production 246
Nuclear power 239, 238
**Arizona** 656
Admission, area, capital 542, 543, 656
Agriculture 156-61
Altitudes (high, low) 541
Birth, death statistics 963
Budget 135
Congressional representation 111, 112-13, 380
Courts, U.S. 190
Crime, prisons, death penalty 959, 960, 961
Energy consumption 237
Federally owned land 545
Governor, state officials 124, 125
Hazardous waste sites 228
Health insurance coverage 971
Immigrants admitted (1995) 383
Indians, American 550
Interest laws, rates 721, 722
Marriage, divorce laws 728, 729
Mineral production 151
Motor vehicles 245, 248
Name origin, nickname 544, 656
Population 380-81, 384
Cities, towns 390-91, 691, 693, 695
Counties, county seats 421
Poverty rates 388
Presidential elections 76, 78, 106
Schools and libraries 252-53, 257
Taxes 245, 735
Temperature, precipitation 222, 224
Unemployment benefits 165
Welfare assistance 389
**Arkansas** 656-57
Admission, area, capital 542, 543, 656
Agriculture 156-61
Altitudes (high, low) 541
Birth, death statistics 963
Budget 135
Congressional representation 111, 113, 380
Courts, U.S. 190
Crime, prisons, death penalty 959, 960, 961
Energy consumption 237
Federally owned land 545
Governor, state officials 124, 125
Hazardous waste sites 228
Health insurance coverage 971
Immigrants admitted (1995) 383
Indians, American 550
Interest laws, rates 722
Marriage, divorce laws 728, 729
Motor vehicles 245, 248
Name origin, nickname 544, 656
Population 380-81, 384
Cities, towns 391
Counties, county seats 421-22
Poverty rates 388
Presidential elections 76, 78, 106
Schools and libraries 252-53, 257
Taxes 245, 735
Temperature, precipitation 222, 224
Tucker indictment, conviction (1995-96) 48, 51, 53, 56, 62, 510
Unemployment benefits 165
Welfare assistance 389
**Arkansas River** 596
**Arlington National Cemetery** (VA) 685
**Arlington, TX** 121, 386, 416, 686
**Armed forces** (general)
Leaders, notable past 343-44
Military strength (by country) 182
Per 1,000 persons (by country) 182
*see also specific countries*
**Armed forces, U.S.** 176-84
Academies, service 178, 268
Address, forms of 641
Addresses for information 182
Battlefields and parks, national 547-48
Black troops 180
Casualties, by wars 184
Chronology (1995-96)
Bosnia peacekeeping mission 42, 45, 49, 510, *779*
Iraqi Kurdish incursion 66-67
Liberian civil strife 54
U.S. installation bombings 43, 60, 306, 510, *779*
Commands 176
Defense contracts 180
Expenditures 129
Generals 176
Homosexual issues (1993) 509
Insignia 178
Joint Chiefs of Staff (1989) 508
Chairmen 186, 176, 183
Leaders, notable past 343-44
Medal of Honor 181
Military strength 181, 182
Pay scales 183
Personnel 176, 179, 180, 181, 182
Salutes 177
Secretaries 186, 202-3
Time, 24-hour 479
Training centers 176-77
Troop strength, by wars 184
Units 177
Veterans 180, 181
Women, active duty 180
First generals (1970) 506
*see also* Weapons; *specific branches, ranks*
**Armenia** 239, 481, 740, 840, 846
**Arms control** 183
Limitations of Armaments Conference (1921) 502
Mid-range missiles ban 183
Nuclear test-ban treaty (1963) 183, 505
Pacifist pacts (1920s) 570
SALT (1972, 1979) 183
START (1991, 1993) 183
**Army, Department of the** 169, 186
**Army, U.S.**
Academy (West Point) 178, 268
Address for information 182
Generals 176
Address, form of 641
Salutes, honors 177
Women, first (1970) 506
Insignia 178
Leaders, notable past 343-44
Personnel, active duty 179
Training centers 176
Units 177
Women, active duty 179, 180
**Arson** 957, 961, 969
Black church burnings (1996) 58, *197*

**Art**
Abstract 570, 571
Artists, notable 336-39
Baroque 562
Beaux Arts 567
Gothic 560, 565
Impressionist 567
Neoclassical 564
Pop 574
Renaissance 561, 562
Rococo 564
Romanesque 560
Romanticism 565
**Artemis, Temple at Ephesus** 555
**Arthur, Chester A.** 109, 110, 533
*see also* Presidents, U.S.
**Articles of Confederation** (1777) 498, 514
**Artillery salutes** 177
**Artists, notable** 336-39
**Aruba** 592, 803
**Ascension Island** 592, 831
**ASEAN.** *See* Association of Southeast Asian Nations
**Ashmore and Cartier Islands** 741
**Ash Wednesday** 647, 648
**Asia** 838-39
AIDS cases 840
Commercial fishing 164
Highest, lowest points 597
Lakes 598
Languages 642-43
Maps 491, 492-93
Mountain peaks 590, 591
Religious adherents 646
Trade 240
Volcanoes 589
Waterfalls 599
*see also specific countries*
**Asians, U.S.** 377, 378, 379, 965, 975
**Asia-Pacific Economic Cooperation Group** 842
**Assassinations** 307-8
Attempts 308
Clinton, Bill (1994) 308
Ford, Gerald R. (1975) 308
John Paul II, Pope (1981, 1982) 308
Mubarak, Hosni (1995) 308
Reagan, Ronald (1981) 308, 507
Truman, Harry S. (1950) 308, 504
Wallace, George C. (1972) 308, 506
International
Gandhi, Indira (1984) 307, 576
Gandhi, Rajiv (1991) 307
Karami, Rashid (1987) 307, 576
Ngo Dinh Diem (1963) 307, 505
Palme, Olaf (1986) 307
Rabin, Yitzhak (1995, 1996) 42-43, 52, 75, 307
Sadat, Anwar al- (1981) 307, 576
Presidents, U.S., 539
Garfield, James A. (1881) 307, 501, 533
Kennedy, John F. (1963) 307, 505, 536
Lincoln, Abraham (1865) 307, 500, 532
McKinley, William (1901) 307, 502, 534
United States
Kennedy, Robert F. (1968) 307, 506
King, Martin Luther (1968) 307, 506
Lennon, John (1980) 507
Long, Huey (1935) 307, 503
**Assemblies of God** 645
**Association of Southeast Asian Nations,** 240, 842
**Associations and societies** 620-31
Health care 617-19
Sports 904
**Asthma** 616, 617
**Astrological signs** 456
**Astronauts**
First on moon (1969) 506
First orbit (1962) 505
First women (1983) 309, 310, 311, 508
Hall of Fame 314-15
Lucid in-space record (1996) 66, *199*, 312
Missions 309-12
Numbers of 313
U.S.-Russian space linkup (1995) 311, 510
**Astronomy** 440-74
Auroras 454
Calendar (1997) 463-74
Celestial highlights (1997) 440-43
Comets *199*, 440, 443
Constants 450
Constellations 451
Earth 455, 457-60
Eclipses (1997) 454
Eclipses, total (1950-2010) 461-62
Moon 462, 440-43, 454, 456-57
Planets 444-49, 455
Configurations 440-43
Rising, setting 452-53
Positions, celestial bodies 443
Star tables 450
Morning, evening 449
Sun 462, 444, 454, 455-56
Time 458, 450
Twilight 460-61
**Athletics.** *See* Sports; *specific sports*
**Atlanta, GA.** *See* Cities, U.S.
**Atlantic cable, first** (1858) 500
**Atlantic Charter** (1941) 503
**Atlantic Ocean** 593
Coasts, U.S.
Highest point 540
Length 541
Ports 242, 243
Commercial fishing 164
Crossings, notable (1819) 316, 499
**Atlantis** (space shuttle) (1995) 311, 312, 510
**Atmosphere** (air pressure) 607
**Atmosphere** (Earth's) 458
**Atolls** 592, 683
**Atomic bomb** (1945) 504, 572
*see also* Nuclear arms
**Atomic clock** 460
**Atomic energy.** *See* Nuclear energy
**Atomic weights** 218-19
**Attila** 557
**Attorneys general, U.S.** 185, 186, 203
**Auction, Kennedy memorabilia** 53, 200
**Aunu'u Island** 681
**Aurora, CO** 121, 386, 686
**Auroras** 454, 555
**Austin, TX.** *See* Cities, U.S.
**Australia** 568, 740-41
Ambassadors, envoys 846
Area 838
Chronology (1996) 55
Flag, map 481, 496
Gold production 153
Great Barrier Reef 555
Gross domestic product 134
Highest, lowest points 597
Lakes 598
Merchant fleet 243
Motor vehicle production 246
Mountain peaks 590
Population 838-39
Territories 741
Unemployment rates 166
Wages, hourly 171
Waterfalls 599
**Australian Antarctic** 741
**Australian Open** (tennis) 930
**Austral Islands** 765
**Austria** 741
Ambassadors, envoys 846
Flag 481
Gross domestic product 134
History 561, 565, 569
Motor vehicle production 246
Rulers 581
Wages, hourly 171
**Authors, notable.** *See* Writers, notable
**Automobiles**
Accidents, deaths 168, 964, 967
Colors, most popular 247
Drivers
Licensed (by age) 247
By state 245
Exports, imports 241, 242
First cross-country trip (1903) 502
Fuel
Consumption 245
Prices, retail 53-54, 238
Tax 245
Inventions 215
Production 244, 246
Registration 245
Safety belt laws, U.S. 245
Sales 245-47
Speed limits (1995) 38, 42, 248
Theft 957, 959, 961
**Auto racing** 930-32
One-mile speed records 931
**Autumn** 459
**Autumnal Equinox** 442, 459
**Aviation**
Accidents 299-300, 314, 968
Brown plane crash (1996) 53, 65, 74, *197*, 300
Dubroff plane crash (1996) 55
TWA Flight 800 crash (1996) 61, 63-64, 66, *198*
ValuJet crash (1996) 55-56, 59, *198*
Air cargo 314
Air Commerce Act (1926) 503
Aircraft operation statistics 314
Airlines, leading U.S. 314
Air mail 315, 634, 635-36
Air mileage, between world cities 250
Airplane exports, imports 241
Airships 299, 316
Fatalities 168, 968
Safety record (1980-95) 314
Federal agency 187, 188
Firsts, notable 315
Jet, U.S. passenger (1958) 505
Transatlantic flight (1919) 316, 502
Transatlantic nonstop flight (1927) 316, 503
Transcontinental flight (1911) 502
Flights, notable 316
Earhart lost (1937) 503
Hall of Fame 314-15
Inventions 215
Wright brothers (1903) 315, 502, 568
Pilots, personnel 315
Traffic 313
Traffic controllers strike (1981) 507
**Avoirdupois measures** 601, 602, 603
**Awards, prizes** 317-33
Baseball 939, 942, 943
Broadcasting (TV, radio) 328, 329-30, 333
Football 872, 876, 879, 886
Hockey, ice 894-96
Journalism 319-23, 328
Literature 39, 318-19, 324-26, 327-28
Medal of Honor 181
Miscellaneous 329
Miss America 329
Movies 330-32, 333, *780*
Music 326-27, 333
Nobel Prizes 39, 317-19
Pulitzer Prizes 319-27
Recording 292-93, 333, *781*
Spingarn Medal 328-29
Theater 330, *781*
Video, music 292, 293
**Azerbaijan** 481, 742, 840, 846
**Azores** 592, 810
**Aztecs** 563, 586, 798

— B—

**Badminton** 850
**Baha'i Faith** 644, 645, 646
**Bahamas** 742
Ambassadors, envoys 846
Area 592
Flag 481
Gross domestic product 134
Merchant fleet 243
**Bahrain** 134, 481, 592, 742-43, 846
**Baker Islands** 683
**Bakersfield, CA** 121, 387, 686
**Balance of trade** 154, 240, 241
**Balearic Islands** 592, 819
**Bali** 592
**Balkan War** (1995, 1996) 510, 779
**Ballet**
Companies, U.S. 287
Notable figures 357-58
**Baltic Sea** 592, 593
**Baltimore, MD.** *See* Cities, U.S.
**Bangladesh** 134, 481, 743, 846
**Bankruptcy** 134
**Banks**
Charter, first (1781) 498
Closed (1933) 503
Deposit insurance 136
Deposits, U.S. 137
Failures 138
Farm credit 160
Financial panics (1873, 1893, 1907) 501, 502
Gold reserves (world) 146
International 845
Largest 137
Modern, beginning of 562
Mortgages 727
Number, U.S. 137
Savings and loan crisis (1989) 39, 136, 508
Supreme Court decisions (1995-96) 39
*see also* Federal Reserve System
**Baptist churches** 652-53
Membership 644
**Barbados** 481, 592, 743, 846
**Barley production** 160, 161, 162
**Baseball** 937-56
Addresses, team 903
All-Star games 950
Batting records 941-942
Cy Young Award 942
First black major league player (1947) 504
Franchise moves, additions 955
Gold Glove Awards (1996) 939
Hall of Fame 944
Home run leaders 937, 939-40, 951
Leaders
All-time 954
League (1996) 951

Little League . . . 955
Most Valuable Players . . . 943
NCAA champions . . . 955
Olympic champions (1996) . . . 850
Pennant, division winners . . . 937-38
American League (1996) . . . 947-49
National League (1996) . . . 944-46
Pitching records . . . 951, 954
Players' strike (1994, 1995) . . . 509, 510
RBI leaders . . . 940-41
Stadiums . . . 954
World Series . . . 41, 69, 849, 952-53
**Basketball**
Hall of Fame . . . 913
NBA . . . 849, 906-13
Addresses, team . . . 903
All-time leaders . . . 912
Arenas . . . 913
Champions (1947-96) . . . 907-8
Championship (1996) . . . 60, *784*, 906
Coaches . . . 908, 913
Most Valuable Players . . . 907
Player draft picks . . . 912
Player statistics, by team (1995-96) . . . 909-11
Rookies of the Year (1954-96) . . . 909
Scoring leaders (1947-96) . . . 907
Season highs, leaders (1995-96) . . . 906, 908-9
NCAA . . . 914-19
All-time scorers . . . 917
All-time winningest teams . . . 915
Coaches, Division I . . . 918
Conference standings (1995-96) 914-15
Tournament champions . . . 55, 849, 915-17
Wade Trophy . . . 919
Women's champions . . . 849, 919
Wooden Award . . . 917
Olympic champions (1996) . . . 850
**Baton Rouge, LA.** *See* Cities, U.S.
**Battlefields, national** . . . 547
**Beans.** *See* Legumes
**Beef**
Livestock population . . . 156
"Mad cow disease" (1996) . . . 52, 54, *778*
Nutritive value . . . 610
Prices, farm . . . 162
Production, consumption . . . 157
**Belarus** . . . 481, 743-44, 846
**Belep Archipelago** . . . 765
**Belgium** . . . 744
Ambassadors, envoys . . . 846
Flag . . . 481
Gold reserves . . . 146
Gross domestic product . . . 134
Motor vehicle production . . . 246
Nuclear power . . . 238, 239
Rulers, royal family . . . 376, 583, 744
Wages, hourly . . . 171
**Belize** . . . 481, 744, 846
**Bell, Alexander Graham** (1915) . . 348, 502
**Belmont Stakes** . . . 898
**Benin** . . . 481, 744-45, 846
**Bering, Vitus** (1740-41) . . . 497, 587
**Bering Sea** . . . 593
**Berlin, Germany**
Blockade, airlift (1948) . . . 504, 572
Wall built, opened (1961, 1989) . . . 574, 576, 767, 768
**Bermuda** . . . 243, 592, 831
**Beverages**
Nutritive value . . . 610, 611
*see also specific kinds*
**Bhutan** . . . 481, 745, 840, 846
**Biathlon** . . . 863-64
**Bible, books of the** . . . 649
**Biblical measures** . . . 605
**Bicycles.** *See* Cycling
**Bill of Rights** (1791) . . . 498, 519
**Biology**
Animal, plant classification . . . 231
Discoveries . . . 217-18
**Birmingham, AL.** *See* Cities, U.S.
**Births**
Certificates, records . . . 727
Infant mortality rates . . . 962, 963, 964
Life expectancy . . . 973
Notable personalities, birth dates . 334-76
Number, rate . . . 962
By country (*see specific countries*)
By states . . . 963
**Birthstones** . . . 727
**Black Death** . . . 561
**Black Friday** (1869) . . . 501
**Blacks**
AIDS incidence . . . 975
Bus boycott (1955) . . . 505
Cigarette use . . . 965
Civil rights amendments . . . 520-21
Civil rights legislation (1875, 1957, 1964) . . . 501, 505, 573
Civil rights workers (1964) . . . 505
Companies owned . . . 143, 377
Education . . . 254, 255
As elected officials . . . 377
Employment, unemployment . . 172, 167, 170
First astronauts . . . 310, 311
First governor since Reconstruction (1989) . . . 508
First in colonies (1619) . . . 497
First Joint Chiefs chairman (1989) . . . 508
First major league baseball player (1947) . . . 504
First senator since Reconstruction (1966) . . . 506
First Supreme Court justice (1967) . . 506
First woman representative (1968) . . 506
Health insurance coverage . . . 971
Households . . . 965
Income distribution . . . 389
Ku Klux Klan (1866, 1921) . . . 501, 503
Life expectancy . . . 973
March on Washington (1963) . . . 505
Million Man March (1995) . . . 40, 510
Notable personalities . . . 339-40
Population . . . 377, 378, 379, 382
Poverty rates . . . 172, 388
Race riots (1943, 1965, 1967, 1992) . . . 504, 506, 509
Salaries and wages . . . 172, 167, 170
Sit-ins (1960) . . . 505
Spingarn Medal . . . 328-29
Suicide rate . . . 965
Voting rights (1957, 1965) . . . 505, 506
War service . . . 180
*see also* Desegregation; Slavery
**Black Sea** . . . 593
**Blindness** . . . 615, 617
Income tax deduction . . . 733
**Blizzards**
Characteristics . . . 220
Notable . . . 302
Eastern U.S. (1996) . . . 46, *196*
Great (1888) . . . 302, 501
**Blood pressure** . . . 616
**Blues artists, notable** . . . 358-59
**Boat racing**
America's Cup . . . 936
Olympic champions (1996) . . . 853
Power boat . . . 936
**Bobsledding** . . . 863
**Body weight tables** . . . 612
**Boer War** (1899-1902) . . . 567, 818
**Boiling points** . . . 605
**Bolivia** . . . 745-46
Ambassadors, envoys . . . 846
Flag . . . 481
History . . . 573, 575
**Bombings.** *See* Terrorism
**Bonaire** . . . 803
**Bonaparte, Napoleon** (1798, 1803) . . . 499, 564, 565
**Bonds**
Defined . . . 154, 155
Portraits on U.S. . . . 139
Yields . . . 148
**Books**
Awards . . . 318-19, 324-26, 327-28
Best-selling (1995) . . . 289
Copyright law, U.S. . . . 724-25
Notable (1996) . . . 288-89
Postal rates . . . 633
*see also* Writers, notable
**Boorda, Jeremy** (1996) . . . 56, 74
**Booth, John Wilkes** (1865) . 307, 500, 532
**Borneo** . . . 592
**Bosnia and Herzegovina** . . . 746
Ambassadors, envoys . . . 846
Chronology (1995-96)
National elections . . . 33, 67
Peace agreement . . . 42, 45, 510
Peacekeeping efforts . . . 42, 45, 47, 49, 52, 510, *779*
War crimes tribunal . . . 40, 43, 49, 52, 57, 60, 62
Flag, map . . . 481, 490
Refugees from . . . 840
**Boston, MA** . . . 687
Education, compulsory (1636) . . . 497
Historical sites . . . 546, 547
Marathon . . . 956
*News Letter* (1704) . . . 497
Tea Party (1773) . . . 498
*see also* Cities, U.S.
**Botany,** Plant classification . . . 231
**Botswana** . . . 481, 746, 846
**Boundary lines, U.S.** . . . 543
**Bourbon, House of** . . . 580
**Bowl games** (football)
College . . . 48, 849, 881-83
Super Bowl . . . 48, *784*, 849, 872, 879
**Bowling** . . . 900-901
**Boxer Rebellion** (1900) . . . 501
**Boxing** . . . 933-35
Champions (by class) . . . 933
Heavyweight title bouts . . . 935
Olympic champions . . . 850, 862
**Boy Scouts**
Address . . . 621
Founded (1910) . . . 502
**Brady Bill** (1993) . . . 509
**Branch Davidians** (1993, 1994) . . . 509
**Brazil** . . . 746-47
Ambassadors, envoys . . . 846
Cities (largest) . . . 838
Flag . . . 481
Gross domestic product . . . 134
History . . . 563, 565
Merchant fleet . . . 243
Military strength . . . 182
Motor vehicle production . . . 246
Nuclear power . . . 239, 238
Rio de Janiero harbor . . . 555
**Bread,** Nutritive value . . . 610
**Breeders' Cup** . . . 899
**Brethren churches** . . . 644, 645
**Bridge** (card game) . . . 607
**Bridges** . . . 540, 702-5
**Britain.** *See* United Kingdom
**British Antarctic Territory** . . . 831
**British Honduras.** *See* Belize
**British Indian Ocean Territory** . . . 831
**British Isles.** *See* United Kingdom
**British West Indies** . . . 831
**Broadcasting.** *See* Radio; Television
**Broadway.** *See* Theater
**Bronx, NY** . . . 233, 431
**Brooklyn, NY** (Kings County) . . . 384, 431
**Brooklyn Bridge** (1883) . . . 501, 702
**Brown, Ron** (1996) . . . 53, 65, 74, *197*, 300
**Brunei** . . . 134, 481, 747, 846
**Bubonic plague** . . . 561
**Buchanan, James** . . . 107, 109, 532, 539
*see also* Presidents, U.S.
**Buddhism** . . . 654
Address, U.S. headquarters . . . 645
Adherents, world, U.S. . . . 644, 646
History . . . 554, 562, 575
**Budget**
Economic terms defined . . . 154-55
Federal . . . 129-30
Balanced-budget legislation (1995) . 510
Chronology (1995-96) . . . 40, 41
Congressional stalemate . . . 38, 41-42, 44, 46, 53, *196*, 510
Deficit . . . 130, 131
Deficit reduction legislation (1993) . 509
First trillion-dollar (1987) . . . 508
Line-item veto (1996) . . . 38, 51
Proposed 1997 fiscal year . . . 51, 55
States . . . 135-36
**Buffalo, NY.** *See* Cities, U.S.
**Buildings, tall** . . . 540, 696-702
**Bulgaria** . . . 576, 747-48
Ambassadors, envoys . . . 846
Flag . . . 481
Merchant fleet . . . 243
Nuclear power . . . 238, 239
**Bull Run, Battle of** (1861) . . . 500
**Bunker Hill, Battle of** (1775) . . . 498
**Burglaries** . . . 957, 959, 958, 961
**Burkina Faso** . . . 481, 748, 846
**Burma.** *See* Myanmar
**Burns, George** (1996) . . . 74, *781*
**Burr, Aaron** (1804) . . . 109, 110, 499
**Burundi** . . . 481, 748-49, 840, 846
**Bush, George** . . . 105, 107, 109, 110, 537
**Business**
Advertising expenditures . . . 297
Air travel . . . 314
Black-owned . . . 143, 377
Charitable contributions . . . 713
Consumer products, parent company . 720
Corporate tax rates . . . 144
Defense contracts . . . 180
Directory . . . 714-19
Empowerment zones . . . 731
Franchises, fastest growing (1995) . . . 143
International transactions, U.S. . . . 146
Internet addresses . . . 211
Leaders, notable past . . . 340-41
Leading companies (1995) . . . 141-42
Leave law impact . . . 172
Mergers/acquisitions . . . 142
Occupational injuries . . . 168
Ownership profile, U.S. . . . 377
Patents granted . . . 218
Profits (by industry) . . . 143
Rotary club, first (1905) . . . 502

Sherman Antitrust Act (1890) . . . . . . . 501
Tax deductions . . . . . . . . . . . . 730, 731
Tobacco industry lawsuits (1996) . . 51, 56, 64
U.S. investments abroad . . . . . . . . . . 145
Workers employed . . . . . . . . . . . . . . 377
*see also* Banks; Economics; Industries, U.S.; Stocks
**Butter,** Nutritive value . . . . . . . . . 609, 610
**Byzantine Empire** . . . . . . . . . . . . . . 558

—C—

**Cabinet, U.S.** . . . . . . . . . . . . . . . . 201-5
Address, form of . . . . . . . . . . . . . . 641
Clinton administration . . . . . . . . . . 201-5
Personal salutes, honors . . . . . . . . . . 177
Salute (artillery) . . . . . . . . . . . . . . . 177
**Cable** (measure) . . . . . . . . . . . . . . . 601
**Cable television**
Advertising expenditures . . . . . . . . . . 297
Networks
Addresses, phone numbers . . . . . . 294
Internet addresses . . . . . . . . . . . . 294
Top 20 (1996) . . . . . . . . . . . . . . 294
Penetration . . . . . . . . . . . . . . . 293, 295
Program rating initiatives (1996) . . . . . 49
Reform legislation (1996) . . . . . . . 38, 48
Subscribers, U.S. . . . . . . . . . . . 294, 295
Systems, U.S. . . . . . . . . . . . . . . . . . 294
Viewing shares . . . . . . . . . . . . . . . . 295
**Cabot, John** (1497) . . . . . . . . . . 497, 586
**Cabrera Island** . . . . . . . . . . . . . . . . 819
**Caicos Island** . . . . . . . . . . . . . . . . . 831
**Calcium** (dietary) . . . . . . . 609, 610-11, 612
**Calendar**
Celestial (1997) . . . . . . . . . . . . . . 440-43
Daily astronomical (1997) . . . . . . . 463-74
Days between two dates . . . . . . . . . . 478
Episcopal Church . . . . . . . . . . . . . . 647
Eras, cycles (1997) . . . . . . . . . . . . . 460
Greek Orthodox Church . . . . . . . . . . 647
Gregorian . . . . . . . . . . . . . . . . . . . 475
Islamic . . . . . . . . . . . . . . . . . . . . . 647
Jewish . . . . . . . . . . . . . . . . . . . . . 648
Julian . . . . . . . . . . . . . . . . . . 475, 478
Leap years . . . . . . . . . . . . . . . . . . . 475
Lenten . . . . . . . . . . . . . . . . . . 647, 648
Lunar . . . . . . . . . . . . . . . . . . . . . . 478
Perpetual . . . . . . . . . . . . . . . . . 476-77
Twilight (1997) . . . . . . . . . . . . . 460-61
Year . . . . . . . . . . . . . . . . . . . . . . 458
**Caliber** (measure) . . . . . . . . . . . . . . 604
**California** . . . . . . . . . . . . . . . . . . . 657
Admission, area, capital . . . . . . 542, 657
Agriculture . . . . . . . . . . . . . . . . 156-61
Altitudes (high, low) . . . . . . . . . . . . 541
Birth, death statistics . . . . . . . . . . . . 963
Budget . . . . . . . . . . . . . . . . . . . . . 135
Coastline . . . . . . . . . . . . . . . . . . . 541
Congressional representation . . . 111, 113, 380
Courts, U.S. . . . . . . . . . . . . . . . . . . 190
Crime, prisons, death penalty . . . 959, 960, 961
Desert Protection Act (1994) . . . . . . . 510
Earthquake (1994) . . . . . . . . . . . . . . 509
Energy consumption . . . . . . . . . . . . 237
Federally owned land . . . . . . . . . . . . 545
Governor, state officials . . . . . . 124, 125
Hazardous waste sites . . . . . . . . . . . 228
Health insurance coverage . . . . . . . . 971
Immigrants admitted (1995) . . . . . . . . 383
Indians, American . . . . . . . . . . . . . . 550
Interest laws, rates . . . . . . . . . . 721, 722
Marriage, divorce laws . . . . . . . 728, 729
Mineral production . . . . . . . . . . . . . 151
Motor vehicles . . . . . . . . . . . . 245, 248
Name origin, nickname . . . . . . . 544, 657
Population . . . . . . . . . . . . . . 380-81, 384
Cities, towns . . . 391-94, 686, 689, 690, 692, 693, 694, 695
Counties, county seats . . . . . . . . . 422
Port traffic . . . . . . . . . . . . . . . . . . 242
Poverty rates . . . . . . . . . . . . . . . . . 388
Presidential elections . . . . . . 76, 79, 106
Schools and libraries . . . . . . 252-53, 257
Taxes . . . . . . . . . . . . . . . . . . 245, 735
Temperature, precipitation . . . . . 222, 224
Unemployment benefits . . . . . . . . . . 165
Welfare assistance . . . . . . . . . . . . . 389
**California, Gulf of** . . . . . . . . . . . . . . 593
**Calories** (dietary) . . . . . . . . . . 609, 610-11
Labels, nutrition . . . . . . . . . . . . . . . 612
**Calvin, John** . . . . . . . . . . . . . . . 344, 562
**Cambodia** . . . . . . . . . . . . . . . . . . . . 749
Ambassadors, envoys . . . . . . . . . . . 846
Flag . . . . . . . . . . . . . . . . . . . . . . 481
History . . . . . . . . . . . . . . . . . 573, 575
*Mayaguez* seized (1975) . . . . . . . . . 507
U.S. invasion (1970) . . . . . . . . . . . . 506
**Cameroon** . . . . . . . . . . . 481, 749-50, 846
**Canada** . . . . . . . . . . . . . . . . . . . 750-51
Ambassadors, envoys . . . . . . . . . . . 846
Buildings, tall . . . . . . 696, 698, 699, 701-2
Chronology (1995-96) . . . . . . . . . . . . 40
Consumer price changes . . . . . . . . . 133
Distances to ports . . . . . . . . . . . . . 243
Energy production, consumption . . . . 236
Flag, maps . . . . . . . . . 481, 485, 486-87
Football . . . . . . . . . . . . . . . . . . . . 880
French and Indian War (1754-63) . . . 497
Gold production, reserves . . . . . 146, 153
Gross domestic product . . . . . . . . . . 134
Islands . . . . . . . . . . . . . . . . . . . . 592
Lakes, largest . . . . . . . . . . . . . . . . 598
Latitudes, longitudes, altitudes . . . 594-95
Libraries, public . . . . . . . . . . . . . . . 257
Mineral resources . . . . . . . . . . 151, 152
Motor vehicle production, exports 246, 242
Mountain peaks . . . . . . . . . . . . . . . 590
Newspaper circulation . . . . . . . . . . . 290
Nuclear power . . . . . . . . . . . . . 238, 239
Postal codes, rates . . . . . . . . . . 634, 635
Prime ministers . . . . . . . . . . . . . . . 751
Provinces, territories . . . . . . . . . . . . 750
Religions . . . . . . . . . . . . . . . . . . . 651
Rivers . . . . . . . . . . . . . . . . . . . 596-97
St. Lawrence Seaway (1959) . . . . . . 505
Trade . . . . . . . . . . . . . . . 240, 377, 750
Unemployment rates . . . . . . . . . . . . 166
U.S. immigrants from . . . . . . . . 377, 383
Wages, hourly . . . . . . . . . . . . . . . . 171
Waterfalls . . . . . . . . . . . . . . . . . . . 599
Zoos . . . . . . . . . . . . . . . . . . . . . . 233
**Canadian Football League** . . . . . . . . 880
**Canals**
Erie (1825) . . . . . . . . . . . . . . . . . . 499
Panama (1978) . . . . . . . . . . . . 507, 807
Suez . . . . . . . . . . . . . . . . . . . 573, 761
**Canary Islands** . . . . . . . . . . . . 592, 819
**Cancer**
Carcinogenic pollutants . . . . . . . . . . 228
Deaths, new cases . . . . . . . . . . 964, 974
Help organizations . . . . . . . . . . . . . 617
Prevention . . . . . . . . . . . . . . . 613, 614
Warning signals . . . . . . . . . . . . . . . 614
**Canoeing** . . . . . . . . . . . . . . . . . . . 850
**Cape Verde** . . . . . . . . . 481, 592, 751, 846
**Capital gains** . . . . . . . . . . . . . . 144, 154
**Capital punishment.** *See* Death penalty
**Capitals**
States, U.S. . . . . . . . . . . . . . . . . . 542
U.S. (*see* Washington, DC)
World (*see specific countries*)
**Capitol, U.S.** . . . . . . . . . . . . . . . . . 684
Burned (1814) . . . . . . . . . . . . . . . . 499
**Carat** (measure) . . . . . . . . . . . . . . . 604
**Carbohydrates** . . . . . . . . . . . 609, 610-11
**Carbon monoxide emmissions** . . 228, 229
**Cardinals, Roman Catholic** . . . . . . . . 649
**Cardiovascular disease** . . . . . . . . . . 974
**Cards, playing** (odds) . . . . . . . . . . . 607
**Caribbean Community and Common Market** . . . . . . . . . . . . . . . . . . . 842
**Caribbean Sea**
Area, depth . . . . . . . . . . . . . . . . . . 593
Islands, area . . . . . . . . . . . . 592, 682-83
Maps . . . . . . . . . . . . . . . . . . . 485, 488
Volcanoes . . . . . . . . . . . . . . . . . . . 589
**CARICOM.** *See* Caribbean Community and Common Market
**Carlsbad Caverns** (NM) . . . . . . . 546, 670
**Carolingian dynasty** . . . . . . . . . . . . 581
**Cars.** *See* Automobiles
**Carter, Jimmy** . . . . 105, 107, 109, 110, 537
**Cartier and Ashmore Islands** . . . . . . 741
**Cartoonists**
Awards . . . . . . . . . . . . . . . . 322-23, 328
Notable American . . . . . . . . . . . . . . 341
**Castro, Fidel** . . . . . . . . . . . . . 573, 757
**Casualties, U.S. wars** . . . . . . . . . . . 184
**Catacombs** (Egypt) . . . . . . . . . . . . . 555
**Cat breeds** . . . . . . . . . . . . . . . . . . 234
**Catholic Church.** *See* Roman Catholicism
**Cattle.** *See* Beef; Livestock; Meats
**Caucasus Mountains** . . . . . . . . . . . . 591
**Caves, U.S.** . . . . . . . . . . . . . . . . . . 546
**Cayman Islands** . . . . . . . . . . . . . . . 831
**CD-ROM**
School usage . . . . . . . . . . . . . . . . . 251
Software, top selling . . . . . . . . . . . . 212
**Celebes** . . . . . . . . . . . . . . . . . . . . 592
**Celebrities.** *See* Notable personalities; *specific fields*
**Celestial events** (1997) . . . . . . . . . 440-43
**Celestial Longitude** (astronomical position) . . . . . . . . . . . . . . . . . . . 443
**Celsius scale** . . . . . . . . . . . . . . . . . 605
**Cemeteries**
Arlington National (VA) . . . . . . . . . . 685
Presidential burial sites . . . . . . . . . . 539
**Census.** *See* Population, U.S.; Population, world
**Census, Bureau of the** . . . . 187, 188, 129, 210, 378
**Census Act** (1790) . . . . . . . . . . . . . . 498
**Census of U.S. Governments** (1992) . . 125
**Central African Republic** . 481, 751-52, 846
**Central America** . . . . . . . . . . . . . . . 576
Maps . . . . . . . . . . . . . . . . . . . 485, 488
Trade . . . . . . . . . . . . . . . . . . . . . . 240
Volcanoes . . . . . . . . . . . . . . . . . . . 589
*see also specific countries*
**Central American Common Market** . . . 240
**Central Intelligence Agency** . . . . . . . . 188
Ames spy case (1994) . . . . . . . . . . . 509
Directors . . . . . . . . . . . . . . . . 188, 206
Internet address . . . . . . . . . . . . . . . 210
**Century, defined** . . . . . . . . . . . . . . . 475
**Cereals,** Nutritive value . . . . . . . 609, 610
**Ceuta** . . . . . . . . . . . . . . . . . . . . . . 819
**Ceylon.** *See* Sri Lanka
**Chad** . . . . . . . . . . . . . . . . . . . . . . 752
Ambassadors, envoys . . . . . . . . . . . 846
Flag . . . . . . . . . . . . . . . . . . . . . . 481
History . . . . . . . . . . . . . . . . . 560, 575
**Challenger** (space shuttle) (1983, 1984, 1986) . . . . . . . . . . . . 310, 311, 508
**Chambers of Commerce.** *See* Cities, U.S.; States, U.S.
**Champlain, Samuel de** (1609) . . . 497, 586
**Channel Islands** . . . . . . . . . . . . 592, 830
**Chapter 11** (bankruptcy) . . . . . . . . . . 134
**Charitable contributions** . . . . . . . 713, 731
**Charlemagne** . . . . . . . . . . . . . . 558, 579
**Charles, Prince of Wales** (1996) . . . 46, 50, 62, *200*
**Charlotte, NC.** *See* Cities, U.S.
**Chatham Islands** . . . . . . . . . . . . 592, 803
**Chechnya revolt** (1996) . . . . 47, 54-55, 57, 61, 65, *777*
**Cheese,** Nutritive value . . . . . . . . 609, 610
**Chemicals**
Exports, imports . . . . . . . . . . . . . . . 241
Toxic . . . . . . . . . . . . . . . . . . . . . . 228
**Chemistry**
Discoveries . . . . . . . . . . . . . . . . 217-18
Elements (atomic weights, numbers) 218-19
Nobel Prizes . . . . . . . . . . . . 39, 317-18
**Chesapeake, VA** . . . . . . 121, 387, 418, 687
**Chess** . . . . . . . . . . . . . . . . . . . . . 956
**Chiang Kai-shek** . . . . . . . . . . . . 345, 570
**Chicago, IL** . . . . . . . . . . . . . . . . . . 687
Fire (1871) . . . . . . . . . . . . . . . 304, 501
*see also* Cities, U.S.
**Chicago Board of Trade** . . . . . . . . . . 148
**Chicken**
Nutritive value . . . . . . . . . . . . . . . . 610
Prices, farm . . . . . . . . . . . . . . . . . 162
**Children**
AIDS incidence . . . . . . . . . . . . . . . 975
Cost of raising . . . . . . . . . . . . . . . . 727
Health insurance coverage . . . . . . . . 971
Immunization schedule . . . . . . . . . . 613
Internet addresses . . . . . . . . . . . . . 211
Living arrangements . . . . . . . . . . . . 965
Population . . . . . . . . . . 377, 378, 379, 387
Poverty rates . . . . . . . . . . . . . . . . . 388
Single-parent families . . . . . . . . 377, 965
Social Security benefits . . . . . . . . . . 709
Taxes, federal . . . . . . . . . . . . 730, 731
Welfare assistance . . . . . . . . . . . . . 389
**Children's books**
Awards . . . . . . . . . . . . . . . . . . . 327-28
Notable (1996) . . . . . . . . . . . . . . 288-89
**Chile** . . . . . . . . . . . . . . . . . . . . . . 752
Ambassadors, envoys . . . . . . . . . . . 846
Commercial fishing . . . . . . . . . . . . . 164
Flag . . . . . . . . . . . . . . . . . . . . . . 481
History . . . . . . . . . . . . . . . . . . . . 575
Rulers . . . . . . . . . . . . . . . . . . . . . 584
**China, dynastic** . . . . . . . . . 566, 567, 568
Boxer Rebellion (1900) . . . . . . . . . . 501
Great Wall . . . . . . . . . . . . . . . 554, 555
Kuomintang . . . . . . . . 569, 570, 571, 572
Open Door Policy (1899) . . . . . . . . . 501
Opium War (1839-1842) . . . . . . . . . . 565
Revolution (1911) . . . . . . . . . . . . . . 569
Ruling dynasties . . . . 552, 554, 556, 559, 560, 562, 563, 569, 585
Seven Wonders, Middle Ages . . . . . . 555
**China, People's Republic of** . . . . . 753-54
Ambassadors, envoys . . . . . . . . . . . 846
Chronology (1996) . 52, 57, 59-60, 62, 69
Cities (largest) . . . . . . . . . . . . . . . . 838
Commercial fishing . . . . . . . . . . . . . 164
Energy production, consumption . . . . 236
Flag, map . . . . . . . . . . . . . . 481, 492-93
Gold production . . . . . . . . . . . . . . . 153
Gross domestic product . . . . . . . . . . 134
History . . . 572, 573, 574-75, 576, 753-54
Leaders . . . . . . . . . . . . . . . . 585, 753-54
Maoism . . . . . . . . . . . . . . . . . 574-75, 753
Merchant fleet . . . . . . . . . . . . . . . . 243

Military strength 182
Motor vehicle production 246
Nixon visit (1972) 506
Nuclear power 239
Population, world's greatest 838
Tiananmen Square 576, 754
Trade 240, 377
U.S. immigrants from 377, 383
**China, Republic of.** *See* Taiwan
**China Sea** 593
**Chinese lunar calendar** 478
**Choate, Pat** (1996) 65
**Cholesterol**
Heart disease 616
Labels, nutrition 612
**Choreographers, notable** 357-58
**Christ.** *See* Jesus Christ
**Christianity**
Denominations 644-47, 652-53
History 556-57, 559-60, 562
Population, world 646
**Christmas Day** 480
**Christmas Island** 592, 741
**Chromium** 151, 152
**Chronological eras, cycles** (1997) 460
**Chronology of 1995-96** 40-69
**Churches**
Addresses, U.S. headquarters 645-46
Black church arsons (1996) 58, *197*
Calendars 647-48
Denominations 644-47, 652-53
Feast, fast, holy days 647-48
Membership
Canada 651
U.S. 644-45
Worldwide 646
**Churchill, Sir Winston** (1945) 346, 504
**Church of Christ, Scientist** 644, 645
**Church of England** 829
**Church of Jesus Christ of Latter-Day Saints.** *See* Latter-Day Saints, Church of
**CIA.** *See* Central Intelligence Agency
**Cigarettes.** *See* Smoking
**Cincinnati, OH.** *See* Cities, U.S.
**Cinema.** *See* Movies
**CIO.** *See* American Federation of Labor and Congress of Industrial Organizations
**Circle,** Mathematical formulas 607
**Circulation** (newspapers, magazines) 288, 290
**Circumference,** Formula 607
**Circumnavigation** 316
**CIS.** *See* Commonwealth of Independent States
**Cities, U.S.** 686-95
Air quality 229
Airport traffic 313
Area codes, telephone 390-420
Buildings, tall 540, 696-702
Climatological data 226, 221-25
Consumer price indexes 132
Crime index 957
Farthest east, north, south, west 540
Housing prices 726
Immigrants (1995) 383
Internet addresses 686-95
Latitudes, longitudes, altitudes 594-95
Libraries, public 257
Mayors 121-24
Mileage tables
Air 250
Road 249
Newspaper circulation 290
Orchestras, opera companies 286-87
Population 377, 382, 390-420, 686-95
Fastest-growing 377
Metropolitan areas (1990-94) 385
100 largest 386-87
Ports 242
Precipitation 221, 223
Stadiums, arenas 879, 913, 954
Temperatures 221, 223
Theater companies 285-86
Time differences 480
Wind velocities 223, 226
ZIP codes 390-420
**Cities, world**
Air mileage 250
Air traffic 313
Bridges, buildings 702, 705
Latitudes, longitudes, altitudes 593
Population (by country) 737-837
Population of largest 838
Port distances 243
Temperatures, precipitation 225
Time differences 479
**Citizenship, U.S.**
American Indians (1924) 503
14th Amendment 520-21
Naturalization process 841
**Civil rights**
Bill vetoed (1990) 509
Commission, U.S. 188
Constitutional amendments 520-21, 522
Disabilities Act (1990) 509
Legislation (1875, 1957, 1964) 501, 505, 573
Supreme Court rulings (1995-96) 39
*see also* Desegregation; Elections, voting rights; Women
**Civil War, U.S.** (1861-65) 500
Amnesty Act (1872) 501
Appomattox Court House (1865) 500, 546
Battlefields 547
Bull Run (1861) 500
Casualties, numbers serving 180, 184
Confederate States (1861) 500, 523
Costs 181
Draft riots (1863) 500
Emancipation Proclamation (1863) 500
Ft. Sumter (1861) 500
Gettysburg Address (1863) 500, 523
Historical parks, sites 546, 547-48
Lincoln assassination (1865) 307, 500, 532
Military leaders 343-44
Secession of states 523
Sherman's March (1864) 500
**Classical music** 355-56
**Classification, animal/plant** 231
**Clergy, forms of address** 641
**Cleveland, Grover** 107, 109, 533, 539
*see also* Presidents, U.S.
**Cleveland, OH.** *See* Cities, U.S.
**Climate, U.S.** 221-25, 226
**Clinton, Bill**
Administration 109, 185-88, 110, 538
Assassination attempt (1994) 308, 538
Cabinet 185, 201-5
Chronology (1995-96) 40, 43, 45, 49, 50, 51, 52, 54, 56, 57, 61, 64, 66
Budget stalemate 38, 41-42, 44, 46, 53, *196*, 510
Sexual harassment suit (1994) 46, 55, 509
Travelgate case 42, 58
Whitewater investigation (1994) 44-45, 46, 48-49, 53, 56, 59, 62, 509, 510
Foster suicide (1993, 1995) 509, 510
Health-care reform (1993, 1994) 509
Inauguration (1993) 509
Next 4 years 35
Presidential elections
1992 76-105, 105, 107, 509
Popular, electoral votes 76-105, 108
1996 33-34, 60, 63, 64, 65-66, 68, *193*, *195*
Salary 185
State of the Union (1996) 47
Vetoes (1995-96) 44, 46, 53, 55, 58, 120, 510
*see also* Presidents, U.S.
**Clinton, Hillary Rodham** 538, 539
Health-care reform (1993) 509
Presidential campaign (1996) 64, *195*
Whitewater investigation (1994, 1995, 1996) 44-45, 46, 51, 59, *196*, 509, 510
**Clothing**
Exports, imports 241
Personal expenditures 150
Price index 131, 132
**Clubs, organizations** 620-31
**Coal**
Exports, imports 235, 241
Mining strikes (1922, 1946) 503, 504
Production, consumption 235
**Coast Guard, U.S.** 188
Academy 178
Address for information 182
Commandants 187, 176
Insignia 178
Personnel, active duty 179
Women, active duty 180
**Coastlines, U.S.** 541
**Cobalt** 151, 152
**Cocoa,** Exports, imports 241
**Cocos (Keeling) Island** 741
**Coffee,** Exports, imports 241
**Coinage** 139, 140
**Cold War** 572, 575-76
**Colleges and universities** 254-56, 258-82
ACT scores 255
Addresses 258-82
Citadel female cadets (1995, 1996) 64, 510
Coeducation, first (1833) 499
Desegregation (1962) 505
Drug abuse 965
Enrollment 254, 258-82
Faculty 256, 258-82
Founding dates 258-82
Four-year 258-72
Freshman attitudes (1995) 282
Governing officials 258-82
Graduates 377
Land Grant Act (1862) 500
SAT scores 255, 256
Sports
Baseball 937-56
Basketball 55, 849, 914-19
Football 48, 849, 881-88
Ice hockey 896
Lacrosse 896
Team nicknames, colors 884-86
Wrestling 904
State military college ruling (1996) 39
State university, first (1795) 498
Tuition and costs 254
Two-year 272-82
Women's, first (1821) 499
**Colombia** 754
Ambassadors, envoys 846
Flag 481
Gold production 153
Gross domestic product 134
Rulers 584
**Colorado** 657-58
Admission, area, capital 542, 543, 657
Agriculture 156-61
Altitudes (high, low) 541
Birth, death statistics 963
Budget 135
Congressional representation 111, 113, 380
Courts, U.S. 190
Crime, prisons, death penalty 959, 960
Energy consumption 237
Federally owned land 545
Governor, state officials 124, 125
Hazardous waste sites 228
Health insurance coverage 971
Immigrants admitted (1995) 383
Indians, American 550
Interest laws, rates 721, 722
Marriage, divorce laws 728, 729
Motor vehicles 245, 248
Name origin, nickname 544, 657
Population 380-81, 384
Cities, towns 394, 686, 687, 688
Counties, county seats 422
Poverty rates 388
Presidential elections 76, 79-80, 106
Schools and libraries 252-53, 257
Taxes 245, 735, 736
Temperature, precipitation 222, 224
Unemployment benefits 165
Welfare assistance 389
**Colorado River** 586, 596
**Colorado Springs, CO.** *See* Cities, U.S.
**Colors**
Colleges, universities 884-86
Of spectrum 606
**Colosseum** (Rome) 555
**Colossus of Rhodes** 555
**Columbia** (space shuttle) (1981, 1982) 310, 312, 311, 507, 508
**Columbia River** 596
**Columbium** 151, 152
**Columbus, Christopher** (1492) 497, 561, 586
**Columbus, GA** 121, 387, 688
**Columbus, OH.** *See* Cities, U.S.
**Columbus Day** 480
**Comecon** 573
**Comets** *199*, 440, 443
**Commands, U.S.** 176
**Commerce.** *See* Commodities; Exports, imports; Shipping
**Commerce, Department of** 186-87
Employees, payroll 169
Expenditures 129
Internet address 210
Secretaries 185, 186, 204-5
Brown plane crash (1996) 53, 65, 74, *197*, 300
**Commission on Civil Rights** 188
**Committee for Industrial Organization.** *See* American Federation of Labor and Congress of Industrial Organizations
**Commodities**
Exports, imports 241
Price indexes 131
Production 157, 160, 161, 162
**Common Market.** *See* European Community
**Common Sense** (Paine) Excerpt 511
**Commonwealth, The** (British Commonwealth) 43, 842
**Commonwealth of Independent States** 246, 842
**Communications**
Inventions 215-17
Reform legislation (1996) 38, 48
Satellite, first (1962) 505
*see also specific communications media*

**Communism**
Post-World War II . . . 572
Russian revolution (1917) . . . 569
Soviet Bloc breakup (1989) . . . 576
U.S.
Red scare (1920) . . . 502
Trials, convictions (1949) . . . 504
*see also* Cold War
**Communist China.** *See* China, People's Republic of
**Community colleges** . . . 272-82
**Comoros** . . . 481, 754-55, 846
**Compact discs.** *See* Recordings
**Composers, notable** . . . 355-57
**Compound interest table** . . . 605
**Computers** . . . 207-14
CD-ROM software . . . 212
Exports, imports . . . 241
Glossary of terms . . . 212-13
Sales, ownership . . . 212
School usage . . . 251
Software, top-selling . . . 212
Tax deductions . . . 731
*see also* Internet; Intranet
**Concentration camps** . . . 571, 572
**Concerts, top-grossing** (1985-95; 1995) 291
**Cone,** Volume formula . . . 607
**Confederate States of America**
Amnesty Act (1872) . . . 501
Battlefield memorials . . . 547
Civil War (1861-65) . . . 500
Casualties, numbers serving . . . 184
Costs . . . 181
Flags . . . 523
Government . . . 523
**Confucianism**
Adherents . . . 646
Confucius (551 BC) . . . 344, 554
**Congo, Democratic Republic of.** *See* Zaire
**Congo, Republic of** . . . 481, 755, 846
**Congo (Zaire) River** . . . 596
**Congregational churches** . . . 644
**Congress, U.S.** . . . 111-20
Address, forms of . . . 641
Apportionment . . . 380
Bill-into-law process . . . 522
Chronology (1995-96) . . . 42, 56
Budget stalemate . . . 38, 41-42, 44, 46, 53, *196*, 510
Legislator retirements . . . 41, 44, 47
Waldholtz campaign fraud . . . 45, 58
Committees . . . 119
Constitutional powers . . . 516
Contract With America (1995) . . . 38, 510
Elections . . . 111-18
Republican control (1994) . . . 44, 510
Employees, payroll . . . 169
Expenditures . . . 129
House of Representatives . . . 112-18, 119
Committees . . . 119
Constitutional powers . . . 515, 516
First woman (1916) . . . 502
Floor leaders . . . 112
Members . . . 112-18
Party representation . . . 120
Revenue bill origination . . . 516
Salaries, term . . . 112
Speakers (1995) . . . 38, 112, 206, 510
Internet addresses . . . 210
Legislative actions (1995-96) . . . 38
Nonvoting members . . . 118
Political division (1901-96) . . . 120
Presidential vetoes (1789-96) . . . 120
Presidents, vice presidents . . . 109-10
Qualifications . . . 515
Salary amendment (1992) . . . 509, 522
Senate . . . 111-12
Committees . . . 119
Election of senators . . . 515, 521
Floor leaders (1995) . 38, 111, 206, 510
Members . . . 111-12
Party representation . . . 120
Salaries, term . . . 111
States' rights ruling (1996) . . . 39
Term limits
Legislation (1995) . . . 510
Supreme Court rulings . . . 524
Visitors, admission of . . . 684
Women members (1916) . . . 502
*see also* Continental Congress; Library of Congress
**Congress of Industrial Organizations.** *See* American Federation of Labor and Congress of Industrial Organizations
**Congress of Vienna** (1814-15) . . . 565
**Conjunction** (astronomical position) . . . 443
**Connecticut** . . . 658
Admission, area, capital . . . 542, 658
Agriculture . . . 156-61
Altitudes (high, low) . . . 541
Birth, death statistics . . . 963
Budget . . . 135
Coastline . . . 541
Congressional representation . . 111, 113, 380
Courts, U.S. . . . 190
Crime, prisons, death penalty . . . 959, 960
Energy consumption . . . 237
Federally owned land . . . 545
Governor, state officials . . . 124, 126
Hazardous waste sites . . . 228
Health insurance coverage . . . 971
Immigrants admitted (1995) . . . 383
Indians, American . . . 550
Interest laws, rates . . . 721, 722
Marriage, divorce laws . . . 728, 729
Motor vehicles . . . 245, 248
Name origin, nickname . . . 544, 658
Population . . . 380-81, 384
Cities, towns . . . 394-95
Counties, county seats . . . 422
Poverty rates . . . 388
Presidential elections . . . 76, 80, 106
Schools and libraries . . . 252-53, 257
Taxes . . . 245, 735, 736
Temperature, precipitation . . . 222, 224
Unemployment benefits . . . 165
Welfare assistance . . . 389
**Conservation.** *See* Environment
**Constantinople** . . . 558
**Constants, astronomical** . . . 450
**Constellations** . . . 451
**Constitution, U.S.** . . . 514-22
Amendments . . . 519-22
Balanced budget (1995) . . . 510
ERA proposed (1972, 1982) . . 506, 508
Poll tax barred . . . 522
Procedure for . . . 518
Prohibition (1917, 1933) . 502, 503, 521
Reconstruction . . . 520-21
Slavery abolished (1865) . . . 500, 520
27th ratified (1992) . . . 509
Voting age (1971) . . . 506, 522
Bill of Rights . . . 519
Internet address . . . 210
Origin . . . 514
Preamble . . . 515
Ratification (1787) . . . 498, 514
Supreme Court rulings (1995-96) . . . 39
**Constitutional Convention** (1787) 498, 514
**Construction industry,** Occupational injuries . . . 168
**Consumer electronics products** . . . 293
**Consumer Price Indexes** . . . 131, 132
Chronology (1995-96) . . 41, 48, 55, 63, 66
**Consumer Product Safety Commission** . . . 188
**Consumers and consumption** . . . 713-27
At-home shopping tips, rights . . . 713
Business directory . . . 714-19
Charitable giving . . . 713, 731
*Consumer Information Catalog* . . . 713
Credit . . . 721-22
Debt outstanding . . . 140
Electronics products . . . 293
Energy . . . 235, 236, 237
Food
Labeling, nutrition . . . 612
Meats . . . 157
Nutritive values . . . 609-11
Housing prices . . . 726
Loan rates . . . 721
Mortgages . . . 727, 731
Personal expenditures . . . 150
Price change percentages . . . 133
Price indexes . . . 131, 132
Products
Parent companies . . . 720
Pure Food and Drug Act (1906) . . . 502
Safety Commission . . . 188
Transportation . . . 245, 246
**Continental Congress**
Articles of Confederation (1777) . . 498, 514
Declaration of Independence (1776) . 498, 512-13
First (1774) . . . 498
Great Seal of the U.S. . . . 525
Northwest Ordinance (1787) . . . 498
Presidents, meetings . . . 511
Stars and Stripes (1777) . . . 498, 525-26
**Continental Divide** . . . 542
**Continents** . . . 838
Altitudes (highest, lowest) . . . 597
Explorations . . . 586-88
Lakes . . . 598
Maps . . . 485-96
Mountain peaks . . . 590-91
Religious adherents . . . 646
Rivers . . . 596-97
Volcanoes . . . 588-89
Waterfalls . . . 599
*see also specific continents*
**Contract With America** (1995) . . . 38, 510
**Convention sites, political** . . . 106
Democratic Party (1996) . . . 64, *195*
Reform Party (1996) . . . 64, *195*
Republican Party (1996) . . . 63, *194*
**Cook Islands** . . . 803
**Coolidge, Calvin** . . . 107, 109, 110, 535
**Cooperstown** (NY) (Baseball Hall of Fame) . . . 671, 950
**Copper** . . . 151, 152, 153
**Copyright law, U.S.** . . . 724-25
Chinese compliance (1996) . . . 59-60
**Corn**
Exports, imports . . . 163, 241
Nutritive value . . . 611
Prices, farm . . . 162
Production . . . 160, 161, 163
**Coronado, Francisco** (1540) . . . 497, 586
**Corporation for Public Broadcasting** . . 130
**Corporations**
Bond yields . . . 148
Charitable contributions . . . 713
Internet addresses . . . 211
Leading (1995) . . . 141-42
Mergers and acquisitions . . . 142
Patents received (1995) . . . 218
Profits (by industry) . . . 143
Revenues, largest (1995) . . . 142
Tax rates . . . 144
*see also* Business
**Corpus Christi, TX.** *See* Cities, U.S.
**Corsica** . . . 592, 765
**Cortes, Hernando** . . . 563, 586
**Cosmonauts,** (1995, 1996) . . . 66, *199*, 309-11, 313, 510
**Costa Rica** . . . 481, 755, 846
**Cote d'Ivoire (Ivory Coast)** . . 481, 756, 846
**Cotton**
Exports, imports . . . 241
Prices, farm . . . 162
Production . . . 160, 161
**Cotton Bowl** . . . 882
**Counterfeiting** . . . 961
**Counties, U.S.**
Areas and county seats . . . 421-39
Elections (1992, 1996) . . . 77-105
Largest, by population . . . 384
Largest, smallest . . . 540
**Country music, notable artists** . . . 359
**Courts.** *See* Judiciary, U.S.; World Court
**Courts of Appeal, U.S.,** 190
**CPI.** *See* Consumer Price Indexes
**Credit**
Consumer outstanding . . . 140
Farm . . . 160
Laws, rates . . . 721, 722
Compound interest table . . . 605
Mortgages . . . 727
Rating (how to check) . . . 722
**Credit cards** . . . 39, 721, 722
**Crime** . . . 957-61
Arrests . . . 961
Assassinations . . . 307-8, 539, 576
Chronology (1995-96)
Dunblane kindergarten slaying . 52, *779*
Menendez brothers verdict . . . 52-53
Unabomber case . . . 53, 59, *197*, 510, 961
Crime bills (1994) . . . 509
Death penalty (1890, 1977) . . . 39, 501, 507, 960, 961
Index, by crime, population, region . 957-58
Law enforcement officers . . . 958
Prison population . . . 960, 961
Rates, by type, region, state . . . 959
Sentences versus time served . . . 960
Simpson murder case (1994, 1995) . . . 509, 510
Supreme Court decisions (1995-96) . . . 39
*see also* Terrorism; War crimes; *specific types*
**Crimean War** (1853-56) . . . 566
**Croatia** . . . 481, 756, 840, 846
Chronology (1995-96) . . 42, 43, 45, 47, 49
**Crozet Archipelago** . . . 765
**Crude oil.** *See* Petroleum
**Crusades** . . . 559
**Cuba** . . . 756-57, 846
Area . . . 592
Bay of Pigs (1961) . . . 505, 573, 757
Castro, revolution (1959) . . . 573, 757
Flag, map . . . 481, 488
Missile crisis (1962) . . . 505, 757
Spanish-American War (1898) . . . 501
U.S. immigrants from . . . 377, 383
U.S. plane downings, sanctions (1996) . . . 50, 52
**Cube,** Volume formula . . . 607
**Curacao** . . . 592, 803
**Currency, U.S.**
Circulation, amount in . . . 140

Denominations . . . . . . . . . . . . 139, 140
Design, new . . . . . . . . . . . . . . . . . . 139
Engraving, printing . . . . . . . . . . . . . . 684
Foreign exchange rates . . . . . . 144, 146
Gold Standard dropped (1933) . . . . . . 503
Mint, U.S. . . . . . . . . . . . . . . . . . . . 139
Portraits on . . . . . . . . . . . . . . . . . . 139
Silver coinage . . . . . . . . . . . . 139, 140
**Customs, U.S.**, 186, 188
Exemptions, advice . . . . . . . . . . . . . 722
U.S. receipts . . . . . . . . . . . . . . . . . 129
**Cycles, chronological** (1997) . . . . . . . 460
**Cycling**
Olympic champions . . . . . . . . . . . . . 850
Tour de France (1996) . . . . . . . . . . . 932
**Cyclones** . . . . . . . . . . . . . . . . 220, 302
**Cylinder,** Volume formula . . . . . . . . . . 607
**Cyprus** . . . . . . . . . . . . . . . . . . . 757-58
Ambassadors, envoys . . . . . . . . . . . 846
Area . . . . . . . . . . . . . . . . . . . . . . . 592
Flag . . . . . . . . . . . . . . . . . . . . . . . 481
Gross domestic product . . . . . . . . . . 134
Merchant fleet . . . . . . . . . . . . . . . . 243
**Cy Young awards** . . . . . . . . . . . . . . . 942
**Czechoslovakia** . . . . . . 570, 571, 576, 758
**Czech Republic** . . . 239, 246, 481, 758, 846

— D—

**Dahomey.** *See* Benin
**Dairy products**
Exports, imports . . . . . . . . . . . . . . . 241
Nutritive value . . . . . . . . . . . . . 609, 610
Prices, farm . . . . . . . . . . . . . . . . . . 162
**Dallas, TX.** *See* Cities, U.S.
**Dams, major** . . . . . . . . . . . . . . . . . 706-7
**Dance**
Companies, U.S. . . . . . . . . . . . . . . . 287
Notable figures . . . . . . . . 357-58, 360-72
**Dates**
Days between two . . . . . . . . . . . . . . 478
Days of week, to find . . . . . . . . . 476-77
Gregorian calendar . . . . . . . . . . . . . 475
History, U.S. . . . . . . . . . . . . . . 497-510
History, world . . . . . . . . . . . . . . 551-76
International line . . . . . . . . . . . 479, 484
Julian calendar . . . . . . . . . . . . . . . . 475
Julian period . . . . . . . . . . . . . . . . . 478
**Davis, Jefferson** (1861) . . . . 346, 500, 523
**Davis Cup** (tennis) . . . . . . . . . . . . . . 929
**Daylight Saving Time** . . . . . . . . . . . . 479
**Days**
Between two dates . . . . . . . . . . . . . 478
Holidays . . . . . . . . . . . . . . . . . . . . 480
Length of . . . . . . . . . . . . . . . . . . . 479
Names, non-English languages . . . . . 640
**Daytona 500** (auto race) . . . . . . . . . . 932
**Dayton, OH.** *See* Cities, U.S.
**Death penalty**
Electrocution, first (1890) . . . . . . . . . 501
Gilmore execution (1977) . . . . . . . . . 507
Rates, U.S. . . . . . . . . . . . . . . . . . . 960
States with . . . . . . . . . . . . . . . 960, 961
Supreme Court rulings (1996) . . . . . . 39
**Death records, sources** . . . . . . . . . . . 727
**Deaths**
Accidental . . . . . . . . . . . . 964, 967, 968
AIDS . . . . . . . . . . . . . . . . . . . 964, 975
Aviation . . . . . . . 168, 299-300, 314, 968
Cancer . . . . . . . . . . . . . . . . . . 964, 974
Cardiovascular disease . . . . . . . 964, 974
Critical illness, state laws . . . . . . . . . 615
By execution . . . . . . . . . . . . . . 960, 961
Firearms . . . . . . . . . . . . . . . . 967, 968
Fires . . . . . . . . 168, 304-5, 967, 968, 969
Infant rates . . . . . . . . . . . 962, 963, 964
Leading causes . . . . . . . . . . . . . . . 964
Motor vehicles . . . . . . . . . . 168, 964, 967
Obituaries (1995-96) . . . . . . . . . . . 74-75
Occupational . . . . . . . . . . . . . . . . . 168
Presidents, U.S. (dates) . . . . . . . . . . 109
Rates, U.S. . . . . . . . . . . . 962, 963, 964
Suicides . . . . . . . . . . 168, 964, 965, 968
Survivor benefits . . . . . . . . . . . . . . 709
*see also* Accidents and disasters; Murders
**Debt**
Consumer . . . . . . . . . . . . . . . . . . . 140
Farm, U.S. . . . . . . . . . . . . . . . . . . 160
National . . . . . . . . . . . 38, 130, 131, 155
State . . . . . . . . . . . . . . . . . . . . . . 135
**Decathlon**
Olympic champions . . . . . . *783*, 852, 857
World record . . . . . . . . . . . . . . . . . 867
**Decibel** (measure) . . . . . . . . . . . . . . 604
**Decimals** . . . . . . . . . . . . . . . . . . . . 606
**Declaration of Independence**
Adopted (1776) . . . . . . . . . . . . 498, 512
Signers . . . . . . . . . . . . . . . . . . 513-14
Text . . . . . . . . . . . . . . . . . . . . 512-13
**Defense, Department of** . . . . . . . . . . . 186
Employees, payroll . . . . . . . . . . . . . 169
Expenditures . . . . . . . . . . . . . . . . . 129
Internet address . . . . . . . . . . . . . . . 210
Pentagon . . . . . . . . . . . . . . . . . . . 685
Personal salutes, honors . . . . . . . . . 177
Secretaries . . . . . . . . . . . 185, 186, 202
**Defense, national.** *See* Armed forces, U.S.; Weapons
**Defense contracts** . . . . . . . . . . . . . . 180
**Deficits, U.S. budget** (1993). 130, 131, 509
**Delaware** . . . . . . . . . . . . . . . . . . 658-59
Admission, area, capital . . . . . . . 542, 658
Agriculture . . . . . . . . . . . . . . . . 156-61
Altitudes (high, low) . . . . . . . . . . . . 541
Birth, death statistics . . . . . . . . . . . . 963
Budget . . . . . . . . . . . . . . . . . . . . . 135
Coastline . . . . . . . . . . . . . . . . . . . 541
Congressional representation . 111, 113, 380
Courts, U.S. . . . . . . . . . . . . . . . . . 190
Crime, prisons, death penalty . 959, 960, 961
Energy consumption . . . . . . . . . . . . 237
Federally owned land . . . . . . . . . . . 545
Governor, state officials . . . . . . . 124, 126
Hazardous waste sites . . . . . . . . . . . 228
Health insurance coverage . . . . . . . . 971
Immigrants admitted (1995) . . . . . . . 383
Indians, American . . . . . . . . . . . . . . 550
Interest laws, rates . . . . . . . . . . 721, 722
Marriage, divorce laws . . . . . . . 728, 729
Motor vehicles . . . . . . . . . . . . . 245, 248
Name origin, nickname . . . . . . . 544, 658
Population . . . . . . . . . . . . . . . 380-81, 384
Cities, towns . . . . . . . . . . . . . . . . 395
Counties, county seats . . . . . . . . . 422
Poverty rates . . . . . . . . . . . . . . . . . 388
Presidential elections . . . . . . 76, 80, 106
Prot traffic . . . . . . . . . . . . . . . . . . 242
Schools and libraries . . . . . . . 252-53, 257
Taxes . . . . . . . . . . . . . . . 245, 735, 736
Temperature, precipitation . . . . . 222, 224
Unemployment benefits . . . . . . . . . . 165
Welfare assistance . . . . . . . . . . . . . 389
**Democratic Party**
Chronology (1995-96) . . . . . . . . . . 46-47
Congressional members (1901-96) . . 120
Convention sites . . . . . . . . . . . . . . 106
Presidential campaign (1996) . . . . . . *193*
National convention . . . . . . . . . 64, *195*
Presidential elections (by county) . 77-105
Presidential, vice presidential candidates . . . . . . . . . . . . . . . 107
**Denmark** . . . . . . . . . . . . . . . . . . 758-59
Ambassadors, envoys . . . . . . . . . . . 846
Flag . . . . . . . . . . . . . . . . . . . . . . 481
Gross domestic product . . . . . . . . . . 134
Merchant fleet . . . . . . . . . . . . . . . . 243
Rulers, royal family . . . . . . . . . . 376, 582
Wages, hourly . . . . . . . . . . . . . . . . 171
**Denominations, religious** . 644-47, 652-53
**Density**
Air . . . . . . . . . . . . . . . . . . . . 458, 605
Earth . . . . . . . . . . . . . . . . 455, 457-58
Gases . . . . . . . . . . . . . . . . . . . . . 605
Planets . . . . . . . . . . . . . . . . . . . . 455
Sun . . . . . . . . . . . . . . . . . . . . . . 455
**Denver, CO.** *See* Cities, U.S.
**Departments, U.S.**
Employees, payrolls . . . . . . . . . . . . 169
Executive personnel . . . . . . . . . . 185-88
Expenditures . . . . . . . . . . . . . . . . . 129
Secretaries . . . . . . . . . . . 201-5, 185-88
*see also specific departments, name inverted*
**Depression, economic**
Defined . . . . . . . . . . . . . . . . . . . . 154
Panics (1873, 1893) . . . . . . . . . . . . 501
Stock Market crash (1929) . . . . . 503, 570
Worldwide (1929-39) . . . . . . . . . . 570-71
**Desegregation**
Baseball (1947) . . . . . . . . . . . . . . . 504
Bus boycott (1955) . . . . . . . . . . . . . 505
Mississippi, University of (1962) . . . . 505
Public schools (1954) . . . . . . . . . . . 505
Sit-ins (1960) . . . . . . . . . . . . . . . . 505
Supreme Court rulings (1954, 1955, 1956) . . . . . . . . . . . . 505, 524
**Deserts, world** . . . . . . . . . . . . . . . . 599
**Des Moines, IA.** *See* Cities, U.S.
**De Soto, Hernando** (1539) . . . . . . 497, 586
**Detroit, MI.** *See* Cities, U.S.
Riots (1943, 1967) . . . . . . . . . . 504, 506
**Diabetes** . . . . . . . . . . . 614-15, 618, 964
**Diana, Princess of Wales** (1996) . . 46, 50, 62, *200*
**Dice** (odds) . . . . . . . . . . . . . . . . . . 607
**Diet.** *See* Nutrition
**Dinosaurs** . . . . . . . . . . . . . . . 36-37, *199*
**Directories.** *See* Addresses
**Dirigibles**
Hindenburg burned (1937) . . . . . . . . 299
Notable trips . . . . . . . . . . . . . . . . . 316
**Disability insurance** . . . . . . . . . . . 708-12
**Disabled people** . . . . . . . . . . . . . . . *194*
Anti-discrimination act (1990) . . . . . . 509
Help organizations . . . . . . . . . . . . . 618
School programs . . . . . . . . . . . . . . 251
**Disasters.** *See* Accidents and disasters
**Disciples of Christ Church** . . . . . . 652-53
Address, headquarters . . . . . . . . . . . 645
Membership . . . . . . . . . . . . . . . . . 644
**Discoveries** . . . . . . . . . . . . 217-19, 348-49
Chemical elements . . . . . . . . . . . 218-19
Drugs . . . . . . . . . . . . . . . . . . . 217-18
Explorers . . . . . . . . . . . . . . . . . 586-88
Medical procedures . . . . . . . . . . . 217-18
**Discus throw**
Olympic champions . . . . . . 852, 856, 858
World records . . . . . . . . . . . . . 867, 868
**Diseases.** *See* Health and medicine; *specific diseases*
**District Courts, U.S.** . . . . . . . . . . . 190-92
**District of Columbia.** *See* Washington, DC
**Diving** . . . . . . . . . . . . . . 850, 860, 861-62
**Divorce**
Laws (by states) . . . . . . . . . . . . . . . 729
Rates, patterns . . . . . . . . . . . . . . . 962
**Djibouti** . . . . . . . . . . . . 481, 575, 759, 846
**Doctors**
Age, sex, specialty . . . . . . . . . . . . . 969
Patient visits . . . . . . . . . . . . . . . . . 972
**Documents.** *See* Laws and documents
**Dogs**
American Kennel Club . . . . . . . . . . . 234
Iditarod sled race . . . . . . . . . . . . . . 936
Westminster Kennel Club . . . . . . . . . 936
**Dole, Elizabeth** . . . . . . . . . . . . . . 63, *194*
**Dole, Robert**
Chronology (1995-96) . . . . . . . 41-42, 47, 53-54, 57, 61, 67
Resignation from Senate . . . . . . 38, 56, 58, *194*
Presidential campaign (1996) . . 33-34, 60, 63, 64, 65-66, 68, *193*, *194*
Popular, electoral votes
Primaries, caucuses . . . . . . . . 42, 49, 50
Senate Majority Leader (1995) . . . . . 510
**Domain Name System** (Internet) . . . . . 207
**Dominica** . . . . . . . . . . . 481, 592, 759, 846
**Dominican Republic** . . . . . . . . . . . 759-60
Ambassadors, envoys . . . . . . . . . . . 846
Flag . . . . . . . . . . . . . . . . . . . . . . 481
U.S. immigrants from . . . . . . . . . 377, 383
U.S. involvement in (1916, 1965) . 502, 506
**Dow Jones Industrial Average** . . . . . . 154
Components . . . . . . . . . . . . . . . . . 149
Milestones . . . . . . . . . . . . . . . . . . 149
Close above 6,000 (1996) . . . . . 68, 149
Record drop (1987) . . . . . . . . . . . 508
Performance (1961-96) . . . 44, 51, 55, 60, 63, 66, 149
**Draft, U.S.**
NYC riots (1863) . . . . . . . . . . . . . . 500
Peacetime, first (1940) . . . . . . . . . . 503
Selective Service System . . . . . . . . . 188
Vietnam-era end (1973) . . . . . . . . . . 506
Vietnam evaders pardoned (1977) . . . 507
**Drake, Sir Francis** (1579) . . . . . . . 497, 586
**Dram** (measure) . . . . . . 601, 602, 603, 604
**Drama.** *See* Theater
**Dred Scott decision** (1857) . . . . . 500, 523
**Drownings** . . . . . . . . . . . . . . . . . . . 967
**Drug abuse**
Arrests . . . . . . . . . . . . . . . . . . . . 961
Election campaign issues (1996) . . . . . 64
Help organizations . . . . . . . . . . . . . 617
Usage overview . . . . . . . . . . . . . . . 966
**Drugs, therapeutic**
AIDS (1986) . . . . . . . . . . . . . . . . . 508
Consumer protection (1906) . . . . . . . 502
Discoveries . . . . . . . . . . . . . . . . 217-18
Most frequently prescribed . . . . . . . . 973
**Dry measures** . . . . . . . . . . 601, 602, 604
**Dutch East Indies.** *See* Indonesia
**Duties.** *See* Customs, U.S.
**Duty-free imports** . . . . . . . . . . . . . . 722

— E—

**Earhart, Amelia** (1937) . . . . . . . . . 316, 503
**Earnings.** *See* Salaries and wages
**Earth** . . . . . . . . . . . . . . . . . . 455, 457-60
Area . . . . . . . . . . . . . . . . . . . . . . 457
Atmosphere . . . . . . . . . . . . . . . . . . 458
Climate zones . . . . . . . . . . . . . . 458-59
Dimensions . . . . . . . . . . . . . . . . 457-58
Latitude, longitude . . . . . . . . . . . . . 458
Poles . . . . . . . . . . . . . . . . . . . . . 459
Rotation . . . . . . . . . . . . . . . . . . 459-60
Seasons . . . . . . . . . . . . . . . . . . . 459
Sun, distance from . . . . . . . . . . 444, 455
Time . . . . . . . . . . . . . . . . . . . . . . 458
**Earthquakes, major** . . . . . . . . . . . . 303-4
Japan (1995) . . . . . . . . . . . . . . . . . 304
Los Angeles (1994) . . . . . . . . . . 304, 509

San Francisco (1906, 1989) 303, 304, 502, 508
**East China Sea** 593
**Eastern Atoll** 683
**Eastern Europe** 571, 573, 574, 575-76
*see also specific countries*
**Eastern Orthodox churches** 644, 652-53
Addresses, U.S. headquarters 645, 646
Church calendar 647
Russian church established 560
**Easter Sunday** 647, 648
**East Germany.** *See* Germany
**EC.** *See* European Community
**Eclipse Awards** 899-900
**Eclipses** 443, 454, 461-62
**Ecology.** *See* Environment
**Economic indicators, leading**
Chronology (1995-96) 41, 44, 47, 53, 55, 58, 60, 63, 66
Defined 133, 155
**Economics**
Banking statistics 137-38
Bankruptcy 134
Budget, U.S. 129-30
Business leaders, notable past 340-41
Chronology (1995-96) 44, 48, 51, 60, 63, 66
Consumer credit 140
Consumer Price Indexes 131, 132
Depressions (1873, 1893, 1929) 501, 503, 570-71
Dow Jones Average 68, 149, 154
Economists, notable 319, 342-43
GDP, GNP 133, 134
Glossary of terms 154-55
Gold reserves 146
Income, national 133, 147
Investments abroad 145
Nobel Prizes 39, 319
Reagan boom (1980s) 576
State finances 135-36
Stocks, bonds 148-50
U.S. net receipts 129-30
World Bank 845
*see also* Stocks
**Ecuador** 481, 760, 846
**Edison, Thomas A.** (1878, 1894) 348, 501
**Education** 251-82
Attainment
Annual earnings correlate 167
By labor-force status, occupation 171
Awards 329
Black enrollment 254, 255
Computer software, top-selling 212
Computers, technology in schools 251
Day schools, full-time 252
Desegregation, Supreme Court rulings (1954, 1955, 1956) 505, 524
Disabled students 251
Educators, notable past 350
Enrollment 251, 252, 254
Food program costs 158
Graduates, high school 253, 254, 377
Historical summary (1949-94) 251
Personal expenditures 150
Revenues and expenditures, public schools 251, 252, 253
SAT, ACT scores 255-56
School prayer ban (1963) 505
Tax deductions 730, 731
*see also* Colleges and universities
**Education, Department of** 187-88
Employees, payroll 169
Expenditures 129
Internet address 210
Secretaries 205, 185, 187
**EEC.** *See* European Community
**EEOC.** *See* Equal Employment Opportunity Commission
**EFTA.** *See* European Free Trade Association
**Eggs**
Exports, imports 241
Nutritive value 609, 610
Prices
Farm 162
Per dozen, by state 157
Production, by state 157
**Egypt** 760-61
Ambassadors, envoys 846
Ancient 552, 554
Seven Wonders 555
Chronology (1996) 54
Distances to ports 243
Flag 481
Gross domestic product 134
Middle Ages 555
Military strength 182
Sadat assassination (1981) 307, 576, 761
**Eisenhower, Dwight D.** 105, 107, 109, 110, 536
*see also* Presidents, U.S.
**Elba** 565, 592, 786
**Elderly** (over 65)
AIDS incidence 975
Alzheimer's disease 615, 617
Help organizations 617
Living arrangements 379, 965
Medicare 710
Enacted (1966) 506
Population 377, 378, 379, 387
Poverty level 387
Social Security 708-12
Tax considerations (1996) 51, 730, 734
**Election Day** 480
**Elections**
Campaign spending ruling (1996) 39
Congressional 33-34, 41, 111-20
Presidential
Electoral College 106
1996 campaign 47, 65-66, *193-95*
Contenders for office (1995, 1996) 41, 60-61, 510
Primaries, conventions 42, 49, 50, 63, 64, *194*, *195*
Party nominees (1856-92) 107
Popular, electoral vote (1789-1996) 76-105, 108
Third parties (1996) 60-61, 64, *195*, 107
Voter participation (1932-92) 105
Voting rights
Act signed (1965) 506
Black males 521
18-year-olds (1971) 506, 522
Minority-district gerrymandering ruling (1996) 39
Motor-voter bill (1993) 509
Turnout (1932-92) 105
Washington (DC) residents (1961) 522, 681
Women (1869, 1920) 501, 502, 521
**Electoral College** 106
Apportionment 380
Constitution on 516-17, 520
Map 106
**Electrical appliance use** 237
**Electric power**
Blackout, northeastern U.S. (1965) 506
Hydroelectric plants 706
Nuclear plants 239
Production, consumption 235, 237, 238
Unit measurements 604
**Electronics products, consumer** 293
**Elements, chemical** 218-19
**Elevations, mountain** 590-91
**Elizabeth II, Queen** (UK) (1996) 46, 578, 829
**Ellice Islands.** *See* Tuvalu
**Ellis Island** (NYC) 529
**Elongation** (astronomical position) 443
**El Paso, TX.** *See* Cities, U.S.
**El Salvador** 761-62
Ambassadors, envoys 846
Flag 481
History 576
U.S. immigrants from 377, 383
**Em** (measure) 604
**E-mail** (Internet) 207
**Emancipation Proclamation** (1863) 500
**Emigration.** *See* Immigration, emigration; *specific countries*
**Emmy Awards** 329-30
**Empire State Building** (NYC)
Height 699
Opened (1931) 503
**Employment** 165-75, 377
Age discrimination ruling (1996) 39
Agricultural 156, 166, 167
Benefit programs 167, 172
By cities (selected) 686-95
Earnings 170, 173, 170
By educational attainment 167, 171
Full, defined 154
Government 169
Immigration based on 840-41
Insurance 165, 167
Military 179, 180, 181
By nation (*see specific country*)
Occupational injuries, fatalities 168
Occupations 166, 167
Rates (1940-95) 165
Social Security benefits 708-12
Women 172, 173, 166, 167, 170
*see also* Labor unions; Salaries and wages; Unemployment
**Endangered species** 230
***Endeavour*** (space shuttle) (1993) 312, 311, 509
**Energy** 235-39
Consumption 235, 236, 237
Exports, imports 235, 236, 241
Production 235, 236, 238
*see also specific countries, sources, types*
**Energy, Department of** 187
Employees, payroll 169
Expenditures 129
Internet address 210
Secretaries 185, 187, 205
**England**
History 561, 563, 564, 567, 829-30
Poets laureate 351
Prime ministers 579
Rulers 577-78
*see also* United Kingdom
**Engraving and Printing, Bureau of** 186, 684
**Enlightenment** (18th century) 563
**Entertainers**
Awards 329-33
Birthplaces, birth dates 360-71
Notable past 372-75
Original names 375-76
*see also* Actors, actresses
**Environment** 228-34
Endangered species 230
Hazardous waste sites 228
Legislation (1994, 1996) 38, 510
Pollutant emissions 228-29
Toxic releases 228
Water usage 234
**Environmental Protection Agency** 188
Employees, payroll 169
Expenditures 129
Internet address 210
**Envoys.** *See* Ambassadors and envoys
**EPA.** *See* Environmental Protection Agency
**Ephemeris time** 458
**Episcopal Church** 644, 652-53
Address, headquarters 645
Calendar, fast days 647
Church of England 829
Liturgical colors 647
**Eponyms** 637
**Equal Employment Opportunity Commission** 188, 130
**Equal Rights Amendment** (1972, 1982) 506, 508
**Equatorial Guinea** 481, 762, 846
**Equestrian sports** 850
**Equinoxes** (1997) 441, 442, 459
**ERA.** *See* Equal Rights Amendment
**Eras, chronological** (1997) 460
**Erie, Lake** 598
**Erie Canal** (1825) 499
**Eriksson, Leif** 559
**Eritrea** 481, 762, 840, 846
**Eskimos** 377, 378, 379, 550
**Estonia** 481, 762-63, 846
**Ethiopia** 763
Ambassadors, envoys 846
Flag 482
History 558, 561, 567, 571, 575
Refugees from 840
**Ethnic, racial distribution** (U.S.) 377, 382, 388, 550
**Etna, Mt.** 589, 786
**EU.** *See* European Union
**Europe** 838-39
AIDS cases 840
Commercial fishing 164
Highest, lowest points 597
Islands 592
Lakes 598
Languages 642-43
Map 490
Motor vehicle production 246
Mountain peaks 590-91
Religious adherents 646
Rivers 596
Rulers, royal families 376, 577-84
Trade, U.S. 240
Volcanoes 588, 589
Waterfalls 599
*see also specific countries*
**European Community** 573, 575, 576, 842
**European Free Trade Association** 240, 573, 575, 842
**European Union** (1996) 54, 240, 842
**Evangelical churches** 575, 644, 645
**Evening stars** (1997) 449
**Events and anniversaries.** *See* Anniversaries; Chronology of 1995-96
**Everest, Mt.** 555, 590, 591, 597
**Evolution theory** 566
**Exchange rates, foreign** 144, 146
**Executions, U.S.** *See* Death penalty
**Executive agencies, U.S.** 185
**Executive Office of the President** 185, 129
**Exercise,** Heart rate 609
**Expenditures, federal** 129-30
**Explorations, expeditions**
Antarctic 587-88
Arctic 586-87
Space 309-13

Western Hemisphere . . . . . 559, 561, 563
Major explorers . . . . . . . . . . . . . . 586
**Explosions** . . . . . . . . . . . . . . . 168, 305-6
*see also* Terrorism
**Exports, imports** . . . . . . . . . . . . . 240-42
Agricultural . . . . . . . . . . . . 159, 163, 241
Automobiles . . . . . . . . . . . . . . 241, 242
Balance of trade . . . . . . . . 154, 240, 241
Coal, coke . . . . . . . . . . . . . . . . . . . 241
Commodities. . . . . . . . . . . . . . . . . 241
Energy. . . . . . . . . . . . . . . 235, 236, 241
International trade court, U.S. . . . . . . 192
International transactions, U.S. . . . . . 146
Manufactures . . . . . . . . . . . . . . . . 241
Merchant fleets . . . . . . . . . . . . . 243-44
Petroleum. . . . . . . . . . . . . 235, 236, 241
**Express Mail**. . . . . . . . . . . . . . . . . . 632

— F—

**FAA.** *See* Federal Aviation Administration
**Faeroe Islands** . . . . . . . . . . . . . 592, 759
**Fahrenheit scale** . . . . . . . . . . . . . . . 605
**Falkland Islands** . . . . . . . . . . . . 592, 831
**Families** . . . . . . . . . . . . . . . . . 377, 378
Immigrant preference system. . . . 840-41
One-parent. . . . . . . . . . . . 172, 377, 378
Poverty rates, levels. . . . . . 377, 387, 388
Welfare assistance. . . . . . . . . . . . . . 389
*see also* Households
**Family and Medical Leave Act** . . . . . . 172
**FAO.** *See* Food and Agriculture Organization
**Farms.** *See* Agriculture
**Fathom** (measurement). . . . . . . . . . . . 601
**Fats and oils**. . . . . . . . . . . . . 609, 610-11
Labels, nutrition. . . . . . . . . . . . . . . 612
Olestra approval (1996) . . . . . . . . . . 48
**FBI.** *See* Federal Bureau of Investigation
**FCC.** *See* Federal Communications Commission
**FDIC.** *See* Federal Deposit Insurance Corporation
**Federal agencies**
Budget receipts, outlays . . . . . . . 129-30
Civilian employment. . . . . . . . . . . . . 169
Directory . . . . . . . . . . . . . . . . . . . 188
Internet addresses . . . . . . . . . . . . . 210
*see also specific agencies*
**Federal Aviation Administration** . . 59, 129, 187, 188
**Federal Bureau of Investigation**
Chronology (1996)
"Filegate" investigation. . . . . . . . . . 58
Freemen group standoff. . . . . . . 51, 58
Olympic park bombing. . . . . . . . 61, 68
Weaver shootout . . . . . . . . . . . . . 68
Directors . . . . . . . . . . . . . . . . . . . 186
Expenditures. . . . . . . . . . . . . . . . . 129
Headquarters . . . . . . . . . . . . . 188, 684
**Federal Claims Court, U.S.** . . . . . . . . 192
**Federal Communications Commission** . . . . . . . . . . 188, 130
**Federal Deposit Insurance Corporation** . 188, 136, 130, 154, 169
**Federal government.** *See* Government, U.S.
**Federal Reserve System** . . . 188, 138, 154
Board actions (1996) . . . . . . . . . . . . 47
Discount rate . . . . . . . . . . . . . . . . 138
Formed (1913) . . . . . . . . . . . . . . . 502
**Federal taxes.** *See* Taxes, federal
**Federal Trade Commission** . 188, 130, 210
**Fencing** (sport) . . . . . . . . . . . . . . . . 851
**Fertility rate** . . . . . . . . . . . . . . . . . . 962
**Fiber,** Labels, nutrition. . . . . . . . . . . . 612
**Field hockey**. . . . . . . . . . . . . . . . . . 851
**Fiesta Bowl** (1996). . . . . . . . . 48, 849, 882
**Figure skating.** *See under* Skating
**Fiji**. . . . . . . . . . . . . . . 482, 592, 763, 846
**Fillmore, Millard** . . . . . . . . 109, 110, 532
*see also* Presidents, U.S.
**Films.** *See* Movies
**Finance.** *See* Banks; Business; Economics; Stocks
**Finland**. . . . . . . . . . . . . . . . . . . . . 764
Ambassadors, envoys . . . . . . . . . . . 846
Flag . . . . . . . . . . . . . . . . . . . . . . 482
Gross domestic product . . . . . . . . . . 134
Nuclear power. . . . . . . . . . . . . 238, 239
Trade. . . . . . . . . . . . . . . . . . . . . . 240
Wages, hourly. . . . . . . . . . . . . . . . 171
**Firearms**
Deaths involving . . . . . . . . . . . 968, 967
Gun control legislation (1993, 1994) . . 509
Gun gauge, caliber. . . . . . . . . . . . . . 604
*see also* Shooting (sport)
**Fires** . . . . . . . . . . . . . . . . . . . . . . 969
Chicago, IL (1871) . . . . . . . . . . 304, 501
Deaths. . . . . . . 168, 304-5, 967, 968, 969
Major. . . . . . . . . . . . . . . . . . . . . 304-5
Property damage, loss . . . . . . . . . . . 969
*see also* Arson
**First aid** . . . . . . . . . . . . . . . . . . . . 608
**First ladies** . . . . . . . . . . . . . . . . 210, 538
Clinton, Hillary Rodham . . . . . . . 538, 539
**Fish and fishing**
Commercial. . . . . . . . . . . . . . . . . . 164
Endangered species . . . . . . . . . . . . 230
Exports, imports. . . . . . . . . . . . . . . 241
Game fish records . . . . . . . . . . . 920-21
Nutritive food values . . . . . . . . . 609, 610
Venomous species . . . . . . . . . . . . . 232
*see also specific countries*
**Flags**
Confederacy . . . . . . . . . . . . . . . . . 523
United States. . . . . . . . . . . . . . . 525-27
Display . . . . . . . . . . . . . . . . . . 526-27
History . . . . . . . . . . . . . . . . . . 525-26
Pledge to . . . . . . . . . . . . . . . . . . 527
21-gun-salute to . . . . . . . . . . . . . 177
World (color) . . . . . . . . . . . . . . . 481-84
**Flaxseed production** . . . . . . . . . . . . 161
**Fleets, merchant** . . . . . . . . . . . . . 243-44
**Flights.** *See* Aviation
**Floods**
Characteristics. . . . . . . . . . . . . . . . 220
Johnstown (PA) (1889) . . . . . . . 303, 501
Mississippi River (1993) . . . . . . 303, 509
Worldwide. . . . . . . . . . . . . . . . . . . 303
**Florida** . . . . . . . . . . . . . . . . . . . . . 659
Accession (1819) . . . . . . . 499, 545, 659
Admission, area, capital. . . 542, 543, 659
Agriculture . . . . . . . . . . . . . . . . 156-61
Altitudes (high, low) . . . . . . . . . . . . 541
Birth, death statistics. . . . . . . . . . . . 963
Budget . . . . . . . . . . . . . . . . . . . . . 135
Coastline . . . . . . . . . . . . . . . . . . . 541
Congressional representation. . . . . . 111, 113-14, 380
Courts, U.S. . . . . . . . . . . . . . . . . . 191
Crime, prisons, death penalty . . . . . . 959, 960, 961
Energy consumption . . . . . . . . . . . . 237
Federally owned land . . . . . . . . . . . 545
Governor, state officials. . . . . . . 124, 126
Hazardous waste sites . . . . . . . . . . 228
Health insurance coverage. . . . . . . . 971
Immigrants admitted (1995) . . . . . . . 383
Indians, American. . . . . . . . . . . . . . 550
Interest laws, rates . . . . . . . . . . 721, 722
Marriage, divorce laws . . . . . . . 728, 729
Mineral production . . . . . . . . . . . . . 151
Motor vehicles . . . . . . . . . . . . . 245, 248
Name origin, nickname . . . . . . . 544, 659
Population. . . . . . . . . . . . . 380-81, 384
Cities, towns. . . . . . . 395-97, 689, 690, 691, 694, 695
Counties, county seats . . . . . . . . . 423
Port traffic. . . . . . . . . . . . . . . . . . . 242
Poverty rates. . . . . . . . . . . . . . . . . 388
Presidential elections . . . . 76, 80-81, 106
Schools and libraries. . . . . . . 252-53, 257
Taxes. . . . . . . . . . . . . . . . . . . . . . 245
Temperature, precipitation . . . . . 222, 224
Toxic chemical pollution. . . . . . . . . . 228
Unemployment benefits. . . . . . . . . . 165
Welfare assistance. . . . . . . . . . . . . 389
**Florida Citrus (Tangerine) Bowl** . . . . 883
**Fluid measures** . . . 600, 601, 602, 604, 605
**Folger Shakespeare Library** (DC). . . . 684
**Food** . . . . . . . . . . . . . . . . . . . . . 609-12
Exports, imports. . . . . . . . . . . . 163, 241
Federal assistance programs . . . . . . 158
Help organizations . . . . . . . . . . . . . 618
Internet addresses . . . . . . . . . . . . . 211
Labels, nutrition . . . . . . . . . . . . . . . 612
Nutritive values . . . . . . . . . . . . . 609-11
Dietary allowances . . . . . . . . . 609, 612
Olestra approval (1996). . . . . . . . . . . 48
Personal expenditures. . . . . . . . . . . 150
Price indexes. . . . . . . . . . . . . . 131, 132
Pure Food and Drug Act (1906) . . . . 502
**Food and Agriculture Organization** (UN). . . . . . . . . . . . . . . . . . . 845
**Food stamp program** . . . . . . . . . . . . 158
Expenditures . . . . . . . . . . . . . . . . . 129
**Football, Canadian**. . . . . . . . . . . . . . 880
**Football, college** . . . . . . . . . . . . . 881-88
Bowl games . . . . . . . . . . . . . . . 881-83
Coaches. . . . . . . . . . . 884-86, 887, 888
Conference champions . . . . . . . . . . 888
Heisman Trophy. . . . . . . . . . . . . . . 886
National champions . . . . . . . . . . 48, 887
Outland Award. . . . . . . . . . . . . . . . 886
Poll leaders, final standings (1995) . . 888
Teams, Division I . . . . . . . . . . . . 884-86
Winning percentage leaders. . . . . . . 887
**Football, pro** . . . . . . . . . . . . . . . . 869-79
Addresses, teams. . . . . . . . . . . . . . 904
All-pro team (1995). . . . . . . . . . . . . 879
All-time records . . . . . . . . . . . . . 878-79
Champions (1933-95) . . . . . . . . . 869-71
Coaching victories, all-time . . . . . . . 878
George Halas Trophy . . . . . . . . . . . 876
Hall of Fame . . . . . . . . . . . . . . . . . 877
Head coaches (1996) . . . . . . . . . . . 876
Jim Thorpe Trophy . . . . . . . . . . . . . 876
Player draft
First round selections (1996) . . . . . 877
Number one choice (1936-96) . . . . 877
Rookies of the Year (1964-1995) . . . . 876
Stadiums. . . . . . . . . . . . . . . . . . . . 879
Standings, final (1995) . . . . . . . . . . 869
Statistical leaders (1995) . . . . . . . 875-76
Statistical leaders (by years). . . . . 873-74
Super Bowl . . . . . 48, *784*, 849, 872, 879
**Force, measures of**. . . . . . . . . . . . . . 607
**Ford, Gerald R.** 105, 107, 109, 110, 537, 539
Presidential library . . . . . . . . . . . . 539
*see also* Presidents, U.S.
**Foreign investment**
By U.S. abroad. . . . . . . . . . . . . . . . 145
In U.S. companies. . . . . . . . . . . . . . 145
**Foreign trade.** *See* Exports, imports
**Foreign words, phrases** . . . . . . . . . . 638
**Forests,** Champion trees (U.S.) . . . . . . 234
**Forgery**. . . . . . . . . . . . . . . . . . . . . 961
**Formentera** . . . . . . . . . . . . . . . . . . 819
**Forms of address**. . . . . . . . . . . . . . . 641
**Formulas, mathematical** . . . . . . . . . . 607
**Fort Wayne, IN.** *See* Cities, U.S.
**Fort Worth, TX.** *See* Cities, U.S.
**Foster, Vincent** (1993, 1995, 1996) . . . 44, 59, 509, 510
**Four Freedoms** (1941). . . . . . . . . . . . 503
**Fractions-to-decimals reduction** . . . . 606
**France**. . . . . . . . . . . . . . . . . . . . 764-65
Ambassadors, envoys . . . . . . . . . . . 846
Chronology (1995-96) . . . . . . . . . 43, 48
Consumer price changes . . . . . . . . . 133
Departments, territories . . . . . . . . . . 765
Energy consumption . . . . . . . . . . . . 236
Flag . . . . . . . . . . . . . . . . . . . . . . 482
Gold reserves. . . . . . . . . . . . . . . . . 146
Gross domestic product . . . . . . . . . . 134
History . . . . . . . 561, 563, 564, 565, 567, 571, 575, 576
French and Indian War (1754-63) . . 497
French Revolution (1789) . . . . . . . 564
New World settlements (1699) . . . . 497
Merchant fleet . . . . . . . . . . . . . . . . 243
Military strength . . . . . . . . . . . . . . . 182
Motor vehicle production, exports 246, 242
Nuclear power . . . . . . . . . . . . . 238, 239
Rulers. . . . . . . . . . . . . 563, 564, 579-80
Trade . . . . . . . . . . . . . . . . . . . 240, 377
Unemployment rates . . . . . . . . . . . . 166
Wages, hourly . . . . . . . . . . . . . . . . 171
**Franchises**. . . . . . . . . . . . . . . . . . . 143
**Franconia, House of**. . . . . . . . . . . . . 581
**Franklin, Benjamin** (1732, 1752) . . 346, 497
**Freedom Statue** (U.S. Capitol) . . . . . . 684
**Freemen** (antitax group) (1996) . . . . 51, 58
**Freezing point, water** . . . . . . . . . . . 605
**Freight statistics**
Air cargo . . . . . . . . . . . . . . . . . . . 314
Merchant marine. . . . . . . . . . . . . 243-44
**Fremont, John C.** (1856) . . . . . . . . . . 500
**Fremont, CA** . . . . . . . . . . . 122, 387, 689
**French and Indian War** (1754-63) . . . . 497
**French Antarctica**. . . . . . . . . . . . . . . 765
**French Guiana** . . . . . . . . . . . . . . . . 765
**French Open** (tennis). . . . . . . . . . . . . 930
**French Polynesia** . . . . . . . . . . . . . . . 765
**French Revolution** (1789) . . . . . . . . . 564
**Fresno, CA.** *See* Cities, U.S.
**Friends, Society of** (Quakers). . . . 644, 645
**Fruits**
Exports, imports . . . . . . . . . . . . . . . 241
Nutritive values. . . . . . . . . . . . . 609, 610
Prices, farm . . . . . . . . . . . . . . . . . 162
Production. . . . . . . . . . . . . . . . . . . 161
**FTC.** *See* Federal Trade Commission
**Fuel.** *See* Energy; *specific kinds*
**Fulton, Robert** (1807) . . . . . . . . . . . . 499
**Futuna-Alofi Island**. . . . . . . . . . . . . . 765
**Futures** (stock) . . . . . . . . . . . . . 148, 155

— G—

**Gabon**. . . . . . . . . . . 240, 482, 765-66, 846
**Gadsden Purchase**. . . . . . . . . . . . . . 545
**Galapagos Islands** . . . . . . . . . . . 592, 760
**Gambia** . . . . . . . . . . . . . . . 482, 766, 846
**Gambier Islands**. . . . . . . . . . . . . . . . 765
**Gandhi, Indira** . . . . . . . 307, 346, 576, 774
**Gandhi, Mohandas**. 307, 346, 571, 572, 773
**GAO.** *See* General Accounting Office
**Garfield, James A.** . . . . . . . 107, 109, 533
Assassinated (1881) . . 307, 501, 533, 539
*see also* Presidents, U.S.
**Garland, TX** . . . . . . . . . . . . 122, 386, 689
**Gas, natural.** *See* Natural gas
**Gas appliance use** . . . . . . . . . . . . . . 237
**Gases**
Densities. . . . . . . . . . . . . . . . . . . . 605

Pollutant emmissions . . . . . . . . 228, 229
**Gasoline**
Arab embargo (1973) . . . . . . . . . . . 507
Automobile consumption . . . . . . . . . . 245
Prices, retail (1996) . . . . . . . . 53-54, 238
Taxes (by state) . . . . . . . . . . . . . . 245
**Gator Bowl** . . . . . . . . . . . . . . . . . 882
**GATT.** *See* General Agreement on Tariffs and Trade
**Gauge** (measure) . . . . . . . . . . . . . . . 604
**Gays.** *See* Homosexuality
**Gaza.** *See* Israel; Palestine
**GDP.** *See* Gross Domestic Product
**General Accounting Office** . . . . . 188, 169
**General Agreement on Tariffs and Trade** (1994) . . . . . . . . . . . . 241, 510, 573
*see also* World Trade Organization
**Generals, U.S.** . . . . . . . . . . . . . . . . 176
Address, form of . . . . . . . . . . . . . . 641
Insignia . . . . . . . . . . . . . . . . . . . 178
Pay scale . . . . . . . . . . . . . . . . . . 183
Personal salutes, honors . . . . . . . . . . 177
Women, first (1970) . . . . . . . . . . . . 506
**General Services Administration** . . . 188, 129, 169
**Geneva Conventions** . . . . . . . . . . . . 845
**Geodetic datum point** . . . . . . . . . . . 540
**Geographic mobility, U.S.** (1960-94) . . 387
**Geography** . . . . . . . . . . . . 540-45, 586-99
Geographic centers, U.S. . . . . . . . . . 543
International boundary lines, U.S. . . . 543
Superlative statistics, U.S. . . . . . . . . 540
**George Halas Trophy** . . . . . . . . . . . . 876
**George Washington Bridge** (NY-NJ) . . 702
**Georgia** . . . . . . . . . . . . . . . . . . 659-60
Admission, area, capital . . . . . . 542, 659
Agriculture . . . . . . . . . . . . . . . . 156-61
Altitudes (high, low) . . . . . . . . . . . . 541
Birth, death statistics . . . . . . . . . . . 963
Budget . . . . . . . . . . . . . . . . . . . . 135
Coastline . . . . . . . . . . . . . . . . . . . 541
Congressional representation . . . 111, 114, 380
Courts, U.S. . . . . . . . . . . . . . . . . . 191
Crime, prisons, death penalty . 959, 960, 961
Energy consumption . . . . . . . . . . . . 237
Federally owned land . . . . . . . . . . . 545
Governor, state officials . . . . . . 124, 126
Hazardous waste sites . . . . . . . . . . . 228
Health insurance coverage . . . . . . . . 971
Immigrants admitted (1995) . . . . . . . . 383
Indians, American . . . . . . . . . . . . . 550
Interest laws, rates . . . . . . . . . 721, 722
Marriage, divorce laws . . . . . . . 728, 729
Mineral production . . . . . . . . . . . . . 151
Motor vehicles . . . . . . . . . . . . 245, 248
Name origin, nickname . . . . . . . 544, 659
Population . . . . . . . . . . . . . . 380-81, 384
Cities, towns . . . . . . . 397-98, 686, 688
Counties, county seats . . . . . . . 423-24
Port traffic . . . . . . . . . . . . . . . . . 242
Poverty rates . . . . . . . . . . . . . . . . 388
Presidential elections . . . . 76, 81-82, 106
Schools and libraries . . . . . . 252-53, 257
Taxes . . . . . . . . . . . . . . . 245, 735, 736
Temperature, precipitation . . . . . 222, 224
Unemployment benefits . . . . . . . . . . 165
Welfare assistance . . . . . . . . . . . . . 389
**Georgia, Republic of** . . . . . . 43, 482, 491, 766-67, 846
**Germany** . . . . . . . . . . . . . . . . . 767-68
Ambassadors, envoys . . . . . . . . . . . 846
Consumer price changes . . . . . . . . . 133
Energy consumption . . . . . . . . . . . . 236
Flag . . . . . . . . . . . . . . . . . . . . . 482
Gold reserves . . . . . . . . . . . . . . . . 146
Gross domestic product . . . . . . . . . . 134
History . . . . . . . 559, 561, 564, 565, 566, 567, 571, 576
Munich Olympics (1972) . . . . . . . . 575
Reunification (1990) . . . . . . . . . . . 768
Third Reich (1945) . . . . 504, 571, 572, 581, 767
Weimar Republic . . . . . . . . . 570, 767
World War I (1917) . . . . . . . . 502, 569
Merchant fleet . . . . . . . . . . . . . . . . 243
Military strength . . . . . . . . . . . . . . 182
Motor vehicle production, exports 246, 242
Nuclear power . . . . . . . . . . . . 238, 239
Rulers . . . . . . . . . . . 559, 561, 581, 767
Trade . . . . . . . . . . . . . . . . . 240, 377
Unemployment rates . . . . . . . . . . . . 166
U.S. immigrants from . . . . . . . . 377, 383
Wages, hourly . . . . . . . . . . . . . . . . 171
*see also* Berlin, Germany
**Gestation** (animal) . . . . . . . . . . . . . . 231
**Gettysburg Address** (1863) . . . . 500, 523
**Ghana** . . . . . . . . . . . . . . . . . . . . . 768
Ambassadors, envoys . . . . . . . . . . . 846
Flag . . . . . . . . . . . . . . . . . . . . . 482
Gold production . . . . . . . . . . . . . . . 153
History . . . . . . . . . . . . . . . . . 558, 572
**GI Bill of Rights** (1944) . . . . . . . . . . . 504
**Gibraltar** . . . . . . . . . . . . . . . . . . . . 831
**Gingrich, Newt** (1995) . . . 38, 112, 206, 510
Budget stalemate (1995-96) . . . . . . 41-42
Ethics Committee investigation (1995-96) . . . . . . . . . . . . . . 44, 51
**Girl Scouts**
Address . . . . . . . . . . . . . . . . . . . 624
Founded (1912) . . . . . . . . . . . . . . . 502
**Glenn, John H., Jr.** (1962) . . . . . . 309, 505
**GNP.** *See* Gross National Product
**Gold**
Black Friday (1869) . . . . . . . . . . . . 501
Carats in pure . . . . . . . . . . . . . . . 604
Discovered, U.S. (1835, 1848) . . 499, 500
Production . . . . . . . . . . . 151, 152, 153
Reserves . . . . . . . . . . . . . . . 146, 151
**Golden Gate Bridge** (CA) . . . . . . . . . 702
**Golden Globe Awards** . . . . . . . . . . . 330
**Golf** . . . . . . . . . . . . . . . . . . 849, 922-24
**Good Friday** . . . . . . . . . . . . . . 480, 647
**Gorbachev, Mikhail** . . . . 575-76, 585, 812
Nobel Peace Prize . . . . . . . . . . . . . 319
Summit talks (1987) . . . . . 183, 508, 576
**Gore, Albert, Jr.** . . . . . . . . . 185, 207, 110
Campaign (1996) . . . . . . . . . . . . 64, *195*
**Gore, Tipper** (1996) . . . . . . . . . . . . *195*
**Government, U.S.**
Federal . . . . . . . . . . . . . . . . . . . 185-92
Agencies . . . . . . . . . . . . . . . 169, 188
Branches . . . . . . . . . . . . . . . . . . 185
Clinton administration . . . . . . . . 185-88
Elected officials profile . . . . . . . . . 377
Internet addresses . . . . . . . . . 210, 378
Publications catalog . . . . . . . . . . . 713
Revenue and expenditures . . . . 129-30
Shutdown (1995-96) . . . 38, 41-42, 44, 46, *196*, 510
Local . . . . . . . . . . . . . . . . . . . . 121-24
State . . . . . . . . . . . . . . . . . . . . 124-28
**Governors, state** . . . . . . . . . . . . . 124-28
Address, form of . . . . . . . . . . . . . . 641
First women (1924) . . . . . . . . . . . . 503
1996 election results . . . . . . . . . . . 125
**Grains**
Exports, imports . . . . . . . . . . . 163, 241
Nutritive value . . . . . . . . . . 609, 610-11
Prices, farm . . . . . . . . . . . . . . . . . 162
Production, U.S. . . . . . . . 160, 161, 163
Production, world (by country) . . . . . 163
Storage capacities . . . . . . . . . . . . . 162
**Grammy Awards** . . . . . . . . . . . . 333, *781*
**Grand Canyon** (AZ) . . . . . . 546, 555, 656
**Grand Coulee Dam** . . . . . . . . . . . . . 707
**Grand Rapids, MI** . . . . . . . . 122, 386, 689
**Grant, Ulysses S.** . . . . . . . 107, 109, 533
*see also* Presidents, U.S.
**Gravity**
Atmosphere, effect on . . . . . . . . . . . 458
Planets (relative) . . . . . . . . . . . . . . 455
**Great Barrier Reef** . . . . . . . . . . . . . 555
**Great Britain.** *See* United Kingdom
**Great Lakes** . . . . . . . . . . . . . . . . . . 598
Commercial fishing . . . . . . . . . . . . 164
**Great Seal of the U.S.** . . . . . . . . . . . 525
**Great Wall** . . . . . . . . . . . . . . . 554, 555
**Great White Fleet** (1907) . . . . . . . . . . 502
**Greece** . . . . . . . . . . . . . . . . . . . . . 769
Ambassadors, envoys . . . . . . . . . . . 846
Chronology (1996) . . . . . . . . . . . . . . 48
Flag . . . . . . . . . . . . . . . . . . . . . 482
History . . . . . . . . . . . . . . . . . 565, 575
Merchant fleet . . . . . . . . . . . . . . . . 243
Wages, hourly . . . . . . . . . . . . . . . . 171
**Greece, ancient**
City-states . . . . . . . . . . . . . . . . . . 552
Hellenistic Era . . . . . . . . . . . . 554, 556
Leading figures . . . . . . . . . . . . . . . 577
Measures . . . . . . . . . . . . . . . . . . . 605
Minoan civilization . . . . . . . . . . . . . 552
Philosophers . . . . . . . . . . . . . . . . . 552
Seven Wonders . . . . . . . . . . . . . . . 555
**Greek Orthodox Church.** *See* Eastern Orthodox churches
**Greenland** . . . . . . . . . . . . . 559, 592, 759
**Greensboro, NC** . . . . . . . . . 122, 386, 689
**Greenwich meridian** . . . . . . . . . 479, 484
**Greenwich sidereal time** (1997) . . . . . 450
**Gregorian calendar** . . . . . . . . . . . . . 475
**Grenada** . . . . . . . . . . . . . . . . . . . . 769
Ambassadors, envoys . . . . . . . . . . . 846
Flag . . . . . . . . . . . . . . . . . . . . . 482
Invasion (1983) . . . . . . . . . 508, 576, 769
**Grenadines.** *See* St. Vincent and the Grenadines
**Grey Cup** . . . . . . . . . . . . . . . . . . . 880
**Gross domestic product**
By country . . . . . . . . . . . . . . . . 737-837
Highest rates . . . . . . . . . . . . . . . . 134
Defined . . . . . . . . . . . . . . . . . . . . 154
U.S. (1995-96) . . . . . 40, 48, 63, 133, 134
**Gross national product, U.S.** . . . . . . 133
**Group of Seven (G-7)** (1996) . . . . 60, 842
**Guadalcanal** (1942) . . . . . . . 503, 572, 592
**Guadeloupe** . . . . . . . . . . . . . . . 592, 765
**Guam** . . . . . . . . . . . . . . . . . . . . . . 682
Accession (1898) . . . . . . . . . . . 501, 545
Altitudes (high, low) . . . . . . . . . . . . 541
Area . . . . . . . . . . . . . . . . 439, 545, 592
Congressional delegate . . . . . . . . . . 118
Courts, U.S. . . . . . . . . . . . . . . . . . 192
Immigrants admitted (1995) . . . . . . . 383
Population . . . . . . . . . . . . . . . . . . 439
Welfare assistance . . . . . . . . . . . . . 389
Zip codes . . . . . . . . . . . . . . . . . . 439
**Guangxi** . . . . . . . . . . . . . . . . . . . . 754
**Guatemala** . . . . . . . . . . . 482, 769-70, 846
**Guernsey** . . . . . . . . . . . . . . . . . . . 830
**Guiana, French** . . . . . . . . . . . . . . . 765
**Guinea, Republic of** . . . . . . 482, 770, 846
**Guinea-Bissau** . . . . . . . . . 482, 770-71, 846
**Gulf Coast,** Length . . . . . . . . . . . . . 541
**Gulfs** . . . . . . . . . . . . . . . . . . . . . . 593
**Gulf War.** *See* Persian Gulf War
**Guns.** *See* Firearms
**Guyana** . . . . . . . . . . . . . . . 482, 771, 846
**Gymnastics**
Olympic champions (1996) . . . . . *782*, 851
Rhythmic . . . . . . . . . . . . . . . . . . . 851

—H—

**Hagia Sophia Mosque** . . . . . . . . . . . 555
**Haiti** . . . . . . . . . . . . . . . . . . . 565, 771
Ambassadors, envoys . . . . . . . . . . . 846
Flag, map . . . . . . . . . . . . . . . 482, 488
Peacekeeping efforts (1995) . . . . 46, 510
Presidential election (1995) . . . . . . 45-46
U.S. occupation (1915, 1934) . . . 502, 503
**Halas Trophy** . . . . . . . . . . . . . . . . . 876
**Hale, Nathan** (1776) . . . . . . . . . . . . . 498
**Hale-Bopp Comet** . . . . . . . . . . . 440, 443
**Halicarnassus Mausoleum** . . . . . . . . 555
**Hall of Fame**
Aviation . . . . . . . . . . . . . . . . . . 314-15
Baseball . . . . . . . . . . . . . . . . . . . 950
Basketball . . . . . . . . . . . . . . . . . . 913
Bowling . . . . . . . . . . . . . . . . . . . . 900
Football, pro. . . . . . . . . . . . . . . . . 877
**Hambletonian** (horse race) . . . . . . . . . 900
**Hammer throw**
Olympic champions . . . . . . . . . 852, 856
World record . . . . . . . . . . . . . . . . 867
**Hammurabi** . . . . . . . . . . . . . . . . . . 551
**Handball** . . . . . . . . . . . . . . . . . . . 852
**Hanging Gardens of Babylon** . . . . . . 555
**Hanover, House of** . . . . . . . . . . . . . 578
**Hapsburg dynasty** . . . . . . . 561, 566, 581
**Harbors.** *See* Ports
**Harding, Warren G.** . 107, 109, 110, 535, 539
*see also* Presidents, U.S.
**Harness racing** . . . . . . . . . . . . . . . . 900
**Harrison, Benjamin** . . . . . . . 107, 109, 534
*see also* Presidents, U.S.
**Harrison, William Henry** . . . 109, 531, 539
*see also* Presidents, U.S.
**Hartford, CT** . . . . . . . . . . . . . . 122, 698
**Hart Memorial Trophy** . . . . . . . . . . . 896
**Harvest moon** . . . . . . . . . . . . . . . . 457
**Hawaii** . . . . . . . . . . . . . . . . . . . . . 660
Accession (1898) . . . . . . . . . . . 501, 545
Admission, area, capital 542, 543, 592, 660
Agriculture . . . . . . . . . . . . . . . . 156-61
Altitudes (high, low) . . . . . . . . . . . . 541
Birth, death statistics . . . . . . . . . . . 963
Budget . . . . . . . . . . . . . . . . . . . . 135
Coastline . . . . . . . . . . . . . . . . . . . 541
Commercial fishing . . . . . . . . . . . . 164
Congressional representation . . 111, 114, 380
Courts, U.S. . . . . . . . . . . . . . . . . . 191
Crime, prisons, death penalty . . . 959, 960
Energy consumption . . . . . . . . . . . . 237
Federally owned land . . . . . . . . . . . 545
Governor, state officials . . . . . . . 124, 126
Hazardous waste sites . . . . . . . . . . . 228
Health insurance coverage . . . . . . . . 971
Immigrants admitted (1995) . . . . . . . 383
Indians, American . . . . . . . . . . . . . 550
Interest laws, rates . . . . . . . . . 721, 722
Marriage, divorce laws . . . . . . . 728, 729
Motor vehicles . . . . . . . . . . . . 245, 248
Name origin, nickname . . . . . . . 544, 660
Population . . . . . . . . . . . . . . 380-81, 384
Cities, towns . . . . . . . . . . . . . 398, 689
Counties, county seats . . . . . . . . . 424
Port traffic . . . . . . . . . . . . . . . . . 242
Poverty rates . . . . . . . . . . . . . . . . 388
Presidential elections . . . . . . . 76, 82, 106
Schools and libraries . . . . . . 252-53, 257
Taxes . . . . . . . . . . . . . . . 245, 735, 736
Temperature, precipitation . . . . . 222, 224

Unemployment benefits . . . . . . . . . . 165
Volcanoes . . . . . . . . . . . . . . . . . . 589
Welfare assistance. . . . . . . . . . . . . 389
Wettest spot, U.S. . . . . . . . . . 222, 540
**Hayes, Rutherford B.** . . . . . 107, 109, 533
*see also* Presidents, U.S.
**Hay fever** . . . . . . . . . . . . . . . . . . . . 616
**Hay production** . . . . . . . . . 160, 161, 162
**Hazardous waste sites**. . . . . . . . . . . 228
**Health and Human Services, Department of** . . . . . . . . . . . . 187
Employees, payroll. . . . . . . . . . . . . 169
Expenditures. . . . . . . . . . . . . . . . . 129
Internet address . . . . . . . . . . . . . . 210
Secretaries. . . . . . . . . . . 185, 187, 205
Surgeon General . . . . . . . . . . 187, 188
*see also* Social Security Administration
**Health and medicine**
AIDS (1986, 1994, 1996). . . . 57, 62, 508, 840, 964, 975
Allergies, asthma. . . . . . . . . . . . . . 616
Alzheimer's disease. . . . . . . . . 615, 617
Anesthesia (1842) . . . . . . . . . . . . . 500
Black Death . . . . . . . . . . . . . . . . . 561
Cancer. . . . . . . . 228, 613, 614, 964, 974
Confidentiality ruling (1996) . . . . . . . . 39
Critical illness, state laws . . . . . . . . 615
Diabetes . . . . . . . . . . . 614-15, 618, 964
Doctor-office visits . . . . . . . . . . . . . 972
Doctors . . . . . . . . . . . . . . . . . . . . . 969
Drug abuse. . . . . . . . . . . . . . . . . . . 966
Emergency room visits . . . . . . . . . . 972
Expenditures. . . . . . . . . . . . . . . . . 970
First aid . . . . . . . . . . . . . . . . . . . . 608
Health maintenance organizations . . . 973
Heart, blood vessels. . . . . 615, 616, 618, 964, 974
Artificial implant (1982) . . . . . . . . 508
Rate targets. . . . . . . . . . . . . . . . 609
Help organizations. . . . . . . . . . . 617-19
High blood pressure . . . . . . . . . 616, 974
Immunization . . . . . . . . . . . . . . . . 613
Internet addresses . . . . . . . . . . . . . 211
Leave law impact. . . . . . . . . . . . . . 172
Legionnaires' disease (1976) . . . . . . 507
Life expectancy . . . . . . . . . . . . . . . 973
"Mad cow disease" (1996) . . . 52, 54, *778*
Medical discoveries . . . . . . . . . . 217-18
Nobel Prizes. . . . . . . . . . . . . . . 39, 318
Nursing school, first (1873) . . . . . . . 501
Occupational injuries, fatalities . . . . . 168
Patient characteristics (1987-94) . . . . 972
Personal expenditures . . . . . . . . . . 150
Price Indexes . . . . . . . . . . . . . 131, 132
Smoking risk reduction . . . . . . . . . . 613
Weight ranges. . . . . . . . . . . . . . . . 612
*see also* Deaths
**Health, Education, and Welfare, Department of** . . . . . . . . . . . . 205
*see also* Education, Department of; Health and Human Services, Department of
**Health insurance**
Coverage
Benefits portability (1996). . . . 38, 62-63
By state . . . . . . . . . . . . . . . . . . 971
Uninsured persons . . . . . . . . . . . 971
Disability benefits. . . . . . . . . . . 708-12
Medicare (1966) . . . . . . . . . . . 506, 710
Personal expenditures . . . . . . . . . . 150
Reform efforts (1993, 1994). . . . . . . 509
Taxes, federal . . . . . . . . . . . . . . . . 730
**Health maintenance organizations** . . . 973
**Heart disease** . . . . 615, 616, 618, 964, 974
**Heart rate** . . . . . . . . . . . . . . . . . . . . 609
**Heat index** . . . . . . . . . . . . . . . . . . . 227
**Hebrews.** *See* Judaism
**Hebrides** . . . . . . . . . . . . . . . . . 592, 830
**Height, weight ranges** . . . . . . . . . . . 612
**Heimlich maneuver** . . . . . . . . . . . . . 608
**Heisman Trophy** . . . . . . . . . . . . . . . 886
**Helgoland**. . . . . . . . . . . . . . . . . . . . 768
**Henry, Patrick** (1775) . . . . . . 346, 498, 511
**Heptathlon** . . . . . . . . . . . . 852, 858, 868
**Herzegovina.** *See* Bosnia and Herzegovina
**Hialeah, FL**. . . . . . . . . . . . 122, 386, 689
**Hieroglyphic writing** . . . . . . . . . . . . 552
**High blood pressure** . . . . . . . . . 616, 974
**High jump**
Olympic champions . . . . 852, 855-56, 858
World records . . . . . . . . . . . . . 867, 868
**High schools**
Computer, technology usage . . . . . . . 251
Drug abuse. . . . . . . . . . . . . . . . . . . 966
Enrollment . . . . . . . . . . . . . . . . . . 251
Graduates . . . . . . . . 251, 253, 254, 377
SAT, ACT scores. . . . . . . . . . . . 255-56
**Highways.** *See* Roads
**Hindenburg** (dirigible). . . . . . . . . 299, 316
**Hinduism** . . . . . . . . . . . . . . . . . . . . 654
Adherents, U.S. . . . . . . . . . . . . . . . 644
Population, world. . . . . . . . . . . . . . 646
**Hiroshima bombing** (1945) . . . . . 504, 572
**Hispanics**
AIDS incidence . . . . . . . . . . . . . . . 975
Business ownership . . . . . . . . . . . . 377
Cigarette use. . . . . . . . . . . . . . . . . 965
Education . . . . . . . . . . . . . . . . . . . 254
As elected officials . . . . . . . . . . . . . 377
Employment, unemployment . . . 167, 172
Health insurance coverage. . . . . . . . 971
Households. . . . . . . . . . . . . . . . . . 965
Population. . . . . . . . . . . . 377, 378, 379
Poverty rates. . . . . . . . . . . . . 172, 388
Salaries and wages . . . . . 167, 170, 172
**Hiss, Alger** (1948) . . . . . . . . . . . . . . 504
**Historic sites, national** . . . . . . . . . 547-48
**History**
Anniversaries . . . . . . . . . . . . . . . 72-73
Historians, notable past. . . . . . . . 342-43
Leading figures . . . . . . . . . . . . . 577-85
Parks, national. . . . . . . . . . . . . . 546-48
Pulitzer Prizes . . . . . . . . . . . . . . 324-25
U.S. . . . . . . . . . . . . . . . . . . . . 497-510
World. . . . . . . . . . . . . . . . . . . . 551-76
**Hitler, Adolf**. . . . . . . . . 346, 571, 581, 767
**HMOs.** *See* Health maintenance organizations
**Hockey, field** . . . . . . . . . . . . . . . . . 851
**Hockey, ice** . . . . . . . . . . . . . . . . 889-96
NCAA champions. . . . . . . . . . . . . . 896
NHL. . . . . . . . . . . . . . . . . . . . . 889-96
Addresses, teams . . . . . . . . . . . 903-4
All-time scorers. . . . . . . . . . . . . . 894
Individual leaders (1995-96) . . 890, 894
Individual scoring, by team (1995-96) . . . . . . . . . . . . . 890-93
Most goals in a season. . . . . . . . . 896
Stanley Cup . . . . . . . 60, *784*, 849, 889
Trophy winners. . . . . . . . . . . . 894-96
Olympic champions . . . . . . . . . . . . 864
**Hog production** . . . . . . . . . 156, 157, 162
**Holidays**
International, selected. . . . . . . . . . . 480
Legal, public (U.S.). . . . . . . . . . . . . 480
Flag display . . . . . . . . . . . . . . . . 526
Religious . . . . . . . . . . . . . . . . . 647-48
**Holland.** *See* Netherlands
**Holocaust Memorial Museum** . . . . . . 684
**Holy days** . . . . . . . . . . . . . . . . . 647-48
**Holy Roman Empire**. . . . . . . . . . . . . 559
**Home accident deaths** . . . . . . . . . . 968
**Homes.** *See* Housing
**Homestead Act** (1862) . . . . . . . . . . . 500
**Homosexuality**
Equal rights ruling (1996). . . . . . . . . . 39
Marriage sanction legislation (1996). 38, 66
Military conduct (1993) . . . . . . . . . . 509
**Honduras** . . . . . . . . . . . . . 482, 772, 846
**Honduras, British.** *See* Belize
**Hong Kong** . . . . . 171, 243, 377, 592, 831
**Honolulu, HI.** *See* Cities, U.S.
**Hoover, Herbert**. . . 105, 107, 109, 110, 535
*see also* Presidents, U.S.
**Hoover Dam** . . . . . . . . . . . . . . . 706, 707
**Horsepower** (measure) . . . . . . . . . . . 604
**Horse racing**
American thoroughbred. . . . . . . 897-900
Belmont Stakes . . . . . . . . . . . . . . . 898
Breeders' Cup . . . . . . . . . . . . . . . . 899
Eclipse awards . . . . . . . . . . . . 899-900
Horses of Year. . . . . . . . . . . . . . . . 900
Jockey, annual leading . . . . . . . . . . 898
Kentucky Derby . . . . . . . . . . . . . . . 897
Preakness. . . . . . . . . . . . . . . . . 897-98
Triple Crown winners . . . . . . . . . . . 897
Trotting, pacing . . . . . . . . . . . . . . . 900
*see also* Equestrian sports
**Household furnishings**
Appliances in use. . . . . . . . . . . . . . 237
Consumer electronics products. . . . . 293
Personal expenditures. . . . . . . . . . . 150
Price index . . . . . . . . . . . . . . . . . . 132
**Households**
Composition of. . . . . . . . . . . . . 377, 378
Median income . . . . . . . . . . . . . . . 377
Population (by type) . . . . . . . . . . . . 379
Poverty rates, levels . . . . . 377, 387, 388
Single-parent. . . . . 172, 377, 378, 388, 965
Single-person . . . . . . . . . 377, 378, 379
**House of Representatives.** *See* Congress, U.S.
**Housing**
Mortgages. . . . . . . . . . . . . . . . 727, 731
Personal expenditures. . . . . . . . . . . 150
Price Indexes . . . . . . . . . . . . . 131, 132
Prices. . . . . . . . . . . . . . . . . . . . . . 726
Tax deductions . . . . . . . . . . . . . . . 731
**Housing and Urban Development, Department of** . . . . . . . . . . . . 187
Employees, payroll . . . . . . . . . . . . . 169
Expenditures . . . . . . . . . . . . . . . . . 129
Internet address. . . . . . . . . . . . . . . 210
Secretaries . . . . . . . . . . . 185, 187, 205
**Houston, TX**
**Howland Island** . . . . . . . . . . . . . . . . 683
**Hubble Space Telescope** (1993) . . 311, 509
**HUD.** *See* Housing and Urban Development, Department of
**Hudson, Henry** (1609) . . . . . . . . . 497, 586
**Hudson Bay**. . . . . . . . . . . . . . . . . . . 593
**Hudson River**. . . . . . . . . . . . . . . . . . 596
**Humanitarians, notable**. . . . . . . . . . . 350
**Hundred Years' War** (1337-1453) . . . . 561
**Hungary** . . . . . . . . . . . . . . . . . . . . . 772
Ambassadors, envoys . . . . . . . . . . . 846
Flag . . . . . . . . . . . . . . . . . . . . . . . 482
History . . . . . . . . . . 559, 561, 562, 569, 570, 571, 573, 576
Nuclear power . . . . . . . . . . . . . 238, 239
Rulers. . . . . . . . . . . . . . . . . . . . . . 581
**Hunter's moon** . . . . . . . . . . . . . . . . 457
**Huntington Beach, CA.** *See* Cities, U.S.
**Huon Islands** . . . . . . . . . . . . . . . . . 765
**Huron, Lake**. . . . . . . . . . . . . . . . . . . 598
**Hurricanes**. . . . . . . . . . . . . . . . . . . 302
Characteristics . . . . . . . . . . . . . . . 220
Classifications . . . . . . . . . . . . . . . . 225
Names of (1997). . . . . . . . . . . . . . . 226
1996 storm damage . . . . . . . . . . . . . 67
Notable . . . . . . . . . . . . . . . . . . . . 302
**Hussein, Saddam** . . . . . . . . . . . . . . 776
**Hyakutake** (comet) . . . . . . . *199*, 440, 443
**Hydroelectric plants** . . . . . . . . . 235, 706
**Hydrogen bomb** (1950, 1952) . . . . 504, 573
*see also* Nuclear arms
**Hypertension** . . . . . . . . . . . . . . 616, 974

— I —

**IAEA.** *See* International Atomic Energy Agency
**Ibiza** . . . . . . . . . . . . . . . . . . . . . . . 819
**ICAO.** *See* International Civil Aviation Organization
**ICC.** *See* Interstate Commerce Commission
**Ice hockey.** *See* Hockey, ice
**Iceland** . . . . . 134, 482, 559, 592, 773, 846
**Ice skating.** *See* Skating
**IDA.** *See* International Development Association
**Idaho**. . . . . . . . . . . . . . . . . . . . . 660-61
Admission, area, capital . . . 542, 543, 660
Agriculture. . . . . . . . . . . . . . . . 156-61
Altitudes (high, low). . . . . . . . . . . . 541
Birth, death statistics . . . . . . . . . . . 963
Budget . . . . . . . . . . . . . . . . . . . . . 135
Congressional representation . . 111, 114, 380
Courts, U.S. . . . . . . . . . . . . . . . . . 191
Crime, prisons, death penalty. . 959, 960, 961
Energy consumption . . . . . . . . . . . . 237
Federally owned land. . . . . . . . . . . . 545
Governor, state officials . . . . . . . 124, 126
Hazardous waste sites. . . . . . . . . . . 228
Health insurance coverage . . . . . . . . 971
Immigrants admitted (1995) . . . . . . . 383
Indians, American . . . . . . . . . . . . . . 550
Interest laws, rates . . . . . . . . . . 721, 722
Marriage, divorce laws. . . . . . . . 728, 729
Motor vehicles . . . . . . . . . . . . . 245, 248
Name origin, nickname . . . . . . . 544, 660
Population . . . . . . . . . . . . . 380-81, 384
Cities, towns . . . . . . . . . . . . . . . . 398
Counties, county seats . . . . . . . . . 424
Poverty rates . . . . . . . . . . . . . . . . . 388
Presidential elections. . . . . 76, 82-83, 106
Schools and libraries . . . . . . . 252-53, 257
Taxes . . . . . . . . . . . . . . . . . . . 245, 735
Temperature, precipitation . . . . . 222, 224
Unemployment benefits . . . . . . . . . . 165
Welfare assistance . . . . . . . . . . . . . 389
**Idioms**. . . . . . . . . . . . . . . . . . . . . . . 640
**Iditarod sled race** . . . . . . . . . . . . . . . 936
**IFC.** *See* International Finance Corporation
**Illinois**. . . . . . . . . . . . . . . . . . . . . . . 661
Admission, area, capital . . . 542, 543, 661
Agriculture. . . . . . . . . . . . . . . . 156-61
Altitudes (high, low). . . . . . . . . . . . 541
Birth, death statistics . . . . . . . . . . . 963
Budget . . . . . . . . . . . . . . . . . . . . . 135
Congressional representation . . 114, 111, 380
Courts, U.S. . . . . . . . . . . . . . . . . . 191
Crime, prisons, death penalty . . 959, 960, 961
Energy consumption . . . . . . . . . . . . 237
Federally owned land. . . . . . . . . . . . 545
Governor, state officials . . . . . . . 124, 126
Hazardous waste sites. . . . . . . . . . . 228
Health insurance coverage . . . . . . . . 971
Immigrants admitted (1995) . . . . . . . 383
Indians, American . . . . . . . . . . . . . . 550
Interest laws, rates . . . . . . . . . . 721, 722
Marriage, divorce laws. . . . . . . . 728, 729

Motor vehicles 245, 248
Name origin, nickname 544, 661
Population 380-81, 384
Cities, towns 398-99, 687
Counties, county seats 424-25
Port traffic 242
Poverty rates 388
Presidential elections 76, 83, 106
Schools and libraries 252-53, 257
Taxes 245, 735
Temperature, precipitation 222, 224
Toxic chemical pollution 228
Unemployment benefits 165
Welfare assistance 389
**ILO.** *See* International Labor Organization
**IMF.** *See* International Monetary Fund
**Immigration and Naturalization Act** (1952) 504
**Immigration, emigration**
Ellis Island (1892) 501, 529
Illegal aliens amnesty (1988) 508
Immigrants admitted
Country of origin 377, 383
Intended residence area 383
Naturalization 841
Quota system (1921, 1965) 502, 506
Rates of 377
Regulations, U.S. 840-41
**Immunization schedule** 613
**IMO.** *See* International Maritime Organization
**Impeachment** 515, 517
Johnson, Andrew (1868) 501, 533
Nixon hearings (1974) 507, 536
**Imports.** *See* Exports, imports
**Incomes**
Disposable, defined 154
Distribution 389
Farm 159
Mean amounts received 389
Median household 377
Minimum wage
Enacted (1938) 503
Hourly rates (1950-96) 170
Increase (1996) 38, 56, 63
National, U.S. 133, 147
Pay differentials 167
Per capita income
Defined 155
By foreign countries 737-837
By U.S. states 655-80
Personal, U.S. 133
Distribution of total 147
Poverty levels 377, 387
Wage, salary workers 170, 173
Welfare assistance, by states 389
**Income taxes** 730-36
Federal 730-34
Amendment authorizing 521
Audits 734
Children 730, 731
Deductions 730-31, 732-33
Earned income credit 734
Estimated 731
Filing, forms 734
Health insurance 730
Household employees 731
Individual rates (1996) 730, 732-33
Paycheck withholding (1943) 504
Recent changes, developments 730-31
Reform Law (1986) 508
Retirement plan withdrawals 730
Revenues 129
Social Security 708, 731, 734
Taxpayers' rights 734
State 735-36
**Incubation** (animal) 231
**Index numbers**
Consumer prices 131, 132
Economic indicators 133, 155
Heat 227
Ultraviolet 227
**India** 773-74
Ambassadors, envoys 846
Chronology (1996) 57, 59
Cities (largest) 838
Commercial fishing 164
Energy production, consumption 236
Flag, map 482, 492
Gross domestic product 134
History 552, 556, 560, 561, 564-65, 566, 567, 569, 571, 572, 575
Merchant fleet 243
Military strength 182
Motor vehicle production 246
Nuclear power 239, 238
Population 838
Trade 240
**Indiana** 661-62
Admission, area, capital 542, 543, 661, 662
Agriculture 156-61
Altitudes (high, low) 541
Birth, death statistics 963
Budget 135
Congressional representation 111, 114, 380
Courts, U.S. 191
Crime, prisons, death penalty 959, 960, 961
Energy consumption 237
Federally owned land 545
Governor, state officials 124, 126
Hazardous waste sites 228
Health insurance coverage 971
Immigrants admitted (1995) 383
Indians, American 550
Interest laws, rates 721, 722
Marriage, divorce laws 728, 729
Motor vehicles 245, 248
Name origin, nickname 544, 661
Population 380-81, 384
Cities, towns 399-400, 688, 689
Counties, county seats 425
Port traffic 242
Poverty rates 388
Presidential elections 76, 83-84, 106
Schools and libraries 252-53, 257
Taxes 245, 735
Temperature, precipitation 222, 224
Unemployment benefits 165
Welfare assistance 389
**Indianapolis, IN.** *See* Cities, U.S.
**Indianapolis 500** (auto race) 930
**Indian Ocean** 593
Commercial fishing 164
Islands, areas 592
**Indians, American**
AIDS incidence 975
Cigarette use 965
Custer's last stand (1876) 501
As elected officials 377
Geronimo surrender (1886) 501
Gold discovered (1835) 499
Population 377, 378, 550
Reservations, trust lands 550
Sacagawea (1804) 499
Sand Creek Massacre (1864) 500
Seminole War (1835) 499
Tribes 550
U.S. citizenship (1924) 503
Wounded Knee, Battle of (1890) 501
**Individual Retirement Accounts** 154, 733
**Indochina.** *See* Cambodia; Laos; Vietnam
**Indochina War** (1953) 504, 573
**Indonesia** 774
Ambassadors, envoys 846
Commercial fishing 164
East Timor issue 39, 69
Flag, maps 482, 493, 496
Gross domestic product 134
Merchant fleet 243
Military strength 182
Trade 240
Volcanoes 588, 589
**Industrialists, notable** 340-41
**Industrial Revolution** 564, 566
**Industries, U.S.**
Advertising expenditures 297
Business directory 714-19
Corporate tax rates 144
Employees 166, 170
Mineral production 151-53
National income by 147
Occupational injuries, fatalities 168
Profits 143
Toxic releases 228
*see also* Business; *specific types*
**Infant mortality** 962, 963, 964
**Information superhighway.** *See* Internet
**Injuries**
Accidental 967, 968
Cost of unintentional 968
Fire-related 969
Occupational
Fatalities 168
By industry, type 168
**Inner Mongolia** 754
**Insects, venomous** 232
**Insignia, military** 178
**Insurance**
Bank deposits 136
Life 970
Medical 150, 712, 730, 971
Coverage portability (1996) 38, 62-63
Medicare (1966) 506, 710
Reform efforts (1993, 1994) 509
Social Security 708-12
Unemployment 165, 167
**Interest**
Compound, table of 605
Discount rate 138
Laws, rates 721, 722
Tax deductions 731
**Interior, Department of the** 186
Employees, payroll 169
Expenditures 129
Internet address 210
Secretaries 185, 186, 204
**Internal Revenue Service** 186, 188
Audits 734
Expenditures 129
Internet address 730
*see also* Income taxes
**International Atomic Energy Agency** 845
**International Bank for Reconstruction and Development** 845
**International boundary lines, U.S.** 543
**International Civil Aviation Organization** 845
**International Court of Justice** 845
**International Criminal Police Organization** 842
**International Date Line** 479, 484
**International Development Association** 845
**International Finance Corporation** 845
**International Fund for Agricultural Development** 845
**International Labor Organization** 845
**International Maritime Organization** 845
**International Monetary Fund** 845
**International organizations** 842-45
**International postage** 635-36
**International System** (measurement) 600
**International Telecommunication Union** 845
**Internet** 207-11
Abbreviations, lingo 210
Accessing, searching 207, 208
Glossary of terms 209
Intranet 208, 211
Online services, commercial 207, 210
Resources available 207-8
Security 208
Site addresses 210-11
Cities, U.S. 686-95
Government, U.S. 210, 378
Internal Revenue Service 730
Presidential libraries 539
Sports organizations 903-4
States, U.S. 655-81
Television, cable networks 294
**Interpol.** *See* International Criminal Police Organization
**Interstate Commerce Commission** 38, 130
**Intolerable Acts** (1774) 498
**Intranet** 208, 209, 211
**Inventions** 215-17
Awards 329
**Investment**
Foreign
By U.S. companies 145
In U.S. companies 145
Glossary of terms 154-55
*see also* Business; Stocks
**Iowa** 662
Admission, area, capital 542, 543, 662
Agriculture 156-61
Altitudes (high, low) 541
Birth, death statistics 963
Budget 135
Congressional representation 111, 114, 380
Courts, U.S. 191
Crime, prisons, death penalty 959, 960
Energy consumption 237
Federally owned land 545
Governor, state officials 124, 126
Hazardous waste sites 228
Health insurance coverage 971
Immigrants admitted (1995) 383
Indians, American 550
Interest laws, rates 721, 722
Marriage, divorce laws 728, 729
Motor vehicles 245, 248
Name origin, nickname 544, 662
Population 380-81, 384
Cities, towns 400, 688
Counties, county seats 425-26
Poverty rates 388
Presidential elections 76, 84-85, 106
Schools and libraries 252-53, 257
Taxes 245, 735, 736
Temperature, precipitation 222, 224
Unemployment benefits 165
Welfare assistance 389
**IRA.** *See* Individual Retirement Accounts
**Iran**
775, 846
Chronology (1996) 64-65
Energy production 236
Flag, map 482, 492
Gross domestic product 134
Merchant fleet 243
Military strength 182

Nuclear power. . . . . . . . . . . . . . . . . . 239
Persia . . . . . . . . 554, 557, 560, 561, 570
Revolution (1979-80) . . . . . . . . 575, 775
Terrorism, international . . . . . . . . . . . 576
U.S. embassy seizure (1979, 1980, 1981) . . . . . . . . . . . 507, 775
**Iran-contra affair** (1986, 1987, 1989, 1991) . . . . . . . . . . . 508, 509
**Iran-Iraq War** (1980-88) . . . . . . . 576, 775
**Iraq** . . . . . . . . . . . . . . . . . . 775-76, 846
Chronology (1996)
Hussein family murders . . . . . . . . . 50
Kurdish incursion . . . . . . . . . 65, 66-67
Oil-export agreement. . . . . . . . . . . 57
Flag, map. . . . . . . . . . . . . . . 482, 492
Gulf War (1991). . . 509, 776, 790-91, 815
Kuwait invasion (1990) 509, 776, 790, 815
Military strength. . . . . . . . . . . . . . . 182
Refugees from . . . . . . . . . . . . . . . . 840
**Ireland, Northern**. . . . . . . . . . . . . . . 830
Area . . . . . . . . . . . . . . . . . . . . . . . 592
Chronology (1995-96). . . . . 43, 48, 49-50, 52, 59
History. . . . . . . . . . . . . . . . . . . . . 575
Map . . . . . . . . . . . . . . . . . . . . . . 490
**Ireland, Republic of**. . . . . . . . . . 776, 785
Ambassadors, envoys . . . . . . . . . . . 846
Area . . . . . . . . . . . . . . . . . . . . . . . 592
Chronology (1995-96). . . . . . . . . . . . 43
Flag, map. . . . . . . . . . . . . . . . 482, 490
Gross domestic product . . . . . . . . . 134
History. . . . . . . . . . . . . . . . . . 558, 569
Wages, hourly. . . . . . . . . . . . . . . . 171
**Iron** (dietary) . . . . . . . . . . 609, 610-11, 612
**Iron** (metal)
Exports, imports . . . . . . . . . . . . . . 241
Production . . . . . . . . . . . . 151, 152, 153
Reserve base, world. . . . . . . . . . . . 151
**IRS.** *See* Internal Revenue Service
**Islam** . . . . . . . . . . . . . . . . . . . . . . . 654
Address, U.S. headquarters. . . . . . . . 645
Adherents, U.S. . . . . . . . . . . . . . . 644
History. . . . . . . . . . . 557, 558, 560, 575
Holy days . . . . . . . . . . . . . . . . . . . 647
Population, world . . . . . . . . . . . . . . 646
**Islamic Jihad** (1995). . . . . . . . . . . . . . 40
**Islands**
Area, ownership . . . . . . . . . . . . . . 592
*see also specific islands*
**Isle of Man** . . . . . . . . . . . . . 243, 592, 830
**Isle of Pines** . . . . . . . . . . . . . . . . . . 765
**Isle of Skye**. . . . . . . . . . . . . . . . 592, 830
**Israel** . . . . . . . . . . . . . . . . . . . . 785-86
Ambassadors, envoys . . . . . . . . . . . 846
Chronology (1995-96)
Netanyahu election . . . . . . 57, 59, *778*
Palestine settlement expansion . . . . 65
Palestinian clashes . . . . . . . . . 67, 69
Palestinian self-rule. . . 45, 47-48, 55, 786
Rabin assassination . . 42-43, 52, 75, 307
Retaliatory actions . . . . . . . . 54, 56-57
Suicide bombings . . . . 50, 52, 306, *778*
Summit. . . . . . . . . . . . . . . . . . . . 69
Flag, map. . . . . . . . . . . . . . . 482, 492
Formed (1948) . . . . . . . . . . . . . . . 572
Gross domestic product . . . . . . . . . 134
Jordanian peace treaty (1994) . . 786, 788
Military strength. . . . . . . . . . . . . . . 182
Palestinian militancy, uprisings. . . 33, 575, 576, 785
Wages, hourly. . . . . . . . . . . . . . . . 171
**Israeli-Arab wars.** *See* Arab-Israeli conflict
**Italy** . . . . . . . . . . . . . . . . . . . . . . . 786
Ambassadors, envoys . . . . . . . . . . . 846
Chronology (1995-96). . . . . . . 43, 54, 57
Consumer price changes . . . . . . . . . 133
Energy consumption. . . . . . . . . . . . 236
Flag . . . . . . . . . . . . . . . . . . . . . . 482
Gold reserves . . . . . . . . . . . . . . . . 146
Gross domestic product . . . . . . . . . 134
History. . . . . . . . 561, 566, 570, 571, 576
Merchant fleet . . . . . . . . . . . . . . . . 243
Military strength. . . . . . . . . . . . . . . 182
Motor vehicle production, exports 246, 242
Rulers . . . . . . . . . . . . . . . . . . . 583-84
Trade. . . . . . . . . . . . . . . . . . . . . . 240
Unemployment rates . . . . . . . . . . . 166
Wages, hourly. . . . . . . . . . . . . . . . 171
**ITU.** *See* International Telecommunication Union
**Ivory Coast.** *See* Cote d'Ivoire
**Iwo Jima**
Area . . . . . . . . . . . . . . . . . . . . . . 592
Battle (1945). . . . . . . . . . . . . . 504, 572
Memorial (statue). . . . . . . . . . . . . . 685

—J—

**Jackson, Andrew** . . . . . . . . . . . 109, 531
*see also* Presidents, U.S.
**Jackson, MS.** *See* Cities, U.S.
**Jacksonville, FL.** *See* Cities, U.S.
**Jamaica** . . . . . . . . . . . . . . . . . . . 786-87
Ambassadors, envoys. . . . . . . . . . . 846
Area. . . . . . . . . . . . . . . . . . . . . . 592
Flag . . . . . . . . . . . . . . . . . . . . . . 482
U.S. immigrants from . . . . . . . . 377, 383
**Japan** . . . . . . . . . . . . . . . . . . . . 787-88
Ambassadors, envoys. . . . . . . . . . . 846
Automobile production, exports. . . . 244, 246, 242
Chronology (1996) . . . . . . . . . . . 47, 54
Cities (largest) . . . . . . . . . . . . . . . 838
Commercial fishing . . . . . . . . . . . . 164
Consumer price changes . . . . . . . . . 133
Elections. . . . . . . . . . . . . . . . . . . . 69
Energy consumption . . . . . . . . . . . 236
Flag, map . . . . . . . . . . . . . . . 482, 493
Gold reserves . . . . . . . . . . . . . . . 146
Gross domestic product. . . . . . . . . . 134
History . . . . . 558-59, 562, 563, 566, 567, 568, 571, 576, 579
Peace treaty, U.S. (1951) . . . . 504, 787
Perry treaty (1853) . . . . . . . . . . . 500
World War II (1941-45). . . . 503-4, 572
Islands, areas . . . . . . . . . . . . . . . 592
Merchant fleet . . . . . . . . . . . . . . . 243
Military strength . . . . . . . . . . . . . . 182
Nuclear power. . . . . . . . . . . . . 238, 239
Trade. . . . . . . . . . . . . . . . . . . 240, 377
Unemployment rates. . . . . . . . . . . . 166
Wages, hourly . . . . . . . . . . . . . . . 171
**Japan, Sea of** . . . . . . . . . . . . . . . . . 593
**Jarvis Island** . . . . . . . . . . . . . . . . . 683
**Java** . . . . . . . . . . . . . . . . . . . . 592, 774
**Javelin throw**
Olympic champions . . . . . 852, 856, 858
World records . . . . . . . . . . . . . 867, 868
**Jazz artists, notable**. . . . . . . . . . . 358-59
**Jefferson, Thomas**. . . . 109, 110, 530, 539
Declaration of Independence . . . . . . 512
*see also* Presidents, U.S.
**Jefferson Memorial** (DC). . . . . . . . . . 684
**Jehovah's Witnesses** . . . 644, 645, 652-53
**Jersey, Isle of** . . . . . . . . . . . . . 592, 830
**Jersey City, NJ.** *See* Cities, U.S.
**Jerusalem**. . . . . . . . . . . . . . . . . 554, 785
**Jesuits** . . . . . . . . . . . . . . . . . . . . . 562
**Jesus Christ** . . . . . . . . . . . . . . . . . . 557
**Jewell, Richard** (1996) . . . . . . . . . . 61, 68
**Jewelry**
Birthstones . . . . . . . . . . . . . . . . . 727
Carat weight, gold . . . . . . . . . . . . 604
Wedding anniversaries . . . . . . . . . . 727
**Jewish people.** *See* Judaism
**Jim Thorpe Trophy** . . . . . . . . . . . . . 876
**Jobs.** *See* Employment
**Jockeys, leading** . . . . . . . . . . . . . . . 898
**John Paul II, Pope** . . . . . . . . . . . 649, 833
Assassination attempts (1981, 1982) . 308
**Johnson, Andrew** . . 107, 109, 110, 532-33
Impeachment (1868). . . . . . . . . . . . 501
*see also* Presidents, U.S.
**Johnson, Lyndon B.** 105, 107, 109, 110, 536
*see also* Presidents, U.S.
**Johnston Atoll**. . . . . . . . . . . . . . 439, 683
**Johnstown (PA) flood** (1889). . . . . . . 501
**Joint Chiefs of Staff**
Chairmen . . . . . . . . . . . . 176, 183, 186
Personal salutes, honors . . . . . . . . . 177
**Jordan** . . . . . . . . . . . . . . . . . . . . . 788
Ambassadors, envoys. . . . . . . . . . . 846
Flag, map . . . . . . . . . . . . . . . 482, 492
Israeli peace treaty (1994) . . . . . 786, 788
**Joule** (electrical unit) . . . . . . . . . . . . 604
**Journalism awards** . . . . . . . . . 319-23, 328
*see also* Magazines; Newspapers
**Judaism** . . . . . . . . . . . . . . . . . . . . 654
Addresses, U.S. headquarters . . . . . 646
Ancient Hebrews . . . . . . . 552, 554, 605
Clergy, form of address . . . . . . . . . 641
Holy days . . . . . . . . . . . . . . . . . . 648
Population, U.S., world . . . . . . . 644, 646
**Judiciary, U.S.**
Address, forms of. . . . . . . . . . . . . 641
Court addresses, judges . . . . . . . 189-92
Employment, payroll . . . . . . . . . . . 169
Expenditures . . . . . . . . . . . . . . . . 129
Salaries . . . . . . . . . . . . . 189, 190, 192
*see also* Supreme Court, U.S.
**Judo** . . . . . . . . . . . . . . . . . . . . . . 851
**Julian calendar** . . . . . . . . . . . . . . . 475
**Julian Period**. . . . . . . . . . . . . . . . . 478
**Junior colleges** . . . . . . . . . . . . . 272-82
**Jupiter** (planet). . . . . . . . . . . . 446-47, 455
Morning, evening stars . . . . . . . . . 449
Position by month. . . . . . . . . . . 440-43
Rises, sets . . . . . . . . . . . . . . . . . 453
Sun, distance from . . . . . . . . . . 455, 444
**Justice, Department of**. . . . . . . . . . . 186
Attorneys general. . . . . . . 185, 186, 203
First woman (1993) . . . . . . . . . . . 509
Employees, payroll . . . . . . . . . . . . 169
Expenditures . . . . . . . . . . . . . . . . 129
Internet address . . . . . . . . . . . . . . 210

—K—

**Kaczynski, Theodore** (1996) . . 33, 53, 59, *197*, 961
**Kampuchea.** *See* Cambodia
**Kansas** . . . . . . . . . . . . . . . . . . . 662-63
Admission, area, capital . . . . . 542, 543, 662, 663
Agriculture . . . . . . . . . . . . . . . . 156-61
Altitudes (high, low). . . . . . . . . . . . 541
Birth, death statistics . . . . . . . . . . . 963
Budget . . . . . . . . . . . . . . . . . . . . 135
Congressional representation . . 111, 114, 380
Courts, U.S. . . . . . . . . . . . . . . . . 191
Crime, prisons, death penalty . . . 959, 960
Energy consumption . . . . . . . . . . . 237
Federally owned land. . . . . . . . . . . 545
Governor, state officials . . . . . . . 124, 126
Hazardous waste sites. . . . . . . . . . . 228
Health insurance coverage . . . . . . . . 971
Immigrants admitted (1995) . . . . . . . 383
Indians, American . . . . . . . . . . . . . 550
Interest laws, rates . . . . . . . . . . 721, 722
Marriage, divorce laws. . . . . . . . 728, 729
Motor vehicles . . . . . . . . . . . . 245, 248
Name origin, nickname . . . . . . . 544, 662
Population . . . . . . . . . . . . . . 380-81, 384
Cities, towns . . . . . . . . . 400-401, 695
Counties, county seats . . . . . . . . . 426
Poverty rates . . . . . . . . . . . . . . . . 388
Presidential elections. . . . . 76, 85-86, 106
Schools and libraries . . . . . . 252-53, 257
Taxes . . . . . . . . . . . . . . . 245, 735, 736
Temperatures, record . . . . . . . . . . . 224
Unemployment benefits . . . . . . . . . . 165
Welfare assistance . . . . . . . . . . . . . 389
**Kansas City, MO.** *See* Cities, U.S.
**Kansas-Nebraska Act** (1854) . . . . . . . 500
**Kashmir** . . . . . . . . . . . . . . . . . . . . 774
**Kayaking** . . . . . . . . . . . . . . . . . . . . 850
**Kazakstan** . . . . . . 239, 482, 491, 788, 846
**Kellogg-Briand Pact** (1928) . . . . . . . . 570
**Kemp, Jack** (1996) . . . . . . . . . . . . 63, *194*
**Kennedy, John F.** . 105, 107, 109, 110, 536
Assassination (1963) . . 307, 505, 536, 539
Warren Commission (1964) . . . . . . 505
Auction . . . . . . . . . . . . . . . . . . . . 55
*see also* Presidents, U.S.
**Kennedy, John F., Center for the Performing Arts** (DC) . . . . . . . . 684
**Kennedy, John F., Jr.** (1996) . . . . . 55, 67
**Kennedy, Robert F.**
Assassinated (1968) . . . . . . . . . 307, 506
Burial site . . . . . . . . . . . . . . . . . . 685
**Kentucky**. . . . . . . . . . . . . . . . . . . . 663
Admission, area, capital. . . . . . . 542, 663
Agriculture. . . . . . . . . . . . . . . . 156-61
Altitudes (high, low). . . . . . . . . . . . 541
Birth, death statistics . . . . . . . . . . . 963
Budget . . . . . . . . . . . . . . . . . . . . 135
Congressional representation . . . . . 111, 114-15, 380
Courts, U.S. . . . . . . . . . . . . . . . . 191
Crime, prisons, death penalty . . . 959, 960
Energy consumption . . . . . . . . . . . 237
Federally owned land. . . . . . . . . . . 545
Governor, state officials . . . . . . . 124, 126
Hazardous waste sites. . . . . . . . . . . 228
Health insurance coverage . . . . . . . . 971
Immigrants admitted (1995) . . . . . . . 383
Indians, American. . . . . . . . . . . . . 550
Interest laws, rates . . . . . . . . . . 721, 722
Marriage, divorce laws. . . . . . . . 728, 729
Motor vehicles . . . . . . . . . . . . 245, 248
Name origin, nickname . . . . . . . 544, 663
Population . . . . . . . . . . . . . 380-81, 384
Cities, towns . . . . . . . . . . . . 401, 690
Counties, county seats . . . . . . . 426-27
Poverty rates . . . . . . . . . . . . . . . . 388
Presidential elections. . . . . . . 76, 86, 106
Schools and libraries . . . . . . 252-53, 257
Taxes . . . . . . . . . . . . . . . . . . 245, 735
Temperature, precipitation . . . . . 222, 224
Unemployment benefits . . . . . . . . . . 165
Welfare assistance . . . . . . . . . . . . . 389
**Kentucky Derby** . . . . . . . . . . . . . . . 897
First (1875) . . . . . . . . . . . . . . . . . 501
**Kenya** . . . . . . . . . . . . . 482, 788-89, 846
**Kerguelen Archipelago** . . . . . . . . . . . 765
**Key, Francis Scott** . . . . . . . . . . . . . 527
**Khmer Empire** . . . . . . . . . . . . . . . . 559
**Khrushchev, Nikita S.** (1959) . . . 346, 505, 573, 585, 812
**Kidnappings** . . . . . . . . . . . . . . . . . 308
Hearst, Patty (1975) . . . . . . . . 308, 507
Lindbergh baby (1932) . . . . . . 308, 503
Sentences served . . . . . . . . . . . . . . 960
**Kilowatt-hour** (electrical unit) . . . . . . . 604

**King, Martin Luther, Jr.** 339
Assassinated (1968) 307, 506
Birthday (legal holiday) (1986) 480, 508
"I have a dream" speech (1963) 505
**Kingman Reef** 683
**Kiribati** 482, 789, 846
**Knot** (measure) 604
**Koran** 557, 654
**Korea, North (Democratic People's Republic of)** 789-90, 846
Chronology (1995-96) 45
Established 572
Flag, map 482, 493
Military strength 182
*Pueblo* incident (1968) 506
South Korea invaded (1950) 504, 573
**Korea, South (Republic of)** 790
Ambassadors, envoys 847
Chronology (1995-96) 40, 43, 45, 54, 65
Commercial fishing 164
Established 572
Flag, map 482, 493
Gross domestic product 134
Invaded by North Korea (1950) 504, 573
Merchant fleet 243
Military strength 182
Motor vehicle production, exports 246, 242
Nuclear power 238, 239
Trade 377
U.S. force (1945-1950) 504, 573
Wages, hourly 171
**Korean War** (1950-53) 573
Beginning (1950) 504, 573
Casualties, U.S. forces 184
Costs 181
MacArthur removal (1951) 504
Medals of Honor 181
Veteran population 180
**Korean War Memorial** (DC) 684
**Kosovo** 836
**Krakatau volcano** 588, 589
**Kublai Khan** 346, 560
**Ku Klux Klan** (1866, 1921) 501, 503
**Kuomintang** (China) 569, 570, 571, 572, 753
**Kuwait** 790-91
Ambassadors, envoys 847
Flag, map 482, 492
Gross domestic product 134
Gulf War (1991) 509, 776, 790-91, 815
Iraqi invasion (1990) 509, 776, 790, 815
Merchant fleet 243
**Kyrgyzstan** 482, 491, 791, 847

—L—

**Labor.** *See* Employment; Labor unions
**Labor, Department of** 187
Employees, payroll 169
Expenditures 129
Internet address 210
Secretaries 185, 187, 204
**Labor unions** 566
AFL-CIO merger (1955) 505
AFL formed (1886) 501
CIO formed (1935) 503
Contracts, first major (1937) 503
Directory 174-75
Haymarket riot (1886) 501
Knights of Labor (1869) 501
Membership (1930-95) 175
Salary, wage correlate 173
Sweeney election (1995) 40
Taft-Hartley Act (1947) 504
*see also* Strikes
**Lacrosse** 896
**LAFTA.** *See* Latin American Free Trade Association
**Lake Champlain, Battle of** (1814) 499
**Lakes** 598
**Lamb**
Nutritive value 610
Prices, farm 162
Production, consumption 157
**Land** (public)
California Desert Protection Bill (1994) 510
Federally owned, by state 545
Homestead Act (1862) 500
Land Grant Act (1862) 500
National recreation areas 545
**Language** 637-43
Abbreviations, common 639
Animal names 638, 639
Commonly confused words 640
Commonly misspelled words 641
Computer glossary 212-13
Days of week 640
Economic, financial glossary 154-55
Eponyms 637
Forms of address 641
Idioms 640
Internet, Intranet terms, lingo 209-10
National Spelling Bee 637
New words, English 637
World languages 638, 640, 642-43
**Laos** 482, 573, 575, 791, 847
**Lard** 157
**La Salle, Sieur de** (1682) 497, 586
**Las Vegas, NV.** *See* Cities, U.S.
**Latin America.** *See* Central America; South America
**Latin American Free Trade Association** 240
**Latinos.** *See* Hispanics
**Latitude**
Cities (U.S., world) 593-95
Position, reckoning 458
**Latter-Day Saints, Church of** 652-53
Address, headquarters 645
Membership 644
Organized (1830) 499
Utah (1846) 500
**Latvia** 482, 791-92, 847
**Law enforcement**
Crime bills (1994) 509
Officers 958
**Laws and documents**
Bill of Rights (1791) 498, 519
Civil rights (1875, 1964, 1990) 501, 505, 509, 573
Constitution 515-22
Consumer finance 721
Copyright 724-25
Crime bill (1994) 509
Declaration of Independence (1776) 498, 512-13
Disabilities, anti-discrimination (1990) 509
Divorce (by states) 729
Immigration (1952, 1990) 504, 840-41
Legislation, major (1995-96) 38, 53, 61, 62-63
Lend-Lease (1941) 503
Line-item veto (1996) 38, 51
Marriage (by states) 728
Mayflower Compact (1620) 497, 511
Personal records, obtaining 727
Safety belt 245
Social Security (1935) 503, 708-12
Supreme Court
Landmark decisions 523-24
Notable rulings (1995-96) 39
Tax reform (1986) 508, 730-31
Voting rights (1957, 1965) 505, 506
**Lazarus, Emma** 529
**Lead** (metal) 151, 152, 153, 228, 229
**League of Arab States** 573, 842
**League of Nations** (1920) 502, 569
**Leaning Tower of Pisa** 555
**Leap years** 475
**Lebanon** 792
Ambassadors, envoys 847
Chronology (1996) 54, 56-57
Flag 482
Israeli-Palestinian conflicts 575, 576, 785, 792
Terrorism (1983) 508, 792
**Lee, Robert E.** (1865) 343, 500
**Leeward Islands** 831
**Legal holidays** 480
**Legislation.** *See* Laws and documents
**Legislatures, state** 125-28
**Legumes**
Nutritive value 609, 611
Production 161
**Lend-Lease Act** (1941) 503
**Lent** 647, 648
**Lesotho** 482, 792-93, 847
**Lewis and Clark expedition** (1804) 499
**Lexington, KY**
**Liberia** 243, 793
Ambassadors, envoys 847
Civil strife (1996) 54
Flag 482
Refugees from 840
**Liberty Bell** 528-29
**Liberty Bowl** 883
**Libraries** 257
Awards 329
Postal rates 633
Presidential 539
**Library of Congress** 188, 684
Employees, payroll 169
Internet address 210
Librarians 206
**Libya** (1996) 64-65, 482, 576, 793-94, 846
**Liechtenstein** 134, 376, 482, 794, 846
**Life expectancy**
Animal longevity 231
Humans 973
**Life insurance** 970
**Light, speed of** 450
**Lincoln, Abraham** 107, 109, 532
Assassinated (1865) 307, 500, 532, 539
Emancipation Proclamation (1863) 500
Gettysburg Address (1863) 500, 523
*see also* Presidents, U.S.
**Lincoln, NE.** *See* Cities, U.S.
**Lincoln Memorial** (DC) *196*, 684
**Lindbergh, Charles A.** 316, 503
Son kidnapped (1932) 308, 503
**Linear measures** 600, 601, 603, 605
**Lipari Islands** 786
**Liquid measures** 600, 601, 602, 604, 605
**Liquor**
Abuse 965
Help organizations 617, 620
Consumption, recommended 609
Duty-free 722
Exports, imports 241
Measures 606
Nutritive value 611
Prohibition (1917, 1933) 502, 503, 521, 570
**Liter** (measure) 600, 602, 604
**Literature**
Awards 318-19, 324-26, 327-28
Best-selling books (1995) 289
Notable (1996) 288-89
*see also* Writers, notable
**Lithuania** 239, 238, 482, 794, 847
**Little Big Horn, Battle of** (1876) 501
**Little Rock, AR** 505
**Livestock** 156, 157, 159, 162, 241
"Mad cow disease" (1996) 52, 54, *778*
*see also* Dairy products; Meats
**Living wills** 615
**Lizards, poisonous** 232
**Loans.** *See* Credit
**Long Beach, CA.** *See* Cities, U.S.
**Longevity, animal** 231
**Long Island, NY** (1776) 498, 592
**Longitude**
Cities (U.S., world) 593-95
Position, reckoning 458
**Long jump**
Olympic champions *783*, 852, 856, 858
World records 867, 868
**Los Angeles, CA** 690
Earthquake (1994) 304, 509
*see also* Cities, U.S.
**Louisiana** 663-64
Admission, area, capital 542, 543, 663, 664
Agriculture 156-61
Altitudes (high, low) 541
Birth, death statistics 963
Budget 135
Coastline 541
Congressional representation 111, 115, 380
Courts, U.S. 191
Crime, prisons, death penalty 959, 960, 961
Energy consumption 237
Federally owned land 545
Governor, state officials 124, 126
Hazardous waste sites 228
Health insurance coverage 971
Immigrants admitted (1995) 383
Indians, American 550
Interest laws, rates 721, 722
Marriage, divorce laws 728, 729
Motor vehicles 245, 248
Name origin, nickname 544, 663
Population 380-81, 384
Cities, towns 401-2, 687, 692, 694
Parishes, parish seats 427
Port traffic 242
Poverty rates 388
Presidential elections 76, 87, 106
Schools and libraries 252-53, 257
Taxes 245, 735, 736
Temperature, precipitation 222, 224
Toxic chemical pollution 228
Unemployment benefits 165
Welfare assistance 389
**Louisiana Purchase** (1803) 499, 545
**Louisville, KY.** *See* Cities, U.S.
**Loyalty Islands** 765
**Lubbock, TX.** *See* Cities, U.S.
**Lucid, Shannon** (1996) 66, *199*, 312
**Luge** (sledding) 863
**Lunar calendar** 478
**Luther, Martin** 345, 562, 652
**Lutheran churches** 652-53
Addresses, headquarters 645
Membership 644
**Luxembourg** 794
Ambassadors, envoys 847
Flag 482
Gross domestic product 134
Royal family 376
Wages, hourly 171
**Lyricists, notable** 357

—M—

**MacArthur, Douglas** (1945, 1951) 343, 504

**Macau** . . . 810
**Macedonia** . . . 482, 487, 554, 795
**Mach** (measure) . . . 606
**Madagascar** . . . 482, 592, 795, 847
**"Mad cow disease"** (1996) . . . 52, 54, *778*
**Madeira Islands** . . . 592, 810
**Madison, James** . . . 109, 530
*see also* Presidents, U.S.
**Madison, WI** . . . 122, 386, 691
**Madura** . . . 592
**Magazines**
Advertising expenditures . . . 297
Best-selling (1995) . . . 288
Journalism awards . . . 328
Postal rates . . . 632
**Magna Carta** (1215) . . . 561
**Magnetic poles** . . . 459
**Mailing information** . . . 632-36
**Maine** . . . 664
Admission, area, capital . . . 542, 664
Agriculture . . . 156-61
Altitudes (high, low) . . . 541
Birth, death statistics . . . 963
Budget . . . 135
Coastline . . . 541
Congressional representation . . . 111, 115, 380
Courts, U.S. . . . 191
Crime, prisons, death penalty . . . 959, 960
Energy consumption . . . 237
Federally owned land . . . 545
Governor, state officials . . . 124, 126
Hazardous waste sites . . . 228
Health insurance coverage . . . 971
Immigrants admitted (1995) . . . 383
Indians, American . . . 550
Interest laws, rates . . . 721, 722
Marriage, divorce laws . . . 728, 729
Motor vehicles . . . 245, 248
Name origin, nickname . . . 544, 664
Population . . . 380-81, 384
Cities, towns . . . 402
Counties, county seats . . . 427
Port traffic . . . 242
Poverty rates . . . 388
Presidential elections . . . 76, 87, 106
Schools and libraries . . . 252-53, 257
Taxes . . . 245, 735, 736
Temperature, precipitation . . . 222, 224
Unemployment benefits . . . 165
Welfare assistance . . . 389
**Majorca** . . . 819
**Major League Soccer** . . . 849
**Malagasy Republic.** *See* Madagascar
**Malawi** . . . 482, 795-96, 847
**Malaysia** . . . 796
Ambassadors, envoys . . . 847
Flag . . . 482
Gross domestic product . . . 134
Merchant fleet . . . 243
Motor vehicle production . . . 246
Trade . . . 240
**Maldives** . . . 482, 796, 847
**Mali** . . . 482, 796-97, 847
**Malta** . . . 797
Ambassadors, envoys . . . 847
Area . . . 592
Flag . . . 482
Gross domestic product . . . 134
Merchant fleet . . . 243
**Man, Isle of** . . . 243, 592, 830
**Management and Budget, Office of**
Director . . . 185
Employees, payroll . . . 169
Expenditures . . . 129
**Manchuria** . . . 754
**Mandela, Nelson** . . . 819
**Manganese** . . . 151, 152
**Manhattan, NY** (New York County) (1626) . . . 384, 431, 497
**Manu'a Islands** . . . 681
**Manufactures**
Employees (by industry) . . . 166
Exports, imports . . . 241
Personal consumption expenditures . . . 150
Workers' statistics . . . 165-75
Occupational injuries . . . 168
*see also specific industries*
**Mao Zedong** (Mao Tse-tung) . . . 347, 574-75, 585, 753
**Maps, world** (color) . . . 485-96
Time zones . . . 484
**Marathon**
Boston . . . 956
New York . . . 956
Olympic champions . . . 852, 855, 858
World records . . . 867, 868
**Mariana Islands.** *See* Northern Mariana Islands
**Marine Corps, U.S.**
Address for information . . . 182
Generals (active duty) . . . 176
Insignia . . . 178
Organization bases . . . 177
Personnel, active duty . . . 179
Training centers . . . 177
War memorial . . . 685
Women, active duty . . . 180
**Marine warnings, advisories** . . . 220
**Marquesas Islands** . . . 592, 765
**Marriage**
Age, lawful (by states) . . . 728
Blood test requirements . . . 728
Number, rate . . . 377, 378, 962
Records, obtaining . . . 727
Same-sex unions legislation (1996) . . . 38, 66
Spousal Social Security benefits . . . 709
Wedding anniversaries . . . 727
**Mars** (planet) . . . 455, 445-46
Morning, evening stars . . . 449
Position by month . . . 440-43
Primitive life-form discovery (1996) . . . 65
Rises, sets . . . 452
Sun, distance from . . . 455, 444
**Marshall, Thurgood** (1967) . . . 506
**Marshall Islands** . . . 797
Ambassadors, envoys . . . 847
Area . . . 592
Flag . . . 482
Merchant fleet . . . 244
**Martinique** . . . 592, 765
**Maryland** . . . 664-65
Admission, area, capital . . . 542, 664, 665
Agriculture . . . 156-61
Altitudes (high, low) . . . 541
Birth, death statistics . . . 963
Budget . . . 135
Coastline . . . 541
Congressional representation . . . 111, 115, 380
Courts, U.S. . . . 191
Crime, prisons, death penalty . . . 959, 960, 961
Energy consumption . . . 237
Federally owned land . . . 545
Governor, state officials . . . 124, 126
Hazardous waste sites . . . 228
Health insurance coverage . . . 971
Immigrants admitted (1995) . . . 383
Indians, American . . . 550
Interest laws, rates . . . 721, 722
Marriage, divorce laws . . . 728, 729
Motor vehicles . . . 245, 248
Name origin, nickname . . . 544, 664
Population . . . 380-81, 384
Cities, towns . . . 402-3, 686
Counties, county seats . . . 427-28
Port traffic . . . 242
Poverty rates . . . 388
Presidential elections . . . 76, 87-88, 106
Schools and libraries . . . 252-53, 257
Taxes . . . 245, 735
Temperature, precipitation . . . 222, 224
Unemployment benefits . . . 165
Welfare assistance . . . 389
**Mass, units of** . . . 600, 602, 603, 605
**Massachusetts** . . . 665
Admission, area, capital . . . 542, 665
Agriculture . . . 156-61
Altitudes (high, low) . . . 541
Birth, death statistics . . . 963
Budget . . . 135
Coastline . . . 541
Congressional representation . . . 111, 115, 380
Courts, U.S. . . . 191
Crime, prisons, death penalty . . . 959, 960
Energy consumption . . . 237
Federally owned land . . . 545
Governor, state officials . . . 124, 127
Hazardous waste sites . . . 228
Health insurance coverage . . . 971
Immigrants admitted (1995) . . . 383
Indians, American . . . 550
Interest laws, rates . . . 721, 722
Marriage, divorce laws . . . 728, 729
Motor vehicles . . . 245, 248
Name origin, nickname . . . 544, 665
Population . . . 380-81, 384
Cities, towns . . . 403-4, 687
Counties, county seats . . . 428
Port traffic . . . 242
Poverty rates . . . 388
Presidential elections . . . 76, 88, 106
Schools and libraries . . . 252-53, 257
Taxes . . . 245, 735, 736
Temperature, precipitation . . . 222, 224
Unemployment benefits . . . 165
Welfare assistance . . . 389
**Mathematics**
Formulas . . . 607
Fractions, decimals . . . 606
**Mauritania** . . . 482, 575, 797-98, 847
**Mauritius** . . . 482, 592, 798, 847
**Mayans** . . . 554, 559
**Mayflower Compact** (1620) . . . 497, 511
**Mayors**
Address, form of . . . 641
By city . . . 121-24
First black (1967) . . . 506
**Mayotte** . . . 765
**McDougal, James** (1994, 1995) . . . 48, 51, 53, 56, 62, 509, 510
**McDougal, Susan** (1995, 1996) . . . 48, 51, 53, 56, 62, 66, 510
**McKinley, Mt.** . . . 540, 541, 590, 597
**McKinley, William** . . . 107, 109, 534
Assassinated (1901) . . . 307, 502, 534, 539
*see also* Presidents, U.S.
**McVeigh, Timothy** (1995, 1996) . . . 49, 510
**Mean time** . . . 458
**Measures** . . . 600-607
**Meats**
Consumption . . . 157
Exports, imports . . . 241
Inspection Act (1906) . . . 502
"Mad cow disease" (1996) . . . 52, 54, *778*
Nutritive values . . . 609, 610
Prices, farm . . . 162
Production . . . 156, 157
**Medal of Honor** . . . 181
**Media.** *See* Cable television; Magazines; Newspapers; Radio; Television
**Medicaid** . . . 971
**Medicare**
Bankruptcy forecasts (1996) . . . 58
Enacted (1966) . . . 506
Program summary . . . 710
**Medicine.** *See* Health and medicine
**Mediterranean Sea**
Area, depth . . . 593
Islands, areas . . . 592
**Melilla** . . . 819
**Memorial Day** . . . 480
**Memorials, national** . . . 547, 684-85
**Memphis, TN.** *See* Cities, U.S.
**Men**
AIDS incidence . . . 975
Cancer cases, deaths . . . 974
Cigarette use . . . 965
Educational level . . . 254
Employment, unemployment . . . 166, 167
Life expectancy . . . 973
Marital status . . . 377
One-parent families . . . 377, 965
Population (1790-1994) . . . 379, 382
Poverty rates . . . 388
Salaries and wages . . . 167, 170, 173
Suicide rates . . . 965, 968
**Mennonite churches** . . . 644, 645
**Mercantilism** . . . 563
**Merchant Marine**
Academy . . . 178
Fleets, by country . . . 243-44
**Mercury** (planet) . . . 444, 455
Morning, evening stars . . . 449
Position by month . . . 440-43
Sun, distance from . . . 444, 455
**Mergers**
Corporate, largest . . . 142
Labor unions (1955) . . . 505
Sherman Antitrust Act (1890) . . . 501
**Mesa, AZ.** *See* Cities, U.S.
**Metals**
Exports, imports . . . 241
Production . . . 151, 152, 153
Reserve base, world . . . 151
**Meteorology** . . . 220-27
**Methodist churches** . . . 652-53
Addresses, U.S. headquarters . . . 646
Membership . . . 644
**Metric measures** . . . 600-604
**Metropolitan areas, U.S.**
Air quality . . . 229
Average annual salaries . . . 171
Immigrants' intended residence . . . 383
Population (1990-94) . . . 385
**Mexican War** (1846-48) . . . 500
Casualties, U.S. forces . . . 184
Costs . . . 181
**Mexico** . . . 798-99
Ambassadors, envoys . . . 847
Cession to U.S. (1846) . . . 500, 545
Energy production . . . 236
Flag, maps . . . 483, 485, 486-87
Gold production . . . 153
Gross domestic product . . . 134
History . . . 552, 559, 563, 586
Military strength . . . 182
Motor vehicle production, exports 246, 242
Mountain peaks . . . 590
Nuclear power . . . 239, 238
Paricutin volcano . . . 555

Revolution (1910) . . . . . . . . . . . . . . 569
Trade. . . . . . . . . . . . . . . . . . . 240, 377
U.S. foreign aid (1995) . . . . . . . . . . 510
U.S. immigrants from . . . . . . . . 377, 383
Wages, hourly. . . . . . . . . . . . . . . . . 171
**Mexico, Gulf of** . . . . . . . . . . . . . . . . . 593
**Mexico City, Mex.** . . . . . . . . . . . . . . . 838
**Miami, FL**
**Michigan** . . . . . . . . . . . . . . . . . 665-66
Admission, area, capital 542, 543, 665, 666
Agriculture . . . . . . . . . . . . . . . . 156-61
Altitudes (high, low) . . . . . . . . . . . . 541
Birth, death statistics . . . . . . . . . . . 963
Budget. . . . . . . . . . . . . . . . . . . . . 135
Congressional representation 115, 111, 380
Courts, U.S. . . . . . . . . . . . . . . . . . 191
Crime, prisons, death penalty. . . 959, 960, 961
Energy consumption. . . . . . . . . . . . 237
Federally owned land . . . . . . . . . . . 545
Governor, state officials . . . . . . 124, 127
Hazardous waste sites . . . . . . . . . . . 228
Health insurance coverage . . . . . . . . 971
Immigrants admitted (1995) . . . . . . . 383
Indians, American . . . . . . . . . . . . . 550
Interest laws, rates. . . . . . . . . . 721, 722
Marriage, divorce laws . . . . . . . 728, 729
Mineral production . . . . . . . . . . . . 151
Motor vehicles. . . . . . . . . . . . . 245, 248
Name origin, nickname . . . . . . . 544, 665
Population . . . . . . . . . . . . . 380-81, 384
Cities, towns . . . . . . . 404-5, 688, 689
Counties, county seats . . . . . . . . . 428
Port traffic . . . . . . . . . . . . . . . . . . 242
Poverty rates . . . . . . . . . . . . . . . . 388
Presidential elections . . . . 76, 88-89, 106
Schools and libraries . . . . . . 252-53, 257
Taxes . . . . . . . . . . . . . . . . . . 245, 735
Temperature, precipitation. . . . . 222, 224
Toxic chemical pollution . . . . . . . . . 228
Unemployment benefits . . . . . . . . . . 165
Welfare assistance. . . . . . . . . . . . . 389
**Michigan, Lake** . . . . . . . . . . . . . . . . 598
**Micronesia** . . . . . . . . . 483, 592, 799, 847
**Middle East**
History. . . . . . . . . . . 557, 558, 570, 574
*see also* Arab-Israeli conflict; Persian Gulf War; *specific countries*
**Midway, Battle of** (1942). . . . . . . 503, 572
**Midway Atoll**. . . . . . . . . . . . . . . 439, 683
**MIGA.** *See* Multilateral Investment Guarantee Agency
**Mileage**
Air . . . . . . . . . . . . . . . . . . . . . . 250
Road . . . . . . . . . . . . . . . . . . . . . 249
Sea lanes. . . . . . . . . . . . . . . . . . . 243
**Miles** (measurement) . . . . . . 600, 601, 603
**Military.** *See* Armed forces, U.S.; *specific branches*
**Military Academy, U.S.** (West Point, NY) . . . . . . . . 178, 268
**Military leaders, notable**. . . . . . . . 343-44
**Military parks, national** . . . . . . . . . . 547
**Military strength**
By country . . . . . . . . . . . . . . . . . 182
U.S. . . . . . . . . . . . . . . . . . . . 181, 182
**Military time** (24-hour) . . . . . . . . . . . 479
**Military training centers**. . . . . . . . 176-77
**Milk**
Nutritive value. . . . . . . . . . . . . 609, 610
Prices, farm . . . . . . . . . . . . . . . . . 162
**Million Man March** (1995) . . . . . . . 40, 510
**Milwaukee, WI.** *See* Cities, U.S.
**Minerals** (dietary). . . . . . . 609, 610-11, 612
**Minerals** (industrial) . . . . . . . . 151-53, 241
**Minimum wage, U.S.**
Enacted (1938) . . . . . . . . . . . . . . . 503
Hourly rates (1950-96) . . . . . . . . . . 170
Increase (1996). . . . . . . . . . . 38, 56, 63
**Mining**
Coal . . . . . . . . . . . . . . . . . . . . . . 235
Disasters, U.S. . . . . . . . . . . . . . . . 301
Gold, silver. . . . . . . . . . . . 151, 152, 153
Occupational injuries . . . . . . . . . . . 168
**Minneapolis, MN.** *See* Cities, U.S.
**Minnesota** . . . . . . . . . . . . . . . . . . . 666
Admission, area, capital . . . 542, 543, 666
Agriculture . . . . . . . . . . . . . . . 156-61
Altitudes (high, low) . . . . . . . . . . . . 541
Birth, death statistics . . . . . . . . . . . 963
Budget. . . . . . . . . . . . . . . . . . . . . 135
Congressional representation. . . 111, 115, 380
Courts, U.S. . . . . . . . . . . . . . . . . . 191
Crime, prisons, death penalty. . . 959, 960, 961
Energy consumption. . . . . . . . . . . . 237
Federally owned land . . . . . . . . . . . 545
Governor, state officials . . . . . . 124, 127
Hazardous waste sites . . . . . . . . . . . 228
Health insurance coverage . . . . . . . . 971
Immigrants admitted (1995) . . . . . . . 383
Indians, American. . . . . . . . . . . . . 550
Interest laws, rates . . . . . . . . . . 721, 722
Marriage, divorce laws . . . . . . . 728, 729
Mineral production . . . . . . . . . . . . 151
Motor vehicles . . . . . . . . . . . . . 245, 248
Name origin, nickname . . . . . . . 544, 666
Population. . . . . . . . . . . . . . 380-81, 384
Cities, towns. . . . . . . . 405-6, 691, 693
Counties, county seats . . . . . . . 428-29
Port traffic . . . . . . . . . . . . . . . . . . 242
Poverty rates . . . . . . . . . . . . . . . . 388
Presidential elections . . . . 76, 89-90, 106
Schools and libraries. . . . . . . 252-53, 257
Taxes. . . . . . . . . . . . . . . . 245, 735, 736
Temperature, precipitation . . . . . 222, 224
Unemployment benefits . . . . . . . . . . 165
Welfare assistance . . . . . . . . . . . . . 389
**Minoans** . . . . . . . . . . . . . . . . . . . . 552
**Minorca** . . . . . . . . . . . . . . . . . . . . 819
**Mint, Bureau of the** . . . . . . 186, 188, 139
**Minuit, Peter** (1626) . . . . . . . . . . . . 497
**Miquelon Island**. . . . . . . . . . . . . . . 765
**Miscellaneous facts** . . . . . . . . . . . . . 71
**Miss America** . . . . . . . . . . . . . . . . 329
**Missiles, rockets.** *See* Nuclear arms; Space developments
**Mississippi** . . . . . . . . . . . . . . . . 666-67
Admission, area, capital. . . . . 542, 543, 666, 667
Agriculture . . . . . . . . . . . . . . . 156-61
Altitudes (high, low) . . . . . . . . . . . 541
Birth, death statistics. . . . . . . . . . . 963
Budget . . . . . . . . . . . . . . . . . . . . 135
Coastline . . . . . . . . . . . . . . . . . . 541
Congressional representation . . 111, 115, 380
Courts, U.S. . . . . . . . . . . . . . . . . 191
Crime, prisons, death penalty . . 959, 960, 961
Energy consumption . . . . . . . . . . . 237
Federally owned land . . . . . . . . . . 545
Governor, state officials. . . . . . . 124, 127
Hazardous waste sites . . . . . . . . . . 228
Health insurance coverage. . . . . . . . 971
Immigrants admitted (1995) . . . . . . . 383
Indians, American. . . . . . . . . . . . . 550
Interest laws, rates . . . . . . . . . . 721, 722
Marriage, divorce laws . . . . . . . 728, 729
Motor vehicles . . . . . . . . . . . . . 245, 248
Name origin, nickname . . . . . . . 544, 666
Population. . . . . . . . . . . . . . 380-81, 384
Cities, towns. . . . . . . . . . . . 406, 690
Counties, county seats . . . . . . . . 429
Port traffic . . . . . . . . . . . . . . . . . . 242
Poverty rates. . . . . . . . . . . . . . . . 388
Presidential elections . . . . . . 76, 90, 106
Schools and libraries. . . . . . . 252-53, 257
Taxes. . . . . . . . . . . . . . . . . . . 245, 735
Temperature, precipitation . . . . . 222, 224
Toxic chemical pollution. . . . . . . . . 228
Unemployment benefits. . . . . . . . . . 165
Welfare assistance . . . . . . . . . . . . 389
**Mississippi River**. . . . . . . . . . . . 596, 597
Bridges spanning . . . . . . . . . . . 703, 704
First railroad crossing (1855) . . . . . 500
Commerce . . . . . . . . . . . . . . . . . . 242
Discovered (1541) . . . . . . . . . . 497, 586
Floods (1993) . . . . . . . . . . . . . 303, 509
**Missouri** . . . . . . . . . . . . . . . . . . . . 667
Admission, area, capital. . . 542, 543, 667
Agriculture . . . . . . . . . . . . . . . 156-61
Altitudes (high, low) . . . . . . . . . . . 541
Birth, death statistics. . . . . . . . . . . 963
Budget . . . . . . . . . . . . . . . . . . . . 135
Congressional representation . . 111, 115, 380
Courts, U.S. . . . . . . . . . . . . . . . . 191
Crime, prisons, death penalty . . 959, 960, 961
Energy consumption . . . . . . . . . . . 237
Federally owned land . . . . . . . . . . 545
Governor, state officials. . . . . . . 124, 127
Hazardous waste sites . . . . . . . . . . 228
Health insurance coverage. . . . . . . . 971
Immigrants admitted (1995) . . . . . . . 383
Indians, American. . . . . . . . . . . . . 550
Interest laws, rates . . . . . . . . . . 721, 722
Marriage, divorce laws . . . . . . . 728, 729
Mineral production . . . . . . . . . . . . 151
Motor vehicles . . . . . . . . . . . . . 245, 248
Name origin, nickname . . . . . . . 544, 667
Population. . . . . . . . . . . . . . 380-81, 384
Cities, towns. . . . . . . . 406-7, 690, 693
Counties, county seats . . . . . . . 429-30
Port traffic . . . . . . . . . . . . . . . . . . 242
Poverty rates. . . . . . . . . . . . . . . . 388
Presidential elections . . . . 76, 90-91, 106
Schools and libraries. . . . . . . 252-53, 257
Taxes. . . . . . . . . . . . . . . . . . . 245, 735
Temperature, precipitation . . . . . 222, 224
Unemployment benefits . . . . . . . . . . 165
U.S. center of population . . . . . . . . . 381
Welfare assistance . . . . . . . . . . . . . 389
**Missouri Compromise** (1820). . . . . . . 499
**Missouri River** . . . . . . . . . . . . . 596, 597
Bridges spanning . . . . . . . . . . . 703, 704
**Mobile, AL.** *See* Cities, U.S.
**Mobility, geographic, U.S.** (1960-94) . . 387
**Mohammed.** *See* Muhammad
**Moldova** . . . . . . . . . . . . . 483, 799, 847
**Moluccas**. . . . . . . . . . . . . . . . . . . . 592
**Monaco** . . . . . . . . . . . . 134, 376, 483, 799
**Money.** *See* Currency, U.S.; Exchange rates, foreign
**Mongolia** . . . . . . . . . . . 483, 799-800, 847
**Mongolia, Inner** . . . . . . . . . . . . . . . 754
**Mongols** . . . . . . . . . . . . . . . . . . . . 560
**Monroe, James** . . . . . . . 109, 530-31, 539
*see also* Presidents, U.S.
**Monroe Doctrine** (1823). . . . . . . . . . . 499
**Montana** . . . . . . . . . . . . . . . . . . . . 668
Admission, area, capital. . . 542, 543, 668
Agriculture. . . . . . . . . . . . . . . . 156-61
Altitudes (high, low). . . . . . . . . . . . 541
Birth, death statistics . . . . . . . . . . . 963
Budget . . . . . . . . . . . . . . . . . . . . 135
Congressional representation 111, 115, 380
Courts, U.S. . . . . . . . . . . . . . . . . . 191
Crime, prisons, death penalty . . . 959, 960
Energy consumption . . . . . . . . . . . . 237
Federally owned land. . . . . . . . . . . 545
Governor, state officials . . . . . . . 124, 127
Hazardous waste sites. . . . . . . . . . . 228
Health insurance coverage . . . . . . . . 971
Immigrants admitted (1995) . . . . . . . 383
Indians, American . . . . . . . . . . . . . 550
Interest laws, rates . . . . . . . . . . 721, 722
Marriage, divorce laws. . . . . . . . 728, 729
Motor vehicles . . . . . . . . . . . . 245, 248
Name origin, nickname . . . . . . . 544, 668
Population . . . . . . . . . . . . . 380-81, 384
Cities, towns . . . . . . . . . . . . . . . 407
Counties, county seats . . . . . . . . . 430
Poverty rates . . . . . . . . . . . . . . . . 388
Presidential elections. . . . . 76, 91-92, 106
Schools and libraries . . . . . . 252-53, 257
Taxes . . . . . . . . . . . . . . . 245, 735, 736
Temperature, precipitation . . . . . 222, 224
Unemployment benefits . . . . . . . . . . 165
Welfare assistance . . . . . . . . . . . . . 389
**Montgomery, AL.** *See* Cities, U.S.
**Montserrat**. . . . . . . . . . . . . . . . . . . 831
**Monuments, national** . . . . 548-49, 684-85
Utah scenic area (1996). . . . . . . . . . . 66
**Moon** . . . . . . . . . . . . . . . . . . . . 456-57
Apogee, perigee . . . . . . . . . . . . . . 457
Apollo missions (1969). . . . . . 309-10, 506
Chinese lunar calendar . . . . . . . . . . 478
Conjunctions . . . . . . . . . . . . . . 440-43
Eclipses (1997). . . . . . . . . . . . . . . 454
First man on (1969) . . . . . . . . . . 309, 506
Full. . . . . . . . . . . . . . . . . . . . . 463-74
Harvest, Hunter's . . . . . . . . . . . . . 457
Occultations. . . . . . . . . . . . . . . 440-43
Phases of . . . . . . . . . . . . . 457, 463-74
Position by month . . . . . . . . . . . 440-43
Rises, sets (1997). . . . . . . . . . . . 462-74
Tides, effects on . . . . . . . . . . . . 226, 457
**Moravian churches**. . . . . . . . . . . . . 645
**Mormons.** *See* Latter-Day Saints, Church of
**Morning stars** (1997). . . . . . . . . . . . 449
**Morocco** . . . . . . . . . . . 182, 483, 800, 847
**Morris, Dick** (1996) . . . . . . . . . . . . . . 64
**Mortgages**
Farm. . . . . . . . . . . . . . . . . . . . . . 160
Payment tables. . . . . . . . . . . . . . . 727
Tax deductions. . . . . . . . . . . . . . . 731
**Motion pictures.** *See* Movies
**Motorcycle racing** (1996). . . . . . . . . . 932
**Motor vehicles**
Accidents and deaths . . . . 168, 964, 967
Exports, imports . . . . . . . . . . . . 241, 242
Production. . . . . . . . . . . . . . . . 246, 244
Speed limits (1996) . . . . . . . . 38, 42, 248
Tax deductions. . . . . . . . . . . . . 730, 731
*see also* Automobiles
**Motto, U.S.** . . . . . . . . . . . . . . . . . . 525
**Mountains** . . . . . . . . . . . . . . . . . 590-91
Highest, Canada. . . . . . . . . . . . . . 590
Highest, U.S. . . . . . . . 540, 541, 590, 591
Volcanoes . . . . . . . . . . . . . . . . 588-89
**Mt. Etna**. . . . . . . . . . . . . . . . . . 589, 786
**Mt. Everest** . . . . . . . . . . 555, 590, 591, 597
**Mt. McKinley** . . . . . . . . 540, 541, 590, 597
**Mt. Rushmore** . . . . . . . . . . . . . . 547, 676
**Mt. St. Helens** (1980). . . . . . . 507, 588, 589
**Mt. Vesuvius** . . . . . . . . . . . . . . . . . 588
**Mount Vernon** (VA). . . . . . . . . . . . . . 685
**Mouth-to-mouth resuscitation** . . . . . . 608
**Movies** . . . . . . . . . . . . . . . . . . . . . 568
Awards . . . . . . . . . . . . . . . . 330-32, 333

Kinetoscope (1894) . . . . . . . . . . . . . 501
National Film Registry . . . . . . . . 284-85
Notable (1995-96) . . . . . . . . . . 283, *780*
Sound-on-film, first (1923) . . . . . . . . . 503
Stars, directors . . . . . . . . . . 283, 360-76
Talking (1927) . . . . . . . . . . . . . . . . 503
Top 50 films (1995) . . . . . . . . . . . . 283
Top grossing, all-time . . . . . . . . . . . 284
Top videos (1995; all-time) . . . . . . . . 284
**Mozambique** . . . . . . . . . 483, 800-801, 847
**MSA.** *See* Metropolitan Areas
**Muhammad** . . . . . . . . . 345, 557, 647, 654
**Multilateral Investment Guarantee Agency** . . . . . . . . . . . . . . . . . 845
**Municipal bonds** . . . . . . . . . . . . 148, 155
**Murders**
Arrests, sentences . . . . . . . . . . 960, 961
Assassinations . . . . . . . 307-8, 539, 576
With firearms . . . . . . . . . . . . . . . 968
Incidence . . . . . . . . . . . . 957, 958, 959
Workplace . . . . . . . . . . . . . . . . . 168
**Museums,** Washington, DC . . . . . . 684-85
**Music and musicians**
Awards . . . . . . . . . . . 326-27, 333, *781*
Classical . . . . . . . . . . . . . . . 355-56
Composers, works . . . . . . . . . . . 355-57
Concerts, top-grossing (1985-95) . . . . 291
Country music artists . . . . . . . . . . . 359
Dance companies . . . . . . . . . . . . . 287
Jazz, blues artists . . . . . . . . . . . 358-59
Lyricists . . . . . . . . . . . . . . . . . . 357
Musicians, singers . . . . . . . . 358-76, *781*
Opera, operetta . . . 286-87, 355-57, 358
Recordings . . . . . . . . . . . . . 291-93, 333
Rock & roll notables . . . . 333, 359-60, *781*
Symphony orchestras . . . . . . . . . . . 286
Theater . . . . . . . . . . . . . . 356-57, *781*
Videos . . . . . . . . . . . . . . . . 291-92, 293
**Muslims.** *See* Islam
**Mutual funds** . . . . . . . . . . . . . . 148, 155
**Myanmar** (Burma) . . . . . . . . 182, 572, 801
Ambassadors, envoys . . . . . . . . . . . 847
Flag . . . . . . . . . . . . . . . . . . . . . 483
Refugees from . . . . . . . . . . . . . . . 840


— N—


**NAACP.** *See* National Association for the Advancement of Colored People
**Nader, Ralph** (1996) . . . . . . . . . . . . . 64
**NAFTA.** *See* North American Free Trade Agreement
**Nagasaki bombing** (1945) . . . . . . 504, 572
**Names**
Animals . . . . . . . . . . . . . . . . . 638-39
Days, foreign languages . . . . . . . . . 640
Original, entertainers . . . . . . . . . 375-76
Pen names . . . . . . . . . . . . . . . . . 642
States, origin and nicknames . 544, 655-80
**Namibia** . . . . . . . . . . . . 483, 801-2, 847
**Napoleon Bonaparte** (1798, 1803) . . . 499, 564, 565
**NASA.** *See* National Aeronautics and Space Administration
**NASCAR** (auto racing) . . . . . . . . 931, 932
**NASDAQ Stock Exchange** . . . . . . . . . 149
**Nashville, TN.** *See* Cities, U.S.
**National Aeronautics and Space Administration** . . . . . . . . . . . . . 188
Employees, payroll . . . . . . . . . . . . . 169
Expenditures . . . . . . . . . . . . . . . . 129
Internet address . . . . . . . . . . . . . . 210
**National Anthem**
Composed (1814) . . . . . . . . . . 499, 527
Text . . . . . . . . . . . . . . . . . . . . . 528
**National Archives** . . . . . . . . . . . 130, 685
**National Association for the Advancement of Colored People**
Director sworn in (1996) . . . . . . . . . . 49
Founding (1909) . . . . . . . . . . . . . . 502
Spingarn Medal . . . . . . . . . . . . 328-29
**National Basketball Association** . . . . . 60, *784*, 849, 906-13
Addresses, teams . . . . . . . . . . . . . 903
**National debt** . . . . . . . . 38, 130, 131, 155
**National Film Registry** . . . . . . . . . 284-85
**National Football League** . 48, *784*, 869-79
Addresses, teams . . . . . . . . . . . . . 904
**National Foundation on the Arts and Humanities** . . . . . . . . . . . . . . . 130
**National Gallery of Art** (DC) . . . . . . . . 685
**National historic sites** . . . . . . . . 547-48
**National Hockey League** . . . 60, *784*, 849, 889-96
Addresses, teams . . . . . . . . . . . . 903-4
**National Income, U.S.** . . . . . . . . 133, 147
**National Invitation Tournament** . . . . . 915
**National Labor Relations Board** . . 130, 188
**National monuments** . . . . . 548-49, 684-85
**National park system, U.S.** . . . 540, 546-49
Visitors, number (1995) . . . . . . . . . . 549
**National recreation areas** . . . . . . 545, 549
**National Science Foundation** 188, 130, 207
**National seashores** . . . . . . . . . . . . 549
**National Spelling Bee** . . . . . . . . . . . 637
**Nations of the World** . . . . . . . . . 737-848
Ambassadors and envoys . . . . . . 846-48
Cities (largest) . . . . . . . . . . . . . . . 838
Consumer price changes . . . . . . . . . 133
Daylight Saving Time . . . . . . . . . . . 479
Direct dialing codes . . . . . . . . . . . . 848
Embassies . . . . . . . . . . . . . . . 737-837
Energy production, consumption . 236, 238
Exchange rates . . . . . . . . . . . . . . . 144
Flags . . . . . . . . . . . . . . . . . . . 481-84
Grain production . . . . . . . . . . . . . . 163
Gross domestic product . . . . . . . . . . 134
Investment in U.S. . . . . . . . . . . . . . 145
Maps . . . . . . . . . . . . . . . . . . . 485-96
Merchant fleets . . . . . . . . . . . . . 243-44
Military strength . . . . . . . . . . . . . . 182
Motor vehicle production . . . . . . . . . 246
Nuclear power . . . . . . . . . . . . 238, 239
Population projections (2010, 2020) 838-39
Refugees . . . . . . . . . . . . . . . . . . 840
Rulers . . . . . . . . . . . . . . . . . . 577-85
Stock exchanges . . . . . . . . . . . . . . 144
Trade . . . . . . . . . . . . . . . . . . . . 240
UN members . . . . . . . . . . . . . . 843-44
**Native Americans.** *See* Indians, American
**NATO.** *See* North Atlantic Treaty Organization
**Natural gas**
Exports, imports . . . . . . . . . . . 235, 241
Production, consumption . . . . . . . . . 235
Reserves . . . . . . . . . . . . . . . . . . 238
**Naturalization** . . . . . . . . . . . . . 504, 841
*see also* Aliens
**Nauru** . . . . . . . . . . . . . 483, 592, 802, 847
**Nautilus** (nuclear submarine) (1954) . . 504
**Naval Academy, U.S.** (Annapolis, MD) . . . . . . . . . . . . . . . . . . 178, 268
**Naval disasters** . . . . . . . . . . . . . 298-99
**Naval leaders, notable** . . . . . . . . . 343-44
**Navassa Island** . . . . . . . . . . . . . . . 683
**Navigation Act** (1660) . . . . . . . . . . . . 497
**Navy, Department of the** . . . . . . . . . 169
Secretaries . . . . . . . . . . . . . 186, 202-3
**Navy, U.S.**
Academy . . . . . . . . . . . . . . . . 178, 268
Address for information . . . . . . . . . . 182
Admirals (active duty) . . . . . . . . . . . 176
Boorda suicide (1996) . . . . . . . . . . 56, 74
Insignia . . . . . . . . . . . . . . . . . . . 178
Leaders, notable past . . . . . . . . . 343-44
Personnel, active duty . . . . . . . . . . . 179
Training centers . . . . . . . . . . . . . . 177
Women, active duty . . . . . . . . . . . . 180
**Nazis** . . . . . . . . . . . . 504, 571, 572, 767
**NBA.** *See* National Basketball Association
**Nebraska** . . . . . . . . . . . . . . . . . . . 668
Admission, area, capital . . . 542, 543, 668
Agriculture . . . . . . . . . . . . . . . . 156-61
Altitudes (high, low) . . . . . . . . . . . . 541
Birth, death statistics . . . . . . . . . . . 963
Budget . . . . . . . . . . . . . . . . . . . . 135
Congressional representation . . 111, 116, 380
Courts, U.S. . . . . . . . . . . . . . . . . . 191
Crime, prisons, death penalty . . 959, 960, 961
Energy consumption . . . . . . . . . . . . 237
Federally owned land . . . . . . . . . . . 545
Governor, state officials . . . . . . . 124, 127
Hazardous waste sites . . . . . . . . . . . 228
Health insurance coverage . . . . . . . . 971
Immigrants admitted (1995) . . . . . . . 383
Indians, American . . . . . . . . . . . . . 550
Interest laws, rates . . . . . . . . . . 721, 722
Marriage, divorce laws . . . . . . . 728, 729
Motor vehicles . . . . . . . . . . . . . 245, 248
Name origin, nickname . . . . . . . 544, 668
Population . . . . . . . . . . . . . 380-81, 384
Cities, towns . . . . . . . . . . 407, 690, 692
Counties, county seats . . . . . . . 430-31
Poverty rates . . . . . . . . . . . . . . . . 388
Presidential elections . . . . . . 76, 92, 106
Schools and libraries . . . . . . . 252-53, 257
Taxes . . . . . . . . . . . . . . . 245, 735, 736
Temperature, precipitation . . . . . 222, 224
Unemployment benefits . . . . . . . . . . 165
Welfare assistance . . . . . . . . . . . . . 389
**Necrology** (1995-96) . . . . . . . . . . . 74-75
**Neolithic Revolution** . . . . . . . . . . . . 551
**Nepal** . . . . . . . . . . . . . . . . 483, 802, 847
**Neptune** (planet) . . . . . . . . . . . . 448, 455
Morning, evening stars . . . . . . . . . . 449
Position by month . . . . . . . . . . . 440-43
Sun, distance from . . . . . . . . . . 444, 455
**Netanyahu, Benjamin** (1996) . . . . . 43, 57, 59, 67, 69, *778*
**Netherlands** . . . . . . . . . . . . . . . 802-3
Ambassadors, envoys . . . . . . . . . . . 847
Flag . . . . . . . . . . . . . . . . . . . . . 483
Gold reserves . . . . . . . . . . . . . . . . 146
Gross domestic product . . . . . . . . . . 134
History . . . . . . . . . . . . . . 497, 561, 563
Merchant fleet . . . . . . . . . . . . . . . 244
Motor vehicle production . . . . . . . . . 246
Nuclear power . . . . . . . . . . . . 239, 238
Rulers, royal family . . . . . . . . . . 376, 583
Wages, hourly . . . . . . . . . . . . . . . 171
**Netherlands Antilles** . . . . . . . . . . . . 803
**Nevada** . . . . . . . . . . . . . . . . . . . . 669
Admission, area, capital . . . 542, 543, 669
Agriculture . . . . . . . . . . . . . . . . 156-61
Altitudes (high, low) . . . . . . . . . . . . 541
Birth, death statistics . . . . . . . . . . . 963
Budget . . . . . . . . . . . . . . . . . . . . 135
Congressional representation . . 111, 116, 380
Courts, U.S. . . . . . . . . . . . . . . . . . 191
Crime, prisons, death penalty 959, 960, 961
Energy consumption . . . . . . . . . . . . 237
Federally owned land . . . . . . . . . . . 545
Governor, state officials . . . . . . . 124, 127
Hazardous waste sites . . . . . . . . . . . 228
Health insurance coverage . . . . . . . . 971
Immigrants admitted (1995) . . . . . . . 383
Indians, American . . . . . . . . . . . . . 550
Interest laws, rates . . . . . . . . . . 721, 722
Marriage, divorce laws . . . . . . . 728, 729
Mineral production . . . . . . . . . . . . . 151
Motor vehicles . . . . . . . . . . . . . 245, 248
Name origin, nickname . . . . . . . 544, 669
Population . . . . . . . . . . . . . 380-81, 384
Cities, towns . . . . . . . . . . . . . 407, 690
Counties, county seats . . . . . . . . . 431
Poverty rates . . . . . . . . . . . . . . . . 388
Presidential elections . . . . . 76, 92-93, 106
Schools and libraries . . . . . . 252-53, 257
Taxes . . . . . . . . . . . . . . . . . . . . 245
Temperature, precipitation . . . . . 222, 224
Unemployment benefits . . . . . . . . . . 165
Welfare assistance . . . . . . . . . . . . . 389
**Nevis.** *See* St. Kitts and Nevis
**New Amsterdam** (1626, 1664) . . . . . . . 497
**Newark, NJ**
Riots (1967) . . . . . . . . . . . . . . . . . 506
*see also* Cities, U.S.
**Newbery Medal** . . . . . . . . . . . . . . 327-28
**New Britain** . . . . . . . . . . . . . . . . . 592
**New Caledonia** . . . . . . . . . . . . . 592, 765
**New Deal** (1933) . . . . . . . . . . . . 503, 571
**Newfoundland** . . . . . . . . . . . . . . . . 592
**New Guinea.** *See* Papua New Guinea
**New Hampshire** . . . . . . . . . . . . . . . 669
Admission, area, capital . . . . . . 542, 669
Agriculture . . . . . . . . . . . . . . . . 156-61
Altitudes (high, low) . . . . . . . . . . . . 541
Birth, death statistics . . . . . . . . . . . 963
Budget . . . . . . . . . . . . . . . . . . . . 135
Coastline . . . . . . . . . . . . . . . . . . . 541
Congressional representation . . 111, 116, 380
Courts, U.S. . . . . . . . . . . . . . . . . . 191
Crime, prisons, death penalty . . 959, 960, 961
Energy consumption . . . . . . . . . . . . 237
Federally owned land . . . . . . . . . . . 545
Governor, state officials . . . . . . . 124, 127
Hazardous waste sites . . . . . . . . . . . 228
Health insurance coverage . . . . . . . . 971
Immigrants admitted (1995) . . . . . . . 383
Indians, American . . . . . . . . . . . . . 550
Interest laws, rates . . . . . . . . . . 721, 722
Marriage, divorce laws . . . . . . . 728, 729
Motor vehicles . . . . . . . . . . . . . 245, 248
Name origin, nickname . . . . . . . 544, 669
Population . . . . . . . . . . . . . 380-81, 384
Cities, towns . . . . . . . . . . . . . . . 407
Counties, county seats . . . . . . . . . 431
Poverty rates . . . . . . . . . . . . . . . . 388
Presidential elections . . . . . . . 76, 93, 106
Schools and libraries . . . . . . 252-53, 257
Taxes . . . . . . . . . . . . . . . . . . 245, 735
Temperatures, record . . . . . . . . . . . 224
Unemployment benefits . . . . . . . . . . 165
Welfare assistance . . . . . . . . . . . . . 389
**New Ireland** . . . . . . . . . . . . . . . . . 592
**New Jersey** . . . . . . . . . . . . . . . . 669-70
Admission, area, capital . . . . . . 542, 670
Agriculture . . . . . . . . . . . . . . . . 156-61
Altitudes (high, low) . . . . . . . . . . . . 541
Birth, death statistics . . . . . . . . . . . 963
Budget . . . . . . . . . . . . . . . . . . . . 135
Coastline . . . . . . . . . . . . . . . . . . . 541
Congressional representation 112, 116, 380
Courts, U.S. . . . . . . . . . . . . . . . . . 191
Crime, prisons, death penalty . . . 959, 960
Energy consumption . . . . . . . . . . . . 237
Federally owned land . . . . . . . . . . . 545
Governor, state officials . . . . . . . 124, 127
Hazardous waste sites . . . . . . . . . . . 228

Health insurance coverage 971
Immigrants admitted (1995) 383
Indians, American 550
Interest laws, rates 721, 722
Marriage, divorce laws 728, 729
Motor vehicles 245, 248
Name origin, nickname 544, 669
Population 380-81, 384
Cities, towns 407-9, 690, 692
Counties, county seats 431
Port traffic 242
Poverty rates 388
Presidential elections 76, 93, 106
Schools and libraries 252-53, 257
Taxes 245, 735, 736
Temperature, precipitation 222, 224
Unemployment benefits 165
Welfare assistance 389
**New Mexico** 670-71
Admission, area, capital 542, 543, 670
Agriculture 156-61
Altitudes (high, low) 541
Birth, death statistics 963
Budget 135
Congressional representation 112, 116, 380
Courts, U.S. 191
Crime, prisons, death penalty 959, 960, 961
Energy consumption 237
Federally owned land 545
Governor, state officials 124, 127
Hazardous waste sites 228
Health insurance coverage 971
Immigrants admitted (1995) 383
Indians, American 550
Interest laws, rates 721, 722
Marriage, divorce laws 728, 729
Motor vehicles 245, 248
Name origin, nickname 544, 670
Population 380-81, 384
Cities, towns 409, 686
Counties, county seats 431
Poverty rates 388
Presidential elections 76, 93-94, 106
Schools and libraries 252-53, 257
Taxes 245, 735, 736
Temperature, precipitation 222, 224
Unemployment benefits 165
Welfare assistance 389
**New Orleans, LA.** *See* Cities, U.S.
**Newport News, VA** 123, 242, 387, 692
**Newspapers**
Advertising expenditures 297
*Boston News Letter* (1704) 497
Dailies
First U.S. (1784) 498
Top U.S., Canadian 290
Journalism awards 328
Pulitzer Prize winners 319-23
Muckrakers 568
**News photos** (1996) *193-200, 777-84*
**New Testament** 649
**New words in English** 637
**New World**
Central, South America 563
Explorers 559, 561, 563, 586
Jamestown (VA) colony (1607) 497
Mayflower Compact (1620) 497, 511
New Netherland colony (1664) 497
**New Year, Chinese** 478
**New Year, Jewish** 648
**New Year, Tet** 478
**New Year's Day** 480
**New York** (state) 671
Admission, area, capital 542, 671
Agriculture 156-61
Altitudes (high, low) 541
Birth, death statistics 963
Budget 135
Coastline 541
Congressional representation 112, 116-88, 380
Courts, U.S. 191
Crime, prisons, death penalty 959, 960, 961
Energy consumption 237
Federally owned land 545
Governor, state officials 124, 127
Hazardous waste sites 228
Health insurance coverage 971
Immigrants admitted (1995) 383
Indians, American 550
Interest laws, rates 721, 722
Marriage, divorce laws 728, 729
Motor vehicles 245, 248
Name origin, nickname 544, 671
Population 380-81, 384
Cities, towns 409-11, 687, 692, 693, 695
Counties, county seats 431-32
Port traffic 242
Poverty rates 388
Presidential elections 76, 94, 106
Schools and libraries 252-53, 257
Taxes 245, 735, 736
Temperature, precipitation 222, 224
Unemployment benefits 165
Welfare assistance 389
**New York City** 692
Airport traffic 313
Bridges, tunnels 702, 703, 704
Buildings, tall 699-700
Ellis Island 529
Marathon 956
Mayor 123
Mileage to foreign ports 243
Population 377, 384, 386, 410, 692, 838
Port traffic 242
Statue of Liberty (1886) 501, 529
Theater openings (1995-96) 285, *781*
United Nations 843
World Trade Center bombing (1993, 1994) 509
**New York Stock Exchange**
Address 630
Volume, transactions 149
*see also* Stocks
**New Zealand** 568, 803
Ambassadors, envoys 847
Flag 483
Gross domestic product 134
Islands, areas 592
Mountain peaks 590
Wages, hourly 171
**Niagara Falls** 599
**Nicaragua** 69, 483, 576, 804, 847
**Nichols, Terry** (1995, 1996) 49, 510
**Nickel** (metal) 151, 152
**Nicknames**
College football teams 884-86
U.S. states 655-80
**Niger** 483, 804, 847
**Nigeria** 804-5
Ambassadors, envoys 847
Chronology (1995) 43
Flag 483
Gross domestic product 134
History 554, 560, 572
Trade 240
**Nile River** 596
**NIT.** *See* National Invitation Tournament
**Nitrogen oxide emissions** 228, 229
**Niue Island** 803
**Nixon, Richard M.** 105, 107, 109, 110, 536, 539
China visit (1972) 506
Impeachment hearings (1974) 507, 536
Moscow summit (1972) 506
Resignation (1974) 507, 574
Watergate (1973, 1974) 507
*see also* Presidents, U.S.
**Nobel Prizes** 39, 69, 317-19
**Nobility, forms of address** 641
**Norfolk, VA.** *See* Cities, U.S.
**Norfolk Island** 741
**Normandy, House of** 577
**Normandy invasion** (1944) 504
**North America** 838-39
AIDS cases 840
Bridges 702-5
Buildings, tall 540, 696-702
Cities 386-87, 594-95, 686-95
Time differences 480
Commercial fishing 164
Explorations 586
Gold production 153
Highest, lowest points 597
Lakes 598
Map 485
Mountain peaks 590, 591
Religious adherents 646
Rivers 596-97
Trade 240
Tunnels 705
Volcanoes 588, 589
Waterfalls 599
**North Atlantic Treaty Organization** 842-43
Bosnia peacekeeping mission (1995-96) 42, 45, 49, *779*
Established (1949) 504, 572
International commands 176
**North Carolina** 671-72
Admission, area, capital 542, 671, 672
Agriculture 156-61
Altitudes (high, low) 541
Birth, death statistics 963
Budget 135
Coastline 541
Congressional representation 112, 116, 380
Courts, U.S. 192
Crime, prisons, death penalty 959, 960, 961
Energy consumption 237
Federally owned land 545
Governor, state officials 124, 127
Hazardous waste sites 228
Health insurance coverage 971
Immigrants admitted (1995) 383
Indians, American 550
Interest laws, rates 721, 722
Marriage, divorce laws 728, 729
Motor vehicles 245, 248
Name origin, nickname 544, 671
Population 380-81, 384
Cities, towns 411, 687, 689, 693
Counties, county seats 432
Poverty rates 388
Presidential elections 76, 94-95, 106
Schools and libraries 252-53, 257
Taxes 245, 735, 736
Temperature, precipitation 222, 224
Toxic chemical pollution 228
Unemployment benefits 165
Welfare assistance 389
**North Dakota** 672
Admission, area, capital 542, 543, 672
Agriculture 156-61
Altitudes (high, low) 541
Birth, death statistics 963
Budget 135
Congressional representation 112, 116, 380
Courts, U.S. 192
Crime, prisons, death penalty 959, 960, 961
Energy consumption 237
Federally owned land 545
Governor, state officials 124, 127
Hazardous waste sites 228
Health insurance coverage 971
Immigrants admitted (1995) 383
Indians, American 550
Interest laws, rates 721, 722
Marriage, divorce laws 728, 729
Motor vehicles 245, 248
Name origin, nickname 544, 672
Population 380-81, 384
Cities, towns 411
Counties, county seats 432
Poverty rates 388
Presidential elections 76, 95-96, 106
Schools and libraries 252-53, 257
Taxes 245, 735, 736
Temperature, precipitation 222, 224
Unemployment benefits 165
Welfare assistance 389
**Northern Cyprus, Turkish Republic of** 758
**Northern Ireland.** *See* Ireland, Northern
**Northern Lights** 454, 555
**Northern Mariana Islands** 545, 682
Area 439, 592
Courts, U.S. 192
Immigrants admitted (1995) 383
Population 439
Zip codes 439
**North Island** 592, 803
**North Korea.** *See* Korea, North (Democratic People's Republic of)
**North Pole**
Discovery (1909) 502
Explorations 587
Magnetic force 459
**North Sea** 593
**Northwest Ordinance** (1787) 498
**Northwest Territory, U.S.** (1787) 498, 543
**Norway** 805
Ambassadors, envoys 847
Flag 483
Gross domestic product 134
Merchant fleet 244
Rulers, royal family 376, 582
Trade 240
Wages, hourly 171
**Notable personalities** 334-76
Obituaries (1995-96) 74-75
Sports 925-27
**NRC.** *See* Nuclear Regulatory Commission
**Nubia** 554
**Nuclear arms**
A-bomb
Dropped (1945) 504, 572
Experiments (1939) 503
H-bomb (1950, 1952) 504, 573
*Nautilus* submarine (1954) 504
Treaties, negotiations (1963-93, 1996) 47, 54, 67, 183, 505, 506, 508
Underground testing (1996) 48, 62
**Nuclear energy**
Accidents, major 306, 507, 574
First chain reaction (1942) 504
North Korea agreement (1995) 45
Power production 235, 238, 239

By U.S. states . . . . . . . . . . . . 655-80
**Nuclear Regulatory Commission** 188, 130
**Numbers, large** . . . . . . . . . . . . . . . . . 607
**Numerals, roman** . . . . . . . . . . . . . . . . 607
**Nutrition** . . . . . . . . . . . . . . . . . . . 609-12
Federal program costs . . . . . . . . . . . 158
Food labels . . . . . . . . . . . . . . . . . . . 612
Help organizations . . . . . . . . . . . . . . 618
Internet addresses . . . . . . . . . . . . . . 211
**Nuts**
Nutritive value . . . . . . . . . . . . . 609, 611
Prices, farm . . . . . . . . . . . . . . . . . . 162
Production . . . . . . . . . . . . . . . . . . . 161

— O—

**Oakland, CA.** *See* Cities, U.S.
**OAS.** *See* Organization of American States
**Oat production** . . . . . . . . . . 160, 161, 162
**OAU.** *See* Organization of African Unity
**Obesity** . . . . . . . . . . . . . . . . . . 612, 616
**Obituaries** (1995-96) . . . . . . . . . . . 74-75
**Occultation** (astronomical position) . . . . 443
Moon . . . . . . . . . . . . . . . . . . . 440-43
**Occupations**
Educational attainment . . . . . . . 167, 171
Injuries, fatalities . . . . . . . . . . . . . . . 168
By sex . . . . . . . . . . . . . . . . . . . . . . 166
**Oceans and seas**
Areas, depths . . . . . . . . . . . . . . . . . 593
Commercial fishing . . . . . . . . . . . . . 164
Crossings, notable . . . . . . . . . . . . . . 316
Islands . . . . . . . . . . . . . . . . . . . . . . 592
Marine warnings, advisories . . . . . . . 220
Territorial extent, U.S. . . . . . . . . . . . 545
**Odds** (cards, dice) . . . . . . . . . . . . . . . 607
**OECD.** *See* Organization for Economic Cooperation and Development
**Offbeat news stories** (1996) . . . . . . . . 71
**Ofu Island** . . . . . . . . . . . . . . . . . . . . 681
**Ohio** . . . . . . . . . . . . . . . . . . . . 672-73
Admission, area, capital 542, 543, 672, 673
Agriculture . . . . . . . . . . . . . . . . 156-61
Altitudes (high, low) . . . . . . . . . . . . . 541
Births, death statistics . . . . . . . . . . . . 963
Budget . . . . . . . . . . . . . . . . . . . . . . 135
Congressional representation . . . . . . 112, 116-17, 380
Courts, U.S. . . . . . . . . . . . . . . . . . . 192
Crime, prisons, death penalty . . . 959, 960, 961
Energy consumption . . . . . . . . . . . . . 237
Federally owned land . . . . . . . . . . . . 545
Governor, state officials . . . . . . 124, 127
Hazardous waste sites . . . . . . . . . . . 228
Health insurance coverage . . . . . . . . 971
Immigrants admitted (1995) . . . . . . . . 383
Indians, American . . . . . . . . . . . . . . 550
Interest laws, rates . . . . . . . . . . 721, 722
Marriage, divorce laws . . . . . . . 728, 729
Motor vehicles . . . . . . . . . . . . . 245, 248
Name origin, nickname . . . . . . . 544, 672
Population . . . . . . . . . . . . . 380-81, 384
Cities, towns 411-13, 686, 687, 688, 695
Counties, county seats . . . . . . 432-33
Port traffic . . . . . . . . . . . . . . . . . . . 242
Poverty rates . . . . . . . . . . . . . . . . . 388
Presidential elections . . . . . . 76, 96, 106
Schools and libraries . . . . . . 252-53, 257
Taxes . . . . . . . . . . . . . . 245, 735, 736
Temperature, precipitation . . . . . 222, 224
Toxic chemical pollution . . . . . . . . . 228
Unemployment benefits . . . . . . . . . . 165
Welfare assistance . . . . . . . . . . . . . . 389
**Ohio River** . . . . . . . . . . . . . . . 596, 597
**Ohm** (electrical unit) . . . . . . . . . . . . . 604
**Oil.** *See* Petroleum
**Oil spills** (1989) . . . . . . . . . . . . 306, 508
**Okhotsk, Sea of** . . . . . . . . . . . . . . . 593
**Okinawa Island** (1996) . . 54, 572, 592, 787
**Oklahoma** . . . . . . . . . . . . . . . . . . . . 673
Admission, area, capital . . . 542, 543, 673
Agriculture . . . . . . . . . . . . . . . . 156-61
Altitudes (high, low) . . . . . . . . . . . . . 541
Birth, death statistics . . . . . . . . . . . . 963
Budget . . . . . . . . . . . . . . . . . . . . . . 135
Congressional representation . . . 112, 117, 380
Courts, U.S. . . . . . . . . . . . . . . . . . . 192
Crime, prisons, death penalty . . . 959, 960, 961
Energy consumption . . . . . . . . . . . . . 237
Federally owned land . . . . . . . . . . . . 545
Governor, state officials . . . . 124, 127-28
Hazardous waste sites . . . . . . . . . . . 228
Health insurance coverage . . . . . . . . 971
Immigrants admitted (1995) . . . . . . . . 383
Indians, American . . . . . . . . . . . . . . 550
Interest laws, rates . . . . . . . . . . 721, 722
Marriage, divorce laws . . . . . . . 728, 729
Motor vehicles . . . . . . . . . . . . . 245, 248
Name origin, nickname . . . . . . . 544, 673
Population . . . . . . . . . . . . . . 380-81, 384
Cities, towns . . . . . . . . . 413, 692, 695
Counties, county seats . . . . . . . . . 433
Poverty rates . . . . . . . . . . . . . . . . . 388
Presidential elections . . . . 76, 96-97, 106
Schools and libraries . . . . . . . 252-53, 257
Taxes . . . . . . . . . . . . . . . 245, 735, 736
Temperatures, record . . . . . . . . . . . 224
Unemployment benefits . . . . . . . . . . 165
Welfare assistance . . . . . . . . . . . . . 389
**Oklahoma City, OK**
Bombing (1995, 1996) . . . . . . . . . 49,510
*see also* Cities, U.S.
**Old-age insurance.** *See* Social Security Administration
**Old Ironsides** (1797) . . . . . . . . . . . . . 498
**Old Testament** . . . . . . . . . . . . . . . . . 649
**Olosega Island** . . . . . . . . . . . . . . . . 681
**Olympic Games**
History, symbolism . . . . . . . . . . 853, 867
Summer . 33, 62, 65, *782-83*, 849, 849-62
Centennial Park bombing (1996) . . . 61, 68, *782*
Games sites . . . . . . . . . . . . . . . . 853
Medal standings (1996) . . . . . . . . 849
Medal winners (1996) . . . . . . . . 850-53
Winter . . . . . . . . . . . . . . . . . . . 863-67
Games sites . . . . . . . . . . . . . . . . 863
Medal standings (1994) . . . . . . . . 863
*see also under specific sports*
**Olympics, Special** . . . . . . . . . . . . . . 955
**Omaha, NE.** *See* Cities, U.S.
**Oman** . . . . . . . . . . . . 134, 483, 805-6, 847
**Omnibus Violent Crime Control and Prevention Act** (1994) . . . . . . . 509
**Onassis, Jacqueline Kennedy** (1996) . . . . . . . . . . . . . . . . . . 55, *200*
**Online services, commercial** (Internet) . . . . . . . . . . . . . . 207, 210
**Ontario, Lake** . . . . . . . . . . . . . . . . . 598
**OPEC.** *See* Organization of Petroleum Exporting Countries
**Open Door Policy** (1899) . . . . . . . . . . 501
**Opera**
Companies, U.S. . . . . . . . . . . . . 286-87
Composers . . . . . . . . . . . . . . . . 355-57
Singers . . . . . . . . . . . . . . . . . . . . . 358
**Opium War** . . . . . . . . . . . . . . . . . . . 565
**Opposition** (astronomical position) . . . 443
**Options** (stock) . . . . . . . . . . . . . . . . 148
**Orange Bowl** . . . . . . . . . . . . . . . . . . 881
**Orbits, planetary** . . . . . . . . . . . . . . . 455
**Orchestras, symphony** (U.S.) . . . . . . 286
**Oregon** . . . . . . . . . . . . . . . . . . . 673-74
Accession . . . . . . . . . . . . . . . . . . . . 545
Admission, area, capital . . . 542, 543, 674
Agriculture . . . . . . . . . . . . . . . . 156-61
Altitudes (high, low) . . . . . . . . . . . . 541
Birth, death statistics . . . . . . . . . . . . 963
Budget . . . . . . . . . . . . . . . . . . . . . 135
Coastline . . . . . . . . . . . . . . . . . . . . 541
Congressional representation . . 112, 117, 380
Courts, U.S. . . . . . . . . . . . . . . . . . 192
Crime, prisons, death penalty . . 959, 960, 961
Energy consumption . . . . . . . . . . . . 237
Federally owned land . . . . . . . . . . . 545
Governor, state officials . . . . . . . 124, 128
Hazardous waste sites . . . . . . . . . . 228
Health insurance coverage . . . . . . . . 971
Immigrants admitted (1995) . . . . . . . 383
Indians, American . . . . . . . . . . . . . 550
Interest laws, rates . . . . . . . . . . 721, 722
Marriage, divorce laws . . . . . . . 728, 729
Motor vehicles . . . . . . . . . . . . . 245, 248
Name origin, nickname . . . . . . . 544, 673
Population . . . . . . . . . . . . . . 380-81, 384
Cities, towns . . . . . . . . . . . 413-14, 693
Counties, county seats . . . . . . . 433-34
Port traffic . . . . . . . . . . . . . . . . . . 242
Poverty rates . . . . . . . . . . . . . . . . . 388
Presidential elections . . . . . . 76, 97, 106
Schools and libraries . . . . . . . 252-53, 257
Taxes . . . . . . . . . . . . . . . 245, 735, 736
Temperature, precipitation . . . . . 222, 224
Unemployment benefits . . . . . . . . . . 165
Welfare assistance . . . . . . . . . . . . . 389
**Organization for Economic Cooperation and Development** . . . 240, 236, 843
**Organization for Security and Cooperation in Europe** . . . . . . . . . . . . . . . 843
**Organization of African Unity** . . . . . . 843
**Organization of American States** (1948) . . . . . . . . . . . 504, 572, 843
**Organization of Petroleum Exporting Countries** . . . . . . . . . 240, 235, 843
**Organizations.** *See* Associations and societies; International organizations
**Orinoco River** . . . . . . . . . . . . . . . . . 596
**Orkney Islands** . . . . . . . . . . . . . 592, 830
**Orlando, FL** . . . . . . . . . . . . 123, 396, 700
**Orleans, House of** . . . . . . . . . . . . . . 580
**Orthodox churches.** *See* Eastern Orthodox churches
**Oscars.** *See* Academy Awards
**OSCE.** *See* Organization for Security and Cooperation in Europe
**Ottoman Empire** . . . . . . . . . 560, 566, 568
**Outland Award** . . . . . . . . . . . . . . . . 886
**Outlying areas, U.S.,** 681-83
Population . . . . . . . . . . . . . . . . . . 439

— P—

**Pacific Islanders, U.S.** . . . . . . . 377, 378, 379, 965, 975
**Pacific Ocean** . . . . . . . . . . . . . . . . . 593
Coast, U.S.
Length . . . . . . . . . . . . . . . . . . . . 541
Ports, cargo, volume . . . . . . . 242, 243
Commercial fishing . . . . . . . . . . . . 164
Crossings, notable . . . . . . . . . . . . 316
Discovery . . . . . . . . . . . . . . . . . . 586
Islands
Areas . . . . . . . . . . . . . . . . . . . . 592
U.S. . . . . . . . . . . . . . . . . 592, 681-83
Map . . . . . . . . . . . . . . . . . . . . . . 496
**Pacing, trotting** . . . . . . . . . . . . . . . 900
**Paine, Thomas** . . . . . . . . . . . . . . . . 511
**Painters, notable** . . . . . . . . . . . . 336-39
**Pakistan** . . . . . . . . . . . . . . . . . . . 806-7
Ambassadors, envoys . . . . . . . . . . . 847
Flag, map . . . . . . . . . . . . . . . 483, 492
Gross domestic product . . . . . . . . . . 134
History . . . . . . . . . . . . . . . . . 572, 575
Military strength . . . . . . . . . . . . . . 182
Nuclear power . . . . . . . . . . . . . . . . 239
**Palau** . . . . . . . . . . . . . 483, 592, 807, 847
**Paleontology** . . . . . . . . . . . . . . . . . 553
**Palestine**
History . . . . . . . . . . . . . . . . . 570, 572
Israeli gunfire clashes (1996) . . . . . . . 67
Israeli settlement expansion (1996) . . . 65
Militancy, uprisings . . . . . . 575, 576, 785
Refugees from . . . . . . . . . . . . . . . . 840
Self-rule (1995-96) . . . 45, 47-48, 55, 786
**Palestine Liberation Organization** . . . 788
Gaza, West Bank self-rule. . 47-48, 785, 786
**Palm Sunday** . . . . . . . . . . . . . . . . . 647
**Palmyra** (atoll) . . . . . . . . . . . . . . . . 683
**Panama** . . . . . . . . . . . . . . . . . . . . . 807
Ambassadors, envoys . . . . . . . . . . . 847
Distances to ports . . . . . . . . . . . . . 243
Flag . . . . . . . . . . . . . . . . . . . . . . . 483
Merchant fleet . . . . . . . . . . . . . . . . 244
Treaties, U.S. (1903, 1978) . 502, 507, 807
U.S. invasion (1989) . . . . . . . . . 508, 807
**Panama Canal** . . . . . . . . . . . . . . . . 807
Employees, federal . . . . . . . . . . . . . 169
Opened (1914) . . . . . . . . . . . . . . . . 502
Treaties (1903, 1978) . . . . 502, 507, 807
**Pantelleria Island** . . . . . . . . . . . . . . 786
**Paper**
Exports, imports . . . . . . . . . . . . . . 241
Invention . . . . . . . . . . . . . . . . . . . 556
Measures . . . . . . . . . . . . . . . . . . . 604
**Papua New Guinea** . . 483, 592, 807-8, 847
**Paraguay** . . . . . . . . . . . . . . 483, 808, 847
**Parcel post rates** . . . . . . . . . . . . 632-36
**Parenthood** . . . . . . . . . . . . . . . . . . 727
*see also* Households
**Paricutin volcano** . . . . . . . . . . . . . . 555
**Parks, national** (1994) . . . 510, 540, 546-49
Utah scenic area (1996) . . . . . . . . . . . 66
**Parliament**
British . . . . . . . . . . . . . . . . . . . . . 829
Oldest (Iceland) . . . . . . . . . . . . . . 773
**Parthenon** . . . . . . . . . . . . . . . . . . . 552
**Parthians** . . . . . . . . . . . . . . . . . . . 556
**Passport regulations, U.S.** . . . . . . . . 723
**Patents, U.S.** . . . . . . . . . . . . . . . . . 218
**Patrick, Saint** . . . . . . . . . . . . . 345, 558
**Peace Prizes, Nobel** . . . . . . . . . . 39, 319
**Peale Atoll** . . . . . . . . . . . . . . . . . . 683
**Peanut production** . . . . . . . . . . 161, 162
**Pearl Harbor** (1941) . . . . . . . . . . . . . 503
**Peary, Robert E.** (1909) . . . . . . . 502, 587
**Peloponnesian Wars** . . . . . . . . . . . . 552
**Pemba** . . . . . . . . . . . . . . . . . . 592, 824
**Penghu** (Pescadores) . . . . . . . . . . . . 823
**Pen names** . . . . . . . . . . . . . . . . . . 642
**Pennsylvania** . . . . . . . . . . . . . . . 674-75
Admission, area, capital . . . . . . . 542, 674
Agriculture . . . . . . . . . . . . . . . . 156-61
Altitudes (high, low) . . . . . . . . . . . . 541
Birth, death statistics . . . . . . . . . . . 963
Budget . . . . . . . . . . . . . . . . . . . . . 135
Coastline . . . . . . . . . . . . . . . . . . . 541
Congressional representation. . 117, 112, 380
Courts, U.S. . . . . . . . . . . . . . . . . . 192
Crime, prisons, death penalty . . 959, 960, 961

Energy consumption. . . . . . . . . . . . . 237
Federally owned land . . . . . . . . . . . 545
Governor, state officials . . . . . . 124, 128
Hazardous waste sites . . . . . . . . . . . 228
Health insurance coverage . . . . . . . . 971
Immigrants admitted (1995) . . . . . . . . 383
Indians, American . . . . . . . . . . . . . 550
Interest laws, rates. . . . . . . . . . 721, 722
Marriage, divorce laws . . . . . . . 728, 729
Motor vehicles. . . . . . . . . . . . 245, 248
Name origin, nickname . . . . . . . 544, 674
Population . . . . . . . . . . . . . 380-81, 384
Cities, towns . . . . . . . 414-15, 692, 693
Counties, county seats . . . . . . . . . 434
Port traffic . . . . . . . . . . . . . . . . . 242
Poverty rates . . . . . . . . . . . . . . . . 388
Presidential elections . . . . 76, 97-98, 106
Schools and libraries . . . . . . 252-53, 257
Taxes . . . . . . . . . . . . . . . . . 245, 735
Temperature, precipitation. . . . . 222, 224
Unemployment benefits . . . . . . . . . . 165
Welfare assistance. . . . . . . . . . . . . 389
**Pensions**
Veterans . . . . . . . . . . . . . . . . . . . 181
*see also* Social Security Administration
**Pentagon** (Defense Department) . . . . . 685
**Pentagon Papers** (1971). . . . . . . . . . . 506
**Pentathlon** . . . . . . . . . . . . . . . . . . . 851
**Pentecostal churches** . . . . . . . . . 652-53
Addresses, U.S. headquarters . . . . . . 646
Membership . . . . . . . . . . . . . . . . . 645
**Per capita income.** *See under* Incomes
**Perigee of moon** . . . . . . . . . . . . . . . 457
**Perihelion.** *See* Aphelion, perihelion
**Perón, Juan** . . . . . . . . . . . . 347, 573, 740
**Perot, H. Ross** (1995). . . . . . . . . . . . . 509
Presidential campaigns
1992. . . . . . . . . 76-105, 105, 107, 108
1996. . . 33-34, 60, 64, 65, 67, *193, 195*
Popular, electoral votes . . . . 76-105
**Perpetual calendar** . . . . . . . . . . . 476-77
**Perry, Matthew C.** (1853) . . . . . . . . . . 500
**Perry, Oliver H.** (1813) . . . . . . . . . . . . 499
**Pershing, John J.** (1916) . . . . . . . . . . 502
**Persia.** *See under* Iran
**Persian Gulf**
Area, depth. . . . . . . . . . . . . . . . . . 593
Map . . . . . . . . . . . . . . . . . . . . . . 492
**Persian Gulf War** (1991) . . . . . . . 509, 776, 790-91, 815
Black troops . . . . . . . . . . . . . . . . . 180
Casualties, U.S. forces . . . . . . . . . . 184
Kuwait invaded (1990) 509, 776, 790, 815
Veteran population. . . . . . . . . . . . . 180
**Personal consumption, U.S** . . . . 150, 131
**Personal income, U.S.** . . . . . . . . 133, 147
**Personalities, notable.** *See* Notable personalities
**Peru** . . . . . . . . . . . . . . . . . 575, 808-9
Ambassadors, envoys . . . . . . . . . . 847
Ancient civilizations . . . . . . . . . . . . 554
Commercial fishing . . . . . . . . . . . . 164
Flag . . . . . . . . . . . . . . . . . . . . . . 483
Rulers . . . . . . . . . . . . . . . . . . . . . 584
**Pescadores** (Penghu) . . . . . . . . . . . . 823
**Petroleum**
Arab embargo (1973) . . . . . . . . . . . 507
Exports, imports . . . . . . . . 235, 236, 241
First well (PA) (1859) . . . . . . . . . . . 500
Oil spills (1989) . . . . . . . . . . . 306, 508
OPEC . . . . . . . . . . . . . . 240, 235, 843
Production, consumption, U.S. . . . . . 235
Reserves, crude oil . . . . . . . . . . . . 238
U.S. dependence on. . . . . . . . . 235, 236
*see also* Gasoline
**Pharos of Alexandria**. . . . . . . . . . . . . 555
**Phases of moon** . . . . . . . . . . 457, 463-74
**Philadelphia, PA** . . . . . . . . . . . . . . . 692
Capital of U.S. (1790) . . . . . . . . . . . 498
Liberty Bell . . . . . . . . . . . . . . . 528-29
*see also* Cities, U.S.
**Philanthropists, notable**. . . . . . . . 340-41
**Philippines, Republic of the** . . . . . . . . 809
Accession, U.S. (1898) . . . . . . . 501, 809
Ambassadors, envoys . . . . . . . . . . . 847
Flag, map. . . . . . . . . . . . . . . . 483, 493
Gold production. . . . . . . . . . . . . . . 153
Gross domestic product . . . . . . . . . . 134
Independence (1946) . . . . . 504, 572, 809
Insurrection (1899). . . . . . . . . . . . . . 501
Islands, areas . . . . . . . . . . . . . . . . 592
Merchant fleet. . . . . . . . . . . . . . . . 244
Trade. . . . . . . . . . . . . . . . . . . . . 240
U.S. immigrants from . . . . . . . . 377, 383
World War II (1944) . . . . . . 504, 572, 809
**Philosophers, notable** . . . 344-45, 552, 564
**Phoenicians** . . . . . . . . . . . . . . . . . . 551
**Phoenix, AZ.** *See* Cities, U.S.
**Phosphorus** (dietary) . . . . . . . . . 609, 612
**Photographers, notable** . . . . . 323, 336-39
**Photographs of the year** (1996) . . *193-200, 777-84*
**Photography**
Inventions, notable . . . . . . . . . . 215, 216
Pulitzer Prizes . . . . . . . . . . . . . . . . 323
**Physicians.** *See* Doctors
**Physics**
Discoveries . . . . . . . . . . . . . . . . 217-18
Nobel Prizes . . . . . . . . . . . . . . 39, 317
**Physiology,** Nobel Prizes. . . . . . . . 39, 318
**Pierce, Franklin** . . . . . . . . . . . . . 109, 532
*see also* Presidents, U.S.
**Pig iron production** . . . . . . . . . . . . . 153
**Pilots, airplane** . . . . . . . . . . . . . . . . 315
**Ping-Pong.** *See* Table tennis
**Pinochle** (odds) . . . . . . . . . . . . . . . . 607
**Pisa, Leaning Tower of**. . . . . . . . . . . 555
**Pistol champions** (1996) . . . . . . . . . . 924
**Pitcairn Island** . . . . . . . . . . . . . . . . 831
**Pittsburgh, PA.** *See* Cities, U.S.
**Pizarro, Francisco** . . . . . . . . . . . 563, 586
**Planets** . . . . . . . . . . . 455, 440-43, 444-49
Configurations . . . . . . . . . . . . . . 440-43
Earth . . . . . . . . . . . . . . . . . 455, 457-60
Morning, evening stars . . . . . . . . . . 449
Rising, setting . . . . . . . . . . . . . . 452-53
Sun relationship . . . . . . . . . . . . 455, 444
*see also* Space developments
**Plantagenet, House of** . . . . . . . . . . . 577
**Plants**
Classification. . . . . . . . . . . . . . . . . 231
Endangered species . . . . . . . . . . . . 230
Exports, imports. . . . . . . . . . . . . . . 241
**Platinum** . . . . . . . . . . . . . . . . . . . . 151
**Playing cards** (odds). . . . . . . . . . . . . 607
**Plays.** *See* Theater
**Playwrights, notable** . 330, 350-51, 351-55
Pulitzer Prizes . . . . . . . . . . . . . . . 324
**Pledge of Allegiance** . . . . . . . . . . . . 527
**PLO.** *See* Palestine Liberation Organization
**Pluto** (planet) . . . . . . . . . . . . . 455, 448-49
Position by month. . . . . . . . . . . . 440-43
Sun, distance from . . . . . . . . . . 444, 455
**Plymouth colony** (1620) . . . . . . . 497, 563
**Poets, notable** . . . . . . . . . . . . . . . 351-55
Awards. . . . . . . . . . . . 318-19, 326, 327
Laureates . . . . . . . . . . . . . . . . . . 351
**Poisons**
Animals, venomous . . . . . . . . . . . . 232
Chemical pollution . . . . . . . . . . . . . 228
Death rates . . . . . . . . . . . . . . . 967, 968
**Poker odds** . . . . . . . . . . . . . . . . . . 607
**Poland** . . . . . . . . . . . . . . . . . . . . 809-10
Ambassadors, envoys. . . . . . . . . . . 847
Chronology (1995) . . . . . . . . . . . . . 43
Flag . . . . . . . . . . . . . . . . . . . . . . 483
Gross domestic product. . . . . . . . . . 134
History . . . . . . . . 559, 563, 564, 565, 576
Merchant fleet . . . . . . . . . . . . . . . 244
Military strength . . . . . . . . . . . . . . 182
Motor vehicle production . . . . . . . . . 246
Rulers . . . . . . . . . . . . . . . . . . . . . 582
Solidarity . . . . . . . . . . . . . . . . 576, 810
U.S. immigrants from . . . . . . . . 377, 383
World War II . . . . . . . . . . . . . . 571, 810
**Polar explorations** . . . . . . . . . . . . 586-88
**Poles of the earth** . . . . . . . . . . . . . . 459
**Pole vault**
Olympic champions . . . . . . . . . 852, 856
World records . . . . . . . . . . . . 867, 868
**Police** . . . . . . . . . . . . . . . . . . . . . . 958
**Political convention sites** (1996) . . . . . 63, 64, *194, 195*, 106
**Political leaders, notable** . . . . . . . 345-48
**Political parties**
Campaign spending ruling (1996) . . . . 39
Independent (1996) . . 60-61, 64, 76-105, *195*, 107
*see also* Democratic Party; Republican Party
**Polk, James K.** . . . . . . . . . . . . 109, 531-32
*see also* Presidents, U.S.
**Pollution.** *See* Environment
**Polynesia, French** . . . . . . . . . . . . . . 765
**Ponce de Leon** (1513). . . . . . . . . 497, 586
**Pony Express** (1860) . . . . . . . . . . . . 500
***Poor Richard's Almanac*** (1732) . . . . . 497
**Popes** . . . . . . . . . . . . . . . . . . . 649, 650
*see also* John Paul II, Pope
**Population, U.S.** . . . . . . . . . . . . . 377-439
Age, median (1790-1996) . . . . . 377, 382
Asian-Pacific Islander . . . . 377, 378, 379
Birth, death statistics. . . . 962, 963, 964
Black . . . . . . . . . . . . 377, 378, 379, 382
Census (1790-1990) . . . . . . . . . . 380-81
Census Act (1790) . . . . . . . . . . . . . 498
Census Bureau . . . . . . . . 187, 188, 378
Center of (1790-1990) . . . . . . . . . . 381
Children . . . . . . . . . . . . . 377, 379, 387
Cities . . . . . . . . 386-87, 390-420, 686-95
Colonies (1630-1780) . . . . . . . . . . . 378
Congressional apportionment . . . . . . 380
Counties . . . . . . . . . . . . . . 421-39, 384
Density (by state) . . . . . . . . . . . . . 384
Drug use . . . . . . . . . . . . . . . . . . . . 966
Educational level. . . . . . . . . . . . 253, 377
Elderly (over 65) . . . . . 377, 378, 379, 387
Ethnic, racial distribution . . 377, 378, 379, 382, 388, 550
Farm. . . . . . . . . . . . . . . . . . . . 156, 377
Foreign-born percentage (1990-95) . . 383
Gender distribution . . . . . . . . . . 379, 382
Geographic mobility (1960-94) . . . . . 387
Hispanic . . . . . . . . . . . . . 377, 378, 379
Immigration . . . . . . . . . . . . . . . 377, 383
Indian, American. . . . . 377, 378, 379, 550
Marital status . . . . . . . . . . . . . . 377, 962
Metropolitan areas (1990-94) . . . . . . 385
More than 5,000 (by state) . . . . . 390-420
Poverty statistics. . . . . . . . . . 377, 387-88
Projections . . . . . . . . . . . . . . . . . . 839
By age . . . . . . . . . . . . . . . . . 378, 387
By race . . . . . . . . . . . . . . . . . . . 378
Religious groups. . . . . . . . . . . . . 644-45
Residence type. . . . . . . . . . . . . . . . 379
States . . . . . . . . . . . 384, 421-39, 655-80
Census (1790-1990). . . . . . . . . 380-81
Veterans . . . . . . . . . . . . . . . . . . . . 180
Youth (under age 18) . . . . . 377, 378, 387
**Population, world**
Cities
By country . . . . . . . . . . . . . . 737-837
By largest. . . . . . . . . . . . . . . . . . 838
Continents . . . . . . . . . . . . . . . . . . 838
Growth (AD 1-1996) . . . . . . . . . . . . . 553
Growth rate (by country). . . . . . . 737-837
Projections (2010, 2020) . . . . . . . 838-39
Religious adherents. . . . . . . . . . . . . 646
**Porcelain Tower of Nanking** . . . . . . . 555
**Pork**
Nutritive value . . . . . . . . . . . . . . . 610
Prices, farm . . . . . . . . . . . . . . . . . 162
Production, consumption . . . . . . . . . 157
**Portland, OR.** *See* Cities, U.S.
**Ports** . . . . . . . . . . . . . . . . . . . . 243, 242
**Portugal** . . . . . . . . . . . . . . . . . . . . . 810
Ambassadors, envoys . . . . . . . . . . . 847
Flag . . . . . . . . . . . . . . . . . . . . . . 483
Gross domestic product . . . . . . . . . . 134
History . . . . . . . . . . . . . . 569, 570, 575
Wages, hourly . . . . . . . . . . . . . . . . 171
**Possessions, U.S.** . . . . . . . . . . . . . 681-83
Courts, U.S. . . . . . . . . . . . . . . . . . 192
Governors . . . . . . . . . . . . . . . . . . 124
Populations . . . . . . . . . . . . . . . . . 439
ZIP codes . . . . . . . . . . . . . . . . . . 439
**Postage stamps** (1847) . . . . . . . . . . . 500
**Postal cards**
First U.S. (1873) . . . . . . . . . . . . . . 501
International rates . . . . . . . . . . . . . 635
**Postal information** . . . . . . . . . . . . 632-36
Abbreviations . . . . . . . . . . . . . . . . 634
Domestic rates . . . . . . . . . . . . . 632-34
Express and Priority Mail . . . . . . . . . 632
International rates . . . . . . . . . . . 635-36
Parcel post rates. . . . . . . . . . . . . 632-36
ZIP codes . . . . . . . . . . . . 390-420, 439
**Postal Service, U.S.** . . . . . . . . 188, 632-36
Abbreviations . . . . . . . . . . . . . . . . 634
Employees, payroll . . . . . . . . . . . . 169
Established (1970) . . . . . . . . . 506, 632
Internet address . . . . . . . . . . . . . . 210
Rates . . . . . . . . . . . . . . . . . . . . 632-36
**Potatoes**
Nutritive value . . . . . . . . . . . . . . . 611
Prices, farm . . . . . . . . . . . . . . . . . 162
Production. . . . . . . . . . . . . . . . 160, 161
**Poultry products**
Egg production . . . . . . . . . . . . . . . 157
Nutritive value . . . . . . . . . . . . 609, 610
Prices
Egg (per dozen, by state) . . . . . . . 157
Farm . . . . . . . . . . . . . . . . . . . . . 162
**Pound** (measure) . . . . . . . . . 601, 602, 603
**Poverty**
Rates, levels . . . . . . . . 172, 377, 387-88
Welfare assistance, by state . . . . . . . 389
**Powell, Colin** (1989, 1995) 41, 183, 508, 510
**Power-boat racing** . . . . . . . . . . . . . . 936
**Preakness Stakes**. . . . . . . . . . . . . . 897-98
**Precipitation**
International. . . . . . . . . . . . . . . . . . 225
U.S.
Cities. . . . . . . . . . . . . . . . . . . 221, 223
States . . . . . . . . . . . . . . . . . . . . 222
Wettest spot. . . . . . . . . . . . . . 222, 540
*see also* Blizzards
**Presbyterian churches** . . . . . . . . . . 652-53
Addresses, U.S. headquarters. . . . . . 646
Membership. . . . . . . . . . . . . . . . . . 645
**Presidential elections** . . . . . . . . . . 76-108
Electoral College. . . 380, 106, 516-17, 520
Independent parties (1996). . . . . . 60-61, 64, *195*, 107

National convention sites . . . . . . . . . 106
1996 campaign . . . . . . 47, 65-66, *193-95*
Contenders for office (1995, 1996). . 41, 60-61, 510
Primaries, conventions . 42, 49, 50, 63, 64, *194, 195*
Party nominees . . . . . . . . . . . . . . . 107
Popular, electoral votes . . . . . . . 76, 108
Returns (by states, counties) . . . . 77-105
Voter participation (1932-92) . . . . . . . 105
**Presidents, U.S.**
Address, form of . . . . . . . . . . . . . . . 641
Ages . . . . . . . . . . . . . . . . . . . . . . . 109
Aides . . . . . . . . . . . . . . . . . . . . . . . 185
Appointment powers. . . . . . . . . . . . . 517
Assassinations . 307, 500, 501, 502, 505, 532, 533, 534, 536, 539
Biographies . . . . . . . . . . . . . . 530-38
Birth, death dates . . . . . . . . . . . . . 109
Burial sites . . . . . . . . . . . . . . . . . . 539
Cabinets . . . . . . . . . . . . . . 185, 201-5
Children, number of . . . . . . . . . . . . 538
Clinton administration . . . . . . . . . 185-88
Congresses . . . . . . . . . . . . . . . 109-10
Constitutional powers . . . . . . . . . . . 517
Disability . . . . . . . . . . . . . . . . 517, 525
Election (*see* Presidential elections)
Inauguration date. . . . . . . . . . . . . . . 521
Internet addresses . . . . . . . . . . 210, 539
Libraries. . . . . . . . . . . . . . . . . . . . . 539
Notable facts. . . . . . . . . . . . . . . . . . 539
Oath of office . . . . . . . . . . . . . 517, 525
Party . . . . . . . . . . . . . . . . . . . . . . . 107
Popular, electoral votes . . . . . . . 76,108
Salary . . . . . . . . . . . . . . . . . . . . . . 185
Salutes, honors . . . . . . . . . . . . . . . 177
Succession law . . . . . . . . . . . . 522, 525
Term beginning, limit . . . . . . 185, 521-22
Vetoes . . . . . . . . . . . . . . . . . . . . . . 120
Vice presidents . . . . . . . . . . . . . 109-10
White House. . . . . . . . . . . . . . 185, 685
Wives . . . . . . . . . . . . . . . . . . 538, 539
**Press.** *See* Magazines; Newspapers
**Pressure, measures of.** . . . . . . . . . . 607
**Price indexes, consumer** . . . . . . 131, 132
**Priest, form of address** . . . . . . . . . . 641
**Primaries, 1996 presidential.** *See under* Presidential elections
**Prime Meridian** . . . . . . . . . . . . 479, 484
**Príncipe.** *See* Sao Tomé and Príncipe
**Printer's measures** . . . . . . . . . . . . . 604
**Priority Mail** . . . . . . . . . . . . . . . . . 632
**Prism,** Volume formula . . . . . . . . . . . 607
**Prisoners of war,** Geneva Conventions . 845
**Prison population** . . . . . . . . . . . 960, 961
**Prizes.** *See* Awards, prizes
**Probability** (cards, dice) . . . . . . . . . . 607
**Prohibition** (1917, 1933) . . . 502, 503, 521, 570
**Protein**. . . . . . . . . . . . . 609, 610-11, 612
**Protestant churches** . . . . . . . . . . 652-53
Books of the Bible . . . . . . . . . . . . . . 649
Clergy, forms of address . . . . . . . . . . 641
Membership . . . . . . . . . 644-45, 646, 651
Reformation . . . . . . . . . . . . . . . . . . 562
*see also specific denominations*
**Protestant Episcopal Church.** *See* Episcopal Church
**Providence, RI** . . . . . . . . . . . . . 123, 701
**Prussia.** *See* Germany
**Public debt**. . . . . . . . . . . . . 131, 130, 155
**Public holidays** . . . . . . . . . . . . . . . . 480
**Public libraries, U.S., Canada** . . . . . . . 257
**Public schools.** *See* Education
**Puerto Rico** . . . . . . . . . . . . . . . . 682-83
Accession (1898). . . . . . . . . . . . 501, 545
Altitudes (high, low) . . . . . . . . . . . . . 541
Area . . . . . . . . . . . . . . . . 439, 545, 592
Cities (population) . . . . . . . . . . . . . . 439
Congressional delegate . . . . . . . . . . . 118
Courts, U.S. . . . . . . . . . . . . . . . . . . 192
Government . . . . . . . . . . . . . . . . . . 683
Governor . . . . . . . . . . . . . . . . . . . . 124
Immigrants admitted (1995) . . . . . . . . 383
Interest laws, rates. . . . . . . . . . . 721, 722
Marriage, divorce laws . . . . . . . 728, 729
Name origin . . . . . . . . . . . . . . . . . . 544
Port traffic . . . . . . . . . . . . . . . . . . . 242
Unemployment benefits . . . . . . . . . . . 165
Welfare assistance. . . . . . . . . . . . . . 389
ZIP codes. . . . . . . . . . . . . . . . . . . . 439
**Pulitzer Prizes**. . . . . . . . . . . . . 319-27, *781*
**Pure Food and Drug Act** (1906). . . . . . 502
**Pyramid,** Volume formula . . . . . . . . . . 607
**Pyramids** (Egypt) . . . . . . . . . . . . . . . 555
**Pyrenees** . . . . . . . . . . . . . . . . . . . . 591

— Q—

**Qatar** . . . . . . . . . . . . 134, 483, 811, 847
**Quadrature** (astronomical position) . . . . 443
**Quakers** (Society of Friends) . . . . 644, 645
**Queen Anne's War** (1701-13). . . . . . . 497
**Queens County, NY** . . . . . . . . . . 384, 431
**Quemoy** . . . . . . . . . . . . . . . . . 592, 823
**Quire** (measure) . . . . . . . . . . . . . . . . 604
**Quotes, notable** (1996) . . . . . . . . . . . . 70

— R—

**Rabin, Yitzhak** (1995, 1996). . . . . . 42-43, 52, 75, 307, 347, 786
**Race**
Distribution . . . . . . . . 377, 379, 382, 550
By state. . . . . . . . . . . . . . . . . 655-80
Poverty rates. . . . . . . . . . . . . . . . . 388
*see also* Aleuts, U.S.; Asians, U.S.; Blacks; Hispanics; Indians, American; Pacific Islanders, U.S.
**Racing**
Automobile . . . . . . . . . . . . . . . . 930-32
Bicycle . . . . . . . . . . . . . . . . . . . . . 850
Bobsled . . . . . . . . . . . . . . . . . . . . 863
Harness . . . . . . . . . . . . . . . . . . . . 900
Motorcycle . . . . . . . . . . . . . . . . . . 932
Power boat . . . . . . . . . . . . . . . . . . 936
Rowing. . . . . . . . . . . . . . . . . . 850, 851
Skiing. . . . . . . . . . . . . . . . . 864-66, 919
Sled dog . . . . . . . . . . . . . . . . . . . . 936
Speed skating . . . . . . . . . . . . . . 866-67
Swimming . . . . . . . *782*, 852, 858-61, 905
Thoroughbred horse . . . . . . . . . 897-900
Track and field. . *783*, 852, 853-58, 867-68
Yacht . . . . . . . . . . . . . . . . . . . . . . 936
**Radio**
Advertising expenditures . . . . . . . . . 297
Awards. . . . . . . . . . . . . . . . . . . . . 328
Broadcast, first (1920). . . . . . . . . . . 502
Commercial stations . . . . . . . . . . . . 291
Inventions, notable . . . . . . . . . . . . . 216
Notable personalities . . . . . . . . . 360-76
Reform legislation (1996). . . . . . . . 38, 48
Transatlantic, first (1901) . . . . . . . . . 568
*War of the Worlds* scare (1938) . . . . 503
**Railroads, U.S.**
Accidents, deaths. . . . . . . . 168, 300-301
First Mississippi R. crossing (1855) . . 500
First passenger (1828) . . . . . . . . . . 499
Growth (19th century) . . . . . . . . . . . 566
Transcontinental (1869). . . . . . . . . . 501
**Railroads, world**
Accidents, deaths. . . . . . . . . . . 300-301
Growth (19th century) . . . . . . . . . . . 566
Tunnels, longest. . . . . . . . . . . . . . . 706
**Rainfall.** *See* Precipitation
**Raleigh, NC.** *See* Cities, U.S.
**Ramayana**. . . . . . . . . . . . . . . . 554, 654
**Rape**. . . . . . . . . . . 957, 958, 959, 960, 961
***Reader's Digest*** (1922). . . . . . . . . . . 503
**Reagan, Ronald** . 105, 107, 109, 110, 537, 539
*see also* Presidents, U.S.
**Ream** (measure). . . . . . . . . . . . . . . . 604
**Recommended Daily Dietary Allowances** . . . . . . . . . . . 609, 612
**Reconstruction Era** (1866) . . . . . . . . 501
Constitutional amendments . . . . . 520-21
**Recordings**
Awards. . . . . . . . . . . . 292-93, 333, *781*
Chinese copyright violations (1996) . 59-60
Sales . . . . . . . . . . . . . . . . . . . . 291-92
**Recreation, personal expenditures** . . 150
**Recreation areas, national** . . . . . 545, 549
**Rectangle,** Area formula . . . . . . . . . . 607
**Red Sea** . . . . . . . . . . . . . . . . . . . . 593
**Reformation, Protestant**. . . . . . . . . . 562
**Reformed churches** . . . . . . . . . . 645, 646
**Reform Party** (1996) 60, 64, 65, 76-105, *195*
**Refrigerators**. . . . . . . . . . . . . . . . . 237
**Refugees, world** . . . . . . . . . . . . . . 840
**Religion** . . . . . . . . . . . . . . . . . 644-54
Addresses, U.S. headquarters . . . 645-46
Adherents
Canada . . . . . . . . . . . . . . . . . . . 651
U.S. . . . . . . . . . . . . . . . . . . . 644-45
Worldwide . . . . . . . . . . . . . . . . . 646
Beliefs, practices . . . . . . . . . . . 652-54
Bible . . . . . . . . . . . . . . . . . . . . . . 649
Christian denominations . . . . . . . 652-53
Holy days . . . . . . . . . . . . . . . . 647-48
Major world . . . . . . . . . . . . . . . 652-54
Religious figures . . . . . . . . . 329, 344-45
School prayer banned (1963) . . . . . . 505
*see also specific faiths, denominations*
**Renaissance** . . . . . . . . . . . . . . 561, 562
**Reno, Janet** (1993, 1994). . . . . . . . . . 509
**Rents,** Consumer price index . . . . 131, 132
**Reporters.** *See* Journalism awards
**Republican Party**
Congressional elections (1994). . . . . 510
Congressional members (1901-96) . . 120
Contract With America (1995). . . . 38, 510
Convention sites . . . . . . . . . . . . . . 106
Democratic defectors (1995) . . . . . 41, 44
First presidential nominee (1856) . . . 500
Formed (1854) . . . . . . . . . . . . . . . . 500
Presidential campaign (1996) . 47, 60, *193*
National convention . . . . . . . . 63, *194*
Primaries, caucuses . . . . . . . 42, 49, 50
Presidential elections (by county). . 77-105
Presidential, vice presidential candidates. . . . . . . . . . . . . . . . 107
**Reservoirs, major**. . . . . . . . . . . . . . 707
**Réunion Island**. . . . . . . . . . . . . 592, 765
**Revenue sharing** . . . . . . . . . . . . 129-30
**Revere, Paul** (1775). . . . . . . . . . . . . 498
**Revolutionary War.** *See* American Revolution
**Rheumatic heart disease**. . . . . . . . . . 974
**Rhode Island** . . . . . . . . . . . . . . . . 675
Admission, area, capital . . . . . . . 542, 675
Agriculture . . . . . . . . . . . . . . . . 156-61
Altitudes (high, low). . . . . . . . . . . . . 541
Birth, death statistics . . . . . . . . . . . . 963
Budget . . . . . . . . . . . . . . . . . . . . . 135
Coastline. . . . . . . . . . . . . . . . . . . . 541
Congressional representation . . 112, 117, 380
Courts, U.S. . . . . . . . . . . . . . . . . . 192
Crime, prisons, death penalty . . . 959, 960
Energy consumption . . . . . . . . . . . . 237
Federally owned land. . . . . . . . . . . . 545
Governor, state officials . . . . . . . 124, 128
Hazardous waste sites. . . . . . . . . . . 228
Health insurance coverage . . . . . . . . 971
Immigrants admitted (1995) . . . . . . . 383
Indians, American . . . . . . . . . . . . . . 550
Interest laws, rates . . . . . . . . . . 721, 722
Marriage, divorce laws. . . . . . . . 728, 729
Motor vehicles . . . . . . . . . . . . . 245, 248
Name origin, nickname . . . . . . . 544, 675
Population . . . . . . . . . . . . 380-81, 384
Cities, towns . . . . . . . . . . . . . . . . 415
Counties, county seats . . . . . . . . . 434
Poverty rates . . . . . . . . . . . . . . . . . 388
Presidential elections. . . . . . . 76, 98, 106
Schools and libraries . . . . . . . 252-53, 257
Taxes . . . . . . . . . . . . . . . . . . . 245, 735
Temperature, precipitation . . . . . 222, 224
Unemployment benefits . . . . . . . . . . 165
Welfare assistance . . . . . . . . . . . . . 389
**Rhodesia.** *See* Zimbabwe
**Rice** . . . . . . . . . . . . . . 161, 162, 163, 241
**Richmond, VA.** *See* Cities, U.S.
**Richmond County, NY** (Staten Island) . 431
**Ride, Sally** (1983) . . . . . . . . . . . . 310, 508
**Rifle champions** (1996) . . . . . . . . . . . 924
**Right ascension** (astronomical position) 443
**Rig Veda** . . . . . . . . . . . . . . . . . 552, 654
**Ring of Fire volcanoes** . . . . . . . . . . . 588
**Rio de Janiero, Brazil** . . . . . . . . . 555, 838
**Rio Grande** . . . . . . . . . . . . . . . 596, 597
**Riots**
Coal miner's strike (1922). . . . . . . . . 503
Detroit (1943, 1967) . . . . . . . . . . 504, 506
Haymarket (1886). . . . . . . . . . . . . . . 501
Los Angeles (1965, 1992). . . . . . . 506, 509
Newark (NJ) (1967). . . . . . . . . . . . . . 506
New York City (1863, 1943) . . . . 500, 504
Slave revolt (1712) . . . . . . . . . . . . . 497
**Rivers**
North American . . . . . . . . . . . . . 596-97
World . . . . . . . . . . . . . . . . . . . . . . 596
*see also specific rivers*
**Riverside, CA.** *See* Cities, U.S.
**Roads**
Interstate system (1956). . . . . . . . . . 505
Mileage between cities. . . . . . . . . . . 249
**Robberies** . . . . . . . . . . . 957, 958, 959, 961
**Rochester, NY.** *See* Cities, U.S.
**Rock & roll**
Concerts, top-grossing (1985-95; 1995) . . . . . . . . . . . . . . . . . . 291
Notable personalities . . . 333, 359-60, *781*
**Rockets.** *See* Nuclear arms; Space developments
**Rodeo champions** . . . . . . . . . . . . . . 936
***Roe* v. *Wade*** (1973). . . . . . . . . . . 506, 524
**Rogers, Will** (1935) . . . . . . . . . . . . . . 503
**Roman Catholicism** . . . . . . . . . . . 652-53
Address, U.S. headquarters . . . . . . . 646
Books of the Bible. . . . . . . . . . . . . . 649
Clergy, forms of address . . . . . . . . . 641
Hierarchy. . . . . . . . . . . . . . . . . . . . 649
Pope John Paul II (1981, 1982) . . . . 308, 649, 833
Popes (chronological list) . . . . . . . . . 650
Population, U.S., world. . . . 645, 646, 651
Vatican City . . . . . . . . . . . . . . . 833, 848
**Romania** . . . . . . . . . . . . . . . . . . . . 811
Ambassadors, envoys . . . . . . . . . . . 847
Flag . . . . . . . . . . . . . . . . . . . . . . . 483
History . . . . . . . . . . . . . . . . . . 570, 576
Merchant fleet . . . . . . . . . . . . . . . . 244
Military strength . . . . . . . . . . . . . . . 182
Nuclear power . . . . . . . . . . . . . . . . 239

**Roman numerals** . . . 607
**Romans, ancient**
Historical figures . . . 577
Measures . . . 605
Rulers, emperors . . . 556, 583
**Rome**
Founding . . . 556
Seven Wonders, Middle Ages . . . 555
**Roosevelt, Franklin D.** . . . 105, 107, 109, 110, 535, 539
New Deal (1933) . . . 503, 571
World War II (1939, 1941, 1945) . . 503, 504
*see also* Presidents, U.S.
**Roosevelt, Theodore** . 107, 109, 110, 534, 539
*see also* Presidents, U.S.
**Rose Bowl** . . . 881
**Rose Island** . . . 681
**Ross, Betsy** . . . 526
**Ross Dependency** . . . 803
**Rostenkowski, Dan** (1996) . . . 53
**Rowing** . . . 851
**Royalty** . . . 577-85
Address, forms of . . . 641
European families . . . 376
Charles, Diana divorce (1996) . . 46, 50, 62, *200*
**Rushmore, Mt.** *See* Mt. Rushmore
**Russia** . . . 811-13
Ambassadors, envoys . . . 847
Area, world's largest country . . . 838
Chronology (1995-96)
Bosnia peacekeeping efforts . . . 47
Chechen revolt . . . 47, 54-55, 57, 61, 65, *777*
Legislative elections . . . 45
Nuclear arms pact . . . 47
Presidential election . . . 59, 61, 65, *777*
Commercial fishing . . . 164
Energy production, consumption . . . 236
Flag, map . . . 483, 491
Gold production . . . 153
Gross domestic product . . . 134
Islands, areas . . . 592
Leaders . . . 585
Merchant fleet . . . 244
Military strength . . . 182
Mineral resources . . . 151, 152
Nuclear power . . . 238, 239
Russian Federation . . . 812-13
Space exploration (1995, 1996) . . *199*, 311, 312, 510
Trade . . . 240
Yeltsin, Boris . . . 33, 59, 61, 65, 777
*see also* Soviet Union
**Russian Empire** (pre-1917) . . . 560
Alaska (1741, 1867) . . . 497, 501
Congress of Vienna . . . 565
Crimean War (1853-56) . . . 566
Japanese War (1904-5) . . . 568
Orthodox Church . . . 560
Tsars . . . 560, 585
*see also* Russia; Soviet Union (*for later history*)
**Russian Federation.** *See* Russia
**Russian Orthodox churches.** *See* Eastern Orthodox churches
**Russian Revolution** (1917) . . . 569
**Russo-Japanese War** (1904-5) . . . 568
**Rwanda** . . . 813
Ambassadors, envoys . . . 847
Flag . . . 483
Refugees from . . . 840
**Rye production** . . . 161

—S—

**Saba Island** . . . 803
**SAC.** *See* Strategic Air Command
**Sacco-Vanzetti case** (1920) . . . 502
**Sacramento, CA.** *See* Cities, U.S.
**Sadat, Anwar al-** (1981) . . 307, 347, 576, 761
**Saints.** *See name, inverted*
**St. Croix Island** . . . 439, 683
**St. Eustatius Island** . . . 803
**St. Helena Island** . . . 592, 831
**St. Helens volcano** (1980) . . 507, 545, 588, 589
**St. John Island** . . . 439, 683
**St. Kitts and Nevis** . . . 483, 813, 847
**St. Lawrence River**
Discovered . . . 586
Length, outflow . . . 596, 597
**St. Lawrence Seaway** (1959) . . . 505
**St. Louis, MO.** *See* Cities, U.S.
**St. Lucia** . . . 483, 813-14, 847
**St. Maarten** . . . 803
**St. Paul, MN.** *See* Cities, U.S.
**St. Petersburg, FL.** *See* Cities, U.S.
**St. Pierre and Miquelon** . . . 765
**St. Thomas Island** . . . 439, 683
**St. Valentine's Day Massacre** (1929) . . 503
**St. Vincent and the Grenadines** . . 244, 483, 814, 847
**Salaries and wages**
Armed Forces scale . . . 183
Average . . . 167, 171
College professors . . . 256
Earnings . . . 173, 167, 170
Governors, state officials . . . 124-28
Hourly rate distribution . . . 170
Hourly rates, by country . . . 171
Judges, U.S. . . . 190, 192
Minimum wage
Enacted (1938) . . . 503
Hourly rates . . . 170
Increase (1996) . . . 38, 56, 63
Pay, average . . . 171, 173
Paycheck withholding tax (1943) . . . 504
Pay differentials . . . 167
President, U.S. . . . 185
Representatives, U.S. . . . 112
Senators, U.S. . . . 111
Supreme Court justices . . . 189
Teachers . . . 252, 256
Vice president, U.S. . . . 185
*see also* Income taxes
**SALT I and II.** *See* Strategic Arms Limitation Treaty, I and II
**Salt Lake City, UT** . . . 123, 418, 701
**Salutations, persons of rank** . . . 641
**Salutes and honors** . . . 177
**Salvation Army** . . . 645, 646
**Samoa, American** . . . 681-82
Accession . . . 545
Altitudes (high, low) . . . 541
Area . . . 439, 545, 592
Congressional delegate . . . 118
Population . . . 439
ZIP code . . . 439
**Samoa, Western** . . . 484, 592, 834-35, 848
**San Antonio, TX.** *See* Cities, U.S.
**San Bernardino, CA** . . . 123, 384, 387, 393
**Sand Atoll** . . . 683
**Sand Creek Massacre** (1864) . . . 500
**San Diego, CA.** *See* Cities, U.S.
**San Francisco, CA**
Earthquakes (1906, 1989) . . . 303, 304, 502, 508
Mileage to foreign ports . . . 243
*see also* Cities, U.S.
**San Jose, CA.** *See* Cities, U.S.
**San Marino** . . . 134, 483, 814
**Santa Ana, CA.** *See* Cities, U.S.
**Sao Tomé and Príncipe** . . . 483, 814, 847
**Sardinia** . . . 592, 786
**Sark Island** . . . 592, 830
**Satellites, space.** *See* Space developments
**Saturn** (planet) . . . 455, 447
Morning, evening stars . . . 449
Position by month . . . 440-43
Rises, sets . . . 453
Sun, distance from . . . 455, 444
**Saudi Arabia** . . . 814-15
Ambassadors, envoys . . . 847
Energy production . . . 236
Flag, map . . . 483, 492
Gross domestic product . . . 134
History . . . 570, 574
Merchant fleet . . . 244
Persian Gulf War (1991) . . . 509, 815
Trade . . . 240
U.S. installation bombings (1995, 1996) . . . 43, 60, 306, 510, *779*
**Savings and loan crisis** (1989) . . . 39, 136, 508
**Savings bonds, U.S.** . . . 139
**Scandinavia** . . . 559
*see also* Denmark; Norway; Sweden
**Scholastic Aptitude Testing (SAT) Program** . . . 255-56
**School prayer ban** (1963) . . . 505
**Schools.** *See* Education
**Science and technology** . . . 215-19, *199*
Awards . . . 317-18, 329
Chemical elements . . . 218-19
Inventions, discoveries . . . 215-18
Mars primitive life-form discovery (1996) . . . 65
Scientific Revolution (1500-1700) . . . 562
Scientists, notable . . . 317-18, 348-49
*see also* Computers; Internet
**Scorpions, poisonous** . . . 232
**Scotland** . . . 578, 830
Dunblane kindergarten slaying (1996) . . . 52, *779*
*see also* United Kingdom
**Sculptors, notable** . . . 336-39
**Sea creatures, venomous** . . . 232
**Seas.** *See* Oceans and seas
**Seashores, national** . . . 549
**Seasons** . . . 459
**SEATO.** *See* Southeast Asia Treaty Organization
**Seattle, WA.** *See* Cities, U.S.
**Secret Service, U.S.** . . . 186, 188
**Securities and Exchange Commission** . . . 188, 130
**Seeds** . . . 241, 611
**Segregation.** *See* Desegregation
**Selective Service System.** *See* Draft, U.S.
**Self-employment**
Social Security benefits . . . 709
Taxes, federal . . . 730
**Seminole War** (1835) . . . 499
**Senate.** *See* Congress, U.S.
**Senegal** . . . 483, 815, 847
**Sentences, prison** . . . 960
**Serbia** (1995-96) . . . 40, 42, 43, 45, 47, 49, 52, 57, 60, 62
**Seventh-Day Adventists** . . . 644
**Seven Wonders of the World** . . . 555
**Sexual harassment**
Clinton accuser (1994, 1996) . 46, 55, 509
Thomas accuser (1991) . . . 509
**Seychelles** . . . 483, 592, 815-16, 847
**Shakespeare, William** . . . 354, 561
Folger Library . . . 684
**Shalikashvili, John** . . . 176, 183, 186
**Shay's Rebellion** (1787) . . . 498
**Sheep** . . . 156, 157, 162
**Shepard, Alan B., Jr.** (1961) . . . 309, 505
**Sherman, William** (1864, 1865) . . . 500
**Sherman Antitrust Act** (1890) . . . 501
**Shetland Islands** . . . 592, 830
**Shi'ites.** *See* Islam
**Shintoism** . . . 558, 646
**Shipping**
Distances between ports . . . 243
Merchant fleets . . . 243-44
Tonnage at ports . . . 242, 243-44
**Ships**
Disasters (1915, 1989) . . 298-99, 502, 508
Frigates, famous U.S. (1797) . . . 498
Great White Fleet (1907) . . . 502
Steamboats
First Atlantic crossing (1819) . . . 499
Fulton's (1807) . . . 499
Inventors . . . 216
*see also* Submarines
**Shipwrecks** . . . 298-99
**Shooting** (sport)
Olympic champions (1996) . . . 851
Rifle, pistol champions (1996) . . . 924
**Shot put**
Olympic champions . . . 852, 856, 858
World records . . . 867, 868
**Shreveport, LA.** *See* Cities, U.S.
**Siam.** *See* Thailand
**Sicily** . . . 592, 786
**Sidereal day, year, time** . . . 458, 450
**Sierra Leone** . . . 483, 816, 840, 847
**Sign language** . . . 643
**Signs and symbols**
Chemical elements . . . 218-19
Internet . . . 210
Zodiac . . . 456
**Sikhism** . . . 561, 565, 646
**Sikkim** . . . 774
**Silver**
Coinage, U.S. . . . 139
Production . . . 151, 152, 153
Reserve base, world . . . 151
**Simpson, O. J.** . . . 69, 509, 510
**Singapore** . . . 816
Ambassadors, envoys . . . 847
Distances to ports . . . 243
Flag . . . 483
Gross domestic product . . . 134
Merchant fleet . . . 244
Trade . . . 240, 377
Wages, hourly . . . 171
**Singers, notable** . . . 358-76
**Single-parent households** . . . 172, 377, 378, 388, 965
**Sioux Indian War** (1876) . . . 501
**Skating**
Figure
Olympic champions (1908-94) . . . 864
U.S., world champions . . . 902
Speed, Olympic champions (1924-94) . . . 866-67
**Skiing**
Olympic champions (1924-94) . . . 864-66
World Cup Alpine Champions . . . 919
**Skye, Isle of** . . . 592, 830
**Skylab** . . . 310
**Slavery**
Abolished, 13th Amendment (1865) . . . 500, 520
Abolitionist raids (1856, 1859) . . . 500
*Dred Scott* decision (1857) . . . 500, 523
Emancipation Proclamation (1863) . . . 500
Importation outlawed (1808) . . . 499
Introduced into America (1619) . . . 497
Kansas-Nebraska Act (1854) . . . 500
Missouri Compromise (1820) . . . 499

Rebellions (1712, 1831) . . . . . . 497, 499
**Slovakia** . . . . . . . . . . . 239, 483, 817, 847
**Slovenia** . . . . . . . . . . . 239, 483, 817, 847
**Small Business Administration** . . . . 129, 169, 188
**Smith, Adam** . . . . . . . . . . . . . . 342, 564
**Smith, John** (1607) . . . . . . . . . . . . . 497
**Smithsonian Institution** 130, 169, 188, 685
**Smoking**
By adults . . . . . . . . . . . . . . . . . . . 965
Anti-smoking campaign (1996) . . . . 58, 64
Benefits of quitting . . . . . . . . . . . . . 613
Heart disease . . . . . . . . . . . . . . . . 616
By high school students . . . . . . . . . 966
Lung cancer, how caused . . . . . . . . . 69
Tobacco industry suits (1996) . 51, 56, 64
**Smythe Trophy** . . . . . . . . . . . . . . . . 896
**Snakes, poisonous** . . . . . . . . . . . . . 232
**Snowfall**
Blizzards
Characteristics . . . . . . . . . . . . . . 220
Notable (1888, 1996). 46, *196*, 302, 501
Cities, U.S. . . . . . . . . . . . . . . . . . 223
Mean annual . . . . . . . . . . . . . . . . . 222
**Soccer**
Olympic champions (1996) . . . . . . . . 851
U.S. professional league . . . . . . . . . 956
World Cup . . . . . . . . . . . . . . . . . . 956
**Social reformers, notable** . . . . . . . . . 350
**Social scientists, notable** . . . . . . 342-43
**Social Security Administration** 188, 708-12
Act passed (1935) . . . . . . . . . . . . . 503
Employees, payroll . . . . . . . . . . . . . 169
Expenditures . . . . . . . . . . . . . . . . . 129
Internet address . . . . . . . . . . . . . . 210
Medicare (1966) . . . . . . . . . . . 506, 710
Retiree earnings increase (1996) . . . . 51
Tax revenues . . . . . . . . . . . . . . . . 129
**Societies.** *See* Associations and societies
**Sodium** (dietary)
Labels, nutrition . . . . . . . . . . . . . . . 612
Nutritive value . . . . . . . . . . . . . . 610-11
**Softball** . . . . . . . . . . . . . . . . . . . . . 851
**Software, computer** . . . . . . . . . . . . . 212
**Solar day** . . . . . . . . . . . . . . . . . . . 458
**Solar system** . . . . . . . . . . . . . . . 440-60
**Solidarity** (Poland) . . . . . . . . . . 576, 810
**Solomon Islands** . . . . . . . . 483, 817, 847
**Solstices** (1997) . . . . . . . . . 441, 443, 459
**Somalia** . . . . . . . . . . . . . . . . . . 817-18
Chronology (1996) . . . . . . . . . . . . . . 64
Flag, map . . . . . . . . . . . . . . 483, 494-95
Medals of Honor awarded . . . . . . . . . 181
Peacekeeping troop withdrawal (1995) 510
Refugees from . . . . . . . . . . . . . . . . 840
**Somerset Island** . . . . . . . . . . . . . . . 592
**Sorghum production** . . . . . . . . . 161, 162
**Sound**
Measurements . . . . . . . . . . . . . . . . 604
Speed of . . . . . . . . . . . . . . . . . . . 606
**South Africa** . . . . . . . . . . . . . . . 818-19
Ambassadors, envoys . . . . . . . . . . . 847
Apartheid . . . . . . . . . . . . . . . 576, 818
Boer War (1899-1902) . . . . . . . . . . . 818
Chronology (1996) . . . . . . . . . . . . . . 57
Distances to ports . . . . . . . . . . . . . 243
Flag, map . . . . . . . . . . . . . . . 483, 495
Gold production . . . . . . . . . . . . . . . 153
Gross domestic product . . . . . . . . . . 134
Nuclear power . . . . . . . . . . . . 238, 239
Self-government (1910) . . . . . . . . . . 568
U.S. sanctions (1986) . . . . . . . . . . . 508
**South America** . . . . . . . . . . . . . . 838-39
AIDS cases . . . . . . . . . . . . . . . . . . 840
Commercial fishing . . . . . . . . . . . . . 164
Explorations . . . . . . . . . . . . . . . . . 586
Gold production . . . . . . . . . . . . . . . 153
Highest, lowest points . . . . . . . . . . . 597
Lakes . . . . . . . . . . . . . . . . . . . . . 598
Languages . . . . . . . . . . . . . . . . 642-43
Largest country . . . . . . . . . . . . . 746-47
Liberation wars, leaders . . . . . . 573, 584
Map . . . . . . . . . . . . . . . . . . . . 488-89
Mountain peaks . . . . . . . . . . . . . . . 590
Religious adherents . . . . . . . . . . . . 646
Trade . . . . . . . . . . . . . . . . . . . . . 240
Volcanoes . . . . . . . . . . . . . . . . . . 589
Waterfalls . . . . . . . . . . . . . . . . . . 599
*see also specific countries*
**South Carolina** . . . . . . . . . . . . . 675-76
Admission, area, capital . . . . . . 542, 675
Agriculture . . . . . . . . . . . . . . . . 156-61
Altitudes (high, low) . . . . . . . . . . . . 541
Birth, death statistics . . . . . . . . . . . 963
Budget . . . . . . . . . . . . . . . . . . . . 135
Coastline . . . . . . . . . . . . . . . . . . . 541
Congressional representation . . . . . . 112, 117, 380
Courts, U.S. . . . . . . . . . . . . . . . . . 192
Crime, prisons, death penalty . . . 959, 960, 961
Energy consumption . . . . . . . . . . . . 237
Federally owned land . . . . . . . . . . . 545
Governor, state officials . . . . . . . 124, 128
Hazardous waste sites . . . . . . . . . . . 228
Health insurance coverage . . . . . . . . 971
Immigrants admitted (1995) . . . . . . . 383
Indians, American . . . . . . . . . . . . . 550
Interest laws, rates . . . . . . . . . . 721, 722
Marriage, divorce laws . . . . . . . 728, 729
Motor vehicles . . . . . . . . . . . . . 245, 248
Name origin, nickname . . . . . . . 544, 675
Population . . . . . . . . . . . . . . 380-81, 384
Cities, towns . . . . . . . . . . . . . . 415-16
Counties, county seats . . . . . . . . . 434
Poverty rates . . . . . . . . . . . . . . . . . 388
Presidential elections . . . . 76, 98-99, 106
Schools and libraries . . . . . . . 252-53, 257
Taxes . . . . . . . . . . . . . . . . . . 245, 735
Temperature, precipitation . . . . . 222, 224
Unemployment benefits . . . . . . . . . . 165
Welfare assistance . . . . . . . . . . . . . 389
**South China Sea** . . . . . . . . . . . . . . 593
**South Dakota** . . . . . . . . . . . . . . . . 676
Admission, area, capital . . . 542, 543, 676
Agriculture . . . . . . . . . . . . . . . . 156-61
Altitudes (high, low) . . . . . . . . . . . . 541
Birth, death statistics . . . . . . . . . . . 963
Budget . . . . . . . . . . . . . . . . . . . . 135
Congressional representation . . 112, 117, 380
Courts, U.S. . . . . . . . . . . . . . . . . . 192
Crime, prisons, death penalty . . . 959, 960
Energy consumption . . . . . . . . . . . . 237
Federally owned land . . . . . . . . . . . 545
Governor, state officials . . . . . . . 124, 128
Hazardous waste sites . . . . . . . . . . . 228
Health insurance coverage . . . . . . . . 971
Immigrants admitted (1995) . . . . . . . 383
Indians, American . . . . . . . . . . . . . 550
Interest laws, rates . . . . . . . . . . 721, 722
Marriage, divorce laws . . . . . . . 728, 729
Motor vehicles . . . . . . . . . . . . . 245, 248
Name origin, nickname . . . . . . . 544, 676
Population . . . . . . . . . . . . . . 380-81, 384
Cities, towns . . . . . . . . . . . . . . . . 416
Counties, county seats . . . . . . . 434-35
Poverty rates . . . . . . . . . . . . . . . . . 388
Presidential elections . . . . . . 76, 99, 106
Schools and libraries . . . . . . . 252-53, 257
Taxes . . . . . . . . . . . . . . . . . . . . . 245
Temperature, precipitation . . . . . 222, 224
Unemployment benefits . . . . . . . . . . 165
Welfare assistance . . . . . . . . . . . . . 389
**Southeast Asia**
Map . . . . . . . . . . . . . . . . . . . . . . 493
*see also* Vietnam War; *specific countries*
**Southeast Asia Treaty Organization** (1954) . . . . . . . . . . . . . . . 505, 572
**South Island** . . . . . . . . . . . . . . 592, 803
**South Korea.** *See* Korea, South (Republic of)
**South Pole**
Exploration . . . . . . . . . . . . . . . . 587-88
Magnetic force . . . . . . . . . . . . . . . . 459
**South Yemen.** *See* Yemen
**Soviet Union** . . . . . . . . . . . . . . . . . 812
Berlin blockade (1948) . . . . . . . . . . 504
Chernobyl disaster (1986) . . . . . . . . 306
Cold War . . . . . . . . . . . . . . 572, 575-76
Cuban missle crisis (1962) . . . . . . . . 505
Eastern Bloc revolt (1989) . . . . . . 575-76
*Glasnost* and *perestroika* . . . . 575-76, 812
Gold production . . . . . . . . . . . . . . . 153
History . . . . . . . . . . . . . . . 569, 570, 571
Hungarian revolt (1956) . . . . . . . . . . 573
Leaders . . . . . . . . . . . . . . . . . . . . 585
Nixon visit (1972) . . . . . . . . . . . . . . 506
Space exploration . . . . . . . . . 309-11, 573
Summit talks (1972, 1985, 1987). 506, 508
World War I . . . . . . . . . . . . . . . . . . 569
World War II (1945) . . . . . . . 504, 571-72
*see also* Arms control; Russia; Russian Empire; *former republics*
**Soybeans** . . . . . . . . . . 160, 161, 162, 241
**Space developments** . . . . . . . . . . 309-13
Apollo missions (1969) . . . . . 309-10, 506
Astronauts . . . . . . . . . . . . . . 309-12, 313
First men in space (1961) . . . . 309, 505
First women in space (1983) . . . . . 309, 310, 311, 508
Lucid in-space record (1996) . . 66, *199*, 312
Cosmonauts . . . . . . 66, *199*, 309-11, 313
*Explorer 1* (1958) . . . . . . . . . . . . . . 505
Hall of Fame . . . . . . . . . . . . . . . 314-15
Hubble telescope (1993) . . . . . . 311, 509
Missions, proposed . . . . . . . . . . . . . 313
Moonwalk, U.S. (1969) . . . . . . . 309, 506
Outer Space Treaty (1967) . . . . . . . . 183
Payloads, worldwide . . . . . . . . . . . . 313
Planetary missions, U.S. . . . . 312, 444-48
Skylab . . . . . . . . . . . . . . . . . . . . . 310
Space shuttles
*Atlantis* (1995) . . . . . . . . 311, 312, 510
*Challenger* (1983, 1984, 1986) . . . 310, 311, 508
*Columbia* (1981, 1982) . . . . . 310, 311, 312, 507, 508
*Discovery* . . . . . . . . . . . . . . . 310, 311
*Endeavour* (1993) . . . . . 311, 312, 509
Missions . . . . . . . . . . . . . . . . . 310-12
Sputnik satellite . . . . . . . . . . . . . . . 573
U.S.-Russian linkup (1995) . . . . . 311, 510
**Spain** . . . . . . . . . . . . . . . . . . . . . 819
Ambassadors, envoys . . . . . . . . . . . 847
Chronology (1996) . . . . . . . . . . . 52, 56
Consumer price changes . . . . . . . . . 133
Flag . . . . . . . . . . . . . . . . . . . . . . 483
Gross domestic product . . . . . . . . . . 134
History . . . . . . 558, 559, 561, 571, 575
Military strength . . . . . . . . . . . . . . 182
Motor vehicle production . . . . . . . . . 246
Nuclear power . . . . . . . . . . . . 238, 239
Rulers, royal family . . . . . . . . . 376, 584
Wages, hourly . . . . . . . . . . . . . . . . 171
**Spanish-American War** (1898) . . . 501, 567
Casualties, U.S. forces . . . . . . . . . . 184
Costs . . . . . . . . . . . . . . . . . . . . . 181
**Spanish Civil War** (1936-39) . . . . . . . . 571
**Spanish Sahara** . . . . . . . . . . . . . . . 575
**Special Olympics** . . . . . . . . . . . . . . 955
**Spectrum, colors of** . . . . . . . . . . . . . 606
**Speech, freedom of** . . . . . . . . . . 39, 519
**Speed**
Of animals . . . . . . . . . . . . . . . . . . 231
Automobile, one-mile records . . . . . . 931
Highway limits, U.S. (1995) . . . 38, 42, 248
Of light . . . . . . . . . . . . . . . . . . . . 450
Of sound . . . . . . . . . . . . . . . . . . . 606
**Speedboat racing** . . . . . . . . . . . . . . 936
**Speed skating.** *See under* Skating
**Spelling**
Commonly misspelled words . . . . . . . 641
Spelling Bee, National . . . . . . . . . . 637
**Sphere,** Mathematical formulas . . . . . . 607
**Spiders, poisonous** . . . . . . . . . . . . . 232
**Spingarn Medal** . . . . . . . . . . . . . 328-29
**Spokane, WA** . . . . . . . . . 123, 387, 694-95
**Sports**
Directory . . . . . . . . . . . . . . . . . . 903-4
Dramatic events (1995-96) . . . . . . . . 849
Highlights (1996) . . . . . . . . . . . . *782-84*
Personalities, notable . . . . . . . . . 925-27
*see also specific sports*
**Spring** (season) . . . . . . . . . . . . . . . 459
**Sputnik** (1957) . . . . . . . . . . . . . . . . 573
**Square,** Area formula . . . . . . . . . . . . 607
**Sri Lanka** (Ceylon) . . . . . . . . . . . . . 820
Ambassadors, envoys . . . . . . . . . . . 847
Area . . . . . . . . . . . . . . . . . . . . . . 592
Chronology (1996) . . . . . . . . . . . . . . 48
Flag . . . . . . . . . . . . . . . . . . . . . . 483
Trade . . . . . . . . . . . . . . . . . . . . . 240
Wages, hourly . . . . . . . . . . . . . . . . 171
**Stadiums, arenas**
Baseball . . . . . . . . . . . . . . . . . . . 954
Basketball . . . . . . . . . . . . . . . . . . 913
Football . . . . . . . . . . . . . . . . . . . . 879
**Stalin, Joseph V.** . . . . . . . . . . . 347, 812
**Stamp Act** (1765) . . . . . . . . . . . . . . 497
**Stamps.** *See* Postage stamps
**Standard time** . . . . . . . . . . . . . 479, 480
**Stanley Cup** . . . . . . . . . . 60, *784*, 849, 889
**Stars**
Constellations . . . . . . . . . . . . . . . . 451
Morning, evening . . . . . . . . . . . . . . 449
Tables . . . . . . . . . . . . . . . . . . . . . 450
**"Star-Spangled Banner"** (1814) . . 499, 528
**START I and II.** *See* Strategic Arms Reduction Treaty, I and II
**State, Department of** . . . . . . . . . . . . 185
Employees, payroll . . . . . . . . . . . . . 169
Expenditures . . . . . . . . . . . . . . . . . 129
Internet address . . . . . . . . . . . . . . 210
Secretaries . . . . . . . . . . . . . . 185, 201
**States, U.S.** . . . . . . . . . . . . . . . 655-81
Abbreviations, postal . . . . . . . . . . . 634
Admission of new (law) . . . . . . . . . . 518
Admitted to Union . . . . . 542, 543, 655-80
Agriculture . . . . . . . . . . . . . . . . 156-61
Altitudes (high, low) . . . . . . . . . . . . 541
Area, rank . . . . . . . . . . . . . . . 540, 542
Area codes, telephone . . . . . . . . 390-420
Automobile data . . . . . . . . . . . . . . . 245
Births, deaths . . . . . . . . . . . . . . . . 963
Bridges . . . . . . . . . . . . . . . . . . . 702-5
Budgets . . . . . . . . . . . . . . . . . . 135-36
Capitals . . . . . . . . . . . . . . . . . . . . 542
Census . . . . . . . . . 380-81, 380-439, 384
Chambers of Commerce . . . . . . . 655-80
Climate . . . . . . . . . . . . . . . . 222, 224-25
Coastline, in miles . . . . . . . . . . . . . 541
Congressional representation . . . . 111-18

Construction, value of. . . . . . . . . 655-80
Contiguous. . . . . . . . . . . . . . . . 48, 540
Counties, county seats . . . . . 384, 421-39
Courts, U.S. . . . . . . . . . . . . . . 190-92
Crime, prisons, death penalty. . . 959, 960, 961
Critical illness, laws regarding . . . . . . 615
Deaths, births . . . . . . . . . . . . . . . . . 963
Education. . . . . . . . . . . . . 252, 253, 256
Electoral votes . . . . . . . . . . . . . 76, 106
Energy consumption. . . . . . . . . . . . . 237
Famous natives. . . . . . . . . . . . . 655-81
Federally owned land . . . . . . . . . . . 545
Finances . . . . . . . . . . . . . . . . 135-36
Forested land . . . . . . . . . . . . . 655-80
Geographic centers . . . . . . . . . . . . 543
Governors, state officials. . . . . . . 124-28
Hazardous waste sites . . . . . . . . . . 228
Health insurance coverage . . . . . . . . 971
Highway speed limits . . . . . . . . . . . 248
Immigrants admitted. . . . . . . . . . . . 383
Income, per capita . . . . . . . . . . . 655-80
Indians, American . . . . . . . . . . . . . 550
Inland water area. . . . . . . . . . . . . . 542
Internet addresses . . . . . . . . . . . 655-81
Legislatures . . . . . . . . . . . . . . . 125-28
Marriage, divorce laws . . . . . . . 728, 729
Mineral production . . . . . . . . . . . . . 151
Motor vehicle registration . . . . . . . . . 245
Mountain peaks. . . . . . . . . . . . 590, 591
Names, origin of . . . . . . . . . . . . . . 544
Nicknames . . . . . . . . . . . . . . . 655-80
Original . . . . . . . . . . . . . . 13, 378, 542
Population, by state . 380-81, 384, 655-80
Cities, more than 5,000 . . . . . 390-420
Ethnic, racial distribution . . 550, 655-80
Poverty rates . . . . . . . . . . . . . . . . 388
Precipitation . . . . . . . . . . . . . . . . 222
Presidential elections . . . . . . . . . 76-105
Public lands
Parks . . . . . . . . . . . . . . . . . . 546-49
Recreation areas . . . . . . . . . 545, 549
Public libraries. . . . . . . . . . . . . . . . 257
Rivers . . . . . . . . . . . . . . . . . . 596-97
Secession . . . . . . . . . . . . . . . . . . 523
Settlement dates . . . . . . . . . . . . . . 542
States' rights ruling (1996). . . . . . . . . 39
Taxes . . . . . . . . . . . . . . . 245, 735-36
Temperatures . . . . . . . . . . . 222, 224-25
Tourist attractions . . . . . . . . . . . 655-81
Toxic chemical pollution . . . . . . . . . . 228
Unemployment benefits . . . . . . . . . . 165
Union entry dates . . . . . . . . . . 542, 543
Volcanoes . . . . . . . . . . . . . . . . . . 589
Welfare assistance. . . . . . . . . . . . . . 389
ZIP codes. . . . . . . . . . . . . . . . 390-420
**Statesmen and stateswomen, notable** . . . . . . . . . . . . 319, 345-48
**Statistical Abstract of the United States**. . . . . . . . . . . . . . 540
**Statue of Liberty** . . . . . . . . . . . . . . 529
Dedicated (1886). . . . . . . . . . . . . . 501
Ellis Island . . . . . . . . . . . . . . . . . 529
**Steamships** (1807, 1819) . . . . . . 216, 499
**Steel**
Exports, imports . . . . . . . . . . . . . . 241
Inventions. . . . . . . . . . . . . . . . . . 216
Production . . . . . . . . . . . . . . . . . 153
Strikes (1892, 1952). . . . . . . . . 501, 504
**Steeplechase** (track and field)
Olympic champions . . . . . . . . . 852, 855
World record. . . . . . . . . . . . . . . . . 867
**Stewart Island**. . . . . . . . . . . . . 592, 803
**Stocks** . . . . . . . . . . . . . . . . . . 148-50
Dow Jones Average . . . . . . . 68, 149, 154
Performance (1995-96) . . . . 51, 55, 60, 63, 66, 68
Exchanges, global . . . . . . . . . . . . . 144
Exchanges, U.S. . . . . . . . . 148, 149, 630
Foreign, U.S. holdings . . . . . . . . . . . 150
Glossary of terms . . . . . . . . . . . 154-55
Market crashes (1929, 1987) . . . 503, 508, 570-71
Most active (1995) . . . . . . . . . . . . . 149
Mutual funds. . . . . . . . . . . . . . 155, 148
**Stockton, CA** . . . . . . . . . . . 123, 386, 695
**Stonehenge** . . . . . . . . . . . . . . . . . 555
**Storms**
Classifications. . . . . . . . . . . . . . . . 225
Notable . . . . . . . . . . . . . . . . . . . 302
Watches, warnings, advisories . . . . . . 220
**Strategic Air Command** . . . . . . . . . . . 176
**Strategic Arms Limitation Treaty, I and II** (1972, 1979). . . . . . . . . . . . . . . . 183
**Strategic Arms Reduction Treaty, I and II** (1991, 1993). . . . . . . . . . 183
**Stratosphere**. . . . . . . . . . . . . . . . . . 458
**Strikes**
Air traffic controllers (1981) . . . . . . . . 507
Baseball players (1994, 1995) . . 509, 510
Coal miners (1922, 1946) . . . . . 503, 504
Number, days idle (1960-95) . . . . . . 173
Steel mill seizure (1952) . . . . . . . . . 504
Steel workers (1892). . . . . . . . . . . . 501
Women weavers (1824). . . . . . . . . . 499
**Strokes**
Deaths . . . . . . . . . . . . . . . . . 964, 974
Diabetes. . . . . . . . . . . . . . . . . . . 615
Help organizations . . . . . . . . . . . . 618
Warning signs . . . . . . . . . . . . . . . 616
**Stuart, House of** . . . . . . . . . . . . . . 578
**Students.** *See* Colleges and universities; Education; High schools
**Submarines**
Inventions. . . . . . . . . . . . . . . . . . 216
*Nautilus* (1954) . . . . . . . . . . . . . . 504
Sinkings . . . . . . . . . . . . . . . . . 298-99
Warfare (1917) . . . . . . . . . . . . 502, 569
**Subway accidents** . . . . . . . . . . . 300-301
**Succession, presidential** . . . . . . 522, 525
**Sudan**. . . . . . . . . . . 483, 820-21, 840, 847
**Suez Canal** . . . . . . . . . . . . . . . 573, 761
**Suffrage, women's,** Amendment (1920) . . . . . . . . . . . . . . 502, 521
**Sugar**
Exports, imports. . . . . . . . . . . . . . 241
Labels, nutrition . . . . . . . . . . . . . . 612
Nutritive value . . . . . . . . . . . . . . . 611
Production . . . . . . . . . . . . . . . . . 161
**Sugar Bowl** . . . . . . . . . . . . . . . . . . 881
**Suicides**
Doctor-assisted (1996) . . . . . . . . . 50, 66
By firearms . . . . . . . . . . . . . . . . . 968
Number . . . . . . . . . . . . . . . . 964, 965
Workplace. . . . . . . . . . . . . . . . . . 168
**Sullivan Trophy** . . . . . . . . . . . . . . . 902
**Sumatra** . . . . . . . . . . . . . . . . . . . . 592
**Sumeria** . . . . . . . . . . . . . . . . . . . . 551
**Summer** (season). . . . . . . . . . . . . . . 459
**Summer Olympics.** *See under* Olympic games
**Summer solstice** . . . . . . . . . . . . 441, 459
**Sun** . . . . . . . . . . . . . . . . . . . . 455-56
Eclipses . . . . . . . . . . . . . . 454, 461-62
Planets' distance from. . . . . . . . 444, 455
Rises, sets (1997) . . . . . . . . . . . 462-74
Twilight. . . . . . . . . . . . . . . . . . 460-61
Ultraviolet index . . . . . . . . . . . . . . 227
**Sun Bowl** . . . . . . . . . . . . . . . . . . . 882
**Sunspots** . . . . . . . . . . . . . . . . . . . 456
**Super Bowl** . . . . . . 48, *784*, 849, 872, 879
**Superior, Lake**. . . . . . . . . . . . . . . . 598
**Superlative statistics, U.S.,** 540
**Supplemental Security Income (SSI)** . 711
**Supreme Court, U.S.**
Abortion legalization (1973) . . . . 506, 524
Address, form of. . . . . . . . . . . . . . 641
Appointments, salaries . . . . . . . . . . 189
Created (1789). . . . . . . . . . . . . . . 498
Decisions, notable . . . . . . . . . . . 523-24
*Dred Scott* (1857) . . . . . . . . . 500, 523
*Marbury* v. *Madison* (1803) . . . 499, 523
1995-96 term . . . . . . . . . . . . . . . . 39
*Plessy* v. *Ferguson* (1896) . . . 501, 523
Employees, payroll . . . . . . . . . . . . 169
Internet address . . . . . . . . . . . . . . 210
Judicial powers (constitutional) . . . . . 517
Justices . . . . . . . . . . . . . . . . . . . 189
First black (1967) . . . . . . . . . . . . 506
First woman (1981) . . . . . . . . . . . 507
Schools
Desegregation (1954, 1955, 1956) . . . . . . . . . . . . . . . 505, 524
Prayer ban (1963) . . . . . . . . . . . . 505
**Surgeon General, U.S.** . . . . . . . . 187, 188
**Suriname** . . . . . . . . . . . . . 483, 821, 847
**Surveyor's chain measure** . . . . . . . . 601
**Survivor insurance** . . . . . . . . . . 709, 711
**Svalbard Islands** . . . . . . . . . . . 592, 805
**Swains Island** . . . . . . . . . . . . . . . . 681
**Swaziland** . . . . . . . . . . . . . 483, 821, 847
**Sweden**. . . . . . . . . . . . . . . . . . . 821-22
Ambassadors, envoys. . . . . . . . . . . . 847
Consumer price changes . . . . . . . . . 133
Flag . . . . . . . . . . . . . . . . . . . . . . 483
Gross domestic product. . . . . . . . . . 134
History . . . . . . . . . . . . . . 559, 563, 575
Merchant fleet . . . . . . . . . . . . . . . 244
Motor vehicle production, exports 246, 242
Nuclear power . . . . . . . . . . . . 238, 239
Rulers, royal family. . . . . . . . . . 376, 582
Trade . . . . . . . . . . . . . . . . . . . . . 240
Unemployment rates. . . . . . . . . . . . 166
Wages, hourly . . . . . . . . . . . . . . . 171
**Sweet potato production** . . . . . . . . . 161
**Swimming**
Olympic champions . . . *782*, 852, 858-61
Synchronized. . . . . . . . . . . . . . . . 852
World records . . . . . . . . . . . . . . . 905
**Switzerland** . . . . . . . . . . . . . . . . . . 822
Alps . . . . . . . . . . . . . . . . . . . 590-91
Ambassadors, envoys. . . . . . . . . . . 847
Consumer price changes . . . . . . . . . 133
Flag . . . . . . . . . . . . . . . . . . . . . . 483
Gold reserves. . . . . . . . . . . . . . . . 146
Gross domestic product . . . . . . . . . . 134
Nuclear power . . . . . . . . . . . . . 238, 239
Trade . . . . . . . . . . . . . . . . . . . . . 240
Wages, hourly . . . . . . . . . . . . . . . . 171
**Symbols.** *See* Signs and symbols
**Symphony orchestras, U.S.** . . . . . . . . 286
**Syria** . . . . . . . . . . . . 182, 483, 822-23, 847

— T —

**Table tennis**. . . . . . . . . . . . . . . . . . 852
**Tacoma, WA** . . . . . . . . . 123, 242, 387, 695
**Taft, William H.** . . . . . . . 107, 109, 534, 539
*see also* Presidents, U.S.
**Taft-Hartley Act** (1947) . . . . . . . . . . . 504
**Tahiti** . . . . . . . . . . . . . . . . . . . 592, 765
**Taiwan** . . . . . . . . . . . . . . . . . . 823, 846
Area . . . . . . . . . . . . . . . . . . . . . . 592
Chronology (1996) . . . . . . . . . . . . . . 52
Flag, map . . . . . . . . . . . . . . . . 483, 493
Gross domestic product . . . . . . . . . . 134
Merchant fleet . . . . . . . . . . . . . . . . 244
Military strength . . . . . . . . . . . . . . 182
Motor vehicle production . . . . . . . . . 246
Nuclear power . . . . . . . . . . . . . 238, 239
Trade . . . . . . . . . . . . . . . . . . . 240, 377
U.S. immigrants from. . . . . . . . . . . . 377
Wages, hourly . . . . . . . . . . . . . . . . 171
**Tajikistan**. . . . . . 484, 491, 823-24, 840, 847
**Taj Mahal**. . . . . . . . . . . . . . . . . . . . 561
**Tall buildings**. . . . . . . . . . . 540, 696-702
**Talmud** . . . . . . . . . . . . . . . . . . . . . 557
**Tampa, FL.** *See* Cities, U.S.
**Tanganyika** . . . . . . . . . . . . . . . . . . 824
**Tantalum**. . . . . . . . . . . . . . . . . . 151, 152
**Tanzania** . . . . . . . . . . . . . . . 484, 824, 847
**Taoism** . . . . . . . . . . . . . . . . . . . 554, 556
**Tariff of Abominations** (1828) . . . . . . 499
**Tariffs.** *See* Customs, U.S.
**Ta'u Island**. . . . . . . . . . . . . . . . . . . 681
**Taxes, federal.** *See* Income taxes, Federal.
**Taxes, state**
Gasoline . . . . . . . . . . . . . . . . . . . . 245
Income (by states) . . . . . . . . . . . 735-36
Per capita . . . . . . . . . . . . . . . . . . . 135
**Taylor, Zachary** . . . . . . . . . 109, 532, 539
*see also* Presidents, U.S.
**Teachers**
Awards . . . . . . . . . . . . . . . . . . . . . 329
College, university. . . . . . . . . 256, 258-82
Pay, average . . . . . . . . . . . . . . 252, 256
Public schools . . . . . . . . . . . . . 251, 252
**Technology.** *See* Science and technology
**Telegraph**
Atlantic cable (1858) . . . . . . . . . . . . 500
First message (1844). . . . . . . . . . . . 500
Inventions . . . . . . . . . . . . . . . . 216, 566
Transcontinental (1861) . . . . . . . . . . 500
**Telephone**
Area codes . . . . . . . . . . . . . . . 390-420
AT&T breakup (1982) . . . . . . . . . . . 507
First exchange (1878) . . . . . . . . 501, 566
First transcontinental talk (1915) . . . . 502
International direct dial codes . . . . . . 848
Inventions . . . . . . . . . . . . . . . . . . . 216
Reform legislation (1996) . . . . . . . 38, 48
Tax deductions. . . . . . . . . . . . . . . . 731
Transatlantic cable (1956) . . . . . . . . 505
**Television** . . . . . . . . . . . . . . . . . *780*, *781*
Actors, actresses . . . . . . . . . . . . 360-76
Advertising expenditures . . . . . . . . . 297
Awards . . . . . . . . . . . . . 328, 329-30, 333
Internet addresses . . . . . . . . . . . . . 294
Inventions . . . . . . . . . . . . . . . . . . . 216
Network addresses, phone numbers . 294
Program rating initiatives (1996) . . . . . 49
Programs, favorite. . . . . . . . . . . . 295-96
Reform legislation (1996) . . . . . . . 38, 48
Set ownership profile . . . . . . . . . . . . 293
Time spent viewing . . . . . . . . . . . . . 294
Transcontinental, first (1951). . . . . . . 504
Viewing shares. . . . . . . . . . . . . . . . 295
*see also* Cable television; Videos
**Temperature** (weather)
Celsius-Fahrenheit conversion . . . . . 605
Heat index. . . . . . . . . . . . . . . . . . . 227
Heat wave deaths (1995) . . . . . . . . . 510
Highest, lowest recorded . . . . . . . . . 222
International. . . . . . . . . . . . . . . . . . 225
U.S. normal, highs, lows. . . . . . . . 221-25
**Temperature,** Boiling, freezing points . . 605
**Ten Commandments** . . . . . . . . . . . . 649
**Tennessee**. . . . . . . . . . . . . . . . . . 676-77
Admission, area, capital . . . 542, 543, 676
Agriculture. . . . . . . . . . . . . . . . . 156-61
Altitudes (high, low) . . . . . . . . . . . . 541
Birth, death statistics . . . . . . . . . . . . 963
Budget . . . . . . . . . . . . . . . . . . . . . 135

Congressional representation . . . 112, 117, 380
Courts, U.S. . . . 192
Crime, prisons, death penalty . . . 959, 960
Energy consumption . . . 237
Federally owned land . . . 545
Governor, state officials . . . 124, 128
Hazardous waste sites . . . 228
Health insurance coverage . . . 971
Immigrants admitted (1995) . . . 383
Indians, American . . . 550
Interest laws, rates . . . 721, 722
Marriage, divorce laws . . . 728, 729
Motor vehicles . . . 245, 248
Name origin, nickname . . . 544, 676
Population . . . 380-81, 384
Cities, towns . . . 416, 691
Counties, county seats . . . 435
Port traffic . . . 242
Poverty rates . . . 388
Presidential elections . . . 76, 99-100, 106
Schools and libraries . . . 252-53, 257
Taxes . . . 245, 735
Temperature, precipitation . . . 222, 224
Toxic chemical pollution . . . 228
Unemployment benefits . . . 165
Welfare assistance . . . 389
**Tennessee Valley Authority** . . 188, 130, 169
**Tennis** . . . 849
Australian Open . . . 930
Davis Cup . . . 929
French Open . . . 930
Olympic champions (1996) . . . 852
U.S. Open (1996) . . . 67, 928
Wimbledon (1996) . . . 62, 929
**Territorial sea, U.S.** . . . 545
**Territories, U.S.**
Accession of . . . 545
Altitudes (high, low) . . . 541
Areas . . . 439
Courts, U.S. . . . 192
External . . . 439, 681-83
Populations . . . 439
Statehood . . . 543
ZIP codes . . . 439
**Terrorism**
Chronology (1995-96)
Greek tourist slayings . . . 54
G-7 antiterrorism proposals . . . 60
Israel suicide bombings . . . 50, 52, 306, *778*
Northern Ireland bombings 49-50, 52, 59
Oklahoma City bombing . . . 49, 510
Olympic park bombing . . . 61, 68, *782*
Paris subway bombing . . . 40
Unabomber case . . 53, 59, *197*, 510, 961
UN bombing plot conviction . . . 47, 510
U.S. airliner bombing plot convictions . . 66
U.S. installation bombings . . . 43, 60, 306, 510, *779*
U.S. paramilitary group arrests . . . 60
International (1980-89) . . . 576
Lebanon (1983) . . . 508, 792
Legislation, sanctions, U.S. (1996) . . . 53, 64-65
World Trade Center bombing (1993, 1994) . . . 509
*see also* Assassinations
**Tet New Year** . . . 478
**Texas** . . . 677
Admission, area, capital . . . 542, 677
Agriculture . . . 156-61
Altitudes (high, low) . . . 541
Birth, death statistics . . . 963
Budget . . . 135
Coastline . . . 541
Congressional representation . . . 112, 117-18, 380
Courts, U.S. . . . 192
Crime, prisons, death penalty . . . 959, 960, 961
Energy consumption . . . 237
Federally owned land . . . 545
Governor, state officials . . . 124, 128
Hazardous waste sites . . . 228
Health insurance coverage . . . 971
Immigrants admitted (1995) . . . 383
Indians, American . . . 550
Interest laws, rates . . . 721, 722
Marriage, divorce laws . . . 728, 729
Mineral production . . . 151
Motor vehicles . . . 245, 248
Name origin, nickname . . . 544, 677
Population . . . 380-81, 384
Cities, towns . . . 416-18, 686, 688, 689, 691, 694
Counties, county seats . . . 435-37
Port traffic . . . 242
Poverty rates . . . 388
Presidential elections . . . 76, 100-101, 106
Schools and libraries . . . 252-53, 257
Taxes . . . 245
Temperature, precipitation . . . 222, 225
Toxic chemical pollution . . . 228
Unemployment benefits . . . 165
Welfare assistance . . . 389
**Thailand** (Siam) . . . 824-25
Ambassadors, envoys . . . 847
Commercial fishing . . . 164
Flag . . . 484
Gross domestic product . . . 134
Merchant fleet . . . 244
Military strength . . . 182
Trade . . . 240
**Thames River** . . . 596
**Thanksgiving Day** . . . 480
**Theater** . . . 285-86
Actors, actresses . . . 360-76
Awards . . . 330
Composers . . . 356-57
Dance companies . . . 287
First in colonies (1716) . . . 497
Long runs . . . 285
Notable openings (1995-96) . . . 285, *781*
Playwrights . . . 330, 350-51, 351-55
Pulitzer Prizes . . . 324, *781*
**Theft** . . . 957, 958, 959, 960, 961
**Third parties** . . . 107
Presidential election (1996) . . . 60-61, 64, 76-105, *195*
**Third Reich.** *See under* Germany
**Thirteen colonies** . . . 378, 542
**Thirty Years War** (1618-48) . . . 562
**Thorpe Trophy** . . . 876
**Thunderstorm characteristics** . . . 220
**Tibet** . . . 754, 840
**Ticonderoga, Ft.** (1777) . . . 498
**Tidal waves** . . . 303
**Tides** . . . 226, 457
**Tierra del Fuego** . . . 592, 752
**Tilden, Samuel J.** (1876) . . . 501
**Timbuktu** . . . 560, 797
**Time**
Cities . . . 479, 480
Computation . . . 458
Daylight Saving . . . 479
Differences, cities . . . 479, 480
Earth's rotation . . . 458, 459-60
Greenwich . . . 479, 450
International Date Line . . . 479, 484
Mean, apparent . . . 458
Military . . . 479
Sidereal . . . 458, 450
Solar . . . 458
Standard . . . 479, 480
24-hour . . . 479
Zones (map) . . . 484
**Timor** . . . 592
**Titanium** . . . 151
**Tobacco**
Exports, imports . . . 241
Production . . . 160, 161
*see also* Smoking
**Tobago.** *See* Trinidad and Tobago
**Togo** . . . 484, 825, 847
**Tokelau Island** . . . 803
**Tokyo, Japan** . . . 838
**Toledo, OH.** *See* Cities, U.S.
**Ton** (measure) . . . 601, 602, 603
**Tonga** . . . 484, 825, 847
**Tonkin Resolution** (1964) . . . 505
**Tonnage, gross, deadweight** . . . 243-44
**Tony Awards** . . . 330
**Top Ten News Stories 1996** . . . 33
**Tornadoes**
Characteristics . . . 220
Classifications . . . 225
Notable . . . 302
**Tour de France** (1996) . . . 932
**Tourism**
Customs exemptions . . . 722
Expenditures (by states) . . . 655-80
Foreign to U.S. . . . 145
Internet addresses . . . 211
National parks, monuments . . . 546-49
Passports, visas . . . 723
States, territories, cities . . . 655-85
Washington (DC) sites . . . 684-85
**Townshend Acts** (1767) . . . 497
**Toxic chemical pollution** . . . 228
**Track and field**
Olympic champions . . . *783*, 852, 853-58
World indoor, outdoor records . . . 867-68
*see also* Marathon
**Trade** . . . 240-44
Antiterrorism economic sanctions (1996) . . . 64-65
Court, U.S. . . . 192
Deficit, U.S. (1995-96) . . . 40, 41, 47, 48, 53, 55, 63, 66
Leading U.S. partners . . . 377
*see also* Exports, imports
**Traffic**
Airline . . . 313, 314
Motor vehicle accidents . . . 964, 967
Ports, major U.S. . . . 242
**Trails, national scenic** . . . 549
**Trains.** *See* Railroads, U.S.; Railroads, world; Subways
**Transportation** . . . 240-50
Expenditures, consumer . . . 150
Occupational injuries, fatalities . . . 168
Price Indexes . . . 131, 132
*see also specific types*
**Transportation, Department of** . . . 187
Employees, payroll . . . 169
Expenditures . . . 129
Internet address . . . 210
Secretaries . . . 185, 187, 205
**Trans World Airlines** (1996) . . . 61, 63-64, 66, *198*, 300
**Trapezoid,** Area formula . . . 607
**Travel, foreign.** *See* Tourism
**Treasury, Department of** . . . 186
Bonds . . . 148, 139
Employees, payroll . . . 169
Expenditures . . . 129
Internet address . . . 210
Secretaries . . . 185, 186, 201-2
Waco (TX) standoff (1993, 1994) . . . 509
*see also* Currency; *specific bureaus*
**Treaties.** *See* Arms control; *specific treaties*
**Trees**
Champion (U.S.) . . . 234
Official, by states . . . 655-80
**Triangle,** Area formula . . . 607
**Trinidad and Tobago** . . . 134, 484, 592, 825-26, 847
**Triple Crown winners** (horse racing) . . 897
**Triple jump**
Olympic champions . . . 852, 856, 858
World records . . . 867, 868
**Tripoli-U.S. War** (1801) . . . 499
**Tristan da Cunha** . . . 592, 831
**Tropical year** . . . 458
**Trotsky, Leon** . . . 307, 348
**Trotting, pacing** . . . 900
**Troy weight** (measure) . . . 601, 602, 603
**Trucks.** *See* Motor vehicles
**Truman, Harry S.** . 105, 107, 109, 110, 535-36
Presidential library . . . 539
*see also* Presidents, U.S.
**Trust funds, Social Security** . . . 711-12
**Tsars, Russian** . . . 560, 585
**Tucker, Jim Guy** (1995-96) . . . 48, 51, 53, 56, 62, 510
**Tucson, AZ.** *See* Cities, U.S.
**Tudor, House of** . . . 561, 578
**Tuition, U.S. college** . . . 254
**Tulsa, OK.** *See* Cities, U.S.
**Tunisia** . . . 484, 826, 847
**Tunnels** . . . 705-6
**Turkey** . . . 826-27
Ambassadors, envoys . . . 847
Chronology (1996) . . . 62
Flag . . . 484
Gross domestic product . . . 134
History . . . 560, 566, 568, 570, 575
Merchant fleet . . . 244
Military strength . . . 182
Motor vehicle production . . . 246
**Turkey** (meat) . . . 162
**Turkmenistan** . . . 484, 491, 827, 847
**Turks and Caicos Islands** . . . 831
**Turner, Nat** (1831) . . . 499
**Tutuila Island** . . . 681
**Tuvalu** . . . 484, 827, 847
**TV.** *See* Television
**TVA.** *See* Tennessee Valley Authority
**21st century, start of** . . . 475
**24-hour time** . . . 479
**21-gun salute** . . . 177
**Twilight** . . . 460-61
**2-year colleges** . . . 272-82
**Tyler, John** . . . 109, 110, 531
*see also* Presidents, U.S.
**Typhoons** . . . 302

—U—

**Uganda** . . . 484, 827-28, 847
**Ukraine** . . . 828
Ambassadors, envoys . . . 847
Flag, map . . . 484, 491
Gross domestic product . . . 134
Merchant fleet . . . 244
Military strength . . . 182
Nuclear power . . . 238, 239
**Ulster.** *See* Northern Ireland
**Ultraviolet index** . . . 227
**UN.** *See* United Nations
**Unabomber case** (1995, 1996) . . . 33, 53, 59, *197*, 510, 961
**Unemployment, U.S.**
AT&T layoffs (1996) . . . 46

By educational attainment . . . . . . . . . 171
Rates, indicators . . . . . . . . 165, 166, 167
Chronology (1995-96) . . 41, 44, 48, 50, 53, 55, 58, 60, 63, 66
Highest (1982) . . . . . . . . . . . . . . 508
**Unemployment insurance** . . . . . 165, 167
**UNESCO.** *See* United Nations Educational, Scientific, and Cultural Organization
**UNICEF.** *See* United Nations Children's Fund
**Unified defense commands, U.S.,** 176
**Union of Soviet Socialist Republics.** *See* Soviet Union
**Unions.** *See* Labor unions
**Unitarian churches** . . . . . . . . . . 645, 646
**United Arab Emirates** . 134, 484, 828, 847
**United Arab Republic.** *See* Egypt
**United Church of Christ** . . 645, 646, 652-53
**United Kingdom** . . . . . . . . . . . . . 829-31
Ambassadors, envoys . . . . . . . . . . . 847
Commonwealth . . . . . . . . . . . . . . . 842
Consumer price changes . . . . . . . . . 133
Energy production, consumption . . . . . 236
Flag . . . . . . . . . . . . . . . . . . . . . . 484
Gold reserves . . . . . . . . . . . . . . . . 146
Gross domestic product . . . . . . . . . . 134
History . . . . . . . . . . . . . . . 568, 570, 576
World War I . . . . . . . . . . . . . . . . 569
World War II (1945) . . . . . . 504, 571-72
Islands, areas . . . . . . . . . . . . . . . . 592
"Mad cow disease" (1996) . . . 52, 54, *778*
Merchant fleet . . . . . . . . . . . . . . . . 244
Military strength . . . . . . . . . . . . . . . 182
Monarchs . . . . . . . . . . . . . . 577-78, 829
Motor vehicle production, exports 246, 242
Northern Ireland (1995, 1996)43, 48, 49-50, 52, 59, 575, 592, 830
Nuclear power . . . . . . . . . . . . . 238, 239
Poets laureate . . . . . . . . . . . . . . . . 351
Prime ministers . . . . . . . . . . . . . . . 579
Royal family . . . . . . . . . . . . . . . . . 376
Charles, Diana divorce . 46, 50, 62, *200*
Scotland . . . . . . . . . . . . . . . . . 578, 830
Stonehenge . . . . . . . . . . . . . . . . . . 555
Trade . . . . . . . . . . . . . . . . . . . . . . 377
Unemployment rates . . . . . . . . . . . . 166
U.S. immigrants from . . . . . . . . 377, 383
Wages, hourly . . . . . . . . . . . . . . . . 171
Wales . . . . . . . . . . . . . . . . . . . . . 830
*see also* England
**United Mine Workers**
Membership . . . . . . . . . . . . . . . . . 174
Strikes (1922, 1946) . . . . . . . . . 503, 504
**United Nations** . . . . . . . . . . . . . . 843-45
Agencies . . . . . . . . . . . . . . . . . . . 845
Charter (1945) . . . . . . . . . . . . . 572, 843
Chronology (1995-96)
Bomb plot conviction . . . . . . . . 47, 510
50th anniversary celebration . . . . . . 40
Iraqi Kurdish incursion . . . . . . . . 66-67
Iraq oil-export agreement . . . . . . . . 57
Nuclear test-ban treaty . . . . . . . . . 67
Headquarters . . . . . . . . . . . . . . . . 843
Members . . . . . . . . . . . . . . . . . 843-44
Peacekeeping efforts
Bosnia (1995-96) . . . . . . . . 42, 45, 47
Haiti (1995) . . . . . . . . . . . . . . 46, 510
Somalia (1995) . . . . . . . . . . . . . . 510
Secretaries General . . . . . . . . . . . . 844
U.S. Representatives . . . . . . . . . . . . 844
**United Nations Children's Fund** . . . . . 845
**United Nations Educational, Scientific, and Cultural Organization** . . . . . 845
**United Nations High Commissioner for Refugees** . . . . . . . . . . . . . . . . 845
**United States of America** . . . . . . . 831-32
Accessions . . . . . . . . . . . . . . . . . . 545
Agencies, government . . . . . . . . . . . 188
Altitudes (highest, lowest) . . . . . . . . . 541
Ambassadors, envoys . . . . . . . . . 846-48
Anthem, national . . . . . . . . . . . . 527-28
Area codes . . . . . . . . . . . . . . . 390-420
Areas (square miles) . . . . . 382, 540, 542
Banks . . . . . . . . . . . . . . . . . . . 137, 138
Bicentennial (1976) . . . . . . . . . . . . . 507
Births, deaths . . . . . . . . . . . . . . 962-64
Boundaries . . . . . . . . . . . . . . . . . . 543
Budget . . . . . . . . . . . . . . . . . . . 129-30
Cabinets, presidential . . . . . . . 185, 201-5
Capital . . . . . . . . . . . . . 681, 684-85, 695
Cities . . . . . . . . . . . . 386-87, 686-95, 838
Latitudes, longitudes, altitudes . 594-95
State capitals . . . . . . . . . . . . . 655-80
Clinton administration . . . . . . . . . 185-88
Coastline (by states) . . . . . . . . . . . . 541
Congress . . . . . . . . . . . . . . . . . 111-20
Constitution . . . . . . . . . . . . . . . 515-22
Consumer prices . . . . . . . . . . . . 131-33
Contiguous . . . . . . . . . . . . . . . . 48, 540
Continental Divide . . . . . . . . . . . . . 542
Copyright law . . . . . . . . . . . . . . 724-25
Courts . . . . . . . . . . . . . . . . . . . 189-92
Crime . . . . . . . . . . . . . . . . . . . . 957-61
Currency . . . . . . . . . . . . . . . . . . 139-40
Customs (traveler exemptions) . . . . . 722
Dams and reservoirs . . . . . . . . . . . 706-7
Debt, national . . . . . . . 38, 130, 131, 155
Declaration of Independence . . . . . 512-13
Education . . . . . . . . . . . . . . . . . 251-82
Energy . . . . . . . . . . . . 235, 236, 237, 238
Federally owned land . . . . . . . . . . . 545
Flag . . . . . . . . . . . . . . . . . . 484, 525-27
Foreign investment in . . . . . . . . . . . 145
Foreign relations (*see* State, Department of; *specific countries*)
Geographic centers . . . . . . . . . . . . 543
Geographic superlatives . . . . . . . . . 540
Gold production, reserves . . . . . 153, 146
Government . . . . . . . . . . . . . . . 185-92
Government employment, payroll . . . 169
Gross national/domestic products 133, 134
Historic parks, sites . . . . . . . . . . 546-49
History . . . . . . . . . . . . . . . . . . 497-510
Holidays . . . . . . . . . . . . . . . . . . . . 480
Immigration . . . . . . . . . 377, 383, 840-41
Income, national . . . . . . . . . . . 133, 147
Income taxes . . . . . . . . . . . . . . 730-36
Indians, American . . . . . . . . . . . . . 550
Investments abroad . . . . . . . . . . . . 145
Islands, areas . . . . . . . . . . . . . . . . 592
Joint Chiefs of Staff . . . . . 186, 176, 183
Judiciary . . . . . . . . . . . . . . . . . . 189-92
Labor force . . . . . . . . . . . . . . . . . . 166
Lakes . . . . . . . . . . . . . . . . . . . . . . 598
Land, federally owned . . . . . . . . . . . 545
Libraries, public . . . . . . . . . . . . . . . 257
Maps . . . . . . . . . . . . . . . . . 485, 486-87
Memorials, national . . . . . . . . . . . . . 547
Merchant fleet . . . . . . . . . . . . . . . . 243
Military . . . . . . . . . . . . . . . . . . . 176-84
Mineral production . . . . . . . . . . . 151-53
Monuments, national . . . . . . . . . . 548-49
Motto, national . . . . . . . . . . . . . . . . 525
Mountains . . . . . . . . . . . . . . . . 590, 591
Naturalization process . . . . . . . . . . . 841
Nuclear arms treaties . . . . . . . . . . . 183
Nuclear power . . . . . . . . . . . . . 238, 239
Outlying areas . . . . . . . . . . . 439, 681-83
Parks, national . . . . . . . . . . . 546-47, 549
Passports . . . . . . . . . . . . . . . . . . . 723
Petroleum production, consumption . . 235
Poets laureate . . . . . . . . . . . . . . . . 351
Population . . . . . . . . . . . . . . 377-439, 839
Postal information . . . . . . 390-420, 632-36
Presidential elections . . . . . . . . . 76-108
Presidents . . . . . . . . . . . . 109-10, 530-39
Recreation areas . . . . . . . . . . . 545, 549
Religions . . . . . . . . . . . . . . . . . 644-46
Social Security . . . . . . . . . . . . . 708-12
Space program . . . . . . . . . . . . . 309-13
Statehood dates . . . . . . 542, 543, 655-80
States, individual . . . . . . . . . . . . 655-81
Superlative statistics . . . . . . . . . . . 540
Trade . . . . . . . . . . . . . . . . . . . . 240-42
Veterans . . . . . . . . . . . . . . . . . 180, 181
Vice presidents . . . . . . . . . . . . . 109-10
Vital statistics . . . . . . . . . . . . . . 962-75
Wars
American Revolution . . . 180, 498, 564
Casualties . . . . . . . . . . . . . . . . . 184
Civil War . . . . . . . . . . . . . . . 180, 500
Costs in dollars . . . . . . . . . . . . . . 181
Gulf War . . . . . 180, 509, 776, 790, 815
Korean War . . . . . . . . . . 180, 504, 573
Mexican War . . . . . . . . . . . . . . . 500
Spanish-American War . . . . . . 501, 567
Vietnam War . . . . 180, 505-6, 574, 834
War of 1812, 499
World War I . . . . . . . . . 180, 502, 569
World War II . . . . . . . . 180, 503-4, 572
Water area . . . . . . . . . . . . . . . 382, 542
Waterfalls . . . . . . . . . . . . . . . . . . 599
Weather . . . . . . . . . . . . . . . 226, 221-25
ZIP codes . . . . . . . . . . . . . . 390-420, 439
**Units**
Electrical . . . . . . . . . . . . . . . . . . . 604
Of measurement . . . . . . . . . . . 600-607
**Universal Postal Union** . . . . . . . . . . 845
**Universities.** *See* Colleges and universities
**Unknown Soldier's Tomb** . . . . . . . . . 685
**Upanishads** . . . . . . . . . . . . . . . 554, 654
**Upper Volta.** *See* Burkina Faso
**UPU.** *See* Universal Postal Union
**Uranus** (planet) . . . . . . . . . . . 455, 447-48
Morning, evening stars . . . . . . . . . . 449
Position by month . . . . . . . . . . . 440-43
Sun, distance from . . . . . . . . . . 444, 455
**Urban areas.** *See* Cities; Metropolitan areas, U.S.
**Urban Development, Department of.** *See* Housing and Urban Development, Department of
**Uruguay** . . . . . . . . . . . . . . 484, 832, 847
**U.S. Open** (tennis) (1996) . . . . . . . 67, 928
**USSR.** *See* Soviet Union
**Utah** 677-78
Admission, area, capital . . . 542, 543, 677
Agriculture . . . . . . . . . . . . . . . . . 156-61
Altitudes (high, low) . . . . . . . . . . . . . 541
Birth, death statistics . . . . . . . . . . . 963
Budget . . . . . . . . . . . . . . . . . . . . . 135
Congressional representation . . . . . 112, 118, 380
Courts, U.S. . . . . . . . . . . . . . . . . . . 192
Crime, prisons, death penalty . . . . . 959, 960, 961
Energy consumption . . . . . . . . . . . . 237
Federally owned land . . . . . . . . . . . 545
Governor, state officials . . . . . . . 124, 128
Hazardous waste sites . . . . . . . . . . . 228
Health insurance coverage . . . . . . . . 971
Immigrants admitted (1995) . . . . . . . 383
Indians, American . . . . . . . . . . . . . 550
Interest laws, rates . . . . . . . . . . 721, 722
Marriage, divorce laws . . . . . . . . 728, 729
Mineral production . . . . . . . . . . . . . 151
Motor vehicles . . . . . . . . . . . . . 245, 248
Name origin, nickname . . . . . . . 544, 677
Population . . . . . . . . . . . . . . 380-81, 384
Cities, towns . . . . . . . . . . . . . . . . 418
Counties, county seats . . . . . . . . . 437
Poverty rates . . . . . . . . . . . . . . . . . 388
Presidential elections . . . . . . 76, 102, 106
Schools and libraries . . . . . . . 252-53, 257
Taxes . . . . . . . . . . . . . . . 245, 735, 736
Temperature, precipitation . . . . . 222, 225
Unemployment benefits . . . . . . . . . . 165
Welfare assistance . . . . . . . . . . . . . 389
**UV index** . . . . . . . . . . . . . . . . . . . 227
**Uzbekistan** . . . . . . . . . . 484, 491, 832, 847

— V—

**Valdez, AK** . . . . . . . . . . . . . . . . . . 242
**Valois, House of** . . . . . . . . . . . . . . 580
**ValuJet Airlines** (1996) . . . . . . . 55-56, 59, *198*, 300
**Vanadium** . . . . . . . . . . . . . . . . . . . 151
**Van Buren, Martin** . . . . . . . 109, 110, 531
*see also* Presidents, U.S.
**Vanuatu** . . . . . . 244, 484, 592, 832-33, 847
**Varangians** . . . . . . . . . . . . . . . . . . 559
**Vatican City** . . . . . . . . . . . . . . . . . 833
Ambassadors, envoys . . . . . . . . . . . 848
Flag . . . . . . . . . . . . . . . . . . . . . . . 484
Popes . . . . . . . . . . . . . . . . . . . 649, 650
**Veal**
Nutritive value . . . . . . . . . . . . . . . 610
Prices, farm . . . . . . . . . . . . . . . . . 162
Production, consumption . . . . . . . . . 157
**Vegetables**
Nutritive value . . . . . . . . . . . . . 609, 611
Production . . . . . . . . . . . . . . . . . . 161
**Venezuela** . . . . . . . . . . . . . . . . . . 833
Ambassadors, envoys . . . . . . . . . . . 848
Energy production . . . . . . . . . . . . . 236
Flag . . . . . . . . . . . . . . . . . . . . . . . 484
Gross domestic product . . . . . . . . . . 134
Rulers . . . . . . . . . . . . . . . . . . . . . 584
Trade . . . . . . . . . . . . . . . . . . . . . . 240
**Venomous animals** . . . . . . . . . . . . . 232
**Venus** (planet) . . . . . . . . . . . 455, 444-45
Morning, evening stars . . . . . . . . . . 449
Position by month . . . . . . . . . . . 440-43
Rises, sets . . . . . . . . . . . . . . . . . . 452
Sun, distance from . . . . . . . . . . 455, 444
**Vermont** . . . . . . . . . . . . . . . . . . . . 678
Admission, area, capital . . . . . . 542, 678
Agriculture . . . . . . . . . . . . . . . . . 156-61
Altitudes (high, low) . . . . . . . . . . . . . 541
Birth, death statistics . . . . . . . . . . . 963
Budget . . . . . . . . . . . . . . . . . . . . . 135
Congressional representation . . 112, 118, 380
Courts, U.S. . . . . . . . . . . . . . . . . . . 192
Crime, prisons, death penalty . . . 959, 960
Energy consumption . . . . . . . . . . . . 237
Federally owned land . . . . . . . . . . . 545
Governor, state officials . . . . . . . 124, 128
Hazardous waste sites . . . . . . . . . . . 228
Health insurance coverage . . . . . . . . 971
Immigrants admitted (1995) . . . . . . . 383
Indians, American . . . . . . . . . . . . . 550
Interest laws, rates . . . . . . . . . . 721, 722
Marriage, divorce laws . . . . . . . . 728, 729
Motor vehicles . . . . . . . . . . . . . 245, 248
Name origin, nickname . . . . . . . 544, 678
Population . . . . . . . . . . . . . . 380-81, 384
Cities, towns . . . . . . . . . . . . . . . . 418
Counties, county seats . . . . . . . . . 437
Poverty rates . . . . . . . . . . . . . . . . . 388
Presidential elections . . . . . . 76, 102, 106
Schools and libraries . . . . . . . 252-53, 257
Taxes . . . . . . . . . . . . . . . . . . . 245, 735
Temperature, precipitation . . . . . 222, 225

Unemployment benefits 165
Welfare assistance 389
**Vernal Equinox** 441, 459
**Verrazano, Giovanni da** (1524) 497, 586
**Versailles conference** (1919) 569
**Vesuvius** 588
**Veterans, U.S.** 180, 181
Agent Orange suit (1984) 508
Court of Appeals 192
GI Bill (1944) 504
**Veterans Affairs, Department of** 188
Employees, payroll 169
Expenditures 129
Internet address 210
Secretaries 205, 185, 188
**Veterans' Day** 480
**Vezina Trophy** 895
**Vice presidents, U.S.** 109-10
Address, form of 641
Internet address 210
1996 campaign 63, 64, *194*, *195*
Nominees 107
Presidential succession 522, 525
Salary 185
Salutes, honors 177
**Victoria Falls** 555
**Videos**
Games, top-selling (1995) 293
Movies, most popular (1995; all-time) 284
Music
Awards 293, 292
Sales 291-92
**Vietnam** 834
Ambassadors, envoys 848
Division (1954) 573
Flag 484
Indochina War (1953) 504, 573
Military strength 182
Nam-Viet Kingdom 559
Refugees from (1975) 507, 575, 840
Tet New Year 478
U.S. advisers, aid (1950) 504
U.S. relations normalized (1994, 1995) 509, 510
**Vietnam Veterans Memorial** (DC) 685
**Vietnam War** 574, 834
Agent Orange suit (1984) 508
Black troops 180
Bombings (1965, 1966, 1971, 1972) 505, 506
Casualties, U.S. forces 184
Costs 181
Demonstrations against (1969) 506
End (1975) 507, 575
Medals of Honor 181
Mylai massacre (1969, 1971) 506
Peace talks, pacts (1969, 1973) 506
Pentagon Papers (1971) 506
Tet offensive (1968) 506
Tonkin Resolution (1964) 505
Troop withdrawal (1973) 506
Veteran population 180
**Vikings** 559, 586
**Virginia** 539, 678-79
Admission, area, capital 542, 678
Agriculture 156-61
Altitudes (high, low) 541
Birth, death statistics 963
Budget 135
Coastline 541
Congressional representation 112, 118, 380
Courts, U.S. 192
Crime, prisons, death penalty 959, 960, 961
Energy consumption 237
Federally owned land 545
Governor, state officials 124, 128
Hazardous waste sites 228
Health insurance coverage 971
Immigrants admitted (1995) 383
Indians, American 550
Interest laws, rates 721, 722
Marriage, divorce laws 728, 729
Memorials, monuments 685
Motor vehicles 245, 248
Name origin, nickname 544, 678
Population 380-81, 384
Cities, towns 418-19, 687, 692, 693, 695
Counties, county seats 437-38
Port traffic 242
Poverty rates 388
Presidential elections 76, 102-3, 106
Schools and libraries 252-53, 257
Taxes 245, 735
Temperature, precipitation 222, 225
Unemployment benefits 165
Welfare assistance 389
**Virginia Beach, VA.** *See* Cities, U.S.
**Virgin Islands, British** 592, 831
**Virgin Islands, U.S.** 683
Accession (1916) 502, 545
Altitudes (high, low) 541
Area, capital, population 439, 545, 592, 683
Cities (population) 439
Citizenship 683
Congressional delegate 118
Courts, U.S. 192
Immigrants admitted (1995) 383
Unemployment benefits 165
Welfare assistance 389
ZIP codes 439
**Visas, travel** 723
**Vital statistics** 962-75
**Vitamins** 609, 610-11, 612
**Vojvodina** 836
**Volcanoes** 588-89
Mt. St. Helens (1980) 507, 588, 589
Paricutin 555
**Volleyball** 850, 853
**Volume**
Mathematical formulas 607
Measures (dry, fluid) 600, 601, 602, 604
Sun and planets 455
**Voting rights.** *See* Elections
**Voting Rights Act** (1965) 506

—W—

**Waco (TX) standoff** (1993, 1994) 509
**Wade Trophy** 919
**Wages.** *See* Salaries and wages
**Wake Atoll** 439, 683
**Wales** 830
**Walesa, Lech** (1995) 43, 576, 810
**Walking,** Olympic champions 852, 855
**Wallis and Futuna Islands** 765
**Wall Street.** *See* Stocks
**War, Department of** 202
*see also* Defense, Department of
**War crimes**
Bosnia conflict (1995-96) 40, 43, 49, 52, 57, 60, 62
Geneva Conventions 845
Nuremberg trials (1946) 572
**Warehouse Act** (1916) 502
**War of 1812** (1812-15) 499
Casualties, numbers serving 184
Costs 181
**War of the Worlds** (broadcast) (1938) 503
**Warren Commission** (1964) 505
**Wars**
Battlefields, military parks 547
Casualties, U.S. 184
Costs, U.S. dollars 181
Geneva Conventions 845
Veterans, U.S. 180, 181
*see also specific wars*
**Wars of the Roses** (1455-85) 561
**Washington** (state) 679
Admission, area, capital 542, 543, 679
Agriculture 156-61
Altitudes (high, low) 541
Birth, death statistics 963
Budget 135
Coastline 541
Congressional representation 118, 112, 380
Courts, U.S. 192
Crime, prisons, death penalty 959, 960
Energy consumption 237
Federally owned land 545
Governor, state officials 124, 128
Hazardous waste sites 228
Health insurance coverage 971
Immigrants admitted (1995) 383
Indians, American 550
Interest laws, rates 721, 722
Marriage, divorce laws 728, 729
Motor vehicles 245, 248
Name origin, nickname 544, 679
Population 380-81, 384
Cities, towns 419-20, 694, 695
Counties, county seats 438
Port traffic 242
Poverty rates 388
Presidential elections 76, 103-4, 106
Schools and libraries 252-53, 257
Taxes 245
Temperature, precipitation 222, 225
Unemployment benefits 165
Welfare assistance 389
**Washington, Booker T.** (1881) 340, 501
**Washington, DC** 681, 695
Altitudes (high, low) 541
Area, population 422, 542, 681
Birth, death statistics 963
British burning of (1814) 499
Budget 130
Congressional delegate 118
Courts 191
Crime, prisons, death penalty 959, 960
Energy consumption 237
Federally owned land 545
Federal workers 169
Health insurance coverage 971
Immigrants admitted (1995) 383
Indians, American 550
Interest laws, rates 721, 722
Marches
Antiwar (1969) 506
Black civil rights (1963) 505
Million Man (1995) 40, 510
Marriage, divorce laws 728, 729
Mayor 124
Memorials, monuments 684-85
Motor vehicles 245, 248
Museums, libraries 684-85
Name origin 544
Population 380-81, 384, 386, 395, 422, 695
Poverty rates 388
Presidential elections 76, 80, 106
Public buildings 684-85
Schools and libraries 252-53, 257
Taxes 245, 735, 736
Temperature, precipitation 222, 224
Unemployment benefits 165
Voting rights 522, 681
Welfare assistance 389
White House 185, 685
**Washington, George** 109, 530
Birthday (legal holiday) 480
Commander-in-chief (1775) 498
Constitutional convention (1787) 498
Delaware crossing (1776) 498
Farewell Address (1796) 498
Mount Vernon 685
*see also* Presidents, U.S.
**Washington Monument** (DC) 685
**Water**
Area (U.S.) 382, 542
Boiling, freezing points 605
Dams, reservoirs 706-7
Drinking water safety act 38
Health, nutrition 609
Oceans, seas, gulfs 593
Pollution 228
Usage 234
Weight, mass 605
**Waterfalls** 540, 599
**Watergate** 536, 574
Break-in (1972) 506
Convictions (1973) 506
Cover-up (1973, 1975) 507
Impeachment hearings (1974) 507
Nixon resignation (1974) 507, 574
"Plumbers" (1974) 507
Tapes (1973, 1974) 507
**Waterloo, Battle of** (1815) 565
**Water polo** 853
**Waterways.** *See* Canals
**Watt** (electrical unit) 604
**Weapons**
Arrests, sentences 961
Defense contracts 180
*see also* Firearms; Nuclear arms
**Weather** 220-27
Annual climatological data 223
Blizzards 220, 302
Eastern U.S. (1996) 46, *196*
By cities, foreign 225
By cities and states, U.S. 226, 221-25
Floods (1993) 220, 303, 509
Hurricanes (1996) 67, 220, 225, 226, 302
Marine warnings, advisories 220
Precipitation 225, 221-23
Wettest spot 222, 540
Storms 302
Classifications 225
Watches, warnings 220
Temperatures 221-25
Heat index 227
Heat wave deaths (1995) 510
Highest, lowest recorded 222
Thunderstorms 220
Tornadoes 220, 225, 302
Typhoons 302
Ultraviolet index 227
Wind chill 227
Winds, velocities 226, 223, 225
**Webster, Noah** (1783, 1828) 498, 499
**Wedding anniversaries** 727
**Weight, body** 612, 616
**Weight lifting** 853
**Weights, measures, numbers** 600-607
Atomic 218-19
Electrical units 604
Energy measures 604
Equivalents, table of 601-2
Gases 605
Human 612, 616
Metric 600-604
Temperature 605

U.S. Customary System . . . . . . 600-601
Water . . . . . . . . . . . . . . . . . . . . . 605
**Weimar Republic** (1919) . . . . . . . 570, 767
**Welfare**
Aid to Families with Dependent Children (by state) . . . . . . . . . . . 389
Federal food programs . . . . . . . . . . . 158
Reform legislation (1995-96) . . 38, 45, 46, 56, 61
Supplemental Security Income . . . . . . 711
**West Bank.** *See* Israel; West Bank
**Western Samoa.** *See* Samoa, Western
**West Germany.** *See* Germany
**West Indies, British** . . . . . . . . . . . . . 831
**Westminster Kennel Club** . . . . . . . . . 936
**West Point Military Academy** . . . 178, 268
**West Virginia** . . . . . . . . . . . . . . . 679-80
Admission, area, capital . . . . . . 542, 679
Agriculture . . . . . . . . . . . . . . . . 156-61
Altitudes (high, low) . . . . . . . . . . . . 541
Birth, death statistics . . . . . . . . . . . . 963
Budget . . . . . . . . . . . . . . . . . . . . . 135
Congressional representation . . . 112, 118, 380
Courts, U.S. . . . . . . . . . . . . . . . . . 192
Crime, prisons, death penalty . . . 959, 960
Energy consumption . . . . . . . . . . . . 237
Federally owned land . . . . . . . . . . . 545
Governor, state officials . . . . . . 124, 128
Hazardous waste sites . . . . . . . . . . . 228
Health insurance coverage . . . . . . . . 971
Immigrants admitted (1995) . . . . . . . . 383
Indians, American . . . . . . . . . . . . . 550
Interest laws, rates . . . . . . . . . . 721, 722
Marriage, divorce laws . . . . . . . 728, 729
Motor vehicles . . . . . . . . . . . . . 245, 248
Name origin, nickname . . . . . . . 544, 679
Population . . . . . . . . . . . . . 380-81, 384
Cities, towns . . . . . . . . . . . . . . . . 420
Counties, county seats . . . . . . . . . 438
Port traffic . . . . . . . . . . . . . . . . . . 242
Poverty rates . . . . . . . . . . . . . . . . . 388
Presidential elections . . . . . . 76, 104, 106
Schools and libraries . . . . . . 252-53, 257
Taxes . . . . . . . . . . . . . . . 245, 735, 736
Temperatures, record . . . . . . . . . . . 225
Unemployment benefits . . . . . . . . . . 165
Welfare assistance . . . . . . . . . . . . . 389
**Wheat**
Exports, imports . . . . . . . . . . . 163, 241
Prices, farm . . . . . . . . . . . . . . . . . 162
Production . . . . . . . . . . . . 160, 161, 163
**Whiskey Rebellion** (1794) . . . . . . . . . . 498
**White House** . . . . . . . . . . . . . . . . . . 685
Burning (1814) . . . . . . . . . . . . . . . 499
Employees, payroll . . . . . . . . . . . . . 169
Expenditures . . . . . . . . . . . . . . . . . 129
Internet addresses . . . . . . . . . . . . . 210
Staff . . . . . . . . . . . . . . . . . . . . . . 185
**Whitewater investigation** (1994, 1995, 1996) . . . 44-45, 46, 48-49, 51, 53, 56, 59, 62, 66, *196*, 509, 510
**Whitney, Eli** (1793) . . . . . . . . . . . . . 498
**WHO.** *See* World Health Organization
**Wichita, KS.** *See* Cities, U.S.
**Wilkes Atoll** . . . . . . . . . . . . . . . . . . 683
**Williams, Roger** (1636) . . . . . . . . . . . 497
**William the Conqueror** . . . . . . . . 559, 577
**Wills, living** . . . . . . . . . . . . . . . . . . 615
**Wilson, Woodrow** . . . . . . 107, 109, 534-35
*see also* Presidents, U.S.
**Wimbledon** (tennis tournament) (1996) . . . . . . . . . . . . . . . . 62, 929
**Wind chill factor** . . . . . . . . . . . . . . . 227
**Windsor, House of** . . . . . . . 376, 578, 829
Charles, Diana divorce . . . 46, 50, 62, *200*
**Wind speeds, U.S.** . . . . . . . . 223, 225, 226
**Windward Islands.** *See* Dominica; St. Lucia; St. Vincent and the Grenadines
**Winston Cup** (auto racing) . . . . . . 931, 932
**Winston-Salem, NC** . . . . . . . . . . 124, 702
**Winter** (season) . . . . . . . . . . . . . . . . 459
**Winter Olympics.** *See under* Olympic Games
**Winter solstice** . . . . . . . . . . . . . 443, 459
**WIPO.** *See* World Intellectual Property Organization
**Wisconsin** . . . . . . . . . . . . . . . . . . . 680
Admission, area, capital . . . 542, 543, 680
Agriculture . . . . . . . . . . . . . . . . 156-61
Altitudes (high, low) . . . . . . . . . . . . 541
Birth, death statistics . . . . . . . . . . . . 963
Budget . . . . . . . . . . . . . . . . . . . . . 135
Congressional representation . . . 112, 118, 380
Courts, U.S. . . . . . . . . . . . . . . . . . 192
Crime, prisons, death penalty . . . 959, 960 961
Energy consumption . . . . . . . . . . . . 237
Federally owned land . . . . . . . . . . . 545
Governor, state officials . . . . . . 124, 128
Hazardous waste sites . . . . . . . . . . . 228
Health insurance coverage . . . . . . . . 971
Immigrants admitted (1995) . . . . . . . 383
Indians, American . . . . . . . . . . . . . 550
Interest laws, rates . . . . . . . . . . 721, 722
Marriage, divorce laws . . . . . . . 728, 729
Motor vehicles . . . . . . . . . . . . . 245, 248
Name origin, nickname . . . . . . . 544, 680
Population . . . . . . . . . . . . . 380-81, 384
Cities, towns . . . . . . . . . . . . . 420, 691
Counties, county seats . . . . . . . 438-39
Port traffic . . . . . . . . . . . . . . . . . . 242
Poverty rates . . . . . . . . . . . . . . . . . 388
Presidential elections . . . . 76, 104-5, 106
Schools and libraries . . . . . . . 252-53, 257
Taxes . . . . . . . . . . . . . . . 245, 735, 736
Temperature, precipitation . . . . . 222, 225
Unemployment benefits . . . . . . . . . . 165
Welfare assistance . . . . . . . . . . . . . 389
**WMO.** *See* World Meteorological Organization
**Women**
AIDS incidence . . . . . . . . . . . . . . . 975
Armed forces . . . . . . . . . . . . . . 179, 180
Generals, first U.S. (1970) . . . . . . 506
Vietnam memorial . . . . . . . . . . . . 685
Astronauts
First (1983) . . . . . . 309, 310, 311, 508
Lucid record (1996) . . . . . 66, *199*, 312
Attorney general, first (1993) . . . . . . 509
Business ownership . . . . . . . . . . . . 377
Cancer cases, deaths . . . . . . . . . . . 974
Cigarette use . . . . . . . . . . . . . . . . 965
Colleges
Citadel female cadets (1995, 1996) . . . . . . . . . . . . . . . . 64, 510
First (1821) . . . . . . . . . . . . . . . . 499
State military school ruling (1996) . . . 39
Congresswoman, first (1916) . . . . . . 502
Educational level . . . . . . . . . . . . . . 254
As elected officials . . . . . . . . . . . . 377
Employment . . . . . . . . . . 166, 167, 172
Equal Rights Amendment (1972, 1982) . . . . . . . . . . . . . . . 506, 508
Equal rights convention (1848) . . . . . 500
First ladies . . . . . . . . . . . . . . 538, 539
Governor, first U.S. (1924) . . . . . . . . 503
Health help organizations . . . . . . . . . 619
Life expectancy . . . . . . . . . . . . . . . 973
Marital status . . . . . . . . . . . . . . . . 377
Nobel Prize winners . . . . . . . . . . 317-19
Population (1790-1994) . . . . . . . 379, 382
Poverty rates . . . . . . . . . . . . . . 172, 388
Salaries and wages . . . . . . . . . 167, 172
Hourly rates . . . . . . . . . . . . . . . . 170
Weekly earnings median . . . . . 173, 172
Single household heads . . 172, 377, 388, 965
Strikers, first (1824) . . . . . . . . . . . 499
Suicide rates . . . . . . . . . . . . . 965, 968
Supreme Court justices (1981, 1993) . . . . . . . . . . . . . . . 507, 509
Vice-presidential nominee (1984) . . . 508
Voting rights (1869, 1920) . 501, 502, 521
**Wooden Award** . . . . . . . . . . . . . . . 917
**Wool** . . . . . . . . . . . . . . . . . . . . . . 162
**Woolworth's Five and Dime** (1879) . . 501
**Words, new** . . . . . . . . . . . . . . . . . 637
**Workers.** *See* Employment
***World Almanac, The***
First (1868) . . . . . . . . . . . . . . . . . 501
Internet address . . . . . . . . . . . . . . 207
**World Bank** . . . . . . . . . . . . . . . . . 845
**World Court** . . . . . . . . . . . . . . . . . 845
**World Cup**
Skiing . . . . . . . . . . . . . . . . . . . . . 919
Soccer . . . . . . . . . . . . . . . . . . . . 956
**World Health Organization** . . . . . . . . 845
**World history** . . . . . . . . . . . . . 551-76
**World Intellectual Property Organization** . . . . . . . . . . . . 845
**World Meteorological Organization** . . 845
**World Series** . . . . . . . . . . . . . . . 952-53
**World Trade Center bombing** (1993, 1994) . . . . . . . . . . . . . . . . 509
**World Trade Organization** . . . . . . 241, 845
**World War I** (1914-18) . . . . . . . . . . . 569
Armistice (1918) . . . . . . . . . . . . . . 502
Black troops . . . . . . . . . . . . . . . . 180
Casualties, U.S. forces . . . . . . . . . . 184
Costs . . . . . . . . . . . . . . . . . . . . . 181
Medals of Honor . . . . . . . . . . . . . . 181
Troop strength . . . . . . . . . . . . . . . 184
U.S. neutrality (1914) . . . . . . . . . . . 502
Versailles conference (1919) . . . . . . 569
Veteran population . . . . . . . . . . . . . 180
**World War II** (1939-45) . . . . 503-4, 571-72
Atomic bombs (1945) . . . . . . . . 504, 572
Black troops . . . . . . . . . . . . . . . . 180
Casualties, U.S. forces . . . . . . . . . . 184
Costs . . . . . . . . . . . . . . . . . . . . . 181
Medals of Honor . . . . . . . . . . . . . . 181
Peace treaties, Japan (1951) . . . . . . 504
Pearl Harbor attack (1941) . . . . . . . . 503
Troop strength . . . . . . . . . . . . . . . 184
Veteran population . . . . . . . . . . . . . 180
**World Wide Web** . . . . . . 211, 207, 208, 378
**Wounded Knee, Battle of** (1890) . . . . . 501
**Wrestling**
NCAA champions . . . . . . . . . . . . . 904
Olympic champions (1996) . . . . . . . 853
**Wright brothers** (1903) . . . . 315, 502, 568
**Writers, notable** . . . . . . . . . . . . . 350-55
Best-selling books (1995) . . . . . . . . 289
Children's books . . . . . . . 288-89, 327-28
Newbery Medal . . . . . . . . . . . . 327-28
Nobel Prizes . . . . . . . . . . . . 39, 318-19
Noteworthy literature (1996) . . . . . . . 288
Pen names . . . . . . . . . . . . . . . . . 642
Poets laureate . . . . . . . . . . . . . . . 351
Pulitzer Prizes . . . . . . . . . . . . . 320-23
Special awards . . . . . . . . . . . . . . . 327
**WTO.** *See* World Trade Organization
**Wyoming** . . . . . . . . . . . . . . . . . . 680-81
Admission, area, capital . . . 542, 543, 680
Agriculture . . . . . . . . . . . . . . . . 156-61
Altitudes (high, low) . . . . . . . . . . . . 541
Birth, death statistics . . . . . . . . . . . 963
Budget . . . . . . . . . . . . . . . . . . . . . 135
Congressional representation 112, 118, 380
Courts, U.S. . . . . . . . . . . . . . . . . . 192
Crime, prisons, death penalty . . 959, 960, 961
Energy consumption . . . . . . . . . . . . 237
Federally owned land . . . . . . . . . . . 545
Governor, state officials . . . . . . . 124, 128
Hazardous waste sites . . . . . . . . . . . 228
Health insurance coverage . . . . . . . . 971
Immigrants admitted (1995) . . . . . . . 383
Indians, American . . . . . . . . . . . . . 550
Interest laws, rates . . . . . . . . . . 721, 722
Marriage, divorce laws . . . . . . . 728, 729
Motor vehicles . . . . . . . . . . . . . 245, 248
Name origin, nickname . . . . . . . 544, 680
Population . . . . . . . . . . . . . 380-81, 384
Cities, towns . . . . . . . . . . . . . . . . 420
Counties, county seats . . . . . . . . . 439
Poverty rates . . . . . . . . . . . . . . . . 388
Presidential elections . . . . . 76, 105, 106
Schools and libraries . . . . . . 252-53, 257
Taxes . . . . . . . . . . . . . . . . . . . . . 245
Temperature, precipitation . . . . . 222, 225
Unemployment benefits . . . . . . . . . . 165
Welfare assistance . . . . . . . . . . . . . 389


—X—


**Xinjiang** . . . . . . . . . . . . . . . . . . . . 754


—Y—


**Yacht racing**
America's Cup . . . . . . . . . . . . . . . 936
Olympic champions (1996) . . . . . . . . 853
**Yalta Conference** (1945) . . . . . . . . . . 504
**Year**
Calendar, perpetual . . . . . . . . . . . 476-77
Chronological eras . . . . . . . . . . . . . 460
Holidays . . . . . . . . . . . . . . . . . . . 480
Sidereal, tropical . . . . . . . . . . . 458, 450
**Year in pictures** (1996) . . *193-200, 777-84*
**Yellow Sea** . . . . . . . . . . . . . . . . . . 593
**Yellowstone National Park** . . 501, 546, 681
**Yeltsin, Boris** . . . . . . . . . . . . . 33, 812-13
Chronology (1995-96) . . . . . . 54, 69, 510
Health problems . . . . . . . . . 40, 61, 67
Presidential election . . 33, 59, 61, 65, *777*
**Yemen** . . . . . . . . . . . . . . . 484, 835, 848
**Yonkers, NY.** *See* Cities, U.S.
**York, House of** . . . . . . . . . . . . . . . . 578
**Young, Brigham** (1846) . . . . . . . . 345, 500
**Yugoslavia** . . . . . . . . 484, 570, 835-36, 848
**Yukon River** . . . . . . . . . . . . . . . 596, 597


—Z—


**Zaire** . . . . . . . . . . . . . . . . . . . . 836-37
Ambassadors, envoys . . . . . . . . . . . 848
Flag . . . . . . . . . . . . . . . . . . . . . . 484
Gold production . . . . . . . . . . . . . . 153
History . . . . . . . . . . . . . . . . . . . . 575
**Zaire (Congo) River** . . . . . . . . . . . . . 596
**Zambia** . . . . . . . . . . . . . . . . 484, 837, 848
**Zanzibar** . . . . . . . . . . . . . . . . . 592, 824
**Zen Buddhism** . . . . . . . . . . . . . . . . . 562
**Zeppelins** . . . . . . . . . . . . . . . . . . . 316
**Zeus, Statue at Olympia** . . . . . . . . . . 555
**Zimbabwe** . . . . . . . . . . 484, 575, 837, 848
**Zinc** . . . . . . . . . . . . . . . . . 151, 152, 153
**ZIP codes**
Colleges and universities . . . . . . . 258-82
U.S. outlying areas . . . . . . . . . . . . 439
U.S. states . . . . . . . . . . . . . . . . 390-420
**Zodiac signs** . . . . . . . . . . . . . . . . . 456
**Zones**
Temperature . . . . . . . . . . . . . . . 458-59
Time . . . . . . . . . . . . . . . . . . . . . . 484
**Zoological parks** . . . . . . . . . . . . . . . 233
**Zoroaster** . . . . . . . . . . . . . . . . . . . . 55

# The World Almanac

**and Book of Facts 1997**

## The Top 10 News Stories

Bill Clinton was reelected president of the U.S. on Nov. 5, easily defeating his chief opponent, former Senate Majority Leader Bob Dole (R, KS). Clinton won 31 states and the District of Columbia, taking 49% of the popular vote overall, according to preliminary returns. Republicans, however, retained control of Congress.

TWA Flight 800, traveling from New York City to Paris, exploded and crashed into the Atlantic Ocean off the coast of Long Island July 17, killing all 230 people aboard. During a long and painstaking process of retrieving and analyzing wreckage, authorities investigated whether the explosion had been caused by mechanical failure, a terrorist bomb, or a missile.

Overcoming poor health and popular misgivings about the economy, Boris Yeltsin won reelection as president of Russia on July 3, in a runoff against Communist Party candidate Gennadi Zyuganov. As concern over his health continued, he underwent heart bypass surgery Nov. 5.

Theodore Kaczynski was arrested in Apr. and indicted in June as the so-called Unabomber, sought for over 17 years in connection with a series of mail bombs that killed 3 and injured more than 20.

The Arab-Israeli peace process was stalled following a series of terrorist bombings in Israel in late Feb. and early Mar. that killed 60 people. Emphasizing security issues, Benjamin Netanyahu defeated Shimon Peres in the May 29 election for Israeli prime minister. Violence flared between Israeli soldiers and Palestinians in Sept. after Israel opened a new tunnel entrance near a holy Muslim site in Jerusalem.

The Summer Olympic Games, held in Atlanta, GA, July 19-Aug. 4, were marred by a bombing at Centennial Olympic Park on July 27, which directly killed 1 person. Despite this tragedy, the games went on. Highlights of the competition included the gold-medal performance of the U.S. women's gymnastics team, Carl Lewis's 4th consecutive Olympic gold in the long jump, and Michael Johnson's victories in both the 400-meter and 200-meter races.

Troops from the U.S. and other countries monitored implementation of a peace accord between the 3 warring factions in Bosnia and Herzegovina, including elections for a new collective presidency and legislators on Sept. 14.

In July and August the U.S. Congress passed, and Pres. Bill Clinton signed, a sweeping measure revamping the nation's welfare system and ending Aid to Families With Dependent Children as a federal entitlement program.

On Sept. 26, astronaut Shannon Lucid ended a 188-day stay in space—longer than any other American or any other woman. Most of that time was spent aboard the Russian space station *Mir*, as part of a long-term cooperative U.S.-Russian space venture.

Britain's Prince Charles and Princess Diana were divorced, Aug. 28, ending an unhappy 15-year marriage.

## Election '96

By Donald Young

In a strong victory that had seemed almost impossible a few years earlier, Pres. Bill Clinton (D) carried 31 states and the District of Columbia to win reelection on Nov. 5, 1996. Clinton and his running mate, Vice Pres. Al Gore, won 379 electoral votes (109 more than needed) and, according to preliminary results, took 49% of the popular vote overall.

Clinton's main rival, former Senate Majority Leader Bob Dole (R, KS)—who had retired from the Senate to concentrate on the campaign—never overcame a deficit in the polls; he and his running mate, former Rep. Jack Kemp (R, NY), ended up with the remaining 159 electoral votes and 41% of the popular vote. Ross Perot, the Texas billionaire who founded the Reform Party and ran on its ticket, trailed with 8% of the popular vote; minor-party candidates shared the other 2%.

Despite the Clinton victory, Republicans retained control of both houses of Congress. In the House, where all 435 seats were at stake, the GOP, in nearly complete returns, had secured 222 seats, to 204 for Democrats. Two independents were elected, and results in 7 congressional districts remained in doubt, with runoff elections scheduled for 3 districts in Texas. The Republicans went into the election holding 235 seats; they needed 218 seats to maintain control.

In the Senate, where 34 of the 100 seats were being filled, the Republicans made a small gain; they emerged with at least 54 seats, one more than before, with one seat undecided. With many incumbents retiring, the new Senate looked more conservative than the old one.

Only 11 states, most of them small, elected governors. Republicans held a 32–17 majority (with one independent) before the election and retained that identical advantage as a result of the Nov. 5 voting.

### Analysis of the Results

Elected in 1992 with 43% of the popular vote, Pres. Clinton had sought a broader mandate in 1996. In this he was partially successful, though he apparently fell short of an absolute majority. He ran well ahead of Dole in the East, Midwest, and West. Dole ran ahead in the South and in the wheat belt and mountain states, which yielded only a small harvest of electoral votes.

The coastal anchors of the Clinton strategy were New York, a natural Democratic stronghold, and California—the biggest prize of all, with its 54 electoral votes. Despite a strong push by Dole in California, Clinton carried both states easily; he supported many initiatives to aid the California economy and seemed more in tune with the electorate, with its laid-back, youth-oriented, trend-setting culture, than did Dole. While Dole carried Texas and Georgia, he failed to catch on in the crucial industrial Midwest, where Clinton took the 3 biggest prizes, Illinois, Michigan, and Ohio—the last a state without which no Republican has ever been elected president.

Exit polls showed that voters who rated the economy, Medicare, or education as their most important issue went overwhelmingly for Clinton. Clinton won 2 states that he lost in 1992—Florida and Arizona, both of which have large populations of senior citizens. A majority of voters in exit polls did not regard Clinton as honest and trustworthy, but this apparently did not hurt him greatly. Dole ran well ahead among voters who said they were most concerned about taxes or the federal budget deficits, but many doubted he could cut taxes by 15% and still shrink the deficit, as he promised. The so-called gender gap remained a major factor in the voting, with Clinton getting 54% of the votes of women but only 44% support from men.

In 1994, the Republicans had won a majority in the House for the first time in 40 years; in the 1996 election they suffered some slippage, principally within the 71-member "freshman class" that had been swept into office in the nationwide GOP tide of 1994. But, aided by gains in the once-solidly-Democratic South, the GOP held on—an achievement, considering the big Clinton victory and the charges of extremism leveled against many Republican members. The combative House Speaker Newt Gingrich (R, GA) easily held on to his seat.

Senate elections appeared immune to any national trends. The Democrats lost open seats in Alabama, Colorado, and Arkansas. They unseated one incumbent Republican, Larry Pressler of South Dakota. In the contest for an open seat in Oregon, Republican Gordon Smith and Democrat Tom Bruggere were running neck and neck in preliminary returns. Several Senate incumbents survived strong challenges, among them the dean of the Senate, Strom Thurmond (R, SC), who was reelected at the age of 93 (at the end of his new term he would serve just past his 100th birthday). Jesse Helms (R, NC), perhaps the most outspoken conservative senator, defeated Harvey Gantt, his unsuccessful opponent 6 years earlier, who had hoped to become the South's first black senator since Reconstruction. On the Democratic side, Paul Wellstone (MN), arguably the Senate's most outspoken liberal, survived a rematch against former Sen. Rudy Boschwitz.

In a widely watched race, Democrat John Kerry of Massachusetts turned back that state's popular governor, William Weld. And Rep. Robert Torricelli (D) defeated Dick Zimmer (R) for the Senate seat held by retiring New Jersey Sen. Bill Bradley, in a hard fought campaign that featured "negative advertising" on both sides.

In Washington state, Gary Locke, a Democrat, became the first Asian-American to be elected governor outside Hawaii.

### Issues in the Campaign

In 1992, a sign reading "It's the economy, stupid" was put up in Clinton campaign headquarters to remind his strategists to stay focused on this key issue. In 1996, Clinton and the Democrats could boast that 10 million jobs had been created during the past 4 years and that the unemployment rate was barely above 5%, the lowest in many years. Also, inflation and interest rates were low, and stock prices had surged to new heights. Dole and the Republicans countered with figures showing that economic growth was sluggish and that many new jobs were low paying. They blamed slow growth on the 1993 Clinton economic plan, which passed without the support of any Republican in Congress, and which raised taxes, mostly on wealthier Americans. The president responded that the 1993 plan and ongoing budget cuts that he supported had resulted in sharp declines in the size of the annual federal budget deficits. Clinton had promised to cut the deficits by 50% and he had exceeded that goal by 1996.

The Republicans endorsed an across-the-board 15% tax cut, which Dole said would lift consumer spending and create jobs. Following a philosophy long championed by Kemp, he argued that increased tax collections would partly cover the loss from lower rates, but he was not specific as to how the rest of the shortfall would be covered. Clinton ridiculed Dole's plan, offering smaller, targeted tax cuts instead. Democrats claimed that Republicans wanted to "cut" Medicare, the health-insurance program for the elderly; Republicans responded that they merely sought to reduce the rate of future growth in Medicare spending and noted that Clinton himself supported such a cut, though of less magnitude.

The Republicans had long stressed social issues, especially those relating to "family values," but their advantage was somewhat undermined in 1996. Abortion was a divisive issue but its electoral impact was uncertain and the presidential candidates largely avoided discussing it. Clinton pointed to many of his initiatives as being pro-family, including his support for the Family and Medical Leave Act, student loans, and an increase in the minimum wage. The president also claimed credit for a decline in the rate of violent crime, citing his support for gun-control measures and a commitment to putting more police officers on the streets.

Dole and the Republicans sought to paint the president as a liberal, but Clinton had positioned himself near the center on some "hot-button" issues. To the distress of many liberal Democrats, the president joined with congressional Republicans to reform welfare by shifting responsibility to the states, restricting benefits, and ending the entitlement to assistance.

The issue of drugs cut both ways. The Republicans blamed a sharp increase in drug use by teenagers on an indifferent White House that was itself populated by some former drug users. Clinton, meanwhile, issued regulations aimed at preventing young people from taking up cigarette smoking, and Democrats noted that large donations from tobacco companies flowed largely to Republicans.

Late in the campaign, Dole sought to make character and integrity an issue. Clinton was embarrassed by a steady drip of revelations relevant to numerous scandals involving the White House, his years as governor of Arkansas, and his personal life. Perot warned of a "constitutional crisis" in a 2d Clinton term, which he said would cause a national trauma similar to Watergate. Perot, in particular, and Dole zeroed in on reports that the Democrats had taken large donations, some illegal, from foreigners. Immense sums of so-called soft money, which could be spent without legal restraint to "educate" the public (but not actually endorse a candidate), were accepted by both major parties.

Most Americans apparently found the campaign boring, in part because a Clinton victory was widely assumed. Televised debates between Clinton and Dole, on Oct. 6 and Oct. 16, attracted media attention but low audience ratings. (Some said that Perot, who was excluded from the debates, could have added a new dimension to them.) A debate between Kemp and Gore, on Oct. 9, had a similar result. Much of the energy in the campaign was generated by ostensibly nonpartisan bodies, such as labor unions (which spent $35 million, mostly for Democrats) and the Christian Coalition, whose sympathies lay mostly with Republicans.

Dole's age (73) was not addressed directly by Clinton, though the president did express concern about "the age of his ideas." Dole showed that he was willing and able to take bold and daring actions—such as a sweeping tax cut, and the choice of a popular rival, Jack Kemp, as his running mate. But it was to no avail.

### Nomination of the Candidates

Clinton's prospects for reelection had been poor after the failure of his comprehensive, and expensive, health-reform plan in 1994, and the loss of Congress by the Democrats. Obliged to deny that he was "irrelevant," he rebounded, raised an immense amount of campaign money, and was not challenged in the Democratic presidential primaries.

Dole, who had also sought the presidential nomination in 1980 and 1988, benefited from the fact that his potentially most serious challenger, Gen. Colin Powell (ret.), chose not to run. Magazine publisher Steve Forbes ran for the nomination as an advocate of a flat tax, and commentator Pat Buchanan waged a colorful campaign that stressed opposition to abortion and international trade policies that allegedly cost American jobs. But Dole had the near-unanimous support of the GOP establishment and wrapped up the nomination after a shaky start.

Perot used his own money to launch the Reform Party and defeated former Gov. Richard Lamm (D, CO) for its nomination. But he did not come close to equaling his showing at the polls in 1992.

# The Next Four Years

By Geoffrey M. Horn

*Geoffrey M. Horn is a freelance editor and writer who often writes about politics.*

Carrying 31 states, on Election Day 1996, Bill Clinton became only the 14th of the 42 U.S. presidents to win election to two successive terms. In this century, only two other Democrats did it: Woodrow Wilson in 1916 and Franklin D. Roosevelt in 1936—the second of FDR's four consecutive presidential election victories. Unlike Wilson and FDR, however, Clinton failed to carry Congress.

### Lame Ducks

Fear of another FDR-style presidency had led Republicans to press for a constitutional amendment to bar presidents from serving more than two elected terms. Because of the 22d Amendment, ratified in 1951, the moment the champagne corks popped on election night, Bill Clinton became a lame duck. Did he shake all those hands and raise all that money just so he could spend four years in the Oval Office fine-tuning the blueprints for his presidential library?

It's a mistake to underestimate the powers of the president in working with Congress and promoting his own agenda—especially one with such superb communication skills and sensitive political antennae. But voters who wanted to know what four more years of Clinton might look like could take little comfort from his immediate two-term predecessors. Ronald Reagan beat Walter Mondale in a 59-41% blowout in 1984, then saw much of his second term blighted by the Iran-contra scandal. Richard Nixon's 1972 victory margin over George McGovern was even wider—23%. Less than two years later, Nixon had to resign.

### Think Small

What happens when an activist president confronts the frustrations of his first term and the diminished horizons of a second? Clinton's acceptance speech to the Democratic National Convention in August 1996 showed he knows how to do more with less.

The domestic agenda for a second term was crafted in large part to reassure the elderly and to attract "soccer moms"—mostly white, mostly suburban—who juggle the demands of home, job, kids, and car pools. These voters didn't want grand themes and "risky" schemes. With inflation, unemployment, and interest rates low and incomes inching upward, they wanted modest changes that would ease some of their anxieties. In his address, Clinton promised to aid education and the environment, protect Medicare and Medicaid, provide tax breaks for college tuition and home ownership, toughen gun-control laws, tighten restrictions on advertising and sales of cigarettes to children, and clean up toxic waste dumps. He said he wanted to build "a bridge to the 21st century." But what he promised, mainly, were better onramps and guardrails.

### On the Bench

Clinton's judicial selections played a marginal role in the 1996 campaign, but in a second term they may have much greater impact. According to an Associated Press survey, Clinton had already placed 185 judges on the federal bench when Congress adjourned in October. At that rate, by the end of his second term, nearly half of all federal district court judges will be Clinton appointees. He may also have an opportunity for a major impact on the Supreme Court, especially if the conservative Chief Justice William H. Rehnquist, who turned 72 in Oct. 1996, decides to step down.

### The World Stage

In domestic matters, a president is more likely to be held in check by a hostile or independent-minded Congress. In foreign affairs, the president has a much freer hand. Bob Dole carped about Clinton's "photo-op foreign policy." But Clinton understands that every successful president bolsters his domestic image by making use of the world stage.

Progress toward peace in Bosnia, Northern Ireland, and the Middle East represented an important, if shaky, legacy of Clinton's first term. Protecting the peace processes and propping up the elected government in Haiti may absorb much of his energy and add to his accomplishments. But there are obvious hazards. Some of America's least-favorite leaders remained in power in Iraq, Libya, Cuba, and North Korea. The uncertain state of Boris Yeltsin's health raised the specter of instability in Russia. Hong Kong, reverting from Britain to China in 1997, was another potential trouble spot.

### Personnel Matters

The dropout rate among Clinton's first-term aides and cabinet officers was alarmingly high. Commerce Secretary Ron Brown died in a plane crash. Scandals claimed others. Deputy White House Counsel Vincent Foster committed suicide. Other Arkansas friends and cronies wilted in the Washington media glare.

Typically, in the first few months of a second term, at least a half dozen top-level executive posts change hands. Secretary of State Warren Christopher and chief of staff Leon Panetta were among top officials who indicated they were leaving the Clinton administration.

An especially delicate question concerns the role of First Lady Hillary Rodham Clinton. During 1993-94 she was the First Co-President, directing the ill-fated health care reform effort. During 1996 she played the part of First Wife and First Mom, galvanizing support for a Democratic "family values" agenda. The Clinton campaign said little about what her responsibilities might be in a second term.

### Starr Chambers

On that matter, as on so many others, Whitewater independent counsel Kenneth Starr and the grand juries under his direction may have a decisive voice. After former Clinton associates James and Susan McDougal and Arkansas Gov. Jim Guy Tucker were convicted on felony charges on May 28, 1996, Starr began pressing them to tell what they know about both Clintons' possible involvement in fraudulent Whitewater financial dealings.

Starr's mandate now includes not just Whitewater but the White House travel office firings and the administration's mishandling of hundreds of FBI files. In an interview in September with broadcaster Jim Lehrer, the president left no doubt he thought Starr was out to get him. Controversies about grand jury subpoenas, congressional inquiries, and, perhaps, presidential pardons will likely dog both Clintons during a second term.

The case of *Clinton* v. *Jones*, which the Supreme Court accepted on June 24, 1996, poses another threat to the president. If the justices agree to let a civil trial go forward, Clinton could conceivably have to defend himself in open court against Paula Jones's lurid charges that he sexually harassed her while he was Arkansas governor and she was a state employee.

Finally, Washington was already gearing up for an investigation of Democratic fundraising during the 1996 campaign. Congressional committees, political watchdog groups, the press, and the courts will want to know whether the Clinton administration or party officials solicited or accepted cash from foreign sources or broke any other campaign finance laws.

### The Last Campaign?

First elected state attorney general in 1976, when he was only 30 years old, Bill Clinton has been running for something for most of his adult life. His 1996 campaign probably marks the last time he will ever seek elective office.

But that doesn't mean Clinton has run his last race. The most gifted Democratic politician of the last three decades will want to take an active role in the 1998 congressional contests, trying to limit the losses the party that holds the White House usually suffers in an off-year election.

The presidential campaign of the year 2000 will give Clinton the opportunity to repay Al Gore for his loyal and effective service as vice president. One of Clinton's most important steps on the road to reelection was to choke off any challenge within his own party. The White House will most likely try to secure for Gore the same clear path to a presidential inaugural in 2001.

# The Fascination of Dinosaurs

By Stephen Jay Gould

*Stephen Jay Gould teaches biology, geology, and the history of science at Harvard University, where he is Curator for Invertebrate Paleontology of the Museum of Comparative Zoology. He has received numerous awards for his books and articles in paleontology and other areas of science.*

Dinosaurs recently celebrated their 150th birthday in human consciousness—65 million years after their actual extinction. Public fascination has always gone hand in hand with scientific study. Dinosaurs received their name in the early 1840s, in a technical paper by the great British anatomist Richard Owen. Just ten years later, the first full-scale models of dinosaurs, built by sculptor Waterhouse Hawkins, graced London's Crystal Place Exhibition, the greatest public fair that had ever been held. This fascination, with the ups and downs common to all fads, has persisted to the present day, and has surely peaked in our premillennial decade of the 1990s, the age of *Jurassic Park* and its sequelae.

I do not pretend to know all the reasons why dinosaurs fascinate so many people, particularly our children. They did dominate the terrestrial environments of large-bodied vertebrates for about 150 million years during the Mesozoic Era, which ended with their extinction 65 million years ago.

Early mammals evolved at the same time and lived throughout the age of dinosaurs. But the largest mammal never got much bigger than a rat while dinosaurs still lived, and the great success of our group came only after the death of the dinosaurs. Thus, for some reason, dinosaurs enjoyed persistently greater evolutionary success than mammals throughout their long period of joint existence. I once asked a prominent child psychologist why dinosaurs fascinated young people so much—and he replied simply: "big, fierce, and extinct." Perhaps we will let the issue go at that.

As a result of such intense fascination, the public focuses on every new detail of dinosaur lore. Thus, discoveries that might strike a professional paleontologist as interesting for local or particular reasons often get reported in the press as epoch-making generalities capable of revising our entire view of life and evolution. For example, during the past year, we learned that carnivorous dinosaurs as big as, or bigger than, *Tyrannosaurus rex* lived in both Africa and South America, and that the Mongolian eggs discovered by the American naturalist Roy Chapman Andrews in the 1920s, and always attributed to the herbivorous dinosaur *Protoceratops*, probably belonged to the small carnivore *Oviraptor*. I am delighted to have both these bits of new information, but they must be kept in perspective. They are descriptive details and do not substantially revise our view of life, or even of dinosaurs.

## Dinosaurs Are Not What They Used to Be

The fact remains, however, that during the generation that has separated my own childhood love of dinosaurs from my present status as a professional paleontologist, our general view of dinosaurs has been completely revised—and this change does imply an important rereading of life's history and the direction of evolution. The dinosaurs of my youth were big and fierce, but they were also slow, inefficient, and dumbwitted. The giant sauropods hung out in ponds, supposedly unable to hold up their huge bodies for long on land. All popular literature emphasized the supposed stupidity of dinosaurs as revealed by small brains. The most famous dinosaur poem of my youth was a humorous verse by a Chicago journalist, Bert Leston Taylor, who ridiculed poor *Diplodocus* for its tiny brain and made great fun of a peculiar idea, then somewhat popular but now known to be wrong, that this giant beast must have had a second brain in its pelvic region. The poem ended: "No problem bothered him a bit./He made both head and tail of it."

The final proof of dinosaurian unworthiness presumably lay in their extinction, accompanied by mammalian survival. Didn't this pattern prove our inherent superiority, even as the little rat-sized creatures of our early days? This old and traditional opprobrium persists in ordinary English usage, even in the face of our revised view. So often we refer to a failed business, or a defeated politician, as a "dinosaur," thus heaping the insult of supposed unworthiness upon the injury of actual demise. But consider the utter inappropriateness of such an image. Dinosaurs were among the most successful creatures that ever lived, and any comparison with them should be viewed as a badge of honor. While they ruled terrestrial environments for 150 million years, the domination of mammals, by contrast, has endured only for 65 million—and I am not laying enormous odds on a long continuation, especially given the power and frequently poor judgment of the brainiest mammal of them all, *Homo sapiens*.

The revisionary theme can be summarized in a sentence: dinosaurs were anatomically efficient, adequately intelligent, metabolically advanced, behaviorally complex vertebrates fully equal to any challenge of their times, and not at all like our conventional image of a torpid and slithering reptile. The four major aspects to this general revision are summarized in the following four sections; together, they well describe our new view of dinosaurs—the greatest change in our conception of these animals since Owen gave the name and Hawkins built the first statues.

## Dinosaur Anatomy: Not So Slow and Dumb

During the past 20 years, new reconstructions of skeletons and inferred musculature indicate that dinosaurs could move efficiently, rapidly, and with relative agility, given their admitted bulk. Mobility varied, to be sure, and the smaller, lighter, two-legged dinosaurs like *Velociraptor* and *Deinonychus* surely ran more rapidly, and with more precision, than the large sauropods, stegosaurs, and ankylosaurs. But all dinosaurs carried their legs under their bodies, not splayed out to the sides as in older reconstructions—thus providing an efficient and more mammallike gait.

Dinosaurs, admittedly, did not have large brains. At any comparable body size, the average mammal has a substantially larger brain than the average dinosaur. Nonetheless, dinosaurs do not depart at all from reptilian expectations. Dinosaurs had brains of predicted size for reptiles of their body weight. That is, if we study the relationship of brain weight to body weight in modern reptiles, and then scale this relationship into the size range of dinosaurs, expected brain size matches the volumes actually found in dinosaurs.

The most widely discussed theme in revising the anatomy and physiology of dinosaurs, a staple of debate during the past 20 years, has not been resolved: were dinosaurs warm-blooded? The jury is still out on this issue, and will probably remain hung until some substantially new sources of evidence appear. Nonetheless, and even with this issue in limbo, we can be confident that dinosaurs were fully efficient and adequately intelligent creatures—more than a good enough match for any contemporary mammal.

## Dinosaur Society

The dinosaurs of my youth were too dumb to do much beyond grunting, eating, trying to make a catch (for carnivores), or trying to run away (for herbivores). They certainly exhibited no parental or familial behavior. Females just laid their eggs, covered them up, walked away, and hoped for the best.

Two new modes of study—the careful excavation of buried communities rather than just individuals and the discovery and analysis of large numbers of eggs and juvenile skeletons—have completely revised our view in favor of substantial behavioral complexity, more reminiscent of "advanced" mammals than of our prejudicial image of reptilian monotony. First of all, many odd features of dinosaurs—the thick heads of pachycephalosaurs, the elaborate crests of some ornithopods, and the frills and horns of ceratopsians—have been sensibly reinterpreted as devices for display or combat in complex rituals of competition for mates: thick heads to butt, crests to bellow, frills to lock arms in the quest.

Second, the study of herds and communities shows that dinosaurs lived in structured societies, not merely as independent individuals. The inferred group behavior indicates a level of social complexity previously unsuspected for dinosaurs. For example, in some trackways (sets of footprints showing the migration of an entire herd rather than only of an individual), the small prints of juveniles appear in the center, with the prints of large adults at the periphery—a common social adaptation in modern mammals, serving to protect the vulnerable young from predators by placing the strong adults around them.

Third, studies of eggs and juvenile skeletons reveal a surprising degree of maternal rearing and protection; mothers did not invariably "walk away" after laying the eggs. These eggs are often found in careful arrangement within well-protected nests. Moreover, at least one small dinosaur has been found preserved in a sitting posture atop a nest of eggs, thus persisting in a primary duty, even as a sandstorm swept the area and buried both parent and eggs.

### From Dinosaurs to Birds

Dinosaurs may have been "reptiles" in some general features of structural organization (they had scales rather than hair and laid eggs rather than giving birth to live young), but they are not linearly related to any modern group of reptiles (turtles, snakes, lizards, or alligators). They did, however, spawn one prominent group of linear descendants: the birds. For a variety of technical reasons, with the case recently cinched by a study of bones in the shoulder region, birds almost surely evolved from a lineage of small dinosaurs. The conclusion is not nearly so implausible as it might seem at first glance. We have known for a century that bird feathers represent the same organ, much modified of course, as reptilian scales. Moreover, the warm-bloodedness of birds, with characteristic body temperatures even higher than those of mammals, may not be an innovation if dinosaurs were also warm-blooded.

This discovery, while interesting, means less than a common formulation, promoted in press and movies, would suggest. The derivation of birds from dinosaurs does not mean that dinosaurs did not become extinct and that they still dwell among us in hidden form—the *Tyrannosaurus* of the trees, so to speak. The survival of an evolutionary descendant does not translate to the continued existence of an ancestor. First of all, birds did not evolve from our standard image of a large and terrifying monster; their dinosaurian ancestors were small-bodied creatures quite unlike the traditional icon. Second, and more important, birds modifed their dinosaurian features substantially in becoming adapted to such a new mode of life (no dinosaurs could fly; the flying pterosaurs are not dinosaurs, but reptiles of an entirely distinct lineage). After all, we do not say that rhipidistean fishes (the ancestors of all terrestrial vertebrates) are still alive because I am now sitting here writing this article. Similarly, dinosaurs are not still alive simply because a descendant lineage, which later evolved in a quite different direction, persists. Nonetheless, for those who love them, some solace may be gained from the thought that dinosaurs spawned some highly successful offspring, and that an evolutionary legacy still exists.

### An Unfortunate Accident

The very fact that seemed to seal the case for dinosaurian inadequacy—their extinction accompanied by mammalian survival—must be radically reinterpreted in the light of a new theory for the causes of this extinction. (We must also remember, as mentioned before, that dinosaurs had ruled for 150 million years, far longer than mammals have dominated subsequently, and that such longevity must count as phenomenal success. All lineages eventually perish on the long time scales of geology and evolution.)

We have known for a century that dinosaurs died during a major episode of mass extinction also leading to the death of some 50 percent of invertebrate species in the sea—thus marking the event as global. Previous theories, following traditional preferences for gradual change, tried to spread this episode over a few million years and attempted to identify an ordinary earthly cause, perhaps only accelerated in rate or intensity (rising or falling temperatures, leading to extensive climatic change, for example). But we are now fairly confident on the basis of strong evidence—including chemical signatures in sediments deposited at the time of extinction and, especially, the discovery of a large crater of appropriate age in the Gulf of Mexico, just off the Yucatan Peninsula—that the dinosaurs' extinction was triggered by a truly catastrophic event: the impact of a large extraterrestrial object, some 5 miles in diameter. (Luis Alvarez, the great physicist who helped to develop this theory, calculated that an object this size would strike our planet with 10,000 times the megatonnage of all the nuclear weapons now stockpiled on earth.)

We do not know what set of climatic consequences actually killed the dinosaurs and so many other creatures, but we can be sure that the trigger was cataclysmic. In such extreme and unanticipatable circumstances, whether a species survives or is wiped out represents more of a crapshoot than a predictable mark of evolutionary superiority or inadequacy. Dinosaurs probably died, while mammals survived, more by the luck of the draw than for any reason that could possibly measure higher or lower evolutionary status. In fact, we have no idea why mammals "made it," and dinosaurs perished after one of the most successful "runs" in the history of life. Many plausible reasons, admittedly in the realm of speculation, attribute mammalian survival to incidental features that convey no sense of general superiority. For example, creatures of small body size tend to survive better in episodes of mass extinction—perhaps because small creatures generally have larger populations (the "more ants than elephants" principle) or more flexibility in choice of foodstuff and habitats. (The smallest dinosaur, though no giant, was still a few feet tall, and substantially larger than the biggest mammal of the time.) Mammalian smallness cannot, however, be an adaptation for extended survival (a lineage, obviously, cannot prepare evolutionarily for a meteoritic impact 10 million years down the road). If anything, mammalian smallness represented a negative feature in comparison with dinosaurs, a sign that mammals could not successfully compete with dinosaurs in regimes of large body size. Thus, and ironically, mammals might have survived as a fortuitous consequence of their *lack* of success (at least versus dinosaurs) during ordinary times, providing them with the lucky gift of small size to weather an unpredictable catastrophe.

In short, dinosaurs "ruled" their age with as much "authority," and as much excellence in adaptation and design, as mammals now possess in our own times. The history of life is not a tale of predictable and progressive advance, necessarily culminating in a creature like us. Major lineages often die more by luck, and in catastrophic episodes, than by inferior design through eons of competition with superior replacements. If we generalize these messages, we might read an important lesson for our current age, and for our own assessments of human strength and status. A little evolutionary humility never hurts.

# Major Actions of the 104th Congress

When the 104th Congress convened Jan. 4, 1995, Republicans controlled both the House and the Senate for the first time in 40 years. Newt Gingrich (R, GA) was sworn in as House speaker, and Bob Dole (R,KS), Senate majority leader. The agenda for most of 1995 was dominated by the "Contract With America," a legislative program endorsed by most GOP House candidates during the 1994 campaign. A budget deadlock between Congress and the White House led to two partial shutdowns of the federal government, Nov. 14-20, 1995, and Dec. 16, 1995-Jan. 4, 1996.

On June 11, 1996, Dole gave up his Senate seat and majority leadership post to run for president full-time. Trent Lott (R, MS) was elected Senate majority leader June 12. Congress adjourned for the 1996 elections Oct. 4.

The following is a summary of major actions of the 104th Congress during Bill Clinton's 3d and 4th years as president. Measures that have become law are followed by the Public Law (PL) number. Detailed information on each piece of legislation may be accessed via the Internet at http://thomas.loc.gov

## 1995

**Congressional Accountability Act.** The 1st law passed by the 104th Congress, as called for in the "Contract With America." Extends to congressional employees various civil rights and employment protections that already covered most Americans. Passed by the House Jan. 17, 390-0; passed by the Senate Jan. 11, 98-1; signed by Pres. Clinton Jan. 23 (PL 104-1).

**Balanced Budget Amendment.** Would have amended the Constitution to require a balanced federal budget. Passed the House Jan. 26, 300-132; in the Senate received 65-35 vote, Mar. 2, short of the two-thirds vote need for passage; also failed in the Senate, 64-35, on June 6.

**Unfunded Mandate Reform Act.** Bars Congress from imposing new requirements on states and localities without providing funds to implement them. Passed by the House Mar. 16, 394-28; passed by the Senate Mar. 15, 91-9; signed by Pres. Clinton Mar. 22 (PL 104-4).

**Congressional Term Limits.** Would have amended the Constitution to limit the number of terms served by Senate and House members. Four term-limit proposals all rejected by the House, Mar. 29.

**Interstate Commerce Commission.** Congress abolished the 108-year-old Interstate Commerce Commission as of Jan. 1, 1996. Its remaining responsibilities were transferred to the U.S. Department of Transportation. Passed by the House Nov. 14, 417-8; passed the Senate Nov. 28 by voice vote; signed by Pres. Clinton Dec. 29 (PL 104-88).

**Speed Limits.** A provision of the National Highway System Designation Act repeals national highway speed limits. Passed unanimously by the House Nov. 18; passed by the Senate Nov. 17, 80-16; signed by Pres. Clinton Nov. 28 (PL 104-59).

**Lobbying Disclosure Act.** Toughens regulations on lobbyists. Requires more lobbyists to register with Congress and to report whom they represent and how much they are paid. Passed the House by voice vote Nov. 29; passed by the Senate July 25, 98-0; signed by Pres. Clinton Dec. 19 (PL 104-65).

## 1996

**Telecommunications Reform Act.** Landmark measure substantially deregulates telephone, mobile phone, and cable TV services. Provides for installation in new TV sets of the V-chip, permitting objectionable material to be blocked electronically. Seeks to halt transmission of "indecent" materials via the Internet. Passed by the House Feb. 1, 414-16; passed by the Senate Feb. 1, 91-5; signed by Pres. Clinton Feb. 8 (PL 104-104).

**Abortion.** Measure would have banned an abortion method known as late-term or partial-birth abortion. Passed by the House Mar. 27, 286-129; passed by the Senate Dec. 7, 1995, 54-44; vetoed by Pres. Clinton Apr. 10; motion to override passed the House Sept. 19, 285-137; failed in the Senate Sept., 26, 58-40 (a two-thirds majority is required).

**National Debt.** Congress raised the public debt limit to $5.5 trillion. Passed by the House Mar. 28, 328-91; passed the Senate Mar. 28 by unanimous consent; signed by Pres. Clinton Mar. 29 (PL 104-121).

**Line-Item Veto.** Authorizes the president to eliminate specific items in spending and tax bills, subject to congressional override. Exempts major entitlement programs, such as Social Security, and tax breaks affecting more than 100 taxpayers. Passed by the House Mar. 28 without objection; passed by the Senate Mar. 27, 69-31; signed by Pres. Clinton Apr. 9 (PL 104-130).

**Freedom to Farm Act.** Ends government controls over which crops may be planted and how much land must be left idle. Replaces subsidies with "transition payments" that decline over 7 years. Passed by the House Mar. 29, 318-89; passed by the Senate Mar. 28, 74-26; signed by Pres. Clinton Apr. 4 (PL 104-127).

**Product Liability.** Legislation would have limited damage awards in product liability lawsuits. Passed by the House Mar. 29, 259-158; passed by the Senate Mar. 21, 59-40; vetoed by Pres. Clinton May 2; motion to override failed in the House May 9, 258-163.

**Defense of Marriage Act.** Frees states and localities from any obligation to recognize same-sex marriages accepted in other jurisdictions. Passed by the House July 12, 342-67; passed by the Senate Sept. 10, 85-14; signed by Pres. Clinton Sept. 21 (PL 104-199).

**Welfare.** Landmark welfare-reform legislation. Authorizes states to establish their own welfare programs using block grants from the federal government. Requires most adult recipients to find work within 2 years. Establishes a lifetime limit of 5 years on welfare. Abolishes federal Aid to Families with Dependent Children (AFDC), effectively ending welfare as an entitlement program. Authorizes cuts in benefits to noncitizens. Passed by the House July 31, 328-101; passed by the Senate Aug. 1, 78-21; signed by Pres. Clinton Aug. 22 (PL 104-193).

**Health Insurance Portability and Accountability Act.** Formerly known as the Kennedy-Kassebaum bill. Allows workers who change jobs to maintain coverage. Prevents insurers from withholding coverage from people with pre-existing medical conditions. Passed by the House Aug. 1, 421-2; passed by the Senate Aug. 2, 98-0; signed by Pres. Clinton Aug. 21 (PL 104-191).

**Safe Drinking Water.** Requires municipal water systems to report on levels of contaminants. Establishes fund for upgrading water systems. Passed by the House Aug. 2, 392-30; passed by the Senate Aug. 2, 98-0; signed by Pres. Clinton Aug. 6 (PL 104-182).

**Minimum Wage.** Raises the hourly minimum wage for most employees from $4.25 to $4.75 as of Oct. 1, 1996, and to $5.15 as of Sept. 1, 1997. Passed by the House Aug. 2, 354-72; passed by the Senate Aug. 2, 76-22; signed by Pres. Clinton Aug. 20 (PL 104-188).

**Omnibus Consolidated Appropriations Act.** Comprehensive measure enacted just before adjournment, averting another government shutdown. Appropriates $244 billion for defense and $356 billion for nonmilitary programs for the 1997 fiscal year. Intensifies U.S. efforts against illegal immigration. Provides $1.1 billion for new antiterrorism measures. Boosts funding for education programs. Bars anyone convicted of domestic violence from owning a handgun. Passed by the House Sept. 28, 370-37; passed by the Senate Sept. 30 by voice vote; signed by Pres. Clinton Sept. 30 (PL 104-208).

# Notable Supreme Court Decisions, 1995-96

The Supreme Court term that began Oct. 2, 1995, and ended July 1, 1996, marked William H. Rehnquist's 10th year as chief justice. The Court issued signed opinions in only 75 cases, 7 fewer than in 1994-95, and its lightest caseload in more than 40 years. The full Court ruled unanimously in 34 cases, or 45% of the total; 12 cases, or 16%, were decided by a 5-4 vote.

Two moderate conservatives, Justices Sandra Day O'Connor and Anthony M. Kennedy, held the balance of power. O'Connor dissented only 6 times, Kennedy 5; each voted with the majority in 75% of the 5-4 decisions. Justice John Paul Stevens, a moderate liberal, was the Court's most frequent dissenter, siding with the minority in 19 of the 41 cases where the Court did not reach a unanimous verdict. The Court's most conservative member, Justice Antonin Scalia, also dissented frequently, and often did so vehemently, hurling some of his sharpest barbs in high-profile First Amendment and equal rights cases.

**Banking and Commerce:** In a ruling that could cost U.S. taxpayers up to $10 billion, the Court held, 7-2, that the federal government had breached its contract with savings and loan institutions when Congress changed accounting rules and in effect pushed many S&Ls into insolvency. (*U.S.* v. *Winstar*; decision issued July 1). A 9-0 ruling upheld the right of banks to charge late fees on out-of-state credit card accounts even when cardholders' home states ban or limit such fees (*Smiley* v. *Citicorp*; June 3). The Court, 5-4, struck down as "grossly excessive" a $4 million punitive-damage award for a car sold as new that had been repainted. (*BMW* v. *Gore*; May 20).

**Confidentiality:** By a 7-2 vote, the Court held that mental health professionals, including clinical social workers, may not be compelled to reveal details of counseling sessions with patients (*Jaffee* v. *Redmond*; June 13).

**Criminal Law:** The Court strengthened the hand of law-enforcement officials against drug traffickers by upholding the government's right both to seek criminal penalties against a defendant and to seize the same person's property. Writing for an 8-1 majority, Chief Justice Rehnquist maintained that such civil forfeiture did not violate the constitutional ban on double jeopardy (*U.S.* v. *Ursery*; June 24). Another important 8-1 decision ruled out purely statistical claims that the federal government's prosecution of crack-cocaine cases was racially biased (*U.S.* v. *Armstrong*; May 13). In *Whren* v. *U.S.* (June 10), the Court was unanimous in granting the police wide latitude to use even a minor traffic violation as a reason for stopping a vehicle and searching it for drugs.

**Death Penalty:** The Court unanimously upheld the use of capital punishment by the military justice system (*Loving* v. *U.S.*; June 3) and a federal law restricting appeals by death-row inmates (*Felker* v. *Turpin*; June 28).

**Equal Rights:** The Court struck down, 6-3, a controversial state constitutional amendment in Colorado that specifically excluded homosexuals from civil rights protections (*Romer* v. *Evans*; May 20).

The Court ruled, 7-1, that women cannot be barred from a state-supported military college (*U.S.* v. *Virginia*; June 26). The majority opinion by Justice Ruth Bader Ginsburg applied the standard of "skeptical scrutiny" to government actions treating men and women differently. Justice Clarence Thomas did not participate because his son attended Virginia Military Institute, the college in question.

The Court held unanimously that a worker may sue for age discrimination even if replaced by someone also over 40 years old (*O'Connor* v. *Consolidated Coin Caterers*; Apr. 1).

**Federal Authority and States' Rights:** A 5-4 decision in *Seminole Tribe* v. *Florida* (Mar. 27) curtailed the power of Congress to pass laws allowing states to be sued in federal court. The Court unanimously upheld the results of the 1990 Census against a challenge by New York and other large cities that sought a statistical adjustment for undercounting (*Wisconsin* v. *New York*; Mar. 20).

**First Amendment:** A divided Court underscored the primacy of political speech by holding that political parties may spend as much they want to support candidates, as long as such spending is "independent" of the candidates' campaigns (*Colorado Republican Federal Campaign Committee* v. *Federal Election Commission*; June 26). Four justices said they would be willing to outlaw all limitations on political parties' campaign spending.

In two patronage cases decided June 28, the Court ruled, 7-2, that the First Amendment protects government contractors from losing business because they supported a particular candidate, party, or political position (*Board of County Commissioners* v. *Umbehr*; *O'Hare Truck Services* v. *City of Northlake*). In a stinging dissent, Justice Scalia wrote: "The Court must be living in another world. Day by day, case by case, it is busy designing a Constitution for a country I do not recognize."

In a fragmented ruling that involved 6 separate opinions, the Court held that certain provisions of a 1992 law that allowed cable television providers to decide whether to show sexually explicit programs violated free-speech guarantees (*Denver Area Consortium* v. *Federal Communications Commission*; June 28). The Court strengthened commercial speech rights when it unanimously overturned a state law that banned advertising liquor prices (*44 Liquormart* v. *Rhode Island*; May 13).

**Voting Rights:** In parallel 5-4 rulings issued June 13, the Court invalidated one majority black congressional district in North Carolina (*Shaw* v. *Hunt*) and 3 majority black and Hispanic districts in Texas (*Bush* v. *Vera*) as the product of race-based gerrymandering. In her plurality opinion in the Texas case, Justice O'Connor argued that the 14th Amendment required "a commitment to eliminate unnecessary and excessive governmental use and reinforcement of racial stereotypes."

# The 1996 Nobel Prizes

The 1996 Nobel Prize winners were announced in October. Each prize consisted of a large solid gold medal and a cash award worth more than $1 million.

**Chemistry:** Harold W. Kroto, British, and two Americans—Robert F. Curl Jr. and Richard E. Smalley—shared the prize for their discovery of a new class of carbon molecules (called "buckyballs").

**Memorial Prize in Economic Science:** James A. Mirrlees, British, and Canadian-born American William Vickrey won the prize for their theories on economic incentives for situations in which decisions are made with differing or incomplete information. (Vickrey died on Oct. 11, 1996, 3 days after winning the prize.)

**Literature:** Wislawa Szymborska, a Polish poet whose works deal with the personal sphere, including the anomalies of daily life and relationships, won the prize. Her poetry collections include *Salt, No End of Fun, A Large Number,* and *The End and the Beginning.*

**Peace:** Two Timorese, Bishop Carlos Ximenes Belo and José Ramos-Horta, won the prize. Ramos-Horta (in exile) and Belo have fought against human rights abuses in East Timor, a Portuguese colony annexed by Indonesia in 1975.

**Physics:** Three Americans, David M. Lee, Douglas D. Osheroff, and Robert C. Richardson, shared the prize for their discovery that helium-3, a rare form of the element, flows without resistance at very low temperatures.

**Physiology or Medicine:** Peter C. Doherty, an Australian, and Rolf M. Zinkernagel, a Swiss, shared the prize for their discovery of how the immune system identifies cells infected with viruses.

# CHRONOLOGY OF THE YEAR'S EVENTS

## Reported Month by Month in 3 Categories: National, International, and General

## Oct. 16, 1995, to Oct. 31, 1996

## OCTOBER 1995

### National

**Blacks Attend "Million Man March"**—Hundreds of thousands of black men participated in a "Million Man March" and rally in Washington, DC, **Oct. 16**, to demonstrate a commitment to responsible personal behavior and support for their families and communities. The organizer of the event, Nation of Islam leader Rev. Louis Farrakhan, called it a "holy day of atonement and reconcilation." While there was wide support for the march, Farrakhan himself remained controversial; critics accused him of being a racist and anti-Semitic. Pres. Bill Clinton expressed approval for the objectives of the rally, but characterized Farrakhan implicitly as a man of "malice and division." The National Park Service initially estimated rally attendance at 400,000. Farrakhan blamed racism for a too-low estimate, and the Park Service later said attendance might have been as high as 600,000. Based on aerial photographs, the Boston University Center for Remote Sensing estimated that some 837,000 had attended.

**Senate, House Approve Budget Bills**—The long-anticipated confrontation between Pres. Bill Clinton and Congress over the federal budget moved closer in Oct. when the Senate and House each approved a budget reconciliation bill. Clinton surprised many, **Oct. 17**, when he said in Houston that he had raised taxes "too much" in 1993. Democrats in Congress had put their careers on the line by supporting the budget package, which included a tax increase. On **Oct. 19**, Clinton said he had meant to say that nobody enjoyed raising taxes. Clinton also said that the Republican goal of a balanced budget in 7 years was attainable, provided the GOP cut the projected size of its reductions in expenditures for education, health, and the environment. The House, **Oct. 26**, 227–203, and the Senate, **Oct. 28**, 52–47, approved a budget bill, but differences in their respective plans were left to be worked out in a conference committee. Voting was nearly along party lines.

Both bills sought to achieve a balanced budget by 2002, with two-thirds of reduced expenditures coming out of entitlement programs. Both bills aimed to reduce projected outlays for Medicare, the health insurance program for the elderly, by $270 bil. Medicaid, the federal health plan for low-income persons, would be scrapped in favor of block grants, or lump sums, to states to run their own programs. Both houses approved the elimination of the federal Aid to Families With Dependent Children program in favor of block grants to the states. Both bills provided for $245 bil in tax cuts over 7 years, mostly in the form of a $500 tax credit per child for families; the House credits would go to families earning up to $200,000 a year, but the Senate drew the line at $110,000 a year for dual-income families.

**Trade Deficit Shrinks**—The Commerce Dept. reported, **Oct. 18**, that the trade deficit in Aug. was $8.82 bil, the lowest to date for any month in 1995. The Commerce Dept. reported, **Oct. 27**, that the gross domestic product had grown at an annual rate of 4.2% in the 3d quarter, up sharply from the 1.3% expansion in the 2d quarter.

**AFL-CIO Picks New President**—The national labor federation, the AFL-CIO, chose a new president in Oct., its 3d in 3 months. Lane Kirkland had stepped down in Aug. after 16 years at the helm. His interim successor, Thomas Donahue, sought a full term at the federation's convention, **Oct. 25**, but was defeated, by a margin of 56% to 44%, by John J. Sweeney, who had headed the Service Employees International Union for 15 years. Sweeney had vowed to boost the AFL-CIO's declining membership and increase its influence in the political arena.

### International

**Terrorist Bombers Strike Again in Paris**—A bomb exploded, **Oct. 17**, on an underground commuter train in Paris, injuring 29 people. This was the 8th in a series of bombings that authorities believed were the work of Algerian terrorists. Turmoil in Algeria had grown since 1992, when the military government canceled elections that Islamic fundamentalists were expected to win. A civil war had then broken out and had claimed 30,000 to 40,000 lives. The fundamentalists opposed French support for the government of Algeria, a former French colony.

**UN Commemorates 50th Anniversary**—Leaders from around the world came to New York City in Oct. to join in a commemoration of the 50th anniversary of the founding of the UN. In an address to the General Assembly, **Oct. 22**, Pres. Bill Clinton called for a crackdown on international crime, including terrorism and drug smuggling. Pres. Boris Yeltsin of Russia, **Oct. 22**, asserted in an address that NATO was overplaying its hand in Bosnia and Herzegovina and should be more firmly under control of the UN Security Council. Pres. Fidel Castro of Cuba, in the U.S. for the first time since 1979, addressed the UN **Oct. 22**, as did Yasir Arafat, chairman of the Palestine Liberation Organization. Pres. Jiang Zemin of China, in an **Oct. 24** address, warned the U.S. not to use human rights as an excuse to meddle in China's internal affairs. In a declaration, **Oct. 24**, member nations pledged to modernize and bring financial reform to the UN.

**Yeltsin Hospitalized Again**—Pres. Boris Yeltsin of Russia was hospitalized with a heart condition **Oct. 25**, for the 2d time in 4 months. On **Oct. 23**, he had met with Pres. Bill Clinton in Hyde Park, NY, at a summit that produced little of substance aside from a display of jovial friendship between the 2 leaders.

**Islamic Jihad Leader Assassinated**—Fathi al-Shiqaqi, leader in the Gaza Strip of the Islamic Jihad, an extremist anti-Israel organization, was shot and killed, **Oct. 26**, by 2 men on a motorcycle, in the town of Sliema, Malta. Israeli Foreign Minister Shimon Peres, **Oct. 29**, called Shiqaqi "an archmurderer," but Israel did not claim responsibility.

**Ex-Korean President Admits Taking Money**—Roh Tae Woo, president of South Korea (1988–93), admitted, **Oct. 27**, that while in office he had accepted the equivalent of $650 mil in illegal campaign donations. Lee Hyun Woo, director of the National Security Planning Agency in the Roh administration, had also admitted accepting and keeping large sums. Roh's successor, the current president, Kim Young Sam, said, **Oct. 30**, that he had not received money from Roh's slush fund, but that it was possible Democratic Liberal Party funds had come from Roh.

**Quebec Votes Not to Secede From Canada**—In a referendum in Quebec, **Oct. 30**, voters narrowly rejected sovereignty, despite the urgings of secessionists in the predominantly French-speaking province. Many French speakers believed that their language, culture, and system of justice were being submerged in a country that was largely of English heritage. In the voting, 49.4% supported sovereignty, while 50.6% opposed it. Premier Jacques Parizeau of Quebec, leader of the separatists, announced, **Oct. 31**, that he would resign in Dec.

**Tribunal Indicts 3 Serb Officers**—In The Hague, the Netherlands, **Oct. 30**, the Yugoslav War Crimes Tribunal indicted 3 senior officers in the Yugoslav army for their part in a 1991 atrocity. The tribunal said that the 3, all Serbs, had been responsible for removing 260 Croat men from a hospital and in their beatings and executions.

## General

**Atlanta Braves Win Their First World Series**—The Atlanta Braves won the National League pennant, **Oct. 14**, by completing a 4-game sweep of the Cincinnati Reds, 6–0, in Atlanta. Right fielder Mike Devereaux hit a 3-run homer, and pitcher Steve Avery gave up only 2 hits in the 6 innings he pitched to earn the victory. The Cleveland Indians also qualified for the series by defeating the Seattle Mariners, 4–0, **Oct. 17**, in Seattle, to take the American League championship series, 4 games to 2. Dennis Martinez pitched 7 innings for the victory. In a dramatic World Series between the Braves and Indians, 5 of the 6 games were decided by one run. Atlanta wrapped up the title, 4 games to 2, **Oct. 28**, with a 1-0 victory, as Tom Glavine and his 9th-inning reliever, Mark Wohlers, gave up just one hit. Right fielder Dave Justice accounted for the game's only run with a home run in the 6th inning off reliever Jim Poole.

**Killer of Popular Singer Convicted**—The killer of Selena, the popular Mexican–American singer who had been shot to death in Corpus Christi, TX, in Mar., was convicted of murder in Houston, **Oct. 23**. Selena Quintanilla Perez, who performed a music style called Tejano, had been thought to be at the point of stardom. On the day of her death she met at a motel with Yolanda Saldivar, founder of her fan club, who had been dismissed after allegedly embezzling $30,000 from a boutique owned by Selena's family. Saldivar shot Selena fatally, and later contended that her gun had gone off by accident. The Houston jury, **Oct. 26**, sentenced Saldivar to life in prison.

# NOVEMBER 1995

## National

**More Members of Congress Retire**—Throughout the fall, members of the Senate and House announced decisions not to seek reelection in 1996. On **Oct. 23**, Rep. Charles Wilson (D, TX) had announced his retirement. Rep. Gerry Studds (D, MA), former chairman of the Merchant Marine and Fisheries Committee, had announced **Oct. 28** that he was retiring. Rep. Cardiss Collins (D, IL), who had served longer in the House—12 terms—than any other black woman, said, **Nov. 8**, that she would not seek reelection. Meanwhile, Rep. Mike Parker (MS) announced, **Nov. 10**, that he was switching from the Democratic to the Republican Party. Rep. Andrew Jacobs (D, IN), a member of the House for 3 decades, said, **Nov. 15**, that he was stepping down. On **Nov. 20**, Sen. Nancy Kassebaum (R, KS) said she would not run for a 4th term. The daughter of former Kansas Gov. Alf Landon, Kassebaum had been the first woman to serve as chair of a major committee, the Labor and Human Resources Committee. Rep. Pat Schroeder (D, CO), who had served in the House since 1972, announced her retirement, **Nov. 28.** A liberal who was a sharp critic of the Pentagon, she had explored a possible bid for president in 1988.

**Economic Indicators Continue Downward Trend**—The index of leading economic indicators declined by 0.1% in Sept., the Commerce Dept. reported, **Nov. 1**. The index, a gauge of future economic activity, had been down in 7 of 9 months so far in 1995. The Labor Dept. reported, **Nov. 3**, that the unemployment rate in Oct. had edged slightly downward to 5.5%. The department said, **Nov. 15**, that an index of consumer prices had risen 0.3% in Oct. On Wall Street, the Dow Jones closed **Nov. 21** at 5,023.55, its first close ever above 5,000. The Commerce Dept. reported, **Nov. 22**, that the U.S. trade deficit in Sept. stood at $8.35 bil, the lowest level of the year.

**Colin Powell Won't Seek Presidency**—Gen. Colin Powell (ret.) announced **Nov. 8** that he was a Republican but that he would not seek the GOP nomination for president in 1996. A Vietnam war veteran and the first black to serve as chairman of the Joint Chiefs of Staff, Powell, a moderate, was widely admired for his leadership qualities and was seen as someone who could improve the status of race relations in the U.S. He had said he would make a decision on running for president after completing the tour to promote his new book, *My American Journey*. On **Nov. 2**, a number of leading conservatives declared that they opposed his candidacy, though some other conservatives were urging him to run. In his announcement, Powell said he did not have the "passion and commitment" to run for president.

**GOP Tide Slows in Off-Year Voting**—Results of widely scattered elections held on **Nov. 7** indicated no further surge in Republican fortunes. In a hard-fought and close contest, Lt. Gov. Paul Patton retained the Kentucky governorship for the Democrats; he edged out Republican Larry Forgy by 51% to 49%. In Mississippi, Gov. Kirk Fordice, a conservative Republican, was reelected, but the Democrats captured the office of lieutenant-governor. A major effort by the GOP to win control of the Virginia legislature failed. In Maine, voters defeated, 53%-47%, a ballot proposition that would have prohibited enactment of laws designed specifically to protect homosexual rights. The Republicans did pick up a governorship in Louisiana on **Nov. 18**. Gov. Edwin Edwards (D) had decided not to seek a 5th term, and in a runoff election, State Sen. Mike Foster, a Republican and conservative businessman, defeated U.S. Rep. Cleo Fields, a Democrat, by 64% to 36%.

**Clinton's Conflict With Congress Continues**—The dispute between Pres. Bill Clinton and the Republican-led Congress over budgetary priorities continued in Nov. The Senate, **Nov. 9**, 49-47, and the House, **Nov. 10**, 219-185, passed legislation that would increase the national-debt ceiling from $4.9 tril to $4.967 tril. The legislation, however, had provisions Clinton resisted, including one that would require balancing of the federal budget in 7 years using Congressional Budget Office estimates. The House, **Nov. 10**, 224-172, and the Senate, **Nov. 13**, by voice vote, approved a continuing resolution to fund government agencies for the rest of the month. Congress had sent Clinton only 5 of 13 appropriations bills that funded the agencies. The continuing resolution bill, however, also contained provisions that displeased the president, including an increase in premiums for Medicare. Clinton vetoed both these bills, **Nov. 13**, and it was apparent Congress did not have enough votes to override.

To avoid default on government loans—in the absence of a debt-ceiling increase—Sec. of the Treasury Robert Rubin said, **Nov. 13**, that he would draw from 2 federal retirement funds to repay principal and interest due later that week. Without money to pay them, 770,000 federal employees were sent home, **Nov. 14**. Some 1.9 mil employees continued to work, either because their work was classified as essential or because their agencies had been funded by bills previously signed.

House Speaker Newt Gingrich (R, GA) said, **Nov. 15**, that he had been especially tough in the confrontation with the White House because he had been offended by his treatment on the plane that had taken Clinton, Gingrich, and Senate Majority Leader Robert Dole (R, KS) to and from the funeral of Israeli Prime Min. Yitzhak Rabin. He said that Clinton had declined to negotiate on the budget crisis during the long flights, and that the 2 Republican leaders had been required to leave the plane by the back door. Gingrich was criticized for voicing these complaints.

The House, **Nov. 16**, 277-151, and the Senate, **Nov. 16**, 60-37, passed a 2d continuing-resolution bill that omitted the Medicare premiums increase, but did include the commitment to a 7-year balanced budget using CBO numbers. Both houses, **Nov. 17**, passed a balanced-budget bill that Clinton quickly promised to veto. Clinton signed the continuing-resolution bill, **Nov. 20**, but only after getting Dole and Gingrich to modify it to include wording committing Congress to "adequate" funding for Medicare, Medicaid, education, and the environment. The bill provided money to pay federal workers who had been furloughed; they returned to work **Nov. 20**.

**House Bans Gifts to Members**—The House of Representatives, **Nov. 16**, voted, 422-6, to prohibit members and members' staffs from accepting any gifts except from close relatives and friends. In July, the Senate had restricted gifts to its members to those worth less than $50. An amendment to permit House members to accept expense-paid invitations to charity events was defeated, 276-154, **Nov. 16**. These events are often sponsored by big corporations, who utilize them to gain access to members of Congress.

**Ex-White House Official Acquitted**—Billy Dale, former director of the White House travel office, was acquitted of embezzlement **Nov. 16.** The travel office was responsible for scheduling trips by members of the media who travel with the president. Shortly after Bill Clinton became president in 1993, the office had come under criticism for alleged mismanagement, and Dale and 6 other employees were summarily dismissed. Dale was replaced by Catherine Cornelius, a distant relative of Clinton, who, with his wife, was criticized for the dismissals. The matter darkened when it appeared to have distressed White House Counsel Vincent Foster, who committed suicide in July 1993. Dale, who was indicted, admitted having transferred $68,000 to a personal account, but said he used the money only to pay for official expenses. A federal jury in Washington, DC, acquitted him of all charges.

**Federal Speed Limit Repealed**—The federal 55-miles-per-hour speed limit was repealed in Nov. The limit had been enacted in 1974 in an effort to conserve fuel during an international oil embargo. Congress had modified it in 1987 by raising the limit to 65 on interstates in sparsely populated areas. For years, most motorists on major highways had disregarded the official limits. As sentiment grew for returning power to the states, both houses of Congress approved bills lifting the federal limit, and the Senate, **Nov. 17**, 80-16, and the House, **Nov. 18**, by unanimous consent, approved a compromise bill. Pres. Bill Clinton signed it, **Nov. 28**. Many states subsequently raised their speed limits, and Montana voted to have no daytime limit at all.

**Dole Wins Florida GOP Presidential Poll**—Senate Majority Leader Robert Dole (R, KS), considered to be the front-runner for the 1996 Republican presidential nomination, placed first in a straw poll of delegates to a GOP convention in Orlando, FL, **Nov. 18**. The poll was considered a key indicator of party sentiment in the South. With 3,325 delegates voting, Dole received 33%, followed most closely by Sen. Phil Gramm (TX) with 26% and former Gov. Lamar Alexander (TN) with 23%. On **Nov. 21**, Sen. Arlen Specter (PA) suspended his campaign for the nomination. Specter, the only supporter of abortion rights in the GOP field, and a frequent critic of the religious right, said a lack of funds had forced his decision. Dole, **Nov. 27**, was endorsed by Gov. Tommy Thompson of Wisconsin, and now had the support of 16 Republican governors. House Speaker Newt Gingrich, principal architect of the Republican revolution in Congress, announced, **Nov. 27**, that he would not seek the GOP presidential nomination.

**Regulation of Lobbyists to Become Law**—Congress completed action on a bill that would impose some regulations on lobbyists' activities. The Senate had passed a bill in July, and on **Nov. 29** the House approved the same bill by voice vote. Pres. Bill Clinton signed it Dec. 19. Under a broader definition of lobbying, more lobbyists than in the past would be required to register, disclose their clients, and state how much they were paid. Lobbyists would have to list what issues they were working on and whom they had lobbied.

## International

**U.S. Troops to Enforce Bosnia Peace Accord**—The warring parties in Bosnia and Herzegovina reached an agreement in Nov. to end their conflict, and Pres. Bill Clinton said that securing the peace required sending 20,000 U.S. troops into the storm-tossed country. A resurgence during the summer by Bosnian government forces, who were mostly Muslim, and their Croatian allies, plus bombing of Serb positions by NATO airplanes, had produced a military stalemate. In addition, international trade sanctions had devastated the economy of Serbia. In this context, the Bosnian Serbs agreed to negotiate with their adversaries in talks that opened, **Nov. 1**, at Wright-Patterson Air Force Base outside Dayton, OH. Presidents Alija Izetbegovic and Franjo Tudjman of Croatia attended, as did Pres. Slobodan Milosevic of Serbia, who spoke for the Bosnian Serbs. Radovan Karadzic, leader of the Bosnian Serbs, had been indicted for war crimes and did not attend. The U.S., Britain, Germany, Russia, France, and the European Union also attended the Dayton talks.

The parties, **Nov. 21**, finally reached a comprehensive agreement. Sec. of State Warren Christopher initialed the pact for the U.S. The agreement established Sarajevo as the unified capital under control of the central government. Bosnian Serbs would have to give up control of neighborhoods and suburbs of Sarajevo, from which they had attacked government positions during the war. The agreement established a national presidency and a legislature, with the Muslims and Croats having a two-thirds majority in both. The Muslim–Croat Federation and the Serbs would also elect their own presidents and legislatures within their own territories. The national government would handle foreign policy, monetary policy, and foreign trade. The sub-states would be responsible for taxation and economic and welfare activities. The agreement barred anyone indicted for war crimes from holding political office. It permitted refugees to return to their homes or receive compensation.

On **Nov. 22**, the UN Security Council, effective Mar. 1996, lifted a longstanding arms embargo against all the republics of the former Yugoslavia. After meeting with Milosevic in Belgrade, Karadzic and other Serb leaders initialed the pact, **Nov. 23**. On **Nov. 25**, Serbs living in and near Sarajevo demonstrated against the agreement, with many proclaiming they would not live under control of the Muslim–Croat Federation.

In a televised address, **Nov. 27**, Pres. Clinton asked for congressional and public support for the deployment of 20,000 U.S. troops in Bosnia as part of the NATO mission aimed at enforcing the treaty. He estimated that the deployment in Bosnia would last approximately one year. Clinton met, **Nov. 28**, with leaders of Congress, although he was not required to obtain congressional approval of the deployment. Germany's government, **Nov. 28**, agreed to provide 4,000 troops—the largest military unit outside Germany since World War II. Russia agreed, **Nov. 28**, to send 1,500 troops. Senate Majority Leader Robert Dole (R, KS) supported the U.S. deployment, **Nov. 30**, but public opinion leaned in the other direction, with polls showing a majority opposed to the commitment. The UN Security Council, **Nov. 30**, approved the withdrawal of its peacekeepers from Bosnia and Croatia by the end of Jan., to make way for the NATO force. Some 1,100 UN troops would stay in Macedonia.

**Prime Min. Rabin of Israel Assassinated**—Prime Min. Yitzhak Rabin of Israel, a wartime hero who later shared the 1994 Nobel Peace Prize for his efforts to end the long conflict between his country and its neighbors, was shot to death in Tel Aviv, **Nov. 4**. A bodyguard was wounded. The gunman, seized immediately, was Yigal Amir, 25, a strong opponent of the peace settlement with the Palestinians. Amir, who shot Rabin 3 times as he was leaving the site of a speech to more than 100,000 persons at City Hall, asserted that he was acting on God's orders. Rabin was succeeded by Foreign Minister Shimon Peres, who had worked closely with the prime minister during negotiations with the Palestinians and other Middle Eastern states.

Rabin was chosen leader of the Labor Party in 1974 and became prime minister 2 months later. A scandal brought down his government in 1977, but his fortunes revived after he became defense minister in 1984 and then dealt firmly with the Palestinian uprising beginning in 1987. After returning as prime minister in 1992, he sought peace with Israel's neighbors, and in 1993 his government and the Palestine Liberation Organization reached an agreement on Palestinian self-rule. Rabin signed a second-stage agreement in Washington, DC, in Sept. 1995.

The latter accord set in motion the Israeli withdrawal from much of the West Bank and the onset of Palestinian control. Israeli settlers in West Bank towns were intensely opposed, claiming that the region was part of the biblical land of Israel. Political debate reached an intense level in Israel, and Amir's violent deed occurred in this charged atmosphere. Amir, a law student, gave a detailed confession, **Nov. 5**.

Many world leaders, including Pres. Bill Clinton, King Hussein of Jordan, Pres. Hosni Mubarak of Egypt, Prime Min. John Major of Britain, and former U.S. presidents Jimmy Carter and George Bush, attended Rabin's funeral in Jerusalem, **Nov. 6**. PLO leader Yasir Arafat did not attend, but paid warm tribute to the prime minister.

Between **Nov. 6** and **10**, authorities arrested Amir's brother Hagai, and 4 men with nationalist-oriented religious views, on suspicion of involvement in the assassination. On **Nov. 7**, Rabin's widow, Leah, said she blamed Benjamin Netanyahu, leader of the opposition Likud bloc, for contributing to overheated rhetoric that she said had led to the tragedy. Investigators said, **Nov. 10**, that Yigal Amir had belonged to a terrorist group guided by an unnamed spiritual leader who encouraged violence. Meanwhile, the Israelis, **Nov. 13**, withdrew from the West Bank city of Jenin. On **Nov. 14**, authorities said they had rounded up more than 50 other right-wing militants, though not on charges directly related to the assassination.

**Ex-Premier of Italy Indicted for Murder**—Giulio Andreotti, who had served as premier of Italy 7 times, was indicted, **Nov. 4**, in the 1979 murder of a magazine editor, Carmine Pecorelli, who may have been attempting to blackmail him. Four others, including 2 Mafia figures and the alleged hit man, were also indicted. Earlier in the year, Andreotti was indicted on other Mafia-related charges.

**Georgians Elect Shevardnadze President**—Eduard Shevardnadze, who had been chairman of the parliament of Georgia and the country's head of state, was elected president of the former Soviet republic of Georgia, **Nov. 5**, under the new constitution. He received 74% of the vote.

**France Gets New Government**—France got a new government in Nov., though under the same prime minister, Alain Juppe. Pres. Jacques Chirac decided to overhaul the cabinet prior to moving forward with sweeping economic reforms. Chirac's popularity had been tumbling, in part because of controversy over France's nuclear tests in the Pacific. The new cabinet was unveiled **Nov. 7**. Chirac said, **Nov. 8**, that the government would aim to reduce unemployment through elimination of the country's large budget deficit.

**Hague Tribunal Indicts Serbs, Croats**—The Yugoslav War Crimes Tribunal in The Hague, the Netherlands, announced new indictments in Nov. On **Nov. 13**, 6 Bosnian Croats were charged with persecuting Muslim civilians; 2 were accused of responsibility in the destruction of 14 towns and for participating in a massacre in which about 120 persons were killed. The tribunal, **Nov. 16**, indicted Radovan Karadzic and Gen. Ratko Mladic, the civilian and military leaders of the Bosnian Serbs, in connection with inhumane treatment of Muslim civilians during and after the capture of Srebrenica in July. Up to 8,000 civilians had died. Both men had previously been indicted on similar charges.

**Nigeria Hangs 9, Stirs World Outcry**—The Nigerian government, **Nov. 10**, hanged Ken Saro-Wiwa, a critic of the military regime and an advocate of minority and environmental rights, along with 8 of his allies. The 9 had been convicted of inciting the killing of 4 progovernment leaders of the Ogoni ethnic group, to which the accused also belonged. Saro-Wiwa and the others maintained their innocence. Saro-Wiwa had long criticized the environmental practices and economic exploitation of Royal Dutch/Shell Group, the leading producer of oil in the Ogoni region. At a meeting in New Zealand, **Nov. 11**, the 52-member Commonwealth of Nations condemned the executions and threatened to expel Nigeria from membership.

**2 Bombs in Saudi Capital Kill 7**—Five Americans were among 7 people killed, **Nov. 13**, when 2 bombs exploded at a military training and communications center in Riyadh, the capital of Saudi Arabia. About 60 persons were injured. Many of the 200 persons at the complex were U.S. military and civilian advisers. One of the dead Americans was a soldier, and 4 were civilians.

**Amid Strife, Algerian President Reelected**—Pres. Liamine Zeroual was reelected, **Nov. 16**, to a 5-year term, with 61% of the vote. The Algerian government was engaged in a civil war with Islamic fundamentalists that had taken 30,000 to 40,000 lives. Despite intimidation by the fundamentalists, almost 75% of eligible voters cast ballots in the election. Zeroual during the campaign had signaled support for a role in Algerian politics for moderate Islamic opponents of the government.

**South Korea's Ex-President Arrested**—Roh Tae Woo, president of South Korea from 1988 to 1993, was arrested, **Nov. 16**, on charges of having accepted the equivalent of $650 mil in bribes. He had acknowledged in Oct. that he had taken the money.

**Walesa Loses Presidency of Poland**—Lech Walesa, leader of the trade-union movement that had been instrumental in bringing an end to Communist rule in Poland, and president of Poland since 1990, was defeated for reelection, **Nov. 19**. The winner, with 51.7% of the vote in a runoff election, was Aleksander Kwasniewski, 41, leader of the Democratic Left Alliance (SLD). He had been an active Communist figure for many years but now supported democratic reforms and industrial privatization.

**Irish Voters End Ban on Divorce**—By a narrow margin, **Nov. 24**, voters in Ireland ended the country's constitutional ban on divorce. The margin in the referendum was just 50.3% to 49.7%—only about 9,100 votes out of 1.6 mil cast. The issue had been intensely debated for years in the largely Roman Catholic country. The government of Prime Min. John Bruton had called for an end to the divorce ban, while the Church had urged its retention. Under Irish law, a couple could now obtain a divorce after living apart for 4 years and showing that there was no chance for a reconciliation.

**Clinton Visits Northern Ireland**—Prime Mins. John Bruton of Ireland and John Major of Great Britain, **Nov. 28**, announced an agreement aimed at restarting talks on the future of Northern Ireland. Britain had insisted that the Irish Republican Army decommission its weapons before talks began, while the IRA said it would do so only after negotiations began. The compromise plan provided for an international commission to be headed by former U.S. Sen. George Mitchell (D, ME) that would make recommendations concerning the IRA's arms. Pres. Bill Clinton, in London, **Nov. 29**, endorsed the peace agreement and also addressed Britain's Parliament, reiterating his support for the NATO force being sent into Bosnia and Herzegovina. The first president to come to Northern Ireland, Clinton, **Nov. 30**, visited Belfast and Londonderry, and met with both republican and unionist leaders. Clinton visited Dublin, Dec. 1.

# DECEMBER 1995

## National

**Senators Hatfield, Simpson Retire**—The lengthening list of retiring members of Congress expanded in Dec. to include 2 of the most prominent Republican members of the Senate. On **Dec. 1**, Mark Hatfield (OR) announced that he would not seek reelection in 1996. On **Dec. 2,** Alan Simpson (WY) also said that he would not run again.

**Republicans Add to Advantage in House**—On **Dec. 1**, Rep. Jimmy Hayes of Louisiana switched to the GOP from the Democratic side; he was the 5th House Democrat to cross the aisle since the GOP romp in the 1994 election. On **Dec. 12**, California State Sen. Tom Campbell, a moderate Republican, won an election to fill the vacancy resulting from the resignation in Sept. of Rep. Norman Mineta (D). Meanwhile, Jesse Jackson Jr., son of the civil rights leader, was elected to the House, **Dec. 12**, in a special election held to fill the vacancy created by the resignation of Mel Reynolds, who had been sentenced to prison in a sex case. Both men were Democrats.

**Clinton Vetoes GOP's 7-Year Budget Bill**—Pres. Bill Clinton, **Dec. 6**, vetoed the budget reconciliation bill pushed through Congress by the Republicans. The centerpiece of the GOP's legislative agenda, the bill was designed to achieve a balanced federal budget in 7 years. It reduced projected future spending for both Medicare and Medicaid and turned over to the states many programs that were currently federal responsibilities. The bill would also cut government revenue by $245 bil over 7 years.

Clinton, **Dec. 7**, put out his own 7-year balanced-budget plan. It contained smaller reductions in spending and smaller tax cuts. Cuts in projected Medicare and Medicaid spending came to $178 bil, compared to $433.4 bil in the GOP bill. The plan would require states to continue Medicaid to all those who currently qualified for federal benefits. Arguing that Republican tax cuts largely favored corporations and the rich, Clinton proposed reductions of only $98 bil. The federal government experienced a new partial shutdown, beginning **Dec. 16**, after expiration of a continuing resolution funding some of the departments.

The Interior Dept. appropriations bill drew a presidential veto, **Dec. 18**. Clinton opposed the bill's moratorium on new listings of endangered species, the increase in timber cuts in Alaska's Tongass National Forest, the delay in the Energy Dept.'s implementation of new rules for energy efficiency, and cuts in funding for the National Endowments for the Arts and the Humanities. Clinton, **Dec. 18**, vetoed another bill that would have cut discretionary spending for the Environmental Protection Agency by 21% and killed the AmeriCorps community service program, a favorite of the president's, which gave participants money for college expenses. On **Dec. 19**, Clinton vetoed a bill that would have killed funding provided in the 1994 anticrime law to add 100,000 police officers across the country; the Republican bill instead provided for block grants to the states to help fight crime.

It appeared, **Dec. 19**, that Clinton had agreed to negotiate with Republican congressional leaders on the basis of a commitment to a 7-year balanced budget using the more conservative Congressional Budget Office figures. After Vice Pres. Al Gore made a statement leaving Clinton's commitments in doubt, the House, by voice vote, **Dec. 20**, approved a resolution requiring a firm agreement before they would pass another continuing resolution to fund furloughed agencies. Clinton, **Dec. 28**, vetoed the defense authorization bill, objecting to provisions reviving the missile defense system and limiting his ability to deploy troops abroad. The White House and Republican leaders resumed budget negotiations, **Dec. 29**.

**Gingrich Faces New Investigation**—On **Dec. 6**, the House Committee on Ethics voted unanimously to have an independent counsel investigate allegations that Speaker Newt Gingrich (R, GA) had violated tax laws. In 1994, former Rep. Ben Jones (D, GA) had charged that Gingrich's college course, "Renewing American Civilization," which was televised by satellite across the country, promoted the agenda of the Republican Party and was funded, improperly, by tax-deductible donations. The Ethics Committee, consisting of 5 members from each party, found that Gingrich had misused public funds to benefit his own business interests when he promoted his college-course videotape during televised House proceedings. The committee also said that Gingrich's book deal with HarperCollins, which was owned by Rupert Murdoch, who had a major interest in pending congressional action, created "the impression of exploiting one's office for personal gain." Gingrich had accepted, and then given up, a $4.5 mil advance against royalties for the book. The committee took no action, however, on several other ethical complaints lodged against the Speaker.

**1995 Is Banner Year on Wall Street**—The leading economic indicators declined for the 8th time in 10 months in Oct., the Commerce Dept. said, **Dec. 6**; this time the drop was 0.5%. The Federal Reserve Board said, **Dec. 6**, that the economy continued to expand, but at a somewhat slower pace. The Labor Dept. said, **Dec. 8**, that unemployment had edged upward to 5.6% in Nov. from 5.5% in Oct. On Wall Street, the Dow Jones Industrial Average closed, **Dec. 13**, at an all-time high of 5,216.47. The Federal Reserve Board, **Dec. 19**, announced a reduction in the federal funds rate—the interest rate banks charged on overnight loans to each other—from 5.75% to 5.50%. Many banks promptly cut their prime lending rate from 8.75% to 8.5%. On the final trading day of 1995, **Dec. 29**, the dollar stood at 103.40 against the Japanese yen, up from 99.60 at the end of 1994, and at 1.4366 German marks, down from 1.5498 marks a year earlier. These figures represented significant recoveries for the dollar, compared with sharp plunges against the yen and mark in the spring of 1995. The Dow Jones average closed, **Dec. 29**, at 5117.12, not far below its record high. For the year, the Dow was up 33.5%, one of its best performances ever.

**White House Releases Subpoenaed Notes**—The White House in Dec. handed over to the Senate Whitewater Committee the notes from a Nov. 1993 meeting that the committee had requested, then subpoenaed. Two White House lawyers, Bruce Lindsey and David Kennedy, had invoked lawyer–client privilege when they testified before the committee on **Nov. 29** and **Dec. 5**, respectively. In response, the committee, **Dec. 8**, voted, 10–8, to subpoena documents that included notes taken during the meeting by Kennedy. Other White House lawyers and personal attorneys of Pres. Bill Clinton and First Lady Hillary Rodham Clinton had attended the meeting. Republicans on the Whitewater committee said they wanted to learn to what extent White House lawyers had gained information on the status of investigations by the Treasury Dept. and the Small Business Administration into the Whitewater affair.

On a related matter, Sen. Alphonse D'Amato (R, NY), chairman of the committee, said, **Dec. 11**, that the committee had uncovered a "smoking gun" showing that the late White House Counsel Vincent Foster had files relating to Hillary Clinton's legal work for Madison Guarantee, the failed savings and loan linked to Whitewater. The evidence was contained in a letter by David Kendall, the Clintons' personal attorney, to the Rose Law Firm, where Hillary Clinton had been a partner, stating that he was returning documents on Madison from Foster's files that "appear to me to be files" of the Rose firm. Kendall testified, **Dec. 11**, that so far as he knew the documents were never at Foster's White House office. Margaret Williams, the First Lady's chief of staff, testified, **Dec. 11**, that neither she nor Mrs. Clinton had removed or destroyed any documents in Foster's office. When the White House, **Dec. 12**, initially refused to hand over the subpoened documents, D'Amato said it was an attempt to impede the investigation. Notes taken by Susan Thomases, a lawyer and friend of the Clintons, in 1992 had indicated that Hillary Clinton had had "numerous conferences" with Madison officials during their negotiations with state regulators appointed by her husband, then-Gov. Clinton. In testimony, **Dec. 18**, Thomases said she could not recall much about the events in question. Kendall stated that Thomases' notes did not contradict previous testimony by the First Lady, to the effect that her work for Madison had been minimal.

The full Senate, **Dec. 20**, voted, 51–45, along party lines, to subpoena the Nov. 1993 notes. The White House agreed, **Dec. 21**, to hand over the notes after the investigators agreed not to consider the release as a waiver of lawyer–client privilege. The notes appeared to show no clear evidence of wrongdoing, but Republicans said they were intrigued by several passages, and especially by the phrase, "vacuum Rose Law files." Kennedy contended, **Dec. 22**, that this was a reference to an information vacuum confronting anyone seeking answers on the Clintons' Whitewater investment.

**Congresswoman Describes Financing Violation**—At a 5-hour press conference in Salt Lake City, **Dec. 11**, Rep. Enid Greene Waldholtz (R, UT) admitted that her 1994 campaign for the House had violated federal election rules limiting donations from any individual to any one candidate to $1,000. In 1994, in her successful effort to win a House seat, she spent $1.8 mil that came from her father, D. Forrest Greene. She said she had believed that the money was part of a $5 mil wedding gift from her husband, Joseph Waldholtz. At her press conference, she claimed that, in fact, Joseph Waldholtz (from whom she was seeking a divorce) had bilked her father of $4 mil, exchanging bogus real-estate holdings for the money. Joseph Waldholtz, who served as treasurer of his wife's campaign, had temporarily disappeared in Nov. 1995. He returned to face charges he had written $250,000 in bad checks.

**Congress Passes Welfare Bill**—The House, **Dec. 21**, 245–178, and the Senate, **Dec. 22**, 52–47, approved identical bills intended to reform the nation's welfare system. The voting was essentially along party lines. This Republican plan would eliminate federal cash assistance to poor families and substitute block grants to the states. The bill required the states to limit recipients to 2 years of payments unless they found work; a 5-year limit for any assistance was imposed. Under this legislation, states would also be prohibited from increasing benefits to mothers who had additional children while on welfare.

## International

**U.S. Troops Deployed in Bosnia**—The deployment of troops from the U.S. and other nations in Bosnia and Herzegovina, aimed at guaranteeing the new peace treaty, got underway in Dec. On **Dec. 2**, during his European trip, Pres. Bill Clinton told Bosnia-bound soldiers of the U.S. Army's 1st Armored Division, stationed in Germany, that they would be authorized to use "decisive force" against any attackers. NATO units began arriving in Sarajevo, capital of Bosnia, in force, **Dec. 4**. Senate and House resolutions opposing the deployment of U.S. troops were defeated. The Senate, **Dec. 13**, approved, 69–30, a resolution supporting the deployment providing that it last no more than about one year. The resolution also called on the U.S. to train and arm the Bosnian government army. The House, **Dec. 13**, in a 287–141 vote, declared that it strongly supported the U.S. forces that were to be deployed, but explicitly opposed Clinton's decision to send them. The House resolution opposed U.S. support for the government army. According to public opinion polls, Americans remained opposed to the deployment. In a nonbinding referendum, **Dec. 12**, 90% of Serbs living in and near Sarajevo voted against the peace treaty.

In Paris, **Dec. 14**, the presidents of Bosnia, Croatia, and Serbia signed the peace treaty agreed to in Nov. Clinton, who was among those who signed as witnesses, said that the U.S. would provide $85.6 mil in economic aid immediately and that he would ask Congress to provide $600 mil more over the next few years. A large-scale landing of U.S. troops began **Dec. 18**. On **Dec. 20**, Gen. Bernard Janvier of France, commander of UN peacekeeping forces in Bosnia, turned over control of international operations to the NATO commander in Southern Europe, U.S. Adm. Leighton Smith. U.S. Army Engineers, **Dec. 31**, completed a bridge across the Sava River from Croatia to Bosnia, across which U.S. soldiers would enter Bosnia.

**2 Korean Presidents Face New Charges**—Two former presidents of South Korea, Chun Doo Hwan and Roh Tae Woo, faced new legal difficulties in Dec. On **Dec. 3**, Chun was charged with having staged the 1979 military coup that put him in power. Roh was indicted, **Dec. 5**, for having accepted bribes while president. On **Dec. 18**, the trial of Roh and 14 others began. Roh, in court, admitted having taken bribes and kickbacks, but said he had destroyed records and could not remember who had given him the money. Legislation passed by parliament, **Dec. 19**, opened the way for Chun and Roh to be prosecuted in connection with the 1980 massacre of prodemocracy demonstrators in Kwangju. Chun and Roh were indicted, **Dec. 21**, in connection with the 1979 coup.

**Israel Continues Withdrawal**—Implementation of the Israeli–Palestinian peace agreement continued, **Dec. 11**, as Israel withdrew from Nablus, the largest city on the West Bank. Palestinian police immediately assumed control. On **Dec. 11-12**, Israeli Prime Min. Shimon Peres, in Washington, DC, met with Pres. Bill Clinton and addressed a joint session of Congress. Israeli troops withdrew from Bethlehem, **Dec. 21.** After 4 days of meetings with representatives of the Palestinian National Authority (PNA), the Islamic group Hamas said, **Dec. 21**, that it would not participate in Palestinian elections or stop attacking Israelis. Hamas promised, however, that it would not attempt to disrupt the Jan. voting.

**North Korea Signs Nuclear Agreement**—North Korea and a consortium that included the U.S., Japan, and South Korea signed an agreement, **Dec. 15**, that formalized an accord reached in 1994. Under the terms of the agreement, the consortium, the Korean Peninsula Energy Development Organization, would replace North Korea's nuclear reactors with 2 light-water reactors that would produce far less weapons-grade plutonium. South Korea would finance 70% of the cost, and Japan most of the rest. North Korea would repay interest-free loans over 20 years. The U.S. would supply a contractor and engineers.

**Communists Score Big Gains in Russian Voting**—In a **Dec. 17** election, Communists greatly increased their membership in the State Duma, the lower house of the Russian parliament. Pres. Boris Yeltsin, who was recuperating from a heart ailment at a rest home near Moscow, had spoken on television, **Dec. 15**, recalling times of famine and mass persecution under Communism. Voters, however, were unhappy with Russia's declining influence in world affairs and with the stresses related to the movement toward a market economy. In the election, the Communists polled 22% of the vote and won 157 of 450 seats in the Duma, up from 45. The ultranationalist Liberal Democratic Party drew 11%; Our Home Is Russia, the party of Premier Viktor Chernomyrdin, 10%; and the pro-economic reform Yabloko party, 7%. Yeltsin returned to work at the Kremlin, **Dec. 29**.

**New President Elected in Haiti**—Haiti, a nation in crisis for years, completed a peaceful presidential election **Dec. 17**. The incumbent president, Jean-Bertrand Aristide, who had been restored to power in 1994 with U.S. intervention, had announced that he would not seek another term. On **Dec. 15**, he endorsed one of the candidates, René

Préval of the Lavalas party, an agronomist and a former premier. Préval won 88% of the vote. UN peacekeeping troops and Haitian police provided security. Only about one-fourth of the nation's registered voters participated.

### General

**Queen Asks Charles, Diana to Divorce**—Buckingham Palace announced, **Dec. 20**, that Queen Elizabeth II had asked Prince Charles, the heir to the throne, and Princess Diana to obtain a divorce. The couple had been married in 1981 and have 2 sons, Prince William, 13, and Prince Harry, 11. They had separated in 1992. Charles had admitted to having an affair with Camilla Parker-Bowles, a friend of long standing, who was also married at the time. Diana had stated in a BBC television interview broadcast Nov. 20 that she, too, had had an affair, and she described the palace as her "enemy." She said that she did not want a divorce because of her concern about the impact on her children but that she would follow her husband's wishes. A palace spokesperson said Charles favored a divorce.

## JANUARY 1996

### National

**AT&T to Cut Payroll by 40,000**—AT&T Corp. announced, **Jan. 2**, that it would reduce its payroll by 40,000 (out of a total of 300,000) within 3 years. The company had previously announced that by the end of 1996 it would split into 3 separate companies engaged in communications services, telecommunications equipment, and computers, respectively. Richard Miller, AT&T's chief financial officer, said that the cutbacks were necessary to make the spinoff companies "successful competitors in their respective industries." The announcement promptly triggered a runup in the price of AT&T.

**Whitewater Grand Jury Hears From First Lady**—Responding to a subpoena, First Lady Hillary Rodham Clinton testified in Jan. before a grand jury investigating the Whitewater affair. The White House, **Jan. 3**, had released to the Senate committee investigating Whitewater a 1993 internal memorandum written by former White House aide David Watkins, stating that Mrs. Clinton played a central role in the dismissal of the employees of the White House travel office. She had previously told investigators that she had had nothing to do with the dismissals. Watkins, testifying to the Senate committee, **Jan. 17**, said he had felt a lot of internal pressure from Pres. and Mrs. Clinton to deal with the travel office, though he said she had never directly told him to dismiss the employees.

Long-sought records released by the White House **Jan. 5** showed that Mrs. Clinton, while working for the Rose Law Firm in Little Rock, had done 60 hours of work for Madison Guaranty Savings and Loan. David Kendall, attorney for the Clintons, said, **Jan. 5**, that the records, which had been subpoenaed in 1994 and whose whereabouts had been unaccounted for for some time, had been found the previous day in the White House by Carolyn Huber, an aide to Mrs. Clinton. Republicans contended that the 60 hours was inconsistent with her assertion that she had done little work for the now-defunct S&L. In a **Jan. 8** column concerning the Rose firm documents and the White House travel office, *New York Times* columnist William Safire labeled Mrs. Clinton a "congenital liar." Michael McCurry, chief spokesman for the White House, said the following day that the president wished he could punch Safire on the nose for his verbal assault on the first lady.

Huber, testifying **Jan. 18**, said she had first discovered the Rose Law Firm documents in a room in the Clintons' private quarters in the White House in Aug. 1995, and—assuming she was to file them—had taken them to her office. She did not realize their significance, she said, until she examined them earlier in Jan. Some Republicans charged that the Clintons knowingly had the documents in their possession and that the Clintons' failure to provide them to the committee constituted obstruction of justice.

The White House announced, **Jan. 22**, that the Whitewater independent counsel, Kenneth Starr, had subpoenaed Mrs. Clinton to testify before the grand jury concerning the documents. Kendall was also subpoenaed. She appeared before the grand jury, **Jan. 26**, the first time a first lady had ever done so. Media coverage of her arrival and departure was heavy, but the proceedings were secret.

**Longest-Ever Government Shutdown Ends**—The longest shutdown in U.S. government history, 21 days, ended in Jan. Some 280,000 federal workers had been furloughed in mid-Dec. because of the budget impasse between Pres. Bill Clinton and Congress. Both houses of Congress, **Jan. 5**, passed a stopgap spending bill that would allow workers to return. The bill required that Clinton submit a 7-year balanced budget using Congressional Budget Office projections. Clinton submitted such a budget proposal, **Jan. 6**, and then signed the bill. The president's proposal to balance the budget contained much smaller cuts in projected Medicare and Medicaid spending, as well as tax cuts totaling $87 bil—far less than the tax cuts of $245 bil favored by the Republicans in Congress. The 2 sides were divided not only by numbers but also by the Republicans' philosophical desire to transfer administration of many programs to the states. Negotiations continued.

The early-Jan. agreement covered only a 3-week period, and the House, **Jan. 25**, and the Senate, **Jan. 26**, passed another stopgap spending bill to fund the government through mid-Mar. Clinton signed the bill **Jan. 26**. Congressional approval of this latest stopgap bill appeared to signal an end to Republican attempts to use the threat of a government shutdown as a means of forcing White House concessions in budget negotiations.

**Blizzard in East One of Worst Ever**—An immense storm system deposited up to 3 feet of snow onto the Mid-Atlantic and New England states, **Jan. 7** and **8**. The blizzard claimed about 100 lives in all and caused up to $1.5 bil in damages. The snowfall in New York City was as high as 27.5 inches, 3d deepest on record. Schools were closed for 2 days. Federal employees in Washington, DC, many of whom had lost workdays because of the government shutdown over the budget, were out for 3 more days because of the storm. Airports in major Northeastern cities were shut down for 2 days.

**Woman's Suit Against Clinton Allowed to Proceed**—A 3-judge federal panel held **Jan. 9** that a sexual-harassment suit against Pres. Bill Clinton could go forward. The plaintiff, Paula Corbin Jones, had filed a suit in 1994 alleging that in 1991, then-Gov. Bill Clinton of Arkansas had made unwanted advances toward her. In 1994, a federal judge held that Clinton was immune to lawsuits while president, because they would distract him from official duties. By a 2-1 vote, the 3-judge panel of the 8th Circuit Court of Appeals in St. Louis reversed that ruling.

**Clinton Vetoes Shift of Welfare to States**—Pres. Bill Clinton, **Jan. 9**, vetoed a welfare-reform bill supported by Republicans in Congress that would have shifted responsibility to the states, imposed work requirements, and limited benefits. In his veto message, Clinton charged that the GOP approach would not encourage recipients to find work and that poor children would suffer.

**Democrats Capture Senate Seat in Oregon**—The Democrats, in a minority in the Senate since the 1994 election, picked up an Oregon seat previously held by Bob Packwood, a Republican. Packwood had resigned in Oct. 1995 after a Senate committee found he had engaged in sexual misconduct. The first congressional election conducted entirely by mail began **Jan. 9**. U.S. Rep. Ron Wyden, the Democratic candidate, was declared the winner **Jan. 30**, the closing date for receiving ballots, with 48% of the vote. Nearly two-thirds of registered voters participated, and the state saved $1 mil by utilizing the mails. Wyden's victory cut the GOP majority in the Senate to 53-47.

**"Flat Tax" Foremost Issue in GOP Race**—Federal taxation policy was the dominant issue in Jan. in the contest for the Republican presidential nomination. Steve Forbes, publisher of *Forbes Magazine* and a candidate for the nomination, proposed a flat 17% tax on wages and salaries, after an exemption ($36,000 for a family of 4). Forbes proposed to eliminate the deductions for mortgage-interest payments, property taxes, and charitable gifts. Because he had declined to accept federal matching funds, Forbes—who was thought to have a net worth of $500 mil—was able to spend any amount of his own money and he advertised heavily on television. At a debate among 9 presidential candidates in Des Moines, IA, **Jan. 13**, Sen. Phil Gramm (TX) said that Forbes' plan would create deep budget deficits. Former Gov. Lamar Alexander (TN) opposed the elimination of the mortgage deduction. Because the plan would not include taxes on capital gains, commentator Patrick Buchanan said it must have been "cooked up by the boys at the yacht basin." Gramm, **Jan. 17**, unveiled a flat-tax proposal of his own, but with more personal deductions. A Republican-supported private commission also endorsed a flat tax, **Jan. 17**.

**13th Senator to Retire**—Sen. William Cohen (R, ME) announced, **Jan. 16**, that he would retire at the end of his 3d term in 1996. He was the 13th senator to announce his retirement in the current election cycle, an all-time record.

**10 Sentenced in Plot to Bomb UN**—Ten Muslims who were convicted in Oct. 1995 of conspiracy to bomb the UN and other New York City landmarks, and to assassinate public figures, were sentenced **Jan. 17**, in U.S. District Court in New York City. Sheik Omar Abdel Rahman, the alleged ringleader, was sentenced to life in prison plus 65 years for directing the plot and for plotting to kill Pres. Hosni Mubarak of Egypt. El Sayyid Nosair was sentenced to life in prison for the 1990 assassination of Rabbi Meir Kahane, an Israeli militant. He had previously been acquitted in a state trial. Judge Michael Mukasey sentenced the 8 others to prison terms of 25 years or more.

**Trade Deficit Continues to Shrink**—The U.S. trade deficit continued to decline in Oct., to $8.04 bil, the Commerce Dept. said, **Jan. 17**. This was the 4th straight monthly drop, and was the smallest monthly total of 1995. The Conference Board, a research group based in New York City, reported, **Jan. 17**, that the leading economic indicators had declined again in Nov., by 0.3%. Amid indications that the U.S. economy was slowing down, the Federal Reserve Board, **Jan. 31**, lowered 2 short-term interest rates by 0.25% each—the federal funds rate (the rate banks charges on overnight loans to each other) to 5.25%, and the discount rate (the rate the Fed charged to commercial banks) to 5%. The Labor Dept. said, **Jan. 31**, that prices charged by producers for finished goods had risen only 2.2% in all of 1995.

**State of the Union Address Taps GOP Ideas**—Pres. Bill Clinton, **Jan. 23**, delivered his annual State of the Union address before a joint session of Congress. Declaring that "The era of big government is over," Clinton embraced a number of objectives more often advanced by Republicans, including the balancing the budget, fighting crime, and protecting the family. He also stressed some traditional Democratic issues, including education and the environment. The president urged Congress not to scrap the 1994 ban on assault weapons. He admonished Congress to "never—ever—shut the federal government again" and urged quick approval of portions of the balanced-budget bill on which he and Congress had reached an agreement.

In his response for the Republicans, Sen. Majority Leader Robert Dole (KS) stressed a need to eliminate the federal budget deficit.

**Senate Ratifies Nuclear Pact With Russia**—The Senate, **Jan. 26**, approved, 87–4, the Second Strategic Arms Reduction Treaty. Pres. Boris Yeltsin of Russia and Pres. George Bush had signed the agreement in Jan. 1993. Under it, both countries agreed to eliminate all land-based intercontinental ballistic missiles with multiple warheads. By 2003, the total number of missile- and bomber-based warheads deployed by each side would be no more than 3,500.

## International

**Hashimoto Elected Premier of Japan**—Premier Tomiichi Murayama of Japan announced his resignation, **Jan. 5**, after 18 months in office. Japan's first Socialist premier since 1948, he had headed a coalition government during a period of slow economic growth. The Diet, **Jan. 11**, elected Ryutaro Hashimoto, head of the Liberal Democratic Party, to replace Murayama. Hashimoto installed a 4-member cabinet dominated by the LDP. He had served as minister of transportation, health and welfare, finance, and trade.

**Bosnian Combatants Withdraw Forces**—According to the terms of the peace agreement, military forces of opposing factions in Bosnia and Herzegovina pulled back from the cease-fire line in Jan. Earlier, on **Jan. 8**, the UN Security Council rebuked Croatia for killing or driving out the Serbs who remained in the Krajina region of Croatia, which Croat forces had taken from rebel Serbs in 1995. On **Jan. 12**, 150 Russian paratroopers—the first of 1,600 Russian troops coming to Bosnia—joined U.S. troops on patrol in northeastern Bosnia. Pres. Bill Clinton, **Jan. 13**, met with Pres. Franjo Tudjman of Croatia in the latter's capital, Zagreb, and then went to Tuzla, the U.S. headquarters in Bosnia, where he addressed 500 soldiers and toured some frontline positions. The UN Security Council, **Jan. 15**, authorized a 5,000-member force to monitor the situation in Eastern Slavonia, in Croatia, where rebel Serbs were giving up control to the Croatian government. The Bosnian government said, **Jan. 15**, that it would not participate in the exchange of prisoners with Bosnian Serbs until the latter disclosed the whereabouts of more than 24,000 missing Muslims. However, Bosnian Muslims and Serbs, **Jan. 19**, freed 225 prisoners in time for a treaty-imposed deadline. The opposing sides met the **Jan. 19** deadline for withdrawing their heavy weapons and most of their troops from the 2.5-mile-wide zone of separation. In many places, though, heavy artillery pieces were placed just beyond the separation zone. U.S. Asst. Sec. of State John Shattuck, **Jan. 21**, headed a group of investigators who inspected a frozen site near Srebrenica that may have contained mass graves of Muslims killed by Serbs.

**Russians, Chechens Battle Over Hostages**—The conflict between Russian military forces and Chechen rebels flared anew in Jan. On **Jan. 9**, Chechen guerrillas crossed the Chechen border into the Dagestan region and occupied the town of Kizlyar, taking 2,000 hostages at a hospital and in nearby homes. On **Jan. 10**, the Chechens released all but about 130 hostages, and the Russians allowed the rebels to flee toward Chechnya with their captives. Just short of the border, the Russians attacked the convoy, and the Chechens responded by taking over the town of Pervomayskoye and seizing more hostages. Some hostages were freed, and a 5-day standoff ended, **Jan. 15**, when the Russians launched a major air, tank, and artillery attack. The assault leveled the village. Some hostages escaped, but many were killed. The Russian Interior Ministry said, **Jan. 17**, that 26 Russian soldiers and 153 Chechens had been killed in the fighting.

**Arafat Elected President of Palestine Authority**—Yasir Arafat, chairman of the Palestine Liberation Organization, was elected president **Jan. 20** of the Palestine National Authority, which was assuming control of territory previously occupied by Israel. Israel had freed 812 Palestinians from jails, **Jan. 10**, in a gesture apparently intended to help Arafat's chances. In the voting, Arafat defeated his only opponent, with 88% of the vote. Al-Fatah, the PLO faction led by Arafat, won about three-fourths of the seats in the Palestinian legislature. The turnout was large, despite nonparticipation by militant Islamic organizations.

**Papandreou Steps Down in Greece**—Prime Min. Andreas Papandreou of Greece, who was seriously ill with lung and kidney infections, resigned **Jan. 15**. The leader of Greece from 1981 to 1989, he had lost office in the midst of a financial and personal scandal, then won reelection in 1993. On **Jan. 18**, the ruling Panhellenic Socialist Movement, which he led, chose former Industry Minister Costas Simitis to be the new premier. He was sworn into office on **Jan. 22**.

**Panel Offers Advice on Ulster Impasse**—An international panel headed by former Sen. George Mitchell (D, ME) recommended, **Jan. 24**, that all-party talks aimed at resolving the future status of Ulster, or Northern Ireland, should begin before the disarmament of the Irish Republican Army.

**France Ends Nuclear Tests in Pacific**—On **Jan. 27**, France conducted the 6th of a planned total of 8 underwater nuclear tests in the South Pacific. The explosion was about 6 times as powerful as the bomb that devastated the Japanese city of Hiroshima in 1945. In the face of widespread international condemnation, French Pres. Jacques Chirac had defended the tests as militarily necessary. On **Jan. 29**, however, Chirac announced that the test 2 days earlier would be the last one.

**Sri Lanka Bomber Kills 86, Injures 1,400**—The long and violent civil war in Sri Lanka claimed another heavy death toll on **Jan. 31**, when a suicide bomber drove a truck loaded with more than 400 pounds of explosives into the gates of the Central Bank in Colombo, the capital. The ensuing blast killed 86 persons and injured more than 1,400. Later, authorities arrested 2 suspects who were members of the Liberation Tigers of Tamil Eelam. The Tigers began fighting in 1983 to establish a separate homeland for the Tamil minority in Sri Lanka. By 1996 the conflict had claimed some 40,000 lives.

### General

**Nebraska Repeats as College Football Champs**—The Nebraska Cornhuskers won the Division I collegiate football championship for the 2d year in a row, **Jan. 2**, when they defeated the Florida Gators, 62–24, in the Fiesta Bowl in Tempe, AZ. With their Bowl victory, Nebraska boasted a 24–0 record over the 2 seasons. Quarterback Tommie Frazier, named the game's most valuable player, ran for 199 yards, and running back Lawrence Phillips ran for 165 yards and 3 touchdowns. The rout was Florida's first loss of the season. No other team got through the season unbeaten, and polls of coaches and media members, announced **Jan. 3**, gave the national title to Nebraska.

**Dallas Defeats Pittsburgh in Super Bowl**—The Dallas Cowboys captured their 5th Super Bowl championship in Jan. Dallas qualified to compete for the National Football League title by defeating the Green Bay Packers, 38–27, on **Jan. 14** in the National Football Conference championship game. Also on **Jan. 14**, the Pittsburgh Steelers won the American Football Conference championship game against the Indianapolis Colts, 20–16, when a Colts receiver was unable to hold on to a pass in the end zone on the last play of the game.

Dallas defeated Pittsburgh, 27–17, in Super Bowl XXX in Tempe, AZ, **Jan. 28**. Cowboy cornerback Larry Brown, named the game's most valuable player, intercepted 2 passes and returned them for 77 yards. In an aerial duel, Cowboy quarterback Troy Aikman completed 15 of 23 passes for 209 yards, and Steeler quarterback Neil O'Donnell completed 28 of 49 passes for 239 yards.

**Olestra Approved as Fat Substitute**—The U.S. Food and Drug Administration, **Jan. 24**, approved use of a fat substitute that is also free of calories. The synthetic compound of sugar and vegetable oil, called olestra, passes through the digestive system without being absorbed. Proctor & Gamble Co. would make and market the substance and license it to other companies, while using it in its own Pringles brand potato chips and other snack foods. The FDA required that foods containing olestra carry a label warning that the substance can cause "abdominal cramping and loose stools." Because olestra was found to inhibit absorption of some nutrients, it was fortified with 4 vitamins. Some scientists protested the approval of olestra, arguing that the potential side effects—including the loss of nutrients that helped protect the body against heart disease and cancer—outweighed its benefits.

## FEBRUARY 1996

### National

**Telecommunications Bill Signed Into Law**—The Senate, 91–5, and House, 414–16, gave final approval, **Feb. 1**, to a sweeping revision of U.S. communications laws. Under one provision, telephone companies offering long-distance service, such as AT&T, could compete in regional markets now controlled by the so-called Baby Bells—companies formed during the breakup in 1984 of AT&T. The Baby Bells, on the other hand, would now be allowed to offer national long-distance service. The bill increased from 25% to 35% the proportion of U.S. households that could receive broadcasts from television stations owned by a single company. It eliminated a requirement that a company could own no more than 12 TV stations and no more than 20 AM band and 20 FM band radio stations.

The telecommunications bill required that new TV sets contain a so-called v-chip, which would permit parents to lock their children out of violent programs. Except for restrictions on charges for basic services, cable companies would be freed from present rate caps. The legislation also imposed criminal penalties for distribution of "indecent" material over computer networks and forbade dissemination of information about abortion. Pres. Bill Clinton signed it into law **Feb. 8**.

**Inflation Low, Economic Growth Slowed, in 1995**—The Labor Dept. reported, **Feb. 1**, that consumer prices had risen 0.2% in Dec. and 2.5% for all of 1995. Inflation was thus slightly lower than the 2.7% rate reported for both 1993 and 1994, and fell under 3% for the 4th straight year. Prices had not been so stable since the early 1960s. The department said, **Feb. 2**, that unemployment stood at 5.8% in Jan., up from 5.6% for the 2 previous months. In the greatest monthly decline in payroll employment in almost 5 years, 201,000 nonfarm jobs disappeared in that month. Much of the decline was blamed on the early-Jan. blizzard in the East. The Commerce Dept. said, **Feb. 7**, that the U.S. trade deficit stood in Nov. at $7.06 bil, the 5th straight monthly decline to the lowest level in 20 months.

The Commerce Dept. announced, **Feb. 23**, that the gross domestic product had grown by only 2.1% during 1995, the lowest annual rate since 1991. This figure suggested that the economy was weaker than many had thought.

The Labor Dept. reported, **Feb. 28**, that consumer prices were up 0.4% in Jan., the biggest monthly increase in more than 2 years. The Commerce Dept. said, **Feb. 28**, that the U.S. had recorded a trade deficit of $111 bil during all of 1995, the highest since 1988. However, the deficit with Japan had declined by almost one-tenth during 1995.

**President to Testify at Whitewater Trial**—U.S. District Judge George Howard Jr., **Feb. 5**, ordered Pres. Bill Clinton to testify in the trial of Susan McDougal, one of his former partners in the now-defunct Whitewater Development Corp. Susan McDougal; her former husband, James McDougal; and Gov. Jim Guy Tucker of Arkansas were to go on trial in Mar. on charges that they had conspired and made false statements in order to get millions of dollars in U.S.-backed loans.

The Whitewater independent counsel, Kenneth Starr, **Feb. 20**, indicted Robert Hill and Herby Branscum Jr., owners of the Perry County Bank in Perryville, AR, for fraud and conspiracy. The charges related to the handling of money they had donated to Bill Clinton's gubernatorial reelection campaign. The bank's former president, Neal Ainley, had pleaded guilty to charges linked to the loans.

The Federal Deposit Insurance Corp. notified Congress, **Feb. 28**, that a legal technicality would probably prevent the winning of damages from the Rose Law Firm, in Little Rock, for fraud or other misconduct in connection with the collapse of Madison Guaranty. In stating that it would not sue the firm, the FDIC said that, although the firm and its attorneys had engaged in impermissible conflicts of interest, there was no convincing evidence that Rose itself had committed fraud.

**Republican Presidential Voting Begins**—None of the candidates for the Republican presidential nomination took a decisive lead in the early caucuses and primaries. Columnist Pat Buchanan, winning two-thirds of the votes of religious conservatives, was the surprise winner, **Feb. 6**, in the Louisiana caucuses, finishing ahead of Sen. Phil Gramm, from the next-door state of Texas. On **Feb. 12**, in the Iowa caucuses, Sen. Robert Dole (KS) placed first, though he was supported by only 26% of the caucus attendees in this farm belt-state. Buchanan had the backing of 23% of the participants, followed by former Tennessee Gov. Lamar Alexander (18%), magazine publisher Steve Forbes (10%), and Gramm (9%). In the contest for the support of social conservatives, Buchanan had again prevailed over Gramm, and the latter, **Feb. 14**, announced that he was abandoning his well-financed campaign. The wealthy Forbes spent $4 mil of his own money in Iowa, almost all on radio and television ads, many of which were attacks on his opponents.

Buchanan, campaigning in New Hampshire prior to the **Feb. 20** primary there, denounced recent international trade agreements that, he said, were costing Americans thousands of jobs as U.S. companies sought out cheap labor elsewhere. He backed higher tariffs for goods imported from Japan and China and favored building a fence along the southern U.S. border, if necessary, to stop illegal immigration from Mexico. In a surprise, Buchanan won New Hampshire with 27% of the vote, followed by Dole (26%), Alexander (23%), and Forbes (12%).

Forbes's support for a flat tax found favor **Feb. 24** in Delaware, where he won the primary and all 12 delegates. On **Feb. 27**, in Arizona, the biggest state to vote so far, where sympathy for tax reform and small government ran high, Forbes won again with 111,000 votes to 101,000 for Dole, pocketing the state's 39 delegates. Buchanan's anti-immigration theme brought him only 3d place. Also on **Feb. 27**, Dole won primaries in North Dakota and South Dakota. By one count, at month's end, Forbes had captured 57 delegates to the national convention, Buchanan 31, and Dole 27. A total of 996 were needed for the nomination.

**Programs to Be Rated for Sex, Violence**—Pres. Bill Clinton, **Feb. 8**, asked television network and cable executives to come to the White House to work out a means of rating television programs that had a violent or sexual content. At the meeting with the president, **Feb. 29**, the heads of the 4 major networks and the leading cable companies agreed to take steps to implement use of the so-called v-chip (for "violence") that parents could install in their sets. The chip, which was mandated in the telecommunications law just passed by Congress, would "read" a program's rating, and television owners would have the option of blocking out programs with certain ratings.

**Oklahoma Bomb Trial Moved to Colorado**— In a decision publicly released **Feb. 20**, a federal judge granted a defense motion requesting that the trial of 2 suspects in the bombing of a federal building in Oklahoma City be moved to Colorado. The bomb that had exploded in Apr. 1995 had killed 168 people. Subsequently, 2 men, Timothy McVeigh and Terry Nichols, had been charged in the crime. Judge Richard Matsch noted that while relatives of the victims wanted to attend the trial, prejudice against the accused ran high in Oklahoma.

**Mfume Takes Office as NAACP Leader**—Former U.S. Rep. Kweisi Mfume (D, MD) was sworn in **Feb. 20** as president and chief executive officer of the National Assocation for the Advancement of Colored People. Mfume, who replaced director Benjamin Chevis (ousted in a scandal over alleged misuse of funds), vowed to lead a "reinvigorated" NAACP.

## International

**Path Toward Peace in Bosnia Still Rocky**—The NATO mission continued its efforts to bring peace to Bosnia and Herzegovina. Sniper attacks on NATO personnel in the vicinity of Sarajevo, the capital, were being reported almost daily, and on **Feb. 1**, in the first fatal exchange of gunfire, French troops killed a sniper. The mission's first American fatality occurred, **Feb. 3**, when Army Sgt. Donald Dugan was killed as a piece of undetonated ammunition exploded after he picked it up. In all, by **Feb. 3**, 9 soldiers in the multinational NATO force had been killed, and 44, including 3 Americans, had been wounded.

The Serb siege of Sarajevo was effectively lifted, **Feb. 3**, when Bosnian Serbs, Croats, and Muslims met the deadline for withdrawal from most of the 1,500 square miles of lands that they were to swap in compliance with the Dec. 1995 peace treaty. Many bridges and roads linking the capital and its suburbs were opened for the first time in 4 years. Meeting with Pres. Alija Izetbegovic in Sarajevo, **Feb. 3**, Sec. of State Warren Christopher reportedly urged the Bosnian president to see to it that Muslim guerrilla fighters from other countries were expelled. At a meeting, **Feb. 4**, Christopher told Pres. Slobodan Milosevic of Serbia he must cooperate with the prosecution of Serbian war criminals or face continuation of international trade sanctions. After Bosnian government forces detained 8 Serb officers as war-crimes suspects, the Bosnian Serbs, **Feb. 6**, suspended relations with the government. Justice Richard Goldstone, head of the international war-crimes tribunal, **Feb. 7**, urged that the officers be held until the tribunal determined whether they should be indicted.

At a meeting in Rome, **Feb. 18**, Izetbegovic, Milosevic, and Pres. Franjo Tudjman of Croatia pledged to resolve any remaining difficulties over implementation of the peace treaty. The Bosnian Serbs said that they would not attempt to delay the Mar. deadline for the transfer of Serb-held suburbs of Sarajevo to the Muslim–Croat federation. The U.S. agreed to seek the lifting of UN economic sanctions against Serbia. The Bosnian government promised to expel all foreign Muslim military personnel from its territory. All factions agreed to help the investigation of war crimes.

**2 IRA Bombs Shatter Cease-Fire on Ireland**—Recent progress in the efforts to resolve the conflict over the future of Northern Ireland, or Ulster, seemed in jeopardy following the detonation of 2 bombs. In Aug. 1994, the Irish Republican Army had declared a cease-fire, setting in motion informal discussions that seemed likely to lead soon to all-party negotiations on Ulster. Then, on **Feb. 9**, a bomb, estimated at 500 to 1,000 pounds in weight, exploded beneath an elevated railroad station in London, killing 2 people and injuring about 100. The IRA, declaring an end to its cease-fire, **Feb. 9**, and claiming responsibility for the latest bombing, **Feb. 10**, blamed its decision on the failure of the government of British Prime Min. John Major to resolve the Ulster dispute. Gerry Adams, head of Sinn Fein, the political wing of the IRA, said, **Feb. 10**, that he had been surprised by the bombing. Pres. Bill Clinton, who had met with Adams at the White House in Mar. 1995, said, **Feb. 10**, that he would continue to seek peace in Northern

Ireland. Major said, **Feb. 12**, that he had suspended all contacts with the IRA.

A second bomb exploded on a bus in London, **Feb. 18**, killing 1 and injuring 9. The IRA claimed responsibility, **Feb. 19**, and said, **Feb. 21**, that the person killed had been an IRA member who was carrying the explosive. British government officials and Sinn Fein leaders met, **Feb. 26**, for the first time since the end of the cease-fire. Major and Prime Min. John Bruton of Ireland announced, **Feb. 28**, that all-party talks would start **June 10**, providing that the IRA reinstated the cease-fire and that Ulster elect its negotiators. IRA disarmament was no longer a precondition.

**2 Sons-in-Law of Iraqi Ruler Killed**—Two brothers who were married to daughters of Pres. Saddam Hussein of Iraq were shot to death in Baghdad, shortly after returning from exile in Jordan. Lt. Col. Hussein Kamel Hassan al-Majid had once been in charge of Iraq's chemical, biological, and nuclear weapons program. His brother, Lt. Col. Saddam Kamel Hassan al-Majid, had led the Iraqi special forces. In 1995 the brothers, their wives, and a number of senior Iraqi military officers defected and were granted political asylum in Jordan. Hussein Kamel vowed to try to overthrow his father-in-law, but he did not gain support abroad; other exiled opponents of the Iraqi dictatorship resented his links to human rights abuses while in the government. He also threatened to reveal Iraqi military secrets; in apparent response, Iraq provided the UN with long-requested information on its nuclear-weapons program.

After receiving a government pardon, the brothers returned to Iraq on **Feb. 20**. On **Feb. 23**, the government announced that Saddam Hussein's 2 daughters had requested and been given divorces. Hours later, members of the Majid clan who were cousins of the former defectors stormed the brothers' residence in Baghdad and killed them, along with a 3d brother and their father. Two of the attackers were killed in the gunfight. The attackers said they had acted because the defectors had betrayed their homeland.

**Cuban Jets Down 2 U.S. Civilian Planes**—Tensions between the U.S. and Cuba rose again **Feb. 24** after Cuban jets shot down 2 unarmed private planes owned by a Cuban exile organization based in Miami. All 4 persons on the planes were presumed to have been killed. A 3d civilian plane returned safely to Miami. During the past 5 years, this nonviolent organization of exile pilots, Brothers to the Rescue, had flown more than 1,800 times over the Florida Straits, between Florida and Cuba, looking for refugees attempting to escape Cuba in rafts. The organization had also sought to encourage civil disobedience in Cuba. In Jan., after the group had twice dropped leaflets over Havana attacking the Cuban regime, the government threatened to take "all necessary measures" to prevent future incursions.

Sec. of State Warren Christopher said, **Feb. 25**, that the attacks had occurred over international waters, while Cuba said, **Feb. 26**, that radar tapes and recorded cockpit conversations proved the planes had flown over Cuba's territorial waters, or within 12 miles of Cuba's coast. Cuban air traffic controllers warned the exile pilots, but cockpit tapes showed that the jet pilots did not subsequently warn of the imminent attack and apparently took pleasure in it. Pres. Bill Clinton, **Feb. 26**, suspended charter flights between the U.S. and Cuba. Cuban Foreign Minister Roberto Robaina said, **Feb. 27**, that after more than 25 violations of Cuban sovereignty, his government had run out of alternatives to downing the planes. Clinton, **Feb. 28**, backed a bill just passed by Congress that required congressional approval for any modification made by the president in the U.S. embargo of Cuba.

**Bombs Kill 27 in Israel**—Two bombs exploded in Israel, **Feb. 25**, killing 27 people. The first bomb exploded on a bus in West Jerusalem, killing 25 people, including the man carrying the bomb. Two American Jewish students were among the dead. Later, an explosion in Ashkelon killed the bomber and a soldier. Hamas, the militant Islamic resistance organization, claimed responsibility, **Feb. 25**, for the bombings, which came in response to the killing of a Hamas leader in Jan., presumably by Israeli agents. Prime Min. Shimon Peres promised to continue peace talks, but he temporarily closed borders between Israel and the Palestinian territories.

### General

**Prince Charles, Princess Diana to Divorce**—The unhappy 15-year marriage of Britain's Prince Charles and Princess Diana came close to its conclusion in Feb. Apparently incompatible, the royal couple had drifted apart, with both admitting to extramarital affairs. The final decision to divorce was apparently reached at a meeting between Charles and Diana, **Feb. 28**. Later that day, a spokeswoman for Diana said she had agreed to a divorce.

## MARCH 1996

### National

**Doctor Present at Suicides Is Acquitted**—Dr. Jack Kevorkian, a retired pathologist who since 1990 had been present at the suicide of 27 persons, was acquitted **Mar. 8** in Michigan of having violating a since-expired state law against doctor-assisted suicides in 1993. Kevorkian testified at the trial, **Mar. 1**, that he had not sought to help patients end their lives, only to help end their suffering, and that he had actually urged patients not to take their lives. When a jury in Pontiac, MI, found him not guilty, this was the 3d acquittal for Kevorkian. He was also awaiting trial in 2 1991 deaths that preceded the state assisted-suicide law but were prosecuted on the basis that assisted suicide violated common laws. (On May 14, in the same court, he was acquitted in that case as well.)

Meanwhile, in San Francisco, **Mar. 6**, the 9th Circuit Court of Appeals struck down a Washington state law prohibiting doctors from helping patients commit suicide. The court held, 8–3, that an individual's right to control the time and manner of his or her death outweighed the state's obligation to preserve life. In response, the American Medical Assn., **Mar. 7**, called doctor-assisted suicide "fundamentally incompatible with the physician's role as healer and caregiver."

**Dole Wraps Up GOP Presidential Nomination**—Sen. Robert Dole (KS), the Senate majority leader, won enough delegates in Mar. to ensure that he would receive the Republican nomination for president at the Aug. GOP convention. Dole's triumph came abruptly, considering that the voting in primaries and caucuses in Feb. had failed to produce a front-runner. In a vote that foreshadowed sentiment in the South, Dole won the **Mar. 2** South Carolina primary with the strong support of the state organization. He led commentator Pat Buchanan, 45% to 29%, with other candidates trailing badly. After winning the Puerto Rico primary, **Mar. 3**, Dole swept 5 New England states, **Mar. 5**, as well as Colorado, Maryland, and Georgia. In Georgia, a state critical to Buchanan, the latter trailed Dole 41% to 29%. On **Mar. 6**, former Gov. Lamar Alexander of Tennessee, who had also counted on a strong Southern showing, withdrew and endorsed Dole. Sen. Dick Lugar (IN) also dropped out, and backed Dole, **Mar. 6**. Magazine publisher Steve Forbes campaigned for an upset in New York, but Dole won handily, again with strong organization support, taking all 93 delegates, **Mar. 7**.

In the so-called Super Tuesday voting in 7 states, including Texas and Florida, on **Mar. 12**, Dole won everywhere and collected 349 of 362 delegates at stake. Forbes, after having spent $25 mil or more of his own money, dropped out, **Mar. 14**, and endorsed Dole. On **Mar. 19**, the senator also won in 4 Great Lakes states—Illinois, Ohio, Michigan, and Wisconsin. He nailed down the nomination, **Mar. 26**, by capturing California's 165 delegates with nearly 1.5 mil votes, 66% of the total cast.

**Stocks Suffer Sharp, Brief Drop in Value**—The stock market slumped dramatically, **Mar. 8**. The Labor Dept. had reported a decline in the unemployment rate, from 5.8% in Jan. to 5.5% in Feb., and also said that 705,000 nonfarm jobs had been created in Feb.—the largest one-month increase in 13 years. Investors apparently concluded from these figures that the economy was heating up and that no further reductions in interest rates would be announced. The Dow Jones industrial average declined by 171.24 points and closed at 5470.45. The decline of 3.04% was the greatest for any trading day since 1991. By **Mar. 18**, the stock market had recovered from the sharp decline 10 days earlier; the Dow Jones industrial average closed that day at an all-time high of 5,683.60.

**Whitewater Trial Opens in Little Rock**—The trial of 3 major figures in the Whitewater affair opened in Little Rock in Mar. The defendants included Gov. Jim Guy Tucker of Arkansas and James and Susan McDougal (by then divorced), who had been partners with then-Gov. Bill Clinton and Hillary Rodham Clinton in the Whitewater Development Corp. The defendants were accused of having borrowed $3 mil under false pretenses from Capital Management, an investment firm that made loans subsidized by the U.S. Small Business Administration, and from Madison Guaranty Savings and Loan, an institution owned by James McDougal that later failed. Ray Jahn, the prosecutor, in his opening argument, **Mar. 11**, called the defendants collaborators in a scheme to enrich themselves through loans for which they were not legally eligible. A panel of the 8th U.S. Circuit Court of Appeals, **Mar. 15**, reinstated a separate indictment against Tucker that had been tossed out by a U.S. district judge in Sept. Judge George Howard, who was presiding at the Little Rock trial, ruled **Mar. 20** that Pres. Clinton could testify by videotape. Attorneys for Susan McDougal had subpoenaed Clinton to testify and rebut charges by David Hale, a former municipal judge who had pleaded guilty to arranging fraudulent loans through Capital Management that had cost the federal government $2 mil. Hale claimed that in 1986 Gov. Clinton had pressured him to make a $300,000 personal loan to Susan McDougal that was misrepresented as a business loan to qualify for federal subsidies. On **Mar. 25**, in Little Rock, U.S. District Judge Stephen Reasoner sentenced Hale to 28 months in prison, fined him $10,000, and ordered him to pay $2.4 mil in restitution.

**Clinton Submits Budget for 1997**—Even though he had not yet reached an agreement with Congress on the 1996 federal budget, Pres. Bill Clinton, **Mar. 19,** submitted his budget for the 1997 fiscal year, which would begin Oct. 1, 1996. Earlier, on **Mar. 12**, to avert a default on government loans, he signed a bill temporarily increasing the federal debt limit of $4.9 tril. In presenting his $1.64 tril 1997 budget to Congress, Clinton said it was on course toward a balanced budget by 2002. The deficit for 1997 was projected at $140 bil. The budget offered tax cuts for middle-class families, tightened business-tax loopholes, and maintained approximate current levels of spending for domestic programs that Clinton had been defending in the 1996 budget debate.

**Tobacco Firm Settles Suits, Agrees to Pay**—The nation's 5th-largest tobacco company reached a settlement in Mar. in a class-action lawsuit against the industry. In doing so, the Liggett Group Inc. broke ranks with the other tobacco companies. Liggett, **Mar. 13**, agreed to contribute 5% of its annual pretax income—to a maximum of $50 mil—for 25 years to programs to help smokers give up their habit. Liggett, **Mar. 15**, also agreed to give 5 states $5 mil plus 2.5% of its pretax profits for 25 years. The states had sued the industry to recover Medicaid costs linked to smoking-related illnesses. On **Mar. 18**, the Food and Drug Administration released affidavits from 3 former employees of Philip Morris Cos. Inc. who charged that the company intentionally used cigarettes as a vehicle for delivering nicotine, a chemical generally recognized as addictive.

**Abortion-Clinic Gunman Found Guilty**—John Salvi 3d, an abortion opponent, was found guilty of murder, **Mar. 18**, in the killing of 2 receptionists and of armed assault with intent to murder in the wounding of 5 other persons at 2 abortion clinics in Brookline, MA, in Dec. 1994. The lawyer for Salvi had contended that the defendant was not guilty by reason of insanity. Superior Court Judge Barbara Dortch-Okara, **Mar. 18**, sentenced Salvi to 2 consecutive life terms without parole, plus 18 to 20 years on the assault charges.

**FBI Surrounds Antitax Group's Farm**—Agents of the Federal Bureau of Investigation began a confrontation, **Mar. 25**, with the Freemen, an antigovernment antitax group in Montana. The Freemen occupied a farm complex near Jordan; some 20 persons, including family members, were thought to be there. Two brothers, Richard and Emmett Clark, had owned the farm and had remained on it after they lost it in a tax foreclosure. Prosecutors had warrants for the arrest of several people at the farm. LeRoy Schweitzer and Daniel Petersen were arrested nearby, **Mar. 25**. They were charged, **Mar. 28**, with making a death threat against a judge. The indictment said that the Freemen had defrauded banks and other companies of $1.8 mil and had held seminars for 800 people on how to conduct fraud.

**Congress Grants President Line-Item Veto**—The Senate, **Mar. 27**, and the House, **Mar. 28**, approved a bill allowing the president to veto parts of a spending bill while approving the rest of the bill. This so-called line-item veto, which passed with the support of most Republicans and some Democrats, had long been promoted by reformers as a means of eliminating "pork" from spending bills. Under the bill the president, like many state governors, could eliminate (though not raise or just reduce) dollar amounts for specific items in a spending bill. Entitlement programs such as Medicare and Social Security were exempt. Broad-based tax cuts would also be exempt, but the president could kill a tax break affecting up to 100 individuals or 10 businesses. Pres. Clinton signed it Apr. 9.

**Congress Backs Overhaul of Farm Subsidies**—The Senate, **Mar. 28**, and the House, **Mar. 29**, approved a bill that would sharply curtail the farm subsidy program. As part of the broadest overhaul in farm subsidies since the 1930s, growers of corn, wheat, rice, and cotton would no longer be paid not to plant these crops. They would receive transition payments that would decline and end in 7 years. The subsidies were designed to prevent large crop surpluses that would in turn cause a plunge in prices. Small farmers were the major beneficiaries of subsidies, and the new approach was seen by some as a potential threat to family farming. The bill also provided $200 mil for restoration of the Florida Everglades. Despite reservations over the elimination of subsidies, Pres. Bill Clinton signed the bill Apr. 4.

**Debt Limit Raised, Social Security Rule Changed**—A bill increasing the federal debt limit to $5.5 trillion was signed by Pres. Bill Clinton **Mar. 29.** The bill included a provision permitting retirees who were 65 to 69 years old to earn more money and still receive full Social Security benefits. Under the previous law, they could earn up to $11,520 and collect full benefits. The new law provided for a gradual increase in that amount until it peaked at $30,000 in 2002.

**2d Gingrich Violation of House Rules Cited**—The House Ethics Committee concluded, for the 2d time in 3 months, that Speaker Newt Gingrich (R, GA) had violated House rules. In a letter to Gingrich, **Mar. 29**, the committee said that the activities in Gingrich's office of a wealthy Republican donor with financial interests in cable television and Internet "were not provided as part of a clearly defined education program," as required by the rules. The committee did not recommend any penalty.

## International

**Serb General Charged With War Crimes**—The UN International War Crimes Tribunal, **Mar. 1**, charged Gen. Djordje Djukic of the Bosnian Serb army with war crimes. The tribunal's prosecutor, Judge Richard Goldstone, alleged, **Mar. 1**, that Djukic had coordinated the bombardment of civilians in Sarajevo during the siege of the capital by Serb forces. Djukic, who had been captured by Bosnian government troops in Jan., pleaded not guilty, **Mar. 4**. The government of Bosnia and Herzegovina, **Mar. 19**, completed the process of taking control of the suburbs surrounding the capital of Sarajevo. Under the peace treaty, the capital area was to be in the hands of the Muslim-dominated government. Djukic, Apr. 24, was released from UN custody after doctors concluded that he was near death from pancreatic cancer; he died in Belgrade, May 18.

**Law Tightens Embargo Against Cuba**—Pres. Bill Clinton, **Mar. 12,** signed a bill that strengthened the U.S. economic embargo against Cuba. Earlier, on **Mar. 2**, supporters of Brothers to the Rescue, the group of Cuban exile aviators, organized a flotilla of 35 boats to honor the pilots who were killed when their planes were downed by Cuban jets in Feb. In Miami, 60,000 gathered to remember the pilots. The embargo bill, enacted in response to the Feb. incident, denied U.S. entry visas to executives of companies that trafficked in property expropriated by the Communist government in Cuba after 1959. The law also allowed U.S. citizens to sue, in U.S. courts, foreigners who trafficked in such properties.

**33 More Die in Israel in Suicide Attacks**—Suicide bombers from Hamas, the radical Palestinian organization, took another heavy toll of life in Israel in Mar. A bomb that exploded on a bus in West Jerusalem, **Mar. 3**, killed 19. Prime Min. Shimon Peres of Israel said that barricades would be built between Israel and the Palestine territories to deter Islamic militants from entering Israel. A communiqué purportedly from the Hamas leadership, **Mar. 3**, said that the bombing was the last retaliation for the killing of a Hamas leader in Jan. But then, on **Mar. 4**, a bomb exploded at a shopping mall in Tel Aviv, killing 14. The 2 bombers were among the total of 33 victims.

Leaders from 27 countries, meeting in Cairo, **Mar. 13**, reaffirmed their support for the Arab–Israeli peace process. They pledged to work together to prevent terrorists from raising funds, recruiting members, and trafficking in arms. Attendees included Peres, Pres. Bill Clinton, Pres. Boris Yeltsin of Russia, Prime Min. John Major of Britain, Chancellor Helmut Kohl of Germany, Pres. Jacques Chirac of France, Pres. Hosni Mubarak of Egypt, and King Hussein of Jordan. Yasir Arafat, head of the Palestinian National Authority, also attended. In Israel, **Mar. 14**, Clinton pledged to give the Israelis $100 mil for training and technical assistance to fight terrorism.

**Rabin's Assassin Receives Life Sentence**—Yigal Amir, who had shot and killed Prime Min. Yitzhak Rabin of Israel in Nov. 1995, was found fit to stand trial and, on **Mar. 27**, was found guilty of premeditated murder. Amir had acknowledged shooting Rabin, but said that he would have been satisfied if the prime minister had only been injured and forced from office. He said his goal was to stop the peace process between Israel and the Palestinians. In handing down its verdict, a 3-judge panel in Tel Aviv District Court also sentenced Amir to prison for life.

**Spanish Parliamentary Election Inconclusive**—The voting in Spain's parliamentary election, **Mar. 3**, left in doubt who would be the country's next prime minister. Felipe Gonzalez, who had led the government since 1982, had suffered a loss of public support because of corruption scandals and an economic slump. In the voting, the conservative Popular Party of Jose Maria Aznar won 156 seats in the 350-member lower house of parliament, to 141 for the ruling Socialist Party. Aznar began negotiations in an effort to form a majority.

**China Seeks to Intimidate Taiwan**—China resorted to military means in Mar. in an apparent effort to intimidate Taiwan in advance of the island's first direct presidential election. China had made known its displeasure with Pres. Lee Teng-hui, who was seeking reelection, and had been especially irritated by Lee's visit to the U.S. in 1995. On **Mar. 8**, China fired 3 unarmed missiles at targets in waters off 2 Taiwanese port cities. U.S. Sec. of State Warren Christopher said, **Mar. 10**, that the U.S. would move a naval battle group nearer to Taiwan. On **Mar. 12**, China began naval exercises off the coast of Taiwan that utilized live firing, and China fired another missile into water near a Taiwanese port **Mar. 13**. The U.S., **Mar. 19**, approved a request from Taiwan to purchase surface-to-air missiles. On **Mar. 23**, Lee was reelected, winning 54% of the vote in a 4-way contest. By **Mar. 24**, 2 U.S. aircraft carrier battle groups, one from the Persian Gulf, arrived in waters around Taiwan. On **Mar. 25**, China announced that its military exercises in the Taiwan Strait had been completed.

**Northern Ireland Peace Plan Proposed**— Prime Min. John Major of Britain, **Mar. 21**, announced a plan for the election of negotiators from Northern Ireland, or Ulster, who would participate in all-party talks on the future of the province. The Irish government, **Mar. 22**, gave its qualified support to the plan, but the Irish Republican Army, **Mar. 22**, rejected it. Meanwhile, the IRA, which had abandoned its cease-fire in Feb., claimed responsibility for a bomb that exploded in West London, **Mar. 9**. No one was injured.

**"Mad Cow Disease" Alarms Britain**—A report released by the British government **Mar. 20** raised serious questions about the safety of beef consumption in Britain. After 10 teenagers and young adults were stricken with a variant of the rare Creutzfeldt-Jakob Disease, the government ordered the inquiry to determine any relationship between it and bovine spongiform encephalopathy, or "mad cow disease." The report concluded that beef consumption was the most likely cause for the human infections. Five European nations, **Mar. 21**, banned importation of British beef. Other countries soon joined the list. McDonald's announced, **Mar. 24**, that it would no longer sell British meat at its British restaurants. The European Commission, executive body of the European Union, banned, worldwide, the export of British beef products, **Mar. 27**. Britain, **Mar. 28**, banned the sale domestically of all beef from cattle that were more than 30 months old and barred the feeding of meat and bonemeal to cattle—a suspected cause of the spread of the disease.

## General

**16 Kindergarten Children, Teacher Shot to Death**—A gun collector who reportedly was angry because he had not been reinstated as a Boy Scout leader opened fire on a kindergarten class in a school gymnasium in Dunblane, Scotland, **Mar. 13**, killing 16 children and their teacher, while wounding many others. He then shot himself fatally. Of the 29 children, only one escaped injury. The killer, Thomas Hamilton, used 4 hand guns, which were licensed. Queen Elizabeth and Princess Anne visited the town to **Mar. 17**, to offer sympathy to the injured children and to relatives of those killed.

**Brothers Guilty of Killing Parents**—Two California brothers who had shot their wealthy parents to death in 1989 were convicted of murder **Mar. 20.** The brothers, Lyle and Erik Menendez, had initially denied killing Jose Menendez, an entertainment executive, and Kitty Menendez, but they were eventually arrested and charged with having committed the crimes in order to obtain their inheritance. During their first trials, conducted separately, the brothers admitted the killings, but contended they had acted in response to years of sexual and emotional abuse. Both trials ended in hung juries in 1994. But in a single retrial in a Van Nuys, CA, superior court, Lyle and Erik—now 28 and 25, respectively—were found guilty of first-degree murder. The jury, Apr. 17, recommended that they be sentenced to prison for life without parole; the judge was bound by the recommendation.

# APRIL 1996

## National

**Leading Economic Indicators up Sharply**—The Conference Board, a business-research organization, reported, **Apr. 2**, that the leading economic indicators had jumped 1.3% in Feb., the largest increase in 20 years. The Labor Dept. reported, **Apr. 5**, that 140,000 nonfarm jobs had been created in Mar., but the unemployment rate had edged upward to 5.6%, from 5.5% in Feb. The trade deficit declined in Feb. to $8.19 bil, the Commerce Dept. reported **Apr. 23**.

**Commerce Secretary Among 35 Dead in Crash**—U.S. Commerce Secretary Ron Brown was killed **Apr. 3**, when the U.S. Air Force jet in which he was flying crashed into a mountain in bad weather near Dubrovnik, Croatia. All 35 on the plane, including other government officials and business leaders, were killed. One crew member survived the crash but died en route to a hospital.

Brown became chairman of the Democratic National Committee in 1989, the first black to head a major party, and helped Bill Clinton win the presidency in 1992. As secretary of commerce since 1993, he had traveled the world, helping win contracts for U.S. companies. It was while on such a trip, to get U.S. contracts for the rebuilding of the war-torn Balkans, that he died.

On **Apr. 12**, Clinton named U.S. trade representative Mickey Kantor to succeed Brown as commerce secretary. This "recess appointment," made while Congress was not in session, allowed Kantor to serve until the end of 1996 before he would need approval by the Senate.

**Ex-Professor Is Suspect in Unabomber Case**—On **Apr. 3**, federal agents seized a former college professor at his cabin in a remote area of western Montana. They believed that he was the notorious Unabomber, though at first, on **Apr. 4**, he was charged only with possessing components for a "destructive device." The Unabomb case—so named because the bomber's initial targets were universities and airlines—dated back as far as 1978. Since then the bomber's mailed explosives had killed 3 people and injured 23 others. The bomber was an opponent of modern technology, and in 1995 the *Washington Post* had published his 35,000-word manifesto on that subject in return for a promise that he would curtail future acts of violence.

The man seized in Montana, Theodore Kaczynski, had received degrees in mathematics from Harvard and the University of Michigan and had taught math at the University of California–Berkeley until abruptly leaving in 1969. Kaczynski's brother, David, thought that some of Theodore's writings resembled those of the Unabomber, and notified the FBI. Authorities said they had found 2 live bombs and bomb-making manuals in Kaczynski's cabin. On **Apr. 7**, they said that hotel records showed he had been in Sacramento, CA, on days when bombs were mailed from there. On **Apr. 12**, the authorities reported finding the manuscript of the bomber's manifesto.

**Rostenkowski Pleads Guilty to 2 Charges**—Dan Rostenkowski, former congressman from Illinois and former chairman of the House Ways and Means Committee, pleaded guilty, **Apr. 9**, in U.S. District Court, to 2 counts of mail fraud. Indicted on 17 charges in 1994, Rostenkowski had been accused of crimes that included padding his payroll with employees who did little work, buying gifts with money from his expense account, and attempting to obstruct justice. In exchange for his guilty pleas, the prosecution dropped the other charges. Judge Norma Johnson, **Apr. 9**, fined Rostenkowski $100,000 and sentenced him to 17 months in prison. Rostenkowski told reporters he had been punished for behavior that was routine in Congress.

**Clinton Vetoes Bill on "Partial-Birth" Abortions**—On **Apr. 10**, Pres. Bill Clinton vetoed a bill that would have banned so-called partial-birth abortions. In this late-term procedure, the fetus is killed by crushing its skull or suctioning out its brains after the head has emerged from the birth canal. Clinton said that the procedure was important for a small but vulnerable number of women—"just a few hundred"—each year and that he would have supported a ban that made an exception for cases in which the mother's health was at risk. Reflecting the views of abortion opponents, who strongly denounced the veto, Sen. Robert Dole (KS) said that the procedure "blurs the line between abortion and infanticide."

**President Clinton Testifies on Whitewater**—Pres. Bill Clinton provided testimony in Apr. in the trial of Gov. Jim Guy Tucker of Arkansas and James and Susan McDougal, who faced charges related to the Whitewater affair. Earlier, in testimony concluding **Apr. 11**, former Judge David Hale, who had pleaded guilty to fraud, testified that in 1986 then-Gov. Clinton had pressured him to make a fraudulent $300,000 loan to Susan McDougal. Hale owned Capital Management Services, which could make business loans subsidized by the Small Business Administration. Clinton publicly denied Hale's allegations. In the White House, **Apr. 28**, Clinton also testified on videotape for 3½ hours as a defense witness. The text was not made public.

**Congress Approves Bill to Fight Terrorists**—The Senate, **Apr. 17**, and the House, **Apr. 18**, approved a bill aimed at terrorism in the U.S. It provided $1 bil, over 4 years, to combat terrorism. The government could deny entry to foreigners who were members of terrorist groups. Fundraisers for, and contributors to, terrorist groups could face prosecution. Opportunities for death-row inmates to utilize the habeas corpus process, seeking federal review of convictions, would be curtailed. Pres. Bill Clinton signed the bill **Apr. 24**.

**Impasse Over 1996 Budget Finally Ends**—On **Apr. 25**, with only about 5 months left in the 1996 fiscal year, Congress finally approved a spending bill for the rest of the year that Pres. Bill Clinton could accept. The $159.4 bil omnibus bill covered the executive departments—all but 5—whose budgets had not been approved already. Although the measure abolished 200 federal programs, in many cases with Clinton's support, funding for departments dealing with domestic affairs was approved at a far higher level than the Republicans had wanted. The bill kept $400 mil for the AmeriCorps national service program and $350 mil for Goals 2000 education initiatives; the GOP had wanted to kill both of these Clinton projects. The bill also funded the president's plan to put 100,000 additional police on the streets; Republicans had wanted to give the states block grants to spend on crime as they chose.

With respect to the environment, the bill ended a GOP-supported moratorium on listing endangered species, preserved the power of the Environmental Protection Agency to nullify permits to drain wetlands, granted new funds to clean up toxic waste sites, and allowed the president to stop implementation of accelerated logging in the nation's only temperate rain forest, the Tongass National Forest in Alaska. As part of the bill, the Republicans agreed to rescind a recent policy requiring that the military services discharge anyone infected with the virus that causes AIDS. Clinton signed the bill **Apr. 26**.

**Rise in Cost of Gas Stirs Political Response**—Drivers were fuming in Apr. as gasoline prices rose to their highest levels in 5 years. The average increase in just 2 months had been 12%, but gas had gone up 21% in California. The runup was attributed to increased demand, the growing popularity of vehicles that were not fuel efficient, and greater highway speeds following repeal of the federal speed limit. On **Apr. 26**, Sen. Robert Dole (R, KS), the prospective Republican nominee for president, called for repeal of the 4.3-cents-per-gallon gasoline tax that Congress had approved in 1993 as part of the Clinton administration's deficit-reduction package. Pres. Bill Clinton said, **Apr. 29**, that he had approved the sale of 12 mil barrels of oil from the nation's Strategic Petroleum Reserve, in a move to bring down prices.

## International

**Britain Plans Massive Slaughter of Cows**—In an attempt to rid the country of the so-called mad cow disease, which had been linked to a serious though rare disease in humans, Britain, on **Apr. 1**, proposed to slaughter hundreds of thousands of cows and asked the European Union for financial support. The EU, **Apr. 3**, said it would cover 70% of the cost. British Agriculture Minister Douglas Hogg insisted, **Apr. 16**, that British beef was safe to eat. The EU told Britain, **Apr. 30**, that the worldwide ban on British beef would be lifted gradually as the slaughter of cattle got underway. On Sept. 19, however, the British government, citing a study that disputed the necessity of large-scale slaughter, announced it would not carry out the plan, though officials indicated that a smaller number of cows considered most vulnerable to the disease might be culled. The EU vowed to continue the ban on beef as long as Britain declined to carry out the plan.

**Foreigners Flee Strife in Liberia**—Monrovia, the capital of Liberia, was caught up in Apr. in the civil strife that had plagued the country for years. Since 1989, the conflict had claimed 150,000 lives. The factions had agreed on a peace plan in 1995. Fighting began in the capital, **Apr. 6**, after the Council of State ordered the arrest on murder charges of D. Roosevelt Johnson, one of the factional leaders, who had recently been ousted as minister of rural development. The U.S. military, **Apr. 9**, began evacuating U.S. citizens and other foreign nationals, but the helicopter flights were suspended temporarily after the copters were fired upon, **Apr. 10**. U.S. forces, **Apr. 11**, turned back Liberian rebels who had broken into the U.S. Embassy's housing annex. Up to 20,000 Liberian civilians took refuge in the annex. Pres. Bill Clinton, **Apr. 11**, sent 1,500 Marines to the Liberian coast. As looting spread in the capital, **Apr. 12**, and cholera and other diseases began to proliferate, representatives of the Red Cross and the UN pulled out. Helicopter flights were halted, **Apr. 14**, after 500 Americans and 1,100 other foreigners had been evacuated. A cease-fire was announced, **Apr. 18**. The first contingent of Marines arrived off the coast, **Apr. 20**, and numbered 5,000 by **Apr. 23**. Returning fire, U.S. Marines shot and killed 3 Liberians near the American Embassy, **Apr. 30**.

**Israeli Retaliation Takes Heavy Toll**—Israel struck back in Apr. at Hezbollah guerrillas who had been shelling settlements in northern Israel. The retaliation, begun **Apr. 11**, and known by the Israelis as Operation Grapes of Wrath, killed many civilians. By **Apr. 13**, Israeli warships positioned off the coast had imposed a virtual blockade of Lebanon. On **Apr. 13**, rockets fired by an Israeli helicopter struck an ambulance and killed 6 civilians, including 4 children. On **Apr. 18**, Israeli artillery shells struck a UN refugee camp near Tyre, killing more than 100 civilians and wounding about 100. The refugees had sought protection from Israeli attacks. Israel said it had targeted guerrillas several hundred yards from the camp. Also on **Apr. 18**, an air strike near Nabatiye al-Fawqa destroyed an apartment building and killed 11 people. Prime Min. Shimon Peres of Israel, who, it was said, had launched the retaliatory campaign to show his firmness prior to the Israeli election in May, said, **Apr. 18**, that he would now accept a cease-fire from Hezbollah. Syria, which had 35,000 troops in Lebanon, was seen as being influential in determining what happened next in the area. Israel and Lebanon, **Apr. 26**, announced a cease-fire agreement "in consultation with Syria." In Washington, **Apr. 30**, Peres and Pres. Bill Clinton signed an antiterrorism agreement that committed their countries to closer cooperation on security matters.

**Clinton Meets Leaders of South Korea and Japan**—Pres. Bill Clinton visited South Korea and Japan, **Apr. 16-18**, signing agreements with both nations. In South Korea, **Apr. 16**, Clinton and Pres. Kim Young Sam proposed that the 2 Koreas, China, and the U.S. undertake talks aimed at reaching a permanent peace agreement; no treaty had ever been signed formally concluding the Korean War. Prior to Pres. Clinton's Far East trip, the U.S. and Japan reached an agreement over the U.S. occupation of the Japanese island of Okinawa. The Japanese had long resented the presence of U.S. troops on Japanese soil, and tensions had grown in late 1995 after 3 American servicemen had raped a 12-year-old girl in Okinawa. The 3 had later been sentenced to prison. Prime Min. Ryutaro Hashimoto and U.S. Ambassador Walter Mondale announced, **Apr. 12**, that the Futenma Marine Corps Air Station would be returned to Japan, and the 2 countries, **Apr. 15**, signed an agreement under which all or part of 11 Okinawan military installations would be returned to Japan within 7 years. In Tokyo, **Apr. 17**, Clinton and Hashimoto signed a declaration on joint security. The U.S. said it would maintain its force of 100,000 troops in the Far East, and Japan, which had contended that its participation in any joint military operation would violate its constitution, agreed to review its role in the event that fighting involving U.S. troops broke out. Addressing the Japanese Diet (parliament), **Apr. 18**, Clinton urged Japan to continue to lower its trade barriers. He said Americans profoundly regretted the assault on the girl in Okinawa.

**Militants Kill 17 Greek Tourists in Egypt**—Islamic militants wielding automatic weapons shot and killed 17 Greek tourists at a hotel near the pyramids in Giza, Egypt, **Apr. 18**. A hotel employee was also killed, and 15 tourists were wounded. The Muslim Brotherhood, Egypt's largest Islamic organization, denounced the attack, **Apr. 18**. The Gamaa al-Islamiya, **Apr. 20**, claimed responsibility. The act was the worst yet since the fundamentalists had begun attacking tourists as a means of undermining the secular government of Egypt.

**Yeltsin Hosts Industrial Nations' Leaders**—Leaders of the world's 7 wealthiest industrial nations went to Moscow in Apr. as guests of Pres. Boris Yeltsin of Russia. They focused on issues relating to nuclear weapons and nuclear power. Yeltsin, **Apr. 19**, backed the Group of 7 nations' call for a comprehensive nuclear test ban; the G-7 nations and Russia, **Apr. 20**, called for an international treaty to be ready for signing by Sept. Yeltsin agreed to cooperate with worldwide efforts to prevent weapons-grade nuclear material from being smuggled from the nations of the former Soviet Union. Radical nations and terrorists, it was feared, had been exploiting the chaos that followed the collapse of the Soviet Union to secure such material. Clinton, **Apr. 21**, met privately with Yeltsin and then with Gennadi Zyuganov, the Communist Party's presidential candidate in the June election.

**Italian Political Pendulum Swings to Left**—The Olive Tree coalition, a left-of-center alliance, comprised most prominently of former Communists in the Democratic Party of the Left, won 284 of 630 seats in Italy's Chamber of Deputies, the lower house of parliament, on **Apr. 21.** The more conservative Freedom Alliance, led by Forza Italia, won 246 seats.

**Mystery Surrounds Fate of 2 Chechen Leaders**—Pres. Dzhokhar Dudayev of Russia's breakaway republic of Chechnya was reportedly killed, **Apr. 21**, but the manner of his death, assuming that it had occurred at all, could not be confirmed. As Russian forces pounded Chechen positions, in an apparent violation of a cease-fire, Chechens said, **Apr. 24**, that Dudayev had been killed when a Russian rocket struck his jeep. The rebels claimed that the rocket had homed in on the jeep when Dudayev was using his cellular phone to talk with a Russian mediator acting as a decoy. The Russian commander in Chechnya denied any role by his troops in Dudayev's death. Outside Chechnya, speculation lingered that he had died in factional fighting among Chechens, or that he had faked his death and was in hiding. In any event, he was succeeded by Zelimkhan Yandarbiyev. On **Apr. 29** the official Russian news agency said Yandarbiyev himself had been killed during factional fighting among the rebels, but another news agency reported that he was still alive.

**Palestinians Drop Vow to Destroy Israel**—In 1995, as the peace process in the Middle East moved forward, Palestinian leader Yasir Arafat had promised that clauses in the Palestine National Council's charter calling for guerrilla warfare against Israel and for its destruction would be rescinded. The Council, meeting in Gaza City, **Apr. 24**, voted, 504 to 54, to delete the clauses. Although the Palestinian leadership had long made clear that it no longer favored Israel's demise, Prime Min. Shimon Peres of Israel hailed the official vote as representing an important step.

## General

**Kentucky Wins NCAA Basketball Title**—The University of Kentucky Wildcats won their 6th national college basketball championship **Apr. 1**. Only UCLA had won more often. The semifinals and final, involving 4 regional winners, were played in East Rutherford, NJ. One semifinal game, Mar. 30, paired Massachusetts and Kentucky, ranked 1st and 2d during the regular season, and the Wildcats prevailed, 81-74. In the other semifinal, Syracuse defeated Mississippi State, 77–69. In the final, **Apr. 1**, Kentucky set a title-game record by hitting 12 three-point shots. The Wildcats led underdog Syracuse only 64–62 with 4:46 to go, but pulled away to win, 76–67, and finished the season at 34–2. Kentucky's senior guard Tony Delk, who scored 24 points in the final, was named the tournament's most outstanding player.

**Plane Crash Kills 7-Year-Old Pilot**—A 7-year-old girl who was trying to become the youngest person ever to pilot a plane across the U.S. was killed **Apr. 11** when her plane crashed. Because of the concern that ever-younger and unqualified persons might seek to pilot planes, the *Guinness Book of Records* and the U.S. government had stopped recording such achievements. The girl, Jessica Dubroff, accompanied by her father, Lloyd Dubroff, and a flight instructor, Joe Reid, had taken off from Half Moon Bay, CA, on **Apr. 10**, in a single-engine Cessna equipped with dual controls. The 3-day trip was to end in Falmouth, MA. After a first-night stop in Cheyenne, WY, the plane took off **Apr. 11**, from the Cheyenne airport while heavy rain, sleet, and gusty winds were occurring in the vicinity. The Cessna quickly stalled and nose-dived into a residential area of the city. All 3 on board were killed.

**Jacqueline Onassis Auction Brings $34 Mil**—An auction of some 5,900 items owned by former First Lady Jacqueline Kennedy Onassis created great excitement in Apr. Mrs. Onassis had died in 1994, and the property was put up for sale by her children, John F. Kennedy Jr. and Caroline Kennedy Schlossberg. The auction house, Sotheby's Holdings, Inc., had made a $5 mil estimate for all the lots, which included works of art and everyday items, but interest in owning a memento from the Camelot period of American history drove prices far higher. Some 2,000 persons attended the auction in New York, **Apr. 23–26**, and thousands of bids were phoned in and mailed in. The highest bid was $2.4 mil, for a 40-carat diamond ring that the Greek shipping owner, Aristotle Onassis, had given to his future bride. Actor Arnold Schwarzenegger, husband of Maria Shriver, niece of former Pres. John F. Kennedy, won a set of the former president's golf clubs with a bid of $772,500. The Louis XVI mahogany desk at which Kennedy signed the nuclear test-ban treaty went for $1,432,500. A rocking chair of the type favored by the president, who had a bad back, sold for $453,500. All together, the lots brought in more than $34 mil.

**Gunman Kills 35 in Tasmania**—A man carrying a semiautomatic rifle opened fire in a crowded cafe in Port Arthur, in the Australian state of Tasmania, **Apr. 28**. After fatally shooting 20 people there, he killed 12 more at a nearby tourist attraction, the ruins of a colonial prison. He then took 3 hostages, set afire the cottage in which he held them, **Apr. 29**, and fled from the flames. The hostages also died, bringing the death toll to 35; 18 were injured. Police apprehended Martin Bryant, who was initially charged with one count of murder, **Apr. 30**; he was described as a loner with mental problems.

# MAY 1996

## National

**Economic Indicators Point to Resurgence**—The Conference Board, a business-research organization, reported, **May 1**, that the leading economic indicators had risen 0.2% in Mar. Of greater interest, the indicators had risen for 2 consecutive months, for the first time since 1994. The Labor Dept. said, **May 3**, that unemployment in Apr. had declined to 5.4%, the lowest in 14 months, from 5.6% in Mar. The department reported, **May 10**, that prices charged by manufacturers and farmers for finished goods had risen 0.4% in Apr. It said, **May 14**, that consumer prices had also risen 0.4% in Apr. The Commerce Dept. announced, **May 17**, that the trade deficit was at $8.92 bil in Mar. On Wall Street, **May 22**, the Dow Jones industrial average closed at an all-time high of 5,778.00. The Commerce Dept. said, **May 30**, that the economy had grown at an annual rate of 2.3% in the first quarter.

**Clinton Vetoes Limit on Punitive Damages**—Pres. Bill Clinton, **May 2**, vetoed a bill that would have limited punitive damages in product-liability cases to either $250,000 or twice the compensatory damage award, whichever was greater.

**Republicans Unveil Budget Plan for 1997**—Republican leaders in Congress, **May 8**, presented their proposal for the federal budget for the 1997 fiscal year. Although it aimed to produce a balanced budget by 2002, it differed from earlier GOP proposals by calling for smaller cuts in taxes and social spending. Cuts in discretionary spending over 6 years were put at $295 bil, lower than the previous GOP proposal of $348 bil, but still above the $228 bil in cuts supported by Pres. Bill Clinton. The proposal included a $500-per-child tax credit for families earning up to $110,000. Clinton said the Republicans were moving in the right direction. The House, **May 16**, rejected the president's 1997 budget plan, 117-304, and then approved the Republican plan, 226-195. The Senate, in a party-line vote of 53-46, **May 23**, approved a similar plan. The proposals approved by the House and Senate were, in effect, blueprints for the detailed crafting of departmental budgets, and were not going to Clinton for his approval.

**Clinton Legal Ploy in Sex Case Draws GOP Attack**—A panel of the U.S. Court of Appeals in St. Louis, **May 8**, refused, 2–1, to allow further delay in the trial proceedings in a sexual harassment case against Pres. Bill Clinton by Paula Corbin Jones, a former Arkansas state employee. In a brief filed, **May 15**, with the Supreme Court, the president's attorneys contended that "absent exceptional circumstances," a president in office should not have to submit to civil suits. The Supreme Court, June 24, agreed to hear Clinton's appeal; the practical political effect of the ruling was that the case would not come to trial at least prior to the Nov. election.

**Florida Crash Fatal to 110 Raises Questions**—A commercial jet crash in May that killed all 110 aboard provoked questions and much debate over the safety of air travel. The plane, a DC-9 operated by ValuJet, a small but growing regional airline offering deeply discounted fares, plunged into an Everglades swamp 20 miles northwest of Miami International Airport, **May 11**. The plane was en route from Miami to Atlanta. A few minutes after takeoff, the copilot reported that the cockpit and cabin were filled with smoke. Soon thereafter, the plane hit the surface, angled almost straight down, and disappeared under water and mud. The pilot, Candalyn Kubeck, was the first female captain to be killed in a U.S. commercial jet crash.

Salvage operations were handicapped by the presence of alligators and poisonous snakes and the threat of contamination from leaking jet fuel. The flight-data recorder was found, **May 13**. It was reported, **May 15**, that evidence indicated that there had been a fire and, possibly, an explosion. The cockpit voice recorder was recovered, **May 26**, and investigators said that the tapes supported their belief that a fire in the cargo hold had played a part in the crash.

ValuJet, whose fares were a fraction of those charged by the major airlines, was one of many small discount carriers that had sprung up in recent years. Its fleet of planes was older than that of the major carriers, and the plane that crashed was 27 years old. Because of safety problems, it had returned to airports 7 times in the past 2 years. To save money, ValuJet utilized outside contractors to handle plane maintenance. The Federal Aviation Administration was currently investigating the airline.

**Dole to Leave Senate to Campaign**—Sen. Robert Dole (KS), who had locked up the 1996 Republican presidential nomination, announced in May that he would leave the Senate in order to concentrate on his campaign against Pres. Bill Clinton. Dole came to Washington in 1961, first serving in the House for 8 years. Elected to the Senate in 1968, he had been reelected 4 times. The Republican Senate leader since 1985, Dole had held that position longer than anyone else, and had been majority leader twice (1985–87 and 1995–96). Known as a legislative craftsman, Dole often got complex legislation passed as a result of negotiation and compromise. He had hoped his leadership role in Congress would enhance his presidential bid, but he became ensnarled in disputes with Democrats on Capitol Hill and with the White House, and he trailed Clinton badly in current polls. In announcing, **May 15**, that he would resign officially within a month, Dole said he had an obligation to the people "to leave behind all the trappings of power" and campaign as a private citizen. Clinton praised Dole's record of service. Sen. Christopher Dodd (CT), general chairman of the Democratic Party, said Dole was departing because the public disapproved of what the Republican Congress was doing. Gov. Bill Graves of Kansas, a Republican, said, **May 24**, that he would appoint Lt. Gov. Sheila Frahm to replace Dole in the Senate.

**Top Admiral Commits Suicide**—Adm. Jeremy Boorda, Chief of Naval Operations, the highest-ranking admiral in the Navy, took his life with a pistol outside his home in Washington, DC, in May. Boorda, the first Naval chief to begin his career as an enlisted man, had risen through the ranks during 40 years of service. Bill Clinton named him the Navy's top admiral in 1994. In 1995, the National Security News Service sought information concerning 2 Vietnam combat decorations that Boorda wore. Doubts were raised about whether he had been in a combat zone and under fire, and Boorda then stopped wearing the decorations. On **May 16**, Boorda was told that *Newsweek* wanted to question him about the decorations. He then left his office, and took his life a little later.

**Clinton, Dole Advocate Welfare Reform**—Debate over the nation's welfare policies heated up in May. Pres. Bill Clinton, **May 18**, spoke favorably of a welfare plan proposed by Wisconsin, in which cash payments would be replaced by job training and placement programs, utilizing federal welfare funds. Those who didn't get jobs would be paid for community work. Sen. Robert Dole (KS), **May 21**, called for distribution of money for welfare to the states in lump-sum payments, or block grants; the states could then make most decisions on the use of the money. Dole said his plan would also probably include these elements: individuals would generally be limited to 5 years on welfare; healthy recipients would have to find jobs within 2 years in order to continue getting benefits; states could deny benefits to unmarried teen-age mothers; illegal immigrants would be denied most benefits.

**House Acts on Gas Tax, Minimum Wage**—Responding to a runup in the cost of gasoline at the pump, the House, **May 21**, voted, 301–108, to repeal temporarily the 4.3 cents-per-gallon increase in the gasoline tax that the Clinton administration had pushed through in 1993. In an agreement between leaders of the 2 parties and the White House, Republicans, in turn, allowed an increase in the minimum wage to pass, **May 23**, 281–144. Under the House bill, supported by 93 Republicans, the minimum wage would rise from $4.25 to $5.15 an hour.

**Tobacco Industry Wins Round in Legal Fight**—On **May 23**, in New Orleans, a 3-judge panel of the 5th U.S. Circuit Court of Appeals unanimously invalidated a huge class-action lawsuit against 7 tobacco companies and the Tobacco Institute. The plaintiffs, represented by almost 60 law firms, alleged that the defendants had concealed evidence that smoking was addictive and had manipulated nicotine levels in tobacco products. The panel held that there were too many differences in the circumstances of the plaintiffs and too many conflicts in state laws for the case to proceed. The suit would continue, limited to Diane Castano, for whom the so-called Castano case had been named, and 3 other original plaintiffs.

**Clintons' Whitewater Partners Convicted**—James McDougal and Susan McDougal, former business partners of Bill and Hillary Rodham Clinton, were convicted **May 28** of fraud and conspiracy. Gov. Jim Guy Tucker (D) of Arkansas was convicted of similar charges by the same jury. The McDougals and the Clintons had been partners in the Whitewater Development Corp. in the 1980s, while Bill Clinton was governor. James McDougal then owned Madison Guaranty Savings and Loan. The prosecution contended that the defendants, seeking to enrich themselves, had issued $3 mil in fraudulent loans. David Hale, who had owned Capital Management Services, had pleaded guilty to making fraudulent loans, and had testified that Gov. Clinton had pressured him to make a fraudulent loan to Susan McDougal. Pres. Clinton, in taped testimony for the McDougal-Tucker trial, denied Hale's assertions. Taxpayers covered losses suffered by the 2 companies. James McDougal was convicted by the federal jury in Little Rock of 18 counts of conspiracy, fraud, and making false statements; Susan McDougal of 4 counts of mail fraud, making false statements, and misapplication of funds; and Tucker of one count each of conspiracy and mail fraud. Tucker said, **May 28**, that he would resign as governor. The defendants said they would appeal.

## International

**Spain Gets New Premier**—Jose Maria Aznar was approved by parliament as the new premier of Spain, **May 4**. His Popular Party had won a plurality of seats in the Mar. general election, but his premiership was not assured until he received the backing of the Catalan nationalist party. King Juan Carlos swore in Aznar, **May 5**. The new premier had been elected to parliament in 1982, and worked to break the Popular Party's ties to Franco and move it toward the center. He became his party's leader in 1989.

**Report Critical of Israel in Lethal Shelling**—A report sponsored by the UN was sharply critical of Israel for its Apr. artillery attack on a UN base in southern Lebanon that killed more than 100 civilians. Israel said, **May 5**, that gunners relying on outdated maps had fired on the base by mistake. The UN report, issued **May 7** by European military experts, did not specifically accuse Israel of having knowingly fired on civilians, but stated it was unlikely that mistakes had led to the shelling of the compound.

**New Indian Government Lasts Only 2 Weeks**—Inconclusive results in a national parliamentary election led to governmental chaos in India in May. The voting, which had ended **May 7**, constituted a stinging rebuff for the long-dominant Congress (I) Party of Prime Min. P. V. Narisimha Rao, which won only 135 seats. Rao was under a bribery investigation. The Bharatiya Janata Party, which supported establishment of India as a Hindu state, won 185 seats, but that was far short of a majority in the 545-seat lower house of parliament. Rao resigned, **May 10**, and Pres. Shankar Dayal Sharma, **May 15**, asked the BJP to form a new coalition government. Sharma, **May 16**, swore in BJP Pres. Atal Behari Vajpayee as prime minister. Vajpayee, was considered a comparative moderate in the BJP leadership, which had a reputation for hostility toward India's Muslims and for opposition to economic liberalization and the presence of multinational corporations in India. Vajpayee announced an interim cabinet, **May 16**. However, on **May 28**, facing defeat on a vote of confidence motion, he resigned. Sharma immediately asked H. D. Deve Gowda, a member of the centrist Janata Dai Party, to attempt to form a new government.

**South Africa Adopts Permanent Constitution**—The Constitutional Assembly in South Africa, **May 8**, approved a new constitution to replace the 1993 interim constitution. Under the interim charter, which ended the era of racial separation, or apartheid, the leading black and white parties had joined in a coalition government. The new constitution's bill of rights banned discrimination on the basis of race, gender, age, marital status, pregnancy, and sexual orientation. All citizens were guaranteed freedom of speech, movement, and political activity, as well as adequate housing, food, health care, and education. Deputy Pres. F. W. de Klerk, who had led the last white government, announced, **May 9**, that his National Party, while supporting the new constitution, would pull out of the ruling coalition and go into opposition.

**Clinton Backs Favored Trade Status for China**—Pres. Bill Clinton said on **May 20** that he would authorize renewal of most-favored-nation (MFN) trade status with China, which would thus remain eligible for lower tariff rates on exports to the U.S. Many had urged the president not to grant the status because of China's poor record on human rights, export of nuclear-weapons technology, and piracy of copyrighted products. Sen. Robert Dole (KS), the prospective Republican nominee for president, said, **May 9**, that he also supported MFN status for China, but Dole went on to criticize Clinton's Asian policy as weak and vacillating.

**Bosnian Serb Leader Ousts Moderate Premier**—Premier Rajko Kasagic of the self-styled Serb Republic within Bosnia, who had cooperated with other countries in furthering the peace process, was ousted, **May 15**, by Radovan Karadzic, hardline leader of the Bosnian Serbs. Carl Bildt, the mediator implementing the Bosnian peace plan, called on Pres. Slobodan Milosevic of Serbia to turn over Karadzic, who had been indicted for war crimes, to the UN international war crimes tribunal. The parliament of the Republika Serb Republic, **May 18**, chose an ally of Karadzic, Gojko Klickovic, as the new premier.

On **May 31**, at the war crimes tribunal at The Hague, Drazen Erdemovic, an ethnic Croat who had fought with the Bosnian Serbs, pleaded guilty to having helped massacre Muslims after the fall of Srebrenica in 1995. The first person to be convicted by the tribunal, Erdemovic was cooperating with the investigation. He said that his commanders had given him no choice but to kill or be killed.

**Romano Prodi Becomes Premier of Italy**—Romano Prodi, leader of the Olive Tree coalition, which won a plurality in Italian parliamentary elections Apr. 21, was named prime minister **May 16.** An economics professor and businessman, with no ties to recent and pervasive political scandals, Prodi had been asked to head the Olive Tree coalition in 1995. For the most part, Prodi did not give top appointments in his government to members of the Party of the Democratic Left, ex-communists who had been the most popular component of the left-center coalition in the Apr. voting.

**UN, Iraq Sign Oil-Export Agreement**—For the first time since Iraq invaded Kuwait in 1990, an agreement was signed potentially allowing Iraq to export oil. The United Nations had imposed trade sanctions on Iraq after the latter's defeat in the 1991 Gulf War, and Iraq subsequently faced serious shortages of food and medicine. In an agreement with the UN, signed **May 20**, Iraq would be permitted to sell up to $2 bil of oil within 6 months, provided that UN inspectors could verify that food and medicine were reaching needy Iraqis. A portion of the proceeds from the sale of oil would be set aside for the victims of Iraq's invasion of Kuwait and for Iraq's Kurdish population, which was under UN protection.

**Russia, Chechnya Sign Cease-Fire Accord**—Premier Viktor Chernomyrdin of Russia and the Chechnyan rebel leader, Zelimkhan Yandarbiyev, signed a cease-fire agreement in Moscow on **May 27**. The pact provided for a prisoner exchange, but talks on greater autonomy or sovereignty for Chechnya were put off until later. Up to 40,000 had been killed by then in the 17-month civil war. Pres. Boris Yeltsin went to the airport in the Chechen capital of Grozny, **May 28**. He spoke to Russian soldiers and signed a decree abolishing conscription in the army, effective in 2000. Yeltsin also made service in combat voluntary, effective immediately.

**Critic of Peace Process Upsets Peres in Israel**—Benjamin Netanyahu, leader since 1992 of the conservative Likud Party and a critic of some aspects of the Labor government's efforts to achieve a regional peace in the Middle East, was elected prime minister of Israel **May 29**. He defeated Shimon Peres, who had succeeded the assassinated Yitzhak Rabin as prime minister in Nov. 1995. Labor had supported creation of a Palestinian National Authority on Israeli-occupied land. Under a Labor government, Israel had also signed a peace agreement with Jordan, and had made tentative moves toward a settlement with another neighbor, Syria. Netanyahu contended that the peace process had put Israel's security at risk, and several deadly suicide bombings by fanatic Palestinians opposed to peace with Israel gave weight to his concerns. Netanyahu also opposed creation of a Palestinian state and supported expansion of Israeli settlements in Palestinian territory. Peres, for his part, did not enjoy the same popularity as Rabin, who was a national military hero.

For the first time, Israel chose its prime minister in a direct vote. The result was dramatically close, with Netanyahu receiving 1,501,023 votes to 1,471,566 for Peres, a margin of less than 1%. In the 120-seat Knesset, Labor won 34 seats and Likud 32. Nine other parties won seats, with religious parties sympathetic to Netanyahu showing greater strength.

## General

**Scientists Hail Breakthrough in Fight Against AIDS**—Scientists at the National Institute of Allergy and Infectious Diseases said in May that they had found a protein whose presence was necessary to allow the AIDS virus to enter human immune system cells. Although a receptor molecule, CD–4, embedded in the surface of some cells, is the primary target of the virus, scientists knew that another protein had to be present to allow access. Scientists said, **May 9**, that they had identified the "co-factor" protein, which they called fusin because it helps the virus fuse with the cell's outer membrane and inject its genetic material. Scientists said that the discovery might open important new lines of research.

# JUNE 1996

## National

**White House Obtained FBI Files**—On May 30, Jack Quinn, the White House counsel, gave the House Government Reform and Oversight Committee 1,000 documents that the committee had requested for its investigation of the dismissal of 7 employees of the White House travel office. (He declined to provide 2,000 more requested documents, citing the president's claim of executive privilege.) The documents provided included a form letter, dated Dec. 20, 1993, and bearing the printed name of then–White House counsel Bernard Nussbaum, to the FBI asking for the bureau's file on Billy Dale, the dismissed head of the travel office. Republicans speculated that the White House hoped to get information on Dale's past that would justify his dismissal. Nussbaum, **June 5**, denied having personally authorized the letter or having reviewed Dale's file. The White House said, **June 5**, that no one had reviewed Dale's records. FBI Director Louis Freeh, **June 5**, ordered the bureau to investigate.

On **June 7**, the White House said FBI files had been obtained on 329 other people whose names began with A through G, including leading Republicans, to update clearance reviews of people having passes to enter the White House. Anthony Marceca, a White House employee at the time, said, **June 10**, that he had been given an out-of-date list of passholders that he had used to request the files. Marceca said he had looked for "derogatory information" in the files and had given 3 to his superior, Craig Livingstone, head of the personnel security office. Freeh, **June 14**, said he and the FBI had been "victimized" by the White House, which, he said, would now have to obtain written permission from each person whose files it requested.

Attorney Gen. Janet Reno, **June 20**, asked that Kenneth Starr, the independent counsel investigating the Whitewater affair, be granted authority to investigate the matter of the FBI files; a panel of 3 federal judges granted her request, **June 21**. Congress, on **June 19**, opened hearings on "Filegate." The House committee, **June 25**, obtained computer disks showing that the White House security office had acquired more than 600 files in all. Livingstone, testifying **June 26**, said he had resigned as head of the security office. While accepting responsibility for the acquisition of the files, he denied any political motive. William Kennedy, former White House assistant counsel and Livingstone's immediate superior, testified, **June 26**, that he had no idea who had hired Livingstone. Livingstone and Marceca both had reputations as political operatives. Marceca, **June 28**, declined to answer questions before the Senate Judiciary Committee on grounds of possible self-incrimination.

**Virginia GOP Renominates Sen. Warner**—Sen. John Warner (R, VA), who had earned the wrath of some Republicans when he refused to endorse Oliver North, the 1994 GOP nominee for a U.S. Senate seat from Virginia, was up for renomination himself in 1996. Virginia conservatives viewed Warner as too liberal, and delegates to the Republican state convention, ending **June 1**, gave their Senate endorsement to James Miller, White House budget director under Pres. Ronald Reagan. However, Warner defeated Miller in the primary election, **June 11**, taking 65% of the votes and winning nomination. He had encouraged support from Democrats and independents, who were permitted to vote in the Republican primary.

**Antitax Group Surrenders to Authorities**—The Montana antitax group known as the Freemen surrendered in June after a standoff with federal agents that had lasted nearly 3 months. During that time a number of the occupants, including minors, of the remote ranch near Jordan, MT, had come out without incident. The FBI, **June 3**, cut off electricity to the ranch to increase pressure on the Freemen. The 16 remaining holdouts gave up, **June 13**, ending the 81-day standoff. All but 2 of them were in a federal court in Billings, **June 14**, to face various charges. Some were defiant and denied that the court had any jurisdiction over them.

**Economic Indicators Rise Again**—The Conference Board, a business-research organization, reported, **June 3**, that leading economic indicators rose 0.3% in Apr., in their 3d straight monthly advance. The Labor Dept. said, **June 7**, that the unemployment rate had risen from 5.4% in April to 5.6% in May, but that 348,000 nonfarm jobs had been created in that month.

**Congresswoman's Husband Pleads Guilty**—Joseph Waldholtz, husband of Rep. Enid Waldholtz (R, UT), pleaded guilty to fraud in U.S. District Court in Washington, DC, **June 5**. As part of a plea bargain, Waldholtz admitted having written $250,000 in bad checks, made false statements to the Federal Election Commission, helped his wife file a false income-tax return, and created phony contributors to put $60,000 into her campaign for the House. The couple was granted a divorce, **June 5**, in Salt Lake City. Enid Waldholtz had previously announced that she would not seek reelection.

**Medicare Bankruptcy by 2001 Forecast**—The trustees of the Medicare Hospital Insurance Trust Fund said, **June 5**, that the fund would be bankrupt by 2001 unless changes were made. Medicare provides insurance to 30 mil elderly and disabled people. Pres. Bill Clinton had vetoed a bill cutting the growth in Medicare spending, saying that the cuts were too great and were linked to a tax cut for the wealthy.

**Dole Resigns His Seat**—Following up his May announcement, Sen. Robert Dole, the prospective Republican nominee for president, resigned from the Senate, **June 11**. In his farewell Senate speech, he recalled some of the many pieces of legislation on which he had worked and urged the members to seek compromise when possible. On **June 12**, the Republican senators chose Sen. Trent Lott (MS) as the new majority leader; Lott defeated his fellow Mississippian, Thad Cochran, 44–8. Sen. Don Nickles (OK) was elected majority whip.

Earlier, on **June 6**, Dole sought to mollify pro-choice Republicans by favoring the inclusion in the platform—which was expected to call, once again, for a constitutional amendment barring abortion—of a "declaration of tolerance" for party members who supported abortion rights.

**Use of Tobacco Debated in Presidential Race**—Robert Dole, the GOP nominee-to-be, said, **June 13**, that he did not think the Food and Drug Administration had the authority to regulate tobacco and did not think tobacco was addictive for all smokers. On **June 14**, while urging children not to smoke, he remarked that "other things," including alcohol, also posed dangers. He added, "Some would say milk's not good." Pres. Bill Clinton said, **June 15**, that "some political leaders" followed the "tobacco company line," and his campaign noted the industry had given $383,350 to Dole's campaigns. Former Surgeon Gen. C. Everett Koop said, **June 21**, that Dole had shown "an abysmal lack of knowledge of nicotine addiction"; Dole, replied, **June 28**, that while he would discourage tobacco use as president, the states should enact any laws on the subject.

**Church Burnings Prompt Federal Inquiry**—For years, predominantly black churches in the South had been burning with apparent increased frequency, and arson was suspected in many cases. After the burnings came to national attention in the spring of 1996, some 200 agents of the Federal Bureau of Investigation and the Bureau of Alcohol, Tobacco, and Firearms began investigating, but the Dept. of Justice was unable to establish any kind of regional or national conspiracy. On **June 12**, in Greeleyville, SC, at the dedication of a new sanctuary for the Mt. Zion African Methodist Episcopal Church, replacing one that had burned in 1995, Pres. Bill Clinton vowed that Americans would not tolerate any return of the violence that had plagued the South prior to the civil rights movement.

**Airline Whose Plane Crashed Shuts Down**—ValuJet Airlines, operator of the plane that crashed in Florida in May, killing all 110 aboard, voluntarily suspended operations, **June 17**, for an indefinate period, at the request of the Federal Aviation Administration. The FAA had found that ValuJet had not always performed repairs properly or documented them, had ignored FAA directives on safety, and had flown planes known to have maintenance problems. The FAA said ValuJet had not effectively monitored maintenance work assigned to outside contractors. Investigators believed that oxygen generators, mislabeled as empty and loaded onto the doomed plane, had caused a fire that resulted in the crash.

**Senators Issue Reports on Whitewater**—The Republican majority and the Democratic minority on the Senate Whitewater Committee issued final reports, **June 18**, based on their investigation. The Republicans concluded that First Lady Hillary Rodham Clinton and some White House officials had obstructed a federal investigation into the Whitewater Development Corp. and its connection with Pres. Bill Clinton and Mrs. Clinton. The Republicans viewed with suspicion Mrs. Clinton's role in the financing of Castle Grande, a real-estate development in Arkansas financed by Madison Guaranty Savings & Loan. The majority report also concluded that she had sought to prevent "unfettered access" by investigators into the office of Vince Foster, the assistant White House counsel, who committed suicide in 1993 and who, Republicans believed, had "damaging evidence" related to Whitewater and the dismissal of 7 employees of the White House travel office. The Republicans also asserted that Mrs. Clinton had probably held subpoenaed billing records from the Rose Law Firm for 2 years before they surfaced in Jan. 1996 in the White House. Their report said that then-White House Counsel Bernard Nussbaum, former Associate Attorney Gen. Webster Hubbell, Mrs. Clinton's chief of staff Margaret Williams, and her friend Susan Thomases had testified inaccurately about events following Foster's death.

The Democratic report contended that Mrs. Clinton was unaware of any illegal conduct relating to Castle Grande. Their report said that law enforcement officials had testified that they had not been denied access to Foster's files and that it was impossible to determine, based on the evidence, when and how the billing records had come to the White House.

At the 2d Whitewater trial, underway in Little Rock, prosecutors, **June 19**, named Bruce Lindsay, deputy White House counsel, as an unindicted coconspirator in the case.

**Suspect in Unabomber Case Charged in 2 Deaths**—Theodore Kaczynski, who had been arrested in Apr., was charged with 10 felony counts in June as the alleged Unabomber. Over 17 years, the so-called Unabomber had killed 3 men and injured 23 people with small bombs sent through the mail. After his arrest in Montana, Kaczynski had been charged with one count of possessing bomb components. On **June 18**, a federal grand jury in Sacramento charged him in connection with 2 deaths and 2 injuries caused by bombs mailed from that city. The bomb-possession charge was dropped, **June 21**. Kaczynski, **June 23**, was transferred to Sacramento. On **June 25**, he pleaded not guilty to all counts.

## International

**Coalition Government Takes Over in India**—A month of turmoil in India, following the inconclusive result of parliamentary elections, ended in early June. After one attempt to form a government had failed, a coalition headed by H. D. Deve Gowda was formed in parliament, **June 1**. His 13-party coalition of leftist and regional parties was supported by the Congress (I) Party, which had led India until slumping badly in the May voting. Most of the cabinet apppointments made by Prime Min. Gowda were drawn from the lower castes, and only one minister was from the high-ranking Brahmin caste—circumstances without precedent in the 49 years of Indian independence.

**Talks on Northern Ireland's Future Open**—Negotiations that sought to bring peace to Northern Ireland, or Ulster, and determine its future status opened in Belfast, **June 10**. Participants had been chosen in elections conducted in May. However, the British and Irish governments barred negotiators from Sinn Fein, the political wing of the Irish Republican Army, until the IRA reinstated the cease-fire that it had abandoned earlier in the year. Former U.S. Sen. George Mitchell headed the talks. The Ulster Unionist Party accepted Mitchell, **June 11**, after expressing concern that he would be biased toward the unification of Northern Ireland with the Republic of Ireland because his father was Irish. A bomb exploded outside a shopping center in Manchester, England, **June 15**, injuring 206 people. Gerry Adams, head of Sinn Fein, said, **June 17**, that Sinn Fein was an organization separate from the IRA and not to blame in any way for the bombing. The IRA, **June 19**, claimed responsibility for the attack.

**Yeltsin in Runoff for President of Russia**—Pres. Boris Yeltsin led the first round of voting, in June, for president of Russia. Early in the campaign it had been thought that Yeltsin, who was in uncertain health and whose behavior was sometimes erratic, had little chance for reelection. The Communist Party had already gained ground in parliamentary voting in 1995, and its candidate, Gennadi Zyuganov, appealed effectively to memories of the old days of Soviet world power and Communist domestic order. But Yeltsin campaigned vigorously, vowing to complete the political and economic reforms that he had launched.

In the voting, **June 16**, Yeltsin received 35% and Zyuganov 32%, leaving them to compete in the July runoff. Gen. Aleksandr Lebed (ret.) was third with 14.5%. The other 7 candidates included former Pres. Mikhail Gorbachev, who had presided over the collapse of the Soviet empire and who now was unpopular with both Communists and reformers; though his place in history was secure, Gorbachev polled only 0.5% in the 1996 election.

On **June 18**, Yeltsin dismissed Defense Minister Pavel Grachev, who had been criticized for his conduct of the civil war with Chechnya, and replaced him with Lebed. On **June 20**, he removed 3 other top aides who had supported prosecution of the war.

**New Israeli Leader Forms Cabinet**—Benjamin Netanyahu, the first prime minister of Israel to be chosen by direct popular vote, formed and won approval for his cabinet, **June 18**, after negotiations with religious parties and others. On **June 16**, he had issued policy guidelines, indicating he would promote a free-market economy, deregulate business and industry, and reduce government expenditures; the guidelines also reaffirmed Likud opposition to Palestinian statehood and pledged to maintain control of East Jerusalem and the Golan Heights. Negotiations with the largest Orthodox parties, **June 16-17**, assured Netanyahu of majority support in the Israeli Knesset, or parliament. The Yisrael Ba-Aliya party led by Natan Sharansky, a former Soviet dissident, also joined the coalition, with the promise of 2 cabinet seats. Under pressure on the right from David Levy, who threatened otherwise to withdraw from the cabint, he included Gen. Ariel Sharon (ret.) in his cabinet, giving him the newly-created post in charge of national infrastructure, where he would be in a position to promote expansion of Jewish settlements in occupied territories.

**U.S., China Act Again to Stop Piracy of Property**—For the 2d time in 2 years, **June 17**, the U.S. and China took steps aimed at stopping the manufacture and sale in China of pirated intellectual property. In 1995, China had agreed to enforce copyright laws and close down companies turning out music, motion pictures, and computer software copied from other countries. The U.S. believed that China's subsequent efforts had not been effective, although the Chinese had closed 15 factories and confiscated 80,000 pirated compact discs. Under the new agreement, every CD would carry a registry number to establish that it had been produced legally. The import of CD presses would be regulated, and authorities would monitor factories around the clock.

**Bomb in Saudi Arabia Kills 19 U.S. Servicemen**—A bomb exploded at a military complex near Dhahran, in Saudi Arabia, in June, killing 19 American servicemen and wounding several hundred people. The incident occurred 7 months after another bomb exploded in Riyadh, the Saudi capital, in Nov., killing 7 people, including 5 Americans. Subsequently, 4 Saudi men had confessed to the bombing and been executed. On **June 25**, Saudi police investigated a fuel truck that had stopped at the perimeter of the complex in Khobar. The driver ran from the truck and entered another vehicle, which left the scene. The police had little time to warn people nearby before the bomb exploded. All the dead were in an 8-story apartment house. The explosion dug a crater 35 feet deep. Pres. Bill Clinton ordered the FBI to send investigators to Saudi Arabia.

**War Crimes Tribunal Indicts 8 for Rape**—Treating rape as a war crime for the first time, the War Crimes Tribunal at The Hague, **June 27**, indicted 8 Bosnian Serb policemen and soldiers for allegedly commiting a series of assaults on Muslim women and girls in southeastern Bosnia. According to reports, Serb soldiers had raped many thousands of Muslim women during the war in Bosnia and Herzegovina.

**Group of 7 Confronts Terrorism**—The "Group of 7," the presidents and prime ministers of the world's largest industrial nations, met in Paris at the end of June. The bombing of a U.S. military complex in Saudi Arabia just before the meeting focused attention on the problem of terrorism. In a communiqué, **June 28**, the leaders backed a package of antiterrorism proposals that included broadening extradition treaties, controlling the import and export of firearms, and controlling money laundering. However, several leaders expressed concern about a bill in the U.S. Congress to impose economic sanctions on foreign companies that invested in Iran or Libya, with whom many countries did significant business. On **June 29**, the leaders warned Serbia that it faced renewal of economic sanctions unless Radovan Karadzic, an indicted war criminal, resigned as president of the Bosnian Serb republic.

## General

**Colorado Wins Hockey's Stanley Cup**—The Colorado Avalanche won the championship of the National Hockey League in June, and possession of the Stanley Cup. In the championship series, Colorado won 4 straight games from the Florida Panthers. Neither team had reached the finals before, a circumstance that had not occurred since the league's first season in 1918. The Colorado franchise had been moved from Quebec prior to the current season. After Colorado won the first 3 games, the 4th, in Miami, proved to be a 5-hour marathon that began **June 10** and ended after midnight, **June 11**. In the third overtime of a scoreless tie, Uwe Krupp of the Avalanche hit a slap shot past the Florida goalie, John Vanbiesbrouck, for a 1–0 victory. Patrick Roy, the Colorado goalie, gave up only 4 goals in the series. The Avalanche center, Joe Sakic, was named most valuable player in the playoffs.

**Chicago Bulls End Great Season With NBA Title**—The Chicago Bulls, arguably the greatest team in the history of basketball, capped a record-breaking season in June by capturing the championship of the National Basketball Assn. Chicago was led by Michael Jordan, who had returned from retirement toward the end of the previous season. The Bulls posted a 72–10 won–lost record during the regular 1995–96 season, the best in league history. Chicago romped through the first 3 rounds of the playoffs and met the Seattle SuperSonics in the final. After winning the first 3 games, Chicago lost twice, but took the title, **June 16**, defeating Seattle in Chicago, 87–75. Jordan was named most valuable player in the finals for the 4th time, a record. Other Chicago starters were Dennis Rodman, Scottie Pippen, Ron Harper, and Luc Longley.

# JULY 1996

## National

**12 Charged in Alleged Plot to Bomb Buildings**—Twelve members of a paramilitary group were arrested in the Phoenix, AZ, area, **July 1**, thwarting what federal authorities said was a plot to bomb 7 government buildings. Authorities confiscated weapons and materials to make bombs. All or some of them were charged, **July 1**, with conspiracy to manufacture and possess unregistered destructive devices, conspiracy to instruct others in the use of explosive devices to cause disorder, and illegal possession of automatic weapons. Evidence cited included a videotape showing 7 targeted buildings and information on how and where to place bombs. All 12 pleaded not guilty.

**Sharp Declines Occur on Wall Street**—The Conference Board, a business-research organization, reported, **July 2**, that the leading economic indicators had risen in May by 0.3%—the 4th straight monthly advance. The Labor Dept. announced, **July 5**, that the unemployment rate had declined in June to 5.3% (from 5.6%), the lowest rate in 6 years. Also in June, 239,000 nonfarm jobs had been created. The news caused stock investors to fear that the economy might be gathering momentum too quickly and that the Fed might raise short-term interest rates. As a result, the Dow Jones industrial average fell 114.88 points, or 2%, **July 5**. The Dow average fell another 161.05 points, **July 15**, closing at 5,349.51, some 430 points below the all-time high posted in May.

**Pre-Convention Campaigns Heat Up**—Although the party nominating conventions had not yet been held, the prospective major-party nominees were campaigning hard in July. Former Sen. Robert Dole appeared, **July 9**, to be backing away from support for a repeal of the ban on assault weapons that Congress had passed in 1994. Pres. Bill Clinton, **July 10**, told the convention of the National Association for the Advancement of Colored People that he would veto any attempt to repeal the assault-weapons ban. Dole, **July 11**, having already declined an invitation to speak to the NAACP, asserted that the organization's president, Kweisi Mfume, a former House member from Maryland, was a "very liberal Democrat" who was "trying to set me up."

On **July 12**, Dole, shifting position, dropped previous support for a statement in the party's platform plank on abortion that would call for tolerance for party members supporting abortion rights. Instead, Dole supported a declaration of tolerance in a separate plank. On **July 17**, setting forth his views on education, Dole said Clinton had become a pet of the "militant teachers' unions" who, he said, perpetuated incompetence in education. Dole urged that children have greater choice as to which schools they would attend and proposed to provide poor children with financial assistance to help them attend private or parochial schools.

**Perot and Others Focus on Presidency**— On **July 9**, former Gov. Richard Lamm (D) of Colorado announced he would seek the presidential nomination of the Reform Party. Lamm warned that growing outlays for entitlement programs could bankrupt the country; he also advocated restraints on immigration. The Reform Party was founded in 1995 by Texas billionaire Ross Perot, who had sought the presidency as an independent in 1992. Perot, who captured 19% of the vote then, announced, **July 11**, that he himself would seek the nomination of his party in 1996.

On **July 6**, the Libertarian Party held its presidential nominating convention in Washington, DC. The Libertarians, who opposed governmental intrusion into the private lives of citizens, nominated Harry Browne, author of best-selling books on financial investment; he called for the elimination of most taxes, the phaseout of Medicare and Medicaid, and the replacement of Social Security with a privately run pension system.

**TWA Jet Crashes Into Ocean, Killing 230**—A Trans World Airlines jetliner crashed into the Atlantic Ocean, **July 17**, killing all 230 aboard.

Bound for Paris, TWA Flight 800 took off from John F. Kennedy International Airport in New York City at 8:19 PM. The Boeing 747, carrying 212 passengers and a crew of 18, disappeared from radar screens at 8:48 PM. The plane was about 50 mi east of the airport and had attained an altitude of 13,700 ft. It plunged into the ocean about 10 mi south of East Moriches, Long Island. Witnesses described seeing 2 explosions and a fireball falling into the sea. The U.S. Coast Guard, supported by operators of small boats, began a rescue effort, but no one was found alive. The passengers included 16 members of a high-school French club and 5 adult chaperons from Montoursville, PA.

Retrieval and analysis of the wreckage was a protracted process, and the investigation, headed by the National Transportation Safety Board, continued for months. A mechanical failure was one possibility investigated, and a terrorist bomb aboard the aircraft was another; in addition, some witnesses said they saw a streak of light going toward the plane before the explosion, suggesting the possibility that a missile had struck it. On **July 24**, the U.S. Navy recovered the flight data recorder and cockpit voice recorder. A brief unidentified sound was heard on the voice recorder just before it stopped recording; the conversation in the cockpit gave no indication of danger.

Pres. Bill Clinton met with 300 relatives and friends of the victims in New York City, **July 25**. He announced new federal rules tightening the inspection of carry-on and checked luggage. For international flights, searches of a plane's cockpit, cabin, and cargo area were ordered.

**Bomb Explodes in Atlanta During Olympics**—A homemade pipe bomb exploded in a park in downtown Atlanta on **July 27**, directly killing one person and injuring more than 100. In addition, a Turkish television cameraman died of a heart attack while rushing to the scene of the explosion. The blast, at 1:25 AM, came while the Centennial Olympic Park was filled with thousands of persons attending a concert; many of those injured had come to Atlanta to attend the Olympic Games, which were in progress.

A man who did not identify himself made an emergency 911 call from a phone booth near the park at about 12:58 AM. At about 1:00 AM, a security guard, Richard Jewell, pointed out an unattended knapsack to a Georgia Bureau of Investigation agent. Jewell and others began to clear the area, and explosives experts were brought in to examine the bag. At the time of the explosion, which occurred from within the knapsack, word of the 911 call had not been brought to the scene. The explosion killed Alice Hawthorne of Albany, GA. Hawthorne and those injured in the blast were struck by fragments of the pipe and by nails and screws packed into the pipe.

The FBI said, **July 27**, that the voice on the 911 message was that of a white American male without a distinguishable accent. Members of the media reported, **July 30**, that law-enforcement officials viewed Jewell as a leading suspect in the case. Jewell was questioned by the FBI, and authorities searched his apartment, **July 31**. Although no charges were made against Jewell, camera crews and reporters pursued him wherever he appeared. In Oct. the FBI said Jewell was no longer a suspect.

**Congress Revamps Welfare System**—During his campaign for president in 1992, Bill Clinton promised to "end welfare as we know it." It was the Republican-controlled Congress, however, that twice passed a major overhaul of welfare in 1995, and Clinton vetoed both bills.

In 1996, with both Clinton and Capitol Hill eager to point to a major accomplishment in an election year, Congress made a 3d attempt. The Senate, **July 30**, 78–21, and the House, **July 31**, 328–101, approved a compromise bill. Under this bill, Aid to Families With Dependent Children was replaced by block grants to the states, ending the federal guarantee of subsidies to poor people with children. To maintain its full grant each state would have to continue to spend 80% of what it spent on welfare in 1994. States got wide latitude in dispersing funds, but it was required that the head of household in a welfare family find a job within 2 years, and no benefits from federal funds could generally be paid to a family for more than 5 years (lifetime limit). States were allowed to exempt up to 20% of families on welfare from the 5-year time limit, on grounds of hardship. Future legal immigrants who are not U.S. citizens would be ineligible for most benefits during their first 5 years in the U.S. The bill gave states the option of requiring that heads of welfare households perform community service. It cut spending on food stamps by $24 bil over 6 years and tightened eligibility for SSI programs. Altogether, $55 bil was expected to be saved under the reconstituted system.

As the bill moved through the legislative process, administration officials sought changes to make it acceptable to the president. As a result, $14 bil was included over 6 years for child-care services to families on welfare, which would permit parents to work outside the home. (At the same time, a woman would not be penalized for failing to work if she could not find child care for a child under 6.) Another provision guaranteed poor people needing health care continued access to Medicaid.

This measure did not restrict states from paying more money to a parent with children, and unwed teenaged mothers could be eligible for benefits, but only those who attend school and live with an adult. States in which the rates of childbirth among unwed mothers decline would receive bonus payments. States were required to reduce benefits to women who failed to help identify fathers of their children. Federal block grants would be reduced for states that fail to have half of all single parents on welfare employed or in work-related activity by the year 2002.

Almost all the votes cast against the bill in Congress were by Democrats, who were deeply divided over the measure. Clinton signed it, Aug. 22, though he said he still opposed some provisions, especially the cutback in funding for food stamps and the denial of most benefits to legal immigrants. Robert Dole, the prospective Republican presidential nominee, congratulated Clinton for "finally climbing on board" welfare reform. However, Sen. Daniel Patrick Moynihan (D, NY), a leading opponent of the bill in Congress, painted a grim picture of thousands of children abandoned in the streets.

## International

**Yeltsin Wins Runoff for President of Russia**—Pres. Boris Yeltsin of Russia retained his office, **July 3**, when he defeated the Communist Party candidate, Gennadi Zyuganov, in a runoff election. The margin was 54% to 40%, with the rest of the voters voting "against all." For most of the week before the runoff, Yeltsin was nowhere to be seen, prompting new rumors about his health. Joining many other world leaders, Pres. Bill Clinton hailed Yeltsin's victory, saying, "The Russian people have turned their backs on tyranny." Yeltsin, **July 4**, asked Premier Viktor Chernomyrdin to form a new government. Meanwhile, the conflict in Chechnya flared up after rebels ignored a **July 8** ultimatum to free 1,000 Russian prisoners. Russian troops, **July 9**, began an attack on a village 20 miles from the Chechen capital of Grozny. Yeltsin, **July 15**, canceled an appointment with U.S. Vice Pres. Al Gore. But the 2 men met, **July 16**, at a sanatorium near Moscow, where Yeltsin, still apparently in shaky health, had begun a 2-week vacation.

**Pressure Grows on Indicted Serb Leaders**—On **July 11**, the UN International Criminal Tribunal at The Hague issued international arrest warrants for Ratko Mladic, the Bosnian Serb military commander, and Radovan Karadzic, political leader of the Bosnian Serbs, citing them for crimes against humanity. Richard Holbrooke, former U.S. assistant secretary of state, and Pres. Slobodan Milosevic of Serbia, **July 17–19**, negotiated the resignation of Karadzic as president of the Bosnian Serb republic and as chairman of the dominant party. The 1995 peace agreement for Bosnia and Herzegovina required that those indicted for war crimes must leave office, and could not be candidates in the forthcoming election. Holbrooke, **July 19**, said that Karadzic might try to hold power behind the scenes.

**Islamic Party Member Is Premier of Turkey**—In July, for the first time since Turkey became a republic in 1923, a member of an Islamic party was chosen as the premier. Necmettin Erbakan, leader of the Welfare Party, became premier when the National Assembly, **July 8**, approved, 278–265, with 7 abstentions, a coalition government that also included the True Path Party, led by former Premier Tansu Ciller. The Welfare Party had won a plurality in the Dec. 1995 elections. Turkey had long been allied with the West, but the Welfare Party viewed Western nations with distrust. In the newly formed government the key ministries of defense and foreign affairs remained in the hands of True Path.

**China Declares Moratorium**—China conducted an underground nuclear test, **July 29**, and then declared a moratorium on future tests. Negotiations resumed in Geneva, **July 29**, on an international nuclear test-ban treaty.

## General

**AIDS Spreading More Quickly Among Women**—The UN reported, **July 5**, that 21.8 mil people around the world had developed AIDS or were infected with the virus (HIV) that causes AIDS. Of these, 42% were women, and the UN report said that "the proportion is growing." Some 5.8 mil people had died of AIDS. Sub-Saharan Africa had by far the most people living with HIV infection: 63% of the world total. South and Southeast Asia accounted for 23%, and Latin America 6%. Only 3.7% were found in North America and 2.2% in Western Europe.

The 11th International Conference on AIDS drew more than 15,000 people to Vancouver, B.C., **July 7–11**. Researchers reported on progress in treatment, especially with a combination of drugs that included both older drugs such as AZT and the newer drug nevirapine. The latter is a so-called protease inhibitor. Such drugs, used in combination, have been found to reduce high levels of HIV in the bloodstream to undetectable levels in many patients.

**Graf Wins 7th Wimbledon Singles Title**—Steffi Graf of Germany won the women's singles title at the All-England Tennis Championship (Wimbledon) for the 7th time, on **July 6**, defeating Arantxa Sánchez Vicario of Spain, 6–3, 7–5. The men's singles competition was marked by many upsets, and on **July 7** the final, for the first time ever, featured 2 players who had not been seeded in the top 16. The winner, Richard Krajicek of the Netherlands, defeated MaliVai Washington, of the U.S., 6–3, 6–4, 6–3. Krajicek brought the title to the Netherlands for the first time, and Washington was the first black male finalist since Arthur Ashe in 1975.

**Charles, Diana Agree on Terms of Divorce**—Prince Charles, heir to the British throne, and Princess Diana, his estranged wife, reached an agreement in July on the terms for their divorce. Their announcement, **July 12**, did not include details of their financial agreement, which had been negotiated for several months. The *Times* of London reported, **July 13**, that Diana was likely to get the equivalent of $23 mil to $26 mil from the royal family immediately, and $600,000 a year thereafter. Diana would no longer be called Her Royal Highness, and would never become queen, but would continue to be known as the Princess of Wales. Charles and Diana would have equal custody of their 2 sons. They were granted a preliminary divorce decree **July 15**; the decree was made final Aug. 28.

**197 Nations in Atlanta Centennial Olympics**—The 100th anniversary of the founding of the modern Olympic Games was celebrated at the opening ceremonies for the games of the 26th Olympiad, in Atlanta, **July 19**. All 197 invited countries sent athletes to the games, by far the most nations ever to participate. Security was tight, but the games were nevertheless marred by a bombing in adjacent Centennial Olympic Park, **July 27**, that directly killed 1 person and injured many. The Olympic torch, which had been carried for 15,000 miles throughout the U.S., was taken up by Muhammad Ali, who lit the flame ushering in the 1996 games. Ali had won the Olympic heavyweight boxing title at the 1960 Rome Olympics, and later became world heavyweight boxing champion.

In swimming finals held **July 20–26**, Michelle Smith of Ireland won 3 gold medals and a bronze. Amy Van Dyken won 4 swimming gold medals, **July 22–26**, the most ever for an American woman in one Olympics. Naim Suleymanoglu, a Turkish weightlifter, nicknamed Pocket Hercules because he was only 4' 11" tall, won his 3d Olympic gold medal, **July 22**, in the 141-lb class, lifting a world record 738¼ lbs. Russian gymnasts won the men's team competition in that sport, **July 22**. Kerri Strug became a popular favorite in the U.S., **July 23**, completing her team gymnastics competition despite having dislocated her ankle. The U.S. women's team won the gold medal, but Strug was carried off the floor and was unable to compete in individual events. Li Xiaoshuang of China won the men's individual gymnastics title, **July 24**, and Liliya Podkopayeva of Ukraine, the women's crown, **July 25**.

Donovan Bailey of Canada claimed the title of world's fastest human, **July 27**, capturing the 100 meters on the track in a world-record 9.84 sec. American Gail Devers, **July 27**, won the women's 100 meters in a photo-finish time of 10.94 seconds. Fatuma Roma of Ethiopia won the women's marathon, **July 28**. Carl Lewis of the United States won the Olympic long jump for the 4th consecutive time, **July 29**. He was the 2d person ever to win 4 straight golds in the same event, and his total of 9 gold medals was one of the highest ever. A 2-run homer by Dot Richardson, an orthopedic surgeon, **July 30**, lifted the U.S. women's softball team to a 3–1 gold-medal victory over China.

# AUGUST 1996

## National

**Defendants in 2d Arkansas Trial Not Guilty; Others Sentenced**—Two Arkansas bankers prosecuted by Kenneth Starr, the independent counsel investigating the Whitewater affair, were found not guilty on some charges **Aug. 1**. The defendants, Robert Hill and Herby Branscum Jr., had been accused of conspiring to conceal large cash withdrawals made by the 1990 reelection campaign of then-Gov. Bill Clinton. They were also accused of stealing from their bank, in Perryville, to repay themselves for donations to the Clinton campaign. Pres. Clinton, in taped testimony in July, denied he had appointed them to state agencies as a thank-you for campaign contributions. Jurors acquitted the defendants on the conspiracy charges and on 2 of 9 fraud charges but were deadlock on the other charges.

On **Aug. 19**, U.S. District Judge George Howard Jr. sentenced former Gov. Jim Guy Tucker of Arkansas to 4 years probation; Tucker was reported to be in failing health. Susan McDougal, **Aug. 20**, was sentenced to 2 years in prison; James McDougal, who was not sentenced, was reported to be cooperating with the independent counsel. Tucker and the McDougals had been convicted on Whitewater-related charges in May.

**Health Insurance Bill Becomes Law**—On **Aug. 1-2** Congress approved a measure intended to make it easier for workers to carry their health insurance from job to job. It also limited the power of companies to withhold insurance coverage because of preexisting medical conditions. The legislation, initially known as the Kennedy-Kassebaum bill, was sponsored in the Senate by Edward Kennedy (D, MA) and Nancy Landon Kassebaum (R, KS). Clinton signed the bill **Aug. 21**.

**Economic Growth Jumps in 2d Quarter**—The Commerce Dept. said, **Aug. 1**, that the gross domestic product had grown at an annual rate of 4.2% during the 2d quarter, the fastest rate in 2 years. The Labor Dept. reported, **Aug. 2**, that unemployment had edged upward in July to 5.4%, from 5.3% in June. Investors took these figures to mean that the economy was not overheating, and the Dow Jones industrial average rose 85.08 points, or 1.5%, **Aug. 2**. The Conference Board, a business research organization, said, **Aug. 5**, that the leading economic indicators had risen 0.5% in June; this 5th straight monthly advance was seen as a strong signal that the economy would continue to expand. The Labor Dept. said, **Aug. 13**, that consumer prices had risen 0.3% in July. The Commerce Dept. reported, **Aug. 20**, that the trade deficit in June had been $8.11 bil.

**Increase in Minimum Wage Becomes Law**—On **Aug. 2**, both the House, 354–72, and the Senate, 76–22, approved legislation that increased the minimum wage for the first time since 1991. Congress had struggled for months over the proposal, which was strongly backed by the Clinton administration. Republican leaders in Congress opposed it, but GOP defectors preparing to join with Democratic supporters ultimately ensured its passage. The new increase, tacked onto the Small Business Job Protection Act, raised the minimum wage, in 2 steps, from $4.25 an hour to $5.15 an hour. Another provision in the bill increased the amount businesses could write off in annual equipment costs. The bill also granted a $5,000-per-child credit for families who adopted children. A related provision barred adoption agencies that receive federal funds from determining child placements on the basis of race. The bill also allowed higher contributions to tax-deferred retirement accounts. Pres. Bill Clinton signed the legislation **Aug. 20**.

**Dole Proposes $548 Billion Tax Cut**—Robert Dole, the prospective Republican presidential nominee, introduced a dramatic new element into the campaign, **Aug. 5**, when he announced his support for tax cuts totaling $548 billion. He proposed to stimulate what he called an anemic economy with an across-the-board tax cut totaling 15% over 3 years. This reduction by itself would cost the federal government more than $400 bil. His plan also included a reduction in the capital gains tax rate from 28% to 14% and a $500-per-child tax credit for each family. In addition, Dole called for reducing the percentage of Social Security benefits subject to taxation from 85% to 50%. He backed a "fairer, flatter" tax code but did not endorse outright the concept of a flat tax. Dole, long known as a "deficit hawk" who was opposed to federal red ink, did not provide details as to how the revenue shortfall would be made up. But he did say he would not cut defense or reduce Medicare beyond what Republicans were supporting in Congress, and he asserted that faster economic growth after the tax plan was instituted would produce more income from taxes.

Pres. Bill Clinton, **Aug. 5**, rejected Dole's plan, saying he opposed repeating "the mistake we made before and having big tax cuts that are not paid for."

**GOP Adopts Conservative Platform**—A platform generally reflecting the views of conservative Republicans was adopted **Aug. 12** by delegates to the Republican National Convention. The draft platform called for a constitutional amendment barring abortions. A related issue was whether it would include a declaration of tolerance for party members who held different positions, especially those who held a pro-choice position on abortion. Robert Dole, the prospective presidential nominee, had supported an explicit tolerance plank; opponents of abortion, **Aug. 5**, gained approval for language that party members "have deeply held and sometimes differing views" but not explicitly expressing "tolerance." The draft supported an end to most public benefits to illegal aliens and called for a constitutional amendment denying citizenship to children born in the U.S. to illegal immigrants. Pat Buchanan, who had sought the presidential nomination but was not given a speaking slot at the Republican National Convention, spoke at a rally in Escondido, CA, **Aug. 11;** he said the draft platform showed that the GOP was becoming a "Buchanan party." He had threatened to run for president as a 3d-party candidate, but instead endorsed Dole, **Aug. 12**.

**Jack Kemp Tapped for 2d Spot on GOP Ticket**—On **Aug. 10**, at a rally in his hometown of Russell, KS, Robert Dole announced his choice of Jack Kemp, a former professional football star and later a member of Congress and cabinet member, for the vice presidential nomination on the Republican ticket. Dole had considered a number of other prominent Republicans, and had been interested in attracting Gen. Colin Powell (ret.), who, however, declined to be considered. Kemp was an energetic proponent of "supply side economics," a theory which holds that increased tax revenue generated by economic growth can make up in large part for a reduction in rates. He also was known for his concern for inner-city problems and was an advocate of affirmative action. A onetime quarterback for the Buffalo Bills, Kemp represented the Buffalo (NY) area in the U.S. House from 1971 to 1989. Kemp's economic ideas were incorporated into the tax policy implemented by Pres. Ronald Reagan. After a failed try for the 1988 Republican presidential nomination, Kemp was secretary of Housing and Urban Development in the Bush administration.

**Republicans Nominate Dole for President**—Delegates to the Republican National Convention in San Diego nominated former Sen. Robert Dole (KS) for president **Aug. 14.** Dole had wrapped up the nomination by winning most of the primaries and caucuses held in the late winter and spring. He had resigned from the Senate in June to campaign full-time. Gen. Colin Powell (ret.) spoke on **Aug. 12**, the opening night of the convention; he urged a policy of inclusion for the party and mentioned his own support for abortion rights and affirmative action programs. Former Presidents Gerald Ford and George Bush addressed the delegates, **Aug. 12**, and former First Lady Nancy Reagan described the struggle of ex-Pres. Ronald Reagan, afflicted with Alzheimer's disease. In her keynote speech, **Aug. 13**, Rep. Susan Molinari (R, NY), who was married to Rep. Bill Paxon (R, NY) and had a baby daughter, sought to enhance the appeal of the party to working mothers.

Elizabeth Dole, wife of Robert Dole, spoke **Aug. 14**. She left the podium and walked among the delegates as she shared information about her husband's personal life, including his long painful ordeal after being seriously wounded in Italy during World War II. In the balloting for the presidential nomination, Dole received 1,928 votes, and Pat Buchanan, the columnist and commentator, received 43. Four votes were scattered and 15 uncast. Former Representative Jack Kemp was officially nominated for vice president by voice vote.

On **Aug. 15**, Kemp and Dole gave acceptance speeches. Dole reiterated his support for an across-the-board 15% cut in taxes. He pledged to maintain a strong national defense. He said that as a member of an older generation he could serve as a bridge to a previous time of tranquility and faith. He said America had been better: "I know, because I was there." In contrast, he said that Clinton administration elitists "never grew up, never did anything real, never sacrificed, never suffered, and never learned . . . ."

**Investigation of TWA Crash Continues**—In the investigation of the Flight 800 crash, the FBI confirmed, **Aug. 23**, that microscopic traces of a chemical explosive had been found on a piece of wreckage from a center section of the plane, but did not consider this conclusive proof of an explosion. By month's end, 211 of 230 bodies and 60% of the plane had been recovered.

**Reform Party Picks Nominees**—Ross Perot, the Texas billionaire who had run for president as an independent in 1992, was declared, **Aug. 17**, to have won the presidential nomination of the new Reform Party. Perot's money had largely funded the party, which was on the ballot in every state. The voting was conducted by mail and phone and on the Internet among party adherents. While 1.13 mil ballots were sent out, only 49,226 people cast ballots that were found to be valid. In the end, Perot defeated his only challenger, former Gov. Richard Lamm of Colorado, 65% to 35%. At the party's convention in Valley Forge, Pa., **Aug. 18**, Lamm declined to endorse Perot. Accepting the nomination, Perot deplored the proposal by Robert Dole, the Republican nominee, to cut taxes by 15%, as a threat to fiscal solvency. He also blamed the North American Free Trade Agreement, which Dole and Pres. Bill Clinton supported, for the loss of 500,000 jobs to Mexico.

The Green Party nominated its first presidential candidate, Ralph Nader, **Aug. 19** at its convention in Los Angeles. In his acceptance speech, Nader, a consumer advocate who had gained fame as a critic of safety defects in automobiles, denounced corporate influence over the major parties.

**Rise in Teen Drug Use Becomes Issue**—The government reported, **Aug. 20**, that the use of illicit drugs among young people 12 to 17 had more than doubled between 1992 and 1995. Robert Dole, the GOP presidential nominee, charged, **Aug. 31**, that the Clinton administration had been indifferent to the threat posed by drugs to young people, and cited a White House acknowledgement that it had hired people with a drug history. Dole said, **Sept. 1**, that he would end trade with and impose sanctions on nations that produced drugs and beef up protection of U.S. borders against drug-runners, possibly using the U.S. military.

**Clinton Approves Regulations on Tobacco**—Pres. Bill Clinton, **Aug. 23**, approved regulations on tobacco products recommended by the Food and Drug Admin. The regulations, aimed at curbing the marketing and sale of tobacco products to young people, had been drafted in 1995 and had been the target of lawsuits filed by publishers, advertisers, and the tobacco industry. As finally approved, they prohibited the sale of tobacco products from vending machines and self-service displays unless situated in places generally inaccessible to young people. Free samples and the sale of cigarettes in quantities under 20 were banned. Most billboard ads and much magazine advertising were banned outright, and the rest limited to black-and-white and text only. Brand-name ads were banned on clothing and at athletic and musical events.

Earlier, on **Aug. 9**, a state circuit court jury in Jacksonville, FL, ordered Brown & Williamson Tobacco Company to pay $750,000 to Grady Carter, a longtime smoker who contracted lung cancer. Carter began smoking Lucky Strike cigarettes in 1947; the brand was purchased in 1994 by Brown & Willliamson, a British firm. The suit was based on internal documents which showed that tobacco company executives had known of the addictiveness and danger of smoking while publicly stating otherwise.

**4 Women Enter Citadel**—The long dispute over the admission of women to The Citadel, the military academy in Charleston, SC, ended on **Aug. 24** when the institution admitted 4 women. In June, the U.S. Supreme Court had ordered Virginia Military Institute, another all-male school supported by the state, to admit women. At that point, The Citadel dropped its own opposition to female cadets and agreed to admit them. The women began training **Aug. 26**.

**Democrats Renominate Clinton and Gore**—Pres. Bill Clinton and Vice Pres. Al Gore were renominated for 2d terms at the Democratic National Convention in Chicago, **Aug. 26-29**. Clinton, **Aug. 25**, began a 4-day train trip to the convention, making speeches in West Virginia, Kentucky, Ohio, Michigan, and Indiana. On the opening night of the convention, **Aug. 26**, Sarah and James Brady praised the president for his support of the Brady bill, which required a 5-day waiting period for the purchase of handguns. James Brady had been badly wounded in the attempt on Pres. Ronald Reagan's life in 1981. Actor Christopher Reeve, who had been paralyzed in a fall from a horse, called for more funding for medical research.

The party platform, more moderate in tone than in the recent past, was adopted **Aug. 27**. It gave cautious approval to the new welfare law, which had divided the party, but called for amendments. Given Clinton's shift to the center on some issues, forthrightly liberal speeches by the Rev. Jesse Jackson and former New York Gov. Mario Cuomo, **Aug. 27**, seemed like echoes of the past. First Lady Hillary Rodham Clinton, **Aug. 27**, received an enthusiastic welcome as she stressed pro-family themes. Gov. Evan Bayh of Indiana gave a middle-of-the-road keynote speech, **Aug. 27**. Gore, **Aug. 28**, described how his sister, who had started smoking at age 13, died of lung cancer, and he vowed to work to prevent young people from starting to smoke. Clinton and Gore were renominated without opposition, **Aug. 28**.

In his acceptance speech, **Aug. 29**, Clinton restated support for several tax cuts designed to help families. He charged that tax cuts proposed by Robert Dole, the Republican presidential nominee, would "explode the deficit" and force deep cuts in Medicare and other programs. He announced initiatives in education, including a $10,000-a-year tax deduction for families with children in college. As achievements in his first term Clinton claimed credit for job creation, a decline in crime, a sharp decline in federal budget deficits, cuts in inflation and unemployment, and the passage of a minimum-wage law, health-insurance reform, the Family and Medical Leave Act, and the Brady gun-control bill. Clinton also claimed achievements in foreign affairs, including progress in negotiations between Israel and the Palestinians and in the establishment of a democratic government in Haiti.

**Clinton Aide Quits After Being Linked to Prostitute**—Dick Morris, the architect of the strategy that had seen Pres. Bill Clinton move toward the center of the political spectrum, resigned **Aug. 29**, after the *New York Post* reported that another newspaper, the tabloid *Star*, would soon reveal that he had been seeing a prostitute. Morris, a consultant, had first worked for Clinton during the 1978 Arkansas gubernatorial campaign, and had advised many other political figures, both Democrats and Republicans. His resignation came on the day that Clinton accepted the nomination for president. The *Post* said that the prostitute, Sherry Rowlands, had checks from Morris and tapes of his phone messages. She said Morris had let her listen in on his phone conversations with the president.

## International

**Somali Clan Leader Killed by Opponents**—Gen. Mohammed Farah Aidid, the factional leader who had been a major figure in the long and violent civil war in Somalia, died, **Aug. 1**, of gunshot wounds suffered in a battle with opponents. It was during a search for Aidid, whose arrest had been ordered by the UN, that 18 U.S. troops in the Somali peacekeeping force had been killed in 1993. Aidid's son, Hussein Aided, was chosen **Aug. 4** as the new leader of the clan, the United Somali Congress—Somali National Alliance.

**U.S. Sanctions Law Annoys Allies**—Pres. Bill Clinton, **Aug. 5**, signed a law providing for economic sanctions against foreign companies that invested in energy projects in Iran or Libya. Clinton called the 2 countries "dangerous supporters of terrorism." France and Germany denounced the policy, and the European Union, **Aug. 8**, filed a protest with the U.S. State Dept.

**Air Force Reprimands 16 in Crash of Plane**—The U.S. Air Force said, **Aug. 6**, that 2 generals and 14 other officers had been reprimanded in connection with the Apr. crash of a transport plane in Croatia that killed Commerce Secretary Ron Brown and all 34 others on board. Brig. Gen. William Stevens and Col. John Mazurowski were the subjects of the most serious charge, dereliction of duty, for not ensuring that the Dubrovnik airport, to which the plane was headed, and other East European airports had undergone safety inspections.

**Agreement Stops New Fighting in Chechnya**—Rebels in Chechnya struck back in Aug. against Russian troops who had disregarded a cease-fire and attacked 2 Chechen towns in July. The Chechens attacked Grozny, the republic's capital, **Aug. 6**, and on **Aug. 9** they seized its main government building. Some 7,000 Russian troops were trapped inside the city. Aleksandr Lebed, the Russian government's security council secretary, negotiated a new cease-fire agreement with the rebels, **Aug. 22**. It was agreed that the Russians would withdraw from the capital and then from Chechnya and that the rebels would then disarm. On **Aug. 31**, Lebed and Gen. Aslan Maskhadov, the Chechen commander, reached an agreement under which the Chechens would defer their demands for independence for 5 years and a joint commission would oversee a complete Russian withdrawal from Chechnya.

**Yeltsin Sworn in as President of Russia**—For the first time ever, **Aug. 9**, a head of state chosen in a democratic election was inaugurated as the leader of Russia. Boris Yeltsin, who had held the presidency since 1991, had been elected to a new term in July. The ceremony, held at a time when Yeltsin was believed to be ill, was brief and subdued. Parliament, **Aug. 10**, approved the reappointment of Viktor Chernomyrdin as premier.

**Iraq Seizes Kurdish Town Under UN Protection**—The Iraqi regime of Pres. Saddam Hussein appeared to be moving toward a new confrontation with the international community in Aug. Iraq, which had been routed by the U.S. and its Persian Gulf allies in 1991 after it had invaded Kuwait, had been warned not to attack its population of Kurds, an ethnic minority that also occupied parts of Turkey and Iran. Kurdish factions had been fighting among themselves, and on **Aug. 17** one group backed by Iran attacked another. Cease-fires brokered by the U.S., **Aug. 23** and **28**, failed to hold. Responding to an appeal from the Kurds who were on the defensive, Iraqi troops began to move north, drawing a warning from the U.S., **Aug. 28**. On **Aug. 31**, the Iraqi forces seized Arbil, a city that the Kurds had designated as their capital and which was under UN protection.

**Ex-President of South Korea Sentenced to Die**—A criminal court in Seoul, South Korea, convicted and sentenced former Pres. Chun Doo Hwan to death, **Aug. 26**, for his part in a coup that brought him to power in 1979 and for the subsequent massacre of at least 240 pro-democracy demonstrators by army troops in 1980. Chun, who was president from 1980 to 1988, was also convicted of bribery. Roh Tae Woo, president from 1988 to 1993, was convicted, **Aug. 26**, for his support of the coup and for accepting bribes. He was sentenced to 22½ years in prison. A number of business executives, generals, and former government officials were also convicted and sentenced.

**Palestinians Protest Expansion of Settlement**—The Israeli government, **Aug. 27**, approved expanding the settlement of Kiryat Sefer, in the Israeli-occupied West Bank,. ending a freeze on expansion of settlements in Palestinian territories, in place since 1992. Palestinian leader Yasir Arafat denounced the plan, **Aug. 28**, and the Palestinian Legislative Council backed a general strike, which took place **Aug. 29.**

## General

**Olympic Games Conclude in Atlanta**—The centennial Olympic Games concluded in Atlanta **Aug. 4.** Michael Johnson of the U.S. won the 400-meter run, July 29, and the 200 meters, **Aug. 1**, in world-record time of 19.32 seconds. He was the first man to win both these events at the same Olympics. Dan O'Brien of the U.S. won the decathlon, **Aug. 1.** Cuba repeated as the gold medalist in baseball, defeating Japan, 13–9, **Aug. 2**. The U.S. men's basketball team, once more consisting mostly of professional stars and again nicknamed the Dream Team, won the gold medal again, defeating Yugoslavia, 95–69, in the final game, **Aug. 3**. By defeating Brazil, 111–87, **Aug. 4**, the U.S. women's basketball team also won a gold medal. Josia Thugwane, **Aug. 4**, became the first black athlete from South Africa to win a gold medal, finishing 3 seconds ahead of South Korea's Lee Bong-ju in the closest marathon race in Olympic history. In all, the U.S. won 44 gold medals and a total of 101 medals, more than any other country. Germany won 65 medals and Russia 63.

**Primitive Life Form Reportedly Detected on Mars**—Scientific evidence pointing to the possible existence of life beyond Earth was announced **Aug. 6** by Daniel Goldin, administrator of the U.S. National Aeronautics and Space Administration.The reputed evidence of "a primitive form of microscopic life" was contained in a 4.5-lb meteorite that reportedly originated on Mars 4.5 bil years ago and struck Antarctica 13,000 years ago. U.S. spacecraft that landed on Mars had detected no sign of life but had brought back rock samples that permitted identification of the meteorite as Martian. Utilizing electron microscopes, scientists believe they identified fossil remains of microorganisms in the meteorite. Researchers also discovered organic compounds having rings of carbon atoms like those found on Earth that often had biological origins. They also found carbonate globules from 3.6 bil years ago, when Mars was probably warmer and wetter.

# SEPTEMBER 1996

## National

**Fall Election Campaign Gets Underway**—Although the presidential candidates had been on the campaign trail for months, the 1996 race for the White House got started in earnest in Sept., along with contests for Congress and thousands of state and local offices.

As in 1992, Ross Perot, the Reform Party presidential nominee, used 30-minute TV "infomercials" to promote his candidacy. On **Sept. 1**, he warned that Medicare and Medicaid were headed for insolvency, and that Social Security should be privatized if it was to be saved. On **Sept. 10**, Perot announced he had chosen Pat Choate, an economist and author who, like Perot, was a critic of recent international trade agreements, as his vice-presidential running mate.

The Family and Medical Leave Act, which allowed workers time off after a child's birth or to deal with serious family illness, and which Pres. Bill Clinton championed, was criticized, **Sept. 7**, by Bob Dole, the Republican presidential nominee, as antibusiness and as an example of Clinton's use of government to intervene in people's lives. Clinton, **Sept. 13**, released an 11-page summary of his medical records after the Dole campaign had demanded that he provide more information on his health. The report indicated that Clinton was in good health; he did not, however, release medical records themselves, as Dole did. At the Christian Coalition convention, Dole, **Sept. 14**, told the cheering delegates that as president he would sign a bill banning a procedure called partial-birth abortion; Clinton had vetoed such a bill.

Dole, stressing drugs and crime, promised, **Sept. 16**, that he would cut drug use by teen-agers in half during his first term. Clinton, **Sept. 16**, received the endorsement of the Fraternal Order of Police, a 270,000-member union that had never previously supported a Democrat for president. The Commission on Presidential Debates, **Sept. 17**, announced that only Clinton and Dole would participate in televised presidential debates. An advisory board had recommended that no other candidates be included because none had a "realistic chance" of winning.

**Economic Data Give Lift to Clinton**—Statistics released in Sept. appeared to strengthen the claim by Pres. Bill Clinton that the economy was doing well. The Conference Board said, **Sept. 3**, that the leading economic indicators had risen by 0.2% in July, the 6th consecutive monthly advance. The Labor Dept. reported, **Sept. 6**, that in August the unemployment rate had hit a 7-year low of 5.1%; as well, 250,000 nonfarm jobs had been created. The department announced, **Sept. 12**, that prices charged by manufacturers and farmers for finished goods had risen 0.3% in August. It reported, **Sept. 13**, that consumer prices had edged upward by only 0.1% in August. This small increase plus a report that retail sales were weak persuaded Wall Street that the economy was not overheating, and the Dow Jones industrial average, **Sept. 13**, closed at an all-time high of 5,838.52—a dramatic rebound from a summer slump. The Commerce Dept., **Sept. 18**, reported that the trade deficit had soared to $11.7 bil in July, the highest since monthly levels had first been calculated in 1992.

**Whitewater Defendant Jailed for Contempt**—On **Sept. 4**, prosecutors handling the Whitewater affair called Susan McDougal, who had been convicted in a trial in May, to testify before a grand jury in Little Rock that was continuing to consider related matters. She was offered immunity from further prosecution. McDougal refused to testify and, on **Sept. 4**, was held in contempt by U.S. District Judge Susan Webber Wright. McDougal said that she did not trust the prosecutors and that she believed they were trying to get something on Pres. and Mrs. Bill Clinton. She was sent to jail for contempt, **Sept. 9**, 3 weeks before the scheduled beginning of her jail term for fraud and conspiracy.

**3 Convicted in Plot to Bomb U.S. Airliners**—Three Muslim radicals were convicted in federal district court in New York City, **Sept. 5**, of plotting to blow up 12 U.S. airliners over the Pacific Ocean. Prosecutors said that Ramzi Ahmed Yousef, described as the mastermind, planned to have 5 people each smuggle bombs onto 12 planes departing East Asian cities within 48 hours in Jan. 1995. The 3 men on trial were all Muslims, and the plot was hatched to protest U.S. support for Israel. Yousef was also found guilty of planting a bomb on a Philippine Airlines plane in 1994 that killed one passenger.

**Kevorkian Attends 40th Suicide**—During the spring and summer, Dr. Jack Kevorkian attended suicides frequently, with 10 reported from May, when he was acquitted for the 3d time on charges related to assisted suicide, through Aug. On **Sept. 6**, police in Southfield, MI, broke in on a meeting between Kevorkian and Isabel Correa, a California woman who was paralyzed. With Kevorkian present for the 40th time at a suicide, Correa took her life, **Sept. 7**. Kevorkian's critics contended that some of his patients would not have chosen to die if they had been treated for pain and depression.

**Same-Sex Marriages Are Set Back by New Law**—Following the lead of the House in July, the Senate, **Sept. 10**, voted, 85–14, in favor of the Defense of Marriage bill, which would bar federal benefits to cohabiting people of the same sex and allow a state to disregard any such union legally recognized in another state. The U.S. Constitution requires that a state accept the "acts, records, and judicial proceedings of every other state"; it was anticipated that Hawaii might soon become the first state to legalize same-sex marriages. Also on **Sept. 10**, the Senate, voting, 50–49, rejected a bill to ban discrimination against homosexuals in the workplace. Pres. Bill Clinton, **Sept. 21**, signed the Defense of Marriage Act.

**Clinton Protects Vast Scenic Area in Utah**—Pres. Bill Clinton, **Sept. 18**, issued an executive order creating the Grand Staircase-Escalante National Monument in southern Utah. Under the Antiquities Act of 1906, the president had the power to protect, as national monuments, federal lands of "historic or scientific interest." Clinton signed the order at the rim of the Grand Canyon in Arizona, southwest from the new monument, which, at 1.7 million acres, would be one of the largest units in the national park system. The area included deep twisting canyons and a sequence of exposed rock strata of many colors and fanciful shapes. Clinton's order thwarted plans by Andalex Resources, a Dutch company, to mine for coal on the Kaiparowits Plateau, and was criticized by Utah political leaders who supported development.

**U.S. Woman Completes 6 Months in Space**—Dr. Shannon Lucid completed a space voyage of 188 days in Sept. The astronaut, a 53-year-old biochemist, had spent more time in space than any other U.S. astronaut and more than any other woman from any country. She spent most of her time above the Earth in the Russian space station *Mir*. On **Sept. 18-19**, the *Mir* linked up with the U.S. shuttle *Atlantis*. This permitted her to change from *Mir* to *Atlantis* and land at Cape Canaveral, FL, **Sept. 26**.

**TWA Crash Inquiry Takes New Twist**—Investigators believed in Aug. that they had achieved a breakthrough when they found traces of explosives on pieces of the TWA plane that crashed off Long Island, NY, in July. But federal officials said, **Sept. 20**, that packages containing the same explosives may have been placed on the plane in June in a test to see if a trained dog could sniff them out. The test was conducted in St. Louis when the plane was present, although it was not certain that this particular plane was used. The traces could have remained, and thus did not prove that a bomb caused the crash.

**Defense Bill Has Anti-Stalking Provision**—Pres. Bill Clinton, **Sept. 23**, signed a $256.6 billion defense-spending authorization bill for fiscal year 1997; it provided a 3% pay increase for military personnel and increased total defense expenditures by $1.3 billion over 1996. A key provision of the bill that was unrelated to the military made it a crime to cross state lines to stalk someone.

**Congress Passes Omnibus Spending Bill, With Provisions That Seek to Slow Illegal Immigration**—In late Sept. Congress enacted an omnibus spending bill appropriating $595 bil in federal expenditures for fiscal year 1997. The measure increased funding for education and included $1.1 bil for antiterrorism measures; it also contained a provision barring anyone convicted of domestic violence from owning a handgun.

The spending bill incorporated a major immigration bill that had been separate. It provided for hiring 1,000 new Border Patrol agents over 5 years, authorized construction of a fence along the U.S.-Mexico border south of San Diego, and stepped up penalties for smuggling in illegal aliens. The bill also provided for 1,200 new investigators for the Immigration and Naturalization Service, partly to track down employers hiring illegal aliens. Income requirements for sponsors of legal immigrants were tightened. A controversial amendment that would have denied public education to children of illegal immigrants was dropped in the face of opposition. In the end, the omnibus spending bill was passed by the House, **Sept. 28**, 370–37, and the Senate, **Sept. 30**, 84–15. Pres. Bill Clinton signed it **Sept. 30**.

## International

**U.S. Missiles Strike at Iraqi Military Sites**—The UN and U.S. responded in Sept. to the Iraqi army's advance into Kurdish territory in late Aug. On **Sept. 1**, UN Secretary General Boutros Boutros-Ghali froze an agreement under which Iraq was to be allowed to sell some oil to relieve a shortage of food and medical supplies. Iraqi forces, **Sept. 2**, began to pull out of Arbil, the Kurdish city they had seized to assist the Kurdish Democratic Party (KDP), which had come under attack from another faction. Iraqi troops had reportedly killed hundreds of people in house-to-house searches there. The United States launched 27 missile attacks against Iraq, **Sept. 3**. They came not in northern Iraq, in the Kurdish area, but on air-defense sites in the south. U.S. Defense Secretary William Perry said, **Sept. 3**, that the targets had been chosen because the policies of Pres. Saddam Hussein threatened oil-producing countries south of Iraq.

Britain, Germany, and Japan supported the U.S. action, but Russia, China, and most Arab countries opposed it, **Sept. 3**. Tariq Aziz, Iraq's deputy premier, said, **Sept. 3**, that Iraq was within its rights in coming to the aid of the Kurds. The United States, **Sept. 3**, extended the southern "no-fly zone" northward from the 32d to the 33d parallel. Bob Dole, the Republican presidential nominee, who had criticized the Clinton administration's handling of Iraq the previous day, backed the U.S. military moves in the Gulf region, **Sept. 3**. The United States launched 17 more missile attacks, **Sept. 4**.

The KDP captured Sulaimaniya, the Kurdish cultural capital, from their rivals, the Iranian-backed Patriotic Union of Kurdistan, **Sept. 9**. The Iraqis fired at 2 U.S. jets that were surveying the northern no-fly zone, **Sept. 11**. The United States responded by moving more air and sea forces into the Gulf region.

**After Peace Moves, Israelis and Palestinians Clash**—Fighting between Israelis and Palestinians took a heavy toll of life in Sept. Earlier, Israeli Prime Minister Benjamin Netanyahu met with Yasir Arafat, leader of the Palestinian National Authority, at the border of Israel and the Gaza Strip, **Sept. 4**. The meeting marked the renewal of peace talks stalled since Netanyahu's election in May. The 2 leaders affirmed their commitment to carry out the interim agreement, and Netanyahu said Israel would increase the number of Palestinians allowed to enter Israel to work each day. Hard-liners in Israel's ruling Likud Party, **Sept. 5**, sharply criticized Netanyahu's meeting with Arafat. In Washington, **Sept. 9**, Netanyahu discussed with Pres. Bill Clinton the possibility of opening negotiations with Syria.

On **Sept. 24**, Israel opened a 2d entrance to an archaeological tunnel near the Temple Mount, a site sacred to both Jews and Muslims. The move angered Palestinians, who responded with demonstrations and rock-throwing familiar in years past, but the confrontation took on a new dimension, **Sept. 25**, as Israeli soldiers and police from the new Palestinian Authority exchanged gunfire. As violence mounted, Israel evacuated a West Bank settlement, **Sept. 26**. Fighting ranged through West Bank cities, Gaza, and Jerusalem. Netanyahu, **Sept. 27**, blamed Arafat for inciting the Palestinians. The prime minister acknowledged, **Sept. 27**, that the 2d entrance to the tunnel had been opened not just to accommodate tourists but also to help establish Israel's claim to all of Jerusalem. By **Sept. 29**, the fighting had subsided, with 54 Palestinians and 14 Israelis dead, and hundreds wounded.

**Yeltsin to Undergo Heart Surgery**—Pres. Boris Yeltsin of Russia said, **Sept, 5**, that he would soon undergo heart surgery. He had appeared ill at his inauguration in August, and had been out of public sight since. He had a condition called ischemia, which restricted the flow of blood to the heart. On **Sept. 20**, Russian medical personnel said that Yeltsin had problems that might complicate his bypass surgery and that he had had a heart attack before the presidential runoff election in July.

**Bosnia's "Collective Presidency" Elected**—Pursuant to the peace agreement negotiated in the United States in 1995, voters in Bosnia and Herzegovina participated in Sept. in an election of national and parliamentary leaders. The peace agreement had divided Bosnia into a Muslim–Croat entity and another controlled by Bosnian Serbs. Voting separately, **Sept. 14**, the 3 ethnic groups chose their representatives on the so-called collective presidency. The 3 successful candidates were Alija Izetbegovic (Muslim), who was named head of the collective presidency; Kresimir Zubak (Croat); and Momcilo Krajisnik (Serb). U.S. Sec. of State Warren Christopher said, **Sept. 18**, that U.S. peacekeepers would leave Bosnia in Dec., as planned, but that an "international presence" would be required there after all the NATO troops left.

**Nuclear Test-Ban Treaty Approved by UN**—The UN General Assembly, **Sept. 10**, approved the comprehensive nuclear test-ban treaty. The vote was 158–3, with Bhutan, India, and Libya opposed. Pakistan, which was thought to be capable of building a nuclear weapon, voted for the treaty but did not promise to ratify it.

**Taliban Guerrillas Seize Afghan Capital**—Militant guerrillas in Afghanistan captured the capital, Kabul, in Sept. and quickly moved to impose an authoritarian fundamentalist Muslim regime. The rebels, who had gradually occupied two-thirds of the country, had begun an offensive earlier in the month, taking the city of Jalalabad. On **Sept. 26**, troops loyal to Pres. Burhanuddin Rabbani pulled out of Kabul, and the guerrillas, members of the Taliban militia, occupied the city, **Sept. 27**. The rebels seized and hanged Najibullah, a former president, and his brother, Shahpur Ahmadzi, once the nation's security chief. Other leaders fled the capital and joined resistance forces. Within days, the victors had closed places of entertainment in Kabul and demanded that women wear traditional clothing covering all but their eyes.

### General

**Hurricanes Flog Caribbean, East Coast**—On **Sept. 6**, Hurricane Fran struck land at Cape Fear, NC, with winds of 115 miles an hour. Moving north, it released heavy rain and spun off tornadoes. It claimed 28 lives, and damage was estimated at as high as $1 billion. On **Sept. 10**, Hurricane Hortense struck Puerto Rico and the Dominican Republic with 85-mile-an-hour winds, and released up to 20 inches of rain. In Puerto Rico, most homes and businesses lost electricity and running water. Twenty died in Puerto Rico, where damage was estimated at $200 million.

**Sampras, Graf Keep U.S. Open Tennis Titles**—Pete Sampras, an American, won the U.S. Open men's singles tennis crown in New York City, **Sept. 8**. It was his 2d straight title and 4th overall, making him the 3d man to claim that many championships. He defeated Michael Chang, 6–1, 6–4, 7–6. On **Sept. 8**, Steffi Graf of Germany also retained her Open title and won her 5th championship overall, defeating Monica Seles, 7–5, 6–4.

**John F. Kennedy Jr. Marries**—John F. Kennedy Jr., son of the 35th president, married his girlfriend, Carolyn Bessette, **Sept. 21**. Kennedy was editor and cofounder of *George*, a magazine containing political commentary. He had been proclaimed The Sexiest Man Alive and America's Most Eligible Bachelor. Ms. Bessette had been on the staff of Calvin Klein, Ltd. The couple was married in a private, unannounced ceremony on Cumberland Island, GA, with only about 40 relatives and close friends attending.

## OCTOBER 1996

### National

**Debates Highlight Presidential Campaign**—Debates between the major-party presidential and vice-presidential candidates dominated the campaign in Oct. On **Oct. 1**, Federal Judge Thomas Hogan dismissed a suit by Ross Perot, presidential candidate of the Reform Party, who had sought to be in the debates, from which he had been barred. Hogan said the courts had no authority to decide who should be included. He rejected a similar suit by John Hagelin, candidate of the Natural Law Party.

In the first presidential debate, **Oct. 6** in Hartford, CT, Bob Dole, the Republican nominee, sought to define himself with regard to Pres. Bill Clinton, asserting, "The difference is, I trust the people. The president trusts the government." He said that average people had become worse off, economically, during the past 4 years and that they would prosper with his major tax cut. Clinton dismissed Dole's tax program as a "scheme" and argued instead for smaller, more targeted tax cuts. He noted that Dole had opposed "the family and medical leave bill, the Brady bill, the assault weapons ban, the program to put 100,000 police on the street."

Perot, **Oct. 7**, asked Clinton to say he would not pardon former associates and appointees who had been convicted or faced the possibility of trial on various charges. He suggested Clinton might use his pardon power to prevent others from implicating himself or Hillary Clinton in plea bargains. Dole, who had refrained from going after Clinton on ethical issues, began to shift strategy, **Oct. 8**, saying, "The president promised us the most ethical administration in American history," and noting that many associated with Clinton had been immersed in scandal.

The economy was the principal issue in the vice presidential debate in St. Petersburg, FL, **Oct. 9**. Jack Kemp, the GOP nominee, said the administration was trying to frighten older Americans into believing that Republicans would wreck Medicare. He also stressed concern for economic problems of the inner city. Vice Pres. Al Gore recalled that Kemp had once said Dole—long known for his concern about balancing the budget—"never met a tax that he didn't hike."

Clinton and Dole debated for the 2d and last time, **Oct. 16**, in San Diego, in a town-meeting-style format, with questions from the audience. Dole stepped up his criticism on ethics, asserting that "30-some" people around Clinton had resigned under a cloud, been convicted, or were under investigation. He said that Americans "see scandals on almost a daily basis," causing cynicism. Clinton generally brushed aside the attacks. Asked if he thought Dole, at 73, was too old to be president, Clinton said, "It's the age of his ideas that I question," to which Dole responded, "When you don't have any ideas, I guess you say the other person's ideas are old."

The Democratic National Committee acted on another scandal, **Oct. 18**, suspending the fund-raising activities of John Huang, a vice-chairman for finance, who had solicited an illegal contribution of $250,000 from a South Korean conglomerate. That gift had been returned. Huang had organized a fund-raising event at a Buddhist temple near Los Angeles, which had brought in $140,000, some of it from monks who had taken vows of poverty. News reports had linked Huang to millions of dollars in gifts to the Democrats from a wealthy family in Indonesia. Dole and Perot excoriated Clinton for the foreign contributions. It was reported, **Oct. 23**, that the Democratic National Committee had returned a $20,000 donation from a convicted drug dealer who had also been to a White House dinner.

In a move that surprised many, Scott Reed, Dole's campaign manager, met with Perot, **Oct. 23**, and asked him to withdraw and back Dole. A recent New York Times/CBS poll had shown these results: Clinton 55%, Dole 33%, Perot 5%. Perot, **Oct. 24**, rejected the Dole overture as "weird" and said he was in the race "to the bitter end."

Stepping up his attacks, **Oct. 25**, and adding the press as a target, Dole said, "We've got to stop the liberal bias in this country," and he asked, referring to scandals, "Where is the outrage?" Clinton, **Oct. 27**, intensified his appeal to women, citing efforts to fight breast cancer and support for family leave, Head Start, and student loans. Dole said, **Oct. 28**, that he supported an initiative on the ballot in California that would prohibit state affirmative action programs; the GOP candidate said he opposed quotas and set asides to redress racial discrimination in hiring and education.

Dole warned, **Oct. 30**, that new figures showing a slow growth rate for the economy in the 3d quarter foreshadowed a recession. He said that the 1993 tax increase supported by the administration was responsible.

**Dow Jones Industrial Average Tops 6,000**—The Conference Board said, **Oct. 1**, that the leading economic indicators has risen 0.2% in Aug., the 7th consecutive monthly gain. The Labor Dept. reported, **Oct. 4**, that the unemployment rate had edged upward in Sept. from 5.1% to 5.2% and that payroll employment had declined by 40,000. The department said, **Oct. 11**, that prices charged by manufacturers for finished goods had risen 0.2% in Sept. The small advance was seen to mean that inflation remained under control. Data showing slow, steady growth reassured Wall Street. On **Oct. 14**, the Dow Jones industrial average closed above 6,000 for the first time—at 6,010. Continuing improvement in corporate profits had further buttressed the market. The Labor Dept. reported, **Oct. 16**, that consumer prices had risen 0.3% in Sept. The Commerce Dept. said, **Oct. 18**, that the trade deficit had declined only slightly, to $10.8 billion in August, from its high in July.

Pres. Bill Clinton, **Oct. 28**, hailed the news that the federal budget deficit for the fiscal year ending in Sept. had been $107.3 billion, lowest since 1981, and a fulfillment of his vow to reduce the deficit by half; in fact, it was down 63% during his presidency. In other news, the Commerce Dept. reported, **Oct. 30**, that economic growth at an annual rate had been only 2.2% in the 3d quarter, half the rate in the 2d quarter.

**Archer Daniels Midland Co. Fined $100 Million**—The Archer Daniels Midland Company announced, **Oct. 14**, that it had agreed to pay a fine of $100 million for conspiring with competitors to fix the prices of 2 agricultural products. The fine was by far the largest ever obtained by the U.S. Justice Dept. in a price-fixing case. The food-processing corporation, which describes itself as Supermarket to the World, admitted that it had fixed the prices of lysine, a feed additive, and citric acid, which is used in foods and beverages.

**Security Guard Cleared in Atlanta Bombing**—The Justice Dept. said in Oct. that a security guard was no longer a suspect in the bombing in Atlanta's Centennial Olympic Park in July. The explosion, at a concert held in conjunction with the Olympic games, directly caused 1 death and injured more than 100 people. The guard, Richard Jewell, was first hailed as a hero for helping to clear the area before a suspicious bag exploded, but then the media reported he was a suspect. He passed a polygraph test, however, and an intense FBI investigation failed to produce evidence against him. Meanwhile, reporters and the FBI dogged him relentlessly, making a normal life impossible. In the letter to his lawyer, **Oct. 20**, the FBI did not offer an apology.

**FBI Official Destroyed Report on Fatal Shootout**—A top executive in the Federal Bureau of Investigation pleaded guilty in Oct. to obstructing justice for destroying a document relevant to a violent shootout. A confrontation in rural Idaho in 1992 between Randall Weaver and law enforcement officials had resulted in the fatal shootings of a federal Marshall and Weaver's young son and wife. E. Michael Kahoe, then head of the FBI's violent crime and major offenders' section, was asked by prosecutors in Idaho to provide any reports of evaluations and critiques of FBI conduct in the incident, which had come under widespread criticism. Instead, Kahoe had a report destroyed that referred to problems in FBI conduct. On **Oct. 30**, in federal district court in Washington, DC, Kahoe pleaded guilty to obstructing justice.

## International

**Summit Fails to End Mideast Tension**—Prime Min. Benjamin Netanyahu of Israel and Yasir Arafat, head of the Palestinian National Authority, met with Pres. Bill Clinton at the White House, **Oct. 1** and **2**, following the deadly violence of late Sept. King Hussein of Jordan also attended the meetings. Little progress was reported, however. Netanyahu declined to set a deadline for Israeli withdrawal from the city of Hebron or to agree on a date to begin talks on the future status of Jerusalem. He also declined to close an entrance to the tunnel near the Al–Aksa mosque in Jerusalem that was the focal point of the Sept. unrest. Three weeks of intense negotiations over Hebron appeared, **Oct. 28**, to have reached an impasse, when the U.S. mediator, Dennis Ross, left the talks.

**2 From East Timor Win Peace Prize**—The Nobel Peace Price was awarded, **Oct. 11**, to 2 individuals who had led the opposition to the occupation of East Timor by Indonesia and the subsequent abuses of human rights there. East Timor, one-half of the island of Timor in the Indonesian Archipelago, was a former Portuguese colony that was annexed by Indonesia in the 1970s. The Nobel Prize was awarded to Jose Ramos-Horta, who from exile in Australia was the leading international spokesman for the independence movement, and to Roman Catholic Bishop Carlos Ximenes Belo, who lived in East Timor and who was thought to be in danger because of his frequent denunciations of the regime. The award citation said "it has been estimated that one-third of the population of East Timor lost their lives due to starvation, epidemics, war, and terror" under the Indonesians.

**Yeltsin Fires Popular Aide for Insubordination**—The struggle for power in Russia took a dramatic turn in Oct., as the day drew near for Pres. Boris Yeltsin to undergo heart surgery. Yeltsin dismissed Aleksandr Lebed, his national security chief, charging the outspoken former general with insubordination. Lebed, a retired general, had placed third in the first round of voting for president in June, and Yeltsin had then brought him into his administration, improving his chances in the July runoff, which he won. Lebed's popularity rose after he negotiated a truce in Chechnya, succeeding where others had failed. Lebed openly criticized other top aides to Yeltsin, including potential successors, whom he regarded as corrupt and inept. In removing Lebed, Yeltsin, **Oct. 17**, said that the country must be led by a united team. Responding, Lebed said that the army was demoralized and the nation faced a "hot autumn," but he said that he would utilize only constitutional means in any future action he might take.

**Japan's Ruling Party Tightens Grip in Voting**—The Liberal Democratic Party reestablished its primacy in Japanese politics in the parliamentary election held **Oct. 20**. The LDP, the most conservative of the leading parties, had led Japan for 38 years until 1993, when widespread scandals involving many of its leaders brought defeat at the polls. Within a year, however, the winning coalition in that election, which was committed to government reform, collapsed, and the LDP returned to tenuous power in another coalition. In the voting, the LDP increased its seats in the 500-member Diet from 211 to 239, nearly a majority. The New Frontier Party won 156 seats. Among the smaller parties, the Communists rose from 15 to 26 seats.

**Sandinistas Rebuffed by Nicaraguan Voters**—The Sandinista National Liberation Front failed in Oct. to recapture the presidency of Nicaragua. The Sandinista guerrilla fighters had seized power from the dictatorial Somoza regime in 1979, then moved sharply to the political left. A long struggle with so-called contras, backed by the United States, led ultimately to the defeat of the Sandinistas in a presidential election in 1990 that was won by Violeta Barrios de Chamorro. She was ineligible for a 2d term. In the **Oct. 20** voting, Arnoldo Aleman of the Liberal Alliance, and a former mayor of Managua, the capital, was elected president. Aleman, a strong advocate of free enterprise and close ties with the United States, defeated Daniel Ortega Saavedra, who had been president in the Sandinista years.

**Chinese Dissident Sentenced in Beijing**—Wang Dan, a prominent dissident and leader in the 1989 Tiananmen Square democracy protests, was convicted **Oct. 30** of "plotting to subvert the government," for writings in foreign publications that criticized the regime and for association with other dissidents in China, in the period from 1993 to 1995. After a trial before the Intermediate People's Court that lasted only 4 hours, from which the Western media were barred, he was sentenced to 11 years in prison and deprived of political rights for 2 years. Wang Dan had already served 4 years in prison for his role in the Tiananmen demonstrations.

## General

**Civil Trial in Simpson Case Begins**—The civil trial got underway in Santa Monica, CA, in the wrongful death suit brought against former football star O. J. Simpson, as a largely white jury was sworn in **Oct. 17**. Families of Nicole Brown Simpson, O. J. Simpson's former wife, and her friend, Ronald Goldman, were seeking unspecified damages from Simpson, contending that he had committed the murders of which he had been acquitted in a sensational 1995 trial.

Earlier, on **Oct. 2**, Mark Fuhrman, a retired detective in the Los Angeles Police Dept., pleaded no contest to one count of perjury in connection with his 1995 testimony during the criminal trial. Fuhrman, a witness for the prosecution who had described evidence he said he had found at the home of O. J. Simpson, had testified that he had never used a racial slur in reference to blacks during the previous 10 years. A tape recording had been produced that showed the contrary.

**Pope's Appendix Removed**—Pope John Paul II's appendix was removed, **Oct. 8**, in an operation in Rome. The pope had been in evident pain during recent months, and had suffered from an inflamed appendix digestive system problems, and fever. Doctors said they had found no evidence of any other serious ailment.

**Researchers Find Smoking-Cancer Link**—A long-sought explanation for how smoking causes lung cancer was announced on **Oct. 17** in the journal *Science.* Although a statistical association between smoking and lung cancer had long been apparent, the scientific connection had not been established. In the paper published in the journal, researchers from the University of Texas and Beckman Research Institute of the City of Hope said they had studied the effects of a cigarette-smoke ingredient on gene p53, which suppresses the uncontrolled growth of cells that cause tumors. They wrote that a chemical in smoke damaged the gene, preventing it from playing its protective role.

**Yankees Win World Series With Big Comeback**—The New York Yankees won their 23d World Series in late Oct., claiming their first title since 1978. In defeating the defending champions, the Atlanta Braves, the Yankees staged a dramatic comeback after losing the first 2 games at home, 12–1 and 4–0. The Yankees then swept 3 games in Atlanta, and won their 4th and deciding game in New York, 3–2, on **Oct. 26**. After scoring 3 runs in the 3d inning, the Yankees held off the Braves, who scored once in the 4th and again in the 9th. With the tying run on 2d and the lead run on 1st, and John Wetteland pitching in relief, Mark Lemke fouled out for the final out. Joe Torre was the Yankee manager. Adding drama to the series for the Yankees was the heart transplant operation in New York on the day before the final game for Frank Torre, Joe's brother, who had played first base for the Milwaukee Braves when they won the World Series in 1957.

# Notable Quotes in 1996

"We have a bridge to build [to the 21st century], and I'm ready if you are. Today the American people have spoken. They have affirmed our course. They have told us to go forward."
Pres. *Bill Clinton*, speaking to supporters in Little Rock, AR, after his reelection victory, Nov. 5.

"I was thinking on the way down the elevator [that] tomorrow will be the first time in my life I don't have anything to do."
Former Sen. and Republican presidential candidate *Bob Dole*, in his concession speech on the night of Nov. 5.

"Americans of all political persuasions are coming to the sad realization that our First Lady. . . is a congenital liar."
New York *Times* columnist *William Safire*, about First Lady Hillary Rodham Clinton and White House scandals.

"The president, if he were not the president, would have delivered a more forceful response to that on the bridge of Mr. Safire's nose."
White House spokesman *Mike McCurry*, on Safire's column.

"I will seek the presidency with nothing to fall back on but the judgment of the people, and nowhere to go but the White House or home."
*Bob Dole*, announcing his resignation from the Senate.

"The best way to have a party for 36 teenagers is to have the Secret Service and the military there."
*Hillary Rodham Clinton*, on daughter Chelsea's birthday party.

"People who didn't know me well thought I was frozen stiff."
*Vice President Al Gore*, on venturing outside during a cold spell in Washington, DC.

"When the voter speaks, I listen. Especially when the voter is saying someone else's name."
*Sen. Phil Gramm*, announcing his withdrawal from the GOP presidential race.

"If you're not going to send me a check for $5,000, I can't stay on the phone long."
*Mel Sembler*, a Tampa shopping center developer who was calling prospective donors to the campaign of cash-strapped GOP presidential candidate Lamar Alexander.

"We've got a strong candidate, I'm trying to think of his name."
*Sen. Christopher Dodd*, Democratic National Committee chairman, on Elliott Close, who subsequently lost a Senate race in South Carolina to 93-year-old incumbent Sen. Strom Thurmond.

"Well, maybe the butler did it."
*Sen. Lauch Faircloth*, on how Whitewater documents turned up in the White House living quarters last summer.

"I'd tell you what I really thought about the national media, but, as my good friend Dana Carvey would say, 'Wouldn't be prudent. Not gonna do it'."
Former Pres. *George Bush*, speaking in Texas.

"I get these invitations to speak on some campus and find that the students don't really want me, don't know what it's all about. But there's always about 10 faculty people who invited me and want me to talk about the old days."
*Eugene J. McCarthy*, about recollections of his 1968 presidential campaign.

"She says she wants to eat junk food and drink diet Cokes and be cross at us. She said it's a lot of work to stay in a good mood all the time."
*Michael Lucid*, about his mother, Dr. Shannon Lucid, who was heading home after 6 months in space.

"Wow, what did I do?"
Twelve-year old Yankee fan *Jeff Maier*, after his catch turned New York shortstop Derek Jeter's fly ball into a game-tying home run—and sent the first game of the AL championship into extra innings for an eventual Yankee victory over the Orioles.

"The Bible says life is a vapor. For them, it was. They were old and gone at 15."
*The Rev. Gary Finn*, in Montoursville, PA, commenting on the death of 16 young people from the town's French club in the crash of TWA Flight 800.

"Do you hear the rain? Do you hear the rain?"
Seven-year-old pilot *Jessica Dubroff*, speaking to her mother by telephone as the engines revved for takeoff from Cheyenne, WY. The plane crashed minutes later in the storm.

"Evil visited us yesterday, and we don't know why."
*Ron Taylor*, headmaster of the school in Scotland where a gunman killed 16 kindergarten children and their teacher.

"Everybody knows he was good at the beginning, but he just went too far."
Cincinnati Reds owner *Marge Schott*, about Adolf Hitler.

"And so it has come to pass that South Africa today undergoes her rebirth, cleansed of a horrible past, matured from a tentative beginning, and reaching out to the future with confidence. Our pledge is: Never and never again shall the laws of our land rend our people apart or legalize their oppression and repression."
Pres. *Nelson Mandela*, speaking on the adoption of a new South African constitution.

"Sometimes a kiss is just a kiss."
National Women's Law Center attorney *Verna Williams*, on Queens, NY, 7-year-old De'Andrea Dearinge, a boy in the news in late 1996 after being suspended for "sexual harassment" for kissing a girl in school.

"Remember the bar scene from *Star Wars* with all the animals? That's what it looked like."
*Jon Koncak*, of the Orlando Magic, on the basketball team's getting stranded during a winter storm in the Allentown, PA, airport with the cast of *Sesame Street Live* and a rock-and-roll band called Marilyn Manson.

"It's not like he's shining shoes so roughly that it knocks people off the stand."
*Ron Corbett*, speaker of the Iowa statehouse, on an effort by lawmakers to help the operator of a shoeshine stand avoid having to buy a $1 million liability insurance policy.

"Got a lawyer?"
Attorney turned author *John Grisham*, joking with a reporter who tripped and fell while covering Grisham's successful court case in Brookhaven, MS—his first in 7 years.

"Somewhere up there, Elvis is smiling."
*An unnamed music-industry insider* on Lisa Marie Presley's announcement that she would divorce Michael Jackson.

"Our show is the reality. There is never a happy ending for Iraqis."
*Mahmoud Abu al-Abbas*, creator of a hit Baghdad adaptation of *My Fair Lady* in which the Eliza Doolittle character, a belly dancer, jilts Henry Higgins and returns to her home village.

"In the wrong hands, this is like giving your kids matches in a fuel-storage facility."
*Jonathan Pond*, a Boston financial planner, on new platinum Visa and MasterCards that have $100,000 credit limits.

"How do you score a disembowelment? That's very tricky."
Composer *James Horner*, on his Academy Award-nominated musical score for the film *Braveheart.*

"I guess this means you tolerate me, you really tolerate me."
The notoriously temperamental *Sean Penn*, accepting best-actor honors at the Independent Spirit movie awards.

"We have found a common cause, and it's your money."
*Johnny Rotten*, of the Sex Pistols, on why the 1970s punk band decided to reunite for a 20th-anniversary tour.

"It always does my heart good when men become secretaries."
Acting U.S. Trade Representative *Charlene Barshefsky*, on her former boss Mickey Kantor's appointment as commerce secretary.

"I've been here laboring for 5 years and now we have a sock talking at our commencement. It's kind of upsetting."
Graduate *Samantha Chie*, on Southampton College of Long Island University's decision to bestow an honorary degree on Kermit the Frog to publicize the school's marine-studies program.

"I just hope he doesn't start dialing long distance."
*Gail Curtis*, whose cat Tipper was choking on his flea collar and managed to hit speed dial and reach 911. Police succeeded in locating the cat and loosening his collar.

## Offbeat News Stories

**Mother Love**—When a 3-year-old boy fell a horrifying 20 feet onto the cement floor of the gorilla pit in the Brookfield, IL, zoo, Aug. 16, he was rescued by an unlikely bystander—one of the gorillas. The 8-year-old Binti Jua, while carrying her own baby on her back, cradled the injured boy in her arms, rocking him softly, and carried him to a door where he could be reached by paramedics. (The boy spent 4 days in the hospital, where he was treated for cuts, bruises, and a broken left hand.)

**Gibberish?**—The editors of a trendy academic journal called *Social Text* apparently made a boner when they published an esoteric article in May by New York University physicist Alan Sokal, entitled "Transgressing the Boundaries: Toward a Transformative Hermeneutics of Quantum Gravity." Fed up with what he regarded as sloppy thinking and obscure jargon in academic journals, Sokal had actually written a spoof, sprinkled with errors, poor logic, and intentional nonsense—and the *Social Text* editors failed to spot the difference. While they made excuses, Sokal made the newspapers, and apparently made his point.

**Jet Suit**—Seattle student John Leonard, 21, stunned PepsiCo attorneys when he demanded that the company give him a $70 million Harrier jet plane. PepsiCo, in what it later called a joke, had offered on TV to give away a Harrier jet, as the biggest prize in a contest, to anyone who accumulated enough Pepsi Points from bottles and cans of Pepsi. Winning enough for a jet plane would take nearly 17 million cans or bottles, but Leonard claimed he was also allowed under the rules to buy Pepsi Points for 10 cents each. He racked up 15 points in Pepsi cans, got 5 investors to chip in, and wrote a $700,008.50 check to cover the remaining points plus "shipping and handling." PepsiCo called his claim frivolous and countersued him.

**Kiss and Tell**—In the first of several similar incidents reported in the press, Johnathan Prevette, a first-grader from Lexington, NC, was removed from class, and kept out of an ice-cream party for kids with perfect attendance records, after kissing a girl on the cheek. School authorities, deluged by phone calls, defended the reaction, citing a rule against "unwelcome touching;" they also pointed out, contrary to popular perception, that Johnathan had not been accused of sexual harassment as such. Still, pundits everywhere debated the case, and Johnathan emerged as a national celebrity, with his picture in the papers and appearances on CNN and NBC's *Today Show.*

**World's Oldest Rapper**—Jeanne Calment, the French woman who first won fame in 1995, when she turned 120 and was billed as the oldest person alive, celebrated her next birthday, in Feb. 1996, by releasing a record album, with her speaking voice backed up by rap and techno rhythms. It's entitled *The March of Time.* "I waited 120 years to become famous," she told an interviewer, "and I intend to take advantage of that as long as possible."

**Gift From Heaven**—When Eduardo Sierra stopped in an otherwise empty church one day, he found that a deceased stranger was being waked there. Sierra said a prayer for him and signed his name in a blank condolence book. Little did he know that the recently departed Swedish real estate dealer had left a will stipulating that whoever prayed for his soul would get all his belongings. Sierra was the only person to sign the book, and became the sole inheritor of the millionaire's estate.

**Dumber and Dumbest**—The year had its share of klutzy crooks. For example, Robert Franklin Devoe, 33, was arrested for bank robbery in Toronto after a suspicious shopkeeper saw him weighing bundles of $100 bills on an electronic scale on sale in a store. Also, MacArthur Wheeler, 46, was convicted of bank robbery after his face was caught clearly in a surveillance camera; he and his partners had rubbed lemon juice on their faces in the belief that it would blur their image and make masks unnecessary. In another caper, Wesley Steny, 16, and Jeanis Caty, 18, were nabbed for allegedly robbing a Food Spot store in Miami, after they went to a hospital for treatment of gunshot wounds. According to police, Caty, while reaching over the store counter for cash, had accidentally discharged his gun, wounding Steny, who fell against a third robber, causing the latter's gun to go off and hit Caty. "I knew there was a mistake," the Food Spot clerk said later. "They were the only ones bleeding."

## Miscellaneous Facts

—The *Guinness Book of Records* recently certified that Brazil's Ryoki Inoue is the world's most prolific, if not most celebrated, novelist. Inoue's name is not a household word. But under a variety of pen names, writing in Portuguese, he has churned out well over 1,000 novels in the decade since he cast aside a medical career for the author's craft. He specializes in pulp fiction, mostly westerns, and when he gets going can write 3 modest-size novels in a day. Of course, this leaves little time for recreation. "Truthfully," he told one reporter, " I haven't even read all the books I've written."

—According to a poll of 801 adults for *Good Housekeeping* magazine, 33% would rather have dinner with Gen. Colin Powell than Pres. Bill Clinton, the first runner-up, who drew 24%.

—A recent study of 202 drivers in Lithuania who had rear end collisions made a strange discovery: not a single driver reported suffering from whiplash. In fact, most Lithuanians appeared never to have heard of such a thing. There's no evidence that the Lithuanians have strong necks or high pain thresholds—but it so happens that, at the time of the study, personal injury insurance did not exist in Lithuania. The authors of the study, published in *The Lancet,* the British medical journal, were researchers from Norway, which has one of the highest whiplash rates in the world. An organization of whiplash patients there soon threatened to sue them, and most medical experts assert that whiplash is indeed real. The authors themselves did not deny the existence of short-term whiplash symptoms, but they're more skeptical about long-term injuries that drag on through the hospitals, and the courts.

—The first McDonald's restaurant in India, which opened late in 1996, was also the only McDonalds's in the world that's beef-free, in keeping with Hindu religious beliefs. The Indian equivalent of a Big Mac is the Maharajah Mac, made of mutton.

—According to the American Automobile Association, the average cost of owning and driving a new car in 1996 was 42.6 cents a mile, or $6,389 a year, up $204 from the year before.

—California's Jan. 17, 1994, earthquake officially killed 61 people. But a study released in 1996 by researchers at Good Samaritan Hospital in Los Angeles found that 24 people in the county died of observed sudden heart attacks that day—far more than the normal average of 5. In the 6 days following the quake, on the other hand, sudden cardiac deaths were below average. Researchers theorized that the stress of the event triggered many deaths, especially among people who already had serious heart problems and were at risk of dying during that week.

—Switzerland, which lost its watch-making dominance in the 1970s to Japan with its precision quartz watches, won back the lead in the mid-1990s. Figures for 1995 show that the Swiss that year turned out some 39 million timepieces, compared to 30 million made in Japan. The Swiss have been gaining customers around the world by putting the stress on fashion and luxury watches.

# Historical Anniversaries

## 1897 — 100 Years Ago

A period of prosperity begins as wheat prices rise and news of Klondike gold discoveries sparks a gold rush, yielding $22 million worth of gold by year's end.

The Olney-Paunceforte Treaty, signed by the U.S. and Great Britain, **Jan. 11,** establishes arbitration as the means of solving territorial disputes between the two nations.

The U.S. endorses the gold standard, **Jan. 12,** at the National Monetary Conference.

The National Congress of Mothers, forerunner of the Parent Teachers Assn. (PTA), is organized, **Feb. 17**.

William McKinley is inaugurated, **Mar. 4,** as the 25th president of the U.S.

Congress appropriates $50,000, **May 22**, for relief of U.S. citizens in Cuba. War fever grows as U.S. sensationalist press stirs public outcry against Spain's alleged human rights violations in Cuba.

The Hawaiian government and Sec. of State John Sherman sign a treaty, **June 16,** starting a process that leads to formal U.S. annexation of Hawaii.

Klondike gold worth $750,000 arrives in San Francisco, **July 14,** aboard the *Excelsior*.

The first U.S. subway line—between the Public Gardens and Park Street in Boston—begins service **Sept. 1**.

More than 20 miners are killed by deputy sheriffs, **Sept. 10**, during a coal-miners' strike. The strike ends the next day as miners win an 8-hour day, among other gains.

Queen Victoria celebrates her Diamond Jubilee, **June 22**.

**Inventions.** The cathode-ray oscilloscope—forerunner of the first television tube—is invented by German physicist Karl Braun.

**Art.** Henri Rousseau's *The Sleeping Gypsy*, Camille Pissarro's *Boulevard des Italiens, Morning, Sunlight.*

**Literature.** *The Invisible Man* by H. G. Wells, *Captains Courageous* by Rudyard Kipling, *Dracula* by Bram Stoker.

**Theater.** *John Gabriel Borkman* by Henrik Ibsen, *The Devil's Disciple* by George Bernard Shaw, *Cyrano de Bergerac* by Edmond Rostand.

**Musicals.** *The Belle of New York,* music by Gustave A. Kecker, book and lyrics by Hugh Martin.

**Popular Songs.** "Stars and Stripes Forever" by John Philip Sousa; "On the Banks of the Wabash Far Away" by Paul Dresser; "Take Back Your Gold" by Monroe H. Rosenfeld, lyrics by Louis W. Pritzkow.

**Journalism.** Cartoonist Rudolph Dirks's "Katzenjammer Kids" debuts in the *New York Journal. New York Sun* editor Francis Church replies, "Yes, Virginia, there is a Santa Claus," in an editorial addressed to Virginia O'Hanlon, age 8, who had written to ask whether Santa Claus really exists.

**Sports.** The first Boston Marathon is run **Apr. 19**; John J. McDermott wins the then-25-mi race with a time of 2 hr, 55 min, 10 sec.

**Miscellaneous.** Steeplechase Park opens at Coney Island, NY. Cheyenne, WY, celebrates the first Frontier Day, starting an annual rodeo tradition. New York's Waldorf-Astoria Hotel is opened by John Jacob Astor IV. Jell-O dessert and Lifebuoy soap go on the market. Grape Nuts cereal is introduced by C. W. Post as a health food.

## 1947 — 50 Years Ago

Fear of Communism spurs federal government action at home and abroad. College enrollments boom as more than 2.5 million students enroll; half are veterans responding to the G.I. Bill, which provides tuition assistance.

Pres. Harry S. Truman, **Mar. 12,** asks a joint session of Congress to approve $400 million in aid to Greece and Turkey for economic recovery and defense against Soviet Communism. Called the Truman Doctrine, the bill is approved by Congress and signed into law, **May 22**.

Reflecting a rising fear of Communism, the Loyalty Program is established by executive order, **Mar. 22,** requiring security clearance for all executive-branch employees.

Nearly 600 people are killed, **Apr. 16,** after an explosion on the nitrate-laden French freighter *Grandcamp* at Texas City, TX.

At Harvard University's commencement, **June 5,** Sec. of State George Marshall proposes a plan (dubbed the Marshall Plan) for European economic recovery.

Pan American becomes the first airline to offer round-the-world service, **June 17**; the fare is $1,700.

The Taft-Hartley Act, restricting labor union power, becomes law, **June 23,** as Congress overrides Pres. Truman's veto.

Pres. Truman signs the Presidential Succession Act, **July 18,** which designates the speaker of the House and president pro tempore of the Senate next in line after the vice president.

Pres. Truman signs a law, **July 26,** uniting the army, navy, and air force as the National Military Establishment, directed by the secretary of defense, and creating the National Security Council and Central Intelligence Agency.

Norwegian anthropologist Thor Heyerdahl completes a 101-day journey, **Aug. 7**, across more than 4,000 miles of the Pacific on a balsa raft named *Kon-Tiki.*

India gains independence from Great Britain, **Aug. 15.** It is divided into two dominions, with Jawaharlal Nehru becoming the first prime minister of Hindu India and Muhammad Ali Jinnah president of Muslim Pakistan.

In the first-ever televised presidential speech to the nation, **Oct. 5,** Pres. Truman discusses the world food crisis.

U.S. Air Force Capt. Chuck Yeager becomes the first person to break the sound barrier, **Oct. 14** (in an X-1 rocket plane).

The House Un-American Activities Committee begins investigations, **Oct. 18,** into Communist influence in the movie industry. Ten motion picture professionals are blacklisted by industry leaders for supposed Communist ties.

Princess Elizabeth Alexandra, heir to the British throne, and Lt. Philip Mountbatten are married, **Nov. 20**.

The New York City area is paralyzed, **Dec. 26,** by a 16-hr, 25.8-in. snowfall, the heaviest since the blizzard of 1888, when 20.9 inches were recorded.

**Art.** Pablo Picasso's *Ulysses With His Sirens*, Henri Matisse's *Young English Girl*, Jackson Pollock's *Full Fathom Five*, Arshile Gorky's *Betrothal II*, Alberto Giacometti's *Man Pointing*.

**Literature.** *The Proper Bostonians* by Cleveland Amory, *The Plague* by Albert Camus, *Tales of the South Pacific* by James Michener, *The Setting Sun* by Osamu Dazai, *The Pearl* by John Steinbeck, *The Age of Anxiety* by W. H. Auden.

**Theater.** *A Streetcar Named Desire* by Tennessee Williams, *All My Sons* by Arthur Miller.

**Musicals.** *Finian's Rainbow* with Ella Logan, David Wayne, music by Burton Lane, lyrics by E. Y. Harburg; *Brigadoon* with James Mitchell, David Brooks, music by Frederick Loewe, book and lyrics by Alan Jay Lerner; *High Button Shoes* with Phil Silvers, Nanette Fabray, music by Jule Styne, lyrics by Sammy Cahn.

**Movies.** *Gentlemen's Agreement* with Gregory Peck, Dorothy McGuire, John Garfield, Celeste Holm; *Black Narcissus* with Deborah Kerr, Jean Simmons; *Miracle on 34th Street* with Edmund Gwenn, Maureen O'Hara, Natalie Wood; *The Farmer's Daughter* with Loretta Young, Joseph Cotten; *The Ghost and Mrs. Muir* with Gene Tierney, Rex Harrison; *Monsieur Verdoux* with Charlie Chaplin.

**Television.** *Howdy Doody, Meet the Press*, and *Kraft Television Theater* debut.

**Popular Songs.** "Autumn Leaves" by Joseph Kosma, English lyrics by Johnny Mercer; "Ballerina" by Carl Sigman, lyrics by Bob Russell; "Golden Earrings" by Ray

Evans and Victor Young, lyrics by Jay Livingston; "Ivy" by Hoagy Carmichael.

**Journalism.** Milton Caniff's "Steve Canyon" debuts on newspaper cartoon pages.

**Sports.** Jackie Robinson signs with the Brooklyn Dodgers and becomes the first black major-league baseball player. In the first World Series broadcast on TV, the New York Yankees beat the Dodgers 4 games to 3.

**Miscellaneous.** The American Theater Wing establishes the Antoinette Perry "Tony" Awards for outstanding contributions to American theater. Ajax cleanser is introduced by Colgate-Palmolive-Peet. The first commercial microwave oven is introduced by the Raytheon Co. Reddi-Wip whipped cream, the first major U.S. aerosol food product, goes on the market. B. F. Goodrich makes the first tubeless automobile tires, which seal themselves when punctured.

## 1972 — 25 Years Ago

A break-in at Democratic Party headquarters in the Watergate complex sets off a chain of events that will ultimately lead to Pres. Richard Nixon's resignation, but in Nov. 1972, he is reelected in a landslide. U.S. involvement in the Vietnam war changes character, as U.S. bombing attacks heat up and U.S. ground-troop involvement winds down.

Pres. Nixon approves a $5.5 bil program, **Jan. 5,** for the development of a space shuttle that will lift off like a rocket but land back on Earth like an airplane.

Pres. Nixon makes a historic visit to China, **Feb. 21-28,** where he meets with Chairman Mao Zedong and Premier Zhou Enlai; both powers pledge to work for "normalization of relations."

Author Clifford Irving admits, **Mar. 13,** that his purported interviews with and subsequent biography of multimillionaire Howard Hughes were hoaxes.

The Equal Rights Amendment, prohibiting discrimination on grounds of gender, is approved by the Senate, **Mar. 22**. Passed by the House in Oct. 1971, it went to the states for ratification (which it did not receive).

North Vietnamese forces launch the biggest attacks in 4 years across the demilitarized zone **Mar. 30**. The U.S. responds by resumption of bombing of Hanoi and Haiphong after a 4-year lull.

The 11-week trial of the antiwar "Harrisburg 7" activists ends in mistrial, **Apr. 5,** as the jury declares itself deadlocked.

Canada's Prime Minister Pierre Elliott Trudeau and Pres. Nixon sign, **Apr. 13-15,** a landmark treaty to clean up the Great Lakes.

J. Edgar Hoover, 77, director of the Federal Bureau of Investigation (FBI) for all of its 48 years, dies, **May 2.**

The U.S. begins mining Haiphong and other North Vietnamese ports, **May 9**.

While campaigning for the presidency at a Laurel, MD, shopping center, Alabama Gov. George C. Wallace is shot and seriously disabled, **May 15**. Arthur H. Bremer is sentenced to 63 years for shooting Wallace and 3 bystanders.

In the first visit of a U.S. president to Moscow, Richard Nixon arrives, **May 22,** for a week of summit talks that culminate in a landmark strategic arms pact.

Five men are arrested, **June 17,** for breaking into the offices of the Democratic National Committee in the Watergate complex in Washington, DC.

Hurricane Agnes hits Florida and goes on a 10-day rampage up the Eastern Seaboard in **June**, causing 118 deaths and more than $3 bil in damage.

The U.S. Supreme Court, in *Furman* v. *Georgia*, rules the death penalty unconstitutional, **June 29**.

The Democratic National Convention is held in Miami, FL, **July 10-13,** and nominates Sen. George McGovern as the presidential candidate and Sen. Thomas Eagleton as the vice-presidential candidate. Because of controversy over Eagleton's past treatment for depression, he is replaced, **Aug. 8**, by R. Sargent Shriver.

As the U.S. ends its Vietnam ground combat role with the withdrawal of the last U.S. combat troops, **Aug. 11,** the heaviest U.S. Air Force bombing of the war takes place.

Eight Arab guerrillas, members of the Black September terrorist group, invade the Israeli dormitory of the Olympic village in Munich, **Sept. 5,** killing 2 Israelis and taking 9 hostages. All 9, along with 5 terrorists, are killed the next day during a shootout with police.

Two former White House aides, G. Gordon Liddy and E. Howard Hunt, are indicted along with 5 others, **Sept. 15,** on charges stemming from the break-in at Democratic headquarters in the Watergate complex.

Japan's Prime Minister Kakuei Tanaka and China's Premier Zhou Enlai sign an accord, **Sept. 29,** to end the technical state of war existing between their countries since 1937 and renew diplomatic relations.

Pres. Nixon wins a landslide victory in the presidential election, **Nov. 7,** over Democratic candidate George McGovern.

Full-scale bombing of North Vietnam resumes, **Dec. 18,** after Paris peace negotiations reached an impasse.

Harry S. Truman, 33d president of the U.S., dies, **Dec. 26**; he was 88 years old.

**Art.** Andy Warhol's *Mao*; in Rome, Michelangelo's *Pietà* is seriously damaged by a deranged man who attacks it with a hammer.

**Literature.** *August 1914* by Aleksandr Solzhenitsyn, *The Manticore* by Robertson Davies, *The Optimist's Daughter* by Eudora Welty, *Watership Down* by Richard George Adams, *The Terminal Man* by Michael Crichton, *The Exorcist* by William P. Blatty, *The Day of the Jackal* by Frederick Forsyth.

**Theater.** *Sticks and Bones* by David Rabe, *Small Craft Warnings* by Tennessee Williams, *That Championship Season* by Jason Miller, *6 Rooms Riv Vu* by Bob Randall, *The River Niger* by Joseph A. Walker, *The Sunshine Boys* by Neil Simon, *Jumpers* by Tom Stoppard.

**Musicals.** *Sugar* with Robert Morse, Cyril Ritchard, music by Jule Styne, lyrics by Bob Merrill; *Don't Bother Me, I Can't Cope* by Micki Grant; *Grease* by Jim Jacobs and Warren Casey; *Pippin* with John Rubinstein, Ben Vereen, music and lyrics by Stephen Schwartz.

**Movies.** *Cabaret* with Liza Minnelli, Joel Grey; *Butterflies Are Free* with Goldie Hawn, Eddie Albert; *Deliverance* with Jon Voight, Burt Reynolds, Ned Beatty; *Sleuth* with Laurence Olivier, Michael Caine; *Sounder* with Cicely Tyson, Paul Winfield, Kevin Hooks; *The Godfather* with Marlon Brando, Al Pacino, James Caan, Diane Keaton; *Play It Again, Sam* with Woody Allen, Diane Keaton.

**Television.** Comedy/drama series *M*A*S*H* and rural Depression-era drama *The Waltons* premiere.

**Popular Songs.** "American Pie" by Don McLean; "The First Time Ever I Saw Your Face" by Ewan MacColl; "I Am Woman" by Helen Reddy; "Operator" by Jim Croce; "Rocket Man" by Elton John.

**Journalism.** *Ms* magazine debuts in **July**, with Gloria Steinem as editor. After 36 years, *Life* magazine ceases weekly publication. *Washington Post* reporters Bob Woodward and Carl Bernstein report a link between the Watergate break-in and the Committee for the Re-Election of the President (CREEP).

**Sports.** Baseball's American League sanctions the "designated hitter"—a tenth player who hits in place of the pitcher. U.S. swimmer Mark Spitz wins a record 7 gold medals at the Summer Olympics in Munich, Germany. Bobby Fischer becomes the first American to win the world chess title, defeating Soviet grandmaster Boris Spassky, at Reykjavik, Iceland.

**Miscellaneous.** The first offices are opened in one of two 110-story towers in New York's World Trade Center. Federal Express is founded by Memphis businessman Frederick W. Smith. Edwin H. Land introduces the Polaroid SX-70 instant camera.

# OBITUARIES

Deaths, Oct. 16, 1995—Oct. 31, 1996

### A

**Agnew, Spiro T.,** 77, former Maryland governor and outspoken conservative who was Richard Nixon's vice president from 1969 until he resigned in 1973 after pleading guilty to tax evasion; Berlin, MD, Sept. 17, 1996.

**Allen, Mel,** 83, longtime "voice of the [New York] Yankees"; he and Red Barber were the first announcers inducted into the Baseball Hall of Fame; Greenwich, CT, June 16, 1996.

**Amis, Kingsley,** 73, prize-winning British satiric novelist; knighted in 1990; London, England, Oct. 22, 1995.

**Amsterdam, Morey,** 81(?), wisecracking jokester of vaudeville, radio, and TV; he played a comedy writer on *The Dick Van Dyke Show.* Los Angeles, CA, Oct. 18, 1996.

**Andrews, Maxene,** 79, one of the famous singing sisters trio of the 1940s; Cape Cod, MA, Oct. 21, 1995.

### B

**Balsam, Martin,** 76, award-winning character actor; his films include *On the Waterfront, Psycho,* and *A Thousand Clowns*; found dead in Rome, Italy, Feb. 13, 1996.

**Bell, Terrel H.,** 74, former education commissioner (1981-85) and senator (1970-76) who commissioned the 1983 report, "A Nation at Risk"; Salt Lake City, UT, June 22, 1996.

**Belli, Melvin,** 88, flamboyant lawyer who brought personal injury settlements to new heights; his famous clients included Jack Ruby; San Francisco, CA, July 9, 1996.

**Beltrán, Lola,** 65(?), Mexican singer who as Lola la Grande recorded more than 100 albums of soulful music; Mexico City, Mexico, Mar. 24, 1996.

**Beradino, John,** 79, actor who played Dr. Steve Hardy on TV soap *General Hospital* for 33 years; Los Angeles, CA, May 19, 1996.

**Bombeck, Erma,** 69, housewife-humorist whose newspaper columns and best-selling books lightly reflected ordinary American life; San Francisco, CA, Apr. 22, 1996.

**Boorda, Jeremy M.,** 57, four-star admiral and chief of U.S. naval operations; first sailor to rise from the lowest enlisted rank to the top rank in the navy; committed suicide, Washington, DC, May 16, 1996.

**Brodkey, Harold,** 65, poet, critic, and novelist; his magnum opus was *Runaway Soul* (1991); New York, NY, Jan. 26, 1996.

**Brodsky, Joseph,** 55, Russian expatriate poet; denounced by Soviet authorities, he emigrated, won the 1987 Nobel Prize for literature, and was 1991 U.S. poet laureate; Brooklyn, NY, Jan. 28, 1996.

**Brown, Edmund G. (Pat),** 90, former governor of California (1959-67) who inspired the state's modernization, building highways, water systems, and public universities; Feb. 16, 1996, Beverly Hills, CA.

**Brown, Ronald (Ron),** 54, U.S. secretary of commerce since 1993, and former Democratic Party National Committee chairman, 1989-93, in a plane crash near Dubrovnik, Croatia, Apr. 3, 1996.

**Burke, Arleigh,** 94, highly decorated U.S. admiral whose Squadron 23 devastated Japanese warships in the Pacific during World War II; Bethesda, MD, Jan. 1, 1996.

**Burns, George,** 100, legendary vaudevillian, radio and TV comedian, and Oscar-winning actor who entertained generations of Americans; Beverly Hills, CA, Mar. 9, 1996.

### C

**Chancellor, John,** 68, pioneer of TV journalism who reported from more than 50 countries as a correspondent for NBC News; he anchored *NBC Nightly News* from 1970 to 1982; Princeton, NJ, July 12, 1996.

**Colbert, Claudette,** 92, stage and film actress whose career spanned 7 decades; she won an Oscar for *It Happened One Night* (1934); Barbados, July 30, 1996.

**Colby, William E.,** 76, former head of U.S. intelligence operations in Vietnam (1962-67) and CIA director (1973-76); found dead May 6, 1996, in Wicomico River, MD.

**Condon, Richard,** 81, best-selling author of such books as *The Manchurian Candidate* (1959) and *Prizzi's Honor* (1982); Dallas, TX, Apr. 9, 1996.

**Corrigan, Douglas "Wrong-Way,"** 88, aviator who in 1938 became famous when he made a solo flight from New York to Ireland, instead of to California as announced; Orange, CA, Dec. 9, 1995.

**Cray, Seymour,** 71, electrical engineer, father of the supercomputer; Colorado Springs, CO, Oct. 5, 1996.

### D

**Davies, Robertson,** 82, Canadian novelist known for such works as the 1970s Deptford trilogy; Orangeville, Ontario, Dec. 2, 1995.

**Duras, Marguerite,** 81, prolific and popular French novelist; author of *The Lover* (1985); Paris, France, Mar. 3, 1996.

### E

**Eberhart, Mignon,** 97, prolific writer who authored more than 50 mystery novels; Greenwich, CT, Oct. 8, 1996.

**Edwards, Vince,** 69, actor who portrayed 1960s TV doctor Ben Casey; Los Angeles, CA, Mar. 11, 1996.

**Egan, Eddie,** 65, New York police detective whose undercover exploits were the basis of the 1971 film *The French Connection*; Miami, FL, Nov. 4, 1995.

**Elytis, Odysseus,** 84, Greek poet best known for his epic *The Axion Esti;* winner of a 1979 Nobel Prize; Athens, Greece, Mar. 18, 1996.

**Erdos, Paul,** 83, Hungarian-born mathematician considered one of the 20th century's greatest; Warsaw, Poland, Sept. 20, 1996.

### F

**Factor, Max,** 91, cosmetics mogul and movie make-up artist; he introduced waterproof mascara and smudge-proof lipstick; Los Angeles, CA, June 7, 1996.

**Finley, Charles O.,** 77, controversial former owner of the Oakland A's who inspired bright-colored uniforms, night games, and the designated hitter; Chicago, IL, Feb. 19, 1996.

**Fitzgerald, Ella,** 79, renowned jazz vocalist and "first lady of song," known for her sweet versatile voice and scat improvisation; Beverly Hills, CA, June 15, 1996.

### G

**Garson, Greer,** 92, screen actress who earned a best actress Oscar for her role in *Mrs. Miniver* (1942); Dallas, TX, Apr. 6, 1996.

**Goodman, Linda,** 70, author of *Sun Signs* (1968) and other best-sellers on astrology; Colorado Springs, CO, Oct. 21, 1995.

**Gordone, Charles,** 70, first black playwright to win a Pulitzer Prize (1970), for *No Place to Be Somebody*; College Station, TX, Nov. 17, 1995.

**Gould, Morton,** 82, prizewinning popular conductor and composer of musicals, ballets, and symphonies; Orlando, FL, Feb. 21, 1996.

**Gray, Georgia Neese Clark,** 95, first woman to serve as treasurer of the U.S. (1949-53); Topeka, KS, Oct. 26, 1995.

**Grinkov, Sergei,** 28, Russian pairs figure skater who, with his wife and partner, won 2 Olympic gold medals (1988, 1994); Lake Placid, NY, Nov. 20, 1995.

**Gullikson, Tim,** 44, champion tennis player of the 70s and 80s and coach who guided the careers of such greats as Martina Navratolova and Pete Sampras; Wheaton, IL, May 3, 1996.

### H

**Hansen, Austin,** 85, African-American photojournalist who recorded Harlem life; New York, NY, Jan. 23, 1996.

**Hemingway, Margaux,** 41, actress and 1970s supermodel; her 1975 $1 million contract with Fabergé was said to be the largest to that date for a woman; found dead, Santa Monica, CA, July 1, 1996.

**Hunter, Ross,** 75, movie producer responsible for such hits as *Pillow Talk* (1959) and *Airport (1970)*; Los Angeles, CA, Mar. 10, 1996.

### J

**Jacobs, Bernard B.,** 80, American theater mogul who was president of the Shubert Organization for 24 years; Roslyn, NY, Aug. 27, 1996.

**Jenco, Rev. Lawrence M.,** 61, former head of Catholic Relief Services in Beirut; held hostage in Lebanon by Islamic rebels for 594 days during the 1980s; Hillside, IL, July 19, 1996.

**Johnson, Ben,** 75, actor who portrayed characters from the American West and earned an Oscar for his supporting role in *The Last Picture Show (1971)*; Mesa, AZ, Apr. 8, 1996.

**Jordan, Barbara,** 59, congresswoman (D, TX), scholar, and passionate orator; the first black woman to deliver a keynote address at a Democratic National Convention (1976); Austin, TX, Jan. 17, 1996.

### K

**Kelly, Gene,** 83, innovative actor, dancer, and choreographer, celebrated for his splashy dance in the movie *Singin' in the Rain* (1952) and graceful ballet in *An American in Paris* (1951); Beverly Hills, CA, Feb. 2, 1996.

**Kirstein, Lincoln,** 88, ballet promoter; cofounded the New York City Ballet (1948); New York, NY, Jan. 5, 1996.

**Krol, Cardinal John,** 85, leading conservative Catholic prelate; former archbishop of Philadelphia (1961-88); Philadelphia, PA, Mar. 3, 1996.

**Kuhn, Thomas S.,** 73, historian of science whose 1962 study, *The Structure of Scientific Revolutions,* was vastly influential; Cambridge, MA, June 17, 1996.

L

**Lamour, Dorothy,** 81, actress famous for her sarong and "Road" movies with Bob Hope and Bing Crosby; known as the "bond bombshell" for her efforts in selling U.S. bonds during WW2; North Hollywood, CA, Sept. 22, 1996.

**LaRue, Lash (Alfred),** 78, tough B-movie Western star of the 1940s and 1950s; Burbank, CA, May 21, 1996.

**Leary, Timothy,** 75, clinical psychologist and 1960s psychedelic guru who advised followers to "turn on, tune in, and drop out," while promoting the use of such hallucinogens as LSD; Beverly Hills, CA, May 31, 1996.

**Lewis, Henry,** 63, first black conductor of a major American orchestra, the New Jersey Symphony (1968); New York, NY, Jan. 26, 1996.

**Lindfors, Viveca,** 74, award-winning Swedish stage and film actress; Upsala, Sweden, Oct. 25, 1995.

M

**Madison, Guy,** 74, Hollywood actor who played Wild Bill Hickok on radio and TV in the 1950s; Palm Springs, CA, Feb. 6, 1996.

**Malle, Louis,** 63, French director whose films included *Pretty Baby* (1978), *Atlantic City* (1980), and *Au Revoir les Enfants* (1987); Beverly Hills, CA, Nov. 23, 1995.

**Martin, Dean,** 78, pop singer, and actor who first teamed with comic Jerry Lewis; he later became one of Frank Sinatra's "Rat Pack"; Beverly Hills, CA, Dec. 25, 1995.

**McGhee, Brownie, 80,** Piedmont-blues guitarist and song writer; Oakland, CA, Feb. 16, 1996.

**McNeill, Don,** 88, creator and host for 33 years of *Don McNeill's Breakfast Club* on radio; Evanston, IL, May 7, 1996.

**McQueen, Butterfly,** 84, actress best known for her role as Scarlett O'Hara's maid in *Gone With the Wind* (1939); Augusta, GA, Dec. 22, 1995.

**Meadows, Audrey,** 71, actress who played Jackie Gleason's spunky wife, Alice Kramden, on TV's *The Honeymooners*; Los Angeles, CA, Feb. 3, 1996.

**Milne, Christopher Robin,** 75, son of writer A. A. Milne; inspired the character Christopher Robin in his father's Winnie the Pooh books; London, England, Apr. 20, 1996.

**"Minnesota Fats"** (Rudolf Wanderone, Jr.), 82(?), pool hustler who claimed to be the prototype for Jackie Gleason's character in the 1961 film *The Hustler;* Nashville, TN, Jan. 18, 1996.

**Mitterrand, François,** 79, French political leader and former president (1981-95) who helped revive the Socialist Party and championed European unity; Paris, France, Jan. 9, 1996.

**Mitford, Jessica,** 78, muckraking writer and polemicist, best-known for her exposé of the funeral industry, *The American Way of Death* (1963); Oakland, CA, July 23, 1996.

**Monroe, Bill,** 84, mandolin-playing tenor recognized as the father of bluegrass music; Springfield, TN, Sept. 9, 1996.

**Morris, Greg,** 61, one of the first black actors to star on TV—in the popular *Mission Impossible* (1966-73); Las Vegas, NV, Aug. 27, 1996.

**Mulligan, Gerry,** 68, saxophonist and composer known for his "cool school" jazz; Darien, CT; Jan. 20, 1996.

**Muskie, Edmund S.,** 81, former Maine governor, U.S. senator, and U.S. secretary of state; Hubert Humphrey's 1968 vice-presidential running mate; Washington, DC, Mar. 26, 1996.

N

**Najibullah (Najibullah Ahmadzl),** 49, Soviet-backed president of Afghanistan (1987-92); hanged by Islamic regime in Kabul, Sept. 27, 1996.

**Ngor, Haing S.,** 55, expatriate Cambodian physician and sometime actor who won an Oscar for his supporting role in *The Killing Fields;* murdered in Los Angeles, CA, Feb. 25, 1996.

**Niarchos, Stavros,** 86, Greek shipping tycoon and rival of Aristotle Onassis; Zurich, Switzerland, Apr. 15, 1996.

P

**Packard, David,** 83, electronics pioneer who cofounded the Hewlett-Packard Company; San Francisco, CA, Mar. 26, 1996.

**Papandreou, Andreas,** 77, leftist Greek premier (1981-89, 1993-96) who founded the Panhellenic Socialist Movement, Pasok, and introduced liberal social reforms; Athens, Greece, June 23, 1996.

**Patrick, John,** 90, playwright who earned a Pulitzer Prize for *Teahouse of the August Moon* (1953); Delray Beach, FL, Nov. 7, 1995.

**Pearl, Minnie** (Sarah Cannon), 83, comedian of Grand Ole Opry fame known for her wisecracking, hayseed routine; Nashville, TN, Mar. 5, 1996.

**Peterson, Roger Tory,** 87, ornithologist, artist, and author of the classic *Field Guide to the Birds*; Old Lyme, CT, July 28, 1996.

**Prowse, Juliet,** 59, dancer of nightclub, musical, and TV fame; shocked Soviet leader Nikita Khrushchev in 1959 with her performance of the cancan; Los Angeles, CA, Sept. 14, 1996.

R

**Rabin, Yitzhak,** 73, Israeli prime minister (1974-77, 1992-95); shared the 1994 Nobel Peace Prize for his peace efforts in the Middle East; assassinated, Tel Aviv, Israel, Nov. 4, 1995.

**Reston, James "Scotty",** 86, highly influential prize-winning journalist who had extraordinary access to Washington's inner circle; Washington, DC, Dec. 6, 1995.

**Rettig, Tommy, 54,** the first boy to play Lassie's master on the '50s TV show *Lassie*; Los Angeles, CA, Feb. 15, 1996.

**Roker, Roxie,** 66, actress who broke the color barrier with her interracial marriage on TV's *The Jeffersons* (1975-84); Los Angeles, CA, Dec. 2, 1995.

**Rouse, James, W.,** 81, real estate developer who built malls, planned cities (Columbia, MD), and Boston's "festival marketplace" Faneuil Hall; Columbia, MD, Apr. 9, 1996.

**Riggs, Bobby,** 77, 2-time U.S. Open winner and 1939 Wimbledon champ; lost a 1973 "battle of the sexes" tennis match with Billie Jean King; Leucadia, CA, Oct. 25, 1995.

S

**Schapiro, Meyer,** 91, highly eminent Lithuanian-born art historian and critic; New York, NY, Mar. 3, 1996.

**Scribner, Charles, Jr.,** 74, gentlemanly publisher who headed Charles Scribner's Sons (1952-84); New York, NY, Nov. 11, 1995.

**Shakur, Tupac,** 25, actor and chart-topping rap artist whose life and music personified violence; died of wounds from a shooting; Las Vegas, NV, Sept. 13, 1996.

**Siegel, Jerry,** 81, Superman co-creator who sold his rights to the superhero for a mere $130 in 1938; Los Angeles, CA, Jan. 28, 1996.

**Snyder, Jimmy (the Greek),** 76, expert oddsmaker and sports commentator, Las Vegas, NV, Apr. 21, 1996.

**Southern, Terry,** 71, novelist and screenwriter whose films included *Dr. Strangelove* (1964) and *Easy Rider* (1969); New York, NY, Oct. 29, 1995.

**Stevenson, McLean,** 66, television actor who played the affable Lt. Col. Henry Blake on *M*A*S*H*; Feb. 15, 1996, Tarzana, CA.

**Stokes, Carl,** 68, former mayor of Cleveland, 1968-71, and first African American to become mayor of a major U.S. city; Cleveland, OH, Apr. 3, 1996.

**Suenens, Cardinal Leo,** 91, Belgian archbishop, considered a key voice for reform in the Second Vatican Council; Brussels, Belgium, May 6, 1996.

T

**Takemitsu, Toru,** 65, innovative Japanese composer whose music bridged East and West; Tokyo, Japan, Feb. 20, 1996.

**Thompson, Mary,** 120, daughter of slaves who was thought to be the oldest living American; Orlando, FL, Aug. 3, 1996.

**Toumanova, Tamara,** 77, Russian-born ballerina dominant in the 1930s; she helped make the Ballets Russes world-famous and was a favorite of many choreographers; Santa Monica, CA, May 29, 1996.

**Travers, P. L.,** 96, British writer who created the children's book character Mary Poppins; London, England, Apr. 23, 1996.

**Trilling, Diana, 91,** esteemed essayist, literary critic, and editor; widow of Lionel Trilling; New York, NY, Oct. 23, 1996.

V

**Van Fleet, Jo,** 81, stage and film actress who won an Oscar for her supporting role in *East of Eden* (1955); New York, NY, June 10, 1996.

**Vickrey, William,** 82, economist who won a 1996 Nobel Prize in economics 3 days before his death; Harrison, NY, Oct. 10, 1996.

W

**Walker, Junior,** 53, saxophonist and leader of pop music's Junior Walker and the All Stars; Battle Creek, MI, Nov. 23, 1995.

**Wallenda, Helen,** 85, last of the original Flying Wallendas trapeze artists; Sarasota, FL, May 9, 1996.

**Whittle, Sir Frank,** 89, British engineer who, in the 1930s, invented the jet engine; Columbia, MD, Aug. 8, 1996.

# PRESIDENTIAL ELECTIONS

## Popular and Electoral Vote, 1992 and 1996

**Source:** Voter News Service; Federal Election Commission; 1996 totals are preliminary

| | 1996 | | | | | | 1992 | | | | | |
|---|---|---|---|---|---|---|---|---|---|---|---|---|
| | Electoral Vote | | | Democrat | Republican | Reform | Electoral Vote | | | Democrat | Republican | Independent |
| State | Clinton | Dole | Perot | Clinton | Dole | Perot | Clinton | Bush | Perot | Clinton | Bush | Perot |
| AL | 0 | 9 | 0 | 658,308 | 771,529 | 91,357 | 0 | 9 | 0 | 690,080 | 804,283 | 183,109 |
| AK | 0 | 3 | 0 | 66,508 | 101,234 | 21,536 | 0 | 3 | 0 | 78,294 | 102,000 | 73,481 |
| AZ | 8 | 0 | 0 | 612,412 | 576,126 | 104,712 | 0 | 8 | 0 | 543,050 | 572,086 | 353,741 |
| AR | 6 | 0 | 0 | 465,362 | 320,323 | 67,245 | 6 | 0 | 0 | 505,823 | 337,324 | 99,132 |
| CA | 54 | 0 | 0 | 4,639,935 | 3,412,563 | 667,702 | 54 | 0 | 0 | 5,121,325 | 3,630,574 | 2,296,006 |
| CO | 0 | 8 | 0 | 670,854 | 691,290 | 99,510 | 8 | 0 | 0 | 629,681 | 562,850 | 366,010 |
| CT | 8 | 0 | 0 | 712,603 | 481,047 | 137,784 | 8 | 0 | 0 | 682,318 | 578,313 | 348,771 |
| DE | 3 | 0 | 0 | 140,209 | 98,906 | 28,693 | 3 | 0 | 0 | 126,054 | 102,313 | 59,213 |
| DC | 3 | 0 | 0 | 152,031 | 16,637 | 3,479 | 3 | 0 | 0 | 192,619 | 20,698 | 9,681 |
| FL | 25 | 0 | 0 | 2,533,502 | 2,226,117 | 482,237 | 0 | 25 | 0 | 2,071,651 | 2,171,781 | 1,052,481 |
| GA | 0 | 13 | 0 | 1,047,214 | 1,078,972 | 146,031 | 13 | 0 | 0 | 1,008,966 | 995,252 | 309,657 |
| HI | 4 | 0 | 0 | 205,012 | 113,943 | 27,358 | 4 | 0 | 0 | 179,310 | 136,822 | 53,003 |
| ID | 0 | 4 | 0 | 165,545 | 256,406 | 62,506 | 0 | 4 | 0 | 137,013 | 202,645 | 130,395 |
| IL | 22 | 0 | 0 | 2,299,476 | 1,577,930 | 344,311 | 22 | 0 | 0 | 2,453,350 | 1,734,096 | 840,515 |
| IN | 0 | 12 | 0 | 874,668 | 995,082 | 218,739 | 0 | 12 | 0 | 848,420 | 989,375 | 455,934 |
| IA | 7 | 0 | 0 | 615,499 | 489,776 | 104,401 | 7 | 0 | 0 | 586,353 | 504,891 | 253,468 |
| KS | 0 | 6 | 0 | 384,439 | 578,572 | 92,093 | 0 | 6 | 0 | 390,434 | 449,951 | 312,358 |
| KY | 8 | 0 | 0 | 635,804 | 622,339 | 118,768 | 8 | 0 | 0 | 665,104 | 617,178 | 203,944 |
| LA | 9 | 0 | 0 | 928,983 | 710,240 | 122,981 | 9 | 0 | 0 | 815,971 | 733,386 | 211,478 |
| ME | 4 | 0 | 0 | 326,217 | 190,711 | 88,082 | 4 | 0 | 0 | 263,420 | 206,504 | 206,820 |
| MD | 10 | 0 | 0 | 924,284 | 651,682 | 113,684 | 10 | 0 | 0 | 988,571 | 707,094 | 281,414 |
| MA | 12 | 0 | 0 | 1,532,917 | 693,866 | 219,525 | 12 | 0 | 0 | 1,318,639 | 805,039 | 630,731 |
| MI | 18 | 0 | 0 | 1,911,553 | 1,413,812 | 319,095 | 18 | 0 | 0 | 1,871,182 | 1,554,940 | 824,813 |
| MN | 10 | 0 | 0 | 1,096,320 | 751,860 | 252,952 | 10 | 0 | 0 | 1,020,997 | 747,841 | 562,506 |
| MS | 0 | 7 | 0 | 385,005 | 434,547 | 51,500 | 0 | 7 | 0 | 400,258 | 487,793 | 85,626 |
| MO | 11 | 0 | 0 | 1,024,679 | 889,684 | 217,101 | 11 | 0 | 0 | 1,053,873 | 811,159 | 518,741 |
| MT | 0 | 3 | 0 | 167,169 | 178,957 | 55,017 | 3 | 0 | 0 | 154,507 | 144,207 | 107,225 |
| NE | 0 | 5 | 0 | 231,863 | 355,562 | 76,103 | 0 | 5 | 0 | 216,864 | 343,678 | 174,104 |
| NV | 4 | 0 | 0 | 203,388 | 198,775 | 43,855 | 4 | 0 | 0 | 189,148 | 175,828 | 132,580 |
| NH | 4 | 0 | 0 | 245,260 | 196,740 | 48,140 | 4 | 0 | 0 | 209,040 | 202,484 | 121,337 |
| NJ | 15 | 0 | 0 | 1,599,932 | 1,080,041 | 257,979 | 15 | 0 | 0 | 1,436,206 | 1,356,865 | 521,829 |
| NM | 5 | 0 | 0 | 252,215 | 210,791 | 30,978 | 5 | 0 | 0 | 261,617 | 212,824 | 91,895 |
| NY | 33 | 0 | 0 | 3,513,191 | 1,861,198 | 485,547 | 33 | 0 | 0 | 3,444,450 | 2,346,649 | 1,090,721 |
| NC | 0 | 14 | 0 | 1,099,123 | 1,211,655 | 164,512 | 0 | 14 | 0 | 1,114,042 | 1,134,661 | 357,864 |
| ND | 0 | 3 | 0 | 106,360 | 124,507 | 32,566 | 0 | 3 | 0 | 99,168 | 136,244 | 71,084 |
| OH | 21 | 0 | 0 | 2,100,799 | 1,823,873 | 470,707 | 21 | 0 | 0 | 1,984,942 | 1,894,310 | 1,036,426 |
| OK | 0 | 8 | 0 | 488,102 | 582,310 | 130,788 | 0 | 8 | 0 | 473,066 | 592,929 | 319,878 |
| OR | 7 | 0 | 0 | 325,225 | 255,452 | 73,011 | 7 | 0 | 0 | 621,314 | 475,757 | 354,091 |
| PA | 23 | 0 | 0 | 2,206,241 | 1,793,568 | 430,082 | 23 | 0 | 0 | 2,239,164 | 1,791,841 | 902,667 |
| RI | 4 | 0 | 0 | 243,027 | 108,401 | 44,468 | 4 | 0 | 0 | 213,299 | 131,601 | 105,045 |
| SC | 0 | 8 | 0 | 495,458 | 564,387 | 63,300 | 0 | 8 | 0 | 479,514 | 577,507 | 138,872 |
| SD | 0 | 3 | 0 | 139,295 | 150,508 | 31,248 | 0 | 3 | 0 | 124,888 | 136,718 | 73,295 |
| TN | 11 | 0 | 0 | 905,599 | 860,809 | 105,577 | 11 | 0 | 0 | 933,521 | 841,300 | 199,968 |
| TX | 0 | 32 | 0 | 2,455,735 | 2,731,998 | 377,530 | 0 | 32 | 0 | 2,281,815 | 2,496,071 | 1,354,781 |
| UT | 0 | 5 | 0 | 220,197 | 359,394 | 66,100 | 0 | 5 | 0 | 183,429 | 322,632 | 203,400 |
| VT | 3 | 0 | 0 | 138,400 | 80,043 | 30,912 | 3 | 0 | 0 | 133,590 | 88,122 | 65,985 |
| VA | 0 | 13 | 0 | 1,070,990 | 1,119,974 | 158,707 | 0 | 13 | 0 | 1,038,650 | 1,150,517 | 348,639 |
| WA | 11 | 0 | 0 | 899,645 | 639,743 | 161,642 | 11 | 0 | 0 | 993,037 | 731,234 | 541,780 |
| WV | 5 | 0 | 0 | 324,394 | 231,908 | 70,853 | 5 | 0 | 0 | 331,001 | 241,974 | 108,829 |
| WI | 11 | 0 | 0 | 1,071,859 | 845,172 | 227,426 | 11 | 0 | 0 | 1,041,066 | 930,855 | 544,479 |
| WY | 0 | 3 | 0 | 77,897 | 105,347 | 25,854 | 0 | 3 | 0 | 68,160 | 79,347 | 51,263 |
| **Total** | **379** | **159** | **0** | **45,590,703** | **37,816,307** | **7,866,284** | **370** | **168** | **0** | **44,908,254** | **39,102,343** | **19,741,065** |

# Presidential Election Returns by Counties

**All 1996 results are preliminary. Results for New England states are for selected cities or towns because county results are not available. Totals are always statewide. In Alaska, individual election districts not available. Preliminary 1996 county or city/town figures may not add to state totals. D-Democrat; R-Republican; RF-Reform; I-Independent. (In 1996, Ross Perot was on the ballot in some states as "Independent".)**

**Source:** Voter News Service; Federal Election Commission

## Alabama

| County | 1996 Clinton (D) | 1996 Dole (R) | 1996 Perot (RF) | 1992 Clinton (D) | 1992 Bush (R) | 1992 Perot (I) |
|---|---|---|---|---|---|---|
| Autauga . . | 5,011 | 9,504 | 811 | 4,819 | 8,715 | 1,916 |
| Baldwin . . | 12,744 | 39,845 | 4,426 | 12,195 | 26,270 | 7,656 |
| Barbour . . | 4,787 | 3,627 | 515 | 4,836 | 4,475 | 1,020 |
| Bibb . . . . | 2,775 | 3,037 | 455 | 2,900 | 3,124 | 686 |
| Blount . . . | 5,060 | 9,049 | 985 | 5,433 | 8,882 | 1,949 |
| Bullock . . | 3,078 | 1,154 | 111 | 3,259 | 1,253 | 266 |
| Butler . . . | 3,826 | 3,365 | 516 | 4,021 | 3,494 | 867 |
| Calhoun . . | 15,694 | 18,088 | 2,613 | 16,453 | 20,623 | 4,717 |
| Chambers | 5,515 | 4,707 | 812 | 5,938 | 5,682 | 1,427 |
| Cherokee . | 4,399 | 3,048 | 898 | 4,222 | 2,745 | 846 |
| Chilton . . | 5,342 | 7,903 | 927 | 4,946 | 8,126 | 1,363 |
| Choctaw . | 4,074 | 2,623 | 413 | 3,941 | 3,069 | 489 |
| Clarke . . . | 4,831 | 4,775 | 476 | 5,023 | 5,495 | 872 |
| Clay . . . . | 2,306 | 2,694 | 538 | 2,073 | 2,859 | 652 |
| Cleburne . | 1,737 | 2,063 | 385 | 2,144 | 2,425 | 630 |
| Coffee . . . | 5,168 | 7,805 | 1,042 | 5,776 | 7,591 | 2,021 |
| Colbert . . | 10,216 | 8,305 | 1,696 | 12,206 | 8,073 | 2,098 |
| Conecuh . | 2,904 | 2,002 | 445 | 3,155 | 2,463 | 552 |
| Coosa . . . | 2,121 | 1,721 | 262 | 2,330 | 1,973 | 476 |
| Covington | 4,543 | 6,035 | 1,098 | 5,004 | 6,840 | 1,880 |
| Crenshaw | 2,172 | 1,939 | 317 | 2,404 | 2,339 | 485 |
| Cullman . . | 9,544 | 14,308 | 2,440 | 10,451 | 14,411 | 4,113 |
| Dale . . . . | 4,732 | 8,288 | 1,216 | 5,098 | 8,123 | 2,423 |
| Dallas . . . | 10,507 | 7,003 | 539 | 11,053 | 7,394 | 1,110 |
| DeKalb . . | 6,776 | 10,194 | 1,648 | 8,245 | 10,519 | 2,741 |
| Elmore . . | 6,530 | 12,937 | 1,368 | 6,223 | 11,356 | 2,765 |
| Escambia . | 4,653 | 5,340 | 869 | 4,809 | 5,955 | 1,616 |
| Etowah . . | 17,976 | 16,835 | 2,529 | 20,558 | 17,467 | 4,277 |
| Fayette . . | 3,381 | 3,191 | 590 | 3,830 | 3,604 | 1,012 |
| Franklin . . | 5,028 | 4,442 | 966 | 5,953 | 4,794 | 1,075 |
| Geneva . . | 3,174 | 4,725 | 857 | 3,622 | 4,843 | 1,323 |
| Greene . . | 3,526 | 796 | 55 | 3,865 | 805 | 194 |
| Hale . . . . | 3,372 | 1,893 | 190 | 3,481 | 2,001 | 486 |
| Henry . . . | 3,013 | 3,082 | 515 | 2,804 | 2,970 | 667 |
| Houston . . | 8,791 | 17,476 | 1,653 | 8,857 | 17,360 | 3,492 |
| Jackson . . | 8,204 | 5,650 | 1,573 | 10,628 | 5,711 | 2,462 |
| Jefferson . | 120,201 | 130,956 | 7,994 | 125,889 | 149,832 | 22,191 |
| Lamar . . . | 2,880 | 3,011 | 624 | 2,849 | 3,262 | 763 |
| Lauderdale | 13,619 | 14,058 | 2,574 | 15,936 | 13,728 | 4,009 |
| Lawrence . | 5,254 | 3,889 | 964 | 6,364 | 3,576 | 1,624 |
| Lee . . . . . | 12,919 | 17,985 | 1,949 | 13,770 | 16,885 | 4,572 |
| Limestone. | 8,025 | 10,841 | 1,656 | 8,087 | 9,862 | 3,584 |
| Lowndes . | 3,970 | 1,369 | 80 | 3,500 | 1,328 | 284 |
| Macon . . . | 7,018 | 987 | 150 | 7,253 | 1,134 | 283 |
| Madison . . | 40,607 | 49,413 | 6,861 | 38,974 | 51,444 | 16,989 |
| Marengo . | 4,900 | 4,022 | 346 | 5,632 | 4,470 | 919 |
| Marion . . | 5,049 | 4,742 | 904 | 6,167 | 5,692 | 1,389 |
| Marshall . . | 8,572 | 12,040 | 2,379 | 10,421 | 12,249 | 3,795 |
| Mobile . . . | 54,507 | 66,553 | 7,523 | 54,962 | 72,935 | 15,105 |
| Monroe . . | 3,815 | 4,382 | 486 | 3,872 | 4,919 | 759 |
| Montgomery | 38,382 | 37,784 | 2,036 | 37,342 | 40,742 | 7,647 |
| Morgan . . | 14,607 | 21,764 | 3,348 | 15,091 | 21,073 | 7,683 |
| Perry . . . . | 4,053 | 1,703 | 119 | 3,712 | 1,829 | 213 |
| Pickens . . | 4,018 | 3,322 | 403 | 3,783 | 3,634 | 690 |
| Pike . . . . | 4,514 | 5,281 | 503 | 4,688 | 5,423 | 1,024 |
| Randolph . | 3,023 | 3,304 | 603 | 3,318 | 3,813 | 919 |
| Russell . . | 7,835 | 5,028 | 792 | 8,647 | 5,587 | 1,360 |
| St. Clair . . | 6,186 | 12,756 | 1,417 | 6,517 | 12,447 | 2,614 |
| Shelby . . . | 9,361 | 29,935 | 1,679 | 10,317 | 32,736 | 5,022 |
| Sumter . . | 4,706 | 1,561 | 172 | 4,810 | 1,807 | 388 |
| Talladega . | 10,377 | 10,927 | 1,335 | 10,695 | 12,661 | 2,629 |
| Tallapoosa | 6,071 | 7,627 | 1,038 | 5,703 | 8,140 | 1,562 |
| Tuscaloosa | 23,067 | 27,939 | 3,048 | 23,495 | 27,454 | 7,011 |
| Walker . . | 12,929 | 9,837 | 2,012 | 14,831 | 11,301 | 3,344 |
| Washington | 3,935 | 2,900 | 820 | 4,046 | 3,270 | 829 |
| Wilcox . . . | 3,285 | 1,448 | 71 | 3,439 | 1,671 | 174 |
| Winston . . | 3,113 | 4,716 | 722 | 3,415 | 5,550 | 1,110 |
| **Totals . . .** | **658,308** | **771,529** | **91,357** | **690,080** | **804,283** | **183,109** |

### Alabama Vote Since 1948

1948, Thurmond, States' Rights, 171,443; Dewey, Rep., 40,930; Wallace, Prog., 1,522; Watson, Proh., 1,085.

1952, Eisenhower, Rep., 149,231; Stevenson, Dem., 275,075; Hamblen, Proh., 1,814.

1956, Stevenson, Dem., 290,844; Eisenhower, Rep., 195,694; Independent electors, 20,323.

1960, Kennedy, Dem., 324,050; Nixon, Rep., 237,981; Faubus, States' Rights, 4,367; Decker, Proh., 2,106; King, Afro-Americans, 1,485; scattering, 236.

1964, Dem. (electors unpledged), 209,848; Goldwater, Rep., 479,085; scattering, 105.

1968, Nixon, Rep., 146,923; Humphrey, Dem., 196,579; Wallace, 3d Party, 691,425; Munn, Proh., 4,022.

1972, Nixon, Rep., 728,701; McGovern, Dem., 219,108 plus 37,815 Natl. Demo. Party of Alabama; Schmitz, Conservative, 11,918; Munn., Proh., 8,551.

1976, Carter, Dem., 659,170; Ford, Rep., 504,070; Maddox, Amer. Ind., 9,198; Bubar, Proh., 6,669; Hall, Com., 1,954; MacBride, Libertarian, 1,481.

1980, Reagan, Rep., 654,192; Carter, Dem., 636,730; Anderson, Independent, 16,481; Rarick, Amer. Ind., 15,010; Clark, Libertarian, 13,318; Bubar, Statesman, 1,743; Hall, Com., 1,629; DeBerry, Soc. Workers, 1,303; McReynolds, Socialist, 1,006; Commoner, Citizens, 517.

1984, Reagan, Rep., 872,849; Mondale, Dem., 551,899; Bergland, Libertarian, 9,504.

1988, Bush, Rep., 815,576; Dukakis, Dem., 549,506; Paul, Lib., 8,460; Fulani, Ind., 3,311.

1992, Bush, Rep., 804,283; Clinton, Dem., 690,080; Perot, Ind., 183,109; Marrou, Libertarian, 5,737; Fulani, New Alliance, 2,161.

1996, Dole, Rep., 771,529; Clinton, Dem., 658,308; Perot, Ind. (Ref.), 91,357; Browne, Libertarian, 5,470; Phillips, Ind., 2,229; Hagelin, Natural Law, 1,672; Harris, Ind., 535.

## Alaska

| Election District | 1996 Clinton (D) | 1996 Dole (R) | 1996 Perot (RF) | 1992 Clinton (D) | 1992 Bush (R) | 1992 Perot (I) |
|---|---|---|---|---|---|---|
| No. 1 . . . . | | | | 2,055 | 2,495 | 2,120 |
| No. 2 . . . . | | | | 2,565 | 2,916 | 2,137 |
| No. 3 . . . . | | | | 4,064 | 2,447 | 1,424 |
| No. 4 . . . . | | | | 2,688 | 2,894 | 1,561 |
| No. 5 . . . . | | | | 2,095 | 1,844 | 1,684 |
| No. 6 . . . . | | | | 1,546 | 2,345 | 1,748 |
| No. 7 . . . . | | | | 2,088 | 2,173 | 2,244 |
| No. 8 . . . . | | | | 1,509 | 2,499 | 2,325 |
| No. 9 . . . . | | | | 1,540 | 2,349 | 2,368 |
| No. 10. . . . | | | | 1,947 | 3,548 | 1,899 |
| No. 11. . . . | | | | 2,009 | 2,730 | 2,081 |
| No. 12. . . . | | | | 1,831 | 2,999 | 2,039 |
| No. 13. . . . | | | | 3,001 | 2,963 | 1,907 |
| No. 14. . . . | | | | 1,423 | 3,013 | 1,599 |
| No. 15. . . . | | | | 2,389 | 1,842 | 1,591 |
| No. 16. . . . | | | | 1,814 | 1,375 | 1,320 |
| No. 17. . . . | | | | 1,749 | 2,623 | 1,958 |
| No. 18. . . . | | | | 2,483 | 3,629 | 2,134 |
| No. 19. . . . | | | | 1,931 | 2,539 | 1,840 |
| No. 20. . . . | | | | 2,383 | 2,914 | 1,823 |
| No. 21. . . . | | | | 2,386 | 2,437 | 1,693 |
| No. 22. . . . | | | | 2,253 | 3,164 | 1,713 |
| No. 23. . . . | | | | 1,139 | 2,127 | 1,217 |
| No. 24. . . . | | | | 1,876 | 3,441 | 1,930 |
| No. 25. . . . | | | | 1,513 | 3,197 | 2,122 |
| No. 26. . . . | | | | 1,439 | 2,675 | 2,419 |
| No. 27. . . . | | | | 1,625 | 2,757 | 2,401 |
| No. 28. . . . | | | | 1,522 | 2,459 | 2,825 |
| No. 29. . . . | | | | 3,216 | 2,205 | 2,026 |
| No. 30. . . . | | | | 1,860 | 2,434 | 1,912 |
| No. 31. . . . | | | | 1,969 | 2,223 | 1,992 |
| No. 32. . . . | | | | 1,150 | 2,339 | 1,724 |
| No. 33. . . . | | | | 1,712 | 3,100 | 2,278 |
| No. 34. . . . | | | | 1,455 | 3,408 | 2,201 |
| No. 35. . . . | | | | 1,572 | 2,525 | 2,139 |
| No. 36. . . . | | | | 1,748 | 2,081 | 1,322 |
| No. 37. . . . | | | | 1,822 | 1,689 | 925 |
| No. 38. . . . | | | | 1,897 | 2,011 | 850 |
| No. 39. . . . | | | | 1,797 | 1,777 | 860 |
| No. 40. . . . | | | | 1,211 | 1,786 | 1,122 |
| **Totals. . . .** | **66,508** | **101,234** | **21,536** | **78,294** | **102,000** | **73,481** |

### Alaska Vote Since 1960

1960, Kennedy, Dem., 29,809; Nixon, Rep., 30,953.

1964, Johnson, Dem., 44,329; Goldwater, Rep., 22,930.

1968, Nixon, Rep., 37,600; Humphrey, Dem., 35,411; Wallace, 3d Party, 10,024.

1972, Nixon, Rep., 55,349; McGovern, Dem., 32,967; Schmitz, Amer., 6,903.

1976, Carter, Dem., 44,058; Ford, Rep., 71,555; MacBride, Libertarian, 6,785.

1980, Reagan, Rep., 86,112; Carter, Dem., 41,842; Clark, Libertarian, 18,479; Anderson, Ind., 11,155; write-in, 857.

1984, Reagan, Rep., 138,377; Mondale, Dem., 62,007; Bergland, Libertarian, 6,378.

1988, Bush, Rep., 119,251; Dukakis, Dem., 72,584; Paul, Lib., 5,484; Fulani, New Alliance, 1,024.

1992, Bush, Rep., 102,000; Clinton, Dem., 78,294; Perot, Ind., 73,481; Gritz, Populist/America First, 1,379; Marrou, Libertarian, 1,378.
1996, Dole, Rep., 101,234; Clinton, Dem., 66,508; Perot, Ref., 21,536; Nader, Green, 6,178; Browne, Libertarian, 1,873; Phillips, Taxpayers, 764; Hagelin, Natural Law, 583.

## Arizona

| County | 1996 Clinton (D) | 1996 Dole (R) | 1996 Perot (RF) | 1992 Clinton (D) | 1992 Bush (R) | 1992 Perot (I) |
|---|---|---|---|---|---|---|
| Apache . . | 12,258 | 4,686 | 1,278 | 11,218 | 4,588 | 1,979 |
| Cochise . . | 13,737 | 14,299 | 3,329 | 12,701 | 12,202 | 7,857 |
| Coconino . | 18,055 | 11,728 | 3,268 | 18,888 | 13,769 | 9,363 |
| Gila . . . . . | 8,454 | 6,319 | 2,176 | 7,571 | 5,781 | 4,694 |
| Graham . . | 3,931 | 4,196 | 1,030 | 3,391 | 4,169 | 1,860 |
| Greenlee . | 1,755 | 1,159 | 426 | 1,695 | 1,451 | 794 |
| La Paz . . | 1,964 | 1,902 | 597 | 1,808 | 1,599 | 1,488 |
| Maricopa . | 337,034 | 353,417 | 53,800 | 285,457 | 360,049 | 221,475 |
| Mohave . . | 15,107 | 15,526 | 5,746 | 13,255 | 13,684 | 12,706 |
| Navajo . . | 12,902 | 9,255 | 2,458 | 10,882 | 7,994 | 4,787 |
| Pima . . . . | 131,263 | 98,864 | 17,810 | 128,569 | 97,036 | 53,925 |
| Pinal . . . . | 19,211 | 12,809 | 3,902 | 15,468 | 11,669 | 9,231 |
| Santa Cruz | 5,241 | 2,256 | 600 | 3,512 | 3,024 | 1,447 |
| Yavapai . . | 19,233 | 26,697 | 6,135 | 18,268 | 23,419 | 16,409 |
| Yuma . . . | 12,267 | 13,013 | 2,157 | 10,367 | 11,652 | 5,726 |
| **Totals . . .** | **612,412** | **576,126** | **104,712** | **543,050** | **572,086** | **353,741** |

### Arizona Vote Since 1948

1948, Truman, Dem., 95,251; Dewey, Rep., 77,597; Wallace, Prog., 3,310; Watson, Proh., 786; Teichert, Soc. Labor, 121.
1952, Eisenhower, Rep., 152,042; Stevenson, Dem., 108,528.
1956, Eisenhower, Rep., 176,990; Stevenson, Dem., 112,880; Andrews, Ind. 303.
1960, Kennedy, Dem., 176,781; Nixon, Rep., 221,241; Hass, Soc. Labor, 469.
1964, Johnson, Dem., 237,753; Goldwater, Rep., 242,535; Hass, Soc. Labor, 482.
1968, Nixon, Rep., 266,721; Humphrey, Dem., 170,514; Wallace, 3d Party, 46,573; McCarthy, New Party, 2,751; Halstead, Soc. Workers, 85; Cleaver, Peace and Freedom, 217; Blomen, Soc. Labor, 75.
1972, Nixon, Rep., 402,812; McGovern, Dem., 198,540; Schmitz, Amer., 21,208; Soc. Workers, 30,945. Due to ballot peculiarities in 3 counties (particularly Pima), thousands of voters cast ballots for the Soc. Workers Party *and* one of the major candidates. Court ordered both votes counted as official.
1976, Carter, Dem., 295,602; Ford, Rep., 418,642; McCarthy, Ind., 19,229; MacBride, Libertarian, 7,647; Camejo, Soc. Workers, 928; Anderson, Amer., 564; Maddox, Amer. Ind., 85.
1980, Reagan, Rep., 529,688; Carter, Dem., 246,843; Anderson, Ind., 76,952; Clark, Libertarian, 18,784; De Berry, Soc. Workers, 1,100; Commoner, Citizens, 551; Hall, Com., 25; Griswold, Workers World, 2.
1984, Reagan, Rep., 681,416; Mondale, Dem., 333,854; Bergland, Libertarian, 10,585.
1988, Bush, Rep., 702,541; Dukakis, Dem., 454,029; Paul, Lib., 13,351; Fulani, New Alliance, 1,662.
1992, Bush, Rep., 572,086; Clinton, Dem., 543,050; Perot, Ind., 353,741; Gritz, Populist/America First, 8,141; Marrou, Libertarian, 6,759; Hagelin, Natural Law, 2,267.
1996, Clinton, Dem., 612,412; Dole, Rep., 576,126; Perot, Ref., 104,712; Browne, Libertarian, 13,458.

## Arkansas

| County | 1996 Clinton (D) | 1996 Dole (R) | 1996 Perot (RF) | 1992 Clinton (D) | 1992 Bush (R) | 1992 Perot (I) |
|---|---|---|---|---|---|---|
| Arkansas . | 4,220 | 1,910 | 463 | 4,709 | 2,594 | 639 |
| Ashley . . | 5,011 | 2,428 | 704 | 5,876 | 2,686 | 931 |
| Baxter . . . | 6,703 | 6,877 | 1,572 | 6,991 | 5,640 | 2,938 |
| Benton . . . | 14,274 | 20,064 | 3,740 | 15,774 | 21,126 | 6,128 |
| Boone . . . | 5,744 | 6,093 | 1,132 | 6,128 | 6,094 | 2,079 |
| Bradley . . | 2,553 | 1,146 | 220 | 2,954 | 1,482 | 391 |
| Calhoun . . | 1,306 | 727 | 237 | 1,389 | 1,047 | 257 |
| Carroll . . . | 3,689 | 3,957 | 986 | 3,769 | 3,535 | 1,500 |
| Chicot . . . | 3,090 | 1,056 | 233 | 3,504 | 1,242 | 347 |
| Clark . . . . | 5,281 | 2,112 | 567 | 5,767 | 2,403 | 714 |
| Clay. . . . . | 3,848 | 1,512 | 464 | 4,848 | 1,647 | 568 |
| Cleburne . | 4,466 | 3,797 | 1,019 | 5,090 | 3,580 | 1,263 |
| Cleveland . | 1,741 | 990 | 268 | 1,893 | 1,127 | 337 |
| Columbia . | 4,727 | 3,375 | 678 | 4,747 | 3,702 | 1,090 |
| Conway . . | 4,052 | 2,305 | 745 | 4,898 | 2,719 | 803 |
| Craighead. | 13,168 | 9,103 | 175 | 13,931 | 9,104 | 2,274 |
| Crawford . | 6,528 | 6,893 | 1,629 | 6,656 | 6,882 | 2,442 |
| Crittenden. | 4,345 | 4,902 | 242 | 9,683 | 5,910 | 848 |
| Cross. . . . | 3,631 | 1,999 | 465 | 4,058 | 2,303 | 602 |
| Dallas . . . | 2,118 | 1,041 | 236 | 2,107 | 1,458 | 345 |
| Desha . . . | 3,230 | 978 | 247 | 3,815 | 1,279 | 392 |
| Drew . . . . | 3,570 | 1,657 | 395 | 3,748 | 1,938 | 596 |
| Faulkner. . | 11,844 | 10,178 | 1,476 | 13,000 | 9,491 | 2,437 |
| Franklin . . | 3,163 | 2,113 | 639 | 3,217 | 2,495 | 987 |
| Fulton . . . | 2,361 | 1,351 | 455 | 2,827 | 1,258 | 631 |
| Garland . . | 19,199 | 13,659 | 2,767 | 18,811 | 12,886 | 3,475 |
| Grant. . . . | 2,948 | 1,925 | 557 | 3,190 | 2,272 | 702 |
| Greene. . . | 6,622 | 3,757 | 1,041 | 7,541 | 3,510 | 1,213 |
| Hempstead | 4,796 | 1,949 | 488 | 5,476 | 2,387 | 1,022 |
| Hot Spring | 6,002 | 2,863 | 1,123 | 6,308 | 3,036 | 1,209 |
| Howard . . | 2,737 | 1,477 | 369 | 2,764 | 1,728 | 466 |
| Independence | 6,030 | 3,885 | 1,081 | 7,083 | 4,232 | 1,444 |
| Izard . . . . | 2,818 | 1,678 | 540 | 3,419 | 1,532 | 606 |
| Jackson . . | 4,300 | 1,525 | 611 | 4,944 | 1,864 | 673 |
| Jefferson . | 19,324 | 6,283 | 1,281 | 21,819 | 7,525 | 2,067 |
| Johnson . . | 3,585 | 2,367 | 757 | 3,951 | 2,563 | 1,013 |
| Lafayette . | 2,465 | 971 | 374 | 2,273 | 1,188 | 504 |
| Lawrence . | 3,652 | 1,823 | 609 | 4,146 | 2,124 | 636 |
| Lee . . . . . | 3,267 | 1,013 | 257 | 3,436 | 1,293 | 308 |
| Lincoln . . . | 2,517 | 907 | 221 | 2,805 | 1,142 | 390 |
| Little River | 3,183 | 1,409 | 480 | 3,327 | 1,483 | 890 |
| Logan . . . | 3,832 | 2,966 | 1,048 | 3,995 | 3,408 | 1,220 |
| Lonoke. . . | 7,785 | 6,174 | 1,325 | 7,963 | 6,253 | 1,554 |
| Madison . . | 2,503 | 2,303 | 461 | 2,415 | 2,238 | 598 |
| Marion . . . | 2,735 | 2,312 | 764 | 2,757 | 2,023 | 1,327 |
| Miller . . . . | 6,465 | 4,871 | 1,043 | 7,050 | 5,273 | 2,249 |
| Mississippi | 8,299 | 3,914 | 1,016 | 10,046 | 4,697 | 981 |
| Monroe . . | 2,247 | 973 | 202 | 2,578 | 1,324 | 355 |
| Montgomery | 1,830 | 1,137 | 427 | 1,904 | 1,205 | 576 |
| Nevada . . | 2,279 | 976 | 345 | 2,242 | 1,217 | 455 |
| Newton . . | 1,631 | 1,927 | 498 | 1,765 | 1,730 | 608 |
| Ouachita . | 6,632 | 3,128 | 733 | 7,411 | 3,711 | 1,238 |
| Perry . . . . | 1,873 | 1,143 | 395 | 1,906 | 1,162 | 412 |
| Phillips . . . | 5,725 | 2,216 | 463 | 6,456 | 2,695 | 634 |
| Pike. . . . . | 2,360 | 1,399 | 441 | 2,168 | 1,577 | 472 |
| Poinsett . . | 4,686 | 2,033 | 647 | 5,341 | 2,425 | 761 |
| Polk. . . . . | 2,821 | 2,947 | 876 | 3,162 | 2,757 | 1,225 |
| Pope . . . . | 8,433 | 8,243 | 1,891 | 7,704 | 8,056 | 1,989 |
| Prairie . . . | 2,211 | 1,025 | 305 | 2,366 | 1,154 | 434 |
| Pulaski. . . | 74,003 | 44,141 | 5,964 | 79,482 | 47,789 | 8,751 |
| Randolph . | 3,233 | 1,796 | 562 | 3,921 | 1,766 | 578 |
| St. Francis | 5,561 | 2,523 | 506 | 6,548 | 3,289 | 766 |
| Saline . . . | 14,027 | 11,695 | 2,612 | 12,671 | 10,105 | 2,751 |
| Scott . . . . | 2,259 | 1,426 | 513 | 2,228 | 1,695 | 610 |
| Searcy . . . | 1,669 | 1,786 | 381 | 1,679 | 1,772 | 503 |
| Sebastian . | 15,508 | 16,479 | 2,899 | 16,570 | 16,817 | 6,023 |
| Sevier . . . | 2,553 | 1,378 | 446 | 2,558 | 1,592 | 643 |
| Sharp. . . . | 3,572 | 2,635 | 687 | 3,761 | 2,486 | 921 |
| Stone. . . . | 2,227 | 1,526 | 579 | 2,622 | 1,672 | 697 |
| Union. . . . | 8,373 | 6,054 | 1,059 | 8,786 | 7,305 | 1,919 |
| Van Buren | 3,521 | 2,345 | 756 | 3,819 | 2,612 | 888 |
| Washington | 20,407 | 19,461 | 3,130 | 22,029 | 20,292 | 5,304 |
| White. . . . | 10,202 | 8,657 | 1,828 | 10,494 | 8,538 | 2,366 |
| Woodruff . | 2,044 | 568 | 186 | 2,589 | 676 | 227 |
| Yell . . . . . | 3,748 | 2,111 | 714 | 4,165 | 2,506 | 940 |
| **Totals . . .** | **465,362** | **320,323** | **67,245** | **505,823** | **337,324** | **99,132** |

### Arkansas Vote Since 1948

1948, Truman, Dem., 149,659; Dewey, Rep., 50,959; Thurmond, States' Rights, 40,068; Thomas, Soc., 1,037; Wallace, Prog., 751; Watson, Proh., 1.
1952, Eisenhower, Rep., 177,155; Stevenson, Dem., 226,300; Hamblen, Proh., 886; MacArthur, Christian Nationalist, 458; Hass, Soc. Labor, 1.
1956, Stevenson, Dem., 213,277; Eisenhower, Rep., 186,287; Andrews, Ind., 7,008.
1960, Kennedy, Dem., 215,049; Nixon, Rep., 184,508; Natl. States' Rights, 28,952.
1964, Johnson, Dem., 314,197; Goldwater, Rep., 243,264; Kasper, Natl. States' Rights, 2,965.
1968, Nixon, Rep., 189,062; Humphrey, Dem., 184,901; Wallace, 3d Party, 235,627.
1972, Nixon, Rep., 445,751; McGovern, Dem., 198,899; Schmitz, Amer., 3,016.
1976, Carter, Dem., 498,604; Ford, Rep., 267,903; McCarthy, Ind., 639; Anderson, Amer., 389.
1980, Reagan, Rep., 403,164; Carter, Dem., 398,041; Anderson, Ind., 22,468; Clark, Libertarian, 8,970; Commoner, Citizens, 2,345; Bubar, Statesman, 1,350; Hall, Com., 1,244.
1984, Reagan, Rep., 534,774; Mondale, Dem., 338,646; Bergland, Libertarian, 2,220.
1988, Bush, Rep., 466,578; Dukakis, Dem., 349,237; Duke, Chr. Pop., 5,146; Paul, Lib., 3,297.
1992, Clinton, Dem., 505,823; Bush, Rep., 337,324; Perot, Ind., 99,132; Phillips, U.S. Taxpayers, 1,437; Marrou, Libertarian, 1,261; Fulani, New Alliance, 1,022.
1996, Clinton, Dem., 465,362; Dole, Rep., 320,323; Perot, Ref., 67,245; Nader, Ind., 3,539; Browne, Ind., 3,039; Phillips, Ind., 2,004; Forbes, Ind., 851; Collins, Ind., 753; Masters, Ind., 737; Hagelin, Ind., 711; Moorehead, Ind., 690; Hollis, Ind., 535; Dodge, Ind., 384.

## California

| County | 1996 Clinton (D) | 1996 Dole (R) | 1996 Perot (RF) | 1992 Clinton (D) | 1992 Bush (R) | 1992 Perot (I) |
|---|---|---|---|---|---|---|
| Alameda. . | 279,040 | 96,942 | 22,623 | 334,224 | 109,292 | 81,643 |
| Alpine . . . | 258 | 263 | 63 | 215 | 222 | 186 |
| Amador . . | 5,675 | 6,647 | 1,218 | 5,286 | 5,477 | 4,553 |
| Butte . . . . | 26,243 | 32,179 | 5,509 | 32,489 | 31,608 | 20,231 |
| Calaveras. | 5,999 | 7,392 | 1,435 | 5,989 | 6,006 | 4,848 |
| Colusa . . . | 2,023 | 2,977 | 400 | 1,798 | 2,589 | 1,206 |
| Contra Costa | 182,346 | 113,056 | 18,936 | 194,960 | 112,965 | 72,518 |
| Del Norte . | 3,605 | 3,589 | 1,193 | 3,639 | 3,083 | 2,575 |
| El Dorado . | 21,543 | 30,354 | 4,745 | 21,012 | 25,906 | 17,503 |
| Fresno . . . | 71,885 | 78,038 | 8,656 | 92,418 | 89,137 | 36,299 |
| Glenn. . . . | 2,815 | 5,001 | 780 | 2,666 | 3,812 | 2,278 |
| Humboldt . | 20,104 | 15,505 | 4,815 | 28,854 | 18,299 | 12,340 |
| Imperial . . | 14,149 | 9,336 | 1,726 | 11,109 | 9,759 | 4,247 |
| Inyo. . . . . | 2,482 | 3,668 | 787 | 2,695 | 3,689 | 1,999 |
| Kern . . . . | 55,170 | 80,995 | 12,049 | 60,510 | 80,762 | 36,891 |
| Kings . . . . | 4,382 | 7,681 | 833 | 9,982 | 10,673 | 4,899 |
| Lake . . . . | 9,748 | 6,837 | 2,372 | 10,548 | 6,678 | 5,797 |
| Lassen. . . | 3,202 | 5,015 | 1,035 | 3,388 | 3,836 | 3,004 |
| Los Angeles | 1,310,438 | 672,089 | 146,561 | 1,446,529 | 799,607 | 488,624 |
| Madera . . | 10,907 | 16,005 | 2,128 | 10,863 | 13,066 | 6,156 |
| Marin. . . . | 64,148 | 31,081 | 6,279 | 76,158 | 30,479 | 22,986 |
| Mariposa . | 2,823 | 3,835 | 698 | 3,023 | 2,982 | 2,211 |
| Mendocino | 14,199 | 9,233 | 3,948 | 18,344 | 7,958 | 9,753 |
| Merced. . . | 21,257 | 20,131 | 3,332 | 20,133 | 17,981 | 10,914 |
| Modoc . . . | 1,339 | 2,213 | 519 | 1,489 | 1,803 | 1,269 |
| Mono . . . . | 1,547 | 1,848 | 444 | 1,489 | 1,570 | 1,248 |
| Monterey . | 53,120 | 36,305 | 36,305 | 54,861 | 36,461 | 24,472 |
| Napa . . . . | 22,052 | 15,087 | 3,804 | 24,215 | 15,662 | 13,150 |
| Nevada . . | 14,520 | 20,298 | 3,125 | 15,433 | 17,343 | 11,072 |
| Orange. . . | 295,037 | 403,207 | 60,948 | 306,930 | 426,613 | 232,394 |
| Placer . . . | 29,795 | 41,468 | 5,548 | 30,783 | 38,298 | 21,741 |
| Plumas. . . | 3,391 | 4,702 | 859 | 3,742 | 3,599 | 2,551 |
| Riverside . | 151,387 | 156,262 | 31,909 | 166,241 | 159,457 | 102,233 |
| Sacramento. | 191,818 | 156,292 | 22,605 | 197,540 | 160,366 | 91,412 |
| San Benito | 6,209 | 4,798 | 901 | 5,354 | 4,112 | 3,182 |
| San Bernardino | 176,068 | 171,578 | 37,643 | 183,634 | 176,563 | 109,183 |
| San Diego. | 345,615 | 349,389 | 56,007 | 367,397 | 352,125 | 259,249 |
| San Francisco | 188,858 | 39,974 | 8,693 | 233,263 | 57,352 | 29,018 |
| San Joaquin | 63,180 | 60,959 | 9,050 | 63,655 | 58,355 | 31,205 |
| San Luis Obispo . . | 34,052 | 37,710 | 7,039 | 40,136 | 36,384 | 27,314 |
| San Mateo | 135,972 | 64,944 | 13,603 | 149,232 | 75,080 | 50,465 |
| Santa Barbara | 62,627 | 54,686 | 8,396 | 69,215 | 57,375 | 35,105 |
| Santa Clara. | 266,728 | 147,337 | 31,714 | 296,265 | 170,870 | 128,895 |
| Santa Cruz | 48,922 | 22,646 | 5,499 | 66,183 | 24,916 | 21,615 |
| Shasta . . . | 19,737 | 32,629 | 5,570 | 21,605 | 28,190 | 17,990 |
| Sierra. . . . | 573 | 877 | 170 | 653 | 691 | 519 |
| Siskiyou . . | 6,548 | 8,095 | 1,758 | 8,254 | 6,660 | 5,567 |
| Solano . . . | 60,755 | 37,680 | 8,180 | 64,320 | 38,883 | 27,851 |
| Sonoma . . | 91,544 | 48,089 | 12,594 | 104,334 | 47,619 | 43,859 |
| Stanislaus. | 47,765 | 45,938 | 7,333 | 52,415 | 47,275 | 27,651 |
| Sutter. . . . | 7,976 | 13,125 | 1,432 | 7,883 | 12,956 | 4,881 |
| Tehama . . | 7,125 | 10,024 | 2,256 | 7,508 | 7,419 | 5,884 |
| Trinity . . . | 2,198 | 2,525 | 853 | 1,967 | 1,886 | 2,092 |
| Tulare . . . | 28,682 | 39,289 | 4,478 | 31,188 | 40,482 | 16,430 |
| Tuolumne . | 8,410 | 9,786 | 1,789 | 9,216 | 8,525 | 6,294 |
| Ventura . . | 94,855 | 89,470 | 20,288 | 99,011 | 94,911 | 71,844 |
| Yolo. . . . . | 31,446 | 17,809 | 2,992 | 33,297 | 17,574 | 11,073 |
| Yuba . . . . | 5,643 | 7,675 | 1,277 | 5,785 | 7,333 | 3,637 |
| **Totals . . .** | **4,639,935** | **3,412,563** | **667,702** | **5,121,325** | **3,630,574** | **2,296,006** |

### California Vote Since 1948

1948, Truman, Dem., 1,913,134; Dewey, Rep., 1,895,269; Wallace, Prog., 190,381; Watson, Proh., 16,926; Thomas, Soc., 3,459; Thurmond, States' Rights, 1,228; Teichert, Soc. Labor, 195; Dobbs, Soc. Workers, 133.

1952, Eisenhower, Rep., 2,897,310; Stevenson, Dem., 2,197,548; Hallinan, Prog., 24,106; Hamblen, Proh., 15,653; MacArthur, (Tenny Ticket), 3,326; (Kellems Ticket) 178; Hass, Soc. Labor, 273; Hoopes, Soc., 206; scattered, 3,249.

1956, Eisenhower, Rep., 3,027,668; Stevenson, Dem., 2,420,136; Holtwick, Proh., 11,119; Andrews, Constitution, 6,087; Hass, Soc. Labor, 300; Hoopes, Soc., 123; Dobbs, Soc. Workers, 96; Smith, Christian Natl., 8.

1960, Kennedy, Dem., 3,224,099; Nixon, Rep., 3,259,722; Decker, Proh., 21,706; Hass, Soc. Labor, 1,051.

1964, Johnson, Dem., 4,171,877; Goldwater, Rep., 2,879,108; Hass, Soc. Labor, 489; DeBerry, Soc. Workers, 378; Munn, Proh., 305; Hensley, Universal, 19.

1968, Nixon, Rep., 3,467,664; Humphrey, Dem., 3,244,318; Wallace, 3d Party, 487,270; Peace and Freedom, 27,707; McCarthy, Alternative, 20,721; Gregory, write-in, 3,230; Mitchell, Com., 260; Munn, Proh., 59; Blomen, Soc. Labor, 341; Soeters, Defense, 17.

1972, Nixon, Rep., 4,602,096; McGovern, Dem., 3,475,847; Schmitz, Amer., 232,554; Spock, Peace and Freedom, 55,167; Hall, Com., 373; Hospers, Libertarian, 980; Munn, Proh., 53; Fisher, Soc. Labor, 197; Jenness, Soc. Workers, 574; Green, Universal, 21.

1976, Carter, Dem., 3,742,284; Ford, Rep., 3,882,244; MacBride, Libertarian, 56,388; Maddox, Amer. Ind., 51,098; Wright, People's, 41,731; Camejo, Soc. Workers, 17,259; Hall, Com., 12,766; write-in, McCarthy, 58,412; other write-in, 4,935.

1980, Reagan, Rep. 4,524,858; Carter, Dem., 3,083,661; Anderson, Ind., 739,833; Clark, Libertarian, 148,434; Commoner, Ind., 61,063; Smith, Peace and Freedom, 18,116; Rarick, Amer. Ind., 9,856.

1984, Reagan, Rep. 5,305,410; Mondale, Dem., 3,815,947; Bergland, Libertarian, 48,400.

1988, Bush, Rep., 5,054,917; Dukakis, Dem., 4,702,233; Paul, Lib., 70,105; Fulani, Ind., 31,181.

1992, Clinton, Dem., 5,121,325; Bush, Rep., 3,630,575; Perot, Ind., 2,296,006; Marrou, Libertarian, 48,139; Daniels, Ind., 18,597; Phillips, U.S. Taxpayers, 12,711.

1996, Clinton, Dem., 4,639,935; Dole, Rep., 3,412,563; Perot, Ref., 667,702; Nader, Green, 214,392; Browne, Libertarian, 66,482; Feinland, Peace & Freedom, 22,593; Phillips, Amer. Ind., 18,932; Hagelin, Natural Law, 13,712.

## Colorado

| County | 1996 Clinton (D) | 1996 Dole (R) | 1996 Perot (RF) | 1992 Clinton (D) | 1992 Bush (R) | 1992 Perot (I) |
|---|---|---|---|---|---|---|
| Adams . . . | 48,314 | 36,666 | 7,206 | 45,357 | 30,856 | 26,379 |
| Alamosa . . | 2,295 | 1,997 | 425 | 1,928 | 1,572 | 1,089 |
| Arapahoe . | 68,306 | 82,778 | 8,476 | 66,607 | 72,221 | 44,363 |
| Archuleta . | 997 | 1,963 | 360 | 819 | 1,242 | 741 |
| Baca . . . . | 659 | 1,321 | 203 | 726 | 1,240 | 647 |
| Bent . . . . | 1,046 | 917 | 209 | 985 | 759 | 506 |
| Boulder . . | 63,316 | 41,922 | 6,840 | 64,567 | 33,553 | 27,762 |
| Chaffee . . | 2,768 | 3,052 | 538 | 2,284 | 2,419 | 1,549 |
| Cheyenne. | 328 | 739 | 91 | 301 | 615 | 292 |
| Clear Creek. | 1,863 | 1,746 | 365 | 1,744 | 1,356 | 1,308 |
| Conejos . . | 1,718 | 1,150 | 245 | 1,705 | 1,160 | 578 |
| Costilla. . . | 1,168 | 333 | 108 | 1,180 | 366 | 199 |
| Crowley . . | 559 | 680 | 114 | 570 | 602 | 276 |
| Custer . . . | 412 | 920 | 164 | 343 | 651 | 368 |
| Delta . . . . | 3,584 | 6,047 | 1,060 | 3,424 | 4,359 | 2,627 |
| Denver. . . | 120,430 | 58,508 | 8,735 | 121,961 | 55,418 | 37,298 |
| Dolores . . | 276 | 417 | 95 | 242 | 315 | 285 |
| Douglas . . | 16,232 | 32,120 | 2,662 | 9,991 | 18,592 | 11,329 |
| Eagle. . . . | 4,883 | 4,532 | 1,154 | 3,870 | 3,100 | 3,821 |
| Elbert. . . . | 1,767 | 3,794 | 492 | 1,237 | 2,205 | 1,567 |
| El Paso . . | 55,815 | 102,396 | 11,175 | 45,827 | 86,044 | 34,346 |
| Fremont . . | 5,344 | 7,437 | 1,438 | 5,356 | 5,961 | 3,709 |
| Garfield . . | 5,722 | 6,281 | 1,561 | 5,082 | 4,404 | 4,408 |
| Gilpin. . . . | 799 | 682 | 184 | 726 | 462 | 545 |
| Grand . . . | 2,010 | 2,264 | 473 | 1,678 | 1,763 | 1,454 |
| Gunnison . | 2,810 | 2,230 | 571 | 2,389 | 1,662 | 1,671 |
| Hinsdale. . | 185 | 289 | 56 | 151 | 188 | 136 |
| Huerfano . | 1,483 | 996 | 210 | 1,224 | 685 | 385 |
| Jackson . . | 222 | 486 | 107 | 216 | 422 | 326 |
| Jefferson . | 89,494 | 101,517 | 12,967 | 80,834 | 82,705 | 58,404 |
| Kiowa . . . | 246 | 549 | 74 | 290 | 472 | 267 |
| Kit Carson | 1,073 | 2,068 | 235 | 925 | 1,801 | 919 |
| Lake . . . . | 1,338 | 728 | 274 | 1,426 | 605 | 863 |
| La Plata . . | 6,507 | 8,036 | 1,399 | 5,913 | 5,522 | 4,083 |
| Larimer . . | 40,965 | 45,935 | 6,823 | 38,232 | 35,995 | 24,879 |
| Las Animas | 3,611 | 1,905 | 427 | 3,847 | 1,739 | 953 |
| Lincoln. . . | 729 | 1,267 | 164 | 640 | 1,079 | 581 |
| Logan . . . | 2,764 | 4,032 | 609 | 2,718 | 3,420 | 2,184 |
| Mesa. . . . | 17,114 | 24,761 | 3,707 | 15,162 | 18,169 | 10,474 |
| Mineral. . . | 192 | 179 | 69 | 171 | 159 | 117 |
| Moffat . . . | 1,635 | 2,466 | 649 | 1,386 | 1,809 | 1,875 |
| Montezuma | 2,578 | 4,175 | 827 | 2,270 | 3,124 | 2,205 |
| Montrose . | 4,019 | 6,730 | 1,187 | 3,713 | 4,847 | 3,093 |
| Morgan . . | 3,347 | 4,557 | 687 | 2,985 | 3,724 | 2,175 |
| Otero. . . . | 3,386 | 3,356 | 581 | 3,485 | 3,120 | 1,590 |
| Ouray . . . | 569 | 984 | 167 | 461 | 653 | 466 |
| Park . . . . | 1,844 | 2,661 | 534 | 1,307 | 1,530 | 1,396 |
| Philips . . . | 706 | 1,284 | 156 | 692 | 1,075 | 525 |
| Pitkin. . . . | 3,949 | 1,969 | 535 | 3,820 | 1,686 | 1,907 |
| Prowers . . | 1,745 | 2,504 | 342 | 1,770 | 2,371 | 1,184 |
| Pueblo . . . | 28,791 | 17,402 | 3,374 | 30,261 | 16,120 | 9,841 |
| Rio Blanco | 731 | 1,697 | 243 | 778 | 1,231 | 794 |
| Rio Grande | 1,699 | 2,109 | 377 | 1,541 | 1,927 | 1,043 |
| Routt . . . . | 3,659 | 3,016 | 859 | 3,188 | 2,358 | 2,564 |
| Saguache. | 969 | 712 | 160 | 1,011 | 675 | 471 |
| San Juan . | 133 | 153 | 50 | 147 | 118 | 183 |
| San Miguel | 1,536 | 770 | 230 | 1,380 | 628 | 634 |
| Sedgwick . | 519 | 715 | 101 | 397 | 447 | 295 |
| Summit . . | 3,970 | 3,261 | 823 | 3,344 | 2,256 | 2,715 |
| Teller. . . . | 2,312 | 4,458 | 707 | 1,873 | 3,050 | 1,927 |
| Washington | 649 | 1,566 | 190 | 660 | 1,266 | 671 |
| Weld . . . . | 21,325 | 26,517 | 4,347 | 19,295 | 20,958 | 13,571 |
| Yuma. . . . | 1,439 | 2,588 | 319 | 1,269 | 2,019 | 1,197 |
| **Totals . . .** | **670,854** | **691,290** | **99,510** | **629,681** | **562,850** | **366,010** |

### Colorado Vote Since 1948

1948, Truman, Dem., 267,288; Dewey, Rep., 239,714; Wallace, Prog., 6,115; Thomas, Soc., 1,678; Dobbs, Soc. Workers, 228; Teichert, Soc. Labor, 214.

1952, Eisenhower, Rep., 379,782; Stevenson, Dem., 245,504; MacArthur, Constitution, 2,181; Hallinan, Prog., 1,919; Hoopes, Soc., 365; Hass, Soc. Labor, 352.

1956, Eisenhower, Rep., 394,479; Stevenson, Dem., 263,997; Hass, Soc. Lab., 3,308; Andrews, Ind., 759; Hoopes, Soc., 531.

1960, Kennedy, Dem., 330,629; Nixon, Rep., 402,242; Hass, Soc. Labor, 2,803; Dobbs, Soc. Workers, 572.

1964, Johnson, Dem., 476,024; Goldwater, Rep., 296,767; Hass, Soc. Labor, 302; DeBerry, Soc. Workers, 2,537; Munn, Proh., 1,356.

1968, Nixon, Rep., 409,345; Humphrey, Dem., 335,174; Wallace, 3d Party, 60,813; Blomen, Soc. Labor, 3,016; Gregory, New-party, 1,393; Munn, Proh., 275; Halstead, Soc. Workers, 235.

1972, Nixon, Rep., 597,189; McGovern, Dem., 329,980; Fisher, Soc. Labor, 4,361; Hospers, Libertarian, 1,111; Hall, Com., 432; Jenness, Soc. Workers, 555; Munn, Proh., 467; Schmitz, Amer., 17,269; Spock, Peoples, 2,403.

1976, Carter, Dem., 460,353; Ford, Rep., 584,367; McCarthy, Ind., 26,107; MacBride, Libertarian, 5,330; Bubar, Proh., 2,882.

1980, Reagan, Rep., 652,264; Carter, Dem., 367,973; Anderson, Ind., 130,633; Clark, Libertarian, 25,744; Commoner, Citizens, 5,614; Bubar, Statesman, 1,180; Pulley, Socialist, 520; Hall, Com., 487.

1984, Reagan, Rep., 821,817; Mondale, Dem., 454,975; Bergland, Libertarian, 11,257.

1988, Bush, Rep., 728,177; Dukakis, Dem., 621,453; Paul, Lib., 15,482; Dodge, Proh., 4,604.

1992, Clinton, Dem., 629,681; Bush, Rep., 562,850; Perot, Ind., 366,010; Marrou, Libertarian, 8,669; Fulani, New Alliance, 1,608.

1996, Dole, Rep., 691,290; Clinton, Dem., 670,854; Perot, Ref., 99,510; Nader, Green, 25,045; Browne, Libertarian, 12,380; Collins, Ind., 2,799; Phillips, Amer. Constitution, 2,791; Hagelin, Natural Law, 2,544; Hollis, Soc., 668; Moorehead, Workers World, 609; Templin, Amer., 584; Dodge, Proh., 374; Harris, Soc. Workers, 248.

## Connecticut

| City | 1996 Clinton (D) | 1996 Dole (R) | 1996 Perot (RF) | 1992 Clinton (D) | 1992 Bush (R) | 1992 Perot (I) |
|---|---|---|---|---|---|---|
| Bridgeport. | 22,883 | 6,785 | 2,367 | 22,321 | 13,149 | 6,263 |
| Hartford . . | 2,291 | 3,082 | 1,010 | 26,971 | 6,180 | 3,390 |
| New Britain | 14,322 | 4,911 | 1,717 | 14,159 | 7,040 | 4,983 |
| New Haven | 24,678 | 4,632 | 1,434 | 29,774 | 8,931 | 4,130 |
| Norwalk . . | 17,354 | 10,800 | 2,237 | 16,488 | 14,743 | 6,046 |
| Stamford . | 25,005 | 14,696 | 2,594 | 23,185 | 19,809 | 6,763 |
| Waterbury. | 18,901 | 12,075 | 3,169 | 16,366 | 16,155 | 9,188 |
| West Hartford | 19,037 | 10,781 | 1,892 | 19,623 | 12,266 | 5,017 |
| Other . . . . | 536,345 | 387,740 | 114,660 | 513,431 | 480,040 | 302,991 |
| **Totals . . .** | **680,816** | **455,502** | **131,080** | **682,318** | **578,313** | **348,771** |

### Connecticut Vote Since 1948

1948, Truman, Dem., 423,297; Dewey, Rep., 437,754; Wallace, Prog., 13,713; Thomas, Soc., 6,964; Teichert, Soc. Labor, 1,184; Dobbs, Soc. Workers, 606.

1952, Eisenhower, Rep., 611,012; Stevenson, Dem., 481,649; Hoopes, Soc., 2,244; Hallinan, Peoples, 1,466; Hass, Soc. Labor, 535; write-in, 5.

1956, Eisenhower, Rep., 711,837; Stevenson, Dem., 405,079; scattered, 205.

1960, Kennedy, Dem., 657,055; Nixon, Rep., 565,813.

1964, Johnson, Dem., 826,269; Goldwater, Rep., 390,996; scattered, 1,313.

1968, Nixon, Rep., 556,721; Humphrey, Dem., 621,561; Wallace, 3d Party, 76,650; scattered, 1,300.

1972, Nixon, Rep., 810,763; McGovern, Dem., 555,498; Schmitz, Amer., 17,239; scattered, 777.

1976, Carter, Dem., 647,895; Ford, Rep., 719,261; Maddox, George Wallace Party, 7,101; LaRouche, U.S. Labor, 1,789.

1980, Reagan, Rep., 677,210; Carter, Dem., 541,732; Anderson, Ind., 171,807; Clark, Libertarian, 8,570; Commoner, Citizens, 6,130; scattered, 836.

1984, Reagan, Rep., 890,877; Mondale, Dem., 569,597.

1988, Bush, Rep., 750,241; Dukakis, Dem., 676,584; Paul, Lib., 14,071; Fulani, New Alliance, 2,491.

1992, Clinton, Dem., 682,318; Bush, Rep., 578,313; Perot, Ind., 348,771; Marrou, Libertarian, 5,391; Fulani, New Alliance, 1,363.

1996, Clinton, Dem., 712,603; Dole, Rep., 481,047; Perot, Ref., 137,784; Nader, Green, 23,600; Browne, Libertarian, 5,890; Phillips, Concerned Citizens, 3,749; Hagelin, Natural Law, 1,679.

## Delaware

| County | 1996 Clinton (D) | 1996 Dole (R) | 1996 Perot (RF) | 1992 Clinton (D) | 1992 Bush (R) | 1992 Perot (I) |
|---|---|---|---|---|---|---|
| Kent. . . . . | 18,311 | 15,926 | 4,703 | 15,364 | 15,562 | 8,916 |
| New Castle | 98,718 | 60,808 | 17,725 | 91,516 | 66,311 | 37,581 |
| Sussex. . . | 23,180 | 22,172 | 6,265 | 19,174 | 20,440 | 12,716 |
| **Totals . . .** | **140,209** | **98,906** | **28,693** | **126,054** | **102,313** | **59,213** |

### Delaware Vote Since 1948

1948, Truman, Dem., 67,813; Dewey, Rep., 69,688; Wallace, Prog., 1,050; Watson, Proh., 343; Thomas, Soc., 250; Teichert, Soc. Labor, 29.

1952, Eisenhower, Rep., 90,059; Stevenson, Dem., 83,315; Hass, Soc. Labor, 242; Hamblen, Proh., 234; Hallinan, Prog., 155; Hoopes, Soc., 20.

1956, Eisenhower, Rep., 98,057; Stevenson, Dem., 79,421; Oltwick, Proh., 400; Hass, Soc. Labor, 110.

1960, Kennedy, Dem., 99,590; Nixon, Rep., 96,373; Faubus, States' Rights, 354; Decker, Proh., 284; Hass, Soc. Labor, 82.

1964, Johnson, Dem., 122,704; Goldwater, Rep., 78,078; Hass, Soc. Labor, 113; Munn, Proh., 425.

1968, Nixon, Rep., 96,714; Humphrey, Dem., 89,194; Wallace, 3d Party, 28,459.

1972, Nixon, Rep., 140,357; McGovern, Dem., 92,283; Schmitz, Amer., 2,638; Munn, Proh., 238.

1976, Carter, Dem., 122,596; Ford, Rep., 109,831; McCarthy, non-partisan, 2,437; Anderson, Amer., 645; LaRouche, U.S. Labor, 136; Bubar, Proh., 103; Levin, Soc. Labor, 86.

1980, Reagan, Rep., 111,252; Carter, Dem., 105,754; Anderson, Ind., 16,288; Clark, Libertarian, 1,974; Greaves, Amer., 400.

1984, Reagan, Rep., 152,190; Mondale, Dem., 101,656; Bergland, Libertarian, 268.

1988, Bush, Rep., 139,639; Dukakis, Dem., 108,647; Paul, Lib., 1,162; Fulani, New Alliance, 443.

1992, Clinton, Dem., 126,054; Bush, Rep., 102,313; Perot, Ind., 59,213; Fulani, New Alliance, 1,105.

1996, Clinton, Dem., 140,209; Dole, Rep., 98,906; Perot, Ind. (Ref.), 28,693; Browne, Libertarian, 2,050; Phillips, Taxpayers, 348; Hagelin, Natural Law, 272.

## District of Columbia

| | 1996 Clinton (D) | 1996 Dole (R) | 1996 Perot (RF) | 1992 Clinton (D) | 1992 Bush (R) | 1992 Perot (I) |
|---|---|---|---|---|---|---|
| **Totals . . .** | **152,031** | **16,637** | **3,479** | **192,619** | **20,698** | **9,681** |

### District of Columbia Vote Since 1964

1964, Johnson, Dem., 169,796; Goldwater, Rep., 28,801.

1968, Nixon, Rep., 31,012; Humphrey, Dem., 139, 566.

1972, Nixon, Rep., 35,226; McGovern, Dem., 127,627; Reed, Soc. Workers, 316; Hall, Com., 252.

1976, Carter, Dem., 137,818; Ford, Rep., 27,873; Camejo, Soc. Workers, 545; MacBride, Libertarian, 274; Hall, Com., 219; LaRouche, U.S. Labor, 157.

1980, Reagan, Rep., 23,313; Carter, Dem., 130,231; Anderson, Ind., 16,131; Commoner, Citizens, 1,826; Clark, Libertarian, 1,104; Hall, Com., 369; DeBerry, Soc. Workers, 173; Griswold, Workers World, 52; write-ins, 690.

1984, Mondale, Dem., 180,408; Reagan, Rep., 29,009; Bergland, Libertarian, 279.

1988, Bush, Rep., 27,590; Dukakis, Dem., 159,407; Fulani, New Alliance, 2,901; Paul, Lib., 554.

1992, Clinton, Dem., 192,619; Bush, Rep., 20,698; Perot, Ind., 9,681; Fulani, New Alliance, 1,459; Daniels, Ind., 1,186.

1996, Clinton, Dem., 152,031; Dole, Rep., 16,637; Perot, Ref., 3,479; Nader, Green, 4,592; Browne, Libertarian, 565; Hagelin, Natural Law, 270; Harris, Soc. Workers, 249.

## Florida

| County | 1996 Clinton (D) | 1996 Dole (R) | 1996 Perot (RF) | 1992 Clinton (D) | 1992 Bush (R) | 1992 Perot (I) |
|---|---|---|---|---|---|---|
| Alachua . . | 40,144 | 25,303 | 8,072 | 37,876 | 22,806 | 15,293 |
| Baker. . . . | 2,273 | 3,684 | 667 | 1,974 | 3,417 | 1,315 |
| Bay . . . . . | 16,950 | 28,188 | 5,916 | 12,830 | 22,820 | 9,702 |
| Bradford . . | 3,356 | 4,038 | 819 | 3,040 | 3,671 | 1,572 |
| Brevard . . | 80,410 | 87,981 | 25,251 | 61,070 | 84,545 | 49,491 |
| Broward . . | 320,389 | 142,594 | 38,928 | 276,309 | 164,782 | 90,923 |
| Calhoun . . | 1,642 | 1,572 | 603 | 1,665 | 1,721 | 1,176 |
| Charlotte . | 27,121 | 27,836 | 7,783 | 22,904 | 24,302 | 14,711 |
| Citrus. . . . | 22,042 | 20,114 | 7,244 | 15,935 | 16,402 | 12,310 |
| Clay. . . . . | 13,246 | 30,332 | 3,281 | 10,597 | 26,313 | 8,414 |
| Collier . . . | 23,182 | 42,590 | 6,320 | 18,794 | 38,447 | 14,514 |
| Columbia . | 6,691 | 7,588 | 1,970 | 5,526 | 6,489 | 2,906 |
| Dade . . . . | 317,378 | 209,634 | 24,722 | 254,444 | 235,149 | 53,957 |
| De Soto . . | 3,219 | 3,272 | 965 | 2,646 | 3,070 | 1,687 |
| Dixie . . . . | 1,731 | 1,398 | 652 | 1,855 | 1,401 | 1,094 |
| Duval. . . . | 103,498 | 113,587 | 13,156 | 92,010 | 123,480 | 33,335 |
| Escambia . | 37,768 | 60,839 | 8,587 | 32,018 | 52,775 | 19,868 |
| Flagler . . . | 9,583 | 8,232 | 2,185 | 6,692 | 6,241 | 3,387 |
| Franklin . . | 2,095 | 1,563 | 878 | 1,534 | 1,660 | 1,143 |
| Gadsden . | 9,405 | 3,813 | 938 | 8,478 | 3,975 | 1,871 |
| Gilchrist . . | 1,985 | 1,939 | 841 | 1,511 | 1,395 | 1,090 |
| Glades . . . | 1,530 | 1,361 | 521 | 1,305 | 1,185 | 878 |

| County | 1996 Clinton (D) | 1996 Dole (R) | 1996 Perot (RF) | 1992 Clinton (D) | 1992 Bush (R) | 1992 Perot (I) |
|---|---|---|---|---|---|---|
| Gulf. . . . . | 2,480 | 2,424 | 1,054 | 1,938 | 2,650 | 1,245 |
| Hamilton. . | 1,734 | 1,518 | 406 | 1,622 | 1,402 | 695 |
| Hardee. . . | 2,417 | 2,926 | 851 | 2,017 | 2,898 | 1,498 |
| Hendry. . . | 3,882 | 3,855 | 1,135 | 2,690 | 3,279 | 2,032 |
| Hernando . | 28,520 | 22,039 | 7,272 | 19,171 | 17,896 | 11,845 |
| Highlands . | 14,244 | 15,608 | 3,739 | 11,234 | 14,497 | 6,592 |
| Hillsborough | 144,022 | 136,361 | 25,136 | 115,261 | 130,611 | 63,037 |
| Holmes . . | 2,147 | 3,027 | 1,165 | 1,877 | 3,196 | 1,426 |
| Indian River | 16,373 | 22,709 | 4,635 | 12,359 | 19,137 | 12,375 |
| Jackson . . | 6,665 | 7,181 | 1,602 | 5,481 | 6,720 | 2,447 |
| Jefferson . | 2,543 | 1,851 | 20 | 2,270 | 1,506 | 894 |
| Lafayette . | 829 | 1,166 | 316 | 866 | 1,037 | 612 |
| Lake . . . . | 29,750 | 35,087 | 8,813 | 23,199 | 30,818 | 15,606 |
| Lee . . . . . | 65,692 | 80,882 | 18,389 | 53,656 | 73,423 | 38,446 |
| Leon . . . . | 50,058 | 33,914 | 6,672 | 47,770 | 31,964 | 17,207 |
| Levy . . . . | 4,938 | 4,299 | 1,774 | 4,330 | 3,796 | 2,784 |
| Liberty . . . | 868 | 913 | 376 | 820 | 1,126 | 617 |
| Madison . . | 2,791 | 2,195 | 578 | 2,644 | 2,006 | 1,174 |
| Manatee . . | 41,835 | 44,059 | 10,360 | 33,826 | 42,708 | 23,282 |
| Marion . . . | 37,033 | 41,397 | 11,340 | 30,823 | 35,438 | 20,524 |
| Martin . . . | 20,853 | 28,516 | 5,005 | 14,778 | 24,768 | 13,433 |
| Monroe . . | 15,219 | 12,021 | 4,817 | 10,435 | 9,891 | 8,306 |
| Nassau . . | 7,276 | 12,134 | 1,657 | 5,497 | 9,364 | 3,251 |
| Okaloosa . | 16,434 | 40,631 | 5,432 | 12,003 | 32,755 | 16,649 |
| Okeechobee | 4,824 | 3,415 | 1,666 | 3,418 | 3,298 | 2,645 |
| Orange. . . | 105,050 | 105,564 | 18,143 | 82,656 | 108,738 | 44,827 |
| Osceola . . | 21,870 | 18,335 | 6,091 | 15,009 | 19,139 | 11,021 |
| Palm Beach | 228,869 | 131,874 | 30,559 | 187,840 | 140,317 | 76,223 |
| Pasco . . . | 66,472 | 48,346 | 18,011 | 53,125 | 47,721 | 34,650 |
| Pinellas . . | 184,715 | 152,112 | 36,989 | 160,217 | 158,733 | 101,150 |
| Polk. . . . . | 66,735 | 67,943 | 14,991 | 51,442 | 65,952 | 28,198 |
| Putnam . . | 12,008 | 9,781 | 3,272 | 10,707 | 8,909 | 5,975 |
| St. Johns . | 16,703 | 27,298 | 4,203 | 12,284 | 20,173 | 7,397 |
| St. Lucie. . | 36,168 | 28,892 | 8,482 | 23,873 | 24,397 | 19,813 |
| Santa Rosa | 10,922 | 26,242 | 4,957 | 6,526 | 17,229 | 8,735 |
| Sarasota. . | 63,648 | 69,198 | 14,939 | 54,536 | 66,831 | 34,281 |
| Seminole . | 45,003 | 59,679 | 9,348 | 35,649 | 57,085 | 24,477 |
| Sumter. . . | 7,014 | 5,960 | 2,375 | 5,027 | 4,366 | 2,901 |
| Suwannee | 4,478 | 5,742 | 1,874 | 3,985 | 4,571 | 2,790 |
| Taylor . . . | 3,583 | 3,188 | 1,140 | 2,568 | 2,693 | 1,929 |
| Union. . . . | 1,388 | 1,636 | 425 | 1,247 | 1,543 | 770 |
| Volusia. . . | 78,876 | 63,043 | 17,313 | 65,213 | 59,155 | 30,813 |
| Wakulla . . | 3,054 | 2,931 | 1,091 | 2,319 | 2,586 | 1,790 |
| Walton . . . | 5,341 | 7,706 | 2,342 | 3,886 | 5,719 | 3,886 |
| Washington | 2,540 | 3,061 | 1,183 | 2,544 | 3,694 | 1,596 |
| **Totals . . .** | **2,533,502** | **2,226,117** | **482,237** | **2,071,651** | **2,171,781** | **1,052,481** |

## Florida Vote Since 1948

1948, Truman, Dem., 281,988; Dewey, Rep., 194,280; Thurmond, States' Rights, 89,755; Wallace, Prog., 11,620.

1952, Eisenhower, Rep., 544,036; Stevenson, Dem., 444,950; scattered, 351.

1956, Eisenhower, Rep., 643,849; Stevenson, Dem., 480,371.

1960, Kennedy, Dem., 748,700; Nixon, Rep., 795,476.

1964, Johnson, Dem., 948,540; Goldwater, Rep., 905,941.

1968, Nixon, Rep., 886,804; Humphrey, Dem., 676,794; Wallace, 3d Party, 624,207.

1972, Nixon, Rep., 1,857,759; McGovern, Dem., 718,117; scattered, 7,407.

1976, Carter, Dem., 1,636,000; Ford, Rep., 1,469,531; McCarthy, Ind., 23,643; Anderson, Amer., 21,325.

1980, Reagan, Rep., 2,046,951; Carter, Dem., 1,419,475; Anderson, Ind., 189,692; Clark, Libertarian, 30,524; write-ins, 285.

1984, Reagan, Rep., 2,728,775; Mondale, Dem., 1,448,344.

1988, Bush, Rep., 2,616,597; Dukakis, Dem., 1,655,851; Paul, Lib., 19,796, Fulani, New Alliance, 6,655.

1992, Bush, Rep., 2,171,781; Clinton, Dem., 2,071,651; Perot, Ind., 1,052,481; Marrou, Libertarian, 15,068.

1996, Clinton, Dem., 2,533,502; Dole, Rep., 2,226,117; Perot, Ref., 482,237; Browne, Libertarian, 24,185.

# Georgia

| County | 1996 Clinton (D) | 1996 Dole (R) | 1996 Perot (RF) | 1992 Clinton (D) | 1992 Bush (R) | 1992 Perot (I) |
|---|---|---|---|---|---|---|
| Appling. . . | 2,070 | 2,572 | 446 | 2,455 | 2,514 | 1,047 |
| Atkinson . . | 823 | 784 | 215 | 1,056 | 779 | 342 |
| Bacon . . . | 1,360 | 1,580 | 402 | 1,423 | 1,301 | 604 |
| Baker. . . . | 955 | 408 | 105 | 864 | 391 | 210 |
| Baldwin . . | 5,959 | 4,570 | 849 | 5,813 | 4,262 | 1,679 |
| Banks . . . | 1,533 | 1,924 | 592 | 1,530 | 1,551 | 583 |
| Barrow . . . | 3,928 | 5,342 | 942 | 3,991 | 4,328 | 1,633 |
| Bartow . . . | 6,853 | 9,250 | 1,770 | 6,675 | 7,742 | 2,500 |
| Ben Hill . . | 2,198 | 1,516 | 361 | 2,348 | 1,476 | 619 |
| Berrien. . . | 2,066 | 1,950 | 525 | 2,103 | 1,637 | 796 |
| Bibb. . . . . | 26,727 | 20,778 | 2,268 | 28,070 | 19,847 | 6,021 |
| Bleckley . . | 1,365 | 1,632 | 300 | 1,710 | 1,570 | 662 |
| Brantley . . | 1,494 | 1,738 | 386 | 1,883 | 1,541 | 840 |
| Brooks . . . | 1,977 | 1,738 | 314 | 1,895 | 1,779 | 630 |
| Bryan. . . . | 2,152 | 3,577 | 513 | 2,031 | 2,789 | 1,095 |
| Bulloch. . . | 5,396 | 6,646 | 939 | 4,903 | 5,690 | 2,020 |
| Burke. . . . | 3,915 | 2,590 | 389 | 3,647 | 2,390 | 807 |
| Butts . . . . | 2,272 | 2,027 | 416 | 2,448 | 1,768 | 619 |
| Calhoun . . | 1,217 | 541 | 106 | 1,301 | 464 | 248 |
| Camden . . | 3,644 | 4,222 | 557 | 2,952 | 3,517 | 1,077 |
| Candler . . | 1,097 | 1,131 | 264 | 1,192 | 1,014 | 541 |
| Carroll . . . | 8,436 | 11,156 | 2,002 | 8,404 | 10,750 | 3,358 |
| Catoosa . . | 5,185 | 8,237 | 1,257 | 4,817 | 7,599 | 2,290 |
| Charlton . . | 1,368 | 1,374 | 280 | 1,127 | 1,333 | 427 |
| Chatham . | 35,781 | 31,997 | 3,028 | 31,533 | 31,925 | 8,269 |
| Chattahoochee. | 565 | 398 | 115 | 604 | 413 | 177 |
| Chattooga. | 3,003 | 2,513 | 796 | 2,976 | 2,439 | 965 |
| Cherokee . | 10,041 | 22,593 | 2,611 | 8,113 | 16,054 | 4,950 |
| Clarke . . . | 15,206 | 10,504 | 1,201 | 15,403 | 10,459 | 2,987 |
| Clay. . . . . | 787 | 293 | 62 | 778 | 264 | 155 |
| Clayton . . | 30,686 | 20,625 | 3,494 | 25,890 | 23,965 | 7,942 |
| Clinch . . . | 973 | 789 | 182 | 759 | 790 | 286 |
| Cobb . . . . | 73,750 | 114,188 | 10,438 | 63,960 | 103,734 | 28,747 |
| Coffee . . . | 3,407 | 3,934 | 711 | 3,275 | 3,778 | 1,256 |
| Colquitt . . | 4,135 | 4,847 | 957 | 3,891 | 4,680 | 1,682 |
| Columbia . | 8,601 | 21,290 | 1,709 | 7,115 | 16,657 | 4,379 |
| Cook . . . . | 1,780 | 1,354 | 267 | 1,731 | 1,318 | 537 |
| Coweta . . | 7,794 | 13,058 | 1,949 | 7,093 | 9,814 | 3,587 |
| Crawford . | 1,534 | 1,290 | 270 | 1,648 | 974 | 549 |
| Crisp . . . . | 2,504 | 2,321 | 445 | 2,610 | 2,253 | 823 |
| Dade . . . . | 1,737 | 2,295 | 618 | 1,782 | 2,191 | 823 |
| Dawson . . | 1,434 | 2,342 | 473 | 1,399 | 1,696 | 790 |
| Decatur . . | 3,245 | 3,035 | 497 | 3,198 | 3,142 | 1,068 |
| DeKalb. . . | 131,903 | 60,255 | 6,742 | 124,559 | 70,282 | 19,741 |
| Dodge . . . | 2,596 | 2,478 | 587 | 3,002 | 2,287 | 978 |
| Dooly. . . . | 1,951 | 990 | 207 | 1,993 | 1,034 | 350 |
| Dougherty. | 15,600 | 11,144 | 1,072 | 15,236 | 12,455 | 3,178 |
| Douglas . . | 9,631 | 14,495 | 2,109 | 8,869 | 13,349 | 4,362 |
| Early . . . . | 1,648 | 1,374 | 246 | 1,970 | 1,457 | 652 |
| Echols . . . | 308 | 335 | 97 | 312 | 361 | 238 |
| Effingham . | 3,031 | 5,022 | 769 | 2,690 | 3,814 | 1,443 |
| Elbert. . . . | 2,900 | 2,393 | 552 | 3,025 | 2,372 | 757 |
| Emanuel. . | 2,947 | 2,451 | 450 | 2,951 | 2,662 | 755 |
| Evans . . . | 1,117 | 1,206 | 204 | 1,230 | 1,244 | 480 |
| Fannin . . . | 2,741 | 3,373 | 782 | 2,902 | 3,255 | 1,028 |
| Fayette. . . | 9,872 | 21,004 | 2,015 | 8,430 | 17,576 | 5,598 |
| Floyd . . . . | 10,464 | 12,426 | 2,345 | 11,614 | 12,378 | 3,779 |
| Forsyth . . | 5,957 | 15,013 | 1,889 | 4,936 | 8,652 | 3,453 |
| Franklin . . | 2,338 | 2,364 | 665 | 2,505 | 2,391 | 1,014 |
| Fulton . . . | 143,306 | 89,809 | 7,720 | 147,459 | 85,451 | 23,578 |
| Gilmer . . . | 2,464 | 3,121 | 725 | 2,311 | 2,661 | 879 |
| Glascock . | 348 | 532 | 128 | 316 | 516 | 180 |
| Glynn. . . . | 8,058 | 12,305 | 1,137 | 8,581 | 11,242 | 3,053 |
| Gordon. . . | 4,239 | 5,232 | 1,284 | 4,103 | 5,265 | 1,818 |
| Grady . . . | 2,862 | 2,674 | 634 | 2,520 | 2,370 | 1,126 |
| Greene. . . | 2,115 | 1,702 | 173 | 2,259 | 1,307 | 483 |
| Gwinnett. . | 53,819 | 96,610 | 10,236 | 44,253 | 81,822 | 23,926 |
| Habersham | 3,170 | 4,730 | 1,149 | 3,098 | 4,569 | 1,444 |
| Hall . . . . . | 10,352 | 19,280 | 2,291 | 11,214 | 16,108 | 5,043 |
| Hancock. . | 2,135 | 438 | 71 | 2,461 | 506 | 189 |
| Haralson . | 2,850 | 3,260 | 808 | 3,281 | 3,142 | 1,167 |
| Harris. . . . | 2,779 | 3,775 | 489 | 2,679 | 3,316 | 954 |
| Hart. . . . . | 3,486 | 2,884 | 767 | 3,614 | 2,607 | 1,376 |
| Heard . . . | 1,248 | 1,170 | 406 | 1,456 | 1,190 | 617 |
| Henry. . . . | 9,501 | 16,972 | 2,320 | 7,817 | 12,634 | 3,769 |
| Houston . . | 12,757 | 17,049 | 2,729 | 12,270 | 14,119 | 6,263 |
| Irwin . . . . | 1,225 | 1,085 | 224 | 1,366 | 973 | 465 |
| Jackson . . | 3,746 | 4,782 | 899 | 3,792 | 3,976 | 1,381 |
| Jasper . . . | 1,553 | 1,423 | 243 | 1,485 | 1,153 | 373 |
| Jeff Davis . | 1,576 | 1,796 | 428 | 2,031 | 1,947 | 958 |
| Jefferson . | 3,404 | 2,077 | 298 | 3,220 | 2,077 | 685 |
| Jenkins . . | 1,336 | 955 | 166 | 1,401 | 929 | 394 |
| Johnson . . | 1,194 | 815 | 242 | 1,473 | 1,314 | 502 |
| Jones. . . . | 3,195 | 3,272 | 497 | 3,338 | 2,770 | 1,159 |
| Lamar . . . | 2,125 | 1,988 | 409 | 2,065 | 1,707 | 600 |
| Lanier . . . | 818 | 519 | 160 | 811 | 600 | 298 |
| Laurens . . | 5,792 | 6,118 | 818 | 6,184 | 6,146 | 1,602 |
| Lee . . . . . | 2,005 | 3,983 | 506 | 1,811 | 3,061 | 1,024 |
| Liberty . . . | 4,462 | 3,042 | 580 | 3,853 | 2,832 | 1,176 |
| Lincoln. . . | 1,334 | 1,391 | 208 | 1,327 | 1,149 | 479 |
| Long . . . . | 936 | 791 | 236 | 874 | 719 | 355 |
| Lowndes. . | 9,470 | 10,578 | 1,518 | 9,019 | 10,276 | 2,864 |
| Lumpkin . . | 1,949 | 2,576 | 588 | 2,010 | 1,972 | 1,035 |
| McDuffie. . | 2,725 | 3,254 | 395 | 2,640 | 2,955 | 860 |
| McIntosh . | 1,927 | 1,219 | 293 | 1,925 | 1,027 | 550 |
| Macon . . . | 2,618 | 1,006 | 159 | 2,491 | 944 | 363 |
| Madison . . | 2,571 | 3,992 | 868 | 2,393 | 3,351 | 1,129 |
| Marion . . . | 977 | 678 | 159 | 1,145 | 711 | 198 |
| Meriwether | 3,492 | 2,259 | 480 | 4,002 | 2,364 | 942 |
| Miller . . . . | 909 | 847 | 235 | 934 | 826 | 455 |
| Mitchell . . | 3,165 | 2,032 | 372 | 3,052 | 1,917 | 818 |
| Monroe . . | 2,768 | 3,054 | 488 | 2,774 | 2,423 | 949 |
| Montgomery | 1,233 | 1,163 | 284 | 1,185 | 1,009 | 416 |
| Morgan . . | 2,111 | 2,118 | 364 | 2,057 | 1,797 | 596 |
| Murray. . . | 2,861 | 3,289 | 938 | 2,764 | 3,256 | 1,186 |
| Muscogee. | 24,867 | 19,360 | 1,891 | 25,476 | 21,386 | 4,327 |
| Newton . . | 6,759 | 7,273 | 1,258 | 5,811 | 5,804 | 1,998 |
| Oconee . . | 2,995 | 5,119 | 616 | 2,745 | 4,125 | 1,182 |
| Oglethorpe | 1,570 | 1,825 | 369 | 1,491 | 1,590 | 620 |
| Paulding. . | 5,699 | 10,152 | 1,603 | 5,212 | 7,180 | 2,654 |
| Peach . . . | 3,582 | 2,675 | 471 | 3,677 | 2,327 | 947 |
| Pickens . . | 2,693 | 3,041 | 783 | 2,359 | 2,332 | 1,037 |
| Pierce . . . | 1,420 | 2,319 | 333 | 1,852 | 1,899 | 708 |

| County | 1996 Clinton (D) | 1996 Dole (R) | 1996 Perot (RF) | 1992 Clinton (D) | 1992 Bush (R) | 1992 Perot (I) |
|---|---|---|---|---|---|---|
| Pike. . . . . | 1,474 | 2,054 | 357 | 1,651 | 1,822 | 623 |
| Polk. . . . . | 4,298 | 4,130 | 1,076 | 4,872 | 4,158 | 1,598 |
| Pulaski. . . | 1,554 | 1,201 | 268 | 1,756 | 1,075 | 614 |
| Putnam . . | 2,372 | 2,346 | 494 | 2,149 | 1,756 | 775 |
| Quitman . . | 514 | 224 | 59 | 523 | 284 | 113 |
| Rabun . . . | 1,943 | 2,213 | 585 | 1,878 | 1,902 | 825 |
| Randolph . | 1,438 | 816 | 106 | 1,756 | 887 | 315 |
| Richmond. | 30,738 | 23,670 | 2,310 | 28,910 | 24,227 | 6,290 |
| Rockdale . | 7,656 | 13,006 | 1,750 | 7,003 | 11,945 | 3,664 |
| Schley . . . | 576 | 470 | 123 | 601 | 511 | 180 |
| Screven . . | 2,042 | 1,862 | 263 | 1,940 | 1,705 | 709 |
| Seminole . | 1,265 | 1,003 | 250 | 1,193 | 850 | 468 |
| Spalding. . | 6,017 | 7,376 | 1,059 | 6,392 | 7,262 | 2,044 |
| Stephens . | 3,072 | 3,890 | 979 | 2,976 | 4,047 | 1,448 |
| Stewart . . | 1,537 | 525 | 152 | 1,540 | 1,186 | 175 |
| Sumter. . . | 4,239 | 3,358 | 451 | 4,489 | 3,616 | 1,046 |
| Talbot . . . | 1,579 | 652 | 111 | 1,768 | 671 | 238 |
| Taliaferro . | 615 | 235 | 36 | 755 | 269 | 80 |
| Tattnall. . . | 2,369 | 2,518 | 541 | 2,360 | 2,566 | 996 |
| Taylor . . . | 1,450 | 952 | 195 | 1,508 | 1,078 | 281 |
| Telfair . . . | 1,856 | 1,143 | 322 | 2,238 | 1,324 | 613 |
| Terrell . . . | 1,509 | 1,111 | 129 | 1,942 | 1,143 | 384 |
| Thomas . . | 5,183 | 5,649 | 667 | 4,841 | 5,500 | 1,591 |
| Tift. . . . . . | 4,198 | 5,613 | 729 | 3,930 | 4,485 | 1,139 |
| Toombs . . | 2,763 | 3,646 | 602 | 2,648 | 3,609 | 1,210 |
| Towns . . . | 1,664 | 2,030 | 459 | 1,487 | 1,674 | 537 |
| Treutlen . . | 912 | 723 | 122 | 1,116 | 898 | 318 |
| Troup. . . . | 5,940 | 8,716 | 1,090 | 6,412 | 8,118 | 2,488 |
| Turner . . . | 1,272 | 924 | 246 | 1,669 | 936 | 370 |
| Twiggs . . . | 1,927 | 958 | 210 | 2,097 | 853 | 432 |
| Union. . . . | 2,174 | 2,675 | 622 | 2,304 | 2,533 | 804 |
| Upson . . . | 3,491 | 3,783 | 731 | 3,740 | 4,053 | 1,186 |
| Walker . . . | 6,743 | 8,817 | 1,969 | 6,217 | 8,489 | 2,748 |
| Walton . . . | 5,617 | 7,931 | 1,322 | 4,821 | 5,619 | 1,923 |
| Ware . . . . | 4,171 | 4,746 | 636 | 4,573 | 4,573 | 1,263 |
| Warren. . . | 1,230 | 735 | 83 | 1,239 | 751 | 180 |
| Washington | 4,057 | 2,348 | 488 | 3,508 | 2,384 | 820 |
| Wayne . . . | 2,692 | 3,665 | 660 | 3,052 | 3,381 | 1,107 |
| Webster . . | 529 | 235 | 59 | 600 | 208 | 103 |
| Wheeler . . | 751 | 460 | 141 | 880 | 601 | 214 |
| White . . . . | 1,864 | 2,960 | 556 | 1,756 | 2,477 | 981 |
| Whitfield . . | 7,799 | 12,539 | 1,662 | 7,335 | 12,003 | 2,866 |
| Wilcox . . . | 1,067 | 882 | 171 | 1,365 | 916 | 433 |
| Wilkes . . . | 1,971 | 1,417 | 184 | 1,955 | 1,535 | 464 |
| Wilkinson . | 2,278 | 1,332 | 287 | 2,286 | 1,232 | 520 |
| Worth. . . . | 2,300 | 2,752 | 521 | 2,578 | 2,344 | 905 |
| **Totals . . .** | **1,047,214** | **1,078,972** | **146,031** | **1,008,966** | **995,252** | **309,657** |

## Georgia Vote Since 1948

1948, Truman, Dem., 254,646; Dewey, Rep., 76,691; Thurmond, States' Rights, 85,055; Wallace, Prog., 1,636; Watson, Proh., 732.

1952, Eisenhower, Rep., 198,979; Stevenson, Dem., 456,823; Liberty Party, 1.

1956, Stevenson, Dem., 444,388; Eisenhower, Rep., 222,778; Andrews, Ind., write-in, 1,754.

1960, Kennedy, Dem., 458,638; Nixon, Rep., 274,472; write-in, 239.

1964, Johnson, Dem., 522,557; Goldwater, Rep., 616,600.

1968, Nixon, Rep., 380,111; Humphrey, Dem., 334,440; Wallace, 3d Party, 535,550; write-in, 162.

1972, Nixon, Rep., 881,496; McGovern, Dem., 289,529; scattered, 2,935; Schmitz, Amer., 812.

1976, Carter, Dem., 979,409; Ford, Rep., 483,743; write-in, 4,306.

1980, Reagan, Rep., 654,168; Carter, Dem., 890,955; Anderson, Ind., 36,055; Clark, Libertarian, 15,627.

1984, Reagan, Rep., 1,068,722; Mondale, Dem., 706,628.

1988, Bush, Rep., 1,081,331; Dukakis, Dem., 714,792; Paul, Lib., 8,435; Fulani, New Alliance, 5,099.

1992, Clinton, Dem., 1,008,966; Bush, Rep., 995,252; Perot, Ind., 309,657; Marrou, Libertarian, 7,110.

1996, Dole, Rep., 1,078,972; Clinton, Dem., 1,047,214; Perot, Ref., 146,031; Browne, Libertarian, 18,222.

# Hawaii

| County | 1996 Clinton (D) | 1996 Dole (R) | 1996 Perot (RF) | 1992 Clinton (D) | 1992 Bush (R) | 1992 Perot (I) |
|---|---|---|---|---|---|---|
| Hawaii. . . . | 27,262 | 13,516 | 5,137 | 25,725 | 15,460 | 8,889 |
| Honolulu . . | 143,793 | 85,779 | 17,389 | 123,908 | 103,937 | 35,728 |
| Kauai . . . . | 13,357 | 5,325 | 1,568 | 10,715 | 6,274 | 1,756 |
| Maui . . . . . | 20,600 | 9,323 | 3,264 | 18,962 | 11,151 | 6,630 |
| **Totals. . . .** | **205,012** | **113,943** | **27,358** | **179,310** | **136,822** | **53,003** |

## Hawaii Vote Since 1960

1960, Kennedy, Dem., 92,410; Nixon, Rep., 92,295.

1964, Johnson, Dem., 163,249; Goldwater, Rep., 44,022.

1968, Nixon, Rep., 91,425; Humphrey, Dem., 141,324; Wallace, 3d Party, 3,469.

1972, Nixon, Rep., 168,865; McGovern, Dem., 101,409.

1976, Carter, Dem., 147,375; Ford, Rep., 140,003; MacBride, Libertarian, 3,923.

1980, Reagan, Rep., 130,112; Carter, Dem., 135,879; Anderson, Ind., 32,021; Clark, Libertarian, 3,269; Commoner, Citizens, 1,548; Hall, Com., 458.

1984, Reagan, Rep., 184,934; Mondale, Dem., 147,098; Bergland, Libertarian, 2,167.

1988, Bush, Rep., 158,625; Dukakis, Dem., 192,364; Paul, Lib., 1,999; Fulani, New Alliance, 1,003.

1992, Clinton, Dem., 179,310; Bush, Rep., 136,822; Perot, Ind., 53,003; Gritz, Populist/America First, 1,452; Marrou, Libertarian, 1,119.

1996, Clinton, Dem., 205,012; Dole, Rep., 113,943; Perot, Ref., 27,358; Nader, Green, 10,386; Browne, Libertarian, 2,493; Hagelin, Natural Law, 570; Phillips, Taxpayers, 358.

# Idaho

| County | 1996 Clinton (D) | 1996 Dole (R) | 1996 Perot (RF) | 1992 Clinton (D) | 1992 Bush (R) | 1992 Perot (I) |
|---|---|---|---|---|---|---|
| Ada . . . . . | 43,040 | 61,811 | 11,171 | 31,941 | 49,000 | 28,192 |
| Adams . . | 537 | 1,053 | 311 | 457 | 754 | 695 |
| Bannock. . | 12,805 | 14,059 | 4,157 | 11,091 | 12,016 | 8,116 |
| Bear Lake | 807 | 1,583 | 377 | 562 | 1,419 | 684 |
| Benewah . | 1,488 | 1,667 | 701 | 1,270 | 1,223 | 1,165 |
| Bingham. . | 4,304 | 8,391 | 2,021 | 3,565 | 7,333 | 4,144 |
| Blaine . . . | 3,840 | 3,003 | 1,193 | 2,865 | 2,243 | 2,831 |
| Boise . . . | 879 | 1,384 | 440 | 623 | 912 | 754 |
| Bonner. . . | 5,394 | 6,207 | 2,669 | 4,995 | 3,937 | 4,645 |
| Bonneville. | 9,013 | 19,977 | 3,921 | 7,014 | 16,557 | 10,241 |
| Boundary . | 1,194 | 1,937 | 626 | 1,095 | 1,479 | 1,136 |
| Butte . . . . | 507 | 741 | 233 | 433 | 602 | 392 |
| Camas . . | 156 | 283 | 95 | 134 | 202 | 145 |
| Canyon . . | 11,800 | 23,988 | 3,956 | 9,095 | 19,220 | 8,974 |
| Caribou . . | 841 | 1,740 | 501 | 562 | 1,350 | 1,088 |
| Cassia . . . | 1,596 | 4,663 | 976 | 1,351 | 4,052 | 1,785 |
| Clark . . . . | 117 | 266 | 45 | 95 | 195 | 119 |
| Clearwater | 1,507 | 1,658 | 650 | 1,433 | 1,152 | 1,098 |
| Custer . . . | 635 | 1,249 | 400 | 564 | 829 | 729 |
| Elmore . . . | 2,324 | 3,668 | 845 | 1,858 | 3,087 | 1,867 |
| Franklin . . | 807 | 2,435 | 589 | 524 | 2,115 | 890 |
| Fremont . | 1,114 | 3,040 | 630 | 903 | 2,333 | 1,349 |
| Gem . . . . | 1,968 | 3,365 | 833 | 1,609 | 2,455 | 1,555 |
| Gooding . . | 1,503 | 2,637 | 980 | 1,530 | 2,178 | 1,591 |
| Idaho . . . . | 1,980 | 3,873 | 1,083 | 1,974 | 2,709 | 1,900 |
| Jefferson . | 1,427 | 4,925 | 994 | 978 | 3,471 | 2,164 |
| Jerome. . . | 1,679 | 3,358 | 1,014 | 1,739 | 2,972 | 1,768 |
| Kootenai. . | 13,627 | 18,740 | 6,083 | 11,553 | 13,065 | 11,261 |
| Latah . . . . | 7,741 | 6,311 | 1,828 | 7,233 | 5,353 | 3,602 |
| Lemhi . . . | 1,015 | 2,334 | 461 | 996 | 1,540 | 1,175 |
| Lewis . . . | 674 | 861 | 314 | 674 | 593 | 491 |
| Lincoln . . | 478 | 744 | 319 | 514 | 656 | 441 |
| Madison . | 1,216 | 5,705 | 744 | 741 | 4,591 | 1,920 |
| Minidoka . | 1,977 | 4,008 | 977 | 1,815 | 3,304 | 1,875 |
| Nez Perce | 7,491 | 6,675 | 2,385 | 7,069 | 5,431 | 4,363 |
| Oneida . . | 429 | 993 | 285 | 351 | 713 | 590 |
| Owyhee . . | 895 | 2,033 | 364 | 686 | 1,469 | 862 |
| Payette . . | 2,119 | 3,901 | 906 | 1,656 | 2,895 | 2,055 |
| Power . . . | 1,070 | 1,501 | 344 | 837 | 1,352 | 697 |
| Shoshone. | 2,981 | 1,588 | 1,283 | 3,182 | 1,441 | 1,878 |
| Teton . . . | 866 | 1,251 | 326 | 472 | 762 | 608 |
| Twin Falls. | 6,826 | 12,393 | 3,383 | 6,593 | 10,335 | 6,043 |
| Valley . . . | 1,564 | 2,089 | 568 | 1,259 | 1,548 | 1,313 |
| Washington | 1,314 | 2,318 | 525 | 1,122 | 1,802 | 1,204 |
| **Totals . . .** | **165,545** | **256,406** | **62,506** | **137,013** | **202,645** | **130,395** |

## Idaho Vote Since 1948

1948, Truman, Dem., 107,370; Dewey, Rep., 101,514; Wallace, Prog., 4,972; Watson, Proh., 628; Thomas, Soc., 332.

1952, Eisenhower, Rep., 180,707; Stevenson, Dem., 95,081; Hallinan, Prog., 443; write-in, 23.

1956, Eisenhower, Rep., 166,979; Stevenson, Dem., 105,868; Andrews, Ind., 126; write-in, 16.

1960, Kennedy, Dem., 138,853; Nixon, Rep., 161,597.

1964, Johnson, Dem., 148,920; Goldwater, Rep., 143,557.

1968, Nixon, Rep., 165,369; Humphrey, Dem., 89,273; Wallace, 3d Party, 36,541.

1972, Nixon, Rep., 199,384; McGovern, Dem., 80,826; Schmitz, Amer., 28,869; Spock, Peoples, 903.

1976, Carter, Dem., 126,549; Ford, Rep., 204,151; Maddox, Amer., 5,935; MacBride, Libertarian, 3,558; LaRouche, U.S. Labor, 739.

1980, Reagan, Rep., 290,699; Carter, Dem., 110,192; Anderson, Ind., 27,058; Clark, Libertarian, 8,425; Rarick, Amer., 1,057.

1984, Reagan, Rep., 297,523; Mondale, Dem., 108,510; Bergland, Libertarian, 2,823.

1988, Bush, Rep., 253,881; Dukakis, Dem., 147,272; Paul, Lib., 5,313; Fulani, Ind., 2,502.

1992, Clinton, Dem., 137,013; Bush, Rep., 202,645; Perot, Ind., 130,395; Gritz, Populist/America First, 10,281; Marrou, Libertarian, 1,167.

1996, Dole, Rep., 256,406; Clinton, Dem., 165,545; Perot, Ref., 62,506; Browne, Libertarian, 3,318; Phillips, Taxpayers, 2,231; Hagelin, Natural Law, 1,620.

# Illinois

| County | 1996 Clinton (D) | 1996 Dole (R) | 1996 Perot (RF) | 1992 Clinton (D) | 1992 Bush (R) | 1992 Perot (I) |
|---|---|---|---|---|---|---|
| Adams . . . | 11,336 | 13,836 | 3,069 | 11,748 | 13,529 | 6,157 |
| Alexander . | 2,753 | 1,212 | 321 | 2,566 | 1,301 | 474 |
| Bond . . . . | 3,213 | 3,018 | 685 | 3,428 | 2,715 | 1,373 |
| Boone . . . | 5,345 | 6,181 | 1,377 | 5,114 | 5,589 | 2,880 |
| Brown . . . | 997 | 1,053 | 237 | 1,146 | 1,029 | 504 |
| Bureau . . . | 7,651 | 6,528 | 1,798 | 7,551 | 6,836 | 3,465 |
| Calhoun . . | 1,676 | 941 | 363 | 1,519 | 745 | 532 |
| Carroll . . . | 2,926 | 3,029 | 792 | 2,854 | 3,297 | 1,502 |
| Cass . . . . | 2,834 | 2,214 | 589 | 3,200 | 2,162 | 1,072 |
| Champaign | 32,454 | 28,232 | 4,806 | 35,003 | 27,096 | 13,571 |
| Christian . . | 7,431 | 5,563 | 1,727 | 9,042 | 5,087 | 3,401 |
| Clark . . . . | 2,995 | 3,409 | 781 | 3,338 | 3,175 | 1,450 |
| Clay. . . . . | 2,750 | 2,703 | 719 | 2,962 | 2,471 | 1,193 |
| Clinton . . . | 6,104 | 6,065 | 1,580 | 6,686 | 5,771 | 3,315 |
| Coles . . . . | 8,950 | 8,038 | 2,137 | 9,402 | 8,098 | 4,707 |
| Cook . . . . | 1,111,208 | 452,610 | 94,587 | 1,249,533 | 605,300 | 281,999 |
| Crawford. . | 3,627 | 3,965 | 1,057 | 3,964 | 3,606 | 2,062 |
| Cumberland | 1,776 | 2,002 | 657 | 2,111 | 1,860 | 1,209 |
| DeKalb. . . | 12,715 | 12,380 | 3,009 | 13,744 | 12,655 | 7,680 |
| DeWitt . . . | 2,878 | 2,978 | 694 | 3,009 | 3,164 | 1,543 |
| Douglas . . | 2,955 | 3,272 | 740 | 3,341 | 3,309 | 1,600 |
| DuPage . . | 129,709 | 164,630 | 27,419 | 114,564 | 178,271 | 76,839 |
| Edgar. . . . | 3,552 | 3,746 | 935 | 4,014 | 3,790 | 1,930 |
| Edwards . . | 1,089 | 1,613 | 384 | 1,299 | 1,601 | 634 |
| Effingham . | 4,825 | 7,696 | 1,555 | 5,221 | 6,329 | 3,354 |
| Fayette. . . | 3,887 | 3,881 | 964 | 4,833 | 3,508 | 1,730 |
| Ford. . . . . | 2,065 | 3,077 | 590 | 2,175 | 3,046 | 1,222 |
| Franklin . . | 9,814 | 5,354 | 2,096 | 12,744 | 5,504 | 3,180 |
| Fulton . . . | 8,857 | 5,155 | 1,610 | 9,725 | 5,062 | 2,874 |
| Gallatin. . . | 2,113 | 856 | 527 | 2,371 | 990 | 568 |
| Greene. . . | 2,547 | 2,102 | 852 | 3,164 | 2,391 | 1,461 |
| Grundy. . . | 6,759 | 6,177 | 1,860 | 6,122 | 6,346 | 3,724 |
| Hamilton. . | 2,242 | 1,677 | 560 | 2,582 | 1,521 | 862 |
| Hancock . . | 4,001 | 3,961 | 1,148 | 4,213 | 3,714 | 2,091 |
| Hardin . . . | 1,323 | 790 | 485 | 1,665 | 985 | 515 |
| Henderson | 1,953 | 1,233 | 408 | 2,013 | 1,310 | 715 |
| Henry. . . . | 11,201 | 8,393 | 2,194 | 11,077 | 8,989 | 4,231 |
| Iroquois . . | 4,559 | 6,564 | 1,522 | 4,440 | 6,948 | 3,073 |
| Jackson . . | 12,214 | 7,422 | 2,082 | 13,373 | 6,899 | 3,995 |
| Jasper . . . | 2,038 | 2,234 | 641 | 2,284 | 1,996 | 1,160 |
| Jefferson . | 7,263 | 5,937 | 1,647 | 8,665 | 5,497 | 3,403 |
| Jersey . . . | 4,275 | 3,211 | 1,186 | 4,749 | 2,933 | 2,363 |
| Jo Daviess | 4,171 | 3,915 | 1,131 | 4,044 | 4,249 | 2,102 |
| Johnson . . | 2,009 | 2,241 | 640 | 2,299 | 2,124 | 944 |
| Kane . . . . | 36,210 | 46,606 | 9,442 | 44,568 | 55,684 | 27,179 |
| Kankakee . | 16,820 | 14,595 | 3,574 | 17,229 | 15,411 | 7,264 |
| Kendall. . . | 6,499 | 8,958 | 2,055 | 5,423 | 8,521 | 4,394 |
| Knox . . . . | 4,854 | 3,655 | 1,018 | 12,524 | 8,331 | 4,357 |
| Lake . . . . | 93,315 | 93,149 | 16,640 | 81,693 | 99,000 | 42,384 |
| LaSalle. . . | 21,643 | 15,299 | 5,259 | 23,276 | 16,078 | 10,434 |
| Lawrence . | 2,871 | 2,568 | 916 | 3,270 | 2,681 | 1,498 |
| Lee . . . . . | 5,895 | 6,677 | 1,520 | 5,530 | 6,652 | 3,191 |
| Livingston . | 5,641 | 7,653 | 1,409 | 6,007 | 8,004 | 3,029 |
| Logan. . . . | 4,618 | 6,518 | 1,141 | 5,169 | 6,567 | 2,420 |
| McDonough | 5,632 | 5,049 | 1,217 | 5,814 | 5,297 | 2,770 |
| McHenry. . | 31,240 | 41,136 | 10,082 | 24,783 | 41,356 | 21,817 |
| McLean . . | 12,320 | 15,571 | 2,282 | 23,090 | 25,726 | 10,282 |
| Macon . . . | 24,256 | 18,161 | 4,540 | 27,449 | 18,684 | 9,236 |
| Macoupin . | 11,107 | 7,235 | 2,532 | 12,050 | 6,518 | 5,018 |
| Madison . . | 53,568 | 35,758 | 10,121 | 58,484 | 32,167 | 23,110 |
| Marion . . . | 7,792 | 5,999 | 1,825 | 9,669 | 5,764 | 3,407 |
| Marshall . . | 2,640 | 2,453 | 586 | 2,819 | 2,491 | 1,169 |
| Mason . . . | 3,385 | 2,430 | 600 | 3,969 | 2,473 | 1,245 |
| Massac . . | 2,841 | 2,507 | 675 | 3,347 | 2,754 | 892 |
| Menard. . . | 2,204 | 3,106 | 534 | 2,264 | 2,834 | 1,179 |
| Mercer . . . | 4,278 | 2,688 | 889 | 3,990 | 2,983 | 1,535 |
| Monroe. . . | 4,798 | 5,350 | 1,276 | 4,894 | 4,807 | 2,813 |
| Montgomery | 6,338 | 4,770 | 1,436 | 7,424 | 4,407 | 2,956 |
| Morgan. . . | 6,150 | 6,352 | 1,633 | 6,351 | 6,566 | 3,317 |
| Moultrie . . | 2,629 | 2,199 | 596 | 3,056 | 2,065 | 1,322 |
| Ogle. . . . . | 6,765 | 9,558 | 1,876 | 6,512 | 9,008 | 4,455 |
| Peoria . . . | 15,046 | 12,534 | 2,792 | 38,099 | 30,718 | 12,195 |
| Perry . . . . | 5,347 | 3,237 | 1,262 | 6,009 | 3,105 | 1,955 |
| Piatt. . . . . | 3,274 | 3,264 | 818 | 3,520 | 3,076 | 1,822 |
| Pike. . . . . | 3,604 | 3,225 | 1,039 | 4,016 | 3,342 | 1,643 |
| Pope . . . . | 915 | 850 | 277 | 1,063 | 951 | 391 |
| Pulaski . . . | 1,524 | 1,036 | 235 | 1,987 | 1,169 | 379 |
| Putnam . . | 1,425 | 987 | 322 | 1,574 | 969 | 752 |
| Randolph . | 7,419 | 5,422 | 1,698 | 8,529 | 4,899 | 3,092 |
| Richland . . | 2,679 | 3,137 | 927 | 3,286 | 3,053 | 1,689 |
| Rock Island | 34,822 | 20,626 | 5,135 | 37,412 | 23,212 | 10,416 |
| St. Clair . . | 41,069 | 32,788 | 6,926 | 57,625 | 31,951 | 17,592 |
| Saline . . . | 6,156 | 3,693 | 1,752 | 7,258 | 3,667 | 2,302 |
| Sangamon | 14,368 | 19,099 | 3,086 | 40,052 | 39,641 | 16,861 |
| Schuyler . . | 1,636 | 1,597 | 483 | 1,650 | 1,512 | 815 |
| Scott . . . . | 1,012 | 1,112 | 396 | 1,057 | 1,132 | 588 |
| Shelby . . . | 4,249 | 4,215 | 1,262 | 5,101 | 3,631 | 2,401 |
| Stark . . . . | 1,262 | 1,278 | 312 | 1,336 | 1,384 | 625 |
| Stephenson | 7,145 | 8,871 | 1,940 | 7,899 | 9,005 | 4,677 |
| Tazewell. . | 24,139 | 24,395 | 4,814 | 26,428 | 23,469 | 9,927 |
| Union . . . . | 4,252 | 3,147 | 832 | 4,681 | 3,003 | 1,373 |
| Vermilion . | 9,531 | 7,506 | 2,556 | 18,383 | 11,703 | 8,162 |
| Wabash . . | 2,177 | 2,381 | 683 | 2,436 | 2,485 | 1,302 |
| Warren. . . | 3,500 | 2,974 | 742 | 3,661 | 3,325 | 1,436 |
| Washington | 2,744 | 3,339 | 790 | 2,986 | 3,003 | 1,542 |
| Wayne . . . | 3,054 | 4,029 | 999 | 3,332 | 3,809 | 1,702 |
| White. . . . | 3,553 | 2,878 | 888 | 4,308 | 3,057 | 1,428 |
| Whiteside . | 11,913 | 8,859 | 2,436 | 12,329 | 10,146 | 4,589 |
| Will . . . . . | 69,354 | 62,506 | 15,485 | 59,633 | 58,337 | 32,788 |
| Williamson | 12,510 | 9,734 | 2,877 | 14,361 | 9,462 | 4,779 |
| Winnebago | 20,579 | 22,068 | 4,606 | 48,298 | 42,221 | 21,227 |
| Woodford . | 5,270 | 8,527 | 1,170 | 5,490 | 8,032 | 2,733 |
| **Totals . . .** | **2,299,476** | **1,577,930** | **344,311** | **2,453,350** | **1,734,096** | **840,515** |

## Illinois Vote Since 1948

1948, Truman, Dem., 1,994,715; Dewey, Rep., 1,961,103; Watson, Proh., 11,959; Thomas, Soc., 11,522; Teichert, Soc. Labor, 3,118.

1952, Eisenhower, Rep., 2,457,327; Stevenson, Dem., 2,013,920; Hass, Soc. Labor, 9,363; write-in, 448.

1956, Eisenhower, Rep., 2,623,327; Stevenson, Dem., 1,775,682; Hass, Soc. Labor, 8,342; write-in, 56.

1960, Kennedy, Dem., 2,377,846; Nixon, Rep., 2,368,988; Hass, Soc. Labor, 10,560; write-in, 15.

1964, Johnson, Dem., 2,796,833; Goldwater, Rep., 1,905,946; write-in, 62.

1968, Nixon, Rep., 2,174,774; Humphrey, Dem., 2,039,814; Wallace, 3d Party, 390,958; Blomen, Soc. Labor, 13,878; write-in, 325.

1972, Nixon, Rep. 2,788,179; McGovern, Dem., 1,913,472; Fisher, Soc. Labor, 12,344; Schmitz, Amer., 2,471; Hall, Com., 4,541; others, 2,229.

1976, Carter, Dem., 2,271,295; Ford, Rep., 2,364,269; McCarthy, Ind., 55,939; Hall, Com., 9,250; MacBride, Libertarian, 8,057; Camejo, Soc. Workers, 3,615; Levin, Soc. Labor, 2,422; LaRouche, U.S. Labor, 2,018; write-in, 1,968.

1980, Reagan, Rep., 2,358,049; Carter, Dem., 1,981,413; Anderson, Ind., 346,754; Clark, Libertarian, 38,939; Commoner, Citizens, 10,692; Hall, Com., 9,711; Griswold, Workers World, 2,257; DeBerry, Soc. Workers, 1,302; write-ins, 604.

1984, Reagan, Rep., 2,707,103; Mondale, Dem., 2,086,499; Bergland, Libertarian, 10,086.

1988, Bush, Rep., 2,310,939; Dukakis, Dem., 2,215,940; Paul, Lib., 14,944; Fulani, Solid., 10,276.

1992, Clinton, Dem., 2,453,350; Bush, Rep., 1,734,096; Perot, Ind., 840,515; Marrou, Libertarian, 9,218; Fulani, New Alliance, 5,267; Gritz, Populist/America First, 3,577; Hagelin, Natural Law, 2,751; Warren, Soc. Workers, 1,361.

1996, Clinton, Dem., 2,299,476; Dole, Rep., 1,577,930; Perot, Ref., 344,311; Browne, Libertarian, 22,134; Phillips, Taxpayers, 7,523; Hagelin, Natural Law, 4,534.

# Indiana

| County | 1996 Clinton (D) | 1996 Dole (R) | 1996 Perot (RF) | 1992 Clinton (D) | 1992 Bush (R) | 1992 Perot (I) |
|---|---|---|---|---|---|---|
| Adams . . . | 4,247 | 6,960 | 1,346 | 3,708 | 6,078 | 2,865 |
| Allen . . . . | 39,784 | 56,379 | 8,623 | 39,629 | 55,003 | 25,809 |
| Bartholomew | 9,301 | 13,188 | 2,815 | 8,284 | 13,146 | 5,882 |
| Benton. . . | 1,311 | 1,947 | 609 | 1,221 | 2,030 | 1,056 |
| Blackford . | 2,335 | 2,070 | 681 | 2,088 | 2,347 | 1,319 |
| Boone . . . | 4,625 | 11,338 | 1,498 | 3,982 | 9,485 | 3,826 |
| Brown . . . | 2,413 | 2,988 | 802 | 2,029 | 2,633 | 1,635 |
| Carroll . . . | 2,747 | 4,062 | 1,171 | 2,561 | 3,800 | 2,173 |
| Cass . . . . | 5,419 | 8,020 | 2,029 | 4,757 | 7,421 | 3,944 |
| Clark . . . . | 16,018 | 12,821 | 0 | 17,460 | 13,333 | 5,653 |
| Clay. . . . . | 3,605 | 4,858 | 1,406 | 3,306 | 4,696 | 2,134 |
| Clinton . . . | 3,787 | 5,907 | 1,309 | 3,490 | 6,141 | 2,535 |
| Crawford . | 2,324 | 1,759 | 700 | 2,260 | 1,903 | 819 |
| Daviess . . | 3,230 | 5,531 | 994 | 3,201 | 5,591 | 1,695 |
| Dearborn . | 6,269 | 8,318 | 1,731 | 5,116 | 6,974 | 3,384 |
| Decatur . . | 3,190 | 4,782 | 1,389 | 2,774 | 5,195 | 2,299 |
| Dekalb. . . | 4,840 | 6,851 | 1,534 | 4,652 | 6,682 | 3,554 |
| Delaware . | 20,385 | 18,126 | 6,042 | 19,556 | 20,473 | 10,453 |
| Dubois. . . | 6,499 | 6,840 | 1,777 | 5,878 | 6,785 | 3,195 |
| Elkhart. . . | 16,598 | 28,770 | 5,133 | 14,660 | 27,920 | 9,450 |
| Fayette. . . | 3,822 | 4,091 | 1,137 | 3,969 | 4,376 | 2,299 |
| Floyd . . . . | 13,814 | 12,473 | 2,609 | 13,166 | 11,932 | 4,421 |
| Fountain. . | 2,327 | 3,984 | 1,033 | 2,829 | 3,391 | 2,162 |
| Franklin . . | 2,808 | 4,167 | 943 | 2,456 | 3,831 | 1,858 |
| Fulton . . . | 2,956 | 3,934 | 1,143 | 2,552 | 3,982 | 1,963 |
| Gibson. . . | 6,488 | 5,392 | 1,585 | 6,909 | 5,172 | 2,680 |
| Grant. . . . | 9,818 | 13,443 | 3,008 | 9,211 | 13,806 | 5,597 |
| Greene. . . | 5,277 | 5,746 | 1,689 | 5,431 | 5,410 | 2,610 |
| Hamilton. . | 14,153 | 42,792 | 4,234 | 10,215 | 34,622 | 10,365 |
| Hancock. . | 6,123 | 12,907 | 2,258 | 4,752 | 11,072 | 4,752 |
| Harrison . . | 5,900 | 6,073 | 1,839 | 5,768 | 5,403 | 2,469 |
| Hendricks . | 9,392 | 22,293 | 3,405 | 7,071 | 18,373 | 7,519 |
| Henry. . . . | 7,667 | 8,537 | 2,381 | 6,794 | 8,720 | 4,416 |
| Howard . . | 11,999 | 16,771 | 4,172 | 10,288 | 15,306 | 8,575 |

| County | 1996 Clinton (D) | 1996 Dole (R) | 1996 Perot (RF) | 1992 Clinton (D) | 1992 Bush (R) | 1992 Perot (I) |
|---|---|---|---|---|---|---|
| Huntington | 4,287 | 8,275 | 1,400 | 3,855 | 9,093 | 2,967 |
| Jackson . . | 5,868 | 6,755 | 1,861 | 5,663 | 7,246 | 3,148 |
| Jasper . . . | 3,554 | 5,173 | 1,271 | 3,033 | 4,809 | 2,019 |
| Jay . . . . . | 3,356 | 3,584 | 1,022 | 3,208 | 3,609 | 1,994 |
| Jefferson . | 5,441 | 4,827 | 1,438 | 5,510 | 4,937 | 2,565 |
| Jennings. . | 4,223 | 4,461 | 1,629 | 3,471 | 4,392 | 2,370 |
| Johnson . . | 11,278 | 23,733 | 3,975 | 8,712 | 20,353 | 8,246 |
| Knox . . . . | 7,003 | 6,395 | 2,022 | 6,718 | 6,683 | 3,719 |
| Kosciusko. | 6,166 | 15,084 | 2,531 | 5,307 | 14,179 | 5,115 |
| LaGrange . | 2,704 | 4,033 | 949 | 2,093 | 3,584 | 1,736 |
| Lake . . . . | 99,150 | 47,629 | 14,978 | 102,778 | 53,867 | 28,635 |
| LaPorte . . | 19,879 | 14,106 | 5,133 | 17,717 | 14,962 | 9,641 |
| Lawrence . | 5,703 | 8,107 | 2,063 | 5,557 | 7,712 | 3,452 |
| Madison . . | 23,772 | 23,151 | 6,447 | 22,276 | 23,479 | 13,100 |
| Marion . . . | 117,473 | 126,714 | 20,299 | 122,234 | 141,369 | 57,878 |
| Marshall . . | 4,486 | 8,158 | 1,698 | 4,912 | 8,048 | 3,522 |
| Martin . . . | 1,848 | 2,281 | 485 | 2,018 | 2,523 | 883 |
| Miami. . . . | 4,260 | 6,719 | 1,657 | 3,967 | 6,416 | 3,428 |
| Monroe . . | 18,531 | 16,744 | 3,179 | 19,712 | 16,661 | 6,943 |
| Montgomery. | 3,825 | 7,705 | 1,766 | 3,371 | 7,602 | 3,511 |
| Morgan . . | 5,812 | 12,872 | 2,755 | 4,690 | 10,939 | 5,375 |
| Newton . . | 1,897 | 2,075 | 801 | 1,757 | 2,295 | 1,274 |
| Noble. . . . | 5,101 | 6,782 | 1,521 | 4,411 | 5,883 | 3,328 |
| Ohio . . . . | 1,083 | 1,098 | 281 | 970 | 1,009 | 527 |
| Orange. . . | 2,930 | 3,287 | 907 | 2,948 | 3,738 | 1,296 |
| Owen. . . . | 2,244 | 3,056 | 874 | 2,207 | 2,753 | 1,563 |
| Parke. . . . | 2,453 | 3,151 | 981 | 2,429 | 2,953 | 1,696 |
| Perry . . . . | 4,426 | 2,554 | 913 | 4,829 | 2,973 | 1,560 |
| Pike. . . . . | 2,780 | 2,174 | 884 | 2,960 | 2,156 | 1,238 |
| Porter . . . | 24,044 | 22,931 | 7,169 | 21,022 | 22,644 | 13,096 |
| Posey . . . | 4,965 | 4,638 | 1,304 | 4,632 | 4,435 | 2,357 |
| Pulaski. . . | 2,010 | 2,693 | 634 | 1,950 | 2,712 | 1,214 |
| Putnam . . | 3,962 | 5,958 | 1,619 | 3,487 | 5,341 | 3,174 |
| Randolph . | 4,087 | 4,708 | 1,557 | 3,870 | 4,937 | 2,939 |
| Ripley . . . | 4,142 | 5,280 | 1,208 | 3,480 | 5,033 | 2,406 |
| Rush . . . . | 2,578 | 3,827 | 973 | 2,168 | 3,873 | 1,948 |
| St. Joseph | 45,720 | 38,265 | 8,371 | 46,203 | 38,934 | 18,828 |
| Scott . . . . | 3,798 | 2,620 | 760 | 4,085 | 2,649 | 1,092 |
| Shelby . . . | 4,714 | 7,103 | 1,812 | 4,560 | 8,075 | 3,521 |
| Spencer . . | 3,906 | 3,628 | 711 | 4,301 | 3,789 | 1,464 |
| Starke . . . | 3,854 | 3,108 | 1,094 | 3,695 | 3,100 | 1,885 |
| Steuben . . | 4,124 | 5,513 | 1,390 | 3,630 | 4,868 | 2,896 |
| Sullivan . . | 4,076 | 3,207 | 436 | 4,211 | 3,052 | 1,857 |
| Switzerland | 1,496 | 1,266 | 403 | 1,535 | 1,211 | 636 |
| Tippecanoe | 17,232 | 22,556 | 5,394 | 17,343 | 23,050 | 9,684 |
| Tipton . . . | 2,478 | 3,980 | 861 | 2,125 | 3,906 | 1,816 |
| Union . . . | 1,019 | 1,334 | 364 | 898 | 1,394 | 664 |
| Vanderburgh | 30,934 | 28,509 | 6,132 | 33,799 | 30,271 | 12,513 |
| Vermillion . | 3,251 | 2,334 | 1,029 | 3,652 | 2,360 | 1,794 |
| Vigo. . . . . | 17,972 | 15,751 | 4,500 | 18,050 | 15,834 | 8,141 |
| Wabash . . | 4,575 | 6,990 | 1,294 | 4,518 | 7,062 | 3,424 |
| Warren. . . | 1,394 | 1,678 | 560 | 1,367 | 1,601 | 1,020 |
| Warrick . . | 9,285 | 9,221 | 2,471 | 8,612 | 8,087 | 3,862 |
| Washington | 3,819 | 4,066 | 1,264 | 4,092 | 4,043 | 1,846 |
| Wayne . . . | 10,905 | 12,188 | 2,525 | 9,960 | 12,221 | 5,095 |
| Wells . . . . | 3,752 | 6,322 | 1,157 | 3,282 | 5,799 | 2,890 |
| White. . . . | 3,396 | 4,642 | 1,610 | 2,988 | 4,622 | 2,582 |
| Whitley. . . | 4,176 | 5,965 | 1,392 | 3,569 | 5,217 | 3,195 |
| **Totals . . .** | **874,668** | **995,082** | **218,739** | **848,420** | **989,375** | **455,934** |

## Indiana Vote Since 1948

1948, Truman, Dem., 807,833; Dewey, Rep., 821,079; Watson, Proh., 14,711; Wallace, Prog., 9,649; Thomas, Soc., 2,179; Teichert, Soc. Labor, 763.

1952, Eisenhower, Rep., 1,136,259; Stevenson, Dem., 801,530; Hamblen, Proh., 15,335; Hallinan, Prog., 1,222; Hass, Soc. Labor, 979.

1956, Eisenhower, Rep., 1,182,811; Stevenson, Dem., 783,908; Holtwick, Proh., 6,554; Hass, Soc. Labor, 1,334.

1960, Kennedy, Dem., 952,358; Nixon, Rep., 1,175,120; Decker, Proh., 6,746; Hass, Soc. Labor, 1,136.

1964, Johnson, Dem., 1,170,848; Goldwater, Rep., 911,118; Munn, Proh., 8,266; Hass, Soc. Labor, 1,374.

1968, Nixon, Rep., 1,067,885; Humphrey, Dem., 806,659; Wallace, 3d Party, 243,108; Munn, Proh., 4,616; Halstead, Soc. Workers, 1,293; Gregory, write-in, 36.

1972, Nixon, Rep., 1,405,154; McGovern, Dem., 708,568; Reed, Soc. Workers, 5,575; Fisher, Soc. Labor, 1,688; Spock, Peace and Freedom, 4,544.

1976, Carter, Dem., 1,014,714; Ford, Rep., 1,185,958; Anderson, Amer., 14,048; Camejo, Soc. Workers, 5,695; LaRouche, U.S. Labor, 1,947.

1980, Reagan, Rep., 1,255,656; Carter, Dem., 844,197; Anderson, Ind., 111,639; Clark, Libertarian, 19,627; Commoner, Citizens, 4,852; Greaves, Amer., 4,750; Hall, Com., 702; DeBerry, Soc., 610.

1984, Reagan, Rep., 1,377,230; Mondale, Dem., 841,481; Bergland, Libertarian, 6,741.

1988, Bush, Rep., 1,297,763; Dukakis, Dem., 860,643; Fulani, New Alliance, 10,215.

1992, Bush, Rep., 989,375; Clinton, Dem., 848,420; Perot, Ind., 455,934; Marrou, Libertarian, 7,936; Fulani, New Alliance, 2,583.

1996, Dole, Rep., 995,082; Clinton, Dem., 874,668; Perot, Ref., 218,739; Browne, Libertarian, 16,239.

# Iowa

| County | 1996 Clinton (D) | 1996 Dole (R) | 1996 Perot (RF) | 1992 Clinton (D) | 1992 Bush (R) | 1992 Perot (I) |
|---|---|---|---|---|---|---|
| Adair . . . . | 1,795 | 1,648 | 455 | 1,655 | 1,713 | 814 |
| Adams . . . | 1,068 | 918 | 320 | 1,034 | 863 | 679 |
| Allamakee | 2,543 | 2,452 | 678 | 2,362 | 2,627 | 1,543 |
| Appanoose | 2,747 | 2,232 | 554 | 2,810 | 2,346 | 1,161 |
| Audubon. . | 1,823 | 1,307 | 313 | 1,589 | 1,373 | 887 |
| Benton . . . | 5,541 | 3,829 | 845 | 4,467 | 3,469 | 2,454 |
| Black Hawk | 29,588 | 19,263 | 3,616 | 29,584 | 21,398 | 10,182 |
| Boone . . . | 6,438 | 4,276 | 985 | 5,913 | 4,148 | 2,070 |
| Bremer. . . | 5,012 | 4,208 | 860 | 4,774 | 4,482 | 2,338 |
| Buchanan . | 4,990 | 3,038 | 836 | 4,166 | 3,313 | 2,126 |
| Buena Vista | 3,412 | 3,623 | 827 | 3,374 | 3,863 | 1,955 |
| Butler. . . . | 3,060 | 3,033 | 359 | 2,548 | 3,209 | 1,333 |
| Calhoun . . | 2,186 | 2,070 | 458 | 2,140 | 2,169 | 946 |
| Carroll . . . | 4,325 | 3,381 | 997 | 3,800 | 3,439 | 2,192 |
| Cass . . . . | 2,612 | 3,378 | 807 | 2,231 | 3,176 | 1,608 |
| Cedar . . . | 3,847 | 2,958 | 749 | 3,296 | 2,965 | 1,945 |
| Cerro Gordo. | 11,893 | 7,390 | 1,678 | 11,415 | 8,250 | 4,498 |
| Cherokee . | 2,850 | 2,627 | 832 | 2,590 | 2,768 | 1,503 |
| Chickasaw | 3,355 | 2,199 | 757 | 2,913 | 2,129 | 1,566 |
| Clarke . . . | 2,053 | 1,399 | 440 | 1,921 | 1,417 | 899 |
| Clay. . . . . | 3,653 | 3,125 | 786 | 3,346 | 3,011 | 1,964 |
| Clayton . . | 4,275 | 3,091 | 910 | 3,742 | 3,044 | 2,309 |
| Clinton . . . | 11,353 | 7,612 | 2,290 | 11,683 | 8,746 | 4,414 |
| Crawford . | 3,128 | 2,673 | 783 | 3,004 | 2,693 | 1,905 |
| Dallas . . . | 7,992 | 6,619 | 1,195 | 6,554 | 5,587 | 2,665 |
| Davis. . . . | 1,889 | 1,443 | 379 | 1,962 | 1,344 | 718 |
| Decatur . . | 1,844 | 1,283 | 0 | 1,866 | 1,316 | 786 |
| Delaware . | 3,806 | 3,061 | 674 | 3,093 | 3,195 | 2,144 |
| Des Moines | 8,815 | 4,895 | 2,311 | 11,309 | 6,378 | 3,386 |
| Dickinson . | 3,562 | 3,129 | 901 | 3,106 | 3,196 | 1,974 |
| Dubuque . | 20,792 | 13,328 | 3,301 | 20,539 | 14,007 | 8,208 |
| Emmet. . . | 2,264 | 1,634 | 467 | 2,239 | 1,749 | 1,010 |
| Fayette. . . | 4,817 | 3,838 | 888 | 4,412 | 3,879 | 2,493 |
| Floyd . . . . | 3,658 | 2,312 | 671 | 3,688 | 2,404 | 1,611 |
| Franklin . . | 2,211 | 2,045 | 414 | 2,049 | 2,137 | 1,045 |
| Fremont . . | 1,473 | 1,573 | 477 | 1,422 | 1,459 | 1,003 |
| Greene. . . | 2,327 | 1,723 | 405 | 2,422 | 1,952 | 956 |
| Grundy. . . | 2,321 | 2,925 | 399 | 1,895 | 3,160 | 1,069 |
| Guthrie. . . | 2,509 | 2,002 | 499 | 2,234 | 1,962 | 1,216 |
| Hamilton. . | 3,452 | 3,104 | 661 | 3,262 | 3,031 | 1,348 |
| Hancock. . | 2,430 | 2,341 | 514 | 2,175 | 2,428 | 1,170 |
| Hardin . . . | 4,043 | 3,490 | 712 | 3,792 | 3,590 | 1,547 |
| Harrison . . | 2,572 | 3,064 | 819 | 2,349 | 2,763 | 1,691 |
| Henry. . . . | 3,786 | 3,455 | 907 | 3,544 | 3,435 | 1,522 |
| Howard . . | 2,299 | 1,527 | 553 | 2,099 | 1,516 | 1,193 |
| Humboldt . | 2,077 | 2,232 | 585 | 1,765 | 2,299 | 1,093 |
| Ida . . . . . | 1,528 | 1,610 | 408 | 1,449 | 1,714 | 1,061 |
| Iowa . . . . | 3,342 | 3,036 | 574 | 2,560 | 2,656 | 1,709 |
| Jackson . . | 4,605 | 2,829 | 936 | 4,421 | 2,673 | 2,096 |
| Jasper . . . | 8,773 | 6,398 | 1,259 | 8,120 | 6,866 | 2,972 |
| Jefferson . | 2,591 | 2,536 | 570 | 2,562 | 2,541 | 1,241 |
| Johnson . . | 27,710 | 13,339 | 2,287 | 28,656 | 14,041 | 8,625 |
| Jones. . . . | 4,662 | 3,074 | 765 | 3,508 | 3,071 | 2,306 |
| Keokuk. . . | 2,524 | 2,065 | 423 | 2,329 | 1,981 | 1,238 |
| Kossuth . . | 4,023 | 3,466 | 931 | 3,660 | 3,464 | 1,906 |
| Lee . . . . . | 8,819 | 4,919 | 1,731 | 9,366 | 4,777 | 2,920 |
| Linn. . . . . | 45,283 | 30,797 | 5,572 | 38,567 | 30,215 | 19,643 |
| Louisa . . . | 2,079 | 1,564 | 589 | 2,091 | 1,691 | 1,044 |
| Lucas. . . . | 2,166 | 1,583 | 431 | 2,072 | 1,734 | 848 |
| Lyon . . . . | 1,486 | 3,390 | 422 | 1,331 | 3,272 | 1,068 |
| Madison . . | 3,059 | 2,541 | 649 | 2,525 | 2,421 | 1,168 |
| Mahaska . | 3,727 | 4,461 | 654 | 3,714 | 4,953 | 1,508 |
| Marion . . . | 5,959 | 6,071 | 867 | 5,531 | 6,062 | 1,896 |
| Marshall . . | 8,640 | 6,993 | 1,452 | 8,303 | 6,784 | 3,100 |
| Mills. . . . . | 2,062 | 2,949 | 680 | 1,798 | 2,699 | 1,638 |
| Mitchell . . | 2,590 | 1,868 | 558 | 2,177 | 1,933 | 1,199 |
| Monona . . | 1,948 | 1,669 | 579 | 1,939 | 1,660 | 1,231 |
| Monroe . . | 1,882 | 1,268 | 328 | 1,829 | 1,323 | 612 |
| Montgomery | 1,907 | 2,582 | 663 | 1,599 | 2,404 | 1,341 |
| Muscatine. | 7,629 | 5,825 | 1,692 | 7,089 | 6,087 | 3,583 |
| O'Brien. . . | 2,225 | 3,870 | 576 | 2,122 | 3,869 | 1,557 |
| Osceola . . | 1,007 | 1,731 | 274 | 990 | 1,756 | 813 |
| Page . . . . | 2,213 | 4,020 | 749 | 1,951 | 3,670 | 1,669 |
| Palo Alto . | 2,366 | 1,812 | 465 | 2,374 | 1,789 | 1,186 |
| Plymouth . | 3,737 | 5,104 | 993 | 3,171 | 5,196 | 2,039 |
| Pocahontas | 1,877 | 1,602 | 430 | 1,919 | 1,743 | 942 |
| Polk. . . . . | 83,100 | 60,388 | 9,400 | 78,585 | 63,708 | 24,155 |
| Pottawattamie | 13,218 | 15,575 | 3,514 | 13,228 | 15,671 | 8,035 |
| Poweshiek | 4,168 | 3,211 | 650 | 4,056 | 3,245 | 1,680 |
| Ringgold. . | 1,432 | 962 | 308 | 1,341 | 967 | 551 |
| Sac . . . . . | 2,162 | 2,199 | 578 | 1,896 | 2,138 | 1,157 |
| Scott . . . . | 32,657 | 26,723 | 4,984 | 33,765 | 28,844 | 11,423 |
| Shelby . . . | 2,173 | 3,043 | 670 | 2,094 | 2,809 | 1,614 |
| Sioux. . . . | 2,387 | 10,948 | 718 | 2,226 | 10,637 | 1,771 |
| Story . . . . | 17,166 | 12,412 | 2,082 | 17,118 | 12,702 | 6,275 |
| Tama. . . . | 3,984 | 2,980 | 710 | 3,573 | 2,948 | 1,748 |
| Taylor . . . | 1,456 | 1,417 | 377 | 1,430 | 1,200 | 910 |
| Union. . . . | 2,781 | 2,154 | 659 | 2,565 | 2,224 | 1,280 |
| Van Buren | 1,532 | 1,455 | 345 | 1,464 | 1,418 | 811 |
| Wapello . . | 8,415 | 4,818 | 1,376 | 8,670 | 4,852 | 2,513 |

| County | Clinton (D) 1996 | Dole (R) 1996 | Perot (RF) 1996 | Clinton (D) 1992 | Bush (R) 1992 | Perot (I) 1992 |
|---|---|---|---|---|---|---|
| Warren. . . | 9,061 | 6,850 | 1,259 | 8,612 | 7,242 | 3,217 |
| Washington | 3,808 | 3,592 | 634 | 3,384 | 3,576 | 1,994 |
| Wayne . . . | 1,644 | 1,290 | 303 | 1,632 | 1,299 | 642 |
| Webster . . | 8,335 | 6,257 | 1,578 | 8,562 | 6,992 | 3,272 |
| Winnebago | 2,673 | 2,204 | 588 | 2,322 | 2,407 | 1,329 |
| Winneshiek | 4,113 | 3,527 | 971 | 3,791 | 3,331 | 2,416 |
| Woodbury. | 17,175 | 16,324 | 3,391 | 17,398 | 18,148 | 7,182 |
| Worth. . . . | 2,247 | 1,255 | 396 | 2,009 | 1,382 | 1,044 |
| Wright . . . | 2,907 | 2,467 | 536 | 2,776 | 2,708 | 1,151 |
| **Totals . . .** | **615,499** | **489,776** | **104,401** | **586,353** | **504,891** | **253,468** |

## Iowa Vote Since 1948

1948, Truman, Dem., 522,380; Dewey, Rep., 494,018; Wallace, Prog., 12,125; Teichert, Soc. Labor, 4,274; Watson, Proh., 3,382; Thomas, Soc., 1,829; Dobbs, Soc. Workers, 26.

1952, Eisenhower, Rep., 808,906; Stevenson, Dem., 451,513; Hallinan, Prog., 5,085; Hamblen, Proh., 2,882; Hoopes, Soc., 219; Hass, Soc. Labor, 139; scattering, 29.

1956, Eisenhower, Rep., 729,187; Stevenson, Dem., 501,858; Andrews (A.C.P. of Iowa), 3,202; Hoopes, Soc., 192; Hass, Soc. Labor, 125.

1960, Kennedy, Dem., 550,565; Nixon, Rep., 722,381; Hass, Soc. Labor, 230; write-in, 634.

1964, Johnson, Dem., 733,030; Goldwater, Rep., 449,148; Hass, Soc. Labor, 182; DeBerry, Soc. Workers, 159; Munn, Proh., 1,902.

1968, Nixon, Rep., 619,106; Humphrey, Dem., 476,699; Wallace, 3d Party, 66,422; Munn, Proh., 362; Halstead, Soc. Workers, 3,377; Cleaver, Peace and Freedom, 1,332; Blomen, Soc. Labor, 241.

1972, Nixon, Rep., 706,207; McGovern, Dem., 496,206; Schmitz, Amer., 22,056; Jenness, Soc. Workers, 488; Fisher, Soc. Labor, 195; Hall, Com., 272; Green, Universal, 199; scattered, 321.

1976, Carter, Dem., 619,931; Ford, Rep., 632,863; McCarthy, Ind., 20,051; Anderson, Amer., 3,040; MacBride, Libertarian, 1,452.

1980, Reagan, Rep., 676,026; Carter, Dem., 508,672; Anderson, Ind., 115,633; Clark, Libertarian, 13,123; Commoner, Citizens, 2,273; McReynolds, Socialist, 534; Hall, Com., 298; DeBerry, Soc. Workers, 244; Greaves, Amer., 189; Bubar, Statesman, 150; scattering, 519.

1984, Reagan, Rep., 703,088; Mondale, Dem., 605,620; Bergland, Libertarian, 1,844.

1988, Bush, Rep., 545,355; Dukakis, Dem., 670,557; LaRouche, Ind., 3,526; Paul, Lib., 2,494.

1992, Clinton, Dem., 586,353; Bush, Rep., 504,891; Perot, Ind., 253,468; Hagelin, Natural Law, 3,079; Gritz, Populist/America First, 1,177; Marrou, Libertarian, 1,076.

1996, Clinton, Dem., 615,499; Dole, Rep., 489,776; Perot, Ref., 104,401; Nader, Green, 6,102; Hagelin, Natural Law, 3,514; Browne, Libertarian, 2,161; Phillips, Taxpayers, 2,119; Harris, Soc. Workers, 322.

# Kansas

| County | Clinton (D) 1996 | Dole (R) 1996 | Perot (RF) 1996 | Clinton (D) 1992 | Bush (R) 1992 | Perot (I) 1992 |
|---|---|---|---|---|---|---|
| Allen . . . . | 2,294 | 2,790 | 792 | 2,312 | 2,351 | 1,746 |
| Anderson . | 1,363 | 1,631 | 444 | 1,178 | 1,218 | 1,282 |
| Atchison . . | 2,894 | 2,793 | 719 | 2,959 | 2,521 | 2,020 |
| Barber . . . | 726 | 1,684 | 272 | 759 | 1,225 | 893 |
| Barton . . . | 3,107 | 7,807 | 992 | 3,846 | 5,113 | 4,574 |
| Bourbon . . | 2,841 | 3,745 | 865 | 2,509 | 2,876 | 1,763 |
| Brown . . . | 1,518 | 2,583 | 445 | 1,476 | 2,203 | 1,603 |
| Butler. . . . | 7,201 | 13,767 | 2,243 | 7,029 | 9,166 | 7,355 |
| Chase . . . | 496 | 771 | 257 | 470 | 610 | 600 |
| Chautauqua | 553 | 1,127 | 219 | 598 | 853 | 607 |
| Cherokee . | 3,766 | 4,136 | 1,069 | 4,083 | 3,589 | 2,067 |
| Cheyenne | 422 | 1,211 | 174 | 407 | 863 | 477 |
| Clark . . . . | 332 | 845 | 99 | 293 | 676 | 341 |
| Clay . . . . | 961 | 2,781 | 388 | 947 | 2,198 | 1,434 |
| Cloud. . . . | 1,604 | 2,706 | 598 | 1,720 | 2,131 | 1,578 |
| Coffey . . . | 1,118 | 2,368 | 572 | 1,021 | 1,824 | 1,443 |
| Comanche | 296 | 690 | 130 | 325 | 636 | 324 |
| Cowley. . . | 5,562 | 7,813 | 1,877 | 5,405 | 5,422 | 4,911 |
| Crawford . | 7,429 | 6,381 | 1,764 | 7,366 | 5,468 | 3,706 |
| Decatur . . | 416 | 1,249 | 156 | 576 | 940 | 565 |
| Dickinson . | 2,397 | 5,117 | 871 | 2,518 | 3,851 | 2,833 |
| Doniphan . | 1,046 | 1,958 | 442 | 1,177 | 1,579 | 1,200 |
| Douglas . . | 17,602 | 15,691 | 2,545 | 19,439 | 12,949 | 9,630 |
| Edwards . | 539 | 1,088 | 180 | 567 | 769 | 584 |
| Elk . . . . . | 483 | 928 | 200 | 485 | 748 | 503 |
| Ellis. . . . . | 4,085 | 6,700 | 871 | 4,544 | 3,985 | 3,887 |
| Ellsworth . | 897 | 2,078 | 242 | 1,010 | 1,197 | 1,020 |
| Finney . . . | 2,378 | 6,105 | 797 | 2,612 | 5,278 | 3,011 |
| Ford . . . . | 2,596 | 5,650 | 902 | 2,635 | 4,342 | 3,341 |
| Franklin . . | 3,490 | 4,923 | 1,139 | 2,968 | 3,699 | 3,184 |
| Geary . . . | 2,417 | 3,652 | 609 | 2,559 | 2,928 | 2,057 |
| Gove . . . . | 342 | 1,123 | 141 | 379 | 792 | 532 |
| Graham . . | 432 | 1,041 | 152 | 554 | 752 | 603 |
| Grant . . . | 615 | 1,735 | 245 | 619 | 1,561 | 835 |
| Gray . . . . | 400 | 1,448 | 164 | 443 | 1,039 | 686 |
| Greeley . . | 161 | 567 | 47 | 191 | 504 | 175 |
| Greenwood | 1,105 | 1,924 | 549 | 1,262 | 1,411 | 1,167 |
| Hamilton . | 342 | 811 | 84 | 386 | 716 | 271 |
| Harper . . . | 833 | 1,936 | 351 | 845 | 1,371 | 1,151 |
| Harvey. . . | 4,911 | 8,371 | 1,021 | 5,047 | 6,259 | 3,653 |
| Haskell . . | 304 | 1,136 | 96 | 336 | 1,023 | 462 |
| Hodgeman | 251 | 808 | 99 | 258 | 625 | 343 |
| Jackson . . | 1,965 | 2,664 | 730 | 1,639 | 1,970 | 1,927 |
| Jefferson . | 2,745 | 3,763 | 1,025 | 2,538 | 2,569 | 2,642 |
| Jewell . . . | 417 | 1,374 | 188 | 546 | 1,050 | 698 |
| Johnson . . | 67,437 | 109,166 | 10,294 | 59,573 | 85,418 | 49,136 |
| Kearny . . | 333 | 1,037 | 105 | 384 | 943 | 376 |
| Kingman. . | 1,006 | 2,659 | 409 | 1,100 | 1,680 | 1,370 |
| Kiowa . . . | 330 | 1,254 | 169 | 355 | 1,057 | 475 |
| Labette. . . | 3,931 | 4,283 | 1,091 | 4,196 | 3,368 | 2,577 |
| Lane . . . . | 271 | 865 | 86 | 265 | 674 | 356 |
| Leavenworth | 8,990 | 10,663 | 2,368 | 8,077 | 7,738 | 7,306 |
| Lincoln . . | 522 | 1,368 | 210 | 612 | 893 | 657 |
| Linn. . . . . | 1,578 | 2,063 | 534 | 1,353 | 1,413 | 1,358 |
| Logan . . . | 296 | 1,155 | 112 | 355 | 905 | 446 |
| Lyon . . . . | 4,796 | 6,478 | 1,554 | 4,811 | 5,090 | 4,717 |
| McPherson | 3,530 | 8,117 | 1,110 | 3,645 | 5,745 | 3,561 |
| Marion . . . | 1,656 | 4,143 | 485 | 1,627 | 3,142 | 1,557 |
| Marshall . . | 1,920 | 2,759 | 704 | 2,022 | 2,030 | 1,786 |
| Meade . . . | 420 | 1,426 | 168 | 430 | 1,135 | 592 |
| Miami. . . . | 4,215 | 5,215 | 1,324 | 3,835 | 3,528 | 3,701 |
| Mitchell . . | 833 | 2,430 | 246 | 938 | 1,601 | 1,098 |
| Montgomery. | 5,269 | 7,428 | 1,528 | 5,453 | 6,848 | 3,570 |
| Morris . . . | 961 | 1,549 | 453 | 957 | 1,071 | 1,071 |
| Morton . . | 376 | 1,063 | 122 | 398 | 915 | 350 |
| Nemaha . . | 1,639 | 2,999 | 667 | 1,580 | 2,220 | 1,804 |
| Neosho . . | 2,513 | 3,342 | 895 | 2,799 | 2,926 | 2,136 |
| Ness . . . . | 425 | 1,329 | 185 | 565 | 967 | 678 |
| Norton . . . | 640 | 1,811 | 264 | 779 | 1,469 | 815 |
| Osage . . . | 2,491 | 3,460 | 1,091 | 2,297 | 2,561 | 2,532 |
| Osborne . | 605 | 1,555 | 189 | 779 | 1,003 | 819 |
| Ottawa . . | 750 | 1,841 | 260 | 764 | 1,284 | 762 |
| Pawnee . . | 925 | 1,913 | 273 | 1,118 | 1,357 | 1,097 |
| Phillips . . | 756 | 1,987 | 240 | 843 | 1,579 | 955 |
| Pottawatomie | 1,971 | 4,460 | 1,016 | 2,099 | 3,106 | 2,759 |
| Pratt . . . . | 1,353 | 2,556 | 392 | 1,466 | 1,779 | 1,528 |
| Rawlins . . | 335 | 1,392 | 146 | 393 | 1,023 | 517 |
| Reno . . . . | 9,096 | 14,219 | 2,659 | 9,257 | 11,377 | 7,636 |
| Republic . | 685 | 2,267 | 268 | 939 | 1,767 | 1,084 |
| Rice. . . . . | 1,413 | 2,783 | 473 | 1,555 | 2,158 | 1,543 |
| Riley . . . . | 6,589 | 10,909 | 1,438 | 7,933 | 8,394 | 5,387 |
| Rooks . . . | 650 | 1,864 | 251 | 771 | 1,249 | 1,063 |
| Rush . . . . | 547 | 1,239 | 185 | 689 | 756 | 665 |
| Russell. . . | 700 | 3,334 | 162 | 1,178 | 1,434 | 1,395 |
| Saline . . . | 7,634 | 12,315 | 2,143 | 7,890 | 8,565 | 7,108 |
| Scott . . . . | 456 | 1,745 | 154 | 480 | 1,426 | 621 |
| Sedgwick . | 59,133 | 92,758 | 11,770 | 62,670 | 75,577 | 47,238 |
| Seward . . | 1,304 | 3,794 | 395 | 1,488 | 3,477 | 1,818 |
| Shawnee . | 32,573 | 34,634 | 7,251 | 31,972 | 29,344 | 20,653 |
| Sheridan . | 261 | 1,048 | 95 | 347 | 739 | 546 |
| Sherman . | 736 | 2,110 | 220 | 810 | 1,630 | 828 |
| Smith . . . | 636 | 1,625 | 213 | 789 | 1,236 | 816 |
| Stafford . . | 641 | 1,576 | 266 | 777 | 1,064 | 910 |
| Stanton . . | 185 | 620 | 59 | 224 | 556 | 214 |
| Stevens . . | 401 | 1,531 | 209 | 390 | 1,408 | 674 |
| Sumner . . | 3,592 | 5,934 | 1,254 | 3,564 | 4,087 | 3,887 |
| Thomas . . | 852 | 2,695 | 288 | 932 | 1,849 | 1,129 |
| Trego . . . | 546 | 1,198 | 204 | 608 | 727 | 574 |
| Wabaunsee | 965 | 1,884 | 479 | 851 | 1,254 | 1,258 |
| Wallace . . | 160 | 734 | 65 | 164 | 679 | 219 |
| Washington | 796 | 2,388 | 326 | 893 | 1,740 | 1,054 |
| Wichita . . | 239 | 796 | 80 | 241 | 681 | 303 |
| Wilson . . . | 1,284 | 2,433 | 555 | 1,331 | 1,925 | 1,365 |
| Woodson . | 594 | 947 | 265 | 590 | 662 | 604 |
| Wyandotte | 31,046 | 13,957 | 3,911 | 34,397 | 12,872 | 13,620 |
| **Totals . . .** | **384,439** | **578,572** | **92,093** | **390,434** | **449,951** | **312,358** |

## Kansas Vote Since 1948

1948, Truman, Dem., 351,902; Dewey, Rep., 423,039; Watson, Proh., 6,468; Wallace, Prog., 4,603; Thomas, Soc., 2,807.

1952, Eisenhower, Rep., 616,302; Stevenson, Dem., 273,296; Hamblen, Proh., 6,038; Hoopes, Soc., 530.

1956, Eisenhower, Rep., 566,878; Stevenson. Dem., 296,317; Holtwick, Proh., 3,048.

1960, Kennedy, Dem., 363,213; Nixon, Rep., 561,474; Decker, Proh., 4,138.

1964, Johnson, Dem., 464,028; Goldwater, Rep., 386,579; Munn, Proh., 5,393; Hass, Soc. Labor, 1,901.

1968, Nixon, Rep., 478,674; Humphrey, Dem., 302,996; Wallace, 3d Party, 88,921; Munn, Proh., 2,192.

1972, Nixon, Rep., 619,812; McGovern, Dem., 270,287; Schmitz, Conservative, 21,808; Munn, Proh., 4,188.

1976, Carter, Dem., 430,421; Ford, Rep., 502,752; McCarthy, Ind., 13,185; Anderson, Amer., 4,724; MacBride, Libertarian, 3,242; Maddox, Conservative, 2,118; Bubar, Proh., 1,403.

1980, Reagan, Rep., 566,812; Carter, Dem., 326,150; Anderson, Ind., 68,231; Clark, Libertarian, 14,470; Shelton, Amer., 1,555; Hall, Com., 967; Bubar, Statesman, 821; Rarick, Conservative, 789.

1984, Reagan, Rep., 674,646; Mondale, Dem., 332,471; Bergland, Libertarian, 3,585.

1988, Bush, Rep., 554,049; Dukakis, Dem., 422,636; Paul, Ind., 12,553; Fulani, Ind., 3,806.

1992, Clinton, Dem., 390,434; Bush, Rep., 449,951; Perot, Ind., 312,358; Marrou, Libertarian, 4,314.

1996, Dole, Rep., 578,572; Clinton, Dem., 384,439; Perot, Ref., 92,093; Browne, Libertarian, 4,544; Phillips, Ind., 3,489; Hagelin, Ind., 1,679.

# Kentucky

| | 1996 | | | 1992 | | |
|---|---|---|---|---|---|---|
| County | Clinton (D) | Dole (R) | Perot (RF) | Clinton (D) | Bush (R) | Perot (I) |
| Adair . . . . | 1,821 | 3,878 | 790 | 2,044 | 3,740 | 617 |
| Allen . . . . | 1,781 | 3,032 | 393 | 2,040 | 2,747 | 606 |
| Anderson . | 2,898 | 2,972 | 751 | 2,491 | 2,731 | 1,219 |
| Ballard . . . | 2,255 | 1,064 | 411 | 2,268 | 1,108 | 500 |
| Barren . . . | 5,044 | 5,700 | 1,065 | 5,688 | 5,467 | 1,778 |
| Bath. . . . . | 1,886 | 1,229 | 428 | 2,229 | 1,259 | 694 |
| Bell . . . . . | 5,058 | 3,917 | 940 | 5,745 | 4,501 | 1,193 |
| Boone . . . | 8,379 | 15,085 | 1,900 | 6,514 | 12,306 | 4,676 |
| Bourbon . . | 3,030 | 2,592 | 577 | 2,895 | 2,707 | 1,290 |
| Boyd . . . . | 9,668 | 7,054 | 2,070 | 10,496 | 7,387 | 3,195 |
| Boyle . . . . | 3,877 | 4,157 | 709 | 3,894 | 4,019 | 1,335 |
| Bracken . . | 1,055 | 1,371 | 271 | 1,259 | 1,162 | 500 |
| Breathitt . . | 3,047 | 1,131 | 392 | 3,496 | 1,303 | 515 |
| Breckinridge. | 2,956 | 3,151 | 670 | 3,113 | 2,941 | 945 |
| Bullitt . . . . | 7,648 | 8,695 | 1,973 | 7,830 | 7,745 | 3,333 |
| Butler. . . . | 1,260 | 2,531 | 348 | 1,468 | 2,729 | 596 |
| Caldwell . . | 2,434 | 2,067 | 637 | 3,000 | 1,966 | 670 |
| Calloway . | 5,281 | 4,989 | 1,223 | 6,181 | 4,654 | 1,853 |
| Campbell . | 11,957 | 16,640 | 2,312 | 10,673 | 16,382 | 5,659 |
| Carlisle. . . | 1,355 | 816 | 245 | 1,383 | 844 | 309 |
| Carroll . . . | 1,689 | 1,170 | 351 | 2,119 | 1,046 | 566 |
| Carter . . . | 3,728 | 3,240 | 781 | 4,224 | 3,305 | 989 |
| Casey . . . | 1,106 | 3,187 | 525 | 1,409 | 3,317 | 542 |
| Christian. . | 6,843 | 8,285 | 1,064 | 6,709 | 7,737 | 1,789 |
| Clark . . . . | 4,987 | 4,739 | 1,095 | 4,892 | 4,625 | 1,955 |
| Clay. . . . . | 2,135 | 3,716 | 478 | 2,012 | 4,747 | 648 |
| Clinton . . . | 1,072 | 2,521 | 350 | 1,241 | 2,830 | 348 |
| Crittenden. | 1,480 | 1,509 | 400 | 1,740 | 1,576 | 495 |
| Cumberland | 753 | 1,654 | 227 | 917 | 1,866 | 268 |
| Daviess . . | 15,366 | 15,844 | 3,344 | 16,592 | 14,936 | 5,112 |
| Edmonson | 1,595 | 2,619 | 298 | 1,653 | 2,486 | 438 |
| Elliott . . . . | 1,298 | 411 | 284 | 1,796 | 444 | 273 |
| Estill . . . . | 1,724 | 2,220 | 479 | 1,837 | 2,453 | 736 |
| Fayette. . . | 43,632 | 42,930 | 5,345 | 38,306 | 41,908 | 14,215 |
| Fleming . . | 1,913 | 2,313 | 522 | 2,257 | 2,045 | 815 |
| Floyd . . . . | 9,655 | 3,139 | 1,518 | 13,351 | 3,540 | 1,723 |
| Franklin . . | 11,251 | 7,132 | 1,873 | 9,896 | 7,591 | 3,340 |
| Fulton . . . | 1,614 | 863 | 223 | 1,813 | 1,073 | 306 |
| Gallatin . . | 1,189 | 838 | 299 | 1,171 | 699 | 445 |
| Garrard . . | 1,486 | 2,540 | 337 | 1,730 | 2,359 | 697 |
| Grant . . . . | 2,541 | 2,697 | 661 | 2,097 | 2,128 | 1,149 |
| Graves. . . | 6,991 | 5,130 | 1,538 | 8,001 | 5,311 | 1,943 |
| Grayson . . | 2,716 | 4,249 | 677 | 2,909 | 4,533 | 993 |
| Green . . . | 1,285 | 2,763 | 475 | 1,760 | 2,709 | 500 |
| Greenup . . | 6,883 | 5,370 | 1,627 | 7,214 | 4,975 | 2,188 |
| Hancock. . | 1,547 | 1,356 | 418 | 1,714 | 1,261 | 551 |
| Hardin . . . | 11,031 | 12,642 | 2,815 | 9,417 | 12,299 | 4,026 |
| Harlan . . . | 5,874 | 3,437 | 885 | 6,796 | 3,970 | 1,391 |
| Harrison . . | 2,934 | 2,433 | 801 | 2,795 | 2,148 | 1,225 |
| Hart. . . . . | 2,527 | 2,701 | 501 | 2,852 | 2,401 | 579 |
| Henderson | 8,051 | 5,092 | 1,556 | 8,270 | 5,125 | 2,678 |
| Henry. . . . | 2,324 | 2,110 | 564 | 2,838 | 1,640 | 720 |
| Hickman . . | 1,220 | 695 | 247 | 1,296 | 861 | 294 |
| Hopkins . . | 7,359 | 6,442 | 1,539 | 8,881 | 6,032 | 2,565 |
| Jackson . . | 960 | 3,045 | 299 | 776 | 3,398 | 341 |
| Jefferson . | 144,207 | 114,860 | 19,413 | 152,728 | 116,566 | 39,822 |
| Jessamine | 4,428 | 6,686 | 1,040 | 3,764 | 6,474 | 2,059 |
| Johnson . . | 3,348 | 3,262 | 1,010 | 3,669 | 3,614 | 1,118 |
| Kenton . . . | 19,407 | 28,575 | 3,680 | 16,344 | 27,261 | 9,336 |
| Knott . . . . | 4,682 | 1,174 | 496 | 5,500 | 1,243 | 560 |
| Knox . . . . | 3,736 | 4,502 | 811 | 3,787 | 5,011 | 972 |
| Larue. . . . | 2,040 | 2,140 | 469 | 2,190 | 2,154 | 582 |
| Laurel . . . | 4,306 | 9,454 | 1,211 | 4,560 | 8,583 | 1,859 |
| Lawrence . | 2,195 | 1,812 | 481 | 2,400 | 2,084 | 557 |
| Lee . . . . . | 1,023 | 1,302 | 181 | 1,170 | 1,617 | 356 |
| Leslie. . . . | 1,466 | 2,296 | 304 | 1,591 | 2,879 | 450 |
| Letcher. . . | 4,160 | 2,222 | 790 | 5,817 | 3,011 | 1,206 |
| Lewis. . . . | 1,415 | 2,365 | 561 | 1,713 | 2,493 | 673 |
| Lincoln . . . | 2,550 | 3,006 | 318 | 2,532 | 2,624 | 762 |
| Livingston . | 2,228 | 1,258 | 449 | 2,386 | 1,339 | 578 |
| Logan . . . | 4,181 | 3,888 | 704 | 4,064 | 3,710 | 1,043 |
| Lyon . . . . | 1,641 | 999 | 284 | 1,583 | 820 | 293 |
| McCracken | 12,670 | 10,221 | 2,268 | 13,341 | 10,657 | 3,077 |
| McCreary . | 1,710 | 2,527 | 488 | 1,934 | 3,588 | 624 |
| McLean . . | 1,834 | 1,368 | 385 | 2,223 | 1,355 | 529 |
| Madison . . | 8,142 | 9,212 | 1,613 | 8,005 | 8,719 | 3,038 |
| Magoffin . . | 2,249 | 1,434 | 337 | 3,261 | 1,992 | 440 |
| Marion . . . | 2,922 | 2,013 | 757 | 3,403 | 2,091 | 805 |
| Marshall . . | 6,054 | 4,579 | 1,391 | 6,576 | 4,368 | 1,773 |
| Martin . . . | 1,807 | 1,612 | 401 | 1,715 | 1,961 | 393 |
| Mason . . . | 2,444 | 2,588 | 484 | 2,657 | 2,432 | 916 |
| Meade . . . | 3,653 | 2,855 | 912 | 3,387 | 2,641 | 1,298 |
| Menifee . . | 979 | 608 | 179 | 1,311 | 557 | 254 |
| Mercer . . . | 3,179 | 3,264 | 738 | 3,010 | 3,211 | 1,298 |
| Metcalfe . . | 1,349 | 1,651 | 355 | 1,703 | 1,683 | 409 |
| Monroe . . | 1,114 | 3,300 | 415 | 1,515 | 3,776 | 480 |
| Montgomery. | 3,372 | 2,681 | 705 | 3,686 | 2,590 | 1,308 |
| Morgan . . | 1,843 | 1,439 | 380 | 2,655 | 1,239 | 498 |
| Muhlenberg | 6,564 | 3,569 | 1,218 | 7,901 | 3,551 | 1,624 |
| Nelson . . . | 5,392 | 4,645 | 1,067 | 5,437 | 4,495 | 1,638 |
| Nicholas . . | 1,092 | 950 | 265 | 1,341 | 894 | 513 |
| Ohio . . . . | 3,487 | 3,475 | 1,076 | 4,022 | 3,385 | 1,423 |
| Oldham . . | 5,734 | 9,545 | 1,473 | 5,457 | 8,263 | 2,855 |
| Owen. . . . | 1,603 | 1,709 | 454 | 1,830 | 1,108 | 613 |
| Owsley . . | 647 | 875 | 153 | 678 | 1,437 | 209 |
| Pendleton . | 1,926 | 2,177 | 462 | 1,740 | 1,810 | 1,086 |
| Perry . . . . | 6,015 | 3,382 | 894 | 6,619 | 4,128 | 1,308 |
| Pike. . . . . | 13,885 | 6,982 | 2,128 | 17,358 | 8,212 | 2,444 |
| Powell . . . | 2,156 | 1,526 | 523 | 2,323 | 1,809 | 874 |
| Pulaski . . . | 5,340 | 11,945 | 142 | 5,465 | 11,423 | 2,449 |
| Robertson | 360 | 368 | 117 | 439 | 329 | 170 |
| Rockcastle | 1,160 | 3,106 | 338 | 1,144 | 3,287 | 446 |
| Rowan . . . | 3,215 | 2,309 | 724 | 3,558 | 2,469 | 1,212 |
| Russell. . . | 1,582 | 4,017 | 837 | 1,950 | 4,641 | 673 |
| Scott . . . . | 4,258 | 4,349 | 977 | 3,639 | 3,810 | 1,800 |
| Shelby . . . | 4,630 | 5,307 | 780 | 4,398 | 4,550 | 1,451 |
| Simpson. . | 2,749 | 2,186 | 401 | 2,834 | 2,280 | 708 |
| Spencer . . | 1,404 | 1,614 | 341 | 1,383 | 1,305 | 466 |
| Taylor . . . | 2,897 | 4,573 | 829 | 3,518 | 4,319 | 1,044 |
| Todd . . . . | 1,744 | 1,912 | 424 | 1,858 | 1,691 | 612 |
| Trigg . . . . | 2,087 | 1,975 | 394 | 2,438 | 1,820 | 573 |
| Trimble. . . | 1,245 | 999 | 308 | 1,413 | 789 | 413 |
| Union. . . . | 2,913 | 1,554 | 598 | 3,325 | 1,605 | 794 |
| Warren. . . | 11,642 | 15,784 | 1,835 | 11,529 | 14,748 | 3,533 |
| Washington | 1,639 | 2,116 | 383 | 2,008 | 2,098 | 542 |
| Wayne . . . | 2,422 | 3,122 | 481 | 2,516 | 3,412 | 560 |
| Webster . . | 2,852 | 1,568 | 660 | 3,380 | 1,408 | 854 |
| Whitley. . . | 4,174 | 5,402 | 1,027 | 4,600 | 5,998 | 1,533 |
| Wolfe. . . . | 1,297 | 772 | 202 | 1,674 | 697 | 297 |
| Woodford . | 3,910 | 4,270 | 746 | 3,161 | 3,992 | 1,535 |
| **Totals . . .** | **635,804** | **622,339** | **2,202** | **665,104** | **617,178** | **203,944** |

## Kentucky Vote Since 1948

1948, Truman, Dem., 466,756; Dewey, Rep., 341,210; Thurmond, States' Rights, 10,411; Wallace, Prog., 1,567; Thomas, Soc., 1,284; Watson, Proh., 1,245; Teichert, Soc. Labor, 185.

1952, Eisenhower, Rep., 495,029; Stevenson, Dem., 495,729; Hamblen, Proh., 1,161; Hass, Soc. Labor, 893; Hallinan, Proh., 336.

1956, Eisenhower, Rep., 572,192; Stevenson, Dem., 476,453; Byrd, States' Rights, 2,657; Holtwick, Proh., 2,145; Hass, Soc. Labor, 358.

1960, Kennedy, Dem., 521,855; Nixon, Rep., 602,607.

1964, Johnson, Dem., 669,659; Goldwater, Rep., 372,977; Kasper, Natl. States Rights, 3,469.

1968, Nixon, Rep., 462,411; Humphrey, Dem., 397,547; Wallace, 3d Party, 193,098; Halstead, Soc. Workers, 2,843.

1972, Nixon, Rep., 676,446; McGovern, Dem., 371,159; Schmitz, Amer., 17,627; Jenness, Soc. Workers, 685; Hall, Com., 464; Spock, Peoples, 1,118.

1976, Carter, Dem., 615,717; Ford, Rep., 531,852; Anderson, Amer., 8,308; McCarthy, Ind., 6,837; Maddox, Amer. Ind., 2,328; MacBride, Libertarian, 814.

1980, Reagan, Rep., 635,274; Carter, Dem., 616,417; Anderson, Ind., 31,127; Clark, Libertarian, 5,531; McCormack, Respect For Life, 4,233; Commoner, Citizens, 1,304; Pulley, Socialist, 393; Hall, Com., 348.

1984, Reagan, Rep., 815,345; Mondale, Dem., 536,756.

1988, Bush, Rep., 734,281; Dukakis, Dem., 580,368; Duke, Pop., 4,494; Paul, Lib., 2,118.

1992, Clinton, Dem., 665,104; Bush, Rep., 617,178; Perot, Ind., 203,944; Marrou, Libertarian, 4,513.

1996, Clinton, Dem., 635,804; Dole, Rep., 622,339; Perot, Ref., 118,768; Browne, Libertarian, 4,022; Phillips, Taxpayers, 2,202; Hagelin, Natural Law, 1,545.

# Louisiana

| Parish | 1996 Clinton (D) | 1996 Dole (R) | 1996 Perot (RF) | 1992 Clinton (D) | 1992 Bush (R) | 1992 Perot (I) |
|---|---|---|---|---|---|---|
| Acadia | 12,300 | 9,246 | 2,234 | 12,276 | 9,017 | 3,145 |
| Allen | 4,834 | 2,491 | 1,134 | 5,626 | 3,069 | 1,245 |
| Ascension | 15,263 | 10,885 | 3,027 | 13,036 | 10,275 | 4,295 |
| Assumption | 6,416 | 2,698 | 904 | 5,639 | 2,928 | 1,358 |
| Avoyelles | 9,689 | 4,433 | 1,937 | 8,696 | 4,851 | 2,139 |
| Beauregard | 4,866 | 5,524 | 1,831 | 5,037 | 5,119 | 2,103 |
| Bienville | 4,343 | 2,397 | 457 | 3,899 | 2,412 | 832 |
| Bossier | 15,504 | 16,852 | 2,660 | 11,313 | 15,628 | 4,863 |
| Caddo | 55,543 | 38,445 | 4,821 | 47,733 | 42,665 | 11,830 |
| Calcasieu | 38,238 | 26,494 | 8,281 | 33,570 | 24,847 | 10,980 |
| Caldwell | 2,117 | 1,842 | 506 | 2,061 | 1,752 | 653 |
| Cameron | 2,103 | 1,365 | 594 | 1,985 | 1,329 | 995 |
| Catahoula | 2,487 | 1,765 | 608 | 2,570 | 1,976 | 773 |
| Claiborne | 3,609 | 2,500 | 530 | 3,263 | 2,599 | 926 |
| Concordia | 4,565 | 3,134 | 855 | 4,283 | 3,223 | 1,317 |
| DeSoto | 6,073 | 3,356 | 621 | 5,671 | 3,643 | 1,358 |
| E. Baton Rouge | 83,489 | 77,529 | 8,008 | 68,622 | 81,072 | 16,102 |
| East Carroll | 2,149 | 1,008 | 186 | 1,835 | 1,142 | 283 |
| East Feliciana | 4,714 | 2,949 | 660 | 4,093 | 2,813 | 932 |
| Evangeline | 7,847 | 5,279 | 1,447 | 8,564 | 5,147 | 2,124 |
| Franklin | 3,871 | 3,854 | 771 | 4,127 | 3,889 | 1,311 |
| Grant | 2,980 | 3,117 | 1,055 | 3,122 | 3,214 | 1,174 |
| Iberia | 15,087 | 12,014 | 2,448 | 13,040 | 11,905 | 4,337 |
| Iberville | 9,136 | 3,978 | 1,041 | 8,218 | 5,211 | 1,543 |
| Jackson | 3,371 | 3,028 | 601 | 3,370 | 3,072 | 882 |
| Jefferson | 80,407 | 92,820 | 9,667 | 64,302 | 100,493 | 21,278 |
| Jefferson Davis | 6,897 | 4,311 | 1,518 | 7,022 | 4,513 | 2,221 |
| Lafayette | 32,504 | 36,420 | 4,631 | 28,583 | 32,406 | 9,124 |
| Lafourche | 18,810 | 12,105 | 2,984 | 16,182 | 12,744 | 5,077 |
| LaSalle | 2,543 | 2,925 | 947 | 2,389 | 3,068 | 993 |
| Lincoln | 7,903 | 6,973 | 761 | 7,205 | 7,220 | 1,751 |
| Livingston | 13,276 | 16,159 | 4,150 | 11,499 | 14,808 | 4,971 |
| Madison | 3,085 | 1,591 | 315 | 2,773 | 1,702 | 469 |
| Morehouse | 6,160 | 5,193 | 963 | 6,013 | 5,364 | 1,727 |
| Natchitoches | 8,296 | 5,471 | 1,014 | 6,974 | 5,694 | 1,606 |
| Orleans | 144,673 | 39,575 | 3,805 | 133,261 | 52,019 | 10,889 |
| Ouachita | 24,525 | 28,659 | 3,586 | 20,835 | 27,600 | 6,612 |
| Plaquemines | 5,348 | 4,493 | 856 | 4,467 | 5,018 | 1,729 |
| Pointe Coupee | 6,808 | 3,545 | 840 | 6,512 | 3,563 | 1,157 |
| Rapides | 22,962 | 21,515 | 4,656 | 20,873 | 22,783 | 6,599 |
| Red River | 2,641 | 1,344 | 268 | 2,360 | 1,649 | 566 |
| Richland | 4,143 | 3,765 | 645 | 3,706 | 3,808 | 1,054 |
| Sabine | 4,263 | 3,475 | 1,015 | 4,173 | 3,586 | 1,219 |
| St. Bernard | 14,310 | 13,548 | 2,663 | 12,305 | 16,131 | 4,308 |
| St. Charles | 10,616 | 9,207 | 1,307 | 8,810 | 9,158 | 2,593 |
| St. Helena | 3,682 | 1,455 | 417 | 3,416 | 1,515 | 589 |
| St. James | 7,247 | 2,829 | 608 | 6,609 | 3,339 | 993 |
| St. John the Baptist | 9,937 | 6,025 | 966 | 8,977 | 6,730 | 1,922 |
| St. Landry | 20,636 | 12,274 | 2,293 | 20,383 | 11,882 | 4,266 |
| St. Martin | 15,490 | 6,296 | 1,607 | 11,252 | 5,909 | 2,573 |
| St. Mary | 12,405 | 8,018 | 1,850 | 10,648 | 8,792 | 3,257 |
| St. Tammany | 24,201 | 44,557 | 4,741 | 19,735 | 37,839 | 9,005 |
| Tangipahoa | 18,280 | 14,413 | 3,016 | 15,194 | 14,128 | 4,612 |
| Tensas | 1,882 | 1,000 | 176 | 1,666 | 1,153 | 353 |
| Terrebonne | 18,550 | 13,944 | 3,459 | 13,325 | 14,662 | 5,505 |
| Union | 4,174 | 4,216 | 680 | 4,005 | 4,434 | 1,209 |
| Vermilion | 12,609 | 7,653 | 1,954 | 12,324 | 7,062 | 3,127 |
| Vernon | 6,195 | 5,449 | 2,068 | 6,005 | 5,912 | 2,313 |
| Washington | 9,603 | 6,642 | 1,643 | 9,095 | 7,227 | 2,303 |
| Webster | 9,688 | 6,153 | 1,316 | 8,380 | 6,640 | 2,629 |
| W. Baton Rouge | 5,697 | 3,254 | 799 | 5,131 | 3,522 | 1,249 |
| West Carroll | 1,853 | 2,366 | 457 | 2,068 | 2,082 | 771 |
| West Feliciana | 2,311 | 1,616 | 388 | 2,328 | 1,501 | 516 |
| Winn | 3,779 | 2,803 | 735 | 3,537 | 2,932 | 843 |
| **Totals** | **928,983** | **710,240** | **122,981** | **815,971** | **733,386** | **211,478** |

## Louisiana Vote Since 1948

1948, Thurmond, States' Rights, 204,290; Truman, Dem., 136,344; Dewey, Rep., 72,657; Wallace, Prog., 3,035.

1952, Eisenhower, Rep., 306,925; Stevenson, Dem., 345,027.

1956, Eisenhower, Rep., 329,047; Stevenson, Dem., 243,977; Andrews, States' Rights, 44,520.

1960, Kennedy, Dem., 407,339; Nixon, Rep., 230,890; States' Rights (unpledged), 169,572.

1964, Johnson, Dem., 387,068; Goldwater, Rep., 509,225.

1968, Nixon, Rep., 257,535; Humphrey, Dem., 309,615; Wallace, 3d Party, 530,300.

1972, Nixon, Rep., 686,852; McGovern, Dem., 298,142; Schmitz, Amer., 52,099; Jenness, Soc. Workers, 14,398.

1976, Carter, Dem., 661,365; Ford, Rep., 587,446; Maddox, Amer., 10,058; Hall, Com., 7,417; McCarthy, Ind., 6,588; MacBride, Libertarian, 3,325.

1980, Reagan, Rep., 792,853; Carter, Dem., 708,453; Anderson, Ind., 26,345; Rarick, Amer. Ind., 10,333; Clark, Libertarian, 8,240; Commoner, Citizens, 1,584; DeBerry, Soc. Work., 783.

1984, Reagan, Rep., 1,037,299; Mondale, Dem., 651,586; Bergland, Libertarian, 1,876.

1988, Bush, Rep., 883,702; Dukakis, Dem., 717,460; Duke, Pop., 18,612; Paul, Lib., 4,115.

1992, Clinton, Dem., 815,971; Bush, Rep., 733,386; Perot, Ind., 211,478; Gritz, Populist/America First, 18,545; Marrou, Libertarian, 3,155; Daniels, Ind., 1,663; Phillips, U.S. Taxpayers, 1,552; Fulani, New Alliance, 1,434; LaRouche, Ind., 1,136.

1996, Clinton, Dem., 928,983; Dole, Rep., 710,240; Perot, Ref., 122,981; Browne, Libertarian, 7,559; Nader, Liberty, Ecology, Community, 4,706; Phillips, Taxpayers, 3,431; Hagelin, Natural Law, 3,069; Moorehead, Workers World, 1,678.

# Maine

| City | 1996 Clinton (D) | 1996 Dole (R) | 1996 Perot (RF) | 1992 Clinton (D) | 1992 Bush (R) | 1992 Perot (I) |
|---|---|---|---|---|---|---|
| Auburn | 5,750 | 3,060 | 1,484 | 5,025 | 3,653 | 3,964 |
| Augusta | 4,082 | 1,778 | 825 | 4,657 | 3,003 | 3,002 |
| Bangor | 7,550 | 4,438 | 1,377 | 6,826 | 5,185 | 4,689 |
| Bidderford | 5,653 | 1,768 | 1,019 | 4,945 | 2,533 | 2,717 |
| Brewer | 2,301 | 1,730 | 532 | 1,788 | 1,907 | 1,625 |
| Lewiston | 10,275 | 3,182 | 2,113 | 9,265 | 4,372 | 6,180 |
| Old Town | 2,442 | 976 | 407 | 2,272 | 1,173 | 1,302 |
| Rockland | 1,538 | 978 | 442 | 1,192 | 1,081 | 1,059 |
| Saco | 4,506 | 2,140 | 834 | 4,000 | 2,769 | 2,303 |
| Sanford | 4,368 | 2,239 | 1,524 | 3,854 | 3,030 | 3,215 |
| South Portland | 6,785 | 3,245 | 906 | 5,933 | 3,999 | 2,734 |
| Waterville | 4,219 | 1,478 | 750 | 3,868 | 1,832 | 2,257 |
| Westbrook | 4,373 | 2,186 | 874 | 3,665 | 2,904 | 2,512 |
| Other | 262,375 | 161,513 | 74,995 | 183,241 | 157,719 | 159,778 |
| **Totals** | **326,217** | **190,711** | **88,082** | **263,420** | **206,504** | **206,820** |

## Maine Vote Since 1948

1948, Truman, Dem., 111,916; Dewey, Rep., 150,234; Wallace, Prog., 1,884; Thomas, Soc., 547; Teichert, Soc. Labor, 206.

1952, Eisenhower, Rep., 232,353; Stevenson, Dem., 118,806; Hallinan, Prog., 332; Hass, Soc. Labor, 156; Hoopes, Soc., 138; scattered, 1.

1956, Eisenhower, Rep., 249,238; Stevenson, Dem., 102,468.

1960, Kennedy, Dem., 181,159; Nixon, Rep., 240,608.

1964, Johnson, Dem., 262,264; Goldwater, Rep., 118,701.

1968, Nixon, Rep., 169,254; Humphrey, Dem., 217,312; Wallace, 3d Party, 6,370.

1972, Nixon, Rep., 256,458; McGovern, Dem., 160,584; scattered, 229.

1976, Carter, Dem., 232,279; Ford, Rep., 236,320; McCarthy, Ind., 10,874; Bubar, Proh., 3,495.

1980, Reagan, Rep., 238,522; Carter, Dem., 220,974; Anderson, Ind., 53,327; Clark, Libertarian, 5,119; Commoner, Citizens, 4,394; Hall, Com., 591; write-ins, 84.

1984, Reagan, Rep., 336,500; Mondale, Dem., 214,515.

1988, Bush, Rep., 307,131; Dukakis, Dem., 243,569; Paul, Lib., 2,700; Fulani, New Alliance, 1,405.

1992, Clinton, Dem., 263,420; Perot, Ind., 206,820; Bush, Rep., 206,504; Marrou, Libertarian, 1,681.

1996, Clinton, Dem., 326,217; Dole, Rep., 190,711; Perot, Ref., 88,082; Nader, Green, 14,508; Browne, Libertarian, 2,867; Phillips, Taxpayers, 1,458; Hagelin, Natural Law, 800.

# Maryland

| County | 1996 Clinton (D) | 1996 Dole (R) | 1996 Perot (RF) | 1992 Clinton (D) | 1992 Bush (R) | 1992 Perot (I) |
|---|---|---|---|---|---|---|
| Allegany | 10,570 | 11,659 | 2,653 | 11,501 | 13,862 | 5,081 |
| Anne Arundel | 69,417 | 80,063 | 14,023 | 68,629 | 81,467 | 35,191 |
| Baltimore | 128,142 | 110,096 | 20,148 | 143,498 | 126,728 | 51,757 |
| Calvert | 9,606 | 11,064 | 1,899 | 8,619 | 10,026 | 4,499 |
| Caroline | 3,133 | 3,740 | 927 | 2,822 | 3,856 | 1,729 |
| Carroll | 16,402 | 29,201 | 4,818 | 15,447 | 28,405 | 10,965 |
| Cecil | 9,797 | 10,428 | 3,080 | 10,232 | 10,784 | 6,115 |
| Charles | 15,293 | 16,678 | 2,300 | 14,498 | 17,293 | 6,501 |
| Dorchester | 4,434 | 4,147 | 994 | 3,933 | 4,934 | 2,010 |
| Frederick | 24,110 | 33,295 | 4,917 | 21,848 | 31,290 | 11,373 |
| Garrett | 2,920 | 5,115 | 1,167 | 2,856 | 5,714 | 1,987 |
| Harford | 28,594 | 38,029 | 7,825 | 27,164 | 36,350 | 17,002 |
| Howard | 44,889 | 38,764 | 5,826 | 44,763 | 38,594 | 16,182 |
| Kent | 3,041 | 2,865 | 661 | 3,093 | 3,094 | 1,411 |
| Montgomery | 188,243 | 111,699 | 14,080 | 199,757 | 119,705 | 41,971 |
| Prince George's | 171,091 | 50,498 | 8,962 | 168,691 | 62,955 | 23,355 |
| Queen Anne's | 4,822 | 6,814 | 1,294 | 4,668 | 6,829 | 2,958 |

| County | 1996 Clinton (D) | 1996 Dole (R) | 1996 Perot (RF) | 1992 Clinton (D) | 1992 Bush (R) | 1992 Perot (I) |
|---|---|---|---|---|---|---|
| St. Mary's . | 9,494 | 11,237 | 1,786 | 8,931 | 11,485 | 4,550 |
| Somerset . | 3,420 | 2,811 | 604 | 3,210 | 3,450 | 1,230 |
| Talbot . . . | 4,586 | 6,556 | 891 | 4,642 | 6,774 | 2,233 |
| Washington | 15,689 | 20,431 | 3,868 | 16,495 | 21,977 | 7,537 |
| Wicomico . | 11,855 | 12,187 | 2,127 | 11,481 | 13,560 | 5,140 |
| Worcester. | 7,144 | 7,075 | 1,563 | 6,040 | 7,237 | 3,256 |
| **City** | | | | | | |
| Baltimore . . | 137,592 | 27,230 | 7,271 | 185,753 | 40,725 | 17,381 |
| **Totals . . . .** | **924,284** | **651,682** | **113,684** | **988,571** | **707,094** | **281,414** |

## Maryland Vote Since 1948

1948, Truman, Dem., 286,521; Dewey, Rep., 294,814; Wallace, Prog., 9,983; Thomas, Soc., 2,941; Thurmond, States' Rights, 2,476; Wright, write-in, 2,294.

1952, Eisenhower, Rep., 499,424; Stevenson, Dem., 395,337; Hallinan, Prog., 7,313.

1956, Eisenhower, Rep., 559,738; Stevenson, Dem., 372,613.

1960, Kennedy, Dem., 565,800; Nixon, Rep., 489,538.

1964, Johnson, Dem., 730,912; Goldwater, Rep., 385,495; write-in, 50.

1968, Nixon, Rep., 517,995; Humphrey, Dem., 538,310; Wallace, 3d Party, 178,734.

1972, Nixon, Rep., 829,305; McGovern, Dem., 505,781; Schmitz, Amer., 18,726.

1976, Carter, Dem., 759,612; Ford, Rep., 672,661.

1980, Reagan, Rep., 680,606; Carter, Dem., 726,161; Anderson, Ind., 119,537; Clark, Libertarian, 14,192.

1984, Reagan, Rep., 879,918; Mondale, Dem., 787,935; Bergland, Libertarian, 5,721.

1988, Bush, Rep., 876,167; Dukakis, Dem., 826,304; Paul, Lib., 6,748; Fulani, New Alliance, 5,115.

1992, Clinton, Dem., 988,571; Bush, Rep., 707,094; Perot, Ind., 281,414; Marrou, Libertarian, 4,715; Fulani, New Alliance, 2,786.

1996, Clinton, Dem., 924,284; Dole, Rep., 651,682; Perot, Ref., 113,684; Browne, Libertarian, 9,018; Phillips, Taxpayers, 3,275; Hagelin, Natural Law, 2,299.

# Massachusetts

| City | 1996 Clinton (D) | 1996 Dole (R) | 1996 Perot (RF) | 1992 Clinton (D) | 1992 Bush (R) | 1992 Perot (I) |
|---|---|---|---|---|---|---|
| Boston . . . | 123,844 | 32,993 | 8,384 | 114,260 | 41,868 | 25,189 |
| Brockton . . | 16,185 | 6,920 | 2,715 | 13,209 | 8,863 | 7,579 |
| Cambridge | 29,913 | 4,976 | 1,415 | 30,737 | 5,847 | 4,106 |
| Fall River . | 22,796 | 4,287 | 2,612 | 18,652 | 5,456 | 6,922 |
| Framingham . | 22,796 | 4,287 | 2,612 | 15,165 | 8,114 | 6,089 |
| Lawrence . | 16,630 | 6,594 | 1,685 | 7,698 | 5,079 | 3,245 |
| Lowell . . . | 8,613 | 2,804 | 1,096 | 14,492 | 8,467 | 8,893 |
| Lynn. . . . . | 16,908 | 5,891 | 2,911 | 15,275 | 7,350 | 7,665 |
| New Bedford. | 23,604 | 4,148 | 2,547 | 20,880 | 5,255 | 6,965 |
| Newton. . . | 29,991 | 8,497 | 1,674 | 29,136 | 9,623 | 5,685 |
| Quincy . . . | 23,172 | 9,819 | 3,064 | 18,891 | 12,306 | 9,068 |
| Somerville. | 20,171 | 3,981 | 1,455 | 19,792 | 5,883 | 4,416 |
| Springfield. | 31,235 | 9,107 | 3,403 | 27,302 | 12,200 | 10,361 |
| Worcester. | 35,296 | 12,767 | 3,894 | 32,326 | 17,228 | 10,488 |
| Other . . . . | 1,111,763 | 576,795 | 180,058 | 940,824 | 651,500 | 514,060 |
| **Totals . . .** | **1,532,917** | **693,866** | **219,525** | **1,318,639** | **805,039** | **630,731** |

## Massachusetts Vote Since 1948

1948, Truman, Dem., 1,151,788; Dewey, Rep., 909,370; Wallace, Prog., 38,157; Teichert, Soc. Labor, 5,535; Watson, Proh., 1,663.

1952, Eisenhower, Rep., 1,292,325; Stevenson, Dem., 1,083,525; Hallinan, Prog., 4,636; Hass, Soc. Labor, 1,957; Hamblen, Proh., 886; scattered, 69; blanks, 41,150.

1956, Eisenhower, Rep., 1,393,197; Stevenson, Dem., 948,190; Hass, Soc. Labor, 5,573; Holtwick, Proh., 1,205; others, 341.

1960, Kennedy, Dem., 1,487,174; Nixon, Rep., 976,750; Hass, Soc. Labor, 3,892; Decker, Proh., 1,633; others, 31; blank and void, 26,024.

1964, Johnson, Dem., 1,786,422; Goldwater, Rep., 549,727; Hass, Soc. Labor, 4,755; Munn, Proh., 3,735; scattered, 159; blank, 48,104.

1968, Nixon, Rep., 766,844; Humphrey, Dem., 1,469,218; Wallace, 3d Party, 87,088; Blomen, Soc. Labor, 6,180; Munn, Proh., 2,369; scattered, 53; blanks, 25,394.

1972, Nixon, Rep., 1,112,078; McGovern, Dem., 1,332,540; Jenness, Soc. Workers, 10,600; Fisher, Soc. Labor, 129; Schmitz, Amer., 2,877; Spock, Peoples, 101; Hall, Com., 46; Hospers, Libertarian, 43; scattered, 342.

1976, Carter, Dem., 1,429,475; Ford, Rep., 1,030,276; McCarthy, Ind., 65,637; Camejo, Soc. Workers, 8,138; Anderson, Amer., 7,555; La Rouche, U.S. Labor, 4,922; MacBride, Libertarian, 135.

1980, Reagan, Rep., 1,057,631; Carter, Dem., 1,053,802; Anderson, Ind., 382,539; Clark, Libertarian, 22,038; DeBerry, Soc. Workers, 3,735; Commoner, Citizens, 2,056; McReynolds, Soc., 62; Bubar, Statesman, 34; Griswold, Workers World, 19; scattered, 2,382.

1984, Reagan, Rep., 1,310,936; Mondale, Dem., 1,239,606.

1988, Bush, Rep., 1,194,635; Dukakis, Dem., 1,401,415; Paul, Lib., 24,251; Fulani, New Alliance, 9,561.

1992, Clinton, Dem., 1,318,639; Bush, Rep., 805,039; Perot, Ind., 630,731; Marrou, Libertarian, 9,021; Fulani, New Alliance, 3,172; Phillips, U.S. Taxpayers, 2,218; Hagelin, Natural Law, 1,812; LaRouche, Ind., 1,027.

1996, Clinton, Dem., 1,532,917; Dole, Rep., 693,866; Perot, Ref., 219,525; Browne, Libertarian, 20,720; Hagelin, Natural Law, 5,202; Moorehead, Workers World, 3,276.

# Michigan

| County | 1996 Clinton (D) | 1996 Dole (R) | 1996 Perot (RF) | 1992 Clinton (D) | 1992 Bush (R) | 1992 Perot (I) |
|---|---|---|---|---|---|---|
| Alcona . . . | 2,619 | 2,227 | 669 | 2,383 | 2,247 | 1,117 |
| Alger . . . . | 2,229 | 1,429 | 537 | 2,144 | 1,471 | 941 |
| Allegan. . . | 14,395 | 20,874 | 3,205 | 12,823 | 19,077 | 8,742 |
| Alpena . . . | 7,114 | 4,525 | 1,730 | 6,894 | 4,878 | 3,236 |
| Antrim . . . | 4,226 | 4,630 | 1,129 | 3,431 | 3,984 | 2,528 |
| Arenac. . . | 3,472 | 2,247 | 844 | 3,244 | 2,330 | 1,608 |
| Baraga. . . | 1,601 | 1,209 | 460 | 1,695 | 1,160 | 754 |
| Barry . . . . | 10,049 | 11,049 | 2,312 | 8,652 | 9,489 | 6,303 |
| Bay . . . . . | 27,796 | 16,024 | 5,404 | 26,492 | 16,383 | 11,258 |
| Benzie . . . | 3,081 | 2,856 | 763 | 2,715 | 2,438 | 1,657 |
| Berrien. . . | 24,326 | 27,836 | 5,843 | 25,840 | 29,252 | 14,056 |
| Branch. . . | 6,592 | 6,332 | 1,769 | 5,850 | 5,976 | 4,683 |
| Calhoun . . | 26,285 | 21,053 | 4,765 | 25,542 | 19,791 | 13,058 |
| Cass . . . . | 8,269 | 7,412 | 2,250 | 8,047 | 7,391 | 4,756 |
| Charlevoix | 4,689 | 4,864 | 1,303 | 4,063 | 4,017 | 3,360 |
| Cheboygan | 5,018 | 4,244 | 1,462 | 4,459 | 3,864 | 2,495 |
| Chippewa . | 11,679 | 5,146 | 1,455 | 5,434 | 5,462 | 2,706 |
| Clare . . . . | 6,311 | 3,741 | 1,530 | 5,346 | 3,916 | 2,812 |
| Clinton . . . | 11,944 | 13,690 | 2,697 | 10,116 | 12,216 | 7,877 |
| Crawford . | 2,666 | 2,157 | 840 | 2,252 | 2,193 | 1,442 |
| Delta . . . . | 8,291 | 5,953 | 1,531 | 8,387 | 6,027 | 3,485 |
| Dickinson . | 5,614 | 4,408 | 1,478 | 5,689 | 4,273 | 3,022 |
| Eaton. . . . | 19,800 | 20,128 | 4,354 | 16,752 | 18,669 | 12,208 |
| Emmet. . . | 4,892 | 6,002 | 1,512 | 4,245 | 5,312 | 3,576 |
| Genesee . | 106,065 | 49,332 | 17,671 | 105,156 | 47,834 | 46,259 |
| Gladwin . . | 5,494 | 3,670 | 1,466 | 4,457 | 3,616 | 2,649 |
| Gogebic . . | 4,436 | 2,769 | 917 | 4,792 | 2,838 | 1,543 |
| Grand Traverse . | 12,983 | 16,342 | 3,523 | 11,148 | 13,629 | 9,495 |
| Gratiot . . . | 6,751 | 6,129 | 1,761 | 5,678 | 6,280 | 3,866 |
| Hillsdale . . | 5,955 | 7,947 | 2,262 | 5,244 | 7,579 | 4,968 |
| Houghton . | 5,957 | 5,941 | 1,571 | 6,558 | 5,575 | 2,945 |
| Huron . . . | 6,827 | 6,126 | 1,778 | 6,023 | 6,491 | 4,064 |
| Ingham. . . | 63,646 | 43,114 | 8,645 | 61,596 | 43,926 | 27,683 |
| Ionia . . . . | 9,261 | 9,574 | 2,354 | 8,370 | 9,135 | 6,211 |
| Iosco . . . . | 6,240 | 4,410 | 1,710 | 5,369 | 4,912 | 3,131 |
| Iron . . . . . | 3,232 | 2,014 | 755 | 3,648 | 1,971 | 1,344 |
| Isabella . . | 9,635 | 7,460 | 2,069 | 8,784 | 7,706 | 5,434 |
| Jackson . . | 21,598 | 21,050 | 5,131 | 23,686 | 25,424 | 15,194 |
| Kalamazoo | 45,226 | 40,313 | 5,803 | 43,568 | 38,035 | 21,666 |
| Kalkaska . | 2,523 | 2,346 | 869 | 2,297 | 2,173 | 1,915 |
| Kent . . . . | 85,758 | 121,119 | 14,102 | 82,305 | 115,285 | 43,707 |
| Keweenaw | 572 | 491 | 169 | 582 | 378 | 212 |
| Lake . . . . | 2,606 | 1,213 | 552 | 2,351 | 1,194 | 981 |
| Lapeer . . . | 14,308 | 13,369 | 4,793 | 11,982 | 12,326 | 10,541 |
| Leelanau . | 4,019 | 5,155 | 924 | 3,445 | 3,993 | 2,685 |
| Lenawee . | 14,978 | 12,632 | 3,628 | 15,399 | 14,297 | 9,517 |
| Livingston. | 18,150 | 25,965 | 5,137 | 17,851 | 27,539 | 15,971 |
| Luce . . . . | 1,112 | 967 | 366 | 972 | 958 | 660 |
| Mackinac . | 2,782 | 2,284 | 742 | 2,293 | 2,278 | 1,379 |
| Macomb . . | 120,167 | 97,352 | 24,697 | 130,732 | 147,795 | 67,954 |
| Manistee . | 5,383 | 3,807 | 1,280 | 5,193 | 3,491 | 2,923 |
| Marquette. | 15,168 | 8,805 | 2,492 | 16,038 | 9,665 | 5,768 |
| Mason . . . | 5,597 | 5,066 | 1,525 | 4,829 | 5,102 | 3,096 |
| Mecosta . . | 6,364 | 5,288 | 1,372 | 6,097 | 6,047 | 3,612 |
| Menominee | 4,787 | 3,996 | 1,189 | 4,559 | 3,995 | 2,487 |
| Midland . . | 15,177 | 16,547 | 3,964 | 13,382 | 16,149 | 8,945 |
| Missaukee | 2,256 | 3,012 | 719 | 1,893 | 2,829 | 1,306 |
| Monroe . . | 26,072 | 19,678 | 6,315 | 24,957 | 20,250 | 13,551 |
| Montcalm . | 10,053 | 8,679 | 2,530 | 8,730 | 8,420 | 5,504 |
| Montmorency | 2,120 | 1,760 | 682 | 1,903 | 1,794 | 1,077 |
| Muskegon. | 34,534 | 21,415 | 5,544 | 32,515 | 23,769 | 15,268 |
| Newaygo . | 7,614 | 7,868 | 2,047 | 6,455 | 7,333 | 4,056 |
| Oakland . . | 240,838 | 219,468 | 36,630 | 214,733 | 242,160 | 94,911 |
| Oceana . . | 4,419 | 3,947 | 1,286 | 3,846 | 3,944 | 2,713 |
| Ogemaw. . | 4,725 | 2,904 | 1,369 | 4,016 | 2,936 | 2,122 |
| Ontonagon | 2,080 | 1,523 | 604 | 2,451 | 1,463 | 805 |
| Osceola . . | 4,085 | 3,855 | 1,078 | 3,529 | 3,606 | 2,199 |
| Oscoda . . | 1,652 | 1,545 | 503 | 1,471 | 1,583 | 755 |
| Otsego. . . | 3,460 | 3,785 | 1,298 | 3,129 | 3,393 | 2,635 |
| Ottawa. . . | 26,373 | 61,685 | 6,108 | 22,180 | 56,862 | 16,855 |

| County | 1996 Clinton (D) | 1996 Dole (R) | 1996 Perot (RF) | 1992 Clinton (D) | 1992 Bush (R) | 1992 Perot (I) |
|---|---|---|---|---|---|---|
| Presque Isle. | 3,449 | 2,463 | 932 | 3,308 | 2,398 | 1,612 |
| Roscommon. | 6,092 | 4,135 | 1,510 | 5,243 | 4,170 | 2,551 |
| Saginaw . . | 47,464 | 31,545 | 8,074 | 43,819 | 32,103 | 20,523 |
| St. Clair . . | 7,088 | 7,823 | 2,265 | 23,385 | 24,508 | 18,523 |
| St. Joseph | 2,192 | 1,203 | 461 | 7,817 | 9,836 | 6,209 |
| Sanilac. . . | 14,761 | 11,820 | 3,716 | 5,868 | 7,891 | 4,894 |
| Schoolcraft | 28,235 | 22,032 | 8,054 | 2,139 | 1,253 | 721 |
| Shiawassee | 8,530 | 9,764 | 2,319 | 12,629 | 10,930 | 8,632 |
| Tuscola . . | 10,314 | 9,154 | 2,986 | 9,138 | 8,636 | 6,765 |
| Van Buren | 13,350 | 11,347 | 2,942 | 12,466 | 10,357 | 7,255 |
| Washtenaw | 71,004 | 39,349 | 8,019 | 73,325 | 41,386 | 21,889 |
| Wayne . . . | 467,568 | 144,558 | 34,659 | 508,464 | 227,002 | 102,074 |
| Wexford . . | 5,510 | 4,866 | 1,386 | 4,894 | 4,696 | 2,923 |
| **Totals . . .** | **1,911,553** | **1,413,812** | **319,095** | **1,871,182** | **1,554,940** | **824,813** |

## Michigan Vote Since 1948

1948, Truman, Dem., 1,003,448; Dewey, Rep., 1,038,595; Wallace, Prog., 46,515; Watson, Proh., 13,052; Thomas, Soc., 6,063; Teichert, Soc. Labor, 1,263; Dobbs, Soc. Workers, 672.

1952, Eisenhower, Rep., 1,551,529; Stevenson, Dem., 1,230,657; Hamblen, Proh., 10,331; Hallinan, Prog., 3,922; Hass, Soc. Labor, 1,495; Dobbs, Soc. Workers, 655; scattered, 3.

1956, Eisenhower, Rep., 1,713,647; Stevenson, Dem., 1,359,898; Holtwick, Proh., 6,923.

1960, Kennedy, Dem., 1,687,269; Nixon, Rep., 1,620,428; Dobbs, Soc. Workers, 4,347; Decker, Proh., 2,029; Daly, Tax Cut, 1,767; Hass, Soc. Labor, 1,718; Ind. Amer., 539.

1964, Johnson, Dem., 2,136,615; Goldwater, Rep., 1,060,152; DeBerry, Soc. Workers, 3,817; Hass, Soc. Labor, 1,704; Proh. (no candidate listed), 699; scattering, 145.

1968, Nixon, Rep., 1,370,665; Humphrey, Dem., 1,593,082; Wallace, 3d Party, 331,968; Halstead, Soc. Workers, 4,099; Blomen, Soc. Labor, 1,762; Cleaver, New Politics, 4,585; Munn, Proh., 60; scattering, 29.

1972, Nixon, Rep., 1,961,721; McGovern, Dem., 1,459,435; Schmitz, Amer., 63,321; Fisher, Soc. Labor, 2,437; Jenness, Soc. Workers, 1,603; Hall, Com., 1,210.

1976, Carter, Dem., 1,696,714; Ford, Rep., 1,893,742; McCarthy, Ind., 47,905; MacBride, Libertarian, 5,406; Wright, People's, 3,504; Camejo, Soc. Workers, 1,804; LaRouche, U.S. Labor, 1,366; Levin, Soc. Labor, 1,148; scattering, 2,160.

1980, Reagan, Rep., 1,915,225; Carter, Dem., 1,661,532; Anderson, Ind., 275,223; Clark, Libertarian, 41,597; Commoner, Citizens, 11,930; Hall, Com., 3,262; Griswold, Workers World, 30; Greaves, Amer., 21; Bubar, Statesman, 9.

1984, Reagan, Rep., 2,251,571; Mondale, Dem., 1,529,638; Bergland, Libertarian, 10,055.

1988, Bush, Rep., 1,965,486; Dukakis, Dem., 1,675,783; Paul, Lib., 18,336; Fulani, Ind., 2,513.

1992, Clinton, Dem., 1,871,182; Bush, Rep., 1,554,940; Perot, Ind., 824,813; Marrou, Libertarian, 10,175; Phillips, U.S. Taxpayers, 8,263; Hagelin, Natural Law, 2,954.

1996, Clinton, Dem., 1,911,553; Dole, Rep., 1,413,812; Perot, Ref., 319,095; Browne, Libertarian, 26,459; Hagelin, Natural Law, 4,454; Moorehead, Workers World, 3,032; White, Soc. Equality, 1,547.

# Minnesota

| County | 1996 Clinton (D) | 1996 Dole (R) | 1996 Perot (RF) | 1992 Clinton (D) | 1992 Bush (R) | 1992 Perot (I) |
|---|---|---|---|---|---|---|
| Aitkin . . . . | 3,720 | 2,327 | 1,153 | 3,400 | 2,151 | 1,951 |
| Anoka . . . | 63,751 | 41,743 | 16,446 | 54,621 | 39,458 | 35,140 |
| Becker . . . | 5,911 | 5,461 | 1,813 | 4,958 | 5,430 | 3,238 |
| Beltrami . . | 7,775 | 5,628 | 1,586 | 7,210 | 5,204 | 3,473 |
| Benton . . . | 6,006 | 4,835 | 2,133 | 5,156 | 5,053 | 4,048 |
| Big Stone . | 1,619 | 990 | 368 | 1,610 | 1,052 | 740 |
| Blue Earth. | 12,227 | 8,941 | 3,231 | 11,531 | 8,813 | 7,299 |
| Brown . . . | 4,866 | 5,580 | 1,786 | 4,278 | 5,390 | 3,845 |
| Carlton . . . | 8,052 | 4,034 | 1,591 | 7,736 | 3,922 | 3,005 |
| Carver . . . | 11,554 | 12,380 | 3,781 | 8,349 | 10,201 | 7,942 |
| Cass . . . . | 5,437 | 4,794 | 1,620 | 4,901 | 4,276 | 2,939 |
| Chippewa . | 3,178 | 2,119 | 782 | 2,929 | 2,143 | 1,505 |
| Chisago . . | 8,611 | 5,984 | 2,812 | 7,077 | 4,813 | 5,098 |
| Clay. . . . . | 10,475 | 8,763 | 1,732 | 9,845 | 9,666 | 3,835 |
| Clearwater | 1,513 | 1,350 | 450 | 1,587 | 1,315 | 841 |
| Cook . . . . | 1,169 | 1,010 | 246 | 1,005 | 878 | 704 |
| Cottonwood | 2,737 | 2,633 | 741 | 2,382 | 2,481 | 1,749 |
| Crow Wing | 11,120 | 10,057 | 3,412 | 8,896 | 9,112 | 6,367 |
| Dakota . . . | 77,297 | 57,244 | 17,095 | 63,660 | 52,312 | 40,244 |
| Dodge . . . | 3,233 | 2,888 | 1,223 | 2,620 | 3,049 | 2,231 |
| Douglas . . | 6,450 | 6,747 | 2,091 | 5,252 | 6,356 | 4,138 |
| Faribault . . | 3,817 | 3,272 | 1,103 | 3,339 | 3,439 | 2,322 |
| Fillmore . . | 4,733 | 3,466 | 1,575 | 3,977 | 3,583 | 3,011 |
| Freeborn. . | 8,458 | 5,166 | 2,106 | 7,759 | 5,089 | 4,878 |
| Goodhue . | 9,930 | 7,293 | 2,806 | 7,916 | 7,321 | 5,790 |
| Grant. . . . | 1,806 | 1,284 | 434 | 1,561 | 1,201 | 885 |
| Hennepin . | 280,199 | 166,964 | 46,931 | 278,648 | 179,581 | 123,659 |
| Houston . . | 4,153 | 3,674 | 1,439 | 3,744 | 3,853 | 2,697 |
| Hubbard . . | 3,802 | 3,593 | 1,141 | 3,362 | 3,227 | 1,949 |
| Isanti . . . . | 6,041 | 4,451 | 2,242 | 5,386 | 3,988 | 3,898 |
| Itasca. . . . | 10,705 | 6,502 | 2,885 | 9,621 | 5,952 | 5,147 |
| Jackson . . | 2,727 | 2,153 | 908 | 2,481 | 1,824 | 1,918 |
| Kanabec. . | 2,927 | 1,924 | 996 | 2,532 | 1,876 | 1,836 |
| Kandiyohi . | 9,009 | 7,119 | 2,229 | 7,914 | 6,784 | 4,869 |
| Kittson . . . | 1,394 | 1,055 | 270 | 1,307 | 1,098 | 558 |
| Koochiching | 3,472 | 2,080 | 1,098 | 3,474 | 1,954 | 1,993 |
| LacQuiParle | 2,420 | 1,447 | 561 | 2,342 | 1,435 | 1,163 |
| Lake . . . . | 3,383 | 1,682 | 750 | 3,415 | 1,465 | 1,437 |
| Lake of the Woods . . | 888 | 814 | 287 | 794 | 762 | 629 |
| Le Sueur. . | 5,457 | 3,902 | 1,699 | 4,662 | 3,858 | 3,363 |
| Lincoln . . . | 1,641 | 1,199 | 504 | 1,555 | 1,084 | 967 |
| Lyon . . . . | 5,062 | 4,932 | 1,351 | 4,481 | 4,591 | 3,180 |
| McLeod . . | 6,025 | 5,473 | 2,401 | 4,919 | 5,422 | 4,933 |
| Mahnomen | 1,026 | 877 | 270 | 1,035 | 854 | 483 |
| Marshall . . | 2,333 | 2,068 | 720 | 2,309 | 2,136 | 1,306 |
| Martin . . . | 4,718 | 4,303 | 1,405 | 4,019 | 4,438 | 3,089 |
| Meeker. . . | 4,532 | 3,428 | 1,572 | 3,861 | 3,497 | 3,120 |
| Mille Lacs . | 4,336 | 2,948 | 1,467 | 3,648 | 2,814 | 2,615 |
| Morrison . . | 5,729 | 5,055 | 2,310 | 5,588 | 5,038 | 3,710 |
| Mower . . . | 10,413 | 4,994 | 2,464 | 9,935 | 5,147 | 5,001 |
| Murray . . . | 2,174 | 1,907 | 753 | 1,993 | 1,609 | 1,588 |
| Nicollet. . . | 6,772 | 5,057 | 1,737 | 6,055 | 5,091 | 3,799 |
| Nobles . . . | 4,106 | 3,769 | 1,132 | 3,756 | 3,548 | 2,586 |
| Norman . . | 1,875 | 1,392 | 425 | 1,784 | 1,541 | 776 |
| Olmsted . . | 22,818 | 22,804 | 5,636 | 19,039 | 23,404 | 13,806 |
| Otter Tail . | 10,519 | 11,808 | 3,191 | 9,176 | 11,074 | 6,274 |
| Pennington | 2,814 | 2,129 | 910 | 2,578 | 2,155 | 1,598 |
| Pine. . . . . | 5,432 | 3,080 | 1,597 | 4,929 | 2,841 | 2,952 |
| Pipestone . | 1,999 | 2,096 | 599 | 1,773 | 1,953 | 1,429 |
| Polk. . . . . | 6,369 | 5,563 | 1,502 | 5,850 | 5,817 | 3,176 |
| Pope . . . . | 2,803 | 1,992 | 665 | 2,619 | 1,886 | 1,390 |
| Ramsey . . | 134,716 | 67,433 | 20,581 | 130,932 | 68,206 | 50,757 |
| Red Lake . | 1,053 | 695 | 334 | 1,020 | 691 | 472 |
| Redwood . | 2,997 | 3,700 | 1,053 | 2,740 | 3,408 | 2,710 |
| Renville . . | 3,957 | 2,889 | 1,314 | 3,414 | 2,852 | 2,598 |
| Rice. . . . . | 12,821 | 7,016 | 2,876 | 10,908 | 7,015 | 6,057 |
| Rock . . . . | 2,143 | 2,170 | 555 | 2,006 | 2,065 | 1,244 |
| Roseau . . | 2,759 | 2,988 | 1,081 | 2,346 | 2,785 | 2,099 |
| St. Louis. . | 41,318 | 18,040 | 7,393 | 61,813 | 24,579 | 21,714 |
| Scott . . . . | 14,657 | 12,734 | 4,886 | 11,225 | 10,936 | 9,881 |
| Sherburne. | 10,551 | 8,699 | 3,665 | 7,843 | 7,339 | 6,534 |
| Sibley. . . . | 2,767 | 2,591 | 1,226 | 2,421 | 2,315 | 2,407 |
| Stearns . . | 24,238 | 21,474 | 8,150 | 21,451 | 22,502 | 14,834 |
| Steele . . . | 6,961 | 5,615 | 2,189 | 5,152 | 5,964 | 4,542 |
| Stevens . . | 2,741 | 2,141 | 467 | 2,466 | 2,229 | 1,086 |
| Swift . . . . | 3,054 | 1,541 | 690 | 2,980 | 1,603 | 1,359 |
| Todd . . . . | 4,520 | 4,078 | 1,958 | 4,059 | 3,990 | 2,976 |
| Traverse. . | 1,135 | 775 | 295 | 1,053 | 841 | 582 |
| Wabasha . | 4,523 | 3,452 | 1,474 | 3,736 | 3,397 | 3,012 |
| Wadena . . | 2,480 | 2,696 | 801 | 2,340 | 2,492 | 1,535 |
| Waseca . . | 3,820 | 3,171 | 1,385 | 3,146 | 3,118 | 2,621 |
| Washington | 45,118 | 31,219 | 10,105 | 35,820 | 26,568 | 22,585 |
| Watonwan. | 2,634 | 1,997 | 711 | 2,100 | 1,871 | 1,574 |
| Wilkin. . . . | 1,319 | 1,498 | 358 | 1,122 | 1,626 | 748 |
| Winona. . . | 10,272 | 7,956 | 2,908 | 9,707 | 8,585 | 5,993 |
| Wright . . . | 15,542 | 13,174 | 5,550 | 12,465 | 11,650 | 10,829 |
| Yellow Medicine | 2,741 | 2,006 | 818 | 2,593 | 1,909 | 1,645 |
| **Totals . . .** | **1,096,320** | **751,860** | **252,952** | **1,020,997** | **747,841** | **562,506** |

## Minnesota Vote Since 1948

1948, Truman, Dem., 692,966; Dewey, Rep., 483,617; Wallace, Prog., 27,866; Thomas, Soc., 4,646; Teichert, Soc. Labor, 2,525; Dobbs, Soc. Workers, 606.

1952, Eisenhower, Rep., 763,211; Stevenson, Dem., 608,458; Hallinan, Prog., 2,666; Hass, Soc. Labor, 2,383; Hamblen, Proh., 2,147; Dobbs, Soc. Workers, 618.

1956, Eisenhower, Rep., 719,302; Stevenson, Dem., 617,525; Hass, Soc. Labor (Ind. Gov.), 2,080; Dobbs, Soc. Workers, 1,098.

1960, Kennedy, Dem., 779,933; Nixon, Rep., 757,915; Dobbs, Soc. Workers, 3,077; Industrial Gov., 962.

1964, Johnson, Dem., 991,117; Goldwater, Rep., 559,624; DeBerry, Soc. Workers, 1,177; Hass, Industrial Gov., 2,544.

1968, Nixon, Rep., 658,643; Humphrey, Dem., 857,738; Wallace, 3d Party, 68,931; scattered, 2,443; Halstead, Soc. Workers, 808; Blomen, Ind. Gov't., 285; Mitchell, Com., 415; Cleaver, Peace, 935; McCarthy, write-in, 585; scattered, 170.

1972, Nixon, Rep., 898,269; McGovern, Dem., 802,346; Schmitz, Amer., 31,407; Spock, Peoples, 2,805; Fisher, Soc. Labor, 4,261; Jenness, Soc. Workers, 940; Hall, Com., 662; scattered, 962.

1976, Carter, Dem., 1,070,440; Ford, Rep., 819,395; McCarthy, Ind., 35,490; Anderson, Amer., 13,592; Camejo, Soc. Workers, 4,149; MacBride, Libertarian, 3,529; Hall, Com., 1,092.

1980, Reagan, Rep., 873,268; Carter, Dem., 954,173; Anderson, Ind., 174,997; Clark, Libertarian, 31,593; Commoner, Citizens, 8,406; Hall, Com., 1,117; DeBerry, Soc. Workers, 711; Griswold, Workers World, 698; McReynolds, Soc., 536; write-ins, 281.

1984, Reagan, Rep., 1,032,603; Mondale, Dem., 1,036,364; Bergland, Libertarian, 2,996.

1988, Bush, Rep., 962,337; Dukakis, Dem., 1,109,471; McCarthy, Minn. Prog., 5,403; Paul, Lib., 5,109.

1992, Clinton, Dem., 1,020,997; Bush, Rep., 747,841; Perot, Ind., 562,506; Marrou, Libertarian, 3,373; Gritz, Populist/America First, 3,363; Hagelin, Natural Law, 1,406.

1996, Clinton, Dem., 1,096,320; Dole, Rep., 751,860; Perot, Ref., 252,952; Nader, Green, 24,283; Browne, Libertarian, 7,974; Peron, Grass Roots, 4,798; Phillips, Taxpayers, 3,262; Hagelin, Natural Law, 1,749; Birrenbach, Ind. Grass Roots, 894; Harris, Soc. Workers, 681; White, Soc. Equality, 344.

## Mississippi

| County | 1996 Clinton (D) | 1996 Dole (R) | 1996 Perot (RF) | 1992 Clinton (D) | 1992 Bush (R) | 1992 Perot (I) |
|---|---|---|---|---|---|---|
| Adams . . . | 7,952 | 5,222 | 747 | 8,255 | 5,831 | 1,753 |
| Alcorn . . . | 5,191 | 4,950 | 918 | 6,373 | 6,249 | 1,349 |
| Amite. . . . | 2,818 | 2,512 | 351 | 2,608 | 2,561 | 498 |
| Attala. . . . | 3,052 | 3,087 | 379 | 3,015 | 3,520 | 529 |
| Benton . . . | 1,944 | 993 | 207 | 2,402 | 1,253 | 293 |
| Bolivar . . . | 8,387 | 3,998 | 306 | 8,801 | 4,752 | 593 |
| Calhoun . . | 1,967 | 2,378 | 323 | 2,462 | 3,191 | 607 |
| Carroll . . . | 2,041 | 2,629 | 245 | 1,182 | 1,695 | 200 |
| Chickasaw | 2,945 | 2,508 | 393 | 3,220 | 3,150 | 629 |
| Choctaw. . | 1,171 | 1,667 | 222 | 1,435 | 2,026 | 298 |
| Claiborne . | 3,666 | 784 | 103 | 3,302 | 935 | 161 |
| Clarke . . . | 2,315 | 3,457 | 365 | 2,259 | 4,207 | 450 |
| Clay. . . . . | 4,261 | 2,943 | 337 | 4,620 | 3,297 | 626 |
| Coahoma . | 5,663 | 3,413 | 252 | 6,409 | 4,120 | 518 |
| Copiah . . . | 4,387 | 4,123 | 372 | 4,397 | 4,600 | 409 |
| Covington . | 2,593 | 3,192 | 414 | 2,775 | 3,525 | 654 |
| DeSoto. . . | 10,282 | 18,135 | 2,399 | 8,833 | 16,104 | 2,569 |
| Forrest. . . | 7,897 | 11,197 | 1,090 | 8,333 | 12,432 | 1,909 |
| Franklin . . | 1,365 | 1,574 | 327 | 1,587 | 1,942 | 393 |
| George. . . | 1,885 | 3,302 | 708 | 2,650 | 4,141 | 1,335 |
| Greene. . . | 1,339 | 1,941 | 318 | 1,664 | 2,406 | 559 |
| Grenada. . | 4,379 | 4,500 | 467 | 4,203 | 4,721 | 609 |
| Hancock. . | 4,281 | 5,805 | 1,136 | 4,651 | 6,422 | 2,302 |
| Harrison . . | 18,414 | 25,036 | 3,647 | 15,268 | 25,049 | 6,855 |
| Hinds. . . . | 43,514 | 34,668 | 2,818 | 43,434 | 45,031 | 5,341 |
| Holmes . . | 4,572 | 1,517 | 139 | 4,092 | 1,694 | 203 |
| Humphreys | 2,303 | 1,381 | 110 | 2,696 | 1,721 | 258 |
| Issaquena. | 544 | 269 | 42 | 550 | 298 | 79 |
| Itawamba . | 2,982 | 3,474 | 731 | 3,635 | 4,142 | 918 |
| Jackson . . | 13,239 | 24,274 | 2,853 | 13,017 | 25,321 | 6,484 |
| Jasper . . . | 3,109 | 2,600 | 351 | 3,059 | 2,789 | 568 |
| Jefferson . | 2,525 | 489 | 89 | 2,796 | 562 | 156 |
| Jefferson Davis . . . | 2,660 | 1,890 | 263 | 2,991 | 2,228 | 382 |
| Jones. . . . | 7,347 | 13,015 | 1,361 | 8,035 | 13,824 | 2,523 |
| Kemper . . | 2,035 | 1,524 | 188 | 2,243 | 1,830 | 278 |
| Lafayette . | 4,646 | 4,753 | 580 | 5,224 | 5,251 | 861 |
| Lamar . . . | 3,154 | 8,558 | 919 | 3,208 | 8,259 | 1,543 |
| Lauderdale | 8,626 | 15,015 | 1,024 | 8,489 | 17,098 | 1,659 |
| Lawrence . | 2,464 | 2,384 | 470 | 2,582 | 2,689 | 765 |
| Leake. . . . | 2,902 | 3,017 | 407 | 3,333 | 3,943 | 497 |
| Lee . . . . . | 8,237 | 11,508 | 1,318 | 7,710 | 12,231 | 2,041 |
| Leflore . . . | 6,791 | 4,219 | 225 | 6,374 | 5,298 | 611 |
| Lincoln . . . | 4,255 | 5,914 | 778 | 4,744 | 7,040 | 1,281 |
| Lowndes. . | 6,105 | 9,022 | 733 | 6,552 | 10,509 | 1,716 |
| Madison . . | 8,948 | 13,836 | 745 | 9,386 | 12,810 | 1,478 |
| Marion . . . | 4,270 | 4,954 | 576 | 4,654 | 5,776 | 1,162 |
| Marshall . . | 7,285 | 3,141 | 478 | 7,913 | 3,847 | 689 |
| Monroe. . . | 5,151 | 5,191 | 887 | 4,933 | 5,994 | 1,255 |
| Montgomery. | 1,946 | 1,918 | 192 | 2,076 | 2,324 | 370 |
| Neshoba. . | 2,637 | 4,527 | 539 | 3,090 | 6,135 | 794 |
| Newton. . . | 2,163 | 4,223 | 464 | 2,146 | 5,128 | 494 |
| Noxubee. . | 2,753 | 1,267 | 130 | 3,188 | 1,623 | 203 |
| Oktibbeha. | 5,867 | 6,099 | 388 | 5,726 | 6,381 | 984 |
| Panola . . . | 5,359 | 3,683 | 509 | 6,066 | 4,644 | 729 |
| Pearl River | 4,796 | 8,044 | 1,150 | 4,683 | 7,726 | 2,352 |
| Perry . . . . | 1,379 | 2,146 | 443 | 1,490 | 2,538 | 462 |
| Pike. . . . . | 6,233 | 5,310 | 662 | 6,279 | 6,005 | 1,380 |
| Pontotoc. . | 2,582 | 4,275 | 771 | 2,965 | 4,595 | 777 |
| Prentiss . . | 3,036 | 3,453 | 570 | 3,385 | 4,317 | 781 |
| Quitman . . | 2,174 | 1,119 | 125 | 2,422 | 1,451 | 210 |
| Rankin . . . | 8,614 | 24,585 | 2,093 | 8,155 | 24,537 | 3,454 |
| Scott . . . . | 3,150 | 4,004 | 461 | 3,349 | 5,268 | 691 |
| Sharkey . . | 1,557 | 904 | 69 | 1,526 | 1,008 | 145 |
| Simpson. . | 2,851 | 4,455 | 525 | 3,213 | 5,358 | 726 |
| Smith. . . . | 1,858 | 3,371 | 522 | 1,968 | 4,106 | 680 |
| Stone. . . . | 1,546 | 2,279 | 416 | 1,447 | 2,295 | 447 |
| Sunflower . | 4,879 | 2,898 | 288 | 5,050 | 3,726 | 600 |
| Tallahatchie | 2,907 | 1,669 | 255 | 2,902 | 2,213 | 380 |
| Tate. . . . . | 3,195 | 3,694 | 406 | 3,519 | 4,196 | 634 |
| Tippah . . . | 2,978 | 3,235 | 656 | 3,475 | 4,444 | 802 |
| Tishomingo | 2,678 | 2,749 | 604 | 3,910 | 3,393 | 751 |
| Tunica . . . | 1,244 | 556 | 52 | 1,451 | 693 | 96 |
| Union. . . . | 3,308 | 4,365 | 785 | 3,714 | 5,173 | 816 |
| Walthall . . | 2,240 | 2,238 | 441 | 2,476 | 2,728 | 711 |
| Warren. . . | 8,470 | 9,093 | 1,225 | 8,175 | 10,209 | 2,146 |
| Washington | 9,876 | 6,661 | 428 | 10,588 | 7,598 | 795 |
| Wayne . . . | 2,613 | 3,191 | 584 | 3,064 | 3,874 | 824 |
| Webster . . | 1,362 | 2,228 | 252 | 1,746 | 2,791 | 444 |
| Wilkinson . | 275 | 1,012 | 226 | 3,210 | 1,399 | 307 |
| Winston . . | 3,434 | 3,470 | 429 | 3,953 | 4,311 | 688 |
| Yalobusha | 2,437 | 1,711 | 332 | 2,617 | 2,179 | 438 |
| Yazoo . . . | 4,749 | 4,156 | 397 | 4,880 | 5,113 | 669 |
| **Totals . . .** | **385,005** | **434,547** | **51,500** | **400,258** | **487,793** | **85,626** |

## Mississippi Vote Since 1948

1948, Thurmond, States' Rights, 167,538; Truman, Dem., 19,384; Dewey, Rep., 5,043; Wallace, Prog., 225.

1952, Eisenhower, Ind. vote pledged to Rep. candidate, 112,966; Stevenson, Dem., 172,566.

1956, Eisenhower, Rep., 56,372; Stevenson, Dem., 144,498; Black and Tan Grand Old Party, 4,313; total, 60,685; Byrd, Ind., 42,966.

1960, Kennedy, Dem., 108,362; Democratic unpledged electors, 116,248; Nixon, Rep., 73,561. Mississippi's victorious slate of 8 unpledged Democratic electors cast their votes for Sen. Harry F. Byrd (D, VA).

1964, Johnson, Dem., 52,618; Goldwater, Rep., 356,528.

1968, Nixon, Rep., 88,516; Humphrey, Dem., 150,644; Wallace, 3d Party, 415,349.

1972, Nixon, Rep., 505,125; McGovern, Dem., 126,782; Schmitz, Amer., 11,598; Jenness, Soc. Workers, 2,458.

1976, Carter, Dem., 381,309; Ford, Rep., 366,846; Anderson, Amer., 6,678; McCarthy, Ind., 4,074; Maddox, Ind., 4,049; Camejo, Soc. Workers, 2,805; MacBride, Libertarian, 2,609.

1980, Reagan, Rep., 441,089; Carter, Dem., 429,281; Anderson, Ind., 12,036; Clark, Libertarian, 5,465; Griswold, Workers World, 2,402; Pulley, Soc. Workers, 2,347.

1984, Reagan, Rep., 582,377; Mondale, Dem., 352,192; Bergland, Libertarian, 2,336.

1988, Bush, Rep., 557,890; Dukakis, Dem., 363,921; Duke, Ind., 4,232; Paul, Lib., 3,329.

1992, Bush, Rep., 487,793; Clinton, Dem., 400,258; Perot, Ind., 85,626; Fulani, New Alliance, 2,625; Marrou, Libertarian, 2,154; Phillips, U.S. Taxpayers, 1,652; Hagelin, Natural Law, 1,140.

1996, Dole, Rep., 434,547; Clinton, Dem., 385,005; Perot, Ind. (Ref.), 51,500; Browne, Libertarian, 2,750; Phillips, Taxpayers, 2,331; Hagelin, Natural Law, 1,424; Collins, Ind., 1,224.

## Missouri

| County | 1996 Clinton (D) | 1996 Dole (R) | 1996 Perot (RF) | 1992 Clinton (D) | 1992 Bush (R) | 1992 Perot (I) |
|---|---|---|---|---|---|---|
| Adair . . . . | 4,441 | 4,656 | 1,170 | 4,232 | 4,141 | 2,224 |
| Andrew . . | 2,807 | 3,281 | 964 | 2,675 | 2,652 | 2,151 |
| Atchison. . | 1,266 | 1,327 | 367 | 1,208 | 1,140 | 840 |
| Audrain . . | 4,690 | 3,955 | 1,046 | 4,731 | 3,798 | 2,099 |
| Barry . . . . | 4,352 | 5,855 | 1,494 | 4,791 | 5,565 | 2,381 |
| Barton . . . | 1,625 | 2,812 | 563 | 1,433 | 2,775 | 971 |
| Bates. . . . | 3,222 | 2,903 | 948 | 2,993 | 2,499 | 2,225 |
| Benton . . . | 2,996 | 2,895 | 764 | 3,195 | 2,511 | 1,551 |
| Bollinger. . | 2,044 | 2,420 | 506 | 2,150 | 2,289 | 909 |
| Boone . . . | 24,986 | 22,047 | 4,080 | 26,176 | 19,405 | 12,040 |
| Buchanan. | 15,848 | 12,610 | 4,248 | 16,570 | 11,275 | 9,404 |
| Butler. . . . | 5,780 | 6,996 | 1,414 | 6,602 | 6,450 | 2,189 |
| Caldwell . . | 1,487 | 1,464 | 468 | 1,456 | 1,295 | 1,283 |
| Callaway . | 5,880 | 5,567 | 1,530 | 5,799 | 4,880 | 3,266 |
| Camden . . | 5,566 | 7,190 | 1,809 | 5,140 | 5,554 | 3,891 |
| Cape Girardeau | 9,948 | 15,552 | 1,861 | 9,605 | 13,464 | 5,199 |
| Carroll . . . | 2,080 | 1,839 | 580 | 2,100 | 1,774 | 1,495 |
| Carter . . . | 1,172 | 1,180 | 301 | 1,169 | 1,101 | 405 |
| Cass . . . . | 11,743 | 13,495 | 3,474 | 10,246 | 10,349 | 9,216 |
| Cedar . . . | 2,027 | 2,484 | 658 | 2,064 | 2,085 | 1,173 |
| Chariton . . | 2,072 | 1,512 | 423 | 2,141 | 1,378 | 1,067 |
| Christian. . | 6,627 | 9,477 | 2,301 | 6,242 | 7,422 | 3,422 |
| Clark . . . . | 1,749 | 1,081 | 458 | 1,815 | 1,039 | 725 |
| Clay. . . . . | 32,559 | 28,901 | 7,033 | 30,565 | 23,798 | 20,951 |
| Clinton . . . | 3,445 | 2,780 | 848 | 3,400 | 2,391 | 2,423 |
| Cole . . . . | 10,862 | 16,139 | 2,121 | 10,201 | 15,270 | 5,770 |
| Cooper. . . | 2,753 | 2,900 | 891 | 2,709 | 2,867 | 1,735 |
| Crawford . | 3,349 | 2,990 | 1,223 | 3,515 | 2,831 | 2,002 |
| Dade . . . . | 1,243 | 1,822 | 447 | 1,332 | 1,577 | 834 |
| Dallas . . . | 2,277 | 2,554 | 787 | 2,533 | 2,116 | 1,392 |
| Daviess . . | 1,534 | 1,321 | 466 | 1,477 | 1,107 | 1,143 |

| County | 1996 Clinton (D) | 1996 Dole (R) | 1996 Perot (RF) | 1992 Clinton (D) | 1992 Bush (R) | 1992 Perot (I) |
|---|---|---|---|---|---|---|
| DeKalb. . . | 1,675 | 1,626 | 492 | 1,630 | 1,318 | 1,207 |
| Dent . . . . | 2,234 | 2,539 | 693 | 2,689 | 2,125 | 1,049 |
| Douglas . . | 1,744 | 2,601 | 775 | 2,126 | 2,569 | 1,081 |
| Dunklin. . . | 5,428 | 3,766 | 934 | 6,277 | 4,024 | 1,166 |
| Franklin . . | 13,908 | 13,715 | 5,517 | 13,431 | 11,477 | 11,043 |
| Gasconade | 2,104 | 2,997 | 820 | 1,952 | 2,690 | 1,672 |
| Gentry . . . | 1,492 | 1,361 | 416 | 1,519 | 1,272 | 921 |
| Greene. . . | 39,300 | 48,193 | 8,569 | 41,137 | 46,457 | 17,770 |
| Grundy. . . | 2,073 | 1,883 | 631 | 1,968 | 1,749 | 1,372 |
| Harrison . . | 1,628 | 1,737 | 404 | 1,590 | 1,563 | 1,059 |
| Henry. . . . | 4,574 | 3,257 | 1,230 | 4,232 | 2,681 | 2,807 |
| Hickory. . . | 1,858 | 1,491 | 531 | 1,929 | 1,259 | 864 |
| Holt . . . . . | 1,144 | 1,323 | 314 | 1,050 | 1,202 | 781 |
| Howard . . | 2,014 | 1,545 | 568 | 2,085 | 1,253 | 1,090 |
| Howell . . . | 5,261 | 5,991 | 2,066 | 5,492 | 5,360 | 2,650 |
| Iron . . . . . | 2,221 | 1,328 | 568 | 2,507 | 1,276 | 841 |
| Jackson . . | 139,839 | 85,501 | 21,069 | 145,999 | 78,611 | 66,142 |
| Jasper . . . | 11,462 | 18,361 | 3,545 | 11,727 | 17,592 | 6,440 |
| Jefferson . | 32,072 | 23,877 | 8,893 | 32,569 | 20,637 | 20,057 |
| Johnson . . | 6,217 | 6,275 | 1,911 | 5,546 | 5,032 | 4,578 |
| Knox . . . . | 891 | 862 | 254 | 1,010 | 724 | 523 |
| Laclede . . | 4,044 | 5,883 | 1,458 | 4,179 | 5,176 | 2,852 |
| Lafayette . | 6,118 | 5,489 | 1,516 | 5,213 | 4,651 | 3,561 |
| Lawrence . | 4,465 | 6,099 | 1,613 | 4,666 | 5,608 | 2,570 |
| Lewis. . . . | 2,050 | 1,453 | 644 | 2,196 | 1,461 | 892 |
| Lincoln . . . | 5,644 | 4,897 | 1,881 | 5,453 | 3,718 | 3,572 |
| Linn . . . . . | 2,967 | 2,097 | 781 | 2,916 | 1,967 | 1,524 |
| Livingston . | 2,913 | 2,384 | 777 | 2,505 | 2,370 | 1,976 |
| McDonald . | 1,980 | 3,008 | 923 | 2,281 | 3,010 | 1,551 |
| Macon . . . | 2,937 | 2,634 | 848 | 3,194 | 2,256 | 1,697 |
| Madison . . | 2,351 | 1,595 | 625 | 2,501 | 1,673 | 899 |
| Maries . . . | 1,540 | 1,560 | 516 | 1,732 | 1,356 | 915 |
| Marion . . . | 4,923 | 4,649 | 1,081 | 5,156 | 4,762 | 1,841 |
| Mercer . . . | 700 | 660 | 208 | 843 | 626 | 378 |
| Miller . . . | 3,110 | 4,387 | 1,185 | 2,905 | 4,175 | 2,391 |
| Mississippi | 3,235 | 1,595 | 380 | 3,226 | 1,675 | 776 |
| Moniteau . | 2,129 | 2,603 | 693 | 2,018 | 2,566 | 1,499 |
| Monroe. . . | 1,938 | 1,333 | 532 | 2,060 | 1,153 | 969 |
| Montgomery . | 2,277 | 2,124 | 772 | 2,063 | 1,974 | 1,266 |
| Morgan. . . | 3,005 | 3,059 | 1,006 | 2,906 | 2,819 | 2,028 |
| New Madrid | 4,451 | 2,417 | 663 | 4,883 | 2,431 | 962 |
| Newton. . . | 5,840 | 10,067 | 1,995 | 5,987 | 8,804 | 3,567 |
| Nodaway . . | 3,966 | 3,362 | 1,043 | 3,723 | 3,147 | 2,484 |
| Oregon. . . | 1,795 | 1,502 | 475 | 2,258 | 1,402 | 564 |
| Osage . . . | 2,045 | 2,890 | 608 | 1,860 | 2,784 | 1,423 |
| Ozark. . . . | 1,433 | 1,859 | 591 | 1,581 | 1,772 | 906 |
| Pemiscot . | 3,371 | 1,820 | 458 | 3,924 | 2,161 | 670 |
| Perry . . . . | 2,517 | 3,427 | 777 | 2,525 | 3,205 | 1,498 |
| Pettis . . . . | 6,049 | 7,331 | 1,715 | 5,314 | 6,823 | 4,278 |
| Phelps . . . | 6,405 | 6,990 | 1,703 | 6,852 | 6,040 | 3,774 |
| Pike. . . . . | 3,495 | 2,209 | 916 | 3,609 | 2,255 | 1,464 |
| Platte . . . . | 12,705 | 13,332 | 3,035 | 10,920 | 9,380 | 9,062 |
| Polk. . . . . | 3,307 | 4,521 | 1,169 | 3,316 | 3,465 | 1,879 |
| Pulaski . . . | 3,783 | 4,089 | 1,141 | 4,113 | 3,793 | 2,057 |
| Putnam . . | 868 | 1,091 | 276 | 838 | 1,143 | 522 |
| Ralls . . . . | 1,998 | 1,513 | 520 | 2,158 | 1,349 | 880 |
| Randolph . | 4,502 | 3,274 | 1,130 | 4,951 | 3,025 | 2,212 |
| Ray . . . . . | 4,714 | 2,884 | 1,113 | 4,457 | 2,563 | 2,567 |
| Reynolds . | 1,631 | 903 | 386 | 2,014 | 776 | 532 |
| Ripley . . . | 2,079 | 1,988 | 530 | 2,300 | 1,814 | 739 |
| St. Charles | 41,369 | 47,705 | 11,591 | 37,263 | 38,673 | 30,351 |
| St. Clair . . | 1,974 | 1,815 | 650 | 1,965 | 1,555 | 1,083 |
| St. Francois | 9,034 | 6,200 | 2,266 | 9,367 | 5,889 | 3,635 |
| St. Louis . . | 225,751 | 196,060 | 34,887 | 235,760 | 188,285 | 109,099 |
| Ste. Genevieve | 3,597 | 2,078 | 942 | 3,795 | 1,780 | 1,547 |
| Saline . . . | 4,765 | 2,928 | 1,098 | 4,643 | 2,688 | 2,815 |
| Schuyler . . | 857 | 777 | 287 | 936 | 742 | 487 |
| Scotland . . | 990 | 773 | 326 | 1,070 | 798 | 617 |
| Scott . . . . | 7,011 | 6,641 | 1,483 | 7,452 | 6,265 | 2,763 |
| Shannon. . | 1,882 | 1,339 | 524 | 2,135 | 1,224 | 579 |
| Shelby . . . | 1,410 | 1,213 | 413 | 1,435 | 1,169 | 786 |
| Stoddard . | 4,883 | 5,020 | 1,185 | 5,720 | 4,608 | 1,977 |
| Stone. . . . | 3,497 | 5,223 | 1,353 | 3,256 | 4,035 | 1,884 |
| Sullivan . . | 1,402 | 1,275 | 340 | 1,510 | 1,326 | 596 |
| Taney . . . | 4,623 | 6,844 | 1,580 | 4,682 | 6,081 | 2,395 |
| Texas. . . . | 3,897 | 4,065 | 1,335 | 4,597 | 3,470 | 1,900 |
| Vernon. . . | 3,363 | 3,123 | 1,135 | 3,546 | 2,851 | 1,890 |
| Warren. . . | 3,443 | 3,768 | 1,254 | 3,213 | 2,953 | 2,471 |
| Washington | 4,315 | 2,259 | 1,169 | 4,211 | 2,157 | 1,618 |
| Wayne . . . | 2,754 | 2,172 | 674 | 3,073 | 2,101 | 837 |
| Webster . . | 3,855 | 4,958 | 1,214 | 4,149 | 4,361 | 2,108 |
| Worth. . . . | 572 | 540 | 150 | 599 | 483 | 328 |
| Wright . . . | 2,280 | 3,754 | 890 | 2,814 | 3,427 | 1,425 |
| **City** | | | | | | |
| St. Louis . | 90,306 | 21,942 | 7,229 | 102,356 | 25,441 | 18,864 |
| **Totals . . .** | **1,024,679** | **889,684** | **217,101** | **1,053,873** | **811,159** | **518,741** |

## Missouri Vote Since 1948

1948, Truman, Dem., 917,315; Dewey, Rep., 655,039; Wallace, Prog., 3,998; Thomas, Soc., 2,222.

1952, Eisenhower, Rep., 959,429; Stevenson, Dem., 929,830; Hallinan, Prog., 987; Hamblen, Proh., 885; MacArthur, Christian Nationalist, 302; America First, 233; Hoopes, Soc., 227; Hass, Soc. Labor, 169.

1956, Stevenson, Dem., 918,273; Eisenhower, Rep., 914,299.

1960, Kennedy, Dem., 972,201; Nixon, Rep., 962,221.

1964, Johnson, Dem., 1,164,344; Goldwater, Rep., 653,535.

1968, Nixon, Rep., 811,932; Humphrey, Dem., 791,444; Wallace, 3d Party, 206,126.

1972, Nixon, Rep., 1,154,058; McGovern, Dem., 698,531.

1976, Carter, Dem., 999,163; Ford, Rep., 928,808; McCarthy, Ind., 24,329.

1980, Reagan, Rep., 1,074,181; Carter, Dem., 931,182; Anderson, Ind., 77,920; Clark, Libertarian, 14,422; DeBerry, Soc. Workers, 1,515; Commoner, Citizens, 573; write-ins, 31.

1984, Reagan, Rep., 1,274,188; Mondale, Dem., 848,583.

1988, Bush, Rep., 1,084,953; Dukakis, Dem., 1,001,619; Fulani, New Alliance, 6,656; Paul, write-in, 434.

1992, Clinton, Dem., 1,053,873; Bush, Rep., 811,159; Perot, Ind., 518,741; Marrou, Libertarian, 7,497.

1996, Clinton, Dem., 1,024,679; Dole, Rep., 889,684; Perot, Ref., 217,101; Phillips, Taxpayers, 11,494; Browne, Libertarian, 10,511; Hagelin, Natural Law, 2,267.

# Montana

| County | 1996 Clinton (D) | 1996 Dole (R) | 1996 Perot (RF) | 1992 Clinton (D) | 1992 Bush (R) | 1992 Perot (I) |
|---|---|---|---|---|---|---|
| Beaverhead | 1,164 | 2,414 | 412 | 1,098 | 1,746 | 1,202 |
| Big Horn. . | 2,453 | 1,337 | 424 | 2,154 | 1,377 | 840 |
| Blaine . . . | 1,316 | 1,127 | 435 | 1,355 | 971 | 699 |
| Broadwater | 603 | 1,029 | 318 | 491 | 830 | 505 |
| Carbon. . . | 1,854 | 2,146 | 713 | 1,549 | 1,562 | 1,482 |
| Carter . . . | 150 | 522 | 89 | 154 | 497 | 220 |
| Cascade. . | 15,707 | 14,290 | 4,749 | 14,719 | 12,494 | 9,151 |
| Chouteau . | 1,039 | 1,640 | 434 | 959 | 1,380 | 870 |
| Custer . . . | 2,115 | 2,467 | 695 | 1,968 | 2,105 | 1,505 |
| Daniels. . . | 510 | 558 | 240 | 457 | 496 | 402 |
| Dawson . . | 1,903 | 1,890 | 842 | 1,785 | 1,679 | 1,370 |
| Deer Lodge | 3,331 | 883 | 772 | 3,174 | 832 | 1,207 |
| Fallon . . . | 452 | 778 | 276 | 446 | 731 | 427 |
| Fergus . . . | 1,866 | 3,671 | 605 | 1,615 | 2,736 | 1,934 |
| Flathead. . | 10,521 | 16,585 | 4,817 | 9,746 | 11,699 | 9,109 |
| Gallatin . . | 10,972 | 14,559 | 3,146 | 9,535 | 11,109 | 7,711 |
| Garfield . . | 107 | 562 | 69 | 125 | 403 | 281 |
| Glacier. . . | 2,293 | 1,270 | 491 | 2,076 | 1,222 | 997 |
| Golden Valley . | 128 | 284 | 73 | 142 | 192 | 157 |
| Granite. . . | 429 | 733 | 228 | 358 | 556 | 386 |
| Hill . . . . . | 3,517 | 2,601 | 950 | 3,618 | 2,408 | 2,017 |
| Jefferson . | 1,775 | 2,248 | 729 | 1,415 | 1,541 | 1,172 |
| Judith Basin | 452 | 766 | 126 | 409 | 610 | 415 |
| Lake . . . . | 3,744 | 4,118 | 1,697 | 3,938 | 3,596 | 2,878 |
| Lewis & Clark | 11,463 | 11,605 | 3,125 | 11,117 | 9,351 | 5,560 |
| Liberty . . . | 379 | 634 | 144 | 321 | 512 | 363 |
| Lincoln. . . | 2,705 | 3,552 | 1,425 | 2,765 | 2,799 | 2,637 |
| McCone . . | 390 | 615 | 244 | 424 | 528 | 395 |
| Madison . . | 950 | 1,984 | 508 | 779 | 1,415 | 1,043 |
| Meagher. . | 150 | 284 | 59 | 260 | 422 | 310 |
| Mineral. . . | 658 | 549 | 383 | 664 | 403 | 543 |
| Missoula. . | 21,686 | 16,003 | 5,565 | 20,347 | 12,898 | 9,735 |
| Musselshell | 652 | 1,121 | 291 | 648 | 876 | 691 |
| Park . . . . | 2,564 | 3,837 | 959 | 2,258 | 2,846 | 2,182 |
| Petroleum . | 62 | 186 | 36 | 61 | 135 | 95 |
| Phillips . . . | 705 | 1,392 | 401 | 634 | 1,026 | 949 |
| Pondera . . | 1,148 | 1,480 | 395 | 1,046 | 1,252 | 855 |
| Powder River | 236 | 663 | 137 | 258 | 547 | 340 |
| Powell . . . | 952 | 1,274 | 531 | 989 | 1,058 | 872 |
| Prairie . . . | 259 | 417 | 99 | 260 | 412 | 179 |
| Ravalli . . . | 5,200 | 8,132 | 2,713 | 4,644 | 5,392 | 4,573 |
| Richland. . | 1,614 | 2,021 | 906 | 1,440 | 1,760 | 1,525 |
| Roosevelt . | 2,118 | 1,207 | 642 | 1,827 | 1,212 | 1,089 |
| Rosebud. . | 1,681 | 1,413 | 547 | 1,669 | 1,130 | 1,099 |
| Sanders . . | 1,573 | 2,043 | 990 | 1,689 | 1,361 | 1,378 |
| Sheridan. . | 1,187 | 832 | 408 | 1,077 | 795 | 782 |
| Silver Bow | 11,199 | 3,909 | 2,447 | 9,960 | 3,491 | 4,570 |
| Stillwater . | 1,282 | 1,870 | 618 | 1,178 | 1,390 | 1,056 |
| Sweet Grass | 469 | 1,209 | 186 | 395 | 880 | 507 |
| Teton. . . . | 1,188 | 1,701 | 416 | 1,043 | 1,364 | 969 |
| Toole. . . . | 874 | 1,203 | 386 | 854 | 943 | 903 |
| Treasure . | 171 | 237 | 87 | 157 | 206 | 178 |
| Valley . . . | 1,674 | 1,892 | 645 | 1,715 | 1,497 | 1,320 |
| Wheatland | 391 | 563 | 127 | 384 | 478 | 284 |
| Wibaux. . . | 197 | 284 | 128 | 195 | 234 | 173 |
| Yellowstone | 22,991 | 26,367 | 6,139 | 20,163 | 22,822 | 13,133 |
| **Totals . . .** | **167,169** | **178,957** | **55,017** | **154,507** | **144,207** | **107,225** |

## Montana Vote Since 1948

1948, Truman, Dem., 119,071; Dewey, Rep., 96,770; Wallace, Prog., 7,313; Thomas, Soc., 695; Watson, Proh., 429.

1952, Eisenhower, Rep., 157,394; Stevenson, Dem., 106,213; Hallinan, Prog., 723; Hamblen, Proh., 548; Hoopes, Soc., 159.

1956, Eisenhower, Rep., 154,933; Stevenson, Dem., 116,238.

1960, Kennedy, Dem., 134,891; Nixon, Rep., 141,841; Decker, Proh., 456; Dobbs, Soc. Workers, 391.

1964, Johnson, Dem., 164,246; Goldwater, Rep., 113,032; Kasper, Natl. States' Rights, 519; Munn, Proh., 499; DeBerry, Soc. Workers, 332.
1968, Nixon, Rep., 138,835; Humphrey, Dem., 114,117; Wallace, 3d Party, 20,015; Halstead, Soc. Workers, 457; Munn, Proh., 510; Caton, New Reform, 470.
1972, Nixon, Rep., 183,976; McGovern, Dem., 120,197; Schmitz, Amer., 13,430.
1976, Carter, Dem., 149,259; Ford, Rep., 173,703; Anderson, Amer., 5,772.
1980, Reagan, Rep., 206,814; Carter, Dem., 118,032; Anderson, Ind., 29,281; Clark, Libertarian, 9,825.
1984, Reagan, Rep., 232,450; Mondale, Dem., 146,742; Bergland, Libertarian, 5,185.
1988, Bush, Rep., 190,412; Dukakis, Dem., 168,936; Paul, Lib., 5,047; Fulani, New Alliance, 1,279.
1992, Clinton, Dem., 154,507; Bush, Rep., 144,207; Perot, Ind., 107,225; Gritz, Populist/America First, 3,658.
1996, Dole, Rep., 178,957; Clinton, Dem., 167,169; Perot, Ref., 55,017; Browne, Libertarian, 2,524; Hagelin, Natural Law, 1,775.

## Nebraska

| | | 1996 | | | 1992 | |
|---|---|---|---|---|---|---|
| County | Clinton (D) | Dole (R) | Perot (RF) | Clinton (D) | Bush (R) | Perot (I) |
| Adams . . . | 3,874 | 6,829 | 1,487 | 3,445 | 6,346 | 3,273 |
| Antelope . . | 879 | 1,986 | 455 | 650 | 1,979 | 1,134 |
| Arthur. . . . | 25 | 184 | 45 | 18 | 148 | 97 |
| Banner . . . | 62 | 304 | 26 | 68 | 284 | 128 |
| Blaine . . . | 53 | 262 | 39 | 64 | 256 | 130 |
| Boone . . . | 804 | 1,681 | 424 | 604 | 1,588 | 956 |
| Box Butte . | 1,768 | 2,433 | 691 | 1,935 | 2,198 | 1,508 |
| Boyd . . . . | 368 | 771 | 177 | 353 | 744 | 468 |
| Brown . . . | 353 | 1,085 | 282 | 311 | 999 | 525 |
| Buffalo . . . | 4,250 | 9,897 | 1,468 | 3,742 | 9,708 | 4,083 |
| Burt . . . . . | 1,228 | 1,690 | 493 | 1,224 | 1,667 | 1,009 |
| Butler. . . . | 1,091 | 2,026 | 505 | 1,087 | 1,881 | 1,157 |
| Cass . . . . | 3,432 | 4,818 | 1,218 | 2,949 | 4,314 | 2,657 |
| Cedar. . . . | 1,216 | 2,142 | 738 | 1,007 | 1,981 | 1,507 |
| Chase . . . | 360 | 1,264 | 195 | 398 | 1,000 | 674 |
| Cherry . . . | 547 | 1,887 | 329 | 563 | 1,707 | 730 |
| Cheyenne . | 1,001 | 2,418 | 264 | 967 | 2,197 | 1,061 |
| Clay. . . . . | 865 | 1,956 | 417 | 802 | 1,818 | 952 |
| Colfax . . . | 1,062 | 1,937 | 490 | 1,011 | 1,915 | 1,197 |
| Cuming . . | 1,021 | 2,502 | 503 | 835 | 2,711 | 1,192 |
| Custer . . . | 1,234 | 3,278 | 587 | 1,126 | 3,180 | 1,492 |
| Dakota . . . | 2,558 | 2,541 | 702 | 2,322 | 2,771 | 1,307 |
| Dawes . . . | 1,098 | 1,976 | 442 | 987 | 1,961 | 1,103 |
| Dawson . . | 2,156 | 4,729 | 1,026 | 1,739 | 4,710 | 2,305 |
| Deuel. . . . | 240 | 624 | 111 | 232 | 558 | 327 |
| Dixon . . . . | 930 | 1,464 | 415 | 830 | 1,484 | 726 |
| Dodge . . . | 5,078 | 7,331 | 8,141 | 4,665 | 7,269 | 4,432 |
| Douglas . . | 69,170 | 89,927 | 14,569 | 67,003 | 93,421 | 38,641 |
| Dundy . . . | 224 | 743 | 112 | 244 | 664 | 332 |
| Fillmore . . | 1,043 | 1,668 | 318 | 988 | 1,495 | 993 |
| Franklin . . | 477 | 999 | 214 | 477 | 967 | 527 |
| Frontier . . | 305 | 892 | 164 | 302 | 785 | 479 |
| Furnas . . . | 630 | 1,475 | 205 | 624 | 1,365 | 804 |
| Gage . . . . | 3,951 | 4,375 | 1,325 | 3,309 | 3,995 | 2,726 |
| Garden. . . | 277 | 839 | 153 | 212 | 697 | 385 |
| Garfield . . | 246 | 619 | 110 | 221 | 595 | 270 |
| Gosper. . . | 273 | 607 | 150 | 254 | 492 | 297 |
| Grant . . . . | 84 | 255 | 55 | 75 | 247 | 124 |
| Greeley . . | 467 | 633 | 154 | 435 | 587 | 395 |
| Hall . . . . . | 6,620 | 10,015 | 2,360 | 5,519 | 9,264 | 5,822 |
| Hamilton. . | 1,068 | 2,408 | 441 | 992 | 2,379 | 1,213 |
| Harlan . . . | 516 | 1,098 | 195 | 488 | 991 | 623 |
| Hayes . . . | 87 | 436 | 39 | 85 | 362 | 207 |
| Hitchcock . | 404 | 964 | 172 | 359 | 824 | 540 |
| Holt . . . . . | 1,082 | 3,377 | 651 | 835 | 3,131 | 1,714 |
| Hooker. . . | 114 | 302 | 82 | 70 | 283 | 102 |
| Howard . . | 837 | 1,275 | 412 | 778 | 1,138 | 940 |
| Jefferson . | 1,499 | 1,952 | 469 | 1,506 | 1,783 | 1,177 |
| Johnson . . | 762 | 998 | 308 | 822 | 885 | 642 |
| Kearney . . | 774 | 1,937 | 290 | 644 | 1,751 | 844 |
| Keith . . . . | 811 | 2,451 | 449 | 731 | 2,019 | 1,130 |
| Keya Paha | 94 | 382 | 46 | 105 | 368 | 158 |
| Kimball. . . | 486 | 915 | 196 | 408 | 931 | 440 |
| Knox . . . . | 1,260 | 2,113 | 530 | 968 | 2,112 | 1,166 |
| Lancaster . | 42,123 | 43,409 | 8,291 | 41,207 | 41,400 | 21,783 |
| Lincoln . . . | 5,021 | 7,327 | 1,972 | 5,142 | 7,025 | 3,384 |
| Logan . . . | 79 | 291 | 72 | 80 | 271 | 98 |
| Loup . . . . | 71 | 225 | 28 | 58 | 233 | 96 |
| McPherson | 49 | 231 | 33 | 49 | 217 | 62 |
| Madison . . | 2,966 | 7,760 | 1,513 | 2,352 | 7,851 | 3,486 |
| Merrick. . . | 982 | 2,042 | 447 | 864 | 1,854 | 1,072 |
| Morrill . . . | 612 | 1,275 | 262 | 577 | 1,184 | 752 |
| Nance . . . | 580 | 885 | 235 | 559 | 851 | 569 |
| Nemaha . . | 1,217 | 1,864 | 482 | 1,110 | 1,696 | 1,020 |
| Nuckolls . . | 753 | 1,374 | 303 | 834 | 1,277 | 825 |
| Otoe . . . . | 2,255 | 3,250 | 861 | 2,038 | 2,960 | 1,800 |
| Pawnee . . | 574 | 754 | 199 | 566 | 670 | 565 |
| Perkins . . | 349 | 1,007 | 160 | 300 | 842 | 522 |
| Phelps . . . | 1,058 | 2,975 | 465 | 829 | 2,748 | 1,298 |
| Pierce . . . | 695 | 1,915 | 446 | 611 | 1,853 | 1,084 |
| Platte. . . . | 2,953 | 7,802 | 1,322 | 2,409 | 7,712 | 3,656 |
| Polk. . . . . | 799 | 1,489 | 263 | 661 | 1,435 | 812 |
| Red Willow | 1,335 | 3,075 | 491 | 1,164 | 2,488 | 1,660 |
| Richardson | 1,485 | 2,035 | 615 | 1,513 | 2,050 | 1,356 |
| Rock . . . . | 178 | 562 | 134 | 162 | 588 | 233 |
| Saline . . . | 2,476 | 1,903 | 673 | 2,425 | 1,740 | 1,576 |
| Sarpy. . . . | 12,497 | 22,456 | 3,627 | 10,720 | 20,482 | 9,270 |
| Saunders . | 2,746 | 4,463 | 1,217 | 2,509 | 4,037 | 2,567 |
| Scotts Bluff | 4,439 | 7,459 | 1,212 | 4,173 | 7,213 | 3,514 |
| Seward . . | 2,403 | 3,420 | 721 | 2,118 | 3,044 | 1,722 |
| Sheridan. . | 566 | 1,811 | 289 | 535 | 1,698 | 751 |
| Sherman . | 565 | 814 | 263 | 568 | 736 | 582 |
| Sioux. . . . | 138 | 546 | 75 | 148 | 445 | 206 |
| Stanton . . | 571 | 1,444 | 384 | 496 | 1,274 | 786 |
| Thayer . . . | 916 | 1,673 | 326 | 923 | 1,387 | 1,077 |
| Thomas . . | 63 | 299 | 62 | 69 | 283 | 115 |
| Thurston. . | 954 | 826 | 291 | 865 | 898 | 487 |
| Valley . . . | 710 | 1,245 | 264 | 716 | 1,173 | 693 |
| Washington | 2,219 | 4,326 | 947 | 2,108 | 4,035 | 2,148 |
| Wayne . . . | 1,034 | 2,130 | 440 | 921 | 2,122 | 1,047 |
| Webster . . | 613 | 1,078 | 235 | 624 | 972 | 657 |
| Wheeler . . | 103 | 259 | 45 | 88 | 246 | 127 |
| York . . . . | 1,602 | 4,193 | 548 | 1,385 | 3,783 | 1,825 |
| **Totals . . .** | **231,863** | **355,562** | **76,103** | **216,864** | **343,678** | **174,104** |

### Nebraska Vote Since 1948

1948, Truman, Dem., 224,165; Dewey, Rep., 264,774.
1952, Eisenhower, Rep., 421,603; Stevenson, Dem., 188,057.
1956, Eisenhower, Rep., 378,108; Stevenson, Dem., 199,029.
1960, Kennedy, Dem., 232,542; Nixon, Rep., 380,553.
1964, Johnson, Dem., 307,307; Goldwater, Rep., 276,847.
1968, Nixon, Rep., 321,163; Humphrey, Dem., 170,784; Wallace, 3d Party, 44,904.
1972, Nixon, Rep., 406,298; McGovern, Dem., 169,991; scattered, 817.
1976, Carter, Dem., 233,287; Ford, Rep., 359,219; McCarthy, Ind., 9,383; Maddox, Amer. Ind., 3,378; MacBride, Libertarian, 1,476.
1980, Reagan, Rep., 419,214; Carter, Dem., 166,424; Anderson, Ind., 44,854; Clark, Libertarian, 9,041.
1984, Reagan, Rep., 459,135; Mondale, Dem., 187,475; Bergland, Libertarian, 2,075.
1988, Bush, Rep., 397,956; Dukakis, Dem., 259,235; Paul, Lib., 2,534; Fulani, New Alliance, 1,740.
1992, Bush, Rep., 343,678; Clinton, Dem., 216,864; Perot, Ind., 174,104; Marrou, Libertarian, 1,340.
1996, Dole, Rep., 355,562; Clinton, Dem., 231,863; Perot, Ref., 76,103; Browne, Libertarian, 2,651; Phillips, Ind., 1,877; Hagelin, Natural Law, 1,143.

## Nevada

| | | 1996 | | | 1992 | |
|---|---|---|---|---|---|---|
| County | Clinton (D) | Dole (R) | Perot (RF) | Clinton (D) | Bush (R) | Perot (I) |
| Churchill. . | 2,282 | 4,369 | 821 | 1,770 | 3,789 | 1,964 |
| Clark . . . . | 127,963 | 103,431 | 23,177 | 124,586 | 97,403 | 75,364 |
| Douglas . . | 5,109 | 8,828 | 1,486 | 3,928 | 6,182 | 4,814 |
| Elko. . . . . | 3,149 | 6,512 | 1,539 | 2,782 | 5,208 | 3,628 |
| Esmeralda | 140 | 277 | 91 | 118 | 221 | 220 |
| Eureka . . . | 158 | 411 | 90 | 129 | 330 | 214 |
| Humboldt . | 1,467 | 2,334 | 603 | 810 | 1,505 | 1,149 |
| Lander . . . | 660 | 1,107 | 361 | 423 | 885 | 652 |
| Lincoln . . . | 499 | 936 | 255 | 511 | 890 | 394 |
| Lyon . . . . | 3,419 | 4,753 | 1,104 | 2,777 | 3,509 | 2,716 |
| Mineral. . . | 1,068 | 858 | 372 | 909 | 918 | 746 |
| Nye . . . . . | 3,300 | 3,979 | 1,544 | 2,561 | 2,743 | 2,501 |
| Pershing. . | 565 | 743 | 203 | 467 | 643 | 429 |
| Storey . . . | 604 | 695 | 242 | 488 | 458 | 550 |
| Washoe . . | 44,420 | 49,076 | 9,854 | 39,500 | 42,636 | 30,974 |
| White Pine | 1,316 | 1,298 | 522 | 1,354 | 1,206 | 1,070 |
| **City** | | | | | | |
| Carson City | 7,269 | 9,168 | 1,591 | 6,035 | 7,302 | 5,195 |
| **Totals . . .** | **203,388** | **198,775** | **43,855** | **189,148** | **175,828** | **132,580** |

### Nevada Vote Since 1948

1948, Truman, Dem., 31,291; Dewey, Rep., 29,357; Wallace, Prog., 1,469.
1952, Eisenhower, Rep., 50,502; Stevenson, Dem., 31,688.
1956, Eisenhower, Rep., 56,049; Stevenson, Dem., 40,640.
1960, Kennedy, Dem., 54,880; Nixon, Rep., 52,387.
1964, Johnson, Dem., 79,339; Goldwater, Rep., 56,094.
1968, Nixon, Rep., 73,188; Humphrey, Dem., 60,598; Wallace, 3d Party, 20,432.

1972, Nixon, Rep., 115,750; McGovern, Dem., 66,016.
1976, Carter, Dem., 92,479; Ford, Rep., 101,273; MacBride, Libertarian, 1,519; Maddox, Amer. Ind., 1,497; scattered, 5,108.
1980, Reagan, Rep., 155,017; Carter, Dem., 66,666; Anderson, Ind., 17,651; Clark, Libertarian, 4,358.
1984, Reagan, Rep., 188,770; Mondale, Dem., 91,655; Bergland, Libertarian, 2,292.
1988, Bush, Rep., 206,040; Dukakis, Dem., 132,738; Paul, Lib., 3,520; Fulani, New Alliance, 835.
1992, Clinton, Dem., 189,148; Bush, Rep., 175,828; Perot, Ind., 132,580; Gritz, Populist/America First, 2,892; Marrou, Libertarian, 1,835.
1996, Clinton, Dem., 203,388; Dole, Rep., 198,775; Perot, Ref., 43,855; "None of These Candidates," 5,575; Nader, Green, 4,710; Browne, Libertarian, 4,451; Phillips, Ind. Amer., 1,727; Hagelin, Natural Law, 543.

# New Hampshire

| | | 1996 | | | 1992 | |
|---|---|---|---|---|---|---|
| City | Clinton (D) | Dole (R) | Perot (RF) | Clinton (D) | Bush (R) | Perot (I) |
| Berlin City. | 2,771 | 1,047 | 672 | 2,680 | 1,272 | 1,162 |
| Claremont. | 2,662 | 1,694 | 518 | 2,650 | 1,822 | 904 |
| Concord . . | 9,643 | 5,042 | 1,147 | 8,325 | 5,651 | 2,843 |
| Dover. . . . | 6,332 | 3,752 | 930 | 5,449 | 4,197 | 2,246 |
| Keene . . . | 5,401 | 2,910 | 621 | 5,210 | 3,257 | 1,736 |
| Laconia . . | 2,865 | 2,842 | 508 | 2,390 | 3,033 | 1,496 |
| Manchester | 19,857 | 14,492 | 3,029 | 16,627 | 16,298 | 7,441 |
| Nashua . . | 16,584 | 11,479 | 2,858 | 14,777 | 12,514 | 8,306 |
| Portsmouth | 6,343 | 3,014 | 661 | 6,132 | 3,563 | 2,088 |
| Rochester. | 5,430 | 4,181 | 1,097 | 4,588 | 4,272 | 2,541 |
| Other. . . . | 163,848 | 143,241 | 36,123 | 140,212 | 147,999 | 90,574 |
| **Totals . . .** | **245,260** | **196,740** | **48,140** | **209,040** | **202,484** | **121,337** |

## New Hampshire Vote Since 1948

1948, Truman, Dem., 107,995; Dewey, Rep., 121,299; Wallace, Prog., 1,970; Thomas, Soc., 86; Teichert, Soc. Labor, 83; Thurmond, States' Rights, 7.
1952, Eisenhower, Rep., 166,287; Stevenson, Dem., 106,663.
1956, Eisenhower, Rep., 176,519; Stevenson, Dem., 90,364; Andrews, Const., 111.
1960, Kennedy, Dem., 137,772; Nixon, Rep., 157,989.
1964, Johnson, Dem., 182,065; Goldwater, Rep., 104,029.
1968, Nixon, Rep., 154,903; Humphrey, Dem., 130,589; Wallace, 3d Party, 11,173; New Party, 421; Halstead, Soc. Workers, 104.
1972, Nixon, Rep., 213,724; McGovern, Dem., 116,435; Schmitz, Amer., 3,386; Jenness, Soc. Workers, 368; scattered, 142.
1976, Carter, Dem., 147,645; Ford, Rep., 185,935; McCarthy, Ind., 4,095; MacBride, Libertarian, 936; Reagan, write-in, 388; La Rouche, U.S. Labor, 186; Camejo, Soc. Workers, 161; Levin, Soc. Labor, 66; scattered, 215.
1980, Reagan, Rep., 221,705; Carter, Dem., 108,864; Anderson, Ind., 49,693; Clark, Libertarian, 2,067; Commoner, Citizens, 1,325; Hall, Com., 129; Griswold, Workers World, 76; DeBerry, Soc. Workers, 72; scattered, 68.
1984, Reagan, Rep., 267,051; Mondale, Dem., 120,377; Bergland, Libertarian, 735.
1988, Bush, Rep., 281,537; Dukakis, Dem., 163,696; Paul, Lib., 4,502; Fulani, New Alliance, 790.
1992, Clinton, Dem., 209,040; Bush, Rep., 202,484; Perot, Ind., 121,337; Marrou, Libertarian, 3,548.
1996, Clinton, Dem., 245,260; Dole, Rep., 196,740; Perot, Ref., 48,140; Browne, Libertarian, 3,897; Phillips, Taxpayers, 1,255.

# New Jersey

| | | 1996 | | | 1992 | |
|---|---|---|---|---|---|---|
| County | Clinton (D) | Dole (R) | Perot (RF) | Clinton (D) | Bush (R) | Perot (I) |
| Atlantic. . . | 42,341 | 27,891 | 8,046 | 39,633 | 34,279 | 15,890 |
| Bergen . . . | 179,460 | 142,842 | 24,506 | 171,104 | 178,223 | 52,082 |
| Burlington . | 80,082 | 53,636 | 17,741 | 72,845 | 63,709 | 35,322 |
| Camden . . | 108,951 | 50,200 | 16,636 | 104,915 | 67,205 | 37,144 |
| Cape May. | 18,651 | 17,877 | 4,915 | 17,324 | 21,502 | 9,798 |
| Cumberland | 25,456 | 14,622 | 5,313 | 22,220 | 19,253 | 9,901 |
| Essex . . . | 166,823 | 62,405 | 9,223 | 158,130 | 89,146 | 26,961 |
| Gloucester | 51,435 | 31,803 | 14,179 | 42,425 | 37,335 | 24,132 |
| Hudson . . . | 111,158 | 37,351 | 8,748 | 99,799 | 66,505 | 14,569 |
| Hunterdon. | 18,424 | 26,358 | 5,680 | 15,423 | 25,130 | 12,736 |
| Mercer . . . | 76,977 | 40,312 | 10,435 | 71,383 | 50,473 | 22,503 |
| Middlesex. | 149,171 | 85,301 | 25,690 | 128,824 | 108,701 | 45,055 |
| Monmouth | 120,252 | 99,762 | 22,471 | 101,750 | 117,715 | 45,445 |
| Morris . . . | 77,060 | 91,673 | 15,060 | 67,593 | 108,431 | 32,447 |
| Ocean . . . | 93,623 | 82,106 | 22,723 | 75,431 | 95,984 | 41,668 |
| Passaic . . | 82,882 | 51,414 | 10,759 | 70,030 | 71,147 | 21,494 |
| Salem . . . | 11,833 | 9,068 | 4,057 | 10,062 | 10,363 | 7,274 |
| Somerset . | 47,479 | 48,849 | 8,085 | 42,867 | 56,044 | 21,014 |
| Sussex. . . | 19,454 | 26,665 | 6,673 | 14,775 | 29,510 | 12,537 |
| Union. . . . | 103,669 | 62,804 | 12,066 | 96,671 | 87,742 | 23,991 |
| Warren. . . | 14,751 | 17,102 | 4,973 | 13,002 | 18,468 | 9,866 |
| **Totals . . .** | **1,599,932** | **1,080,041** | **257,979** | **1,436,206** | **1,356,865** | **521,829** |

## New Jersey Vote Since 1948

1948, Truman, Dem., 895,455; Dewey, Rep., 981,124; Wallace, Prog., 42,683; Watson, Proh., 10,593; Thomas, Soc., 10,521; Dobbs, Soc. Workers, 5,825; Teichert, Soc. Labor, 3,354.
1952, Eisenhower, Rep., 1,373,613; Stevenson, Dem., 1,015,902; Hoopes, Soc., 8,593; Hass, Soc. Labor, 5,815; Hallinan, Prog., 5,589; Krajewski, Poor Man's, 4,203; Dobbs, Soc. Workers, 3,850; Hamblen, Proh., 989.
1956, Eisenhower, Rep., 1,606,942; Stevenson Dem., 850,337; Holtwick, Proh., 9,147; Hass, Soc. Labor, 6,736; Andrews, Cons., 5,317; Dobbs, Soc. Workers, 4,004; Krajewski, Amer. Third Party, 1,829.
1960, Kennedy, Dem., 1,385,415; Nixon, Rep., 1,363,324; Dobbs, Soc. Workers, 11,402; Lee, Cons., 8,708; Hass, Soc. Labor, 4,262.
1964, Johnson, Dem., 1,867,671; Goldwater, Rep., 963,843; DeBerry, Soc. Workers, 8,181; Hass, Soc. Labor, 7,075.
1968, Nixon, Rep., 1,325,467; Humphrey, Dem., 1,264,206; Wallace, 3d Party, 262,187; Halstead, Soc. Workers, 8,667; Gregory, Peace and Freedom, 8,084; Blomen, Soc. Labor, 6,784.
1972, Nixon, Rep., 1,845,502; McGovern, Dem., 1,102,211; Schmitz, Amer., 34,378; Spock, Peoples, 5,355; Fisher, Soc. Labor, 4,544; Jenness, Soc. Workers, 2,233; Mahalchik, Amer. First, 1,743; Hall, Com., 1,263.
1976, Carter, Dem., 1,444,653; Ford, Rep., 1,509,688; McCarthy, Ind., 32,717; MacBride, Libertarian, 9,449; Maddox, Amer., 7,716; Levin, Soc. Labor, 3,686; Hall, Com., 1,662; LaRouche, U.S. Labor, 1,650; Camejo, Soc. Workers, 1,184; Wright, People's, 1,044; Bubar, Proh., 554; Zeidler, Soc., 469.
1980, Reagan, Rep., 1,546,557; Carter, Dem., 1,147,364; Anderson, Ind., 234,632; Clark, Libertarian, 20,652; Commoner, Citizens, 8,203; McCormack, Right to Life, 3,927; Lynen, Middle Class, 3,694; Hall, Com., 2,555; Pulley, Soc. Workers, 2,198; McReynolds, Soc., 1,973; Gahres, Down With Lawyers, 1,718; Griswold, Workers World, 1,288; Wendelken, Ind., 923.
1984, Reagan, Rep., 1,933,630; Mondale, Dem., 1,261,323; Bergland, Libertarian, 6,416.
1988, Bush, Rep., 1,740,604; Dukakis, Dem., 1,317,541; Lewin, Peace and Freedom, 9,953; Paul, Lib., 8,421.
1992, Clinton, Dem., 1,436,206; Bush, Rep., 1,356,865; Perot, Ind., 521,829; Marrou, Libertarian, 6,822; Fulani, New Alliance, 3,513; Phillips, U.S. Taxpayers, 2,670; LaRouche, Ind., 2,095; Warren, Soc. Workers, 2,011; Daniels, Ind., 1,996; Gritz, Populist/America First, 1,867; Hagelin, Natural Law, 1,353.
1996, Clinton, Dem., 1,599,932; Dole, Rep., 1,080,041; Perot, Ref., 257,979; Nader, Green, 32,441; Browne, Libertarian, 14,387; Hagelin, Natural Law, 3,952; Phillips, Taxpayers, 3,502; Harris, Soc. Workers, 3,182; Moorehead, Workers World, 1,675; White, Soc. Equality, 720.

# New Mexico

| | | 1996 | | | 1992 | |
|---|---|---|---|---|---|---|
| County | Clinton (D) | Dole (R) | Perot (RF) | Clinton (D) | Bush (R) | Perot (I) |
| Bernalillo . | 69,049 | 57,887 | 7,531 | 90,863 | 77,304 | 31,241 |
| Catron . . . | 423 | 923 | 114 | 465 | 771 | 289 |
| Chaves . . | 6,922 | 9,922 | 1,256 | 6,360 | 8,872 | 3,590 |
| Cibola . . . | 4,030 | 2,243 | 488 | 3,334 | 2,051 | 847 |
| Colfax . . . | 2,659 | 1,975 | 411 | 2,607 | 1,730 | 871 |
| Curry. . . . | 4,112 | 7,373 | 840 | 3,699 | 6,831 | 2,056 |
| De Baca. . | 509 | 489 | 86 | 451 | 526 | 204 |
| Dona Ana . | 22,723 | 17,525 | 2,269 | 19,894 | 16,308 | 7,682 |
| Eddy . . . . | 8,959 | 8,534 | 1,297 | 7,409 | 7,313 | 3,430 |
| Grant. . . . | 5,855 | 3,989 | 778 | 5,603 | 2,917 | 1,685 |
| Guadalupe | 1,223 | 436 | 79 | 1,225 | 691 | 173 |
| Harding . . | 264 | 321 | 28 | 268 | 312 | 98 |
| Hidalgo . . | 942 | 789 | 209 | 995 | 871 | 442 |
| Lea . . . . . | 5,358 | 7,574 | 1,447 | 5,047 | 7,921 | 3,233 |
| Lincoln . . . | 2,195 | 3,358 | 660 | 1,730 | 2,669 | 1,431 |
| Los Alamos | 3,983 | 4,996 | 560 | 3,897 | 4,320 | 2,339 |
| Luna . . . . | 3,000 | 2,615 | 598 | 2,637 | 2,166 | 1,445 |
| McKinley . | 10,123 | 4,470 | 650 | 9,405 | 4,720 | 1,304 |
| Mora . . . . | 1,649 | 564 | 131 | 1,555 | 668 | 188 |
| Otero. . . . | 5,938 | 9,044 | 1,096 | 5,377 | 7,481 | 3,257 |
| Quay . . . . | 1,829 | 1,943 | 377 | 1,758 | 1,759 | 755 |
| Rio Arriba . | 7,846 | 2,510 | 557 | 7,832 | 2,680 | 984 |
| Roosevelt . | 2,097 | 3,245 | 467 | 2,172 | 3,215 | 1,085 |

| County | 1996 Clinton (D) | 1996 Dole (R) | 1996 Perot (RF) | 1992 Clinton (D) | 1992 Bush (R) | 1992 Perot (I) |
|---|---|---|---|---|---|---|
| Sandoval . | 12,708 | 10,729 | 1,441 | 10,951 | 8,491 | 3,954 |
| San Juan . | 12,061 | 17,471 | 2,355 | 11,302 | 13,415 | 5,351 |
| San Miguel | 6,999 | 1,944 | 405 | 6,186 | 2,183 | 965 |
| Santa Fe . | 25,628 | 10,848 | 1,845 | 27,189 | 9,684 | 5,656 |
| Sierra. . . . | 1,910 | 2,120 | 428 | 1,771 | 1,562 | 1,055 |
| Socorro . . | 3,373 | 2,315 | 455 | 2,908 | 2,186 | 918 |
| Taos . . . . | 6,632 | 2,126 | 545 | 7,051 | 2,260 | 1,300 |
| Torrance. . | 2,056 | 2,131 | 328 | 1,662 | 1,667 | 810 |
| Union. . . . | 519 | 995 | 125 | 519 | 975 | 355 |
| Valencia . . | 8,641 | 7,387 | 1,122 | 7,495 | 6,305 | 2,902 |
| **Totals . . .** | **252,215** | **210,791** | **30,978** | **261,617** | **212,824** | **91,895** |

## New Mexico Vote Since 1948

1948, Truman, Dem., 105,464; Dewey, Rep., 80,303; Wallace, Prog., 1,037; Watson, Proh., 127; Thomas, Soc., 83; Teichert, Soc. Labor, 49.

1952, Eisenhower, Rep., 132,170; Stevenson, Dem., 105,661; Hamblen, Proh., 297; Hallinan, Ind. Prog., 225; MacArthur, Christian National, 220; Hass, Soc. Labor, 35.

1956, Eisenhower, Rep., 146,788; Stevenson, Dem., 106,098; Holtwick, Proh., 607; Andrews, Ind., 364; Hass, Soc. Labor, 69.

1960, Kennedy, Dem., 156,027; Nixon, Rep., 153,733; Decker, Proh., 777; Hass, Soc. Labor, 570.

1964, Johnson, Dem., 194,017; Goldwater, Rep., 131,838; Hass, Soc. Labor, 1,217; Munn, Proh., 543.

1968, Nixon, Rep., 169,692; Humphrey, Dem., 130,081; Wallace, 3d Party, 25,737; Chavez, 1,519; Halstead, Soc. Workers, 252.

1972, Nixon, Rep., 235,606; McGovern, Dem., 141,084; Schmitz, Amer., 8,767; Jenness, Soc. Workers, 474.

1976, Carter, Dem., 201,148; Ford, Rep., 211,419; Camejo, Soc. Workers, 2,462; MacBride, Libertarian, 1,110; Zeidler, Soc., 240; Bubar, Proh., 211.

1980, Reagan, Rep., 250,779; Carter, Dem., 167,826; Anderson, Ind., 29,459; Clark, Libertarian, 4,365; Commoner, Citizens, 2,202; Bubar, Statesman, 1,281; Pulley, Soc. Workers, 325.

1984, Reagan, Rep., 307,101; Mondale, Dem., 201,769; Bergland, Libertarian, 4,459.

1988, Bush, Rep., 270,341; Dukakis, Dem., 244,497; Paul, Lib., 3,268; Fulani, New Alliance, 2,237.

1992, Clinton, Dem., 261,617; Bush, Rep., 212,824; Perot, Ind., 91,895; Marrou, Libertarian, 1,615.

1996, Clinton, Dem., 252,215; Dole, Rep., 210,791; Perot, Ref., 30,978; Nader, Green, 12,276; Browne, Libertarian, 2,743; Phillips, Taxpayers, 676; Hagelin, Natural Law, 607.

# New York

| County | 1996 Clinton (D) | 1996 Dole (R) | 1996 Perot (RF) | 1992 Clinton (D) | 1992 Bush (R) | 1992 Perot (I) |
|---|---|---|---|---|---|---|
| Albany . . . | 51,068 | 30,616 | 9,078 | 80,641 | 49,452 | 24,064 |
| Allegany . . | 6,178 | 7,491 | 2,640 | 4,848 | 8,976 | 4,703 |
| Bronx. . . . | 236,954 | 31,890 | 7,139 | 225,038 | 63,310 | 15,115 |
| Broome . . | 40,810 | 29,137 | 8,591 | 43,444 | 34,653 | 21,280 |
| Cattaraugus | 12,165 | 12,481 | 5,014 | 10,150 | 13,944 | 10,662 |
| Cayuga . . | 14,560 | 10,218 | 4,320 | 13,088 | 12,065 | 10,279 |
| Chautauqua | 25,185 | 19,843 | 7,117 | 22,645 | 21,222 | 18,455 |
| Chemung . | 16,499 | 13,990 | 3,875 | 15,099 | 16,088 | 7,493 |
| Chenango. | 8,064 | 6,824 | 2,669 | 8,017 | 8,114 | 5,356 |
| Clinton . . . | 14,825 | 9,688 | 3,422 | 12,881 | 13,455 | 5,389 |
| Columbia . | 12,694 | 10,509 | 3,422 | 11,368 | 11,568 | 5,829 |
| Cortland . . | 8,575 | 7,084 | 2,361 | 7,815 | 7,782 | 5,098 |
| Delaware . | 8,362 | 7,374 | 2,500 | 7,152 | 8,829 | 4,404 |
| Dutchess . | 46,463 | 41,649 | 11,989 | 41,655 | 46,709 | 26,320 |
| Erie . . . . . | 214,615 | 127,404 | 43,732 | 196,233 | 129,444 | 123,358 |
| Essex . . . | 7,850 | 6,246 | 2,352 | 6,717 | 8,278 | 3,784 |
| Franklin . . | 7,822 | 4,636 | 2,393 | 7,654 | 6,635 | 3,857 |
| Fulton . . . | 9,229 | 7,428 | 3,257 | 8,400 | 9,137 | 5,120 |
| Genesee . | 9,773 | 10,491 | 2,953 | 8,071 | 11,663 | 6,192 |
| Greene. . . | 8,153 | 8,647 | 2,645 | 6,924 | 9,390 | 4,689 |
| Hamilton. . | 1,198 | 1,800 | 484 | 963 | 2,038 | 793 |
| Herkimer . | 10,882 | 9,260 | 3,991 | 10,880 | 12,052 | 6,866 |
| Jefferson . | 15,386 | 11,325 | 4,350 | 13,380 | 14,227 | 9,461 |
| Kings . . . . | 402,306 | 78,372 | 14,511 | 411,183 | 133,344 | 33,014 |
| Lewis. . . . | 3,979 | 3,520 | 1,562 | 3,676 | 4,101 | 3,164 |
| Livingston . | 10,739 | 10,754 | 2,831 | 8,648 | 12,122 | 5,775 |
| Madison . . | 11,666 | 11,152 | 3,312 | 10,099 | 11,293 | 7,391 |
| Monroe. . . | 156,380 | 111,643 | 23,360 | 141,502 | 134,021 | 63,229 |
| Montgomery. | 9,867 | 6,778 | 3,265 | 9,509 | 8,802 | 5,020 |
| Nassau . . | 292,062 | 192,721 | 35,523 | 282,593 | 246,881 | 77,097 |
| New York . | 351,332 | 61,898 | 10,309 | 416,142 | 84,501 | 27,689 |
| Niagara . . | 43,389 | 31,027 | 12,156 | 35,649 | 30,401 | 30,126 |
| Oneida . . . | 41,071 | 34,328 | 10,560 | 40,966 | 43,806 | 22,717 |
| Onondaga. | 97,944 | 73,359 | 17,316 | 90,645 | 77,642 | 45,175 |
| Ontario. . . | 19,014 | 17,239 | 4,473 | 16,064 | 18,995 | 9,571 |
| Orange. . . | 51,605 | 43,508 | 11,349 | 45,946 | 53,493 | 22,499 |
| Orleans . . | 6,141 | 6,782 | 1,966 | 4,927 | 7,468 | 4,275 |
| Oswego . . | 19,785 | 16,764 | 7,396 | 16,990 | 18,530 | 14,853 |
| Otsego. . . | 10,699 | 8,153 | 3,120 | 10,471 | 10,141 | 5,841 |
| Putnam . . | 15,229 | 16,478 | 3,909 | 14,048 | 18,934 | 8,011 |
| Queens . . | 346,874 | 102,560 | 21,236 | 349,520 | 157,561 | 46,014 |
| Rensselaer | 32,545 | 22,208 | 8,304 | 29,793 | 28,937 | 15,198 |
| Richmond. | 61,126 | 50,788 | 8,564 | 56,901 | 70,707 | 19,678 |
| Rockland . | 59,291 | 38,359 | 6,591 | 56,759 | 49,608 | 15,026 |
| St. Lawrence | 21,262 | 10,470 | 5,128 | 18,197 | 13,901 | 9,758 |
| Saratoga . | 39,988 | 34,363 | 9,915 | 33,011 | 36,917 | 19,091 |
| Schenectady | 34,294 | 21,513 | 7,772 | 32,335 | 26,258 | 14,838 |
| Schoharie. | 5,523 | 4,973 | 1,724 | 4,997 | 5,678 | 3,327 |
| Schuyler. . | 3,272 | 3,093 | 1,031 | 2,859 | 3,226 | 2,051 |
| Seneca . . | 6,410 | 4,679 | 1,813 | 5,810 | 5,432 | 3,660 |
| Steuben . . | 14,154 | 17,385 | 5,381 | 12,043 | 19,761 | 9,378 |
| Suffolk . . . | 251,243 | 180,819 | 50,819 | 220,811 | 229,467 | 112,973 |
| Sullivan . . | 16,029 | 9,027 | 3,400 | 13,717 | 11,396 | 6,336 |
| Tioga . . . . | 8,641 | 9,274 | 2,667 | 7,791 | 9,287 | 5,867 |
| Tompkins . | 19,312 | 10,749 | 2,537 | 23,197 | 11,520 | 6,704 |
| Ulster. . . . | 34,601 | 25,624 | 9,027 | 32,886 | 29,223 | 17,952 |
| Warren. . . | 10,327 | 10,159 | 3,454 | 9,820 | 12,260 | 6,401 |
| Washington | 8,806 | 8,237 | 3,555 | 8,429 | 10,305 | 6,143 |
| Wayne . . . | 14,906 | 15,668 | 4,522 | 11,866 | 18,019 | 9,188 |
| Westchester. | 183,664 | 119,444 | 17,353 | 184,300 | 151,990 | 39,933 |
| Wyoming . | 6,435 | 7,478 | 2,382 | 4,045 | 7,324 | 4,837 |
| Yates. . . . | 3,970 | 3,821 | 1,160 | 3,242 | 4,366 | 2,354 |
| **Totals . . .** | **3,513,191** | **1,861,198** | **485,547** | **3,444,450** | **2,346,649** | **1,090,721** |

## New York Vote Since 1948

1948, Truman, Dem., 2,557,642; Liberal, 222,562; total, 2,780,204; Dewey, Rep., 2,841,163; Wallace, Amer. Lab., 509,559; Thomas, Soc., 40,879; Teichert, Ind. Gov't., 2,729; Dobbs, Soc. Workers, 2,675.

1952, Eisenhower, Rep., 3,952,815; Stevenson, Dem., 2,687,890; Liberal, 416,711; total, 3,104,601; Hallinan, Amer. Lab., 64,211; Hoopes, Soc., 2,664; Dobbs, Soc. Workers, 2,212; Hass, Ind. Gov't., 1,560; scattering, 178; blank and void, 87,813.

1956, Eisenhower, Rep., 4,340,340; Stevenson, Dem., 2,458,212; Liberal, 292,557; total, 2,750,769; write-in votes for Andrews, 1,027; Werdel, 492; Hass, 150; Hoopes, 82; others, 476.

1960, Kennedy, Dem., 3,423,909; Liberal, 406,176; total, 3,830,085; Nixon, Rep., 3,446,419; Dobbs, Soc. Workers, 14,319; scattering, 256; blank and void, 88,896.

1964, Johnson, Dem., 4,913,156; Goldwater, Rep., 2,243,559; Hass, Soc. Labor, 6,085; DeBerry, Soc. Workers, 3,215; scattering, 188; blank and void, 151,383.

1968, Nixon, Rep., 3,007,932; Humphrey, Dem., 3,378,470; Wallace, 3d Party, 358,864; Blomen, Soc. Labor, 8,432; Halstead, Soc. Workers, 11,851; Gregory, Freedom and Peace, 24,517; blank, void, and scattering, 171,624.

1972, Nixon, Rep., 3,824,642; Cons., 368,136; McGovern, Dem., 2,767,956; Liberal, 183,128; Reed, Soc. Workers, 7,797; Fisher, Soc. Labor, 4,530; Hall, Com., 5,641; blank, void, or scattered, 161,641.

1976, Carter, Dem., 3,389,558; Ford, Rep., 3,100,791; MacBride, Libertarian, 12,197; Hall, Com., 10,270; Camejo, Soc. Workers, 6,996; LaRouche, U.S. Labor, 5,413; blank, void, or scattered, 143,037.

1980, Reagan, Rep., 2,893,831; Carter, Dem., 2,728,372; Anderson, Ind., 467,801; Clark, Libertarian, 52,648; McCormack, Right To Life, 24,159; Commoner, Citizens, 23,186; Hall, Com., 7,414; DeBerry, Soc. Workers, 2,068; Griswold, Workers World, 1,416; scattering, 1,064.

1984, Reagan, Rep., 3,664,763; Mondale, Dem., 3,119,609; Bergland, Libertarian, 11,949.

1988, Bush, Rep., 3,081,871; Dukakis, Dem., 3,347,882; Marra, Right to Life, 20,497; Fulani, New Alliance, 15,845.

1992, Clinton, Dem., 3,444,450; Bush, Rep., 2,346,649; Perot, Ind., 1,090,721; Warren, Soc. Workers, 15,472; Marrou, Libertarian, 13,451; Fulani, New Alliance, 11,318; Hagelin, Natural Law, 4,420.

1996, Clinton, Dem., 3,513,191; Dole, Rep., 1,861,198; Perot, Ind. (Ref.), 485,547; Nader, Green, 66,393; Phillips, Right to Life, 23,669; Browne, Libertarian, 12,556; Hagelin, Natural Law, 5,678; Harris, Soc. Workers, 4,886; Moorehead, Workers World, 4,011.

# North Carolina

| County | 1996 Clinton (D) | 1996 Dole (R) | 1996 Perot (RF) | 1992 Clinton (D) | 1992 Bush (R) | 1992 Perot (I) |
|---|---|---|---|---|---|---|
| Alamance . | 15,564 | 22,059 | 3,320 | 15,521 | 20,637 | 6,444 |
| Alexander. | 6,120 | 7,320 | 1,202 | 4,849 | 6,764 | 2,002 |

| County | Clinton (D) | 1996 Dole (R) | Perot (RF) | Clinton (D) | 1992 Bush (R) | Perot (I) |
|---|---|---|---|---|---|---|
| Alleghany . | 1,801 | 1,936 | 458 | 2,271 | 1,853 | 600 |
| Anson . . . | 4,847 | 2,181 | 526 | 5,269 | 2,334 | 921 |
| Ashe . . . . | 3,824 | 5,101 | 864 | 4,624 | 5,200 | 1,220 |
| Avery. . . . | 1,581 | 3,858 | 654 | 1,755 | 3,895 | 1,123 |
| Beaufort . . | 6,138 | 8,154 | 808 | 6,445 | 7,337 | 2,174 |
| Bertie. . . . | 4,201 | 1,743 | 316 | 4,382 | 1,756 | 600 |
| Bladen . . . | 4,871 | 3,313 | 653 | 5,700 | 3,214 | 1,248 |
| Brunswick. | 10,011 | 10,025 | 1,809 | 10,177 | 8,833 | 3,349 |
| Buncombe | 31,546 | 30,415 | 6,225 | 32,955 | 30,892 | 11,481 |
| Burke. . . . | 11,614 | 13,740 | 2,632 | 12,565 | 13,397 | 4,124 |
| Cabarrus . | 14,339 | 22,896 | 3,583 | 13,513 | 21,281 | 6,251 |
| Caldwell . . | 8,011 | 12,606 | 2,093 | 9,033 | 12,543 | 3,965 |
| Camden . . | 1,183 | 1,074 | 292 | 1,153 | 1,039 | 479 |
| Carteret . . | 7,554 | 11,713 | 1,461 | 8,028 | 10,334 | 3,401 |
| Caswell . . | 4,309 | 3,310 | 510 | 4,725 | 2,793 | 827 |
| Catawba. . | 15,217 | 26,406 | 3,542 | 16,334 | 25,466 | 7,523 |
| Chatham . | 9,294 | 7,665 | 999 | 9,520 | 6,568 | 2,425 |
| Cherokee . | 3,118 | 3,876 | 777 | 3,686 | 4,021 | 1,040 |
| Chowan . . | 2,232 | 1,658 | 358 | 2,136 | 1,661 | 700 |
| Clay. . . . . | 1,450 | 1,755 | 378 | 1,600 | 1,890 | 465 |
| Cleveland . | 12,647 | 13,013 | 1,803 | 13,037 | 13,650 | 3,784 |
| Columbus . | 8,631 | 5,396 | 1,024 | 11,469 | 5,462 | 1,963 |
| Craven. . . | 10,143 | 13,173 | 1,526 | 9,998 | 11,575 | 3,679 |
| Cumberland | 32,284 | 29,434 | 3,581 | 30,291 | 27,139 | 6,792 |
| Currituck. . | 2,271 | 2,564 | 765 | 1,935 | 2,188 | 1,163 |
| Dare . . . . | 4,517 | 4,974 | 1,257 | 3,925 | 4,357 | 2,388 |
| Davidson . | 13,570 | 24,745 | 3,665 | 16,462 | 24,869 | 8,324 |
| Davie. . . . | 3,520 | 8,128 | 912 | 3,675 | 6,796 | 1,903 |
| Duplin . . . | 5,969 | 5,196 | 756 | 6,816 | 5,286 | 1,636 |
| Durham . . | 48,873 | 27,699 | 3,076 | 47,331 | 27,581 | 7,504 |
| Edgecombe | 10,539 | 5,994 | 655 | 11,174 | 6,275 | 2,175 |
| Forsyth. . . | 46,490 | 59,084 | 5,733 | 49,006 | 52,787 | 14,262 |
| Franklin . . | 6,414 | 5,663 | 887 | 6,517 | 4,669 | 2,062 |
| Gaston. . . | 18,176 | 30,570 | 3,711 | 19,121 | 34,714 | 7,490 |
| Gates. . . . | 2,149 | 1,066 | 304 | 2,206 | 1,158 | 466 |
| Graham . . | 1,205 | 1,804 | 276 | 1,551 | 1,919 | 403 |
| Granville. . | 6,588 | 5,338 | 423 | 6,178 | 4,538 | 1,321 |
| Greene. . . | 2,221 | 2,687 | 278 | 2,768 | 2,180 | 780 |
| Guilford . . | 68,871 | 67,533 | 9,708 | 66,319 | 60,140 | 19,601 |
| Halifax . . . | 9,527 | 5,777 | 813 | 9,960 | 5,769 | 2,047 |
| Harnett. . . | 8,706 | 11,534 | 1,280 | 8,473 | 9,751 | 2,684 |
| Haywood . | 9,350 | 7,995 | 2,596 | 10,385 | 7,292 | 3,303 |
| Henderson | 10,617 | 18,885 | 2,671 | 10,747 | 17,010 | 5,260 |
| Hertford . . | 4,839 | 1,818 | 356 | 4,609 | 2,208 | 846 |
| Hoke . . . . | 3,442 | 1,875 | 471 | 3,730 | 1,711 | 887 |
| Hyde . . . . | 1,109 | 780 | 143 | 1,206 | 740 | 340 |
| Iredell. . . . | 12,979 | 21,116 | 2,961 | 13,263 | 19,411 | 6,204 |
| Jackson . . | 5,178 | 4,201 | 959 | 5,753 | 4,275 | 1,516 |
| Johnston . | 11,155 | 18,260 | 2,159 | 11,284 | 15,418 | 4,939 |
| Jones. . . . | 1,805 | 1,673 | 171 | 1,962 | 1,438 | 444 |
| Lee . . . . . | 6,215 | 7,321 | 963 | 5,852 | 6,658 | 2,125 |
| Lenoir . . . | 8,609 | 9,417 | 818 | 8,793 | 8,932 | 2,107 |
| Lincoln . . . | 7,563 | 11,336 | 1,593 | 8,150 | 11,018 | 3,142 |
| McDowell . | 4,166 | 5,220 | 1,112 | 5,309 | 6,090 | 1,881 |
| Macon . . . | 3,334 | 3,110 | 538 | 4,624 | 4,797 | 1,829 |
| Madison . . | 4,486 | 3,585 | 442 | 3,980 | 3,121 | 857 |
| Martin . . . | 4,486 | 3,584 | 444 | 4,069 | 2,958 | 981 |
| Mecklenburg | 102,497 | 97,015 | 10,322 | 97,065 | 99,496 | 31,283 |
| Mitchell . . | 1,487 | 3,867 | 548 | 1,727 | 4,405 | 877 |
| Montgomery. | 3,849 | 3,376 | 585 | 4,422 | 3,543 | 1,185 |
| Moore . . . | 9,684 | 14,578 | 1,728 | 9,649 | 12,448 | 4,448 |
| Nash . . . . | 11,105 | 15,303 | 1,744 | 10,809 | 14,446 | 4,544 |
| New Hanover | 22,451 | 27,439 | 3,434 | 20,291 | 24,338 | 7,401 |
| Northampton | 4,995 | 1,671 | 382 | 5,195 | 1,845 | 916 |
| Onslow. . . | 8,636 | 13,320 | 1,835 | 8,045 | 11,842 | 4,387 |
| Orange. . . | 28,654 | 15,139 | 1,490 | 28,595 | 13,009 | 5,535 |
| Pamlico . . | 2,198 | 2,266 | 294 | 2,229 | 1,929 | 809 |
| Pasquotank | 4,212 | 2,987 | 558 | 4,709 | 3,419 | 1,434 |
| Pender. . . | 5,382 | 5,501 | 842 | 5,825 | 4,857 | 1,725 |
| Perquimans | 2,069 | 1,561 | 369 | 1,818 | 1,429 | 624 |
| Person. . . | 4,535 | 4,870 | 595 | 4,323 | 4,460 | 1,431 |
| Pitt . . . . . | 17,429 | 18,161 | 1,886 | 17,959 | 16,609 | 5,262 |
| Polk. . . . . | 2,699 | 3,512 | 491 | 2,939 | 3,448 | 1,134 |
| Randolph . | 10,728 | 22,864 | 3,566 | 11,274 | 20,697 | 6,870 |
| Richmond . | 7,447 | 3,919 | 1,137 | 9,163 | 4,356 | 2,015 |
| Robeson. . | 17,305 | 8,128 | 2,104 | 19,378 | 7,777 | 3,277 |
| Rockingham | 11,962 | 14,110 | 2,410 | 13,880 | 12,678 | 4,671 |
| Rowan . . . | 13,402 | 22,654 | 2,882 | 14,308 | 21,297 | 7,053 |
| Rutherford | 7,099 | 9,703 | 1,570 | 7,855 | 9,748 | 2,695 |
| Sampson . | 8,024 | 8,154 | 818 | 8,698 | 8,007 | 1,852 |
| Scotland . . | 4,222 | 2,755 | 517 | 5,175 | 2,980 | 1,196 |
| Stanly . . . | 7,124 | 11,434 | 1,687 | 7,735 | 11,030 | 2,855 |
| Stokes . . . | 4,738 | 9,400 | 1,014 | 6,463 | 7,979 | 2,183 |
| Surry . . . . | 7,255 | 10,977 | 1,508 | 9,392 | 10,866 | 3,164 |
| Swain. . . . | 1,865 | 1,441 | 399 | 2,117 | 1,640 | 568 |
| Transylvania. | 4,835 | 6,725 | 1,175 | 5,120 | 5,984 | 2,006 |
| Tyrrell . . . | 907 | 485 | 109 | 928 | 553 | 189 |
| Union. . . . | 11,466 | 18,650 | 2,470 | 10,789 | 16,542 | 4,601 |
| Vance . . . | 6,373 | 4,650 | 496 | 6,598 | 4,747 | 1,444 |
| Wake. . . . | 101,788 | 107,268 | 11,567 | 88,979 | 86,798 | 31,140 |
| Warren. . . | 4,211 | 1,861 | 316 | 4,656 | 1,767 | 693 |
| Washington | 2,776 | 1,552 | 119 | 2,902 | 1,780 | 563 |
| Watauga. . | 7,327 | 8,131 | 1,408 | 8,262 | 7,899 | 3,007 |
| Wayne . . . | 11,519 | 16,634 | 1,169 | 10,307 | 14,397 | 2,798 |
| Wilkes . . . | 6,759 | 12,359 | 1,953 | 7,991 | 12,547 | 3,307 |
| Wilson . . . | 9,778 | 10,517 | 1,100 | 10,105 | 10,176 | 2,630 |
| Yadkin . . . | 2,913 | 8,400 | 908 | 3,913 | 7,311 | 1,725 |
| Yancey. . . | 3,950 | 3,967 | 718 | 4,285 | 3,994 | 917 |
| **Totals . . .** | **1,099,123** | **1,211,655** | **164,512** | **1,114,042** | **1,134,661** | **357,864** |

## North Carolina Vote Since 1948

1948, Truman, Dem., 459,070; Dewey, Rep., 258,572; Thurmond, States' Rights, 69,652; Wallace, Prog., 3,915.

1952, Eisenhower, Rep., 558,107; Stevenson, Dem., 652,803.

1956, Eisenhower, Rep., 575,062; Stevenson, Dem., 590,530.

1960, Kennedy, Dem., 713,136; Nixon, Rep., 655,420.

1964, Johnson, Dem., 800,139; Goldwater, Rep., 624,844.

1968, Nixon, Rep., 627,192; Humphrey, Dem., 464,113; Wallace, 3d Party, 496,188.

1972, Nixon, Rep., 1,054,889; McGovern, Dem., 438,705; Schmitz, Amer., 25,018.

1976, Carter, Dem., 927,365; Ford, Rep., 741,960; Anderson, Amer., 5,607; MacBride, Libertarian, 2,219; LaRouche, U.S. Labor, 755.

1980, Reagan, Rep., 915,018; Carter, Dem., 875,635; Anderson, Ind., 52,800; Clark, Libertarian, 9,677; Commoner, Citizens, 2,287; DeBerry, Soc. Workers, 416.

1984, Reagan, Rep., 1,346,481; Mondale, Dem., 824,287; Bergland, Libertarian, 3,794.

1988, Bush, Rep., 1,237,258; Dukakis, Dem., 890,167; Fulani, New Alliance, 5,682; Paul, write-in, 1,263.

1992, Clinton, Dem., 1,114,042; Bush, Rep., 1,134,661; Perot, Ind., 357,864; Marrou, Libertarian, 5,171.

1996, Dole, Rep., 1,211,655; Clinton, Dem., 1,099,123; Perot, Ref., 164,512; Browne, Libertarian, 8,910; Hagelin, Natural Law, 2,895.

# North Dakota

| County | Clinton (D) | 1996 Dole (R) | Perot (RF) | Clinton (D) | 1992 Bush (R) | Perot (I) |
|---|---|---|---|---|---|---|
| Adams . . . | 365 | 575 | 200 | 469 | 647 | 499 |
| Barnes . . . | 2,283 | 2,428 | 656 | 2,124 | 2,728 | 1,568 |
| Benson . . | 917 | 853 | 366 | 1,126 | 874 | 610 |
| Billings . . . | 116 | 281 | 107 | 123 | 279 | 270 |
| Bottineau . | 1,277 | 1,682 | 536 | 1,266 | 1,787 | 1,036 |
| Bowman. . | 488 | 710 | 261 | 506 | 712 | 678 |
| Burke. . . . | 415 | 482 | 176 | 458 | 551 | 506 |
| Burleigh . . | 10,604 | 15,353 | 3,519 | 8,940 | 16,484 | 6,780 |
| Cass . . . . | 21,583 | 24,121 | 4,102 | 18,077 | 25,312 | 9,513 |
| Cavalier . . | 939 | 1,178 | 352 | 866 | 1,527 | 723 |
| Dickey . . . | 953 | 1,416 | 276 | 918 | 1,514 | 616 |
| Divide . . . | 637 | 487 | 209 | 634 | 515 | 456 |
| Dunn . . . . | 586 | 829 | 304 | 667 | 784 | 637 |
| Eddy . . . . | 553 | 513 | 200 | 575 | 591 | 432 |
| Emmons. . | 544 | 1,147 | 441 | 595 | 1,047 | 774 |
| Foster . . . | 668 | 789 | 265 | 565 | 803 | 556 |
| Golden Valley. | 235 | 520 | 161 | 255 | 503 | 352 |
| Grand Forks. | 11,346 | 11,567 | 2,657 | 10,930 | 13,705 | 6,349 |
| Grant. . . . | 297 | 754 | 294 | 415 | 900 | 629 |
| Griggs . . . | 669 | 730 | 162 | 647 | 773 | 330 |
| Hettinger . | 418 | 765 | 238 | 465 | 854 | 500 |
| Kidder . . . | 434 | 689 | 242 | 468 | 739 | 489 |
| La Moure . | 879 | 1,219 | 276 | 797 | 1,270 | 679 |
| Logan . . . | 360 | 704 | 254 | 383 | 703 | 390 |
| McHenry . | 1,096 | 1,185 | 453 | 1,173 | 1,321 | 886 |
| McIntosh . | 470 | 1,005 | 295 | 450 | 1,134 | 454 |
| McKenzie . | 928 | 1,337 | 428 | 787 | 1,324 | 969 |
| McLean . . | 1,753 | 1,982 | 617 | 1,808 | 2,124 | 1,330 |
| Mercer . . . | 1,297 | 1,949 | 763 | 1,323 | 2,274 | 1,378 |
| Morton . . . | 3,738 | 4,689 | 1,564 | 3,594 | 5,042 | 2,787 |
| Mountrail . | 1,273 | 963 | 360 | 1,393 | 1,017 | 861 |
| Nelson . . . | 827 | 743 | 206 | 841 | 864 | 486 |
| Oliver. . . . | 333 | 499 | 183 | 306 | 503 | 407 |
| Pembina. . | 1,187 | 1,670 | 400 | 1,186 | 1,917 | 991 |
| Pierce . . . | 670 | 1,014 | 270 | 761 | 1,099 | 554 |
| Ramsey . . | 2,121 | 2,076 | 549 | 2,008 | 2,516 | 1,507 |
| Ransom . . | 1,197 | 919 | 303 | 1,166 | 1,102 | 625 |
| Renville . . | 559 | 576 | 210 | 580 | 655 | 429 |
| Richland. . | 2,887 | 3,337 | 782 | 2,688 | 3,873 | 1,698 |
| Rolette . . . | 2,299 | 820 | 448 | 2,002 | 895 | 660 |
| Sargent . . | 1,001 | 811 | 241 | 961 | 816 | 463 |
| Sheridan. . | 207 | 476 | 92 | 276 | 589 | 304 |
| Sioux . . . . | 393 | 207 | 82 | 463 | 264 | 244 |
| Slope. . . . | 123 | 259 | 60 | 145 | 226 | 162 |
| Stark . . . . | 3,089 | 4,080 | 1,456 | 3,003 | 4,491 | 3,123 |
| Steele . . . | 618 | 486 | 115 | 598 | 503 | 267 |
| Stutsman . | 3,581 | 3,774 | 1,141 | 3,313 | 4,039 | 2,580 |
| Towner. . . | 649 | 540 | 187 | 748 | 600 | 402 |
| Traill . . . . | 1,816 | 1,819 | 379 | 1,638 | 2,019 | 875 |
| Walsh . . . | 2,078 | 2,221 | 599 | 1,936 | 2,544 | 1,384 |
| Ward . . . . | 8,637 | 10,513 | 2,584 | 7,856 | 12,056 | 5,856 |

| County | 1996 Clinton (D) | 1996 Dole (R) | 1996 Perot (RF) | 1992 Clinton (D) | 1992 Bush (R) | 1992 Perot (I) |
|---|---|---|---|---|---|---|
| Wells . . . . | 962 | 1,190 | 373 | 888 | 1,171 | 850 |
| Williams . . | 3,005 | 3,575 | 1,172 | 3,008 | 3,664 | 3,180 |
| **Totals . . .** | **106,360** | **124,507** | **32,566** | **99,168** | **136,244** | **71,084** |

## North Dakota Vote Since 1948

1948, Truman, Dem., 95,812; Dewey, Rep., 115,139; Wallace, Prog., 8,391; Thomas, Soc., 1,000; Thurmond, States' Rights, 374.

1952, Eisenhower, Rep., 191,712; Stevenson, Dem., 76,694; MacArthur, Christian Nationalist, 1,075; Hallinan, Prog., 344; Hamblen, Proh., 302.

1956, Eisenhower, Rep., 156,766; Stevenson, Dem., 96,742; Andrews, Amer., 483.

1960, Kennedy, Dem., 123,963; Nixon, Rep., 154,310; Dobbs, Soc. Workers, 158.

1964, Johnson, Dem., 149,784; Goldwater, Rep., 108,207; DeBerry, Soc. Workers, 224; Munn, Proh., 174.

1968, Nixon, Rep., 138,669; Humphrey, Dem., 94,769; Wallace, 3d Party, 14,244; Halstead, Soc. Workers, 128; Munn, Prohibition, 38; Troxell, Ind., 34.

1972, Nixon, Rep., 174,109; McGovern, Dem., 100,384; Jenness, Soc. Workers, 288; Hall, Com., 87; Schmitz, Amer., 5,646.

1976, Carter, Dem., 136,078; Ford, Rep., 153,470; Anderson, Amer., 3,698; McCarthy, Ind., 2,952; Maddox, Amer. Ind., 269; MacBride, Libertarian, 256; scattering, 371.

1980, Reagan, Rep., 193,695; Carter, Dem., 79,189; Anderson, Ind., 23,640; Clark, Libertarian, 3,743; Commoner, Libertarian, 429; McLain, Natl. People's League, 296; Greaves, Amer., 235; Hall, Com., 93; DeBerry, Soc. Workers, 89; McReynolds, Soc., 82; Bubar, Statesman, 54.

1984, Reagan, Rep., 200,336; Mondale, Dem., 104,429; Bergland, Libertarian, 703.

1988, Bush, Rep., 166,559; Dukakis, Dem., 127,739; Paul, Lib., 1,315; LaRouche, Natl. Econ. Recovery, 905.

1992, Clinton, Dem., 99,168; Bush, Rep., 136,244; Perot, Ind., 71,084.

1996, Dole, Rep., 124,507; Clinton, Dem., 106,360; Perot, Ref., 32,566; Browne, Libertarian, 843; Phillips, Ind., 739; Hagelin, Natural Law, 373.

# Ohio

| County | 1996 Clinton (D) | 1996 Dole (R) | 1996 Perot (RF) | 1992 Clinton (D) | 1992 Bush (R) | 1992 Perot (I) |
|---|---|---|---|---|---|---|
| Adams . . . | 4,244 | 4,677 | 1,196 | 3,998 | 4,722 | 1,993 |
| Allen . . . . | 15,218 | 23,839 | 3,701 | 13,777 | 25,322 | 8,131 |
| Ashland . . | 6,448 | 10,215 | 2,573 | 5,985 | 9,864 | 4,950 |
| Ashtabula . | 18,696 | 12,807 | 5,473 | 18,843 | 13,254 | 10,765 |
| Athens . . . | 12,258 | 6,577 | 2,622 | 13,423 | 7,184 | 5,074 |
| Auglaize . . | 6,458 | 9,884 | 2,557 | 4,960 | 10,455 | 4,840 |
| Belmont . . | 17,517 | 8,111 | 4,368 | 18,527 | 8,614 | 6,142 |
| Brown . . . | 6,204 | 6,861 | 1,904 | 5,540 | 5,912 | 3,676 |
| Butler. . . . | 42,567 | 65,391 | 10,185 | 39,682 | 63,375 | 27,527 |
| Carroll . . . | 4,726 | 4,381 | 2,375 | 4,731 | 4,224 | 3,434 |
| Champaign | 5,843 | 6,423 | 2,143 | 5,201 | 7,004 | 3,992 |
| Clark . . . . | 27,467 | 22,000 | 6,948 | 26,692 | 24,011 | 12,571 |
| Clermont . | 21,011 | 35,871 | 5,688 | 17,558 | 32,065 | 14,279 |
| Clinton . . . | 5,209 | 7,355 | 1,546 | 4,638 | 7,290 | 3,402 |
| Columbiana | 20,488 | 15,210 | 6,993 | 19,765 | 15,016 | 12,611 |
| Coshocton | 5,933 | 5,937 | 2,141 | 6,212 | 5,705 | 4,081 |
| Crawford . | 7,309 | 8,607 | 2,999 | 6,351 | 8,618 | 5,764 |
| Cuyahoga. | 330,264 | 159,467 | 49,068 | 337,548 | 187,186 | 112,352 |
| Darke. . . . | 8,660 | 10,542 | 3,037 | 7,016 | 11,098 | 6,217 |
| Defiance. . | 6,199 | 7,313 | 1,870 | 5,735 | 7,195 | 4,187 |
| Delaware . | 13,234 | 23,740 | 3,391 | 9,263 | 18,225 | 9,244 |
| Erie . . . . . | 16,395 | 12,013 | 4,115 | 14,531 | 12,459 | 8,720 |
| Fairfield . . | 18,570 | 26,440 | 4,587 | 14,249 | 24,125 | 12,246 |
| Fayette. . . | 3,601 | 4,732 | 1,016 | 2,976 | 4,916 | 2,162 |
| Franklin . . | 188,466 | 174,655 | 24,723 | 176,656 | 186,324 | 79,049 |
| Fulton . . . | 6,555 | 8,567 | 2,348 | 5,576 | 8,358 | 4,798 |
| Gallia. . . . | 5,265 | 5,071 | 1,796 | 5,350 | 5,776 | 2,549 |
| Geauga . . | 13,986 | 19,420 | 4,774 | 11,466 | 18,200 | 10,577 |
| Greene. . . | 24,378 | 29,853 | 5,078 | 20,139 | 27,651 | 11,459 |
| Guernsey . | 6,495 | 5,758 | 2,182 | 6,428 | 5,749 | 4,103 |
| Hamilton. . | 156,491 | 183,026 | 20,766 | 148,409 | 192,447 | 60,145 |
| Hancock. . | 9,137 | 17,032 | 2,791 | 7,944 | 16,821 | 7,002 |
| Hardin . . . | 4,855 | 5,356 | 1,334 | 4,364 | 5,851 | 2,867 |
| Harrison . . | 3,680 | 2,293 | 1,291 | 3,830 | 2,289 | 1,679 |
| Henry. . . . | 4,676 | 6,310 | 1,508 | 3,933 | 6,196 | 3,178 |
| Highland. . | 5,732 | 6,999 | 1,595 | 4,866 | 7,020 | 3,315 |
| Hocking . . | 4,535 | 3,932 | 1,518 | 3,935 | 3,761 | 2,831 |
| Holmes . . | 2,482 | 5,120 | 1,244 | 1,969 | 5,079 | 1,945 |
| Huron. . . . | 8,779 | 8,584 | 3,389 | 7,930 | 9,480 | 6,751 |
| Jackson . . | 5,425 | 4,871 | 1,487 | 5,016 | 5,422 | 2,389 |
| Jefferson . | 19,138 | 10,057 | 4,664 | 20,978 | 10,764 | 6,910 |
| Knox . . . . | 7,458 | 9,992 | 2,113 | 7,259 | 9,044 | 5,282 |
| Lake . . . . | 42,652 | 40,479 | 12,257 | 37,682 | 40,766 | 26,878 |
| Lawrence . | 11,467 | 8,773 | 3,182 | 12,325 | 10,044 | 4,536 |
| Licking . . . | 22,164 | 27,637 | 6,339 | 18,898 | 26,918 | 13,806 |
| Logan . . . | 6,282 | 8,156 | 2,194 | 4,889 | 9,364 | 4,472 |
| Lorain . . . | 54,426 | 34,275 | 14,526 | 50,962 | 36,803 | 30,425 |
| Lucas. . . . | 102,327 | 57,052 | 16,740 | 99,989 | 63,297 | 38,108 |
| Madison . . | 4,995 | 6,789 | 1,348 | 3,998 | 6,865 | 3,170 |
| Mahoning . | 71,893 | 31,030 | 13,022 | 64,731 | 31,191 | 29,417 |
| Marion . . . | 10,262 | 10,904 | 2,825 | 9,444 | 11,675 | 6,471 |
| Medina. . . | 23,491 | 25,729 | 8,583 | 18,995 | 24,090 | 17,290 |
| Meigs. . . . | 4,212 | 3,577 | 1,425 | 4,226 | 3,916 | 2,098 |
| Mercer . . . | 6,250 | 8,736 | 2,327 | 4,883 | 8,683 | 4,913 |
| Miami. . . . | 15,188 | 19,022 | 4,446 | 12,547 | 19,741 | 10,544 |
| Monroe . . | 3,874 | 1,833 | 1,104 | 4,235 | 1,823 | 1,505 |
| Montgomery. | 113,144 | 93,398 | 17,740 | 108,017 | 104,751 | 47,854 |
| Morgan . . | 2,359 | 2,541 | 914 | 2,402 | 2,719 | 1,551 |
| Morrow. . . | 4,574 | 5,563 | 1,706 | 3,907 | 5,208 | 3,623 |
| Muskingum | 13,536 | 13,614 | 4,740 | 11,670 | 14,168 | 8,731 |
| Noble. . . . | 2,320 | 2,158 | 881 | 2,201 | 2,223 | 1,429 |
| Ottawa. . . | 9,095 | 6,820 | 2,358 | 8,128 | 6,782 | 4,832 |
| Paulding. . | 3,501 | 3,724 | 1,283 | 3,293 | 3,652 | 2,510 |
| Perry . . . . | 5,728 | 4,536 | 1,827 | 4,972 | 4,712 | 3,810 |
| Pickaway . | 6,924 | 8,525 | 1,657 | 5,765 | 8,690 | 4,319 |
| Pike. . . . . | 5,475 | 3,720 | 1,374 | 5,057 | 4,094 | 2,192 |
| Portage . . | 28,957 | 18,652 | 9,012 | 26,325 | 18,447 | 17,065 |
| Preble . . . | 6,502 | 8,018 | 2,191 | 5,557 | 8,023 | 4,460 |
| Putnam . . | 4,935 | 9,230 | 1,746 | 3,962 | 9,338 | 3,648 |
| Richland. . | 20,284 | 23,081 | 5,964 | 19,606 | 23,532 | 13,370 |
| Ross . . . . | 12,453 | 10,152 | 2,594 | 10,452 | 10,825 | 5,616 |
| Sandusky . | 11,356 | 9,882 | 3,556 | 9,878 | 10,772 | 6,682 |
| Scioto . . . | 14,683 | 11,433 | 4,282 | 14,715 | 11,931 | 6,860 |
| Seneca . . | 9,855 | 9,585 | 3,414 | 9,280 | 9,763 | 6,967 |
| Shelby . . . | 6,590 | 8,598 | 2,603 | 5,262 | 8,854 | 5,835 |
| Stark . . . . | 71,760 | 58,976 | 22,420 | 70,064 | 61,863 | 42,413 |
| Summit . . | 110,226 | 72,304 | 27,223 | 107,881 | 77,530 | 55,151 |
| Trumbull. . | 54,578 | 24,420 | 13,266 | 54,591 | 25,831 | 26,791 |
| Tuscarawas | 15,011 | 13,146 | 5,511 | 14,787 | 13,179 | 8,785 |
| Union. . . . | 4,923 | 8,164 | 1,569 | 3,465 | 7,818 | 3,433 |
| Van Wert . | 4,365 | 6,876 | 1,445 | 3,822 | 7,227 | 3,102 |
| Vinton . . . | 2,321 | 1,660 | 715 | 2,308 | 1,975 | 1,050 |
| Warren. . . | 16,839 | 32,560 | 4,559 | 13,542 | 27,998 | 11,115 |
| Washington | 10,766 | 11,784 | 2,766 | 10,380 | 12,204 | 5,415 |
| Wayne . . . | 14,616 | 19,344 | 5,662 | 13,953 | 18,350 | 9,482 |
| Williams . . | 5,393 | 7,606 | 2,064 | 4,862 | 7,614 | 4,902 |
| Wood. . . . | 22,592 | 20,121 | 4,931 | 20,754 | 20,579 | 11,682 |
| Wyandot. . | 3,603 | 4,401 | 1,319 | 3,031 | 4,411 | 2,929 |
| **Totals . . .** | **2,100,799** | **1,823,873** | **470,707** | **1,984,942** | **1,894,310** | **1,036,426** |

## Ohio Vote Since 1948

1948, Truman, Dem., 1,452,791; Dewey, Rep., 1,445,684; Wallace, Prog., 37,596.

1952, Eisenhower, Rep., 2,100,391; Stevenson, Dem., 1,600,367.

1956, Eisenhower, Rep., 2,262,610; Stevenson, Dem., 1,439,655.

1960, Kennedy, Dem., 1,944,248; Nixon, Rep., 2,217,611.

1964, Johnson, Dem., 2,498,331; Goldwater, Rep., 1,470,865.

1968, Nixon, Rep., 1,791,014; Humphrey, Dem., 1,700,586; Wallace, 3d Party, 467,495; Gregory, 372; Munn, Proh., 19; Blomen, Soc. Labor, 120; Halstead, Soc. Workers, 69; Mitchell, Com., 23.

1972, Nixon, Rep., 2,441,827; McGovern, Dem., 1,558,889; Fisher, Soc. Labor, 7,107; Hall, Com., 6,437; Schmitz, Amer., 80,067; Wallace, Ind., 460.

1976, Carter, Dem., 2,011,621; Ford, Rep., 2,000,505; McCarthy, Ind., 58,258; Maddox, Amer. Ind., 15,529; MacBride, Libertarian, 8,961; Hall, Com., 7,817; Camejo, Soc. Workers, 4,717; LaRouche, U.S. Labor, 4,335; scattered, 130.

1980, Reagan, Rep., 2,206,545; Carter, Dem., 1,752,414; Anderson, Ind., 254,472; Clark, Libertarian, 49,033; Commoner, Citizens, 8,564; Hall, Com., 4,729; Congress, Ind., 4,029; Griswold, Workers World, 3,790; Bubar, Statesman, 27.

1984, Reagan, Rep., 2,678,559; Mondale, Dem., 1,825,440; Bergland, Libertarian, 5,886.

1988, Bush, Rep., 2,416,549; Dukakis, Dem., 1,939,629; Fulani, Ind., 12,017; Paul, Ind., 11,926.

1992, Clinton, Dem., 1,984,942; Bush, Rep., 1,894,310; Perot, Ind., 1,036,426; Marrou, Libertarian, 7,252; Fulani, New Alliance, 6,413; Gritz, Populist/America First, 4,699; Hagelin, Natural Law, 3,437; LaRouche, Ind., 2,446.

1996, Clinton, Dem., 2,100,799; Dole, Rep., 1,823,873; Perot, Ref., 470,707; Browne, Ind., 12,150; Moorehead, Ind., 10,467; Hagelin, Natural Law, 9,083; Phillips, Ind., 7,064.

# Oklahoma

| County | 1996 Clinton (D) | 1996 Dole (R) | 1996 Perot (RF) | 1992 Clinton (D) | 1992 Bush (R) | 1992 Perot (I) |
|---|---|---|---|---|---|---|
| Adair . . . . | 2,792 | 2,956 | 751 | 2,645 | 2,994 | 914 |
| Alfalfa . . . | 796 | 1,504 | 348 | 741 | 1,567 | 722 |

| County | Clinton (D) | 1996 Dole (R) | Perot (RF) | Clinton (D) | 1992 Bush (R) | Perot (I) |
|---|---|---|---|---|---|---|
| Atoka. . . . | 2,281 | 1,542 | 532 | 2,336 | 1,561 | 1,255 |
| Beaver. . . | 515 | 1,892 | 199 | 580 | 1,699 | 565 |
| Beckham . | 2,797 | 2,912 | 817 | 2,947 | 2,913 | 1,929 |
| Blaine . . . | 1,832 | 2,127 | 563 | 1,564 | 2,209 | 1,258 |
| Bryan. . . . | 5,962 | 3,943 | 1,396 | 6,259 | 3,452 | 3,713 |
| Caddo . . . | 4,844 | 3,422 | 1,358 | 4,861 | 3,664 | 2,911 |
| Canadian . | 8,977 | 18,139 | 3,297 | 7,215 | 16,756 | 8,985 |
| Carter . . . | 6,979 | 6,769 | 1,997 | 7,171 | 5,947 | 5,188 |
| Cherokee . | 6,817 | 5,046 | 1,777 | 6,794 | 4,977 | 3,297 |
| Choctaw. . | 3,198 | 1,580 | 589 | 3,413 | 1,641 | 1,298 |
| Cimarron . | 361 | 985 | 102 | 395 | 965 | 254 |
| Cleveland . | 26,038 | 36,457 | 6,785 | 24,404 | 35,561 | 20,352 |
| Coal. . . . . | 1,205 | 734 | 323 | 1,448 | 714 | 618 |
| Comanche | 12,841 | 14,461 | 2,819 | 12,237 | 15,704 | 7,463 |
| Cotton . . . | 1,258 | 1,042 | 381 | 1,314 | 910 | 853 |
| Craig . . . . | 2,649 | 2,058 | 758 | 2,780 | 2,106 | 1,316 |
| Creek. . . . | 9,674 | 9,861 | 2,837 | 9,118 | 10,055 | 5,984 |
| Custer . . . | 4,027 | 4,723 | 1,101 | 3,540 | 5,362 | 2,741 |
| Delaware . | 5,094 | 5,230 | 1,573 | 4,842 | 4,840 | 2,689 |
| Dewey . . . | 816 | 1,179 | 292 | 845 | 1,244 | 684 |
| Ellis . . . . . | 619 | 1,090 | 279 | 594 | 1,072 | 632 |
| Garfield . . | 7,504 | 11,712 | 2,523 | 6,720 | 13,095 | 5,559 |
| Garvin . . . | 4,639 | 3,745 | 1,345 | 4,811 | 3,983 | 3,014 |
| Grady. . . . | 6,256 | 7,228 | 2,048 | 6,177 | 6,997 | 4,528 |
| Grant. . . . | 867 | 1,382 | 384 | 864 | 1,311 | 871 |
| Greer. . . . | 1,240 | 905 | 361 | 1,162 | 964 | 640 |
| Harmon . . | 729 | 448 | 143 | 783 | 496 | 326 |
| Harper . . . | 511 | 1,036 | 219 | 486 | 1,038 | 501 |
| Haskell. . . | 2,762 | 1,442 | 590 | 3,069 | 1,461 | 995 |
| Hughes . . | 2,748 | 1,510 | 730 | 2,850 | 1,522 | 1,158 |
| Jackson . . | 3,244 | 4,422 | 892 | 3,273 | 3,893 | 2,227 |
| Jefferson . | 1,430 | 865 | 337 | 1,580 | 671 | 758 |
| Johnston . | 1,998 | 1,229 | 532 | 2,096 | 1,191 | 1,040 |
| Kay . . . . . | 6,882 | 9,741 | 2,785 | 6,643 | 9,115 | 6,984 |
| Kingfisher . | 1,626 | 3,423 | 621 | 1,379 | 3,479 | 1,534 |
| Kiowa. . . . | 1,973 | 1,638 | 510 | 2,143 | 1,635 | 1,114 |
| Latimer. . . | 2,222 | 1,189 | 578 | 2,606 | 1,212 | 1,049 |
| Le Flore . . | 6,831 | 5,689 | 1,721 | 7,843 | 5,850 | 3,021 |
| Lincoln . . . | 4,332 | 5,243 | 1,500 | 3,904 | 5,315 | 3,160 |
| Logan . . . | 4,854 | 5,949 | 1,410 | 4,453 | 6,071 | 3,239 |
| Love . . . . | 1,675 | 1,224 | 385 | 1,708 | 922 | 1,033 |
| McClain . . | 3,753 | 4,363 | 1,289 | 3,378 | 4,377 | 2,996 |
| McCurtain . | 4,350 | 3,892 | 1,483 | 5,082 | 3,519 | 2,852 |
| McIntosh . | 4,219 | 2,400 | 1,044 | 4,184 | 2,225 | 1,469 |
| Major. . . . | 900 | 2,188 | 410 | 731 | 2,154 | 857 |
| Marshall . . | 2,624 | 1,605 | 663 | 2,519 | 1,478 | 1,486 |
| Mayes . . . | 6,377 | 5,268 | 1,617 | 6,432 | 5,445 | 3,235 |
| Murray . . . | 2,620 | 1,712 | 723 | 2,594 | 1,536 | 1,447 |
| Muskogee. | 12,963 | 8,974 | 3,163 | 13,619 | 8,782 | 5,454 |
| Noble. . . . | 1,756 | 2,318 | 694 | 1,333 | 2,474 | 1,449 |
| Nowata. . . | 1,788 | 1,457 | 586 | 1,912 | 1,531 | 1,063 |
| Okfuskee . | 2,074 | 1,380 | 536 | 2,141 | 1,580 | 889 |
| Oklahoma. | 80,438 | 120,429 | 18,411 | 76,271 | 126,788 | 56,139 |
| Okmulgee. | 7,555 | 4,246 | 1,487 | 7,767 | 4,586 | 3,013 |
| Osage . . . | 7,342 | 5,827 | 1,938 | 6,894 | 5,891 | 4,477 |
| Ottawa . . . | 5,844 | 4,126 | 1,496 | 6,304 | 4,141 | 2,721 |
| Pawnee . . | 2,663 | 2,560 | 756 | 2,612 | 2,675 | 1,656 |
| Payne . . . | 9,985 | 11,686 | 2,472 | 9,886 | 13,032 | 7,852 |
| Pittsburg. . | 8,475 | 5,966 | 2,217 | 8,523 | 5,659 | 4,594 |
| Pontotoc. . | 6,470 | 5,366 | 1,712 | 6,350 | 5,206 | 3,916 |
| Pottawatomie | 9,141 | 9,800 | 2,724 | 8,616 | 10,350 | 6,520 |
| Pushmataha. | 2,270 | 1,458 | 588 | 2,553 | 1,319 | 1,000 |
| Roger Mills | 733 | 959 | 233 | 767 | 890 | 505 |
| Rogers. . . | 9,544 | 12,883 | 3,022 | 8,257 | 12,455 | 7,101 |
| Seminole . | 4,225 | 2,935 | 1,041 | 4,624 | 3,253 | 2,330 |
| Sequoyah . | 5,665 | 4,733 | 1,673 | 6,092 | 4,925 | 2,486 |
| Stephens . | 7,248 | 8,144 | 2,312 | 7,644 | 7,085 | 5,692 |
| Texas. . . . | 1,408 | 4,139 | 518 | 1,487 | 4,059 | 1,417 |
| Tillman. . . | 1,827 | 1,346 | 471 | 1,749 | 1,377 | 1,039 |
| Tulsa . . . . | 76,924 | 111,243 | 18,201 | 71,165 | 117,465 | 49,760 |
| Wagoner . | 7,749 | 9,392 | 2,357 | 7,041 | 9,053 | 5,381 |
| Washington | 6,730 | 11,605 | 2,255 | 6,593 | 11,342 | 5,664 |
| Washita . . | 1,913 | 1,994 | 748 | 1,929 | 1,912 | 1,468 |
| Woods . . . | 1,431 | 2,151 | 497 | 1,361 | 2,225 | 1,167 |
| Woodward | 2,403 | 4,093 | 963 | 2,063 | 4,006 | 2,411 |
| **Totals . . .** | **488,102** | **582,310** | **130,788** | **473,066** | **592,929** | **319,878** |

## Oklahoma Vote Since 1948

1948, Truman, Dem., 452,782; Dewey, Rep., 268,817.

1952, Eisenhower, Rep., 518,045; Stevenson, Dem., 430,939.

1956, Eisenhower, Rep., 473,769; Stevenson, Dem., 385,581.

1960, Kennedy, Dem., 370,111; Nixon, Rep., 533,039.

1964, Johnson, Dem., 519,834; Goldwater, Rep., 412,665.

1968, Nixon, Rep., 449,697; Humphrey, Dem., 301,658; Wallace, 3d Party, 191,731.

1972, Nixon, Rep., 759,025; McGovern, Dem., 247,147; Schmitz, Amer., 23,728.

1976, Carter, Dem., 532,442; Ford, Rep., 545,708; McCarthy, Ind., 14,101.

1980, Reagan, Rep., 695,570; Carter, Dem., 402,026; Anderson, Ind., 38,284; Clark, Libertarian, 13,828.

1984, Reagan, Rep., 861,530; Mondale, Dem., 385,080; Bergland, Libertarian, 9,066.

1988, Bush, Rep., 678,367; Dukakis, Dem., 483,423; Paul, Lib., 6,261; Fulani, New Alliance, 2,985.

1992, Clinton, Dem., 473,066; Bush, Rep., 592,929; Perot, Ind., 319,878; Marrou, Libertarian, 4,486.

1996, Dole, Rep., 582,310; Clinton, Dem., 488,102; Perot, Ref., 130,788; Browne, Libertarian, 5,505.

# Oregon

| County | Clinton (D) | 1996 Dole (R) | Perot (RF) | Clinton (D) | 1992 Bush (R) | Perot (I) |
|---|---|---|---|---|---|---|
| Baker. . . . | 916 | 1,627 | 425 | 2,395 | 2,862 | 2,191 |
| Benton . . . | 10,972 | 6,558 | 1,659 | 17,966 | 11,550 | 8,103 |
| Clackamas | 34,448 | 28,151 | 7,603 | 60,310 | 53,724 | 39,776 |
| Clatsop . . | 3,564 | 2,308 | 863 | 7,700 | 4,683 | 4,316 |
| Columbia . | 5,834 | 3,682 | 1,702 | 8,298 | 5,227 | 5,670 |
| Coos . . . . | 8,260 | 6,691 | 2,506 | 12,072 | 9,284 | 7,989 |
| Crook. . . . | 1,328 | 1,606 | 580 | 2,508 | 2,703 | 2,024 |
| Curry . . . . | 2,865 | 2,901 | 1,037 | 3,841 | 3,809 | 3,310 |
| Deschutes | 9,792 | 10,197 | 3,473 | 15,693 | 15,655 | 12,293 |
| Douglas . . | 9,599 | 11,774 | 3,139 | 14,137 | 19,011 | 12,377 |
| Gilliam . . . | 485 | 398 | 143 | 374 | 377 | 283 |
| Grant. . . . | 617 | 1,090 | 242 | 1,135 | 1,496 | 1,302 |
| Harney. . . | 978 | 1,944 | 505 | 973 | 1,350 | 1,024 |
| Hood River | 3,552 | 2,687 | 689 | 3,106 | 2,453 | 2,235 |
| Jackson . . | 20,530 | 20,357 | 5,772 | 29,146 | 28,704 | 18,633 |
| Jefferson . | 1,688 | 1,434 | 570 | 2,161 | 1,962 | 1,741 |
| Josephine. | 7,031 | 8,760 | 2,464 | 11,007 | 13,003 | 8,426 |
| Klamath . . | 4,206 | 6,053 | 1,708 | 7,918 | 11,864 | 6,636 |
| Lake . . . . | 942 | 2,127 | 359 | 1,019 | 1,791 | 980 |
| Lane . . . . | 35,838 | 22,223 | 6,540 | 74,083 | 41,789 | 34,906 |
| Lincoln. . . | 2,596 | 1,637 | 830 | 9,603 | 5,716 | 6,127 |
| Linn. . . . . | 11,924 | 11,320 | 3,638 | 15,399 | 16,461 | 13,256 |
| Malheur . . | 2,020 | 4,178 | 602 | 2,539 | 5,374 | 2,654 |
| Marion . . . | 14,160 | 13,147 | 3,357 | 41,137 | 42,145 | 26,156 |
| Morrow. . . | 1,061 | 958 | 387 | 1,174 | 1,187 | 1,089 |
| Multnomah | 68,990 | 27,939 | 8,760 | 165,081 | 72,326 | 58,236 |
| Polk. . . . . | 7,110 | 6,660 | 1,521 | 9,551 | 10,082 | 5,818 |
| Sherman . | 280 | 333 | 93 | 362 | 424 | 326 |
| Tillamook . | 2,045 | 1,486 | 596 | 5,040 | 3,359 | 2,997 |
| Umatilla . . | 8,576 | 9,448 | 2,436 | 6,787 | 7,095 | 5,581 |
| Union. . . . | 1,292 | 1,767 | 452 | 3,990 | 4,223 | 3,305 |
| Wallowa . . | 413 | 724 | 193 | 1,203 | 1,630 | 1,209 |
| Wasco . . . | 2,720 | 1,975 | 622 | 4,663 | 3,242 | 3,008 |
| Washington | 32,359 | 24,801 | 5,907 | 67,528 | 57,146 | 41,575 |
| Wheeler . . | 158 | 215 | 74 | 267 | 357 | 227 |
| Yamhill. . . | 6,950 | 6,944 | 1,818 | 11,148 | 11,693 | 8,312 |
| **Totals . . .** | **325,225** | **255,452** | **73,011** | **621,314** | **475,757** | **354,091** |

## Oregon Vote Since 1948

1948, Truman, Dem., 243,147; Dewey, Rep., 260,904; Wallace, Prog., 14,978; Thomas, Soc., 5,051.

1952, Eisenhower, Rep., 420,815; Stevenson, Dem., 270,579; Hallinan, Ind., 3,665.

1956, Eisenhower, Rep., 406,393; Stevenson, Dem., 329,204.

1960, Kennedy, Dem., 367,402; Nixon, Rep., 408,060.

1964, Johnson, Dem., 501,017; Goldwater, Rep., 282,779; write-in, 2,509.

1968, Nixon, Rep., 408,433; Humphrey, Dem., 358,866; Wallace, 3d Party, 49,683; write-in, McCarthy, 1,496; N. Rockefeller, 69; others, 1,075.

1972, Nixon, Rep., 486,686; McGovern, Dem., 392,760; Schmitz, Amer., 46,211; write-in, 2,289.

1976, Carter, Dem., 490,407; Ford, Rep., 492,120; McCarthy, Ind., 40,207; write-in, 7,142.

1980, Reagan, Rep., 571,044; Carter, Dem., 456,890; Anderson, Ind., 112,389; Clark, Libertarian, 25,838; Commoner, Citizens, 13,642; scattered, 1,713.

1984, Reagan, Rep., 658,700; Mondale, Dem., 536,479.

1988, Bush, Rep., 560,126; Dukakis, Dem., 616,206; Paul, Lib., 14,811; Fulani, Ind., 6,487.

1992, Clinton, Dem., 621,314; Bush, Rep., 475,757; Perot, Ind., 354,091; Marrou, Libertarian, 4,277; Fulani, New Alliance, 3,030.

1996, Clinton, Dem., 325,225; Dole, Rep., 255,452; Perot, Ref., 73,011; Nader, Pacific, 28,012; Browne, Libertarian, 5,196; Phillips, Taxpayers, 1,784; Hagelin, Natural Law, 1,567; Hollis, Soc., 998.

# Pennsylvania

| County | Clinton (D) | 1996 Dole (R) | Perot (RF) | Clinton (D) | 1992 Bush (R) | Perot (I) |
|---|---|---|---|---|---|---|
| Adams . . . | 10,760 | 15,294 | 3,179 | 9,576 | 13,552 | 6,313 |
| Allegheny . | 282,884 | 203,310 | 42,039 | 324,004 | 183,035 | 103,470 |
| Armstrong. | 11,111 | 11,011 | 3,448 | 12,995 | 9,122 | 6,166 |
| Beaver. . . | 39,301 | 25,759 | 8,211 | 44,877 | 21,361 | 15,954 |
| Bedford . . | 5,953 | 10,065 | 2,042 | 5,840 | 9,216 | 3,731 |

| | | 1996 | | | 1992 | |
|---|---|---|---|---|---|---|
| County | Clinton (D) | Dole (R) | Perot (RF) | Clinton (D) | Bush (R) | Perot (I) |
| Berks. . . . | 49,636 | 55,939 | 13,745 | 46,031 | 52,939 | 31,663 |
| Blair. . . . . | 15,000 | 21,182 | 4,009 | 14,857 | 21,447 | 8,284 |
| Bradford . . | 7,701 | 10,340 | 2,700 | 6,903 | 10,221 | 5,452 |
| Bucks . . . | 102,684 | 94,440 | 24,357 | 97,902 | 94,584 | 53,931 |
| Butler. . . . | 21,969 | 32,007 | 6,141 | 22,303 | 23,656 | 15,013 |
| Cambria . . | 30,181 | 20,245 | 7,828 | 34,334 | 20,770 | 11,070 |
| Cameron . | 822 | 1,113 | 283 | 824 | 1,173 | 676 |
| Carbon. . . | 9,443 | 7,185 | 2,981 | 9,072 | 7,243 | 5,222 |
| Centre . . . | 21,146 | 20,942 | 4,173 | 21,177 | 20,478 | 9,356 |
| Chester . . | 64,724 | 76,930 | 14,057 | 59,643 | 74,002 | 34,536 |
| Clarion . . . | 5,935 | 6,898 | 2,063 | 5,584 | 6,477 | 3,619 |
| Clearfield . | 11,993 | 12,991 | 3,758 | 12,247 | 11,553 | 6,989 |
| Clinton . . . | 5,612 | 4,284 | 1,409 | 5,397 | 4,471 | 2,654 |
| Columbia . | 8,356 | 8,198 | 3,650 | 8,261 | 9,742 | 5,683 |
| Crawford . | 12,815 | 14,630 | 3,511 | 12,813 | 14,112 | 7,392 |
| Cumberland | 28,674 | 43,809 | 5,655 | 26,635 | 43,447 | 14,344 |
| Dauphin . . | 40,840 | 44,310 | 6,954 | 36,990 | 45,479 | 16,063 |
| Delaware . | 117,053 | 92,000 | 21,852 | 111,210 | 108,587 | 43,728 |
| Elk. . . . . . | 5,749 | 4,889 | 2,293 | 5,016 | 4,908 | 3,885 |
| Erie . . . . . | 57,419 | 39,765 | 10,358 | 56,381 | 39,283 | 21,510 |
| Fayette. . . | 26,336 | 13,949 | 5,687 | 30,577 | 12,820 | 10,162 |
| Forest . . . | 944 | 882 | 319 | 890 | 801 | 448 |
| Franklin . . | 14,895 | 25,199 | 4,112 | 13,440 | 23,387 | 6,941 |
| Fulton . . . | 1,620 | 2,665 | 554 | 1,588 | 2,558 | 869 |
| Greene. . . | 7,603 | 3,981 | 1,995 | 8,438 | 3,482 | 3,186 |
| Huntingdon | 5,285 | 7,324 | 1,813 | 5,153 | 7,249 | 3,273 |
| Indiana. . . | 13,832 | 12,828 | 3,665 | 15,194 | 10,966 | 7,089 |
| Jefferson . | 5,830 | 8,126 | 2,318 | 5,998 | 7,271 | 4,403 |
| Juniata. . . | 2,891 | 4,119 | 910 | 2,601 | 3,980 | 1,819 |
| Lackawanna. | 46,413 | 26,790 | 9,224 | 45,054 | 33,443 | 15,667 |
| Lancaster . | 48,971 | 92,712 | 11,536 | 44,255 | 88,447 | 26,807 |
| Lawrence . | 18,993 | 13,088 | 4,002 | 20,830 | 12,359 | 7,950 |
| Lebanon . . | 14,160 | 21,831 | 4,220 | 12,350 | 21,512 | 9,005 |
| Lehigh . . . | 48,492 | 45,048 | 10,953 | 46,711 | 42,631 | 24,853 |
| Luzerne . . | 59,993 | 43,474 | 12,377 | 56,623 | 49,285 | 21,007 |
| Lycoming . | 13,715 | 21,610 | 3,837 | 13,315 | 20,536 | 9,170 |
| McKean . . | 5,505 | 6,815 | 2,306 | 5,331 | 6,965 | 4,019 |
| Mercer . . . | 23,152 | 17,205 | 4,977 | 23,264 | 16,081 | 10,277 |
| Mifflin. . . . | 5,323 | 6,883 | 1,392 | 4,946 | 6,300 | 3,382 |
| Monroe. . . | 16,503 | 17,274 | 4,648 | 13,468 | 14,557 | 9,257 |
| Montgomery. | 143,040 | 120,372 | 24,386 | 136,572 | 125,704 | 53,738 |
| Montour . . | 2,183 | 2,785 | 784 | 2,150 | 3,096 | 1,373 |
| Northampton | 43,764 | 34,472 | 9,405 | 42,203 | 34,429 | 20,234 |
| North-umberland | 13,401 | 13,488 | 5,019 | 12,814 | 15,057 | 7,782 |
| Perry . . . . | 4,595 | 8,124 | 1,606 | 4,086 | 7,871 | 3,334 |
| Philadelphia | 407,209 | 85,154 | 29,489 | 434,904 | 133,328 | 65,455 |
| Pike. . . . . | 5,498 | 6,680 | 1,868 | 4,382 | 6,084 | 3,019 |
| Potter. . . . | 2,142 | 3,698 | 924 | 1,892 | 3,452 | 1,687 |
| Schuylkill . | 24,801 | 22,829 | 8,462 | 23,679 | 25,780 | 13,398 |
| Snyder . . . | 3,405 | 6,742 | 1,451 | 2,952 | 6,934 | 2,686 |
| Somerset . | 12,719 | 14,733 | 3,968 | 12,493 | 13,858 | 6,333 |
| Sullivan . . | 1,073 | 1,356 | 418 | 1,030 | 1,340 | 731 |
| Susquehanna | 5,687 | 6,991 | 2,163 | 5,368 | 7,356 | 3,946 |
| Tioga . . . . | 4,910 | 7,304 | 1,981 | 4,868 | 7,823 | 3,804 |
| Union. . . . | 3,658 | 6,567 | 1,431 | 3,623 | 6,362 | 2,255 |
| Venango. . | 8,204 | 8,396 | 2,777 | 8,230 | 8,545 | 4,695 |
| Warren. . . | 7,290 | 7,050 | 2,516 | 6,972 | 6,585 | 4,795 |
| Washington | 40,872 | 27,627 | 8,647 | 46,143 | 21,977 | 16,083 |
| Wayne . . . | 5,904 | 8,058 | 2,117 | 4,817 | 8,184 | 3,727 |
| Westmoreland | 63,553 | 61,895 | 16,099 | 69,817 | 47,315 | 37,036 |
| Wyoming . | 4,050 | 4,948 | 1,414 | 3,158 | 5,143 | 2,525 |
| York. . . . . | 50,066 | 64,960 | 11,616 | 46,113 | 60,130 | 27,743 |
| **Totals . . .** | **2,206,241** | **1,793,568** | **430,082** | **2,239,164** | **1,791,841** | **902,667** |

## Pennsylvania Vote Since 1948

1948, Truman, Dem., 1,752,426; Dewey, Rep., 1,902,197; Wallace, Prog., 55,161; Thomas, Soc., 11,325; Watson, Proh., 10,338; Dobbs, Militant Workers, 2,133; Teichert, Ind. Gov., 1,461.

1952, Eisenhower, Rep., 2,415,789; Stevenson, Dem., 2,146,269; Hamblen, Proh., 8,771; Hallinan, Prog., 4,200; Hoopes, Soc., 2,684; Dobbs, Militant Workers, 1,502; Hass, Ind. Gov., 1,347; scattered, 155.

1956, Eisenhower, Rep., 2,585,252; Stevenson, Dem., 1,981,769; Hass, Soc. Labor, 7,447; Dobbs, Militant Workers, 2,035.

1960, Kennedy, Dem., 2,556,282; Nixon, Rep., 2,439,956; Hass, Soc. Labor, 7,185; Dobbs, Soc. Workers, 2,678; scattering, 440.

1964, Johnson, Dem., 3,130,954; Goldwater, Rep., 1,673,657; DeBerry, Soc. Workers, 10,456; Hass, Soc. Labor, 5,092; scattering, 2,531.

1968, Nixon, Rep., 2,090,017; Humphrey, Dem., 2,259,405; Wallace, 3d Party, 378,582; Blomen, Soc. Labor, 4,977; Halstead, Soc. Workers, 4,862; Gregory, Peace and Freedom, 7,821; others, 2,264.

1972, Nixon, Rep., 2,714,521; McGovern, Dem., 1,796,951; Schmitz, Amer., 70,593; Jenness, Soc. Workers, 4,639; Hall, Com., 2,686; others, 2,715.

1976, Carter, Dem., 2,328,677; Ford, Rep., 2,205,604; McCarthy, Ind., 50,584; Maddox, Constitution, 25,344; Camejo, Soc. Workers, 3,009; LaRouche, U.S. Labor, 2,744; Hall, Com., 1,891; others, 2,934.

1980, Reagan, Rep., 2,261,872; Carter, Dem., 1,937,540; Anderson, Ind., 292,921; Clark, Libertarian, 33,263; DeBerry, Soc. Workers, 20,291; Commoner, Consumer, 10,430; Hall, Com., 5,184.

1984, Reagan, Rep., 2,584,323; Mondale, Dem., 2,228,131; Bergland, Libertarian, 6,982.

1988, Bush, Rep., 2,300,087; Dukakis, Dem., 2,194,944; McCarthy, Consumer, 19,158; Paul, Lib., 12,051.

1992, Clinton, Dem., 2,239,164; Bush, Rep., 1,791,841; Perot, Ind., 902,667; Marrou, Libertarian, 21,477; Fulani, New Alliance, 4,661.

1996, Clinton, Dem., 2,206,241; Dole, Rep., 1,793,568; Perot, Ref., 430,082; Browne, Libertarian, 29,061; Phillips, Constitutional, 20,454; Hagelin, Natural Law, 6,371.

# Rhode Island

| | | 1996 | | | 1992 | |
|---|---|---|---|---|---|---|
| City | Clinton (D) | Dole (R) | Perot (RF) | Clinton (D) | Bush (R) | Perot (I) |
| Cranston . . | 19,831 | 8,760 | 2,840 | 18,589 | 12,450 | 8,331 |
| East Providence. . . . | 12,301 | 3,954 | 1,927 | 11,701 | 5,843 | 4,661 |
| Pawtucket . | 14,038 | 3,694 | 2,438 | 14,177 | 6,322 | 6,244 |
| Providence. | 26,923 | 6,629 | 2,411 | 32,536 | 11,519 | 7,816 |
| Warwick . . | 22,435 | 10,046 | 4,503 | 20,504 | 13,348 | 10,526 |
| Other . . . . | 147,499 | 75,318 | 30,349 | 115,792 | 82,119 | 67,467 |
| **Totals. . . .** | **243,027** | **108,401** | **44,468** | **213,299** | **131,601** | **105,045** |

## Rhode Island Vote Since 1948

1948, Truman, Dem., 188,736; Dewey, Rep., 135,787; Wallace, Prog., 2,619; Thomas, Soc., 429; Teichert, Soc. Labor, 131.

1952, Eisenhower, Rep., 210,935; Stevenson, Dem., 203,293; Hallinan, Prog., 187; Hass, Soc. Labor, 83.

1956, Eisenhower, Rep., 225,819; Stevenson, Dem., 161,790.

1960, Kennedy, Dem., 258,032; Nixon, Rep., 147,502.

1964, Johnson, Dem., 315,463; Goldwater, Rep., 74,615.

1968, Nixon, Rep., 122,359; Humphrey, Dem., 246,518; Wallace, 3d Party, 15,678; Halstead, Soc. Workers, 383.

1972, Nixon, Rep., 220,383; McGovern, Dem., 194,645; Jenness, Soc. Workers, 729.

1976, Carter, Dem., 227,636; Ford, Rep., 181,249; MacBride, Libertarian, 715; Camejo, Soc. Workers, 462; Hall, Com., 334; Levin, Soc. Labor, 188.

1980, Reagan, Rep., 154,793; Carter, Dem., 198,342; Anderson, Ind., 59,819; Clark, Libertarian, 2,458; Hall, Com., 218; McReynolds, Soc., 170; DeBerry, Soc. Workers, 90; Griswold, Workers World, 77.

1984, Reagan, Rep., 212,080; Mondale, Dem., 197,106; Bergland, Libertarian, 277.

1988, Bush, Rep., 177,761; Dukakis, Dem., 225,123; Paul, Lib., 825; Fulani, New Alliance, 280.

1992, Clinton, Dem., 213,299; Bush, Rep., 131,601; Perot, Ind., 105,045; Fulani, New Alliance, 1,878.

1996, Clinton, Dem., 243,027; Dole, Rep., 108,401; Perot, Ref., 44,468; Nader, Green, 5,572; Browne, Libertarian, 969; Phillips, Taxpayers, 962; Hagelin, Natural Law, 404; Moorehead, Workers World, 181.

# South Carolina

| | | 1996 | | | 1992 | |
|---|---|---|---|---|---|---|
| County | Clinton (D) | Dole (R) | Perot (RF) | Clinton (D) | Bush (R) | Perot (I) |
| Abbeville . | 3,482 | 3,038 | 633 | 3,968 | 3,317 | 1,036 |
| Aiken . . . . | 14,232 | 26,410 | 1,973 | 14,802 | 25,731 | 6,056 |
| Allendale . | 2,222 | 941 | 87 | 2,159 | 1,049 | 212 |
| Anderson . | 17,418 | 24,093 | 3,889 | 16,072 | 24,793 | 6,966 |
| Bamberg . | 3,366 | 1,713 | 292 | 3,426 | 1,906 | 360 |
| Barnwell . . | 3,620 | 3,808 | 310 | 3,344 | 4,026 | 752 |
| Beaufort . . | 13,374 | 17,467 | 1,817 | 11,466 | 14,735 | 4,966 |
| Berkeley . . | 12,644 | 16,693 | 1,788 | 12,533 | 18,048 | 4,632 |
| Calhoun . . | 2,707 | 2,513 | 316 | 2,770 | 2,418 | 564 |
| Charleston | 43,210 | 48,469 | 3,494 | 40,095 | 47,403 | 10,354 |
| Cherokee . | 5,807 | 6,675 | 1,055 | 5,453 | 6,887 | 2,186 |
| Chester . . | 5,096 | 3,150 | 756 | 5,458 | 3,451 | 1,350 |
| Chesterfield | 5,734 | 4,028 | 768 | 5,691 | 4,183 | 1,315 |
| Clarendon. | 5,933 | 3,844 | 394 | 6,033 | 4,147 | 744 |
| Colleton . . | 5,010 | 4,273 | 538 | 5,455 | 4,545 | 1,245 |
| Darlington. | 8,888 | 8,196 | 890 | 9,090 | 8,912 | 1,863 |
| Dillon . . . . | 3,873 | 2,662 | 268 | 4,953 | 3,575 | 831 |
| Dorchester | 9,874 | 15,233 | 1,586 | 9,160 | 15,004 | 3,648 |
| Edgefield . | 3,574 | 3,638 | 244 | 3,433 | 3,339 | 596 |

| County | 1996 Clinton (D) | 1996 Dole (R) | 1996 Perot (RF) | 1992 Clinton (D) | 1992 Bush (R) | 1992 Perot (I) |
|---|---|---|---|---|---|---|
| Fairfield . . | 4,719 | 2,414 | 284 | 4,867 | 2,518 | 652 |
| Florence . . | 15,792 | 18,480 | 1,562 | 15,569 | 19,802 | 3,499 |
| Georgetown | 8,249 | 6,976 | 947 | 7,494 | 6,870 | 1,840 |
| Greenville . | 41,548 | 71,120 | 6,748 | 34,651 | 65,066 | 13,699 |
| Greenwood | 7,464 | 8,015 | 931 | 7,621 | 9,079 | 2,101 |
| Hampton . | 4,806 | 2,111 | 344 | 4,332 | 2,402 | 564 |
| Horry . . . . | 23,694 | 26,111 | 4,438 | 18,896 | 23,489 | 8,472 |
| Jasper . . . | 4,048 | 2,021 | 347 | 3,453 | 1,725 | 549 |
| Kershaw . . | 6,749 | 8,490 | 994 | 6,585 | 8,499 | 2,150 |
| Lancaster . | 8,749 | 7,540 | 1,597 | 8,307 | 7,757 | 2,563 |
| Laurens . . | 2,376 | 2,563 | 469 | 6,638 | 8,347 | 2,157 |
| Lee . . . . . | 3,588 | 1,971 | 320 | 4,454 | 2,730 | 611 |
| Lexington . | 18,865 | 39,598 | 3,697 | 18,312 | 41,759 | 8,652 |
| McCormick | 1,848 | 1,103 | 148 | 1,846 | 899 | 295 |
| Marion . . . | 6,348 | 3,595 | 363 | 5,843 | 3,647 | 822 |
| Marlboro . . | 4,823 | 1,957 | 474 | 5,111 | 2,526 | 895 |
| Newberry . | 4,804 | 5,668 | 682 | 4,896 | 5,980 | 1,393 |
| Oconee . . | 7,365 | 10,461 | 1,956 | 6,617 | 10,379 | 3,405 |
| Orangeburg | 18,560 | 10,481 | 1,110 | 18,440 | 11,328 | 2,383 |
| Pickens . . | 8,347 | 17,098 | 2,204 | 8,275 | 17,008 | 4,128 |
| Richland . . | 51,905 | 38,837 | 3,139 | 53,648 | 43,744 | 7,918 |
| Saluda . . . | 2,592 | 2,980 | 373 | 2,393 | 2,968 | 833 |
| Spartanburg | 26,743 | 35,877 | 3,868 | 25,488 | 37,707 | 8,900 |
| Sumter . . . | 12,157 | 12,047 | 929 | 11,852 | 12,576 | 2,062 |
| Union . . . . | 5,504 | 3,971 | 752 | 4,644 | 4,647 | 1,371 |
| Williamsburg. | 6,977 | 3,957 | 374 | 8,077 | 5,289 | 864 |
| York . . . . . | 16,774 | 22,101 | 3,152 | 15,844 | 21,297 | 6,418 |
| **Totals . . .** | **495,458** | **564,387** | **63,300** | **479,514** | **577,507** | **138,872** |

## South Carolina Vote Since 1948

1948, Thurmond, States' Rights, 102,607; Truman, Dem., 34,423; Dewey, Rep., 5,386; Wallace, Prog., 154; Thomas, Soc., 1.

1952, Eisenhower ran on two tickets. Under state law vote cast for two Eisenhower slates of electors could not be combined. Eisenhower, Ind., 158,289; Rep., 9,793; total, 168,082; Stevenson, Dem., 173,004; Hamblen, Proh., 1.

1956, Eisenhower, Rep., 75,700; Stevenson, Dem., 136,372; Byrd, Ind., 88,509; Andrews, Ind., 2.

1960, Kennedy, Dem., 198,129; Nixon, Rep., 188,558; write-in, 1.

1964, Johnson, Dem., 215,700; Goldwater, Rep., 309,048; write-ins: Nixon, 1, Wallace, 5; Powell, 1; Thurmond, 1.

1968, Nixon, Rep., 254,062; Humphrey, Dem., 197,486; Wallace, 3d Party, 215,430.

1972, Nixon, Rep., 477,044; McGovern, Dem., 184,559; United Citizens, 2,265; Schmitz, Amer., 10,075; write-in, 17.

1976, Carter, Dem., 450,807; Ford, Rep., 346,149; Anderson, Amer., 2,996; Maddox, Amer. Ind., 1,950; write-in, 681.

1980, Reagan, Rep., 439,277; Carter, Dem., 428,220; Anderson, Ind., 13,868; Clark, Libertarian, 4,807; Rarick, Amer. Ind., 2,086.

1984, Reagan, Rep., 615,539; Mondale, Dem., 344,459; Bergland, Libertarian, 4,359.

1988, Bush, Rep., 606,443; Dukakis, Dem., 370,554; Paul, Lib., 4,935; Fulani, United Citizens, 4,077.

1992, Clinton, Dem., 479,514; Bush, Rep., 577,507; Perot, Ind., 138,872; Marrou, Libertarian, 2,719; Phillips, U.S. Taxpayers, 2,680; Fulani, New Alliance, 1,235.

1996, Dole, Rep., 564,387; Clinton, Dem., 495,458; Perot, Ref./Patriot, 63,300; Browne, Libertarian, 4,210; Phillips, Taxpayers, 1,995; Hagelin, Natural Law, 1,225.

# South Dakota

| County | 1996 Clinton (D) | 1996 Dole (R) | 1996 Perot (RF) | 1992 Clinton (D) | 1992 Bush (R) | 1992 Perot (I) |
|---|---|---|---|---|---|---|
| Aurora . . . . | 663 | 709 | 201 | 680 | 594 | 435 |
| Beadle . . . . | 3,984 | 3,670 | 842 | 3,925 | 3,363 | 1,819 |
| Bennett . . . | 507 | 539 | 93 | 413 | 556 | 221 |
| Bon Homme. | 1,569 | 1,428 | 391 | 1,294 | 1,212 | 836 |
| Brookings . . | 5,105 | 5,112 | 979 | 4,645 | 4,698 | 2,614 |
| Brown . . . . | 7,913 | 6,801 | 1,622 | 7,521 | 6,665 | 3,812 |
| Brule . . . . . | 1,091 | 981 | 281 | 1,060 | 908 | 687 |
| Buffalo . . . . | 445 | 134 | 35 | 282 | 137 | 72 |
| Butte . . . . . | 1,132 | 1,947 | 541 | 973 | 1,674 | 1,039 |
| Campbell . . | 202 | 623 | 140 | 222 | 574 | 252 |
| Chas. Mix . . | 1,913 | 1,711 | 390 | 1,639 | 1,570 | 886 |
| Clark . . . . . | 956 | 998 | 272 | 799 | 803 | 761 |
| Clay . . . . . | 2,980 | 2,008 | 505 | 2,826 | 1,869 | 1,303 |
| Codington . . | 4,718 | 4,982 | 1,237 | 3,701 | 3,943 | 3,262 |
| Corson . . . . | 538 | 533 | 216 | 444 | 483 | 321 |
| Custer . . . . | 1,122 | 1,740 | 418 | 1,078 | 1,422 | 845 |
| Davison . . . | 3,364 | 3,371 | 737 | 3,285 | 3,111 | 1,706 |
| Day . . . . . . | 1,840 | 1,280 | 395 | 1,578 | 1,161 | 973 |
| Deuel . . . . . | 1,090 | 955 | 275 | 880 | 778 | 761 |
| Dewey . . . . | 1,114 | 657 | 195 | 766 | 642 | 340 |
| Douglas . . . | 524 | 1,210 | 161 | 481 | 1,175 | 403 |
| Edmunds . . | 973 | 1,055 | 263 | 894 | 944 | 415 |
| Fall River . . | 1,357 | 1,636 | 417 | 1,416 | 1,533 | 792 |
| Faulk . . . . . | 493 | 725 | 165 | 488 | 658 | 281 |
| Grant . . . . . | 1,805 | 1,787 | 471 | 1,484 | 1,595 | 1,018 |
| Gregory . . . | 923 | 1,208 | 286 | 879 | 1,027 | 688 |
| Haakon . . . | 284 | 887 | 110 | 209 | 860 | 245 |
| Hamlin . . . . | 1,092 | 1,347 | 285 | 826 | 1,133 | 774 |
| Hand . . . . . | 803 | 1,187 | 250 | 785 | 1,130 | 624 |
| Hanson . . . | 541 | 801 | 170 | 566 | 522 | 341 |
| Harding . . . | 151 | 524 | 90 | 139 | 515 | 225 |
| Hughes . . . | 2,788 | 4,469 | 531 | 2,578 | 4,325 | 1,160 |
| Hutchinson . | 1,285 | 2,177 | 409 | 1,211 | 2,002 | 920 |
| Hyde . . . . . | 309 | 493 | 94 | 301 | 440 | 211 |
| Jackson/ Washabaugh | 423 | 646 | 88 | 351 | 627 | 184 |
| Jerauld . . . | 656 | 530 | 151 | 600 | 518 | 346 |
| Jones . . . . | 184 | 463 | 75 | 166 | 454 | 154 |
| Kingsbury . . | 1,357 | 1,297 | 320 | 1,267 | 1,113 | 744 |
| Lake . . . . . | 2,526 | 1,966 | 593 | 2,388 | 1,890 | 1,299 |
| Lawrence . . | 3,568 | 4,430 | 1,308 | 3,157 | 3,770 | 2,673 |
| Lincoln . . . . | 3,643 | 4,201 | 682 | 2,943 | 3,365 | 1,593 |
| Lyman . . . . | 646 | 726 | 130 | 486 | 669 | 311 |
| McCook . . . | 1,167 | 1,292 | 245 | 1,167 | 1,177 | 617 |
| McPherson . | 463 | 1,080 | 182 | 478 | 945 | 322 |
| Marshall . . . | 1,185 | 861 | 189 | 1,056 | 810 | 427 |
| Meade . . . . | 2,955 | 4,974 | 1,132 | 2,694 | 4,724 | 2,611 |
| Mellette . . . | 302 | 417 | 67 | 277 | 417 | 140 |
| Miner . . . . . | 739 | 571 | 170 | 698 | 543 | 332 |
| Minnehaha . | 29,790 | 27,432 | 4,425 | 27,016 | 25,081 | 11,496 |
| Moody . . . . | 1,443 | 1,024 | 284 | 1,473 | 898 | 715 |
| Pennington . | 12,784 | 19,293 | 3,149 | 11,106 | 18,052 | 8,358 |
| Perkins . . . | 460 | 983 | 225 | 566 | 872 | 541 |
| Potter . . . . | 534 | 979 | 181 | 493 | 901 | 375 |
| Roberts . . . | 2,186 | 1,646 | 474 | 1,716 | 1,437 | 954 |
| Sanborn . . . | 647 | 630 | 151 | 632 | 595 | 376 |
| Shannon . . | 1,926 | 253 | 87 | 1,267 | 225 | 137 |
| Spink . . . . . | 1,636 | 1,651 | 360 | 1,732 | 1,527 | 839 |
| Stanley . . . | 454 | 795 | 121 | 427 | 719 | 240 |
| Sully . . . . . | 321 | 592 | 106 | 273 | 565 | 167 |
| Todd . . . . . | 1,380 | 482 | 108 | 915 | 456 | 246 |
| Tripp . . . . . | 1,088 | 1,680 | 337 | 1,046 | 1,459 | 848 |
| Turner . . . . | 1,682 | 1,970 | 385 | 1,507 | 1,906 | 867 |
| Union . . . . | 2,378 | 2,234 | 555 | 2,210 | 1,784 | 1,085 |
| Walworth . . | 939 | 1,461 | 366 | 829 | 1,439 | 628 |
| Yankton . . . | 3,776 | 3,889 | 1,073 | 3,404 | 3,430 | 2,511 |
| Ziebach . . . | 483 | 375 | 62 | 280 | 328 | 117 |
| **Totals . . . .** | **139,295** | **150,508** | **31,248** | **124,888** | **136,718** | **73,295** |

## South Dakota Vote Since 1948

1948, Truman, Dem., 117,653; Dewey, Rep., 129,651; Wallace, Prog., 2,801.

1952, Eisenhower, Rep., 203,857; Stevenson, Dem., 90,426.

1956, Eisenhower, Rep., 171,569; Stevenson, Dem., 122,288.

1960, Kennedy, Dem., 128,070; Nixon, Rep., 178,417.

1964, Johnson, Dem., 163,010; Goldwater, Rep., 130,108.

1968, Nixon, Rep., 149,841; Humphrey, Dem., 118,023; Wallace, 3d Party, 13,400.

1972, Nixon, Rep., 166,476; McGovern, Dem., 139,945; Jenness, Soc. Workers, 994.

1976, Carter, Dem., 147,068; Ford, Rep., 151,505; MacBride, Libertarian, 1,619; Hall, Com., 318; Camejo, Soc. Workers, 168.

1980, Reagan, Rep., 198,343; Carter, Dem., 103,855; Anderson, Ind., 21,431; Clark, Libertarian, 3,824; Pulley, Soc. Workers, 250.

1984, Reagan, Rep., 200,267; Mondale, Dem., 116,113.

1988, Bush, Rep., 165,415; Dukakis, Dem., 145,560; Paul, Lib., 1,060; Fulani, New Alliance, 730.

1992, Clinton, Dem., 124,888; Bush, Rep., 136,718; Perot, Ind., 73,295.

1996, Dole, Rep., 150,508; Clinton, Dem., 139,295; Perot, Ref., 31,248; Browne, Libertarian, 1,469; Phillips, Taxpayers, 912; Hagelin, Natural Law, 316.

# Tennessee

| County | 1996 Clinton (D) | 1996 Dole (R) | 1996 Perot (RF) | 1992 Clinton (D) | 1992 Bush (R) | 1992 Perot (I) |
|---|---|---|---|---|---|---|
| Anderson . | 13,457 | 11,943 | 1,817 | 13,482 | 11,838 | 3,149 |
| Bedford . . | 5,736 | 4,634 | 823 | 5,978 | 3,836 | 1,541 |
| Benton . . . | 3,294 | 1,890 | 570 | 3,896 | 1,625 | 559 |
| Bledsoe . . | 1,621 | 1,626 | 251 | 1,884 | 1,776 | 352 |
| Blount . . . | 14,686 | 19,307 | 2,553 | 14,655 | 18,415 | 4,468 |
| Bradley . . | 9,095 | 15,478 | 1,856 | 9,889 | 16,528 | 3,212 |
| Campbell . | 6,119 | 4,394 | 775 | 6,756 | 4,897 | 1,240 |
| Cannon . . | 2,318 | 1,488 | 361 | 2,593 | 1,229 | 495 |
| Carroll . . . | 4,912 | 4,206 | 697 | 5,741 | 4,842 | 1,139 |
| Carter . . . | 6,218 | 10,540 | 1,383 | 6,502 | 10,712 | 1,898 |
| Cheatham . | 4,882 | 4,281 | 705 | 4,817 | 3,496 | 1,433 |
| Chester . . | 1,922 | 2,746 | 203 | 2,317 | 2,834 | 439 |

| County | 1996 Clinton (D) | 1996 Dole (R) | 1996 Perot (RF) | 1992 Clinton (D) | 1992 Bush (R) | 1992 Perot (I) |
|---|---|---|---|---|---|---|
| Claiborne | 3,681 | 4,023 | 727 | 4,509 | 4,065 | 860 |
| Clay | 1,559 | 1,108 | 315 | 1,922 | 1,072 | 223 |
| Cocke | 3,328 | 4,481 | 788 | 3,495 | 5,298 | 1,124 |
| Coffee | 7,951 | 7,038 | 1,205 | 8,534 | 6,047 | 2,420 |
| Crockett | 2,256 | 1,872 | 201 | 2,657 | 2,180 | 507 |
| Cumberland | 6,676 | 8,098 | 1,398 | 6,393 | 7,116 | 2,200 |
| Davidson | 110,591 | 78,170 | 9,002 | 106,355 | 76,567 | 20,184 |
| Decatur | 2,262 | 1,712 | 229 | 2,633 | 1,667 | 351 |
| De Kalb | 3,213 | 1,696 | 324 | 4,382 | 1,714 | 608 |
| Dickson | 7,458 | 5,289 | 986 | 7,863 | 4,450 | 1,730 |
| Dyer | 5,602 | 5,059 | 676 | 5,845 | 5,668 | 1,241 |
| Fayette | 4,655 | 4,406 | 416 | 4,211 | 3,713 | 657 |
| Fentress | 2,332 | 2,307 | 386 | 2,730 | 2,391 | 606 |
| Franklin | 6,922 | 5,296 | 1,057 | 7,773 | 4,507 | 1,837 |
| Gibson | 8,851 | 6,614 | 891 | 9,555 | 7,161 | 1,536 |
| Giles | 4,861 | 3,212 | 731 | 5,601 | 2,827 | 1,309 |
| Grainger | 2,162 | 2,875 | 382 | 2,242 | 2,772 | 513 |
| Greene | 6,896 | 9,879 | 1,604 | 7,857 | 9,912 | 2,930 |
| Grundy | 2,596 | 1,094 | 326 | 2,997 | 1,004 | 366 |
| Hamblen | 7,006 | 9,797 | 1,106 | 7,114 | 8,898 | 1,760 |
| Hamilton | 48,008 | 55,205 | 6,699 | 46,770 | 53,476 | 14,400 |
| Hancock | 759 | 1,252 | 116 | 1,000 | 1,274 | 151 |
| Hardeman | 4,859 | 2,961 | 346 | 4,832 | 3,122 | 594 |
| Hardin | 3,504 | 3,978 | 593 | 3,922 | 3,875 | 734 |
| Hawkins | 6,367 | 8,164 | 1,282 | 6,623 | 7,758 | 1,847 |
| Haywood | 3,565 | 2,293 | 154 | 3,511 | 2,518 | 331 |
| Henderson | 2,841 | 4,002 | 408 | 3,502 | 4,719 | 785 |
| Henry | 6,153 | 4,372 | 994 | 6,797 | 3,661 | 1,588 |
| Hickman | 3,917 | 2,002 | 460 | 4,093 | 1,820 | 795 |
| Houston | 1,868 | 742 | 182 | 2,012 | 648 | 280 |
| Humphreys | 3,075 | 1,892 | 423 | 3,875 | 1,641 | 609 |
| Jackson | 2,889 | 916 | 289 | 3,208 | 708 | 332 |
| Jefferson | 4,688 | 6,446 | 882 | 4,740 | 6,184 | 1,385 |
| Johnson | 1,698 | 3,137 | 489 | 1,781 | 3,170 | 574 |
| Knox | 60,064 | 69,412 | 6,354 | 59,702 | 66,607 | 15,669 |
| Lake | 1,273 | 589 | 110 | 1,449 | 680 | 151 |
| Lauderdale | 4,349 | 2,481 | 308 | 4,452 | 2,928 | 561 |
| Lawrence | 6,188 | 6,115 | 934 | 6,816 | 5,608 | 1,403 |
| Lewis | 1,971 | 1,298 | 316 | 2,491 | 1,218 | 434 |
| Lincoln | 4,361 | 4,547 | 761 | 5,063 | 3,814 | 1,371 |
| Loudon | 5,552 | 7,106 | 889 | 5,414 | 6,444 | 1,602 |
| McMinn | 5,987 | 7,655 | 1,033 | 6,682 | 7,453 | 1,812 |
| McNairy | 4,050 | 3,960 | 519 | 4,691 | 4,093 | 774 |
| Macon | 2,240 | 2,482 | 411 | 2,961 | 2,299 | 443 |
| Madison | 13,577 | 14,908 | 968 | 13,629 | 14,869 | 2,634 |
| Marion | 5,194 | 3,166 | 768 | 5,589 | 3,262 | 1,186 |
| Marshall | 4,447 | 2,781 | 603 | 4,491 | 2,516 | 1,050 |
| Maury | 10,367 | 8,737 | 1,366 | 9,997 | 7,440 | 2,821 |
| Meigs | 1,476 | 1,228 | 245 | 1,673 | 1,355 | 453 |
| Monroe | 4,872 | 5,257 | 713 | 5,384 | 6,025 | 936 |
| Montgomery | 16,498 | 15,133 | 1,781 | 14,507 | 13,011 | 3,753 |
| Moore | 935 | 846 | 177 | 1,151 | 661 | 327 |
| Morgan | 2,767 | 2,070 | 446 | 3,190 | 2,306 | 658 |
| Obion | 6,256 | 4,310 | 914 | 6,497 | 4,812 | 1,494 |
| Overton | 3,800 | 1,756 | 431 | 4,489 | 1,657 | 468 |
| Perry | 1,445 | 747 | 178 | 1,889 | 708 | 317 |
| Pickett | 901 | 1,046 | 116 | 1,144 | 1,094 | 121 |
| Polk | 2,450 | 1,910 | 377 | 2,583 | 1,584 | 419 |
| Putnam | 10,047 | 9,093 | 1,487 | 10,858 | 7,998 | 2,473 |
| Rhea | 3,969 | 4,476 | 694 | 4,289 | 4,860 | 1,163 |
| Roane | 9,744 | 9,044 | 1,437 | 9,812 | 8,719 | 2,396 |
| Robertson | 8,465 | 6,695 | 993 | 8,498 | 5,271 | 1,978 |
| Rutherford | 22,794 | 24,538 | 3,775 | 21,084 | 18,877 | 7,005 |
| Scott | 2,506 | 2,645 | 430 | 2,730 | 3,011 | 643 |
| Sequatchie | 1,598 | 1,391 | 288 | 1,754 | 1,381 | 405 |
| Sevier | 7,136 | 11,847 | 1,650 | 6,719 | 11,714 | 2,760 |
| Shelby | 179,532 | 136,168 | 8,287 | 191,322 | 153,310 | 20,223 |
| Smith | 3,811 | 1,857 | 346 | 5,061 | 1,482 | 486 |
| Stewart | 2,962 | 1,306 | 386 | 2,779 | 1,046 | 487 |
| Sullivan | 20,569 | 29,290 | 3,555 | 20,935 | 28,801 | 6,730 |
| Sumner | 19,112 | 20,434 | 2,777 | 19,387 | 17,401 | 5,177 |
| Tipton | 6,596 | 7,585 | 799 | 5,652 | 6,757 | 1,279 |
| Trousdale | 1,615 | 683 | 190 | 1,846 | 565 | 243 |
| Unicoi | 2,131 | 3,122 | 447 | 2,375 | 3,344 | 709 |
| Union | 2,421 | 2,253 | 385 | 2,478 | 2,274 | 580 |
| Van Buren | 1,010 | 504 | 128 | 1,329 | 555 | 191 |
| Warren | 6,396 | 4,227 | 913 | 7,189 | 3,704 | 1,415 |
| Washington | 13,147 | 18,841 | 2,225 | 13,071 | 18,206 | 4,002 |
| Wayne | 1,574 | 2,715 | 317 | 1,868 | 2,955 | 424 |
| Weakley | 5,657 | 4,622 | 873 | 5,691 | 4,800 | 1,355 |
| White | 3,592 | 2,498 | 505 | 4,102 | 2,118 | 821 |
| Williamson | 15,231 | 27,698 | 2,071 | 13,053 | 22,015 | 5,026 |
| Wilson | 13,655 | 13,816 | 1,840 | 13,861 | 12,061 | 3,848 |
| **Totals** | **905,599** | **860,809** | **105,577** | **933,521** | **841,300** | **199,968** |

## Tennessee Vote Since 1948

1948, Truman, Dem., 270,402; Dewey, Rep., 202,914; Thurmond, States' Rights, 73,815; Wallace, Prog., 1,864; Thomas, Soc., 1,288.

1952, Eisenhower, Rep., 446,147; Stevenson, Dem., 443,710; Hamblen, Proh., 1,432; Hallinan, Prog., 885; MacArthur, Christian Nationalist, 379.

1956, Eisenhower, Rep., 462,288; Stevenson, Dem., 456,507; Andrews, Ind., 19,820; Holtwick, Proh., 789.

1960, Kennedy, Dem., 481,453; Nixon, Rep., 556,577; Faubus, States' Rights, 11,304; Decker, Proh., 2,458.

1964, Johnson, Dem., 635,047; Goldwater, Rep., 508,965; write-in, 34.

1968, Nixon, Rep., 472,592; Humphrey, Dem., 351,233; Wallace, 3d Party, 424,792.

1972, Nixon, Rep., 813,147; McGovern, Dem., 357,293; Schmitz, Amer., 30,373; write-in, 369.

1976, Carter, Dem., 825,879; Ford, Rep., 633,969; Anderson, Amer., 5,769; McCarthy, Ind., 5,004; Maddox, Amer. Ind., 2,303; MacBride, Libertarian, 1,375; Hall, Com., 547; LaRouche, U.S. Labor, 512; Bubar, Proh., 442; Miller, Ind., 316; write-in, 230.

1980, Reagan, Rep., 787,761; Carter, Dem., 783,051; Anderson, Ind., 35,991; Clark, Libertarian, 7,116; Commoner, Citizens, 1,112; Bubar, Statesman, 521; McReynolds, Soc., 519; Hall, Com., 503; DeBerry, Soc. Workers, 490; Griswold, Workers World, 400; write-ins, 152.

1984, Reagan, Rep., 990,212; Mondale, Dem., 711,714; Bergland, Libertarian, 3,072.

1988, Bush, Rep., 947,233; Dukakis, Dem., 679,794; Paul, Ind., 2,041; Duke, Ind., 1,807.

1992, Clinton, Dem., 933,521; Bush, Rep., 841,300; Perot, Ind., 199,968; Marrou, Libertarian, 1,847.

1996, Clinton, Dem., 905,599; Dole, Rep., 860,809; Perot, Ind. (Ref.), 105,577; Nader, Ind., 6,383; Browne, Ind., 4,914; Phillips, Ind., 1,791; Collins, Ind., 672; Hagelin, Ind., 631; Michael, Ind., 407; Dodge, Ind., 317.

# Texas

| County | 1996 Clinton (D) | 1996 Dole (R) | 1996 Perot (RF) | 1992 Clinton (D) | 1992 Bush (R) | 1992 Perot (I) |
|---|---|---|---|---|---|---|
| Anderson | 5,692 | 6,456 | 1,170 | 5,322 | 5,598 | 3,519 |
| Andrews | 1,181 | 2,360 | 431 | 1,081 | 2,266 | 875 |
| Angelina | 11,347 | 11,806 | 2,160 | 10,318 | 9,722 | 6,204 |
| Aransas | 2,964 | 3,769 | 655 | 2,246 | 2,826 | 1,676 |
| Archer | 1,235 | 1,974 | 437 | 1,284 | 1,560 | 1,106 |
| Armstrong | 272 | 582 | 75 | 278 | 561 | 187 |
| Atascosa | 4,259 | 4,102 | 813 | 3,766 | 3,806 | 2,035 |
| Austin | 2,719 | 4,669 | 577 | 2,278 | 4,015 | 1,585 |
| Bailey | 706 | 1,246 | 109 | 677 | 1,308 | 376 |
| Bandera | 1,383 | 3,700 | 520 | 1,059 | 2,674 | 1,537 |
| Bastrop | 6,773 | 6,323 | 1,342 | 6,252 | 4,980 | 3,240 |
| Baylor | 955 | 860 | 252 | 990 | 611 | 529 |
| Bee | 4,561 | 3,611 | 539 | 4,083 | 3,633 | 1,367 |
| Bell | 22,638 | 30,348 | 3,666 | 18,684 | 24,936 | 11,026 |
| Bexar | 180,308 | 161,619 | 17,822 | 172,513 | 168,816 | 72,110 |
| Blanco | 1,028 | 1,919 | 330 | 891 | 1,370 | 830 |
| Borden | 93 | 201 | 45 | 106 | 184 | 87 |
| Bosque | 2,397 | 2,840 | 732 | 2,173 | 2,300 | 1,999 |
| Bowie | 13,659 | 12,751 | 2,760 | 11,825 | 11,776 | 6,659 |
| Brazoria | 22,959 | 36,392 | 5,869 | 21,861 | 30,384 | 18,954 |
| Brazos | 13,968 | 22,082 | 2,215 | 14,819 | 23,943 | 10,372 |
| Brewster | 1,643 | 1,438 | 299 | 1,383 | 1,127 | 712 |
| Briscoe | 408 | 416 | 45 | 430 | 360 | 164 |
| Brooks | 2,945 | 414 | 108 | 2,856 | 585 | 318 |
| Brown | 4,138 | 6,524 | 1,081 | 4,264 | 5,313 | 3,034 |
| Burleson | 2,419 | 2,174 | 347 | 2,511 | 2,013 | 1,179 |
| Burnet | 4,123 | 5,744 | 1,108 | 3,638 | 4,272 | 2,865 |
| Caldwell | 3,914 | 3,258 | 549 | 3,794 | 2,749 | 1,776 |
| Calhoun | 2,753 | 2,832 | 507 | 2,550 | 2,640 | 1,579 |
| Callahan | 1,666 | 2,480 | 534 | 1,694 | 2,134 | 1,452 |
| Cameron | 34,891 | 18,434 | 2,757 | 29,435 | 20,123 | 9,286 |
| Camp | 1,912 | 1,488 | 252 | 1,938 | 1,219 | 821 |
| Carson | 742 | 1,742 | 225 | 825 | 1,647 | 578 |
| Cass | 5,691 | 4,066 | 1,038 | 5,476 | 3,999 | 2,168 |
| Castro | 1,107 | 1,231 | 144 | 1,113 | 1,307 | 485 |
| Chambers | 2,876 | 4,101 | 818 | 2,832 | 3,398 | 2,122 |
| Cherokee | 5,185 | 6,483 | 971 | 5,003 | 5,847 | 3,273 |
| Childress | 700 | 1,072 | 165 | 881 | 1,033 | 421 |
| Clay | 1,636 | 1,917 | 465 | 1,919 | 1,586 | 1,397 |
| Cochran | 511 | 662 | 127 | 454 | 750 | 255 |
| Coke | 573 | 777 | 157 | 580 | 640 | 393 |
| Coleman | 1,489 | 1,804 | 349 | 1,579 | 1,462 | 1,095 |
| Collin | 37,854 | 83,750 | 10,443 | 24,508 | 60,514 | 43,287 |
| Collingsworth | 553 | 694 | 118 | 635 | 697 | 265 |
| Colorado | 2,795 | 3,381 | 574 | 2,442 | 3,286 | 1,421 |
| Comal | 7,132 | 16,763 | 1,903 | 6,312 | 12,651 | 5,841 |
| Comanche | 2,257 | 2,192 | 516 | 2,296 | 1,666 | 1,281 |
| Concho | 434 | 488 | 107 | 489 | 414 | 329 |
| Cooke | 3,782 | 7,320 | 1,150 | 3,105 | 5,299 | 4,658 |
| Coryell | 5,299 | 7,141 | 1,443 | 4,157 | 6,144 | 3,974 |
| Cottle | 404 | 330 | 77 | 542 | 245 | 235 |
| Crane | 627 | 993 | 201 | 514 | 918 | 412 |
| Crockett | 684 | 714 | 147 | 653 | 623 | 368 |
| Crosby | 1,122 | 968 | 189 | 1,010 | 1,006 | 313 |
| Culberson | 746 | 327 | 99 | 424 | 251 | 171 |
| Dallam | 493 | 970 | 170 | 434 | 922 | 325 |
| Dallas | 255,766 | 260,058 | 36,759 | 231,412 | 256,007 | 170,571 |
| Dawson | 1,601 | 2,315 | 233 | 1,639 | 2,691 | 518 |
| Deaf Smith | 1,655 | 3,051 | 294 | 1,642 | 3,137 | 772 |
| Delta | 849 | 744 | 138 | 864 | 599 | 551 |

| County | 1996 | | | 1992 | | |
|---|---|---|---|---|---|---|
| | Clinton (D) | Dole (R) | Perot (RF) | Clinton (D) | Bush (R) | Perot (I) |
| Denton | 36,138 | 65,313 | 9,294 | 27,891 | 48,492 | 39,653 |
| DeWitt | 2,074 | 3,577 | 483 | 2,127 | 3,238 | 1,346 |
| Dickens | 509 | 421 | 117 | 536 | 373 | 250 |
| Dimmit | 2,242 | 604 | 128 | 3,172 | 844 | 361 |
| Donley | 495 | 988 | 97 | 578 | 893 | 260 |
| Duval | 3,958 | 543 | 136 | 4,006 | 698 | 326 |
| Eastland | 2,594 | 3,272 | 705 | 2,738 | 2,830 | 1,698 |
| Ector | 12,017 | 17,746 | 2,511 | 11,130 | 18,161 | 6,668 |
| Edwards | 437 | 511 | 60 | 254 | 460 | 171 |
| Ellis | 10,832 | 16,046 | 2,750 | 9,537 | 13,564 | 10,303 |
| El Paso | 83,964 | 43,255 | 6,300 | 67,715 | 47,224 | 19,738 |
| Erath | 3,664 | 4,750 | 1,134 | 3,531 | 3,835 | 3,046 |
| Falls | 3,256 | 2,260 | 479 | 2,761 | 1,826 | 1,185 |
| Fannin | 4,276 | 3,495 | 980 | 4,164 | 2,510 | 2,919 |
| Fayette | 3,119 | 4,195 | 708 | 2,923 | 3,789 | 2,088 |
| Fisher | 1,142 | 537 | 170 | 1,242 | 539 | 442 |
| Floyd | 1,121 | 1,530 | 126 | 947 | 1,676 | 385 |
| Foard | 326 | 162 | 37 | 435 | 207 | 152 |
| Fort Bend | 38,163 | 49,945 | 4,363 | 29,992 | 41,039 | 16,853 |
| Franklin | 1,484 | 1,575 | 386 | 1,338 | 1,058 | 942 |
| Freestone | 2,638 | 2,888 | 568 | 2,445 | 2,316 | 1,596 |
| Frio | 2,593 | 1,225 | 253 | 2,377 | 1,275 | 654 |
| Gaines | 1,012 | 1,812 | 353 | 1,095 | 2,138 | 696 |
| Galveston | 38,458 | 35,251 | 5,897 | 38,623 | 31,303 | 20,103 |
| Garza | 703 | 946 | 103 | 558 | 982 | 345 |
| Gillespie | 1,655 | 5,867 | 542 | 1,600 | 4,712 | 2,018 |
| Glasscock | 70 | 382 | 30 | 100 | 379 | 93 |
| Goliad | 1,135 | 1,335 | 148 | 1,069 | 1,236 | 521 |
| Gonzales | 2,110 | 2,687 | 354 | 2,006 | 2,502 | 1,018 |
| Gray | 2,114 | 6,102 | 568 | 2,426 | 6,105 | 1,810 |
| Grayson | 14,338 | 17,169 | 3,745 | 12,547 | 12,322 | 13,327 |
| Gregg | 13,659 | 21,611 | 2,079 | 12,797 | 20,542 | 8,437 |
| Grimes | 2,584 | 2,564 | 538 | 2,594 | 2,402 | 1,213 |
| Guadalupe | 8,066 | 14,251 | 1,810 | 6,567 | 10,818 | 5,618 |
| Hale | 3,204 | 5,905 | 605 | 2,761 | 6,098 | 1,357 |
| Hall | 747 | 626 | 94 | 819 | 631 | 263 |
| Hamilton | 1,200 | 1,493 | 323 | 1,100 | 1,232 | 921 |
| Hansford | 343 | 1,493 | 105 | 345 | 1,660 | 398 |
| Hardeman | 750 | 610 | 168 | 954 | 614 | 362 |
| Hardin | 7,179 | 8,529 | 2,112 | 6,753 | 5,885 | 4,129 |
| Harris | 382,291 | 416,512 | 42,015 | 360,171 | 406,778 | 172,922 |
| Harrison | 10,307 | 9,835 | 1,427 | 9,538 | 8,733 | 4,371 |
| Hartley | 463 | 1,242 | 101 | 406 | 1,081 | 308 |
| Haskell | 1,374 | 964 | 225 | 1,438 | 852 | 562 |
| Hays | 11,577 | 12,863 | 1,990 | 10,842 | 10,008 | 6,252 |
| Hemphill | 330 | 944 | 104 | 479 | 989 | 232 |
| Henderson | 10,081 | 10,340 | 2,273 | 9,105 | 8,368 | 6,746 |
| Hidalgo | 55,783 | 24,235 | 3,526 | 51,205 | 26,976 | 9,757 |
| Hill | 3,988 | 4,401 | 1,052 | 3,929 | 3,669 | 2,752 |
| Hockley | 2,170 | 4,230 | 519 | 2,301 | 4,261 | 1,291 |
| Hood | 5,459 | 7,575 | 1,445 | 4,359 | 5,313 | 4,457 |
| Hopkins | 4,522 | 4,341 | 1,034 | 4,085 | 3,398 | 3,147 |
| Houston | 3,383 | 3,443 | 585 | 3,250 | 3,067 | 1,690 |
| Howard | 3,732 | 5,007 | 1,037 | 3,735 | 5,129 | 1,984 |
| Hudspeth | 427 | 367 | 92 | 364 | 325 | 178 |
| Hunt | 8,801 | 10,746 | 2,225 | 7,452 | 9,739 | 7,387 |
| Hutchinson | 2,553 | 6,350 | 864 | 2,833 | 6,034 | 1,993 |
| Irion | 213 | 386 | 86 | 256 | 283 | 290 |
| Jack | 1,019 | 1,162 | 301 | 1,254 | 1,041 | 1,045 |
| Jackson | 1,785 | 2,533 | 309 | 1,722 | 2,451 | 976 |
| Jasper | 5,039 | 4,523 | 1,041 | 5,658 | 3,870 | 2,539 |
| Jeff Davis | 370 | 482 | 99 | 321 | 360 | 187 |
| Jefferson | 45,854 | 32,821 | 5,319 | 48,405 | 29,622 | 17,242 |
| Jim Hogg | 1,437 | 307 | 64 | 1,520 | 478 | 107 |
| Jim Wells | 7,116 | 2,989 | 430 | 7,812 | 3,311 | 1,413 |
| Johnson | 12,817 | 16,246 | 3,250 | 12,030 | 13,473 | 11,573 |
| Jones | 2,375 | 2,316 | 603 | 2,400 | 2,088 | 1,436 |
| Karnes | 2,154 | 1,869 | 291 | 1,897 | 1,990 | 802 |
| Kaufman | 7,383 | 8,697 | 1,831 | 6,498 | 6,578 | 5,913 |
| Kendall | 2,092 | 5,940 | 620 | 1,374 | 4,162 | 1,773 |
| Kenedy | 133 | 71 | 4 | 87 | 69 | 18 |
| Kent | 260 | 187 | 67 | 271 | 175 | 163 |
| Kerr | 4,192 | 11,173 | 1,236 | 3,707 | 8,787 | 3,790 |
| Kimble | 521 | 898 | 131 | 467 | 790 | 354 |
| King | 46 | 97 | 29 | 54 | 79 | 56 |
| Kinney | 503 | 650 | 97 | 598 | 634 | 299 |
| Kleberg | 5,136 | 3,408 | 398 | 5,109 | 3,897 | 1,470 |
| Knox | 785 | 599 | 149 | 854 | 521 | 438 |
| Lamar | 6,075 | 6,393 | 1,198 | 6,328 | 5,778 | 4,093 |
| Lamb | 1,676 | 2,590 | 283 | 1,737 | 2,998 | 709 |
| Lampasas | 1,819 | 3,008 | 509 | 1,508 | 2,233 | 1,432 |
| LaSalle | 1,522 | 570 | 85 | 1,522 | 586 | 211 |
| Lavaca | 2,575 | 3,697 | 551 | 2,700 | 3,362 | 1,696 |
| Lee | 2,008 | 2,354 | 421 | 1,847 | 2,108 | 1,088 |
| Leon | 2,217 | 2,839 | 499 | 2,042 | 2,212 | 1,251 |
| Liberty | 6,877 | 7,784 | 2,011 | 7,036 | 6,959 | 4,311 |
| Limestone | 3,339 | 2,783 | 721 | 3,188 | 2,358 | 1,505 |
| Lipscomb | 357 | 875 | 115 | 338 | 839 | 270 |
| Live Oak | 1,454 | 1,929 | 292 | 1,345 | 1,805 | 806 |
| Llano | 2,653 | 4,290 | 762 | 2,409 | 3,056 | 1,799 |
| Loving | 14 | 48 | 15 | 20 | 31 | 45 |
| Lubbock | 22,786 | 47,304 | 3,996 | 22,240 | 48,847 | 11,618 |
| Lynn | 903 | 1,151 | 136 | 902 | 1,233 | 291 |
| McCulloch | 1,231 | 1,465 | 292 | 1,393 | 1,108 | 986 |
| McLennan | 27,050 | 30,666 | 5,131 | 25,903 | 28,473 | 15,505 |
| McMullen | 117 | 274 | 35 | 78 | 274 | 89 |
| Madison | 1,470 | 1,576 | 293 | 1,553 | 1,544 | 778 |

| County | 1996 | | | 1992 | | |
|---|---|---|---|---|---|---|
| | Clinton (D) | Dole (R) | Perot (RF) | Clinton (D) | Bush (R) | Perot (I) |
| Marion | 2,028 | 1,260 | 353 | 2,156 | 1,245 | 882 |
| Martin | 640 | 966 | 140 | 641 | 986 | 356 |
| Mason | 618 | 948 | 151 | 570 | 776 | 364 |
| Matagorda | 5,373 | 5,869 | 1,190 | 4,759 | 5,328 | 3,045 |
| Maverick | 5,307 | 1,050 | 202 | 4,540 | 2,002 | 771 |
| Medina | 3,880 | 5,710 | 715 | 3,650 | 4,912 | 2,167 |
| Menard | 490 | 443 | 102 | 553 | 354 | 367 |
| Midland | 9,514 | 25,384 | 2,079 | 9,160 | 24,143 | 7,880 |
| Milam | 3,869 | 3,019 | 657 | 3,542 | 2,414 | 1,495 |
| Mills | 752 | 1,057 | 230 | 753 | 702 | 530 |
| Mitchell | 1,213 | 949 | 232 | 1,353 | 1,128 | 604 |
| Montague | 2,718 | 3,029 | 842 | 2,885 | 2,304 | 2,330 |
| Montgomery | 20,722 | 51,011 | 6,065 | 18,551 | 39,976 | 19,203 |
| Moore | 1,358 | 3,353 | 359 | 1,361 | 3,147 | 976 |
| Morris | 2,973 | 1,449 | 402 | 3,028 | 1,400 | 1,138 |
| Motley | 164 | 380 | 56 | 256 | 446 | 117 |
| Nacogdoches | 7,640 | 10,356 | 1,352 | 6,937 | 9,864 | 4,803 |
| Navarro | 6,078 | 5,236 | 1,140 | 6,006 | 4,897 | 3,800 |
| Newton | 2,548 | 1,409 | 473 | 3,249 | 1,212 | 1,032 |
| Nolan | 2,582 | 2,166 | 613 | 2,490 | 1,993 | 1,455 |
| Nueces | 50,107 | 37,635 | 5,062 | 46,317 | 36,781 | 17,374 |
| Ochiltree | 466 | 2,448 | 167 | 557 | 2,419 | 576 |
| Oldham | 208 | 523 | 77 | 225 | 583 | 177 |
| Orange | 13,741 | 12,560 | 2,836 | 15,305 | 9,793 | 7,321 |
| Palo Pinto | 3,938 | 3,666 | 1,011 | 3,392 | 2,852 | 3,010 |
| Panola | 4,168 | 4,008 | 177 | 3,950 | 3,473 | 1,906 |
| Parker | 9,447 | 14,580 | 2,703 | 7,934 | 10,321 | 9,148 |
| Parmer | 676 | 2,042 | 160 | 637 | 1,829 | 564 |
| Pecos | 1,816 | 1,730 | 369 | 1,778 | 1,836 | 895 |
| Polk | 6,360 | 6,473 | 1,347 | 5,942 | 5,390 | 2,884 |
| Potter | 9,273 | 14,995 | 1,799 | 9,527 | 13,510 | 4,655 |
| Presidio | 1,205 | 383 | 111 | 1,189 | 400 | 290 |
| Rains | 1,265 | 1,123 | 335 | 1,108 | 975 | 890 |
| Randall | 9,177 | 28,266 | 1,985 | 9,119 | 24,971 | 6,340 |
| Reagan | 407 | 645 | 101 | 337 | 651 | 259 |
| Real | 414 | 845 | 178 | 463 | 787 | 386 |
| Red River | 2,346 | 1,783 | 433 | 2,686 | 1,735 | 1,228 |
| Reeves | 2,279 | 1,007 | 245 | 2,569 | 1,244 | 734 |
| Refugio | 1,635 | 1,376 | 222 | 1,531 | 1,469 | 716 |
| Roberts | 119 | 420 | 40 | 126 | 391 | 99 |
| Robertson | 2,912 | 1,944 | 315 | 2,927 | 1,707 | 963 |
| Rockwall | 3,289 | 8,319 | 1,121 | 2,397 | 6,427 | 4,393 |
| Runnels | 1,423 | 1,949 | 396 | 1,401 | 1,653 | 1,279 |
| Rusk | 5,988 | 8,423 | 1,072 | 5,391 | 7,560 | 3,575 |
| Sabine | 1,913 | 1,660 | 334 | 2,288 | 1,490 | 894 |
| San Augustine | 1,853 | 1,262 | 324 | 1,737 | 1,243 | 667 |
| San Jacinto | 2,771 | 2,878 | 810 | 2,846 | 2,494 | 1,653 |
| San Patricio | 8,132 | 7,678 | 1,085 | 8,202 | 7,456 | 3,178 |
| San Saba | 826 | 991 | 194 | 716 | 723 | 660 |
| Schleicher | 505 | 588 | 111 | 420 | 452 | 355 |
| Scurry | 2,099 | 2,929 | 813 | 1,609 | 2,670 | 1,826 |
| Shackelford | 502 | 792 | 169 | 484 | 623 | 422 |
| Shelby | 3,720 | 3,482 | 815 | 3,986 | 3,217 | 1,487 |
| Sherman | 243 | 809 | 89 | 261 | 851 | 256 |
| Smith | 18,265 | 32,171 | 2,933 | 17,514 | 27,753 | 13,569 |
| Somervell | 993 | 1,099 | 273 | 782 | 872 | 903 |
| Starr | 6,312 | 756 | 157 | 7,668 | 1,209 | 345 |
| Stephens | 1,218 | 1,714 | 336 | 1,115 | 1,573 | 1,062 |
| Sterling | 186 | 394 | 86 | 127 | 322 | 182 |
| Stonewall | 487 | 323 | 105 | 561 | 242 | 322 |
| Sutton | 508 | 688 | 102 | 524 | 687 | 387 |
| Swisher | 1,222 | 1,155 | 195 | 1,413 | 989 | 541 |
| Tarrant | 170,431 | 208,312 | 28,715 | 156,230 | 183,387 | 129,998 |
| Taylor | 13,213 | 23,682 | 2,912 | 12,382 | 22,614 | 10,331 |
| Terrell | 278 | 185 | 47 | 325 | 176 | 128 |
| Terry | 1,272 | 2,013 | 269 | 1,461 | 2,309 | 619 |
| Throckmorton | 285 | 360 | 90 | 401 | 389 | 228 |
| Titus | 4,834 | 4,483 | 846 | 3,625 | 3,024 | 2,146 |
| Tom Green | 11,777 | 18,112 | 2,757 | 11,437 | 14,989 | 10,244 |
| Travis | 128,970 | 98,454 | 14,008 | 130,546 | 88,105 | 56,158 |
| Trinity | 2,774 | 2,058 | 460 | 2,784 | 1,988 | 1,133 |
| Tyler | 3,300 | 2,804 | 645 | 3,465 | 2,357 | 1,529 |
| Upshur | 5,032 | 5,174 | 1,086 | 4,776 | 4,511 | 2,896 |
| Upton | 424 | 685 | 88 | 489 | 908 | 313 |
| Uvalde | 3,397 | 3,494 | 403 | 3,482 | 3,635 | 1,387 |
| Val Verde | 5,623 | 4,357 | 548 | 4,748 | 4,102 | 2,093 |
| Van Zandt | 5,752 | 7,453 | 1,756 | 5,310 | 5,810 | 5,239 |
| Victoria | 8,238 | 14,457 | 1,177 | 7,604 | 13,086 | 5,136 |
| Walker | 6,008 | 7,177 | 1,186 | 5,619 | 6,662 | 3,619 |
| Waller | 4,535 | 3,557 | 499 | 4,270 | 3,065 | 1,692 |
| Ward | 1,644 | 1,620 | 446 | 1,695 | 1,769 | 948 |
| Washington | 3,460 | 6,319 | 601 | 3,283 | 5,817 | 1,738 |
| Webb | 18,997 | 4,712 | 936 | 14,509 | 7,789 | 2,517 |
| Wharton | 5,176 | 6,163 | 871 | 4,643 | 5,503 | 2,624 |
| Wheeler | 703 | 1,332 | 174 | 938 | 1,458 | 367 |
| Wichita | 15,775 | 20,495 | 3,371 | 17,021 | 17,956 | 11,478 |
| Wilbarger | 1,730 | 2,037 | 465 | 1,924 | 1,959 | 1,453 |
| Willacy | 3,787 | 1,328 | 241 | 3,359 | 1,490 | 652 |
| Williamson | 24,175 | 36,836 | 4,931 | 19,437 | 26,208 | 15,415 |
| Wilson | 3,713 | 4,530 | 760 | 3,711 | 3,766 | 2,105 |
| Winkler | 872 | 1,009 | 218 | 942 | 1,173 | 582 |
| Wise | 5,056 | 6,330 | 1,516 | 4,478 | 4,555 | 4,485 |
| Wood | 4,711 | 6,228 | 1,184 | 4,084 | 4,708 | 3,494 |
| Yoakum | 738 | 1,485 | 218 | 595 | 1,486 | 484 |
| Young | 2,304 | 3,535 | 639 | 2,464 | 2,894 | 2,302 |
| Zapata | 1,786 | 521 | 131 | 2,052 | 866 | 326 |
| Zavala | 2,629 | 463 | 91 | 3,058 | 571 | 237 |
| **Totals** | **2,455,735** | **2,731,998** | **377,530** | **2,281,815** | **2,496,071** | **1,354,781** |

## Texas Vote Since 1948

1948, Truman, Dem., 750,700; Dewey, Rep., 282,240; Thurmond, States' Rights, 106,909; Wallace, Prog., 3,764; Watson, Proh., 2,758; Thomas, Soc., 874.
1952, Eisenhower, Rep., 1,102,878; Stevenson, Dem., 969,228; Hamblen, Proh., 1,983; MacArthur, Christian Nationalist, 833; MacArthur, Constitution, 730; Hallinan, Prog., 294.
1956, Eisenhower, Rep., 1,080,619; Stevenson, Dem., 859,958; Andrews, Ind., 14,591.
1960, Kennedy, Dem., 1,167,932; Nixon, Rep., 1,121,699; Sullivan, Constitution, 18,169; Decker, Proh., 3,870; write-in, 15.
1964, Johnson, Dem., 1,663,185; Goldwater, Rep., 958,566; Lightburn, Constitution, 5,060.
1968, Nixon, Rep., 1,227,844; Humphrey, Dem., 1,266,804; Wallace, 3d Party, 584,269; write-in, 489.
1972, Nixon, Rep., 2,298,896; McGovern, Dem., 1,154,289; Schmitz, Amer., 6,039; Jenness, Soc. Workers, 8,664; others, 3,393.
1976, Carter, Dem., 2,082,319; Ford, Rep., 1,953,300; McCarthy, Ind., 20,118; Anderson, Amer., 11,442; Camejo, Soc. Workers, 1,723; write-in, 2,982.
1980, Reagan, Rep., 2,510,705; Carter, Dem., 1,881,147; Anderson, Ind., 111,613; Clark, Libertarian, 37,643; write-in, 528.
1984, Reagan, Rep., 3,433,428; Mondale, Dem., 1,949,276.
1988, Bush, Rep., 3,036,829; Dukakis, Dem., 2,352,748; Paul, Lib., 30,355; Fulani, New Alliance, 7,208.
1992, Clinton, Dem., 2,281,815; Bush, Rep., 2,496,071; Perot, Ind., 1,354,781; Marrou, Libertarian, 19,699.
1996, Dole, Rep., 2,731,998; Clinton, Dem., 2,455,735; Perot, Ind. (Ref.), 377,530; Browne, Libertarian, 20,226; Phillips, Taxpayers, 7,520; Hagelin, Natural Law, 4,424.

# Utah

| County | 1996 Clinton (D) | 1996 Dole (R) | 1996 Perot (RF) | 1992 Clinton (D) | 1992 Bush (R) | 1992 Perot (I) |
|---|---|---|---|---|---|---|
| Beaver . . . | 686 | 1,162 | 217 | 668 | 1,040 | 330 |
| Box Elder . | 3,166 | 8,360 | 1,577 | 2,186 | 7,712 | 4,507 |
| Cache . . . | 6,526 | 16,685 | 2,382 | 4,973 | 15,971 | 8,032 |
| Carbon. . . | 4,167 | 2,342 | 951 | 4,480 | 2,038 | 2,002 |
| Daggett . . | 131 | 233 | 53 | 122 | 172 | 117 |
| Davis . . . . | 19,259 | 42,651 | 7,483 | 14,924 | 39,087 | 24,105 |
| Duchesne . | 892 | 2,634 | 563 | 772 | 1,983 | 1,229 |
| Emery . . . | 1,368 | 2,018 | 661 | 1,349 | 1,643 | 1,138 |
| Garfield . . | 278 | 1,308 | 221 | 309 | 1,235 | 355 |
| Grand . . . | 1,189 | 1,375 | 431 | 1,160 | 1,100 | 991 |
| Iron . . . . . | 1,783 | 6,279 | 689 | 1,537 | 5,616 | 1,693 |
| Juab . . . . | 925 | 1,287 | 353 | 823 | 1,237 | 616 |
| Kane . . . . | 298 | 1,653 | 286 | 295 | 1,241 | 534 |
| Millard . . . | 934 | 2,656 | 501 | 742 | 2,496 | 1,064 |
| Morgan. . . | 859 | 1,649 | 337 | 520 | 1,339 | 851 |
| Piute . . . . | 176 | 473 | 53 | 169 | 429 | 146 |
| Rich. . . . . | 175 | 521 | 88 | 154 | 525 | 187 |
| Salt Lake . | 117,240 | 127,369 | 27,476 | 100,082 | 117,247 | 91,968 |
| San Juan . | 1,669 | 2,120 | 279 | 1,639 | 2,004 | 576 |
| Sanpete . . | 1,565 | 3,622 | 801 | 1,302 | 2,995 | 1,742 |
| Sevier . . . | 1,327 | 4,018 | 670 | 1,039 | 3,160 | 1,671 |
| Summit . . | 4,139 | 3,835 | 970 | 3,013 | 3,133 | 3,060 |
| Tooele . . . | 3,970 | 3,848 | 1,237 | 3,270 | 3,676 | 3,011 |
| Uintah . . . | 1,711 | 4,720 | 898 | 1,374 | 3,505 | 2,250 |
| Utah . . . . | 18,027 | 68,763 | 8,006 | 14,090 | 61,398 | 24,558 |
| Wasatch. . | 1,366 | 2,212 | 556 | 1,042 | 1,822 | 1,234 |
| Washington | 4,768 | 17,508 | 2,056 | 3,364 | 11,310 | 4,623 |
| Wayne . . . | 265 | 735 | 114 | 236 | 706 | 251 |
| Weber . . . | 21,338 | 27,358 | 6,191 | 17,795 | 26,812 | 20,559 |
| **Totals . . .** | **220,197** | **359,394** | **66,100** | **183,429** | **322,632** | **203,400** |

## Utah Vote Since 1948

1948, Truman, Dem., 149,151; Dewey, Rep., 124,402; Wallace, Prog., 2,679; Dobbs, Soc. Workers, 73.
1952, Eisenhower, Rep., 194,190; Stevenson, Dem., 135,364.
1956, Eisenhower, Rep., 215,631; Stevenson, Dem., 118,364.
1960, Kennedy, Dem., 169,248; Nixon, Rep., 205,361; Dobbs, Soc. Workers, 100.
1964, Johnson, Dem., 219,628; Goldwater, Rep., 181,785.
1968, Nixon, Rep., 238,728; Humphrey, Dem., 156,665; Wallace, 3d Party, 26,906; Halstead, Soc. Workers, 89; Peace and Freedom, 180.
1972, Nixon, Rep., 323,643; McGovern, Dem., 126,284; Schmitz, Amer., 28,549.
1976, Carter, Dem., 182,110; Ford, Rep., 337,908; Anderson, Amer., 13,304; McCarthy, Ind., 3,907; MacBride, Libertarian, 2,438; Maddox, Amer. Ind., 1,162; Camejo, Soc. Workers, 268; Hall, Com., 121.
1980, Reagan, Rep., 439,687; Carter, Dem., 124,266; Anderson, Ind., 30,284; Clark, Libertarian, 7,226; Commoner, Citizens, 1,009; Greaves, Amer., 965; Rarick, Amer. Ind., 522; Hall, Com., 139; DeBerry, Soc. Workers, 124.
1984, Reagan, Rep., 469,105; Mondale, Dem., 155,369; Bergland, Libertarian, 2,447.
1988, Bush, Rep., 428,442; Dukakis, Dem., 207,352; Paul, Lib., 7,473; Dennis, Amer., 2,158.
1992, Clinton, Dem., 183,429; Bush, Rep., 322,632; Perot, Ind., 203,400; Gritz, Populist/America First, 28,602; Marrou, Libertarian, 1,900; Hagelin, Natural Law, 1,319; LaRouche, Ind., 1,089.
1996, Dole, Rep., 359,394; Clinton, Dem., 220,197; Perot, Ref., 66,100; Nader, Green, 4,601; Browne, Libertarian, 4,104; Phillips, Taxpayers, 2,610; Templin, Ind. Amer., 1,291; Crane, Ind., 1,105; Hagelin, Natural Law, 1,085; Moorehead, Workers World, 298; Harris, Soc. Workers, 238; Dodge, Proh., 110.

# Vermont

| City | 1996 Clinton (D) | 1996 Dole (R) | 1996 Perot (RF) | 1992 Clinton (D) | 1992 Bush (R) | 1992 Perot (I) |
|---|---|---|---|---|---|---|
| Barre City. . | 1,890 | 1,107 | 376 | 1,807 | 1,508 | 1,035 |
| Bennington . | 3,454 | 1,654 | 960 | 3,646 | 2,151 | 1,536 |
| Brattleboro . | 3,006 | 1,194 | 393 | 3,519 | 1,447 | 847 |
| Burlington. . | 11,600 | 3,762 | 1,309 | 12,508 | 4,462 | 3,241 |
| Montpelier . | 2,348 | 1,058 | 253 | 2,490 | 1,407 | 657 |
| Rutland City | 3,687 | 2,239 | 834 | 3,888 | 2,915 | 1,722 |
| St. Albans City . . . . . | 1,514 | 655 | 337 | 1,455 | 887 | 744 |
| St. Johnsbury . | 1,367 | 968 | 414 | 1,249 | 1,243 | 836 |
| South Burlington . | 3,929 | 2,274 | 351 | 3,730 | 2,131 | 1,359 |
| Winooski . . | 1,480 | 568 | 300 | 1,462 | 733 | 646 |
| Other. . . . . | 103,899 | 64,399 | 25,330 | 97,836 | 69,238 | 53,362 |
| **Totals . . . .** | **138,400** | **80,043** | **30,912** | **133,590** | **88,122** | **65,985** |

## Vermont Vote Since 1948

1948, Truman, Dem., 45,557; Dewey, Rep., 75,926; Wallace, Prog., 1,279; Thomas, Soc., 585.
1952, Eisenhower, Rep., 109,717; Stevenson, Dem., 43,355; Hallinan, Prog., 282; Hoopes, Soc., 185.
1956, Eisenhower, Rep., 110,390; Stevenson, Dem., 42,549; scattered, 39.
1960, Kennedy, Dem., 69,186; Nixon, Rep., 98,131.
1964, Johnson, Dem., 107,674; Goldwater, Rep., 54,868.
1968, Nixon, Rep., 85,142; Humphrey, Dem., 70,255; Wallace, 3d Party, 5,104; Halstead, Soc. Workers, 295; Gregory, New Party, 579.
1972, Nixon, Rep., 117,149; McGovern, Dem., 68,174; Spock, Liberty Union, 1,010; Jenness, Soc. Workers, 296; scattered, 318.
1976, Carter, Dem., 77,798; Carter, Ind. Vermonter, 991; Ford, Rep., 100,387; McCarthy, Ind., 4,001; Camejo, Soc. Workers, 430; LaRouche, U.S. Labor, 196; scattered, 99.
1980, Reagan, Rep., 94,598; Carter, Dem., 81,891; Anderson, Ind., 31,760; Commoner, Citizens, 2,316; Clark, Libertarian, 1,900; McReynolds, Liberty Union, 136; Hall, Com., 118; DeBerry, Soc. Workers, 75; scattering, 413.
1984, Reagan, Rep., 135,865; Mondale, Dem., 95,730; Bergland, Libertarian, 1,002.
1988, Bush, Rep., 124,331; Dukakis, Dem., 115,775; Paul, Lib., 1,000; LaRouche, Ind., 275.
1992, Clinton, Dem., 133,590; Bush, Rep., 88,122; Perot, Ind., 65,985.
1996, Clinton, Dem., 138,400; Dole, Rep., 80,043; Perot, Ref., 30,912; Nader, Green, 5,511; Browne, Libertarian, 1,231; Peron, Grass Roots, 675; Hagelin, Natural Law, 498; Phillips, Taxpayers, 366; Hollis, Liberty Union, 316; Harris, Soc. Workers, 196.

# Virginia

| County | 1996 Clinton (D) | 1996 Dole (R) | 1996 Perot (RF) | 1992 Clinton (D) | 1992 Bush (R) | 1992 Perot (I) |
|---|---|---|---|---|---|---|
| Accomack. | 5,127 | 5,008 | 1,217 | 4,950 | 5,666 | 2,304 |
| Albemarle . | 14,087 | 15,242 | 1,533 | 13,886 | 13,894 | 3,855 |
| Alleghany . | 2,386 | 2,085 | 606 | 2,396 | 2,294 | 926 |
| Amelia . . . | 1,625 | 2,119 | 323 | 1,534 | 2,062 | 574 |
| Amherst . . | 4,864 | 5,094 | 835 | 4,101 | 5,482 | 1,268 |
| Appomattox | 2,223 | 2,601 | 508 | 1,919 | 2,830 | 801 |
| Arlington. . | 43,184 | 25,058 | 2,734 | 47,756 | 26,376 | 7,992 |
| Augusta . . | 5,966 | 13,456 | 1,916 | 5,190 | 12,896 | 3,397 |
| Bath. . . . . | 922 | 847 | 247 | 855 | 1,075 | 354 |

| County | 1996 Clinton (D) | 1996 Dole (R) | 1996 Perot (RF) | 1992 Clinton (D) | 1992 Bush (R) | 1992 Perot (I) |
|---|---|---|---|---|---|---|
| Bedford . . | 8,849 | 12,944 | 2,188 | 6,792 | 10,496 | 3,251 |
| Bland . . . . | 939 | 1,167 | 385 | 1,001 | 1,368 | 408 |
| Botetourt. . | 4,576 | 6,404 | 1,137 | 4,349 | 5,904 | 1,819 |
| Brunswick. | 3,442 | 2,059 | 340 | 3,687 | 2,480 | 479 |
| Buchanan . | 6,551 | 2,783 | 815 | 7,405 | 3,297 | 815 |
| Buckingham . | 2,274 | 1,874 | 392 | 2,193 | 2,368 | 459 |
| Campbell . | 6,772 | 10,230 | 1,503 | 5,999 | 10,931 | 2,553 |
| Caroline . . | 3,897 | 2,816 | 521 | 3,770 | 2,947 | 965 |
| Carroll . . . | 3,613 | 5,088 | 1,158 | 3,790 | 5,664 | 1,388 |
| Charles City . | 1,842 | 729 | 178 | 2,010 | 729 | 251 |
| Charlotte. . | 2,004 | 2,103 | 431 | 2,098 | 2,293 | 640 |
| Chesterfield | 30,209 | 56,641 | 6,004 | 28,028 | 56,626 | 16,898 |
| Clarke . . . | 1,906 | 2,201 | 379 | 1,811 | 1,994 | 802 |
| Craig . . . . | 895 | 979 | 262 | 965 | 1,008 | 304 |
| Culpeper. . | 3,524 | 4,965 | 704 | 3,444 | 5,226 | 1,640 |
| Cumberland | 1,303 | 1,544 | 275 | 1,284 | 1,643 | 372 |
| Dickenson. | 3,912 | 2,227 | 660 | 4,839 | 2,574 | 660 |
| Dinwiddie . | 3,871 | 3,503 | 666 | 3,624 | 3,648 | 1,198 |
| Essex. . . . | 1,668 | 1,627 | 188 | 1,583 | 1,897 | 382 |
| Fairfax . . . | 156,673 | 162,251 | 15,370 | 160,186 | 170,488 | 53,012 |
| Fauquier. . | 6,759 | 11,062 | 1,287 | 6,600 | 10,497 | 3,464 |
| Floyd . . . . | 1,409 | 2,374 | 545 | 2,026 | 2,575 | 672 |
| Fluvanna. . | 2,676 | 3,442 | 457 | 2,134 | 2,811 | 871 |
| Franklin . . | 7,298 | 7,382 | 2,015 | 6,590 | 6,724 | 2,232 |
| Frederick . | 5,986 | 10,607 | 1,599 | 4,942 | 9,425 | 2,981 |
| Giles . . . . | 3,196 | 2,566 | 841 | 3,346 | 3,023 | 1,142 |
| Gloucester | 4,710 | 6,447 | 1,266 | 4,058 | 6,461 | 2,640 |
| Goochland | 2,776 | 4,119 | 424 | 2,589 | 3,834 | 994 |
| Grayson . . | 2,661 | 3,004 | 675 | 2,615 | 3,378 | 860 |
| Greene. . . | 1,440 | 2,351 | 346 | 1,353 | 2,265 | 627 |
| Greensville | 2,384 | 1,176 | 263 | 2,237 | 1,335 | 360 |
| Halifax . . . | 5,598 | 6,486 | 876 | 4,752 | 5,199 | 1,140 |
| Hanover . . | 9,879 | 22,086 | 2,447 | 8,021 | 20,336 | 5,674 |
| Henrico. . . | 41,039 | 54,439 | 5,944 | 36,807 | 56,910 | 14,720 |
| Henry. . . . | 9,061 | 9,111 | 2,370 | 9,296 | 9,005 | 3,212 |
| Highland . . | 446 | 631 | 134 | 494 | 686 | 212 |
| Isle of Wight | 4,952 | 5,416 | 893 | 4,380 | 5,370 | 1,536 |
| James City | 7,247 | 10,120 | 1,036 | 6,536 | 8,781 | 2,675 |
| King and Queen . . | 1,393 | 1,073 | 213 | 1,811 | 2,570 | 918 |
| King George . | 1,875 | 2,597 | 341 | 1,363 | 1,206 | 323 |
| King William . | 1,765 | 2,346 | 339 | 1,822 | 2,591 | 758 |
| Lancaster . | 1,844 | 2,709 | 324 | 1,812 | 2,841 | 739 |
| Lee . . . . . | 4,443 | 3,225 | 822 | 5,215 | 3,504 | 1,002 |
| Loudoun . . | 18,886 | 24,428 | 2,988 | 14,462 | 19,290 | 7,391 |
| Louisa . . . | 3,754 | 3,746 | 692 | 3,399 | 3,461 | 1,381 |
| Lunenburg. | 1,762 | 1,613 | 271 | 2,082 | 2,227 | 505 |
| Madison . . | 1,734 | 2,296 | 360 | 1,700 | 2,341 | 653 |
| Mathews . . | 1,602 | 2,206 | 403 | 1,402 | 2,179 | 884 |
| Mecklenburg. | 4,409 | 4,937 | 789 | 4,273 | 5,401 | 1,128 |
| Middlesex . | 1,704 | 2,141 | 348 | 1,597 | 2,224 | 768 |
| Montgomery . | 10,867 | 10,517 | 2,594 | 10,658 | 10,606 | 3,449 |
| Nelson . . . | 2,753 | 1,988 | 401 | 2,586 | 2,159 | 748 |
| New Kent . | 1,859 | 2,852 | 520 | 1,738 | 2,708 | 1,017 |
| Northampton. | 2,569 | 1,763 | 522 | 2,568 | 2,088 | 844 |
| Northum- berland . . | 1,976 | 2,613 | 377 | 1,862 | 2,667 | 729 |
| Nottoway . | 2,327 | 2,416 | 347 | 2,411 | 2,610 | 606 |
| Orange. . . | 3,590 | 4,435 | 750 | 3,348 | 4,092 | 1,425 |
| Page . . . . | 2,868 | 3,876 | 640 | 3,010 | 4,203 | 1,163 |
| Patrick . . . | 2,302 | 3,547 | 719 | 2,465 | 3,521 | 1,026 |
| Pittsylvania | 7,676 | 12,122 | 1,469 | 7,675 | 11,467 | 2,296 |
| Powhatan . | 2,254 | 4,679 | 626 | 1,950 | 3,832 | 1,232 |
| Prince Edward . . | 2,823 | 2,444 | 433 | 2,775 | 2,858 | 635 |
| Prince George . . | 3,498 | 5,113 | 698 | 3,087 | 4,799 | 1,459 |
| Prince William . . | 33,459 | 39,296 | 4,881 | 26,486 | 35,432 | 13,190 |
| Pulaski . . . | 5,333 | 5,387 | 1,399 | 5,633 | 6,148 | 2,066 |
| Rappahan- nock . . . . | 1,405 | 1,505 | 213 | 1,273 | 1,410 | 487 |
| Richmond . | 1,101 | 1,424 | 201 | 1,034 | 1,609 | 366 |
| Roanoke . . | 15,387 | 20,700 | 2,934 | 14,704 | 20,667 | 5,477 |
| Rockbridge | 3,116 | 3,272 | 760 | 2,908 | 3,228 | 1,254 |
| Rockingham . | 5,857 | 14,615 | 1,320 | 5,407 | 13,016 | 2,839 |
| Russell . . . | 5,437 | 3,696 | 862 | 6,480 | 3,891 | 958 |
| Scott . . . . | 3,448 | 4,097 | 798 | 3,979 | 4,515 | 957 |
| Shenandoah. | 4,223 | 7,440 | 1,353 | 3,956 | 7,746 | 2,063 |
| Smyth . . . | 4,990 | 4,776 | 1,407 | 4,924 | 6,128 | 1,618 |
| Southampton | 3,454 | 2,275 | 564 | 3,199 | 2,844 | 754 |
| Spotsylvania . | 9,943 | 13,109 | 1,799 | 8,133 | 11,829 | 3,918 |
| Stafford . . | 9,901 | 14,098 | 1,855 | 7,718 | 12,528 | 4,481 |
| Surry . . . . | 1,753 | 944 | 181 | 1,823 | 1,046 | 364 |
| Sussex. . . | 2,089 | 1,382 | 256 | 2,193 | 1,527 | 446 |
| Tazewell . . | 7,499 | 6,128 | 1,554 | 8,586 | 6,375 | 1,872 |
| Warren. . . | 3,792 | 4,657 | 904 | 3,554 | 4,319 | 1,650 |
| Washington | 6,941 | 9,098 | 1,666 | 7,269 | 9,150 | 2,288 |
| Westmoreland. | 2,949 | 2,333 | 427 | 2,758 | 2,554 | 818 |
| Wise . . . . | 6,712 | 4,316 | 1,479 | 7,681 | 5,144 | 1,835 |
| Wythe . . . | 3,275 | 4,272 | 955 | 3,616 | 5,121 | 1,557 |
| York. . . . . | 7,731 | 11,396 | 1,469 | 6,218 | 10,197 | 3,426 |
| **Cities** | | | | | | |
| Alexandria. | 27,925 | 15,533 | 1,471 | 30,784 | 16,700 | 4,934 |
| Bedford . . | 1,065 | 990 | 212 | 963 | 1,091 | 313 |
| Bristol. . . . | 2,586 | 2,983 | 429 | 2,948 | 3,616 | 851 |
| Buena Vista | 1,090 | 713 | 216 | 1,023 | 849 | 291 |
| Charlottesville | 7,916 | 4,091 | 565 | 8,685 | 4,705 | 1,397 |
| Chesapeake . | 28,711 | 29,248 | 4,323 | 23,495 | 28,909 | 9,237 |
| Clifton Forge . | 974 | 486 | 147 | 958 | 632 | 251 |
| Colonial Heights . . | 1,780 | 4,631 | 518 | 1,721 | 5,298 | 1,312 |
| Covington . | 1,394 | 763 | 255 | 1,442 | 995 | 402 |
| Danville . . | 8,168 | 9,254 | 762 | 8,134 | 9,584 | 1,679 |
| Emporia . . | 1,103 | 835 | 98 | 1,048 | 1,094 | 157 |
| Fairfax . . . | 3,652 | 4,072 | 413 | 3,884 | 4,333 | 1,439 |
| Falls Church . | 2,875 | 1,926 | 237 | 2,864 | 1,912 | 599 |
| Franklin . . | 1,962 | 1,200 | 207 | 1,696 | 1,347 | 272 |
| Fredericks- burg . . . . | 3,215 | 2,579 | 300 | 3,266 | 2,819 | 738 |
| Galax. . . . | 1,033 | 910 | 221 | 957 | 1,087 | 276 |
| Hampton. . | 24,485 | 16,591 | 2,783 | 23,395 | 19,219 | 6,581 |
| Harrisonburg. | 3,346 | 4,945 | 434 | 3,414 | 4,935 | 1,162 |
| Hopewell . | 2,864 | 3,489 | 549 | 2,863 | 3,818 | 1,227 |
| Lexington . | 1,059 | 850 | 112 | 1,128 | 894 | 228 |
| Lynchburg. | 10,280 | 11,441 | 1,155 | 9,587 | 12,518 | 2,545 |
| Manassas . | 4,378 | 5,799 | 670 | 3,647 | 5,453 | 1,971 |
| Manassas Park . . . . | 748 | 916 | 151 | 567 | 792 | 356 |
| Martinsville | 2,993 | 2,400 | 382 | 3,073 | 2,690 | 748 |
| Newport News . . . | 27,155 | 23,556 | 3,095 | 25,743 | 26,779 | 8,217 |
| Norfolk . . . | 37,653 | 18,699 | 3,424 | 37,602 | 22,362 | 8,732 |
| Norton . . . | 802 | 416 | 138 | 871 | 472 | 182 |
| Petersburg | 7,514 | 1,939 | 379 | 8,671 | 3,125 | 834 |
| Poquoson . | 1,409 | 3,422 | 400 | 1,086 | 3,354 | 960 |
| Portsmouth | 22,132 | 10,678 | 2,242 | 20,416 | 12,575 | 4,360 |
| Radford . . | 2,113 | 1,742 | 381 | 2,183 | 1,996 | 582 |
| Richmond . | 41,133 | 20,231 | 2,714 | 47,642 | 24,341 | 6,992 |
| Roanoke. . | 17,268 | 12,245 | 2,177 | 17,724 | 13,443 | 3,753 |
| Salem . . . | 4,282 | 4,936 | 796 | 4,028 | 5,143 | 1,430 |
| South Boston[1] . . | — | — | — | 1,051 | 1,435 | 252 |
| Staunton. . | 3,162 | 4,526 | 605 | 2,851 | 4,989 | 1,146 |
| Suffolk . . . | 10,436 | 8,140 | 1,246 | 9,196 | 8,697 | 2,150 |
| Virginia Beach. . . | 52,134 | 63,730 | 9,326 | 44,294 | 68,936 | 24,087 |
| Waynesboro . | 2,397 | 3,466 | 462 | 2,302 | 3,758 | 961 |
| Williamsburg. | 1,826 | 1,561 | 162 | 1,856 | 1,349 | 445 |
| Winchester | 3,023 | 3,680 | 434 | 2,768 | 3,833 | 1,048 |
| **Totals . . .** | **1,070,990** | **1,119,974** | **158,707** | **1,038,650** | **1,150,517** | **348,639** |

(1) South Boston merged with Halifax County in July 1996.

## Virginia Vote Since 1948

1948, Truman, Dem., 200,786; Dewey, Rep., 172,070; Thurmond, States' Rights, 43,393; Wallace, Prog., 2,047; Thomas, Soc., 726; Teichert, Soc. Labor, 234.

1952, Eisenhower, Rep., 349,037; Stevenson, Dem., 268,677; Hass, Soc. Labor, 1,160; Hoopes, Social Dem., 504; Hallinan, Prog., 311.

1956, Eisenhower, Rep., 386,459; Stevenson, Dem., 267,760; Andrews, States' Rights, 42,964; Hoopes, Soc. Dem., 444; Hass, Soc. Labor, 351.

1960, Kennedy, Dem., 362,327; Nixon, Rep., 404,521; Coiner, Cons., 4,204; Hass, Soc. Labor, 397.

1964, Johnson, Dem., 558,038; Goldwater, Rep., 481,334; Hass, Soc. Labor, 2,895.

1968, Nixon, Rep., 590,319; Humphrey, Dem., 442,387; Wallace, 3d Party, *320,272; Blomen, Soc. Labor, 4,671; Munn, Proh., 601; Gregory, Peace and Freedom, 1,680.

*10,561 votes for Wallace were omitted in the count.

1972, Nixon, Rep., 988,493; McGovern, Dem., 438,887; Schmitz, Amer., 19,721; Fisher, Soc. Labor, 9,918.

1976, Carter, Dem., 813,896; Ford, Rep., 836,554; Camejo, Soc. Workers, 17,802; Anderson, Amer., 16,686; LaRouche, U.S. Labor, 7,508; MacBride, Libertarian, 4,648.

1980, Reagan, Rep., 989,609; Carter, Dem., 752,174; Anderson, Ind., 95,418; Commoner, Citizens, 14,024; Clark, Libertarian, 12,821; DeBerry, Soc. Workers, 1,986.

1984, Reagan, Rep., 1,337,078; Mondale, Dem., 796,250.

1988, Bush, Rep., 1,309,162; Dukakis, Dem., 859,799; Fulani, Ind., 14,312; Paul, Lib., 8,336.

1992, Clinton, Dem., 1,038,650; Bush, Rep., 1,150,517; Perot, Ind., 348,639; LaRouche, Ind., 11,937; Marrou, Libertarian, 5,730; Fulani, New Alliance, 3,192.

1996, Dole, Rep., 1,119,974; Clinton, Dem., 1,070,990; Perot, Ref., 158,707; Phillips, Taxpayers, 13,660; Browne, Libertarian, 8,887; Hagelin, Natural Law, 4,514.

# Washington

| County | 1996 Clinton (D) | 1996 Dole (R) | 1996 Perot (RF) | 1992 Clinton (D) | 1992 Bush (R) | 1992 Perot (I) |
|---|---|---|---|---|---|---|
| Adams. . . | 1,566 | 2,084 | 398 | 1,449 | 2,087 | 1,010 |
| Asotin . . . | 3,251 | 2,769 | 915 | 3,239 | 2,425 | 1,849 |

| County | 1996 Clinton (D) | 1996 Dole (R) | 1996 Perot (RF) | 1992 Clinton (D) | 1992 Bush (R) | 1992 Perot (I) |
|---|---|---|---|---|---|---|
| Benton . . . | 17,733 | 22,291 | 4,690 | 16,459 | 22,883 | 12,878 |
| Chelan . . . | 7,556 | 10,476 | 2,035 | 7,860 | 10,716 | 4,606 |
| Clallam. . . | 10,331 | 9,733 | 2,613 | 10,820 | 9,765 | 7,775 |
| Clark . . . . | 41,783 | 36,009 | 7,669 | 42,648 | 36,906 | 26,163 |
| Columbia . | 712 | 883 | 210 | 668 | 761 | 466 |
| Cowlitz. . . | 15,615 | 9,368 | 2,872 | 15,052 | 10,000 | 9,246 |
| Douglas . . | 3,156 | 4,323 | 865 | 3,731 | 4,920 | 2,315 |
| Ferry . . . . | 914 | 810 | 276 | 963 | 773 | 762 |
| Franklin . . | 3,704 | 4,007 | 703 | 3,743 | 4,486 | 2,597 |
| Garfield . . | 346 | 440 | 84 | 473 | 620 | 222 |
| Grant. . . . | 7,003 | 9,021 | 2,171 | 7,278 | 9,503 | 4,898 |
| Grays Harbor | 12,234 | 6,391 | 3,246 | 12,599 | 6,904 | 7,460 |
| Island. . . . | 9,998 | 9,690 | 2,388 | 9,555 | 9,526 | 7,889 |
| Jefferson . | 6,018 | 3,696 | 1,137 | 6,148 | 3,467 | 3,168 |
| King. . . . . | 337,849 | 170,989 | 41,810 | 391,050 | 212,986 | 167,216 |
| Kitsap . . . | 33,905 | 26,255 | 6,568 | 34,442 | 29,340 | 23,873 |
| Kittitas . . . | 5,008 | 4,430 | 1,023 | 5,432 | 4,078 | 2,778 |
| Klickitat . . | 2,827 | 2,182 | 761 | 2,758 | 2,085 | 1,938 |
| Lewis. . . . | 9,118 | 11,206 | 2,935 | 7,810 | 12,316 | 6,684 |
| Lincoln . . . | 1,412 | 1,954 | 411 | 1,653 | 2,152 | 1,098 |
| Mason . . . | 8,186 | 5,687 | 2,343 | 8,076 | 5,776 | 5,577 |
| Okanogan. | 3,816 | 4,488 | 1,400 | 5,015 | 4,265 | 3,541 |
| Pacific . . . | 4,822 | 2,404 | 1,069 | 4,587 | 2,243 | 2,351 |
| Pend Oreille. | 1,879 | 1,757 | 618 | 1,798 | 1,528 | 1,340 |
| Pierce . . . | 80,070 | 56,391 | 13,876 | 102,243 | 77,410 | 59,523 |
| San Juan . | 3,073 | 2,068 | 411 | 3,353 | 1,901 | 1,776 |
| Skagit . . . | 15,563 | 13,203 | 4,218 | 15,936 | 13,388 | 10,973 |
| Skamania . | 1,609 | 1,237 | 410 | 1,474 | 1,102 | 1,050 |
| Snohomish | 86,493 | 62,425 | 18,097 | 88,643 | 69,137 | 65,838 |
| Spokane. . | 61,674 | 55,283 | 14,919 | 69,526 | 59,984 | 38,251 |
| Stevens . . | 4,280 | 5,676 | 1,776 | 4,960 | 5,706 | 3,769 |
| Thurston. . | 38,142 | 24,308 | 6,037 | 38,293 | 25,643 | 19,551 |
| Wahkiakum | 829 | 575 | 189 | 696 | 488 | 584 |
| Walla Walla | 7,214 | 7,969 | 1,701 | 7,325 | 7,894 | 4,507 |
| Whatcom . | 22,940 | 20,543 | 3,816 | 26,619 | 23,801 | 12,455 |
| Whitman. . | 6,094 | 5,436 | 1,160 | 7,637 | 6,428 | 3,220 |
| Yakima. . . | 20,922 | 21,286 | 3,822 | 21,026 | 25,841 | 10,583 |
| **Totals . . .** | **899,645** | **639,743** | **161,642** | **993,037** | **731,234** | **541,780** |

## Washington Vote Since 1948

1948, Truman, Dem., 476,165; Dewey, Rep., 386,315; Wallace, Prog., 31,692; Watson, Proh., 6,117; Thomas, Soc., 3,534; Teichert, Soc. Labor, 1,133; Dobbs, Soc. Workers, 103.

1952, Eisenhower, Rep., 599,107; Stevenson, Dem., 492,845; MacArthur, Christian Nationalist, 7,290; Hallinan, Prog., 2,460; Hass, Soc. Labor, 633; Hoopes, Soc., 254; Dobbs, Soc. Workers, 119.

1956, Eisenhower, Rep., 620,430; Stevenson, Dem., 523,002; Hass, Soc. Labor, 7,457.

1960, Kennedy, Dem., 599,298; Nixon, Rep., 629,273; Hass, Soc. Labor, 10,895; Curtis, Constitution, 1,401; Dobbs, Soc. Workers, 705.

1964, Johnson, Dem., 779,699; Goldwater, Rep., 470,366; Hass, Soc. Labor, 7,772; DeBerry, Freedom Soc., 537.

1968, Nixon, Rep., 588,510; Humphrey, Dem., 616,037; Wallace, 3d Party, 96,990; Blomen, Soc. Labor, 488; Cleaver, Peace and Freedom, 1,609; Halstead, Soc. Workers, 270; Mitchell, Free Ballot, 377.

1972, Nixon, Rep., 837,135; McGovern, Dem., 568,334; Schmitz, Amer., 58,906; Spock, Ind., 2,644; Fisher, Soc. Labor, 1,102; Jenness, Soc. Workers, 623; Hall, Com., 566; Hospers, Libertarian, 1,537.

1976, Carter, Dem., 717,323; Ford, Rep., 777,732; McCarthy, Ind., 36,986; Maddox, Amer. Ind., 8,585; Anderson, Amer., 5,046; MacBride, Libertarian, 5,042; Wright, People's, 1,124; Camejo, Soc. Workers, 905; LaRouche, U.S. Labor, 903; Hall, Com., 817; Levin, Soc. Labor, 713; Zeidler, Soc., 358.

1980, Reagan, Rep., 865,244; Carter, Dem., 650,193; Anderson, Ind., 185,073; Clark, Libertarian, 29,213; Commoner, Citizens, 9,403; DeBerry, Soc. Workers, 1,137; McReynolds, Soc., 956; Hall, Com., 834; Griswold, Workers World, 341.

1984, Reagan, Rep., 1,051,670; Mondale, Dem., 798,352; Bergland, Libertarian, 8,844.

1988, Bush, Rep., 903,835; Dukakis, Dem., 933,516; Paul, Lib., 17,240; LaRouche, Ind., 4,412.

1992, Clinton, Dem., 993,037; Bush, Rep., 731,234; Perot, Ind., 541,780; Marrou, Libertarian, 7,533; Gritz, Populist/America First, 4,854; Hagelin, Natural Law, 2,456; Phillips, U.S. Taxpayers, 2,354; Fulani, New Alliance, 1,776; Daniels, Ind., 1,171.

1996, Clinton, Dem., 899,645; Dole, Rep., 639,743; Perot, Ref., 161,642; Nader, Ind., 48,162; Browne, Libertarian, 9,704; Hagelin, Natural Law, 4,725; Phillips, Taxpayers, 3,480; Collins, Ind., 1,780; Moorehead, Workers World, 1,673; Harris, Soc. Workers, 629.

# West Virginia

| County | 1996 Clinton (D) | 1996 Dole (R) | 1996 Perot (RF) | 1992 Clinton (D) | 1992 Bush (R) | 1992 Perot (I) |
|---|---|---|---|---|---|---|
| Barbour . . | 3,062 | 2,144 | 778 | 3,467 | 2,322 | 1,153 |
| Berkeley. . | 8,152 | 9,548 | 2,232 | 7,159 | 9,134 | 3,645 |
| Boone . . . | 6,002 | 1,891 | 918 | 6,576 | 2,021 | 1,037 |
| Braxton . . | 2,981 | 1,431 | 518 | 3,396 | 1,535 | 823 |
| Brooke. . . | 5,320 | 2,729 | 1,369 | 5,693 | 2,582 | 2,103 |
| Cabell . . . | 16,003 | 12,952 | 2,904 | 15,111 | 13,203 | 5,311 |
| Calhoun . . | 1,391 | 992 | 303 | 1,627 | 1,095 | 537 |
| Clay. . . . . | 2,056 | 1,125 | 350 | 1,928 | 1,255 | 462 |
| Doddridge. | 862 | 1,329 | 377 | 968 | 1,500 | 515 |
| Fayette. . . | 9,312 | 3,607 | 1,529 | 9,574 | 3,991 | 2,002 |
| Gilmer . . . | 1,386 | 929 | 312 | 1,576 | 1,085 | 484 |
| Grant. . . . | 1,189 | 2,566 | 476 | 1,011 | 2,762 | 519 |
| Greenbrier | 6,224 | 4,398 | 1,405 | 5,784 | 4,442 | 1,898 |
| Hampshire | 2,335 | 2,810 | 603 | 2,365 | 2,767 | 1,022 |
| Hancock. . | 7,480 | 4,246 | 2,149 | 7,830 | 3,897 | 3,267 |
| Hardy. . . . | 1,898 | 1,875 | 431 | 1,917 | 2,144 | 602 |
| Harrison . . | 14,545 | 8,723 | 3,079 | 15,480 | 9,687 | 5,131 |
| Jackson . . | 4,813 | 4,184 | 1,260 | 5,102 | 4,192 | 1,908 |
| Jefferson . | 6,145 | 5,151 | 1,275 | 5,363 | 4,656 | 2,114 |
| Kanawha . | 39,867 | 28,865 | 6,315 | 38,315 | 31,358 | 11,778 |
| Lewis. . . . | 2,847 | 2,265 | 969 | 2,931 | 2,413 | 1,197 |
| Lincoln . . . | 4,895 | 2,489 | 685 | 4,502 | 2,637 | 787 |
| Logan . . . | 11,107 | 2,584 | 1,486 | 11,095 | 3,336 | 1,835 |
| McDowell . | 5,925 | 1,530 | 642 | 7,019 | 1,941 | 803 |
| Marion . . . | 12,897 | 6,172 | 2,956 | 14,042 | 6,380 | 4,736 |
| Marshall . . | 6,990 | 4,429 | 2,182 | 7,298 | 4,463 | 3,402 |
| Mason . . . | 5,264 | 3,565 | 1,525 | 5,331 | 3,808 | 2,045 |
| Mercer . . . | 8,684 | 7,723 | 2,135 | 9,511 | 7,888 | 2,817 |
| Mineral. . . | 3,411 | 4,283 | 1,138 | 3,992 | 4,837 | 1,884 |
| Mingo . . . | 7,519 | 2,196 | 1,020 | 7,342 | 2,584 | 915 |
| Monongalia | 13,200 | 10,023 | 2,997 | 14,142 | 9,831 | 4,576 |
| Monroe . . | 2,336 | 2,114 | 549 | 2,418 | 2,311 | 685 |
| Morgan . . | 1,918 | 2,580 | 597 | 1,854 | 2,585 | 886 |
| Nicholas. . | 4,717 | 2,617 | 1,057 | 5,042 | 2,959 | 1,495 |
| Ohio . . . . | 8,646 | 7,174 | 2,035 | 9,522 | 7,421 | 3,632 |
| Pendleton . | 1,582 | 1,423 | 256 | 1,626 | 1,589 | 362 |
| Pleasants . | 1,471 | 1,259 | 414 | 1,387 | 1,248 | 731 |
| Pocahontas | 1,786 | 1,231 | 423 | 1,741 | 1,401 | 627 |
| Preston . . | 4,215 | 4,232 | 1,756 | 3,933 | 4,429 | 2,109 |
| Putnam . . | 7,936 | 8,664 | 1,880 | 6,817 | 7,653 | 2,910 |
| Raleigh . . | 12,247 | 8,343 | 2,310 | 13,171 | 8,700 | 3,247 |
| Randolph . | 5,459 | 3,343 | 1,184 | 5,097 | 3,496 | 1,582 |
| Ritchie . . . | 1,366 | 1,883 | 518 | 1,474 | 2,184 | 745 |
| Roane . . . | 2,558 | 2,064 | 618 | 2,607 | 2,207 | 1,009 |
| Summers . | 2,388 | 1,497 | 434 | 2,650 | 1,652 | 565 |
| Taylor . . . | 2,673 | 1,951 | 834 | 2,843 | 2,022 | 1,242 |
| Tucker . . . | 1,639 | 1,204 | 418 | 1,805 | 1,261 | 550 |
| Tyler . . . . | 1,450 | 1,725 | 557 | 1,587 | 1,593 | 1,013 |
| Upshur. . . | 2,995 | 3,289 | 1,018 | 3,161 | 3,505 | 1,558 |
| Wayne . . . | 8,245 | 5,524 | 1,596 | 8,392 | 5,729 | 2,199 |
| Webster . . | 2,281 | 649 | 365 | 2,320 | 811 | 436 |
| Wetzel . . . | 3,202 | 2,017 | 1,000 | 3,753 | 2,271 | 1,550 |
| Wirt . . . . . | 902 | 918 | 276 | 1,043 | 939 | 394 |
| Wood. . . . | 13,145 | 15,328 | 3,640 | 13,529 | 15,441 | 6,998 |
| Wyoming . | 5,475 | 2,125 | 800 | 5,782 | 2,821 | 996 |
| **Totals . . .** | **324,394** | **231,908** | **70,853** | **331,001** | **241,974** | **108,829** |

## West Virginia Vote Since 1948

1948, Truman, Dem., 429,188; Dewey, Rep., 316,251; Wallace, Prog., 3,311.

1952, Eisenhower, Rep., 419,970; Stevenson, Dem., 453,578.

1956, Eisenhower, Rep., 449,297; Stevenson, Dem., 381,534.

1960, Kennedy, Dem., 441,786; Nixon, Rep., 395,995.

1964, Johnson, Dem., 538,087; Goldwater, Rep., 253,953.

1968, Nixon, Rep., 307,555; Humphrey, Dem., 374,091; Wallace, 3d Party, 72,560.

1972, Nixon, Rep., 484,964; McGovern, Dem., 277,435.

1976, Carter, Dem., 435,864; Ford, Rep., 314,726.

1980, Reagan, Rep., 334,206; Carter, Dem., 367,462; Anderson, Ind., 31,691; Clark, Libertarian, 4,356.

1984, Reagan, Rep., 405,483; Mondale, Dem., 328,125.

1988, Bush, Rep., 310,065; Dukakis, Dem., 341,016; Fulani, New Alliance, 2,230.

1992, Clinton, Dem., 331,001; Bush, Rep., 241,974; Perot, Ind., 108,829; Marrou, Libertarian, 1,873.

1996, Clinton, Dem., 324,394; Dole, Rep., 231,908; Perot, Ref., 70,853; Browne, Libertarian, 3,020.

# Wisconsin

| County | 1996 Clinton (D) | 1996 Dole (R) | 1996 Perot (RF) | 1992 Clinton (D) | 1992 Bush (R) | 1992 Perot (I) |
|---|---|---|---|---|---|---|
| Adams . . . | 4,119 | 2,450 | 1,122 | 3,539 | 2,465 | 2,003 |
| Ashland . . | 3,808 | 1,853 | 861 | 4,213 | 2,372 | 1,746 |
| Barron . . . | 8,025 | 6,158 | 2,692 | 8,063 | 6,572 | 5,479 |
| Bayfield . . | 3,896 | 2,250 | 899 | 3,873 | 2,393 | 1,786 |
| Brown . . . | 42,823 | 38,563 | 8,036 | 37,513 | 42,352 | 22,395 |

| County | 1996 Clinton (D) | 1996 Dole (R) | 1996 Perot (RF) | 1992 Clinton (D) | 1992 Bush (R) | 1992 Perot (I) |
|---|---|---|---|---|---|---|
| Buffalo . . . | 2,681 | 1,805 | 972 | 2,996 | 2,029 | 1,889 |
| Burnet . . . | 3,625 | 2,457 | 962 | 3,172 | 2,340 | 1,855 |
| Calumet . . | 6,940 | 7,049 | 2,112 | 5,701 | 7,541 | 5,055 |
| Chippewa . | 9,647 | 7,520 | 3,563 | 10,487 | 8,215 | 6,408 |
| Clark . . . . | 5,543 | 4,617 | 2,472 | 5,540 | 4,977 | 4,284 |
| Columbia . | 10,336 | 8,377 | 2,377 | 9,348 | 9,099 | 5,439 |
| Crawford. . | 3,658 | 2,149 | 1,060 | 3,540 | 2,390 | 1,797 |
| Dane . . . . | 109,327 | 59,480 | 12,430 | 114,724 | 61,957 | 31,874 |
| Dodge . . . | 12,625 | 12,890 | 3,322 | 11,438 | 14,971 | 9,136 |
| Door. . . . . | 5,590 | 4,948 | 1,475 | 4,735 | 5,468 | 3,506 |
| Douglas . . | 10,976 | 5,167 | 2,000 | 12,319 | 5,679 | 4,150 |
| Dunn . . . . | 7,536 | 4,917 | 2,555 | 7,965 | 5,283 | 4,809 |
| Eau Claire. | 20,757 | 14,296 | 5,293 | 21,221 | 15,915 | 9,783 |
| Florence . . | 869 | 927 | 331 | 978 | 942 | 719 |
| Fond du Lac. | 15,542 | 16,488 | 4,204 | 13,757 | 19,785 | 10,660 |
| Forest . . . | 2,092 | 1,166 | 678 | 1,904 | 1,393 | 1,062 |
| Grant . . . . | 9,203 | 7,026 | 2,597 | 8,914 | 7,678 | 6,405 |
| Green. . . . | 6,136 | 4,697 | 1,532 | 5,467 | 4,887 | 3,735 |
| Green Lake | 3,152 | 3,565 | 1,025 | 2,772 | 3,897 | 2,827 |
| Iowa. . . . . | 4,691 | 2,866 | 1,071 | 4,467 | 3,288 | 2,341 |
| Iron . . . . . | 1,725 | 1,260 | 469 | 1,762 | 1,273 | 835 |
| Jackson . . | 3,705 | 2,262 | 1,163 | 3,681 | 2,644 | 2,040 |
| Jefferson. . | 13,188 | 12,681 | 3,177 | 11,593 | 13,072 | 7,960 |
| Juneau . . . | 4,332 | 3,226 | 1,393 | 4,177 | 4,051 | 2,670 |
| Kenosha . . | 27,964 | 18,296 | 6,557 | 27,341 | 19,854 | 14,232 |
| Kewaunee. | 4,311 | 3,431 | 1,161 | 4,050 | 3,570 | 2,700 |
| La Crosse . | 23,647 | 16,482 | 4,844 | 22,838 | 18,891 | 10,224 |
| La Fayette. | 3,261 | 2,177 | 944 | 3,143 | 2,582 | 2,079 |
| Langlade. . | 4,074 | 3,206 | 1,249 | 3,630 | 3,890 | 2,444 |
| Lincoln . . . | 6,133 | 4,040 | 1,787 | 5,297 | 4,321 | 3,605 |
| Manitowoc. | 16,750 | 13,239 | 3,941 | 15,903 | 14,008 | 11,179 |
| Marathon . | 24,012 | 19,874 | 6,749 | 21,482 | 20,948 | 14,600 |
| Marinette . | 8,413 | 7,231 | 2,367 | 7,626 | 7,984 | 5,412 |
| Marquette . | 2,859 | 2,208 | 915 | 2,533 | 2,322 | 1,818 |
| Menominee | 992 | 230 | 107 | 691 | 244 | 221 |
| Milwaukee. | 216,628 | 119,410 | 26,027 | 235,521 | 151,314 | 76,039 |
| Monroe. . . | 6,856 | 5,368 | 2,081 | 6,427 | 6,118 | 4,183 |
| Oconto . . . | 6,685 | 5,389 | 1,646 | 5,898 | 5,720 | 4,405 |
| Oneida . . . | 7,620 | 6,337 | 2,604 | 7,160 | 6,725 | 4,782 |
| Outagamie | 28,815 | 27,758 | 7,338 | 23,735 | 30,370 | 18,479 |
| Ozaukee. . | 13,269 | 22,078 | 2,774 | 11,879 | 22,805 | 8,002 |
| Pepin . . . . | 1,585 | 1,007 | 456 | 1,673 | 1,098 | 781 |
| Pierce . . . | 7,970 | 4,604 | 2,030 | 7,824 | 4,844 | 4,492 |
| Polk . . . . . | 8,334 | 5,396 | 2,364 | 7,746 | 5,446 | 4,753 |
| Portage . . | 15,900 | 9,636 | 3,410 | 15,553 | 10,914 | 7,083 |
| Price . . . . | 3,523 | 2,545 | 1,218 | 3,575 | 2,654 | 2,286 |
| Racine . . . | 38,567 | 30,105 | 7,600 | 34,875 | 32,310 | 20,227 |
| Richland . . | 3,504 | 2,647 | 906 | 3,458 | 3,144 | 1,899 |
| Rock . . . . | 32,450 | 20,096 | 6,800 | 31,154 | 21,942 | 15,700 |
| Rusk . . . . | 2,944 | 2,222 | 1,308 | 3,376 | 2,430 | 2,085 |
| St. Croix . . | 11,384 | 8,253 | 3,180 | 10,281 | 8,114 | 7,125 |
| Sauk . . . . | 9,889 | 7,448 | 2,469 | 9,128 | 8,886 | 5,280 |
| Sawyer. . . | 2,873 | 2,603 | 962 | 2,796 | 2,658 | 1,861 |
| Shawano . | 6,856 | 6,395 | 2,071 | 6,062 | 7,253 | 4,540 |
| Sheboygan | 22,029 | 20,084 | 4,157 | 20,568 | 22,526 | 11,295 |
| Taylor. . . . | 3,253 | 3,108 | 1,436 | 3,305 | 3,415 | 2,590 |
| Trempealeau | 5,848 | 3,035 | 1,688 | 6,218 | 3,577 | 3,160 |
| Vernon . . . | 5,572 | 3,796 | 1,523 | 5,673 | 4,072 | 2,890 |
| Vilas . . . . | 3,702 | 4,209 | 1,528 | 3,764 | 4,616 | 2,827 |
| Walworth . | 13,283 | 15,099 | 3,729 | 11,825 | 15,727 | 9,029 |
| Washburn . | 3,231 | 2,703 | 925 | 3,080 | 2,586 | 1,978 |
| Washington | 17,154 | 25,829 | 4,786 | 13,339 | 22,739 | 13,045 |
| Waukesha. | 57,344 | 91,701 | 13,103 | 50,270 | 91,461 | 36,622 |
| Waupaca . | 7,796 | 8,670 | 2,462 | 6,666 | 10,252 | 6,088 |
| Waushara . | 3,824 | 3,573 | 1,264 | 3,402 | 4,045 | 2,829 |
| Winnebago | 29,558 | 27,878 | 6,518 | 27,234 | 33,709 | 16,140 |
| Wood . . . . | 14,650 | 12,666 | 4,599 | 13,208 | 13,843 | 8,822 |
| **Totals . . .** | **1,071,859** | **845,172** | **227,426** | **1,041,066** | **930,855** | **544,479** |

## Wisconsin Vote Since 1948

1948, Truman, Dem., 647,310; Dewey, Rep., 590,959; Wallace, Prog., 25,282; Thomas, Soc., 12,547; Teichert, Soc. Labor, 399; Dobbs, Soc. Workers, 303.

1952, Eisenhower, Rep., 979,744; Stevenson, Dem., 622,175; Hallinan, Ind., 2,174; Dobbs, Ind., 1,350; Hoopes, Ind., 1,157; Hass, Ind., 770.

1956, Eisenhower, Rep., 954,844; Stevenson, Dem., 586,768; Andrews, Ind., 6,918; Hoopes, Soc., 754; Hass, Soc. Labor, 710; Dobbs, Soc. Workers, 564.

1960, Kennedy, Dem., 830,805; Nixon, Rep., 895,175; Dobbs, Soc. Workers, 1,792; Hass, Soc. Labor, 1,310.

1964, Johnson, Dem., 1,050,424; Goldwater, Rep., 638,495; DeBerry, Soc. Workers, 1,692; Hass, Soc. Labor, 1,204.

1968, Nixon, Rep., 809,997; Humphrey, Dem., 748,804; Wallace, 3d Party, 127,835; Blomen, Soc. Labor, 1,338; Halstead, Soc. Workers, 1,222; scattered, 2,342.

1972 Nixon, Rep., 989,430; McGovern, Dem., 810,174; Schmitz, Amer., 47,525; Spock, Ind., 2,701; Fisher, Soc. Labor, 998; Hall, Com., 663; Reed, Ind., 506; scattered, 893.

1976, Carter, Dem., 1,040,232; Ford, Rep., 1,004,987; McCarthy, Ind., 34,943; Maddox, Amer. Ind., 8,552; Zeidler, Soc., 4,298; MacBride, Libertarian, 3,814; Camejo, Soc. Workers, 1,691; Wright, People's, 943; Hall, Com., 749; LaRouche, U.S. Lab., 738; Levin, Soc. Labor, 389; scattered, 2,839.

1980, Reagan, Rep., 1,088,845; Carter, Dem., 981,584; Anderson, Ind., 160,657; Clark, Libertarian, 29,135; Commoner, Citizens, 7,767; Rarick, Constitution, 1,519; McReynolds, Soc., 808; Hall, Com., 772; Griswold, Workers World, 414; DeBerry, Soc. Workers, 383; scattering, 1,337.

1984, Reagan, Rep., 1,198,584; Mondale, Dem., 995,740; Bergland, Libertarian, 4,883.

1988, Bush, Rep., 1,047,499; Dukakis, Dem., 1,126,794; Paul, Lib., 5,157; Duke, Pop., 3,056.

1992, Clinton, Dem., 1,041,066; Bush, Rep., 930,855; Perot, Ind., 544,479; Marrou, Libertarian, 2,877; Gritz, Populist/America First, 2,311; Daniels, Ind., 1,883; Phillips, U.S. Taxpayers, 1,772; Hagelin, Natural Law, 1,070.

1996, Clinton, Dem., 1,071,859; Dole, Rep., 845,172; Perot, Ref., 227,426; Nader, Green, 28,587; Phillips, Taxpayers, 8,805; Browne, Libertarian, 7,923; Hagelin, Natural Law, 1,379; Moorehead, Workers World, 1,363; Hollis, Soc., 855; Harris, Soc. Workers, 516.

# Wyoming

| County | 1996 Clinton (D) | 1996 Dole (R) | 1996 Perot (RF) | 1992 Clinton (D) | 1992 Bush (R) | 1992 Perot (I) |
|---|---|---|---|---|---|---|
| Albany . . . | 6,370 | 5,940 | 1,329 | 5,713 | 4,176 | 2,862 |
| Big Horn. . | 1,438 | 2,821 | 545 | 1,216 | 2,216 | 1,236 |
| Campbell . | 3,468 | 6,382 | 1,954 | 2,709 | 5,315 | 3,133 |
| Carbon. . . | 2,684 | 2,923 | 850 | 2,737 | 2,320 | 1,579 |
| Converse . | 1,520 | 2,702 | 639 | 1,307 | 2,159 | 1,260 |
| Crook. . . . | 651 | 1,698 | 394 | 568 | 1,377 | 718 |
| Fremont . . | 5,445 | 7,550 | 1,781 | 4,765 | 5,387 | 3,594 |
| Goshen . . | 1,923 | 2,989 | 547 | 1,754 | 2,395 | 1,144 |
| Hot Springs | 779 | 1,348 | 287 | 740 | 978 | 652 |
| Johnson . . | 814 | 2,071 | 378 | 656 | 1,614 | 844 |
| Laramie . . | 13,676 | 16,924 | 2,958 | 12,177 | 12,890 | 6,607 |
| Lincoln . . . | 1,803 | 3,764 | 906 | 1,430 | 2,595 | 1,495 |
| Natrona . . | 11,240 | 13,182 | 3,521 | 9,817 | 9,717 | 7,647 |
| Niobrara. . | 325 | 757 | 209 | 298 | 635 | 355 |
| Park . . . . | 3,240 | 7,430 | 1,318 | 2,771 | 5,218 | 3,145 |
| Platte. . . . | 1,631 | 2,155 | 578 | 1,398 | 1,668 | 956 |
| Sheridan. . | 4,594 | 5,892 | 1,414 | 4,139 | 4,303 | 3,035 |
| Sublette . . | 677 | 1,829 | 401 | 536 | 1,168 | 828 |
| Sweetwater | 7,088 | 5,588 | 2,792 | 6,417 | 4,476 | 3,879 |
| Teton. . . . | 4,042 | 3,918 | 839 | 3,120 | 2,854 | 2,340 |
| Uinta . . . . | 2,414 | 3,471 | 1,240 | 2,047 | 2,701 | 2,041 |
| Washakie . | 1,205 | 2,250 | 470 | 1,118 | 1,720 | 1,084 |
| Weston . . | 870 | 1,763 | 504 | 727 | 1,465 | 829 |
| **Totals . . .** | **77,897** | **105,347** | **25,854** | **68,160** | **79,347** | **51,263** |

## Wyoming Vote Since 1948

1948, Truman, Dem., 52,354; Dewey, Rep., 47,947; Wallace, Prog., 931; Thomas, Soc., 137; Teichert, Soc. Labor, 56.

1952, Eisenhower, Rep., 81,047; Stevenson, Dem., 47,934; Hamblen, Proh., 194; Hoopes, Soc., 40; Haas, Soc. Labor, 36.

1956, Eisenhower, Rep., 74,573; Stevenson, Dem., 49,554.

1960, Kennedy, Dem., 63,331; Nixon, Rep., 77,451.

1964, Johnson, Dem., 80,718; Goldwater, Rep., 61,998.

1968, Nixon, Rep., 70,927; Humphrey, Dem., 45,173; Wallace, 3d Party, 11,105.

1972, Nixon, Rep., 100,464; McGovern, Dem., 44,358; Schmitz, Amer., 748.

1976, Carter, Dem., 62,239; Ford, Rep., 92,717; McCarthy, Ind., 624; Reagan, Ind., 307; Anderson, Amer., 290; MacBride, Libertarian, 89; Brown, Ind., 47; Maddox, Amer. Ind., 30.

1980, Reagan, Rep., 110,700; Carter, Dem., 49,427; Anderson, Ind., 12,072; Clark, Libertarian, 4,514.

1984, Reagan, Rep., 133,241; Mondale, Dem., 53,370; Bergland, Libertarian, 2,357.

1988, Bush, Rep., 106,867; Dukakis, Dem., 67,113; Paul, Lib., 2,026; Fulani, New Alliance, 545.

1992, Clinton, Dem., 68,160; Bush, Rep., 79,347; Perot, Ind., 51,263.

1996, Dole, Rep., 105,347; Clinton, Dem., 77,897; Perot, Ind. (Ref.), 25,854; Browne, Libertarian, 1,735; Hagelin, Natural Law, 582.

## Electoral Votes for President

(based on 1990 Census)

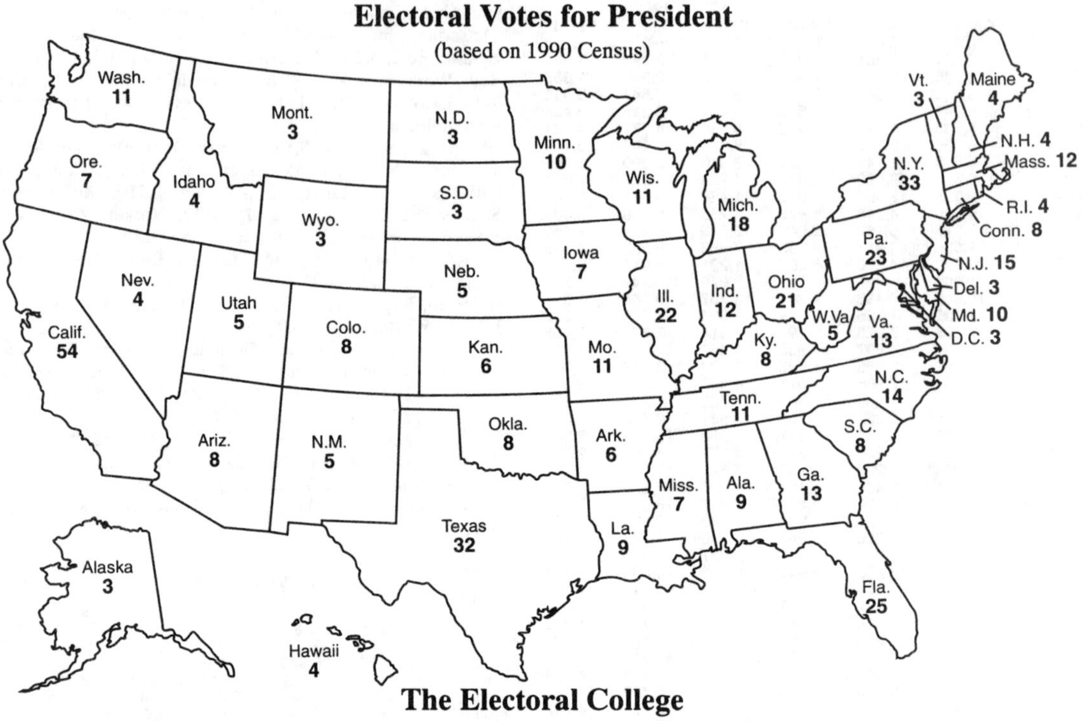


## The Electoral College

The president and the vice president are the only elective federal officials not chosen by direct vote of the people. They are elected by the members of the Electoral College, an institution provided for in the U.S. Constitution.

On presidential election day, the first Tuesday after the first Monday in Nov. of every 4th year, each state chooses as many electors as it has senators and representatives in Congress. In 1964, for the first time, as provided by the 23d Amendment to the Constitution, the District of Columbia voted for 3 electors. Thus, with 100 senators and 435 representatives, there are 538 members of the Electoral College, with a majority of 270 electoral votes needed to elect the president and vice president.

Although political parties were not part of the original plan created by the Founding Fathers, today political parties customarily nominate their lists of electors at their respective state conventions. Some states print the names of the candidates for president and vice president at the top of the Nov. ballot; others list only the names of the electors. In either case, the electors of the party receiving the highest vote are elected.

The electors meet on the first Monday after the 2d Wednesday in Dec. in their respective state capitals or in some other place prescribed by state legislatures. By long-established custom, they vote for their party nominees, although this is not required by law.

The Constitution requires electors to cast a ballot for at least one person who is not an inhabitant of that elector's home state. This ensures that presidential and vice presidential candidates from the same party will not be from the same state. Also, an elector cannot be a member of Congress or hold federal office.

Certified and sealed lists of the votes of the electors in each state are sent to the president of the U.S. Senate, who then opens them in the presence of the members of the Senate and House of Representatives in a joint session held on Jan. 6 (the next day if that falls on a Sunday), and the electoral votes of all the states are then officially counted.

If no candidate for president has a majority, the House of Representatives chooses a president from among the 3 highest candidates, with all representatives from each state combining to cast one vote for that state. The House decided the outcome of the presidential elections of 1800 and 1824. If no candidate for vice president has a majority, the Senate chooses from the top 2, with the senators voting as individuals. The Senate chose the vice president following the 1836 election.

Under the electoral college system, a candidate who fails to be the top vote getter in the popular vote may still win a majority of electoral votes. This happened in the elections of 1876 and 1888.

## National Political Convention Sites, 1856-1996[1]

| Year | Democrats | Republicans | Year | Democrats | Republicans | Year | Democrats | Republicans |
|---|---|---|---|---|---|---|---|---|
| 1856 | Cincinnati | Philadelphia | 1904 | St. Louis | Chicago | 1952 | Chicago | Chicago |
| 1860 | Baltimore[2] | Chicago | 1908 | Denver | Chicago | 1956 | Chicago | San Francisco |
| 1864 | Chicago | Baltimore | 1912 | Baltimore | Chicago | 1960 | Los Angeles | Chicago |
| 1868 | New York City | Chicago | 1916 | St. Louis | Chicago | 1964 | Atlantic City | San Francisco |
| 1872 | Baltimore | Philadelphia | 1920 | San Francisco | Chicago | 1968 | Chicago | Miami Beach |
| 1876 | St. Louis | Cincinnati | 1924 | New York City | Cleveland | 1972 | Miami Beach | Miami Beach |
| 1880 | Cincinnati | Chicago | 1928 | Houston | Kansas City | 1976 | New York City | Kansas City, MO |
| 1884 | Chicago | Chicago | 1932 | Chicago | Chicago | 1980 | New York City | Detroit |
| 1888 | St. Louis | Chicago | 1936 | Philadelphia | Cleveland | 1984 | San Francisco | Dallas |
| 1892 | Chicago | Minneapolis | 1940 | Chicago | Philadelphia | 1988 | Atlanta | New Orleans |
| 1896 | Chicago | St. Louis | 1944 | Chicago | Chicago | 1992 | New York City | Houston |
| 1900 | Kansas City, MO | Philadelphia | 1948 | Philadelphia | Philadelphia | 1996 | Chicago | San Diego |

(1) The first Democratic National Convention was held in 1832. All conventions prior to 1856 were held in Baltimore. The first Republican National Convention was held in 1856. Chicago has hosted more conventions (25) than any other city. (2) An earlier convention, held in Charleston, SC, had resulted in a split in the party. The official nomination was made at the Baltimore convention.

# Third-Party and Independent Presidential Candidates

Although many "third party" candidates or independents have pursued the presidency, only 8 of these have polled more than a million votes. In most elections since 1860, fewer than one vote in 20 has been cast for a third-party candidate. In only 6 presidential elections since then have all non-major-party candidates combined polled more than 10% of the vote. The major vote setters in those elections were James B. Weaver (People's Party), 1892; former President Theodore Roosevelt (Progressive Party), 1912; Robert M. La Follette (Progressive Party), 1924; Strom Thurmond, States' Rights (Dixiecrat) candidate in 1948; George C. Wallace (American Independent Party), 1968; and H. Ross Perot, an independent in 1992.

Roosevelt outpolled the Republican candidate, William Howard Taft, in 1912, capturing 28% of the popular vote and 88 electoral votes. In 1948, Thurmond was able to capture 39 electoral votes (from 5 Southern states); however, all third parties received only 5.75% of the popular vote in the election. Twenty years later, George Wallace's popularity in the same region allowed him to get 46 electoral votes. In 1992 Perot was able to capture 19% of the popular vote; however, he did not win a single state. In 1996, according to preliminary returns, Perot (as the candidate of his newly formed Reform Party) won 8% of the vote; all third-party candidates won 10%.

Despite the difficulty in winning the presidency, independent and third-party candidates sometimes succeed in winning other offices and often bring the attention of all presidential candidates to particular issues.

## Notable Independent Party Presidential Candidates

| Party | Presidential nominee | Year | Issues | Strength in . . . |
|---|---|---|---|---|
| Anti-Masonic | William Wirt | 1832 | Against secret societies and oaths | PA, VT |
| Liberty | James G. Birney | 1844 | Anti-slavery | North |
| Free Soil | Martin Van Buren | 1848 | Anti-slavery | NY, OH |
| American (Know-Nothing) | Millard Fillmore | 1856 | Anti-immigrant | Northeast, South |
| Greenback | Peter Cooper | 1876 | For "cheap money," labor rights | National |
| Greenback | James B. Weaver | 1880 | For "cheap money," labor rights | National |
| Prohibition | John P. St. John | 1884 | Anti-liquor | National |
| Populist | James B. Weaver | 1892 | For "cheap money," end of national banks | South, West |
| Socialist | Eugene V. Debs | 1900-12; 1920 | For public ownership | National |
| Progressive (Bull Moose) | Theodore Roosevelt | 1912 | Against high tariffs | Midwest, West |
| Progressive | Robert M. La Follette | 1924 | Farmer and labor rights | Midwest, West |
| Socialist | Norman Thomas | 1928-48 | Liberal reforms | National |
| Union | William Lemke | 1936 | Anti-New Deal | National |
| States' Rights (Dixiecrats) | Strom Thurmond | 1948 | For states' rights | South |
| Progressive | Henry A. Wallace | 1948 | Anti-Cold War | NY, CA |
| American Independent | George C. Wallace | 1968 | For states' rights | South |
| American | John G. Schmitz | 1972 | For "law and order" | Far West, OH, LA |
| None (Independent) | John B. Anderson | 1980 | A 3d choice | National |
| None (Independent) | H. Ross Perot | 1992 | Federal budget deficit | National |
| Reform | H. Ross Perot | 1996 | Deficit; campaign finance | National |

## Major-Party Nominees for President and Vice President

Asterisk (*) denotes winning ticket

| | Democratic | | Republican | |
|---|---|---|---|---|
| Year | President | Vice President | President | Vice President |
| 1856 | James Buchanan* | John Breckinridge | John Frémont | William Dayton |
| 1860 | Stephen A. Douglas[1] | Herschel V. Johnson | Abraham Lincoln* | Hannibal Hamlin |
| 1864 | George McClellan | G.H. Pendleton | Abraham Lincoln* | Andrew Johnson |
| 1868 | Horatio Seymour | Francis Blair | Ulysses S. Grant* | Schuyler Colfax |
| 1872 | Horace Greeley | B. Gratz Brown | Ulysses S. Grant* | Henry Wilson |
| 1876 | Samuel J. Tilden | Thomas Hendricks | Rutherford B. Hayes* | William Wheeler |
| 1880 | Winfield Hancock | William English | James A. Garfield* | Chester A. Arthur |
| 1884 | Grover Cleveland* | Thomas Hendricks | James Blaine | John Logan |
| 1888 | Grover Cleveland | A.G. Thurman | Benjamin Harrison* | Levi Morton |
| 1892 | Grover Cleveland* | Adlai Stevenson | Benjamin Harrison | Whitelaw Reid |
| 1896 | William J. Bryan | Arthur Sewall | William McKinley* | Garret Hobart |
| 1900 | William J. Bryan | Adlai Stevenson | William McKinley* | Theodore Roosevelt |
| 1904 | Alton Parker | Henry Davis | Theodore Roosevelt* | Charles Fairbanks |
| 1908 | William J. Bryan | John Kern | William H. Taft* | James Sherman |
| 1912 | Woodrow Wilson* | Thomas Marshall | William H. Taft | James Sherman[2] |
| 1916 | Woodrow Wilson* | Thomas Marshall | Charles Hughes | Charles Fairbanks |
| 1920 | James M. Cox | Franklin D. Roosevelt | Warren G. Harding* | Calvin Coolidge |
| 1924 | John W. Davis | Charles W. Bryan | Calvin Coolidge* | Charles G. Dawes |
| 1928 | Alfred E. Smith | Joseph T. Robinson | Herbert Hoover* | Charles Curtis |
| 1932 | Franklin D. Roosevelt* | John N. Garner | Herbert Hoover | Charles Curtis |
| 1936 | Franklin D. Roosevelt* | John N. Garner | Alfred M. Landon | Frank Knox |
| 1940 | Franklin D. Roosevelt* | Henry A. Wallace | Wendell L. Willkie | Charles McNary |
| 1944 | Franklin D. Roosevelt* | Harry S. Truman | Thomas E. Dewey | John W. Bricker |
| 1948 | Harry S. Truman* | Alben W. Barkley | Thomas E. Dewey | Earl Warren |
| 1952 | Adlai E. Stevenson | John J. Sparkman | Dwight D. Eisenhower* | Richard M. Nixon |
| 1956 | Adlai E. Stevenson | Estes Kefauver | Dwight D. Eisenhower* | Richard M. Nixon |
| 1960 | John F. Kennedy* | Lyndon B. Johnson | Richard M. Nixon | Henry Cabot Lodge |
| 1964 | Lyndon B. Johnson* | Hubert H. Humphrey | Barry M. Goldwater | William E. Miller |
| 1968 | Hubert H. Humphrey | Edmund S. Muskie | Richard M. Nixon* | Spiro T. Agnew |
| 1972 | George S. McGovern | R. Sargent Shriver Jr. | Richard M. Nixon* | Spiro T. Agnew |
| 1976 | Jimmy Carter* | Walter F. Mondale | Gerald R. Ford | Bob Dole |
| 1980 | Jimmy Carter | Walter F. Mondale | Ronald Reagan* | George Bush |
| 1984 | Walter F. Mondale | Geraldine Ferraro | Ronald Reagan* | George Bush |
| 1988 | Michael S. Dukakis | Lloyd Bentsen | George Bush* | Dan Quayle |
| 1992 | Bill Clinton* | Al Gore | George Bush | Dan Quayle |
| 1996 | Bill Clinton* | Al Gore | Bob Dole | Jack Kemp |

(1) Douglas and Johnson were nominated at the Baltimore convention. An earlier convention, which had failed to reach a consensus, had nominated John Breckinridge for president and Joseph Lane for vice president. (2) Died Oct. 30; replaced on ballot by Nicholas Butler.

# Popular and Electoral Vote for President

(D) Democrat; (DR) Democratic Republican; (F) Federalist; (LR) Liberal Republican; (NR) National Republican; (P) People's; (PR) Progressive; (R) Republican; (RF) Reform; (SR) States' Rights; (W) Whig; Asterisk (*)—See notes.

| Year | President elected | Popular | Elec. | Major losing candidate(s) | Popular | Elec. |
|---|---|---|---|---|---|---|
| 1789 | George Washington (F) | Unknown | 69 | No opposition | — | — |
| 1792 | George Washington (F) | Unknown | 132 | No opposition | — | — |
| 1796 | John Adams (F) | Unknown | 71 | Thomas Jefferson (DR) | Unknown | 68 |
| 1800* | Thomas Jefferson (DR) | Unknown | 73 | Aaron Burr (DR) | Unknown | 73 |
| 1804 | Thomas Jefferson (DR) | Unknown | 162 | Charles Pinckney (F) | Unknown | 14 |
| 1808 | James Madison (DR) | Unknown | 122 | Charles Pinckney (F) | Unknown | 47 |
| 1812 | James Madison (DR) | Unknown | 128 | DeWitt Clinton (F) | Unknown | 89 |
| 1816 | James Monroe (DR) | Unknown | 183 | Rufus King (F) | Unknown | 34 |
| 1820 | James Monroe (DR) | Unknown | 231 | John Quincy Adams (DR) | Unknown | 1 |
| 1824* | John Quincy Adams (DR) | 105,321 | 84 | Andrew Jackson (DR) | 155,872 | 99 |
| | | | | Henry Clay (DR) | 46,587 | 37 |
| | | | | William H. Crawford (DR) | 44,282 | 41 |
| 1828 | Andrew Jackson (D) | 647,231 | 178 | John Quincy Adams (NR) | 509,097 | 83 |
| 1832 | Andrew Jackson (D) | 687,502 | 219 | Henry Clay (NR) | 530,189 | 49 |
| 1836 | Martin Van Buren (D) | 762,678 | 170 | William H. Harrison (W) | 548,007 | 73 |
| 1840 | William H. Harrison (W) | 1,275,017 | 234 | Martin Van Buren (D) | 1,128,702 | 60 |
| 1844 | James K. Polk (D) | 1,337,243 | 170 | Henry Clay (W) | 1,299,068 | 105 |
| 1848 | Zachary Taylor (W) | 1,360,101 | 163 | Lewis Cass (D) | 1,220,544 | 127 |
| | | | | Martin Van Buren (Free Soil) | 291,501 | — |
| 1852 | Franklin Pierce (D) | 1,601,474 | 254 | Winfield Scott (W) | 1,386,578 | 42 |
| 1856 | James Buchanan (D) | 1,927,995 | 174 | John C. Fremont (R) | 1,391,555 | 114 |
| | | | | Millard Fillmore (American) | 873,053 | 8 |
| 1860 | Abraham Lincoln (R) | 1,866,352 | 180 | Stephen A. Douglas (D) | 1,375,157 | 12 |
| | | | | John C. Breckinridge (D) | 845,763 | 72 |
| | | | | John Bell (Const. Union) | 589,581 | 39 |
| 1864 | Abraham Lincoln (R) | 2,216,067 | 212 | George McClellan (D) | 1,808,725 | 21 |
| 1868 | Ulysses S. Grant (R) | 3,015,071 | 214 | Horatio Seymour (D) | 2,709,615 | 80 |
| 1872* | Ulysses S. Grant (R) | 3,597,070 | 286 | Horace Greeley (D-LR) | 2,834,079 | — |
| 1876* | Rutherford B. Hayes (R) | 4,033,950 | 185 | Samuel J. Tilden (D) | 4,284,757 | 184 |
| 1880 | James A. Garfield (R) | 4,449,053 | 214 | Winfield S. Hancock (D) | 4,442,030 | 155 |
| 1884 | Grover Cleveland (D) | 4,911,017 | 219 | James G. Blaine (R) | 4,848,334 | 182 |
| 1888* | Benjamin Harrison (R) | 5,444,337 | 233 | Grover Cleveland (D) | 5,540,050 | 168 |
| 1892 | Grover Cleveland (D) | 5,554,414 | 277 | Benjamin Harrison (R) | 5,190,802 | 145 |
| | | | | James Weaver (P) | 1,027,329 | 22 |
| 1896 | William McKinley (R) | 7,035,638 | 271 | William J. Bryan (D-P) | 6,467,946 | 176 |
| 1900 | William McKinley (R) | 7,219,530 | 292 | William J. Bryan (D) | 6,358,071 | 155 |
| 1904 | Theodore Roosevelt (R) | 7,628,834 | 336 | Alton B. Parker (D) | 5,084,491 | 140 |
| 1908 | William H. Taft (R) | 7,679,006 | 321 | William J. Bryan (D) | 6,409,106 | 162 |
| 1912 | Woodrow Wilson (D) | 6,286,214 | 435 | Theodore Roosevelt (PR) | 4,216,020 | 88 |
| | | | | William H. Taft (R) | 3,483,922 | 8 |
| 1916 | Woodrow Wilson (D) | 9,129,606 | 277 | Charles E. Hughes (R) | 8,538,221 | 254 |
| 1920 | Warren G. Harding (R) | 16,152,200 | 404 | James M. Cox (D) | 9,147,353 | 127 |
| 1924 | Calvin Coolidge (R) | 15,725,016 | 382 | John W. Davis (D) | 8,385,586 | 136 |
| | | | | Robert M. La Follette (PR) | 4,822,856 | 13 |
| 1928 | Herbert Hoover (R) | 21,392,190 | 444 | Alfred E. Smith (D) | 15,016,443 | 87 |
| 1932 | Franklin D. Roosevelt (D) | 22,821,857 | 472 | Herbert Hoover (R) | 15,761,841 | 59 |
| 1936 | Franklin D. Roosevelt (D) | 27,751,597 | 523 | Alfred Landon (R) | 16,679,583 | 8 |
| 1940 | Franklin D. Roosevelt (D) | 27,243,466 | 449 | Wendell Willkie (R) | 22,304,755 | 82 |
| 1944 | Franklin D. Roosevelt (D) | 25,602,505 | 432 | Thomas E. Dewey (R) | 22,006,278 | 99 |
| 1948 | Harry S. Truman (D) | 24,105,812 | 303 | Thomas E. Dewey (R) | 21,970,065 | 189 |
| | | | | Strom Thurmond (SR) | 1,169,021 | 39 |
| | | | | Henry A. Wallace (PR) | 1,157,172 | — |
| 1952 | Dwight D. Eisenhower (R) | 33,936,252 | 442 | Adlai E. Stevenson (D) | 27,314,992 | 89 |
| 1956* | Dwight D. Eisenhower (R) | 35,585,316 | 457 | Adlai E. Stevenson (D) | 26,031,322 | 73 |
| 1960* | John F. Kennedy (D) | 34,227,096 | 303 | Richard M. Nixon (R) | 34,108,546 | 219 |
| 1964 | Lyndon B. Johnson (D) | 43,126,506 | 486 | Barry M. Goldwater (R) | 27,176,799 | 52 |
| 1968 | Richard M. Nixon (R) | 31,785,480 | 301 | Hubert H. Humphrey (D) | 31,275,166 | 191 |
| | | | | George C. Wallace (3d party) | 9,906,473 | 46 |
| 1972* | Richard M. Nixon (R) | 47,165,234 | 520 | George S. McGovern (D) | 29,170,774 | 17 |
| 1976* | Jimmy Carter (D) | 40,828,929 | 297 | Gerald R. Ford (R) | 39,148,940 | 240 |
| 1980 | Ronald Reagan (R) | 43,899,248 | 489 | Jimmy Carter (D) | 35,481,435 | 49 |
| | | | | John B. Anderson (independent) | 5,719,437 | — |
| 1984 | Ronald Reagan (R) | 54,281,858 | 525 | Walter F. Mondale (D) | 37,457,215 | 13 |
| 1988* | George Bush (R) | 48,881,221 | 426 | Michael S. Dukakis (D) | 41,805,422 | 111 |
| 1992 | Bill Clinton (D) | 44,908,254 | 370 | George Bush (R) | 39,102,343 | 168 |
| | | | | H. Ross Perot (independent) | 19,741,065 | — |
| 1996* | Bill Clinton (D) | 45,590,703 | 379 | Bob Dole (R) | 37,816,307 | 159 |
| | | | | H. Ross Perot (RF) | 7,866,284 | — |

**1800**—Elected by House of Representatives because of tied electoral vote. **1824**—Elected by House of Representatives. No candidate polled a majority. In 1824, the Democratic Republicans had become a loose coalition of competing political groups. By 1828, the supporters of Jackson were known as Democrats, and the John Q. Adams and Henry Clay supporters as National Republicans. **1872**—Greeley died Nov. 29, 1872. His electoral votes were split among 4 individuals. **1876**—FL, LA, OR, and SC election returns were disputed. Congress in joint session (Mar. 2, 1877) declared Hayes and Wheeler elected president and vice president. **1888**—Cleveland had more votes than Harrison, but the 233 electoral votes cast for Harrison against the 168 for Cleveland elected Harrison president. **1956**—Democrats elected 74 electors, but one from Alabama refused to vote for Stevenson. **1960**—Sen. Harry F. Byrd (D, VA) received 15 electoral votes. **1972**—John Hospers of California and Theodora Nathan of Oregon received one vote from an elector of Virginia. **1976**—Ronald Reagan of CA received one vote from an elector of Washington. **1988**—Sen. Lloyd Bentsen (D, TX) received 1 electoral vote. **1996**—Preliminary totals.

# Presidents of the U.S.

| No. | Name | Politics | Born | In | Inaug. | at age | Died | at age |
|---|---|---|---|---|---|---|---|---|
| 1 | George Washington | Fed. | 1732, Feb. 22 | VA | 1789 | 57 | 1799, Dec. 14 | 67 |
| 2 | John Adams | Fed. | 1735, Oct. 30 | MA | 1797 | 61 | 1826, July 4 | 90 |
| 3 | Thomas Jefferson | Dem.-Rep. | 1743, Apr. 13 | VA | 1801 | 57 | 1826, July 4 | 83 |
| 4 | James Madison | Dem.-Rep. | 1751, Mar. 16 | VA | 1809 | 57 | 1836, June 28 | 85 |
| 5 | James Monroe | Dem.-Rep. | 1758, Apr. 28 | VA | 1817 | 58 | 1831, July 4 | 73 |
| 6 | John Quincy Adams | Dem.-Rep. | 1767, July 11 | MA | 1825 | 57 | 1848, Feb. 23 | 80 |
| 7 | Andrew Jackson | Dem. | 1767, Mar. 15 | SC | 1829 | 61 | 1845, June 8 | 78 |
| 8 | Martin Van Buren | Dem. | 1782, Dec. 5 | NY | 1837 | 54 | 1862, July 24 | 79 |
| 9 | William Henry Harrison | Whig | 1773, Feb. 9 | VA | 1841 | 68 | 1841, Apr. 4 | 68 |
| 10 | John Tyler | Whig | 1790, Mar. 29 | VA | 1841 | 51 | 1862, Jan. 18 | 71 |
| 11 | James Knox Polk | Dem. | 1795, Nov. 2 | NC | 1845 | 49 | 1849, June 15 | 53 |
| 12 | Zachary Taylor | Whig | 1784, Nov. 24 | VA | 1849 | 64 | 1850, July 9 | 65 |
| 13 | Millard Fillmore | Whig | 1800, Jan. 7 | NY | 1850 | 50 | 1874, Mar. 8 | 74 |
| 14 | Franklin Pierce | Dem. | 1804, Nov. 23 | NH | 1853 | 48 | 1869, Oct. 8 | 64 |
| 15 | James Buchanan | Dem. | 1791, Apr. 23 | PA | 1857 | 65 | 1868, June 1 | 77 |
| 16 | Abraham Lincoln | Rep. | 1809, Feb. 12 | KY | 1861 | 52 | 1865, Apr. 15 | 56 |
| 17 | Andrew Johnson | (1) | 1808, Dec. 29 | NC | 1865 | 56 | 1875, July 31 | 66 |
| 18 | Ulysses Simpson Grant | Rep. | 1822, Apr. 27 | OH | 1869 | 46 | 1885, July 23 | 63 |
| 19 | Rutherford Birchard Hayes | Rep. | 1822, Oct. 4 | OH | 1877 | 54 | 1893, Jan. 17 | 70 |
| 20 | James Abram Garfield | Rep. | 1831, Nov. 19 | OH | 1881 | 49 | 1881, Sept. 19 | 49 |
| 21 | Chester Alan Arthur | Rep. | 1830, Oct. 5 | VT | 1881 | 50 | 1886, Nov. 18 | 56 |
| 22 | Grover Cleveland | Dem. | 1837, Mar. 18 | NJ | 1885 | 47 | 1908, June 24 | 71 |
| 23 | Benjamin Harrison | Rep. | 1833, Aug. 20 | OH | 1889 | 55 | 1901, Mar. 13 | 67 |
| 24 | Grover Cleveland | Dem. | 1837, Mar. 18 | NJ | 1893 | 55 | 1908, June 24 | 71 |
| 25 | William McKinley | Rep. | 1843, Jan. 29 | OH | 1897 | 54 | 1901, Sept. 14 | 58 |
| 26 | Theodore Roosevelt | Rep. | 1858, Oct. 27 | NY | 1901 | 42 | 1919, Jan. 6 | 60 |
| 27 | William Howard Taft | Rep. | 1857, Sept. 15 | OH | 1909 | 51 | 1930, Mar. 8 | 72 |
| 28 | Woodrow Wilson | Dem. | 1856, Dec. 28 | VA | 1913 | 56 | 1924, Feb. 3 | 67 |
| 29 | Warren Gamaliel Harding | Rep. | 1865, Nov. 2 | OH | 1921 | 55 | 1923, Aug. 2 | 57 |
| 30 | Calvin Coolidge | Rep. | 1872, July 4 | VT | 1923 | 51 | 1933, Jan. 5 | 60 |
| 31 | Herbert Clark Hoover | Rep. | 1874, Aug. 10 | IA | 1929 | 54 | 1964, Oct. 20 | 90 |
| 32 | Franklin Delano Roosevelt | Dem. | 1882, Jan. 30 | NY | 1933 | 51 | 1945, Apr. 12 | 63 |
| 33 | Harry S. Truman | Dem. | 1884, May 8 | MO | 1945 | 60 | 1972, Dec. 26 | 88 |
| 34 | Dwight David Eisenhower | Rep. | 1890, Oct. 14 | TX | 1953 | 62 | 1969, Mar. 28 | 78 |
| 35 | John Fitzgerald Kennedy | Dem. | 1917, May 29 | MA | 1961 | 43 | 1963, Nov. 22 | 46 |
| 36 | Lyndon Baines Johnson | Dem. | 1908, Aug. 27 | TX | 1963 | 55 | 1973, Jan. 22 | 64 |
| 37 | Richard Milhous Nixon (2) | Rep. | 1913, Jan. 9 | CA | 1969 | 56 | 1994, Apr. 22 | 81 |
| 38 | Gerald Rudolph Ford | Rep. | 1913, July 14 | NE | 1974 | 61 | | |
| 39 | Jimmy (James Earl) Carter | Dem. | 1924, Oct. 1 | GA | 1977 | 52 | | |
| 40 | Ronald Reagan | Rep. | 1911, Feb. 6 | IL | 1981 | 69 | | |
| 41 | George Bush | Rep. | 1924, June 12 | MA | 1989 | 64 | | |
| 42 | Bill Clinton | Dem. | 1946, Aug. 19 | AR | 1993 | 46 | | |

(1) Andrew Johnson was a Democrat, nominated vice president by Republicans, and elected with Lincoln on National Union ticket.
(2) Resigned Aug. 9, 1974.

# U.S. Presidents, Vice Presidents, Congresses

| | President | Service | | Vice President | Congress |
|---|---|---|---|---|---|
| 1 | George Washington | Apr. 30, 1789—Mar. 3, 1797 | 1 | John Adams | 1, 2, 3, 4 |
| 2 | John Adams | Mar. 4, 1797—Mar. 3, 1801 | 2 | Thomas Jefferson | 5, 6 |
| 3 | Thomas Jefferson | Mar. 4, 1801—Mar. 3, 1805 | 3 | Aaron Burr | 7, 8 |
| | " | Mar. 4, 1805—Mar. 3, 1809 | 4 | George Clinton | 9, 10 |
| 4 | James Madison | Mar. 4, 1809—Mar. 3, 1813 | | " (1) | 11, 12 |
| | " | Mar. 4, 1813—Mar. 3, 1817 | 5 | Elbridge Gerry[2] | 13, 14 |
| 5 | James Monroe | Mar. 4, 1817—Mar. 3, 1825 | 6 | Daniel D. Tompkins | 15, 16, 17, 18 |
| 6 | John Quincy Adams | Mar. 4, 1825—Mar. 3, 1829 | 7 | John C. Calhoun | 19, 20 |
| 7 | Andrew Jackson | Mar. 4, 1829—Mar. 3, 1833 | | " (3) | 21, 22 |
| | " | Mar. 4, 1833—Mar. 3, 1837 | 8 | Martin Van Buren | 23, 24 |
| 8 | Martin Van Buren | Mar. 4, 1837—Mar. 3, 1841 | 9 | Richard M. Johnson | 25, 26 |
| 9 | William Henry Harrison[4] | Mar. 4, 1841—Apr. 4, 1841 | 10 | John Tyler | 27 |
| 10 | John Tyler | Apr. 6, 1841—Mar. 3, 1845 | | | 27, 28 |
| 11 | James K. Polk | Mar. 4, 1845—Mar. 3, 1849 | 11 | George M. Dallas | 29, 30 |
| 12 | Zachary Taylor[4] | Mar. 5, 1849—July 9, 1850 | 12 | Millard Fillmore | 31 |
| 13 | Millard Fillmore | July 10, 1850—Mar. 3, 1853 | | | 31, 32 |
| 14 | Franklin Pierce | Mar. 4, 1853—Mar. 3, 1857 | 13 | William R. King[5] | 33, 34 |
| 15 | James Buchanan | Mar. 4, 1857—Mar. 3, 1861 | 14 | John C. Breckinridge | 35, 36 |
| 16 | Abraham Lincoln | Mar. 4, 1861—Mar. 3, 1865 | 15 | Hannibal Hamlin | 37, 38 |
| | " (4) | Mar. 4, 1865—Apr. 15, 1865 | 16 | Andrew Johnson | 39 |
| 17 | Andrew Johnson | Apr. 15, 1865—Mar. 3, 1869 | | | 39, 40 |
| 18 | Ulysses S. Grant | Mar. 4, 1869—Mar. 3, 1873 | 17 | Schuyler Colfax | 41, 42 |
| | " | Mar. 4, 1873—Mar. 3, 1877 | 18 | Henry Wilson[6] | 43, 44 |
| 19 | Rutherford B. Hayes | Mar. 4, 1877—Mar. 3, 1881 | 19 | William A. Wheeler | 45, 46 |
| 20 | James A. Garfield[4] | Mar. 4, 1881—Sept. 19, 1881 | 20 | Chester A. Arthur | 47 |
| 21 | Chester A. Arthur | Sept. 20, 1881—Mar. 3, 1885 | | | 47, 48 |
| 22 | Grover Cleveland[7] | Mar. 4, 1885—Mar. 3, 1889 | 21 | Thomas A. Hendricks[8] | 49, 50 |
| 23 | Benjamin Harrison | Mar. 4, 1889—Mar. 3, 1893 | 22 | Levi P. Morton | 51, 52 |
| 24 | Grover Cleveland[7] | Mar. 4, 1893—Mar. 3, 1897 | 23 | Adlai E. Stevenson | 53, 54 |
| 25 | William McKinley | Mar. 4, 1897—Mar. 3, 1901 | 24 | Garret A. Hobart[9] | 55, 56 |
| | " (4) | Mar. 4, 1901—Sept. 14, 1901 | 25 | Theodore Roosevelt | 57 |
| 26 | Theodore Roosevelt | Sept. 14, 1901—Mar. 3, 1905 | | | 57, 58 |
| | " | Mar. 4, 1905—Mar. 3, 1909 | 26 | Charles W. Fairbanks | 59, 60 |
| 27 | William H. Taft | Mar. 4, 1909—Mar. 3, 1913 | 27 | James S. Sherman[10] | 61, 62 |
| 28 | Woodrow Wilson | Mar. 4, 1913—Mar. 3, 1921 | 28 | Thomas R. Marshall | 63, 64, 65, 66 |

*(continued)*

## U.S. Presidents, Vice Presidents, Congresses (*continued*)

| | President | Service | | Vice President | Congress |
|---|---|---|---|---|---|
| 29 | Warren G. Harding[4] | Mar. 4, 1921—Aug. 2, 1923 | 29 | Calvin Coolidge | 67 |
| 30 | Calvin Coolidge | Aug. 3, 1923—Mar. 3, 1925 | | | 68 |
| | " | Mar. 4, 1925—Mar. 3, 1929 | 30 | Charles G. Dawes | 69, 70 |
| 31 | Herbert C. Hoover | Mar. 4, 1929—Mar. 3, 1933 | 31 | Charles Curtis | 71, 72 |
| 32 | Franklin D. Roosevelt[11] | Mar. 4, 1933—Jan. 20, 1941 | 32 | John N. Garner | 73, 74, 75, 76 |
| | " | Jan. 20, 1941—Jan. 20, 1945 | 33 | Henry A. Wallace | 77, 78 |
| | " (4) | Jan. 20, 1945—Apr. 12, 1945 | 34 | Harry S. Truman | 79 |
| 33 | Harry S. Truman | Apr. 12, 1945—Jan. 20, 1949 | | | 79, 80 |
| | " | Jan. 20, 1949—Jan. 20, 1953 | 35 | Alben W. Barkley | 81, 82 |
| 34 | Dwight D. Eisenhower | Jan. 20, 1953—Jan. 20, 1961 | 36 | Richard M. Nixon | 83, 84, 85, 86 |
| 35 | John F. Kennedy[4] | Jan. 20, 1961—Nov. 22, 1963 | 37 | Lyndon B. Johnson | 87, 88 |
| 36 | Lyndon B. Johnson | Nov. 22, 1963—Jan. 20, 1965 | | | 88 |
| | " | Jan. 20, 1965—Jan. 20, 1969 | 38 | Hubert H. Humphrey | 89, 90 |
| 37 | Richard M. Nixon | Jan. 20, 1969—Jan. 20, 1973 | 39 | Spiro T. Agnew[12] | 91, 92, 93 |
| | " (13) | Jan. 20, 1973—Aug. 9, 1974 | 40 | Gerald R. Ford[14] | 93 |
| 38 | Gerald R. Ford[15] | Aug. 9, 1974—Jan. 20, 1977 | 41 | Nelson A. Rockefeller[16] | 93, 94 |
| 39 | Jimmy (James Earl) Carter | Jan. 20, 1977—Jan. 20, 1981 | 42 | Walter F. Mondale | 95, 96 |
| 40 | Ronald Reagan | Jan. 20, 1981—Jan. 20, 1989 | 43 | George Bush | 97, 98, 99, 100 |
| 41 | George Bush | Jan. 20, 1989—Jan. 20, 1993 | 44 | Dan Quayle | 101, 102 |
| 42 | Bill Clinton | Jan. 20, 1993— | 45 | Al Gore | 103, 104[17] |

(1) Died Apr. 20, 1812. (2) Died Nov. 23, 1814. (3) Resigned Dec. 28, 1832, to become U.S. senator. (4) Died in office. (5) Died Apr. 18, 1853. (6) Died Nov. 22, 1875. (7) Terms not consecutive. (8) Died Nov. 25, 1885. (9) Died Nov. 21, 1899. (10) Died Oct. 30, 1912. (11) First president to be inaugurated under 20th Amendment, Jan. 20, 1937. (12) Resigned Oct. 10, 1973. (13) Resigned Aug. 9, 1974. (14) First nonelected vice president, chosen under 25th Amendment procedure. (15) First nonelected president. (16) Second nonelected vice president, chosen under 25th Amendment procedure. (17) Through 1996.

# Vice Presidents of the U.S.

The numerals given vice presidents do not coincide with those given presidents, because some presidents had none and some had more than one.

| Name | Birthplace | Year | Home | Inaug. | Politics | Place of death | Year | Age |
|---|---|---|---|---|---|---|---|---|
| 1 John Adams | Quincy, MA | 1735 | MA | 1789 | Fed. | Quincy, MA | 1826 | 90 |
| 2 Thomas Jefferson | Shadwell, VA | 1743 | VA | 1797 | Dem.-Rep. | Monticello, VA | 1826 | 83 |
| 3 Aaron Burr | Newark, NJ | 1756 | NY | 1801 | Dem.-Rep. | Staten Island, NY | 1836 | 80 |
| 4 George Clinton | Ulster Co., NY | 1739 | NY | 1805 | Dem.-Rep. | Washington, DC | 1812 | 73 |
| 5 Elbridge Gerry | Marblehead, MA | 1744 | MA | 1813 | Dem.-Rep. | Washington, DC | 1814 | 70 |
| 6 Daniel D. Tompkins | Scarsdale, NY | 1774 | NY | 1817 | Dem.-Rep. | Staten Island, NY | 1825 | 51 |
| 7 John C. Calhoun(1) | Abbeville, SC | 1782 | SC | 1825 | Dem.-Rep. | Washington, DC | 1850 | 68 |
| 8 Martin Van Buren | Kinderhook, NY | 1782 | NY | 1833 | Dem. | Kinderhook, NY | 1862 | 79 |
| 9 Richard M. Johnson(2) | Louisville, KY | 1780 | KY | 1837 | Dem. | Frankfort, KY | 1850 | 70 |
| 10 John Tyler | Greenway, VA | 1790 | VA | 1841 | Whig | Richmond, VA | 1862 | 71 |
| 11 George M. Dallas | Philadelphia, PA | 1792 | PA | 1845 | Dem. | Philadelphia, PA | 1864 | 72 |
| 12 Millard Fillmore | Summerhill, NY | 1800 | NY | 1849 | Whig | Buffalo, NY | 1874 | 74 |
| 13 William R. King | Sampson Co., NC | 1786 | AL | 1853 | Dem. | Dallas Co., AL | 1853 | 67 |
| 14 John C. Breckinridge | Lexington, KY | 1821 | KY | 1857 | Dem. | Lexington, KY | 1875 | 54 |
| 15 Hannibal Hamlin | Paris, ME | 1809 | ME | 1861 | Rep. | Bangor, ME | 1891 | 81 |
| 16 Andrew Johnson | Raleigh, NC | 1808 | TN | 1865 | (3) | Carter Co., TN | 1875 | 66 |
| 17 Schuyler Colfax | New York, NY | 1823 | IN | 1869 | Rep. | Mankato, MN | 1885 | 62 |
| 18 Henry Wilson | Farmington, NH | 1812 | MA | 1873 | Rep. | Washington, DC | 1875 | 63 |
| 19 William A. Wheeler | Malone, NY | 1819 | NY | 1877 | Rep. | Malone, NY | 1887 | 68 |
| 20 Chester A. Arthur | Fairfield, VT | 1830 | NY | 1881 | Rep. | New York, NY | 1886 | 57 |
| 21 Thomas A. Hendricks | Muskingum Co., OH | 1819 | IN | 1885 | Dem. | Indianapolis, IN | 1885 | 66 |
| 22 Levi P. Morton | Shoreham, VT | 1824 | NY | 1889 | Rep. | Rhinebeck, NY | 1920 | 96 |
| 23 Adlai E. Stevenson(4) | Christian Co., KY | 1835 | IL | 1893 | Dem. | Chicago, IL | 1914 | 78 |
| 24 Garret A. Hobart | Long Branch, NJ | 1844 | NJ | 1897 | Rep. | Paterson, NJ | 1899 | 55 |
| 25 Theodore Roosevelt | New York, NY | 1858 | NY | 1901 | Rep. | Oyster Bay, NY | 1919 | 60 |
| 26 Charles W. Fairbanks | Unionville Centre, OH | 1852 | IN | 1905 | Rep. | Indianapolis, IN | 1918 | 66 |
| 27 James S. Sherman | Utica, NY | 1855 | NY | 1909 | Rep. | Utica, NY | 1912 | 57 |
| 28 Thomas R. Marshall | N. Manchester, IN | 1854 | IN | 1913 | Dem. | Washington, DC | 1925 | 71 |
| 29 Calvin Coolidge | Plymouth, VT | 1872 | MA | 1921 | Rep. | Northampton, MA | 1933 | 60 |
| 30 Charles G. Dawes | Marietta, OH | 1865 | IL | 1925 | Rep. | Evanston, IL | 1951 | 85 |
| 31 Charles Curtis | Topeka, KS | 1860 | KS | 1929 | Rep. | Washington, DC | 1936 | 76 |
| 32 John Nance Garner | Red River Co., TX | 1868 | TX | 1933 | Dem. | Uvalde, TX | 1967 | 98 |
| 33 Henry Agard Wallace | Adair County, IA | 1888 | IA | 1941 | Dem. | Danbury, CT | 1965 | 77 |
| 34 Harry S. Truman | Lamar, MO | 1884 | MO | 1945 | Dem. | Kansas City, MO | 1972 | 88 |
| 35 Alben W. Barkley | Graves County, KY | 1877 | KY | 1949 | Dem. | Lexington, VA | 1956 | 78 |
| 36 Richard M. Nixon | Yorba Linda, CA | 1913 | CA | 1953 | Rep. | New York, NY | 1994 | 81 |
| 37 Lyndon B. Johnson | Johnson City, TX | 1908 | TX | 1961 | Dem. | San Antonio, TX | 1973 | 64 |
| 38 Hubert H. Humphrey | Wallace, SD | 1911 | MN | 1965 | Dem. | Waverly, MN | 1978 | 66 |
| 39 Spiro T. Agnew(5) | Baltimore, MD | 1918 | MD | 1969 | Rep. | Berlin, MD | 1996 | 77 |
| 40 Gerald R. Ford(6) | Omaha, NE | 1913 | MI | 1973 | Rep. | | | |
| 41 Nelson A. Rockefeller(7) | Bar Harbor, ME | 1908 | NY | 1974 | Rep. | New York, NY | 1979 | 70 |
| 42 Walter F. Mondale | Ceylon, MN | 1928 | MN | 1977 | Dem. | | | |
| 43 George Bush | Milton, MA | 1924 | TX | 1981 | Rep. | | | |
| 44 Dan Quayle | Indianapolis, IN | 1947 | IN | 1989 | Rep. | | | |
| 45 Al Gore | Washington, DC | 1948 | TN | 1993 | Dem. | | | |

(1) John C. Calhoun resigned Dec. 28, 1832, having been elected to the Senate to fill a vacancy. (2) Richard M. Johnson was the only vice president to be chosen by the Senate because of a tied vote in the Electoral College. (3) Andrew Johnson was a Democrat, nominated vice president by Republicans, and elected with Lincoln on the National Union Ticket. (4) Adlai E. Stevenson, 23d vice president, was grandfather of Democratic candidate for president, 1952 and 1956. (5) Resigned Oct. 10, 1973. (6) First nonelected vice president, chosen under the 25th Amendment procedure. (7) Second nonelected vice president, chosen under the 25th Amendment procedure.

# The One Hundred and Fifth Congress

## With Preliminary 1996 Election Results

**Source:** Voter News Service; World Almanac research; data subject to change, pending official election results

The 105th Congress convenes on Jan. 7, 1997.

## The Senate

**Rep., 54; Dem., 45; Undecided, 1; Total, 100. *Incumbent. Boldface denotes the 1996 election winner.**

Terms are for 6 years and end Jan. 3 of the year preceding the senator's name in the following table. Annual salary, $133,600; President Pro Tempore, Majority Leader, and Minority Leader, $148,400. To be eligible for the U.S. Senate, a person must be at least 30 years of age, a citizen of the United States for at least 9 years, and a resident of the state from which he or she is chosen. The Congress must meet annually on Jan. 3, unless it has, by law, appointed a different day.

The ZIP code of the Senate is 20510; the telephone number is 202-224-3121.

**Senate officials in 1995-97 (104th Congress) were:** President Pro Tempore, Strom Thurmond; Majority Leader, Bob Dole (1995-96), Trent Lott (1996); Majority Whip, Trent Lott (1995-96), Don Nickles (1996); Minority Leader, Tom Daschle; Minority Whip, Wendell Ford.

**D-Democrat; R-Republican; ACP-A Connecticut Party; GR-Green; I-Independent; L-Liberal; C-Conservative**

| Term ends | Senator (Party)/Service from[1] | 1996 Election |
|---|---|---|
| | **Alabama** | |
| 1999 | Richard C. Shelby (R)[2]/1/6/87 | |
| 2003 | **Jeff Sessions** (R)/1/7/97 | **779,415** |
| | Roger Bedford (D) | 685,556 |
| | **Alaska** | |
| 1999 | Frank H. Murkowski (R)/1981 | |
| 2003 | **Ted Stevens*** (R)/12/24/68 | **149,475** |
| | Jed Whittaker (GR) | 24,219 |
| | Theresa Nangle Obermeyer (D) | 19,402 |
| | **Arizona** | |
| 1999 | John McCain (R)/1/6/87 | |
| 2001 | Jon Kyl (R)/1/4/95 | |
| | **Arkansas** | |
| 1999 | Dale Bumpers (D)/1975 | |
| 2003 | **Tim Hutchinson** (R)/1/7/97 | **437,546** |
| | Winston Bryant (D) | 394,112 |
| | **California** | |
| 1999 | Barbara Boxer (D)/1993 | |
| 2001 | Dianne Feinstein (D)/11/10/92 | |
| | **Colorado** | |
| 1999 | Ben Nighthorse Campbell (R)[3]/1993 | |
| 2003 | **Wayne Allard** (R)/1/7/97 | **748,515** |
| | Tom Strickland (D) | 677,151 |
| | **Connecticut** | |
| 1999 | Christopher J. Dodd (D)/1981 | |
| 2001 | Joe Lieberman (D,ACP)/1989 | |
| | **Delaware** | |
| 2001 | William V. Roth, Jr. (R)/1/1/71 | |
| 2003 | **Joseph R. Biden, Jr.*** (D)/1973 | **165,241** |
| | Raymond J. Clatworthy (R) | 104,982 |
| | **Florida** | |
| 1999 | Bob Graham (D)/1/6/87 | |
| 2001 | Connie Mack (R)/1989 | |
| | **Georgia** | |
| 1999 | Paul Coverdell (R)/1993 | |
| 2003 | **Max Cleland** (D)/1/7/97 | **1,100,732** |
| | Guy W. Millner (R) | 1,073,297 |
| | **Hawaii** | |
| 1999 | Daniel K. Inouye (D)/1963 | |
| 2001 | Daniel K. Akaka (D)/4/28/90 | |
| | **Idaho** | |
| 1999 | Dirk Kempthorne (R)/1993 | |
| 2003 | **Larry E. Craig*** (R)/1991 | **283,530** |
| | Walt Minnick (D) | 198,415 |
| | **Illinois** | |
| 1999 | Carol Moseley-Braun (D)/1993 | |
| 2003 | **Richard J. Durbin** (D)/1/7/97 | **2,340,655** |
| | Al Salvi (R) | 1,718,856 |
| | **Indiana** | |
| 1999 | Daniel R. Coats (R)/1989 | |
| 2001 | Richard G. Lugar (R)/1977 | |
| | **Iowa** | |
| 1999 | Charles E. Grassley (R)/1981 | |
| 2003 | **Tom Harkin*** (D)/1985 | **628,961** |
| | Jim Ross Lightfoot (R) | 568,097 |
| | **Kansas** | |
| 1999 | **Sam Brownback** (R)[4]/1/7/97 | **569,157** |
| | Jill Docking (D) | 457,540 |
| 2003 | **Pat Roberts** (R)/1/7/97 | **647,612** |
| | Sally Thompson (D) | 359,474 |
| | **Kentucky** | |
| 1999 | Wendell H. Ford (D)/12/28/74 | |
| 2003 | **Mitch McConnell*** (R)/1985 | **722,525** |
| | Steven L. Beshear (D) | 558,621 |
| | **Louisiana** | |
| 1999 | John B. Breaux (D)/1/6/87 | |
| 2003 | **Mary L. Landrieu** (D)/1/7/97 | **852,622** |
| | Louis "Woody" Jenkins (R) | 840,342 |
| | **Maine** | |
| 2001 | Olympia J. Snowe (R)/1/4/95 | |
| 2003 | **Susan M. Collins** (R)/1/7/97 | **290,800** |
| | Joseph E. Brennan (D) | 259,902 |
| | **Maryland** | |
| 1999 | Barbara A. Mikulski (D)/1/6/87 | |
| 2001 | Paul S. Sarbanes (D)/1977 | |
| | **Massachusetts** | |
| 2001 | Edward M. Kennedy (D)/11/7/62 | |
| 2003 | **John F. Kerry*** (D)/1/2/85 | **1,327,524** |
| | William F. Weld (R) | 1,140,472 |
| | **Michigan** | |
| 2001 | Spencer Abraham (R)/1/4/95 | |
| 2003 | **Carl Levin*** (D)/1979 | **2,104,678** |
| | Ronna Romney (R) | 1,436,750 |
| | **Minnesota** | |
| 2001 | Rod Grams (R)/1/4/95 | |
| 2003 | **Paul David Wellstone*** (D)/1991 | **1,063,280** |
| | Rudy Boschwitz (R) | 880,707 |
| | **Mississippi** | |
| 2001 | Trent Lott (R)/1989 | |
| 2003 | **Thad Cochran*** (R)/12/27/78 | **616,160** |
| | James W. (Bootie) Hunt (D) | 235,990 |
| | **Missouri** | |
| 1999 | Christopher "Kit" Bond (R)/1/6/87 | |
| 2001 | John Ashcroft (R)/1/4/95 | |
| | **Montana** | |
| 2001 | Conrad Burns (R)/1989 | |
| 2003 | **Max Baucus*** (D)/12/15/78 | **198,248** |
| | Dennis Rehberg (R) | 179,235 |
| | **Nebraska** | |
| 2001 | Bob Kerrey (D)/1989 | |
| 2003 | **Chuck Hagel** (R)/1/7/97 | **371,930** |
| | Ben Nelson (D) | 276,030 |

| Term ends | Senator (Party)/Service from[1] | 1996 Election |
|---|---|---|
| | **Nevada** | |
| 1999 | Harry M. Reid (D)/1/6/87 | |
| 2001 | Richard H. Bryan (D)/1989 | |
| | **New Hampshire** | |
| 1999 | Judd Gregg (R)/1993 | |
| 2003 | **Robert Smith*** (R)/12/7/90 | **241,862** |
| | "Dick" Swett (D) | 226,616 |
| | **New Jersey** | |
| 2001 | Frank R. Lautenberg (D)/12/27/82 | |
| 2003 | **Robert G. Torricelli** (D)1/7/97 | **1,464,404** |
| | Dick Zimmer (R) | 1,185,421 |
| | **New Mexico** | |
| 2001 | Jeff Bingaman (D)/1983 | |
| 2003 | **Pete V. Domenici*** (R)/1973 | **326,053** |
| | Art Trujillo (D) | 152,742 |
| | **New York** | |
| 1999 | Alfonse M. D'Amato (R)/1981 | |
| 2001 | Daniel Patrick Moynihan (D,L)/1977 | |
| | **North Carolina** | |
| 1999 | Lauch Faircloth (R)/1993 | |
| 2003 | **Jesse Helms*** (R)/1973 | **1,331,353** |
| | Harvey B. Gantt (D) | 1,160,448 |
| | **North Dakota** | |
| 1999 | Byron L. Dorgan (D)/12/14/92 | |
| 2001 | Kent Conrad (D)/1/6/87 | |
| | **Ohio** | |
| 1999 | John Glenn (D)/12/24/74 | |
| 2001 | Mike Dewine (R)/1/4/95 | |
| | **Oklahoma** | |
| 1999 | Don Nickles (R)/1981 | |
| 2003 | **James M. Inhofe*** (R)[5]/11/21/94 | **670,609** |
| | Jim Boren (D) | 474,161 |
| | **Oregon** | |
| 1999 | Ron Wyden (D)[6] | |
| 2003[7] | Gordon Smith (R) | 333,275 |
| | Tom Bruggere (D) | 317,387 |
| | **Pennsylvania** | |
| 1999 | Arlen Specter (R)/1981 | |
| 2001 | Rick Santorum (R)/1/4/95 | |
| | **Rhode Island** | |
| 2001 | John H. Chafee (R)/12/29/76 | |
| 2003 | **John F. Reed** (D)/1/7/97 | **212,909** |
| | Nancy J. Mayer (R) | 118,358 |
| | **South Carolina** | |
| 1999 | Ernest F. "Fritz" Hollings (D)/11/9/66 | |
| 2003 | **Strom Thurmond*** (R)/11/7/56 | **607,097** |
| | Elliot Springs Close (D) | 502,202 |
| | **South Dakota** | |
| 1999 | Thomas A. Daschle (D)/1/6/87 | |
| 2003 | **Tim Johnson** (D)/1/7/97 | **166,511** |
| | Larry Pressler* (R)/1979 | 157,912 |
| | **Tennessee** | |
| 2001 | Bill Frist (R)/1/4/95 | |
| 2003 | **Fred Thompson*** (R)/12/9/94 | **1,088,364** |
| | Houston Gordon (D) | 652,754 |
| | **Texas** | |
| 2001 | Kay Bailey Hutchison (R)/6/5/93 | |
| 2003 | **Phil Gramm*** (R)/1985 | **3,028,504** |
| | Victor M. Morales (D) | 2,428,998 |
| | **Utah** | |
| 1999 | Robert F. Bennett (R)/1993 | |
| 2001 | Orrin G. Hatch (R)/1977 | |
| | **Vermont** | |
| 1999 | Patrick J. Leahy (D)/1975 | |
| 2001 | Jim Jeffords (R)/1989 | |
| | **Virginia** | |
| 2001 | Charles S. Robb (D)/1989 | |
| 2003 | **John W. Warner*** (R)/1/2/79 | **1,221,508** |
| | Mark R. Warner (D) | 1,098,440 |
| | **Washington** | |
| 1999 | Patty Murray (D)/1993 | |
| 2001 | Slade Gorton (R)/1989 | |
| | **West Virginia** | |
| 2001 | Robert C. Byrd (D)/1959 | |
| 2003 | **John D. Rockefeller IV*** (D)/1/15/85 | **450,903** |
| | Betty A. Burks (R) | 137,240 |
| | **Wisconsin** | |
| 1999 | Russell D. Feingold (D)/1993 | |
| 2001 | Herbert H. Kohl (D)/1989 | |
| | **Wyoming** | |
| 2001 | Craig Thomas (R)/1/4/95 | |
| 2003 | **Michael B. Enzi** (R)/1/7/97 | **114,071** |
| | Kathy Karpan (D) | 89,056 |

(1) Jan. 3, unless otherwise noted. (2) Democratic Sen. Richard C. Shelby announced Nov. 9, 1994, that he changed his party designation to Republican. (3) Democratic Sen. Ben Nighthorse Campbell announced Mar. 3, 1995, that he changed his party designation to Republican. (4) Senator Bob Dole resigned June 11, 1996, to run for president. Republican Sam Brownback will serve out the remainder of Dole's term. (5) James M. Inhofe won a special election held Nov. 8, 1994, to fill the seat left vacant by the resignation of Sen. David Boren (D). (6) Ron Wyden won a special election (by mail) Jan. 30, 1996, to fill the seat left vacant when Republican Senator Bob Packwood resigned, Oct. 1, 1995, after the Senate Ethics Committee had concluded that Packwood had engaged in sexual and official misconduct while a senator. This was the first time a U.S. senator was elected by a mail-in vote. (7) Because the totals were so close, no winner had been declared as of Nov. 7, 1996.

## The House of Representatives

**Rep., 222; Dem., 204; Ind., 2; Undecided, 7; Total, 435. *Incumbent. Boldface denotes the 1996 election winner.**

Members' terms to Jan. 3, 1999. Annual salary, $133,600; Speaker of the House, $171,500; Majority Leader and Minority Leader, $148,400. To be eligible for membership, a person must be at least 25 years of age, a U.S. citizen for at least 7 years, and a resident of the state from which he or she is chosen. The ZIP code of the House is 20515; the telephone number is 202-225-3121.

**House officials in 1995-97 (104th Congress) were:** Speaker, Newt Gingrich; Majority Leader, Dick Armey; Majority Whip, Tom DeLay; Minority Leader, Richard A. Gephardt; Minority Whip, David E. Bonior.

**D-Democrat; R-Republican; ACP-A Connecticut Party; LB-Libertarian; C-Conservative; F-Freedom; I-Independent; IC-Independence; L-Liberal; NL-Natural Law; PS-Protect Seniors; S-Save Medicare; T-Right to Life.**

| Dist. | Representative (Party) | 1996 Election |
|---|---|---|
| | **Alabama** | |
| 1. | **H. L. "Sonny" Callahan*** (R) | **132,086** |
| | Don Womack (D) | 69,322 |
| 2. | **Terry Everett*** (R) | **132,596** |
| | Bob Gaines (D) | 74,330 |
| 3. | **Bob Riley** (R) | **102,923** |
| | T. D. (Ted) Little (D) | 94,927 |
| 4. | **Robert Aderholt** (R) | **102,879** |
| | Robert T. (Bob) Wilson, Jr. (D) | 99,356 |
| 5. | **Bud Cramer*** (D) | **126,705** |
| | Wayne Parker (R) | 94,334 |
| 6. | **Spencer Bachus*** (R) | **181,313** |
| | Mary Lynn Bates (D) | 70,072 |
| 7. | **Earl F. Hilliard*** (D) | **136,634** |
| | Joe Powell (R) | 52,084 |
| | **Alaska** | |
| | **Don Young*** (R) | **115,480** |
| | Georgianna "Georg" Lincoln (D) | 72,448 |
| | **Arizona** | |
| 1. | **Matt Salmon*** (R) | **123,527** |
| | John Cox (D) | 82,547 |

| Dist. | Representative (Party) | 1996 Election |
|---|---|---|
| 2. | **Ed Pastor*** (D) | **78,090** |
| | Jim Buster (R) | 37,486 |
| 3. | **Bob Stump*** (R) | **156,847** |
| | Alexander "Big Al" Schneider (D) | 79,423 |
| 4. | **John Shadegg*** (R) | **137,639** |
| | Maria Elena Milton (D) | 69,176 |
| 5. | **Jim Kolbe*** (R) | **171,064** |
| | Mort Nelson (D) | 64,660 |
| 6. | **J. D. Hayworth*** (R) | **113,545** |
| | Steve Owens (D) | 112,955 |

**Arkansas**

| Dist. | Representative (Party) | 1996 Election |
|---|---|---|
| 1. | **Marion Berry** (D) | **102,567** |
| | Warren Dupwe (R) | 86,028 |
| 2. | **Vic Snyder** (D) | **113,786** |
| | Bud Cummins (R) | 103,793 |
| 3. | **Asa Hutchinson** (R) | **132,303** |
| | Ann Henry (D) | 99,975 |
| 4. | **Jay Dickey*** (R) | **125,568** |
| | Vincent Tolliver (D) | 72,066 |

**California**

| Dist. | Representative (Party) | 1996 Election |
|---|---|---|
| 1. | **Frank Riggs*** (R) | **96,622** |
| | Michela Alioto (D) | 86,997 |
| 2. | **Wally Herger*** (R) | **131,749** |
| | Roberts A. Braden (D) | 73,965 |
| 3. | **Vic Fazio*** (D) | **112,590** |
| | Tim Lefever (R) | 86,204 |
| 4. | **John T. Doolittle*** (R) | **147,879** |
| | Katie Hirning (D) | 89,178 |
| 5. | **Robert T. Matsui*** (D) | **134,802** |
| | Robert S. Dinsmore (R) | 49,820 |
| 6. | **Lynn Woolsey*** (D) | **145,364** |
| | Duane C. Hughes (R) | 79,317 |
| 7. | **George Miller*** (D) | **128,249** |
| | Norman H. Reece (R) | 39,514 |
| 8. | **Nancy Pelosi*** (D) | **158,533** |
| | Justin Raimondo (R) | 22,828 |
| 9. | **Ronald V. Dellums*** (D) | **140,638** |
| | Deborah Wright (R) | 33,201 |
| 10. | **Ellen O. Tauscher** (D) | **126,868** |
| | Bill Baker* (R) | 121,332 |
| 11. | **Richard Pombo*** (R) | **100,404** |
| | Jason Silva (D) | 61,573 |
| 12. | **Tom Lantos*** (D) | **133,583** |
| | Storm Jenkins (R) | 43,809 |
| 13. | **Fortney "Pete" Stark*** (D) | **106,467** |
| | James S. Fay (R) | 49,141 |
| 14. | **Anna G. Eshoo*** (D) | **131,595** |
| | Ben Brink (R) | 62,334 |
| 15. | **Tom Campbell*** (R)[1] | **115,434** |
| | Dick Lane (D) | 70,691 |
| 16. | **Zoe Lofgren*** (D) | **85,082** |
| | Chuck Wojslaw (R) | 38,205 |
| 17. | **Sam Farr*** (D) | **100,658** |
| | Jess Brown (R) | 65,648 |
| 18. | **Gary A. Condit*** (D) | **98,517** |
| | Bill Conrad (R) | 47,890 |
| 19. | **George P. Radanovich*** (R) | **114,211** |
| | Paul Barile (D) | 47,565 |
| 20. | **Cal Dooley*** (D) | **46,427** |
| | Trice Harvey (R) | 33,939 |
| 21. | **Bill Thomas*** (R) | **111,105** |
| | Deborah A. Vollmer (D) | 45,230 |
| 22. | **Walter Holden Capps** (D) | **102,915** |
| | Andrea Seastrand* (R) | 90,374 |
| 23. | **Elton Gallegly*** (R) | **98,369** |
| | Robert R. Unruhe (D) | 60,388 |
| 24. | **Brad Sherman** (D) | **96,641** |
| | Rich Sybert (R) | 81,428 |
| 25. | **Howard "Buck" McKeon*** (R) | **110,998** |
| | Diane Trautman (D) | 59,602 |
| 26. | **Howard L. Berman*** (D) | **61,963** |
| | Bill Glass (R) | 26,734 |
| 27. | **James E. Rogan** (R) | **84,642** |
| | Doug Kahn (D) | 73,679 |
| 28. | **David Dreier*** (R) | **103,939** |
| | David Levering (D) | 63,972 |
| 29. | **Henry A. Waxman*** (D) | **132,206** |
| | Paul Stepanek (R) | 46,667 |
| 30. | **Xavier Becerra*** (D) | **52,673** |
| | Patricia Jean Parker (R) | 13,216 |
| 31. | **Matthew G. Martinez*** (D) | **63,553** |
| | John V. Flores (R) | 26,041 |
| 32. | **Julian C. Dixon*** (D) | **114,584** |
| | Larry Ardito (R) | 16,712 |
| 33. | **Lucille Roybal-Allard*** (D) | **43,788** |
| | John P. Leonard (R) | 7,308 |
| 34. | **Esteban E. Torres*** (D) | **87,803** |
| | David G. Nunez (R) | 33,677 |
| 35. | **Maxine Waters*** (D) | **86,878** |
| | Eric Carlson (R) | 11,930 |
| 36. | **Jane Harman*** (D) | **107,738** |
| | Susan Brooks (R) | 88,909 |
| 37. | **Juanita M. McDonald*** (D)[2] | **81,695** |
| | Michael E. Voetee (R) | 14,115 |
| 38. | **Steve Horn*** (R) | **81,372** |
| | Rick Zbur (D) | 65,882 |
| 39. | **Ed Royce*** (R) | **110,201** |
| | R. O. "Bob" Davis (D) | 56,723 |
| 40. | **Jerry Lewis*** (R) | **93,750** |
| | Robert "Bob" Conaway (D) | 42,117 |
| 41. | **Jay C. Kim*** (R) | **77,578** |
| | Richard L. Waldron (D) | 44,425 |
| 42. | George E. Brown, Jr.* (D)[3] | 49,907 |
| | Linda M. Wilde (R)[3] | 48,757 |
| 43. | **Ken Calvert*** (R) | **85,172** |
| | Guy C. Kimbrough (D) | 60,516 |
| 44. | **Sonny Bono*** (R) | **97,522** |
| | Anita Rufus (D) | 66,750 |
| 45. | **Dana Rohrabacher*** (R) | **113,827** |
| | Sally J. Alexander (D) | 62,569 |
| 46. | Robert K. "Bob" Dornan* (R)[3] | 41,308 |
| | Loretta Sanchez (D)[3] | 41,075 |
| 47. | **Christopher Cox*** (R) | **143,383** |
| | Tina Louise Laine (D) | 63,877 |
| 48. | **Ron Packard*** (R) | **128,066** |
| | Dan Farrell (D) | 53,381 |
| 49. | **Brian P. Bilbray*** (R) | **94,850** |
| | Peter Navarro (D) | 77,482 |
| 50. | **Bob Filner*** (D) | **65,246** |
| | Jim Baize (R) | 33,722 |
| 51. | **Randy "Duke" Cunningham*** (R) | **127,961** |
| | Rita Tamerius (D) | 57,917 |
| 52. | **Duncan Hunter*** (R) | **103,231** |
| | Darity Wesley (D) | 47,676 |

**Colorado**

| Dist. | Representative (Party) | 1996 Election |
|---|---|---|
| 1. | **Diana DeGette** (D) | **112,555** |
| | Joe Rogers (R) | 79,536 |
| 2. | **David Skaggs*** (D) | **145,894** |
| | Patricia (Pat) Miller (R) | 97,865 |
| 3. | **Scott McInnis*** (R) | **183,062** |
| | Albert L. Gurule (D) | 82,544 |
| 4. | **Bob Schaffer** (R) | **136,579** |
| | Guy Kelley (D) | 92,680 |
| 5. | **Joel Hefley*** (R) | **188,795** |
| | Mike Robinson (D) | 73,654 |
| 6. | **Dan Schaefer*** (R) | **146,018** |
| | Joan Fitz-Gerald (D) | 88,600 |

**Connecticut**

| Dist. | Representative (Party) | 1996 Election |
|---|---|---|
| 1. | **Barbara Bailey Kennelly*** (D,ACP) | **159,312** |
| | Kent Sleath (R) | 53,678 |
| 2. | **Sam Gejdenson*** (D,ACP) | **114,453** |
| | Edward W. Munster (R) | 100,008 |
| 3. | **Rosa L. DeLauro*** (D,ACP) | **149,212** |
| | John Coppola (R) | 59,093 |
| 4. | **Christopher Shays*** (R) | **121,658** |
| | Bill Finch (D) | 75,181 |
| 5. | **James H. Maloney** (D,ACP) | **110,844** |
| | Gary A. Franks* (R) | 97,725 |
| 6. | **Nancy L. Johnson*** (R) | **113,020** |
| | Charlotte Koskoff (D,ACP) | 111,396 |

**Delaware**

| Dist. | Representative (Party) | 1996 Election |
|---|---|---|
| | **Michael N. Castle*** (R) | **185,341** |
| | Dennis E. Williams (D) | 73,177 |

**Florida**

| Dist. | Representative (Party) | 1996 Election |
|---|---|---|
| 1. | **Joe Scarborough*** (R) | **175,382** |
| | Kevin Beck (D) | 66,243 |
| 2. | **Allen Boyd** (D) | **137,213** |
| | Bill Sutton (R) | 93,519 |

| Dist. | Representative (Party) | 1996 Election |
|---|---|---|
| 3. | **Corrine Brown*** (D) | **97,972** |
| | Preston James Fields (R) | 62,128 |
| 4. | **Tillie K. Fowler*** (R) | **Unopposed** |
| 5. | **Karen L. Thurman*** (D) | **161,027** |
| | Dave Gentry (R) | 100,023 |
| 6. | **Clifford "Cliff" B. Stearns*** (R) | **161,461** |
| | Newell O'Brien (D) | 78,886 |
| 7. | **John L. Mica*** (R) | **143,503** |
| | George Stuart, Jr. (D) | 87,773 |
| 8. | **Bill McCollum*** (R) | **136,133** |
| | Al Krulick (D) | 65,528 |
| 9. | **Michael Bilirakis*** (R) | **161,649** |
| | Jerry Provenzano (D) | 73,779 |
| 10. | **C. W. Bill Young*** (R) | **114,418** |
| | Henry Green (D) | 57,359 |
| 11. | **Jim Davis** (D) | **108,454** |
| | Mark Sharpe (R) | 78,680 |
| 12. | **Charles T. Canady*** (R) | **122,531** |
| | Mike Canady (D) | 76,490 |
| 13. | **Dan Miller*** (R) | **173,570** |
| | Sanford Gordon (D) | 96,049 |
| 14. | **Porter J. Goss*** (R) | **176,961** |
| | Jim Nolan (D) | 63,833 |
| 15. | **Dave Weldon** (R) | **138,965** |
| | John L. Byron (D) | 115,952 |
| 16. | **Mark Foley** (R) | **176,670** |
| | Jim Stuber (D) | 98,823 |
| 17. | **Carrie P. Meek*** (D) | **114,170** |
| | Wellington Rolle (R) | 14,428 |
| 18. | **Ileana Ros-Lehtinen*** (R) | **Unopposed** |
| 19. | **Robert Wexler** (D) | **188,693** |
| | Beverly Kennedy (R) | 99,015 |
| 20. | **Peter Deutsch*** (D) | **159,053** |
| | Jim Jacobs (R) | 85,620 |
| 21. | **Lincoln Diaz-Balart*** (R) | **Unopposed** |
| 22. | **E. Clay Shaw, Jr.*** (R) | **136,967** |
| | Kenneth D. Cooper (D) | 84,451 |
| 23. | **Alcee L. Hastings*** (D) | **102,063** |
| | Robert Paul Brown (R) | 36,881 |
| | **Georgia** | |
| 1. | **Jack Kingston*** (R) | **108,557** |
| | Rosemary D. Kaszans (D) | 50,516 |
| 2. | **Sanford Bishop*** (D) | **88,253** |
| | Darrel Bush Ealum (R) | 75,686 |
| 3. | **Michael Allen "Mac" Collins*** (R) | **120,254** |
| | Jim Chafin (D) | 76,537 |
| 4. | **Cynthia McKinney*** (D) | **127,157** |
| | John M. Mitnick (R) | 92,985 |
| 5. | **John Lewis*** (D) | **Unopposed** |
| 6. | **Newt Gingrich*** (R) | **174,152** |
| | Michael Coles (D) | 127,132 |
| 7. | **Bob Barr*** (R) | **109,452** |
| | Charlie Watts (D) | 79,905 |
| 8. | **Saxby Chambliss*** (R) | **93,432** |
| | Jim Wiggins (D) | 84,175 |
| 9. | **John Nathan Deal*** (R)[4] | **130,380** |
| | McCracken "Ken" Poston (D) | 68,963 |
| 10. | **Charles Norwood, Jr.*** (R) | **94,690** |
| | David Bell (D) | 88,104 |
| 11. | **John Linder*** (R) | **145,813** |
| | Tommy Stephenson (D) | 81,030 |
| | **Hawaii** | |
| 1. | **Neil Abercrombie*** (D) | **86,732** |
| | Orson Swindle (R) | 80,053 |
| 2. | **Patsy Takemoto Mink*** (D) | **109,178** |
| | Tom Pico, Jr. (R) | 55,729 |
| | **Idaho** | |
| 1. | **Helen Chenoweth*** (R) | **132,340** |
| | Dan Williams (D) | 125,893 |
| 2. | **Mike Crapo*** (R) | **157,643** |
| | John D. Seidl (D) | 67,620 |
| | **Illinois** | |
| 1. | **Bobby L. Rush*** (D) | **164,163** |
| | Noel Naughton (R) | 25,335 |
| 2. | **Jesse L. Jackson, Jr.*** (D)[5] | **168,086** |
| | Frank H. Stratman (LB) | 10,706 |
| 3. | **William O. Lipinski*** (D) | **134,846** |
| | Jim Nalepa (R) | 66,365 |
| 4. | **Luis V. Gutierrez*** (D) | **81,298** |
| | William Passmore (B) | 5,602 |
| 5. | **Rod R. Blagojevich** (D) | **111,608** |
| | Michael Patrick Flanagan* (R) | 62,588 |
| 6. | **Henry J. Hyde*** (R) | **131,948** |
| | Stephen de la Rosa (D) | 68,567 |
| 7. | **Danny K. Davis** (D) | **139,973** |
| | Randy Borow (R) | 26,088 |
| 8. | **Philip M. Crane*** (R) | **127,763** |
| | Elizabeth Anne "Betty" Hull (D) | 74,068 |
| 9. | **Sidney R. Yates*** (D) | **120,354** |
| | Joseph Walsh (R) | 69,785 |
| 10. | **John E. Porter*** (R) | **145,626** |
| | Philip R. Torf (D) | 65,144 |
| 11. | **Gerald C. "Jerry" Weller** (R) | **109,135** |
| | Clem Balanoff (D) | 101,839 |
| 12. | **Jerry F. Costello*** (D) | **150,005** |
| | Shapley R. Hunter (R) | 55,690 |
| 13. | **Harris W. Fawell*** (R) | **141,119** |
| | Susan W. Hynes (D) | 94,274 |
| 14. | **J. Dennis Hastert*** (R) | **134,432** |
| | Doug Mains (D) | 74,332 |
| 15. | **Thomas W. Ewing*** (R) | **121,019** |
| | Laurel Lunt Prussing (D) | 90,065 |
| 16. | **Donald A. Manzullo*** (R) | **137,523** |
| | Catherine M. Lee (D) | 90,575 |
| 17. | **Lane A. Evans*** (D) | **120,008** |
| | Mark Baker (R) | 109,240 |
| 18. | **Ray LaHood*** (R) | **143,110** |
| | Mike Curran (D) | 98,413 |
| 19. | **Glenn Poshard*** (D) | **158,668** |
| | Brent Winters (R) | 75,751 |
| 20. | **John M. Shimkus** (R) | **120,749** |
| | Jay C. Hoffman (D) | 119,496 |
| | **Indiana** | |
| 1. | **Peter J. Visclosky*** (D) | **132,430** |
| | Michael Edward Petyo (R) | 56,205 |
| 2. | **David M. McIntosh*** (R) | **122,288** |
| | R. Marc Carmichael (D) | 83,478 |
| 3. | **Tim Roemer*** (D) | **109,756** |
| | Joe Zakas (R) | 77,952 |
| 4. | **Mark Edward Souder*** (R) | **118,344** |
| | Gerald L. Houseman (D) | 76,152 |
| 5. | **Steve Buyer*** (R) | **133,604** |
| | Douglas L. Clark (D) | 67,125 |
| 6. | **Dan Burton*** (R) | **189,461** |
| | Carrie Jean Dillard-Trammell (D) | 58,362 |
| 7. | **Edward A. Pease** (R) | **130,010** |
| | Robert F. Hellman (D) | 72,705 |
| 8. | **John N. Hostettler*** (R) | **109,582** |
| | Jonathan Weinzapfel (D) | 106,134 |
| 9. | **Lee H. Hamilton*** (D) | **128,885** |
| | Jean Leising (R) | 97,747 |
| 10. | **Julia M. Carson** (D) | **80,869** |
| | Virginia Blankenbaker (R) | 69,248 |
| | **Iowa** | |
| 1. | **Jim Leach*** (R) | **128,684** |
| | Bob Rush (D) | 111,190 |
| 2. | **Jim Nussle*** (R) | **127,357** |
| | Donna L. Smith (D) | 109,383 |
| 3. | **Leonard L. Boswell** (D) | **113,811** |
| | Mike Mahaffey (R) | 110,507 |
| 4. | **Greg Ganske*** (R) | **132,396** |
| | Connie McBurney (D) | 118,909 |
| 5. | **Tom Latham*** (R) | **146,581** |
| | MacDonald Smith (D) | 75,522 |
| | **Kansas** | |
| 1. | **Jerry Moran** (R) | **191,050** |
| | John Divine (D) | 63,537 |
| 2. | **Jim Ryun** (R) | **130,927** |
| | John Frieden (D) | 114,051 |
| 3. | **Vince Snowbarger** (R) | **137,598** |
| | Judy Hancock (D) | 125,389 |
| 4. | **Todd Tiahrt*** (R) | **127,166** |
| | Randall Rathbun (D) | 118,689 |
| | **Kentucky** | |
| 1. | **Edward Whitfield*** (R) | **111,483** |
| | Dennis L. Null (D) | 96,640 |

| Dist. | Representative (Party) | 1996 Election |
|---|---|---|
| 2. | **Ron Lewis*** (R) | **125,430** |
| | Joe Wright (D) | 90,208 |
| 3. | **Anne Meagher Northup** (R) | **126,625** |
| | Mike Ward* (D) | 125,326 |
| 4. | **Jim Bunning*** (R) | **147,997** |
| | Denny Bowman (D) | 68,661 |
| 5. | **Harold "Hal" Rogers*** (R) | **Unopposed** |
| 6. | **Scotty Baesler*** (D) | **125,908** |
| | Ernest Fletcher (R) | 100,234 |
| | **Louisiana** | |
| 1. | **Robert L. "Bob" Livingston*** (R) | |
| 2. | **William J. Jefferson*** (D) | |
| 3. | **W. J. "Billy" Tauzin*** (R)[6] | |
| 4. | **Cleo Fields*** (D) | |
| 5. | **John Cooksey** (R) | **135,699** |
| | Francis Thompson (D) | 96,717 |
| 6. | **Richard Baker*** (R) | |
| 7. | **Chris John** (D) | **128,263** |
| | Hunter Lundy (D) | 113,235 |

In Louisiana, all candidates of all parties run against each other in an open primary, unless they are unopposed incumbents, in which case they are declared elected. All candidates who receive more than 50 percent of the primary vote are also declared elected and do not appear on the general election ballot. In 1996, candidates in Districts 1, 2, 3, 4, and 6 were declared elected.

| Dist. | Representative (Party) | 1996 Election |
|---|---|---|
| | **Maine** | |
| 1. | **Thomas H. Allen** (D) | **165,815** |
| | James B. Longley, Jr.* (R) | 133,501 |
| 2. | **John E. Baldacci*** (D) | **197,177** |
| | Paul R. Young (R) | 68,420 |
| | **Maryland** | |
| 1. | **Wayne T. Gilchrest*** (R) | **124,687** |
| | Steve R. Eastaugh (D) | 78,865 |
| 2. | **Robert L. Ehrlich, Jr.*** (R) | **137,746** |
| | Connie Galiazzo DeJuliis (D) | 85,526 |
| 3. | **Benjamin L. Cardin*** (D) | **123,237** |
| | Patrick L. McDonough (R) | 60,655 |
| 4. | **Albert R. Wynn*** (D) | **137,100** |
| | John B. Kimble (R) | 23,373 |
| 5. | **Steny H. Hoyer*** (D) | **116,611** |
| | John S. Morgan (R) | 88,111 |
| 6. | **Roscoe Bartlett*** (R) | **127,415** |
| | Stephen Crawford (D) | 96,592 |
| 7. | **Elijah E. Cummings*** (D)[7] | **110,473** |
| | Kenneth Kondner (R) | 22,386 |
| 8. | **Constance A. Morella*** (R) | **144,125** |
| | Donald Mooers (D) | 91,173 |
| | **Massachusetts** | |
| 1. | **John W. Olver*** (D) | **129,020** |
| | Jane Maria Swift (R) | 115,712 |
| 2. | **Richard E. Neal*** (D) | **162,890** |
| | Mark Steele (R) | 49,858 |
| 3. | **James P. McGovern** (D) | **134,780** |
| | Peter Blute* (R) | 115,477 |
| 4. | **Barney Frank*** (D) | **183,629** |
| | Jonathan P. Raymond (R) | 72,670 |
| 5. | **Martin T. Meehan* (D)** | **Unopposed** |
| 6. | **John F. Tierney** (D) | **132,868** |
| | Peter G. Torkildsen* (R) | 132,268 |
| 7. | **Edward J. Markey*** (D) | **176,592** |
| | Patricia H. Long (R) | 76,275 |
| 8. | **Joseph P. Kennedy, II*** (D) | **145,949** |
| | R. Philip Hyde (R) | 27,271 |
| 9. | **John Joseph Moakley*** (D) | **171,749** |
| | Paul V. Gryska (R) | 65,608 |
| 10. | **William D. Delahunt** (D) | **160,486** |
| | Edward B. Teague, III (R) | 123,261 |
| | **Michigan** | |
| 1. | **Bart Stupak*** (D) | **180,389** |
| | Bob Carr (R) | 69,970 |
| 2. | **Peter Hoekstra*** (R) | **165,330** |
| | Dan Kruszynski (D) | 82,562 |
| 3. | **Vernon J. Ehlers*** (R) | **169,021** |
| | Betsy J. Flory (D) | 72,685 |
| 4. | **Dave Camp*** (R) | **158,816** |
| | Lisa A. Donaldson (D) | 79,333 |
| 5. | **James A. Barcia*** (D) | **162,531** |
| | Lawrence H. Sims (R) | 65,513 |
| 6. | **Fred Upton*** (R) | **145,056** |
| | Clarence J. Annen (D) | 65,814 |
| 7. | **Nick Smith*** (R) | **107,552** |
| | Kim H. Tunnicliff (D) | 89,487 |
| 8. | **Debbie Stabenow** (D) | **136,781** |
| | Dick Chrysler* (R) | 110,307 |
| 9. | **Dale E. Kildee*** (D) | **136,129** |
| | Patrick M. Nowak (R) | 89,522 |
| 10. | **David E. Bonior*** (D) | **117,894** |
| | Susy Heintz (R) | 93,848 |
| 11. | **Joe Knollenberg*** (R) | **154,293** |
| | Morris Frumin (D) | 88,213 |
| 12. | **Sander Levin*** (D) | **116,007** |
| | John Pappageorge (R) | 78,153 |
| 13. | **Lynn Nancy Rivers*** (D) | **67,302** |
| | Joe Fitzsimmons (R) | 37,676 |
| 14. | **John Conyers, Jr.*** (D) | **150,926** |
| | William A. Ashe (R) | 15,195 |
| 15. | **Carolyn Cheeks Kilpatrick** (D) | **131,723** |
| | Stephen Hume (R) | 11,478 |
| 16. | **John D. Dingell*** (D) | **80,068** |
| | James R. DeSana (R) | 52,599 |
| | **Minnesota** | |
| 1. | **Gil Gutknecht*** (R) | **136,304** |
| | Mary Rieder (D) | 122,401 |
| 2. | **David Minge*** (D) | **144,186** |
| | Gary B. Revier (R) | 107,533 |
| 3. | **Jim Ramstad*** (R) | **201,060** |
| | Stanley J. Leino (D) | 85,444 |
| 4. | **Bruce F. Vento*** (D) | **145,790** |
| | Dennis Newinski (R) | 94,012 |
| 5. | **Martin Olav Sabo*** (D) | **155,576** |
| | Jack Uldrich (R) | 68,601 |
| 6. | **Bill Luther*** (D) | **164,915** |
| | Tad Jude (R) | 129,986 |
| 7. | **Collin C. Peterson*** (D) | **170,335** |
| | Darrell McKigney (R) | 79,907 |
| 8. | **James L. Oberstar*** (D) | **155,689** |
| | Andy Larson (R) | 62,966 |
| | **Mississippi** | |
| 1. | **Roger F. Wicker*** (R) | **122,554** |
| | Henry Boyd, Jr. (D) | 55,200 |
| 2. | **Bennie G. Thompson*** (D) | **99,754** |
| | Danny Covington (R) | 63,989 |
| 3. | **Charles W. "Chip" Pickering, Jr.** (R) | **114,379** |
| | John Arthur Eaves, Jr. (D) | 67,957 |
| 4. | **Mike Parker*** (R) | **110,895** |
| | Kevin Antoine (D) | 64,823 |
| 5. | **Gene Taylor*** (D) | **101,832** |
| | Dennis Dollar (R) | 69,990 |
| | **Missouri** | |
| 1. | **William "Bill" Clay*** (D) | **131,125** |
| | Daniel F. O'Sullivan, Jr. (R) | 51,969 |
| 2. | **James M. Talent*** (R) | **165,984** |
| | Joan Kelly Horn (D) | 100,539 |
| 3. | **Richard A. Gephardt*** (D) | **136,869** |
| | Deborah Lynn "Debbie" Wheelehan (R) | 89,951 |
| 4. | **Ike Skelton*** (D) | **154,116** |
| | Bill Phelps (R) | 81,806 |
| 5. | **Karen McCarthy*** (D) | **143,761** |
| | Penny Bennett (R) | 61,769 |
| 6. | **Pat "Patsy Ann" Danner*** (D) | **168,935** |
| | Jeff Bailey (R) | 72,139 |
| 7. | **Roy Blunt** (R) | **162,529** |
| | Ruth Bamberger (D) | 79,298 |
| 8. | **Jo Ann Emerson** (I) | **112,473** |
| | Richard Kline (R) | 23,459 |
| | Emily Firebaugh (D) | 83,074 |
| 9. | **Kenny Hulshof** (R) | **123,579** |
| | Harold L. Volkmer* (D) | 117,684 |
| | **Montana** | |
| | **Rick Hill** (R) | **210,302** |
| | Bill Yellowtail (D) | 173,416 |

| Dist. | Representative (Party) | 1996 Election |
|---|---|---|
| | **Nebraska** | |
| 1. | **Doug Bereuter*** (R) | **153,794** |
| | Patrick J. Combs (D) | 65,896 |
| 2. | **Jon Christensen*** (R) | **122,017** |
| | James Martin Davis (D) | 86,702 |
| 3. | **Bill Barrett*** (R) | **164,565** |
| | John Webster (D) | 48,563 |
| | **Nevada** | |
| 1. | **John Ensign*** (R) | **84,958** |
| | Bob Coffin (D) | 73,925 |
| 2. | **Jim Gibbons** (R) | **161,633** |
| | Thomas "Spike" Wilson (D) | 97,241 |
| | **New Hampshire** | |
| 1. | **John E. Sununu** (R) | **123,616** |
| | "Joe" Keefe (D) | 114,930 |
| 2. | **Charles Bass*** (R) | **122,931** |
| | Deborah Arnie Arnesen (D) | 105,764 |
| | **New Jersey** | |
| 1. | **Robert E. Andrews*** (D) | **154,486** |
| | Mel Suplee (R) | 42,500 |
| 2. | **Frank A. LoBiondo*** (R) | **128,308** |
| | Ruth Katz (D) | 81,141 |
| 3. | **Jim Saxton*** (R) | **151,748** |
| | John Leonardi (D) | 78,756 |
| 4. | **Christopher H. Smith*** (R) | **143,412** |
| | Kevin John Meara (D) | 75,851 |
| 5. | **Marge Roukema*** (R) | **172,464** |
| | Bill Auer (D) | 59,798 |
| 6. | **Frank Pallone, Jr.*** (D) | **125,448** |
| | Steven J. Corodemus (R) | 73,035 |
| 7. | **Bob Franks*** (R) | **125,952** |
| | Larry Lerner (D) | 96,367 |
| 8. | **William J. Pascrell, Jr.** (D) | **94,086** |
| | Bill Martini* (R) | 88,683 |
| 9. | **Steven R. Rothman** (D) | **102,810** |
| | Kathleen A. Donovan (R) | 81,715 |
| 10. | **Donald M. Payne*** (D) | **121,684** |
| | Vanessa Williams (R) | 21,612 |
| 11. | **Rodney P. Frelinghuysen*** (R) | **160,067** |
| | Chris Evangel (D) | 75,350 |
| 12. | **Mike Pappas** (R) | **134,452** |
| | David M. DelVecchio (D) | 125,111 |
| 13. | **Robert Menendez*** (D) | **110,231** |
| | Carlos E. Munoz (R) | 23,955 |
| | **New Mexico** | |
| 1. | **Steven H. Schiff*** (R) | **82,694** |
| | John Wertheim (D) | 57,745 |
| 2. | **Joe Skeen*** (R) | **94,546** |
| | E. Shirley Baca (D) | 74,294 |
| 3. | **Bill Richardson*** (D) | **123,894** |
| | Bill Redmond (R) | 55,893 |
| | **New York** | |
| 1. | **Michael P. Forbes*** (R,C,IC,T) | **113,330** |
| | Nora L. Bredes (D,S) | 92,767 |
| 2. | **Rick A. Lazio*** (R,C) | **107,875** |
| | Kenneth J. Herman (D,IC) | 56,347 |
| 3. | **Peter T. King*** (R,C,F) | **124,941** |
| | Dal A. Lamagna (D,IC) | 94,208 |
| 4. | **Carolyn McCarthy** (D,IC) | **123,228** |
| | Daniel Frisa (R,C,F) | 87,695 |
| 5. | **Gary L. Ackerman*** (D,IC,L) | **120,739** |
| | Grant M. Lally (R,C,F) | 67,105 |
| 6. | **Floyd H. Flake*** (D) | **94,626** |
| | Jorawar Misir (R,C,IC,F) | 16,714 |
| 7. | **Thomas J. Manton*** (D) | **72,351** |
| | Rose Birtley (R,C,IC) | 30,135 |
| 8. | **Jerrold L. Nadler*** (D,L) | **115,476** |
| | Michael Benjamin (R,F) | 23,359 |
| 9. | **Charles E. Schumer*** (D,L) | **99,450** |
| | Robert J. Verga (R,IC,F) | 29,378 |
| 10. | **Edolphus Towns*** (D,L) | **91,848** |
| | Amelia Smith-Parker (R,C,F) | 8,056 |
| 11. | **Major R. Owens*** (D,L) | **81,950** |
| | Claudette Hayle (R,C,IC,F) | 7,606 |
| 12. | **Nydia M. Velázquez*** (D,L) | **54,851** |
| | Miguel I. Prado (R,C,T) | 9,241 |
| 13. | **Susan Molinari*** (R,C,F) | **89,884** |
| | Tyrone G. Butler (D,L) | 50,464 |
| 14. | **Carolyn B. Maloney*** (D,L) | **113,433** |
| | Jeffrey E. Livingston (R) | 36,978 |
| 15. | **Charles B. Rangel*** (D,L) | **102,840** |
| | Edward R. Adams (R) | 5,526 |
| 16. | **José E. Serrano*** (D,L) | **89,227** |
| | Rodney Torres (R) | 2,662 |
| 17. | **Eliot L. Engel*** (D,L) | **95,966** |
| | Denis McCarthy (R,C,T) | 15,392 |
| 18. | **Nita M. Lowey*** (D) | **110,327** |
| | Kerry J. Katsorhis (R,C) | 56,343 |
| 19. | **Sue W. Kelly** (R,F) | **97,666** |
| | Richard S. Klein (D,L) | 83,333 |
| 20. | **Benjamin A. Gilman*** (R) | **115,066** |
| | Yash P. Aggarwal (D,L) | 76,324 |
| 21. | **Michael R. McNulty*** (D,C,IC) | **148,984** |
| | Nancy Norman (R,F) | 60,365 |
| 22. | **Gerald B. H. Solomon*** (R,C,T,F) | **97,911** |
| | Steve James (D) | 62,005 |
| 23. | **Sherwood L. Boehlert*** (R,F) | **115,053** |
| | Bruce W. Hapanowicz (D) | 46,875 |
| 24. | **John M. McHugh*** (R,C) | **118,976** |
| | Donald Ravenscroft (D) | 41,303 |
| 25. | **James T. Walsh*** (R,C,IC,F) | **123,441** |
| | Marty Mack (D) | 99,860 |
| 26. | **Maurice D. Hinchey*** (D,L) | **115,426** |
| | Sue Wittig (R,C,T,F) | 88,912 |
| 27. | **Bill Paxon*** (R,C,T,F) | **137,292** |
| | Thomas M. Fricano (D,S) | 91,404 |
| 28. | **Louise M. Slaughter*** (D) | **125,425** |
| | Geoff H. Rosenberger (R,C,F) | 94,647 |
| 29. | **John J. LaFalce*** (D,L) | **128,272** |
| | David B. Callard (R,C,T,F) | 78,938 |
| 30. | **Jack Quinn*** (R,C,IC,F) | **117,414** |
| | Francis J. Pordum (D,PS) | 96,435 |
| 31. | **Amo Houghton*** (R,C,F) | **132,896** |
| | Bruce D. MacBain (D) | 47,327 |
| | **North Carolina** | |
| 1. | **Eva M. Clayton*** (D) | **104,867** |
| | Ted Tyler (R) | 53,237 |
| 2. | **Bob Etheridge** (D) | **113,371** |
| | David Funderburk* (R) | 98,317 |
| 3. | **Walter B. Jones, Jr.*** (R) | **117,641** |
| | George Parrott (D) | 67,647 |
| 4. | **David E. Price** (D) | **155,163** |
| | Fred Heineman* (R) | 124,882 |
| 5. | **Richard M. Burr*** (R) | **129,575** |
| | Neil Grist Cashion, Jr. (D) | 73,961 |
| 6. | **Howard Coble*** (R) | **166,846** |
| | Mark Costley (D) | 57,701 |
| 7. | **Mike McIntyre** (D) | **86,489** |
| | Bill Caster (R) | 74,883 |
| 8. | **W. G. "Bill" Hefner*** (D) | **101,777** |
| | Curtis Blackwood (R) | 81,487 |
| 9. | **Sue Myrick*** (R) | **143,040** |
| | Michel C. (Mike) Daisley (D) | 81,297 |
| 10. | **T. Cass Ballenger*** (R) | **156,875** |
| | Ben Neill (D) | 64,653 |
| 11. | **Charles H. Taylor*** (R) | **132,203** |
| | James Mark Ferguson (D) | 90,758 |
| 12. | **Mel Watt*** (D) | **123,899** |
| | Joseph A. "Joe" Martino (R) | 46,406 |
| | **North Dakota** | |
| | Earl **Pomeroy*** (D) | **144,235** |
| | Kevin Cramer (R) | 113,134 |
| | **Ohio** | |
| 1. | **Steve Chabot*** (R) | **116,003** |
| | Mark P. Longabaugh (D) | 92,197 |
| 2. | **Rob Portman*** (R) | **183,167** |
| | Thomas R. Chandler (D) | 57,548 |
| 3. | **Tony P. Hall*** (D) | **141,471** |
| | David A. Westbrock (R) | 74,128 |
| 4. | **Michael G. Oxley*** (R) | **143,706** |
| | Paul McClain (D) | 67,747 |

| Dist. | Representative (Party) | 1996 Election |
|---|---|---|
| 5. | **Paul E. Gillmor*** (R) | **143,375** |
| | Annie Saunders (D) | 79,885 |
| 6. | **Ted Strickland** (D) | **114,961** |
| | Frank A. Cremeans* (R) | 109,626 |
| 7. | **David L. Hobson*** (R) | **155,067** |
| | Richard K. Blain (D) | 60,234 |
| 8. | **John A. Boehner*** (R) | **161,938** |
| | Jeffrey D. Kitchen (D) | 60,115 |
| 9. | **Marcy Kaptur*** (D) | **166,671** |
| | Randy Whitman (R) | 44,846 |
| 10. | **Dennis J. Kucinich** (D) | **107,986** |
| | Martin R. Hoke* (R) | 102,149 |
| 11. | **Louis Stokes*** (D) | **148,346** |
| | James J. Sykora (R) | 28,143 |
| 12. | **John R. Kasich*** (R) | **199,361** |
| | Cynthia L. Ruccia (D) | 91,493 |
| 13. | **Sherrod Brown*** (D) | **144,198** |
| | Kenneth C. Blair, Jr. (R) | 85,807 |
| 14. | **Thomas C. Sawyer*** (D) | **121,650** |
| | Joyce George (R) | 93,725 |
| 15. | **Deborah Pryce*** (R) | **164,208** |
| | Cliff Arnebeck (D) | 66,626 |
| 16. | **Ralph Regula*** (R) | **156,034** |
| | Thomas E. Burkhart (D) | 63,593 |
| 17. | **James A. Traficant, Jr.*** (D) | **215,114** |
| | James M. Cahaney (NL) | 21,378 |
| 18. | **Bob Ney*** (R) | **115,153** |
| | Robert L. Burch (D) | 106,583 |
| 19. | **Steven C. LaTourette*** (R) | **131,624** |
| | Thomas J. Coyne, Jr. (D) | 98,023 |
| | **Oklahoma** | |
| 1. | **Steve Largent*** (R) | **143,415** |
| | Randolph John Amen (D) | 57,996 |
| 2. | **Tom A. Coburn*** (R) | **112,272** |
| | Glen D. Johnson (D) | 90,120 |
| 3. | **Wes Watkins** (R) | **98,525** |
| | Darryl Roberts (D) | 86,646 |
| 4. | **J. C. Watts, Jr.*** (R) | **106,923** |
| | Ed Crocker (D) | 73,950 |
| 5. | **Ernest Istook*** (R) | **148,362** |
| | James L. Forsythe (D) | 57,594 |
| 6. | **Frank D. Lucas*** (R) | **113,499** |
| | Paul M. Barby (D) | 64,173 |
| | **Oregon** | |
| 1. | Elizabeth Furse* (D)[3] | 68,566 |
| | Bill Witt (R)[3] | 52,856 |
| 2. | **Robert F. (Bob) Smith** (R) | **99,128** |
| | Mike Dugan (D) | 65,374 |
| 3. | **Earl Blumenauer*** (D)[8] | **74,779** |
| | Scott Bruun (R) | 27,321 |
| 4. | **Peter A. DeFazio*** (D) | **104,302** |
| | John D. Newkirk (R) | 40,345 |
| 5. | Jim Bunn* (R)[3] | 59,013 |
| | Darlene Hooley (D)[3] | 51,462 |
| | **Pennsylvania** | |
| 1. | **Thomas M. Foglietta*** (D) | **142,304** |
| | James D. Cella (R) | 20,584 |
| 2. | **Chaka Fattah*** (D) | **166,626** |
| | Larry G. Murphy (R) | 22,533 |
| 3. | **Robert A. Borski*** (D) | **120,106** |
| | Joseph M. McColgan (R) | 54,334 |
| 4. | **Ron Klink*** (D) | **142,207** |
| | Paul T. Adametz (R) | 79,217 |
| 5. | **John E. Peterson** (R) | **116,072** |
| | Ruth C. Rudy (D) | 76,605 |
| 6. | **Tim Holden*** (D) | **114,977** |
| | Christian Y. Leinbach (R) | 79,714 |
| 7. | **Curt Weldon*** (R) | **165,692** |
| | John F. Innelli (D) | 79,864 |
| 8. | **Jim Greenwood*** (R) | **133,183** |
| | John P. Murray (D) | 79,410 |
| 9. | **Bud Shuster*** (R) | **141,676** |
| | Monte Kemmler (D) | 50,572 |
| 10. | **Joseph M. McDade*** (R) | **124,711** |
| | Joe Cullen (D) | 76,771 |
| 11. | **Paul E. Kanjorski*** (D) | **127,253** |
| | Stephen A. Urban (R) | 58,586 |

| Dist. | Representative (Party) | 1996 Election |
|---|---|---|
| 12. | **John P. Murtha*** (D) | **136,406** |
| | Bill Choby (R) | 58,628 |
| 13. | **Jon D. Fox*** (R) | **120,297** |
| | Joseph M. Hoeffel (D) | 120,287 |
| 14. | **William J. Coyne*** (D) | **122,440** |
| | Bill Ravotti (R) | 78,800 |
| 15. | **Paul McHale*** (D) | **109,377** |
| | Bob Kilbanks (R) | 80,784 |
| 16. | **Joseph R. Pitts** (R) | **124,560** |
| | James G. Blaine (D) | 78,572 |
| 17. | **George W. Gekas*** (R) | **150,559** |
| | Paul Kettl (D) | 57,874 |
| 18. | **Mike Doyle*** (D) | **120,181** |
| | David B. Fawcett (R) | 86,816 |
| 19. | **Bill Goodling*** (R) | **130,552** |
| | Scott L. Chronister (D) | 74,755 |
| 20. | **Frank R. Mascara*** (D) | **113,302** |
| | Mike McCormick (R) | 97,037 |
| 21. | **Phil English*** (R) | **106,421** |
| | Ronald A. DiNicola (D) | 103,675 |
| | **Rhode Island** | |
| 1. | **Patrick J. Kennedy*** (D) | **115,733** |
| | Giovanni D. Cicione (R) | 47,266 |
| 2. | **Robert A. Weygand** (D) | **110,345** |
| | Richard E. Wild (R) | 53,837 |
| | **South Carolina** | |
| 1. | **Mark Sanford*** (R) | **136,576** |
| | Joseph F. Innella (NL) | 4,999 |
| 2. | **Floyd D. Spence*** (R) | **157,685** |
| | Maurice T. Raiford (NL) | 17,624 |
| 3. | **Lindsey Graham*** (R) | **106,862** |
| | Debbie Dorn (D) | 67,660 |
| 4. | **Bob Inglis*** (R) | **137,386** |
| | Darrell E. Curry (D) | 53,837 |
| 5. | **John M. Spratt*** (D) | **96,390** |
| | Larry L. Bigham (R) | 80,950 |
| 6. | **James E. Clyburn*** (D) | **120,012** |
| | Gary McLeod (R) | 52,096 |
| | **South Dakota** | |
| | **John R. Thune** (R) | **186,330** |
| | Rick Weiland (D) | 119,406 |
| | **Tennessee** | |
| 1. | **William L. "Bill" Jenkins** (R) | **117,922** |
| | Kay. C. Smith (D) | 61,346 |
| 2. | **John J. Duncan, Jr.*** (R) | **149,205** |
| | Stephen Smith (D) | 60,267 |
| 3. | **Zach Wamp*** (R) | **113,411** |
| | Charles N. "Chuck" Jolly (D) | 85,678 |
| 4. | **Van Hilleary*** (R) | **102,993** |
| | Mark Stewart (D) | 72,950 |
| 5. | **Bob Clement*** (D) | **140,025** |
| | Steven L. Edmondson (R) | 45,988 |
| 6. | **Bart Gordon*** (D) | **123,786** |
| | Steve Gill (R) | 94,572 |
| 7. | **Ed Bryant*** (R) | **136,720** |
| | Don Trotter (D) | 73,752 |
| 8. | **John Tanner*** (D) | **121,993** |
| | Tom Watson (R) | 54,499 |
| 9. | **Harold E. Ford, Jr.** (D) | **116,304** |
| | Rod DeBerry (R) | 70,886 |
| | **Texas** | |
| 1. | **Max Sandlin** (D) | **103,924** |
| | Ed Merritt (R) | 94,107 |
| 2. | **Jim Turner** (D) | **102,868** |
| | Brian Babin (R) | 89,810 |
| 3. | **Sam Johnson*** (R) | **142,325** |
| | Lee Cole (D) | 47,654 |
| 4. | **Ralph M. Hall*** (D) | **132,128** |
| | Jerry Ray Hall (R) | 71,065 |
| 5. | **Pete Sessions** (R) | **80,311** |
| | John Pouland (D) | 71,065 |
| 6. | **Joe Barton*** (R) | **160,800** |
| | Janet Carroll "Skeet" Richardson (I) | 26,713 |
| 7. | **Bill Archer*** (R) | **151,997** |
| | Al J. K. Siegmund (D) | 28,186 |
| 8. | Kevin Brady (R)[9] | 80,334 |
| | Gene Fontenot (R)[9] | 75,398 |

| Dist. | Representative (Party) | 1996 Election |
|---|---|---|
| 9. | Steve Stockman* (R)[9] | 88,171 |
| | Nick Lampson (D)[9] | 83,781 |
| 10. | **Lloyd Doggett*** (D) | **132,066** |
| | Teresa Doggett (R) | 97,204 |
| 11. | **Chet Edwards*** (D) | **100,107** |
| | Jay Mathis (R) | 74,712 |
| 12. | **Kay Granger** (R) | **98,349** |
| | Hugh Parmer (D) | 69,859 |
| 13. | **William M. "Mac" Thornberry*** (R) | **115,899** |
| | Samuel Brown Silverman (D) | 55,743 |
| 14. | **Ron Paul** (R) | **99,970** |
| | Charles "Lefty" Morris (D) | 93,326 |
| 15. | **Ruben Hinojosa** (D) | **85,442** |
| | Tom Haughey (R) | 50,608 |
| 16. | **Silvestre Reyes** (D) | **90,260** |
| | Rick Ledesma (R) | 35,271 |
| 17. | **Charles W. Stenholm*** (D) | **99,458** |
| | Rudy Izzard (R) | 91,197 |
| 18. | **Sheila Jackson Lee*** (D) | **106,097** |
| | Lary White (R) | 13,955 |
| 19. | **Larry Combest*** (R) | **156,845** |
| | John W. Sawyer (D) | 38,283 |
| 20. | **Henry B. Gonzalez*** (D) | **88,190** |
| | James Walker (R) | 47,616 |
| 21. | **Lamar Smith*** (R) | **205,829** |
| | Gordon H. Wharton (D) | 60,338 |
| 22. | **Tom DeLay*** (R) | **126,054** |
| | Scott Douglas Cunningham (D) | 59,029 |
| 23. | **Henry Bonilla*** (R) | **101,340** |
| | Charles P. Jones (D) | 59,549 |
| 24. | **Martin Frost*** (D) | **77,847** |
| | Ed Harrison (R) | 54,551 |
| 25. | Ken Bentsen* (D)[9] | 43,693 |
| | Dolly Madison McKenna (R)[9] | 21,898 |
| | Beverley Clark (D)[9] | 21,698 |
| 26. | **Dick Armey*** (R) | **163,708** |
| | Jerry Frankel (D) | 58,623 |
| 27. | **Solomon P. Ortiz*** (D) | **97,251** |
| | Joe Gardner (R) | 50,962 |
| 28. | **Frank Tejeda*** (D) | **110,143** |
| | Mark L. Cude (R) | 34,190 |
| 29. | **Gene Green*** (D) | **61,872** |
| | Jack Rodriguez (R) | 28,535 |
| 30. | **Eddie Bernice Johnson*** (D) | **61,723** |
| | John Hendry (R) | 20,664 |

**Utah**

| Dist. | Representative (Party) | 1996 Election |
|---|---|---|
| 1. | **James V. Hansen*** (R) | **149,216** |
| | Gregory J. Sanders (D) | 65,515 |
| 2. | **Merrill Cook** (R) | **129,339** |
| | Ross C. Anderson (D) | 99,689 |
| 3. | **Christopher B. Cannon** (R) | **105,297** |
| | Bill Orton* (D) | 97,416 |

**Vermont**

| Dist. | Representative (Party) | 1996 Election |
|---|---|---|
| | **Bernie Sanders*** (I) | **139,756** |
| | Susan W. Sweetser (R) | 82,351 |
| | Jack Long (D) | 23,839 |

**Virginia**

| Dist. | Representative (Party) | 1996 Election |
|---|---|---|
| 1. | **Herbert H. "Herb" Bateman*** (R) | **Unopposed** |
| 2. | **Owen B. Pickett*** (D) | **106,208** |
| | John F. Tate (R) | 56,682 |
| 3. | **Robert C. "Bobby" Scott*** (D) | **117,399** |
| | Elsie Goodwyn Holland (R) | 25,471 |
| 4. | **Norman Sisisky*** (D) | **157,807** |
| | Anthony J. "Tony" Zevgolis (R) | 43,237 |
| 5. | **Virgil H. Goode, Jr.** (D) | **118,949** |
| | George C. Landrith, III (R) | 72,000 |
| 6. | **Robert W. "Bob" Goodlatte*** (R) | **132,599** |
| | Jeffrey W. Grey (D) | 61,398 |
| 7. | **Thomas J. "Tom" Bliley, Jr.*** (R) | **188,626** |
| | Roderic H. Slayton (D) | 50,839 |
| 8. | **James P. Moran, Jr.*** (D) | **145,140** |
| | John E. Otey (R) | 62,126 |
| 9. | **Frederick C. "Rick" Boucher*** (D) | **122,866** |
| | Patrick C. Muldoon (R) | 58,038 |
| 10. | **Frank R. Wolf*** (R) | **163,593** |
| | Robert L. "Bob" Weinberg (D) | 57,845 |
| 11. | **Thomas M. Davis, III*** (R) | **129,807** |
| | Thomas J. "Tom" Horton (D) | 69,886 |

**Washington**

| Dist. | Representative (Party) | 1996 Election |
|---|---|---|
| 1. | **Rick White*** (R) | **106,372** |
| | Jeff Coopersmith (D) | 97,711 |
| 2. | **Kevin Quigley** (D) | **99,155** |
| | Jack Metcalf* (R) | 96,826 |
| 3. | **Brian Baird** (D) | **102,044** |
| | Linda Smith* (R) | 99,397 |
| 4. | **Doc Hastings*** (R) | **87,033** |
| | Rick Locke (D) | 80,352 |
| 5. | **George R. Nethercutt, Jr.*** (R) | **110,338** |
| | Judy Olson (D) | 90,612 |
| 6. | **Norm Dicks*** (D) | **123,815** |
| | Bill Tinsley (R) | 51,179 |
| 7. | **Jim McDermott*** (D) | **173,668** |
| | Frank Kleschen (R) | 37,456 |
| 8. | **Jennifer Dunn*** (R) | **121,550** |
| | Dave Little (D) | 69,757 |
| 9. | **Adam Smith** (D) | **81,029** |
| | Randy Tate* (R) | 72,367 |

**West Virginia**

| Dist. | Representative (Party) | 1996 Election |
|---|---|---|
| 1. | **Alan B. Mollohan*** (D) | **Unopposed** |
| 2. | **Bob Wise*** (D) | **139,778** |
| | Greg Morris (R) | 63,036 |
| 3. | **Nick Joe Rahall*** (D) | **Unopposed** |

**Wisconsin**

| Dist. | Representative (Party) | 1996 Election |
|---|---|---|
| 1. | **Mark W. Neumann*** (R) | **118,397** |
| | Lydia C. Spottswood (D) | 113,850 |
| 2. | **Scott L. Klug*** (R) | **154,553** |
| | Paul R. Soglin (D) | 110,560 |
| 3. | **Ron Kind** (D) | **122,462** |
| | James E. Harsdorf (R) | 112,686 |
| 4. | **Gerald D. Kleczka*** (D) | **134,017** |
| | Tom Reynolds (R) | 98,398 |
| 5. | **Tom Barrett*** (D) | **140,697** |
| | Paul D. Melotik (R) | 47,274 |
| 6. | **Thomas E. Petri*** (R) | **168,941** |
| | Al Lindskoog (D) | 55,047 |
| 7. | **David R. Obey*** (D) | **136,397** |
| | Scott West (R) | 102,807 |
| 8. | **Jay Johnson** (D) | **129,544** |
| | David Prosser (R) | 119,666 |
| 9. | **F. James Sensenbrenner, Jr.*** (R) | **197,929** |
| | Floyd Brenholt (D) | 67,744 |

**Wyoming**

| Dist. | Representative (Party) | 1996 Election |
|---|---|---|
| | **Barbara Cubin*** (R) | **115,664** |
| | Pete Maxfield (D) | 85,742 |

Nonvoting members (104th Congress): Carlos A. Romero Barceló (D), resident commissioner, Puerto Rico; Eleanor Holmes Norton (D), District of Columbia; Robert Underwood (D), Guam; Eni F. H. Faleomavaega (D), American Samoa; Victor O. Frazer (I), Virgin Islands.

(1) Tom Campbell won a Dec. 12, 1995, special election to replace Norman Y. Mineta who resigned. (2) Juanita M. McDonald won a Mar. 26, 1996, special election to replace Walter R. Tucker, who resigned after a bribery conviction. (3) No winner had been declared as of Nov. 7, 1996. (4) John Nathan Deal changed his party designation to Republican in 1995. (5) Jesse Jackson, Jr. won a Dec. 12, 1995, special election to replace Mel Reynolds, who resigned after his criminal conviction relating to his having had sex with a minor. (6) W. J. "Billy" Tauzin changed his party designation to Republican in 1995. (7) Elijah E. Cummings won an Apr. 16, 1996, special election to replace Kweisi Mfume, who resigned to become president of the NAACP. (8) Earl Blumenauer won a May 21, 1996, special election to replace Ron Wyden, who was elected to fill the Senate seat of Bob Packwood. (9) Based on a 1996 Federal decision, the lines of 13 Texas districts were redrawn. A candidate had to receive a majority of the vote to win in the Nov. 5, 1996, election. In these 3 districts, no candidate received a majority, so the top 2 vote-getters will compete in a runoff on Dec. 10, 1996.

# Congressional Committees

## Senate Standing Committees

(as of Oct. 31, 1996)

**Agriculture, Nutrition, and Forestry**
Chairman: Richard G. Lugar, IN
Ranking Dem.: Patrick J. Leahy, VT

**Appropriations**
Chairman: Mark O. Hatfield, OR
Ranking Dem.: Robert C. Byrd, WV

**Armed Services**
Chairman: Strom Thurmond, SC
Ranking Dem.: Sam Nunn, GA

**Banking, Housing, and Urban Affairs**
Chairman: Alfonse M. D'Amato, NY
Ranking Dem.: Paul S. Sarbanes, MD

**Budget**
Chairman: Pete V. Domenici, NM
Ranking Dem.: J. James Exon, NE

**Commerce, Science, and Transportation**
Chairman: Larry Pressler, SD
Ranking Dem.: Ernest F. "Fritz" Hollings, SC

**Energy and Natural Resources**
Chairman: Frank H. Murkowski, AK
Ranking Dem.: J. Bennett Johnston, LA

**Environment and Public Works**
Chairman: John H. Chafee, RI
Ranking Dem.: Max Baucus, MT

**Finance**
Chairman: William V. Roth, Jr., DE
Ranking Dem.: Daniel Patrick Moynihan, NY

**Foreign Relations**
Chairman: Jesse Helms, NC
Ranking Dem.: Claiborne Pell, RI

**Governmental Affairs**
Chairman: Ted Stevens, AK
Ranking Dem.: John Glenn, OH

**Indian Affairs**
Chairman: John McCain, AZ
Ranking Dem.: Daniel K. Inouye, HI

**Judiciary**
Chairman: Orrin G. Hatch, UT
Ranking Dem.: Joseph R. Biden, Jr., DE

**Labor and Human Resources**
Chairman: Nancy Landon Kassebaum, KS
Ranking Dem.: Edward M. Kennedy, MA

**Rules and Administration**
Chairman: John W. Warner, VA
Ranking Dem.: Wendell H. Ford, KY

**Small Business**
Chairman: Christopher "Kit" Bond, MO
Ranking Dem.: Dale Bumpers, AR

**Veterans' Affairs**
Chairman: Alan K. Simpson, WY
Ranking Dem.: John D. Rockefeller IV, WV

## Senate Select Committees

(as of Oct. 31, 1996)

**Aging**
Chairman: William S. Cohen, ME
Ranking Dem.: David H. Pryor, AR

**Ethics**
Chairman: Mitch McConnell, KY
Ranking Dem.: Byron L. Dorgan, ND

**Intelligence**
Chairman: Arlen Specter, PA
V. Chairman: Bob Kerrey, NE

## House Select Committee

(as of Oct. 31, 1996)

**Intelligence**
Chairman: Larry Combest, TX
Ranking Dem.: Norman Dicks, WA

## Joint Committees of Congress

(as of Oct. 31, 1996)

**Economic**
Chairman: Sen. Connie Mack, FL
V. Chairman: Rep. Jim Saxton, NJ

**Library**
Chairman: Sen. Mark O. Hatfield, OR
V. Chairman: Rep. Bill Thomas, CA

**Printing**
Chairman: Rep. Bill Thomas, CA
V. Chairman: Sen. John W. Warner, VA

**Taxation**
Chairman: Rep. Bill Archer, TX
V. Chairman: Sen. William V. Roth, Jr., DE

## House Standing Committees

(as of Oct. 31, 1996)

**Agriculture**
Chairman: Pat Roberts, KS
Ranking Dem.: E. "Kika" de la Garza, TX

**Appropriations**
Chairman: Robert L. "Bob" Livingston, LA
Ranking Dem.: David R. Obey, WI

**Banking and Financial Services**
Chairman: Jim Leach, IA
Ranking Dem.: Henry B. Gonzalez, TX

**Budget**
Chairman: John R. Kasich, OH
Ranking Dem.: Martin Olav Sabo, MN

**Commerce**
Chairman: Thomas J. "Tom" Bliley, Jr., VA
Ranking Dem.: John D. Dingell, MI

**Economic and Educational Opportunities**
Chairman: Bill Goodling, PA
Ranking Dem.: William "Bill" Clay, Sr., MO

**Government Reform and Oversight**
Chairman: William F. "Bill" Clinger, Jr., PA
Ranking Dem.: Cardiss Collins, IL

**House Oversight**
Chairman: Bill Thomas, CA
Ranking Dem.: Vic Fazio, CA

**International Relations**
Chairman: Benjamin A. Gilman, NY
Ranking Dem.: Lee H. Hamilton, IN

**Judiciary**
Chairman: Henry J. Hyde, IL
Ranking Dem.: John Conyers, Jr., MI

**National Security**
Chairman: Floyd D. Spence, SC
Ranking Dem.: Ronald V. Dellums, CA

**Resources**
Chairman: Don Young, AK
Ranking Dem.: George Miller, CA

**Rules**
Chairman: Gerald B. H. Solomon, NY
Ranking Dem.: John Joseph Moakley, MA

**Science**
Chairman: Robert S. Walker, PA
Ranking Dem.: George E. Brown, Jr., CA

**Small Business**
Chairman: Jan Meyers, KS
Ranking Dem.: John J. LaFalce, NY

**Standards of Official Conduct**
Chairman: Nancy L. Johnson, CT
Ranking Dem.: Jim McDermott, WA

**Transportation and Infrastructure**
Chairman: Bud Shuster, PA
Ranking Dem.: James L. Oberstar, MN

**Veterans' Affairs**
Chairman: Bob Stump, AZ
Ranking Dem.: G. V. "Sonny" Montgomery, MS

**Ways and Means**
Chairman: Bill Archer, TX
Ranking Dem.: Sam M. Gibbons, FL

# Political Divisions of the U.S. Senate and House of Representatives, 1901-96

**Source:** Clerk of the House of Representatives; Secretary of the Senate; Voter News Service

| | | Senate | | | | | House of Representatives | | | | |
|---|---|---|---|---|---|---|---|---|---|---|---|
| Congress | Years | No. of Sen | Demo-crats | Repub-licans | Other parties | Vacant | No. of Rep | Demo-crats | Repub-licans | Other parties | Vacant |
| 57th | 1901-03 | 90 | 29 | 56 | 3 | 2 | 357 | 153 | 198 | 5 | 1 |
| 58th | 1903-05 | 90 | 32 | 58 | | | 386 | 178 | 207 | | 1 |
| 59th | 1905-07 | 90 | 32 | 58 | | | 386 | 136 | 250 | | |
| 60th | 1907-09 | 92 | 29 | 61 | | 2 | 386 | 164 | 222 | | |
| 61st | 1909-11 | 92 | 32 | 59 | | 1 | 391 | 172 | 219 | | |
| 62d | 1911-13 | 92 | 42 | 49 | | 1 | 391 | 228 | 162 | | |
| 63d | 1913-15 | 96 | 51 | 44 | 1 | | 435 | 290 | 127 | 18 | |
| 64th | 1915-17 | 96 | 56 | 39 | 1 | | 435 | 231 | 193 | 8 | 3 |
| 65th | 1917-19 | 96 | 53 | 42 | 1 | | 435 | 210[1] | 216 | 9 | |
| 66th | 1919-21 | 96 | 47 | 48 | 1 | | 435 | 191 | 237 | 7 | |
| 67th | 1921-23 | 96 | 37 | 59 | | | 435 | 132 | 300 | 1 | 2 |
| 68th | 1923-25 | 96 | 43 | 51 | 2 | | 435 | 207 | 225 | 3 | |
| 69th | 1925-27 | 96 | 40 | 54 | 1 | 1 | 435 | 183 | 247 | 5 | |
| 70th | 1927-29 | 96 | 47 | 48 | 1 | | 435 | 195 | 237 | 3 | |
| 71st | 1329-31 | 96 | 39 | 56 | 1 | | 435 | 163 | 267 | 1 | 4 |
| 72d | 1931-33 | 96 | 47 | 48 | 1 | | 435 | 216[2] | 218 | 1 | |
| 73d | 1933-35 | 96 | 59 | 36 | 1 | | 435 | 313 | 117 | 5 | |
| 74th | 1935-37 | 96 | 69 | 25 | 2 | | 435 | 322 | 103 | 10 | |
| 75th | 1937-39 | 96 | 75 | 17 | 4 | | 435 | 333 | 89 | 13 | |
| 76th | 1939-41 | 96 | 69 | 23 | 4 | | 435 | 262 | 169 | 4 | |
| 77th | 1941-43 | 96 | 66 | 28 | 2 | | 435 | 267 | 162 | 6 | |
| 78th | 1943-45 | 96 | 57 | 38 | 1 | | 435 | 222 | 209 | 4 | |
| 79th | 1945-47 | 96 | 57 | 38 | 1 | | 435 | 243 | 190 | 2 | |
| 80th | 1947-49 | 96 | 45 | 51 | | | 435 | 188 | 246 | 1 | |
| 81st | 1949-51 | 96 | 54 | 42 | | | 435 | 263 | 171 | 1 | |
| 82d | 1951-53 | 96 | 48 | 47 | 1 | | 435 | 234 | 199 | 2 | |
| 83d | 1953-55 | 96 | 46 | 48 | 2 | | 435 | 213 | 221 | 1 | |
| 84th | 1955-57 | 96 | 48 | 47 | 1 | | 435 | 232 | 203 | | |
| 85th | 1957-59 | 96 | 49 | 47 | | | 435 | 234 | 201 | | |
| 86th | 1959-61 | 98 | 64 | 34 | | | 436[3] | 283 | 153 | | |
| 87th | 1961-63 | 100 | 64 | 36 | | | 437[4] | 262 | 175 | | |
| 88th | 1963-65 | 100 | 67 | 33 | | | 435 | 258 | 176 | | 1 |
| 89th | 1965-67 | 100 | 68 | 32 | | | 435 | 295 | 140 | | |
| 90th | 1967-69 | 100 | 64 | 36 | | | 435 | 248 | 187 | | |
| 91st | 1969-71 | 100 | 58 | 42 | | | 435 | 243 | 192 | | |
| 92d | 1971-73 | 100 | 54 | 44 | 2 | | 435 | 255 | 180 | | |
| 93d | 1973-75 | 100 | 56 | 42 | 2 | | 435 | 242 | 192 | 1 | |
| 94th | 1975-77 | 100 | 61 | 37 | 2 | | 435 | 291 | 144 | | |
| 95th | 1977-79 | 100 | 61 | 38 | 1 | | 435 | 292 | 143 | | |
| 96th | 1979-81 | 100 | 58 | 41 | 1 | | 435 | 276 | 159 | | |
| 97th | 1981-83 | 100 | 46 | 53 | 1 | | 435 | 242 | 190 | | 3 |
| 98th | 1983-85 | 100 | 46 | 54 | | | 435 | 269 | 166 | | |
| 99th | 1985-87 | 100 | 47 | 53 | | | 435 | 253 | 182 | | |
| 100th | 1987-89 | 100 | 54 | 46 | | | 435 | 258 | 177 | | |
| 101st | 1989-91 | 100 | 57 | 43 | | | 435 | 262 | 173 | | |
| 102d | 1991-93 | 100 | 57 | 43 | | | 435 | 266 | 164 | 1 | 4 |
| 103d | 1993-95 | 100 | 56 | 44 | | | 435 | 256 | 178 | 1 | |
| 104th | 1995-97 | 100 | 47 | 53 | | | 435 | 197 | 235 | 1 | 2 |
| 105th | 1997-99 | 100 | 45[5] | 54[5] | | | 435 | 204[5] | 222[5] | 2[5] | |

(1) Democrats organized House with help of other parties. (2) Democrats organized House due to Republican deaths. (3) Proclamation declaring AK a State issued Jan. 3, 1959. (4) Proclamation declaring HI a State issued Aug. 21, 1959. (5) As of Nov. 7, 1996.

# Congressional Bills Vetoed, 1789-1996

**Source:** Senate Library

| | Regular vetoes | Pocket vetoes | Total vetoes | Vetoes overridden |
|---|---|---|---|---|
| Washington | 2 | — | 2 | — |
| John Adams | — | — | — | — |
| Jefferson | — | — | — | — |
| Madison | 5 | 2 | 7 | — |
| Monroe | 1 | — | 1 | — |
| John Q. Adams | — | — | — | — |
| Jackson | 5 | 7 | 12 | — |
| Van Buren | — | 1 | 1 | — |
| William Harrison | — | — | — | — |
| Tyler | 6 | 4 | 10 | 1 |
| Polk | 2 | 1 | 3 | — |
| Taylor | — | — | — | — |
| Fillmore | — | — | — | — |
| Pierce | 9 | — | 9 | 5 |
| Buchanan | 4 | 3 | 7 | — |
| Lincoln | 2 | 5 | 7 | — |
| Andrew Johnson | 21 | 8 | 29 | 15 |
| Grant | 45 | 48 | 93 | 4 |
| Hayes | 12 | 1 | 13 | 1 |
| Garfield | — | — | — | — |
| Arthur | 4 | 8 | 12 | 1 |
| Cleveland | 304 | 110 | 414 | 2 |
| Benjamin Harrison | 19 | 25 | 44 | 1 |
| Cleveland | 42 | 128 | 170 | 5 |
| McKinley | 6 | 36 | 42 | — |
| Theodore Roosevelt | 42 | 40 | 82 | 1 |
| Taft | 30 | 9 | 39 | 1 |
| Wilson | 33 | 11 | 44 | 6 |
| Harding | 5 | 1 | 6 | — |
| Coolidge | 20 | 30 | 50 | 4 |
| Hoover | 21 | 16 | 37 | 3 |
| Franklin Roosevelt | 372 | 263 | 635 | 9 |
| Truman | 180 | 70 | 250 | 12 |
| Eisenhower | 73 | 108 | 181 | 2 |
| Kennedy | 12 | 9 | 21 | — |
| Lyndon Johnson | 16 | 14 | 30 | — |
| Nixon | 26 | 17 | 43 | 7 |
| Ford | 48 | 18 | 66 | 12 |
| Carter | 13 | 18 | 31 | 2 |
| Reagan | 39 | 39 | 78 | 9 |
| Bush[1] | 29 | 15 | 44 | 1 |
| Clinton[2] | 17 | — | 17 | 1 |
| **Total[1]** | **1,464** | **1,065** | **2,530** | **105** |

(1) Excluded from the figures are 2 additional bills, which Pres. Bush claimed to be vetoed but Congress considered enacted into law because the president failed to return them to Congress during a recess period. (2) As of Oct. 30, 1996.

# STATE AND LOCAL GOVERNMENT

## Mayors of Selected U.S. Cities

Reflects Nov. 5, 1996, elections (preliminary results)

D, Democrat; R, Republican; N-P, Non-Partisan; I, Independent

| City | Name | Next Election |
|---|---|---|
| Abilene, TX | Gary McCaleb, N-P | 1999, May |
| Akron, OH | Donald L. Plusquellic, D | 1999, Nov. |
| Alameda, CA | Ralph J. Appezato, N-P | 1998, Nov. |
| Albany, GA | Thomas Coleman, D | 1997, Nov. |
| Albany, NY | Gerald D. Jennings, D | 1997, Nov. |
| Albuquerque, NM | Martin Chavez, D | 1997, Oct. |
| Alexandria, LA | Edward Randolph Jr., D | 1998, Oct. |
| Alexandria, VA | Kerry J. Donley, D | 1997, May |
| Alhambra, CA | Paul Talbot, N-P | ([1]) |
| Allentown, PA | William Heydt, R | 1997, Nov. |
| Amarillo, TX | Kel Seliger, N-P | 1997, May |
| Ames, IA | Larry R. Curtis, N-P | 1997, Nov. |
| Anaheim, CA | Tom Daly, N-P | 1998, Nov. |
| Anchorage, AK | Rick Mystrom, R | 1997, July |
| Anderson, IN | J. Mark Lawler, D | 1999, Nov. |
| Anderson, SC | Darwin Wright, D | 1998, June |
| Ann Arbor, MI | Ingrid B. Sheldon, R | 1998, Nov. |
| Annapolis, MD | Alfred A. Hopkins, D | 1997, Nov. |
| Appleton, WI | Richard De Broux, N-P | 2000, Apr. |
| Arcadia, CA | Barbara D. Kuhn, N-P | 1997, Apr. |
| Arlington, MA | Charles Lyons, D | 1998, Nov. |
| Arlington, TX | Richard Greene, N-P | 1997, May |
| Arlington Hts., IL | Arlene J. Mulder, N-P | 1997, Apr. |
| Arvada, CO | Robert G. Frie, N-P | 1999, Nov. |
| Asheville, NC | Russel Martin, N-P | 1997, Nov. |
| Athens, GA | Gwenn O'Looney, D | 1998, Nov. |
| Atlanta, GA | Bill Campbell, D | 1997, Nov. |
| Atlantic City, NJ | Jim Whelan, N-P | 1998, June |
| Augusta, GA | Larry Sconyers, N-P | 1999, Nov. |
| Augusta, ME | John C. Bridge, R | 1998, Nov. |
| Aurora, CO | Paul E. Tauer, N-P | 1999, Nov. |
| Aurora, IL | David L. Pierce, N-P | 1997, Apr. |
| Austin, TX | Bruce Todd, N-P | 1997, May |
| Bakersfield, CA | Bob Price, N-P | 2000, Mar. |
| Baldwin Park, CA | Fidel A. Vargas, N-P | 1997, Mar. |
| Baltimore, MD | Kurt Schmoke, D | 1999, Nov. |
| Baton Rouge, LA | Tom E. McHugh, D | 1997, Nov. |
| Battle Creek, MI | Ted Dearing, N-P | 1996, Nov.[2] |
| Bayonne, NJ | Leonard P. Kiczek, N-P | 1998, May |
| Baytown, TX | Pete C. Alfaro, N-P | 1998, May |
| Beaumont, TX | David W. Moore, N-P | 1998, May |
| Belleville, IL | Roger C. Cook, I | 1997, Apr. |
| Bellevue, WA | Ron Smith, I | 1998, Nov. |
| Bellingham, WA | Mark Asmundson, N-P | 1999, Nov. |
| Bellflower, CA | Randy Boomgaars, N-P | 1997, Jan. |
| Berkeley, CA | Shirley Dean, N-P | 1998, Dec. |
| Bethlehem, PA | Kenneth R. Smith, R | 1997, Nov. |
| Beverly Hills, CA | Thomas S. Levyn, D | 1997, Apr. |
| Billings, MT | Charles F. Tooley, N-P | 1997, Nov. |
| Biloxi, MS | A. J. Holloway, R | 1997, June |
| Binghamton, NY | Richard A. Bucci, R | 1997, Nov. |
| Birmingham, AL | Richard Arrington Jr., D | 1999, Oct. |
| Bismarck, ND | Bill Sorensen, R | 1998, June |
| Bloomfield, NJ | James P. Norton, R | 1998, Nov. |
| Bloomington, IL | Jesse Smart, R | 1997, Apr. |
| Bloomington, IN | John Fernandez, D | 1999, Nov. |
| Bloomington, MN | Carol Houle, N-P | 1997, Nov. |
| Boca Raton, FL | Carol G. Hanson, N-P | 1997, Apr. |
| Boise, ID | Brent Coles, N-P | 1997, Nov. |
| Bossier City, LA | George Dement, N-P | 1997, Apr. |
| Boston, MA | Thomas M. Menino, D | 1997, Nov. |
| Boulder, CO | Leslie L. Durgin, N-P | 1997, Nov. |
| Bridgeport, CT | Joseph Ganim, D | 1997, Nov. |
| Bristol, CT | Frank N. Nicastro, D | 1997, Nov. |
| Brockton, MA | John T. Yunits Jr., D | 1997, Nov. |
| Broken Arrow, OK | Jim Reynolds, N-P | 1999, Apr. |
| Brooklyn Park, MN | Grace Arborgast | 1998, Nov. |
| Brownsville, TX | Henry Gonzalez, N-P | 1999, May |
| Bryan, TX | Lonnie Stabler, N-P | 1997, May |
| Buena Park, CA | Patsy Marshall, N-P | 1996, Dec. |
| Buffalo, NY | Anthony M. Masiello, D | 1997, Nov. |
| Burbank, CA | Dave Golonski, N-P | 1997, May |
| Burlington, VT | Peter Clavelle, Prog. Coalition | 1997, Mar. |
| Calumet City, IL | Gerome P. Genova, I | 1997, Apr. |
| Camarillo, CA | Michael D. Morgan, N-P | 1998, Dec. |
| Cambridge, MA | Sheila Doyle Russell, D | 1998, Jan. |
| Camden, NJ | Arnold Webster, D | 1997, Nov. |
| Canton, OH | Richard Watkins, R | 1999, Nov. |
| Cape Coral, FL | Roger G. Butler, N-P | 2000, Nov. |
| Carlsbad, CA | Claude Lewis, N-P | 1998, Nov. |
| Carson, CA | Michael Mitoma, N-P | 1998, May. |
| Carson City, NV | Ray Maysako, N-P | 2000, Nov. |
| Casper, WY | Owen Jones, N-P | 1997, Jan. |
| Cedar Rapids, IA | Lee R. Clancey, N-P | 1997, Nov. |
| Champaign, IL | Dan McCollum, N-P | 1999, Apr. |
| Chandler, AZ | Jay Tibshraeny, N-P | 1998, Mar. |
| Charleston, SC | Joseph P. Riley Jr., D | 1999, Nov. |
| Charleston, WV | G. Kemp Melton, D | 1999, Apr. |
| Charlotte, NC | Pat McCrory, R | 1997, Nov. |
| Charlottesville, VA | Kay Slaughter, D | 1998, May |
| Chattanooga, TN | Gene Roberts, R | 1997, Mar. |
| Chesapeake, VA | William E. Ward, N-P | 2000, May |
| Chester, PA | Aaron Wilson, R | 1999, Nov. |
| Cheyenne, WY | Leo Pando, N-P | 1997, Nov. |
| Chicago, IL | Richard M. Daley, D | 1999, Apr. |
| Chicopee, MA | Joseph J. Chessey, Jr., D | 1997, Nov. |
| Chino, CA | Eunice M. Ulloa, R | 2000, Nov. |
| Chula Vista, CA | Shirley Horton, I | 1998, Jun. |
| Cicero, IL | Betty Loren-Maltese, R | 1997, Apr. |
| Cincinnati, OH | Roxanne Qualls, D | 1999, Nov. |
| Clarksville, TN | Donald W. Trotter, N-P | 1998, Nov. |
| Clearwater, FL | Rita Garvey, N-P | 2000, Apr. |
| Cleveland, OH | Michael R. White, D | 1997, Nov. |
| Cleveland Hts., OH | Carol Edwards, N-P | 1997, Jan. |
| Clinton, IA | La Metta Wynn, N-P | 1999, Nov. |
| Clifton, NJ | James Anzaldi, R | 1998, May |
| Colorado Spgs., CO | Robert M. Isaac, N-P | 1999, Apr. |
| Columbia, MO | Darwin Hindman, N-P | 1998, Apr. |
| Columbia, SC | Robert D. Coble, N-P | 1998, Apr. |
| Columbus, GA | Bobby Peters, D | 1998, Nov. |
| Columbus, OH | Gregory S. Lashutka, R | 1999, Nov. |
| Compton, CA | Omar Bradley, N-P | 1997, June |
| Concord, CA | Lou Rosas, N-P | 1996, Nov.[3] |
| Concord, NH | William Veroneau, N-P | 1997, Nov. |
| Coon Rapids, MN | William Thompson, N-P | 1997, Nov. |
| Coral Gables, FL | Raul Valdes-Sauli, N-P | 1997, Mar. |
| Coral Springs, FL | John Sommerer, N-P | 1998, Mar. |
| Corona, CA | Andrea M. Puga, N-P | 1996, Dec. |
| Corpus Christi, TX | Mary Rhodes, N-P | 1997, Apr. |
| Costa Mesa, CA | Joe Erickson, N-P | 1996, Dec. |
| Council Bluffs, IA | Tom Hanafan, N-P | 1997, Nov. |
| Covington, KY | Denny Bowman, D | 1999, Nov. |
| Cranston, RI | Michael A. Traficante, R | 1998, Nov. |
| Cuyahoga Falls, OH | Donald L. Robart, R | 1997, Nov. |
| Dallas, TX | Ronald Kirk, N-P | 1998, June |
| Daly City, CA | Michael Guingona, N-P | 1996, Dec. |
| Danbury, CT | Gene Eriquez, D | 1997, Nov. |
| Danville, VA | E. Linwood Wright, N-P | 1998, July |
| Davenport, IA | Patrick J. Gibbs, R | 1997, Nov. |
| Davis, CA | Lois Wolk, N-P | 1998, Apr. |
| Dayton, OH | Michael R. Turner, N-P | 1997, Nov. |
| Daytona Beach, FL | Baron H. Asher, N-P | 1997, Oct. |
| Dearborn, MI | Michael Guido, N-P | 1997, Nov. |
| Dearborn Hts., MI | Ruth A. Canfield, N-P | 1997, Nov. |
| Decatur, IL | Terry M. Howley, N-P | 1999, May |
| Delray Beach, FL | Jay Alperin, N-P | 1998, Mar. |
| Denton, TX | Jack Miller, N-P | 1998, May |
| Denver, CO | Wellington Webb, N-P | 1999, May |
| Des Moines, IA | Arthur Davis, N-P | 1997, Nov. |
| Des Plaines, IL | Ted Sherwood, N-P | 1997, Apr. |
| Detroit, MI | Dennis W. Archer, D | 1997, Nov. |
| Dothan, AL | Alfred Saliba, N-P | 1997, July |
| Dover, DE | James L. Hutchinson, N-P | 1998, Apr. |
| Downey, CA | Barbara Riley, N-P | 1998, July |
| Dubuque, IA | Terrance M. Duggan, N-P | 1997, Nov. |
| Duluth, MN | Gary L. Doty, N-P | 1999, Nov. |
| Durham, NC | Sylvia S. Kerckhoff, N-P | 1997, Nov. |
| East Hartford, CT | Robert DeCrescenzo, D | 1997, Nov. |
| East Lansing, MI | Douglas B. Jester, N-P | 1997, Nov. |
| East Orange, NJ | Cardell Cooper, D | 1997, Nov. |
| Edison, NJ | George Spadoro, D | 1997, Nov. |
| Edmond, OK | Robert Rudkin, N-P | 1997, Apr. |
| El Cajon, CA | Joan Shoemaker, N-P | 1998, Nov. |
| Elgin, IL | Kevin Kelly, N-P | 1999, Apr. |
| Elizabeth, NJ | J. C. Bollwage, D | 2000, Mar. |
| Elkhart, IN | James P. Perron, D | 1999, Nov. |
| El Monte, CA | Patricia Wallach, D | 1997, Mar. |
| El Paso, TX | Larry Francis, N-P | 1997, June |
| Elyria, OH | Michael B. Keys, D | 1999, Nov. |
| Enfield, CT | Mary Lou Strom, R | 1997, Nov. |
| Enid, OK | Mike Cooper, N-P | 1997, Apr. |
| Erie, PA | Joyce Savocchio, D | 1997, Nov. |
| Escondido, CA | Sid Hollins, N-P | 1998, Nov.[4] |
| Euclid, OH | Paul Oyaski, D | 1999, Nov. |

*(continued)*

| City | Name | Next Election |
|---|---|---|
| Eugene, OR | Ruth Bascom, N-P | 1997, Jan. |
| Evanston, IL | Lorraine Morton, N-P | 1997, Apr. |
| Evansville, IN. | Frank F. McDonald II, D | 1999, Nov. |
| Everett, WA | Edward D. Hansen, N-P | 1997, Nov. |
| Fairbanks, AK | James C. Hayes | 1998, Oct. |
| Fairfield, CA | Chuck Hamond, N-P | 1997, Nov. |
| Fairfield, CT. | Paul A. Audley, R | 1997, Nov. |
| Fall River, MA | Edward Lambert Jr., D | 1997, Nov. |
| Fargo, ND | Bruce Furness, N-P | 1998, Apr. |
| Farmington Hills, MI | Aldo Vagnozzi, N-P | 1997, Nov. |
| Fayetteville, NC | J. L. Dawkins, N-P | 1997, Nov. |
| Fitchburg, MA | Jeffrey Bean, D | 1997, Jan. |
| Flagstaff, AZ | Christopher Bavasi, N-P | 2000, Apr. |
| Flint, MI. | Woodrow Stanley, D | 1999, Nov. |
| Florissant, MO | James J. Eagan, N-P | 1999, Apr. |
| Fontana, CA | David Eshleman, D | 1998, Nov. |
| Ft. Collins, CO | Ann Azari, N-P | 1997, Apr. |
| Ft. Lauderdale, FL | Jim Naugle, N-P | 1997, Mar. |
| Ft. Smith, AR. | Ray Baker, N-P | 1998, Nov. |
| Ft. Wayne, IN | Paul Helmke, R | 1999, Nov. |
| Ft. Worth, TX. | Kenneth L. Barr, N-P | 1997, May |
| Fountain Valley, CA | George Scott, N-P | 1996, Dec. |
| Frankfort, KY | William I. May Jr., N-P | 1999, Nov. |
| Fremont, CA | Gus Morrison, N-P | 2000, Nov. |
| Fresno, CA | Jim Patterson, N-P | 1997, Apr. |
| Fullerton, CA | Chris Norby, N-P | 1996, Dec. |
| Gadsden, AL. | Steve Means, N-P | 1998, Oct. |
| Gainesville, FL. | Edward Jennings Sr., N-P | 1997, May |
| Galveston, TX | Henry Freudenburg III, N-P | 1998, May |
| Gardena, CA | Donald L. Dear, N-P | 1997, Mar. |
| Garden Grove, CA | Bruce Broadwater, N-P | 1996, Dec. |
| Garland, TX. | James B. Ratliff, N-P | 1998, May |
| Gary, IN | Scott King, D | 1999, Nov. |
| Gastonia, NC. | James B. Garland, N-P | 1997, Nov. |
| Glendale, AZ | Elaine Scruggs, N-P | 1998, Mar. |
| Glendale, CA. | Richard M. Reyes, N-P | 1997, Apr. |
| Grand Forks, ND | Patricia Owens, N-P | 2000, June |
| Grand Prairie, TX. | Charles V. England, N-P | 1997, May |
| Grand Rapids, MI. | John Logie, N-P | 1999, Nov. |
| Greeley, CO | LaVern C. Nelson, N-P | 1997, Nov. |
| Green Bay, WI | Paul F. Jadin, N-P | 1999, Apr. |
| Greenville, SC | Knox White, R | 1999, Nov. |
| Greensboro, NC | Carolyn Allen, N-P | 1997, Nov. |
| Greenwich, CT. | Tom R. Ragland, R | 1997, Nov. |
| Groton, CT | Dolores Hauber, N-P | 1997, Nov. |
| Gulfport, MS | Ken Combs, R | 1997, June |
| Hamden, CT | Lillian D. Clayman, D | 1997, Nov. |
| Hamilton, OH. | Gregory V. Jolivette, N-P | 1997, Nov. |
| Hammond, IN | Duane W. Dadelow Jr. R | 1999, Nov. |
| Hampton, VA. | James L. Eason, N-P | 2000, May |
| Harrisburg, PA | Stephen Reed, D | 1997, Nov. |
| Hartford, CT | Michael P. Peters, N-P | 1997, Dec. |
| Haverhill, MA | James A. Rurak, D | 1997, Nov. |
| Hawthorne, CA | Larry Guidi, N-P | 1997, Nov. |
| Hayward, CA | Roberta Cooper, N-P | 1998, Mar. |
| Helena, MT | Colleen McCarthy, N-P | 1997, Nov. |
| Henderson, NV | Robert Groesbeck, N-P | 1997, June |
| Hialeah, FL | Raul Martinez, R | 1997, Nov. |
| High Point, NC | Rebecca R. Smothers, N-P | 1998, Nov. |
| Hoboken, NJ | Anthony Russo, N-P | 1997, June |
| Hollywood, FL | Mara Giulianti, N-P | 1998, Mar. |
| Holyoke, MA | Daniel Szostkiewicz, D | 1997, Nov. |
| Honolulu, HI | Jeremy Harris, N-P | 2000, Nov. |
| Houston, TX | Bob Lanier, N-P | 1997, Nov. |
| Huntington, WV | Jean Dean, R | 1997, June |
| Huntington Beach, CA | Ralph Bauer, N-P | 1997, Dec. |
| Huntington Park, CA | Tom Jackson, N-P | 1997, Apr. |
| Huntsville, AL | Loretta Spencer, N-P | 2000, Aug. |
| Idaho Falls, ID | Linda Milam, N-P | 1997, Nov. |
| Independence, MO | Ron Stewart, N-P | 1998, Apr. |
| Indianapolis, IN | Stevphen Goldsmith, R | 1999, Nov. |
| Inglewood, CA | Edward Vincent, D | 1999, Jan. |
| Iowa City, IA | Naomi Novick, N-P | 1998, Jan. |
| Irvine, CA | Christina Shea, N-P | 1998, Nov. |
| Irving, TX | Morris Parrish, N-P | 1997, May |
| Irvington, NJ | Sara A. Bost, D | 1998, May |
| Jackson, MS | Kane Ditto, D | 1997, June |
| Jacksonville, FL | John A. Delaney, R | 1999, May |
| Janesville, WI | Bill Schneider, N-P | 2000, Apr. |
| Jefferson City, MO | Duane Schreimann, D | 1999, Apr. |
| Jersey City, NJ | Bret Schundler, R | 1997, May |
| Johnson City, TN | Mickii Carter, N-P | 1997, May |
| Joliet, IL | Arthur Schultz, N-P | 1999, Apr. |
| Juneau, AK | Dennis Egan, D | 1997, Oct. |
| Kalamazoo, MI | Barbara Larson, N-P | 1997, Nov. |
| Kansas City, KS | Carol Marinovich, N-P | 1999, Apr. |
| Kansas City, MO | Emanuel Cleaver II, D | 1999, Apr. |
| Kenner, LA | Louis J. Congemi, R | 1998, Apr. |
| Kenosha, WI. | John Antaramian, D | 2000, Apr. |
| Kettering, OH | Richard Hartmann, R | 1997, Nov. |
| Killeen, TX | Raul G. Villaronga, N-P | 1997, May |
| Knoxville, TN | Victor Ashe, R | 2000, Nov. |
| Kokomo, IN | James Trobaugh, R | 1999, Nov. |
| LaCrosse, WI | Patrick T. Zielke, N-P | 1997, Apr. |
| Lafayette, IN. | Dave Heath, R | 1999, Nov. |
| La Habra, CA | Steve Anderson, N-P | 1996, Dec. |
| Lake Charles, LA | Willie L. Mount, D | 1997, May |
| Lakeland, FL | Ralph L. Fletcher, N-P | 2000, Sept. |
| Lakewood, CA | Robert Wagner, N-P | 1997, Mar. |
| Lakewood, CO | Linda Morton, N-P | 1999, Nov. |
| Lakewood, OH | Madeline Cain, D | 1999, Nov. |
| La Mesa, CA | Arthur Madrid, N-P | 1998, Nov. |
| La Mirada, CA | Wayne Rew, N-P | 1997, Apr. |
| Lancaster, CA. | Frank Roberts, N-P. | 1997, Apr. |
| Lancaster, PA. | Janice C. Stork, D | 1997, Nov. |
| Lansing, MI | David Hollister, N-P | 1997, Nov. |
| Laredo, TX. | Saul N. Ramirez Jr., N-P. | 1998, May |
| Largo, FL. | Thomas Feaster, N-P | 1997, Apr. |
| Las Cruces, NM | Ruben A. Smith, D | 1999, Nov. |
| Las Vegas, NV | Jan Laverty Jones, D | 1999, June |
| Lawrence, KS. | John Nalbaudian, N-P. | 1997, Apr. |
| Lawrence, MA | Mary Claire Kennedy, N-P | 1997, Apr. |
| Lawton, OK | John T. Marley, N-P | 1997, Jan. |
| Lexington, KY. | Pam Miller, N-P | 1998, Nov. |
| Lima, OH | David J. Berger, N-P. | 1997, Nov. |
| Lincoln, NE. | Mike Johanns, R | 1999, May |
| Little Rock, AR | Jim Dailey, N-P | 1999, Jan. |
| Livermore, CA | Cathie Brown, N-P | 1997, Nov. |
| Livonia, MI | Jack Kirksey, N-P. | 1999, Nov. |
| Lodi, CA. | David P. Warner, N-P | 1996, Dec. |
| Long Beach, CA | Beverly O'Neill, N-P | 1998, July |
| Longmont,CO | Leona Stoecker, N-P | 1997, Nov. |
| Longview, TX | I. J. Patterson Jr., N-P. | 1997, May |
| Lorain, OH | Joe Koziura | 1999, Nov. |
| Los Angeles, CA. | Richard Riordan, N-P | 1997, June |
| Louisville, KY | Jerry E. Abramson, D | 1998, Nov. |
| Lowell, MA | Edward Caufield, N-P | 1998, Jan. |
| Lubbock, TX. | David R. Langston, N-P | 1998, May |
| Lynchburg, VA | James S. Whitaker, N-P | 1998, July |
| Lynn, MA | Patrick J. McManus, D | 1997, Nov. |
| Lynwood, CA | Paul Richards, III, N-P | 1996, Dec. |
| Macon, GA. | Jim Marshall, D | 1999, Nov. |
| Madison, WI | Paul R. Soglin, D | 1999, Apr. |
| Malden, MA | Richard Howard, D. | 1997, Nov. |
| Manchester, CT | Stephen T. Cassano, N-P | 1997, Nov. |
| Manchester, NH | Ray J. Wieczorek, R | 1997, Nov. |
| Mansfield, OH. | Lydia J. Reid, D | 1999, Nov. |
| Marietta, GA. | Ansley L. Meaders, D | 1997, Nov. |
| McAllen, TX | Othal E. Brand Sr., R | 1997, May |
| Medford, MA. | Michael J. McGlynn, D | 1997, Nov. |
| Medford, OR. | Jerry Lausman, N-P | 1998, Nov. |
| Melbourne, FL | John Buckley, N-P | 2000, Nov. |
| Memphis, TN | Willie W. Herenton, D | 1999, Oct. |
| Mentor, OH | Edward Walsh, N-P | 1998, Jan. |
| Merced, CA | Richard Bernasconi, N-P. | 1997, Nov. |
| Meriden, CT | Joseph Marinan Jr., N-P | 1997, Dec. |
| Meridian, MS | John Robert Smith, R | 1997, June |
| Mesa, AZ | Willie Wong, N-P | 1998, May |
| Mesquite, TX | Cathye Ray, N-P | 1997, May |
| Miami, FL. | Joe Carollo, N-P. | 1997, Nov. |
| Miami Beach, FL. | Seymour Gelber, D. | 1997, Nov. |
| Midland, TX | Robert E. Burns, N-P | 1998, May |
| Midwest City, OK | Eddie O. Reed, N-P | 1998, Apr. |
| Milford, CT. | Frederick Lisman, R | 1997, Nov. |
| Milpitas, CA | Henry Manayan, N-P | 1998, Nov. |
| Milwaukee, WI | John O. Norquist, D | 2000, Apr. |
| Minneapolis, MN | Sharon Sayles Belton, D | 1997, Nov. |
| Minnetonka, MN | Karen J. Anderson, N-P | 1997, Nov. |
| Mobile, AL | Michael Dow, R, I | 1997, Oct. |
| Modesto, CA | Richard Lang, N-P | 1999, Nov. |
| Monroe, LA | Robert E. Powell, D | 2000, Apr. |
| Montclair, NJ | William Farlie Jr., N-P | 2000, May |
| Montebello, CA. | Arnold Alvarez-Glasman, N-P | 1997, Nov. |
| Monterey Park, CA | Fred Balderrama, N-P. | 1997, Mar. |
| Montgomery, AL | Emory Folmar, R | 1999, Oct. |
| Montpelier, VT | Charles Kaparis, N-P | 1998, Mar. |
| Moreno Valley, CA | Denise Lanning, N-P | 1996, Dec. |
| Mt. Prospect, IL | Gerald "Skip" Farley, N-P | 1997, Apr. |
| Mt. Vernon, NY. | Ernest D. Davis, D | 1999, Nov. |
| Mountain View, CA | Ralph Faravelli, N-P | 1997, Jan. |
| Muncie, IN | Dan Cannan | 1999, Nov. |
| Muskogee, OK | James Bushnell, N-P | 1998, Apr. |
| Napa, CA. | Ed Solomon, R. | 2000, July |
| Naperville, IL | George Pradel, N-P | 1999, Apr. |
| Nashua, NH | Donald Davidson, N-P | 1999, Nov. |

| City | Name | Next Election |
|---|---|---|
| Nashville, TN | Philip N. Bredesen, D | 1998, Aug. |
| National City, CA | George H. Waters, R | 1998, Nov. |
| Newark, NJ | Sharpe James, D | 1998, May |
| New Bedford, MA | Rosemary Tierney, D | 1997, Nov. |
| New Britain, CT | Lucian Pawlak, D | 1997, Nov. |
| New Haven, CT | John DeStafano, D | 1997, Dec. |
| New Orleans, LA | Marc H. Morial, D | 1998, Feb. |
| Newport Beach, CA | John Hedges, N-P | 1996, Dec. |
| Newport News, VA | Joe S. Frank, N-P | 1998, June |
| New Rochelle, NY | Timothy Idoni, D | 1999, Nov. |
| Newton, MA | Thomas Concannon Jr., N-P | 1997, Nov. |
| New York, NY | Rudolph Giuliani, R | 1997, Nov. |
| Niagara Falls, NY | James Galie, D | 1999, Nov. |
| Norfolk, VA | Paul D. Fraim, N-P | 1998, July |
| Norman, OK | Dr. William Nation, N-P | 1998, Mar. |
| North Charleston, SC | R. Keith Summey, R | 1999, July |
| N. Little Rock, AR | Patrick Hays, N-P | 2000, Nov. |
| Norwalk, CA | Judith Brennan, N-P | 1997, Apr. |
| Norwalk, CT | Frank J. Esposito, R | 1997, Nov. |
| Novato, CA | Ernest Gray, N-P | 1996, Nov.[2] |
| Oakland, CA | Elihu Mason Harris, N-P | 1999, Jan. |
| Oak Park, IL | Lawrence Christmas, N-P | 1997, Apr. |
| Oceanside, CA | Dick Lyon, N-P | 2000, Nov. |
| Odessa, TX | Mike Atkins, N-P | 1998, May |
| Ogden, UT | Glenn J. Mecham, N-P | 1999, Nov. |
| Oklahoma City, OK | Ronald J. Norick, N-P | 1998, Apr. |
| Olympia, WA | Bob Jacobs, N-P | 1999, Nov. |
| Omaha, NE | Hal Daub, R | 1997, May |
| Ontario, CA | Gus James Skropos, N-P | 1998, Nov. |
| Orange, CA | Joanne Coontz, N-P | 1998, Nov. |
| Orlando, FL | Glenda E. Hood, N-P | 2000, Apr. |
| Oshkosh, WI | William Castle Jr., N-P | 1997, Apr. |
| Overland Park, KS | Ed Eilert, R | 1997, Apr. |
| Owensboro, KY | Waymund Morris, N-P | 1999, Nov. |
| Oxnard, CA | Manuel M. Lopez, N-P | 1998, Nov. |
| Palm Springs, CA | William G. Kleindienst, N-P | 1999, Nov. |
| Palo Alto, CA | Lanie Wheeler, N-P | 1998, Jan. |
| Parma, OH | Gerald M. Boldt, D | 1999, Nov. |
| Pasadena, CA | William M. Paparian, N-P | 1997, Mar. |
| Pasadena, TX | Johnny Isbell, N-P | 1997, May |
| Passaic, NJ | Margie Semler, N-P | 1997, May |
| Paterson, NJ | William J. Pascrell Jr., D | 1997, May |
| Pawtucket, RI | Robert E. Metivier, D | 1997, Nov. |
| Peabody, MA | Peter Torigian, D | 1997, Nov. |
| Pembroke Pines, FL | Alex G. Fekete, N-P | 2000, Mar. |
| Pensacola, FL | John Fogg, N-P | 1997, May |
| Peoria, IL | James A. Maloof, N-P | 1997, Apr. |
| Philadelphia, PA | Edward Rendell, D | 1999, Nov. |
| Phoenix, AZ | Skip Rimza, N-P | 1999, Oct. |
| Pico Rivera, CA | John G. Chavez, N-P | 1997, Mar. |
| Pierre, SD | Gary Drewes, N-P | 1999, Apr. |
| Pine Bluff, AR | Jerry Taylor, N-P | 2000, Nov. |
| Pittsburgh, PA | Tom Murphy, D | 1997, Nov. |
| Pittsfield, MA | Edward Reilly, N-P | 1997, Nov. |
| Plainfield, NJ | Mark Fury, N-P | 1997, Nov. |
| Plano, TX | John Longstreet, N-P | 1998, May |
| Plantation, FL | Frank Veltri, D | 1999, Mar. |
| Pocatello, ID | Peter J. Angstadt, N-P | 1997, Nov. |
| Pomona, CA | Eddie Cortez, N-P | 1997, Mar. |
| Pompano Beach, FL | William F Griffin, N-P | 1997, Mar. |
| Pontiac, MI | Walter Moore, N-P | 1997, Nov. |
| Port Arthur, TX | Robert T. Morgan, D | 1998, May |
| Portland, ME | John F. McDonough, N-P | 1997, May |
| Portland, OR | Vera Katz, N-P | 2000, Nov. |
| Portsmouth, VA | Dr. James W. Holley, N-P | 2000, May |
| Providence, RI | Vincent Cianci Jr., R, I | 1998, Nov. |
| Provo, UT | George O. Stewart, N-P | 1997, Nov. |
| Quincy, IL | Charles W. Scholz, D | 1997, Apr. |
| Quincy, MA | James A. Sheets, D | 1997, Nov. |
| Racine, WI | James M. Smith, N-P | 1999, Apr. |
| Raleigh, NC | Tom Fetzer, N-P | 1997, Oct. |
| Rancho Cucamonga, CA | William Alexander, N-P | 1998, Nov. |
| Rapid City, SD | Edward McLaughlin, N-P | 1999, Apr. |
| Reading, PA | Paul Angstadt, R | 1999, Nov. |
| Redding, CA | David McGeorge, N-P | 1997, Mar. |
| Redondo Beach, CA | Brad Parton, N-P | 1997, Apr. |
| Redwood City, CA | Jim Hartnett, N-P | 1997, Nov. |
| Reno, NV | Jeff Griffin, N-P | 1999, June |
| Rialto, CA | John Longville, N-P | 2000, Nov. |
| Richardson, TX | Gary Slagel, N-P | 1997, May |
| Richmond, CA | Rosemary Corbin, D | 1997, Nov. |
| Richmond, VA | Larry Chavis, N-P | 1998, July |
| Riverside, CA | Ronald O. Loveridge, N-P | 1997, Dec. |
| Roanoke, VA | David A. Bowers, D | 2000, May |
| Rochester, MN | Chuck Caulfield, N-P | 1999, Nov. |
| Rochester, NY | William A. Johnson Jr., D | 1997, Nov. |
| Rochester Hills, MI | Kenneth D. Snell, N-P | 1999, Nov. |
| Rock Hill, SC | Elizabeth D. Rhea, N-P | 1998, Apr. |
| Rock Island, IL | Mark W. Schwiebert, N-P | 1997, Apr. |
| Rockford, IL | Charles Box, D | 1997, Apr. |
| Rockville, MD | Rose G. Krasnow, N-P | 1997, Nov. |
| Rome, NY | Joseph A. Griffo, R | 1999, Nov. |
| Rosemead, CA | Margaret Clark, N-P | 1997, Mar. |
| Roseville, MI | Gerald K. Alsip, N-P | 1997, Nov. |
| Roswell, NM | Thomas E. Jennings, N-P | 1998, Mar. |
| Royal Oak, MI | Dennis G. Cowan, N-P | 1997, Nov. |
| Sacramento, CA | Joseph Serna Jr., N-P | 2000, June |
| Saginaw, MI | Gary L. Loster, N-P | 1997, Nov. |
| St. Charles, MO | Robert L. Moeller, N-P | 1999, Apr. |
| St. Clair Shores, MI | Curtis L. Dumas, N-P | 1999, Nov. |
| St. Cloud, MN | Charles Winkleman, N-P | 1997, Nov. |
| St. Joseph, MO | Larry Stobbs, N-P | 1998, Apr. |
| St. Louis, MO | Freeman R. Bosley Jr., D | 1997, Apr. |
| St. Louis Park, MN | Gail Dorfman, N-P | 1999, Nov. |
| St. Paul, MN | Norm Coleman, N-P | 1997, Nov. |
| St. Petersburg, FL | David Fischer, N-P | 1997, Mar. |
| Salem, OR | Michael Swaim, N-P | 1998, Nov. |
| Salinas, CA | Alan Styles, N-P | 1997, June |
| Salt Lake City, UT | Deedee Corradini, D | 1999, Nov. |
| San Angelo, TX | Dick Funk, N-P | 1997, May |
| San Antonio, TX | William Thornton, N-P | 1997, May |
| San Bernardino, CA | Tom Minor, R | 1997, Nov. |
| San Diego, CA | Susan Golding, R | 2000, Nov. |
| Sandy, UT | Thomas M. Dolan, N-P | 1997, Nov. |
| San Francisco, CA | Willie Brown, N-P | 1999, Jan. |
| San Jose, CA | Susan Hammer | 1999, Jan. |
| San Leandro, CA | Ellen M. Corbett, N-P | 1998, May |
| San Mateo, CA | Paul Gumbinger, N-P | 1996, Dec. |
| San Rafael, CA | Albert J. Boro, N-P | 1999, Nov. |
| Santa Ana, CA | Miguel Pulido, N-P | 1998, Nov. |
| Santa Barbara, CA | Harriet Miller, N-P | 1999, Nov. |
| Santa Clara, CA | Judy Nadler, N-P | 1998, Nov. |
| Santa Clarita, CA | Carl Boyer, N-P | 1996 Dec. |
| Santa Cruz, CA | Mike Rotkin, N-P | 1996, Nov.[5] |
| Santa Fe, NM | Debbie Jaramillo, N-P | 1998, Mar. |
| Santa Maria, CA | Roger Bunch, N-P | 1998, Nov.[4] |
| Santa Monica, CA | Paul Rosenstein, N-P | 1996, Dec. |
| Santa Rosa, CA | Sharon Wright, N-P | 1996, Dec. |
| Sarasota, FL | Mollie Cardamone, N-P | 1997, Apr. |
| Savannah, GA | Floyd Adams Jr., N-P | 1999, Nov. |
| Schaumburg, IL | Al Larson, N-P | 1999, Apr. |
| Schenectady, NY | Albert Jurczynski, R | 1999, Nov. |
| Scottsdale, AZ | Herbert Drinkwater, R | 2000, Apr. |
| Scranton, PA | James P. Connors, R | 1997, Nov. |
| Seattle, WA | Norman B. Rice, D | 1997, Nov. |
| Sheboygan, WI | Richard J. Schneider, N-P | 1997, Apr. |
| Shreveport, LA | Robert W. Williams, R | 1998, Nov. |
| Simi Valley, CA | Greg Stratton, N-P | 1998, Nov. |
| Sioux City, IA | Robert Scott, N-P | 1998, Jan. |
| Sioux Falls, SD | Gary Hanson, N-P | 1999, Jan. |
| Skokie, IL | Jacqueline B. Gorell, N-P | 1997, Apr. |
| Somerville, MA | Michael E. Capuano, D | 1997, Nov. |
| South Bend, IN | Joseph Kernan, D | 1999, Nov. |
| South Gate, CA | Jerry M. Garcia, N-P | 1997, Apr. |
| Southfield, MI | Donald F. Fracassi, R | 1997, Nov. |
| Sparks, NV | Bruce Breslow, N-P | 1999, June |
| Spartanburg, SC | James E. Talley, N-P | 1997, Nov. |
| Spokane, WA | Jack Geraghty, N-P | 1997, Nov. |
| Springfield, IL | Karen Hasara, N-P | 1999, Apr. |
| Springfield, MA | Michael Albano, D | 1997, Nov. |
| Springfield, MO | Leland L. Gannaway, N-P | 1997, Apr. |
| Springfield, OH | Kevin O'Neill, N-P | 1998, Jan. |
| Stamford, CT | Dannel P. Malloy, D | 1997, Dec. |
| Sterling Hts., MI | Richard J. Notte, N-P | 1997, Nov. |
| Stockton, CA | Gary Podesto, N-P | 2000, Nov. |
| Stratford, CT | Clement F. Naples, N-P | 1997, Nov. |
| Sunnyvale, CA | Robin Parker, N-P | 1997, Nov. |
| Suffolk, VA | Thomas Underwood, N-P | 1998, July |
| Sunrise, FL | Steve Effman, N-P | 1997, Mar. |
| Syracuse, NY | Roy A. Bernardi, R | 1997, Nov. |
| Tacoma, WA | Brian Ebersole, N-P | 1999, Nov. |
| Tallahassee, FL | Ron Weaver, N-P | 1997, Mar. |
| Tampa, FL | Dick Greco, N-P | 1999, Mar. |
| Taunton, MA | Robert Nunes, D | 1997, Nov. |
| Taylor, MI | Cameron G. Priebe, D | 1997, Nov. |
| Tempe, AZ | Neil Giuliano, N-P | 1998, Apr. |
| Temple, TX | J. W. Perry, N-P | 1998, May |
| Terre Haute, IN | James Jenkins, D | 1999, Nov. |
| Thornton, CO | Margaret Carpenter, N-P | 1999, Nov. |
| Thousand Oaks, CA | Andrew P. Fox, N-P | 1996, Dec. |
| Titusville, FL | Larry D. Bartley, N-P | 1998, Nov. |
| Toledo, OH | Carty Finkbeiner, N-P | 1997, Nov. |
| Topeka, KS | Harry Felker, R | 1997, Apr. |
| Torrance, CA | Dee Hardison, N-P | 1998, Mar. |
| Trenton, NJ | Douglas H. Palmer, N-P | 1998, May |

| City | Name | Next Election |
|---|---|---|
| Troy, MI | Jeanne M. Stine, N-P | 1998, Apr. |
| Troy, NY | Mark Pattison, D | 1998, Jan. |
| Tucson, AZ | George Miller, D | 1999, Nov. |
| Tulsa, OK | M. Susan Savage, D | 1998, Mar. |
| Tuscaloosa, AL | Alvin DuPont, D | 1997, Oct. |
| Tyler, TX | Kevin Eltise, N-P | 1998, May |
| Union City, NJ | Bruce D. Walter, D | 2000, May |
| Upland, CA | Robert R. Nolan, N-P | 2000, Nov. |
| Utica, NY | Edward Hanna, I | 1999, Nov. |
| Vacaville, CA | David A. Fleming, N-P | 1998, Nov. |
| Vallejo, CA | Gloria Exlin, N-P | 1999, Nov. |
| Vancouver, WA | Royce Pollard, N-P | 1997, Nov. |
| Vineland, NJ | Anthony Campanella, R | 2000, June |
| Virginia Beach, VA | Meyera E. Oberndorf, I | 2000, May |
| Visalia, CA | Mary Louise Vivier, N-P | 1997, Nov. |
| Vista, CA | Gloria McClellan, R | 1998, Dec. |
| Waco, TX | Mike Morrison, N-P | 1997, May |
| Walnut Creek, CA | Gwen Regalia, N-P | 1996, Dec. |
| Waltham, MA | William F. Stanley, D | 1999, Nov. |
| Warren, MI | Mark Steenburgh, N-P | 1999, Nov. |
| Warren, OH | Henry Angelo, D | 1999, Nov. |
| Warwick, RI | Lincoln D. Chafee, R | 1998, Nov. |
| Washington, DC | Marion Barry, D | 1999, Jan. |
| Waterbury, CT | Philip Giordino, R | 1997, Nov. |
| Waterloo, IA | John R. Rooff III, R | 1997, Nov. |
| Waukegan, IL | William F. Durkin, D | 1997, Apr. |
| Waukesha, WI | Carol Opel, N-P | 1998, Apr. |
| Wauwatosa, WI | Maricolette Walsh, N-P | 2000, Mar. |
| W. Allis, WI | Jeannette Bell, N-P | 2000, Mar. |
| W. Covina, CA | Michael R. Touhey, N-P | 1997, Mar. |
| W. Hartford, CT | Nan Glass, D | 1997, Nov. |
| W. Haven, CT | H. Richard Borer Jr., D | 1997, Dec. |
| W. Palm Beach, FL | Nancy M. Graham, N-P | 1999, Mar. |
| Westland, MI | Robert J. Thomas, D | 1997, Nov. |
| Westminster, CA | Frank Fry, N-P | 1998, Nov. |
| Westminster, CO | Nancy Heil, N-P | 1997, Nov. |
| Wheaton, IL | C. James Carr, N-P | 1999, Apr. |
| White Plains, NY | S. J. Schulman, D | 1997, Nov. |
| Whittier, CA | Janet Henke, N-P | 1998, Apr. |
| Wichita, KS | Bob Knight, N-P | 1999, Apr. |
| Wichita Falls, TX | Kay Yeager, N-P | 1998, May |
| Wilkes-Barre, PA | Thomas McGroarty, D | 1997, Nov. |
| Wilmington, DE | James H. Sills Jr., D | 2000, Nov. |
| Wilmington, NC | Don Betz, N-P | 1997, Nov. |
| Winston-Salem, NC | Martha S. Wood, N-P | 1997, Nov. |
| Woodbridge, NJ | James McGreevey, D | 1999, Nov. |
| Woonsocket, RI | Susan D. Menard, N-P | 1997, Nov. |
| Worcester, MA | Raymond Mariano, N-P | 1997, Nov. |
| Wyandotte, MI | James R. DeSana, D | 1997, Apr. |
| Wyoming, MI | Jack Magnuson, N-P | 1997, Nov. |
| Yakima, WA | Lynn Buchanan, N-P | 1998, Jan. |
| Yonkers, NY | John Spencer, R | 1999, Nov. |
| York, PA | Charles Robertson, D | 1997, Nov. |
| Youngstown, OH | Patrick J. Ungaro, D | 1997, Nov. |
| Yuma, AZ | Marilyn R. Young, N-P | 1997, Nov. |

(1) Position of mayor is rotated among City Council members every 9 months. (2) City Council to elect mayor on Nov. 12, 1996. (3) City Council to elect mayor on Nov. 19, 1996. (4) Incumbent listed; sought reelection Nov. 5, 1996; race undecided as of Nov. 7. (5) City Council to elect mayor on Nov. 26, 1996.

# Governors of States and Puerto Rico

As of Jan. 1997, including results of Nov. 1996 elections (preliminary results)

| State | Capital, Zip Code | Governor | Party | Term years | Term expires | Annual salary[1] |
|---|---|---|---|---|---|---|
| Alabama | Montgomery 36130 | Fob James Jr. | Rep. | 4 | Jan. 1999 | $87,643 |
| Alaska | Juneau 99811 | Tony Knowles | Dem. | 4 | Dec. 1998 | 81,648 |
| Arizona | Phoenix 85007 | Fife Symington | Rep. | 4 | Jan. 1999 | 75,000 |
| Arkansas | Little Rock 72201 | Mike Huckabee | Rep. | 4 | Jan. 1999 | 60,000 |
| California | Sacramento 95814 | Pete Wilson | Rep. | 4 | Jan. 1999 | 120,000 |
| Colorado | Denver 80203 | Roy Romer | Dem. | 4 | Jan. 1999 | 70,000 |
| Connecticut | Hartford 06106 | John G. Rowland | Rep. | 4 | Jan. 1999 | 78,000 |
| Delaware[1] | Dover 19901 | Thomas R. Carper | Dem. | 4 | Jan. 2001 | 95,000 |
| Florida | Tallahassee 32399 | Lawton Chiles | Dem. | 4 | Jan. 1999 | 104,817 |
| Georgia | Atlanta 30334 | Zell Miller | Dem. | 4 | Jan. 1999 | 103,074 |
| Hawaii | Honolulu 96813 | Ben Cayetano | Dem. | 4 | Dec. 1998 | 94,780 |
| Idaho | Boise 83720 | Phil Batt | Rep. | 4 | Jan. 1999 | 85,000 |
| Illinois | Springfield 62706 | Jim Edgar | Rep. | 4 | Jan. 1999 | 123,022 |
| Indiana[1] | Indianapolis 46204 | Frank O'Bannon | Dem. | 4 | Jan. 2001 | 77,200 |
| Iowa | Des Moines 50319 | Terry E. Branstad | Rep. | 4 | Jan. 1999 | 98,200 |
| Kansas | Topeka 66612 | Bill Graves | Rep. | 4 | Jan. 1999 | 80,340 |
| Kentucky | Frankfort 40601 | Paul Patton | Dem. | 4 | Dec. 1999 | 86,352 |
| Louisiana | Baton Rouge 70804 | M. J. Foster | Rep. | 4 | Jan. 2000 | 95,000 |
| Maine | Augusta 04333 | Angus King Jr. | Ind. | 4 | Jan. 1999 | 69,992 |
| Maryland | Annapolis 21401 | Parris N. Glendening | Dem. | 4 | Jan. 1999 | 120,000 |
| Massachusetts | Boston 02113 | William F. Weld | Rep. | 4 | Jan. 1999 | 90,000 |
| Michigan | Lansing 48909 | John Engler | Rep. | 4 | Jan. 1999 | 121,166 |
| Minnesota | St. Paul 55155 | Arne H. Carlson | Rep. | 4 | Jan. 1999 | 114,506 |
| Mississippi | Jackson 39205 | Kirk Fordice | Rep. | 4 | Jan. 2000 | 83,160 |
| Missouri[1] | Jefferson City 65102 | Mel Carnahan | Dem. | 4 | Jan. 2001 | 94,563 |
| Montana[1] | Helena 59620 | Marc Racicot | Rep. | 4 | Jan. 2001 | 59,310 |
| Nebraska | Lincoln 68509 | Ben Nelson | Dem. | 4 | Jan. 1999 | 65,000 |
| Nevada | Carson City 89710 | Bob Miller | Dem. | 4 | Jan. 1999 | 90,000 |
| New Hampshire[1] | Concord 03301 | Jeanne Shaheen | Dem. | 2 | Jan. 1999 | 86,235 |
| New Jersey | Trenton 08625 | Christine Todd Whitman | Rep. | 4 | Jan. 1998 | 85,000 |
| New Mexico | Santa Fe 87503 | Gary Johnson | Rep. | 4 | Jan. 1999 | 90,000 |
| New York | Albany 12224 | George E. Pataki | Rep. | 4 | Jan. 1999 | 130,000 |
| North Carolina[1] | Raleigh 27603 | James B. Hunt Jr. | Dem. | 4 | Jan. 2001 | 103,012 |
| North Dakota[1] | Bismarck 58505 | Edward T. Schafer | Rep. | 4 | Jan. 2001 | 71,042 |
| Ohio | Columbus 43215 | George V. Voinovich | Rep. | 4 | Jan. 1999 | 115,762 |
| Oklahoma | Oklahoma City 73105 | Frank Keating | Rep. | 4 | Jan. 1999 | 70,000 |
| Oregon | Salem 97310 | John Kitzhaber | Dem. | 4 | Jan. 1999 | 80,000 |
| Pennsylvania | Harrisburg 17120 | Tom Ridge | Rep. | 4 | Jan. 1999 | 105,000 |
| Rhode Island | Providence 02903 | Lincoln C. Almond | Rep. | 4 | Jan. 1999 | 69,900 |
| South Carolina | Columbia 29211 | David Beasley | Rep. | 4 | Jan. 1999 | 106,078 |
| South Dakota | Pierre 57501 | William J. Janklow | Rep. | 4 | Jan. 1999 | 79,875 |
| Tennessee | Nashville 37243 | Don Sundquist | Rep. | 4 | Jan. 1999 | 85,000 |
| Texas | Austin 78711 | George W. Bush | Rep. | 4 | Jan. 1999 | 99,122 |
| Utah[1] | Salt Lake City 84114 | Michael O. Leavitt | Rep. | 4 | Jan. 2001 | 77,250 |
| Vermont[1] | Montpelier 05609 | Howard Dean | Dem. | 2 | Jan. 1999 | 80,730 |
| Virginia | Richmond 23219 | George F. Allen | Rep. | 4 | Jan. 1998 | 110,000 |
| Washington[1] | Olympia 98504 | Gary Locke | Dem. | 4 | Jan. 2001 | 121,000 |
| West Virginia[1] | Charleston 25305 | Cecil H. Underwood | Rep. | 4 | Jan. 2001 | 90,000 |
| Wisconsin | Madison 53707 | Tommy G. Thompson | Rep. | 4 | Jan. 1999 | 101,861 |
| Wyoming | Cheyenne 82002 | Jim Geringer | Rep. | 4 | Jan. 1999 | 95,000 |
| Puerto Rico[1] | San Juan 00936 | Pedro J. Rossello | NPP[2] | 4 | Jan. 2001 | 70,000 |

(1) Elected Nov. 5, 1996. (2) New Progressive Party.

# Races for Governor, 1996

**Source:** Voter News Service

In 1996, there were 11 state governors races, 7 of which went to the incumbent candidate. Control of the statehouses changed hands from one party to another in 2 states—New Hampshire and West Virginia. The next party breakdown remained the same. Vote totals below are preliminary.

| State | Democrat | Vote | Republican | Vote | Other | Vote |
|---|---|---|---|---|---|---|
| DE | **Thomas R.Carper*** | 188,323 | Janet C. Rzewnicki | 82,653 | | |
| IN | **Frank O'Bannon** | 1,075,342 | Stephen Goldsmith | 977,505 | Steve Dillon, (LB) | 35,053 |
| MO | **Mel Carnahan*** | 1,223,315 | Margaret Kelly | 865,932 | J. Mark Oglesby, (LB) | 51,414 |
| MT | Judy Jacobson | 69,925 | **Marc Racicot*** | 272,013 | | |
| NH | **Jeanne Shaheen** | 283,592 | Ovide M. Lamontagne | 195,903 | Fred Bramante (IR) | 9,712 |
| NC | **James B. Hunt Jr.*** | 1,423,351 | Robin Hayes | 1,088,113 | Scott D. Yost, (LB) | 17,304 |
| ND | Lee Kaldor | 89,078 | **Edward T. Schafer*** | 174,337 | | |
| UT | Jim Bradley | 155,294 | **Michael O. Leavitt*** | 500,293 | Ken Larsen, (IA) | 4,709 |
| VT | **Howard Dean*** | 178,032 | John L. Gropper | 56,993 | Mary Alice Herbert, (LU) | 4,121 |
| WA | **Gary Locke** | 1,038,108 | Ellen Craswell | 721,944 | | |
| WV | Charlotte Pritt | 284,398 | **Cecil H. Underwood** | 320,502 | Wallace Johnson, (LB) | 15,958 |
| | **New Progressive Party** | | **Popular Democratic Party** | | **Puerto Rican Independent Party** | |
| Puerto Rico | **Pedro Rossello*** | 1,000,941 | Hector Luis Acevedo | 868,945 | David Noriega Rodriquez | 74,595 |

* Denotes incumbent. **Boldface** denotes winner. (LB)=Libertarian, (IR)=Reform, (IA)=Independent American, (LU)=Liberty Union

# 1992 Census of U.S. Governments—Popularly Elected Officials

**Source:** U.S. Dept. of Commerce, Economics and Statistics Administration; Bureau of the Census

A census of U.S. governments is taken at 5-year intervals (beginning in 1957). One of the major subject areas includes popularly elected officials. The term *elected officials* refers to officials who are directly elected by the voters, plus the president and the vice president of the U.S., who are elected by presidential electors rather than direct election by the people. Officials who are selected by the governing body of one or more governments are not classified as elected officials.

There were 85,006 governments in the U.S. as of Jan. 1992. In addition to the federal government and the 50 state governments, there were 84,955 units of local government. Of these, 38,978 are general-purpose local governments—3,043 county governments, and 35,935 subcounty general-purpose governments (including 19,279 municipal governments and 16,656 town or township governments). The remainder, more than half the total number, are special-purpose local governments, including 14,422 school district governments and 31,555 special district governments.

The 85,006 governments in the U.S. in 1992 had 513,200 elected officials—approximately one elected official for every 485 inhabitants. There were 542 federal and 18,828 state elected officials, which accounted for only 3.8% of the total. The majority were officials of the various local governments.

# State Officials, Salaries, Party Membership

As of mid-1996; † ind. or other party.

### Alabama

**Governor** — Fob James Jr., R, $87,643
**Lt. Gov.** — Don Siegelman, D, $12 per day, plus $50 per day expenses, plus $3,780 per mo expenses
**Sec. of State** — Jim Bennett, D, $61,779
**Atty. Gen.** — Jeff Sessions, R, $115,695
**Treasurer** — Lucy Baxley, D, $61,779
**Legislature:** meets annually at Montgomery the 3d Tues. in Apr., 1st year of term of office; 1st Tues. in Feb., 2d and 3d yr; 2d Tues. in Jan., 4th yr. Members receive $10 per day salary, plus $50 per day expenses, plus $2,280 per mo expenses.
**Senate** — Dem., 22; Rep., 12, 1 vacancy . Total, 34
**House** — Dem., 83; Rep., 22. Total, 105

### Alaska

**Governor** — Tony Knowles, D, $81,648
**Lt. Gov.** — Fran Ulmer, D, $76,188
**Atty. General** — Bruce Botelho, D, $84,000
**Legislature:** meets annually in Jan. at Juneau for 120 days with a 10-day extension possible upon 2/3 vote. First session in odd years. Members receive $24,120 annually, plus per diem as follows: beginning of session to Apr. 29, $148 per day; Apr. 30 to end of session, $160 per day.
**Senate** — Dem., 8; Rep., 12. Total, 20
**House** — Dem., 17; Rep., 22; 1 other. Total, 40

### Arizona

**Governor** — J. Fife Symington III, R, $75,000
**Sec. of State** — Jane Dee Hull, R, $54,600
**Atty. Gen.** — Grant Woods, R, $76,440
**Treasurer** — Tony West, R, $54,600
**Legislature:** meets annually in Jan. at Phoenix. Each member receives an annual salary of $15,000.
**Senate** — Dem., 11; Rep., 19. Total, 30
**House** — Dem., 22; Rep., 38. Total, 60

### Arkansas

**Governor** — Mike Huckabee, R, $60,000
**Lt. Gov.** — Vacant, $29,000
**Sec. of State** — Sharon Priest, D, $37,500
**Atty. Gen.** — Winston Bryant, D, $50,000
**Treasurer** — Jimmie Lou Fisher, D, $37,500
**Auditor** — Gus Wingfield, D, $37,500
**General Assembly:** meets odd years in Jan. at Little Rock. Members receive $12,500 annually.
**Senate** — Dem., 28; Rep., 7. Total, 35
**House** — Dem., 89; Rep., 11; Total, 100

### California

**Governor** — Pete Wilson, R, $120,000
**Lt. Gov.** — Gray Davis, D, $90,000
**Sec. of State** — Bill Jones, R, $90.000
**Controller** — Kathleen Connell, D, $90,000
**Atty. Gen.** — Dan Lungren, R, $102,000
**Legislature:** meets at Sacramento on the 1st Mon. in Dec. of even-numbered years; each session lasts 2 years. Members receive $52,500 annually, plus $101 per diem.
**Senate** — Dem., 22; Rep., 16; 2 ind. Total, 40
**Assembly** — Dem., 36; Rep., 41. Reform party, 1; 2 vacancies, Total, 80

### Colorado

**Governor** — Roy Romer, D, $70,000
**Lt. Gov.** — Gail Schoettler, D, $48,500
**Sec. of State** — Victoria (Vikki) Buckley, R, $48,500
**Atty. Gen.** — Gale Norton, R, $60,000
**Treasurer** — Bill Owens, $48,500
**General Assembly:** meets annually in Jan. at Denver. Members receive $17,500 annually.
**Senate** — Dem., 16; Rep., 19. Total, 35
**House** — Dem., 24; Rep., 41. Total, 65

## State Officials, Salaries, Party Membership (*continued*)

### Connecticut

**Governor** — John G. Rowland, R, $78,000
**Lt. Gov.** — M. Jodi Rell, R, $55,000
**Sec. of State** — Miles S. Rapoport, D, $50,000
**Treasurer** — Christopher B. Burnham, R, $50,000
**Comptroller** — Nancy S. Wyman, D, $50,000
**Atty. Gen.** — Richard Blumenthal, D, $60,000
**General Assembly:** meets annually odd years in Jan. and even years in Feb., at Hartford. Members receive $15,200 annually, plus $4,500 (senator), $3,500 (representative) per yr for expenses.
**Senate** — Dem., 17; Rep., 19. Total, 36
**House** — Dem., 91; Rep., 60. Total, 151

### Delaware

**Governor** — Thomas R. Carper, D, $95,000
**Lt. Gov.** — Ruth Ann Minner, D, $41,500
**Sec. of State** — Edward J. Freel, D, $87,300
**Atty. Gen.** — M. Jane Brady, R, $96,200
**Treasurer** — Janet C. Rzewnicki, R, $77,400
**General Assembly:** meets annually the 2d Tues. in Jan. and continues until June 30. Members receive $27,500 annually, plus $5,500 expense allowance.
**Senate** — Dem., 13; Rep., 8. Total, 21
**House** — Dem., 14; Rep., 27. Total, 41

### Florida

**Governor** — Lawton Chiles, D, $104,817
**Lt. Gov.** — Kenneth "Buddy" McKay, D, $100,403
**Sec. of State** — Sandra Mortham, R, $103,757
**Comptroller** — Robert R. Milligan, R, $103,757
**Atty. Gen.** — Robert Butterworth, D, $103,757
**Treasurer** — Bill Nelson, D, $103,757
**Legislature:** meets annually at Tallahassee. Members receive $24,180 annually, plus expense allowance for official business.
**Senate** — Dem., 18; Rep., 22. Total, 40
**House** — Dem., 63; Rep., 57. Total, 120

### Georgia

**Governor** — Zell Miller, D, $103,074
**Lt. Gov.** — Pierre Howard, D, $67,319
**Sec. of State** — Lewis Massey, D, $82,786
**Atty. Gen.** — Michael J. Bowers, R, $94,500
**General Assembly:** meets annually in Atlanta. Members receive $11,125 annually ($59 per diem and $4,800 expense reimbursement).
**Senate** — Dem., 35; Rep., 21. Total, 56
**House** — Dem., 112; Rep., 68. Total, 180

### Hawaii

**Governor** — Benjamin Cayetano, D, $94,780
**Lt. Gov.** — Mazie K. Hirono, D, $90,041
**Atty. Gen.** — Margery Bronster, $85,302
**Comptroller** — Sam Callejo, $85,302
**Dir. of Budget & Finance** — Earl Anzai, $85,302
**Legislature:** meets annually on 3d Wed. in Jan. at Honolulu. Members receive $32,000 annually, plus expenses.
**Senate** — Dem., 23; Rep., 2. Total, 25
**House** — Dem., 44; Rep., 7. Total, 51

### Idaho

**Governor** — Philip E. Batt, R, $85,000
**Lt. Gov.** — C. L. "Butch" Otter, R, $22,500
**Sec. of State** — Pete T. Cenarrusa, R, $67,500
**Treasurer** — Lydia Justice Edwards, R, $67,500
**Atty. Gen.** — Alan Lance, R, $75,000
**Legislature:** meets annually the Mon. on or nearest Jan. 9 at Boise. Members receive $12,360 annually, plus $75 per day during session if required to maintain a 2d residence, $40 if no 2d residence; plus $50 per day when engaged in legislative business when legislature is not in session.
**Senate** — Dem., 8; Rep., 27. Total, 35
**House** — Dem., 13; Rep., 57. Total, 70

### Illinois

**Governor** — Jim Edgar, R, $123,022
**Lt. Gov.** — Bob Kustra, R, $86,839
**Sec. of State** — George H. Ryan, R, $108,549
**Comptroller** — Loleta A. Didrickson, R, $94,076
**Atty. Gen.** — Jim Ryan, R, $108,549
**Treasurer** — Judy Baar Topinka, R, $94,076
**General Assembly:** meets annually in Jan. at Springfield. Members receive $47,309 annually.
**Senate** — Dem., 26; Rep., 33. Total, 59
**House** — Dem., 54; Rep., 64. Total, 118

### Indiana

**Governor** — Evan Bayh, D, $77,200
**Lt. Gov.** — Frank O'Bannon, D, $64,000
**Sec. of State** — Sue Anne Gilroy, R, $46,000
**Atty. Gen.** — Pamela Carter, D, $59,200
**Treasurer** — Joyce Brinkman, R, $46,000
**Auditor** — Morris Wooden, R, $46,000
**General Assembly:** meets annually in Jan. Members receive $11,600 annually, plus $105 per day while in session, $25 per day while not in session.
**Senate** — Dem., 19; Rep., 31. Total, 50
**House** — Dem., 45; Rep., 55. Total, 100

### Iowa

**Governor** — Terry E. Branstad, R, $98,200
**Lt. Gov.** — Joy Corning, R, $68,740
**Sec. of State** — Paul D. Pate, R, $78,050
**Atty. Gen.** — Tom Miller, D, $93,520
**Treasurer** — Michael L. Fitzgerald, D, $78,050
**Auditor** — Richard D. Johnson, R, $78,050
**Sec. of Agriculture** — Dale M. Cochran, D, $78,050
**General Assembly:** meets annually in Jan. at Des Moines. Members receive $18,100 annually, plus expense allowance.
**Senate** — Dem., 27; Rep., 23. Total, 50
**House** — Dem., 37; Rep., 63. Total, 100

### Kansas

**Governor** — Bill Graves, R, $80,340
**Lt. Gov.** — Sheila Frahm, R, $81,600
**Sec. of State** — Ron Thornburgh, R, $62, 412
**Atty. Gen.** — Carla Stovall, R, $71,772
**Treasurer** — Sally Thompson, D, $62,412
**Legislature:** meets annually in Jan. at Topeka. Members receive $63 per day salary, plus $73 per day expenses while in session, $600 per month while not in session.
**Senate** — Dem., 13; Rep., 27. Total, 40
**House** — Dem., 44; Rep., 81. Total, 125

### Kentucky

**Governor** — Paul Patton, D, $86,352
**Lt. Gov.** — Steve Henry, D, $77,294
**Sec. of State** — John Y. Brown III, D, $77,294
**Atty. Gen.** —A. B. Chandler III, D, $77,294
**Treasurer** — John Kennedy Hamilton, D, $77,294
**Auditor** — Ed Hatchett, D, $77,294
**General Assembly:** meets even years in Jan. at Frankfort. Members receive $100 per day, plus $75 per day expenses during session and $950 per month for expenses for interim.
**Senate** — Dem., 20; Rep., 17; 1 vacancy. Total, 38
**House** — Dem., 63; Rep., 36; 1 vacancy. Total, 100

### Louisiana

**Governor** — M. J. "Mike" Foster, R, $95,000
**Lt. Gov.** — Kathleen Babineaux Blanco, D, $85,000
**Sec. of State** — W. Fox McKeithen, R, $85,000
**Atty. Gen.** — Richard Ieyoub, D, $85,000
**Treasurer** — Ken Duncan, D, $85,000
**Legislature:** meets in odd-numbered years on last Mon. in Mar. for 60 legislative days of 85 calendar days; meets in even-numbered years on last Mon. in Apr. for 30 legislative days of 45 calendar days. Members receive $16,800 annually, plus $75 per day expenses while in session.
**Senate** — Dem., 24; Rep., 14; 1 vacancy. Total, 39.
**House** — Dem., 77; Rep., 27;, 1 vacancy. Total, 105.

### Maine

**Governor** — Angus King Jr. † $69,992
**Sec. of State** — G. William Diamond, D, $60,000
**Atty. Gen.** — Andrew Ketterer, $66,123
**Treasurer** — Samuel Shapiro, D, $69,000
**Legislature:** meets annually at Augusta the first Wed. in Dec. and the Wed. after the first Tues. in Jan., in even numbered years. Members receive $10,500 for first regular session, $7,500 for second regular session, plus expenses; presiding officers receive 50% more.
**Senate** — Dem., 16; Rep., 18; 1 ind. Total, 35
**House** — Dem., 76; Rep., 75. Total, 151

### Maryland

**Governor** — Parris N. Glendening, D, $120,000
**Lt. Gov.** — Kathleen Kennedy Townsend, D, $100,000
**Comptroller** — Louis L. Goldstein, D, $100,000
**Atty. Gen.** — J. Joseph Curran Jr., D, $100,000
**Sec. of State** — John Willis, D, $70,000
**Treasurer** —Richard N. Dixon, D, $100,000
**General Assembly:** meets 90 consecutive days annually beginning on the 2d Wed. in Jan. in Annapolis. Members receive $29,700 annually, plus expenses.
**Senate** — Dem., 32; Rep., 15. Total, 47
**House** — Dem., 100; Rep., 41. Total, 141

### Massachusetts

**Governor** — William F. Weld, R, $90,000[1]
**Lt. Gov.** — A. Paul Cellucci, R, $75,000
**Sec. of State** — William Francis Galvin, D, $75,000
**Atty. Gen.** — L. Scott Harshbarger, D, $80,000
**Treasurer** — Joseph Malone, R, $75,000
**Auditor** — A. Joseph DeNucci, D, $75,000
**General Court (legislature):** meets Jan. biennially in Boston. Members receive $46,410 annually.
**Senate** — Dem., 31; Rep., 9. Total, 40
**House** — Dem., 124; Rep., 35; 1 ind. Total, 160

### Michigan

**Governor** — John Engler, R, $121,166
**Lt. Gov.** — Connie Binsfeld, R, $89,450
**Sec. of State** — Candice S. Miller, R, $112,000
**Atty. Gen.** — Frank J. Kelley, D, $112,000
**Treasurer** — Douglas B. Roberts, (appointed), $97,000
**Legislature:** meets annually in Jan. in Lansing. Members receive $50,629 annually.
**Senate** — Dem., 16; Rep., 22. Total, 38
**House** — Dem., 54; Rep., 56. Total, 110

### Minnesota

(DFL means Democratic-Farmer-Labor Party)
**Governor** — Arne H. Carlson, R, $114,506
**Lt. Gov.** — Joanne E. Benson, R, $62,980
**Sec. of State** — Joan Anderson Growe, DFL, $62,980
**Atty. Gen.** — Hubert H. Humphrey 3d, DFL, $89,454
**Treasurer** — Michael McGrath, DFL, $62,980
**Auditor** — Judith H. Dutcher, R, $68,709
**Legislature:** meets for a total of 120 days within every 2 years, at St. Paul. Members receive $29,657 annually, plus expense allowance during session.
**Senate** — DFL, 43; R, 24. Total, 67
**House** — DFL, 69; R, 65. Total, 134

### Mississippi

**Governor** — Kirk Fordice, R, $83,160
**Lt. Gov.** — Ronnie Musgrove, D, $40,800
**Sec. of State** — Eric Clark, D, $59,400
**Atty. Gen.** — Mike Moore, D, $68,400
**Treasurer** — Marshall Bennett, D, $59,400
**Auditor** — Steve Patterson, $59,400
**Legislature:** meets annually in Jan. at Jackson. Members receive $10,000 per regular session, plus travel allowance, and $800 per month while not in session.
**Senate** — Dem., 35; Rep., 17. Total, 52
**House** — Dem., 85; Rep., 34; 3 ind. Total, 122

### Missouri

**Governor** — Mel Carnahan, D, $94,563
**Lt. Gov.** — Roger Wilson, D, $57,145
**Sec. of State** — Rebecca McDowell Cook, D, $75,854
**Atty. Gen.** — Jeremiah W. Nixon, D, $82,090
**Treasurer** — Bob Holden, D, $75,854
**State Auditor** — Margaret Kelly, R, $75,854
**General Assembly:** meets annually in Jefferson City on the first Wed. after first Mon. in Jan. Members receive $24,313 annually.
**Senate** — Dem., 19; Rep., 15. Total, 34
**House** — Dem., 87; Rep., 76. Total, 163

### Montana

**Governor** — Marc Racicot, R, $59,310
**Lt. Gov.** — Dennis Rehberg, R, $43,242
**Sec. of State** — Mike Cooney, D, $40,101
**Atty. Gen.** — Joe Mazurek, D, $54,329
**Legislative Assembly:** meets odd years in Jan. at Helena. Members receive $55.50 per legislative day, plus $50 per day for expenses while in session.
**Senate** — Dem., 19; Rep., 31. Total, 50
**House** — Dem., 33; Rep., 67. Total, 100

### Nebraska

**Governor** — Ben Nelson, D, $65,000
**Lt. Gov.** — Kim Robak, D, $47,000
**Sec. of State** — Scott Moore, R, $52,000
**Atty. Gen.** — Don Stenberg, R, $64,500
**Treasurer** — David Heineman, R, $49,500
**Legislature:** Unicameral body composed of 49 members who are elected on a nonpartisan ballot and are called senators; meets annually in Jan. at Lincoln. Members receive $12,000 annually, plus expenses.

### Nevada

**Governor** — Bob Miller, D, $90,000
**Lt. Gov.** — Lonnie Hammargren, R, $20,000
**Sec. of State** — Dean Heller, R, $62,500
**Comptroller** — Darrel Daines, R, $62,500
**Atty. Gen.** — Frankie Sue Del Papa, D, $85,000
**Treasurer** — Bob Seale, R, $62,500
**Legislature:** meets at Carson City odd years third Mon. in Jan. for 60 days. Members receive $130 per day salary, plus $66 per day expenses, while in session
**Senate** — Dem., 8; Rep., 13. Total, 21
**Assembly** — Dem., 21; Rep., 21. Total, 42

### New Hampshire

**Governor** — Steve Merrill, R, $86,235
**Sec. of State** — William M. Gardner, D, $68,768
**Atty. Gen.** — Jeffrey Howard, R, $76,983
**Treasurer** — Georgie A. Thomas, R, $68,768.
**General Court (Legislature):** meets every year in Jan. at Concord. Members receive $200, presiding officers $250, annually.
**Senate** — Dem., 6; Rep., 18. Total, 24
**House** — Rep., 279; Dem., 112; 1 ind.; 1 lib.; 7 vac. Total, 400

### New Jersey

**Governor** — Christine Todd Whitman, R, $85,000
**Sec. of State** — Lonna R. Hooks, R, $100,225
**Atty. Gen.** — Deborah T. Poritz, R, $100,225
**Treasurer** — Bryan W. Clymer, R, $100,225
**Legislature:** meets throughout the year at Trenton. Members receive $35,000 annually, except president of Senate and speaker of Assembly, who receive 1/3 more.
**Senate** — Dem., 16; Rep., 24. Total, 40
**Assembly** — Dem., 30; Rep., 50. Total, 80

### New Mexico

**Governor** — Gary Johnson, R, $90,000
**Lt. Gov.** — Walter Bradley, R, $65,000
**Sec. of State** — Stephanie Gonzales, D, $65,000
**Atty. Gen.** — Tom Udall, D, $72,500
**Treasurer** — Michael A. Montoya, D, $65,000
**Legislature:** meets on the 3d Tues. in Jan. at Santa Fe; odd years for 60 days, even years for 30 days. Members receive $75 per day while in session.
**Senate** — Dem., 27; Rep., 15. Total, 42
**House** — Dem., 46; Rep., 24. Total, 70

### New York

**Governor** — George E. Pataki, R, $130,000
**Lt. Gov.** — Elizabeth McCaughey, R, $110,000
**Sec. of State** — Alexander F. Treadwell, R, $90,832
**Comptroller** — H. Carl McCall, D, $110,000
**Atty. Gen.** — Dennis Vacco, R, $110,000
**Legislature:** meets annually in Jan. at Albany. Members receive $57,500 annually, plus $89 per day expenses.
**Senate** — Dem., 25; Rep., 36. Total, 61
**Assembly** — Dem., 94; Rep., 56; Total, 150

### North Carolina

**Governor** — James B. Hunt Jr., D, $103,012
**Lt. Gov.** — Dennis Wicker, D, $90,915, plus expenses
**Sec. of State** — Janice H. Faulkner, D, $90,915
**Atty. Gen.** — Michael Easley, D, $90,915
**Treasurer** — Harlan E. Boyles, D, $90,915
**General Assembly:** meets odd years in Jan. at Raleigh. Members receive $13,951 annually and an expense allowance of $559 per month, plus subsistence and travel allowance while in session.
**Senate** — Dem., 26; Rep., 24. Total, 50
**House** — Dem., 52; Rep., 68. Total, 120

### North Dakota

**Governor** — Edward T. Schafer, R, $71,042
**Lt. Gov.** — Rosemarie Myrdal, R, $57,338
**Sec. of State** — Alvin A. Jaeger, R, $53,843
**Atty. Gen.** — Heidi Heitkamp, D, $60,768
**Treasurer** — Kathi Gilmore, D, $53,843
**Legislative Assembly:** meets odd years in Jan. at Bismarck. Members receive $480 per month salary, plus $90 per day salary and $35 per day expenses during session.
**Senate** — Dem., 20; Rep., 29. Total, 49
**House** — Dem., 23; Rep., 75. Total, 98

### Ohio

**Governor** — George V. Voinovich, R, $115,762
**Lt. Gov.** — Nancy P. Hollister, R, $59,861
**Sec. of State** — Bob Taft, R, $85,516
**Atty. Gen.** — Betty Montgomery, R, $85,516
**Treasurer** — J. Kenneth Blackwell, R, $85,516
**Auditor** — Jim Petro, $85,516
**General Assembly:** meets odd years at Columbus on 1st Mon. in Jan.; no limit on session. Members receive $42,426 annually.
**Senate** — Dem., 13; Rep., 20. Total, 33
**House** — Dem., 43; Rep., 56. Total, 99

### Oklahoma

**Governor** — Frank Keating, R, $70,000
**Lt. Gov.** — Mary Fallin, R, $62,500
**Sec. of State** — Tom Cole, R, $43,700

*(continued)*

**Atty. Gen.** — Drew Edmondson, D, $75,000
**Treasurer** — Robert Butkin, D, $70,000
**Auditor**— Clifton Scott, D, $70,000
**Legislature:** meets annually the first Mon. in Feb. at Oklahoma City. Members receive $32,000 annually.
**Senate** — Dem., 35; Rep., 13. Total, 48
**House** — Dem., 64; Rep., 36; 1 vacancy. Total, 101

### Oregon

**Governor** — John Kitzhaber, D, $80,000
**Sec. of State** — Phil Keisling, D, $61,500
**Atty. Gen.** — Ted Kulongoski, D, $66,000
**Treasurer** — Jim Hill, D, $61,500
**Legislative Assembly:** meets odd years in Jan. at Salem. Members receive $1,092 monthly, plus $77 expenses per day both during and out of session.
**Senate** — Dem., 11; Rep., 19. Total, 30
**House** — Dem., 26; Rep., 34. Total, 60

### Pennsylvania

**Governor** — Tom Ridge, R, $105,000
**Lt. Gov.** — Mark Schweiker, R, $83,000
**Sec. of the Commonwealth** — Yvette Kane, $72,000
**Atty. Gen.** — Thomas W. Corbett Jr., R, $84,000
**Treasurer** — Catherine Baker Knoll, D, $84,000
**General Assembly** — convenes annually in Jan. at Harrisburg. Members receive $47,000 annually, plus expenses.
**Senate** — Dem., 20; Rep., 29; 1 vacancy. Total, 50.
**House** — Dem., 101; Rep., 102. Total, 203

### Rhode Island

**Governor** — Lincoln C. Almond, R, $69,900
**Lt. Gov.** — Robert A. Weygand, D, $52,000
**Sec. of State** — James R. Langevin, D, $52,000
**Atty. Gen.** — Jeffrey B. Pine, R, $55,000
**Treasurer** — Nancy J. Mayer, R, $52,000
**General Assembly:** meets annually in Jan. at Providence. Members receive $10,000 annually.
**Senate** — Dem., 40; Rep., 10. Total, 50
**House** — Dem., 84; Rep., 16. Total, 100

### South Carolina

**Governor** — David M. Beasley, R, $106,078
**Lt. Gov.** — Robert L. Peeler, R, $46,545
**Sec. of State** — Jim Miles, R, $92,007.
**Comptroller Gen.** — Earle E. Morris Jr., D, $92,007
**Atty. Gen.** — Charles M. Condon, R, $92,007
**Treasurer** — Richard Eckstrom, R, $92,007
**General Assembly:** meets annually in Jan. at Columbia. Members receive $10,400 annually, plus $88 per day for expenses.
**Senate** — Dem., 25; Rep., 20; 1 ind. Total, 46
**House** — Dem.,62; Rep., 54; 4 ind.; 4 vacancy. Total, 124

### South Dakota

**Governor** — William Janklow, R, $79,875
**Lt. Gov.** — Carole Hillard, R, $10,581
**Sec. of State** — Joyce Hazeltine, R, $54,272
**Treasurer** — Dick Butler, D, $54,272
**Atty. Gen.** — Mark Barnett, R, $67,841
**Auditor** — Vernon Larson, R, $54,272
**Legislature:** meets annually in Jan. at Pierre. Members receive $4,267 for 40-day session in odd-numbered years, and $3,733 for 35-day session in even-numbered years, plus $75 per legislative day.
**Senate** — Dem., 16; Rep., 19. Total, 35
**House** — Dem., 24; Rep., 46. Total, 70

### Tennessee

**Governor** — Don Sundquist, R, $85,000
**Lt. Gov.** — John S. Wilder, D, $49,500
**Sec. of State** — Riley C. Darnell, D, $80,700
**Comptroller** — William Snodgrass, D, $80,700
**Atty. Gen.** — Charles W. Burson, D, $101,820
**General Assembly:** meets annually in Jan. at Nashville. Members receive $16,500 annual salary, plus $78 per day expenses while in session.
**Senate** — Dem., 16; Rep., 17. Total, 33
**House** — Dem., 59; Rep., 40. Total, 99

### Texas

**Governor** — George W. Bush, R, $99,122
**Lt. Gov.** — Bob Bullock, D, $7,200
**Sec. of State** — Antonio Garza Jr., R, $76,966
**Comptroller** — John Sharp, D, $79,247
**Atty. Gen.** — Dan Morales, D, $79,247
**Railroad Commissioners** — Carole Keeton Rylander, R, Chair; Barry Williamson, R; Charles R. Matthews, R; $79,247
**Legislature:** meets odd years in Jan. at Austin. Members receive $7,200 annually, plus $95 per day expenses while in session.
**Senate** — Dem., 17; Rep., 14. Total, 31
**House** — Dem., 88; Rep., 62. Total, 150

### Utah

**Governor** — Michael O. Leavitt, R, $77,250
**Lt. Gov.** — Olene S. Walker, R, $60,000
**Atty. Gen.** — Jan Graham, D, $65,000
**Treasurer** — Edward T. Alter, R, $60,000
**Legislature:** convenes for 45 days on 2d Mon. in Jan. each year; Members receive $85 per day, plus $35 a day expenses.
**Senate** — Dem., 10; Rep., 19. Total, 29
**House** — Dem., 20; Rep., 55. Total, 75

### Vermont

**Governor** — Howard Dean, D, $80,730
**Lt. Gov.** — Barbara W. Snelling, R, $33,655
**Sec. of State** — Jim Milne, R, $58,598
**Atty. Gen.** — Jeff Amestoy, R, $70,382
**Treasurer** — James Douglas, R, $58,598
**Auditor** -Edward Flanagan, D, $58,598
**General Assembly:** meets in Jan. at Montpelier (annual and biennial session). Members receive $510 per week while in session plus $100 per day for special session, plus expenses.
**Senate** — Dem., 12; Rep., 18. Total, 30
**House** — Dem., 86; Rep., 61; Prog. Coalition, 1; 2 ind. Total, 150

### Virginia

**Governor** — George F. Allen, R, $110,000
**Lt. Gov.** — Donald S. Beyer Jr., D, $32,000
**Atty. Gen.** — James S. Gilmore III, R, $97,500
**Sec. of the Commonwealth** — Elizabeth Beamer, R, $73,023
**Treasurer** — Ronald L. Tillett, $89,500
**General Assembly:** meets annually in Jan. at Richmond. Members receive $18,000 (senate), $17,640 (assembly) annually, plus expense and mileage allowances.
**Senate** — Dem., 20; Rep., 20. Total, 40
**House** — Dem., 52; Rep., 47; 1 ind. Total, 100

### Washington

**Governor** — Mike Lowry, D, $121,000
**Lt. Gov.** — Joel Pritchard, R, $62,700
**Sec. of State** — Ralph Munro, R, $64,300
**Atty. Gen.** — Christine Gregoire, D, $92,000
**Treasurer** — Daniel K. Grimm, D, $79,500
**Legislature:** meets annually in Jan. at Olympia. Members receive $25,900 annually, plus $66 per diem while in session, and $66 per diem for attending meetings during interim.
**Senate** — Dem., 24; Rep., 24; 1 vacancy. Total, 49
**House** — Dem., 37; Rep., 61. Total, 98

### West Virginia

**Governor** — Gaston Caperton, D, $90,000
**Sec. of State** — Ken Hechler, D, $65,000
**Atty. Gen.** — Darrell McGraw, D, $75,000
**Treasurer** — Larrie Bailey, D, $65,000
**Comm. of Agric.** — Gus Douglass, D, $70,000
**Auditor** — Glen B. Gainer 3d, D, $70,000
**Legislature:** meets annually in Jan. at Charleston. Members receive $15,000 annually.
**Senate** — Dem., 32; Rep., 2. Total, 34
**House** — Dem., 79; Rep., 21. Total, 100

### Wisconsin

**Governor** — Tommy G. Thompson, R, $101,861
**Lt. Gov.** — Scott McCallum, R, $54,795
**Sec. of State** — Douglas La Follette, D, $49,719
**Treasurer** — Jack Voight, R, $49,719
**Atty. Gen.** — James E. Doyle, D, $97,756
**Legislature:** meets in Jan. at Madison. Members receive $35,070 annually, plus $75 per day expenses.
**Senate** — Dem., 17; Rep., 16. Total, 33
**Assembly** — Dem., 47; Rep., 51; 1 vacancy. Total, 99

### Wyoming

**Governor** — Jim Geringer, R, $95,000
**Sec. of State** — Diana J. Ohman, R, $77,000
**Atty. Gen.** — William U. Hill, no statutory salary
**Treasurer** — Stan Smith, R, $77,000
**Auditor** — Dave Ferrari, R, $77,000
**Legislature:** meets odd years in Jan., even years in Feb., at Cheyenne. Members receive $125 per day while in session, plus $80 per day for expenses.
**Senate** — Dem., 10; Rep., 20. Total, 30.
**House** — Dem., 13; Rep., 47. Total, 60.

(1) Gov. Weld has declined a recent increase and draws his former $75,000 salary.

# ECONOMICS

## U.S. Budget Receipts and Outlays, 1992-95

**Source:** Financial Management Service, U.S. Dept. of the Treasury

(Fiscal year ends Sept. 30)

(millions of dollars; some figures may not add because of independent rounding; outlays incl. selected depts. and agencies)

| Classification | Fiscal 1992 | Fiscal 1993 | Fiscal 1994 | Fiscal 1995 |
|---|---|---|---|---|
| **Net Receipts** | | | | |
| Individual income taxes | $475,964 | $509,680 | $543,055 | $590,157 |
| Corporation income taxes | 100,270 | 117,520 | 140,385 | 157,088 |
| Social insurance taxes and contributions: | | | | |
| Federal old-age and survivors insurance | 273,137 | 281,735 | 302,607 | 284,091 |
| Federal disability insurance | 29,289 | 30,199 | 32,419 | 66,989 |
| Federal hospital insurance | 79,108 | 81,224 | 90,062 | 96,025 |
| Railroad retirement fund | 3,957 | 3,781 | 3,723 | 3,942 |
| **Total employment taxes and contributions** | **385,491** | **396,939** | **428,810** | **451,046** |
| Other insurance and retirement: | | | | |
| Unemployment | 23,410 | 26,556 | 28,004 | 28,878 |
| Federal employees retirement | 4,683 | 4,709 | 4,563 | 4,461 |
| Non-federal employees | 105 | 96 | 98 | 89 |
| **Total social insurance taxes and contributions** | **413,689** | **428,300** | **461,475** | **484,474** |
| Excise taxes | 45,569 | 48,057 | 55,225 | 57,485 |
| Estate and gift taxes | 11,143 | 12,577 | 15,225 | 14,764 |
| Customs duties | 17,359 | 18,802 | 20,099 | 19,300 |
| Deposits of earnings by Federal Reserve Banks | 22,920 | 14,908 | 18,023 | 23,378 |
| All other miscellaneous receipts | 3,538 | 3,382 | 3,965 | 3,928 |
| **Net Budget Receipts** | **$1,090,453** | **$1,153,226** | **$1,257,451** | **$1,350,576** |
| **Net Outlays** | | | | |
| Legislative Branch | $2,677 | $2,406 | $2,552 | $2,621 |
| The Judiciary | 2,308 | 2,628 | 2,659 | 2,903 |
| Executive Office of the President: | | | | |
| The White House Office | 36 | 40 | 40 | 37 |
| Office of Management and Budget | 54 | 55 | 57 | 56 |
| **Total Executive Office** | **186** | **194** | **229** | **213** |
| Funds appropriated to the President: | | | | |
| International security assistance | 7,203 | 7,322 | 6,306 | 4,952 |
| Multilateral assistance | 1,717 | 1,547 | 1,753 | 2,194 |
| Agency for International Development | 2,142 | 2,099 | 2,544 | 3,252 |
| International Development Assistance | 4,029 | 3,855 | 4,445 | 5,557 |
| **Total funds appropriated to the President** | **11,113** | **11,526** | **10,511** | **11,164** |
| Agriculture Department: | | | | |
| Food stamp program | 22,800 | 24,602 | 25,549 | 25,554 |
| Farm Service Agency | NA | NA | 14,627 | 9,123 |
| Forest Service | 3,293 | 3,292 | 3,353 | 3,415 |
| **Total Agriculture Department** | **56,436** | **63,112** | **60,753** | **56,667** |
| Commerce Department: | | | | |
| Bureau of the Census | 302 | 346 | 250 | 293 |
| **Total Commerce Department** | **2,567** | **2,798** | **2,915** | **3,403** |
| Defense Department (military): | | | | |
| Military personnel | 81,171 | 75,904 | 73,137 | 70,807 |
| Operation and maintenance | 92,042 | 94,121 | 87,880 | 90,851 |
| Procurement | 74,881 | 69,936 | 61,769 | 54,984 |
| Research, development, test, evaluation | 34,632 | 36,968 | 34,786 | 34,710 |
| Military construction | 4,262 | 4,831 | 4,979 | 6,826 |
| **Total Defense Department** (military) | **286,632** | **278,586** | **268,646** | **259,565** |
| Defense Department (civil) | 28,270 | 29,266 | 30,407 | 31,664 |
| Education Department | 26,047 | 30,290 | 24,699 | 31,321 |
| Energy Department | 15,439 | 16,801 | 17,840 | 17,618 |
| Health and Human Services Department: | | | | |
| Food and Drug Administration | 752 | 733 | 801 | 858 |
| National Institutes of Health | 8,376 | 9,543 | 10,165 | 10,875 |
| Public Health Service | 17,447 | 18,872 | 19,760 | 20,982 |
| Health Care Financing Adm. | 239,366 | 266,452 | 285,117 | 310,657 |
| **Total Health and Human Services Dept.** | **257,293** | **282,781** | **278,901** | **303,075** |
| Housing and Urban Development Department | 24,470 | 25,181 | 25,845 | 29,045 |
| Interior Department | 6,555 | 6,720 | 6,900 | 7,415 |
| Justice Department: | | | | |
| Federal Bureau of Investigation | 1,832 | 1,975 | 2,106 | 2,041 |
| **Total Justice Department** | **9,802** | **10,170** | **10,005** | **10,781** |
| Labor Department: | | | | |
| Unemployment Trust Fund | 41,294 | 39,869 | 30,458 | 25,282 |
| **Total Labor Department** | **47,163** | **44,738** | **37,130** | **32,169** |
| State Department | 5,007 | 5,385 | 5,718 | 5,347 |
| Transportation Department: | | | | |
| Federal Aviation Administration | 8,155 | 8,800 | 8,784 | 9,206 |
| **Total Transportation Department** | **32,510** | **34,457** | **37,228** | **38,776** |
| Treasury Department: | | | | |
| Internal Revenue Service | 17,403 | 18,437 | 21,810 | 25,579 |
| Interest on the public debt | 292,323 | 292,502 | 296,278 | 332,414 |
| **Total Treasury Department** | **292,964** | **298,802** | **307,577** | **348,441** |
| Veterans Affairs Department | 33,897 | 35,487 | 37,401 | 37,769 |
| Environmental Protection Agency | 5,932 | 5,930 | 5,855 | 6,349 |
| General Services Administration | 469 | 743 | 334 | 708 |
| National Aeronautics and Space Administration | 13,961 | 14,305 | 13,695 | 13,377 |
| Office of Personnel Management | 35,596 | 36,794 | 38,596 | 41,279 |
| Small Business Administration | 546 | 785 | 779 | 678 |
| Social Security Administration[1] | 307,819 | 328,028 | 345,817 | 362,226 |

*(continued)*

| Classification | Fiscal 1992 | Fiscal 1993 | Fiscal 1994 | Fiscal 1995 |
|---|---|---|---|---|
| Other independent agencies: | | | | |
| Board for International Broadcasting | $ 210 | $ 246 | $ 213 | $ 239 |
| Corporation for Natl. and Community Service[2] | 194 | 208 | 211 | 424 |
| Corporation for Public Broadcasting | 327 | 319 | 275 | 286 |
| District of Columbia | 691 | 698 | 698 | 714 |
| Equal Employment Opportunity Commission | 209 | 218 | 229 | 234 |
| Export-Import Bank of the U.S. | –119 | –747 | –832 | –53 |
| Federal Communications Commission | 78 | 94 | 49 | 6 |
| Federal Deposit Insurance Corporation | 11,843 | –8,412 | –11,396 | –6,922 |
| Federal Trade Commission | 71 | 64 | 69 | 31 |
| Interstate Commerce Commission | 40 | 41 | 43 | 37 |
| Legal Services Corporation | 329 | 389 | 375 | 429 |
| National Archives & Records Adm. | 225 | 269 | 261 | 219 |
| National Foundation on the Arts and Humanities | 332 | 343 | 354 | 355 |
| National Labor Relations Board | 155 | 171 | 173 | 174 |
| National Science Foundation | 2,249 | 2,452 | 2,642 | 2,847 |
| Nuclear Regulatory Commission | 50 | –19 | 46 | 28 |
| Railroad Retirement Board | 4,843 | 4,782 | 4,780 | 4,282 |
| Securities and Exchange Commission | 117 | 99 | 68 | 122 |
| Smithsonian Institution | 378 | 395 | 422 | 432 |
| Tennessee Valley Authority | 1,469 | 1,629 | 1,210 | 1,313 |
| U.S. Information Agency | 1,050 | 1,088 | 1,165 | 1,160 |
| Total other independent agencies | 18,648 | –9,992 | 11,030 | –2,555 |
| Undistributed offsetting receipts | –117,111 | –119,711 | –123,469 | –137,631 |
| **Net Budget Outlays** | **$1,380,794** | **$1,408,532** | **$1,460,553** | **$1,514,389** |
| Less net receipts | 1,090,543 | 1,153,226 | 1,257,451 | 1,350,576 |
| **Deficit** | **$–290,340** | **$–255,306** | **$–203,102** | **$–163,813** |

(1) The Social Security Administration (SSA), formerly a part of the Dept. of Health and Human Services, became an independent agency, Mar. 31, 1995; figures given prior to 1994 are sums of outlays originally listed under the Health and Human Services Dept. total with the heading "Social Security (Off Budget)" plus other administrative SSA outlays. (2) Formerly Action. NA=not applicable.

## Summary of Receipts, Outlays, and Surpluses or Deficits, 1936-91

**Source:** Financial Management Service, U.S. Dept. of the Treasury

(millions of dollars)

| Fiscal Year[1] | Receipts | Total Outlays | Surplus or Deficit (–)[2] |
|---|---|---|---|
| 1936 | $3,923 | $8,228 | $–4,304 |
| 1937 | 5,387 | 7,580 | –2,193 |
| 1938 | 6,751 | 6,840 | –89 |
| 1939 | 6,295 | 9,141 | –2,846 |
| 1940 | 6,548 | 9,468 | –2,920 |
| 1941 | 8,712 | 13,653 | –4,941 |
| 1942 | 14,634 | 35,137 | –20,503 |
| 1943 | 24,001 | 78,555 | –54,554 |
| 1944 | 43,747 | 91,304 | –47,557 |
| 1945 | 45,159 | 92,712 | –47,553 |
| 1946 | 39,296 | 55,232 | –15,936 |
| 1947 | 38,514 | 34,496 | 4,018 |
| 1948 | 41,560 | 29,764 | 11,796 |
| 1949 | 39,415 | 38,835 | 580 |
| 1950 | 39,443 | 42,562 | –3,119 |
| 1951 | 51,616 | 45,514 | 6,102 |
| 1952 | 66,167 | 67,686 | –1,519 |
| 1953 | 69,608 | 76,101 | –6,493 |
| 1954 | 69,701 | 70,855 | –1,154 |
| 1955 | 65,451 | 68,444 | –2,993 |
| 1956 | 74,587 | 70,640 | 3,947 |
| 1957 | 79,990 | 76,578 | 3,412 |
| 1958 | 79,636 | 82,405 | –2,769 |
| 1959 | 79,249 | 92,098 | –12,849 |
| 1960 | 92,492 | 92,191 | 301 |
| 1961 | 94,388 | 97,723 | –3,335 |
| 1962 | 99,676 | 106,821 | –7,146 |
| 1963 | 106,560 | 111,316 | –4,756 |
| 1964 | 112,613 | 118,528 | –5,915 |
| 1965 | $116,817 | $118,228 | $ –1,411 |
| 1966 | 130,835 | 134,532 | –3,698 |
| 1967 | 148,822 | 157,464 | –8,643 |
| 1968 | 152,973 | 178,134 | –25,161 |
| 1969 | 186,882 | 183,640 | 3,242 |
| 1970 | 192,807 | 195,649 | –2,842 |
| 1971 | 187,139 | 210,172 | –23,033 |
| 1972 | 207,309 | 230,681 | –23,373 |
| 1973 | 230,799 | 245,707 | –14,908 |
| 1974 | 263,224 | 269,359 | –6,135 |
| 1975 | 279,090 | 332,332 | –53,242 |
| 1976 | 298,060 | 371,779 | –73,719 |
| Transition quarter[3] | 81,232 | 95,973 | –14,741 |
| 1977 | 355,559 | 409,203 | –53,644 |
| 1978 | 399,561 | 458,729 | –59,168 |
| 1979 | 463,302 | 503,464 | –40,162 |
| 1980 | 517,112 | 590,920 | –73,808 |
| 1981 | 599,272 | 678,209 | –78,936 |
| 1982 | 617,766 | 745,706 | –127,940 |
| 1983 | 600,562 | 808,327 | –207,764 |
| 1984 | 666,457 | 851,781 | –185,324 |
| 1985 | 734,057 | 946,316 | –212,260 |
| 1986 | 769,091 | 990,231 | –221,140 |
| 1987 | 854,143 | 1,003,804 | – 149,661 |
| 1988 | 908,166 | 1,063,318 | –155,151 |
| 1989 | 990,701 | 1,144,020 | –153,319 |
| 1990 | 1,031,308 | 1,251,776 | –220,469 |
| 1991 | 1,054,265 | 1,323,757 | –269,492 |

(1) Fiscal years 1936 to 1976 ending June 30; after 1976, fiscal years end Sept. 30. (2) May not exactly equal difference between figures shown, because of rounding. (3) Transition quarter covers July 1, 1976-Sept. 30, 1976.

## Net Receipts and Outlays, 1789-1935

**Source:** U.S. Dept. of the Treasury; annual statements for years ending June 30 unless otherwise noted

(thousands of dollars)

| Yearly Average | Receipts | Outlays |
|---|---|---|
| 1789-1800[1] | $ 5,717 | $ 5,776 |
| 1801-1810[2] | 13,056 | 9,086 |
| 1811-1820[2] | 21,032 | 23,943 |
| 1821-1830[2] | 21,928 | 16,162 |
| 1831-1840[2] | 30,461 | 24,495 |
| 1841-1850[2] | 28,545 | 34,097 |
| 1851-1860 | 60,237 | 60,163 |
| 1861-1865 | 160,907 | 683,785 |
| 1866-1870 | $447,301 | $377,642 |
| 1871-1875 | 336,830 | 287,460 |
| 1876-1880 | 288,124 | 255,598 |
| 1881-1885 | 366,961 | 257,691 |
| 1886-1890 | 375,448 | 279,134 |
| 1891-1895 | 352,891 | 363,599 |
| 1896-1900 | 434,877 | 457,451 |
| 1901-1905 | $ 559,481 | $ 535,559 |
| 1906-1910 | 628,507 | 639,178 |
| 1911-1915 | 710,227 | 720,252 |
| 1916-1920 | 3,483,652 | 8,065,333 |
| 1921-1925 | 4,306,673 | 3,578,989 |
| 1926-1930 | 4,069,138 | 3,182,807 |
| 1931-1935 | 2,770,973 | 5,214,874 |

(1) Average for period March 4, 1789, to Dec. 31, 1800. (2) Years ended Dec. 31, 1801 to 1842; average for 1841-1850 is for the period Jan. 1, 1841, to June 30, 1850.

## Public Debt of the U.S.

**Source:** Bureau of Public Debt, U.S. Dept. of the Treasury

| Fiscal year | Debt (billions) | Debt per. cap. (dollars) | Interest paid (billions) | % of federal outlays | Fiscal year | Debt (billions) | Debt per. cap. (dollars) | Interest paid (billions) | % of federal outlays |
|---|---|---|---|---|---|---|---|---|---|
| 1870 | $2.4 | $61.06 | — | — | 1979 | $826.5 | $3,669 | $59.8 | 11.9 |
| 1880 | 2.0 | 41.60 | — | — | 1980 | 907.7 | 3,985 | 74.9 | 12.7 |
| 1890 | 1.1 | 17.80 | — | — | 1981 | 997.9 | 4,338 | 95.6 | 14.1 |
| 1900 | 1.2 | 16.60 | — | — | 1982 | 1,142.0 | 4,913 | 117.4 | 15.7 |
| 1910 | 1.1 | 12.41 | — | — | 1983 | 1,377.2 | 5,870 | 128.8 | 15.9 |
| 1920 | 24.2 | 228 | — | — | 1984 | 1,572.3 | 6,640 | 153.8 | 18.1 |
| 1930 | 16.1 | 131 | — | — | 1985 | 1,823.1 | 7,598 | 178.9 | 18.9 |
| 1940 | 43.0 | 325 | $1.0 | 10.5 | 1986 | 2,125.3 | 8,774 | 190.2 | 19.2 |
| 1945 | 258.7 | 1,849 | 3.8 | 4.1 | 1987 | 2,350.3 | 9,615 | 195.4 | 19.5 |
| 1950 | 256.1 | 1,688 | 5.7 | 13.4 | 1988 | 2,602.3 | 10,534 | 214.1 | 20.1 |
| 1955 | 272.8 | 1,651 | 6.4 | 9.4 | 1989 | 2,857.4 | 11,545 | 240.9 | 21.0 |
| 1960 | 284.1 | 1,572 | 9.2 | 10.0 | 1990 | 3,233.3 | 13,000 | 264.8 | 21.1 |
| 1965 | 313.8 | 1,613 | 11.3 | 9.6 | 1991 | 3,665.3 | 14,436 | 285.5 | 21.6 |
| 1970 | 370.1 | 1,814 | 19.3 | 9.9 | 1992 | 4,064.6 | 15,846 | 292.3 | 21.2 |
| 1975 | 533.2 | 2,475 | 32.7 | 9.8 | 1993 | 4,411.5 | 17,105 | 292.5 | 20.8 |
| 1976 | 620.4 | 2,852 | 37.1 | 10.0 | 1994 | 4,692.8 | 18,025 | 296.3 | 20.3 |
| 1977 | 698.8 | 3,170 | 41.9 | 10.2 | 1995 | 4,974.0 | 18,930 | 332.4 | 22.0 |
| 1978 | 771.5 | 3,463 | 48.7 | 10.6 | | | | | |

**Note:** Through 1976 the fiscal year ended June 30. From 1977 on, the fiscal year ends Sept. 30.

## Consumer Price Index

The Consumer Price Index (CPI) is a measure of the average change in prices over time of basic consumer goods and services. From Jan. 1978, the Bureau of Labor Statistics began publishing CPI's for 2 population groups: (1) a CPI for all urban consumers (CPI-U), which covers about 80% of the total population; and (2) a CPI for urban wage earners and clerical workers (CPI-W), which covers about 32% of the total population. The CPI-U includes, in addition to wage earners and clerical workers, groups such as professional, managerial, and technical workers, the self-employed, short-term workers, the unemployed, retirees, and others not in the labor force.

The CPI is based on prices of food, clothing, shelter, and fuels; transportation fares; charges for doctors' and dentists' services, drug prices; and prices of the other goods and services bought for day-to-day living. The index currently measures price changes from a designated reference period, 1982-84, which equals 100.0.

Use of this reference period began in Jan. 1988.

## Consumer Price Indexes, First Half 1996

**Source:** Bureau of Labor Statistics, U.S. Dept. of Labor

(Data are semiannual averages of monthly figures)

| | CPI-U (all urban consumers) | | CPI-W (urban wage-earners/clerical) | |
|---|---|---|---|---|
| (1982-84=100) | 1st half 1996 | % change 2d half 1995 to 1st half 1996 | 1st half 1996 | % change 2d half 1995 to 1st half 1996 |
| **All items** | **155.8** | **1.7** | **153.1** | **1.6** |
| Food, beverages | 152.2 | 1.8 | 151.6 | 1.8 |
| Housing | 151.7 | 1.5 | 148.5 | 1.4 |
| Apparel and upkeep | 132.6 | 0.7 | 131.8 | 0.9 |
| Transportation | 142.2 | 2.1 | 142.0 | 2.2 |
| Medical care | 226.7 | 1.9 | 226.1 | 1.9 |
| Entertainment | 158.4 | 2.2 | 156.1 | 2.2 |
| Other goods, services | 213.2 | 1.8 | 210.1 | 1.7 |
| Services | 172.6 | 1.5 | 169.9 | 1.5 |
| **Special indexes** | | | | |
| All items less food | 156.5 | 1.6 | 153.4 | 1.7 |
| Commodities less food | 132.4 | 1.8 | 132.6 | 1.8 |
| Nondurables | 142.7 | 2.1 | 142.4 | 2.2 |
| Energy | 108.7 | 3.1 | 108.3 | 3.3 |
| All items less energy | 162.1 | 1.6 | 159.4 | 1.5 |

## Consumer Price Indexes (CPI-U),[1] Annual Percent Change, 1984-95

**Source:** Bureau of Labor Statistics, U.S. Dept. of Labor

| | 1984[2] | 1985 | 1986 | 1987 | 1988 | 1989 | 1990 | 1991 | 1992 | 1993 | 1994 | 1995 |
|---|---|---|---|---|---|---|---|---|---|---|---|---|
| **All items** | **4.3** | **3.6** | **1.9** | **3.6** | **4.1** | **4.8** | **5.4** | **4.2** | **3.0** | **3.0** | **2.6** | **2.8** |
| Food | 3.8 | 2.3 | 3.2 | 4.1 | 4.1 | 5.8 | 5.8 | 2.9 | 1.2 | 2.2 | 2.4 | 2.8 |
| Shelter | 4.9 | 5.6 | 5.5 | 4.7 | 4.8 | 4.5 | 5.4 | 4.5 | 3.3 | 3.0 | 3.1 | 3.2 |
| Rent, residential | 5.2 | 6.2 | 5.8 | 4.1 | 3.8 | 3.9 | 5.6 | 6.1 | 2.5 | 2.3 | 2.5 | 2.5 |
| Fuel and other utilities | 4.6 | 1.6 | −2.3 | −1.1 | −1.4 | 3.3 | 3.5 | 3.3 | 2.2 | 3.0 | 1.0 | 0.7 |
| Apparel and upkeep | 1.9 | 2.8 | 0.9 | 4.4 | 4.3 | 2.8 | 4.6 | 3.7 | 2.5 | 1.4 | −0.2 | −1.0 |
| Private transportation | 4.3 | 2.5 | −4.7 | −3.0 | 3.3 | 4.9 | 5.2 | 2.6 | 2.2 | 2.3 | 3.1 | 3.7 |
| New cars | 2.9 | 3.2 | 4.2 | 3.6 | 2.0 | 2.0 | 1.8 | 3.8 | 2.5 | 2.4 | 3.4 | 2.2 |
| Gasoline | −1.6 | 0.8 | −21.9 | −4.0 | 0.9 | 9.5 | 14.1 | −1.8 | −0.2 | −1.3 | 0.5 | 1.6 |
| Public transportation | 6.2 | 4.5 | 5.9 | 3.5 | 1.8 | 5.0 | 10.1 | 4.4 | 1.7 | 10.3 | 3.0 | 2.3 |
| Medical care | 6.2 | 6.3 | 7.5 | 6.6 | 6.5 | 7.7 | 9.0 | 8.7 | 7.4 | 5.9 | 4.8 | 4.5 |
| Entertainment | 3.7 | 3.9 | 3.4 | 3.3 | 4.3 | 5.2 | 4.7 | 4.5 | 2.8 | 2.5 | 2.9 | 2.5 |
| Commodities | 3.4 | 2.1 | −0.9 | 3.2 | 3.5 | 4.7 | 5.2 | 4.2 | 2.0 | 1.9 | 1.7 | 1.9 |

(1) The Consumer Price Index CPI-U measures the average change in prices of goods and services purchased by all urban consumers. (2) Change from 1983.

# Consumer Price Indexes for Selected Items and Groups, 1970-95

**Source:** Bureau of Labor Statistics, U.S. Dept. of Labor

(1982-84 = 100. Annual averages of monthly figures. For all urban consumers.)

| | 1970 | 1975 | 1980 | 1985 | 1990 | 1993 | 1994 | 1995 |
|---|---|---|---|---|---|---|---|---|
| **All Items** | **38.8** | **53.8** | **82.4** | **107.6** | **130.7** | **144.5** | **148.2** | **152.4** |
| **Food and beverages** | **40.1** | **60.2** | **86.7** | **105.6** | **132.1** | **141.6** | **144.9** | **148.9** |
| Food | 39.2 | 59.8 | 86.8 | 105.6 | 132.4 | 140.9 | 144.3 | 148.4 |
| Food at home | 39.9 | 61.8 | 88.4 | 104.3 | 132.3 | 140.1 | 144.1 | 148.8 |
| Cereals and bakery products | 37.1 | 62.9 | 83.9 | 107.9 | 140.0 | 156.6 | 163.0 | 167.5 |
| Meats, poultry, fish, and eggs | 44.6 | 67.0 | 92.0 | 100.1 | 130.0 | 135.5 | 137.2 | 138.8 |
| Dairy products | 44.7 | 62.6 | 90.9 | 103.2 | 126.5 | 129.4 | 131.7 | 132.8 |
| Fruits and vegetables | 37.8 | 56.9 | 82.1 | 106.4 | 149.0 | 159.0 | 165.0 | 177.7 |
| Sugar and sweets | 30.5 | 65.3 | 90.5 | 105.8 | 124.7 | 133.4 | 135.2 | 137.5 |
| Fats and oils | 39.2 | 73.5 | 89.3 | 106.9 | 126.3 | 130.0 | 133.5 | 137.3 |
| Nonalcoholic beverages | 27.1 | 41.3 | 91.4 | 104.3 | 113.5 | 114.6 | 123.2 | 131.7 |
| Other prepared foods | 39.6 | 58.9 | 83.6 | 106.4 | 131.2 | 143.7 | 147.5 | 151.1 |
| Food away from home | 37.5 | 54.5 | 83.4 | 108.3 | 133.4 | 143.2 | 145.7 | 149.0 |
| Alcoholic beverages | 52.1 | 65.9 | 86.4 | 106.4 | 129.3 | 149.6 | 151.5 | 153.9 |
| **Housing** | **36.4** | **50.7** | **81.1** | **107.7** | **128.5** | **141.2** | **144.8** | **148.5** |
| Shelter | 35.5 | 48.8 | 81.0 | 109.8 | 140.0 | 155.7 | 160.5 | 165.7 |
| Rent | 46.5 | 58.0 | 80.9 | 111.8 | 146.7 | 165.0 | 169.4 | 174.3 |
| Maintenance and repairs | 35.8 | 54.1 | 82.4 | 106.5 | 122.2 | 130.6 | 130.8 | 135.0 |
| Fuel and other utilities | 29.1 | 45.4 | 75.4 | 106.5 | 111.6 | 121.3 | 122.8 | 123.7 |
| Energy services | 31.8 | 50.0 | 75.8 | 106.9 | 117.4 | 118.5 | 119.2 | 119.2 |
| Household furnishings & operation | 46.8 | 63.4 | 86.3 | 103.8 | 113.3 | 119.3 | 121.0 | 123.0 |
| House furnishings | 55.5 | 69.8 | 88.5 | 101.7 | 106.7 | 109.5 | 111.0 | 111.2 |
| **Apparel and upkeep** | **59.2** | **72.5** | **90.9** | **105.0** | **124.1** | **133.7** | **133.4** | **132.0** |
| Apparel commodities | 63.3 | 76.7 | 92.9 | 104.0 | 122.0 | 131.0 | 130.4 | 127.0 |
| Men's and boys' | 62.2 | 75.5 | 89.4 | 105.0 | 120.4 | 127.5 | 126.4 | 126.2 |
| Women's and girls' | 71.8 | 85.5 | 96.0 | 104.9 | 122.6 | 132.6 | 130.9 | 126.9 |
| Footwear | 56.8 | 69.6 | 91.8 | 102.3 | 117.4 | 125.9 | 126.0 | 125.4 |
| **Transportation** | **37.5** | **50.1** | **83.1** | **106.4** | **120.5** | **130.4** | **134.3** | **139.1** |
| Private | 37.5 | 50.6 | 84.2 | 106.2 | 118.8 | 127.5 | 131.4 | 136.3 |
| New cars | 53.0 | 62.9 | 88.4 | 106.1 | 121.4 | 131.5 | 136.0 | 139.0 |
| Used cars | 31.2 | 43.8 | 62.3 | 113.7 | 117.6 | 133.9 | 141.7 | 156.5 |
| Gasoline | 27.9 | 45.1 | 97.5 | 98.6 | 101.0 | 97.7 | 98.2 | 99.8 |
| Public | 35.2 | 43.5 | 69.0 | 110.5 | 142.6 | 167.0 | 172.0 | 175.9 |
| **Medical care** | **34.0** | **47.5** | **74.9** | **113.5** | **162.8** | **201.4** | **211.0** | **220.5** |
| **Entertainment** | **47.5** | **62.0** | **83.6** | **107.9** | **132.4** | **145.8** | **150.1** | **153.9** |
| **Other goods and services** | **40.9** | **53.9** | **75.2** | **114.5** | **159.0** | **192.9** | **198.5** | **206.9** |
| Tobacco products | 43.1 | 54.7 | 72.0 | 116.7 | 181.5 | 228.4 | 220.0 | 225.7 |
| Personal care | 43.5 | 57.9 | 81.9 | 106.3 | 130.4 | 141.5 | 144.6 | 147.1 |
| Toilet goods and personal care appliances | 42.7 | 58.0 | 79.6 | 107.6 | 128.2 | 139.0 | 141.5 | 143.1 |
| Personal care services | 44.2 | 57.7 | 83.7 | 108.9 | 132.8 | 144.0 | 147.9 | 151.5 |
| Personal, educational expenses | 35.5 | 48.7 | 70.9 | 119.1 | 170.2 | 210.7 | 223.2 | 235.5 |

# Consumer Price Index by Region and Selected Cities, 1995-96

**Source:** Bureau of Labor Statistics, U.S. Dept. of Labor

| | CPI-U Indexes[1] | | | % change | CPI-W Indexes[2] | | | % change |
|---|---|---|---|---|---|---|---|---|
| (1982-84 = 100) | Avg. 1995 | July 1996 | Aug. 1996 | Aug. 1995-Aug. 1996 | Avg. 1995 | July 1996 | Aug. 1996 | Aug. 1995-Aug. 1996 |
| **U.S. city average** | **152.4** | **157.0** | **157.3** | **2.9** | **149.8** | **154.3** | **154.5** | **2.9** |
| **Northeast urban** | **159.1** | **163.4** | **164.0** | **2.7** | **156.6** | **160.9** | **161.4** | **2.7** |
| More than 1,200,000 | 159.7 | 164.1 | 164.7 | 2.7 | 156.2 | 160.5 | 161.0 | 2.7 |
| 500,000 to 1,200,000 | 157.1 | 161.8 | 162.2 | 2.7 | 155.0 | 159.7 | 160.0 | 2.8 |
| 50,000 to 500,000 | 157.5 | 161.5 | 161.8 | 2.1 | 159.1 | 162.9 | 163.2 | 2.1 |
| **North central urban** | **148.4** | **153.2** | **153.4** | **3.0** | **145.2** | **149.8** | **149.9** | **3.0** |
| More than 1,200,000 | 149.3 | 153.7 | 154.0 | 2.8 | 145.4 | 149.7 | 149.9 | 2.8 |
| 360,000 to 1,200,000 | 147.2 | 152.4 | 152.8 | 3.4 | 143.6 | 148.3 | 148.7 | 3.3 |
| 50,000 to 360,000 | 149.8 | 154.6 | 154.7 | 3.2 | 147.2 | 151.9 | 151.9 | 3.1 |
| Less than 50,000 | 144.7 | 150.4 | 150.4 | 3.2 | 142.9 | 148.5 | 148.5 | 3.1 |
| **South urban** | **149.0** | **154.0** | **154.1** | **2.9** | **147.6** | **152.6** | **152.7** | **3.0** |
| More than 1,200,000 | 148.7 | 153.2 | 153.1 | 2.5 | 146.9 | 151.6 | 151.4 | 2.6 |
| 450,000 to 1,200,000 | 151.3 | 156.7 | 156.9 | 3.2 | 147.8 | 152.9 | 153.1 | 3.2 |
| 50,000 to 450,000 | 148.4 | 153.7 | 154.0 | 3.1 | 148.4 | 153.6 | 153.9 | 3.0 |
| Less than 50,000 | 147.7 | 152.5 | 152.6 | 3.2 | 148.0 | 152.8 | 153.1 | 3.2 |
| **West urban** | **153.5** | **157.9** | **158.0** | **2.8** | **150.5** | **154.9** | **154.9** | **2.8** |
| More than 1,250,000 | 154.0 | 158.0 | 158.1 | 2.6 | 149.6 | 153.4 | 153.4 | 2.5 |
| 50,000 to 330,000 | 156.6 | 162.4 | 162.6 | 3.6 | 153.7 | 159.3 | 159.5 | 3.6 |
| **Selected areas** | | | | | | | | |
| Chicago, IL–Gary–Lake County, IL–IN–WI | 153.3 | 157.7 | 158.1 | 2.8 | 148.4 | 152.7 | 152.9 | 2.8 |
| L.A.–Anaheim–Riverside, CA | 154.6 | 157.6 | 157.3 | 1.9 | 149.4 | 152.3 | 151.9 | 1.8 |
| New York, NY–Northern NJ–Long Island, NY–NJ–CT | 162.2 | 166.7 | 167.2 | 2.7 | 158.3 | 162.8 | 163.3 | 2.8 |
| Phila.–Wilm.–Trenton, PA–NJ–DE–MD | 158.7 | 162.8 | 163.6 | 2.5 | 158.3 | 162.1 | 163.0 | 2.4 |
| San Francisco–Oakland–San Jose, CA | 151.6 | 155.9 | 155.6 | 2.7 | 149.3 | 153.4 | 153.0 | 2.5 |
| Baltimore, MD | 150.7 | 155.7 | — | 2.8* | 149.7 | 154.6 | — | 2.7* |
| Boston–Lawrence–Salem, MA–NH | 158.6 | 162.0 | — | 2.7* | 157.4 | 160.9 | — | 2.7* |
| Cleveland–Akron–Lorain, OH | 147.9 | 152.1 | — | 2.7* | 140.2 | 144.3 | — | 2.9* |
| Miami–Ft. Lauderdale, FL | 148.9 | 152.4 | — | 2.8* | 146.9 | 150.8 | — | 2.9* |
| St. Louis–East St. Louis, MO–IL | 145.2 | 149.9 | — | 3.0* | 144.7 | 149.0 | — | 2.6* |
| Washington, DC–MD–VA | 155.3 | 160.1 | — | 2.6* | 152.7 | 157.6 | — | 2.7* |
| Dallas–Fort Worth, TX | 144.9 | — | 149.5 | 3.0 | 144.6 | — | 149.5 | 3.2 |
| Detroit–Ann Arbor, MI | 148.6 | — | 152.7 | 2.6 | 143.9 | — | 148.0 | 2.8 |
| Houston–Galveston–Brazoria, TX | 139.8 | — | 142.8 | 1.9 | 139.4 | — | 142.2 | 1.7 |
| Pittsburgh–Beaver Valley, PA | 149.2 | — | 153.6 | 2.3 | 142.9 | — | 147.2 | 2.4 |

*From July 1995 to July 1996. (1) For all urban consumers. (2) For urban wage-earners and clerical workers.

# Percentage Change in Consumer Prices in Selected Countries

**Source:** International Monetary Fund

(annual averages)

| Country | 1975-1980 | 1980-1985 | 1989-1990 | 1991-1992 | 1992-1993 | 1993-1994 | 1994-1995 |
|---|---|---|---|---|---|---|---|
| Canada | 8.7 | 7.4 | 4.8 | 1.5 | 1.8 | 0.2 | 2.2 |
| France | 10.5 | 9.6 | 3.4 | 2.4 | 2.1 | 1.7 | 1.8 |
| Germany | 4.1 | 3.9 | 2.7 | 4.0 | 4.1 | 3.0 | 1.8 |
| Italy | 16.3 | 13.7 | 6.4 | 5.1 | 4.5 | 4.0 | 5.2 |
| Japan | 6.5 | 2.7 | 3.1 | 1.7 | 1.3 | 0.7 | –0.1 |
| Spain | 18.6 | 12.2 | 6.7 | 5.9 | 4.6 | 4.7 | 4.7 |
| Sweden | 10.5 | 9.0 | 10.5 | 2.3 | 4.6 | 2.2 | 2.5 |
| Switzerland | 2.3 | 4.3 | 5.4 | 4.1 | 3.3 | 0.8 | 1.8 |
| United Kingdom | 14.4 | 7.2 | 9.5 | 3.7 | 1.6 | 2.5 | 3.4 |
| United States | 8.9 | 5.5 | 5.4 | 3.0 | 3.0 | 2.6 | 2.8 |

# Index of Leading Economic Indicators

**Source:** The Conference Board

The index of leading economic indicators is used to project the U.S. economy's performance. The index is made up of 11 measurements of economic activity that tend to change direction in advance of the overall economy. The index has predicted economic downturns from 8 to 20 months in advance and recoveries from 1 to 10 months in advance; however, it can be inconsistent, and has occasionally shown "false signals" of recessions.

## Components

Average weekly hours of production workers in manufacturing
Average weekly initial claims for unemployment insurance, state programs
Manufacturers' new orders for consumer goods and materials, adjusted for inflation
Vendor performance (slower deliveries diffusion index)
Contracts and orders for plant and equipment, adj. for inflation
New private housing units authorized by local building permits
Change in manufacturers' unfilled orders, adjusted for inflation, durable goods industries
Change in sensitive-materials prices
Stock prices, 500 common stocks
Money supply: M-2, adjusted for inflation
Consumer expectations (researched by Univ. of Michigan)

# Gross Domestic Product, Gross National Product, Net National Product, National Income, and Personal Income

**Source:** Bureau of Economic Analysis, U.S. Dept. of Commerce

(billions of dollars)

| | 1960 | 1970 | 1980 | 1990 | 1994 | 1995 |
|---|---|---|---|---|---|---|
| **Gross domestic product** | — | — | — | $5,546.1 | $6,935.7 | $7,253.8 |
| **Gross national product** | $515.3 | $1,015.5 | $2,732.0 | 5,567.8 | 6,931.9 | 7,246.7 |
| Less: Capital consumption allowances | 46.4 | 88.8 | 303.8 | 602.7 | 818.8 | 825.9 |
| **Equals: Net national product** | 468.9 | 926.6 | 2,428.1 | 4,965.1 | 6,113.2 | 6,420.8 |
| Less: Indirect business tax and nontax liability | 45.3 | 94.0 | 213.3 | 444.0 | 572.5 | 595.5 |
| Business transfer payments | 2.0 | 4.1 | 12.1 | 26.8 | 30.1 | 30.8 |
| Statistical discrepancy | –2.8 | –1.1 | 4.9 | 7.8 | 34.1 | –0.9 |
| Plus: Subsidies less current surplus of government enterprises | 0.4 | 2.9 | 5.7 | 4.5 | 25.1 | 18.2 |
| **Equals: National income** | 424.9 | 832.6 | 2,203.5 | 4,491.0 | 5,501.6 | 5,813.5 |
| Less: Corporate profits with inventory valuation and capital consumption adjustments | 49.5 | 74.7 | 177.2 | 380.6 | 529.5 | 586.6 |
| Net interest | 11.3 | 41.2 | 200.9 | 463.7 | 394.9 | 403.6 |
| Contributions for social insurance | 21.9 | 62.2 | 216.5 | 503.1 | 628.3 | 660.0 |
| Wage accruals less disbursements | 0.0 | 0.0 | 0.0 | 0.1 | 15.5 | 2.7 |
| Plus: Government transfer payments to persons | 27.5 | 81.8 | 312.6 | 666.3 | 933.8 | 1,000.0 |
| Personal interest income | 24.9 | 69.3 | 271.9 | 698.2 | 663.7 | 717.1 |
| Personal dividend income | 12.9 | 22.2 | 52.9 | 144.4 | 199.6 | 214.8 |
| Business transfer payments | 2.0 | 4.1 | 12.1 | 21.3 | 22.6 | 22.6 |
| **Equals: Personal income** | 409.4 | 831.8 | 2,258.5 | 4,673.8 | 5,753.1 | 6,115.1 |

# Gross Domestic Product

**Source:** Bureau of Economic Analysis, U.S. Dept. of Commerce

(billions of dollars)

| | 1994 | 1995 | First Quarter 1996[1] |
|---|---|---|---|
| **Gross domestic product** | $6,935.7 | $7,253.8 | $7,426.8 |
| **Personal consumption expenditures** | 4,700.9 | 4,924.9 | 5,060.5 |
| Durable goods | 580.9 | 606.4 | 625.2 |
| Nondurable goods | 1,429.7 | 1,485.9 | 1,522.1 |
| Services | 2,690.3 | 2,832.6 | 2,913.2 |
| **Gross private domestic investment** | 1,014.4 | 1,065.3 | 1,068.9 |
| Fixed investment | 954.9 | 1,028.2 | 1,070.7 |
| Nonresidential | 667.2 | 738.5 | 769.0 |
| Structures | 180.2 | 199.7 | 208.4 |
| Producers' durable equipment | 487.0 | 538.8 | 560.6 |
| Residential | 287.7 | 289.8 | 301.7 |
| Change in business inventories | 59.5 | 37.0 | –1.7 |
| **Net exports of goods and services** | $–94.4 | $–94.7 | $–86.3 |
| Exports | 719.1 | 807.4 | 839.5 |
| Goods | 509.1 | 581.4 | 603.6 |
| Services | 210.1 | 225.9 | 235.9 |
| Imports | 813.5 | 902.0 | 925.8 |
| Goods | 677.0 | 757.0 | 776.7 |
| Services | 136.4 | 145.1 | 149.2 |
| **Government consumption expenditures and gross investment** | 1,314.7 | 1,358.3 | 1,383.7 |
| Federal | 516.4 | 516.6 | 518.6 |
| National defense | 352.0 | 345.5 | 343.9 |
| Nondefense | 164.3 | 171.0 | 174.7 |
| State and local | 798.4 | 841.7 | 865.1 |

(1) Seasonally adjusted at annual rates.

# Countries With Highest Gross Domestic Product and Per Capita GDP[1]

**Source:** Central Intelligence Agency, *The World Factbook 1995*; Bureau of Economic Analysis, Dept. of Commerce

**Gross Domestic Product[2]**
(billions of dollars; 1994 estimates)

| | | | |
|---|---|---|---|
| 1. United States | $6,935.7 | 21. Argentina | $270.8 |
| 2. China | 2,978.8[4] | 22. Taiwan | 257.0 |
| 3. Japan | 2,527.4 | 23. Pakistan | 248.5 |
| 4. Germany | 1,344.6 | 24. South Africa | 194.3 |
| 5. India | 1,253.9 | 25. Poland | 191.1 |
| 6. France | 1,080.1 | 26. Ukraine | 189.2[4] |
| 7. UK | 1,045.2 | 27. Belgium | 181.5 |
| 8. Italy | 998.9 | 28. Venezuela | 178.3 |
| 9. Brazil | 886.3 | 29. Saudi Arabia | 173.1 |
| 10. Mexico | 728.7 | 30. Colombia | 172.4 |
| 11. Russia | 721.2[4] | 31. Malaysia | 166.8 |
| 12. Canada | 639.8 | 32. Sweden | 163.1 |
| 13. Indonesia | 619.4 | 33. Philippines | 161.4 |
| 14. Spain | 515.8 | 34. Egypt | 151.5 |
| 15. South Korea | 508.3 | 35. Switzerland | 148.4 |
| 16. Australia | 374.6 | 36. Austria | 139.3 |
| 17. Thailand | 355.2 | 37. Bangladesh | 130.1 |
| 18. Iran | 310.0 | 38. Nigeria | 122.6 |
| 19. Turkey | 305.2 | 39. Portugal | 107.3 |
| 20. Netherlands | 275.8 | 40. Denmark | 103.0 |

**Per Capita Gross Domestic Product[3]**
(dollars; 1994 estimates)

| | | | |
|---|---|---|---|
| 1. United States | $26,640 | 21. Italy | $17,180 |
| 2. Luxembourg | 22,830 | 22. Kuwait | 16,900 |
| 3. Canada | 22,760 | 23. New Zealand | 16,640 |
| 4. U.A.E. | 22,480 | 24. Germany | 16,580 |
| 5. Liechtenstein | 22,300[5] | 25. Finland | 16,140 |
| 6. Norway | 22,170 | 26. Brunei | 16,000 |
| 7. Switzerland | 22,080 | 27. Bahamas | 15,900 |
| 8. Qatar | 20,820 | 28. San Marino | 15,800[6] |
| 9. Australia | 20,720 | 29. Ireland | 14,060 |
| 10. Japan | 20,200 | 30. Andorra | 14,000[7] |
| 11. Singapore | 19,940 | 31. Israel | 13,880 |
| 12. Denmark | 19,860 | 32. Spain | 13,120 |
| 13. France | 18,670 | 33. Cyprus | 12,500[8] |
| 14. Sweden | 18,580 | 34. Bahrain | 12,100 |
| 15. Belgium | 18,040 | 35. Taiwan | 12,070 |
| 16. Monaco | 18,000[6] | 36. Trin. & Tob. | 11,280 |
| 17. UK | 17,980 | 37. South Korea | 11,270 |
| 18. Netherlands | 17,940 | 38. Malta | 10,760 |
| 19. Austria | 17,500 | 39. Portugal | 10,190 |
| 20. Iceland | 17,250 | 40. Oman | 10,020 |

(1) International data are from CIA's *The World Factbook;* U.S. data are supplied by the Bureau of Economic Analysis. International GDP estimates are derived from purchasing power parity calculations, which involve the use of intl. dollar price weights applied to the quantities of goods and services produced in a given economy. (2) Does not include the territory of Hong Kong (UK): $136.1 billion. (3) Does not include the following territories: Bermuda (UK) $28,000, Hong Kong (UK) $24,530, Cayman Islands (UK, 1993) $23,000, Aruba (Neth., 1993) $17,000, British Virgin Islands (UK) $10,600, N. Mariana Islands (U.S.) $10,500. (4) 1994 estimate as extrapolated from World Bank estimate for 1992. (5) 1990 estimate. (6) 1993 estimate. (7) 1992 estimate. (8) Does not include Turkish-held area.

# Chapter 11

Chapter 11 refers to the provisions in the Federal Bankruptcy Code for court-supervised reorganization of debtor companies. A company files for Chapter 11 protection when it can no longer pay its creditors or when it expects future liabilities it cannot hope to pay, such as product liability damage awards. In 1991, the U.S. Supreme Court ruled that the provision of federal bankruptcy law that permits corporations to reorganize while continuing to operate was also available for use by individuals. The Bankruptcy Reform Act of 1994 further amended Chapter 11.

## Process

**1. Bankruptcy filing imposes an automatic stay.**

- Creditors generally cannot file or continue suits for repayment.
- Debts are frozen and creditors generally must stop collection actions. This is called the "automatic stay."
- Debtor's day-to-day operations continue.
- Spending, borrowing, and asset sales outside of the debtor's normal course of business must be approved by the court.
- Secured creditors can ask the court for exemption from the automatic stay to undertake or continue to recover the collateral that secures their claim.

**2. Unsecured creditors form a committee.**

- The U.S. trustee appoints the committee, which ordinarily consists of the 7 largest unsecured creditors who are willing to serve on the panel.
- The U.S. trustee can appoint additional committees to represent other creditors and shareholders.
- The committee chooses representatives to deal with the debtor company.
- The committee and U.S. trustee oversee the debtor's business operations.
- Creditors and the U.S. trustee can ask the court to appoint an examiner to investigate possible fraud or mismanagement.
- Creditors and the U.S. trustee can ask the court to order the appointment of a case trustee to run the debtor company.
- If the court orders the appointment, the U.S. trustee selects the case trustee unless a party asks that creditors be allowed to elect the case trustee.

**3. The committee, other creditors, and the debtor company negotiate a reorganization plan.**

- Parties negotiate a plan for the reorganization of the debtor's business and repayment of frozen debts. This step can take months or years.
- Only the debtor can file a reorganization plan with the court for the first 120 days of the bankruptcy case. The court can extend the so-called "exclusivity" period and often does so.
- If the debtor does not file a plan during the exclusivity period, if the debtor's plan is not approved by the court, or if a trustee is appointed, any party can file a plan.
- The proponent of the plan prepares a disclosure statement, which must be approved by the court at a separate hearing.

**4. Creditors and shareholders vote on the plan.**

- Only creditors and shareholders whose claims and interests are impaired or affected by the plan vote on it.
- A class of creditors accepts the plan if the plan is approved by creditors who hold more than half of the claims in the class by number and at least two-thirds of the claims by amount.
- A class of shareholders accepts the plan if the plan is approved by shareholders who hold at least two-thirds of the equity interest in the class by amount.

**5. Judge considers the plan.**

- The bankruptcy judge approves the plan if it complies with the Bankruptcy Code and all impaired classes approve.
- If at least one of the impaired classes approves the plan and it meets certain statutory tests, the judge can confirm the plan in a so-called "cramdown," even if not all impaired classes approve.

**6. Reorganized company emerges.**

- Generally, the debtor's debts are discharged.
- The debtor and creditors must comply with the confirmed plan.
- The automatic stay ends and a permanent injunction goes into effect against any effort to collect prepetition debts other than as provided in the plan.
- The reorganized debtor operates like a normal company.
- Only 17% of the debtors who file Chapter 11 cases get their plans confirmed.

## Expedited Procedure for Small Businesses

- The Bankruptcy Reform Act of 1994 included an expedited confirmation process to be used in Chapter 11 cases filed by small businesses.
- The debtor can elect to use the new process if it has less than $2 million in debts and its primary business is not owning or operating real estate.
- The court can order that a creditors' committee not be appointed.
- Unless the court orders otherwise, the debtor's exclusivity period for filing a plan is shortened to 100 days and all plans must be filed within 160 days.
- The court may conditionally approve the disclosure statement. This saves time by combining the court hearing on the disclosure statement with the hearing on confirmation of the plan.

# State Finances

## Revenue, Expenditures, Debt, and Taxes

**Source:** Census Bureau, U.S. Dept. of Commerce

(fiscal year 1994)

| State | Revenue (millions) | Expenditures (millions) | Debt (millions) | Per capita[1] debt | Per capita[1] taxes | Per capita[1] expenditures |
|---|---|---|---|---|---|---|
| Alabama | $11,599 | $10,815 | $3,854 | $913 | $1,130 | $2,563 |
| Alaska | 6,203 | 5,752 | 3,585 | 5,916 | 2,047 | 9,491 |
| Arizona | 11,749 | 10,522 | 3,170 | 778 | 1,388 | 2,582 |
| Arkansas | 6,870 | 6,078 | 1,812 | 739 | 1,295 | 2,478 |
| California | 115,228 | 105,831 | 48,120 | 1,531 | 1,581 | 3,367 |
| Colorado | 10,425 | 8,903 | 3,263 | 892 | 1,136 | 2,435 |
| Connecticut | 11,993 | 12,964 | 13,599 | 4,152 | 2,073 | 3,958 |
| Delaware | 3,237 | 2,617 | 3,397 | 4,812 | 2,045 | 3,707 |
| Florida | 34,805 | 32,284 | 14,565 | 1,044 | 1,276 | 2,314 |
| Georgia | 18,265 | 16,823 | 5,174 | 733 | 1,245 | 2,385 |
| Hawaii | 5,698 | 5,806 | 5,146 | 4,365 | 2,539 | 4,924 |
| Idaho | 3,628 | 2,989 | 1,281 | 1,130 | 1,427 | 2,638 |
| Illinois | 31,897 | 29,449 | 20,355 | 1,732 | 1,317 | 2,506 |
| Indiana | 15,813 | 15,048 | 5,572 | 969 | 1,266 | 2,616 |
| Iowa | 8,961 | 8,101 | 1,990 | 704 | 1,460 | 2,864 |
| Kansas | 7,474 | 6,654 | 1,103 | 432 | 1,439 | 2,605 |
| Kentucky | 11,730 | 10,541 | 6,744 | 1,762 | 1,488 | 2,754 |
| Louisiana | 13,524 | 12,936 | 8,782 | 2,035 | 1,016 | 2,998 |
| Maine | 4,098 | 3,902 | 2,993 | 2,414 | 1,423 | 3,147 |
| Maryland | 15,581 | 14,203 | 9,130 | 1,824 | 1,515 | 2,837 |
| Massachusetts | 22,298 | 22,454 | 26,681 | 4,417 | 1,824 | 3,717 |
| Michigan | 31,814 | 29,305 | 11,505 | 1,212 | 1,624 | 3,086 |
| Minnesota | 17,182 | 15,278 | 4,351 | 953 | 1,894 | 3,345 |
| Mississippi | 7,697 | 6,796 | 2,066 | 774 | 1,246 | 2,546 |
| Missouri | 13,359 | 11,549 | 6,512 | 1,225 | 1,112 | 2,173 |
| Montana | 3,166 | 2,778 | 2,108 | 2,462 | 1,356 | 3,245 |
| Nebraska | 4,446 | 3,991 | 1,468 | 905 | 1,321 | 2,459 |
| Nevada | 4,767 | 4,203 | 1,685 | 1,156 | 1,634 | 2,884 |
| New Hampshire | 3,081 | 3,179 | 5,651 | 4,970 | 736 | 2,796 |
| New Jersey | 29,808 | 29,606 | 22,894 | 2,897 | 1,707 | 3,746 |
| New Mexico | 6,709 | 5,995 | 1,735 | 1,049 | 1,826 | 3,625 |
| New York | 82,202 | 76,871 | 65,078 | 3,582 | 1,806 | 4,231 |
| North Carolina | 21,051 | 19,040 | 4,538 | 642 | 1,488 | 2,693 |
| North Dakota | 2,289 | 2,083 | 757 | 1,186 | 1,387 | 3,266 |
| Ohio | 40,836 | 33,422 | 12,117 | 1,091 | 1,278 | 3,010 |
| Oklahoma | 9,184 | 8,493 | 3,873 | 1,189 | 1,308 | 2,607 |
| Oregon | 10,886 | 9,104 | 5,645 | 1,829 | 1,309 | 2,950 |
| Pennsylvania | 38,252 | 37,818 | 13,671 | 1,134 | 1,422 | 3,138 |
| Rhode Island | 4,131 | 3,745 | 5,544 | 5,561 | 1,440 | 3,757 |
| South Carolina | 11,268 | 11,209 | 4,972 | 1,357 | 1,229 | 3,059 |
| South Dakota | 2,041 | 1,826 | 1,680 | 2,331 | 914 | 2,532 |
| Tennessee | 12,725 | 11,940 | 2,627 | 508 | 1,108 | 2,307 |
| Texas | 45,035 | 40,967 | 9,378 | 510 | 1,059 | 2,229 |
| Utah | 5,907 | 5,132 | 2,103 | 1,102 | 1,266 | 2,690 |
| Vermont | 2,026 | 1,913 | 1,570 | 2,707 | 1,435 | 3,298 |
| Virginia | 17,295 | 15,523 | 7,912 | 1,208 | 1,227 | 2,369 |
| Washington | 19,379 | 19,577 | 8,266 | 1,547 | 1,816 | 3,664 |
| West Virginia | 6,349 | 6,190 | 2,525 | 1,386 | 1,402 | 3,397 |
| Wisconsin | 19,617 | 15,281 | 7,748 | 1,525 | 1,658 | 3,007 |
| Wyoming | 2,308 | 1,975 | 702 | 1,476 | 1,553 | 4,149 |
| **United States** | **$845,887** | **$779,459** | **$410,998** | **$1,582** | **$1,439** | **$3,001** |

(1) Per capita amounts are based on population figures of the resident U.S. population (excluding the District of Columbia) as of July 1, 1994.

## State and Local Government Receipts and Current Expenditures

**Source:** Bureau of Economic Analysis, U.S. Dept. of Commerce

(billions of dollars)

| | 1994 | 1995 | First Quarter 1996[1] |
|---|---|---|---|
| **Receipts** | **$946.4** | **$996.1** | **$1,023.0** |
| Personal tax and nontax receipts | 170.0 | 179.4 | 185.3 |
| Income taxes | 125.7 | 133.5 | 138.1 |
| Nontaxes | 23.4 | 23.9 | 24.4 |
| Other | 20.9 | 22.0 | 22.8 |
| Corporate profits tax accruals | 30.9 | 34.4 | 36.9 |
| Indirect business tax and nontax accruals | 479.9 | 504.3 | 519.7 |
| Sales taxes | 227.4 | 238.3 | 245.9 |
| Property taxes | 205.1 | 216.3 | 222.2 |
| Other | 47.4 | 49.7 | 51.6 |
| Contributions for social insurance | 69.7 | 71.9 | 73.4 |
| Federal grants-in-aid | 195.9 | 206.1 | 207.6 |
| **Current expenditures** | **846.6** | **901.1** | **932.0** |
| Consumption expenditures | 651.7 | 682.6 | 701.3 |
| Transfer payments to persons | 267.4 | 291.6 | 302.9 |

| | 1994 | 1995 | First Quarter 1996[1] |
|---|---|---|---|
| Net interest paid | $–49.8 | $–47.4 | $–45.7 |
| Interest paid | 64.2 | 64.0 | 63.9 |
| Less: Interest received by government | 114.0 | 111.4 | 109.6 |
| Less: Dividends received by government | 11.4 | 12.6 | 13.3 |
| Subsidies less current surplus of government enterprises | –11.2 | –13.1 | –13.1 |
| Subsidies | 0.4 | 0.4 | 0.4 |
| Less: Current surplus of government enterprises | 11.6 | 13.5 | 13.5 |
| Less: Wage accruals less disbursements | 0.0 | 0.0 | 0.0 |
| **Surplus or deficit (–), national income and product accounts** | **99.7** | **95.0** | **91.0** |

(1) Seasonally adjusted at annual rates.

# State and Local Government Current Expenditures and Gross Investment, by Function

**Source:** Bureau of Economic Analysis, U.S. Dept. Of Commerce

(millions of dollars)

| | 1993 | | | 1994 | | |
|---|---|---|---|---|---|---|
| | Total[1] | Current Expenditures | Gross Investment | Total[1] | Current Expenditures | Gross Investment |
| **Total** | **$942,059** | **$802,174** | **$139,885** | **$993,277** | **$846,634** | **$146,643** |
| **Central executive, legislative, and judicial activities** | **54,270** | **52,422** | **1,848** | **63,491** | **61,480** | **2,011** |
| Administrative, legislative, and judicial activities | 29,770 | 28,614 | 1,156 | 30,792 | 29,540 | 1,252 |
| Tax collection and financial management | 24,500 | 23,808 | 692 | 32,699 | 31,940 | 759 |
| **Civilian safety** | **89,279** | **83,262** | **6,017** | **94,708** | **88,408** | **6,300** |
| Police | 39,496 | 37,872 | 1,624 | 41,644 | 39,891 | 1,753 |
| Fire | 16,586 | 15,425 | 1,161 | 17,609 | 16,384 | 1,225 |
| Correction | 33,197 | 29,965 | 3,232 | 35,455 | 32,133 | 3,322 |
| **Education** | **337,781** | **305,286** | **32,495** | **353,275** | **318,845** | **34,430** |
| Elementary and secondary | 257,322 | 234,519 | 22,803 | 268,971 | 244,719 | 24,252 |
| Higher | 61,257 | 52,434 | 8,823 | 63,860 | 54,604 | 9,256 |
| Libraries | 4,598 | 4,066 | 532 | 4,807 | 4,245 | 562 |
| Other | 14,604 | 14,267 | 337 | 15,637 | 15,277 | 360 |
| **Health and hospitals** | **29,958** | **25,075** | **4,883** | **29,325** | **24,264** | **5,061** |
| Health | 22,210 | 20,963 | 1,247 | 23,157 | 21,858 | 1,299 |
| Hospitals | 7,748 | 4,112 | 3,636 | 6,168 | 2,406 | 3,762 |
| **Income support, social security, and welfare** | **205,976** | **205,523** | **453** | **220,395** | **219,911** | **484** |
| Government employees retirement and disability | –9,351 | –9,351 | ... | –7,570 | –7,570 | ... |
| Workers' compensation and temporary disability insurance | 10,086 | 10,086 | ... | 8,648 | 8,648 | ... |
| Medical care | 135,131 | 135,131 | ... | 146,596 | 146,596 | ... |
| Welfare and social services | 70,110 | 69,657 | 453 | 72,721 | 72,237 | 484 |
| **Veterans' benefits and services** | **198** | **169** | **29** | **184** | **158** | **26** |
| **Housing and community services** | **25,544** | **2,649** | **22,895** | **26,149** | **1,766** | **24,383** |
| Housing, community development, and urban renewal | 4,664 | 623 | 4,041 | 5,034 | 640 | 4,394 |
| Water | 4,599 | –2,838 | 7,437 | 4,654 | –3,214 | 7,868 |
| Sewerage | 9,726 | –395 | 10,121 | 9,933 | –833 | 10,766 |
| Sanitation | 6,555 | 5,259 | 1,296 | 6,528 | 5,173 | 1,355 |
| **Recreational and cultural activities** | **14,609** | **10,818** | **3,761** | **15,018** | **11,184** | **3,834** |
| **Energy** | **–627** | **–6,432** | **5,805** | **–1,001** | **–6,438** | **5,437** |
| Gas utilities | 23 | –390 | 413 | 78 | –356 | 434 |
| Electric utilities | –650 | –6,042 | 5,392 | –1,079 | –6,082 | 5,003 |
| **Agriculture** | **4,260** | **4,042** | **218** | **4,155** | **3,924** | **231** |
| **Natural resources** | **8,870** | **7,380** | **1,490** | **8,845** | **7,329** | **1,516** |
| **Transportation** | **108,271** | **56,564** | **51,707** | **112,131** | **57,550** | **54,581** |
| Highways | 86,668 | 45,942 | 40,726 | 89,652 | 46,370 | 43,282 |
| Water | 1,211 | –109 | 1,320 | 1,226 | –125 | 1,351 |
| Air | 2,589 | –1,410 | 3,999 | 2,563 | –1,540 | 4,103 |
| Transit and railroad | 17,803 | 12,141 | 5,662 | 18,690 | 12,845 | 5,845 |
| **Economic development, regulation, and services** | **6,960** | **6,753** | **207** | **6,728** | **6,512** | **216** |
| **Labor training and services** | **5,733** | **5,575** | **158** | **5,432** | **5,288** | **144** |
| **Commercial activities** | **–9,601** | **–9,873** | **272** | **–10,368** | **–10,649** | **281** |
| Publicly owned liquor store systems | –480 | –487 | 7 | –419 | –425 | 6 |
| Government-administered lotteries and parimutuels | –9,361 | –9,361 | ... | –10,196 | –10,196 | ... |
| Other | 240 | –25 | 265 | 247 | –28 | 275 |
| **Net interest paid[2]** | **8,305** | **8,305** | **...** | **10,827** | **10,827** | **...** |
| **Other and unallocable** | **52,273** | **44,656** | **7,617** | **53,983** | **46,275** | **7,708** |

(1) Sum of current expenditures and gross investment. (2) Excludes interest received by social insurance funds, which is netted against expenditures for the appropriate functions.

# Federal Deposit Insurance Corporation (FDIC)

The Federal Deposit Insurance Corporation (FDIC) is the independent deposit insurance agency created by Congress to maintain stability and public confidence in the nation's banking system. In its unique role as deposit insurer of banks and savings associations, and in cooperation with other federal and state regulatory agencies, the FDIC promotes the safety and soundness of insured depository institutions in the U.S. financial system by identifying, monitoring, and addressing risks to the deposit insurance funds. The FDIC promotes public understanding and sound public policies by providing financial and economic information and analyses. It minimizes disruptive effects from the failure of banks and savings associations. It ensures fairness in the sale of financial products and the provision of financial services. The FDIC's income consists of assessments on insured banks and income from investments; it receives no appropriations from Congress. The Corporation may borrow from the U.S. Treasury, not to exceed $30 billion outstanding, but the agency has made no such borrowings since it was organized in 1933. The FDIC's Bank Insurance Fund was $25.8 billion (unaudited) and the Savings Association Insurance Fund stood at $3.9 billion (unaudited), as of June 30, 1996.

# The Savings and Loan Crisis

Congress authorized $105 billion in funding for the Resolution Trust Corporation (RTC) for resolving insolvent savings institutions that failed between 1989 and June 30, 1995. The sunset date for the RTC was Dec. 31, 1995. The RTC concluded the S&L cleanup at a cost of $87.9 billion, not including $60 billion spent before 1989. The remaining business of the RTC shifted to the FDIC on Jan. 1, 1996.

## Banks in the U.S.—Number, Deposits

**Source:** Federal Deposit Insurance Corp. (as of Dec. 31; 1996 data as of June 30)

Comprises all FDIC-insured commercial and savings banks, including savings and loan institutions (S&Ls).

| | Number of banks | | | | | Total deposits (millions of dollars) | | | | |
|---|---|---|---|---|---|---|---|---|---|---|
| | | Commercial banks[1] | | | | | Commercial banks[1] | | | |
| **Year** | **Total** | **Natl.** | **State** | **Non-members** | **All savings** | **Total** | **Natl.** | **State** | **Non-members** | **All savings** |
| 1935 . . . . | **15,295** | 5,386 | 1,001 | 7,735 | 1,173 | **$ 45,102**[2] | $ 24,802 | $ 13,653 | $ 5,669 | $ 978[2] |
| 1940 . . . . | **15,772** | 5,144 | 1,342 | 6,956 | 2,330 | **67,494** | 35,787 | 20,642 | 7,040 | 4,025 |
| 1945 . . . . | **15,969** | 5,017 | 1,864 | 6,421 | 2,667 | **151,524** | 77,778 | 41,865 | 16,307 | 15,574 |
| 1950 . . . . | **16,500** | 4,958 | 1,912 | 6,576 | 3,054 | **171,963** | 84,941 | 41,602 | 19,726 | 25,694 |
| 1955 . . . . | **17,001** | 4,692 | 1,847 | 6,698 | 3,764 | **235,211** | 102,796 | 55,739 | 26,198 | 50,478 |
| 1960 . . . . | **17,549** | 4,530 | 1,641 | 6,955 | 4,423 | **310,262** | 120,242 | 65,487 | 34,369 | 90,164 |
| 1965 . . . . | **18,384** | 4,815 | 1,405 | 7,327 | 4,837 | **467,633** | 185,334 | 78,327 | 51,982 | 151,990 |
| 1970 . . . . | **18,205** | 4,621 | 1,147 | 7,743 | 4,694 | **686,901** | 285,436 | 101,512 | 95,566 | 204,367 |
| 1975 . . . . | **18,792** | 4,744 | 1,046 | 8,595 | 4,407 | **1,157,648** | 450,308 | 143,409 | 187,031 | 376,900 |
| 1980 . . . . | **18,763** | 4,425 | 997 | 9,013 | 4,328 | **1,832,716** | 656,752 | 191,183 | 344,311 | 640,470 |
| 1985 . . . . | **18,033** | 4,959 | 1,070 | 8,378 | 3,626 | **3,140,827** | 1,241,875 | 354,585 | 521,628 | 1,022,739 |
| 1990 . . . . | **15,158** | 3,979 | 1,009 | 7,355 | 2,815 | **3,637,292** | 1,558,915 | 397,797 | 693,438 | 987,142 |
| 1993 . . . . | **13,220** | 3,304 | 969 | 6,685 | 2,262 | **3,528,487** | 1,576,725 | 476,093 | 701,512 | 774,157 |
| 1994 . . . . | **12,603** | 3,075 | 976 | 6,400 | 2,152 | **3,611,618** | 1,630,171 | 533,261 | 711,006 | 737,180 |
| 1995 . . . . | **11,970** | 2,858 | 1,042 | 6,040 | 2,030 | **3,769,477** | 1,695,817 | 614,924 | 716,829 | 741,907 |
| 1996 . . . . | **11,670** | 2,763 | 1,024 | 5,902 | 1,981 | **3,788,905** | 1,795,110 | 567,809 | 698,497 | 727,489 |

(1) "Nonmembers" are banks that are not members of the Federal Reserve System; "National" and "State" institutions are members. (2) Figures do not include data for S&Ls, which were unavailable for 1935.

## Largest U.S. Commercial Banks

**Source:** *American Banker* (as of Dec. 31, 1995)

| **Bank** | **Assets (millions)** |
|---|---|
| Citibank, New York, NY | $220,110 |
| Bank of America, San Francisco, CA | 163,398 |
| Chemical Bank, New York, NY | 147,120 |
| Morgan Guaranty Trust Co., New York, NY | 143,397 |
| Chase Manhattan Bank, New York, NY | 100,352 |
| NationsBank (Carolinas), Charlotte, NC | 79,179 |
| Bankers Trust Co., New York, NY | 79,100 |
| First National Bank, Chicago, IL | 49,360 |
| Wells Fargo Bank, San Francisco, CA | 49,092 |
| NationsBank of Texas, Dallas | 48,368 |
| Bank of New York, NY | 42,712 |
| PNC Bank, Pittsburgh, PA | 41,905 |
| First National Bank, Boston, MA | 40,274 |
| NationsBank, South, Atlanta, GA | 37,610 |
| First Union National Bank of Florida, Jacksonville | 36,591 |
| Mellon Bank, Pittsburgh, PA | 35,565 |
| Republic National Bank of New York, NY | 34,580 |
| First Fidelity Bank, Elkton, MD | 32,687 |
| NBD Bank, Detroit, MI | 29,462 |
| NatWest Bank, Jersey City, NJ | 28,489 |
| Comerica Bank, Detroit, MI | 28,394 |
| First Union National Bank of North Carolina, Charlotte | 27,415 |
| Wachovia Bank of North Carolina, Winston-Salem | 26,865 |
| First Interstate Bank of California, Los Angeles | 26,556 |
| State Street Bank & Trust Co., Boston, MA | 25,558 |
| Society National Bank, Cleveland, OH | $22,307 |
| CoreStates Bank, Philadelphia, PA | 21,577 |
| Marine Midland Bank, Buffalo, NY | 20,342 |
| Texas Commerce Bank, Houston | 19,990 |
| Union Bank, San Francisco, CA | 19,518 |
| Bank One, Texas, Dallas | 18,798 |
| Norwest Bank Minnesota, Minneapolis | 18,234 |
| Shawmut Bank Connecticut, Hartford | 18,129 |
| Wachovia Bank of Georgia, Atlanta | 17,346 |
| Seattle-First National Bank, WA | 17,151 |
| First Bank, Minneapolis, MN | 16,376 |
| Bank of America Illinois, Chicago | 16,171 |
| Branch Banking & Trust Co., Winston-Salem, NC | 15,992 |
| Key Bank of New York, Albany | 15,373 |
| Northern Trust Co., Chicago, IL | 15,231 |
| Fleet Bank of New York, Albany | 14,621 |
| Huntington National Bank, Columbus, OH | 14,425 |
| Integra Bank, Pittsburgh, PA | 13,979 |
| Shawmut Bank, Boston, MA | 13,868 |
| Crestar Bank, Richmond, VA | 13,558 |
| First of America Bank-Michigan, Grand Rapids | 13,338 |
| Midlantic Bank, Newark, NJ | 13,290 |
| United Jersey Bank, Hackensack, NJ | 13,129 |
| Bank One, Arizona, Phoenix | 13,081 |
| Banco Popular de Puerto Rico, San Juan | 12,931 |

**Note:** On Mar. 31, 1996, Chemical Banking Corp. completed the acquisition of Chase Manhattan Corp. and changed its title to Chase Manhattan Corp., becoming the largest bank in the U.S.

## World's Largest Banking Companies[1]

**Source:** *American Banker* (as of Dec. 31, 1995; Japan data as of Mar. 31, 1996)

| **Banks** | **Assets (millions)** |
|---|---|
| Deutsche Bank, AG, Frankfurt, Germany | $502,279 |
| Sanwa Bank Ltd., Osaka, Japan | 500,026 |
| Sumitomo Bank Ltd., Osaka | 498,917 |
| Dai-Ichi Kangyo Bank Ltd., Tokyo, Japan | 497,612 |
| Fuji Bank, Ltd., Tokyo | 486,351 |
| Sakura Bank, Ltd., Tokyo | 477,079 |
| Mitsubishi Bank Ltd., Tokyo | 474,045 |
| Norinchukin Bank, Tokyo | 428,644 |
| Credit Agricole Mutuel, Paris, France | 384,340 |
| Industrial Bank of Japan, Ltd., Tokyo | 360,638 |
| HSBC Holdings, Plc., London, United Kingdom | 351,568 |
| ABN-AMRO Bank, N.V., Amsterdam, Netherlands | 339,393 |
| Credit Lyonnais, Paris | 337,595 |
| Union Bank of Switzerland, Zurich | 335,303 |
| Dresdner Bank, Frankfurt | 332,148 |
| Mitsubishi Trust & Banking Corp., Tokyo | 330,076 |
| Societe Generale, Paris | 324,776 |
| Banque Nationale de Paris | 323,526 |
| Sumitomo Trust & Banking Co., Ltd., Osaka | 299,209 |
| Tokai Bank Ltd., Nagoya, Japan | 297,705 |
| Long-Term Credit Bank of Japan Ltd., Tokyo | 297,430 |
| Westdeutsche Landesbank Girozentrale, Dusseldorf, Ger. | 290,648 |
| Mitsui Trust & Banking Co., Ltd., Tokyo | 283,711 |
| Commerzbank, Frankfurt | 280,743 |
| Compagnie Financiere de Paribas, Paris | 270,771 |
| Asahi Bank, Ltd., Tokyo | $265,969 |
| National Westminster Bank Plc., London | 257,838 |
| Citicorp, New York, United States | 255,311 |
| Barclays Bank Plc., London | 254,485 |
| Swiss Bank Corp., Basel, Switzerland | 249,906 |
| Daiwa Bank, Ltd., Osaka | 248,274 |
| Bayerische Vereinsbank, Munich, Germany | 247,082 |
| Bank of Tokyo, Ltd. | 237,255 |
| BankAmerica Corp., San Francisco, United States | 230,151 |
| Yasuda Trust & Banking Co., Ltd., Tokyo | 224,186 |
| Credit Suisse, Zurich | 212,022 |
| Bayerische Landesbank Girozentrale, Munich | 211,192 |
| Bayerische Hypotheken und Wechsel Bank, Munich | 207,458 |
| Lloyds TSB Group, Inc., London | 204,213 |
| Deutsche Genossenschaftsbank, Frankfurt | 199,681 |
| Bankgesellschaft Berlin, AG, Berlin | 194,450 |
| Toyo Trust & Banking Co. Ltd., Tokyo | 189,723 |
| NationsBank Corp., Charlotte, NC, United States | 186,380 |
| J. P. Morgan & Co., Inc., New York | 184,642 |
| Rabobank Nederland, Utrecht, Netherlands | 182,273 |
| Chemical Banking Corp., New York | 181,747 |
| Generale Bank, Brussels, Belgium | 161,131 |
| Sanpaolo Bank Holding, Turin, Italy | 160,389 |
| ING Bank, Amsterdam | 153,484 |
| Abbey National, Plc., London | 151,302 |

(1) Includes bank holding companies and commercial and savings banks. **Notes:** Data for U.S. companies listed include assets not included in "Largest U.S. Commercial Banks" table. On Apr. 1, 1996, Mitsubishi Bank Ltd. merged with Bank of Tokyo, Ltd., to form Bank of Tokyo/Mitsubishi Ltd., becoming the largest bank in the world.

# Bank Failures

**Source:** Federal Deposit Insurance Corp.

| Year | Closed or assisted | Year | Closed or assisted | Year | Closed or assisted | Year | Closed or assisted | Year | Closed or assisted |
|---|---|---|---|---|---|---|---|---|---|
| 1934 | 61 | 1960 | 2 | 1970 | 8 | 1980 | 11 | 1988 | 221 |
| 1935 | 32 | 1961 | 9 | 1971 | 6 | 1981 | 10 | 1989 | 207 |
| 1936 | 72 | 1963 | 2 | 1972 | 3 | 1982 | 42 | 1990 | 169 |
| 1937 | 84 | 1964 | 8 | 1973 | 6 | 1983 | 48 | 1991 | 127 |
| 1938 | 81 | 1965 | 9 | 1975 | 14 | 1984 | 80 | 1992 | 122 |
| 1939 | 72 | 1966 | 8 | 1976 | 17 | 1985 | 120 | 1993 | 41 |
| 1940 | 48 | 1967 | 4 | 1978 | 7 | 1986 | 145 | 1994 | 13 |
| 1955 | 5 | 1969 | 9 | 1979 | 10 | 1987 | 203 | 1995 | 6 |
| 1959 | 3 | | | | | | | | |

# Federal Reserve Board Discount Rate

The discount rate is the rate of interest set by the Federal Reserve that member banks are charged when borrowing money through the Federal Reserve System. Data are as of Oct. 1996.

| Effective date | Rate |
|---|---|
| **1980:** | |
| Feb. 15 | 13 |
| May 30 | 12 |
| June 13 | 11 |
| July 28 | 10 |
| Sept. 26 | 11 |
| Nov. 17 | 12 |
| Dec. 5 | 13 |
| **1981:** | |
| May 5 | 14 |
| Nov. 2 | 13 |
| Dec. 4 | 12 |
| **1982:** | |
| July 20 | 11½ |
| Aug. 2 | 11 |
| Aug. 16 | 10½ |
| Aug. 27 | 10 |
| Oct. 12 | 9½ |
| Nov. 22 | 9 |
| Dec. 15 | 8½ |
| **1984:** | |
| April 9 | 9 |
| Nov. 21 | 8½ |
| Dec. 24 | 8 |
| **1985:** | |
| May 20 | 7½ |
| **1986:** | |
| March 7 | 7 |
| April 21 | 6½ |
| July 11 | 6 |
| Aug. 21 | 5½ |
| **1987:** | |
| Sept. 4 | 6 |
| **1988:** | |
| Aug. 9 | 6½ |
| **1989:** | |
| Feb. 24 | 7 |
| **1990:** | |
| Dec. 18 | 6½ |
| **1991:** | |
| Apr. 30 | 5½ |
| Sept. 13 | 5 |
| Nov. 6 | 4½ |
| Dec. 20 | 3½ |
| **1992:** | |
| July 3 | 3 |
| **1994:** | |
| May 17 | 3½ |
| Aug. 16 | 4 |
| Nov. 15 | 4¾ |
| **1995:** | |
| Feb. 1 | 5¼ |
| **1996:** | |
| Jan. 31 | 5 |

# Federal Reserve System

(as of Sept. 1996)

The Federal Reserve System is the central bank for the U.S. The system was established on Dec. 23, 1913, originally to give the country an elastic currency, to provide facilities for discounting commercial paper, and to improve the supervision of banking. Since then, the system's responsibilities have been broadened. Over the years, stability and growth of the economy, a high level of employment, stability in the purchasing power of the dollar, and reasonable balance in transactions with other countries have come to be recognized as primary objectives of governmental economic policy.

The Federal Reserve System consists of the Board of Governors, the 12 District Reserve Banks and their branch offices, and the Federal Open Market Committee. Several advisory councils help the board meet its varied responsibilities.

The hub of the system is the 7-member Board of Governors in Washington. The members of the board are appointed by the president and confirmed by the Senate, to serve 14-year terms. The president also appoints the chairman and vice chairman of the board from among the board members for 4-year terms that may be renewed. As of Sept. 1996 the board members were: Alan Greenspan, Chairman; Alice H. Rivlin, Vice Chair; Edward W. Kelley Jr.; Lawrence B. Lindsey; Susan M. Phillips; Janet Yellen; and Laurence H. Meyer.

The board is the policy-making body. In addition to its policy-making responsibilities, it supervises the budget and operations of the Reserve Banks, approves the appointments of their presidents, and appoints 3 of each District Bank's directors, including the chairman and vice chairman of each Reserve Bank's board.

The 12 Reserve Banks and their branch offices serve as the decentralized portion of the system, carrying out day-to-day operations such as circulating currency and coin and providing fiscal agency functions and payments mechanism services. The District Banks are in Boston, New York, Philadelphia, Cleveland, Richmond, Atlanta, Chicago, St. Louis, Minneapolis, Kansas City, Dallas, and San Francisco.

The system's principal function is monetary policy, which it controls using 3 tools: reserve requirements, the discount rate, and open market operations. Uniform reserve requirements, set by the board, are applied to the transaction accounts and nonpersonal time deposits of all depository institutions. Responsibility for setting the discount rate (the interest rate at which depository institutions can borrow money from the Reserve Banks) is shared by the Board of Governors and the Reserve Banks. Changes in the discount rate are recommended by the individual boards of directors of the Reserve Banks and are subject to approval by the Board of Governors. The most important tool of monetary policy is open market operations (the purchase and sale of government securities). Responsibility for influencing the cost and availability of money and credit through the purchase and sale of government securities lies with the Federal Open Market Committee (FOMC). The FOMC is composed of the 7 members of the Board of Governors, the president of the Federal Reserve Bank of New York, and 4 other Federal Reserve Bank presidents, who serve one-year terms on a rotating basis. The committee bases its decisions on economic and financial developments and outlook, setting yearly growth objectives for key measures of money supply and credit. The decisions of the committee are carried out by the Domestic Trading Desk of the Federal Reserve Bank of New York.

The Federal Reserve Act prescribes a Federal Advisory Council, consisting of one member from each Federal Reserve District, who is elected annually by the Board of Directors of each of the 12 Federal Reserve Banks. The council meets with the Federal Reserve Board 4 times a year to discuss business and financial conditions and to make advisory recommendations.

The Consumer Advisory Council is a statutory body, including both consumer and creditor representatives, which advises the Board of Governors on its implementation of consumer regulations and other consumer-related matters.

Following the passage of the Monetary Control Act of 1980, the Board of Governors established the Thrift Institutions Advisory Council to provide information and views on the special needs and problems of thrift institutions. The group is composed of representatives of mutual savings banks, savings and loan associations, and credit unions.

# United States Mint

**Source:** United States Mint, U.S. Dept. of the Treasury

The United States Mint was created by an act of Congress on Apr. 2, 1792, which established the U.S. national coinage system. Supervision of the mint was a function of the secretary of state, but in 1799 the mint became an independent agency reporting directly to the president. The mint was made a statutory bureau of the Treasury Department in 1873, with a director appointed by the President to oversee its operations.

The mint manufactures and ships all U.S. coins for circulation to the Federal Reserve banks and branches, which issue coins to the public and the business community through depository institutions. The mint also safeguards the Treasury Department's stored gold and silver and other monetary assets.

The composition of dimes, quarters, and half dollars, traditionally produced from silver, was changed by the Coinage Act of 1965, which mandated that these coins be minted from a cupronickel-clad alloy and reduced the silver content of the half dollar to 40%. In 1970, legislative action mandated that the half dollar and a dollar coin be minted from the same alloy.

The Eisenhower dollar was minted from 1971 through 1978, when legislation called for the minting of the smaller Susan B. Anthony dollar coin. The Anthony dollar, which was minted from 1979 through 1981, marked the first time that a woman, other than a mythical figure, appeared on a U.S. coin produced for general circulation.

Mint headquarters is in Washington, DC. Mint production facilities are in Philadelphia, Denver, San Francisco, and West Point, NY. In addition, the mint is responsible for the U.S. Bullion Depository at Fort Knox, KY.

Proof coin sets, silver proof coin sets, and uncirculated coin sets are available annually from the mint. The mint also produces ongoing series of national and historic medals in honor of outstanding persons or events and sites of special meaning to the American people.

Since 1982, the mint has produced the following congressionally authorized commemorative coins: the 1982 George Washington commemorative half dollar; 1984 U.S. Olympic coins; 1986 U.S. Statue of Liberty coins; 1987 Bicentennial of the U.S. Constitution coins; 1989 U.S. Congressional coins; the 1990 Eisenhower Centennial coin; the 1991 United Services Organization 59th Anniversary coin; the 1991 Korean War Memorial coin; 1991 Mount Rushmore Anniversary coins; 1992 U.S. Olympic coins; the 1992 White House 200th Anniversary coin; 1992 Christopher Columbus Quincentenary coins; 1993 Bill of Rights coins; 1993 World War II 50th Anniversary coins; 1994 World Cup USA coins; the Thomas Jefferson 250th Anniversary coin; U.S. Veterans Commemorative coins (featuring the Prisoner of War coin, the Vietnam Veterans Memorial coin, and the Women in Military Service for America coin); the Bicentennial of the U.S. Capitol Commemorative Silver Dollar; 1995 Civil War Battlefield coins, and 1995 and 1996 Atlanta Centennial Olympic coins.

Other commemorative coins available from the mint in 1996 are the National Community Service Silver Dollar, which will benefit innovative community service programs at U.S. universities, and Smithsonian 150th Anniversary Coins in gold and silver, which will support the National Numismatic Collection as well as the enhancement and expansion of all Smithsonian collections.

The congressionally authorized American eagle gold and silver bullion coins produced by the mint are available through dealers worldwide. The gold eagles are sold in one-ounce, half-ounce, quarter-ounce, and one-tenth-ounce sizes; the price of the coins fluctuates with the daily market value of gold. The American eagle silver bullion coin contains one troy ounce of .999 fine silver and is priced according to the daily market value of silver. These coins also are available in proof condition, separately priced.

The mint offers free public tours and operates sales centers at the U.S. mints in Denver and Philadelphia, and also operates a sales center at Union Station in Washington, DC.

Information about mint programs and products is available from the United States Mint, Customer Service Center, 10003 Derekwood Lane, Lanham, MD 20706. Telephone: (202) 283-COIN.

# Portraits on U.S. Treasury Bills, Bonds, Notes, and Savings Bonds

| Denomination | Savings bonds | Treasury bills* | Treasury bonds* | Treasury notes* |
|---|---|---|---|---|
| 50 | Washington | | Jefferson | |
| 75 | Adams | | | |
| 100 | Jefferson | | Jackson | |
| 200 | Madison | | | |
| 500 | Hamilton | | Washington | |
| 1,000 | Franklin | H. McCulloch | Lincoln | Lincoln |
| 5,000 | Revere | J. G. Carlisle | Monroe | Monroe |
| 10,000 | J. Wilson | J. Sherman | Cleveland | Cleveland |
| 50,000 | | C. Glass | | |
| 100,000 | | A. Gallatin | Grant | Grant |
| 1,000,000 | | O. Wolcott | T. Roosevelt | T. Roosevelt |
| 100,000,000 | | | | Madison |
| 500,000,000 | | | | McKinley |

*The U.S. Treasury discontinued issuing treasury bill, bond, and note certificates in 1986. Since then, all issues of marketable treasury securities have been available only in book-entry form, although some certificates remain in circulation.

# Denominations of U.S. Currency

Since 1969 the largest denomination of U.S. currency that has been issued is the $100 bill. As larger-denomination bills reach the Federal Reserve Bank, they are removed from circulation. Because some discontinued currency is expected to be in the hands of holders for many years, the description of the various denominations below is continued.

| Amt. | Portrait | Embellishment on back | Amt. | Portrait | Embellishment on back |
|---|---|---|---|---|---|
| $ 1 | Washington | Great Seal of U.S. | $ 100 | Franklin | Independence Hall |
| 2 | Jefferson | Signers of Declaration | 500 | McKinley | Ornate denominational marking |
| 5 | Lincoln | Lincoln Memorial | 1,000 | Cleveland | Ornate denominational marking |
| 10 | Hamilton | U.S. Treasury | 5,000 | Madison | Ornate denominational marking |
| 20 | Jackson | White House | 10,000 | Chase | Ornate denominational marking |
| 50 | Grant | U.S. Capitol | 100,000* | W. Wilson | Ornate denominational marking |

*For use only in transactions between Federal Reserve System and Treasury Department.

# New U.S. Currency Design

In 1996, the U.S. issued a redesigned $100 note that incorporated many new and modified anticounterfeiting features. The note, issued Mar. 25, was the first of the U.S. currency series to be redesigned. The new currency is scheduled to be issued at a rate of one denomination per year. Old notes are being removed from circulation as they are returned to the Federal Reserve, but all U.S. currency will continue to be honored at full face value. The new $100 bill has the following features: a larger portrait, moved off-center to create space to incorporate a watermark; a watermark (seen only when held up to the light) to the right of the portrait, depicting the same historical figure; a security thread (to be located in a unique position on each denomination) that glows red when exposed to ultraviolet light in a dark environment; color-shifting ink that changes from green to black when viewed at different angles, to appear in the numeral on the lower, front right-hand corner of the bill; microprinting in the numeral in the note's lower, front left-hand corner and on the portrait (on Benjamin Franklin's lapel); and other features for security, machine authentication, and processing of the currency. Some or all of these features are expected to appear in the subsequent denominations. A new $50 note will be issued sometime in 1997. More information on the new currency is available on the U.S. Treasury's official internet site: http://www.ustreas.gov

# U.S. Currency and Coin

**Source:** Financial Management Service, U.S. Dept. of the Treasury (Mar. 31, 1996)

## Amounts Outstanding and in Circulation

| Currency | Total currency and coin | Total currency | Federal Reserve notes[1] | U.S. notes | Currency no longer issued |
|---|---|---|---|---|---|
| Amounts outstanding | $530,413,463,732 | $506,724,922,834 | $506,144,368,026 | $322,083,116 | $258,471,692 |
| Less amounts held by: | | | | | |
| Treasury | 312,859,519 | 55,425,292 | 11,701,637 | 43,527,339 | 196,316 |
| Federal Reserve banks | 113,819,921,781 | 113,240,812,348 | 113,240,808,673 | — | 3,675 |
| Amounts in circulation | $416,280,682,432 | $393,428,685,194 | $392,891,857,716 | $278,555,777 | $258,271,701 |

| Coins[2] | Total | Dollars[3] | Fractional coins |
|---|---|---|---|
| Amounts outstanding | $23,688,540,898 | $2,024,703,898 | $21,663,837,000 |
| Less amounts held by: | | | |
| Treasury | 257,434,227 | 169,407,002 | 88,027,225 |
| Federal Reserve banks | 579,109,433 | 53,593,603 | 525,515,830 |
| Amounts in circulation | $22,851,997,238 | $1,801,703,293 | $21,050,293,945 |

## Currency in Circulation by Denominations

| Denomination | Total currency in circulation | Federal Reserve notes[1] | U.S. notes | Currency no longer issued |
|---|---|---|---|---|
| $1 | $6,046,024,130 | $5,897,666,092 | $143,481 | $148,214,557 |
| $2 | 1,049,874,404 | 917,235,364 | 132,626,466 | 12,574 |
| $5 | 7,140,614,620 | 6,996,954,260 | 110,716,810 | 32,943,550 |
| $10 | 13,278,560,500 | 13,255,581,890 | 5,950 | 22,972,660 |
| $20 | 80,101,119,140 | 80,081,015,360 | 3,380 | 20,100,400 |
| $50 | 47,779,383,800 | 47,767,891,950 | — | 11,491,850 |
| $100 | 237,714,698,500 | 237,657,651,300 | 35,059,600 | 21,987,600 |
| $500 | 144,959,500 | 144,771,500 | — | 188,000 |
| $1,000 | 168,230,000 | 168,025,000 | — | 205,000 |
| $5,000 | 1,770,000 | 1,715,000 | — | 55,000 |
| $10,000 | 3,450,000 | 3,350,000 | — | 100,000 |
| Fractional parts | 485 | — | — | 485 |
| Partial notes[4] | 115 | — | 90 | 25 |
| **Total currency** | **$393,428,685,194** | **$392,891,857,716** | **$278,555,777** | **$258,271,701** |

## Comparative Totals of Money in Circulation — Selected Dates

| Date | Dollars (in millions) | Per capita[5] | Date | Dollars (in millions) | Per capita[5] | Date | Dollars (in millions) | Per capita[5] |
|---|---|---|---|---|---|---|---|---|
| Mar. 31, 1996 | 416,280.0 | 1,573.15 | June 30, 1975 | 81,196.4 | 380.08 | June 30, 1940 | 7,847.5 | 59.40 |
| Mar. 31, 1995 | 401,610.0 | 1,531.39 | June 30, 1970 | 54,351.0 | 265.39 | June 30, 1935 | 5,567.1 | 43.75 |
| Mar. 31, 1994 | 371,466.0 | 1,428.37 | June 30, 1965 | 39,719.8 | 204.14 | June 30, 1930 | 4,522.0 | 36.74 |
| Mar. 31, 1993 | 332,822.7 | 1,293.58 | June 30, 1960 | 32,064.6 | 177.47 | June 30, 1925 | 4,815.2 | 41.56 |
| Mar. 31, 1990 | 257,664.4 | 1,028.71 | June 30, 1955 | 30,229.3 | 182.90 | June 30, 1920 | 5,467.6 | 51.36 |
| June 30, 1985 | 185,890.7 | 778.58 | June 30, 1950 | 27,156.3 | 179.03 | June 30, 1915 | 3,319.6 | 33.01 |
| June 30, 1980 | 127,097.2 | 558.28 | June 30, 1945 | 26,746.4 | 191.14 | June 30, 1910 | 3,148.7 | 34.07 |

(1) Issued on and after July 1, 1929. (2) Excludes coin sold to collectors at premium prices. (3) Includes $481,781,898 in standard silver dollars. (4) Represents value of certain partial denominations not presented for redemption. (5) Based on Bureau of the Census estimates of population.

The requirement for a gold reserve against U.S. notes was repealed by Public Law 90-269, approved Mar. 18, 1968. Silver certificates issued on and after July 1, 1929, became redeemable from the general fund on June 24, 1968. The amount of security after those dates has been reduced accordingly.

# Consumer Credit Outstanding, 1993-95

**Source:** Federal Reserve System

(billions of dollars)

Estimated amounts of credit outstanding as of end of year. Not seasonally adjusted.

| | 1993[R] | 1994[R] | 1995 |
|---|---|---|---|
| **Total** | **$863.9** | **$988.8** | **$1,131.9** |
| Ratio to disposable personal income[1] (percent) | 18.0 | 19.7 | 21.3 |
| By major holder | | | |
| Commercial banks | 399.7 | 462.9 | 507.8 |
| Finance companies | 116.5 | 134.8 | 152.6 |
| Credit unions | 101.6 | 119.6 | 131.9 |
| Savings institutions | 37.9 | 38.5 | 40.1 |
| Nonfinancial business | 77.2 | 86.6 | 85.1 |
| Pools of securitized assets[2] | 131.1 | 147.8 | 214.4 |
| By major type of credit[3] | | | |
| Automobile | $281.5 | $319.7 | $354.1 |
| Commercial banks | $122.0 | $141.9 | $149.1 |
| Finance companies | 56.1 | 61.6 | 70.6 |
| Pools of securitized assets[2] | 39.6 | 36.4 | 44.4 |
| Revolving | 302.2 | 357.3 | 435.7 |
| Commercial banks | 149.9 | 182.0 | 210.3 |
| Finance companies | 50.1 | 56.8 | 53.5 |
| Pools of securitized assets[2] | 80.2 | 96.1 | 147.9 |
| Other | 280.2 | 313.2 | 342.2 |
| Commercial banks | 127.8 | 139.0 | 148.4 |
| Finance companies | 60.4 | 73.2 | 82.0 |
| Nonfinancial business | 27.1 | 29.8 | 31.5 |
| Pools of securitized assets[2] | 11.3 | 15.3 | 22.1 |

(1) Based on 4th quarter seasonally adjusted disposable personal income at annual rates as published by the U.S. Bureau of Economic Analysis. (2) Outstanding balances of pools upon which securities have been issued; these balances are no longer carried on the balance sheets of the loan originator. (3) Totals include estimates for certain holders for which only consumer credit totals are available. (R) Revised.

# Leading U.S. Businesses in 1995

Source: *FORTUNE* Magazine

(millions of dollars in revenues)

### Aerospace

| | |
|---|---|
| Lockheed Martin | $22,853 |
| United Technologies | 22,802 |
| Boeing | 19,515 |
| AlliedSignal | 14,346 |
| McDonnell Douglas | 14,332 |
| Textron | 9,973 |
| Northrop Grumman | 6,818 |
| General Dynamics | 3,544 |
| B.F. Goodrich | 2,409 |
| Sundstrand | 1,473 |

### Airlines

| | |
|---|---|
| AMR | $16,910 |
| UAL | 14,943 |
| Delta Air Lines | 12,194 |
| Northwest Airlines | 9,085 |
| USAir Group | 7,474 |
| Continental Airlines | 5,825 |
| Trans World Airlines | 3,317 |
| Southwest Airlines | 2,873 |
| America West Airlines | 1,551 |
| Alaska Air Group | 1,418 |

### Apparel

| | |
|---|---|
| Levi Strauss Associates | $6,708 |
| VF | 5,062 |
| Fruit of the Loom | 2,403 |
| Liz Claiborne | 2,082 |
| Kellwood | 1,365 |
| Russell | 1,153 |
| Warnaco Group | 916 |

### Beverages

| | |
|---|---|
| Coca-Cola | $18,018 |
| Anheuser-Busch | 12,326 |
| Coca-Cola Enterprises | 6,773 |
| Whitman | 2,947 |
| Adolph Coors | 1,675 |
| Brown-Forman | 1,420 |
| Canandaigua Wine | 907 |

### Brokerage

| | |
|---|---|
| Merrill Lynch | $21,513 |
| Lehman Brothers Holdings | 13,476 |
| Salomon | 8,933 |
| Paine Webber Group | 5,320 |
| Bear Stearns | 3,754 |
| Charles Schwab | 1,777 |
| A.G. Edwards & Sons | 1,178 |

### Building Materials, Glass

| | |
|---|---|
| Corning | $5,346 |
| Owens-Illinois | 3,763 |
| Owens-Corning | 3,612 |
| Manville | 2,734 |
| Armstrong World Ind. | 2,635 |
| USG | 2,444 |

### Chemicals

| | |
|---|---|
| E. I. Du Pont De Nemours | $37,607 |
| Dow Chemical | 20,957 |
| Occidental Petroleum | 10,423 |
| Monsanto | 8,962 |
| PPG Industries | 7,058 |
| Union Carbide | 5,888 |
| W.R. Grace | 5,784 |
| Eastman Chemical | 5,040 |
| Lyondell Petrochemical | 4,936 |
| FMC | 4,567 |

### Commercial Banks

| | |
|---|---|
| Citicorp | $31,690 |
| Bankamerica Corp. | 20,386 |
| Nationsbank Corp. | 16,298 |
| Chemical Banking Corp. | 14,884 |
| J.P. Morgan & Co. | 13,838 |
| Chase Manhattan Corp. | 11,336 |
| First Chicago NBD Corp. | 10,681 |
| First Union Corp. | 10,583 |
| Banc One Corp. | 8,971 |
| Bankers Trust N.Y. Corp. | 8,600 |

### Computer and Data Services

| | |
|---|---|
| Unisys | $6,460 |
| Microsoft | 5,937 |
| Dun & Bradstreet | 5,415 |
| First Data | 4,081 |
| Computer Sciences | 3,373 |

### Computers, Office Equipment

| | |
|---|---|
| IBM | $71,940 |
| Hewlett-Packard | 31,519 |
| Compaq Computer | 14,755 |
| Digital Equipment | 13,813 |
| Apple Computer | 11,062 |
| Sun Microsystems | 5,902 |
| Dell Computer | 5,296 |
| Seagate Technology | 4,540 |
| Pitney Bowes | 3,861 |
| Gateway 2000 | 3,676 |

### Diversified Financials

| | |
|---|---|
| Fed. Natl. Mortgage Assn. | $22,246 |
| American Express | 15,841 |
| Morgan Stanley Group | 10,949 |
| Fed. Home Loan Mortgage | 10,915 |
| College Ret. Equities Fund | 7,951 |
| Dean Witter Discover | 7,934 |
| American General | 6,495 |
| Household International | 5,144 |
| Berkshire Hathaway | 4,488 |
| Student Loan Mrktg. Assn. | 3,917 |

### Electric and Gas Utilities

| | |
|---|---|
| Pacific Gas & Electric | $9,622 |
| Southern | 9,180 |
| Edison International | 8,405 |
| UNICOM | 6,910 |
| Con. Edison of New York | 6,402 |
| Entergy | 6,274 |
| Public Service Entr. Group | 6,164 |
| American Electric Power | 5,670 |
| Texas Utilities | 5,639 |
| FPL Group | 5,592 |

### Electronics, Electrical Equip.

| | |
|---|---|
| General Electric | $70,028 |
| Motorola | 27,037 |
| Intel | 16,202 |
| Texas Instruments | 13,128 |
| Rockwell International | 13,009 |
| Raytheon | 11,716 |
| Emerson Electric | 10,013 |
| Westinghouse Electric | 9,605 |
| Whirlpool | 8,347 |
| Loral | 5,484 |

### Entertainment

| | |
|---|---|
| Walt Disney | $12,112 |
| Viacom | 11,780 |
| Time Warner | 8,067 |
| Turner Broadcasting | 3,437 |

### Food

| | |
|---|---|
| ConAgra | $24,109 |
| Sara Lee | 17,719 |
| RJR Nabisco Holdings | 16,008 |
| Archer Daniels Midland | 12,672 |
| IBP | 12,668 |
| CPC International | 8,431 |
| General Mills | 8,394 |
| H. J. Heinz | 8,087 |
| Campbell Soup | 7,278 |
| Farmland Industries | 7,257 |

### Food and Drug Stores

| | |
|---|---|
| Kroger | $23,938 |
| American Stores | 18,309 |
| Safeway | 16,398 |
| Albertson's | 12,585 |
| Winn-Dixie Stores | 11,788 |
| Walgreen | 10,395 |
| Publix Super Markets | 9,471 |
| Vons | 5,071 |
| Eckerd | 4,997 |
| Thrifty Payless Holdings | 4,659 |

### Food Services

| | |
|---|---|
| Pepsico | $30,421 |
| McDonald's | 9,795 |
| Aramark | 5,601 |
| Flagstar | 2,894 |
| Wendy's International | 1,746 |
| Shoney's | 1,140 |
| Family Restaurants | 1,122 |
| Brinker International | 1,042 |
| Morrison Restaurants | 1,035 |
| Foodmaker | 1,019 |

### Forest and Paper Products

| | |
|---|---|
| International Paper | $19,797 |
| Georgia-Pacific | 14,292 |
| Kimberly-Clark | 13,789 |
| Weyerhaeuser | 11,788 |
| Stone Container | 7,351 |
| Champion International | 6,972 |
| James River Corp. of VA | 6,800 |
| Mead | 5,179 |
| Boise Cascade | 5,058 |
| Union Camp | 4,212 |

### Furniture

| | |
|---|---|
| Leggett & Platt | $2,059 |
| Herman Miller | 1,083 |
| Interco | 1,074 |
| Kimball International | 896 |
| Hon Industries | 893 |

### General Merchandisers

| | |
|---|---|
| Wal-Mart Stores | $93,627 |
| Sears Roebuck | 35,181 |
| Kmart | 34,654 |
| Dayton Hudson | 23,516 |
| J. C. Penney | 21,419 |
| Federated Dept. Stores | 15,049 |
| May Department Stores | 12,187 |
| Dillard Dept. Stores | 6,097 |
| Nordstrom | 4,114 |
| Fred Meyer | 3,429 |

### Industrial and Farm Equip.

| | |
|---|---|
| Caterpillar | $16,072 |
| Deere | 10,291 |
| Ingersoll-Rand | 5,729 |
| Dresser Industries | 5,629 |
| Black & Decker | 5,566 |
| Cummins Engine | 5,245 |
| American Standard | 5,221 |
| Case | 5,105 |
| Dover | 3,746 |
| Parker Hannifin | 3,214 |

### Insurance (Life and Health)

| | |
|---|---|
| Prudential Ins. of America (Mutual) | $41,330 |
| Metropolitan Life Ins. (Mutual) | 27,977 |
| Cigna (Stock) | 18,955 |
| New York Life Ins. (Mutual) | 16,202 |
| Aetna Life & Casualty (Stock) | 12,978 |

### Insurance (Property and Casualty)

| | |
|---|---|
| State Farm Group (Mutual) | $40,180 |
| American Intl. Group (Stock) | 25,874 |
| Allstate (Stock) | 22,793 |
| Loews (Stock) | 18,770 |
| Travelers Group (Stock) | 16,583 |

### Metal Products

| | |
|---|---|
| Gillette | $6,795 |
| Crown Cork & Seal | 5,054 |
| Masco | 4,779 |
| Tyco International | 4,535 |
| Illinois Tool Works | 4,152 |
| U.S. Industries | 2,908 |
| Stanley Works | 2,624 |
| Ball | 2,592 |
| Newell | 2,498 |
| Mascotech | 1,678 |

### Metals

| | |
|---|---|
| Alcoa | $12,655 |
| Reynolds Metals | 7,252 |
| Bethlehem Steel | 4,868 |
| Inland Steel Industries | 4,781 |
| LTV | 4,283 |
| Phelps Dodge | 4,185 |
| Nucor | 3,462 |
| Alumax | 2,926 |
| Maxxam | 2,565 |
| AK Steel Holding | 2,257 |

### Motor Vehicles and Parts

| | |
|---|---|
| General Motors | $168,829 |
| Ford Motor | 137,137 |
| Chrysler | 53,195 |
| TRW | 10,172 |
| Tenneco | 8,899 |
| ITT Industries | 8,884 |
| Johnson Controls | 8,330 |
| Dana | 7,795 |
| Eaton | 6,822 |
| Navistar International | 6,342 |

**Petroleum Refining**

| | |
|---|---|
| Exxon | $110,009 |
| Mobil | 66,724 |
| Texaco | 36,787 |
| Chevron | 32,094 |
| Amoco | 27,665 |
| USX | 18,214 |
| Atlantic Richfield | 16,739 |
| Phillips Petroleum | 13,521 |
| Ashland | 11,251 |
| Coastal | 10,223 |

**Pharmaceuticals**

| | |
|---|---|
| Johnson & Johnson | $18,842 |
| Merck | 16,681 |
| Bristol-Myers Squibb | 13,767 |
| American Home Products | 13,376 |
| Pfizer | 10,021 |
| Abbott Laboratories | 10,012 |
| Eli Lilly | 7,535 |
| Pharmacia & Upjohn | 7,095 |
| Warner-Lambert | 7,040 |
| Schering-Plough | 5,151 |

**Publishing & Printing**

| | |
|---|---|
| R.R. Donnelley & Sons | $6,512 |
| Gannett | 4,007 |
| Times Mirror | 3,491 |
| Reader's Digest Assn. | 3,069 |
| McGraw-Hill | 2,935 |
| Tribune | 2,864 |
| Knight-Ridder | 2,752 |
| New York Times | 2,409 |
| Dow Jones | 2,284 |
| American Greetings | 1,878 |

**Railroads**

| | |
|---|---|
| CSX | $10,504 |
| Union Pacific | 8,942 |
| Burlington Northern Santa Fe | 6,183 |
| Norfolk Southern | 4,668 |
| Conrail | 3,686 |
| Southern Pacific Rail | 3,151 |

**Rubber and Plastic Prods.**

| | |
|---|---|
| Goodyear Tire & Rubber | $13,166 |
| Premark International | 3,574 |
| Rubbermaid | 2,344 |
| M. A. Hanna | 1,957 |
| Mark IV Industries | 1,603 |

**Scientific, Photographic, and Control Equipment**

| | |
|---|---|
| Xerox | $18,963 |
| Minnesota Mining & Mfg. | 16,105 |
| Eastman Kodak | 15,269 |
| Baxter International | 9,730 |
| Honeywell | 6,731 |
| Becton Dickinson | 2,713 |
| Polaroid | 2,237 |
| Thermo Electron | 2,207 |
| EG&G | 2,079 |
| Bausch & Lomb | 1,933 |

**Soaps, Cosmetics**

| | |
|---|---|
| Procter & Gamble | $33,434 |
| Colgate-Palmolive | 8,358 |
| Avon Products | 4,492 |
| Dial | 3,575 |
| Estée Lauder | 2,899 |
| Clorox | 1,984 |
| Intl. Flavors & Fragrances | 1,439 |
| Alberto-Culver | 1,358 |
| Helene Curtis Industries | 1,266 |

**Specialist Retailers**

| | |
|---|---|
| Price/Costco | $18,247 |
| Home Depot | 15,470 |
| Melville | 11,516 |
| Toys "R" Us | 9,427 |
| Woolworth | 8,224 |
| Limited | 7,881 |
| Lowe's | 7,075 |
| Tandy | 5,839 |
| Circuit City Stores | 5,583 |
| Office Depot | 5,313 |

**Telecommunications**

| | |
|---|---|
| AT&T | $79,609 |
| GTE | 19,957 |
| BellSouth | 17,886 |
| MCI Communications | 15,265 |
| Sprint | 13,600 |
| Bell Atlantic | 13,430 |
| Ameritech | 13,428 |
| NYNEX | 13,407 |
| SBC Communications | 12,670 |
| US West | 11,746 |

**Textiles**

| | |
|---|---|
| Shaw Industries | $2,870 |
| Springs Industries | 2,233 |
| Burlington Industries | 2,209 |
| Westpoint Stevens | 1,650 |
| Mohawk Industries | 1,649 |

**Tobacco**

| | |
|---|---|
| Philip Morris | $53,139 |
| American Brands | 5,905 |
| Universal | 3,281 |
| Dimon | 1,928 |
| UST | 1,300 |

**Toys, Sporting Goods**

| | |
|---|---|
| Mattel | $3,639 |
| Hasbro | 2,858 |
| Coleman Holdings | 934 |

**Transportation Equipment**

| | |
|---|---|
| Brunswick | $3,077 |
| Trinity Industries | 2,315 |
| Harley-Davidson | 1,794 |
| Outboard Marine | 1,229 |
| Polaris Industries | 1,114 |

**Wholesalers**

| | |
|---|---|
| Fleming | $17,502 |
| Supervalu | 16,564 |
| McKesson | 13,326 |
| Sysco | 12,118 |
| Alco Standard | 9,892 |

## U.S. Corporations With Largest Revenues in 1995

**Source:** *FORTUNE* Magazine

(millions of dollars)

| Company, headquarters | Revenues |
|---|---|
| General Motors, Detroit, MI | $168,829 |
| Ford Motor, Dearborn, MI | 137,137 |
| Exxon, Irving, TX | 110,009 |
| Wal-Mart Stores, Bentonville, AR | 93,627 |
| AT&T, New York, NY | 79,609 |
| IBM, Armonk, NY | 71,940 |
| General Electric, Fairfield, CT | 70,028 |
| Mobil, Fairfax, VA | 66,724 |
| Chrysler, Auburn Hills, MI | 53,195 |
| Philip Morris, New York, NY | 53,139 |
| Prudential Insurance Co. of America, Newark, NJ | $41,330 |
| State Farm Group, Bloomington, IL | 40,809 |
| E. I. Du Pont de Nemours, Wilmington, DE | 37,607 |
| Texaco, White Plains, NY | 36,787 |
| Sears Roebuck, Hoffman Estates, IL | 35,181 |
| Kmart, Troy, MI | 34,654 |
| Procter & Gamble, Cincinnati, OH | 33,434 |
| Chevron, San Francisco, CA | $32,094 |
| Citicorp, New York, NY | 31,690 |
| Hewlett-Packard, Palo Alto, CA | 31,519 |
| Pepsico, Purchase, NY | 30,421 |
| Metropolitan Life Insurance, New York, NY | 27,977 |
| Amoco, Chicago, IL | 27,665 |
| Motorola, Schaumberg, IL | 27,037 |
| American International Group, New York, NY | 25,874 |

## Largest Corporate Mergers or Acquisitions in U.S.

**Source:** Securities Data Co.

(as of Oct. 1996; *italics* denotes that a merger or acquisition may not be complete; year = year announced)

| Company | Acquirer | Dollars | Year |
|---|---|---|---|
| RJR Nabisco | Kohlberg Kravis Roberts | 30.6 bil | 1988 |
| Electronic Data Systems | shareholders | 28.0 bil | 1995 |
| Lucent Technologies | shareholders | 24.1 bil | 1995 |
| *NYNEX* | *Bell Atlantic* | *21.3 bil* | *1996* |
| McCaw Cellular Communications | AT&T | 18.9 bil | 1993 |
| Capital Cities/ABC | Walt Disney | 18.9 bil | 1995 |
| *Pacific Telesis Group* | *SBC Communications* | *16.5 bil* | *1996* |
| Warner Communications | Time | 14.1 bil | 1989 |
| Kraft | Philip Morris | 13.4 bil | 1988 |
| Gulf Oil | Standard Oil of CA | 13.4 bil | 1984 |
| *MFS Communications* | *WorldCom* | *13.4 bil* | *1996* |
| Squibb | Bristol-Myers | 12.1 bil | 1989 |
| *Continental Cablevision* | *US West Media Group* | *11.8 bil* | *1996* |
| Allstate | shareholders | 11.8 bil | 1994 |
| First Interstate Bancorp | Wells Fargo | 10.9 bil | 1995 |
| Getty Oil | Texaco | 10.1 bil | 1984 |
| Chase Manhattan | Chemical Banking | 9.9 bil | 1995 |
| Paramount | Viacom | 9.6 bil | 1993 |
| American Cyanamid | American Home Products | 9.6 bil | 1994 |
| *Boatmen's Bancshares* | *NationsBank, Charlotte, NC* | *9.5 bil* | *1996* |
| US West Media Grp. | shareholders | 9.3 bil | 1995 |
| Loral | Lockheed Martin | 8.8 bil | 1996 |
| US Healthcare | Aetna Life & Casualty | 8.8 bil | 1996 |
| PacTel | shareholders | 8.6 bil | 1992 |
| Blockbuster | Viacom | 8.0 bil | 1994 |
| SmithKline Beckman | Beecham Group | 7.9 bil | 1989 |
| NCR | AT&T | 7.9 bil | 1990 |
| Standard Oil | British Petroleum | 7.9 bil | 1987 |
| Conoco | Du Pont | 7.6 bil | 1981 |
| MCA | Matsushita Electric Industrial | 7.4 bil | 1990 |
| Marion Merrell Dow | Hoechst AG | 7.1 bil | 1995 |
| Duracell Intl. | Gillette | 7.0 bil | 1996 |
| Turner Broadcasting System | Time Warner | 6.9 bil | 1995 |
| Scott Paper | Kimberly-Clark | 6.8 bil | 1995 |
| US West-Domestic Cellular | AirTouch Communications | 6.8 bil | 1994 |
| RCA | General Electric | 6.6 bil | 1985 |
| Federated Dept. Stores | Campeau | 6.5 bil | 1988 |
| NYNEX-Cellular Phone Bus. | Bell Atlantic | 6.5 bil | 1994 |
| Marathon Oil | U.S. Steel | 6.4 bil | 1981 |
| Contel | GTE | 6.2 bil | 1990 |
| Medco | Merck | 6.2 bil | 1993 |
| Marion Laboratories | Dow Chemical | 6.2 bil | 1989 |
| Beatrice | BCI Holdings | 6.1 bil | 1985 |

# U.S. Corporate Profits by Industry[1]

**Source:** Bureau of Economic Analysis, U.S. Dept. of Commerce

(billions of dollars)

| | 1994 | 1995 | First quarter 1996[2] |
|---|---|---|---|
| **Corporate profits with inventory valuation and capital consumption adjustments** | **529.5** | **586.6** | **645.1** |
| **Domestic industries** | **465.3** | **510.0** | **562.0** |
| Financial | 100.7 | 125.4 | 141.7 |
| Nonfinancial | 364.6 | 384.6 | 420.3 |
| **Rest of the world** | **64.3** | **76.7** | **83.2** |
| Receipts from rest of world | 88.5 | 111.1 | 122.2 |
| Less: Payments to rest of world | 24.3 | 34.5 | 39.0 |
| **Corporate profits with inventory valuation adjustment** | **517.9** | **570.8** | **624.8** |
| **Domestic industries** | **453.7** | **494.1** | **541.6** |
| Financial | 94.4 | 119.1 | 134.9 |
| Federal Reserve banks | 17.8 | 21.9 | 21.5 |
| Other | 76.6 | 97.3 | 113.4 |
| Nonfinancial | 359.3 | 375.0 | 406.7 |
| Manufacturing | 142.7 | 145.7 | 161.3 |
| Durable goods | 77.2 | 77.2 | 89.5 |
| Primary metal industries | 0.7 | 3.0 | 2.3 |
| Fabricated metal prods. | 10.7 | 11.1 | 13.9 |
| Industrial machinery, equip. | 9.0 | 12.1 | 14.3 |
| Electronic, other electric equip. | 22.5 | 25.6 | 27.1 |
| Motor vehicles and equip. | 10.2 | 4.4 | 8.1 |
| Other | 24.1 | 20.9 | 23.8 |
| Nondurable goods | 65.5 | 68.5 | 71.8 |
| Food and kindred prods. | 19.1 | 17.7 | 15.7 |
| Chemicals and allied prods. | 18.0 | 20.9 | 20.7 |
| Petroleum and coal prods. | –0.1 | 0.8 | –4.5 |
| Other | 28.4 | 29.1 | 39.9 |
| Transportation and public utils. | 81.3 | 94.8 | 95.6 |
| Transportation | 10.8 | 14.4 | 13.1 |
| Communications | 36.7 | 41.0 | 43.3 |
| Electric, gas, sanitary srvcs. | 33.8 | 39.4 | 39.3 |
| Wholesale trade | 34.5 | 29.6 | 37.5 |
| Retail trade | 42.2 | 38.7 | 41.7 |
| Other | 58.6 | 66.2 | 70.6 |
| **Rest of the world** | **64.3** | **76.7** | **83.2** |

(1) Figures are rounded; therefore, some totals may not add. (2) Seasonally adjusted at annual rates.

# Fastest Growing Franchises in 1995[1]

**Source:** Reprinted with permission from *Entrepreneur* Magazine, Jan. 1996

| Company | Business | Minimum start-up cost[2] |
|---|---|---|
| Subway | sandwiches, salads | $ 54,270 |
| 7-Eleven Convenience Stores | convenience stores | varies |
| Burger King Corp. | hamburgers | 320,000 |
| McDonald's | hamburgers, chicken, salads | 363,000 |
| Dunkin' Donuts | donuts, baked goods | 181,600 |
| Yogen Fruz | frozen yogurt, ice cream | 55,000 |
| Baskin-Robbins USA Co. | ice cream, yogurt | 42,200 |
| Jani-King | commercial cleaning | 1,800 |
| Coverall Cleaning Concepts | commercial cleaning | 350 |
| CleanNet USA Inc. | commercial cleaning | 425 |
| Snap-On Tools | professional tools & equipment | 104,900 |
| Thrifty Rent-A-Car System Inc. | vehicle rentals, leasing, & parking | varies |
| Mail Boxes Etc. | postal, business, communications srvcs. | 68,500 |
| Blimpie Intl. Inc. | sandwiches, salads | 63,920 |
| Jackson Hewitt Tax Service | computer tax prep./ filing services | 10,020 |
| Chem-Dry Carpet Drapery & Upholstery Cleaning | carpet/fabric cleaning & care | $ 8,400 |
| ServiceMaster | commercial cleaning | 4,150 |
| GNC Franchising Inc. | vitamin/nutrition stores | 75,000 |
| Dairy Queen | soft-serve dairy prods., sandwiches | 370,000 |
| Futurekids Inc. | children's computer learning centers | 65,000 |
| Re/Max Intl. Inc. | real estate services | 10,000 |
| Super 8 Motels Inc. | economy motels | 240,000 |
| Papa John's Pizza | pizza | 148,500 |
| KFC | chicken | 950,000 |
| Furniture Medic | furniture restoration & repair service | 7,260 |
| Holiday Inn Worldwide | hotels | varies |
| Great Clips Inc. | family hair salons | 64,050 |
| Realty Executives | real estate services | 17,550 |
| Applebee's Neighborhood Grill & Bar | restaurants | 1,700,000 |
| The Prudential Real Estate Affiliates Inc. | real estate brokerage | 12,500 |

(1) Based on the number of new franchise units added. (2) Not including franchise fee, which varies.

# Largest U.S. Black-Owned Companies in 1995

**Source:** *Black Enterprise* Magazine

| Company, Location (Business) | Sales (millions) |
|---|---|
| TLC Beatrice International Holdings Inc., New York, NY (international food processor and distributor) | $2,100.0 |
| Johnson Publishing Co. Inc., Chicago, IL (publishing, broadcasting, TV production, cosmetics, hair care) | 316.2 |
| Philadelphia Coca-Cola Bottling Co. Inc., Philadelphia, PA | 315.0 |
| H. J. Russell & Co., Atlanta, GA (construction, airport concessions, real estate development) | 172.8 |
| Pulsar Data Systems Inc., Lanham, MD (systems integration, office automation, computer reseller) | 165.1 |
| Uniworld Group Inc., New York, NY (advertising, public relations, event marketing, TV programs) | 133.7 |
| Burrell Communications Group, Chicago, IL (advertising, public relations, consumer promotions, printing) | 127.9 |
| The Anderson-Dubose Co., Solon, OH (food distributor) | 119.5 |
| Granite Broadcasting Co., New York, NY (network TV affiliates) | 119.5 |
| BET Holdings, Washington, DC (cable TV network, magazine publishing) | $115.0 |
| Mays Chemical Co., Indianapolis, IN (industrial chemical distributors) | 107.0 |
| Envirotest Systems Corp., Phoenix, AZ (vehicle emissions testing) | 104.8 |
| The Bing Group, Detroit, MI (steel processing; metal stamping distribution) | 101.0 |
| RMS Technologies, Marlton, NJ (computer and technical services) | 95.0 |
| Soft Sheen Products, Chicago, IL (hair care products manufacturer) | 92.8 |
| Midwest Stamping, Bowling Green, OH (metal stamping and assemblies) | 90.2 |
| Sylvest Management Systems Corp., Lanham, MD (computer systems and engineering) | 84.0 |
| Essence Communications, New York, NY (magazine publishing; licensing; TV production) | 80.1 |
| Thacker Engineering, Atlanta, GA (construction; construction management; engineering) | 76.8 |
| Wesley Industries, Flint MI (industrial coatings; grey iron foundry products) | 75.7 |

# Capital Gains Tax

**Source:** U.S. Chamber of Commerce; as of Sept. 1996

The following shows how the maximum tax rate on net long-term capital gains for individuals has changed since 1960.

| Year | Maximum rate (percentage) | Year | Maximum rate (percentage) | Year | Maximum rate (percentage) | Year | Maximum rate (percentage) | Year | Maximum rate (percentage) |
|---|---|---|---|---|---|---|---|---|---|
| 1960 | 25.0 | 1971 | 32.5 | 1978 | 28.0 | 1987 | 28.0 | 1990 | 28.0[3] |
| 1970 | 29.5 | 1972 | 35.0[1] | 1981 | 20.0 | 1988 | 33.0[2] | | |

(1) From 1972 to 1976, the interplay of minimum tax and maximum tax resulted in a marginal rate of 49.125%. (2) Statutory maximum of 28%, but "phase-out" notch increased marginal rate to 33%; interplay of all "phase outs" could have increased marginal rate to 49.5%. (3) The Budget Act of 1990 increased the statutory rate to 31%, and capped the marginal rate at 28%; however, some taxpayers will face effective marginal rates of more than 34% because of the phase out of personal exemptions and itemized deductions.

# 1996 Federal Corporate Tax Rates

| Taxable Income Amount | Tax Rate | Taxable Income Amount | Tax Rate |
|---|---|---|---|
| Not more than $50,000 | 15% | $335,001 to $10,000,000 | 34% |
| $50,001 to $75,000 | 25% | $10,000,001 to $15,000,000 | 35% |
| $75,001 to $100,000 | 34% | $15,000,001 to $18,333,333 | 38% |
| $100,001 to $335,000 | 39% | More than $18,333,333 | 35% |

Personal service corporations (used by professional individuals such as attorneys and doctors) pay a flat rate of 35%.

# Global Stock Markets

**Source:** The Conference Board; not seasonally adjusted

| Stock price indexes (1967=100): | 1994 | 1995 | 1996 Jan. | Feb. | Mar. | Apr. | May | June |
|---|---|---|---|---|---|---|---|---|
| United States | 500.8 | 589.2 | 668.4 | 706.6 | 703.9 | 704.0 | 719.3 | 727.2 |
| Japan | 1,449.6 | 1,251.6 | 1,449.1 | 1,445.1 | 1,421.4 | 1,520.3 | 1,518.3 | 1,532.1 |
| Germany | 376.8 | 361.2 | 396.2 | 405.4 | 413.0 | 420.4 | 420.2 | 425.9 |
| France | 1,034.4 | 940.4 | 976.7 | 990.6 | 998.1 | 1,052.6 | 1,062.1 | 1,061.7 |
| United Kingdom | 1,478.3 | 1,538.6 | 1,672.1 | 1,694.0 | 1,701.3 | 1,760.8 | 1,753.5 | 1,742.0 |
| Italy | 717.2 | 656.9 | 633.8 | 646.8 | 628.2 | 654.4 | 702.1 | 699.3 |

# Foreign Exchange Rates, 1970-95

**Source:** International Monetary Fund

(National currency units per dollar except as indicated; data are annual averages)

| Year | Australia[1] (dollar) | Austria (schilling) | Belgium (franc) | Canada (dollar) | Denmark (krone) | France (franc) | Germany[2] (deutsche mark) | Greece (drachma) |
|---|---|---|---|---|---|---|---|---|
| 1970 | 1.1136 | 25.880 | 49.680 | 1.0103 | 7.489 | 5.5200 | 3.6480 | 30.00 |
| 1975 | 1.3077 | 17.443 | 36.799 | 1.0175 | 5.748 | 4.2876 | 2.4613 | 32.29 |
| 1980 | 1.1400 | 12.945 | 29.237 | 1.1693 | 5.634 | 4.2250 | 1.8175 | 42.62 |
| 1985 | 0.7003 | 20.690 | 59.378 | 1.3655 | 10.596 | 8.9852 | 2.9440 | 138.12 |
| 1988 | 0.7842 | 12.348 | 36.768 | 1.2307 | 6.732 | 5.9569 | 1.7562 | 141.86 |
| 1989 | 0.7925 | 13.231 | 39.404 | 1.1840 | 7.310 | 6.3801 | 1.8800 | 162.42 |
| 1990 | 0.7813 | 11.370 | 33.418 | 1.1668 | 6.189 | 5.4453 | 1.6157 | 158.51 |
| 1991 | 0.7791 | 11.676 | 34.148 | 1.1457 | 6.396 | 5.6421 | 1.6595 | 182.27 |
| 1992 | 0.7353 | 10.989 | 32.150 | 1.2087 | 6.036 | 5.2938 | 1.5617 | 190.62 |
| 1993 | 0.6801 | 11.632 | 34.597 | 1.2901 | 6.484 | 5.6632 | 1.6533 | 229.25 |
| 1994 | 0.7317 | 11.422 | 33.456 | 1.3656 | 6.361 | 5.5520 | 1.6228 | 242.60 |
| 1995 | 0.7415 | 10.081 | 29.480 | 1.3724 | 5.602 | 4.9915 | 1.4331 | 231.66 |

| Year | India (rupee) | Ireland[1] (pound) | Italy (lira) | Japan (yen) | Malaysia (ringgit) | Mexico (new peso) | Netherlands (guilder) | Norway (kroner) |
|---|---|---|---|---|---|---|---|---|
| 1970 | 7.576 | 2.3959 | 623 | 357.60 | 3.0900 | — | 3.5970 | 7.1400 |
| 1975 | 8.409 | 2.2216 | 653 | 296.78 | 2.4030 | — | 2.5293 | 5.2282 |
| 1980 | 7.887 | 2.0577 | 856 | 226.63 | 2.1767 | — | 1.9875 | 4.9381 |
| 1985 | 12.369 | 1.0656 | 1,909 | 238.54 | 2.4830 | — | 3.3214 | 8.5972 |
| 1988 | 13.917 | 1.5261 | 1,302 | 128.15 | 2.6188 | 2.2731 | 1.9766 | 6.5170 |
| 1989 | 16.226 | 1.4190 | 1,372 | 137.96 | 2.7088 | 2.4615 | 2.1207 | 6.9045 |
| 1990 | 17.504 | 1.6585 | 1,198 | 144.79 | 2.7049 | 2.8126 | 1.8209 | 6.2597 |
| 1991 | 22.742 | 1.6155 | 1,241 | 134.71 | 2.7501 | 3.0184 | 1.8697 | 6.4829 |
| 1992 | 25.918 | 1.7053 | 1,232 | 126.65 | 2.5474 | 3.0949 | 1.7585 | 6.2145 |
| 1993 | 30.493 | 1.4671 | 1,574 | 111.20 | 2.5741 | 3.1156 | 1.8573 | 7.0941 |
| 1994 | 31.374 | 1.4978 | 1,612 | 102.21 | 2.6243 | 3.3751 | 1.8200 | 7.0576 |
| 1995 | 32.427 | 1.6038 | 1,629 | 94.06 | 2.5044 | 6.4194 | 1.6057 | 6.3352 |

| Year | Portugal (escudo) | Singapore (dollar) | South Korea (won) | Spain (peseta) | Sweden (krona) | Switzerland (franc) | Thailand (baht) | United[1] Kingdom (pound) |
|---|---|---|---|---|---|---|---|---|
| 1970 | 28.75 | 3.0800 | 310.57 | 69.72 | 5.1700 | 4.3160 | 21.000 | 2.3959 |
| 1975 | 25.51 | 2.3713 | 484.00 | 57.43 | 4.1530 | 2.5839 | 20.379 | 2.2216 |
| 1980 | 50.08 | 2.1412 | 607.43 | 71.76 | 4.2309 | 1.6772 | 20.476 | 2.3243 |
| 1985 | 170.39 | 2.2002 | 870.02 | 170.04 | 8.6039 | 2.4571 | 27.159 | 1.2963 |
| 1988 | 143.95 | 2.0124 | 731.47 | 116.49 | 6.1272 | 1.4633 | 25.294 | 1.7814 |
| 1989 | 157.46 | 1.9503 | 671.46 | 118.38 | 6.4469 | 1.6359 | 25.702 | 1.6397 |
| 1990 | 142.55 | 1.8125 | 707.76 | 101.93 | 5.9188 | 1.3892 | 25.585 | 1.7847 |
| 1991 | 144.48 | 1.7276 | 733.35 | 103.91 | 6.0475 | 1.4340 | 25.517 | 1.7694 |
| 1992 | 135.00 | 1.6290 | 780.65 | 102.38 | 5.8238 | 1.4062 | 25.400 | 1.7655 |
| 1993 | 160.80 | 1.6158 | 802.67 | 127.26 | 7.7834 | 1.4776 | 25.319 | 1.5020 |
| 1994 | 165.99 | 1.5274 | 803.45 | 133.96 | 7.7160 | 1.3677 | 25.150 | 1.5316 |
| 1995 | 151.11 | 1.4174 | 771.27 | 124.69 | 7.1333 | 1.1825 | NA | 1.5785 |

(1) Value of one unit of foreign currency in dollars. (2) West Germany prior to 1991. NA=not available.

## Tourism: International Visitors to the U.S., 1995

**Source:** International Trade Administration, Dept. of Commerce

| Country of origin | Visitors (thousands) | Expenditures (millions) | Expenditures per visitor |
|---|---|---|---|
| Canada | 14,663 | $6,207.0 | $423 |
| Mexico | 8,083 | 2,857.0 | 353 |
| Japan | 4,598 | 11,189.0 | 2,433 |
| United Kingdom | 2,888 | 6,422.0 | 2,224 |
| Germany | 1,848 | 4,023.0 | 2,177 |
| France | 922 | 1,830.0 | 1,985 |
| Brazil | 838 | NA | — |
| South Korea | 592 | NA | — |
| Italy | 525 | $1,234.0 | $2,350 |
| Venezuela | 511 | 1,437.0 | 2,812 |
| All countries | 43,385 | 61,137.0 | 1,409 |

**Note:** Excludes international passenger fare payments and cruise travel. NA=not available.

## Foreign Direct Investment[1] in the U.S. by Selected Countries and Territories

**Source:** Bureau of Economic Analysis; U.S. Dept. of Commerce

(millions of dollars)

| | 1994 | 1995 |
|---|---|---|
| **All countries[2]** | **$502,410** | **$560,088** |
| Canada | 42,133 | 46,005 |
| Europe[2] | 309,415 | 360,762 |
| Austria | 853 | 1,635 |
| Belgium | 3,882 | 3,637 |
| Denmark | 1,913 | 3,043 |
| Finland | 1,787 | 2,498 |
| France | 34,139 | 38,240 |
| Germany | 40,297 | 47,907 |
| Ireland | 4,354 | 7,146 |
| Italy | 2,387 | 2,258 |
| Luxembourg | 2,457 | 4,636 |
| Netherlands | 68,212 | 67,654 |
| Norway | 1,469 | 1,931 |
| Spain | 1,777 | 2,568 |
| Sweden | 8,891 | 11,740 |
| Switzerland | 25,342 | 33,070 |
| United Kingdom | 111,058 | 132,273 |
| South and Central America[2] | 6,966 | 7,278 |
| Brazil | 712 | 864 |
| Mexico | $ 2,342 | $ 1,952 |
| Panama | 3,751 | 4,061 |
| Other Western Hemisphere[2] | 18,075 | 15,438 |
| Bahamas | 1,071 | –2,159 |
| Bermuda | 2,060 | 1,859 |
| Netherlands Antilles | 8,349 | 7,159 |
| UK islands, Caribbean[2] | 6,365 | 8,515 |
| Africa[2] | 925 | 936 |
| Middle East[2] | 5,565 | 5,053 |
| Israel | 2,188 | 2,168 |
| Kuwait | 1,581 | 1,420 |
| Saudi Arabia | 1,668 | 1,353 |
| Asia and Pacific[2] | 119,331 | 124,615 |
| Australia | 7,928 | 7,788 |
| Hong Kong | 1,614 | 1,387 |
| Japan | 104,529 | 108,582 |
| Malaysia | 465 | 429 |
| Singapore | 1,139 | 1,338 |
| South Korea | 1,279 | 1,914 |
| Taiwan | 1,451 | 2,117 |

(1) The book value of foreign direct investors' equity in, and net outstanding loans to, their U.S. affiliates. A U.S. affiliate is a U.S. business enterprise in which a single foreign direct investor owns at least 10% of the voting securities or the equivalent. (2) Totals include countries or territories not shown.

## U.S. Direct Investment[1] Abroad in Selected Countries and Territories

**Source:** Bureau of Economic Analysis, U.S. Dept. of Commerce

(millions of dollars)

| | 1990 | 1994 | 1995 |
|---|---|---|---|
| **All countries[2]** | **$424,086** | **$621,044** | **$711,621** |
| Canada | 67,033 | 74,987 | 81,387 |
| Europe[2] | 211,194 | 310,031 | 363,527 |
| Austria | 889 | 1,577 | 2,094 |
| Belgium | 9,050 | 14,213 | 17,785 |
| Denmark | 1,597 | 1,983 | 2,251 |
| Finland | 551 | 621 | 830 |
| France | 18,874 | 27,860 | 32,645 |
| Germany | 27,259 | 39,622 | 43,001 |
| Greece | 288 | 447 | 437 |
| Ireland | 6,880 | 10,159 | 10,970 |
| Italy | 13,117 | 14,578 | 16,718 |
| Luxembourg | 1,390 | 6,112 | 7,661 |
| Netherlands | 22,658 | 25,127 | 37,421 |
| Norway | 3,815 | 4,282 | 4,904 |
| Portugal | 598 | 1,465 | 1,712 |
| Spain | 7,704 | 8,316 | 9,689 |
| Sweden | 1,600 | 2,675 | 12,226 |
| Switzerland | 25,199 | 34,351 | 36,342 |
| Turkey | 494 | 1,079 | 1,167 |
| United Kingdom | 68,224 | 111,255 | 119,938 |
| Eastern Europe[2] | NA | 3,159 | 4,490 |
| South America[2] | 23,760 | 37,841 | 46,970 |
| Argentina | 2,956 | 5,945 | 7,962 |
| Brazil | 14,918 | 18,798 | 23,590 |
| Chile | 1,368 | 4,384 | 5,510 |
| Colombia | 1,728 | 3,282 | 3,414 |
| Ecuador | 387 | 736 | 830 |
| Peru | 410 | 819 | 1,213 |
| Venezuela | 1,490 | 2,991 | 3,372 |
| Central America[2] | 17,719 | 30,408 | 31,408 |
| Costa Rica | NA | 566 | 790 |
| Honduras | NA | 186 | 236 |
| Mexico | $ 9,398 | $15,714 | $14,037 |
| Panama | 7,409 | 13,538 | 15,908 |
| Other Western Hemishere[2] | 30,113 | 43,978 | 44,387 |
| Bahamas | 3,309 | 2,736 | 1,566 |
| Barbados | NA | 551 | 792 |
| Bermuda | 21,737 | 27,561 | 27,807 |
| Dominican Republic | NA | 1,191 | 1,274 |
| Jamaica | 604 | 1,259 | 1,400 |
| Netherlands Antilles | –2,229 | 1,823 | 2,473 |
| Trinidad and Tobago | 508 | 771 | 813 |
| UK islands, Caribbean[2] | 4,800 | 7,327 | 7,615 |
| Africa[2] | 4,861 | 5,530 | 6,516 |
| Egypt | 1,465 | 1,412 | 1,409 |
| Nigeria | 161 | 322 | 595 |
| South Africa | 956 | 1,013 | 1,269 |
| Middle East[2] | 3,973 | 6,794 | 7,982 |
| Israel | 756 | 1,357 | 1,574 |
| Saudi Arabia | 1,981 | 2,655 | 3,371 |
| United Arab Emirates | 519 | 531 | 675 |
| Asia and Pacific[2] | 61,869 | 108,075 | 125,968 |
| Australia | 14,846 | 19,900 | 24,713 |
| China | NA | 1,656 | 1,997 |
| Hong Kong | 6,187 | 13,018 | 13,780 |
| India | 513 | 783 | 836 |
| Indonesia | 3,226 | 4,885 | 7,050 |
| Japan | 20,997 | 36,677 | 39,198 |
| Malaysia | 1,384 | 2,343 | 3,653 |
| New Zealand | 3,131 | 3,622 | 4,530 |
| Philippines | 1,629 | 2,324 | 2,648 |
| Singapore | 3,385 | 10,310 | 12,570 |
| South Korea | 2,178 | 4,081 | 5,322 |
| Taiwan | 2,014 | 3,878 | 4,391 |
| Thailand | 1,585 | 3,741 | 4,596 |

(1) The book value of U.S. direct investors' equity in, and net outstanding loans to, their foreign affiliates. A foreign affiliate is a foreign business enterprise in which a single U.S. investor owns at least 10% of the voting securities or the equivalent. (2) Total includes countries not shown. NA = not available.

# U.S. International Transactions

**Source:** Bureau of Economic Analysis, U.S. Dept. of Commerce; revised as of July 1996

(millions of dollars)

| | 1965 | 1970 | 1975 | 1980 | 1985 | 1990 | 1994 | 1995 |
|---|---|---|---|---|---|---|---|---|
| **Exports of goods, services, and income[1]** | **$42,722** | **$68,387** | **$157,936** | **$344,440** | **$382,747** | **$697,083** | **$840,006** | **$969,189** |
| Merchandise, adjusted, excluding military[2] | 26,461 | 42,469 | 107,088 | 224,250 | 215,915 | 389,307 | 502,463 | 575,940 |
| Services | 8,824 | 14,171 | 25,497 | 47,584 | 73,155 | 147,477 | 195,839 | 210,590 |
| Income receipts on U.S. assets abroad | 7,437 | 11,748 | 25,351 | 72,606 | 93,677 | 160,300 | 141,704 | 182,659 |
| **Imports of goods, services, and income** | **–32,708** | **–59,901** | **–132,745** | **–333,774** | **–484,037** | **–756,522** | **–948,544** | **–1,082,268** |
| Merchandise, adjusted, excluding military[2] | –21,510 | –39,866 | –98,185 | –249,750 | –338,088 | –498,337 | –668,584 | –749,364 |
| Services | –9,111 | –14,520 | –21,996 | –41,491 | –72,862 | –118,783 | –134,097 | –142,230 |
| Income payments on foreign assets in the U.S. | –2,088 | –5,515 | –12,564 | –42,532 | –73,087 | –139,402 | –145,863 | –190,674 |
| **Unilateral transfers, net** | **–4,583** | **–6,156** | **–7,075** | **–8,349** | **–22,954** | **–35,219** | **–39,866** | **–35,075** |
| **U.S. assets abroad, net (increase/capital outflow [–])** | **–5,716** | **–9,337** | **–39,703** | **–86,967** | **–39,889** | **–74,011** | **–150,695** | **–307,856** |
| U.S. official reserve assets, net | 1,225 | 2,481 | –849 | –8,155 | –3,858 | –2,158 | 5,346 | –9,742 |
| U.S. government assets, other than official reserve assets, net | –1,605 | –1,589 | –3,474 | –5,162 | –2,821 | 2,307 | –341 | –280 |
| U.S. private assets, net | –5,336 | –10,229 | –35,380 | –73,651 | –33,211 | –74,160 | –155,700 | –297,834 |
| **Foreign assets in the U.S., net (increase/capital inflow [+])** | **742** | **6,359** | **15,670** | **58,112** | **141,183** | **122,192** | **285,376** | **424,462** |
| **Statistical discrepancy (sum of above items with sign reversed)** | **–457** | **–219** | **5,917** | **25,386** | **22,950** | **46,476** | **13,724** | **31,548** |
| **Memorandum:** | | | | | | | | |
| Balance on current account | 5,431 | 2,331 | 18,116 | 2,317 | –124,243 | –94,657 | –148,405 | –148,154 |

(1) Excludes transfers of goods and services under U.S. military grant programs. (2) Excludes exports of goods under U.S. military agency sales contracts identified in Census export documents, excludes imports of goods under direct defense expenditures identified in Census import documents, and reflects various other adjustments.

# Gold Reserves of Central Banks and Governments

**Source:** *International Financial Statistics,* IMF; million fine troy ounces

| Year end | All countries[1] | United States | Canada | Japan | Belgium | France | Germany | Italy | Netherlands | Switzerland | United Kingdom |
|---|---|---|---|---|---|---|---|---|---|---|---|
| 1975 | 1,018.71 | 274.71 | 21.95 | 21.11 | 42.17 | 100.93 | 117.61 | 82.48 | 54.33 | 83.20 | 21.03 |
| 1976 | 1,014.23 | 274.68 | 21.62 | 21.11 | 42.17 | 101.02 | 117.61 | 82.48 | 54.33 | 83.28 | 21.03 |
| 1977 | 1,029.19 | 277.55 | 22.01 | 21.62 | 42.45 | 101.67 | 118.30 | 82.91 | 54.63 | 83.28 | 22.23 |
| 1978 | 1,036.82 | 276.41 | 22.13 | 23.97 | 42.59 | 101.99 | 118.64 | 83.12 | 54.78 | 83.28 | 22.83 |
| 1979 | 944.44 | 264.60 | 22.18 | 24.23 | 34.21 | 81.92 | 95.25 | 66.71 | 43.97 | 83.28 | 18.25 |
| 1980 | 952.99 | 264.32 | 20.98 | 24.23 | 34.18 | 81.85 | 95.18 | 66.67 | 43.94 | 83.28 | 18.84 |
| 1981 | 953.72 | 264.11 | 20.46 | 24.23 | 34.18 | 81.85 | 95.18 | 66.67 | 43.94 | 83.28 | 19.03 |
| 1982 | 949.16 | 264.03 | 20.26 | 24.23 | 34.18 | 81.85 | 95.18 | 66.67 | 43.94 | 83.28 | 19.01 |
| 1983 | 947.84 | 263.39 | 20.17 | 24.23 | 34.18 | 81.85 | 95.18 | 66.67 | 43.94 | 83.28 | 19.01 |
| 1984 | 946.79 | 262.79 | 20.14 | 24.23 | 34.18 | 81.85 | 95.18 | 66.67 | 43.94 | 83.28 | 19.03 |
| 1985 | 949.39 | 262.65 | 20.11 | 24.33 | 34.18 | 81.85 | 95.18 | 66.67 | 43.94 | 83.28 | 19.03 |
| 1986 | 949.11 | 262.04 | 19.72 | 24.23 | 34.18 | 81.85 | 95.18 | 66.67 | 43.94 | 83.28 | 19.01 |
| 1987 | 944.49 | 262.38 | 18.52 | 24.23 | 33.63 | 81.85 | 95.18 | 66.67 | 43.94 | 83.28 | 19.01 |
| 1988 | 946.65 | 261.87 | 17.14 | 24.23 | 33.67 | 81.85 | 95.18 | 66.67 | 43.94 | 83.28 | 19.00 |
| 1989 | 941.04 | 261.93 | 16.10 | 24.23 | 30.23 | 81.85 | 95.18 | 66.67 | 43.94 | 83.28 | 18.99 |
| 1990 | 939.01 | 261.91 | 14.76 | 24.23 | 30.23 | 81.85 | 95.18 | 66.67 | 43.94 | 83.28 | 18.94 |
| 1991 | 938.01 | 261.91 | 12.96 | 24.23 | 30.23 | 81.85 | 95.18 | 66.67 | 43.94 | 83.28 | 18.89 |
| 1992 | 927.55 | 261.84 | 9.94 | 24.23 | 25.04 | 81.85 | 95.18 | 66.67 | 43.94 | 83.28 | 18.61 |
| 1993 | 920.93 | 261.79 | 6.05 | 24.23 | 25.04 | 81.85 | 95.18 | 66.67 | 35.05 | 83.28 | 18.45 |
| 1994 | 916.58 | 261.73 | 3.89 | 24.23 | 25.04 | 81.85 | 95.18 | 66.67 | 34.77 | 83.28 | 18.44 |
| 1995 | 907.42 | 261.70 | 3.41 | 24.23 | 20.54 | 81.85 | 95.18 | 66.67 | 34.77 | 83.28 | 18.44 |

(1) Covers IMF members with reported gold holdings. For countries not listed above, see *International Financial Statistics.*

# Trade-Weighted Index of Foreign Currency Value of the Dollar

**Source:** Office of Foreign Exchange Operations, U.S. Dept. of the Treasury

These indexes are presented to provide measures of the general foreign exchange value of the dollar that are broader than those provided by single exchange rate levels. They do not purport to represent a guide to measuring the impact of exchange rate levels on U.S. international transactions. The indexes are computed as geometric averages of individual currency levels with weights derived from the share of each country's trade with the U.S. during 1982-83.

| End of period (Dec. 1980 = 100) | Index of industrial country currencies[1] | End of period (Dec. 1980 = 100) | Index of industrial country currencies[1] | End of period (Dec. 1980 = 100) | Index of industrial country currencies[1] |
|---|---|---|---|---|---|
| 1985 | 127.8 | 1989 | 100.0 | 1993 | 103.3 |
| 1986 | 114.4 | 1990 | 94.4 | 1994 | 99.0 |
| 1987 | 97.8 | 1991 | 93.7 | 1995 | 97.1 |
| 1988 | 98.4 | 1992 | 101.1 | | |

(r)=revised. (1) Each index covers (a) 22 currencies of countries represented in the Organization for Economic Cooperation and Development (OECD): Australia, Austria, Belgium-Luxembourg, Canada, Denmark, Finland, France, Germany, Greece, Iceland, Ireland, Italy, Japan, the Netherlands, New Zealand, Norway, Portugal, Spain, Sweden, Switzerland, Turkey, and the United Kingdom; and (b) currencies of 4 major trading economies outside the OECD: Hong Kong, South Korea, Singapore, and Taiwan. Exchange rates are drawn from the International Monetary Fund's *International Financial Statistics* when available.

## National Income by Industry[1]

**Source:** Bureau of Economic Analysis, U.S. Dept. of Commerce

(billions of dollars)

| | 1960 | 1970 | 1975 | 1980 | 1990 | 1994 | 1995 |
|---|---|---|---|---|---|---|---|
| **National income without capital consumption adjustment** | **$428.6** | **$835.1** | **$1,315.0** | **$2,263.9** | **$4,513.6** | **$5,534.9** | **5,825.1** |
| **Domestic industries** | **425.1** | **827.8** | **1,297.4** | **2,216.3** | **4,492.0** | **5,538.7** | **5,832.2** |
| **Private industries** | **371.6** | **695.4** | **1,088.3** | **1,894.5** | **3,830.2** | **4,743.0** | **5,011.9** |
| Agriculture, forestry, fisheries | 17.8 | 25.9 | 46.5 | 61.4 | 98.0 | 97.4 | 94.0 |
| Mining | 5.6 | 8.4 | 21.2 | 43.8 | 36.8 | 42.4 | 43.6 |
| Construction | 22.5 | 47.4 | 69.9 | 126.6 | 222.0 | 250.6 | 263.6 |
| Manufacturing | 125.3 | 215.6 | 317.5 | 532.1 | 859.5 | 991.2 | 1,026.3 |
| Durable goods | 73.4 | 127.7 | 185.0 | 313.7 | 483.1 | 574.1 | 597.1 |
| Nondurable goods | 52.0 | 87.9 | 132.5 | 218.4 | 376.3 | 417.1 | 429.3 |
| Transportation, public utilities | 35.8 | 64.4 | 101.1 | 177.3 | 326.3 | 422.8 | 451.0 |
| Transportation | 18.5 | 31.5 | 48.0 | 85.8 | 139.2 | 176.9 | 189.4 |
| Communications | 8.2 | 17.6 | 26.8 | 48.1 | 91.6 | 125.9 | 136.6 |
| Electric, gas, sanitary services | 9.1 | 86.8 | 90.2 | 43.4 | 95.5 | 119.9 | 125.0 |
| Wholesale trade | 25.0 | 47.5 | 83.0 | 143.3 | 261.7 | 312.1 | 327.0 |
| Retail trade | 41.3 | 79.9 | 123.1 | 189.4 | 392.3 | 457.0 | 478.6 |
| Finance, insurance, real estate | 51.3 | 96.4 | 143.9 | 279.5 | 684.2 | 938.8 | 991.9 |
| Services | 46.9 | 109.8 | 182.1 | 341.0 | 949.4 | 1,230.7 | 1,335.9 |
| **Government** | **53.5** | **132.4** | **209.1** | **321.8** | **661.1** | **795.7** | **820.3** |

(1) Figures may not add because of rounding.

## National Income by Type of Income[1]

**Source:** Bureau of Economic Analysis, U.S. Dept. of Commerce

(billions of dollars)

| | 1960 | 1970 | 1980 | 1990 | 1993 | 1994 | 1995 |
|---|---|---|---|---|---|---|---|
| **National income[2]** | **$424.9** | **$832.6** | **$2,203.5** | **$4,491.0** | **$5,195.3** | **$5,501.6** | **$5,813.5** |
| **Compensation of employees** | **296.7** | **618.3** | **1,638.2** | **3,297.6** | **3,809.5** | **4,009.8** | **4,222.7** |
| Wages and salaries | 272.8 | 551.5 | 1,372.0 | 2,745.0 | 3,095.3 | 3,257.3 | 3,433.2 |
| Government | 49.2 | 117.1 | 260.1 | 516.0 | 584.2 | 602.5 | 621.7 |
| Other | 223.7 | 434.3 | 1,111.8 | 2,229.0 | 2,511.1 | 2,654.8 | 2,811.5 |
| Supplements to wages and salaries | 23.8 | 66.8 | 266.3 | 552.5 | 714.2 | 752.4 | 789.5 |
| Employer contrib. for social ins. | 12.6 | 34.3 | 127.9 | 278.3 | 333.3 | 350.2 | 365.5 |
| Other labor income | 11.2 | 32.5 | 138.4 | 274.3 | 380.9 | 402.2 | 424.0 |
| **Proprietors' income with adjustments** | **52.1** | **80.2** | **180.7** | **363.3** | **420.0** | **450.9** | **478.3** |
| Farm | 11.6 | 14.7 | 20.5 | 41.9 | 32.0 | 35.0 | 29.0 |
| Nonfarm | 40.5 | 65.4 | 160.1 | 321.4 | 388.1 | 415.9 | 449.3 |
| **Rental income of persons, with capital consumption adjustment** | **15.3** | **18.2** | **6.6** | **–14.2** | **102.5** | **116.6** | **122.2** |
| **Corp. profits with inventory adjustment** | **49.8** | **69.5** | **194.0** | **354.7** | **457.7** | **517.9** | **570.8** |
| Corp. profits before tax | 49.9 | 76.0 | 237.1 | 365.7 | 464.3 | 531.2 | 598.9 |
| Corp. profits tax liability | 22.7 | 34.4 | 84.8 | 138.7 | 163.8 | 195.3 | 218.7 |
| Corp. profits after tax | 27.2 | 41.7 | 152.3 | 227.1 | 300.5 | 335.9 | 380.2 |
| Dividends | 12.9 | 22.5 | 54.7 | 153.5 | 197.3 | 211.0 | 227.4 |
| Undistributed profits | 14.3 | 19.2 | 97.6 | 73.6 | 103.2 | 124.8 | 152.8 |
| Inventory valuation adjustment | –0.2 | –6.6 | –43.1 | –11.0 | –6.6 | –13.3 | –28.1 |
| **Net interest** | **11.3** | **41.2** | **200.9** | **463.7** | **398.9** | **394.9** | **403.6** |

(1) Figures may not add because of rounding. (2) National income is the aggregate of labor and property earnings that arises in the current production of goods and services. It is the sum of employee compensation, proprietors' income, rental income, corporate profits, and net interest. It measures the total factor costs of the goods and services produced by the economy. Income is measured before deduction of taxes on income. Total national income figures include adjustments not itemized below.

## Distribution of Total Personal Income[1]

**Source:** Bureau of Economic Analysis, U.S. Dept. of Commerce

(billions of dollars)

| | | | | | Personal Savings | |
|---|---|---|---|---|---|---|
| Year | Personal income | Personal taxes | Disposable personal income | Personal outlays | Amount | As pct. of disposable income |
| 1960 | $ 411.7 | $48.7 | $ 362.9 | $339.6 | $23.3 | 6.4% |
| 1965 | 555.8 | 61.9 | 493.9 | 456.2 | 37.8 | 7.6 |
| 1970 | 836.1 | 109.0 | 727.1 | 666.1 | 61.0 | 8.4 |
| 1975 | 1,315.6 | 156.4 | 1,159.2 | 1,054.8 | 104.4 | 9.0 |
| 1980 | 2,285.7 | 312.4 | 1,973.3 | 1,811.5 | 161.8 | 8.2 |
| 1981 | 2,560.4 | 360.2 | 2,200.2 | 2,001.1 | 199.1 | 9.1 |
| 1982 | 2,718.7 | 371.4 | 2,347.3 | 2,141.8 | 205.5 | 8.8 |
| 1983 | 2,891.7 | 369.3 | 2,522.4 | 2,355.5 | 167.0 | 6.6 |
| 1984 | 3,205.5 | 395.5 | 2,810.0 | 2,574.4 | 235.7 | 8.4 |
| 1985 | 3,439.6 | 437.7 | 3,002.0 | 2,795.8 | 206.2 | 6.9 |
| 1986 | 3,647.5 | 459.9 | 3,187.6 | 2,991.1 | 196.5 | 6.2 |
| 1987 | 3,877.3 | 514.2 | 3,363.1 | 3,194.7 | 168.4 | 5.0 |
| 1988 | 4,172.8 | 532.0 | 3,640.8 | 3,451.7 | 189.1 | 5.2 |
| 1989 | 4,489.3 | 594.9 | 3,894.5 | 3,706.7 | 187.8 | 4.8 |
| 1990 | 4,791.6 | 624.8 | 4,166.8 | 3,958.1 | 208.7 | 5.0 |
| 1991 | 4,968.5 | 624.8 | 4,343.7 | 4,097.4 | 246.4 | 5.7 |
| 1992 | 5,264.2 | 650.5 | 4,613.7 | 4,341.0 | 272.6 | 5.9 |
| 1993 | 5,480.1 | 689.9 | 4,790.2 | 4,575.8 | 214.4 | 4.5 |
| 1994 | 5,753.1 | 731.4 | 5,021.7 | 4,832.3 | 189.4 | 3.8 |
| 1995 | 6,115.1 | 794.3 | 5,320.8 | 5,071.5 | 249.3 | 4.7 |

(1) Figures may not add because of rounding.

# Average Yields of Long-Term Treasury, Corporate, and Municipal Bonds

**Source:** Office of Market Finance, U.S. Dept. of the Treasury

| Period | Treasury 30-year bonds | New Aa corporate bonds[1] | New Aa municipal bonds[2] |
|---|---|---|---|
| **1985** | | | |
| June | 10.45 | 11.33 | 8.46 |
| Dec. | 9.54 | 10.42 | 8.44 |
| **1986** | | | |
| June | 7.57 | 9.39 | 7.75 |
| Dec. | 7.37 | 8.87 | 6.70 |
| **1987** | | | |
| June | 8.57 | 9.64 | 7.69 |
| Dec. | 9.12 | 10.22 | 7.83 |
| **1988** | | | |
| June | 9.00 | 10.08 | 7.67 |
| Dec. | 9.01 | 10.05 | 7.40 |
| **1989** | | | |
| June | 8.27 | 9.24 | 6.94 |
| Dec. | 7.90 | 9.23 | 6.76 |
| **1990** | | | |
| June | 8.46 | 9.69 | 6.98 |
| Dec. | 8.24 | 9.55 | 6.85 |
| **1991** | | | |
| June | 8.47 | 9.37 | 6.90 |
| Dec. | 7.70 | 8.55 | 6.43 |
| **1992** | | | |
| June | 7.84 | 8.45 | 6.32 |
| Dec. | 7.44 | 8.12 | 6.02 |

| Period | Treasury 30-year bonds | New Aa corporate bonds[1] | New Aa municipal bonds[2] |
|---|---|---|---|
| **1993** | | | |
| June | 6.81 | 7.48 | 5.54 |
| Dec. | 6.25 | 7.22 | 5.27 |
| **1994** | | | |
| June | 7.40 | 8.16 | 5.96 |
| Dec. | 7.87 | 8.66 | 6.63 |
| **1995** | | | |
| Jan. | 7.85 | 8.59 | 6.48 |
| Feb. | 7.61 | 8.39 | 6.09 |
| Mar. | 7.45 | 8.23 | 5.91 |
| Apr. | 7.36 | 8.10 | 5.80 |
| May | 6.95 | 7.68 | 5.75 |
| June | 6.57 | 7.42 | 5.61 |
| July | 6.72 | 7.54 | 5.69 |
| Aug. | 6.86 | 7.75 | 5.81 |
| Sept. | 6.55 | 7.42 | 5.75 |
| Oct. | 6.37 | 7.29 | 5.80 |
| Nov. | 6.26 | 7.20 | 5.56 |
| Dec. | 6.06 | 7.02 | 5.46 |
| **1996** | | | |
| Jan. | 6.05 | 7.00 | 5.41 |
| Feb. | 6.24 | 7.14 | 5.41 |
| Mar. | 6.60 | 7.57 | 5.57 |

(1) Treasury series based on 3-week moving average of reoffering yields of new corporate bonds rated Aa by Moody's Investors Service with an original maturity of at least 20 years. (2) Index of new reoffering yields on 20-year general obligations rated Aa by Moody's Investors Service.

# Performance of Mutual Funds by Type

**Source:** CDA/Wiesenberger, Rockville, MD, 800-232-2285

(data for period ending Aug. 31, 1996)

| Fund type | Fund objective | 1-Yr Total return No. | 1-Yr Total return Avg. | 5-Yr Annual return No. | 5-Yr Annual return Avg. |
|---|---|---|---|---|---|
| **Stock** | Natural resources | 38 | 23.22 | 18 | 10.48 |
| | Equity income | 147 | 16.14 | 58 | 12.27 |
| | Financial services | 16 | 19.06 | 10 | 22.73 |
| | Precious metals | 49 | 15.67 | 30 | 10.96 |
| | Growth and current income | 508 | 15.19 | 206 | 12.29 |
| | Health care | 16 | 24.24 | 10 | 12.33 |
| | Long-term growth | 895 | 13.16 | 367 | 12.67 |
| | Max. capital gain | 139 | 11.16 | 68 | 13.00 |
| | Other specialized | 46 | 13.71 | 29 | 13.16 |
| | Small company | 371 | 15.20 | 116 | 15.02 |
| | Technology | 33 | –1.61 | 14 | 18.37 |
| | Utilities | 97 | 10.89 | 24 | 10.75 |
| **International stock** | Emerging markets | 110 | 9.90 | 6 | 11.80 |
| | Global | 482 | 11.72 | 128 | 9.34 |
| | European | 51 | 15.31 | 16 | 11.73 |
| **International stock** | Pacific area | 51 | 3.82 | 14 | 9.80 |
| | Other foreign | 396 | 9.47 | 77 | 9.33 |
| **Hybrid** | Asset allocation | 132 | 10.60 | 36 | 10.29 |
| | Balanced | 271 | 10.57 | 86 | 10.25 |
| | Flexible income | 67 | 10.57 | 34 | 11.86 |
| **Bond** | Corporate bond | 613 | 4.33 | 198 | 7.11 |
| | Corporate high yield | 163 | 10.97 | 75 | 11.98 |
| | Govt. mortgage-backed | 178 | 4.06 | 66 | 5.61 |
| | Govt. securities | 502 | 3.08 | 176 | 6.34 |
| | International | 227 | 11.33 | 70 | 6.90 |
| **Municipal bond** | National | 513 | 4.38 | 201 | 6.64 |
| | California | 164 | 5.26 | 60 | 6.81 |
| | New York | 144 | 4.27 | 57 | 6.81 |
| | Other state | 999 | 4.64 | 242 | 6.80 |

# Chicago Board of Trade, Contracts Traded 1986-95

| | 1986 | 1995 | Percent change 1986-95 |
|---|---|---|---|
| **Futures group** | | | |
| Agricultural | 20,757,202 | 41,493,622 | 99.9 |
| Financial | 57,963,696 | 124,016,379 | 114.0 |
| Stock index | 1,778,951 | — | — |
| Metals | 635,785 | 106,176 | –83.3 |
| **Total futures** | **81,135,634** | **165,616,177** | **104.1** |
| **Options group** | | | |
| Agricultural | 1,360,087 | 8,767,223 | 544.6 |
| Financial | 18,315,031 | 36,283,780 | 98.1 |
| Metals | 3,081 | 1,476 | –52.1 |
| Insurance | — | 3,324 | — |
| PCS insurance | — | 1,064 | — |
| **Total options** | **19,678,199** | **45,056,867** | **129.0** |
| **Combined futures and options** | | | |
| Agricultural | 22,117,289 | 50,260,845 | 127.2 |
| Financial | 76,278,727 | 160,300,159 | 110.2 |
| Stock index | 1,778,951 | — | — |
| Metals | 638,866 | 107,652 | –83.1 |
| Insurance | — | 3,324 | — |
| PCS insurance | — | 1,064 | — |
| **Grand total** | **100,813,833** | **210,673,044** | **109.0** |

# Dow Jones Industrial Average Since 1961

| High | | | Year | Low | | | High | | | Year | Low | | |
|---|---|---|---|---|---|---|---|---|---|---|---|---|---|
| Dec. | 13 | 734.91 | **1961** | Jan. | 3 | 610.25 | Oct. | 5 | 897.61 | **1979** | Nov. | 7 | 796.67 |
| Jan. | 3 | 726.01 | **1962** | June | 26 | 535.76 | Nov. | 20 | 1000.17 | **1980** | Apr. | 21 | 759.13 |
| Dec. | 18 | 767.21 | **1963** | Jan. | 2 | 646.79 | Apr. | 27 | 1024.05 | **1981** | Sept. | 25 | 824.01 |
| Nov. | 18 | 891.71 | **1964** | Jan. | 2 | 766.08 | Dec. | 27 | 1070.55 | **1982** | Aug. | 12 | 776.92 |
| Dec. | 31 | 969.26 | **1965** | June | 28 | 840.59 | Nov. | 29 | 1287.20 | **1983** | Jan. | 3 | 1027.04 |
| Feb. | 9 | 995.15 | **1966** | Oct. | 7 | 744.32 | Jan. | 6 | 1286.64 | **1984** | July | 24 | 1086.57 |
| Sept. | 25 | 943.08 | **1967** | Jan. | 3 | 786.41 | Dec. | 16 | 1553.10 | **1985** | Jan. | 4 | 1184.96 |
| Dec. | 3 | 985.21 | **1968** | Mar. | 21 | 825.13 | Dec. | 2 | 1955.57 | **1986** | Jan. | 22 | 1502.29 |
| May | 14 | 968.85 | **1969** | Dec. | 17 | 769.93 | Aug. | 25 | 2722.42 | **1987** | Oct. | 19 | 1738.74 |
| Dec. | 29 | 842.00 | **1970** | May | 6 | 631.16 | Oct. | 21 | 2183.50 | **1988** | Jan. | 20 | 1879.14 |
| Apr. | 28 | 950.82 | **1971** | Nov. | 23 | 797.97 | Oct. | 9 | 2791.41 | **1989** | Jan. | 3 | 2144.64 |
| Dec. | 11 | 1036.27 | **1972** | Jan. | 26 | 889.15 | July | 16 | 2999.75 | **1990** | Oct. | 11 | 2365.10 |
| Jan. | 11 | 1051.70 | **1973** | Dec. | 5 | 788.31 | Dec. | 31 | 3168.83 | **1991** | Jan. | 9 | 2470.30 |
| Mar. | 13 | 891.66 | **1974** | Dec. | 6 | 577.60 | June | 1 | 3413.21 | **1992** | Oct. | 9 | 3136.58 |
| July | 15 | 881.81 | **1975** | Jan. | 2 | 632.04 | Dec. | 29 | 3794.33 | **1993** | Jan. | 20 | 3241.95 |
| Sept. | 21 | 1014.79 | **1976** | Jan. | 2 | 858.71 | Jan. | 31 | 3978.36 | **1994** | Apr. | 4 | 3593.35 |
| Jan. | 3 | 999.75 | **1977** | Nov. | 2 | 800.85 | Dec. | 13 | 5216.47 | **1995** | Jan. | 30 | 3832.08 |
| Sept. | 8 | 907.74 | **1978** | Feb. | 28 | 742.12 | Oct. | 14 | 6010.00 | **1996*** | Jan. | 10 | 5032.94 |

*As of Oct. 15

# Components of the Dow Jones Averages

(as of Oct. 1996)

## Dow Jones Industrial Average

AlliedSignal
Aluminum Co. of America (Alcoa)
American Express
AT&T
Bethlehem Steel
Boeing
Caterpillar
Chevron
Coca-Cola
Disney
DuPont
Eastman Kodak
Exxon
General Electric
General Motors
Goodyear
IBM
International Paper
McDonald's
Merck
Minnesota Mining & Manufacturing
Morgan (J.P.)
Philip Morris
Procter & Gamble
Sears
Texaco
Union Carbide
United Technologies
Westinghouse
Woolworth

## Dow Jones Transportation Average

Airborne Freight
Alaska Air Group
AMR
APL Limited
Burlington Northern Santa Fe
Caliber Systems
Conrail
Consolidated Freightways
CSX
Delta Air Lines
Federal Express
Illinois Central
Norfolk Southern
Ryder System
Southwest Air Lines
UAL (United Air Lines)
Union Pacific
USAir Group
XTRA
Yellow Corp.

## Dow Jones Utility Average

American Electric Power
Centerior Energy
Consolidated Edison of New York
Consolidated Natural Gas
DTE Energy
Edison International
Houston Industries
Niagara Mohawk Power
NorAm Energy
Pacific Gas & Electric
PanEnergy
PECO Energy
Peoples Energy
Public Service Enterprise Group
Unicom

# Milestones of the Dow Jones Industrial Average

| First close over... | |
|---|---|
| 100 | Jan. 12, 1906 |
| 500 | Mar. 12, 1956 |
| 1,000 | Nov. 14, 1972 |
| 1,500 | Dec. 11, 1985 |
| 2,000 | Jan. 8, 1987 |
| 2,500 | July 17, 1987 |
| 3,000 | April 17, 1991 |
| 3,500 | May 19, 1993 |
| 4,000 | Feb. 23, 1995 |
| 4,500 | June 16, 1995 |
| 5,000 | Nov. 21, 1995 |
| 5,500 | Feb. 8, 1996 |
| 5,600 | Feb. 12, 1996 |
| 5,700 | May 20, 1996 |
| 5,800 | Sept. 13, 1996 |
| 5,900 | Oct. 1, 1996 |
| 6,000 | Oct. 14, 1996 |

# Most Active Common Stocks in 1995

**New York Exchange**

| | Volume (millions of shares) |
|---|---|
| Teléfonos de Mexico | 1,006.4 |
| Micron Technology | 849.5 |
| Ford Motor | 679.1 |
| Motorola | 669.6 |
| IBM | 659.2 |
| Compaq Computer | 632.6 |
| Wal-Mart Stores | 624.6 |
| AT&T | 572.1 |
| Kmart | 540.7 |
| Merck | 517.9 |
| General Motors | 477.9 |
| Chrysler | 472.3 |
| Hanson | 457.9 |
| Citicorp | 447.0 |
| EMC | 445.1 |

**American Exchange**

| | Volume (millions of shares) |
|---|---|
| Viacom B | 368.4 |
| XCL Limited | 209.3 |
| Echo Bay Mines | 161.8 |
| Ivax | 160.8 |
| Interdigital Communications | 138.7 |
| Cheyenne Software | 116.6 |
| Royal Oak Mines | 110.5 |
| Amdahl | 94.5 |
| Gaylord Container | 87.0 |
| Greyhound Lines | 83.8 |
| Autotote | 82.5 |
| Standard & Poor's Depository Receipts (SPDR) | 81.3 |
| First Australia Prime Income | 69.6 |
| Pegasus Gold | 64.9 |
| Organogenesis | 60.9 |

**NASDAQ**

| | Volume (millions of shares) |
|---|---|
| Intel | 2,106.3 |
| Microsoft | 1,204.2 |
| Novell | 1,106.5 |
| Cisco Systems | 1,082.2 |
| Oracle | 818.5 |
| MCI Communications | 755.1 |
| Tele-Communications "A" | 697.9 |
| Applied Materials | 694.1 |
| Sun Microsystems | 670.4 |
| Apple Computer | 663.2 |
| Sybase | 635.5 |
| 3Com | 596.8 |
| DSC Communications | 559.9 |
| Cirrus Logic | 525.2 |
| U.S. Healthcare | 524.5 |

## U.S. Holdings of Foreign Stocks

**Source:** Bureau of Economic Analysis, U.S. Dept. Of Commerce

(billions of dollars)

| | 1994 | 1995 | | 1994 | 1995 |
|---|---|---|---|---|---|
| Total holdings | 324.0 | 411.1 | Canada | 25.0 | 29.0 |
| Western Europe | 142.1 | 186.8 | Japan | 69.1 | 90.4 |
| Of which: United Kingdom | 44.5 | 58.1 | Latin America | 22.6 | 20.3 |
| Germany | 25.5 | 30.0 | Of which: Mexico | 15.9 | 12.8 |
| Netherlands | 20.0 | 26.3 | Other countries | 65.2 | 84.6 |
| France | 17.3 | 21.0 | | | |

## Selected Personal Consumption Expenditures in the U.S., 1989-95

**Source:** Bureau of Economic Analysis, U.S. Dept. of Commerce

(billions of dollars)

| | 1989 | 1990 | 1991 | 1992 | 1993 | 1994 | 1995 |
|---|---|---|---|---|---|---|---|
| **Food & Tobacco** | **605.6** | **648.2** | **693.8.8** | **709.5** | **732.7** | **763.3** | **794.4** |
| Food purchased for off-premise consumption | 373.7 | 400.2 | 419.1 | 423.3 | 434.9 | 449.1 | 466.8 |
| Purchased meals and beverages | 180.6 | 193.1 | 223.1 | 228.6 | 242.9 | 258.4 | 271.9 |
| Tobacco products | 40.5 | 43.4 | 43.8 | 49.6 | 47.0 | 47.7 | 47.2 |
| **Clothing, accessories, jewelry** | **248.7** | **259.3** | **265.7** | **283.5** | **296.6** | **310.5** | **320.2** |
| Shoes | 30.1 | 31.4 | 31.9 | 33.6 | 34.4 | 35.5 | 36.2 |
| Clothing and accessories less shoes | 170.1 | 175.7 | 179.3 | 191.7 | 201.2 | 212.3 | 218.1 |
| Jewelry and watches | 29.7 | 31.3 | 31.4 | 33.2 | 35.6 | 36.7 | 38.8 |
| **Personal care** | **55.8** | **59.2** | **59.1** | **63.1** | **65.1** | **67.7** | **70.0** |
| Toilet articles, preparations | 34.1 | 36.8 | 39.4 | 41.4 | 43.1 | 45.1 | 46.7 |
| Barber shops, beauty parlors, health clubs | 21.6 | 22.4 | 19.7 | 21.8 | 22.0 | 22.6 | 23.4 |
| **Housing** | **514.4** | **547.5** | **616.5** | **646.8** | **673.2** | **706.6** | **743.7** |
| Owner-occupied nonfarm dwellings—space rent | 355.8 | 379.5 | 434.1 | 457.8 | 481.1 | 502.6 | 528.5 |
| Tenant-occupied nonfarm dwellings—rent | 132.6 | 141.1 | 155.8 | 160.5 | 162.3 | 172.5 | 181.6 |
| Rental value of farm dwellings | 5.0 | 5.2 | 5.2 | 5.3 | 5.5 | 5.7 | 5.8 |
| **Household operation** | **422.6** | **437.3** | **448.4** | **470.6** | **503.5** | **528.1** | **554.3** |
| Furniture, including bedding | 36.9 | 36.7 | 38.4 | 39.8 | 42.6 | 45.4 | 47.7 |
| Kitchen and other household appliances | 25.7 | 26.4 | 21.6 | 22.2 | 23.9 | 25.9 | 27.3 |
| China, glassware, tableware, utensils | 17.9 | 18.7 | 18.9 | 20.7 | 22.0 | 23.5 | 24.7 |
| Other durable house furnishings | 40.2 | 42.0 | 42.3 | 45.5 | 48.2 | 52.1 | 53.8 |
| Semidurable house furnishings | 20.4 | 21.2 | 21.6 | 23.2 | 24.9 | 26.9 | 28.8 |
| Household utilities | 134.1 | 136.7 | 145.4 | 148.6 | 160.2 | 162.2 | 166.2 |
| Telephone, telegraph | 51.7 | 53.8 | 63.5 | 70.3 | 74.1 | 79.8 | 85.6 |
| **Medical care** | **536.4** | **597.8** | **668.7** | **733.2** | **787.1** | **833.7** | **883.1** |
| Drug preparations, sundries | 55.0 | 60.6 | 70.9 | 75.0 | 77.9 | 81.7 | 85.7 |
| Physicians | 121.6 | 133.8 | 152.1 | 167.2 | 172.9 | 179.8 | 189.8 |
| Dentists | 30.0 | 31.6 | 34.7 | 38.5 | 40.9 | 43.8 | 46.6 |
| Hospitals and nursing homes | 209.5 | 231.3 | 293.4 | 320.0 | 344.4 | 363.8 | 383.6 |
| Health insurance | 31.2 | 36.6 | 37.3 | 42.7 | 51.7 | 57.0 | 61.3 |
| **Personal business** | **272.2** | **296.0** | **318.9** | **341.7** | **354.0** | **361.9** | **373.4** |
| Brokerage charges, investment counseling | 21.6 | 22.0 | 25.3 | 30.4 | 35.6 | 36.1 | 37.0 |
| Bank service charges, trust services, safe deposit box | 22.0 | 23.7 | 25.7 | 28.0 | 30.5 | 31.0 | 32.8 |
| Legal services | 45.5 | 49.2 | 42.9 | 46.5 | 47.9 | 48.6 | 50.3 |
| Funeral, burial expenses | 7.9 | 8.5 | 9.4 | 10.1 | 10.8 | 11.1 | 11.7 |
| **Transportation** | **437.3** | **453.9** | **436.8** | **471.5** | **503.8** | **536.6** | **554.8** |
| User-operated transportation | 399.6 | 414.0 | 401.4 | 435.7 | 465.4 | 498.0 | 514.2 |
| New autos | 99.9 | 96.6 | 75.3 | 82.1 | 86.5 | 91.3 | 84.6 |
| Used autos | 32.5 | 33.1 | 32.0 | 35.5 | 40.8 | 46.1 | 52.7 |
| Repair, greasing, washing, parking, storage, rental, leasing | 79.1 | 82.6 | 85.2 | 94.4 | 102.0 | 113.0 | 121.2 |
| Gasoline and oil | 96.2 | 108.4 | 103.9 | 106.6 | 108.1 | 109.9 | 114.6 |
| Tolls | 2.1 | 2.0 | 2.1 | 2.3 | 2.5 | 2.5 | 2.6 |
| Insurance premiums less claims paid | 16.8 | 18.1 | 22.6 | 25.5 | 26.8 | 27.3 | 28.0 |
| Purchased local transportation | 8.1 | 8.9 | 7.9 | 8.0 | 8.3 | 8.6 | 8.8 |
| Mass transit systems | 5.3 | 5.7 | 5.3 | 5.4 | 5.5 | 5.6 | 5.8 |
| Taxicab | 2.8 | 3.2 | 2.6 | 2.6 | 2.8 | 2.9 | 3.0 |
| Purchased intercity transportation | 29.5 | 30.9 | 27.5 | 27.9 | 30.1 | 30.0 | 31.8 |
| Railway (excl. commutation) | 0.7 | 0.7 | 0.8 | 0.8 | 0.8 | 0.7 | 0.7 |
| Bus | 1.7 | 1.4 | 1.1 | 1.1 | 0.9 | 0.8 | 0.9 |
| Airline | 24.7 | 26.4 | 23.0 | 23.3 | 25.5 | 25.3 | 26.9 |
| **Recreation** | **266.0** | **285.7** | **292.0** | **310.8** | **339.0** | **374.8** | **401.7** |
| Books, maps | 15.8 | 17.5 | 16.9 | 17.7 | 19.0 | 20.1 | 20.9 |
| Magazines, newspapers, sheet music | 22.0 | 23.8 | 21.9 | 21.6 | 22.6 | 24.0 | 25.6 |
| Nondurable toys and sport supplies | 30.0 | 32.1 | 32.8 | 34.2 | 36.5 | 40.1 | 42.7 |
| Wheel goods, sports and photographic equipment, boats, pleasure aircraft | 31.0 | 31.3 | 29.5 | 29.9 | 32.6 | 39.1 | 43.8 |
| Video & audio prods., computers, musical instruments | 47.3 | 50.4 | 57.3 | 61.2 | 68.8 | 80.0 | 88.3 |
| Flowers, seeds, potted plants | 10.1 | 10.3 | 11.3 | 12.3 | 12.8 | 14.0 | 14.2 |
| Admissions to specified spectator amusements | 12.1 | 14.0 | 15.7 | 16.6 | 18.2 | 19.5 | 19.9 |
| Motion picture theaters | 3.9 | 4.7 | 5.3 | 5.0 | 5.2 | 5.5 | 5.6 |
| Legitimate theater, opera | 3.9 | 4.5 | 6.0 | 6.8 | 7.9 | 8.7 | 9.0 |
| Spectator sports | 4.3 | 4.9 | 4.5 | 4.8 | 5.1 | 5.3 | 5.3 |
| Clubs, fraternal organizations | 8.0 | 8.4 | 9.6 | 10.3 | 11.2 | 12.1 | 12.9 |
| Commercial participant amusements | 20.5 | 23.1 | 23.8 | 27.2 | 31.4 | 34.9 | 37.0 |
| **Education and research** | **79.4** | **86.2** | **86.1** | **93.1** | **99.3** | **105.4** | **110.7** |
| Higher education | 40.3 | 44.0 | 48.0 | 52.0 | 55.9 | 59.7 | 63.5 |
| Nursery, elementary, and secondary schools | 19.2 | 19.8 | 18.0 | 19.3 | 20.2 | 21.2 | 20.7 |
| **Religious and welfare activities** | **92.7** | **101.6** | **104.1** | **115.6** | **121.3** | **131.2** | **137.4** |
| **Total personal consumption expenditures** | **$3,523.1** | **$3,761.2** | **$3,975.1** | **$4,219.8** | **$4,454.1** | **$4,700.9** | **$4,924.9** |

# Minerals

**Source:** U.S. Geological Survey, U.S. Dept. of the Interior; as of mid-1996

**Aluminum:** the second most abundant metallic element in the earth's crust. Bauxite is the main source of aluminum; convert to aluminum equivalent by multiplying by 0.232. Guinea and Australia have 49% of the world's reserves. Aluminum is used in the U.S. principally in transportation (32%), packaging (28%), and building (15%).

**Chromium:** some two-thirds of the world's production of chromite, the chief source of chromium, is in Kazakstan and South Africa. The chemical and metallurgical industries use about 90% of the chromite consumed in the world.

**Cobalt:** used in superalloys for jet engines, chemicals (paint driers, catalysts, magnetic coatings), permanent magnets, and cemented carbides for cutting tools. More than 90% of the world's cobalt is produced in Canada, Finland, Norway, Russia, Zaire, and Zambia. The U.S. uses about one-third of total world consumption. Although its resources are relatively large, the U.S. has not produced cobalt since 1971; most U.S. cobalt resources are low grade, and production from these deposits is not economically feasible.

**Columbium:** used mostly as an additive in steelmaking and in superalloys. Brazil and Canada are the world's leading columbium raw materials (feedstock) producers. There is no U.S. columbium mining industry.

**Copper:** uses of copper in the U.S. are in building construction (42%), electrical and electronic products (24%), industrial machinery and equipment (13%), transportation (11%), and consumer and general products (10%). The leading producer is Chile, followed by the U.S., Canada, Russia, Australia, Zambia, Poland, and China. Principal mining states are Arizona, New Mexico, and Utah.

**Gold:** used in the U.S. in jewelry and the arts (70%), electronics and other industries (23%), and dentistry (7%). South Africa has about half the world's resources; significant quantities are also present in the U.S., Australia, Canada, the former Soviet Union, and Brazil. Gold is mined in nearly all the Western U.S. states and in Alaska.

**Iron ore:** the source of primary iron for the world's iron and steel industries. Major iron ore producers include Australia, Brazil, China, and the former Soviet Union.

**Lead:** the U.S., Australia, China, Peru, and Canada are the world's largest producers of lead. Transportation accounts for the major end use in the U.S., with 85% used in batteries, bearings, casting metals, and solders. Other uses include emergency power supply batteries, construction sheeting, sporting ammunition, and power cable coverings. The U.S. produces and consumes more than 20% of the world's lead metal.

**Manganese:** essential to iron and steel production. The U.S., Japan, and Western Europe have exhausted nearly all of their economically minable manganese. South Africa and the former Soviet Union have about 80% of the world's reserves.

**Nickel:** vital to the stainless steel industry; played a key role in the development of the chemical and aerospace industries. Leading producers include Russia, Canada, Australia, New Caledonia, and Indonesia.

**Platinum-Group Metals:** the platinum group consists of 6 closely related metals: platinum, palladium, rhodium, ruthenium, iridium, and osmium. They commonly occur together in nature and are among the scarcest of the metallic elements. They are consumed in the U.S. by the following industries: automotive, electrical and electronic, chemical, and dental and medical. The automotive, chemical, and petroleum-refining industries use platinum-group metals mainly as catalysts. The former Soviet Union and South Africa have nearly all the world's reserves.

**Silver:** used in the following U.S. industries: photography, electrical and electronic products, sterlingware, electroplated ware, and jewelry. Silver is mined in more than 60 countries. Nevada produces more than 50% of U.S. silver, Idaho 12%.

**Tantalum:** a refractory metal with unique electrical, chemical, and physical properties; used in the U.S. mostly to produce electronic components, mainly tantalum capacitors. Australia, Brazil, and Canada are the leading tantalum raw-material producers. There is no U.S. tantalum mining industry.

**Titanium:** as a metal, titanium is used mostly in commercial and military aerospace applications. Titanium metal is produced primarily in China, Japan, Kazakstan, Russia, and the U.S.

**Vanadium:** used as an alloying element in steel and aerospace titanium alloys, as a catalyst in the production of maleic and phthalic anhydride, and in the production of sulfuric acid. China, South Africa, and Russia are the world's largest producers of vanadium-bearing ores and concentrates.

**Zinc:** used as a protective coating on steel, as diecastings, as an alloying metal with copper to make brass, and as a component of chemical compounds in rubber and paints. It is mined in more than 50 countries. Canada is the leading producer, followed by China, Australia, Peru, the U.S., and Mexico. In the U.S., mine production comes mostly from Alaska, Tennessee, New York, and Missouri.

# World Mineral Reserve Base

**Source:** U.S. Geological Survey, U.S. Dept. of the Interior; as of mid-1996

| Mineral | Reserve Base[1] | Mineral | Reserve Base[1] |
|---|---|---|---|
| Aluminum | 28,000 mil metric tons[2] | Manganese | 5,000 mil metric tons |
| Chromium | 7,400 mil metric tons | Nickel | 110 mil metric tons |
| Cobalt | 8.8 mil metric tons | Platinum-Group Metals | 66 mil kilograms |
| Columbium | 4,200 mil kilograms | Silver | 420,000 metric tons |
| Copper | 610 mil metric tons | Tantalum | 35 mil kilograms |
| Gold | 61,000 metric tons | Titanium | 600 mil metric tons[4] |
| Iron ore | 230,000 mil metric tons[3] | Vanadium | 27 mil metric tons |
| Lead | 120 mil metric tons | Zinc | 330 mil metric tons |

(1) Includes demonstrated resources that are currently economic (reserves) or marginally economic (marginal reserves) and some that are currently subeconomic. (2) Bauxite. (3) Crude ore. (4) Titanium dioxide ($TiO_2$) content.

# U.S. Nonfuel Mineral Production—10 Leading States in 1995

**Source:** U.S. Geological Survey, U.S. Dept. of the Interior

| Rank/State | Value (millions) | Percent of U.S. total | Principal minerals |
|---|---|---|---|
| 1. Arizona | $4,150 | 11.00 | Copper, sand & gravel (construction), molybdenum, cement |
| 2. Nevada | 2,920 | 7.79 | Gold, silver, sand & gravel (construction), diatomite |
| 3. California | 2,680 | 7.14 | Cement, sand & gravel (construction), boron minerals, gold |
| 4. Utah | 1,810 | 4.83 | Copper, gold, magnesium metal, molybdenum |
| 5. Georgia | 1,670 | 4.45 | Clays, stone (crushed), cement, sand & gravel (construction) |
| 6. Texas | 1,620 | 4.31 | Cement, stone (crushed), sand & gravel (construction), magnesium metal |
| 7. Minnesota | 1,490 | 3.96 | Iron ore, sand & gravel (construction), stone (crushed), sand & gravel (industrial) |
| 8. Michigan | 1,460 | 3.89 | Iron ore, cement, sand & gravel (construction), stone (crushed) |
| 9. Florida | 1,390 | 3.69 | Phosphate rock, stone (crushed), cement, sand & gravel (construction) |
| 10. Missouri | 1,110 | 2.95 | Stone (crushed), lead, cement, lime |

# U.S. Nonfuel Mineral Production

**Source:** U.S. Geological Survey, U.S. Dept. of the Interior

Production as measured by mine shipments, sales, or marketable production (including consumption by producers)

| | | 1990 | 1991 | 1992 | 1993 | 1994 | 1995 |
|---|---|---|---|---|---|---|---|
| Beryllium (metal equivalent) | metric tons | 182 | 174 | 193 | 198 | 173 | 202 |
| Copper (recoverable content of ores, etc.) | thousand metric tons | 1,588 | 1,630 | 1,760 | 1,800 | 1,850 | 1,850 |
| Gold (recoverable content of ores, etc.) | metric tons | 294.2 | 294.1 | 330.2 | 331.0 | 326.2 | 320.0[E] |
| Iron ore, usable (includes byproduct material) | million metric tons | 56.4 | 56.8 | 55.6 | 55.7 | 58.4 | 62.5 |
| Lead (in concentrate) | thousand metric tons | 497 | 477 | 407 | 362 | 370 | 394 |
| Magnesium metal (primary) | thousand metric tons | 139 | 131 | 137 | 132 | 128 | 142 |
| Molybdenum (content of ore and concentrate) | metric tons | 61,611 | 53,364 | 49,725 | 36,803 | 46,810 | 58,000 |
| Nickel (content of ore and concentrate) | metric tons | 330 | 5,523 | 6,671 | 2,464 | — | 1,700[P] |
| Silver (recoverable content of ores, etc.) | metric tons | 2,120 | 1,860 | 1,800 | 1,640 | 1,480 | 1,540 |
| Zinc (recoverable content of ores, etc.) | thousand metric tons | 515 | 518 | 523 | 488 | 570 | 601 |
| Asbestos | thousand metric tons | W | 20 | 16 | 14 | 10 | W |
| Barite | thousand metric tons | 430 | 448 | 326 | 315 | 583 | 543 |
| Boron minerals | thousand metric tons | 608 | 626 | 554 | 574 | 550 | 796 |
| Bromine | million kilograms | 177 | 170 | 171 | 177 | 195 | 218 |
| Cement (portland, masonry, etc.) | thousand metric tons | 78,199 | 68,999 | 69,203 | 74,079 | 80,490 | 79,000[E] |
| Clays | thousand metric tons | 42,904 | 41,017 | 40,237 | 40,700 | 42,200 | 43,000[E] |
| Diatomite | thousand metric tons | 631 | 610 | 595 | 599 | 613 | 687 |
| Feldspar | thousand metric tons | 630 | 580 | 725 | 770 | 765 | 880 |
| Fluorspar | thousand metric tons | 64 | 58 | 51 | 56 | 49 | 51 |
| Garnet (industrial) | metric tons | 47,000 | 50,900 | 54,100 | 44,000 | 51,000 | 53,000 |
| Gemstones | million dollars | 52.9 | 84.4 | 66.2 | 57.7 | 50.5 | 75.0 |
| Gypsum | thousand metric tons | 14,900 | 14,000 | 14,900 | 15,800 | 17,200 | 17,500 |
| Helium (extracted from natural gas) | million cubic meters | 64.6 | 86.4 | 92.0 | 99.3 | 112.0 | 117.0[E] |
| Helium (Grade A sold) | million cubic meters | 84.8 | 88.1 | 94.4 | 95.6 | 100.0 | 104.0[E] |
| Iodine | thousand kilograms | 1,973 | 1,999 | 1,995 | 1,935 | 1,630 | 1,800[E] |
| Lime | thousand metric tons | 15,832 | 15,667 | 16,199 | 16,932 | 17,393 | 18,530 |
| Mica (scrap & flake) | thousand metric tons | 109 | 103 | 85 | 88 | 110 | 105 |
| Peat | thousand metric tons | 692 | 632 | 599 | 616 | 574 | 660 |
| Perlite (sold and used by producers) | thousand metric tons | 576 | 514 | 541 | 569 | 644 | 700 |
| Phosphate rock (marketable product) | thousand metric tons | 46,343 | 48,096 | 46,965 | 35,494 | 41,115 | 43,500 |
| Potash ($K_2O$ equivalent) | thousand metric tons | 1,713 | 1,749 | 1,705 | 1,506 | 1,400 | 1,480 |
| Pumice and pumicite | thousand metric tons | 443 | 401 | 481 | 469 | 490 | 529 |
| Salt | thousand metric tons | 36,916 | 35,902 | 34,784 | 38,770 | 39,483 | 39,900[E] |
| Sand and gravel (construction) | thousand metric tons | 829,000 | 708,000 | 834,000 | 869,000 | 891,000 | 879,000[E] |
| Sand and gravel (industrial) | thousand metric tons | 25,769 | 23,224 | 25,195 | 26,220 | 27,900 | 28,900 |
| Soda ash (sodium carbonate) | thousand metric tons | 9,156 | 9,005 | 9,379 | 8,959 | 9,321 | 10,100 |
| Sodium sulfate (natural) | thousand metric tons | 349 | 354 | 337 | 322 | 298 | 327 |
| Stone (crushed) | million metric tons | 1,110 | 997 | 1,050 | 1,120 | 1,230 | 1,250[P] |
| Stone (dimension)[1] | thousand metric tons | 1,118 | 1,160 | 1,140 | 1,280 | 1,190 | 1,320 |
| Sulfur (in all forms) | thousand metric tons | 11,560 | 10,820 | 10,663 | 10,959 | 11,500 | 11,800 |
| Talc | thousand metric tons | 1,267[2] | 1,037 | 997 | 968 | 935 | 1,060 |
| Vermiculite | thousand metric tons | 209[E] | 180 | 190 | 190 | 180 | 170[E] |

(E) Estimated. (P) Preliminary figure. (W) Withheld to avoid disclosing company proprietary data. (—) No production. (1) After 1990 production includes Puerto Rico. (2) Includes pyrophyllite.

# U.S. Reliance on Foreign Supplies of Minerals

**Source:** U.S. Geological Survey, U.S. Dept. of the Interior

| Mineral | Percent imported in 1995 | Major sources (1991-1995) | Major uses |
|---|---|---|---|
| Arsenic | 100% | China, Chile, Mexico | Wood preservatives, glass manufacturing, agricultural chemicals |
| Columbium | 100 | Brazil, Canada, Germany | Steelmaking, superalloys |
| Graphite (natural) | 100 | Mexico, Canada, China, Madagascar, Brazil | Refractories, brake linings, packings |
| Manganese | 100 | South Africa, Gabon, France, Brazil | Steelmaking |
| Mica, sheet (natural) | 100 | India, Brazil, Finland, China | Electronic and electrical equipment |
| Strontium (celestite) | 100 | Mexico | Television picture tubes, ferrite magnets, pyrotechnics |
| Yttrium | 100 | China, UK, Hong Kong, Japan, France | Color television phosphors, fluorescent lights, temperature sensors |
| Bauxite and alumina | 99 | Australia, Jamaica, Guinea, Brazil | Aluminum production, abrasives, refractories |
| Gemstones | 98 | Israel, India, Belgium, UK | Jewelry, carvings, gem and mineral collections |
| Fluorspar | 92 | China, South Africa, Mexico | Hydrofluoric acid production, steelmaking |
| Tungsten | 87 | China, Germany, Bolivia, Peru | Machinery, lamps and lighting |
| Tin | 84 | Brazil, Bolivia, Indonesia, China | Cans and containers, electrical, transportation |
| Cobalt | 82 | Zambia, Norway, Canada, Zaire, Finland | Aerospace alloys, catalysts, paint driers, magnetic alloys |
| Tantalum | 80 | Australia, Germany, Canada, Thailand | Electronic components |
| Chromium | 78 | South Africa, Turkey, Zimbabwe, Russia, Finland | Ferroalloys, chemicals, refractories |
| Potash | 74 | Canada, Belarus, Germany, Israel, Russia | Fertilizer |
| Barite | 65 | China, India, Mexico | Oil and gas well drilling fluids |
| Iodine | 62 | Japan, Chile | Animal feed supplements, catalysts, inks, disinfectants |
| Nickel | 61 | Canada, Norway, Australia, Dominican Rep. | Stainless steel, other alloys |
| Antimony | 60 | China, Mexico, South Africa, Hong Kong | Flame retardants, batteries |
| Stone (dimension) | 57 | Italy, Spain, India, Canada | Construction |
| Peat | 55 | Canada | Horticulture/agriculture |
| Magnesium compounds | 50 | China, Canada, Mexico, Greece, Austria | Refractories, agriculture, chemicals |

# U.S. Copper, Lead, and Zinc Production, 1950-95

Source: U.S. Geological Survey, U.S. Dept. of the Interior

| Year | Copper Quantity (metric tons) | Copper Value ($1,000) | Lead Quantity (metric tons) | Lead Value ($1,000) | Zinc Quantity (metric tons) | Zinc Value ($1,000) |
|---|---|---|---|---|---|---|
| 1950 | 827 | 379,122 | 390,839 | 113,078 | 565,516 | 167,000 |
| 1960 | 1,037 | 733,706 | 223,774 | 57,722 | 395,013 | 112,365 |
| 1965 | 1,226 | 957,028 | 273,196 | 93,959 | 554,429 | 178,284 |
| 1970 | 1,560 | 1,984,484 | 518,698 | 178,609 | 484,560 | 163,650 |
| 1975 | 1,282 | 1,814,763 | 563,783 | 267,230 | 425,792 | 366,097 |
| 1980 | 1,181 | 2,666,931 | 550,366 | 515,189 | 317,103 | 261,671 |
| 1985 | 1,105 | 1,631,000 | 413,955 | 174,008 | 226,545 | 201,607 |
| 1989 | 1,497 | 4,323,000 | 410,915 | 356,476 | 275,883 | 499,103 |
| 1990 | 1,586 | 4,310,000 | 483,704 | 490,750 | 515,355 | 847,485 |
| 1991 | 1,630 | 3,931,000 | 465,931 | 343,907 | 517,804 | 602,426 |
| 1992 | 1,760 | 4,167,000 | 397,076 | 307,337 | 523,430 | 673,800 |
| 1993 | 1,800 | 3,635,000 | 355,185 | 248,540 | 488,283 | 496,795 |
| 1994 | 1,850 | 5,647,000 | 363,000 | 298,000 | 570,162 | 619,195 |
| 1995 | 1,850 | 4,523,000 | 386,000 | 359,000 | 601,000[E] | 653,000[E] |

(E) Estimated.

# U.S. Pig Iron and Raw Steel Output, 1940-95

Source: American Iron and Steel Institute

(net tons)

| Year | Total pig iron | Raw steel |
|---|---|---|
| 1940 | 46,071,666 | 66,982,686 |
| 1945 | 53,223,169 | 79,701,648 |
| 1950 | 64,586,907 | 96,836,075 |
| 1955 | 76,857,417 | 117,036,085 |
| 1960 | 66,480,648 | 99,281,601 |
| 1965 | 88,184,901 | 131,461,601 |
| 1970 | 91,435,000 | 131,514,000 |
| 1975 | 79,923,000 | 116,642,000 |
| 1980 | 68,721,000 | 111,835,000 |
| 1985 | 50,446,000 | 88,259,000 |
| 1988 | 55,745,000 | 99,924,000 |
| 1989 | 55,873,000 | 97,943,000 |
| 1990 | 54,750,000 | 98,906,000 |
| 1991 | 48,637,000 | 87,896,000 |
| 1992 | 52,224,000 | 92,949,000 |
| 1993 | 53,082,000 | 97,877,000 |
| 1994 | 54,426,000 | 100,579,000 |
| 1995 | 56,097,000 | 104,930,000 |

Steel figures include only that portion of the capacity and production of steel for castings used by foundries that were operated by companies producing steel ingots.

# World Gold Production, 1972-95

Source: U.S. Geological Survey, U.S. Dept. of the Interior

(troy ounces)

| | | Africa | | | North and South America | | | | Other | | | |
|---|---|---|---|---|---|---|---|---|---|---|---|---|
| Year | World prod. | South Africa | Ghana | Zaire[R] | United States | Canada | Mexico | Colombia | Australia | China | Philip-pines | USSR |
| 1972 | 44,843,374 | 29,245,273 | 724,051 | 80,377 | 1,449,943 | 2,078,567 | 146,061 | 188,137 | 754,866 | NA | 606,730 | NA |
| 1975 | 38,476,371 | 22,937,820 | 523,889 | 115,743 | 1,052,252 | 1,653,611 | 144,710 | 308,864 | 526,821 | NA | 502,577 | NA |
| 1978 | 38,983,019 | 22,648,558 | 402,034 | 32,151 | 998,832 | 1,735,077 | 202,003 | 246,446 | 647,579 | NA | 586,531 | NA |
| 1980 | 39,197,315 | 21,669,468 | 353,000 | 96,452 | 969,782 | 1,627,477 | 195,991 | 510,439 | 547,591 | NA | 753,452 | 8,425,000 |
| 1982 | 43,082,814 | 21,355,111 | 331,000 | 135,033 | 1,465,686 | 2,081,230 | 214,349 | 472,674 | 866,815 | 1,800,000 | 834,439 | 8,550,000 |
| 1984 | 46,929,444 | 21,860,933 | 287,000 | 321,507 | 2,084,615 | 2,682,786 | 270,998 | 730,670 | 1,295,963 | 1,900,000 | 827,149 | 8,650,000 |
| 1985 | 49,283,691 | 21,565,230 | 299,363 | 257,206 | 2,427,232 | 2,815,118 | 265,693 | 1,142,385 | 1,881,491 | 1,950,000 | 1,062,997 | 8,700,000 |
| 1986 | 51,534,056 | 20,513,665 | 287,127 | 257,206 | 3,739,015 | 3,364,700 | 250,615 | 1,285,878 | 2,413,842 | 2,100,000 | 1,296,400 | 8,850,000 |
| 1987 | 53,033,614 | 19,176,500 | 327,598 | 385,809 | 4,947,040 | 3,724,000 | 256,822 | 853,600 | 3,558,954 | 2,300,000 | 1,048,081 | 8,850,000 |
| 1988 | 60,308,973 | 19,965,611 | 355,620 | 401,884 | 6,459,534 | 4,334,338 | 292,508 | 932,822 | 5,046,059 | 2,507,758 | 980,019 | 8,925,046 |
| 1989 | 65,335,998 | 19,530,290 | 429,470 | 340,798 | 8,543,449 | 5,127,850 | 276,914 | 948,640 | 6,544,702 | 2,893,567 | 964,265 | 9,773,826 |
| 1990 | 70,206,932 | 19,454,414 | 541,419 | 299,002 | 9,458,395 | 5,446,722 | 311,283 | 943,689 | 7,849,186 | 3,215,074 | 790,619 | 9,709,524 |
| 1991 | 70,422,599 | 19,326,133 | 845,918 | 282,927 | 9,454,311 | 5,676,278 | 326,073 | 1,120,260 | 7,530,283 | 3,858,089 | 833,219 | 8,359,193 |
| 1992 | 73,529,583 | 19,742,838 | 997,702 | 225,055 | 10,616,561 | 5,189,194 | 318,003 | 1,032,618 | 7,825,491 | 4,501,104 | 729,886 | 8,231,554* |
| 1993 | 74,210,568 | 19,907,772 | 1,261,434 | 192,904 | 10,642,314 | 4,916,781 | 356,873 | 883,149 | 7,947,535 | 5,144,119 | 508,818 | 8,228,179* |
| 1994 | 73,618,833 | 18,637,078 | 1,430,869 | 34,562 | 10,488,247 | 4,694,008 | 446,895 | 883,149 | 8,236,634 | 5,144,119 | 469,754 | 8,172,719* |
| 1995[E] | 73,200,000 | 16,800,000 | 1,680,000 | 305,000 | 10,300,000 | 4,830,000 | 652,000 | 680,000 | 8,150,000 | 4,500,000 | 873,000 | 4,270,000† |

NA=not available. (R) Revised to reflect improved data. (E) Estimated. (*) USSR as constituted prior to Dec. 1991. (†) Russia only.

# U.S. and World Silver Production, 1930-95

Source: U.S. Geological Survey, U.S. Dept. of the Interior

(metric tons)

| Year[1] | United States | World | Year[1] | United States | World | Year[1] | United States | World |
|---|---|---|---|---|---|---|---|---|
| 1930 | 1,578 | 7,736 | 1965 | 1,238 | 8,007 | 1989 | 2,008 | 16,041 |
| 1935 | 1,428 | 6,865 | 1970 | 1,400 | 9,670 | 1990 | 2,120 | 16,600 |
| 1940 | 2,164 | 8,565 | 1975 | 1,087 | 9,428 | 1991 | 1,860 | 15,600 |
| 1945 | 904 | 5,039 | 1980 | 1,006 | 10,556 | 1992 | 1,800 | 14,600 |
| 1950 | 1,347 | 6,323 | 1985 | 1,227 | 13,051 | 1993 | 1,640 | 14,300 |
| 1955 | 1,134 | 6,967 | 1987 | 1,241 | 14,019 | 1994 | 1,480 | 14,000 |
| 1960 | 1,120 | 7,505 | 1988 | 1,661 | 15,484 | 1995 | 1,540 | 14,500[E] |

(1) Largest production of silver in the United States was in 1915—2,332 metric tons. (E) Estimated.

# Aluminum Summary, 1980-95

Source: U.S. Geological Survey, U.S. Dept. of the Interior

| Item | Unit | 1980 | 1985 | 1990 | 1991 | 1992 | 1993 | 1994 | 1995 |
|---|---|---|---|---|---|---|---|---|---|
| U.S. production | 1,000 metric tons | 6,231 | 5,262 | 6,441 | 6,407 | 6,798 | 6,639 | 6,385 | 6,563 |
| Primary aluminum | 1,000 metric tons | 4,654 | 3,500 | 4,048 | 4,121 | 4,042 | 3,695 | 3,299 | 3,375 |
| Secondary aluminum[1] | 1,000 metric tons | 1,577 | 1,762 | 2,393 | 2,286 | 2,756 | 2,944 | 3,086 | 3,188 |
| Primary aluminum value | Billion dollars | 7.8 | 3.8 | 6.6 | 5.4 | 5.1 | 4.3 | 5.2 | 6.4 |
| Price (Primary alum.)[2] | Cents/lb. | 76.1 | 48.8 | 74.0 | 59.5 | 57.5 | 53.3 | 71.2 | 85.9 |
| Imports for consumption[3] | 1,000 metric tons | 647 | 1,420 | 1,514 | 1,490 | 1,725 | 2,544 | 3,382 | 2,975 |
| Exports[3] | 1,000 metric tons | 1,346 | 908 | 1,659 | 1,762 | 1,453 | 1,207 | 1,365 | 1,610 |
| World production | 1,000 metric tons | 15,383 | 15,398 | 19,299 | 19,652 | 19,488 | 19,765 | 19,166 | 19,403[E] |

(1) Recoverable metal content from purchased scrap, old and new. (2) Average prices for primary aluminum, quoted by *Metals Week*. (3) Crude and semicrude (including metal and alloys, plates, bars, etc., and scrap). (E) Estimated.

# Economic and Financial Glossary

**Source:** Reviewed by Daniel Raff, Associate Professor of Management, The Wharton School

**Acquisition:** The purchase of one company by another.

**Arbitrage:** A form of hedged investment meant to capture slight differences in the prices of two related securities—for example, buying gold in London and selling it at a higher price in New York. Distinct from *risk arbitrage.*

**Balanced budget:** A budget is balanced when receipts equal current expenditure.

**Balance of payments:** The difference between all payments, for some categories of transactions, made to and from foreign countries over a set period of time. A *favorable* balance exists when more payments are coming in than going out; an *unfavorable* balance, when the reverse is true. Payments may include gold, the cost of merchandise and services, interest and dividend payments, money spent by travelers, and repayment of principal on loans.

**Balance of trade (trade gap):** The difference between exports and imports, in both actual funds and credit. A nation's balance of trade is *favorable* when exports exceed imports and *unfavorable* when the reverse is true.

**Bear market:** A market in which prices are falling.

**Bearer bond:** A bond issued in bearer form rather than being registered in a specific owner's name. Ownership is determined by possession.

**Bond:** A written promise or IOU by the issuer to repay a fixed amount of borrowed money on a specified date and generally to make payments of interest at regular intervals in the interim.

**Bull market:** A market in which prices are on the rise.

**Capital gain (loss):** An increase (decrease) in the market value of an asset above (below) the price originally paid, at the time the asset is sold.

**Commercial paper:** An extremely short-term corporate IOU, generally due in 270 days or less. Available in face amounts of $100,000, $250,000, $500,000, $1,000,000 and combinations thereof.

**Convertible bond:** A corporate bond (see below) that may be converted into a stated number of shares of common stock. Its price tends to fluctuate along with fluctuations in the price of the stock and with changes in interest rates.

**Corporate bond:** A bond issued by a corporation. The bond normally has a stated life and pays a fixed rate of interest. Considered safer than the common or preferred stock of the same company.

**Cost of living:** The cost of maintaining a standard of living measured in terms of purchased goods and services. Inflation typically measures changes in the cost of living.

**Cost-of-living benefits:** Benefit payments whose sum in current dollars is regularly adjusted for changes in the cost of living.

**Credit crunch (liquidity crisis):** A situation in which cash for lending is in short supply.

**Debenture:** An unsecured bond backed only by the general credit of the issuing corporation.

**Deficit spending:** Government spending in excess of revenues, generally financed with the sale of bonds.

**Depression:** A long period of economic decline when prices are low, unemployment is high, and there are many business failures.

**Derivatives:** Financial contracts whose values are based on, or *derived* from, the price of an underlying financial asset or price—for example, a stock or an interest rate.

**Devaluation:** The official lowering of a nation's currency, decreasing its value in relation to foreign currencies.

**Discount rate:** The rate of interest set by the Federal Reserve that member banks are charged when borrowing money through the Federal Reserve System.

**Disposable income:** Income after taxes that is available to persons for spending and saving.

**Dividend:** Discretionary payment by a corporation to its shareholders, usually in the form of cash, stock shares, or other property.

**Dow Jones Industrial Average:** An index of stock market prices, based on the prices of 30 leading companies on the New York Stock Exchange.

**Econometrics:** The use of statistical methods to study economic and financial data.

**Federal Deposit Insurance Corporation (FDIC):** A U.S. government-sponsored corporation that insures accounts in national banks and other qualified institutions.

**Federal Reserve System:** The entire banking system of the U.S., incorporating 12 Federal Reserve banks (one in each of 12 Federal Reserve districts), 24 Federal Reserve branch banks, all national banks, and state-chartered commercial banks and trust companies that have been admitted to its membership. The governors of the system greatly influence the nation's monetary and credit policies.

**Full employment:** The economy is said to be at full employment when everyone who wishes to work at the going wage-rate for his or her type of labor is employed, save for only the small amount of unemployment due to the fact that it takes time to switch from one job to another.

**Golden parachute:** Provisions in the employment contracts of executives guaranteeing substantial severance benefits if they lose their position in a corporate takeover.

**Government bond:** A bond issued by the U.S. Treasury, considered the safest security in the investment world. Government bonds are divided into 2 categories—those that are not marketable and those that are. *Savings Bonds* cannot be bought and sold once the original purchase is made. These include the familiar Series EE bonds. You buy them at 50 percent of their face value, and when they mature, 12 years later, they can be cashed in for 100 percent of face value. Another type, Series H, are not discounted, but issued in amounts of $500, $1,000, $5,000, and $10,000 and pay their interest in semiannual checks. Marketable bonds fall into several categories. *Treasury Bills* are short-term U.S. obligations, maturing in 3, 6, or 12 months. They are sold at a discount of the face value, and the minimum denomination is $10,000. *Treasury Notes* mature in up to 10 years. Denominations currently range from $500 to $10,000 and up. *Treasury Bonds* mature in 10 to 30 years. The minimum investment is $1,000.

**Greenmail:** A company buying back its own shares for more than the going market price to avoid a threatened hostile takeover.

**Gross domestic product (GDP):** The market value of all goods and services that have been bought for final use during a year. It became the official measure of the size of the U.S. economy in 1991, replacing the *Gross National Product (GNP),* which had been in use since 1941. GDP covers workers and capital employed within the nation's borders. GNP covers production by American residents, regardless of where it takes place. The switch aligned the U.S. with most other industrialized countries, making exact comparisons easier.

**Hedge fund:** A flexible investment fund for a limited number of large investors (the minimum investment is typically $1 million). Hedge funds use almost all investment techniques, including those forbidden to mutual funds, such as short-selling and heavy leveraging.

**Hedging:** Taking 2 positions whose gains and losses will offset each other if prices change, in order to limit financial risk.

**Individual retirement account (IRA):** A self-funded retirement plan that allows employed individuals to contribute up to a maximum yearly sum toward their retirement while deferring tax on the interest until retirement.

**Inflation:** An increase in the level of prices.

**Insider information:** Important facts about the condition or plans of a corporation that have not been released to the general public.

**Interest:** The cost of borrowing money.

**Investment bank:** A financial institution that arranges the initial issuance of stocks and bonds and offers companies advice about acquisitions and divestitures.

**Junk bonds:** Bonds issued by companies with low credit ratings. They typically pay relatively high interest rates because of the fear of default.

**Leading indicators:** A series of 11 indicators from different segments of the economy used by the Commerce Department to predict when changes in the level of economic activity will occur.

**Leverage:** The extent to which a purchase was paid for with borrowed money. Amplifies the potential gain or loss for the purchaser.

**Leveraged buy-out:** An acquisition of a company in which much of the purchase price is borrowed, with the debt to be repaid from future profits or by subsequently selling off company assets. Typically carried out by a small group of investors, often including incumbent management.

**Liquid assets:** Assets that include cash or those items that are easily converted into cash.

**Margin account:** A brokerage account that allows a person to trade securities on credit. A **margin call** is a demand for more collateral on the account.

**Money supply:** The currency held by the public, plus checking accounts in commercial banks and savings institutions.

**Mortgage-backed securities:** Created when a bank, builder, or government agency gathers together a group of mortgages and then sells bonds to other institutions and the public. The investors receive their proportionate share of the interest payments on the loans as well as the principal payments. Usually, the mortgages in question are guaranteed by the government.

**Municipal bond:** Issued by governmental units such as states, cities, local taxing authorities, and other agencies. Interest is exempt from U.S.—and sometimes state and local—income tax. *Municipal Bond Unit Investment Trusts* offer a portfolio of many different municipal bonds chosen by professionals. The income is exempt from federal income taxes.

**Mutual fund:** A portfolio of professionally bought and managed financial assets in which you pool your money along with thousands of other people. A share price is based on net asset value, or the value of all the investments owned by the funds, less any debt, and divided by the total number of shares. The major advantage, relative to investing individually only in a small number of stocks, is less risk—the holdings are spread out over many assets and if one or two do badly the remainder may shield you from the losses. *Bond Funds* are mutual funds that deal in the bond market exclusively. *Money Market Mutual Funds* buy in the so-called "Money Market"—institutions that need to borrow large sums of money for short terms. Usually the individual investor cannot afford the denominations required in the "Money Market" (e.g., treasury bills, commercial paper, certificates of deposit), but through a money market mutual fund he or she can take advantage of these instruments when interest rates are high as well as get the diversification advantages. These funds often offer special checking account advantages.

**National debt:** The debt of the national government as distinguished from the debts of the political subdivisions of the nation and private business and individuals.

**National debt ceiling:** Total borrowing limit set by Congress beyond which the national debt cannot rise. This limit is periodically raised by congressional vote.

**Option:** A type of contractual agreement between a buyer and a seller to buy or sell shares of a security. A **Call** option contract gives the right to purchase shares of a specific stock at a stated price within a given period of time. A **Put** option contract gives the buyer the right to sell shares of a specific stock at a stated price within a given period of time.

**Per capita income:** The nation's total income divided by the number of people in the nation.

**Prime interest rate:** The rate charged by banks on short-term loans to large commercial customers with the highest credit rating.

**Producer price index:** A statistical measure of the change in the price of wholesale goods. It is reported for 3 different stages of the production chain: crude, intermediate, and finished goods.

**Program trading:** A term for trading techniques involving large numbers and large blocks of stocks, usually used in conjunction with computer programs. Techniques include *Index Arbitrage,* in which traders profit from price differences between stocks and futures contracts on stock indexes, and *Portfolio Insurance,* which is the use of stock-index futures to protect stock investors from large losses when the market drops.

**Public debt:** The total of the nation's debts owed by state, local, and national government. Increases in this sum, reflected in public-sector deficits, indicate how much of the nation's spending is financed by borrowing rather than by taxation.

**Recession:** A mild decrease in economic activity marked by a decline in real GDP, employment, and trade, usually lasting 6 months to a year, and marked by widespread decline in many sectors of the economy.

**Risk arbitrage:** The purchase and/or selling of the securities of companies expected to be involved in takeover situations, in order to realize a profit.

**Savings Association Insurance Fund (SAIF):** Created in 1989 to insure accounts in savings and loan associations up to $100,000.

**Seasonal adjustment:** Statistical changes made to compensate for regular fluctuations in data that are so great they tend to distort the statistics and make comparisons meaningless. For instance, seasonal adjustments are made in midwinter for a slowdown in housing construction and for the rise in farm income in the fall after the summer crops are harvested.

**Short-selling:** Borrowing shares of stock from a brokerage firm and selling them, hoping to buy the shares back at a lower price, return them, and realize a profit from the decline in prices.

**Stagnation:** Economic slowdown in which there is little growth in GDP, capital investment, and real income.

**Stock:** *Common Stocks* are shares of ownership in a corporation; they are the most direct way to participate in the fortunes of a company. There can be wide swings in the prices of this kind of stock. *Preferred Stock* is a type of stock on which a fixed dividend must be paid before holders of common stock are issued their share of the issuing corporation's earnings. Prices are higher and yields lower than comparable bonds. However, preferred stock is attractive to corporate investors because 85% of preferred dividends are tax exempt to corporations. *Convertible Preferred Stock* can be converted into the common stock of the company that issued the preferred. This stock has the advantage of producing a higher yield than common stock; it also has appreciation potential. *Over-the-Counter Stock* is not traded on the major or regional exchanges, but rather through dealers from whom you buy directly. *Blue Chip* stocks are so called because they have been leading stocks for a long time. *Growth* stocks are those whose earnings are expected to grow over several years.

**Stock-index futures:** A futures contract is an agreement to buy or sell a specific amount of a commodity or financial instrument at a particular price at a set date in the future. Futures based on a stock index (such as the Dow Jones Industrial Average) are bets on the future price of that group of stocks.

**Supply-side economics:** A school of thinking about economic policy holding that lowering income tax rates will inevitably lead to enhanced economic growth and general revitalization of the economy.

**Takeover:** Acquisition of one company by another company or group by sale or merger. A friendly takeover occurs when the acquired company's management is agreeable to the merger; when management is opposed to the merger, it is an unfriendly takeover.

**Tender offer:** A public offer to buy a company's stock; usually priced at a premium above the market.

**Zero coupon bond:** A corporate or government bond that is issued at a deep discount from the maturity value and pays no interest during the life of the bond. It is redeemable at face value.

# AGRICULTURE

## The U.S. Farm Population

**Source:** Margaret Butler, U.S. Dept. of Agriculture, Economic Research Service

When first separately counted in the 1920 census, the farm population was defined as people living on farms, regardless of occupation or source of income. Many people who live on farms today have no one in the household employed primarily in agriculture, and those employed in agriculture often do not live on farms. Thirty-five percent of persons in farm operator or manager households did not live on a farm in 1992, and 38% of farm residents were members of households in which no one operated or managed a farm or received farm self-employment income. Thus, the conventional farm residence definition has lost some of its former validity and has been discontinued.

In 1994, about 5 million people lived in households associated with the operation of farms, as indicated by a household member's occupation or source of income. This farm population definition is now identified as the farm entrepreneurial population. The Midwest was home to a larger proportion of that population—44%—than any other region of the country.

## Persons in Farm Occupations, 1850-1994

**Source:** U.S. Dept. of Agriculture, Economic Research Service

(in thousands)

| Year | Total workers* | Farm occupations Number | Farm occupations % of total |
|---|---|---|---|
| 1850 | 7,697 | 4,902 | 63.7 |
| 1870 | 12,925 | 6,850 | 53.0 |
| 1900 | 29,030 | 10,888 | 37.5 |
| 1920 | 42,206 | 11,390 | 27.0 |
| 1930 | 48,686 | 10,321 | 21.2 |
| 1940 | 51,742 | 8,995 | 17.4 |
| 1950 | 59,230 | 6,858 | 11.6 |
| 1960 | 67,990 | 4,132 | 6.1 |
| 1970 | 79,802 | 2,881 | 3.6 |
| 1980 | 104,058 | 2,818 | 2.7 |
| 1985 (Mar.) | 106,214 | 2,949 | 2.8 |
| 1990 (Mar.) | 117,491 | 2,864 | 2.4 |
| 1991 (Mar.) | 116,000 | 2,848 | 2.5 |
| 1992 (Mar.) | 116,442 | 2,936 | 2.5 |
| 1993 (Mar.) | 117,238 | 2,988 | 2.5 |
| 1994 (Mar.) | 120,383 | 3,038 | 2.5 |

* Total workers for 1985 to 1994 are employed workers ages 15 years and older; total workers for 1970 and 1980 are members of the experienced civilian labor force ages 16 years and older; total workers for 1900 to 1960 are members of the experienced civilian labor force ages 14 years and older; total workers for 1850 to 1890 are gainfully employed workers ages 10 years and older.

## U.S. Farms–Number and Acreage by State, 1985 and 1995

**Source:** National Agricultural Statistics Service, U.S. Dept. of Agriculture

| State | Farms (1,000) 1985 | Farms (1,000) 1995 | Acreage (mil) 1985 | Acreage (mil) 1995 | Acreage per farm 1985 | Acreage per farm 1995 |
|---|---|---|---|---|---|---|
| **U.S.** | **2,275** | **2,072** | **1,014** | **972** | **446** | **469** |
| Alabama | 54 | 47 | 12 | 10 | 213 | 217 |
| Alaska | 1 | 1 | 1 | 1 | 2,132 | 1,769 |
| Arizona | 9 | 7 | 38 | 35 | 4,412 | 4,784 |
| Arkansas | 53 | 43 | 16 | 15 | 302 | 349 |
| California | 79 | 80 | 33 | 30 | 416 | 375 |
| Colorado | 27 | 25 | 34 | 33 | 1,288 | 1,308 |
| Connecticut | 4 | 4 | (Z) | (Z) | 120 | 100 |
| Delaware | 4 | 3 | 1 | 1 | 186 | 228 |
| Florida | 39 | 39 | 13 | 10 | 333 | 264 |
| Georgia | 50 | 45 | 14 | 12 | 270 | 267 |
| Hawaii | 5 | 5 | 2 | 2 | 424 | 331 |
| Idaho | 25 | 22 | 15 | 14 | 589 | 628 |
| Illinois | 90 | 77 | 29 | 28 | 319 | 365 |
| Indiana | 80 | 62 | 16 | 16 | 205 | 256 |
| Iowa | 111 | 100 | 34 | 33 | 303 | 332 |
| Kansas | 72 | 66 | 48 | 48 | 667 | 724 |
| Kentucky | 100 | 89 | 15 | 14 | 145 | 157 |
| Louisiana | 36 | 27 | 10 | 9 | 281 | 315 |
| Maine | 8 | 8 | 2 | 1 | 195 | 178 |
| Maryland | 18 | 14 | 3 | 2 | 149 | 154 |
| Massachusetts | 6 | 6 | 1 | 1 | 113 | 95 |
| Michigan | 62 | 54 | 11 | 11 | 184 | 198 |
| Minnesota | 96 | 87 | 30 | 30 | 317 | 343 |
| Mississippi | 48 | 42 | 14 | 13 | 294 | 310 |
| Missouri | 115 | 105 | 31 | 30 | 268 | 286 |
| Montana | 24 | 22 | 61 | 60 | 2,563 | 2,714 |
| Nebraska | 59 | 56 | 47 | 47 | 800 | 839 |
| Nevada | 3 | 3 | 9 | 9 | 3,520 | 3,520 |
| New Hampshire | 3 | 2 | 1 | (Z) | 159 | 191 |
| New Jersey | 9 | 9 | 1 | 1 | 108 | 94 |
| New Mexico | 14 | 14 | 45 | 44 | 3,261 | 3,259 |
| New York | 44 | 36 | 9 | 8 | 207 | 214 |
| N. Carolina | 76 | 58 | 11 | 9 | 142 | 159 |
| N. Dakota | 34 | 32 | 41 | 40 | 1,203 | 1,259 |
| Ohio | 89 | 74 | 16 | 15 | 178 | 205 |
| Oklahoma | 71 | 71 | 33 | 34 | 465 | 479 |
| Oregon | 37 | 39 | 18 | 18 | 486 | 455 |
| Pennsylvania | 58 | 50 | 9 | 8 | 150 | 154 |
| Rhode Island | 1 | 1 | (Z) | (Z) | 97 | 90 |
| S. Carolina | 28 | 22 | 6 | 5 | 200 | 230 |
| S. Dakota | 37 | 33 | 45 | 44 | 1,219 | 1,333 |
| Tennessee | 98 | 81 | 13 | 12 | 137 | 148 |
| Texas | 177 | 202 | 136 | 129 | 766 | 639 |
| Utah | 14 | 13 | 12 | 11 | 835 | 828 |
| Vermont | 7 | 6 | 2 | 1 | 229 | 228 |
| Virginia | 54 | 47 | 10 | 9 | 171 | 185 |
| Washington | 38 | 36 | 16 | 16 | 424 | 439 |
| W. Virginia | 21 | 20 | 4 | 4 | 173 | 185 |
| Wisconsin | 83 | 80 | 18 | 17 | 213 | 211 |
| Wyoming | 9 | 9 | 35 | 35 | 3,867 | 3,761 |

(Z) Fewer than 500,000 acres

## Livestock on Farms in the U.S., 1900-96

**Source:** National Agricultural Statistics Service, U.S. Dept. of Agriculture

(in thousands)

| Year (On Jan. 1) | All cattle | Milk cows | Sheep | Hogs[1] |
|---|---|---|---|---|
| 1900 | 59,739 | 16,544 | 48,105 | 51,055 |
| 1910 | 58,993 | 19,450 | 50,239 | 48,072 |
| 1920 | 70,400 | 21,455 | 40,743 | 60,159 |
| 1925 | 63,373 | 22,575 | 38,543 | 55,770 |
| 1930 | 61,003 | 23,032 | 51,565 | 55,705 |
| 1935 | 68,846 | 26,082 | 51,808 | 39,066 |
| 1940 | 68,309 | 24,940 | 52,107 | 61,165 |
| 1945 | 85,573 | 27,770 | 46,520 | 59,373 |
| 1950 | 77,963 | 23,853 | 29,826 | 58,937 |
| 1955 | 96,592 | 23,462 | 31,582 | 50,474 |
| 1960 | 96,236 | 19,527 | 33,170 | 59,026 |
| 1965[2] | 109,000 | 16,981 | 25,127 | 56,106 |
| 1970 | 112,369 | 12,091 | 20,423 | 57,046 |
| 1980 | 111,242 | 10,758 | 12,699 | 67,318 |
| 1985 | 109,582 | 10,777 | 10,716 | 54,073 |
| 1990* | 95,816 | 10,015 | 11,358 | 53,788 |
| 1991* | 96,393 | 9,966 | 11,174 | 54,416 |
| 1992* | 97,556 | 9,728 | 10,797 | 57,649 |
| 1993* | 99,176 | 9,658 | 10,201 | 58,202 |
| 1994* | 100,988 | 9,528 | 9,742 | 57,904 |
| 1995 | 102,755 | 9,487 | 8,886 | 59,990 |
| 1996[3] | 103,819 | 9,412 | 8,457 | 58,700 |

* Figures revised by USDA NASS, Jan. 1996. (1) As of Dec. 1 of preceding year. (2) From 1966, milk cows and heifers that have calved. (3) Total estimated value on farms as of Jan. 1, 1996, was (avg. value per head in parentheses): cattle $52,159,765,000 ($502.00); sheep $731,360,000 ($86.50); hogs $4,225,087,000 ($70.70).

## U.S. Farms, 1940-95

**Source:** National Agricultural Statistics Service, U.S. Dept. of Agriculture

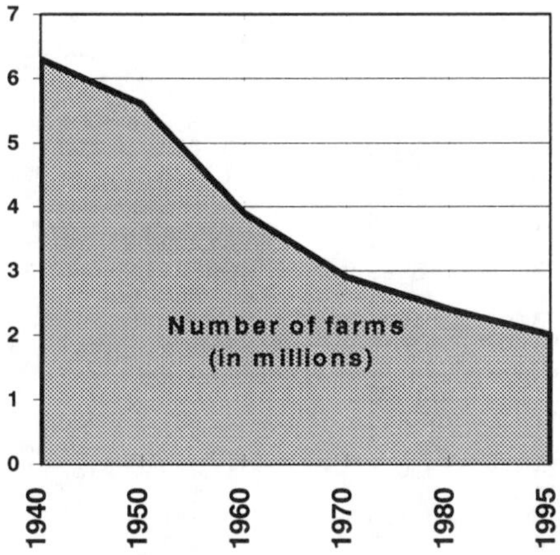


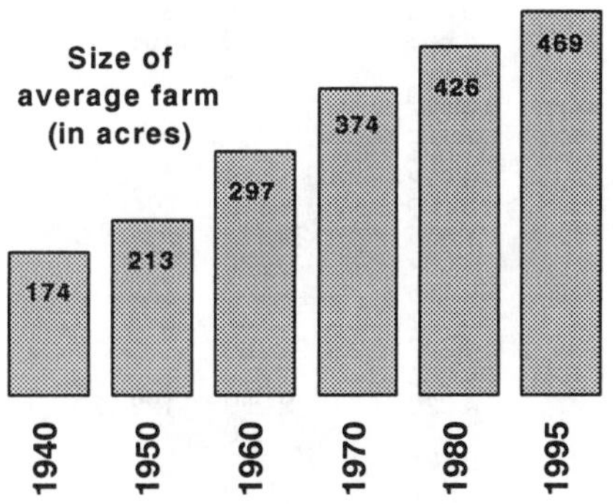


## Eggs: U.S. Production, Price, and Value, 1994-95[1]

**Source:** National Agricultural Statistics Service, U.S. Dept. of Agriculture

| State | Eggs produced[2] 1994 (mil) | Eggs produced[2] 1995 (mil) | Price per dozen[2] 1994 (cents) | Price per dozen[2] 1995 (cents) | Value of production 1994 (1,000 dollars) | Value of production 1995 (1,000 dollars) |
|---|---|---|---|---|---|---|
| AL | 2,732 | 2,693 | 90.2 | 96.1 | 205,355 | 215,664 |
| AK | 0.5 | | 171.0 | | 71 | |
| AZ | 81 | | 49.1 | | 3,314 | |
| AR | 3,803 | 3,608 | 104.0 | 97.9 | 329,593 | 294,353 |
| CA | 6,602 | 6,444 | 46.4 | 53.7 | 255,277 | 288,369 |
| CO | 778 | 805 | 66.0 | 70.6 | 42,790 | 47,361 |
| CT | 972 | 944 | 99.7 | 104.0 | 80,757 | 81,813 |
| DE | 152 | 138 | 108.0 | 108.0 | 13,680 | 12,995 |
| FL | 2,538 | 2,374 | 46.5 | 48.1 | 98,348 | 95,158 |
| GA | 4,543 | 4,376 | 74.5 | 79.4 | 282,045 | 289,545 |
| HI | 195 | 186 | 85.9 | 87.2 | 13,959 | 13,516 |
| ID | 254 | 238 | 64.8 | 60.7 | 13,716 | 12,039 |
| IL | 768 | 762 | 64.0 | 68.4 | 40,960 | 43,434 |
| IN | 5,452 | 5,496 | 50.8 | 51.6 | 230,801 | 236,328 |
| IA | 3,808 | 4,032 | 39.8 | 43.4 | 126,299 | 145,824 |
| KS | 352 | 325 | 38.8 | 38.8 | 11,381 | 11,917 |
| KY | 680 | 679 | 63.7 | 65.4 | 36,097 | 37,006 |
| LA | 442 | 472 | 111.0 | 98.4 | 40,885 | 38,704 |
| ME | 1,403 | 1,364 | 92.2 | 97.1 | 107,797 | 110,370 |
| MD | 852 | 1,003 | 63.7 | 64.0 | 45,227 | 53,493 |
| MA | 207 | 133 | 98.7 | 102.0 | 17,026 | 11,305 |
| MI | 1,435 | 1,387 | 42.5 | 43.5 | 50,823 | 50,279 |
| MN | 2,669 | 2,823 | 40.0 | 41.8 | 88,967 | 98,335 |
| MS | 1,515 | 1,443 | 96.4 | 99.0 | 121,544 | 119,048 |
| MO | 1,713 | 1,705 | 43.3 | 49.0 | 61,811 | 69,621 |
| MT | 99 | 104 | 55.0 | 57.0 | 4,538 | 4,940 |
| NE | 2,027 | 2,364 | 36.0 | 38.0 | 60,810 | 74,860 |
| NV | 1.4 | | 43.8 | | 51 | |
| NH | 39 | 44 | 97.0 | 109.0 | 3,153 | 3,997 |
| NJ | 451 | 444 | 71.0 | 74.6 | 26,684 | 27,602 |
| NM | 301 | 303 | 59.8 | 64.8 | 15,000 | 16,362 |
| NY | 1,049 | 1,071 | 57.2 | 62.6 | 50,002 | 55,871 |
| NC | 3,214 | 3,152 | 73.5 | 77.3 | 196,858 | 203,041 |
| ND | 51 | 47 | 36.0 | 38.4 | 1,530 | 1,504 |
| OH | 5,644 | 5,964 | 48.7 | 50.9 | 229,052 | 252,973 |
| OK | 799 | 897 | 89.9 | 86.0 | 59,858 | 64,285 |
| OR | 708 | 709 | 78.3 | 81.6 | 46,197 | 48,212 |
| PA | 5,597 | 5,655 | 51.1 | 56.2 | 238,339 | 264,843 |
| RI | 56 | 34 | 94.9 | 99.6 | 4,429 | 2,822 |
| SC | 1,326 | 1,289 | 63.7 | 65.8 | 70,389 | 70,680 |
| SD | 525 | 481 | 32.5 | 34.5 | 14,219 | 13,829 |
| TN | 256 | 254 | 72.0 | 79.0 | 15,360 | 16,722 |
| TX | 3,860 | 3,950 | 61.6 | 66.3 | 198,147 | 218,238 |
| UT | 491 | 513 | 45.1 | 47.1 | 18,453 | 20,135 |
| VT | 20 | 21 | 99.3 | 105.0 | 1,655 | 1,838 |
| VA | 940 | 916 | 88.5 | 89.5 | 69,325 | 68,318 |
| WA | 1,371 | 1,455 | 73.0 | 76.9 | 83,403 | 93,241 |
| WV | 250 | 239 | 115.0 | 118.0 | 23,958 | 23,502 |
| WI | 883 | 849 | 41.0 | 43.3 | 30,169 | 30,635 |
| WY | 2.8 | 2.4 | 67.6 | 74.1 | 158 | 148 |
| Other[3] | 84 | 74 | 49.7 | 64.1 | 3,477 | 3,901 |
| **U.S.[4]** | **73,866** | **74,268** | **61.4** | **64.0** | **3,780,377** | **3,958,976** |

(1) Estimates cover the 12-month period from Dec. 1 of the previous year through Nov. 30. (2) Average of all eggs sold by producers, including hatching eggs. (3) AK, AZ and NV combined to avoid disclosure of individual operations. AK price estimates discontinued in 1995. AZ and NV listed under "other." (4) Total states may not equal U.S. total because of rounding.

## U.S. Meat Production and Consumption, 1940-95

**Source:** Economic Research Service, U.S. Dept. of Agriculture

(in millions of pounds)

| Year | Beef Production | Beef Consumption[2] | Veal Production | Veal Consumption[2] | Lamb and mutton Production | Lamb and mutton Consumption[2] | Pork (exclud. lard) Production | Pork (exclud. lard) Consumption[2] | All meats[1] Production | All meats[1] Consumption[2] | Lard Production | Lard Consumption[3] |
|---|---|---|---|---|---|---|---|---|---|---|---|---|
| 1940 | 7,175 | 7,257 | 981 | 981 | 876 | 873 | 10,044 | 9,701 | 19,076 | 18,812 | 2,288 | 1,901 |
| 1950 | 9,534 | 9,529 | 1,230 | 1,206 | 597 | 596 | 10,714 | 10,390 | 22,075 | 21,721 | 2,631 | 1,891 |
| 1960 | 14,728 | 15,465 | 1,109 | 1,118 | 769 | 857 | 13,905 | 14,057 | 30,511 | 31,497 | 2,562 | 1,358 |
| 1970 | 21,684 | 23,451 | 588 | 613 | 551 | 669 | 14,699 | 14,957 | 37,522 | 39,689 | 1,913 | 939 |
| 1980 | 21,643 | 23,560 | 400 | 420 | 318 | 351 | 16,617 | 16,838 | 38,978 | 41,701 | 1,207 | 588 |
| 1990 | 22,743 | 24,031 | 327 | 325 | 363 | 397 | 15,354 | 16,031 | 38,787 | 40,784 | [4] | [4] |
| 1991 | 22,917 | 24,113 | 306 | 305 | 363 | 396 | 15,999 | 16,399 | 39,585 | 41,214 | [4] | [4] |
| 1992 | 23,086 | 24,261 | 310 | 312 | 348 | 388 | 17,233 | 17,474 | 40,977 | 42,435 | [4] | [4] |
| 1993 | 23,049 | 24,006 | 285 | 286 | 337 | 381 | 17,088 | 18,213 | 40,759 | 42,092 | [4] | [4] |
| 1994 | 24,386 | 25,125 | 293 | 291 | 308 | 345 | 17,696 | 17,829 | 42,683 | 43,592 | [4] | [4] |
| 1995 | 25,222 | 25,533 | 319 | 319 | 287 | 348 | 17,850 | 17.785 | 43,678 | 43,986 | [4] | [4] |

(1) Meats may not add to total. (2) Includes shipments. (3) Direct use. Excludes lard used in such products as table spreads and shortenings. (4) Data collection discontinued.

# Government Agricultural Payments by State, 1995[1]

**Source:** Economic Research Service, U.S. Dept. of Agriculture

(in thousands of dollars)

| State | Feed Grains | Wheat | Rice | Cotton[2] | Wool Act | Conservation[3] | Miscellaneous | Total |
|---|---|---|---|---|---|---|---|---|
| Alabama | $ 3,368 | $ 1,740 | $ 0 | $1,611 | $ 42 | $31,713 | $14,912 | $53,388 |
| Alaska | 57 | 0 | 0 | 0 | 1 | 1,056 | 621 | 1,735 |
| Arizona | 1,904 | 2,115 | 0 | 2,166 | 771 | 1,787 | 756 | 9,501 |
| Arkansas | 6,332 | 9,759 | 312,711 | 1,307 | 128 | 15,330 | 37,698 | 383,265 |
| California | 8,606 | 11,743 | 155,898 | 5,276 | 5,797 | 15,379 | 35,059 | 237,760 |
| Colorado | 43,505 | 21,733 | 0 | 0 | 4,838 | 83,149 | 13,828 | 167,053 |
| Connecticut | 720 | 0 | 0 | 0 | 20 | 382 | 1,260 | 2,382 |
| Delaware | 2,178 | 151 | 0 | 0 | 1 | 373 | 406 | 3,109 |
| Florida | 1,638 | 215 | 163 | 14 | 4 | 10,249 | 43,433 | 55,716 |
| Georgia | 9,812 | 3,713 | 0 | –176 | 27 | 32,169 | 20,921 | 66,466 |
| Hawaii | 0 | 0 | 0 | 0 | 0 | 400 | 541 | 947 |
| Idaho | 7,555 | 22,513 | 0 | 0 | 3,078 | 40,914 | 15,476 | 89,536 |
| Illinois | 453,034 | 9,270 | 0 | 0 | 384 | 66,018 | 15,029 | 543,735 |
| Indiana | 200,255 | 4,348 | 0 | 0 | 180 | 35,744 | 5,539 | 246,066 |
| Iowa | 590,872 | 87 | 0 | 0 | 1,391 | 183,685 | 8,604 | 784,639 |
| Kansas | 154,847 | 96,786 | 0 | -3 | 911 | 157,489 | 12,991 | 423,021 |
| Kentucky | 34,005 | 2,618 | 33 | 0 | 94 | 28,217 | 2,406 | 67,373 |
| Louisiana | 4,320 | 2,259 | 122,172 | 2,187 | 14 | 9,045 | 17,318 | 157,315 |
| Maine | 577 | 0 | 0 | 0 | 54 | 3,575 | 9,874 | 14,080 |
| Maryland | 9,724 | 667 | 0 | 0 | 85 | 2,370 | 2,301 | 15,147 |
| Massachusetts | 425 | 0 | 0 | 0 | 38 | 498 | 1,497 | 2,458 |
| Michigan | 86,348 | 5,190 | 0 | 0 | 475 | 22,829 | 36,167 | 151,009 |
| Minnesota | 268,636 | 27,763 | 0 | 0 | 1,057 | 106,098 | 64,347 | 467,901 |
| Mississippi | 3,438 | 2,588 | 61,397 | 4,471 | 16 | 38,555 | 18,696 | 129,161 |
| Missouri | 84,974 | 11,379 | 25,097 | 340 | 588 | 119,044 | 14,574 | 255,996 |
| Montana | 18,141 | 46,841 | 0 | 0 | 6,983 | 104,194 | 9,172 | 185,331 |
| Nebraska | 382,887 | 20,308 | 0 | 0 | 817 | 81,412 | 21,923 | 507,347 |
| Nevada | 108 | 342 | 0 | 0 | 732 | 785 | 2,298 | 4,265 |
| New Hampshire | 267 | 0 | 0 | 0 | 32 | 575 | 309 | 1,183 |
| New Jersey | 2,209 | 129 | 0 | 0 | 28 | 402 | 2,724 | 5,492 |
| New Mexico | 7,977 | 3,412 | 0 | –82 | 4,753 | 20,615 | 18,483 | 55,158 |
| New York | 25,951 | 1,367 | 0 | 0 | 306 | 6,157 | 10,067 | 43,488 |
| North Carolina | 19,860 | 1,944 | 0 | –666 | 67 | 9,213 | 9,741 | 40,159 |
| North Dakota | 48,132 | 88,001 | 0 | 0 | 1,761 | 113,714 | 44,594 | 296,202 |
| Ohio | 121,510 | 7,604 | 0 | 0 | 792 | 28,865 | 8,536 | 167,307 |
| Oklahoma | 9,631 | 55,781 | 227 | 945 | 932 | 52,854 | 44,304 | 164,674 |
| Oregon | 2,641 | 12,104 | 0 | 0 | 1,853 | 28,800 | 6,652 | 52,050 |
| Pennsylvania | 16,538 | 432 | 0 | 0 | 434 | 9,638 | 14,013 | 41,055 |
| Rhode Island | 5 | 0 | 0 | 0 | 4 | 206 | 103 | 318 |
| South Carolina | 10,165 | 2,937 | 0 | 671 | 5 | 12,995 | 7,009 | 33,782 |
| South Dakota | 104,102 | 28,629 | 0 | 0 | 5,614 | 75,900 | 30,790 | 245,035 |
| Tennessee | 13,236 | 2,652 | 177 | 496 | 52 | 25,807 | 4,918 | 47,338 |
| Texas | 128,230 | 40,614 | 106,755 | 11,397 | 38,284 | 174,099 | 143,499 | 642,878 |
| Utah | 1,622 | 1,839 | 0 | 0 | 4,759 | 10,510 | 5,777 | 24,507 |
| Vermont | 796 | 0 | 0 | 0 | 100 | 1,783 | 1,643 | 4,322 |
| Virginia | 9,645 | 1,261 | 0 | –36 | 466 | 6,526 | 7,531 | 25,393 |
| Washington | 9,709 | 33,311 | 0 | 0 | 507 | 55,912 | 16,488 | 115,927 |
| West Virginia | 1,470 | 29 | 0 | 0 | 245 | 1,635 | 1,857 | 5,236 |
| Wisconsin | 110,848 | 717 | 0 | 0 | 354 | 51,180 | 20,741 | 183,840 |
| Wyoming | 2,113 | 1,714 | 0 | 0 | 8,403 | 11,717 | 7,279 | 31,226 |
| **United States** | **$3,024,563** | **$588,605** | **$784,630** | **$29,920** | **$98,277** | **$1,891,588** | **$834,707** | **$7,252,270** |

(1) Includes both cash payments and payment-in-kind (PIK) for fiscal year. (2) Negatives indicate that the current year's Advanced Deficiency Payments were less than refunds from producers to government because advances paid in the previous year were too high. (3) Includes amount paid under agriculture and conservation programs (Conservation Reserve, Agriculture Conservation, Emergency Conservation, and Great Plains Program).

# U.S. Federal Food Assistance Programs, 1986-95[1]

**Source:** Food and Nutrition Service, U.S. Dept. of Agriculture

(in millions of dollars)

| Program | 1986 | 1987 | 1988 | 1989 | 1990 | 1991 | 1992 | 1993 | 1994 | 1995 |
|---|---|---|---|---|---|---|---|---|---|---|
| Food stamps[2] | $11,638 | $11,605 | $12,317 | $12,932 | $15,491 | $18,769 | $22,462 | $23,653 | $24,492 | $24,621 |
| Puerto Rico nutrition asst.[3] | 820 | 853 | 879 | 908 | 937 | 963 | 1,002 | 1,040 | 1,079 | 1,131 |
| Natl. school lunch[4] | 3,537 | 3,685 | 3,730 | 3,769 | 3,834 | 4,224 | 4,564 | 4,751 | 4,964 | 5,160 |
| School breakfast[5] | 406 | 447 | 482 | 513 | 596 | 685 | 787 | 869 | 959 | 1,048 |
| WIC[6] | 1,583 | 1,680 | 1,798 | 1,911 | 2,122 | 2,301 | 2,597 | 2,829 | 3,170 | 3,430 |
| Summer food service[4] | 115 | 129 | 133 | 146 | 164 | 182 | 204 | 220 | 230 | 237 |
| Child/adult care[4] | 496 | 548 | 628 | 697 | 813 | 945 | 1,104 | 1,223 | 1,354 | 1,464 |
| Special milk | 16 | 15 | 19 | 18 | 19 | 20 | 20 | 19 | 18 | 17 |
| Nutrition for the elderly[4] | 137 | 139 | 146 | 146 | 142 | 144 | 151 | 150 | 153 | 151 |
| Food distrib. to Indian reserv. | 60 | 63 | 62 | 65 | 66 | 65 | 62 | 62 | 65 | 65 |
| Commodity supp. food prog.[4,7] | 48 | 56 | 62 | 73 | 85 | 93 | 105 | 112 | 107 | 99 |
| Food dist.—charitable inst.[8] | 240 | 158 | 159 | 136 | 104 | 93 | 116 | 92 | 106 | 64 |
| Emergency food assistance | 895 | 895 | 645 | 276 | 257 | 256 | 236 | 238 | 218 | 89 |
| Soup kitchens/food banks | 0 | 0 | 0 | 34 | 77 | 45 | 36 | 35 | 48 | 46 |
| Other costs[9] | 60 | 62 | 58 | 68 | 71 | 78 | 92 | 107 | 120 | 117 |
| **Total[10]** | **$20,051** | **$20,335** | **$21,118** | **$21,692** | **$24,776** | **$28,863** | **$33,538** | **$35,400** | **$37,136** | **$37,739** |

(1) Data are for fiscal (not calendar) years. (2) Includes the federal share of state administrative expenses and other federal costs. (3) Puerto Rico participated in the Food Stamp Program from FY 1975 until July 1982, when it initiated a separate grant program. (4) Includes the value of commodities (entitlement, bonus, and cash in lieu). (5) Excludes startup costs. (6) Includes program studies and the WIC Farmers Market Nutrition Program. (7) Includes elderly feeding projects. (8) Includes summer camps. (9) Includes child nutrition state administration expenses, nutrition studies, nutrition education and training, Northern Marianas nutrition assistance grant, and commodity disaster relief. (10) Excludes food program administration costs.

# U.S. Farm Marketings by State, 1994-95

**Source:** Economic Research Service, U.S. Dept. of Agriculture

(in thousands of dollars)

| | 1995 Farm marketings | | | 1994 Farm marketings | | |
|---|---|---|---|---|---|---|
| State/Rank | Total | Crops | Livestock and products | Total | Crops | Livestock and products |
| Alabama (26) | $ 2,951,334 | $ 801,784 | $2,149,550 | $ 2,908,347 | $ 740,772 | $2,167,575 |
| Alaska (50) | 27,935 | 21,890 | 6,045 | 30,119 | 24,380 | 5,739 |
| Arizona (29) | 1,853,669 | 1,049,326 | 804,343 | 2,256,444 | 1,446,126 | 810,318 |
| Arkansas (13) | 5,394,516 | 2,249,765 | 3,144,751 | 5,065,456 | 2,042,233 | 3,023,223 |
| California (1) | 21,281,547 | 15,792,837 | 5,488,710 | 22,261,109 | 16,712,582 | 5,548,527 |
| Colorado (17) | 4,051,357 | 1,287,188 | 2,764,169 | 3,984,525 | 1,360,834 | 2,623,691 |
| Connecticut (41) | 477,791 | 224,242 | 253,549 | 484,490 | 227,679 | 256,811 |
| Delaware (40) | 657,594 | 152,222 | 505,372 | 675,613 | 159,124 | 516,489 |
| Florida (9) | 5,984,249 | 4,792,116 | 1,192,133 | 5,848,907 | 4,719,097 | 1,129,810 |
| Georgia (14) | 4,688,737 | 2,017,742 | 2,670,995 | 5,166,101 | 2,376,917 | 2,789,184 |
| Hawaii (42) | 507,609 | 430,788 | 76,821 | 483,468 | 411,656 | 71,812 |
| Idaho (22) | 2,955,215 | 1,756,147 | 1,199,068 | 3,166,248 | 1,945,204 | 1,221,044 |
| Illinois (5) | 7,945,732 | 5,896,508 | 2,049,224 | 7,887,034 | 6,176,908 | 1,710,126 |
| Indiana (14) | 4,664,044 | 2,930,321 | 1,733,723 | 4,981,458 | 3,240,106 | 1,741,352 |
| Iowa (3) | 9,999,410 | 4,769,337 | 5,230,073 | 10,958,874 | 5,891,122 | 5,067,752 |
| Kansas (6) | 7,626,389 | 2,868,415 | 4,757,974 | 7,521,311 | 2,828,527 | 4,692,784 |
| Kentucky (25) | 3,220,241 | 1,571,305 | 1,648,936 | 3,059,463 | 1,443,913 | 1,615,550 |
| Louisiana (32) | 2,028,702 | 1,329,095 | 699,607 | 2,024,862 | 1,395,025 | 629,837 |
| Maine (43) | 457,905 | 187,744 | 270,161 | 479,230 | 198,159 | 281,071 |
| Maryland (36) | 1,339,209 | 540,508 | 798,701 | 1,402,319 | 571,829 | 830,490 |
| Massachusetts (45) | 459,517 | 342,080 | 117,437 | 430,377 | 327,055 | 103,322 |
| Michigan (20) | 3,381,239 | 1,992,076 | 1,389,163 | 3,520,756 | 2,196,837 | 1,323,919 |
| Minnesota (7) | 6,407,645 | 2,959,643 | 3,448,002 | 7,001,667 | 3,550,943 | 3,450,724 |
| Mississippi (24) | 2,870,975 | 1,180,604 | 1,690,371 | 3,126,153 | 1,441,265 | 1,684,888 |
| Missouri (16) | 4,561,575 | 2,098,225 | 2,463,350 | 4,399,227 | 2,133,772 | 2,265,455 |
| Montana (33) | 1,884,628 | 1,028,968 | 855,660 | 1,845,168 | 1,047,254 | 797,914 |
| Nebraska (4) | 8,524,549 | 3,119,834 | 5,404,715 | 8,690,446 | 3,503,152 | 5,187,294 |
| Nevada (47) | 299,221 | 109,588 | 189,633 | 285,614 | 122,042 | 163,572 |
| New Hampshire (48) | 150,955 | 87,453 | 63,502 | 152,167 | 88,150 | 64,017 |
| New Jersey (38) | 769,991 | 589,332 | 180,659 | 773,151 | 572,673 | 200,478 |
| New Mexico (35) | 1,527,909 | 426,365 | 1,101,544 | 1,415,176 | 451,786 | 963,390 |
| New York (27) | 2,867,681 | 979,338 | 1,888,343 | 2,877,474 | 1,012,139 | 1,865,335 |
| North Carolina (8) | 6,439,341 | 3,110,371 | 3,328,970 | 6,986,814 | 3,251,476 | 3,735,338 |
| North Dakota (23) | 3,028,022 | 2,403,427 | 624,595 | 3,153,765 | 2,588,112 | 565,653 |
| Ohio (15) | 4,438,388 | 2,874,796 | 1,563,592 | 4,576,009 | 2,986,816 | 1,589,193 |
| Oklahoma (19) | 3,898,466 | 1,199,059 | 2,699,407 | 3,704,737 | 1,133,469 | 2,571,268 |
| Oregon (28) | 2,650,706 | 1,929,627 | 721,079 | 2,719,992 | 2,054,775 | 665,217 |
| Pennsylvania (18) | 3,769,178 | 1,164,194 | 2,604,984 | 3,738,250 | 1,186,204 | 2,552,046 |
| Rhode Island (49) | 80,422 | 68,335 | 12,087 | 80,059 | 70,051 | 10,008 |
| South Carolina (34) | 1,383,281 | 768,243 | 615,038 | 1,441,296 | 830,313 | 610,983 |
| South Dakota (21) | 3,335,563 | 1,633,924 | 1,701,639 | 3,383,637 | 1,707,340 | 1,676,297 |
| Tennessee (31) | 2,171,600 | 1,199,891 | 971,709 | 2,126,727 | 1,258,284 | 868,443 |
| Texas (2) | 12,929,651 | 4,817,398 | 8,112,253 | 13,287,680 | 4,833,844 | 8,453,836 |
| Utah (37) | 826,942 | 229,841 | 597,101 | 815,400 | 222,957 | 592,443 |
| Vermont (44) | 478,746 | 88,642 | 390,104 | 472,314 | 92,277 | 380,037 |
| Virginia (30) | 2,194,166 | 784,735 | 1,409,431 | 2,248,012 | 854,832 | 1,393,180 |
| Washington (12) | 4,768,986 | 3,143,459 | 1,625,527 | 5,157,957 | 3,563,581 | 1,594,376 |
| West Virginia (46) | 400,384 | 69,406 | 330,978 | 386,335 | 74,285 | 312,050 |
| Wisconsin (10) | 5,378,700 | 1,417,171 | 3,961,529 | 5,582,296 | 1,656,284 | 3,926,012 |
| Wyoming (39) | 783,407 | 160,315 | 623,092 | 725,987 | 182,069 | 543,918 |
| **United States** | **$180,775,019** | **$92,645,620** | **$88,129,399** | **$185,750,021** | **$98,906,230** | **$86,843,791** |

# Value of U.S. Agricultural Exports and Imports, 1975-95

**Source:** Economic Research Service, U.S. Dept. of Agriculture

(in billions of dollars, except percent)

| Year | Trade balance | Exports, domestic prods. | Percentage of all exports | Imports for consumption | Percentage of all imports |
|---|---|---|---|---|---|
| 1975 | $12.6 | $21.9 | 21 | $ 9.3 | 10 |
| 1976 | 12.0 | 23.0 | 20 | 11.0 | 9 |
| 1977 | 10.2 | 23.6 | 20 | 13.4 | 9 |
| 1978 | 14.6 | 29.4 | 21 | 14.8 | 9 |
| 1979 | 18.0 | 34.7 | 19 | 16.7 | 8 |
| 1980 | 23.9 | 41.2 | 19 | 17.4 | 7 |
| 1981 | 26.6 | 43.3 | 18 | 16.8 | 6 |
| 1982 | 21.2 | 36.6 | 17 | 15.4 | 6 |
| 1983 | 19.5 | 36.1 | 18 | 16.6 | 6 |
| 1984 | 18.5 | 37.8 | 17 | 19.3 | 6 |
| 1985 | 9.1 | 29.0 | 13 | 20.0 | 6 |
| 1986 | $ 4.8 | $26.2 | 13 | $21.5 | 6 |
| 1987 | 8.3 | 28.7 | 12 | 20.4 | 5 |
| 1988 | 16.1 | 37.1 | 12 | 21.0 | 5 |
| 1989 | 18.2 | 39.9 | 11 | 21.7 | 5 |
| 1990 | 16.6 | 39.4 | 10 | 22.8 | 5 |
| 1991 | 16.5 | 39.2 | 10 | 22.7 | 5 |
| 1992 | 18.3 | 42.9 | 10 | 24.6 | 5 |
| 1993 | 17.6 | 42.6 | 10 | 25.0 | 4 |
| 1994 | 18.9 | 45.7 | 10 | 26.8 | 4 |
| 1995 | 25.8 | 55.8 | 10 | 30.0 | 4 |

# Farm Business Real Estate Debt Outstanding, by Lender Groups,[1] 1960-94

**Source:** Economic Research Service, U.S.Dept. of Agriculture

(in thousands of dollars)

| | | Amounts held by principal lender groups | | | | |
|---|---|---|---|---|---|---|
| Dec. 31 | Total farm real estate debt[2] | Farm Credit System[2] | Farm Services Agency[3] | Life insurance companies[4] | All operating banks | Other[5] |
| 1960 | $11,309,593 | $2,222,301 | $623,895 | $2,651,587 | $1,355,733 | $4,456,068 |
| 1970 | 27,505,932 | 6,420,357 | 2,179,873 | 5,122,291 | 3,328,876 | 10,454,540 |
| 1980 | 89,692,429 | 33,224,684 | 7,435,059 | 11,997,922 | 7,765,058 | 29,269,705 |
| 1985 | 100,076,120 | 42,168,554 | 9,820,913 | 11,272,689 | 10,731,881 | 26,082,096 |
| 1986 | 90,407,602 | 35,592,540 | 9,713,096 | 10,377,063 | 11,942,258 | 22,782,645 |
| 1987 | 82,398,048 | 30,646,143 | 9,430,087 | 9,355,026 | 13,541,447 | 19,425,345 |
| 1988 | 77,832,498 | 28,445,452 | 8,979,749 | 9,039,395 | 14,433,688 | 16,934,218 |
| 1989 | 75,978,245 | 26,895,927 | 8,203,215 | 9,113,109 | 15,685,485 | 16,080,503 |
| 1990 | 74,731,876 | 25,924,490 | 7,639,490 | 9,703,958 | 16,288,128 | 15,175,805 |
| 1991 | 74,943,893 | 25,305,300 | 7,040,851 | 9,545,804 | 17,416,527 | 15,635,414 |
| 1992 | 75,421,255 | 25,407,547 | 6,394,446 | 8,765,021 | 18,756,852 | 16,097,400 |
| 1993 | 76,025,860 | 24,889,079 | 5,837,377 | 8,985,489 | 19,594,554 | 16,719,356 |
| 1994 | 77,641,681 | 24,582,844 | 5,462,679 | 9,022,832 | 21,070,317 | 17,503,009 |

(1) Figures revised as of 1996; exclude operator households. (2) Includes data for joint stock land banks and real estate loans by Agricultural Credit Assn. (3) Includes loans made directly by Farm Services Agency for farm ownership, soil and water loans to individuals, Native American tribe land acquisition, grazing associations, and half of economic emergency loans. Also includes loans for rural housing on farm tracts and labor housing. (4) American Council of Life Insurance. (5) Estimated by ERS, USDA. Includes Commodity Credit Corporation storage and drying facility loans.

# Grain, Hay, Potato, Cotton, Soybean, Tobacco Production, by State, 1995

**Source:** National Agricultural Statistics Service, U.S. Dept. of Agriculture

| 1995 State | Barley (1,000 bu) | Corn, grain (1,000 bu) | Cotton lint (1,000 b) | All hay (1,000 t) | Oats (1,000 bu) | Potatoes (1,000 cwt) | Soybeans (1,000 bu) | Tobacco (1,000 lb) | All wheat (1,000 bu) |
|---|---|---|---|---|---|---|---|---|---|
| Alabama | — | 16,500 | 460.0 | 1,512 | 805 | 1,539 | 5,400 | — | 2,880 |
| Alaska | — | — | — | — | — | — | — | — | — |
| Arizona | 1,890 | 3,740 | 864.0 | 1,392 | — | 1,755 | — | — | 10,354 |
| Arkansas | — | 9,775 | 1,460.0 | 2,011 | 1,530 | — | 86,700 | — | 47,000 |
| California | 14,000 | 24,000 | 2,515.0 | 9,000 | 2,550 | — | — | — | 32,725 |
| Colorado | 10,000 | 92,130 | — | 3,978 | 2,046 | 14,620 | — | — | 105,260 |
| Connecticut | — | NE | — | 142 | — | 26,404 | — | 3,347 | — |
| Delaware | 2,960 | 14,595 | — | 31 | — | — | 4,660 | — | 4,352 |
| Florida | — | 5,400 | 100.0 | 575 | — | 1,475 | 728 | 17,352 | 384 |
| Georgia | — | 31,500 | 1,970.0 | 1,500 | 1,750 | 9,003 | 8,370 | 84,000 | 11,400 |
| Hawaii | — | — | — | — | — | — | — | — | — |
| Idaho | 60,800 | 4,900 | — | 5,080 | 1,600 | 131,274 | — | — | 103,320 |
| Illinois | — | 1,130,000 | — | 3,598 | 5,360 | 1,485 | 373,450 | — | 68,110 |
| Indiana | — | 598,900 | — | 2,400 | 2,040 | 1,196 | 194,220 | 13,650 | 39,600 |
| Iowa | — | 1,402,200 | — | 5,665 | 14,625 | 232 | 398,180 | — | 1,225 |
| Kansas | 315 | 244,280 | 1.2 | 6,555 | 3,760 | — | 51,250 | — | 286,000 |
| Kentucky | 1,050 | 123,120 | — | 5,790 | — | — | 41,400 | 375,150 | 24,380 |
| Louisiana | — | 23,205 | 1,375.0 | 744 | — | — | 26,000 | — | 2,880 |
| Maine | — | NE | — | 419 | 1,440 | 17,160 | — | — | — |
| Maryland | 5,022 | 42,000 | — | 552 | 366 | 360 | 11,730 | 11,475 | 14,400 |
| Massachusetts | — | NE | — | 192 | — | 858 | — | 851 | — |
| Michigan | 1,150 | 249,550 | — | 5,025 | 5,130 | 16,500 | 59,600 | — | 37,200 |
| Minnesota | 29,000 | 731,850 | — | 6,943 | 18,000 | 20,790 | 232,000 | — | 71,849 |
| Mississippi | — | 26,125 | 1,845.0 | 1,668 | — | — | 37,800 | — | 6,270 |
| Missouri | — | 149,940 | 525.0 | 6,818 | 1,363 | 1,587 | 130,500 | 5,670 | 47,970 |
| Montana | 62,400 | 1,920 | — | 5,360 | 4,720 | 2,940 | — | — | 195,750 |
| Nebraska | 222 | 854,700 | — | 6,975 | 4,500 | 4,934 | 99,450 | — | 86,100 |
| Nevada | 320 | — | — | 1,505 | — | 2,774 | — | — | 850 |
| New Hampshire | — | NE | — | 137 | — | — | — | — | — |
| New Jersey | 325 | 7,254 | — | 285 | — | — | 3,036 | — | 1,824 |
| New Mexico | — | 11,680 | 100.0 | 1,515 | — | 702 | — | — | 3,300 |
| New York | — | 64,050 | — | 3,448 | 5,310 | 3,759 | — | — | 6,875 |
| North Carolina | 1,800 | 74,900 | 830.0 | 1,286 | 1,950 | 7,695 | 26,750 | 483,720 | 28,160 |
| North Dakota | 101,250 | 40,290 | — | 5,095 | 21,600 | 3,177 | 18,560 | — | 300,078 |
| Ohio | — | 375,100 | — | 4,035 | 6,900 | 25,410 | 153,140 | 17,347 | 73,810 |
| Oklahoma | 90 | 16,250 | 125.0 | 4,174 | 780 | 1,404 | 5,500 | — | 109,200 |
| Oregon | 7,220 | 3,360 | — | 3,300 | 3,395 | 23,760 | — | — | 63,678 |
| Pennsylvania | 5,175 | 94,080 | — | 4,409 | 9,440 | 4,080 | 9,450 | 15,685 | 10,175 |
| Rhode Island | — | NE | — | 14 | — | 239 | — | — | — |
| South Carolina | 210 | 24,115 | 390.0 | 720 | 1,575 | — | 12,720 | 105,000 | 8,960 |
| South Dakota | 6,080 | 193,550 | — | 9,050 | 11,500 | 988 | 75,000 | — | 90,736 |
| Tennessee | — | 63,720 | 730.0 | 3,920 | — | — | 34,560 | 104,344 | 15,980 |
| Texas | 322 | 216,600 | 4,551.0 | 8,136 | 5,040 | 2,570 | 6,000 | — | 75,600 |
| Utah | 8,370 | 2,000 | — | 2,644 | 630 | 1,224 | — | — | 8,950 |
| Vermont | — | NE | — | 559 | — | — | — | — | — |
| Virginia | 6,720 | 30,525 | 130.0 | 2,571 | — | 2,040 | 11,280 | 81,807 | 17,600 |
| Washington | 20,880 | 19,380 | — | 3,278 | 1,120 | 80,850 | — | — | 153,770 |
| West Virginia | — | 4,000 | — | 1,056 | 210 | — | — | 3,400 | 624 |
| Wisconsin | 3,456 | 347,700 | — | 6,820 | 18,700 | 27,135 | 34,400 | 6,200 | 8,070 |
| Wyoming | 8,075 | 4,992 | — | 2,904 | 2,112 | 390 | — | — | 7,890 |
| **United States** | **359,102** | **7,373,876** | **17,971.2** | **154,786** | **161,847** | **442,309** | **2,151,834** | **1,328,998** | **2,185,539** |

NE = Not estimated. bu = bushels, b=bales (480-lbs), t = tons, cwt =hundredweight.

# Production of Principal U.S. Crops, 1986-95

**Source:** National Agricultural Statistics Service, U.S. Dept. of Agriculture

| Year | Corn for grain (1,000 bu) | Oats (1,000 bu) | Barley (1,000 bu) | Sorghum for grain (1,000 bu) | All wheat (1,000 bu) | Rye (1,000 bu) | Flax-seed (1,000 bu) | Cotton lint (1,000 b) | Cotton-seed (1,000 t) |
|---|---|---|---|---|---|---|---|---|---|
| 1986 | 8,225,764 | 384,996 | 608,532 | 938,869 | 2,090,570 | 19,067 | 11,538 | 9,731.1 | 3,800.9 |
| 1987 | 7,131,300 | 373,713 | 521,499 | 730,809 | 2,107,685 | 19,526 | 7,444 | 14,760.9 | 5,769.2 |
| 1988 | 4,928,681 | 217,600 | 289,994 | 576,686 | 1,812,201 | 14,689 | 1,615 | 15,412.5 | 6,061.8 |
| 1989 | 7,525,493 | 373,587 | 404,203 | 615,420 | 2,036,618 | 13,647 | 1,215 | 12,196.6 | 4,677.4 |
| 1990 | 7,934,028 | 357,524 | 422,196 | 573,303 | 2,736,428 | 10,176 | 3,812 | 15,505.4 | 5,968.5 |
| 1991 | 7,475,480 | 243,451 | 464,326 | 584,860 | 1,981,139 | 9,761 | 6,200 | 17,614.3 | 6,925.5 |
| 1992 | 9,476,698 | 294,229 | 455,090 | 875,022 | 2,466,798 | 11,440 | 3,288 | 16,219.5 | 6,230.1 |
| 1993 | 6,336,470 | 206,770 | 398,041 | 534,172 | 2,396,440 | 10,340 | 3,480 | 16,134.6 | 6,343.2 |
| 1994 | 10,102,735 | 229,008 | 374,862 | 649,206 | 2,320,981 | 11,341 | 2,922 | 19,662.0 | 7,603.9 |
| 1995 | 7,373,876 | 161,847 | 359,102 | 460,373 | 2,185,539 | 9,928 | 2,211 | 17,971.2 | 7,373.7 |

| Year | Tobacco (1,000 lb) | All hay (1,000 t) | Beans, dry edible (1,000 cwt) | Peas, dry edible (1,000 cwt) | Peanuts (1,000 lb) | Soy-beans (1,000 bu) | Potatoes (1,000 cwt) | Sweet potatoes (1,000 cwt) |
|---|---|---|---|---|---|---|---|---|
| 1986 | 1,161,940 | 155,385 | 22,960 | 3,196 | 3,697,085 | 1,942,558 | 361,511 | 12,368 |
| 1987 | 1,188,868 | 147,319 | 26,031 | 3,385 | 3,616,010 | 1,938,087 | 385,774 | 11,611 |
| 1988 | 1,369,500 | 126,010 | 19,253 | 3,868 | 3,980,917 | 1,548,841 | 356,438 | 10,945 |
| 1989 | 1,367,188 | 145,512 | 23,729 | 3,883 | 3,989,995 | 1,923,666 | 370,444 | 11,358 |
| 1990 | 1,626,380 | 146,820 | 32,379 | 2,372 | 3,602,770 | 1,925,947 | 402,110 | 12,594 |
| 1991 | 1,664,372 | 153,325 | 33,765 | 3,715 | 4,926,570 | 1,986,539 | 417,622 | 11,203 |
| 1992 | 1,721,671 | 146,903 | 22,615 | 2,535 | 4,284,416 | 2,190,354 | 425,367 | 12,005 |
| 1993 | 1,613,319 | 146,799 | 21,913 | 3,292 | 3,392,415 | 1,870,958 | 428,693 | 11,053 |
| 1994 | 1,582,896 | 150,060 | 29,028 | 2,255 | 4,247,455 | 2,516,694 | 467,924 | 13,395 |
| 1995 | 1,328,998 | 154,786 | 31,032 | 3,749 | 3,477,760 | 2,151,834 | 442,309 | 12,883 |

| Year | Rice (1,000 cwt) | Sugar-cane (1,000 t) | Sugar beets (1,000 t) | Pecans (1,000 t) | Almonds (1,000 t) | Wal-nuts (1,000 t) | Hazel-nuts[1] (1,000 t) | Oranges[2] (1,000 bx) | Grape-fruit[2] (1,000 bx) |
|---|---|---|---|---|---|---|---|---|---|
| 1986 | 133,356 | 30,311 | 25,150 | 136.4 | 201.3 | 180.0 | 15.1 | 175,440 | 57,870 |
| 1987 | 129,603 | 29,218 | 28,072 | 131.1 | 519.0 | 247.0 | 21.8 | 181,175 | 63,775 |
| 1988 | 159,897 | 29,904 | 24,810 | 154.1 | 451.9 | 209.0 | 16.5 | 200,250 | 68,700 |
| 1989 | 154,487 | 29,426 | 25,131 | 125.3 | 394.7 | 229.0 | 13.0 | 209,050 | 69,500 |
| 1990 | 156,088 | 28,136 | 27,513 | 102.5 | 519.7 | 227.0 | 21.7 | 184,415 | 49,300 |
| 1991 | 157,457 | 30,252 | 28,203 | 149.5 | 385.8 | 259.0 | 25.5 | 178,950 | 55,500 |
| 1992 | 179,658 | 30,363 | 29,143 | 83.0 | 454.4 | 203.0 | 27.7 | 209,610 | 55,265 |
| 1993 | 156,110 | 31,101 | 26,249 | 182.5 | 401.0 | 260.0 | 41.0 | 255,760 | 68,375 |
| 1994 | 197,779 | 30,929 | 31,853 | 99.5 | 584.3 | 232.0 | 21.1 | 240,450 | 65,100 |
| 1995 | 173,871 | 30,944 | 27,954 | 134.0 | 304.3 | 234.0 | 39.0 | 263,605 | 71,050 |

NA=Not available. (1) Formerly called filberts. (2) Crop year ending in year cited.

# Principal U.S. Crops: Area Planted and Harvested, 1993-95

**Source:** National Agricultural Statistics Service, U.S. Dept. of Agriculture

(in thousand acres)

| State | Area planted[1] 1993 | 1994 | 1995 | Area harvested[1] 1993 | 1994 | 1995 | State | Area planted[1] 1993 | 1994 | 1995 | Area harvested[1] 1993 | 1994 | 1995 |
|---|---|---|---|---|---|---|---|---|---|---|---|---|---|
| AL | 2,256 | 2,289 | 2,204 | 2,116 | 2,170 | 2,093 | NE | 18,532 | 19,043 | 18,280 | 17,718 | 18,619 | 17,769 |
| AZ | 710 | 750 | 795 | 695 | 744 | 787 | NV | 530 | 497 | 516 | 527 | 491 | 512 |
| AR | 8,755 | 8,360 | 8,435 | 8,305 | 8,160 | 8,188 | NH | 109 | 98 | 85 | 107 | 96 | 83 |
| CA | 4,791 | 5,119 | 5,351 | 4,402 | 4,674 | 4,791 | NJ | 456 | 458 | 452 | 413 | 410 | 413 |
| CO | 6,052 | 6,103 | 6,104 | 5,661 | 5,632 | 5,748 | NM | 1,276 | 1,252 | 1,282 | 986 | 985 | 869 |
| CT | 117 | 130 | 112 | 111 | 123 | 107 | NY | 3,187 | 3,119 | 3,045 | 3,101 | 3,071 | 2,981 |
| DE | 512 | 510 | 507 | 499 | 494 | 499 | NC | 4,482 | 4,731 | 4,644 | 4,168 | 4,489 | 4,341 |
| FL | 1,133 | 1,090 | 1,079 | 1,077 | 1,048 | 1,036 | ND | 21,982 | 21,714 | 20,706 | 19,832 | 20,719 | 20,114 |
| GA | 4,068 | 4,276 | 4,237 | 3,551 | 3,874 | 3,862 | OH | 10,231 | 10,408 | 10,025 | 10,009 | 10,277 | 9,884 |
| HI | 70 | 67 | 50 | 70 | 67 | 50 | OK | 10,690 | 10,826 | 10,631 | 8,780 | 8,788 | 8,628 |
| ID | 4,506 | 4,402 | 4,483 | 4,322 | 4,244 | 4,306 | OR | 2,317 | 2,318 | 2,436 | 2,240 | 2,240 | 2,292 |
| IL | 23,533 | 23,801 | 23,221 | 21,241 | 23,393 | 22,526 | PA | 4,111 | 4,154 | 2,146 | 4,035 | 4,063 | 4,050 |
| IN | 12,038 | 12,237 | 11,942 | 11,768 | 12,071 | 11,785 | RI | 13 | 12 | 11 | 13 | 12 | 11 |
| IA | 23,662 | 24,207 | 23,502 | 22,001 | 23,967 | 22,872 | SC | 1,837 | 2,042 | 1,973 | 1,602 | 1,926 | 1,871 |
| KS | 21,899 | 22,540 | 22,428 | 20,485 | 21,724 | 21,363 | SD | 15,231 | 16,391 | 14,334 | 14,073 | 15,714 | 13,947 |
| KY | 5,600 | 5,558 | 5,716 | 5,375 | 5,353 | 5,461 | TN | 4,690 | 4,658 | 4,897 | 4,458 | 4,396 | 4,535 |
| LA | 3,947 | 3,896 | 3,857 | 3,811 | 3,810 | 3,786 | TX | 22,012 | 21,817 | 22,600 | 18,108 | 17,529 | 17,870 |
| ME | 379 | 349 | 364 | 364 | 339 | 355 | UT | 1,083 | 1,114 | 1,099 | 1,032 | 1,050 | 1,042 |
| MD | 1,627 | 1,569 | 1,548 | 1,569 | 1,506 | 1,463 | VT | 413 | 418 | 387 | 404 | 409 | 379 |
| MA | 138 | 141 | 134 | 133 | 135 | 131 | VA | 2,854 | 2,906 | 2,910 | 2,682 | 2,749 | 2,749 |
| MI | 6,726 | 7,013 | 6,790 | 6,554 | 6,815 | 6,647 | WA | 4,378 | 4,057 | 4,130 | 4,227 | 3,922 | 3,997 |
| MN | 19,277 | 20,077 | 19,577 | 16,940 | 19,534 | 18,972 | WV | 630 | 646 | 650 | 621 | 636 | 642 |
| MS | 4,841 | 4,881 | 4,850 | 4,709 | 4,813 | 4,739 | WI | 8,020 | 8,438 | 8,195 | 7,511 | 8,074 | 7,793 |
| MO | 12,749 | 12,674 | 12,055 | 11,483 | 12,466 | 11,687 | WY | 1,890 | 1,713 | 1,898 | 1,806 | 1,637 | 1,835 |
| MT | 9,378 | 9,357 | 9,697 | 8,816 | 8,988 | 9,245 | **U.S.[2]** | **319,553** | **324,256** | **318,458** | **295,529** | **308,474** | **301,186** |

(1) Crops included in area planted are corn, sorghum, oats, barley, winter wheat, rye, durum wheat, other spring wheat, rice, soybeans, peanuts, sunflower, cotton, dry edible beans, potatoes, and sugar beets. Harvested acreage is used for all hay, tobacco, and sugarcane in computing total area planted. Includes double-cropped acres and unharvested small grains planted as cover crops. (2) State figures do not add to U.S. totals because of sunflower and sugar-beet unallocated acreage.

# Average Prices Received by U.S. Farmers, 1940-94

**Source:** Natl. Agricultural Statistics Service, U.S. Dept. of Agriculture

Figures below represent dollars per 100 lb for hogs, beef cattle, veal calves, sheep, lamb, and milk (wholesale); dollars per head for milk cows; cents per lb for chickens, broilers, turkeys, and wool; cents per dozen for eggs; weighted calendar year prices for livestock and livestock products other than wool. For 1943-63, wool prices are weighted on marketing year basis. The marketing year was changed in 1964 from a calendar year to a Dec.-Nov. basis for hogs, chickens, broilers, and eggs.

| Year | Hogs | Cattle (beef) | Calves (veal) | Sheep | Lambs | Milk cows | Milk | Chickens (excl. broilers) | Broilers | Turkeys | Eggs | Wool |
|---|---|---|---|---|---|---|---|---|---|---|---|---|
| 1940 | 5.39 | 7.56 | 8.83 | 3.95 | 8.10 | 61 | 1.82 | 13.0 | 17.3 | 15.2 | 18.0 | 28.4 |
| 1950 | 18.00 | 23.30 | 26.30 | 11.60 | 25.10 | 198 | 3.89 | 22.2 | 27.4 | 32.8 | 36.3 | 62.1 |
| 1960 | 15.30 | 20.40 | 22.90 | 5.61 | 17.90 | 223 | 4.21 | 12.2 | 16.9 | 25.4 | 36.1 | 42.0 |
| 1970 | 22.70 | 27.10 | 34.50 | 7.51 | 26.40 | 332 | 5.71 | 9.1 | 13.6 | 22.6 | 39.1 | 35.4 |
| 1975 | 46.10 | 32.20 | 27.20 | 11.30 | 42.10 | 412 | 8.75 | 9.9 | 26.3 | 34.8 | 54.5 | 44.8 |
| 1979 | 41.80 | 66.10 | 88.80 | 26.30 | 66.70 | 1,040 | 12.00 | 14.4 | 25.9 | 41.3 | 58.3 | 86.3 |
| 1980 | 38.00 | 62.40 | 76.80 | 21.30 | 63.60 | 1,190 | 13.05 | 11.0 | 27.7 | 41.3 | 56.3 | 88.1 |
| 1984 | 47.10 | 57.30 | 59.90 | 16.40 | 60.10 | 895 | 13.46 | 15.9 | 33.7 | 48.9 | 72.3 | 79.5 |
| 1985 | 44.00 | 53.70 | 62.10 | 23.90 | 67.70 | 860 | 12.76 | 14.8 | 30.1 | 49.1 | 57.1 | 63.3 |
| 1986 | 49.30 | 52.60 | 61.10 | 25.60 | 69.00 | 820 | 12.51 | 12.5 | 34.5 | 47.1 | 61.6 | 66.8 |
| 1987 | 51.20 | 61.10 | 78.50 | 29.50 | 77.60 | 920 | 12.54 | 11.0 | 28.7 | 34.8 | 54.9 | 91.7 |
| 1988 | 42.30 | 66.60 | 89.20 | 25.60 | 69.10 | 990 | 12.26 | 9.2 | 33.1 | 38.6 | 52.8 | 138.0 |
| 1989 | 42.50 | 69.50 | 90.80 | 24.40 | 66.10 | 1,030 | 13.56 | 14.9 | 36.6 | 40.9 | 68.9 | 124.0 |
| 1990 | 53.70 | 74.60 | 95.60 | 23.20 | 55.50 | 1,160 | 13.74 | 9.3 | 32.6 | 39.4 | 70.9 | 80.0 |
| 1991 | 49.10 | 72.70 | 98.00 | 19.70 | 52.20 | 1,100 | 12.27 | 7.1 | 30.8 | 38.4 | 67.8 | 55.0 |
| 1992 | 41.60 | 71.30 | 89.00 | 25.80 | 59.50 | 1,130 | 13.15 | 8.6 | 31.8 | 37.7 | 57.6 | 74.0 |
| 1993 | 45.20 | 72.60 | 91.20 | 28.60 | 64.40 | 1,160 | 12.84 | 10.0 | 34.0 | 39.0 | 63.4 | 51.0 |
| 1994 | 39.90 | 66.70 | 87.20 | 30.90 | 65.60 | 1,170 | 13.01 | 7.6 | 35.0 | 40.4 | 61.4 | 78.0 |
| 1995 | 40.50 | 61.80 | 73.10 | 28.00 | 78.20 | 1,130 | 12.78 | 6.4 | 34.4 | 41.6 | 64.0 | 104.0 |

Figures below represent cents per lb for cotton, apples, and peanuts; dollars per bushel for oats, wheat, corn, barley, and soybeans; dollars per 100 lb for rice, sorghum, and potatoes; dollars per ton for cottonseed and baled hay; weighted crop year prices.

Crop years are as follows: apples, June-May; wheat, oats, barley, hay, and potatoes, July-June; cotton, rice, peanuts, and cottonseed, Aug.-July; soybeans, Sept.-Aug.; and corn and sorghum grain, Oct.-Sept.

| Year | Corn | Wheat | Upland cotton* | Oats | Barley | Rice | Soy-beans | Sor-ghum | Pea-nuts | Cotton-seed | Hay | Pota-toes | Apples |
|---|---|---|---|---|---|---|---|---|---|---|---|---|---|
| 1940 | 0.62 | 0.67 | 9.8 | 0.30 | 0.39 | 1.80 | 0.89 | 0.87 | 3.7 | 21.70 | 9.78 | 0.85 | NA |
| 1950 | 1.52 | 2.00 | 39.9 | 0.79 | 1.19 | 5.09 | 2.47 | 1.88 | 10.9 | 86.60 | 21.10 | 1.50 | NA |
| 1960 | 1.00 | 1.74 | 30.1 | 0.60 | 0.84 | 4.55 | 2.13 | 1.49 | 10.0 | 42.50 | 21.70 | 2.00 | 2.7 |
| 1970 | 1.33 | 1.33 | 21.9 | 0.62 | 0.97 | 5.17 | 2.85 | 2.04 | 12.8 | 56.40 | 26.10 | 2.21 | 6.5 |
| 1975 | 2.54 | 3.55 | 51.1 | 1.45 | 2.42 | 8.35 | 4.92 | 4.21 | 19.0 | 97.00 | 52.10 | 4.48 | 8.8 |
| 1979 | 2.52 | 3.78 | 62.3 | 1.36 | 2.29 | 10.50 | 6.28 | 4.18 | 20.6 | 121.00 | 59.50 | 3.43 | 15.4 |
| 1980 | 3.11 | 3.91 | 74.4 | 1.79 | 2.86 | 12.80 | 7.57 | 5.25 | 25.1 | 129.00 | 71.00 | 6.55 | 12.1 |
| 1984 | 2.63 | 3.39 | 58.7 | 1.67 | 2.29 | 8.04 | 5.84 | 4.15 | 27.9 | 99.50 | 72.70 | 5.69 | 15.5 |
| 1985 | 2.23 | 3.08 | 56.8 | 1.23 | 1.98 | 6.53 | 5.05 | 3.45 | 24.4 | 66.00 | 67.60 | 3.92 | 17.3 |
| 1986 | 1.50 | 2.42 | 51.5 | 1.21 | 1.61 | 3.75 | 4.78 | 2.45 | 29.2 | 80.00 | 59.70 | 5.03 | 19.1 |
| 1987 | 1.94 | 2.57 | 63.7 | 1.56 | 1.81 | 7.27 | 5.88 | 3.04 | 28.0 | 82.50 | 65.00 | 4.38 | 12.7 |
| 1988 | 2.54 | 3.72 | 55.6 | 2.61 | 2.80 | 6.83 | 7.42 | 4.05 | 28.0 | 118.00 | 85.20 | 6.02 | 17.4 |
| 1989 | 2.36 | 3.72 | 63.6 | 1.49 | 2.42 | 7.35 | 5.69 | 3.75 | 28.0 | 105.00 | 85.40 | 7.36 | 13.9 |
| 1990 | 2.28 | 2.61 | 67.1 | 1.14 | 2.14 | 6.68 | 5.74 | 3.79 | 34.7 | 121.00 | 80.60 | 6.08 | 20.9 |
| 1991 | 2.37 | 3.00 | 56.8 | 1.21 | 2.10 | 7.58 | 5.58 | 4.01 | 28.3 | 71.00 | 71.20 | 4.96 | 25.1 |
| 1992 | 2.07 | 3.24 | 53.7 | 1.32 | 2.04 | 5.89 | 5.56 | 3.38 | 30.0 | 97.50 | 74.30 | 5.52 | 19.5 |
| 1993 | 2.50 | 3.26 | 58.1 | 1.36 | 1.99 | 7.98 | 6.40 | 4.13 | 30.4 | 113.00 | 84.70 | 6.18 | 18.4 |
| 1994 | 2.26 | 3.45 | 72.0 | 1.22 | 2.03 | 6.78 | 5.48 | 3.80 | 28.9 | 101.00 | 86.70 | 5.58 | 18.6 |
| 1995 | 3.20 | 4.55 | 75.9 | 1.68 | 2.89 | 8.95 | 6.75 | 5.70 | 29.3 | 107.00 | 82.10 | 6.35 | 23.8 |

*Beginning in 1964, 480-lb net weight bales. NA = Not available.

# Grain Storage Capacity at Principal U.S. Grain Centers, Aug. 1996

**Source:** Chicago Board of Trade Market Information Dept.

(in bushels)

| | Capacity |
|---|---|
| **Atlantic Coast** | 12,800,000 |
| **Great Lakes** | |
| Toledo, OH | 63,100,000 |
| Duluth, MN | 57,600,000 |
| Chicago, IL | 52,400,000 |
| Buffalo, NY | 15,200,000 |
| Milwaukee, WI | NA |
| **River Points** | |
| Kansas City, MO | 95,200,000 |
| Minneapolis, MN | 78,900,000 |
| St. Joseph, MO | 22,300,000 |
| Atchison, KS | 20,100,000 |
| St. Louis, MO | 10,300,000 |
| Omaha-Council Bluffs, NE | 8,400,000 |
| Sioux City, IA | 7,500,000 |

| | Capacity |
|---|---|
| **Southwest** | |
| Texas High Plains | 72,900,000 |
| Fort Worth, TX | 68,000,000 |
| Enid, OK | NA |
| **Gulf Points** | |
| South Mississippi Region | 46,600,000 |
| Texas Gulf | 46,700,000 |
| **Plains** | |
| Topeka, KS | 53,300,000 |
| Salina, KS | 50,600,000 |
| Wichita, KS | 34,300,000 |
| Lincoln, NE | 33,700,000 |
| Hutchinson, KS | 29,600,000 |
| Hastings-Grand Island, NE | 42,400,000 |
| **Pacific NW** | |
| Puget Sound (incl. Portland) | 32,100,000 |
| California Ports | NA |

NA= Not available.

**Atlantic Coast** — Albany, NY; Philadelphia, PA; Baltimore, MD; Norfolk, VA. **Gulf Points, South Mississippi Region** — New Orleans, Baton Rouge, Ama, Belle Chasse, LA; Mobile, AL. **Texas Gulf** — Houston, Galveston, Beaumont, Port Arthur, Corpus Christi, Brownsville, TX. **Pacific NW** — Seattle, Tacoma, WA; Portland, OR; Columbia River. **Texas High Plains** — Amarillo, Lubbock, Hereford, Plainview, TX.

# World Wheat, Rice, and Corn Production, 1995

**Source:** UN Food and Agriculture Organization

(in thousands of metric tons)

| Country | Wheat | Rice | Corn | Country | Wheat | Rice | Corn |
|---|---|---|---|---|---|---|---|
| Afghanistan | 2,170F | 300F | 530F | Laos | — | 1,409 | 82F |
| Argentina | 8,656 | 926 | 11,396 | Madagascar | 14* | 2,596* | 169* |
| Australia | 16,623 | 1,137 | 259 | Malaysia | — | 2,126 | 43* |
| Austria | 1,301 | — | 1,474 | Mexico | 3,809 | 454 | 16,187 |
| Bangladesh | 1,200* | 24,659* | 3F | Morocco | 1,090 | 35* | 50 |
| Belgium-Lux | 1,536 | — | 230* | Myanmar | 145 | 20,109 | 272 |
| Brazil | 1,516 | 11,236 | 36,276 | Nepal | 942 | 2,906 | 1,302 |
| Bulgaria | 3,523* | 6* | 1,200 | Netherlands | 1,213 | — | 85F |
| Cambodia | — | 1,817F | 50F | New Zealand | 250 | — | 145 |
| Canada | 25,432 | — | 7,251 | Nigeria | 36 | 2,548 | 1,240 |
| Chile | 1,384 | 136 | 984 | Pakistan | 17,002 | 5,714 | 1,275* |
| China | 102,207 | 185,226 | 112,331 | Panama | — | 200F | 120F |
| Colombia | 86* | 1,749* | 1,084* | Peru | 125 | 1,142 | 715 |
| Croatia | 1,008 | — | 1,600F | Philippines | — | 11,002 | 4,161 |
| Cuba | — | 95F | 85F | Poland | 8,668 | — | 239 |
| Czech Rep. | 3,823 | — | 113 | Portugal | 259 | 119 | 732 |
| Denmark | 4,420 | — | — | Romania | 7,667 | 24 | 9,923 |
| Ecuador | 20 | 1,291 | 688* | Russia | 30,118 | 462 | 1,739 |
| Egypt | 5,722 | 4,822F | 5,500* | Slovakia | 1,938 | — | 597 |
| Ethiopia | 1,571F | — | 2,189F | South Africa | 2,125 | 3F | 4,670 |
| Finland | 380 | — | — | Spain | 2,958 | 327 | 2,560 |
| France | 30,878 | 126 | 12,784 | Sri Lanka | — | 2,684F | 32F |
| Germany | 17,816 | — | 2,133 | Sweden | 1,554 | — | — |
| Greece | 2,000* | 202* | 1,912* | Switzerland | 623 | — | 243 |
| Hungary | 4,600 | 20F | 4,597 | Syria | 4,193 | 100F | 215* |
| India | 63,007 | 122,372* | 9,800* | Thailand | 7F | 21,130 | 3,965 |
| Indonesia | — | 49,860 | 8,223 | Turkey | 18,015 | 230 | 1,900 |
| Iran | 11,200F | 2,300F | 700* | Turkmenistan | 800* | 90* | 149* |
| Iraq | 1,320* | 403* | 127* | Ukraine | 16,273 | 80 | 3,392 |
| Ireland | 588 | — | — | United Kingdom | 14,400 | — | — |
| Israel | 242 | — | 3 | United States | 59,494 | 7,888 | 187,300 |
| Italy | 7,995 | 1,284 | 8,446 | Uruguay | 410* | 631 | 109 |
| Japan | 580* | 12,625* | 420F | Uzbekistan | 1.700* | 550* | 240* |
| Kazakstan | 7,029 | 238 | 179 | Venezuela | 300F | 643* | 1,100* |
| Kenya | 330* | 60F | 2,750* | Vietnam | — | 24,000 | 1,200 |
| Korea, North | 125* | 2,580 | 2,350 | Yugoslavia | 3,002* | — | 5,000* |
| Korea, South | 2F | 6,519* | 90* | **World, total** | **541,120** | **550,193** | **514,507** |

**Note:** * Unofficial figure. F=Food and Agriculture Organization (FAO) estimate. Where production is small or nonexistent, — is indicated. Because not all countries are reported on this table, country totals do not add to world totals.

# Wheat, Rice, and Corn—Exports and Imports of 10 Leading Countries

**Source:** UN Food and Agriculture Organization

(in thousands of metric tons)

| Leading exporters | Exports[1] | | | Leading importers | Imports[1] | | |
|---|---|---|---|---|---|---|---|
| | | **Wheat** | | | | **Wheat** | |
| | **1992** | **1993** | **1994** | | **1992** | **1993** | **1994** |
| U.S. | 33,877 | 35,666 | 30,571 | China | 11,475 | 7,332 | 8,079 |
| Canada | 23,645 | 18,210 | 21,378 | Egypt | 5,300 | 4,080 | 6,597 |
| Australia | 8,097 | 9,487 | 12,730 | Japan | 5,979 | 5,814 | 6,352 |
| France | 17,355 | 18,259 | 12,670 | Brazil | 4,404 | 5,615 | 6,123 |
| Germany | 4,764 | 3,812 | 5,377 | South Korea | 3,546 | 4,939 | 6,057 |
| Argentina | 6,072 | 5,777 | 5,172 | Italy | 6,314 | 5,023 | 4,880 |
| United Kingdom | 3,975 | 3,898 | 3,493 | Iran | 2,453 | 2,450 | 3,960 |
| Turkey | 3,805 | 649 | 980 | Algeria | 2,329 | 2,588 | 3,800 |
| Saudi Arabia | 1,181 | 1,569 | 895 | Indonesia | 2,456 | 2,526 | 3,297 |
| Greece | 957 | 699 | 826 | U.S. | 1,475 | 1,812 | 2,521 |
| | | **Rice** | | | | **Rice** | |
| | **1992** | **1993** | **1994** | | **1992** | **1993** | **1994** |
| Thailand | 5,151 | 4,989 | 4,859 | Japan | 18 | 108 | 2,536 |
| U.S. | 2,164 | 2,680 | 2,822 | Brazil | 584 | 701 | 987 |
| Vietnam | 1,946 | 1,765 | 1,970 | Indonesia | 610 | 24 | 630 |
| China | 1,034 | 1,507 | 1,630 | China | 107 | 100 | 517 |
| Pakistan | 1,512 | 1,032 | 984 | Iran | 944 | 1,159 | 475 |
| India | 580 | 768 | 891 | Saudi Arabia | 490 | 577 | 434 |
| Myanmar | 205 | 209 | 643 | South Africa | 362 | 385 | 431 |
| Italy | 739 | 574 | 619 | Hong Kong | 400 | 373 | 358 |
| Australia | 519 | 482 | 585 | Nigeria | 350 | 350 | 350 |
| Uruguay | 328 | 505 | 408 | United Arab Em | 362 | 370 | 350 |
| | | **Corn** | | | | **Corn** | |
| | **1992** | **1993** | **1994** | | **1992** | **1993** | **1994** |
| U.S. | 43,236 | 40,365 | 35,877 | Japan | 16,382 | 16,863 | 15,930 |
| China | 10,340 | 11,098 | 8,740 | South Korea | 6,612 | 6,207 | 5,749 |
| France | 7,042 | 7,758 | 8,013 | China | 5,355 | 5,466 | 5,601 |
| Argentina | 6,092 | 4,871 | 4,154 | Mexico | 1,306 | 211 | 2,747 |
| South Africa | 524 | 216 | 4,000 | Spain | 1,790 | 2,401 | 2,339 |
| Belgium-Lux | 98 | 414 | 488 | Netherlands | 1,911 | 1,136 | 2,171 |
| Canada | 399 | 357 | 381 | Egypt | 1,444 | 2,148 | 2,021 |
| Germany | 254 | 219 | 308 | Malaysia | 1,816 | 2,058 | 1,969 |
| Greece | 653 | 141 | 246 | United Kingdom | 1,690 | 1,508 | 1,602 |
| Netherlands | 14 | 213 | 198 | Belgium-Lux | 947 | 1,284 | 1,557 |

(1) By marketing years.

## World Commercial Catch of Fish, Crustaceans, and Mollusks,[1] by Major Fishing Areas, 1989-94

**Source:** U.S. Dept. of Commerce, Natl. Oceanic and Atmospheric Admin., Natl. Marine Fisheries Service

(in thousands of metric tons; live weight)

| Area | 1989 | 1990 | 1991 | 1992 | 1993 | 1994 |
|---|---|---|---|---|---|---|
| **Marine** | | | | | | |
| Pacific Ocean | 54,678 | 52,939 | 52,011 | 51,782 | 53.569 | 59,355 |
| Atlantic Ocean | 25,314 | 23,552 | 23,760 | 24,204 | 23,391 | 23,545 |
| Indian Ocean | 6,198 | 6,199 | 6,689 | 7,089 | 7,289 | 7,512 |
| **Total** | **86,190** | **82,690** | **82,460** | **83,075** | **84,249** | **90,412** |
| **Inland Waters** | | | | | | |
| N. America | 546 | 552 | 548 | 600 | 584 | 562 |
| S. America | 340 | 335 | 331 | 363 | 387 | 399 |
| Europe | 520 | 511 | 484 | 494 | 487 | 501 |
| Former USSR | 1,030 | 988 | 824 | 700 | 595 | 524 |
| Asia | 9,658 | 10,402 | 10,920 | 11,756 | 13,301 | 15,278 |
| Africa | 1,807 | 1,930 | 1,812 | 1,772 | 1,792 | 1,881 |
| Oceania | 24 | 24 | 23 | 25 | 23 | 28 |
| **Total** | **13,925** | **14,742** | **14,942** | **15,710** | **17,169** | **19,173** |
| **Grand total** | **100,115** | **97,432** | **97,402** | **98,785** | **101,418** | **109,585** |

(1) Does not include marine mammals and aquatic plants.

## World Commercial Catch of Fish, Crustaceans, and Mollusks,[1] by Country, 1989-94

**Source:** U.S. Dept. of Commerce, Natl. Oceanic and Atmospheric Admin., Natl. Marine Fisheries Service

(in thousands of metric tons; live weight)

| Country | 1989 | 1990 | 1991 | 1992 | 1993 | 1994 |
|---|---|---|---|---|---|---|
| China | 11,220 | 12,095 | 13,135 | 15,007 | 17,568 | 20,719 |
| Peru | 6,854 | 6,875 | 6,949 | 6,871 | 8,451 | 11,587 |
| Japan | 11,173 | 10,354 | 9,301 | 8,502 | 8,128 | 7,363 |
| Chile | 6,454 | 5,195 | 6,003 | 6,502 | 6,038 | 7,841 |
| United States[2,3] | 5,775 | 5,868 | 5,486 | 5,588 | 5,939 | 5,941 |
| Russia | NA | NA | 7,047 | 5,611 | 4,461 | 3,781 |
| India | 3,640 | 3,794 | 4,044 | 4,232 | 4,324 | 4,540 |
| Indonesia | 2,948 | 3,044 | 3,252 | 3,442 | 3,638 | 3,954 |
| Thailand | 2,700 | 2,786 | 2,968 | 3,240 | 3,348 | 3,432 |
| South Korea | 2,841 | 2,843 | 2,521 | 2,696 | 2,649 | 2,700 |

(1) Does not include marine mammals and aquatic plants. (2) Includes weight of clam, oyster, scallop, and other mollusk shells. (3) Quantities caught by recreational anglers in the U.S. are excluded. NA = Not available.

## U.S. Commercial Landings of Fish and Shellfish, 1985-95[1]

**Source:** U.S. Dept. of Commerce, Natl. Oceanic and Atmospheric Admin., Natl. Marine Fisheries Service

| Year | Landings for human food | | Landings for industrial purposes[2] | | Total | |
|---|---|---|---|---|---|---|
| | mil lb | mil dollars | mil lb | mil dollars | mil lb | mil dollars |
| 1985 | 3,294 | $2,198 | 2,964 | $128 | 6,258 | $2,326 |
| 1986 | 3,393 | 2,641 | 2,638 | 122 | 6,031 | 2,763 |
| 1987 | 3,946 | 2,979 | 2,950 | 136 | 6,896 | 3,115 |
| 1988 | 4,588 | 3,362 | 2,604 | 158 | 7,192 | 3,520 |
| 1989 | 6,204 | 3,111 | 2,259 | 127 | 8,463 | 3,238 |
| 1990 | 7,041 | 3,366 | 2,363 | 156 | 9,404 | 3,522 |
| 1991 | 7,031 | 3,169 | 2,453 | 139 | 9,484 | 3,308 |
| 1992 | 7,618 | 3,531 | 2,019 | 147 | 9,637 | 3,678 |
| 1993 | 8,214 | 3,317 | 2,253 | 154 | 10,467 | 3,471 |
| 1994 | 7,936 | 3,751 | 2,525 | 95 | 10,461 | 3,846 |
| 1995 | 7,783 | 3,625 | 2,121 | 145 | 9,904 | 3,770 |

**Note:** Data do not include landings outside the 50 states or products of aquaculture, except oysters and clams.

(1) Statistics on landings are shown in round weight for all items except univalve and bivalve mollusks such as clams, oysters, and scallops, which are shown in weight of meats (excluding the shell). All data are preliminary. (2) Processed into meal, oil, solubles, and shell products or used as bait or animal food.

## U.S. Domestic Landings, by Regions, 1994-95[1]

**Source:** U.S. Dept. of Commerce, Natl. Oceanic and Atmospheric Admin., Natl. Marine Fisheries Service

| Region | 1994 | | 1995 | |
|---|---|---|---|---|
| | 1,000 lb | 1,000 dollars | 1,000 lb | 1,000 dollars |
| New England | 558,046 | $ 583,228 | 592,665 | $ 580,957 |
| Middle Atlantic | 253,237 | 148,741 | 240,413 | 179,747 |
| Chesapeake | 648,442 | 161,748 | 845,632 | 174,229 |
| South Atlantic | 286,674 | 214,997 | 277,035 | 238,112 |
| Gulf | 2,152,719 | 806,270 | 1,464,718 | 724,619 |
| Pacific Coast and Alaska | 6,505,716 | 1,849,695 | 6,424,412 | 1,791,396 |
| Great Lakes | 29,464 | 19,268 | 29,432 | 21,413 |
| Hawaii | 27,090 | 62,451 | 29,892 | 59,847 |
| **Total** | **10,461,388** | **$3,846,398** | **9,904,199** | **$3,770,320** |

(1) Landings are reported in round (live) weight for all items except univalve and bivalve mollusks such as clams, oysters, and scallops, which are reported in weight of meats (excluding shell). Landings for Mississippi River Drainage Area states are not available.

# EMPLOYMENT

## Employment and Unemployment in the U.S., 1940-95

**Source:** Bureau of Labor Statistics, U.S. Dept. of Labor

(civilian labor force, persons 16 years of age and older; annual averages; in thousands)

| Year[1] | Employed | Unemployed | Unemployment rate | Year[1] | Employed | Unemployed | Unemployment rate |
|---|---|---|---|---|---|---|---|
| 1940[2] | 47,520 | 8,120 | 14.6% | 1987 | 112,440 | 7,425 | 6.2% |
| 1950 | 58,918 | 3,288 | 5.0 | 1988 | 114,988 | 6,701 | 5.5 |
| 1960 | 65,778 | 3,852 | 5.5 | 1989 | 117,342 | 6,528 | 5.3 |
| 1970 | 78,678 | 4,093 | 4.9 | 1990[3] | 118,793 | 7,047 | 5.6 |
| 1980 | 99,303 | 7,637 | 7.1 | 1991 | 117,718 | 8,628 | 6.8 |
| 1983 | 100,834 | 10,717 | 9.6 | 1992 | 118,482 | 9,613 | 7.5 |
| 1984 | 105,005 | 8,539 | 7.5 | 1993 | 120,259 | 8,940 | 6.9 |
| 1985 | 107,150 | 8,312 | 7.2 | 1994[4] | 123,060 | 7,996 | 6.1 |
| 1986 | 109,597 | 8,237 | 7.0 | 1995[4] | 124,900 | 7,404 | 5.6 |

(1) **Early unemployment rates:** 1915, 9.7; 1916, 4.8; 1917, 4.8; 1918, 1.4; 1919, 2.3; 1920, 4.0; 1921, 11.9; 1922, 7.6; 1923, 3.2; 1924, 5.5; 1925, 4.0; 1926, 1.9; 1927, 4.1; 1928, 4.4; 1929, 3.2; 1930, 8.7; 1931, 15.9; 1932, 23.6; 1933, 24.9; 1934, 21.7; 1935, 20.1; 1936, 16.9; 1937, 14.3; 1938, 19.0; 1939, 17.2. (2) Persons 14 years of age and older. (3) Beginning in 1990, data incorporate 1990 census-based population controls, adjusted for the estimated undercount. (4) Not strictly comparable with prior years, because of a major redesign of the survey used.

## Selected Unemployment Insurance Data, by State, 1995

**Source:** Employment and Training Admin., U.S. Dept. of Labor; state programs only

| State | Monetarily eligible claimants | First payments | Final payments | Initial claims | Benefits paid | Average weekly benefit amount | Employers subject to state law |
|---|---|---|---|---|---|---|---|
| AL | 175,464 | 148,924 | 27,037 | 354,105 | $184,455,292 | $138.51 | 83,157 |
| AK | 50,910 | 46,832 | 19,480 | 100,741 | 113,639,511 | 172.88 | 15,093 |
| AZ | 99,808 | 74,264 | 25,277 | 154,528 | 154,303,551 | 148.57 | 90,244 |
| AR | 109,425 | 88,797 | 24,261 | 225,122 | 162,316,515 | 167.73 | 56,206 |
| CA | 1,574,468 | 1,224,056 | 520,105 | 3,420,295 | 3,085,152,310 | 153.55 | 765,407 |
| CO | 103,477 | 71,188 | 27,361 | 136,835 | 178,233,380 | 202.49 | 108,017 |
| CT | 152,714 | 142,036 | 44,891 | 248,716 | 458,031,909 | 214.29 | 92,745 |
| DE | 29,945 | 24,142 | 4,376 | 54,760 | 61,441,065 | 195.34 | 21,229 |
| DC | 28,832 | 24,081 | 12,674 | 38,531 | 106,644,601 | 231.75 | 23,355 |
| FL | 345,196 | 271,217 | 118,525 | 482,759 | 657,801,939 | 171.94 | 341,022 |
| GA | 273,121 | 191,584 | 53,536 | 401,368 | 281,118,511 | 161.67 | 160,347 |
| HI | 52,661 | 47,533 | 16,152 | 96,587 | 198,269,360 | 270.03 | 26,894 |
| ID | 57,090 | 48,219 | 15,291 | 120,333 | 96,094,152 | 175.14 | 32,758 |
| IL | 400,349 | 337,575 | 115,335 | 696,407 | 1,162,650,422 | 207.62 | 264,703 |
| IN | 186,379 | 121,040 | 33,091 | 265,946 | 223,323,200 | 178.71 | 118,856 |
| IA | 100,605 | 78,467 | 14,774 | 144,552 | 162,383,983 | 194.11 | 66,001 |
| KS | 72,904 | 58,503 | 16,754 | 125,150 | 149,593,950 | 195.95 | 62,745 |
| KY | 140,788 | 123,253 | 19,910 | 310,898 | 218,800,205 | 167.26 | 76,759 |
| LA | 109,653 | 81,791 | 21,160 | 199,486 | 137,001,184 | 121.38 | 86,857 |
| ME | 54,213 | 50,381 | 15,983 | 113,594 | 106,872,519 | 166.10 | 34,150 |
| MD | 170,549 | 117,126 | 37,046 | 243,006 | 343,435,343 | 185.76 | 120,882 |
| MA | 244,601 | 203,099 | 72,280 | 389,842 | 790,345,319 | 244.40 | 152,824 |
| MI | 498,856 | 364,888 | 88,126 | 781,290 | 884,219,407 | 221.04 | 201,272 |
| MN | 133,361 | 116,098 | 32,929 | 212,265 | 364,352,903 | 228.22 | 111,238 |
| MS | 104,559 | 74,150 | 16,466 | 199,172 | 113,536,961 | 134.06 | 48,676 |
| MO | 209,684 | 146,007 | 41,185 | 390,097 | 273,475,096 | 152.46 | 122,182 |
| MT | 34,565 | 27,880 | 9,240 | 60,967 | 54,370,097 | 159.56 | 27,215 |
| NE | 36,709 | 27,008 | 7,091 | 57,404 | 45,871,100 | 156.89 | 42,154 |
| NV | 75,929 | 55,406 | 18,001 | 116,760 | 142,755,491 | 189.98 | 34,429 |
| NH | 30,727 | 22,391 | 3,299 | 47,787 | 32,920,104 | 147.58 | 33,849 |
| NJ | 352,988 | 306,687 | 137,603 | 582,889 | 1,280,600,625 | 252.63 | 207,341 |
| NM | 37,123 | 28,186 | 9,688 | 58,996 | 69,625,893 | 153.05 | 38,919 |
| NY | 635,947 | 582,840 | 247,234 | 1,163,213 | 2,225,217,549 | 207.71 | 435,436 |
| NC | 335,932 | 232,924 | 31,574 | 801,833 | 342,038,675 | 189.62 | 147,781 |
| ND | 18,652 | 14,953 | 4,988 | 28,463 | 29,583,672 | 166.08 | 18,482 |
| OH | 329,306 | 259,354 | 61,103 | 585,324 | 681,274,140 | 196.78 | 221,586 |
| OK | 69,101 | 47,598 | 17,256 | 117,562 | 108,108,010 | 172.52 | 70,292 |
| OR | 158,205 | 138,439 | 45,149 | 345,985 | 362,884,758 | 183.97 | 91,242 |
| PA | 574,960 | 479,269 | 133,540 | 1,173,345 | 1,590,729,197 | 219.48 | 235,069 |
| PR | 129,322 | 125,924 | 66,163 | 240,620 | 215,362,607 | 91.85 | 45,497 |
| RI | 63,348 | 57,046 | 24,456 | 127,375 | 189,251,971 | 225.73 | 30,716 |
| SC | 168,692 | 108,839 | 24,080 | 330,229 | 178,386,452 | 161.55 | 76,840 |
| SD | 12,029 | 8,448 | 840 | 19,546 | 12,238,666 | 144.92 | 20,735 |
| TN | 228,787 | 167,755 | 43,946 | 431,752 | 265,832,733 | 150.11 | 103,611 |
| TX | 493,161 | 366,346 | 164,656 | 729,190 | 1,012,873,267 | 186.97 | 359,093 |
| UT | 41,680 | 29,991 | 7,990 | 52,130 | 63,057,251 | 191.74 | 41,518 |
| VT | 27,695 | 23,013 | 4,158 | 45,021 | 51,218,145 | 165.82 | 19,560 |
| VA | 183,981 | 119,975 | 29,095 | 349,482 | 201,350,958 | 169.63 | 147,270 |
| VI | 5,721 | 5,920 | 1,474 | 7,798 | 11,948,298 | 162.71 | 4,644 |
| WA | 315,863 | 237,365 | 81,661 | 571,962 | 832,515,700 | 204.53 | 160,100 |
| WV | 69,332 | 60,567 | 13,014 | 100,419 | 138,941,472 | 172.07 | 37,787 |
| WI | 245,437 | 213,327 | 36,757 | 474,430 | 445,791,772 | 198.84 | 114,549 |
| WY | 17,415 | 12,527 | 3,712 | 25,907 | 30,556,308 | 179.63 | 17,133 |
| **U.S.** | **10,172,219** | **8,035,229** | **2,661,773** | **18,552,774** | **21,282,797,499** | **187.29** | **6,066,460** |

# Unemployment Rates, by Selected Country, 1975-96

**Source:** Bureau of Labor Statistics, U.S. Dept. of Labor; civilian labor force, seasonally adjusted; Aug. 1996

| Time period | U.S. | Canada | Australia | Japan | France | Germany[1] | Italy[2] | Sweden | United Kingdom |
|---|---|---|---|---|---|---|---|---|---|
| 1975 | 8.5 | 6.9 | 4.9 | 1.9 | 4.2 | 3.4 | 3.4 | 1.6 | 4.6 |
| 1980 | 7.1 | 7.5 | 6.1 | 2.0 | 6.5 | 2.8 | 4.4 | 2.0 | 7.0 |
| 1981 | 7.6 | 7.6 | 5.8 | 2.2 | 7.6 | 4.0 | 4.9 | 2.5 | 10.5 |
| 1982 | 9.7 | 11.0 | 7.2 | 2.4 | 8.3 | 5.6 | 5.4 | 3.1 | 11.3 |
| 1983 | 9.6 | 11.9 | 10.0 | 2.7 | 8.6 | 6.9[3] | 5.9 | 3.5 | 11.8 |
| 1984 | 7.5 | 11.3 | 9.0 | 2.8 | 10.0 | 7.1 | 5.9 | 3.1 | 11.8 |
| 1985 | 7.2 | 10.5 | 8.3 | 2.6 | 10.5 | 7.2 | 6.0 | 2.8 | 11.2 |
| 1986 | 7.0 | 9.6 | 8.1 | 2.8 | 10.6 | 6.6 | 7.5[3] | 2.6 | 11.2 |
| 1987 | 6.2 | 8.9 | 8.1 | 2.9 | 10.8 | 6.3 | 7.9 | 2.2[3] | 10.3 |
| 1988 | 5.5 | 7.8 | 7.2 | 2.5 | 10.3 | 6.3 | 7.9 | 1.9 | 8.6 |
| 1989 | 5.3 | 7.5 | 6.2 | 2.3 | 9.6 | 5.7 | 7.8 | 1.6 | 7.3 |
| 1990 | 5.6[3] | 8.1 | 6.9 | 2.1 | 9.1 | 5.0 | 7.0 | 1.8 | 7.0 |
| 1991 | 6.8 | 10.4 | 9.6 | 2.1 | 9.6 | 4.3P | 6.9[3] | 3.1 | 8.9 |
| 1992 | 7.5 | 11.3 | 10.8 | 2.2 | 10.4R[3] | 4.6P | 7.3P | 5.6 | 10.1 |
| 1993 | 6.9 | 11.2 | 10.9 | 2.5 | 11.8R | 5.7P | 10.2P[3] | 9.3 | 10.5 |
| 1994 | 6.1[3] | 10.4 | 9.7 | 2.9 | 12.3R | 6.5P | 11.3P | 9.6 | 9.6P |
| 1995 | 5.6 | 9.5 | 8.5 | 3.2 | 11.5R | 6.5P | 12.0P | 9.1 | 8.8P |
| 1st quarter | 5.5 | 9.7 | 8.8 | 3.0 | 11.5R | 6.5P | 12.0P | 9.1 | 8.9P |
| 2d quarter | 5.7 | 9.5 | 8.4 | 3.2 | 11.4R | 6.5P | 12.1P | 9.0 | 8.8P |
| 3d quarter | 5.6 | 9.5 | 8.4 | 3.2 | 11.4R | 6.6P | 11.9P | 8.9 | 8.8P |
| 4th quarter | 5.5 | 9.4 | 8.4 | 3.4 | 11.6R | 6.7P | 11.9P | 9.3 | 8.6P |
| 1996 | | | | | | | | | |
| 1st quarter | 5.6 | 9.5 | 8.5 | 3.3 | 11.9R | 7.0P | 12.0P | 9.0 | 8.4P,R |
| 2d quarter | 5.4 | 9.6 | 8.6 | 3.5 | NA | NA | 12.5P | 9.4 | 8.3P |

NA=Not available. P=Preliminary. R=Revised. **Note:** For the sake of making comparisions, U.S. unemployment rate concepts were applied to unemployment data collected from Canada, Australia, Japan, France, Germany, Italy, Sweden, and the United Kingdom. Quarterly and monthly figures for France and Germany were calculated by applying annual adjustment factors to current published data and therefore should be viewed as less precise indicators of unemployment under U.S. concepts than the annual figures. (1) All figures for region of former West Germany. (2) Quarterly rates are for the first month of the quarter. (3) As a result of revisions in survey methodology, there are breaks in the data series for the U.S. (1990, 1994), France (1992), Germany (1983), Italy (1986, 1991, 1993), and Sweden (1987); data prior to a survey change are not fully comparable to data released after a survey change.

# Employed Persons, by Occupation and Sex, 1994-95

**Source:** Bureau of Labor Statistics, U.S. Dept. of Labor

(in thousands)

| Occupation | Total 16 years and older | | Men 16 years and older | | Women 16 years and older | |
|---|---|---|---|---|---|---|
| | 1994 | 1995 | 1994 | 1995 | 1994 | 1995 |
| **Total** | **123,060** | **124,900** | **66,450** | **67,377** | **56,610** | **57,523** |
| Managerial and professional specialty | 33,847 | 35,318 | 17,583 | 18,378 | 16,264 | 16,940 |
| Executive, administrative, and managerial | 16,312 | 17,186 | 9,298 | 9,840 | 7,014 | 7,346 |
| Officials and administrators, public administration | 673 | 710 | 375 | 371 | 298 | 339 |
| Other executive, administrative, and managerial | 11,364 | 12,151 | 6,941 | 7,471 | 4,422 | 4,680 |
| Management-related occupations | 4,269 | 4,325 | 1,977 | 1,998 | 2,291 | 2,327 |
| Professional specialty | 17,536 | 18,132 | 8,285 | 8,539 | 9,250 | 9,593 |
| Engineers | 1,866 | 1,934 | 1,711 | 1,771 | 155 | 163 |
| Mathematical and computer scientists | 1,186 | 1,195 | 787 | 813 | 399 | 382 |
| Natural scientists | 535 | 519 | 369 | 377 | 166 | 142 |
| Health diagnosing occupations | 932 | 1,002 | 731 | 773 | 200 | 229 |
| Health assessment and treating occupations | 2,708 | 2,762 | 375 | 393 | 2,333 | 2,369 |
| Teachers, college and university | 838 | 846 | 482 | 464 | 356 | 382 |
| Teachers, except college and university | 4,330 | 4,507 | 1,087 | 1,142 | 3,244 | 3,365 |
| Lawyers and judges | 861 | 926 | 648 | 684 | 213 | 242 |
| Other professional specialty occupations | 4,279 | 4,440 | 2,095 | 2,122 | 2,184 | 2,318 |
| Technical, sales, and administrative support | 37,306 | 37,417 | 13,322 | 13,310 | 23,984 | 24,107 |
| Technicians and related support | 3,869 | 3,909 | 1,856 | 1,900 | 2,013 | 2,009 |
| Sales occupations | 14,817 | 15,119 | 7,543 | 7,634 | 7,273 | 7,485 |
| Administrative support, including clerical | 18,620 | 18,389 | 3,923 | 3,776 | 14,697 | 14,613 |
| Service occupations | 16,912 | 16,930 | 6,840 | 6,774 | 10,072 | 10,155 |
| Precision production, craft, and repair | 13,489 | 13,524 | 12,241 | 12,323 | 1,248 | 1,201 |
| Mechanics and repairers | 4,419 | 4,423 | 4,219 | 4,248 | 201 | 175 |
| Construction trades | 5,008 | 5,098 | 4,900 | 4,978 | 108 | 120 |
| Other precision production, craft, and repair | 4,062 | 4,004 | 3,123 | 3,097 | 939 | 907 |
| Operators, fabricators, and laborers | 17,876 | 18,068 | 13,535 | 13,675 | 4,341 | 4,393 |
| Machine operators, assemblers, and inspectors | 7,754 | 7,907 | 4,800 | 4,958 | 2,954 | 2,949 |
| Transportation and material moving occupations | 5,136 | 5,171 | 4,654 | 4,682 | 483 | 490 |
| Motor vehicle operators | 3,882 | 3,904 | 3,454 | 3,474 | 428 | 429 |
| Other transportation and material moving occupations | 1,254 | 1,268 | 1,200 | 1,207 | 54 | 60 |
| Handlers, equipment cleaners, helpers, and laborers | 4,986 | 4,990 | 4,081 | 4,035 | 904 | 955 |
| Constuction laborers | 740 | 780 | 714 | 754 | 27 | 26 |
| Other handlers, equipment cleaners, etc. | 4,245 | 4,210 | 3,368 | 3,281 | 878 | 929 |
| Farming, forestry, and fishing | 3,629 | 3,642 | 2,928 | 2,916 | 701 | 726 |

# Unemployment Insurance

**Source:** Unemployment Insurance Service, U.S. Dept. of Labor; September 1996

Unlike old-age and survivors insurance, which is entirely a federal program, the unemployment insurance program is a federal-state system that provides insured wage earners partial replacement for lost wages during a period of involuntary unemployment. The program protects most workers. During fiscal year 1995, an estimated 113 million workers in commerce, industry, agriculture, and government, including the armed forces, were covered under the federal-state system.

Each state, as well as the District of Columbia, Puerto Rico, and the Virgin Islands, has its own law and operates its own program. The amount and duration of the weekly benefits are determined by state laws, based on prior wages and length of employment. States are required to extend the duration of benefits when unemployment rises to and remains above specified state levels; costs of extended benefits are shared by the state and federal governments.

Under the Federal Unemployment Tax Act, the federal tax rate is 6.2% on the first $7,000 paid to each employee of employers with one or more employees in 20 weeks of the year or with a quarterly payroll of $1,500 or more. A credit of up to 5.4% is allowed for taxes paid under state unemployment insurance laws that meet certain criteria, leaving the net federal rate at 0.8% of taxable wages. Subject employers also pay a state unemployment tax.

The secretary of labor certifies states for administrative grants to operate the program (under the Social Security Act) and for employer tax credit (under the Federal Unemployment Tax Act).

Benefits are financed solely by employer contributions, except in Alaska, Pennsylvania, and New Jersey, where employees also contribute. Benefits are paid through the states' public employment offices, at which unemployed workers must register for work and to which they must report regularly for referral to a possible job during the time when they are drawing weekly benefit payments. During fiscal year 1995, $20.9 billion in benefits was paid under state unemployment insurance programs (including the state share of extended benefit programs) to 7.9 million beneficiaries. Beneficiaries received an average weekly payment of $186.15 for total unemployment, which lasted an average of 14.9 weeks.

# U.S. Unemployment Rates by Selected Characteristics, 1993-96

**Source:** Bureau of Labor Statistics, U.S. Dept. of Labor; seasonally adjusted, quarterly averages

| | 1993 | | | 1994 | | | | 1995 | | | | 1996 | |
|---|---|---|---|---|---|---|---|---|---|---|---|---|---|
| Characteristic | II | III | IV | I | II | III | IV | I | II | III | IV | I | II |
| **Total (all civilian workers)** | 7.1 | 6.6 | 6.6 | 6.6 | 6.2 | 6.0 | 5.6 | 5.5 | 5.7 | 5.6 | 5.5 | 5.6 | 5.4 |
| Men, 20 years and older | 6.5 | 6.4 | 6.0 | 6.0 | 5.4 | 5.3 | 4.9 | 4.8 | 4.9 | 4.8 | 4.7 | 4.9 | 4.7 |
| Women, 20 years and older | 6.0 | 5.8 | 5.8 | 5.8 | 5.5 | 5.3 | 4.9 | 4.9 | 5.0 | 5.0 | 4.8 | 4.9 | 4.8 |
| Both sexes, 16 to 19 years | 19.7 | 18.3 | 18.4 | 18.2 | 18.1 | 17.5 | 16.7 | 16.8 | 17.2 | 17.7 | 17.6 | 17.4 | 16.0 |
| White | 6.2 | 6.0 | 5.9 | 5.7 | 5.4 | 5.2 | 4.9 | 4.8 | 4.8 | 4.9 | 4.9 | 4.9 | 4.7 |
| Black and other | 12.2 | 11.3 | 11.0 | 11.4 | 10.6 | 10.2 | 9.9 | 9.4 | 9.5 | 10.0 | 9.3 | 9.5 | 9.2 |
| Black | 13.5 | 12.5 | 12.1 | 12.9 | 11.6 | 10.8 | 10.6 | 10.2 | 10.4 | 10.9 | 9.9 | 10.7 | 10.3 |
| Hispanic origin | 10.5 | 10.2 | 10.9 | 10.3 | 10.3 | 10.0 | 9.1 | 9.4 | 9.2 | 8.2 | 9.3 | 9.7 | 9.2 |
| Married men, spouse present | 4.5 | 4.4 | 4.2 | 4.2 | 3.7 | 3.4 | 3.3 | 3.2 | 3.3 | 3.4 | 3.2 | 3.1 | 3.0 |
| Married women, spouse present | 4.8 | 4.6 | 4.6 | 4.4 | 4.1 | 4.0 | 3.8 | 3.8 | 4.0 | 4.0 | 3.8 | 3.8 | 3.7 |
| Women who maintain families | 9.8 | 9.4 | 9.8 | 9.5 | 8.9 | 8.5 | 8.7 | 8.4 | 8.4 | 7.8 | 7.5 | 7.8 | 7.7 |
| **Occupation** | | | | | | | | | | | | | |
| Managerial and professional specialty | 3.0 | 2.8 | 2.9 | 2.8 | 2.7 | 2.6 | 2.4 | 2.4 | 2.4 | 2.5 | 2.5 | 2.4 | 2.4 |
| Technical, sales, and administrative support | 5.5 | 5.4 | 5.3 | 5.6 | 5.1 | 4.8 | 4.5 | 4.5 | 4.6 | 4.4 | 4.4 | 4.5 | 4.4 |
| Precision production, craft, and repair | 8.4 | 7.7 | 7.4 | 7.1 | 6.4 | 5.8 | 5.7 | 5.5 | 6.0 | 6.3 | 6.1 | 5.7 | 5.3 |
| Operators, fabricators, and laborers | 10.1 | 10.1 | 9.4 | 9.6 | 9.1 | 8.8 | 8.3 | 7.9 | 8.8 | 8.3 | 8.2 | 8.4 | 8.1 |
| Farming, forestry, and fishing | 8.2 | 8.0 | 8.5 | 9.3 | 7.4 | 8.7 | 8.0 | 7.8 | 8.4 | 7.3 | 7.9 | 8.0 | 8.3 |
| **Industry** | | | | | | | | | | | | | |
| Nonagricultural private wage and salary workers | 7.3 | 7.0 | 6.8 | 6.9 | 6.4 | 6.1 | 5.8 | 5.6 | 5.8 | 5.9 | 5.8 | 5.8 | 5.6 |
| Goods-producing industries | 9.0 | 9.0 | 8.2 | 7.7 | 7.0 | 6.6 | 6.3 | 6.1 | 6.6 | 6.5 | 6.6 | 6.4 | 6.1 |
| Mining | 7.9 | 6.6 | 7.2 | 5.3 | 6.1 | 5.6 | 4.5 | 5.2 | 4.4 | 3.8 | 7.9 | 6.1 | 3.8 |
| Construction | 14.9 | 15.1 | 13.3 | 13.2 | 11.8 | 10.8 | 10.9 | 11.0 | 11.6 | 11.9 | 11.7 | 10.6 | 9.9 |
| Manufacturing | 7.3 | 7.3 | 6.7 | 6.2 | 5.6 | 5.4 | 4.9 | 4.6 | 5.1 | 5.0 | 4.9 | 5.1 | 5.0 |
| Durable goods | 7.3 | 7.0 | 6.5 | 5.7 | 5.3 | 5.3 | 4.4 | 4.2 | 4.5 | 4.3 | 4.4 | 4.9 | 4.7 |
| Nondurable goods | 7.4 | 7.6 | 6.9 | 7.0 | 6.0 | 5.5 | 5.6 | 5.2 | 5.9 | 5.9 | 5.7 | 5.2 | 5.3 |
| Service-producing industries | 6.6 | 6.2 | 6.3 | 6.6 | 6.2 | 5.9 | 5.6 | 5.4 | 5.6 | 5.6 | 5.6 | 5.5 | 5.4 |
| Transportation and public utilities | 5.2 | 5.1 | 5.4 | 5.1 | 5.0 | 4.8 | 4.5 | 4.6 | 4.4 | 4.5 | 4.4 | 3.9 | 4.3 |
| Wholesale and retail trade | 8.2 | 7.5 | 7.7 | 8.0 | 7.4 | 7.2 | 7.0 | 6.5 | 6.5 | 6.7 | 6.4 | 6.7 | 6.5 |
| Finance, insurance, and real estate | 4.2 | 4.0 | 3.8 | 3.5 | 3.5 | 3.9 | 3.4 | 3.2 | 3.4 | 3.3 | 3.2 | 2.5 | 2.5 |
| Services | 6.1 | 5.8 | 6.0 | 6.4 | 6.0 | 5.7 | 5.3 | 5.3 | 5.5 | 5.5 | 5.5 | 5.6 | 5.5 |
| Government workers | 3.4 | 3.2 | 3.2 | 3.7 | 3.5 | 3.4 | 3.0 | 3.0 | 3.0 | 2.9 | 2.8 | 2.8 | 3.0 |
| Agricultural wage/salary workers | 11.6 | 11.7 | 11.6 | 13.2 | 9.3 | 11.7 | 10.9 | 10.3 | 11.5 | 10.3 | 12.3 | 10.7 | 10.0 |

**Note:** Data beginning with 1994 not directly comparable with earlier data because of survey redesign.

# Annual Earnings, by Educational Attainment, Sex, Race, and Hispanic Origin, 1994

**Source:** Bureau of the Census, U.S. Dept. of Commerce; averages per person, ages 18 and over

| Characteristic | Total | Not a high school graduate | High school graduate | Some college or an associate degree | Bachelor's degree | Advanced degree |
|---|---|---|---|---|---|---|
| Total | $25,852 | $13,697 | $20,248 | $22,226 | $37,224 | $56,105 |
| Male | 32,087 | 16,633 | 25,038 | 27,636 | 46,278 | 67,032 |
| Female | 18,684 | 9,189 | 14,995 | 16,928 | 26,483 | 39,905 |
| White | 26,696 | 13,941 | 20,911 | 22,648 | 37,996 | 56,475 |
| Black | 19,772 | 12,705 | 16,446 | 19,631 | 30,938 | 48,653 |
| Hispanic origin[1] | 18,568 | 13,733 | 17,323 | 21,041 | 29,165 | 51,898 |

(1) May be of any race.

# Occupational Illnesses, by Industry and Type of Illness, 1994

**Source:** Bureau of Labor Statistics, U.S. Dept. of Labor

(incidence rate per total injuries and illnesses)

| | | Goods producing | | | | Service producing | | | | |
|---|---|---|---|---|---|---|---|---|---|---|
| **Occupational illness** | **Private sector[1]** | **Agri-culture[2]** | **Min-ing[3]** | **Con-struc-tion** | **Manu-facturing** | **Trans. and pub. utilities** | **Whole-sale** | **Retail** | **Fi-nance[4]** | **Service** |
| **Total [2,236,600 cases]** | **100.0** | **100.0** | **100.0** | **100.0** | **100.0** | **100.0** | **100.0** | **100.0** | **100.0** | **100.0** |
| **Nature of injury, illness:** | | | | | | | | | | |
| Sprains, strains | 43.1 | 36.2 | 39.7 | 37.0 | 38.2 | 51.0 | 45.0 | 42.0 | 36.6 | 49.0 |
| Bruises, contusions | 9.5 | 8.9 | 12.6 | 7.5 | 9.3 | 10.9 | 9.1 | 10.6 | 7.9 | 9.2 |
| Cuts, lacerations | 7.4 | 11.0 | 6.5 | 9.3 | 8.4 | 3.3 | 6.6 | 11.1 | 5.2 | 4.7 |
| Fractures | 6.2 | 7.2 | 10.2 | 9.7 | 6.2 | 5.7 | 6.7 | 5.1 | 8.3 | 5.2 |
| Carpal tunnel syndrome | 1.7 | 0.8 | 0.3 | 0.7 | 3.0 | 1.1 | 1.4 | 1.3 | 4.7 | 1.3 |
| Heat burns | 1.7 | 0.7 | 1.6 | 1.4 | 1.6 | 0.5 | 0.7 | 3.7 | 0.6 | 1.3 |
| Tendinitis | 1.1 | 0.6 | — | 0.4 | 2.3 | 0.4 | 1.1 | 0.8 | 1.6 | 0.8 |
| Chemical burns | 0.7 | 0.6 | 1.2 | 0.8 | 1.0 | 0.3 | 0.8 | 0.7 | 0.7 | 0.7 |
| Amputations | 0.5 | 0.9 | 1.0 | 0.5 | 1.1 | 0.2 | 0.7 | 0.3 | 0.2 | 0.2 |
| Multiple injuries | 3.2 | 3.1 | 5.9 | 3.3 | 2.8 | 3.1 | 4.2 | 2.8 | 3.8 | 3.3 |
| **Source of injury, illness:** | | | | | | | | | | |
| Chemicals/chem. products | 1.9 | 1.5 | 8.2 | 1.5 | 2.5 | 0.9 | 1.5 | 1.7 | 2.1 | 2.0 |
| Containers | 14.7 | 9.2 | 5.3 | 4.9 | 14.1 | 22.5 | 22.4 | 21.6 | 10.9 | 9.4 |
| Furniture, fixtures | 3.6 | 0.7 | 0.6 | 1.7 | 2.6 | 1.8 | 2.7 | 5.7 | 6.2 | 5.3 |
| Machinery | 6.9 | 7.3 | 12.1 | 5.9 | 11.0 | 2.9 | 6.9 | 7.2 | 5.6 | 4.0 |
| Parts and materials | 11.2 | 7.8 | 17.0 | 24.8 | 17.7 | 7.8 | 11.9 | 6.3 | 4.4 | 3.7 |
| Worker motion or position | 14.8 | 14.9 | 3.8 | 12.2 | 18.8 | 14.7 | 13.3 | 12.5 | 19.8 | 13.8 |
| Floor, ground surface | 16.1 | 15.5 | 17.1 | 17.9 | 10.2 | 17.1 | 13.9 | 19.5 | 24.5 | 18.8 |
| Tools, instruments, equip. | 6.0 | 9.1 | 8.6 | 10.5 | 6.6 | 3.1 | 4.1 | 6.1 | 4.7 | 4.9 |
| Vehicles | 7.4 | 8.8 | 7.0 | 4.7 | 4.5 | 16.7 | 11.9 | 6.3 | 6.3 | 6.8 |
| Health care patient | 4.2 | — | — | — | — | 0.6 | — | — | 0.7 | 17.7 |
| **Event or exposure:** | | | | | | | | | | |
| Contact with object/equip. | 27.1 | 32.6 | 39.9 | 33.3 | 33.6 | 21.2 | 28.2 | 28.4 | 18.6 | 18.7 |
| Struck by object | 13.1 | 15.7 | 20.0 | 17.5 | 14.2 | 10.8 | 14.2 | 15.0 | 8.9 | 9.2 |
| Struck against object | 7.3 | 8.3 | 9.4 | 8.4 | 8.1 | 5.4 | 6.9 | 8.4 | 6.3 | 5.8 |
| Caught in object | 4.3 | 4.9 | 9.1 | 3.1 | 8.0 | 2.7 | 4.7 | 3.1 | 1.8 | 2.2 |
| Fall to lower level | 5.0 | 7.5 | 9.4 | 11.3 | 3.0 | 6.0 | 5.7 | 3.9 | 7.1 | 4.0 |
| Fall to same level | 11.9 | 9.2 | 9.5 | 8.4 | 7.8 | 11.3 | 8.9 | 16.5 | 18.7 | 15.3 |
| Slips, trips (without fall) | 3.2 | 3.8 | 1.0 | 3.1 | 2.8 | 3.9 | 3.0 | 3.3 | 3.3 | 3.6 |
| Overexertion | 27.4 | 17.2 | 26.2 | 22.8 | 26.0 | 29.4 | 30.7 | 25.5 | 20.2 | 32.1 |
| Overexertion in lifting | 16.4 | 9.8 | 10.3 | 13.0 | 14.7 | 17.6 | 20.0 | 17.8 | 12.3 | 18.3 |
| Repetitive motion | 4.1 | 1.7 | 0.5 | 1.5 | 8.4 | 2.3 | 2.8 | 2.7 | 9.1 | 2.6 |
| Exposed to harmful substance | 5.0 | 5.2 | 4.6 | 4.5 | 5.4 | 3.1 | 3.1 | 6.2 | 4.7 | 5.2 |
| Transportation accidents | 3.6 | 5.1 | 3.0 | 2.8 | 1.6 | 8.2 | 5.1 | 2.6 | 4.3 | 4.0 |
| Fires, explosions | 0.2 | 0.3 | 0.5 | 0.3 | 0.2 | 0.1 | 0.2 | 0.2 | 0.1 | 0.2 |
| Assault, by person | 0.9 | 0.3 | — | 0.1 | 0.1 | 0.4 | 0.3 | 0.8 | 1.6 | 2.7 |

**Note:** Dashes (—) indicate data that are not available or data that do not meet publication guidelines. Because of rounding and classifications not shown, percentages may not add to 100. All injuries and illnesses reported involved days away from work. (1) Private sector includes all industries except government, but excludes farms with fewer than 11 employees. (2) Agriculture includes forestry and fishing, but excludes farms with fewer than 11 employees. (3) Data conforming to OSHA definition for mining operators in coal, metal, and nonmetal mining and for employers in railroad transportation are provided to the Bureau of Labor Statistics by the Mine Safety and Health Administration, U.S. Dept. of Labor; and by the Federal Railroad Administration, U.S. Dept. of Transportation. Independent mining contractors are excluded from the coal, metal, and nonmetal industries. (4) Finance includes insurance and real estate.

# Fatal Occupational Injuries, 1995

**Source:** Bureau of Labor Statistics, U.S. Dept. of Labor

| | Fatalities | |
|---|---|---|
| **Event or exposure** | **Number** | **Percentage** |
| **Transportation incidents** | **2,560** | **41** |
| Highway | 1,329 | 21 |
| Collision between vechicles | 634 | 10 |
| Vehicle struck stationary object | 268 | 4 |
| Noncollision | 350 | 6 |
| Nonhighway (farm, industrial premises) | 388 | 6 |
| Aircraft | 278 | 4 |
| Worker struck by a vehicle | 385 | 6 |
| Water vehicle | 84 | 1 |
| Railway | 82 | 1 |
| **Assaults and violent acts** | **1,262** | **20** |
| Homicide | 1,024 | 16 |
| Shooting | 754 | 12 |
| Stabbing | 67 | 1 |
| Self-inflicted injury | 215 | 3 |
| **Falls** | **643** | **10** |
| Fall to lower level | 573 | 9 |
| Fall on same level | 50 | 1 |
| **Contact with objects and equipment** | **915** | **15** |
| Struck by object | 546 | 9 |
| Struck by falling object | 340 | 5 |
| Struck by flying object | 63 | 1 |
| Caught in or compressed by equipment or objects | 255 | 4 |
| Caught in or crushed in collapsing materials | 99 | 2 |
| **Exposure to harmful substances or environments** | **598** | **10** |
| Contact with electric current | 347 | 6 |
| Contact with temperature extremes | 55 | 1 |
| Exposure to caustic, noxious, or allergenic substances | 101 | 2 |
| Oxygen deficiency | 94 | 2 |
| **Fires and explosions** | **208** | **3** |
| **Other events or exposures** | **24** | **–** |
| **Total** | **6,210** | **100** |

**Note:** Totals for major categories may include subcategories not shown separately. Percentages, based on incidence rate per total fatalities, may not add to totals because of rounding.

# Civilian Employment of the Federal Government, May 1996

**Source:** Statistical Analysis and Services Division, U.S. Office of Personnel Management

(payroll in thousands of dollars, for May 1996)

| Agency | All Areas Employ-ment | All Areas Payroll | United States Employ-ment | United States Payroll | Wash., DC, MSA Employ-ment | Wash., DC, MSA Payroll | Overseas Employ-ment | Overseas Payroll |
|---|---|---|---|---|---|---|---|---|
| **Total, all agencies[1]** | **2,880,999** | **$9,485,618** | **2,773,179** | **$9,154,994** | **344,086** | **$1,418,619** | **107,820** | **$330,624** |
| **Legislative Branch** | **32,441** | **121,357** | **32,430** | **121,289** | **30,971** | **115,169** | **11** | **68** |
| Congress | 17,623 | 63,509 | 17,623 | 63,509 | 17,623 | 63,509 | — | — |
| U.S. Senate | 7,071 | 24,545 | 7,071 | 24,545 | 7,071 | 24,545 | — | — |
| House of Representatives | 10,536 | 38,909 | 10,536 | 38,909 | 10,536 | 38,909 | — | — |
| Comm. on Scty & Coop in Eur | 16 | 55 | 16 | 55 | 16 | 55 | — | — |
| Architect of the Capitol | 1,957 | 5,747 | 1,957 | 5,747 | 1,957 | 5,747 | — | — |
| Botanical Garden | 50 | 152 | 50 | 152 | 50 | 152 | — | — |
| Comm. on Immigration Reform | 15 | 136 | 15 | 136 | 15 | 136 | — | — |
| Comm. Prot. & Reduc. Govt. Sec | 8 | 10 | 8 | 10 | 8 | 10 | — | — |
| Competit. Policy Council | 7 | 41 | 7 | 41 | 7 | 41 | — | — |
| Congressional Budget Ofc | 232 | 1,182 | 232 | 1,182 | 232 | 1,182 | — | — |
| General Accounting Ofc | 3,743 | 18,596 | 3,739 | 18,571 | 2,696 | 13,622 | 4 | 25 |
| Government Printing Ofc. | 3,821 | 13,337 | 3,821 | 13,337 | 3,437 | 12,286 | — | — |
| John C. Stennis Ctr Pub Dev. | 5 | 15 | 5 | 15 | — | — | — | — |
| Library of Congress | 4,554 | 16,437 | 4,547 | 16,394 | 4,526 | 16,335 | 7 | 43 |
| Natl Bankruptcy Rev Comm. | 4 | 33 | 4 | 33 | 3 | 11 | — | — |
| Ofc of Compliance | 13 | 44 | 13 | 44 | 13 | 44 | — | — |
| Physician Payment Rev. Comm. | 18 | 139 | 18 | 139 | 18 | 139 | — | — |
| Prospect. Paymt Assessmt Comm. | 16 | 151 | 16 | 151 | 16 | 151 | — | — |
| U.S. Court of Vets Appeals | 78 | 327 | 78 | 327 | 78 | 327 | — | — |
| U.S. Tax Court | 297 | 1,501 | 297 | 1,501 | 292 | 1,477 | — | — |
| **Judicial Branch** | **29,025** | **111,244** | **28,693** | **110,047** | **1,843** | **8,641** | **332** | **1,197** |
| Supreme Court | 382 | 1,799 | 382 | 1,799 | 382 | 1,799 | — | — |
| U.S. Courts | 28,643 | 109,445 | 28,311 | 108,248 | 1,461 | 6,842 | 332 | 1,197 |
| **Executive Branch** | **2,819,533** | **9,253,017** | **2,712,056** | **8,923,658** | **311,272** | **1,294,809** | **107,477** | **329,359** |
| Exec Ofc of the President | 1,571 | 9,324 | 1,564 | 9,282 | 1,564 | 9,282 | 7 | 42 |
| White House Office | 396 | 2,062 | 396 | 2,062 | 396 | 2,062 | — | — |
| Ofc of Vice President | 21 | 143 | 21 | 143 | 21 | 143 | — | — |
| Ofc of Mgmt & Budget | 539 | 3,513 | 539 | 3,513 | 539 | 3,513 | — | — |
| Office of Administration | 183 | 905 | 183 | 905 | 183 | 905 | — | — |
| Council Economic Advisors | 27 | 158 | 27 | 158 | 27 | 158 | — | — |
| Council on Environ Qual | 16 | 116 | 16 | 116 | 16 | 116 | — | — |
| Ofc of Policy Development | 31 | 186 | 31 | 186 | 31 | 186 | — | — |
| Exec Residence at WH | 86 | 409 | 86 | 409 | 86 | 409 | — | — |
| National Security Council | 43 | 245 | 43 | 245 | 43 | 245 | — | — |
| Ofc of Natl Drug Control | 38 | 265 | 38 | 265 | 38 | 265 | — | — |
| Ofc of Sci & Tech Policy | 34 | 257 | 34 | 257 | 34 | 257 | — | — |
| Ofc of U.S. Trade Rep. | 157 | 1,065 | 150 | 1,023 | 150 | 1,023 | 7 | 42 |
| **Executive Departments** | **1,744,295** | **6,002,969** | **1,656,761** | **5,725,304** | **232,001** | **966,941** | **87,534** | **277,665** |
| State | 24,608 | 104,319 | 8,779 | 37,118 | 7,669 | 31,895 | 15,829 | 67,201 |
| Treasury | 161,278 | 523,215 | 160,195 | 518,497 | 22,783 | 98,733 | 1,083 | 4,718 |
| Defense, Total | 811,618 | 2,725,167 | 749,259 | 2,548,761 | 79,694 | 305,320 | 62,359 | 176,406 |
| Defense, Mil Funct Total | 782,718 | 2,648,632 | 720,437 | 2,472,507 | 78,595 | 301,754 | 62,281 | 176,125 |
| Defense, Civ Funct Total | 28,900 | 76,535 | 28,822 | 76,254 | 1,099 | 3,566 | 78 | 281 |
| Dept of the Army | 268,554 | 774,992 | 242,247 | 695,618 | 22,635 | 52,458 | 26,307 | 79,374 |
| Army, Mil Funct Total | 239,655 | 698,458 | 213,426 | 619,365 | 21,536 | 48,892 | 26,229 | 79,093 |
| Army, Civil Funct Total | 28,899 | 76,534 | 28,821 | 76,253 | 1,099 | 3,566 | 78 | 281 |
| Corps of Engineers | 28,799 | 76,170 | 28,721 | 75,889 | 999 | 3,202 | 78 | 281 |
| Cemeterial Expenses | 100 | 364 | 100 | 364 | 100 | 364 | — | — |
| Dept of the Navy | 227,791 | 896,034 | 216,753 | 862,254 | 32,010 | 136,287 | 11,038 | 33,780 |
| Dept of the Air Force | 177,909 | 575,897 | 169,952 | 562,067 | 5,730 | 25,581 | 7,957 | 13,830 |
| Defense Log Agcy | 48,638 | 174,556 | 47,418 | 174,471 | 2,910 | 13,574 | 1,220 | 85 |
| Other Def Act (excl DLA) | 88,726 | 303,688 | 72,889 | 254,351 | 16,409 | 77,420 | 15,837 | 49,337 |
| Justice | 107,277 | 426,043 | 105,277 | 417,919 | 20,727 | 94,123 | 2,000 | 8,124 |
| Interior | 71,338 | 217,214 | 71,026 | 216,259 | 7,975 | 30,691 | 312 | 955 |
| Agriculture | 105,463 | 315,473 | 104,099 | 312,073 | 11,849 | 46,611 | 1,364 | 3,400 |
| Commerce | 35,956 | 129,968 | 35,097 | 125,577 | 19,269 | 79,025 | 859 | 4,391 |
| Labor | 15,412 | 58,060 | 15,377 | 57,887 | 5,368 | 21,828 | 35 | 173 |
| Health and Human Services | 58,671 | 225,517 | 58,472 | 224,651 | 26,970 | 112,214 | 199 | 866 |
| Housing & Urban Dev. | 11,466 | 44,991 | 11,372 | 44,635 | 3,203 | 14,955 | 94 | 356 |
| Transportation | 62,869 | 316,390 | 62,360 | 313,878 | 9,856 | 50,015 | 509 | 2,512 |
| Energy | 18,555 | 89,518 | 18,549 | 89,474 | 6,619 | 38,044 | 6 | 44 |
| Education | 4,743 | 19,273 | 4,737 | 19,247 | 3,220 | 13,613 | 6 | 26 |
| Veterans Affairs | 255,041 | 807,821 | 252,162 | 799,328 | 6,799 | 29,874 | 2,879 | 8,493 |
| **Independent Agencies[1]** | **1,073,667** | **3,240,724** | **1,053,731** | **3,189,072** | **77,707** | **318,586** | **19,936** | **51,652** |
| Environmtl Protect Agcy | 17,109 | 72,603 | 17,082 | 72,486 | 5,635 | 26,819 | 27 | 117 |
| Federal Deposit Ins Corp. | 10,900 | 51,528 | 10,895 | 51,500 | 2,922 | 16,401 | 5 | 28 |
| Fed Emergency Mgmt Agcy | 4,903 | 15,454 | 4,712 | 15,041 | 1,873 | 6,691 | 191 | 413 |
| General Svcs Admin. | 15,765 | 57,253 | 15,682 | 57,040 | 5,253 | 21,695 | 83 | 213 |
| Natl Aero & Space Admin | 21,328 | 97,072 | 21,305 | 96,941 | 4,758 | 23,152 | 23 | 131 |
| Office of Personnel Mgmt | 4,202 | 11,848 | 4,183 | 11,822 | 1,845 | 6,990 | 19 | 26 |
| Panama Canal Comm. | 9,022 | 22,682 | 19 | 84 | 7 | 42 | 9,003 | 22,598 |
| Small Business Admin | 4,755 | 16,803 | 4,624 | 16,555 | 785 | 3,500 | 131 | 248 |
| Smithsonian Inst. (total) | 5,325 | 16,271 | 5,149 | 15,797 | 4,747 | 14,396 | 176 | 474 |
| Social Security Admin. | 64,568 | 207,663 | 64,085 | 206,240 | 1,440 | 5,673 | 483 | 1,423 |
| Tennessee Valley Auth. | 16,433 | 79,087 | 16,433 | 79,087 | 8 | 50 | — | — |
| U.S. Information Agency | 7,052 | 20,397 | 3,545 | 15,664 | 3,363 | 14,534 | 3,507 | 4,733 |
| U.S. Postal Service | 856,480 | 2,412,978 | 852,504 | 2,399,903 | 23,676 | 73,862 | 3,976 | 13,075 |

(1) Included in totals are other independent agencies with fewer than 4,000 employees.

## Distribution of Wage and Salary Workers Paid Hourly Rates, 1995

**Source:** Bureau of Labor Statistics, U.S. Dept. of Labor; unpublished tabulations from Current Population Survey

(in thousands)

| | Total hourly workers | $4.25[1] or less | Less than $10.00 | $10.00 or more |
|---|---|---|---|---|
| **Sex and age** | | | | |
| **Total, 16 years and older** | **68,354** | **3,655** | **42,113** | **26,241** |
| 16 to 24 years | 15,567 | 1,978 | 14,149 | 1,418 |
| 20 to 24 years | 9,779 | 839 | 8,485 | 1,294 |
| 25 years and older | 52,786 | 1,677 | 27,963 | 24,823 |
| 25 to 54 years | 46,077 | 1,374 | 24,017 | 22,060 |
| 25 to 34 years | 18,156 | 709 | 10,838 | 7,318 |
| 35 to 44 years | 16,963 | 421 | 8,077 | 8,886 |
| 45 to 54 years | 10,958 | 244 | 5,102 | 5,856 |
| 55 years and older | 6,710 | 304 | 3,948 | 2,762 |
| 55 to 64 years | 5,229 | 156 | 2,813 | 2,416 |
| 65 years and older | 1,481 | 148 | 1,135 | 346 |
| Men, 16 years and older | 34,420 | 1,338 | 18,231 | 16,189 |
| 16 to 24 years | 8,156 | 825 | 7,203 | 953 |
| 20 to 24 years | 5,244 | 339 | 4,380 | 864 |
| 25 years and older | 26,264 | 513 | 11,028 | 15,236 |
| Women, 16 years and older | 33,934 | 2,318 | 23,882 | 10,052 |
| 16 to 24 years | 7,411 | 1,154 | 6,946 | 465 |
| 20 to 24 years | 4,534 | 501 | 4,105 | 429 |
| 25 years and older | 26,523 | 1,164 | 16,936 | 9,587 |
| **Race and Hispanic origin** | | | | |
| White | | | | |
| Total, 16 years and older | 56,475 | 2,994 | 34,062 | 22,413 |
| Men | 28,609 | 1,078 | 14,652 | 13,957 |
| Women | 27,866 | 1,916 | 19,410 | 8,456 |
| Black | | | | |
| Total, 16 years and older | 8,957 | 498 | 6,128 | 2,829 |
| Men | 4,281 | 190 | 2,650 | 1,631 |
| Women | 4,676 | 308 | 3,478 | 1,198 |
| Hispanic origin | | | | |
| Total, 16 years and older | 7,624 | 566 | 5,630 | 1,994 |
| Men | 4,637 | 289 | 3,221 | 1,416 |
| Women | 2,987 | 277 | 2,409 | 578 |
| **Full- and part-time status** | | | | |
| Full-time workers | | | | |
| Total, 16 years and older | 51,347 | 1,347 | 28,067 | 23,280 |
| Men | 29,200 | 582 | 13,691 | 15,509 |
| Women | 22,147 | 765 | 14,376 | 7,771 |
| Part-time workers | | | | |
| Total, 16 years and older | 16,898 | 2,301 | 13,982 | 2,916 |
| Men | 5,162 | 751 | 4,509 | 653 |
| Women | 11,736 | 1,550 | 9,473 | 2,263 |

**Note:** Data exclude the incorporated self-employed. (1) $4.25 = minimum wage, Apr. 1, 1991-Sept. 30, 1996.

## Federal Minimum Hourly Wage Rates Since 1950

**Source:** Bureau of Labor Statistics, U.S. Dept. of Labor

The Fair Labor Standards Act of 1938 and subsequent amendments provide for minimum wage-coverage applicable to workers in specified nonsupervisory employment categories. Exempt from coverage are executives and administrators or professionals. Under legislation signed by Pres. Bill Clinton, Aug. 20, 1996, the federal minimum was raised by 90 cents an hour in two steps, effective Oct. 1, 1996, and Sept. 1, 1997.

| | Nonfarm Workers | | | Farm Workers[4] |
|---|---|---|---|---|
| Effective date | Under laws prior to 1966[1] | Percent, of avg earnings[2] | Under 1966 and later provis.[3] | |
| Jan. 25, 1950 | $0.75 | 54 | NA | NA |
| Mar. 1, 1956 | 1.00 | 52 | NA | NA |
| Sept. 3, 1961 | 1.15 | 50 | NA | NA |
| Sept. 3, 1963 | 1.25 | 51 | NA | NA |
| Feb. 1, 1967 | 1.40 | 50 | $1.00 | $1.00 |
| Feb. 1, 1968 | 1.60 | 54 | 1.15 | 1.15 |
| Feb. 1, 1969 | (5) | (5) | 1.30 | 1.30 |
| Feb. 1, 1970 | (5) | (5) | 1.45 | (5) |
| Feb. 1, 1971 | (5) | (5) | 1.60 | (5) |
| May 1, 1974 | 2.00 | 46 | 1.90 | 1.60 |
| Jan. 1, 1975 | $2.10 | 45 | $2.00 | $1.80 |
| Jan. 1, 1976 | 2.30 | 46 | 2.20 | 2.00 |
| Jan. 1, 1977 | (5) | (5) | 2.30 | 2.20 |
| Jan. 1, 1978 | 2.65 | 44 | 2.65 | 2.65 |
| Jan. 1, 1979 | 2.90 | 45 | 2.90 | 2.90 |
| Jan. 1, 1980 | 3.10 | 43 | 3.10 | 3.10 |
| Jan. 1, 1981 | 3.35 | 42 | 3.35 | 3.35 |
| Apr. 1, 1990 | 3.80[6] | 35 | 3.80[6] | 3.80[6] |
| Apr. 1, 1991 | 4.25[6] | 38 | 4.25[6] | 4.25[6] |
| Oct. 1, 1996 | 4.75[7] | NA | 4.75[7] | 4.75[7] |

NA = not applicable. (1) Applies to workers covered prior to 1961 Amendments and, after Sept. 1965, to workers covered by 1961 Amendments. Rates set by 1961 Amendments were: Sept. 1961, $1.00; Sept. 1964, $1.15; and Sept. 1965, $1.25. (2) Percent of gross average hourly earnings of production workers in manufacturing. (3) Applies to workers newly covered by Amendments of 1966, 1974, and 1977, and Title IX of Education Amendments of 1972. (4) Included in coverage as of 1966, 1974, and 1977 Amendments. (5) No change in rate. (6) Training wage for workers age 16-19 in first six months of first job: Apr. 1, 1990, $3.35; Apr. 1, 1991, $3.62. The training wage expired Mar. 31, 1993. (7) Under 1996 legislation, a subminimum training wage of $4.25 an hour was established for employees under 20 years of age during their first 90 consecutive calendar days of employment with an employer. The minimum wage increases to $5.15 an hour on Sept. 1, 1997. For workers receiving gratuities, the minimum wage remained $2.13 per hour.

## Hourly Compensation Costs, by Selected Country, 1975-94

**Source:** Bureau of Labor Statistics, U.S. Dept. of Labor

(in U.S. dollars, compensation for production workers in manufacturing)

| Country/Territory | 1975 | 1985 | 1990 | 1994 |
|---|---|---|---|---|
| United States | $6.36 | $13.01 | $14.91 | $17.10 |
| Canada | 5.96 | 10.94 | 15.83 | 15.68 |
| Mexico | 1.47 | 1.59 | 1.64 | 2.61 |
| Australia | 5.62 | 8.20 | 13.07 | 13.66 |
| Hong Kong | 0.76 | 1.73 | 3.20 | 4.80 |
| Israel | 2.25 | 4.06 | 8.55 | 9.14 |
| Japan | 3.00 | 6.34 | 12.80 | 21.42 |
| Korea, South | 0.32 | 1.23 | 3.71 | 6.25 |
| New Zealand | 3.21 | 4.47 | 8.33 | 8.93 |
| Singapore | 0.84 | 2.47 | 3.78 | 6.29 |
| Sri Lanka | 0.28 | 0.28 | 0.35 | NA |
| Taiwan | 0.40 | 1.50 | 3.95 | 5.55 |
| Austria | 4.51 | 7.58 | 17.75 | 21.73 |
| Belgium | 6.41 | 8.97 | 19.22 | 22.97 |
| Denmark | 6.28 | 8.13 | 17.96 | 20.44 |
| Finland | $4.61 | $8.16 | $21.03 | $18.89 |
| France | 4.52 | 7.52 | 15.23 | 17.04 |
| Germany[1] | 6.35 | 9.60 | 21.96 | 27.31 |
| Greece | 1.69 | 3.66 | 6.71 | NA |
| Ireland | 3.03 | 5.92 | 11.76 | NA |
| Italy | 4.67 | 7.63 | 17.74 | 16.16 |
| Luxembourg | 6.35 | 7.72 | 16.37 | NA |
| Netherlands | 6.58 | 8.75 | 18.29 | 20.91 |
| Norway | 6.77 | 10.37 | 21.47 | 20.91 |
| Portugal | 1.58 | 1.53 | 3.77 | 4.57 |
| Spain | 2.53 | 4.66 | 11.33 | 11.45 |
| Sweden | 7.18 | 9.66 | 20.93 | 18.81 |
| Switzerland | 6.09 | 9.66 | 20.86 | 24.83 |
| United Kingdom | 3.37 | 6.27 | 12.71 | 13.62 |

NA=Not available. (1) Former West Germany.

## Top 15 Metropolitan Areas, by Average Annual Salary, 1994

**Source:** Bureau of Labor Statistics, U.S. Dept. of Labor

| Rank | Metropolitan area | Average annual salary[1] |
|---|---|---|
| 1. | New York, NY | $39,933 |
| 2. | San Jose, CA | 39,127 |
| 3. | Middlesex–Somerset–Hunterdon, NJ | 36,690 |
| 4. | San Francisco, CA | 36,510 |
| 5. | Newark, NJ | 35,910 |
| 6. | New Haven–Bridgeport–Stamford–Danbury–Waterbury, CT | 35,535 |
| 7. | Trenton, NJ | 35,345 |
| 8. | Bergen–Passaic, NJ | $34,675 |
| 9. | Anchorage, AK | 34,098 |
| 10. | Washington, DC–MD–VA | 33,949 |
| 11. | Kokomo, IN | 33,231 |
| 12. | Flint, MI | 33,219 |
| 13. | Detroit, MI | 33,203 |
| 14. | Hartford, CT | 33,172 |
| 15. | Jersey City, NJ | 33,012 |

**Note:** Jacksonville, NC, recorded the **lowest annual pay level** among metropolitan statistical areas in 1994—$16,334—followed by Myrtle Beach, SC ($17,498), McAllen–Edinburg–Mission, TX ($17,683), Brownsville–Harlingen–San Benito, TX ($17,952), and Yuma, AZ ($17,996). The average annual salary in the 5 bottom-ranked metropolitan areas averaged 36-42% below the nationwide metropolitan average of $28,128. A total of 20 metropolitan areas reported average pay levels below $20,000 annually. (1) Data are preliminary and include workers covered by Unemployment Insurance and Unemployment Compensation for Federal Employees programs.

## Average Hours and Earnings of Production Workers, 1967-95[1]

**Source:** Bureau of Labor Statistics, U.S. Dept. of Labor

(annual averages)

| | Weekly hours | Hourly earnings | Weekly earnings |
|---|---|---|---|
| 1967 | 38.0 | $2.68 | $ 101.84 |
| 1968 | 37.8 | 2.85 | 107.73 |
| 1969 | 37.7 | 3.04 | 114.61 |
| 1970 | 37.1 | 3.23 | 119.83 |
| 1971 | 36.9 | 3.45 | 127.31 |
| 1972 | 37.0 | 3.70 | 136.90 |
| 1973 | 36.9 | 3.94 | 145.39 |
| 1974 | 36.5 | 4.24 | 154.76 |
| 1975 | 36.1 | 4.53 | 163.53 |
| 1976 | 36.1 | 4.86 | 175.45 |
| 1977 | 36.0 | 5.25 | 189.00 |
| 1978 | 35.8 | 5.69 | 203.70 |
| 1979 | 35.7 | 6.16 | 219.91 |
| 1980 | 35.3 | 6.66 | 235.10 |
| 1981 | 35.2 | 7.25 | 255.20 |
| 1982 | 34.8 | $ 7.68 | $267.26 |
| 1983 | 35.0 | 8.02 | 280.70 |
| 1984 | 35.2 | 8.32 | 292.86 |
| 1985 | 34.9 | 8.57 | 299.09 |
| 1986 | 34.8 | 8.76 | 304.85 |
| 1987 | 34.8 | 8.98 | 312.50 |
| 1988 | 34.7 | 9.28 | 322.02 |
| 1989 | 34.6 | 9.66 | 334.24 |
| 1990 | 34.5 | 10.01 | 345.35 |
| 1991 | 34.3 | 10.32 | 353.98 |
| 1992 | 34.4 | 10.57 | 363.61 |
| 1993 | 34.5 | 10.83 | 373.64 |
| 1994 | 34.7 | 11.12 | 385.86 |
| 1995 | 34.5 | 11.44 | 394.68 |

(1) Data relate to private-industry production workers in mining and manufacturing; construction workers in construction; and nonsupervisory workers in transportation and public utilities; wholesale and retail trade; finance, insurance, and real estate; and services.

## Educational Attainment by Labor-Force Status and Occupation, March 1995

**Source:** Bureau of the Census, Dept. of Commerce

| Characteristics | Number of persons (1,000) | Percentage with: High school degree or more | Some college or more | Bachelor's degree or more |
|---|---|---|---|---|
| **Civilian labor force, 25 years and older** | **110,357** | **88.8** | **55.7** | **28.1** |
| Employed | 105,163 | 89.4 | 56.4 | 28.7 |
| Not employed | 5,193 | 77.4 | 41.3 | 15.2 |
| Not in the labor force | 55,309 | 67.1 | 31.5 | 12.7 |
| **Total, employed persons, 25-64 years old** | **101,454** | **89.8** | **56.8** | **28.9** |
| Executive, admin., and managerial | 15,161 | 97.5 | 77.2 | 49.0 |
| Professional specialty occupations | 16,645 | 99.3 | 93.6 | 76.5 |
| Technicians and related support occupations | 3,402 | 98.6 | 78.7 | 31.1 |
| Sales occupations | 11,010 | 94.2 | 59.7 | 29.5 |
| Administrative support occupations, includ. clerical | 14,963 | 96.5 | 54.5 | 14.4 |
| Private household occupations | 582 | 61.5 | 20.4 | 5.7 |
| Other service occupations | 11,562 | 80.7 | 37.4 | 8.4 |
| Farming, forestry, and fishing | 2,446 | 70.1 | 31.2 | 12.1 |
| Precision products, craft, and repair | 11,530 | 83.6 | 36.0 | 6.6 |
| Machine operators, assemblers, and inspectors | 6,668 | 72.6 | 23.1 | 3.9 |
| Transportation and material moving | 4,314 | 79.8 | 29.9 | 5.8 |
| Handlers, equip. cleaners, helpers, and laborers | 3,171 | 73.3 | 23.6 | 4.9 |

# Impact of the Family and Medical Leave Law

**Source:** Commission on Family and Medical Leave, Dept. of Labor

The Family and Medical Leave Act (FMLA) took effect in Aug. 1993. It required businesses with 50 or more employees to grant workers up to 12 weeks of unpaid leave to address their own serious health condition; the serious illness of a child, parent, or spouse; or the birth or adoption of a child. According to studies conducted for the bipartisan Commission on Family and Medical Leave, slightly fewer than half (46.5%) of all American workers employed in the private sector were covered under FMLA, and between 2% and 4% of these employees in FMLA-covered firms actually took leave under the new law in the 18-month period from Jan. 1994 to July 1995, which was the time period that was measured by the studies.

The studies also found that:

- Approximately 58% of leave takers were women.
- The largest group of leave takers were 35-49 years old.
- The most common reason cited by employees for leave was to address their own serious health condition (58.8% of respondents).
- Caring for a seriously ill child, spouse, or parent was the next most common reason for taking leave (18.9%).
- Half of those who took leave used fewer than 10 days of leave.
- Leaves to care for an ill child, spouse, or parent were of the shortest average duration.
- About two-thirds of FMLA-covered firms (66%) changed their leave policies to comply with the 1993 law. Other FMLA-covered firms already had policies consistent with the 1993 law.
- Of the 66% that changed their policies, about three-fourths (76.9%) had expanded the number of reasons employees could take leave; 69.3% allowed male employees to take leave to care for sick, newborn, or newly adopted children; 66.4% had expanded the length of leave available; 54.8% provided job-guaranteed leave; and 52.9% continued health insurance during leave.
- Overall, 86.5% of employers that are covered by FMLA reported knowledge of the 1993 law, and about 90% of these firms reported no costs or small costs associated with administration, hiring and training, and continuation of benefits under FMLA.
- At least 85% of establishments covered by the FMLA reported "no noticeable effect" on employee turnover, absences, and productivity. Large firms (defined as those with more than 250 employees) were more likely to report "noticeable effects" than smaller FMLA-covered firms.
- Nearly 40% of employers (39.2%) said that it was very or somewhat difficult to manage the intermittent leave allowed under the FMLA.
- Nearly half (46%) of small businesses (defined as those with fewer than 50 employees) that were not covered by the FMLA predicted a negative effect on business productivity and profitability if the law were to be extended to them. This finding appeared more negative than the actual experience of companies that had implemented the FMLA during the last 2 years.

# 10 Facts About Women Workers

**Source:** Women's Bureau, U.S. Dept. of Labor

1. Of the 103 million women 16 years or older in the U.S., 61 million were labor-force participants (working or looking for work) during 1995. Women accounted for 59% of labor-force growth between 1985 and 1995.
2. Women represented 46% of all persons in the civilian labor force in 1995. Women are projected to comprise 48% of the labor force by the year 2005.
3. Teenage women (16-19 years old) are not as active in the labor force as adult women (20 years of age and older). In all, 52% of teenage women were participants in the labor force, compared with 59% of adult women. Teenage women's unemployment rate was 3 times as high as that of adult women—16.1%, as against 4.9%.
4. The unemployment rate for all women in the labor force was 5.6% in 1995. Teenage black and Hispanic women continued to experience much higher unemployment rates—34.3% and 22.6%, respectively.
5. Of the 58 million employed women in the U.S. in 1995, 42 million worked full time (35 or more hours per week); nearly 16 million, or 28% of all women workers, held part-time jobs. Two-thirds (68%) of all part-time workers were women.
6. Women have made substantial progress in obtaining jobs in virtually all managerial and professional specialty occupations. In 1985 they held 43% (11 million) of these high-paying jobs; in 1995 they held 48% (16.9 million). Women employed in managerial and professional specialty occupations had 1995 median weekly earnings between $303 and $958.
7. Women are still overrepresented in relatively low-paying jobs. Two-fifths (42%) of employed women work in technical, sales, and administrative support positions—24 million women. Even though the earnings gap between men and women is slowly closing, women still earn only 75 cents for every dollar earned by men when considering 1995 median weekly earnings of full-time workers ($406 for women and $538 for men). The 5 most lucrative occupations for women are: lawyer, physician, engineer, physical therapist, and computer systems analyst and scientist. (This list excludes any occupation at which fewer than 50,000 females are employed.)
8. Median income for female high school graduates age 25 and older (with no college) working year-round, full time in 1994 was less than that of fully employed men who were high school dropouts—$20,373 and $22,048, respectively. During the 10-year period ending in 1994, the income gap between the 2 groups slowly declined from $4,551 to $1,675. Female high school graduates (with no college) continue to have incomes substantially lower than their male counterparts—$20,373 versus $28,037. In addition, men with an associate's degree working year-round, full time had incomes a little higher than similarly employed women with a bachelor's degree—$35,794 and $35,378, respectively.
9. Of the approximately 69 million families in the U.S. in 1994, 12 million (18%) were maintained by women. In black families, women maintained 46%; in Hispanic families, 24%; and in white families, 14%. The 1994 median income of families maintained by women was $18,236, compared with $44,959 for married-couple families and $27,751 for families maintained by men, no wife present.
10. In 1994 women represented 62% of all persons 18 years and older who were living below the poverty level. The poverty rate for families maintained by women with no husband present was nearly 5 times as high as for married-couple families—38.6% and 7.4%, respectively. Women maintained half of all poor families in 1994. Women maintained 77% of poor black families, about 40% of poor Hispanic families, and 39% of poor white families.

# Median Weekly Earnings of Full-Time Wage and Salary Workers by Age, Sex, and Union Affiliation, 1994-95

**Source:** Bureau of Labor Statistics, U.S. Dept. of Labor

| Sex and age | 1994 Total | 1994 Members of unions[1] | 1994 Represented by unions[2] | 1994 Non-union | 1995 Total | 1995 Members of unions[1] | 1995 Represented by unions[2] | 1995 Non-union |
|---|---|---|---|---|---|---|---|---|
| Total, 16 years and older | $467 | $592 | $587 | $432 | $479 | $602 | $598 | $447 |
| 16 to 24 years | 286 | 366 | 364 | 281 | 292 | 375 | 373 | 287 |
| 25 years and older | 500 | 603 | 599 | 474 | 510 | 613 | 610 | 486 |
| 25 to 34 years | 439 | 532 | 522 | 421 | 451 | 542 | 534 | 433 |
| 35 to 44 years | 537 | 623 | 618 | 508 | 550 | 621 | 619 | 520 |
| 45 to 54 years | 566 | 639 | 636 | 520 | 582 | 665 | 663 | 536 |
| 55 to 64 years | 501 | 588 | 589 | 472 | 514 | 614 | 614 | 482 |
| 65 years and older | 384 | 549 | 549 | 361 | 389 | 509 | 506 | 362 |
| Men, 16 years and older | 522 | 621 | 620 | 495 | 538 | 640 | 638 | 507 |
| 16 to 24 years | 294 | 374 | 371 | 288 | 303 | 388 | 388 | 298 |
| 25 years and older | 576 | 635 | 635 | 544 | 588 | 654 | 652 | 563 |
| 25 to 34 years | 479 | 572 | 566 | 460 | 490 | 583 | 579 | 475 |
| 35 to 44 years | 617 | 657 | 656 | 603 | 624 | 665 | 663 | 612 |
| 45 to 54 years | 671 | 685 | 684 | 661 | 685 | 705 | 706 | 670 |
| 55 to 64 years | 603 | 617 | 624 | 591 | 623 | 655 | 659 | 607 |
| 65 years and older | 441 | 608 | 604 | 405 | 441 | 615 | 619 | 400 |
| Women, 16 years and older | 399 | 522 | 517 | 377 | 406 | 527 | 523 | 386 |
| 16 to 24 years | 276 | 350 | 348 | 271 | 275 | 349 | 345 | 272 |
| 25 years and older | 421 | 535 | 527 | 401 | 428 | 539 | 536 | 408 |
| 25 to 34 years | 397 | 483 | 478 | 385 | 403 | 492 | 488 | 393 |
| 35 to 44 years | 448 | 570 | 560 | 419 | 453 | 553 | 552 | 427 |
| 45 to 54 years | 450 | 573 | 572 | 415 | 464 | 595 | 593 | 423 |
| 55 to 64 years | 398 | 506 | 504 | 374 | 403 | 501 | 501 | 383 |
| 65 years and older | 336 | 458 | 450 | 323 | 353 | 435 | 425 | 333 |

**Note:** Data refer to the sole or principal job of full-time workers. Excluded are self-employed workers whose businesses are incorporated, although they technically qualify as wage and salary workers. (1) Data refer to members of a labor union or an employee association similar to a union. (2) Data refer to members of a labor union or an employee association similar to a union, as well as to workers who report no union affiliation but whose jobs are covered by a union or an employee association contract.

# Work Stoppages (Strikes and Lockouts) in the U.S., 1960-95

**Source:** Bureau of Labor Statistics, U.S. Dept. of Labor; involving 1,000 workers or more

| Year | Number stoppages[1] | Workers involved[1] (thousands) | Work days idle[1] (thousands) |
|---|---|---|---|
| 1960 | 222 | 896 | 13,260 |
| 1965 | 268 | 999 | 15,140 |
| 1970 | 381 | 2,468 | 52,761 |
| 1971 | 298 | 2,516 | 35,538 |
| 1972 | 250 | 975 | 16,764 |
| 1973 | 317 | 1,400 | 16,260 |
| 1974 | 424 | 1,796 | 31,809 |
| 1975 | 235 | 965 | 17,563 |
| 1976 | 231 | 1,519 | 23,962 |
| 1977 | 298 | 1,212 | 21,258 |
| 1978 | 219 | 1,006 | 23,774 |
| 1979 | 235 | 1,021 | 20,409 |
| 1980 | 187 | 795 | 20,844 |
| 1981 | 145 | 729 | 16,908 |
| 1982 | 96 | 656 | 9,061 |
| 1983 | 81 | 909 | 17,461 |
| 1984 | 62 | 376 | 8,499 |
| 1985 | 54 | 324 | 7,079 |
| 1986 | 69 | 533 | 11,861 |
| 1987 | 46 | 174 | 4,481 |
| 1988 | 40 | 118 | 4,381 |
| 1989 | 51 | 452 | 16,996 |
| 1990 | 44 | 185 | 5,926 |
| 1991 | 40 | 392 | 4,584 |
| 1992 | 35 | 364 | 3,989 |
| 1993 | 35 | 182 | 3,981 |
| 1994 | 45 | 322 | 5,020 |
| 1995 | 31 | 192 | 5,771 |

(1) The number of stoppages and workers relate to stoppages that began in the year. Days of idleness include all stoppages in effect. Workers are counted more than once if they were involved in more than one stoppage during the year.

# Work Stoppages Involving 5,000 Workers or More, Beginning in 1995

**Source:** Bureau of Labor Statistics, U.S. Dept. of Labor

| Employer, location, and union | Began | Ended | Workers involved[1] | Estimated days idle in 1995[1] |
|---|---|---|---|---|
| **General Motors Corp.**, Flint, MI; Automobile Workers (UAW) | 1/18 | 1/20 | 37,700 | 64,500 |
| **Southern Pennsylvania Transportation Authority,** Philadelphia, PA, area; Transport Workers (TWU) | 3/28 | 4/10 | 5,200 | 52,000 |
| **Chrysler Corp.**, Kokomo, IN; Automobile Workers (UAW) | 3/31 | 3/31 | 5,700 | 5,700 |
| **General Motors Corp.**, Pontiac East truck plant, Pontiac, MI; Automobile Workers (UAW) | 3/31 | 4/5 | 5,500 | 22,000 |
| **Retail grocery chains—Safeway, Lucky Stores, and Save Mart,** Northern California, Food and Commercial Workers (UFCW) | 4/7 | 4/15 | 32,000 | 192,000 |
| **Oregon State,** Oregon; Service Employees (SEIU) | 5/8 | 5/14 | 14,000 | 50,000 |
| **Pacific Maritime Association,** West Coast ports; Longshoremen and Warehousemen (ILWU) | 8/7 | 8/7 | 7,500 | 7,500 |
| **Ryder Systems, Inc.**, interstate; Teamsters (IBT) | 9/7 | 10/7 | 5,000 | 110,000 |
| **Boeing Co.,** Wichita, KS; Portland, OR; and Seattle, WA; Machinists (IAM) | 10/6 | 12/14 | 33,000 | 1,551,000 |

(1) Workers and days idle are rounded to the nearest 100.

# Labor Union Directory

Source: Bureau of Labor Statistics, U.S. Dept. of Labor; AFL-CIO; World Almanac questionnaire

(*) Independent union; all others affiliated with AFL-CIO.

**American Federation of Labor & Congress of Industrial Organizations (AFL-CIO),** 815 16th St. NW, Washington, DC 20006; founded 1955; John J. Sweeney, Pres. (since 1995); 13.1 mil. members.

**Actors and Artistes of America, Associated (AAAA),** 165 W 46th St., New York, NY 10036; founded 1919; Theodore Bikel, Pres.; no individual members, 7 National Performing Arts Unions are affiliates; approx. 100,000 combined membership.

**Actors' Equity Association,** 165 W 46th St., New York, NY 10036; founded 1913; Ron Silver, Pres. (since 1991); 39,000 active members.

**Air Line Pilots Association,** 535 Herndon Parkway, PO Box 1169, Herndon, VA 22070; founded 1931; J. Randolph Babbitt, Pres. (since 1990); 45,000 members.

**Aluminum, Brick & Glass Workers International Union (ABGWIU),** 3362 Hollenberg Drive, Bridgeton, MO 63044; founded 1953; Ernie J. LaBaff, Pres. (since 1985); 40,000 members, 300 locals.

**Automobile, Aerospace & Agricultural Implement Workers of America, International Union, United (UAW),** 8000 E Jefferson Ave., Detroit, MI 48214; founded 1935; Stephen P. Yokich, Pres. (since 1995); 1.3 mil. members, 1,130 locals.

**Bakery, Confectionery & Tobacco Workers International Union (BC&T),** 10401 Connecticut Ave., Kensington, MD 20895; founded 1886; Frank Hurt, Pres. (since 1992); 125,000 members.

**Boilermakers, Iron Shipbuilders, Blacksmiths, Forgers and Helpers, International Brotherhood of (IBBISB/BF&H),** 753 State Ave., Suite 570, Kansas City, KS 66101; founded 1880; Charles W. Jones, Pres. (since 1983); 82,419 members, 337 locals.

**Bricklayers and Allied Craftworkers, International Union of,** 815 15th St. NW, Washington, DC 20005; founded 1865; John T. Joyce, Pres. (since 1979); 100,000 members, 400 locals.

**Carpenters and Joiners of America, United Brotherhood of,** 101 Constitution Ave. NW, Washington, DC 20001; founded 1881; Douglas J. McCarron, Gen. Pres. (since 1995); 500,000 members, 1,000 locals.

**Chemical Workers Union, International (ICWU),** 1655 W Market St., Akron, OH 44313; founded 1944 (merged with Food and Commercial Workers, July 1, 1996).

**Clothing and Textile Workers Union, Amalgamated (ACTWU),** 15 Union Square, New York, NY 10003; founded 1976 (merged with International Ladies' Garment Workers' to form Needletrades, Industrial, and Textile Employees, June 1995.

**Communications Workers of America (CWA),** 501 3d St. NW, Washington, DC 20001; founded 1938; Morton Bahr, Pres. (since 1985); 600,000 members, 2,000 locals.

**Distillery, Wine & Allied Workers International Union (DWU),** 66 Grand Ave., Englewood, NJ 07631; founded 1940 (merged with Food and Commercial Workers, Oct. 1, 1995).

***Education Association, National,** 1201 16th St. NW, Washington, DC 20036; founded 1857; Bob Chase, Pres. (since 1996); 2 mil. members, 13,500 affiliates.

**Electrical Workers, International Brotherhood of (IBEW),** 1125 15th St. NW, Washington, DC 20005; founded 1891; John J. Barry, Intl Pres. (since 1986); 800,000 members, 1,134 locals.

**Electronic, Electrical, Salaried, Machine and Furniture Workers, International Union of (IUE),** 1126 16th St. NW, Washington, DC 20036; founded 1949; William H. Bywater, Pres. (since 1982); 130,000 members, 450 locals.

**Engineers, International Union of Operating (IUOE),** 1125 17th St. NW, Washington, DC 20036; founded 1896; Frank Hanley, Gen. Pres.; 400,000 members, 183 locals.

**Farm Workers of America, United (UFW),** 29700 Woodford Tehachapi Rd., PO Box 62, Keene, CA 93531; founded 1962; Arturo S. Rodríguez, Pres. (since 1993); 50,000 members.

***Federal Employees, National Federation of (NFFE),** 1016 16th St. NW, Suite 300, Washington, DC 20036; founded 1917; Gary W. Divine, Pres. (since 1996); 150,000 members, 350 locals.

**Fire Fighters, International Association of,** 1750 New York Ave. NW, Washington, DC 20006; founded 1918; Alfred K. Whitehead, Pres. (since 1988); 200,000 members, 2,280 locals.

**Firemen and Oilers, International Brotherhood of,** 1100 Circle 75 Parkway, Suite 350, Atlanta, GA 30339; founded 1899; Jimmy L. Walker, Pres.; 26,000 members, 210 locals.

**Flight Attendants, Association of,** 1625 Massachusetts Ave. NW, Washington, DC 20036-2212; founded 1945; Patricia A. Friend, Pres.; 40,000 members.

**Food and Commercial Workers International Union, United (UFCW),** 1775 K St. NW, Washington, DC 20006-1598; founded 1979 following merger; Douglas H. Dority, Intl Pres. (since 1994); 1.4 mil. members, 997 locals.

**Garment Workers of America, United (UGWA),** 4207 Lebanon Rd., Hermitage, TN 37076; founded 1891 (merged with Food and Commercial Workers, Dec. 1, 1994).

**Garment Workers' Union, International Ladies' (ILGWU),** 1710 Broadway, New York, NY 10019; founded 1900 (merged with Amalgamated Clothing and Textile Workers to form Needletrades, Industrial, and Textile Employees, June 1995.

**Glass, Molders, Pottery, Plastics & Allied Workers Intl. Union (GMP),** 608 E Baltimore Pike, PO Box 607, Media, PA 19063; founded 1842; Frank Carter, Intl Pres. (since 1994); 68,000 members, 390 locals.

**Government Employees, American Federation of (AFGE),** 80 F St. NW, Washington, DC 20001; founded 1932; John N. Sturdivant, Natl. Pres. (since 1988); 210,000 members, 1,200 locals.

**Grain Millers, American Federation of (AFGM),** 4949 Olson Memorial Hwy., Minneapolis, MN 55422; founded 1936; Larry R. Jackson, Gen. Pres. (since 1991); 27,000 members, 200 locals.

**Graphic Communications International Union (GCIU),** 1900 L St. NW, Washington, DC 20036; founded 1983; James J. Norton, Pres. (since 1985); 160,000 members, 450 locals.

**Hotel Employees and Restaurant Employees International Union,** 1219 28th St. NW, Washington, DC 20007; Edward T. Henley, Gen. Pres.(since 1973); 400,000 members, 190 locals.

**Iron Workers, International Association of Bridge, Structural and Ornamental,** 1750 New York Ave. NW, Suite 400, Washington, DC 20006; founded 1896; Jake West, Gen. Pres. (since 1989); 120,000 members, 242 locals.

**Laborers' International Union of North America (LIUNA),** 905 16th St. NW, Washington, DC 20006-1765; founded 1903; Arthur A. Coia, Gen. Pres. (since 1993); 750,000 members, 624 locals.

**Leather Goods, Plastics Novelty and Service Workers' Union, International,** 265 W 14th St., New York, NY 10011; Andrew McKenzie, Gen. Pres. (since 1992); 6,000 members, 85 locals.

**Letter Carriers, National Association of (NALC),** 100 Indiana Ave. NW, Washington, DC 20001-2144; founded 1889; Vincent R. Sombrotto, Pres. (since 1978); 320,000 members, 3,100 locals.

***Locomotive Engineers, Brotherhood of (BLE),** The Standard Bldg. Mezzanine, 1370 Ontario St., Cleveland, OH 44113-1702; founded 1863; Clarence V. Monin, Intl Pres. (since 1996); 55,000 members, 615 divisions.

**Longshoremen's Association, International (ILA),** 17 Battery Pl., New York, NY 10004; John Bowers, Pres., (since 1987); 65,000 members, 340 locals.

***Longshoremen's & Warehousemen's Union, International (ILWU),** 1188 Franklin St., San Francisco, CA 94109-6800; founded 1937; Brian McWilliams, Pres. (since 1994); 60,000 members, 74 locals.

**Machinists and Aerospace Workers, International Association of (IAM),** 9000 Machinists Pl., Upper Marlboro, MD 20772-2687; founded 1888; George J. Kourpias, Intl Pres. (since 1989); 731,780 members, 1,370 locals.

**Maintenance of Way Employees, Brotherhood of (BMWE),** 26555 Evergreen Rd., Suite 200, Southfield, MI 48076; founded 1887; Mac A. Fleming, Pres. (since 1990); 50,000 members, 790 locals.

**Marine Engineer Beneficial Assn. (MEBA),** 444 N Capitol St. NW, Suite 800, Washington, DC 20001; founded 1875; Alex Shandrowsky, Pres. (since 1996); 4,242 members, 25 locals.

**Maritime Union, National (NMU),** 30 Montgomery St., 8th floor, Jersey City, NJ 07302; Louis Parise, Pres.; 50,000 members.

***Mine Workers of America, United (UMWA),** 900 15th St. NW, Washington, DC 20005; founded 1890; Cecil Roberts, Intl Pres. (since 1996); 240,000 members, 900 locals.

**Musicians of the United States and Canada, American Federation of (AF of M),** 1501 Broadway, Suite 600, New York, NY 10036; founded 1896; Steve Young, Pres. (since 1995); 125,000 members, 324 locals.

**Needletrades, Industrial, and Textile Employees, Union of (UNITE),** 1710 Broadway, New York, NY 10019; founded 1995; Jay Mazur, Pres (since 1995); 285,000 members, 1,138 locals.

**Newspaper Guild, The (TNG),** 8611 Second Ave., Silver Spring, MD 20910; founded 1933; Linda Foley, Pres. (since 1995); 34,000 members, 72 locals.

***Nurses Association, American (ANA),** 600 Maryland Ave. SW, Suite 100W, Washington, DC 20024-2571; founded 1897; Beverly L. Malone, PhD, RN, FAAN, Pres. (since 1996); 200,000 members, 53 constituent state & territorial assns.

**Office and Professional Employees International Union (OPEIU),** 265 W 14th St., Suite 610, New York, NY 10011; founded 1945 (AFL Charter); Michael Goodwin, Intl Pres. (since 1994); 110,334 members, 200 locals.

**Oil, Chemical and Atomic Workers International Union (OCAW),** 255 Union Blvd., PO Box 281200, Lakewood, CO 80228-8200; Robert E. Wages, Pres. (since 1991); 87,000 members, 350 locals.

**Painters and Allied Trades, International Brotherhood of (IBPAT),** 1750 New York Ave. NW, Washington, DC 20006; founded 1887; A. L. "Mike" Monroe, Gen. Pres.; 128,243 members, 550 locals.

**Paperworkers International Union, United (UPIU),** 3340 Perimeter Hill Dr., Nashville, TN 37211; founded 1884; Boyd Young, Pres. (since 1996); 255,000 members, 1,300 locals.

***Plant Guard Workers of America, International Union, United (UPGWA),** 25510 Kelly Rd., Roseville, MI 48066; founded 1948; Gene McConville, Pres.; 20,000 members, 180 locals.

**Plasterers' and Cement Masons' International Association of the United States & Canada, Operative,** 1125 17th St. NW, 6th floor, Washington, DC 20036; founded 1864; Dominic A. Martell, Gen. Pres.; 50,000 members, 135 locals.

**Plumbing and Pipe Fitting Industry of the United States and Canada, United Association of Journeymen and Apprentices of the,** 901 Massachusetts Ave. NW, Washington, DC 20001; founded 1889; Marvin J. Boede, Pres. (since 1982); 292,000 members, 417 locals.

***Police, Fraternal Order of,** 1410 Donelson Pike, A-17, Nashville, TN 37217; Gilbert G. Gallegos, Natl. Pres. (since 1995); 270,000 members, 1,992 affiliates.

**Police Associations, International Union of,** 1421 Prince St., Suite 330, Alexandria, VA 22314; Sam A. Cabral, Pres (since 1995); 50,000 members, 400 locals.

***Postal Supervisors, National Association of,** 1727 King St., Suite 400, Alexandria, VA 22314-2753; Vincent Palladino, Pres. (since 1992); 36,000 members, 400 locals.

**Postal Workers Union, American (APWU),** 1300 L St. NW, Washington, DC 20005; founded 1971; Moe Biller, Pres. (since 1980); 350,000 members, 1,850 locals.

**Retail, Wholesale and Department Store Union,** 30 E 29th St., New York, NY 10016; Lenore Miller, Pres.; 100,000 members, 157 locals.

**Roofers, Waterproofers & Allied Workers, United Union of,** 1660 L St. NW, Suite 800, Washington, DC 20036; founded 1906; Earl J. Kruse, Pres. (since 1985); 25,000 members, 110 locals.

**Rubber, Cork, Linoleum and Plastic Workers of America, United (URW),** 570 White Pond Dr., Akron, OH 44320-1156; founded 1935 (merged with Steelworkers, July 1, 1995).

***Rural Letter Carriers' Association, National,** 1630 Duke St., 4th floor, Alexandria, VA 22314; founded 1903; Scottie B. Hicks, Pres. (since 1994); 93,000 members; 50 state org.

**Seafarers International Union of North America (SIUNA),** 5201 Auth Way, Camp Springs, MD 20746; founded 1938; Michael Sacco, Pres. (since 1988); 85,000 members, 18 locals.

**Service Employees International Union (SEIU),** 1313 L St. NW, Washington, DC 20005; founded 1921; Andrew L. Stern, Pres. (since 1996); 1,084,720 members, 493 locals.

**Sheet Metal Workers' International Association (SMWIA),** 1750 New York Ave. NW, Washington, DC 20006; founded 1888; Arthur Moore, Gen. Pres. (since 1993); 150,000 members, 203 locals.

**State, County and Municipal Employees, American Federation of (AFSCME),** 1625 L St. NW, Washington, DC 20036; Gerald McEntee, Pres. (since 1981); 1.3 mil. members, 3,617 locals.

**Steelworkers of America, United (USWA),** 5 Gateway Center, Pittsburgh, PA 15222; founded 1936; George Becker, Intl Pres. (since 1994); 550,000 members, 2,300 locals.

**Teachers, American Federation of (AFT),** 555 New Jersey Ave. NW, Washington, DC 20001; founded 1916; Albert Shanker, Pres. (since 1974); 900,000 members, 2,378 locals.

**Teamsters, Chauffeurs, Warehousemen and Helpers of America, International Brotherhood of (IBT),** 25 Louisiana Ave. NW, Washington, DC 20001; founded 1903; Ronald R. Carey, Pres. (since 1992); 1.4 mil. members, 559 locals.

**Television and Radio Artists, American Federation of,** 260 Madison Ave., 7th floor, New York, NY 10016; founded 1937; Shelby Scott, Pres. (since 1993); 75,000 members, 30 locals.

**Textile Workers of America, United (UTWA),** 2 Echelon Plaza, Suite 200, Laurel Rd., Voorhees, NJ 08043; founded 1901 (merged with Food and Commercial Workers, Nov. 1, 1995).

**Theatrical Stage Employees, Moving Picture Technicians, Artists and Allied Crafts of the United States and Canada, International Alliance of (IATSE),** 1515 Broadway, Suite 601, New York, NY 10036; founded 1893; Thomas C. Short, Intl Pres. (since 1994); 90,000 members, 555 locals.

**Transit Union, Amalgamated (ATU),** 5025 Wisconsin Ave. NW, Washington, DC 20016; founded 1892; James LaSala, Intl Pres. (since 1986); 155,000 members, 275 locals.

**Transportation-Communications International Union (TCU),** 3 Research Place, Rockville, MD 20850; founded 1899; Robert A. Scardelletti, Intl Pres. (since 1991); 125,000 members, 450 locals.

**Transportation Union, United (UTU),** 14600 Detroit Ave., Cleveland, OH 44107; founded 1969; Charles L. Little, Pres. (since 1995); 80,000 members, 688 locals.

**Transport Workers Union of America,** 80 West End Ave., New York, NY 10023; founded 1934; Sonny Hall, Intl Pres. (since 1993); 125,000 members, 92 locals.

***Treasury Employees Union, National (NTEU),** 901 E St. NW, Suite 600, Washington, DC 20004; founded 1938; Robert M. Tobias, Natl. Pres. (since 1983); 150,000 represented, 226 chapters.

***University Professors, American Association of (AAUP),** 1012 14th St. NW, Washington, DC 20005; founded 1915; James Perley, Pres.; 44,000 members, 850 chapters.

**Utility Workers Union of America (UWUA),** 815 16th St. NW, Suite 605, Washington, DC 20006; founded 1945; Donald E. Wightman, Natl. Pres. (since 1996); 50,000 members, 225 locals.

## U.S. Union Membership, 1930-95

**Source:** Bureau of Labor Statistics, U.S. Dept. of Labor

| Year | Labor force[1] (thousands) | Union members[2] (thousands) | Percentage of labor force | Year | Labor force[1] (thousands) | Union members[2] (thousands) | Percentage of labor force |
|---|---|---|---|---|---|---|---|
| 1930 | 29,424 | 3,401 | 11.6 | 1985 | 94,521 | 16,996 | 18.0 |
| 1935 | 27,053 | 3,584 | 13.2 | 1986 | 96,903 | 16,975 | 17.5 |
| 1940 | 32,376 | 8,717 | 26.9 | 1987 | 99,303 | 16,913 | 17.0 |
| 1945 | 40,394 | 14,322 | 35.5 | 1988 | 101,407 | 17,002 | 16.8 |
| 1950 | 45,222 | 14,267 | 31.5 | 1989 | 103,480 | 16,960 | 16.4 |
| 1955 | 50,675 | 16,802 | 33.2 | 1990 | 103,905 | 16,740 | 16.1 |
| 1960 | 54,234 | 17,049 | 31.4 | 1991 | 102,786 | 16,568 | 16.1 |
| 1965 | 60,815 | 17,299 | 28.4 | 1992 | 103,688 | 16,390 | 15.8 |
| 1970 | 70,920 | 19,381 | 27.3 | 1993 | 105,067 | 16,598 | 15.8 |
| 1975 | 76,945 | 19,611 | 25.5 | 1994 | 107,989 | 16,748 | 15.5 |
| 1980 | 90,564 | 19,843 | 21.9 | 1995 | 110,038 | 16,360 | 14.9 |

(1) Does not include agricultural employment; from 1985, does not include self-employed or unemployed persons. (2) From 1930 to 1980 data are the number of dues-paying members of traditional trade unions, with members counted regardless of employment status; from 1985, figures also include members of employee associations that engage in collective bargaining with employers.

# NATIONAL DEFENSE

Data as of mid-1996

Chairman, Joint Chiefs of Staff
**Gen. John M. Shalikashvili**
Vice Chairman
**Gen. Joseph W. Ralston**

The Joint Chiefs of Staff consists of the Chairman and Vice Chairman of the Joint Chiefs of Staff; the Chief of Staff, U.S. Army; the Chief of Naval Operations; the Chief of Staff, U.S. Air Force; and the Commandant of the Marine Corps.

## Army

**Chief of Staff**—Gen. Dennis J. Reimer

| Generals | Date of Rank |
|---|---|
| Clark , Wesley K. | June 21, 1996 |
| Crouch, William W. | Jan. 1, 1995 |
| Griffith, Ronald H. | June 6, 1995 |
| Hartzog, William W. | Dec. 1, 1994 |
| Joulwan, George A. | Nov. 21, 1990 |
| Luck, Gary E. | July 1, 1993 |
| Peay, J. H. Binford, III. | Mar. 26, 1993 |
| Shalikashvili, John M. | June 24, 1992 |
| Shelton, Henry H. | Mar. 1, 1996 |
| Tilelli, John H., Jr. | July 19, 1994 |
| Wilson, Johnnie E. | May 1, 1996 |

## Air Force

**Chief of Staff**—Gen. Ronald R. Fogleman

| Generals | Date of Rank |
|---|---|
| Boles, Billy J. | July 1, 1995 |
| Estes, Howell M., III | Oct. 1, 1996 |
| Habiger, Eugene E. | Mar. 1, 1996 |
| Hawley, Richard E. | Aug. 1, 1995 |
| Jamerson, James L. | Sept. 1, 1994 |
| Kross, Walter | Aug. 1, 1996 |
| Lorber, John G. | Oct. 12, 1994 |
| Moorman, Thomas S., Jr. | Aug. 1, 1994 |
| Ralston, Joseph W. | July 1, 1995 |
| Ryan, Michael E. | Apr. 4, 1996 |
| Viccellio, Henry, Jr. | Dec. 10, 1992 |

## Navy

**Chief of Naval Operations**
Adm. Jay L. Johnson (aviator)

| Admirals | Date of Rank |
|---|---|
| Bowman, Frank L. (submariner) | Oct. 1, 1996 |
| Flanagan, William J., Jr. (surface warfare) | Nov. 1, 1994 |
| Gehman, Harold W., Jr. (surface warfare) | Oct. 1, 1996 |
| Larson, Charles R. (submariner) | Mar. 1, 1990 |
| Lopez, Thomas J. (surface warfare) | July 31, 1996 |
| Prueher, Joseph W. (aviator) | June 1, 1995 |
| Zlatoper, Ronald J. (aviator) | Oct. 5, 1994 |

## Marine Corps

**Commandant of the Marine Corps (CMC)**
Gen. Charles C. Krulak . . . . . . . . . . . July 1, 1995

**Assistant Commandant of the Marine Corps (ACMC)**
Gen. Richard I. Neal . . . . . . . . . . . . . Sept. 27, 1996

## Coast Guard

**Commandant, with rank of Admiral**
Robert E. Kramek . . . . . . . . . . . . . . . June 1, 1994

**Vice Commandant, with rank of Vice Admiral**
Richard D. Herr . . . . . . . . . . . . . . . . . June 30, 1994

## Unified Defense Commands Commanders in Chief

(as of mid-1996)

**U.S. European Command,** Stuttgart-Vaihingen, Germany — Gen. George A. Joulwan (USA) (concurrently NATO Supreme Allied Commander, Europe)

**U.S. Pacific Command,** Honolulu, Hawaii — Adm. Joseph W. Prueher (USN)

**U.S. Atlantic Command,** Norfolk, Virginia — Gen. John J. Sheehan (USMC) (concurrently NATO Supreme Allied Commander, Atlantic)

**U.S. Special Operations Command,** MacDill AFB, Florida — Gen. Henry H. Shelton (USA)

**U.S. Transportation Command,** Scott AFB, Illinois — Gen. Walter Kross (USAF)

**U.S. Central Command,** MacDill AFB, Florida — Gen. J. H. Binford Peay III (USA)

**U.S. Southern Command,** Quarry Heights, Panama — Gen. Wesley K. Clark (USA)

**U.S. Space Command,** Peterson AFB, Colorado — Gen. Howell M. Estes III (USAF)

**U.S. Strategic Command,** Offutt AFB, Nebraska — Gen. Eugene E. Habiger (USAF)

## North Atlantic Treaty Organization International Commands

(as of mid-1996)

**Supreme Allied Commander, Europe (SACEUR)** — Gen. George A. Joulwan (USA)

**Deputy Supreme Allied Commander, Europe (DSACEUR)** — Gen. Sir Jeremy MacKenzie (UKA)

**Supreme Allied Commander, Atlantic** — Gen John J. Sheehan (USMC)

**Commander in Chief, Allied Forces Southern Europe** — Adm. Thomas J. Lopez (USN)

**Commander in Chief, Allied Forces Central Europe** — Gen. D. Stoeckmann (GEA)

**Commander in Chief, Allied Forces Northwestern Europe** — Air Chief Marshal Sir Richard Jones (UKAF)

**Chairman, NATO Military Committee** — Gen. Klaus Naumann (GEA)

## Principal U.S. Military Training Centers

### Army

| Name, P.O. address | Zip | Nearest city |
|---|---|---|
| Aberdeen Proving Ground, MD | 21005 | Aberdeen |
| Carlisle Barracks, PA | 17013 | Carlisle |
| Fort Benning, GA | 31905 | Columbus |
| Fort Bliss, TX | 79916 | El Paso |
| Fort Bragg, NC | 28307 | Fayetteville |
| Fort Devens, MA | 01433 | Ayer |
| Fort Eustis, VA | 23604 | Newport News |
| Fort Gordon, GA | 30905 | Augusta |
| Fort Huachuca, AZ | 85613 | Sierra Vista |
| Fort Jackson, SC | 29207 | Columbia |
| Fort Knox, KY | 40121 | Louisville |
| Fort Leavenworth, KS | 66027 | Leavenworth |
| Fort Lee, VA | 23801 | Petersburg |
| Fort McClellan, AL | 36205 | Anniston |
| Fort Rucker, AL | 36362 | Dothan |
| Fort Sill, OK | 73503 | Lawton |
| Fort Leonard Wood, MO | 65473 | Rolla |
| Joint Readiness, Ft. Chaffee, AR | 72905 | Fort Smith |
| National Training Center | 92311 | Barstow, CA |
| The Judge Advocate General School, VA | 22901 | Charlottesville |

### Navy

| Name | Zip | Nearest city | Name | Zip | Nearest city |
|---|---|---|---|---|---|
| Naval Education & Training Ctr. | 32508 | Pensacola, FL | Naval Education & Training Ctr. | 02841 | Newport, RI |
| Naval Air Training Center | 78419 | Corpus Christi,TX | Naval Post Graduate School | 93943 | Monterey, CA |
| Training Command, Atlantic Fleet | 23511 | Norfolk, VA | Naval Submarine School | 06349 | Groton, CT |
| Training Command, Pacific Fleet | 92143 | San Diego, CA | Naval Training Ctr., Great Lakes | 60088 | N. Chicago, IL |
| Naval Aviation Schools Command | 32508 | Pensacola, FL | Naval War College | 02841 | Newport, RI |

### Marine Corps

| Name, P.O. address | Zip | Nearest city | Name, P.O. address | Zip | Nearest city |
|---|---|---|---|---|---|
| MCB Camp Lejeune, NC | 28542 | Jacksonville | MCAS Cherry Point, NC | 28533 | Havelock |
| MCB Camp Pendleton, CA | 92055 | Oceanside | MCAS El Toro, CA | 92709 | Santa Ana |
| MCB Kaneohe Bay, HI | 96863 | Kailua | MCAS New River, NC | 28545 | Jacksonville |
| MCAGCC Twentynine Palms, CA | 92278 | Palm Springs | MCAS Beaufort, SC | 29904 | Beaufort |
| MCCDC Quantico, VA | 22134 | Quantico | MCAS Yuma, AZ | 85369 | Yuma |
| MCRD Parris Island, SC | 29905 | Beaufort | MCMWTC Bridgeport, CA | 93517 | Bridgeport |
| MCRD San Diego, CA | 92140 | San Diego | | | |

MCB = Marine Corps Base. MCCDC = Marine Corps Combat Development Command. MCAS = Marine Corps Air Station. MCRD = Marine Corps Recruit Depot. MCAGCC = Marine Corps Air-Ground Combat Center. MCMWTC = Marine Corps Mountain Warfare Training Center.

### Air Force

| Name, P.O. address | Zip | Nearest city | Name, P.O. address | Zip | Nearest city |
|---|---|---|---|---|---|
| Goodfellow AFB, TX | 76908 | San Angelo | Maxwell AFB, AL | 36112 | Montgomery |
| Keesler AFB, MS | 39534 | Biloxi | Sheppard AFB, TX | 76311 | Wichita Falls |
| Lackland AFB, TX | 78236 | San Antonio | | | |

All are Air Education and Training Command Bases.

## Personal Salutes and Honors

The United States national salute, 21 guns, is also the salute to a national flag. The independence of the U.S. is commemorated by the salute to the Union — one gun for each state — fired at noon on July 4, at all military posts provided with suitable artillery.

A 21-gun salute on arrival and departure, with 4 ruffles and flourishes, is rendered to the president of the United States, to an ex-president, and to a president-elect. The national anthem or "Hail to the Chief," as appropriate, is played for the president, and the national anthem for the others. A 21-gun salute on arrival and departure, with 4 ruffles and flourishes, also is rendered to the sovereign or chief of state of a foreign country or a member of a reigning royal family; the national anthem of his or her country is played. The music is considered an inseparable part of the salute and immediately follows the ruffles and flourishes without pause. Regarding the Honors March, generals receive the "General's March," admirals receive the "Admiral's March," and all others receive the 32-bar medley of "The Stars and Stripes Forever."

| Grade, title, or office | Salute — guns Arrive | Salute — guns Leave | Ruffles and flourishes | Music |
|---|---|---|---|---|
| Vice President of United States | 19 | | 4 | Hail, Columbia |
| Speaker of the House | 19 | | 4 | Honors March |
| American or foreign ambassador | 19 | | 4 | Nat. anthem of official |
| Premier or prime minister | 19 | | 4 | Nat. anthem of official |
| Secretary of Defense, Army, Navy, or Air Force | 19 | 19 | 4 | Honors March |
| Other Cabinet members, Senate President pro tempore, Governor, or Chief Justice of U.S. | 19 | | 4 | Honors March |
| Chairman, Joint Chiefs of Staff | 19 | 19 | 4 | |
| Army Chief of Staff, Chief of Naval Operations, Air Force Chief of Staff, Marine Commandant | 19 | 19 | 4 | Honors March |
| General of the Army, General of the Air Force, Fleet Admiral | 19 | 19 | 4 | |
| Generals, Admirals | 17 | 17 | 4 | |
| Assistant secretaries of Defense, Army, Navy, or Air Force | 17 | 17 | 4 | Honors March |
| Chairman of a committee of Congress | 17 | | 4 | Honors March |

**Other salutes** (on arrival only) include 15 guns, along with 3 ruffles and flourishes, for U.S. envoys or ministers and foreign envoys or ministers accredited to the U.S.; 15 guns, for a lieutenant general or vice admiral; 13 guns, along with 2 ruffles and flourishes, for a major general or rear admiral (upper half) and for U.S. ministers resident and ministers resident accredited to the U.S.; 11 guns, along with 1 ruffle and flourish, for a brigadier general or rear admiral (lower half) and for U.S. charges d'affaires and like officials accredited to the U.S.; and 11 guns, and no ruffles and flourishes, for consuls general accredited to the U.S.

## Military Units, U.S. Army and Air Force

**Army Units. Squad:** In infantry usually 10 enlisted personnel under a staff sergeant. **Platoon:** In infantry 4 squads under a lieutenant. **Company:** Headquarters section and 4 platoons under a captain. (Company-size unit in the artillery is a battery; in the cavalry, a troop.) **Battalion:** Hdqts. and 4 or more companies under a lieutenant colonel. (Battalion-size unit in the cavalry is a squadron.) **Brigade:** Hdqts. and 3 or more battalions under a colonel. **Division:** Hdqts. and 3 brigades with artillery, combat support, and combat service support units under a major general. **Army Corps:** Two or more divisions with corps troops under a lieutenant general. **Field Army:** Hdqts. and two or more corps with field Army troops under a general.

**Air Force Units. Flight:** Numerically designated flights are the lowest level unit in the Air Force. They are used primarily where there is a need for small mission elements to be incorporated into an organized unit. **Squadron:** A squadron is the basic unit in the Air Force. It is used to designate the mission units in operational commands. **Group:** The group is a flexible unit composed of two or more squadrons whose functions may be operational, support, or administrative in nature. **Wing:** An operational wing normally has two or more assigned mission squadrons in an area such as combat, flying training, or airlift. **Numbered Air Forces:** Normally an operationally oriented agency, the numbered air force is designed for the control of two or more wings with the same mission and/or geographical location. **Major Command:** A major subdivision of the Air Force that is assigned a major segment of the USAF mission.

# The Federal Service Academies

**U.S. Military Academy, West Point, NY.** Founded 1802. Awards BS degree and Army commission for a 5-year service obligation. For admissions information, write Admissions Office, USMA, West Point, NY 10996.

**U.S. Naval Academy, Annapolis, MD.** Founded 1845. Awards BS degree and Navy or Marine Corps commission for a 5-year service obligation. For admissions information, write Dean of Admissions, Naval Academy, Annapolis, MD 21402.

**U.S. Air Force Academy, Colorado Springs, CO.** Founded 1954. Awards BS degree and Air Force commission for a 6-year service obligation. For admissions information, write Registrar, U.S. Air Force Academy, CO 80840-5025.

**U.S. Coast Guard Academy, New London, CT.** Founded 1876. Awards BS degree and Coast Guard commission for a 5-year service obligation. For admissions information, write Director of Admissions, Coast Guard Academy, New London, CT 06320.

**U.S. Merchant Marine Academy, Kings Point, NY.** Founded 1943. Awards BS degree, a license as a deck, engineer, or dual officer, and a U.S. Naval Reserve commission. Service obligations vary according to options taken by the graduate. For admissions information, write Admission Office, U.S. Merchant Marine Academy, Kings Point, NY 11024.

# U.S. Army, Navy, Air Force, Marine Corps, and Coast Guard Insignia

**Source:** Dept. of the Army, Dept. of the Navy, Dept. of the Air Force, U.S. Dept. of Defense

## Army

**General of the Armies** — General John J. Pershing, the only person to have held this rank, was authorized to prescribe his own insignia, but never wore in excess of four stars. The rank originally was established by Congress for George Washington in 1799, and he was promoted to the rank by joint resolution of Congress, approved by Pres. Gerald Ford, Oct. 19, 1976.

**General of the Army** — Five silver stars fastened together in a circle and the coat of arms of the United States in gold color metal with shield and crest enameled.

| | |
|---|---|
| **General** | Four silver stars |
| **Lieutenant General** | Three silver stars |
| **Major General** | Two silver stars |
| **Brigadier General** | One silver star |
| **Colonel** | Silver eagle |
| **Lieutenant Colonel** | Silver oak leaf |
| **Major** | Gold oak leaf |
| **Captain** | Two silver bars |
| **First Lieutenant** | One silver bar |
| **Second Lieutenant** | One gold bar |

### Warrant Officers

**Grade Five** — Silver bar with 4 enamel silver squares
**Grade Four** — Silver bar with 4 enamel black squares
**Grade Three** — Silver bar with 3 enamel black squares
**Grade Two** — Silver bar with 2 enamel black squares
**Grade One** — Silver bar with 1 enamel black squares

### Noncommissioned Officers

**Sergeant Major of the Army** (E-9) — Same as Command Sergeant Major (below) but with 2 stars. Also wears distinctive red and white shield on lapel.

**Command Sergeant Major** (E-9) — Three chevrons above 3 arcs with a 5-pointed star with a wreath around the star between the chevrons and arcs.

**Sergeant Major** (E-9) — Three chevrons above 3 arcs with a 5-pointed star between the chevrons and arcs.

**First Sergeant** (E-8) — Three chevrons above 3 arcs with a lozenge between the chevrons and arcs.

**Master Sergeant** (E-8) — Three chevrons above 3 arcs.
**Sergeant First Class** (E-7) — Three chevrons above 2 arcs.
**Staff Sergeant** (E-6) — Three chevrons above 1 arc.
**Sergeant** (E-5) — Three chevrons.
**Corporal** (E-4) — Two chevrons.

### Specialists

**Specialist** (E-4) — Eagle device only.

### Other enlisted

**Private First Class** (E-3) — One chevron above one arc.
**Private** (E-2) — One chevron.
**Private** (E-1) — None.

## Air Force

Insignia for Air Force officers are identical to those of the Army. Insignia for enlisted personnel are worn on both sleeves and consist of a star and an appropriate number of rockers. Chevrons appear above 5 rockers for the top 3 noncommissioned officer ranks, as follows (in ascending order): Master Sergeant, 1 chevron; Senior Master Sergeant, 2 chevrons; and Chief Master Sergeant, 3 chevrons. The insignia of the Chief Master Sergeant of the Air Force has 3 chevrons and a wreath around the star design.

## Navy

**Stripes and corps device are of gold embroidery.**

| Rank | Stripes |
|---|---|
| **Fleet Admiral** | 1 two inch with 4 one-half inch |
| **Admiral** | 1 two inch with 3 one-half inch |
| **Vice Admiral** | 1 two inch with 2 one-half inch |
| **Rear Admiral (upper half)** | 1 two inch with 1 one-half inch |
| **Rear Admiral (lower half)** | 1 two inch |
| **Captain** | 4 one-half inch |
| **Commander** | 3 one-half inch |
| **Lieutenant Commander** | 2 one-half inch with 1 one-quarter inch between |
| **Lieutenant** | 2 one-half inch |
| **Lieutenant (j.g.)** | 1 one-half inch with one-quarter inch above |
| **Ensign** | 1 one-half inch |

**Warrant Officers**—One ½″ broken with ½″ intervals of blue as follows:

**Warrant Officer W-4** — 1 break
**Warrant Officer W-3** — 2 breaks, 2″ apart
**Warrant Officer W-2** — 3 breaks, 2″ apart

The breaks are symmetrically centered on outer face of the sleeve.

**Enlisted personnel** (noncommissioned petty officers)—A rating badge worn on the upper left arm, consisting of a spread eagle, appropriate number of chevrons, and centered specialty mark.

## Marine Corps

Marine Corps' distinctive cap and collar ornament is the Marine Corps Emblem—a combination of the American eagle, a globe, and an anchor. Marine Corps and Army officer insignia are similar. Marine Corps enlisted insignia, although basically similar to Army's, feature crossed rifles beneath the chevrons. Marine Corps enlisted rank insignia are as follows:

**Sergeant Major of the Marine Corps** (E-9) — Same as Sergeant Major (below) but with Marine Corps emblem in the center instead of the star.

**Sergeant Major** (E-9) — Three chevrons above 4 rockers with a 5-pointed star in the center.

**Master Gunnery Sergeant** (E-9) — Three chevrons above 4 rockers with a bursting bomb insignia in the center.

**First Sergeant** (E-8) — Three chevrons above 3 rockers with a diamond in the middle.

**Master Sergeant** (E-8) — Three chevrons above 3 rockers with crossed rifles in the middle.

**Gunnery Sergeant** (E-7) — Three chevrons above 2 rockers with crossed rifles in the middle.

**Staff Sergeant** (E-6) —Three chevrons above 1 rocker with crossed rifles in the middle.

**Sergeant** (E-5) — Three chevrons above crossed rifles.
**Corporal** (E-4) — Two chevrons above crossed rifles.
**Lance Corporal** (E-3) — One chevron above crossed rifles.
**Private First Class** (E-2) — One chevron.
**Private** (E-1) — None.

## Coast Guard

Coast Guard insignia follow Navy custom, with certain minor changes such as the officer cap insignia. The Coast Guard shield is worn on both sleeves of officers and on the right sleeve of all enlisted personnel.

# U.S. Army Personnel on Active Duty[1]

**Source:** Department of the Army, U.S. Dept. of Defense

| | | Commissioned officers | | | Warrant officers | | Enlisted personnel | | |
|---|---|---|---|---|---|---|---|---|---|
| **Date**[2] | **Total strength** | **Total** | **Male** | **Female**[3] | **Male**[4] | **Female** | **Total** | **Male** | **Female** |
| 1940 | 267,767 | 17,563 | 16,624 | 939 | 763 | — | 249,441 | 249,441 | — |
| 1942 | 3,074,184 | 203,137 | 190,662 | 12,475 | 3,285 | — | 2,867,762 | 2,867,762 | — |
| 1943 | 6,993,102 | 557,657 | 521,435 | 36,222 | 21,919 | 0 | 6,413,526 | 6,358,200 | 55,325 |
| 1944 | 7,992,868 | 740,077 | 692,351 | 47,726 | 36,893 | 10 | 7,215,888 | 7,144,601 | 71,287 |
| 1945 | 8,266,373 | 835,403 | 772,511 | 62,892 | 56,216 | 44 | 7,374,710 | 7,283,930 | 90,780 |
| 1946 | 1,889,690 | 257,300 | 240,643 | 16,657 | 9,826 | 18 | 1,622,546 | 1,605,847 | 16,699 |
| 1950 | 591,487 | 67,784 | 63,375 | 4,409 | 4,760 | 22 | 518,921 | 512,370 | 6,551 |
| 1955 | 1,107,606 | 111,347 | 106,173 | 5,174 | 10,552 | 48 | 985,659 | 977,943 | 7,716 |
| 1960 | 871,348 | 91,056 | 86,832 | 4,224 | 10,141 | 39 | 770,112 | 761,833 | 8,279 |
| 1965 | 967,049 | 101,812 | 98,029 | 3,783 | 10,285 | 23 | 854,929 | 846,409 | 8,520 |
| 1970 | 1,319,735 | 143,704 | 138,469 | 5,235 | 23,005 | 13 | 1,153,013 | 1,141,537 | 11,476 |
| 1975 | 781,316 | 89,756 | 85,184 | 4,572 | 13,214 | 22 | 678,324 | 640,621 | 37,703 |
| 1980 (Sept. 30) | 772,661 | 85,339 | 77,843 | 7,496 | 13,265 | 113 | 673,944 | 612,593 | 61,351 |
| 1985 (Sept. 30) | 776,244 | 94,103 | 83,563 | 10,540 | 15,296 | 288 | 666,557 | 598,639 | 67,918 |
| 1990 (Mar. 31) | 746,220 | 91,330 | 79,520 | 11,810 | 15,177 | 470 | 639,713 | 567,015 | 72,698 |
| 1992 (Mar. 31) | 661,391 | 85,953 | 74,326 | 11,627 | 13,840 | 494 | 561,104 | 496,335 | 64,769 |
| 1993 (Mar. 31) | 590,324 | 76,714 | 66,336 | 10,378 | 12,359 | 441 | 500,810 | 443,942 | 56,868 |
| 1994 | 553,627 | 74,956 | 64,281 | 10,675 | 12,448 | 535 | 465,688 | 405,664 | 60,024 |
| 1995 | 521,036 | 72,646 | 62,250 | 10,396 | 12,053 | 599 | 435,807 | 377,832 | 57,975 |
| 1996 (May 31) | 493,330 | 68,850 | 58,875 | 9,975 | 11,456 | 660 | 408,511 | 351,669 | 56,842 |

(1) Represents strength of the active Army, including Philippine Scouts, retired Regular Army personnel on extended active duty, and National Guard and Reserve personnel on extended active duty; excludes U.S. Military Academy cadets, contract surgeons, and National Guard and Reserve personnel not on extended active duty.
(2) June 30, unless otherwise noted; data for 1940 to 1946 include personnel in the Army Air Forces and its predecessors (Air Service and Air Corps).
(3) Includes women doctors, dentists, and Medical Service Corps officers for 1946 and subsequent years, women in the Army Nurse Corps for all years, and the Women's Army Corps and Women's Medical Specialists Corps (dietitians, physical therapists, and occupational specialists) for 1943 and subsequent years.
(4) Act of Congress approved Apr. 27, 1926, directed the appointment as warrant officers of field clerks still in active service. Includes flight officers as follows: 1943, 5,700; 1944, 13,615; 1945, 31,117; 1946, 2,580.

# U.S. Navy Personnel on Active Duty

| Date | Officers | Nurses | Enlisted | Officer Candidates | Total |
|---|---|---|---|---|---|
| 1940 (June) | 13,162 | 442 | 144,824 | 2,569 | 160,997 |
| 1945 (June) | 320,293 | 11,086 | 2,988,207 | 61,231 | 3,380,817 |
| 1950 (June) | 42,687 | 1,964 | 331,860 | 5,037 | 381,538 |
| 1960 (June) | 67,456 | 2,103 | 544,040 | 4,385 | 617,984 |
| 1970 (June) | 78,488 | 2,273 | 605,899 | 6,000 | 692,660 |
| 1980 (June)[1] | 63,100 | — | 464,100 | — | 527,200 |
| 1990 (Sept.) | 74,429 | — | 530,133 | — | 604,562 |
| 1992 (Mar.) | 71,826 | — | 500,459 | — | 572,285 |
| 1993 (Mar.) | 66,787 | — | 445,409 | — | 512,196 |
| 1994 (Apr.) | 64,430 | — | 418,378 | — | 482,808 |
| 1995 (May) | 61,075 | — | 402,626 | — | 463,701 |
| 1996 (June) | 60,013 | — | 376,595 | — | 436,608 |

(1) Starting in 1980, "Nurses" are included with "Officers," and "Officer Candidates" are included with "Enlisted."

# U.S. Marine Corps Personnel on Active Duty

(midyear personnel figures)

| Year | Officers | Enlisted | Total | Year | Officers | Enlisted | Total | Year | Officers | Enlisted | Total |
|---|---|---|---|---|---|---|---|---|---|---|---|
| 1940 | 1,800 | 26,545 | 28,345 | 1970 | 24,941 | 234,796 | 259,737 | 1993 | 18,878 | 161,205 | 180,083 |
| 1945 | 37,067 | 437,613 | 474,680 | 1980 | 18,198 | 170,271 | 188,469 | 1994 | 18,430 | 159,949 | 178,379 |
| 1950 | 7,254 | 67,025 | 74,279 | 1990 | 19,958 | 176,694 | 196,652 | 1995 | 18,017 | 153,929 | 171,946 |
| 1960 | 16,203 | 154,418 | 170,621 | 1992 | 19,132 | 165,397 | 184,529 | 1996 | 18,146 | 154,141 | 172,287 |

# U.S. Air Force Personnel on Active Duty

| Year[1] | Strength | Year[1] | Strength | Year[1] | Strength | Year[1] | Strength |
|---|---|---|---|---|---|---|---|
| 1907 | 3 | 1942 | 764,415 | 1960 | 814,213 | 1992 | 470,315 |
| 1918 | 195,023 | 1943 | 2,197,114 | 1970 | 791,078 | 1993 | 444,351 |
| 1920 | 9,050 | 1944 | 2,372,292 | 1980 | 557,969 | 1994 | 426,327 |
| 1930 | 13,531 | 1945 | 2,282,259 | 1986 | 608,200 | 1995 | 400,051 |
| 1940 | 51,165 | 1950 | 411,277 | 1990 | 535,233 | 1996 | 389,400 |
| 1941 | 152,125 | | | | | | |

(1) Prior to 1947, data are for U.S. Army Air Corps and Air Service of the Signal Corps.

# U.S. Coast Guard Personnel on Active Duty

| Year | Total | Officers | Cadets | Enlisted | Year | Total | Officers | Cadets | Enlisted |
|---|---|---|---|---|---|---|---|---|---|
| 1970 | 37,689 | 5,512 | 653 | 31,524 | 1987 | 38,576 | 6,644 | 859 | 31,073 |
| 1975 | 36,788 | 5,630 | 1,177 | 29,981 | 1988 | 37,723 | 6,530 | 887 | 30,306 |
| 1980 | 39,381 | 6,463 | 877 | 32,041 | 1990 | 37,308 | 6,475 | 820 | 29,860 |
| 1981 | 39,760 | 6,519 | 981 | 32,260 | 1991 | 38,280 | 7,095 | 900 | 30,285 |
| 1982 | 38,248 | 6,431 | 902 | 30,915 | 1992 | 39,185 | 7,348 | 919 | 30,918 |
| 1983 | 39,708 | 6,535 | 811 | 32,362 | 1993 | 38,832 | 7,724 | 691 | 30,417 |
| 1984 | 38,705 | 6,790 | 759 | 31,156 | 1994 | 37,284 | 7,401 | 881 | 29,002 |
| 1985 | 38,595 | 6,775 | 733 | 31,087 | 1995 | 36,731 | 7,489 | 841 | 28,401 |
| 1986 | 37,284 | 6,577 | 754 | 29,953 | | | | | |

# Defense Contracts

**Source:** U.S. Dept. of Defense

(in thousands of dollars)

The 50 companies (including their subsidiaries) receiving the largest dollar volume of prime contract awards from the Department of Defense during fiscal year 1995.

| | | | | | |
|---|---|---|---|---|---|
| Lockheed Martin | $10,482,787 | Computer Sciences | $656,135 | Carlyle Partners Lev. Cap. | $386,706 |
| McDonnell Douglas | 8,020,868 | ITT Industries | 647,888 | Boeing Sikorsky Comanche Team JV | 372,556 |
| Tenneco | 3,709,810 | GTE | 633,070 | Mitre | 370,277 |
| General Motors | 2,992,929 | Fulcrum II Ltd. Partnership | 563,480 | Rolls-Royce PLC | 350,469 |
| Northrop-Grumman | 2,913,072 | Texas Instruments | 554,389 | MIT | 343,644 |
| Raytheon | 2,890,409 | Tracor | 510,465 | Chrysler | 340,266 |
| General Electric | 2,103,657 | AlliedSignal | 503,032 | United Defense LP | 319,667 |
| Loral | 1,967,305 | FMC | 485,551 | Logicon | 317,293 |
| Boeing | 1,780,287 | Alliant Techsystems | 472,974 | Federal Express | 302,221 |
| United Technologies | 1,774,835 | Exxon | 471,859 | Honeywell | 300,760 |
| General Dynamics | 1,695,254 | Olin | 468,753 | OHM | 289,231 |
| Litton Industries | 1,237,209 | Dyncorp | 448,409 | Motorola | 286,350 |
| Westinghouse Electric | 1,225,438 | Stewart & Stevenson Srvcs. | 442,144 | Halliburton | 276,180 |
| Rockwell International | 1,209,971 | Black & Decker | 434,060 | Harris | 275,654 |
| Textron | 1,069,000 | IBM | 425,566 | Johns Hopkins University | 274,258 |
| Science Applications | 931,391 | AT&T | 422,289 | Draker Charles Stark | 271,525 |
| TRW | 866,963 | Unisys | 393,315 | | |

# Women in the Armed Forces

**Source:** U.S. Dept. of Defense

Women in the Army, Navy, Air Force, Marines, and Coast Guard are fully integrated with male personnel. Expansion of military women's programs began in the Department of Defense in fiscal year 1973.

Admission of women to the service academies began in the fall of 1976.

Under rules instituted in 1993, women are allowed to fly combat aircraft and to serve aboard warships. Women are still restricted from service in ground combat units.

Between Apr. 1993 and July 1994, almost 260,000 positions in the armed forces had been opened to women. In July 1994, 80.2% of all jobs and 92% of all career fields in the military had been opened to women. As of June 30, 1996, women made up 13.0% of the armed forces.

**Women Active Duty Troops in 1996**

| Service | % Women |
|---|---|
| Army (May 31) | 13.8 |
| Navy | 12.6 |
| Marines | 4.9 |
| Air Force | 16.3 |
| Coast Guard (1995) | 9.1 |

**Women on Active Duty, All Services*: 1973-95**

| Year | % Women | Year | % Women |
|---|---|---|---|
| 1973 | 2.5 | 1987 | 10.2 |
| 1975 | 4.6 | 1993 | 11.6 |
| 1981 | 8.9 | 1996 | 13.0 |

*Not including the Coast Guard, which is a part of the Dept. of Transportation.

# African American Service in U.S. Wars

**American Revolution.** About 5,000 blacks served in the Continental Army, mostly in integrated units, some in all-black combat units.

**Civil War.** Some 200,000 blacks served in the Union Army; 38,000 were killed, 22 won the Medal of Honor (the nation's highest award).

**World War I.** About 367,000 blacks served in the armed forces, 100,000 in France.

**World War II.** More than 1 million blacks served in the armed forces; all-black fighter and bomber AAF units and infantry divisions gave distinguished service. (By 1954, the armed forces were completely desegregated.)

**Vietnam War.** 274,937 blacks served in the armed forces (1965-74); 5,681 were killed in combat.

**Persian Gulf War.** About 104,000 blacks served in the Kuwaiti theater—20% of U.S. soldiers, compared with 8.7% for World War II and 9.8% for Vietnam.

# Veteran Population

**Source:** U.S. Dept. of Veterans Affairs; as of July 1995

(in thousands)

| | |
|---|---|
| **Total veterans in civilian life[a,b]** | **26,198** |
| **Total wartime veterans** | **20,169** |
| Total Persian Gulf War | 1,450 |
| Persian Gulf War with service in Vietnam era | 244 |
| Persian Gulf War with no prior wartime service | 1,206 |
| Total Vietnam era | 8,273 |
| Vietnam era with service in Korean conflict | 520 |
| Vietnam era with no prior wartime service | 7,753 |
| Total Korean conflict | 4,499 |
| Korean conflict with service in WWII | 735 |
| Korean conflict with no prior wartime service | 3,764 |
| World War II | 7,433 |
| World War I | 13 |
| **Total peacetime veterans** | **6,029** |
| Total post-Vietnam era | 3,041 |
| Service between Korean conflict and Vietnam era only | 2,830 |
| Other peacetime | 158 |

**Note:** Detail may not add to total shown due to rounding. (a) The category "wartime veterans" equals the sum of Persian Gulf War (no service in Vietnam era), Vietnam era (no service in Korean conflict), Korean conflict (no service in World War II), World War II, and World War I. The data refer only to veterans living in the U.S. and Puerto Rico since data on veterans living elsewhere are not available. (b) There are an indeterminate number of Mexican Border period veterans, 24 of whom were receiving benefits in July 1996.

# Veterans Compensation and Pension Case Payments

**Source:** 1900-1980: Dept. of Veterans Affairs; 1990-1995: Natl. Center for Veteran Analysis and Statistics

| Fiscal year | Living veteran cases | Deceased veteran cases | Total cases | Total expenditures (dollars) |
|---|---|---|---|---|
| 1900 | 752,510 | 241,019 | 993,529 | $138,462,130 |
| 1910 | 602,622 | 318,461 | 921,083 | 159,974,056 |
| 1920 | 419,627 | 349,916 | 769,543 | 316,418,030 |
| 1930 | 542,610 | 298,223 | 840,833 | 418,432,809 |
| 1940 | 610,122 | 239,176 | 849,298 | 429,138,465 |
| 1950 | 2,368,238 | 658,123 | 3,026,361 | 2,009,462,298 |
| 1960 | 3,008,935 | 950,802 | 3,959,737 | 3,314,761,383 |
| 1970 | 3,127,338 | 1,487,176 | 4,614,514 | $5,253,839,611 |
| 1980 | 3,195,395 | 1,450,785 | 4,646,180 | 11,046,637,368 |
| 1990 | 2,746,329 | 837,596 | 3,583,925 | 14,674,411,000 |
| 1992 | 2,673,833 | 753,981 | 3,427,814 | 16,281,864,000 |
| 1993 | 2,660,030 | 713,758 | 3,373,788 | 16,881,938,000 |
| 1994 | 2,658,704 | 683,200 | 3,341,904 | 17,188,447,000 |
| 1995 | 2,668,576 | 661,679 | 3,330,255 | 17,765,045,000 |

# Active Duty U.S. Military Personnel Strengths, Worldwide

**Source:** U.S. Dept. of Defense

(as of Mar. 31, 1996)

| | |
|---|---|
| **U.S. Territories & Special Locations** | |
| U.S., 48 contiguous states | 1,018,072 |
| Alaska | 16,872 |
| Hawaii | 37,616 |
| Guam | 5,420 |
| Johnston Atoll | 259 |
| Puerto Rico | 2,501 |
| Transients | 40,761 |
| Afloat | 135,318 |
| **Total[1]** | **1,256,866** |
| **Europe** | |
| Belgium | 1,656 |
| Germany | 50,167 |
| Greece | 477 |
| Greenland | 128 |
| Iceland | 1,943 |
| Italy | 11,913 |
| Macedonia | 540 |
| Netherlands | 736 |
| Norway | 194 |
| Portugal | 1,070 |
| Spain | 2,676 |
| Turkey | 3,055 |
| United Kingdom | 11,962 |
| Afloat | 4,117 |
| **Total[1]** | **117,327** |
| **East Asia & Pacific** | |
| Australia | 319 |
| Japan | 43,804 |
| Korea, South | 34,662 |
| Philippines | 130 |
| Singapore | 162 |
| Thailand | 109 |
| Afloat | 14,813 |
| **Total[1]** | **94,189** |
| **North Africa, Middle East & South Asia** | |
| Bahrain | 504 |
| Diego Garcia | 905 |
| Egypt | 652 |
| Kuwait | 1,751 |
| Saudi Arabia | 1,260 |
| Afloat | 3,590 |
| **Total[1]** | **8,930** |
| **Sub-Saharan Africa** | |
| Somalia | NA |
| Afloat | 2,754 |
| **Total[1]** | **3,015** |
| **Other Western Hemisphere** | |
| Bermuda | NA |
| Canada | NA |
| Cuba (Guantánamo) | 2,173 |
| Haiti | 197 |
| Honduras | 216 |
| Panama | 7,170 |
| Afloat | 1,371 |
| **Total[1]** | **12,032** |
| **Total Worldwide[2]** | **1,493,391** |

(1) Regional totals include countries with fewer than 100 assigned U.S. military members. (2) Total worldwide includes U.S. military personnel stationed in former Soviet republics and Antarctica, as well as undistributed personnel. NA=not available.

# Estimates of Total Dollar Costs of American Wars

**Source:** *The Military Budget and National Economic Priorities,* revised and updated by James L. Clayton

(millions of dollars, except percent)

| Item | World War II | Vietnam Conflict | Korean Conflict | World War I | Civil War: Union | Civil War: Confed-eracy | Spanish American War | American Revolution | War of 1812 | Mexican War |
|---|---|---|---|---|---|---|---|---|---|---|
| Original increment, direct costs:[1] | | | | | | | | | | |
| Current dollars | 360,000 | 140,600 | 50,000 | 32,700 | 2,300 | 1,000 | 270 | 100-140 | 89 | 82 |
| Constant (1967) dollars | 816,300 | 148,800 | 69,300 | 100,000 | 8,500 | 3,700 | 1,100 | 400-680 | 170 | 300 |
| Percent 1 year's GNP | 188 | 14 | 15 | 43 | 74 | 123 | 2 | 10 | 14 | 4 |
| Service-connected veterans' benefits[2] | 96,666 | 32,288 | 19,512 | 19,580 | 3,290 | — | 2,111 | 28 | 20 | 26 |
| Interest, pmts. on war loans[3] | (5) | (5) | (5) | 11,000 | 1,200 | (5) | 60 | 20 | 14 | 10 |
| Current cost to 1990[4] | 466,000 | 179,000 | 72,000 | 63,500 | 6,790 | (5) | 2,441 | 170 | 120 | 120 |

**Note:** The U.S. Department of Defense reported that, as of 1991, the total cost of the **Persian Gulf War** was $61.1 billion; this figure includes $7.4 billion from the U.S. and $53.7 billion in contributions from other countries.

(1) Figures are rounded and taken from Claudia D. Goldin, *Encyclopedia of American Economic History.* (2) Total cost to Oct. 1, 1990. For World War I and later wars, benefits are actual service-connected figures from *Annual Report* of Veterans Administration. For earlier wars, service-connected veterans' benefits are estimated at 40% of total, the approximate ratio of service-connected to total benefits since World War I. (3) Total cost to 1990. Interest payments are a very rough approximation based on the percentage of the original costs of each war financed by money creation and debt, the difference between the level of public debt at the beginning of the war and at its end, and the approximate time required to pay off the war debts. (4) Figures are rounded estimates. (5) Unknown.

# The Medal of Honor

The Medal of Honor is the highest military award for bravery that can be given to any individual in the United States. The first Army Medals were awarded on Mar. 25, 1863, and the first Navy Medals went to sailors and Marines on Apr. 3, 1863.

The Medal of Honor, established by Joint Resolution of Congress, July 12, 1862 (amended by Acts of Congress, July 9, 1918, and July 25, 1963), is awarded in the name of Congress to a person who, while a member of the Armed Forces, distinguishes himself or herself conspicuously by gallantry and intrepidity at the risk of life above and beyond the call of duty while engaged in an action against any enemy of the United States; while engaged in military operations involving conflict with an opposing foreign force; or while serving with friendly foreign forces engaged in an armed conflict against an opposing armed force in which the United States is not a belligerent party. The deed performed must have been one of personal bravery or self-sacrifice so conspicuous as to clearly distinguish the individual above his or her comrades and must have involved risk of life. Incontestable proof of the performance of service is required, and each recommendation for award of this decoration is considered on the standard of extraordinary merit.

Prior to World War I, the 2,625 Army Medal of Honor awards up to that time were reviewed to determine which past awards met new stringent criteria. The Army removed 911 names from the list, most of them former members of a volunteer infantry group during the Civil War who had been induced to extend their enlistments when they were promised the medal.

Since that review, Medals of Honor have been awarded in the following numbers:

| | | | |
|---|---|---|---|
| World War I | 124 | Korean War | 131 |
| Peacetime (1920-40) | 18 | Vietnam War | 239 |
| World War II | 433 | Somalia | 2 |

## For Further Information on the U.S. Armed Forces

**Army** — Office of the Chief of Public Affairs, 1500 Army Pentagon, Wash., DC 20310-1500.

**Navy** — Chief of Information, 1200 Navy Pentagon, Wash., DC 20350-1200.

**Air Force** — Office of Public Affairs, 1690 Air Force Pentagon, Wash., DC 20330-1690.

**Marine Corps** — Commandant of the Marine Corps (Code PA), Headquarters, U.S. Marine Corps, Wash., DC 20380-1775.

**Coast Guard** — Commandant (G-CP), U.S. Coast Guard, 2100 Second St. SW, Wash., DC 20593-0001.

Additional information on all the U.S. Armed Forces branches, as well as many other related organizations, can be accessed through DefenseLINK, the official Internet site of the Dept. of Defense: http://www.dtic.dla.mil/defenselink

## Armed Forces per 1,000 Persons, 1994[1]

**Source:** U.S. Arms Control and Disarmament Agency

| Country | Per 1,000 |
|---|---|
| Afghanistan | 2.3 |
| Albania | 22.2 |
| Argentina | 2.0 |
| Australia | 3.3 |
| Austria | 5.7 |
| Belarus | 8.6 |
| Belgium | 5.3 |
| Bolivia | 3.6 |
| Bosnia and Herzegovina | 22.0 |
| Brazil | 1.2 |
| Bulgaria | 9.1 |
| Cambodia | 6.8 |
| Canada | 2.7 |
| Chile | 7.3 |
| China | 2.5 |
| Colombia | 4.1 |
| Croatia | 17.2 |
| Cuba | 12.9 |
| Czech Republic | 8.6 |
| Denmark | 5.4 |
| Egypt | 7.0 |
| El Salvador | 5.2 |
| Finland | 6.9 |
| France | 8.7 |
| Germany | 4.5 |
| Greece | 19.5 |
| Haiti | 0 |
| Hungary | 5.8 |
| India | 1.4 |
| Indonesia | 1.4 |
| Iran | 8.4 |
| Iraq | 21.4 |
| Israel | 36.6 |
| Italy | 7.5 |
| Japan | 1.9 |
| Jordan | 25.0 |
| Korea, North | 52.0 |
| Korea, South | 16.6 |
| Kuwait | 8.9 |
| Lebanon | 13.8 |
| Libya | 15.8 |
| Mexico | 1.9 |
| Mongolia | 8.6 |
| Morocco | 6.8 |
| Netherlands | 5.0 |
| Nicaragua | 3.4 |
| Norway | 2.8 |
| Oman | 15.1 |
| Pakistan | 4.2 |
| Philippines | 1.5 |
| Poland | 6.6 |
| Portugal | 11.6 |
| Qatar | 19.3 |
| Romania | 8.6 |
| Russia | 9.3 |
| Rwanda | 4.8 |
| Saudi Arabia | 9.1 |
| Singapore | 19.6 |
| Slovakia | 8.7 |
| South Africa | 2.3 |
| Spain | 5.4 |
| Sweden | 8.0 |
| Switzerland | 5.5 |
| Syria | 21.5 |
| Taiwan | 20.0 |
| Thailand | 4.9 |
| Turkey | 13.0 |
| Ukraine | 9.5 |
| United Arab Emirates | 21.5 |
| United Kingdom | 4.4 |
| Venezuela | 3.6 |
| Vietnam | 11.7 |
| Yugoslavia | 12.6 |
| Zaire | 1.2 |

(1) Includes active-duty personnel performing national security functions. Does not include reserves or paramilitary forces.

## Nations With Largest Armed Forces, by Active-Duty Troop Strength, 1995

**Source:** *The Military Balance, 1995-96* (International Institute for Strategic Studies, published by Brassey's U.K.)

| | | Troop strength | | | | Navy | | | |
|---|---|---|---|---|---|---|---|---|---|
| | | Active troops (thousands) | Reserve troops (thousands) | Defense expend. ($bil)[1] | Tanks (MBT) (army only) | Cruisers/ Frigates/ Destroyers | Sub-marines | Combat aircraft FGA (air force only) | Combat aircraft fighters (air force only) |
| 1 | **China** | 2,930.0 | 1,200+ | 28.5 | 7,500-8,000 | 32F/18D | 52 | 400+ | 4000 est. |
| 2 | **U.S.** | 1,547.3 | 2,045.0 | 270.6[3] | 12,245 | 32C/49F/46D* | 100 | 52 tactical ftr. sqn | |
| 3 | **Russia** | 1,520.0 | 20,000 | 98.0 | 19,000 | 25C/102F/22D* | 183 | 750 | 425 |
| 4 | India | 1,145.0 | 655.0 | 7.4 | 2,400 | 18F/5D* | 15 | 22 sqn | 20 sqn |
| 5 | N. Korea | 1,128.0 | 4,700.0 | 5.6 | 3,400 | 3F | 25 | 509 total FGA/ftr. | |
| 6 | S. Korea | 633.0 | 4,500.0 | 13.5 | 2,050 | 33F/7D | 3 | 255 | 130 |
| 7 | Pakistan | 587.0 | 513.0 | 3.3[2] | 2,050+ | 8F/3D | 9 | 123 | 243 |
| 8 | Vietnam | 572.0 | 3-4,000 | 0.7[2] | 1,300 | 7F | — | 65 | 125 |
| 9 | Iran | 513.0 | 350.0 | 4.9[2] | 1,440 | 3F/2D | 2 | 144 | 115 |
| 10 | Turkey | 507.8 | 378.7 | 5.4 | 4,280 | 16F/5D | 16 | 13 sqn | 5 sqn |
| 11 | Ukraine[4] | 452.5 | 1,000.0 | 0.8[2] | 4,775 | — | — | 200 | 482 |
| 12 | Egypt | 436.0 | 254.0 | 2.5[2] | 3,500 | 6F/1D | 4 | 135 | 339 |
| 13 | Syria | 423.0 | 650.0 | 2.4[2] | 4,600 | 2F | 1 | 154 | 300 |
| 14 | **France** | 409.0 | 337.0 | 35.9 | 1,016 | 1C/35F/4D* | 18 | 9 sqn | 7 sqn |
| 15 | Iraq | 382.5 | 650.0 | 2.7 | 2,700 | 1F | — | 130 | 180 |
| 16 | Taiwan | 376.0 | 1,657.5 | 11.3 | 570+ | 16F/22D | 4 | 365 total FGA/ftr. | |
| 17 | Germany | 339.9 | 414.7 | 29.1 | 2,695 | 10F/3D | 20 | 8 sqn | 7 sqn |
| 18 | Italy | 328.7 | 584.0 | 16.5[2] | 1,319 | 1C/26F/4D* | 9 | 8 sqn | 8 sqn |
| 19 | Brazil | 295.0 | 1,115.0 | 6.4 | † | 15F/5D* | 5 | 84 | 16 |
| 20 | Myanmar | 286.0 | NA | 0.4[2] | 62 | — | — | 24 | 36 |
| 21 | Poland | 278.6 | 465.5 | 2.3 | 1,752 | 1F/1D | 3 | 119 | 265 |
| 22 | Indonesia | 274.5 | 400.0 | 2.0[2] | † | 13F | 2 | 49 | 12 |
| 23 | Thailand | 259.0 | 200.0 | 3.1[2] | 253+ | 10F | — | 22 | 37 |
| 24 | Japan | 239.5 | 47.9 | NA | 1,160 | 55F/8D | 18 | 50 | 290 |
| 25 | **UK** | 236.9 | 332.9 | 34.9 | 506 | 23F/12D* | 16 | 11 sqn | 6 sqn |
| 26 | Romania | 217.4 | 427.0 | 0.6[2] | 1,843 | 5F/1D | 1 | 155 | 176 |
| 27 | Spain | 206.0 | 438.0 | 6.2 | 668 | 17F* | 8 | 4 sqn | 8 sqn |
| 28 | Morocco | 195.5 | 150.0 | 1.1[2] | 524 | 1F | — | 30 | 15 |
| 29 | Mexico | 175.0 | 300.0 | 1.6 | — | 2F/3D | — | — | 9 |
| 30 | Israel | 172.0 | 430.0 | 6.2[2] | 4,095 | — | 2 | 413 total FGA/ftr. | |

**Boldface** denotes nations with known strategic nuclear capability. MBT=main battle tank. FGA=fighter, ground attack. sqn= squadron (12-24 aircraft). †=light tanks only. *Denotes navies with aircraft carriers, as follows: Russia 1, U.S. 12, India 2, France 2, Brazil 1, Italy 1, UK 3, Spain 1. (1) 1994 figures unless otherwise noted. (2) 1993. (3) 1995. (4) Ukraine transferred the last of its nuclear warheads to Russia, June 1, 1996. NA = not available.

## Nuclear Arms Treaties and Negotiations: An Historical Overview

**Aug. 5, 1963—Limited Test Ban Treaty** signed in Moscow by the U.S., USSR, and Great Britain; prohibited testing of nuclear weapons in space, above ground, and under water.

**Jan. 27, 1967—Outer Space Treaty** banned the introduction of nuclear weapons and other weapons of mass destruction into orbit around the earth, their installation on the moon or other celestial body, or their station in space.

**July 1, 1968—Nuclear Nonproliferation Treaty,** with U.S., USSR, and Great Britain as major signers, limited the spread of nuclear material and technology for military purposes by agreement not to assist nonnuclear nations in getting or making nuclear weapons. Extended indefinitely, May 11, 1995.

**May 26, 1972—Strategic Arms Limitation Treaty (SALT I)** signed in Moscow by U.S. and USSR. An interim short-term agreement putting a ceiling on numbers of offensive nuclear weapons delivery vehicles. The treaty imposed a 5-year freeze on testing and deployment of intercontinental ballistic missiles (ICBMs) and submarine-launched ballistic missiles (SLBMs). SALT I was in effect until Oct. 3, 1977. In the area of defensive nuclear weapons, the separate **ABM Treaty** limited antiballistic missiles to 2 sites of 100 antiballistic missile launchers in each country (amended in 1974 to one site in each country).

**July 3, 1974—ABM Treaty Revision** (protocol on antiballistic missile systems) and **Threshold Test Ban Treaty** on limiting underground testing of nuclear weapons to 150 kilotons were signed by U.S. and USSR in Moscow.

**Sept. 1977—U.S. and USSR** agreed to continue to abide by SALT I, despite its expiration date.

**June 18, 1979—SALT II,** signed in Vienna by the U.S. and USSR, constrained offensive nuclear weapons, limiting each side to 2,400 missile launchers and heavy bombers with that ceiling to apply until Jan. 1, 1985. The treaty also set a subceiling of 1,320 ICBMs and SLBMs with multiple warheads on each side. Although approved by the U.S. Senate Foreign Relations Committee, the treaty never reached the Senate floor for ratification because Pres. Jimmy Carter withdrew his support for the treaty following the Dec. 1979 invasion of Afghanistan by Soviet troops.

**Dec. 8, 1987—Intermediate-Range Nuclear Forces (INF) Treaty** signed in Washington, D.C., by USSR leader Mikhail Gorbachev and U.S. Pres. Ronald Reagan, eliminating all U.S. and Soviet intermediate- and shorter-range nuclear missiles from Europe and Asia; ratified with conditions by U.S. Senate on May 27, 1988.

**July 31, 1991—Strategic Arms Reduction Treaty (START I)** signed in Moscow by Soviet Pres. Mikhail Gorbachev and U.S. Pres. George Bush to reduce strategic offensive arms by approximately 30% in 3 phases over 7 years. START I was the first treaty to mandate reductions by the superpowers. The treaty was approved by the U.S. Senate Oct. 1, 1992. With the breakup of the Soviet Union in Dec. 1991, 4 former Soviet republics became independent nations with strategic nuclear weapons on their territory—Russia, Ukraine, Kazakstan, and Belarus. The last 3 agreed in principle in 1992 to transfer their nuclear weapons to Russia and ratify START I. The Russian Supreme Soviet voted to ratify Nov. 4, 1992, but Russia decided not to provide the instruments of ratification until the other three republics each ratified START I and acceded to the Nuclear Nonproliferation Treaty (NPT) as nonnuclear nations. By late 1993, Belarus and Kazakstan had ratified START I and acceded to the nonproliferation treaty. In Feb. 1994, Ukraine ratified START I and subsequently acceded to the NPT, which entered into force on Dec. 5, 1994. As of Oct. 1996, Belarus was the last of the three republics not to have eliminated its nuclear weapons.

**Jan. 3, 1993—START II** signed in Moscow by U.S. Pres. George Bush and Russian Pres. Boris Yeltsin. Potentially the broadest disarmament pact in history, it called for both sides to reduce their long-range nuclear arsenals to about one-third of their then-current levels within a decade and would entirely eliminate land-based multiple-warhead missiles. START II required ratification only by the U.S. Senate and the legislature of Russia (under the guidelines for START I finalization, the only remaining nuclear republic of the former Soviet Union). The U.S. ratified START II on Jan. 26, 1996; Russia has yet to do so.

## Monthly Military Pay Scale

**Source:** U.S. Dept. of Defense; effective Jan. 1, 1996

| | Years of Service | | | | | | |
|---|---|---|---|---|---|---|---|
| **Rank/Grade** | **2** | **4** | **8** | **12** | **16** | **20** | **26** |
| General—0-10 | $7,397.10 | $7,397.10 | $7,681.20 | $8,106.60 | $8,686.50 | $9,268.20 | $9,845.40 |
| Lt. General—0-9 | 6,498.90 | 6,637.50 | 6,806.10 | 7,089.30 | 7,681.20 | 8,106.60 | 8,686.50 |
| Major General—0-8 | 5,908.20 | 6,048.30 | 6,498.90 | 6,806.10 | 7,089.30 | 7,681.20 | 7,870.50 |
| Brig. General—0-7 | 5,090.40 | 5,090.40 | 5,318.70 | 5,626.80 | 6,498.90 | 6,945.90 | 6,945.90 |
| Colonel—0-6 | 3,881.10 | 4,135.50 | 4,135.50 | 4,135.50 | 4,952.40 | 5,318.70 | 6,102.60 |
| Lt. Colonel—0-5 | 3,317.40 | 3,546.90 | 3,546.90 | 3,851.10 | 4,416.60 | 4,811.40 | 4,979.40 |
| Major—0-4 | 2,900.10 | 3,093.60 | 3,289.80 | 3,711.90 | 4,051.80 | 4,163.10 | 4,163.10 |
| Captain—0-3 | 2,474.40 | 2,926.80 | 3,176.70 | 3,514.50 | 3,600.60 | 3,600.60 | 3,600.60 |
| 1st Lt.—0-2 | 2,107.50 | 2,617.20 | 2,671.50 | 2,671.50 | 2,671.50 | 2,671.50 | 2,671.50 |
| 2d Lt.—0-1 | 1,743.90 | 2,107.50 | 2,107.70 | 2,107.50 | 2,107.50 | 2,107.50 | 2,107.50 |
| Chief Warrant—W-4 | 2,419.20 | 2,474.40 | 2,700.90 | 3,011.10 | 3,261.60 | 3,456.90 | 3,851.10 |
| Warrant Officer—W-1 | 1,714.50 | 1,857.60 | 2,025.00 | 2,194.50 | 2,362.80 | 2,532.30 | 2,532.30 |
| Sgt. Major—E-9 | 0.00 | 0.00 | 0.00 | 2,682.00 | 2,805.60 | 2,924.10 | 3,377.10 |
| Master Sgt.—E-8 | 0.00 | 0.00 | 2,199.60 | 2,322.30 | 2,445.60 | 2,562.90 | 3,015.90 |
| Sgt. 1st class—E-7 | 1,658.10 | 1,779.60 | 1,898.70 | 2,020.80 | 2,172.00 | 2,261.40 | 2,713.50 |
| Staff Sgt.—E-6 | 1,440.30 | 1,563.90 | 1,680.90 | 1,832.40 | 1,950.90 | 1,980.60 | 1,980.60 |
| Sergeant—E-5 | 1,262.10 | 1,380.90 | 1,531.80 | 1,650.90 | 1,680.90 | 1,680.90 | 1,680.90 |
| Corporal—E-4 | 1,142.10 | 1,302.60 | 1,354.20 | 1,354.20 | 1,354.20 | 1,354.20 | 1,354.20 |
| Pvt. 1st class—E-3 | 1,074.90 | 1,161.90 | 1,161.90 | 1,161.90 | 1,161.90 | 1,161.90 | 1,161.90 |
| Private—E-2 | 980.70 | 980.70 | 980.70 | 980.70 | 980.70 | 980.70 | 980.70 |
| Recruit—E-1 | 874.80 | 874.80 | 874.80 | 874.80 | 874.80 | 874.80 | 874.80 |

## Chairmen of the Joint Chiefs of Staff

| | |
|---|---|
| Gen. of the Army Omar N. Bradley, USA | 8/16/49–8/14/ 53 |
| Adm. Arthur W. Radford, USN | 8/15/53– 8/14/ 57 |
| Gen. Nathan F. Twining, USAF | 8/15/57 – 9/30/ 60 |
| Gen. Lyman L. Lemnitzer, USA | 10/1/60 – 10/30/62 |
| Gen. Maxwell D. Taylor, USA | 10/1/62 – 7/3/64 |
| Gen. Earle G. Wheeler, USA | 7/3/64 – 7/2/70 |
| Adm. Thomas H. Moorer, USN | 7/3/70 – 6/30/74 |
| Gen. George S. Brown, USAF | 7/1/74 – 6/20/78 |
| Gen. David C. Jones, USAF | 6/21/78 – 6/18/82 |
| Gen. John W. Vessey Jr., USA | 6/18/82 – 9/30/85 |
| Adm. William J. Crowe, Jr., USN | 10/1/85 – 9/30/89 |
| Gen. Colin L. Powell, USA | 10/1/89 – 9/30/93 |
| Gen. John M. Shalikashvili, USA | 10/1/93 – |

# Casualties in Principal Wars of the U.S.

**Source:** U.S. Dept. of Defense

Data prior to World War I are based on incomplete records in many cases. Casualty data are confined to dead and wounded personnel and therefore exclude personnel captured or missing in action who were subsequently returned to military control. Dash (—) indicates information is not available.

| War | Branch of service | Number serving | Casualties: Battle deaths | Other deaths | Wounds not mortal[7] | Total |
|---|---|---|---|---|---|---|
| **Revolutionary War** | **Total** | **—** | **4,435** | **—** | **6,188** | **—** |
| 1775-83 | Army | 184,000 | 4,044 | — | 6,004 | — |
| | Navy | to | 342 | — | 114 | — |
| | Marines | 250,000 | 49 | — | 70 | — |
| **War of 1812** | **Total** | **286,730[8]** | **2,260** | **—** | **4,505** | **6,765** |
| 1812-15 | Army | — | 1,950 | — | 4,000 | 5,950 |
| | Navy | — | 265 | — | 439 | 704 |
| | Marines | — | 45 | — | 66 | 111 |
| **Mexican War** | **Total** | **78,718[8]** | **1,733** | **11,550** | **4,152** | **17,435** |
| 1846-48 | Army | — | 1,721 | 11,500 | 4,102 | 17,373 |
| | Navy | — | 1 | — | 3 | 4 |
| | Marines | — | 11 | — | 47 | 58 |
| **Civil War** | **Total** | **2,213,363[8]** | **140,414** | **224,097** | **281,881** | **646,392** |
| Union forces | Army | 2,128,948 | 138,154 | 221,374 | 280,040 | 639,568 |
| 1861-65 | Navy | — | 2,112 | 2,411 | 1,710 | 6,233 |
| | Marines | 84,415 | 148 | 312 | 131 | 591 |
| Confederate forces | **Total** | **—** | **74,524** | **59,297** | **—** | **133,821** |
| (estimate)[1] | Army | 600,000 | — | — | — | — |
| 1863-66 | Navy | to | — | — | — | — |
| | Marines | 1,500,000 | — | — | — | — |
| **Spanish-American** | **Total** | **306,760** | **385** | **2,061** | **1,662** | **4,108** |
| War | Army[3] | 280,564 | 369 | 2,061 | 1,594 | 4,024 |
| 1898 | Navy | 22,875 | 10 | 0 | 47 | 57 |
| | Marines | 3,321 | 6 | 0 | 21 | 27 |
| **World War I** | **Total** | **4,743,826** | **53,513** | **63,195** | **204,002** | **320,710** |
| April 6, 1917- | Army[4] | 4,057,101 | 50,510 | 55,868 | 193,663 | 300,041 |
| Nov. 11, 1918 | Navy | 599,051 | 431 | 6,856 | 819 | 8,106 |
| | Marines | 78,839 | 2,461 | 390 | 9,520 | 12,371 |
| | Coast Guard | 8,835 | 111 | 81 | — | 192 |
| **World War II** | **Total** | **16,353,659** | **292,131** | **115,185** | **670,846** | **1,078,162** |
| Dec. 7, 1941- | Army[5] | 11,260,000 | 234,874 | 83,400 | 565,861 | 884,135 |
| Dec. 31, 1946[2] | Navy[6] | 4,183,466 | 36,950 | 25,664 | 37,778 | 100,392 |
| | Marines | 669,100 | 19,733 | 4,778 | 67,207 | 91,718 |
| | Coast Guard | 241,093 | 574 | 1,343 | — | 1,917 |
| **Korean War[9]** | **Total** | **5,764,143** | **33,651** | **—** | **103,284** | **—** |
| June 25, 1950- | Army | 2,834,000 | 27,709 | — | 77,596 | — |
| July 27, 1953 | Navy | 1,177,000 | 474 | 176 | 1,576 | 2,226 |
| | Marines | 424,000 | 4,270 | 339 | 23,744 | 28,353 |
| | Air Force | 1,285,000 | 1,198 | 298 | 368 | 1,864 |
| | Coast Guard | 44,143 | — | — | — | — |
| **Vietnam War[10]** | **Total** | **8,744,000** | **47,369** | **10,799** | **153,303** | **211,471** |
| Aug. 4, 1964- | Army | 4,368,000 | 30,911 | 7,274 | 96,802 | 134,987 |
| Jan. 27, 1973 | Navy | 1,842,000 | 1,631 | 927 | 4,178 | 6,736 |
| | Marines | 794,000 | 13,083 | 1,754 | 51,392 | 66,229 |
| | Air Force | 1,740,000 | 1,739 | 842 | 931 | 3,512 |
| | Coast Guard | — | 5 | 2 | — | 7 |
| **Persian Gulf War** | **Total** | **467,539[11]** | **148** | **145** | **467** | **760** |
| 1991 | Army | 246,682 | 98 | 105 | — | — |
| | Navy | 98,852 | 6 | 8 | — | — |
| | Marines | 71,254 | 24 | 26 | — | — |
| | Air Force | 50,751 | 20 | 6 | — | — |

(1) Authoritative statistics for the Confederate forces are not available. An estimated 26,000-31,000 Confederate personnel died in Union prisons.
(2) Data are for the period Dec. 1, 1941 through Dec. 31, 1946, when hostilities were officially terminated by Presidential Proclamation, but few battle deaths or wounds not mortal were incurred after the Japanese acceptance of Allied peace terms on Aug. 14, 1945. Numbers serving Dec. 1, 1941-Aug. 31, 1945 were: Total—14,903,213; Army—10,420,000; Navy—3,883,520; and Marine Corps—599,693.
(3) Number serving covers the period April 21-Aug. 13, 1898, while dead and wounded data are for the period May 1-Aug. 31, 1898. Active hostilities ceased on Aug. 13, 1898, but ratifications of the treaty of peace were not exchanged between the United States and Spain until April 11, 1899.
(4) Includes Army Air Forces battle deaths and wounds not mortal, as well as casualties suffered by American forces in Northern Russia to Aug. 25, 1919, and in Siberia to April 1, 1920. Other deaths covered the period April 1, 1917-Dec. 31, 1918.
(5) Includes Army Air Forces.
(6) Battle deaths and wounds not mortal include casualties incurred in Oct. 1941 due to hostile action.
(7) Marine Corps data for World War II, the Spanish-American War, and prior wars represent the number of individuals wounded, whereas all other data in this column represent the total number (incidence) of wounds.
(8) As reported by the Commissioner of Pensions in his Annual Report for Fiscal Year 1903.
(9) Battle deaths and other deaths associated with the conflict differ from previously reported figures due to a reexamination of individual files by the U.S. Dept. of Defense.
(10) Number serving covers the period Aug. 4, 1964-Jan. 27, 1973 (date of ceasefire). Number of casualties incurred in connection with the conflict in Vietnam covers the period Jan. 1, 1961-Sept. 30, 1977. Includes casualties incurred in Mayaguez Incident. Wounds not mortal exclude 150,375 persons not requiring hospital care.
(11) Estimated, because deployment figures changed continually.

# UNITED STATES GOVERNMENT

| EXECUTIVE BRANCH | LEGISLATIVE BRANCH | JUDICIAL BRANCH |
|---|---|---|
| **PRESIDENT**<br>**Vice President**<br>**Executive Office of the President**<br>White House Office<br>Office of the Vice President<br>Council of Economic Advisers<br>Council on Environmental Quality<br>National Security Council<br>Office of Administration<br>Office of Management and Budget<br>Office of National Drug Control Policy<br>Office of Policy Development<br>Office of Science and Technology Policy<br>Office of the U.S. Trade Representative | **CONGRESS**<br>**Senate House**<br>Architect of the Capitol<br>U.S. Botanic Garden<br>General Accounting Office<br>Government Printing Office<br>Library of Congress<br>Congressional Budget Office<br><br>**See Pages 111-120** | **Supreme Court of the United States**<br>Courts of Appeals<br>District Courts<br>Territorial Courts<br>Court of International Trade<br>Court of Federal Claims<br>Court of Appeals for the Armed Forces<br>Tax Court<br>Court of Veterans Appeals<br>Administrative Office of the Courts<br>Federal Judicial Center<br>Sentencing Commission |

## The Clinton Administration

As of Oct. 15, 1996; all mailing addresses listed are for Washington, DC

Terms of office of the president and vice president: Jan. 20, 1993, to Jan. 20, 1997. No person may be elected president of the United States for more than two 4-year terms.

**President** — Bill Clinton of Arkansas receives a salary of $200,000 taxable, as well as an annual expense allowance of $50,000 to assist in defraying costs resulting from his official duties. In addition, up to $100,000 a year (nontaxable) may be spent on travel expenses and $20,000 for official entertainment, available for allocation within the Executive Office of the President.

**Vice President** — Albert Gore Jr. of Tennessee receives an annual salary of $171,500, plus $10,000 for expenses, all of which is taxable.

### The Cabinet Department Heads

(Salary: $148,400 per year)

**Secretary of State** — Warren M. Christopher
**Secretary of the Treasury** — Robert E. Rubin
**Secretary of Defense** — William J. Perry
**Attorney General** — Janet Reno
**Secretary of the Interior** — Bruce Babbitt
**Secretary of Agriculture** — Dan Glickman
**Secretary of Commerce** — Mickey Kantor
**Secretary of Labor** — Robert B. Reich
**Secretary of Health and Human Services** — Donna E. Shalala
**Secretary of Housing and Urban Development** — Henry G. Cisneros
**Secretary of Transportation** — Federico F. Peña
**Secretary of Energy** — Hazel R. O'Leary
**Secretary of Education** — Richard W. Riley
**Secretary of Veterans Affairs** — Jesse Brown

### The White House Staff

1600 Pennsylvania Ave. NW 20500

**Chief of Staff** — Leon Panetta
**Asst. to the President & Deputy Chief of Staff for Policy and Political Affairs** — Harold Ickes
**Asst. to the President & Deputy Chief of Staff for White House Operations** — Evelyn S. Lieberman
**Counselor to the President** — Thomas F. McLarty 3d
**Senior Adviser on Policy & Strategy** — George Stephanopoulos
**Assistants to the President:**
- **Counsel to the President** — Jack Quinn
- **Domestic Policy Council** — Carol Rasco
- **Presidential Personnel** — Bob Nash
- **Press Secretary** — Michael McCurry
- **Legislative Affairs** — John Hilley
- **Strategic Planning** — Don Baer
- **National Economic Policy** — Laura D'Andrea Tyson
- **Intergovernmental Affairs** — Marcia Hale
- **National Security** — W. Anthony Lake
- **Staff Secretary** — Todd Stern
- **Political Affairs** — Doug Sosnik
- **Public Liaison** — Alexis Herman
- **Management & Administration** — Jodie R. Torkelson

### Executive Agencies

**Council of Economic Advisers** — Joseph Stiglitz, chmn.
**Office of Administration** — Franklin S. Reeder, dir.
**Office of Science & Technology Policy** — John H. Gibbons
**Office of National AIDS Policy** — Patricia Fleming
**Office of National Drug Control Policy** — Barry R. McCaffrey
**Office of Management and Budget** — Alice M. Rivlin, dir.
**U.S. Trade Representative** — Charlene Barshefsky, act.
**Council on Environmental Quality** — Kathleen McGinty, chmn.

### Department of State

2201 C St. NW 20520

**Secretary of State** — Warren M. Christopher
**Deputy Secretary** — Strobe Talbott
**Chief of Staff & Asst. Sec. for Public Affairs** — Thomas E. Donilon
**U.S. Ambassador to the United Nations** — Madeleine K. Albright
**Under Sec. for Political Affairs** — Peter Tarnoff
**Under Sec. for Management** — Richard M. Moose
**Under Sec. for Global Affairs** — Timothy E. Wirth
**Under Sec. for Economic, Business, & Agricultural Affairs** — Joan E. Spero
**Under Sec. for Arms Control & International Security Affairs** — Lynn E. Davis
**Policy Planning Director** — James B. Steinberg
**Chief of Protocol** — Molly M. Raiser
**Inspector General** — Jacqueline L. Williams-Bridgers
**Legal Adviser** — Conrad K. Harper
**Director Gen. of the Foreign Service & Dir. of Personnel** — Anthony C. E. Quainton
**Assistant Secretaries for:**
- **Administration** — Patrick F. Kennedy
- **African Affairs** — George E. Moose
- **Consular Affairs** — Mary A. Ryan
- **Democracy, Human Rights, & Labor** — John Shattuck
- **Diplomatic Security** — Eric J. Boswell
- **East Asian & Pacific Affairs** — Winston Lord
- **Economic & Business Affairs** — Alan Larson
- **European & Canadian Affairs** — vacant
- **Intelligence & Research** — Toby T. Gati
- **Inter-American Affairs** — Jeffery Davidow, act.
- **International Narcotics & Law** — Robert S. Gelbard
- **International Organization Affairs** — Princeton Lyman
- **Legislative Affairs** — Barbara Larkin, act.
- **Near Eastern Affairs** — Robert H. Pelletreau
- **Oceans, International Environmental, & Scientific Affairs** — Eileen B. Claussen
- **Politico-Military Affairs** — Thomas E. McNamara
- **Population, Refugees, & Migration** — Phyllis E. Oakley

## Department of the Treasury

1500 Pennsylvania Ave. NW 20220

**Secretary of the Treasury** — Robert E. Rubin
**Deputy Sec. of the Treasury** — Lawrence Summers
**Under Sec. for Domestic Finance** — John Hawke
**Under Sec. for International Affairs** — Jeff Shafer
**Under Sec. for Enforcement** — Raymond Kelly
**General Counsel** — Edward Knight
**Inspector General** — Valerie Lau
**Assistant Secretaries for:**
- **Economic Policy** — Joshua Gotbaum
- **Enforcement** — James Johnson
- **Fiscal Affairs** — Gerald Murphy
- **International Affairs** — David Lipton
- **Legislative Affairs** — Linda Robertson
- **Public Affairs** — Howard Schloss
- **Tax Policy** — Donald Lubick
- **Management** — George Muñoz
- **Financial Institutions** — Richard Carnell

**Treasurer of the U.S.** — Mary Ellen Withrow
**Bureaus:**
- **Alcohol, Tobacco, & Firearms** — John W. Magaw, dir.
- **Comptroller of the Currency** — Eugene A. Ludwig, comm.
- **Customs** — George J. Weise, comm.
- **Engraving & Printing** — Larry Rolufs, dir.
- **Federal Law Enforcement Training Center** — Charles F. Rinkevich, dir.
- **Financial Management Service** — Russell Morris, comm.
- **Internal Revenue Service** — Margaret Milner Richardson, comm.
- **Mint** — Philip Diehl, dir.
- **Public Debt** — Richard L. Gregg, comm.
- **U.S. Secret Service** — Eljay B. Bowron, dir.
- **Office of Thrift Supervision** — vacant

## Department of Defense

The Pentagon 20301

**Secretary of Defense** — William J. Perry
**Deputy Secretary** — John P. White
**Under Sec. for Acquisition and Technol.** — Paul Kaminski
**Under Sec. for Policy** — Walter B. Slocombe
**Assistant Secretaries for:**
- **Command, Control, Communications, & Intelligence** — Emmett Paige Jr.
- **Personnel & Readiness** — Edwin Dorn
- **Health Affairs** — Stephen C. Joseph
- **International Security Policy** — Ashton B. Carter
- **Legislative Affairs** — Sandra Stuart
- **Program Analysis & Evaluation** — William J. Lynn III
- **Public Affairs** — Kenneth Bacon
- **Reserve Affairs** — Deborah Lee
- **Special Operations & Low Intensity Conflict**— H. Allen Holmes

**Comptroller**— John Hamre
**General Counsel** — Judith Miller
**Administration** — Ann Reese, dir.
**Operational Test & Evaluation** — Phillip E. Coyle III
**Chairman, Joint Chiefs of Staff** — Gen. John Shalikashvili
**Secretary of the Army** — Togo West
**Secretary of the Navy** — John Dalton
**Secretary of the Air Force** — Sheila Widnall

## Department of Justice

Constitution Ave. & 10th St. NW 20530

**Attorney General** — Janet Reno
**Deputy Attorney General** — Jamie S. Gorelick
**Associate Attorney General** — John R. Schmidt
**Solicitor General** — Walter A. Dellinger, act.
**Office of Inspector General** — Michael R. Bromwich
**Assistants:**
- **Antitrust Division** — Anne K. Bingaman
- **Civil Division** — Frank W. Hunger
- **Civil Rights Division** — Deval L. Patrick
- **Criminal Division** — John C. Keeney, act.
- **Environment & Natural Resources Division** — Lois J. Schiffer
- **Justice Programs** — Laurie Robinson
- **Legal Counsel** — Christopher H. Schroeder, act.
- **Policy Development** — Eleanor D. Acheson
- **Legislative Affairs** — Andrew Fois
- **Administration** — Stephen R. Colgate
- **Tax Division** — Loretta C. Argrett

**Executive Secretariat** — Anna Gatons
**Office of Public Affairs** — Carl Stern
**Office of Information & Privacy** — Richard L. Huff/Daniel J. Metcalf
**Community Oriented Policing Services** — Joseph Brann, dir.
**Fed. Bureau of Investigation** — Louis J. Freeh, dir.
**Exec. Off. for Immigration Review** — Tony Moscato, dir.
**Bureau of Prisons** — Kathleen M. Hawk, dir.
**Comm. Relations Service** — Rose Ochi, act. dir.
**Drug Enforcement Adm.** — Tom Constantine
**Office of Intelligence Policy & Review** — James McAdams, counsel
**Exec. Off. for National Security** — Frederick Baron, dir.
**Off. of Professional Responsibility** — Michael E. Shaheen Jr.
**Exec. Off. for U.S. Trustees** — Joseph Patchan, dir.
**Foreign Claims Comm.** — Delissa Ridgeway, comm.
**Exec. Off. for U.S. Attorneys** — Carol DiBattiste, dir.
**Immigration & Naturalization Service** — Doris Meissner, comm.
**Pardon Attorney** — Margaret C. Love
**U.S. Parole Commission** — Edward F. Reilly Jr., chmn.
**U.S. Marshals Service** — Eduardo Gonzalez, dir.
**U.S. Natl. Central Bureau of INTERPOL** — James Christensen, act. chief
**Office of Public Liaison** — Nick Gess
**Office of Tribal Justice** — Herbert A. Becker
**Violence Against Women Act** — Bonnie Campbell

## Department of the Interior

1849 C St. NW 20240

**Secretary of the Interior** — Bruce Babbitt
**Deputy Secretary** — John Garamendi
**Assistant Secretaries for:**
- **Fish, Wildlife, & Parks** — George T. Frampton Jr.
- **Indian Affairs** — Ada E. Deer
- **Land & Minerals** — Robert Armstrong
- **Policy, Budget, & Management** — Bonnie R. Cohen
- **Intergovernmental Affairs** — Leslie Turner
- **Water & Science** — Patricia J. Beneke

**Bureau of Land Management** — Michael Dombeck, act. dir.
**Bureau of Reclamation** — Eluid L. Martinez, comm.
**Fish & Wildlife Service** — John Rogers, act. dir.
**Geological Survey** — Gordon P. Eaton, dir.
**National Park Service** — Roger Kennedy, dir.
**Surface Mining Reclamation & Enforcement** — Kay Henry, act. dir.
**Communications** — Michael Gauldin, dir.
**Office of Congressional & Legisl. Affairs** — Melanie Bellar
**Solicitor** — John D. Leshy
**External Affairs** — Ken Smith
**Exec. Secretariat & Regulatory Affairs** — Julie Faulkner

## Department of Agriculture

14th St. and Independence Ave. SW 20250

**Secretary of Agriculture** — Dan Glickman
**Deputy Secretary** — Richard Rominger
**Assistant Secretaries for:**
- **Administration** — Wardell Townsend Jr.
- **Congressional Relations** — Dave Carlin
- **Research, Educ., & Economics** — Catherine Woteki, act.
- **Food, Nutrition, & Consumer Services** — Ellen Haas
- **Food Safety** — Mike Taylor, act.
- **Farm & Foreign Agriculture Services** — Eugene Moos
- **Marketing & Regulatory Program**— Mike Dunn
- **Natural Resources & Environment** — James Lyons
- **Rural Development** — Jill John-Thompson, undersec.

**General Counsel** — James Gilliland
**Inspector General** — Roger Vladero
**Communications** — Tom Amontree, act.
**Press Secretary** — Tom Amontree

## Department of Commerce

14th St. between Constitution & Pennsylvania Ave. NW 20230

**Secretary of Commerce** — Mickey Kantor
**Chief of Staff** — Peter Scher
**General Counsel** — Susan Esserman, act.
**Assistant Secretaries:**
- **Chief Financial Officer & Asst. for Administration** — Ray Kammer, act.
- **Economic Development Adm.** — Phillip Singerman
- **Export Admin.** — Sue Eckert
- **Export Enforcement** — John Despres
- **Import Administration** — Robert LaRussa, act.
- **Legislative Affairs** — Jane Bobbitt

**Market Access & Compliance** — William W. Ginsberg, act.
**Natl. Telecommunications Information Adm.** — Clarence Irving Jr.
**Oceans & Atmosphere** — Douglas K. Hall
**Patent & Trademark Office & Comm.** — Bruce Lehman
**Trade Development** — Raymond Vickery Jr.
**U.S. & Foreign Commercial Service** — Lauri Fitz-Pegado
**Bureau of the Census** — Martha Farnsworth Riche
**Bureau of Economic Analysis** — J. Steven Landerfeld, act. dir.
**Under Sec. for Oceans & Atmosphere** — Dr. James Baker
**Under Sec. for Export Admin.** — William Reinsch
**Under Sec. for International Trade** — Stuart Eizenstat
**Under Sec. for Econ. Affairs** — Everett Ehrlich
**Under Sec. for Technology** — Mary Lowe Good
**Natl. Technical Info. Service** — Donald Johnson
**Natl. Institute for Standards & Technology** — Arati Prabhakar, dir.
**Minority Business Development Agency** — Joan Parrott-Fonseca
**Public Affairs and Press Secretary** — Anne Luzzatto

## Department of Labor

200 Constitution Ave. NW 20210

**Secretary of Labor** — Robert B. Reich
**Deputy Secretary** — Cynthia A. Metzler
**Chief of Staff** — Vince Trivelli
**Assistant Secretaries for:**
**Admin. & Management** — Patricia W. Lattimore, act.
**Congressional & Intergovernmental Affairs** — Geri Palast
**Employment & Training** — Timothy Barnicle
**Employment Standards** — Bernard E. Anderson
**Occupational Safety & Health** — Joseph A. Dear
**Mine Safety & Health**—Davitt McAteer
**Pension & Welfare Benefits** — E. Olena Berg
**Policy** — Anne H. Lewis
**Public Affairs** — Susan R. King, act.
**Veterans Employment & Training** — Preston M. Taylor Jr.
**Solicitor of Labor** — Davitt McAteer, act.
**Bureau of International Affairs** — Joaquin F. Otero
**Women's Bureau** — Ida Castro
**Inspector General** — Charles C. Masten
**Bureau of Labor Statistics** — Katharine G. Abraham

## Department of Health and Human Services

200 Independence Ave. SW 20201

**Secretary of HHS** — Donna E. Shalala, Ph.D.
**Deputy Secretary** — vacant
**Chief of Staff** — Kevin L. Thurm
**Assistant Secretaries for:**
**Health** — Philip Lee, M.D.
**Legislation** — vacant
**Management & Budget** — John Callahan
**Planning & Evaluation** — Peter Edelman
**Public Affairs** — Melissa Skolfield, act.
**General Counsel** — Harriet Rabb
**Inspector General** — June Gibbs Brown
**Surgeon General** — Audrey Manley, act.
**Office of Consumer Affairs** — Bernice Friedlander
**Administration on Aging**— vacant
**Health Care Financing Adm.** — Bruce C. Vladeck
**Administration for Children & Families** — Mary Jo Bane

## Department of Housing and Urban Development

451 7th St. SW 20410

**Secretary of Housing & Urban Development** — Henry G. Cisneros
**Deputy Secretary** — Dwight P. Robinson
**Assistant Secretaries for:**
**Administration** — Marilynn A. Davis
**Community Planning & Development** — Andrew M. Cuomo
**Fair Housing & Equal Opportunity** — Elizabeth K. Julian
**Housing & Federal Housing Commissioner** — Nicolas P. Retsinas
**Congressional & Intergovernmental Relations** — Halbert C. DeCell III
**Policy Development & Research** — Michael A. Stegman
**Public Affairs** — vacant
**Public & Indian Housing** — vacant
**General Counsel** — Nelson A. Diaz
**Inspector General** — Susan M. Gaffney
**Chief Financial Officer** — John A. Knubel
**Government National Mortgage Assn.** — Kevin G. Chavers, pres.
**Off. of Federal Housing Enterprise Oversight** — Aida Alvarez, dir.

## Department of Transportation

400 7th St. SW 20590

**Secretary of Transportation** — Federico F. Peña
**Deputy Secretary** — Mortimer L. Downey
**Assistant Secretaries for:**
**Administration** — Melissa Spillenkothen
**Budget & Programs** — Louise F. Stoll
**Governmental Affairs** — Steven O. Palmer
**Aviation & International Affairs** — Charles Hunnicutt
**Transportation**—Frank E. Kreusi
**Public Affairs** — Steve Akey
**U.S. Coast Guard Commandant** — Adm. Robert E. Kramek
**Federal Aviation Admin.** — David R. Hinson
**Federal Highway Admin.** — Rodney E. Slater
**Federal Railroad Admin.** — Jolene Molitoris
**Maritime Admin.** — Albert Herberger
**National Highway Traffic Safety Adm.** — Ricardo Martinez
**Federal Transit Admin.** — Gordon J. Linton
**Research & Special Programs Admin.** — Dharmendra K. Sahama
**Saint Lawrence Seaway Development Corp.** — Gail McDonald

## Department of Energy

1000 Independence Ave. SW 20585

**Secretary of Energy** — Hazel R. O'Leary
**Deputy Secretary** — Charles B. Curtis
**Under Secretary** — Thomas Grumbly
**Chief of Staff** — Dan Reicher
**Deputy Chief of Staff** — Jonathan Miller
**General Counsel** — Robert Nordhaus
**Inspector General** — John C. Layton
**Assistant Secretaries for:**
**Congressional, Public, & Intergovernmental Affairs** — Dick Forrister
**Energy Efficiency & Renewable Energy** — Christine Ervin
**Defense Programs** — Victor Reis
**Policy, Planning, & Program Evaluation** — Marc Chupka, act.
**Environmental Restoration & Waste Management** — Alvin Alm
**Administration & Human Resource Management** — Archer L. Durham
**Environment, Safety, & Health** — Tara Jeanne O'Toole
**Fossil Energy** — Patricia Godley
**Nuclear Energy** — Terry Lash, dir.
**Energy Information Adm.** — Jay E. Hakes, adm.
**Economic Impact & Diversity** — Corlis Moody, dir.
**Hearings & Appeals** — George Breznay, dir.
**Energy Research** — Martha Krebs, dir.
**Civilian Radioactive Waste Management** — Daniel A. Dreyfus, dir.
**Nonproliferation & National Security** — Joan Rohlfing, dir.
**Chief Financial Officer** — Don Pearman, act.
**Field Management** —Don Pearman
**Quality Management** — Nancy K. Weidenfeller, dir.
**Energy Advisory Board** — David Chaney, act. dir.

## Department of Education

600 Independence Ave. SW 20202

**Secretary of Education** — Richard W. Riley
**Deputy Secretary** — vacant
**Under Secretary** — Marshall S. Smith
**Chief of Staff** — Frank Holleman
**Inspector General** — Thomas R. Bloom
**General Counsel** — Judith Winston
**Assistant Secretaries for:**
**Adult & Vocational Education** — Patricia McNeil
**Civil Rights** — Norma V. Cantu
**Educational Research & Improvement** — Sharon Porter Robinson
**Elementary & Secondary Educ.** — Gerald N. Tirozzi
**Intergovernmental & Interagency Affairs** — Mario Moreno
**Legislation & Congressional Affairs** — Kay Casstevens
**Management** — vacant
**Postsecondary Education** — David Longanecker
**Special Educ. & Rehab. Services** — Judith Heumann
**Bilingual & Minority Language Affairs** — Delia Pompa
**Rehab. Services Admin.** — Frederic K. Schroeder, comm.

## Department of Veterans Affairs

810 Vermont Ave. NW 20420

**Secretary of Veterans Affairs** — Jesse Brown
**Deputy** — Hershel W. Gober
**Assistant Secretaries for:**
**Congressional Affairs** — Edward P. Scott
**Management** — D. Mark Catlett
**Human Resources & Adm.** — Eugene Brickhouse
**Policy & Planning** — Dennis Duffy
**Public & Intergovernmental Affairs** — Kathy E. Jurado
**Inspector General** — vacant
**Under Sec. for Benefits** — R. John Vogel
**Under Sec. for Health** — Kenneth W. Kizer, M.D.
**National Cemetery System** — Jerry W. Bowen, dir.
**General Counsel** — Mary Lou Keener
**Board of Veterans Appeals** — Charles L. Cragin, chmn.
**Board of Contract Appeals** — Guy H. McMichael III, chmn.
**Small & Disadvantaged Business Utilization** — Scott S. Denniston, dir.
**Veterans Service Organization Liaison** — Allen F. Kent

# Notable U.S. Government Agencies

**Source:** *The U.S. Government Manual*, National Archives and Records Administration; World Almanac research

All addresses are Washington, DC, unless otherwise noted; as of mid-1996; * = independent agency

**Bureau of Alcohol, Tobacco, and Firearms** — John W. Magaw, dir. (Dept. of Treas., 650 Mass. Ave NW, 20226).

**Bureau of the Census** — Martha Farnsworth Riche, dir. (Dept. of Commerce, 4700 Silver Hill Rd., Suitland, MD 20746).

**Bureau of Economic Analysis** — J. Steven Landerfeld, dir. (Dept. of Commerce, 1441 L St. NW, 20230).

**Bureau of Indian Affairs** — Ada E. Deer, asst. sec. (Dept. of the Interior, 1849 C St. NW, 20240).

**Bureau of Prisons** — Kathleen M. Hawk, dir. (Dept. of Justice, 320 First St. NW, 20534).

**Centers for Disease Control & Prevention** — David Satcher, dir. (Dept. of HHS, 1600 Clifton Rd. NE, Atlanta, GA 30333).

***Central Intelligence Agency** — John M. Deutch, dir. (Wash., DC 20505).

***Commission on Civil Rights** — Mary Frances Berry, chmn. (624 9th St. NW, 20425).

***Commodity Futures Trading Commision** — Brooksley Born, chmn. (3 Lafayette Center, 1155 21st St. NW, 20581).

***Consumer Product Safety Commission** — Ann Brown, chmn. (East West Towers, 4330 East West Hwy., Bethesda, MD 20814).

***Environmental Protection Agency** — Carol M. Browner, adm. (401 M St. SW, 20460).

***Equal Employment Opportunity Commission** — Gilbert Casellas, chmn. (1801 L St. NW, 20507).

***Export-Import Bank of the United States** — Martin A. Kamarck, pres. and chmn. (811 Vermont Ave. NW, 20571).

***Farm Credit Administration** — Marsha P. Martin, chmn., Farm Credit Administration Board (1501 Farm Credit Drive, McLean, VA 22102).

**Federal Aviation Administration** — David R. Hinson, adm. (Dept. of Trans., 800 Independence Ave. SW, 20591).

**Federal Bureau of Investigation** — Louis J. Freeh, dir. (Dept. of Justice, 935 Pennsylvania Ave. NW, 20535).

***Federal Communications Commission** — Reed E. Hundt, chmn. (1919 M St. NW, 20554).

***Federal Deposit Insurance Corporation** — Ricki R. Tigert-Halfer, chmn. (550 17th St. NW, 20429).

***Federal Election Commission** — Lee Ann Elliott, chmn. (999 E St. NW, 20463).

***Federal Emergency Management Agency** — James Lee Witt, dir. (500 C St. SW, 20472).

**Federal Energy Regulatory Commission** — Elizabeth A. Moler, chair (888 1st St. NE, 20426).

**Federal Highway Administration** — Rodney E. Slater, adm. (Dept. of Trans., 400 7th St. SW, 20590).

***Federal Maritime Commission** — Harold J. Creel Jr., chmn. (800 N. Capitol St. NW, 20573).

***Federal Mine Safety & Health Review Commission** — Mary Lu Jordan, chmn. (1730 K St. NW, 20006).

***Federal Reserve System** — Alan Greenspan, chmn., Board of Governors (20th St. & C St. NW, 20551).

***Federal Trade Commission** — Robert Pitofsky, chmn. (Pennsylvania Ave. at 6th St. NW, 20580).

**Fish & Wildlife Service** — John Rogers, act. dir. (Dept. of the Interior, 1849 C St. NW, 20240).

**Food and Drug Administration** — David A. Kessler, comm. (Dept. of HHS, 5600 Fishers Ln., Rockville, MD 20857).

**Forest Service** — Jack W. Thomas,[1] chief (Dept. of Agriculture, PO Box 96090, 20090).

**General Accounting Office** — (congressional agency) Charles A. Bowsher, comptroller gen. (441 G St. NW, 20548).

***General Services Administration** — David Barram, adm. (18th St. & F St. NW, 20405).

**Government Printing Office** — (congressional agency) Michael F. DiMario, public printer (732 N. Capitol St. NW, 20401).

**Immigration & Naturalization Service** — Doris Meissner, comm. (Dept. of Justice, 425 I St. NW, 20536).

***Inter-American Foundation** — Maria Otero, chmn. (901 N Stuart St., 10th floor, Arlington, VA 22203).

**Internal Revenue Service** — Margaret Milner Richardson, comm. (Dept. of Treas., 1111 Constitution Ave. NW, 20224).

**Library of Congress** — (congressional agency) James H. Billington, Librarian of Congress (101 Independence Ave. SE, 20540).

***National Aeronautics and Space Administration** — Daniel S. Goldin, adm. (300 E St. SW, 20546).

***National Archives & Records Administration** — John W. Carlin, archivist (700 Pennsylvania Ave. NW, 20408).

***National Endowment for the Arts** — Jane Alexander, chmn. (1100 Pennsylvania Ave. NW, 20506).

***National Endowment for the Humanities** — Sheldon Hackney, chmn. (1100 Pennsylvania Ave. NW, 20506).

**National Institutes of Health** — Harold E. Varmus, dir. (Dept. of HHS, 9000 Rockville Pike, Bethesda, MD 20892).

***National Labor Relations Board** — William B. Gould IV, chmn. (1099 14th St. NW, 20570).

**National Oceanic and Atmospheric Administration** — D. James Baker, undersec. (Dept. of Commerce, 14th & Constitution Ave. NW, 20230).

**National Park Service** — Roger G. Kennedy, dir. (Dept. of the Interior, 1849 C St. NW, 20240).

***National Railroad Passenger Corporation (Amtrak)** — Thomas M. Downs, chmn. (60 Massachusetts Ave. NE, 20002).

***National Science Foundation** — Richard Zare, chmn., National Science Board (4201 Wilson Blvd., Arlington, VA 22230).

***National Transportation Safety Board** — Jim Hall, chmn. (490 L'Enfant Plaza SW, 20594).

***Nuclear Regulatory Commission** — Shirley A. Jackson, chmn. (11555 Rockville Pike, Rockville, MD 20852).

**Occupational Safety & Health Administration** — Joseph A. Dear, asst. sec. (Dept. of Labor, 200 Constitution Ave. NW, 20210).

***Occupational Safety & Health Review Commission** — Stuart E. Weisberg, chmn. (1120 20th St. NW, 20036).

***Office of Government Ethics** — Stephen D. Potts, dir. (1201 New York Ave. NW, Suite 500, 20005).

***Office of Personnel Management** — James B. King, dir. (1900 E St. NW, 20415-0001).

***Office of Special Counsel** — Kathleen Day Koch, sp. counsel (1730 M St. NW, Suite 216, 20036).

***Peace Corps** — Mark Gearan, dir. (1990 K St. NW, 20526).

***Postal Rate Commission** — Edward J. Gleiman, chmn. (1333 H St. NW, 20268).

***Securities and Exchange Commission** — Arthur Levitt, chmn. (450 5th St. NW, 20549).

***Selective Service System** — Gil Coronado, dir. (National Headquarters, 1515 Wilson Blvd., Arlington, VA 22209-2425).

***Small Business Administration** — Philip Lader, adm. (409 Third St. SW, 20416).

**Smithsonian Institution** — (quasi-official agency) Ira M. Hayman, sec. (1000 Jefferson Dr. SW, 20560).

***Social Security Administration** — Shirley S. Chater, comm. (6401 Security Blvd., Baltimore, MD 21235).

**Surgeon General** — Audrey F. Manley, act. (Pub. Health Service, HHS, Parklawn Bldg. 5600 Fishers Ln., Rockville, MD 20857).

***Tennessee Valley Authority** — Craven Crowell, chmn., Board of Directors (400 W. Summit Hill Dr., Knoxville, TN 37902, and One Mass. Ave. NW, Suite 300, 20444).

***Trade and Development Agency** — J. Joseph Grandmaison, dir. (State Annex 16, Room 309, 20523).

***United States Arms Control & Disarmament Agency** — John D. Holum, dir. (320 21st St. NW, 20451).

**United States Coast Guard** — Adm. Robert E. Kramek, commandant (Dept. of Trans., 2100 2d St. SW, 20593).

**United States Customs Service** — George J. Weise, comm. (Dept. of Treas., 1301 Constitution Ave. NW, 20229).

***United States Information Agency** — Joseph D. Duffey, dir. (301 4th St. SW, 20547).

***United States International Trade Commission** — Marcia E. Miller, chmn. (500 E St. SW, 20436).

**United States Mint** — Philip N. Diehl, dir. (Dept. of Treas., 633 3d St. NW, 20220).

***United States Postal Service** — Marvin Runyon, Postmaster General (475 L'Enfant Plaza SW, 20260).

**United States Secret Service** — Eljay B. Bowron, dir. (Dept. of Treas., 1800 G St. NW, 20223).

(1) Retirement announced Oct. 1996.

# Judiciary of the U.S.

(data as of Oct. 1996)

## Justices of the United States Supreme Court

The Supreme Court comprises the chief justice of the U.S. and 8 associate justices, all appointed by the president with advice and consent of the Senate. Salaries: chief justice, $171,500 annually; associate justice, $164,100 annually. The Supreme Court is at the U.S. Supreme Court Bldg., 1 First St. NE, Washington, DC 20543.

**Members of the Supreme Court at the start of the 1996–97 term (Oct. 7, 1996):** Chief justice: William H. Rehnquist; associate justices: Stephen G. Breyer, Ruth Bader Ginsburg, Anthony M. Kennedy, Sandra Day O'Connor, Antonin Scalia, David H. Souter, John Paul Stevens, Clarence Thomas.

| Name,[1] apptd from | Service Term | Yrs | Born | Died |
|---|---|---|---|---|
| *John Jay,* NY | 1789-1795 | 5 | 1745 | 1829 |
| John Rutledge, SC | 1789-1791 | 1 | 1739 | 1800 |
| William Cushing, MA | 1789-1810 | 20 | 1732 | 1810 |
| James Wilson, PA | 1789-1798 | 8 | 1742 | 1798 |
| John Blair, VA | 1789-1796 | 6 | 1732 | 1800 |
| James Iredell, NC | 1790-1799 | 9 | 1751 | 1799 |
| Thomas Johnson, MD | 1791-1793 | 1 | 1732 | 1819 |
| William Paterson, NJ | 1793-1806 | 13 | 1745 | 1806 |
| *John Rutledge,*[2] SC | 1795 | — | 1739 | 1800 |
| Samuel Chase, MD | 1796-1811 | 15 | 1741 | 1811 |
| *Oliver Ellsworth,* CT | 1796-1800 | 4 | 1745 | 1807 |
| Bushrod Washington, VA | 1798-1829 | 31 | 1762 | 1829 |
| Alfred Moore, NC | 1799-1804 | 4 | 1755 | 1810 |
| *John Marshall,* VA | 1801-1835 | 34 | 1755 | 1835 |
| William Johnson, SC | 1804-1834 | 30 | 1771 | 1834 |
| Henry B. Livingston, NY | 1806-1823 | 16 | 1757 | 1823 |
| Thomas Todd, KY | 1807-1826 | 18 | 1765 | 1826 |
| Joseph Story, MA | 1811-1845 | 33 | 1779 | 1845 |
| Gabriel Duval, MD | 1811-1835 | 22 | 1752 | 1844 |
| Smith Thompson, NY | 1823-1843 | 20 | 1768 | 1843 |
| Robert Trimble, KY | 1826-1828 | 2 | 1777 | 1828 |
| John McLean, OH | 1829-1861 | 32 | 1785 | 1861 |
| Henry Baldwin, PA | 1830-1844 | 14 | 1780 | 1844 |
| James M. Wayne, GA | 1835-1867 | 32 | 1790 | 1867 |
| *Roger B. Taney,* MD | 1836-1864 | 28 | 1777 | 1864 |
| Philip P. Barbour, VA | 1836-1841 | 4 | 1783 | 1841 |
| John Catron, TN | 1837-1865 | 28 | 1786 | 1865 |
| John McKinley, AL | 1837-1852 | 15 | 1780 | 1852 |
| Peter V. Daniel, VA | 1841-1860 | 19 | 1784 | 1860 |
| Samuel Nelson, NY | 1845-1872 | 27 | 1792 | 1873 |
| Levi Woodbury, NH | 1845-1851 | 5 | 1789 | 1851 |
| Robert C. Grier, PA | 1846-1870 | 23 | 1794 | 1870 |
| Benjamin R. Curtis, MA | 1851-1857 | 6 | 1809 | 1874 |
| John A. Campbell, AL | 1853-1861 | 8 | 1811 | 1889 |
| Nathan Clifford, ME | 1858-1881 | 23 | 1803 | 1881 |
| Noah H. Swayne, OH | 1862-1881 | 18 | 1804 | 1884 |
| Samuel F. Miller, IA | 1862-1890 | 28 | 1816 | 1890 |
| David Davis, IL | 1862-1877 | 14 | 1815 | 1886 |
| Stephen J. Field, CA | 1863-1897 | 34 | 1816 | 1899 |
| *Salmon P. Chase,* OH | 1864-1873 | 8 | 1808 | 1873 |
| William Strong, PA | 1870-1880 | 10 | 1808 | 1895 |
| Joseph P. Bradley, NJ | 1870-1892 | 21 | 1813 | 1892 |
| Ward Hunt, NY | 1872-1882 | 9 | 1810 | 1886 |
| *Morrison R. Waite,* OH | 1874-1888 | 14 | 1816 | 1888 |
| John M. Harlan, KY | 1877-1911 | 34 | 1833 | 1911 |
| William B. Woods, GA | 1880-1887 | 6 | 1824 | 1887 |
| Stanley Matthews, OH | 1881-1889 | 7 | 1824 | 1889 |
| Horace Gray, MA | 1881-1902 | 20 | 1828 | 1902 |
| Samuel Blatchford, NY | 1882-1893 | 11 | 1820 | 1893 |
| Lucius Q.C. Lamar, MS | 1888-1893 | 5 | 1825 | 1893 |
| *Melville W. Fuller,* IL | 1888-1910 | 21 | 1833 | 1910 |
| David J. Brewer, KS | 1889-1910 | 20 | 1837 | 1910 |
| Henry B. Brown, MI | 1890-1906 | 15 | 1836 | 1913 |
| George Shiras Jr, PA | 1892-1903 | 10 | 1832 | 1924 |
| Howell E. Jackson, TN | 1893-1895 | 2 | 1832 | 1895 |
| Edward D. White, LA | 1894-1910 | 16 | 1845 | 1921 |
| Rufus W. Peckham, NY | 1895-1909 | 13 | 1838 | 1909 |
| Joseph McKenna, CA | 1898-1925 | 26 | 1843 | 1926 |
| Oliver W. Holmes, MA | 1902-1932 | 29 | 1841 | 1935 |
| William R. Day, OH | 1903-1922 | 19 | 1849 | 1923 |
| William H. Moody, MA | 1906-1910 | 3 | 1853 | 1917 |
| Horace H. Lurton, TN | 1909-1914 | 4 | 1844 | 1914 |
| Charles E. Hughes, NY | 1910-1916 | 5 | 1862 | 1948 |
| Willis Van Devanter, WY | 1910-1937 | 26 | 1859 | 1941 |
| Joseph R. Lamar, GA | 1910-1916 | 5 | 1857 | 1916 |
| *Edward D. White,* LA | 1910-1921 | 10 | 1845 | 1921 |
| Mahlon Pitney, NJ | 1912-1922 | 10 | 1858 | 1924 |
| James C. McReynolds, TN | 1914-1941 | 26 | 1862 | 1946 |
| Louis D. Brandeis, MA | 1916-1939 | 22 | 1856 | 1941 |
| John H. Clarke, OH | 1916-1922 | 5 | 1857 | 1945 |
| *William H. Taft,* CT | 1921-1930 | 8 | 1857 | 1930 |
| George Sutherland, UT | 1922-1938 | 15 | 1862 | 1942 |
| Pierce Butler, MN | 1922-1939 | 16 | 1866 | 1939 |
| Edward T. Sanford, TN | 1923-1930 | 7 | 1865 | 1930 |
| Harlan F. Stone, NY | 1925-1941 | 16 | 1872 | 1946 |
| *Charles E. Hughes,* NY | 1930-1941 | 11 | 1862 | 1948 |
| Owen J. Roberts, PA | 1930-1945 | 15 | 1875 | 1955 |
| Benjamin N. Cardozo, NY | 1932-1938 | 6 | 1870 | 1938 |
| Hugo L. Black, AL | 1937-1971 | 34 | 1886 | 1971 |
| Stanley F. Reed, KY | 1938-1957 | 19 | 1884 | 1980 |
| Felix Frankfurter, MA | 1939-1962 | 23 | 1882 | 1965 |
| William O. Douglas, CT | 1939-1975 | 36 | 1898 | 1980 |
| Frank Murphy, MI | 1940-1949 | 9 | 1890 | 1949 |
| *Harlan F. Stone,* NY | 1941-1946 | 5 | 1872 | 1946 |
| James F. Byrnes, SC | 1941-1942 | 1 | 1879 | 1972 |
| Robert H. Jackson, NY | 1941-1954 | 12 | 1892 | 1954 |
| Wiley B. Rutledge, IA | 1943-1949 | 6 | 1894 | 1949 |
| Harold H. Burton, OH | 1945-1958 | 13 | 1888 | 1964 |
| *Fred M. Vinson,* KY | 1946-1953 | 7 | 1890 | 1953 |
| Tom C. Clark, TX | 1949-1967 | 18 | 1899 | 1977 |
| Sherman Minton, IN | 1949-1956 | 7 | 1890 | 1965 |
| *Earl Warren,* CA | 1953-1969 | 16 | 1891 | 1974 |
| John Marshall Harlan, NY | 1955-1971 | 16 | 1899 | 1971 |
| William J. Brennan Jr, NJ | 1956-1990 | 33 | 1906 | — |
| Charles E. Whittaker, MO | 1957-1962 | 5 | 1901 | 1973 |
| Potter Stewart, OH | 1958-1981 | 23 | 1915 | 1985 |
| Byron R. White, CO | 1962-1993 | 31 | 1917 | — |
| Arthur J. Goldberg, IL | 1962-1965 | 3 | 1908 | 1990 |
| Abe Fortas, TN | 1965-1969 | 4 | 1910 | 1982 |
| Thurgood Marshall, NY | 1967-1991 | 24 | 1908 | 1993 |
| *Warren E. Burger,* VA | 1969-1986 | 17 | 1907 | 1995 |
| Harry A. Blackmun, MN | 1970-1994 | 24 | 1908 | — |
| Lewis F. Powell Jr, VA | 1972-1987 | 15 | 1907 | — |
| William H. Rehnquist, AZ | 1972-1986 | 14 | 1924 | — |
| John Paul Stevens, IL | 1975- | — | 1920 | — |
| Sandra Day O'Connor, AZ | 1981- | — | 1930 | — |
| *William H. Rehnquist,* AZ | 1986- | — | 1924 | — |
| Antonin Scalia, VA | 1986- | — | 1936 | — |
| Anthony M. Kennedy, CA | 1988- | — | 1936 | — |
| David H. Souter, NH | 1990- | — | 1939 | — |
| Clarence Thomas, VA | 1991- | — | 1948 | — |
| Ruth Bader Ginsburg, DC | 1993- | — | 1933 | — |
| Stephen Breyer, MA | 1994- | — | 1938 | — |

(1) Chief justices in italics. (2) Rejected Dec. 15, 1795.

## U.S. Courts of Appeals

(Salaries, $141,700. CJ means Chief Judge)

**Federal Circuit** — Glenn L. Archer Jr, CJ; Giles S. Rich, Wilson Cowen, Bryon G. Skelton, Marion T. Bennett, Daniel M. Friedman, Edward S. Smith, Pauline Newman, H. Robert Mayer, Paul R. Michel, S. Jay Plager, Alan D. Lourie, Raymond C. Clevenger III, Randall R. Rader, Alvin A. Schall, William C. Bryson; Clerk's Office, Washington, DC 20439.

**District of Columbia** —Harry T. Edwards, CJ; Patricia M. Wald, Laurence H. Silberman, James L. Buckley, Stephen F. Williams, Douglas Ginsburg, David B. Sentelle, Karen LeCraft Henderson, A. Raymond Randolph, Judith W. Rogers, David S. Tatel; Clerk's Office, Washington, DC 20001.

**First Circuit** (ME, MA, NH, RI, Puerto Rico) — Juan R. Torruella, CJ; Bruce M. Selya, Conrad K. Cyr, Michael Boudin, Norman H. Stahl, Sandra Lynch; Clerk's Office, Boston, MA 02109.

**Second Circuit** (CT, NY, VT) — Jon O. Newman, CJ; Amalya Lyle Kearse, Ralph K. Winter, Roger J. Miner, J. Daniel Mahoney, John M. Walker Jr, Joseph M. McLaughlin, Dennis G. Jacobs, Pierre N. Leval, Guido Calabresi, José A. Cabranes, Fred I. Parker; Clerk's Office, New York, NY 10007.

**Third Circuit** (DE, NJ, PA, Virgin Islands) — Dolores K. Sloviter, CJ; Edward R. Becker, Walter K. Stapleton, Carol Los Mansmann, Morton I. Greenberg, Anthony J. Scirica, Robert E. Cowen, Richard L. Nygaard, Samuel A. Alito Jr, Jane R. Roth, Timothy K. Lewis, Theodore A. McKee; Clerk's Office, Philadelphia, PA 19106.

**Fourth Circuit** (MD, NC, SC, VA, WV) — J. Harvie Wilkinson III, CJ; Donald Stuart Russell, H. Emory Widener Jr, Kenneth K. Hall, Francis D. Murnaghan Jr, Sam J. Ervin III, William W. Wilkins Jr, Paul V. Niemeyer, Clyde H. Hamilton, J. Michael Luttig, Karen J. Williams, M. Blane Michael, Diana G. Motz; Clerk's Office, Richmond, VA 23219.

**Fifth Circuit** (LA., MS, TX) — Henry A. Politz, CJ; Carolyn Dineen King, Will Garwood, E. Grady Jolly, Patrick E. Higginbotham, W. Eugene Davis, Edith H. Jones, Jerry E. Smith, John M. Duhé Jr, Jacques L. Wiener Jr, Rhesa A. Barksdale, Emilio M. Garza, Harold R. DeMoss Jr, Fortunato P. Benavides, Carl E. Stewart, Robert M. Parker, James L. Dennis; Clerk's Office, New Orleans, LA 70130.

**Sixth Circuit** (KY, MI, OH, TN) — Boyce F. Martin Jr, CJ, Gilbert S. Merritt; Cornelia G. Kennedy, H. Ted Milburn, David A. Nelson, James L. Ryan, Danny J. Boggs, Alan E. Norris, Richard H. Suhrheinrich, Eugene E. Siler Jr, Alice M. Batchelder, Martha Craig Daughtrey, Karen Nelson Moore, R. Guy Cole; Clerk's Office, Cincinnati, OH 45202.

**Seventh Circuit** (IL, IN, WI) — Richard A. Posner, CJ, Thomas E. Fairchild; Walter J. Cummings, Wilbur F. Pell Jr, William J. Bauer, Harlington Wood, Richard D. Cudahy, Jesse E. Eschbach, John L. Coffey, Joel M. Flaum, Frank H. Easterbrook, Kenneth F. Ripple, Daniel A. Manion, Michael S. Kanne, Ilana D. Rovner, Diane P. Wood, Terence T. Evans; Clerk's Office, Chicago, IL 60604.

**Eighth Circuit** (AR, IA, MN, MO, NE, ND, SD) — Richard S. Arnold, CJ; Theodore McMillian, George G. Fagg, Pasco M. Bowman, Roger L. Wollman, Frank J. Magill, C. Arlen Beam, James B. Loken, David R. Hansen, Morris S. Arnold, Diana E. Murphy; Clerk's Office, St. Louis, MO 63101.

**Ninth Circuit** (AK, AZ, CA, HI, ID, MT, NV, OR, WA, Guam, N. Mariana Islands) — Procter Hug Jr, CJ; James R. Browning, Mary M. Schroeder, Betty Binns Fletcher, Harry Pregerson, Stephen Reinhardt, Cynthia Holcomb Hall, Charles E. Wiggins, Melvin Brunetti, Alex Kozinski, John T. Noonan Jr, Sidney R. Thomas, David R. Thompson, Diarmuid F. O'Scannlain, Edward Leavy, Stephen S. Trott, Ferdinand F. Fernandez, Pamela Ann Rymer, Thomas G. Nelson, Andrew J. Kleinfeld, Michael D. Hawkins, A. Wallace Tashima; Clerk's Office, San Francisco, CA 94119.

**Tenth Circuit** (CO, KS, NM, OK, UT, WY) — Stephanie K. Seymour, CJ; John C. Porfilio, Stephen H. Anderson, Deanell R. Tacha, Bobby R. Baldock, Wade Brorby, David M. Ebel, Paul J. Kelly Jr, Robert H. Henry, Mary Beck Briscoe, Carlos Lucero, Michael R. Murphy; Clerk's Office, Denver, CO 80294.

**Eleventh Circuit** (AL, FL, GA)— Joseph W. Hatchett, CJ; Gerald B. Tjoflat, Phyllis A. Kravitch, R. Lanier Anderson III, J. L. Edmondson, Emmett R. Cox, Stanley F. Birch Jr, Joel F. Dubina, Susan H. Black, Edward E. Carnes, Rosemary Barkett; Clerk's Office, Atlanta GA 30303.

## U.S. District Courts

(Salaries, $133,600. CJ means Chief Judge)

**Alabama** — **Northern:** Sam C. Pointer Jr, CJ; U. W. Clemon, Edwin L. Nelson, Sharon Lovelace Blackburn, C. Lynwood Smith Jr; Clerk's Office, Birmingham 35203. **Middle:** Myron H. Thompson, CJ; W. Harold Albritton, Ira Dement; Clerk's Office, Montgomery 36101. **Southern:** Charles R. Butler Jr, CJ; Richard W. Vollmer Jr; Clerk's Office, Mobile 36602.

**Alaska** — James K. Singleton, CJ; H. Russel Holland, John W. Sedwick; Clerk's Office, Anchorage 99513.

**Arizona** — Robert C. Bloomfield, CJ; William D. Browning, Paul G. Rosenblat, Roger G. Strand, Stephen M. McNamee, John M. Roll, Roslyn Silver, Frank R. Zappata; Clerk's Office, Phoenix 85025.

**Arkansas** — **Eastern:** Stephen M. Reasoner, CJ; Henry Woods, George Howard Jr, Susan Webber Wright, G. Thomas Eisele, Elsijane Trimble Roy, William R. Wilson Jr, James M. Moody; Clerk's Office, Little Rock 72201-3325. **Western:** H. Franklin Waters, CJ; Jimm Larry Hendren, Harry F. Barnes; Clerk's Office, Fort Smith 72902.

**California** — **Northern:** Thelton E. Henderson, CJ; Stanley A. Weigel, Samuel Conti, Spencer Williams, William H. Orrick Jr, William A. Ingram, William W Schwarzer, Robert P. Aguilar, Marilyn H. Patel, Eugene F. Lynch, Charles A. Legge, D. Lowell Jensen, Fern M. Smith, Vaughn R. Walker, James Ware, Saundra Brown Armstrong, Ronald M. Whyte, Claudia Wilken, Maxine M. Chesney, Susan Illston; Clerk's Office, San Francisco 94102. **Eastern:** William B. Shubb, CJ; Robert E. Coyle, Lawrence K. Karlton, CJ Emeritus; Edward J. Garcia, David F. Levi, Oliver W. Wanger, Garland E. Burrell Jr; Clerk's Office, Sacramento 95814. **Central:** Wm. Matthew Byrne Jr, CJ; Manuel L. Real, Robert M. Takasugi, Mariana R. Pfaelzer, Terry J. Hatter Jr, Consuelo B. Marshall, Harry L. Hupp, Alicemarie H. Stotler, William J. Rea, James M. Ideman, William D. Keller, Stephen V. Wilson, J. Spencer Letts, Dickran M. Tevrizian, John G. Davies, Ronald S. W. Lew, Gary L. Taylor, Lourdes G. Baird, Linda H. McLaughlin, Audrey B. Collins, Richard A. Paez, Robert J. Timlin, George H. King, Kim M. Wardlaw, Dean D. Pregerson; Clerk's Office, Los Angeles 90012. **Southern:** Judith N. Keep, CJ; Rudi M. Brewster, Marilyn L. Huff, Irma E. Gonzalez, Napoleon A. Jones Jr, Barry T. Moskowitz, Edward J. Schwartz, Howard B. Turrentine, Gordon Thompson Jr, Leland C. Nielsen, William B. Enright, John S. Rhoades, Earl B. Gilliam; Clerk's Office, San Diego 92101.

**Colorado** — Richard P. Matsch, CJ; Zita L. Weinshienk, Lewis T. Babcock, Edward W. Nottingham, Daniel B. Sparr, Wiley Y. Daniel, Miller D. Walker; Clerk's Office, Denver 80294.

**Connecticut** — Peter C. Dorsey, CJ; Alan H. Nevas, Alfred V. Covello, Robert N. Chatigny, Dominic J. Squatrito, Alvin W. Thompson, Janet Bond Arterton; Clerk's Office, New Haven 06510.

**Delaware** — Joseph J. Farnan Jr, CJ; Joseph J. Longobardi, Sue L. Robinson, Roderick R. McKelvie; Clerk's Office, Wilmington 19801.

**District of Columbia** — John Garrett Penn, CJ; Charles R. Richey, Norma Holloway Johnson, Thomas P. Jackson, Thomas F. Hogan, Stanley Sporkin, Royce C. Lamberth, Gladys Kessler, Paul L. Friedman, Ricardo M. Urbina, Emmet G. Sullivan, James Robertson; Clerk's Office, Washington DC 20001.

**Florida** — **Northern:** Maurice M. Paul, CJ; C. Roger Vinson, Lacey A. Collier, William H. Stafford, Robert L. Hinkle; Clerk's Office, Tallahassee 32301. **Middle:** Elizabeth A. Kovachevich, CJ; Wm. Terrell Hodges, George Kendall Sharp, Patricia C. Fawsett, Harvey E. Schlesinger, Ralph W. Nimmons Jr, Anne C. Conway, Steven D. Merryday, Susan C. Bucklew, Henry L. Adams Jr; Clerk's Office, Jacksonville 32201. **Southern:** Norman C. Roettger, CJ; Jose A. Gonzalez Jr, Edward B. Davis, Lenore C. Nesbitt, Stanley Marcus, William J. Zloch, Kenneth L. Ryskamp, Federico A. Moreno, Shelby Highsmith, Donald L. Graham, K. Michael Moore, Ursula Ungaro-Benages, Wilkie D. Ferguson Jr, Daniel T. K. Hurley, Joan A. Lenard; Clerk's Office, Miami 33128.

**Georgia** — **Northern:** G. Ernest Tidwell, CJ; Robert L. Vining Jr, William C. O'Kelley, Harold L. Murphy, Orinda D. Evans, J. Owen Forrester, Jack T. Camp, Julie E. Carnes, Clarence Cooper, Frank M. Hull, Willis B. Hunt Jr; Clerk's Office, Atlanta 30303. **Middle:** Duross Fitzpatrick, CJ; Wilbur D. Owens Jr, J. Robert Elliott, W. Louis Sands, Hugh Lawson; Clerk's Office, Macon 31202. **Southern:** B. Avant Edenfield, CJ; Dudley H. Bowen Jr, William T. Moore Jr; Clerk's Office, Savannah 31412.

**Hawaii** — Alan B. Kay, CJ; David A. Ezra, Helen Gillmor; Clerk's Office, Honolulu 96850.

**Idaho** — Edward J. Lodge, CJ; B. Lynn Winmill; Clerk's Office, Boise 83724.

**Illinois** — **Northern:** Marvin E. Aspen, CJ; Charles P. Kocoras, William T. Hart, Paul E. Plunkett, Charles R. Norgle Sr, James F. Holderman, Ann C. Williams, Brian Barnett Duff, Harry D. Leinenweber, James B. Zagel, James H. Alesia, Suzanne B. Conlon, George M. Marovich, George W. Lindberg, Wayne R. Andersen, Philip G. Reinhard, Ruben Castillo, Blanche M. Manning, David H. Coar, Robert W. Gettleman, Elaine E. Bucklo, Joan B. Gottschall; Clerk's Office, Chicago 60604. **Central:** Michael M. Mihm, CJ; Richard Mills, Joe Billy McDade; Clerk's Office, Springfield 62701. **Southern:** J. Phil Gilbert, CJ; William D. Stiehl, Paul E. Riley, James L. Foreman, William L. Beatty; Clerk's Office, East St. Louis 62201.

**Indiana** — **Northern:** Allen Sharp, CJ; William C. Lee, James T. Moody, Robert L. Miller Jr, Rudy Lozano; Clerk's Office, South Bend 46601. **Southern:** Sarah E. Barker, CJ; Gene E. Brooks, S. Hugh Dillin, Larry J. McKinney, John Daniel Tinder, David F. Hamilton; Clerk's Office, Indianapolis 46204.

**Iowa** — **Northern:** Michael J. Melloy, CJ; Mark W. Bennett, Edward J McManus, Donald E. O'Brien; Clerk's Office, Cedar Rapids 52401. **Southern:** Charles R. Wolle, CJ; Harold D. Vietor, R. E. Longstaff; Clerk's Office, Des Moines 50309.

**Kansas** — G. Thomas Van Bebber, CJ; Sam A. Crow, John W. Lungstrum, Monti L. Belot, Kathryn H. Vratil, John T. Marten; Clerk's Office, Wichita 67202.

**Kentucky** — **Eastern:** William Bertelsman, CJ; Henry R. Wilhoit Jr, Karl S. Forester, Joseph M. Hood, Jennifer B. Coffman; Clerk's Office, Lexington 40596-3074. **Western:** Charles R. Simpson III, CJ; John G. Heyburn II, Jennifer B. Coffman, Thomas B. Russell, Joseph P. McKinley Jr; Clerk's Office, Louisville 40202.

**Louisiana** — **Eastern:** Morley L. Sear, CJ; A. J. McNamara, Martin L. C. Feldman, Marcel Livaudais Jr, Edith Brown Clement, Ginger Berrigan, Stanwood R. Duval Jr, Eldon E. Fallon, Sarah S. Vance, Mary Ann Viel Lemmo, G. Thomas Porteous Jr; Clerk's Office, New Orleans 70130. **Middle:** John V. Parker, CJ; Frank J. Polozola; Clerk's Office, Baton Rouge 70801. **Western:** John M. Shaw, CJ; Rebecca F. Doherty, Richard T. Haik Sr, F. A. Little Jr, James T. Trimble, Donald E. Walter, Tucker L. Melançon; Clerk's Office, Shreveport 71101.

**Maine** — D. Brock Hornby, CJ; Gene Carter, Morton A. Brody; Clerk's Office, Portland 04101.

**Maryland** — J. Frederick Motz, CJ; Frederic N. Smalkin, William M. Nickerson, Marvin J. Garbis, Benson Everett Legg, Catherine C. Blake, Andre M. Davis, Deborah K. Chasanow, Peter J. Messitte, Alexander Williams Jr; Clerk's Office, Baltimore 21201.

**Massachusetts** — Joseph L. Tauro, CJ; Robert E. Keeton, William G. Young, Mark L. Wolf, Douglas P. Woodlock, Edward F. Harrington, Nathaniel M. Gorton, Richard G. Stearns, Reginald C. Lindsay, Patti B. Saris, Nancy Gertner, George A. O'Toole, Nathaniel M. Gorton, Michael A. Ponsor; Clerk's Office, Boston 02109.

**Michigan** — **Eastern:** Julian A. Cook Jr, CJ; Avern Cohn, Anna Diggs Taylor, Barbara K. Hackett, Lawrence P. Zatkoff, Patrick J. Duggan, Bernard A. Friedman, Paul V. Gadola, Gerald E. Rosen, Robert H. Cleland, Nancy G. Edmunds, Denise Page-Hood, Paul D. Borman, John Corbett O'Meara; Clerk's Office, Detroit 48226. **Western:** Richard A. Enslen, CJ; Robert H. Bell, David W. McKeague, Gordon J. Quist; Clerk's Office, Grand Rapids 49503.

**Minnesota** — Paul A. Magnuson, CJ; James M. Rosenbaum, David S. Doty, Richard H. Kyle, Michael J. Davis, John R. Tunheim, Ann D. Montgomery; Clerk's Office, St. Paul 55101.

**Mississippi** — **Northern:** L. T. Senter Jr, CJ; Neal Biggers, Glen H. Davidson; Clerk's Office, Oxford 38655. **Southern:** Tom S. Lee, CJ; William H. Barbour Jr, Henry T. Wingate, Walter J. Gex III, Charles W. Pickering Sr, David Bramlette; Clerk's Office, Jackson 39201.

**Missouri** — **Eastern:** Jean Hamilton, CJ; George F. Gunn Jr, Donald J. Stohr, Carol E. Jackson, Charles A. Shaw, Catherine D. Perry, E. Richard Webber; Clerk's Office, St. Louis 63101. **Western:** D. Brook Bartlett, CJ; Dean Whipple, Fernando J. Gaitan Jr, Ortrie D. Smith, Gary A. Fenner, Nanette Laughery; Clerk's Office, Kansas City 64106.

**Montana** — Jack D. Shanstrom, CJ; Charles C. Lovell, Donald W. Molloy; Clerk's Office, Billings 59101.

**Nebraska** — William G. Cambridge, CJ; Richard G. Kopf, Thomas M. Shanahan; Clerk's Office, Omaha 68101.

**Nevada** — Lloyd D. George, CJ; Howard D. McKibben, Philip M. Pro, David W. Hagen; Clerk's Office, Las Vegas 89101, Reno 89509.

**New Hampshire** — Joseph A. DiClerico, CJ; Paul J. Barbadoro, Steven J. McAuliffe; Clerk's Office, Concord 03301.

**New Jersey** — Anne E. Thompson, CJ; John W. Bissell, Maryanne Trump Barry, Joseph H. Rodriguez, Garrett E. Brown Jr, A. J. Lechner Jr, Nicholas H. Politan, Alfred M. Wolin, John C. Lifland, William G. Bassler, Mary Little Parell, Joseph E. Irenas, Jerome E. Simandle, William H. Walls, Stephen M. Orlofsky, Joseph A. Greenaway; Clerk's Office, Newark 07101.

**New Mexico** — John E. Conway, CJ; James A. Parker, C. Leroy Hansen, Martha Vazquez, Bruce D. Black; Clerk's Office, Albuquerque 87103.

**New York** — **Northern:** Thomas J. McAvoy, CJ; Frederick J. Scullin Jr, Rosemary S. Pooler, Lawrence E. Kahn; Clerk's Office, Syracuse 13261-7367. **Eastern:** Charles P. Sifton, CJ; Thomas C. Platt Jr, Raymond J. Dearie, Edward R. Korman, Reena Raggi, Arthur D. Spatt, Carol Bagley Amon, Sterling Johnson Jr, Denis R. Hurley, David G. Trager, Joanna Seybert, Allyne Ross, John Gleeson, Fredric Block; Clerk's Office, Brooklyn 11201. **Southern:** Thomas P. Griesa, CJ; Charles L. Brieant, Kevin Thomas Duffy, John E. Sprizzo, John F. Keenan, Peter K. Leisure, Miriam G. Cedarbaum, Lewis A. Kaplan, Michael B. Mukasey, Kimba Wood, Robert P. Patterson Jr, Lawrence McKenna, John S. Martin Jr, Loretta A. Preska, Sonia Sotomayer, Harold Baer Jr, Deborah A. Batts, Denny Chin, Denise L. Cote, John Koeltl, Allen G. Schwartz, Barrington D. Parker Jr, Shira A. Scheindlin, Sidney H. Stein, Jed S. Rakoff; Clerk's Office New York City 10007. **Western:** David G. Larimer, CJ; Michael A. Telesca; Richard J. Arcara, William M. Skretny, John T. Curtin, John T. Elfvin; Clerk's Office, Buffalo 14202.

*(continued)*

**North Carolina — Eastern:** James C. Fox, CJ; W. Earl Britt, Terrence W. Boyle, Malcolm J. Howard; Clerk's Office, Raleigh 27611. **Middle:** Frank W. Bullock, CJ; N. Carlton Tilley Jr, William L. Osteen Sr, James A. Beaty Jr; Clerk's Office, Greensboro 27402. **Western:** Richard L. Voorhees, CJ; Graham C. Mullen, Lacy H. Thornburg; Clerk's Office, Asheville 28801.

**North Dakota** — Rodney S. Webb, CJ; Patrick A. Conmy; Judge; Clerk's Office, Bismarck 58502.

**Ohio — Northern:** George W. White, CJ; Sam H. Bell, Paul R. Matia, Lesley Brooks Wells, James G. Carr, Solomon Oliver Jr, David A. Katz, Kathleen McDonald O'Malley, Peter C. Economus, Donald C. Nugent, Patricia A. Gaughan; Clerk's Office, Cleveland 44114. **Southern:** Walter Herbert Rice, CJ; John D. Holschuh, Herman J. Weber, James L. Graham, George C. Smith, S. Arthur Spiegel, Sandra S. Beckwith, Edmund A. Sargus Jr, Susan J. Dlott, Joseph P. Kinneary; Clerk's Office, Columbus 43215.

**Oklahoma — Northern:** Terry C. Kern, CJ; Sven Erik Holmes, Michael Burrage; Clerk's Office, Tulsa 74103. **Eastern:** Michael Burrage CJ; Frank H. Seay; Clerk's Office, Muskogee 74401. **Western:** David L. Russell, CJ; Ralph G. Thompson, Wayne E. Alley, Robin J. Cauthron, Tim Leonard, Michael Burrage, Vicki Miles-LaGrange; Clerk's Office, Oklahoma City 73102.

**Oregon** — Michael R. Hogan, CJ; Malcolm F. Marsh, Robert E. Jones, Ancer L. Haggerty; Clerk's Office, Portland 97205.

**Pennsylvania — Eastern:** Edward N. Cahn, CJ; Norma L. Shapiro, James T. Giles, James McGirr Kelly, Thomas N. O'Neill Jr, Marvin Katz, Edmund V. Ludwig, Robert F. Kelly, Franklin S. Van Antwerpen, Robert S. Gawthrop III, Lowell A. Reed Jr, Jan E. Dubois, Herbert J. Hutton, Jay C. Waldman, Ronald L. Buckwalter, Stewart Dalzell, William H. Yohn Jr, Harvey Bartle III, John R. Padova, J. Curtis Joyner, Eduardo C. Robreno, Anita B. Brody, Marjorie O. Rendell; Clerk's Office, Philadelphia 19106. **Middle:** Sylvia H. Rambo, CJ; James F. McClure Jr, Thomas I. Vanaskie; Clerk's Office, Scranton 18501. **Western:** Donald E. Ziegler, CJ; Alan N. Bloch, William L. Standish, D. Brooks Smith, Donald J. Lee, Donetta W. Ambrose, Gary L. Lancaster, Robert J. Cindrich, Sean J. McLaughlin; Clerk's Office, Pittsburgh 15230.

**Rhode Island** — Ronald R. Lagueux, CJ; Ernest C. Torres, Mary M. Lisi; Clerk's Office, Providence 02903.

**South Carolina** — C. Weston Houck, CJ; G. Ross Anderson Jr, Joseph F. Anderson Jr, David C. Norton, Dennis W. Shedd, Henry M. Herlong Jr, William B. Traxler, Cameron M. Currie, Patrick Michael Duffy; Clerk's Office, Columbia 29201.

**South Dakota** — Richard H. Battey, CJ; Lawrence L. Piersol, Charles B. Kornmann; Clerk's Office, Sioux Falls 57102.

**Tennessee — Eastern:** James H. Jarvis, CJ; Thomas G. Hull, R. Allan Edgar, Leon Jordan, Curtis Collier; Clerk's Office, Knoxville 37901. **Middle:** John T. Nixon, CJ; Thomas A. Higgins, Robert L. Echols, Todd J. Campbell; Clerk's Office, Nashville 37203. **Western:** Julia S. Gibbons, CJ; James D. Todd, Jerome Turner, John Phipps McCalla, Bernice B. Donald; Clerk's Office, Memphis 38103.

**Texas — Northern:** Jerry Buchmeyer, CJ; Mary Lou Robinson, A. Joe Fish, Robert B. Maloney, Sidney A. Fitzwater, Samuel R. Cummings, John H. McBryde, Jorge A. Solis, Terry Means, Joe Kendall; Clerk's Office, Dallas 75242. **Southern:** Norman W. Black, CJ; George P. Kazen, Filemon B. Vela, Hayden W. Head Jr, Ricardo H. Hinojosa, Lynn N. Hughes, David Hittner, Kenneth M. Hoyt, Sim Lake, Melinda Harmon, John D. Rainey, Samuel B. Kent, Ewing Werlein Jr, Lee H. Rosenthal, Janis Graham Jack, Vanessa D. Gilmore, Nancy F. Atlas; Clerk's Office, Houston 77208. **Eastern:** Richard A. Schell, CJ; William Wayne Justice, Howell Cobb, Paul N. Brown, John Hannah Jr, David Folsom, Thad Heartfield; Clerk's Office, Tyler 75702. **Western:** Harry Lee Hudspeth, CJ; David Briones, Hipolito F. Garcia, Edward C. Prado, Fred Biery, Orlando L. Garcia, James R. Nowlin, Sam Sparks, Walter S. Smith Jr, W. Royal Furgeson; Clerk's Office, San Antonio 78206.

**Utah** — David K. Winder, CJ; J. Thomas Greene, David Sam, Dee Benson, Tena Campbell; Clerk's Office, Salt Lake City 84101.

**Vermont** — J. Garvan Murtha, CJ, William K. Sessions III; Clerk's Office, Burlington 05402.

**Virginia — Eastern:** James C. Cacheris, CJ; Claude M. Hilton, James R. Spencer, Thomas S. Ellis III, Rebecca Beach Smith, Henry Coke Morgan Jr, Robert E. Payne, Raymond A. Jackson, Leonie M. Brinkema; Clerk's Office, Alexandria 22314. **Western:** Jackson L. Kiser, CJ; James P. Jones, James C. Turk, Samuel G. Wilson; Clerk's Office, Roanoke 24006.

**Washington — Eastern:** William Fremming Nielsen, CJ; Alan A. McDonald, Fred Van Sickle, Robert H. Whaley; Clerk's Office, Spokane 99210. **Western:** Carolyn R. Dimmick, CJ; Barbara J. Rothstein, John C. Coughenour, Robert J. Bryan, William L. Dwyer, Thomas Zilly, Franklin D. Burgess; Clerk's Office, Seattle 98104.

**West Virginia — Northern:** Frederick P. Stamp Jr, CJ; Irene M. Keeley, W. Craig Broadwater; Clerk's Office, Wheeling 26003. **Southern:** Charles H. Haden II, CJ; John T. Copenhaver Jr, Elizabeth V. Hallanan, David A. Faber, Joseph R. Goodwin; Clerk's Office, Charleston 25329.

**Wisconsin — Eastern:** J. P. Stadtmueller, CJ; Thomas J. Curran, Rudolph T. Randa, Charles N. Clevert; Clerk's Office, Milwaukee 53202. **Western:** John C. Shabaz; CJ; Barbara B. Crabb, Clerk's Office, Madison 53701.

**Wyoming** — Alan B. Johnson, CJ; Clarence A. Brimmer, William F. Downes; Clerk's Office, Cheyenne 82001.

## U.S. Territorial District Courts

**Guam** — John S. Unpingco, CJ; Clerk's Office, Agana 96910.

**Northern Mariana Islands** — Alex R. Munson, CJ; Clerk's Office, Saipan MP 96950.

**Puerto Rico** — Carmen Consuelo Cerezo, CJ; Juan M. Perez-Gimenez, Hector M. Laffitte, Jose Antonio Fuste, Salvador Casellas, Daniel Dominguez; Clerk's Office, Hato Rex 00918.

**Virgin Islands** — Thomas K. Moore, CJ; Raymond L. Finch; Clerk's Office, St. Croix 00820.

## U.S. Court of International Trade

New York, NY 10278-0001 (Salaries, $133,600)

**Chief Judge** — Dominick L. DiCarlo.

**Judges** — Gregory W. Carman, Jane A. Restani, Thomas J. Aquilino Jr, Nicholas Tsoucalas, R. Kenton Musgrave, Richard W. Goldberg, Donald C. Pogue, Evan J. Wallach.

## U.S. Court of Federal Claims

Washington, DC 20005 (Salaries, $133,600)

**Chief Judge** — Loren A. Smith.

**Judges** — James F. Merow, John P. Wiese, Robert J. Yock, Lawrence S. Margolis, Christine Odell Cook Miller, Moody R. Tidwell 3d, Marian Blank Horn, Eric G. Bruggink, Bohdan A. Futey, Wilkes C. Robinson, Roger B. Andewelt, James T. Turner, Robert H. Hodges Jr, Diane Gilbert Weinstein.

## U.S. Tax Court

Washington, DC 20217 (Salaries, $133,600)

**Chief Judge** — Mary Ann Cohen

**Judges** — Renato Beghe, Herbert L. Chabot, John O. Colvin, Joel Gerber, Julien I. Jacobs, Carolyn Miller Parr, Robert P. Ruwe, James S. Halpern, Carolyn P. Chiechi, David Laro, Stephen Swift, Thomas Wells, Laurence J. Whalen, Lawrence A. Wright, Maurice B. Foley, Juan F. Vasquez, Joseph H. Gale.

## U.S. Court of Veterans Appeals

Washington, D.C. 20004 (Salaries, $133,600)

**Chief Judge** — Frank Q. Nebeker.

**Judges** — Kenneth B. Kramer, John J. Farley 3d, Ronald M. Holdaway, Donald L. Ivers, Jonathan R. Steinberg.

# 1996 IN PICTURES

L. DOWNING/SYGMA

PORTER GIFFORD/GAMMA LIAISON

Politics was big news in 1996, as Bill Clinton and Bob Dole, plus third-party candidate Ross Perot, campaigned to win the next four years in the White House.

# CAMPAIGN '96

© MARK PETERSON/SABA

Bob Dole (R, KS), with his wife and daughter, takes leave of the Senate; he resigned June 11 to concentrate on his presidential campaign, ending 35 years in Congress and 11 as his party's leader in the Senate.

At the Republican National Convention, Aug.12-15 in San Diego, CA, Elizabeth Dole turned her speech into a conversation with delegates on the floor; here she greets Kansan Tim Steininger, who inspired her husband to start a foundation to aid the disabled.

GERRY GROPP/SIPA PRESS

BROOKS KRAFT/SYGMA

Just before the convention, Dole went back to his hometown of Russell, KS, where he introduced his running mate, at left, former U.S. Rep. Jack Kemp (NY).

The Democratic National Convention, held Aug. 26-29 in Chicago, ended in a rain of confetti, as family, friends, and supporters thronged the podium. In front at left are Vice President Al Gore and his wife, Tipper; at right is Pres. Clinton, with First Lady Hillary Rodham Clinton and daughter Chelsea.

© JOE TRAVER/GAMMA LIAISON

Before appearing in Chicago to accept his party's nomination, Pres. Clinton took to the train for a four-day campaign trip, starting in Huntington, WV. Below, accompanied by his daughter, Chelsea, he makes a stop to preach the Democratic message.

MARGARET BAILEY/SIPA PRESS

ALLAN TANNENBAUM/SYGMA

Texas billionaire Ross Perot, the founder and presidential candidate of the Reform Party, gives his acceptance speech, Aug. 18, at the party convention in Valley Forge, PA.

# NATIONAL SCENE

Hillary Rodham Clinton arrives at court, Jan. 26, to testify before a grand jury investigating the Whitewater affair.

ERIK FREELAND/U.S. NEWS & WORLD REPORT

PORTER GIFFORD/GAMMA LIAISON

Eastern states were snowed in early in January by the "Blizzard of '96," during one of the nation's harshest winters. Above, cross-country skiers in New York City.

BRAD MARKEL/GAMMA LIAISON

A stalemate between Pres. Bill Clinton and the Republican-controlled Congress over the federal budget led to a record 21-day partial shutdown of the federal government, closing many offices and public buildings, including the Lincoln Memorial (right).

Commerce Secretary Ron Brown (center) at a power plant near the Bosnian city of Tuzla, during a tour to promote U.S. business investment. Later the same day, Apr. 3, he was killed, with 34 others, in a plane crash in Croatia.

VADIM GHIRDA/AP/WIDE WORLD PHOTOS

NEIL REDMOND/AP/WIDE WORLD PHOTOS

Arson investigators comb through charred remains of a sanctuary at the Matthews Murkland Presbyterian Church in Charlotte, NC, after a June 7 fire. During 1996 there was an upsurge in arson fires at Southern black churches.

BOTH PHOTOS, ELAINE THOMPSON/AP/WIDE WORLD PHOTOS

"Unabomber" suspect Theodore Kaczynski was arrested after a tip by his brother and a raid on his Montana cabin, above, allegedly linked him to a series of deadly bombings over two decades.

# AIR DISASTERS

CANDACE BARBOT/MIAMI HERALD/GAMMA LIAISON

On May 11, a ValuJet plane crashed in the Florida Everglades, killing all 110 people aboard (at left, a search through the crash site for clues); the airline was temporarily grounded for safety lapses. On July 17, TWA Flight 800, bound for Paris, crashed after takeoff from New York, killing 230. As wreckage (below) and bodies were slowly retrieved from the sea, relatives of the victims mourned.

BEBETO MATTHEWS/AP/WIDE WORLD PHOTOS

RICK MAIMAN/SYGMA

# SCIENCE AND TECHNOLOGY

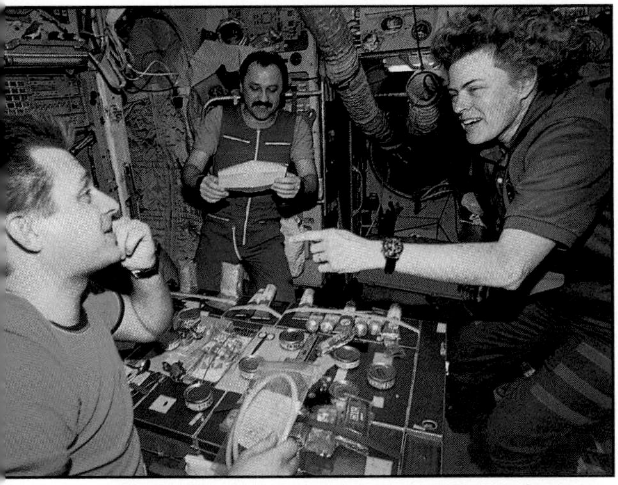

NASA

Shannon Lucid (above, right) became the first American woman to work aboard the Russian *Mir* space station; here, Lucid, who set an American record for longevity in space, joins two cosmonauts in checking food supplies.

The true king of carnivorous dinosaurs may be the newly discovered *Carcharodontosaurus saharicus.* Its skull is bigger than that of any T. Rex yet found—and much bigger than a human's.

HANS LARRSON, DAVID CHRISTOPHER, PAUL SERENO

NASA/GAMMA LIAISON

The showy Comet Hyakutake (above, left) was discovered by a Japanese astronomer in late January, less than 2 months before coming closer to Earth than any comet since 1983.

# PEOPLE

An auction of some 5,900 items owned by the late Jacqueline Kennedy Onassis—from costume jewelry like the pearls in the 1960s photo at left to antiques like the desk, below, at which Pres. Kennedy signed the nuclear test ban treaty—drew throngs of eager buyers in April.

© MARK PETERSON/SABA INSET: JOHN F. KENNEDY LIBRARY

DOUG DAVIES/ALL ACTION/RETNA LTD.

The divorce of Britain's Prince Charles and Diana, Princess of Wales (shown above, with Prince William and Prince Henry, in a 1995 photo), was finalized in the summer of 1996

*Photos continue on page 777*

# CABINETS OF THE U.S.

## Role of the Cabinet

The heads of major executive departments of government constitute the Cabinet. This institution, not provided for in the U.S. Constitution, developed as an advisory body out of the desire of presidents to consult on policy matters. Aside from its advisory role, the Cabinet as such has no function and wields no executive authority. The president may or may not consult it and is not bound by its advice. Most presidents also confer with numerous advisers outside the Cabinet. A group of regular informal advisers to the president has been known in American history as a "kitchen cabinet." The formal Cabinet (which may include other officials besides department heads, as designated by the president) meets at times set by the president. Members of Pres. Bill Clinton's Cabinet listed here are as of Oct. 15, 1996.

## Secretaries of State

The Department of Foreign Affairs was created by act of Congress on July 27, 1789, and the name changed to Department of State on Sept. 15.

| President | Secretary | Home | Apptd. |
|---|---|---|---|
| Washington | Thomas Jefferson | VA | 1789 |
| " | Edmund Randolph | VA | 1794 |
| " | Timothy Pickering | PA | 1795 |
| Adams, J. | Timothy Pickering | PA | 1797 |
| " | John Marshall | VA | 1800 |
| Jefferson | James Madison | VA | 1801 |
| Madison | Robert Smith | MD | 1809 |
| " | James Monroe | VA | 1811 |
| Monroe | John Quincy Adams | MA | 1817 |
| Adams, J.Q. | Henry Clay | KY | 1825 |
| Jackson | Martin Van Buren | NY | 1829 |
| " | Edward Livingston | LA | 1831 |
| " | Louis McLane | DE | 1833 |
| " | John Forsyth | GA | 1834 |
| Van Buren | John Forsyth | GA | 1837 |
| Harrison, W.H. | Daniel Webster | MA | 1841 |
| Tyler | Daniel Webster | MA | 1841 |
| " | Abel P. Upshur | VA | 1843 |
| " | John C. Calhoun | SC | 1844 |
| Polk | John C. Calhoun | SC | 1845 |
| " | James Buchanan | PA | 1845 |
| Taylor | James Buchanan | PA | 1849 |
| " | John M. Clayton | DE | 1849 |
| Fillmore | John M. Clayton | DE | 1850 |
| " | Daniel Webster | MA | 1850 |
| " | Edward Everett | MA | 1852 |
| Pierce | William L. Marcy | NY | 1853 |
| Buchanan | William L. Marcy | NY | 1857 |
| " | Lewis Cass | MI | 1857 |
| " | Jeremiah S. Black | PA | 1860 |
| Lincoln | Jeremiah S. Black | PA | 1861 |
| " | William H. Seward | NY | 1861 |
| Johnson, A. | William H. Seward | NY | 1865 |
| Grant | Elihu B. Washburne | IL | 1869 |
| " | Hamilton Fish | NY | 1869 |
| Hayes | Hamilton Fish | NY | 1877 |
| " | William M. Evarts | NY | 1877 |
| Garfield | William M. Evarts | NY | 1881 |
| " | James G. Blaine | ME | 1881 |
| Arthur | James G. Blaine | ME | 1881 |
| " | F.T. Frelinghuysen | NJ | 1881 |
| Cleveland | F.T. Frelinghuysen | NJ | 1885 |
| " | Thomas F. Bayard | DE | 1885 |
| Harrison, B. | Thomas F. Bayard | DE | 1889 |
| Harrison, B. | James G. Blaine | ME | 1889 |
| " | John W. Foster | IN | 1892 |
| Cleveland | Walter Q. Gresham | IN | 1893 |
| " | Richard Olney | MA | 1895 |
| McKinley | Richard Olney | MA | 1897 |
| " | John Sherman | OH | 1897 |
| " | William R. Day | OH | 1898 |
| " | John Hay | DC | 1898 |
| Roosevelt, T. | John Hay | DC | 1901 |
| " | Elihu Root | NY | 1905 |
| " | Robert Bacon | NY | 1909 |
| Taft | Robert Bacon | NY | 1909 |
| " | Philander C. Knox | PA | 1909 |
| Wilson | Philander C. Knox | PA | 1913 |
| " | William J. Bryan | NE | 1913 |
| " | Robert Lansing | NY | 1915 |
| " | Bainbridge Colby | NY | 1920 |
| Harding | Charles E. Hughes | NY | 1921 |
| Coolidge | Charles E. Hughes | NY | 1923 |
| " | Frank B. Kellogg | MN | 1925 |
| Hoover | Frank B. Kellogg | MN | 1929 |
| " | Henry L. Stimson | NY | 1929 |
| Roosevelt, F.D. | Cordell Hull | TN | 1933 |
| " | E.R. Stettinius Jr. | VA | 1944 |
| Truman | E.R. Stettinius Jr. | VA | 1945 |
| " | James F. Byrnes | SC | 1945 |
| " | George C. Marshall | PA | 1947 |
| " | Dean G. Acheson | CT | 1949 |
| Eisenhower | John Foster Dulles | NY | 1953 |
| " | Christian A. Herter | MA | 1959 |
| Kennedy | Dean Rusk | NY | 1961 |
| Johnson, L.B. | Dean Rusk | NY | 1963 |
| Nixon | William P. Rogers | NY | 1969 |
| " | Henry A. Kissinger | DC | 1973 |
| Ford | Henry A. Kissinger | DC | 1974 |
| Carter | Cyrus R. Vance | NY | 1977 |
| " | Edmund S. Muskie | ME | 1980 |
| Reagan | Alexander M. Haig Jr. | CT | 1981 |
| " | George P. Shultz | CA | 1982 |
| Bush | James A. Baker 3d | TX | 1989 |
| " | Lawrence S. Eagleburger | MI | 1992 |
| Clinton | Warren M. Christopher | CA | 1993 |

## Secretaries of the Treasury

The Treasury Department was organized by act of Congress on Sept. 2, 1789.

| President | Secretary | Home | Apptd. |
|---|---|---|---|
| Washington | Alexander Hamilton | NY | 1789 |
| " | Oliver Wolcott | CT | 1795 |
| Adams, J. | Oliver Wolcott | CT | 1797 |
| " | Samuel Dexter | MA | 1801 |
| Jefferson | Samuel Dexter | MA | 1801 |
| " | Albert Gallatin | PA | 1801 |
| Madison | Albert Gallatin | PA | 1809 |
| " | George W. Campbell | TN | 1814 |
| " | Alexander J. Dallas | PA | 1814 |
| " | William H. Crawford | GA | 1816 |
| Monroe | William H. Crawford | GA | 1817 |
| Adams, J.Q. | Richard Rush | PA | 1825 |
| Jackson | Samuel D. Ingham | PA | 1829 |
| " | Louis McLane | DE | 1831 |
| " | William J. Duane | PA | 1833 |
| " | Roger B. Taney | MD | 1833 |
| " | Levi Woodbury | NH | 1834 |
| Van Buren | Levi Woodbury | NH | 1837 |
| Harrison, W.H. | Thomas Ewing | OH | 1841 |
| Tyler | Thomas Ewing | OH | 1841 |
| " | Walter Forward | PA | 1841 |
| Tyler | John C. Spencer | NY | 1843 |
| " | George M. Bibb | KY | 1844 |
| Polk | Robert J. Walker | MS | 1845 |
| Taylor | William M. Meredith | PA | 1849 |
| Fillmore | Thomas Corwin | OH | 1850 |
| Pierce | James Guthrie | KY | 1853 |
| Buchanan | Howell Cobb | GA | 1857 |
| " | Phillip F. Thomas | MD | 1860 |
| " | John A. Dix | NY | 1861 |
| Lincoln | Salmon P. Chase | OH | 1861 |
| " | William P. Fessenden | ME | 1864 |
| " | Hugh McCulloch | IN | 1865 |
| Johnson, A. | Hugh McCulloch | IN | 1865 |
| Grant | George S. Boutwell | MA | 1869 |
| " | William A. Richardson | MA | 1873 |
| " | Benjamin H. Bristow | KY | 1874 |
| " | Lot M. Morrill | ME | 1876 |
| Hayes | John Sherman | OH | 1877 |
| Garfield | William Windom | MN | 1881 |
| Arthur | Charles J. Folger | NY | 1881 |

*(continued)*

## Secretaries of the Treasury (*continued*)

| President | Secretary | Home | Apptd. |
|---|---|---|---|
| Arthur | Walter Q. Gresham | IN | 1884 |
| " | Hugh McCulloch | IN | 1884 |
| Cleveland | Daniel Manning | NY | 1885 |
| " | Charles S. Fairchild | NY | 1887 |
| Harrison, B. | William Windom | MN | 1889 |
| " | Charles Foster | OH | 1891 |
| Cleveland | John G. Carlisle | KY | 1893 |
| McKinley | Lyman J. Gage | IL | 1897 |
| Roosevelt, T. | Lyman J. Gage | IL | 1901 |
| " | Leslie M. Shaw | IA | 1902 |
| " | George B. Cortelyou | NY | 1907 |
| Taft | Franklin MacVeagh | IL | 1909 |
| Wilson | William G. McAdoo | NY | 1913 |
| " | Carter Glass | VA | 1918 |
| " | David F. Houston | MO | 1920 |
| Harding | Andrew W. Mellon | PA | 1921 |
| Coolidge | Andrew W. Mellon | PA | 1923 |
| Hoover | Andrew W. Mellon | PA | 1929 |
| " | Ogden L. Mills | NY | 1932 |
| Roosevelt, F.D. | William H. Woodin | NY | 1933 |
| " | Henry Morgenthau, Jr. | NY | 1934 |
| Truman | Fred M. Vinson | KY | 1945 |
| " | John W. Snyder | MO | 1946 |
| Eisenhower | George M. Humphrey | OH | 1953 |
| " | Robert B. Anderson | CT | 1957 |
| Kennedy | C. Douglas Dillon | NJ | 1961 |
| Johnson, L.B. | C. Douglas Dillon | NJ | 1963 |
| " | Henry H. Fowler | VA | 1965 |
| " | Joseph W. Barr | IN | 1968 |
| Nixon | David M. Kennedy | IL | 1969 |
| " | John B. Connally | TX | 1971 |
| " | George P. Shultz | IL | 1972 |
| " | William E. Simon | NJ | 1974 |
| Ford | William E. Simon | NJ | 1974 |
| Carter | W. Michael Blumenthal | MI | 1977 |
| " | G. William Miller | RI | 1979 |
| Reagan | Donald T. Regan | NY | 1981 |
| " | James A. Baker 3d | TX | 1985 |
| " | Nicholas F. Brady | NJ | 1988 |
| Bush | Nicholas F. Brady | NJ | 1989 |
| Clinton | Lloyd Bentsen | TX | 1993 |
| " | Robert E. Rubin | NY | 1995 |

## Secretaries of Defense

The Department of Defense, originally designated the National Military Establishment, was created Sept. 18, 1947. It is headed by the secretary of defense, a member of the president's Cabinet. The departments of the army, of the navy, and of the air force function within the Defense Department, and since 1947 their secretaries have not been members of the president's cabinet.

| President | Secretary | Home | Apptd. |
|---|---|---|---|
| Truman | James V. Forrestal | NY | 1947 |
| " | Louis A. Johnson | WV | 1949 |
| " | George C. Marshall | PA | 1950 |
| " | Robert A. Lovett | NY | 1951 |
| Eisenhower | Charles E. Wilson | MI | 1953 |
| " | Neil H. McElroy | OH | 1957 |
| " | Thomas S. Gates Jr. | PA | 1959 |
| Kennedy | Robert S. McNamara | MI | 1961 |
| Johnson, L.B. | Robert S. McNamara | MI | 1963 |
| " | Clark M. Clifford | MD | 1968 |
| Nixon | Melvin R. Laird | WI | 1969 |
| " | Elliot L. Richardson | MA | 1973 |
| " | James R. Schlesinger | VA | 1973 |
| Ford | James R. Schlesinger | VA | 1974 |
| " | Donald H. Rumsfeld | IL | 1975 |
| Carter | Harold Brown | CA | 1977 |
| Reagan | Caspar W. Weinberger | CA | 1981 |
| " | Frank C. Carlucci | PA | 1987 |
| Bush | Richard B. Cheney | WY | 1989 |
| Clinton | Les Aspin | WI | 1993 |
| " | William J. Perry | CA | 1994 |

## Secretaries of War

The War Department (which included jurisdiction over the navy until 1798) was created by act of Congress on Aug. 7, 1789, and Gen. Henry Knox was commissioned secretary of war under that act on Sept. 12, 1789.

| President | Secretary | Home | Apptd. |
|---|---|---|---|
| Washington | Henry Knox | MA | 1789 |
| " | Timothy Pickering | PA | 1795 |
| " | James McHenry | MD | 1796 |
| Adams, J. | James McHenry | MD | 1797 |
| " | Samuel Dexter | MA | 1800 |
| Jefferson | Henry Dearborn | MA | 1801 |
| Madison | William Eustis | MA | 1809 |
| " | John Armstrong | NY | 1813 |
| " | James Monroe | VA | 1814 |
| " | William H. Crawford | GA | 1815 |
| Monroe | John C. Calhoun | SC | 1817 |
| Adams, J.Q. | James Barbour | VA | 1825 |
| " | Peter B. Porter | NY | 1828 |
| Jackson | John H. Eaton | TN | 1829 |
| " | Lewis Cass | MI | 1831 |
| " | Benjamin F. Butler | NY | 1837 |
| Van Buren | Joel R. Poinsett | SC | 1837 |
| Harrison, W.H. | John Bell | TN | 1841 |
| Tyler | John Bell | TN | 1841 |
| " | John C. Spencer | NY | 1841 |
| " | James M. Porter | PA | 1843 |
| " | William Wilkins | PA | 1844 |
| Polk | William L. Marcy | NY | 1845 |
| Taylor | George W. Crawford | GA | 1849 |
| Fillmore | Charles M. Conrad | LA | 1850 |
| Pierce | Jefferson Davis | MS | 1853 |
| Buchanan | John B. Floyd | VA | 1857 |
| " | Joseph Holt | KY | 1861 |
| Lincoln | Simon Cameron | PA | 1861 |
| " | Edwin M. Stanton | PA | 1862 |
| Johnson, A. | Edwin M. Stanton | PA | 1865 |
| " | John M. Schofield | IL | 1868 |
| Grant | John A. Rawlins | IL | 1869 |
| " | William T. Sherman | OH | 1869 |
| " | William W. Belknap | IA | 1869 |
| " | Alphonso Taft | OH | 1876 |
| " | James D. Cameron | PA | 1876 |
| Hayes | George W. McCrary | IA | 1877 |
| " | Alexander Ramsey | MN | 1879 |
| Garfield | Robert T. Lincoln | IL | 1881 |
| Arthur | Robert T. Lincoln | IL | 1881 |
| Cleveland | William C. Endicott | MA | 1885 |
| Harrison, B. | Redfield Proctor | VT | 1889 |
| " | Stephen B. Elkins | WV | 1891 |
| Cleveland | Daniel S. Lamont | NY | 1893 |
| McKinley | Russel A. Alger | MI | 1897 |
| " | Elihu Root | NY | 1899 |
| Roosevelt, T. | Elihu Root | NY | 1901 |
| " | William H. Taft | OH | 1904 |
| " | Luke E. Wright | TN | 1908 |
| Taft | Jacob M. Dickinson | TN | 1909 |
| " | Henry L. Stimson | NY | 1911 |
| Wilson | Lindley M. Garrison | NJ | 1913 |
| " | Newton D. Baker | OH | 1916 |
| Harding | John W. Weeks | MA | 1921 |
| Coolidge | John W. Weeks | MA | 1923 |
| " | Dwight F. Davis | MO | 1925 |
| Hoover | James W. Good | IL | 1929 |
| " | Patrick J. Hurley | OK | 1929 |
| Roosevelt, F.D. | George H. Dern | UT | 1933 |
| " | Harry H. Woodring | KS | 1937 |
| " | Henry L. Stimson | NY | 1940 |
| Truman | Robert P. Patterson | NY | 1945 |
| " | *Kenneth C. Royall | NC | 1947 |

* Last member of the Cabinet with this title. The War Department became the Department of the Army and became a branch of the Department of Defense in 1947.

## Secretaries of the Navy

The Navy Department was created by act of Congress on Apr. 30, 1798.

| President | Secretary | Home | Apptd. |
|---|---|---|---|
| Adams, J. | Benjamin Stoddert | MD | 1798 |
| Jefferson | Benjamin Stoddert | MD | 1801 |
| Jefferson | Robert Smith | MD | 1801 |
| Madison | Paul Hamilton | SC | 1809 |

| President | Secretary | Home | Apptd. |
|---|---|---|---|
| Madison | William Jones | PA | 1813 |
| " | Benjamin W. Crowninshield | MA | 1814 |
| Monroe | Benjamin W. Crowninshield | MA | 1817 |
| " | Smith Thompson | NY | 1818 |
| " | Samuel L. Southard | NJ | 1823 |
| Adams, J.Q. | Samuel L. Southard | NJ | 1825 |
| Jackson | John Branch | NC | 1829 |
| " | Levi Woodbury | NH | 1831 |
| " | Mahlon Dickerson | NJ | 1834 |
| Van Buren | Mahlon Dickerson | NJ | 1837 |
| " | James K. Paulding | NY | 1838 |
| Harrison, W.H. | George E. Badger | NC | 1841 |
| Tyler | George E. Badger | NC | 1841 |
| " | Abel P. Upshur | VA | 1841 |
| " | David Henshaw | MA | 1843 |
| " | Thomas W. Gilmer | VA | 1844 |
| " | John Y. Mason | VA | 1844 |
| Polk | George Bancroft | MA | 1845 |
| " | John Y. Mason | VA | 1846 |
| Taylor | William B. Preston | VA | 1849 |
| Fillmore | William A. Graham | NC | 1850 |
| " | John P. Kennedy | MD | 1852 |
| Pierce | James C. Dobbin | NC | 1853 |
| Buchanan | Isaac Toucey | CT | 1857 |
| Lincoln | Gideon Welles | CT | 1861 |
| Johnson, A. | Gideon Welles | CT | 1865 |
| Grant | Adolph E. Borie | PA | 1869 |
| Grant | George M. Robeson | NJ | 1869 |
| Hayes | Richard W. Thompson | IN | 1877 |
| " | Nathan Goff Jr. | WV | 1881 |
| Garfield | William H. Hunt | LA | 1881 |
| Arthur | William E. Chandler | NH | 1882 |
| Cleveland | William C. Whitney | NY | 1885 |
| Harrison, B. | Benjamin F. Tracy | NY | 1889 |
| Cleveland | Hilary A. Herbert | AL | 1893 |
| McKinley | John D. Long | MA | 1897 |
| Roosevelt, T. | John D. Long | MA | 1901 |
| " | William H. Moody | MA | 1902 |
| " | Paul Morton | IL | 1904 |
| " | Charles J. Bonaparte | MD | 1905 |
| " | Victor H. Metcalf | CA | 1906 |
| " | Truman H. Newberry | MI | 1908 |
| Taft | George von L. Meyer | MA | 1909 |
| Wilson | Josephus Daniels | NC | 1913 |
| Harding | Edwin Denby | MI | 1921 |
| Coolidge | Edwin Denby | MI | 1923 |
| " | Curtis D. Wilbur | CA | 1924 |
| Hoover | Charles Francis Adams | MA | 1929 |
| Roosevelt, F.D. | Claude A. Swanson | VA | 1933 |
| " | Charles Edison | NJ | 1940 |
| " | Frank Knox | IL | 1940 |
| " | James V. Forrestal | NY | 1944 |
| Truman | *James V. Forrestal | NY | 1945 |

* Last member of Cabinet with this title. The Navy Department became a branch of the Department of Defense when the latter was created on Sept. 18, 1947.

## Attorneys General

The office of attorney general was established by act of Congress on Sept. 24, 1789. It officially reached Cabinet rank in Mar. 1792, when the first attorney general, Edmund Randolph, attended his initial Cabinet meeting. The Department of Justice, headed by the attorney general, was created June 22, 1870.

| President | Attorney General | Home | Apptd. |
|---|---|---|---|
| Washington | Edmund Randolph | VA | 1789 |
| " | William Bradford | PA | 1794 |
| " | Charles Lee | VA | 1795 |
| Adams, J. | Charles Lee | VA | 1797 |
| Jefferson | Levi Lincoln | MA | 1801 |
| " | John Breckenridge | KY | 1805 |
| " | Caesar A. Rodney | DE | 1807 |
| Madison | Caesar A. Rodney | DE | 1807 |
| " | William Pinkney | MD | 1811 |
| " | Richard Rush | PA | 1814 |
| Monroe | Richard Rush | PA | 1817 |
| " | William Wirt | VA | 1817 |
| Adams, J.Q. | William Wirt | VA | 1825 |
| Jackson | John M. Berrien | GA | 1829 |
| " | Roger B. Taney | MD | 1831 |
| " | Benjamin F. Butler | NY | 1833 |
| Van Buren | Benjamin F. Butler | NY | 1837 |
| " | Felix Grundy | TN | 1838 |
| " | Henry D. Gilpin | PA | 1840 |
| Harrison, W.H. | John J. Crittenden | KY | 1841 |
| Tyler | John J. Crittenden | KY | 1841 |
| " | Hugh S. Legare | SC | 1841 |
| " | John Nelson | MD | 1843 |
| Polk | John Y. Mason | VA | 1845 |
| " | Nathan Clifford | ME | 1846 |
| " | Isaac Toucey | CT | 1848 |
| Taylor | Reverdy Johnson | MD | 1849 |
| Fillmore | John J. Crittenden | KY | 1850 |
| Pierce | Caleb Cushing | MA | 1853 |
| Buchanan | Jeremiah S. Black | PA | 1857 |
| " | Edwin M. Stanton | PA | 1860 |
| Lincoln | Edward Bates | MO | 1861 |
| " | James Speed | KY | 1864 |
| Johnson, A. | James Speed | KY | 1865 |
| " | Henry Stanbery | OH | 1866 |
| " | William M. Evarts | NY | 1868 |
| Grant | Ebenezer R. Hoar | MA | 1869 |
| " | Amos T. Akerman | GA | 1870 |
| " | George H. Williams | OR | 1871 |
| " | Edwards Pierrepont | NY | 1875 |
| " | Alphonso Taft | OH | 1876 |
| Hayes | Charles Devens | MA | 1877 |
| Garfield | Wayne MacVeagh | PA | 1881 |
| Arthur | Benjamin H. Brewster | PA | 1882 |
| Cleveland | Augustus Garland | AR | 1885 |
| Harrison, B. | William H. H. Miller | IN | 1889 |
| Cleveland | Richard Olney | MA | 1893 |
| " | Judson Harmon | OH | 1895 |
| McKinley | Joseph McKenna | CA | 1897 |
| " | John W. Griggs | NJ | 1898 |
| " | Philander C. Knox | PA | 1901 |
| Roosevelt, T. | Philander C. Knox | PA | 1901 |
| " | William H. Moody | MA | 1904 |
| " | Charles J. Bonaparte | MD | 1906 |
| Taft | George W. Wickersham | NY | 1909 |
| Wilson | J.C. McReynolds | TN | 1913 |
| " | Thomas W. Gregory | TX | 1914 |
| " | A. Mitchell Palmer | PA | 1919 |
| Harding | Harry M. Daugherty | OH | 1921 |
| Coolidge | Harry M. Daugherty | OH | 1923 |
| " | Harlan F. Stone | NY | 1924 |
| " | John G. Sargent | VT | 1925 |
| Hoover | William D. Mitchell | MN | 1929 |
| Roosevelt, F.D. | Homer S. Cummings | CT | 1933 |
| " | Frank Murphy | MI | 1939 |
| " | Robert H. Jackson | NY | 1940 |
| " | Francis Biddle | PA | 1941 |
| Truman | Thomas C. Clark | TX | 1945 |
| " | J. Howard McGrath | RI | 1949 |
| " | J.P. McGranery | PA | 1952 |
| Eisenhower | Herbert Brownell Jr. | NY | 1953 |
| " | William P. Rogers | MD | 1957 |
| Kennedy | Robert F. Kennedy | MA | 1961 |
| Johnson, L.B. | Robert F. Kennedy | MA | 1963 |
| " | N. de B. Katzenbach | IL | 1964 |
| " | Ramsey Clark | TX | 1967 |
| Nixon | John N. Mitchell | NY | 1969 |
| " | Richard G. Kleindienst | AZ | 1972 |
| " | Elliot L. Richardson | MA | 1973 |
| " | William B. Saxbe | OH | 1974 |
| Ford | William B. Saxbe | OH | 1974 |
| " | Edward H. Levi | IL | 1975 |
| Carter | Griffin B. Bell | GA | 1977 |
| " | Benjamin R. Civiletti | MD | 1979 |
| Reagan | William French Smith | CA | 1981 |
| " | Edwin Meese 3d. | CA | 1985 |
| " | Richard Thornburgh | PA | 1988 |
| Bush | Richard Thornburgh | PA | 1989 |
| " | William P. Barr | NY | 1991 |
| Clinton | Janet Reno | FL | 1993 |

## Secretaries of the Interior

The Department of the Interior was created by act of Congress on Mar. 3, 1849.

| President | Secretary | Home | Apptd. |
|---|---|---|---|
| Taylor | Thomas Ewing | OH | 1849 |
| Fillmore | Thomas M. T. McKennan | PA | 1850 |
| " | Alex H. H. Stuart | VA | 1850 |
| Pierce | Robert McClelland | MI | 1853 |
| Buchanan | Jacob Thompson | MS | 1857 |
| Lincoln | Caleb B. Smith | IN | 1861 |
| " | John P. Usher | IN | 1863 |
| Johnson, A. | John P. Usher | IN | 1865 |
| " | James Harlan | IA | 1865 |
| " | Orville H. Browning | IL | 1866 |
| Grant | Jacob D. Cox | OH | 1869 |
| " | Columbus Delano | OH | 1870 |
| " | Zachariah Chandler | MI | 1875 |
| Hayes | Carl Schurz | MO | 1877 |
| Garfield | Samuel J. Kirkwood | IA | 1881 |
| Arthur | Henry M. Teller | CO | 1882 |
| Cleveland | Lucius Q.C. Lamar | MS | 1885 |
| " | William F. Vilas | WI | 1888 |
| Harrison, B. | John W. Noble | MO | 1889 |
| Cleveland | Hoke Smith | GA | 1893 |
| " | David R. Francis | MO | 1896 |
| McKinley | Cornelius N. Bliss | NY | 1897 |
| " | Ethan A. Hitchcock | MO | 1898 |
| Roosevelt, T. | Ethan A. Hitchcock | MO | 1901 |
| " | James R. Garfield | OH | 1907 |
| Taft | Richard A. Ballinger | WA | 1909 |
| Taft | Walter L. Fisher | IL | 1911 |
| Wilson | Franklin K. Lane | CA | 1913 |
| " | John B. Payne | IL | 1920 |
| Harding | Albert B. Fall | NM | 1921 |
| " | Hubert Work | CO | 1923 |
| Coolidge | Hubert Work | CO | 1923 |
| " | Roy O. West | IL | 1929 |
| Hoover | Ray Lyman Wilbur | CA | 1929 |
| Roosevelt, F.D. | Harold L. Ickes | IL | 1933 |
| Truman | Harold L. Ickes | IL | 1945 |
| " | Julius A. Krug | WI | 1946 |
| " | Oscar L. Chapman | CO | 1949 |
| Eisenhower | Douglas McKay | OR | 1953 |
| " | Fred A Seaton | NE | 1956 |
| Kennedy | Stewart L. Udall | AZ | 1961 |
| Johnson, L.B. | Stewart L. Udall | AZ | 1963 |
| Nixon | Walter J. Hickel | AK | 1969 |
| " | Rogers C.B. Morton | MD | 1971 |
| Ford | Rogers C.B. Morton | MD | 1971 |
| " | Stanley K. Hathaway | WY | 1975 |
| " | Thomas S. Kleppe | ND | 1975 |
| Carter | Cecil D. Andrus | ID | 1977 |
| Reagan | James G. Watt | CO | 1981 |
| " | William P. Clark | CA | 1983 |
| " | Donald P. Hodel | OR | 1985 |
| Bush | Manuel Lujan | NM | 1989 |
| Clinton | Bruce Babbitt | AZ | 1993 |

## Secretaries of Agriculture

The Department of Agriculture was created by act of Congress on May 15, 1862. On Feb. 8, 1889, its commissioner was renamed secretary of agriculture and became a member of the Cabinet.

| President | Secretary | Home | Apptd. |
|---|---|---|---|
| Cleveland | Norman J. Colman | MO | 1889 |
| Harrison, B. | Jeremiah M. Rusk | WI | 1889 |
| Cleveland | J. Sterling Morton | NE | 1893 |
| McKinley | James Wilson | IA | 1897 |
| Roosevelt, T. | James Wilson | IA | 1901 |
| Taft | James Wilson | IA | 1909 |
| Wilson | David F. Houston | MO | 1913 |
| " | Edwin T. Meredith | IA | 1920 |
| Harding | Henry C. Wallace | IA | 1921 |
| Coolidge | Henry C. Wallace | IA | 1923 |
| " | Howard M. Gore | WV | 1924 |
| " | William M. Jardine | KS | 1925 |
| Hoover | Arthur M. Hyde | MO | 1929 |
| Roosevelt, F.D. | Henry A. Wallace | IA | 1933 |
| " | Claude R. Wickard | IN | 1940 |
| Truman | Clinton P. Anderson | NM | 1945 |
| Truman | Charles F. Brannan | CO | 1948 |
| Eisenhower | Ezra Taft Benson | UT | 1953 |
| Kennedy | Orville L. Freeman | MN | 1961 |
| Johnson, L.B. | Orville L. Freeman | MN | 1963 |
| Nixon | Clifford M. Hardin | IN | 1969 |
| " | Earl L. Butz | IN | 1971 |
| Ford | Earl L. Butz | IN | 1974 |
| " | John A. Knebel | VA | 1976 |
| Carter | Bob Bergland | MN | 1977 |
| Reagan | John R. Block | IL | 1981 |
| " | Richard E. Lyng | CA | 1986 |
| Bush | Clayton K. Yeutter | NE | 1989 |
| " | Edward Madigan | IL | 1991 |
| Clinton | Mike Espy | MS | 1993 |
| " | Dan Glickman | KS | 1995 |

## Secretaries of Commerce and Labor

The Department of Commerce and Labor, created by Congress on Feb. 14, 1903, was divided by Congress Mar. 4, 1913, into separate departments of Commerce and Labor. The secretary of each was made a Cabinet member.

### Secretaries of Commerce and Labor

| President | Secretary | Home | Apptd. |
|---|---|---|---|
| Roosevelt, T. | George B. Cortelyou | NY | 1903 |
| " | Victor H. Metcalf | CA | 1904 |
| " | Oscar S. Straus | NY | 1906 |
| Taft | Charles Nagel | MO | 1909 |

### Secretaries of Labor

| President | Secretary | Home | Apptd. |
|---|---|---|---|
| Wilson | William B. Wilson | PA | 1913 |
| Harding | James J. Davis | PA | 1921 |
| Coolidge | James J. Davis | PA | 1923 |
| Hoover | James J. Davis | PA | 1929 |
| " | William N. Doak | VA | 1930 |
| Roosevelt, F.D. | Frances Perkins | NY | 1933 |
| Truman | L.B. Schwellenbach | WA | 1945 |
| " | Maurice J. Tobin | MA | 1949 |
| Eisenhower | Martin P. Durkin | IL | 1953 |
| " | James P. Mitchell | NJ | 1953 |
| Kennedy | Arthur J. Goldberg | IL | 1961 |
| " | W. Willard Wirtz | IL | 1962 |
| Johnson, L.B. | W. Willard Wirtz | IL | 1963 |
| Nixon | George P. Shultz | IL | 1969 |
| " | James D. Hodgson | CA | 1970 |
| " | Peter J. Brennan | NY | 1973 |
| Ford | Peter J. Brennan | NY | 1974 |
| " | John T. Dunlop | CA | 1975 |
| " | W.J. Usery Jr. | GA | 1976 |
| Carter | F. Ray Marshall | TX | 1977 |
| Reagan | Raymond J. Donovan | NJ | 1981 |
| " | William E. Brock | TN | 1985 |
| " | Ann D. McLaughlin | DC | 1987 |
| Bush | Elizabeth Hanford Dole | NC | 1989 |
| " | Lynn Martin | IL | 1991 |
| Clinton | Robert B. Reich | MA | 1993 |

### Secretaries of Commerce

| President | Secretary | Home | Apptd. |
|---|---|---|---|
| Wilson | William C. Redfield | NY | 1913 |
| " | Joshua W. Alexander | MO | 1919 |
| Harding | Herbert C. Hoover | CA | 1921 |
| Coolidge | Herbert C. Hoover | CA | 1923 |
| " | William F. Whiting | MA | 1928 |
| Hoover | Robert P. Lamont | IL | 1929 |
| " | Roy D. Chapin | MI | 1932 |

| President | Secretary | Home | Apptd. |
|---|---|---|---|
| Roosevelt, F.D. | Daniel C. Roper . . . | SC . . . . . | 1933 |
| " | Harry L. Hopkins . . | NY . . . . . | 1939 |
| " | Jesse Jones. . . . . . | TX . . . . . | 1940 |
| " | Henry A. Wallace . . | IA. . . . . . | 1945 |
| Truman. . . . . | Henry A. Wallace . . | IA. . . . . . | 1945 |
| " | W. Averell Harriman | NY . . . . . | 1947 |
| " | Charles Sawyer . . . | OH . . . . . | 1948 |
| Eisenhower. . | Sinclair Weeks . . . . | MA . . . . . | 1953 |
| " | Lewis L. Strauss. . . | NY . . . . . | 1958 |
| " | Frederick H. Mueller | MI. . . . . . | 1959 |
| Kennedy. . . . | Luther H. Hodges . . | NC . . . . . | 1961 |
| Johnson, L.B. | Luther H. Hodges . . | NC . . . . . | 1963 |
| " | John T. Connor . . . | NJ . . . . . | 1965 |
| " | Alex B. Trowbridge . | NJ . . . . . | 1967 |
| " | Cyrus R. Smith. . . . | NY . . . . . | 1968 |
| Nixon. . . . . . . | Maurice H. Stans. . . | MN . . . . . | 1969 |
| " | Peter G. Peterson . . | IL. . . . . . . | 1972 |
| " | Frederick B. Dent . . | SC. . . . . . | 1973 |
| Ford . . . . . . . | Frederick B. Dent . . | SC. . . . . . | 1974 |
| " | Rogers C.B. Morton. | MD . . . . . | 1975 |
| " | Elliot L. Richardson . | MA . . . . . | 1975 |
| Carter . . . . . . | Juanita M. Kreps . . . | NC. . . . . . | 1977 |
| " | Philip M. Klutznick . . | IL. . . . . . . | 1979 |
| Reagan . . . . . | Malcolm Baldrige. . . | CT. . . . . . | 1981 |
| " | C. William Verity Jr. . | OH . . . . . | 1987 |
| Bush . . . . . . . | Robert A. Mosbacher | TX. . . . . . | 1989 |
| " | Barbara H. Franklin . | PA. . . . . . | 1992 |
| Clinton. . . . . . | Ronald H. Brown . . . | DC. . . . . . | 1993 |
| " | Mickey Kantor . . . . . | CA. . . . . . | 1996 |

## Secretaries of Housing and Urban Development

The Department of Housing and Urban Development was created by act of Congress on Sept. 9, 1965.

| President | Secretary | Home | Apptd. |
|---|---|---|---|
| Johnson, L.B. | Robert C. Weaver . | WA . . . | 1966 |
| " | Robert C. Wood . . . | MA . . . . | 1969 |
| Nixon . . . . . . | George W. Romney | MI. . . . . | 1969 |
| " | James T. Lynn . . . . | OH . . . . | 1973 |
| Ford . . . . . . . | James T. Lynn . . . . | OH . . . . | 1974 |
| " | Carla Anderson Hills | CA . . . . | 1975 |
| Carter . . . . . . | Patricia Roberts Harris | DC. . . . . | 1977 |
| " | Moon Landrieu . . . . | LA . . . . . | 1979 |
| Reagan . . . . . | Samuel R. Pierce Jr. | NY. . . . . | 1981 |
| Bush . . . . . . . | Jack F. Kemp . . . . . | NY. . . . . | 1989 |
| Clinton. . . . . . | Henry G. Cisneros . | TX. . . . . | 1993 |

## Secretaries of Transportation

The Department of Transportation was created by act of Congress on Oct. 15, 1966.

| President | Secretary | Home | Apptd. |
|---|---|---|---|
| Johnson, L.B. | Alan S. Boyd . . . . . . | FL. . . . . | 1966 |
| Nixon . . . . . . | John A. Volpe . . . . . | MA . . . . | 1969 |
| " | Claude S. Brinegar. . | CA . . . . | 1973 |
| Ford . . . . . . . | Claude S. Brinegar. . | CA . . . . | 1974 |
| " | William T. Coleman Jr. | PA . . . . | 1975 |
| Carter. . . . . . | Brock Adams. . . . . . | WA. . . . | 1977 |
| " | Neil E. Goldschmidt . | OR . . . . | 1979 |
| Reagan . . . . . | Andrew L. Lewis Jr.. | PA. . . . . | 1981 |
| " | Elizabeth Hanford Dole | NC. . . . . | 1983 |
| " | James H. Burnley . . | NC. . . . . | 1987 |
| Bush . . . . . . . | Samuel K. Skinner . | IL. . . . . . | 1989 |
| " | Andrew H. Card Jr. . | MA . . . . | 1992 |
| Clinton . . . . . | Federico F. Peña . . | CO. . . . . | 1993 |

## Secretaries of Energy

The Department of Energy was created by federal law on Aug. 4, 1977.

| President | Secretary | Home | Apptd. |
|---|---|---|---|
| Carter. . . . . . | James R. Schlesinger | VA . . . . . | 1977 |
| " | Charles Duncan Jr. . | WY. . . . . | 1979 |
| Reagan. . . . . | James B. Edwards. . | SC . . . . . | 1981 |
| " | Donald P. Hodel . . . | OR . . . . . | 1982 |
| Reagan . . . . . | John S. Herrington . | CA. . . . . | 1985 |
| Bush . . . . . . . | James D. Watkins. . | CA. . . . . | 1989 |
| Clinton. . . . . . | Hazel R. O'Leary . . | MN . . . . | 1993 |

## Secretaries of Health, Education, and Welfare

The Department of Health, Education, and Welfare was created by Congress on Apr. 11, 1953. On Sept. 27, 1979, it was divided by Congress into separate departments of Education and of Health and Human Services, with the secretary of each being a Cabinet member.

| President | Secretary | Home | Apptd. |
|---|---|---|---|
| Eisenhower. . | Oveta Culp Hobby . . | TX . . . . | 1953 |
| " | Marion B. Folsom. . . | NY . . . . | 1955 |
| " | Arthur S. Flemming . | OH . . . . | 1958 |
| Kennedy. . . . | Abraham A. Ribicoff . | CT . . . . | 1961 |
| " | Anthony J. Celebrezze | OH . . . . | 1962 |
| Johnson, L.B. | Anthony J. Celebrezze | OH . . . . | 1963 |
| " | John W. Gardner . . . | NY . . . . | 1965 |
| " | Wilbur J. Cohen. . . . | MI. . . . . | 1968 |
| Nixon. . . . . . . | Robert H. Finch . . . | CA. . . . . | 1969 |
| " | Elliot L. Richardson. | MA. . . . . | 1970 |
| " | Caspar W. Weinberger | CA. . . . . | 1973 |
| Ford . . . . . . . | Caspar W. Weinberger | CA. . . . . | 1974 |
| " | Forrest D. Mathews. | AL . . . . . | 1975 |
| Carter . . . . . . | Joseph A. Califano Jr. | DC. . . . . | 1977 |
| " | Patricia Roberts Harris | DC. . . . . | 1979 |

## Secretaries of Health and Human Services

| President | Secretary | Home | Apptd. |
|---|---|---|---|
| Carter. . . . . . | Patricia Roberts Harris | DC . . . . | 1979 |
| Reagan. . . . . | Richard S. Schweiker | PA . . . . | 1981 |
| " | Margaret M. Heckler. | MA . . . . | 1983 |
| Reagan . . . . . | Otis R. Bowen . . . . | IN . . . . . | 1985 |
| Bush . . . . . . . | Louis W. Sullivan . . | GA. . . . . | 1989 |
| Clinton. . . . . . | Donna E. Shalala . . | WI . . . . . | 1993 |

## Secretaries of Education

| President | Secretary | Home | Apptd. |
|---|---|---|---|
| Carter. . . . . . | Shirley Hufstedler . . | CA . . . . . | 1979 |
| Reagan. . . . . | Terrel Bell . . . . . . . . | UT . . . . . | 1981 |
| " | William J. Bennett . . | NY . . . . . | 1985 |
| " | Lauro F. Cavazos . . | TX . . . . . | 1988 |
| Bush . . . . . . . | Lauro F. Cavazos . . | TX. . . . . | 1989 |
| " | Lamar Alexander . . | TN. . . . . | 1991 |
| Clinton. . . . . . | Richard W. Riley. . . | SC. . . . . | 1993 |

## Secretaries of Veterans Affairs

The Department of Veterans Affairs was created on Oct. 25, 1988, when Pres. Ronald Reagan signed a bill that made the Veterans Administration into a Cabinet department, effective Mar. 15, 1989.

| President | Secretary | Home | Apptd. |
|---|---|---|---|
| Bush. . . . . . . | Edward J. Derwinski. | IL . . . . . | 1989 |
| Clinton. . . . . . | Jesse Brown. . . . . . | IL. . . . . . | 1993 |

# Directors of the Central Intelligence Agency

In 1942, Pres. Franklin D. Roosevelt established the Office of Strategic Services (OSS); it was disbanded in 1945. In 1946, Pres. Harry Truman established the Central Intelligence Agency Group (CIG) to operate under the National Intelligence Authority (NIA). The National Security Act of 1947 replaced the NIA with the National Security Council and the CIG with the Central Intelligence Agency.

| Director | Served | Appointed by President |
|---|---|---|
| Adm. Sidney W. Souers | 1946 | Truman |
| Gen. Hoyt S. Vandenberg | 1946-1947 | Truman |
| Adm. Roscoe H. Hillenkoetter | 1947-1950 | Truman |
| Gen. Walter Bedell Smith | 1950-1953 | Truman |
| Allen W. Dulles | 1953-1961 | Eisenhower |
| John A. McCone | 1961-1965 | Kennedy |
| Adm. William F. Raborn Jr. | 1965-1966 | Johnson |
| Richard Helms | 1966-1973 | Johnson |
| James R. Schlesinger | 1973 | Nixon |
| William E. Colby | 1973-1976 | Nixon |
| George Bush | 1976-1977 | Ford |
| Adm. Stansfield Turner | 1977-1981 | Carter |
| William J. Casey | 1981-1987 | Reagan |
| William H. Webster | 1987-1991 | Reagan |
| Robert M. Gates | 1991-1993 | Bush |
| R. James Woolsey | 1993-1995 | Clinton |
| John M. Deutch | 1995- | Clinton |

# Speakers of the House of Representatives

(as of Oct. 1996)

Party designations: A, American; D, Democratic; DR, Democratic-Republican; F, Federalist; R, Republican; W, Whig

| Name | Party | State | Tenure |
|---|---|---|---|
| Frederick Muhlenberg | F | PA | 1789-1791 |
| Jonathan Trumbull | F | CT | 1791-1793 |
| Frederick Muhlenberg | F | PA | 1793-1795 |
| Jonathan Dayton | F | NJ | 1795-1799 |
| Theodore Sedgwick | F | MA | 1799-1801 |
| Nathaniel Macon | DR | NC | 1801-1807 |
| Joseph B. Varnum | DR | MA | 1807-1811 |
| Henry Clay | DR | KY | 1811-1814 |
| Langdon Cheves | DR | SC | 1814-1815 |
| Henry Clay | DR | KY | 1815-1820 |
| John W. Taylor | DR | NY | 1820-1821 |
| Philip P. Barbour | DR | VA | 1821-1823 |
| Henry Clay | DR | KY | 1823-1825 |
| John W. Taylor | D | NY | 1825-1827 |
| Andrew Stevenson | D | VA | 1827-1834 |
| John Bell | D | TN | 1834-1835 |
| James K. Polk | D | TN | 1835-1839 |
| Robert M. T. Hunter | D | VA | 1839-1841 |
| John White | W | KY | 1841-1843 |
| John W. Jones | D | VA | 1843-1845 |
| John W. Davis | D | IN | 1845-1847 |
| Robert C. Winthrop | W | MA | 1847-1849 |
| Howell Cobb | D | GA | 1849-1851 |
| Linn Boyd | D | KY | 1851-1855 |
| Nathaniel P. Banks | A | MA | 1856-1857 |
| James L. Orr | D | SC | 1857-1859 |
| William Pennington | R | NJ | 1860-1861 |
| Galusha A. Grow | R | PA | 1861-1863 |
| Schuyler Colfax | R | IN | 1863-1869 |
| Theodore M. Pomeroy | R | NY | 1869 |
| James G. Blaine | R | ME | 1869-1875 |
| Michael C. Kerr | D | IN | 1875-1876 |
| Samuel J. Randall | D | PA | 1876-1881 |
| Joseph W. Keifer | R | OH | 1881-1883 |
| John G. Carlisle | D | KY | 1883-1889 |
| Thomas B. Reed | R | ME | 1889-1891 |
| Charles F. Crisp | D | GA | 1891-1895 |
| Thomas B. Reed | R | ME | 1895-1899 |
| David B. Henderson | R | IA | 1899-1903 |
| Joseph G. Cannon | R | IL | 1903-1911 |
| Champ Clark | D | MO | 1911-1919 |
| Frederick H. Gillett | R | MA | 1919-1925 |
| Nicholas Longworth | R | OH | 1925-1931 |
| John N. Garner | D | TX | 1931-1933 |
| Henry T. Rainey | D | IL | 1933-1935 |
| Joseph W. Byrns | D | TN | 1935-1936 |
| William B. Bankhead | D | AL | 1936-1940 |
| Sam Rayburn | D | TX | 1940-1947 |
| Joseph W. Martin Jr. | R | MA | 1947-1949 |
| Sam Rayburn | D | TX | 1949-1953 |
| Joseph W. Martin Jr. | R | MA | 1953-1955 |
| Sam Rayburn | D | TX | 1955-1961 |
| John W. McCormack | D | MA | 1962-1971 |
| Carl Albert | D | OK | 1971-1977 |
| Thomas P. O'Neill Jr. | D | MA | 1977-1987 |
| James Wright | D | TX | 1987-1989 |
| Thomas S. Foley | D | WA | 1989-1995 |
| Newt Gingrich | R | GA | 1995- |

# Floor Leaders in the U.S. Senate Since the 1920s

**Majority Leaders**

| Name | Party | State | Tenure |
|---|---|---|---|
| Charles Curtis[1] | R | KS | 1925-1929 |
| James E. Watson | R | IN | 1929-1933 |
| Joseph T. Robinson | D | AR | 1933-1937 |
| Alben W. Barkley | D | KY | 1937-1947 |
| Wallace H. White | R | ME | 1947-1949 |
| Scott W. Lucas | D | IL | 1949-1951 |
| Ernest W. McFarland | D | AZ | 1951-1953 |
| Robert A. Taft | R | OH | 1953 |
| William F. Knowland | R | CA | 1953-1955 |
| Lyndon B. Johnson | D | TX | 1955-1961 |
| Mike Mansfield | D | MT | 1961-1977 |
| Robert C. Byrd | D | WV | 1977-1981 |
| Howard H. Baker Jr. | R | TN | 1981-1985 |
| Robert J. Dole | R | KS | 1985-1987 |
| Robert C. Byrd | D | WV | 1987-1989 |
| George J. Mitchell | D | ME | 1989-1995 |
| Robert J. Dole | R | KS | 1995-1996 |
| Trent Lott | R | MS | 1996 |

**Minority Leaders**

| Name | Party | State | Tenure |
|---|---|---|---|
| Oscar W. Underwood[2] | D | AL | 1920-1923 |
| Joseph T. Robinson | D | AR | 1923-1933 |
| Charles L. McNary | R | OR | 1933-1944 |
| Wallace H. White | R | ME | 1944-1947 |
| Alben W. Barkley | D | KY | 1947-1949 |
| Kenneth S. Wherry | R | NE | 1949-1951 |
| Henry Styles Bridges | R | NH | 1951-1953 |
| Lyndon B. Johnson | D | TX | 1953-1955 |
| William F. Knowland | R | CA | 1955-1959 |
| Everett M. Dirksen | R | IL | 1959-1969 |
| Hugh D. Scott | R | PA | 1969-1977 |
| Howard H. Baker Jr. | R | TN | 1977-1981 |
| Robert C. Byrd | D | WV | 1981-1987 |
| Robert J. Dole | R | KS | 1987-1995 |
| Thomas A. Daschle | D | SD | 1995- |

**Note**: Majority and Minority Leaders as of Oct. 1996. (1) First Republican to be designated floor leader. (2) First Democrat to be designated floor leader.

# Librarians of Congress

| Librarian | Served | Appointed by President |
|---|---|---|
| John J. Beckley | 1802-1807 | Jefferson |
| Patrick Magruder | 1807-1815 | Jefferson |
| George Watterston | 1815-1829 | Madison |
| John Silva Meehan | 1829-1861 | Jackson |
| John G. Stephenson | 1861-1864 | Lincoln |
| Ainsworth Rand Spofford | 1864-1897 | Lincoln |
| John Russell Young | 1897-1899 | McKinley |
| Herbert Putnam | 1899-1939 | McKinley |
| Archibald MacLeish | 1939-1944 | F. Roosevelt |
| Luther H. Evans | 1945-1953 | Truman |
| L. Quincy Mumford | 1954-1974 | Eisenhower |
| Daniel J. Boorstin | 1975-1987 | Ford |
| James H. Billington | 1987- | Reagan |

# COMPUTERS

## The Internet

For more details about terms used here, see the Glossary of Internet and Intranet Terms that follows.

### What Is the Internet?

The Internet is a vast computer network of computer networks. Estimates are that more than 30 million computer users populated this electronic global village by late 1996 and that some 8 to 10 million had access to the World Wide Web.

Some other facts about the Internet:

- An average Web page contains about 500 words, and experts put the number of Web pages at somewhere between 30 million and 50 million.
- During 1996, the number of registered commercial sites on the Internet increased more than 500%.
- The average Web user is 33 years old, has a household income of $59,000, and accesses the Web at least once a day.
- The Internet is accessible in more than 100 countries.
- Experts predict that spending for online advertising will exceed $2.6 billion by the year 2000.

The Internet is *not* owned or funded by any one institution, organization, or government. It doesn't have a CEO, and it is not a commercial service. The Internet is, however, directed by the Internet Society (ISOC), which is composed of volunteers. The ISOC appoints a subcouncil, the Internet Architecture Board (IAB), and members of this board work out issues of standards, network resources, network addresses, and so on. Another volunteer group, the Internet Engineering Task Force (IETF), takes care of the day-to-day issues of Internet operation.

Practically speaking, the Internet, also referred to as the Information Superhighway, is composed of people, hardware, and software. With the proper equipment, you can sit at your computer and communicate with someone any place in the world as long as that person also has the proper equipment. You can also use the Internet to access vast amounts of information, including text, graphics, sound, and video. From your computer, you can view masterpieces from the Louvre, take an aerial tour of Hawaii, or dissect a virtual frog. You can search databases at the Library of Congress, send e-mail, receive electronic newsletters, and "chat" with others online.

### How Did It Originate?

In the late 1960s, a group of scientists at the U.S. Department of Defense's Advanced Research Projects Agency (ARPA) wanted to share information with others working on similar research projects, many of whom were government contractors working at large universities. Thus, ARPAnet was spawned. When people at these institutions discovered the enormous utility of a network that linked them with colleagues around the world, the project mushroomed.

As the network expanded throughout the 1970s, members of the computer industry began to participate, and the Internet became an online haven for computer jocks, researchers, and academics. The first commercial online service, CompuServe, started up in 1969 and for several years was itself primarily an online hangout for computer jocks.

In 1986, the National Science Foundation (NSF) created NSFNET to connect supercomputer sites around the U.S. It also connected computers at research sites and schools that were near the supercomputers. Within 2 years, NSFNET had totally replaced ARPAnet.

In 1991, Vice President Al Gore, then a U.S. senator, proposed widening the architecture of NSFNET to include more K-12 schools, community colleges, and 2-year colleges. The resulting legislation expanded NSFNET and renamed it NREN (National Research and Educational Network). This bill also allowed businesses to purchase part of the network for commercial uses. The mass commercialization of today's Internet is the direct result of this legislation.

### How Can You Get There?

First, you need the equipment. You can get basic Internet access with any computer that has a modem that is connected to a phone line. However, to take full advantage of all the Internet has to offer, you need either a Macintosh that has a 68040 or higher CPU or a PC that has an 80486 or higher CPU. With either system, you also need the following:

- At least 4 megabytes of RAM (8 is recommended)
- A 250 megabyte hard drive
- A 14.4 bps modem (28.8 or faster is even better)

You can access the Internet in 4 ways: directly; with a SLIP/PPP account; with a shell, or dial-up, account; and via an Internet service provider (ISP). *Direct access* is primarily the province of large institutions and businesses that have computers that are part of a network that is part of the Internet. *SLIP* (Serial Line Internet Protocol) and *PPP* (Point-to-Point Protocol) accounts attach your computer to a network of computers that is directly attached to the Internet. You use software that you purchase or download off the Net. A *shell account* gives you text-only access through a Unix system.

*An Internet service provider* is a company that provides access to the Internet; some also provide content and e-mail. The best-known ISPs are the commercial online services such as America Online, CompuServe, Prodigy, and MSN (The Microsoft Network), but many national companies (for example, MCI and AT&T) and local and regional companies also provide Internet access. Free installation software is available for most of these services. ISPs generally charge a monthly subscription rate, and some (such as commercial online services) may charge additionally for connect time beyond that included in the monthly rate.

Currently, there are approximately 2,500 Internet service providers in the U.S., but that number is expected to shrink to about 500 by 1998. Internet service providers are consolidating in an attempt to cope with competition from the large telephone companies.

### Internet Resources

What you can do on the Internet depends on which resource you access. The basic resources are e-mail, FAQs, FTP, Gopher, newsgroups, and the World Wide Web.

*E-mail.* Electronic mail is probably the most popular and widely used resource on the Internet. To use it, however, you must know the address of the person or organization. An e-mail address consists of a *username*, a *service*, and a *domain*. For example, The World Almanac's e-mail address is `Walmanac@aol.com`. `Walmanac` is the username, `aol` is the service (in this case, America Online), and `com` is the domain (in this case, a commercial organization). The domains are identified in the Domain Name Service, also known as the Domain Name System. A consortium between AT&T and Network Solutions, called InterNIC (Internet Network Information Center), manages the task of registering addresses, or domain names. In mid-1996 a commercial domain name cost $100 for two years (and $50/year thereafter); `.edu` and `.org` names were free. Domain names can be applied for online at `http://rs.internic.net` or by contacting Network Solutions, InterNIC Registration Services, 505 Huntmar Park Dr., Herndon, VA 22070.

Here are the most familiar domains:

| Domain | What it is |
|---|---|
| com | a commercial organization, business, or company |
| edu | an educational institution |
| int | an international organization |
| gov | a nonmilitary government entity |
| mil | a military organization |
| net | a network administration |
| org | other organizations: nonprofit, nonacademic, or nongovernmental |

Of the 9.4 million registered Internet sites, the `com` domain is the largest group, at more than 2.4 million. The area with the largest number of registered commercial site names is San Francisco. The second largest domain is the `edu` group, at 1.8 million. Outside the U.S., the final part of a domain name represents the name of the country in which the site is located. For example, `jp` for Japan, `uk` for Great Britain, and `ru` for Russia.

*FAQs.* Frequently Asked Questions documents contain the answers to common Internet questions. Reading some of these documents, which can be found in many areas of the Internet, is a first step for anyone new to the Internet.

*FTP.* File Transfer Protocol is a method of transferring files on the Internet and a type of Internet site. Using FTP, you log on to a remote site, usually a server, view the available files, and copy them to your computer. The address for an FPT site begins with `ftp.`

*Gopher.* Developed at the University of Minnesota, home of the Golden Gophers, Gopher is a hierarchy of menus you can use to browse the Internet or search for a specific file. These menus are available on numerous Gopher servers on the Internet. Any Internet address that begins with `gopher` points to a location on a Gopher server.

*Newsgroups.* Newsgroups, a classic institution of the Internet, are found on the part of the Internet called Usenet. In a newsgroup, messages concerning a particular topic are posted in a public forum. You can simply read the postings, or you can post an article yourself.

*The World Wide Web.* The Web may be the most complete realization of the Internet to date. It was developed in the early 1990s at the European Center for Nuclear Research as an environment in which scientists in Geneva, Switzerland, could share information. It has evolved into a medium that consists of text, graphics, audio, animation, and video. The address of a site on the Web usually begins with `http://www.` The World Wide Web is a graphical environment that can be navigated through hyperlinks. From one site you click on hyperlinks to go to any number of related sites.

### Safety and Security on the Internet

The Internet has no governing body through which laws and policies are enforced, and its original inhabitants were known for their opposition to censorship and their strong-held beliefs about free speech. Thus, when President Bill Clinton on Feb. 8, 1996, signed into law the Communications Decency Act (CDA), a broad coalition of free speech and computer industry groups immediately filed a lawsuit. Under the CDA, anyone who makes "indecent" or "patently offensive" material available to a minor through what it calls an "interactive computer service" will be subject to a $250,000 fine and 2 years in jail. In June 1996, 3 federal district and appellate court judges blocked the bill, calling the restrictions a "profound and repugnant" violation of First Amendment rights and arguing that the Internet must have the broadest possible protection against government intrusion. Undoubtedly, the issues raised by this legislation will ultimately be decided by the U.S. Supreme Court.

That said, common sense dictates some basic codes of conduct when you are surfing the Net.

- If you encounter an area that you find offensive, for example, a newsgroup or a chat room, remove that area from your list of places to visit. In fact, any time you feel uncomfortable, remember: The computer is under your control. You can always turn it off.
- If you feel that someone is being threatening or dangerous, you can inform your Internet service provider, which can issue a warning or can even withdraw entirely the person's online privileges.
- Be as conscious of your privacy on the Internet as you would in any other situation in which you interact with strangers. Children, especially, should never give out their home phone number or address or any other personal information.
- Be extremely careful about giving out credit card numbers. The Internet is not 100% secure.

### Searching the Internet

A search engine is a special Web site that you can use to locate Web sites based on specific keywords. Many of the newer search engines actively search the Web, checking that existing URLs in their giant databases still work and adding information about new sites. The programs that do this are called spiders, Web crawlers, or bots (short for robots). Some search engines store only the title and URL of sites; others index every word of a site's content. Below are some of the most popular, a brief description of their content, and their URLs.

**AltaVista**, sponsored by Digital Equipment Corp., processes more than 2.5 million search requests every day. It has cataloged more than 15 billion words on some 30 million Web pages as well as all 13,000 Usenet newsgroups. It collects Web pages at the rate of 2.5 million a day. Find AltaVista at `http://www.altavista.digital.com`

**Excite** has a database of 1.5 million Web pages that you can search by keyword or by concept. In addition, it has a browsable directory of more than 50,000 reviewed Web sites, a Usenet database of more than 1 million articles, and a search of the Usenet classifieds from the last 2 weeks. Find Excite at `http://www.excite.com`

**HotBot** features a menu-driven search engine. You can search by file type, date, geographic location and domain, and Web site. Find HotBot at `http://www.hotbot.com`

**InfoSeek** is a full-text search system with which you can look for Web pages, Usenet newsgroups, and FAQs. A normal, free search is limited to the first 100 matches. If you subscribe to InfoSeek Professional, you can search computer, medical, and business news, press releases, and technical-support databases. Find InfoSeek at `http://www2.infoseek.com`

**Lycos** is used by more than 500,000 people every week and catalogs some 20 million Web pages, FTP sites, and Gopher sites. Find Lycos at `http://www.lycos.com`

**Open Text Index** is a very powerful, multilingual search engine with which you can do a weighted search and receive information that is ranked by relevancy. Find Open Text at `http:www.opentext.com:8080`

**WebCrawler** is a free service from America Online that gives you fast access to a 200 megabyte database of 2 million indexed Web documents. Find WebCrawler at `http://webcrawler.com`

**Yahoo** lists more than 200,000 Web sites in more than 20,000 categories. A utility at this site lets you extend your search to other search engines, such as AltaVista, Lycos, or WebCrawler. Find Yahoo at `http://www.yahoo.com`

### The Intranet

If 1995 was the Year of the Internet, 1996 may well become known as the Year of the Intranet. An Intranet is an internal company network that uses Internet technology to support real business applications and provide departmental, interdepartmental, and companywide communications. An Intranet consists of a Web server and a Web browser connected to a company local area network. Only those within a corporate enterprise can access an Intranet. In some cases, users of an Intranet can also access the Internet, but unauthorized users cannot access the Intranet.

The ways in which an Intranet can be used by industries, corporations, or organizations are as numerous and as varied as the enterprises themselves. Here are some examples:

- At AT&T, employees stay in touch via an Intranet database that contains the phone numbers, addresses, titles, and organizational information for all 300,000 of them.
- At HBO, researchers, programmers, and high-level executives use an Intranet to access a database that contains information on every movie ever made or in the process of being made and tracks a movie's cast, director, distributor, how much money it made, whether it's on videocassette, and when it's schedule to play for the next two years.
- At Ford Motor Co., engineers created the 1996 Taurus with the help of an Intranet that connected design centers in Asia, Europe, and the U.S.

In 1995, sales of Web servers for Intranet use exceeded those for Internet use by 10%. Some experts predict that by the year 2000 sales of Web servers for Intranet usage will exceed those for Internet use by 10 to 1.

# Glossary of Internet and Intranet Terms

For general computer terms, see the Computer Glossary later in this section.

**Archie** A system of servers that searches for publicly available files in FTP archives. *See* **FTP**.

**browser** A tool that you use to explore Internet and Intranet resources.

**CGI** An abbreviation for Common Gateway Interface, a standard way that programs can interface with Web servers and that allows them to run applications such as search engines and to access databases.

**chat room** An area of an online service where people can communicate from their computers in real time.

**client** An application that uses information or services provided by a server. Some common clients are Gopher, FTP, and Web browsers.

**cyberspace** The online culture that the Internet creates.

**dial-up account** A basic access to a text-only Unix system.

**directory service** A provider of online directories of Web sites and search engines. *See* **search engine.**

**domain** The portion of an Internet address that designates the site's type (such as company, or educational institution, or government agency).

**emoticon** A combination of keyboard characters that depicts an emotional response (also called smiley). For example, :-) is a smiley face, indicating happiness. If you don't get it, turn this page sideways and look again.

**FAQ** An abbreviation for Frequently Asked Questions, a document that assembles answers to common questions about sites or areas of the Internet.

**Fetch** A program for finding and accessing FTP files.

**flame** A derisive, possibly insulting message posted on a newsgroup.

**forum** An online gathering place for groups of people with a similar interest.

**FTP** An abbreviation for File Transfer Protocol. As a noun, FTP is a protocol for the transfer of data on the Internet. As a verb, it is a method for transferring data. As an adjective, it is a type of site on the Internet.

**Gopher** A menu-based tool for finding, accessing, and organizing Internet resources.

**home page** The first screen you see when you go to a site on the World Wide Web; also the site itself.

**HTML** An abbreviation for Hypertext Markup Language, the language used to create World Wide Web documents.

**HTTP** An abbreviation for Hypertext Transfer Protocol, the protocol used to manage the links between one hypertext document and another.

**hyperlink** A highlighted (and sometimes underlined) word, phrase, or image in a Web document that connects to another part of the document, another document, or even a document on a different server.

**hypertext** A method of presenting information so that it can be viewed in a nonsequential way.

**Internet service provider** A network, commercial or otherwise, to which you can connect in order to get access to the Internet.

**Java** A programming language designed to create applications for use with special Web browsers.

**Jughead** A Gopher search program that searches a specific set of Gopher menus.

**legacy system** A computer system that has been in use for a long time, either in a corporation (in the case of a mainframe) or in a home or small office (in the case of an older PC system), and that performs essential functions that cannot be disrupted.

**link** *See* **hyperlink.**

**logon** The process of identifying oneself to a computer after connecting to it.

**lurk** To read articles in a newsgroup or e-mail discussion list without joining in. A perfectly acceptable practice for a newbie. *See* **newbie.**

**Lynx** A nongraphical Web browser. With it, you can see text on the World Wide Web and iconic representations of the graphics.

**mailing list** An electronic version of the printed kind. If your name is on a mailing list, you receive, via e-mail, anything that is sent to those on the list.

**moderated** A description of a newsgroup or mailing list whose contents are monitored by a human being.

**Mosaic** Any of several programs that you can use to browse the Web. *See* **browser.**

**Net** Short for the Internet.

**netiquette** The Internet code of conduct

**Netizen** An Internet user.

**newbie** A new or an inexperienced user of the Internet.

**newsgroup** Usenet message areas, each of which focuses on a particular topic.

**password** A unique string of characters that a user types to identify himself or herself when logging on to a protected computer system.

**posting** Submitting an article to a newsgroup; also the article itself. *See* **thread.**

**PPP** An abbreviation for Point-to-Point Protocol, a set of rules or standards for direct Internet access over the phone lines.

**protocol** A set of rules or standards that enables computers to communicate with as little error as possible.

**search engine** Software that finds and retrieves data.

**server** A computer that makes access to files, printing, communications, and other services available to users.

**shell account** A Unix-based Internet access account.

**site** A location on the Internet.

**SLIP** An abbreviation for Serial Line Internet Protocol, a set of rules or standards for direct Internet access over the phone lines.

**smiley** *See* **emoticon.**

**snail mail** Items that travel via the postal service, which in the Information Age is viewed as terribly slow.

**spamming** Sending junk e-mail.

**system administrator** The person who organizes, maintains, troubleshoots, and generally oversees a network.

**TCP/IP** An abbreviation for Transmission Control Protocol/Internet Protocol, the underlying standards that define the Internet and make Intranets possible.

**Telnet** A protocol to log in to remote computers on the Internet. It can be used to access databases or one's own accounts from a remote location.

**thread** A series of newsgroup postings on the same subject. *See* **posting.**

**TIA** An abbreviation for The Internet Adapter, a shareware program that enables you to use a less expensive shell account to access the World Wide Web.

**Unix** A text-based, as opposed to a graphical, operating system in which you must type commands rather than pointing and clicking with a mouse.

**URL** An abbreviation for Uniform Resource Locator, an address or location of a site on the World Wide Web.

**Usenet** An informal, anarchistic worldwide newsgroup network that exchanges public messages on specific topics.

**username** The name that is used in an e-mail address.

**Veronica** A search program for Gophers.

**Web** *See* **World Wide Web**

**Web browser** A World Wide Web client application that you use to look at hypertext documents and follow links to other documents on the Web.

**Web server** A hardware and software package that provides service to Web clients. *See* **client.**

**World Wide Web (WWW)** A huge collection of sites that are connected through hyperlinks; you navigate this graphical environment with a Web browser. *See* **Web browser.**

**Yahoo** A search and reference tool, specific to the World Wide Web.

# Internet Lingo

The following abbreviations are commonly used in Internet documents and in e-mail.

**BTW** By the way
**F2F** Face to face, a personal meeting
**FCOL** For crying out loud
**FWIW** For what it's worth
**FYI** For your information
**GOK** God only knows
**HHOK** Ha, ha—only kidding
**HHOS** Ha, ha—only serious
**IMHO** In my humble opinion
**IMO** In my opinion
**LOL** Laughing out loud
**OTOH** On the other hand
**ROFL** or **ROTFL** Rolling on the floor laughing
**TAFN** That's all for now

Emoticons, or smileys, are a series of typed characters that, when turned sideways, resemble a face and express an emotion. Here are some smileys that are often encountered on the Internet.

:-) Smile
;-) Wink
:-* Kiss
:-( Unhappy
:-o Shouting
:-b... Drooling
=:o Argh!
{*} A hug and a kiss
:p Raz

# Internet Directory to Selected Sites

The e-mail and site addresses listed below are but a small sampling of what is available on the Internet. When you enter an address, you must type it exactly as written, including capital and lowercase letters, any nonalphanumeric characters, and spaces. You may be unable to connect to a site for the following reasons: (1) You have mistyped the address; (2) the site is busy; (3) the site has moved; (4) the site no longer exists.

### U.S. Government

To send e-mail to the president, the vice president, or the first lady, use the following addresses:

`president@whitehouse.gov`
`vice.president@whitehouse.gov`
`first.lady@whitehouse.gov`

To take a virtual tour of the White House, connect to the following site:

`http://www.whitehouse.gov`

The White House FAQ is at the following address:

`http://www.whitehouse.gov/WH/html/faq.html`

To receive White House documents and publications by e-mail, send the message `Send Info` to:
`publications@whitehouse.gov`

To get a complete listing of the e-mail addresses and Web sites of the members of Congress, connect to:

`www.yahoo.com/Government/Legislative_Branch/Congressional_E_Mail_Addresses`

For all kinds of information about the U.S. government and links to many of the sites listed below, connect to the Vote Smart Web site at:

`http://www.vote-smart.org`

**Census Bureau**
`http://www.census.gov`
**Central Intelligence Agency**
`http://www.odci.gov/cia`
**Department of Agriculture**
`http://www.usda.gov`
**Department of Commerce**
`http://www.doc.gov`
**Department of Defense**
`http://www.dtic.dla.mil/defenselink`
**Department of Education**
`http://gopher.ed.gov`
**Department of Energy**
`http://www.doe.gov`
**Department of Health and Human Services**
`http://www.os.dhhs.gov`
**Department of Housing and Urban Development**
`http://www.hud.gov`
**Department of the Interior**
`http://info.er.usgs.gov/doi/doi.html`
**Department of Justice**
`http://www.usdoj.gov`
**Department of Labor**
`http://www.dol.gov`
**Department of State**
`http://www.state.gov/index.html`
**Department of Transportation**
`http://www.dot.gov`
**Department of the Treasury**
`http://www.ustreas.gov`
**Department of Veterans Affairs**
`http://www.va.gov`
**Environmental Protection Agency**
`http://www.epa.gov`
**Federal Trade Commisssion**
`http://www.ftc.gov/Welcome.html`
**Library of Congress**
`http://www.loc.gov`
**NASA**
`http://www.nasa.gov`
**Postal Service**
`http://www.usps.gov`
**Social Security Online**
`http://www.ssa.gov/SSA_Home.html`
**THOMAS: Legislative Information**
`http://thomas.loc.gov`
**U. S Constitution**
At this site, you can access the complete text of the U.S. Constitution:
`http://www.house.gov/Constitution/Constitution.html`
**U.S. House of Representatives**
`http://www.house.gov`
**U.S. Senate**
`http://www.senate.gov`
**U.S. Supreme Court Decisions**
`http://www.law.cornell.edu/supct/supct.table.html`
**U.S. Supreme Court Justices**
For biographical data on and decisions of each justice:
`http://www.law.cornell.edu/supct/justices/fullcourt.html`

### Listings of Internet Server Providers

`http://thelist.com`
`http://wings.buffalo.edu/world`

### Commercial Online Services

**America Online**
`http://www.aol.com`
**CompuServe**
`http://www.compuserve.com`
**The Microsoft Network**
`http://www.msn.com`
**Prodigy**
`http://www.prodigy.com`

### Introduction to the World Wide Web

**The World Wide Web Consortium**
`http://www.w3.org`
**The World Wide Web Frequently Asked Questions List**
`http://www.boutell.com/faq`
**World Wide Web Servers, by Region**
`http://www.w3.org/pub/DataSources/WWW/Servers.html`

### Intranet Resources on the Internet

**The Corporate Intranet**
`http://webcom.com/wordmark/sem_1.html`
**Intranet News and Discussion**
`http://www.intranut.com`
**News and Reviews of Intranet Software**
`http://www.zdnet.com/pcmag/IU/iuser.htm`

### Security Information

**The National Fraud Information Center**
`http://www.fraud.org`
**The Secure Electronic Transaction Standard** (general information about electronic commerce)
`http://www.visa.com/cgi-bin/vee/sf/standard.html?2+0`

### Shopping

**1-800-FLOWERS** (one of the most visually appealing sites on the Internet)
`http://www.1800flowers.com`
**Amazon.com Inc** (a completely Web-based bookstore that has a database of 1.1 million titles)
`http://www.amazon.com`
**eShop Inc** (a small electronic mall)
`http://www.eshop.com`
**Good Stuff Cheap** (manufacturers' closeouts)
`http://www.onramp.net/goodstuf`
**Shoppers Advantage** (online superstore)
`http://www.cuc.com`
**Virtual Vineyards** (wine)
`http://www.virtualvin.com`

### Travel

**city.net**
`http://www.city.net`
**Cyberlopolis Metrosource**
`http://www.cyberlopolis.com`
**Virtual Tourist**
`http://www.vtourist.com/vt`

### Kids' Places

**CRAYON (CReAte Your Own Newspaper)**
`http://crayon.net`
**Interactive Frog Dissection**
`http://teach.virginia.edu/go/frog`
**Lite Board**
`http://asylum.cid.com/lb/lb.html`
**VolcanoWorld**
`http://volcano.und.nodak.edu`

### Health and Fitness

**Multimedia Medical Reference Library**
`http://www.med-library.com`
**The Running Page**
`http://sunsite.unc.edu:80/drears/running/running.html`
**Tennis Server**
`http://www.tennisserver.com/Tennis.html`

### Food and Drink

**CheeseNet**
`http://wgx.com/cheesenet/index.html`
**The Chile-Heads Home Page**
`http://neptune.netimages.com/~chile`
**Cooking and Recipes**
`http://www.yatcom.com/neworl/food/cooktop.html`
**the electronic Gourmet Guide (eGG)**
`http://www.2way.com/food/egg/index.html`
**The Gumbo Pages**
`http://www.Webcom.com/~gumbo/welcome.html`
**Hawaii's Best Espresso Company**
`http://planet-hawaii.com/~bec`
**Mimi's Cyber Kitchen**
`http://www.cyber-kitchen.com`

### Home Improvement

**Black & Decker**
`http://www.blackanddecker.com`
**Hardwareworld**
`http://www.hardwareworld.com`
**Home Depot**
`http://www.homedepot.com`
**Hometime**
`http://www.hometime.com`
**Pella Windows**
`http://www.pella.com`
**This Old House**
`http://www.pathfinder.com/TOH`

### Corporations

**AT&T**
`http://www.att.com`
**Coca-Cola**
`http://www.cocacola.com`
**Federal Express Page**
(track your shipment)
`http://www.fedex.com`
**General Electric**
`http://www.ge.com`
**IBM**
`http://www.ibm.com`
**Kmart**
`http://www.kmart.com`
**Microsoft**
`http://www.microsoft.com`
**Netscape Communications**
`http://www.netscape.com`
**United Parcel Service (UPS)**
(track your shipment)
`http://www.ups.com`
**Wal-Mart Stores**
`http://www.wal-mart.com`

### Reference

**The World-Wide Web Virtual Library: Subject Catalog**
`http://www.w3.org/pub/DataSources/bySubject/Overview.html`
**WWW Meta-Indexes and Search Tools**
`http://lcweb.loc.gov/global/search.html`
**U. Albany Quick Reference**
`http://www.albany.edu/library/newlib/quickref.html`
**Libweb—Library WWW Servers**
`http://sunsite.berkeley.edu/Libweb`
**Global Internet: Net Happenings**
`http://www.gi.net/NET`
**Liszt: Searchable Directory of E-mail Discussion Groups**
`http://www.liszt.com`
**Online Dictionaries**
`http://www.bucknell.edu/~rbeard/diction.html`
**BookWire—The First Place to Look for Book Information**
`http://www.bookwire.com`
**Reference Reviews Europe**
`http://www.library.upenn.edu/ifba`

# Top-Selling Software, 1996

**Source:** PC Data, Reston, VA

(based on average U.S. sales, Jan.-June 1996)

### CD-ROM, All Categories

1. Microsoft Windows 95 Upgrade, Microsoft
2. Turbo Tax Deluxe - Final, Intuit
3. Warcraft II, Davidson
4. Corel Printhouse, Corel
5. Myst, Brøderbund
6. Quicken Deluxe, Intuit
7. Print Shop Deluxe Ensemble, Brøderbund
8. Microsoft Plus, Microsoft
9. Microsoft Encarta Encyclopedia, Microsoft
10. Civilization 2, MicroProse
11. Toy Story Animated Storybook, Disney
12. Duke Nukem 3D, Formgen
13. Star Wars Rebel Assault II, LucasArts
14. Mechwarrior II, Activision
15. Command & Conquer, Virgin

### Windows 95 Software

1. Microsoft Windows 95 Upgrade, Microsoft
2. Microsoft Plus, Microsoft
3. Corel Printhouse, Corel
4. Viruscan, McAfee
5. Netscape Navigator, Netscape
6. Norton Antivirus, Symantec
7. First Aid, Cybermedia
8. Uninstaller, MicroHelp
9. Microsoft Return of the Arcade, Microsoft
10. Microsoft Publisher, Microsoft
11. After Dark '95, Berkeley
12. CleanSweep, Quarterdeck
13. Sim City 2000 Collection, Maxis
14. Mechwarrior II, Activision
15. Fury 3 (cubed), Microsoft

### PC Games (MS-DOS/Windows/Win95)

1. Warcraft II, Davidson
2. Myst, Brøderbund
3. Civilization 2, MicroProse
4. Microsoft Flight Simulator, Microsoft
5. Duke Nukem 3D, Formgen
6. Mechwarrior II, Activision
7. Command & Conquer, Virgin
8. Doom II, GT Interactive
9. Ultimate Doom Thy Flesh, GT Interactive
10. Star Wars Rebel Assault II, LucasArts
11. Wing Commander IV, Electronic Arts
12. Hexen, GT Interactive
13. Descent II, Interplay
14. Need for Speed, Electronic Arts
15. NBA Live '96, Electronic Arts

### Games (Macintosh)

1. Myst, Brøderbund
2. Top Ten Pack, Electronic Arts
3. Warcraft II, Davidson
4. Links Pro, Access
5. X-Wing Collector's CD, LucasArts
6. FA-18 Hornet, Graphic Simulations
7. Doom II, GT Interactive
8. Star Wars Rebel Assault II, LucasArts
9. Ultimate Doom Thy Flesh, GT Interactive
10. The Archives I, LucasArts

### Home Education (MS-DOS/Windows/Win95)

1. Toy Story Animated Storybook, Disney
2. Math Blaster: In Search of Spot, Davidson
3. Pocahontas Animated Storybook, Disney
4. Mathematics Box Set, SofSource
5. Lion King Activity Center, Disney
6. Winnie The Pooh, Disney
7. Fisher Price Ready for School, Davidson
8. Where in the World Is Carmen Sandiego? Brøderbund
9. Dr. Seuss's ABCs, Living Books
10. Microsoft Magic School Bus, Microsoft

### Home Education (Macintosh)

1. Mavis Beacon Teaches Typing, Mindscape
2. Lion King Activity Center, Disney
3. Pocahontas Animated Storybook, Disney
4. Winnie The Pooh, Disney
5. Kid's Mac Pack, Palladium Interactive
6. A.D.A.M. Inside Story, A.D.A.M. Software
7. Where in the USA Is Carmen Sandiego? Brøderbund
8. Mario Teaches Typing, Interplay
9. Oregon Trail, Softkey
10. The Way Things Work, DK Multimedia

### Reference Software

1. Microsoft Encarta, Microsoft
2. Microsoft Bookshelf, Microsoft
3. Compton's Interactive Encyclopedia, SoftKey
4. Grolier Encyclopedia, Grolier
5. Select Phone, Pro CD

### Personal Productivity (MS-DOS/Windows)

1. TurboTax Final, Intuit
2. TurboTax Deluxe - Final, Intuit
3. Quicken, Intuit
4. Quicken Deluxe, Intuit
5. Corel Printhouse, Corel
6. Print Shop Deluxe CD Ensemble, Brøderbund
7. TaxCut - Final, Block Financial
8. Microsoft Publisher, Microsoft
9. Tripmaker, Rand McNally
10. Family Tree Maker Deluxe, Brøderbund
11. Hallmark Connections Card Studio, Micrografx
12. Print Shop Deluxe, Brøderbund
13. State TurboTax CA, Intuit
14. Street Finder, Rand McNally
15. Microsoft Works, Microsoft

### Personal Productivity (Macintosh)

1. Macintax Final, Intuit
2. Quicken, Intuit
3. Print Shop Deluxe CD Ensemble, Brøderbund
4. Quicken Deluxe, Intuit
5. State Macintax CA - Final, Intuit

# U.S. Computer Sales and Ownership, 1983-96

**Source:** Electronic Industries Association, Arlington, VA

(U.S. sales through retail consumer channels)

| Year | Unit sales to dealers (thousands) | Dollar sales to dealers (millions) | Percentage of house-holds with owners | Year | Unit sales to dealers (thousands) | Dollar sales to dealers (millions) | Percentage of house-holds with owners |
|---|---|---|---|---|---|---|---|
| 1983 | 3,750 | $2,070 | 7 | 1990 | 4,000 | $ 4,187 | 22 |
| 1984 | 3,975 | 2,385 | 13 | 1991 | 3,900 | 4,287 | 25 |
| 1985 | 3,200 | 2,175 | 15 | 1992 | 4,875 | 5,573 | 27 |
| 1986 | 2,950 | 3,060 | 16 | 1993 | 5,850 | 6,921 | 30 |
| 1987 | 3,125 | 3,100 | 18 | 1994 | 6,725 | 8,070 | 33 |
| 1988 | 3,500 | 3,340 | 20 | 1995[1] | 8,400 | 10,920 | 37 |
| 1989 | 3,900 | 3,711 | 21 | 1996[1] | 9,825 | 12,773 | 40[2] |

(1) Estimated figures. Sales and households with owners estimated through the end of the calendar year. (2) As of June 1996, an estimated 21% of households had computers with CD-ROM drives, and 18% had modems.

# Glossary of Computer Terms



For additional terms, see the Glossary of Internet and Intranet Terms earlier in this section.

**application** A computer program designed to help people perform a certain type of work. An application can manipulate text, numbers, graphics, or a combination of those elements.

**artificial intelligence (AI)** The branch of computer science that deals with enabling computers to emulate such aspects of intelligence as speech recognition, deduction, inference, creative response, the ability to learn from past experience, and the ability to make reasonable inferences from incomplete information.

**ASCII** (pronounced "askee"); acronym for American Standard Code for Information Interchange, a coding scheme that assigns numeric values to letters, numbers, punctuation marks, and certain other characters.

**backup (noun); back up (verb)** As a noun, a duplicate copy of a program, a disk, or data. As a verb, to make a backup copy.

**bandwidth** In communications, the difference between the highest and lowest frequencies in a given range. In computer networks, greater bandwidth indicates faster data-transfer capability.

**baud rate** Commonly, a reference to the speed at which a modem can transmit data.

**BBS** An abbreviation for bulletin board system, a computer system equipped with one or more modems that serves as an information and message-passing center for dial-up users.

**bit** Short for binary digit; either 1 or 0 in the binary number system. In processing and storage, a bit is the smallest unit of information handled by a computer.

**boot** As a verb, to start up a computer. As a noun, the process of starting or resetting a computer.

**broadband network** A type of local area network on which transmissions travel as radio-frequency signals over separate inbound and outbound channels. Stations on a broadband network are connected by coaxial or fiber-optic cable. The cable itself can be made to carry data, voice, and video simultaneously.

**bug** An error in software or hardware. In software, a bug is an error in coding or logic that causes a program to malfunction or to produce incorrect results.

**bulletin board system** *See* **BBS.**

**byte** Abbreviation for binary term. A unit of information consisting of 8 bits; in computer processing and storage, the equivalent of a single character.

**CD-ROM** Acronym for compact disc read-only memory, a form of storage characterized by high capacity (roughly 600 megabytes) and the use of laser optics rather than magnetic means for reading data.

**central processing unit (CPU)** The computational and control unit of a computer; the device that interprets and executes instructions.

**chip** *See* **integrated circuit.**

**client** On a local area network, a computer that accesses shared network resources provided by another computer (called a server). *See also* **server.**

**computer** Any machine that does three things: accepts structured input, processes it according to prescribed rules, and produces the results as output.

**copy protection** A software "lock" placed on a computer program by its developer to prevent the product from being copied and distributed without approval or authorization.

**CPU** *See* **central processing unit.**

**crash** To fail suddenly. *Crash* is commonly used to describe the failure of either a program or a disk drive.

**cursor** A special on-screen indicator that marks the place at which keystrokes will occur when typed.

**database** Loosely, any aggregation of data; a file consisting of a number of records (or tables), each of which is constructed of fields (columns) of a particular type, together with a collection of operations that facilitate searching, sorting, recombination, and similar activities.

**debug** With software, to detect, locate, and correct logical or syntactical errors in a computer program.

**desktop publishing** The use of a computer and specialized software to combine text and graphics to create a document that can be printed on either a laser printer or a typesetting machine.

**disk** A round, flat piece of flexible plastic (floppy disk) or inflexible metal (hard disk) coated with a magnetic material that can be electrically influenced to hold information recorded in digital (binary) format.

**disk drive** An electromechanical device that reads from and writes to disks.

**disk operating system** Abbreviated DOS. A generic term describing any operating system that is loaded from disk devices when the system is started or rebooted.

**document** As a noun, any self-contained piece of work created with an application program and, if saved on disk, given a filename by which it can be retrieved.

**DOS** *See* **disk operating system.**

**download** In communications, the process of transferring a copy of a file from a remote computer to the requesting computer by means of a modem or network.

**DVD** An abbreviation for digital versatile disc, an optical multimedia platform with a storage capacity of 4.7 to 8.5 gigabytes for single-sided discs and about 17 gigabytes for double-sided discs. This memory capacity allows DVDs to hold more than 2 hours of high-quality video.

**electronic mail (e-mail)** The transmission of messages over a communications network.

**Ethernet** A local area network developed by Xerox in 1976, originally for linking minicomputers at the Palo Alto Research Center.

**field** A location in a record in which a particular type of data is stored.

**file** A complete, named collection of information, such as a program, a set of data used by a program, or a user-created document.

**filename** The set of letters, numbers, and allowable symbols assigned to a file that distinguishes it from all other files in a particular directory on a disk.

**file server** A file-storage device on a local area network that is accessible to all users on the network. On local area networks, a file server is often a computer with a large hard disk that is dedicated only to the task of managing shared files.

**floppy disk** *See* **disk.**

**format** As a noun, the structure or appearance of a unit of data, such as a file, fields in a database record, a cell in a spreadsheet, or the text in a word-processed document. As a verb, to format text or the contents of a cell in a spreadsheet means to change the appearance of the selected material.

**graphical user interface** Abbreviated GUI (pronounced "gooey"). A type of display format that enables the user to choose commands, start programs, and see lists of files and other options by pointing to pictorial representations (icons) and lists of menu items on the screen. *See also* **icon.**

**hacker** Originally, a computerphile—a person totally engrossed in computer programming and computer technology. In the 1980s, the term acquired a pejorative connotation, often referring to someone who secretively invades others' computers.

**hard copy** Printed output on paper, film, or other permanent media. *See* **soft copy.**

**hard disk** *See* **disk.**
**host** The main computer in a system of computers or terminals connected by communications links.
**icon** In graphical environments, a small graphics image displayed on the screen to represent an object that can be manipulated by the user.
**import** To bring information from one system or program into another.
**integrated circuit** Also called a chip. In electronics, the packing of circuit elements, such as transistors and resistors, onto a single chip of silicon crystal or other material.
**interactive** Operating in a back-and-forth, often conversational, manner, as when a user enters a question or command and the system immediately responds.
**kilobyte** Abbreviated KB, K, or Kbyte. 1,024 bytes.
**kludge** Pronounced "klooj." With computers, a term used to describe a piece of hardware or software that basically operates properly but whose construction or design is severely lacking in elegance or logical efficiency.
**LAN** Rhymes with "can." Acronym for local area network, a group of computers and other devices dispersed over a relatively limited area and connected by a communications link that enables any device to interact with any other on the network.
**laptop computer** A portable computer that can be held on the lap.
**mainframe computer** A high-level computer designed for the most intensive computational tasks.
**megabyte** Abbreviated MB. Either 1 million bytes or 1,048,576 bytes ($2^{20}$).
**memory** Circuitry that allows information to be stored and retrieved. In common usage, it refers only to the fast semiconductor storage (RAM) directly connected to the processor. *See* **RAM.**
**menu** A list of options from which a program user can select in order to perform a desired action, such as choosing a command or applying a format.
**microcomputer** A computer built around a microprocessor.
**microprocessor** A central processing unit (CPU) on a single chip. *See also* **integrated circuit.**
**minicomputer** A mid-level computer built to perform complex computations while dealing efficiently with a high level of input and output from users connected via terminals.
**modem** Short for modulator/demodulator, a communications device that enables a computer to transmit information over a standard telephone line.
**monitor** The device on which images generated by the computer's video adapter are displayed.
**motherboard** The main circuit board containing the primary components of a computer system.
**mouse** A common pointing device, popularized by its inclusion as standard equipment with the Apple Macintosh. By moving the mouse on a surface, the user typically controls an on-screen cursor. *See* **cursor.**
**multimedia** The combination of sound, graphics, animation, and video.
**multitasking** A mode of operation offered by an operating system in which a computer works on more than one task at a time.
**network** A group of computers and associated devices that are connected by communications facilities.
**online** Activated and ready for operation; capable of communicating with or being controlled by a computer.
**operating system** The software responsible for controlling the allocation and usage of hardware resources such as memory, central processing unit (CPU) time, disk space, and peripheral devices.
**optical fiber** A thin strand of transparent material used to carry optical signals.
**optical scanner** An input device that uses light-sensing equipment to scan paper or another medium, translating the pattern of light and dark (or color) into a digital signal that can be manipulated by either optical character recognition software or graphics software.
**packet** In general usage, a unit of information transmitted as a whole from one device to another on a network.
**PC** Abbreviation for personal computer.
**Pentium** A microprocessor introduced by Intel Corporation in 1993.
**peripherals** Devices, such as disk drives, printers, modems, and joysticks, that are connected to a computer and are controlled by its microprocessor.
**pixel** Short for picture element; sometimes called a pel.
**port** In computer hardware, a location for passing data in and out of a computing device.
**portable computer** Any computer designed to be moved easily.
**printer** A computer peripheral that puts text or a computer-generated image on paper or on another medium, such as a transparency.
**program** Synonymous with *software;* a sequence of instructions that can be executed by a computer.
**RAM** Pronounced "ram." Acronym for random access memory. Semiconductor-based memory that can be read and written by the microprocessor or other hardware devices.
**server** On a local area network, a computer running administrative software that controls access to all or part of the network and its resources (such as disk drives or printers). *See* **LAN.**
**soft copy** The temporary images presented on a computer display screen. *See* **hard copy.**
**software** Computer programs; instructions that cause the hardware—the machines—to do work.
**spreadsheet program** An application program commonly used for budgets, forecasting, and other finance-related tasks.
**supercomputer** A large, extremely fast, and expensive computer used for complex or sophisticated calculations.
**telecommuting** The practice of working in one location (often, at home) and communicating with a main office in a different location through a personal computer equipped with a modem and communications software.
**teleconferencing** The use of audio, video, or computer equipment linked through a communications system to enable geographically separated individuals to participate in a meeting or discussion.
**Unix** Pronounced "ewe-niks." A multiuser, multitasking operating system originally developed by Ken Thompson and Dennis Ritchie at AT&T Bell Laboratories in 1969 for use on minicomputers.
**upload** In communications, the process of transferring a copy of a file from a local computer to a remote computer by means of a modem or network.
**user-friendly** An adjective meaning easy to learn and easy to use.
**user interface** The portion of a program with which a user interacts.
**virus** A program that "infects" computer files (usually other executable programs) by inserting in those files copies of itself.
**wide area network (WAN)** A communications network that connects geographically separated areas.
**window** In applications and graphical interfaces, a portion of the screen that can contain its own document or message.
**word processor** An application program for manipulating text-based documents; the electronic equivalent of paper, pen, typewriter, eraser, and, most likely, dictionary and thesaurus.
**workstation** In general, a combination of input, output, and computing hardware that can be used for work by an individual.
**WYSIWYG** Pronounced "wizzywig." Acronym for "What you see is what you get." A display method that shows documents and graphics characters on the screen as they will appear when printed, WYSIWYG attempts to duplicate print output as closely as possible.

# SCIENCE AND TECHNOLOGY

## Inventions

| Inventions | Date | Inventor | Nation |
|---|---|---|---|
| Adding machine | **1642** | Pascal | French |
| Adding machine | **1885** | Burroughs | U.S. |
| Aerosol spray | **1926** | Rotheim | Norwegian |
| Air brake | **1868** | Westinghouse | U.S. |
| Air conditioning | **1911** | Carrier | U.S. |
| Air pump | **1654** | Guericke | German |
| Airplane, automatic pilot | **1912** | Sperry | U.S. |
| Airplane, experimental | **1896** | Langley | U.S. |
| Airplane jet engine | **1939** | Ohain | German |
| Airplane with motor | **1903** | Wright bros. | U.S. |
| Airplane, hydro | **1911** | Curtiss | U.S. |
| Airship | **1852** | Giffard | French |
| Airship, rigid dirigible | **1900** | Zeppelin | German |
| Arc welder | **1919** | Thomson | U.S. |
| Aspartame | **1965** | Schlatter | U.S. |
| Autogyro | **1920** | de la Cierva | Spanish |
| Automobile, differential gear | **1885** | Benz | German |
| Automobile, electric | **1892** | Morrison | U.S. |
| Automobile, exp'mtl | **1864** | Marcus | Austrian |
| Automobile, gasoline | **1889** | Daimler | German |
| Automobile, gasoline | **1892** | Duryea | U.S. |
| Automobile magneto | **1897** | Bosch | German |
| Automobile muffler | **1904** | Pope | U.S. |
| Automobile self-starter | **1911** | Kettering | U.S. |
| Babbitt metal | **1839** | Babbitt | U.S. |
| Bakelite | **1907** | Baekeland | Belg., U.S. |
| Balloon | **1783** | Montgolfier | French |
| Barometer | **1643** | Torricelli | Italian |
| Bicycle, modern | **1885** | Starley | English |
| Bifocal lens | **1780** | Franklin | U.S. |
| Block signals, railway | **1867** | Hall | U.S. |
| Bomb, depth | **1916** | Tait | U.S. |
| Bottle machine | **1895** | Owens | U.S. |
| Braille printing | **1829** | Braille | French |
| Burner, gas | **1855** | Bunsen | German |
| Calculating machine | **1833** | Babbage | English |
| Calculator, electronic pocket | **1972** | Merryman, Van Tassel | U.S. |
| Camera, Kodak | **1888** | Eastman, Walker | U.S. |
| Camera, Polaroid Land | **1948** | Land | U.S. |
| Car coupler | **1873** | Janney | U.S. |
| Carburetor, gasoline | **1893** | Maybach | German |
| Card time recorder | **1894** | [illegible] | U.S. |
| Carding machine | **1797** | Whittemore | U.S. |
| Carpet sweeper | **1876** | Bissell | U.S. |
| Cash register | **1879** | Ritty | U.S. |
| Cassette, audio | **1963** | Philips Co. | Dutch |
| Cassette, videotape | **1969** | Sony | Japanese |
| Cathode ray oscilloscope | **1897** | Braun | German |
| Cathode ray tube | **1878** | Crookes | English |
| CAT, or CT, scan (computerized tomography) | **1973** | Hounsfield | English |
| Cellophane | **1908** | Brandenberger | Swiss |
| Celluloid | **1870** | Hyatt | U.S. |
| Cement, Portland | **1824** | Aspdin | English |
| Chronometer | **1761** | Harrison | English |
| Circuit breaker | **1925** | Hilliard | U.S. |
| Circuit, integrated | **1959** | Kilby, Noyce, Texas Instr. | U.S. |
| Clock, pendulum | **1657** | Huygens | Dutch |
| Coaxial cable system | **1929** | Affel, Espensched | U.S. |
| Coke oven | **1893** | Hoffman | Austrian |
| Compressed air rock drill | **1871** | Ingersoll | U.S. |
| Comptometer | **1887** | Felt | U.S. |
| Computer, automatic sequence | **1944** | Aiken, et al. | U.S. |
| Computer, mini | **1960** | Digital Corp | U.S. |
| Condenser microphone (telephone) | **1916** | Wente | U.S. |
| Contraceptive, oral | **1954** | Pincus, Rock | U.S. |
| Corn, hybrid | **1917** | Jones | U.S. |
| Cotton gin | **1793** | Whitney | U.S. |
| Cream separator | **1878** | DeLaval | Swedish |
| Cultivator, disc | **1878** | Mallon | U.S. |
| Cystoscope | **1878** | Nitze | German |
| Diesel engine | **1895** | Diesel | German |
| Disc, compact | **1972** | RCA | U.S. |
| Disk, floppy | **1970** | IBM | U.S. |
| Disc player, compact | **1979** | Sony, Philips Co. | Japan, Dutch |
| Disk, video | **1972** | Philips Co. | Dutch |
| Dynamite | **1866** | Nobel | Swedish |
| Dynamo, continuous current | **1871** | Gramme | Belgian |
| Dynamo, hydrogen cooled | **1915** | Schuler | U.S. |
| Electric battery | **1800** | Volta | Italian |
| Electric fan | **1882** | Wheeler | U.S. |
| Electrocardiograph | **1903** | Einthoven | Dutch |
| Electroencephalograph | **1929** | Berger | German |
| Electromagnet | **1824** | Sturgeon | English |
| Electron spectrometer | **1944** | Deutsch, Elliott, Evans | U.S. |
| Electron tube multigrid | **1913** | Langmuir | U.S. |
| Electroplating | **1805** | Brugnatelli | Italian |
| Electrostatic generator | **1929** | Van de Graaff | U.S. |
| Elevator brake | **1852** | Otis | U.S. |
| Elevator, push button | **1922** | Larson | U.S. |
| Engine, automatic transmission | **1910** | Fottinger | German |
| Engine, coal-gas 4-cycle | **1876** | Otto | German |
| Engine, compression ignition | **1883** | Daimler | German |
| Engine, electric ignition | **1883** | Benz | German |
| Engine, gas, compound | **1926** | Eickemeyer | U.S. |
| Engine, gasoline | **1872** | Brayton, Geo. | U.S. |
| Engine, gasoline | **1889** | Daimler | German |
| Engine, jet | **1930** | Whittle | English |
| Engine, steam, piston | **1705** | Newcomen | English |
| Engine, steam, piston | **1769** | Watt | Scottish |
| Engraving, half-tone | **1852** | Talbot | U.S. |
| Fiberglass | **1938** | Owens-Corning | U.S. |
| Fiber optics | **1955** | Kapany | English |
| Filament, tungsten | **1913** | Coolidge | U.S. |
| Flanged rail | **1831** | Stevens | U.S. |
| Flatiron, electric | **1882** | Seely | U.S. |
| Food, frozen | **1924** | Birdseye | U.S. |
| Freon (low-boiling fluorine compounds) | **1930** | Midgley, et al. | U.S. |
| Furnace (for steel) | **1858** | Siemens | German |
| Galvanometer | **1820** | Sweigger | German |
| Gas discharge tube | **1922** | Hull | U.S. |
| Gas lighting | **1792** | Murdoch | Scottish |
| Gas mantle | **1885** | Welsbach | Austrian |
| Gasoline (lead ethyl) | **1922** | Midgley | U.S. |
| Gasoline, cracked | **1913** | Burton | U.S. |
| Gasoline, high octane | **1930** | Ipatieff | Russian |
| Geiger counter | **1913** | Geiger | German |
| Glass, laminated safety | **1909** | Benedictus | French |
| Glider | **1853** | Cayley | English |
| Gun, breechloader | **1811** | Thornton | U.S. |
| Gun, Browning | **1897** | Browning | U.S. |
| Gun, magazine | **1875** | Hotchkiss | U.S. |
| Gun, silencer | **1908** | Maxim, H.P. | U.S. |
| Guncotton | **1847** | Schoenbein | German |
| Gyrocompass | **1911** | Sperry | U.S. |
| Gyroscope | **1852** | Foucault | French |
| Harvester-thresher | **1818** | Lane | U.S. |
| Heart, artificial | **1982** | Jarvik | U.S. |
| Helicopter | **1939** | Sikorsky | U.S. |
| Hydrometer | **1768** | Baume | French |
| Hydrogen bomb | **1952** | U.S. government scientists | U.S |
| Ice-making machine | **1851** | Gorrie | U.S. |
| Iron lung | **1928** | Drinker, Slaw | U.S. |
| Kaleidoscope | **1817** | Brewster | Scottish |
| Kinetoscope | **1889** | Edison | U.S. |
| Lacquer, nitrocellulose | **1921** | Flaherty | U.S. |
| Lamp, arc | **1847** | Staite | English |
| Lamp, fluorescent | **1938** | General Electric, Westinghouse | U.S. |
| Lamp, incandescent | **1879** | Edison | U.S. |
| Lamp, incand., frosted | **1924** | Pipkin | U.S. |
| Lamp, incand., gas | **1913** | Langmuir | U.S. |
| Lamp, klieg | **1911** | Kliegl, A. & J. | U.S. |
| Lamp, mercury vapor | **1912** | Hewitt | U.S. |
| Lamp, miner's safety | **1816** | Davy | English |
| Lamp, neon | **1909** | Claude | French |
| Lathe, turret | **1845** | Fitch | U.S. |
| Launderette | **1934** | Cantrell | U.S. |
| Lens, achromatic | **1758** | Dollond | English |
| Lens, fused bifocal | **1908** | Borsch | U.S. |
| Leyden jar (condenser) | **1745** | von Kleist | German |
| Lightning rod | **1752** | Franklin | U.S. |
| Linoleum | **1860** | Walton | English |
| Linotype | **1884** | Mergenthaler | U.S. |
| Lock, cylinder | **1851** | Yale | U.S. |
| Locomotive, electric | **1851** | Vail | U.S. |
| Locomotive, exp'mtl | **1802** | Trevithick | English |
| Locomotive, exp'mtl | **1812** | Fenton, et al. | English |
| Locomotive, exp'mtl | **1813** | Hedley | English |
| Locomotive, exp'mtl | **1814** | Stephenson | English |
| Locomotive, practical | **1829** | Stephenson | English |
| Locomotive, 1st U.S. | **1830** | Cooper, P. | U.S. |
| Loom, power | **1785** | Cartwright | English |
| Loudspeaker, dynamic | **1924** | Rice, Kellogg | U.S. |

*(continued)*

## Inventions *(continued)*

| Inventions | Date | Inventor | Nation |
|---|---|---|---|
| Machine gun | 1861 | Gatling | U.S. |
| Machine gun, improved | 1872 | Hotchkiss | U.S. |
| Machine gun (Maxim) | 1883 | Maxim, H.S. | U.S., Eng. |
| Magnet, electro | 1828 | Henry | U.S. |
| Mantle, gas | 1885 | Welsbach | Austrian |
| Mason jar | 1858 | Mason, J. | U.S. |
| Match, friction | 1827 | John Walker | English |
| Mercerized textiles | 1843 | Mercer, J. | English |
| Meter, induction | 1888 | Shallenberg | U.S. |
| Metronome | 1816 | Malezel | German |
| Microcomputer | 1973 | Truong, et al. | French |
| Micrometer | 1636 | Gascoigne | English |
| Microphone | 1877 | Berliner | U.S. |
| Microprocessor | 1971 | Intel Corp. | U.S. |
| Microscope, compound | 1590 | Janssen | Dutch |
| Microscope, electronic | 1931 | Knoll, Ruska | German |
| Microscope, field ion | 1951 | Mueller | German |
| Monitor, warship | 1861 | Ericsson | U.S. |
| Monotype | 1887 | Lanston | U.S. |
| Motor, AC | 1892 | Tesla | U.S. |
| Motor, DC | 1837 | Davenport | U.S. |
| Motor, induction | 1887 | Tesla | U.S. |
| Motorcycle | 1885 | Daimler | German |
| Movie machine | 1894 | Jenkins | U.S. |
| Movie, panoramic | 1952 | Waller | U.S. |
| Movie, talking | 1927 | Warner Bros. | U.S. |
| Mower, lawn | 1831 | Budding, Ferrabee | English |
| Mowing machine | 1822 | Bailey | U.S. |
| Neoprene | 1930 | Carothers | U.S. |
| Nylon synthetic | 1930 | Carothers | U.S. |
| Nylon | 1937 | Du Pont lab | U.S. |
| Oil cracking furnace | 1891 | Gavrilov | Russian |
| Oil filled power cable | 1921 | Emanueli | Italian |
| Oleomargarine | 1869 | Mege-Mouries | French |
| Ophthalmoscope | 1851 | Helmholtz | German |
| Paper | 105 | Lun | Chinese |
| Paper machine | 1809 | Dickinson | U.S. |
| Parachute | 1785 | Blanchard | French |
| Pen, ballpoint | 1888 | Loud | U.S. |
| Pen, fountain | 1884 | Waterman | U.S. |
| Pen, steel | 1780 | Harrison | English |
| Pendulum | 1583 | Galileo | Italian |
| Percussion cap | 1807 | Forsythe | Scottish |
| Phonograph | 1877 | Edison | U.S. |
| Photo, color | 1892 | Ives | U.S. |
| Photo film, celluloid | 1893 | Reichenbach | U.S. |
| Photo film, transparent | 1884 | Eastman, Goodwin | U.S. |
| Photoelectric cell | 1895 | Elster | German |
| Photographic paper | 1835 | Talbot | English |
| Photography | 1835 | Talbot | English |
| Photography | 1835 | Daguerre | French |
| Photography | 1816 | Niepce | French |
| Photophone | 1880 | Bell | U.S.-Scot. |
| Phototelegraphy | 1925 | Bell Labs | U.S. |
| Piano | 1709 | Cristofori | Italian |
| Piano, player | 1863 | Fourneaux | French |
| Pin, safety | 1849 | Hunt | U.S. |
| Pistol (revolver) | 1836 | Colt | U.S. |
| Plow, cast iron | 1785 | Ransome | English |
| Plow, disc | 1896 | Hardy | U.S. |
| Pneumatic hammer | 1890 | King | U.S. |
| Powder, smokeless | 1884 | Vieille | French |
| Printing press, rotary | 1845 | Hoe | U.S. |
| Printing press, web | 1865 | Bullock | U.S. |
| Propeller, screw | 1804 | Stevens | U.S. |
| Propeller, screw | 1837 | Ericsson | Swedish |
| Pulsars | 1967 | Bell | English |
| Punch card accounting | 1889 | Hollerith | U.S. |
| Quasars | 1963 | Schmidt | U.S. |
| Radar | 1940 | Watson-Watt | Scottish |
| Radio amplifier | 1906 | De Forest | U.S. |
| Radio beacon | 1928 | Donovan | U.S. |
| Radio crystal oscillator | 1918 | Nicolson | U.S. |
| Radio receiver, cascade tuning | 1913 | Alexanderson | U.S. |
| Radio receiver, heterodyne | 1913 | Fessenden | U.S. |
| Radio transmitter triode modulation | 1914 | Alexanderson | U.S. |
| Radio tube diode | 1905 | Fleming | English |
| Radio tube oscillator | 1915 | De Forest | U.S. |
| Radio tube triode | 1906 | De Forest | U.S. |
| Radio, signals | 1895 | Marconi | Italian |
| Radio, magnetic detector | 1902 | Marconi | Italian |
| Radio FM, 2-path | 1933 | Armstrong | U.S. |
| Rayon (acetate) | 1895 | Cross | English |
| Rayon (cuprammonium) | 1890 | Despeissis | French |
| Rayon (nitrocellulose) | 1884 | Chardonnet | French |
| Razor, electric | 1917 | Schick | U.S. |
| Razor, safety | 1895 | Gillette | U.S. |
| Reaper | 1834 | McCormick | U.S. |

| Inventions | Date | Inventor | Nation |
|---|---|---|---|
| Record, cylinder | 1887 | Bell, Tainter | U.S. |
| Record, disc | 1887 | Berliner | U.S. |
| Record, long playing | 1947 | Goldmark | U.S. |
| Record, wax cylinder | 1888 | Edison | U.S. |
| Refrigerator car | 1868 | David | U.S. |
| Resin, synthetic | 1931 | Hill | English |
| Richter scale | 1935 | Richter | U.S. |
| Rifle, repeating | 1860 | Spencer | U.S. |
| Rocket engine | 1926 | Goddard | U.S. |
| Rubber, vulcanized | 1839 | Goodyear | U.S. |
| Saccharin | 1879 | Remsen, Fahlberg | U.S. |
| Saw, band | 1808 | Newberry | English |
| Saw, circular | 1777 | Miller | English |
| Sewing machine | 1846 | Howe | U.S. |
| Shoe-sewing machine | 1860 | McKay | U.S. |
| Shrapnel shell | 1784 | Shrapnel | English |
| Shuttle, flying | 1733 | Kay | English |
| Sleeping-car | 1865 | Pullman | U.S. |
| Slide rule | 1620 | Oughtred | English |
| Soap, hardwater | 1928 | Bertsch | German |
| Spectroscope | 1859 | Kirchoff, Bunsen | German |
| Spectroscope (mass) | 1918 | Dempster | U.S. |
| Spinning jenny | c. 1764 | Hargreaves | English |
| Spinning mule | 1779 | Crompton | English |
| Steamboat, exp'mtl | 1778 | Jouffroy | French |
| Steamboat, exp'mtl | 1785 | Fitch | U.S. |
| Steamboat, exp'mtl | 1787 | Rumsey | U.S. |
| Steamboat, exp'mtl | 1788 | Miller | Scottish |
| Steamboat, exp'mtl | 1803 | Fulton | U.S. |
| Steamboat, exp'mtl | 1804 | Stevens | U.S. |
| Steamboat, practical | 1802 | Symington | Scottish |
| Steamboat, practical | 1807 | Fulton | U.S. |
| Steam car | 1770 | Cugnot | French |
| Steam turbine | 1884 | Parsons | English |
| Steel (converter) | 1856 | Bessemer | English |
| Steel alloy | 1891 | Harvey | U.S. |
| Steel alloy, high-speed | 1901 | Taylor, White | U.S. |
| Steel, electric | 1900 | Heroult | French |
| Steel, manganese | 1884 | Hadfield | English |
| Steel, stainless | 1916 | Brearley | English |
| Stereoscope | 1838 | Wheatstone | English |
| Stethoscope | 1819 | Laennec | French |
| Stethoscope, binaural | 1840 | Cammann | U.S. |
| Stock ticker | 1870 | Edison | U.S. |
| Storage battery, rechargeable | 1859 | Plante | French |
| Stove, electric | 1896 | Hadaway | U.S. |
| Submarine | 1891 | Holland | U.S. |
| Submarine, even keel | 1894 | Lake | U.S. |
| Submarine, torpedo | 1776 | Bushnell | U.S. |
| Superconductivity (BCS theory) | 1957 | Bardeen, Cooper, Schreiffer | U.S. |
| Tank, military | 1914 | Swinton | English |
| Tape recorder, magnetic | 1899 | Poulsen | Danish |
| Teflon | 1938 | Du Pont | U.S. |
| Telegraph, magnetic | 1837 | Morse | U.S. |
| Telegraph, quadruplex | 1864 | Edison | U.S. |
| Telegraph, railroad | 1887 | Woods | U.S. |
| Telegraph, wireless high frequency | 1895 | Marconi | Italian |
| Telephone | 1876 | Bell | U.S.-Scot. |
| Telephone amplifier | 1912 | De Forest | U.S. |
| Telephone, automatic | 1891 | Stowger | U.S. |
| Telephone, radio | 1900 | Poulsen, Fessenden | Danish |
| Telephone, radio | 1906 | De Forest | U.S. |
| Telephone, radio, l. d. | 1915 | AT&T | U.S. |
| Telephone, recording | 1898 | Poulsen | Danish |
| Telephone, wireless | 1899 | Collins | U.S. |
| Telescope | 1608 | Lippershey | Neth. |
| Telescope | 1609 | Galileo | Italian |
| Telescope, astronomical | 1611 | Kepler | German |
| Teletype | 1928 | Morkrum, Kleinschmidt | U.S. |
| Television, iconoscope | 1923 | Zworykin | U.S. |
| Television, electronic | 1927 | Farnsworth | U.S. |
| Television, mech. scanner | 1923 | Baird | Scottish |
| Thermometer | 1593 | Galileo | Italian |
| Thermometer | 1730 | Reaumur | French |
| Thermometer, mercury | 1714 | Fahrenheit | German |
| Time recorder | 1890 | Bundy | U.S. |
| Time, self-regulator | 1918 | Bryce | U.S. |
| Tire, double-tube | 1845 | Thomson | Scottish |
| Tire, pneumatic | 1888 | Dunlop | Scottish |
| Toaster, automatic | 1918 | Strite | U.S. |
| Toilet, flush | 1589 | Harington | English |
| Tool, pneumatic | 1865 | Law | English |
| Torpedo, marine | 1804 | Fulton | U.S. |
| Tractor, crawler | 1904 | Holt | U.S. |
| Transformer, AC | 1885 | Stanley | U.S. |
| Transistor | 1947 | Shockley, Brattain, Bardeen | U.S. |

| Inventions | Date | Inventor | Nation |
|---|---|---|---|
| Trolley car, electric | 1884-87 | Van DePoele, Sprague | U.S. |
| Tungsten, ductile | 1912 | Coolidge | U.S. |
| Tupperware | 1945 | Tupper | U.S. |
| Turbine, gas | 1849 | Bourdin | French |
| Turbine, hydraulic | 1849 | Francis | U.S. |
| Turbine, steam | 1884 | Parsons | English |
| Type, movable | 1447 | Gutenberg | German |
| Typewriter | 1867 | Sholes, Soule, Glidden | U.S. |
| Vacuum cleaner, electric | 1907 | Spangler | U.S. |
| Velcro | 1948 | de Mestral | Swiss |
| Video game ("Pong") | 1972 | Buschnel | U.S. |
| Video home system (VHS) | 1975 | Matsushita, JVC | Japanese |
| Washer, electric | 1901 | Fisher | U.S. |
| Welding, atomic hydrogen | 1924 | Langmuir, Palmer | U.S. |
| Welding, electric | 1877 | Thomson | U.S. |
| Wind tunnel | 1912 | Eiffel | French |
| Wire, barbed | 1874 | Glidden | U.S. |
| Wire, barbed | 1875 | Haish | U.S. |
| Wrench, double-acting | 1913 | Owen | U.S. |
| X-ray tube | 1913 | Coolidge | U.S. |

## Discoveries and Innovations: Chemistry, Physics, Biology, Medicine

| | Date | Discoverer | Nation |
|---|---|---|---|
| Acetylene gas | 1862 | Berthelot | French |
| ACTH | 1927 | Evans, Long | U.S. |
| Adrenalin | 1901 | Takamine | Japanese |
| Aluminum, electrolytic process | 1886 | Hall | U.S. |
| Aluminum, isolated | 1825 | Oersted | Danish |
| Anesthesia, ether | 1842 | Long | U.S. |
| Anesthesia, local | 1885 | Koller | Austrian |
| Anesthesia, spinal | 1898 | Bier | German |
| Aniline dye | 1856 | Perkin | English |
| Anti-rabies | 1885 | Pasteur | French |
| Antiseptic surgery | 1867 | Lister | English |
| Antitoxin, diphtheria | 1891 | Von Behring | German |
| Argyrol | 1897 | Bayer | German |
| Arsphenamine | 1910 | Ehrlich | German |
| Aspirin | 1889 | Dresser | German |
| Atabrine | 1932 | Mietzsch, et al. | German |
| Atomic numbers | 1913 | Moseley | English |
| Atomic theory | 1803 | Dalton | English |
| Atomic time clock | 1948 | Lyons | U.S. |
| Atomic time clock, cesium beam | 1948 | Essen | English |
| Atom-smashing theory | 1919 | Rutherford | English |
| Bacitracin | 1945 | Johnson, et al. | U.S. |
| Bacteria (described) | 1676 | Leeuwenhoek | Dutch |
| Barbital | 1903 | Fischer | German |
| Bleaching powder | 1798 | Tennant | English |
| Blood, circulation | 1628 | Harvey | English |
| Bordeaux mixture | 1885 | Millardet | French |
| Bromie from sea | 1924 | Edgar Kramer | U.S. |
| Calcium carbide | 1888 | Wilson | U.S. |
| Calculus | 1670 | Newton | English |
| Camphor synthetic | 1896 | Haller | French |
| Canning (food) | 1804 | Appert | French |
| Carbomycin | 1952 | Tanner | U.S. |
| Carbon oxides | 1925 | Fisher | German |
| Chloamphenicol | 1947 | Burkholder | U.S. |
| Chlorine | 1774 | Scheele | Swedish |
| Chloroform | 1831 | Guthrie, S. | U.S. |
| Chlortetracycline | 1948 | Duggen | U.S. |
| Classification of plants and animals | 1735 | Linnaeus | Swedish |
| Cocaine | 1860 | Niermann | German |
| Combustion explained | 1777 | Lavoisier | French |
| Conditioned reflex | 1914 | Pavlov | Russian |
| Cortisone | 1936 | Kendall | U.S. |
| Cortisone, synthesis | 1946 | Sarett | U.S. |
| Cosmic rays | 1910 | Gockel | Swiss |
| Cyanamide | 1905 | Frank, Caro | German |
| Cyclotron | 1930 | Lawrence | U.S. |
| DDT (not applied as insecticide until 1939) | 1874 | Zeidler | German |
| Deuterium | 1932 | Urey, Brickwedde, Murphy | U.S. |
| DNA (structure) | 1951 | Crick | English |
| | | Watson | U.S. |
| | | Wilkins | English |
| Electric resistance (law) | 1827 | Ohm | German |
| Electric waves | 1888 | Hertz | German |
| Electrolysis | 1852 | Faraday | English |
| Electromagnetism | 1819 | Oersted | Danish |
| Electron | 1897 | Thomson, J. | English |
| Electron diffraction | 1936 | Thomson, G. | English |
| | | Davisson | U.S. |
| Electroshock treatment | 1938 | Cerletti, Bini | Italian |
| Erythromycin | 1952 | McGuire | U.S. |
| Evolution, natural selection | 1858 | Darwin | English |
| Falling bodies, law | 1590 | Galileo | Italian |
| Gases, law of combining volumes | 1808 | Gay-Lussac | French |
| Geometry, analytic | 1619 | Descartes | French |
| Gold (cyanide process for extraction) | 1887 | MacArthur, Forest | British |
| Gravitation, law | 1687 | Newton | English |
| Holograph | 1948 | Gabor | British |
| Human heart transplant | 1967 | Barnard | S. African |
| Human immunodeficiency virus identified | 1984 | Montagnier, Gallo | French, U.S. |
| Indigo, synthesis of | 1880 | Baeyer | German |
| Induction, electric | 1830 | Henry | U.S. |
| Insulin | 1922 | Banting, Best, Macleod | Canadian, Scottish |
| Intelligence testing | 1905 | Binet, Simon | French |
| In vitro fertilization | 1978 | Steptoe, Edwards | English |
| Isoniazid | 1952 | Hoffman-La-Roche | U.S. |
| | | Domagk | German |
| Isotopes, theory | 1912 | Soddy | English |
| Laser (light amplification by stimulated emission of radiation) | 1957 | Gould | U.S. |
| Lasting machine | 1883 | Jan Matzelieger | U.S. |
| Light, velocity | 1675 | Roemer | Danish |
| Light, wave theory | 1690 | Huygens | Dutch |
| Lithography | 1796 | Senefelder | Bohemian |
| Logarithms | 1614 | Napier | Scottish |
| Lobotomy | 1935 | Egas Moniz | Portuguese |
| LSD-25 | 1943 | Hoffman | Swiss |
| Mendelian laws | 1866 | Mendel | Austrian |
| Mercator projection (map) | 1568 | Mercator (Kremer) | Flemish |
| Methanol | 1661 | Boyle | Irish |
| Milk condensation | 1853 | Borden | U.S. |
| Molecular hypothesis | 1811 | Avogadro | Italian |
| Motion, laws of | 1687 | Newton | English |
| Neomycin | 1949 | Waksman, Lechevalier | U.S. |
| Neutron | 1932 | Chadwick | English |
| Nitric acid | 1648 | Glauber | German |
| Nitric oxide | 1772 | Priestley | English |
| Nitroglycerin | 1846 | Sobrero | Italian |
| Oil cracking process | 1891 | Dewar | U.S. |
| Oxygen | 1774 | Priestley | English |
| Oxytetracycline | 1950 | Finlay, et al. | U.S. |
| Ozone | 1840 | Schonbein | German |
| Paper, sulfite process | 1867 | Tilghman | U.S. |
| Paper, wood pulp, sulfate process | 1884 | Dahl | German |
| Penicillin | 1929 | Fleming | Scottish |
| practical use | 1941 | Florey, Chain | English |
| Periodic law and table of elements | 1869 | Mendeleyev | Russian |
| Planetary motion, laws | 1609 | Kepler | German |
| Plutonium fission | 1940 | Kennedy, Wahl, Seaborg, Segre | U.S. |
| Polymyxin | 1947 | Ainsworth | English |
| Positron | 1932 | Anderson | U.S. |
| Proton | 1919 | Rutherford | N. Zealand |
| Psychoanalysis | 1900 | Freud | Austrian |
| Quantum theory | 1900 | Planck | German |
| Quasars | 1963 | Matthews, Sandage | U.S. |
| Quinine synthetic | 1946 | Woodward, Doering | U.S. |
| Radioactivity | 1896 | Becquerel | French |
| Radiocarbon dating | 1947 | Libby | U.S. |

*(continued)*

## Discoveries and Innovations *(continued)*

| | Date | Discoverer | Nation |
|---|---|---|---|
| Radium | 1898 | Curie, Pierre<br>Curie, Marie | French<br>Pol.-Fr. |
| Relativity theory | 1905 | Einstein | German |
| Reserpine | 1949 | Jal Vaikl | Indian |
| Schick test | 1913 | Schick | U.S. |
| Silicon | 1823 | Berzelius | Swedish |
| Smallpox eradication | 1979 | World Health Organization | UN |
| Streptomycin | 1945 | Schatz, Waksman | U.S. |
| Sulfanilamide | 1935 | Bovet, Trefouel | French |
| Sulfanilamide theory | 1908 | Gelmo | German |
| Sulfapyridine | 1938 | Ewins, Phelps | English |
| Sulfathiazole | 1939 | Fosbinder, Walter | U.S. |
| Sulfuric acid | 1831 | Phillips | English |
| Sulfuric acid, lead | 1746 | Roebuck | English |
| Thiacetazone | 1950 | Belmisch, Mietzsch, Domagk | German |
| Tuberculin | 1890 | Koch | German |
| Uranium fission theory | 1939 | Hahn, Meitner, Strassmann<br>Bohr<br>Fermi<br>Einstein, Pegram, Wheeler | German<br>Danish<br>Italian<br>U.S. |
| Uranium fission, atomic reactor | 1942 | Fermi, Szilard | U.S. |
| Vaccine, measles | 1954 | Enders, Peebles | U.S. |
| Vaccine, meningitis (first conjugate) | 1987 | Gordon, et. al., Connaught Lab., Inc. | U.S. |
| Vaccine, polio | 1955 | Salk | U.S. |
| Vaccine, polio, oral | 1955 | Sabin | U.S. |
| Vaccine, rabies | 1885 | Pasteur | French |
| Vaccine, smallpox | 1796 | Jenner | English |
| Vaccine, typhus | 1909 | Nicolle | French |
| Vaccine, varicella | 1974 | Takahashi | Japan |
| Van Allen belts, radiation | 1958 | Van Allen | U.S. |
| Vitamin A | 1913 | McCollum, Davis | U.S. |
| Vitamin B | 1916 | McCollum | U.S. |
| Vitamin C | 1928 | Szent-Gyorgyi, King | U.S. |
| Vitamin D | 1922 | McCollum | U.S. |
| Vitamin K | 1935 | Dam, Doisy | U.S. |
| Wassermann test for syphilis | 1906 | Wassermann | German |
| Xerography | 1938 | Carlson | U.S. |
| X ray | 1895 | Roentgen | German |

## Top 20 Corporations Receiving U.S. Patents in 1995

Source: *Technology Assessment and Forecast Program,* Patent and Trademark Office, U.S. Department of Commerce

| Rank | Company | Number of patents | Rank | Company | Number of patents |
|---|---|---|---|---|---|
| 1. | International Business Machines Corp. | 1,468 | 11. | General Electric Company | 765 |
| 2. | Canon K. K. | 1,169 | 12. | Fujitsu, Ltd. | 732 |
| 3. | Motorola, Inc. | 1,108 | 13. | AT&T Corp. | 654 |
| 4. | NEC Corp. | 1,009 | 14. | Minnesota Mining & Manufacturing Co. | 598 |
| 4. | Toshiba Corp. | 1,009 | 15. | Xerox Corp. | 554 |
| 6. | Mitsubishi Denki K. K. | 975 | 16. | Texas Instruments, Inc. | 529 |
| 7. | Hitachi, Ltd. | 924 | 17. | U.S. Philips Corp. | 527 |
| 8. | Matsushita Electric Industrial Co., Ltd. | 921 | 18. | Hewlett-Packard Corp. | 492 |
| 9. | Sony Corp. | 805 | 19. | E. I. du Pont de Nemours & Co. | 445 |
| 10. | Eastman Kodak Company | 784 | 20. | Sharp K. K. | 435 |

## Chemical Elements, Atomic Weights, Discoverers

Source: Glenn T. Seaborg, Ph.D., Ernest Orlando Lawrence Berkeley National Laboratory, Berkeley, CA

Atomic weights, based on the exact number 12 as the assigned atomic mass of the principal isotope of carbon, carbon 12, are provided through the courtesy of the International Union of Pure and Applied Chemistry and Butterworth Scientific Publications. For the radioactive elements, with the exception of uranium and thorium, the mass number of either the isotope of longest half-life (*) or the better known isotope (**) is given.

| Chemical element | Symbol | Atomic number | Atomic weight | Year discov. | Discoverer |
|---|---|---|---|---|---|
| Actinium | Ac | 89 | 227* | 1899 | Debierne |
| Aluminum | Al | 13 | 26.9815 | 1825 | Oersted |
| Americium | Am | 95 | 243* | 1944 | Seaborg, et al. |
| Antimony | Sb | 51 | 121.75 | 1450 | Valentine |
| Argon | Ar | 18 | 39.948 | 1894 | Rayleigh, Ramsay |
| Arsenic | As | 33 | 74.9216 | 13th c. | Albertus Magnus |
| Astatine | At | 85 | 210* | 1940 | Corson, et al. |
| Barium | Ba | 56 | 137.34 | 1808 | Davy |
| Berkelium | Bk | 97 | 249** | 1949 | Thompson, Ghiorso, Seaborg |
| Beryllium | Be | 4 | 9.0122 | 1798 | Vauquelin |
| Bismuth | Bi | 83 | 208.980 | 15th c. | Valentine |
| Boron | B | 5 | 10.811[a] | 1808 | Gay-Lussac, Thenard |
| Bromine | Br | 35 | 79.904[b] | 1826 | Balard |
| Cadmium | Cd | 48 | 112.40 | 1817 | Stromeyer |
| Calcium | Ca | 20 | 40.08 | 1808 | Davy |
| Californium | Cf | 98 | 251* | 1950 | Thompson, et al. |
| Carbon | C | 6 | 12.01115[a] | BC | unknown |
| Cerium | Ce | 58 | 140.12 | 1803 | Klaproth |
| Cesium | Cs | 55 | 132.905 | 1860 | Bunsen, Kirchhoff |
| Chlorine | Cl | 17 | 35.453[b] | 1774 | Scheele |
| Chromium | Cr | 24 | 51.996[b] | 1797 | Vauquelin |
| Cobalt | Co | 27 | 58.9332 | 1735 | Brandt |
| Copper | Cu | 29 | 63.546[b] | BC | unknown |
| Curium | Cm | 96 | 247* | 1944 | Seaborg, James, Ghiorso |
| Dysprosium | Dy | 66 | 162.50* | 1886 | Boisbaudran |
| Einsteinium | Es | 99 | 254** | 1952 | Ghiorso, et al. |
| Erbium | Er | 68 | 167.26 | 1843 | Mosander |
| Europium | Eu | 63 | 151.96 | 1901 | Demarcay |
| Fermium | Fm | 100 | 257* | 1953 | Ghiorso, et al. |
| Fluorine | F | 9 | 18.9984 | 1771 | Scheele |

| Chemical element | Symbol | Atomic number | Atomic weight | Year discov. | Discoverer |
|---|---|---|---|---|---|
| Francium | Fr | 87 | 223* | 1939 | Perey |
| Gadolinium | Gd | 64 | 157.25 | 1886 | Marignac |
| Gallium | Ga | 31 | 69.72 | 1875 | Boisbaudran |
| Germanium | Ge | 32 | 72.59 | 1886 | Winkler |
| Gold | Au | 79 | 196.967 | BC | unknown |
| Hafnium | Hf | 72 | 178.49 | 1923 | Coster, Hevesy |
| Hahnium | Ha | 105 | 262* | 1970 | Ghiorso, et al. |
| Hassium | Hs | 108 | 265* | 1984 | Münzenberg, et al. |
| Helium | He | 2 | 4.0026 | 1868 | Janssen, Lockyer |
| Holmium | Ho | 67 | 164.930 | 1878 | Soret, Delafontaine |
| Hydrogen | H | 1 | 1.00797[a] | 1766 | Cavendish |
| Indium | In | 49 | 114.82 | 1863 | Reich, Richter |
| Iodine | I | 53 | 126.9044 | 1811 | Courtois |
| Iridium | Ir | 77 | 192.2 | 1804 | Tennant |
| Iron | Fe | 26 | 55.847[b] | BC | unknown |
| Krypton | Kr | 36 | 83.80 | 1898 | Ramsay, Travers |
| Lanthanum | La | 57 | 138.91 | 1839 | Mosander |
| Lawrencium | Lr | 103 | 262* | 1961 | Ghiorso, T. Sikkeland, A.E. Larsh, and R.M. Latimer |
| Lead | Pb | 82 | 207.19 | BC | unknown |
| Lithium | Li | 3 | 6.939 | 1817 | Arfvedson |
| Lutetium | Lu | 71 | 174.97 | 1907 | Welsbach, Urbain |
| Magnesium | Mg | 12 | 24.312 | 1829 | Bussy |
| Manganese | Mn | 25 | 54.9380 | 1774 | Gahn |
| Meitnerium | Mt | 109 | 266* | 1982 | Münzenberg, et al. |
| Mendelevium | Md | 101 | 258* | 1955 | Ghiorso, et al. |
| Mercury | Hg | 80 | 200.59 | BC | unknown |
| Molybdenum | Mo | 42 | 95.94 | 1782 | Hjelm |
| Neodymium | Nd | 60 | 144.24 | 1885 | Welsbach |
| Neon | Ne | 10 | 20.183 | 1898 | Ramsay, Travers |
| Neptunium | Np | 93 | 237* | 1940 | McMillan, Abelson |
| Nickel | Ni | 28 | 58.71 | 1751 | Cronstedt |
| Nielsbohrium | Ns | 107 | 262* | 1981 | Münzenberg, et al. |
| Niobium[1] | Nb | 41 | 92.906 | 1801 | Hatchett |
| Nitrogen | N | 7 | 14.0067 | 1772 | Rutherford |
| Nobelium | No | 102 | 259* | 1958 | Ghiorso, et al. |
| Osmium | Os | 76 | 190.2 | 1804 | Tennant |
| Oxygen | O | 8 | 15.9994[a] | 1774 | Priestley, Scheele |
| Palladium | Pd | 46 | 106.4 | 1803 | Wollaston |
| Phosphorus | P | 15 | 30.9738 | 1669 | Brand |
| Platinum | Pt | 78 | 195.09 | 1735 | Ulloa |
| Plutonium | Pu | 94 | 242** | 1940 | Seaborg, et al. |
| Polonium | Po | 84 | 210** | 1898 | P. and M. Curie |
| Potassium | K | 19 | 39.102 | 1807 | Davy |
| Praseodymium | Pr | 59 | 140.907 | 1885 | Welsbach |
| Promethium | Pm | 61 | 147** | 1945 | Glendenin, Marinsky, Coryell |
| Protactinium | Pa | 91 | 231* | 1917 | Hahn, Meitner |
| Radium | Ra | 88 | 226* | 1898 | P. and M. Curie, Bemont |
| Radon | Rn | 86 | 222* | 1900 | Dorn |
| Rhenium | Re | 75 | 186.2 | 1925 | Noddack, Tacke, Berg |
| Rhodium | Rh | 45 | 102.905 | 1803 | Wollaston |
| Rubidium | Rb | 37 | 85.47 | 1861 | Bunsen, Kirchhoff |
| Ruthenium | Ru | 44 | 101.07 | 1845 | Klaus |
| Rutherfordium | Rf | 104 | 261* | 1969 | Ghiorso, et al. |
| Samarium | Sm | 62 | 150.35 | 1879 | Boisbaudran |
| Scandium | Sc | 21 | 44.956 | 1879 | Nilson |
| Seaborgium | Sg | 106 | 266* | 1974 | Ghiorso, et al. |
| Selenium | Se | 34 | 78.96 | 1817 | Berzelius |
| Silicon | Si | 14 | 28.086[a] | 1823 | Berzelius |
| Silver | Ag | 47 | 107.868[b] | BC | unknown |
| Sodium | Na | 11 | 22.9898 | 1807 | Davy |
| Strontium | Sr | 38 | 87.62 | 1790 | Crawford |
| Sulfur | S | 16 | 32.064[a] | BC | unknown |
| Tantalum | Ta | 73 | 180.948 | 1802 | Ekeberg |
| Technetium | Tc | 43 | 99** | 1937 | Perrier and Segre |
| Tellurium | Te | 52 | 127.60 | 1782 | Von Reichenstein |
| Terbium | Tb | 65 | 158.924 | 1843 | Mosander |
| Thallium | Tl | 81 | 204.37 | 1861 | Crookes |
| Thorium | Th | 90 | 232.038 | 1828 | Berzelius |
| Thulium | Tm | 69 | 168.934 | 1879 | Cleve |
| Tin | Sn | 50 | 118.69 | BC | unknown |
| Titanium | Ti | 22 | 47.90 | 1791 | Gregor |
| Tungsten (Wolfram) | W | 74 | 183.85 | 1783 | d'Elhujar |
| Uranium | U | 92 | 238.03 | 1789 | Klaproth |
| Vanadium | V | 23 | 50.942 | 1830 | Sefstrom |
| Xenon | Xe | 54 | 131.30 | 1898 | Ramsay, Travers |
| Ytterbium | Yb | 70 | 173.04 | 1878 | Marignac |
| Yttrium | Y | 39 | 88.905 | 1794 | Gadolin |
| Zinc | Zn | 30 | 65.37 | BC | unknown |
| Zirconium | Zr | 40 | 91.22 | 1789 | Klaproth |

**Note:** 109 elements are listed here. In addition, elements 110-112 were discovered recently at the Society for Heavy Ion Research accelerator laboratory at Darmstadt, Germany, by a team led by Dr. Peter Armbruster; these elements have not yet been named. Elements 110 and 111, discovered in 1994, have atomic weights 271 and 272, respectively; element 112, discovered in 1996, has atomic weight 277. Because different nomenclature systems were in use, the names of elements 101 through 109 may vary. (1) Formerly Columbium. (a) Atomic weights so designated are known to be variable because of natural variations in isotopic composition. The observed ranges are: hydrogen±0.0001; boron±0.003; carbon±0.005; oxygen±0.0001; silicon±0.001; sulfur±0.003. (b) Atomic weights so designated are believed to have the following experimental uncertainties: chlorine±0.001; chromium±0.001; iron±0.003; copper±0.001; bromine±0.001; silver±0.001.

# METEOROLOGY

## National Weather Service Watches and Warnings

**Source:** National Weather Service, NOAA, U.S. Dept. of Commerce; *Glossary of Meteorology,* American Meteorological Society

National Weather Service forecasters issue a Severe Thunderstorm or Tornado Watch for a specific area where a severe convective storm that usually covers a relatively small geographic area or moves in a narrow path is sufficiently intense to threaten life and/or property. Examples include thunderstorms with large hail, damaging winds, and/or tornadoes. Additionally, excessive localized convective rains are classified as severe storms but are often the product of severe local storms. Such rainfall may result in related phenomena that threaten life and property, such as flash floods. Although cloud-to-ground lightning is not a criterion for severe local storms, it is acknowledged to be highly dangerous and a leading cause of deaths, injuries, and damage from thunderstorms.

A *Watch* alerts people that threatening weather is likely. Under a Watch, persons should remain alert for approaching storms, activate a plan for action, and monitor ongoing events closely. A *Warning* means that severe weather is occurring or has been indicated by radar; **immediate** action should be taken.

**Severe Thunderstorm**—A thunderstorm that produces a tornado, winds of at least 50 knots (58 mph), and/or hail at least 3/4 inch in diameter. A thunderstorm with winds of at least 35 knots (40 mph) and/or hail at least 1/2 inch in diameter is defined as approaching severe. A Severe Thunderstorm Watch is issued for a specific area where such storms are most likely to develop. A Severe Thunderstorm Warning indicates that a severe thunderstorm has been sighted or indicated by radar.

**Tornado**—A violent rotating column of air (winds up to 300 mph), usually pendant to a cumulonimbus cloud, with circulation reaching the ground. A tornado nearly always starts as a funnel cloud and may be accompanied by a loud roaring noise. On a local scale, it is the most destructive of all atmospheric phenomena. Tornado paths have varied in length from a few feet to nearly 300 miles (avg. 5 mi); in diameter from a few feet to more than a mile (avg. 220 yd); average forward speed, 30 mph.

**Cyclone**—An atmospheric circulation of winds rotating counterclockwise in the northern hemisphere and clockwise in the southern hemisphere. Tornadoes, hurricanes, and the lows shown on weather maps are all examples of cyclones of various size and intensity. Cyclones are usually accompanied by precipitation or stormy weather.

**Subtropical Storm**—An atmospheric circulation of one-minute sustained surface winds, 34 knots (39 mph) or more. Depending on its characteristics and intensity, it can develop into a tropical storm or a hurricane.

**Tropical Storm**—An atmospheric circulation of one-minute sustained surface winds within a range of 34 to 63 knots (39 to 73 mph). A *Tropical Storm Watch* is an announcement that a tropical storm or tropical storm conditions may pose a threat to coastal areas generally within 36 hours. A *Tropical Storm Warning* is an announcement that tropical storm conditions pose a threat along a specified segment of coastline within 24 hours.

**Hurricane**—A severe cyclone originating over tropical ocean waters and having one-minute sustained surface winds, 64 knots (73 mph) or higher. (West of the international date line, in the western Pacific, such storms are known as *typhoons.*) The area of hurricane-force winds takes the form of a circle or an oval, sometimes as wide as 300 mi in diameter. In the lower latitudes, hurricanes usually move west or northwest at 10 to 15 mph. When the center approaches 25° to 30° North Latitude, direction of motion often changes to northeast, with increased forward speed.

**Blizzard**—A severe weather condition characterized by strong winds bearing a great amount of snow. The National Weather Service specifies winds of 35 mph or higher and sufficient falling and/or blowing snow to frequently reduce visibility to less than 1/4 mile for a duration of at least 3 hours.

**Flood**—Flooding takes many forms. *River Flood:* A natural process that occurs seasonally when winter or spring rains are coupled with melting snow, filling river basins with too much water, too quickly; torrential rains from decaying hurricanes or tropical systems can also produce river flooding. *Coastal Flooding:* Winds generated from tropical storms and hurricanes or intense offshore low pressure systems can drive ocean water inland and cause significant flooding. Coastal floods can also be produced by sea waves called *Tsunamis,* sometimes referred to as tidal waves; these waves are produced by earthquakes or volcanic activity. *Urban Flooding:* Urbanization increases runoff 2-6 times over what would occur on natural terrain. During periods of urban flooding, streets can become swift-moving rivers, and basements can become death traps as they fill with water. *Flash Flooding:* The result of copious amounts of rain in a short period of time; flash flooding occurs within 6 hours of the rain event. *Ice Jam Flooding:* Ice can accumulate at natural or artificial obstructions and stop the flow of water. As the water flow is stopped, water builds up and flooding occurs.

*Flash Flood or Flood Watch:* Persons should be alert that flash flooding or flooding is possible within a designated area.

*Flash Flood or Flood Warning:* Flash flooding or flooding has been reported, and all necessary precautions should be taken immediately.

*Urban and Small Stream Advisory:* Small streams, streets, and low-lying areas such as railroad underpasses and urban storm drains are flooding.

## National Weather Service Marine Warnings and Advisories

**Small Craft Advisory:** A Small Craft Advisory alerts mariners to sustained (exceeding 2 hours) weather and/or sea conditions, either present or forecast, potentially hazardous to small boats. Although there is no definition of a small craft, hazardous conditions generally include winds of 18 to 33 knots and/or dangerous wave conditions. It is the responsibility of the mariner, based on experience and on the location and size or type of boat, to determine if the conditions are hazardous. When a mariner becomes aware of a Small Craft Advisory, he or she should immediately obtain the latest marine forecast to determine the reason for the advisory.

**Gale Warning** indicates that winds within the range 34 to 47 knots, not directly associated with a tropical storm, are forecast for the area.

**Tropical Storm Warning** indicates that winds of 34 to 63 knots are forecast in a specified coastal area within 24 hours or less. Only issued for winds of tropical weather systems.

**Storm Warning** indicates that winds 48 knots or above, not directly associated with a tropical storm, are forecast for the area.

**Hurricane Warning** indicates that winds 64 knots or greater are forecast for the area. Only issued for winds produced by tropical weather systems.

**Special Marine Warning:** A warning for potentially hazardous weather conditions, usually of short duration (2 hours or less) and producing wind speeds of 34 knots or more, not adequately covered by existing marine warnings.

Primary sources of dissemination are commercial radio, TV, U.S. Coast Guard radio stations, and NOAA VHF-FM broadcasts. These broadcasts on 162.40 to 162.55 MHz can usually be received 20-40 mi from the transmitting antenna site, depending on terrain and quality of the receiver used. Where transmitting antennas are on high ground, the range may be somewhat greater, reaching 60 mi or more.

# Monthly Normal Temperatures, Precipitation

**Source:** National Climatic Data Center, NESDIS, NOAA, U.S. Dept. of Commerce

The normal temperatures below are based on records for the 30-year period 1961-90 inclusive. For stations that did not have continuous records from the same instrument site for the entire 30 years, the means have been adjusted to the record at the present site.

Airport station; *city stations. T, temperature in Fahrenheit; P, precipitation in inches; L, less than 0.05 inch.

| | Jan. | | Feb. | | Mar. | | Apr. | | May | | June | | July | | Aug. | | Sept. | | Oct. | | Nov. | | Dec. | |
|---|---|---|---|---|---|---|---|---|---|---|---|---|---|---|---|---|---|---|---|---|---|---|---|---|
| **Station** | T | P | T | P | T | P | T | P | T | P | T | P | T | P | T | P | T | P | T | P | T | P | T | P |
| Albany, NY | 21 | 2.4 | 24 | 2.3 | 34 | 2.9 | 46 | 3.0 | 58 | 3.4 | 67 | 3.6 | 72 | 3.2 | 70 | 3.5 | 61 | 3.0 | 50 | 2.8 | 40 | 3.2 | 27 | 2.9 |
| Albuquerque, NM | 34 | 0.4 | 40 | 0.5 | 47 | 0.5 | 55 | 0.5 | 64 | 0.5 | 74 | 0.6 | 79 | 1.4 | 76 | 1.6 | 69 | 1.0 | 57 | 0.9 | 44 | 0.4 | 35 | 0.5 |
| Anchorage, AK | 15 | 0.8 | 19 | 0.8 | 26 | 0.7 | 36 | 0.7 | 47 | 0.7 | 54 | 1.1 | 58 | 1.7 | 56 | 2.4 | 48 | 2.7 | 35 | 2.0 | 21 | 1.1 | 16 | 1.1 |
| Asheville, NC | 36 | 3.3 | 39 | 3.9 | 47 | 4.6 | 55 | 3.4 | 63 | 4.4 | 69 | 4.2 | 73 | 4.5 | 72 | 4.7 | 66 | 3.9 | 56 | 3.6 | 48 | 3.6 | 40 | 3.5 |
| Atlanta, GA | 41 | 4.8 | 45 | 4.8 | 54 | 5.8 | 62 | 4.3 | 69 | 4.3 | 76 | 3.6 | 79 | 5.0 | 78 | 3.7 | 73 | 3.4 | 62 | 3.1 | 53 | 3.9 | 45 | 4.3 |
| Atlantic City, NJ | 31 | 3.5 | 33 | 3.1 | 42 | 3.6 | 50 | 3.6 | 60 | 3.3 | 69 | 2.6 | 75 | 3.8 | 73 | 4.1 | 66 | 2.9 | 55 | 2.8 | 46 | 3.6 | 36 | 3.3 |
| Baltimore, MD | 32 | 3.1 | 35 | 3.1 | 44 | 3.4 | 53 | 3.1 | 63 | 3.7 | 73 | 3.7 | 77 | 3.7 | 76 | 3.9 | 69 | 3.4 | 57 | 3.0 | 47 | 3.3 | 37 | 3.4 |
| Barrow, AK | −13 | 0.2 | −18 | 0.2 | −15 | 0.2 | −2 | 0.2 | 19 | 0.2 | 34 | 0.3 | 39 | 0.9 | 38 | 1.0 | 31 | 0.6 | 14 | 0.5 | −2 | 0.3 | −11 | 0.2 |
| Birmingham, AL | 42 | 5.1 | 46 | 4.7 | 54 | 6.2 | 62 | 5.0 | 69 | 4.9 | 76 | 3.7 | 80 | 5.3 | 79 | 3.6 | 73 | 3.9 | 63 | 2.8 | 53 | 4.3 | 45 | 5.1 |
| Bismarck, ND | 9 | 0.5 | 16 | 0.4 | 28 | 0.8 | 43 | 1.7 | 55 | 2.2 | 64 | 2.7 | 71 | 2.1 | 68 | 1.7 | 57 | 1.5 | 46 | 0.9 | 29 | 0.5 | 14 | 0.5 |
| Boise, ID | 29 | 1.5 | 36 | 1.2 | 43 | 1.3 | 49 | 1.2 | 58 | 1.1 | 67 | 1.8 | 74 | 0.4 | 73 | 0.4 | 63 | 0.8 | 52 | 0.8 | 40 | 1.5 | 30 | 1.4 |
| Boston, MA | 29 | 3.6 | 30 | 3.6 | 39 | 3.7 | 48 | 3.6 | 58 | 3.3 | 68 | 3.1 | 74 | 2.8 | 72 | 3.2 | 65 | 3.1 | 55 | 3.3 | 45 | 4.2 | 34 | 4.0 |
| Buffalo, NY | 24 | 2.7 | 25 | 2.3 | 34 | 2.7 | 45 | 2.9 | 57 | 3.1 | 66 | 3.6 | 71 | 3.1 | 69 | 4.2 | 62 | 3.5 | 51 | 3.1 | 41 | 3.8 | 29 | 3.7 |
| Burlington, VT | 16 | 1.8 | 18 | 1.6 | 31 | 2.2 | 44 | 2.8 | 56 | 3.1 | 65 | 3.5 | 71 | 3.7 | 68 | 4.1 | 59 | 3.3 | 48 | 2.9 | 37 | 3.1 | 23 | 2.4 |
| Caribou, ME | 9 | 2.4 | 12 | 1.9 | 25 | 2.4 | 38 | 2.5 | 51 | 3.1 | 61 | 2.9 | 66 | 4.0 | 63 | 4.1 | 54 | 3.5 | 43 | 3.1 | 31 | 3.6 | 15 | 3.2 |
| Charleston, SC | 48 | 3.5 | 51 | 3.3 | 58 | 4.3 | 65 | 2.7 | 73 | 4.0 | 78 | 6.4 | 82 | 6.8 | 81 | 7.2 | 76 | 4.7 | 67 | 2.9 | 58 | 2.5 | 51 | 3.2 |
| Chicago, IL | 21 | 1.5 | 25 | 1.4 | 37 | 2.7 | 49 | 3.6 | 59 | 3.3 | 69 | 3.8 | 73 | 3.7 | 72 | 4.2 | 64 | 3.8 | 53 | 2.4 | 40 | 2.9 | 27 | 2.5 |
| Cleveland, OH | 25 | 2.0 | 27 | 2.2 | 37 | 2.9 | 48 | 3.1 | 58 | 3.5 | 68 | 3.7 | 72 | 3.5 | 70 | 3.4 | 64 | 3.4 | 53 | 2.5 | 43 | 3.2 | 31 | 3.1 |
| Columbus, OH | 26 | 2.2 | 30 | 2.2 | 41 | 3.3 | 51 | 3.2 | 61 | 3.9 | 69 | 4.0 | 73 | 4.3 | 72 | 3.7 | 66 | 3.0 | 54 | 2.2 | 43 | 3.2 | 32 | 2.9 |
| Dallas-Ft. Worth, TX | 43 | 1.8 | 48 | 2.2 | 57 | 2.8 | 66 | 3.5 | 73 | 4.9 | 81 | 3.0 | 85 | 2.3 | 85 | 2.2 | 77 | 3.4 | 67 | 3.5 | 56 | 2.3 | 47 | 1.8 |
| Denver, CO | 30 | 0.5 | 33 | 0.6 | 39 | 1.3 | 48 | 1.7 | 57 | 2.4 | 67 | 1.8 | 74 | 1.9 | 71 | 1.5 | 62 | 1.2 | 51 | 1.0 | 39 | 0.9 | 31 | 0.6 |
| Des Moines, IA | 19 | 1.0 | 25 | 1.1 | 37 | 2.3 | 51 | 3.4 | 62 | 3.7 | 72 | 4.5 | 77 | 3.8 | 74 | 4.2 | 65 | 3.5 | 54 | 2.6 | 39 | 1.8 | 24 | 1.3 |
| Detroit, MI | 23 | 1.8 | 25 | 1.7 | 36 | 2.6 | 47 | 3.0 | 58 | 2.9 | 68 | 3.6 | 72 | 3.2 | 71 | 3.4 | 63 | 2.9 | 51 | 2.1 | 40 | 2.7 | 28 | 2.8 |
| Dodge City, KS | 30 | 0.5 | 35 | 0.6 | 43 | 1.6 | 55 | 2.0 | 64 | 3.0 | 74 | 3.1 | 80 | 3.2 | 78 | 2.7 | 69 | 1.9 | 57 | 1.3 | 43 | 0.8 | 32 | 0.6 |
| Duluth, MN | 7 | 1.2 | 12 | 0.8 | 24 | 1.9 | 39 | 2.3 | 51 | 3.0 | 60 | 3.8 | 66 | 3.6 | 64 | 4.0 | 54 | 3.8 | 44 | 2.5 | 28 | 1.8 | 13 | 1.2 |
| Fairbanks, AK | −10 | 0.5 | −4 | 0.4 | 11 | 0.4 | 31 | 0.3 | 49 | 0.6 | 60 | 1.4 | 63 | 1.9 | 57 | 2.0 | 46 | 1.0 | 25 | 0.9 | 3 | 0.8 | −7 | 0.9 |
| Fresno, CA | 46 | 2.0 | 51 | 1.8 | 55 | 1.9 | 61 | 1.0 | 69 | 0.3 | 77 | 0.1 | 82 | L | 80 | L | 75 | 0.2 | 65 | 0.5 | 54 | 1.4 | 45 | 1.4 |
| Galveston, TX* | 53 | 3.3 | 55 | 2.3 | 62 | 2.2 | 69 | 2.4 | 76 | 3.6 | 81 | 4.4 | 83 | 4.0 | 84 | 4.5 | 80 | 5.9 | 73 | 2.8 | 64 | 3.4 | 56 | 3.5 |
| Grand Junction, CO | 25 | 0.6 | 34 | 0.5 | 43 | 0.9 | 52 | 0.7 | 62 | 0.9 | 72 | 0.5 | 79 | 0.6 | 76 | 0.8 | 67 | 0.8 | 55 | 1.0 | 40 | 0.7 | 29 | 0.6 |
| Grand Rapids, MI | 22 | 1.8 | 24 | 1.4 | 34 | 2.6 | 46 | 3.4 | 58 | 3.1 | 67 | 3.7 | 72 | 3.2 | 70 | 3.6 | 61 | 4.2 | 50 | 2.8 | 38 | 3.3 | 27 | 2.9 |
| Hartford, CT | 25 | 3.4 | 28 | 3.2 | 38 | 3.6 | 49 | 3.9 | 60 | 4.1 | 69 | 3.8 | 74 | 3.2 | 72 | 3.7 | 63 | 3.8 | 52 | 3.6 | 42 | 4.0 | 30 | 3.9 |
| Helena, MT | 20 | 0.6 | 26 | 0.4 | 34 | 0.7 | 43 | 1.0 | 53 | 1.8 | 62 | 1.9 | 69 | 1.1 | 67 | 1.3 | 55 | 1.2 | 45 | 0.6 | 32 | 0.5 | 21 | 0.6 |
| Honolulu, HI | 73 | 3.6 | 73 | 2.2 | 74 | 2.2 | 76 | 1.5 | 78 | 1.1 | 79 | 0.5 | 81 | 0.6 | 81 | 0.4 | 81 | 0.8 | 80 | 2.3 | 77 | 3.0 | 74 | 3.8 |
| Houston, TX | 50 | 3.2 | 54 | 3.3 | 61 | 2.7 | 68 | 4.2 | 75 | 4.7 | 80 | 4.0 | 83 | 3.3 | 82 | 3.7 | 78 | 4.9 | 70 | 3.7 | 61 | 3.4 | 54 | 3.7 |
| Huron, SD | 13 | 0.4 | 19 | 0.8 | 32 | 1.2 | 46 | 2.0 | 58 | 2.7 | 68 | 3.3 | 74 | 2.3 | 72 | 2.0 | 61 | 1.4 | 49 | 1.4 | 32 | 0.7 | 18 | 0.5 |
| Indianapolis, IN | 26 | 2.3 | 30 | 2.5 | 41 | 3.8 | 52 | 3.7 | 63 | 4.0 | 72 | 3.5 | 75 | 4.5 | 73 | 3.6 | 67 | 2.9 | 55 | 2.6 | 43 | 3.2 | 31 | 3.3 |
| Jackson, MS | 44 | 5.2 | 48 | 4.7 | 57 | 5.8 | 65 | 5.6 | 72 | 5.1 | 79 | 3.2 | 82 | 4.5 | 81 | 3.8 | 76 | 3.6 | 65 | 3.3 | 56 | 4.8 | 48 | 5.9 |
| Jacksonville, FL | 52 | 3.3 | 55 | 3.9 | 61 | 3.7 | 67 | 2.8 | 73 | 3.6 | 79 | 5.7 | 82 | 5.6 | 81 | 7.9 | 78 | 7.0 | 70 | 2.9 | 62 | 2.1 | 55 | 2.7 |
| Juneau, AK | 24 | 4.5 | 28 | 3.7 | 33 | 3.3 | 40 | 2.8 | 47 | 3.4 | 53 | 3.1 | 56 | 4.2 | 55 | 5.3 | 49 | 6.7 | 42 | 7.8 | 32 | 4.9 | 27 | 4.4 |
| Kansas City, MO | 26 | 1.1 | 31 | 1.1 | 43 | 2.5 | 55 | 3.1 | 64 | 5.0 | 73 | 4.7 | 79 | 4.4 | 76 | 4.0 | 68 | 4.9 | 57 | 3.3 | 43 | 1.9 | 30 | 1.6 |
| Knoxville, TN | 36 | 4.2 | 40 | 4.1 | 49 | 5.1 | 58 | 3.7 | 65 | 4.1 | 73 | 4.0 | 77 | 4.7 | 76 | 3.1 | 70 | 3.1 | 58 | 2.8 | 49 | 3.8 | 40 | 4.5 |
| Lander, WY | 20 | 0.5 | 25 | 0.6 | 34 | 1.2 | 43 | 2.1 | 53 | 2.3 | 63 | 1.5 | 71 | 0.8 | 69 | 0.5 | 58 | 1.1 | 47 | 1.1 | 31 | 0.8 | 21 | 0.6 |
| Lexington, KY | 31 | 2.9 | 35 | 3.2 | 45 | 4.4 | 55 | 3.9 | 64 | 4.5 | 72 | 3.7 | 76 | 5.0 | 75 | 3.9 | 68 | 3.2 | 57 | 2.6 | 46 | 3.4 | 36 | 4.0 |
| Little Rock, AR | 39 | 3.9 | 44 | 4.4 | 53 | 5.3 | 62 | 6.2 | 70 | 7.0 | 78 | 7.8 | 82 | 8.2 | 81 | 8.1 | 74 | 7.4 | 63 | 6.3 | 52 | 5.2 | 43 | 4.3 |
| Los Angeles, CA* | 58 | 2.9 | 60 | 3.1 | 61 | 2.6 | 63 | 1.0 | 66 | 0.2 | 70 | L | 74 | L | 75 | 0.1 | 74 | 0.5 | 70 | 0.3 | 63 | 2.0 | 58 | 2.0 |
| Louisville, KY | 32 | 2.9 | 36 | 3.3 | 46 | 4.7 | 56 | 4.2 | 65 | 4.6 | 73 | 3.5 | 77 | 4.5 | 76 | 3.5 | 70 | 3.2 | 58 | 2.7 | 47 | 3.7 | 37 | 3.6 |
| Marquette, MI* | 12 | 2.2 | 14 | 1.7 | 24 | 2.8 | 37 | 2.6 | 50 | 3.0 | 59 | 3.5 | 65 | 2.9 | 63 | 3.4 | 54 | 4.1 | 44 | 3.6 | 30 | 2.9 | 17 | 2.6 |
| Memphis, TN | 40 | 3.7 | 44 | 4.4 | 53 | 5.4 | 63 | 5.5 | 71 | 5.0 | 79 | 3.6 | 83 | 3.8 | 81 | 3.4 | 74 | 3.5 | 63 | 3.0 | 53 | 5.1 | 44 | 5.7 |
| Miami, FL | 67 | 2.0 | 69 | 2.1 | 72 | 2.4 | 75 | 2.9 | 79 | 6.2 | 81 | 9.3 | 83 | 5.7 | 83 | 7.6 | 82 | 7.6 | 78 | 5.6 | 74 | 2.7 | 69 | 1.8 |
| Milwaukee, WI | 19 | 1.6 | 23 | 1.5 | 33 | 2.7 | 44 | 3.5 | 55 | 2.8 | 65 | 3.2 | 71 | 3.5 | 69 | 3.5 | 62 | 3.4 | 50 | 2.4 | 38 | 2.5 | 24 | 2.3 |
| Minneapolis, MN | 12 | 1.0 | 18 | 0.9 | 31 | 1.9 | 46 | 2.4 | 59 | 3.4 | 68 | 4.1 | 74 | 3.5 | 71 | 3.6 | 61 | 2.7 | 49 | 2.2 | 33 | 1.6 | 18 | 1.1 |
| Mobile, AL | 50 | 4.8 | 53 | 5.5 | 61 | 6.4 | 68 | 4.5 | 75 | 5.7 | 80 | 5.0 | 82 | 6.9 | 82 | 7.0 | 78 | 5.9 | 68 | 2.9 | 60 | 4.1 | 53 | 5.3 |
| Moline, IL | 20 | 1.5 | 25 | 1.2 | 37 | 3.0 | 50 | 3.9 | 61 | 4.3 | 71 | 4.3 | 75 | 5.0 | 73 | 4.2 | 65 | 4.0 | 53 | 2.9 | 40 | 2.5 | 25 | 2.2 |
| Nashville, TN | 36 | 3.6 | 40 | 3.8 | 50 | 4.9 | 59 | 4.4 | 68 | 4.9 | 76 | 3.6 | 79 | 4.0 | 78 | 3.5 | 72 | 3.5 | 60 | 2.6 | 50 | 4.1 | 41 | 4.6 |
| Newark, NJ | 31 | 3.4 | 33 | 3.0 | 42 | 3.9 | 52 | 3.8 | 63 | 4.1 | 73 | 3.2 | 78 | 4.5 | 76 | 3.9 | 69 | 3.7 | 58 | 3.1 | 47 | 3.9 | 36 | 3.5 |
| New Orleans, LA | 51 | 5.1 | 54 | 6.0 | 62 | 4.9 | 69 | 4.5 | 75 | 4.6 | 80 | 5.8 | 82 | 6.1 | 82 | 6.2 | 78 | 5.5 | 69 | 3.1 | 61 | 4.4 | 55 | 5.8 |
| New York, NY* | 32 | 3.4 | 34 | 3.3 | 42 | 4.1 | 53 | 4.2 | 63 | 4.4 | 72 | 3.7 | 77 | 4.4 | 76 | 4.0 | 68 | 3.9 | 58 | 3.6 | 48 | 4.5 | 37 | 3.9 |
| Norfolk, VA | 39 | 3.8 | 41 | 3.5 | 49 | 3.7 | 57 | 3.1 | 66 | 3.8 | 74 | 3.8 | 78 | 5.1 | 77 | 4.8 | 72 | 3.9 | 61 | 3.2 | 53 | 2.9 | 44 | 3.2 |
| Oklahoma City, OK | 36 | 1.1 | 41 | 1.6 | 50 | 2.7 | 60 | 2.8 | 68 | 5.2 | 77 | 4.3 | 82 | 2.6 | 81 | 2.6 | 73 | 3.8 | 62 | 3.2 | 50 | 2.0 | 39 | 1.4 |
| Omaha, NE | 21 | 0.7 | 27 | 0.8 | 39 | 2.0 | 52 | 2.7 | 62 | 4.5 | 72 | 3.9 | 77 | 3.5 | 74 | 3.2 | 65 | 3.7 | 53 | 2.3 | 39 | 1.5 | 25 | 1.0 |
| Philadelphia, PA | 30 | 3.2 | 33 | 2.8 | 42 | 3.5 | 52 | 3.6 | 63 | 3.8 | 72 | 3.7 | 77 | 4.3 | 76 | 3.8 | 68 | 3.4 | 56 | 2.6 | 46 | 3.3 | 36 | 3.4 |
| Phoenix, AZ | 54 | 0.7 | 58 | 0.7 | 62 | 0.9 | 70 | 0.2 | 79 | 0.1 | 88 | 0.1 | 94 | 0.8 | 92 | 1.0 | 86 | 0.9 | 75 | 0.7 | 62 | 0.7 | 54 | 1.0 |
| Pittsburgh, PA | 26 | 2.5 | 29 | 2.4 | 39 | 3.4 | 50 | 3.2 | 60 | 3.6 | 68 | 3.7 | 72 | 3.8 | 71 | 3.2 | 64 | 3.0 | 52 | 2.4 | 42 | 2.9 | 32 | 2.9 |
| Portland, ME | 21 | 3.5 | 23 | 3.3 | 33 | 3.7 | 43 | 4.1 | 53 | 3.6 | 62 | 3.4 | 69 | 3.1 | 67 | 2.9 | 59 | 3.1 | 49 | 3.9 | 39 | 5.2 | 27 | 4.6 |
| Portland, OR | 40 | 5.4 | 44 | 3.9 | 47 | 3.6 | 51 | 2.4 | 57 | 2.1 | 64 | 1.5 | 68 | 0.6 | 69 | 1.1 | 63 | 1.8 | 55 | 2.7 | 46 | 5.3 | 40 | 6.1 |
| Providence, RI | 28 | 4.1 | 30 | 3.7 | 37 | 4.3 | 47 | 4.0 | 57 | 3.5 | 67 | 2.8 | 73 | 3.0 | 71 | 4.0 | 64 | 3.5 | 54 | 3.8 | 44 | 4.2 | 33 | 4.5 |
| Raleigh, NC | 39 | 3.6 | 42 | 3.4 | 50 | 3.7 | 59 | 2.9 | 67 | 3.7 | 74 | 3.7 | 78 | 4.4 | 77 | 4.4 | 71 | 3.3 | 60 | 2.7 | 51 | 2.9 | 43 | 3.1 |
| Rapid City, SD | 22 | 0.4 | 27 | 0.5 | 34 | 1.0 | 45 | 1.9 | 55 | 2.7 | 65 | 3.1 | 72 | 2.0 | 71 | 1.7 | 60 | 1.2 | 49 | 1.1 | 35 | 0.6 | 24 | 0.5 |
| Reno, NV | 33 | 1.1 | 38 | 1.0 | 43 | 0.7 | 49 | 0.4 | 57 | 0.7 | 65 | 0.5 | 72 | 0.3 | 70 | 0.3 | 60 | 0.4 | 51 | 0.4 | 40 | 0.9 | 33 | 1.0 |
| Richmond, VA | 37 | 3.2 | 39 | 3.2 | 48 | 3.6 | 57 | 3.0 | 66 | 3.8 | 74 | 3.6 | 78 | 5.0 | 77 | 4.4 | 70 | 3.3 | 59 | 3.5 | 50 | 3.2 | 40 | 3.3 |
| St. Louis, MO | 29 | 1.8 | 34 | 2.1 | 45 | 3.6 | 57 | 3.5 | 66 | 4.0 | 75 | 3.7 | 80 | 3.9 | 78 | 2.9 | 70 | 3.1 | 58 | 2.7 | 46 | 3.3 | 34 | 3.0 |
| Salt Lake City, UT | 28 | 1.1 | 34 | 1.2 | 42 | 1.9 | 50 | 2.1 | 59 | 1.8 | 69 | 0.9 | 78 | 0.8 | 76 | 0.9 | 65 | 1.3 | 53 | 1.4 | 41 | 1.3 | 30 | 1.4 |
| San Antonio, TX | 49 | 1.7 | 54 | 1.8 | 62 | 1.5 | 69 | 2.5 | 76 | 4.2 | 82 | 3.8 | 85 | 2.2 | 85 | 2.5 | 79 | 3.4 | 70 | 3.2 | 60 | 2.6 | 52 | 1.5 |
| San Diego, CA | 57 | 1.8 | 59 | 1.5 | 60 | 1.8 | 62 | 0.8 | 64 | 0.2 | 67 | 0.1 | 71 | L | 73 | 0.1 | 71 | 0.2 | 68 | 0.4 | 62 | 1.5 | 57 | 1.6 |
| San Francisco, CA | 49 | 4.4 | 52 | 3.2 | 53 | 3.1 | 56 | 1.4 | 58 | 0.2 | 62 | 0.1 | 63 | L | 64 | 0.1 | 65 | 0.2 | 61 | 1.2 | 55 | 2.9 | 49 | 3.1 |
| San Juan, PR | 77 | 2.8 | 77 | 2.1 | 78 | 2.3 | 79 | 3.8 | 81 | 5.9 | 82 | 4.0 | 83 | 4.4 | 83 | 5.3 | 82 | 5.3 | 82 | 5.7 | 80 | 5.9 | 78 | 4.7 |
| Sault Ste. Marie, MI* | 13 | 2.4 | 14 | 1.7 | 24 | 2.3 | 38 | 2.4 | 51 | 2.7 | 58 | 3.1 | 64 | 2.7 | 63 | 3.6 | 55 | 3.7 | 45 | 3.2 | 33 | 3.5 | 19 | 2.9 |
| Savannah, GA | 49 | 3.6 | 52 | 3.2 | 59 | 3.8 | 66 | 3.0 | 74 | 4.1 | 79 | 5.7 | 82 | 6.4 | 81 | 7.4 | 77 | 4.5 | 67 | 2.4 | 59 | 2.2 | 52 | 3.0 |
| Scottsbluff, NE | 25 | 0.5 | 30 | 0.5 | 36 | 1.1 | 47 | 1.6 | 56 | 2.8 | 67 | 2.6 | 74 | 2.1 | 72 | 1.1 | 61 | 1.1 | 50 | 0.8 | 36 | 0.6 | 26 | 0.6 |
| Seattle, WA | 41 | 5.4 | 44 | 4.0 | 47 | 3.8 | 50 | 2.5 | 56 | 1.8 | 61 | 1.6 | 65 | 0.9 | 66 | 1.2 | 61 | 1.9 | 54 | 3.3 | 46 | 5.7 | 42 | 6.0 |
| Spokane, WA | 27 | 2.0 | 33 | 1.5 | 39 | 1.5 | 46 | 1.2 | 54 | 1.4 | 62 | 1.3 | 69 | 0.7 | 68 | 0.7 | 59 | 0.7 | 47 | 1.0 | 35 | 2.2 | 28 | 2.4 |
| Springfield, MO | 31 | 1.8 | 36 | 2.2 | 46 | 3.9 | 56 | 4.2 | 65 | 4.4 | 73 | 5.1 | 78 | 2.9 | 77 | 3.5 | 69 | 4.6 | 58 | 3.6 | 46 | 3.8 | 35 | 3.2 |
| Syracuse, NY | 22 | 2.3 | 24 | 2.2 | 34 | 2.8 | 46 | 3.3 | 57 | 3.3 | 65 | 3.8 | 70 | 3.8 | 68 | 3.5 | 62 | 3.8 | 51 | 3.2 | 41 | 3.7 | 28 | 3.2 |
| Tampa, FL | 60 | 2.0 | 62 | 3.1 | 67 | 3.0 | 71 | 1.2 | 77 | 3.1 | 81 | 5.5 | 82 | 6.6 | 82 | 7.6 | 81 | 6.0 | 75 | 2.0 | 68 | 1.8 | 62 | 2.2 |
| Washington, DC | 31 | 2.7 | 34 | 2.8 | 43 | 3.2 | 53 | 3.1 | 62 | 4.0 | 71 | 3.9 | 76 | 3.5 | 74 | 3.9 | 67 | 3.4 | 55 | 3.2 | 45 | 3.3 | 35 | 3.2 |
| Wilmington, DE | 31 | 3.0 | 33 | 2.9 | 43 | 3.4 | 52 | 3.4 | 63 | 3.8 | 72 | 3.6 | 76 | 4.2 | 75 | 3.4 | 68 | 3.4 | 56 | 2.9 | 46 | 3.3 | 36 | 3.5 |

# Normal High and Low Temperatures, Precipitation

**Source:** National Climatic Data Center, NESDIS, NOAA, U.S. Dept. of Commerce

The normal temperatures below are based on records for the 30-year period 1961-90. The extreme temperatures (through 1990) are listed for the stations shown and may not agree with the state records shown on page 224.

Airport stations; * city stations. The minus (–) sign indicates temperatures below zero. Fahrenheit thermometer registration.

| State | Station | Normal temperature: January Max. | January Min. | July Max. | July Min. | Extreme temperature: Highest | Lowest | Normal annual precipitation (inches) |
|---|---|---|---|---|---|---|---|---|
| Alabama | Mobile | 60 | 40 | 91 | 73 | 104 | 3 | 63.96 |
| Alaska | Anchorage | 21 | 8 | 65 | 52 | 85 | –34 | 15.91 |
| Alaska | Barrow | –7 | –19 | 45 | 34 | 79 | –56 | 4.49 |
| Arizona | Phoenix | 66 | 41 | 106 | 81 | 122 | 17 | 7.66 |
| Arkansas | Little Rock | 49 | 29 | 92 | 72 | 112 | –5 | 72.10 |
| California | Los Angeles* | 68 | 49 | 84 | 65 | 112 | 28 | 14.77 |
| California | San Diego | 66 | 49 | 76 | 66 | 111 | 29 | 9.9 |
| California | San Francisco | 56 | 42 | 72 | 54 | 106 | 20 | 19.70 |
| Colorado | Denver | 43 | 16 | 88 | 59 | 104 | –30 | 15.40 |
| Connecticut | Hartford | 33 | 16 | 85 | 62 | 102 | –26 | 44.14 |
| Delaware | Wilmington | 39 | 22 | 86 | 67 | 102 | –14 | 40.84 |
| District of Columbia | Washington–National | 42 | 27 | 89 | 71 | 104 | –5 | 38.63 |
| Florida | Jacksonville | 64 | 41 | 91 | 72 | 105 | 7 | 51.32 |
| Florida | Miami | 75 | 59 | 89 | 76 | 98 | 30 | 55.91 |
| Georgia | Atlanta | 50 | 32 | 88 | 70 | 105 | –8 | 50.77 |
| Georgia | Savannah | 60 | 38 | 91 | 72 | 105 | 3 | 49.22 |
| Hawaii | Honolulu | 80 | 66 | 88 | 74 | 94 | 53 | 22.02 |
| Idaho | Boise | 36 | 22 | 90 | 58 | 111 | –25 | 12.11 |
| Illinois | Chicago | 29 | 13 | 84 | 63 | 104 | –27 | 35.82 |
| Illinois | Moline | 28 | 11 | 86 | 65 | 106 | -27 | 39.08 |
| Indiana | Indianapolis | 34 | 17 | 86 | 65 | 104 | –23 | 39.94 |
| Iowa | Des Moines | 28 | 11 | 87 | 67 | 108 | –24 | 33.12 |
| Kentucky | Lexington | 39 | 22 | 86 | 66 | 103 | –21 | 44.55 |
| Kentucky | Louisville | 40 | 23 | 87 | 67 | 105 | –20 | 44.39 |
| Louisiana | New Orleans | 61 | 42 | 91 | 73 | 102 | 11 | 61.88 |
| Maine | Caribou | 19 | –2 | 77 | 55 | 96 | –41 | 36.60 |
| Maine | Portland | 30 | 11 | 79 | 58 | 103 | –39 | 44.34 |
| Maryland | Baltimore | 40 | 23 | 87 | 67 | 105 | –7 | 40.76 |
| Massachusetts | Boston | 36 | 22 | 82 | 65 | 102 | –12 | 41.51 |
| Michigan | Detroit | 30 | 16 | 83 | 61 | 104 | –21 | 32.62 |
| Michigan | Sault Ste. Marie* | 21 | 5 | 76 | 51 | 98 | –36 | 34.23 |
| Minnesota | Duluth | 16 | –2 | 77 | 55 | 97 | –39 | 30.00 |
| Minnesota | Minneapolis-St. Paul | 21 | 3 | 84 | 63 | 105 | –34 | 28.32 |
| Mississippi | Jackson | 56 | 33 | 92 | 71 | 106 | 2 | 55.37 |
| Missouri | Kansas City | 35 | 17 | 89 | 68 | 109 | –23 | 37.62 |
| Missouri | St. Louis | 38 | 21 | 89 | 70 | 107 | –18 | 37.51 |
| Montana | Helena | 30 | 10 | 85 | 53 | 105 | –42 | 11.60 |
| Nebraska | Omaha | 31 | 11 | 88 | 66 | 114 | –23 | 29.86 |
| Nebraska | Scottsbluff | 38 | 12 | 90 | 59 | 109 | –42 | 15.27 |
| Nevada | Reno | 45 | 21 | 92 | 51 | 105 | –16 | 7.53 |
| New Jersey | Atlantic City | 40 | 21 | 85 | 65 | 106 | –11 | 40.29 |
| New Mexico | Albuquerque | 47 | 22 | 93 | 64 | 105 | –17 | 8.88 |
| New York | Albany | 30 | 11 | 84 | 60 | 100 | –28 | 36.17 |
| New York | Buffalo | 30 | 17 | 80 | 62 | 99 | –20 | 38.58 |
| New York | New York–La Guardia | 37 | 26 | 84 | 69 | 107 | –3 | 42.12 |
| North Carolina | Asheville | 47 | 25 | 83 | 62 | 100 | –16 | 47.59 |
| North Carolina | Raleigh | 49 | 29 | 88 | 68 | 105 | –9 | 41.43 |
| North Dakota | Bismarck | 20 | –2 | 84 | 56 | 109 | –44 | 15.47 |
| Ohio | Cleveland | 32 | 18 | 82 | 61 | 104 | –19 | 36.63 |
| Ohio | Columbus | 34 | 19 | 84 | 63 | 102 | –19 | 38.09 |
| Oregon | Portland | 45 | 34 | 80 | 57 | 107 | –3 | 36.30 |
| Pennsylvania | Philadelphia | 38 | 23 | 86 | 67 | 104 | –7 | 41.41 |
| Pennsylvania | Pittsburgh | 34 | 19 | 83 | 62 | 103 | –18 | 36.85 |
| Rhode Island | Providence | 37 | 19 | 82 | 63 | 104 | –13 | 45.53 |
| South Carolina | Charleston | 58 | 38 | 90 | 73 | 104 | 6 | 51.53 |
| South Dakota | Huron | 24 | 2 | 87 | 62 | 112 | –39 | 20.08 |
| South Dakota | Rapid City | 34 | 11 | 86 | 58 | 110 | –30 | 16.64 |
| Tennessee | Memphis | 49 | 31 | 92 | 73 | 108 | –13 | 52.10 |
| Tennessee | Nashville | 46 | 27 | 90 | 69 | 107 | –17 | 47.30 |
| Texas | Galveston* | 58 | 47 | 87 | 79 | 101 | 8 | 42.28 |
| Texas | Houston | 61 | 40 | 93 | 72 | 107 | 7 | 46.07 |
| Utah | Salt Lake City | 36 | 19 | 92 | 64 | 107 | –30 | 16.18 |
| Vermont | Burlington | 25 | 8 | 81 | 60 | 101 | –30 | 34.47 |
| Virginia | Norfolk | 47 | 31 | 86 | 70 | 104 | –3 | 44.64 |
| Virginia | Richmond | 46 | 26 | 88 | 68 | 105 | –12 | 43.16 |
| Washington | Seattle-Tacoma | 45 | 35 | 75 | 55 | 99 | 0 | 37.19 |
| Washington | Spokane | 33 | 21 | 83 | 54 | 108 | –25 | 16.49 |
| Wisconsin | Milwaukee | 26 | 12 | 80 | 62 | 103 | –26 | 32.93 |
| Wyoming | Lander | 31 | 8 | 86 | 56 | 101 | –37 | 13.01 |

**Mean Annual Snowfall** (inches) based on record through 1990: Boston, MA, 42; Sault Ste. Marie, MI, 113; Albany, NY, 65.2; Burlington, VT, 78.6; Lander, WY, 66; Juneau, AK, 105.8.

**Wettest Spot:** Mount Waialeale, HI, on the island of Kauai, is the rainiest place in the world, according to the National Geographic Society, with an average annual rainfall of 460 inches.

**Highest Temperature:** A temperature of 136° F observed at Azizia (Al Aziziyah), near Tripoli, Libya, on Sept. 13, 1922, is generally accepted as the world's highest temperature recorded under standard conditions.

The record high in the United States was 134° F in Death Valley, CA, July 10, 1913.

**Lowest Temperature:** A record low temperature of –128.6° F was recorded at the Soviet Antarctica station Vostok on July 21, 1983.

The record low in the United States was –80° F at Prospect Creek, AK, Jan. 23, 1971.

The lowest official temperature on the North American continent was recorded at –81° F in Feb. 1947, at a lonely airport in the Yukon called Snag.

These are the meteorological champions—the official temperature extremes—but there are plenty of other claimants to thermometer fame. However, sun readings are unofficial records, since meteorological data to qualify officially must be taken on instruments in a sheltered and ventilated location.

# Annual Climatological Data

**Source:** National Climatic Data Center, NESDIS, NOAA, U.S. Dept. of Commerce

| 1995 | | Temperature °F | | | | Precipitation[1] | | | | | | Fastest[2] wind | | No. of days | | | |
|---|---|---|---|---|---|---|---|---|---|---|---|---|---|---|---|---|---|
| | | | | | | | | | Sleet or snow | | | | | | | | |
| Station | Elev. ft | Highest | Date | Lowest | Date | Total (in.) | Greatest in 24 hours | Date | Total (in.) | Greatest in 24 hours | Date | MPH | Date | Clear* | Cloudy* | Prec. .01 in. or more | Snow, sleet 1 in. or more |
| Albany, NY | 275 | 99 | 7/14 | –18 | 2/7 | 34.08 | 2.67 | 10/20 | 54.8 | 13.3 | 2/4 | 47 | 8/31 | — | — | 118 | 14 |
| Albuquerque, NM | 5,311 | 103 | 7/28 | 16 | 12/26 | 5.68 | 0.99 | 9/7 | 9.8 | 4.5 | 1/4 | 41 | 3/28 | 151 | 91 | 50 | 3 |
| Anchorage, AK | 114 | 78 | 6/11 | –15 | 1/13 | 13.76 | 1.02 | 8/12 | 52.0 | 12.0 | 3/16 | 43 | 2/14 | 61 | 244 | 93 | 14 |
| Asheville, NC | 2,140 | 93 | 8/18 | 6 | 2/9 | 55.39 | 4.22 | 10/4 | 3.5 | 3.1 | 2/7 | 33 | 10/5 | 72 | 179 | 123 | 2 |
| Atlanta, GA | 1,010 | 102 | 8/15 | 13 | 12/10 | 52.77 | 7.27 | 10/3 | 0.4 | 0.4 | 2/6 | 41 | 5/15 | — | — | 115 | 0 |
| Atlantic City, NJ[3] | 64 | 100 | 7/15 | 6 | 2/6 | 35.70 | 3.06 | 8/5 | 0.8 | 0.4 | 2/15 | 47 | 11/11 | — | — | 100 | 23 |
| Baltimore, MD | 148 | 102 | 7/15 | 5 | 2/6 | 36.93 | 2.76 | 8/5 | 11.3 | 7.2 | 2/3 | 36 | 2/5 | 96 | 175 | 118 | 2 |
| Barrow, AK | 31 | 64 | 7/8 | –51 | 2/1 | 2.75 | 0.42 | 7/5 | 24.0 | 2.0 | 3/17 | 38 | 12/19 | 40 | 213 | 51 | 6 |
| Birmingham, AL | 620 | 103 | 8/18 | 13 | 12/10 | 55.12 | 6.94 | 10/3 | 1.0 | 0.8 | 2/6 | — | — | — | — | 121 | 0 |
| Bismarck, ND | 1,647 | 98 | 8/17 | –28 | 3/8 | 18.90 | 1.80 | 5/8 | 64.2 | 7.7 | 1/16 | 48 | 7/12 | 78 | 186 | 104 | 19 |
| Boise, ID | 2,838 | 102 | 7/28 | 9 | 1/2 | 14.02 | 0.75 | 5/1 | 14.5 | 4.8 | 2/12 | 38 | 4/7 | — | — | 109 | 3 |
| Boston, MA | 15 | 100 | 7/14 | 1 | 2/7 | 35.10 | 3.31 | 10/5 | 41.5 | 11.0 | 12/19 | 43 | 4/4 | 106 | 178 | 127 | 11 |
| Buffalo, NY | 705 | 97 | 7/15 | –1 | 2/12 | 33.99 | 2.22 | 10/5 | 142.8 | 37.9 | 12/9 | 39 | 12/9 | — | — | 169 | 29 |
| Burlington, VT | 332 | 100 | 7/14 | –13 | 2/6 | 32.19 | 1.88 | 8/3 | 102.5 | 17.7 | 2/4 | 35 | 11/11 | 69 | 197 | 154 | 30 |
| Caribou, ME[4] | 624 | 93 | 8/10 | –33 | 1/11 | 34.41 | 2.58 | 10/27 | — | 21.2 | 2/4 | 32 | 4/5 | — | — | 159 | 35 |
| Charleston, SC | 40 | 102 | 8/14 | 19 | 2/9 | 49.59 | 2.55 | 8/23 | T | T | 11/5 | 36 | 1/7 | — | — | 131 | 0 |
| Chicago, IL | 658 | 104 | 7/13 | –4 | 12/9 | 32.88 | 2.57 | 11/10 | 30.9 | 3.7 | 1/21 | 36 | 4/18 | 96 | 163 | 121 | 13 |
| Cleveland, OH | 777 | 98 | 7/14 | –1 | 2/12 | 39.05 | 2.53 | 1/15 | 82.1 | 12.0 | 12/19 | 45 | 3/20 | — | — | 149 | 23 |
| Columbus, OH | 813 | 97 | 7/15 | –3 | 2/12 | 45.30 | 3.22 | 8/4 | 34.9 | 4.3 | 12/19 | 32 | 4/11 | 70 | 204 | 142 | 15 |
| Dallas-Ft. Worth, TX | 551 | 105 | 7/28 | 16 | 12/10 | 35.40 | 3.68 | 3/12 | T | T | 11/28 | 39 | 7/5 | — | — | 73 | 0 |
| Denver, CO | 5,282 | 99 | 8/8 | –7 | 1/1 | 18.27 | 1.13 | 7/13 | — | — | — | 45 | 3/22 | — | — | 94 | — |
| Des Moines, IA[3] | 938 | 101 | 7/13 | –6 | 12/10 | 31.03 | 2.54 | 5/8 | 24.7 | 8.1 | 1/5 | 38 | 12/8 | — | — | 109 | 8 |
| Detroit, MI | 637 | 100 | 7/14 | –2 | 2/5 | 28.82 | 1.45 | 7/26 | 29.7 | 5.1 | 1/6 | 39 | 7/13 | — | — | 136 | 11 |
| Duluth, MN | 1,428 | 94 | 7/30 | –22 | 12/11 | 34.30 | 2.71 | 8/24 | 123.6 | 12.1 | 12/13 | 41 | 7/31 | 66 | 207 | 149 | 38 |
| Fairbanks, AK | 436 | 88 | 5/11 | –48 | 1/26 | 8.85 | 1.07 | 6/25 | 28.9 | 3.7 | 2/10 | 25 | 8/29 | 71 | 189 | 79 | 12 |
| Fresno, CA | 328 | 108 | 7/28 | 32 | 1/2 | 17.29 | 2.43 | 3/9 | T | T | 6/15 | 29 | 1/4 | — | — | 71 | 0 |
| Grand Rapids, MI | 793 | 98 | 6/20 | –7 | 2/12 | 35.25 | 2.73 | 6/2 | 83.6 | 5.8 | 11/11 | 36 | 10/27 | — | — | 148 | 26 |
| Hartford, CT | 169 | 100 | 7/15 | –9 | 2/7 | 40.92 | 2.71 | 10/5 | 43.2 | 9.7 | 2/4 | 44 | 11/12 | 87 | 186 | 120 | 11 |
| Helena, MT | 3,828 | 98 | 8/6 | –21 | 12/8 | 12.37 | 1.18 | 5/11 | 27.2 | 5.1 | 4/9 | 51 | 6/15 | — | — | 102 | 7 |
| Honolulu, HI | 7 | 94 | 7/15 | 56 | 2/12 | 13.60 | 3.96 | 2/27 | 0.0 | 0.0 | — | 28 | 4/17 | 86 | 92 | 81 | 0 |
| Houston, TX | 96 | 103 | 7/28 | 27 | 12/10 | 44.63 | 4.14 | 12/17 | T | T | 1/2 | 35 | 3/7 | 100 | 161 | 104 | 0 |
| Huron, SD | 1,281 | 98 | 7/11 | –18 | 3/8 | 29.97 | 2.02 | 5/26 | 67.9 | 8.6 | 10/23 | 38 | 12/8 | 82 | 180 | 103 | 16 |
| Indianapolis, IN | 795 | 99 | 7/14 | –1 | 12/9 | 35.46 | 2.39 | 5/13 | 29.7 | 8.0 | 12/19 | 43 | 6/21 | 82 | 185 | 119 | 10 |
| Jackson, MS[3] | 291 | 100 | 7/28 | 18 | 12/29 | 59.03 | 4.32 | 4/22 | 0.0 | 0.0 | — | 37 | 11/11 | — | — | 102 | 0 |
| Jacksonville, FL | 26 | 100 | 7/16 | 20 | 2/9 | 50.25 | 4.52 | 8/24 | T | T | 12/22 | 32 | 5/19 | 87 | 144 | 127 | 0 |
| Kansas City, MO | 979 | 99 | 7/11 | –4 | 1/7 | 34.69 | 3.39 | 5/16 | 10.4 | 3.4 | 12/8 | 38 | 10/23 | — | — | 101 | 2 |
| Knoxville, TN[5] | 979 | 100 | 8/16 | 8 | 2/9 | 42.83 | 2.30 | 5/18 | 3.7 | 2.0 | 1/30 | 45 | 11/11 | — | — | 121 | 2 |
| Lander, WY | 5,557 | 97 | 7/29 | –10 | 1/1 | 19.68 | 1.29 | 5/26 | 105.5 | 13.7 | 10/21 | 39 | 3/21 | 118 | 134 | 95 | 31 |
| Lexington, KY | 966 | 97 | 7/14 | 1 | 2/12 | 50.08 | 4.25 | 6/26 | 12.4 | 3.0 | 3/8 | 31 | 11/11 | 80 | 189 | 123 | 3 |
| Little Rock, AR | 257 | 105 | 8/20 | 13 | 12/10 | 37.01 | 2.18 | 10/2 | 8.1 | 7.0 | 1/22 | — | — | — | — | 98 | 1 |
| Los Angeles, CA | 97 | 93 | 10/2 | 44 | 3/24 | 23.28 | 3.50 | 1/3 | 0.0 | 0.0 | — | 29 | 1/5 | 132 | 120 | 42 | 0 |
| Louisville, KY | 477 | 96 | 8/31 | 4 | 12/10 | 40.89 | 2.68 | 5/17 | 6.0 | 2.6 | 2/7 | 39 | 8/8 | — | — | 116 | 3 |
| Marquette, MI | 1,415 | 96 | 6/18 | –17 | 12/13 | 38.96 | 2.09 | 9/6 | 223.6 | 16.2 | 2/3 | — | — | — | — | 173 | 53 |
| Memphis, TN | 258 | 100 | 8/19 | 13 | 12/10 | 56.90 | 4.12 | 6/30 | 3.7 | 2.5 | 2/6 | — | — | — | — | 101 | 1 |
| Miami, FL | 7 | 97 | 8/15 | 39 | 2/9 | 79.30 | 5.02 | 6/20 | 0.0 | 0.0 | — | 33 | 5/17 | 71 | 123 | 138 | 0 |
| Milwaukee, WI | 679 | 103 | 7/13 | –5 | 12/9 | 31.34 | 2.65 | 8/16 | 46.2 | 9.7 | 11/27 | 47 | 8/28 | — | — | 130 | 13 |
| Minn.-St. Paul, MN | 834 | 101 | 7/13 | –11 | 2/11 | 25.66 | 1.85 | 8/5 | 40.3 | 7.1 | 12/8 | 40 | 7/14 | 74 | 210 | 132 | 12 |
| Mobile, AL | 211 | 99 | 8/16 | 22 | 12/10 | 80.49 | 8.86 | 5/9 | T | T | 12/22 | 38 | 10/4 | 96 | 149 | 107 | 0 |
| Moline, IL | 592 | 100 | 7/13 | –5 | 1/5 | 34.27 | 2.92 | 5/23 | 37.3 | 15.1 | 1/19 | 38 | 10/23 | — | — | 113 | 7 |
| Nashville, TN | 590 | 99 | 8/30 | 9 | 12/10 | 48.84 | 3.05 | 9/12 | 3.3 | 1.0 | 2/7 | 29 | 11/11 | 93 | 149 | 119 | 2 |
| Newark, NJ | 7 | 104 | 7/15 | 5 | 2/6 | 37.67 | 3.63 | 7/17 | 26.1 | 9.5 | 12/19 | 41 | 4/4 | 88 | 161 | 115 | 6 |
| New Orleans, LA | 4 | 100 | 8/20 | 26 | 12/11 | 65.33 | 12.40 | 5/8 | T | T | 12/22 | 35 | 11/11 | 112 | 142 | 101 | 0 |
| New York, NY | 132 | 102 | 7/15 | 6 | 2/6 | 40.42 | 3.36 | 7/17 | 26.2 | 10.8 | 2/4 | 29 | 11/14 | — | — | 118 | 6 |
| Norfolk, VA | 24 | 101 | 7/15 | 15 | 2/7 | 35.82 | 2.29 | 6/12 | 0.3 | 0.3 | 2/8 | 29 | 4/10 | 110 | 157 | 108 | 0 |
| Oklahoma City, OK | 1,285 | 102 | 9/3 | 11 | 12/10 | 36.77 | 3.31 | 5/26 | 14.0 | 4.0 | 1/22 | 74 | 7/23 | — | — | 87 | 3 |
| Philadelphia, PA | 5 | 103 | 7/15 | 5 | 2/6 | 31.53 | 1.81 | 10/27 | 14.0 | 8.8 | 2/3 | 36 | 10/14 | — | — | 108 | 4 |
| Phoenix, AZ | 1,109 | 121 | 7/28 | 37 | 12/23 | 9.51 | 1.59 | 8/20 | 0.0 | 0.0 | — | 41 | 7/30 | — | — | 31 | 0 |
| Pittsburgh, PA | 1,137 | 100 | 7/15 | –4 | 2/12 | 28.89 | 2.12 | 7/17 | 49.7 | 7.1 | 11/14 | 35 | 11/11 | 68 | 209 | 145 | 12 |
| Portland, ME | 43 | 96 | 7/14 | –10 | 2/7 | 41.29 | 2.73 | 11/14 | 73.5 | 13.1 | 2/4 | 45 | 2/4 | — | — | 135 | 17 |
| Portland, OR[3] | 21 | 99 | 7/17 | 16 | 2/14 | 43.33 | 2.82 | 11/10 | 4.0 | 3.6 | 2/12 | 51 | 12/12 | — | — | 158 | 1 |
| Providence, RI[3] | 51 | 99 | 7/15 | 1 | 2/7 | 38.24 | 2.87 | 10/5 | 15.5 | 7.5 | 2/4 | 38 | 11/12 | — | — | 125 | 3 |
| Raleigh, NC | 416 | 100 | 8/14 | 12 | 2/9 | 48.59 | 4.24 | 10/4 | 2.2 | 1.0 | 2/7 | 37 | 5/19 | 112 | 144 | 109 | 1 |
| Rapid City, SD | 3,162 | 102 | 8/17 | –15 | 12/9 | 19.65 | 1.63 | 6/21 | 41.2 | 8.5 | 3/3 | 52 | 12/8 | — | — | 116 | 10 |
| Reno, NV[3] | 4,404 | 100 | 8/4 | 10 | 12/25 | 12.56 | 1.85 | 12/11 | 13.1 | 4.2 | 1/4 | 48 | 3/9 | — | — | 64 | 5 |
| Richmond, VA[6] | 164 | 100 | 7/15 | 9 | 2/7 | 34.44 | 1.88 | 3/8 | 3.9 | 1.9 | 1/29 | 40 | 3/8 | — | — | 99 | 2 |
| St. Louis, MO | 535 | 101 | 8/18 | 4 | 12/9 | 41.68 | 6.55 | 5/16 | 14.4 | 5.3 | 12/19 | 40 | 10/26 | 100 | 168 | 122 | 4 |
| Salt Lake City, UT | 4,221 | 106 | 7/29 | 11 | 2/15 | 16.92 | 1.01 | 9/29 | 40.3 | 7.0 | 2/11 | 43 | 6/5 | 115 | 160 | 96 | 13 |
| San Antonio, TX | 788 | 103 | 7/28 | 25 | 12/10 | 22.66 | 3.87 | 9/19 | T | T | 1/2 | 34 | 7/3 | — | — | 74 | 0 |
| San Diego, CA | 13 | 90 | 2/19 | 43 | 1/18 | 17.04 | 2.30 | 1/4 | 0.0 | 0.0 | — | 32 | 1/4 | 138 | 118 | 47 | 0 |
| San Francisco, CA | 8 | 95 | 6/25 | 38 | 2/15 | 27.42 | 3.18 | 12/11 | T | T | 3/23 | 54 | 12/12 | 137 | 144 | 87 | 0 |
| San Juan, PR | 13 | 96 | 9/18 | 66 | 3/16 | 55.95 | 3.95 | 5/15 | 0.0 | 0.0 | — | 32 | 9/6 | 128 | 77 | 197 | 0 |
| Sault Ste. Marie, MI | 718 | 90 | 6/18 | –20 | 2/5 | 45.84 | 4.11 | 8/30 | 208.8 | 27.8 | 12/10 | 38 | 4/3 | 60 | 227 | 190 | 49 |
| Savannah, GA | 46 | 100 | 8/18 | 20 | 2/9 | 51.11 | 8.71 | 8/25 | T | T | 2/7 | 40 | 5/15 | 103 | 157 | 113 | 0 |
| Scottsbluff, NE | 3,943 | 103 | 8/7 | –22 | 1/4 | 16.70 | 1.31 | 5/16 | 44.4 | 9.1 | 1/16 | 45 | 12/4 | — | — | 100 | 18 |
| Seattle, WA | 400 | 96 | 6/30 | 22 | 2/14 | 42.60 | 2.30 | 11/28 | 0.2 | 0.2 | 2/12 | 41 | 12/12 | 66 | 215 | 144 | 0 |
| Spokane, WA[7] | 2,356 | 93 | 7/20 | 2 | 2/14 | 19.85 | 1.08 | 3/14 | 9.0 | 3.3 | 2/14 | 46 | 12/12 | — | — | 111 | 14 |
| Springfield, MO | 1,278 | 101 | 8/31 | –5 | 12/10 | 41.86 | 2.54 | 4/10 | 24.8 | 13.5 | 1/18 | 38 | 11/6 | — | — | 118 | 5 |
| Syracuse, NY | 410 | 96 | 8/3 | –11 | 2/7 | 31.34 | 2.98 | 10/21 | 136.8 | 10.1 | 11/14 | 41 | 7/6 | — | — | 159 | 37 |
| Tampa, FL | 19 | 97 | 8/15 | 28 | 2/9 | 54.13 | 5.29 | 6/24 | 0.0 | 0.0 | — | 40 | 11/8 | — | — | 118 | 0 |
| Washington, DC | 10 | 99 | 7/15 | 7 | 2/6 | 39.80 | 3.36 | 10/14 | 11.9 | 4.5 | 2/3 | 37 | 11/11 | 93 | 168 | 105 | 4 |
| Wilmington, DE | 74 | 99 | 7/15 | 4 | 2/6 | 39.27 | 2.57 | 10/14 | 18.6 | 7.5 | 2/3 | 46 | 4/9 | — | — | 116 | 4 |

*To get partly cloudy days, deduct the total of clear and cloudy days from 365 (1 yr). (T) Trace. (—) Data not available or incomplete. (1) Date shown is the starting date of the storm (in some cases it lasted more than one day). (2) Sustained for at least 1 minute, not peak gust. (3) Snow/sleet data compiled through Nov. (4) Snow/sleet data not available for Jan. (5) Snow/sleet data not available for Nov. (6) Snow/sleet and wind data compiled through Nov. (7) Snow/sleet data compiled through Sept.

## Record Temperatures by State Through 1995

**Source:** National Climatic Data Center, NESDIS, NOAA, U.S. Dept. of Commerce

| State | Lowest °F | Highest °F | Latest date | Station | Approximate elevation in feet |
|---|---|---|---|---|---|
| Alabama | –27 | | Jan. 30, 1966 | New Market | 760 |
| | | *112* | *Sept. 5, 1925* | *Centerville* | *345* |
| Alaska | –80 | | Jan. 23, 1971 | Prospect Creek | 1,100 |
| | | *100* | *June 27, 1915* | *Fort Yukon* | *420* |
| Arizona | –40 | | Jan. 7, 1971 | Hawley Lake | 8,180 |
| | | *128* | *June 29, 1994*[1] | *Lake Havasu City* | *505* |
| Arkansas | –29 | | Feb. 13, 1905 | Pond | 1,250 |
| | | *120* | *Aug. 10, 1936* | *Ozark* | *396* |
| California | –45 | | Jan. 20, 1937 | Boca | 5,532 |
| | | *134* | *July 10, 1913* | *Greenland Ranch* | *–178* |
| Colorado | –61 | | Feb. 1, 1985 | Maybell | 5,920 |
| | | *118* | *July 11, 1888* | *Bennett* | *5,484* |
| Connecticut | –32 | | Feb. 16, 1943 | Falls Village | 585 |
| | | *106* | *July 15, 1995* | *Danbury* | *450* |
| Delaware | –17 | | Jan. 17, 1893 | Millsboro | 20 |
| | | *110* | *July 21, 1930* | *Millsboro* | *20* |
| District of Columbia | –15 | | Feb. 11, 1899 | Washington | 112 |
| | | *106* | *July 20, 1930* | *Washington* | *112* |
| Florida | –2 | | Feb. 13, 1899 | Tallahassee | 193 |
| | | *109* | *June 29, 1931* | *Monticello* | *207* |
| Georgia | –17 | | Jan. 27, 1940 | CCC Camp F-16 | 1,000 |
| | | *112* | *July 24, 1952* | *Louisville* | *132* |
| Hawaii | 12 | | May 17, 1979 | Mauna Kea Obs. 111.2 | 13,770 |
| | | *100* | *Apr. 27, 1931* | *Pahala* | *850* |
| Idaho | –60 | | Jan. 18, 1943 | Island Park Dam | 6,285 |
| | | *118* | *July 28, 1934* | *Orofino* | *1,027* |
| Illinois | –35 | | Jan. 22, 1930 | Mount Carroll | 817 |
| | | *117* | *July 14, 1954* | *East St. Louis* | *410* |
| Indiana | –36 | | Jan. 19, 1994 | New Whiteland | 785 |
| | | *116* | *July 14, 1936* | *Collegeville* | *672* |
| Iowa | –47 | | Jan. 12, 1912 | Washta | 1,157 |
| | | *118* | *July 20, 1934* | *Keokuk* | *614* |
| Kansas | –40 | | Feb. 13, 1905 | Lebanon | 1,812 |
| | | *121* | *July 24, 1936*[1] | *Alton (near)* | *1,651* |
| Kentucky | –37 | | Jan. 19, 1994 | Shelbyville | 730 |
| | | *114* | *July 28, 1930* | *Greensburg* | *581* |
| Louisiana | –16 | | Feb. 13, 1899 | Minden | 194 |
| | | *114* | *Aug. 10, 1936* | *Plain Dealing* | *268* |
| Maine | –48 | | Jan. 19, 1925 | Van Buren | 510 |
| | | *105* | *July 10, 1911*[1] | *North Bridgton* | *450* |
| Maryland | –40 | | Jan. 13, 1912 | Oakland | 2,461 |
| | | *109* | *July 10, 1936*[1] | *Cumberland; Frederick* | *623; 325* |
| Massachusetts | –35 | | Jan. 12, 1981 | Chester | 640 |
| | | *107* | *Aug. 2, 1975* | *Chester; New Bedford* | *640; 120* |
| Michigan | –51 | | Feb. 9, 1934 | Vanderbilt | 785 |
| | | *112* | *July 13, 1936* | *Mio* | *963* |
| Minnesota | –59 | | Feb. 16, 1903[1] | Pokegama Dam | 1,280 |
| | | *114* | *July 6, 1936*[1] | *Moorhead* | *904* |
| Mississippi | –19 | | Jan. 30, 1966 | Corinth | 420 |
| | | *115* | *July 29, 1930* | *Holly Springs* | *600* |
| Missouri | –40 | | Feb. 13, 1905 | Warsaw | 700 |
| | | *118* | *July 14, 1954*[1] | *Warsaw; Union* | *705; 560* |
| Montana | –70 | | Jan. 20, 1954 | Rogers Pass | 5,470 |
| | | *117* | *July 5, 1937* | *Medicine Lake* | *1,950* |
| Nebraska | –47 | | Feb. 12, 1899 | Camp Clarke | 3,700 |
| | | *118* | *July 24, 1936*[1] | *Minden* | *2,169* |
| Nevada | –50 | | Jan. 8, 1937 | San Jacinto | 5,200 |
| | | *125* | *June 29, 1994*[1] | *Laughlin* | *605* |
| New Hampshire | –46 | | Jan. 28 1925 | Pittsburg | 1,575 |
| | | *106* | *July 4, 1911* | *Nashua* | *125* |
| New Jersey | –34 | | Jan. 5, 1904 | River Vale | 70 |
| | | *110* | *July 10, 1936* | *Runyon* | *18* |
| New Mexico | –50 | | Feb. 1, 1951 | Gavilan | 7,350 |
| | | *122* | *June 27, 1994* | *Waste Isolat. Pilot Plt.* | *3,418* |
| New York | –52 | | Feb. 18, 1979[1] | Old Forge | 1,720 |
| | | *108* | *July 22, 1926* | *Troy* | *35* |
| North Carolina | –34 | | Jan. 21, 1985 | Mt. Mitchell | 6,525 |
| | | *110* | *Aug. 21, 1983* | *Fayetteville* | *213* |
| North Dakota | –60 | | Feb. 15, 1936 | Parshall | 1,929 |
| | | *121* | *July 6, 1936* | *Steele* | *1,857* |
| Ohio | –39 | | Feb. 10, 1899 | Milligan | 800 |
| | | *113* | *July 21, 1934*[1] | *Gallipolis (near)* | *673* |
| Oklahoma | –27 | | Jan. 18, 1930 | Watts | 958 |
| | | *120* | *June 27, 1994*[1] | *Tipton* | *1,350* |
| Oregon | –54 | | Feb. 10, 1933[1] | Seneca | 4,700 |
| | | *119* | *Aug. 10, 1898* | *Pendleton* | *1,074* |
| Pennsylvania | –42 | | Jan. 5, 1904 | Smethport | 1,500 |
| | | *111* | *July 10, 1936*[1] | *Phoenixville* | *100* |
| Rhode Island | –23 | | Jan. 11, 1942 | Kingston | 100 |
| | | *104* | *Aug. 2, 1975* | *Providence* | *51* |
| South Carolina | –19 | | Jan. 21, 1985 | Caesars Head | 3,115 |
| | | *111* | *June 28, 1954*[1] | *Camden* | *170* |
| South Dakota | –58 | | Feb. 17, 1936 | McIntosh | 2,277 |
| | | *120* | *July 5, 1936* | *Gannvalley* | *1,750* |
| Tennessee | –32 | | Dec. 30, 1917 | Mountain City | 2,471 |
| | | *113* | *Aug. 9, 1930*[1] | *Perryville* | *377* |

| State | Lowest °F | Highest °F | Latest date | Station | Approximate elevation in feet |
|---|---|---|---|---|---|
| Texas | -23 | | Feb. 8, 1933[1] | Seminole | 3,275 |
| | | *120* | *Aug. 12, 1936* | *Seymour* | *1,291* |
| Utah | -69 | | Feb. 1, 1985 | Peter's Sink | 8,092 |
| | | *117* | *Jul. 5, 1985* | *Saint George* | *2,880* |
| Vermont | -50 | | Dec. 30, 1933 | Bloomfield | 915 |
| | | *105* | *July 4, 1911* | *Vernon* | *310* |
| Virginia | -30 | | Jan. 22, 1985 | Mountain Lake Bio. Station | 3,870 |
| | | *110* | *July 15, 1954* | *Balcony Falls* | *725* |
| Washington | -48 | | Dec. 30, 1968 | Mazama; Winthrop | 2,120; 1,755 |
| | | *118* | *Aug. 5, 1961*[1] | *Ice Harbor Dam* | *475* |
| West Virginia | -37 | | Dec. 30, 1917 | Lewisburg | 2,200 |
| | | *112* | *July 10, 1936*[1] | *Martinsburg* | *435* |
| Wisconsin | -54 | | Jan. 24, 1922 | Danbury | 908 |
| | | *114* | *July 13, 1936* | *Wisconsin Dells* | *900* |
| Wyoming | -66 | | Feb. 9, 1933 | Riverside R.S. | 6,650 |
| | | *114* | *July 12, 1900* | *Basin* | *3,500* |

(1) Also on earlier dates at the same or other places.

# International Temperature and Precipitation

**Source:** World Meteorological Organization

Average daily maximum and minimum temperatures and annual precipitation are based on records for the 30-year period 1961-90. The length of record of extreme temperatures includes all available years of data for a given location and is usually for a longer period; record temperatures may have been measured at a different location within the city. Surface elevations are supplied by the WMO and may differ from city elevation figures in other sections of *The World Almanac.* NA=not available.

| Station | Surface elevation (feet) | Temperature °F — Average Daily — January Max. | January Min. | July Max. | July Min. | Extreme Max. | Extreme Min. | Average annual precipitation (inches) |
|---|---|---|---|---|---|---|---|---|
| Algiers, Algeria | 82 | 61.7 | 42.6 | 87.1 | 65.3 | NA | NA | 27.0 |
| Athens, Greece | 49 | 56.1 | 44.6 | 88.9 | 73.0 | NA | NA | 14.6 |
| Auckland, New Zealand | 20 | 74.8 | 61.2 | 58.5 | 46.4 | NA | NA | 49.4 |
| Bangkok, Thailand | 66 | 89.6 | 69.8 | 90.9 | 77.0 | 104 | 51 | 59.0 |
| Berlin, Germany | 190 | 35.2 | 26.8 | 73.6 | 55.2 | 107 | –4 | 23.3 |
| Bogotá, Colombia | 8,357 | 67.3 | 41.7 | 64.6 | 45.5 | 75 | 21 | 32.4 |
| Bombay (Mumbai), India | 36 | 85.3 | 66.7 | 86.2 | 77.5 | 110 | 46 | 85.4 |
| Bucharest, Romania | 298 | 34.7 | 22.1 | 83.8 | 60.1 | 105 | -18 | 23.4 |
| Budapest, Hungary | 456 | 34.2 | 24.8 | 79.7 | 59.7 | 103 | -10 | 20.3 |
| Buenos Aires, Argentina | 82 | 85.8 | 67.3 | 59.7 | 45.7 | 104 | 22 | 45.2 |
| Cairo, Egypt | 243 | 65.8 | 48.2 | 93.9 | 71.1 | 118 | 34 | 1.0 |
| Cape Town, South Africa | 138 | 79.0 | 60.3 | 63.3 | 44.6 | 105 | 28 | 20.5 |
| Caracas, Venezuela | 2,739 | 79.9 | 60.8 | 81.3 | 66.0 | 96 | 45 | 36.1 |
| Casablanca, Morocco | 203 | 62.8 | 47.1 | 77.7 | 66.7 | NA | NA | 16.8 |
| Copenhagen, Denmark | 16 | 35.6 | 28.4 | 68.9 | 55.0 | NA | NA | NA |
| Damascus, Syria | 2,004 | 54.3 | 32.9 | 97.2 | 61.9 | NA | NA | 5.6 |
| Dublin, Ireland | 279 | 45.7 | 36.5 | 66.0 | 52.5 | 86 | 8 | 28.8 |
| Geneva, Switzerland | 1,364 | 38.3 | 27.9 | 76.3 | 53.2 | 101 | -3 | 35.6 |
| Havana, Cuba | 164 | 78.4 | 65.5 | 88.3 | 74.8 | NA | NA | 46.9 |
| Hong Kong | 203 | 65.5 | 56.5 | 88.7 | 79.9 | 97 | 32 | 87.2 |
| Istanbul, Turkey | 108 | 47.8 | 37.2 | 82.8 | 65.3 | 105 | 7 | 27.4 |
| Jerusalem, Israel | 2,483 | 53.4 | 39.4 | 83.8 | 63.0 | 107 | 26 | 23.2 |
| Lagos, Nigeria | 125 | 90.0 | 72.3 | 82.8 | 72.1 | NA | NA | 59.3 |
| Lima, Peru | 43 | 79.0 | 66.9 | 66.4 | 59.4 | NA | NA | 0.2 |
| London, England | 203 | 44.1 | 32.7 | 71.1 | 52.3 | 99 | 2 | 29.7 |
| Manila, Philippines | 79 | 85.8 | 74.8 | 89.1 | 76.8 | NA | NA | 49.6 |
| Mexico City, Mexico | 7,570 | 70.3 | 43.7 | 73.8 | 53.2 | NA | NA | 33.4 |
| Montreal, Canada | 118 | 21.6 | 5.2 | 79.2 | 59.7 | 100 | -36 | 37.0 |
| Nairobi, Kenya | 5,897 | 77.9 | 50.9 | 71.6 | 48.6 | NA | NA | 41.9 |
| Paris, France | 213 | 42.8 | 33.6 | 75.2 | 55.2 | 105 | -1 | 25.6 |
| Prague, Czech Republic | 1,197 | 32.7 | 22.5 | 73.9 | 53.2 | 98 | -16 | 20.7 |
| Reykjavik, Iceland | 200 | 35.4 | 26.6 | 55.9 | 46.9 | 76 | -3 | 31.5 |
| Rome, Italy | 79 | 53.8 | 35.4 | 88.2 | 62.1 | NA | NA | 33.0 |
| San Salvador, El Salvador | 2,037 | 86.5 | 61.3 | 86.2 | 66.4 | 105 | 45 | 68.3 |
| Sao Paolo, Brazil | 2,598 | 81.1 | 65.7 | 71.2 | 53.1 | NA | NA | 57.4 |
| Shanghai, China | 23 | 45.9 | 32.9 | 88.9 | 76.6 | 104 | 10 | 43.8 |
| Singapore | 52 | 85.8 | 73.6 | 87.4 | 75.6 | NA | NA | 84.6 |
| Stockholm, Sweden | 171 | 30.7 | 23.0 | 71.4 | 56.1 | 97 | -26 | 21.2 |
| Sydney, Australia | 10 | 79.5 | 65.5 | 62.4 | 43.9 | 114 | 32 | 46.4 |
| Tehran, Iran | 3,906 | 45.0 | 30.0 | 98.2 | 75.2 | 109 | -5 | 9.1 |
| Tokyo, Japan | 118 | 49.1 | 34.2 | 83.8 | 72.1 | NA | NA | 55.4 |
| Toronto, Canada | 567 | 27.5 | 12.0 | 80.2 | 57.6 | 105 | -26 | 30.8 |

# Hurricane and Tornado/Wind Storm Classifications

**Source:** National Weather Service, NOAA, U.S. Dept. of Commerce

The Saffir-Simpson Hurricane Scale is a 1-5 rating based on a hurricane's present intensity. The scale is used to give an estimate of the potential property damage and flooding expected along the coast from a hurricane landfall. Wind speed is the determining factor in the scale. The Fujita (or F) Scale, created by T. Theodore Fujita, is used to classify tornadoes or other severe wind storms. The F Scale uses rating numbers from 0-5, based on the amount and type of wind damage.

**Saffir-Simpson Scale (Hurricanes)**

| Category | Wind Speed | Severity | Storm Surge[1] |
|---|---|---|---|
| 1 | 74-95 MPH | Weak | 4-5 feet |
| 2 | 96-110 MPH | Moderate | 6-8 feet |
| 3 | 111-130 MPH | Strong | 9-12 feet |
| 4 | 131-155 MPH | Very Strong | 13-18 feet |
| 5 | > 155 MPH | Devastating | > 18 feet |

(1) Above normal tides.

**Fujita Scale (Tornadoes/Wind Storms)**

| Rank | Wind Speed | Damage | Strength |
|---|---|---|---|
| F-0 | Up to 72 MPH | Light | Weak |
| F-1 | 73-112 MPH | Moderate | Weak |
| F-2 | 113-157 MPH | Considerable | Strong |
| F-3 | 158-206 MPH | Severe | Strong |
| F-4 | 207-260 MPH | Devastating | Violent |
| F-5 | > 261 MPH | Incredible | Violent |

# Hurricane Names in 1997

**Source:** National Weather Service, NOAA, U.S. Dept. of Commerce

**Names assigned to Atlantic hurricanes, 1997 —** Ana, Bill, Claudette, Danny, Erika, Fabian, Grace, Henri, Isabel, Juan, Kate, Larry, Mindy, Nicholas, Odette, Peter, Rose, Sam, Teresa, Victor, Wanda.

**Names assigned to Eastern Pacific hurricanes, 1997 —** Andres, Blanca, Carlos, Dolores, Enrique, Felicia, Guillermo, Hilda, Ignacio, Jimena, Kevin, Linda, Marty, Nora, Olaf, Pauline, Rick, Sandra, Terry, Vivian, Waldo, Xina, York, Zelda.

# Tides and Their Causes

**Source:** U.S. Dept. of Commerce, Natl. Oceanic & Atmospheric Admin. (NOAA), Natl. Ocean Service (NOS)

The tides are a natural phenomenon involving the alternating rise and fall in the large fluid bodies of the earth caused by the combined gravitational attraction of the sun and moon. The combination of these two variable force influences produces the complex recurrent cycle of the tides. Tides may occur in both oceans and seas, to a limited extent in large lakes, the atmosphere and, to a very minute degree, in the earth itself. The period between succeeding tides varies as the result of many factors and force influences.

The tide-generating force represents the difference between (1) the centrifugal force produced by the revolution of the earth around the common center-of-gravity of the earth-moon system and (2) the gravitational attraction of the moon acting upon the earth's overlying waters. Since, on the average, the moon is only 238,852 miles from the earth compared with the sun's much greater distance of 92,956,000 miles, this closer distance outranks the much smaller mass of the moon compared with that of the sun, and the moon's tide-raising force is, accordingly, 2.5 times that of the sun.

The effect of the tide-generating forces of the moon and sun acting tangentially to the earth's surface (the so-called "tractive force") tends to cause a maximum accumulation of the waters of the oceans at two diametrically opposite positions on the surface of the earth and to withdraw compensating amounts of water from all points 90° removed from the positions of these tidal bulges. As the earth rotates beneath the maxima and minima of these tide-generating forces, a sequence of two high tides, separated by two low tides, ideally is produced each day (semidiurnal tide).

Twice in each lunar month, when the sun, moon, and earth are directly aligned, with the moon between the earth and the sun (at new moon) or on the opposite side of the earth from the sun (at full moon), the sun and the moon exert their gravitational force in a mutual or additive fashion. The highest high tides and lowest low tides are produced at these times. These are called *spring* tides. At two positions 90° in between, the gravitational forces of the moon and sun—imposed at right angles—tend to counteract each other to the greatest extent, and the range between high and low tides is reduced. These are called *neap* tides. This semi-monthly variation between the spring and neap tides is called the *phase inequality*.

The inclination of the moon's monthly orbit to the equator and the inclination of the sun during the earth's yearly orbit to the equator produce a difference in the height of succeeding high tides and in the extent of depression of succeeding low tides that is known as the diurnal inequality. In most cases, this produces a type of tide called a mixed tide. In extreme cases, these phenomena can result in only one high tide and one low tide each (diurnal tide). There are also other monthly and yearly variations in the tide due to the elliptical shape of the orbits themselves.

The datum for Charting and Predictions is Mean Lower Low Water (MLLW). This became effective January 1989 according to the convention of 1980, which prescribed that data on all United States coastlines would be the same; namely, Mean Higher High Water (MHHW), Mean High Water (MHW), Mean Tide Level (MTL), Mean Sea Level (MSL), Mean Low Water (MLW), Mean Lower Low Water (MLLW). Diurnal range of tide is the difference in height between MHHW and MLLW. Mean range of tide is the difference in height between MHW and MLW.

The actual range of tide in the waters of the open oceans may amount to only one to three feet. However, as the ocean tide approaches shoal waters and its effects are augmented the tidal range may be greatly increased. In Nova Scotia along the narrow channel of the Bay of Fundy, the range of tides, or difference between high and low waters, may reach 43-1/2 feet or more (under spring tide conditions) due to resonant amplification.

At New Orleans, the periodic rise and fall of the diurnal tide is affected by the seasonal stages of the Mississippi River, being about 10 inches at low stage and zero at high. The Canadian Tide Tables for 1972 gave a maximum range of nearly 50 feet at Leaf Basin, Ungava Bay, Quebec.

In every case, actual high or low tide can vary considerably from the average, due to weather conditions such as strong winds, abrupt barometric pressure changes, or prolonged periods of extreme high or low pressure.

## The Average Rise and Fall of Tides[1]

| Places | Ft. | In. | Places | Ft. | In. | Places | Ft. | In. |
|---|---|---|---|---|---|---|---|---|
| Baltimore, MD | 1 | 8 | Hampton Roads, VA | 2 | 10 | St. John's, Nfld. | 2 | 7[2] |
| Boston, MA | 10 | 4 | Key West, FL | 1 | 10 | St. Petersburg, FL | 2 | 3 |
| Charleston, SC | 5 | 10 | Mobile, AL | 1 | 6 | San Diego, CA | 5 | 9 |
| Cristobal, Panama | 1 | 1 | New London, CT | 3 | 1 | Sandy Hook, NJ | 5 | 2 |
| Eastport, ME | 19 | 4 | Newport, RI | 3 | 11 | San Francisco, CA | 5 | 10 |
| Ft. Pulaski, GA | 7 | 6 | New York, NY | 5 | 1 | Seattle, WA | 11 | 4 |
| Galveston, TX | 1 | 5 | Philadelphia, PA | 6 | 9 | Vancouver, B.C. | 10 | 6 |
| Halifax, N.S. | 4 | 5[2] | Portland, ME | 9 | 11 | Washington, DC | 3 | 2 |

(1) Diurnal range. (2) Mean range.

# Speed of Winds in the U.S.

**Source:** National Climatic Data Center, NESDIS, NOAA, U.S. Dept. of Commerce

Miles per hour — average through 1994. High through 1994. Wind velocities in true values.

| Station | Avg. | High | Station | Avg. | High | Station | Avg. | High |
|---|---|---|---|---|---|---|---|---|
| Albuquerque, NM | 8.9 | (b)90 | Helena, MT | 7.7 | 73 | Mt. Washington, NH | 35.3 | 231 |
| Anchorage, AK | 7.1 | 75 | Honolulu, HI | 11.3 | (b)67 | New Orleans, LA | 8.2 | (b)98 |
| Atlanta, GA | 9.1 | 60 | Houston, TX | 7.9 | 51 | New York, NY(c) | 9.4 | (b)70 |
| Baltimore, MD | 9.1 | 80 | Indianapolis, IN | 9.6 | 46 | Omaha, NE | 10.5 | (b)109 |
| Bismarck, ND | 10.2 | (b)72 | Jacksonville, FL | 7.9 | (b)82 | Philadelphia, PA | 9.5 | 73 |
| Boston, MA | 12.5 | (b)61 | Kansas City, MO | 10.8 | (b)70 | Phoenix, AZ | 6.2 | (b)86 |
| Buffalo, NY | 11.9 | 91 | Lexington, KY | 9.2 | 46 | Pittsburgh, PA | 9.1 | 58 |
| Cape Hatteras, NC | 11.1 | (b)110 | Little Rock, AR | 7.8 | 65 | Portland, OR | 7.9 | 88 |
| Casper, WY | 12.9 | 81 | Los Angeles, CA | 6.2 | 49 | St. Louis, MO | 9.7 | (b)60 |
| Chicago, IL | 10.4 | (b)84 | Louisville, KY | 8.3 | (b)61 | Salt Lake City, UT | 8.8 | 71 |
| Cleveland, OH | 10.5 | (b)74 | Memphis, TN | 8.9 | 51 | San Diego, CA | 7.0 | 56 |
| Dallas-Ft. Worth, TX | 10.7 | 73 | Miami, FL | 9.3 | (a)86 | San Francisco, CA | 8.7 | 47 |
| Denver, CO | 8.6 | 46 | Milwaukee, WI | 11.5 | 54 | Seattle, WA | 8.9 | 63 |
| Detroit, MI | 10.4 | 48 | Minn.-St. Paul, MN | 10.5 | (b)92 | Spokane, WA | 8.9 | 59 |
| Galveston, TX | 11.0 | (d)100 | Mobile, AL | 8.9 | 63 | Washington, DC | 9.4 | (b)78 |

(a) Highest velocity ever recorded in Miami area was 132 mph, at former station in Miami Beach in September 1926. (b) Previous location. (c) Data for Central Park; Battery Place data through 1960, avg. 14.5, high 113. (d) Recorded before anemometer blew away. Estimated high 120.

# Wind Chill Table

**Source:** National Weather Service, NOAA, U.S. Dept. of Commerce

Both temperature and wind cause heat loss from body surfaces. A combination of cold and wind makes a body feel colder than the actual temperature. The table shows, for example, that a temperature of 20 degrees Fahrenheit, plus a wind of 20 miles per hour, causes a body heat loss equal to that in minus 10 degrees with no wind. In other words, a 20-mph wind makes 20 degrees feel like minus 10.

Top line of figures shows actual temperatures in degrees Fahrenheit. Column at left shows wind speeds. (Wind speeds greater than 45 mph have little additional chilling effect.)

| MPH | 35 | 30 | 25 | 20 | 15 | 10 | 5 | 0 | -5 | -10 | -15 | -20 | -25 | -30 | -35 | -40 | -45 |
|---|---|---|---|---|---|---|---|---|---|---|---|---|---|---|---|---|---|
| **5** | 33 | 27 | 21 | 16 | 12 | 7 | 0 | -5 | -10 | -15 | -21 | -26 | -31 | -36 | -42 | -47 | -52 |
| **10** | 22 | 16 | 10 | 3 | -3 | -9 | -15 | -22 | -27 | -34 | -40 | -46 | -52 | -58 | -64 | -71 | -77 |
| **15** | 16 | 9 | 2 | -5 | -11 | -18 | -25 | -31 | -38 | -45 | -51 | -58 | -65 | -72 | -78 | -85 | -92 |
| **20** | 12 | 4 | -3 | -10 | -17 | -24 | -31 | -39 | -46 | -53 | -60 | -67 | -74 | -81 | -88 | -95 | -103 |
| **25** | 8 | 1 | -7 | -15 | -22 | -29 | -36 | -44 | -51 | -59 | -66 | -74 | -81 | -88 | -96 | -103 | -110 |
| **30** | 6 | -2 | -10 | -18 | -25 | -33 | -41 | -49 | -56 | -64 | -71 | -79 | -86 | -93 | -101 | -109 | -116 |
| **35** | 4 | -4 | -12 | -20 | -27 | -35 | -43 | -52 | -58 | -67 | -74 | -82 | -89 | -97 | -105 | -113 | -120 |
| **40** | 3 | -5 | -13 | -21 | -29 | -37 | -45 | -53 | -60 | -69 | -76 | -84 | -92 | -100 | -107 | -115 | -123 |
| **45** | 2 | -6 | -14 | -22 | -30 | -38 | -46 | -54 | -62 | -70 | -78 | -85 | -93 | -102 | -109 | -117 | -125 |

# Heat Index

The heat index is a measure of the contribution that high humidity makes with abnormally high temperatures in reducing the body's ability to cool itself. For example, the index shows that for an actual air temperature of 100 degrees Fahrenheit and a relative humidity of 50%, the effect on the human body would be same as 120 degrees. Sunstroke and heat exhaustion are likely when the heat index reaches 105. This index is a measure of what hot weather "feels like" to the average person for various temperatures and relative humidities.

| | Air Temperature* | | | | | | | | | | |
|---|---|---|---|---|---|---|---|---|---|---|---|
| **Relative Humidity** | **70** | **75** | **80** | **85** | **90** | **95** | **100** | **105** | **110** | **115** | **120** |
| | **Apparent Temperature*** | | | | | | | | | | |
| **0%** | 64 | 69 | 73 | 78 | 83 | 87 | 91 | 95 | 99 | 103 | 107 |
| **10%** | 65 | 70 | 75 | 80 | 85 | 90 | 95 | 100 | 105 | 111 | 116 |
| **20%** | 66 | 72 | 77 | 82 | 87 | 93 | 99 | 105 | 112 | 120 | 130 |
| **30%** | 67 | 73 | 78 | 84 | 90 | 96 | 104 | 113 | 123 | 135 | 148 |
| **40%** | 68 | 74 | 79 | 86 | 93 | 101 | 110 | 123 | 137 | 151 | |
| **50%** | 69 | 75 | 81 | 88 | 96 | 107 | 120 | 135 | 150 | | |
| **60%** | 70 | 76 | 82 | 90 | 100 | 114 | 132 | 149 | | | |
| **70%** | 70 | 77 | 85 | 93 | 106 | 124 | 144 | | | | |
| **80%** | 71 | 78 | 86 | 97 | 113 | 136 | | | | | |
| **90%** | 71 | 79 | 88 | 102 | 122 | | | | | | |
| **100%** | 72 | 80 | 91 | 108 | | | | | | | |

*Degrees Fahrenheit.

# Ultraviolet (UV) Index Forecast

**Source:** National Weather Service, NOAA, U.S. Dept. of Commerce

The National Weather Service (NWS), the Environmental Protection Agency (EPA), and the Centers for Disease Control and Prevention (CDC) developed the UV Index in an effort to raise the visibility of the risks associated with prolonged exposure to ultraviolet radiation. The NWS, EPA, and CDC began offering an experimental UV index on a limited basis on June 28, 1994, in response to increasing incidence of skin cancer, cataracts, and other effects from exposure to the sun's harmful rays. The NWS UV Index is now a regular element of atmospheric forecasts.

**UV Index number and forecast.** The UV Index number, ranging between 0 and 10+, is an indication of the amount of UV radiation reaching the earth's surface over the one-hour period around noon. The lower the number, the less the amount of UV radiation. The UV Index forecast is produced by the NWS Climate Analysis Center, Camp Springs, MD, about a day in advance of the time for which the forecast is effective. The forecast is based on several factors: latitude, day of year, time of day, total ozone in the atmosphere, elevation, and predicted cloud conditions at solar noon time. A forecast is given for 58 listed cities. The index is valid for a radius of about 30 miles around a listed city; however, adjustments should be made for a number of factors.

***Ozone.*** Total ozone is measured by a NOAA polar orbiting satellite. This measurement is combined with the aforementioned factors to help determine how much atmosphere the UV rays must pass through to reach the surface; the greater the distance and more ozone, the lower the UV radiation at the surface.

***Cloudiness.*** Rapid changes in cloud amount can alter the predicted UV Index. Increased cloudiness will lower the index number.

***Reflectivity.*** Reflective surfaces will intensify UV exposure to varying degrees. For example, grass reflects 2.5% to 3% of the UV radiation reaching the surface; sand, 20% to 30%; snow and ice, 80% to 90%; water, up to 100% (depending on the angle of reflection).

***Elevation.*** Trips to the mountains and to the beach will increase exposure to UV radiation. At higher elevations, the distance by which UV radiation has to travel to reach the surface is shortened, so there is less atmosphere to absorb the rays. For every 4,000 ft. one travels above sea level, the UV Index increases by 1 unit. The presence of snow and the lack of pollutants in the atmoshere also intensify UV exposure at higher altitudes. At the beach, several factors increase UV exposure: light-colored sand and water reflect UV rays, and people usually wear less clothing and often lie in a horizontal position.

***Latitude.*** The closer someone is to the equator, the higher the UV radiation level. It makes good sense to cover exposed areas and wear sunglasses when traveling in tropical regions. (A person can suffer a bad sunburn in the Tropics even during winter.).

**Accuracy.** By gathering data from 20 UV sensors (June-Oct. 1994), the NWS determined 32% of UV Index forecasts were correct, 76% were within plus or minus 1 UV Index unit, and about 90% were within plus or minus 2 units. Unpredictable cloudiness, haze, and pollution contribute to forecast error.

**SPF number.** The UV Index is not linked in any way to the SPF number found on suntan lotions and sunscreens. For an explanation of the SPF factor for a particular product, contact the manufacturer or the Food and Drug Administration.

**Further information.** For questions about health aspects or what precautions to take after learning the UV Index number, call the U.S. EPA hot line (800-296-1996) or a doctor/optometrist. For questions about scientific aspects, call the NWS at 301-713-0622.

# ENVIRONMENT

## Hazardous Waste Sites in the U.S., 1996

**Source:** Environmental Protection Agency, *National Priorities List,* June 1996

| State | Final Gen | Final Fed | Proposed Gen | Proposed Fed | Total |
|---|---|---|---|---|---|
| Alabama | 9 | 3 | 1 | 0 | 13 |
| Alaska | 2 | 6 | 0 | 0 | 8 |
| Arizona | 7 | 3 | 0 | 0 | 10 |
| Arkansas | 12 | 0 | 0 | 0 | 12 |
| California | 69 | 23 | 3 | 0 | 96 |
| Colorado | 13 | 3 | 2 | 0 | 18 |
| Connecticut | 14 | 1 | 0 | 0 | 15 |
| Delaware | 18 | 1 | 0 | 0 | 19 |
| District of Columbia | 0 | 0 | 0 | 0 | 0 |
| Florida | 46 | 5 | 2 | 0 | 53 |
| Georgia | 11 | 2 | 1 | 0 | 14 |
| Hawaii | 1 | 3 | 0 | 0 | 4 |
| Idaho | 6 | 2 | 2 | 0 | 10 |
| Illinois | 33 | 4 | 1 | 0 | 38 |
| Indiana | 32 | 0 | 1 | 0 | 33 |
| Iowa | 15 | 1 | 1 | 0 | 17 |
| Kansas | 8 | 1 | 1 | 1 | 11 |
| Kentucky | 16 | 1 | 0 | 0 | 17 |
| Louisiana | 13 | 1 | 3 | 0 | 17 |
| Maine | 8 | 3 | 1 | 0 | 12 |
| Maryland | 8 | 5 | 1 | 0 | 14 |
| Massachusetts | 22 | 8 | 0 | 0 | 30 |
| Michigan | 71 | 0 | 3 | 1 | 75 |
| Minnesota | 31 | 3 | 0 | 0 | 34 |
| Mississippi | 1 | 0 | 2 | 0 | 3 |
| Missouri | 19 | 3 | 0 | 0 | 22 |
| Montana | 8 | 0 | 1 | 0 | 9 |
| Nebraska | 8 | 1 | 1 | 0 | 10 |
| Nevada | 1 | 0 | 0 | 0 | 1 |
| New Hampshire | 16 | 1 | 0 | 0 | 17 |
| New Jersey | 99 | 6 | 2 | 0 | 107 |
| New Mexico | 8 | 2 | 1 | 0 | 11 |
| New York | 74 | 4 | 1 | 0 | 79 |
| North Carolina | 21 | 2 | 0 | 0 | 23 |
| North Dakota | 2 | 0 | 0 | 0 | 2 |
| Ohio | 31 | 3 | 2 | 2 | 38 |
| Oklahoma | 9 | 1 | 1 | 0 | 11 |
| Oregon | 9 | 2 | 1 | 0 | 12 |
| Pennsylvania | 95 | 6 | 2 | 0 | 103 |
| Rhode Island | 10 | 2 | 0 | 0 | 12 |
| South Carolina | 23 | 2 | 0 | 0 | 25 |
| South Dakota | 2 | 1 | 1 | 0 | 4 |
| Tennessee | 11 | 3 | 0 | 1 | 15 |
| Texas | 23 | 4 | 0 | 0 | 27 |
| Utah | 8 | 4 | 4 | 0 | 16 |
| Vermont | 8 | 0 | 0 | 0 | 8 |
| Virginia | 18 | 6 | 0 | 1 | 25 |
| Washington | 35 | 17 | 0 | 0 | 52 |
| West Virginia | 4 | 2 | 1 | 0 | 7 |
| Wisconsin | 40 | 0 | 1 | 0 | 41 |
| Wyoming | 2 | 1 | 0 | 0 | 3 |
| **Totals**[1] | **1,074** | **153** | **42** | **7** | **1,276** |

Note: Gen = general superfund sites; Fed = Federal facility sites.
(1) State figures do not add up to listed totals because the latter include some outlying areas of the U.S.

## Toxics Release Inventory, 1993-94

**Source:** Environmental Protection Agency

Reported industrial releases of toxic chemicals into the environment by major manufacturing facilities (excluding power plants and mining facilities) decreased 8.6% from the 1993 figure and 44.1% from the figure for 1988, the baseline year.

| Pollutant releases | 1993 mil lb | 1994 mil lb |
|---|---|---|
| Air releases | 1,672 | 1,556 |
| Underground injection | 576 | 349 |
| Land releases | 289 | 289 |
| Water releases | 271 | 66 |
| **Total** | **2,808** | **2,260** |
| **Pollutant transfers** | | |
| To recycling | 3,252 | 2,456 |
| To energy recovery | 487 | 464 |
| To treatment | 328 | 319 |
| To disposal/other | 325 | 298 |
| To publicly owned treatment works | 314 | 255 |
| **Total** | **4,706** | **3,792** |

| Top industries, total releases | 1993 mil lb | 1994 mil lb |
|---|---|---|
| Chemicals | 1,316 | 851 |
| Primary metals | 329 | 313 |
| Paper | 216 | 246 |
| Transportation equipment | 136 | 122 |
| Plastics | 127 | 119 |
| **Carcinogens, air/water/land releases** | | |
| Dichloromethane | 64 | 63 |
| Styrene | 33 | 40 |
| Chloroform | 14 | 11 |
| Formaldehyde | 12 | 12 |
| Tetrachloroethylene | 12 | 10 |
| Benzene | 11 | 10 |

## Top 10 States, Total Releases 1993-94

**Source:** Environmental Protection Agency

(air, water, land, and underground injection)

| State | 1993 mil lb | 1994 mil lb |
|---|---|---|
| Texas | 352 | 250 |
| Tennessee | 188 | 156 |
| Louisiana (#1 in 1993) | 451 | 153 |
| Mississippi | 118 | 122 |
| Ohio | 138 | 117 |
| Illinois | 101 | 98 |
| Alabama | 106 | 95 |
| Florida (#12 in 1993) | 69 | 94 |
| North Carolina | 91 | 89 |
| Michigan (#11 in 1993) | 82 | 83 |

## Emissions of Principal Pollutants 1985-1994

**Source:** U.S. Environmental Protection Agency, Office of Air Quality Planning and Standards

(in thousand short tons)

| Source | 1985 | 1986 | 1987 | 1988 | 1989 | 1990 | 1991 | 1992 | 1993 | 1994 |
|---|---|---|---|---|---|---|---|---|---|---|
| Carbon monoxide[1] | 114,690 | 109,199 | 108,012 | 115,849 | 103,144 | 100,650 | 97,376 | 94,043 | 94,133 | 98,017 |
| Lead | 20.1 | 7.3 | 6.9 | 6.5 | 6.0 | 5.7 | 5.3 | 4.9 | 4.9 | 5.0 |
| Nitrogen oxides[2] | 22,860 | 22,348 | 22,403 | 23,618 | 23,222 | 23,038 | 22,672 | 22,847 | 23,276 | 23,615 |
| Volatile organic compounds[2] | 25,799 | 24,991 | 24,777 | 25,720 | 23,934 | 23,600 | 22,876 | 22,422 | 25,575 | 23,174 |
| Particulate matter | 3,220 | 3,092 | 2,964 | 3,067 | 3,036 | 2,704 | 2,674 | 2,725 | 2,666 | 2,688 |
| Sulfur oxides | 23,230 | 22,442 | 22,204 | 22,647 | 22,785 | 22,433 | 22,068 | 21,836 | 21,517 | 21,118 |
| **Total** | **189,819** | **184,079** | **180,366** | **190,907** | **176,127** | **172,430** | **167,671** | **163,877** | **167,171** | **168,617** |

(1) The observed increase in carbon monoxide emissions between 1993 and 1994 is attributed to 2 sources: transportation emissions (up 2%) and wildfire emissions (up 160%). (2) Ozone, a major air pollutant and the primary constituent of smog, is not emitted directly to the air but is formed by sunlight acting on emissions of nitrogen oxides and volatile organic compounds.

# U.S. Carbon Monoxide Emissions, 1985-94

**Source:** U.S. Environmental Protection Agency, Office of Air Quality Planning and Standards

(estimated; in thousand short tons)

| Source | 1985 | 1986 | 1987 | 1988 | 1989 | 1990 | 1991 | 1992 | 1993 | 1994 |
|---|---|---|---|---|---|---|---|---|---|---|
| Fuel combustion | 8,486 | 7,548 | 6,960 | 7,372 | 7,441 | 5,064 | 5,356 | 5,601 | 4,954 | 4,884 |
| Industrial processes | 7,215 | 7,067 | 6,851 | 7,033 | 7,013 | 6,914 | 6,815 | 6,910 | 7,009 | 7,160 |
| Transportation | 91,094 | 87,330 | 85,381 | 85,581 | 80,568 | 77,500 | 76,675 | 74,759 | 75,471 | 76,727 |
| Natural sources | 0 | 0 | 0 | 0 | 0 | 0 | 0 | 0 | 0 | 0 |
| Miscellaneous | 7,895 | 7,254 | 8,820 | 15,863 | 8,121 | 11,173 | 8,530 | 6,774 | 6,700 | 9,245 |
| **Total[1]** | **114,690** | **109,199** | **108,012** | **115,849** | **103,144** | **100,650** | **97,376** | **94,043** | **94,133** | **98,017** |

(1) Totals may not add because of rounding.

# U.S. Lead Emission Estimates, 1985-94

**Source:** U.S. Environmental Protection Agency, Office of Air Quality Planning and Standards

(in short tons)

| Source | 1985 | 1986 | 1987 | 1988 | 1989 | 1990 | 1991 | 1992 | 1993 | 1994 |
|---|---|---|---|---|---|---|---|---|---|---|
| Fuel combustion | 515 | 516 | 510 | 511 | 505 | 500 | 495 | 491 | 491 | 493 |
| Industrial processes | 3,402 | 2,972 | 3,004 | 3,090 | 3,161 | 3,278 | 3,081 | 2,771 | 2,866 | 2,868 |
| Transportation | 16,207 | 3,808 | 3,343 | 2,911 | 2,368 | 1,888 | 1,704 | 1,637 | 1,580 | 1,596 |
| Natural sources | 0 | 0 | 0 | 0 | 0 | 0 | 0 | 0 | 0 | 0 |
| Miscellaneous | 0 | 0 | 0 | 0 | 0 | 0 | 0 | 0 | 0 | 0 |
| **Total[1]** | **20,124** | **7,296** | **6,857** | **6,513** | **6,034** | **5,666** | **5,279** | **4,899** | **4,938** | **4,956** |

(1) Totals may not add because of rounding.

# National Nitrogen Oxides Emission Estimates, 1985-94

**Source:** U.S. Environmental Protection Agency, Office of Air Quality Planning and Standards

(in thousand short tons)

| Source | 1985 | 1986 | 1987 | 1988 | 1989 | 1990 | 1991 | 1992 | 1993 | 1994 |
|---|---|---|---|---|---|---|---|---|---|---|
| Fuel Combustion | 10,836 | 10,668 | 10,897 | 11,457 | 11,552 | 11,483 | 11,382 | 11,421 | 11,696 | 11,728 |
| Industrial Processes | 891 | 873 | 840 | 860 | 851 | 850 | 838 | 852 | 866 | 888 |
| Transportation | 10,823 | 10,550 | 10,315 | 10,575 | 10,526 | 10,331 | 10,170 | 10,325 | 10,495 | 10,624 |
| Natural sources | 0 | 0 | 0 | 0 | 0 | 0 | 0 | 0 | 0 | 0 |
| Miscellaneous | 309 | 257 | 351 | 726 | 292 | 373 | 283 | 249 | 219 | 374 |
| **Total** | **22,860** | **22,348** | **22,403** | **23,618** | **23,222** | **23,038** | **22,672** | **22,847** | **23,276** | **23,615** |

# Air Quality of Selected U.S. Metropolitan Areas[1], 1986-94

**Source:** U.S. Environmental Protection Agency, Office of Air Quality Planning and Standards

| Metropolitan statistical area | 1986 | 1987 | 1988 | 1989 | 1990 | 1991 | 1992 | 1993 | 1994 |
|---|---|---|---|---|---|---|---|---|---|
| Atlanta, GA | 18 | 27 | 21 | 3 | 17 | 6 | 5 | 17 | 4 |
| Bakersfield, CA | 54 | 70 | 85 | 56 | 48 | 48 | 16 | 49 | 45 |
| Baltimore, MD | 23 | 28 | 43 | 9 | 12 | 20 | 5 | 14 | 17 |
| Boston, MA | 2 | 5 | 15 | 4 | 1 | 3 | 1 | 3 | 1 |
| Chicago, IL | 9 | 17 | 22 | 4 | 3 | 8 | 7 | 1 | 8 |
| Dallas, TX | 9 | 13 | 14 | 7 | 8 | 1 | 3 | 5 | 1 |
| Denver, CO | 49 | 37 | 19 | 11 | 9 | 7 | 7 | 3 | 2 |
| Detroit, MI | 5 | 9 | 17 | 10 | 3 | 8 | 0 | 2 | 8 |
| El Paso, TX | 43 | 32 | 16 | 33 | 27 | 10 | 13 | 6 | 10 |
| Fresno, CA | 37 | 49 | 29 | 45 | 22 | 32 | 27 | 27 | 11 |
| Hartford, CT | 7 | 20 | 27 | 11 | 7 | 14 | 9 | 9 | 10 |
| Houston, TX | 55 | 67 | 61 | 42 | 61 | 42 | 31 | 26 | 29 |
| Las Vegas, NV | 40 | 7 | 30 | 46 | 21 | 15 | 5 | 8 | 12 |
| Los Angeles/Long Beach, CA | 226 | 201 | 239 | 226 | 178 | 182 | 185 | 146 | 136 |
| Miami, FL | 4 | 4 | 5 | 4 | 1 | 2 | 0 | 0 | 0 |
| Minneapolis/St. Paul, MN/WI | 13 | 7 | 1 | 5 | 1 | 0 | 1 | 0 | 3 |
| New Haven/Meriden, CT | 7 | 17 | 16 | 7 | 10 | 22 | 3 | 11 | 8 |
| New York, NY | 58 | 44 | 46 | 18 | 18 | 22 | 4 | 6 | 8 |
| Orange County, CA | 66 | 58 | 65 | 66 | 47 | 42 | 43 | 25 | 14 |
| Phoenix/Mesa, AZ | 88 | 42 | 26 | 30 | 9 | 4 | 9 | 7 | 7 |
| Pittsburgh, PA | 8 | 13 | 25 | 9 | 11 | 4 | 2 | 5 | 2 |
| Riverside/San Bernardino, CA | 170 | 171 | 180 | 177 | 143 | 141 | 150 | 139 | 122 |
| San Diego, CA | 70 | 61 | 84 | 90 | 60 | 39 | 37 | 17 | 16 |
| Sacramento, CA | 69 | 52 | 76 | 60 | 43 | 44 | 21 | 10 | 11 |
| Salt Lake City, UT | 36 | 8 | 11 | 17 | 6 | 19 | 10 | 3 | 10 |
| San Francisco, CA | 4 | 1 | 2 | 1 | 1 | 0 | 0 | 0 | 0 |
| Seattle/Bellevue/Everett, WA | 13 | 14 | 20 | 8 | 5 | 2 | 1 | 0 | 0 |
| St. Louis, MO/IL | 13 | 17 | 18 | 13 | 8 | 6 | 3 | 5 | 11 |
| Ventura, CA | 84 | 54 | 83 | 59 | 36 | 49 | 25 | 16 | 24 |
| Washington, DC/MD/VA/WV | 12 | 26 | 37 | 8 | 5 | 17 | 2 | 13 | 7 |

(1) Data indicate the number of days metropolitan statistical areas failed to meet acceptable air-quality standards. (Pollutant Standards Index rating over 100).

# U.S. List of Endangered and Threatened Species

**Source:** Fish and Wildlife Service, U.S. Dept. of Interior; as of June 30, 1996

| Group | Endangered | | Threatened | | | |
|---|---|---|---|---|---|---|
| | U.S. only | Foreign only | U.S. only | Foreign only | Total listed species | Species with recovery plans |
| Mammals | 55 | 252 | 9 | 19 | 335 | 40 |
| Birds | 76 | 178 | 16 | 6 | 274 | 73 |
| Reptiles | 14 | 65 | 19 | 15 | 113 | 31 |
| Amphibians | 7 | 8 | 6 | 1 | 22 | 11 |
| Fishes | 65 | 11 | 40 | 0 | 116 | 72 |
| Snails | 15 | 1 | 7 | 0 | 23 | 18 |
| Clams | 51 | 2 | 6 | 0 | 59 | 42 |
| Crustaceans | 14 | 0 | 3 | 0 | 17 | 4 |
| Insects | 20 | 4 | 9 | 0 | 33 | 20 |
| Arachnids | 5 | 0 | 0 | 0 | 5 | 4 |
| **Animals, subtotal** | **320** | **521** | **115** | **41** | **997** | **315** |
| Flowering plants | 403 | 1 | 92 | 0 | 496 | 270 |
| Conifers | 2 | 0 | 0 | 2 | 4 | 1 |
| Ferns and others | 26 | 0 | 2 | 0 | 28 | 15 |
| **Plant, subtotal** | **431** | **1** | **94** | **2** | **528** | **286** |
| **Grand total** | **751** | **522** | **209** | **43** | **1,525[1]** | **601[2]** |

(1)When separate populations of a species are listed as endangered and as threatened, those species are tallied twice. Those species are the argali, chimpanzee, leopard, gray wolf, piping plover, roseate tern, green sea turtle, saltwater/Nile crocodile, and olive ridley sea turtle. (2)There are 424 approved recovery plans. Some recovery plans cover more than one species, and a few species have separate plans covering different parts of their ranges. Recovery plans are drawn up only for listed species that occur in the U.S.

# Some Endangered Species

**Source:** Fish and Wildlife Service, U.S. Dept. of Interior

| Common name | Scientific name | Range |
|---|---|---|
| Armadillo, giant | Pridontes maximus (giganteus) | Venezuela, Guyana to Argentina |
| Bat, gray | Myotis grisescens | Central, southeastern U.S. |
| Bison, wood | Bison bison athabascae | Canada, northwestern U.S. |
| Bobcat | Felis rufus escuinapae | Central Mexico |
| Camel, Bactrian | Camelus bactrianus | Mongolia, China |
| Caribou, woodland | Rangifer tarandus caribou | U.S., Canada |
| Cheetah | Acinonyx jubatus | Africa to India |
| Chimpanzee, pygmy | Pan Paniscus | Zaire |
| Condor, California | Gymnogyps californianus | U.S. (OR, CA), Mexico (Baja) |
| Cougar, eastern | Felis concolor couguar | Eastern N America |
| Crane, hooded | Grus monacha | Japan, Russia |
| Crane, whooping | Grus americana | Canada, Mexico, U.S. (Rocky Mts. to Carolinas) |
| Crocodile, American | Crocodylus acutus | U.S. (FL), Mexico, C and S America |
| Curlew, Eskimo | Numenius borealis | Alaska, N Canada to Argentina |
| Dolphin, Chinese river | Lipotes vexillifer | China |
| Elephant, Asian | Elephas maximus | S central & SE Asia |
| Falcon, American peregrine | Falco peregrinus anatum | Canada to Mexico |
| Fox, northern swift | Vulpes velox hebes | U.S., Canada |
| Frog, Israel painted | Discoglossus nigriventer | Israel |
| Gorilla | Gorilla gorilla | Central & W Africa |
| Hawk, Hawaiian | Buteo solitarius | U.S. (HI) |
| Hyena, brown | Hyaena brunnea | Southern Africa |
| Kangaroo, Tasmanian forester | Macropus giganteus tasmaniensis | Australia, Tasmania |
| Leopard | Panthera pardus | Africa & Asia |
| Lion, Asiatic | Panthera leo persica | Turkey to India |
| Macaw, indigo | Anodorhynchus leari | Brazil |
| Manatee, West Indian (Florida) | Trichechus manatus | U.S. (SE), Caribbean Sea, S America |
| Ocelot | Felis pardalis | U.S. (TX, AZ) to Central & S America |
| Ostrich, West African | Struthio camelus spatzi | W Sahara |
| Otter, marine | Lutra felina | Peru south to Straits of Magellan |
| Panda, giant | Ailuropoda melanoleuca | China |
| Panther, Florida | Felis concolor coryi | U.S. (LA, AR east to SC, FL) |
| Parakeet, golden | Aratinga guarouba | Brazil |
| Parrot, imperial | Amazona imperialis | West Indies (Dominica) |
| Python, Indian | Python molurus molurus | Sri Lanka, India |
| Rhinoceros, black | Diceros bicornis | Sub-Saharan Africa |
| Rhinoceros, northern white | Ceratotherium simum cottoni | Zaire, Sudan, Uganda, Central African Rep. |
| Salamander, Chinese giant | Andrias davidanus davidianus | Western China |
| Sea turtle, leatherback | Dermochelys coriacea | Tropical, temperate, & subpolar seas |
| Squirrel, Carolina northern flying | Glaucomys sabrinus coloratus | U.S. (NC, TN) |
| Stork, Oriental white | Ciconia ciconia boyciana | China, Japan, Korea, Russia |
| Tiger | Panthera tigris | Asia |
| Tortoise, Galapagos | Geochelone elephantopus | Ecuador (Galapagos Islands) |
| Turtle, Plymouth red-bellied | Pseudemys rubiventris bangsi | U.S. (MA) |
| Whale, gray | Eschrichtius robustus | N Pacific Ocean |
| Whale, humpback | Megaptera novaeangliae | Oceania |
| Wolf, red | Canis rufus | Southeastern U.S. to central TX |
| Woodpecker, ivory-billed | Campephilus principalis | S central and southeastern U.S., Cuba |
| Yak, wild | Bos grunniens mutus | China (Tibet), India |
| Zebra, mountain | Equus zebra zebra | S Africa |

# Classification

**Source:** *Funk & Wagnalls New Encyclopedia*

In biology, classification is the identification, naming, and grouping of organisms into a formal system. The 2 fields that are most directly concerned with classification are taxonomy and systematics. Although the 2 disciplines overlap considerably, taxonomy is more concerned with nomenclature (naming) and with constructing hierarchical systems, and systematics with uncovering evolutionary relationships. Two kingdoms of living forms, Plantae and Animalia, have been recognized since Aristotle established the first taxonomy in the 4th century BC. In addition, there are the following 3 kingdoms: Protista (one-celled organisms), Monera (bacteria and blue-green algae; also known as the kingdom Procaryotae), and Fungi. The 7 basic categories of classification (from most general to most specific) are: kingdom, phylum (or division), class, order, family, genus, and species. Below are 2 examples:

Zoological hierarchy

| Kingdom | Phylum | Class | Order | Family | Genus | Species Name | Common name |
|---|---|---|---|---|---|---|---|
| Animalia | Chordata | Mammalia | Primates | Hominidae | Homo | Homo sapiens | Human |

Botanical hierarchy

| Kingdom | Division* | Class | Order | Family | Genus | Species Name | Common name |
|---|---|---|---|---|---|---|---|
| Plantae | Magnoliophyta | Magnoliopsida | Magnoliales | Magnoliaceae | Magnolia | M. virginiana | Sweet Bay |

* In botany, the division is generally used in place of the phylum.

# Gestation, Longevity, and Incubation of Animals

Information reviewed and updated by Ronald M. Nowak, ed. *Walker's Mammals of the World* (5th ed., Johns Hopkins University Press, 1991). Average longevity figures supplied by Ronald T. Reuther. These apply to animals in captivity; the potential life span of animals is rarely attained in nature. Figures on gestation and incubation are averages based on estimates by leading authorities.

| Animal | Gestation (days) | Average longevity (years) | Maximum longevity (yr-mo) |
|---|---|---|---|
| Ass | 365 | 12 | 47 |
| Baboon | 187 | 20 | 45 |
| Bear: Black | 219 | 18 | 36-10 |
| Grizzly | 225 | 25 | 50 |
| Polar | 240 | 20 | 38 |
| Beaver | 105 | 5 | 50 |
| Bison | 285 | 15 | 40 |
| Camel (Bactrian) | 406 | 12 | 50 |
| Cat (domestic) | 63 | 12 | 28 |
| Chimpanzee | 230 | 20 | 53 |
| Chipmunk | 31 | 6 | 8 |
| Cow | 284 | 15 | 30 |
| Deer (white-tailed) | 201 | 8 | 20 |
| Dog (domestic) | 61 | 12 | 20 |
| Elephant (African) | 660 | 35 | 70 |
| Elephant (Asian) | 645 | 40 | 77 |
| Elk | 250 | 15 | 26-8 |
| Fox (red) | 52 | 7 | 14 |
| Giraffe | 425 | 10 | 33-7 |
| Goat (domestic) | 151 | 8 | 18 |
| Gorilla | 258 | 20 | 54 |
| Guinea pig | 68 | 4 | 8 |
| Hippopotamus | 238 | 41 | 54-4 |
| Horse | 330 | 20 | 50 |
| Kangaroo (gray) | 36 | 7 | 24 |
| Leopard | 98 | 12 | 23 |
| Lion | 100 | 15 | 30 |
| Monkey (rhesus) | 166 | 15 | 37 |
| Moose | 240 | 12 | 27 |
| Mouse (meadow) | 21 | 3 | 4 |
| Mouse (dom. white | 19 | 3 | 6 |
| Opossum (American) | 13 | 1 | 5 |
| Pig (domestic) | 112 | 10 | 27 |
| Puma | 90 | 12 | 20 |
| Rabbit (domestic) | 31 | 5 | 13 |
| Rhinoceros (black) | 450 | 15 | 45 |
| Rhinoceros (white) | 480 | 20 | 50 |
| Sea lion (California) | 350 | 12 | 30 |
| Sheep (domestic) | 154 | 12 | 20 |
| Squirrel (gray) | 44 | 10 | 23-6 |
| Tiger | 105 | 16 | 26-3 |
| Wolf (maned) | 63 | 5 | 13 |
| Zebra (Grant's) | 365 | 15 | 50 |

**Incubation time** (days)

| | |
|---|---|
| Chicken | 21 |
| Duck | 30 |
| Goose | 30 |
| Pigeon | 18 |
| Turkey | 26 |

# Speeds of Animals

**Source:** *Natural History* magazine, Mar. 1974. Copyright © The American Museum of Natural History, 1974

| Animal | mph |
|---|---|
| Cheetah | 70 |
| Pronghorn antelope | 61 |
| Wildebeest | 50 |
| Lion | 50 |
| Thomson's gazelle | 50 |
| Quarterhorse | 47.5 |
| Elk | 45 |
| Cape hunting dog | 45 |
| Coyote | 43 |
| Gray fox | 42 |
| Hyena | 40 |
| Zebra | 40 |
| Mongolian wild ass | 40 |
| Greyhound | 39.35 |
| Whippet | 35.50 |
| Rabbit (domestic) | 35 |
| Mule deer | 35 |
| Jackal | 35 |
| Reindeer | 32 |
| Giraffe | 32 |
| White-tailed deer | 30 |
| Wart hog | 30 |
| Grizzly bear | 30 |
| Cat (domestic) | 30 |
| Human | 27.89 |
| Elephant | 25 |
| Black mamba snake | 20 |
| Six-lined race runner | 18 |
| Wild turkey | 15 |
| Squirrel | 12 |
| Pig (domestic) | 11 |
| Chicken | 9 |
| Spider (Tegenaria atrica) | 1.17 |
| Giant tortoise | 0.17 |
| Three-toed sloth | 0.15 |
| Garden snail | 0.03 |

Most of these measurements are for maximum speeds over approximate quarter-mile distances. Exceptions are the lion and elephant, whose speeds were clocked in the act of charging; the whippet, which was timed over a 200-yd course; the cheetah, timed over a 100-yd distance; the human, timed for a 15-yd segment of a 100-yd run (of 13.6 sec); and the black mamba, six-lined race runner, spider, giant tortoise, three-toed sloth, and garden snail, which were measured over various small distances.

# Major Venomous Animals

## Snakes

**Asian pit viper** — from 2 ft to 5 ft long; throughout Asia; reactions and mortality vary, but most bites cause tissue damage, and mortality is generally low.

**Australian brown snake** — 4 ft to 7 ft long; very slow onset of cardiac or respiratory distress; moderate mortality, but because death can be sudden and unexpected, it is the most dangerous of the Australian snakes; antivenom.

**Barba Amarilla or fer-de-lance** — up to 7 ft long; from tropical Mexico to Brazil; severe tissue damage common; moderate mortality; antivenom.

**Black mamba** — up to 14 ft long, fast-moving; S and C Africa; rapid onset of dizziness, difficulty breathing, erratic heartbeat; mortality high, nears 100% without antivenom.

**Boomslang** — less than 6 ft long; in African savannahs; rapid onset of nausea and dizziness, often followed by slight recovery and then sudden death from internal hemorrhaging; bites rare, mortality high; antivenom.

**Bushmaster** — up to 12 ft long; wet tropical forests of C and S America; few bites occur, but mortality rate is high.

**Common or Asian cobra** — 4 ft to 8 ft long; throughout southern Asia; considerable tissue damage, sometimes paralysis; mortality probably not more than 10%; antivenom.

**Copperhead** — less than 4 ft long; from New England to Texas; pain and swelling; very seldom fatal; antivenom seldom needed.

**Coral snake** — 2 ft to 5 ft long; in Americas south of Canada; bite may be painless; slow onset of paralysis, impaired breathing; mortalities rare, but high without antivenom and mechanical respiration.

**Cottonmouth water moccasin** — up to 5 ft long; wetlands of southern U.S. from Virginia to Texas. Rapid onset of severe pain, swelling; mortality low, but tissue destruction can be extensive; antivenom.

**Death adder** — less than 3 ft long; Australia; rapid onset of faintness, cardiac and respiratory distress; at least 50% mortality without antivenom.

**Desert horned viper** — in dry areas of Africa and western Asia; swelling and tissue damage; low mortality; antivenom.

**European viper** —1 ft to 3 ft long; bleeding and tissue damage; mortality low; antivenom.

**Gaboon viper** — more than 6 ft long, fat; 2-in. fangs; south of the Sahara; massive tissue damage, internal bleeding; few recorded bites.

**King cobra** — up to 16 ft long; throughout southern Asia; rapid swelling, dizziness, loss of consciousness, difficulty breathing, erratic heartbeat; mortality varies sharply with amount of venom involved, but most bites involve nonfatal amounts; antivenom.

**Krait** — up to 5 ft long; in SE Asia; rapid onset of sleepiness; numbness; as much as 50% mortality even with use of antivenom.

**Puff adder** — up to 5 ft long; fat; south of the Sahara and throughout the Middle East; rapid large swelling, great pain, dizziness; moderate mortality, often from internal bleeding; antivenom.

**Rattlesnake** — 2 ft to 6 ft long; throughout W Hemisphere; rapid onset of severe pain, swelling; mortality low, but amputation of affected digits is sometimes necessary; antivenom. Mojave rattler may produce temporary paralysis.

**Ringhals, or spitting, cobra** — 5 ft to 7 ft long; southern Africa; squirts venom through holes in front of fangs as a defense; venom is severely irritating, can cause blindness.

**Russell's viper or tic-polonga** — more than 5 ft long; throughout Asia; internal bleeding; moderate mortality rate; bite reports common; antivenom.

**Saw-scaled or carpet viper** — as much as 2 ft long; in dry areas from India to Africa; severe bleeding, fever; high mortality, causes more human fatalities than any other snake; antivenom.

**Sea snakes** — throughout Pacific, Indian oceans except NE Pacific; almost painless bite, variety of muscle pain, paralysis; mortality rate low, many bites not envenomed; some antivenoms.

**Sharp-nosed pit viper or one hundred pace snake** — up to 5 ft long; in S Vietnam, Taiwan, and China; the most toxic of Asian pit vipers; very rapid onset of swelling and tissue damage, internal bleeding; moderate mortality; antivenom.

**Taipan** — up to 11 ft long; in Australia and New Guinea; rapid paralysis with severe breathing difficulty; mortality nears 100% without antivenom.

**Yellow or Cape cobra** — 7 ft long; in S Africa; most toxic venom of any cobra; rapid onset of swelling, breathing and cardiac difficulties; mortality is high without treatment; antivenom.

**Tiger snake** — 2 ft to 6 ft long; S Australia; pain, numbness, mental disturbances with rapid onset of paralysis; may be the most deadly of all land snakes, although antivenom is quite effective.

*Note:* Not all bites by venomous snakes are actually envenomed. Any animal bite, however, carries the danger of tetanus, and anyone suffering a venomous snake bite should seek medical attention. Antivenoms do not cure; they are only an aid in the treatment of bites. Mortality rates above are for envenomed bites; low mortality, c. 2% or less; moderate, 2%-5%; high, 5%-15%.

## Lizards

**Gila monster** — as much as 24 in. long, with heavy body and tail; in high desert in SW U.S. and N Mexico; immediate severe pain and transient low blood pressure; no recent mortality.

**Mexican beaded lizard** — similar to Gila monster, Mexican west coast; reaction and mortality rate similar to Gila monster.

## Insects

**Ants, bees, wasps, hornets, etc.** Global distribution. Usual reaction is piercing pain in area of sting. Not directly fatal, except in cases of massive multiple stings. However, many people suffer allergic reactions — swelling and rashes — and a few may die within minutes from severe sensitivity to the venom (anaphylactic shock).

## Spiders, Scorpions

**Atrax spider** — also known as funnel whip spider; several varieties, often large; in Australia; slow onset of breathing, circulation difficulties; low mortality; antivenom.

**Black widow** — small, round-bodied with red hourglass marking; the widow and its relatives are found in tropical and temperate zones; severe musculoskeletal pain, weakness, breathing difficulty, convulsions; may be more serious in small children; low mortality; antivenom. The **redback** spider of Australia has the hourglass marking on its back, rather than on its front, but is otherwise identical to the black widow.

**Brown recluse, or fiddleback, spider** — small, oblong body; throughout U.S.; pain with later ulceration at place of bite; in severe cases fever, nausea, and stomach cramps; ulceration may last months; very low mortality.

**Scorpion** — crablike body with stinger in tail, various sizes, many varieties throughout tropical and subtropical areas; various symptoms may include severe pain spreading from the wound, numbness, severe agitation, cramps; severe reaction may include respiratory failure; low mortality, usually in children; antivenoms.

**Tarantula** — large, hairy spider found around the world; the American tarantula, and probably all other tarantulas, are harmless to humans, though their bite may cause some pain and swelling.

## Sea Life

**Cone-shell** — mollusk in small, beautiful shell; in the S Pacific and Indian oceans; shoots barbs into victims; paralysis; low mortality.

**Octopus** — global distribution, usually in warm waters; all varieties produce venom, but only a few can cause death; rapid onset of paralysis with breathing difficulty.

**Portuguese man-of-war** — jellyfishlike, with tentacles up to 70 ft long; in most warm water areas; immediate severe pain; not directly fatal, though shock may cause death in rare cases.

**Sea wasp** — jellyfish, with tentacles up to 30 ft long, in the S Pacific; very rapid onset of circulatory problems; high mortality because of speed of toxic reaction; antivenom.

**Stingray** — several varieties of differing sizes; found in tropical and temperate seas and some fresh water; severe pain, rapid onset of nausea, vomiting, breathing difficulties; wound area may ulcerate, gangrene may appear; seldom fatal.

**Stonefish** — brownish fish that lies motionless as a rock on bottom in shallow water; throughout S Pacific and Indian oceans; extraordinary pain, rapid paralysis; low mortality; antivenom available, amount determined by number of puncture wounds; warm water relieves pain.

## Major U.S. Public Zoological Parks

**Source:** *World Almanac* questionnaire, 1996; budget and attendance in millions

| Zoo | Budget | Atten-dance | Acres | Species | Some major attractions |
|---|---|---|---|---|---|
| Albuquerque Biological Park | 14.5 | 0.6 | 210 | 271 | Sea lion pool, white Bengal tigers *for further information: (505) 764-6200.* |
| Arizona-Sonora Desert Museum (Tucson) | 5.8 | 0.6 | 30 | 1,703 | Desert grasslands, Hummingbird aviary *for further information: (520) 883-3019.* |
| Atlanta | $9.5 | 0.9 | 38.5 | 218 | Masai Mara, Ford African Rain Forest *for further information: (404) 624-5630.* |
| Audubon (New Orleans) | 10.0 | 0.9 | 58 | 360 | White alligators, Louisiana Swamp, Reptile Encounter *for further information: (504) 861-2537 x-366.* |
| Baltimore | 7.9 | 0.6 | 180 | 250 | Children's zoo, Chimpanzee Forest, Leopard Lair Exhibit *for further information: (410)-366-LION.* |
| Bronx (NYC) | 38.1 | 2.0 | 265 | 600+ | Himalayan Highlands, Jungle World, World of Darkness *for further information: (718) 367-1010.* |
| Buffalo | 3.8 | 0.5 | 23.5 | 180 | Gorilla Habitat, World of Wildlife Building *for further information: (716) 837-3900 x-104.* |
| Chicago (Brookfield) | 35.0 | 2.0 | 216 | 400 | 7 Seas Panorama, Tropic World, Habitat Africa! *for further information: (708) 485-0263, x-352.* |
| Cincinnati | NA | 1.3 | 67 | 750 | Gorilla World, Wings of the World, Jungle Trails *for further information: 1-(800) 944-4770.* |
| Cleveland | 8.7 | 1.2 | 165 | 574 | Rain forest, Nothern Trek, Wolf Wilderness *for further information: (216) 661-6500 x-233.* |
| Columbus (Powell, OH) | 13.0 | 2.5 | 404 | 600 | Discovery Reef, Gorilla habitat, All of N. America *for further information: (614)-645-3400.* |
| Dallas | 6.9 | 0.4 | 70 | 377 | Wilds of Africa with monorail, Reptile Discovery Center. *for further information: (214) 670-6842.* |
| Denver | 9.0 | 1.7 | 80 | 600 | Tropical Discovery, Primate Panorama, Northern Shores *for further information: (303) 331-4100.* |
| Detroit | 9.0 | 1.0 | 125 | 277 | Penguinarium, Chimps of Harambee, Interpretive Gallery *for further information: (810) 398-0903, x-3166.* |
| Houston | 6.6 | 1.5 | 55 | 721 | McGovern Mammal Marina, rain-forest birds in free flight *for further information: (713) 520-3200.* |
| Lincoln Park (Chicago) | 12.0 | 2.0 | 35 | 233 | Great Ape house, polar bear pool, Farm-in-the-Zoo *for further information: (312) 742-2000.* |
| Los Angeles | 17.2 | 1.3 | 80 | 400 | Tiger Falls, Great ape families, Walk through aviary *for further information: (213) 666-4650 x-275.* |
| Metro Washington Park (Portland, OR) | 15 | 1.1 | 64 | 188 | Asian elephants, Alaska Tundra, African rain forest *for further information: (503) 226-1561.* |
| Miami Metrozoo | 6.9 | 5.6 | 740 | 163 | African Plains, Children's Zoo, Koalas, Gorillas *for further information: (305) 251-0401.* |
| Milwaukee | 15.1 | 1.4 | 200 | 300 | Aquatic and Reptile Center, wolf woods, bear dens *for further information: (414) 256-5412.* |
| Minnesota | 13.7 | 1.2 | 500 | 389 | Dolphin shows, World of Birds, Discovery Bay (6/97) *for further information: (612) 431-9322.* |
| National (Washington, DC) | 23.0 | 3.0 | 163 | 500 | Think Tank, Amazonia, Panda Exhibit *for further information: (202) 673-4666.* |
| Oklahoma City | 8.3 | 0.6 | 110 | 648 | Aquaticus, Great EscApe (gorillas, chimps, orangutans). *for further information: (405) 424-0280.* |
| Omaha/Henry Doorly Zoo | 11.0 | 1.6 | 110 | 595 | Indoor rain forest, Cat complex, aquarium *for further information: (402) 733-8401.* |
| Point Defiance (Tacoma, WA) | 6.9 | .5 | 29 | 295 | Arctic Tundra, Southeast Asia, Discovery Reef, The Farm *for further information: (206)-591-5337.* |
| Philadelphia | 15.5 | 1.3 | 42 | 437 | Carnivore Kingdom, white lions, red pandas *for further information: (215) 243-1100.* |
| Phoenix | NA | 1.0 | 125 | NA | Africa Trail, The Forest of Uco (1/19/96) *for further information: (602) 914-4346.* |
| Riverbanks (Columbia, SC) | 4.2 | 0.9 | 170 | 500 | Aquarium Reptile Complex, Botanical Garden *for further information: (803) 779-8717, x-1117.* |
| St. Louis | 21.0 | 2.5 | 91 | 759 | Big Cat Country, Bear Pits, Jungle of the Apes, herpetarium *for further information: (314) 781-0900, x–239.* |
| San Diego | 70.0 | 3.2 | 100 | 900 | Tiger River, Gorilla Tropics,Polar Bear Plunge *for further information: (619) 234-1515, x-9.* |
| San Diego (Wild Animal Park) | 24.0 | 1.3 | 1,800 | 374 | Bushline monorail tour, Mombassa Lagoon, Bird show *for further information: (619) 738-5046.* |
| San Francisco | 12.0 | 0.9 | 125 | 270 | Primate Discovery Center, Big Cat feeding, Gorilla World *for further information: (415) 753-7080.* |
| Toledo | 9.0 | 0.9 | 31 | 525 | Hippoquarium, aquarium, Kingdom of the Apes *for further information: (419) 385-5721.* |
| Woodland Park (Seattle) | 9.6 | 1.1 | 92 | 260 | Tropical rain forest, Elephant Forest, Trail of Vines *for further information: (206) 684-4838.* |

Note: NA = Not Available.

## Major Canadian Public Zoological Parks

**Source:** *World Almanac* questionnaire, 1996; budget in millions of dollars (Canadian), attendance in millions

| Zoo | Budget | Atten-dance | Acres | Species | Major attractions |
|---|---|---|---|---|---|
| Calgary | 11.8 | 0.8 | 170 | 304 | Canadian Wilds, Prehistoric Park, Aspen Woodlands *for further information: (403) 232-9319.* |
| Granby (Quebec) | 4.5 | 0.4 | 70 | 230 | Reptile House, Bear Mountain, Big Cats Pavilion *for further information: (514) 372-9113 x-102.* |
| Toronto | 19.1 | 1.3 | 710 | 559 | Edge of Night Pavilion, Polar Bears, Underground Zoo *for further information: (416) 392-5941.* |
| Vancouver Aquarium | 9.0 | 0.9 | 2 | 612 | Pacific North West, Amazon Gallery, Arctic Canada *for further information: (604) 231-2505.* |
| Winnipeg (Assiniboine Park) | 2.4 | 0.5 | 54 | 250 | Kinsmen Discovery Center,Tropical House *for further information: (204) 986-6922.* |

## Trees of the U.S.

**Source:** American Forests, Washington, DC, 1996

Approximately 850 native and naturalized species of trees are grown in the U.S. The oldest living tree is believed to be a bristlecone pine tree in California named Methusalah, estimated to be 4,700 years old. The world's largest known living tree, the General Sherman giant sequoia in California, weighs more than 6,167 tons—as much as 41 blue whales or 740 elephants.

American Forests recognizes and lists the "National Champion" (largest known, by total mass) of each U.S. tree species. Anyone can nominate candidates for this National Register of Big Trees; for information, write to American Forests, PO Box 2000, Washington, DC 20013. Listed below, in alphabetical order, are ten National Champion trees selected by American Forests as worthy of note.

### Selected National Champion Trees

| Tree Type | Girth at 4.5 ft. (in.) | Height (ft.) | Crown Spread (ft.) | Total Points | Location |
|---|---|---|---|---|---|
| American Elm | 313 | 87 | 76 | 419 | Louisville, KS |
| Black Willow | 400 | 76 | 92 | 499 | Grand Traverse County, MI |
| Coast Douglas-Fir | 438 | 329 | 60 | 782 | Coos County, CA |
| Coast Redwood | 845 | 313 | 101 | 1,183 | Prairie Creek, CA |
| Giant Sequoia | 998 | 275 | 107 | 1,300 | Sequoia National Park, CA |
| Loblolly Pine | 188 | 148 | 83 | 357 | Warren, AZ |
| Pinyon Pine | 213 | 69 | 52 | 295 | Cuba, NM |
| Sugar Maple | 233 | 87 | 100 | 345 | Kingston, NH |
| Sugar Pine | 442 | 232 | 29 | 681 | Dorrington, CA |
| White Oak | 374 | 79 | 102 | 479 | Wye Mills State Park, MD |

## Top 50 American Kennel Club Registrations

**Source:** American Kennel Club, New York, NY; dogs registered during calendar year shown

| Breed | Rank 1995 | Number registered 1995 | Rank 1994 | Number registered 1994 |
|---|---|---|---|---|
| Labrador Retriever | 1 | 132,051 | 1 | 126,393 |
| Rottweiler | 2 | 93,656 | 2 | 102,596 |
| German Shepherd Dog | 3 | 78,088 | 3 | 78,999 |
| Golden Retriever | 4 | 64,107 | 4 | 64,322 |
| Beagle | 5 | 57,063 | 7 | 59,215 |
| Poodle | 6 | 54,784 | 5 | 61,775 |
| Cocker Spaniel | 7 | 48,065 | 6 | 60,888 |
| Dachshund | 8 | 44,680 | 8 | 46,129 |
| Pomeranian | 9 | 37,894 | 10 | 39,947 |
| Yorkshire Terrier | 10 | 36,881 | 11 | 38,626 |
| Dalmatian | 11 | 36,714 | 9 | 42,621 |
| Shih Tzu | 12 | 34,947 | 12 | 37,017 |
| Shetland Sheepdog | 13 | 33,721 | 13 | 36,853 |
| Chihuahua | 14 | 33,542 | 15 | 32,705 |
| Boxer | 15 | 31,894 | 16 | 30,629 |
| Miniature Schnauzer | 16 | 30,256 | 14 | 33,344 |
| Siberian Husky | 17 | 24,291 | 18 | 25,415 |
| Doberman Pinscher | 18 | 18,141 | 19 | 19,822 |
| Miniature Pinscher | 19 | 17,810 | 23 | 16,538 |
| Chow Chow | 20 | 17,722 | 17 | 25,415 |
| Maltese | 21 | 16,179 | 22 | 17,030 |
| Basset Hound | 22 | 16,055 | 20 | 18,043 |
| Boston Terrier | 23 | 16,031 | 24 | 16,453 |
| Pug | 24 | 15,927 | 26 | 15,464 |
| English Springer Spaniel | 25 | 15,039 | 21 | 17,404 |
| German Shorthaired Pointer | 26 | 14,113 | 29 | 14,154 |
| Chinese Shar-Pei | 27 | 13,174 | 25 | 15,834 |
| Pekingese | 28 | 13,081 | 27 | 15,306 |
| Collie | 29 | 12,850 | 30 | 14,073 |
| Bulldog | 30 | 12,092 | 33 | 11,357 |
| Lhasa Apso | 31 | 12,060 | 28 | 14,504 |
| Brittany | 32 | 11,618 | 31 | 12,741 |
| Great Dane | 33 | 11,015 | 34 | 11,155 |
| Bichon Frise | 34 | 10,817 | 32 | 11,363 |
| Akita | 35 | 10,661 | 35 | 11,014 |
| West Highland White Terrier | 36 | 7,773 | 36 | 8,441 |
| St. Bernard | 37 | 6,537 | 39 | 6,063 |
| Pembroke Welsh Corgi | 38 | 6,520 | 37 | 6,554 |
| Weimaraner | 39 | 6,312 | 41 | 5,678 |
| Australian Shepherd | 40 | 5,940 | 40 | 6,906 |
| Scottish Terrier | 41 | 5,311 | 38 | 6,091 |
| Chesapeake Bay Retriever | 42 | 5,089 | 42 | 5,198 |
| Alaskan Malamute | 43 | 4,510 | 44 | 4,855 |
| Great Pyrenees | 44 | 4,465 | 46 | 4,273 |
| Mastiff | 45 | 4,245 | 48 | 3,884 |
| Cairn Terrier | 46 | 4,102 | 45 | 4,653 |
| Samoyed | 47 | 4,088 | 43 | 5,017 |
| Airedale Terrier | 48 | 3,307 | 49 | 3,798 |
| Schipperke | 49 | 3,162 | 50 | 3,562 |
| Keeshond | 50 | 3,119 | 47 | 4,002 |

## Cat Breeds

**Source:** Cat Fanciers' Assn., Manasquan, NJ

Only a small percentage of house cats in the U.S. are pedigreed or registered with one of the official registering bodies, the largest of which is the Cat Fanciers' Assn., sponsor of more than 600 clubs. The Cat Fanciers' Assn. recognized 36 breeds as of Dec. 31, 1995 (in order of registration totals): Persian, Maine Coon, Siamese, Abyssinian, Exotic, Scottish Fold, Oriental Shorthair, American Shorthair, Birman, Burmese, Ocicat, Tonkinese, Cornish Rex, Russian Blue, Devon Rex, Somali, Manx, Colorpoint Shorthair, British Shorthair, Ragdoll, Norwegian Forest Cat, Egyptian Mau, Balinese, Japanese Bobtail, American Curl, Chartreux, Turkish Angora, Javanese, Singapura, Korat, Bombay, American Wirehair, Selkirk Rex, Havana Brown, Turkish Van, and European Burmese.

## Water Usage

**Source:** American Water Works Association; U.S. Geological Survey

Total freshwater withdrawals for all offstream uses in the U.S. were estimated to be 339 bil gal per day during 1990, about the same as during 1985. Offstream use means withdrawn or diverted from a ground- or surface-water source for public water supply; domestic, commercial, or industrial use; irrigation; livestock; mining; or thermoelectric power.

Total water withdrawals in 1990 from lakes, reservoirs, streams, wells, and springs were estimated at 408 bil gal per day, including 69 bil gal per day of salt water.

Here are some typical examples of water usage, by volume:

In the average residence during a year: 110,000 gal
By an average person daily: 100 gal
To flush a non low-flow toilet: 5-7 gal
To take a shower: 15-30 gal or 5-10 gal per min
To brush your teeth (water running): 1-2 gal
To shave (water running): 10-15 gal
To wash dishes by hand: 20 gal
To run a dishwasher: 10-25 gal
By a dripping faucet: 1,000 gal or more per year
To manufacture a new car: 39,090 gal

# ENERGY

## U.S. Energy Summary, 1995

**Source:** Energy Information Administration, U.S. Dept. of Energy, *Annual Energy Review 1995*

In 1995, a reviving domestic economy, generally low energy prices, a heat wave in July and August, and very cold weather in November and December contributed to the fourth consecutive year of growth in total U.S. energy consumption, which rose to an all-time high of nearly 91 quadrillion Btu. The increase resulted from a rise in the consumption of natural gas, coal, nuclear electric power, and renewable energy; the use of petroleum declined by 0.3%. Renewable energy consumption rose 9.3% to a record high of 6.9 quadrillion Btu; conventional hydroelectric power accounted for a little more than half of the renewable energy consumed. Electric utilities' preference for other energy sources and a slight increase in crude oil prices led to the decrease in petroleum consumption, which fell 0.02 million barrels per day from the 1994 level to 17.7 million barrels per day. Consumption of petroleum by electric utilities fell 33% and industrial consumption declined 1.7% in 1995, offsetting increases by the residential and commercial sectors of 1.7% and 1.8%, respectively.

The energy intensity of the economy, which is measured in terms of energy consumption per dollar of gross domestic product, declined for the fourth consecutive year. About 13,000 Btu of energy were consumed for each 1992 dollar in 1995, compared with about 19,000 Btu in the early 1970s.

U.S. total energy production rose 0.8% to 71.2 quadrillion Btu in 1995. Most of the increase was attributed to growth in production of renewable energy and nuclear electric power. Nuclear electricity net generation grew 5.2% to a record 673 billion kilowatt-hours. Fossil fuel production fell in 1995; coal and natural gas fell 0.16 and 0.04 quadrillion Btu, respectively, and crude oil (including lease condensate) dropped almost 0.3 quadrillion Btu to 13.8 quadrillion Btu, its lowest level in 41 years.

U.S. net imports of energy fell to 17.8 quadrillion Btu in 1995, a decrease of 3.9% from the record 1994 level. Petroleum net imports fell 1.8% to 16.9 quadrillion Btu, and coal net exports increased 27% to 2.1 quadrillion Btu, while natural gas net imports rose 4.4% to 2.6 quadrillion Btu. U.S. net imports of petroleum totaled 7.9 million barrels per day in 1995. Members of OPEC supplied 4.2 million barrels per day, more than half the total. Coal remained the primary U.S. energy export. Coal exports rose 24% to 89 million short tons in 1995.

## U.S. Energy Overview, 1960-95

**Source:** Energy Information Administration, U.S. Dept. of Energy, *Annual Energy Review 1995*

(in quadrillion Btu)

| Activity and energy source | 1960 | 1970 | 1975 | 1980 | 1985 | 1990[1] | 1992 | 1993 | 1994 | 1995[P] |
|---|---|---|---|---|---|---|---|---|---|---|
| **Production** | **41.49** | **62.07** | **59.86** | **64.76** | **64.87** | **70.75[R]** | **69.96[R]** | **68.32** | **70.62[R]** | **71.16** |
| Fossil fuels | 39.87 | 59.19 | 54.73 | 59.01 | 57.54 | 58.56 | 57.55 | 55.71[R] | 57.83[R] | 57.40 |
| Coal | 10.82 | 14.61 | 14.99 | 18.60 | 19.33 | 22.46 | 21.59 | 20.22 | 22.07[R] | 21.91 |
| Natural gas (dry) | 12.66 | 21.67 | 19.64 | 19.91 | 16.98 | 18.36 | 18.38 | 18.58[R] | 19.27[R] | 19.23 |
| Crude oil[2] | 14.93 | 20.40 | 17.73 | 18.25 | 18.99 | 15.57 | 15.22 | 14.49 | 14.10[R] | 13.82 |
| Natural gas plant liquids | 1.46 | 2.51 | 2.37 | 2.25 | 2.24 | 2.17 | 2.36 | 2.41 | 2.39 | 2.44 |
| Nuclear electric power | 0.01 | 0.24 | 1.90 | 2.74 | 4.15 | 6.16 | 6.61 | 6.52 | 6.84[R] | 7.19 |
| Hydroelectric pumped storage[3] | (4) | (4) | (4) | (4) | (4) | –0.04 | –0.04 | –0.04 | –0.03[R] | –0.03 |
| Renewable energy | 1.61 | 2.65 | 3.23 | 3.01 | 3.18 | 6.06[R] | 5.84[R] | 6.13[R] | 5.99[R] | 6.60 |
| Conventional hydroelectric power[5] | 1.61 | 2.63 | 3.15 | 2.90 | 2.97 | 3.01 | 2.61 | 2.88 | 2.67 | 3.20 |
| Geothermal energy | (*) | 0.01 | 0.07 | 0.11 | 0.20 | 0.34[R] | 0.37[R] | 0.38[R] | 0.38[R] | 0.36 |
| Biofuels[6] | (*) | (*) | (*) | (*) | 0.01 | 2.63 | 2.79[R] | 2.78[R] | 2.85[R] | 2.94 |
| Solar energy | 0 | 0 | 0 | 0 | 0 | 0.07 | 0.07 | 0.07 | 0.07 | 0.07 |
| Wind energy | 0 | 0 | 0 | 0 | (*) | 0.02 | 0.03 | 0.03 | 0.04 | 0.04 |
| **Imports** | **4.23** | **8.39** | **14.11** | **15.97** | **12.10** | **18.99** | **19.66[R]** | **21.54[R]** | **22.71[R]** | **22.44** |
| Natural gas | 0.16 | 0.85 | 0.98 | 1.01 | 0.95 | 1.55 | 2.16 | 2.40 | 2.68[R] | 2.80 |
| Crude oil[7] | 2.20 | 2.81 | 8.72 | 11.19 | 6.81 | 12.77 | 13.25 | 14.75 | 15.34[R] | 15.74 |
| Petroleum products[8] | 1.80 | 4.66 | 4.23 | 3.46 | 3.80 | 4.35 | 3.71 | 3.76 | 3.91[R] | 3.20 |
| Other[9] | 0.07 | 0.07 | 0.19 | 0.31 | 0.54 | 0.32 | 0.53[R] | 0.63[R] | 0.78[R] | 0.70 |
| **Exports** | **1.48** | **2.66** | **2.36** | **3.72** | **4.23** | **4.91** | **5.02** | **4.35** | **4.12[R]** | **4.58** |
| Coal | 1.02 | 1.94 | 1.76 | 2.42 | 2.44 | 2.77 | 2.68 | 1.96 | 1.88 | 2.32 |
| Crude oil | 0.43 | 0.55 | 0.44 | 1.16 | 1.66 | 1.82 | 2.01 | 2.12 | 1.99 | 1.99 |
| Other[10] | 0.03 | 0.18 | 0.16 | 0.14 | 0.14 | 0.31 | 0.33 | 0.27 | 0.26[R] | 0.27 |
| **Adjustments[11]** | **–0.43** | **–1.37** | **–1.07** | **–1.05** | **1.24** | **–0.67** | **0.65[R]** | **1.51[R]** | **–0.32[R]** | **1.59** |
| **Consumption[12]** | **43.80** | **66.43** | **70.55** | **75.96** | **73.98** | **84.17[R]** | **85.26[R]** | **87.03[R]** | **88.90[R]** | **90.62** |
| Fossil fuels | 42.14 | 63.52 | 65.35 | 69.98 | 66.22 | 71.96 | 72.55 | 74.12[R] | 75.64[R] | 76.47 |
| Coal | 9.84 | 12.26 | 12.66 | 15.42 | 17.48 | 19.10 | 18.87 | 19.43 | 19.54 | 19.62 |
| Coal coke net imports | –0.01 | –0.06 | 0.01 | –0.04 | –0.01 | (*) | 0.03 | 0.02 | 0.02 | 0.03 |
| Natural gas[13] | 12.39 | 21.79 | 19.95 | 20.39 | 17.83 | 19.30 | 20.13 | 20.83[R] | 21.34[R] | 22.20 |
| Petroleum[14] | 19.92 | 29.52 | 32.73 | 34.20 | 30.92 | 33.55 | 33.53 | 33.84 | 34.73[R] | 34.62 |
| Nuclear electric power | 0.01 | 0.24 | 1.90 | 2.74 | 4.15 | 6.16 | 6.61 | 6.52 | 6.84[R] | 7.19 |
| Hydroelectric pumped storage[3] | (4) | (4) | (4) | (4) | (4) | –0.04 | –0.04 | –0.04 | –0.03[R] | –0.03 |
| Renewable energy | 1.66 | 2.67 | 3.29 | 3.23 | 3.61 | 6.16[R] | 6.11[R] | 6.40[R] | 6.30[R] | 6.88 |
| Conventional hydroelectric power[5,15] | 1.66 | 2.65 | 3.22 | 3.12 | 3.40 | 3.10 | 2.85[R] | 3.14[R] | 2.96[R] | 3.46 |
| Geothermal energy[16] | (*) | 0.01 | 0.07 | 0.11 | 0.20 | 0.34[R] | 0.37[R] | 0.38[R] | 0.38[R] | 0.36 |
| Biofuels[6] | (*) | (*) | (*) | (*) | 0.01 | 2.63 | 2.79[R] | 2.78[R] | 2.85[R] | 2.94 |
| Solar energy | 0 | 0 | 0 | 0 | 0 | 0.07 | 0.07 | 0.07 | 0.07 | 0.07 |
| Wind energy | 0 | 0 | 0 | 0 | (*) | 0.02 | 0.03 | 0.03 | 0.04 | 0.04 |

(1) Starting in 1990, expanded coverage of nonelectric utility use of renewable energy resulted an increase in total energy production and consumption figures. (2) Includes lease condensate. (3) Total pumped storage facility production minus energy used for pumping. (4) Before 1990, pumped storage is included in conventional hydroelectric power. (5) Starting in 1990, pumped storage is removed and expanded coverage of industrial use of hydroelectric power is included. (6) These include wood, wood waste, peat, wood liquors, railroad ties, pitch, wood sludge, municipal solid waste, agricultural waste, straw, tires, landfill gases, fish oils, and/or other waste. (7) Includes imports of crude oil for the Strategic Petroleum Reserve, which began in 1977. (8) Include imports of unfinished oils and natural gas plant liquids. (9) Coal, electricity, and coal coke. (10) Natural gas, petroleum products, electricity, and coal coke. (11) A balancing item. Includes stock changes, losses, gains, miscellaneous blending components, and unaccounted-for supply. (12) Starting in 1990, "Consumption" includes the part of net imports of electricity derived from nonrenewable energy sources. (13) Includes supplemental gaseous fuels. (14) Petroleum products supplied, including natural gas plant liquids and crude oil burned as fuel. (15) Starting in 1990, includes only the part of net imports of electricity derived from hydroelectric power. (16) Includes electricity imports from Mexico derived from geothermal energy. R=revised data. P=preliminary data. (*)=Less than 0.005 quadrillion Btu. **Note:** Totals may not equal sum of components as a result of independent rounding.

## World Energy Consumption and Production Trends

**Source:** Energy Information Administration, U.S. Dept. of Energy, International Database, Aug. 1996

The world's consumption of primary energy—petroleum, natural gas, coal, and net hydroelectric, nuclear, geothermal, solar, and wind electric power—increased from 349 quadrillion Btu in 1993 to 352 quadrillion Btu in 1994. The 25 countries of the Organization for Economic Cooperation and Development (OECD), which includes some of the world's largest economies (the United States, Japan, Germany), continued to dominate global energy use. OECD nations accounted for more than 54% of the world's primary energy consumption in 1994. World production of primary energy increased from 347 quadrillion Btu in 1993 to 352 quadrillion Btu in 1994. World production of petroleum in 1994 was about 66.7 million barrels per day, or 139 quadrillion Btu; petroleum remained the most heavily used source of energy.

In 1994, 3 countries—the United States, Russia, and China—were the world's leading producers (40%) and consumers (42%) of energy. Russia and the United States alone supplied 31% of the world total. The United States alone accounted for 24% of the world's total energy consumption. The United States consumed 27% more energy than it produced—an imbalance of almost 18.3 quadrillion Btu.

## World's Major Producers of Primary Energy, 1994

**Source:** Energy Information Administration, U.S. Dept. of Energy, International Database, Aug. 1996; quadrillion Btu

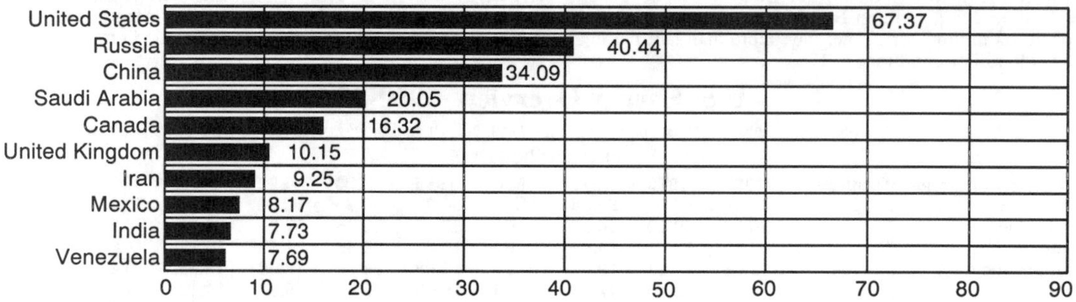


## World's Major Consumers of Primary Energy, 1994

**Source:** Energy Information Administration, U.S. Dept. of Energy, International Database, Aug. 1996; quadrillion Btu

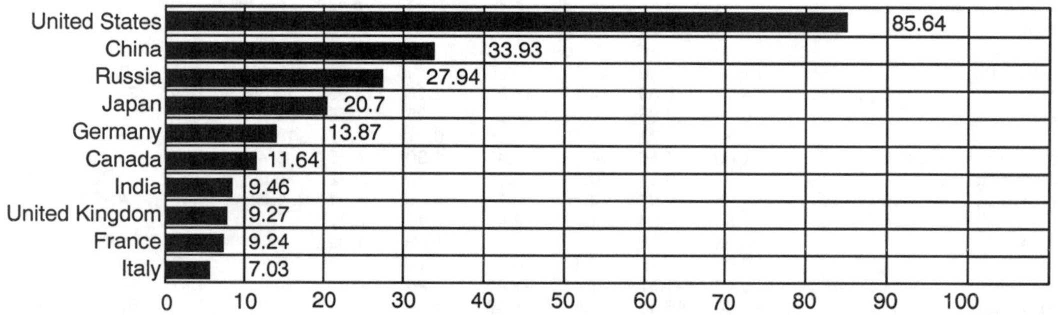


## U.S. Petroleum Trade, 1973-95

**Source:** Energy Information Administration, U.S. Dept. of Energy, *Monthly Energy Review,* June 1996

(in thousands of barrels per day; average for the year)

| Year | Imports from Persian Gulf[1] | Total imports | Total exports | Net imports[2] | Petroleum products supplied | Year | Imports from Persian Gulf[1] | Total imports | Total exports | Net imports[2] | Petroleum products supplied |
|---|---|---|---|---|---|---|---|---|---|---|---|
| 1973 | 848 | 6,256 | 231 | 6,025 | 17,308 | 1985 | 311 | 5,067 | 781 | 4,286 | 15,726 |
| 1974 | 1,039 | 6,112 | 221 | 5,892 | 16,653 | 1986 | 912 | 6,224 | 785 | 5,439 | 16,281 |
| 1975 | 1,165 | 6,056 | 209 | 5,846 | 16,322 | 1987 | 1,077 | 6,678 | 764 | 5,914 | 16,665 |
| 1976 | 1,840 | 7,313 | 223 | 7,090 | 17,461 | 1988 | 1,541 | 7,402 | 815 | 6,587 | 17,283 |
| 1977 | 2,448 | 8,807 | 243 | 8,565 | 18,431 | 1989 | 1,861 | 8,061 | 859 | 7,202 | 17,325 |
| 1978 | 2,219 | 8,363 | 362 | 8,002 | 18,847 | 1990 | 1,966 | 8,018 | 857 | 7,161 | 16,988 |
| 1979 | 2,069 | 8,456 | 471 | 7,985 | 18,513 | 1991 | 1,845 | 7,627 | 1,001 | 6,626 | 16,714 |
| 1980 | 1,519 | 6,909 | 544 | 6,365 | 17,056 | 1992 | 1,778 | 7,888 | 950 | 6,938 | 17,033 |
| 1981 | 1,219 | 5,996 | 595 | 5,401 | 16,058 | 1993 | 1,782 | 8,620 | 1,003 | 7,618 | 17,237 |
| 1982 | 696 | 5,113 | 815 | 4,298 | 15,296 | 1994 | 1,728 | 8,996 | 942 | 8,054 | 17,718 |
| 1983 | 442 | 5,051 | 739 | 4,312 | 15,231 | 1995 | 1,573 | 8,835 | 949 | 7,886 | 17,725 |
| 1984 | 506 | 5,437 | 722 | 4,715 | 15,726 | | | | | | |

(1) Bahrain, Iran, Iraq, Kuwait, Qatar, Saudi Arabia, and the United Arab Emirates. (2) Net imports are imports minus exports; figures may not add as a result of independent rounding. **Notes:** Beginning in Oct. 1977, imports for the Strategic Petroleum Reserves are included. U.S. geographic coverage includes the 50 states and the District of Columbia. U.S. exports include shipments to U.S. territories, and imports include receipts from U.S. territories.

# Appliance Use in U.S. Households, 1978-93

**Source:** Energy Information Administration, U.S. Dept. of Energy, *Annual Energy Review 1995*

(percentage of households)

| Appliance | 1978 | 1980 | 1982 | 1984 | 1987 | 1990 | 1993 | Change 1980-93 |
|---|---|---|---|---|---|---|---|---|
| **Total households** | 100 | 100 | 100 | 100 | 100 | 100 | 100 | — |
| **Type of appliances** | | | | | | | | |
| **Electric appliances** | | | | | | | | |
| Television set (color) | NA | 82 | 85 | 88 | 93 | 96 | 98 | 16 |
| Television set (B/W) | NA | 51 | 47 | 43 | 36 | 31 | 20 | –31 |
| Clothes washer | 75 | 75 | 72 | 74 | 76 | 76 | 77 | 2 |
| Range (stove-top burner) | 53 | 54 | 53 | 54 | 57 | 58 | 61 | 7 |
| Oven, regular or microwave | 54 | 59 | 59 | 63 | 79 | 88 | 91 | 32 |
| Oven, microwave | 8 | 14 | 21 | 34 | 61 | 79 | 84 | 70 |
| Clothes dryer | 45 | 47 | 45 | 46 | 51 | 53 | 57 | 10 |
| Separate freezer | 35 | 38 | 37 | 37 | 34 | 35 | 35 | –3 |
| Dishwasher | 35 | 37 | 36 | 38 | 43 | 45 | 45 | 8 |
| Dehumidifier | NA | 9 | 9 | 9 | 10 | 12 | 9 | (1) |
| Waterbed heaters | NA | NA | NA | 10 | 14 | 15 | 12 | NA |
| Window or ceiling fan | NA | NA | 28 | 35 | 46 | 51 | 60 | NA |
| Whole house fan | NA | NA | 8 | 8 | 9 | 10 | 4 | NA |
| Evaporative cooler | NA | 4 | 4 | 4 | 3 | 4 | 3 | –1 |
| Pump for well water | NA | NA | NA | NA | NA | 15 | 13 | NA |
| Swimming-pool pump[2] | NA | 4 | 3 | NA | NA | 5 | 5 | 1 |
| **Gas appliances[3]** | | | | | | | | |
| Range (stove-top burner) | 48 | 46 | 47 | 45 | 43 | 42 | 38 | –8 |
| Oven | 47 | 42 | 42 | 42 | 41 | 41 | 36 | –6 |
| Clothes dryer | 14 | 14 | 15 | 16 | 15 | 16 | 15 | 1 |
| Outdoor gas grill | NA | 9 | 11 | 13 | 20 | 26 | 29 | 20 |
| Outdoor gas light | 2 | 2 | 2 | 1 | 1 | 1 | 1 | –1 |
| Swimming pool heater[4] | NA | NA | NA | 1 | 1 | 2 | 1 | NA |
| **Refrigerators[5]** | | | | | | | | |
| One | 86 | 86 | 86 | 88 | 86 | 84 | 85 | –1 |
| Two or more | 14 | 14 | 13 | 12 | 14 | 15 | 15 | 1 |
| **Air conditioning** | | | | | | | | |
| Central[6] | 23 | 27 | 28 | 30 | 36 | 39 | 44 | 17 |
| Individual room units[6] | 33 | 30 | 30 | 30 | 30 | 29 | 25 | –5 |
| None | 44 | 43 | 42 | 40 | 36 | 32 | 32 | –11 |
| **Portable kerosene heaters** | **(1)** | **(1)** | **3** | **6** | **6** | **5** | **2** | **2** |

(1) Less than 0.5%. (2) All reported swimming pools were assumed to have an electric pump for filtering and circulating the water, except for 1993, when a filtering system was made explicit. (3) Includes natural gas or liquefied petroleum gases. (4) In 1984 and 1987, also includes heaters for jacuzzis and hot tubs. (5) Fewer than 0.5% of the households did not have a refrigerator. (6) Households with both central and individual room units are counted only under "Central." NA= not available. **Note:** Percentages may not add because of independent rounding.

# Energy Consumption and Consumption per Capita by State, 1994

**Source:** Energy Information Administration, U.S. Dept. of Energy, State Energy Data System; preliminary data

**Consumption**

| Rank | State | Trillion Btu | Rank | State | Trillion Btu |
|---|---|---|---|---|---|
| 1. | Texas | 10,388.5 | 28. | Colorado | 1,050.5 |
| 2. | California | 7,556.9 | 29. | Oregon | 1,038.2 |
| 3. | Ohio | 3,968.4 | 30. | Iowa | 1,034.7 |
| 4. | New York | 3,868.0 | 31. | Arizona | 1,033.8 |
| 5. | Pennsylvania | 3,832.2 | 32. | Arkansas | 956.5 |
| 6. | Louisiana | 3,817.8 | 33. | West Virginia | 817.2 |
| 7. | Illinois | 3,708.1 | 34. | Connecticut | 797.2 |
| 8. | Florida | 3,382.4 | 35. | Alaska | 633.3 |
| 9. | Michigan | 3,090.3 | 36. | Utah | 594.8 |
| 10. | New Jersey | 2,546.8 | 37. | New Mexico | 590.8 |
| 11. | Indiana | 2,528.2 | 38. | Nebraska | 560.1 |
| 12. | Georgia | 2,377.7 | 39. | Maine | 546.9 |
| 13. | North Carolina | 2,215.0 | 40. | Nevada | 514.4 |
| 14. | Washington | 2,088.5 | 41. | Idaho | 441.3 |
| 15. | Virginia | 1,996.7 | 42. | Wyoming | 410.8 |
| 16. | Tennessee | 1,955.4 | 43. | Montana | 368.8 |
| 17. | Alabama | 1,883.5 | 44. | North Dakota | 344.5 |
| 18. | Wisconsin | 1,714.4 | 45. | New Hampshire | 285.5 |
| 19. | Kentucky | 1,705.3 | 46. | Delaware | 265.4 |
| 20. | Missouri | 1,613.3 | 47. | Hawaii | 259.6 |
| 21. | Minnesota | 1,562.7 | 48. | Rhode Island | 248.1 |
| 22. | Massachusetts | 1,487.5 | 49. | South Dakota | 232.5 |
| 23. | Oklahoma | 1,381.6 | 50. | District of Columbia | 176.0 |
| 24. | South Carolina | 1,359.6 | 51. | Vermont | 152.6 |
| 25. | Maryland | 1,283.0 | | **Total U.S.** | **88,886.3** |
| 26. | Kansas | 1,071.9 | | | |
| 27. | Mississippi | 1,062.9 | | | |

**Consumption per Capita**

| Rank | State | Million Btu | Rank | State | Million Btu |
|---|---|---|---|---|---|
| 1. | Alaska | 1,050.8 | 28. | Georgia | 336.9 |
| 2. | Louisiana | 884.5 | 29. | Oregon | 336.3 |
| 3. | Wyoming | 862.8 | 30. | Michigan | 325.6 |
| 4. | Texas | 564.2 | 31. | New Jersey | 322.3 |
| 5. | North Dakota | 538.9 | 32. | South Dakota | 321.5 |
| 6. | West Virginia | 448.1 | 33. | Pennsylvania | 317.7 |
| 7. | Alabama | 446.3 | 34. | Illinois | 315.3 |
| 8. | Kentucky | 445.5 | 35. | North Carolina | 313.3 |
| 9. | Maine | 441.3 | 36. | Utah | 311.6 |
| 10. | Indiana | 439.3 | 37. | District of Columbia | 310.3 |
| 11. | Montana | 430.8 | 38. | Missouri | 305.6 |
| 12. | Oklahoma | 424.2 | 39. | Virginia | 304.8 |
| 13. | Kansas | 420.2 | 40. | Colorado | 286.9 |
| 14. | Mississippi | 398.0 | 41. | Vermont | 263.0 |
| 15. | Washington | 391.2 | 42. | Maryland | 256.6 |
| 16. | Arkansas | 389.9 | 43. | Arizona | 253.5 |
| 17. | Idaho | 389.0 | 44. | New Hampshire | 251.4 |
| 18. | Tennessee | 377.8 | 45. | Rhode Island | 249.5 |
| 19. | Delaware | 374.9 | 46. | Massachusetts | 246.2 |
| 20. | South Carolina | 373.2 | 47. | Connecticut | 243.4 |
| 21. | Iowa | 365.5 | 48. | Florida | 242.3 |
| 22. | Ohio | 357.4 | 49. | California | 240.6 |
| 23. | New Mexico | 356.9 | 50. | Hawaii | 220.3 |
| 24. | Nevada | 351.8 | 51. | New York | 213.1 |
| 25. | Nebraska | 344.8 | | **Total U.S.** | **341.4** |
| 26. | Minnesota | 342.1 | | | |
| 27. | Wisconsin | 337.3 | | | |

# World Crude Oil and Natural Gas Reserves, Jan. 1, 1995

**Sources:** Energy Information Administration, U.S. Dept. of Energy, *Annual Energy Review 1995; Oil and Gas Journal,* PennWell Publishing Co., Dec. 1994; *World Oil,* Gulf Publishing Co., Aug. 1995

| Region and country | Crude oil (billion barrels) *Oil and Gas Journal* | Crude oil (billion barrels) *World Oil* | Natural gas (trillion cubic feet) *Oil and Gas Journal* | Natural gas (trillion cubic feet) *World Oil* |
|---|---|---|---|---|
| **North America** | **78.3** | **78.1** | **312.7** | **312.4** |
| Canada | 5.0 | 5.8 | 79.2 | 80.1 |
| Mexico | 50.8 | 49.8 | 69.7 | 68.4 |
| United States | 22.5 | 22.5 | 163.8 | 163.8 |
| **Central and South America** | **78.3** | **82.0** | **189.1** | **204.4** |
| Argentina | 2.2 | 2.2 | 18.2 | 19.6 |
| Bolivia | 0.1 | 0.1 | 4.5 | 3.8 |
| Brazil | 3.8 | 4.2 | 4.9 | 5.5 |
| Colombia | 3.4 | 5.0 | 7.9 | 10.0 |
| Ecuador | 2.0 | 3.0 | 3.8 | 3.9 |
| Peru | 0.8 | 1.2 | 7.0 | 7.1 |
| Trinidad and Tobago | 0.5 | 0.6 | 8.5 | 10.8 |
| Venezuela | 64.5 | 64.9 | 130.4 | 140.0 |
| Other | 1.0 | 0.8 | 4.0 | 3.7 |
| **Western Europe** | **16.8** | **35.5** | **194.3** | **271.9** |
| Denmark | 0.7 | 0.8 | 4.3 | 4.9 |
| Germany | 0.4 | 0.3 | 10.7 | 12.5 |
| Italy | 0.6 | 0.7 | 13.2 | 11.1 |
| Netherlands | 0.1 | 0.4 | 66.2 | 70.5 |
| Norway | 9.4 | 17.0 | 70.9 | 101.2 |
| United Kingdom | 4.5 | 15.5 | 22.2 | 67.6 |
| Other | 1.0 | 0.8 | 6.7 | 4.2 |
| **Eastern Europe and Former USSR** | **59.0** | **192.4** | **1,999.0** | **1,951.8** |
| Hungary | 0.1 | 0.1 | 3.5 | 3.5 |
| Romania | 1.6 | 1.0 | 12.3 | 4.6 |
| Former USSR | 57.0 | 191.1 | 1,977.0 | 1,937.0 |
| Other[1] | 0.2 | 0.2 | 6.3 | 6.7 |
| **Middle East** | **660.3** | **597.6** | **1,594.3** | **1,383.7** |
| Bahrain | 0.2 | 0.1 | 5.3 | 5.6 |
| Iran | 89.3 | 58.7 | 741.6 | 620.0 |
| Iraq | 100.0 | 99.4 | 109.5 | 108.0 |
| Kuwait | 96.5 | 97.7 | 52.9 | 51.1 |
| Oman | 4.8 | 5.0 | 22.2 | 25.3 |
| Qatar | 3.7 | 4.9 | 250.0 | 164.0 |
| Saudi Arabia | 261.2 | 262.5 | 185.9 | 188.9 |
| Syria | 2.5 | 2.7 | 7.0 | 7.0 |
| United Arab Emirates | 98.1 | 63.4 | 204.6 | 198.7 |
| Yemen | 4.0 | 3.4 | 15.0 | 15.0 |
| Other | 0.0 | 0.0 | 0.2 | 0.2 |
| **Africa** | **62.2** | **72.8** | **341.6** | **316.6** |
| Algeria | 9.2 | 10.2 | 128.0 | 102.0 |
| Angola | 5.4 | 2.0 | 1.8 | 2.0 |
| Cameroon | 0.4 | 0.3 | 3.9 | 3.9 |
| Congo | 0.8 | 0.6 | 2.7 | 2.7 |
| Egypt | 3.3 | 3.4 | 19.3 | 21.0 |
| Libya | 22.8 | 36.6 | 45.8 | 45.2 |
| Nigeria | 17.9 | 17.2 | 120.0 | 120.8 |
| Tunisia | 0.4 | 0.3 | 1.1 | 1.2 |
| Other | 2.0 | 2.3 | 19.0 | 17.8 |
| **Far East and Oceania** | **44.5** | **52.9** | **350.6** | **309.0** |
| Australia | 1.6 | 1.9 | 19.6 | 20.8 |
| Brunei | 1.4 | 1.2 | 14.0 | 12.9 |
| China | 24.0 | 30.2 | 59.0 | 45.5 |
| India | 5.8 | 5.8 | 25.0 | 24.2 |
| Indonesia | 5.8 | 6.3 | 64.4 | 64.9 |
| Malaysia | 4.3 | 5.1 | 68.0 | 80.8 |
| New Zealand | 0.1 | 0.1 | 3.0 | 2.9 |
| Pakistan | 0.2 | 0.2 | 27.5 | 21.1 |
| Papua New Guinea | 0.2 | 0.5 | 15.0 | 0.0 |
| Thailand | 0.2 | 0.2 | 6.2 | 5.9 |
| Other | 0.8 | 1.5 | 49.0 | 30.0 |
| **World** | **999.3** | **1,111.3** | **4,981.7** | **4,749.8** |

(1) Albania, Bulgaria, former Czechoslovakia, and Poland. **Notes:** Data for Kuwait and Saudi Arabia include one-half of the reserves in the Neutral Zone between Kuwait and Saudi Arabia. All reserve figures except those for the former USSR and natural gas reserves in Canada are proved reserves recoverable with present technology and prices. Former USSR figures are "explored reserves," which include proved, probable, and some partially possible. The Canadian natural gas figure includes proved and some probable. The latest Energy Information Administration data for the U.S. are for Dec. 31, 1994. Totals may not equal sum of components as a result of independent rounding.

# Gasoline Retail Prices, U.S. City Average, 1973-95

**Source:** Energy Information Administration, U.S. Dept. of Energy, *Monthly Energy Review,* June 1996

(cents per gallon, including taxes)

| Average | Leaded regular | Unleaded regular | Unleaded premium | All types[1] |
|---|---|---|---|---|
| 1973 | 38.8 | NA | NA | NA |
| 1974 | 53.2 | NA | NA | NA |
| 1975 | 56.7 | NA | NA | NA |
| 1976 | 59.0 | 61.4 | NA | NA |
| 1977 | 62.2 | 65.6 | NA | NA |
| 1978 | 62.6 | 67.0 | NA | 65.2 |
| 1979 | 85.7 | 90.3 | NA | 88.2 |
| 1980 | 119.1 | 124.5 | NA | 122.1 |
| 1981[2] | 131.1 | 137.8 | 147.0[3] | 135.3 |
| 1982 | 122.2 | 129.6 | 141.5 | 128.1 |
| 1983 | 115.7 | 124.1 | 138.3 | 122.5 |
| 1984 | 112.9 | 121.2 | 136.6 | 119.8 |
| 1985 | 111.5 | 120.2 | 134.0 | 119.6 |
| 1986 | 85.7 | 92.7 | 108.5 | 93.1 |
| 1987 | 89.7 | 94.8 | 109.3 | 95.7 |
| 1988 | 89.9 | 94.6 | 110.7 | 96.3 |
| 1989 | 99.8 | 102.1 | 119.7 | 106.0 |
| 1990 | 114.9 | 116.4 | 134.9 | 121.7 |
| 1991 | NA | 114.0 | 132.1 | 119.6 |
| 1992 | NA | 112.7 | 131.6 | 119.0 |
| 1993 | NA | 110.8 | 130.2 | 117.3 |
| 1994 | NA | 111.2 | 130.5 | 117.4 |
| 1995 | NA | 114.7 | 133.6 | 120.5 |

(1) Also includes types of motor gasoline not shown separately. (2) In Sept. 1981, the Bureau of Labor Statistics changed the weights used in the calculation of average motor gasoline prices. Starting in Sept. 1981, gasohol is included in the average for all types, and unleaded premium is weighted more heavily. (3) Based on Sept. through Dec. data only. **Notes:** Geographic coverage for 1973-77 is 56 urban areas; for 1978 and later, 85 urban areas. NA = not available.

# Nuclear Electricity Gross Generation by Selected Country, Mar. 1996

**Source:** Energy Information Administration, U.S. Dept. of Energy; *Monthly Energy Review,* June 1996

(billion kilowatt-hours; E = estimate)

| | | | | | | | |
|---|---|---|---|---|---|---|---|
| Argentina | 0.7 | France | 35.8 | Lithuania | 1.6 | Sweden | 7.5 |
| Belgium | 3.9 | Germany | 13.1 | Mexico | 0.9 | Switzerland | 2.4 |
| Brazil | 0.6 | Hungary | 1.3 | Netherlands | 0.2 | Taiwan | 2.9 |
| Bulgaria | 2.3 | India | 0.8 | Russia | 11.2 | Ukraine | 8.3 |
| Canada | 10.2 | Japan | 25.1 | South Africa | 1.1 | United Kingdom | 7.5[E] |
| Finland | 1.8 | Korea, South | 6.2 | Spain | 4.9 | United States | 57.8[E] |

# World Nuclear Power

**Source:** International Atomic Energy Agency, Dec. 31, 1995

| | Reactors in operation | | Reactors under construction | | Nuclear electricity supplied in 1995 | | Total operating experience to Dec. 31, 1995 | |
|---|---|---|---|---|---|---|---|---|
| Country | No. of units | Total MW(e) | No. of units | Total MW(e) | TW(e).h[1] | % of total | Years | Months |
| Argentina | 2 | 935 | 1 | 692 | 7.07 | 11.79 | 34 | 7 |
| Armenia | 1 | 376 | — | — | — | — | 28 | 4 |
| Belgium | 7 | 5,631 | — | — | 39.20 | 55.52 | 135 | 7 |
| Brazil | 1 | 626 | 1 | 1,245 | 2.50 | 0.97 | 13 | 9 |
| Bulgaria | 6 | 3,538 | — | — | 17.26 | 46.43 | 83 | 1 |
| Canada | 21 | 14,907 | — | — | 92.31 | 17.26 | 348 | 9 |
| China | 3 | 2,167 | — | — | 12.38 | 1.24 | 8 | 5 |
| Czech Republic | 4 | 1,648 | 2 | 1,824 | 12.23 | 20.10 | 38 | 8 |
| Finland | 4 | 2,310 | — | — | 18.13 | 29.91 | 67 | 4 |
| France | 56 | 58,493 | 4 | 5,810 | 358.60 | 76.14 | 878 | 10 |
| Germany | 20 | 22,017 | — | — | 154.14 | 29.09 | 510 | 7 |
| Hungary | 4 | 1,729 | — | — | 13.20 | 42.30 | 42 | 2 |
| India | 10 | 1,695 | 4 | 808 | 6.46 | 1.89 | 129 | 1 |
| Iran | — | — | 2 | 2,146 | — | — | — | — |
| Japan | 51 | 39,893 | 3 | 3,757 | 286.90 | 33.40 | 704 | 5 |
| Kazakstan | 1 | 70 | — | — | 0.08 | 0.13 | 22 | 6 |
| Korea, South | 11 | 9,120 | 5 | 3,870 | 63.68 | 36.10 | 100 | 10 |
| Lithuania | 2 | 2,370 | — | — | 10.64 | 85.59 | 20 | 6 |
| Mexico | 2 | 1,308 | — | — | 8.44 | 6.00 | 7 | 11 |
| Netherlands | 2 | 504 | — | — | 3.70 | 4.86 | 49 | 9 |
| Pakistan | 1 | 125 | 1 | 300 | 0.46 | 0.88 | 24 | 3 |
| Romania | — | — | 2 | 1,300 | — | — | — | — |
| Russia | 29 | 19,843 | 4 | 3,375 | 99.38 | 11.79 | 526 | 6 |
| Slovakia | 4 | 1,632 | 4 | 1,552 | 11.44 | 44.14 | 61 | 5 |
| Slovenia | 1 | 632 | — | — | 4.56 | 39.46 | 14 | 3 |
| South Africa | 2 | 1,842 | — | — | 11.28 | 6.48 | 22 | 3 |
| Spain | 9 | 7,124 | — | — | 53.10 | 34.06 | 147 | 2 |
| Sweden | 12 | 10,002 | — | — | 66.70 | 46.61 | 219 | 2 |
| Switzerland | 5 | 3,050 | — | — | 23.49 | 39.92 | 103 | 10 |
| Taiwan | 6 | 4,884 | — | — | 33.93 | 28.79 | 86 | 1 |
| Ukraine | 16 | 13,629 | 5 | 4,750 | 65.64 | 37.83 | 174 | 2 |
| United Kingdom | 35 | 12,908 | — | — | 77.64 | 24.99 | 1,063 | 4 |
| United States | 109 | 98,784 | 1 | 1,165 | 673.40 | 22.49 | 2,028 | 8 |
| **Total** | **437** | **343,792** | **39** | **32,594** | **2,227.94** | **—** | **7,696** | **2** |

(1) 1 terawatt-hour [TW(e).h] = $10^6$ megawatt-hour [MW(e).h]. For an average power plant, 1 TW(e).h = 0.39 megatonnes of coal equivalent (input) and 0.23 megatonnes of oil equivalent (input). **Note:** In 1995, 2 reactors were shut down—1 in Canada (which can restart in the future) and 1 in Germany.

# U.S. Nuclear Power Plant Operations

**Source:** Energy Information Administration, U.S. Dept. of Energy, *Monthly Energy Review,* June 1996

| | Operable reactors (number) | Nuclear-based electricity generation (million net kilowatt-hours) | Nuclear portion of domestic electricity generation (percent) |
|---|---|---|---|
| 1976 | 61 | 191,104 | 9.4 |
| 1977 | 65 | 250,883 | 11.8 |
| 1978 | 70 | 276,403 | 12.5 |
| 1979 | 68 | 255,155 | 11.4 |
| 1980 | 70 | 251,116 | 11.0 |
| 1981 | 74 | 272,674 | 11.9 |
| 1982 | 77 | 282,773 | 12.6 |
| 1983 | 80 | 293,677 | 12.7 |
| 1984 | 86 | 327,634 | 13.6 |
| 1985 | 95 | 383,691 | 15.5 |
| 1986 | 100 | 414,038 | 16.6 |
| 1987 | 107 | 455,270 | 17.7 |
| 1988 | 108 | 526,973 | 19.5 |
| 1989 | 110 | 529,355 | 19.0 |
| 1990 | 111 | 576,862 | 20.5 |
| 1991 | 111 | 612,565 | 21.7 |
| 1992 | 109 | 618,776 | 22.1 |
| 1993 | 109 | 610,291 | 21.2 |
| 1994 | 109 | 640,440 | 22.0 |
| 1995 | 109 | 673,402 | 22.5 |

# Status of U.S. Nuclear Reactor Units

**Source:** Energy Information Administration, U.S. Dept. of Energy, *Monthly Energy Review,* June 1996

(number of reactor units)

| | Licensed for operation | | Construction permits | | | | | |
|---|---|---|---|---|---|---|---|---|
| | Operable | In startup | Granted | Pending | On order | Announced | Total | Total design capacity (million net kilowatts) |
| 1980 | 70 | 1 | 82 | 12 | 3 | 0 | 168 | 162 |
| 1981 | 74 | 0 | 76 | 11 | 2 | 0 | 163 | 157 |
| 1982 | 77 | 2 | 60 | 3 | 2 | 0 | 144 | 134 |
| 1983 | 80 | 3 | 53 | 0 | 2 | 0 | 138 | 129 |
| 1984 | 86 | 6 | 38 | 0 | 2 | 0 | 132 | 123 |
| 1985 | 95 | 3 | 30 | 0 | 2 | 0 | 130 | 121 |
| 1986 | 100 | 7 | 19 | 0 | 2 | 0 | 128 | 119 |
| 1987 | 107 | 4 | 14 | 0 | 2 | 0 | 127 | 119 |
| 1988 | 108 | 3 | 12 | 0 | 0 | 0 | 123 | 115 |
| 1989 | 110 | 1 | 10 | 0 | 0 | 0 | 121 | 113 |
| 1990 | 111 | 0 | 8 | 0 | 0 | 0 | 119 | 111 |
| 1991 | 111 | 0 | 8 | 0 | 0 | 0 | 119 | 111 |
| 1992 | 109 | 0 | 8 | 0 | 0 | 0 | 117 | 111 |
| 1993 | 109 | 0 | 7 | 0 | 0 | 0 | 116 | 110 |
| 1994 | 109 | 0 | 7 | 0 | 0 | 0 | 116 | 110 |
| 1995 | 109 | 1 | 6 | 0 | 0 | 0 | 116 | 110 |

# TRADE AND TRANSPORTATION

## U.S. Trade With Selected Countries and Major Areas, 1995

**Source:** Office of Trade and Economic Analysis, U.S. Dept. of Commerce

(millions of dollars)

| Country/Area | U.S. trade balance with | Rank | Exports to | Rank | Imports from | Rank |
|---|---|---|---|---|---|---|
| Japan | –59,136.5 | 1 | 64,342.6 | 2 | 123,479.1 | 2 |
| China | –33,789.6 | 2 | 11,753.6 | 13 | 45,543.2 | 4 |
| Canada | –18,122.7 | 3 | 127,226.1 | 1 | 145,348.7 | 1 |
| Mexico | –15,392.5 | 4 | 46,292.1 | 3 | 61,684.6 | 3 |
| Germany | –14,449.8 | 5 | 22,394.3 | 6 | 36,844.0 | 5 |
| Taiwan | –9,682.2 | 6 | 19,289.6 | 7 | 28,971.8 | 6 |
| Malaysia | –8,636.6 | 7 | 8,816.1 | 17 | 17,452.8 | 10 |
| Italy | –7,486.7 | 8 | 8,861.6 | 16 | 16,348.3 | 12 |
| Venezuela | –5,080.4 | 9 | 4,640.4 | 24 | 9,720.8 | 15 |
| Thailand | –4,683.1 | 10 | 6,665.0 | 18 | 11,348.1 | 13 |
| Nigeria | –4,197.7 | 11 | 602.8 | 60 | 4,800.5 | 26 |
| Indonesia | –4,075.7 | 12 | 3,359.6 | 29 | 7,435.3 | 19 |
| Singapore | –2,337.8 | 13 | 13,019.9 | 10 | 15,357.7 | 10 |
| Sweden | –3,176.6 | 14 | 3,079.8 | 31 | 6,256.4 | 22 |
| France | –3,080.2 | 15 | 14,245.2 | 10 | 17,209.4 | 11 |
| India | –2,430.5 | 16 | 3,295.8 | 30 | 5,726.2 | 24 |
| Saudi Arabia | –2,082.1 | 17 | 6,154.9 | 20 | 8,237.0 | 17 |
| Angola | –1,952.8 | 18 | 259.6 | 75 | 2,212.4 | 35 |
| Norway | –1,793.7 | 19 | 1,293.0 | 49 | 3,086.7 | 33 |
| Philippines | –1,711.7 | 20 | 5,294.8 | 23 | 7,006.5 | 20 |
| Gabon | –1,395.0 | 21 | 54.4 | 121 | 1,449.4 | 47 |
| Switzerland | –1,366.4 | 22 | 6,227.5 | 19 | 7,593.8 | 18 |
| Russia | –1,206.6 | 23 | 2,823.3 | 34 | 4,030.0 | 28 |
| Finland | –1,020.3 | 24 | 1,249.7 | 51 | 2,270.0 | 34 |
| Sri Lanka | –980.5 | 25 | 279.1 | 73 | 1,259.7 | 50 |
| North America | –33,515.2 | NA | 173,518.1 | NA | 207,033.3 | NA |
| Western Europe | –10,456.9 | NA | 134,863.2 | NA | 145,320.0 | NA |
| European Union (EU) | –8,163.4 | NA | 123,671.2 | NA | 131,834.5 | NA |
| European Free Trade Association | –3,333.5 | NA | 7,706.0 | NA | 11,039.4 | NA |
| Eastern Europe | –1,318.8 | NA | 5,700.8 | NA | 7,019.6 | NA |
| Former Soviet Republics | –1,088.2 | NA | 3,807.3 | NA | 4,895.5 | NA |
| Organization for Economic Cooperation & Development (OECD) in Europe | –10,523.6 | NA | 134,161.6 | NA | 144,685.2 | NA |
| Pacific Rim Countries | –108,131.1 | NA | 180,551.8 | NA | 288,682.9 | NA |
| Asia—Middle East | 1,121.4 | NA | 17,537.2 | NA | 16,415.9 | NA |
| Asia—Newly Industrialized Countries (NICS) | –7,773.4 | NA | 74,234.1 | NA | 82,007.5 | NA |
| South Asia | –4,686.4 | NA | 4,855.2 | NA | 9,541.6 | NA |
| Assn. of Southeast Asian Nations (ASEAN) | –22,183.0 | NA | 39,658.6 | NA | 61,841.6 | NA |
| South/Central America | 7,737.3 | NA | 49,992.0 | NA | 42,254.7 | NA |
| Twenty Latin American Republics | –10,126.3 | NA | 90,698.4 | NA | 100,824.7 | NA |
| Central American Common Market | 160.3 | NA | 6,022.3 | NA | 5,862.1 | NA |
| Latin American Free Trade Association (LAFTA) | –11,411.1 | NA | 79,715.8 | NA | 91,126.8 | NA |
| North Atlantic Treaty Organization (NATO) Allies | –23,058.7 | NA | 244,673.5 | NA | 267,732.2 | NA |
| Organization of Petroleum Exporting Countries (OPEC) | –15,663.6 | NA | 19,533.3 | NA | 35,196.9 | NA |
| Unidentified[1] | 564.8 | NA | 564.8 | NA | (–) | NA |
| **Total** | **$–158,703.0** | **NA** | **$584,742.0** | **NA** | **$743,445.0** | **NA** |

(1) The export totals reflect shipments of certain grains, oilseeds, and satellites that are not included in the country/area totals. NA – Not applicable. **Note:** Details may not equal totals because of rounding.

Definitions of areas as used in the above table:

**North America**—Canada, Mexico.
**Western Europe**—Andorra, Austria, Belgium, Bosnia and Herzegovina, Croatia, Cyprus, Denmark, Faeroe Islands, Finland, France, Germany, Gibraltar, Greece, Iceland, Ireland, Italy, Liechtenstein, Luxembourg, Macedonia, Malta, Monaco, Netherlands, Norway, Portugal, San Marino, Slovenia, Spain, Svalbard/Jan Mayen Island, Sweden, Switzerland, Turkey, United Kingdom, Vatican City, Yugoslavia.
**European Union**—Statistics cover Belgium, Denmark, France, Germany, Greece, Ireland, Italy, Luxembourg, Netherlands, Portugal, Spain, United Kingdom.
**European Free Trade Association** —Austria, Finland, Iceland, Liechtenstein, Norway, Sweden, Switzerland.
**Eastern Europe**—Albania, Armenia, Azerbaijan, Belarus, Bulgaria, Czech Republic, Estonia, Georgia, Hungary, Kazakstan, Kyrgyzstan, Latvia, Lithuania, Moldova, Poland, Romania, Russia, Slovakia, Tajikistan, Turkmenistan, Ukraine, Uzbekistan.
**Former Soviet Republics**—Armenia, Azerbaijan, Belarus, Estonia, Georgia, Kazakstan, Kyrgyzstan, Latvia, Lithuania, Moldova, Russia, Tajikistan, Turkmenistan, Ukraine, Uzbekistan.
**OECD**—Austria, Belgium, Denmark, Finland, France, Germany, Greece, Iceland, Ireland, Italy, Liechtenstein, Luxembourg, Monaco, Netherlands, Norway, Portugal, San Marino, Spain, Svalbard/Jan Mayen Island, Sweden, Switzerland, Turkey, United Kingdom.
**Pacific Rim Countries**—Australia, Brunei, China, Hong Kong, Indonesia, Japan, South Korea, Macao, Malaysia, New Zealand, Papua New Guinea, Philippines, Singapore, Taiwan.
**Asia—Middle East**—Bahrain, Iran, Iraq, Israel, Jordan, Kuwait, Lebanon, Oman, Qatar, Saudi Arabia, Syria, United Arab Emirates, Yemen.
**Asia—Newly Industrialized Countries (NICS)**—Hong Kong, South Korea, Singapore, Taiwan.
**South Asia**—Afghanistan, Bangladesh, India, Nepal, Pakistan, Sri Lanka.
**ASEAN**—Statistics cover Brunei, Indonesia, Malaysia, Philippines, Singapore, Thailand.
**South/Central America**—Anguilla, Antigua and Barbuda, Argentina, Aruba, Bahamas, Barbados, Belize, Bermuda, Bolivia, Brazil, British Virgin Islands, Cayman Islands, Chile, Colombia, Costa Rica, Cuba, Dominica, Dominican Republic, Ecuador, El Salvador, Falkland Islands, French Guiana, Grenada, Guadeloupe, Guatemala, Guyana, Haiti, Honduras, Jamaica, Martinique, Montserrat, Netherland Antilles, Nicaragua, Panama, Paraguay, Peru, St. Kitts and Nevis, St. Lucia, St. Vincent and the Grenadines, Suriname, Trinidad and Tobago, Turks and Caicos Islands, Uruguay, Venezuela.
**Twenty Latin American Republics**—Argentina, Bolivia, Brazil, Chile, Colombia, Costa Rica, Cuba, Dominican Republic, Ecuador, El Salvador, Guatemala, Haiti, Honduras, Mexico, Nicaragua, Panama, Paraguay, Peru, Uruguay, Venezuela.
**Central American Common Market**—Costa Rica, El Salvador, Guatemala, Honduras, Nicaragua.
**LAFTA**—Argentina, Bolivia, Brazil, Chile, Colombia, Ecuador, Mexico, Paraguay, Peru, Uruguay, Venezuela.
**NATO Allies**—Belgium, Canada, Denmark, France, Germany, Greece, Iceland, Ireland, Italy, Liechtenstein, Luxembourg, Monaco, Netherlands, Norway, Portugal, San Marino, Spain, Svalbard Jan Mayan Island, Sweden, Switzerland, Turkey, United Kingdom.
**OPEC**—Algeria, Gabon, Indonesia, Iran, Iraq, Kuwait, Libya, Nigeria, Qatar, Saudi Arabia, United Arab Emirates, Venezuela.

## U.S. Exports and Imports by Principal Commodity Groupings, 1995

**Source:** Office of Trade and Economic Analysis, U.S. Dept. of Commerce

(millions of dollars)

| Item | Exports | Imports |
|---|---|---|
| **Total** | **$584,742** | **$743,445** |
| **Agricultural commodities** | **54,850** | **29,258** |
| Animal feeds | 3,667 | 472 |
| Bulbs | 110 | 283 |
| Cereal flour | 1,163 | 1,082 |
| Cocoa | 39 | 722 |
| Coffee | 15 | 2,985 |
| Corn | 7,521 | 66 |
| Cotton, raw and linters | 3,711 | 29 |
| Dairy products; eggs | 776 | 820 |
| Fur skins, raw | 127 | 59 |
| Grains, unmilled | 721 | 176 |
| Hides and skins | 1,621 | 140 |
| Live animals | 521 | 1,729 |
| Meat and preparations | 6,450 | 2,317 |
| Oils/fats, animal | 789 | 24 |
| Oils/fats, vegetable | 1,293 | 1,157 |
| Plants | 120 | 130 |
| Rice | 994 | 121 |
| Seeds | 321 | 172 |
| Soybeans | 5,422 | 32 |
| Sugar | 5 | 682 |
| Tobacco, unmanufactured | 1,397 | 555 |
| Vegetables and fruit | 7,096 | 6,581 |
| Wheat | 6,464 | 238 |
| Other agricultural | 5,504 | 8,887 |
| **Manufactured goods** | **451,826** | **829,685** |
| ADP equipment; office mach. | 36,410 | **62,73** |
| Airplanes | 13,836 | 3,651 |
| Airplane parts | 10,349 | 2,616 |
| Aluminum | 3,775 | 5,819 |
| Artwork/antiques | 1,071 | 2,666 |
| Basketware, etc. | 1,996 | 2,942 |
| Chemicals - cosmetics | 3,835 | 2,307 |
| Chemicals - dyeing | 2,585 | 2,079 |
| Chemicals - fertilizers | 3,219 | 1,391 |
| Chemicals - inorganic | 4,541 | 4,658 |
| Chemicals - medicinal | 6,434 | 5,543 |
| Chemicals - organic | 16,106 | 13,334 |
| Chemicals - plastics | 14,958 | 7,155 |
| Chemicals - other | 9,131 | 3,925 |
| Clothing | 6,482 | 39,523 |
| Copper | 1,728 | 2,983 |
| Electrical machinery | 58,139 | 75,051 |
| Footwear | 671 | 12,098 |
| Furniture and parts | 3,125 | 8,338 |
| Gem diamonds | 171 | 5,951 |
| General industrial mach. | 24,394 | 24,125 |
| Glass | 1,644 | 1,468 |
| Glassware | 630 | 1,333 |
| Gold, nonmonetary | 5,055 | 2,155 |
| Iron and steel mill products | 5,349 | 12,279 |
| Lighting, plumbing | $1,293 | $2,284 |
| Metal manufactures | 8,060 | 10,010 |
| Metalworking machinery | 4,626 | 5,926 |
| Motorcycles, bicycles | 1,786 | 2,825 |
| Nickel | 284 | 1,197 |
| Optical goods | 1,113 | 1,197 |
| Paper and paperboard | 9,572 | 2,148 |
| Photographic equipment | 3,351 | 12,470 |
| Plastic articles | 3,847 | 5,145 |
| Platinum | 318 | 5,101 |
| Pottery | 99 | 1,694 |
| Power generating mach. | 21,856 | 1,667 |
| Printed materials | 4,325 | 20,493 |
| Records/magnetic media | 6,263 | 2,584 |
| Rubber articles | 888 | 3,896 |
| Rubber tires and tubes | 14,858 | 1,415 |
| Scientific instruments | 18,616 | 5,144 |
| Ships, boats | 1,176 | 11,581 |
| Silver and bullion | 663 | 816 |
| Spacecraft | 655 | 580 |
| Specialized ind. mach. | 23,311 | 169 |
| Telecommunications equip. | 19,005 | 18,972 |
| Textile yarn, fabric | 7,192 | 34,457 |
| Toys/games/sporting goods | 3,560 | 9,960 |
| Travel goods | 253 | 19,074 |
| Vehicles/new cars - Canada | 7,187 | 3,406 |
| Vehicles/new cars - Japan | 2,642 | 24,623 |
| Vehicles/new cars - other | 5,100 | 21,441 |
| Vehicles/trucks | 5,646 | 16,041 |
| Vehicles/chassis/bodies | 441 | 11,284 |
| Vehicles/parts | 23,354 | 436 |
| Watches/clocks/parts | 248 | 20,132 |
| Wood manufactures | 1,633 | 2,785 |
| Zinc | 58 | 3,687 |
| Other manufactured goods | 30,911 | 44,933 |
| **Mineral fuel** | **10,358** | **59,109** |
| Coal | 3,714 | 703 |
| Crude oil | 6 | 42,814 |
| Petroleum preparations | 3,244 | 9,096 |
| Liquefied propane/butane | 316 | 852 |
| Natural gas | 266 | 3,182 |
| Electricity | 57 | 858 |
| Other mineral fuels | 2,755 | 1,606 |
| **Selected commodities:** | | |
| Fish and preparations | 3,177 | 6,739 |
| Cork, wood, lumber | 5,637 | 6,149 |
| Pulp and waste paper | 6,206 | 3,827 |
| Metal ores; scrap | 6,564 | 4,004 |
| Crude fertilizers | 1,525 | 1,164 |
| Cigarettes | 4,770 | 64 |
| Alcoholic bev., distilled | 390 | 1,844 |
| **All other** | **3,857** | **1,602** |

**Note:** Details may not equal totals as a result of rounding.

## U.S. Exports and Imports, 1950-95

**Source:** Office of Trade and Economic Analysis, U.S. Dept. of Commerce

(millions of dollars)

| Year | Exports | Imports | Year | Exports | Imports | Year | Exports | Imports |
|---|---|---|---|---|---|---|---|---|
| 1950 | $ 9,997 | $ 8,954 | 1975 | $107,652 | $ 98,503 | 1992 | $448,164 | $532,665 |
| 1955 | 14,298 | 11,566 | 1980 | 220,626 | 244,871 | 1993 | 465,091 | 580,659 |
| 1960 | 19,659 | 15,073 | 1985 | 213,133 | 345,276 | 1994 | 512,626 | 663,256 |
| 1965 | 26,742 | 21,520 | 1990 | 394,030 | 495,042 | 1995 | 584,742 | 743,445 |
| 1970 | 42,681 | 40,356 | 1991 | 421,730 | 485,453 | | | |

## World Trade Organization

Following World War II, the major economic powers of the world, recognizing that obstacles to trade hindered economic development and growth, negotiated a set of rules for reducing and limiting barriers to trade and for settling trade disputes. These rules were called the General Agreement on Tariffs and Trade (GATT). Headquarters to oversee the administration of the GATT were established in Geneva, Switzerland.

Periodically, rounds of multilateral trade negotiations under the GATT have been carried out since the late 1940s. The 8th round began in 1986 in Punta del Este, Uruguay, and is usually referred to as the Uruguay Round. The Uruguay Round concluded on Dec. 15, 1993, when 117 countries completed a new trade-liberalization agreement. One of the provisions of the agreement changed the name of the GATT to the World Trade Organization (WTO).

The agreement required ratification by the legislatures of many countries, including the U.S. The U.S. House of Representatives approved legislation to implement the Uruguay Round on Nov. 29, 1994, by a vote of 288-146, and the Senate voted 76-24 to approve it on Dec. 1, 1994. Pres. Bill Clinton signed the legislation Dec. 8, 1994. The World Trade Organization formally took effect on Jan. 1, 1995. As of Aug. 1996, the European Union and 122 nations were members of the WTO.

# New Passenger Cars Imported Into the U.S., by Country of Origin,[1] 1968-95

**Source:** Bureau of the Census, U.S. Dept. of Commerce

| | Japan | Germany[2] | Italy | United Kingdom | Sweden | France | South Korea | Mexico | Canada | Total[3] |
|---|---|---|---|---|---|---|---|---|---|---|
| 1968 . . . | 169,849 | 707,972 | 33,843 | 96,787 | 52,515 | 39,551 | NA | NA | 500,881 | 1,620,452 |
| 1969 . . . | 260,005 | 642,157 | 41,569 | 104,050 | 41,008 | 24,457 | NA | NA | 691,146 | 1,846,717 |
| 1970 . . . | 381,338 | 674,945 | 42,523 | 76,257 | 57,844 | 37,114 | NA | NA | 692,783 | 2,013,420 |
| 1971 . . . | 703,672 | 770,807 | 51,469 | 106,710 | 61,925 | 23,316 | NA | 0 | 802,281 | 2,587,484 |
| 1972 . . . | 697,788 | 676,967 | 64,614 | 72,038 | 64,541 | 14,713 | NA | 9 | 842,300 | 2,485,901 |
| 1973 . . . | 624,805 | 677,465 | 56,102 | 64,140 | 58,626 | 8,219 | NA | 4,469 | 871,557 | 2,437,345 |
| 1974 . . . | 791,791 | 619,757 | 107,071 | 72,512 | 60,817 | 21,331 | NA | 3,914 | 817,559 | 2,572,557 |
| 1975 . . . | 695,573 | 370,012 | 102,344 | 67,106 | 51,993 | 15,647 | NA | 0 | 733,766 | 2,074,653 |
| 1976 . . . | 1,128,936 | 349,804 | 82,500 | 77,190 | 37,466 | 21,916 | NA | 0 | 825,590 | 2,536,749 |
| 1977 . . . | 1,341,530 | 423,492 | 55,437 | 56,889 | 39,370 | 19,215 | NA | NA | 849,814 | 2,790,144 |
| 1978 . . . | 1,563,047 | 416,231 | 69,689 | 54,478 | 56,140 | 28,502 | NA | 6 | 833,061 | 3,024,982 |
| 1979 . . . | 1,617,328 | 495,565 | 72,456 | 46,911 | 65,907 | 27,887 | NA | 4 | 677,008 | 3,005,523 |
| 1980 . . . | 1,991,502 | 338,711 | 46,899 | 32,517 | 61,496 | 47,386 | NA | 1 | 594,770 | 3,116,448 |
| 1981 . . . | 1,911,525 | 234,052 | 21,635 | 12,728 | 68,042 | 42,477 | NA | 1 | 563,943 | 2,856,286 |
| 1982 . . . | 1,801,185 | 259,385 | 9,402 | 13,023 | 89,231 | 50,032 | NA | 27 | 702,495 | 2,926,407 |
| 1983 . . . | 1,871,192 | 239,807 | 5,442 | 17,261 | 114,726 | 40,823 | NA | 2 | 835,665 | 3,133,836 |
| 1984 . . . | 1,948,714 | 335,032 | 8,582 | 19,833 | 114,854 | 37,788 | NA | NA | 1,073,425 | 3,559,427 |
| 1985 . . . | 2,527,467 | 473,110 | 8,689 | 24,474 | 142,640 | 42,882 | NA | 13,647 | 1,144,805 | 4,397,679 |
| 1986 . . . | 2,618,711 | 451,699 | 11,829 | 27,506 | 148,700 | 10,869 | 169,309 | 41,983 | 1,162,226 | 4,691,297 |
| 1987 . . . | 2,417,509 | 377,542 | 8,648 | 50,059 | 138,565 | 26,707 | 399,856 | 126,266 | 926,927 | 4,589,010 |
| 1988 . . . | 2,123,051 | 264,249 | 6,053 | 31,636 | 108,006 | 15,990 | 455,741 | 148,065 | 1,191,357 | 4,450,213 |
| 1989 . . . | 2,051,525 | 216,881 | 9,319 | 29,378 | 101,571 | 4,885 | 270,609 | 133,049 | 1,151,122 | 4,042,728 |
| 1990 . . . | 1,867,794 | 245,286 | 11,045 | 27,271 | 93,084 | 1,976 | 201,475 | 215,986 | 1,220,221 | 3,944,602 |
| 1991 . . . | 1,762,347 | 171,097 | 2,886 | 14,862 | 62,905 | 1,727 | 186,740 | 249,498 | 1,109,248 | 3,612,665 |
| 1992 . . . | 1,598,919 | 205,248 | 1,791 | 10,997 | 76,832 | 65 | 130,110 | 266,111 | 1,119,223 | 3,447,200 |
| 1993 . . . | 1,501,953 | 180,383 | 1,178 | 20,029 | 58,742 | 23 | 122,943 | 299,634 | 1,371,856 | 3,604,361 |
| 1994 . . . | 1,488,159 | 178,774 | 1,010 | 28,217 | 63,867 | 58 | 213,962 | 360,367 | 1,525,746 | 3,909,079 |
| 1995 . . . | 1,114,360 | 204,932 | 1,031 | 42,450 | 82,593 | 14 | 131,718 | 462,800 | 1,552,691 | 3,624,428 |

(1) Excludes passenger cars assembled in U.S. foreign trade zones. (2) Figures prior to 1991 are for West Germany. (3) Includes countries not shown separately.

# 50 Busiest U.S. Ports, 1994

**Source:** Corps of Engineers, Dept. of the Army, U.S. Dept. of Defense

(ports ranked by tonnage handled; all figures in tons)

| Rank | Port | Total | Domestic | Foreign | Imports | Exports |
|---|---|---|---|---|---|---|
| 1 | South Louisiana, LA, Port of . . . . . . . . . | 184,855,712 | 96,349,005 | 86,506,707 | 30,085,083 | 56,421,624 |
| 2 | Houston, TX . . . . . . . . . . . . . . . . . . | 143,662,625 | 63,508,777 | 80,153,846 | 54,856,552 | 25,297,296 |
| 3 | New York, NY and NJ. . . . . . . . . . . . . | 126,100,614 | 76,891,347 | 49,209,267 | 41,530,540 | 7,678,727 |
| 4 | Baton Rouge, LA . . . . . . . . . . . . . . . . | 86,245,856 | 44,646,309 | 41,599,547 | 31,353,868 | 10,245,649 |
| 5 | Valdez, AK . . . . . . . . . . . . . . . . . . . | 85,096,176 | 85,074,144 | 22,032 | 1 | 22,031 |
| 6 | Corpus Christi, TX . . . . . . . . . . . . . . . | 78,138,462 | 24,535,796 | 53,602,666 | 47,364,665 | 6,238,001 |
| 7 | New Orleans, LA . . . . . . . . . . . . . . . . | 73,332,939 | 37,705,782 | 35,627,157 | 20,494,075 | 15,133,082 |
| 8 | Plaquemine, LA, Port of . . . . . . . . . . . | 64,758,624 | 43,983,292 | 20,775,332 | 8,915,554 | 11,859,778 |
| 9 | Long Beach, CA. . . . . . . . . . . . . . . . . | 56,522,167 | 23,564,435 | 32,957,732 | 16,247,256 | 16,710,476 |
| 10 | Tampa, FL. . . . . . . . . . . . . . . . . . . . | 51,902,190 | 31,456,771 | 20,445,419 | 6,296,725 | 14,148,694 |
| 11 | Pittsburgh, PA . . . . . . . . . . . . . . . . . | 49,056,218 | 49,056,218 | 0 | 0 | 0 |
| 12 | Lake Charles, LA . . . . . . . . . . . . . . . . | 48,331,277 | 20,632,155 | 27,699,122 | 22,643,525 | 5,055,597 |
| 13 | Norfolk Harbor, VA. . . . . . . . . . . . . . . | 45,773,648 | 10,232,784 | 35,540,864 | 5,097,656 | 30,443,208 |
| 14 | Port Arthur, TX. . . . . . . . . . . . . . . . . | 45,586,136 | 6,193,952 | 39,392,184 | 34,297,737 | 5,094,447 |
| 15 | Mobile, AL. . . . . . . . . . . . . . . . . . . . | 44,996,849 | 24,480,908 | 20,515,941 | 10,657,196 | 9,858,745 |
| 16 | Texas City, TX. . . . . . . . . . . . . . . . . | 44,350,803 | 19,788,156 | 24,562,647 | 23,734,256 | 828,391 |
| 17 | Los Angeles, CA . . . . . . . . . . . . . . . . | 43,139,632 | 17,562,058 | 25,577,574 | 13,897,659 | 11,679,915 |
| 18 | Duluth-Superior, MN & WI. . . . . . . . . . | 41,819,417 | 32,384,355 | 9,435,062 | 2,045,208 | 7,389,854 |
| 19 | Baltimore, MD . . . . . . . . . . . . . . . . . | 41,450,422 | 15,175,369 | 26,275,053 | 15,348,901 | 10,926,152 |
| 20 | Philadelphia, PA . . . . . . . . . . . . . . . . | 40,745,690 | 14,299,063 | 26,446,627 | 25,965,989 | 480,638 |
| 21 | Marcus Hook, PA. . . . . . . . . . . . . . . . | 30,420,459 | 13,845,949 | 16,574,510 | 16,496,857 | 77,653 |
| 22 | Portland, OR . . . . . . . . . . . . . . . . . . | 30,164,479 | 12,734,874 | 17,429,605 | 3,373,503 | 14,056,102 |
| 23 | Pascagoula, MS. . . . . . . . . . . . . . . . . | 30,048,859 | 10,099,010 | 19,949,849 | 16,582,650 | 3,367,199 |
| 24 | Chicago, IL . . . . . . . . . . . . . . . . . . . | 29,421,566 | 25,497,467 | 3,924,099 | 3,687,546 | 236,553 |
| 25 | St. Louis, MO & IL . . . . . . . . . . . . . . | 29,418,967 | 29,418,967 | 0 | 0 | 0 |
| 26 | Huntington, WV . . . . . . . . . . . . . . . . | 25,629,485 | 25,629,485 | 0 | 0 | 0 |
| 27 | Paulsboro, NJ . . . . . . . . . . . . . . . . . | 24,667,782 | 10,887,171 | 13,780,611 | 13,710,006 | 70,605 |
| 28 | Richmond, CA . . . . . . . . . . . . . . . . . | 24,093,993 | 18,005,931 | 6,088,062 | 3,237,808 | 2,850,254 |
| 29 | Seattle, WA. . . . . . . . . . . . . . . . . . . | 22,335,514 | 6,793,746 | 15,541,768 | 7,483,433 | 8,058,335 |
| 30 | Beaumont, TX . . . . . . . . . . . . . . . . . | 21,200,684 | 13,869,242 | 7,331,442 | 5,698,874 | 1,632,568 |
| 31 | Jacksonville, FL. . . . . . . . . . . . . . . . | 18,910,150 | 10,470,156 | 8,439,994 | 6,871,504 | 1,568,490 |
| 32 | Boston, MA . . . . . . . . . . . . . . . . . . . | 18,869,586 | 9,071,468 | 9,798,118 | 9,152,923 | 645,195 |
| 33 | Detroit, MI . . . . . . . . . . . . . . . . . . . | 18,718,014 | 12,703,764 | 6,014,250 | 5,494,396 | 519,854 |
| 34 | Port Everglades, FL . . . . . . . . . . . . . | 18,135,257 | 11,466,557 | 6,668,700 | 5,399,378 | 1,269,322 |
| 35 | Tacoma, WA . . . . . . . . . . . . . . . . . . | 17,615,819 | 6,305,492 | 11,310,327 | 4,240,597 | 7,069,730 |
| 36 | Freeport, TX . . . . . . . . . . . . . . . . . . | 17,450,109 | 4,917,085 | 12,533,024 | 10,809,458 | 1,723,566 |
| 37 | San Juan, PR . . . . . . . . . . . . . . . . . | 16,299,654 | 10,190,664 | 6,108,990 | 5,376,486 | 732,504 |
| 38 | Indiana Harbor, IN . . . . . . . . . . . . . . | 16,144,862 | 15,738,969 | 405,893 | 399,933 | 5,960 |
| 39 | Savannah, GA. . . . . . . . . . . . . . . . . . | 15,904,910 | 3,132,727 | 12,772,183 | 6,254,094 | 6,518,089 |
| 40 | Memphis, TN. . . . . . . . . . . . . . . . . . | 15,679,999 | 15,679,999 | 0 | 0 | 0 |
| 41 | Newport News, VA. . . . . . . . . . . . . . . | 15,671,052 | 4,994,521 | 10,676,531 | 935,963 | 9,740,568 |
| 42 | Cleveland, OH . . . . . . . . . . . . . . . . . | 15,284,407 | 12,228,198 | 3,056,209 | 2,739,956 | 316,253 |
| 43 | Lorain, OH. . . . . . . . . . . . . . . . . . . . | 14,748,165 | 14,678,251 | 69,914 | 69,914 | 0 |
| 44 | New Castle, DE . . . . . . . . . . . . . . . . | 14,738,190 | 6,089,209 | 8,648,981 | 8,633,939 | 15,042 |
| 45 | Portland, ME . . . . . . . . . . . . . . . . . . | 14,245,338 | 1,586,229 | 12,659,109 | 12,555,677 | 103,432 |
| 46 | Toledo, OH . . . . . . . . . . . . . . . . . . . | 13,203,884 | 7,426,387 | 5,777,497 | 1,480,930 | 4,296,667 |
| 47 | Cincinnati, OH . . . . . . . . . . . . . . . . . | 13,192,767 | 13,192,767 | 0 | 0 | 0 |
| 48 | Anacortes, WA. . . . . . . . . . . . . . . . . | 12,950,108 | 10,689,652 | 2,260,456 | 796,384 | 1,464,072 |
| 49 | Oakland, CA . . . . . . . . . . . . . . . . . . | 12,914,086 | 2,486,790 | 10,427,296 | 4,924,275 | 5,503,021 |
| 50 | Honolulu, HI . . . . . . . . . . . . . . . . . . | 11,672,245 | 9,915,153 | 1,757,092 | 1,455,988 | 301,104 |

## Shortest Navigable Distances[1] Between Ports

**Source:** Defense Mapping Agency, Hydrographic/Topographic Center, July 1996

Distances shown are in nautical mi (1,852 m, or about 6,076.115 ft). For statute mi, multiply by 1.15.

| From | To | Distance |
|---|---|---|
| **New York, New York** | Barcelona, Spain | 3,714 |
| " | Cape Town, South Africa | 6,786 |
| " | Cherbourg, France | 3,134 |
| " | Copenhagen, Denmark | 3,720 |
| " | Galveston, Texas | 1,935 |
| " | Glasgow, Scotland | 3,210 |
| " | Hamburg, Germany | 3,654 |
| " | Havana, Cuba | 1,186 |
| " | Helsinki, Finland | 4,257 |
| " | Oslo, Norway | 3,644 |
| " | Piraeus, Greece | 4,688 |
| " | Southampton, England | 3,169 |
| **Montreal, Canada** | Algiers, Algeria | 3,842 |
| " | Barcelona, Spain | 3,939 |
| " | Cape Town, South Africa | 7,118 |
| " | Gibraltar[2] | 3,429 |
| " | Halifax, Nova Scotia | 895 |
| " | Havana, Cuba | 3,326 |
| " | Istanbul, Turkey | 5,226 |
| " | Kingston, Jamaica | 3,269 |
| " | Lagos, Nigeria | 6,505 |
| " | Marseille, France | 4,116 |
| " | Naples, Italy | 4,406 |
| " | Oslo, Norway | 3,957 |
| " | Piraeus, Greece | 4,856 |
| " | Port Said, Egypt | 5,348 |
| " | Southampton, England | 3,397 |
| **Colón,[3] Panama** | Buenos Aires, Argentina | 5,385 |
| " | Galveston, Texas | 1,508 |
| " | Gibraltar[2] | 4,332 |
| " | Hamburg, Germany | 5,061 |
| " | Helsinki, Finland | 5,970 |
| " | Lagos, Nigeria | 5,050 |
| " | Lisbon, Portugal | 4,152 |
| " | Oslo, Norway | 5,053 |
| " | Piraeus, Greece | 5,759 |
| " | Port Said, Egypt | 6,251 |
| " | St. John's, Nfld. | 2,695 |
| " | Southampton, England | 4,576 |
| **San Francisco, Calif.** | Bombay, India | 9,794 |
| " | Calcutta, India | 9,384 |
| " | Colón, Panama | 3,285 |
| **Vancouver, Canada** | Calcutta, India | 8,727 |
| " | Melbourne, Australia | 7,365 |
| **Panama, Panama** | Jakarta, Indonesia | 10,603 |
| **Port Said, Egypt** | Ho Chi Minh City, Vietnam | 5,684 |
| " | Hong Kong | 6,489 |
| " | Manila, Philippines | 6,365 |
| " | Melbourne, Australia | 7,886 |
| " | Singapore | 5,035 |
| " | Yokohama, Japan | 7,924 |
| **Cape Town,[4] S. Africa** | Jakarta, Indonesia | 5,276 |
| " | Melbourne, Australia | 6,600 |
| " | Singapore | 5,614 |
| **Singapore** | Jakarta, Indonesia | 525 |

(1) Traveling through station points. (2) Gibraltar (port) is 24 nautical mi E of the Strait of Gibraltar. (3) Colón, on the Atlantic, is 44 nautical mi from Panama (port) on the Pacific. (4) Cape Town is 35 nautical mi NW of the Cape of Good Hope.

## Major Merchant Fleets of the World

**Source:** Maritime Administration, U.S. Dept of Commerce

Fleets of oceangoing steam and motor ships totaling 1,000 gross tons or more as of Jan. 1996. Excludes ships operating exclusively on the Great Lakes and inland waterways and special types such as channel ships, icebreakers, cable ships, and merchant ships owned by any military force. Gross tonnage is a volume measurement; each cargo gross ton represents 100 cubic ft of enclosed space. Deadweight (Dwt) tonnage is carrying capacity of a ship in long tons (2,240 lb). Tonnage figures may not add, because of rounding.

(tonnage in thousands)

| | Total | | | Type of vessel | | | | | | | | |
|---|---|---|---|---|---|---|---|---|---|---|---|---|
| | | | | General cargo | | | Bulk carriers | | | Tankers | | |
| | No. of ships | Gross tons | Dwt tons | No. of ships | Gross tons | Dwt tons | No. of ships | Gross tons | Dwt tons | No. of ships | Gross tons | Dwt tons |
| All countries[1] | 25,608 | 444,909 | 695,698 | 10,991 | 71,050 | 88,029 | 5,474 | 148,905 | 260,528 | 6,080 | 166,801 | 293,668 |
| United States | 509 | 13,318 | 18,585 | 145 | 1,927 | 2,529 | 20 | 533 | 925 | 181 | 6,283 | 11,028 |
| Privately owned | 319 | 10,600 | 15,052 | 33 | 639 | 794 | 20 | 533 | 925 | 153 | 5,792 | 10,142 |
| Government owned | 190 | 2,718 | 3,533 | 112 | 1,288 | 1,735 | — | — | — | 28 | 491 | 886 |
| Antigua & Barbuda | 357 | 1,632 | 2,120 | 258 | 847 | 1,100 | 8 | 103 | 165 | 11 | 27 | 40 |
| Australia | 66 | 2,351 | 3,336 | 4 | 45 | 59 | 29 | 1,010 | 1,683 | 24 | 1,117 | 1,413 |
| Bahamas | 930 | 22,739 | 35,689 | 419 | 4,544 | 5,722 | 140 | 4,440 | 7,741 | 243 | 11,165 | 20,747 |
| Bermuda | 65 | 2,993 | 4,754 | 13 | 168 | 151 | 9 | 247 | 436 | 32 | 2,411 | 4,009 |
| Brazil | 198 | 4,881 | 8,332 | 34 | 176 | 248 | 60 | 2,096 | 3,709 | 83 | 2,249 | 3,973 |
| Bulgaria | 108 | 1,108 | 1,595 | 45 | 258 | 330 | 33 | 501 | 781 | 16 | 222 | 356 |
| China | 1,454 | 15,286 | 23,311 | 768 | 4,818 | 6,799 | 337 | 6,487 | 10,877 | 216 | 2,299 | 3,738 |
| Cyprus | 1,473 | 24,076 | 39,683 | 611 | 4,565 | 6,365 | 566 | 12,943 | 22,669 | 161 | 4,710 | 8,726 |
| Denmark | 333 | 4,835 | 7,001 | 166 | 508 | 622 | 12 | 507 | 941 | 82 | 1,857 | 3,278 |
| France | 65 | 1,564 | 2,583 | 11 | 121 | 175 | 2 | 11 | 17 | 33 | 1,137 | 2,127 |
| Germany | 404 | 4,961 | 6,170 | 192 | 900 | 1,102 | 8 | 235 | 393 | 38 | 318 | 509 |
| Greece | 952 | 28,615 | 51,758 | 146 | 1,185 | 1,767 | 461 | 12,868 | 22,889 | 275 | 13,555 | 26,201 |
| Hong Kong | 239 | 8,697 | 14,947 | 47 | 696 | 842 | 131 | 6,389 | 11,849 | 21 | 711 | 1,263 |
| India | 299 | 6,591 | 11,076 | 70 | 553 | 782 | 134 | 3,168 | 5,303 | 87 | 2,775 | 4,875 |
| Indonesia | 432 | 1,906 | 2,948 | 282 | 901 | 1,393 | 17 | 208 | 321 | 112 | 699 | 1,117 |
| Iran | 119 | 2,763 | 4,856 | 42 | 456 | 622 | 47 | 1,024 | 1,700 | 27 | 1,278 | 2,527 |
| Isle of Man | 85 | 2,026 | 3,270 | 20 | 201 | 226 | 10 | 415 | 774 | 29 | 1,015 | 1,910 |
| Italy | 389 | 5,470 | 8,071 | 61 | 207 | 281 | 37 | 1,533 | 2,829 | 220 | 2,476 | 4,043 |
| Japan | 762 | 15,705 | 23,478 | 154 | 914 | 721 | 189 | 5,372 | 9,916 | 305 | 7,310 | 11,250 |
| Korea, South | 417 | 6,098 | 9,700 | 149 | 616 | 728 | 124 | 3,661 | 6,658 | 87 | 492 | 888 |
| Kuwait | 45 | 2,016 | 3,228 | 14 | 277 | 364 | — | — | — | 28 | 1,652 | 2,772 |
| Liberia | 1,584 | 59,328 | 97,015 | 263 | 3,808 | 3,823 | 464 | 16,488 | 28,736 | 648 | 33,595 | 59,950 |
| Malaysia | 254 | 3,064 | 4,540 | 100 | 415 | 647 | 39 | 980 | 1,752 | 83 | 1,276 | 1,690 |
| Malta | 1,006 | 16,939 | 28,542 | 396 | 2,719 | 3,780 | 315 | 6,748 | 11,668 | 244 | 6,779 | 12,458 |

*(continued)*

## Major Merchant Fleets of the World (*continued*)

| | Total | | | Type of vessel | | | | | | | | |
|---|---|---|---|---|---|---|---|---|---|---|---|---|
| | | | | General cargo | | | Bulk carriers | | | Tankers | | |
| | No. of ships | Gross tons | Dwt tons | No. of ships | Gross tons | Dwt tons | No. of ships | Gross tons | Dwt tons | No. of ships | Gross tons | Dwt tons |
| Marshall Islands | 78 | 3,067 | 5,101 | 23 | 151 | 163 | 31 | 719 | 1,213 | 10 | 1,503 | 3,005 |
| Netherlands | 406 | 3,909 | 4,544 | 282 | 1,349 | 1,752 | 6 | 168 | 262 | 66 | 1,101 | 1,397 |
| Norway | 630 | 18,352 | 29,385 | 173 | 2,051 | 2,259 | 115 | 4,006 | 7,124 | 285 | 10,785 | 19,149 |
| Panama | 3,692 | 70,246 | 107,030 | 1,507 | 11,189 | 12,051 | 924 | 26,804 | 46,645 | 826 | 22,772 | 39,712 |
| Philippines | 516 | 8,185 | 13,127 | 198 | 1,482 | 1,666 | 224 | 6,186 | 10,876 | 60 | 158 | 245 |
| Poland | 131 | 2,149 | 3,194 | 50 | 501 | 569 | 69 | 1,452 | 2,400 | 5 | 105 | 186 |
| Romania | 220 | 2,257 | 3,477 | 161 | 956 | 1,341 | 39 | 853 | 1,412 | 10 | 375 | 670 |
| Russia | 1,426 | 8,990 | 11,847 | 1,090 | 4,640 | 5,215 | 83 | 1,775 | 2,859 | 190 | 2,019 | 3,197 |
| Saint Vincent | 640 | 5,787 | 9,155 | 395 | 2,000 | 2,778 | 113 | 2,356 | 4,036 | 89 | 1,152 | 2,067 |
| Saudi Arabia | 65 | 1,034 | 1,316 | 20 | 282 | 355 | 1 | 12 | 20 | 30 | 344 | 571 |
| Singapore | 655 | 13,032 | 20,132 | 163 | 1,873 | 1,955 | 111 | 3,562 | 6,224 | 280 | 5,562 | 9,777 |
| Sweden | 184 | 2,311 | 2,171 | 61 | 478 | 335 | 9 | 42 | 61 | 64 | 637 | 1,068 |
| Taiwan | 202 | 5,898 | 9,092 | 44 | 165 | 244 | 53 | 2,429 | 4,526 | 19 | 957 | 1,657 |
| Thailand | 251 | 1,538 | 2,403 | 148 | 909 | 1,372 | 28 | 388 | 651 | 67 | 176 | 299 |
| Turkey | 475 | 5,754 | 9,733 | 227 | 802 | 1,269 | 160 | 3,878 | 6,776 | 68 | 868 | 1,563 |
| Ukraine | 428 | 3,707 | 4,807 | 312 | 2,312 | 2,894 | 39 | 826 | 1,387 | 31 | 93 | 127 |
| United Kingdom | 148 | 3,140 | 3,493 | 30 | 85 | 111 | 7 | 69 | 109 | 63 | 1,306 | 2,042 |
| Vanuatu | 112 | 1,728 | 2,149 | 51 | 487 | 386 | 39 | 861 | 1,436 | 15 | 155 | 228 |

(1) Includes combination passenger & cargo ships and other type of vessels not listed separately.

## Passenger Car Production, U.S. Plants

**Source:** American Automobile Manufacturers Assn.

| | 1995 | 1994 |
|---|---|---|
| **Chrysler Corp.** | | |
| Neon | 116,584 | 119,955 |
| Acclaim | 0 | 28,210 |
| Sundance | 0 | 21,472 |
| Breeze | 7,987 | 0 |
| **Total Plymouth** | **124,571** | **169,637** |
| Cirrus | 83,401 | 29,558 |
| LeBaron Sedan | 0 | 7,932 |
| LeBaron J Coupe | 23,227 | 40,465 |
| Concorde | 14,344 | 38 |
| **Total Chrysler-Plymouth** | **245,593** | **247,630** |
| Neon | 130,863 | 122,757 |
| Shadow | 0 | 30,908 |
| Spirit | 0 | 27,577 |
| Stratus | 114,514 | 2,912 |
| Intrepid | 84,792 | 116,709 |
| Viper | 1,0841 | 2,815 |
| **Total Dodge** | **331,253** | **303,678** |
| **Total Chrysler Corp.** | **576,846** | **551,308** |
| **Ford Motor Co.** | | |
| Contour | 146,536 | 57,108 |
| Thunderbird | 94,027 | 146,848 |
| Taurus | 410,409 | 431,755 |
| Tempo | 0 | 73,562 |
| Escort | 216,086 | 312,191 |
| Mustang | 143,947 | 199,048 |
| **Total Ford** | **1,011,005** | **1,220,512** |
| Cougar | 48,830 | 81,936 |
| Mystique | 51,595 | 25,930 |
| Sable | 124,883 | 121,237 |
| Topaz | 0 | 31,148 |
| Lincoln Town Car | 99,291 | 121,078 |
| Mark | 15,961 | 26,666 |
| Continental | 42,332 | 32,843 |
| Tracer | 1,813 | 0 |
| **Total Lincoln-Mercury** | **384,705** | **440,838** |
| **Total Ford Motor Co.** | **1,395,710** | **1,661,350** |
| **General Motors Corp.** | | |
| Caprice | 89,056 | 110,534 |
| Corvette | 19,478 | 25,390 |
| Beretta-Corsica | 221,484 | 230,761 |
| Cavalier | 241,496 | 170,135 |
| Geo Prizm | 94,441 | 114,827 |
| **Total Chevrolet** | **665,955** | **651,647** |
| Grand Prix | 144,330 | 138,115 |
| Grand Am | 266,046 | 288,740 |
| Bonneville H | 80,565 | 107,982 |
| Sunbird | 0 | 57,677 |
| Sunfire | 83,514 | 4,623 |
| **Total Pontiac** | **574,455** | **597,137** |
| Aurora | 28,496 | 27,558 |

(1) Not all models are listed.

| | 1995 | 1994 |
|---|---|---|
| Delta 88 | 71,594 | 86,937 |
| Oldsmobile 98 | 18,785 | 27,542 |
| Achieva | 49,119 | 69,591 |
| Cutlass Supreme | 93,126 | 124,420 |
| Ciera | 130,096 | 145,404 |
| **Total Oldsmobile** | **391,216** | **481,452** |
| LeSabre | 149,866 | 165,063 |
| Roadmaster | 24,840 | 43,483 |
| Park Avenue | 47,932 | 64,395 |
| Riviera | 25,660 | 24,235 |
| Century | 93,012 | 124,373 |
| Skylark | 52,569 | 61,480 |
| **Total Buick** | **393,879** | **483,029** |
| DeVille (K) | 110,273 | 138,108 |
| Fleetwood | 13,445 | 20,551 |
| Eldorado | 23,670 | 25,942 |
| Seville | 38,725 | 41,528 |
| Allante | 0 | 7 |
| **Total Cadillac** | **186,113** | **226,136** |
| Saturn | 301,540 | 280,363 |
| **Total General Motors Corp.** | **2,515,136** | **2,719,764** |
| **Diamond Star** | | |
| Mitsubishi Eclipse | 60,695 | 57,019 |
| Mitsubishi Galant | 55,523 | 64,958 |
| Dodge Avenger | 42,326 | 13,849 |
| Plymouth Laser | 0 | 1,031 |
| Chrysler Sebring | 39,402 | 1,103 |
| Eagle Talon | 20,215 | 31,869 |
| **Total Mitsubishi Motor** | **218,161** | **169,829** |
| **Honda** | | |
| Accord | 373,227 | 360,591 |
| Civic | 179,768 | 138,119 |
| **Total Honda** | **552,995** | **498,710** |
| **Auto Alliance** | | |
| Probe | 50,653 | 113,849 |
| Mazda MX-6/626 | 98,909 | 133,142 |
| **Total Auto Alliance** | **149,562** | **246,991** |
| **Nissan** | | |
| Altima | 164,522 | 173,416 |
| Sentra | 121,037 | 137,968 |
| 200 SX | 47,675 | 1,291 |
| **Total Nissan** | **333,234** | **312,675** |
| **Subaru Legacy** | **80,660** | **54,002** |
| **Toyota** | | |
| Avalon | 105,611 | 11,768 |
| Corolla | 135,112 | 114,576 |
| Camry | 275,834 | 272,997 |
| **Total Toyota** | **516,557** | **399,341** |
| **Total Passenger Cars[1]** | **6,350,733** | **6,613,970** |

# Selected Motor Vehicle Statistics

**Source:** Federal Highway Administration; U.S. Dept. of Transportation; Insurance Institute for Highway Safety; 1994 figures where not otherwise specified.

| State | Driver's age Jan. 1, 1996 (1) Regular | (2) Juvenile | State gas tax cents/ gal. (July 1, 1996) | Safety belt use law[3] (Sept. 1, 1996) | Licensed drivers per 1,000 resident pop. | Registered motor vehicles per 1,000 resident pop. | Licensed drivers per registered motor vehicle | Gallons of fuel used per vehicle | Miles per gallon | Annual miles driven per vehicle | Vehicle miles per licensed driver |
|---|---|---|---|---|---|---|---|---|---|---|---|
| Alabama | 16 | - | 18 | S | 678 | 753 | 0.90 | 906 | 17.00 | 15,412 | 17,113 |
| Alaska | 16 | - | 8 | S | 719 | 880 | 0.82 | 569 | 13.66 | 7,779 | 9,525 |
| Arizona | 16 | - | 18 | S | 699 | 690 | 1.01 | 840 | 16.41 | 13,782 | 13,608 |
| Arkansas | 16 | - | 18.7 | S | 721 | 639 | 1.13 | 1,122 | 14.19 | 15,923 | 14,108 |
| California | 16-18 | 14 | 18 | P | 641 | 711 | 0.90 | 670 | 18.17 | 12,174 | 13,492 |
| Colorado | 16 | 16 | 22 | S | 748 | 752 | 0.99 | 697 | 17.58 | 12,257 | 12,334 |
| Connecticut | 16-18 | - | 37 | P | 708 | 794 | 0.89 | 583 | 17.91 | 10,440 | 11,705 |
| Delaware | 16-18 | - | 23 | S | 727 | 818 | 0.89 | 704 | 17.26 | 12,153 | 13,683 |
| Dist. of Col. | 18 | - | 20 | S | 635 | 436 | 1.45 | 766 | 18.09 | 13,859 | 9,529 |
| Florida | 16 | - | 12.5 | S | 789 | 735 | 1.07 | 713 | 16.69 | 11,899 | 11,084 |
| Georgia | 16 | - | 7.5 | P | 683 | 849 | 0.80 | 831 | 16.64 | 13,827 | 17,195 |
| Hawaii | 15 | - | 16 | P | 632 | 661 | 0.96 | 535 | 19.04 | 10,188 | 10,645 |
| Idaho | 17 | 15 | 25 | S | 707 | 913 | 0.77 | 666 | 16.92 | 11,261 | 14,556 |
| Illinois | 16-18 | - | 19 | S | 638 | 740 | 0.86 | 640 | 16.58 | 10,614 | 12,305 |
| Indiana | 16-18 | - | 15 | S | 671 | 850 | 0.79 | 755 | 16.83 | 12,705 | 16,089 |
| Iowa | 16-18 | - | 20 | P | 670 | 978 | 0.69 | 640 | 14.55 | 9,305 | 13,571 |
| Kansas | 16 | 14-15 | 18 | S | 694 | 816 | 0.85 | 717 | 16.53 | 11,848 | 13,930 |
| Kentucky | 16 | - | 16.4 | S | 658 | 697 | 0.94 | 937 | 15.94 | 14,939 | 15,825 |
| Louisiana | 15-17 | 15 | 20 | P | 601 | 794 | 0.76 | 680 | 16.08 | 10,924 | 14,426 |
| Maine | 16-17 | 16 | 19 | S | 737 | 763 | 0.97 | 776 | 16.98 | 13,184 | 13,648 |
| Maryland | 16-18 | 16 | 23.5 | S | 661 | 727 | 0.91 | 671 | 18.08 | 12,132 | 13,351 |
| Massachusetts | 18 | 16½ | 21 | S | 740 | 667 | 1.11 | 667 | 17.49 | 11,669 | 10,509 |
| Michigan | 16-18 | 14 | 15 | S | 695 | 798 | 0.87 | 675 | 16.66 | 11,247 | 12,903 |
| Minnesota | 16-18 | 15 | 20 | S | 592 | 888 | 0.67 | 635 | 16.81 | 10,676 | 16,010 |
| Mississippi | 16 | - | 18.4 | S | 626 | 773 | 0.81 | 837 | 16.54 | 13,838 | 17,077 |
| Missouri | 16 | - | 17 | S | 641 | 797 | 0.80 | 837 | 16.27 | 13,614 | 16,939 |
| Montana | 15-16 | 13 | 27 | S | 614 | 1,109 | 0.55 | 633 | 15.16 | 9,601 | 17,338 |
| Nebraska | 16 | 14 | 26 | S | 706 | 898 | 0.79 | 700 | 15.16 | 10,611 | 13,490 |
| Nevada | 16 | 14 | 24 | S | 691 | 676 | 1.02 | 911 | 14.52 | 13,221 | 12,926 |
| New Hampshire | 16-18 | 16 | 18.7 | No | 772 | 872 | 0.88 | 596 | 17.77 | 10,588 | 11,967 |
| New Jersey | 17 | 16 | 10.5 | S | 687 | 739 | 0.93 | 682 | 15.18 | 10,355 | 11,129 |
| New Mexico | 15-16 | - | 18.875 | P | 706 | 860 | 0.82 | 762 | 18.89 | 14,398 | 17,542 |
| New York | 17-18 | 16 | 21.79 | P | 571 | 561 | 1.02 | 616 | 17.98 | 11,080 | 10,887 |
| North Carolina | 16-18 | - | 21.7 | P | 685 | 770 | 0.89 | 783 | 16.87 | 13,215 | 14,861 |
| North Dakota | 16 | 14 | 20 | S | 689 | 1,073 | 0.64 | 667 | 13.87 | 9,257 | 14,427 |
| Ohio | 16-18 | 14 | 22 | S | 643 | 870 | 0.74 | 605 | 16.79 | 10,162 | 13,749 |
| Oklahoma | 16 | - | 17 | S | 719 | 861 | 0.84 | 780 | 16.90 | 13,180 | 15,779 |
| Oregon | 16 | 14 | 24 | P | 824 | 892 | 0.92 | 636 | 16.83 | 10,700 | 11,583 |
| Pennsylvania | 17-18 | 16 | 22.35 | S | 673 | 704 | 0.96 | 680 | 16.01 | 10,887 | 11,380 |
| Rhode Island | 16-18 | - | 29 | S | 691 | 701 | 0.98 | 579 | 17.51 | 10,149 | 10,307 |
| South Carolina | 16 | 15 | 16 | S | 680 | 749 | 0.91 | 881 | 15.41 | 13,579 | 14,946 |
| South Dakota | 16 | 14 | 18 | S | 705 | 1,067 | 0.66 | 695 | 14.28 | 9,918 | 15,019 |
| Tennessee | 16 | 14 | 20 | S | 739 | 977 | 0.76 | 654 | 16.49 | 10,778 | 14,252 |
| Texas | 16-18 | 15 | 20 | P | 659 | 741 | 0.89 | 762 | 17.17 | 13,089 | 14,727 |
| Utah | 16 | - | 19 | S | 653 | 741 | 0.88 | 721 | 17.72 | 12,779 | 14,518 |
| Vermont | 18 | 16 | 16 | S | 768 | 844 | 0.91 | 763 | 16.48 | 12,570 | 13,807 |
| Virginia | 16-19 | - | 17.5 | S | 702 | 841 | 0.84 | 695 | 17.66 | 12,277 | 14,694 |
| Washington | 16-18 | - | 23 | S | 707 | 836 | 0.85 | 657 | 16.16 | 10,622 | 12,564 |
| West Virginia | 16-18 | 16 | 25.35 | S | 713 | 803 | 0.89 | 719 | 16.27 | 11,702 | 13,179 |
| Wisconsin | 16-18 | 14 | 23.7 | S | 699 | 773 | 0.91 | 704 | 18.20 | 12,806 | 14,145 |
| Wyoming | 16 | 14 | 9 | S | 718 | 1,070 | 0.67 | 995 | 13.20 | 13,137 | 19,575 |
| **Average** | | | | | **674** | **761** | **0.89** | **707** | **16.84** | **11,916** | **13,455** |

(1) Unrestricted operation of private passenger car. When 2 ages are shown, license issued at lower age on completion of approved driver education course. (2) Juvenile license issued with consent of parent or guardian. (3) P = officer may stop vehicle for a violation (primary); S = an officer may issue seat belt citation only when vehicle is stopped for another moving violation (secondary).

# U.S. Car Sales by Vehicle Size and Type, 1985-95

**Source:** American Automobile Manufacturers Assn.

| Year | Small (%) | Midsize (%) | Large (%) | Luxury (%) | Total (%) |
|---|---|---|---|---|---|
| 1995 | 27.1 | 48.5 | 10.8 | 13.6 | 100.0 |
| 1994 | 29.2 | 45.6 | 11.7 | 13.5 | 100.0 |
| 1993 | 32.8 | 43.3 | 11.1 | 12.8 | 100.0 |
| 1992 | 32.9 | 44.5 | 9.2 | 13.4 | 100.0 |
| 1991 | 33.0 | 44.9 | 8.3 | 13.9 | 100.0 |
| 1990 | 32.8 | 44.8 | 9.4 | 13.0 | 100.0 |
| 1989 | 36.6 | 41.9 | 11.9 | 11.6 | 100.0 |
| 1988 | 37.6 | 42.5 | 10.0 | 9.9 | 100.0 |
| 1987 | 38.4 | 42.3 | 9.1 | 10.2 | 100.0 |
| 1986 | 37.6 | 42.5 | 9.8 | 10.1 | 100.0 |
| 1985 | 37.9 | 42.1 | 9.8 | 10.2 | 100.0 |

## U.S. Car Sales by Type of Buyer, 1980-95

**Source:** American Automobile Manufacturers Assn.

| Year | Sales in thousands: Consumer | Business | Government | Total | % of total sales: Consumer | Business |
|---|---|---|---|---|---|---|
| 1995 | 4,308 | 4,204 | 160 | 8,672 | 49.9 | 48.7 |
| 1994 | 4,624 | 4,496 | 115 | 9,235 | 51.3 | 47.3 |
| 1993 | 4,669 | 3,941 | 108 | 8,718 | 53.6 | 45.2 |
| 1992 | 4,558 | 3,683 | 113 | 8,354 | 54.6 | 44.1 |
| 1991 | 4,538 | 3,752 | 97 | 8,387 | 54.1 | 44.8 |
| 1990 | 5,768 | 3,567 | 149 | 9,484 | 60.8 | 37.6 |
| 1989 | 6,375 | 3,402 | 136 | 9,913 | 64.3 | 34.3 |
| 1988 | 6,802 | 3,699 | 138 | 10,639 | 63.9 | 34.8 |
| 1987 | 6,748 | 3,395 | 135 | 10,278 | 65.7 | 33.0 |
| 1986 | 7,658 | 3,666 | 127 | 11,450 | 66.9 | 32.0 |
| 1985 | 7,083 | 3,822 | 134 | 11,039 | 64.2 | 34.6 |
| 1984 | 6,590 | 3,669 | 135 | 10,394 | 63.4 | 35.3 |
| 1983 | 6,054 | 3,006 | 119 | 9,179 | 66.0 | 32.7 |
| 1982 | 5,285 | 2,593 | 102 | 7,980 | 66.2 | 32.5 |
| 1981 | 5,623 | 2,787 | 116 | 8,535 | 66.0 | 32.7 |
| 1980 | 6,062 | 2,791 | 126 | 8,979 | 67.5 | 31.1 |

## Domestic and Imported Retail Car Sales in the U.S., 1980-95

**Source:** American Automobile Manufacturers Assn.

| Calendar year | Domestic | Imports: From Japan | From Germany | From other countries | Total imports | Total U.S. sales | Import %: Total | Japan | U.S.-sponsored imports |
|---|---|---|---|---|---|---|---|---|---|
| 1980 | 6,581,307 | 1,905,968 | 305,219 | 186,700 | 2,397,887 | 8,979,194 | 26.7 | 21.2 | 223,310 |
| 1981 | 6,208,760 | 1,858,896 | 282,881 | 185,502 | 2,327,279 | 8,536,039 | 27.3 | 21.8 | 174,665 |
| 1982 | 5,758,586 | 1,801,969 | 247,080 | 174,508 | 2,223,557 | 7,982,143 | 27.9 | 22.6 | 139,767 |
| 1983 | 6,795,295 | 1,915,621 | 279,748 | 191,403 | 2,386,772 | 9,182,067 | 26.0 | 20.9 | 136,798 |
| 1984 | 7,951,523 | 1,906,206 | 344,416 | 188,220 | 2,438,842 | 10,390,365 | 23.5 | 18.3 | 116,965 |
| 1985 | 8,204,542 | 2,217,837 | 423,983 | 195,925 | 2,837,745 | 11,042,287 | 25.7 | 20.1 | 206,252 |
| 1986 | 8,214,897 | 2,382,614 | 443,721 | 418,286 | 3,244,621 | 11,459,518 | 28.3 | 20.8 | 314,358 |
| 1987 | 7,080,858 | 2,190,405 | 347,881 | 657,465 | 3,195,751 | 10,276,609 | 31.1 | 21.3 | 348,154 |
| 1988 | 7,526,038 | 2,022,602 | 280,099 | 700,991 | 3,003,692 | 10,529,730 | 28.5 | 19.2 | 393,412 |
| 1989 | 7,072,902 | 1,897,143 | 248,561 | 553,660 | 2,699,364 | 9,772,266 | 27.6 | 19.4 | 340,425 |
| 1990 | 6,896,888 | 1,719,384 | 265,116 | 418,823 | 2,403,323 | 9,300,211 | 25.8 | 18.5 | 296,778 |
| 1991 | 6,136,757 | 1,500,309 | 192,776 | 344,814 | 2,037,899 | 8,174,656 | 24.9 | 18.4 | 280,673 |
| 1992 | 6,276,557 | 1,451,766 | 200,851 | 283,938 | 1,936,555 | 8,213,112 | 23.6 | 17.7 | 228,927 |
| 1993 | 6,741,667 | 1,328,445 | 186,177 | 261,570 | 1,776,192 | 8,517,859 | 20.9 | 15.6 | 185,284 |
| 1994 | 7,255,303 | 1,239,450 | 192,241 | 303,489 | 1,735,180 | 8,990,483 | 19.3 | 13.8 | 95,399 |
| 1995 | 7,128,712 | 981,462 | 207,555 | 317,269 | 1,606,296 | 8,634,998 | 17.4 | 11.4 | 99,657 |

## World Motor Vehicle Production, 1950-95

**Source:** American Automobile Manufacturers Assn.

(in thousands)

| Year | United States | Canada | Europe | Japan | Other | World total | U.S. % of world total |
|---|---|---|---|---|---|---|---|
| 1995 | 11,985 | 2,417 | 16,897 | 10,196 | 8,374 | 49,863 | 24.0 |
| 1994 | 12,263 | 2,322 | 16,028 | 10,554 | 8,526 | 49,693 | 24.7 |
| 1993 | 10,898 | 2,246 | 14,825 | 11,228 | 7,205 | 46,402 | 23.5 |
| 1992 | 9,729 | 1,961 | 17,307 | 12,499 | 6,269 | 47,765 | 24.5 |
| 1991 | 8,811 | 1,888 | 17,563 | 13,245 | 5,180 | 46,687 | 18.9 |
| 1990 | 9,783 | 1,928 | 18,651 | 13,487 | 4,496 | 48,345 | 20.2 |
| 1985 | 11,653 | 1,933 | 16,015 | 12,271 | 2,939 | 44,811 | 26.0 |
| 1980 | 8,010 | 1,324 | 15,445 | 11,043 | 2,692 | 38,514 | 20.8 |
| 1970 | 8,284 | 1,160 | 13,033 | 5,289 | 1,637 | 29,403 | 28.2 |
| 1960 | 7,905 | 398 | 6,837 | 482 | 866 | 16,488 | 47.9 |
| 1950 | 8,006 | 388 | 1,991 | 32 | 160 | 10,577 | 75.7 |

**Note:** As far as can be determined, production refers to vehicles locally manufactured.

## Motor Vehicle Production by Selected Countries, 1995

**Source:** American Automobile Manufacturers Assn.

| Country | Passenger cars | Commercial vehicles | Total |
|---|---|---|---|
| Argentina | 226,504 | 58,768 | 285,272 |
| Australia | 314,142 | 29,709 | 343,851 |
| Austria | 43,466 | 3,217 | 46,683 |
| Belgium | 385,894 | 81,555 | 467,449 |
| Brazil | 1,531,989 | 92,152 | 1,624,141 |
| Canada | 1,339,474 | 1,077,702 | 2,417,176 |
| China | 320,578 | 1,114,210 | 1,434,788 |
| Commonwealth of Indep. States | 890,000 | 192,000 | 1,082,000 |
| Czech Republic | 189,434 | 26,589 | 216,023 |
| France | 3,050,929 | 423,776 | 3,474,705 |
| Germany | 4,360,235 | 307,129 | 4,667,364 |
| India | 324,721 | 240,366 | 565,087 |
| Italy | 1,422,359 | 244,911 | 1,667,270 |
| Japan | 7,610,533 | 2,585,003 | 10,195,536 |
| Korea, South | 1,985,578 | 540,822 | 2,526,400 |
| Malaysia | 240,887 | 5,521 | 246,408 |
| Mexico | 699,312 | 235,705 | 935,017 |
| Netherlands | 100,434 | 32,036 | 132,470 |
| Poland | 258,000 | 5,000 | 263,000 |
| Spain | 1,958,789 | 374,998 | 2,333,787 |
| Sweden | 387,659 | 102,483 | 490,142 |
| Taiwan | 282,006 | 124,474 | 406,480 |
| Turkey | 233,412 | 49,028 | 282,440 |
| United Kingdom | 1,532,084 | 233,001 | 1,765,085 |
| United States | 6,350,367 | 5,634,724 | 11,985,091 |
| **Total** | **36,064,286** | **13,816,379** | **49,862,665** |

# Top-Selling Passenger Cars in the U.S. by Calendar Year, 1992-95 (Domestic and Import)

**Source:** American Automobile Manufacturers Assn.

### 1995

| | | |
|---|---|---|
| 1. | Ford Taurus | 366,266 |
| 2. | Honda Accord | 341,384 |
| 3. | Toyota Camry | 328,595 |
| 4. | Honda Civic | 289,435 |
| 5. | Saturn | 285,674 |
| 6. | Ford Escort | 285,570 |
| 7. | Dodge/Plymouth Neon | 240,189 |
| 8. | Pontiac Grand Am | 234,226 |
| 9. | Chevrolet Lumina | 214,595 |
| 10. | Toyota Corolla | 213,636 |
| 11. | Chevrolet Cavalier | 212,767 |
| 12. | Chevrolet Corsica/Beretta | 192,361 |
| 13. | Ford Contour | 174,214 |
| 14. | Nissan Altima | 148,172 |
| 15. | Dodge Intrepid | 147,576 |
| 16. | Buick LeSabre | 141,410 |
| 17. | Ford Mustang | 136,962 |
| 18. | Nissan Sentra | 134,854 |
| 19. | Pontiac Grand Prix | 131,747 |
| 20. | Oldsmobile Ciera | 128,860 |

### 1994

| | | |
|---|---|---|
| 1. | Ford Taurus | 397,031 |
| 2. | Honda Accord | 367,615 |
| 3. | Ford Escort | 336,967 |
| 4. | Toyota Camry | 321,979 |
| 5. | Saturn | 286,003 |
| 6. | Honda Civic | 267,023 |
| 7. | Pontiac Grand Am | 262,310 |
| 8. | Chevrolet Corsica/Beretta | 222,129 |
| 9. | Toyota Corolla | 210,926 |
| 10. | Chevrolet Cavalier | 187,263 |

### 1993

| | | |
|---|---|---|
| 1. | Ford Taurus | 360,448 |
| 2. | Honda Accord | 330,030 |
| 3. | Toyota Camry | 299,737 |
| 4. | Chevrolet Cavalier | 273,617 |
| 5. | Ford Escort | 269,034 |
| 6. | Honda Civic | 255,579 |
| 7. | Saturn | 229,356 |
| 8. | Chevrolet Lumina | 219,683 |
| 9. | Ford Tempo | 217,644 |
| 10. | Pontiac Grand Am | 214,761 |

### 1992

| | | |
|---|---|---|
| 1. | Ford Taurus | 409,751 |
| 2. | Honda Accord | 393,477 |
| 3. | Toyota Camry | 286,602 |
| 4. | Ford Escort | 236,622 |
| 5. | Honda Civic/CRX | 219,228 |
| 6. | Chevrolet Lumina | 218,114 |
| 7. | Chevrolet Cavalier | 212,374 |
| 8. | Pontiac Grand Am | 210,332 |
| 9. | Ford Tempo | 207,173 |
| 10. | Saturn | 196,126 |

# The Most Popular Colors, by Type of Vehicle, 1995 Model Year

**Source:** American Automobile Manufacturers Assn.

| Luxury cars | | Full size/ intermediate cars | | Compact/sports cars | | Light trucks and vans | |
|---|---|---|---|---|---|---|---|
| Color | Percentage | Color | Percentage | Color | Percentage | Color | Percentage |
| White | 14.9 | White | 18.9 | Dark green | 15.2 | White | 23.8 |
| Light brown | 13.4 | Dark green | 17.3 | White | 14.4 | Dark green | 15.9 |
| Dark green | 13.0 | Medium red | 11.2 | Medium red | 11.3 | Black | 9.1 |
| Black | 9.7 | Light brown | 9.7 | Black | 11.2 | Bright red | 8.5 |
| Medium red | 9.1 | Black | 5.9 | Bright red | 9.5 | Medium red | 7.5 |
| White metallic | 7.8 | Silver | 5.4 | Purple | 7.8 | Teal/Aqua | 7.4 |
| Silver | 7.7 | Teal/Aqua | 4.6 | Teal/Aqua | 6.6 | Medium/Dark blue | 5.2 |
| Light green | 4.7 | Medium blue | 4.4 | Silver | 6.3 | Light brown | 5.1 |
| Dark red | 4.5 | Bright red | 4.4 | Light brown | 4.4 | Silver | 4.3 |
| Dark blue | 3.9 | Light blue | 4.3 | Dark blue | 3.7 | Dark red | 2.8 |
| Medium gray | 3.2 | Purple | 3.5 | Light green | 3.0 | Bright blue | 2.6 |
| Light blue | 2.9 | Light green | 2.6 | Bright blue | 2.3 | Light green | 2.6 |
| Other | 5.2 | Other | 7.8 | Other | 4.3 | Other | 5.2 |

# Licensed Drivers, by Age

**Source:** Federal Highway Administration, U.S. Dept. of Transportation

| Age | 1994 Male | 1994 Female | 1994 Total | Percent Male (1994) | Estimated 1995 Male (1,000) | Estimated 1995 Female (1,000) | Estimated 1995 Total (1,000) | Percent change total drivers 1984 -94 |
|---|---|---|---|---|---|---|---|---|
| Under 16 | 29,493 | 26,828 | 56,321 | 52.37 | 30 | 27 | 57 | –48.33 |
| 16 | 765,937 | 704,584 | 1,470,521 | 52.09 | 775 | 713 | 1,488 | –12.42 |
| 17 | 1,147,918 | 1,052,924 | 2,200,842 | 52.16 | 1,161 | 1,065 | 2,226 | –8.26 |
| 18 | 1,311,200 | 1,181,937 | 2,493,137 | 52.59 | 1,326 | 1,196 | 2,522 | –11.68 |
| 19 | 1,436,846 | 1,291,126 | 2,727,972 | 52.67 | 1,453 | 1,306 | 2,760 | –14.64 |
| (19 and under) | 4,691,394 | 4,257,399 | 8,948,793 | 52.42 | 4,746 | 4,307 | 9,052 | –12.32 |
| 20 | 1,483,343 | 1,352,749 | 2,836,091 | 52.30 | 1,500 | 1,368 | 2,869 | –18.53 |
| 21 | 1,517,155 | 1,404,366 | 2,921,521 | 51.93 | 1,535 | 1,421 | 2,955 | –20.76 |
| 22 | 1,618,962 | 1,511,063 | 3,130,025 | 51.72 | 1,638 | 1,529 | 3,166 | –18.57 |
| 23 | 1,796,150 | 1,686,492 | 3,482,642 | 51.57 | 1,817 | 1,706 | 3,523 | –13.13 |
| 24 | 1,859,410 | 1,749,570 | 3,608,980 | 51.52 | 1,881 | 1,770 | 3,651 | –10.67 |
| (20-24) | 8,275,019 | 7,704,240 | 15,979,259 | 51.79 | 8,371 | 7,793 | 16,164 | –16.17 |
| 25-29 | 9,294,140 | 8,806,159 | 18,100,299 | 51.35 | 9,401 | 8,908 | 18,310 | –10.79 |
| 30-34 | 10,743,221 | 10,147,503 | 20,890,724 | 51.43 | 10,867 | 10,265 | 21,132 | 11.13 |
| 35-39 | 10,340,903 | 10,131,633 | 20,472,537 | 50.51 | 10,460 | 10,249 | 20,709 | 23.68 |
| 40-44 | 9,321,870 | 9,164,014 | 18,485,884 | 50.43 | 9,430 | 9,270 | 18,700 | 42.21 |
| 45-49 | 8,159,613 | 8,009,774 | 16,169,387 | 50.46 | 8,254 | 8,103 | 16,356 | 53.34 |
| 50-54 | 6,349,025 | 6,195,086 | 12,544,111 | 50.61 | 6,422 | 6,267 | 12,689 | 28.37 |
| 55-59 | 5,092,733 | 4,939,940 | 10,032,673 | 50.76 | 5,152 | 4,997 | 10,149 | 1.68 |
| 60-64 | 4,567,868 | 4,419,678 | 8,987,547 | 50.82 | 4,621 | 4,471 | 9,091 | –1.29 |
| 65-69 | 4,280,619 | 4,247,325 | 8,527,944 | 50.20 | 4,330 | 4,297 | 8,627 | 16.77 |
| 70-74 | 3,577,798 | 3,649,303 | 7,227,101 | 49.51 | 3,619 | 3,692 | 7,311 | 48.89 |
| 75-79 | 2,421,968 | 2,486,334 | 4,908,302 | 49.34 | 2,450 | 2,515 | 4,965 | (1) |
| 80-84 | 1,340,945 | 1,379,120 | 2,720,065 | 49.30 | 1,356 | 1,395 | 2,752 | (1) |
| 85 and over | 736,823 | 672,017 | 1,408,840 | 52.30 | 745 | 680 | 1,425 | (1) |
| **Total** | **89,193,940** | **86,209,525** | **175,403,465** | **50.85** | **90,224** | **87,208** | **177,432** | **12.85** |

(1) Separate totals for these age brackets not available for 1984.

# Highway Speed Limits, by State

**Source:** National Highway Safety Commission, unpublished data

Under the National Highway System Designation Act, signed Nov. 28, 1995, by Pres. Clinton, states were allowed to set their own highway speed limits, as of Dec. 8, 1995. Under federal legislation enacted in 1974 during the energy crisis, states had been restricted to a National Maximum Speed Limit (NMSL) of 55 miles per hour (raised in 1987 to 65 mph on rural interstates). New maximum speed limits by state are given in the table below; all speeds are miles per hour. Most data current as of July 1, 1996.

| | | | Current Speed Limits | | | | |
|---|---|---|---|---|---|---|---|
| | | | Cars | | Trucks | | |
| State | Pre-NMSL Max. | Above NMSL | Inter-state | Other Primary | Inter-state | Other Primary | Notes |
| AL | 70 | Y | 70 | 55 | 70 | 55 | 70 mph on interstates, 65 on other 4-lane highways. |
| AK | 70 | N | 65 | 55 | 65 | 55 | |
| AZ | 75 | Y | 75/55 | 55 | 75/55 | 55 | 75 mph on rural interstates; urban interstates remain 55. |
| AR | 75 | N | 65 | 55 | 65 | 55 | State Hwy Transp. Dept. watching changes in other states. |
| CA | 70 | Y | 70 | 65 | 55 | 55 | Raised to 70 mph eff. 1/1/96. |
| CO | 70 | Y | 75 | 55 | 75 | 55 | Eff. 5/28/96: commonly 55 mph for 2-lane, 65 for 4-lane, but max. can be 75 for any highway; to be determined by late 1997. |
| CT | 60 | N | 55 | 55 | 55 | 55 | |
| DE | 60 | Y | 65 | 50 | 65 | 50 | 65 mph applies to I-495 and part of US 1 (1/26/95). |
| DC | 60 | N | 55 | 50 | 50 | 50 | Only part of Woodrow Wilson Bridge eligible for increase. No change currently being considered. |
| FL | 70 | Y | 70 | 55 | 65 | 55 | Eff. 4/8/96 only on part of Interstate 10 (Jacksonville to Pensacola); additional segments of I-75 and I-95 pending. |
| GA | 70 | Y | 70/65 | 55 | 70/65 | 55 | Eff. 7/1/96: 70 mph on rural interstates, 65 on urban interstates; 65 mph on physically divided hwys lacking controlled access. |
| HI | 70 | N | 55 | 55 | 55 | 55 | |
| ID | 70 | Y | 75 | 65 | 75 | 65 | Eff. 5/1/96 |
| IL | 70 | Y | 65/55 | 55 | 55 | 55 | Some urban interstates raised to 65 mph; restricted unmarked county and township roads to 55 (1/26/96). |
| IN | 70 | N | 65 | 55 | 60 | 55 | Legislation to raise limits defeated in House (1/96). |
| IA | 75 | Y | 65/55 | 55 | 65/55 | 55 | State Transp. Dept. can raise limits up to 65 mph on selected 4-lane divided hwys. Urban interstates remain 55. |
| KS | 75 | Y | 70 | 65 | 70 | 65 | Eff. 3/22/96 |
| KY | 70 | N | 65 | 55 | 65 | 55 | No bills passed. Gov. stated he would veto any bill to raise limits. |
| LA | 70 | N | 65 | 55 | 65 | 55 | Gov. declared postponement of changes to 5/30/97; considering 70 mph for controlled access, 60 for noncontrolled access. |
| ME | 70 | N | 65 | 55 | 65 | 55 | |
| MD | 70 | N | 65 | 55 | 65 | 55 | |
| MA | 65 | Y | 65 | 55 | 65 | 55 | Raised to 65 mph on 13 major interstates and highways, 2 sections of Mass. Turnpike (1/29/96). |
| MI | 70 | N | 65 | 55 | 65 | 55 | 6/25/96, gov. signed legislation raising to 65 mph on most freeways; experimental 70-mph limit on selected hwys. |
| MN | 65 | N | 65 | 55 | 65` | 55 | Hearing held and bills considered; action failed. Task force formed, public mtgs held, findings sent to DOT Commissioner. |
| MS | 70 | Y | 70 | 65 | 70 | 65 | Eff. 3/12/96 |
| MO | 70 | Y | 70/60 | 65 | 70/60 | 65 | Eff. 3/13/96, state can raise any road to 70 mph with safety study. |
| MT | none | Y | See note | See note | See note | See note | Eff. 12/8/95, no max. posted limit, only "reasonable and prudent" (cars/day); 65 mph interstate, 55 all other (cars/night); trucks max. 65 day/night on interstates; triple truck combo 55 all roads. |
| NE | 75 | Y | 75/60 | 60 | 75 | 60 | Gov. signed bill, eff. 6/1/96, increasing interstates to 75 mph (urban 60 mph); eff 9/1/96, 2-lane roads 60, 4-lane expressways usually 65; substantial increase in fines. |
| NV | none | Y | 75 | 70 | 75 | 55 | 75 and 70 mph, eff. 12/8/95 |
| NH | 70 | N | 65 | 55 | 65 | 55 | |
| NJ | 70 | N | 55 | 50 | 55 | 50 | |
| NM | 70 | Y | 65 | 55 | 65 | 55 | Eff. 5/13/96: 75 mph on interstates; 70 on 4-lane highways with shoulders; 65 on 2-lane with shoulders; 60 on 2-lane without shoulders. |
| NY | 55 | N | 65 | 55 | 65 | 55 | |
| NC | 70 | N | 65 | 55 | 65 | 55 | Eff. Oct 1, 1996, speed limits on non-interstate controlled access roads raised to 70 mph based on DOT studies. The Dept. already had authority to set limits up to 70 on interstates. |
| ND | 75 | Y | 70 | 65 | 70 | 65 | 5/24/96, most interstates 70 mph (urban Fargo and Bismark 55 mph); US 2, 83, 85, 281, 65 day (55 night most segments). Eff. when posted. |
| OH | 70 | Y | 65 | 55 | 55 | 55 | Eff. 2/29/96: if DOT, DPS, and local municipality agree, can automatically raise interstates and freeways to 65 after 120 days, rural, divided, multilane hwys to 65 after 360 days. |
| OK | 70 | Y | 75/70 | 65/55 | 75/70 | 55 | Gov. raised limit to 70 mph on interstates (60 for urban) and other 4-lane divided; 65 (55, nights) on other state roads and hwys; Turnpike Auth. raised limit to 75 rural (min. 50), 65 urban (min. 40). |
| OR | 75 | N | 65 | 55 | 55 | 55 | |
| PA | 65 | Y | 65 | 65 | 65 | 65 | Parts of US 15, 22/232, 119, 220, 222, 422, PA 43 raised to 65 mph. |
| RI | 60 | Y | 65 | 55 | 65 | 55 | Eff. 5/12/96: Increased to 65 mph on c. 45 mi. of interstate hwys. |
| SC | 70 | N | 65 | 55 | 65 | 55 | Bill to raise interstate to 70 mph pending. |
| SD | 75 | Y | 75 | 65 | 75 | 65 | Eff. 4/1/96: 75 mph interstates, 65 major 2-lane highways. (40 counties will keep 55, 11 increase to 65, rest undecided.) |
| TE | 75 | Y | 65 | 55 | 65 | 55 | Eff. 4/22/96: Legislature approved raising some urban interstates to 65 mph. Eff. 7/1/96: divided 4-lane limited access to 65. |
| TX | 70 | Y | 70 | 70 | 65 | 60 | Cars-70 mph day/65 night; 60 day/55 night for trucks, on all roads, 12/8/95. Govt. studies indicate about 23,000 mi. will be 70 mph (3/25/96). |
| UT | 70 | Y | 75 | 55 | 75 | 55 | Gov. signed bill 3/13/96, eff. when posted. |
| VT | 65 | N | 65 | 50 | 65 | 50 | |
| VA | 70 | Y | 65/55 | 55 | 65/55 | 55 | Dulles Greenway raised to 65 mph. |
| WA | 70 | Y | 70 | 55 | 60 | 55 | Eff. 3/11/96 |
| WV | 70 | N | 65 | 55 | 65 | 55 | Legislation introduced to allow commissioner to raise to 70 mph (2/96). |
| WI | 70 | N | 65 | 55 | 65 | 55 | Possible increase to 65 mph on multilane roads after study. |
| WY | 75 | Y | 75 | 65 | 75 | 65 | 75 mph, rural interstates; 60, urban interstates; 65 on 4- and 2-lane roads; some secondary and mountainous roads remain at 55. |

# Road Mileage Between Selected U.S. Cities

| | Atlanta | Boston | Chicago | Cincin-nati | Cleve-land | Dallas | Denver | Des Moines | Detroit | Houston |
|---|---|---|---|---|---|---|---|---|---|---|
| Atlanta, Ga. | ... | 1,037 | 674 | 440 | 672 | 795 | 1,398 | 870 | 699 | 789 |
| Boston, Mass. | 1,037 | ... | 963 | 840 | 628 | 1,748 | 1,949 | 1,280 | 695 | 1,804 |
| Chicago, Ill. | 674 | 963 | ... | 287 | 335 | 917 | 996 | 327 | 266 | 1,067 |
| Cincinnati, Oh. | 440 | 840 | 287 | ... | 244 | 920 | 1,164 | 571 | 259 | 1,029 |
| Cleveland, Oh. | 672 | 628 | 335 | 244 | ... | 1,159 | 1,321 | 652 | 170 | 1,273 |
| Dallas Tex. | 795 | 1,748 | 917 | 920 | 1,159 | ... | 781 | 684 | 1,143 | 243 |
| Denver, Col. | 1,398 | 1,949 | 996 | 1,164 | 1,321 | 781 | ... | 669 | 1,253 | 1,019 |
| Detroit, Mich. | 699 | 695 | 266 | 259 | 170 | 1,143 | 1,253 | 584 | ... | 1,265 |
| Houston, Tex. | 789 | 1,804 | 1,067 | 1,029 | 1,273 | 243 | 1,019 | 905 | 1,265 | ... |
| Indianapolis, Ind. | 493 | 906 | 181 | 106 | 294 | 865 | 1,058 | 465 | 278 | 987 |
| Kansas City, Mo. | 798 | 1,391 | 499 | 591 | 779 | 489 | 600 | 195 | 743 | 710 |
| Los Angeles, Cal. | 2,182 | 2,979 | 2,054 | 2,179 | 2,367 | 1,387 | 1,059 | 1,727 | 2,311 | 1,538 |
| Memphis, Tenn. | 371 | 1,296 | 530 | 468 | 712 | 452 | 1,040 | 599 | 713 | 561 |
| Milwaukee, Wis. | 761 | 1,050 | 87 | 374 | 422 | 991 | 1,029 | 361 | 353 | 1,142 |
| Minneapolis, Minn. | 1,068 | 1,368 | 405 | 692 | 740 | 936 | 841 | 252 | 671 | 1,157 |
| New Orleans, La. | 479 | 1,507 | 912 | 786 | 1,030 | 496 | 1,273 | 978 | 1,045 | 356 |
| New York, N.Y. | 841 | 206 | 802 | 647 | 473 | 1,552 | 1,771 | 1,119 | 637 | 1,608 |
| Omaha, Neb. | 986 | 1,412 | 459 | 693 | 784 | 644 | 537 | 132 | 716 | 865 |
| Philadelphia, Pa. | 741 | 296 | 738 | 567 | 413 | 1,452 | 1,691 | 1,051 | 573 | 1,508 |
| Pittsburgh, Pa. | 687 | 561 | 452 | 287 | 129 | 1,204 | 1,411 | 763 | 287 | 1,313 |
| Portland Ore. | 2,601 | 3,046 | 2,083 | 2,333 | 2,418 | 2,009 | 1,238 | 1,786 | 2,349 | 2,205 |
| St. Louis, Mo. | 541 | 1,141 | 289 | 340 | 529 | 630 | 857 | 333 | 513 | 779 |
| San Francisco | 2,496 | 3,095 | 2,142 | 2,362 | 2,467 | 1,753 | 1,235 | 1,815 | 2,399 | 1,912 |
| Seattle, Wash. | 2,618 | 2,976 | 2,013 | 2,300 | 2,348 | 2,078 | 1,307 | 1,749 | 2,279 | 2,274 |
| Tulsa, Okla. | 772 | 1,537 | 683 | 736 | 925 | 257 | 681 | 443 | 909 | 478 |
| Washington, DC | 608 | 429 | 671 | 481 | 346 | 1,319 | 1,616 | 984 | 506 | 1,375 |

| | India-napolis | Kansas City | Los Angeles | Louis-ville | Memphis | Mil-waukee | Minne-apolis | New Orleans | New York | Omaha |
|---|---|---|---|---|---|---|---|---|---|---|
| Atlanta, Ga. | 493 | 798 | 2,182 | 382 | 371 | 761 | 1,068 | 479 | 841 | 986 |
| Boston, Mass. | 906 | 1,391 | 2,979 | 941 | 1,296 | 1,050 | 1,368 | 1,507 | 206 | 1,412 |
| Chicago, Ill. | 181 | 499 | 2,054 | 292 | 530 | 87 | 405 | 912 | 802 | 459 |
| Cincinnati, Oh. | 106 | 591 | 2,179 | 101 | 468 | 374 | 692 | 786 | 647 | 693 |
| Cleveland Oh. | 294 | 779 | 2,367 | 345 | 712 | 422 | 740 | 1,030 | 473 | 784 |
| Dallas, Tex. | 865 | 489 | 1,387 | 819 | 452 | 991 | 936 | 496 | 1,552 | 644 |
| Denver, Col. | 1,058 | 600 | 1,059 | 1,120 | 1,040 | 1,029 | 841 | 1,273 | 1,771 | 537 |
| Detroit, Mich. | 278 | 743 | 2,311 | 360 | 713 | 353 | 671 | 1,045 | 637 | 716 |
| Houston, Tex. | 987 | 710 | 1,538 | 928 | 561 | 1,142 | 1,157 | 356 | 1,608 | 865 |
| Indianapolis, Ind. | ... | 485 | 2,073 | 111 | 435 | 268 | 586 | 796 | 713 | 587 |
| Kansas City, Mo. | 485 | ... | 1,589 | 520 | 451 | 537 | 447 | 806 | 1,198 | 201 |
| Los Angeles, Cal. | 2,073 | 1,589 | ... | 2,108 | 1,817 | 2,087 | 1,889 | 1,883 | 2,786 | 1,595 |
| Memphis, Tenn. | 435 | 451 | 1,817 | 367 | ... | 612 | 826 | 390 | 1,100 | 652 |
| Milwaukee, Wis. | 268 | 537 | 2,087 | 379 | 612 | ... | 332 | 994 | 889 | 493 |
| Minneapolis, Minn. | 586 | 447 | 1,889 | 697 | 826 | 332 | ... | 1,214 | 1,207 | 357 |
| New Orleans, La. | 796 | 806 | 1,883 | 685 | 390 | 994 | 1,214 | ... | 1,311 | 1,007 |
| New York, N.Y. | 713 | 1,198 | 2,786 | 748 | 1,100 | 889 | 1,207 | 1,311 | ... | 1,251 |
| Omaha, Neb. | 587 | 201 | 1,595 | 687 | 652 | 493 | 357 | 1,007 | 1,251 | ... |
| Philadelphia, Pa. | 633 | 1,118 | 2,706 | 668 | 1,000 | 825 | 1,143 | 1,211 | 100 | 1,183 |
| Pittsburgh, Pa. | 353 | 838 | 2,426 | 388 | 752 | 539 | 857 | 1,070 | 368 | 895 |
| Portland, Ore. | 1,227 | 1,809 | 959 | 2,320 | 2,259 | 2,010 | 1,678 | 2,505 | 2,885 | 1,654 |
| St. Louis, Mo. | 235 | 257 | 1,845 | 263 | 285 | 363 | 552 | 673 | 948 | 449 |
| San Francisco | 2,256 | 1,835 | 379 | 2,349 | 2,125 | 2,175 | 1,940 | 2,249 | 2,934 | 1,683 |
| Seattle, Wash. | 2,194 | 1,839 | 1,131 | 2,305 | 2,290 | 1,940 | 1,608 | 2,574 | 2,815 | 1,638 |
| Tulsa, Okla. | 631 | 248 | 1,452 | 659 | 401 | 757 | 695 | 647 | 1,344 | 387 |
| Washington, DC | 558 | 1,043 | 2,631 | 582 | 867 | 758 | 1,076 | 1,078 | 233 | 1,116 |

| | Phila-delphia | Pitts-burgh | Port-land | St. Louis | Salt Lake City | San Fran-cisco | Seattle | Toledo | Tulsa | Wash., DC |
|---|---|---|---|---|---|---|---|---|---|---|
| Atlanta, Ga. | 741 | 687 | 2,601 | 541 | 1,878 | 2,496 | 2,618 | 640 | 772 | 608 |
| Boston, Mass. | 296 | 561 | 3,046 | 1,141 | 2,343 | 3,095 | 2,976 | 739 | 1,537 | 429 |
| Chicago, Ill. | 738 | 452 | 2,083 | 289 | 1,390 | 2,142 | 2,013 | 232 | 683 | 671 |
| Cincinnati, Oh. | 567 | 287 | 2,333 | 340 | 1,610 | 2,362 | 2,300 | 200 | 736 | 481 |
| Cleveland Oh. | 413 | 129 | 2,418 | 529 | 1,715 | 2,467 | 2,348 | 111 | 925 | 346 |
| Dallas, Tex. | 1,452 | 1,204 | 2,009 | 630 | 1,242 | 1,753 | 2,078 | 1,084 | 257 | 1,319 |
| Denver, Col. | 1,691 | 1,411 | 1,238 | 857 | 504 | 1,235 | 1,307 | 1,218 | 681 | 1,616 |
| Detroit, Mich. | 576 | 287 | 2,349 | 513 | 1,647 | 2,399 | 2,279 | 59 | 909 | 506 |
| Houston, Tex. | 1,508 | 1,313 | 2,205 | 779 | 1,438 | 1,912 | 2,274 | 1,206 | 478 | 1,375 |
| Indianapolis, Ind. | 633 | 353 | 2,227 | 235 | 1,504 | 2,256 | 2,194 | 219 | 631 | 558 |
| Kansas City, Mo. | 1,118 | 838 | 1,809 | 257 | 1,086 | 1,835 | 1,839 | 687 | 248 | 1,043 |
| Los Angeles, Cal. | 2,706 | 2,426 | 959 | 1,845 | 715 | 379 | 1,131 | 2,276 | 1,452 | 2,631 |
| Memphis, Tenn. | 1,000 | 752 | 2,259 | 285 | 1,535 | 2,125 | 2,290 | 654 | 401 | 867 |
| Milwaukee, Wis. | 825 | 539 | 2,010 | 363 | 1,423 | 2,175 | 1,940 | 319 | 757 | 758 |
| Minneapolis, Minn. | 1,143 | 857 | 1,678 | 552 | 1,186 | 1,940 | 1,608 | 637 | 695 | 1,076 |
| New Orleans, La. | 1,211 | 1,070 | 2,505 | 673 | 1,738 | 2,249 | 2,574 | 986 | 647 | 1,078 |
| New York, N.Y. | 100 | 368 | 2,885 | 948 | 2,182 | 2,934 | 2,815 | 578 | 1,344 | 233 |
| Omaha, Neb. | 1,183 | 895 | 1,654 | 449 | 931 | 1,683 | 1,638 | 681 | 387 | 1,116 |
| Philadelphia, Pa. | ... | 288 | 2,821 | 868 | 2,114 | 2,866 | 2,751 | 514 | 1,264 | 133 |
| Pittsburgh, Pa. | 288 | ... | 2,535 | 588 | 1,826 | 2,578 | 2,465 | 228 | 984 | 221 |
| Portland, Ore. | 2,821 | 2,535 | ... | 2,060 | 767 | 636 | 172 | 2,315 | 1,913 | 2,754 |
| St. Louis, Mo. | 868 | 588 | 2,060 | ... | 1,337 | 2,089 | 2,081 | 454 | 396 | 793 |
| San Francisco | 2,866 | 2,578 | 636 | 2,089 | 752 | ... | 808 | 2,364 | 1,760 | 2,799 |
| Seattle, Wash. | 2,751 | 2,465 | 172 | 2,081 | 836 | 808 | ... | 2,245 | 1,982 | 2,684 |
| Tulsa, Okla. | 1,264 | 984 | 1,913 | 396 | 1,172 | 1,760 | 1,982 | 850 | ... | 1,189 |
| Washington, DC | 133 | 221 | 2,754 | 793 | 2,047 | 2,799 | 2,684 | 447 | 1,189 | ... |

# Air Distances Between Selected World Cities in Statute Miles

Point-to-point measurements are usually from City Hall.

| | Bangkok | Beijing | Berlin | Cairo | Cape Town | Caracas | Chicago | Hong Kong | Honolulu | Lima |
|---|---|---|---|---|---|---|---|---|---|---|
| Bangkok | ... | 2,046 | 5,352 | 4,523 | 6,300 | 10,555 | 8,570 | 1,077 | 6,609 | 12,244 |
| Beijing | 2,046 | ... | 4,584 | 4,698 | 8,044 | 8,950 | 6,604 | 1,217 | 5,077 | 10,349 |
| Berlin | 5,352 | 4,584 | ... | 1,797 | 5,961 | 5,238 | 4,414 | 5,443 | 7,320 | 6,896 |
| Cairo | 4,523 | 4,698 | 1,797 | ... | 4,480 | 6,342 | 6,141 | 5,066 | 8,848 | 7,726 |
| Cape Town | 6,300 | 8,044 | 5,961 | 4,480 | ... | 6,366 | 8,491 | 7,376 | 11,535 | 6,072 |
| Caracas | 10,555 | 8,950 | 5,238 | 6,342 | 6,366 | ... | 2,495 | 10,165 | 6,021 | 1,707 |
| Chicago | 8,570 | 6,604 | 4,414 | 6,141 | 8,491 | 2,495 | ... | 7,797 | 4,256 | 3,775 |
| Hong Kong | 1,077 | 1,217 | 5,443 | 5,066 | 7,376 | 10,165 | 7,797 | ... | 5,556 | 11,418 |
| Honolulu | 6,609 | 5,077 | 7,320 | 8,848 | 11,535 | 6,021 | 4,256 | 5,556 | ... | 5,947 |
| London | 5,944 | 5,074 | 583 | 2,185 | 5,989 | 4,655 | 3,958 | 5,990 | 7,240 | 6,316 |
| Los Angeles | 7,637 | 6,250 | 5,782 | 7,520 | 9,969 | 3,632 | 1,745 | 7,240 | 2,557 | 4,171 |
| Madrid | 6,337 | 5,745 | 1,165 | 2,087 | 5,308 | 4,346 | 4,189 | 6,558 | 7,872 | 5,907 |
| Melbourne | 4,568 | 5,643 | 9,918 | 8,675 | 6,425 | 9,717 | 9,673 | 4,595 | 5,505 | 8,059 |
| Mexico City | 9,793 | 7,753 | 6,056 | 7,700 | 8,519 | 2,234 | 1,690 | 8,788 | 3,789 | 2,639 |
| Montreal | 8,338 | 6,519 | 3,740 | 5,427 | 7,922 | 2,438 | 745 | 7,736 | 4,918 | 3,970 |
| Moscow | 4,389 | 3,607 | 1,006 | 1,803 | 6,279 | 6,177 | 4,987 | 4,437 | 7,047 | 7,862 |
| New York | 8,669 | 6,844 | 3,979 | 5,619 | 7,803 | 2,120 | 714 | 8,060 | 4,969 | 3,639 |
| Paris | 5,877 | 5,120 | 548 | 1,998 | 5,786 | 4,732 | 4,143 | 5,990 | 7,449 | 6,370 |
| Rio de Janeiro | 9,994 | 10,768 | 6,209 | 6,143 | 3,781 | 2,804 | 5,282 | 11,009 | 8,288 | 2,342 |
| Rome | 5,494 | 5,063 | 737 | 1,326 | 5,231 | 5,195 | 4,824 | 5,774 | 8,040 | 6,750 |
| San Francisco | 7,931 | 5,918 | 5,672 | 7,466 | 10,248 | 3,902 | 1,859 | 6,905 | 2,398 | 4,518 |
| Singapore | 883 | 2,771 | 6,164 | 5,137 | 6,008 | 11,402 | 9,372 | 1,605 | 6,726 | 11,689 |
| Stockholm | 5,089 | 4,133 | 528 | 2,096 | 6,423 | 5,471 | 4,331 | 5,063 | 6,875 | 7,166 |
| Tokyo | 2,865 | 1,307 | 5,557 | 5,958 | 9,154 | 8,808 | 6,314 | 1,791 | 3,859 | 9,631 |
| Warsaw | 5,033 | 4,325 | 322 | 1,619 | 5,935 | 5,559 | 4,679 | 5,147 | 7,366 | 7,215 |
| Washington, DC | 8,807 | 6,942 | 4,181 | 5,822 | 7,895 | 2,047 | 596 | 8,155 | 4,838 | 3,509 |

| | London | Los Angeles | Madrid | Melbourne | Mexico City | Montreal | Moscow | New Delhi | New York | Paris |
|---|---|---|---|---|---|---|---|---|---|---|
| Bangkok | 5,944 | 7,637 | 6,337 | 4,568 | 9,793 | 8,338 | 4,389 | 1,813 | 8,669 | 5,877 |
| Beijing | 5,074 | 6,250 | 5,745 | 5,643 | 7,753 | 6,519 | 3,607 | 2,353 | 6,844 | 5,120 |
| Berlin | 583 | 5,782 | 1,165 | 9,918 | 6,056 | 3,740 | 1,006 | 3,598 | 3,979 | 548 |
| Cairo | 2,185 | 7,520 | 2,087 | 8,675 | 7,700 | 5,427 | 1,803 | 2,758 | 5,619 | 1,998 |
| Cape Town | 5,989 | 9,969 | 5,308 | 6,425 | 8,519 | 7,922 | 6,279 | 5,769 | 7,803 | 5,786 |
| Caracas | 4,655 | 3,632 | 4,346 | 9,717 | 2,234 | 2,438 | 6,177 | 8,833 | 2,120 | 4,732 |
| Chicago | 3,958 | 1,745 | 4,189 | 9,673 | 1,690 | 745 | 4,987 | 7,486 | 714 | 4,143 |
| Hong Kong | 5,990 | 7,240 | 6,558 | 4,595 | 8,788 | 7,736 | 4,437 | 2,339 | 8,060 | 5,990 |
| Honolulu | 7,240 | 2,557 | 7,872 | 5,505 | 3,789 | 4,918 | 7,047 | 7,412 | 4,969 | 7,449 |
| London | ... | 5,439 | 785 | 10,500 | 5,558 | 3,254 | 1,564 | 4,181 | 3,469 | 214 |
| Los Angeles | 5,439 | ... | 5,848 | 7,931 | 1,542 | 2,427 | 6,068 | 7,011 | 2,451 | 5,601 |
| Madrid | 785 | 5,848 | ... | 10,758 | 5,643 | 3,448 | 2,147 | 4,530 | 3,593 | 655 |
| Melbourne | 10,500 | 7,931 | 10,758 | ... | 8,426 | 10,395 | 8,950 | 6,329 | 10,359 | 10,430 |
| Mexico City | 5,558 | 1,542 | 5,643 | 8,426 | ... | 2,317 | 6,676 | 9,120 | 2,090 | 5,725 |
| Montreal | 3,254 | 2,427 | 3,448 | 10,395 | 2,317 | ... | 4,401 | 7,012 | 331 | 3,432 |
| Moscow | 1,564 | 6,068 | 2,147 | 8,950 | 6,676 | 4,401 | ... | 2,698 | 4,683 | 1,554 |
| New York | 3,469 | 2,451 | 3,593 | 10,359 | 2,090 | 331 | 4,683 | 7,318 | ... | 3,636 |
| Paris | 214 | 5,601 | 655 | 10,430 | 5,725 | 3,432 | 1,554 | 4,102 | 3,636 | ... |
| Rio de Janeiro | 5,750 | 6,330 | 5,045 | 8,226 | 4,764 | 5,078 | 7,170 | 8,753 | 4,801 | 5,684 |
| Rome | 895 | 6,326 | 851 | 9,929 | 6,377 | 4,104 | 1,483 | 3,684 | 4,293 | 690 |
| San Francisco | 5,367 | 347 | 5,803 | 7,856 | 1,887 | 2,543 | 5,885 | 7,691 | 2,572 | 5,577 |
| Singapore | 6,747 | 8,767 | 7,080 | 3,759 | 10,327 | 9,203 | 5,228 | 2,571 | 9,534 | 6,673 |
| Stockholm | 942 | 5,454 | 1,653 | 9,630 | 6,012 | 3,714 | 716 | 3,414 | 3,986 | 1,003 |
| Tokyo | 5,959 | 5,470 | 6,706 | 5,062 | 7,035 | 6,471 | 4,660 | 3,638 | 6,757 | 6,053 |
| Warsaw | 905 | 5,922 | 1,427 | 9,598 | 6,337 | 4,022 | 721 | 3,277 | 4,270 | 852 |
| Washington, DC | 3,674 | 2,300 | 3,792 | 10,180 | 1,885 | 489 | 4,876 | 7,500 | 205 | 3,840 |

| | Rio de Janeiro | Rome | San Francisco | Singapore | Stockholm | Tehran | Tokyo | Vienna | Warsaw | Wash., DC |
|---|---|---|---|---|---|---|---|---|---|---|
| Bangkok | 9,994 | 5,494 | 7,931 | 883 | 5,089 | 3,391 | 2,865 | 5,252 | 5,033 | 8,807 |
| Beijing | 10,768 | 5,063 | 5,918 | 2,771 | 4,133 | 3,490 | 1,307 | 4,648 | 4,325 | 6,942 |
| Berlin | 6,209 | 737 | 5,672 | 6,164 | 528 | 2,185 | 5,557 | 326 | 322 | 4,181 |
| Cairo | 6,143 | 1,326 | 7,466 | 5,137 | 2,096 | 1,234 | 5,958 | 1,481 | 1,619 | 5,822 |
| Cape Town | 3,781 | 5,231 | 10,248 | 6,008 | 6,423 | 5,241 | 9,154 | 5,656 | 5,935 | 7,895 |
| Caracas | 2,804 | 5,195 | 3,902 | 11,402 | 5,471 | 7,320 | 8,808 | 5,372 | 5,559 | 2,047 |
| Chicago | 5,282 | 4,824 | 1,859 | 9,372 | 4,331 | 6,502 | 6,314 | 4,698 | 4,679 | 596 |
| Hong Kong | 11,009 | 5,774 | 6,905 | 1,605 | 5,063 | 3,843 | 1,791 | 5,431 | 5,147 | 8,155 |
| Honolulu | 8,288 | 8,040 | 2,398 | 6,726 | 6,875 | 8,070 | 3,859 | 7,632 | 7,366 | 4,838 |
| London | 5,750 | 895 | 5,367 | 6,747 | 942 | 2,743 | 5,959 | 771 | 905 | 3,674 |
| Los Angeles | 6,330 | 6,326 | 347 | 8,767 | 5,454 | 7,682 | 5,470 | 6,108 | 5,922 | 2,300 |
| Madrid | 5,045 | 851 | 5,803 | 7,080 | 1,653 | 2,978 | 6,706 | 1,128 | 1,427 | 3,792 |
| Melbourne | 8,226 | 9,929 | 7,856 | 3,759 | 9,630 | 7,826 | 5,062 | 9,790 | 9,598 | 10,180 |
| Mexico City | 4,764 | 6,377 | 1,887 | 10,327 | 6,012 | 8,184 | 7,035 | 6,320 | 6,337 | 1,885 |
| Montreal | 5,078 | 4,104 | 2,543 | 9,203 | 3,714 | 5,880 | 6,471 | 4,009 | 4,022 | 489 |
| Moscow | 7,170 | 1,483 | 5,885 | 5,228 | 716 | 1,532 | 4,660 | 1,043 | 721 | 4,876 |
| New York | 4,801 | 4,293 | 2,572 | 9,534 | 3,986 | 6,141 | 6,757 | 4,234 | 4,270 | 205 |
| Paris | 5,684 | 690 | 5,577 | 6,673 | 1,003 | 2,625 | 6,053 | 645 | 852 | 3,840 |
| Rio de Janeiro | ... | 5,707 | 6,613 | 9,785 | 6,683 | 7,374 | 11,532 | 6,127 | 6,455 | 4,779 |
| Rome | 5,707 | ... | 6,259 | 6,229 | 1,245 | 2,127 | 6,142 | 477 | 820 | 4,497 |
| San Francisco | 6,613 | 6,259 | ... | 8,448 | 5,399 | 7,362 | 5,150 | 5,994 | 5,854 | 2,441 |
| Singapore | 9,785 | 6,229 | 8,448 | ... | 5,936 | 4,103 | 3,300 | 6,035 | 5,843 | 9,662 |
| Stockholm | 6,683 | 1,245 | 5,399 | 5,936 | ... | 2,173 | 5,053 | 780 | 494 | 4,183 |
| Tokyo | 11,532 | 6,142 | 5,150 | 3,300 | 5,053 | 4,775 | ... | 5,689 | 5,347 | 6,791 |
| Warsaw | 6,455 | 820 | 5,854 | 5,843 | 494 | 1,879 | 5,689 | 347 | ... | 4,472 |
| Washington, DC | 4,779 | 4,497 | 2,441 | 9,662 | 4,183 | 6,341 | 6,791 | 4,438 | 4,472 | ... |

# EDUCATION

## Historical Overview of Public Elementary and Secondary Schools

**Source:** National Center for Education Statistics, U.S. Dept. of Education

| Pupils and teachers (thousands) | 1949-50 | 1959-60[1] | 1969-70[1] | 1979-80[1] | 1989-90[1] | 1990-91[1] | 1991-92[1] | 1992-93[1] | 1993-94[1] |
|---|---|---|---|---|---|---|---|---|---|
| Total U.S. population | 149,199 | 179,323 | 201,385 | 224,567 | 246,819 | 249,402 | 252,137 | 255,028 | 257,783 |
| Population 5-17 years of age | 30,223 | 43,881 | 52,386 | 48,041 | 44,947 | 45,306 | 45,918 | 46,662 | 47,419 |
| Percentage 5-17 years of age | 20.3 | 24.5 | 26 | 21.4 | 18.2 | 18.2 | 18.2 | 18.3 | 18.4 |
| **Enrollment (thousands)** | | | | | | | | | |
| Elementary and secondary | 25,112 | 36,087 | 45,550 | 41,651 | 40,543 | 41,217 | 42,047 | 42,816 | 43,465 |
| Kindergarten & grades 1-8 | 19,387 | 27,602 | 32,513 | 28,034 | 29,152 | 29,878 | 30,506 | 31,081 | 31,504 |
| Grades 9-12 | 5,725 | 8,485 | 13,037 | 13,616 | 11,390 | 11,338 | 11,541 | 11,735 | 11,961 |
| Percentage pop. 5-17 enrolled | 83.1 | 82.2 | 87 | 86.7 | 90.2 | 91.0 | 91.6 | 91.8 | 91.7 |
| Percentage in high schools | 22.8 | 23.5 | 28.6 | 32.7 | 28.1 | 27.5 | 27.4 | 27.4 | 27.5 |
| High school graduates (thousands) | 1,063 | 1,627 | 2,589 | 2,748 | 2,320 | 2,235 | 2,212 | 2,233 | 2,221 |
| Average school term (in days) | 177.9 | 178.0 | 178.9 | 178.5 | * | 179.8 | * | * | * |
| Total instructional staff (thousands) | 963 | 1,457 | 2,286 | 2,406 | 2,986 | 3,051 | 3,104 | 3,140 | 3,209 |
| Teachers, librarians, and other nonsupervisory instructional staff (thousands) | 920 | 1,393 | 2,195 | 2,300 | 2,860 | 2,924 | 2,975 | 3,017 | 3,088 |
| **Revenue & expenditures (millions)** | | | | | | | | | |
| Total revenue | $5,437 | $14,747 | $40,267 | $96,881 | $208,548 | $223,341 | $234,486 | $247,626 | $260,142 |
| Total expenditures | 5,838 | 15,613 | 40,683 | 95,962 | 212,473 | 229,430 | 241,567 | 252,935 | 265,285 |
| Current elem. and secondary | 4,687 | 12,239 | 34,218 | 86,984 | 187,933 | 202,038 | 211,216 | 220,948 | 231,521 |
| Capital outlay | 1,014 | 2,662 | 4,659 | 6,506 | 17,781 | 19,771 | 20,797 | 22,172 | 23,747 |
| Interest on school debt | 101 | 490 | 1,171 | 1,874 | 3,776 | 4,325 | 5,162 | 5,437 | 5,335 |
| Other | 36 | 133 | 636 | 598 | 2,983 | 3,296 | 4,392 | 4,379 | 4,682 |
| **Salaries and pupil cost** | | | | (data in unadjusted dollars) | | | | | |
| Aug. annual salary of instruct. staff[2] | $3,010 | $5,174 | $9,047 | $16,715 | $32,638 | $34,412 | $35,550 | $36,454 | $37,383 |
| Expenditure per capita total pop. | 39 | 87 | 202 | 427 | 861 | 920 | 958 | 992 | 1,029 |
| Current expenditure per pupil ADA[3] | 210 | 375 | 816 | 2,272 | 4,972 | 5,258 | 5,421 | 5,584 | 5,767 |

(1) Because of a modification in scope, data on expenditures for elementary and secondary schools for 1959-60 and later years are not entirely comparable with data for prior years. (2) Includes supervisors, principals, teachers, and nonsupervisory instructional staff. (3) ADA means average daily attendance in elementary and secondary day schools. * = Data not collected. **Note:** Because of rounding, details may not add to totals.

## Programs for the Disabled,[1] 1985-94

**Source:** Office of Special Education and Rehabilitative Services, U.S. Dept. of Education

(Number of children up to 21 years old served annually in educational programs for the disabled; in thousands.)

| Type of Disability | 1985-86 | 1986-87 | 1987-88 | 1988-89 | 1989-90 | 1990-91 | 1991-92 | 1992-93 | 1993-94 |
|---|---|---|---|---|---|---|---|---|---|
| All disabilities | 4,317 | 4,374 | 4,446 | 4,544 | 4,641 | 4,771 | 4,949 | 5,125 | 5,318 |
| Learning disabilities | 1,862 | 1,914 | 1,928 | 1,987 | 2,050 | 2,130 | 2,234 | 2,354 | 2,424 |
| Speech impairments | 1,125 | 1,136 | 953 | 967 | 973 | 987 | 997 | 996 | 1,005 |
| Mental retardation | 660 | 643 | 582 | 564 | 548 | 536 | 538 | 519 | 536 |
| Serious emotional disturbance | 375 | 383 | 373 | 376 | 381 | 391 | 399 | 401 | 413 |
| Hearing impairments | 66 | 65 | 56 | 56 | 57 | 58 | 60 | 60 | 63 |
| Orthopedic impairments | 57 | 57 | 47 | 47 | 48 | 49 | 51 | 52 | 56 |
| Visual impairments | 27 | 26 | 22 | 23 | 22 | 23 | 24 | 23 | 24 |
| Other health impairments | 57 | 52 | 45 | 43 | 52 | 55 | 58 | 65 | 82 |
| Multiple disabilities | 86 | 97 | 77 | 85 | 86 | 96 | 97 | 102 | 108 |
| Deafness/blindness | 2 | 2 | 12 | 2 | 2 | 1 | 1 | 1 | 1 |
| Autism and other | * | * | * | * | * | * | 5 | 19 | 24 |
| Preschool disabilities[2] | [3] | [3] | 361 | 394 | 422 | 441 | 484 | 531 | 582 |

**Note:** Counts are based on reports from the 50 states, the District of Columbia, and Puerto Rico. Increases since 1987-88 are due in part to new legislation enacted in fall 1986, which mandates public school special education services for all disabled children ages 3-5. Details may not add to totals because of rounding.* = Data not collected.

(1) Includes students served under Chapter I and Individuals With Disabilities Education Act (IDEA). (2) Includes preschool children 3-5 years and 0-5 years served under Chapter I and IDEA respectively. (3) Prior to 1987-88, these students were included in the counts by disabling condition. Beginning in 1987-88, states were no longer required to report disabled preschool students (0-5 years) by disabling condition.

## Technology in Public Schools, 1993-96

**Source:** Quality Education Data, Inc., Denver, CO

| Technology | Number of schools | | | | Percentage of schools | | | |
|---|---|---|---|---|---|---|---|---|
| | 1993 | 1994 | 1995 | 1996 | 1993 | 1994 | 1995 | 1996 |
| **Schools with interactive videodisc players[1]** | **11,729** | **17,489** | **24,534** | **28,497** | **14.0** | **21.0** | **29.1** | **29.3** |
| Elementary[2] | 5,986 | 9,247 | 13,292 | 15,447 | 12.0 | 18.0 | 26.0 | 25.2 |
| Junior high[3] | 2,386 | 3,580 | 4,924 | 5,766 | 18.0 | 26.0 | 36.0 | 38.9 |
| Senior high[4] | 3,129 | 4,548 | 5,990 | 6,933 | 19.0 | 27.0 | 35.4 | 36.6 |
| **Schools with modems[1]** | **18,471** | **22,611** | **30,768** | **37,889** | **22.0** | **27.0** | **37.0** | **39.0** |
| Elementary[2] | 8,492 | 10,878 | 16,010 | 20,250 | 17.0 | 21.0 | 31.0 | 33.0 |
| Junior high[3] | 3,431 | 4,246 | 5,652 | 6,929 | 26.0 | 31.0 | 41.1 | 46.7 |
| Senior high[4] | 6,371 | 7,402 | 8,790 | 10,277 | 38.0 | 44.0 | 52.0 | 54.2 |
| **Schools with networks[1]** | **11,657** | **17,522** | **24,604** | **29,875** | **14.0** | **21.0** | **29.2** | **30.7** |
| Elementary[2] | 4,683 | 7,545 | 11,693 | 14,868 | 9.0 | 15.0 | 23.0 | 24.2 |
| Junior high[3] | 2,030 | 3,220 | 4,599 | 5,590 | 15.0 | 24.0 | 33.4 | 37.7 |
| Senior high[4] | 4,895 | 6,576 | 8,159 | 9,166 | 29.0 | 39.0 | 48.3 | 48.4 |
| **Schools with CD-ROMs[1]** | **11,021** | **20,943** | **34,480** | **43,499** | **13.0** | **25.0** | **41.0** | **44.7** |
| Elementary[2] | 4,457 | 9,791 | 18,343 | 24,353 | 9.0 | 19.0 | 36.0 | 39.7 |
| Junior high[3] | 2,326 | 4,261 | 6,510 | 7,952 | 17.0 | 31.0 | 47.4 | 53.6 |
| Senior high[4] | 4,168 | 6,713 | 9,327 | 10,756 | 25.0 | 40.0 | 55.2 | 56.7 |

(1) Includes schools for special and adult education, not shown separately. (2) Includes K-12, preschool, preschool through 3, K-6, and K-8. (3) Includes schools with grade spans of 4-8 and 7-9. (4) Includes 7-12, 9-12, 10-12, vocational technical, and alternative high schools.

# Enrollment and Teachers in Full-Time Public Elementary and Secondary Day Schools, Fall 1994

**Source:** National Center for Education Statistics, U.S. Dept. of Education; National Education Association

| | Local school districts | Classroom teachers | Total enrollment | Pupils per teacher | Teacher's average pay (1994-95)[1] | Instructional aides | Expenditure per pupil |
|---|---|---|---|---|---|---|---|
| **U.S.** | **14,881** | **2,552,199** | **44,108,775** | **17.3** | **$36,802** | **$473,408** | **$5,767** |
| Alabama | 127 | 42,789 | 736,472 | 17.2 | 31,144 | 6,678 | 4,037 |
| Alaska | 56 | 7,205 | 127,057 | 17.6 | 47,951 | 1,842 | 8,882 |
| Arizona | 228 | 38,132 | 737,424 | 19.3 | 32,175 | 9,049 | 4,611 |
| Arkansas | 315 | 26,181 | 447,565 | 17.1 | 28,934 | 2,572 | 4,280 |
| California | 1,002 | 225,001 | 5,407,043 | 24.0 | 41,078 | 56,391 | 4,921 |
| Colorado | 176 | 34,894 | 640,521 | 18.4 | 34,571 | 5,440 | 5,097 |
| Connecticut | 166 | 35,316 | 506,824 | 14.4 | 50,045 | 6,822 | 8,473 |
| Delaware | 19 | 6,416 | 106,813 | 16.6 | 39,076 | 829 | 6,621 |
| District of Columbia | 1 | 6,110 | 80,450 | 13.2 | 43,700 | 359 | 10,180 |
| Florida | 67 | 110,674 | 2,108,968 | 19.1 | 32,588 | 22,243 | 5,516 |
| Georgia | 181 | 77,914 | 1,270,948 | 16.3 | 32,633 | 21,172 | 4,915 |
| Hawaii | 1 | 10,240 | 183,795 | 17.9 | 38,518 | 790 | 5,879 |
| Idaho | 113 | 12,582 | 240,448 | 19.1 | 29,783 | 1,805 | 3,844 |
| Illinois | 922 | 110,830 | 1,916,172 | 17.3 | 39,431 | 19,470 | 5,893 |
| Indiana | 294 | 55,496 | 968,933 | 17.5 | 36,785 | 14,372 | 5,630 |
| Iowa | 397 | 31,775 | 499,550 | 15.7 | 31,511 | 5,346 | 5,288 |
| Kansas | 304 | 30,579 | 460,838 | 15.1 | 34,652 | 4,451 | 5,659 |
| Kentucky | 176 | 38,784 | 657,642 | 17.0 | 32,257 | 9,784 | 5,107 |
| Louisiana | 66 | 47,599 | 797,933 | 16.8 | 26,461 | 10,177 | 4,519 |
| Maine | 282 | 15,404 | 212,601 | 13.8 | 31,972 | 3,726 | 6,069 |
| Maryland | 24 | 46,565 | 790,938 | 17.0 | 40,661 | 7,255 | 6,958 |
| Massachusetts | 351 | 60,489 | 893,727 | 14.8 | 42,174 | 11,714 | 6,959 |
| Michigan | 558 | 80,522 | 1,614,784 | 20.1 | 47,360[1] | 13,412 | 6,658 |
| Minnesota | 405 | 46,958 | 821,693 | 17.5 | 35,948 | 6,088 | 5,720 |
| Mississippi | 149 | 28,866 | 505,962 | 17.5 | 26,818 | 8,930 | 3,660 |
| Missouri | 541 | 56,606 | 878,541 | 15.5 | 31,189 | 6,909 | 5,114 |
| Montana | 495 | 10,079 | 164,341 | 16.3 | 28,785 | 1,841 | 5,598 |
| Nebraska | 695 | 19,774 | 287,100 | 14.5 | 30,922 | 3,370 | 5,651 |
| Nevada | 17 | 13,414 | 250,747 | 18.7 | 34,836 | 1,643 | 5,049 |
| New Hampshire | 178 | 12,109 | 189,319 | 15.6 | 34,720 | 3,098 | 5,723 |
| New Jersey | 608 | 85,258 | 1,174,206 | 13.8 | 46,087 | 13,274 | 9,677 |
| New Mexico | 88 | 19,025 | 327,248 | 17.2 | 28,491 | 4,269 | 4,261 |
| New York | 714 | 182,273 | 2,766,208 | 15.2 | 47,612 | 27,390 | 9,175 |
| North Carolina | 121 | 71,592 | 1,156,767 | 16.2 | 30,793 | 21,766 | 4,894 |
| North Dakota | 260 | 7,796 | 119,288 | 15.3 | 26,327 | 1,343 | 4,674 |
| Ohio | 661 | 109,085 | 1,814,290 | 16.6 | 36,802 | 9,884 | 5,971 |
| Oklahoma | 554 | 39,406 | 609,718 | 15.5 | 28,172 | 7,205 | 4,697 |
| Oregon | 280 | 26,208 | 521,945 | 19.9 | 38,590 | 5,501 | 6,263 |
| Pennsylvania | 501 | 102,988 | 1,765,891 | 17.1 | 44,510 | 13,680 | 6,983 |
| Rhode Island | 36 | 10,066 | 147,487 | 14.7 | 40,729 | 1,272 | 7,333 |
| South Carolina | 95 | 39,437 | 648,673 | 16.4 | 30,279 | 7,268 | 4,761 |
| South Dakota | 178 | 9,985 | 143,482 | 14.4 | 25,994 | 1,905 | 4,586 |
| Tennessee | 140 | 47,406 | 881,355 | 18.6 | 32,477 | 9,574 | 4,149 |
| Texas | 1,046 | 234,213 | 3,677,171 | 15.7 | 31,223 | 41,317 | 4,898 |
| Utah | 40 | 19,524 | 474,675 | 24.3 | 29,082 | 4,665 | 3,439 |
| Vermont | 285 | 7,566 | 104,533 | 13.8 | 35,406 | 2,776 | 6,600 |
| Virginia | 141 | 72,853 | 1,060,809 | 14.6 | 33,998 | 11,692 | 5,109 |
| Washington | 296 | 46,439 | 938,314 | 20.2 | 36,151 | 8,480 | 5,751 |
| West Virginia | 55 | 21,024 | 310,511 | 14.8 | 31,944 | 2,867 | 5,713 |
| Wisconsin | 427 | 54,054 | 860,686 | 15.9 | 37,746 | 8,442 | 6,717 |
| Wyoming | 49 | 6,698 | 100,369 | 15.0 | 31,285 | 1,260 | 5,899 |

(1) National Education Association estimate.

# Revenues for Public Schools by Source, 1990-96

**Source:** National Education Association

(in thousands)

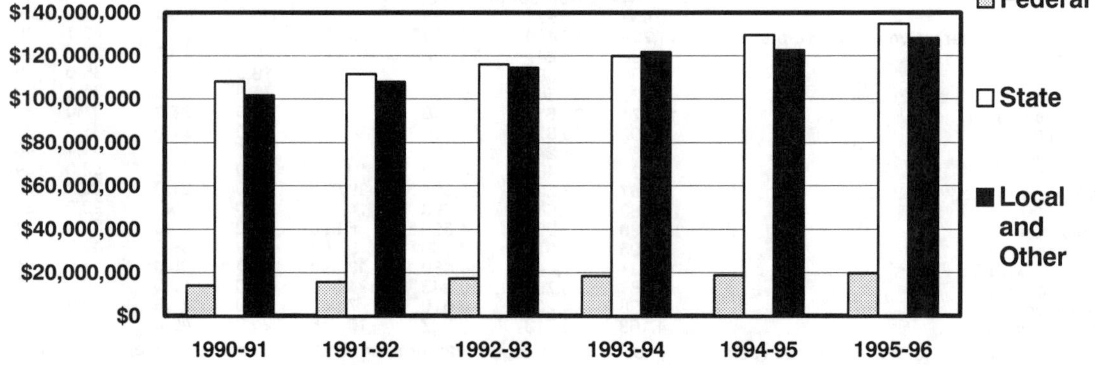

# Estimated Revenues[1] for Public Elementary and Secondary Schools, by State, 1995-96

**Source:** National Education Association

(in thousands)

| State | Total | Federal Amount | Federal % | State Amount | State % | Local and intermediate Amount | Local and intermediate % |
|---|---|---|---|---|---|---|---|
| **U.S.** | **$282,954,229** | **$19,822,759** | **7.0** | **$134,989,140** | **47.7** | **$128,142,330** | **45.3** |
| Alabama | 3,394,989 | 338,155 | 10.0 | 2,406,898 | 70.9 | 649,936 | 19.1 |
| Alaska | 1,097,402* | 137,897* | 12.6* | 697,610* | 63.6* | 261,895* | 23.9* |
| Arizona | 3,904,815* | 340,568* | 8.7* | 1,639,596* | 42.0* | 1,924,651* | 49.3* |
| Arkansas | 2,173,953 | 183,929 | 8.5 | 1,422,700 | 65.4 | 567,324 | 26.1 |
| California | 30,724,041 | 2,670,678 | 8.7 | 17,541,387 | 57.1 | 10,511,976 | 34.2 |
| Colorado | 3,672,517* | 211,180* | 5.8* | 1,672,530* | 45.5* | 1,788,807* | 48.7* |
| Connecticut | 4,665,591 | 216,416 | 4.6 | 1,871,967 | 40.1 | 2,577,208 | 55.2 |
| Delaware | 822,600 | 67,097 | 8.2 | 536,216 | 65.2 | 219,287 | 26.7 |
| District of Columbia | 566,800 | 75,800 | 13.4 | — | — | 491,000 | 86.6 |
| Florida | 13,493,049 | 971,203 | 7.2 | 6,684,689 | 49.5 | 5,837,157 | 43.3 |
| Georgia | 7,494,995* | 577,517* | 7.7* | 3,816,811* | 50.9* | 3,100,667* | 41.4* |
| Hawaii | 1,274,031 | 107,132 | 8.4 | 1,140,839 | 89.5 | 26,060 | 2.0 |
| Idaho | 1,117,123* | 86,397* | 7.7 | 683,123* | 61.2* | 347,603* | 31.1* |
| Illinois | 12,301,244 | 1,082,098 | 8.8 | 3,682,222 | 29.9 | 7,536,924 | 61.3 |
| Indiana | 6,374,276 | 332,569 | 5.2 | 3,331,785 | 52.3 | 2,709,922 | 42.5 |
| Iowa | 2,925,145 | 148,289 | 5.1 | 1,450,600 | 49.6 | 1,326,256 | 45.3 |
| Kansas | 2,735,439 | 156,570 | 5.7 | 1,653,119 | 60.4 | 925,750 | 33.8 |
| Kentucky | 3,582,265 | 319,916 | 8.9 | 2,406,656 | 67.2 | 855,693 | 23.9 |
| Louisiana | 3,873,731 | 510,097 | 13.2 | 2,105,711 | 54.4 | 1,257,923 | 32.5 |
| Maine | 1,362,622 | 94,600 | 6.9 | 647,638 | 47.5 | 620,384 | 45.5 |
| Maryland | 5,536,328 | 320,498 | 5.8 | 2,177,261 | 39.3 | 3,038,569 | 54.9 |
| Massachusetts | 6,703,338* | 378,522* | 5.6* | 2,424,510* | 36.1* | 3,903,306* | 58.2* |
| Michigan | 12,101,778* | 462,542* | 3.8* | 7,091,538* | 58.6* | 4,547,698* | 37.6* |
| Minnesota | 5,818,841* | 268,019* | 4.6* | 2,938,700* | 50.5* | 2,612,122* | 44.9* |
| Mississippi | 2,201,677* | 337,728* | 15.3* | 1,223,732* | 55.6* | 641,217* | 29.1* |
| Missouri | 4,953,604* | 338,761* | 6.8* | 1,849,302* | 37.3* | 2,765,541* | 55.8* |
| Montana | 934,232 | 93,000 | 10.0 | 451,000 | 48.3 | 390,232 | 41.8 |
| Nebraska | 1,542,639 | 73,079 | 4.7 | 598,538 | 38.8 | 871,022 | 56.5 |
| Nevada | 1,441,774 | 66,730 | 4.6 | 478,666 | 33.2 | 896,378 | 62.2 |
| New Hampshire | 1,276,879 | 40,745 | 3.2 | 99,224 | 7.8 | 1,136,910 | 89.0 |
| New Jersey | 12,070,876 | 439,520 | 3.6 | 4,867,200 | 40.3 | 6,764,156 | 56.0 |
| New Mexico | 1,801,170 | 193,499 | 10.7 | 1,339,116 | 74.3 | 268,555 | 14.9 |
| New York | 26,512,566 | 1,597,000 | 6.0 | 9,907,220 | 37.4 | 15,008,346 | 56.6 |
| North Carolina | 6,155,260 | 530,260 | 8.6 | 4,094,000 | 66.5 | 1,531,000 | 24.9 |
| North Dakota | 613,506 | 76,959 | 12.5 | 265,486 | 43.3 | 271,061 | 44.2 |
| Ohio | 10,748,165 | 679,270 | 6.3 | 4,482,878 | 41.7 | 5,586,017 | 52.0 |
| Oklahoma | 2,946,535 | 265,000 | 9.0 | 1,886,535 | 64.0 | 795,000 | 27.0 |
| Oregon | 3,081,800 | 218,600 | 7.1 | 1,741,100 | 56.5 | 1,122,100 | 36.4 |
| Pennsylvania | 14,255,176 | 798,414 | 5.6 | 5,958,015 | 41.8 | 7,498,747 | 52.6 |
| Rhode Island | 1,125,184 | 45,007 | 4.0 | 461,326 | 41.0 | 618,851 | 55.0 |
| South Carolina | 3,430,003 | 320,428 | 9.3 | 1,594,586 | 46.5 | 1,514,989 | 44.2 |
| South Dakota | 727,140* | 73,714* | 10.1* | 187,303* | 25.8* | 466,123* | 64.1* |
| Tennessee | 4,026,403 | 351,989 | 8.7 | 2,026,092 | 50.3 | 1,648,322 | 40.9 |
| Texas | 21,208,476 | 1,858,455 | 8.8 | 9,232,959 | 43.5 | 10,117,062 | 47.7 |
| Utah | 2,000,727 | 128,408 | 6.4 | 1,167,962 | 58.4 | 704,357 | 35.2 |
| Vermont | 756,712 | 38,753 | 5.1 | 224,507 | 29.7 | 493,452 | 65.2 |
| Virginia | 6,108,876 | 325,912 | 5.3 | 2,217,823 | 36.3 | 3,565,141* | 58.4* |
| Washington | 6,209,444 | 390,561 | 6.3 | 4,311,329 | 69.4 | 1,507,554 | 24.3 |
| West Virginia | 2,165,414 | 168,014 | 7.8 | 1,266,835 | 58.5 | 730,565 | 33.7 |
| Wisconsin | 6,279,078 | 272,264 | 4.3 | 2,710,300 | 43.2 | 3,296,514 | 52.5 |
| Wyoming | 663,000 | 43,000 | 6.5 | 325,000 | 49.0 | 295,000 | 44.5 |

* Indicates NEA estimate. (1) Included as revenue receipts are all appropriations from general funds of federal, state, county, and local governments; receipts from taxes levied for school purposes; income from permanent school funds and endowments; and income from leases of school lands and miscellaneous sources (interest on bank deposits, tuition, gifts, school lunch charges, etc.).

# Public High School Graduation Rates, 1993-94

**Source:** National Center for Education Statistics, U.S. Dept. of Education

| State | Graduation rate (%)[1] | Rank | State | Graduation rate (%)[1] | Rank | State | Graduation rate (%)[1] | Rank |
|---|---|---|---|---|---|---|---|---|
| **U.S.** | **70.11** | | Kentucky | 75.5 | 24 | Ohio | 75.0 | 25 |
| Alabama | 60.1 | 46 | Louisiana | 58.5 | 50 | Oklahoma | 76.1 | 22T |
| Alaska | 70.8 | 34 | Maine | 74.0 | 28 | Oregon | 72.7 | 31 |
| Arizona | 68.6 | 36 | Maryland | 74.7 | 27 | Pennsylvania | 78.9 | 14T |
| Arkansas | 76.4 | 21 | Massachusetts | 78.0 | 17T | Rhode Island | 73.4 | 29 |
| California | 66.3 | 40 | Michigan | 70.0 | 35 | South Carolina | 57.5 | 51 |
| Colorado | 74.9 | 26 | Minnesota | 87.9 | 2 | South Dakota | 91.4 | 1 |
| Connecticut | 78.9 | 14T | Mississippi | 62.4 | 45 | Tennessee | 63.0 | 44 |
| Delaware | 66.5 | 39 | Missouri | 73.2 | 30 | Texas | 59.6 | 47 |
| DC | 64.7 | 42 | Montana | 84.4 | 8 | Utah | 80.2 | 11 |
| Florida | 59.3 | 49 | Nebraska | 85.1 | 6 | Vermont | 84.6 | 7 |
| Georgia | 59.4 | 48 | Nevada | 67.4 | 37 | Virginia | 72.4 | 32 |
| Hawaii | 76.1 | 22T | New Hampshire | 78.3 | 16 | Washington | 76.7 | 20 |
| Idaho | 79.7 | 12 | New Jersey | 85.3 | 5 | West Virginia | 78.0 | 17T |
| Illinois | 77.2 | 19 | New Mexico | 66.6 | 38 | Wisconsin | 81.9 | 10 |
| Indiana | 71.3 | 33 | New York | 64.5 | 43 | Wyoming | 84.3 | 9 |
| Iowa | 87.0 | 4 | North Carolina | 66.0 | 41 | | | |
| Kansas | 79.0 | 13 | North Dakota | 87.7 | 3 | | | |

**Note:** T=Tied in rank with one or more states. (1) Graduates as percentage of fall 1990 9th-grade enrollment.

# College Enrollment Rates of High School Graduates, by Race/Ethnicity and Sex, 1986-95

**Source:** American College Testing Program; Bureau of the Census, U.S. Department of Commerce; U.S. Department of Labor

(in thousands)

| | High school graduates[1] | | | | | | Enrolled in college[2] | | | | | |
|---|---|---|---|---|---|---|---|---|---|---|---|---|
| Year | Total | Male | Female | White[3] | Black[3,4] | Hisp.[4] | Total | Male | Female | White[3] | Black[3,4] | Hisp.[4] |
| 1986... | 2,786 | 1,331 | 1,455 | 2,307 | 386 | 169 | 1,499 | 744 | 755 | 1,292 | 141 | 75 |
| 1987... | 2,647 | 1,278 | 1,369 | 2,207 | 337 | 176 | 1,503 | 746 | 757 | 1,249 | 175 | 59 |
| 1988... | 2,673 | 1,334 | 1,339 | 2,187 | 382 | 179 | 1,575 | 761 | 814 | 1,328 | 172 | 102 |
| 1989... | 2,454 | 1,208 | 1,245 | 2,051 | 337 | 168 | 1,463 | 696 | 767 | 1,238 | 178 | 93 |
| 1990... | 2,355 | 1,169 | 1,185 | 1,921 | 341 | 112 | 1,410 | 676 | 735 | 1,182 | 158 | 53 |
| 1991... | 2,276 | 1,139 | 1,137 | 1,867 | 320 | 154 | 1,420 | 656 | 763 | 1,207 | 146 | 88 |
| 1992... | 2,398 | 1,216 | 1,182 | 1,900 | 353 | 199 | 1,479 | 725 | 754 | 1,204 | 169 | 109 |
| 1993... | 2,338 | 1,118 | 1,219 | 1,910 | 302 | 200 | 1,464 | 668 | 797 | 1,200 | 168 | 125 |
| 1994... | 2,517 | 1,244 | 1,273 | 2,065 | 318 | 178 | 1,559 | 754 | 805 | 1,313 | 162 | 87 |
| 1995... | 2,599 | 1,238 | 1,361 | 2,088 | 356 | 288 | 1,610 | 775 | 835 | 1,308 | 183 | 155 |

(1) Individuals age 16 to 24 who graduated from high school during the preceding 12 months. (2) Enrollment in college as of Oct. of each year for individuals age 16 to 24 who graduated from high school during the preceding 12 months. (3) Includes persons of Hispanic origin. (4) Because of the small sample size, data are subject to relatively large sampling errors.

# Institutions of Higher Education–Charges, 1969-70 to 1995-96

**Source:** National Center for Education Statistics, U.S. Dept. of Education; The College Board

Data are for the entire academic year ending in calendar year shown. Figures for 1969-70 are average charges for full-time resident degree-credit students; figures for later years are average charges per full-time equivalent student. Room and board are based on full-time students. All figures are enrollment-weighted, intended to reflect costs that students face at various types of institutions.

| | Tuition and required fees | | | Board rates (7-day basis)[1] | | | Dormitory charges | | |
|---|---|---|---|---|---|---|---|---|---|
| Academic control and year | All institu-tions | 2-yr | 4-yr | All institu-tions | 2-yr | 4-yr | All institu-tions | 2-yr | 4-yr |
| **Public (in-state)** | | | | | | | | | |
| 1969-70 ..... | $323 | $178 | $427 | $511 | $465 | $540 | $ 369 | $ 308 | $395 |
| 1979-80 ..... | 583 | 355 | 840 | 867 | 894 | 898 | 715 | 572 | 749 |
| 1989-90 ..... | 1,356 | 756 | 2,035 | 1,635 | 1,581 | 1,728 | 1,513 | 962 | 1,561 |
| 1990-91 ..... | 1,454 | 824 | 2,159 | 1,691 | 1,594 | 1,767 | 1,612 | 1,050 | 1,658 |
| 1991-92 ..... | 1,624 | 937 | 2,410 | 1,780 | 1,612 | 1,852 | 1,731 | 1,074 | 1,789 |
| 1992-93 ..... | 1,782 | 1,025 | 2,349 | 1,841 | 1,668 | 1,854 | 1,756 | 1,106 | 1,816 |
| 1993-94 ..... | 1,942 | 1,125 | 2,537 | 1,880 | 1,681 | 1,895 | 1,873 | 1,190 | 1,934 |
| 1994-95[2]..... | 2,057 | 1,194 | 2,689 | 1,947 | 1,716 | 1,964 | 1,959 | 1,239 | 2,021 |
| 1995-96[3]..... | NA | 1,330 | 2,811 | NA | —[4] | 3,932[5] | NA | —[5] | —[5] |
| **Private** | | | | | | | | | |
| 1969-70 ..... | 1,533 | 1,034 | 1,809 | 561 | 546 | 608 | 436 | 413 | 503 |
| 1979-80 ..... | 3,130 | 2,062 | 3,811 | 955 | 924 | 1,078 | 827 | 769 | 999 |
| 1989-90 ..... | 8,147 | 5,196 | 10,348 | 1,948 | 1,811 | 2,339 | 1,923 | 1,663 | 2,411 |
| 1990-91 ..... | 8,772 | 5,570 | 11,379 | 2,074 | 1,989 | 2,470 | 2,063 | 1,744 | 2,654 |
| 1991-92 ..... | 9,434 | 5,752 | 12,192 | 2,252 | 2,090 | 2,727 | 2,221 | 1,789 | 2,860 |
| 1992-93 ..... | 9,942 | 6,059 | 10,294 | 2,344 | 1,875 | 2,354 | 2,348 | 1,970 | 2,362 |
| 1993-94 ..... | 10,572 | 6,370 | 10,952 | 2,434 | 1,970 | 2,445 | 2,490 | 2,067 | 2,506 |
| 1994-95[2]..... | 11,128 | 6,865 | 11,522 | 2,508 | 2,028 | 2,520 | 2,586 | 2,166 | 2,604 |
| 1995-96[3]..... | NA | 6,339 | 12,216 | NA | 4,063[5] | 5,166[5] | NA | —[5] | —[5] |

(1) Data for 1989-90 through 1993-94 reflect 20 meals per week rather than 7 days per week. (2) Preliminary data based on fall 1993 enrollment weights. (3) 1995-96 figures supplied by the College Board; earlier figures from National Center for Educational Statistics. (4) Sample too small to provide meaningful information. (5) Board and dormitory figures for 1995-96 and 1996-97 are combined. NA = not available.

# Tuition and College Costs, 1996-97

Based on the Peterson's Guides Annual Survey of Undergraduate Institutions, the average cost of tuition, mandatory fees, and college room and board at four-year private colleges for 1996-97 is $15,880. The average cost at four-year public colleges is $7,020 for state residents and $11,799 for nonresidents. Two-year public colleges are the least expensive group of institutions; tuition and fees average $1,752 for state residents and $4,380 for nonresidents. Tuition and fees at two-year private colleges average $6,316.

The most expensive four-year institutions, including tuition, mandatory fees, and college room and board, are Sarah Lawrence College ($29,446); Harvard University ($28,896); Hampshire College ($28,890); Brandeis University ($28,827); Barnard College ($28,698); Brown University ($28,658); New York University ($28,638); University of Pennsylvania ($28,630); Yale University ($28,600); Tufts University ($28,497). The least expensive four-year undergraduate institutions are the United States service academies, which are all free.

# American College Testing (ACT) Program Mean Scores and Characteristics of College-Bound Students, 1986-95

**Source:** The American College Testing Program

(for school year ending in year shown)

| Type of test and mean test scores[1] | Unit | 1986[2] | 1987[2] | 1988[2] | 1989[2] | 1990[2] | 1991[2] | 1992[2] | 1993[2] | 1994[2] | 1995[2] |
|---|---|---|---|---|---|---|---|---|---|---|---|
| **Composite** | **Points** | **20.8** | **20.8** | **20.8** | **20.6** | **20.6** | **20.6** | **20.6** | **20.7** | **20.8** | **20.8** |
| Male | Points | 19.6 | 19.5 | 19.6 | 19.3 | 21.0 | 20.9 | 20.9 | 21.0 | 20.9 | 21.0 |
| Female | Points | 18.1 | 18.1 | 18.1 | 18.0 | 20.3 | 20.4 | 20.5 | 20.5 | 20.7 | 20.7 |
| **English** | **Points** | **18.5** | **18.4** | **18.5** | **18.4** | **20.5** | **20.3** | **20.2** | **20.3** | **20.3** | **20.2** |
| Male | Points | 17.9 | 17.9 | 18.0 | 17.8 | 20.1 | 19.8 | 19.8 | 19.8 | 19.8 | 19.8 |
| Female | Points | 18.9 | 18.9 | 19.0 | 18.9 | 20.9 | 20.7 | 20.6 | 20.6 | 20.7 | 20.6 |
| **Math** | **Points** | **17.3** | **17.2** | **17.2** | **17.1** | **19.9** | **20.0** | **20.0** | **20.1** | **20.2** | **20.2** |
| Male | Points | 18.8 | 18.6 | 18.4 | 18.3 | 20.7 | 20.6 | 20.7 | 20.8 | 20.8 | 20.9 |
| Female | Points | 16.0 | 16.1 | 16.1 | 16.1 | 19.3 | 19.4 | 19.5 | 19.6 | 19.6 | 19.7 |
| **Participants** | | | | | | | | | | | |
| **Total** | **1,000** | **730** | **777** | **842** | **855** | **817** | **796** | **832** | **875** | **892** | **945** |
| Male | Percent | 46 | 46 | 46 | 46 | 46 | 45 | 45 | 45 | 45 | 44 |
| White | Percent | 82 | 81 | 81 | 80 | 79 | 79 | 79 | 79 | 79 | 80 |
| Black | Percent | 8 | 8 | 9 | 9 | 9 | 9 | 9 | 9 | 9 | 9 |
| **Obtaining composite scores of** | | | | | | | | | | | |
| 27 or above | Percent | 14 | 14 | 14 | 14 | 12 | 11 | 12 | 12 | 13 | 13 |
| 18 or below | Percent | 31 | 31 | 31 | 32 | 35 | 35 | 35 | 35 | 34 | 34 |

(1) Minimum score, 1; maximum score, 36. Test scores and characteristics of college-bound students are based on the performance of all ACT-tested students who graduated in the spring of a given school year and who took the ACT Assessment during junior or senior year of high school. (2) Beginning with the Oct. 1989 test (1990 scores), an entirely new ACT Assessment was introduced. The Enhanced ACT Assessment increases the emphasis on rhetorical skills in the measurement of writing proficiency, increases the number of advanced math items, and includes a new reading test that features inferential and reasoning skills and a test designed to measure science reasoning. The Enhanced ACT also provides subscores in English, mathematics, and reading. The composite scores for 1986-89 have been converted to provide a basis of comparison; all 1990-95 scores are for the Enhanced ACT. It is not possible to compare directly these data and data from earlier years.

# Recentering of the Scholastic Aptitude Test SAT I Scores

**Source:** The College Board

The SAT-I is a 3-hour test of both verbal and mathematical abilities which, like the ACT test, is used for evaluating applicants to colleges and universities. In 1995, the College Board which creates and administers the SAT-I, as well as other tests such as the SAT-II achievement tests in individual subjects, recentered the scoring scale for the SAT I. It did so by reestablishing the original mean score of 500 on the 200-800 scale. This scale had not been adjusted since 1941, when it reflected only the norm of some 10,000 students, mostly from private secondary schools and applying to the nation's most selective private colleges and universities.

Over the years, the mean score had shifted below 500 as a larger number of students were taking the test, and verbal and math scores had become not directly comparable. The recentering of the score scale was implemented to adjust for these factors. Now the scores represent a more diverse college-bound population that encompasses approximately 2 million students nationwide.

The rank order of scores, expressed as percentiles, has not been affected by the recentering. Students' relative standing in respect to one another and the difficulty level of the test remain unchanged, and now a direct comparison can be drawn between the verbal test and the math test. However, numerical scores are not directly comparable to scores originally reported in years before the recentering. The scores listed in the following tables concerning the SATs have been recentered and, therefore, are not the actual scores that were reported for the years shown.

To obtain a free score converter, while supplies last, individuals can write to SAT Score Converter, 45 Columbus Ave., New York, NY 10023. Further information on the SAT can be obtained at the College Board web site—http://www.collegeboard.org

# SAT Mean Verbal and Math Scores of College-Bound Seniors, 1986-96[1]

**Source:** The College Board

(Recentered scale)

| Type of test and characteristic | Unit | 1986 | 1987 | 1988 | 1989 | 1990 | 1991 | 1992 | 1993 | 1994 | 1995 | 1996 |
|---|---|---|---|---|---|---|---|---|---|---|---|---|
| **Test scores** | | | | | | | | | | | | |
| **Verbal, total** | **Points** | **509** | **507** | **505** | **504** | **500** | **499** | **500** | **500** | **499** | **504** | **505** |
| Male | Points | 515 | 512 | 512 | 510 | 505 | 503 | 504 | 504 | 501 | 505 | 507 |
| Female | Points | 504 | 502 | 499 | 498 | 496 | 495 | 496 | 497 | 497 | 502 | 503 |
| **Math, total** | **Points** | **500** | **501** | **501** | **502** | **501** | **500** | **501** | **503** | **504** | **506** | **508** |
| Male | Points | 523 | 523 | 521 | 523 | 521 | 520 | 521 | 524 | 523 | 525 | 527 |
| Female | Points | 479 | 481 | 483 | 482 | 483 | 482 | 484 | 484 | 487 | 490 | 492 |

(1) For 1986, a formula was applied to the original mean and standard deviation to convert the mean to the recentered scale. For 1987-95, individual student scores were converted to the recentered score and then the mean was recomputed. For 1996, most students received scores on the recentered scale. (Any score on the original scale was converted to the recentered score prior to computing the mean.)

# SAT Mean Scores by State, 1987 and 1993-96

**Source:** The College Board

(Recentered scale)

| | 1987 | | 1993 | | 1994 | | 1995 | | 1996 | | % Graduates Taking |
|---|---|---|---|---|---|---|---|---|---|---|---|
| | Verbal | Math | Verbal | Math | Verbal | Math | Verbal | Math | Verbal | Math | SAT[1] |
| Alabama | 553 | 535 | 554 | 545 | 556 | 547 | 565 | 555 | 565 | 558 | 8 |
| Alaska | 521 | 504 | 514 | 502 | 510 | 502 | 521 | 513 | 521 | 513 | 47 |
| Arizona | 539 | 526 | 520 | 520 | 519 | 519 | 524 | 520 | 525 | 521 | 28 |
| Arkansas | 556 | 540 | 553 | 539 | 552 | 537 | 556 | 542 | 566 | 550 | 6 |
| California | 500 | 507 | 491 | 508 | 489 | 506 | 492 | 509 | 495 | 511 | 45 |
| Colorado | 542 | 535 | 530 | 530 | 532 | 534 | 538 | 538 | 536 | 538 | 30 |
| Connecticut | 515 | 499 | 506 | 498 | 502 | 497 | 507 | 502 | 507 | 504 | 79 |
| Delaware | 517 | 496 | 506 | 491 | 505 | 491 | 505 | 494 | 508 | 495 | 66 |
| Dist. of Columbia | 482 | 462 | 479 | 466 | 479 | 468 | 485 | 471 | 489 | 473 | 50 |
| Florida | 501 | 497 | 493 | 492 | 490 | 492 | 497 | 496 | 498 | 496 | 48 |
| Georgia | 478 | 470 | 475 | 474 | 474 | 474 | 483 | 477 | 484 | 477 | 63 |
| Hawaii | 481 | 502 | 477 | 502 | 477 | 504 | 483 | 507 | 485 | 510 | 54 |
| Idaho | 548 | 524 | 541 | 528 | 537 | 529 | 544 | 532 | 543 | 536 | 15 |
| Illinois | 539 | 540 | 550 | 558 | 553 | 562 | 563 | 574 | 564 | 575 | 14 |
| Indiana | 492 | 487 | 487 | 487 | 488 | 493 | 492 | 494 | 494 | 494 | 57 |
| Iowa | 588 | 586 | 593 | 595 | 580 | 586 | 589 | 595 | 590 | 600 | 5 |
| Kansas | 572 | 562 | 568 | 564 | 568 | 565 | 576 | 571 | 579 | 571 | 9 |
| Kentucky | 554 | 538 | 551 | 542 | 549 | 543 | 552 | 542 | 549 | 544 | 12 |
| Louisiana | 548 | 530 | 556 | 546 | 556 | 549 | 560 | 552 | 559 | 550 | 9 |
| Maine | 510 | 493 | 499 | 490 | 497 | 490 | 504 | 497 | 504 | 498 | 68 |
| Maryland | 513 | 502 | 507 | 503 | 505 | 503 | 506 | 503 | 507 | 504 | 64 |
| Massachusetts | 511 | 500 | 503 | 500 | 502 | 500 | 505 | 502 | 507 | 504 | 80 |
| Michigan | 534 | 533 | 544 | 546 | 547 | 554 | 559 | 565 | 557 | 565 | 11 |
| Minnesota | 548 | 549 | 564 | 570 | 569 | 576 | 580 | 591 | 582 | 593 | 9 |
| Mississippi | 561 | 540 | 555 | 540 | 559 | 546 | 572 | 557 | 569 | 557 | 4 |
| Missouri | 549 | 538 | 556 | 550 | 560 | 554 | 569 | 566 | 570 | 569 | 9 |
| Montana | 555 | 548 | 535 | 537 | 540 | 542 | 549 | 553 | 546 | 547 | 21 |
| Nebraska | 563 | 562 | 554 | 560 | 557 | 559 | 568 | 570 | 567 | 568 | 9 |
| Nevada | 516 | 508 | 509 | 512 | 506 | 508 | 511 | 508 | 508 | 507 | 31 |
| New Hampshire | 527 | 512 | 518 | 511 | 515 | 510 | 520 | 515 | 520 | 514 | 70 |
| New Jersey | 502 | 493 | 494 | 498 | 494 | 500 | 496 | 503 | 498 | 505 | 69 |
| New Mexico | 559 | 544 | 553 | 544 | 550 | 546 | 559 | 549 | 554 | 548 | 12 |
| New York | 501 | 495 | 492 | 496 | 492 | 497 | 495 | 498 | 497 | 499 | 73 |
| North Carolina | 477 | 468 | 483 | 481 | 482 | 482 | 488 | 482 | 490 | 486 | 59 |
| North Dakota | 583 | 573 | 590 | 594 | 570 | 573 | 587 | 602 | 596 | 599 | 5 |
| Ohio | 532 | 521 | 530 | 527 | 533 | 531 | 536 | 535 | 536 | 535 | 24 |
| Oklahoma | 560 | 539 | 557 | 548 | 557 | 554 | 565 | 553 | 566 | 557 | 8 |
| Oregon | 521 | 509 | 518 | 515 | 513 | 515 | 525 | 522 | 523 | 521 | 50 |
| Pennsylvania | 505 | 491 | 495 | 487 | 494 | 489 | 496 | 489 | 498 | 492 | 71 |
| Rhode Island | 509 | 492 | 496 | 490 | 496 | 488 | 502 | 490 | 501 | 491 | 69 |
| South Carolina | 474 | 466 | 473 | 472 | 473 | 473 | 478 | 473 | 480 | 474 | 57 |
| South Dakota | 587 | 577 | 576 | 572 | 558 | 563 | 579 | 576 | 574 | 566 | 5 |
| Tennessee | 563 | 543 | 561 | 549 | 562 | 553 | 571 | 560 | 563 | 552 | 14 |
| Texas | 493 | 486 | 490 | 498 | 489 | 500 | 495 | 501 | 495 | 500 | 48 |
| Utah | 577 | 557 | 573 | 565 | 582 | 573 | 585 | 576 | 583 | 575 | 4 |
| Vermont | 518 | 500 | 503 | 493 | 504 | 498 | 506 | 499 | 506 | 500 | 70 |
| Virginia | 511 | 499 | 502 | 495 | 501 | 495 | 504 | 494 | 507 | 496 | 68 |
| Washington | 532 | 519 | 511 | 510 | 511 | 512 | 519 | 517 | 519 | 519 | 47 |
| West Virginia | 534 | 519 | 516 | 510 | 516 | 507 | 525 | 509 | 526 | 506 | 17 |
| Wisconsin | 550 | 551 | 560 | 566 | 562 | 572 | 574 | 585 | 577 | 586 | 8 |
| Wyoming | 557 | 551 | 539 | 528 | 535 | 541 | 551 | 544 | 544 | 544 | 11 |
| **National Average** | **507** | **501** | **500** | **503** | **499** | **504** | **504** | **506** | **505** | **508** | **41** |

(1) Based on number of high school graduates in 1996, as projected by the Western Interstate Commission for Higher Education, and number of students in the class of 1996 who took the SAT. **Note:** Comparing states or ranking them on the basis of SAT scores alone is invalid, and the College Entrance Examination Board strongly discourages doing so.

# Salaries of College Professors, 1995-96

**Source:** American Association of University Professors

| | Men Type of institution | | | Women Type of institution | | |
|---|---|---|---|---|---|---|
| Academic rank | Public | Private/ Independent | Church-related | Public | Private/ Independent | Church-related |
| **Doctoral level** | | | | | | |
| Professor | $70,590 | $89,250 | $76,580 | $63,780 | $80,190 | $70,820 |
| Associate | 51,400 | 59,420 | 55,320 | 48,240 | 55,980 | 52,140 |
| Assistant | 43,750 | 50,570 | 45,900 | 40,760 | 46,910 | 43,270 |
| **Master's level** | | | | | | |
| Professor | 58,990 | 64,300 | 61,990 | 56,480 | 59,800 | 56,590 |
| Associate | 47,600 | 50,050 | 48,870 | 45,360 | 47,960 | 45,810 |
| Assistant | 39,860 | 41,030 | 40,290 | 38,000 | 39,430 | 37,920 |
| **General 4-year** | | | | | | |
| Professor | 52,970 | 60,630 | 48,730 | 50,490 | 56,850 | 45,920 |
| Associate | 43,870 | 46,120 | 40,370 | 42,460 | 44,550 | 38,610 |
| Assistant | 37,000 | 37,890 | 34,110 | 35,670 | 37,000 | 33,180 |
| **2-year** | | | | | | |
| Professor | 52,850 | 42,480 | 35,690 | 49,040 | 38,010 | 33,570 |
| Associate | 44,250 | 38,290 | 31,130 | 41,660 | 33,540 | 30,280 |
| Assistant | 38,100 | 35,650 | 27,440 | 36,010 | 30,670 | 25,650 |

# Top 50 Public Libraries in the U.S. and Canada

**Source:** World Almanac questionnaire; Public Library Association

Ranked at end of the 1995 fiscal year by population served.

| Population served | Library name and location | No. of branches[1] | No. of holdings | Circulation | Annual acquisition expenditures |
|---|---|---|---|---|---|
| 3,433,600 | Los Angeles Public Library (CA) | 66 | 5,000,000* | 8,000,000* | $6,178,838* |
| 3,280,020 | Los Angeles Public Library, County of ( CA) | 84 | 6,404,353 | 11,875,807 | 9,365,813 |
| 3,070,302 | New York Public Library, The Branch Libraries (NY) | 79 | 11,661,064 | 11,509,390 | 7,556,000 |
| 2,783,726 | Chicago Public Library (IL) | 81 | 7,095,735 | 7,585,960 | 9,100,000 |
| 2,300,664 | Brooklyn Public Library (NY) | 59 | 6,134,045 | 9,851,840 | 7,262,338 |
| 1,951,598 | Queens Borough Public Library (NY) | 62 | 7,963,171 | 15,031,092* | 8,000,000* |
| 1,684,608 | Miami-Dade Public Library System (FL) | 31 | 3,863,700 | 10,015,492 | 5,081,883 |
| 1,630,180 | Houston Public Library (TX) | 35 | 6,551,173 | 6,136,811 | 2,823,900 |
| 1,585,577 | Free Library of Philadelphia (PA) | 53 | 7,881,335 | 6,374,491 | 5,925,594 |
| 1,400,000 | Orange County Public Library (CA) | 27 | 2,300,000 | 5,322,194 | 2,639,127 |
| 1,371,946 | Broward County Library System (FL) | 32 | 2,151,075 | 6,831,601 | 4,614,203 |
| 1,336,449 | Carnegie Library of Pittsburgh (PA) | 18 | 2,024,988* | 2,903,052* | 2,002,920* |
| 1,233,096 | San Antonio Public Library (TX) | 18 | 1,680,000* | 3,200,000* | 2,400,000* |
| 1,197,000 | San Diego Public Library (CA) | 32 | 2,380,714* | 6,442,096 | 2,053,619 |
| 1,148,920 | Phoenix Public Library (AZ) | 11 | 519,051 | 5,504,053 | 2,495,875 |
| 1,108,361 | Sacramento Public Library (CA) | 22 | 1,707,189 | 3,365,822 | 1,665,858 |
| 1,104,740 | Riverside City and County Public Library (CA) | 23 | 1,593,134 | 3,590,583* | 369,755* |
| 1,096,265 | King County Library System (WA) | 39 | 3,000,000* | 12,700,000* | 6,000,000* |
| 1,047,265 | Harris County Public Library (TX) | 24 | 1,429,041 | 5,032,493 | 1,520,398 |
| 1,030,678 | Montréal, Bibliothèque Municipale De (Quebec) | 24 | 2,057,828* | 4,729,033 | 3,685,100*,[2] |
| 1,030,150 | Dallas Public Library (TX) | 21 | 2,538,930 | 4,180,638 | 1,637,680 |
| 1,027,974 | Detroit Public Library (MI) | 25 | 2,718,469 | 1,644,486 | 2,504,415 |
| 1,003,464 | Providence Public Library (RI) | 9 | 1,159,421 | 708,405 | 345,028 |
| 1,000,000 | San Bernardino County Library (CA) | 27 | 1,315,098 | 2,999,087 | 567,306 |
| 968,584 | Buffalo & Erie County Public Library (NY) | 52 | 3,600,000* | 8,600,000* | 3,000,000* |
| 903,302 | San Diego County Library (CA) | 32 | 1,059,667 | 2,673,464 | 1,023,804 |
| 879,069 | Tampa-Hillsborough County Public Library (FL) | 17 | 1,789,213 | 2,968,936 | 3,001,300* |
| 878,400 | Fairfax County Public Library (VA) | 23 | 2,067,572* | 9,224,102* | 2,963,910* |
| 866,228 | Cincinnati & Hamilton County, Public Library of (OH) | 41 | 4,782,418* | 12,167,290 | 6,866,642* |
| 846,000 | San Jose Public Library System (CA) | 17 | 1,324,500 | 4,816,079 | 1,365,317 |
| 844,000 | Memphis Shelby County Public Library (TN) | 21 | 1,733,549 | 3,737,504 | 1,836,537 |
| 843,000 | St. Louis County Library (MO) | 17 | 2,891,656 | 9,113,997 | 3,332,438 |
| 811,857 | Las Vegas Clark County Library District (NV) | 24 | 1,800,000 | 4,576,861 | 4,667,534 |
| 810,000 | Montgomery County Dept. of Public Libraries (MD) | 23 | 2,517,409 | 8,756,912 | 4,160,750 |
| 790,400 | Contra Costa County Library (Pleasant Hill, CA) | 22 | 1,010,492* | 3,529,707* | 827,260* |
| 770,684 | Indianapolis-Marion County Public Library (IN) | 21 | 1,961,464 | 7,120,430 | 5,212,831 |
| 768,000 | Jacksonville Public Libraries (FL) | 17 | 2,518,994 | 3,616,753 | 2,125,059 |
| 764,053 | Prince George's County Memorial Library System (MD) | 19 | 1,734,697 | 4,891,234 | 1,437,192 |
| 749,073 | Calgary Public Library (Alberta) | 14 | 2,154,894 | 10,097,613 | 2,746,955 |
| 747,500 | Fresno County Library (CA) | 33 | 896,303 | 1,586,819 | 298,592 |
| 746,770 | Tucson-Pima Library (AZ) | 18 | 1,177,400* | 4,900,000* | 1,926,000* |
| 736,014 | Enoch Pratt Free Library (Baltimore, MD) | 28 | 2,200,000* | 1,700,000* | 2,152,479 |
| 733,607 | Columbus Metropolitan Library (OH) | 19 | 2,310,808 | 11,158,107 | 6,111,615 |
| 718,277 | Atlanta-Fulton Public Library (GA) | 34 | 2,119,443 | 2,645,722 | 1,898,732 |
| 717,400 | Macomb County Library (MI) | | 165,657 | 279,000 | 299,794 |
| 706,874 | Orange County Library System (FL) | 11 | 1,642,370 | 4,369,364 | 2,041,007 |
| 703,526 | Baltimore County Public Library (MD) | 15 | 1,901,894 | 10,985,632 | 3,732,116 |
| 690,193 | Hennepin County Library (MN) | 26 | 1,750,581 | 9,682,484 | 3,989,738 |
| 664,937 | Louisville Free Public Library (KY) | 15 | 1,017,000* | 3,104,300* | 1,972,000* |
| 635,395 | Toronto Public Library (Ontario) | 33 | 2,170,247 | 8,370,922 | 2,212,148 |

**Note:** Holdings, circulation, and annual acquisition expenditure figures are for fiscal year 1994-95 except where an asterisk (*) is used, indicating figures are for 1995-96. (1) Main branch not included. (2) Canadian dollars.

# Number of Public Libraries and Operating Income, by State, Fiscal Year 1993

**Source:** U.S. Dept. of Education; National Center for Education Statistics

(operating income in thousands)

| State | No. of libraries | Operating income[1] | State | No. of libraries | Operating income[1] | State | No. of libraries | Operating income[1] |
|---|---|---|---|---|---|---|---|---|
| Alabama | 208 | $42,165 | Kentucky | 116 | 43,483 | Ohio | 250 | 381,506 |
| Alaska | 85 | 17,913 | Louisiana | 65 | 62,048 | Oklahoma | 110 | 33,928 |
| Arizona | 39 | 63,127 | Maine | 225 | 17,382[2] | Oregon | 124 | 59,467 |
| Arkansas | 36 | 19,848 | Maryland | 24 | 116,358 | Pennsylvania | 448 | 163,127[2] |
| California | 169 | 602,394 | Massachusetts | 374 | 128,241 | Rhode Island | 51 | 18,631 |
| Colorado | 120 | 82,415 | Michigan | 377 | 171,733[2] | S. Carolina | 40 | 42,528 |
| Connecticut | 194 | 88,195 | Minnesota | 132 | 104,545 | S. Dakota | 113 | 9,910 |
| Delaware | 29 | 7,842 | Mississippi | 47 | 22,565 | Tennessee | 137 | 51,631 |
| District of Columbia | 1 | 20,819 | Missouri | 148 | 90,533 | Texas | 498 | 175,821[2] |
| Florida | 100 | 225,779 | Montana | 83 | 10,541 | Utah | 69 | 32,651 |
| Georgia | 54 | 85,846 | Nebraska | 269 | 24,632[2] | Vermont | 201 | 7,894[2] |
| Hawaii | 1 | 24,918 | Nevada | 26 | 41,520 | Virginia | 90 | 122,487 |
| Idaho | 107 | 13,967 | New Hampshire | 229 | 21,123 | Washington | 70 | 136,838 |
| Illinois | 606 | 351,151 | New Jersey | 310 | 233,541 | W. Virginia | 97 | 16,970 |
| Indiana | 238 | 151,990 | New Mexico | 69 | 18,355 | Wisconsin | 380 | 108,125 |
| Iowa | 517 | 47,364 | New York | 758 | 600,407 | Wyoming | 23 | 10,168 |
| Kansas | 320 | 46,850 | N. Carolina | 74 | 91,593 | **U.S. Total** | **8,929** | **$5,068,999** |
| | | | N. Dakota | 78 | 6,132 | | | |

(1) Total income represents data for libraries that reported total operating income and/or all sources of income. Totals may be underestimated because of nonresponse. (2) Data reported are for fiscal year 1992.

# American Colleges and Universities

## General Information for the 1995–96 Academic Year

## Source: Peterson's, Copyright 1996

These listings include all accredited undergraduate degree-granting institutions in the United States and U.S. territories that have a total institutional enrollment of 1,000 or more. Four-year colleges (those that award a bachelor's as their highest undergraduate degree) are listed first, followed by two-year colleges (those that award an associate as their highest or primary undergraduate degree).

All institutions are coeducational except those where the zip code is directly followed by: (1)–men only, (2)–primarily men, (3)–women only, (4)–primarily women.

Year is that of founding.

Governing official is the chief executive officer.

Institutional control: 1–independent (nonprofit), 2–independent-religious, 3–proprietary (profit making), 4–federal, 5–state, 6–commonwealth (Puerto Rico), 7–territory (U.S. territories), 8–county, 9–district, 10–city, 11–state and local, 12–state related.

Highest degree offered: B–bachelor's, M–master's, F–first professional, D–doctorate.

Enrollment is the total number of matriculated undergraduate and (if applicable) graduate students.

Faculty is the total number of faculty members teaching undergraduate courses and (if available) graduate courses.

Any data not reported are indicated as NR.

Data reported for institutions that provided updated information on Peterson's Annual Survey of Undergraduate Institutions for the 1995–96 academic year.

## Four-Year Colleges

| Name, address | Year | Governing official, control, and highest degree offered | | Enrollment | Faculty |
|---|---|---|---|---|---|
| Abilene Christian U, Abilene, TX 79699 | 1906 | Dr. Royce Money | 2-F | 4,436 | 270 |
| Acad of Art Coll, San Francisco, CA 94105-3410 | 1929 | Ms. Elisa Stephens | 3-M | 4,050 | 455 |
| Adams State Coll, Alamosa, CO 81102 | 1921 | Dr. J. Thomas Gilmore | 5-M | 2,546 | 154 |
| Adelphi U, Garden City, NY 11530 | 1896 | Dr. Peter Diamandopoulos | 1-D | 7,003 | 631 |
| Alabama A&M U, Normal, AL 35762-1357 | 1875 | Dr. David B. Henson | 5-D | 5,400 | 366 |
| Alabama State U, Montgomery, AL 36101-0271 | 1867 | Dr. William H. Harris | 5-M | 5,416 | 350 |
| Albany State U, Albany, GA 31705-2717 | 1903 | Dr. Billy C. Black | 5-M | 3,151 | 150 |
| Albion Coll, Albion, MI 49224-1831 | 1835 | Dr. Melvin L. Vulgamore | 2-B | 1,548 | 125 |
| Albright Coll, Reading, PA 19612-5234 | 1856 | Dr. Ellen S. Hurwitz | 2-B | 1,072 | 107 |
| Alcorn State U, Lorman, MS 39096-9402 | 1871 | Dr. Rudolph E. Waters | 5-M | 3,033 | 206 |
| Alfred U, Alfred, NY 14802-1205 | 1836 | Dr. Edward G. Coll, Jr. | 1-D | 2,405 | 200 |
| Allegheny Coll, Meadville, PA 16335 | 1815 | Dr. Daniel F. Sullivan | 2-B | 1,838 | 190 |
| Allentown Coll of St Francis de Sales, Center Valley, PA 18034-9568 | 1962 | Rev. Daniel Gambet, OSFS | 2-M | 2,220 | 95 |
| Alma Coll, Alma, MI 48801-1599 | 1886 | Dr. Alan J. Stone | 2-B | 1,418 | 140 |
| Alvernia Coll, Reading, PA 19607-1799 | 1958 | Dr. Daniel N. DeLucca | 2-B | 1,300 | 112 |
| Alverno Coll, Milwaukee, WI 53234-3922 (3) | 1887 | Sr. Joel Read | 2-B | 2,084 | 199 |
| Amber U, Garland, TX 75041-5595 | 1971 | Dr. Douglas W. Warner | 2-M | 1,610 | 65 |
| American International Coll, Springfield, MA 01109-3189 | 1885 | Dr. Harry J. Courniotes | 1-D | 1,913 | 93 |
| American U, Washington, DC 20016-8001 | 1893 | Dr. Benjamin Ladner | 2-D | 9,630 | 976 |
| Amherst Coll, Amherst, MA 01002 | 1821 | Dr. Tom Gerety | 1-B | 1,600 | 200 |
| Anderson U, Anderson, IN 46012-3462 | 1917 | Dr. James L. Edwards | 2-D | 2,261 | 225 |
| Andrews U, Berrien Springs, MI 49104 | 1874 | Dr. Niels-Erik Andreasen | 2-D | 3,014 | 312 |
| Angelo State U, San Angelo, TX 76909 | 1928 | Dr. E. James Hindman | 5-M | 6,103 | 249 |
| Anna Maria Coll, Paxton, MA 01612 | 1946 | Dr. William R. Dill | 2-M | 1,611 | 84 |
| Appalachian State U, Boone, NC 28608 | 1899 | Dr. Francis T. Borkowski | 5-D | 11,477 | 730 |
| Aquinas Coll, Grand Rapids, MI 49506-1799 | 1886 | Mr. R. Paul Nelson | 2-M | 2,422 | 181 |
| Arizona State U, Tempe, AZ 85287 | 1885 | Dr. Lattie F. Coor | 5-D | 42,040 | 1,947 |
| Arizona State U West, Phoenix, AZ 85069-7100 | 1984 | Dr. Ben R. Forsyth | 5-M | 2,968 | 293 |
| Arkansas State U, State University, AR 72467 | 1909 | Dr. Leslie Wyatt | 5-D | 9,807 | 453 |
| Arkansas Tech U, Russellville, AR 72801-2222 | 1909 | Dr. Robert C. Brown | 5-M | 4,593 | 273 |
| Armstrong State Coll, Savannah, GA 31419-1997 | 1935 | Dr. Robert A. Burnett | 5-M | 5,348 | 348 |
| Art Ctr Coll of Design, Pasadena, CA 91103-1999 | 1930 | Mr. David R. Brown | 1-M | 1,334 | 427 |
| Asbury Coll, Wilmore, KY 40390-1198 | 1890 | Dr. David J. Gyertson | 2-B | 1,206 | 110 |
| Ashland U, Ashland, OH 44805-3702 | 1878 | Dr. G. William Benz | 2-M | 5,608 | 213 |
| Assumption Coll, Worcester, MA 01615-0005 | 1904 | Dr. Joseph H. Hagan | 2-M | 2,606 | 208 |
| Athens State Coll, Athens, AL 35611-1902 | 1822 | Dr. Jerry F. Bartlett | 5-B | 3,200 | 135 |
| Auburn U, Auburn University, AL 36849-0001 | 1856 | Dr. William V. Muse | 5-D | 22,122 | 1,244 |
| Auburn U at Montgomery, Montgomery, AL 36117-3596 | 1967 | Dr. Roy H. Saigo | 5-M | 5,882 | 360 |
| Audrey Cohen Coll, New York, NY 10013 | 1964 | Dr. Audrey C. Cohen | 1-M | 1,150 | 53 |
| Augsburg Coll, Minneapolis, MN 55454-1351 | 1869 | Dr. Charles S. Anderson | 2-M | 2,858 | 303 |
| Augustana Coll, Rock Island, IL 61201-2296 | 1860 | Dr. Thomas Tredway | 2-B | 2,197 | 171 |
| Augustana Coll, Sioux Falls, SD 57197 | 1860 | Dr. Ralph H. Wagoner | 2-M | 1,778 | 162 |
| Augusta State U, Augusta, GA 30904-2200 | 1925 | Dr. William A. Bloodworth, Jr. | 5-M | 5,759 | 271 |
| Aurora U, Aurora, IL 60506-4892 | 1893 | Dr. Thomas H. Zarle | 1-M | 2,025 | 240 |
| Austin Coll, Sherman, TX 75090-4440 | 1849 | Dr. Oscar C. Page | 2-M | 1,083 | 100 |
| Austin Peay State U, Clarksville, TN 37044-0001 | 1927 | Dr. Sal D. Rinella | 5-M | 7,556 | 452 |
| Averett Coll, Danville, VA 24541-3692 | 1859 | Dr. Frank R. Campbell | 2-M | 2,637 | 59 |
| Avila Coll, Kansas City, MO 64145-1698 | 1916 | Dr. Larry Kramer | 2-M | 1,404 | 142 |
| Azusa Pacific U, Azusa, CA 91702-7000 | 1899 | Dr. Richard E. Felix | 2-D | 4,360 | 394 |
| Babson Coll, Babson Park, MA 02157-0310 | 1919 | Mr. William F. Glavin | 1-M | 3,378 | 196 |
| Baker Coll of Flint, Flint, MI 48507-5508 | 1911 | Dr. Julianne T. Princinsky | 1-B | 3,915 | 175 |
| Baker Coll of Muskegon, Muskegon, MI 49442-3497 | 1888 | Dr. Rick Amidon | 1-B | 1,674 | 101 |
| Baker Coll of Owosso, Owosso, MI 48867-4400 | 1984 | NR | 1-B | 1,733 | 101 |
| Baker U, Baldwin City, KS 66006-0065 | 1858 | Dr. Daniel M. Lambert | 2-M | 2,041 | 83 |
| Baldwin-Wallace Coll, Berea, OH 44017-2088 | 1845 | Dr. Neal Malicky | 2-M | 4,789 | 275 |
| Ball State U, Muncie, IN 47306-1099 | 1918 | Dr. John E. Worthen | 5-D | 19,115 | 1,110 |
| Bard Coll, Annandale-on-Hudson, NY 12504 | 1860 | Dr. Leon Botstein | 1-M | 1,249 | 150 |
| Barnard Coll, New York, NY 10027-6598 (3) | 1889 | Prof. Judith R. Shapiro | 1-B | 2,276 | 284 |
| Barry U, Miami Shores, FL 33161-6695 | 1940 | Sr. Jeanne O'Laughlin, OP | 2-D | 7,098 | 500 |
| Barton Coll, Wilson, NC 27893 | 1902 | Dr. James B. Hemby | 2-B | 1,401 | 84 |
| Baruch Coll of the City U of New York, New York, NY 10010-5585 | 1919 | Dr. Matthew Goldstein | 11-D | 15,340 | 770 |
| Bates Coll, Lewiston, ME 04240-6028 | 1855 | Dr. Donald W. Harward | 1-B | 1,636 | 165 |
| Bayamón Central U, Bayamón, PR 00960-1725 | 1970 | Rev. Vincent A. M. Van Rooij, OP | 2-M | 3,136 | 117 |

| Name, address | Year | Governing official, control, and highest degree offered | | Enroll-ment | Faculty |
|---|---|---|---|---|---|
| Bayamón Tech U Coll, Bayamón, PR 00959-1919 | 1971 | Prof. Carmen A. Rivera | 6-B | 5,059 | 247 |
| Baylor U, Waco, TX 76798 | 1845 | Dr. Robert B. Sloan, Jr. | 2-D | 12,202 | 679 |
| Beaver Coll, Glenside, PA 19038-3295 | 1853 | Dr. Bette E. Landman | 2-M | 2,554 | 279 |
| Belhaven Coll, Jackson, MS 39202-1789 | 1883 | Dr. Dan Fredericks | 2-B | 1,350 | 80 |
| Bellarmine Coll, Louisville, KY 40205-0671 | 1950 | Dr. Joseph J. McGowan, Jr. | 2-M | 2,359 | 194 |
| Bellevue U, Bellevue, NE 68005-3098 | 1965 | Dr. John B. Muller | 1-M | 2,303 | 83 |
| Belmont U, Nashville, TN 37212-3757 | 1951 | Dr. William E. Troutt | 2-M | 3,009 | 350 |
| Beloit Coll, Beloit, WI 53511-5596 | 1846 | Mr. Victor E. Ferrall, Jr. | 1-M | 1,259 | 128 |
| Bemidji State U, Bemidji, MN 56601-2699 | 1919 | Dr. M. James Bensen | 5-M | 4,122 | 201 |
| Benedict Coll, Columbia, SC 29204 | 1870 | Dr. David H. Swinton | 2-B | 1,862 | 109 |
| Benedictine Coll, Atchison, KS 66002-1499 | 1859 | Dr. Thomas O. James | 2-M | 1,200 | 89 |
| Benedictine U, Lisle, IL 60532-0900 | 1887 | Dr. William J. Carroll | 2-D | 2,485 | 245 |
| Bentley Coll, Waltham, MA 02154-4705 | 1917 | Dr. Joseph M. Cronin | 1-M | 6,402 | 351 |
| Berea Coll, Berea, KY 40404 | 1855 | Dr. Larry D. Shinn | 1-B | 1,559 | 127 |
| Berklee Coll of Music, Boston, MA 02215-3693 | 1945 | Dr. Lee Eliot Berk | 1-B | 2,685 | 293 |
| Berry Coll, Mount Berry, GA 30149-0159 | 1902 | Dr. Gloria M. Shatto | 1-M | 1,974 | 154 |
| Bethel Coll, Mishawaka, IN 46545-5591 | 1947 | Dr. Norman Bridges | 2-M | 1,352 | 126 |
| Bethel Coll, St Paul, MN 55112-6999 | 1871 | Dr. George K. Brushaber | 2-M | 2,348 | 190 |
| Bethune-Cookman Coll, Daytona Beach, FL 32114-3099 | 1904 | Dr. Oswald P. Bronson, Sr. | 2-B | 2,402 | 190 |
| Biola U, La Mirada, CA 90639-0001 | 1908 | Dr. Clyde Cook | 2-D | 3,039 | 240 |
| Birmingham-Southern Coll, Birmingham, AL 35254 | 1856 | Dr. Neal R. Berte | 2-M | 1,562 | 134 |
| Black Hills State U, Spearfish, SD 57799-9502 | 1883 | Dr. Thomas O. Flickema | 5-M | 2,736 | 121 |
| Bloomfield Coll, Bloomfield, NJ 07003-9981 | 1868 | Dr. John F. Noonan | 2-B | 2,173 | 217 |
| Bloomsburg U of Pennsylvania, Bloomsburg, PA 17815-1905 | 1839 | Dr. Jessica Kozloff | 5-M | 7,312 | 366 |
| Bluffton Coll, Bluffton, OH 45817-1196 | 1899 | Dr. Elmer Neufeld | 2-M | 1,046 | 95 |
| Boise State U, Boise, ID 83725-0399 | 1932 | Dr. Charles Ruch | 5-D | 14,205 | 875 |
| Boricua Coll, New York, NY 10032-1560 | 1974 | Dr. Victor G. Alicea | 1-B | 1,218 | 128 |
| Boston Coll, Chestnut Hill, MA 02167-9991 | 1863 | Rev. J. Donald Monan, SJ | 2-D | 14,695 | 982 |
| Boston U, Boston, MA 02215 | 1839 | Dr. John Silber | 1-D | 29,025 | 2,680 |
| Bowdoin Coll, Brunswick, ME 04011-2546 | 1794 | Mr. Robert H. Edwards | 1-B | 1,530 | 162 |
| Bowie State U, Bowie, MD 20715-3318 | 1865 | Dr. Nathanael Pollard, Jr. | 5-M | 5,258 | 255 |
| Bowling Green State U, Bowling Green, OH 43403 | 1910 | Dr. Sidney A. Ribeau | 5-D | 17,564 | 866 |
| Bradley U, Peoria, IL 61625-0002 | 1897 | Dr. John R. Brazil | 1-M | 5,973 | 454 |
| Brandeis U, Waltham, MA 02254-9110 | 1948 | Dr. Jehuda Reinharz | 1-D | 4,192 | 484 |
| Brenau U, Gainesville, GA 30501-3697 (4) | 1878 | Dr. John S. Burd | 1-M | 2,225 | 224 |
| Brewton-Parker Coll, Mt Vernon, GA 30445 | 1904 | Dr. Y. Lynn Holmes | 2-B | 1,661 | 233 |
| Briar Cliff Coll, Sioux City, IA 51104-2100 | 1930 | Sr. Margaret Wick | 2-B | 1,144 | 71 |
| Bridgewater State Coll, Bridgewater, MA 02325-0001 | 1840 | Dr. Adrian Tinsley | 5-M | 8,393 | 553 |
| Brigham Young U, Provo, UT 84602-1001 | 1875 | Dr. Rex E. Lee | 2-D | 30,465 | 1,736 |
| Brigham Young U–Hawaii Cmps, Laie, Oahu, HI 96762-1294 | 1955 | Dr. Eric B. Shumway | 2-B | 2,096 | 120 |
| Brooklyn Coll of the City U of New York, Brooklyn, NY 11210-2889 | 1930 | Dr. Vernon E. Lattin | 11-M | 13,586 | 771 |
| Brown U, Providence, RI 02912 | 1764 | Dr. Vartan Gregorian | 1-D | 7,641 | 660 |
| Bryant Coll, Smithfield, RI 02917-1287 | 1863 | Dr. William E. Trueheart | 1-M | 3,480 | 132 |
| Bryn Mawr Coll, Bryn Mawr, PA 19010-2899 (3) | 1885 | Dr. Mary Patterson McPherson | 1-D | 1,821 | 221 |
| Bucknell U, Lewisburg, PA 17837 | 1846 | Dr. Wiliam D. Adams | 1-M | 3,558 | 276 |
| Buena Vista U, Storm Lake, IA 50588 | 1891 | Dr. Frederick V. Moore | 2-M | 1,150 | 95 |
| Butler U, Indianapolis, IN 46208-3485 | 1855 | Dr. Geoffrey Bannister | 1-M | 3,866 | 360 |
| Cabrini Coll, Radnor, PA 19087-3698 | 1957 | Dr. Antoinette Iadarola | 2-M | 1,974 | 145 |
| Caldwell Coll, Caldwell, NJ 07006-6195 | 1939 | Sr. Patrice Werner | 2-M | 1,705 | 115 |
| California Baptist Coll, Riverside, CA 92504-3206 | 1950 | Dr. Ron Ellis | 2-M | 1,226 | 92 |
| California Coll for Health Sciences, National City, CA 91950-6605 | 1978 | Mr. Kenneth B. Scheiderman | 3-M | 11,696 | 17 |
| California Coll of Arts and Crafts, Oakland, CA 94618 | 1907 | Mr. Lorne Buchman | 1-M | 1,111 | 235 |
| California Inst of Tech, Pasadena, CA 91125-0001 | 1891 | Dr. Thomas E. Everhart | 1-D | 1,973 | 295 |
| California Inst of the Arts, Valencia, CA 91355-2340 | 1961 | Dr. Steven D. Lavine | 1-M | 1,079 | 212 |
| California Lutheran U, Thousand Oaks, CA 91360-2787 | 1959 | Dr. Luther S. Luedtke | 2-M | 2,611 | 224 |
| California Polytechnic State U, San Luis Obispo, San Luis Obispo, CA 93407 | 1901 | Dr. Warren J. Baker | 5-M | 16,023 | 888 |
| California State Polytechnic U, Pomona, Pomona, CA 91768-2557 | 1938 | Dr. Bob Suzuki | 5-M | 16,605 | 958 |
| California State U, Bakersfield, Bakersfield, CA 93311-1022 | 1970 | Dr. Tomas A. Arciniega | 5-M | 5,319 | 327 |
| California State U, Chico, Chico, CA 95929-0150 | 1887 | Dr. Manuel A. Esteban | 5-M | 13,798 | 816 |
| California State U, Dominguez Hills, Carson, CA 90747-0001 | 1960 | Dr. Robert Detweiler | 5-M | 9,977 | 724 |
| California State U, Fresno, Fresno, CA 93740 | 1911 | Dr. John D. Welty | 5-D | 17,460 | 966 |
| California State U, Fullerton, Fullerton, CA 92634-9480 | 1957 | Dr. Milton A. Gordon | 5-M | 22,097 | 1,013 |
| California State U, Hayward, Hayward, CA 94542-3000 | 1957 | Dr. Norma Rees | 5-M | 12,650 | 688 |
| California State U, Long Beach, Long Beach, CA 90840-0119 | 1949 | Dr. Robert C. Maxson | 5-M | 26,403 | 1,398 |
| California State U, Los Angeles, Los Angeles, CA 90032-8530 | 1947 | Dr. James M. Rosser | 5-M | 18,224 | 946 |
| California State U, Northridge, Northridge, CA 91330 | 1958 | Dr. Blenda J. Wilson | 5-M | 25,020 | 1,453 |
| California State U, Sacramento, Sacramento, CA 95819-6048 | 1947 | Dr. Donald R. Gerth | 5-M | 22,796 | 1,262 |
| California State U, San Bernardino, San Bernardino, CA 92407-2397 | 1965 | Dr. Anthony H. Evans | 5-M | 11,864 | 571 |
| California State U, San Marcos, San Marcos, CA 92096 | 1990 | Dr. Bill W. Stacy | 5-M | 3,642 | 264 |
| California State U, Stanislaus, Turlock, CA 95382 | 1957 | Dr. Marvalene Hughes | 5-M | 5,972 | 335 |
| California U of Pennsylvania, California, PA 15419-1394 | 1852 | Dr. Angelo Armenti, Jr. | 5-M | 6,015 | 355 |
| Calumet Coll of Saint Joseph, Whiting, IN 46394-2195 | 1951 | Dr. Dennis C. Rittenmeyer | 2-B | 1,032 | 110 |
| Calvin Coll, Grand Rapids, MI 49546-4388 | 1876 | Dr. Gaylen J. Byker | 2-M | 3,963 | 296 |
| Cameron U, Lawton, OK 73505-6377 | 1908 | Dr. Don Davis | 5-M | 5,696 | 268 |
| Campbellsville U, Campbellsville, KY 42718-2799 | 1906 | Dr. Kenneth W. Winters | 2-D | 1,366 | 117 |
| Campbell U, Buies Creek, NC 27506 | 1887 | Dr. Norman A. Wiggins | 2-F | 6,814 | 349 |
| Canisius Coll, Buffalo, NY 14208-1098 | 1870 | Rev. Vincent M. Cooke, S.J. | 2-M | 4,836 | 418 |
| Capital U, Columbus, OH 43209-2394 | 1830 | Dr. Josiah H. Blackmore | 2-F | 4,071 | 190 |
| Cardinal Stritch Coll, Milwaukee, WI 53217-3985 | 1937 | Sr. Mary Lea Schneider | 2-M | 5,176 | 572 |
| Carleton Coll, Northfield, MN 55057-4001 | 1866 | Dr. Stephen R. Lewis, Jr. | 1-B | 1,752 | 161 |
| Carlow Coll, Pittsburgh, PA 15213-3165 (4) | 1929 | Dr. Grace Ann Geibel, RSM | 2-M | 2,058 | 203 |
| Carnegie Mellon U, Pittsburgh, PA 15213-3891 | 1900 | Dr. Robert Mehrabian | 1-D | 7,318 | 747 |
| Carroll Coll, Helena, MT 59625-0002 | 1909 | Dr. Matthew J. Quinn | 2-B | 1,412 | 121 |
| Carroll Coll, Waukesha, WI 53186-5593 | 1846 | Dr. Frank Falcone | 2-M | 2,410 | 144 |
| Carson-Newman Coll, Jefferson City, TN 37760 | 1851 | Dr. J. Cordell Maddox | 2-M | 2,207 | 193 |
| Carthage Coll, Kenosha, WI 53140-1994 | 1847 | Dr. F. Gregory Campbell | 2-M | 2,165 | 125 |
| Case Western Reserve U, Cleveland, OH 44106 | 1826 | Dr. Agnar Pytte | 1-D | 9,747 | 1,936 |
| Castleton State Coll, Castleton, VT 05735 | 1787 | Dr. Martha K. Farmer | 5-M | 1,846 | 179 |
| Catawba Coll, Salisbury, NC 28144-2488 | 1851 | Mr. J. Fred Corriher, Jr. | 2-M | 1,102 | 85 |
| The Catholic U of America, Washington, DC 20064 | 1887 | Br. Patrick Ellis, FSC, PhD | 2-D | 6,108 | 670 |
| Cedar Crest Coll, Allentown, PA 18104-6196 (4) | 1867 | Dr. Dorothy Gulbenkian Blaney | 2-B | 1,329 | 141 |
| Cedarville Coll, Cedarville, OH 45314-0601 | 1887 | Dr. Paul H. Dixon | 2-B | 2,454 | 177 |
| Central Coll, Pella, IA 50219-1999 | 1853 | Dr. William M. Wiebenga | 2-B | 1,453 | 123 |
| Central Connecticut State U, New Britain, CT 06050-4010 | 1849 | Dr. Merle W. Harris | 5-M | 9,525 | 742 |
| Central Methodist Coll, Fayette, MO 65248-1198 | 1854 | Dr. Marianne Inman | 2-B | 1,184 | 76 |

| Name, address | Year | Governing official, control, and highest degree offered | | Enroll-ment | Faculty |
|---|---|---|---|---|---|
| Central Michigan U, Mount Pleasant, MI 48859 | 1892 | Dr. Leonard E. Plachta | 5-D | 16,452 | 808 |
| Central Missouri State U, Warrensburg, MO 64093 | 1871 | Dr. Ed Elliott | 5-M | 10,951 | 519 |
| Central State U, Wilberforce, OH 45384 | 1887 | Dr. Herman B. Smith, Jr. | 5-M | 2,596 | 121 |
| Central Washington U, Ellensburg, WA 98926 | 1891 | Dr. Ivory V. Nelson | 5-M | 8,513 | 322 |
| Chadron State Coll, Chadron, NE 69337 | 1911 | Dr. Samuel H. Rankin | 5-M | 3,206 | 146 |
| Chaminade U of Honolulu, Honolulu, HI 96816-1578 | 1955 | Dr. Mary Wesselkamper | 2-M | 2,253 | 190 |
| Chapman U, Orange, CA 92666-1011 | 1861 | Dr. James Doti | 2-F | 3,476 | 343 |
| Charleston Southern U, Charleston, SC 29423-8087 | 1964 | Dr. Jairy C. Hunter, Jr. | 2-M | 2,532 | 129 |
| Charter Oak State Coll, Newington, CT 06111-2646 | 1973 | Dr. Merle W. Harris | 5-B | 1,198 | NR |
| Chestnut Hill Coll, Philadelphia, PA 19118-2695 (3) | 1924 | Dr. Carol J. Vale, SSJ | 2-M | 1,197 | 149 |
| Cheyney U of Pennsylvania, Cheyney, PA 19319 | 1837 | Dr. Douglas Covington | 5-M | 1,386 | 112 |
| Chicago State U, Chicago, IL 60628 | 1867 | Dr. Dolores Cross | 5-M | 9,103 | 482 |
| Christian Brothers U, Memphis, TN 38104-5581 | 1871 | Dr. Michael J. McGinniss, FSC | 2-M | 1,800 | 157 |
| Christopher Newport U, Newport News, VA 23606-2998 | 1961 | Dr. Anthony R. Santoro | 5-M | 4,558 | 340 |
| The Citadel, The Military Coll of South Carolina, Charleston, SC 29409 (1) | 1842 | Lt. Gen. Claudius E. Watts, III | 5-M | 3,600 | 166 |
| City Coll of the City U of New York, New York, NY 10031-6977 | 1847 | Dr. Yolanda T. Moses | 11-D | 14,157 | 1,007 |
| City U, Bellevue, WA 98004-6442 | 1973 | Dr. Michael A. Pastore | 1-M | 9,673 | 1,445 |
| Claflin Coll, Orangeburg, SC 29115 | 1869 | Dr. Henry N. Tisdale | 2-B | 1,001 | 65 |
| Clarion U of Pennsylvania, Clarion, PA 16214 | 1867 | Dr. Diane L. Reinhard | 5-M | 5,860 | 375 |
| Clark Atlanta U, Atlanta, GA 30314 | 1869 | Dr. Thomas Cole, Jr. | 2-D | 5,311 | 442 |
| Clarke Coll, Dubuque, IA 52001-3198 | 1843 | Dr. Catherine Dunn, BVM | 2-M | 1,030 | 106 |
| Clarkson U, Potsdam, NY 13699 | 1896 | Dr. Dennis G. Brown | 1-D | 2,583 | 170 |
| Clark U, Worcester, MA 01610-1477 | 1887 | Dr. Richard P. Traina | 1-D | 2,652 | 168 |
| Clayton State Coll, Morrow, GA 30260-0285 | 1969 | Dr. Richard Skinner | 5-B | 5,020 | 191 |
| Clemson U, Clemson, SC 29634 | 1889 | Dr. Constantine W. Curris | 5-D | 15,434 | 1,419 |
| Cleveland State U, Cleveland, OH 44115 | 1964 | Dr. Claire A. Van Ummersen | 5-D | 15,671 | 834 |
| Coastal Carolina U, Myrtle Beach, SC 29578-1954 | 1954 | Dr. Ronald R. Ingle | 5-M | 4,441 | 252 |
| Coe Coll, Cedar Rapids, IA 52402-5070 | 1851 | Dr. John E. Brown | 2-M | 1,359 | 122 |
| Colby Coll, Waterville, ME 04901 | 1813 | William R. Cotter | 1-B | 1,785 | 155 |
| Colgate U, Hamilton, NY 13346-1386 | 1819 | Dr. Neil R. Grabois | 1-M | 2,939 | 254 |
| Coll for Lifelong Learning of the U System of NH, Concord, NH 03301 | 1972 | Dr. Victor Montana | 11-B | 1,962 | 365 |
| Coll Misericordia, Dallas, PA 18612-1098 | 1924 | Dr. Carol A. Jobe | 2-M | 1,779 | 166 |
| Coll of Charleston, Charleston, SC 29424-0002 | 1770 | Dr. Alexander M. Sanders, Jr. | 5-M | 10,613 | 589 |
| Coll of Insurance, New York, NY 10007-2165 | 1962 | Dr. Ellen Thrower | 1-M | 2,210 | 93 |
| Coll of Mount St Joseph, Cincinnati, OH 45233-1670 | 1920 | Sr. Francis Marie Thrailkill, OSU | 2-M | 2,349 | 223 |
| Coll of Mount Saint Vincent, Riverdale, NY 10471-1093 | 1911 | Dr. Mary C. Stuart | 1-M | 1,454 | 123 |
| The Coll of New Jersey, Trenton, NJ 08650-4700 | 1855 | Dr. Harold Eickhoff | 5-M | 6,666 | 616 |
| Coll of New Rochelle, New Rochelle, NY 10805-2308 (4) | 1904 | Sr. Dorothy Ann Kelly, OSU | 1-M | 2,612 | 219 |
| Coll of Notre Dame, Belmont, CA 94002-1997 | 1851 | Dr. Margaret Huber | 2-M | 1,722 | 194 |
| Coll of Notre Dame of Maryland, Baltimore, MD 21210-2476 (3) | 1873 | Sr. Rosemarie Nassif | 2-M | 2,205 | 85 |
| Coll of Saint Benedict, Saint Joseph, MN 56374 (3) | 1913 | Sr. Colman O'Connell, OSB | 2-B | 1,897 | 155 |
| Coll of St Catherine, St Paul, MN 55105-1789 (3) | 1905 | Dr. Anita Pampusch | 2-M | 2,728 | 212 |
| Coll of Saint Elizabeth, Morristown, NJ 07960-6989 (4) | 1899 | Sr. Jacqueline Burns | 2-M | 1,763 | 155 |
| Coll of St Francis, Joliet, IL 60435-6188 | 1920 | Dr. James A. Doppke | 2-M | 1,200 | 124 |
| Coll of Saint Mary, Omaha, NE 68124-2377 (3) | 1923 | Dr. Kenneth Nielsen | 2-B | 1,096 | 130 |
| The Coll of Saint Rose, Albany, NY 12203-1419 | 1920 | Dr. Louis C. Vaccaro | 1-M | 3,726 | 216 |
| Coll of St Scholastica, Duluth, MN 55811-4199 | 1912 | Dr. Daniel H. Pilon | 2-M | 1,895 | 164 |
| Coll of Santa Fe, Santa Fe, NM 87505 | 1947 | Dr. James A. Fries | 1-M | 1,600 | 147 |
| Coll of Staten Island of the City U of New York, Staten Island, NY 10314-6600 | 1955 | Dr. Marlene Springer | 11-M | 12,196 | 567 |
| Coll of the Holy Cross, Worcester, MA 01610 | 1843 | Rev. Gerard C. Reedy, SJ | 2-B | 2,738 | 259 |
| Coll of the Ozarks, Point Lookout, MO 65726 | 1906 | Dr. Jerry C. Davis | 2-B | 1,509 | 112 |
| The Coll of West Virginia, Beckley, WV 25802-2830 | 1933 | Dr. Charles H. Polk | 1-B | 2,051 | 125 |
| Coll of William and Mary, Williamsburg, VA 23187-8795 | 1693 | Mr. Timothy J. Sullivan | 5-D | 7,709 | 653 |
| The Coll of Wooster, Wooster, OH 44691 | 1866 | Dr. Susanne Woods | 2-B | 1,683 | 147 |
| Colorado Christian U, Lakewood, CO 80226-7499 | 1914 | Dr. Ronald Schmidt | 2-M | 2,672 | 167 |
| The Colorado Coll, Colorado Springs, CO 80903-3294 | 1874 | Dr. Kathryn Mohrman | 1-M | 2,014 | 203 |
| Colorado Sch of Mines, Golden, CO 80401-1887 | 1874 | Dr. George S. Ansell | 5-D | 3,150 | 290 |
| Colorado State U, Fort Collins, CO 80523-0015 | 1870 | Dr. Albert C. Yates | 5-D | 21,914 | 1,291 |
| Colorado Tech U, Colorado Springs, CO 80907-3896 | 1965 | Mr. David D. O'Donnell | 3-D | 1,473 | 97 |
| Columbia Coll, Chicago, IL 60605-1997 | 1890 | Mr. John B. Duff | 1-M | 7,857 | 944 |
| Columbia Coll, New York, NY 10027 | 1754 | Dr. Austin E. Quigley | 1-B | 3,573 | NR |
| Columbia Coll, Columbia, SC 29203-5998 (3) | 1854 | Dr. Peter T. Mitchell | 2-M | 1,310 | 81 |
| Columbia Union Coll, Takoma Park, MD 20912-7794 | 1904 | Dr. Charles Scriven | 2-B | 1,141 | 43 |
| Columbia U, Sch of Engineering & Applied Sci, New York, NY 10027 | 1864 | Dr. Donald Goldfarb | 1-D | 1,044 | 93 |
| Columbia U, Sch of General Studies, New York, NY 10027 | 1754 | Dr. Gillian Lindt | 1-B | 1,300 | 450 |
| Columbia U, Sch of Nursing, New York, NY 10032-3702 (4) | 1892 | Dr. Mary O. Mundinger | 1-D | 600 | 40 |
| Columbus Coll of Art and Design, Columbus, OH 43215-1758 | 1879 | Mr. Charles L. Deihl | 1-B | 1,200 | 140 |
| Columbus State U, Columbus, GA 31907-5645 | 1958 | Dr. Frank D. Brown | 5-M | 5,738 | 228 |
| Concord Coll, Athens, WV 24712-1000 | 1872 | Dr. Jerry L. Beasley | 5-B | 2,631 | 160 |
| Concordia Coll, Moorhead, MN 56562 | 1891 | Dr. Paul J. Dovre | 2-B | 2,958 | 292 |
| Concordia Coll, St Paul, MN 55104-5494 | 1893 | Dr. Robert Holst | 2-M | 1,187 | 94 |
| Concordia U, River Forest, IL 60305-1499 | 1864 | Dr. George C. Heider | 2-M | 2,418 | 195 |
| Concordia U Wisconsin, Mequon, WI 53097-2402 | 1881 | Dr. R. John Buuck | 2-M | 3,719 | 135 |
| Connecticut Coll, New London, CT 06320-4196 | 1911 | Dr. Claire L. Gaudiani | 1-M | 1,913 | 163 |
| Converse Coll, Spartanburg, SC 29302-0006 (3) | 1889 | Dr. Sandra C. Thomas | 1-M | 1,196 | 80 |
| Cooper Union for the Advancement of Science & Art, New York, NY 10003-7120 | 1859 | Dr. John Jay Iselin | 1-M | 1,003 | 192 |
| Coppin State Coll, Baltimore, MD 21216-3698 | 1900 | Dr. Calvin W. Burnett | 5-M | 3,540 | 132 |
| Cornell Coll, Mount Vernon, IA 52314-1098 | 1853 | Dr. Leslie H. Garner, Jr. | 2-B | 1,168 | 120 |
| Cornell U, Ithaca, NY 14853-0001 | 1865 | Dr. Hunter R. Rawlings | 1-D | 18,914 | 1,586 |
| Creighton U, Omaha, NE 68178-0001 | 1878 | Rev. Michael G. Morrison, SJ | 2-D | 6,069 | 1,310 |
| Culver-Stockton Coll, Canton, MO 63435-1299 | 1853 | Dr. Edwin B. Strong, Jr. | 2-B | 1,001 | 74 |
| Cumberland Coll, Williamsburg, KY 40769-1372 | 1889 | Dr. James Taylor | 2-M | 1,505 | 95 |
| Cumberland U, Lebanon, TN 37087-3554 | 1842 | Dr. Clair Eugene Martin | 1-M | 1,040 | 90 |
| Curry Coll, Milton, MA 02186-9984 | 1879 | Dr. Catherine W. Ingold | 1-M | 1,433 | 212 |
| Daemen Coll, Amherst, NY 14226-3592 | 1947 | Dr. Robert S. Marshall | 1-M | 1,938 | 151 |
| Dakota State U, Madison, SD 57042-1799 | 1881 | Dr. Jerald Tunheim | 5-B | 1,356 | 82 |
| Dallas Baptist U, Dallas, TX 75211-9299 | 1965 | Dr. Gary R. Cook | 2-M | 3,102 | 179 |
| Dartmouth Coll, Hanover, NH 03755 | 1769 | Mr. James O. Freedman | 1-D | 5,300 | 488 |
| Davenport Coll of Business, Grand Rapids, MI 49503 | 1866 | Mr. Donald W. Maine | 1-B | 2,719 | 162 |
| Davenport Coll of Business, Kalamazoo Cmps, Kalamazoo, MI 49006-2791 (4) | 1866 | Ms. Patricia Dolly | 1-B | 1,200 | 78 |

| Name, address | Year | Governing official, control, and highest degree offered | | Enroll-ment | Faculty |
|---|---|---|---|---|---|
| Davenport Coll of Business, Lansing Cmps, Lansing, MI 48933-2197 | 1979 | Mr. Don Colizzi | 1-B | 1,188 | 105 |
| David Lipscomb U, Nashville, TN 37204-3951 | 1891 | Dr. Harold Hazelip | 2-M | 2,505 | 176 |
| David N Myers Coll, Cleveland, OH 44115-1096 | 1848 | Dr. John C. Corfias | 1-B | 1,244 | 92 |
| Davidson Coll, Davidson, NC 28036-1719 | 1837 | Dr. John W. Kuykendall | 2-B | 1,616 | 144 |
| Delaware State U, Dover, DE 19901-2277 | 1891 | Dr. William B. DeLauder | 5-M | 3,175 | 174 |
| Delaware Valley Coll, Doylestown, PA 18901-2697 | 1896 | Dr. Joshua Feldstein | 1-B | 2,073 | 129 |
| Delta State U, Cleveland, MS 38733-0001 | 1925 | Dr. F. Kent Wyatt | 5-D | 3,887 | 269 |
| Denison U, Granville, OH 43023 | 1831 | Dr. Michele Tolela Myers | 1-B | 1,995 | 163 |
| Denver Tech Coll, Denver, CO 80224-1658 | 1945 | Mr. Raul Valdez Pages | 3-M | 1,300 | 81 |
| DePaul U, Chicago, IL 60604-2287 | 1898 | Rev. John P. Minogue, CM | 2-D | 17,133 | 1,336 |
| DePauw U, Greencastle, IN 46135-1772 | 1837 | Dr. Robert G. Bottoms | 2-B | 2,082 | 207 |
| Detroit Coll of Business, Dearborn, MI 48126-3799 | 1962 | Dr. James Mendola | 1-B | 3,100 | 195 |
| Detroit Coll of Business, Warren Cmps, Warren, MI 48092-5209 | 1975 | Ms. Janet Guggenheim | 1-B | 1,804 | 85 |
| DeVry Inst of Tech, Phoenix, AZ 85021-2995 | 1967 | Mr. James A. Dugan | 3-B | 2,714 | 90 |
| DeVry Inst of Tech, Pomona, CA 91768-2642 | 1983 | Dr. Rose Marie Dishman | 3-B | 2,988 | 153 |
| DeVry Inst of Tech, Decatur, GA 30030-2198 | 1969 | Dr. Ronald Bush | 3-B | 2,971 | 108 |
| DeVry Inst of Tech, Addison, IL 60101-6106 | 1982 | Mr. Jerry R. Dill | 3-B | 3,116 | 117 |
| DeVry Inst of Tech, Chicago, IL 60618-5994 | 1931 | Dr. E. Arthur Stunnard | 3-B | 2,915 | 157 |
| DeVry Inst of Tech, Kansas City, MO 64131-3698 | 1931 | Mr. Charles R. Levalley | 3-B | 1,965 | 70 |
| DeVry Inst of Tech, Columbus, OH 43209-2764 | 1952 | Mr. Richard A. Czerniak | 3-B | 2,585 | 71 |
| DeVry Inst of Tech, Irving, TX 75063-2440 | 1969 | Dr. Francis V. Cannon | 3-B | 2,315 | 109 |
| Dickinson Coll, Carlisle, PA 17013-2896 | 1773 | Dr. A. Lee Fritschler | 1-B | 1,840 | 183 |
| Dickinson State U, Dickinson, ND 58601-4896 | 1918 | Dr. Philip W. Conn | 5-B | 1,578 | 106 |
| Dillard U, New Orleans, LA 70122-3097 | 1869 | Dr. Samuel DuBois Cook | 2-B | 1,570 | 124 |
| Doane Coll, Crete, NE 68333-2430 | 1872 | Dr. Frederic D. Brown | 2-M | 1,870 | 104 |
| Dominican Coll of Blauvelt, Orangeburg, NY 10962-1210 | 1952 | Sr. Kathleen Sullivan | 1-M | 1,737 | 173 |
| Dominican Coll of San Rafael, San Rafael, CA 94901-2298 | 1890 | Dr. Joseph R. Fink | 2-M | 1,364 | 156 |
| Dordt Coll, Sioux Center, IA 51250-1697 | 1955 | Dr. Carl E. Zylstra | 2-M | 1,209 | 93 |
| Dowling Coll, Oakdale, NY 11769-1999 | 1955 | Dr. Victor P. Meskill | 1-M | 5,855 | 403 |
| Drake U, Des Moines, IA 50311-4516 | 1881 | Dr. Michael R. Ferrari | 1-D | 5,639 | 270 |
| Drew U, Madison, NJ 07940-1493 | 1867 | Mr. Thomas H. Kean | 2-D | 2,111 | 127 |
| Drexel U, Philadelphia, PA 19104-2875 | 1891 | C. R. Pennoni | 1-D | 9,158 | 665 |
| Drury Coll, Springfield, MO 65802-3791 | 1873 | Dr. John E. Moore, Jr. | 1-M | 1,600 | 108 |
| Duke U, Durham, NC 27708-0586 | 1838 | Dr. Nannerl O. Keohane | 2-D | 11,512 | 2,122 |
| Duquesne U, Pittsburgh, PA 15282-0001 | 1878 | Dr. John E. Murray, Jr. | 2-D | 9,285 | 728 |
| D'Youville Coll, Buffalo, NY 14201-1084 | 1908 | Dr. Denise A. Roche, GNSH | 1-M | 1,905 | 146 |
| Earlham Coll, Richmond, IN 47374-4095 | 1847 | Dr. Richard J. Wood | 2-B | 1,017 | 102 |
| East Carolina U, Greenville, NC 27858-4353 | 1907 | Dr. Richard Eakin | 5-D | 16,339 | 1,167 |
| East Central U, Ada, OK 74820-6899 | 1909 | Dr. Bill S. Cole | 5-M | 4,378 | 225 |
| Eastern Coll, St Davids, PA 19087-3696 | 1932 | Dr. Roberta Hestenes | 2-M | 2,155 | 213 |
| Eastern Connecticut State U, Willimantic, CT 06226-2295 | 1889 | Dr. David G. Carter | 5-M | 4,590 | 199 |
| Eastern Illinois U, Charleston, IL 61920-3099 | 1895 | Dr. David L. Jorns | 5-M | 11,424 | 659 |
| Eastern Kentucky U, Richmond, KY 40475-3102 | 1906 | Dr. Hanly Funderburk | 5-M | 16,060 | 855 |
| Eastern Mennonite U, Harrisonburg, VA 22801-2462 | 1917 | Dr. Joseph L. Lapp | 2-F | 1,182 | 114 |
| Eastern Michigan U, Ypsilanti, MI 48197 | 1849 | Dr. William E. Shelton | 5-D | 23,142 | 1,195 |
| Eastern Nazarene Coll, Quincy, MA 02170-2999 | 1918 | Dr. Kent R. Hill | 2-M | 1,260 | 66 |
| Eastern New Mexico U, Portales, NM 88130 | 1934 | Dr. Everett L. Frost | 5-M | 3,632 | 226 |
| Eastern Oregon State Coll, La Grande, OR 97850-2899 | 1929 | Dr. David E. Gilbert | 5-M | 1,847 | 147 |
| Eastern Washington U, Cheney, WA 99004-2431 | 1882 | Dr. Marshall Drummond | 5-M | 8,078 | 454 |
| East Stroudsburg U of Pennsylvania, East Stroudsburg, PA 18301-2999 | 1893 | Dr. James Gilbert | 5-M | 5,491 | 275 |
| East Tennessee State U, Johnson City, TN 37614-0734 | 1911 | Dr. Roy S. Nicks | 5-D | 11,718 | 941 |
| East Texas Baptist U, Marshall, TX 75670-1498 | 1912 | Dr. Bob E. Riley | 2-M | 1,222 | 103 |
| East Texas State U at Texarkana, Texarkana, TX 75505-5518 | 1971 | Dr. Stephen R. Hensley | 5-M | 1,187 | 40 |
| Eckerd Coll, St Petersburg, FL 33711 | 1958 | Dr. Peter H. Armacost | 2-B | 1,366 | 130 |
| Edgewood Coll, Madison, WI 53711-1998 | 1927 | Dr. James A. Ebben | 2-M | 2,056 | 152 |
| Edinboro U of Pennsylvania, Edinboro, PA 16444 | 1857 | Mr. Foster F. Diebold | 5-M | 7,477 | 313 |
| Elizabeth City State U, Elizabeth City, NC 27909-7806 | 1891 | Dr. Jimmy R. Jenkins | 5-B | 2,000 | 149 |
| Elizabethtown Coll, Elizabethtown, PA 17022-2298 | 1899 | Dr. Gerhard E. Spiegler | 2-B | 1,753 | 149 |
| Elmhurst Coll, Elmhurst, IL 60126-3296 | 1871 | Dr. Bryant L. Cureton | 2-B | 2,785 | 215 |
| Elmira Coll, Elmira, NY 14901 | 1855 | Dr. Thomas K. Meier | 1-M | 1,104 | 92 |
| Elms Coll, Chicopee, MA 01013-2839 (3) | 1928 | Sr. Kathleen Keating | 2-M | 1,257 | 106 |
| Elon Coll, Elon College, NC 27244 | 1889 | Dr. J. Fred Young | 2-M | 3,479 | 223 |
| Embry-Riddle Aeronautical U, Prescott, AZ 86301-3720 | 1978 | Dr. Stephen Kahne | 1-B | 1,381 | 88 |
| Embry-Riddle Aeronautical U, Daytona Beach, FL 32114-3900 | 1926 | Dr. Steven M. Sliwa | 1-M | 4,154 | 237 |
| Embry-Riddle Aeronautical U, Extended Cmps, Daytona Beach, FL 32114-3900 | 1970 | Dr. Leon E. Flancher | 1-M | 6,748 | 2,670 |
| Emerson Coll, Boston, MA 02116-1511 | 1880 | Dr. Jacqueline W. Liebergott | 1-D | 3,298 | 275 |
| Emmanuel Coll, Boston, MA 02115 (3) | 1919 | Sr. Janet Eisner, SND | 2-M | 1,553 | 111 |
| Emory U, Atlanta, GA 30322-1100 | 1836 | Dr. William M. Chace | 2-D | 11,308 | 2,404 |
| Emporia State U, Emporia, KS 66801-5087 | 1863 | Dr. Robert E. Glennen | 5-D | 5,913 | 304 |
| Eugene Lang Coll, New Sch for Social Research, New York, NY 10011-8601 | 1978 | Dr. Beatrice Banu | 1-B | 345 | 61 |
| Evangel Coll, Springfield, MO 65802-2191 | 1955 | Dr. Robert H. Spence | 2-B | 1,555 | 122 |
| The Evergreen State Coll, Olympia, WA 98505 | 1967 | Dr. Jane L. Jervis | 5-M | 3,625 | 169 |
| Fairfield U, Fairfield, CT 06430-5195 | 1942 | Rev. Aloysius P. Kelley, SJ | 2-M | 4,980 | 388 |
| Fairleigh Dickinson U, Teaneck-Hackensack Cmps, Teaneck, NJ 07666-1914 | 1942 | Dr. Francis J. Mertz | 1-D | 6,830 | 667 |
| Fairmont State Coll, Fairmont, WV 26554 | 1865 | Dr. Robert J. Dillman | 5-B | 6,547 | 438 |
| Fashion Inst of Tech, New York, NY 10001-5992 | 1944 | Dr. Allan F. Hershfield | 11-M | 8,489 | 919 |
| Faulkner U, Montgomery, AL 36109-3398 | 1942 | Dr. Billy D. Hilyer | 2-F | 2,363 | 125 |
| Felician Coll, Lodi, NJ 07644-2198 | 1942 | Sr. Theresa Martin | 2-M | 1,136 | 97 |
| Ferris State U, Big Rapids, MI 49307 | 1884 | Dr. William Sederburg | 5-F | 9,767 | 611 |
| Ferrum Coll, Ferrum, VA 24088-9001 | 1913 | Dr. Jerry M. Boone | 2-B | 1,093 | 103 |
| Finch U of Health Sciences/Chicago Medical Sch, North Chicago, IL 60064-3037 | 1912 | Mr. Herman M. Finch | 1-D | 1,371 | 23 |
| Fitchburg State Coll, Fitchburg, MA 01420-2697 | 1894 | Dr. Vincent J. Mara | 5-M | 4,351 | 422 |
| Flagler Coll, St Augustine, FL 32085-1027 | 1968 | Dr. William L. Proctor | 1-B | 1,426 | 122 |
| Florida A&M U, Tallahassee, FL 32307 | 1887 | Dr. Frederick Humphries | 5-D | 10,324 | 678 |
| Florida Atlantic U, Boca Raton, FL 33431-0991 | 1961 | Dr. Anthony James Catanese | 5-D | 17,843 | 688 |
| Florida Inst of Tech, Melbourne, FL 32901-6975 | 1958 | Dr. Lynn E. Weaver | 1-D | 4,232 | 441 |
| Florida International U, Miami, FL 33199 | 1965 | Dr. Modesto A. Maidique | 5-D | 23,303 | 1,198 |
| Florida Memorial Coll, Miami, FL 33054 | 1879 | Dr. Albert E. Smith | 2-B | 1,457 | NR |
| Florida Southern Coll, Lakeland, FL 33801-5698 | 1885 | Dr. Thomas L. Reuschling | 2-M | 1,886 | 123 |

| Name, address | Year | Governing official, control, and highest degree offered | | Enroll-ment | Faculty |
|---|---|---|---|---|---|
| Florida State U, Tallahassee, FL 32306 | 1857 | Dr. Talbot D'Alemberte | 5-D | 30,268 | 1,671 |
| Fontbonne Coll, St Louis, MO 63105-3098 | 1917 | Dr. Dennis C. Golden | 2-M | 1,801 | 149 |
| Fordham U, New York, NY 10458 | 1841 | Rev. Joseph A. O'Hare, SJ | 2-D | 13,909 | 765 |
| Fort Hays State U, Hays, KS 67601-4099 | 1902 | Dr. Edward H. Hammond | 5-M | 5,441 | 302 |
| Fort Lewis Coll, Durango, CO 81301-3999 | 1911 | Mr. Joel M. Jones | 5-B | 4,363 | 241 |
| Fort Valley State U, Fort Valley, GA 31030-3262 | 1895 | Dr. Oscar L. Prater | 5-F | 2,978 | 152 |
| Framingham State Coll, Framingham, MA 01701-9101 | 1839 | Dr. Paul F. Weller | 5-M | 4,972 | 215 |
| Franciscan U of Steubenville, Steubenville, OH 43952-6701 | 1946 | Rev. Michael Scanlan, TOR | 2-M | 1,964 | 142 |
| Francis Marion U, Florence, SC 29501-0547 | 1970 | Dr. Lee A. Vickers | 5-M | 3,836 | 219 |
| Franklin and Marshall Coll, Lancaster, PA 17604-3003 | 1787 | Dr. Richard Kneedler | 1-B | 1,866 | 175 |
| Franklin Pierce Coll, Rindge, NH 03461-0060 | 1962 | Dr. Walter Peterson | 1-B | 1,262 | 111 |
| Franklin U, Columbus, OH 43215-5399 | 1902 | Dr. Paul J. Otte | 1-M | 4,073 | 215 |
| Freed-Hardeman U, Henderson, TN 38340-2399 | 1869 | Dr. Milton R. Sewell | 2-M | 1,505 | 101 |
| Fresno Pacific Coll, Fresno, CA 93702-4709 | 1944 | Dr. Richard Kriegbaum | 2-M | 1,543 | 165 |
| Friends U, Wichita, KS 67213 | 1898 | Dr. Biff Green | 1-M | 2,326 | 119 |
| Frostburg State U, Frostburg, MD 21532-2302 | 1898 | Dr. Catherine R. Gira | 5-M | 5,427 | 314 |
| Furman U, Greenville, SC 29613 | 1826 | Dr. David E. Shi | 1-M | 2,673 | 198 |
| Gallaudet U, Washington, DC 20002-3625 | 1864 | Dr. I. King Jordan | 1-D | 2,208 | 330 |
| Gannon U, Erie, PA 16541 | 1925 | Msgr. David A. Rubino, PhD | 2-M | 3,528 | 325 |
| Gardner-Webb U, Boiling Springs, NC 28017 | 1905 | Dr. M. Christopher White | 2-M | 2,511 | 174 |
| Geneva Coll, Beaver Falls, PA 15010-3599 | 1848 | Dr. John H. White | 2-M | 1,697 | 99 |
| George Fox U, Newberg, OR 97132-2697 | 1891 | Dr. Edward F. Stevens | 2-D | 1,718 | 97 |
| George Mason U, Fairfax, VA 22030-4445 | 1957 | Dr. George W. Johnson | 5-D | 24,172 | 1,246 |
| Georgetown Coll, Georgetown, KY 40324-1696 | 1829 | Dr. William H. Crouch, Jr. | 2-M | 1,461 | 106 |
| Georgetown U, Washington, DC 20057 | 1789 | Rev. Leo J. O'Donovan, SJ | 2-D | 12,618 | 2,114 |
| The George Washington U, Washington, DC 20052 | 1821 | Mr. Stephen J. Trachtenberg | 1-D | 19,670 | 2,215 |
| Georgia Coll, Milledgeville, GA 31061 | 1889 | Dr. Edwin G. Speir | 5-M | 5,710 | 336 |
| Georgia Inst of Tech, Atlanta, GA 30332-0001 | 1885 | Dr. Gerald W. Clough | 5-D | 13,036 | 644 |
| Georgian Court Coll, Lakewood, NJ 08701-2697 (4) | 1908 | Sr. Barbara Williams | 2-M | 1,993 | 193 |
| Georgia Southern U, Statesboro, GA 30460 | 1906 | Dr. Nicholas Henry | 5-D | 14,157 | 678 |
| Georgia Southwestern Coll, Americus, GA 31709-4693 | 1906 | Dr. William H. Capitan | 5-M | 2,607 | 133 |
| Georgia State U, Atlanta, GA 30303-3083 | 1913 | Dr. Carl V. Patton | 5-D | 24,316 | 1,381 |
| Gettysburg Coll, Gettysburg, PA 17325-1411 | 1832 | Dr. Gordon A. Haaland | 1-B | 2,000 | 174 |
| Glenville State Coll, Glenville, WV 26351-1200 | 1872 | Dr. William K. Simmons | 5-B | 2,416 | 151 |
| GMI Engineering & Management Inst, Flint, MI 48504-4898 | 1919 | Dr. James E. A. John | 1-M | 3,256 | 150 |
| Golden Gate U, San Francisco, CA 94105-2968 | 1853 | Dr. Thomas M. Stauffer | 1-D | 6,368 | 523 |
| Goldey-Beacom Coll, Wilmington, DE 19808-1999 | 1886 | Mr. William R. Baldt | 1-M | 1,795 | 73 |
| Gonzaga U, Spokane, WA 99258 | 1887 | Rev. Bernard J. Coughlin, SJ | 2-D | 4,785 | 288 |
| Gordon Coll, Wenham, MA 01984-1899 | 1889 | Dr. R. Judson Carlberg | 2-B | 1,229 | 97 |
| Goshen Coll, Goshen, IN 46526-4794 | 1894 | Dr. Victor Stoltzfus | 2-B | 1,071 | 124 |
| Goucher Coll, Baltimore, MD 21204-2794 | 1885 | Dr. Judy Jolley Mohraz | 1-M | 1,276 | 138 |
| Governors State U, University Park, IL 60466 | 1969 | Dr. Paula Wolff | 5-M | 6,073 | 280 |
| Graceland Coll, Lamoni, IA 50140 | 1895 | Dr. William T. Higdon | 2-M | 1,176 | 97 |
| Grambling State U, Grambling, LA 71245 | 1901 | Dr. Raymond A. Hicks | 5-D | 8,000 | 224 |
| Grand Canyon U, Phoenix, AZ 85017-3030 | 1949 | Dr. Bill Williams | 2-M | 2,119 | 196 |
| Grand Valley State U, Allendale, MI 49401-9403 | 1960 | Mr. Arend D. Lubbers | 5-M | 13,887 | 739 |
| Grand View Coll, Des Moines, IA 50316-1599 | 1896 | Dr. Arthur E. Puotinen | 2-B | 1,482 | 135 |
| Greensboro Coll, Greensboro, NC 27401-1875 | 1838 | Dr. Craven E. Williams | 2-B | 1,017 | 90 |
| Grinnell Coll, Grinnell, IA 50112-0805 | 1846 | Dr. Pamela A. Ferguson | 1-B | 1,261 | 161 |
| Grove City Coll, Grove City, PA 16127-2104 | 1876 | Dr. Jerry H. Combee | 2-M | 2,324 | 142 |
| Guilford Coll, Greensboro, NC 27410-4173 | 1837 | Dr. William R. Rogers | 2-B | 1,093 | 104 |
| Gustavus Adolphus Coll, St Peter, MN 56082-1498 | 1862 | Dr. Axel D. Steuer | 2-B | 2,361 | 225 |
| Gwynedd-Mercy Coll, Gwynedd Valley, PA 19437-0901 | 1948 | Dr. Linda M. Bevilacqua, OP | 2-M | 1,816 | 195 |
| Hamilton Coll, Clinton, NY 13323-1218 | 1812 | Dr. Eugene M. Tobin | 1-B | 1,650 | 199 |
| Hamline U, St Paul, MN 55104-1284 | 1854 | Dr. Larry G. Osnes | 2-F | 2,932 | 251 |
| Hampshire Coll, Amherst, MA 01002 | 1965 | Dr. Gregory S. Prince, Jr. | 1-B | 1,073 | 98 |
| Hampton U, Hampton, VA 23668 | 1868 | Dr. William R. Harvey | 1-D | 6,035 | 389 |
| Hanover Coll, Hanover, IN 47243 | 1827 | Dr. Russell L. Nichols | 2-B | 1,087 | 108 |
| Harding U, Searcy, AR 72149-0001 | 1924 | Dr. David B. Burks, Jr. | 2-M | 4,071 | 231 |
| Hardin-Simmons U, Abilene, TX 79698-0001 | 1891 | Dr. Lanny Hall | 2-F | 2,374 | 156 |
| Harris-Stowe State Coll, St Louis, MO 63103-2136 | 1857 | Dr. Henry Givens, Jr. | 5-B | 1,674 | 122 |
| Hartwick Coll, Oneonta, NY 13820-4020 | 1797 | Dr. Richard A. Detweiler | 1-B | 1,522 | 129 |
| Harvard U, Cambridge, MA 02138 | 1636 | Dr. Neil Rudenstine | 1-D | 18,480 | 2,106 |
| Hastings Coll, Hastings, NE 68902-0269 | 1882 | Dr. Richard Hoover | 2-M | 1,089 | 104 |
| Haverford Coll, Haverford, PA 19041-1392 | 1833 | Dr. Tom G. Kessinger | 1-B | 1,115 | 116 |
| Hawaii Pacific U, Honolulu, HI 96813-2785 | 1965 | Mr. Chatt Wright | 1-M | 8,036 | 489 |
| Heidelberg Coll, Tiffin, OH 44883-2462 | 1850 | Dr. William C. Cassell | 2-M | 1,358 | 118 |
| Henderson State U, Arkadelphia, AR 71999-0001 | 1890 | Dr. Charles D. Dunn | 5-M | 3,614 | 187 |
| Heritage Coll, Toppenish, WA 98948-9599 | 1907 | Dr. Kathleen Ross, SNJM | 1-M | 1,061 | 154 |
| High Point U, High Point, NC 27262-3598 | 1924 | Dr. Jacob C. Martinson | 2-M | 2,516 | 137 |
| Hillsdale Coll, Hillsdale, MI 49242-1298 | 1844 | Dr. George C. Roche, III | 1-B | 1,162 | 118 |
| Hofstra U, Hempstead, NY 11550-1090 | 1935 | Dr. James M. Shuart | 1-D | 11,777 | 978 |
| Hollins Coll, Roanoke, VA 24020-1657 (3) | 1842 | Dr. Jane Margaret O'Brien | 1-M | 1,061 | 90 |
| Holy Family Coll, Philadelphia, PA 19114-2094 | 1954 | Sr. Francesca Onley | 2-M | 2,760 | 262 |
| Hood Coll, Frederick, MD 21701-8575 (4) | 1893 | Mrs. Shirley D. Peterson | 2-M | 2,067 | 133 |
| Hope Coll, Holland, MI 49422-9000 | 1866 | Dr. John H. Jacobson, Jr. | 2-B | 2,919 | 269 |
| Houghton Coll, Houghton, NY 14744 | 1883 | Dr. Daniel R. Chamberlain | 2-B | 1,271 | 122 |
| Houston Baptist U, Houston, TX 77074-3298 | 1960 | Dr. E. Douglas Hodo | 2-M | 2,142 | 140 |
| Howard Payne U, Brownwood, TX 76801-2715 | 1889 | Dr. Don Newbury | 2-B | 1,467 | 126 |
| Howard U, Washington, DC 20059-0002 | 1867 | H. Patrick Swygert, Esq. | 1-D | 10,332 | 1,808 |
| Humboldt State U, Arcata, CA 95521-8299 | 1913 | Dr. Alistair W. McCrone | 5-M | 7,427 | 562 |
| Hunter Coll of the City U of New York, New York, NY 10021-5085 | 1870 | Dr. Blanche D. Blank | 11-M | 18,250 | 1,095 |
| Husson Coll, Bangor, ME 04401-2999 | 1898 | Dr. William H. Beardsley | 1-M | 2,036 | 70 |
| ICI U, Irving, TX 75063-2631 | 1967 | Dr. George M. Flattery | 2-M | 8,628 | NR |
| Idaho State U, Pocatello, ID 83209 | 1901 | Dr. Richard Bowen | 5-D | 12,041 | 668 |
| Illinois Inst of Tech, Chicago, IL 60616 | 1890 | Mr. Lewis Collens | 1-D | 7,157 | 600 |
| Illinois State U, Normal, IL 61790-2200 | 1857 | Dr. Thomas P. Wallace | 5-D | 19,294 | 949 |
| Illinois Wesleyan U, Bloomington, IL 61702-2900 | 1850 | Dr. Minor Myers, Jr. | 1-B | 1,875 | 168 |
| Immaculata Coll, Immaculata, PA 19345-0900 (4) | 1920 | Sr. Marie Roseanne Bonfini | 2-D | 2,053 | 143 |
| Indiana Inst of Tech, Fort Wayne, IN 46803-1297 | 1930 | Mr. Donald J. Andorfer | 1-B | 1,175 | 45 |
| Indiana State U, Terre Haute, IN 47809-1401 | 1865 | Dr. John W. Moore | 5-D | 11,184 | 703 |
| Indiana U Bloomington, Bloomington, IN 47405 | 1820 | Dr. Kenneth R. R. Gros Louis | 5-D | 35,059 | 1,628 |
| Indiana U East, Richmond, IN 47374-1289 | 1971 | Dr. David J. Fulton | 5-B | 2,390 | 192 |
| Indiana U Kokomo, Kokomo, IN 46904-9003 | 1945 | Dr. Emita B. Hill | 5-M | 3,065 | 195 |
| Indiana U Northwest, Gary, IN 46408-1197 | 1959 | Dr. Hilda Richards | 5-M | 5,301 | 400 |

| Name, address | Year | Governing official, control, and highest degree offered | | Enrollment | Faculty |
|---|---|---|---|---|---|
| Indiana U of Pennsylvania, Indiana, PA 15705 | 1875 | Dr. Lawrence K. Pettit | 5-D | 13,879 | 826 |
| Indiana U–Purdue U Fort Wayne, Fort Wayne, IN 46805-1499 | 1917 | Dr. Michael A. Wartell | 5-M | 11,011 | 674 |
| Indiana U–Purdue U Indianapolis, Indianapolis, IN 46202-2896 | 1969 | Mr. Gerald L. Bepko | 5-D | 26,939 | 2,113 |
| Indiana U South Bend, South Bend, IN 46634-7111 | 1922 | Dr. Lester C. Lamon | 5-M | 7,544 | 599 |
| Indiana Wesleyan U, Marion, IN 46953-4999 | 1920 | Dr. James Barnes | 2-M | 5,069 | 133 |
| Inter American U of PR, Arecibo Cmps, Arecibo, PR 00614-4050 | 1957 | Dr. Zaida Vega | 1-B | 4,489 | 260 |
| Inter American U of PR, Fajardo Cmps, Fajardo, PR 00738-7003 | 1965 | Mrs. Yolanda Robles Garcia | 1-B | 2,027 | 96 |
| Inter American U of PR, Ponce Cmps, Mercedita, PR 00715-2201 | 1962 | Ms. Marilina Wayland | 1-B | 3,670 | 164 |
| Inter American U of PR, San Germán Cmps, San Germán, PR 00683-5008 | 1912 | Prof. Agnes Mojica | 1-M | 6,392 | 324 |
| Iona Coll, New Rochelle, NY 10801-1890 | 1940 | Br. James A. Liguori, CFC | 1-M | 5,588 | 400 |
| Iowa State U of Science and Tech, Ames, IA 50011 | 1858 | Dr. Martin C. Jischke | 5-D | 24,431 | 1,781 |
| Ithaca Coll, Ithaca, NY 14850-7020 | 1892 | Dr. James J. Whalen | 1-M | 5,695 | 539 |
| Jackson State U, Jackson, MS 39217 | 1877 | Dr. James E. Lyons, Sr. | 5-D | 6,313 | 391 |
| Jacksonville State U, Jacksonville, AL 36265-9982 | 1883 | Dr. Harold J. McGee | 5-M | 7,697 | 339 |
| Jacksonville U, Jacksonville, FL 32211-3394 | 1934 | Dr. James J. Brady | 1-M | 2,416 | 249 |
| James Madison U, Harrisonburg, VA 22807 | 1908 | Dr. Ronald E. Carrier | 5-D | 11,927 | 717 |
| Jamestown Coll, Jamestown, ND 58405 | 1883 | Dr. James Walker | 2-B | 1,064 | 72 |
| Jersey City State Coll, Jersey City, NJ 07305-1957 | 1927 | Dr. Carlos Hernandez | 5-M | 7,356 | 257 |
| John Brown U, Siloam Springs, AR 72761-2121 | 1919 | Dr. A. LeVon Balzer | 2-B | 1,206 | 90 |
| John Carroll U, University Heights, OH 44118-4581 | 1886 | Dr. Frederick Travis, SJ | 2-M | 4,397 | 344 |
| John F Kennedy U, Orinda, CA 94563-2689 | 1964 | Mr. Charles E. Glasser | 1-D | 1,829 | 88 |
| John Jay Coll of Criminal Justice, the City U of NY, New York, NY 10019-1093 | 1964 | Dr. Gerald Lynch | 11-M | 10,030 | 713 |
| Johns Hopkins U, Baltimore, MD 21218-2699 | 1876 | Dr. Daniel Nathans | 1-D | 4,847 | 413 |
| Johnson & Wales U, Providence, RI 02903-3703 | 1914 | Dr. John A. Yena | 1-M | 7,907 | 344 |
| Johnson & Wales U, Charleston, SC 29403 | 1984 | Dr. Barry L. Gleim | 1-B | 1,197 | 62 |
| Johnson C Smith U, Charlotte, NC 28216 | 1867 | Dr. Dorothy Cowser Yancy | 1-B | 1,398 | 88 |
| Johnson State Coll, Johnson, VT 05656-9405 | 1828 | Dr. Robert Hahn | 5-M | 1,618 | 119 |
| Juniata Coll, Huntingdon, PA 16652-2119 | 1876 | Dr. Robert W. Neff | 1-B | 1,065 | 104 |
| Kalamazoo Coll, Kalamazoo, MI 49006-3295 | 1833 | Dr. Lawrence Bryan | 1-B | 1,272 | 108 |
| Kansas Newman Coll, Wichita, KS 67213-2084 | 1933 | Sr. Tarcisia Roths | 2-M | 1,989 | 305 |
| Kansas State U, Manhattan, KS 66506 | 1863 | Dr. Jon Wefald | 5-D | 20,476 | 1,102 |
| Kean Coll of New Jersey, Union, NJ 07083 | 1855 | Dr. Henry J. Ross | 5-M | 11,746 | 824 |
| Keene State Coll, Keene, NH 03435-1701 | 1909 | Dr. Stanley J. Yarosewick | 5-M | 4,042 | 347 |
| Kennesaw State U, Kennesaw, GA 30144 | 1963 | Dr. Betty L. Siegel | 5-M | 12,100 | 484 |
| Kent State U, Kent, OH 44242-0001 | 1910 | Dr. Carol A. Cartwright | 5-D | 20,972 | 1,329 |
| Kentucky State U, Frankfort, KY 40601 | 1886 | Dr. Mary L. Smith | 12-M | 2,579 | 149 |
| Kenyon Coll, Gambier, OH 43022-9623 | 1824 | Dr. Robert A. Oden, Jr. | 1-B | 1,516 | 146 |
| King's Coll, Wilkes-Barre, PA 18711-0801 | 1946 | Rev. James Lackenmier, CSC | 2-M | 2,393 | 180 |
| Knox Coll, Galesburg, IL 61401 | 1837 | Mr. Frederick C. Nahm | 1-B | 1,127 | 111 |
| Kutztown U of Pennsylvania, Kutztown, PA 19530 | 1866 | Dr. David E. McFarland | 5-M | 7,811 | 444 |
| Lafayette Coll, Easton, PA 18042-1798 | 1826 | Mr. Arthur J. Rothkopf | 2-B | 2,219 | 232 |
| LaGrange Coll, LaGrange, GA 30240-2999 | 1831 | Dr. Walter Y. Murphy | 2-M | 1,009 | 85 |
| Lake Forest Coll, Lake Forest, IL 60045-2399 | 1857 | Dr. David Spadafora | 1-M | 1,039 | 113 |
| Lake Superior State U, Sault Sainte Marie, MI 49783-1699 | 1946 | Dr. Robert D. Arbuckle | 5-M | 3,437 | 169 |
| Lamar U, Beaumont, TX 77710 | 1923 | Dr. Rex Cottle | 5-D | 8,356 | 678 |
| Lambuth U, Jackson, TN 38301 | 1843 | Dr. Thomas F. Boyd | 2-B | 1,227 | 90 |
| Lander U, Greenwood, SC 29649-2099 | 1872 | Dr. William C. Moran | 5-M | 2,780 | 166 |
| La Roche Coll, Pittsburgh, PA 15237-5898 | 1963 | Msgr. William Kerr | 2-M | 1,630 | 131 |
| La Salle U, Philadelphia, PA 19141-1199 | 1863 | Br. Joseph Burke | 2-M | 5,449 | 324 |
| La Sierra U, Riverside, CA 92515 | 1922 | Dr. Lawrence T. Geraty | 2-D | 1,509 | 115 |
| Lawrence Tech U, Southfield, MI 48075-1058 | 1932 | Dr. Charles M. Chambers | 1-M | 4,153 | 362 |
| Lawrence U, Appleton, WI 54912-0599 | 1847 | Dr. Richard Warch | 1-B | 1,216 | 149 |
| Lebanon Valley Coll, Annville, PA 17003-0501 | 1866 | Mr. John A. Synodinos | 2-M | 1,884 | 105 |
| Lee Coll, Cleveland, TN 37311-4475 | 1918 | Dr. Paul Conn | 2-B | 2,477 | 187 |
| Lehigh U, Bethlehem, PA 18015-3094 | 1865 | Dr. Peter Likins | 1-D | 6,255 | 504 |
| Lehman Coll of the City U of New York, Bronx, NY 10468-1589 | 1931 | Dr. Ricardo R. Fernandez | 11-M | 9,599 | 693 |
| Le Moyne Coll, Syracuse, NY 13214-1399 | 1946 | Rev. Robert A. Mitchell, SJ | 2-M | 2,425 | 210 |
| LeMoyne-Owen Coll, Memphis, TN 38126-6595 | 1862 | Dr. Burnett Joiner | 2-M | 1,296 | 100 |
| Lenoir-Rhyne Coll, Hickory, NC 28603 | 1891 | Dr. Ryan A. LaHurd | 2-M | 1,555 | 120 |
| Lesley Coll, Cambridge, MA 02138-2790 (3) | 1909 | Ms. Margaret A. McKenna | 1-D | 6,506 | 885 |
| LeTourneau U, Longview, TX 75607-7001 | 1946 | Dr. Alvin O. Austin | 2-M | 2,256 | 151 |
| Lewis & Clark Coll, Portland, OR 97219-7879 | 1867 | Dr. Michael J. Mooney | 1-F | 3,255 | 290 |
| Lewis-Clark State Coll, Lewiston, ID 83501-2698 | 1893 | Dr. James Hottois | 5-B | 3,138 | 303 |
| Lewis U, Romeoville, IL 60446 | 1932 | Br. James Gaffney, FSC | 2-M | 4,348 | 274 |
| Liberty U, Lynchburg, VA 24506-8001 | 1971 | Dr. A. Pierre Guillermin | 2-D | 5,138 | 220 |
| Lincoln Memorial U, Harrogate, TN 37752-1901 | 1897 | Dr. Scott D. Miller | 1-M | 2,000 | 116 |
| Lincoln U, Jefferson City, MO 65102 | 1866 | Dr. Wendell G. Rayburn, Sr. | 5-M | 3,454 | 202 |
| Lincoln U, Lincoln University, PA 19352 | 1854 | Dr. Niara Sudarkasa | 12-M | 1,551 | 138 |
| Lindenwood Coll, St Charles, MO 63301-1695 | 1827 | Dr. Dennis Spellmann | 2-M | 3,660 | 162 |
| Lindsey Wilson Coll, Columbia, KY 42728-1298 | 1903 | Dr. John B. Begley | 2-M | 1,317 | 55 |
| Linfield Coll, McMinnville, OR 97128-6894 | 1849 | Dr. Vivian A. Bull | 2-B | 1,588 | 118 |
| Lock Haven U of Pennsylvania, Lock Haven, PA 17745-2390 | 1870 | Dr. Craig Dean Willis | 5-M | 3,244 | 226 |
| Long Island U, Brooklyn Cmps, Brooklyn, NY 11201-8423 | 1926 | Dr. David J. Steinberg | 1-D | 8,096 | 559 |
| Long Island U, C W Post Cmps, Brookville, NY 11548-1300 | 1954 | Dr. David J. Steinberg | 1-D | 8,060 | 950 |
| Long Island U, Southampton Coll, Southampton, NY 11968-9822 | 1963 | Dr. David J. Steinberg | 1-M | 1,410 | 120 |
| Longwood Coll, Farmville, VA 23909-1800 | 1839 | Dr. William F. Dorrill | 5-M | 3,254 | 248 |
| Loras Coll, Dubuque, IA 52004-0178 | 1839 | Dr. Joachim W. Froehlich | 2-M | 1,809 | 132 |
| Louisiana Coll, Pineville, LA 71359-0001 | 1906 | Dr. Robert L. Lynn | 2-B | 1,024 | 92 |
| Louisiana State U and A&M Coll, Baton Rouge, LA 70803-3103 | 1860 | Dr. William E. Davis | 5-D | 25,897 | 1,291 |
| Louisiana State U in Shreveport, Shreveport, LA 71115-2399 | 1965 | Dr. John R. Darling, Jr. | 5-M | 4,233 | 208 |
| Louisiana State U Medical Ctr, New Orleans, LA 70112-2223 | 1931 | Dr. Mervin L. Trail | 5-D | 3,059 | NR |
| Louisiana Tech U, Ruston, LA 71272 | 1894 | Dr. Daniel D. Reneau | 5-D | 9,667 | 456 |
| Lourdes Coll, Sylvania, OH 43560-2898 | 1958 | Sr. Ann Francis Klimkowski, OSF | 2-B | 1,589 | 132 |
| Loyola Coll, Baltimore, MD 21210-2699 | 1852 | Rev. Harold Ridley, S.J. | 2-D | 6,364 | 334 |
| Loyola Marymount U, Los Angeles, CA 90045-8350 | 1911 | Rev. Thomas P. O'Malley, SJ | 2-F | 6,687 | 524 |
| Loyola U Chicago, Chicago, IL 60611-2196 | 1870 | Rev. John J. Piderit, SJ | 2-D | 14,001 | 961 |
| Loyola U New Orleans, New Orleans, LA 70118-6195 | 1912 | Rev. Bernard Patrick Knoth, SJ | 2-F | 5,234 | 417 |
| Lubbock Christian U, Lubbock, TX 79407-2099 | 1957 | Dr. Ken Jones | 2-M | 1,232 | 97 |
| Luther Coll, Decorah, IA 52101-1045 | 1861 | Dr. H. George Anderson | 2-B | 2,386 | 217 |
| Luther Rice Bible Coll and Sem, Lithonia, GA 30038 (2) | 1962 | NR | 2-D | 1,285 | 33 |
| Lycoming Coll, Williamsport, PA 17701-5192 | 1812 | Dr. James E. Douthat | 2-B | 1,469 | 109 |
| Lynchburg Coll, Lynchburg, VA 24501-3199 | 1903 | Dr. Charles O. Warren, Jr. | 2-M | 1,963 | 170 |
| Lyndon State Coll, Lyndonville, VT 05851 | 1911 | Dr. Margaret R. Williams | 5-M | 1,145 | 108 |

| Name, address | Year | Governing official, control, and highest degree offered | | Enroll- ment | Faculty |
|---|---|---|---|---|---|
| Lynn U, Boca Raton, FL 33431-5598 | 1962 | Dr. Donald E. Ross | 1-M | 1,566 | 125 |
| Macalester Coll, St Paul, MN 55105-1899 | 1874 | Dr. Robert M. Gavin, Jr. | 2-B | 1,768 | 208 |
| Madonna U, Livonia, MI 48150-1173 | 1947 | Sr. Mary Francilene | 2-M | 4,109 | 261 |
| Maharishi U of Management, Fairfield, IA 52557-1155 | 1971 | Dr. Bevan Morris | 1-D | 1,025 | 86 |
| Malone Coll, Canton, OH 44709-3897 | 1892 | Dr. Ronald G. Johnson | 2-M | 1,979 | 165 |
| Manchester Coll, North Manchester, IN 46962-1225 | 1889 | Dr. Parker G. Marden | 2-M | 1,010 | 110 |
| Manhattan Coll, Riverdale, NY 10471 | 1853 | Br. Thomas J. Scanlan | 2-M | 3,121 | 266 |
| Manhattanville Coll, Purchase, NY 10577-2132 | 1841 | Mr. Richard A. Berman | 1-M | 1,500 | 207 |
| Mankato State U, Mankato, MN 56002-8400 | 1868 | Dr. Richard R. Rush | 5-M | 13,175 | 715 |
| Mannes Coll of Music, New Sch for Social Research, New York, NY 10024-4402 | 1916 | Dr. Charles Kaufman | 1-M | 265 | 216 |
| Mansfield U of Pennsylvania, Mansfield, PA 16933 | 1857 | Mr. Rod C. Kelchner | 5-M | 2,954 | 201 |
| Marian Coll, Indianapolis, IN 46222-1997 | 1851 | Dr. Daniel A. Felicetti | 2-B | 1,352 | 135 |
| Marian Coll of Fond du Lac, Fond du Lac, WI 54935-4699 | 1936 | Mr. Matthew G. Flanigan | 2-M | 2,492 | 113 |
| Marietta Coll, Marietta, OH 45750-4000 | 1835 | Dr. Lauren R. Wilson | 1-M | 1,167 | 105 |
| Marist Coll, Poughkeepsie, NY 12601-1387 | 1929 | Dr. Dennis J. Murray | 1-M | 4,308 | 450 |
| Marquette U, Milwaukee, WI 53201-1881 | 1881 | Rev. Albert J. DiUlio, SJ | 2-D | 10,774 | 1,011 |
| Marshall U, Huntington, WV 25755-2020 | 1837 | Dr. J. Wade Gilley | 5-D | 12,468 | 827 |
| Mars Hill Coll, Mars Hill, NC 28754 | 1856 | Dr. Fred B. Bentley | 2-B | 1,056 | 123 |
| Mary Baldwin Coll, Staunton, VA 24401 (4) | 1842 | Dr. Cynthia H. Tyson | 2-M | 1,492 | 122 |
| Marycrest International U, Davenport, IA 52804-4096 | 1939 | Dr. Laurence M. Conner | 1-M | 1,049 | 74 |
| Marygrove Coll, Detroit, MI 48221-2599 (4) | 1905 | Dr. John E. Shay, Jr. | 2-M | 1,800 | 59 |
| Marylhurst Coll, Marylhurst, OR 97036-0261 | 1893 | Dr. Nancy A. Wilgenbusch | 2-M | 1,299 | 278 |
| Marymount Coll, Tarrytown, NY 10591-3796 (4) | 1907 | Dr. Brigid Driscoll, RSHM | 1-B | 1,005 | 126 |
| Marymount Manhattan Coll, New York, NY 10021-4597 | 1936 | Dr. Regina Peruggi | 1-B | 1,896 | 207 |
| Marymount U, Arlington, VA 22207-4299 | 1950 | Sr. Eymard Gallagher, RSHM | 2-M | 4,072 | 382 |
| Maryville U of Saint Louis, St Louis, MO 63141-7299 | 1872 | Dr. Keith Lovin | 1-M | 3,378 | 275 |
| Mary Washington Coll, Fredericksburg, VA 22401-5358 | 1908 | Dr. William M. Anderson, Jr. | 5-M | 3,529 | 235 |
| Marywood Coll, Scranton, PA 18509-1598 | 1915 | Sr. Mary Reap, IHM | 2-D | 2,958 | 261 |
| Massachusetts Coll of Art, Boston, MA 02115-5882 | 1873 | Dr. William F. O'Neil | 5-M | 1,479 | 184 |
| Mass Coll of Pharmacy and Allied Health Sciences, Boston, MA 02115-5896 | 1823 | Dr. Sumner M. Robinson | 1-D | 1,451 | 195 |
| Massachusetts Inst of Tech, Cambridge, MA 02139-4307 | 1861 | Dr. Charles M. Vest | 1-D | 9,960 | 960 |
| McKendree Coll, Lebanon, IL 62254-1299 | 1828 | Dr. James M. Dennis | 2-B | 1,618 | 136 |
| McMurry U, Abilene, TX 79697 | 1923 | Dr. Robert E. Shimp | 2-B | 1,457 | 131 |
| McNeese State U, Lake Charles, LA 70609-2495 | 1939 | Dr. Robert D. Hebert | 5-M | 8,444 | 294 |
| Medical Coll of Georgia, Augusta, GA 30912-1003 | 1828 | Dr. Francis J. Tedesco | 5-D | 2,015 | 782 |
| Medical Coll of Pennsylvania & Hahnemann U, Philadelphia, PA 19102 | 1848 | Mr. Sherif Abdelhak | 1-D | 1,736 | 752 |
| Medical U of South Carolina, Charleston, SC 29425-0002 | 1824 | Dr. James B. Edwards | 5-D | 2,209 | 2,462 |
| Mercer U, Macon, GA 31207-0003 | 1833 | Dr. R. Kirby Godsey | 2-F | 6,728 | 683 |
| Mercer U, Cecil B Day Cmps, Atlanta, GA 30341-4155 | 1968 | Dr. R. Kirby Godsey | 2-D | 1,819 | 38 |
| Mercy Coll, Dobbs Ferry, NY 10522-1189 | 1951 | Dr. Jay Sexter | 1-M | 6,792 | 665 |
| Mercyhurst Coll, Erie, PA 16546 | 1926 | Dr. William P. Garvey | 2-M | 2,504 | 156 |
| Meredith Coll, Raleigh, NC 27607-5298 (3) | 1891 | Dr. John E. Weems | 2-M | 2,477 | 215 |
| Merrimack Coll, North Andover, MA 01845-5800 | 1947 | Mr. Richard J. Santagati | 2-B | 2,804 | 178 |
| Mesa State Coll, Grand Junction, CO 81502-2647 | 1925 | Dr. Ray N. Kieft | 5-B | 4,721 | 285 |
| Messiah Coll, Grantham, PA 17027 | 1909 | Dr. Rodney J. Sawatsky | 2-B | 2,428 | 212 |
| Methodist Coll, Fayetteville, NC 28311-1420 | 1956 | Dr. M. Elton Hendricks | 2-B | 1,806 | 100 |
| Metropolitan State Coll of Denver, Denver, CO 80217-3362 | 1963 | Dr. Sheila Kaplan | 5-B | 16,815 | 880 |
| Metropolitan State U, St Paul, MN 55106-5000 | 1971 | Dr. Susan A. Cole | 5-M | 5,175 | 611 |
| Miami U, Oxford, OH 45056 | 1809 | Dr. Paul G. Risser | 12-D | 15,601 | 982 |
| Michigan State U, East Lansing, MI 48824-1020 | 1855 | Mr. M. Peter McPherson | 5-D | 40,647 | 2,630 |
| Michigan Tech U, Houghton, MI 49931-1295 | 1885 | Dr. Curtis J. Tompkins | 5-D | 6,390 | 386 |
| MidAmerica Nazarene Coll, Olathe, KS 66062-1899 | 1966 | Dr. Richard Spindle | 2-M | 1,453 | 124 |
| Middlebury Coll, Middlebury, VT 05753-6002 | 1800 | Dr. John McCardell | 1-D | 2,041 | 251 |
| Middle Tennessee State U, Murfreesboro, TN 37132 | 1911 | Dr. James E. Walker | 5-D | 17,424 | 953 |
| Midland Lutheran Coll, Fremont, NE 68025-4200 | 1883 | Dr. Carl L. Hansen | 2-B | 1,030 | 70 |
| Midwestern State U, Wichita Falls, TX 76308-2096 | 1922 | Dr. Louis J. Rodriguez | 5-M | 5,833 | 277 |
| Miles Coll, Birmingham, AL 35208 | 1905 | Mr. Albert J. H. Sloan, II | 2-B | 1,957 | 56 |
| Millersville U of Pennsylvania, Millersville, PA 17551-0302 | 1855 | Dr. Joseph A. Caputo | 5-M | 7,510 | 427 |
| Millikin U, Decatur, IL 62522-2084 | 1901 | Dr. Curtis L. McCray | 2-B | 1,883 | 208 |
| Millsaps Coll, Jackson, MS 39210-0001 | 1890 | Dr. George M. Harmon | 2-M | 1,430 | 103 |
| Mills Coll, Oakland, CA 94613-1000 (3) | 1852 | Dr. Janet L. Holmgren | 1-M | 1,169 | 141 |
| Milwaukee Sch of Engineering, Milwaukee, WI 53202-3109 | 1903 | Dr. Hermann Viets | 1-M | 3,007 | 203 |
| Minot State U, Minot, ND 58707-0002 | 1913 | Dr. H. Erik Shaar | 5-M | 3,761 | 233 |
| Mississippi Coll, Clinton, MS 39058 | 1826 | Dr. Howell Todd | 2-F | 3,238 | 234 |
| Mississippi State U, Mississippi State, MS 39762 | 1878 | Dr. Donald W. Zacharias | 5-D | 13,577 | 828 |
| Mississippi U for Women, Columbus, MS 39701-9998 (4) | 1884 | Dr. Clyda S. Rent | 5-M | 3,071 | 190 |
| Mississippi Valley State U, Itta Bena, MS 38941-1400 | 1946 | Dr. William W. Sutton | 5-M | 2,153 | 142 |
| Missouri Baptist Coll, St Louis, MO 63141-8698 | 1968 | Dr. R. Alton Lacey | 2-B | 2,193 | 82 |
| Missouri Southern State Coll, Joplin, MO 64801-1595 | 1937 | Dr. Julio Leon | 5-B | 5,461 | 299 |
| Missouri Valley Coll, Marshall, MO 65340-3197 | 1889 | Dr. J. Kenneth Bryant | 2-B | 1,212 | 68 |
| Missouri Western State Coll, St Joseph, MO 64507-2294 | 1915 | Dr. Janet Gorman Murphy | 5-B | 5,167 | 321 |
| Molloy Coll, Rockville Centre, NY 11571-5002 | 1955 | Dr. Janet A. Fitzgerald, OP | 1-M | 2,346 | 278 |
| Monmouth U, West Long Branch, NJ 07764-1898 | 1933 | Dr. Rebecca Stafford | 1-M | 4,482 | 347 |
| Montana State U–Billings, Billings, MT 59101-9984 | 1927 | Dr. Ronald P. Sexton | 5-M | 3,767 | 224 |
| Montana State U–Bozeman, Bozeman, MT 59717 | 1893 | Dr. Michael P. Malone | 5-D | 11,267 | 663 |
| Montana State U–Northern, Havre, MT 59501-7751 | 1929 | Dr. William Daehling | 5-M | 1,680 | 114 |
| Montana Tech of The U of Montana, Butte, MT 59701-8997 | 1895 | Dr. Lindsay D. Norman, Jr. | 5-D | 1,847 | 123 |
| Montclair State U, Upper Montclair, NJ 07043-1624 | 1908 | Dr. Irvin D. Reid | 5-M | 12,830 | 735 |
| Moody Bible Inst, Chicago, IL 60610-3284 | 1886 | Dr. Joseph M. Stowell, III | 2-M | 1,543 | 134 |
| Moorhead State U, Moorhead, MN 56563-0002 | 1885 | Dr. Roland Barden | 5-M | 6,268 | 341 |
| Moravian Coll, Bethlehem, PA 18018-6650 | 1742 | Dr. Roger Harry Martin | 2-M | 1,989 | 154 |
| Morehead State U, Morehead, KY 40351 | 1922 | Dr. Ronald Eaglin | 5-M | 8,454 | 440 |
| Morehouse Coll, Atlanta, GA 30314 (1) | 1867 | Dr. Walter Massey | 1-B | 2,992 | 178 |
| Morgan State U, Baltimore, MD 21239 | 1867 | Dr. Earl Richardson | 5-D | 6,016 | 340 |
| Morningside Coll, Sioux City, IA 51106-1751 | 1894 | Dr. Jerry Israel | 2-M | 1,117 | 127 |
| Morris Brown Coll, Atlanta, GA 30314-4195 | 1881 | Dr. Samuel D. Jolley, Jr. | 2-B | 1,897 | 125 |
| Mount Aloysius Coll, Cresson, PA 16630-1900 | 1939 | Dr. Edward F. Pierce | 2-B | 1,001 | 120 |
| Mount Holyoke Coll, South Hadley, MA 01075-1414 (3) | 1837 | Dr. Joanne V. Creighton | 1-M | 1,957 | 213 |
| Mount Mary Coll, Milwaukee, WI 53222-4597 (3) | 1913 | Ms. Sally Mahoney | 2-M | 1,444 | 166 |
| Mount Mercy Coll, Cedar Rapids, IA 52402-4797 | 1928 | Dr. Thomas R. Feld | 2-B | 1,224 | 104 |
| Mount Saint Mary Coll, Newburgh, NY 12550-3494 | 1960 | Sr. Ann Sakac | 1-M | 1,913 | 169 |
| Mount St Mary's Coll, Los Angeles, CA 90049-1597 (4) | 1925 | Sr. Karen Kennelly | 2-M | 1,974 | 216 |
| Mount Saint Mary's Coll and Sem, Emmitsburg, MD 21727-7799 | 1808 | Mr. George R. Houston, Jr. | 2-M | 1,900 | 159 |
| Mount Union Coll, Alliance, OH 44601-3993 | 1846 | Dr. Harold M. Kolenbrander | 2-B | 1,583 | 104 |

| Name, address | Year | Governing official, control, and highest degree offered | | Enroll-ment | Faculty |
|---|---|---|---|---|---|
| Mount Vernon Nazarene Coll, Mount Vernon, OH 43050-9509 | 1964 | Dr. E. LeBron Fairbanks | 2-M | 1,458 | 77 |
| Muhlenberg Coll, Allentown, PA 18104-5586 | 1848 | Mr. Arthur R. Taylor | 2-B | 1,874 | 181 |
| Murray State U, Murray, KY 42071-0009 | 1922 | Dr. Kern Alexander | 5-M | 8,166 | 358 |
| Muskingum Coll, New Concord, OH 43762 | 1837 | Dr. Samuel W. Speck, Jr. | 2-M | 1,246 | 98 |
| National–Louis U, Evanston, IL 60201-1730 | 1886 | Dr. Orley R. Herron | 1-D | 7,951 | 285 |
| Nazareth Coll of Rochester, Rochester, NY 14618-3790 | 1924 | Dr. Rose Marie Beston | 1-M | 2,802 | 172 |
| Nebraska Wesleyan U, Lincoln, NE 68504-2796 | 1887 | Dr. John W. White, Jr. | 2-B | 1,584 | 153 |
| Neumann Coll, Aston, PA 19014 | 1965 | Dr. Nan B. Hechenberger | 2-M | 1,214 | 138 |
| New Coll of California, San Francisco, CA 94102-5206 | 1971 | Dr. Peter Gabel | 1-F | 1,600 | 90 |
| New Hampshire Coll, Manchester, NH 03106-1045 | 1932 | Dr. Richard A. Gustafson | 1-M | 5,884 | 236 |
| New Jersey Inst of Tech, Newark, NJ 07102-1982 | 1881 | Dr. Saul K. Fenster | 5-D | 7,885 | 530 |
| New Mexico Highlands U, Las Vegas, NM 87701 | 1893 | Mr. Selimo Rael | 5-M | 2,813 | 169 |
| New Mexico Inst of Mining and Tech, Socorro, NM 87801 | 1889 | Dr. Daniel H. Lopez | 5-D | 1,494 | 108 |
| New Mexico State U, Las Cruces, NM 88003-8001 | 1888 | Dr. J. Michael Orenduff | 5-D | 15,127 | 664 |
| New Orleans Baptist Theological Sem, New Orleans, LA 70126-4858 | 1917 | Dr. Landrum P. Leavell, II | 2-D | 1,854 | 18 |
| New Sch Bach of Arts, New Sch for Social Research, New York, NY 10011-8603 | 1919 | Ms. Elizabeth D. Dickey | 1-D | 320 | 820 |
| New York Inst of Tech, Old Westbury, NY 11568-8000 | 1955 | Dr. Matthew Schure | 1-F | 9,380 | 830 |
| New York U, New York, NY 10012-1019 | 1831 | Dr. L. Jay Oliva | 1-D | 35,825 | 3,995 |
| Niagara U, Niagara University, NY 14109 | 1856 | Rev. Paul L. Golden, CM. | 1-M | 2,865 | 206 |
| Nicholls State U, Thibodaux, LA 70310 | 1948 | Dr. Donald J. Ayo | 5-M | 7,366 | 278 |
| Nichols Coll, Dudley, MA 01571 | 1815 | Dr. Lowell C. Smith | 1-M | 1,688 | 47 |
| North Adams State Coll, North Adams, MA 01247-4100 | 1894 | Dr. Thomas D. Aceto | 5-M | 1,650 | 113 |
| North Carolina Ag and Tech State U, Greensboro, NC 27411 | 1891 | Dr. Edward B. Fort | 5-D | 7,846 | 668 |
| North Carolina Central U, Durham, NC 27707-3129 | 1910 | Mr. Julius L. Chambers | 5-F | 5,470 | 405 |
| North Carolina State U, Raleigh, NC 27695 | 1887 | Dr. Larry K. Monteith | 5-D | 27,537 | 2,623 |
| North Central Bible Coll, Minneapolis, MN 55404-1322 | 1930 | Dr. Gordon L. Anderson | 2-B | 1,100 | 64 |
| North Central Coll, Naperville, IL 60566-7063 | 1861 | Dr. Harold R. Wilde | 2-M | 2,489 | 179 |
| North Dakota State U, Fargo, ND 58105 | 1890 | Dr. Thomas Plough | 5-D | 9,676 | 497 |
| Northeastern Illinois U, Chicago, IL 60625-4699 | 1961 | Dr. Salme H. Steinberg | 5-M | 10,386 | 476 |
| Northeastern State U, Tahlequah, OK 74464-2399 | 1846 | Dr. W. Roger Webb | 5-D | 9,273 | 526 |
| Northeastern U, Boston, MA 02115-5096 | 1898 | Dr. John A. Curry | 1-D | 24,605 | 2,169 |
| Northeast Louisiana U, Monroe, LA 71209-0001 | 1931 | Mr. Lawson L. Swearingen, Jr., JD | 5-D | 11,553 | 568 |
| Northern Arizona U, Flagstaff, AZ 86011 | 1899 | Dr. Clara M. Lovett | 5-D | 20,131 | 543 |
| Northern Illinois U, De Kalb, IL 60115-2854 | 1895 | Dr. John E. LaTourette | 5-D | 22,218 | 1,211 |
| Northern Kentucky U, Highland Heights, KY 41099 | 1968 | Dr. Leon E. Boothe | 5-F | 11,671 | 701 |
| Northern Michigan U, Marquette, MI 49855-5301 | 1899 | Dr. William E. Vandament | 5-M | 7,442 | 362 |
| Northern State U, Aberdeen, SD 57401-7198 | 1901 | Dr. John Hutchinson | 5-M | 2,783 | 135 |
| North Georgia Coll, Dahlonega, GA 30597-1001 | 1873 | Dr. Delmas J. Allen | 5-M | 2,973 | 197 |
| North Park Coll, Chicago, IL 60625-4895 | 1891 | Dr. David G. Horner | 2-D | 1,750 | 86 |
| Northwestern Coll, Orange City, IA 51041-1996 | 1882 | Dr. James E. Bultman | 2-B | 1,198 | 95 |
| Northwestern Coll, St Paul, MN 55113-1598 | 1902 | Dr. Donald Ericksen | 2-B | 1,324 | 132 |
| Northwestern Oklahoma State U, Alva, OK 73717-2799 | 1897 | Dr. Joe J. Struckle | 5-M | 1,861 | 115 |
| Northwestern State U of Louisiana, Natchitoches, LA 71497 | 1884 | Dr. Robert A. Alost | 5-D | 9,040 | 333 |
| Northwestern U, Evanston, IL 60208 | 1851 | Dr. Henry S. Bienen | 1-D | 12,196 | 2,330 |
| Northwest Missouri State U, Maryville, MO 64468-6001 | 1905 | Dr. Dean L. Hubbard | 5-M | 6,133 | 274 |
| Northwest Nazarene Coll, Nampa, ID 83686-5897 | 1913 | Dr. Richard Hagood | 2-M | 1,294 | 79 |
| Northwood U, Midland, MI 48640-2398 | 1959 | Dr. David E. Fry | 1-M | 1,355 | 57 |
| Norwich U, Northfield, VT 05663 | 1819 | Dr. Richard Schneider | 1-M | 2,556 | 179 |
| Notre Dame Coll, Manchester, NH 03104-2299 | 1950 | Dr. Carol J. Descoteaux, CSC | 2-M | 1,316 | 90 |
| Nova Southeastern U, Fort Lauderdale, FL 33314-7721 | 1964 | Dr. Ovid C. Lewis | 1-D | 15,000 | 580 |
| Oakland City U, Oakland City, IN 47660-1099 | 1885 | Dr. James W. Murray | 2-M | 1,008 | 104 |
| Oakland U, Rochester, MI 48309-4401 | 1957 | Dr. Gary D. Russi | 5-D | 13,600 | 619 |
| Oakwood Coll, Huntsville, AL 35896 | 1896 | Dr. Benjamin F. Reaves | 2-B | 1,626 | 124 |
| Oberlin Coll, Oberlin, OH 44074-1090 | 1833 | Dr. Nancy Schrom Dye | 1-B | 2,823 | 217 |
| Occidental Coll, Los Angeles, CA 90041-3392 | 1887 | Dr. John B. Slaughter | 1-M | 1,617 | 197 |
| Oglethorpe U, Atlanta, GA 30319-2797 | 1835 | Dr. Donald S. Stanton | 1-M | 1,313 | 108 |
| Ohio Dominican Coll, Columbus, OH 43219-2099 | 1911 | Sr. Mary Andrew Matesich | 2-B | 1,736 | 104 |
| Ohio Northern U, Ada, OH 45810-1599 | 1871 | Dr. DeBow Freed | 2-F | 2,997 | 247 |
| The Ohio State U, Columbus, OH 43210 | 1870 | Dr. E. Gordon Gee | 5-D | 48,676 | 3,724 |
| The Ohio State U at Marion, Marion, OH 43302-5695 | 1958 | Dr. F. Dominic Dottavio | 5-B | 1,171 | 90 |
| The Ohio State U–Lima Cmps, Lima, OH 45804-3576 | 1960 | Dr. Violet I. Meek | 5-B | 1,244 | 88 |
| Ohio State U–Mansfield Cmps, Mansfield, OH 44906-1547 | 1958 | Dr. John O. Riedl, Jr. | 5-B | 1,359 | 72 |
| Ohio State U–Newark Cmps, Newark, OH 43055-1797 | 1957 | Dr. Rafael L. Cortado | 5-B | 1,548 | 102 |
| Ohio U, Athens, OH 45701-2979 | 1804 | Dr. Robert Glidden | 5-D | 19,143 | 1,109 |
| Ohio U–Chillicothe, Chillicothe, OH 45601-0629 | 1946 | Dr. Delbert Meyer | 5-B | 1,776 | 111 |
| Ohio U–Lancaster, Lancaster, OH 43130-1097 | 1968 | Dr. Charles P. Bird | 5-M | 1,547 | 129 |
| Ohio U–Zanesville, Zanesville, OH 43701-2695 | 1946 | Dr. Craig D. Laubenthal | 5-M | 1,210 | 49 |
| Ohio Wesleyan U, Delaware, OH 43015 | 1842 | Dr. Thomas B. Courtice | 2-B | 1,712 | 161 |
| Oklahoma Baptist U, Shawnee, OK 74801-2558 | 1910 | Dr. Bob R. Agee | 2-M | 2,322 | 150 |
| Oklahoma Christian U of Science and Arts, Oklahoma City, OK 73136-1100 | 1950 | Dr. J. Terry Johnson | 2-M | 1,456 | 127 |
| Oklahoma City U, Oklahoma City, OK 73106-1402 | 1904 | Dr. Jerald C. Walker | 2-F | 4,660 | 368 |
| Oklahoma Panhandle State U, Goodwell, OK 73939-0430 | 1909 | Dr. Carl O. Westbrook | 5-B | 1,171 | 73 |
| Oklahoma State U, Stillwater, OK 74078 | 1890 | Dr. James E. Halligan | 5-D | 19,125 | 905 |
| Old Dominion U, Norfolk, VA 23529 | 1930 | Dr. James V. Koch | 5-D | 17,113 | 1,025 |
| Olivet Nazarene U, Kankakee, IL 60901-0592 | 1907 | Dr. John C. Bowling | 2-M | 2,256 | 148 |
| Oral Roberts U, Tulsa, OK 74171-0001 | 1963 | Mr. Richard L. Roberts | 2-D | 3,682 | 223 |
| Oregon Health Sciences U, Portland, OR 97201-3098 | 1974 | Dr. Peter O. Kohler | 12-D | 1,771 | 76 |
| Oregon Inst of Tech, Klamath Falls, OR 97601-8801 | 1947 | Dr. Lawrence J. Wolf | 5-M | 2,441 | 161 |
| Oregon State U, Corvallis, OR 97331 | 1868 | Dr. John V. Byrne | 5-D | 14,161 | 2,164 |
| Orlando Coll, Orlando, FL 32810-5674 | 1953 | Mrs. Ouida B. Kirby | 3-M | 1,500 | 86 |
| Otterbein Coll, Westerville, OH 43081 | 1847 | Dr. C. Brent DeVore | 2-M | 2,478 | 160 |
| Ouachita Baptist U, Arkadelphia, AR 71998-0001 | 1886 | Dr. Ben M. Elrod | 2-B | 1,440 | 141 |
| Our Lady of Holy Cross Coll, New Orleans, LA 70131-7399 | 1916 | Rev. Thomas E. Chambers, CSC | 2-M | 1,367 | 99 |
| Our Lady of the Lake U of San Antonio, San Antonio, TX 78207-4689 | 1895 | Sr. Elizabeth Anne Sueltenfuss | 2-D | 3,277 | 214 |
| Pace U, New York, NY 10038 | 1906 | Dr. Patricia Ewers | 1-D | 12,534 | 995 |
| Pacific Lutheran U, Tacoma, WA 98447 | 1890 | Dr. Loren J. Anderson | 2-M | 3,579 | 314 |
| Pacific Union Coll, Angwin, CA 94508 | 1882 | Dr. D. Malcolm Maxwell | 2-M | 1,640 | 125 |
| Pacific U, Forest Grove, OR 97116-1797 | 1849 | Dr. Faith Gabelnick | 1-F | 1,840 | 176 |
| Palm Beach Atlantic Coll, West Palm Beach, FL 33416-4708 | 1968 | Dr. Paul R. Corts | 2-M | 1,953 | 147 |
| Palmer Coll of Chiropractic, Davenport, IA 52803-5287 | 1895 | Dr. Virgil V. Strang | 1-F | 1,971 | 128 |
| Park Coll, Parkville, MO 64152-4358 | 1875 | Dr. Donald J. Breckon | 2-M | 1,180 | 117 |

| Name, address | Year | Governing official, control, and highest degree offered | | Enroll-ment | Faculty |
|---|---|---|---|---|---|
| Parsons Sch of Design, New Sch for Social Research, New York, NY 10011-8878 | 1896 | Mr. Charles S. Olton | 1-M | 1,933 | 407 |
| Penn State U at Erie, The Behrend Coll, Erie, PA 16563 | 1948 | Dr. John M. Lilley | 12-M | 3,208 | 204 |
| Penn State U at Harrisburg—The Capital Coll, Middletown, PA 17057-4898 | 1966 | Dr. John G. Bruhn | 12-D | 3,510 | 216 |
| Penn State U Univ Park Cmps, University Park, PA 16802-1503 | 1855 | Dr. Graham B. Spanier | 12-D | 39,646 | 2,186 |
| Pepperdine U, Malibu, CA 90263-0001 | 1937 | Dr. David Davenport | 2-D | 7,833 | 303 |
| Peru State Coll, Peru, NE 68421 | 1867 | Dr. Robert L. Burns | 5-M | 1,739 | 67 |
| Pfeiffer U, Misenheimer, NC 28109-0960 | 1885 | Dr. Zane E. Eargle | 2-M | 1,214 | 91 |
| Philadelphia Coll of Bible, Langhorne, PA 19047-2990 | 1913 | Dr. W. Sherrill Babb | 2-M | 1,124 | 134 |
| Philadelphia Coll of Pharmacy and Science, Philadelphia, PA 19104-4495 | 1821 | Dr. Philip P. Gerbino | 1-D | 2,021 | 205 |
| Philadelphia Coll of Textiles and Science, Philadelphia, PA 19144-5497 | 1884 | Dr. James P. Gallagher | 1-M | 3,386 | 164 |
| Pittsburg State U, Pittsburg, KS 66762-5880 | 1903 | Dr. Tom W. Bryant | 5-M | 6,565 | 293 |
| Plymouth State Coll of the U System of NH, Plymouth, NH 03264-1600 | 1871 | Dr. Donald P. Wharton | 5-M | 4,000 | 200 |
| Point Loma Nazarene Coll, San Diego, CA 92106-2899 | 1902 | Dr. Jim L. Bond | 2-M | 2,459 | 240 |
| Point Park Coll, Pittsburgh, PA 15222-1984 | 1960 | Dr. J. Matthew Simon | 1-M | 2,298 | 207 |
| Polytechnic U, Brooklyn Cmps, Brooklyn, NY 11201-2990 | 1854 | Dr. David C. Chang | 1-D | 2,258 | 293 |
| Pomona Coll, Claremont, CA 91711 | 1887 | Dr. Peter W. Stanley | 1-B | 1,402 | 164 |
| Pontifical Catholic U of Puerto Rico, Ponce, PR 00731-6382 | 1948 | Rev. F. Tosello Giangiacomo | 2-M | 11,786 | 580 |
| Portland State U, Portland, OR 97207-0751 | 1946 | Dr. Judith Ramaley | 5-D | 14,348 | 672 |
| Prairie View A&M U, Prairie View, TX 77446-0188 | 1878 | Dr. Charles A. Hines | 5-M | 5,999 | 329 |
| Pratt Inst, Brooklyn, NY 11205-3899 | 1887 | Dr. Thomas F. Schutte | 1-M | 3,363 | 502 |
| Presbyterian Coll, Clinton, SC 29325 | 1880 | Dr. Kenneth B. Orr | 2-B | 1,186 | 118 |
| Princeton U, Princeton, NJ 08544-1019 | 1746 | Mr. Harold T. Shapiro | 1-D | 6,419 | 886 |
| Providence Coll, Providence, RI 02918 | 1917 | Rev. Philip A. Smith, OP | 2-D | 5,493 | 373 |
| Purchase Coll, State U of NY, Purchase, NY 10577-1400 | 1967 | Mr. Bill Lacy | 5-M | 2,492 | 282 |
| Purdue U, West Lafayette, IN 47907-1968 | 1869 | Dr. Steven C. Beering | 5-D | 34,685 | 2,220 |
| Purdue U Calumet, Hammond, IN 46323-2094 | 1951 | Dr. James Yackel | 5-M | 8,975 | 457 |
| Purdue U North Central, Westville, IN 46391-9543 | 1967 | Dr. Dale W. Alspaugh | 5-M | 3,259 | 233 |
| Queens Coll, Charlotte, NC 28274-0002 | 1857 | Dr. Billy O. Wireman | 2-M | 1,557 | 106 |
| Queens Coll of the City U of New York, Flushing, NY 11367-1597 | 1937 | Dr. Allen Lee Sessoms | 11-M | 17,552 | 988 |
| Quincy U, Quincy, IL 62301-2699 | 1860 | Rev. James Toal, OFM | 2-M | 1,105 | 99 |
| Quinnipiac Coll, Hamden, CT 06518-1904 | 1929 | Dr. John L. Lahey | 1-F | 5,117 | 333 |
| Radford U, Radford, VA 24142 | 1910 | Dr. Douglas Covington | 5-M | 8,687 | 536 |
| Ramapo Coll of New Jersey, Mahwah, NJ 07430-1681 | 1969 | Dr. Robert A. Scott | 5-M | 4,037 | 286 |
| Randolph-Macon Coll, Ashland, VA 23005-5505 | 1830 | Dr. Ladell Payne | 2-B | 1,091 | 152 |
| Reed Coll, Portland, OR 97202-8199 | 1909 | Dr. Steven Koblik | 1-M | 1,290 | 126 |
| Regis Coll, Weston, MA 02193-1571 (3) | 1927 | Dr. Sheila Megley, RSM | 2-M | 1,336 | 121 |
| Regis U, Denver, CO 80221-1099 | 1877 | Rev. Michael J. Sheeran, SJ | 2-M | 6,806 | 89 |
| Rensselaer Polytechnic Inst, Troy, NY 12180-3590 | 1824 | Dr. R. Byron Pipes | 1-D | 6,400 | 342 |
| Research Coll of Nursing–Rockhurst Coll, Kansas City, MO 64110 | 1980 | Dr. Nancy O. DeBasio | 1-B | 2,140 | 46 |
| Rhode Island Coll, Providence, RI 02908-1924 | 1854 | Dr. John Nazarian | 5-M | 9,900 | 502 |
| Rhode Island Sch of Design, Providence, RI 02903-2784 | 1877 | Mr. Roger Mandle | 1-M | 1,987 | 302 |
| Rhodes Coll, Memphis, TN 38112-1690 | 1848 | Dr. James H. Daughdrill, Jr. | 2-M | 1,441 | 147 |
| Rice U, Houston, TX 77005 | 1912 | Dr. Malcolm Gillis | 1-D | 4,051 | 570 |
| The Richard Stockton Coll of New Jersey, Pomona, NJ 08240-9988 | 1971 | Dr. Vera King Farris | 5-B | 5,367 | 287 |
| Rider U, Lawrenceville, NJ 08648-3001 | 1865 | Dr. J. Barton Luedeke | 1-M | 4,941 | 483 |
| Rivier Coll, Nashua, NH 03060-5086 | 1933 | Sr. Jeanne Perreault | 2-M | 2,798 | 190 |
| Roanoke Coll, Salem, VA 24153-3794 | 1842 | Dr. David M. Gring | 2-B | 1,750 | 171 |
| Robert Morris Coll, Chicago, IL 60601-2501 | 1913 | Mr. Michael Viollt | 1-B | 3,100 | 210 |
| Robert Morris Coll, Coraopolis, PA 15108-1189 | 1921 | Dr. Edward A. Nicholson | 1-M | 5,282 | 289 |
| Roberts Wesleyan Coll, Rochester, NY 14624-1997 | 1866 | Dr. William C. Crothers | 2-M | 1,267 | 115 |
| Rochester Inst of Tech, Rochester, NY 14623-5604 | 1829 | Dr. Albert J. Simone | 1-D | 12,600 | 1,095 |
| Rockford Coll, Rockford, IL 61108-2393 | 1847 | Dr. William A. Shields | 1-M | 1,468 | 135 |
| Rockhurst Coll, Kansas City, MO 64110-2561 | 1910 | Rev. Thomas J. Savage, SJ | 2-M | 2,886 | 224 |
| Roger Williams U, Bristol, RI 02809 | 1948 | Mr. Anthony J. Santoro | 1-F | 2,230 | 202 |
| Rollins Coll, Winter Park, FL 32789-4499 | 1885 | Dr. Rita Bornstein | 1-M | 3,281 | 257 |
| Roosevelt U, Chicago, IL 60605-1394 | 1945 | Dr. Theodore L. Gross | 1-M | 4,494 | 508 |
| Rosary Coll, River Forest, IL 60305-1099 | 1901 | Ms. Donna M. Carroll | 2-M | 1,862 | 116 |
| Rose-Hulman Inst of Tech, Terre Haute, IN 47803-3920 | 1874 | Dr. Samuel F. Hulbert | 1-M | 1,520 | 120 |
| Rowan Coll of New Jersey, Glassboro, NJ 08028-1701 | 1923 | Dr. Herman D. James | 5-M | 8,936 | 349 |
| Rush U, Chicago, IL 60612-3832 | 1969 | Dr. Leo M. Henikoff | 1-D | 1,453 | 170 |
| Russell Sage Coll, Troy, NY 12180-4115 (3) | 1916 | Dr. Jeanne K. Neff | 1-B | 1,115 | 113 |
| Rutgers, State U of NJ, Camden Coll of Arts & Scis, Camden, NJ 08102 | 1927 | Dr. Robert A. Catlin | 5-B | 2,361 | NR |
| Rutgers, State U of NJ, Coll of Engineering, Piscataway, NJ 08855-0909 | 1864 | Dr. Ellis H. Dill | 5-B | 2,278 | NR |
| Rutgers, State U of NJ, Coll of Nursing, Newark, NJ 07102-1896 | 1956 | Dr. Dorothy J. DeMaio | 5-D | 371 | NR |
| Rutgers, State U of NJ, Coll of Pharmacy, Piscataway, NJ 08855-0789 | 1927 | Dr. John Louis Colaizzi | 5-D | 983 | NR |
| Rutgers, State U of NJ, Cook Coll, New Brunswick, NJ 08903-0231 | 1921 | Dr. Daryl B. Lund | 5-B | 3,147 | NR |
| Rutgers, State U of NJ, Douglass Coll, New Brunswick, NJ 08903-0270 (3) | 1918 | Dr. Martha A. Cotter | 5-B | 2,973 | NR |
| Rutgers, State U of NJ, Livingston Coll, New Brunswick, NJ 08903 | 1969 | Dr. Arnold G. Hyndman | 5-B | 3,149 | NR |
| Rutgers, State U of NJ, Mason Gross Sch of Arts, New Brunswick, NJ 08903-0270 | 1976 | Dr. Marilyn F. Somville | 5-D | 682 | NR |
| Rutgers, State U of NJ, Newark Coll of Arts & Scis, Newark, NJ 07102-1896 | 1946 | Dr. David Hosford | 5-B | 3,726 | NR |
| Rutgers, State U of NJ, Rutgers Coll, New Brunswick, NJ 08903-2101 | 1766 | Dr. Carl Kirschner | 5-B | 9,573 | NR |
| Rutgers, State U of NJ, U Coll–Camden, Camden, NJ 08102-1401 | 1950 | Dr. Robert A. Catlin | 5-B | 729 | NR |
| Rutgers, State U of NJ, U Coll–Newark, Newark, NJ 07102-1896 | 1934 | Dr. David Hosford | 5-B | 1,915 | NR |
| Rutgers, State U of NJ, U Coll–New Brunswick, New Brunswick, NJ 08903 | 1934 | Dr. Amy Cohen | 5-B | 2,979 | NR |
| Sacred Heart U, Fairfield, CT 06432-1000 | 1963 | Dr. Anthony J. Cernera | 2-M | 5,545 | 349 |
| Saginaw Valley State U, University Center, MI 48710 | 1963 | Dr. Eric R. Gilbertson | 5-M | 7,300 | 394 |
| St Ambrose U, Davenport, IA 52803-2898 | 1882 | Dr. Edward J. Rogalski | 2-M | 2,680 | 200 |
| Saint Anselm Coll, Manchester, NH 03102-1310 | 1889 | Rev. Jonathan DeFelice, OSB | 2-B | 1,910 | 164 |

| Name, address | Year | Governing official, control, and highest degree offered | | Enrollment | Faculty |
|---|---|---|---|---|---|
| Saint Augustine's Coll, Raleigh, NC 27610-2298 | 1867 | Dr. Bernard W. Franklin | 2-B | 1,700 | 92 |
| St Bonaventure U, St Bonaventure, NY 14778-2284 | 1858 | Dr. Robert J. Wickenheiser | 2-M | 2,591 | 117 |
| St Cloud State U, St Cloud, MN 56301-4498 | 1869 | Dr. Bruce Grube | 5-D | 14,128 | 635 |
| St Edward's U, Austin, TX 78704-6489 | 1885 | Dr. Patricia Hayes | 2-M | 3,134 | 243 |
| St Francis Coll, Brooklyn Heights, NY 11201-4398 | 1884 | Br. Donald Sullivan, OSF | 1-B | 2,095 | 154 |
| Saint Francis Coll, Loretto, PA 15940-0600 | 1847 | Rev. Christian R. Oravec | 2-M | 1,886 | 182 |
| St John Fisher Coll, Rochester, NY 14618-3597 | 1948 | Dr. William L. Pickett | 2-M | 2,045 | 164 |
| Saint John's U, Collegeville, MN 56321 (1) | 1857 | Br. Dietrich Reinhart, OSB | 2-M | 1,820 | 177 |
| St John's U, Jamaica, NY 11439 | 1870 | Rev. Donald J. Harrington, CM | 2-D | 17,820 | 1,012 |
| Saint Joseph Coll, West Hartford, CT 06117-2700 (3) | 1932 | Dr. Winifred E. Coleman | 2-M | 1,916 | 173 |
| Saint Joseph's Coll, Standish, ME 04084-5263 | 1912 | Dr. Loring E. Hart | 2-M | 1,087 | 96 |
| St Joseph's Coll, New York, Brooklyn, NY 11205-3688 | 1916 | Sr. George Aquin O'Connor | 1-B | 1,216 | 130 |
| St Joseph's Coll, Suffolk Cmps, Patchogue, NY 11772-2399 | 1916 | Sr. George Aquin O'Connor | 1-M | 2,490 | 335 |
| Saint Joseph's U, Philadelphia, PA 19131-1395 | 1851 | Rev. Nicholas S. Rashford, SJ | 2-M | 6,938 | 380 |
| St Lawrence U, Canton, NY 13617-1455 | 1856 | Dr. Patti McGill Peterson | 1-M | 2,106 | 181 |
| Saint Leo Coll, Saint Leo, FL 33574-2008 | 1889 | Msgr. Frank Mouch | 2-M | 1,461 | 113 |
| Saint Louis U, St Louis, MO 63103-2097 | 1818 | Rev. Lawrence Biondi, SJ | 2-D | 10,719 | 2,928 |
| Saint Mary-of-the-Woods Coll, Saint Mary-of-the-Woods, IN 47876 (3) | 1840 | Dr. Barbara Doherty, SP | 2-M | 1,292 | 55 |
| Saint Mary's Coll, Notre Dame, IN 46556 (3) | 1844 | Dr. William A. Hickey | 2-B | 1,579 | 184 |
| Saint Mary's Coll of California, Moraga, CA 94575 | 1863 | Br. Mel Anderson, FSC | 2-M | 4,318 | 207 |
| St Mary's Coll of Maryland, St Mary's City, MD 20686 | 1840 | Dr. Edward T. Lewis | 5-B | 1,443 | 162 |
| Saint Mary's U of Minnesota, Winona, MN 55987-1399 | 1912 | Br. Louis DeThomasis, FSC | 2-M | 8,075 | 535 |
| St Mary's U of San Antonio, San Antonio, TX 78228-8507 | 1852 | Rev. John Moder, SM | 2-D | 4,171 | 312 |
| Saint Michael's Coll, Colchester, VT 05439 | 1904 | Dr. Paul J. Reiss | 2-M | 2,474 | 189 |
| St Norbert Coll, De Pere, WI 54115-2099 | 1898 | Dr. Thomas A. Manion | 2-M | 2,135 | 163 |
| St Olaf Coll, Northfield, MN 55057-1098 | 1874 | Dr. Mark U. Edwards, Jr. | 2-B | 2,936 | 394 |
| Saint Peter's Coll, Jersey City, NJ 07306 | 1872 | Rev. James N. Loughran, SJ | 2-M | 3,654 | 369 |
| St Thomas Aquinas Coll, Sparkill, NY 10976 | 1952 | Dr. Margaret M. Fitzpatrick, SC | 1-M | 1,692 | 115 |
| St Thomas U, Miami, FL 33054-6459 | 1961 | Rev. Msgr. Franklyn M. Casale | 2-F | 2,500 | 133 |
| Saint Vincent Coll, Latrobe, PA 15650 | 1846 | Rev. John F. Murtha, OSB | 2-M | 1,182 | 104 |
| Saint Xavier U, Chicago, IL 60655-3105 | 1847 | Dr. Richard Yanikoski | 2-M | 4,442 | 261 |
| Salem State Coll, Salem, MA 01970-5353 | 1854 | Dr. Nancy D. Harrington | 5-M | 10,132 | 409 |
| Salisbury State U, Salisbury, MD 21801-6837 | 1925 | Dr. Thomas E. Bellavance | 5-M | 6,010 | 369 |
| Salve Regina U, Newport, RI 02840-4192 | 1934 | Dr. Therese Antone, RSM | 2-D | 1,943 | 192 |
| Samford U, Birmingham, AL 35229-0002 | 1841 | Dr. Thomas E. Corts | 2-F | 4,630 | 450 |
| Sam Houston State U, Huntsville, TX 77341-2448 | 1879 | Dr. Martin J. Anisman | 5-D | 12,439 | 514 |
| San Diego State U, San Diego, CA 92182 | 1897 | Dr. Thomas B. Day | 5-D | 28,724 | 2,228 |
| San Francisco State U, San Francisco, CA 94132-1722 | 1899 | Dr. Robert A. Corrigan | 5-M | 26,791 | 1,437 |
| Santa Clara U, Santa Clara, CA 95053-0001 | 1851 | Rev. Paul L. Locatelli, SJ | 2-D | 7,654 | 555 |
| Sarah Lawrence Coll, Bronxville, NY 10708 | 1926 | Dr. Alice Stone Ilchman | 1-M | 1,279 | 227 |
| Savannah Coll of Art and Design, Savannah, GA 31401-3146 | 1978 | Mr. Richard G. Rowan | 1-M | 2,770 | 145 |
| Savannah State U, Savannah, GA 31404 | 1890 | Dr. John T. Wolfe, Jr. | 5-B | 3,211 | 155 |
| Sch of the Art Inst of Chicago, Chicago, IL 60603-3103 | 1866 | Dr. Carol Becker | 1-M | 2,976 | 373 |
| Sch of Visual Arts, New York, NY 10010-3994 | 1947 | Mr. David Rhodes | 3-M | 3,082 | 650 |
| Seattle Pacific U, Seattle, WA 98119-1997 | 1891 | Dr. Philip W. Eaton | 2-D | 3,437 | 211 |
| Seattle U, Seattle, WA 98122 | 1891 | Rev. William J. Sullivan, SJ | 2-D | 5,988 | 334 |
| Seton Hall U, South Orange, NJ 07079-2697 | 1856 | Rev. Thomas R. Peterson, OP | 2-D | 8,693 | 778 |
| Shawnee State U, Portsmouth, OH 45662-4344 | 1986 | Dr. Clive Veri | 5-B | 3,216 | 239 |
| Shaw U, Raleigh, NC 27601-2399 | 1865 | Dr. Talbert O. Shaw | 2-B | 2,492 | 262 |
| Shenandoah U, Winchester, VA 22601-5195 | 1875 | Dr. James A. Davis | 2-M | 1,751 | 223 |
| Shepherd Coll, Shepherdstown, WV 25443 | 1871 | Dr. Michael P. Riccards | 5-B | 3,602 | 257 |
| Shippensburg U of Pennsylvania, Shippensburg, PA 17257-2299 | 1871 | Dr. Anthony F. Ceddia | 5-M | 6,601 | 373 |
| Shorter Coll, Rome, GA 30165-4298 | 1873 | Dr. Larry Lee McSwain | 2-B | 1,390 | 73 |
| Siena Coll, Loudonville, NY 12211-1462 | 1937 | Fr. William McConville, OFM | 2-M | 3,288 | 230 |
| Siena Heights Coll, Adrian, MI 49221-1796 | 1919 | Dr. Richard Artman | 2-M | 1,130 | 110 |
| Silver Lake Coll, Manitowoc, WI 54220-9319 | 1869 | Sr. Barbara Belinske | 2-M | 1,078 | 128 |
| Simmons Coll, Boston, MA 02115 (3) | 1899 | Dr. Daniel Cheever | 1-D | 3,614 | 364 |
| Simpson Coll, Indianola, IA 50125-1297 | 1860 | Dr. Stephen G. Jennings | 2-B | 1,685 | 153 |
| Skidmore Coll, Saratoga Springs, NY 12866-1632 | 1903 | Dr. David H. Porter | 1-M | 2,183 | 262 |
| Slippery Rock U of Pennsylvania, Slippery Rock, PA 16057 | 1889 | Dr. Robert Aebersold | 5-D | 7,493 | 408 |
| Smith Coll, Northampton, MA 01063 (3) | 1871 | Ms. Ruth Simmons | 1-D | 3,184 | 292 |
| Sonoma State U, Rohnert Park, CA 94928-3609 | 1960 | Dr. Ruben Arminana | 5-M | 6,778 | 433 |
| South Carolina State U, Orangeburg, SC 29117-0001 | 1896 | Dr. Barbara R. Hatton | 5-D | 4,993 | 229 |
| South Dakota Sch of Mines and Tech, Rapid City, SD 57701-3995 | 1885 | Dr. Richard J. Gowen | 5-D | 2,356 | 145 |
| South Dakota State U, Brookings, SD 57007 | 1881 | Dr. Robert T. Wagner | 5-D | 8,840 | NR |
| Southeastern Coll of the Assemblies of God, Lakeland, FL 33801-6099 | 1935 | Dr. James Hennesy | 2-B | 1,065 | 86 |
| Southeastern Louisiana U, Hammond, LA 70402 | 1925 | Dr. G. Warren Smith | 5-M | 14,344 | 606 |
| Southeastern Oklahoma State U, Durant, OK 74701-0609 | 1909 | Dr. Larry Williams | 5-M | 3,912 | 201 |
| Southeast Missouri State U, Cape Girardeau, MO 63701-4799 | 1873 | Dr. Kala M. Stroup | 5-M | 8,118 | 436 |
| Southern Arkansas U–Magnolia, Magnolia, AR 71753 | 1909 | Dr. Steven G. Gamble | 5-M | 2,660 | 221 |
| Southern California Coll, Costa Mesa, CA 92626-6597 | 1920 | Mr. Wayne E. Kraiss | 2-M | 1,200 | 51 |
| Southern Coll of Seventh-day Adventists, Collegedale, TN 37315-0370 | 1892 | Dr. Donald R. Sahly | 2-B | 1,591 | 125 |
| Southern Coll of Tech, Marietta, GA 30060-2896 | 1948 | Dr. Stephen R. Cheshier | 5-M | 3,778 | 197 |
| Southern Connecticut State U, New Haven, CT 06515-1355 | 1893 | Mr. Michael J. Adanti | 5-M | 11,591 | 719 |
| Southern Illinois U at Carbondale, Carbondale, IL 62901-6806 | 1869 | Dr. John C. Guyon | 5-D | 22,418 | 1,539 |
| Southern Illinois U at Edwardsville, Edwardsville, IL 62026-0001 | 1957 | Mr. Ted Sanders | 5-F | 11,047 | 755 |
| Southern Methodist U, Dallas, TX 75275 | 1911 | Dr. R. Gerald Turner | 2-D | 9,172 | 649 |
| Southern Nazarene U, Bethany, OK 73008-2694 | 1899 | Dr. Loren P. Gresham | 2-M | 1,834 | 119 |
| Southern Oregon State Coll, Ashland, OR 97520 | 1926 | Dr. Stephen Reno | 5-M | 4,530 | 279 |
| Southern U and A&M Coll, Baton Rouge, LA 70813 | 1880 | Dr. Marvin L. Yates | 5-D | 9,800 | 603 |
| Southern U at New Orleans, New Orleans, LA 70126-1009 | 1959 | Dr. Robert B. Gex | 5-M | 4,500 | 235 |
| Southern Utah U, Cedar City, UT 84720-2498 | 1897 | Dr. Gerald R. Sherratt | 5-M | 5,159 | 216 |
| Southern Wesleyan U, Central, SC 29630-1020 | 1906 | Dr. David J. Spittal | 2-M | 1,271 | 40 |
| Southwest Baptist U, Bolivar, MO 65613-2597 | 1878 | Dr. Roy Blunt | 2-M | 3,072 | 220 |
| Southwestern Adventist Coll, Keene, TX 76059 | 1894 | Dr. Marvin E. Anderson | 2-M | 1,001 | 80 |
| Southwestern Assemblies of God U, Waxahachie, TX 75165-2342 | 1927 | Dr. Delmer Guynes | 2-B | 1,142 | 28 |
| Southwestern Oklahoma State U, Weatherford, OK 73096-3098 | 1901 | Dr. Joe Anna Hibler | 5-M | 4,623 | 240 |
| Southwestern U, Georgetown, TX 78626 | 1840 | Dr. Roy B. Shilling, Jr. | 2-B | 1,261 | 144 |
| Southwest Missouri State U, Springfield, MO 65804-0094 | 1905 | Dr. John H. Keiser | 5-M | 16,439 | 816 |
| Southwest State U, Marshall, MN 56258-3306 | 1963 | Dr. Doug Sweetland | 5-M | 2,753 | 117 |
| Southwest Texas State U, San Marcos, TX 78666 | 1899 | Dr. Jerome Supple | 5-M | 20,917 | 915 |
| Spalding U, Louisville, KY 40203-2188 | 1814 | Dr. Thomas R. Oates | 2-D | 1,342 | 134 |
| Spelman Coll, Atlanta, GA 30314-4399 (3) | 1881 | Dr. Johnnetta B. Cole | 1-B | 1,961 | 209 |
| Spring Arbor Coll, Spring Arbor, MI 49283-9799 | 1873 | Dr. M. Allen Carden | 2-M | 1,052 | 90 |
| Springfield Coll, Springfield, MA 01109-3797 | 1885 | Dr. Randolph W. Bromery | 1-D | 2,961 | 232 |

| Name, address | Year | Governing official, control, and highest degree offered | | Enroll-ment | Faculty |
|---|---|---|---|---|---|
| Spring Hill Coll, Mobile, AL 36608-1791 | 1830 | Rev. William J. Rewak, SJ | 2-M | 1,331 | 103 |
| Stanford U, Stanford, CA 94305-9991 | 1891 | Mr. Gerhard Casper | 1-D | 14,044 | 1,455 |
| State U of NY at Binghamton, Binghamton, NY 13902-6000 | 1946 | Dr. Lois B. DeFleur | 5-D | 11,952 | 690 |
| State U of NY at Buffalo, Buffalo, NY 14260 | 1846 | Mr. William R. Greiner | 5-D | 24,493 | 1,693 |
| State U of NY at New Paltz, New Paltz, NY 12561-2499 | 1828 | Dr. Alice Chandler | 5-M | 7,897 | 600 |
| State U of NY at Oswego, Oswego, NY 13126 | 1861 | Dr. Stephen Weber | 5-M | 8,734 | 432 |
| State U of NY at Stony Brook, Stony Brook, NY 11794 | 1957 | Dr. Shirley Strum Kenny | 5-D | 17,658 | 1,607 |
| State U of NY Coll at Brockport, Brockport, NY 14420-2997 | 1867 | Dr. John E. Van de Wetering | 5-M | 9,047 | 513 |
| State U of NY Coll at Buffalo, Buffalo, NY 14222-1095 | 1867 | Dr. F. C. Richardson | 5-M | 11,349 | 616 |
| State U of NY Coll at Cortland, Cortland, NY 13045 | 1868 | Dr. Judson H. Taylor | 5-M | 6,224 | 441 |
| State U of NY Coll at Fredonia, Fredonia, NY 14063 | 1826 | Dr. Donald A. MacPhee | 5-M | 4,721 | 295 |
| State U of NY Coll at Geneseo, Geneseo, NY 14454-1401 | 1871 | Dr. Christopher Dahl | 5-M | 5,719 | 333 |
| State U of NY Coll at Old Westbury, Old Westbury, NY 11568-0210 | 1965 | Dr. L. Eudora Pettigrew | 5-B | 3,925 | 232 |
| State U of NY Coll at Oneonta, Oneonta, NY 13820 | 1889 | Dr. Alan B. Donovan | 5-M | 5,568 | 346 |
| State U of NY Coll at Plattsburgh, Plattsburgh, NY 12901 | 1889 | Dr. Horace A. Judson | 5-M | 5,590 | 363 |
| State U of NY Coll at Potsdam, Potsdam, NY 13676 | 1816 | Dr. William Merwin | 5-M | 4,102 | 271 |
| State U of NY Coll of Environ Sci and Forestry, Syracuse, NY 13210-2779 | 1911 | Dr. Ross S. Whaley | 5-D | 1,772 | 127 |
| State U of NY Empire State Coll, Saratoga Springs, NY 12866-4391 | 1971 | Dr. James W. Hall | 5-M | 7,246 | 329 |
| State U of NY Health Science Ctr at Brooklyn, Brooklyn, NY 11203-2098 | 1858 | Dr. Russell L. Miller | 5-D | 1,604 | 156 |
| State U of NY Health Science Ctr at Syracuse, Syracuse, NY 13210-2334 | 1950 | Dr. Gregory L. Eastwood | 5-D | 1,130 | 45 |
| State U of NY Inst of Tech at Utica/Rome, Utica, NY 13504-3050 | 1966 | Dr. Peter J. Cayan | 5-M | 2,578 | 163 |
| State U of West Georgia, Carrollton, GA 30118 | 1933 | Dr. Beheruz N. Sethna | 5-M | 8,650 | 356 |
| Stephen F Austin State U, Nacogdoches, TX 75962 | 1923 | Dr. Daniel D. Angel | 5-D | 11,758 | 679 |
| Stetson U, DeLand, FL 32720-3781 | 1883 | Dr. H. Douglas Lee | 1-F | 2,897 | 197 |
| Stevens Inst of Tech, Hoboken, NJ 07030 | 1870 | Dr. Harold J. Raveche | 1-D | 2,639 | 195 |
| Stonehill Coll, North Easton, MA 02357-0001 | 1948 | Rev. Bartley MacPhaidin, CSC | 2-B | 1,993 | 189 |
| Strayer Coll, Washington, DC 20005-2603 | 1892 | Mr. Ron K. Bailey | 3-M | 7,419 | 458 |
| Suffolk U, Boston, MA 02108-2770 | 1906 | Mr. David J. Sargent | 1-D | 6,156 | 531 |
| Sullivan Coll, Louisville, KY 40232 | 1864 | Mr. A.R. Sullivan | 3-B | 2,167 | 86 |
| Sul Ross State U, Alpine, TX 79832 | 1920 | Dr. R. Vic Morgan | 5-M | 2,458 | 53 |
| Susquehanna U, Selinsgrove, PA 17870-1001 | 1858 | Dr. Joel L. Cunningham | 2-B | 1,568 | 145 |
| Swarthmore Coll, Swarthmore, PA 19081-1397 | 1864 | Dr. Alfred H. Bloom | 1-B | 1,353 | 182 |
| Syracuse U, Syracuse, NY 13244-0003 | 1870 | Dr. Kenneth A. Shaw | 1-D | 14,636 | 1,343 |
| Tarleton State U, Stephenville, TX 76402 | 1899 | Dr. Dennis P. McCabe | 5-M | 6,532 | 329 |
| Taylor U, Upland, IN 46989-1001 | 1846 | Dr. Jay L. Kesler | 2-B | 1,829 | 140 |
| Teikyo Post U, Waterbury, CT 06723-2540 | 1890 | Dr. Phyllis C. DeLeo | 1-B | 1,724 | 166 |
| Temple U, Philadelphia, PA 19122 | 1884 | Mr. Peter J. Liacouras | 12-D | 26,477 | 2,483 |
| Tennessee State U, Nashville, TN 37209-1561 | 1912 | Dr. James A. Hefner | 5-D | 8,464 | 491 |
| Tennessee Tech U, Cookeville, TN 38505 | 1915 | Dr. Angelo A. Volpe | 5-D | 8,166 | 509 |
| Texas A&M International U, Laredo, TX 78041 | 1969 | Dr. Leo Sayavedra | 5-M | 2,510 | 129 |
| Texas A&M U, College Station, TX 77843-1244 | 1876 | Dr. Ray M. Bowen | 5-D | 41,790 | 2,358 |
| Texas A&M U at Galveston, Galveston, TX 77553-1675 | 1962 | Dr. David J. Schmidly | 5-B | 1,241 | 86 |
| Texas A&M U–Commerce, Commerce, TX 75429-3011 | 1889 | Dr. Jerry D. Morris | 5-D | 7,674 | 384 |
| Texas A&M U–Corpus Christi, Corpus Christi, TX 78412-5503 | 1947 | Dr. Robert R. Furgason | 5-D | 5,545 | 343 |
| Texas A&M U–Kingsville, Kingsville, TX 78363 | 1925 | Dr. Manuel L. Ibanez | 5-D | 6,047 | 337 |
| Texas Christian U, Fort Worth, TX 76129-0002 | 1873 | Dr. William E. Tucker | 2-D | 7,050 | 499 |
| Texas Lutheran U, Seguin, TX 78155-5999 | 1891 | Dr. Jon Moline | 2-B | 1,248 | 94 |
| Texas Southern U, Houston, TX 77004-4584 | 1947 | Dr. Joann Horton | 5-D | 9,518 | 524 |
| Texas Tech U, Lubbock, TX 79409 | 1923 | Dr. Robert W. Lawless | 5-D | 24,185 | 954 |
| Texas Wesleyan U, Fort Worth, TX 76105-1536 | 1890 | Dr. Jake B. Schrum | 2-F | 2,811 | 223 |
| Texas Woman's U, Denton, TX 76204 (4) | 1901 | Dr. Carol Surles | 5-D | 9,852 | 763 |
| Thiel Coll, Greenville, PA 16125-2181 | 1866 | Dr. C. Carlyle Haaland | 2-B | 1,008 | 107 |
| Thomas Edison State Coll, Trenton, NJ 08608-1176 | 1972 | Dr. George A. Pruitt | 5-M | 8,500 | 346 |
| Thomas Jefferson U, Philadelphia, PA 19107 | 1824 | Dr. Paul C. Brucker | 1-M | 1,533 | 83 |
| Thomas More Coll, Crestview Hills, KY 41017-3495 | 1921 | Rev. William F. Cleves | 2-M | 1,345 | 127 |
| Tiffin U, Tiffin, OH 44883-2161 | 1888 | Dr. George Kidd, Jr. | 1-M | 1,135 | 70 |
| Tougaloo Coll, Tougaloo, MS 39174 | 1869 | NR | 2-B | 1,105 | 91 |
| Touro Coll, New York, NY 10010 | 1971 | Dr. Bernard Lander | 1-F | 8,876 | 810 |
| Towson State U, Towson, MD 21204-7097 | 1866 | Dr. Hoke L. Smith | 5-M | 14,643 | 955 |
| Trevecca Nazarene U, Nashville, TN 37210-2834 | 1901 | Dr. Millard Reed | 2-M | 1,537 | 81 |
| Trinity Coll, Hartford, CT 06106-3100 | 1823 | Dr. Evan S. Dobelle | 1-M | 2,142 | 260 |
| Trinity Coll, Washington, DC 20017-1094 (3) | 1897 | Ms. Patricia A. McGuire | 2-M | 1,486 | 129 |
| Trinity Coll of Vermont, Burlington, VT 05401-1470 (4) | 1925 | Sr. Janice Ryan | 2-M | 1,084 | 113 |
| Trinity U, San Antonio, TX 78212-7200 | 1869 | Dr. Ronald K. Calgaard | 2-M | 2,482 | 265 |
| Tri-State U, Angola, IN 46703-1764 | 1884 | Dr. R. John Reynolds | 1-B | 1,172 | 97 |
| Troy State U, Troy, AL 36082 | 1887 | Dr. Jack Hawkins, Jr. | 5-M | 5,420 | 349 |
| Troy State U at Dothan, Dothan, AL 36304-0368 | 1961 | Dr. Thomas Harrison | 5-M | 2,500 | 144 |
| Troy State U Montgomery, Montgomery, AL 36103-4419 | 1957 | Dr. Glenda S. McGaha | 5-M | 3,360 | 187 |
| Truman State U, Kirksville, MO 63501-4221 | 1867 | Dr. Jack Magruder | 5-M | 6,287 | 382 |
| Tufts U, Medford, MA 02155 | 1852 | Dr. John A. DiBiaggio | 1-D | 8,097 | 1,093 |
| Tulane U, New Orleans, LA 70118-5669 | 1834 | Dr. Eamon M. Kelly | 1-D | 11,158 | 728 |
| Tusculum Coll, Greeneville, TN 37743-9997 | 1794 | Dr. Robert E. Knott | 2-M | 1,508 | 129 |
| Tuskegee U, Tuskegee, AL 36088 | 1881 | Dr. Benjamin F. Payton | 1-F | 3,100 | 298 |
| Union Coll, Barbourville, KY 40906-1499 | 1879 | Dr. Jack C. Phillips | 2-M | 1,104 | 65 |
| Union Coll, Schenectady, NY 12308-2311 | 1795 | Dr. Roger H. Hull | 1-D | 2,330 | 200 |
| The Union Inst, Cincinnati, OH 45206-1947 | 1964 | Dr. Robert T. Conley | 1-D | 1,740 | 122 |
| Union U, Jackson, TN 38305 | 1823 | Dr. David Dockery | 2-M | 1,973 | 157 |
| United States Air Force Acad, USAF Academy, CO 80840-5025 | 1954 | Lt. Gen. Paul E. Stein | 4-B | 4,117 | 547 |
| United States International U, San Diego, CA 92131-1799 | 1952 | Dr. Garry D. Hays | 1-D | 1,307 | 111 |
| United States Military Acad, West Point, NY 10996 | 1802 | Lt. Gen. Howard D. Graves | 4-B | 4,091 | 529 |
| United States Naval Acad, Annapolis, MD 21402-5000 | 1845 | Adm. Charles Larson | 4-B | 4,080 | 650 |
| Universidad Metropolitana, Río Piedras, PR 00928-1150 | 1980 | Dr. Rene L. Labarca Bonnet | 1-M | 3,200 | NR |
| Universidad Politécnica de Puerto Rico, Hato Rey, PR 00919 | 1966 | Mr. Ernesto Vazquez-Barquet | 1-M | 4,600 | 264 |
| U at Albany, State U of NY, Albany, NY 12222-0001 | 1844 | Dr. Karen R. Hitchcock | 5-D | 14,412 | 1,039 |
| U of Akron, Akron, OH 44325-0001 | 1870 | Dr. Peggy Gordon Elliott | 5-D | 25,098 | 1,737 |
| The U of Alabama, Tuscaloosa, AL 35487 | 1831 | Dr. E. Roger Sayers | 5-D | 18,513 | 995 |
| The U of Alabama at Birmingham, Birmingham, AL 35294 | 1969 | Dr. J. Claude Bennett | 5-D | 16,452 | 1,874 |
| The U of Alabama in Huntsville, Huntsville, AL 35899 | 1950 | Dr. Frank Franz | 5-D | 7,264 | 469 |
| U of Alaska Anchorage, Anchorage, AK 99508-8060 | 1954 | Mr. Edward Lee Gorcuch | 5-M | 13,002 | 1,259 |
| U of Alaska Fairbanks, Fairbanks, AK 99775-7480 | 1917 | Dr. Joan K. Wadlow | 5-D | 7,840 | 717 |
| U of Alaska Southeast, Juneau, AK 99801-8625 | 1972 | Dr. Marshall Lind | 5-M | 2,512 | 134 |
| U of Arizona, Tucson, AZ 85721 | 1885 | Dr. Manuel T. Pacheco | 5-D | 34,777 | 1,588 |

| Name, address | Year | Governing official, control, and highest degree offered | | Enroll-ment | Faculty |
|---|---|---|---|---|---|
| U of Arkansas, Fayetteville, AR 72701-1201 | 1871 | Dr. Daniel E. Ferritor | 5-D | 14,692 | 884 |
| U of Arkansas at Little Rock, Little Rock, AR 72204-1099 | 1927 | Dr. Charles E. Hathaway | 5-D | 11,035 | 740 |
| U of Arkansas at Monticello, Monticello, AR 71656 | 1909 | Dr. Fred J. Taylor | 5-M | 2,051 | 126 |
| U of Arkansas at Pine Bluff, Pine Bluff, AR 71601-2799 | 1873 | Dr. Lawrence A. Davis, Jr. | 5-M | 3,242 | 213 |
| U of Arkansas for Medical Sciences, Little Rock, AR 72205-7199 | 1879 | Dr. Harry P. Ward | 5-D | 1,791 | NR |
| U of Baltimore, Baltimore, MD 21201-5779 | 1925 | Dr. H. Mebane Turner | 5-F | 5,004 | 317 |
| U of Bridgeport, Bridgeport, CT 06601 | 1927 | Dr. Richard L. Robenstein | 1-D | 1,915 | 246 |
| U of California, Berkeley, Berkeley, CA 94720 | 1868 | Dr. Chang-Lin Tien | 5-D | 29,630 | 1,787 |
| U of California, Davis, Davis, CA 95616 | 1905 | Larry N. Vanderhoef | 5-D | 23,092 | 1,548 |
| U of California, Irvine, Irvine, CA 92697 | 1965 | Ms. Laurel L. Wilkening | 5-D | 17,281 | 997 |
| U of California, Los Angeles, Los Angeles, CA 90095 | 1919 | Dr. Charles E. Young | 5-D | 34,713 | 3,275 |
| U of California, Riverside, Riverside, CA 92521-0102 | 1954 | Dr. Raymond L. Orbach | 5-D | 8,906 | 725 |
| U of California, San Diego, La Jolla, CA 92093-5003 | 1959 | Dr. Richard C. Atkinson | 5-D | 18,324 | 1,359 |
| U of California, Santa Barbara, Santa Barbara, CA 93106 | 1909 | Dr. Henry T. Yang | 5-D | 18,224 | 849 |
| U of California, Santa Cruz, Santa Cruz, CA 95064 | 1965 | Dr. Karl S. Pister | 5-D | 9,923 | 530 |
| U of Central Arkansas, Conway, AR 72035-0001 | 1907 | Dr. Winfred L. Thompson | 5-M | 8,882 | 614 |
| U of Central Florida, Orlando, FL 32816 | 1963 | Dr. John C. Hitt | 5-D | 26,174 | 1,278 |
| U of Central Oklahoma, Edmond, OK 73034-5209 | 1890 | Mr. George Nigh | 5-M | 15,334 | 692 |
| U of Central Texas, Killeen, TX 76540-1416 | 1973 | Dr. Jack W. Fuller | 1-M | 1,005 | 57 |
| The U of Charleston, Charleston, WV 25304-1099 | 1888 | Dr. Edwin H. Welch | 1-M | 1,322 | 115 |
| U of Chicago, Chicago, IL 60637-1513 | 1891 | Mr. Hugo F. Sonneschein | 1-D | 11,875 | 1,312 |
| U of Cincinnati, Cincinnati, OH 45221 | 1819 | Dr. Joseph A. Steger | 5-D | 18,373 | 953 |
| U of Colorado at Boulder, Boulder, CO 80309 | 1876 | Dr. Judith E. N. Albino | 5-D | 24,440 | 1,350 |
| U of Colorado at Colorado Springs, Colorado Springs, CO 80933-7150 | 1965 | Dr. Linda Bunnell Shade | 5-D | 5,871 | 379 |
| U of Colorado at Denver, Denver, CO 80217-3364 | 1912 | Mr. John Buechner | 5-D | 9,557 | 564 |
| U of Colorado Health Sciences Ctr, Denver, CO 80262 | 1883 | Dr. Vincent A. Fulginiti | 5-D | 2,260 | 1,094 |
| U of Connecticut, Storrs, CT 06269 | 1881 | Dr. Harry J. Hartley | 5-D | 15,735 | 1,123 |
| U of Dallas, Irving, TX 75062-4799 | 1955 | Dr. Robert F. Sasseen | 2-D | 2,746 | 188 |
| U of Dayton, Dayton, OH 45469-1611 | 1850 | Br. Raymond L. Fitz, SM | 2-D | 9,906 | 781 |
| U of Delaware, Newark, DE 19716 | 1743 | Dr. David P. Roselle | 12-D | 17,892 | 1,009 |
| U of Denver, Denver, CO 80208 | 1864 | Mr. Daniel Ritchie | 1-D | 8,515 | 409 |
| U of Detroit Mercy, Detroit, MI 48219-0900 | 1877 | Sr. Maureen A. Fay, OP | 2-D | 7,524 | 566 |
| U of Evansville, Evansville, IN 47722-0002 | 1854 | Dr. James S. Vinson | 2-M | 3,185 | 183 |
| The U of Findlay, Findlay, OH 45840-3653 | 1882 | Dr. Kenneth E. Zirkle | 2-M | 3,316 | 250 |
| U of Florida, Gainesville, FL 32611-8140 | 1853 | Dr. John V. Lombardi | 5-D | 39,439 | 2,225 |
| U of Georgia, Athens, GA 30602 | 1785 | Dr. Charles B. Knapp | 5-D | 30,149 | 2,179 |
| U of Great Falls, Great Falls, MT 59405 | 1932 | Dr. Frederick W. Gilliard | 2-M | 1,426 | 99 |
| U of Guam, Mangilao, GU 96923 | 1952 | Dr. John C. Salas | 7-M | 3,654 | 230 |
| U of Hartford, West Hartford, CT 06117-1500 | 1877 | Dr. Humphrey Tonkin | 1-D | 7,022 | 714 |
| U of Hawaii at Manoa, Honolulu, HI 96822 | 1907 | Dr. Kenneth P. Mortimer | 5-D | 18,300 | 1,454 |
| U of Houston, Houston, TX 77204 | 1927 | Dr. Glenn A. Goerke | 5-D | 30,757 | 1,960 |
| U of Houston–Clear Lake, Houston, TX 77058-1098 | 1974 | Dr. Glenn A. Goerke | 5-M | 7,095 | 384 |
| U of Houston–Downtown, Houston, TX 77002-1001 | 1974 | Dr. Max Castillo | 5-B | 7,676 | 363 |
| U of Houston–Victoria, Victoria, TX 77901-4450 | 1973 | Dr. Karen S. Haynes | 5-M | 1,548 | 85 |
| U of Idaho, Moscow, ID 83844 | 1889 | Dr. Thomas O. Bell | 5-D | 11,727 | 625 |
| U of Illinois at Chicago, Chicago, IL 60607 | 1946 | Dr. David C. Broski | 5-D | 24,589 | 2,606 |
| U of Illinois at Springfield, Springfield, IL 62794-9243 | 1969 | Dr. Naomi B. Lynn | 5-M | 4,702 | 237 |
| U of Illinois at Urbana-Champaign, Champaign, IL 61820-5711 | 1867 | Dr. Michael Aiken | 5-D | 36,465 | 2,119 |
| U of Indianapolis, Indianapolis, IN 46227-3697 | 1902 | Dr. G. Benjamin Lantz, Jr. | 2-M | 3,891 | 276 |
| The U of Iowa, Iowa City, IA 52242 | 1847 | Dr. Peter E. Nathan | 5-D | 27,597 | 1,803 |
| U of Kansas, Lawrence, KS 66045 | 1866 | Dr. Robert E. Hemenway | 5-D | 27,639 | 2,035 |
| U of Kentucky, Lexington, KY 40506-0032 | 1865 | Dr. Charles T. Wethington, Jr. | 5-D | 23,794 | 2,160 |
| U of La Verne, La Verne, CA 91750-4443 | 1891 | Dr. Stephen Morgan | 1-D | 2,541 | 356 |
| U of Louisville, Louisville, KY 40292-0001 | 1798 | Dr. John W. Shumaker | 5-D | 21,218 | 1,757 |
| U of Maine, Orono, ME 04469-5703 | 1865 | Dr. Frederick E. Hutchinson | 5-D | 9,996 | 647 |
| U of Maine at Farmington, Farmington, ME 04938-1911 | 1863 | Dr. Theodora J. Kalikow | 5-B | 2,178 | 154 |
| U of Maine at Presque Isle, Presque Isle, ME 04769-2888 | 1903 | Dr. W. Michael Easton | 5-B | 1,290 | 106 |
| U of Mary, Bismarck, ND 58504-9652 | 1959 | Sr. Thomas Welder | 2-M | 1,776 | 118 |
| U of Mary Hardin-Baylor, Belton, TX 76513 | 1845 | Dr. Jerry G. Bawcom | 2-M | 2,270 | 156 |
| U of Maryland Baltimore County, Baltimore, MD 21228-5398 | 1963 | Dr. Freeman A. Hrabowski | 5-D | 10,467 | 696 |
| U of Maryland Coll Park, College Park, MD 20742 | 1856 | Dr. William E. Kirwan | 5-D | 30,646 | 1,638 |
| U of Maryland Eastern Shore, Princess Anne, MD 21853 | 1886 | Dr. William P. Hytche | 5-D | 2,878 | 193 |
| U of Maryland U Coll, College Park, MD 20742-1600 | 1947 | Dr. T. Benjamin Massey | 5-M | 34,981 | 1,421 |
| U of Massachusetts Amherst, Amherst, MA 01003-0001 | 1863 | Dr. David K. Scott | 5-D | 22,916 | 1,273 |
| U of Massachusetts Boston, Boston, MA 02125-3393 | 1964 | Dr. Jean F. MacCormack | 5-D | 10,109 | 835 |
| U of Massachusetts Dartmouth, North Dartmouth, MA 02747-2300 | 1895 | Dr. Peter H. Cressy | 5-D | 5,443 | 414 |
| U of Massachusetts Lowell, Lowell, MA 01854-2881 | 1894 | Dr. William T. Hogan | 5-D | 12,731 | 615 |
| The U of Memphis, Memphis, TN 38152 | 1912 | Dr. V. Lane Rawlins | 5-D | 19,977 | 1,162 |
| U of Miami, Coral Gables, FL 33124 | 1925 | Mr. Edward T. Foote, II | 1-D | 13,541 | 2,386 |
| U of Michigan, Ann Arbor, MI 48109 | 1817 | Dr. James J. Duderstadt | 5-D | 36,687 | 3,520 |
| U of Michigan–Dearborn, Dearborn, MI 48128-1491 | 1959 | Dr. James C. Renick | 5-M | 7,534 | 383 |
| U of Michigan–Flint, Flint, MI 48502-2186 | 1956 | Dr. Charlie Nelms | 5-M | 6,236 | 242 |
| U of Minnesota, Duluth, Duluth, MN 55812-2496 | 1947 | Dr. Kathryn A. Martin | 5-M | 7,525 | 437 |
| U of Minnesota, Morris, Morris, MN 56267 | 1959 | Dr. David C. Johnson | 5-B | 1,952 | 142 |
| U of Minnesota, Twin Cities Cmps, Minneapolis, MN 55455-0213 | 1851 | Dr. Nils Hasselmo | 5-D | 36,995 | 2,953 |
| U of Mississippi, University, MS 38677 | 1844 | NR | 5-D | 10,181 | 526 |
| U of Mississippi Medical Ctr, Jackson, MS 39216-4505 | 1955 | Dr. A. Wallace Conerly | 5-D | 1,817 | 644 |
| U of Missouri–Columbia, Columbia, MO 65211 | 1839 | Dr. Charles A. Kiesler | 5-D | 22,313 | 1,599 |
| U of Missouri–Kansas City, Kansas City, MO 64110-2499 | 1929 | Dr. Eleanor B. Schwartz | 5-D | 10,209 | 642 |
| U of Missouri–Rolla, Rolla, MO 65401-0249 | 1870 | Dr. John T. Park | 5-D | 5,426 | 386 |
| U of Missouri–St Louis, St Louis, MO 63121-4499 | 1963 | Dr. Blanche M. Touhill | 5-D | 12,223 | 970 |
| U of Mobile, Mobile, AL 36663-0220 | 1961 | Dr. Michael A. Magnoli | 2-M | 2,156 | 141 |
| The U of Montana–Missoula, Missoula, MT 59812-0002 | 1893 | Dr. George M. Dennison | 5-D | 11,753 | 640 |
| U of Montevallo, Montevallo, AL 35115 | 1896 | Dr. Robert M. McChesney | 5-M | 3,236 | 206 |
| U of Nebraska at Kearney, Kearney, NE 68849-0001 | 1903 | Dr. Gladys Styles Johnston | 5-M | 7,620 | 422 |
| U of Nebraska at Omaha, Omaha, NE 68182 | 1908 | Dr. Del D. Weber | 5-D | 15,216 | 782 |
| U of Nebraska–Lincoln, Lincoln, NE 68588 | 1869 | Dr. Joan Leitzel | 5-D | 24,320 | 1,516 |
| U of Nebraska Medical Ctr, Omaha, NE 68198-0001 | 1869 | Dr. Carol A. Aschenbrener | 5-D | 2,765 | 1,003 |
| U of Nevada, Las Vegas, Las Vegas, NV 89154-9900 | 1957 | Dr. Carol Harter | 5-D | 20,257 | 1,138 |
| U of Nevada, Reno, Reno, NV 89557 | 1874 | Dr. Joseph N. Crowley | 5-D | 11,459 | 616 |
| U of New England, Biddeford, ME 04005-9526 | 1953 | Dr. Sandra Featherman | 1-F | 1,782 | 179 |
| U of New Hampshire, Durham, NH 03824 | 1866 | Mr. Walter R. Peterson | 5-D | 12,414 | 876 |
| U of New Haven, West Haven, CT 06516-1916 | 1920 | Dr. Lawrence J. DeNardis | 1-D | 5,438 | 546 |
| U of New Mexico, Albuquerque, NM 87131-2039 | 1889 | Dr. Richard E. Peck | 5-D | 24,431 | 2,006 |
| U of New Orleans, New Orleans, LA 70148 | 1958 | Dr. Gregory M. St.L. O'Brien | 5-D | 15,483 | 739 |
| U of North Alabama, Florence, AL 35632-0001 | 1872 | Mr. Robert L. Potts | 5-M | 5,437 | 269 |
| U of North Carolina at Asheville, Asheville, NC 28804-3299 | 1927 | Dr. Patsy Reed | 5-M | 3,222 | 256 |

| Name, address | Year | Governing official, control, and highest degree offered | | Enroll-ment | Faculty |
|---|---|---|---|---|---|
| U of North Carolina at Chapel Hill, Chapel Hill, NC 27599 | 1789 | Dr. Michael K. Hooker | 5-D | 24,439 | 2,538 |
| U of North Carolina at Charlotte, Charlotte, NC 28223-0001 | 1946 | Dr. James H. Woodward, Jr. | 5-D | 15,895 | 893 |
| U of North Carolina at Greensboro, Greensboro, NC 27412-0001 | 1891 | Dr. Patricia A. Sullivan | 5-D | 12,644 | 700 |
| U of North Carolina at Pembroke, Pembroke, NC 28372-1510 | 1887 | Dr. Joseph B. Oxendine | 5-M | 3,000 | 214 |
| U of North Carolina at Wilmington, Wilmington, NC 28403-3201 | 1947 | Dr. James R. Leutze | 5-M | 8,601 | 485 |
| U of North Dakota, Grand Forks, ND 58202 | 1883 | Dr. Kendall Baker | 5-D | 11,512 | 737 |
| U of Northern Colorado, Greeley, CO 80639 | 1890 | Dr. Herman D. Lujan | 5-D | 10,352 | 552 |
| U of Northern Iowa, Cedar Falls, IA 50614 | 1876 | Dr. Constantine W. Curris | 5-D | 12,802 | 855 |
| U of North Florida, Jacksonville, FL 32224-2645 | 1965 | Dr. Adam W. Herbert | 5-D | 10,463 | 569 |
| U of North Texas, Denton, TX 76203-6737 | 1890 | Dr. Alfred F. Hurley | 5-D | 25,114 | 1,005 |
| U of Notre Dame, Notre Dame, IN 46556 | 1842 | Rev. Edward A. Malloy, CSC | 2-D | 10,000 | 924 |
| U of Oklahoma, Norman, OK 73019 | 1890 | Mr. David L. Boren | 5-D | 19,964 | 1,022 |
| U of Oklahoma Health Sciences Ctr, Oklahoma City, OK 73190 | 1890 | Dr. Jay H. Stein | 5-D | 2,960 | 961 |
| U of Oregon, Eugene, OR 97403 | 1872 | Mr. David Frohnmayer | 5-D | 17,138 | 825 |
| U of Osteopathic Medicine and Health Sciences, Des Moines, IA 50312-4104 | 1898 | Dr. David Marker | 1-F | 1,350 | 108 |
| U of Pennsylvania, Philadelphia, PA 19104 | 1740 | Dr. Judith Rodin | 1-D | 22,148 | 3,853 |
| U of Phoenix, Phoenix, AZ 85072-2069 | 1976 | Mr. William Gibbs | 3-M | 27,139 | 3,407 |
| U of Pittsburgh, Pittsburgh, PA 15261 | 1787 | Dr. Mark A. Nordenberg | 12-D | 26,083 | 3,410 |
| U of Pittsburgh at Bradford, Bradford, PA 16701-2812 | 1963 | Dr. Richard E. McDowell | 12-B | 1,200 | 109 |
| U of Pittsburgh at Greensburg, Greensburg, PA 15601-5860 | 1963 | Dr. George F. Chambers | 12-B | 1,387 | 90 |
| U of Pittsburgh at Johnstown, Johnstown, PA 15904-2990 | 1927 | Dr. Albert L. Etheridge | 12-B | 3,149 | 195 |
| U of Portland, Portland, OR 97203-5798 | 1901 | Rev. David T. Tyson, CSC | 2-M | 2,331 | 205 |
| U of Puerto Rico, Aguadilla Regional Coll, Aguadilla, PR 00604-0160 | 1972 | Prof. Juana Segarra Jaramillo | 6-B | 2,730 | 133 |
| U of Puerto Rico at Arecibo, Arecibo, PR 00613 | 1967 | Prof. Juan Ramirez Silva | 6-B | 4,531 | 256 |
| U of Puerto Rico at Ponce, Ponce, PR 00732-7186 | 1970 | Ms. Betsabe Perez | 6-B | 3,556 | 181 |
| U of Puerto Rico, Cayey U Coll, Cayey, PR 00737 | 1967 | Jose Luis Monserrate | 6-B | 3,571 | 199 |
| U of Puerto Rico, Humacao U Coll, Humacao, PR 00791 | 1962 | Dr. Roberto Marrero | 6-B | 4,228 | 261 |
| U of Puerto Rico Medical Sciences Cmps, San Juan, PR 00936-5067 | 1950 | Dr. Jorge L. Sanchez | 6-D | 2,881 | 759 |
| U of Puget Sound, Tacoma, WA 98416-0005 | 1888 | Dr. Susan Resneck Pierce | 1-M | 3,073 | 234 |
| U of Redlands, Redlands, CA 92373-0999 | 1907 | Dr. James R. Appleton | 1-M | 3,723 | 661 |
| U of Rhode Island, Kingston, RI 02881 | 1892 | Dr. Robert L. Carothers | 5-D | 13,698 | 665 |
| U of Richmond, Richmond, VA 23173 | 1830 | Dr. Richard L. Morrill | 2-F | 4,320 | 400 |
| U of Rio Grande, Rio Grande, OH 45674 | 1876 | Dr. Barry M. Dorsey | 1-M | 2,057 | 135 |
| U of Rochester, Rochester, NY 14627-0001 | 1850 | Mr. Thomas H. Jackson | 1-D | 8,120 | 1,376 |
| U of St Thomas, St Paul, MN 55105-1089 | 1885 | Rev. Dennis Dease | 2-D | 10,421 | 622 |
| U of St Thomas, Houston, TX 77006-4694 | 1947 | Dr. Joseph M. McFadden | 2-D | 2,502 | 201 |
| U of San Diego, San Diego, CA 92110-2492 | 1949 | Dr. Alice B. Hayes | 2-D | 6,416 | 508 |
| U of San Francisco, San Francisco, CA 94117-1080 | 1855 | Rev. John P. Schlegel, SJ | 2-D | 7,833 | 741 |
| U of Science and Arts of Oklahoma, Chickasha, OK 73018-0001 | 1908 | Dr. Roy Troutt | 5-B | 1,649 | 74 |
| U of Scranton, Scranton, PA 18510-4622 | 1888 | Rev. J. A. Panuska, SJ | 2-M | 4,931 | 405 |
| U of South Alabama, Mobile, AL 36688-0002 | 1963 | Dr. Frederick P. Whiddon | 5-D | 12,254 | 863 |
| U of South Carolina, Columbia, SC 29208 | 1801 | Dr. John M. Palms | 5-D | 26,346 | 1,379 |
| U of South Carolina–Aiken, Aiken, SC 29801-6309 | 1961 | Dr. Robert E. Alexander | 5-M | 3,256 | 241 |
| U of South Carolina–Spartanburg, Spartanburg, SC 29303-4932 | 1967 | Dr. John C. Stockwell | 5-M | 3,420 | 225 |
| U of South Dakota, Vermillion, SD 57069-2390 | 1862 | Dr. Betty Turner Asher | 5-D | 7,329 | 527 |
| U of Southern California, Los Angeles, CA 90089 | 1880 | Dr. Steven B. Sample | 1-D | 27,589 | 2,601 |
| U of Southern Colorado, Pueblo, CO 81001-4901 | 1933 | Dr. Robert Shirley | 5-M | 4,331 | 278 |
| U of Southern Indiana, Evansville, IN 47712-3590 | 1965 | Dr. H. Ray Hoops | 5-M | 7,666 | 406 |
| U of Southern Maine, Portland, ME 04104-9300 | 1878 | Dr. Richard L. Pattenaude | 5-F | 9,721 | 525 |
| U of Southern Mississippi, Hattiesburg, MS 39406-5001 | 1910 | Dr. Aubrey K. Lucas | 5-D | 12,113 | 631 |
| U of South Florida, Tampa, FL 33620-9951 | 1956 | Mrs. Betty Castor | 5-D | 36,146 | 1,652 |
| U of Southwestern Louisiana, Lafayette, LA 70504 | 1898 | Dr. Ray P. Authement | 5-D | 16,902 | 677 |
| The U of Tampa, Tampa, FL 33606-1490 | 1931 | Dr. Ronald L. Vaughn | 1-M | 2,529 | 148 |
| U of Tennessee at Chattanooga, Chattanooga, TN 37403-2598 | 1886 | Dr. Frederick W. Obear | 5-M | 8,331 | 551 |
| The U of Tennessee at Martin, Martin, TN 38238-1000 | 1927 | Dr. Margaret N. Perry | 5-M | 5,812 | 287 |
| U of Tennessee, Knoxville, Knoxville, TN 37996 | 1794 | Dr. William T. Snyder | 5-D | 25,704 | 1,579 |
| U of Tennessee, Memphis, Memphis, TN 38163-0002 | 1911 | Mr. William R. Rice | 5-D | 2,080 | 914 |
| The U of Texas at Arlington, Arlington, TX 76019-0407 | 1895 | Dr. Robert E. Witt | 5-D | 22,121 | 1,253 |
| The U of Texas at Austin, Austin, TX 78712 | 1883 | Dr. Robert M. Berdahl | 5-D | 47,905 | 2,367 |
| The U of Texas at Brownsville, Brownsville, TX 78520-4991 | 1973 | Dr. Juliete Garcia | 5-M | 2,473 | 390 |
| The U of Texas at Dallas, Richardson, TX 75083-0688 | 1969 | Dr. Franklyn G. Jenifer | 5-D | 9,008 | 395 |
| The U of Texas at El Paso, El Paso, TX 79968-0001 | 1913 | Dr. Diana Natalicio | 5-D | 16,275 | 819 |
| The U of Texas at San Antonio, San Antonio, TX 78249 | 1969 | Dr. Samuel A. Kirkpatrick | 5-D | 17,389 | 783 |
| The U of Texas at Tyler, Tyler, TX 75799-0001 | 1971 | Dr. George F. Hamm | 5-M | 3,789 | 219 |
| U of Texas Health Science Ctr at San Antonio, San Antonio, TX 78284-6200 | 1976 | Dr. John P. Howe, III | 5-D | 2,828 | 1,213 |
| U of Texas-Houston Health Science Ctr, Houston, TX 77225-0036 | 1943 | Dr. M. David Low | 5-D | 3,097 | 1,046 |
| U of Texas Medical Branch at Galveston, Galveston, TX 77555 | 1891 | Dr. Thomas N. James | 5-D | 2,249 | 1,213 |
| The U of Texas of the Permian Basin, Odessa, TX 79762-0001 | 1969 | Dr. Charles A. Sorber | 5-M | 2,315 | 120 |
| The U of Texas–Pan American, Edinburg, TX 78539-2999 | 1927 | Dr. Miguel A. Nevarez | 5-D | 13,360 | 478 |
| U of Texas Southwestern Medical Ctr at Dallas, Dallas, TX 75235-9002 | 1943 | Dr. C. Kern Wildenthal | 5-D | 1,687 | 100 |
| U of the Arts, Philadelphia, PA 19102-4944 | 1870 | Mr. Peter Solmssen | 1-M | 1,343 | 264 |
| U of the District of Columbia, Washington, DC 20008-1175 | 1976 | Dr. Tilden J. LeMelle | 9-M | 9,660 | 615 |
| U of the Incarnate Word, San Antonio, TX 78209-6397 | 1881 | Dr. Louis J. Agnese, Jr. | 2-M | 3,076 | 268 |
| U of the Pacific, Stockton, CA 95211-0197 | 1851 | Donald DeRosa | 1-D | 4,174 | 348 |
| U of the South, Sewanee, TN 37383-1000 | 1857 | Dr. Samuel R. Williamson | 2-D | 1,322 | 146 |
| U of the State of NY, Regents Coll, Albany, NY 12203-5159 | 1970 | Mr. C. Wayne Williams | 1-B | 19,443 | NR |
| U of the Virgin Islands, Charlotte Amalie, St Thomas, VI 00802-9990 | 1962 | Dr. Orville Kean | 7-M | 3,054 | 321 |
| U of Toledo, Toledo, OH 43606-3398 | 1872 | Dr. Frank E. Horton | 5-D | 21,991 | 1,450 |
| U of Tulsa, Tulsa, OK 74104-3189 | 1894 | Dr. Robert W. Lawless | 2-D | 4,386 | 405 |
| U of Utah, Salt Lake City, UT 84112 | 1850 | Dr. Arthur K. Smith | 5-D | 25,423 | 1,475 |
| U of Vermont, Burlington, VT 05405-0160 | 1791 | Mr. Thomas P. Salmon | 5-D | 9,111 | 1,002 |
| U of Virginia, Charlottesville, VA 22903 | 1819 | Mr. John T. Casteen, III | 5-D | 18,055 | 2,022 |
| U of Washington, Seattle, WA 98195 | 1861 | Dr. Richard McCormick | 5-D | 33,996 | 3,852 |
| The U of West Alabama, Livingston, AL 35470 | 1835 | Dr. Donald C. Hines | 5-M | 2,320 | 120 |
| U of West Florida, Pensacola, FL 32514-5750 | 1963 | Dr. Morris L. Marx | 5-D | 8,000 | 214 |
| U of Wisconsin–Eau Claire, Eau Claire, WI 54702-4004 | 1916 | Dr. Larry Schnack | 5-M | 10,319 | 521 |
| U of Wisconsin–Green Bay, Green Bay, WI 54311-7001 | 1968 | Dr. Mark L. Perkins | 5-M | 5,190 | 284 |
| U of Wisconsin–La Crosse, La Crosse, WI 54601-3742 | 1909 | Dr. Judith L. Kuipers | 5-M | 8,787 | 446 |
| U of Wisconsin–Madison, Madison, WI 53706-1380 | 1848 | Dr. David Ward | 5-D | 37,890 | 2,475 |
| U of Wisconsin–Milwaukee, Milwaukee, WI 53201-0413 | 1956 | Dr. John H. Schroeder, Jr. | 5-D | 22,342 | 1,354 |
| U of Wisconsin–Oshkosh, Oshkosh, WI 54901-3551 | 1871 | Dr. John E. Kerrigan | 5-M | 10,472 | 704 |

| Name, address | Year | Governing official, control, and highest degree offered | | Enroll-ment | Faculty |
|---|---|---|---|---|---|
| U of Wisconsin–Parkside, Kenosha, WI 53141-2000 | 1968 | Dr. Eleanor J. Smith | 5-M | 4,254 | 275 |
| U of Wisconsin–Platteville, Platteville, WI 53818-3099 | 1866 | Dr. Robert G. Culbertson | 5-M | 4,901 | 280 |
| U of Wisconsin–River Falls, River Falls, WI 54022-5001 | 1874 | Dr. Gary A. Thibodeau | 5-M | 5,259 | 278 |
| U of Wisconsin–Stevens Point, Stevens Point, WI 54481-3897 | 1894 | Dr. Keith R. Sanders | 5-M | 8,402 | 403 |
| U of Wisconsin–Stout, Menomonie, WI 54751 | 1891 | Dr. Charles Sorensen | 5-M | 7,072 | 394 |
| U of Wisconsin–Superior, Superior, WI 54880-2873 | 1893 | Dr. Betty J. Youngblood | 5-M | 2,383 | 160 |
| U of Wisconsin–Whitewater, Whitewater, WI 53190-1790 | 1868 | Dr. H. Gaylon Greenhill | 5-M | 10,441 | 471 |
| U of Wyoming, Laramie, WY 82071 | 1886 | Dr. Terry P. Roark | 5-D | 11,361 | 726 |
| Upper Iowa U, Fayette, IA 52142-1857 | 1857 | Dr. Ralph L. McKay | 1-B | 3,759 | 180 |
| Urbana U, Urbana, OH 43078-2091 | 1850 | Dr. Francis E. Hazard | 2-B | 1,000 | 75 |
| Ursinus Coll, Collegeville, PA 19426-1000 | 1869 | Dr. John Strassburger | 2-B | 1,245 | 135 |
| Ursuline Coll, Pepper Pike, OH 44124-4398 (4) | 1871 | Anne Marie Diederich, OSU, PhD | 2-M | 1,312 | 133 |
| Utah State U, Logan, UT 84322 | 1888 | Dr. George H. Emert | 5-D | 19,861 | 809 |
| Utica Coll of Syracuse U, Utica, NY 13502-4892 | 1946 | Dr. Michael K. Simpson | 1-B | 1,762 | 155 |
| Valdosta State U, Valdosta, GA 31698 | 1906 | Dr. Hugh C. Bailey | 5-D | 9,594 | 472 |
| Valley City State U, Valley City, ND 58072 | 1890 | Dr. Ellen Earle Chaffee | 5-B | 1,118 | 86 |
| Valparaiso U, Valparaiso, IN 46383-6493 | 1859 | Dr. Alan F. Harre | 2-F | 3,524 | 359 |
| Vanderbilt U, Nashville, TN 37240-1001 | 1873 | Mr. Joe B. Wyatt | 1-D | 10,074 | 1,968 |
| Vassar Coll, Poughkeepsie, NY 12601 | 1861 | Dr. Frances D. Fergusson | 1-M | 2,346 | 223 |
| Villa Julie Coll, Stevenson, MD 21153 | 1952 | Dr. Carolyn Manuszak | 1-B | 1,804 | 141 |
| Villanova U, Villanova, PA 19085-1699 | 1842 | Rev. Edmund J. Dobbin, OSA | 2-D | 10,514 | 767 |
| Virginia Commonwealth U, Richmond, VA 23284-9005 | 1838 | Dr. Eugene P. Trani | 5-D | 21,349 | 2,575 |
| Virginia Military Inst, Lexington, VA 24450 (1) | 1839 | Maj. Gen. John W. Knapp | 5-B | 1,196 | 121 |
| Virginia Polytechnic Inst and State U, Blacksburg, VA 24061-0202 | 1872 | Dr. Paul E. Torgersen | 5-D | 23,674 | 1,915 |
| Virginia State U, Petersburg, VA 23806-0001 | 1882 | Mr. Eddie N. Moore, Jr. | 5-M | 3,993 | 265 |
| Virginia Union U, Richmond, VA 23220-1170 | 1865 | Dr. S. Dallas Simmons | 2-D | 1,620 | 104 |
| Virginia Wesleyan Coll, Norfolk, VA 23502-5599 | 1961 | Dr. William T. Greer, Jr. | 2-B | 1,569 | 106 |
| Viterbo Coll, La Crosse, WI 54601-4797 | 1890 | Dr. William J. Medland | 2-M | 1,846 | 153 |
| Wagner Coll, Staten Island, NY 10301 | 1883 | Dr. Norman R. Smith | 1-M | 1,919 | 182 |
| Wake Forest U, Winston-Salem, NC 27109 | 1834 | Dr. Thomas K. Hearn, Jr. | 1-D | 5,913 | 1,510 |
| Walla Walla Coll, College Place, WA 99324-3000 | 1892 | Dr. W. G. Nelson | 2-M | 1,722 | 190 |
| Walsh Coll of Accountancy and Business Admin, Troy, MI 48007-7006 | 1922 | Dr. David A. Spencer | 1-M | 3,428 | 137 |
| Walsh U, North Canton, OH 44720-3396 | 1958 | Rev. Richard Mucowski | 2-M | 1,485 | 88 |
| Wartburg Coll, Waverly, IA 50677-1033 | 1852 | Dr. Robert Vogel | 2-B | 1,433 | 145 |
| Washburn U of Topeka, Topeka, KS 66621 | 1865 | Dr. Hugh Thompson | 10-F | 6,314 | 430 |
| Washington and Jefferson Coll, Washington, PA 15301-4801 | 1781 | Dr. Howard J. Burnett | 1-B | 1,128 | 101 |
| Washington and Lee U, Lexington, VA 24450 | 1749 | Dr. John W. Elrod | 1-F | 1,995 | 167 |
| Washington State U, Pullman, WA 99164 | 1890 | Dr. Samuel H. Smith | 5-D | 19,571 | 1,206 |
| Washington U, St Louis, MO 63130-4899 | 1853 | Dr. Mark S. Wrighton | 1-D | 11,482 | 3,619 |
| Waynesburg Coll, Waynesburg, PA 15370-1222 | 1849 | Mr. Timothy R. Thyreen | 2-M | 1,292 | 113 |
| Wayne State Coll, Wayne, NE 68787 | 1910 | Dr. Donald J. Mash | 5-M | 3,868 | 219 |
| Wayne State U, Detroit, MI 48202 | 1868 | Mr. David Adamany | 5-D | 32,149 | 2,716 |
| Weber State U, Ogden, UT 84408-0002 | 1889 | Dr. Paul H. Thompson | 5-M | 13,996 | 506 |
| Webster U, St Louis, MO 63119-3194 | 1915 | Dr. Richard S. Meyers | 1-D | 11,246 | 749 |
| Wellesley Coll, Wellesley, MA 02181 (3) | 1870 | Ms. Diana Chapman Walsh | 1-B | 2,299 | 320 |
| Wentworth Inst of Tech, Boston, MA 02115-5998 | 1904 | Dr. John F. Van Domelen | 1-B | 2,116 | 120 |
| Wesleyan U, Middletown, CT 06459-0260 | 1831 | Douglas J. Bennet, Jr. | 1-D | 3,244 | 337 |
| Wesley Coll, Dover, DE 19901 | 1873 | Dr. Reed M. Stewart | 2-B | 1,316 | 95 |
| West Chester U of Pennsylvania, West Chester, PA 19383 | 1871 | Dr. Madeleine Wing Adler | 5-M | 11,055 | 672 |
| West Coast U, Los Angeles, CA 90020-1765 | 1909 | Dr. Robert M. L. Baker, Jr. | 1-M | 1,000 | 250 |
| Western Carolina U, Cullowhee, NC 28723 | 1889 | Dr. John W. Bardo | 5-D | 6,651 | 507 |
| Western Connecticut State U, Danbury, CT 06810-6885 | 1903 | Dr. James R. Roach | 5-M | 5,607 | 331 |
| Western Illinois U, Macomb, IL 61455-1390 | 1899 | Dr. Donald S. Spencer | 5-M | 12,115 | 667 |
| Western International U, Phoenix, AZ 85021-2718 | 1978 | Mr. James Haynes | 3-M | 1,431 | 65 |
| Western Kentucky U, Bowling Green, KY 42101-3576 | 1906 | Dr. Thomas C. Meredith | 5-M | 14,721 | 863 |
| Western Maryland Coll, Westminster, MD 21157-4390 | 1867 | Dr. Robert H. Chambers | 1-M | 2,370 | 201 |
| Western Michigan U, Kalamazoo, MI 49008 | 1903 | Dr. Diether H. Haenicke | 5-D | 26,537 | 1,199 |
| Western Montana Coll of The U of Montana, Dillon, MT 59725-3598 | 1893 | Dr. Sheila M. Stearns | 5-B | 1,176 | 75 |
| Western New England Coll, Springfield, MA 01119-2654 | 1919 | Dr. Beverly W. Miller | 1-F | 4,485 | 302 |
| Western New Mexico U, Silver City, NM 88062-0680 | 1893 | Dr. John E. Counts | 5-M | 2,356 | 126 |
| Western Oregon State Coll, Monmouth, OR 97361 | 1856 | Dr. Bill Cowart | 5-M | 3,908 | 282 |
| Western State Coll of Colorado, Gunnison, CO 81231 | 1901 | Dr. Kaye Howe | 5-B | 2,516 | 135 |
| Western Washington U, Bellingham, WA 98225-5996 | 1893 | Dr. Karen Morse | 5-M | 10,708 | 523 |
| Westfield State Coll, Westfield, MA 01086 | 1838 | Dr. Ronald L. Applbaum | 5-M | 4,761 | 280 |
| West Liberty State Coll, West Liberty, WV 26074 | 1837 | Dr. Clyde D. Campbell | 5-B | 2,435 | 141 |
| Westminster Coll, New Wilmington, PA 16172-0001 | 1852 | Dr. Oscar E. Remick | 2-M | 1,672 | 120 |
| Westminster Coll of Salt Lake City, Salt Lake City, UT 84105-3697 | 1875 | Dr. Peggy Stock | 1-M | 2,009 | 207 |
| Westmont Coll, Santa Barbara, CA 93108-1099 | 1940 | Dr. David K. Winter | 2-B | 1,256 | 127 |
| West Texas A&M U, Canyon, TX 79016-0001 | 1909 | Dr. Russell C. Long | 5-M | 6,630 | 336 |
| West Virginia State Coll, Institute, WV 25112-1000 | 1891 | Dr. Hazo W. Carter, Jr. | 5-B | 4,486 | 242 |
| West Virginia U, Morgantown, WV 26506 | 1867 | Mr. David C. Hardesty, Jr. | 5-D | 21,517 | 1,617 |
| West Virginia U Inst of Tech, Montgomery, WV 25136 | 1895 | Dr. John P. Carrier | 5-M | 2,538 | 199 |
| West Virginia Wesleyan Coll, Buckhannon, WV 26201 | 1890 | Mr. William R. Haden | 2-M | 1,679 | 130 |
| Wheaton Coll, Wheaton, IL 60187-5571 | 1860 | Dr. A. Duane Litfin | 2-D | 2,695 | 277 |
| Wheaton Coll, Norton, MA 02766 | 1834 | Dr. Dale Rogers Marshall | 1-B | 1,319 | 110 |
| Wheeling Jesuit Coll, Wheeling, WV 26003-6295 | 1954 | Fr. Thomas S. Acker, SJ | 2-M | 1,500 | 94 |
| Wheelock Coll, Boston, MA 02215 (4) | 1888 | Dr. Marjorie Bakken | 1-M | 1,288 | 183 |
| Whitman Coll, Walla Walla, WA 99362-2083 | 1859 | Dr. Thomas Cronin | 1-B | 1,325 | 174 |
| Whittier Coll, Whittier, CA 90608-0634 | 1887 | Dr. James L. Ash, Jr. | 1-F | 2,167 | 152 |
| Whitworth Coll, Spokane, WA 99251-0001 | 1890 | Dr. William P. Robinson | 2-M | 2,057 | 102 |
| Wichita State U, Wichita, KS 67260 | 1895 | Dr. Eugene Morgan Hughes | 5-D | 14,568 | 728 |
| Widener U, Chester, PA 19013-5792 | 1821 | Dr. Robert J. Bruce | 1-D | 8,630 | 330 |
| Wilkes U, Wilkes-Barre, PA 18766-0002 | 1933 | Dr. Christopher N. Breiseth | 1-M | 2,600 | 225 |
| Willamette U, Salem, OR 97301-3931 | 1842 | Dr. Jerry E. Hudson | 2-F | 2,525 | 247 |
| William Carey Coll, Hattiesburg, MS 39401-5499 | 1906 | Dr. James W. Edwards | 2-M | 2,172 | 172 |
| William Jewell Coll, Liberty, MO 64068-1843 | 1849 | Dr. W. Christian Sizemore | 2-B | 1,250 | 148 |
| William Paterson Coll of New Jersey, Wayne, NJ 07470-8420 | 1855 | Dr. Arnold Speert | 5-M | 9,090 | 326 |
| Williams Coll, Williamstown, MA 01267 | 1793 | Dr. Harry C. Payne | 1-M | 2,104 | 251 |
| William Woods U, Fulton, MO 65251-1098 (4) | 1870 | Dr. Jahnae Barnett | 2-M | 1,170 | 93 |
| Wilmington Coll, New Castle, DE 19720-6491 | 1967 | Dr. Audrey K. Doberstein | 1-D | 3,800 | 430 |
| Wilmington Coll, Wilmington, OH 45177 | 1870 | Dr. Daniel DiBiasio | 2-B | 1,006 | 65 |
| Wingate U, Wingate, NC 28174 | 1896 | Dr. Jerry E. McGee | 2-M | 1,344 | 109 |
| Winona State U, Winona, MN 55987-5838 | 1858 | Dr. Darrell Krueger | 5-M | 7,500 | 350 |
| Winston-Salem State U, Winston-Salem, NC 27110-0003 | 1892 | Dr. Cleon F. Thompson, Jr. | 5-B | 2,863 | 182 |

| Name, address | Year | Governing official, control, and highest degree offered | | Enroll-ment | Faculty |
|---|---|---|---|---|---|
| Winthrop U, Rock Hill, SC 29733 | 1886 | Dr. Anthony DiGiorgio | 5-M | 5,308 | 370 |
| Wittenberg U, Springfield, OH 45501-0720 | 1845 | Dr. L. Baird Tipson | 2-B | 2,050 | 166 |
| Wofford Coll, Spartanburg, SC 29303-3663 | 1854 | Dr. Joab M. Lesesne | 2-B | 1,113 | 94 |
| Woodbury U, Burbank, CA 91510 | 1884 | Dr. Paul E. Sago | 1-M | 1,096 | 139 |
| Worcester Polytechnic Inst, Worcester, MA 01609-2247 | 1865 | Dr. Edward A. Parrish, Jr. | 1-D | 3,593 | 259 |
| Worcester State Coll, Worcester, MA 01602-2597 | 1874 | Dr. Kalyan K. Ghosh | 5-M | 5,505 | 248 |
| Wright State U, Dayton, OH 45435 | 1964 | Dr. Harley E. Flack | 5-D | 16,488 | 950 |
| Xavier U, Cincinnati, OH 45207-5311 | 1831 | Rev. James E. Hoff, SJ | 2-M | 6,127 | 473 |
| Xavier U of Louisiana, New Orleans, LA 70125-1098 | 1925 | Dr. Norman C. Francis | 2-F | 3,467 | 258 |
| Yale U, New Haven, CT 06520 | 1701 | Mr. Richard C. Levin | 1-D | 10,986 | 2,802 |
| Yeshiva U, New York, NY 10033-3201 (1) | 1886 | Dr. Norman Lamm | 1-D | 5,433 | 1,092 |
| York Coll of Pennsylvania, York, PA 17405-7199 | 1787 | Dr. George W. Waldner | 1-M | 5,054 | 310 |
| York Coll of the City U of New York, Jamaica, NY 11451-0001 | 1967 | Dr. Thomas K. Minter | 11-B | 6,111 | 466 |
| Youngstown State U, Youngstown, OH 44555-0002 | 1908 | Dr. Leslie H. Cochran | 5-D | 13,273 | 816 |

## Two-Year Colleges

The highest undergraduate degree offered for all two-year colleges is the associate degree.

| Name, address | Year | Governing official, control, and highest degree offered | | Enroll-ment | Faculty |
|---|---|---|---|---|---|
| Abraham Baldwin Ag Coll, Tifton, GA 31794-2601 | 1933 | Dr. Harold J. Loyd | 5 | 2,592 | 115 |
| Adirondack Comm Coll, Queensbury, NY 12804 | 1960 | Dr. Roger Andersen | 11 | 3,602 | 233 |
| Aiken Tech Coll, Aiken, SC 29802-0600 | 1972 | Dr. Kathleen A. Noble | 11 | 2,258 | 119 |
| Aims Comm Coll, Greeley, CO 80632-0069 | 1967 | Dr. George R. Conger | 9 | 6,958 | 370 |
| Alabama Southern Comm Coll, Monroeville, AL 36460 | 1965 | Dr. John A. Johnson | 5 | 1,800 | 107 |
| Alabama Southern Comm Coll, Thomasville, AL 36784-0489 | 1965 | Dr. John Johnson | 5 | 1,225 | 119 |
| Alamance Comm Coll, Graham, NC 27253-8000 | 1959 | Dr. W. Ronald McCarter | 5 | 3,340 | 145 |
| Albuquerque Tech Vocational Inst, Albuquerque, NM 87106-4096 | 1965 | Dr. Alex A. Sanchez | 5 | 15,021 | 601 |
| Alexandria Tech Coll, Alexandria, MN 56308-3707 | 1961 | Mr. Larry Shellito | 5 | 1,630 | 89 |
| Allan Hancock Coll, Santa Maria, CA 93454-6399 | 1920 | Dr. Ann F. Stephenson | 11 | 7,403 | 404 |
| Allegany Coll of Maryland, Cumberland, MD 21502 | 1961 | Dr. Donald L. Alexander | 11 | 2,844 | 206 |
| Allen County Comm Coll, Iola, KS 66749-1607 | 1923 | Mr. John Masterson | 11 | 1,689 | 135 |
| Allentown Business Sch, Allentown, PA 18103-3880 | 1869 | Ms. Virginia Carpenter | 3 | 1,000 | 50 |
| Alpena Comm Coll, Alpena, MI 49707-1495 | 1952 | Dr. Donald L. Newport | 11 | 1,866 | 89 |
| Alvin Comm Coll, Alvin, TX 77511-4898 | 1949 | Dr. A. Rodney Allbright | 11 | 3,864 | 141 |
| American River Coll, Sacramento, CA 95841-4286 | 1955 | Dr. Marie Smith | 9 | 19,695 | 700 |
| Andover Coll, Portland, ME 04103-2791 | 1966 | Mrs. Brenda J. Berry | 3 | 2,158 | 26 |
| Angelina Coll, Lufkin, TX 75902-1768 | 1968 | Dr. Larry M. Phillips | 11 | 3,984 | 201 |
| Anne Arundel Comm Coll, Arnold, MD 21012-1895 | 1961 | Dr. Martha A. Smith | 11 | 11,890 | 579 |
| Anoka-Ramsey Comm Coll, Coon Rapids, MN 55433-3499 | 1965 | Dr. Patrick M. Johns | 5 | 4,449 | 179 |
| Anson Comm Coll, Polkton, NC 28135-0126 | 1962 | Dr. Donald P. Altieri | 5 | 1,379 | 84 |
| Antelope Valley Coll, Lancaster, CA 93536-5426 | 1929 | Dr. Allan W. Kurki | 11 | 9,027 | 400 |
| Arapahoe Comm Coll, Littleton, CO 80160-9002 | 1965 | Dr. James F. Weber | 5 | 7,346 | 298 |
| Arizona Western Coll, Yuma, AZ 85366-0929 | 1962 | Dr. James R. Carruthers | 11 | 5,837 | 236 |
| Arkansas State U–Beebe Branch, Beebe, AR 72012-1008 | 1927 | Dr. Eugene McKay, Jr. | 5 | 1,999 | 71 |
| Art Inst of Atlanta, Atlanta, GA 30326-1018 | 1949 | Mr. Hal R. Griffith | 3 | 1,408 | 91 |
| Art Inst of Dallas, Dallas, TX 75231-9959 | 1978 | Mr. Thomas M. Hauser | 3 | 1,200 | 84 |
| Art Inst of Fort Lauderdale, Fort Lauderdale, FL 33316-3000 | 1968 | Mr. David Pauldine | 3 | 1,950 | 150 |
| The Art Inst of Houston, Houston, TX 77056-4115 | 1978 | Mr. Steve R. Gregg | 3 | 1,189 | 78 |
| The Art Inst of Philadelphia, Philadelphia, PA 19103-5198 | 1966 | Mr. Robert P. Gioella | 3 | 1,700 | 90 |
| Art Inst of Pittsburgh, Pittsburgh, PA 15222-3269 | 1921 | Ms. Saundra M. Van Dyke | 3 | 2,100 | 107 |
| Art Inst of Seattle, Seattle, WA 98121-1642 | 1982 | Leslie E. Pritchard | 3 | 1,965 | 147 |
| Asheville-Buncombe Tech Comm Coll, Asheville, NC 28801-4897 | 1959 | Mr. K. Ray Bailey | 5 | 4,021 | 407 |
| Asnuntuck Comm-Tech Coll, Enfield, CT 06082-3800 | 1972 | Dr. Harvey S. Irlen | 5 | 2,051 | 112 |
| Athens Area Tech Inst, Athens, GA 30601-1500 | 1958 | Dr. Kenneth C. Easom | 5 | 1,653 | 100 |
| Atlanta Metropolitan Coll, Atlanta, GA 30310-4498 | 1974 | Dr. Harold E. Wade | 5 | 1,811 | 73 |
| Atlantic Comm Coll, Mays Landing, NJ 08330-2699 | 1966 | Dr. John May | 8 | 6,004 | 331 |
| Augusta Tech Inst, Augusta, GA 30906 | 1961 | NR | 5 | 2,325 | 189 |
| Austin Comm Coll, Austin, TX 78752-4342 | 1972 | Dr. Bill Segura | 9 | 25,275 | 1,388 |
| Bainbridge Coll, Bainbridge, GA 31717 | 1972 | Dr. Edward D. Mobley | 5 | 1,180 | 46 |
| Bakersfield Coll, Bakersfield, CA 93305-1299 | 1913 | Dr. Richard Wright | 11 | 12,000 | 496 |
| Baltimore City Comm Coll, Baltimore, MD 21215-7893 | 1947 | Dr. James D. Tschechtelin | 5 | 5,970 | 493 |
| Barstow Coll, Barstow, CA 92311-6699 | 1959 | Dr. Judith Strattan | 11 | 2,632 | 128 |
| Barton County Comm Coll, Great Bend, KS 67530-9283 | 1969 | Dr. Jimmie L. Downing | 11 | 10,000 | 292 |
| Bay de Noc Comm Coll, Escanaba, MI 49829-2511 | 1963 | Dr. Dwight E. Link | 8 | 2,229 | 143 |
| Beaufort County Comm Coll, Washington, NC 27889-1069 | 1967 | Dr. Ron Champion | 5 | 1,154 | 110 |
| Bee County Coll, Beeville, TX 78102-2197 | 1965 | Dr. Norman Wallace | 8 | 2,417 | 134 |
| Belleville Area Coll, Belleville, IL 62221-5899 | 1946 | Dr. Joseph Cipfl | 9 | 15,267 | 893 |
| Bellevue Comm Coll, Bellevue, WA 98007-6484 | 1966 | Mrs. B. Jean Floten | 5 | 10,099 | 619 |
| Belmont Tech Coll, St Clairsville, OH 43950-9766 | 1971 | Dr. Wesley R. Channell | 5 | 1,694 | 101 |
| Bergen Comm Coll, Paramus, NJ 07652-1595 | 1965 | Dr. Judith K. Winn | 8 | 13,207 | 681 |
| Berkeley Coll, West Paterson, NJ 07424-3353 | 1931 | Mr. Kevin L. Luing | 3 | 1,572 | 102 |
| Berkeley Coll, New York, NY 10017-4604 | 1945 | Mr. Robert J. Hurd | 3 | 1,007 | 64 |
| Berkshire Comm Coll, Pittsfield, MA 01201-5786 | 1960 | Dr. Barbara A. Viniar | 5 | 2,388 | 180 |
| Bessemer State Tech Coll, Bessemer, AL 35021-0308 | 1966 | Dr. W. Michael Bailey | 5 | 1,840 | 119 |
| Bevill State Comm Coll, Sumiton, AL 35148 | 1969 | Dr. Harold Wade | 5 | 4,597 | 63 |
| Big Bend Comm Coll, Moses Lake, WA 98837-3299 | 1962 | Dr. William C. Bonaudi | 5 | 1,872 | 148 |
| Bishop State Comm Coll, Mobile, AL 36603-5898 | 1965 | Dr. Yvonne Kennedy | 5 | 4,127 | 257 |
| Bismarck State Coll, Bismarck, ND 58501-1299 | 1939 | Dr. Donna Thigpen | 5 | 2,313 | 117 |
| Black Hawk Coll, Moline, IL 61265-5899 | 1946 | Dr. Judith A. Redwine | 11 | 6,335 | 488 |
| Blackhawk Tech Coll, Janesville, WI 53547-5009 | 1968 | Dr. James C. Catania | 9 | 3,000 | 293 |
| Black River Tech Coll, Pocahontas, AR 72455 | 1972 | Mr. Richard Gaines | 5 | 1,189 | 70 |
| Blinn Coll, Brenham, TX 77833-4049 | 1883 | Dr. Donald E. Voelter | 11 | 9,165 | 370 |
| Blue Mountain Comm Coll, Pendleton, OR 97801-1000 | 1962 | Mr. Ronald L. Daniels | 11 | 3,808 | 245 |
| Blue Ridge Comm Coll, Flat Rock, NC 28731 | 1969 | Dr. David W. Sink | 11 | 2,529 | 176 |
| Blue Ridge Comm Coll, Weyers Cave, VA 24486-0080 | 1965 | Dr. James R. Perkins | 5 | 2,736 | 145 |
| Borough of Manhattan Comm Coll of City U of NY, New York, NY 10007-1079 | 1963 | Dr. Marcia V. Keizs | 11 | 16,334 | 1,204 |
| Bossier Parish Comm Coll, Bossier City, LA 71111-5801 | 1967 | Mr. Thomas N. Carleton | 11 | 4,687 | 134 |
| Bowling Green State U–Firelands Coll, Huron, OH 44839-9791 | 1968 | Dr. R. Darby Williams | 5 | 1,394 | 81 |
| Bramson ORT Tech Inst, Forest Hills, NY 11375-4239 | 1977 | Mr. Barry M. Glotzer | 1 | 1,200 | 57 |
| Brazosport Coll, Lake Jackson, TX 77566-3199 | 1948 | Dr. John R. Grable | 11 | 3,104 | 157 |
| Brevard Comm Coll, Cocoa, FL 32922-6597 | 1960 | Dr. Maxwell C. King | 5 | 14,341 | 1,119 |
| Briarcliffe Coll, Woodbury, NY 11797-2015 | 1966 | Mr. Richard Turan | 3 | 1,243 | 101 |

| Name, address | Year | Governing official, control, and highest degree offered | | Enroll-ment | Faculty |
|---|---|---|---|---|---|
| Bristol Comm Coll, Fall River, MA 02720-7395 | 1965 | Ms. Eileen Farley | 5 | 5,223 | 183 |
| Bronx Comm Coll of City U of NY, Bronx, NY 10453 | 1959 | NR | 11 | 8,450 | 390 |
| Brookdale Comm Coll, Lincroft, NJ 07738-1597 | 1967 | Dr. Peter F. Burnham | 8 | 12,446 | 443 |
| Brookhaven Coll, Farmers Branch, TX 75244-4997 | 1978 | Dr. Walter G. Bumphus | 8 | 9,060 | 525 |
| Broome Comm Coll, Binghamton, NY 13902-1017 | 1946 | Dr. Donald A. Dellow | 11 | 5,986 | 379 |
| Broward Comm Coll, Fort Lauderdale, FL 33301-2298 | 1960 | Dr. Willis N. Holcombe | 5 | 24,600 | 775 |
| Brown Inst, Minneapolis, MN 55407-1932 | 1946 | Dr. Jim Otten | 3 | 1,300 | 96 |
| Brunswick Coll, Brunswick, GA 31520-3644 | 1961 | Dr. Dorothy L. Lord | 5 | 2,085 | 79 |
| Bucks County Comm Coll, Newtown, PA 18940-1525 | 1964 | Dr. James J. Linksz | 8 | 9,500 | 452 |
| Bunker Hill Comm Coll, Boston, MA 02129 | 1973 | Dr. C. Scully Stikes | 5 | 6,002 | 145 |
| Burlington County Coll, Pemberton, NJ 08068-1599 | 1966 | Dr. Robert Messina | 8 | 6,433 | 327 |
| Butler County Comm Coll, El Dorado, KS 67042-3280 | 1927 | Dr. James Stringer | 11 | 7,931 | 573 |
| Butler County Comm Coll, Butler, PA 16003-1203 | 1965 | Dr. Frederick F. Bartok | 8 | 3,133 | 220 |
| Butte Coll, Oroville, CA 95965-8399 | 1966 | Dr. Betty M. Dean | 9 | 11,900 | 561 |
| Cabrillo Coll, Aptos, CA 95003-3194 | 1959 | Mr. John D. Hurd | 9 | 11,805 | 552 |
| Caldwell Comm Coll and Tech Inst, Hudson, NC 28638-2397 | 1964 | Dr. Kenneth A. Boham | 5 | 3,162 | 189 |
| Camden County Coll, Blackwood, NJ 08012-0200 | 1967 | Dr. Phyllis Della Vecchia | 11 | 13,068 | 701 |
| Cañada Coll, Redwood City, CA 94061-1099 | 1968 | Dr. Marie E. Rosenwasser | 9 | 5,261 | 263 |
| Cape Cod Comm Coll, West Barnstable, MA 02668 | 1961 | Dr. Richard A. Kraus | 5 | 3,640 | 259 |
| Cape Fear Comm Coll, Wilmington, NC 28401-3993 | 1959 | Mr. Eric B. McKeithan | 5 | 3,700 | 205 |
| Capital Comm Tech Coll, Hartford, CT 06105-2354 | 1946 | Dr. Conrad L. Mallett | 5 | 2,900 | 174 |
| Carl Albert State Coll, Poteau, OK 74953-5208 | 1934 | Dr. Joe E. White | 5 | 1,933 | 160 |
| Carl Sandburg Coll, Galesburg, IL 61401-9576 | 1967 | Dr. Donald G. Crist | 11 | 3,000 | 208 |
| Carroll Comm Coll, Westminster, MD 21157 | 1996 | Dr. Joseph F. Shields | 11 | 2,532 | 210 |
| Carteret Comm Coll, Morehead City, NC 28557-2989 | 1963 | Dr. Donald W. Bryant | 5 | 1,428 | 93 |
| Casper Coll, Casper, WY 82601-4699 | 1945 | Dr. LeRoy Strausner | 9 | 3,743 | 185 |
| Catawba Valley Comm Coll, Hickory, NC 28602-9699 | 1960 | Dr. Cuyler A. Dunbar | 11 | 3,499 | 235 |
| Catonsville Comm Coll, Catonsville, MD 21228-5381 | 1957 | Dr. Frederick J. Walsh | 8 | 10,240 | 534 |
| Cayuga County Comm Coll, Auburn, NY 13021-3099 | 1953 | Dr. Lawrence H. Poole | 11 | 2,751 | 171 |
| Cecil Comm Coll, North East, MD 21901-1999 | 1968 | Dr. Robert L. Gell | 8 | 1,055 | 158 |
| Cedar Valley Coll, Lancaster, TX 75134-3799 | 1977 | Dr. Carol J. Spencer | 5 | 3,136 | 130 |
| Central Alabama Comm Coll, Alexander City, AL 35011-0699 | 1965 | Dr. James H. Cornell | 5 | 1,917 | 140 |
| Central Carolina Comm Coll, Sanford, NC 27330-9000 | 1962 | Dr. Marvin R. Joyner | 11 | 3,140 | 171 |
| Central Carolina Tech Coll, Sumter, SC 29150-2499 | 1963 | Dr. Herbert C. Robbins | 5 | 2,189 | 144 |
| Central Comm Coll–Grand Island Cmps, Grand Island, NE 68802-4903 | 1976 | Dr. William Giddings | 11 | 1,602 | 165 |
| Central Comm Coll–Hastings Cmps, Hastings, NE 68902-1024 | 1966 | Dr. Judy Dresser | 11 | 1,629 | 111 |
| Central Comm Coll–Platte Cmps, Columbus, NE 68602-1027 | 1968 | Dr. M. Richard Shaink | 11 | 1,511 | 100 |
| Central Florida Comm Coll, Ocala, FL 34478-1388 | 1957 | Dr. William J. Campion | 11 | 6,068 | 219 |
| Centralia Coll, Centralia, WA 98531-4099 | 1925 | Dr. Henry P. Kirk | 5 | 1,800 | 112 |
| Central Lakes Coll, Brainerd, MN 56401-3904 | 1938 | Ms. Sally Jane Ihne | 5 | 1,961 | 98 |
| Central Ohio Tech Coll, Newark, OH 43055-1767 | 1971 | Dr. Rafael L. Cortada | 5 | 1,664 | 103 |
| Central Oregon Comm Coll, Bend, OR 97701-5998 | 1949 | Dr. Robert L. Barber | 9 | 3,240 | 184 |
| Central Piedmont Comm Coll, Charlotte, NC 28235-5009 | 1963 | Dr. Paul A. Zeiss | 11 | 15,614 | 1,630 |
| Central Texas Coll, Killeen, TX 76542-4199 | 1967 | Dr. James R. Anderson | 11 | 8,600 | 328 |
| Central Virginia Comm Coll, Lynchburg, VA 24502-4907 | 1966 | Dr. Belle S. Wheelan | 5 | 4,038 | 200 |
| Central Wyoming Coll, Riverton, WY 82501-2273 | 1966 | Dr. JoAnne McFarland | 11 | 1,510 | 110 |
| Century Comm and Tech Coll, White Bear Lake, MN 55110 | 1970 | Dr. James Meznek | 5 | 1,800 | 95 |
| Cerritos Coll, Norwalk, CA 90650-6298 | 1956 | Dr. Fred Gaskin | 11 | 22,068 | 642 |
| Cerro Coso Comm Coll, Ridgecrest, CA 93555-9571 | 1973 | Dr. Raymond A. McCue | 5 | 5,564 | 262 |
| Chabot Coll, Hayward, CA 94545-5001 | 1961 | Dr. Raul J. Cardoza | 5 | 13,285 | 933 |
| Chaffey Coll, Rancho Cucamonga, CA 91737-3002 | 1883 | Dr. Jerry W. Young | 9 | 12,651 | 540 |
| Champlain Coll, Burlington, VT 05402-0670 | 1878 | Dr. Roger H. Perry | 1 | 2,085 | 128 |
| Chandler-Gilbert Comm Coll, Chandler, AZ 85225-2479 | 1985 | Ms. Arnette S. Ward | 9 | 3,500 | 140 |
| Charles County Comm Coll, La Plata, MD 20646-0910 | 1958 | Dr. John Sine | 11 | 6,077 | 355 |
| Charles Stewart Mott Comm Coll, Flint, MI 48503-2089 | 1923 | Dr. Allen Arnold | 9 | 9,754 | 412 |
| Chattahoochee Tech Inst, Marietta, GA 30060 | 1961 | Dr. Harlon Crimm | 5 | 1,930 | 76 |
| Chattahoochee Valley State Comm Coll, Phenix City, AL 36869-7928 | 1974 | Dr. Richard Federinko | 5 | 2,101 | 107 |
| Chattanooga State Tech Comm Coll, Chattanooga, TN 37406-1018 | 1965 | Dr. James L. Catanzaro | 5 | 8,676 | 599 |
| Chemeketa Comm Coll, Salem, OR 97309-7070 | 1955 | Dr. Gerard Berger | 11 | 9,784 | 883 |
| Chesapeake Coll, Wye Mills, MD 21679-0008 | 1965 | Dr. John R. Kotula | 11 | 2,068 | 141 |
| Chesterfield-Marlboro Tech Coll, Cheraw, SC 29520-1007 | 1967 | Dr. Ronald W. Hampton | 11 | 1,030 | 66 |
| Chipola Jr Coll, Marianna, FL 32446-3065 | 1947 | Dr. H. Dale O'Daniel | 5 | 2,273 | 142 |
| Chippewa Valley Tech Coll, Eau Claire, WI 54701-6120 | 1912 | William A. Ihlenfeldt | 9 | 3,800 | 400 |
| Cincinnati State Tech and Comm Coll, Cincinnati, OH 45223-2690 | 1966 | Dr. James P. Long | 5 | 5,790 | 351 |
| Cisco Jr Coll, Cisco, TX 76437-9321 | 1940 | Dr. Roger C. Schustereit | 11 | 2,553 | 98 |
| Citrus Coll, Glendora, CA 91741-1899 | 1915 | Dr. Louis E. Zellers | 11 | 10,448 | 392 |
| City Colls of Chicago, Harold Washington Coll, Chicago, IL 60601-2420 | 1962 | Ms. Nancy DeSombre | 11 | 7,745 | 681 |
| City Colls of Chicago, Harry S Truman Coll, Chicago, IL 60640-5616 | 1956 | Dr. Donald B. Smith | 11 | 4,620 | 160 |
| City Colls of Chicago, Kennedy-King Coll, Chicago, IL 60621-3733 | 1935 | Dr. Wayne Watson | 11 | 2,539 | 106 |
| City Colls of Chicago, Malcolm X Coll, Chicago, IL 60612-3145 | 1911 | Ms. Zerrie D. Campbell | 11 | 3,480 | 93 |
| City Colls of Chicago, Olive-Harvey Coll, Chicago, IL 60628-1645 | 1970 | Mr. Homer D. Franklin | 11 | 3,419 | 143 |
| City Colls of Chicago, Richard J Daley Coll, Chicago, IL 60652-1242 | 1960 | Dr. Ted Martinez, Jr. | 11 | 4,679 | 155 |
| City Colls of Chicago, Wilbur Wright Coll, Chicago, IL 60634-1591 | 1934 | Mr. Raymond F. LeFevour | 11 | 6,949 | 161 |
| Clackamas Comm Coll, Oregon City, OR 97045-7998 | 1966 | Dr. John S. Keyser | 9 | 6,933 | 506 |
| Clark Coll, Vancouver, WA 98663-3598 | 1933 | Dr. Earl P. Johnson | 5 | 10,300 | 320 |
| Clark State Comm Coll, Springfield, OH 45501-0570 | 1962 | Mr. Albert A. Salerno | 5 | 2,746 | 186 |
| Clatsop Comm Coll, Astoria, OR 97103 | 1958 | Dr. John W. Wubben | 8 | 2,474 | 165 |
| Cleveland Comm Coll, Shelby, NC 28152 | 1965 | Dr. L. Steve Thornburg | 5 | 1,873 | 91 |
| Cleveland Inst of Electronics, Cleveland, OH 44114-3636 (2) | 1934 | Mr. John R. Drinko | 3 | 2,300 | 6 |
| Cleveland State Comm Coll, Cleveland, TN 37320-3570 | 1967 | Dr. Owen Cargol | 5 | 3,670 | 182 |
| Clinton Comm Coll, Clinton, IA 52732-6299 | 1946 | Ms. Karen Vickers | 5 | 1,125 | 75 |
| Clinton Comm Coll, Plattsburgh, NY 12901-9573 | 1969 | Dr. Jay L. Fennell | 11 | 1,662 | 179 |
| Cloud County Comm Coll, Concordia, KS 66901-1002 | 1965 | Dr. James P. Ihrig | 11 | 3,112 | 218 |
| Clovis Comm Coll, Clovis, NM 88101-8381 | 1971 | Dr. Jay Gurley | 5 | 3,920 | 184 |
| Coastal Carolina Comm Coll, Jacksonville, NC 28546-6877 | 1964 | Dr. Ronald K. Lingle, Jr. | 11 | 3,491 | 195 |
| Coastline Comm Coll, Fountain Valley, CA 92708-2597 | 1976 | Dr. Leslie N. Purdy | 11 | 11,950 | 340 |
| Cochise Coll, Douglas, AZ 85607-9724 | 1962 | Dr. Walter S. Patton | 11 | 1,204 | 88 |
| Cochise Coll, Sierra Vista, AZ 85635-2317 | 1977 | Dr. Walter S. Patton | 11 | 2,614 | 253 |
| Coconino County Comm Coll, Flagstaff, AZ 86003 | 1991 | NR | 5 | 1,991 | 201 |
| Coffeyville Comm Coll, Coffeyville, KS 67337-5063 | 1923 | Dr. Ronald E. Thomas | 11 | 2,380 | 86 |
| Colby Comm Coll, Colby, KS 67701-4099 | 1964 | Dr. Mikel Ary | 11 | 1,150 | 63 |

| Name, address | Year | Governing official, control, and highest degree offered | | Enroll-ment | Faculty |
|---|---|---|---|---|---|
| Coll of Alameda, Alameda, CA 94501-2109 | 1970 | Dr. Edward J. Valeau | 11 | 4,858 | 166 |
| Coll of DuPage, Glen Ellyn, IL 60137 | 1967 | Dr. Michael T. Murphy | 11 | 33,920 | 1,819 |
| Coll of Eastern Utah, Price, UT 84501-2699 | 1937 | Dr. Michael A. Petersen | 5 | 3,067 | 122 |
| Coll of Lake County, Grayslake, IL 60030-1198 | 1967 | Dr. Gretchen J. Naff | 9 | 14,865 | 822 |
| Coll of Marin, Kentfield, CA 94904 | 1926 | Dr. James E. Middleton | 11 | 8,845 | 464 |
| Coll of St Catherine–Minneapolis, Minneapolis, MN 55454-1494 | 1964 | Dr. Anita M. Pampusch | 2 | 1,212 | 134 |
| Coll of San Mateo, San Mateo, CA 94402-3784 | 1922 | Mr. Peter Landsberger | 11 | 11,506 | 476 |
| Coll of Southern Idaho, Twin Falls, ID 83303-1238 | 1964 | Mr. Gerald R. Meyerhoeffer | 11 | 4,342 | 248 |
| Coll of The Albemarle, Elizabeth City, NC 27906-2327 | 1960 | Dr. Larry R. Donnithorne | 5 | 1,894 | 118 |
| Coll of the Canyons, Santa Clarita, CA 91355-1899 | 1969 | Dr. Dianne G. Van Hook | 11 | 6,123 | 260 |
| Coll of the Desert, Palm Desert, CA 92260-9305 | 1959 | Dr. David A. George | 11 | 9,638 | 320 |
| Coll of the Mainland, Texas City, TX 77591-2499 | 1967 | Mr. Larry L. Stanley | 11 | 3,564 | 180 |
| Coll of the Redwoods, Eureka, CA 95501-9300 | 1964 | Dr. Cedric A. Sampson | 11 | 6,968 | 376 |
| Coll of the Sequoias, Visalia, CA 93277-2234 | 1925 | Dr. M. Douglas Kechter | 11 | 8,721 | 445 |
| Coll of the Siskiyous, Weed, CA 96094-2899 | 1957 | Dr. Martha Romero | 11 | 2,888 | 146 |
| Collin County Comm Coll, McKinney, TX 75070-2906 | 1985 | Dr. John H. Anthony | 11 | 10,300 | 594 |
| Colorado Inst of Art, Denver, CO 80203-2903 | 1952 | Mr. Elliott B. Jones, Sr. | 3 | 1,478 | 123 |
| Colorado Mountn Coll, Alpine Cmps, Steamboat Springs, CO 80487 | 1965 | Mr. John Vickery | 9 | 1,262 | 132 |
| Columbia Basin Coll, Pasco, WA 99301-3397 | 1955 | Dr. Lee R. Thornton | 5 | 6,580 | 350 |
| Columbia Coll, Sonora, CA 95370 | 1968 | Dr. Kenneth White | 11 | 2,644 | 121 |
| Columbia-Greene Comm Coll, Hudson, NY 12534-0327 | 1969 | Dr. Terry A. Cline | 11 | 1,711 | 115 |
| Columbia State Comm Coll, Columbia, TN 38402-1315 | 1966 | Dr. Paul Sands | 5 | 3,755 | 217 |
| Columbus State Comm Coll, Columbus, OH 43216-1609 | 1963 | Dr. Marvin G. Gutter | 5 | 16,500 | 897 |
| Columbus Tech Inst, Columbus, GA 31904-6572 | | Mr. Eugene Demonet | 5 | 1,964 | NR |
| Comm Coll of Allegheny County Allegheny Cmps, Pittsburgh, PA 15212-6003 | 1966 | Dr. J. David Griffin | 8 | 5,701 | 710 |
| Comm Coll of Allegheny County Boyce Cmps, Monroeville, PA 15146-1348 | 1966 | Dr. Jacqueline D. Taylor | 8 | 3,725 | 321 |
| Comm Coll of Allegheny County North Cmps, Pittsburgh, PA 15237-5353 | 1972 | Dr. Patricia A. McDonald | 8 | 4,374 | 632 |
| Comm Coll of Allegheny County South Cmps, West Mifflin, PA 15122-3029 | 1967 | Dr. Thomas A. Juravich | 8 | 4,567 | 428 |
| Comm Coll of Aurora, Aurora, CO 80011-9036 | 1983 | Dr. Larry Carter | 5 | 4,670 | 197 |
| Comm Coll of Beaver County, Monaca, PA 15061-2588 | 1966 | Dr. Margaret Williams-Betlyn | 5 | 2,497 | 150 |
| Comm Coll of Denver, Denver, CO 80217-3363 | 1970 | Dr. Byron McClenney | 5 | 11,897 | 596 |
| Comm Coll of Philadelphia, Philadelphia, PA 19130-3991 | 1964 | Dr. Frederick W. Capshaw | 11 | 18,713 | 1,182 |
| Comm Coll of Rhode Island, Warwick, RI 02886-1807 | 1964 | Mr. Edward Liston | 5 | 12,184 | 697 |
| Comm Coll of Southern Nevada, North Las Vegas, NV 89030-4296 | 1971 | Dr. Richard Moore | 5 | 20,417 | 860 |
| Comm Coll of the Air Force, Maxwell Air Force Base, AL 36112-6613 | 1972 | Col. Tamzy House | 4 | 410,100 | 6,028 |
| Comm Coll of Vermont, Waterbury, VT 05676-0120 | 1970 | Barbara Murphy | 5 | 3,024 | 517 |
| Connors State Coll, Warner, OK 74469-9700 | 1908 | Dr. Ronald D. Garner | 5 | 2,317 | 121 |
| Contra Costa Coll, San Pablo, CA 94806-3195 | 1948 | Dr. D. Candy Rose | 11 | 9,000 | 222 |
| Copiah-Lincoln Comm Coll, Wesson, MS 39191-0457 | 1928 | Dr. Billy B. Thames | 11 | 1,805 | 116 |
| Corning Comm Coll, Corning, NY 14830-3297 | 1956 | Dr. Eduardo J. Marti | 11 | 3,295 | 176 |
| Cosumnes River Coll, Sacramento, CA 95823-5799 | 1970 | Dr. Merilee R. Lewis | 9 | 11,245 | 425 |
| County Coll of Morris, Randolph, NJ 07869-2086 | 1966 | Dr. Edward J. Yaw | 8 | 9,342 | 541 |
| Cowley County Comm Coll and Voc-Tech Sch, Arkansas City, KS 67005-2662 | 1922 | Dr. Patrick J. McAtee | 11 | 3,054 | 184 |
| Crafton Hills Coll, Yucaipa, CA 92399-1799 | 1972 | Dr. Luis S. Gomez | 11 | 5,041 | 184 |
| Craven Comm Coll, New Bern, NC 28562-4984 | 1965 | Dr. Lewis S. Redd | 5 | 2,254 | 211 |
| Crowder Coll, Neosho, MO 64850-9160 | 1963 | Dr. Kent A. Farnsworth | 11 | 1,698 | 147 |
| Cuesta Coll, San Luis Obispo, CA 93403-8106 | 1964 | Dr. Grace N. Mitchell | 9 | 7,800 | 292 |
| Culinary Inst of America, Hyde Park, NY 12538-1499 | 1946 | Mr. Ferdinand E. Metz | 1 | 2,000 | 124 |
| Cumberland County Coll, Vineland, NJ 08360-0517 | 1963 | Dr. Roland J. Chapdelaine | 11 | 2,484 | 118 |
| Cuyahoga Comm Coll, Eastern Cmps, Highland Hills, OH 44122-6104 | 1971 | Dr. Lawrence Simpson | 11 | 5,382 | 240 |
| Cuyahoga Comm Coll, Metropolitan Cmps, Cleveland, OH 44115-3123 | 1963 | Dr. Alex Johnson | 11 | 6,015 | 351 |
| Cuyahoga Comm Coll, Western Cmps, Parma, OH 44130-5199 | 1966 | Mr. Ronald M. Sobel | 11 | 12,228 | 513 |
| Cuyamaca Coll, El Cajon, CA 92019-4304 | 1978 | Dr. Sherrill L. Amador | 5 | 4,469 | NR |
| Cypress Coll, Cypress, CA 90630-5897 | 1966 | Dr. Christine Johnson | 11 | 14,350 | 434 |
| Dabney S Lancaster Comm Coll, Clifton Forge, VA 24422 | 1964 | Dr. Richard R. Teaff | 5 | 1,722 | 160 |
| Dalton Coll, Dalton, GA 30720-3797 | 1963 | Dr. James A. Burran | 5 | 3,172 | 109 |
| Danville Comm Coll, Danville, VA 24541-4088 | 1967 | Dr. B. Carlyle Ramsey | 5 | 3,869 | 149 |
| Darton Coll, Albany, GA 31707-3098 | 1965 | Dr. Peter J. Sireno | 5 | 2,635 | 152 |
| Davidson County Comm Coll, Lexington, NC 27293-1287 | 1958 | Dr. J. Bryan Brooks | 11 | 2,301 | 140 |
| Daytona Beach Comm Coll, Daytona Beach, FL 32120 | 1958 | Dr. Philip R. Day, Jr. | 5 | 12,001 | 817 |
| Dean Coll, Franklin, MA 02038-1994 | 1865 | Dr. Paula M. Rooney | 1 | 1,950 | 92 |
| De Anza Coll, Cupertino, CA 95014-5793 | 1967 | Dr. Martha J. Kanter | 11 | 23,497 | 890 |
| DeKalb Coll, Decatur, GA 30034-3897 | 1964 | Dr. Jacquelyn Belcher | 5 | 16,073 | 1,050 |
| DeKalb Tech Inst, Clarkston, GA 30021 | | NR | 5 | 4,347 | 492 |
| Delaware County Comm Coll, Media, PA 19063-1094 | 1967 | Dr. Richard D. De Cosmo | 11 | 9,807 | 438 |
| Delaware Tech & Comm Coll, Jack F Owens Cmps, Georgetown, DE 19947 | 1967 | Dr. G. Timothy Kavel | 5 | 3,251 | 164 |
| Delaware Tech & Comm Coll, Stanton/Wilmington Cmps, Newark, DE 19713 | 1968 | Dr. Orlando J. George, Jr. | 5 | 6,552 | 460 |
| Delaware Tech & Comm Coll, Terry Cmps, Dover, DE 19904 | 1972 | Dr. Marguerite M. Johnson | 5 | 1,861 | 119 |
| Delgado Comm Coll, New Orleans, LA 70119-4399 | 1921 | Dr. Ione Elioff | 5 | 13,937 | 1,015 |
| Del Mar Coll, Corpus Christi, TX 78404-3897 | 1935 | Dr. Terry L. Dicianna | 11 | 10,757 | 514 |
| Delta Coll, University Center, MI 48710 | 1961 | Dr. Peter D. Boyse | 9 | 10,446 | 515 |
| Des Moines Area Comm Coll, Ankeny, IA 50021-8995 | 1966 | Dr. Joseph Borgen | 11 | 10,287 | NR |
| DeVry Inst, North Brunswick, NJ 08902-3362 | 1969 | Mr. Robert Bocchino | 3 | 2,536 | 92 |
| Diablo Valley Coll, Pleasant Hill, CA 94523-1544 | 1949 | Dr. Phyllis L. Peterson | 11 | 21,000 | 800 |
| Dixie Coll, St George, UT 84770-3876 | 1911 | Dr. Robert Huddleston | 5 | 2,902 | 152 |
| Dodge City Comm Coll, Dodge City, KS 67801-2399 | 1935 | Dr. Richard Drum | 11 | 2,676 | 163 |
| Doña Ana Branch Comm Coll, Las Cruces, NM 88003-8001 | 1973 | Dr. James L. McLaughlin | 11 | 3,768 | 168 |
| Dundalk Comm Coll, Baltimore, MD 21222-4694 | 1970 | Dr. Harold D. McAninch | 8 | 3,203 | 230 |
| Dunwoody Inst, Minneapolis, MN 55403 | | NR | 1 | 1,191 | 75 |
| Durham Tech Comm Coll, Durham, NC 27703-5023 | 1961 | Dr. Phail Wynn, Jr. | 5 | 4,694 | 443 |
| Dutchess Comm Coll, Poughkeepsie, NY 12601-1595 | 1957 | Dr. D. David Conklin | 11 | 6,284 | 420 |
| Dyersburg State Comm Coll, Dyersburg, TN 38024 | 1969 | Dr. Karen A. Bowyer | 5 | 2,079 | 153 |
| East Arkansas Comm Coll, Forrest City, AR 72335-9598 | 1974 | Dr. George McCormick | 5 | 1,333 | 101 |

| Name, address | Year | Governing official, control, and highest degree offered | | Enroll-ment | Faculty |
|---|---|---|---|---|---|
| East Central Coll, Union, MO 63084-0529 | 1968 | Dr. Dale Gibson | 9 | 2,990 | 181 |
| East Central Comm Coll, Decatur, MS 39327-0129 | 1928 | Dr. Eddie M. Smith | 11 | 1,699 | 102 |
| Eastern Arizona Coll, Thatcher, AZ 85552-0769 | 1888 | Mr. Gherald L. Hoopes, Jr. | 11 | 2,269 | 232 |
| Eastern New Mexico U–Roswell, Roswell, NM 88202-6000 | 1958 | Dr. Loyd R. Hughes | 5 | 2,536 | 150 |
| Eastern Oklahoma State Coll, Wilburton, OK 74578-4999 | 1908 | Dr. Bill Hill | 5 | 2,474 | 54 |
| Eastern Wyoming Coll, Torrington, WY 82240-1699 | 1948 | Dr. Jack L. Bottenfield | 11 | 1,766 | 136 |
| Eastfield Coll, Mesquite, TX 75150-2099 | 1970 | Dr. Robert Aguero | 11 | 8,458 | 105 |
| East Los Angeles Coll, Monterey Park, CA 91754-6001 | 1945 | Mr. Ernest H. Moreno | 11 | 15,100 | 450 |
| East Mississippi Comm Coll, Scooba, MS 39358-0158 | 1927 | Dr. Thomas L. Davis | 11 | 1,535 | 70 |
| Edgecombe Comm Coll, Tarboro, NC 27886-9399 | 1968 | Dr. Hartwell H. Fuller, Jr. | 11 | 1,978 | 135 |
| Edison Comm Coll, Fort Myers, FL 33906-6210 | 1962 | Dr. Kenneth Walker | 11 | 9,836 | 724 |
| Edison State Comm Coll, Piqua, OH 45356-9253 | 1973 | Dr. Kenneth A. Yowell | 5 | 3,297 | 183 |
| Edmonds Comm Coll, Lynnwood, WA 98036-5999 | 1967 | Dr. Carl Opgaard | 11 | 9,194 | 364 |
| Education America–Tampa Tech Inst Cmps, Tampa, FL 33612-8410 | 1948 | Mr. William D. Polmear | 3 | 1,150 | 40 |
| Elaine P Nunez Comm Coll, Chalmette, LA 70043-1249 | 1992 | Dr. Carol S. Hopson | 5 | 1,521 | 103 |
| El Camino Coll, Torrance, CA 90506-0001 | 1947 | Mr. Thomas Fallo | 9 | 21,860 | 533 |
| El Centro Coll, Dallas, TX 75202-3604 | 1966 | Dr. Wright L. Lassiter, Jr. | 8 | 4,593 | 397 |
| Elgin Comm Coll, Elgin, IL 60123-7193 | 1949 | Dr. Roy Flores | 11 | 8,589 | 459 |
| El Paso Comm Coll, El Paso, TX 79998-0500 | 1969 | Dr. Adriana Barrera | 8 | 22,264 | 1,307 |
| Enterprise State Jr Coll, Enterprise, AL 36331-1300 | 1965 | Dr. Stafford L. Thompson | 5 | 1,822 | 125 |
| Erie Comm Coll, City Cmps, Buffalo, NY 14203-2601 | 1971 | Dr. Louis M. Ricci | 11 | 3,112 | 258 |
| Erie Comm Coll, North Cmps, Williamsville, NY 14221-7095 | 1946 | Dr. Louis M. Ricci | 11 | 6,434 | 443 |
| Erie Comm Coll, South Cmps, Orchard Park, NY 14127-2199 | 1974 | Dr. Louis M. Ricci | 11 | 3,391 | 288 |
| Essex Comm Coll, Baltimore, MD 21237-3899 | 1957 | Dr. Donald J. Slowinski | 11 | 9,252 | 525 |
| Essex County Coll, Newark, NJ 07102-1798 | 1966 | Dr. Zachary Yamba | 8 | 8,952 | 270 |
| Eugenio Maria de Hostos Comm Coll of City U of NY, Bronx, NY 10451 | 1968 | Dr. Isaura Santiago | 11 | 4,953 | 403 |
| Everett Comm Coll, Everett, WA 98201-1327 | 1941 | Dr. Susan C. Carroll | 5 | 7,788 | 230 |
| Evergreen Valley Coll, San Jose, CA 95135-1598 | 1975 | Dr. Noella Vela | 11 | 9,002 | 300 |
| Fashion Inst of Design & Merchandising, LA Cmps, Los Angeles, CA 90015-1421 | 1969 | Ms. Tonian Hohberg | 3 | 3,038 | 106 |
| Fashion Inst of Design & Merchandising, SF Cmps, San Francisco, CA 94108-5829 | 1973 | Mrs. Barbara Cupper | 3 | 1,690 | 41 |
| Fayetteville Tech Comm Coll, Fayetteville, NC 28303-0236 | 1961 | Dr. Craig Allen | 5 | 7,118 | 736 |
| Feather River Comm Coll District, Quincy, CA 95971-6023 | 1968 | Dr. Donald Donato | 11 | 1,200 | 92 |
| Fergus Falls Comm Coll, Fergus Falls, MN 56537-1009 | 1960 | Mr. Dan F. True | 5 | 1,299 | 63 |
| Finger Lakes Comm Coll, Canandaigua, NY 14424-8395 | 1965 | Dr. Daniel T. Hayes | 11 | 3,848 | 234 |
| Fiorello H LaGuardia Comm Coll of City U of NY, Long Island City, NY 11101-3071 | 1970 | Dr. Raymond C. Bowen | 11 | 10,675 | 914 |
| Flathead Valley Comm Coll, Kalispell, MT 59901-2622 | 1967 | Dr. David Beyer | 11 | 1,116 | 109 |
| Florence-Darlington Tech Coll, Florence, SC 29501-0548 | 1963 | Dr. Charles W. Gould | 5 | 3,125 | 184 |
| Florida Comm Coll at Jacksonville, Jacksonville, FL 32202-4030 | 1963 | Dr. Charles C. Spence | 5 | 19,211 | 1,533 |
| Florida Keys Comm Coll, Key West, FL 33040-4397 | 1965 | Dr. William A. Seeker | 5 | 2,200 | 94 |
| Florida National Coll, Hialeah, FL 33012 | 1982 | Mr. Jose Regueiro | 3 | 1,100 | 70 |
| Floyd Coll, Rome, GA 30162-1864 | 1970 | Dr. H. Lynn Cundiff | 5 | 3,048 | 66 |
| Foothill Coll, Los Altos Hills, CA 94022-4599 | 1958 | Dr. Bernadine Chuck Fong | 11 | 15,500 | 578 |
| Forsyth Tech Comm Coll, Winston-Salem, NC 27103-5197 | 1964 | Dr. Desna L. Wallin | 5 | 4,895 | 535 |
| Fort Scott Comm Coll, Fort Scott, KS 66701 | 1919 | Dr. Laura Meeks | 11 | 1,651 | 59 |
| Fox Valley Tech Coll, Appleton, WI 54913-2277 | 1967 | Dr. H. Victor Baldi | 11 | 6,370 | 1,241 |
| Frank Phillips Coll, Borger, TX 79008-5118 | 1948 | Dr. William A. Griffin | 11 | 1,108 | 93 |
| Frederick Comm Coll, Frederick, MD 21702-2097 | 1957 | Dr. Lee J. Betts | 11 | 4,378 | 272 |
| Fresno City Coll, Fresno, CA 93741-0002 | 1910 | Dr. Brice W. Harris | 9 | 17,099 | 832 |
| Front Range Comm Coll, Westminster, CO 80030-2105 | 1968 | Dr. Thomas Gonzales | 5 | 11,471 | 517 |
| Fullerton Coll, Fullerton, CA 92632-2095 | 1913 | Dr. Vera M. Martinez | 11 | 18,007 | 678 |
| Fulton-Montgomery Comm Coll, Johnstown, NY 12095-3790 | 1964 | Dr. Priscilla J. Bell | 11 | 1,726 | 94 |
| Gadsden State Comm Coll, Gadsden, AL 35902-0227 | 1985 | Dr. Victor Ficker | 5 | 6,243 | 323 |
| Gainesville Coll, Gainesville, GA 30503-1358 | 1964 | Dr. J. Foster Watkins | 5 | 2,646 | 102 |
| Galveston Coll, Galveston, TX 77550-7496 | 1967 | NR | 11 | 2,218 | 146 |
| Garden City Comm Coll, Garden City, KS 67846-6399 | 1919 | Dr. James H. Tangeman | 9 | 2,204 | 148 |
| Garland County Comm Coll, Hot Springs, AR 71913 | 1973 | Dr. Tom Spencer | 11 | 1,988 | 109 |
| Gaston Coll, Dallas, NC 28034-1499 | 1963 | Dr. Patricia Skinner | 11 | 4,046 | 370 |
| Gateway Comm Coll, Phoenix, AZ 85034-1795 | 1968 | Dr. Phil Randolph | 11 | 6,804 | 300 |
| Gateway Comm-Tech Coll, New Haven, CT 06511-5918 | 1968 | Dr. Antonio Perez | 5 | 4,843 | 248 |
| Gavilan Coll, Gilroy, CA 95020-9599 | 1919 | Dr. Glenn E. Mayle | 11 | 4,029 | 164 |
| Genesee Comm Coll, Batavia, NY 14020-9704 | 1966 | Dr. Stuart Steiner | 11 | 4,346 | 291 |
| George Corley Wallace State Comm Coll, Selma, AL 36702-1049 | 1966 | Dr. Julius Ray Brown | 5 | 1,847 | 78 |
| George C Wallace State Comm Coll, Dothan, AL 36303-9234 | 1949 | Dr. Larry Beaty | 5 | 4,000 | 180 |
| Georgia Military Coll, Milledgeville, GA 31061 | 1879 | Maj Gen. Peter J. Boylam, Jr. | 11 | 3,495 | 179 |
| Germanna Comm Coll, Locust Grove, VA 22508-0339 | 1970 | Dr. Francis S. Turnage | 5 | 2,596 | 135 |
| Glendale Comm Coll, Glendale, AZ 85302-3090 | 1965 | Dr. John R. Waltrip | 11 | 16,235 | 687 |
| Glen Oaks Comm Coll, Centreville, MI 49032-9719 | 1965 | Dr. Philip G. Ward | 11 | 1,190 | 96 |
| Gloucester County Coll, Sewell, NJ 08080 | 1967 | Dr. Richard H. Jones | 8 | 5,047 | 215 |
| Gogebic Comm Coll, Ironwood, MI 49938 | 1932 | Mr. Thomas J. Cuengros | 11 | 1,399 | 91 |
| Golden West Coll, Huntington Beach, CA 92647-2748 | 1966 | Dr. Kenneth D. Yglesias | 11 | 12,415 | 421 |
| Gordon Coll, Barnesville, GA 30204-1762 | 1852 | Dr. Jerry M. Williamson | 5 | 2,204 | 115 |
| Grand Rapids Comm Coll, Grand Rapids, MI 49503-3201 | 1914 | Mr. Richard Calkins | 9 | 13,934 | 549 |
| Grays Harbor Coll, Aberdeen, WA 98520-7599 | 1930 | Dr. Jewell Manspeaker | 5 | 2,815 | 87 |
| Grayson County Coll, Denison, TX 75020-8299 | 1964 | Dr. Jim M. Williams | 11 | 3,286 | 176 |
| Great Basin Coll, Elko, NV 89801-3348 | 1967 | Dr. Ronald K. Remington | 5 | 3,000 | 333 |
| Great Lakes Jr Coll of Business, Saginaw, MI 48607-1158 | 1907 | Mr. William Guerriero | 1 | 1,606 | 124 |
| Greenfield Comm Coll, Greenfield, MA 01301-9739 | 1962 | Mr. Lawrence A. Dean | 5 | 1,863 | 131 |
| Green River Comm Coll, Auburn, WA 98092-3699 | 1965 | Mr. Richard A. Rutkowski | 5 | 8,000 | 342 |
| Greenville Tech Coll, Greenville, SC 29606-5616 | 1962 | Dr. Thomas E. Barton, Jr. | 5 | 8,734 | 539 |
| Grossmont Coll, El Cajon, CA 92020-1799 | 1961 | Dr. Richard M. Sanchez | 11 | 14,500 | 600 |
| Guilford Tech Comm Coll, Jamestown, NC 27282-0309 | 1958 | Dr. Don Cameron | 11 | 6,647 | 385 |
| Gulf Coast Comm Coll, Panama City, FL 32401-1058 | 1957 | Dr. Robert L. McSpadden | 5 | 5,865 | 348 |
| Gwinnett Tech Inst, Lawrenceville, GA 30246-1505 | 1984 | Mr. J. Alvin Wilbanks | 5 | 4,000 | 84 |
| Hagerstown Jr Coll, Hagerstown, MD 21742-6590 | 1946 | Dr. Norman P. Shea | 8 | 3,026 | 177 |
| Halifax Comm Coll, Weldon, NC 27890-0809 | 1967 | Dr. Elton L. Newbern, Jr. | 11 | 1,360 | 68 |
| Harford Comm Coll, Bel Air, MD 21015-1698 | 1957 | Dr. Claudia E. Chiesi | 11 | 4,957 | 358 |
| Harrisburg Area Comm Coll, Harrisburg, PA 17110-2999 | 1964 | Dr. Mary L. Fifield | 11 | 10,726 | 589 |
| Hartnell Coll, Salinas, CA 93901-1697 | 1920 | Dr. Edward J. Valeau | 9 | 7,500 | 363 |
| Hawkeye Comm Coll, Waterloo, IA 50704-8015 | 1967 | Dr. Phillip O. Barry | 11 | 3,530 | 203 |
| Haywood Comm Coll, Clyde, NC 28721-9453 | 1964 | Dr. Dan W. Moore | 11 | 1,322 | 118 |

| Name, address | Year | Governing official, control, and highest degree offered | | Enroll-ment | Faculty |
|---|---|---|---|---|---|
| Heartland Comm Coll, Bloomington, IL 61701 | 1990 | Dr. Jonathon Astroth | 9 | 2,769 | 191 |
| Henry Ford Comm Coll, Dearborn, MI 48128-1495 | 1938 | Dr. Andrew A. Mazzara | 9 | 13,300 | 994 |
| Herkimer County Comm Coll, Herkimer, NY 13350 | 1966 | Dr. Ronald F. Williams | 11 | 2,445 | 123 |
| Hesser Coll, Manchester, NH 03103-7245 | 1900 | Mr. Linwood W. Galeucia | 3 | 3,000 | 99 |
| Hibbing Comm Coll, Hibbing, MN 55746-3300 | 1916 | Dr. Anthony Kuznik | 5 | 1,042 | 65 |
| Highland Comm Coll, Freeport, IL 61032-9341 | 1962 | Dr. Ruth Mercedes Smith | 11 | 2,663 | 169 |
| Highland Comm Coll, Highland, KS 66035-0068 | 1858 | Dr. Betty Stevens | 11 | 2,654 | 195 |
| Highline Comm Coll, Des Moines, WA 98198-9800 | 1961 | Dr. Edward M. Command | 5 | 7,271 | 223 |
| Hill Coll of the Hill Jr Coll District, Hillsboro, TX 76645-0619 | 1923 | Dr. W. R. Auvenshine | 9 | 2,500 | 80 |
| Hillsborough Comm Coll, Tampa, FL 33631-3127 | 1968 | Dr. Andreas A. Paloumpis | 5 | 19,189 | 708 |
| Hinds Comm Coll, Raymond, MS 39154 | 1917 | Dr. Clyde Muse | 11 | 10,743 | 899 |
| Hocking Coll, Nelsonville, OH 45764-9588 | 1968 | Dr. John J. Light | 5 | 6,200 | 265 |
| Holmes Comm Coll, Goodman, MS 39079-0369 | 1928 | Dr. Starkey A. Morgan, Sr. | 11 | 2,553 | 125 |
| Holyoke Comm Coll, Holyoke, MA 01040-1099 | 1946 | Dr. David M. Bartley | 5 | 3,558 | 235 |
| Horry-Georgetown Tech Coll, Conway, SC 29526 | 1965 | Dr. D. Kent Sharples | 11 | 3,194 | 215 |
| Housatonic Comm-Tech Coll, Bridgeport, CT 06608-2453 | 1966 | Dr. Vincent S. Darnowski | 5 | 2,654 | 137 |
| Houston Comm Coll System, Houston, TX 77270-7849 | 1971 | Dr. James Harding | 11 | 39,541 | 2,387 |
| Howard Coll, Big Spring, TX 79720-3702 | 1945 | Dr. Cheryl T. Sparks | 11 | 2,400 | 165 |
| Howard Comm Coll, Columbia, MD 21044-3197 | 1966 | Dr. Dwight A. Burrill | 11 | 5,130 | 315 |
| Hudson County Comm Coll, Jersey City, NJ 07306 | 1974 | Dr. Glen Gabert | 11 | 4,249 | 237 |
| Hudson Valley Comm Coll, Troy, NY 12180-6096 | 1953 | Dr. Stephen M. Curtis | 11 | 10,102 | 511 |
| Huertas Jr Coll, Caguas, PR 00625 | 1945 | Dr. Felix Rodriguez Matos | 3 | 2,220 | 91 |
| Hutchinson Comm Coll and Area Vocational Sch, Hutchinson, KS 67501-5894 | 1928 | Dr. Edward E. Berger | 11 | 3,621 | 264 |
| Illinois Central Coll, East Peoria, IL 61635-0001 | 1967 | Dr. Thomas K. Thomas | 11 | 11,680 | 626 |
| Illinois Eastern Comm Colls, Frontier Comm Coll, Fairfield, IL 62837-2601 | 1976 | Mr. Richard Mason | 11 | 1,904 | 158 |
| Illinois Eastern Comm Colls, Lincoln Trail Coll, Robinson, IL 62454 | 1969 | Dr. John Arabatgis | 11 | 1,127 | 77 |
| Illinois Eastern Comm Colls, Olney Central Coll, Olney, IL 62450 | 1962 | Mr. Ed Covey | 11 | 1,486 | 72 |
| Illinois Eastern Comm Colls, Wabash Valley Coll, Mount Carmel, IL 62863-2657 | 1960 | Dr. Harry K. Benson | 11 | 2,023 | 78 |
| Illinois Valley Comm Coll, Oglesby, IL 61348-9691 | 1924 | Dr. Alfred E. Wisgoski | 9 | 4,281 | 189 |
| Imperial Valley Coll, Imperial, CA 92251-0158 | 1922 | Mr. William Sechrist | 11 | 5,696 | 288 |
| Independence Comm Coll, Independence, KS 67301-0708 | 1925 | Dr. Don Schoening | 5 | 1,848 | 153 |
| Indiana Business Coll, Indianapolis, IN 46204-1108 | 1902 | Mr. Kenneth J. Konesco | 3 | 1,700 | 70 |
| Indian Hills Comm Coll, Ottumwa, IA 52501-1398 | 1966 | Dr. Lyle A. Hellyer | 11 | 3,292 | 137 |
| Indian River Comm Coll, Fort Pierce, FL 34981-5599 | 1960 | Dr. Edwin R. Massey | 5 | 6,919 | 623 |
| Inter American U of PR, Guayama Cmps, Guayama, PR 00785 | 1958 | Dr. Samuel F. Febres-Santiago | 1 | 1,304 | 89 |
| Interboro Inst, New York, NY 10019-3602 | 1888 | Mr. Bruce R. Kalish | 3 | 1,147 | 47 |
| Inver Hills Comm Coll, Inver Grove Heights, MN 55076-3224 | 1969 | Dr. Steve Wallace | 5 | 5,161 | 220 |
| Iowa Central Comm Coll, Fort Dodge, IA 50501-5798 | 1966 | Dr. Robert A. Paxton | 11 | 2,627 | 133 |
| Iowa Lakes Comm Coll, Estherville, IA 51334-2295 | 1967 | Mr. James E. Billings | 11 | 2,068 | 40 |
| Iowa Western Comm Coll, Council Bluffs, IA 51502 | 1966 | Dr. Dan Kinney | 9 | 3,638 | 218 |
| Irvine Valley Coll, Irvine, CA 92720-4399 | 1979 | Dr. Daniel R. Larios | 11 | 10,300 | 344 |
| Isothermal Comm Coll, Spindale, NC 28160-0804 | 1965 | Dr. Willard L. Lewis | 5 | 1,747 | 92 |
| Itasca Comm Coll, Grand Rapids, MN 55744 | 1922 | Dr. James Clark | 5 | 1,138 | 73 |
| Itawamba Comm Coll, Fulton, MS 38843-1099 | 1947 | Dr. David Cole | 11 | 3,500 | 102 |
| Ivy Tech State Coll–Central Indiana, Indianapolis, IN 46206-1763 | 1963 | Dr. Meredith L. Carter | 5 | 5,428 | 326 |
| Ivy Tech State Coll–Columbus, Columbus, IN 47203-1868 | 1963 | Mr. Homer B. Smith | 5 | 2,849 | 200 |
| Ivy Tech State Coll–Eastcentral, Muncie, IN 47302-9448 | 1968 | Dr. Thomas C. Henry | 5 | 2,140 | 249 |
| Ivy Tech State Coll–Kokomo, Kokomo, IN 46903-1373 | 1968 | Dr. Shanon Christiansen | 5 | 1,570 | 141 |
| Ivy Tech State Coll–Lafayette, Lafayette, IN 47903-6299 | 1968 | Dr. Elizabeth J. Doversberger | 5 | 2,187 | 146 |
| Ivy Tech State Coll–Northcentral, South Bend, IN 46619-3837 | 1968 | Dr. Carl F. Lutz | 5 | 2,787 | 226 |
| Ivy Tech State Coll–Northeast, Fort Wayne, IN 46805-1430 | 1969 | Mr. Jon L. Rupright | 5 | 3,411 | 280 |
| Ivy Tech State Coll–Northwest, Gary, IN 46409-1499 | 1963 | NR | 5 | 2,570 | 221 |
| Ivy Tech State Coll–Southcentral, Sellersburg, IN 47172-1829 | 1968 | Mr. James R. Wells | 5 | 1,890 | 128 |
| Ivy Tech State Coll–Southwest, Evansville, IN 47710-3398 | 1963 | NR | 5 | 2,795 | 235 |
| Ivy Tech State Coll–Wabash Valley, Terre Haute, IN 47802 | 1966 | Dr. Sam E. Borden | 5 | 2,447 | 167 |
| Ivy Tech State Coll–Whitewater, Richmond, IN 47374-1220 | 1963 | Mr. James Steck | 5 | 1,028 | 112 |
| Jackson Comm Coll, Jackson, MI 49201-8399 | 1928 | Dr. Lee Howser | 8 | 7,100 | 435 |
| Jackson State Comm Coll, Jackson, TN 38301-3797 | 1967 | Dr. Walter L. Nelms | 5 | 3,438 | 188 |
| James H Faulkner State Comm Coll, Bay Minette, AL 36507-2619 | 1965 | Dr. Gary L. Branch | 5 | 3,042 | 157 |
| James Sprunt Comm Coll, Kenansville, NC 28349-0398 | 1964 | Dr. Donald L. Reichard | 5 | 1,021 | 77 |
| Jamestown Comm Coll, Jamestown, NY 14701-1999 | 1950 | Dr. Gregory T. DeCinque | 11 | 3,660 | NR |
| Jefferson Coll, Hillsboro, MO 63050-2441 | 1963 | Dr. Gregory D. Adkins | 11 | 3,783 | 190 |
| Jefferson Comm Coll, Watertown, NY 13601 | 1961 | Dr. John W. Deans | 11 | 3,200 | 193 |
| Jefferson Comm Coll, Steubenville, OH 43952-3598 | 1966 | Dr. Edward L. Florak | 11 | 1,437 | 114 |
| Jefferson Davis Comm Coll, Brewton, AL 36426 | 1965 | Dr. Richard E. Brogdon | 5 | 1,600 | 66 |
| Jefferson State Comm Coll, Birmingham, AL 35215-3098 | 1965 | Dr. Judy M. Merritt | 5 | 6,749 | 268 |
| John A Logan Coll, Carterville, IL 62918-9900 | 1967 | Dr. Ray Hancock | 11 | 4,897 | 246 |
| John C Calhoun State Comm Coll, Decatur, AL 35609-2216 | 1965 | Dr. Richard Carpenter | 5 | 7,514 | 379 |
| John M Patterson State Tech Coll, Montgomery, AL 36116-2699 | 1962 | Mr. J. L. Taunton | 5 | 1,066 | 63 |
| Johnson County Comm Coll, Overland Park, KS 66210-1299 | 1967 | Dr. Charles J. Carlsen | 11 | 15,477 | 615 |
| Johnston Comm Coll, Smithfield, NC 27577-2350 | 1969 | Dr. John L. Tart | 5 | 2,655 | 269 |
| John Tyler Comm Coll, Chester, VA 23831 | 1967 | Dr. Marshall W. Smith | 5 | 5,367 | 227 |
| John Wood Comm Coll, Quincy, IL 62301-9147 | 1974 | Dr. Robert C. Keys | 9 | 2,300 | 156 |
| Joliet Jr Coll, Joliet, IL 60431-8938 | 1901 | Dr. Raymond A. Pietak | 11 | 10,417 | 496 |
| Jones County Jr Coll, Ellisville, MS 39437-3901 | 1928 | Dr. T. Terrell Tisdale | 11 | 4,430 | 175 |
| J Sargeant Reynolds Comm Coll, Richmond, VA 23285-5622 | 1972 | Dr. S. A. Burnette | 5 | 9,160 | 567 |
| Kalamazoo Valley Comm Coll, Kalamazoo, MI 49003-4070 | 1966 | Dr. Marilyn J. Schlack | 11 | 11,027 | 366 |
| Kankakee Comm Coll, Kankakee, IL 60901-0888 | 1966 | Dr. Larry D. Huffman | 11 | 3,776 | 222 |
| Kansas City Kansas Comm Coll, Kansas City, KS 66112-3003 | 1923 | Dr. Thomas R. Burke | 11 | 6,000 | 357 |
| Kaskaskia Coll, Centralia, IL 62801-7878 | 1966 | Dr. Alice Marie Mumaw | 11 | 2,916 | 220 |
| Kellogg Comm Coll, Battle Creek, MI 49017-3397 | 1956 | Dr. Paul R. Ohm | 11 | 9,012 | 340 |
| Kent State U, Ashtabula Cmps, Ashtabula, OH 44004-2299 | 1958 | Dr. Gary C. Ensign | 5 | 1,100 | 74 |
| Kent State U, Stark Cmps, Canton, OH 44720-7599 | 1967 | Dr. William G. Bittle | 5 | 2,484 | 107 |
| Kent State U, Trumbull Cmps, Warren, OH 44483-1998 | 1954 | Dr. David A. Allen, Jr. | 5 | 1,918 | 100 |
| Kent State U, Tuscarawas Cmps, New Philadelphia, OH 44663-9447 | 1962 | Dr. Gregg L. Andrews | 5 | 1,133 | 86 |
| Kingsborough Comm Coll of City U of NY, Brooklyn, NY 11235 | 1963 | Dr. Leon M. Goldstein | 11 | 15,464 | 842 |
| Kings River Comm Coll, Reedley, CA 93654-2099 | 1926 | Dr. Richard J. Giese | 11 | 6,278 | 221 |
| Kingwood Coll, Kingwood, TX 77339-3801 | 1984 | NR | 11 | 3,400 | 194 |
| Kirkwood Comm Coll, Cedar Rapids, IA 52406-2068 | 1966 | Dr. Norm Nielsen | 11 | 10,025 | 477 |
| Kirtland Comm Coll, Roscommon, MI 48653-9699 | 1966 | Dr. Dorothy N. Franke | 9 | 1,352 | 95 |
| Kishwaukee Coll, Malta, IL 60150 | 1967 | Dr. Norman L. Jenkins | 11 | 3,690 | 198 |

| Name, address | Year | Governing official, control, and highest degree offered | | Enrollment | Faculty |
|---|---|---|---|---|---|
| Labette Comm Coll, Parsons, KS 67357-4299 | 1923 | Mr. Joseph C. Birmingham | 11 | 2,598 | 234 |
| Lake Area Vocational-Tech Inst, Watertown, SD 57201 | 1964 | NR | 5 | 1,044 | 65 |
| Lake City Comm Coll, Lake City, FL 32025 | 1962 | Dr. Muriel Kay Heimer | 5 | 2,700 | 225 |
| Lake Land Coll, Mattoon, IL 61938-9366 | 1966 | Dr. Robert K. Luther | 11 | 4,734 | 424 |
| Lakeland Comm Coll, Kirtland, OH 44094-5198 | 1967 | Dr. Ralph R. Doty | 11 | 8,515 | 544 |
| Lake Michigan Coll, Benton Harbor, MI 49022-1899 | 1946 | Dr. Richard Pappas | 9 | 3,260 | 240 |
| Lakeshore Tech Coll, Cleveland, WI 53015-1414 | 1967 | Dr. Dennis Ladwig | 11 | 2,400 | 336 |
| Lake-Sumter Comm Coll, Leesburg, FL 34788-8751 | 1962 | Dr. Robert Westrick | 11 | 2,700 | 117 |
| Lake Tahoe Comm Coll, South Lake Tahoe, CA 96150-4524 | 1975 | Dr. Guy F. Lease | 11 | 2,700 | 164 |
| Lake Washington Tech Coll, Kirkland, WA 98034 | | Dr. Donald W. Fowler | 9 | 2,787 | 310 |
| Lamar U–Orange, Orange, TX 77630-5899 | 1969 | Dr. J. Michael Shahan | 5 | 1,489 | 63 |
| Lamar U–Port Arthur, Port Arthur, TX 77641-0310 | 1909 | Dr. Sam Monroe | 5 | 2,233 | 129 |
| Lane Comm Coll, Eugene, OR 97405-0640 | 1964 | Dr. Jerry Moskus | 11 | 9,533 | 528 |
| Laney Coll, Oakland, CA 94607-4893 | 1953 | Mr. Earnest C. Crutchfield | 11 | 10,454 | 315 |
| Lansing Comm Coll, Lansing, MI 48901-7210 | 1957 | Dr. Abel B. Sykes, Jr. | 11 | 16,404 | 1,085 |
| Laramie County Comm Coll, Cheyenne, WY 82007-3299 | 1968 | Dr. Charles Bohlen | 8 | 4,282 | 255 |
| Laredo Comm Coll, Laredo, TX 78040-4395 | 1946 | Dr. Roger L. Worsley | 11 | 6,919 | 308 |
| Las Positas Coll, Livermore, CA 94550-7650 | 1988 | Dr. Susan A. Cota | 5 | 5,600 | NR |
| Lassen Coll, Susanville, CA 96130 | 1925 | Dr. Dennis P. Adams | 11 | 2,951 | 204 |
| Lawson State Comm Coll, Birmingham, AL 35221-1798 | 1965 | Dr. Perry W. Ward | 5 | 1,892 | 112 |
| Lee Coll, Baytown, TX 77522-0818 | 1934 | Dr. Jackson N. Sasser | 9 | 5,753 | 333 |
| Lehigh Carbon Comm Coll, Schnecksville, PA 18078-2598 | 1967 | Dr. James R. Davis | 11 | 4,397 | 257 |
| Lenoir Comm Coll, Kinston, NC 28501 | 1960 | Dr. Lonnie H. Blizzard | 5 | 2,069 | 163 |
| Lewis and Clark Comm Coll, Godfrey, IL 62035-2466 | 1970 | Dr. Dale T. Chapman | 9 | 5,303 | 305 |
| Lima Tech Coll, Lima, OH 45804-3597 | 1971 | Dr. James J. Countryman | 5 | 2,591 | 167 |
| Lincoln Land Comm Coll, Springfield, IL 62794-9256 | 1967 | Dr. Norman Stephens, Jr. | 9 | 11,016 | 245 |
| Linn-Benton Comm Coll, Albany, OR 97321 | 1966 | Mr. Jon Carnahan | 11 | 5,453 | 472 |
| Long Beach City Coll, Long Beach, CA 90808-1780 | 1927 | Ms. Barbara A. Adams | 5 | 24,000 | 763 |
| Longview Comm Coll, Lee's Summit, MO 64081-2105 | 1969 | Mr. Aldo W. Leker | 11 | 8,388 | 396 |
| Lorain County Comm Coll, Elyria, OH 44035 | 1963 | Dr. Roy Church | 11 | 7,047 | 347 |
| Lord Fairfax Comm Coll, Middletown, VA 22645-0047 | 1969 | Dr. Marilyn C. Beck | 5 | 3,292 | 148 |
| Los Angeles City Coll, Los Angeles, CA 90029-3590 | 1929 | Mr. Jose Robledo | 9 | 15,217 | 625 |
| Los Angeles Harbor Coll, Wilmington, CA 90744-2311 | 1949 | Mr. James L. Heinselman | 11 | 7,603 | 313 |
| Los Angeles Mission Coll, Sylmar, CA 91342-3200 | 1974 | Dr. William Norlund, EdD | 11 | 6,027 | 115 |
| Los Angeles Pierce Coll, Woodland Hills, CA 91371-0001 | 1947 | Dr. Mary E. Lee | 11 | 18,212 | 519 |
| Los Angeles Southwest Coll, Los Angeles, CA 90047-4810 | 1967 | Dr. Carolyn G. Williams | 11 | 5,802 | 223 |
| Los Angeles Trade-Tech Coll, Los Angeles, CA 90015-4108 | 1925 | Ms. Betty Hartwig, Jr. | 11 | 13,373 | 600 |
| Los Angeles Valley Coll, Van Nuys, CA 91401-4096 | 1949 | Ms. Tyree Wieder | 11 | 17,768 | 482 |
| Los Medanos Coll, Pittsburg, CA 94565-5197 | 1974 | Dr. Helen Spencer | 9 | 7,311 | 236 |
| Louisiana State U at Alexandria, Alexandria, LA 71302-9121 | 1960 | Dr. Robert Cavanaugh | 5 | 2,546 | 87 |
| Louisiana State U at Eunice, Eunice, LA 70535-1129 | 1967 | Dr. Michael Smith | 5 | 2,861 | 120 |
| Lower Columbia Coll, Longview, WA 98632-0310 | 1934 | Dr. Vernon R. Pickett | 5 | 4,081 | 160 |
| Lurleen B Wallace State Jr Coll, Andalusia, AL 36420-1418 | 1969 | Dr. Seth Hammett | 5 | 1,147 | 71 |
| Luzerne County Comm Coll, Nanticoke, PA 18634-9804 | 1966 | Mr. Thomas J. Moran | 8 | 6,407 | 495 |
| Macomb Comm Coll, Warren, MI 48093-3896 | 1954 | Dr. Albert L. Lorenzo | 9 | 24,500 | 841 |
| Macon Coll, Macon, GA 31297 | 1968 | Dr. S. Aaron Hyatt | 5 | 4,500 | 141 |
| Madison Area Tech Coll, Madison, WI 53704-2599 | 1911 | Dr. Beverly S. Simone | 9 | 19,050 | 1,881 |
| Manatee Comm Coll, Bradenton, FL 34206-7046 | 1957 | Dr. Stephen J. Korcheck | 5 | 7,605 | 289 |
| Manchester Comm-Tech Coll, Manchester, CT 06045-1046 | 1963 | Dr. Jonathan M. Daube | 5 | 5,400 | 205 |
| Maple Woods Comm Coll, Kansas City, MO 64156-1299 | 1969 | Dr. Stephen R. Brainard | 11 | 4,572 | 175 |
| Maric Coll of Medical Careers, San Diego, CA 92123-1995 | 1976 | NR | 3 | 1,100 | 65 |
| Marion Tech Coll, Marion, OH 43302-5694 | 1971 | Dr. John Richard Bryson | 12 | 1,800 | 105 |
| Marshalltown Comm Coll, Marshalltown, IA 50158-4760 | 1927 | Dr. William Simpson | 9 | 1,248 | 107 |
| Massachusetts Bay Comm Coll, Wellesley Hills, MA 02181-5359 | 1961 | Mr. Roger A. Van Winkle | 5 | 5,252 | 274 |
| Massasoit Comm Coll, Brockton, MA 02402-3996 | 1966 | Dr. Gerard F. Burke | 5 | 5,602 | 357 |
| McHenry County Coll, Crystal Lake, IL 60012-2761 | 1967 | Mr. Robert C. Bartlett | 11 | 4,933 | 232 |
| McIntosh Coll, Dover, NH 03820-3990 | 1896 | Mr. Robert Decolfmacker | 3 | 1,050 | 27 |
| McLennan Comm Coll, Waco, TX 76708-1499 | 1965 | Dr. Dennis F. Michaelis | 8 | 5,561 | 284 |
| Mendocino Coll, Ukiah, CA 95482-0300 | 1973 | Dr. Carl J. Ehmann | 11 | 3,400 | 169 |
| Merced Coll, Merced, CA 95348-2898 | 1962 | Dr. E. Jan Moser | 11 | 6,327 | 421 |
| Mercer County Comm Coll, Trenton, NJ 08690-1004 | 1966 | Dr. Thomas D. Sepe | 11 | 6,936 | 361 |
| Meridian Comm Coll, Meridian, MS 39307 | 1937 | Dr. William F. Scaggs | 11 | 2,928 | 236 |
| Merritt Coll, Oakland, CA 94619-3196 | 1953 | Mr. Wise Allen | 11 | 5,123 | 201 |
| Mesabi Comm Coll, Virginia, MN 55792-3448 | 1918 | Mr. Jon Harris | 5 | 1,009 | 71 |
| Mesa Comm Coll, Mesa, AZ 85202-4866 | 1965 | Dr. Larry K. Christiansen | 11 | 22,302 | 852 |
| Metropolitan Comm Coll, Omaha, NE 68103-0777 | 1974 | Dr. J. Richard Gilliland | 11 | 10,686 | 549 |
| Metropolitan Comm Coll of East St Louis, East St Louis, IL 62201-1100 | 1969 | Janet Finch | 5 | 1,268 | 83 |
| Miami-Dade Comm Coll, Miami, FL 33132-2296 | 1960 | Dr. Robert H. McCabe | 11 | 51,019 | 2,070 |
| Miami U–Hamilton Cmps, Hamilton, OH 45011-3399 | 1968 | Dr. Jack Rhodes | 5 | 2,384 | 140 |
| Miami U–Middletown Cmps, Middletown, OH 45042-3497 | 1966 | Dr. Michael P. Governanti | 5 | 2,621 | 165 |
| Middle Georgia Coll, Cochran, GA 31014-1599 | 1884 | Dr. Joe Ben Welch | 5 | 2,049 | 82 |
| Middlesex Comm Coll, Bedford, MA 01730-1655 | 1970 | Dr. Carole A. Cowan | 5 | 5,984 | 377 |
| Middlesex Comm– Tech Coll, Middletown, CT 06457-4889 | 1966 | Dr. Leila Gonzalez Sullivan | 5 | 2,785 | 130 |
| Middlesex County Coll, Edison, NJ 08818-3050 | 1964 | Dr. Flora M. Edwards | 8 | 12,500 | 538 |
| Midland Coll, Midland, TX 79705-6399 | 1969 | Dr. David E. Daniel | 11 | 3,763 | 194 |
| Midlands Tech Coll, Columbia, SC 29202-2408 | 1974 | Dr. James L. Hudgins | 11 | 9,834 | 675 |
| Mid Michigan Comm Coll, Harrison, MI 48625-9447 | 1965 | Dr. Charles J. Corrigan | 11 | 3,304 | 227 |
| Mid-Plains Comm Coll, North Platte, NE 69101-9491 | 1965 | Dr. William A. Griffin, Jr. | 9 | 1,824 | 98 |
| Mid-State Tech Coll, Wisconsin Rapids, WI 54494-5599 | 1917 | Mr. Brian Oehler | 11 | 3,104 | 86 |
| Milwaukee Area Tech Coll, Milwaukee, WI 53233-1443 | 1912 | Dr. John R. Birkholz | 9 | 23,099 | 1,759 |
| Mineral Area Coll, Park Hills, MO 63601 | 1922 | Dr. Dixie A. Kohn | 9 | 2,388 | 154 |
| Minneapolis Comm and Tech Coll, Minneapolis, MN 55403-1779 | 1965 | Dr. Mary Retterer | 5 | 4,224 | 192 |
| MiraCosta Coll, Oceanside, CA 92056-3899 | 1934 | Dr. Tim T. L. Dong | 5 | 8,038 | 388 |
| Mission Coll, Santa Clara, CA 95054-1897 | 1977 | Dr. Michael Rao | 11 | 8,750 | 376 |
| Mississippi County Comm Coll, Blytheville, AR 72316-1109 | 1975 | Dr. John P. Sullins | 5 | 2,114 | 88 |
| Mississippi Delta Comm Coll, Moorhead, MS 38761-0668 | 1926 | Dr. Bobby Garvin | 9 | 2,403 | 128 |
| Mississippi Gulf Coast Comm Coll, Perkinston, MS 39573-0047 | 1911 | Dr. Willis H. Lott | 9 | 9,858 | 753 |
| Mitchell Comm Coll, Statesville, NC 28677-5293 | 1852 | Dr. Douglas O. Eason | 5 | 1,550 | 90 |
| Moberly Area Comm Coll, Moberly, MO 65270-1392 | 1927 | Dr. Andrew Komar, Jr. | 11 | 2,014 | 95 |
| Modesto Jr Coll, Modesto, CA 95350-5800 | 1921 | Dr. Maria Sheehan | 11 | 14,774 | 494 |
| Mohave Comm Coll, Kingman, AZ 86401-1299 | 1971 | Dr. Charles W. Hall | 5 | 5,681 | 349 |
| Mohawk Valley Comm Coll, Utica, NY 13501-5394 | 1946 | Dr. Michael I. Schafer | 11 | 6,328 | 353 |
| Monroe Coll, Bronx, NY 10468-5407 | 1933 | Mr. Stephen J. Jerome | 3 | 2,625 | 100 |
| Monroe Comm Coll, Rochester, NY 14623-5780 | 1961 | Dr. Peter A. Spina | 11 | 13,730 | 642 |
| Monroe County Comm Coll, Monroe, MI 48161-9047 | 1964 | Mr. Gerald D. Welch | 8 | 3,923 | 201 |

| Name, address | Year | Governing official, control, and highest degree offered | | Enrollment | Faculty |
|---|---|---|---|---|---|
| Montcalm Comm Coll, Sidney, MI 48885-0300 | 1965 | Dr. Donald C. Burns | 11 | 1,753 | 134 |
| Monterey Peninsula Coll, Monterey, CA 93940-4799 | 1947 | Dr. Edward Orest Gould | 5 | 8,300 | 388 |
| Montgomery Coll, Conroe, TX 77384 | | NR | 11 | 3,196 | 179 |
| Montgomery Coll–Germantown Cmps, Germantown, MD 20876 | 1975 | Dr. Robert E. Parilla | 11 | 3,896 | 185 |
| Montgomery Coll–Rockville Cmps, Rockville, MD 20850-1196 | 1965 | Dr. Robert E. Parilla | 11 | 13,144 | 705 |
| Montgomery Coll–Takoma Park Cmps, Takoma Park, MD 20912 | 1946 | Dr. Robert E. Parilla | 11 | 4,471 | 224 |
| Montgomery County Comm Coll, Blue Bell, PA 19422-0796 | 1964 | Dr. Edward M. Sweitzer | 8 | 8,751 | 514 |
| Moorpark Coll, Moorpark, CA 93021-1695 | 1967 | Dr. Darlene Pacheco | 8 | 10,226 | 450 |
| Moraine Park Tech Coll, Fond du Lac, WI 54936-1940 | 1967 | Dr. John J. Shanahan | 11 | 6,670 | 298 |
| Moraine Valley Comm Coll, Palos Hills, IL 60465-0937 | 1967 | Dr. Vernon O. Crawley | 11 | 12,813 | 592 |
| Morton Coll, Cicero, IL 60650-4398 | 1924 | Dr. John A. Neuhaus | 11 | 4,050 | 214 |
| Motlow State Comm Coll, Tullahoma, TN 37388-8100 | 1969 | Dr. A. Frank Glass | 5 | 3,129 | 205 |
| Mountain Empire Comm Coll, Big Stone Gap, VA 24219-0700 | 1972 | Dr. Robert H. Sandel | 5 | 2,700 | 150 |
| Mountain View Coll, Dallas, TX 75211-6599 | 1970 | Dr. Monique Amerman | 8 | 6,027 | 264 |
| Mt Hood Comm Coll, Gresham, OR 97030-3300 | 1966 | Dr. Paul Kreider | 11 | 7,171 | 547 |
| Mount Ida Coll, Newton Centre, MA 02159-3310 | 1899 | Dr. Bryan E. Carlson | 1 | 2,008 | 211 |
| Mt San Antonio Coll, Walnut, CA 91789-1399 | 1946 | Dr. William H. Feddersen | 9 | 32,000 | 799 |
| Mt San Jacinto Coll, San Jacinto, CA 92583-2399 | 1963 | Dr. Roy B. Mason, II | 11 | 5,627 | 215 |
| Mount Wachusett Comm Coll, Gardner, MA 01440-1000 | 1963 | Dr. Daniel M. Asquino | 5 | 1,900 | 112 |
| Murray State Coll, Tishomingo, OK 73460-3130 | 1908 | Dr. Glen Pedersen | 5 | 1,701 | 70 |
| Muscatine Comm Coll, Muscatine, IA 52761-5396 | 1929 | Dr. Victor G. McAvoy | 5 | 1,250 | 95 |
| Muskegon Comm Coll, Muskegon, MI 49442-1493 | 1926 | Dr. Frank P Marczak | 11 | 5,169 | 150 |
| Muskingum Area Tech Coll, Zanesville, OH 43701-2694 | 1969 | Dr. Lynn H. Willett | 11 | 2,135 | 104 |
| Napa Valley Coll, Napa, CA 94558-6236 | 1942 | Dr. Diane E. Carey | 11 | 7,000 | 304 |
| Nash Comm Coll, Rocky Mount, NC 27804-0488 | 1967 | Dr. J. Reid Parrott, Jr. | 5 | 1,880 | 106 |
| Nashville State Tech Inst, Nashville, TN 37209-4515 | 1970 | Dr. George H. Van Allen | 5 | 6,386 | 294 |
| Nassau Comm Coll, Garden City, NY 11530-6793 | 1959 | Dr. Sean A. Fanelli | 11 | 21,975 | 1,523 |
| National Ed Ctr–Spartan Sch of Aeronautics Cmps, Tulsa, OK 74158-2833 (2) | 1928 | Mr. Ross L. Alloway | 3 | 1,110 | 150 |
| Naugatuck Valley Comm–Tech Coll, Waterbury, CT 06708-3000 | 1967 | Dr. Richard L. Sanders | 5 | 5,533 | 165 |
| Navajo Comm Coll, Tsaile, AZ 86556 | 1968 | Dr. Tommy Lewis, Jr. | 4 | 1,767 | 164 |
| Navarro Coll, Corsicana, TX 75110-4899 | 1946 | Dr. Gerald Burson | 11 | 3,211 | 175 |
| Neosho County Comm Coll, Chanute, KS 66720-2699 | 1936 | Dr. Theodore W. Wischropp | 11 | 1,666 | 96 |
| Newbury Coll, Brookline, MA 02146-5750 | 1962 | Mr. Edward J. Tassinari | 1 | 1,088 | 105 |
| The New England Banking Inst, Boston, MA 02111-2671 | 1909 | Mr. Robert A. Regan | 1 | 1,744 | 360 |
| New England Inst of Tech, Warwick, RI 02886-2244 | 1940 | Dr. Richard I. Gouse | 1 | 2,354 | 168 |
| New Hampshire Tech Inst, Concord, NH 03301-7412 | 1964 | Dr. David E. Larrabee, Sr. | 5 | 1,413 | 145 |
| New Mexico Jr Coll, Hobbs, NM 88240-9123 | 1965 | Dr. Charles D. Hays | 11 | 2,752 | 129 |
| New Mexico State U–Alamogordo, Alamogordo, NM 88310 | 1958 | Dr. Charles R. Reidlinger | 5 | 2,300 | 140 |
| New Mexico State U–Carlsbad, Carlsbad, NM 88220-3509 | 1950 | Dr. Douglas E. Burghan | 5 | 1,151 | 71 |
| New River Comm Coll, Dublin, VA 24084-1127 | 1969 | Dr. Edwin L. Barnes | 5 | 1,554 | 175 |
| Niagara County Comm Coll, Sanborn, NY 14132-9460 | 1962 | Mr. Gerald L. Miller | 11 | 5,361 | 549 |
| Nicolet Area Tech Coll, Rhinelander, WI 54501-0518 | 1968 | Dr. Adrian Lorbetske | 11 | 1,433 | 84 |
| Normandale Comm Coll, Bloomington, MN 55431-4399 | 1968 | Dr. Thomas J. Horak | 5 | 7,718 | 281 |
| Northampton County Area Comm Coll, Bethlehem, PA 18017-7599 | 1967 | Dr. Robert J. Kopecek | 11 | 5,857 | 311 |
| North Arkansas Comm/Tech Coll, Harrison, AR 72601 | 1974 | Dr. Bill Baker | 11 | 1,482 | 116 |
| North Central Michigan Coll, Petoskey, MI 49770-8717 | 1958 | Mr. Robert B. Graham | 8 | 2,032 | 146 |
| North Central Missouri Coll, Trenton, MO 64683-1824 | 1925 | Dr. James Selby | 9 | 1,093 | 69 |
| North Central Tech Coll, Mansfield, OH 44901-0698 | 1961 | Dr. Byron E. Kee | 5 | 2,601 | 182 |
| Northcentral Tech Coll, Wausau, WI 54401-1880 | 1912 | Dr. Robert Ernst | 9 | 3,500 | 211 |
| North Central Texas Coll, Gainesville, TX 76240-4699 | 1924 | Dr. Ronnie Glasscock | 8 | 4,133 | 175 |
| North Country Comm Coll, Saranac Lake, NY 12983-2046 | 1967 | Dr. Gail Rogers Rice | 11 | 1,148 | 140 |
| North Dakota State Coll of Science, Wahpeton, ND 58076 | 1903 | Dr. Jerry Olson | 5 | 2,492 | 156 |
| Northeast Alabama State Comm Coll, Rainsville, AL 35986-0159 | 1963 | Dr. Charles M. Pendley | 5 | 1,589 | 51 |
| Northeast Comm Coll, Norfolk, NE 68702-0469 | 1973 | Dr. James C. Underwood | 11 | 3,413 | 122 |
| Northeastern Jr Coll, Sterling, CO 80751-2344 | 1941 | NR | 11 | 2,734 | 79 |
| Northeastern Oklahoma A&M Coll, Miami, OK 74354-6434 | 1919 | Dr. Jerry D. Carroll | 5 | 2,200 | 100 |
| Northeast Iowa Comm Coll, Peosta Cmps, Peosta, IA 52068-9776 | 1970 | Ms. Karla Berns | 11 | 1,700 | 66 |
| Northeast Mississippi Comm Coll, Booneville, MS 38829 | 1948 | Mr. Joe M. Childers | 5 | 3,000 | 126 |
| Northeast State Tech Comm Coll, Blountville, TN 37617-0246 | 1966 | Dr. R. Wade Powers | 5 | 3,488 | 246 |
| Northeast Texas Comm Coll, Mount Pleasant, TX 75456-1307 | 1985 | Dr. Charles B. Florio | 11 | 1,952 | 114 |
| Northern Essex Comm Coll, Haverhill, MA 01830 | 1960 | Dr. John R. Dimitry | 5 | 6,359 | 457 |
| Northern Oklahoma Coll, Tonkawa, OK 74653-0310 | 1901 | Dr. Joe Kinzer | 5 | 2,350 | 80 |
| Northern Virginia Comm Coll, Annandale, VA 22003-3796 | 1965 | Dr. Richard J. Ernst | 5 | 38,084 | 1,387 |
| North Florida Comm Coll, Madison, FL 32340-1602 | 1958 | Mr. William O. Brazil | 5 | 1,003 | 30 |
| North Harris Coll, Houston, TX 77073-3499 | 1972 | Dr. John E. Pickelman | 11 | 3,080 | 196 |
| North Hennepin Comm Coll, Minneapolis, MN 55445-2231 | 1966 | Dr. Katherine H. Sloan | 5 | 5,527 | 220 |
| North Idaho Coll, Coeur d'Alene, ID 83814-2199 | 1933 | Dr. C. Robert Bennett | 11 | 3,312 | 260 |
| North Iowa Area Comm Coll, Mason City, IA 50401-7299 | 1918 | Dr. David Buettner | 11 | 2,771 | 107 |
| North Lake Coll, Irving, TX 75038-3899 | 1977 | Dr. James F. Horton, Jr. | 8 | 6,400 | 280 |
| Northland Comm and Tech Coll, Thief River Falls, MN 56701 | 1965 | Dr. Orley Gunderson | 5 | 1,150 | 61 |
| Northland Pioneer Coll, Holbrook, AZ 86025-0610 | 1974 | Dr. John H. Anderson | 11 | 4,779 | 400 |
| North Seattle Comm Coll, Seattle, WA 98103-3599 | 1970 | Dr. Constance Rice | 5 | 8,199 | 290 |
| North Shore Comm Coll, Danvers, MA 01923-4093 | 1965 | Dr. George Traicoff | 5 | 5,163 | 361 |
| NorthWest Arkansas Comm Coll, Bentonville, AR 72712 | 1989 | Dr. Bob C. Burns | 11 | 2,245 | 151 |
| Northwest Coll, Powell, WY 82435-1898 | 1946 | Dr. John P. Hanna | 11 | 2,000 | 181 |
| Northwestern Coll, Lima, OH 45805-1498 | 1920 | Mr. Loren R. Jarvis | 1 | 1,800 | 59 |
| Northwestern Connecticut Comm-Tech Coll, Winsted, CT 06098 | 1965 | Dr. R. Eileen Baccus | 5 | 2,116 | 92 |
| Northwestern Michigan Coll, Traverse City, MI 49686-3061 | 1951 | Dr. Timothy G. Quinn | 11 | 3,937 | 97 |
| Northwest Indian Coll, Bellingham, WA 98226 | 1978 | Mr. Robert J. Lorence | 4 | 1,500 | 63 |
| Northwest Mississippi Comm Coll, Senatobia, MS 38668-1701 | 1927 | Dr. David M. Haraway | 11 | 4,200 | 200 |
| Northwest-Shoals Comm Coll, Muscle Shoals, AL 35662 | 1961 | Dr. Larry McCoy | 5 | 4,545 | 176 |
| Northwest State Comm Coll, Archbold, OH 43502-9542 | 1968 | Dr. Larry G. McDougle | 5 | 1,991 | 115 |
| Norwalk Comm-Tech Coll, Norwalk, CT 06854-1655 | 1961 | Dr. William H. Schwab | 5 | 5,352 | 241 |
| Oakland Comm Coll, Bloomfield Hills, MI 48304-2266 | 1964 | Dr. Patsy J. Calkins | 11 | 26,144 | 788 |
| Oakton Comm Coll, Des Plaines, IL 60016-1268 | 1969 | Dr. Thomas TenHoeve | 9 | 10,976 | 625 |
| Ocean County Coll, Toms River, NJ 08754-2001 | 1964 | Dr. Milton Shaw | 8 | 8,122 | 348 |
| Odessa Coll, Odessa, TX 79764-7127 | 1946 | Dr. Vance W. Gipson | 11 | 4,679 | 206 |
| Ohio U–Southern Cmps, Ironton, OH 45638-2214 | 1956 | Dr. Bill Dingus | 5 | 2,236 | 125 |
| Ohlone Coll, Fremont, CA 94539-5884 | 1967 | Dr. Floyd M. Hogue | 11 | 8,400 | 434 |
| Okaloosa-Walton Comm Coll, Niceville, FL 32578-1295 | 1963 | Dr. James R. Richburg | 11 | 5,820 | 297 |
| Oklahoma City Comm Coll, Oklahoma City, OK 73159-4419 | 1969 | Dr. Robert P. Todd | 5 | 10,586 | 342 |
| Oklahoma State U, Oklahoma City, Oklahoma City, OK 73107-6120 | 1961 | Dr. James Hooper | 5 | 4,357 | 205 |
| Oklahoma State U, Okmulgee, Okmulgee, OK 74447-3901 | 1946 | Dr. Robert Klabenes | 5 | 2,188 | 138 |

| Name, address | Year | Governing official, control, and highest degree offered | | Enroll-ment | Faculty |
|---|---|---|---|---|---|
| Olympic Coll, Bremerton, WA 98337-1699 | 1946 | Dr. Wallace A. Simpson | 5 | 7,470 | 323 |
| Onondaga Comm Coll, Syracuse, NY 13215 | 1962 | Dr. Bruce H. Leslie | 11 | 7,400 | 536 |
| Orangeburg-Calhoun Tech Coll, Orangeburg, SC 29118-8299 | 1968 | Dr. Jeffery R. Olson | 11 | 1,768 | 120 |
| Orange Coast Coll, Costa Mesa, CA 92628-5005 | 1947 | Mr. James McIlwain | 11 | 22,009 | 823 |
| Orange County Comm Coll, Middletown, NY 10940-6437 | 1950 | Dr. William F. Messner | 11 | 5,853 | 336 |
| Otero Jr Coll, La Junta, CO 81050-3415 | 1941 | Dr. Joe M. Treece | 5 | 1,000 | 53 |
| Owensboro Comm Coll, Owensboro, KY 42303-1899 | 1986 | Dr. John McGuire | 5 | 2,614 | 124 |
| Owens Comm Coll, Findlay, OH 45840 | 1983 | Mr. Daniel H. Brown | 5 | 1,767 | 102 |
| Owens Comm Coll, Toledo, OH 43699-1947 | 1966 | Mr. Daniel H. Brown | 5 | 9,682 | 752 |
| Oxnard Coll, Oxnard, CA 93033-6699 | 1975 | Dr. Ruth M. Hemming | 8 | 5,073 | 288 |
| Ozarks Tech Comm Coll, Springfield, MO 65802 | | Dr. Norman K. Myers | 9 | 3,507 | 150 |
| Palm Beach Comm Coll, Lake Worth, FL 33461-4796 | 1933 | Dr. Edward M. Eissey | 5 | 16,717 | 772 |
| Palo Alto Coll, San Antonio, TX 78224-2499 | 1987 | Dr. Joel E. Vela | 11 | 7,499 | 317 |
| Palomar Coll, San Marcos, CA 92069-1487 | 1946 | Dr. George R. Boggs | 11 | 22,945 | 1,097 |
| Palo Verde Coll, Blythe, CA 92225-1118 | 1947 | Dr. Wilford J. Beumel | 11 | 1,200 | 69 |
| Paradise Valley Comm Coll, Phoenix, AZ 85032-1200 | 1985 | Dr. Raul Cardenas | 11 | 5,574 | 260 |
| Paris Jr Coll, Paris, TX 75460-6298 | 1924 | Mr. Bobby R. Walters | 11 | 2,450 | 117 |
| Parkland Coll, Champaign, IL 61821-1899 | 1967 | Dr. Zelema M. Harris | 9 | 8,403 | 487 |
| Pasadena City Coll, Pasadena, CA 91106-2041 | 1924 | Dr. James P. Kossler | 11 | 21,756 | 824 |
| Pasco-Hernando Comm Coll, Dade City, FL 33523-7599 | 1972 | Dr. Robert W. Judson, Jr. | 5 | 5,242 | 255 |
| Passaic County Comm Coll, Paterson, NJ 07505-1179 | 1968 | Mr. Elliott Collins | 8 | 3,642 | 267 |
| Patrick Henry Comm Coll, Martinsville, VA 24115-5311 | 1962 | Dr. Max Wingett | 5 | 2,800 | 88 |
| Paul D Camp Comm Coll, Franklin, VA 23851-0737 | 1971 | Dr. Jerome J. Friga | 5 | 1,629 | 59 |
| Pearl River Comm Coll, Poplarville, MS 39470 | 1909 | Dr. Ted J. Alexander | 11 | 2,575 | 167 |
| Peirce Coll, Philadelphia, PA 19102-4603 | 1865 | Dr. Arthur J. Lendo | 1 | 1,154 | 57 |
| Pellissippi State Tech Comm Coll, Knoxville, TN 37933-0990 | 1974 | Dr. Allen G. Edwards | 5 | 7,468 | 448 |
| Peninsula Coll, Port Angeles, WA 98362-2779 | 1961 | Dr. Wallace Sigmar | 5 | 3,550 | 149 |
| Pennsylvania Coll of Tech, Williamsport, PA 17701-5778 | 1965 | Dr. Robert Breuder | 12 | 4,729 | 350 |
| Penn State U Abington-Ogontz Cmps, Abington, PA 19001-3918 | 1950 | Dr. Karen Wiley Sandler | 12 | 3,212 | 173 |
| Penn State U Altoona Cmps, Altoona, PA 16601-3760 | 1929 | Dr. Allen C. Meadors | 12 | 2,919 | 150 |
| Penn State U Berks Cmps, Reading, PA 19610-6009 | 1924 | Dr. Frederick H. Gaige | 12 | 1,771 | 107 |
| Penn State U Delaware County Cmps, Media, PA 19063-5596 | 1966 | Dr. Edward S. J. Tomezsko | 12 | 1,540 | 90 |
| Penn State U Hazleton Cmps, Hazleton, PA 18201-1291 | 1934 | Dr. James J. Staudenmeier | 12 | 1,316 | 75 |
| Penn State U Mont Alto Cmps, Mont Alto, PA 17237-9703 | 1929 | Dr. Corrinne A. Caldwell | 12 | 1,261 | 66 |
| Penn State U Schuylkill Cmps, Schuylkill Haven, PA 17972-2208 | 1934 | Dr. Wayne Lammie | 12 | 1,041 | 62 |
| Penn State U Shenango Cmps, Sharon, PA 16146-1537 | 1965 | Dr. Albert N. Skomra | 12 | 1,005 | 76 |
| Penn State U Worthington Scranton Cmps, Dunmore, PA 18512-1699 | 1923 | Dr. James D. Gallagher | 12 | 1,325 | 80 |
| Penn State U York Cmps, York, PA 17403-3298 | 1926 | Dr. Donald A. Gogniat | 12 | 2,106 | 116 |
| Penn Valley Comm Coll, Kansas City, MO 64111 | 1969 | Dr. E. Paul Williams | 11 | 4,432 | 254 |
| Pensacola Jr Coll, Pensacola, FL 32504-8998 | 1948 | Dr. Horace E. Hartsell | 5 | 12,000 | 819 |
| Phillips Comm Coll, Helena, AR 72342-0785 | 1965 | Dr. Steven Jones | 11 | 1,520 | 107 |
| Piedmont Tech Coll, Greenwood, SC 29648-1467 | 1966 | Dr. Lex D. Walters | 5 | 3,148 | 127 |
| Piedmont Virginia Comm Coll, Charlottesville, VA 22902-7589 | 1972 | Dr. Deborah M. DiCroce | 5 | 4,436 | 262 |
| Pierce Coll, Tacoma, WA 98498-1999 | 1967 | Dr. George Delaney | 5 | 10,294 | 579 |
| Pikes Peak Comm Coll, Colorado Springs, CO 80906-5498 | 1968 | Dr. Marijane Axtell Paulsen | 5 | 6,615 | 479 |
| Pima Comm Coll, Tucson, AZ 85709-1010 | 1966 | Dr. Robert Jensen | 5 | 27,960 | 1,567 |
| Pitt Comm Coll, Greenville, NC 27835-7007 | 1961 | Dr. Charles E. Russell | 11 | 4,712 | 240 |
| Polk Comm Coll, Winter Haven, FL 33881-4299 | 1964 | Dr. Maryly VanLeer Peck | 5 | 6,000 | 260 |
| Porterville Coll, Porterville, CA 93257-6058 | 1927 | Dr. Bonnie L. Rogers | 5 | 2,651 | 128 |
| Portland Comm Coll, Portland, OR 97280-0990 | 1961 | Dr. Daniel F. Moriarty | 11 | 22,840 | 1,215 |
| Potomac State Coll of West Virginia U, Keyser, WV 26726 | 1901 | Dr. Kathryn A. Brailer | 5 | 1,163 | 83 |
| Prairie State Coll, Chicago Heights, IL 60411-1275 | 1958 | Dr. T. Lightfield | 11 | 5,000 | 289 |
| Pratt Comm Coll and Area Voc Sch, Pratt, KS 67124-8317 | 1938 | Dr. William Wojciechowski | 9 | 1,349 | 54 |
| Prince George's Comm Coll, Largo, MD 20774-2199 | 1958 | Dr. Robert I. Bickford | 8 | 12,050 | 554 |
| Pueblo Comm Coll, Pueblo, CO 81004-1499 | 1979 | Dr. Joe May | 5 | 4,127 | 288 |
| Pulaski Tech Coll, North Little Rock, AR 72118 | 1945 | Mr. Benjamin Wyatt | 5 | 1,412 | 88 |
| Queensborough Comm Coll of City U of NY, Bayside, NY 11364 | 1958 | Dr. Kurt R. Schmeller | 11 | 12,000 | 553 |
| Quinebaug Valley Comm-Tech Coll, Danielson, CT 06239-1440 | 1971 | Ms. Dianne E. Williams | 5 | 1,120 | 55 |
| Quinsigamond Comm Coll, Worcester, MA 01606-2092 | 1963 | Dr. Sandra Kurtinitis | 5 | 4,680 | 224 |
| Ramírez Coll of Business and Tech, San Juan, PR 00910-0340 | 1922 | Dr. Rogena Kyles | 3 | 1,364 | NR |
| Rancho Santiago Coll, Santa Ana, CA 92706-3398 | 1915 | Dr. Vivian B. Blevins | 5 | 20,714 | 1,799 |
| Randolph Comm Coll, Asheboro, NC 27204-1009 | 1962 | Dr. Larry K. Linker | 5 | 1,343 | 73 |
| Rappahannock Comm Coll, Glenns, VA 23149-0287 | 1970 | Dr. John H. Upton | 12 | 2,129 | 132 |
| Raritan Valley Comm Coll, Somerville, NJ 08876-1265 | 1965 | Dr. Cary A. Israel | 8 | 5,555 | 276 |
| Reading Area Comm Coll, Reading, PA 19603-1706 | 1971 | Dr. Gust Zogas | 8 | 3,000 | 249 |
| Redlands Comm Coll, El Reno, OK 73036 | 1938 | Dr. Larry F. Devane | 5 | 1,901 | 131 |
| Red Rocks Comm Coll, Lakewood, CO 80401 | 1969 | Dr. Dorothy A. Horrell | 5 | 6,939 | 276 |
| Rend Lake Coll, Ina, IL 62846-9801 | 1967 | Mr. Mark S. Kern | 5 | 3,759 | 201 |
| Richard Bland Coll of the Coll of William and Mary, Petersburg, VA 23805-7100 | 1961 | Dr. James B. McNeer, Jr. | 5 | 1,205 | 48 |
| Richland Coll, Dallas, TX 75243-2199 | 1972 | Dr. Stephen Mittelstet | 11 | 13,391 | 665 |
| Richland Comm Coll, Decatur, IL 62521-8513 | 1971 | Dr. Charles R. Novak | 9 | 3,384 | 224 |
| Richmond Comm Coll, Hamlet, NC 28345-1189 | 1964 | Mr. Joseph W. Grimsley | 5 | 1,146 | 100 |
| Ricks Coll, Rexburg, ID 83460-4107 | 1888 | Dr. Steven D. Bennion | 2 | 7,956 | 387 |
| Rio Hondo Coll, Whittier, CA 90601-1699 | 1960 | Mr. Tim Wood | 11 | 14,500 | 710 |
| Rio Salado Comm Coll, Phoenix, AZ 85003-1558 | 1978 | Dr. Linda Thor | 11 | 8,754 | 446 |
| Riverland Comm Coll, Austin, MN 55912-1407 | 1940 | Dr. Vicky R. Smith | 5 | 1,420 | 73 |
| Riverside Comm Coll, Riverside, CA 92506-1293 | 1916 | Dr. Salvatore Rotella | 11 | 20,000 | 550 |
| Roane State Comm Coll, Harriman, TN 37748-5011 | 1971 | Dr. Sherry L. Hoppe | 5 | 5,803 | 337 |
| Robeson Comm Coll, Lumberton, NC 28359-1420 | 1965 | Mr. Fred W. Williams, Jr. | 5 | 1,322 | 114 |
| Rochester Comm and Tech Coll, Rochester, MN 55904-4999 | 1915 | Dr. Karen E. Nagle | 5 | 3,593 | 225 |
| Rockingham Comm Coll, Wentworth, NC 27375-0038 | 1964 | Dr. N. J. Owens, Jr. | 5 | 1,907 | 114 |
| Rockland Comm Coll, Suffern, NY 10901-3699 | 1959 | Dr. Neal A. Raisman | 11 | 7,240 | 792 |
| Rock Valley Coll, Rockford, IL 61114-5699 | 1964 | Dr. Karl J. Jacobs | 9 | 8,936 | 222 |
| Rogers State Coll, Claremore, OK 74017-3252 | 1909 | Dr. Richard H. Mosier | 5 | 3,204 | 270 |
| Rogue Comm Coll, Grants Pass, OR 97527-9298 | 1970 | Dr. Harvey Bennett | 11 | 1,804 | 279 |
| Rose State Coll, Midwest City, OK 73110-2799 | 1968 | Dr. Larry Nutter | 11 | 9,083 | 402 |
| Rowan-Cabarrus Comm Coll, Salisbury, NC 28145-1595 | 1963 | Dr. Richard L. Brownell | 5 | 3,500 | 130 |
| Roxbury Comm Coll, Roxbury Crossing, MA 02120-3400 | 1973 | Dr. Grace C. Brown | 5 | 3,000 | NR |
| Sacramento City Coll, Sacramento, CA 95822-1386 | 1916 | Dr. Robert M. Harris | 11 | 16,039 | 375 |
| Saddleback Coll, Mission Viejo, CA 92692-3697 | 1967 | Dr. Ned Doffoney | 11 | 16,917 | 635 |
| Saint Augustine Coll, Chicago, IL 60640-3501 | 1980 | Fr. Carlos A. Plazas | 1 | 1,345 | 156 |
| Saint Charles County Comm Coll, St Peters, MO 63376-0975 | 1986 | Dr. Donald D. Shook | 5 | 4,590 | 206 |

| Name, address | Year | Governing official, control, and highest degree offered | | Enroll-ment | Faculty |
|---|---|---|---|---|---|
| St Clair County Comm Coll, Port Huron, MI 48061-5015 | 1923 | Dr. R. Ernest Dear | 8 | 4,264 | 279 |
| St Cloud Tech Coll, St Cloud, MN 56303-1240 | 1948 | Dr. Larry Barnhardt | 5 | 2,431 | 102 |
| St Johns River Comm Coll, Palatka, FL 32177-3807 | 1958 | Dr. R. L. McLendon, Jr. | 5 | 3,500 | 157 |
| St Louis Comm Coll at Florissant Valley, St Louis, MO 63135-1499 | 1963 | Mr. Michael Maguire | 9 | 8,160 | 390 |
| St Louis Comm Coll at Forest Park, St Louis, MO 63110-1316 | 1962 | Dr. Henry D. Shannon | 9 | 8,197 | 366 |
| St Louis Comm Coll at Meramec, Kirkwood, MO 63122-5720 | 1963 | Mr. Richard A. Black | 9 | 13,211 | 570 |
| St Paul Tech Coll, St Paul, MN 55102-1800 | 1922 | Dr. Donovan Schwichtenberg | 12 | 3,401 | 565 |
| St Petersburg Jr Coll, St Petersburg, FL 33781-3489 | 1927 | Dr. Carl M. Kuttler, Jr. | 11 | 19,207 | 976 |
| St Philip's Coll, San Antonio, TX 78203-2098 | 1898 | Dr. Charles A. Taylor | 9 | 72,128 | 334 |
| Salem Comm Coll, Carneys Point, NJ 08069-2799 | 1971 | Dr. Linda C. Jolly | 8 | 1,228 | 74 |
| Salt Lake Comm Coll, Salt Lake City, UT 84130-0808 | 1948 | Dr. Frank W. Budd | 5 | 19,568 | 1,042 |
| San Antonio Coll, San Antonio, TX 78212-4299 | 1925 | Dr. Ruth Burgos-Sasscer | 11 | 21,238 | 896 |
| San Bernardino Valley Coll, San Bernardino, CA 92410-2748 | 1926 | Dr. Donald L. Singer | 11 | 10,673 | 375 |
| Sandhills Comm Coll, Pinehurst, NC 28374-8299 | 1963 | Dr. John Dempsey | 11 | 2,396 | 147 |
| San Diego City Coll, San Diego, CA 92101-4787 | 1914 | Dr. Jerome Hunter | 11 | 12,616 | 250 |
| San Diego Mesa Coll, San Diego, CA 92111-4998 | 1964 | Dr. Constance Carroll | 9 | 22,677 | 676 |
| San Diego Miramar Coll, San Diego, CA 92126-2999 | 1969 | Dr. Louis C. Murillo | 11 | 8,935 | 188 |
| San Jacinto Coll–North Cmps, Houston, TX 77049-4599 | 1974 | Dr. Edwin E. Lehr | 11 | 4,211 | 196 |
| San Jacinto Coll–South Cmps, Houston, TX 77089-6099 | 1979 | Dr. Parker Williams | 11 | 5,411 | 220 |
| San Joaquin Delta Coll, Stockton, CA 95207-6370 | 1935 | Dr. L. H. Horton, Jr. | 9 | 17,860 | 579 |
| San Jose City Coll, San Jose, CA 95128-2797 | 1921 | Dr. Raul Rodriguez | 9 | 10,044 | 390 |
| San Juan Coll, Farmington, NM 87402-4699 | 1958 | Dr. James C. Henderson | 8 | 4,500 | 243 |
| Santa Barbara City Coll, Santa Barbara, CA 93109-2394 | 1908 | Dr. Peter R. MacDougall | 9 | 11,288 | 468 |
| Santa Fe Comm Coll, Gainesville, FL 32606-6200 | 1966 | Dr. Larry W. Tyree | 11 | 12,286 | 587 |
| Santa Monica Coll, Santa Monica, CA 90405-1644 | 1929 | Dr. Piedad F. Robertson | 11 | 22,127 | 664 |
| Santa Rosa Jr Coll, Santa Rosa, CA 95401-4395 | 1918 | Dr. Robert F. Agrella | 11 | 21,651 | 1,130 |
| Sauk Valley Comm Coll, Dixon, IL 61021 | 1965 | Dr. Richard L. Behrendt | 9 | 2,635 | 152 |
| Savannah Tech Inst, Savannah, GA 31499 | | Mr. John D. Stewart | 5 | 2,022 | NR |
| Schenectady County Comm Coll, Schenectady, NY 12305-2294 | 1968 | Dr. Gabriel J. Basil | 11 | 3,692 | 208 |
| Schoolcraft Coll, Livonia, MI 48152-2696 | 1961 | Dr. Richard W. McDowell | 9 | 9,393 | 421 |
| Scott Comm Coll, Bettendorf, IA 52722-6804 | 1966 | Dr. Lenny E. Stone | 11 | 4,000 | 235 |
| Scottsdale Comm Coll, Scottsdale, AZ 85250-2699 | 1969 | Dr. Arthur W. De Cabooter | 11 | 9,765 | 447 |
| Seattle Central Comm Coll, Seattle, WA 98122-2400 | 1966 | Dr. Charles H. Mitchell | 5 | 10,333 | 388 |
| Seminole Comm Coll, Sanford, FL 32773-6199 | 1966 | Dr. Earl S. Weldon | 11 | 6,522 | 502 |
| Seminole Jr Coll, Seminole, OK 74818-0351 | 1931 | Dr. James J. Cook | 5 | 1,700 | 85 |
| Seward County Comm Coll, Liberal, KS 67905-1137 | 1969 | Dr. James Grote | 11 | 1,899 | 147 |
| Shasta Coll, Redding, CA 96049-6006 | 1948 | Dr. Douglas Treadway | 11 | 11,152 | 424 |
| Shawnee Comm Coll, Ullin, IL 62992-9725 | 1967 | Dr. Jack D. Hill | 11 | 2,288 | 176 |
| Shelby State Comm Coll, Memphis, TN 38174-0568 | 1970 | Mr. Mark L. Stansbury | 5 | 6,350 | 342 |
| Shelton State Comm Coll, Tuscaloosa, AL 35405-4093 | 1979 | Dr. Thomas E. Umphrey | 5 | 6,000 | 268 |
| Sheridan Coll, Sheridan, WY 82801-1500 | 1948 | Dr. Stephen Maier | 11 | 2,555 | 215 |
| Shoreline Comm Coll, Seattle, WA 98133-5696 | 1964 | Mr. Gary L. Oertli | 5 | 8,575 | 333 |
| Sierra Coll, Rocklin, CA 95677-3397 | 1936 | Dr. Kevin M. Ramirez | 5 | 13,567 | 518 |
| Sinclair Comm Coll, Dayton, OH 45402-1453 | 1887 | Dr. David H. Ponitz | 11 | 19,817 | 975 |
| Skagit Valley Coll, Mount Vernon, WA 98273-5899 | 1926 | Dr. Lydia Ledesma | 5 | 7,200 | 325 |
| Skyline Coll, San Bruno, CA 94066-1698 | 1969 | Ms. Linda Graef Salter | 8 | 8,104 | 268 |
| Snead State Comm Coll, Boaz, AL 35957 | 1935 | Dr. William H. Osborn | 5 | 1,708 | 81 |
| Snow Coll, Ephraim, UT 84627-1203 | 1888 | Dr. Gerald Day | 5 | 2,491 | 163 |
| Solano Comm Coll, Suisun City, CA 94585-3197 | 1945 | Stan R. Arterberry | 11 | 9,909 | 374 |
| South Arkansas Comm Coll, El Dorado, AR 71731-7010 | 1975 | Dr. Ben Whitfield | 5 | 1,000 | 81 |
| Southeast Arkansas Tech Coll, Pine Bluff, AR 71603 | 1991 | NR | 5 | 1,231 | 100 |
| Southeast Comm Coll, Lincoln Cmps, Lincoln, NE 68520-1299 | 1973 | Mrs. Jeanette Vocker | 9 | 4,555 | 545 |
| Southeastern Baptist Theological Sem, Wake Forest, NC 27588-1889 | 1950 | Dr. Paige Patterson | 2 | 1,098 | 32 |
| Southeastern Comm Coll, Whiteville, NC 28472-0151 | 1964 | Dr. Stephen C. Scott | 5 | 1,750 | 145 |
| Southeastern Comm Coll, North Cmps, West Burlington, IA 52655-0605 | 1968 | Dr. R. Gene Gardner | 11 | 1,791 | 94 |
| Southeastern Illinois Coll, Harrisburg, IL 62946-9804 | 1960 | Dr. Ben Cullers | 5 | 3,382 | 184 |
| Southeast Tech Inst, Sioux Falls, SD 57107 | | NR | 5 | 2,581 | 105 |
| Southern Arkansas U Tech, Camden, AR 71701 | 1968 | Dr. George J. Brown | 5 | 1,197 | 114 |
| Southern Maine Tech Coll, South Portland, ME 04106 | 1946 | Dr. Wayne H. Ross | 5 | 2,524 | 148 |
| Southern State Comm Coll, Hillsboro, OH 45133-9487 | 1975 | Dr. Lawrence N. Dukes | 5 | 1,468 | 117 |
| Southern Union State Comm Coll, Wadley, AL 36276 | 1922 | Dr. Roy W. Johnson | 5 | 6,499 | 217 |
| Southern U at Shreveport–Bossier City Cmps, Shreveport, LA 71107 | 1964 | Dr. Jerome G. Greene, Jr. | 5 | 1,202 | 75 |
| Southern West Virginia Comm and Tech Coll, Mount Gay, WV 25637 | 1971 | Dr. Michael Allkins | 5 | 3,097 | 192 |
| South Florida Comm Coll, Avon Park, FL 33825-9356 | 1965 | Dr. Catherine P. Cornelius | 5 | 1,530 | 202 |
| South Georgia Coll, Douglas, GA 31533-5098 | 1906 | Dr. Edward D. Jackson, Jr. | 5 | 1,171 | 51 |
| South Mountain Comm Coll, Phoenix, AZ 85040 | 1979 | Dr. John A. Cordova | 11 | 2,423 | 184 |
| South Plains Coll, Levelland, TX 79336-6595 | 1958 | Dr. Gary D. McDaniel | 11 | 5,703 | 356 |
| South Puget Sound Comm Coll, Olympia, WA 98512-6292 | 1970 | Dr. Kenneth J. Minnaert | 5 | 5,195 | 229 |
| South Seattle Comm Coll, Seattle, WA 98106-1499 | 1970 | Dr. Peter Ku | 5 | 3,892 | 266 |
| Southside Virginia Comm Coll, Alberta, VA 23821-9719 | 1970 | Dr. John J. Cavan | 5 | 1,697 | 182 |
| South Suburban Coll, South Holland, IL 60473-1270 | 1927 | Dr. Richard Fonte | 11 | 6,185 | 382 |
| Southwestern Coll, Chula Vista, CA 91910-7299 | 1961 | Mr. Joseph M. Conte | 11 | 15,498 | 633 |
| Southwestern Comm Coll, Creston, IA 50801 | 1966 | Dr. Richard L. Byerly | 5 | 1,211 | 86 |
| Southwestern Comm Coll, Sylva, NC 28779 | 1964 | Dr. Barry W. Russell | 5 | 1,517 | 202 |
| Southwestern Michigan Coll, Dowagiac, MI 49047-9793 | 1964 | Mr. David C. Briegel | 11 | 2,551 | 180 |
| Southwestern Oregon Comm Coll, Coos Bay, OR 97420-2911 | 1961 | Dr. Stephen J. Kridelbaugh | 11 | 1,534 | 250 |
| Southwest Mississippi Comm Coll, Summit, MS 39666 | 1918 | Dr. Horace C. Holmes | 9 | 1,650 | 89 |
| Southwest Missouri State U– West Plains, West Plains, MO 65775 | 1963 | NR | 5 | 1,018 | 20 |
| Southwest Texas Jr Coll, Uvalde, TX 78801-6296 | 1946 | Mr. Billy Word | 11 | 3,256 | 166 |
| Southwest Virginia Comm Coll, Richlands, VA 24641 | 1968 | Dr. Charles R. King | 5 | 4,235 | 235 |
| Southwest Wisconsin Tech Coll, Fennimore, WI 53809-9778 | 1967 | Dr. Richard A. Rogers | 11 | 3,870 | 101 |
| Spartanburg Tech Coll, Spartanburg, SC 29305-4386 | 1961 | Dr. Jack A. Powers | 5 | 2,500 | NR |
| Spokane Comm Coll, Spokane, WA 99207-5399 | 1963 | Dr. James Williams | 5 | 5,000 | 342 |
| Spokane Falls Comm Coll, Spokane, WA 99204-5288 | 1967 | Dr. Vern Loland | 5 | 5,300 | 565 |
| Spoon River Coll, Canton, IL 61520-9801 | 1959 | Dr. Felix T. Haynes | 5 | 1,950 | 136 |
| Springfield Tech Comm Coll, Springfield, MA 01105-1296 | 1967 | Dr. Andrew M. Scibelli | 5 | 6,084 | 319 |
| Stanly Comm Coll, Albemarle, NC 28001-7458 | 1971 | Dr. Jan J. Crawford | 5 | 1,660 | 76 |
| Stark Tech Coll, Canton, OH 44720-7299 | 1970 | Dr. John J. McGrath | 11 | 4,164 | 210 |
| State Fair Comm Coll, Sedalia, MO 65301-2199 | 1966 | Dr. Marvin Fielding | 9 | 2,277 | 98 |
| State Tech Inst at Memphis, Memphis, TN 38134-7693 | 1967 | Dr. M. Douglas Call | 5 | 10,569 | 620 |
| State U of NY Coll of A&T at Cobleskill, Cobleskill, NY 12043 | 1916 | Dr. Kenneth E. Wing | 5 | 2,410 | 145 |
| State U of NY Coll of A&T at Morrisville, Morrisville, NY 13408 | 1908 | Dr. Frederick W. Woodward | 5 | 2,890 | 171 |
| State U of NY Coll of Tech at Alfred, Alfred, NY 14802 | 1908 | Dr. William Rezak | 5 | 3,319 | 176 |

| Name, address | Year | Governing official, control, and highest degree offered | | Enroll-ment | Faculty |
|---|---|---|---|---|---|
| State U of NY Coll of Tech at Canton, Canton, NY 13617 | 1906 | Dr. Joseph L. Kennedy | 5 | 2,004 | 107 |
| State U of NY Coll of Tech at Delhi, Delhi, NY 13753 | 1913 | Dr. Mary Ellen Duncan | 5 | 2,098 | NR |
| State U of NY Coll of Tech at Farmingdale, Farmingdale, NY 11735 | 1912 | Dr. Frank A. Cipriani | 5 | 6,209 | 390 |
| Suffolk County Comm Coll–Ammerman Cmps, Selden, NY 11784-2851 | 1962 | Dr. John F. Cooper | 11 | 13,154 | 782 |
| Suffolk County Comm Coll–Eastern Cmps, Riverhead, NY 11901 | 1977 | Ms. Joanne Braxton | 11 | 2,680 | 216 |
| Suffolk County Comm Coll–Western Cmps, Brentwood, NY 11717 | 1974 | Mr. Salvatore J. LaLima | 11 | 6,097 | 349 |
| Sullivan County Comm Coll, Loch Sheldrake, NY 12759-4002 | 1962 | Dr. Jeffrey B. Willens | 11 | 2,085 | 106 |
| Surry Comm Coll, Dobson, NC 27017-0304 | 1965 | Dr. James Reeves | 5 | 3,036 | 98 |
| Sussex County Comm Coll, Newton, NJ 07860 | 1981 | William A. Connor | 11 | 2,293 | 188 |
| Tacoma Comm Coll, Tacoma, WA 98465-1997 | 1965 | Dr. Raymond Needham | 5 | 5,461 | 371 |
| Tallahassee Comm Coll, Tallahassee, FL 32304-2895 | 1966 | Dr. T. K. Wetherall | 11 | 10,084 | 384 |
| Tarrant County Jr Coll, Fort Worth, TX 76102-6599 | 1967 | Mr. C. A. Roberson | 8 | 26,584 | 1,122 |
| Tech Career Institutes, New York, NY 10001-2705 | 1974 | Mr. Eric Biederman | 3 | 3,300 | 152 |
| Temple Coll, Temple, TX 76504-7435 | 1926 | Dr. Marvin R. Felder | 9 | 2,450 | 125 |
| Terra State Comm Coll, Fremont, OH 43420-9670 | 1968 | Dr. Charlotte J. Lee | 5 | 2,628 | 148 |
| Texarkana Coll, Texarkana, TX 75599-0001 | 1927 | Dr. Carl M. Nelson | 11 | 4,038 | 196 |
| Texas Southmost Coll, Brownsville, TX 78520-4991 | 1926 | Dr. Juliet V. Garcia | 9 | 6,564 | 390 |
| Texas State Tech Coll–Harlingen, Harlingen, TX 78550-3697 | 1967 | Dr. J. Gilbert Leal | 5 | 3,056 | 148 |
| Texas State Tech Coll–Waco/Marshall Cmps, Waco, TX 76705-1695 | 1965 | Dr. Fred L. Williams | 5 | 3,313 | 323 |
| Thomas Nelson Comm Coll, Hampton, VA 23670-0407 | 1968 | Dr. Shirley R. Pippins | 5 | 7,192 | 320 |
| Three Rivers Comm Coll, Poplar Bluff, MO 63901-2393 | 1966 | Dr. Stephen M. Poort | 5 | 3,000 | 67 |
| Three Rivers Comm-Tech Coll, Norwich, CT 06360 | 1963 | Dr. Booker T. DeVaughn | 5 | 3,977 | 180 |
| Tidewater Comm Coll, Portsmouth, VA 23703 | 1968 | Dr. Larry Whitworth | 5 | 16,780 | 805 |
| Tomball Coll, Tomball, TX 77375-4036 | 1988 | Dr. Roy Lazenby | 11 | 3,641 | 212 |
| Tompkins Cortland Comm Coll, Dryden, NY 13053-9533 | 1968 | Dr. Carl Haynes | 11 | 2,754 | 196 |
| Treasure Valley Comm Coll, Ontario, OR 97914-3423 | 1962 | Dr. Berton L. Glandon | 11 | 2,348 | 110 |
| Tri-County Tech Coll, Pendleton, SC 29670-0587 | 1962 | Dr. Don C. Garrison | 5 | 3,179 | 250 |
| Trident Tech Coll, Charleston, SC 29423-8067 | 1964 | Dr. Mary Thornley | 11 | 9,110 | 497 |
| Trinidad State Jr Coll, Trinidad, CO 81082-2396 | 1925 | Dr. Harold Deselms | 5 | 2,142 | 111 |
| Trinity Valley Comm Coll, Athens, TX 75751-2765 | 1946 | Mr. Ron Baugh | 11 | 4,786 | 224 |
| Triton Coll, River Grove, IL 60171-9983 | 1964 | Dr. George Jorndt | 5 | 12,050 | 715 |
| Trocaire Coll, Buffalo, NY 14220-2094 | 1958 | Barbara Ciarico, RSM | 1 | 1,044 | 113 |
| Truckee Meadows Comm Coll, Reno, NV 89512-3901 | 1971 | Dr. Rita Gubanich | 5 | 8,346 | 464 |
| Truett-McConnell Coll, Cleveland, GA 30528-9799 | 1946 | Dr. T. Clark Bryan | 2 | 1,957 | 39 |
| Tulsa Jr Coll, Tulsa, OK 74135-6198 | 1968 | Dr. Dean P. VanTrease | 5 | 21,147 | 1,102 |
| Tunxis Comm Tech Coll, Farmington, CT 06032-3026 | 1969 | Dr. Cathryn Addy | 5 | 3,675 | 175 |
| Tyler Jr Coll, Tyler, TX 75711-9020 | 1926 | Dr. William R. Crowe | 11 | 7,984 | 364 |
| Ulster County Comm Coll, Stone Ridge, NY 12484 | 1961 | Mr. Robert T. Brown | 11 | 2,642 | 162 |
| Umpqua Comm Coll, Roseburg, OR 97470-0226 | 1964 | Dr. James M. Kraby | 11 | 2,100 | 145 |
| Union County Coll, Cranford, NJ 07016-1528 | 1933 | Dr. Thomas H. Brown | 11 | 10,046 | 422 |
| The U of Akron–Wayne Coll, Orrville, OH 44667-9192 | 1972 | Dr. Marion Ruebel | 5 | 1,458 | 109 |
| U of Alaska Anchorage, Kenai Peninsula Coll, Soldotna, AK 99669-9798 | 1964 | Ms. Ginger Steffy | 5 | 1,658 | 107 |
| U of Alaska Anchorage, Matanuska-Susitna Coll, Palmer, AK 99645-2889 | 1958 | Mr. Glenn Massay | 5 | 1,654 | 113 |
| U of Alaska, Prince William Sound Comm Coll, Valdez, AK 99686-0097 | 1978 | Dr. Joanne C. McDowell | 5 | 1,508 | 63 |
| U of Alaska Southeast, Sitka Cmps, Sitka, AK 99835-9418 | 1962 | Ms. Elaine Sunde | 5 | 1,470 | 104 |
| U of Cincinnati Clermont Coll, Batavia, OH 45103-1785 | 1972 | Dr. Roger J. Barry | 5 | 1,997 | 143 |
| U of Cincinnati Raymond Walters Coll, Cincinnati, OH 45236-1007 | 1967 | Dr. Barbara A. Bardes | 5 | 2,838 | 236 |
| U of Hawaii–Hawaii Comm Coll, Hilo, HI 96720-4091 | 1954 | Ms. Sandra Sakaguchi | 5 | 2,800 | 98 |
| U of Hawaii–Honolulu Comm Coll, Honolulu, HI 96817-4598 | 1920 | Dr. Peter R. Kessinger | 5 | 4,717 | 285 |
| U of Hawaii–Kapiolani Comm Coll, Honolulu, HI 96816-4421 | 1957 | Mr. John F. Morton | 5 | 7,283 | 317 |
| U of Hawaii–Kauai Comm Coll, Lihue, HI 96766-9591 | 1965 | Mr. David Iha | 5 | 1,143 | 78 |
| U of Hawaii–Leeward Comm Coll, Pearl City, HI 96782-3366 | 1968 | Dr. Barbara B. Polk | 5 | 6,330 | 264 |
| U of Hawaii–Maui Comm Coll, Kahului, HI 96732 | 1967 | Dr. Clyde Sakamoto | 5 | 2,759 | 148 |
| U of Hawaii–Windward Comm Coll, Kaneohe, HI 96744-3528 | 1972 | Dr. Peter T. Dyer | 5 | 1,666 | 80 |
| U of Kentucky, Ashland Comm Coll, Ashland, KY 41101-3683 | 1937 | Dr. Charles Dassance | 5 | 2,560 | 128 |
| U of Kentucky, Elizabethtown Comm Coll, Elizabethtown, KY 42701-3081 | 1964 | Dr. Charles E. Stebbins | 5 | 3,766 | 170 |
| U of Kentucky, Hazard Comm Coll, Hazard, KY 41701-2403 | 1968 | Dr. G. Edward Hughes | 5 | 1,690 | 119 |
| U of Kentucky, Henderson Comm Coll, Henderson, KY 42420-4623 | 1963 | Dr. Patrick R. Lake | 5 | 1,396 | 96 |
| U of Kentucky, Hopkinsville Comm Coll, Hopkinsville, KY 42241-2100 | 1965 | Dr. Jim Kerley | 5 | 2,898 | 158 |
| U of Kentucky, Jefferson Comm Coll, Louisville, KY 40202-2005 | 1968 | Dr. Richard Green | 5 | 9,273 | 490 |
| U of Kentucky, Lexington Comm Coll, Lexington, KY 40506-0235 | 1965 | Dr. Janice N. Friedel | 5 | 5,225 | 302 |
| U of Kentucky, Madisonville Comm Coll, Madisonville, KY 42431-9185 | 1968 | Dr. Arthur D. Stumpf | 5 | 2,533 | 167 |
| U of Kentucky, Maysville Comm Coll, Maysville, KY 41056 | 1967 | Dr. James C. Shires | 5 | 1,409 | 111 |
| U of Kentucky, Paducah Comm Coll, Paducah, KY 42002-7380 | 1932 | Dr. Leonard O'Hara | 5 | 2,833 | 143 |
| U of Kentucky, Prestonsburg Comm Coll, Prestonsburg, KY 41653-1815 | 1964 | Dr. Deborah Lee Floyd | 5 | 2,798 | 121 |
| U of Kentucky, Somerset Comm Coll, Somerset, KY 42501-2973 | 1965 | Dr. Rollin J. Watson | 5 | 2,647 | 153 |
| U of Kentucky, Southeast Comm Coll, Cumberland, KY 40823-1099 | 1960 | Dr. W. Bruce Ayers | 5 | 2,466 | 107 |
| U of Maine at Augusta, Augusta, ME 04330-9410 | 1965 | Charles R. MacRoy | 5 | 6,166 | 272 |
| U of New Mexico–Gallup Branch, Gallup, NM 87301-5603 | 1968 | Dr. Robert Carlson | 5 | 3,000 | 159 |
| U of New Mexico–Los Alamos Branch, Los Alamos, NM 87544-2233 | 1980 | Dr. Carlos B. Ramirez | 5 | 1,023 | 96 |
| U of New Mexico–Valencia Cmps, Los Lunas, NM 87031-7633 | 1981 | Dr. Alice V. Letteney | 5 | 1,440 | 93 |
| U of South Carolina at Beaufort, Beaufort, SC 29902-4601 | 1959 | Dr. Chris P. Plyler | 5 | 1,223 | 81 |
| U of South Carolina at Lancaster, Lancaster, SC 29721-0889 | 1959 | Dr. Joseph Pappin, III | 5 | 1,153 | 52 |
| U of South Carolina at Sumter, Sumter, SC 29150-2498 | 1966 | Dr. C. Leslie Carpenter | 5 | 1,396 | 73 |
| U of Wisconsin Ctr–Fox Valley, Menasha, WI 54952-8002 | 1933 | Dr. James W. Perry | 5 | 1,250 | 58 |
| U of Wisconsin Ctr–Marathon County, Wausau, WI 54401-5396 | 1933 | Dr. G. Dennis Massey | 5 | 1,011 | 71 |
| U of Wisconsin Ctr–Waukesha County, Waukesha, WI 53188-2720 | 1966 | Dr. Mary S. Knudten | 5 | 1,681 | 83 |
| Utah Valley State Coll, Orem, UT 84058-0001 | 1941 | Dr. Kerry D. Romesburg | 5 | 14,041 | 536 |
| Valencia Comm Coll, Orlando, FL 32802-3028 | 1967 | Dr. Paul C. Gianini, Jr. | 5 | 24,121 | 995 |
| Vance-Granville Comm Coll, Henderson, NC 27536-0917 | 1969 | Dr. Ben F. Currin | 5 | 2,434 | 194 |

| Name, address | Year | Governing official, control, and highest degree offered | | Enrollment | Faculty |
|---|---|---|---|---|---|
| Ventura Coll, Ventura, CA 93003-3899 | 1925 | Dr. Larry Calderon | 11 | 10,083 | 541 |
| Vernon Regional Jr Coll, Vernon, TX 76384-4092 | 1972 | Dr. Wade Kirk | 11 | 1,721 | 98 |
| Victoria Coll, Victoria, TX 77901-4494 | 1925 | Dr. Jimmy Goodson | 8 | 3,643 | 120 |
| Victor Valley Coll, Victorville, CA 92392-5849 | 1961 | Dr. Edward O. Gould | 5 | 8,000 | 325 |
| Vincennes U, Vincennes, IN 47591-5202 | 1801 | Dr. Phillip M. Summers | 5 | 6,500 | 400 |
| Vincennes U–Jasper Ctr, Jasper, IN 47546-9393 | 1970 | Dr. Gerald J. Altstadt | 5 | 1,206 | 62 |
| Virginia Highlands Comm Coll, Abingdon, VA 24212-0828 | 1967 | Dr. F. David Wilkin, Jr. | 5 | 1,891 | 131 |
| Virginia Western Comm Coll, Roanoke, VA 24038 | 1966 | Dr. Charles L. Downs | 5 | 6,845 | 202 |
| Vista Comm Coll, Berkeley, CA 94704-5102 | 1974 | Dr. Barbara Beno | 11 | 3,171 | 125 |
| Volunteer State Comm Coll, Gallatin, TN 37066-3188 | 1970 | Dr. Hal R. Ramer | 5 | 6,583 | 404 |
| Wake Tech Comm Coll, Raleigh, NC 27603-5696 | 1958 | Dr. Bruce I. Howell | 11 | 7,340 | 405 |
| Wallace State Comm Coll, Hanceville, AL 35077-2000 | 1966 | Dr. James C. Bailey | 5 | 5,824 | 301 |
| Walla Walla Comm Coll, Walla Walla, WA 99362-9267 | 1967 | Dr. Steven L. VanAusdle | 5 | 4,772 | 268 |
| Walters State Comm Coll, Morristown, TN 37813-6899 | 1970 | Dr. Jack E. Campbell | 5 | 5,824 | 253 |
| Warren County Comm Coll, Washington, NJ 07882-9605 | 1981 | Dr. Vincent De Sanctis | 11 | 1,619 | 56 |
| Washington State Comm Coll, Marietta, OH 45750-9225 | 1971 | Dr. Carson K. Miller | 5 | 2,019 | 132 |
| Washtenaw Comm Coll, Ann Arbor, MI 48106 | 1965 | Dr. Gunder A. Myran | 11 | 10,224 | 759 |
| Waubonsee Comm Coll, Sugar Grove, IL 60554-9799 | 1966 | Dr. John J. Swalec | 9 | 7,460 | 494 |
| Waukesha County Tech Coll, Pewaukee, WI 53072-4601 | 1923 | Dr. Richard T. Anderson | 11 | 4,700 | 520 |
| Wayne Comm Coll, Goldsboro, NC 27533-8002 | 1957 | Dr. Edward H. Wilson, Jr. | 11 | 2,639 | 153 |
| Wayne County Comm Coll, Detroit, MI 48226-3010 | 1967 | Dr. Curtis L. Ivery | 11 | 10,792 | 400 |
| Weatherford Coll, Weatherford, TX 76086-5699 | 1869 | Dr. Jim Boyd | 11 | 2,277 | 94 |
| Wenatchee Valley Coll, Wenatchee, WA 98801-1799 | 1939 | Dr. Woody Ahn | 11 | 3,764 | 203 |
| Westark Comm Coll, Fort Smith, AR 72913-3649 | 1928 | Mr. Joel R. Stubblefield | 11 | 5,323 | 236 |
| Westchester Comm Coll, Valhalla, NY 10595-1698 | 1946 | Dr. Joseph N. Hankin | 11 | 16,914 | 716 |
| Western Iowa Tech Comm Coll, Sioux City, IA 51102-5199 | 1966 | Dr. Robert E. Dunker | 5 | 3,000 | 157 |
| Western Nebraska Comm Coll, Scottsbluff, NE 69361 | 1921 | Dr. Judy Nissen | 11 | 2,291 | 156 |
| Western Nevada Comm Coll, Carson City, NV 89703-7316 | 1971 | Dr. James Randolph | 5 | 4,498 | 358 |
| Western Oklahoma State Coll, Altus, OK 73521-1397 | 1926 | Dr. Ray Brown | 5 | 1,718 | 78 |
| Western Piedmont Comm Coll, Morganton, NC 28655-9978 | 1964 | Dr. Jim A. Richardson | 5 | 2,562 | 132 |
| Western Texas Coll, Snyder, TX 79549-9502 | 1969 | Dr. Harry L. Krenek | 11 | 1,200 | 55 |
| Western Wisconsin Tech Coll, La Crosse, WI 54602-0908 | 1911 | Dr. James Lee Rasch | 9 | 4,458 | 184 |
| Western Wyoming Comm Coll, Rock Springs, WY 82902-0428 | 1959 | Dr. T. L. Boggs | 11 | 3,094 | 232 |
| West Hills Comm Coll, Coalinga, CA 93210-1399 | 1932 | Dr. Frank P. Gornick | 5 | 2,810 | 107 |
| West Los Angeles Coll, Culver City, CA 90230-3500 | 1969 | Dr. Evelyn C. Wong | 11 | 7,400 | 320 |
| Westmoreland County Comm Coll, Youngwood, PA 15697 | 1970 | Dr. Daniel C. Krezenski | 8 | 6,026 | 390 |
| West Shore Comm Coll, Scottville, MI 49454-9716 | 1967 | Dr. William M. Anderson | 9 | 1,617 | 71 |
| West Valley Coll, Saratoga, CA 95070-5697 | 1963 | Dr. Sam Schauerman | 11 | 14,224 | 560 |
| West Virginia Northern Comm Coll, Wheeling, WV 26003 | 1972 | Dr. Linda S. Dunn | 5 | 2,720 | 158 |
| West Virginia U at Parkersburg, Parkersburg, WV 26101-9577 | 1971 | Dr. Eldon L. Miller | 5 | 3,600 | 173 |
| Wharton County Jr Coll, Wharton, TX 77488-3298 | 1946 | Dr. Frank R. Vivelo | 11 | 3,720 | 200 |
| Whatcom Comm Coll, Bellingham, WA 98226-8003 | 1970 | Dr. Harold G. Heiner | 5 | 2,621 | 166 |
| Wilkes Comm Coll, Wilkesboro, NC 28697 | 1965 | Dr. Swanson Richards | 5 | 2,178 | 221 |
| William Rainey Harper Coll, Palatine, IL 60067-7398 | 1965 | Dr. Paul N. Thompson | 11 | 13,744 | 1,018 |
| Willmar Comm Coll, Willmar, MN 56201-0797 | 1961 | Dr. Mary E. Retterer | 5 | 1,318 | 68 |
| Willmar Tech Coll, Willmar, MN 56201-1097 | 1961 | Mr. Ronald Erpelding | 5 | 1,340 | 90 |
| Wilson Tech Comm Coll, Wilson, NC 27893-3310 | 1958 | Dr. Frank L. Eagles | 5 | 1,416 | 79 |
| Wisconsin Indianhead Tech Coll, New Richmond Cmps, New Richmond, WI 54017-1738 | 1972 | Mr. Tim Schreiner | 9 | 1,300 | 65 |
| Wisconsin Indianhead Tech Coll, Rice Lake Cmps, Rice Lake, WI 54868-2435 | 1941 | Mr. Thomas B. Lemler | 9 | 1,136 | 79 |
| Wood Coll, Mathiston, MS 39752-0289 | 1886 | Dr. Robert Sandin | 2 | 1,500 | 35 |
| Wor-Wic Comm Coll, Salisbury, MD 21804 | 1976 | Dr. Arnold H. Maner | 11 | 1,963 | 103 |
| Wytheville Comm Coll, Wytheville, VA 24382-3308 | 1967 | Dr. William F. Snyder | 5 | 2,600 | 137 |
| Yakima Valley Comm Coll, Yakima, WA 98907-1647 | 1928 | Dr. Linda Kaminski | 5 | 4,290 | 374 |
| Yavapai Coll, Prescott, AZ 86301-3297 | 1966 | Dr. Doreen Dailey | 11 | 6,297 | 487 |
| York Tech Coll, Rock Hill, SC 29730-3395 | 1961 | Mr. Dennis F. Merrell | 5 | 3,342 | 236 |
| Yuba Coll, Marysville, CA 95901-7699 | 1927 | Dr. Stephen Epler | 11 | 9,860 | 500 |

# College Freshman Attitudes, 1995

**Source:** *The American Freshman: National Norms for Fall 1995*

According to the 30th annual survey of college freshmen conducted by the American Council on Education and UCLA, interest in "keeping up to date with political affairs" dropped for the 3d straight year, to an all-time low of 28.5%, in 1995, compared with 57.8% in 1966, the first year of the survey. The percentage of freshmen who discuss politics frequently reached an all-time low of 14.8%. Freshmen showed less interest in "influencing social values" (38.2%, down from 43.3% in 1992), "cleaning up the environment" (22.5%, as against 33.6% in 1992), "promoting racial understanding" (33.4%, down from 42.0% in 1992), and "participating in a community action program" (23.0%, versus 26.1% in 1992). Most described their political views as "middle of the road" (54.3%). The percentage labeling themselves as either "far left" or "far right" increased slightly from 1994, reaching a 25-year high of 2.7% for "far left" and an all-time high of 1.6% for "far right."

Support for keeping abortion legal declined for the 3d straight year, to 58.4%. Of the students surveyed, 42.7%, a record low, endorsed the view that "if two people like each other, it's all right for them to have sex even if they've only known each other for a very short time." The belief that homosexual relationships should be prohibited fell to a record low of 30.6%. According to the 1995 survey, 33.8% of college freshmen, the largest percentage in 15 years, supported legalization of marijuana. The percentage who frequently smoke cigarettes rose to 14.6%, the highest level since 1971.

The percentage of freshmen who spent 16 or more hours a week working for pay rose to 38.7%, compared with 35.0% in 1992. The percentage who exercise or play sports more than 16 hours a week rose to 19.1% in 1995, an increase from 15.8% in 1989. Frequent use of personal computers rose dramatically, to 49.6% in 1995, compared with 37.8% in 1993 and 24.9% in 1985, when the question was first asked.

Interest in teaching careers reached its highest level in over 20 years, with 9.7% of freshmen (13.0% of women and 5.8% of men) planning to become elementary or secondary school teachers (the low was 4.9% in 1982). Interest in business careers rose for the first time in 8 years; plans for engineering careers fell to the lowest point since 1975 (6.4%). Plans for a law career declined to an all-time low of 3.4% (the peak was 5.4%, in 1988).

# ARTS AND MEDIA

## Some Notable Movies of the Year, Sept. 1995-Aug. 1996

| Movie | Stars | Director |
|---|---|---|
| Ace Ventura: When Nature Calls | Jim Carrey, Ian McNeice, Simon Callow, Maynard Eziashi, Bob Gunton | Steve Oedekerk |
| The American President | Michael Douglas, Annette Bening, Martin Sheen, Michael J. Fox | Rob Reiner |
| Assassins | Sylvester Stallone, Antonio Banderas, Julianne Moore | Richard Donner |
| A Time to Kill | Sandra Bullock, Samuel L. Jackson, Matthew McConaughey | Joel Schumacher |
| The Birdcage | Robin Williams, Nathan Lane | Mike Nichols |
| The Cable Guy | Jim Carrey, Matthew Broderick | Ben Stiller |
| Casino | Robert DeNiro, Sharon Stone, Joe Pesci | Martin Scorsese |
| City Hall | Al Pacino, John Cusack, Danny Aiello, David Paymer | Harold Becker |
| Courage Under Fire | Denzel Washington, Meg Ryan | Edward Zwick |
| The Craft | Fairuza Balk, Robin Tunney, Neve Campbell, Rachel True | Andrew Fleming |
| Dead Man Walking | Susan Sarandon, Sean Penn | Tim Robbins |
| Dead Presidents | Larenz Tate, Keith David, Chris Tucker | Allen Hughes, Albert Hughes |
| Emma | Gwyneth Paltrow, Toni Collette, Alan Cumming | Doug McGrath |
| Eraser | Arnold Schwarzenegger, James Caan, Vanessa Williams | Charles Russell |
| Fargo | Frances McDormand, William H. Macy, Steve Buscemi | Joel Coen |
| Fear | Mark Wahlberg, Reese Witherspoon, William Petersen | James Foley |
| Flipper | Paul Hogan, Elijah Wood | Alan Shapiro |
| Flirting With Disaster | Ben Stiller, Patricia Arquette, Mary Tyler Moore | David O. Russell |
| From Dusk Till Dawn | Harvey Keitel, George Clooney, Quentin Tarantino | Robert Rodriguez |
| Get Shorty | John Travolta, Gene Hackman, Rene Russo, Danny DeVito | Barry Sonnenfeld |
| Goldeneye | Pierce Brosnan, Sean Bean, Izabella Sorupco, Famke Janssen | Martin Campbell |
| Grumpier Old Men | Jack Lemmon, Walter Matthau, Sophia Loren | Howard Deutch |
| Harriet the Spy | Michelle Trachtenberg, Rosie O'Donnell | Bronwen Hughes |
| Heat | Al Pacino, Robert DeNiro | Michael Mann |
| Home for the Holidays | Holly Hunter, Robert Downey Jr., Anne Bancroft | Jodie Foster |
| How to Make an American Quilt | Winona Ryder, Anne Bancroft, Ellen Burstyn, Maya Angelou, Kate Nelligan, Alfre Woodard | Jocelyn Moorhouse |
| The Hunchback of Notre Dame | Tom Hulce, Demi Moore, Heidi Mollenhauer, Jason Alexander, Tony Jay, Kevin Kline (voices) | Gary Trousdale, Kirk Wise |
| Independence Day | Will Smith, Bill Pullman, Jeff Goldblum | Roland Emmerich |
| James and the Giant Peach | Simon Callow, Richard Dreyfuss, Susan Sarandon (voices) | Henry Selick |
| Jack | Robin Williams | Francis Ford Coppola |
| Jade | David Caruso, Linda Fiorentino, Chazz Palminteri | William Friedkin |
| Jumanji | Robin Williams, Kirsten Dunst, David Alan Grier, Bonnie Hunt | Joe Johnston |
| Leaving Las Vegas | Nicolas Cage, Elisabeth Shue | Mike Figgis |
| Mission: Impossible | Tom Cruise, Emmanuelle Béart, Jon Voight, Jean Reno | Brian De Palma |
| Mr. Holland's Opus | Richard Dreyfuss, Glenne Headley, Olympia Dukakis | Stephen Herek |
| The Nutty Professor | Eddie Murphy, Jada Pinkett, James Coburn, Dave Chappelle | Tom Shadyac |
| Phenomenon | John Travolta, Kyra Sedgwick, Forest Whitaker | Jon Turteltaub |
| Primal Fear | Richard Gere, Laura Linney, John Mahoney, Alfre Woodward | Gregory Hoblit |
| The Rock | Sean Connery, Nicolas Cage, Ed Harris | Michael Bay |
| Sense and Sensibility | Emma Thompson, Alan Rickman, Kate Winslet, Hugh Grant | Ang Lee |
| Seven | Brad Pitt, Morgan Freeman | David Fincher |
| Spy Hard | Leslie Nielsen, Nicollette Sheridan, Andy Griffith, Charles Durning | Rick Friedberg |
| Striptease | Demi Moore, Burt Reynolds, Armand Assante, Ving Rhames | Andrew Bergman |
| The Truth About Cats & Dogs | Uma Thurman, Janeane Garofalo | Michael Lehmann |
| To Die For | Nicole Kidman, Joaquin Phoenix, Matt Dillon | Gus Van Sant |
| To Wong Foo, Thanks for Everything, Julie Newmar | Patrick Swayze, Wesley Snipes, John Leguizamo | Beeban Kidron |
| Toy Story | Tom Hanks, Tim Allen (voices) | John Lasseter |
| Twelve Monkeys | Bruce Willis, Madeleine Stow, Brad Pitt, Christopher Plummer | Terry Gilliam |
| Twister | Helen Hunt, Bill Paxton, Cary Elwes | Jan De Bont |
| Up Close and Personal | Robert Redford, Michelle Pfeiffer | Jon Avnet |
| Waiting to Exhale | Whitney Houston, Angela Bassett | Forest Whitaker |

## Top 50 Movies, 1995

**Source:** *Variety,* Jan. 8-Jan. 14, 1996; box-office grosses in the U.S. and Canada during calendar year 1995

| Rank/Title | Gross (millions) |
|---|---|
| 1. Batman Forever | $184.0 |
| 2. Apollo 13 | 172.1 |
| 3. Toy Story | 146.2 |
| 4. Pocahontas | 141.5 |
| 5. Ace Ventura: When Nature Calls | 104.2 |
| 6. Casper | 100.3 |
| 7. Die Hard With a Vengeance | 100.0 |
| 8. Goldeneye | 92.4 |
| 9. Crimson Tide | 91.4 |
| 10. Waterworld | 88.2 |
| 11. Seven | 87.0 |
| 12. Dangerous Minds | 84.2 |
| 13. While You Were Sleeping | 81.1 |
| 14. Congo | 81.0 |
| 15. Mortal Kombat | 70.4 |
| 16. The Bridges of Madison County | 70.1 |
| 17. Nine Months | $69.7 |
| 18. Get Shorty | 68.6 |
| 19. Dumb & Dumber* | 68.1 |
| 20. Outbreak | 67.8 |
| 21. Braveheart | 67.0 |
| 22. Legends of the Fall* | 66.2 |
| 23. Bad Boys | 65.8 |
| 24. Species | 60.1 |
| 25. Babe | 56.7 |
| 26. Clueless | 56.4 |
| 27. Jumanji | 53.7 |
| 28. Something to Talk About | 50.9 |
| 29. The Net | 50.7 |
| 30. The American President | 50.3 |
| 31. Under Siege 2: Dark Territory | 50.0 |
| 32. A Walk in the Clouds | 50.0 |
| 33. Father of the Bride Part II | 49.9 |
| 34. The Brady Bunch Movie | $46.6 |
| 35. Pulp Fiction* | 45.5 |
| 36. Man of the House | 40.1 |
| 37. Nobody's Fool* | 39.2 |
| 38. French Kiss | 38.9 |
| 39. Higher Learning | 38.3 |
| 40. Mighty Morphin Power Rangers | 37.8 |
| 41. First Knight | 37.6 |
| 42. Casino | 37.1 |
| 43. Just Cause | 36.9 |
| 44. Disclosure* | 36.8 |
| 45. To Wong Foo... | 36.5 |
| 46. The Indian in the Cupboard | 35.6 |
| 47. A Goofy Movie | 35.3 |
| 48. Judge Dredd | 34.7 |
| 49. Heat | 34.5 |
| 50. Money Train | 34.5 |

*1994 release; 1995 gross only.

## All-Time Top 50 American Movies

Source: *Variety*, Feb. 26-Mar. 3, 1996

| Rank/Title/Date | Gross[1] (millions) |
|---|---|
| 1. E.T.: The Extra-Terrestrial (1982) | $399.8 |
| 2. Jurassic Park (1993) | 357.1 |
| 3. Forrest Gump (1994) | 329.7 |
| 4. Star Wars (1977) | 322.7 |
| 5. The Lion King (1993) | 312.9 |
| 6. Home Alone (1990) | 285.8 |
| 7. Return of the Jedi (1983) | 263.7 |
| 8. Jaws (1975) | 260.0 |
| 9. Batman (1989) | 251.2 |
| 10. Raiders of the Lost Ark (1981) | 242.4 |
| 11. Ghostbusters (1984) | 238.6 |
| 12. Beverly Hills Cop (1984) | 234.8 |
| 12. The Empire Strikes Back (1980) | 222.7 |
| 14. Mrs. Doubtfire (1993) | 219.2 |
| 15. Ghost (1990) | 217.6 |
| 16. Aladdin (1992) | 217.4 |
| 17. Back to the Future (1985) | 208.2 |
| 18. Terminator 2 (1991) | 204.8 |
| 19. Indiana Jones and the Last Crusade (1989) | 197.2 |
| 20. Gone With the Wind (1939) | 191.7 |
| 21. Dances With Wolves (1990) | 184.2 |
| 22. Batman Forever (1995) | 184.0 |
| 23. The Fugitive (1993) | 183.9 |
| 24. Toy Story* (1995) | 182.4 |
| 25. Indiana Jones and the Temple of Doom (1984) | 179.9 |
| 26. Pretty Woman (1990) | 178.4 |
| 27. Tootsie (1982) | 177.2 |
| 28. Top Gun (1986) | 176.8 |
| 29. Snow White and the Seven Dwarfs (1937) | 175.3 |
| 30. Crocodile Dundee (1986) | 174.6 |
| 31. Home Alone 2 (1992) | 173.6 |
| 32. Rain Man (1989) | 172.8 |
| 33. Apollo 13 (1995) | 172.1 |
| 34. Thre Men and a Baby (1987) | 167.8 |
| 35. Robin Hood: Prince of Thieves (1991) | 165.5 |
| 36. The Exorcist (1973) | 165.0 |
| 37. Batman Returns (1992) | 162.8 |
| 38. The Sound of Music (1965) | 160.5 |
| 39. The Firm (1993) | 158.3 |
| 40. Fatal Attraction (1987) | 156.6 |
| 41. The Sting (1973) | 156.0 |
| 42. Who Framed Roger Rabbit? (1988) | 154.1 |
| 43. Beverly Hills Cop II (1987) | 153.7 |
| 44. Grease (1978) | 153.1 |
| 45. Rambo: First Blood Part II (1985) | 150.4 |
| 46. Gremlins (1984) | 148.2 |
| 47. Lethal Weapon 2 (1989) | 147.3 |
| 48. True Lies (1994) | 146.3 |
| 49. Beauty and the Beast (1991) | 145.9 |
| 50. The Santa Clause (1994) | 144.8 |

*In release. (1) Gross is in absolute dollars based on box office sales in the U.S. and Canada. Ticket prices favor recent films, but older films have the advantage of reissues.

## Most Popular Movie Videos

Source: Alexander & Associates/Video Flash, New York, NY

**Top 10 Rentals, 1995**

1. Forrest Gump
2. The Lion King
3. True Lies
4. The Mask
5. Speed
6. Dumb and Dumber
7. The Shawshank Redemption
8. The Santa Clause
9. Pulp Fiction
10. Legends of the Fall

**All Time Top 10 Rentals[1]**

1. Top Gun
2. Pretty Woman
3. Home Alone
4. Ghost
5. The Little Mermaid
6. Terminator II: Judgment Day
7. Cinderella
8. Beauty and the Beast
9. Dances With Wolves
10. Batman

**Top 10 Sales, 1995**

1. The Lion King
2. Forrest Gump
3. Cinderella
4. The Santa Clause
5. Snow White and the Seven Dwarfs
6. The Mask
7. Casper
8. Angels in the Outfield
9. Speed
10. Batman Forever

**All Time Top 10 Sales[2]**

1. The Lion King
2. Aladdin
3. Beauty and the Beast
4. Snow White and the Seven Dwarfs
5. Forrest Gump
6. 101 Dalmatians
7. Jurassic Park
8. The Little Mermaid
9. Pinocchio
10. E.T.: The Extra-Terrestrial

(1) Rented Mar. 1, 1987-Jan. 2, 1996. (2) Sold Feb. 16, 1988-Jan. 2, 1996.

## National Film Registry, 1989-95

Source: National Film Registry, Library of Congress

"Culturally, historically, or esthetically significant" films placed on the National Film Registry, Library of Congress. Films selected in 1995 are in **boldface.**

Adam's Rib (1949)
**The Adventures of Robin Hood (1938)**
The African Queen (1951)
All About Eve (1950)
**All That Heaven Allows (1955)**
All Quiet on the Western Front (1930)
An American in Paris (1951)
**American Graffiti (1973)**
Annie Hall (1977)
The Apartment (1960)
Badlands (1973)
**The Band Wagon (1953)**
The Bank Dick (1940)
The Battle of San Pietro (1945)
The Best Years of Our Lives (1946)
Big Business (1929)
The Big Parade (1925)
The Birth of a Nation (1915)
The Black Pirate (1926)
**Blacksmith Scene (1893)**
Blade Runner (1982)
The Blood of Jesus (1941)
Bonnie and Clyde (1967)
Bringing Up Baby (1938)
**Cabaret (1972)**
Carmen Jones (1954)
Casablanca (1942)
Castro Street (1966)
Cat People (1942)
**Chan Is Missing (1982)**
The Cheat (1915)
Chinatown (1974)
Chulas Fronteras (1976)
Citizen Kane (1941)
City Lights (1931)
**The Conversation (1974)**
The Cool World (1963)
A Corner in Wheat (1909)
The Crowd (1928)
David Holzman's Diary (1968)
**The Day the Earth Stood Still (1951)**
Detour (1946)
Dodsworth (1936)
Dog Star Man (1964)
Double Indemnity (1944)
Dr. Strangelove (or, How I Learned to Stop Worrying and Love the Bomb) (1964)
Duck Soup (1933)
Eaux D'Artifice (1953)
**El Norte (1983)**
E.T.: The Extra-Terrestrial (1982)
The Exploits of Elaine (1914)
Fantasia (1940)
**Fatty's Tintype Tangle (1915)**
Footlight Parade (1933)
Force of Evil (1948)
**The Four Horsemen of the Apocalypse (1921)**
Frankenstein (1931)
Freaks (1932)
The Freshman (1925)
**Fury (1936)**
The General (1927)
**Gerald McBoing Boing (1951)**
Gertie the Dinosaur (1914)
Gigi (1958)
The Godfather (1972)
The Godfather, Part II (1974)
The Gold Rush (1925)
Gone With the Wind (1939)
The Grapes of Wrath (1940)
The Great Train Robbery (1903)
Greed (1924)
Harlan County, U.S.A. (1976)
Hell's Hinges (1916)
High Noon (1952)
High School (1968)
His Girl Friday (1940)
Hospital (1970)
**The Hospital (1971)**
How Green Was My Valley (1941)
I Am a Fugitive From a Chain Gang (1932)
Intolerance (1916)
Invasion of the Body Snatchers (1956)
It Happened One Night (1934)
It's a Wonderful Life (1946)
The Italian (1915)
**Jammin' the Blues (1944)**
Killer of Sheep (1977)
King Kong (1933)
The Lady Eve (1941)
Lassie Come Home (1943)
**The Last of the Mohicans (1920)**
Lawrence of Arabia (1962)
The Learning Tree (1969)
Letter From an Unknown Woman (1948)
Louisiana Story (1948)
Love Me Tonight (1932)
The Manchurian Candidate (1962)
**Manhatta (1921)**
Magical Maestro (1952)
The Magnificent Ambersons (1942)
The Maltese Falcon (1941)
March of Time: Inside Nazi Germany—1938 (1938)
Marty (1955)
Meet Me in St. Louis (1944)
Meshes of the Afternoon (1943)
Midnight Cowboy (1969)
Modern Times (1936)
Morocco (1930)
A Movie (1958)
Mr. Smith Goes to Washington (1939)
My Darling Clementine (1946)
Nanook of the North (1922)
Nashville (1975)
A Night at the Opera (1935)
The Night of the Hunter (1955)
Ninotchka (1939)
**North by Northwest (1959)**
Nothing But a Man (1964)
On the Waterfront (1954)
One Flew Over the Cuckoo's Nest (1975)
Out of the Past (1947)
Paths of Glory (1957)
**The Philadelphia Story (1940)**
Pinocchio (1940)

A Place in the Sun (1951)
Point Of Order (1964)
The Poor Little Rich Girl (1917)
Primary (1960)
The Prisoner of Zenda (1937)
Psycho (1960)
Raging Bull (1980)
Rebel Without a Cause (1955)
Red River (1948)
Ride the High Country (1962)
**Rip Van Winkle (1896)**
The River (1937)
Safety Last (1923)
Salesman (1969)
Salt of the Earth (1954)
Scarface (1932)
The Searchers (1956)
**Seventh Heaven (1927)**
Shadow of a Doubt (1943)
Shadows (1959)
Shane (1953)
Sherlock, Jr. (1924)
Singin' in the Rain (1952)
Snow White (1933)
Snow White and the Seven Dwarfs (1937)
Some Like It Hot (1959)
**Stagecoach (1939)**
Star Wars (1977)
Sullivan's Travels (1941)
Sunrise (1927)
Sunset Boulevard (1950)
Sweet Smell of Success (1957)
Tabu (1933)
Taxi Driver (1976)
Tevye (1939)
**To Fly (1976)**
**To Kill a Mockingbird (1962)**
Top Hat (1935)
Touch of Evil (1958)
The Treasure of the Sierra Madre (1948)
Trouble in Paradise (1932)
2001: A Space Odyssey (1968)
Vertigo (1958)
What's Opera, Doc? (1957)
Where Are My Children? (1916)
The Wind (1928)
Within Our Gates (1920)
The Wizard of Oz (1939)
A Woman Under the Influence (1974)
Yankee Doodle Dandy (1942)
Zapruder Film (1963)

## Record Long-Run Broadway Plays[1]

**Source:** *Variety*, July 29-Aug. 4, 1996

| Title | Performances |
|---|---|
| Chorus Line | 6,137 |
| Oh! Calcutta! (revival) | 5,959 |
| *Cats | 5,748 |
| *Les Misérables | 3,845 |
| *Phantom of the Opera | 3,542 |
| 42nd Street | 3,486 |
| Grease | 3,388 |
| Fiddler on the Roof | 3,242 |
| Life With Father | 3,224 |
| Tobacco Road | 3,182 |
| Hello Dolly | 2,844 |
| My Fair Lady | 2,717 |
| Annie | 2,377 |
| Man of La Mancha | 2,328 |
| Abie's Irish Rose | 2,327 |
| Oklahoma! | 2,212 |
| *Miss Saigon | 2,196 |
| Pippin | 1,944 |
| South Pacific | 1,925 |
| Magic Show | 1,920 |
| Deathtrap | 1,792 |
| Gemini | 1,788 |
| Harvey | 1,775 |
| Dancin' | 1,774 |
| La Cage aux Folles | 1,761 |
| Hair | 1,750 |
| The Wiz | 1,672 |
| Born Yesterday | 1,642 |
| Crazy for You | 1,622 |
| Ain't Misbehavin' | 1,604 |
| Best Little Whorehouse in Texas | 1,584 |
| Mary, Mary | 1,572 |
| Evita | 1,567 |
| Voice of the Turtle | 1,557 |
| Barefoot in the Park | 1,530 |
| Dreamgirls | 1,521 |
| Mame | 1,508 |
| Same Time, Next Year | 1,453 |
| Arsenic and Old Lace | 1,444 |
| The Sound of Music | 1,443 |
| How to Succeed in Business Without Really Trying (original) | 1,417 |
| Me and My Girl | 1,412 |
| Hellzapoppin | 1,404 |
| The Music Man | 1,375 |
| Funny Girl | 1,348 |
| Mumenschanz | 1,326 |
| Oh! Calcutta! (original) | 1,314 |
| Brighton Beach Memoirs | 1,299 |
| Angel Street | 1,295 |
| Lightnin' | 1,291 |
| Promises, Promises | 1,281 |
| The King and I | 1,246 |
| Cactus Flower | 1,234 |
| Sleuth | 1,222 |
| Torch Song Trilogy | 1,222 |
| "1776" | 1,217 |
| Equus | 1,209 |
| Sugar Babies | 1,208 |
| Guys and Dolls | 1,200 |
| Amadeus | 1,181 |
| Cabaret | 1,165 |
| Mister Roberts | 1,157 |
| Annie Get Your Gun | 1,147 |

(1) Number of performances through July 21, 1996. * Still running July 21, 1996.

## Some Notable Broadway Theater Openings, 1995-96 Season

**A Funny Thing Happened on the Way to the Forum.** A revival of a musical comedy, set in ancient Rome. Book by Burt Shevelove and Larry Gilbert. Music and lyrics by Stephen Sondheim. Directed by Jerry Zaks. Choreographed by Rob Marshall. With Nathan Lane and Mark Linn-Baker.

**A Midsummer Night's Dream.** The William Shakespeare comedy. Directed by Adrian Noble. With Alex Jennings, Lindsay Duncan, Barry Lynch, and Alfred Burke.

**An Ideal Husband.** Revival of an Oscar Wilde comedy. Directed by Peter Hall. With David Yelland, Penny Downie, Victoria Martin Shaw, Anna Cateret, and Dulcie Gray.

**Big.** A musical adaptation of a 1988 film comedy. Book by John Weidman. Music by David Shire. Lyrics by Richard Maltby Jr. Choreographed by Susan Stroman. Directed by Mike Ockrent. With Daniel Jenkins, Crista Moore, and Jon Cypher.

**Bring in da Noise, Bring in da Funk.** Music and dance revue. Text by Reg E. Gaines. Music by Ann Duquesnay, Zane Mark, and Daryl Waters. Directed by George C. Wolfe. Choreography by Savion Glover. With Glover, Baakari Wilder, and James Tate.

**The King and I.** A revival of a musical comedy based on the real-life experiences of a British woman who was hired to teach English to the King of Siam's children. Book and lyrics by Oscar Hammerstein. Music by Richard Rodgers. Choreographed by Jerome Robbins. Directed by Christopher Renshaw. With Lou Diamond Phillips and Donna Murphy.

**Master Class.** Drama about soprano singer Maria Callas. By Terrence McNally. Directed by Leonard Foglia. With Zoe Caldwell, David Loud, Karen Kay Cody, and Michael Friel.

**Rent.** A rock opera, based on Giacomo Puccini's *La Boheme*, set in New York City's East Village. Book, music, and lyrics by Jonathan Larson. Choreographed by Marlies Yearby. Directed by Michael Greif. With Adam Pascal, Anthony Rapp, and Daphne Rubin-Vega.

**Seven Guitars.** A tragicomedy about black blues musicians. By August Wilson. Directed by Lloyd Richards. With Keith David, Viola Davis, Tommy Hollis, Ruben Santiago-Hudson, Michele Shay, Rosalyn Coleman, and Roger Robinson.

**State Fair.** An adaptation of a film musical. Book by Tom Briggs and Louis Mattioli. Lyrics by Oscar Hammerstein. Music by Richard Rodgers. Directed by James Hammerstein and Randy Skinner. Choreographed by Skinner. With John Davidson, Kathryn Crosby, Andrea McArdle, and Donna McKechnie.

## Some Notable Nonprofit Professional Theater Companies in the U.S.

**Source:** Theatre Communications Group, Inc., July 1996

| Theater Company | City | State |
|---|---|---|
| Actors Theatre of Louisville | Louisville | KY |
| Alabama Shakespeare Festival | Montgomery | AL |
| Alley Theater | Houston | TX |
| Alliance Theatre Company | Atlanta | GA |
| American Conservatory Theatre | San Francisco | CA |
| American Repertory Theatre | Cambridge | MA |
| Arena Stage | Washington | DC |
| Arizona Theatre Company | Tucson | AZ |
| Asolo Theatre Company | Sarasota | FL |
| Berkeley Repertory Theatre | Berkeley | CA |
| Center Stage | Baltimore | MD |
| Children's Theatre Company, The | Minneapolis | MN |
| Cincinnati Playhouse in the Park | Cincinnati | OH |
| Cleveland Play House, The | Cleveland | OH |
| Denver Center Theater Company | Denver | CO |
| GeVa Theatre | Rochester | NY |
| Goodman Theatre | Chicago | IL |
| Great Lakes Theater Festival | Cleveland | OH |
| Guthrie Theater, The | Minneapolis | MN |
| Hartford Stage Company | Hartford | CT |
| Huntington Theatre Company | Boston | MA |
| Indiana Repertory Theatre | Indianapolis | IN |
| La Jolla Playhouse | La Jolla | CA |
| Lincoln Center Theater | New York | NY |
| Long Wharf Theatre | New Haven | CT |
| Manhattan Theatre Club | New York | NY |
| Mark Taper Forum | Los Angeles | CA |
| McCarter Theatre Center for the Performing Arts | Princeton | NJ |

| Theater Company | City | State |
|---|---|---|
| Milwaukee Repertory Theater | Milwaukee | WI |
| Missouri Repertory Theatre | Kansas City | MO |
| Old Globe Theatre | San Diego | CA |
| Oregon Shakespeare Festival | Ashland | OR |
| Pittsburgh Public Theater | Pittsburgh | PA |
| Seattle Repertory Theatre | Seattle | WA |
| Shakespeare Theatre, The | Washington | DC |
| South Coast Repertory | Costa Mesa | CA |
| Steppenwolf Theatre Company | Chicago | IL |
| Studio Arena Theatre | Buffalo | NY |
| TheatreWorks/USA | New York | NY |
| Trinity Repertory Theatre | Providence | RI |

## Some Notable Symphony Orchestras in the U.S.

**Source:** American Symphony Orchestra League, 1156 Fifteenth St. NW, Suite 800, Washington, DC 20005; July 1996

| Symphony Orchestra[1] | Music Director[2] |
|---|---|
| American Composers (NY) | Dennis Russell Davies |
| American (NY) | Leon Botstein |
| Atlanta (GA) | Yoel Levi |
| Austin (TX) | Sung Kwak |
| Baltimore (MD) | David Zinman |
| Baton Rouge (LA) | James Paul |
| Boston (MA) | Seiji Ozawa |
| Brooklyn Philharmonic (NY) | Robert Spano |
| Buffalo Philharmonic (NY) | Maximiano Valdez |
| Cedar Rapids (IA) | Christian Tiemeyer |
| Charleston (SC) | David Stahl |
| Charlotte (NC) | Peter McCoppin |
| Chattanooga, & Opera Assn. (TN) | Robert Bernhardt |
| Chicago (IL) | Daniel Barenboim |
| Cincinnati (OH) | Jesus Lopez-Cobos |
| Cleveland (OH) | Christoph von Dohnanyi |
| Colorado (Denver) | Marin Alsop |
| Colorado Springs (CO) | Yaacov Bergman |
| Columbus (OH) | Alessandro Siciliani |
| Dallas (TX) | Andrew Litton |
| Dayton Philharmonic (OH) | Neal Gittleman |
| Delaware (Wilmington) | Stephen Gunzenhauser |
| Detroit (MI) | Neeme Jarvi |
| The Florida Orchestra (Tampa) | Jahja Ling |
| Florida Philharmonic (Ft. Lauderdale) | James Judd |
| Florida Symphonic Pops (Boca Raton) | Crafton Beck |
| Florida West Coast (FL) | Paul C. Wolfe |
| Fort Wayne Philharmonic (IN) | Edward Chivzel |
| Fort Worth (TX) | John Giordano |
| Grand Rapids (MI) | Catherine Comet |
| Grant Park (Chicago, IL) | Hugh Wolff |
| Greenville (SC) | Davis Pollitt |
| Hartford (CT) | Michael Lankester |
| Houston (TX) | Christoph Eschenbach |
| Hudson Valley Philharmonic (Poughkeepsie, NY) | Randall Craig Fleischer |
| Indianapolis (IN) | Raymond Leppard |
| Jacksonville (FL) | Roger Nierenberg |
| Kansas City (MO) | William McGlaughlin |
| Knoxville (TN) | Kirk Trevor |
| Long Beach (CA) | JoAnn Falletta |
| Long Island Philharmonic (NY) | David Lockington |
| Los Angeles Chamber Orch. (CA) | Christof Perick |
| Los Angeles Philharmonic (CA) | Esa-Pekka Salonen |
| Louisville Orchestra (KY) | Max Bragado-Darman |
| Memphis (TN) | Alan Balter |
| Milwaukee (WI) | Andreas Delfs |
| Minnesota Orch. (Minneapolis) | Eiji Oue |
| Mississippi (Jackson) | Colman Pearce |
| Music of the Baroque (IL) | Thomas S. Wikman |
| Naples Philharmonic (FL) | Christopher Seaman |
| Nashville Symphony (TN) | Kenneth S. Schermerhorn |
| National (Washington, DC) | Leonard Slatkin |
| New Haven (CT) | Michael Palmer |
| New Jersey (Newark) | Zdenek Macal |
| New Mexico (Albuquerque) | David Lockington |
| New World Symphony (Miami Beach, FL) | Michael Tilson Thomas |
| New York Chamber Sym. of the 92nd St. Y (NYC) | Gerard Schwarz |
| New York Philharmonic (NYC) | Kurt Masur |
| New York Pops (NY) | Skitch Henderson |
| North Carolina (Raleigh) | Gerhardt Zimmermann |
| Oklahoma City Philharmonic (OK) | Joel A. Levine |
| Omaha (NE) | Victor Yampolsky |
| Oregon (Portland) | James DePreist |
| Pacific Symphony (Irvine, CA) | Carl St. Clair |
| Philadelphia Orchestra (PA) | Wolfgang Sawallisch |
| Phoenix (AZ) | James L. Sedares |
| Philharmonia Baroque (CA) | Nicholas McGegan |
| Pittsburgh (PA) | Lorin Maazel |
| Portland (ME) | Toshiyuki Shimada |
| Puerto Rico (Santurce) | Eugene Kohn |
| Rhode Island Philharmonic Orch. (Providence) | Larry Rachleff |
| Richmond Symphony (VA) | George Manahan |
| Rochester Philharmonic Orch. (NY) | Robert Bernhardt |
| Sacramento (CA) | Geoffrey Simon |
| St. Louis (MO) | Hans Vonk |
| St. Paul Chamber Orch. (MN) | Hugh Wolff |
| San Antonio (TX) | Christopher P. Wilkins |
| San Francisco (CA) | Michael Tilson Thomas |
| San Jose (CA) | Leonid Grin |
| Santa Barbara (CA) | Gisele Ben-Dor |
| Savannah (GA) | Philip B. Greenberg |
| Seattle (WA) | Gerard Schwarz |
| Shreveport (LA) | Dennis Simons |
| Spokane (WA) | Fabio Mechetti |
| Springfield (MA) | Mark Russell Smith |
| Syracuse (NY) | Fabio Mechetti |
| Toldeo (OH) | Andrew Massey |
| Tucson (AZ) | George Hanson |
| Tulsa Philharmonic Orch. (OK) | Bernard Rubenstein |
| Utah (Salt Lake City) | Joseph Silverstein |
| Virginia Symphony (Norfolk) | JoAnn Falletta |
| West Virginia (Charleston) | Thomas B. Conlin |
| Wichita (KS) | Zuohuang Chen |
| Winston-Salem Piedmont Triad Symphony (NC) | Peter J. Perret |

(1) Orchestra name = place name + Symphony Orchestra, unless otherwise noted. (2) General title; listed is highest-ranking member of conducting personnel.

## U.S. Opera Companies With Budgets of $500,000 or More

**Source:** OPERA America, 1156 15th Street NW, Washington, DC 20005-1704; July 1996

Academy of Vocal Arts Opera Theatre (Philadelphia, PA); K. James McDonnell, dir.
Albuquerque Civic Light Opera (NM); Reuben Murray, exec. dir.
American Music Theater Festival (Phila.); Marjorie Samoff, prod. dir.
American Musical Theater of San José (CA); Dianna Shuster, dir.
Anchorage Opera (AK); Peter Brown, gen. dir.
Arizona Opera Co. (Tucson); Glynn Ross, gen. dir.
Aspen Opera Theatre Center (CO); Edward Sweeney, gen. mgr.
The Atlanta Opera (GA); Alfred Kennedy, exec. dir.
Augusta Opera (GA); Edward Bradberry, gen. dir.
The Austin Lyric Opera (TX); Joseph McClain, gen. dir.
Baltimore Opera Co. (MD); Michael Harrison, gen. dir.
Boston Festival Opera Ltd.; David Spiro, art. dir.
Boston Lyric Opera Co.; Janice Mancini Del Sesto, gen. dir.
Brooklyn Academy of Music; Harvey Lichtenstein, exec. prod.
Central City Opera (Denver, CO); Pelham Pearce, gen. mgr.
Chautauqua Opera (NY); Jay Lesenger, art. dir.
Chicago Opera Theater; Carl Ratner, art. dir.
The Cincinnati Opera; Paul A. Stuhlreyer III, mng. dir.
Cleveland Opera; David Bamberger, gen. dir.
Connecticut Opera (Hartford); George Osborne, gen. dir.
The Dallas Opera; Plato Karayanis, gen. dir.
Dayton Opera Assn. (OH); Paul A. Stuhlreyer III, gen. dir.
Des Moines Metro Opera (Indianola, IA); Jerilee Mace, exec. dir.
Florentine Opera (Milwaukee), Dennis Hanthorn, gen. mgr.
Florida Grand Opera; Robert Heuer, gen. mgr.
Fort Worth Opera; William Walker, gen. dir.
Fullerton Civic Light Opera (CA); Griff Duncan, gen. mgr.
Glimmerglass Opera (Cooperstown, NY); Paul Kellogg, art dir.
Goodspeed Opera House (E. Haddam, CT); Michael Price, exec. dir.
Greater Buffalo Opera (NY); Gary Burgess, gen. dir.
Hawaii Opera Theatre; Henry Akina, gen. dir.
Houston Grand Opera Assn.; David Gockley, gen. dir
Indianapolis Opera; Jeff Maess, mng. dir.
Kentucky Opera Assn. (Louisville); Thomson Smillie, gen. dir.
Knoxville Opera (TN); Robert Lyall, gen. dir.
L.A. Opera; Peter Hemmings, gen. dir.
Light Opera Works (Evanston, IL); Bridget McDonough, mgr. dir.
Long Beach Civic Light Opera (CA); Luke Yankee, prod. art. dir.

Long Beach Opera (CA); Michael Milenski, gen. dir.
Lyric Opera Cleveland (OH); Clara Amster, mng. dir.
Lyric Opera of Chicago; Ardis Krainik, gen. dir.
Lyric Opera of Kansas City (MO); Russell Patterson, gen. dir./art. dir.
Metro Lyric Opera (NJ); Era M. Tognoli, gen. & art. dir.
Metropolitan Opera Assn. (NYC); Joseph Volpe, gen. mgr.
Michigan Opera Theatre (Detroit); David DiChiera, gen. dir.
The Minnesota Opera Co. (St. Paul); Kevin Smith, gen. dir.
Music-Theatre Group (NY & Stockbridge, MA); Lyn Austin, prod. dir.
Nashville Opera Association; Carol Peterman, exec. dir
National Grand Opera, Inc. (NY); Linda Holgers, gen. dir.
Nevada Opera (Reno); Esther Nelson, gen. dir.
New England Marionette Opera (Peterborough, NH); Edward Leach, gen. dir.
New Jersey State Opera (Newark); Alfredo Silipigni, art. dir.
New Orleans Opera Assn.; Arthur Cosenza, gen. dir.
New York City Opera Natl. Co.; Clifford Kellas, tour coordinator
New York City Opera; Paul Kellogg, gen. dir.
New York Gilbert & Sullivan Players, Inc. (NYC); Albert Bergeret, art. dir.
Ohio Light Opera; James Stuart, art. dir.
Opera Carolina (Charlotte, NC); James Wright, gen. dir.
Opera Colorado (Denver); Nathaniel Merrill, art. dir.
Opera Company of Boston; Sarah Caldwell, art. dir.
Opera Company of Philadelphia; Robert B. Driver, gen. dir.
Opera Festival of NJ (Princeton Junction); Deborah S. Sandler, gen. dir.
Opera Grand Rapids (MI); Robert Lyall, gen. dir.
Opera Memphis (TN); Michael Ching, gen./art. dir
Opera Northeast (NY); Donald Westwood, art. dir.
Opera Omaha (NE); Jane Hill, exec. dir.
Opera Orchestra of NY (NYC); Eve Queler, art dir.
Opera Pacific (Irvine, CA); David DiChiera, gen. dir.
Opera San José (CA); Irene Dalis, gen. dir.
Opera Theatre of St. Louis (MO); Charles MacKay, gen. dir.
Opera/Columbus (OH); William F. Russell, gen. dir.
OperaDelaware (Wilmington); Leland Kimball, gen. dir.
Orlando Opera Co. (FL); Robert Swedberg, gen. dir.
Palm Beach Opera (FL); Herbert P. Benn, gen. dir.
The Pennsylvania Opera Theater; Barbara Silverstein, art. dir.
Pittsburgh Civic Light Opera; Charles Gray, exec. dir.
Pittsburgh Opera; Tito Capobianco, gen. dir.
Playwrights Horizons (NYC); Leslie Marcus, mng. dir.
Portland Opera Assn. (OR); Robert Bailey, exec. dir.
Sacramento Opera Assn. (CA); Marianne H. Oaks, gen. dir.
The St. Ann Center for Restoration and the Arts (Brooklyn, NY); Susan Feldman, art. dir.
San Bernardino Civic Light Opera Association (CA); Keith Stava, gen. mgr.
San Diego Civic Light Opera Assn.; Leon Drew, gen. mgr.
San Diego Opera Assn.; Ian Campbell, gen. dir.
San Francisco Opera Center (Western Opera Theater); Susan Webb, dir.
San Francisco Opera; Lotfi Mansouri, gen. dir.
Santa Barbara Civic Light Opera (CA); Paul Iannacone, exec. prod.
The Santa Fe Opera (NM); John Crosby, gen. dir.
Sarasota Opera Assn. (FL); Deane Allyn, exec. dir.
Seattle Opera Assn.; Speight Jenkins, gen. dir.
Skylight Opera Theatre (Milwaukee); Joan Lounsbery, mng. dir.
Southeastern Regional Opera (SC); Einar Anderson, art. dir.
Summer Opera Theatre Company (DC); Elaine Walter, gen. mgr.
Syracuse Opera (NY); Catherine Wolff, gen. dir.
Teatro de la Opera (PR), Alberto Esteves, art. dir.
Tri-Cities Opera (Binghamton, NY); Marilyn Cotter, exec. dir.
Tulsa Opera (OK); Patricia Eaton, exec. dir.
Utah Festival Opera Company; Michael Ballam, gen. dir.
Utah Opera (Salt Lake City); Anne Ewers, gen. dir.
Virginia Opera (Norfolk); Peter Mark, gen. dir.
The Washington Opera (DC); Patricia Mossel, exec. dir.
Wolf Trap Opera (Vienna, VA); Peter Russell, gen. dir.

## Some Notable U.S. Dance Companies

**Source:** Dance/USA, 1156 15th Street NW, Washington, DC 20005-1704; July 1996

African-American Dance Ensemble, Durham, NC
Alvin Ailey American Dance Theater, New York, NY
Aman Folk Ensemble, Los Angeles, CA
American Ballet Theatre, New York, NY
American Repertory Ballet Company, Princeton, NJ
Atlanta Ballet, GA
Avaz International Dance Theatre, Los Angeles, CA
Ballet Arizona, Phoenix, AZ
Ballet Concierto de Puerto Rico, Santurce, PR
Ballet Florida, West Palm Beach, FL
Ballet Hispanico of New York, New York, NY
BalletMet Columbus, Columbus, OH
Ballet Omaha, NE
Ballet West, Salt Lake City, UT
Karen Bamonte Dance Works, Philadelphia, PA
Tandy Beal and Company, Santa Cruz, CA
Maria Benitez Teatro Flamenco, Santa Fe, NM
Boston Ballet, Boston, MA
Trisha Brown Company, New York, NY
Donald Byrd/The Group, New York, NY
Caribbean Dance Company of the Virgin Isl., St. Croix, VI
Chen & Dancers, New York, NY
Lucinda Childs Dance Company, New York, NY
Cincinnati Ballet, Cincinnati, OH
Cleveland San Jose Ballet, Cleveland, OH
Cunningham Dance Foundation, New York, NY
Dallas Black Dance Theatre, Dallas, TX
Dance Alloy, Pittsburgh, PA
Dance Exchange, Washington, DC
Dance Theatre of Harlem, New York, NY
DanceBrazil, New York, NY
Dayton Ballet, Dayton, OH
Dayton Contemporary Dance Company, Dayton, OH
Laura Dean Musicians and Dancers, New York, NY
Eiko & Koma, New York, NY
Eugene Ballet Company, Eugene, OR
Garth Fagan Dance, Rochester, NY
Feld Ballets/NY, New York, NY
Fort Worth Dallas Ballet, Fort Worth, TX
Joe Goode Performance Group, San Francisco, CA
David Gordon/Pick Up Co., New York, NY
Martha Graham Dance Co., New York, NY
Hartford Ballet, Hartford, CT
Erick Hawkins Dance Co., New York, NY
Joseph Holmes Dance Theater, Chicago, IL
Houston Ballet, Houston, TX
Hubbard Street Dance Chicago, Chicago, IL
Indianapolis Ballet Theatre, Indianapolis, IN
Isaacs, McCaleb & Dancers, San Diego, CA
Jazz Tap Ensemble, Los Angeles, CA
Margaret Jenkins Dance Company, San Francisco, CA
The Joffrey Ballet, Chicago, IL
Bill T. Jones/Arnie Zane Company, New York, NY
Ko-Thi Dance Company, Bronx, NY
Lewitzky Dance Company, Los Angeles, CA
Limón Dance Company, New York, NY
LINES Contemporary Ballet, San Francisco, CA
Louisville Ballet, Louisville, KY
Lar Lubovitch Dance Company, New York, NY
Miami City Ballet, Miami Beach, FL
Bebe Miller and Company, New York, NY
Elisa Monte Dance Company, New York, NY
Montgomery Ballet, Montgomery, AL
Mordine & Company, Chicago, IL
Mark Morris Dance Group, New York, NY
Muntu Dance Theatre, Chicago, IL
Nashville Ballet, Nashville, TN
Nevada Dance Theatre, Las Vegas, NV
New York City Ballet, New York, NY
Nikolais and Murray Louis Dance, New York, NY
North Carolina Dance Theatre, Charlotte, NC
Oakland Ballet, Oakland, CA
ODC/San Francisco, San Francisco, CA
Ohio Ballet, Akron, OH
Oregon Ballet Theatre, Portland, OR
Pacific Northwest Ballet, Seattle, WA
The Parsons Dance Company, New York, NY
Pennsylvania Ballet, Philadelphia, PA
Pepatián, Bronx, NY
Philadanco, Philadelphia, PA
Pilobolus Dance Theater, Washington, CT
Stuart Pimsler Dance & Theater, Columbus, OH
Pittsburgh Ballet Theatre, Pittsburgh, PA
Rhythm in Shoes, Spring Valley, OH
Richmond Ballet, Richmond, VA
Ririe-Woodbury Dance Company, Salt Lake City, UT
Cleo Parker Robinson Dance Ensemble, Denver, CO
Betty Salamun's DANCECIRCUS, Milwaukee, WI
San Francisco Ballet, San Francisco, CA
Carlota Santana Spanish Dance Arts Co., New York, NY
James Sewell Dance, Minneapolis, MN
Solomons Company/Dance, New York, NY
State Ballet of Missouri, Kansas City, MO
Elizabeth Streb Ringside, New York, NY
Paul Taylor Dance Company, New York, NY
Tulsa Ballet Theatre, Tulsa, OK
Urban Bush Women, New York, NY
Washington Ballet, Washington, DC
June Watanabe in Company, San Rafael, CA
Zivili Kolo Ensemble, Granville, OH

## 100 Best-Selling U.S. Magazines, 1995

**Source:** Audit Bureau of Circulations, Schaumburg, IL

General magazines, exclusive of groups and comics; also excluding magazines that failed to file reports to ABC by press time. Based on total average paid circulation during the 6 months ending Dec. 31, 1995.

| | Magazine | Circulation |
|---|---|---|
| 1. | Odyssey | 21,100,610 |
| 2. | Modern Maturity | 21,064,030 |
| 3. | Reader's Digest | 15,103,830 |
| 4. | TV Guide | 13,175,549 |
| 5. | National Geographic Magazine | 8,988,444 |
| 6. | Better Homes and Gardens | 7,603,207 |
| 7. | Good Housekeeping | 5,372,786 |
| 8. | Ladies' Home Journal | 5,045,644 |
| 9. | Family Circle | 5,007,542 |
| 10. | Woman's Day | 4,707,330 |
| 11. | McCall's | 4,520,186 |
| 12. | Car & Travel Magazine | 4,150,352 |
| 13. | Time | 4,083,105 |
| 14. | People Weekly | 3,321,198 |
| 15. | Playboy | 3,283,272 |
| 16. | Prevention | 3,252,115 |
| 17. | Redbook | 3,173,313 |
| 18. | Sports Illustrated | 3,157,303 |
| 19. | Newsweek | 3,155,155 |
| 20. | The American Legion Magazine | 2,852,332 |
| 21. | National Enquirer | 2,613,647 |
| 22. | Cosmopolitan | 2,569,186 |
| 23. | Southern Living | 2,471,170 |
| 24. | Star | 2,406,150 |
| 25. | Motorland | 2,334,938 |
| 26. | U.S. News & World Report | 2,220,327 |
| 27. | Home & Away | 2,204,014 |
| 28. | Seventeen | 2,172,923 |
| 29. | YM | 2,165,079 |
| 30. | Smithsonian | 2,151,172 |
| 31. | Glamour | 2,141,752 |
| 32. | V.F.W. Magazine | 2,013,258 |
| 33. | Field & Stream | 2,001,875 |
| 34. | Ebony | 1,927,675 |
| 35. | Money | 1,922,737 |
| 36. | Parents | 1,848,008 |
| 37. | Country Living | 1,838,808 |
| 38. | Popular Science | 1,805,525 |
| 39. | American Rifleman | 1,666,398 |
| 40. | Popular Mechanics | 1,586,137 |
| 41. | Life | 1,556,189 |
| 42. | Golf Digest | 1,501,525 |
| 43. | Sunset | 1,451,846 |
| 44. | Martha Stewart Living | 1,449,744 |
| 45. | Soap Opera Digest | 1,372,316 |
| 46. | Woman's World | 1,363,240 |
| 47. | 'Teen | 1,360,411 |
| 48. | Outdoor Life | 1,358,647 |
| 49. | Discover | 1,320,701 |
| 50. | Men's Health | 1,314,802 |
| 51. | The American Hunter | 1,303,067 |
| 52. | Golf Magazine | 1,283,925 |
| 53. | Mademoiselle | 1,280,169 |
| 54. | The Elks Magazine | 1,269,677 |
| 55. | New Woman | 1,262,003 |
| 56. | Consumers Digest | 1,254,879 |
| 57. | First for Women | 1,237,449 |
| 58. | Boys' Life | 1,229,052 |
| 59. | Cooking Light | 1,213,158 |
| 60. | Self | 1,211,024 |
| 61. | Us | 1,201,377 |
| 62. | Entertainment Weekly | 1,195,926 |
| 63. | Rolling Stone | 1,180,217 |
| 64. | Vanity Fair | 1,173,077 |
| 65. | Vogue | 1,146,037 |
| 66. | Bon Appetit | 1,128,932 |
| 67. | Car and Driver | 1,108,975 |
| 68. | PC Magazine | 1,107,187 |
| 69. | Penthouse | 1,100,679 |
| 70. | The Family Handyman | 1,046,398 |
| 71. | Scouting | 1,038,009 |
| 72. | Scholastic Parent & Child | 1,037,622 |
| 73. | Country Home | 1,030,694 |
| 74. | True Story Plus | 1,028,637 |
| 75. | Endless Vacation | 1,024,287 |
| 76. | Sesame Street Magazine | 1,021,807 |
| 77. | Kiplinger's Personal Finance Magazine | 1,020,931 |
| 78. | PC World | 1,016,889 |
| 79. | Home Mechanix | 1,012,411 |
| 80. | Home | 1,005,916 |
| 81. | Weight Watchers Magazine | 1,001,148 |
| 82. | Essence | 1,000,184 |
| 83. | Travel & Leisure | 988,053 |
| 84. | Globe | 981,889 |
| 85. | House Beautiful | 980,423 |
| 86. | Parenting Magazine | 979,849 |
| 87. | Motor Trend | 968,719 |
| 88. | Jet | 965,870 |
| 89. | PC/Computing | 964,507 |
| 90. | Victoria | 963,277 |
| 91. | Country America | 961,106 |
| 92. | Health | 947,728 |
| 93. | Elle | 922,048 |
| 94. | Gourmet | 896,352 |
| 95. | Business Week | 882,583 |
| 96. | Shape | 865,257 |
| 97. | Nation's Business | 863,156 |
| 98. | Conde Nast Traveler | 850,007 |
| 99. | The New Yorker | 847,201 |
| 100. | Midwest Living | 838,969 |

## Notable Books, 1996

**Source:** American Library Association, Chicago, IL; books published from Nov. 1994 through Oct. 1995

### Fiction

*The First Man,* Albert Camus
*The Point,* Charles D'Ambrosio
*The Paperboy,* Pete Dexter
*The Unconsoled,* Kazuo Ishiguro
*Native Speaker,* Chang-Rae Lee
*All the Days and Nights,* William Maxwell
*The Sharpshooter Blues,* Lewis Nordan
*Snow Angels,* Stewart O'Nan
*The Body Is Water,* Julie Schumacher
*Eveless Eden,* Marianne Wiggins

### Poetry

*Atlantis,* Mark Doty
*The Collected Poems of Langston Hughes,* Langston Hughes
*Passing Through,* Stanley Kunitz

### Nonfiction

*Paula,* Isabel Allende
*Nine Parts of Desire,* Geraldine Brooks
*Salvation on Sand Mountain,* Dennis Covington
*Lincoln,* David Herbert Donald
*Terrible Honesty,* Ann Douglas
*The Last Shot,* Darcy Frey
*Sarajevo Daily,* Tom Gjelten
*Moving Violations,* John Hockenberry
*The Liar's Club,* Mary Karr
*Amazing Grace,* Jonathan Kozol
*The Dying of the Trees,* Charles E. Little
*The End of Education,* Neil Postman
*Walt Whitman's America,* David S. Reynolds

## Notable Books for Children and Young Adults, 1996

**Source:** American Library Association, Chicago, IL; books published from late 1994 through 1995

### All Ages

*Part of Me Died, Too,* Virginia Lynn Fry
*Alphabet City,* Stephen T. Johnson
*Children Just Like Me,* Barnabas Kindersley and Anabel Kindersley
*Chile Fever: A Celebration of Peppers,* Elizabeth King
*Shortcut,* David Macaulay
*Nights of the Pufflings,* Bruce McMillan
*Advice for a Frog,* Alice Schertle
*Math Curse,* Jon Sciezka

### Younger Readers

*Street Music: City Poems,* Arnold Adoff
*The Story of Rosy Dock,* Jeannie Baker
*More Than Anything Else,* Marie Bradby
*That Kookoory!,* Margaret Walden Froehlich
*My Mama Had a Dancing Heart,* Libba Moore Gray
*The Rabbit's Escape,* Suzanne Crowder Han
*Rhymes for Annie Rose,* Shirley Hughes
*Black Swan/White Crow,* J. Patrick Lewis
*Twist Wth a Burger, Jitter With a Bug,* Linda Lowery
*The Matzah That Papa Brought Home,* Fran Manushkin
*Guess How Much I Love You,* Sam McBratney
*Zin! Zin! Zin! A Violin,* Lloyd Moss
*Piggie Pie!,* Margie Palatini
*Officer Buckle and Gloria,* Peggy Rathman
*Mr. Putter and Tabby Pick the Pears,* Cynthia Rylant
*Down the Road,* Alice Schertle
*Carolina Shout!,* Alan Schroeder
*Chato's Kitchen,* Gary Soto
*Tops and Bottoms,* Janet Stevens
*Bad Day at Riverbend,* Chris Van Allsburg
*Whistling Dixie,* Marcia Vaughan
*The Christmas Miracle of Jonathan Toomey,* Susan Wojciechowski
*The Toll-Bridge Troll,* Patricia Rae Wolff
*When the Wind Stops,* Charlotte Zolotow

### Middle Grade Readers

*Poppy,* Avi
*A Boy Called Slow,* Joseph Bruchac
*The Boy Who Lived With the Bears and Other Iroquois Stories,* Joseph Bruchac
*Talking With Artists: Volume Two,* Pat Cummings
*The Watsons Go to Birmingham—1963,* Christopher Paul Curtis
*The Midwife's Apprentice,* Karen Cushman
*Ezra Jack Keats: A Biography With Illustrations,* Dean Engel and Florence B. Freedman
*Fig Pudding,* Ralph Fletcher
*You Want Women to Vote, Lizzie Stanton?,* Jean Frtiz
*Falcon's Egg,* Luli Gray
*Grandaddy's Stars,* Helen V. Griffith
*Star of Fear, Star of Hope,* Jo Hoestlandt
*Songs of Papa's Island,* Barbara Kerley
*Dog Friday,* Hilary McKay
*The Distant Talking Drum: Poems From Nigeria,* Isaac Olaleye

*A School for Pompey Walker*, Michael J. Rosen
*The Van Gogh Café*, Cynthia Rylant
*The Faithful Friend, Robert D. SanSouci*
*Sweet Corn*, James Stevenson
*The Well: David's Story*, Mildred Taylor
*The Forestwife*, Theresa Tomlinson
*In a Circle Long Ago: A Treasury of Native Lore From North America*, Nancy Van Laan
*The Book of Changes*, Tim Wynne-Jones
*The Ballad of the Pirate Queens*, Jane Yolen

### Junior High School Age Readers

*The Arkadians*, Lloyd Alexander
*Navajo: Visions and Voices*, Shonto Begay
*David*, Barbara Cohen
*Rosie the Riveter*, Penny Colman
*What Jamie Saw*, Carolyn Coman
*Trout Summer*, Jane Leslie Conly
*The Middle Passage: White Ships/Black Cargo*, Tom Feelings
*Yolonda's Genius*, Carol Fenner
*Eagle Kite*, Paula Fox
*When Plague Strikes: The Black Death, Smallpox, AIDS*, James Cross Giblin
*Her Stories: African American Folktales, Fairy Tales, and True Tales*, Virginia Hamilton
*The Revenge of the Forty-seven Samurai*, Erik Christian Haugaard
*A Place to Call Home*, Jackie Koller
*Under the Mermaid Angel*, Martha Moore
*The Great Fire*, Jim Murphy
*The Lady With the Hat*, Uri Orlev
*Walt Whitman*, Catherine Reef
*Damned Strong Love: The True Story of Willi G. and Stephen K.*, Lutz van Dikj

### Young Adult (Teenage)—Fiction

*King's Shadow*, Elizabeth Alder
*American Eyes: New Asian-American Short Stories for Young Adults*, Lori M. Carlson, ed.
*Rule of the Bone*, Russell Banks
*Thwonk*, Joan Bauer
*Squared Circle*, James Bennet
*Baby Be-bop*, Francesca Lia Block
*Between a Rock and a Hard Place*, Alden Carter
*I See the Moon*, C. B. Christiansen
*An Island Like You*, Judith Ortiz Cofer
*In the Middle of the Night*, Robert Cormier
*Ironman*, Chris Crutcher
*The Watsons Go to Birmingham—1963*, Christopher Paul Curtis
*The Midwife's Apprentice*, Karen Cushman
*The Longest Memory*, Fred D'Aguiar
*Damned Strong Love: A True Story of Willi G. and Stefan K.*, Lutz van Dijk
*Tears of a Tiger*, Sharon M. Draper
*Midshipman's Hope*, David Feintuch
*Ash*, Lisa R. Fraustino
*Truly Grim Tales*, Priscilla Galloway
*Indio*, Sherry Garland
*Getting Lincoln's Goat*, E. M. Goldman
*Mary Wolf*, Cynthia Grant
*How Far Would You Have Gotten If I Hadn't Called You Back?*, Valerie Hobbs
*A Time for Dancing*, Davida Wills Hurwin
*But Can the Phoenix Sing?*, Crista Laird
*Othello*, Julius Lester
*Third and Indiana*, Steve Lopez
*Slot Machine*, Chris Lynch
*Tomorrow, When the War Began*, John Marsden
*Much Ado About Prom Night*, William D. McCants
*Drummers of Jericho*, Carolyn Meyer
*Under the Mermaid Angel*, Martha Moore
*One Bird*, Kyoko Mori
*War of Jenkins' Ear*, Michael Morpurgo
*The Last Safe Place on Earth*, Richard Peck
*Emperor Mage*, Tamora Pierce
*Dean Duffy*, Randy Powell
*Relic*, Douglas Preston and Child Lincoln
*Only Alien on the Planet*, Kristen Randle
*Math Curse*, Jon Scieszka
*The Bomb*, Theodore Taylor
*Dancing Pink Flamingos and Other Stories*, Maria Testa
*Companions of the Night*, Vivian VandeVelde
*Farm Team*, Will Weaver
*The Road Home*, Ellen E. White
*Like Sisters on the Homefront*, Rita Williams-Garcia
*From the Notebooks of Melanin Sun*, Jacqueline Woodson

## Best-Selling Books, 1995

**Source:** *Publishers Weekly*, Mar. 4, 1996

Rankings are determined by sales figures provided by publishers, based on copies "shipped and billed" in 1995, minus returns through Feb. 16, 1996.

### Hardcover Fiction

1. *The Rainmaker*, John Grisham
2. *The Lost World*, Michael Crichton
3. *Five Days in Paris*, Danielle Steel
4. *The Christmas Box*, Richard Paul Evans
5. *Lightning*, Danielle Steel
6. *The Celestine Prophecy*, James Redfield
7. *Rose Madder*, Stephen King
8. *Silent Night*, Mary Higgins Clark
9. *Politically Correct Holiday Stories*, James Finn Garner
10. *The Horse Whisperer*, Nicholas Evans
11. *Politically Correct Bedtime Stories*, James Finn Garner
12. *Memnoch the Devil*, Anne Rice
13. *Beach Music*, Pat Conroy
14. *From Potter's Field*, Patricia Cornwell
15. *Morning, Noon and Night*, Sidney Sheldon

### Hardcover Nonfiction

1. *Men Are From Mars, Women Are From Venus*, John Gray
2. *My American Journey*, Colin Powell with Joseph Persico
3. *Miss America*, Howard Stern
4. *The Seven Spirtual Laws of Success*, Deepak Chopra
5. *The Road Ahead*, Bill Gates
6. *Charles Kuralt's America*, Charles Kuralt
7. *Mars and Venus in the Bedroom*, John Gray
8. *To Renew America*, Newt Gingrich
9. *My Point. . . And I Do Have One*, Ellen DeGeneres
10. *The Moral Compass*, William J. Bennett
11. *The Book of Virtues*, William J. Bennett
12. *I Want to Tell You*, O.J. Simpson with Laurence Schiller
13. *In the Kitchen With Rosie*, Rosie Daley
14. *Emotional Intelligence*, Daniel Goleman
15. *David Letterman's Book of Top 10 Lists*, David Letterman

### Trade Paperback

1. *2nd Helping of Chicken Soup for the Soul*, eds., Jack Canfield and Mark Hansen
2. *The Calvin and Hobbes Tenth Anniversary Book*, Bill Watterson
3. *The Far Side Gallery 5*, Gary Larson
4. *Ten Stupid Things Women Do to Mess Up Their Lives*, Laura Schlessinger
5. *What to Expect: The Toddler Years*, A. Eisenberg, H. Murkoff, S. Hathaway
6. *The Stone Diaries*, Carol Shields
7. *Microsoft Windows 95 Resource Kit*, orig., Microsoft Press
8. *Aladdin Factor*, Jack Canfield and Mark Victor Hansen
9. *The Promise*, orig., Thomas Nelson
10. *Snow Falling on Cedars*, David Guterson
11. *Illuminata: A Return to Prayer*, Marianne Williamson
12. *Chicken Soup for the Soul Cookbook*, Jack Canfield, Mark Victor Hansen, and Diana von Welanetz Wentworth
13. *Dianetics*, L. Ron Hubbard
14. *The Celestine Prophecy: An Experiential Guide*, James Redfield and Carol Adrienne
15. *Secrets of Fat-Free Cooking*, Sandra Wooduff

### Mass-Market Paperback

1. *The Chamber*, John Grisham
2. *Tom Clancy's Op-Center*, Tom Clancy and Steve Pieczenik
3. *Accident*, Danielle Steel
4. *Wings*, Danielle Steel
5. *Debt of Honor*, Tom Clancy
6. *Insomnia*, Stephen King
7. *Tom Clancy's Op-Center II: Mirror Image*, Tom Clancy and Steve Pieczenik
8. *Nothing Lasts Forever*, Sidney Sheldon
9. *Remember Me*, Mary Higgins Clark
10. *Icebound*, Dean Koontz
11. *The Body Farm*, Patricia Cornwell
12. *Lottery Winner*, Mary Higgins Clark
13. *Key to Midnight*, Dean Koontz
14. *Dark Rivers of the Heart*, Dean Koontz
15. *All That Glitters*, V.C. Andrews

### Almanacs, Atlases, and Annuals

1. *The World Almanac and Book of Facts 1995*, ed. Robert Famighetti
2. *The World Almanac and Book of Facts 1996*, ed. Robert Famighetti
3. *The Ernst & Young Tax Guide, 1995*, orig., Wiley
4. *The Old Farmer's Almanac 1996*, ed. Judson D. Hale
5. *What Color Is Your Parachute? 1996*, Richard Bolles

# Leading U.S. Daily Newspapers, 1995

**Source:** *1996 Editor & Publisher International Yearbook*

(Circulation as of Sept. 30, 1995; m = morning, e = evening)

As of Feb. 1, 1996, the number of U.S. daily newspapers had declined to 1,533, a net loss of 15 since Feb. 1, 1995. Average daily circulation for the 6-month period ending Sept. 30, 1995 was 58,193,391, down 1,112,045 from that for the same period in 1994. The large decrease can be partially attributed to the closing of the large-circulation *Houston Post*, Baltimore *Evening Sun*, *New York Newsday*, and the evening edition of the new Milwaukee *Journal Sentinel*. Although Sunday editions increased by 2 to 888 during 1995, average Sunday circulation for the 6-month period ending Sept. 30, 1995, fell 1,065,503, to 61,229,296. The decline can be partially attributed to the closing of the *Houston Post* and *New York Newsday*.

| | Newspaper | | Circulation |
|---|---|---|---|
| 1. | *Wall Street Journal* (New York, NY) | (m) | 1,763,140 |
| 2. | *USA Today* (Arlington, VA) | (m) | 1,523,610 |
| 3. | *Times* (New York, NY) | (m) | 1,081,541 |
| 4. | *Times* (Los Angeles, CA) | (m) | 1,012,189 |
| 5. | *Post* (Washington, DC) | (m) | 793,660 |
| 6. | *Daily News* (New York, NY) | (m) | 738,091 |
| 7. | *Tribune* (Chicago, IL) | (m) | 684,366 |
| 8. | *Newsday* (Long Island, NY) | (all day) | 634,627 |
| 9. | *Chronicle* (Houston, TX) | (m) | 541,478 |
| 10. | *Free Press* (Detroit, MI) | (m) | 531,825[1] |
| 11. | *Morning News* (Dallas, TX) | (m) | 500,358 |
| 12. | *Globe* (Boston, MA) | (m) | 498,853 |
| 13. | *Chronicle* (San Francisco, CA) | (m) | 489,238 |
| 14. | *Sun-Times* (Chicago, IL) | (m) | 488,405 |
| 15. | *Inquirer* (Philadelphia, PA) | (m) | 469,398 |
| 16. | *Star-Ledger* (Newark, NJ) | (m) | 436,634 |
| 17. | *Post* (New York, NY) | (m) | 413,705 |
| 18. | *Plain Dealer* (Cleveland, OH) | (m) | 396,773 |
| 19. | *Star Tribune* (Minneapolis, MN) | (m) | 389,865 |
| 20. | *Herald* (Miami, FL) | (m) | 383,212 |
| 21. | *Union-Tribune* (San Diego, CA) | (all day) | 379,705 |
| 22. | *Arizona Republic* (Phoenix, AZ) | (m) | 365,979 |
| 23. | *News* (Detroit, MI) | (e) | 354,403[1] |
| 24. | *Register* (Orange County, CA) | (m) | 349,874 |
| 24. | *Times* (St. Petersburg, FL) | (m) | 349,874 |
| 26. | *Sun* (Baltimore, MD) | (m) | 339,493 |
| 27. | *Oregonian* (Portland, OR) | (all day) | 333,654 |
| 28. | *Rocky Mountain News* (Denver, CO) | (m) | 331,044 |
| 29. | *Post-Dispatch* (St. Louis, MO) | (m) | 319,990 |
| 30. | *Journal Sentinel* (Milwaukee, WI) | (m) | 309,137 |
| 31. | *Herald* (Boston, MA) | (m) | 308,077 |
| 32. | *Constitution* (Atlanta, GA) | (m) | 305,457 |
| 33. | *Post* (Denver, CO) | (m) | 303,357 |
| 34. | *Mercury News* (San Jose, CA) | (m) | 286,935 |
| 35. | *Star* (Kansas City, MO) | (m) | 284,675 |
| 36. | *Bee* (Sacramento, CA) | (m) | 279,980 |
| 37. | *News* (Buffalo, NY) | (all day) | 274,614 |
| 38. | *Sentinel* (Orlando, FL) | (all day) | 272,702 |
| 39. | *Times-Picayune* (New Orleans, LA) | (all day) | 267,397 |
| 40. | *Sun-Sentinel* (Fort Lauderdale, FL) | (m) | 264,863 |
| 41. | *Tribune* (Tampa, FL) | (m) | 263,674 |
| 42. | *Dispatch* (Columbus, OH) | (m) | 255,390 |
| 43. | *Post-Gazette* (Pittsburgh, PA) | (m) | 242,723 |
| 44. | *Observer* (Charlotte, NC) | (m) | 239,173 |
| 45. | *Courier-Journal* (Louisville, KY) | (m) | 236,465 |
| 46. | *Times* (Seattle, WA) | (e) | 232,616 |
| 47. | *World-Herald* (Omaha, NE) | (all day) | 232,360 |
| 48. | *Star* (Indianapolis, IN) | (m) | 227,535 |
| 49. | *Star-Telegram* (Fort Worth, TX) | (m) | 225,080 |
| 50. | *Express-News* (San Antonio, TX) | (m) | 221,556 |
| 51. | *Daily Oklahoma* (Oklahoma City, OK) | (m) | 212,382 |
| 52. | *Times-Dispatch* (Richmond, VA) | (m) | 211,589 |
| 53. | *Courant* (Hartford, CT) | (m) | 211,704 |
| 54. | *Pioneer Press* (St. Paul, MN) | (m) | 208,807 |
| 55. | *Post-Intelligencer* (Seattle, WA) | (m) | 204,544 |
| 56. | *Enquirer* (Cincinnati, OH) | (m) | 203,158 |
| 57. | *Daily News* (Los Angeles, CA) | (m) | 201,239 |
| 58. | *Daily News* (Philadelphia, PA) | (m) | 195,447 |
| 59. | *Democrat and Chronicle* (Rochester, NY) | (m) | 194,677 |
| 60. | *Times-Union* (Jacksonville, FL) | (m) | 194,643 |
| 61. | *Investor's Busines Daily* (Los Angeles, CA) | (m) | 193,459 |
| 62. | *Virginian-Pilot* (Norfolk, VA) | (m) | 188,678 |
| 63. | *Journal* (Providence, RI) | (m) | 185,014 |
| 64. | *Commercial Appeal* (Memphis, TN) | (m) | 178,415 |
| 65. | *Register (Des Moines, IA)* | (m) | 177,857 |
| 66. | *American-Statesman* (Austin, TX) | (m) | 177,704 |
| 67. | *Democrat-Gazette* (Little Rock, AR) | (m) | 175,218 |
| 68. | *Palm Beach Post* (West Palm Beach, FL) | (m) | 173,699 |
| 69. | *World* (Tulsa, OK) | (m) | 168,529 |
| 70. | *Press-Enterprise* (Riverside, CA) | (m) | 164,028 |
| 71. | *Daily News* (Dayton, OH) | (m) | 163,187 |
| 72. | *Asbury Park Press* (Neptune, NJ) | (e) | 161,052 |
| 73. | *News* (Birmingham, AL) | (e) | 160,081 |
| 74. | *Record* (Hackensack, NJ) | (m) | 156,726 |
| 75. | *Bee* (Fresno, CA) | (m) | 152,554 |
| 76. | *Beacon Journal* (Akron, OH) | (m) | 152,211 |
| 77. | *Blade* (Toledo, OH) | (m) | 147,526 |
| 78. | *News & Observer* (Raleigh, NC) | (m) | 146,688 |
| 79. | *Tennessean* (Nashville, TN) | (m) | 146,466 |
| 80. | *Press* (Grand Rapids, MI) | (e) | 145,521 |
| 81. | *Review-Journal* (Las Vegas, NV) | (m) | 142,149 |
| 82. | *Morning Call* (Allentown, PA) | (m) | 133,140 |
| 83. | *News Tribune* (Tacoma, WA) | (m) | 128,659 |
| 84. | *Daily Herald* (Arlington Heights, IL) | (m) | 128,172 |
| 85. | *Tribune* (Salt Lake City, UT) | (m) | 126,076 |
| 86. | *State* (Columbia, SC) | (m) | 126,074 |
| 87. | *News Journal* (Wilmington, DE) | (all day) | 125,677 |
| 88. | *Journal* (Atlanta, GA) | (e) | 124,484 |
| 89. | *Spokesman-Review* (Spokane, WA) | (m) | 122,961 |
| 90. | *News-Sentinel* (Knoxville, TN) | (m) | 116,429 |
| 91. | *Examiner* (San Francisco, CA) | (e) | 114,957 |
| 92. | *Herald-Tribune* (Sarasota, FL) | (m) | 114,638 |
| 93. | *Journal* (Albuquerque, NM) | (m) | 113,031 |
| 94. | *Herald-Leader* (Lexington, KY) | (m) | 112,352 |
| 95. | *Telegram & Gazette* (Worcester, MA) | (m) | 111,836 |
| 96. | *Times & World-News* (Roanoke, VA) | (m) | 110,195 |
| 97. | *Clarion-Ledger* (Jackson, MS) | (m) | 110,059 |
| 98. | *Post & Courier* (Charleston, SC) | (m) | 109,520 |
| 99. | *Press-Telegram* (Long Beach, CA) | (m) | 109,029 |
| 100. | *Advertiser* (Honolulu, HI) | (m) | 105,624 |

(1) Because of a subsequent strike that affected circulation, figures are for Mar. 31, 1995.

# Leading Canadian Daily Newspapers, 1995

**Source:** *1996 Editor & Publisher International Yearbook*

(Circulation as of Sept. 30, 1995; m = morning)

For the year ending Feb. 1, 1996, the number of Canadian dailies remained stable at 107. One paper closed, but one paper started up to offset the loss. Canadian daily circulation fell by 142,690, to 4,881,085, in the 6-month period ending Sept. 30, 1995. During the same period, Sunday circulation decreased by 97,118, to 3,109,928.

| Newspaper | | Circulation |
|---|---|---|
| *Star* (Toronto, ON) | (m) | 491,411 |
| *Globe and Mail* (Toronto, ON) | (m) | 306,260 |
| *Le Journal* (Montreal, PQ) | (m) | 270,607 |
| *Sun* (Toronto, ON) | (m) | 240,822 |
| *Sun* (Vancouver, BC) | (m) | 185,535 |
| *La Presse* (Montreal, PQ) | (m) | 179,523 |
| *Province* (Vancouver, BC) | (m) | 153,758 |
| *Gazette* (Montreal, ON) | (m) | 148,777 |
| *Journal* (Edmonton, AB) | (m) | 147,060 |
| *Citizen* (Ottawa, ON) | (all day) | 145,952 |

# U.S. Commercial Radio Stations, by Format, 1990-96

**Source:** M Street Corporation, Nashville, TN © 1996; counts are for Aug. of each year

| Stations, by primary format | 1990 | 1991 | 1992 | 1993 | 1994 | 1995 | 1996 |
|---|---|---|---|---|---|---|---|
| Country | 2,452 | 2,457 | 2,552 | 2,612 | 2,642 | 2,608 | 2,558 |
| Adult Contemporary (AC) | 2,135 | 2,088 | 1,963 | 1,895 | 1,784 | 1,661 | 1,592 |
| News, Talk, Business, Sports | 405 | 527 | 648 | 841 | 1,028 | 1,165 | 1,262 |
| Religion (Teaching and Music) | 745 | 799 | 837 | 915 | 926 | 970 | 996 |
| Rock (Album, Modern, Classic) | 419 | 529 | 592 | 643 | 721 | 808 | 868 |
| Oldies | 659 | 704 | 731 | 734 | 714 | 718 | 725 |
| Spanish and Ethnic | 342 | 370 | 385 | 421 | 470 | 492 | 515 |
| Adult Standards | 383 | 408 | 412 | 421 | 435 | 469 | 474 |
| Urban, Black, Urban AC | 294 | 311 | 313 | 321 | 328 | 342 | 348 |
| Top-40 | 824 | 675 | 578 | 441 | 358 | 324 | 314 |
| Easy Listening | 240 | 210 | 171 | 116 | 106 | 85 | 91 |
| Variety | 97 | 81 | 72 | 68 | 63 | 63 | 65 |
| Jazz and New Age | 68 | 53 | 52 | 45 | 43 | 58 | 54 |
| Classical, Fine Arts | 52 | 51 | 48 | 45 | 44 | 39 | 41 |
| Pre-Teen | 3 | 4 | 3 | 13 | 19 | 26 | 30 |
| Comedy | 1 | 0 | 0 | 0 | 1 | 0 | 0 |
| Off Air | 210 | 308 | 352 | 345 | 369 | 323 | 298 |
| Changing formats/not available | 115 | 19 | 15 | 14 | 6 | 9 | 666 |
| **Total stations** | **9,444** | **9,594** | **9,724** | **9,890** | **10,057** | **10,160** | **10,237** |

# Top-Grossing North American Concert Appearances, 1995

**Source:** Pollstar; Fresno, CA

| Rank | Artist | Venue | Location | Total performances | Total gross (in mils) |
|---|---|---|---|---|---|
| 1. | The Rolling Stones | Autodomo Hermanos Rodriguez | Mexico City, Mex. | 4 | $11.8 |
| 2. | Elton John/Billy Joel | Joe Robbie Stadium | Miami, FL | 2 | 4.4 |
| 3. | The Eagles | Rose Bowl | Pasadena, CA | 1 | 3.9 |
| 4. | The Grateful Dead | Soldier Field Stadium | Chicago, IL | 2 | 3.7 |
| 5. | The Grateful Dead | Sam Boyd Stadium | Las Vegas, NV | 3 | 3.5 |
| 6. | Elton John | Madison Square Garden | New York, NY | 3 | 3.5 |
| 7. | The Grateful Dead | Giants Stadium | East Rutherford, NJ | 2 | 3.4 |
| 8. | The Eagles | Tacoma Dome | Tacoma, WA | 2 | 2.8 |
| 9. | Elton John/Billy Joel | MGM Grand Hotel | Las Vegas, NV | 2 | 2.8 |
| 10. | The Eagles | War Memorial Stadium | Little Rock, AR | 1 | 2.6 |
| 11. | The Eagles | Palace of Auburn Hills | Auburn Hills, MI | 2 | 2.4 |
| 12. | Elton John/Billy Joel | Jack Murphy Stadium | San Diego, CA | 1 | 2.4 |
| 13. | The Eagles | CoreStates Spectrum | Philadelphia, PA | 1 | 2.3 |
| 14. | R.E.M. | Madison Square Garden Arena | New York, NY | 3 | 2.2 |
| 15. | The Eagles | Mile High Stadium | Denver, CO | 1 | 2.2 |
| 16. | The Eagles | Sandstone Amphitheatre | Bonner Springs, KS | 2 | 2.1 |
| 17. | The Grateful Dead | Franklyn County Airport | Highgate, VT | 1 | 2.0 |
| 18. | Elton John/Billy Joel | RCA Dome | Indianapolis, IN | 1 | 2.0 |
| 19. | Elton John/Billy Joel | Clemson Memorial Stadium | Clemson, SC | 1 | 2.0 |
| 20. | The Eagles | Riverbend Music Center | Cincinnati, OH | 2 | 2.0 |

# Top-Grossing North American Concert Tours, 1985-95

**Source:** Pollstar; Fresno, CA

| | Artist (Year) | Total gross[1] | Cities/ Shows |
|---|---|---|---|
| 1. | The Rolling Stones (1994) | $121.2 | 43/60 |
| 2. | Pink Floyd (1994) | 103.5 | 39/59 |
| 3. | The Rolling Stones (1989) | 98.0 | 33/60 |
| 4. | The Eagles (1994) | 79.4 | 32/54 |
| 5. | The New Kids on the Block (1990) | 74.1 | 122/152 |
| 6. | U2 (1992) | 67.0 | 61/73 |
| 7. | The Eagles (1995) | 63.3 | 46/58 |
| 8. | Barbra Streisand (1994) | 58.9 | 6/22 |
| 9. | The Grateful Dead (1994) | 52.4 | 29/84 |
| 10. | Elton John/Billy Joel (1994) | 47.7 | 14/21 |
| 11. | The Grateful Dead (1993) | $45.6 | 29/81 |
| 12. | Boyz II Men (1995) | 43.2 | 133/134 |
| 13. | Billy Joel (1990) | 43.0 | 53/95 |
| 14. | The Who (1989) | 41.7 | 27/39 |
| 15. | Bruce Springsteen & the E St. Band (1985) | 39.1 | 21/40 |
| 16. | R.E.M. (1995) | 38.7 | 63/81 |
| 17. | Paul McCartney (1990) | 37.9 | 21/32 |
| 18. | Bon Jovi (1989) | 36.7 | 129/143 |
| 19. | U2 (1987) | 35.1 | 50/79 |
| 20. | The Grateful Dead (1991) | 34.7 | 27/76 |

(1) In mils. Not adjusted for inflation.

# Sales of Recorded Music and Music Videos, by Genre and Format, 1991-95

**Source:** Recording Industry Assn. of America, New York, NY

| Genre | 1991 | 1992 | 1993 | 1994 | 1995 |
|---|---|---|---|---|---|
| Rock | 34.8 | 31.6 | 30.2 | 35.1 | 33.5 |
| Country | 12.8 | 17.4 | 18.7 | 16.3 | 16.7 |
| Urban Contemp. | 9.9 | 9.8 | 10.6 | 9.6 | 11.3 |
| Pop | 12.1 | 11.5 | 11.9 | 10.3 | 10.1 |
| Rap | 10.0 | 8.6 | 9.2 | 7.9 | 6.7 |
| Gospel | 3.8 | 2.8 | 3.2 | 3.3 | 3.1 |
| Jazz | 4.0 | 3.8 | 3.1 | 3.0 | 3.0 |
| Classical | 3.2 | 3.7 | 3.3 | 3.7 | 2.9 |
| Oldies | NA | 0.8 | 1.0 | 0.8 | 1.0 |
| Soundtracks | 0.7 | 0.7 | 0.7 | 1.0 | 0.9 |
| New Age | NA | 1.2 | 1.0 | 1.0 | 0.7 |
| Children's | 0.3 | 0.5 | 0.4 | 0.4 | 0.5 |
| Other | 6.5 | 5.4 | 4.6 | 5.3 | 7.0 |

| Format | 1991 | 1992 | 1993 | 1994 | 1995 |
|---|---|---|---|---|---|
| Compact disc (CD) | 38.9 | 46.5 | 51.2 | 58.4 | 65.0 |
| CD single | 0.9 | 1.2 | 0.9 | 1.9 | 2.6 |
| Cassette | 49.8 | 43.6 | 38.0 | 32.1 | 25.1 |
| Cassette single | 6.5 | 5.4 | 7.8 | 4.9 | 4.6 |
| LP | 1.7 | 1.3 | 0.3 | 0.8 | 0.5 |
| 7" single | 0.4 | 0.3 | 0.2 | 0.4 | 0.1 |
| 12" single | 1.0 | 0.6 | 0.3 | 0.2 | 0.2 |
| Music video | NA | 1.0 | 1.3 | 0.8 | 0.9 |
| CD-ROM | NA | NA | NA | 0.6 | 1.0 |

NA = Not available. **Note:** As percentage of recorded music sold for calendar year. Totals may not equal 100% because of "Don't know/no answer" responses to survey.

## Sales of Recorded Music and Music Videos, by Units Shipped and Value, 1987-95

**Source:** Recording Industry Assn. of America, New York, NY

(in mils, net after returns)

| Format | 1987 | 1988 | 1989 | 1990 | 1991 | 1992 | 1993 | 1994 | 1995 | % change 1994-95 |
|---|---|---|---|---|---|---|---|---|---|---|
| **Compact disc (CD)** | | | | | | | | | | |
| Units shipped | 102.1 | 149.7 | 207.2 | 286.5 | 333.3 | 407.5 | 495.4 | 662.1 | 727.6 | 9.9 |
| Dollar value | 1,593.6 | 2,089.9 | 2,587.5 | 3,451.6 | 4,337.7 | 5,326.5 | 6,511.4 | 8,464.5 | 9,401.7 | 11.1 |
| **CD single** | | | | | | | | | | |
| Units shipped | NA | 1.6 | –0.1 | 1.1 | 5.7 | 7.3 | 7.8 | 9.3 | 17.2 | 85.0 |
| Dollar value | NA | 9.8 | –0.7 | 6.0 | 35.1 | 45.1 | 45.8 | 56.1 | 88.6 | 57.9 |
| **Cassette** | | | | | | | | | | |
| Units shipped | 410.0 | 450.1 | 446.2 | 442.2 | 360.1 | 366.4 | 339.5 | 345.4 | 272.6 | –21.1 |
| Dollar value | 2,959.7 | 3,385.1 | 3,345.8 | 3,472.4 | 3,019.6 | 3,116.3 | 2,915.8 | 2,976.4 | 2,303.6 | –22.6 |
| **Cassette single** | | | | | | | | | | |
| Units shipped | 5.1[1] | 22.5 | 76.2 | 87.4 | 69.0 | 84.6 | 85.6 | 81.1 | 70.7 | –12.8 |
| Dollar value | 14.3[1] | 57.3 | 194.6 | 257.9 | 230.4 | 298.8 | 298.5 | 274.9 | 236.3 | –14.0 |
| **LP/EP** | | | | | | | | | | |
| Units shipped | 107.0 | 72.4 | 34.6 | 11.7 | 4.8 | 2.3 | 1.2 | 1.9 | 2.2 | 15.8 |
| Dollar value | 793.1 | 532.2 | 220.3 | 86.5 | 29.4 | 13.5 | 10.6 | 17.8 | 25.1 | 41.0 |
| **Vinyl single** | | | | | | | | | | |
| Units shipped | 82.0 | 65.6 | 36.6 | 27.6 | 22.0 | 19.8 | 15.1 | 11.7 | 10.2 | –12.8 |
| Dollar value | 203.3 | 180.4 | 116.4 | 94.4 | 63.9 | 66.4 | 51.2 | 47.2 | 46.7 | –1.1 |
| **Music video** | | | | | | | | | | |
| Units shipped | NA | NA | 6.1 | 9.2 | 6.1 | 7.6 | 11.0 | 11.2 | 12.6 | 12.5 |
| Dollar value | NA | NA | 115.4 | 172.3 | 118.1 | 157.4 | 213.3 | 231.1 | 220.3 | –4.7 |
| **Total units** | **706.8[2]** | **761.9** | **806.7** | **865.7** | **801.0** | **895.5** | **955.6** | **1,122.7** | **1,113.1** | **–0.9** |
| **Total value** | **5,567.5[2]** | **6,254.8** | **6,579.4** | **7,541.1** | **7,834.2** | **9,024.0** | **10,046.6** | **12,068.0** | **12,322.3** | **2.1** |

NA = Not applicable. (1) Cassette singles were introduced in the second half of the year. The figure here represents 6-month sales. (2) Total includes discontinued configurations not itemized in the table.

## Sales of Recorded Music, 1995

**Source:** Recording Industry Assn. of America, New York, NY

Hootie & the Blowfish's debut album *Cracked Rear View* was by far the top-selling album of 1995. At the close of the calendar year *Cracked Rear View* had sold more than 11 mil copies since its release in 1994, putting it in fifth place for best-selling debut album of all time. (By mid-1996 the album had sold 14 million copies, making it the second best-selling debut album ever.)

Other noteworthy sellers in 1995 included Garth Brooks's *The Hits* (8 mil sold), the best selling hits package of the year. Sales of T.L.C.'s second album, *CrazySexyCool* (7 mil sold), made T.L.C. the best selling female group. With the success of "Waterfalls," which went platinum in 1995, T.L.C. also earned the record for most gold singles by a female group (6 by the end of 1995).

Boyz II Men, Motown Records' all-time top-seller, had sold more than 11 mil copies of their hit *II* by the end of 1995; 6 mil of these sales occurred during 1995.

During the course of 1995 the following accumulated sales of 5 mil: Mariah Carey, *Daydream*; Eagles, *Hell Freezes Over*; Kenny G, *Miracles: The Holiday Album*; Pearl Jam, *Vitalogy*; Live, *Throwing Copper*; Green Day, *Dookie*; and Michael Jackson, *HIStory: Past, Present, and Future, Book 1*.

The most successful single of the year was Coolio's "Gangsta' Paradise," which sold 2.5 mil copies.

## Multi-Platinum and Platinum Awards for Recorded Music and Music Videos, 1995

**Source:** Recording Industry Assn. of America, New York, NY

To achieve platinum status, an album must reach a minimum sale of 1 mil units in LPs, tapes, and CDs, with a manufacturer's dollar volume of at least $2 mil based on one-third of the suggested retail list price for each record, tape, or CD sold. To achieve multi-platinum status, an album must reach a minimum sale of at least 2 mil units in LPs, tapes, and CDs, with a manufacturer's dollar volume of at least $4 mil based on one-third of the list price. Singles must sell 1 mil units to achieve a platinum award and at least 2 mil to achieve a multi-platinum award. EP singles count as 2 units. Double-CD sets count as 2 units. Music videos (long form) must sell 100,000 units to qualify for a platinum award and must sell more than 200,000 units for a multi-platinum award. Video singles, which must have a maximum running time of 15 minutes and no more than 2 songs per title, must sell 50,000 units to qualify for a platinum award and at least 100,000 units to qualify for a multi-platinum award.

Awards listed were for albums and singles released in 1995 and for music videos released at any time. No multi-platinum music video singles were awarded in 1995.

### Albums, Multi-Platinum

(number in parentheses = mils sold)

2 Pac, *Me Against the World* (2)
Michael Bolton, *Greatest Hits 1985-1995* (2)
Bone Thugs 'n Harmony, *E. 1999 Eternal* (2)
Bush, *Sixteen Stone* (2)
Mariah Carey, *Daydream* (5)
Janet Jackson, *Design of a Decade* (2)
Michael Jackson, *HIStory of Past, Present, and Future, Book I* (5)
Manheim Steamroller, *Christmas in the Aire* (3)
Tim McGraw, *All I Want* (2)
John Michael Montgomery, *John Michael Montgomery* (2)
Alanis Morissette, *Jagged Little Pill* (4)
Pink Floyd, *Pulse* (2)
Selena, *Dreaming of You* (2)
Soundtrack, *Dangerous Minds* (3)
Soundtrack, *Pocahontas* (3)
Bruce Springsteen, *Greatest Hits* (2)
George Strait, *Strait out of the Box* (2)
Shania Twain, *The Woman in Me* (4)
Van Halen, *Balance* (2)

### Albums, Platinum

AC/DC, *Ballbreaker*
All 4 One, *And the Music Speaks*
Better Than Ezra, *Deluxe*
Bon Jovi, *These Days*
Brownstone, *From the Bottom Up*
Collective Soul, *Collective Soul*
Cypress Hill, *III (Temple of Boom)*
Melissa Etheridge, *Never Enough*
Jeff Foxworthy, *Games Rednecks Play*
Jodeci, *The Show, the After Party, the Hotel*
Elton John, *Made in England*
Montell Jordan, *This is How We Do It*
Alison Krauss, *Now That I've Found You*
Annie Lennox, *Medusa*
Reba McEntire, *Starting Over*
Natalie Merchant, *Tigerlily*

Ozzy Osbourne, *Ozzmosis*
Presidents of the United States of America, *Presidents of the United States of America*
Real McCoy, *Another Night*
Red Hot Chili Peppers, *One Hot Minute*
Silverchair, *Frogstomp*
Soul Asylum, *Let Your Dim Light Shine*
Soul for Real, *Candy Rain*
Soundtrack, *Batman Forever*
Soundtrack, *Boys on the Side*
Soundtrack, *Friday*
Soundtrack, *The Show*
White Zombie, *Astro-Creep 2,000: Songs of Love, Destruction, and Other Synthetic Delusions of the Electric Head*
Xscape, *Off the Hook*

### Singles, Platinum

2 Pac, "Dear Mama"
Brandy, "Baby"
Adina Howard, "Freak Like Me"
Michael Jackson, "You Are Not Alone"
Michael Jackson & Janet Jackson, "Scream"
Montell Jordan, "This Is How We Do It"
Luniz, "I Got 5 on It"
Method Man, "I'll Be There for You"
Monica, "Don't Take It Personal"
Notorious B.I.G., "One More Chance"
Shaggy, "Boombastic/In the Summertime"
TLC, "Waterfalls"
Various, "Pocahontas Read Along"

### Singles, Multi-Platinum

(number in parenthesis = millions sold)

Mariah Carey, "Fantasy" (2)
Coolio, "Gangsta's Paradise" (2)

### Music Videos, Multi-Platinum

(number in parenthesis = units sold)

The Eagles, *Hell Freezes Over* (200,000)
Michael Jackson, *Video Greatest Hits/HIStory* (200,000)
Metallica, *Binge & Purge* (900,000)
Yanni, *Live at the Acropolis* (500,000)

### Music Videos, Platinum

Boyz II Men, *From Then II Now*
The Doors, *A Tribute to Jim Morrison*
Michael Jackson, *Dangerous—The Short Films*
Kiss, *X-Treme Close-Up*
Reba McEntire, *Greatest Hits*
Nirvana, *Live! Tonight! Sold Out!*
Pink Floyd, *Pulse*
Elvis Presley, *Elvis: The Lost Performances*
John Tesh, *Live at Red Rocks*
Various, *Woodstock 1994*
Stevie Ray Vaughan, *Live at the Mocambo*

### Video Singles, Platinum

Jeff Foxworthy, "You Might Be a Redneck If. . ."

## Top-Selling Video Games, 1995

**Source:** The NPD TRSTS Video Games Tracking Service, The NPD Group, Inc., Port Washington, NY; ranked by units sold

| | Title |
|---|---|
| 1. | Super Nintendo Donkey Kong |
| 2. | Super Nintendo Mortal Kombat III |
| 3. | Super Nintendo Killer Instinct |
| 4. | Genesis Mortal Kombat III |
| 5. | Super Nintendo Donkey Kong Country 2 |
| 6. | Super Nintendo Super Mario World 2: Yoshi's Island |
| 7. | Genesis Madden NFL '96 |
| 8. | Genesis NBA Jam Tournament Edition |
| 9. | Super Nintendo NBA Jam Tournament Edition |
| 10. | Genesis Mortal Kombat II |
| 11. | Super Nintendo Lion King |
| 12. | Genesis NBA Live '96 |
| 13. | Genesis NHL '96 |
| 14. | Genesis Lion King |
| 15. | Genesis Toy Story |

## Household Penetration of Some Consumer Electronics Products, 1996

**Source:** Electronic Industries Association Market Research Department; as of Jan. 1996

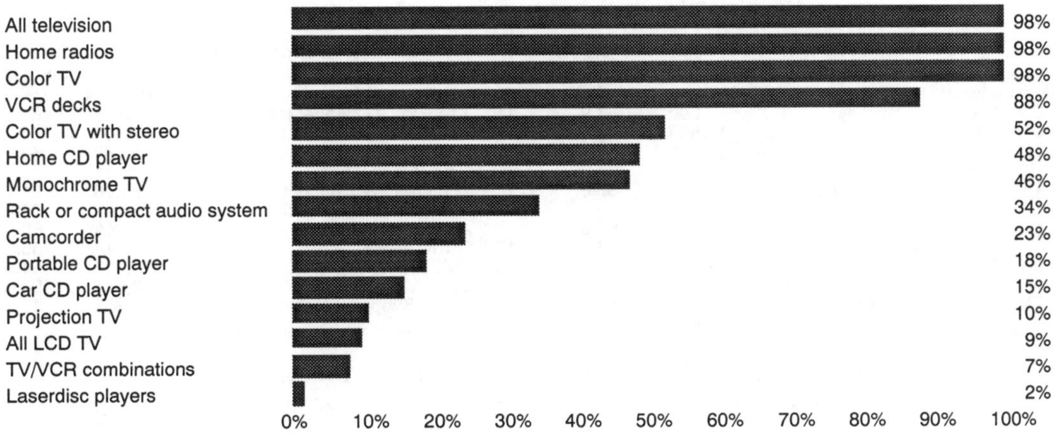


## U.S. Television Set Owners

**Source:** Nielsen Media Research; Dec. 31, 1995

**Of the 95.9 mil homes (98% of U.S. households) that owned at least one TV set in 1995:**

99% had color televisions
38% had 2 TV sets
28% had 3 or more TV sets
81% had a VCR
65% received basic cable
32% received pay cable

# Some Television Addresses, Phone Numbers, Internet Sites

**BROADCAST**

**ABC–American Broadcasting Company**
77 W 66th St.
New York, NY 10023 (212) 456-7777
Web site: http://www.abc.com

**CBS–Columbia Broadcasting System, Inc.**
51 W 52nd St.
New York, NY 10019 (212) 975-4321
Web site: http://www.cbs.com

**NBC–National Broadcasting Company**
30 Rockefeller Plaza
New York, NY 10112 (212) 664-4444
Web site: http://nbc.com

**Fox Television**
205 E 67th St.
New York, NY 10021 (212) 452-5555
Web site: http://www.fox.com/foxtv.htm

**PBS–Public Broadcasting Service**
1320 Braddock Place
Alexandria, VA 22314 (703) 739-5000
Web site: http://www.pbs.org

**CABLE**

**A&E–Arts & Entertainment Network**
235 E 45th St.
New York, NY 10017 (212) 661-4500
Web site: http://www.aetv.com

**AMC–American Movie Classics**
Rainbow Programming Holdings, Inc.
150 Crossways Pk. W
Woodbury, NY 11797 (516) 364-2222
Web site: http://www.amctv.com

**BET–Black Entertainment Television**
1232 31st St. NW
Washington, DC 20007 (202) 608-2000
Web site: http://www.betnetworks.com

**CNBC–Consumer News and Business Channel**
2200 Fletcher Ave.
Fort Lee, NJ 07024 (201) 585-2622
Web site: http://www.cnbc.com

**CNN–Cable News Network**
One CNN Center, Box 105366
Atlanta, GA 30348-5366 (404) 827-1500
Web site: http://www.cnn.com

**C-SPAN–Cable-Satellite Public Affairs Network**
400 N Capitol St. NW, Suite 650
Washington, DC 20001 (202) 737-3220
Web site: http://www.c-span.org

**DIS–The Disney Channel**
3800 W Alameda Ave.
Burbank, CA 91505 (818) 569-7500
Web site: http://www.disneychannel.com

**ESPN–ESPN, Inc.**
ESPN Plaza
Bristol, CT 06010-9454 (860) 585-2000
Web site: http://espnet.sportszone.com

**LIF–Lifetime**
309 W 49th St.
New York, NY 10019 (212) 424-7000
Web site: http://www.lifetimetv.com

**MSNBC**
2200 Fletcher Ave.
Ft. Lee, NJ 07024 (201) 583-5000
Web site: http://www.msnbc.com

**MTV–Music Television**
MTV Networks, Inc.
1515 Broadway
New York, NY 10036 (212) 258-8000
Web site: http://www.mtv.com

**NICK–Nickelodeon/Nick at Nite**
MTV Networks, Inc.
1515 Broadway
New York, NY 10036 (212) 258-8000
Web site: http://www.nick-at-nite.com

**TBS–Turner Broadcasting System**
One CNN Center, Box 105366
Atlanta, GA 30348-5366
(404) 827-1700
Web site: http://www.turner.com/teg.html

**TDC–The Discovery Channel**
Discovery Communications
7700 Wisconsin Ave., Suite 700
Bethesda, MD 20814-3522
(301) 986-0444
Web site: http://www.discovery.com

**USA–USA Network**
USA Networks
1230 Ave. of the Americas
New York, NY 10020 (212) 408-9100
Web site: http://www.usanetwork.com

# Average Television Viewing Time, 1996

**Source:** Nielsen Media Research, May 1996 (hours: minutes per week)

| | Age | Mon.-Fri. 10 AM-4:30 PM | Mon.-Fri. 4:30 PM-7:30 PM | Mon.-Sun. 8-11 PM | Sat. 7 AM-1 PM | Mon.-Fri. 11:30 PM-1 AM |
|---|---|---|---|---|---|---|
| **Total** | | **3:48** | **3:17** | **7:37** | **1:11** | **0:41** |
| Women | 18+ | 5:12 | 3:41 | 8:87 | 1:25 | 0:38 |
| | 18-24 | 4:56 | 2:54 | 6:13 | 1:19 | 0:38 |
| | 25-54 | 4:25 | 4:25 | 3:02 | 8:04 | 1:25 |
| | 55+ | 6:52 | 5:31 | 10:38 | 1:46 | 0:41 |
| Men | 18+ | 3:06 | 2:54 | 7:49 | 1:41 | 0:36 |
| | 18-24 | 2:54 | 2:10 | 4:56 | 1:23 | 0:43 |
| | 25-54 | 2:36 | 2:43 | 7:29 | 1:28 | 0:38 |
| | 55+ | 4:29 | 4:24 | 10:03 | 1:22 | 0:34 |
| Teens | 12-17 | 1:43 | 2:45 | 5:15 | 0:41 | 0:37 |
| Children | 2-5 | 5:04 | 2:44 | 3:45 | 0:19 | 0:59 |
| | 6-11 | 1:38 | 2:45 | 4:41 | 0:22 | 1:01 |

# Top 20 Cable Video Networks, 1996

**Source:** *Cable Television Developments,* Natl. Cable Television Assn., Jan.-Mar. 1996; ranked by number of subscribers

| Rank | Network[1] | Affiliates | Subscribers (mils) |
|---|---|---|---|
| 1. | ESPN (1979) | 27,600 | 67.9 |
| 2. | CNN (1980) | 11,593 | 67.8 |
| 3. | TBS (1976) | 11,668 | 67.6 |
| 4. | USA Network (1980) | 12,500 | 67.2 |
| 5. | The Discovery Channel (1985) | NA | 67.0 |
| 6. | TNT (Turner Network Television) (1988) | 10,260 | 66.6 |
| 7. | C-SPAN (1979) | 5,536 | 66.1 |
| 8. | MTV: Music Television (1981) | 9,176 | 65.9 |
| 9. | Arts & Entertainment Network (1984) | 9,500 | 65.0 |
| 10. | TNN (The Nashville Network) (1983) | 13,639 | 64.8 |
| 11. | The Family Channel (1977) | 10,555 | 64.0 |
| 11. | LIFETIME Television (1984) | 7,600 | 64.0 |
| 11. | Nickelodeon (1979) | 11,788 | 64.0 |
| | Nick at Nite (1985) | 11,711 | |
| 14. | The Weather Channel (1982) | 6,000 | 61.7 |
| 15. | Headline News (1982) | 6,147 | 60.2 |
| 16. | AMC (American Movie Classics) (1984) | NA | 60.0 |
| 17. | CNBC (1989) | NA | 56.0 |
| 18. | QVC Network (1986) | 5,735 | 54.6 |
| 19. | VH-1 (Video Hits One) (1985) | 6,551 | 54.0 |
| 20. | Home Shopping Network (1982) | 2,658 | 47.9 |

NA = Not available. **Note:** Data include noncable affiliates. (1) Date in parentheses is year service began.

# Number of Cable TV Systems and Subscribers, 1973-96

**Source:** *Television and Cable Factbook,* Warren Publishing, Inc., Washington, DC; estimates as of Jan. 1

| Year | Systems | Subscribers[1] | Year | Systems | Subscribers[1] | Year | Systems | Subscribers[1] | Year | Systems | Subscribers[1] |
|---|---|---|---|---|---|---|---|---|---|---|---|
| 1973 | 2,991 | 7.3 | 1979 | 4,150 | 14.1 | 1985 | 6,600 | 32.0 | 1991 | 10,704 | 51.0 |
| 1974 | 3,158 | 8.7 | 1980 | 4,225 | 16.0 | 1986 | 7,500 | 37.5 | 1992 | 11,073 | 53.0 |
| 1975 | 3,506 | 9.8 | 1981 | 4,375 | 18.3 | 1987 | 7,900 | 41.0 | 1993 | 11,108 | 55.0 |
| 1976 | 3,681 | 10.8 | 1982 | 4,825 | 21.0 | 1988 | 8,500 | 44.0 | 1994 | 11,214 | 56.5 |
| 1977 | 3,832 | 11.9 | 1983 | 5,600 | 25.0 | 1989 | 9,050 | 47.5 | 1995 | 11,215 | 58.3 |
| 1978 | 3,875 | 13.0 | 1984 | 6,200 | 29.0 | 1990 | 9,575 | 50.0 | 1996 | 11,220 | 61.7 |

(1) In mils.

## U.S. Households With Cable Television, 1977-95

**Source:** Nielsen Media Research, New York, NY

| Year | Basic cable subscribers | Percentage of households with TVs |
|---|---|---|
| 1977 | 12,168,450 | 16.6 |
| 1978 | 13,391,910 | 17.9 |
| 1979 | 14,814,380 | 19.4 |
| 1980 | 17,671,490 | 22.6 |
| 1981 | 23,219,200 | 28.3 |
| 1982 | 29,340,570 | 35.0 |
| 1983 | 34,113,790 | 40.5 |
| 1984 | 37,290,870 | 43.7 |
| 1985 | 39,872,520 | 46.2 |
| 1986 | 42,237,140 | 48.1 |
| 1987 | 44,970,880 | 50.5 |
| 1988 | 48,636,520 | 53.8 |
| 1989 | 52,564,470 | 57.1 |
| 1990 | 54,871,330 | 59.0 |
| 1991 | 55,786,390 | 60.6 |
| 1992 | 57,211,600 | 61.5 |
| 1993 | 58,834,440 | 62.5 |
| 1994 | 60,483,600 | 63.4 |
| 1995 | 62,620,700 | 65.3 |

## TV Viewing Shares, Broadcast Years 1986/87-1994/95[1]

**Source:** *Cable TV Facts,* Cable Advertising Bureau, New York, NY

| | Total Television Households | | | | | | | | | All Cable Households | | | | | | | | | Pay Cable Households | | | | | | | | |
|---|---|---|---|---|---|---|---|---|---|---|---|---|---|---|---|---|---|---|---|---|---|---|---|---|---|---|---|
| | '86/'87 | '87/'88 | '88/'89 | '89/'90 | '90/'91 | '91/'92 | '92/'93 | '93/'94 | '94/'95 | '86/'87 | '87/'88 | '88/'89 | '89/'90 | '90/'91 | '91/'92 | '92/'93 | '93/'94 | '94/'95 | '86/'87 | '87/'88 | '88/'89 | '89/'90 | '90/'91 | '91/'92 | '92/'93 | '93/'94 | '94/'95 |
| Broadcast Network Affiliates | 64 | 61 | 58 | 55 | 53 | 54 | 53 | 52 | 48 | 53 | 52 | 49 | 46 | 46 | 47 | 46 | 44 | 41 | 48 | 48 | 45 | 43 | 41 | 43 | 42 | 42 | 38 |
| Independent TV Stations[2] | 20 | 20 | 20 | 20 | 21 | 20 | 21 | 21 | 22 | 17 | 17 | 16 | 16 | 17 | 16 | 17 | 17 | 17 | 16 | 17 | 16 | 16 | 16 | 16 | 16 | 17 | 17 |
| Public TV Stations | 4 | 4 | 3 | 3 | 3 | 3 | 4 | 4 | 3 | 3 | 3 | 3 | 3 | 2 | 3 | 3 | 3 | 3 | 3 | 3 | 2 | 2 | 2 | 2 | 2 | 3 | 2 |
| Basic Cable Networks | 13 | 15 | 17 | 21 | 24 | 24 | 25 | 26 | 30 | 23 | 25 | 28 | 32 | 35 | 35 | 36 | 37 | 42 | 23 | 24 | 27 | 30 | 34 | 33 | 35 | 36 | 41 |
| Pay Cable Services | 4 | 7 | 7 | 6 | 6 | 6 | 5 | 5 | 6 | 10 | 11 | 11 | 10 | 9 | 8 | 8 | 8 | 8 | 17 | 18 | 18 | 18 | 17 | 17 | 16 | 15 | 15 |

(1) Share figures refer to percentage of the viewing audience for all television viewing, 24 hours/day. As a result of multiset use and rounding of numbers, share figures add to more than 100. (2) Independent shares include those for Fox.

## Favorite Prime-Time Television Programs, 1995-96

**Source:** Nielsen Media Research

Data are for regularly scheduled network programs (Sept. 18, 1995-May 22, 1996); ranked by average audience percentage. Average audience percentages, or ratings, are estimates of the percentage of TV-owning households watching a program. Audience share percentages are estimates of the percentage of the actual viewing audience tuned into a program.

| Rank | Program | Average audience (%) | Audience share (%) |
|---|---|---|---|
| 1. | E.R. | 22.0 | 36 |
| 2. | Seinfeld | 21.2 | 33 |
| 3. | Friends | 18.7 | 30 |
| 4. | Caroline in the City | 17.9 | 28 |
| 5. | NFL Monday Night Football | 17.1 | 29 |
| 6. | Single Guy | 16.7 | 26 |
| 7. | Home Improvement | 16.2 | 25 |
| 8. | Boston Common | 15.6 | 26 |
| 9. | 60 Minutes | 14.2 | 24 |
| 10. | NYPD Blue | 14.1 | 24 |
| 11. | Frasier | 13.6 | 21 |
| 11. | 20/20 | 13.6 | 24 |
| 13. | Grace Under Fire | 13.2 | 21 |
| 14. | Coach | 12.9 | 20 |
| 14. | NBC Monday Night Movies | 12.9 | 20 |
| 16. | Roseanne | 12.5 | 20 |
| 17. | The Nanny | 12.4 | 20 |
| 18. | Murphy Brown | 12.3 | 18 |
| 18. | Primetime Live | 12.3 | 21 |
| 18. | Walker Texas Ranger | 12.3 | 22 |
| 21. | Champs | 12.2 | 18 |
| 21. | NBC Sunday Night Movie | 12.2 | 20 |
| 23. | 3rd Rock From the Sun | 12.1 | 20 |
| 24. | Chicago Hope | 11.9 | 20 |
| 25. | Can't Hurry Love | 11.4 | 17 |
| 25. | CBS Sunday Movie | 11.4 | 18 |
| 25. | Law and Order | 11.4 | 20 |
| 25. | Naked Truth | 11.4 | 18 |
| 29. | America's Funniest Home Videos | 11.3 | 19 |
| 29. | Dateline NBC-Tues. | 11.3 | 19 |
| 29. | Dateline NBC-Wed. | 11.3 | 18 |
| 32. | Dana Carvey Show | 11.2 | 18 |
| 32. | Fox NFL Sunday-Post Game | 11.2 | 20 |
| 34. | Touched By an Angel | 11.1 | 20 |
| 35. | Wings | 11.0 | 18 |
| 36. | If Not for You | 10.9 | 16 |
| 37. | Mad About You | 10.8 | 17 |
| 38. | Hudson Street | 10.7 | 17 |
| 39. | ABC Sunday Night Movie | 10.6 | 17 |
| 39. | Ellen | 10.6 | 18 |
| 39. | Newsradio | 10.6 | 16 |
| 42. | Family Matters | 10.5 | 19 |
| 42. | John Larroquette Show | 10.5 | 18 |
| 44. | Dateline NBC-Fri. | 10.3 | 17 |
| 44. | Lois & Clark | 10.3 | 18 |
| 46. | ABC Monday Night Movie | 10.2 | 16 |
| 46. | High Society | 10.2 | 15 |
| 48. | Boy Meets World | 10.1 | 18 |
| 48. | Drew Carey Show | 10.1 | 16 |
| 50. | Cybill | 10.0 | 16 |
| 50. | Pursuit of Happiness | 10.0 | 15 |
| 50. | X-Files | 10.0 | 17 |

## Favorite Syndicated Programs, 1995-96

**Source:** Nielsen Media Research, Sept. 4, 1995-May 12, 1996

Average audience percentages, or ratings, are estimates of the percentage of TV-owning households watching a program.

| Rank | Program | Avg. audience (%) |
|---|---|---|
| 1. | Wheel of Fortune (Mon.-Fri.) | 12.5 |
| 2. | Jeopardy | 10.3 |
| 3. | Home Improvement (Mon.-Fri.) | 9.2 |
| 4. | Oprah Winfrey Show | 7.9 |
| 5. | National Geographic on Assignment | 7.4 |
| 5. | Seinfeld (Mon.-Fri.) | 7.3 |
| 7. | ESPN NFL Regular Season | 7.1 |
| 8. | Entertainment Tonight | 6.7 |
| 9. | Star Trek: Deep Space Nine | 6.4 |
| 10. | Buena Vista I | 6.3 |
| 11. | NFL on TNT '95 (regular season) | 6.2 |
| 11. | Wheel of Fortune (weekend) | 6.2 |
| 13. | Simpsons | 6.1 |
| 14. | Journeys of Hercules | 5.9 |
| 14. | Inside Edition | 5.9 |
| 16. | Warner Brothers Volume 3D | 5.8 |
| 16. | WCW Wrestling | 5.8 |
| 18. | Home Improvement (weekend) | 5.7 |
| 19. | Century 16 | 5.6 |
| 20. | Fresh Prince of BelAire (Mon.-Fri.) | 5.2 |
| 20. | Xena | 5.2 |

# All-Time Top Television Programs

**Source:** Nielsen Media Research, Jan. 1961-Apr. 7, 1996

Estimates exclude unsponsored or joint network telecasts or programs under 30 minutes long. Ranked by rating (percentage of TV-owning households tuned in to the program).

| Rank | Program | Telecast date | Network | Rating (%) | Avg. audience (000) |
|---|---|---|---|---|---|
| 1. | M*A*S*H (last episode) | 2/28/83 | CBS | 60.2 | 50,150 |
| 2. | Dallas (Who Shot J.R.?) | 11/21/80 | CBS | 53.3 | 41,470 |
| 3. | Roots-Pt. 8 | 1/30/77 | ABC | 51.1 | 36,380 |
| 4. | Super Bowl XVI | 1/24/82 | CBS | 49.1 | 40,020 |
| 5. | Super Bowl XVII | 1/30/83 | NBC | 48.6 | 40,480 |
| 6. | XVII Winter Olympics - 2d Wed. | 2/23/94 | CBS | 48.5 | 45,690 |
| 7. | Super Bowl XX | 1/26/86 | NBC | 48.3 | 41,490 |
| 8. | Gone With the Wind-Pt. 1 | 11/7/76 | NBC | 47.7 | 33,960 |
| 9. | Gone With the Wind-Pt. 2 | 11/8/76 | NBC | 47.4 | 33,750 |
| 10. | Super Bowl XII | 1/15/78 | CBS | 47.2 | 34,410 |
| 11. | Super Bowl XIII | 1/21/79 | NBC | 47.1 | 35,090 |
| 12. | Bob Hope Christmas Show | 1/15/70 | NBC | 46.6 | 27,260 |
| 13. | Super Bowl XVIII | 1/22/84 | CBS | 46.4 | 38,800 |
| 13. | Super Bowl XIX | 1/20/85 | ABC | 46.4 | 39,390 |
| 15. | Super Bowl XIV | 1/20/80 | CBS | 46.3 | 35,330 |
| 16. | ABC Theater (The Day After) | 11/20/83 | ABC | 46.0 | 38,550 |
| 17. | Roots-Pt. 6 | 1/28/77 | ABC | 45.9 | 32,680 |
| 17. | The Fugitive | 8/29/67 | ABC | 45.9 | 25,700 |
| 19. | Super Bowl XXI | 1/25/87 | CBS | 45.8 | 40,030 |
| 20. | Roots-Pt. 5 | 1/27/77 | ABC | 45.7 | 32,540 |
| 21. | Super Bowl XXVIII | 1/29/94 | NBC | 45.5 | 42,860 |
| 21. | Cheers (last episode) | 5/20/93 | NBC | 45.5 | 42,360 |
| 23. | Ed Sullivan | 2/9/64 | CBS | 45.3 | 23,240 |
| 24. | Super Bowl XXVII | 1/31/93 | NBC | 45.1 | 41,990 |
| 25. | Bob Hope Christmas Show | 1/14/71 | NBC | 45.0 | 27,050 |
| 26. | Roots-Pt. 3 | 1/25/77 | ABC | 44.8 | 31,900 |
| 27. | Super Bowl XI | 1/9/77 | NBC | 44.4 | 31,610 |
| 27. | Super Bowl XV | 1/25/81 | NBC | 44.4 | 34,540 |
| 29. | Super Bowl VI | 1/16/72 | CBS | 44.2 | 27,450 |
| 30. | XVII Winter Olympics - 2d Fri. | 2/25/94 | CBS | 44.1 | 41,540 |
| 30. | Roots-Pt. 2 | 1/24/77 | ABC | 44.1 | 31,400 |
| 32. | Beverly Hillbillies | 1/8/64 | CBS | 44.0 | 22,570 |
| 33. | Roots-Pt. 4 | 1/26/77 | ABC | 43.8 | 31,190 |
| 33. | Ed Sullivan | 2/16/64 | CBS | 43.8 | 22,445 |
| 35. | Super Bowl XXIII | 1/22/89 | NBC | 43.5 | 39,320 |
| 36. | Academy Awards | 4/7/70 | ABC | 43.4 | 25,390 |
| 37. | Thorn Birds-Pt. 3 | 3/29/83 | ABC | 43.2 | 35,990 |
| 38. | Thorn Birds-Pt. 4 | 3/30/83 | ABC | 43.1 | 35,900 |
| 39. | CBS NFC Championship | 1/10/82 | CBS | 42.9 | 34,960 |
| 40. | Beverly Hillbillies | 1/15/64 | CBS | 42.8 | 21,960 |
| 41. | Super Bowl VII | 1/14/73 | NBC | 42.7 | 27,670 |
| 42. | Thorn Birds-Pt. 2 | 3/28/83 | ABC | 42.5 | 35,400 |

# Top-Rated TV Shows of Each Season, 1950-51 to 1995-96

**Source:** Nielsen Media Research; regular series programs, Sept.-May season

| Season | Program | Rating[1] | TV-owning households (in thousands) |
|---|---|---|---|
| 1950-51 | Texaco Star Theatre | 61.6 | 10,320 |
| 1951-52 | Godfrey's Talent Scouts | 53.8 | 15,300 |
| 1952-53 | I Love Lucy | 67.3 | 20,400 |
| 1953-54 | I Love Lucy | 58.8 | 26,000 |
| 1954-55 | I Love Lucy | 49.3 | 30,700 |
| 1955-56 | $64,000 Question | 47.5 | 34,900 |
| 1956-57 | I Love Lucy | 43.7 | 38,900 |
| 1957-58 | Gunsmoke | 43.1 | 41,920 |
| 1958-59 | Gunsmoke | 39.6 | 43,950 |
| 1959-60 | Gunsmoke | 40.3 | 45,750 |
| 1960-61 | Gunsmoke | 37.3 | 47,200 |
| 1961-62 | Wagon Train | 32.1 | 48,555 |
| 1962-63 | Beverly Hillbillies | 36.0 | 50,300 |
| 1963-64 | Beverly Hillbillies | 39.1 | 51,600 |
| 1964-65 | Bonanza | 36.3 | 52,700 |
| 1965-66 | Bonanza | 31.8 | 53,850 |
| 1966-67 | Bonanza | 29.1 | 55,130 |
| 1967-68 | Andy Griffith | 27.6 | 56,670 |
| 1968-69 | Rowan & Martin Laugh-In | 31.8 | 58,250 |
| 1969-70 | Rowan & Martin Laugh-In | 26.3 | 58,500 |
| 1970-71 | Marcus Welby, MD | 29.6 | 60,100 |
| 1971-72 | All in the Family | 34.0 | 62,100 |
| 1972-73 | All in the Family | 33.3 | 64,800 |
| 1973-74 | All in the Family | 31.2 | 66,200 |
| 1974-75 | All in the Family | 30.2 | 68,500 |
| 1975-76 | All in the Family | 30.1 | 69,600 |
| 1976-77 | Happy Days | 31.5 | 71,200 |
| 1977-78 | Laverne & Shirley | 31.6 | 72,900 |
| 1978-79 | Laverne & Shirley | 30.5 | 74,500 |
| 1979-80 | 60 Minutes | 28.2 | 76,300 |
| 1980-81 | Dallas | 31.2 | 79,900 |
| 1981-82 | Dallas | 28.4 | 81,500 |
| 1982-83 | 60 Minutes | 25.5 | 83,300 |
| 1983-84 | Dallas | 25.7 | 83,800 |
| 1984-85 | Dynasty | 25.0 | 84,900 |
| 1985-86 | Bill Cosby Show | 33.8 | 85,900 |
| 1986-87 | Bill Cosby Show | 34.9 | 87,400 |
| 1987-88 | Bill Cosby Show | 27.8 | 88,600 |
| 1988-89 | Roseanne | 25.5 | 90,400 |
| 1989-90 | Roseanne | 23.4 | 92,100 |
| 1990-91 | Cheers | 21.6 | 93,100 |
| 1991-92 | 60 Minutes | 21.7 | 92,100 |
| 1992-93 | 60 Minutes | 21.6 | 93,100 |
| 1993-94 | Home Improvement | 21.9 | 94,200 |
| 1994-95 | Seinfeld | 20.5 | 95,400 |
| 1995-96 | E.R. | 22.0 | 95,900 |

(1) Rating is percent of TV-owning households tuned in to the program. Data prior to 1988-89 exclude Alaska and Hawaii.

# 100 Leading U.S. Advertisers, 1995

**Source:** Competitive Media Reporting and Publishers Information Bureau, New York, © Copyright 1996

(in thousands)

| Rank | Advertiser | Ad spending |
|---|---|---|
| 1. | Procter & Gamble | $1,507,410.1 |
| 2. | General Motors | 1,499,567.7 |
| 3. | Philip Morris | 1,397,679.0 |
| 4. | Chrysler | 954,727.4 |
| 5. | Ford | 891,757.3 |
| 6. | Walt Disney | 777,777.4 |
| 7. | Pepsico | 730,195.9 |
| 8. | AT&T | 675,233.8 |
| 9. | Johnson & Johnson | 601,321.6 |
| 10. | Ford Motor Co. (local dealers) | 586,444.7 |
| 11. | Sears Roebuck & Co. | 557,847.4 |
| 12. | Time Warner | 542,971.2 |
| 13. | Toyota Motor | 513,392.7 |
| 14. | General Motors dealers assn. | 503,744.3 |
| 15. | McDonalds | 490,643.4 |
| 16. | Nestlé | 490,058.3 |
| 17. | Kellogg Co. | 488,205.1 |
| 18. | General Motors (local dealers) | 460,665.7 |
| 19. | Unilever PLC | 442,672.0 |
| 20. | Sony | 430,954.4 |
| 21. | Grand Metropolitan | 418,253.5 |
| 22. | Federated Dept. Stores | 407,640.4 |
| 23. | National Amusements | 404,232.0 |
| 24. | Honda Motor Co. | 388,848.6 |
| 25. | General Mills | 367.678.7 |
| 26. | Nissan Motor Co. | 367,678.7 |
| 27. | American Home Products | 355,524.7 |
| 28. | May Depart. Stores | 339,444.9 |
| 29. | Seagram | 333,102.4 |
| 30. | MCI Communications | 322,615.8 |
| 31. | Anheuser-Busch | 320,473.6 |
| 32. | Ford Motor Co. dealers assn. | $315,565.5 |
| 33. | Warner-Lambert | $308,215.5 |
| 34. | Circuit City Stores | 291,562.7 |
| 35. | IBM | 289,817.6 |
| 36. | Toyota Motor Co. (local dealers) | 280,856.8 |
| 37. | News Corp. | 275,871.2 |
| 38. | JC Penney | 273,872.3 |
| 39. | Dayton Hudson | 259,293.7 |
| 40. | RJR Nabisco Holdings | 243,227.4 |
| 41. | Mazda | 241,283.2 |
| 42. | K Mart | 241,181.3 |
| 43. | Coca-Cola | 238,243.5 |
| 44. | Chrysler Corp. (local dealers) | 231,763.2 |
| 45. | Valassis Communications | 229,238.3 |
| 46. | U.S. Government | 219,909.7 |
| 47. | Bristol-Myers Squibb Co. | 219,367.0 |
| 48. | Sprint | 213,908.6 |
| 49. | American Express | 210,380.6 |
| 50. | Mars | 210,129.1 |
| 51. | Hasbro | 201,658.2 |
| 52. | Sara Lee | 199,049.1 |
| 53. | Mattel | 184,518.1 |
| 54. | Nissan Motor Co. (local dealers) | 179,448.6 |
| 55. | Chrysler Corp. dealer assn. | 175,397.8 |
| 56. | SmithKline Beecham | 173,228.5 |
| 57. | Campbell Soup | 168,954.6 |
| 58. | Wendys Intl. | 161,333.6 |
| 59. | Bayer Group | 160,481.1 |
| 60. | Tandy | 158,256.2 |
| 61. | Clorox | 157,731.6 |
| 62. | Visa Intl. | 154,595.7 |
| 63. | Ralston Purina | 149,979.8 |
| 64. | Turner Broadcasting | 149,542.9 |
| 65. | Microsoft | $147,733.2 |
| 66. | Nike | 146,257.8 |
| 67. | Wal-Mart Stores | 143,166.3 |
| 68. | Credit Lyonnais SA | 136,651.3 |
| 69. | Mitsubishi Motors | 133,578.6 |
| 70. | Darden Restaurants | 133,488.2 |
| 71. | Quaker Oats | 133,131.3 |
| 72. | Honda Motor Co. (local dealers) | 132,709.4 |
| 73. | Benckiser | 131,019.6 |
| 74. | BAT Industries | 128,431.8 |
| 75. | Roll Intl. | 126,197.4 |
| 76. | Kimberly-Clark | 124,830.2 |
| 77. | Wm. Wrigley Jr. Co. | 123247.4 |
| 78. | Gillette | 122,624.7 |
| 79. | Dean Witter Discover | 119,664.7 |
| 80. | Cadbury Schweppes | 116,019.7 |
| 81. | SC Johnson & Sons | 115,555.8 |
| 82. | Montgomery Ward | 115,166.2 |
| 83. | Dillard Dept. Stores | 113,241.8 |
| 84. | Pharmacia & Upjohn | 112,673.5 |
| 85. | Hershey Foods | 111,705.1 |
| 86. | Toyota auto dealers assn. | 109,875.9 |
| 87. | Bertelsmann | 108,759.2 |
| 88. | General Electric | 108,752.6 |
| 89. | Coors Adolph | 108,752.6 |
| 90. | Levi Strauss | 103,984.4 |
| 91. | Schering-Plough | 103,984.4 |
| 92. | Citicorp | 100,967.4 |
| 93. | Conagra | 99,405.4 |
| 94. | Reckitt & Colman | 97,483.4 |
| 95. | Colgate-Palmolive | 96,817.6 |
| 96. | Home Depot | 96,645.7 |
| 97. | National Syndicates | 96,568.2 |
| 98. | Ciba-Geigy | 95,568.2 |
| 99. | Volkswagen | 94,629.6 |
| 100. | Best Buy | 94,021.7 |

# Total U.S. Ad Spending by Category and Medium, 1995

**Source:** Competitive Media Reporting and Publishers Information Bureau, New York, © Copyright 1996

(in thousands, Jan.-Dec. 1995)

| Category | Total ad spending | Magazine | Sunday magazines | Local newspaper | Network TV | Spot TV | Syndicated TV | Cable TV | Network radio |
|---|---|---|---|---|---|---|---|---|---|
| Automotive | $10,625,891.6 | $1,333,190.4 | $47,240.0 | $3,679,782.9 | $1,736,454.9 | $2,937,100.7 | $90,705.5 | $361,826.7 | $134,465.1 |
| Retail | 8,781,375.9 | 258,366.1 | 548,141.5 | 4,463,655.0 | 616,110.7 | 2,478,643.1 | 69,033.0 | 178,990.4 | 343,069.1 |
| Business, consumer services | 6,751,363.6 | 842,506.3 | 36,736.7 | 1,797,630.0 | 1,086,187.6 | 1,547,321.4 | 181,763.9 | 413,145.2 | 243,888.5 |
| Entertainment | 5,289,785.4 | 83,502.7 | 4,091.1 | 1,064,135.8 | 1,542,856.5 | 1,888,469.5 | 158,125.8 | 255,003.1 | 108,708.4 |
| Food | 4,033,054.2 | 675,330.1 | 50,565.8 | 21,102.8 | 1,451,831.0 | 902,435.7 | 437,821.4 | 323,956.0 | 87,276.2 |
| Toiletries & cosmetics | 2,950,466.8 | 868,099.7 | 18,429.1 | 9,332.5 | 1,234,606.5 | 266,520.3 | 261,178.9 | 228,687.7 | 12,274.6 |
| Drugs & remedies | 2,894,345.0 | 497,130.4 | 91,881.0 | 115,105.4 | 1,065,420.0 | 447,633.3 | 261,186.1 | 239,861.9 | 29,548.8 |
| Travel & hotels | 2,363,589.3 | 460,459.9 | 31,728.3 | 975,541.8 | 170,528.8 | 31,18627 | 6,145.9 | 101,817.6 | 58,615.6 |
| Direct response cos. | 1,633,005.7 | 919,422.3 | 384,439.3 | 90,842.3 | 22,186.9 | 28,706.8 | 58,529.8 | 30,319.8 | 12,684.3 |
| Computers, office equip. | 1,626,901.2 | 875,280.8 | 6,393.0 | 54,074.3 | 303,840.5 | 62,960.7 | 14,664.8 | 100,669.5 | 16,356.1 |
| Candy, snacks, & soft drinks | 1,429,949.6 | 69,488.3 | 5,221.8 | 5,343.2 | 644,684.2 | 269,053.5 | 176,008.5 | 165,492.6 | 27,104.6 |
| Insurance & real estate | 1,394,064.7 | 181,272.9 | 15,774.5 | 530,844.9 | 177,331.0 | 269,288.1 | 8,596.4 | 53,197.0 | 41,524.7 |
| Publishing & media | 1,261,417.2 | 290,779.4 | 6,864.6 | 241,959.1 | 53,882.8 | 296,784.4 | 29,504.8 | 112,363.8 | 79,236.3 |
| Sporting goods, toys | 1,177,509.5 | 247,731.7 | 3,153.6 | 5,189.5 | 281,717.2 | 242,195.2 | 205,167.0 | 177,510.8 | 5,969.5 |
| Apparel, footwear | 1,167,796.0 | 582,225.8 | 35,504.9 | 12,742.4 | 305,590.0 | 54,080.0 | 25,328.3 | 121,802.4 | 8,520.5 |
| Household equipment | 822,439.4 | 169,511.8 | 16,616.6 | 6,982.9 | 323,810.6 | 126,116.4 | 67,105.4 | 90,571.9 | 3,427.7 |
| Beer & wine | 806,800.6 | 27,402.6 | 897.1 | 4,219.7 | 379,765.5 | 189,449.9 | 12,665.4 | 84,927.9 | 27,975.1 |
| Electronic equipment | 723,108.6 | 149,583.3 | 18,690.1 | 12,375.8 | 198,776.8 | 147,092.4 | 86,347.6 | 79,205.3 | 9,576.1 |
| Soaps & cleansers | 596,440.9 | 80,592.2 | 2,861.7 | 232.1 | 262,437.4 | 87,467.9 | 77,658.2 | 78,152.3 | 1,573.2 |
| Cigarettes | 504,384.9 | 317,471.5 | 10,689.7 | 21,273.5 | ,552.8 | 337.4 | 71.5 | 338.2 | 220.2 |
| Jewelry, optical | 460,029.0 | 230,334.9 | 12,397.0 | 6,897.7 | 115,864.8 | 31,625.4 | 7,780.9 | 31,093.7 | 5,732.7 |
| Building materials | 427,338.0 | 129,309.3 | 13,059.8 | 30,096.6 | 64,521.7 | 87,412.0 | 13,959.5 | 68,629.7 | 9,633.8 |
| Household furnishings | 340,489.9 | 169,926.7 | 13,279.0 | 23,879.0 | 67,006.3 | 36,187.0 | 13,541.7 | 12,588.0 | 1,389.4 |
| Gasoline & lubricants | 313,889.3 | 18,885.4 | 1,255.6 | 8,699.3 | 60,279.7 | 124,493.2 | 3,179.1 | 25,260.1 | 44,804.8 |
| Horticulture & farming | 283,229.7 | 28,152.7 | 16,007.3 | 53,777.8 | 36,634.8 | 59,894.7 | 29,616.2 | 23,959.6 | 26,917.5 |
| Miscellaneous | 283,065.7 | 109,447.3 | 509.4 | 56,436.4 | 0.0 | 7,911.0 | 0.0 | 39.7 | 0.0 |
| Pets & pet foods | 273,418.9 | 53,140.8 | 2,600.0 | 8,395.0 | 95,085.4 | 149,835.0 | 19,554.9 | 35,485.2 | 6,618.1 |
| Liquor | 233,485.6 | 192,607.7 | 7,641.7 | 3,077.6 | 0.0 | 469.2 | 0.0 | 0.3 | 918.1 |
| Freight, industrial | 171,399.0 | 44,730.1 | 80.0 | 3,443.5 | 64,715.7 | 30,384.2 | 1,024.4 | 6,835.3 | 1,643.2 |
| Industrial materials | 146,382.1 | 56,691.3 | 341.9 | 4,348.5 | 36,994.5 | 15,7443 | 214.2 | 12,277.4 | 1,012.3 |
| Business propositions | 61,836.7 | 38,444.6 | 146.2 | 7,174.0 | 0.0 | 31,85.6 | 0.0 | 3,280.3 | 1,498.8 |
| Airplanes (not travel) | 32,483.9 | 14,458.2 | 130.0 | 6,349.8 | 504.6 | 8,54.7 | 0.0 | 1,174.5 | 76.7 |
| **Total** | **59,887,018.7** | **1,057,776.6** | **955,449.4** | **13,338,635.6** | **1,736,454.9** | **13,017,151.6** | **2,316,800.8** | **3,418,797.3** | **1,352,260.0** |

# DISASTERS

Disasters are reported as of Sept. 1996. Listings are selective and generally do not include disasters having relatively low fatalities in a particular category.

## Some Notable Shipwrecks Since 1854

(Figures indicate estimated lives lost.)

**1854, Mar.—City of Glasgow;** Brit. steamer missing in N Atlantic; 480.

**1854, Sept. 27—Arctic;** U.S. (Collins Line) steamer sunk in collision with French steamer *Vesta* near Cape Race; 285-351.

**1856, Jan. 23—Pacific;** U.S. (Collins Line) steamer missing in N Atlantic; 186-286.

**1858, Sept. 23—Austria;** German steamer destroyed by fire in N Atlantic; 471.

**1863, Apr. 27—Anglo-Saxon;** Brit. steamer wrecked at Cape Race; 238.

**1865, Apr. 27—Sultana;** Mississippi River steamer blew up near Memphis, TN; 1,450.

**1869, Oct. 27—Stonewall;** steamer burned on Mississippi River below Cairo, IL; 200.

**1870, Jan. 25—City of Boston;** Brit. (Inman Line) steamer vanished between New York and Liverpool; 177.

**1870, Oct. 19—Cambria;** Brit. steamer wrecked off N Ireland; 196.

**1872, Nov. 7—Mary Celeste;** U.S. half-brig sailed from New York for Genoa; found abandoned in Atlantic 4 weeks later in mystery of sea; crew never heard from; loss of life unknown.

**1873, Jan. 22—Northfleet;** Brit. steamer foundered off Dungeness, England; 300.

**1873, Apr. 1—Atlantic;** Brit. (White Star) steamer wrecked off Nova Scotia; 585.

**1873, Nov. 23—Ville du Havre;** French steamer sank after collision with Brit. sailing ship *Loch Earn*; 226.

**1875, May 7—Schiller;** German steamer wrecked off Scilly Isles; 312.

**1875, Nov. 4—Pacific;** U.S. steamer sank after collision off Cape Flattery; 236.

**1878, Sept. 3—Princess Alice;** Brit. steamer sank after collision in Thames River; 700.

**1878, Dec. 18—Byzantin;** French steamer sank after collision in Dardanelles; 210.

**1881, May 24—Victoria;** steamer capsized in Thames River, Canada; 200.

**1883, Jan. 19—Cimbria;** German steamer sank in collision with Brit. steamer *Sultan* in North Sea; 389.

**1887, Nov. 15—Wah Yeung;** Brit. steamer burned at sea; 400.

**1890, Feb. 17—Duburg;** Brit. steamer wrecked, China Sea; 400.

**1890, Sept. 19—Ertogrul;** Turkish frigate foundered off Japan; 540.

**1891, Mar. 17—Utopia;** Brit. steamer sank in collision with Brit. ironclad *Anson* off Gibraltar; 562.

**1895, Jan. 30—Elbe;** German steamer sank in collision with Brit. steamer *Craithie* in North Sea; 332.

**1895, Mar. 11—Reina Regenta;** Spanish cruiser foundered near Gibraltar; 400.

**1898, Feb. 15—Maine;** U.S. battleship blown up in Havana Harbor; 260.

**1898, July 4—La Bourgogne;** French steamer sank in collision with Brit. sailing ship *Cromartyshire* off Nova Scotia; 549.

**1898, Nov. 26—Portland;** U.S. steamer wrecked off Cape Cod; 157.

**1904, June 15—General Slocum;** excursion steamer burned in East River, New York City; 1,030.

**1904, June 28—Norge;** Danish steamer wrecked on Rockall Island, Scotland; 620.

**1906, Aug. 4—Sirio;** Italian steamer wrecked off Cape Palos, Spain; 350.

**1908, Mar. 23—Matsu Maru;** Japanese steamer sank in collision near Hakodate, Japan; 300.

**1909, Aug. 1—Waratah;** Brit. steamer, Sydney to London, vanished; 300.

**1910, Feb. 9—General Chanzy;** French steamer wrecked off Minorca, Spain; 200.

**1911, Sept. 25—Liberté;** French battleship exploded at Toulon; 285.

**1912, Mar. 5—Principe de Asturias;** Spanish steamer wrecked off Spain; 500.

**1912, Apr. 14-15—Titanic;** Brit. (White Star) steamer hit iceberg in N Atlantic; 1,503.

**1912, Sept. 28—Kichemaru;** Japanese steamer sank off Japanese coast; 1,000.

**1914, May 29—Empress of Ireland;** Brit. (Canadian Pacific) steamer sunk in collision with Norwegian collier in St. Lawrence River; 1,014.

**1915, May 7—Lusitania;** Brit. (Cunard Line) steamer torpedoed and sunk by German submarine off Ireland; 1,198.

**1915, July 24—Eastland;** excursion steamer capsized in Chicago River; 812.

**1916, Feb. 26—Provence;** French cruiser sank in Mediterranean; 3,100.

**1916, Mar. 3—Principe de Asturias;** Spanish steamer wrecked near Santos, Brazil; 558.

**1916, Aug. 29—Hsin Yu;** Chinese steamer sank off Chinese coast; 1,000.

**1917, Dec. 6—Mont Blanc, Imo;** French ammunition ship and Belgian steamer collided in Halifax Harbor; 1,600.

**1918, Apr. 25—Kiang-Kwan;** Chinese steamer sank in collision off Hankow; 500.

**1918, July 12—Kawachi;** Japanese battleship blew up in Tokayama Bay; 500.

**1918, Oct. 25—Princess Sophia;** Canadian steamer sank off Alaskan coast; 398.

**1919, Jan. 17—Chaonia;** French steamer lost in Straits of Messina, Italy; 460.

**1919, Sept. 9—Valbanera;** Spanish steamer lost off Florida coast; 500.

**1921, Mar. 18—Hong Kong;** steamer wrecked in South China Sea; 1,000.

**1922, Aug. 26—Niitaka;** Japanese cruiser sank in storm off Kamchatka, USSR; 300.

**1924, June 24—USS Mississippi;** U.S. battleship; explosions in gun turret, off San Pedro, CA; 48.

**1925, Sept. 25—S-51;** U.S. submarine sank in collision off Block Island, RI; 37.

**1927, Oct. 25—Principessa Mafalda;** Italian steamer blew up, sank off Porto Seguro, Brazil; 314.

**1927, Dec. 17—S-4;** U.S. submarine sank in collision off Cape Cod, MA; 6.

**1928, Nov. 12—Vestris;** Brit. steamer sank in gale off Virginia; 113.

**1934, Sept. 8—Morro Castle;** U.S. steamer, Havana to New York, burned off Asbury Park, NJ; 134.

**1939, May 23—Squalus;** U.S. submarine sank off Portsmouth, NH; 26.

**1939, June 1—Thetis;** Brit. submarine sank in Liverpool Bay; 99.

**1942, Feb. 18—Truxtun and Pollux;** U.S. destroyer and cargo ship ran aground, sank off Newfoundland; 204.

**1942, Oct. 2—Curacao;** Brit. cruiser sank after collision with liner Queen Mary; 338.

**1944, Dec. 17-18—**3 U.S. Third Fleet destroyers sank during typhoon in Philippine Sea; 790.

**1947, Jan. 19—Himera;** Greek steamer hit a mine off Athens; 392.

**1947, Apr. 16—Grandcamp;** French freighter exploded in Texas City, TX, harbor, starting fires; 510.

**1948, Nov.—**Chinese army evacuation ship exploded and sank off S Manchuria; 6,000.

**1948, Dec. 3—Kiangya;** Chinese refugee ship wrecked in explosion S of Shanghai; 1,100+.

**1949, Sept. 17—Noronic;** Canadian Great Lakes Cruiser burned at Toronto dock; 130.

**1952, Apr. 26—Hobson and Wasp;** U.S. destroyer and aircraft carrier collided in Atlantic; 176.

**1954, May 26—Pennington;** sank off RI coast; 103.

**1954, Sept. 26—Toya Maru;** Japanese ferry sank in Tsugaru Strait, Japan; 1,172.

**1956, July 26—Andrea Doria** and **Stockholm;** Italian liner and Swedish liner collided off Nantucket; 51.

**1957, July 14—Eshghabad;** Soviet ship ran aground in Caspian Sea; 270.

**1960, Dec. 19—Constellation;** U.S. aircraft carrier, caught fire in Brooklyn Navy Yard, NY; 49.

**1961, July 8—Save;** Portuguese ship ran aground off Mozambique; 259.

**1962, Apr. 8—Dara;** Brit. liner exploded and sank in Persian Gulf; 236.

**1963, Apr. 10—Thresher;** U.S. Navy atomic submarine sank in N Atlantic; 129.

**1964, Feb. 10—Voyager** and **Melbourne;** Australian destroyer *Voyager* sank after collision with Australian aircraft carrier *Melbourne* off New South Wales; 82.

**1965, Nov. 13—Yarmouth Castle;** Panamanian registered cruise ship burned and sank off Nassau; 89.

**1967, July 29—Forrestal;** U.S. aircraft carrier caught fire off N Vietnam; 134.

**1968, Jan. 25—Dakar;** Israeli submarine vanished in Mediterranean Sea; 69.

**1968, late May—Scorpion;** U.S. nuclear submarine sank in Atlantic near Azores; 99 (located Oct. 31).
**1969, June 2—Evans;** U.S. destroyer cut in half by Australian carrier *Melbourne*, S China Sea; 74.
**1970, Mar. 4—Eurydice;** French submarine sank in Mediterranean near Toulon; 57.
**1970, Dec. 15—Namyong-Ho;** South Korean ferry sank in Korea Strait; 308.
**1974, May 1**—Motor launch capsized off Bangladesh; 250.
**1974, Sept. 26**—Soviet destroyer burned and sank in Black Sea; 200+.
**1976, Oct. 20—George Prince** and **Frosta;** ferryboat and Norwegian tanker collided on Mississippi R. at Luling, LA; 77.
**1976, Dec. 25—Patria;** Egyptian liner caught fire and sank in the Red Sea; 100.
**1979, Aug. 14**—23 yachts competing in Fastnet yacht race sank or abandoned during storm in S Irish Sea; 18.
**1981, Jan. 27—Tamponas II;** Indonesian passenger ship caught fire and sank in Java Sea; 580.
**1981, May 26—Nimitz;** U.S. Marine combat jet crashed on deck of U.S. aircraft carrier; 14.
**1983, Feb. 12—Marine Electric;** coal freighter sank during storm off Chincoteague, VA; 33.
**1983, May 25—10th of Ramadan;** Nile steamer caught fire and sank in Lake Nasser; 357.
**1986, Apr. 20**—overcrowded ferry sinks near Barisal, Bangladesh; 262.
**1986, Aug. 31**—Soviet passenger ship *Admiral Nakhimov* and Soviet freighter *Pyotr Vasev* collided in Black Sea; 398.
**1987, Mar. 6**—Brit. ferry capsized off Zeebrugge, Belg.; 189.
**1987, Dec. 20**—Philippine ferry *Dona Paz* and oil tanker *Victor* collided in Tablas Strait; 3,000+.
**1988, Aug. 6**—Indian ferry capsized on Ganges R.; 400+.
**1989, Apr. 19—USS Iowa**; U.S. battleship; explosion in gun turret; 47.
**1989, Aug. 20**—Brit. barge *Bowbelle* struck Brit. pleasure cruiser *Marchioness* on Thames R. in central London; 56.
**1989, Sept. 10**—Romanian pleasure boat and Bulgarian barge collided on Danube R.; 161.
**1991, Apr. 10**—Auto ferry and oil tanker collided outside Livorno Harbor, Italy; 140.
**1991, Dec. 14—Salem Express;** ferry rammed coral reef near Safaga, Egypt; 462.
**1993, Feb. 17—Neptune;** ferry capsized off Port-au-Prince, Haiti; 500+.
**1993, Oct. 10—West Sea Ferry;** capsized in Yellow Sea near W South Korea during storm; 285.
**1994, Sept. 28—Estonia;** ferry sank in Baltic Sea when water entered through bow door; 1,049.
**1996, May 21—Bukoba;** ferry sank in Lake Victoria; 500.

## Some Notable Aircraft Disasters Since 1937

| Date | Aircraft | Site of accident | Deaths |
|---|---|---|---|
| 1937, May 6 | German zeppelin Hindenburg | Burned at mooring, Lakehurst, NJ | 36[1] |
| 1944, Aug. 23 | U.S. Air Force B-24 Liberator bomber | Hit school, Freckleton, England | 61[1] |
| 1945, July 28 | U.S. Army B-25 | Hit Empire State Building, New York, NY | 14[1] |
| 1952, Dec. 20 | U.S. Air Force C-124 | Fell, burned, Moses Lake, WA | 87 |
| 1953, Mar. 3 | Canadian Pacific Comet Jet | Karachi, Pakistan | 11[2] |
| 1953, June 18 | U.S. Air Force C-124 | Crashed, burned near Tokyo | 129 |
| 1955, Oct. 6 | United Airlines DC-4 | Crashed in Medicine Bow Peak, WY | 66 |
| 1955, Nov. 1 | United Airlines DC-6B | Exploded, crashed near Longmont, CO | 44[3] |
| 1956, June 20 | Venezuelan Super-Constellation | Crashed in Atlantic off Asbury Park, NJ | 74 |
| 1956, June 30 | TWA Super-Const., United DC-7 | Collided over Grand Canyon, AZ | 128 |
| 1960, Dec. 16 | United DC-8 jet, TWA Super-Constellation | Collided over New York City | 134[4] |
| 1962, Mar. 16 | Flying Tiger Super-Constellation | Vanished in W Pacific | 107 |
| 1962, June 3 | Air France Boeing 707 jet | Crashed on takeoff from Paris | 130 |
| 1962, June 22 | Air France Boeing 707 jet | Crashed in storm, Guadeloupe, W.I. | 113 |
| 1963, June 3 | Chartered Northwest Airlines DC-7 | Crashed in Pacific off British Columbia | 101 |
| 1963, Nov. 29 | Trans-Canada Airlines DC-8F | Crashed after takeoff from Montreal | 118 |
| 1965, May 20 | Pakistani Boeing 720-B | Crashed at Cairo, Egypt, airport | 121 |
| 1966, Jan. 24 | Air India Boeing 707 jetliner | Crashed on Mont Blanc, France-Italy | 117 |
| 1966, Feb. 4 | All-Nippon Boeing 727 | Plunged into Tokyo Bay | 133 |
| 1966, Mar. 5 | BOAC Boeing 707 jetliner | Crashed on Mount Fuji, Japan | 124 |
| 1966, Dec. 24 | U.S. military-chartered CL-44 | Crashed into village in South Vietnam | 129[1] |
| 1967, Apr. 20 | Swiss Britannia turboprop | Crashed at Nicosia, Cyprus | 126 |
| 1967, July 19 | Piedmont Boeing 727, Cessna 310 | Collided in air, Hendersonville, NC | 82 |
| 1968, Apr. 20 | S. African Airways Boeing 707 | Crashed on takeoff, Windhoek, South-West Africa | 122 |
| 1968, May 3 | Braniff International Electra | Crashed in storm near Dawson, TX | 85 |
| 1969, Mar. 16 | Venezuelan DC-9 | Crashed after takeoff from Maracaibo, Venezuela | 155[5] |
| 1969, Dec. 8 | Olympia Airways DC-6B | Crashed near Athens in storm | 93 |
| 1970, Feb. 15 | Dominican DC-9 | Crashed into sea on takeoff from Santo Domingo | 102 |
| 1970, July 3 | British chartered jetliner | Crashed near Barcelona, Spain | 112 |
| 1970, July 5 | Air Canada DC-8 | Crashed near Toronto International Airport | 108 |
| 1970, Aug. 9 | Peruvian turbojet | Crashed after takeoff from Cuzco, Peru | 101[1] |
| 1970, Nov. 14 | Southern Airways DC-9 | Crashed in mountains near Huntington, WV | 75[6] |
| 1971, July 30 | All-Nippon Boeing 727 and Japanese Air Force F-86 | Collided over Morioka, Japan | 162[7] |
| 1971, Sept. 4 | Alaska Airlines Boeing 727 | Crashed into mountain near Juneau, AK | 111 |
| 1972, Aug. 14 | East German Ilyushin-62 | Crashed on takeoff, East Berlin | 156 |
| 1972, Oct. 13 | Aeroflot Ilyushin-62 | Soviet airline crashed near Moscow | 176 |
| 1972, Dec. 3 | Chartered Spanish airliner | Crashed on takeoff, Canary Islands | 155 |
| 1972, Dec. 29 | Eastern Airlines Lockheed Tristar | Crashed on approach to Miami Intl. Airport | 101 |
| 1973, Jan. 22 | Chartered Boeing 707 | Burst into flames during landing, Kano Airport, Nigeria | 176 |
| 1973, Feb. 21 | Libyan jetliner | Shot down by Israeli fighter planes over Sinai | 108 |
| 1973, Apr. 10 | British Vanguard turboprop | Crashed during snowstorm at Basel, Switzerland | 104 |
| 1973, June 3 | Soviet Supersonic TU-144 | Crashed near Goussainville, France | 14[8] |
| 1973, July 11 | Brazilian Boeing 707 | Crashed on approach to Orly Airport, Paris | 122 |
| 1973, July 31 | Delta Airlines jetliner | Crashed, landing in fog at Logan Airport, Boston | 89 |
| 1973, Dec. 23 | French Caravelle jet | Crashed in Morocco | 106 |
| 1974, Mar. 3 | Turkish DC-10 jet | Crashed at Ermenonville near Paris | 346 |
| 1974, Apr. 23 | Pan American 707 jet | Crashed in Bali, Indonesia | 107 |
| 1974, Dec. 1 | TWA-727 | Crashed in storm, Upperville, VA | 92 |
| 1974, Dec. 4 | Dutch-chartered DC-8 | Crashed in storm near Colombo, Sri Lanka | 191 |
| 1975, Apr. 4 | Air Force Galaxy C-5A | Crashed near Saigon, South Vietnam, after takeoff with load of orphans | 172 |
| 1975, June 24 | Eastern Airlines 727 jet | Crashed in storm, JFK Airport, NY | 113 |
| 1975, Aug. 3 | Chartered 707 | Hit mountainside, Agadir, Morocco | 188 |
| 1976, Sept. 10 | British Airways Trident, Yugoslav DC-9 | Collided near Zagreb, Yugoslavia | 176 |
| 1976, Sept. 19 | Turkish 727 | Hit mountain, S Turkey | 155 |
| 1976, Oct. 13 | Bolivian 707 cargo jet | Crashed in Santa Cruz, Bolivia | 100[9] |

(*continued*)

## Some Notable Aircraft Disasters Since 1937 (*continued*)

| Date | Aircraft | Site of accident | Deaths |
|---|---|---|---|
| 1977, Mar. 27 | KLM 747, Pan American 747 | Collided on runway, Tenerife, Canary Islands | 582 |
| 1977, Nov. 19 | TAP Boeing 727 | Crashed on Madeira | 130 |
| 1977, Dec. 4 | Malaysian Boeing 737 | Hijacked, then exploded in mid-air over Straits of Johore | 100 |
| 1977, Dec. 13 | U.S. DC-3 | Crashed after takeoff at Evansville, IN | 29[10] |
| 1978, Jan. 1 | Air India 747 | Exploded, crashed into sea off Bombay | 213 |
| 1978, Sept. 25 | Boeing 727, Cessna 172 | Collided in air, San Diego, CA | 150 |
| 1978, Nov. 15 | Chartered DC-8 | Crashed near Colombo, Sri Lanka | 183 |
| 1979, May 25 | American Airlines DC-10 | Crashed after takeoff at O'Hare Intl. Airport, Chicago | 275[11] |
| 1979, Aug. 17 | Two Soviet Aeroflot jetliners | Collided over Ukraine | 173 |
| 1979, Nov. 26 | Pakistani Boeing 707 | Crashed near Jidda, Saudi Arabia | 156 |
| 1979, Nov. 28 | New Zealand DC-10 | Crashed into mountain in Antarctica | 257 |
| 1980, Mar. 14 | Polish Ilyushin 62 | Crashed making emergency landing, Warsaw | 87[12] |
| 1980, Aug. 19 | Saudi Arabian Tristar | Burned after emergency landing, Riyadh | 301 |
| 1981, Dec. 1 | Yugoslavian DC-9 | Crashed into mountain in Corsica | 174 |
| 1982, Jan. 13 | Air Florida Boeing 737 | Crashed into Potomac R. after takeoff | 78 |
| 1982, July 9 | Pan Am Boeing 727 | Crashed after takeoff in Kenner, LA | 153[13] |
| 1983, Sept. 1 | S. Korean Boeing 747 | Shot down after violating Soviet airspace | 269 |
| 1983, Nov. 27 | Colombian Boeing 747 | Crashed near Barajas Airport, Madrid | 183 |
| 1985, Feb. 19 | Spanish Boeing 727 | Crashed into Mt. Oiz, Spain | 148 |
| 1985, June 23 | Air-India Boeing 747 | Crashed into Atlantic Ocean S of Ireland | 329 |
| 1985, Aug. 2 | Delta Air Lines L-1011 | Crashed at Dallas-Ft. Worth Intl. Airport | 137 |
| 1985, Aug. 12 | Japan Air Lines Boeing 747 | Crashed into Mt. Ogura, Japan | 520[14] |
| 1985, Dec. 12 | Arrow Air DC-8 | Crashed after takeoff in Gander, Newfoundland | 256[15] |
| 1986, Mar. 31 | Mexican Boeing 727 | Crashed NW of Mexico City | 166 |
| 1986, Aug. 31 | Aeromexico DC-9 | Collided with Piper PA-28 over Cerritos, CA | 82[16] |
| 1987, May 9 | Polish Ilyushin 62M | Crashed after takeoff in Warsaw, Poland | 183 |
| 1987, Aug. 16 | Northwest Airlines MD-82 | Crashed after takeoff in Romulus, MI | 156 |
| 1987, Nov. 28 | S. African Boeing 787 | Crashed into Indian Ocean near Mauritius | 159 |
| 1987, Nov. 29 | S. Korean Boeing 767 | Exploded over Thai-Burmese border | 155 |
| 1988, Mar. 17 | Colombian Boeing 707 | Crashed into mountainside near Venezuela border | 137 |
| 1988, July 3 | Iranian A300 Airbus | Shot down by U.S. Navy warship *Vincennes* over Persian Gulf | 290 |
| 1988, Dec. 21 | Pan Am Boeing 747 | Exploded and crashed in Lockerbie, Scotland | 270[17] |
| 1989, Feb. 8 | U.S. Boeing 707 | Crashed into mountain in Azores Islands off Portugual | 144 |
| 1989, June 7 | Suriname DC-8 | Crashed near Paramaribo Airport, Suriname | 168 |
| 1989, July 19 | United Airlines DC-10 | Crashed while landing with a disabled hydraulic system, Sioux City, IA | 111 |
| 1989, Sept. 19 | French DC-10 | Exploded in air over Niger | 171 |
| 1991, May 26 | Lauda-Air Boeing 767-300 | Exploded over rural Thailand | 223 |
| 1991, July 11 | Nigerian DC-8 | Crashed while landing at Jidda, Saudi Arabia | 261 |
| 1991, Oct. 5 | Indonesian military transport | Crashed after takeoff from Jakarta | 137[1] |
| 1992, July 31 | Thai Airbus A-300-310 | Crashed into mountain S. of Kathmandu, Nepal | 113 |
| 1992, Oct. 4 | El Al Boeing 747-200F | Crashed into 2 apartment bldgs., Amsterdam, Netherlands | 120[1] |
| 1994, Jan. 3 | Aeroflot TU-154 | Crashed and exploded after takeoff in Irkhutsk, Russia | 125[18] |
| 1994, Apr. 26 | China Airlines Airbus A-300-600R | Crashed at Japan's Nagoya Airport | 264 |
| 1994, June 16 | China Northwest Airlines TU-154 | Crashed 10 min. after takeoff | 160 |
| 1994, Sept. 8 | USAir Boeing 737-300 | Crashed in Aliquippa, PA, near Pittsburgh Intl. Airport | 132 |
| 1994, Oct. 31 | American Eagle ATR-72-210 | Crashed in field near Roselawn, IN | 68 |
| 1995, Aug. 11 | Aviateca Boeing 737 | Crashed into Chichontepec volcano, El Salvador | 65 |
| 1995, Dec. 20 | American Airlines Boeing 757 | Crashed into mountain 50 mi N of Cali, Colombia | 160 |
| 1996, Jan. 8 | Antonova 32 cargo jet | Crashed into central market, Kinshasa, Zaire | 350+[1] |
| 1996, Feb. 6 | German Boeing 757 | Crashed into Atlantic Ocean, off Dominican Republic | 189 |
| 1996, Apr. 25 | T-43, a military version of a Boeing 737 | Crashed into mountain near Dubrovnik, Croatia | 35[19] |
| 1996, May 11 | ValuJet DC-9 | Crashed into the Florida Everglades after takeoff | 110 |
| 1996, July 17 | Trans World Airlines Boeing 747 | Exploded and crashed in Atlantic Ocean, off Long Isl., NY. | 230 |
| 1996, Aug. 29 | Vnukovo TU-154 | Crashed into mountain on Arctic island of Spitsbergen | 141 |
| 1996, Oct. 2 | Aeroperu Boeing 757 | Crashed in Pacific after takeoff from Lima, Peru | 70 |

(1) Including those on the ground and in buildings. (2) First fatal crash of commercial jet plane. (3) Caused by bomb planted by John G. Graham in insurance plot to kill his mother, a passenger. (4) Including all 128 aboard the planes and 6 on the ground. (5) Killed 84 on the plane and 71 on the ground. (6) Including 43 Marshall University football players and coaches. (7) Airliner-fighter crash; pilot of fighter parachuted to safety, was arrested for negligence. (8) First supersonic plane crash killed 6 crewmen and 8 on the ground; there were no passengers. (9) Crew of 3 killed; 97, mostly children, killed on the ground. (10) Including University of Evansville basketball team. (11) Highest death toll in U.S. aviation history. (12) Including 22 members of U.S. boxing team. (13) Including 8 on the ground. (14) Worst single-plane disaster. (15) Including 248 members of U.S. 101st Airborne Division. (16) Including 15 on the ground. (17) Including 11 on the ground. (18) Including 1 on the ground. (19) Including U.S. Sec. of Commerce Ronald H. Brown.

## Some Notable Railroad Disasters

| Date | Location | Deaths |
|---|---|---|
| 1876, Dec. 29 | Ashtabula, OH | 92 |
| 1880, Aug. 11 | Mays Landing, NJ | 40 |
| 1887, Aug. 10 | Chatsworth, IL | 81 |
| 1888, Oct. 10 | Mud Run, PA | 55 |
| 1891, June 14 | Nr. Basel, Switzerland | 100 |
| 1896, July 30 | Atlantic City, NJ | 60 |
| 1903, Dec. 23 | Laurel Run, PA | 53 |
| 1904, Aug. 7 | Eden, CO | 96 |
| 1904, Sept. 24 | New Market, TN | 56 |
| 1906, Mar. 16 | Florence, CO | 35 |
| 1906, Oct. 28 | Atlantic City, NJ | 40 |
| 1906, Dec. 30 | Washington, DC | 53 |
| 1907, Jan. 2 | Volland, KS | 33 |
| 1907, Jan. 19 | Fowler, IN | 29 |
| 1907, Feb. 16 | New York, NY | 22 |
| 1907, Feb. 23 | Colton, CA | 26 |
| 1907, May 11 | Lompoc, CA | 36 |
| 1907, July 20 | Salem, MI | 33 |
| 1908, Sept. 25 | Young's Point, MT | 21 |
| 1909, Jan. 15 | Dotsero, CO | 21 |
| 1910, Mar. 1 | Wellington, WA | 96 |
| 1910, Mar. 21 | Green Mountain, IA | 55 |
| 1911, Aug. 25 | Manchester, NY | 29 |
| 1912, July 4 | East Corning, NY | 39 |
| 1912, July 5 | Ligonier, PA | 23 |
| 1914, Aug. 5 | Tipton Ford, MO | 43 |
| 1914, Sept. 15 | Lebanon, MO | 28 |
| 1915, May 22 | Nr. Gretna, Scotland | 227 |
| 1916, Mar. 29 | Amherst, OH | 27 |
| 1917, Sept. 28 | Kellyville, OK | 23 |
| 1917, Dec. 12 | Modane, France | 543[1] |
| 1917, Dec. 20 | Shepherdsville, KY | 46 |
| 1918, June 22 | Ivanhoe, IN | 68 |
| 1918, July 9 | Nashville, TN | 101 |
| 1918, Nov. 1 | Brooklyn, NY | 97 |
| 1919, Jan. 12 | South Byron, NY | 22 |
| 1919, Dec. 20 | Onawa, ME | 23 |
| 1921, Feb. 27 | Porter, IN | 37 |

| Date | Location | Deaths |
|---|---|---|
| 1921, Dec. 5 | Woodmont, PA | 27 |
| 1922, Aug. 5 | Sulphur Spring, MO | 34 |
| 1922, Dec. 13 | Humble, TX | 22 |
| 1923, Sept. 27 | Lockett, WY | 31 |
| 1925, June 16 | Hackettstown, NJ | 50 |
| 1925, Oct. 27 | Victoria, MS | 21 |
| 1926, Sept. 5 | Waco, CO | 30 |
| 1928, Aug. 24 | IRT subway, Times Sq., NY | 18 |
| 1937, July 16 | Nr. Patna, India | 107 |
| 1938, June 19 | Saugus, MT | 47 |
| 1939, Aug. 12 | Harney, NV | 24 |
| 1939, Dec. 22 | Near Magdeburg, Germany | 132 |
| 1939, Dec. 22 | Near Friedrichshafen, Germany | 99 |
| 1940, Apr. 19 | Little Falls, NY | 31 |
| 1940, July 31 | Cuyahoga Falls, OH | 43 |
| 1943, Aug. 29 | Wayland, NY | 27 |
| 1943, Sept. 6 | Frankford Junction, Philadelphia, PA | 79 |
| 1943, Dec. 16 | Between Rennert and Buie, NC | 72 |
| 1944, Jan. 16 | Leon Prov., Spain | 500 |
| 1944, Mar. 2 | Salerno, Italy | 521 |
| 1944, July 6 | High Bluff, TN | 35 |
| 1944, Aug. 4 | Near Stockton, GA | 47 |
| 1944, Sept. 14 | Dewey, IN | 29 |
| 1944, Dec. 31 | Bagley, UT | 50 |
| 1945, Aug. 9 | Michigan, ND | 34 |
| 1946, Mar. 20 | Aracaju, Mexco | 185 |
| 1946, Apr. 25 | Naperville, IL | 45 |
| 1947, Feb. 18 | Gallitzin, PA | 24 |
| 1949, Oct. 22 | Nr. Dwor, Poland | 200+ |
| 1950, Feb. 17 | Rockville Centre, NY | 31 |
| 1950, Sept. 11 | Coshocton, OH | 33 |
| 1950, Nov. 22 | Richmond Hill, NY | 79 |
| 1951, Feb. 6 | Woodbridge, NJ | 84 |
| 1951, Nov. 12 | Wyuta, WY | 17 |
| 1951, Nov. 25 | Woodstock, AL | 17 |
| 1952, Mar. 4 | Nr. Rio de Janeiro, Brazil | 119 |
| 1952, July 9 | Rzepin, Poland | 160 |
| 1952, Oct. 8 | Harrow, England | 112 |
| 1953, Mar. 27 | Conneaut, OH | 21 |
| 1955, Apr. 3 | Guadalajara, Mexico | 300 |
| 1956, Jan. 22 | Los Angeles, CA | 30 |
| 1956, Feb. 28 | Swampscott, MA | 13 |
| 1956, Sept. 5 | Springer, NM | 20 |
| 1957, June 11 | Vroman, CO | 12 |
| 1957, Sept. 1 | Kendal, Jamaica | 178 |
| 1957, Sept. 29 | Montgomery, W Pakistan | 250 |
| 1957, Dec. 4 | London, England | 90 |
| 1958, May 8 | Rio de Janeiro, Brazil | 128 |
| 1958, Sept. 15 | Elizabethport, NJ | 48 |
| 1960, Mar. 1 | Bakersfield, CA | 14 |
| 1960, Nov. 14 | Pardubice, Czech. | 110 |
| 1962, Jan. 8 | Woerden, Netherlands | 91 |
| 1962, May 3 | Tokyo, Japan | 163 |
| 1962, July 28 | Steelton, PA | 19 |
| 1964, July 26 | Porto, Portugal | 94 |
| 1966, Dec. 28 | Everett, MA | 13 |
| 1970, Feb. 1 | Buenos Aires, Argentina | 236 |
| 1971, June 10 | Salem, IL | 11 |
| 1972, June 16 | Vierzy, France | 107 |
| 1972, July 21 | Seville, Spain | 76 |
| 1972, Oct. 6 | Saltillo, Mexico | 208 |
| 1972, Oct. 30 | Chicago, IL | 45 |
| 1974, Aug. 30 | Zagreb, Yugoslavia | 153 |
| 1975, Feb. 28 | London subway train | 41 |
| 1977, Jan. 18 | Granville, Australia | 83 |
| 1977, Feb. 4 | Chicago, IL, elevated train | 11 |
| 1981, June 6 | Bihar, India | 500+ |
| 1982, Jan. 27 | El Asnam, Algeria | 130 |
| 1982, July 11 | Tepic, Mexico | 120 |
| 1983, Feb. 19 | Empalme, Mexico | 100 |
| 1987, Jan. 4 | Essex, MD | 16 |
| 1988, Dec. 12 | London, England | 115 |
| 1989, Jan. 15 | Maizdi Khan, Bangladesh | 110+ |
| 1990, Jan. 4 | Sindh Prov., Pakistan | 210+ |
| 1991, May 14 | Shigaraki, Japan | 42 |
| 1993, Sept. 22 | Big Bayou Conot, AL | 47 |
| 1994, Mar. 8 | Nr. Durban, South Africa | 63 |
| 1994, Sept. 22 | Tolunda, Angola | 300 |
| 1995, Mar. 20 | Tokyo subway | 12[2] |
| 1995, Aug. 20 | Firozabad, India | 300+ |
| 1995, Oct. 25 | Fox River Grove, IL | 7[3] |
| 1996, Feb. 16 | Silver Spring, MD | 12 |

(1) World's worst train wreck; passenger train derailed. (2) Sarin nerve gas released in subway. (3) Train hit a school bus.

## Principal U.S. Mine Disasters Since 1900

**Source:** Bureau of Mines, U.S. Dept. of the Interior; Mine Safety and Health Admin., U.S. Dept. of Labor

(Prior to 1968, only disasters with losses of 65 or more lives are listed; since 1968, all disasters in which 5 or more people were killed are listed. All are bituminous-coal mines unless otherwise noted.)

| Date | Location | Deaths |
|---|---|---|
| 1900, May 1 | Scofield, UT | 200 |
| 1902, May 19 | Coal Creek, TN | 184 |
| 1902, July 10 | Johnstown, PA | 112 |
| 1903, June 30 | Hanna, WY | 169 |
| 1904, Jan. 25 | Cheswick, PA | 179 |
| 1905, Feb. 26 | Virginia City, AL | 112 |
| 1907, Jan. 29 | Stuart, WV | 84 |
| 1907, Dec. 6 | Monongah, WV | 361 |
| 1907, Dec. 19 | Jacobs Creek, PA | 239 |
| 1908, Nov. 28 | Marianna, PA | 154 |
| 1909, Jan. 12 | Switchback, WV | 67 |
| 1909, Nov. 13 | Cherry, IL | 259 |
| 1910, Jan. 31 | Primero, CO | 75 |
| 1910, May 5 | Palos, AL | 90 |
| 1910, Nov.8 | Delagua, CO | 79 |
| 1911, Apr. 7 | Throop, PA[1] | 72 |
| 1911, Apr. 8 | Littleton, AL | 128 |
| 1911, Dec.9 | Briceville, TN | 84 |
| 1912, Mar. 20 | McCurtain, OK | 73 |
| 1912, Mar. 26 | Jed, WV | 83 |
| 1913, Apr. 23 | Finleyville, PA | 96 |
| 1913, Oct. 22 | Dawson, NM | 263 |
| 1914, Apr. 28 | Eccles, WV | 181 |
| 1915, Mar. 2 | Layland, WV | 112 |
| 1917, Apr. 27 | Hastings, CO | 121 |
| 1917, June 8 | Butte, MT[2] | 163 |
| 1919, June 5 | Wilkes-Barre, PA[1] | 92 |
| 1922, Nov. 6 | Spangler, PA | 77 |
| 1922, Nov. 22 | Dolomite, AL | 90 |
| 1923, Feb. 8 | Dawson, NM | 120 |
| 1923, Aug. 14 | Kemmerer, WY | 99 |
| 1924, Mar. 8 | Castle Gate, UT | 171 |
| 1924, Apr. 28 | Benwood, WV | 119 |
| 1926, Jan. 13 | Wilburton, OK | 91 |
| 1927, Apr. 30 | Everettville, WV | 97 |
| 1928, May 19 | Mather, PA | 195 |
| 1930, Nov. 5 | Millfield, OH | 79 |
| 1940, Jan. 10 | Bartley, WV | 91 |
| 1940, Mar. 16 | St. Clairsville, OH | 72 |
| 1943, Feb. 27 | Red Lodge, MT | 74 |
| 1944, July 5 | Belmont, OH | 66 |
| 1947, Mar. 25 | Centralia, IL | 111 |
| 1951, Dec. 21 | West Frankfort, IL | 119 |
| 1968, Mar. 6 | Calumet, LA[3] | 21 |
| 1968, Aug. 7 | Greenville, KY | 9 |
| 1968, Nov. 20 | Farmington, WV | 78 |
| 1970, Dec. 30 | Hyden, KY | 38 |
| 1971, Apr. 12 | Rosiclair, IL[3] | 7 |
| 1972, May 2 | Kellogg, ID[2] | 91 |
| 1972, July 22 | Blacksville, WV | 9 |
| 1972, Dec. 16 | Itmann, WV | 5 |
| 1976, Mar. 9, 11 | Oven Fork, KY | 23 |
| 1977, Mar. 1 | Tower City, PA | 9 |
| 1978, Apr. 4 | Duty, VA | 5 |
| 1979, June 8 | Franklin, LA[3] | 5 |
| 1980, Nov. 7 | Clothier, WV | 5 |
| 1981, Apr. 15 | Redstone, CO | 15 |
| 1981, Dec. 7 | Topmost, KY | 8 |
| 1981, Dec. 8 | Whitwell, TN | 13 |
| 1982, Jan. 20 | Craynor, KY | 7 |
| 1983, June 21 | Dante, VA | 7 |
| 1984, Dec. 19 | Huntington, UT | 27 |
| 1986, Feb. 6 | Fairview, WV | 5 |
| 1989, Sept. 13 | Sturgis, KY | 10 |
| 1992, Dec. 7 | Norton, VA | 8 |
| 1995, May 10 | Orkney, South Africa[4] | 100+ |

**Note:** World's worst mine disaster killed 1,549 workers in Honkeiko Colliery in Manchuria, Apr. 25, 1942. (1) Anthracite mine. (2) Metal mine. (3) Nonmetal mine. (4) Gold mine.

## Some Notable U.S. Tornadoes Since 1925

| Date | Location | Deaths |
|---|---|---|
| 1925, Mar. 18 | MO, IL, IN | 689 |
| 1927, Apr. 12 | Rock Springs, TX | 74 |
| 1927, May 9 | AR, Poplar Bluff, MO | 92 |
| 1927, Sept. 29 | St. Louis, MO | 90 |
| 1930, May 6 | Hill, Navarro, Ellis Co., TX | 41 |
| 1932, Mar. 21 | AL (series of tornadoes) | 268 |
| 1936, Apr. 5 | MS, GA | 455 |
| 1936, Apr. 6 | Gainesville, GA | 203 |
| 1938, Sept. 29 | Charleston, SC | 32 |
| 1942, Mar. 16 | Central to NE Mississippi | 75 |
| 1942, Apr. 27 | Rogers and Mayes Co., OK | 52 |
| 1944, June 23 | OH, PA, WV, MD | 150 |
| 1945, Apr. 12 | OK-AR | 102 |
| 1947, Apr. 9 | TX, OK, KS | 169 |
| 1948, Mar. 19 | Bunker Hill and Gillespie, IL | 33 |
| 1949, Jan. 3 | LA and AR | 58 |
| 1952, Mar. 21 | AR, MO, TN (series) | 208 |
| 1953, May 11 | Waco, TX | 114 |
| 1953, June 8 | MI, OH | 142 |
| 1953, June 9 | Worcester and vicinity, MA | 90 |
| 1953, Dec. 5 | Vicksburg, MS | 38 |
| 1955, May 25 | KS, MO, OK, TX | 115 |
| 1957, May 20 | KS, MO | 48 |
| 1958, June, 4 | NW Wisconsin | 30 |
| 1959, Feb. 10 | St. Louis, MO | 21 |
| 1960, May 5, 6 | Southeastern OK, AR | 30 |
| 1965, Apr. 11 | IN, IL, OH, MI, WI | 271 |
| 1966, Mar. 3 | Jackson, MS | 57 |
| 1966, Mar. 3 | MS, AL | 61 |
| 1967, Apr. 21 | IL, MI | 33 |
| 1968, May 15 | Midwest | 71 |
| 1969, Jan. 23 | MS | 32 |
| 1971, Feb. 21 | Mississippi delta | 110 |
| 1973, May 26-27 | South, Midwest (series) | 47 |
| 1974, Apr. 3-4 | AL, GA, TN, KY, OH | 315 |
| 1977, Apr. 4 | AL, MS, GA | 22 |
| 1979, Apr. 10 | TX, OK | 60 |
| 1980, June 3 | Grand Island, NE (series) | 4 |
| 1982, Mar. 2-4 | South, Midwest (series) | 17 |
| 1982, May 29 | Southern IL | 10 |
| 1983, May 18-22 | TX | 12 |
| 1984, Mar. 28 | NC, SC | 57 |
| 1984, Apr. 21-22 | MS | 15 |
| 1984, Apr. 26 | OK-MN (series) | 17 |
| 1985, May 31 | NY, PA, OH, Ont. (series) | 75 |
| 1987, May 22 | Saragosa, TX | 29 |
| 1989, Nov. 15 | Huntsville, AL | 18 |
| 1989, Nov. 16 | Newburgh, NY | 9 |
| 1990, June 2-3 | Midwest, Great Lakes | 13 |
| 1990, Aug. 28 | Northern IL | 25 |
| 1991, Apr. 26 | KS, OK | 23 |
| 1992, Nov. 21-23 | South, Midwest | 26 |
| 1994, Mar. 27-28 | AL, TN, GA, NC, SC (series) | 52 |
| 1994, Apr. 26 | Central TX | 4 |
| 1995, May 6-7 | southern OK, northern TX | 23 |
| 1995, May 19-20 | TX to MD (series) | 4 |
| 1996, Apr. 14 | Northern AR | 7 |
| 1996, Apr. 21 | Western AR (series) | 4 |

## Some Notable Hurricanes, Typhoons, Blizzards, Other Storms

Names of hurricanes and typhoons in italics: H.—hurricane; T.—typhoon

| Date | Location | Deaths |
|---|---|---|
| 1888, Mar. 11-14 | Blizzard, eastern U.S. | 400 |
| 1900, Aug.-Sept. | H., Galveston, TX | 6,000 |
| 1906, Sept. 19-24 | H., LA, MS | 350 |
| 1906, Sept. 18 | Typhoon, Hong Kong | 10,000 |
| 1915, Sept. 29 | H., LA | 500 |
| 1926, Sept. 11-22 | H., FL, AL | 243 |
| 1926, Oct. 20 | H., Cuba | 600 |
| 1928, Sept. 6-20 | H., southern FL | 1,836 |
| 1930, Sept. 3 | H., Dominican Republic | 2,000 |
| 1935, Aug. 29-Sept. 10 | H., Caribbean, southeastern U.S. | 400+ |
| 1938, Sept. 21 | H., Long Island, NY; New England | 600 |
| 1940, Nov. 11-12 | Blizzard, NE, Midwest U.S. | 144 |
| 1942, Oct. 15-16 | H., Bengal, India | 40,000 |
| 1944, Sept. 9-16 | H., NC to New England | 46 |
| 1947, Dec. 26 | Blizzard, New York, NY, N Atlantic states | 55 |
| 1952, Oct. 22 | Typhoon, Philippines | 440 |
| 1954, Aug. 30 | H. *Carol*, northeastern U.S. | 68 |
| 1954, Oct. 5-18 | H. *Hazel*, E Canada, U.S.; Haiti | 347 |
| 1955, Aug. 12-13 | H. *Connie*, NC, SC, VA, MD | 43 |
| 1955, Aug. 7-21 | H. *Diane*, eastern U.S. | 400 |
| 1955, Sept. 19 | H. *Hilda*, Mexico | 200 |
| 1955, Sept. 22-28 | H. *Janet*, Caribbean | 500 |
| 1956, Feb. 1-29 | Blizzard, W Europe | 1,000 |
| 1957, June 25-30 | H. *Audrey*, TX to AL | 390 |
| 1958, Feb. 15-16 | Blizzard, northeastern U.S. | 171 |
| 1959, Sept. 17-19 | T. *Sarah*, Japan, S. Korea | 2,000 |
| 1959, Sept. 26-27 | T. *Vera*, Honshu, Japan | 4,466 |
| 1960, Sept. 4-12 | H. *Donna*, Caribbean, E U.S. | 148 |
| 1961, Sept. 11-14 | H. *Carla*, TX | 46 |
| 1961, Oct. 31 | H. *Hattie*, Br. Honduras | 400 |
| 1963, May 28-29 | Windstorm, Bangladesh | 22,000 |
| 1963, Oct. 4-8 | H. *Flora*, Caribbean | 6,000 |
| 1964, Oct. 4-7 | H. *Hilda*, LA, MS, GA | 38 |
| 1964, June 30 | T. *Winnie*, N Philippines | 107 |
| 1964, Sept. 5 | T. *Ruby*, Hong Kong and China | 735 |
| 1965, May 11-12 | Windstorm, Bangladesh | 17,000 |
| 1965, June 1-2 | Windstorm, Bangladesh | 30,000 |
| 1965, Sept. 7-12 | H. *Betsy*, FL, MS, LA | 74 |
| 1965, Dec. 15 | Windstorm, Bangladesh | 10,000 |
| 1966, June 4-10 | H. *Alma*, Honduras, SE U.S. | 51 |
| 1966, Sept. 24-30 | H. *Inez*, Carib., FL, Mexico | 293 |
| 1967, July 9 | T. *Billie*, SW Japan | 347 |
| 1967, Sept. 5-23 | H. *Beulah*, Carib., Mex., TX | 54 |
| 1967, Dec. 12-20 | Blizzard, Southwest U.S. | 51 |
| 1968, Nov. 18-28 | T. *Nina*, Philippines | 63 |
| 1969, Aug. 17-18 | H. *Camille*, MS, LA | 256 |
| 1970, July 30-Aug. 5 | H. *Celia*, Cuba, FL, TX | 31 |
| 1970, Aug. 20-21 | H. *Dorothy*, Martinique | 42 |
| 1970, Sept. 15 | T. *Georgia*, Philippines | 300 |
| 1970, Oct. 14 | T. *Sening*, Philippines | 583 |
| 1970, Oct. 15 | T. *Titang*, Philippines | 526 |
| 1970, Nov. 13 | Cyclone, Bangladesh | 300,000 |
| 1971, Aug. 1 | T. *Rose*, Hong Kong | 130 |
| 1972, June 19-29 | H. *Agnes*, FL to NY | 118 |
| 1972, Dec. 3 | T. *Theresa*, Philippines | 169 |
| 1973, June-Aug. | Monsoon rains, India | 1,217 |
| 1974, June 11 | Storm Dinah, Luzon Isl., Phil. | 71 |
| 1974, July 11 | T. *Gilda*, Japan, S. Korea | 108 |
| 1974, Sept. 19-20 | H. *Fifi*, Honduras | 2,000 |
| 1974, Dec. 25 | Cyclone leveled Darwin, Austral. | 50 |
| 1975, Sept. 13-27 | H. *Eloise*, Caribbean, NE U.S. | 71 |
| 1976, May 20 | T. *Olga*, floods, Philippines | 215 |
| 1977, July 25, 31 | T. *Thelma*, T. *Vera*, Taiwan | 39 |
| 1978, Oct. 27 | T. *Rita*, Philippines | c. 400 |
| 1979, Aug. 30-Sept. 7 | H. *David*, Caribbean, E U.S. | 1,100 |
| 1980, Aug. 4-11 | H. *Allen*, Caribbean, TX | 272 |
| 1981, Nov. 25 | T. *Irma*, Luzon Isl., Phil. | 176 |
| 1983, June | Monsoon, India | 900 |
| 1983, Aug. 18 | H. *Alicia*, southern TX | 17 |
| 1984, Sept. 2 | T. *Ike*, S Philippines | 1,363 |
| 1985, May 25 | Cyclone, Bangladesh | 10,000 |
| 1985, Oct. 26-Nov. 6 | H. *Juan*, SE U.S. | 97 |
| 1987, Nov. 25 | T. *Nina*, Philippines | 650 |
| 1988, Sept. 10-17 | H. *Gilbert*, Caribbean, Gulf of Mexico | 260 |
| 1989, Sept. 16-22 | H. *Hugo*, Caribbean, SE U.S. | 504 |
| 1990, May 6-11 | Cyclones, SE India | 450 |
| 1991, Apr. 30 | Cyclone, Bangladesh | 139,000 |
| 1991, Nov. 5 | Tropical storm, Samar and Leyte, Philippines | 7,000+ |
| 1992, Aug. 24-26 | H. *Andrew*, southern FL, LA | 14 |
| 1993, Mar. 13-14 | Blizzard, eastern U.S. | 200 |
| 1993, June | Monsoon, Bangladesh | 2,000 |
| 1994, Nov. 8-18 | Storm Gordon, Caribbean, FL | 830 |
| 1995, Sept. 4-6 | H. *Luis*, Caribbean | 14 |
| 1995, Sept. 13-22 | H. *Marilyn*, Virgin Isls., Carib. | 13 |
| 1995, Oct. 2-4 | H. *Opal*, S Mexico, FL, AL | 59 |
| 1995, Nov. 2-3 | T. *Angela*, Philippines | 600+ |
| 1996, Jan. 7-8 | Blizzard, northeastern U.S. | 100 |
| 1996, July 8-13 | H. *Bertha*, Carib., eastern U.S. | 15 |
| 1996, Aug. 22 | Blizzard, Himalayas, N India | 239 |
| 1996, Aug. 29-Sept. 6 | H. *Fran*, Carib., NC, VA, WV | 28 |
| 1996, Sept. 9-10 | H. *Hortense*, Caribbean | 24 |
| 1996, Sept. 9 | T. *Sally*, S China | 114 |

## Some Notable Floods, Tidal Waves

| Date | Location | Deaths |
|---|---|---|
| 1228 | Holland | 100,000 |
| 1642 | China | 300,000 |
| 1883, Aug. 27 | Indonesia | 36,000 |
| 1887 | Huang He River, China | 900,000 |
| 1889, May 31 | Johnstown, PA | 2,209 |
| 1900, Sept. 8 | Galveston, TX | 5,000 |
| 1903, June 15 | Heppner, OR | 325 |
| 1911 | Chang Jiang River, China | 100,000 |
| 1913, Mar. 25-27 | OH, IN | 732 |
| 1915, Aug. 17 | Galveston, TX | 275 |
| 1928, Mar. 13 | Collapse of St. Francis Dam, Saugus, CA | 450 |
| 1928, Sept. 13 | Lake Okeechobee, FL | 2,000 |
| 1931, Aug. | Huang He River, China | 3,700,000 |
| 1937, Jan. 22 | OH, MS Valleys | 250 |
| 1939 | N China | 200,000 |
| 1946, Apr. 1 | HI, AK | 159 |
| 1947, Sept. 20 | Honshu Island, Japan | 1,900 |
| 1951, Aug. | Manchuria | 1,800 |
| 1953, Jan. 31 | W Europe | 2,000 |
| 1954, Aug. 17 | Farahzad, Iran | 2,000 |
| 1955, Oct. 7-12 | India, Pakistan | 1,700 |
| 1959, Nov. 1 | W Mexico | 2,000 |
| 1959, Dec. 2 | Frejus, France | 412 |
| 1960, Oct. 10 | Bangladesh | 6,000 |
| 1960, Oct. 31 | Bangladesh | 4,000 |
| 1962, Feb. 17 | North Sea coast, Germany | 343 |
| 1962, Sept. 27 | Barcelona, Spain | 445 |
| 1963, Oct. 9 | Dam collapse, Vaiont, Italy | 1,800 |
| 1966, Nov. 3-4 | Florence, Venice, Italy | 113 |
| 1967, Jan. 18-24 | E Brazil | 894 |
| 1967, Mar. 19 | Rio de Janeiro, Brazil | 436 |
| 1967, Nov. 26 | Lisbon, Portugal | 464 |
| 1968, Aug. 7-14 | Gujarat State, India | 1,000 |
| 1968, Oct. 7 | NE India | 780 |
| 1969, Jan. 18-26 | Southern CA | 100 |
| 1969, Mar. 17 | Mundau Valley, Alagoas, Brazil | 218 |
| 1969, Aug. 20-22 | Western VA | 189 |
| 1969, Sept. 15 | South Korea | 250 |
| 1969, Oct. 1-8 | Tunisia | 500 |
| 1970, May 20 | Central Romania | 160 |
| 1970, July 22 | Himalayas, India | 500 |
| 1971, Feb. 26 | Rio de Janeiro, Brazil | 130 |
| 1972, Feb. 26 | Buffalo Creek, WV | 118 |
| 1972, June 9 | Rapid City, SD | 236 |
| 1972, Aug. 7 | Luzon Isl., Philippines | 454 |
| 1972, Aug. 19-31 | Pakistan | 1,500 |
| 1974, Mar. 29 | Tubaro, Brazil | 1,000 |
| 1974, Aug. 12 | Monty-Long, Bangladesh | 2,500 |
| 1976, June 5 | Teton Dam collapse, ID | 11 |
| 1976, July 31 | Big Thompson Canyon, CO | 139 |
| 1976, Nov. 17 | East Java, Indonesia | 136 |
| 1977, July 19-20 | Johnstown, PA | 68 |
| 1977, Nov. 6 | Toccoa, GA | 39 |
| 1978, June-Sept. | N India | 1,200 |
| 1979, Jan.-Feb. | Brazil | 204 |
| 1979, July 17 | Lomblem Isl., Indonesia | 539 |
| 1979, Aug. 11 | Morvi, India | 15,000 |
| 1980, Feb. 13-22 | Southern CA, AZ | 26 |
| 1981, Apr. | N China | 550 |
| 1981, July | Sichuan, Hubei Prov., China | 1,300 |
| 1982, Jan. 23 | Nr. Lima, Peru | 600 |
| 1982, May 12 | Guangdong, China | 430 |
| 1982, Sept. 17-21 | El Salvador, Guatemala | 1,300+ |
| 1983, Feb.-Mar. | CA coast | 13 |
| 1983, Apr. 6-12 | AL, LA, MS, TN | 15 |
| 1984, May 27 | Tulsa, OK | 13 |
| 1984, Aug-Sept. | South Korea | 200+ |
| 1985, July 19 | dam burst, N Italy | 361 |
| 1987, Aug.-Sept. | N Bangladesh | 1,000+ |
| 1988, Sept. | N India | 1,000+ |
| 1990, June 14 | Shadyside, OH | 23 |
| 1991, Dec. 18-26 | TX | 18 |
| 1992, Feb. 9-15 | Southern CA | 13 |
| 1993, July-Aug. | Midwest | 48 |
| 1994, July | GA, AL | 32 |
| 1995, Jan. 30-Feb. 9 | NW Europe | 40 |
| 1995, March 8-15 | CA | 15 |
| 1995, July | Hunan Province, China | 1,200 |
| 1995, Aug. 19 | SW Morocco | 136 |
| 1995, Dec. 25 | KwaZulu Natal, South Africa | 166 |
| 1996, Jan. | Northeastern U.S. | 15+ |
| 1996, Feb. 17 | Biak Isl., Indonesia | 105 |
| 1996, April | Afghanistan | 100+ |
| 1996, June-July | S China | 315 |
| 1996, Aug. 7 | Pyrenees Mts., Spain | 71 |

## Major Earthquakes

**Source:** Global Volcanism Network, Smithsonian Institution; U.S. Geological Survey, Dept. of the Interior; World Almanac research

Magnitude of earthquakes (Mag.) is measured on the Richter scale; each higher number represents a tenfold increase in energy measured in ground motion. Adopted in 1935, the scale is applied to earthquakes here as far back as reliable seismograms are available.

| Date | Location | Deaths | Mag. |
|---|---|---|---|
| 526, May 20 | Antioch, Syria | 250,000 | NA |
| 856 | Corinth, Greece | 45,000 | " |
| 1057 | Chihli, China | 25,000 | " |
| 1169, Feb. 11 | Near Mt. Etna, Sicily | 15,000[1] | " |
| 1268 | Cilicia, Asia Minor | 60,000 | " |
| 1290, Sept. 27 | Chihli, China | 100,000 | " |
| 1293, May 20 | Kamakura, Japan | 30,000 | " |
| 1531, Jan. 26 | Lisbon, Portugal | 30,000 | " |
| 1556, Jan. 24 | Shaanxi, China | 830,000 | " |
| 1667, Nov. | Shemaka, Caucasia | 80,000 | " |
| 1693, Jan. 11 | Catania, Italy | 60,000 | " |
| 1730, Dec. 30 | Hokkaido, Japan | 137,000 | " |
| 1737, Oct. 11 | India, Calcutta | 300,000 | " |
| 1755, June 7 | N Persia | 40,000 | " |
| 1755, Nov. 1 | Lisbon, Portugal | 60,000 | 8.75* |
| 1783, Feb. 4 | Calabria, Italy | 30,000 | NA |
| 1797, Feb. 4 | Quito, Ecuador | 41,000 | " |
| 1811-12 | New Madrid, MO (series) | NA | 8.7* |
| 1822, Sept. 5 | Asia Minor, Aleppo | 22,000 | NA |
| 1828, Dec. 28 | Echigo, Japan | 30,000 | " |
| 1868, Aug. 13-15 | Peru, Ecuador | 40,000 | " |
| 1875, May 16 | Venezuela, Colombia | 16,000 | " |
| 1886, Aug. 31 | Charleston, SC | 60 | 6.6 |
| 1896, June 15 | Japan, sea wave | 27,120 | NA |
| 1906, Apr. 18-19 | San Francisco, CA | 503[2] | 8.3 |
| 1906, Aug. 16 | Valparaiso, Chile | 20,000 | 8.6 |
| 1908, Dec. 28 | Messina, Italy | 83,000 | 7.5 |
| 1915, Jan. 13 | Avezzano, Italy | 29,980 | 7.5 |
| 1918, Oct. 11 | Mona Passage, P.R. | 116 | 7.5 |
| 1920, Dec. 16 | Gansu, China | 100,000 | 8.6 |
| 1923, Sept. 1 | Yokohama, Japan | 200,000 | 8.3 |
| 1927, May 22 | Nan-Shan, China | 200,000 | 8.3 |
| 1932, Dec. 26 | Gansu, China | 70,000 | 7.6 |
| 1933, Mar. 2 | Japan | 2,990 | 8.9 |
| 1933, Mar. 10 | Long Beach, CA | 115 | 6.2 |
| 1934, Jan. 15 | India, Bihar-Nepal | 10,700 | 8.4 |
| 1935, May 31 | Quetta, India | 50,000 | 7.5 |
| 1939, Jan. 24 | Chillan, Chile | 28,000 | 8.3 |
| 1939, Dec. 26 | Erzincan, Turkey | 30,000 | 7.9 |
| 1946, Dec. 21 | Honshu, Japan | 2,000 | 8.4 |
| 1948, June 28 | Fukui, Japan | 5,131 | 7.3 |
| 1949, Aug. 5 | Pelileo, Ecuador | 6,000 | 6.8 |
| 1950, Aug. 15 | Assam, India | 1,530 | 8.7 |
| 1953, Mar. 18 | NW Turkey | 1,200 | 7.2 |
| 1956, June 10-17 | N Afghanistan | 2,000 | 7.7 |
| 1957, July 2 | N Iran | 2,500 | 7.4 |
| 1957, Dec. 13 | W Iran | 2,000 | 7.1 |
| 1960, Feb. 29 | Agadir, Morocco | 12,000 | 5.8 |
| 1960, May 21-30 | S Chile | 5,000 | 8.3 |
| 1962, Sept. 1 | NW Iran | 12,230 | 7.1 |
| 1963, July 26 | Skopje, Yugoslavia | 1,100 | 6.0 |
| 1964, Mar. 27 | Alaska | 131 | 8.4 |
| 1966, Aug. 19 | E Turkey | 2,520 | 6.9 |
| 1968, Aug. 31 | NE Iran | 12,000 | 7.4 |
| 1970, Jan. 5 | Yunnan Prov., China | 10,000 | 7.7 |
| 1970, Mar. 28 | W Turkey | 1,086 | 7.4 |
| 1970, May 31 | N Peru | 66,794 | 7.7 |

*(continued)*

## Major Earthquakes *(continued)*

| Date | Location | Deaths | Mag. |
|---|---|---|---|
| 1971, Feb. 9 | San Fernando Valley, CA | 65 | 6.6 |
| 1972, Apr. 10 | S Iran | 5,057 | 6.9 |
| 1972, Dec. 23 | Nicaragua | 5,000 | 6.2 |
| 1974, Dec. 28 | Pakistan (9 towns) | 5,200 | 6.3 |
| 1975, Sept. 6 | Turkey (Lice, etc.) | 2,312 | 6.8 |
| 1976, Feb. 4 | Guatemala | 22,778 | 7.5 |
| 1976, May 6 | NE Italy | 946 | 6.5 |
| 1976, June 26 | Irian Jaya, New Guinea | 443 | 7.1 |
| 1976, July 28 | Tangshan, China | 242,000 | 8.2 |
| 1976, Aug. 17 | Mindanao, Philippines | 8,000 | 7.8 |
| 1976, Nov. 24 | E Turkey | 4,000 | 7.9 |
| 1977, Mar. 4 | Romania | 1,541 | 7.5 |
| 1977, Aug. 19 | Indonesia | 200 | 8.0 |
| 1977, Nov. 23 | NW Argentina | 100 | 8.2 |
| 1978, Sept. 16 | NE Iran | 25,000 | 7.7 |
| 1979, Sept. 12 | Indonesia | 100 | 8.1 |
| 1979, Dec. 12 | Colombia, Ecuador | 800 | 7.9 |
| 1980, Oct. 10 | NW Algeria | 4,500 | 7.3 |
| 1980, Nov. 23 | S Italy | 4,800 | 7.2 |
| 1982, Dec. 13 | N Yemen | 2,800 | 6.0 |
| 1983, May 26 | N Honshu, Japan | 81 | 7.7 |
| 1983, Oct. 30 | E Turkey | 1,300 | 7.1 |
| 1985, Mar. 3 | Chile | 146 | 7.8 |
| 1985, Sept. 19, 21 | Mexico City | 4,200+ | 8.1 |
| 1987, Mar. 5-6 | NE Ecuador | 4,000+ | 7.3 |
| 1988, Aug. 20 | India/Nepal border | 1,000+ | 6.5 |
| 1988, Nov. 6 | China/Burma border | 1,000 | 7.3 |
| 1988, Dec. 7 | NW Armenia | 55,000+ | 6.8 |
| 1989, Oct. 17 | San Francisco Bay area | 62 | 7.1 |
| 1990, May 30 | N Peru | 115 | 6.3 |
| 1990, June 21 | NW Iran | 40,000+ | 7.7 |
| 1990, July 16 | Luzon, Philippines | 1,621 | 7.7 |
| 1991, Feb. 1 | Pakistan, Afghanistan border | 1,200 | 6.8 |
| 1992, Mar. 13, 15 | E Turkey | 4,000 | 6.2/6.0 |
| 1992, June 28 | S California | 1 | 7.5/6.6 |
| 1992, Dec. 12 | Flores Isl., Indonesia | 2,500 | 7.5 |
| 1993, July 12 | off Hokkaido, Japan | 200+ | 7.7 |
| 1993, Sept. 29 | Maharashtra, S India | 9,748[3] | 6.4 |
| 1994, Jan. 17 | Northridge, CA | 61 | 6.8 |
| 1994, Feb. 15 | S Sumatra, Indon. | 215 | 7.0 |
| 1994, June 6 | Cauca, SW Colombia | 1,000 | 6.8 |
| 1994, Aug. 19 | N Algeria | 164 | 6.0 |
| 1995, Jan. 17 | Kobe, Japan | 5,502[4] | 7.2 |
| 1995, May 27 | Sakhalin Isl., Russia | 2,000 | 7.6 |
| 1995, Oct. 1 | SW Turkey | 73 | 6.0 |
| 1995, Oct. 9 | W coast, Mexico | c. 40+ | 7.6 |
| 1996, Feb. 3 | SW China | 200+ | 7.0 |
| 1996, Feb. 17 | Irian Jaya, Indonesia | 53 | 7.5 |

(*) estimated from earthquake intensity. NA=not available. (1) Once thought to have been a volcanic eruption; evidence indicates a destructive earthquake and tsunami occurred on this date. (2) With subsequent fires, death toll rose to 700. (3) Official death toll released by Indian government. Other sources reported 30,000 deaths. (4) Official Japanese death toll as of Mar. 1996.

## Other Recent Earthquakes

**Source:** Global Volcanism Network, Smithsonian Institution; dates are Greenwich Mean Time

| Date | Location | Magnitude |
|---|---|---|
| 1996, June 17 | N of Flores Isl., Indonesia | 7.5 |
| June 11 | Samar Isl., Philippines | 7.0 |
| June 10 | Aleutian Isls. (2) | 7.2/7.7 |
| Apr. 29 | Solomon Isls. | 7.5 |
| Feb. 25 | W Mexico | 6.8 |
| Feb. 7 | Kuril Isls. | 7.0 |
| Jan. 1 | Sulawesi Isl., Indonesia | 7.7 |
| 1995, Dec. 3 | Kuril Isls. | 8.0 |
| Nov. 22 | S of Aqaba, Jordan | 7.2 |
| Nov. 8 | N Sumatra Isl., Indonesia | 7.0 |
| Oct. 18, 19 | Ruykyu Isls., Japan | 6.9/6.9 |
| Oct. 5 | W Sumatra Isl., Indonesia | 6.8 |
| Oct. 3 | Peru-Ecuador border | 6.8 |
| Sept. 14 | S Mexico | 7.2 |
| Aug. 16 | Bougainville Isl., Papua New Guinea (2) | 7.8/6.8 |
| July 30 | N coast, Chile | 7.8 |
| July 11 | E Myanmar | 7.2 |
| July 3 | Kermadec Isls., New Zeal. | 7.1 |

## Some Notable Fires Since 1835

(See also "Some Notable Explosions Since 1910.")

| Date | Location | Deaths |
|---|---|---|
| 1835, Dec. 16 | New York, NY, 500 bldgs. destroyed | — |
| 1845, May | Canton, China, theater | 1,670 |
| 1871, Oct. 8 | Chicago, $196 million loss; 17,000 bldgs. destroyed | 250 |
| 1871, Oct. 8 | Peshtigo, WI, forest fire | 1,182 |
| 1872, Nov. 9 | Boston, 800 bldgs. destroyed | — |
| 1876, Dec. 5 | Brooklyn, NY, theater | 295 |
| 1877, June 20 | St. John, N.B., Canada | 100 |
| 1881, Dec. 8 | Ring Theater, Vienna | 850 |
| 1887, May 25 | Opera Comique, Paris | 200 |
| 1887, Sept. 4 | Exeter, England, theater | 200 |
| 1894, Sept. 1 | MN, forest fire | 413 |
| 1897, May 4 | Paris, charity bazaar | 150 |
| 1900, June 30 | Hoboken, NJ, docks | 326 |
| 1902, Sept. 20 | Birmingham, AL, church | 115 |
| 1903, Dec. 30 | Iroquois Theater, Chicago | 602 |
| 1908, Jan. 13 | Rhoads Theater, Boyertown, PA | 170 |
| 1908, Mar. 4 | Collinwood, OH, school | 176 |
| 1911, Mar. 25 | Triangle Shirtwaist factory, NY, NY | 146 |
| 1913, Oct. 14 | Mid Glamorgan, Wales, colliery | 439 |
| 1918, Apr. 13 | Norman, OK, state hospital | 38 |
| 1918, Oct. 12 | Cloquet, MN, forest fire | 400 |
| 1919, June 20 | Mayagüez Theater, San Juan, Puerto Rico | 150 |
| 1923, May 17 | Camden, SC, school | 76 |
| 1924, Dec. 24 | Babb's Switch, OK, school | 35 |
| 1929, May 15 | Cleveland, OH, clinic | 125 |
| 1930, Apr. 21 | Columbus, OH, penitentiary | 320 |
| 1931, July 24 | Pittsburgh, PA, home for aged | 48 |
| 1934, Dec. 11 | Hotel Kerns, Lansing, MI | 34 |
| 1938, May 16 | Atlanta, GA, Terminal Hotel | 35 |
| 1940, Apr. 23 | Natchez, MS, dance hall | 198 |
| 1942, Nov. 28 | Cocoanut Grove, Boston | 491 |
| 1942, Dec. 12 | St. John's, Nfld., hostel | 100 |
| 1943, Sept. 7 | Gulf Hotel, Houston, TX | 55 |
| 1944, July 6 | Ringling Circus, Hartford, CT | 168 |
| 1946, June 5 | LaSalle Hotel, Chicago | 61 |
| 1946, Dec. 7 | Winecoff Hotel, Atlanta | 119 |
| 1946, Dec. 12 | New York, NY, ice plant, tenement | 37 |
| 1949, Apr. 5 | Effingham, IL, hospital | 77 |
| 1950, Jan. 7 | Davenport, IA, Mercy Hospital | 41 |
| 1953, Mar. 29 | Largo, FL, nursing home | 35 |
| 1953, Apr. 16 | Chicago, metalworking plant | 35 |
| 1957, Feb. 17 | Warrenton, MO, home for aged | 72 |
| 1958, Mar. 19 | New York, NY, loft building | 24 |
| 1958, Dec. 1 | Chicago, parochial school | 95 |
| 1958, Dec. 16 | Bogotà, Colombia, store | 83 |
| 1959, June 23 | Stalheim, Norway, resort hotel | 34 |
| 1960, Mar. 12 | Pusan, Korea, chemical plant | 68 |
| 1960, July 14 | Guatemala City, mental hospital | 225 |
| 1960, Nov. 13 | Amude, Syria, movie theater | 152 |
| 1961, Jan. 6 | Thomas Hotel, San Francisco | 20 |
| 1961, Dec. 8 | Hartford, CT, hospital | 16 |
| 1961, Dec. 17 | Niteroi, Brazil, circus | 323 |
| 1963, May 4 | Diourbel, Senegal, theater | 64 |
| 1963, Nov. 18 | Surfside Hotel, Atlantic City, NJ | 25 |
| 1963, Nov. 23 | Fitchville, OH, rest home | 63 |
| 1963, Dec. 29 | Roosevelt Hotel, Jacksonville, FL | 22 |
| 1964, May 8 | Manila, apartment bldg. | 30 |
| 1964, Dec. 18 | Fountaintown, IN, nursing home | 20 |

| Date | Location | Deaths |
|---|---|---|
| 1965, Mar. 1 | LaSalle, Canada, apartment | 28 |
| 1965, Aug. 11-16 | Watts riot fires, CA | 30+ |
| 1966, Mar. 11 | Numata, Japan, 2 ski resorts | 31 |
| 1966, Aug. 13 | Melbourne, Australia, hotel | 29 |
| 1966, Sept. 12 | Anchorage, AK, hotel | 14 |
| 1966, Oct. 17 | New York, NY, bldg. (firefighters) | 12 |
| 1966, Dec. 7 | Erzurum, Turkey, barracks | 68 |
| 1967, Feb. 7 | Montgomery, AL, restaurant | 25 |
| 1967, May 22 | Brussels, Belgium, store | 322 |
| 1967, July 16 | Jay, FL, state prison | 37 |
| 1968, Feb. 26 | Shrewsbury, England, hospital | 22 |
| 1968, May 11 | Vijayawada, India, wedding hall | 58 |
| 1968, Nov. 18 | Glasgow, Scotland, factory | 24 |
| 1969, Dec. 2 | Notre Dame, Can., nursing home | 54 |
| 1970, Jan. 9 | Marietta, OH, nursing home | 27 |
| 1970, Mar. 20 | Seattle, WA, hotel | 19 |
| 1970, Nov. 1 | Grenoble, France, dance hall | 145 |
| 1970, Dec. 20 | Tucson, AZ, hotel | 28 |
| 1971, Mar. 6 | Burghoezli, Switzerland, psychiatric clinic | 28 |
| 1971, Apr., 20 | Bangkok, Thailand, hotel | 24 |
| 1971, Dec., 25 | Seoul, South Korea, hotel | 162 |
| 1972, May 13 | Osaka, Japan, nightclub | 116 |
| 1972, July 5 | Sherborne, England, hospital | 30 |
| 1973, Feb. 6 | Paris, France, school | 21 |
| 1973, June 24 | New Orleans, LA, bar | 32 |
| 1973, Nov. 6 | Fukui, Japan, train | 28 |
| 1973, Nov. 29 | Kumamoto, Japan, department store | 107 |
| 1973, Dec. 2 | Seoul, South Korea, theater | 50 |
| 1974, Feb. 1 | Sao Paulo, Brazil, bank building | 189 |
| 1974, June 30 | Port Chester, NY, discotheque | 24 |
| 1974, Nov. 3 | Seoul, South Korea, hotel, discotheque | 88 |
| 1975, Dec. 12 | Mina, Saudi Arabia, tent city | 138 |
| 1976, Oct. 24 | Bronx, NY, social club | 25 |
| 1977, Feb. 25 | Moscow, Rossiya hotel | 45 |
| 1977, May 28 | Southgate, KY, nightclub | 164 |
| 1977, June 9 | Abidjan, Ivory Coast, nightclub | 41 |
| 1977, June 26 | Columbia, TN, jail | 42 |
| 1977, Nov. 14 | Manila, Philippines, hotel | 47 |
| 1978, Jan. 28 | Kansas City, Coates House Hotel | 16 |
| 1978, Aug. 19 | Abadan, Iran, movie theater | 425+ |
| 1979, July 14 | Saragossa, Spain, hotel | 80 |
| 1979, Dec. 31 | Chapais, Quebec, social club | 42 |
| 1980, May 20 | Kingston, Jamaica, nursing home | 157 |
| 1980, Nov. 21 | MGM Grand Hotel, Las Vegas | 84 |
| 1980, Dec. 4 | Stouffer Inn, Harrison, NY | 26 |
| 1981, Jan. 9 | Keansburg, NJ, boarding home | 30 |
| 1981, Feb. 10 | Las Vegas Hilton | 8 |
| 1981, Feb. 14 | Dublin, Ireland, discotheque | 44 |
| 1982, Sept. 4 | Los Angeles, apartment house | 24 |
| 1982, Nov. 8 | Biloxi, MS, county jail | 29 |
| 1983, Feb. 13 | Turin, Italy, movie theater | 64 |
| 1983, Dec. 17 | Madrid, Spain, discotheque | 83 |
| 1984, May 11 | Great Adventure Amusement Pk., NJ | 8 |
| 1985, Apr. 21 | Tabaco, Phil., movie theater | 44 |
| 1985, Apr. 26 | Buenos Aires, Arg., hospital | 79 |
| 1985, May 11 | Bradford, England, soccer stadium | 53 |
| 1986, Dec. 31 | Puerto Rico, Dupont Plaza Hotel | 96 |
| 1987, May 6-June 2 | N China, forest fire | 193 |
| 1987, Nov. 17 | London, England, subway | 30 |
| 1988, Mar. 20 | Lashio, Burma, 2,000 buildings | 134 |
| 1990, Mar. 25 | Bronx, NY, social club | 87 |
| 1991, Mar. 3 | Addis Ababa, Ethiopia, munitions dump | 260+ |
| 1991, Sept. 3 | Hamlet, NC, chicken-processing plant | 25 |
| 1991, Oct. 20-21 | Oakland, Berkeley, CA, wildfire | 24 |
| 1993, Apr. 19 | Waco, TX, cult compound | 72 |
| 1994, May 10 | Bangkok, Thailand, toy factory | 213 |
| 1994, July 4-10 | Glenwood Springs, CO (firefighters) | 14 |
| 1994, Dec. 10 | Karamay, China, theater | 300 |
| 1994, Nov. 2 | Durunka, Egypt, burning fuel flood | 500 |
| 1995, Oct. 28 | Baku, Azerbaijan, subway train | 300 |
| 1995, Dec. 23 | Mandi Dabwali, India, school | 500+ |
| 1996, Mar. 19 | Quezon City, Philippines, nightclub | 150+ |
| 1996, Mar. 28 | Bogor, Indonesia, shopping mall | 78 |
| 1996, Apr. 11 | Düsseldorf, Germany, airport | 16 |

# Some Notable Explosions Since 1910

| Date | Location | Deaths |
|---|---|---|
| 1910, Oct. 1 | Los Angeles Times Bldg. | 21 |
| 1913, Mar. 7 | Dynamite, Baltimore harbor | 55 |
| 1915, Sept. 27 | Gasoline tank car, Ardmore, OK | 47 |
| 1917, Apr. 10 | Munitions plant, Eddystone, PA | 133 |
| 1917, Dec. 6 | Halifax Harbor, Canada | 1,654 |
| 1918, May 18 | Chemical plant, Oakdale, PA | 193 |
| 1918, July 2 | Explosives, Split Rock, NY | 50 |
| 1918, Oct. 4 | Shell plant, Morgan Station, NJ | 64 |
| 1919, May 22 | Food plant, Cedar Rapids, IA | 44 |
| 1920, Sept. 16 | Wall Street, NY, NY, bomb | 30 |
| 1921, Sept. 21 | Chem. storage facility, Oppau, Germany | 561 |
| 1924, Jan. 3 | Food plant, Pekin, IL | 42 |
| 1927, May 18 | Bath school, Lansing, MI | 38 |
| 1928, April 13 | Dance hall, West Plains, MO | 40 |
| 1937, Mar. 18 | New London, TX, school | 311 |
| 1940, Sept. 12 | Hercules Powder, Kenvil, NJ | 55 |
| 1942, June 5 | Ordnance plant, Elwood, IL | 49 |
| 1944, Apr. 14 | Bombay, India, harbor | 700 |
| 1944, July 17 | Port Chicago, CA, pier | 322 |
| 1944, Oct. 21 | Liquid gas tank, Cleveland | 135 |
| 1947, Apr. 16 | Texas City, TX, pier | 576 |
| 1948, July 28 | Farben works, Ludwigshafen, Germany | 184 |
| 1950, May 19 | Munitions barges, S. Amboy, NJ | 30 |
| 1956, Aug. 7 | Dynamite trucks, Cali, Colombia | 1,100 |
| 1958, Apr. 18 | Sunken munitions ship, Okinawa, Japan | 40 |
| 1958, May 22 | Nike missiles, Leonardo, NJ | 10 |
| 1959, Apr. 10 | World War II bomb, Philippines | 38 |
| 1959, June 28 | Rail tank cars, Meldrin, GA | 25 |
| 1959, Aug. 7 | Dynamite truck, Roseburg, OR | 13 |
| 1959, Nov. 2 | Jamuri Bazar, India, explosives | 46 |
| 1959, Dec. 13 | Dortmund, Germany., 2 apt. buildings | 26 |
| 1960, Mar. 4 | Belgian munitions ship, Havana, Cuba | 100 |
| 1960, Oct. 25 | Gas, Windsor, Ont., store | 11 |
| 1962, Jan. 16 | Gas pipeline, Edson, Alberta | 8 |
| 1962, Oct. 3 | Telephone Co. office, NY, NY | 23 |
| 1963, Jan. 2 | Packing plant, Terre Haute, IN | 16 |
| 1963, Mar. 9 | Dynamite plant, S. Africa | 45 |
| 1963, Aug. 13 | Explosives dump, Gauhaiti, India | 32 |
| 1963, Oct. 31 | State Fair Coliseum, Indianapolis, IN | 73 |
| 1964, July 23 | Bone, Algeria, harbor munitions | 100 |
| 1965, Mar. 4 | Gas pipeline, Natchitoches, LA | 17 |
| 1965, Aug. 9 | Missile silo, Searcy, AR | 53 |
| 1965, Oct. 21 | Bridge, Tila Bund, Pakistan | 80 |
| 1965, Oct. 30 | Cartagena, Colombia | 48 |
| 1965, Nov. 24 | Armory, Keokuk, IA | 20 |
| 1966, Oct. 13 | Chemical plant, La Salle, Quebec | 11 |
| 1967, Feb. 17 | Chemical plant, Hawthorne, NJ | 11 |
| 1967, Dec. 25 | Apartment bldg., Moscow | 20 |
| 1968, Apr. 6 | Sports store, Richmond, IN | 43 |
| 1970, Apr. 8 | Subway construction, Osaka, Japan | 73 |
| 1971, June 24 | Tunnel, Sylmar, CA | 17 |
| 1971, June 28 | School, fireworks, Puebla, Mexico | 13 |
| 1971, Oct. 21 | Shopping center, Glasgow, Scotland | 20 |
| 1973, Feb., 10 | Liquefied gas tank, Staten Island, NY | 40 |
| 1975, Dec. 27 | Chasnala, India, mine | 431 |
| 1976, Apr. 13 | Lapua, Finland, munitions works | 40 |
| 1977, Nov. 11 | Freight train, Iri, South Korea | 57 |
| 1977, Dec. 22 | Grain elevator, Westwego, LA | 35 |
| 1978, Feb. 24 | Derailed tank car, Waverly, TN | 12 |
| 1978, July 11 | Propylene tank truck, Spanish coastal campsite | 150 |
| 1980, Oct. 23 | School, Ortuella, Spain | 64 |
| 1982, Apr. 25 | Antiques exhibition, Todi, Italy | 33 |
| 1982, Nov. 2 | Salang Tunnel, Afghanistan | 1,000-3,000 |
| 1984, Feb. 25 | Oil pipeline, Cubatao, Brazil | 508 |
| 1984, June 21 | Naval supply depot, Severomorsk, USSR | 200+ |
| 1984, Nov. 19 | Gas storage area, NE Mexico City | 334 |
| 1984, Dec. 3 | Chemical plant, Bhopal, central India | 3,849 |
| 1984, Dec. 5 | Coal mine, Taipei, Taiwan | 94 |
| 1985, June 25 | Fireworks factory, Hallett, OK | 21 |
| 1988, Apr. 10 | Pakistani army ammunitions dump nr. Rawalpindi and Islamabad | 100 |
| 1988, May 5 | Shell Oil Company, Norco, LA | 7 |
| 1988, July 6 | Oil rig, North Sea | 167 |

*(continued)*

## Some Notable Explosions Since 1910 (*continued*)

| Date | Location | Deaths |
|---|---|---|
| 1989, June 3 | Gas pipeline, between Ufa, Asha, USSR | 650+ |
| 1992, Mar. 3 | Coal mine, Kozlu, Turkey | 270+ |
| 1992, Apr. 22 | Sewer, Guadalajara, Mexico | 190 |
| 1992, May 9 | Coal mine, Plymouth, Nova Scotia | 26 |
| 1993, Feb. 26 | World Trade Center, NY, NY | 6 |
| 1994, July 18 | Jewish community center, Buenos Aires | 100 |
| 1995, Apr. 19 | Federal office bldg., Oklahoma City | 168[1] |
| 1995, Apr. 29 | Subway construction, South Korea | 110 |
| 1995, Nov. 13 | 2 bombs explode at military facility in Riyadh, Saudi Arabia | 7 |
| 1996, Jan. 31 | Bank, Colombo, Sri Lanka | 53 |
| 1996, Feb. 25 | 2 suicide bombings, Jerusalem and Ashkelon, Israel | 27 |
| 1996, Mar. 3-4 | Suicide bombings, Jerusalem and Tel Aviv, Israel | 33 |
| 1996, June 25 | U.S. military housing complex, nr. Dhahran, Saudi Arabia | 19 |
| 1996, July 24 | Train, Colombo, Sri Lanka | 54 |

(1) Includes a rescue worker who died during the rescue effort.

# Notable Nuclear Accidents

**Oct. 7, 1957** — A fire in the Windscale plutonium production reactor N of Liverpool, England, spread radioactive material throughout the countryside. In 1983, the British government said that 39 people had probably died of cancer as a result of the accident.

**1957** — A chemical explosion in Kasli, USSR (now in Russia), in tanks containing nuclear waste, spread radioactive material and forced a major evacuation.

**Jan. 3, 1961** — An experimental reactor at a federal installation near Idaho Falls, ID, killed 3 workers—the only deaths in U.S. reactor operations. The plant had high radiation levels, but damage was contained.

**Oct. 5, 1966** — A sodium cooling system malfunction caused a partial core meltdown at the Enrico Fermi demonstration breeder reactor, located near Detroit, MI. Radiation was contained.

**Jan. 21, 1969** — A coolant malfunction from an experimental underground reactor at Lucens Vad, Switzerland, resulted in the release of a large amount of radiation into a cavern, which was then sealed.

**Mar. 22, 1975** — A technician checking for air leaks with a lighted candle caused a $100 million fire at the Brown's Ferry reactor in Decatur, AL. The fire burned out electrical controls, lowering the cooling water to dangerous levels.

**Mar. 28, 1979** — The worst commercial nuclear accident in the U.S. occurred as equipment failures and human mistakes led to a loss of coolant and a partial core meltdown at the Three Mile Island reactor in Middletown, PA.

**Feb. 11, 1981** — Eight workers were contaminated when more than 100,000 gallons of radioactive coolant leaked into the containment building of the TVA's Sequoyah 1 plant in Tennessee.

**Apr. 25, 1981** — Some 100 workers were exposed to radioactive material during repairs of a nuclear plant at Tsuruga, Japan.

**Jan. 6, 1986** — A cylinder of nuclear material burst after being improperly heated at a Kerr-McGee plant at Gore, OK. One worker died, and 100 were hospitalized.

**Apr. 26, 1986** — In the worst accident in the history of the nuclear power industry, fires and explosions resulting from an unauthorized experiment conducted at the Chernobyl nuclear power plant near Kiev, USSR (now in Ukraine), left at least 31 people dead in the immediate aftermath of the disaster and spread significant quantities of radioactive material over much of Europe. An estimated 135,000 people were evacuated from areas around Chernobyl, some of which were rendered uninhabitable for years. As a result of the radiation that was released into the atmosphere, tens of thousands of excess cancer deaths (as well as increased rates of birth defects) were expected in succeeding decades.

# Record Oil Spills

The number of tons can be multiplied by 7 to estimate roughly the number of barrels spilled; the exact number of barrels in a ton varies with the type of oil. Each barrel contains 42 gallons.

| Name, place | Date | Cause | Tons |
|---|---|---|---|
| Ixtoc I oil well, S Gulf of Mexico | June 3, 1979 | Blowout | 600,000 |
| Nowruz oil field, Persian Gulf | Feb. 1983 | Blowout | 600,000 (est.) |
| *Atlantic Empress* & *Aegean Captain*, off Trinidad and Tobago | July 19, 1979 | Collision | 300,000 |
| *Castillo de Bellver*, off Cape Town, South Africa | Aug. 6, 1983 | Fire | 250,000 |
| *Amoco Cadiz*, near Portsall, France | Mar. 16, 1978 | Grounding | 223,000 |
| *Torrey Canyon*, off Land's End, England | Mar. 18, 1967 | Grounding | 119,000 |
| *Sea Star*, Gulf of Oman | Dec. 19, 1972 | Collision | 115,000 |
| *Urquiola*, La Coruna, Spain | May 12, 1976 | Grounding | 100,000 |
| *Hawaiian Patriot*, N Pacific | Feb. 25, 1977 | Fire | 99,000 |
| *Othello*, Tralhavet Bay, Sweden | Mar. 20, 1970 | Collision | 60,000-100,000 |

# Other Notable Oil Spills

| Name, place | Date | Cause | Gallons |
|---|---|---|---|
| Persian Gulf | Jan. 23, 1991 (began) | Spillage by Iraq | 130,000,000[1] |
| *Braer*, off Shetland Islands | Jan. 5, 1993 | Grounding | 26,000,000 |
| Aegean Sea, off N Spain | Dec. 3, 1992 | Unknown | 21,500,000 |
| *Sea Empress*, off SW Wales | Feb. 15, 1996 | Grounding | 18,000,000 |
| *World Glory*, off South Africa | June 13, 1968 | Hull failure | 13,524,000 |
| *Exxon Valdez*, Prince William Sound, AK | Mar. 24, 1989 | Grounding | 10,080,000 |
| *Keo*, off MA | Nov. 5, 1969 | Hull failure | 8,820,000 |
| Storage tank, Sewaren, NJ | Nov. 4, 1969 | Tank rupture | 8,400,000 |
| Ekofisk oil field, North Sea | Apr. 22, 1977 | Well blowout | 8,200,000 |
| *Argo Merchant*, Nantucket, MA | Dec. 15, 1976 | Grounding | 7,700,000 |
| Pipeline, West Delta, LA | Oct. 15, 1967 | Dragging anchor | 6,720,000 |
| Tanker off Japan | Nov. 30, 1971 | Ship broke in half | 6,258,000 |
| *Usinsk*, Russian Arctic | Aug. 12, 1994 | Pipeline rupture | 4,300,000 |
| Storage tank, Monongahela River | Jan. 2, 1988 | Tank rupture | 3,800,000[2] |

(1) Estimated by Saudi Arabia. Some estimates are as low as 25 mln. gallons. (2) Some estimates are as high as 84.6 mln. gallons.

## Historic Assassinations Since 1865

**1865**—Apr. 14. U.S. Pres. Abraham Lincoln shot by John Wilkes Booth in Washington, DC; died Apr. 15.

**1881**—Mar. 13. Alexander II, of Russia.—July 2. U.S. Pres. James A. Garfield shot by Charles J. Guiteau, Washington, DC; died Sept. 19.

**1900**—July 29. Umberto I, king of Italy.

**1901**—Sept. 6. U.S. Pres. William McKinley in Buffalo, NY, died Sept. 14. Leon Czolgosz executed for the crime.

**1913**—Feb. 23. Mex. Pres. Francisco I. Madero and Vice Pres. Jose Pino Suarez.—Mar. 18. George, king of Greece.

**1914**—June 28. Archduke Francis Ferdinand of Austria-Hungary and his wife in Sarajevo, Bosnia (later part of Bosnia and Herzegovina), by Gavrilo Princip.

**1916**—Dec. 30. Grigori Rasputin, politically powerful Russian monk.

**1918**—July 12. Grand Duke Michael of Russia, at Perm.—July 16. Nicholas II, abdicated as czar of Russia; his wife, the Czarina Alexandra; their son, Czarevitch Alexis; their daughters, Grand Duchesses Olga, Tatiana, Marie, Anastasia; and 4 members of their household, executed by Bolsheviks at Ekaterinburg.

**1920**—May 20. Mexican Pres. Gen. Venustiano Carranza in Tlaxcalantongo.

**1922**—Aug. 22. Michael Collins, Irish revolutionary.—Dec. 16. Polish President Gabriel Narutowicz in Warsaw by an anarchist.

**1923**—July 20. Gen. Francisco "Pancho" Villa, ex-rebel leader, in Parral, Mexico.

**1928**—July 17. Gen. Alvaro Obregon, president-elect of Mexico, in San Angel, Mexico.

**1934**—July 25. In Vienna, Austrian Chancellor Engelbert Dollfuss by Nazis.

**1935**—Sept. 8. U.S. Sen. Huey P. Long shot in Baton Rouge, LA, by Dr. Carl Austin Weiss, who was slain by Long's bodyguards; Long died Sept. 10.

**1940**—Aug. 20. Leon Trotsky (Lev Bronstein), 63, exiled Russian war minister, near Mexico City. Killer identified as Ramon Mercador del Rio, a Spaniard; served 20 years in Mexican prison.

**1948**—Jan. 30. Mohandas K. Gandhi, 78, shot in New Delhi, India, by Nathuram Vinayak Godse.— Sept. 17. Count Folke Bernadotte, UN mediator for Palestine, ambushed in Jerusalem.

**1951**—July 20. King Abdullah ibn Hussein of Jordan. —Oct. 16. Prime Min. Liaquat Ali Khan of Pakistan shot in Rawalpindi.

**1956**—Sept. 21. Pres. Anastasio Somoza of Nicaragua, in Leon; died Sept. 29.

**1957**—July 26. Pres. Carlos Castillo Armas of Guatemala, in Guatemala City by one of his own guards.

**1958**—July 14. King Faisal of Iraq; his uncle, Crown Prince Abdullah; and July 15, Premier Nuri as-Said, by rebels in Baghdad.

**1959**—Sept. 25. Prime Minister Solomon Bandaranaike of Ceylon, by Buddhist monk in Colombo.

**1961**—Jan. 17. Ex-Premier Patrice Lumumba of the Congo, in Katanga Province—May 30. Dominican dictator Rafael Leonidas Trujillo Molina shot to death by assassins near Ciudad Trujillo.

**1963**—June 12. Medgar W. Evers, NAACP's Mississippi field secretary, in Jackson, MS.—Nov. 2. Pres. Ngo Dinh Diem of South Vietnam and his brother, Ngo Dinh Nhu, in a military coup.—Nov. 22. U.S. Pres. John F. Kennedy fatally shot in Dallas, TX; accused Lee Harvey Oswald murdered by Jack Ruby while awaiting trial.

**1965**—Jan. 21. Iranian premier Hassan Ali Mansour fatally wounded in Tehran; 4 executed.—Feb. 21. Malcolm X, black nationalist, fatally shot in New York City.

**1966**—Sept. 6. Prime Minister Hendrik F. Verwoerd of South Africa stabbed to death in parliament at Cape Town.

**1968**—Apr. 4. Rev. Dr. Martin Luther King Jr. fatally shot in Memphis, TN, by James Earl Ray.—June 5. Sen. Robert F. Kennedy (D, NY) fatally shot in Los Angeles; Sirhan Sirhan, resident alien, convicted of murder.

**1971**—Nov. 28. Prime Minister Wasfi Tal of Jordan, in Cairo, by Palestinian guerrillas.

**1973**—Mar. 2. U.S. Ambassador Cleo A. Noel Jr., U.S. Charge d'Affaires George C. Moore, and Belgian Charge d'Affaires Guy Eid killed by Palestinian guerrillas in Khartoum, Sudan.

**1974**—Aug. 19. U.S. Ambassador to Cyprus, Rodger P. Davies, killed by sniper's bullet in Nicosia.

**1975**—Feb. 11. Pres. Richard Ratsimandrava, of Madagascar, shot in Tananarive.—Mar. 25. King Faisal of Saudi Arabia shot by nephew Prince Musad Abdel Aziz, in royal palace, Riyadh.— Aug. 15. Bangladesh Pres. Sheik Mujibur Rahman killed in coup.

**1976**—Feb. 13. Nigerian head of state, Gen. Murtala Ramat Mohammed, slain by self-styled "young revolutionaries."

**1977**—Mar. 16. Kamal Jumblat, Lebanese Druse chieftain, shot near Beirut.— Mar. 18. Congo Pres. Marien Ngouabi shot in Brazzaville.

**1978**—July 9. Former Iraqi Premier Abdul Razak Al-Naif shot in London.

**1979**—Feb. 14. U.S. Ambassador Adolph Dubs shot and killed by Afghan Muslim extremists in Kabul.— Aug. 27. Lord Mountbatten, World War II hero, and 2 others killed when a bomb exploded on his fishing boat off the coast of Co. Sligo, Ire. The IRA claimed responsibility. — Oct. 26. South Korean President Park Chung Hee and 6 bodyguards fatally shot by Kim Jae Kyu, head of South Korean CIA, and 5 aides in Seoul.

**1980**—Apr. 12. Liberian President William R. Tolbert slain in military coup.—Sept. 17. Former Nicaraguan President Anastasio Somoza Debayle shot in Paraguay.

**1981**—Oct. 6. Egyptian President Anwar al-Sadat fatally shot by a band of commandos while reviewing a military parade in Cairo.

**1982**—Sept. 14. Lebanese President-elect Bashir Gemayel killed by bomb in east Beirut.

**1983**—Aug. 21. Philippine opposition political leader Benigno Aquino Jr. fatally shot by a gunman at Manila International Airport.

**1984**—Oct. 31. Indian Prime Minister Indira Gandhi shot and killed by 2 of her bodyguards, who were members of the minority Sikh sect, in New Delhi.

**1986**—Feb. 28. Swedish Premier Olof Palme shot and killed by a gunman on Stockholm street.

**1987**—June 1. Lebanese Premier Rashid Karami killed when a bomb exploded aboard a helicopter in which he was traveling.

**1988**—Apr. 16. PLO military chief Khalil Wazir (Abu Jihad) gunned down by Israeli commandos in Tunisia.

**1989**—Aug. 18. Colombian Liberal Party presidential candidate Luis Carlos Galan killed by Medellín cartel drug traffickers at a campaign rally in Bogotà.—Nov. 22. Lebanese President Rene Moawad killed when a bomb exploded next to his motorcade.

**1990**—Mar. 22. Colombian Patriotic Union presidential candidate Bernando Jamamillo Ossa shot by gunman at an airport in Bogotà.

**1991**—May 21. Rajiv Gandhi, former prime minister of India, killed when a bomb exploded during an election rally in Madras.

**1992**—June 29. Mohammed Boudiaf, president of Algeria, shot by a gunman in Annaba.

**1993**—May 1. Ranasinghe Premadasa, president of Sri Lanka, killed by bomb in Colombo.

**1994**—Mar. 23. Luis Donaldo Colosio, Mexican presidential candidate, shot by gunman Mario Aburto Martinez. —Apr. 6. Burundian President Cyprien Ntaryamira and Rwandan President Juvenal Habyarimana killed, with 8 others, when their plane was apparently shot down.

**1995**—Nov. 4. Yitzhak Rabin, prime minister of Israel, shot by gunman Yigal Amir after delivering a speech at a pro-peace rally in Tel Aviv.

# Assassination Attempts

**1912**—Oct. 14. Former U.S. President Theodore Roosevelt shot and seriously wounded by demented man in Milwaukee, WI

**1933**—Feb. 15. In Miami, FL, Joseph Zangara, anarchist, shot at Pres.-elect Franklin D. Roosevelt, but a woman seized his arm, and the bullet fatally wounded Mayor Anton J. Cermak, of Chicago, who died Mar. 6. Zangara was electrocuted on Mar. 20, 1933.

**1950**—Nov. 1. In an attempt to assassinate President Truman, 2 members of a Puerto Rican nationalist movement—Griselio Torresola and Oscar Collazo—tried to shoot their way into Blair House. Torresola was killed, and a guard, Pvt. Leslie Coffelt, was fatally shot. Collazo was convicted, Mar. 7, 1951, of Coffelt's murder.

**1970**—Nov. 27. Pope Paul VI unharmed by knife-wielding assailant who attempted to attack him in Manila airport.

**1972**—May 15. Alabama Gov. George Wallace shot in Laurel, MD, by Arthur Bremer; seriously crippled.

**1975**—Sept. 5. Pres. Gerald R. Ford unharmed when a Secret Service agent grabbed a pistol aimed at him by Lynette (Squeaky) Fromme, a Charles Manson follower, in Sacramento.

**1975**—Sept. 22. Pres. Ford unharmed when Sara Jane Moore fired a revolver at him.

**1980**—May 29. Civil rights leader Vernon E. Jordan Jr. shot and wounded in Ft. Wayne, IN.

**1981**—Jan. 16. Irish political activist Bernadette Devlin McAliskey and her husband shot and seriously wounded by 3 members of a Protestant paramilitary group in Co. Tyrone, Ire.

**1981**—Mar. 30. Pres. Ronald Reagan, along with Press Sec. James Brady, Secret Service agent Timothy J. McCarthy, and Washington, DC, policeman Thomas Delahanty shot and seriously wounded by John W. Hinckley Jr. in Washington, DC

**1981**—May 13. Pope John Paul II and 2 bystanders shot and wounded by Mehmet Ali Agca, an escaped Turkish murderer, in St. Peter's Square, Rome.

**1982**—May 12. Pope John Paul II unharmed when a man with a knife was overpowered by guards, in Fatima, Portugal.

**1984**—Oct. 12. British Prime Minister Margaret Thatcher narrowly escaped injury when a bomb, said to have been planted by the Irish Republican Army, exploded at the Grand Hotel in Brighton, England, during the annual Conservative Party conference. (Four died, including a Conservative member of Parliament.)

**1986**—Sept. 7. Chilean President Gen. Augusto Pinochet Ugarte escaped unharmed when his motorcade was attacked by rebels using rockets, bazookas, grenades, and rifles.

**1994**—Oct. 29. President Bill Clinton unharmed when Francisco Duran, later convicted of attempted assassination, shot at a tourist resembling Clinton outside the White House.

**1995**—June 26. Egyptian President Hosni Mubarak unharmed when gunmen fired on his motorcade in Addis Ababa, Ethiopia. Four died, including two Ethiopian police officers.

# Notable U.S. Kidnappings Since 1924

**Robert Franks,** 13, in Chicago, **May 22, 1924,** by 2 youths, Richard Loeb and Nathan Leopold, who killed boy. Demand for $10,000 ignored. Loeb died in prison; Leopold paroled 1958.

**Charles A. Lindbergh Jr.,** 20 mos. old, in Hopewell, NJ, **Mar. 1, 1932;** found dead **May 12.** Ransom of $50,000 paid to man identified as Bruno Richard Hauptmann, 35, paroled German convict who entered U.S. illegally. Hauptmann was convicted after spectacular trial at Flemington, and electrocuted in Trenton, NJ, prison, **Apr. 3, 1936.**

**William A. Hamm Jr.,** 39, in St. Paul, **June 15, 1933.** $100,000 paid. Alvin Karpis given life, paroled in 1969.

**Charles F. Urschel,** in Oklahoma City, **July 22, 1933.** Released **July 31** after $200,000 paid. George (Machine Gun) Kelly and 5 others given life.

**Brooke L. Hart,** 22, in San Jose, CA. Thomas Thurmond and John Holmes arrested after demanding $40,000 ransom. When Hart's body was found in San Francisco Bay, **Nov. 26, 1933,** a mob attacked the jail at San Jose and lynched the 2 kidnappers.

**George Weyerhaeuser,** 9, in Tacoma, WA, **May 24, 1935.** Returned home **June 1** after $200,000 paid. Kidnappers given 20 to 60 years.

**Charles Mattson,** 10, in Tacoma, WA, **Dec. 27, 1936.** Found dead **Jan. 11, 1937.** Kidnapper asked $28,000, failed to contact.

**Arthur Fried,** in White Plains, NY, **Dec. 4, 1937.** Body not found. Two kidnappers executed.

**Robert C. Greenlease,** 6, taken from Kansas City, MO, school **Sept. 28, 1953,** and held for $600,000. Body found Oct. 7. Bonnie Brown Heady and Carl A. Hall pleaded guilty and were executed.

**Peter Weinberger,** 32 days old, Westbury, NY, **July 4, 1956,** for $2,000 ransom, not paid. Child found dead. Angelo John LaMarca, 31, convicted, executed.

**Lee Crary,** 8, in Everett, WA, **Sept. 22, 1957;** $10,000 ransom, not paid. He escaped after 3 days, led police to George E. Collins, who was convicted.

**Frank Sinatra Jr.,** 19, from hotel room in Lake Tahoe, CA, **Dec. 8, 1963.** Released **Dec. 11** after his father paid $240,000 ransom. Three men sentenced to prison.

**Barbara Jane Mackle,** 20, abducted **Dec. 17, 1968,** from Atlanta, GA, motel; was found unharmed 3 days later, buried in a coffin-like wooden box 18 inches underground, after her father had paid $500,000 ransom; Gary Steven Krist sentenced to life, Ruth Eisenmann-Schier to 7 years.

**Mrs. Roy Fuchs,** 35, and 3 children held hostage 2 hours, **May 14, 1969,** in Long Island, NY, released after her husband, a bank manager, paid kidnappers $129,000 in bank funds; 4 men arrested, ransom recovered.

**Virginia Piper,** 49, abducted **July 27, 1972,** from her home in suburban Minneapolis; found unharmed near Duluth 2 days later after her husband paid $1 million ransom.

**Patricia "Patty" Hearst,** 19, taken from her Berkeley, CA, apartment **Feb. 4, 1974.** "Symbionese Liberation Army" captors demanded her father, publisher Randolph Hearst, give millions to poor. She was identified by FBI as having taken part in a San Francisco bank holdup, **Apr. 15.** FBI, **Sept. 18, 1975,** captured her and others; they were indicted on various charges. Patricia Hearst was convicted of bank robbery, **Mar. 20, 1976;** released from prison under executive clemency, **Feb. 1, 1979.** In 1978, William and Emily Harris were sentenced to 10 years to life for the kidnapping; both paroled in 1983.

**J. Reginald Murphy,** 40, an editor of *Atlanta* (GA) *Constitution,* kidnapped **Feb. 20, 1974;** freed **Feb. 22** after newspaper paid $700,000 ransom. William A. H. Williams arrested; most of the money recovered.

**E. B. Reville,** Hepzibah, GA, banker, and wife, Jean, kidnapped **Sept. 30, 1974.** Ransom of $30,000 paid. He was found alive; Jean Reville was found dead **Oct. 2.**

**Jack Teich,** Kings Point, NY, steel executive, seized **Nov. 12, 1974;** released **Nov. 19** after payment of $750,000.

**Adam Walsh,** 6, abducted from a Hollywood, FL, department store, **July 27, 1981.** Although his severed head was found 2 weeks later at Vero Beach, FL, his body was never recovered. John Walsh, Adam's father, became active in raising awareness about missing children.

**Sidney J. Reso,** oil company executive, seized **Apr. 29, 1992;** died **May 3;** Arthur D. Seale and wife, Irene, arrested **June 19.** Arthur Seale pleaded guilty, sentenced to life in prison; Irene Seale sentenced to 20-year prison term.

**Polly Klaas,** 12, Petaluma, CA, abducted at knife point, **Oct. 1, 1993,** during a slumber party at her home. Police arrested Richard Allen Davis on **Nov. 30;** he led them to her body, found **Dec. 4** in wooded area of Cloverdale, CA. Davis was found guilty **June 18, 1996**, and was sentenced to death **Sept. 26.**

# AEROSPACE

## Memorable Moments in Human Spaceflight

**Sources:** National Aeronautics and Space Administration; Congressional Research Service; World Almanac research

**Note:** U.S. space missions are in boldface. Other missions were sponsored by the Soviet Union or, later, the Commonwealth of Independent States. All dates are Eastern standard time. EVA = extravehicular activity. ASTP = Apollo-Saturn Test Project. Number of total flights by each crew member is given in parentheses when more than 1.

| Dates | Mission[1] | Crew (no. of flights) | Duration (hr:min) | Remarks |
|---|---|---|---|---|
| 4/12/61 | Vostok 1 | Yuri A. Gagarin | 1:48 | 1st human orbital flight |
| **5/5/61** | **Mercury-Redstone 3** | **Alan B. Shepard Jr.** | **0:15** | **1st American in space** |
| **7/21/61** | **Mercury-Redstone 4** | **Virgil I. Grissom** | **0:15** | **Spacecraft sank, Grissom rescued** |
| 8/6/61-8/7/61 | Vostok 2 | Gherman S. Titov | 25:18 | 1st spaceflight of more than 24 hrs |
| **2/20/62** | **Mercury-Atlas 6** | **John H. Glenn Jr.** | **4:55** | **1st American in orbit; 3 orbits** |
| **5/24/62** | **Mercury-Atlas 7** | **M. Scott Carpenter** | **4:56** | **Manual retrofire error caused 250-mi landing overshoot** |
| 8/11/62-8/15/62 | Vostok 3 | Andrian G. Nikolayev | 94:22 | Vostok 3 and 4 made 1st group flight |
| 8/12/62-8/15/62 | Vostok 4 | Pavel R. Popovich | 70:57 | On 1st orbit it came within 3 mi of Vostok 3 |
| **5/15/63-5/16/63** | **Mercury-Atlas 9** | **L. Gordon Cooper** | **34:19** | **1st U.S. evaluation of effects of one day in space on a person; 22 orbits** |
| 6/14/63-6/19/63 | Vostok 5 | Valery F. Bykovsky | 119:06 | Vostok 5 and 6 made 2d group flight |
| 6/16/63-6/19/63 | Vostok 6 | Valentina V. Tereshkova | 70:50 | 1st woman in space; passes within 3 mi of Vostok 5 |
| 10/12/64-10/13/64 | Voskhod 1 | Vladimir M. Komarov, Konstantin P. Feoktistov, Boris B. Yegorov | 24:17 | 1st 3-person orbital flight; 1st without space suits |
| 3/18/65-3/19/65 | Voskhod 2 | Pavel I. Belyayev, Aleksei A. Leonov | 26:02 | Leonov made 1st "space walk" (10 min) |
| **3/23/65** | **Gemini-Titan 3** | **Grissom (2), John W. Young** | **4:53** | **1st piloted spacecraft to change its orbital path** |
| **6/3/65-6/7/65** | **Gemini-Titan 4** | **James A. McDivitt, Edward H. White 2d** | **97:56** | **White was 1st American to "walk in space" (36 min)** |
| **12/15/65-12/16/65** | **Gemini-Titan 6** | **Schirra (2), Thomas P. Stafford** | **25:51** | **Completed 1st U.S. space rendezvous, with Gemini 7** |
| **12/4/65-12/18/65** | **Gemini-Titan 7** | **Frank Borman, James A. Lovell** | **330:35** | **Longest-duration Gemini flight** |
| **3/16/66** | **Gemini-Titan 8** | **Neil A. Armstrong, David R. Scott** | **10:41** | **1st docking of one space vehicle with another; mission aborted, control malfunction; 1st Pacific landing** |
| **7/18/66-7/21/66** | **Gemini-Titan 10** | **Young (2), Michael Collins** | **70:47** | **1st use of Agena target vehicle's propulsion systems; 1st orbital docking** |
| **11/11/66-11/15/66** | **Gemini-Titan 12** | **Lovell (2), Edwin W. "Buzz" Aldrin Jr.** | **94:34** | **Final Gemini mission; 5½ hr EVA** |
| 4/23/67-4/24/67 | Soyuz 1 | Komarov (2) | 26:40 | Crashed on reentry, killing Komarov |
| **10/11/68-10/22/68** | **Apollo-Saturn 7** | **Schirra (3), Donn F. Eisele, R. Walter Cunningham** | **260:09** | **1st piloted flight of Apollo spacecraft command-service module only; live TV footage of crew** |
| **12/21/68-12/27/68** | **Apollo-Saturn 8** | **Borman (2), Lovell (3), William A. Anders** | **147:00** | **1st lunar orbit and piloted lunar return reentry (command-service module only); views of lunar surface televised to Earth** |
| 1/14/69-1/17/69 | Soyuz 4 | Vladimir A. Shatalov | 71:21 | Docked with Soyuz 5 |
| 1/15/69-1/18/69 | Soyuz 5 | Boris V. Volyanov, Aleksei S. Yeliseyev, Yevgeny V. Khrunov | 72:54 | Docked with 4; Yeliseyev and Khrunov transferred to Soyuz 4 via a spacewalk |
| **3/3/69-3/13/69** | **Apollo-Saturn 9** | **McDivitt (2), D. Scott (2), Russell L. Schweickart** | **241:00** | **1st piloted flight of lunar module** |
| **5/18/69-5/26/69** | **Apollo-Saturn 10** | **Stafford (3), Young (3), Cernan(2)** | **192:03** | **1st lunar module orbit of Moon, 50,000 ft from Moon surface** |
| **7/16/69-7/24/69** | **Apollo-Saturn 11** | **Armstrong (2), Collins (2), Aldrin (2)** | **195:18** | **1st lunar landing made by Armstrong and Aldrin (7/20); collected 48.5 lb of soil, rock samples; lunar stay time 21:36:21** |
| 10/11/69-10/16/69 | Soyuz 6 | Georgi S. Shonin, Valery N. Kubasov | 118:43 | 1st welding of metals in space |
| 10/12/69-10/17/69 | Soyuz 7 | Anatoly V. Flipchenko, Vladislav N. Volkov, Viktor V. Gorbatko | 118:40 | Space lab construction test made; Soyuz 6, 7, and 8: 1st time 3 spacecraft, 7 crew members orbited the Earth at once |
| 10/13/69[2] | Soyuz 8 | Shatalov (2), Yeliseyev (2) | 118:51 | Part of space lab construction team |
| **11/14/69-11/24/69** | **Apollo-Saturn 12** | **Conrad (3), Richard F. Gordon Jr. (2), Alan L. Bean** | **244:36** | **Conrad and Bean made 2d Moon landing (11/18); collected 74.7 lb of samples, lunar stay time 31:31** |
| **4/11/70-4/17/70** | **Apollo-Saturn 13** | **Lovell (4), Fred W. Haise Jr., John L. Swigart Jr.** | **142:54** | **Aborted after service module oxygen tank ruptured; crew returned safely using lunar module** |

| Dates | Mission[1] | Crew (no. of flights) | Duration (hr:min) | Remarks |
|---|---|---|---|---|
| **1/31/71-2/9/71** | **Apollo-Saturn 14** | **A. Shepard (2), Stuart A. Roosa, Edgar D. Mitchell** | **216:01** | **Shepard and Mitchell made 3d Moon landing (2/3); collected 96 lb of lunar samples; lunar stay 33:31** |
| 4/19/71[2] | Salyut 1[3] | (Occupied by Soyuz 11 crew) | | 1st space station |
| 4/22/71[2] | Soyuz 10 | Shatalov (3), Yeliseyev (3), Nikolay N. Rukavishnikov | 47:46 | 1st successful docking with a space station; failed to enter space station |
| 6/6/71-6/30/71 | Soyuz 11 | Georgi T. Dobrovolskiy, V. Volkov (2), Viktor I. Patsayev | 570:22 | Docked and entered Salyut 1 space station; orbited in Salyut 1 for 23 days, crew died during reentry from loss of pressurization |
| **7/26/71-8/7/71** | **Apollo-Saturn 15** | **D. Scott (3), James B. Irwin, Alfred M. Worden** | **295:12** | **Scott and Irwin made 4th Moon landing (7/30); 1st lunar rover use; 1st deep space walk; 170 lb of samples; 66:55 stay** |
| **4/16/72-4/27/72** | **Apollo-Saturn 16** | **Young (4), Charles M. Duke Jr., Thomas K. Mattingly 2d** | **265:51** | **Young and Duke made 5th Moon landing (4/20); colleced 213 lb of lunar samples; lunar stay 71:2** |
| **12/7/72-12/19/72** | **Apollo-Saturn 17** | **Cernan (3), Ronald E. Evans, Harrison H. Schmitt** | **301:51** | **Cernan and Schmitt made 6th lunar landing (12/11); collected 243 lb of samples; record lunar stay of more than 75 hr** |
| **5/14/73[2]** | **Skylab 1[4]** | **(Occupied by Skylab 2, 3, and 4 crews)** | | **1st U.S. space station** |
| **5/25/73-6/22/73** | **Skylab 2** | **Conrad (4), Joseph P. Kerwin, Paul J. Weitz** | **672:49** | **1st Amer. piloted orbiting space station; crew repaired damage caused during boost** |
| **7/28/73-9/25/73** | **Skylab 3** | **Bean (2), Owen K. Garriott, Jack R. Lousma** | **1,427:09** | **Crew systems and operational tests; exceeded pre-mission plans for scientific activities; 13 hrs EVA 13:44** |
| **11/16/73-2/8/74** | **Skylab 4** | **Gerald P. Carr, Edward G. Gibson, William Pogue** | **2,017:15** | **Final Skylab mission** |
| 7/15/75-7/21/75 | Soyuz 19 (ASTP) | Leonov (2), Kubasov (2) | 143:31 | U.S.-USSR joint flight; crews linked up in space (7/17), conducted experiments, shared meals, and held a joint news conference |
| **7/15/75-7/24/75** | **Apollo (ASTP)** | **Vance Brand, Stafford (4), Donald K. Slayton** | **217:28** | **Joint flight with Soyuz 19** |
| 12/10/77[2] | Soyuz 26 | Yuri V. Romanenko, Georgiy M. Grechko (2) | 2,314:00 | 1st multiple docking to a space station (Soyuz 26 and 27 docked at Salyut 6) |
| 1/10/78[2] | Soyuz 27 | Vladimir A. Dzhanibekov | 142:59 | *See Soyuz 26* |
| 3/2/78[2] | Soyuz 28 | Aleksei A. Gubarev (2), Vladimir Remek | 190:16 | 1st international crew launch; Remek was 1st Czech in space |
| **4/12/81-4/14/81** | **Columbia (STS-1)** | **Young (5), Robert L. Crippen** | **54:21** | **1st space shuttle flight** |
| **11/11/82-11/16/82** | **Columbia (STS-5)** | **Brand (2), Robert Overmyer, William Lenoir, Joseph Allen** | **122:14** | **1st reuse of space shuttle; 1st 4-person crew** |
| **6/18/83-6/24/83** | **Challenger (STS-7)** | **Crippen (2), Frederick Hauck, Sally K. Ride, John W. Fabian, Norman Thagard** | **146:24** | **Ride was 1st U.S. woman in space; 1st 5-person crew** |
| 6/27/83[2] | Soyuz T-9 | Vladimir A. Lyakhov (2), A. P. Aleksandrov | 3,585:46 | Docked at Salyut 7; 1st construction in space |
| **8/30/83-9/5/83** | **Challenger (STS-8)** | **Truly (2), Daniel Brandenstein, William Thornton, Guion Bluford, Dale Gardner** | **145:09** | **Bluford was 1st U.S. black in space** |
| **11/28/83-12/8/83** | **Columbia (STS-9)** | **Young (6), Brewster Shaw Jr., Robert Parker, Garriott (2), Byron Lichtenberg, Ulf Merbold** | **247:47** | **1st 6-person crew; 1st Spacelab mission** |
| **2/3/84-2/11/84** | **Challenger (41-B)** | **Brand (3), Robert Gibson, Ronald McNair, Bruce McCandless, Robert Stewart** | **191:16** | **1st untethered EVA** |
| **4/6/84-4/13/84** | **Challenger (41-C)** | **Crippen (3), Francis R. Scobee, George D. Nelson, Terry J. Hart, James D. van Hoften** | **167:40** | **1st in-orbit satellite repair** |
| 7/17/84[2] | Soyuz T-12 | Dzhanibekov (4), Svetlana Y. Savitskaya (2), Igor P. Volk, | 283:14 | Docked at Salyut 7; Savitskaya was 1st woman to perform EVA |
| **10/5/84-10/13/84** | **Challenger (41-G)** | **Crippen (4), Jon A. McBride, Kathryn D. Sullivan, Ride (2), Marc Garneau, David C. Leestma, Paul D. Scully-Power** | **197:24** | **1st 7-person crew** |
| **11/8/84-11/16/84** | **Discovery (51-A)** | **Hauck (2); David M. Walker, Dr. Anna L. Fisher, J. Allen (2), D. Gardner (2)** | **191:45** | **1st satellite retrieval/repair** |
| **4/12/85-4/19/85** | **Discovery (51-D)** | **Karol J. Bobko, Donald E. Williams, Jake Garn, Charles D. Walker, Jeffrey A. Hoffman, S. David Griggs, M. Rhea Seddon** | **167:55** | **Garn was 1st senator in space** |
| **6/17/85-6/24/85** | **Discovery (51-G)** | **Brandenstein (2), John O. Creighton, Shannon W. Lucid, Steven R. Nagel, Fabian (2), Prince Sultan Salman al-Saud, Patrick Baudry** | **169:39** | **Launched 3 satellites; Salman al-Saud was 1st Arab in space; Baudry was 1st French person on U.S. mission** |
| **10/3/85-10/7/85** | **Atlantis (51-J)** | **Bobko (3), Ronald J. Grabe, David C. Hilmers, Stewart (2), William A. Pailes** | **97:47** | **1st Atlantis flight** |

| Dates | Mission[1] | Crew (no. of flights) | Duration (hr:min) | Remarks |
|---|---|---|---|---|
| **10/30/85-11/6/85** | **Challenger (61-A)** | **Hartsfield (3), Steven R. Nagel, Buchli (2), Bluford (2), Bonnie J. Dunbar, Wubbo J. Ockels, Richard Furrer, Ernst Messerschmid** | **168:45** | **1st 8-person crew; 1st German Spacelab mission** |
| **11/26/85-12/3/85** | **Atlantis (61-B)** | **Shaw (2), Bryan D. O'Connor, Sherwood C. Spring, Mary L. Cleave, Jerry L. Ross, C. Walker (3), Rodolfo Neri** | **165:05** | **Space structures assembly test; Neri was 1st Mexican in space** |
| **1/12/86-1/18/86** | **Columbia (61-C)** | **R. Gibson (2), Charles F. Bolden Jr., Hawley (2), G. Nelson (2), Franklin R. Chang-Diaz, Robert J. Cenker, Bill Nelson** | **146:04** | **B. Nelson was 1st congressman in space; material and astronomy experiments conducted** |
| **1/28/86** | **Challenger (51-L)** | **Scobee (2), Michael J. Smith, Judith A. Resnik (2), Ellison S. Onizuka (2), Ronald E. McNair, Gregory B. Jarvis, Christa McAuliffe** | | **Exploded 73 sec after liftoff; all were killed** |
| 2/20/86[2] | Mir[3] | Space station with 6 docking ports | | |
| 3/13/86[2] | Soyuz T-15 | Leonid Kizim (3), Vladmir Solovyov (2) | 3,000:01 | Ferry between stations; docked at *Mir* |
| 2/5/87-12/29/87 | Soyuz TM-2 | Romanenko (3), Aleksandr I. Laveikin | 7,835:38 | Romanenko set endurance record, since broken |
| 12/21/87-12/21/88 | Soyuz TM-4 | V. Titov (2), Muso Manarov, Anatoly Levchenko | 8,782:39 | Docked at *Mir* |
| **9/29/88-10/3/88** | **Discovery (STS-26)** | **Hauck (3), Richard O. Covey (2), Hilmers (2), G. Nelson (2), John M. Lounge (2)** | **97:00** | **Redesigned shuttle makes 1st flight** |
| **4/24/90-4/29/90** | **Discovery (STS-31)** | **McCandless (2), Sullivan (2), Loren J. Shriver (2), Bolden (2), Steven A. Hawley (3)** | **121:16** | **Launched Hubble Space Telescope** |
| **5/7/92-5/16/92** | **Endeavour (STS-49)** | **Brandenstein (4), Kevin C. Chilton, Bruce E. Melnick (2), Pierre J. Thuot (2), Richard J. Hieb (2), Kathryn Thornton (2), Tom Akers (2)** | **213:30** | **1st 3-person EVA; satellite recovery and redeployment** |
| **9/12/92-9/21/92** | **Endeavour (STS-47)** | **R. Gibson (4), Curtis L. Brown Jr., Mark Lee (2), Jay Apt (2), N. Jan Davis, Mae Carol Jemison, Mamoru Mohri** | **190:30** | **Jemison was 1st black woman in space; Lee and Davis were 1st married couple to travel together in space; 1st Japanese Spacelab** |
| **4/8/93-4/17/93** | **Discovery (STS-56)** | **Kenneth D. Cameron, Stephen S. Oswald (2), C. Michael Foale (2), Ellen Ochoa, Kenneth D. Cockrell** | **222:08** | **2d atmospheric mission; Ochoa was 1st Hispanic woman in space** |
| **12/2/93-12/13/93** | **Endeavour (STS-61)** | **Covey (3), Kenneth D. Bowersox (2), Claude Nicollier (2), Story Musgrave (5), Akers (3), K. Thornton (3), Hoffman (4)** | **259:58** | **Hubble Space Telescope repaired; Akers set new U.S. EVA duration record (29 hr, 40 min)** |
| **2/3/94-2/11/94** | **Discovery (STS-60)** | **Bolden (3), Kenneth S. Reightier Jr. (2), Davis, (2), Chang-Diaz (3), Ronald M. Sega, Sergei K. Krikalev** | **199:10** | **Krikalev was 1st Russian on U.S. shuttle** |
| **7/8/94-7/23/94** | **Columbia (STS-65)** | **Robert D. Cabana (3), James D. Halsell Jr., Hieb (3), Carl E. Walz (2), Leroy Chiao, Donald A. Thomas; Chiaki Naito-Mukai** | **353:55** | **Studied effects of weightlessness on aquatic animals** |
| **2/3/95-2/11/95** | **Discovery (STS-63)** | **James D. Wetherbee (3), Eileen M. Collins, Bernard A. Harris (2), Foale (3), Janice Voss (2), V. Titov (4)** | **198:29** | ***Discovery* and Russian space station rendezvous** |
| 3/16/95-3/22/95 | Soyuz/Mir-18 | Thagard (2), Vladimir Dezhurov, Gennadi Strekalov | 2,688[5] | Docked with *Mir* 3/16/95; Thagard was the 1st Amer. aboard the Russ. spacecraft; Valery Polyakov returned to Earth, 3/22/95, after a record stay in space (439 days) |
| **3/2/95-3/18/95** | **Endeavour (STS-67)** | **Oswald (3), William G. Gregory, Samuel T. Durrance (2), Ronald Parise (2), Wendy B. Lawrence, Tamara Jenigan (3), John M. Grunsfeld** | **399:09** | **Shuttle data made available on the Internet; astronomy research conducted** |
| **6/27/95-7/7/95** | **Atlantis (STS-71)** | **R. Gibson (5), Charles J. Precourt (2), Ellen S. Baker (3), Gregory J. Harbaugh (3), Dunbar (4), Anatoly Y. Solovyev (4) (to *Mir*), Nikolai M. Budarin (to *Mir*), Thagard (5) (from *Mir*), Strekalov (from *Mir*), Dezhurov (from *Mir*)** | **269:47** | **1st *Mir* docking; exchanged crew members with *Mir*; Thagard, with his stay on *Mir*, had spent 115 days in space** |
| **9/7/95-9/18/95** | **Endeavour (STS-69)** | **D. Walker (3), K. Cockrell (2), James Voss (3), Jim Newman (2), Michael Gernhardt** | **260:29** | **Relayed video images of an Atlantic hurricane to Earth; 2 scientific-studies satellites deployed and retrieved because of malfunctions** |
| **10/20/95-11/5/95** | **Columbia (STS-73)** | **Bowersox (3), Kent Rominger, K. Thornton (4), Catherine Coleman, Michael Lopez-Alegria, Fred Leslie, Albert Sacco** | **381:52** | **Most ever first-time space flyers; near-weightlessness experiments conducted in microgravity laboratory** |
| **11/8/95-11/20/95** | **Atlantis (STS-74)** | **Cameron (3), Halsell (2), Chris Hadfield, Ross (5), William McArthur (2)** | **196:30** | **2d *Mir* docking (11/15-11/18); erected a 15-ft permanent docking tunnel to *Mir* for future use by U.S. orbiters** |
| **1/11/96-1/20/96** | **Endeavour (STS-72)** | **Brian Duffy (3), Brent W. Jett Jr., Winston E. Scott, Chiao (2), Daniel T. Barry, Koichi Wakata** | **214:01** | **Released NASA space probe; retrieved Japanese satellite; 13 hrs EVA** |

| Dates | Mission[1] | Crew (no. of flights) | Duration (hr:min) | Remarks |
|---|---|---|---|---|
| **2/22/96-3/9/96** | **Columbia (STS-75)** | **Andrew M. Allen (3), Scott J. Horowitz, Chang-Diaz (5), Umberto Guidoni, Hoffman (5), Maurizio Cheli, Nicollier (3)** | **377:40** | **Lost an Italian satellite when its tether was severed; microgravity experiments performed; singe marks found on 2 O-rings** |
| **3/22/96-3/31/96** | **Atlantis (STS-76)** | **Chilton (3), Richard A. Searfoss (2), Sega (2), Richard Clifford (3) Linda Godwin (3), Lucid (5) (to *Mir*)** | **221:15** | **3d *Mir* docking (5 days); Lucid to *Mir*; 2-person EVA** |
| **5/19/96-5/29/96** | **Endeavour (STS-77)** | **John Casper (4); Brown (3), Andrew S. W. Thomas, Daniel W. Bursch (3), Mario Runco Jr. (3), Garneau (2)** | **240:39** | **Self-stabilizing satellite studied; commercial experiments conducted** |
| **6/20/96-7/7/96** | **Columbia (STS-78)** | **Terence T. Henricks (4), Kevin R. Kregel (2), Susan J. Helms (3), Richard M. Linnehan, Charles E. Brady, Jean-Jacques Favier, Robert Brent Thirsk** | **405:48** | **Longest-duration shuttle flight; studied weightlessness with the Life/Microgravity Spacelab on board** |
| **9/16/96-9/26/96** | **Atlantis (STS-79)** | **Apt (4), Terry Wilcutt (2), William Readdy (3), Akers (4), Walz (3), Lucid (5) (from *Mir*), John Blaha (5) (to *Mir*)** | **243:19** | **Docked with *Mir* 9/18/96; exchanged crew members, including Lucid, who set U.S. and women's individual duration in space record (188 days).** |

**Note:** As of Sept. 1996, there have been 79 space shuttle flights, 54 since the 1986 *Challenger* explosion. Active shuttles include the *Columbia* (20 flights), the *Discovery* (21), the *Atlantis* (17), and the *Endeavour* (11). (The *Challenger* completed 9 missions.)

Four Soviets died in spaceflights: Komarov was killed on Soyuz 1 (1967) when the parachute lines tangled during descent; the 3-person Soyuz 11 crew (1971) was asphyxiated. Seven Americans died in the *Challenger* explosion, and 3 astronauts—Virgil I. Grissom, Edward H. White, and Roger B. Chaffee—died in the Jan. 27, 1967, Apollo 1 fire on the ground at Cape Kennedy, FL. (1) For space shuttle flights, mission name is in parentheses following the name of the orbiter. (2) Launch date. (3) Space stations, such as the *Salyuts* and *Mir*, have been used to house crews since 1971. (4) Skylab 1 deteriorated and fell from orbit without burning up upon entering the atmosphere. Pieces fell on Australia and the Indian Ocean; however, no one was injured. (5) Approximate crew duration for Thagard's stay. Crew did not return together.

# Notable U.S. Planetary Science Missions

**Source:** National Aeronautics and Space Administration

| Spacecraft | Launch date (GMT) | Mission | Remarks |
|---|---|---|---|
| Mariner 2 | Aug. 27, 1962 | Venus | Passed within 22,000 mi of Venus 12/14/62; contact lost 1/3/63 at 54 million mi |
| Ranger 7 | July 28, 1964 | Moon | Yielded over 4,000 photos of lunar surface |
| Mariner 4 | Nov. 28, 1964 | Mars | Passed behind Mars 7/14/65; took 22 photos from 6,000 mi |
| Ranger 8 | Feb. 17, 1965 | Moon | Yielded over 7,000 photos of lunar surface |
| Surveyor 3 | Apr. 17, 1967 | Moon | Scooped and tested lunar soil |
| Mariner 5 | June 14, 1967 | Venus | In solar orbit; closest Venus fly-by 10/19/67 |
| Mariner 6 | Feb. 24, 1969 | Mars | Came within 2,000 mi of Mars 7/31/69; collected data, photos |
| Mariner 7 | Mar. 27, 1969 | Mars | Came within 2,000 mi of Mars 8/5/69 |
| Mariner 9 | May 30, 1971 | Mars | First craft to orbit Mars 11/13/71; sent back more than 7,000 photos |
| Pioneer 10 | Mar. 2, 1972 | Jupiter | Passed Jupiter 12/3/73; exited the planetary system 6/13/83; still operating in outer solar system |
| Pioneer 11 | Apr. 5, 1973 | Jupiter, Saturn | Passed Jupiter 12/2/74; Saturn 9/1/70; discovered an additional ring and 2 moons around Saturn; operating in outer solar system; transmission planned to end in late 1996 |
| Mariner 10 | Nov. 3, 1973 | Venus, Mercury | Passed Venus 2/5/74; arrived Mercury 3/29/74. First time gravity of one planet (Venus) used to whip spacecraft toward another (Mercury) |
| Viking 1 | Aug. 20, 1975 | Mars | Landed on Mars 7/20/76; did scientific research, sent photos; functioned 6½ years |
| Viking 2 | Sept. 9, 1975 | Mars | Landed on Mars 9/3/76; functioned 3½ years |
| Voyager 1 | Sept. 5, 1977 | Jupiter, Saturn | Encountered Jupiter 3/5/79, provided evidence of Jupiter ring; passed near Saturn 11/12/80 |
| Voyager 2 | Aug. 20, 1977 | Jupiter, Saturn, Uranus, Neptune | Encountered Jupiter 7/9/79; Saturn 8/25/81; Uranus 1/24/86; Neptune 8/25/89 |
| Pioneer Venus 1 | May 20, 1978 | Venus | Entered Venus orbit 12/4/78; spent 14 years studying planet; ceased operating 10/19/92 |
| Pioneer Venus 2 | Aug. 8, 1978 | Venus | Encountered Venus 12/9/78; probes impacted on surface |
| Magellan | May 4, 1989 | Venus | Orbit and map Venus; monitored geological activity on surface; ceased operating 10/12/94 |
| Galileo | Oct. 18, 1989 | Jupiter | Used Earth's gravity to propel it toward Jupiter; encountered Venus Feb. 1991; encountered Jupiter 12/7/95; released probe to Jovian surface |
| Mars Observer | Sept. 25, 1992 | Mars | Communication was lost 8/21/93 |
| Near Earth Asteroid Rendezvous (NEAR) | Feb. 17, 1996 | The asteroid Eros | Expected rendezvous with Eros, early 1999; to orbit and study the asteroid for about 1 year |

## Individuals Who Have Flown in Space, 1961-95

**Source:** Congressional Research Service; as of Dec. 31, 1995

| Country | No. of individs. | Country | No. of individs. | Country | No. of individs. | Country | No. of individs. |
|---|---|---|---|---|---|---|---|
| United States | 216 | Canada[2] | 4 | India[1] | 1 | Romania[1] | 1 |
| Soviet/CIS | 83 | Cuba[1] | 1 | Italy[2] | 1 | Saudi Arabia[2] | 1 |
| Afghanistan[1] | 1 | Czechoslovokia[1] | 1 | Japan[1,2] | 3 | Switzerland[2] | 1 |
| Austria[1] | 1 | France[1,2] | 5 | Mexico[2] | 1 | Syria[1] | 1 |
| Belguim[2] | 1 | Germany[1,2] | 8 | Mongolia[1] | 1 | United Kingdom[1] | 1 |
| Bulgaria[1] | 2 | Hungary[1] | 1 | Netherlands[2] | 1 | Vietnam[1] | 1 |
| | | | | Poland[1] | 1 | **Total** | **339** |

**Note:** "Germany" includes former E and W Germany. (1) On Russian/CIS-sponsored mission. (2) On U.S.-sponsored mission.

## Summary of Worldwide Successful Announced Payloads, 1957-95

**Source:** National Aeronautics and Space Administration

(A payload is something carried into space by a rocket.)

| Year | Total[1] | USSR/ CIS[2] | United States | Japan | China | European Space Agency | France | United Kingdom | India | Germany | Canada |
|---|---|---|---|---|---|---|---|---|---|---|---|
| 1957-59 | 24 | 6 | 18 | — | — | — | — | — | — | — | — |
| 1960-69 | 1,035 | 399 | 614 | — | — | 2 | 4 | 1 | — | — | — |
| 1970-79 | 1,366 | 1,028 | 247 | 18 | 8 | 5 | 14 | 6 | 1 | 3 | 4 |
| 1980-89 | 1,431 | 1,132 | 191 | 26 | 16 | 14 | 5 | 4 | 9 | 7 | 5 |
| 1990 | 159 | 96 | 31 | 7 | 5 | 1 | 2 | 5 | 1 | 1 | 0 |
| 1991 | 157 | 101 | 30 | 2 | 1 | 4 | 6 | 2 | 1 | 1 | 2 |
| 1992 | 128 | 77 | 27 | 3 | 2 | 1 | 3 | 0 | 2 | 1 | 1 |
| 1993 | 104 | 59 | 29 | 1 | 1 | 2 | 2 | 0 | 1 | 0 | 0 |
| 1994 | 109 | 64 | 27 | 4 | 5 | 1 | 0 | 0 | 2 | 2 | 0 |
| 1995 | 87 | 45 | 24 | 2 | 1 | 2 | 3 | 0 | 1 | 1 | 1 |
| **Total** | **4,600** | **3,007** | **1,238** | **63** | **39** | **32** | **39** | **18** | **18** | **16** | **13** |

(1) Includes launches sponsored by countries not shown. (2) Figures for 1986-91 are for the Soviet Union; 1992-95 figures are for the Commonwealth of Independent States.

## Notable Proposed U.S. Space Missions

**Source:** National Aeronautics and Space Administration; as of mid-1996

| Launch date | Mission | Purpose |
|---|---|---|
| Nov. 1996 | Mars Global Surveyor | High-resolution imaging of Martian surface; samples will be collected |
| Dec. 1996 | Mars Pathfinder | On-site measurements of the Martian climate and soil composition |
| Oct. 1997 | Cassini | Study of Saturn's atmosphere, rings, magnetosphere, and moons |
| Oct. 1997 | Lunar Prospector | Search for resources on the Moon, particularly water |
| 1998 | Earth Observing System | Provide long-term data sets of interactions between Earth's land, atmosphere, water, and life |
| 1998 | Landsat-7 | Continue the record of remote-sensing measurements of Earth's land surface |
| 1998 | Advanced X-ray Astrophysics Facility | Study of dark matter, stellar evolution, galactic clusters |
| 1999 | Stardust | Gather samples of dust from the comet Wild-2 and return samples to Earth |
| Not set | Pluto Fast Fly-by | First fly-by of Pluto for photographic survey and other studies |
| 2001 | Space InfraRed Telescope Facility | High-sensitivity observations of celestial sources |

**Note:** All spacecraft to be launched by expendable rockets.

## Traffic at World Airports, 1995

**Source:** Airports Council International-North America

| Airport | Passenger Arrivals and Departures |
|---|---|
| London, UK (Heathrow) | 54,452,634 |
| Tokyo/Haneda, Japan (Tokyo Intl.) | 45,822,503 |
| Frankfurt, Germany (Rhein/Main) | 38,179,543 |
| Seoul, South Korea (Kimpo Intl.) | 30,919,462 |
| Paris, France (Charles De Gaulle) | 28,355,470 |
| Hong Kong (Hong Kong Intl.) | 28,043,338 |
| Paris, France (Orly) | 26,653,878 |
| Amsterdam, Netherlands (Schiphol) | 25,355,007 |
| Tokyo, Japan (Narita) | 24,210,286 |
| Singapore (Changi) | 23,196,242 |
| Bangkok, Thailand (Bangkok Intl.) | 23,124,116 |
| London, UK (Gatwick) | 22,549,296 |
| Toronto, Ontario (Lester B. Pearson Intl.) | 22,353,234 |
| Rome, Italy (Fiumicino) | 21,091,388 |
| Madrid, Spain (Barajas) | 19,956,068 |
| Sydney, Australia (Kingsford Smith) | 18,123,336 |
| Fukuoka, Japan (Fukuoka Intl.) | 16,534,050 |
| Osaka, Japan (Kansai Intl.) | 16,510,325 |
| Mexico City, Mexico (Mexico City) | 15,853,812 |
| Sapporo, Japan (New Chitose) | 15,429,424 |
| Zurich, Switzerland (Zurich) | 15,340,449 |
| Dusseldorf, Germany (Dusseldorf) | 15,146,500 |
| Manchester, UK (Manchester) | 14,987,749 |
| Munich, Germany (Munich) | 14,867,922 |
| Palma de Mallorca, Spain (Palma de Mallorca) | 14,709,800 |

**Note:** Excludes U.S. airports. Includes only those airports participating in the Airports Council International Annual Airport Traffic Statistics collection.

## Traffic at U.S. Airports, 1995

**Source:** Air Transport Association of America

| Airport | Passenger Arrivals and Departures |
|---|---|
| Chicago (O'Hare–ORD) | 67,254,586 |
| Atlanta (Hartsfield Intl.–ATL) | 57,734,755 |
| Dallas/Ft. Worth (DFW) | 54,298,930 |
| Los Angeles (LAX) | 53,909,223 |
| San Francisco (SFO) | 36,260,064 |
| Miami (MIA) | 33,235,658 |
| Denver (Stapleton Intl.–DEN) | 31,028,191 |
| New York (J. F. Kennedy Intl.–JFK) | 30,237,723 |
| Detroit (DTW) | 29,013,260 |
| Las Vegas (McCarran Intl.–LAS) | 28,001,258 |
| Phoenix (Sky Harbor Intl.–PHX) | 27,820,144 |
| Minneapolis/St. Paul (MSP) | 26,782,915 |
| Newark (EWR) | 26,566,948 |
| St. Louis (Lambert St. Louis Intl.–STL) | 25,719,351 |
| Boston (Logan Intl.–BOS) | 24,743,656 |
| Houston (IAH) | 24,724,865 |
| Honolulu (HNL) | 23,580,230 |
| Seattle-Tacoma (SEA) | 22,790,920 |
| Orlando (MCO) | 22,365,503 |
| Charlotte (CLT) | 20,937,233 |

# U.S. Scheduled Airline Traffic, 1993-95

**Source:** Air Transport Association of America

| Passenger traffic | 1993 | 1994 | 1995 |
|---|---|---|---|
| Revenue passengers enplaned (000) | 488,520 | 528,376 | 547,384 |
| Revenue passenger miles (000) | 489,684,421 | 519,381,688 | 540,399,434 |
| Available seat miles (000) | 771,640,648 | 784,330,936 | 806,612,491 |
| Revenue passenger load factor (%) | 63.5 | 66.2 | 67.0 |
| **Cargo traffic (ton miles)** | **14,119,818** | **16,061,707** | **16,911,208** |
| Revenue freight and express (ton miles) | 11,943,595 | 13,729,157 | 14,568,416 |
| Revenue U.S. Mail (ton miles) | 2,176,223 | 2,269,550 | 234,792 |
| **Financial** | | | |
| Passenger revenue ($000) | $63,945,223 | $65,421,539 | $69,484,871 |
| Net profit ($000) | –$2,135,626[1] | –$344,115 | $2,376,763 |
| **Employees** | **537,111** | **539,759** | **546,987** |

(1) Excludes 1993 debt forgiven during bankruptcy proceedings for Continental and Trans World.

# Leading U.S. Passenger Airlines, 1995

**Source:** Air Transport Association of America

(in thousands)

| Airline | Passengers | Airline | Passengers | Airline | Passengers |
|---|---|---|---|---|---|
| Delta | 86,909 | Trans World | 21,551 | Reno | 3,855 |
| American | 79,511 | America West | 16,802 | Horizon Air | 3,796 |
| United | 78,664 | Alaska | 10,084 | Continental Express | 3,656 |
| USAir | 56,674 | ValuJet | 5,145 | Atlantic Southeast | 3,067 |
| Southwest | 50,039 | Aloha | 5,103 | Continental Micronesia | 2,585 |
| Northwest | 49,313 | Simmons | 4,979 | American Trans Air | 2,400 |
| Continental | 35,013 | Hawaiian | 4,776 | | |

# U.S. Airline Safety, Scheduled Commercial Carriers, 1980-95

**Source:** National Transportation Safety Board

| | Departures (millions) | Fatal accidents | Fatalities | Fatal accidents per 100,000 departures | | Departures (millions) | Fatal accidents | Fatalities | Fatal accidents per 100,000 departures |
|---|---|---|---|---|---|---|---|---|---|
| 1980 | 5.4 | 0 | 0 | 0.000 | 1988 | 6.7 | 3[1] | 285 | 0.030[1] |
| 1981 | 5.2 | 4 | 4 | 0.077 | 1989 | 6.6 | 11 | 278 | 0.166 |
| 1982 | 5.0 | 4 | 233 | 0.060 | 1990 | 6.9 | 6 | 39 | 0.087 |
| 1983 | 5.0 | 4 | 15 | 0.079 | 1991 | 6.8 | 4 | 62 | 0.059 |
| 1984 | 5.4 | 1 | 4 | 0.018 | 1992 | 7.1 | 4 | 33 | 0.057 |
| 1985 | 5.8 | 4 | 197 | 0.069 | 1993 | 7.2 | 1 | 1 | 0.014 |
| 1986 | 6.4 | 2 | 5 | 0.016 | 1994 | 7.5 | 4 | 239 | 0.053 |
| 1987 | 6.6 | 4[1] | 231 | 0.046[1] | 1995 | 8.1 | 2 | 166 | 0.025 |

(1) Sabotage-caused accidents are included in the number of fatal accidents, but not in the calculation of accident rates.

# Aircraft Operating Statistics, 1994

**Source:** Air Transport Association of America; figures are averages for most commonly used models

| | Number of seats | Speed airborne (mph) | Flight length (miles) | Fuel (gallons per hour) | Aircraft operating cost per hour |
|---|---|---|---|---|---|
| B747-400 | 396 | 538 | 4,919 | 3,420 | $6,686 |
| B747-100 | 395 | 521 | 3,252 | 3,626 | 6,235 |
| B747-200/300 | 342 | 535 | 4,147 | 3,752 | 7,435 |
| B777 | 291 | 512 | 2,527 | 1,995 | 3,923 |
| DC-10-40 | 288 | 506 | 1,979 | 2,644 | 4,056 |
| L-1011-100/200 | 285 | 490 | 1,317 | 2,356 | 3,861 |
| DC-10-10 | 283 | 503 | 1,629 | 2,226 | 4,690 |
| DC-10-30 | 277 | 523 | 2,883 | 2,663 | 4,861 |
| A300-600 | 267 | 468 | 1,139 | 1,709 | 3,932 |
| MD-11 | 261 | 526 | 3,822 | 2,303 | 4,962 |
| L-1011-500 | 222 | 524 | 3,275 | 2,504 | 4,028 |
| B767-300ER | 219 | 496 | 2,347 | 1,577 | 3,190 |
| B757-200 | 186 | 465 | 1,191 | 1,033 | 2,382 |
| B767-200ER | 180 | 487 | 2,136 | 1,425 | 2,845 |
| A310-300 | 172 | 498 | 2,388 | 1,506 | 3,479 |

# National Aviation Hall of Fame

The National Aviation Hall of Fame at Dayton, OH, is dedicated to honoring the outstanding pioneers of air and space.

Allen, William M.
Andrews, Frank M.
Armstrong, Neil A.
Arnold, Henry H. "Hap"
Atwood, John Leland

Balchen, Bernt
Baldwin, Thomas S.
Beachey, Lincoln
Beech, Olive A.
Beech, Walter H.
Bell, Alexander Graham
Bell, Lawrence D.
Bellanca, Giuseppe Mario
Bendix, Vincent T.
Boeing, William E.
Bong, Richard I.
Borman, Frank
Boyd, Albert
Bradley, Mark E.
Brown, George "Scratchley"
Byrd, Richard E.

Cessna, Clyde V.
Chamberlin, Clarence D.
Chanute, Octave
Chennault, Claire L.
Cochran (Odlum), Jacqueline
Collins, Michael
Combs, Harry B.
Conrad Jr., Charles
Crawford, Frederick C.
Crossfield, A. Scott
Cunningham, Alfred A.
Curtiss, Glenn H.

Davis Jr., Benjamin O.
DeSeversky, Alexander P.
Doolittle, James H.
Douglas, Donald W.
Draper, Charles S.

Eaker, Ira C.
Earhart (Putnam), Amelia
Eielson, C. Benjamin
Ellyson, Theodore G.
Ely, Eugene B.
Everest, Frank K.

Fairchild, Sherman M.
Fleet, Reuben H.
Fokker, Anthony H.G.
Ford, Henry
Foss, Joseph
Foulois, Benjamin D.
Frye, Jack

Gabreski, Francis S.
Gilruth, Robert R.
Gentile, Dominic "Don"
Glenn Jr., John H.
Goddard, George W.
Goddard, Robert H.
Godfrey, Arthur
Goldwater, Barry M.
Grissom, Virgil I.
Gross, Robert E.
Grumman, Leroy R.
Guggenheim, Harry F.

Haughton, Daniel J.
Hegenberger, Albert F.
Heinemann, Edward H.
Hoover, Robert A.
Hughes, Howard R.

Ingalls, David S.
James Jr., Daniel "Chappie"
Jeppesen, Elrey B.
Johnson, Clarence L.
Johnston, Alvin M. "Tex"
Jones, Thomas V.

Kenney, George C.
Kettering, Charles F.
Kindelberger, James H.
Knabenshue, A. Roy
Knight, William J.

Lahm, Frank P.
Langley, Samuel P.
Lear Sr., William P.
LeMay, Curtis E.
LeVier, Anthony W.
Lindbergh, Anne M.
Lindbergh, Charles A.
Link, Edwin A.
Lockheed, Allan H.
Loening, Grover
Luke Jr., Frank

Macready, Carl B.
Macready, John A.
Martin, Glenn L.
McCampbell, David
McDonnell, James S.
Mitscher, Marc A.
Meyer, John C.
Mitchell, William "Billy"
Montgomery, John J.
Moorer, Thomas H.
Moss, Sanford A.

Neumann, Gerhard
Nichols, Ruth R.
Norden, Carl L.
Northrop, John K.

Pangborn, Clyde Edward
Patterson, William A.
Piper Sr., William T.
Pitcairn, Harold Frederick
Post, Wiley H.

Read, Albert C.
Reeve, Robert C.

Rentschler, Frederick B.
Richardson, Holden C.
Rickenbacker, Edward V.
Rodgers, Calbraith P.
Rogers, Will
Rushworth, Robert A.

Rutan, Elbert "Burt" L.
Ryan, T. Claude

Schirra, Walter M.
Schriever, Bernard A.
Selfridge, Thomas E.
Shepard Jr., Alan B.
Sikorsky, Igor I.
Six, Robert F.
Slayton, Donald K. "Deke"
Smith, C.R.
Spaatz, Carl A.
Sperry Sr., Elmer A.
Sperry Sr., Lawrence B.
Stanley, Robert M.
Stapp, John P.
Stearman, Lloyd C.

Taylor, Charles E.
Thomas, Lowell
Tibbets Jr., Paul W.
Towers, John H.
Trippe, Juan T.
Turner, Roscoe
Twining, Nathan F.

Vandenberg, Hoyt
von Braun, Wernher
von Karman, Theodore
von Ohain, Hans P.
Vought, Chance M.

Wade, Leigh
Walden, Henry W.
Wells, Edward
Wilson, Thornton A.
Woolman, Collett Everman "C.E."
Wright, Orville
Wright, Wilbur

Yeager, Charles E.
Young, John W.

# Active Aviation Personnel, 1994-95

**Source:** Federal Aviation Administration, U.S. Dept. of Transportation; as of Dec. 31, 1995

| Category | 1994 | | 1995 | |
|---|---|---|---|---|
| | Total | Percentage women | Total | Percentage women |
| **Total pilots** | **654,088** | **6.0** | **639,184** | **6.0** |
| Student | 96,254 | 12.5 | 101,279 | 12.5 |
| Private | 284,236 | 6.0 | 261,399 | 5.9 |
| Commercial | 138,728 | 4.3 | 133,980 | 4.2 |
| Airline Transport | 117,434 | 2.5 | 123,877 | 2.5 |
| Other[1] | 17,436 | 5.6 | 18,649 | 5.9 |
| **Total nonpilots** | **571,358** | **2.3** | **651,341** | **2.3** |
| Mechanic | 411,071 | 1.3 | 466,527 | 1.2 |
| Ground Instructor | 77,789 | 6.2 | 96,165 | 6.3 |
| Flight Engineer | 59,467 | 2.4 | 60,267 | 6.3 |
| Other[2] | 23,031 | 5.0 | 28,382 | 2.5 |
| **Flight instructors** | **76,171** | **5.9** | **72,147** | **5.5** |

**Note:** Excludes military personnel. (1) Includes helicopter (only), glider (only), and recreational pilot certificates. (2) Includes flight navigators, parachute riggers, and dispatchers.

# Some Notable Aviation Firsts[1]

**1903** — On Dec. 17, near Kitty Hawk, NC, brothers Wilbur and Orville Wright made the first human-carrying, powered flight. Each brother made 2 flights; the longest, about 852 ft, lasted 59 sec.

**1907** — U.S. airplane manufacturing company formed by Glenn H. Curtiss.

**1908** — First airplane passenger, Lt. Frank P. Lahm, rode with Wilbur Wright in a brief (6 min, 24 sec) flight.

**1911** — The first transportation of mail by airplane to be officially approved by the U.S. Postal Service began on Sept. 23. It lasted one week. In 1918, limited scheduled air mail service began. By 1921, scheduled transcontinental airmail service began between New York City and San Francisco.

**1914** — The first scheduled passenger airline service began. It flew between St. Petersburg and Tampa, FL.

**1919** — The first airline food, a basket lunch, was served as part of a commercial airline service.

**1930** — Ellen Church became the first flight attendant.

**1939** — On Aug. 27, the German Heinkel He 178 made the first successful flight powered by a jet engine.

**1947** — Mach 1, the sound barrier, broken by Amer. Charles E. ("Chuck") Yeager in a Bell X-1 rocket-powered aircraft.

**1947** — Largest airplane ever flown, Howard Hughes's "Spruce Goose," flew 1 mi at an altitude of 80 ft.

**1953** — Jacqueline Cochran became the first woman to fly faster than sound.

**1960** — Convair B-58, the first supersonic bomber, is introduced.

**1968** — The supersonic speed of Mach 2 was accomplished for the first time, in a Tupolev Tu-144. The plane had an approximate maximum speed of 1,200 mph.

**1970** — The Tupolev Tu-144, during commercial transport, exceeds Mach 2. It reached about 1,335 mph at 53,475 ft.

**1976** — The Concorde began the first scheduled supersonic commercial service.

(1) Excludes notable around-the-world and international trips.

## Some Notable Around-the-World and Intercontinental Trips

| | From/To | Miles | Time | Date |
|---|---|---|---|---|
| Nellie Bly | New York/New York | | 72d 06h 11m | 1889 |
| George Francis Train | New York/New York | | 67d 12h 03m | 1890 |
| Charles Fitzmorris | Chicago/Chicago | | 60d 13h 29m | 1901 |
| J. W. Willis Sayre | Seattle/Seattle | | 54d 09h 42m | 1903 |
| J. Alcock-A.W. Brown [1] | Newfoundland/Ireland | 1,960 | 16h 12m | June 14-15, 1919 |
| Two U.S. Army airplanes | Seattle/Seattle | 26,103 | 35d 01h 11m | 1924 |
| Richard E. Byrd, Floyd Bennett [2] | Spitsbergen (Nor.)/N. Pole | 1,545 | 15h 30m | May 9, 1926 |
| Amundsen-Ellsworth-Nobile Polar Expedition (in a dirigible) | Spitsbergen (Nor.)/over N. Pole to Teller, Alaska | | 80h | May 11-14,1926 |
| E.S. Evans and L. Wells (*New York World*) | New York/New York | 18,410[3] | 28d 14h 36m 05s | June 16-July 14, 1926 |
| Charles Lindbergh [4] | New York/Paris | 3,610 | 33h 29m 30s | May 20-21, 1927 |
| Amelia Earhart, W. Stultz, L. Gordon | Newfoundland/Wales | | 20h 40m | June 17-18, 1928 |
| Graf Zeppelin | Friedrichshafen, Ger./Lakehurst, NJ | 6,630 | 4d 15h 46m | Oct. 11-15, 1928 |
| Graf Zeppelin | Friedrichshafen, Ger./Lakehurst,NJ | 21,700 | 20d 04h | Aug. 14-Sept. 4, 1929 |
| Wiley Post and Harold Gatty (Monoplane Winnie Mae) | New York/New York | 15,474 | 8d 15h 51m | July 1, 1931 |
| C. Pangborn-H. Herndon Jr. [5] | Misawa, Japan/Wenatchee, Wash. | 4,458 | 41h 34m | Oct. 3-5, 1931 |
| Amelia Earhart [6] | Newfoundland/Ireland | 2,026 | 14h 56m | May 20-21, 1932 |
| Wiley Post (Monoplane Winnie Mae)[7] | New York/New York | 15,596 | 115h 36m 30s | July 15-22, 1933 |
| Hindenburg Zeppelin | Lakehurst, NJ/Frankfort, Ger. | | 42h 53m | Aug. 9-11, 1936 |
| H. R. Ekins (Scripps-Howard Newspapers in race) (Zeppelin Hindenburg to Germany, airplanes from Frankfurt) | Lakehurst, NJ/Lakehurst, NJ | 25,654 | 18d 11h 14m 33s | Sept. 30-Oct. 19, 1936 |
| Howard Hughes and 4 assistants | New York/New York | 14,824 | 3d 19h 08m 10s | July 10-13, 1938 |
| Douglas Corrigan | New York/Dublin | | 28h 13m | July 17-18, 1938 |
| Mrs. Clara Adams (Pan American Clipper) | Port Washington, NY/ Newark, NJ | | 16d 19h 04m | June 28-July 15, 1939 |
| Globester, U.S. Air Transport Command | Washington, DC/Washington, DC | 23,279 | 149h 44m | Oct. 4, 1945 |
| Capt. William P. Odom (A-26 Reynolds Bombshell) | New York/New York | 20,000 | 78h 55m 12s | Apr. 12-16, 1947 |
| America, Pan American 4-engine Lockheed Constellation [8] | New York/New York | 22,219 | 101h 32m | June 17-30, 1947 |
| Col. Edward Eagan | New York/New York | 20,559 | 147h 15m | Dec. 13, 1948 |
| USAF B-50 Lucky Lady II (Capt. James Gallagher) [9] | Ft. Worth, TX/Ft. Worth, TX | 23,452 | 94h 01m | Feb. 26-Mar. 2, 1949 |
| Col. D. Schilling, USAF [10] | England/Limestone, ME. | 3,300 | 10h 01m | Sept. 22, 1950 |
| C.F. Blair Jr. | Norway/Alaska | 3,300 | 10h 29m | May 29, 1951 |
| Two U.S. S-55 | Massachusetts/Scotland | 3,410 | 42h 30m | July 15-31, 1952 |
| Canberra Bomber [11] | N. Ireland/Newfoundland | 2073 | 04h 34m | Aug. 26, 1952 |
| | Newfoundland/N. Ireland | 2073 | 03h 25m | Aug. 26, 1952 |
| Three USAF B-52 Stratofortresses [12] | Merced, CA/CA | 24,325 | 45h 19m | Jan. 15-18, 1957 |
| Max Conrad | Chicago/Rome | 5,000 | 34h 03m | Mar. 5-6, 1959 |
| USSR TU-114 [13] | Moscow/New York | 5,092 | 11h 06m | June 28, 1959 |
| Boeing 707-320 | New York/Moscow | c.5,090 | 08h 54m | July 23, 1959 |
| Peter Gluckmann (solo) | San Francisco/San Francisco | 22,800 | 29d | Aug. 22-Sept. 20, 1959 |
| Sue Snyder | Chicago/Chicago | 21,219 | 62h 59m | June 22-24, 1960 |
| Max Conrad (solo) | Miami/Miami | 25,946 | 8d 18h 35m 57s | Feb. 28-Mar. 8, 1961 |
| Sam Miller & Louis Fodor | New York/New York | | 46h 28m | Aug. 3-4, 1963 |
| Robert & Joan Wallick | Manila/Manila | 23,129 | 5d 06h 17m 10s | June 2-7, 1966 |
| Arthur Godfrey, Richard Merrill Fred Austin, Karl Keller | New York/New York | 23,333 | 86h 9m 01s | June 4-7, 1966 |
| Trevor K. Brougham | Darwin, Australia/Darwin | 24,800 | 5d 05h 57m | Aug. 5-10, 1972 |
| Walter H. Mullikin, Albert Frink, Lyman Watt, Frank Cassaniti, Edward Shields | New York/New York | 23,137 | 1d 22h 50s | May 1-3, 1976 |
| Arnold Palmer | Denver/Denver | 22,985 | 57h 7m 12s | May 17-19, 1976 |
| Boeing 747[14] | San Francisco/San Francisco | 26,382 | 57h 25m 42s | Oct. 28-31, 1977 |
| Richard Rutan & Jeana Yeager[15] | Edwards AFB, CA | 24,986 | 09d 03m 44s | Dec. 14-23, 1986 |
| Concorde | New York/New York | 1,114 mph | 31h 27m 49s | Aug. 15-16, 1995 |
| Col. Douglas L. Raaberg and crew, B1 bomber[16] | Dyess AFB, Abilene, TX/Dyess AFB | 6,250 | 36h 13m 36s | June 3, 1995 |

(1) Nonstop transatlantic flight. (2) Claim of reaching N. Pole in dispute; if claim is untrue, then Amundsen-Ellsworth-Nobile were the first to fly over N. Pole. (3) Includes mileage by train and auto, 4,110; by plane, 6,300; by steamship, 8,000. (4) Solo trans-Atlantic flight in the Ryan monoplane "Spirit of St. Louis." (5) Nonstop trans-Pacific flight. (6) First woman's transoceanic solo flight. (7) First to fly solo around N circumference of the world, also first to fly twice around the world. (8) Inception of regular commercial global air service. (9) First nonstop round-the-world flight, refueled 4 times in flight. (10) Nonstop jet trans-Atlantic flight. (11) Trans-Atlantic round trip on same day. (12) First nonstop global flight by jet planes; refueled in flight by KC-97 aerial tankers; average speed approx. 525 mph. (13) Nonstop between Moscow and New York. (14) Speed record around the world over both Earth's poles. (15) Circled Earth nonstop without refueling. (16) Refueled in flight 6 times. Tested B-1B bomber by bombing 3 pre-arranged target sites on 3 continents.

# AWARDS — MEDALS — PRIZES

## The Alfred B. Nobel Prize Winners

Alfred B. Nobel (1833-96), inventor of dynamite, bequeathed $9,000,000, the interest to be distributed yearly to those who had most benefited humankind in physics, chemistry, medicine-physiology, literature, and promotion of peace. These prizes were first awarded in 1901. The first Nobel Memorial Prize in Economic Science was awarded in 1969, funded by the central bank of Sweden. If the year is omitted, no award was given. In 1995, each prize was worth about $1 mil. For 1996 Nobel Winners, see page 39.

### Physics

1995 Martin Perl, Frederick Reines, both U.S.
1994 Bertram N. Brockhouse, Can.; Clifford G. Shull, U.S.
1993 Joseph H. Taylor, Russell A. Hulse, both U.S.
1992 Georges Charpak, Pol.-Fr.
1991 Pierre-Giles de Gennes, Fr.
1990 Richard E. Taylor, Can.; Jerome I. Friedman, Henry W. Kendall, both U.S.
1989 Norman F. Ramsey, U.S.; Hans G. Dehmelt, Ger.-U.S.; Wolfgang Paul, Ger.
1988 Leon M. Lederman, Melvin Schwartz, Jack Steinberger, all U.S.
1987 K. Alex Müller, Swiss; J. Georg Bednorz, W. Ger.
1986 Ernest Ruska, Ger.; Gerd Binnig, W. Ger.; Heinrich Rohrer, Swiss
1985 Klaus von Klitzing, W. Ger.
1984 Carlo Rubbia, It.; Simon van der Meer, Dutch
1983 Subrahmanyan Chandrasekhar, William A. Fowler, both U.S.
1982 Kenneth G. Wilson, U.S.
1981 Nicolaas Bloembergen, Arthur Schaalow, both U.S.; Kai M. Siegbahn, Swed.
1980 James W. Cronin, Val L. Fitch, both U.S.
1979 Steven Weinberg, Sheldon L. Glashow, both U.S.; Abdus Salam, Pakistani
1978 Pyotr Kapitsa, USSR; Arno Penzias, Robert Wilson, both U.S.
1977 John H. Van Vleck, Philip W. Anderson, both U.S.; Nevill F. Mott, Br.
1976 Burton Richter, Samuel C.C. Ting, both U.S.
1975 James Rainwater, U.S.; Ben Mottelson, U.S.-Dan.; Aage Bohr, Dan.
1974 Martin Ryle, Antony Hewish, both Br.
1973 Ivar Giaever, U.S.; Leo Esaki, Jpn.; Brian D. Josephson, Br.
1972 John Bardeen, Leon N. Cooper, John R. Schrieffer, all U.S.
1971 Dennis Gabor, Br.
1970 Louis Neel, Fr.; Hannes Alfven, Swed.
1969 Murray Gell-Mann, U.S.
1968 Luis W. Alvarez, U.S.
1967 Hans A. Bethe, U.S.
1966 Alfred Kastler, Fr.
1965 Richard P. Feynman, Julian S. Schwinger, both U.S.; Shinichiro Tomonaga, Jpn.
1964 Nikolai G. Basov, Aleksander M. Prochorov, both USSR; Charles H. Townes, U.S.
1963 Maria Goeppert-Mayer, Eugene P. Wigner, both U.S.; J. Hans D. Jensen, Ger.
1962 Lev. D. Landau, USSR
1961 Robert Hofstadter, U.S.; Rudolf L. Mossbauer, Ger.
1960 Donald A. Glaser, U.S.
1959 Owen Chamberlain, Emilio G. Segre, both U.S.
1958 Pavel Cherenkov, Ilya Frank, Igor Y. Tamm, all USSR
1957 Tsung-dao Lee, Chen Ning Yang, both U.S.
1956 John Bardeen, Walter H. Brattain, William Shockley, all U.S.
1955 Polykarp Kusch, Willis E. Lamb, both U.S.
1954 Max Born, Br.; Walter Bothe, Ger.
1953 Frits Zernike, Dutch
1952 Felix Bloch, Edward M. Purcell, both U.S.
1951 Sir John D. Cockroft, Br.; Ernest T. S. Walton, Ir.
1950 Cecil F. Powell, Br.
1949 Hideki Yukawa, Jpn.
1948 Patrick M. S. Blackett, Br.
1947 Sir Edward V. Appleton, Br.
1946 Percy Williams Bridgman, U.S.
1945 Wolfgang Pauli, U.S.
1944 Isidor Isaac Rabi, U.S.
1943 Otto Stern, U.S.
1939 Ernest O. Lawrence, U.S.
1938 Enrico Fermi, It.-U.S.
1937 Clinton J. Davisson, U.S.; Sir George P. Thomson, Br.
1936 Carl D. Anderson, U.S.; Victor F. Hess, Aus.
1935 Sir James Chadwick, Br.
1933 Paul A. M. Dirac, Br.; Erwin Schrodinger, Aus.
1932 Werner Heisenberg, Ger.
1930 Sir Chandrasekhara V. Raman, Indian
1929 Prince Louis-Victor de Broglie, Fr.
1928 Owen W. Richardson, Br.
1927 Arthur H. Compton, U.S.; Charles T. R. Wilson, Br.
1926 Jean B. Perrin, Fr.
1925 James Franck, Gustav Hertz, both Ger.
1924 Karl M. G. Siegbahn, Swed.
1923 Robert A. Millikan, U.S.
1922 Niels Bohr, Dan.
1921 Albert Einstein, Ger.-U.S.
1920 Charles E. Guillaume, Fr.
1919 Johannes Stark, Ger.
1918 Max K. E. L. Planck, Ger.
1917 Charles G. Barkla, Br.
1915 Sir William H. Bragg, Sir William L. Bragg, both Br.
1914 Max von Laue, Ger.
1913 Heike Kamerlingh-Onnes, Dutch
1912 Nils G. Dalen, Swed.
1911 Wilhelm Wien, Ger.
1910 Johannes D. van der Waals, Dutch
1909 Carl F. Braun, Ger.; Guglielmo Marconi, It.
1908 Gabriel Lippmann, Fr.
1907 Albert A. Michelson, U.S.
1906 Sir Joseph J. Thomson, Br.
1905 Philipp E. A. von Lenard, Ger.
1904 John W. Strutt, Lord Rayleigh, Br.
1903 Antoine Henri Becquerel, Pierre Curie, both Fr.; Marie Curie, Pol.-Fr.
1902 Hendrik A. Lorentz, Pieter Zeeman, both Dutch
1901 Wilhelm C. Roentgen, Ger.

### Chemistry

1995 Paul Crutzen, Dutch; Mario Molina, Mex.-U.S.; Sherwood Rowland, U.S.
1994 George A. Olah, U.S.
1993 Kary B. Mullis, U.S.; Michael Smith, Br.-Can.
1992 Rudolph A. Marcus, Can.-U.S.
1991 Richard R. Ernst, Swiss
1990 Elias James Corey, U.S.
1989 Thomas R. Cech, Sidney Altman, both U.S.
1988 Johann Deisenhofer, Robert Huber, Hartmut Michel, all W. Ger.
1987 Donald J. Cram, Charles J. Pedersen, both U.S.; Jean-Marie Lehn, Fr.
1986 Dudley Herschbach, Yuan T. Lee, both U.S.; John C. Polanyi, Can.
1985 Herbert A. Hauptman, Jerome Karle, both U.S.
1984 Bruce Merrifield, U.S.
1983 Henry Taube, Can.
1982 Aaron Klug, S. Afr.
1981 Kenichi Fukui, Jpn.; Roald Hoffmann, U.S.
1980 Paul Berg, Walter Gilbert, both U.S.; Frederick Sanger, Br.
1979 Herbert C. Brown, U.S.; George Wittig, Ger.
1978 Peter Mitchell, Br.
1977 Ilya Prigogine, Belg.
1976 William N. Lipscomb, U.S.
1975 John Cornforth, Austral.-Br.; Vladimir Prelog, Yugo.-Swiss
1974 Paul J. Flory, U.S.
1973 Ernst Otto Fischer, W. Ger.; Geoffrey Wilkinson, Br.
1972 Christian B. Anfinsen, Stanford Moore, William H. Stein, all U.S.
1971 Gerhard Herzberg, Canadian
1970 Luis F. Leloir, Arg.
1969 Derek H. R. Barton, Br.; Odd Hassel, Nor.
1968 Lars Onsager, U.S.
1967 Manfred Eigen, Ger.; Ronald G. W. Norrish, George Porter, both Br.
1966 Robert S. Mulliken, U.S.
1965 Robert B. Woodward, U.S.
1964 Dorothy C. Hodgkin, Br.
1963 Giulio Natta, It.; Karl Ziegler, Ger.
1962 John C. Kendrew, Max F. Perutz, both Br.
1961 Melvin Calvin, U.S.
1960 Willard F. Libby, U.S.
1959 Jaroslav Heyrovsky, Czech.
1958 Frederick Sanger, Br.
1957 Sir Alexander R. Todd, Br.
1956 Sir Cyril N. Hinshelwood, Br.; Nikolai N. Semenov, USSR
1955 Vincent du Vigneaud, U.S.
1954 Linus C. Pauling, U.S.
1953 Hermann Staudinger, Ger.
1952 Archer J. P. Martin, Richard L. M. Synge, both Br.
1951 Edwin M. McMillan, Glenn T. Seaborg, both U.S.
1950 Kurt Alder, Otto P. H. Diels, both Ger.
1949 William F. Giauque, U.S.
1948 Arne W. K. Tiselius, Swed.
1947 Sir Robert Robinson, Br.
1946 James B. Sumner, John H. Northrop, Wendell M. Stanley, all U.S.
1945 Artturi I. Virtanen, Fin.
1944 Otto Hahn, Ger.
1943 Georg de Hevesy, Hung.
1939 Adolf F. J. Butenandt, Ger.; Leopold Ruzicka, Swiss
1938 Richard Kuhn, Ger.
1937 Walter N. Haworth, Br.; Paul Karrer, Swiss
1936 Peter J. W. Debye, Dutch
1935 Frederic & Irene Joliot-Curie, both Fr.
1934 Harold C. Urey, U.S.
1932 Irving Langmuir, U.S.
1931 Friedrich Bergius, Karl Bosch, both Ger.
1930 Hans Fischer, Ger.
1929 Sir Arthur Harden, Br.; Hans von Euler-Chelpin, Swed.
1928 Adolf O. R. Windaus, Ger.
1927 Heinrich O. Wieland, Ger.
1926 Theodor Svedberg, Swed.
1925 Richard A. Zsigmondy, Ger.
1923 Fritz Pregl, Aus.
1922 Francis W. Aston, Br.
1921 Frederick Soddy, Br.
1920 Walther H. Nernst, Ger.
1918 Fritz Haber, Ger.

*(continued)*

## Chemistry *(continued)*

1915 Richard M. Willstatter, Ger.
1914 Theodore W. Richards, U.S.
1913 Alfred Werner, Swiss
1912 Victor Grignard, Paul Sabatier, both Fr.
1911 Marie Curie, Pol.-Fr.
1910 Otto Wallach, Ger.
1909 Wilhelm Ostwald, Ger.
1908 Ernest Rutherford, Br.
1907 Eduard Buchner, Ger.
1906 Henri Moissan, Fr.
1905 Adolf von Baeyer, Ger.
1904 Sir William Ramsay, Br.
1903 Svante A. Arrhenius, Swed.
1902 Emil Fischer, Ger.
1901 Jacobus H. van't Hoff, Dutch

## Physiology or Medicine

1995 Edward B. Lewis, Eric F. Wieschaus, both U.S.; Christiane Nuesslein-Volhard, Ger.
1994 Alfred G. Gilman, Martin Rodbell, both U.S.
1993 Phillip A. Sharp, U.S.; Richard J. Roberts, Br.
1992 Edmond H. Fisher, Edwin G. Krebs, both U.S.
1991 Edwin Neher, Bert Sakmann, both Ger.
1990 Joseph E. Murray, E. Donnall Thomas, both U.S.
1989 J. Michael Bishop, Harold E. Varmus, both U.S.
1988 Gertrude B. Elion, George H. Hitchings, both U.S; Sir James Black, Br.
1987 Susumu Tonegawa, Jpn.
1986 Rita Levi-Montalcini, It.-U.S., Stanley Cohen, U.S.
1985 Michael S. Brown, Joseph L. Goldstein, both U.S.
1984 Cesar Milstein, Br.-Arg.; Georges J. F. Koehler, Ger.; Niels K. Jerne, Br.-Dan.
1983 Barbara McClintock, U.S.
1982 Sune Bergstrom, Bengt Samuelsson, both Swed.; John R. Vane, Br.
1981 Roger W. Sperry, David H. Hubel, Tosten N. Wiesel, all U.S.
1980 Baruj Benacerraf, George Snell, both U.S.; Jean Dausset, Fr.
1979 Allan M. Cormack, U.S.; Godfrey N. Hounsfield, Br.
1978 Daniel Nathans, Hamilton O. Smith, both U.S.; Werner Arber, Swiss
1977 Rosalyn S. Yalow, Roger C.L. Guillemin, Andrew V. Schally, all U.S.
1976 Baruch S. Blumberg, Daniel Carleton Gajdusek, both U.S.
1975 David Baltimore, Howard Temin, both U.S.; Renato Dulbecco, It.-U.S.
1974 Albert Claude, Lux.-U.S.; George Emil Palade, Rom.-U.S.; Christian Rene de Duve, Belg.
1973 Karl von Frisch, Ger.; Konrad Lorenz, Ger.-Aus.; Nikolaas Tinbergen, Br.
1972 Gerald M. Edelman, U.S.; Rodney R. Porter, Br.
1971 Earl W. Sutherland Jr., U.S.
1970 Julius Axelrod, U.S.; Sir Bernard Katz, Br.; Ulf von Euler, Swed.
1969 Max Delbrück, Alfred D. Hershey, Salvador Luria, all U.S.
1968 Robert W. Holley, H. Gobind Khorana, Marshall W. Nirenberg, all U.S.
1967 Ragnar Granit, Swed.; Haldan Keffer Hartline, George Wald, both U.S.
1966 Charles B. Huggins, Francis Peyton Rous, both U.S.
1965 François Jacob, Andre Lwoff, Jacques Monod, all Fr.
1964 Konrad E. Bloch, U.S.; Feodor Lynen, Ger.
1963 Sir John C. Eccles, Austral.; Alan L. Hodgkin, Andrew F. Huxley, both Br.
1962 Francis H. C. Crick, Maurice H. F. Wilkins, both Br.; James D. Watson, U.S.
1961 Georg von Bekesy, U.S.
1960 Sir F. MacFarlane Bumet, Austral.; Peter B. Medawar, Br.
1959 Arthur Kornberg, Severo Ochoa, both U.S.
1958 George W. Beadle, Edward L. Tatum, Joshua Lederberg, all U.S.
1957 Daniel Bovet, It.
1956 Andre F. Cournand, Dickinson W. Richards Jr., both U.S.; Werner Forssmann, Ger.
1955 Alex H. T. Theorell, Swed.
1954 John F. Enders, Frederick C. Robbins, Thomas H. Weller, all U.S.
1953 Hans A. Krebs, Br.; Fritz A. Lipmann, U.S.
1952 Selman A. Waksman, U.S.
1951 Max Theiler, U.S.
1950 Philip S. Hench, Edward C. Kendall, both U.S.; Tadeus Reichstein, Swiss
1949 Walter R. Hess, Swiss; Antonio Moniz, Port.
1948 Paul H. Müller, Swiss
1947 Carl F. Cori, Gerty T. Cori, both U.S.; Bernardo A. Houssay, Arg.
1946 Hermann J. Muller, U.S.
1945 Ernst B. Chain, Sir Alexander Fleming, Sir Howard W. Florey, all Br.
1944 Joseph Erlanger, Herbert S. Gasser, both U.S.
1943 Henrik C. P. Dam, Dan.; Edward A. Doisy, U.S.
1939 Gerhard Domagk, Ger.
1938 Corneille J. F. Heymans, Belg.
1937 Albert Szent-Gyorgyi, Hung.-U.S.
1936 Sir Henry H. Dale, Br.; Otto Loewi, U
1935 Hans Spemann, Ger.
1934 George R. Minot, William P. Murphy, G. H. Whipple, all U.S.
1933 Thomas H. Morgan, U.S.
1932 Edgar D. Adrian, Sir Charles S. Sherrington, both Br.
1931 Otto H. Warburg, Ger.
1930 Karl Landsteiner, U.S.
1929 Christiaan Eijkman, Dutch; Sir Frederick G. Hopkins, Br.
1928 Charles J. H. Nicolle, Fr.
1927 Julius Wagner-Jauregg, Aus.
1926 Johannes A. G. Fibiger, Dan.
1924 Willem Einthoven, Dutch
1923 Frederick G. Banting, Can.; John J. R. Macleod, Scot.
1922 Archibald V. Hill, Br.; Otto F. Meyerhof, Ger.
1920 Schack A. S. Krogh, Dan.
1919 Jules Bordet, Belg.
1914 Robert Barany, Aus.
1913 Charles R. Richet, Fr.
1912 Alexis Carrel, Fr.
1911 Allvar Gullstrand, Swed.
1910 Albrecht Kossel, Ger.
1909 Emil T. Kocher, Swiss
1908 Paul Ehrlich, Ger.; Elie Metchnikoff, Fr.
1907 Charles L. A. Laveran, Fr.
1906 Camillo Golgi, It.; Santiago Ramon y Cajal, Span.
1905 Robert Koch, Ger.
1904 Ivan P. Pavlov, Russ.
1903 Niels R. Finsen, Dan.
1902 Sir Ronald Ross, Br.
1901 Emil A. von Behring, Ger.

## Literature

1995 Seamus Heaney, Ir.
1994 Kenzaburo Oe, Jpn.
1993 Toni Morrison, U.S.
1992 Derek Walcott, W. Ind.
1991 Nadine Gordimer, S. Afr.
1990 Octavio Paz, Mex.
1989 Camilo José Cela, Span.
1988 Naguib Mahfouz, Egy.
1987 Joseph Brodsky, USSR-U.S.
1986 Wole Soyinka, Nig.
1985 Claude Simon, Fr.
1984 Jaroslav Siefert, Czech.
1983 William Golding, Br.
1982 Gabriel Garcia Marquez, Colombian-Mex.
1981 Elias Canetti, Bulg.-Br.
1980 Czeslaw Milosz, Pol.-U.S.
1979 Odysseus Elytis, Gk.
1978 Isaac Bashevis Singer, U.S.
1977 Vicente Aleixandre, Span.
1976 Saul Bellow, U.S.
1975 Eugenio Montale, It.
1974 Eyvind Johnson, Harry Edmund Martinson, both Swed.
1973 Patrick White, Austral.
1972 Heinrich Böll, W. Ger.
1971 Pablo Neruda, Chil.
1970 Aleksandr I. Solzhenitsyn, USSR
1969 Samuel Beckett, Ir.
1968 Yasunari Kawabata, Jpn.
1967 Miguel Angel Asturias, Guate.
1966 Samuel Joseph Agnon, Isr.; Nelly Sachs, Swed.
1965 Mikhail Sholokhov, USSR
1964 Jean Paul Sartre, Fr. (Prize declined)
1963 Giorgos Seferis, Gk.
1962 John Steinbeck, U.S.
1961 Ivo Andric, Yugo.
1960 Saint-John Perse, Fr.
1959 Salvatore Quasimodo, It.
1958 Boris L. Pasternak, USSR (Prize declined)
1957 Albert Camus, Fr.
1956 Juan Ramon Jimenez, Span.
1955 Halldor K. Laxness, Ice.
1954 Ernest Hemingway, U.S.
1953 Sir Winston Churchill, Br.
1952 Francois Mauriac, Fr.
1951 Par F. Lagerkvist, Swed.
1950 Bertrand Russell, Br.
1949 William Faulkner, U.S.
1948 T.S. Eliot, Br.
1947 Andre Gide, Fr.
1946 Hermann Hesse, Ger.-Swiss
1945 Gabriela Mistral, Chil.
1944 Johannes V. Jensen, Dan.
1939 Frans E. Sillanpaa, Fin.
1938 Pearl S. Buck, U.S.
1937 Roger Martin du Gard, Fr.
1936 Eugene O'Neill, U.S.
1934 Luigi Pirandello, It.
1933 Ivan A. Bunin, USSR
1932 John Galsworthy, Br.
1931 Erik A. Karlfeldt, Swed.
1930 Sinclair Lewis, U.S.
1929 Thomas Mann, Ger.
1928 Sigrid Undset, Nor.
1927 Henri Bergson, Fr.
1926 Grazia Deledda, It.
1925 George Bernard Shaw, Ir.-Br.
1924 Wladyslaw S. Reymont, Pol.
1923 William Butler Yeats, Ir.
1922 Jacinto Benavente, Span.
1921 Anatole France, Fr.
1920 Knut Hamsun, Nor.
1919 Carl F. G. Spitteler, Swiss
1917 Karl A. Gjellerup, Henrik Pontoppidan, both Dan.
1916 Verner von Heidenstam, Swed.

1915 Romain Rolland, Fr.
1913 Rabindranath Tagore, Ind.
1912 Gerhart Hauptmann, Ger.
1911 Maurice Maeterlinck, Belg.
1910 Paul J. L. Heyse, Ger.
1909 Selma Lagerlof, Swed.
1908 Rudolf C. Eucken, Ger.
1907 Rudyard Kipling, Br.
1906 Giosue Carducci, It.
1905 Henryk Sienkiewicz, Pol.
1904 Frederic Mistral, Fr.; Jose Echegaray, Span.
1903 Bjornsterne Bjornson, Nor.
1902 Theodor Mommsen, Ger.
1901 Rene F. A. Sully Prudhomme, Fr.

## Peace

1995 Joseph Rotblat, Pol.-Br.; Pugwash Conference
1994 Yasir Arafat, Pal.; Shimon Peres, Yitzhak Rabin, both Isr.
1993 Frederik W. de Klerk, Nelson Mandela, both S. Afr.
1992 Rigoberta Menchú, Guat.
1991 Aung San Suu Kyi, Myanmarese
1990 Mikhail S. Gorbachev, USSR
1989 Dalai Lama, Tib.
1988 United Nations Peacekeeping Forces
1987 Oscar Arias Sanchez, Costa Rican
1986 Elie Wiesel, Rom.-U.S.
1985 Intl. Physicians for the Prevention of Nuclear War, U.S.
1984 Bishop Desmond Tutu, S. Afr.
1983 Lech Walesa, Pol.
1982 Alva Myrdal, Swed.; Alfonso Garcia Robles, Mex.
1981 Office of UN High Commissioner for Refugees
1980 Adolfo Perez Esquivel, Arg.
1979 Mother Teresa of Calcutta, Alb.-Ind.
1978 Anwar Sadat, Egy.; Menachem Begin, Isr.
1977 Amnesty International
1976 Mairead Corrigan, Betty Williams, both N. Ir.
1975 Andrei Sakharov, USSR
1974 Eisaku Sato, Jpn.; Sean MacBride, Ir.
1973 Henry Kissinger, U.S.; Le Duc Tho, N. Viet. (Tho declined)
1971 Willy Brandt, W. Ger.
1970 Norman E. Borlaug, U.S.
1969 Intl. Labor Organization
1968 Rene Cassin, Fr.
1965 UN Children's Fund (UNICEF)
1964 Martin Luther King Jr., U.S.
1963 International Red Cross, League of Red Cross Societies
1962 Linus C. Pauling, U.S.
1961 Dag Hammarskjold, Swed.
1960 Albert J. Luthuli, S. Afr.
1959 Philip J. Noel-Baker, Br.
1958 Georges Pire, Belg.
1957 Lester B. Pearson, Can.
1954 Office of the UN High Commissioner for Refugees
1953 George C. Marshall, U.S.
1952 Albert Schweitzer, Fr.
1951 Leon Jouhaux, Fr.
1950 Ralph J. Bunche, U.S.
1949 Lord John Boyd Orr of Brechin Mearns, Br.
1947 Friends Service Council, Br.; American Friends Service Committee, U.S.
1946 Emily G. Balch, John R. Mott, both U.S.
1945 Cordell Hull, U.S.
1944 International Red Cross
1938 Nansen International Office for Refugees
1937 Viscount Cecil of Chelwood, Br.
1936 Carlos de Saavedra Lamas, Arg.
1935 Carl von Ossietzky, Ger.
1934 Arthur Henderson, Br.
1933 Sir Norman Angell, Br.
1931 Jane Addams, Nicholas Murray Butler, both U.S.
1930 Nathan Soderblom, Swed.
1929 Frank B. Kellogg, U.S.
1927 Ferdinand E. Buisson, Fr.; Ludwig Quidde, Ger.
1926 Aristide Briand, Fr.; Gustav Stresemann, Ger.
1925 Sir J. Austen Chamberlain, Br.; Charles G. Dawes, U.S.
1922 Fridtjof Nansen, Nor.
1921 Karl H. Branting, Swed.; Christian L. Lange, Nor.
1920 Leon V.A. Bourgeois, Fr.
1919 Woodrow Wilson, U.S.
1917 International Red Cross
1913 Henri La Fontaine, Belg.
1912 Elihu Root, U.S.
1911 Tobias M.C. Asser, Dutch; Alfred H. Fried, Aus.
1910 Permanent Intl. Peace Bureau
1909 Auguste M. F. Beernaert, Belg.; Paul H. B. B. d'Estournelles de Constant, Fr.
1908 Klas P. Arnoldson, Swed.; Fredrik Bajer, Dan.
1907 Ernesto T. Moneta, It.; Louis Renault, Fr.
1906 Theodore Roosevelt, U.S.
1905 Baroness Bertha von Suttner, Aus.
1904 Institute of International Law
1903 Sir William R. Cremer, Br.
1902 Elie Ducommun, Charles A. Gobat, both Swiss
1901 Jean H. Dunant, Swiss; Frederic Passy, Fr.

## Nobel Memorial Prize in Economic Science

1995 Robert E. Lucas Jr., U.S.
1994 John C. Harsanyi, John F. Nash, both U.S.
1993 Robert W. Fogel, Douglass C. North, both U.S.
1992 Gary S. Becker, U.S.
1991 Ronald H. Coase, Br.-U.S.
1990 Harry M. Markowitz, William F. Sharpe, Merton H. Miller, all U.S.
1989 Trygve Haavelmo, Nor.
1988 Maurice Allais, Fr.
1987 Robert M. Solow, U.S.
1986 James M. Buchanan, U.S.
1985 Franco Modigliani, It.-U.S.
1984 Richard Stone, Br.
1983 Gerard Debreu, Fr.-U.S.
1982 George J. Stigler, U.S.
1981 James Tobin, U.S.
1980 Lawrence R. Klein, U.S.
1979 Theodore W. Schultz, U.S.; Sir Arthur Lewis, Br.
1978 Herbert A. Simon, U.S.
1977 Bertil Ohlin, Swedish; James E. Meade, Br.
1976 Milton Friedman, U.S.
1975 Tjalling Koopmans, Dutch-U.S.; Leonid Kantorovich, USSR
1974 Gunnar Myrdal, Swed.; Friedrich A. von Hayek, Aus.
1973 Wassily Leontief, U.S.
1972 Kenneth J. Arrow, U.S.; John R. Hicks, Br.
1971 Simon Kuznets, U.S.
1970 Paul A. Samuelson, U.S.
1969 Ragnar Frisch, Norwegian; Jan Tinbergen, Dutch

# Pulitzer Prizes in Journalism, Letters, and Music

The Pulitzer Prizes were endowed by Joseph Pulitzer (1847-1911), publisher of the *New York World*, in a bequest to Columbia University and are awarded annually by the president of the university on recommendation of the Pulitzer Prize Board for work done during the preceding year. The administrator is Seymour Topping of Columbia University. All prizes are now $3,000 (originally $500) in each category, except Meritorious Public Service, for which a gold medal is given. If a year is omitted, no award was given that year.

## Journalism

### Meritorious Public Service

For distinguished and meritorious public service by a United States newspaper.

**1918**—New York Times. Also special award to Minna Lewinson and Henry Beetle Hough
**1919**—Milwaukee Journal
**1921**—Boston Post
**1922**—New York World
**1923**—Memphis Commercial Appeal
**1924**—New York World
**1926**—Enquirer-Sun, Columbus, GA
**1927**—Canton (OH) Daily News
**1928**—Indianapolis Times
**1929**—New York Evening World
**1931**—Atlanta (GA) Constitution
**1932**—Indianapolis (IN) News
**1933**—New York World-Telegram
**1934**—Medford (OR) Mail-Tribune
**1935**—Sacramento (CA) Bee
**1936**—Cedar Rapids (IA) Gazette
**1937**—St.Louis Post-Dispatch
**1938**—Bismarck (ND) Tribune
**1939**—Miami (FL) Daily News
**1940**—Waterbury (CT) Republican and American
**1941**—St.Louis Post-Dispatch
**1942**—Los Angeles Times
**1943**—Omaha World Herald
**1944**—New York Times
**1945**—Detroit Free Press
**1946**—Scranton (PA) Times.
**1947**—Baltimore Sun
**1948**—St. Louis Post-Dispatch
**1949**—Nebraska State Journal
**1950**—Chicago Daily News; St. Louis Post-Dispatch
**1951**—Miami (FL) Herald and Brooklyn Eagle
**1952**—St. Louis Post-Dispatch
**1953**—Whiteville (NC) News Reporter; Tabor City (NC) Tribune

*(continued)*

### Meritorious Public Service *(continued)*

**1954**—Newsday (Long Island, NY)
**1955**—Columbus (GA) Ledger and Sunday Ledger-Enquirer
**1956**—Watsonville (CA) Register-Pajaronian
**1957**—Chicago Daily News
**1958**—Arkansas Gazette, Little Rock
**1959**—Utica (NY) Observer-Dispatch and Utica Daily Press
**1960**—Los Angeles Times
**1961**—Amarillo (TX) Globe-Times
**1962**—Panama City (FL) News-Herald
**1963**—Chicago Daily News
**1964**—St.Petersburg (FL) Times
**1965**—Hutchinson (KS) News
**1966**—Boston Globe
**1967**—Louisville Courier-Journal; Milwaukee Journal
**1968**—Riverside (CA) Press-Enterprise
**1969**—Los Angeles Times
**1970**—Newsday (Long Island, NY)
**1971**—Winston Salem (NC) Journal & Sentinel
**1972**—New York Times
**1973**—Washington Post
**1974**—Newsday (Long Island, NY)
**1975**—Boston Globe
**1976**—Anchorage Daily News
**1977**—Lufkin (TX) News
**1978**—Philadelphia Inquirer
**1979**—Point Reyes (CA) Light
**1980**—Gannett News Service
**1981**—Charlotte (NC) Observer
**1982**—Detroit News
**1983**—Jackson (MS) Clarion-Ledger
**1984**—Los Angeles Times
**1985**—Ft. Worth (TX) Star-Telegram
**1986**—Denver Post
**1987**—Pittsburgh Press
**1988**—Charlotte Observer
**1989**—Anchorage Daily News
**1990**—Philadelphia Inquirer, Gilbert M. Gaul; Washington (NC) Daily News
**1991**—Des Moines Register, Jane Schorer
**1992**—Sacramento Bee, Tom Knudson
**1993**—Miami Herald
**1994**—Akron Beacon Journal
**1995**—The Virgin Islands Daily News, St. Thomas
**1996**—The News & Observer, Raleigh (NC)

### Reporting

This category originally embraced all fields—local, national, and international. Later, separate categories were created for national and international reporting.

**1917**—Herbert Bayard Swope, New York World
**1918**—Harold A. Littledale, New York Evening Post
**1920**—John J. Leary Jr., New York World
**1921**—Louis Seibold, New York World
**1922**—Kirke L. Simpson, Associated Press (AP)
**1923**—Alva Johnston, New York Times
**1924**—Magner White, San Diego Sun
**1925**—James W. Mulroy and Alvin H. Goldstein, Chicago Daily News
**1926**—William Burke Miller, Louisville Courier-Journal
**1927**—John T. Rogers, St. Louis Post-Dispatch
**1929**—Paul Y. Anderson, St. Louis Post-Dispatch
**1930**—Russell D. Owens, New York Times. Also $500 to W.O. Dapping, Auburn (NY) Citizen
**1931**—A.B. MacDonald, Kansas City (MO) Star
**1932**—W.C. Richards, D.D. Martin, J.S. Pooler, F.D. Webb, J.N.W. Sloan, Detroit Free Press
**1933**—Francis A. Jamieson, AP
**1934**—Royce Brier, San Francisco Chronicle
**1935**—William H. Taylor, New York Herald Tribune
**1936**—Lauren D. Lyman, New York Times
**1937**—John J. O'Neill, NY Herald Tribune; William L. Laurence, NY Times; Howard W. Blakeslee, AP; Gobind Behari Lal, Universal Service; and David Dietz, Scripps-Howard Newspapers
**1938**—Raymond Sprigle, Pittsburgh Post-Gazette
**1939**—Thomas L. Stokes, Scripps-Howard Newspaper Alliance
**1940**—S. Burton Heath, New York World-Telegram
**1941**—Westbrook Pegler, New York World-Telegram
**1942**—Stanton Delaplane, San Francisco Chronicle
**1943**—George Weller, Chicago Daily News
**1944**—Paul Schoenstein, New York Journal-American
**1945**—Jack S. McDowell, San Francisco Call-Bulletin
**1946**—William L. Laurence, New York Times
**1947**—Frederick Woltman, New York World-Telegram
**1948**—George E. Goodwin, Atlanta Journal
**1949**—Malcolm Johnson, New York Sun
**1950**—Meyer Berger, New York Times
**1951**—Edward S. Montgomery, San Francisco Examiner
**1952**—George de Carvalho, San Francisco Chronicle

(1) General or Spot; (2) Special or Investigative
**1953**—(1) Providence (RI) Journal and Evening Bulletin; (2) Edward J. Mowery, New York World-Telegram & Sun
**1954**—(1) Vicksburg (MS) Sunday Post-Herald; (2) Alvin Scott McCoy, Kansas City (MO) Star
**1955**—(1) Mrs. Caro Brown, Alice (TX) Daily Echo; (2) Roland K. Towery, Cuero (TX) Record
**1956**—(1) Lee Hills, Detroit Free Press; (2) Arthur Daley, New York Times
**1957**—(1) Salt Lake Tribune; (2) Wallace Turner and William Lambert, Portland Oregonian
**1958**—(1) Fargo, (ND) Forum; (2) George Beveridge, Evening Star, Washington, DC
**1959**—(1) Mary Lou Werner, Washington Evening Star; (2) John Harold Brislin, Scranton (PA) Tribune, and The Scrantonian
**1960**—(1) Jack Nelson, Atlanta Constitution; (2) Miriam Ottenberg, Washington Evening Star
**1961**—(1) Sanche de Gramont, New York Herald Tribune; (2) Edgar May, Buffalo Evening News
**1962**—(1) Robert D. Mullins, Deseret News, Salt Lake City; (2) George Bliss, Chicago Tribune
**1963**—(1) Shared by Sylvan Fox, William Longgood, and Anthony Shannon, New York World-Telegram & Sun; (2) Oscar Griffin Jr., Pecos (TX) Independent and Enterprise
**1964**—(1) Norman C. Miller, Wall Street Journal; (2) Shared by James V. Magee, Albert V. Gaudiosi, and Frederick A. Meyer, Philadelphia Bulletin
**1965**—(1) Melvin H. Ruder, Hungry Horse News, Columbia Falls, MT; (2) Gene Goltz, Houston Post
**1966**—(1) Los Angeles Times Staff; (2) John A. Frasca, Tampa (FL) Tribune
**1967**—(1) Robert V. Cox, Chambersburg (PA) Public Opinion; (2) Gene Miller, Miami Herald
**1968**—(1) Detroit Free Press Staff; (2) J. Anthony Lukas, New York Times
**1969**—(1) John Fetterman, Louisville Courier-Journal and Times; (2) Albert L. Delugach, St. Louis Globe Democrat, and Denny Walsh, Life
**1970**—(1) Thomas Fitzpatrick, Chicago Sun-Times; (2) Harold Eugene Martin, Montgomery Advertiser & Alabama Journal
**1971**—(1) Akron Beacon Journal Staff; (2) William Hugh Jones, Chicago Tribune
**1972**—(1) Richard Cooper and John Machacek, Rochester Times-Union; (2) Timothy Leland, Gerard M. O'Neill, Stephen A. Kurkjian and Anne De Santis, Boston Globe
**1973**—(1) Chicago Tribune; (2) Sun Newspapers of Omaha
**1974**—(1) Hugh F. Hough, Arthur M. Petacque, Chicago Sun-Times; (2) William Sherman, New York Daily News
**1975**—(1) Xenia (OH) Daily Gazette; (2) Indianapolis Star
**1976**—(1) Gene Miller, Miami Herald; (2) Chicago Tribune
**1977**—(1) Margo Huston, Milwaukee Journal; (2) Acel Moore, Wendell Rawls Jr., Philadelphia Inquirer
**1978**—(1) Richard Whitt, Louisville Courier-Journal; (2) Anthony R. Dolan, Stamford (CT) Advocate
**1979**—(1) San Diego (CA) Evening Tribune; (2) Gilbert M. Gaul, Elliot G. Jaspin, Pottsville (PA) Republican
**1980**—(1) Philadelphia Inquirer; (2) Stephen A. Kurkjian, Alexander B. Hawes Jr., Nils Bruzelius, Joan Vennochi, Robert M. Porterfield, Boston Globe
**1981**—(1) Longview (WA) Daily News staff; (2) Clark Hallas and Robert B. Lowe, Arizona Daily Star
**1982**—(1) Kansas City Star, Kansas City Times; (2) Paul Henderson, Seattle Times
**1983**—(1) Fort Wayne (IN) News-Sentinel; (2) Loretta Tofani, Washington Post
**1984**—(1) Newsday (NY); (2) Boston Globe
**1985**—(1) Thomas Turcol, Virginian-Pilot and Ledger-Star, Norfolk, VA; (2) William K. Marimow, Philadelphia Inquirer; Lucy Morgan & Jack Reed, St. Petersburg (FL) Times
**1986**—(1) Edna Buchanan, Miami Herald; (2) Jeffrey A. Marx & Michael M. York, Lexington (KY) Herald-Leader
**1987**—(1) Akron Beacon Journal; (2) Daniel R. Biddle, H.G. Bissinger, Fredric N. Tulsky, Philadelphia Inquirer; John Woestendiek, Philadelphia Inquirer
**1988**—(1) Alabama Journal; Lawrence (MA) Eagle-Tribune; (2) Walt Bogdanich, Wall Street Journal
**1989**—(1) Louisville Courier-Journal; (2) Bill Dedman, Atlanta Journal and Constitution
**1990**—(1) San Jose Mercury News; (2) Lon Kilzer, Chris Ison, Star Tribune, Minneapolis-St. Paul
**1991**—(1) Miami Herald; (2) Joseph T. Hallinan, Susan M. Headden, Indianapolis Star
**1992**—(1) New York Newsday; (2) Lorraine Adams, Dan Malone, Dallas Morning News
**1993**—(1) Los Angeles Times; Jeff Brazil, Steve Berry, Orlando Sentinel
**1994**—(1) New York Times staff; (2) Providence Journal-Bulletin staff
**1995**—(1) Los Angeles Times staff; (2) Brian Donovan, Stephanie Saul, Newsday
**1996**—(1) New York Times, Robert D. McFadden; (2) The Orange County Register staff

## Criticism or Commentary

(1) Criticism; (2) Commentary

**1970**—(1) Ada Louise Huxtable, New York Times; (2) Marquis W. Childs, St. Louis Post-Dispatch
**1971**—(1) Harold C. Schonberg, New York Times; (2) William A. Caldwell, The Record, Hackensack, NJ
**1972**—(1) Frank Peters Jr., St. Louis Post-Dispatch; (2) Mike Royko, Chicago Daily News
**1973**—(1) Ronald Powers, Chicago Sun-Times; (2) David S. Broder, Washington Post
**1974**—(1) Emily Genauer, Newsday (NY); (2) Edwin A. Roberts Jr., National Observer
**1975**—(1) Roger Ebert, Chicago Sun Times; (2) Mary McGrory, Washington Star
**1976**—(1) Alan M. Kriegsman, Washington Post; (2) Walter W. (Red) Smith, New York Times
**1977**—(1) William McPherson, Washington Post; (2) George F. Will, Washington Post Writers Group
**1978**—(1) Walter Kerr, New York Times; (2) William Safire, New York Times
**1979**—(1) Paul Gapp, Chicago Tribune; (2) Russell Baker, New York Times
**1980**—(1) William A. Henry III, Boston Globe; (2) Ellen Goodman, Boston Globe
**1981**—(1) Jonathan Yardley, Washington Star; (2) Dave Anderson, New York Times
**1982**—(1) Martin Bernheimer, Los Angeles Times; (2) Art Buchwald, Los Angeles Times Syndicate
**1983**—(1) Manuela Hoelterhoff, Wall St. Journal; (2) Claude Sitton, Raleigh (NC) News & Observer
**1984**—(1) Paul Goldberger, New York Times; (2) Vermont Royster, Wall St. Journal
**1985**—(1) Howard Rosenberg, Los Angeles Times; (2) Murray Kempton, Newsday (NY)
**1986**—(1) Donal J. Henahan, New York Times; (2) Jimmy Breslin, New York Daily News
**1987**—(1) Richard Eder, Los Angeles Times; (2) Charles Krauthammer, Washington Post
**1988**—(1) Tom Shales, Washington Post; (2) Dave Barry, Miami Herald
**1989**—(1) Michael Skube, News and Observer, Raleigh, NC; (2) Clarence Page, Chicago Tribune
**1990**—(1) Allan Temko, San Francisco Chronicle; (2) Jim Murray, Los Angeles Times
**1991**—(1) David Shaw, Los Angeles Times; (2) Jim Hoagland, Washington Post
**1992**—(1) No award; (2) Anna Quindlen, New York Times
**1993**—(1) Michael Dirda, Washington Post; (2) Liz Balmaseda, Miami Herald
**1994**—(1) Lloyd Schwartz, Boston Phoenix; (2) William Raspberry, Washington Post
**1995**—(1) Margo Jefferson, New York Times; (2) Jim Dwyer, Newsday
**1996**—(1) Robert Campbell, Boston Globe; (2) E.R. Shipp, New York Daily News

## National Reporting

**1942**—Louis Stark, New York Times
**1944**—Dewey L. Fleming, Baltimore Sun
**1945**—James B. Reston, New York Times
**1946**—Edward A. Harris, St. Louis Post-Dispatch
**1947**—Edward T. Folliard, Washington Post
**1948**—Bert Andrews, New York Herald Tribune; Nat S. Finney, Minneapolis Tribune
**1949**—Charles P. Trussell, New York Times
**1950**—Edwin O. Guthman, Seattle Times
**1952**—Anthony Leviero, New York Times
**1953**—Don Whitehead, AP
**1954**—Richard Wilson, Des Moines Register
**1955**—Anthony Lewis, Washington Daily News
**1956**—Charles L. Bartlett, Chattanooga Times
**1957**—James Reston, New York Times
**1958**—Relman Morin, AP; Clark Mollenhoff, Des Moines Register & Tribune
**1959**—Howard Van Smith, Miami (FL) News
**1960**—Vance Trimble, Scripps-Howard, Washington, DC
**1961**—Edward R. Cony, Wall Street Journal
**1962**—Nathan G. Caldwell and Gene S. Graham, Nashville Tennessean
**1963**—Anthony Lewis, New York Times
**1964**—Merriman Smith, United Press Int'l. (UPI)
**1965**—Louis M. Kohlmeier, Wall Street Journal
**1966**—Haynes Johnson, Washington Evening Star
**1967**—Monroe Karmin and Stanley Penn, Wall Street Journal
**1968**—Howard James, Christian Science Monitor; Nathan K. Kotz, Des Moines Register
**1969**—Robert Cahn, Christian Science Monitor
**1970**—William J. Eaton, Chicago Daily News
**1971**—Lucinda Franks & Thomas Powers, UPI
**1972**—Jack Anderson, United Feature Syndicate
**1973**—Robert Boyd and Clark Hoyt, Knight Newspapers
**1974**—James R. Polk, Washington Star-News; Jack White, Providence Journal-Bulletin
**1975**—Donald L. Barlett and James B. Steele, Philadelphia Inquirer
**1976**—James Risser, Des Moines Register
**1977**—Walter Mears, AP
**1978**—Gaylord D. Shaw, Los Angeles Times
**1979**—James Risser, Des Moines Register
**1980**—Charles Stafford, Bette Swenson Orsini, St. Petersburg (FL) Times
**1981**—John M. Crewdson, New York Times
**1982**—Rick Atkinson, Kansas City Times
**1983**—Boston Globe
**1984**—John Noble Wilford, New York Times
**1985**—Thomas J. Knudson, Des Moines Register
**1986**—Craig Flournoy & George Rodrigue, Dallas Morning News; Arthur Howe, Philadelphia Inquirer
**1987**—Miami Herald; New York Times
**1988**—Tim Weiner, Philadelphia Inquirer
**1989**—Donald L. Barlett & James B. Steele, Philadelphia Inquirer
**1990**—Ross Anderson, Bill Dietrich, Mary Ann Gwinn, Eric Nalder, Seattle Times
**1991**—Marjie Lundstrom, Rochelle Sharpe, Gannett News Service
**1992**—Jeff Taylor, Mike McGraw, Kansas City Star
**1993**—David Maraniss, Washington Post
**1994**—Eileen Welsome, Albuquerque Tribune
**1995**—Tony Horwitz, Wall Street Journal
**1996**—Alix M. Freedman, Wall Street Journal

## International Reporting

**1942**—Laurence Edmund Allen, AP
**1943**—Ira Wolfert, North American Newspaper Alliance
**1944**—Daniel DeLuce, AP
**1945**—Mark S. Watson, Baltimore Sun
**1946**—Homer W. Bigart, New York Herald Tribune
**1947**—Eddy Gilmore, AP
**1948**—Paul W. Ward, Baltimore Sun
**1949**—Price Day, Baltimore Sun
**1950**—Edmund Stevens, Christian Science Monitor
**1951**—Keyes Beech and Fred Sparks, Chicago Daily News; Homer Bigart and Marguerite Higgins, New York Herald Tribune; Relman Morin and Don Whitehead, AP
**1952**—John M. Hightower, AP
**1953**—Austin C. Wehrwein, Milwaukee Journal
**1954**—Jim G. Lucas, Scripps-Howard Newspapers
**1955**—Harrison Salisbury, New York Times
**1956**—William Randolph Hearst Jr., Frank Conniff, Hearst Newspapers; Kingsbury Smith, INS
**1957**—Russell Jones, UPI
**1958**—New York Times
**1959**—Joseph Martin and Philip Santora, New York Daily News
**1960**—A.M. Rosenthal, New York Times
**1961**—Lynn Heinzerling, AP
**1962**—Walter Lippmann, New York Herald Tribune Syndicate
**1963**—Hal Hendrix, Miami (FL) News
**1964**—Malcolm W. Browne, AP; David Halberstam, New York Times
**1965**—J.A. Livingston, Philadelphia Bulletin
**1966**—Peter Arnett, AP
**1967**—R. John Hughes, Christian Science Monitor
**1968**—Alfred Friendly, Washington Post
**1969**—William Tuohy, Los Angeles Times
**1970**—Seymour M. Hersh, Dispatch News Service
**1971**—Jimmie Lee Hoagland, Washington Post
**1972**—Peter R. Kann, Wall Street Journal
**1973**—Max Frankel, New York Times
**1974**—Hedrick Smith, New York Times
**1975**—William Mullen and Ovie Carter, Chicago Tribune
**1976**—Sydney H. Schanberg, New York Times
**1978**—Henry Kamm, New York Times
**1979**—Richard Ben Cramer, Philadelphia Inquirer
**1980**—Joel Brinkley, Jay Mather, Louisville (KY) Courier-Journal
**1981**—Shirley Christian, Miami Herald
**1982**—John Darnton, New York Times
**1983**—Thomas L. Friedman, New York Times; Loren Jenkins, Washington Post
**1984**—Karen Elliot House, Wall St. Journal
**1985**—Josh Friedman, Dennis Bell, Ozler Muhammad, Newsday (NY)
**1986**—Lewis M. Simons, Pete Carey, Katherine Ellison, San Jose Mercury News
**1987**—Michael Parks, Los Angeles Times
**1988**—Thomas L. Friedman, New York Times

*(continued)*

### International Reporting *(continued)*

**1989**—Glenn Frankel, Washington Post; Bill Keller, New York Times
**1990**—Nicholas D. Kirstof, Sheryl WuDunn, New York Times
**1991**—Caryle Murphy, Washington Post; Serge Schmemann, New York Times
**1992**—Patrick J. Sloyan, Newsday (NY)
**1993**—John F. Burns, New York Times; Roy Gutman, Newsday (NY)
**1994**—Dallas Morning News team
**1995**—Mark Fritz, AP
**1996**—David Rohde, Christian Science Monitor

### Correspondence

For Washington or foreign correspondence. Category was merged with those in national and international reporting in 1948.

**1929**—Paul Scott Mowrer, Chicago Daily News
**1930**—Leland Stowe, New York Herald Tribune
**1931**—H.R. Knickerbocker, Philadelphia Public Ledger and New York Evening Post
**1932**—Walter Duranty, New York Times, and Charles G. Ross, St. Louis Post-Dispatch
**1933**—Edgar Ansel Mowrer, Chicago Daily News
**1934**—Frederick T. Birchall, New York Times
**1935**—Arthur Krock, New York Times
**1936**—Wilfred C. Barber, Chicago Tribune
**1937**—Anne O'Hare McCormick, New York Times
**1938**—Arthur Krock, New York Times
**1939**—Louis P. Lochner, AP
**1940**—Otto D. Tolischus, New York Times
**1941**—Bronze plaque to commemorate work of American correspondents on war fronts
**1942**—Carlos P. Romulo, Philippines Herald
**1943**—Hanson W. Baldwin, New York Times
**1944**—Ernest Taylor Pyle, Scripps-Howard Newspaper Alliance
**1945**—Harold V. (Hal) Boyle, AP
**1946**—Arnaldo Cortesi, New York Times
**1947**—Brooks Atkinson, New York Times

### Editorial Writing

**1917**—New York Tribune
**1918**—Louisville (KY) Courier-Journal
**1920**—Harvey E. Newbranch, Omaha Evening World-Herald
**1922**—Frank M. O'Brien, New York Herald
**1923**—William Allen White, Emporia Gazette
**1924**—Frank Buxton, Boston Herald, Special Prize; Frank I. Cobb, New York World
**1925**—Robert Lathan, Charleston (SC) News and Courier
**1926**—Edward M. Kingsbury, New York Times
**1927**—F. Lauriston Bullard, Boston Herald
**1928**—Grover C. Hall, Montgomery Advertiser
**1929**—Louis Isaac Jaffe, Norfolk Virginian-Pilot
**1931**—Chas. Ryckman, Fremont (NE) Tribune
**1933**—Kansas City (MO) Star
**1934**—E. P. Chase, Atlantic (IA) News Telegraph
**1936**—Felix Morley, Washington Post; George B. Parker, Scripps-Howard Newspapers
**1937**—John W. Owens, Baltimore Sun
**1938**—W.W. Waymack, Des Moines Register and Tribune
**1939**—Ronald G. Callvert, Portland Oregonian
**1940**—Bart Howard, St. Louis Post-Dispatch
**1941**—Reuben Maury, Daily News, NY
**1942**—Geoffrey Parsons, New York Herald Tribune
**1943**—Forrest W. Seymour, Des Moines Register and Tribune
**1944**—Henry J. Haskell, Kansas City (MO) Star
**1945**—George W. Potter, Providence (RI) Journal-Bulletin
**1946**—Hodding Carter, Greenville (MS) Delta Democrat-Times
**1947**—William H. Grimes, Wall Street Journal
**1948**—Virginius Dabney, Richmond (VA) Times-Dispatch
**1949**—John H. Crider, Boston Herald; Herbert Elliston, Washington Post
**1950**—Carl M. Saunders, Jackson (MI) Citizen-Patriot
**1951**—William H. Fitzpatrick, New Orleans States
**1952**—Louis LaCoss, St. Louis Globe Democrat
**1953**—Vermont C. Royster, Wall Street Journal
**1954**—Don Murray, Boston Herald
**1955**—Royce Howes, Detroit Free Press
**1956**—Lauren K. Soth, Des Moines (IA) Register and Tribune
**1957**—Buford Boone, Tuscaloosa (AL) News
**1958**—Harry S. Ashmore, Arkansas Gazette
**1959**—Ralph McGill, Atlanta Constitution
**1960**—Lenoir Chambers, Norfolk Virginian-Pilot
**1961**—William J. Dorvillier, San Juan (Puerto Rico) Star
**1962**—Thomas M. Storke, Santa Barbara News-Press
**1963**—Ira B. Harkey Jr., Pascagoula (MS) Chronicle
**1964**—Hazel Brannon Smith, Lexington (MS) Advertiser
**1965**—John R. Harrison, Gainesville (FL) Sun
**1966**—Robert Lasch, St. Louis Post-Dispatch
**1967**—Eugene C. Patterson, Atlanta Constitution
**1968**—John S. Knight, Knight Newspapers
**1969**—Paul Greenberg, Pine Bluff (AR) Commercial
**1970**—Philip L. Geyelin, Washington Post
**1971**—Horance G. Davis Jr., Gainesville (FL) Sun
**1972**—John Strohmeyer, Bethlehem (PA) Globe-Times
**1973**—Roger B. Linscott, Berkshire Eagle, Pittsfield, MA
**1974**—F. Gilman Spencer, Trenton (NJ) Trentonian
**1975**—John D. Maurice, Charleston (WV) Daily Mail
**1976**—Philip Kerby, Los Angeles Times
**1977**—Warren L. Lerude, Foster Church, and Norman F. Cardoza, Reno Evening Gazette and Nevada State Journal
**1978**—Meg Greenfield, Washington Post
**1979**—Edwin M. Yoder, Washington Star
**1980**—Robert L. Bartley, Wall Street Journal
**1982**—Jack Rosenthal, New York Times
**1983**—Editorial board, Miami Herald
**1984**—Albert Scardino, Georgia Gazette
**1985**—Richard Aregood, Philadelphia Daily News
**1986**—Jack Fuller, Chicago Tribune
**1987**—Jonathan Freedman, Tribune (San Diego)
**1988**—Jane Healy, Orlando Sentinel
**1989**—Lois Wille, Chicago Tribune
**1990**—Thomas J. Hylton, Pottstown (PA) Mercury
**1991**—Ron Casey, Harold Jackson, Joey Kennedy, Birmingham (AL) News
**1992**—Maria Henson, Lexington (KY) Herald-Leader
**1993**—No award
**1994**—R. Bruce Dold, Chicago Tribune
**1995**—Jeffrey Good, St. Petersburg (FL) Times
**1996**—Robert B. Semple Jr., New York Times

### Editorial Cartooning

**1922**—Rollin Kirby, New York World
**1924**—Jay N. Darling, Des Moines Register
**1925**—Rollin Kirby, New York World
**1926**—D. R. Fitzpatrick, St. Louis Post-Dispatch
**1927**—Nelson Harding, Brooklyn Eagle
**1928**—Nelson Harding, Brooklyn Eagle
**1929**—Rollin Kirby, New York World
**1930**—Charles Macauley, Brooklyn Eagle
**1931**—Edmund Duffy, Baltimore Sun
**1932**—John T. McCutcheon, Chicago Tribune
**1933**—H. M. Talburt, Washington Daily News
**1934**—Edmund Duffy, Baltimore Sun
**1935**—Ross A. Lewis, Milwaukee Journal
**1937**—C. D. Batchelor, New York Daily News
**1938**—Vaughn Shoemaker, Chicago Daily News
**1939**—Charles G. Werner, Daily Oklahoman
**1940**—Edmund Duffy, Baltimore Sun
**1941**—Jacob Burck, Chicago Times
**1942**—Herbert L. Block, Newspaper Enterprise Assn.
**1943**—Jay N. Darling, Des Moines Register
**1944**—Clifford K. Berryman, Washington Star
**1945**—Bill Mauldin, United Feature Syndicate
**1946**—Bruce Alexander Russell, Los Angeles Times
**1947**—Vaughn Shoemaker, Chicago Daily News
**1948**—Reuben L. (Rube) Goldberg, New York Sun
**1949**—Lute Pease, Newark (NJ) Evening News
**1950**—James T. Berryman, Washington Star
**1951**—Reginald W. Manning, Arizona Republic
**1952**—Fred L. Packer, New York Mirror
**1953**—Edward D. Kuekes, Cleveland Plain Dealer
**1954**—Herbert L. Block, Washington Post & Times-Herald
**1955**—Daniel R. Fitzpatrick, St. Louis Post-Dispatch
**1956**—Robert York, Louisville (KY) Times
**1957**—Tom Little, Nashville Tennessean
**1958**—Bruce M. Shanks, Buffalo Evening News
**1959**—Bill Mauldin, St. Louis Post-Dispatch
**1961**—Carey Orr, Chicago Tribune
**1962**—Edmund S. Valtman, Hartford Times
**1963**—Frank Miller, Des Moines Register
**1964**—Paul Conrad, Denver Post
**1966**—Don Wright, Miami News
**1967**—Patrick B. Oliphant, Denver Post
**1968**—Eugene Gray Payne, Charlotte Observer
**1969**—John Fischetti, Chicago Daily News
**1970**—Thomas F. Darcy, Newsday
**1971**—Paul Conrad, Los Angeles Times
**1972**—Jeffrey K. MacNelly, Richmond News-Leader
**1974**—Paul Szep, Boston Globe
**1975**—Garry Trudeau, Universal Press Syndicate
**1976**—Tony Auth, Philadelphia Inquirer
**1977**—Paul Szep, Boston Globe
**1978**—Jeffrey K. MacNelly, Richmond News Leader
**1979**—Herbert L. Block, Washington Post
**1980**—Don Wright, Miami (FL) News
**1981**—Mike Peters, Dayton (OH) Daily News
**1982**—Ben Sargent, Austin American-Statesman
**1983**—Richard Lochner, Chicago Tribune
**1984**—Paul Conrad, Los Angeles Times

**1985**—Jeffrey K. MacNelly, Chicago Tribune
**1986**—Jules Feiffer, Village Voice (NY)
**1987**—Berke Breathed, Washington Post
**1988**—Doug Marlette, Atlanta Constitution, Charlotte Observer
**1989**—Jack Higgins, Chicago Sun-Times
**1990**—Tom Toles, Buffalo News
**1991**—Jim Borgman, Cincinnati Enquirer
**1992**—Signe Wilkinson, Philadelphia Daily News
**1993**—Stephen R. Benson, Arizona Republic
**1994**—Michael P. Ramirez, Commercial Appeal, Memphis, TN
**1995**—Mike Luckovich, Atlanta Constitution
**1996**—Jim Morin, Miami Herald

## Spot News Photography

**1942**—Milton Brooks, Detroit News
**1943**—Frank Noel, AP
**1944**—Frank Filan, AP; Earl L. Bunker, Omaha World-Herald
**1945**—Joe Rosenthal, AP
**1947**—Arnold Hardy, amateur, Atlanta, GA
**1948**—Frank Cushing, Boston Traveler
**1949**—Nathaniel Fein, New York Herald Tribune
**1950**—Bill Crouch, Oakland (CA) Tribune
**1951**—Max Desfor, AP
**1952**—John Robinson and Don Ultang, Des Moines Register and Tribune
**1953**—William M. Gallagher, Flint (MI) Journal
**1954**—Mrs. Walter M. Schau, amateur
**1955**—John L. Gaunt Jr., Los Angeles Times
**1956**—New York Daily News
**1957**—Harry A. Trask, Boston Traveler
**1958**—William C. Beall, Washington Daily News
**1959**—William Seaman, Minneapolis Star
**1960**—Andrew Lopez, UPI
**1961**—Yasushi Nagao, Mainichi Newspapers, Tokyo
**1962**—Paul Vathis, AP
**1963**—Hector Rondon, La Republica, Caracas, Venezuela
**1964**—Robert H. Jackson, Dallas Times-Herald
**1965**—Horst Faas, AP
**1966**—Kyoichi Sawada, UPI
**1967**—Jack R. Thornell, AP
**1968**—Rocco Morabito, Jacksonville Journal
**1969**—Edward Adams, AP
**1970**—Steve Starr, AP
**1971**—John Paul Filo, Valley Daily News & Daily Dispatch of Tarentum & New Kensington, PA
**1972**—Horst Faas and Michel Laurent, AP
**1973**—Huynh Cong Ut, AP
**1974**—Anthony K. Roberts, AP
**1975**—Gerald H. Gay, Seattle Times
**1976**—Stanley Forman, Boston Herald American
**1977**—Neal Ulevich, AP; Stanley Forman, Boston Herald American
**1978**—John H. Blair, UPI
**1979**—Thomas J. Kelly III, Pottstown (PA) Mercury
**1980**—UPI
**1981**—Larry C. Price, Ft. Worth (TX) Star-Telegram
**1982**—Ron Edmonds, AP
**1983**—Bill Foley, AP
**1984**—Stan Grossfeld, Boston Globe
**1985**—The Register, Santa Ana, CA
**1986**—Carol Guzy & Michel duCille, Miami Herald
**1987**—Kim Komenich, San Francisco Examiner
**1988**—Scott Shaw, Odessa (TX) American
**1989**—Ron Olshwanger, St. Louis Post-Dispatch
**1990**—Oakland (CA) Tribune photo staff
**1991**—Greg Marinovich, AP
**1992**—Associated Press staff
**1993**—Ken Geiger, William Snyder, Dallas Morning News
**1994**—Paul Watson, Toronto Star
**1995**—Carol Guzy, Washington Post
**1996**—Charles Porter IV, AP

## Feature Photography

**1968**—Toshio Sakai, UPI
**1969**—Moneta Sleet Jr., Ebony
**1970**—Dallas Kinney, Palm Beach Post
**1971**—Jack Dykinga, Chicago Sun-Times
**1972**—Dave Kennerly, UPI
**1973**—Brian Lanker, Topeka Capitol-Journal
**1974**—Slava Veder, AP
**1975**—Matthew Lewis, Washington Post
**1976**—Louisville Courier-Journal and Louisville Times
**1977**—Robin Hood, Chattanooga News-Free Press
**1978**—J. Ross Baughman, AP
**1979**—Staff photographers, Boston Herald American
**1980**—Erwin H. Hagler, Dallas Times-Herald
**1981**—Taro M. Yamasaki, Detroit Free Press
**1982**—John H. White, Chicago Sun-Times
**1983**—James B. Dickman, Dallas Times-Herald
**1984**—Anthony Suad, Denver Post
**1985**—Stan Grossfeld, Boston Globe; Larry C. Price, Phila. Inquirer
**1986**—Tom Gralish, Philadelphia Inquirer
**1987**—David Peterson, Des Moines Register
**1988**—Michel duCille, Miami Herald
**1989**—Manny Crisostomo, Detroit Free Press
**1990**—David C. Turnley, Detroit Free Press
**1991**—William Snyder, Dallas Morning News
**1992**—John Kaplan, Block Newspapers (Toledo, OH)
**1993**—Associated Press staff
**1994**—Kevin Carter, New York Times
**1995**—Associated Press staff
**1996**—Stephanie Welsh, Newhouse News Service

## Special Citation

**1938**—Edmonton (Alberta) Journal, bronze plaque
**1941**—New York Times
**1944**—Byron Price and Mrs. William Allen White. Also to Richard Rodgers and Oscar Hammerstein 2d, for musical, Oklahoma!
**1945**—Press cartographers for war maps
**1947**—(Pulitzer centennial year) Columbia Univ. and the Graduate School of Journalism; St. Louis Post-Dispatch
**1948**—Dr. Frank Diehl Fackenthal
**1951**—Cyrus L. Sulzberger, New York Times
**1952**—Max Kase, New York Journal-American, Kansas City Star
**1953**—New York Times; Lester Markel
**1957**—Kenneth Roberts, for his historical novels
**1958**—Walter Lippmann, New York Herald Tribune
**1960**—Garrett Mattingly, for The Armada
**1961**—American Heritage Picture History of the Civil War
**1964**—Gannett Newspapers
**1973**—James T. Flexner, for biography of George Washington
**1976**—John Hohenberg, for services to American journalism
**1977**—Alex Haley, for Roots
**1978**—Richard Lee Strout, Christian Science Monitor and New Republic
—E.B. White
**1984**—Theodore Geisel ("Dr. Seuss")
**1985**—William Schuman, composer, educational leader
**1987**—Joseph Pulitzer Jr.
**1992**—Art Spiegelman, for Maus
**1996** Herb Caen, San Francisco Chronicle

## Feature Writing

**1979**—Jon D. Franklin, Baltimore Evening Sun
**1980**—Madeleine Blais, Miami Herald Tropic Magazine;
**1981**—Teresa Carpenter, Village Voice, New York City
**1982**—Saul Pett, AP
**1984**—Peter M. Rinearson, Seattle Times
**1985**—Alice Steinbach, Baltimore Sun
**1986**—John Camp, St. Paul Pioneer Press & Dispatch
**1987**—Steve Twomey, Philadephia Inquirer
**1988**—Jacqui Banaszynski, St. Paul Pioneer Press Dispatch
**1989**—David Zucchino, Philadelphia Inquirer
**1990**—Dave Curtin, Colorado Springs Gazette Telegraph
**1991**—Sheryl James, St. Petersburg Times
**1992**—Howell Raines, New York Times
**1993**—George Lardner Jr., Washington Post
**1994**—Isabel Wilkerson, New York Times
**1995**—Ron Suskind, Wall Street Journal
**1996**—Rick Bragg, New York Times

## Explanatory Journalism

**1985**—Jon Franklin, Baltimore Evening Sun
**1986**—New York Times staff
**1987**—Jeff Lyon & Peter Gorner, Chicago Tribune
**1988**—Daniel Hertzberg, James B. Stewart, Wall Street Journal
**1989**—David Hanners, William Snyder, Karen Blessen, Dallas Morning News
**1990**—David A. Vise, Steve Coll, Washington Post
**1991**—Susan C. Faludi, Wall Street Journal
**1992**—Robert S. Capers, Eric Lipton, Hartford (CT) Courant
**1993**—Mike Toner, Atlanta Journal-Constitution
**1994**—Ronald Kotulak, Chicago Tribune
**1995**—Leon Dash, Lucian Perkins, Washington Post
**1996**—Laurie Garrett, Newsday (Long Island, NY)

## Specialized Reporting (1985-90)

(discontinued category)

**1985**—Randall Savage, Jackie Crosby, Macon (GA) Telegraph & News
**1986**—Andrew Schneider & Mary Pat Flaherty, Pittsburgh Press
**1987**—Alex S. Jones, New York Times
**1988**—Dean Baquet, William Gaines, Ann Marie Lipinski, Chicago Tribune
**1989**—Edward Humes, Orange County (CA) Register
**1990**—Tamar Stieber, Albuquerque Journal

## Beat Reporting

**1991**—Natalie Angier, New York Times
**1992**—Deborah Blum, Sacramento Bee
**1993**—Paul Ingrassia, Joseph B. White, Wall Street Journal
**1994**—Eric Freedman, Jim Mitzelfeld, Detroit News
**1995**—David Shribman, Boston Globe
**1996**—Bob Keeler, Newsday (Long Island, NY)

# Letters

## Fiction

For fiction in book form by an American author, preferably dealing with American life.

**1918**—Ernest Poole, *His Family*
**1919**—Booth Tarkington, *The Magnificent Ambersons*
**1921**—Edith Wharton, *The Age of Innocence*
**1922**—Booth Tarkington, *Alice Adams*
**1923**—Willa Cather, *One of Ours*
**1924**—Margaret Wilson, *The Able McLaughlins*
**1925**—Edna Ferber, *So Big*
**1926**—Sinclair Lewis, *Arrowsmith* (Refused prize)
**1927**—Louis Bromfield, *Early Autumn*
**1928**—Thornton Wilder, *Bridge of San Luis Rey*
**1929**—Julia M. Peterkin, *Scarlet Sister Mary*
**1930**—Oliver LaFarge, *Laughing Boy*
**1931**—Margaret Ayer Barnes, *Years of Grace*
**1932**—Pearl S. Buck, *The Good Earth*
**1933**—T. S. Stribling, *The Store*
**1934**—Caroline Miller, *Lamb in His Bosom*
**1935**—Josephine W. Johnson, *Now in November*
**1936**—Harold L. Davis, *Honey in the Horn*
**1937**—Margaret Mitchell, *Gone With the Wind*
**1938**—John P. Marquand, *The Late George Apley*
**1939**—Marjorie Kinnan Rawlings, *The Yearling*
**1940**—John Steinbeck, *The Grapes of Wrath*
**1942**—Ellen Glasgow, *In This Our Life*
**1943**—Upton Sinclair, *Dragon's Teeth*
**1944**—Martin Flavin, *Journey in the Dark*
**1945**—John Hersey, *A Bell for Adano*
**1947**—Robert Penn Warren, *All the King's Men*
**1948**—James A. Michener, *Tales of the South Pacific*
**1949**—James Gould Cozzens, *Guard of Honor*
**1950**—A. B. Guthrie Jr., *The Way West*
**1951**—Conrad Richter, *The Town*
**1952**—Herman Wouk, *The Caine Mutiny*
**1953**—Ernest Hemingway, *The Old Man and the* Sea
**1955**—William Faulkner, *A Fable*
**1956**—MacKinlay Kantor, *Andersonville*
**1958**—James Agee, *A Death in the Family*
**1959**—Robert Lewis Taylor, *The Travels of Jaimie McPheeters*
**1960**—Allen Drury, *Advise and Consent*
**1961**—Harper Lee, *To Kill a Mockingbird*
**1962**—Edwin O'Connor, *The Edge of Sadness*
**1963**—William Faulkner, *The Reivers*
**1965**—Shirley Ann Grau, *The Keepers of the House*
**1966**—Katherine Anne Porter, *Collected Stories of Katherine Anne Porter*
**1967**—Bernard Malamud, *The Fixer*
**1968**—William Styron, *The Confessions of Nat Turner*
**1969**—N. Scott Momaday, *House Made of Dawn*
**1970**—Jean Stafford, *Collected Stories*
**1972**—Wallace Stegner, *Angle of Repose*
**1973**—Eudora Welty, *The Optimist's Daughter*
**1975**—Michael Shaara, *The Killer Angels*
**1976**—Saul Bellow, *Humboldt's Gift*
**1978**—James Alan McPherson, *Elbow Room*
**1979**—John Cheever, *The Stories of John Cheever*
**1980**—Norman Mailer, *The Executioner's Song*
**1981**—John Kennedy Toole, *A Confederacy of Dunces*
**1982**—John Updike, *Rabbit Is Rich*
**1983**—Alice Walker, *The Color Purple*
**1984**—William Kennedy, *Ironweed*
**1985**—Alison Lurie, *Foreign Affairs*
**1986**—Larry McMurtry, *Lonesome Dove*
**1987**—Peter Taylor, *A Summons to Memphis*
**1988**—Toni Morrison, *Beloved*
**1989**—Anne Tyler, *Breathing Lessons*
**1990**—Oscar Hijuelos, *The Mambo Kings Play Songs of Love*
**1991**—John Updike, *Rabbit at Rest*
**1992**—Jane Smiley, *A Thousand Acres*
**1993**—Robert Olen Butler, *A Good Scent From a Strange Mountain*
**1994**—E. Annie Proulx, *The Shipping News*
**1995**—Carol Shields, *The Stone Diaries*
**1996**—Richard Ford, *Independence Day*

## Drama

For an American play, preferably original and dealing with American life.

**1918**—Jesse Lynch Williams, *Why Marry?*
**1920**—Eugene O'Neill, *Beyond the Horizon*
**1921**—Zona Gale, *Miss Lulu Bett*
**1922**—Eugene O'Neill, *Anna Christie*
**1923**—Owen Davis, *Icebound*
**1924**—Hatcher Hughes, *Hell-Bent for Heaven*
**1925**—Sidney Howard, *They Knew What They Wanted*
**1926**—George Kelly, *Craig's Wife*
**1927**—Paul Green, *In Abraham's Bosom*
**1928**—Eugene O'Neill, *Strange Interlude*
**1929**—Elmer Rice, *Street Scene*
**1930**—Marc Connelly, *The Green Pastures*
**1931**—Susan Glaspell, *Alison's House*
**1932**—George S. Kaufman, Morrie Ryskind, and Ira Gershwin, *Of Thee I Sing*
**1933**—Maxwell Anderson, *Both Your Houses*
**1934**—Sidney Kingsley, *Men in White*
**1935**—Zoe Akins, *The Old Maid*
**1936**—Robert E. Sherwood, *Idiot's Delight*
**1937**—George S. Kaufman and Moss Hart, *You Can't Take It With You*
**1938**—Thornton Wilder, *Our Town*
**1939**—Robert E. Sherwood, *Abe Lincoln in Illinois*
**1940**—William Saroyan, *The Time of Your Life*
**1941**—Robert E. Sherwood, *There Shall Be No Night*
**1943**—Thornton Wilder, *The Skin of Our Teeth*
**1945**—Mary Chase, *Harvey*
**1946**—Russel Crouse and Howard Lindsay, *State of the Union*
**1948**—Tennessee Williams, *A Streetcar Named Desire*
**1949**—Arthur Miller, *Death of a Salesman*
**1950**—Richard Rodgers, Oscar Hammerstein 2d, and Joshua Logan, *South Pacific*
**1952**—Joseph Kramm, *The Shrike*
**1953**—William Inge, *Picnic*
**1954**—John Patrick, *Teahouse of the August Moon*
**1955**—Tennessee Williams, *Cat on a Hot Tin Roof*
**1956**—Frances Goodrich and Albert Hackett, *The Diary of Anne Frank*
**1957**—Eugene O'Neill, *Long Day's Journey Into Night*
**1958**—Ketti Frings, *Look Homeward, Angel*
**1959**—Archibald MacLeish, *J. B.*
**1960**—George Abbott, Jerome Weidman, Sheldon Harnick, and Jerry Bock, *Fiorello*
**1961**—Tad Mosel, *All the Way Home*
**1962**—Frank Loesser and Abe Burrows, *How to Succeed in Business Without Really Trying*
**1965**—Frank D. Gilroy, *The Subject Was Roses*
**1967**—Edward Albee, *A Delicate Balance*
**1969**—Howard Sackler, *The Great White Hope*
**1970**—Charles Gordone, *No Place to Be Somebody*
**1971**—Paul Zindel, *The Effect of Gamma Rays on Man-in-the-Moon Marigolds*
**1973**—Jason Miller, *That Championship Season*
**1975**—Edward Albee, *Seascape*
**1976**—Michael Bennett, James Kirkwood, Nicholas Dante, Marvin Hamlisch, and Edward Kleban, *A Chorus Line*
**1977**—Michael Cristofer, *The Shadow Box*
**1978**—Donald L. Coburn, *The Gin Game*
**1979**—Sam Shepard, *Buried Child*
**1980**—Lanford Wilson, *Talley's Folly*
**1981**—Beth Henley, *Crimes of the Heart*
**1982**—Charles Fuller, *A Soldier's Play*
**1983**—Marsha Norman, *'night, Mother*
**1984**—David Mamet, *Glengarry Glen Ross*
**1985**—Stephen Sondheim and James Lapine, *Sunday in the Park With George*
**1987**—August Wilson, *Fences*
**1988**—Alfred Uhry, *Driving Miss Daisy*
**1989**—Wendy Wasserstein, *The Heidi Chronicles*
**1990**—August Wilson, *The Piano Lesson*
**1991**—Neil Simon, *Lost in Yonkers*
**1992**—Robert Schenkkan, *The Kentucky Cycle*
**1993**—Tony Kushner, *Angels in America: Millennium Approaches*
**1994**—Edward Albee, *Three Tall Women*
**1995**—Horton Foote, *The Young Man From Atlanta*
**1996**—Jonathan Larson, *Rent*

## History

For a book on the history of the United States.

**1917**—J. J. Jusserand, *With Americans of Past and Present Days*
**1918**—James Ford Rhodes, *History of the Civil War*
**1920**—Justin H. Smith, *The War With Mexico*
**1921**—William Sowden Sims, *The Victory at Sea*
**1922**—James Truslow Adams, *The Founding of New England*
**1923**—Charles Warren, *The Supreme Court in United States History*
**1924**—Charles Howard McIlwain, *The American Revolution: A Constitutional Interpretation*
**1925**—Frederick L. Paxton, *A History of the American Frontier*
**1926**—Edward Channing, *A History of the U.S.*
**1927**—Samuel Flagg Bemis, *Pinckney's Treaty*
**1928**—Vernon Louis Parrington, *Main Currents in American Thought*
**1929**—Fred A. Shannon, *The Organization and Administration of the Union Army, 1861-65*

**1930**—Claude H. Van Tyne, *The War of Independence*
**1931**—Bernadotte E. Schmitt, *The Coming of the War, 1914*
**1932**—Gen. John J. Pershing, *My Experiences in the World War*
**1933**—Frederick J. Turner, *The Significance of Sections in American History*
**1934**—Herbert Agar, *The People's Choice*
**1935**—Charles McLean Andrews, *The Colonial Period of American History*
**1936**—Andrew C. McLaughlin, *The Constitutional History of the United States*
**1937**—Van Wyck Brooks, *The Flowering of New England*
**1938**—Paul Herman Buck, *The Road to Reunion, 1865-1900*
**1939**—Frank Luther Mott, *A History of American Magazines*
**1940**—Carl Sandburg, *Abraham Lincoln: The War Years*
**1941**—Marcus Lee Hansen, *The Atlantic Migration, 1607-1860*
**1942**—Margaret Leech, *Reveille in Washington*
**1943**—Esther Forbes, *Paul Revere and the World He Lived In*
**1944**—Merle Curti, *The Growth of American Thought*
**1945**—Stephen Bonsal, *Unfinished Business*
**1946**—Arthur M. Schlesinger Jr., *The Age of Jackson*
**1947**—James Phinney Baxter 3d, *Scientists Against Time*
**1948**—Bernard De Voto, *Across the Wide Missouri*
**1949**—Roy F. Nichols, *The Disruption of American Democracy*
**1950**—O. W. Larkin, *Art and Life in America*
**1951**—R. Carlyle Buley, *The Old Northwest: Pioneer Period 1815-1840*
**1952**—Oscar Handlin, *The Uprooted*
**1953**—George Dangerfield, *The Era of Good Feelings*
**1954**—Bruce Catton, *A Stillness at Appomattox*
**1955**—Paul Horgan, *Great River: The Rio Grande in North American History*
**1956**—Richard Hofstadter, *The Age of Reform*
**1957**—George F. Kennan, *Russia Leaves the War*
**1958**—Bray Hammond, *Banks and Politics in America—From the Revolution to the Civil War*
**1959**—Leonard D. White and Jean Schneider, *The Republican Era; 1869-1901*
**1960**—Margaret Leech, *In the Days of McKinley*
**1961**—Herbert Feis, *Between War and Peace: The Potsdam Conference*
**1962**—Lawrence H. Gibson, *The Triumphant Empire: Thunderclouds Gather in the West*
**1963**—Constance McLaughlin Green, *Washington: Village and Capital, 1800-1878*
**1964**—Sumner Chilton Powell, *Puritan Village: The Formation of a New England Town*
**1965**—Irwin Unger, *The Greenback Era*
**1966**—Perry Miller, *Life of the Mind in America*
**1967**—William H. Goetzmann, *Exploration and Empire: The Explorer and Scientist in the Winning of the American West*
**1968**—Bernard Bailyn, *The Ideological Origins of the American Revolution*
**1969**—Leonard W. Levy, *Origin of the Fifth Amendment*
**1970**—Dean Acheson, *Present at the Creation: My Years in the State Department*
**1971**—James McGregor Burns, *Roosevelt: The Soldier of Freedom*
**1972**—Carl N. Degler, *Neither Black nor White*
**1973**—Michael Kammen, *People of Paradox: An Inquiry Concerning the Origins of American Civilization*
**1974**—Daniel J. Boorstin, *The Americans: The Democratic Experience*
**1975**—Dumas Malone, *Jefferson and His Time*
**1976**—Paul Horgan, *Lamy of Santa Fe*
**1977**—David M. Potter, *The Impending Crisis*
**1978**—Alfred D. Chandler Jr., *The Visible Hand: The Managerial Revolution in American Business*
**1979**—Don E. Fehrenbacher, *The Dred Scott Case: Its Significance in American Law and Politics*
**1980**—Leon F. Litwack, *Been in the Storm So Long*
**1981**—Lawrence A. Cremin, *American Education: The National Experience, 1783-1876*
**1982**—C. Vann Woodward, ed., *Mary Chesnut's Civil War*
**1983**—Rhys L. Issac, *The Transformation of Virginia, 1740-1790*
**1985**—Thomas K. McCraw, *Prophets of Regulation*
**1986**—Walter A. McDougall, *... The Heavens and the Earth*
**1987**—Bernard Bailyn, *Voyagers to the West*
**1988**—Robert V. Bruce, *The Launching of Modern American Science, 1846-1876*
**1989**—Taylor Branch, *Parting the Waters: America in the King Years, 1954-63*; and James M. McPherson, *Battle Cry of Freedom: The Civil War Era*
**1990**—Stanley Karnow, *In Our Image: America's Empire in the Philippines*
**1991**—Laurel Thatcher Ulrich, *A Midwife's Tale: The Life of Martha Ballard,* based on her diary, 1785-1812
**1992**—Mark E. Neely Jr., *The Fate of Liberty: Abraham Lincoln and Civil Liberties*
**1993**—Gordon S. Wood, *The Radicalism of the American Revolution*
**1995**—Doris Kearns Goodwin, *No Ordinary Time: Franklin and Eleanor Roosevelt: The Home Front in World War II*
**1996**—Alan Taylor, *William Cooper's Town: Power and Persuasion on the Frontier of the Early American Republic*

### Biography or Autobiography

For a distinguished biography or autobiography by an American author.

**1917**—Laura E. Richards and Maude Howe Elliott, assisted by Florence Howe Hall, *Julia Ward Howe*
**1918**—William Cabell Bruce, *Benjamin Franklin, Self-Revealed*
**1919**—Henry Adams, *The Education of Henry Adams*
**1920**—Albert J. Beveridge, *The Life of John Marshall*
**1921**—Edward Bok, *The Americanization of Edward Bok*
**1922**—Hamlin Garland, *A Daughter of the Middle Border*
**1923**—Burton J. Hendrick, *The Life and Letters of Walter H. Page*
**1924**—Michael Pupin, *From Immigrant to Inventor*
**1925**—M. A. DeWolfe Howe, *Barrett Wendell and His Letters*
**1926**—Harvey Cushing, *Life of Sir William Osler*
**1927**—Emory Holloway, *Whitman: An Interpretation in Narrative*
**1928**—Charles Edward Russell, *The American Orchestra and Theodore Thomas*
**1929**—Burton J. Hendrick, *The Training of an American: The Earlier Life and Letters of Walter H. Page*
**1930**—Marquis James, *The Raven* (Sam Houston)
**1931**—Henry James, *Charles W. Eliot*
**1932**—Henry F. Pringle, *Theodore Roosevelt*
**1933**—Allan Nevins, *Grover Cleveland*
**1934**—Tyler Dennett, *John Hay*
**1935**—Douglas Southall Freeman, *R. E. Lee*
**1936**—Ralph Barton Perry, *The Thought and Character of William James*
**1937**—Allan Nevins, *Hamilton Fish: The Inner History of the Grant Administration*
**1938**—Divided between Odell Shepard, *Pedlar's Progress* (Bronson Alcott), and Marquis James, *Andrew Jackson*
**1939**—Carl Van Doren, *Benjamin Franklin*
**1940**—Ray Stannard Baker, *Woodrow Wilson, Life and Letters*
**1941**—Ola Elizabeth Winslow, *Jonathan Edwards*
**1942**—Forrest Wilson, *Crusader in Crinoline* (Harriet Beecher Stowe)
**1943**—Samuel Eliot Morison, *Admiral of the Ocean Sea* (Christopher Columbus)
**1944**—Carleton Mabee, *The American Leonardo: The Life of Samuel F. B. Morse*
**1945**—Russell Blaine Nye, *George Bancroft: Brahmin Rebel.*
**1946**—Linny Marsh Wolfe, *Son of the Wilderness* (John Muir)
**1947**—William Allen White, *The Autobiography of William Allen White*
**1948**—Margaret Clapp, *Forgotten First Citizen: John Bigelow*
**1949**—Robert E. Sherwood, *Roosevelt and Hopkins*
**1950**—Samuel Flag Bemis, *John Quincy Adams and the Foundations of American Foreign Policy*
**1951**—Margaret Louise Colt, *John C. Calhoun: American Portrait*
**1952**—Merlo J. Pusey, *Charles Evans Hughes*
**1953**—David J. Mays, *Edmund Pendleton, 1721-1803*
**1954**—Charles A. Lindbergh, *The Spirit of St. Louis*
**1955**—William S. White, *The Taft Story*
**1956**—Talbot F. Hamlin, *Benjamin Henry Latrobe*
**1957**—John F. Kennedy, *Profiles in Courage*
**1958**—Douglas Southall Freeman (Vols. I-VI) and John Alexander Carroll and Mary Wells Ashworth, (Vol. VII), *George Washington*
**1959**—Arthur Walworth, *Woodrow Wilson: American Prophet*
**1960**—Samuel Eliot Morison, *John Paul Jones*
**1961**—David Donald, *Charles Sumner and the Coming of the Civil War*
**1963**—Leon Edel, *Henry James: Vol. II, The Conquest of London, 1870-1881; Vol. III, The Middle Years, 1881-1895*
**1964**—Walter Jackson Bate, *John Keats*
**1965**—Ernest Samuels, *Henry Adams*
**1966**—Arthur M. Schlesinger Jr., *A Thousand Days*
**1967**—Justin Kaplan, *Mr. Clemens and Mark Twain*
**1968**—George F. Kennan, *Memoirs (1925-1950)*
**1969**—B. L. Reid, *The Man From New York: John Quinn and His Friends*
**1970**—T. Harry Williams, *Huey Long*
**1971**—Lawrence Thompson, *Robert Frost: The Years of Triumph, 1915-1938*
**1972**—Joseph P. Lash, *Eleanor and Franklin*
**1973**—W. A. Swanberg, *Luce and His Empire*
**1974**—Louis Sheaffer, *O'Neill, Son and Artist*
**1975**—Robert A. Caro, *The Power Broker: Robert Moses and the Fall of New York*
**1976**—R.W.B. Lewis, *Edith Wharton: A Biography*
**1977**—John E. Mack, *A Prince of Our Disorder: The Life of T. E. Lawrence*
**1978**—Walter Jackson Bate, *Samuel Johnson*
**1979**—Leonard Baker, *Days of Sorrow and Pain: Leo Baeck and the Berlin Jews*

*(continued)*

### Biography or Autobiography *(continued)*

**1980**—Edmund Morris, *The Rise of Theodore Roosevelt*
**1981**—Robert K. Massie, *Peter the Great: His Life and World*
**1982**—William S. McFeely, *Grant: A Biography*
**1983**—Russell Baker, *Growing Up*
**1984**—Louis R. Harlan, *Booker T. Washington*
**1985**—Kenneth Silverman, *The Life and Times of Cotton Mather*
**1986**—Elizabeth Frank, *Louise Bogan: A Portrait*
**1987**—David J. Garrow, *Bearing the Cross: Martin Luther King Jr. and the Southern Christian Leadership Conference*
**1988**—David Herbert Donald, *Look Homeward: A Life of Thomas Wolfe*
**1989**—Richard Ellmann, *Oscar Wilde*
**1990**—Sebastian de Grazia, *Machiavelli in Hell*
**1991**—Steven Naifeh and Gregory White Smith, *Jackson Pollock: An American Saga*
**1992**—Lewis B. Puller Jr., *Fortunate Son: The Healing of a Vietnam Vet*
**1993**—David McCullough, *Truman*
**1994**—David Levering Lewis, *W.E.B. DuBois: Biography of a Race, 1868-1919*
**1995**—Joan D. Hedrick, *Harriet Beecher Stowe: A Life*
**1996**—Jack Miles, *God: A Biography*

### American Poetry

Before this prize was established in 1922, awards were made from gifts provided by the Poetry Society: **1918**—*Love Songs*, by Sara Teasdale; **1919**—*Old Road to Paradise*, by Margaret Widemer; *Corn Huskers*, by Carl Sandburg.

**1922**—Edwin Arlington Robinson, *Collected Poems*
**1923**—Edna St. Vincent Millay, *The Ballad of the Harp-Weaver; A Few Figs From Thistles; Eight Sonnets in American Poetry, 1922; A Miscellany*
**1924**—Robert Frost, *New Hampshire: A Poem With Notes and Grace Notes*
**1925**—Edwin Arlington Robinson, *The Man Who Died Twice*
**1926**—Amy Lowell, *What's O'Clock*
**1927**—Leonora Speyer, *Fiddler's Farewell*
**1928**—Edwin Arlington Robinson, *Tristram*
**1929**—Stephen Vincent Benet, *John Brown's Body*
**1930**—Conrad Aiken, *Selected Poems*
**1931**—Robert Frost, *Collected Poems*
**1932**—George Dillon, *The Flowering Stone*
**1933**—Archibald MacLeish, *Conquistador*
**1934**—Robert Hillyer, *Collected Verse*
**1935**—Audrey Wurdemann, *Bright Ambush*
**1936**—Robert P. Tristram Coffin, *Strange Holiness*
**1937**—Robert Frost, *A Further Range*
**1938**—Marya Zaturenska, *Cold Morning Sky*
**1939**—John Gould Fletcher, *Selected Poems*
**1940**—Mark Van Doren, *Collected Poems*
**1941**—Leonard Bacon, *Sunderland Capture*
**1942**—William Rose Benet, *The Dust Which Is God*
**1943**—Robert Frost, *A Witness Tree*
**1944**—Stephen Vincent Benet, *Western Star*
**1945**—Karl Shapiro, *V-Letter and Other Poems*
**1947**—Robert Lowell, *Lord Weary's Castle*
**1948**—W. H. Auden, *The Age of Anxiety*
**1949**—Peter Viereck, *Terror and Decorum*
**1950**—Gwendolyn Brooks, *Annie Allen*
**1951**—Carl Sandburg, *Complete Poems*
**1952**—Marianne Moore, *Collected Poems*
**1953**—Archibald MacLeish, *Collected Poems*
**1954**—Theodore Roethke, *The Waking*
**1955**—Wallace Stevens, *Collected Poems*
**1956**—Elizabeth Bishop, *Poems, North and South*
**1957**—Richard Wilbur, *Things of This World*
**1958**—Robert Penn Warren, *Promises: Poems 1954-1956*
**1959**—Stanley Kunitz, *Selected Poems 1928-1958*
**1960**—W. D. Snodgrass, *Heart's Needle*
**1961**—Phyllis McGinley, *Times Three: Selected Verse From Three Decades*
**1962**—Alan Dugan, *Poems*
**1963**—William Carlos Williams, *Pictures From Breughel*
**1964**—Louis Simpson, *At the End of the Open Road*
**1965**—John Berryman, *77 Dream Songs*
**1966**—Richard Eberhart, *Selected Poems*
**1967**—Anne Sexton, *Live or Die*
**1968**—Anthony Hecht, *The Hard Hours*
**1969**—George Oppen, *Of Being Numerous*
**1970**—Richard Howard, *Untitled Subjects*
**1971**—William S. Merwin, *The Carrier of Ladders*
**1972**—James Wright, *Collected Poems*
**1973**—Maxine Winokur Kumin, *Up Country*
**1974**—Robert Lowell, *The Dolphin*
**1975**—Gary Snyder, *Turtle Island*
**1976**—John Ashbery, *Self-Portrait in a Convex Mirror*
**1977**—James Merrill, *Divine Comedies*
**1978**—Howard Nemerov, *Collected Poems*
**1979**—Robert Penn Warren, *Now and Then: Poems 1976-1978*
**1980**—Donald Justice, *Selected Poems*
**1981**—James Schuyler, *The Morning of the Poem*
**1982**—Sylvia Plath, *The Collected Poems*
**1983**—Galway Kinnell, *Selected Poems*
**1984**—Mary Oliver, *American Primitive*
**1985**—Carolyn Kizer, *Yin*
**1986**—Henry Taylor, *The Flying Change*
**1987**—Rita Dove, *Thomas and Beulah*
**1988**—William Meredith, *Partial Accounts: New and Selected Poems*
**1989**—Richard Wilbur, *New and Collected Poems*
**1990**—Charles Simic, *The World Doesn't End*
**1991**—Mona Van Duyn, *Near Changes*
**1992**—James Tate, *Selected Poems*
**1993**—Louise Glück, *The Wild Iris*
**1994**—Yusef Komunyakaa, *Neon Vernacular*
**1995**—Philip Levine, *The Simple Truth*
**1996**—Jorie Graham, *The Dream of the Unified Field*

### General Nonfiction

**1962**—Theodore H. White, *The Making of the President 1960*
**1963**—Barbara W. Tuchman, *The Guns of August*
**1964**—Richard Hofstadter, *Anti-Intellectualism in American Life*
**1965**—Howard Mumford Jones, *O Strange New World*
**1966**—Edwin Way Teale, *Wandering Through Winter*
**1967**—David Brion Davis, *The Problem of Slavery in Western Culture*
**1968**—Will and Ariel Durant, *Rousseau and Revolution*
**1969**—Norman Mailer, *The Armies of the Night*; Rene Jules Dubos, *So Human an Animal: How We Are Shaped by Surroundings and Events*
**1970**—Eric H. Erikson, *Gandhi's Truth*
**1971**—John Toland, *The Rising Sun*
**1972**—Barbara W. Tuchman, *Stilwell and the American Experience in China, 1911-1945*
**1973**—Frances FitzGerald, *Fire in the Lake: The Vietnamese and the Americans in Vietnam*; Robert Coles, *Children of Crisis,* Volumes II & III
**1974**—Ernest Becker, *The Denial of Death*
**1975**—Annie Dillard, *Pilgrim at Tinker Creek*
**1976**—Robert N. Butler, *Why Survive? Being Old in America*
**1977**—William W. Warner, *Beautiful Swimmers*
**1978**—Carl Sagan, *The Dragons of Eden*
**1979**—Edward O. Wilson, *On Human Nature*
**1980**—Douglas R. Hofstadter, *Gödel, Escher, Bach: An Eternal Golden Braid*
**1981**—Carl E. Schorske, *Fin-de-Siecle Vienna: Politics and Culture*
**1982**—Tracy Kidder, *The Soul of a New Machine*
**1983**—Susan Sheehan, *Is There No Place on Earth for Me?*
**1984**—Paul Starr, *Social Transformation of American Medicine*
**1985**—Studs Terkel, *The Good War*
**1986**—Joseph Lelyveld, *Move Your Shadow*; J. Anthony Lukas, *Common Ground*
**1987**—David K. Shipler, *Arab and Jew*
**1988**—Richard Rhodes, *The Making of the Atomic Bomb*
**1989**—Neil Sheehan, *A Bright Shining Lie: John Paul Vann and America in Vietnam*
**1990**—Dale Maharidge and Michael Williamson, *And Their Children After Them*
**1991**—Bert Holldobler and Edward O. Wilson, *The Ants*
**1992**—Daniel Yergin, *The Prize: The Epic Quest for Oil*
**1993**—Garry Wills, *Lincoln at Gettysburg*
**1994**—David Remnick, *Lenin's Tomb: The Last Days of the Soviet Empire*
**1995**—Jonathan Weiner, *The Beak of the Finch: A Story of Evolution in Our Time*
**1996**—Tina Rosenberg, *The Haunted Land: Facing Europe's Ghosts After Communism*

## Music

For composition by an American (before 1977, by a composer resident in the U.S.), in the larger forms of chamber, orchestra, or choral music or for an operatic work including ballet. A special posthumous award was granted in 1976 to Scott Joplin.

**1943**—William Schuman, *Secular Cantata No. 2, A Free Song*
**1944**—Howard Hanson, *Symphony No. 4, Op. 34*
**1945**—Aaron Copland, *Appalachian Spring*
**1946**—Leo Sowerby, *The Canticle of the Sun*
**1947**—Charles E. Ives, *Symphony No. 3*
**1948**—Walter Piston, *Symphony No. 3*
**1949**—Virgil Thomson, *Louisiana Story*
**1950**—Gian-Carlo Menotti, *The Consul*
**1951**—Douglas Moore, *Giants in the Earth*
**1952**—Gail Kubik, *Symphony Concertante*

**1954**—Quincy Porter, *Concerto for Two Pianos and Orchestra*
**1955**—Gian-Carlo Menotti, *The Saint of Bleecker Street*
**1956**—Ernest Toch, *Symphony No. 3*
**1957**—Norman Dello Joio, *Meditations on Ecclesiastes*
**1958**—Samuel Barber, *Vanessa*
**1959**—John La Montaine, *Concerto for Piano and Orchestra*
**1960**—Elliott Carter, *Second String Quartet*
**1961**—Walter Piston, *Symphony No. 7*
**1962**—Robert Ward, *The Crucible*
**1963**—Samuel Barber, *Piano Concerto No. 1*
**1966**—Leslie Bassett, *Variations for Orchestra*
**1967**—Leon Kirchner, *Quartet No. 3*
**1968**—George Crumb, *Echoes of Time and The River*
**1969**—Karel Husa, *String Quartet No. 3*
**1970**—Charles W. Wuorinen, *Time's Encomium*
**1971**—Mario Davidovsky, *Synchronisms No. 6*
**1972**—Jacob Druckman, *Windows*
**1973**—Elliott Carter, *String Quartet No. 3*
**1974**—Donald Martino, *Notturno.* (Special Citation) Roger Sessions
**1975**—Dominick Argento, *From the Diary of Virginia Woolf*
**1976**—Ned Rorem, *Air Music*
**1977**—Richard Wernick, *Visions of Terror and Wonder*
**1978**—Michael Colgrass, *Deja Vu for Percussion and Orchestra*
**1979**—Joseph Schwantner, *Aftertones of Infinity*
**1980**—David Del Tredici, *In Memory of a Summer Day*
**1982**—Roger Sessions, *Concerto for Orchestra* (Special Citation) Milton Babbitt
**1983**—Ellen T. Zwilich, *Three Movements for Orchestra*
**1984**—Bernard Rands, *Canti del Sole*
**1985**—Stephen Albert, *Symphony, RiverRun*
**1986**—George Perle, *Wind Quintet IV*
**1987**—John Harbison, *The Flight Into Egypt*
**1988**—William Bolcom, *12 New Etudes for Piano*
**1989**—Roger Reynolds, *Whispers Out of Time*
**1990**—Mel Powell, *Duplicates: A Concerto for Two Pianos and Orchestra*
**1991**—Shulamit Ran, *Symphony*
**1992**—Wayne Peterson, *The Face of the Night, The Heart of the Dark*
**1993**—Christopher Rouse, *Trombone Concerto*
**1994**—Gunther Schuller, *Of Reminiscences and Reflections*
**1995**—Morton Gould, *Stringmusic*
**1996**—George Walker, *Lilacs*

## Miscellaneous Book Awards

Awarded in 1995 or 1996

**Academy of American Poets Awards**, (1996) James Laughlin Award, $5,000: David Rivard, *Wise Poison*; Walt Whitman Award, $1,000: Joshua Clover, *Madonna Anno Domini;* Landon Translation Award, $1,000: Guy Davenport, *7 Greeks*; Frank O'Hara Citation: *The Postman (Il Postino)*

**American Academy of Arts and Letters,** 1996 gold medal for history: Peter Gay; academy awards: in literature, Whitney Balliett, Carol Brightman, Robert Fagles, Robert Hughes, August Kleinzahler, Larry Kramer, Paul Muldoon, David Quammen; Rosenthal Award for Literature, David Long, *Blue Spruce;* Kaufman Prize, $2,500: Peter Landesman, *The Raven;* E. M. Forster Award, $12,500: Jim Crace

**Booker Prize,** British award for fiction, $32,000: Pat Barker, *The Ghost Road*

**Curtis Benjamin Award**, for creative publishing: Robert Bernstein, former Random House chairman

**Caldecott Medal**, by American Library Assn., for most distinguished American picture book: Peggy Rathmann, *Officer Buckle and Gloria*

**Truman Capote Lifetime Achievement Award in Literary Criticism,** awarded every four years, $100,000: Alfred Kazin

**Ruth Lilly Poetry Prize**, by *Poetry* magazine, $75,000: Gerald Stern

**Christopher Awards**, by The Christophers, for expression of highest values of human spirit, bronze medallion each: Johnathon Kozol, *Amazing Grace: The Lives of Children and the Conscience of a Nation*; Lawrence Martin Jenco, O.S.M., *Bound to Forgive: The Pilgrimage to Reconcilliation of a Beirut Hostage*; David Herbert Donald, *Lincoln*; Ruth-Alice von Bismarck and Ulrich Kabbirz, eds.,*Love Letters From Cell 92: The Correspondence Between Dietrich Bonhoeffer and Maria von Wedmeyer 1943-45*; Kathryn Watterson, *Not By the Sword: How the Love of a Cantor and His Family Transformed a Klansman*; Jeff Leeland, *One Small Sparrow*; Eric Lomax, *The Railway Man: A POW's Searing Account of War, Brutality and Forgiveness*

**Society of American Historians**, Francis Parkman Prize: Robert D. Richardson Jr., *Emerson: The Mind on Fire*

**Lincoln Prize**, by Lincoln Soldiers Institute at Gettysburg College, for lifetime contribution to Civil War studies, $35,000 and a bronze bust of Lincoln: *Lincoln,* David Herbert Donald

**National Book Awards,** by National Book Foundation, $10,000 each: nonfiction: Tina Rosenberg, *The Haunted Land: Facing Europe's Ghosts After Communism;* poetry: Stanley Kunitz, *Passing Through: The Later Poems, New and Selected;* fiction: Philip Roth, *Sabbath's Theater;* Medal for Distinguished Contribution to American Letters: David McCullough

**National Book Critics Circle Awards**, fiction: Stanley Elkin, *Mrs. Ted Bliss;* nonfiction: Jonathan Harr, *A Civil Action;* criticism: Robert Darnton, *The Forbidden Best-Sellers of Pre-Revolutionary France;* biography: Robert Polito, *Savage Art: A Biography of Jim Thompson;* poetry: William Matthews, *Time & Money ;* reviewing: Laurie Stone; lifetime achievement in publishing: Alfred Kazin , Elizabeth Hardwick

**Golden Kite Awards**, by Society of Children's Book Writiers and Illustrators: fiction: Christopher Paul Curtis, *The Watsons Go to Birmingham-1963;* nonfiction: Natalie S. Bober, *Abigail Adams;* picture-illustration: Dennis Nolan and Lauren Mills, *Fairy Wings*

**PEN/Faulkner Award**, for fiction, $15,000: Richard Ford, *Independence Day*

**Edgar Allan Poe Awards,** by the Mystery Writers of America: Grand Master award for 1996: Dick Francis; best mystery 1995: Dick Francis, *Come to Grief*

**Whiting Writers' Award**, by the Whiting Foundation for outstanding talent and promise: André Aciman, Michael Cunningham, Lucy Grealy, Suzannah Lessard, Reginald McKnight, James McMichael, Mary Ruefle, Russ Rymer, Matthew Stadler, Melanie Sumner

## Newbery Medal Books

The Newbery Medal is awarded annually by the Association for Library Service to Children, a division of the American Library Association, to the author of the most distinguished contribution to American literature for children.

| Year Awarded | Book, Author |
|---|---|
| 1922 | *The Story of Mankind,* Hendrik Willem van Loon |
| 1923 | *The Voyages of Dr. Dolittle,* Hugh Lofting |
| 1924 | *The Dark Frigate,* Charles Boardman Hawes |
| 1925 | *Tales From Silver Lands,* Charles Joseph Finger |
| 1926 | *Shen of the Sea,* Arthur Bowie Chrisman |
| 1927 | *Smoky, the Cowhorse,* Will James |
| 1928 | *Gay-Neck,* Dhan Gopal Mukerji |
| 1929 | *The Trumpeter of Krakow,* Eric P. Kelly |
| 1930 | *Hitty, Her First Hundred Years,* Rachel Field |
| 1931 | *The Cat Who Went to Heaven,* Elizabeth Coatsworth |
| 1932 | *Waterless Mountain,* Laura Adams Armer |
| 1933 | *Young Fu of the Upper Yangtze,* Elizabeth Foreman Lewis |
| 1934 | *Invincible Louisa,* Cornelia Lynde Meigs |
| 1935 | *Dobry,* Monica Shannon |
| 1936 | *Caddie Woodlawn,* Carol Ryrie Brink |
| 1937 | *Roller Skates,* Ruth Sawyer |
| 1938 | *The White Stag,* Kate Seredy |
| 1939 | *Thimble Summer,* Elizabeth Enright |
| 1940 | *Daniel Boone,* James Daugherty |
| 1941 | *Call It Courage,* Armstrong Sperry |
| 1942 | *The Matchlock Gun,* Walter D. Edmonds |
| 1943 | *Adam of the Road,* Elizabeth Janet Gray |
| 1944 | *Johnny Tremain,* Esther Forbes |
| 1945 | *Rabbit Hill,* Robert Lawson |
| 1946 | *Strawberry Girl,* Lois Lenski |
| 1947 | *Miss Hickory,* Carolyn S. Bailey |
| 1948 | *Twenty-One Balloons,* William Pène Du Bois |
| 1949 | *King of the Wind,* Marguerite Henry |
| 1950 | *The Door in the Wall,* Marguerite de Angeli |
| 1951 | *Amos Fortune, Free Man,* Elizabeth Yates |
| 1952 | *Ginger Pye,* Eleanor Estes |
| 1953 | *Secret of the Andes,* Ann Nolan Clark |
| 1954 | *. . . And Now Miguel,* Joseph Krumgold |
| 1955 | *The Wheel on the School,* Meindert DeJong |
| 1956 | *Carry On, Mr. Bowditch,* Jean Lee Latham |
| 1957 | *Miracles on Maple Hill,* Virginia Sorensen |
| 1958 | *Rifles for Watie,* Harold Keith |
| 1959 | *The Witch of Blackbird Pond,* Elizabeth George Speare |
| 1960 | *Onion John,* Joseph Krumgold |

*(continued)*

## Newbery Medal Books *(continued)*

| Year Awarded | Book, Author |
|---|---|
| 1961 | *Island of the Blue Dolphins,* Scott O'Dell |
| 1962 | *The Bronze Bow,* Elizabeth George Speare |
| 1963 | *A Wrinkle in Time,* Madeleine L'Engle |
| 1964 | *It's Like This, Cat,* Emily Cheney Neville |
| 1965 | *Shadow of a Bull,* Maja Wojciechowska |
| 1966 | *I, Juan de Pareja,* Elizabeth Borton de Trevino |
| 1967 | *Up a Road Slowly,* Irene Hunt |
| 1968 | *From the Mixed-Up Files of Mrs. Basil E. Frankweiler,* E. L. Konigsburg |
| 1969 | *The High King,* Lloyd Alexander |
| 1970 | *Sounder,* William H. Armstrong |
| 1971 | *The Summer of the Swans,* Betsy Byars |
| 1972 | *Mrs. Frisby and the Rats of NIMH,* Robert C. O'Brien |
| 1973 | *Julie of the Wolves,* Jean George |
| 1974 | *The Slave Dancer,* Paula Fox |
| 1975 | *M. C. Higgins the Great,* Virginia Hamilton |
| 1976 | *Grey King,* Susan Cooper |
| 1977 | *Roll of Thunder, Hear My Cry,* Mildred D. Taylor |
| 1978 | *Bridge to Terabithia,* Katherine Paterson |
| 1979 | *The Westing Game,* Ellen Raskin |
| 1980 | *A Gathering of Days,* Joan Blos |
| 1981 | *Jacob Have I Loved,* Katherine Paterson |
| 1982 | *A Visit to William Blake's Inn: Poems for Innocent and Experienced Travelers,* Nancy Willard |
| 1983 | *Dicey's Song,* Cynthia Voigt |
| 1984 | *Dear Mr. Henshaw,* Beverly Cleary |
| 1985 | *The Hero and the Crown,* Robin McKinley |
| 1986 | *Sarah, Plain and Tall,* Patricia MacLachlan |
| 1987 | *The Whipping Boy,* Sid Fleischman |
| 1988 | *Lincoln: A Photobiography,* Russell Freedman |
| 1989 | *Joyful Noise: Poems for Two Voices,* Paul Fleischman |
| 1990 | *Number the Stars,* Lois Lowry |
| 1991 | *Maniac Magee,* Jerry Spinelli |
| 1992 | *Shiloh,* Phyllis Reynolds Naylor |
| 1993 | *Missing May,* Cynthia Rylant |
| 1994 | *The Giver,* Lois Lowry |
| 1995 | *Walk Two Moons,* Sharon Creech |
| 1996 | *The Midwife's Apprentice,* Karen Cushman |

## Journalism

**National Journalism Awards**, by Scripps Howard Foundation, for print journalism: service to literacy, $2,500 each: *The Blade*, Toledo, OH, and *WDEF-TV*, Chattanooga, TN; human interest writing, $2,500: Christine Bertelson, *St. Louis Post-Dispatch*; editorial writing, $2,000: Tom Dennis, *The Times Leader*, Wilkes-Barre, PA; environmental reporting, $2,000 each: *The News & Observer*, Raleigh, NC, and Tony Davis, *The Albuquerque (NM) Tribune*; public service reporting, $2,500 each: Ken Ward, *The Charleston (WV) Gazette,* and *The Orange County (CA) Register*; service to First Amendment, $2,500: *El Vocero de Puerto Rico*, San Juan, PR; college cartoonist, $2,000: Drew Sheneman, Central Michigan University; excellence in broadcast journalism, $2,000 each: *WUAL Radio*, Tuscaloosa, AL; *WHAS Radio*, Louisville, KY; *KXLY-TV*, Spokane, WA; *WSOC-TV*, Charlotte, NC

**National Magazine Awards**, by American Society of Magazine Editors and Columbia Univ. Graduate School of Journalism: general excellence, circulation over 1 million: *Business Week*; 400,000 to 1 million: *Outside*; 100,000 to 400,000: *Civilization*; under 100,000: *The Sciences*; single topic issue: *Bon App tit;* special interests: *Saveur*; feature writing: *GQ*; fiction: *Harper's;* design: *Wired;* photography: *Saveur;* reporting: *The New Yorker;* personal service: *SmartMoney;* public interest: *Texas Monthly;* essays and criticism: *The New Yorker*

**George Foster Peabody Awards,** by the Univ. of Georgia: *Blind Justice: Who Killed Janie Fray?*, WJR Radio, Detroit, MI; *Kevin's Sentence*, Canadian Broadcasting Corporation, Toronto, Can.; *St. Paul Sunday*, Minnesota Public Radio, St. Paul, MN; Oscar Brand, for broadcasting, WNYC, New York, NY; *Wynton Marsalis: Making the Music/Marsalis on Music*, National Public Radio, Washington, DC, and Sony Classical Film and Video for PBS; *The Peavy Investigation*, WFAA-TV, Dallas, TX; *Truth on Trial*, ABC News 20/20, New York, NY; *Target Seven: Armed and Angry*, WXYZ-TV, Detroit, MI; *New York City School Corruption*, WCBS-TV, New York, NY; *50 Years After the War*, Television Broadcasts Ltd., Kowloon, Hong Kong; *Hoop Dreams*, Kartemquin Educational Films and KTCA-TV, St. Paul, MN, presented by PBS; *The Dying Rooms*, A Cinemax Reel Life Presentation of a Lauderville Production for Channel 4, London, England, and Cinemax, New York; *Road Scholar*, Public Policy Productions Inc. with Thirteen/WNET, New York, NY, on PBS; *Rock & Roll*, WGBH-TV, Boston, MA, and BBC Bristol, UK; *Peter Jennings Reporting: Hiroshima: Why the Bomb Was Dropped*, ABC News, New York, NY; *Yugoslavia: The Death of a Nation*, Discovery Journal Special, Discovery Channel, Bethesda, MD, and Brian Lapping Associates for BBC London, England; *CBS Reports: In the Killing Fields of America*, CBS News, New York; *Complaints of a Dutiful Daughter*, P.O.V./Deborah Hoffman, New York, on PBS; *Hank Aaron: Chasing the Dream*, Turner Original Productions, Tollin/Robbins and Mundy Lane with Television Production Partners; *The Private Life of Plants*, Turner Original Productions and BBC Natural History, London, England; *Coming Out Under Fire*, DeepFocus Productions, Los Angeles, on PBS; *Wallace & Gromit*, Aardman Animations with Wallace & Gromit Ltd., BBC Children's International, BBC Bristol and BBC Lionheart; *Frontline: Waco The Inside Story*, Frontline/WGBH-TV, Boston, MA; *Coverage of the assasination of Yitzhak Rabin*, CBS News, New York; *Coverage of The Murrah Building bombing*, KFOR-TV, KOCO-TV, and KWTV-TV, Oklahoma City, OK; *The Politician's Wife*, Producers Films for Channel 4, London, England; *The Tuskegee Airmen*, Price Entertainment Production, HBO, New York; *Homicide: Life on the Street*, NBC, Baltimore Pictures, Reeves Entertainment SL/TMF Productions; *The Boys of St. Vincent*, Les Productions Tele-Action Inc. with the National Film Board of Canada, Canadian Broadcasting Corp., and Telefilm Canada on A&E Television Network, New York; *August Wilson's The Piano Lesson*, CBS, Craig Anderson Productions Inc. with Hallmark Hall of Fame Productions Inc.; *Serving in Silence: The Margarethe Cammermeyer Story*, NBC, Barwood Films Ltd., Story Line Productions Inc., and Trillium Productions with TriStar Television; *The Journey of Christopher Reeve*, ABC News 20/20, New York, NY; Oprah Winfrey, for broadcasting commitment and achievement

**George Polk Awards**, by Long Island Univ., for excellence in journalism: national: Michael Weisskopf, David Maraniss, *Washington Post;* metropolitan: Frank Bruni, Nina Bernstein, Joyce Purnick, Lizette Alvarez, *New York Times;* local: Elizabeth Llorente, *The Record,* Hackensack, NJ; foreign: David Rohde, *Christian Science Monitor*; education: Steve Stecklow, *Wall Street Journal*; medical: *Orange Country Register*, Santa Ana, CA; consumer: Lea Thompson, Lisa Cloherty, Sandra Surles, NBC News "Dateline"; business: Kurt Eichenwald, *New York Times*; magazine reporting: Richard Behar, *Fortune*; local television: Tom Grant, KREM-TV; network television: Jim Clancy, CNN; health care: Chris Adams, *Times-Picayune*, New Orleans; career: John K. Cooley, ABC News

**Reuben Awards,** by National Cartoonists Society: best cartoonist of 1996: Garry Trudeau.

## The Spingarn Medal

The Spingarn Medal has been awarded annually since 1915 by the National Association for the Advancement of Colored People for the highest achievement by a black American. The award is presented for accomplishments in the previous year.

| | |
|---|---|
| 1915 | Ernest E. Just |
| 1916 | Charles Young |
| 1917 | Harry T. Burleigh |
| 1918 | William S. Braithwaite |
| 1919 | Archibald H. Grimké |
| 1920 | W. E. B. Du Bois |
| 1921 | Charles S. Gilpin |
| 1922 | Mary B. Talbert |
| 1923 | George W.Carver |
| 1924 | Roland Hayes |
| 1925 | James W. Johnson |
| 1926 | Carter G. Woodson |
| 1927 | Anthony Overton |
| 1928 | Charles W. Chesnutt |
| 1929 | Mordecai W. Johnson |
| 1930 | Henry A. Hunt |
| 1931 | Richard B. Harrison |
| 1932 | Robert R. Moton |
| 1933 | Max Yergan |
| 1934 | William T. B. Williams |
| 1935 | Mary McLeod Bethune |
| 1936 | John Hope |
| 1937 | Walter White |
| 1938 | no award |
| 1939 | Marian Anderson |
| 1940 | Louis T. Wright |
| 1941 | Richard Wright |
| 1942 | A. Philip Randolph |
| 1943 | William H. Hastie |
| 1944 | Charles Drew |
| 1945 | Paul Robeson |
| 1946 | Thurgood Marshall |
| 1947 | Dr. Percy L. Julian |
| 1948 | Channing H. Tobias |
| 1949 | Ralph J. Bunche |
| 1950 | Charles H. Houston |
| 1951 | Mabel K. Staupers |
| 1952 | Harry T. Moore |
| 1953 | Paul R. Williams |
| 1954 | Theodore K. Lawless |
| 1955 | Carl Murphy |
| 1956 | Jack R. Robinson |
| 1957 | Martin Luther King Jr. |
| 1958 | Daisy Bates and the Little Rock Nine |
| 1959 | Edward Kennedy (Duke) Ellington |
| 1960 | Langston Hughes |
| 1961 | Kenneth B. Clark |
| 1962 | Robert C. Weaver |
| 1963 | Medgar W. Evers |
| 1964 | Roy Wilkins |
| 1965 | Leontyne Price |
| 1966 | John H. Johnson |
| 1967 | Edward W. Brooke |
| 1968 | Sammy Davis Jr. |

| | | | | | | | |
|---|---|---|---|---|---|---|---|
| 1969 | Clarence M. Mitchell Jr. | 1976 | Alvin Ailey | 1983 | Lena Horne | 1990 | L. Douglas Wilder |
| 1970 | Jacob Lawrence | 1977 | Alex Haley | 1984 | Thomas Bradley | 1991 | Gen. Colin L. Powell |
| 1971 | Leon H. Sullivan | 1978 | Andrew Young | 1985 | Bill Cosby | 1992 | Barbara Jordan |
| 1972 | Gordon Parks | 1979 | Mrs. Rosa L. Parks | 1986 | Dr. Benjamin L. Hooks | 1993 | Dorothy I. Height |
| 1973 | Wilson C. Riles | 1980 | Dr. Rayford W. Logan | 1987 | Percy E. Sutton | 1994 | Maya Angelou |
| 1974 | Damon Keith | 1981 | Coleman Young | 1988 | Frederick D. Patterson | 1995 | John Hope Franklin |
| 1975 | Henry (Hank) Aaron | 1982 | Dr. Benjamin E. Mays | 1989 | Jesse Jackson | 1996 | A. Leon Higginbotham |

# Miscellaneous Awards

**American Academy of Arts and Letters,** 1996 gold medal in architecture: Philip Johnson; award of merit, for sculpture, $5,000: George Trakas; academy award in Architecture, Maya Lin; in Art, Jack Beal, John Moore, Jim Nutt, Otto Piene; in Music, Ronald Caltabiano, Richard Danielpour, Anthony Davis, Scott Lindroth; Rosenthal Award, $5,000: for Art, Diana Horowitz; Academy Fellowship prize, $20,000: Jay Wright

**Charles Frankel Prizes,** by National Endowment for the Humanities, for those who have increased public awareness of the humanities (1995), $5,000 each: Charles Kuralt, William Ferris, David Macaulay, David McCullough, and Bernice Johnson Reagon

**National Inventor of the Year Awards,** by Intellectual Property Owners: Eastman Kodak Company, SRAM Corp.

**John F. Kennedy Center for the Performing Arts Awards,** for contribution to U.S. cultural life (1995): Jacques d'Amboise, Marilyn Horne, B. B. King, Sidney Poitier, Neil Simon

**National Medal of Arts,** by White House, for outstanding contributions to cultural life in the U.S. (1995): Bob Hope, Licia Albanese, Gwendolyn Brooks, Roy Lichtenstein, B. Gerald Cantor, Iris Cantor, Ossie Davis, Ruby Dee, David Diamond, James Ingo Freed, Arthur Mitchell, William S. Monroe, Urban Gateways

**Pritzker Architecture Prize,** by the Hyatt Foundation, $100,000: Jose Rafael Moneo

**1996 Teacher of the Year,** by the Council of Chief State School Officers and Scholastic Inc.: Mary Beth Blegen, Worthington, MN

**Library of the Year Award,** by Gale Research, Inc., and Library Journal, $10,000 grant: Broward County Library, Ft. Lauderdale, FL

**Templeton Prize for Progress in Religion**, by Templeton Foundation, about $1 million: Bill Bright, founder and president of the international ministry Campus Crusade for Christ

**Westinghouse Talent Search,** 1st place, $40,000 scholarship: Jacob Lurie, Bethesda, MD; 2d place, $30,000 scholarship: Ting Luo, Woodside, Queens; 3d place, $20,000 scholarship: Matthew Graham, Orange Park, Fl; 4th place, $15,000 scholarship: Bruce Haggerty, New York, NY; 5th place, $15,000 scholarship: Aaron Einbond, New York, NY; 6th place, $15,000 scholarship: Daniel Weitz, Morristown, NJ; 7th place, $10,000 scholarship: Brian Hafler, West Newton, MA; 8th place, $10,000 scholarship: Simon DeDeo, New York, NY; 9th place, $10,000 scholarship: Sidney Chang, Dix Hills, NY; 10th place, $10,000 scholarship: Vezen Wu, Jacksonville, FL

# Miss America Winners

| | |
|---|---|
| 1921 | Margaret Gorman, Washington, DC |
| 1922-23 | Mary Campbell, Columbus, Ohio |
| 1924 | Ruth Malcolmson, Philadelphia, Pennsylvania |
| 1925 | Fay Lamphier, Oakland, California |
| 1926 | Norma Smallwood, Tulsa, Oklahoma |
| 1927 | Lois Delander, Joliet, Illinois |
| 1933 | Marion Bergeron, West Haven, Connecticut |
| 1935 | Henrietta Leaver, Pittsburgh, Pennsylvania |
| 1936 | Rose Coyle, Philadelphia, Pennsylvania |
| 1937 | Bette Cooper, Bertrand Island, New Jersey |
| 1938 | Marilyn Meseke, Marion, Ohio |
| 1939 | Patricia Donnelly, Detroit, Michigan |
| 1940 | Frances Marie Burke, Philadelphia, Pennsylvania |
| 1941 | Rosemary LaPlanche, Los Angeles, California |
| 1942 | Jo-Caroll Dennison, Tyler, Texas |
| 1943 | Jean Bartel, Los Angeles, California |
| 1944 | Venus Ramey, Washington, D.C. |
| 1945 | Bess Myerson, New York City, New York |
| 1946 | Marilyn Buferd, Los Angeles, California |
| 1947 | Barbara Walker, Memphis, Tennessee |
| 1948 | BeBe Shopp, Hopkins, Minnesota |
| 1949 | Jacque Mercer, Litchfield, Arizona |
| 1951 | Yolande Betbeze, Mobile, Alabama |
| 1952 | Coleen Kay Hutchins, Salt Lake City, Utah |
| 1953 | Neva Jane Langley, Macon, Georgia |
| 1954 | Evelyn Margaret Ay, Ephrata, Pennsylvania |
| 1955 | Lee Meriwether, San Francisco, California |
| 1956 | Sharon Ritchie, Denver, Colorado |
| 1957 | Marian McKnight, Manning, South Carolina |
| 1958 | Marilyn Van Derbur, Denver, Colorado |
| 1959 | Mary Ann Mobley, Brandon, Mississippi |
| 1960 | Lynda Lee Mead, Natchez, Mississippi |
| 1961 | Nancy Fleming, Montague, Michigan |
| 1962 | Maria Fletcher, Asheville, North Carolina |
| 1963 | Jacquelyn Mayer, Sandusky, Ohio |
| 1964 | Donna Axum, El Dorado, Arkansas |
| 1965 | Vonda Kay Van Dyke, Phoenix, Arizona |
| 1966 | Deborah Irene Bryant, Overland Park, Kansas |
| 1967 | Jane Anne Jayroe, Laverne, Oklahoma |
| 1968 | Debra Dene Barnes, Moran, Kansas |
| 1969 | Judith Anne Ford, Belvidere, Illinois |
| 1970 | Pamela Anne Eldred, Birmingham, Michigan |
| 1971 | Phyllis Ann George, Denton, Texas |
| 1972 | Laurie Lea Schaefer, Columbus, Ohio |
| 1973 | Terry Anne Meeuwsen, DePere, Wisconsin |
| 1974 | Rebecca Ann King, Denver, Colorado |
| 1975 | Shirley Cothran, Fort Worth, Texas |
| 1976 | Tawney Elaine Godin, Yonkers, New York |
| 1977 | Dorothy Kathleen Benham, Edina, Minnesota |
| 1978 | Susan Perkins, Columbus, Ohio |
| 1979 | Kylene Barker, Galax, Virginia |
| 1980 | Cheryl Prewitt, Ackerman, Mississippi |
| 1981 | Susan Powell, Elk City, Oklahoma |
| 1982 | Elizabeth Ward, Russellville, Arkansas |
| 1983 | Debra Maffett, Anaheim, California |
| 1984 | Vanessa Williams, Milwood, New York* |
| | Suzette Charles, Mays Landing, New Jersey |
| 1985 | Sharlene Wells, Salt Lake City, Utah |
| 1986 | Susan Akin, Meridian, Mississippi |
| 1987 | Kellye Cash, Memphis, Tennessee |
| 1988 | Kaye Lani Rae Rafko, Monroe, Michigan |
| 1989 | Gretchen Carlson, Anoka, Minnesota |
| 1990 | Debbye Turner, Columbia, Missouri |
| 1991 | Marjorie Vincent, Oak Park, Illinois |
| 1992 | Carolyn Suzanne Sapp, Honolulu, Hawaii |
| 1993 | Leanza Cornett, Jacksonville, Florida |
| 1994 | Kimberly Aiken, Columbia, South Carolina |
| 1995 | Heather Whitestone, Birmingham, Alabama |
| 1996 | Shawntel Smith, Muldrow, Oklahoma |
| 1997 | Tara Dawn Holland, Overland Park, Kansas |

* Resigned July 23, 1984.

# Entertainment Awards

## 1995-96 Emmy Awards

### Prime-Time Emmy Awards

Drama series: *E.R.*, NBC
Comedy series: *Frasier*, NBC
Miniseries: *Gulliver's Travels*,
Television movie: *Truman*, HBO
Variety, music, comedy special: *The Kennedy Center Honors*, CBS
Variety, music, comedy series: *Dennis Miller Live*, HBO
Lead actor, drama series: Dennis Franz, *N.Y.P.D. Blue*, ABC
Lead actress, drama series: Kathy Baker, *Picket Fences*, CBS
Lead actor, comedy series: John Lithgow, *Third Rock From the Sun*, NBC
Lead actress, comedy series: Helen Hunt, *Mad About You*, NBC
Lead actor, miniseries/special: Alan Rickman, *Rasputin*, HBO
Lead actress, miniseries/special: Helen Mirren, *Prime Suspect: Scent of Darkness*, PBS
Supporting actor, drama series: Ray Walston, *Picket Fences*, CBS
Supporting actress, drama series: Tyne Daly, *Christy*, CBS
Supporting actor, comedy series: Rip Torn, *The Larry Sanders Show*, HBO
Supporting actress, comedy series: Julia Louis-Dreyfus, *Seinfeld*, NBC
Supporting actor, miniseries/special: Tom Hulce, *The Heidi Chronicles*, TNT
Supporting actress, miniseries/special: Greta Scacchi, *Rasputin*, HBO
Individual performance, variety/music program: Tony Bennett, *Tony Bennett Live by Request: A Valentine Special*, A&E
Directing, drama series: Jeremy Kagan, *Chicago Hope: Leave of Absence*, CBS

*(continued)*

### Prime-Time Emmy Awards *(continued)*

Directing, comedy series: Michael Lembeck, *Friends: The One After the Superbowl*, NBC
Directing, miniseries/special: John Frankenheimer, *Andersonville*, TNT
Directing, variety/music program: Louis J. Horvitz, *The Kennedy Center Honors*, CBS
Writing, drama series: Darin Morgan, *The X-Files: Clyde Bruckman's Final Repose*, FOX
Writing, comedy series: Joe Keenan, Christopher Lloyd, Rob Greenberg, Jack Burditt, Chuck Ranberg, Anne Flett-Giordano, Linda Morris and Vic Rauseo, *Frasier: Moon Dance*, NBC
Writing, miniseries/special: Simon Moore, *Gulliver's Travels*
Writing, variety/music program: Dennis Miller, *Dennis Miller Live*, HBO
President's Award: *Blacklist: Hollywood on Trial*, AMC

### Daytime Emmy Awards

Drama series: *General Hospital*, ABC
Actress: Erika Slezak, *One Life to Live*, ABC
Actor: Charles Keating, *Another World*, NBC
Supporting actress: Anna Holbrook, *Another World*, NBC
Supporting actor: Jerry Ver Dorn, *Guiding Light*, CBS
Directing team: *The Young and the Restless*, CBS
Writing team: *All My Children*, ABC
Game/Audience participation show: *The Price Is Right*, CBS
Game show host: Bob Barker
Children's series: *Reading Rainbow*, PBS
Animated children's program: *Animaniacs*, WB
Outstanding talk show: *The Oprah Winfrey Show*, SYN
Talk show host: Montel Williams

## 1995-96 Tony (Antoinette Perry) Awards

Play: *Master Class*, by Terrence McNally
Musical: *Rent*
Actor, play: George Grizzard, *A Delicate Balance*
Actress, play: Zoe Caldwell, *Master Class*
Actor, musical: Nathan Lane, *A Funny Thing Happened on the Way to the Forum*
Actress, musical: Donna Murphy, *The King and I*
Musical score: *Rent*
Director, play: Gerald Gutierrez, *A Delicate Balance*
Director, musical: George C. Wolfe, *Bring in 'da Noise, Bring in 'da Funk*
Play revival: *A Delicate Balance*
Musical revival: *The King and I*
Featured actor, play: Ruben Santiago-Hudson, *Seven Guitars*
Featured actress, play: Audra McDonald, *Master Class*
Featured actor, musical: Wilson Jermaine Heredia, *Rent*
Featured actress, musical: Ann Duquesnay, *Bring in 'da Noise, Bring in 'da Funk*
Choreography: Savion Glover, *Bring in 'da Noise, Bring in 'da Funk*
Costume design: Roger Kirk, *The King and I*
Scenic design: Brian Thomson, *The King and I*
Lighting design: Jules Fisher and Peggy Eisenhauer, *Bring in 'da Noise, Bring in 'da Funk*
Regional Theatre: Alley Theater, Houston

## Golden Globe Awards

**Movies**
Drama: *Sense and Sensibility*
Musical/comedy: *Babe*
Actress, drama: Sharon Stone, *Casino*
Actor, drama: Nicolas Cage, *Leaving Las Vegas*
Actress, musical/comedy: Nicole Kidman, *To Die For*
Actor, musical/comedy: John Travolta, *Get Shorty*
Supporting actress, drama: Mira Sorvino, *Mighty Aphrodite*
Supporting actor, drama: Brad Pitt, *12 Monkeys*
Director: Mel Gibson, *Braveheart*
Screenplay: Emma Thompson, *Sense and Sensibility*
Foreign-language film: *Les Misérables*
Original Score: Maurice Jarre, *A Walk in the Clouds*
Original song: *Colors of the Wind*, from *Pocahontas*
Cecil B. De Mille Award: Sean Connery

**Television**
Series, drama: *Party of Five*
Actress, drama: Jane Seymour, *Dr. Quinn, Medicine Woman*
Actor, drama: Jimmy Smits, *N.Y.P.D. Blue*
Series, musical/comedy: *Cybill*
Actress, musical/comedy: Cybill Shepherd, *Cybill*
Actor, musical/comedy: Kelsey Grammer, *Frasier*
Miniseries, movie made for TV: *Indictment: The McMartin Trial*
Actress, miniseries, movie made for TV: Jessica Lange, *A Streetcar Named Desire*
Actor, miniseries, movie made for TV: Gary Sinise, *Truman*
Supporting actress, miniseries, movie made for TV: Shirley Knight, *Indictment: The McMartin Trial*
Supporting actor, miniseries, movie made for TV: Donald Sutherland, *Citizen X*

## Academy Awards (Oscars)

**1927-28**
Picture: *Wings*, Paramount
Actor: Emil Jannings, *The Way of All Flesh*
Actress: Janet Gaynor, *Seventh Heaven*
Director: Frank Borzage, *Seventh Heaven*; Lewis Milestone, *Two Arabian Knights*

**1928-29**
Picture: *Broadway Melody*, MGM
Actor: Warner Baxter, *In Old Arizona*
Actress: Mary Pickford, *Coquette*
Director: Frank Lloyd, *The Divine Lady*

**1929-30**
Picture: *All Quiet on the Western Front*, Universal
Actor: George Arliss, *Disraeli*
Actress: Norma Shearer, *The Divorcee*
Director: Lewis Milestone, *All Quiet on the Western Front*

**1930-31**
Picture: *Cimarron*, RKO
Actor: Lionel Barrymore, *Free Soul*
Actress: Marie Dressler, *Min and Bill*
Director: Norman Taurog, *Skippy*

**1931-32**
Picture: *Grand Hotel*, MGM
Actor: Fredric March, *Dr. Jekyll and Mr. Hyde*; Wallace Beery, *The Champ* (tie)
Actress: Helen Hayes, *The Sin of Madelon Claudet*
Director: Frank Borzage, *Bad Girl*
Special: Walt Disney, *Mickey Mouse*

**1932-33**
Picture: *Cavalcade*, Fox
Actor: Charles Laughton, *The Private Life of Henry VIII*
Actress: Katharine Hepburn, *Morning Glory*
Director: Frank Lloyd, *Cavalcade*

**1934**
Picture: *It Happened One Night*, Columbia
Actor: Clark Gable, *It Happened One Night*
Actress: Claudette Colbert, *It Happened One Night*
Director: Frank Capra, *It Happened One Night*

**1935**
Picture: *Mutiny on the Bounty*, MGM
Actor: Victor McLaglen, *The Informer*
Actress: Bette Davis, *Dangerous*
Director: John Ford, *The Informer*

**1936**
Picture: *The Great Ziegfeld*, MGM
Actor: Paul Muni, *Story of Louis Pasteur*
Actress: Luise Rainer, *The Great Ziegfeld*
Sup. Actor: Walter Brennan, *Come and Get It*
Sup. Actress: Gale Sondergaard, *Anthony Adverse*
Director: Frank Capra, *Mr. Deeds Goes to Town*

**1937**
Picture: *Life of Emile Zola*, Warner
Actor: Spencer Tracy, *Captains Courageous*
Actress: Luise Rainer, *The Good Earth*
Sup. Actor: Joseph Schildkraut, *Life of Emile Zola*
Sup. Actress: Alice Brady, *In Old Chicago*
Director: Leo McCarey, *The Awful Truth*

**1938**
Picture: *You Can't Take It With You*, Columbia
Actor: Spencer Tracy, *Boys Town*
Actress: Bette Davis, *Jezebel*
Sup. Actor: Walter Brennan, *Kentucky*
Sup. Actress: Fay Bainter, *Jezebel*
Director: Frank Capra, *You Can't Take It With You*

**1939**
Picture: *Gone With the Wind*, Selznick International
Actor: Robert Donat, *Goodbye, Mr. Chips*
Actress: Vivien Leigh, *Gone With the Wind*
Sup. Actor: Thomas Mitchell, *Stage Coach*
Sup. Actress: Hattie McDaniel, *Gone With the Wind*
Director: Victor Fleming, *Gone With the Wind*

**1940**
Picture: *Rebecca*, Selznick International
Actor: James Stewart, *The Philadelphia Story*
Actress: Ginger Rogers, *Kitty Foyle*
Sup. Actor: Walter Brennan, *The Westerner*
Sup. Actress: Jane Darwell, *The Grapes of Wrath*
Director: John Ford, *The Grapes of Wrath*

**1941**
Picture: *How Green Was My Valley*, 20th Cent.-Fox
Actor: Gary Cooper, *Sergeant York*
Actress: Joan Fontaine, *Suspicion*
Sup. Actor: Donald Crisp, *How Green Was My Valley*
Sup. Actress: Mary Astor, *The Great Lie*
Director: John Ford, *How Green Was My Valley*

**1942**
Picture: *Mrs. Miniver*, MGM
Actor: James Cagney, *Yankee Doodle Dandy*
Actress: Greer Garson, *Mrs. Miniver*
Sup. Actor: Van Heflin, *Johnny Eager*
Sup. Actress: Teresa Wright, *Mrs. Miniver*
Director: William Wyler, *Mrs. Miniver*

**1943**
Picture: *Casablanca,* Warner
Actor: Paul Lukas, *Watch on the Rhine*
Actress: Jennifer Jones, *The Song of Bernadette*
Sup. Actor: Charles Coburn, *The More the Merrier*
Sup. Actress: Katina Paxinou, *For Whom the Bell Tolls*
Director: Michael Curtiz, *Casablanca*

**1944**
Picture: *Going My Way,* Paramount
Actor: Bing Crosby, *Going My Way*
Actress: Ingrid Bergman, *Gaslight*
Sup. Actor: Barry Fitzgerald, *Going My Way*
Sup. Actress: Ethel Barrymore, *None But the Lonely Heart*
Director: Leo McCarey, *Going My Way*

**1945**
Picture: *The Lost Weekend,* Paramount
Actor: Ray Milland, *The Lost Weekend*
Actress: Joan Crawford, *Mildred Pierce*
Sup. Actor: James Dunn, *A Tree Grows in Brooklyn*
Sup. Actress: Anne Revere, *National Velvet*
Director: Billy Wilder, *The Lost Weekend*

**1946**
Picture: *The Best Years of Our Lives,* Goldwyn, RKO
Actor: Fredric March, *The Best Years of Our Lives*
Actress: Olivia de Havilland, *To Each His Own*
Sup. Actor: Harold Russell, *The Best Years of Our Lives*
Sup. Actress: Anne Baxter, *The Razor's Edge*
Director: William Wyler, *The Best Years of Our Lives*

**1947**
Picture: *Gentleman's Agreement,* 20th Cent.-Fox
Actor: Ronald Colman, *A Double Life*
Actress: Loretta Young, *The Farmer's Daughter*
Sup. Actor: Edmund Gwenn, *Miracle on 34th Street*
Sup. Actress: Celeste Holm, *Gentleman's Agreement*
Director: Elia Kazan, *Gentleman's Agreement*

**1948**
Picture: *Hamlet,* Two Cities Film, Universal International
Actor: Laurence Olivier, *Hamlet*
Actress: Jane Wyman, *Johnny Belinda*
Sup. Actor: Walter Huston, *Treasure of Sierra Madre*
Sup. Actress: Claire Trevor, *Key Largo*
Director: John Huston, *Treasure of Sierra Madre*

**1949**
Picture: *All the King's Men,* Columbia
Actor: Broderick Crawford, *All the King's Men*
Actress: Olivia de Havilland, *The Heiress*
Sup. Actor: Dean Jagger, *Twelve O'Clock High*
Sup. Actress: Mercedes McCambridge, *All the King's Men*
Director: Joseph L. Mankiewicz, *Letter to Three Wives*

**1950**
Picture: *All About Eve,* 20th Century-Fox
Actor: Jose Ferrer, *Cyrano de Bergerac*
Actress: Judy Holliday, *Born Yesterday*
Sup. Actor: George Sanders, *All About Eve*
Sup. Actress: Josephine Hull, *Harvey*
Director: Joseph L. Mankiewicz, *All About Eve*

**1951**
Picture: *An American in Paris,* MGM
Actor: Humphrey Bogart, *The African Queen*
Actress: Vivien Leigh, *A Streetcar Named Desire*
Sup. Actor: Karl Malden, *A Streetcar Named Desire*
Sup. Actress: Kim Hunter, *A Streetcar Named Desire*
Director: George Stevens, *A Place in the Sun*

**1952**
Picture: *The Greatest Show on Earth,* C.B. DeMille, Paramount
Actor: Gary Cooper, *High Noon*
Actress: Shirley Booth, *Come Back, Little Sheba*
Sup. Actor: Anthony Quinn, *Viva Zapata!*
Sup. Actress: Gloria Grahame, *The Bad and the Beautiful*
Director: John Ford, *The Quiet Man*

**1953**
Picture: *From Here to Eternity,* Columbia
Actor: William Holden, *Stalag 17*
Actress: Audrey Hepburn, *Roman Holiday*
Sup. Actor: Frank Sinatra, *From Here to Eternity*
Sup. Actress: Donna Reed, *From Here to Eternity*
Director: Fred Zinnemann, *From Here to Eternity*

**1954**
Picture: *On the Waterfront,* Horizon-American, Columbia
Actor: Marlon Brando, *On the Waterfront*
Actress: Grace Kelly, *The Country Girl*
Sup. Actor: Edmond O'Brien, *The Barefoot Contessa*
Sup. Actress: Eva Marie Saint, *On the Waterfront*
Director: Elia Kazan, *On the Waterfront*

**1955**
Picture: *Marty,* Hecht and Lancaster's Steven Prods., U.A.
Actor: Ernest Borgnine, *Marty*
Actress: Anna Magnani, *The Rose Tattoo*
Sup. Actor: Jack Lemmon, *Mister Roberts*
Sup. Actress: Jo Van Fleet, *East of Eden*
Director: Delbert Mann, *Marty*

**1956**
Picture: *Around the World in 80 Days,* Michael Todd, U.A.
Actor: Yul Brynner, *The King and I*
Actress: Ingrid Bergman, *Anastasia*
Sup. Actor: Anthony Quinn, *Lust for Life*
Sup. Actress: Dorothy Malone, *Written on the Wind*
Director: George Stevens, *Giant*

**1957**
Picture: *The Bridge on the River Kwai,* Columbia
Actor: Alec Guinness, *The Bridge on the River Kwai*
Actress: Joanne Woodward, *The Three Faces of Eve*
Sup. Actor: Red Buttons, *Sayonara*
Sup. Actress: Miyoshi Umeki, *Sayonara*
Director: David Lean, *The Bridge on the River Kwai*

**1958**
Picture: *Gigi,* Arthur Freed Production, MGM
Actor: David Niven, *Separate Tables*
Actress: Susan Hayward, *I Want to Live*
Sup. Actor: Burl Ives, *The Big Country*
Sup. Actress: Wendy Hiller, Separate Tables
Director: Vincente Minnelli, *Gigi*

**1959**
Picture: *Ben-Hur,* MGM
Actor: Charlton Heston, *Ben-Hur*
Actress: Simone Signoret, *Room at the Top*
Sup. Actor: Hugh Griffith, *Ben-Hur*
Sup. Actress: Shelley Winters, *Diary of Anne Frank*
Director: William Wyler, *Ben-Hur*

**1960**
Picture: *The Apartment,* Mirisch Co., U.A.
Actor: Burt Lancaster, *Elmer Gantry*
Actress: Elizabeth Taylor, *Butterfield 8*
Sup. Actor: Peter Ustinov, *Spartacus*
Sup. Actress: Shirley Jones, *Elmer Gantry*
Director: Billy Wilder, *The Apartment*

**1961**
Picture: *West Side Story,* United Artists
Actor: Maximilian Schell, *Judgment at Nuremberg*
Actress: Sophia Loren, *Two Women*
Sup. Actor: George Chakiris, *West Side Story*
Sup. Actress: Rita Moreno, *West Side Story*
Director: Jerome Robbins, Robert Wise, *West Side Story*

**1962**
Picture: *Lawrence of Arabia,* Columbia
Actor: Gregory Peck, *To Kill a Mockingbird*
Actress: Anne Bancroft, *The Miracle Worker*
Sup. Actor: Ed Begley, *Sweet Bird of Youth*
Sup. Actress: Patty Duke, *The Miracle Worker*
Director: David Lean, *Lawrence of Arabia*

**1963**
Picture: *Tom Jones,* Woodfall Prod., U.A.-Lopert Pictures
Actor: Sidney Poitier, *Lilies of the Field*
Actress: Patricia Neal, *Hud*
Sup. Actor: Melvyn Douglas, *Hud*
Sup. Actress: Margaret Rutherford, *The V.I.P.s*
Director: Tony Richardson, *Tom Jones*

**1964**
Picture: *My Fair Lady,* Warner Bros.
Actor: Rex Harrison, *My Fair Lady*
Actress: Julie Andrews, *Mary Poppins*
Sup. Actor: Peter Ustinov, *Topkapi*
Sup. Actress: Lila Kedrova, *Zorba the Greek*
Director: George Cukor, *My Fair Lady*

**1965**
Picture: *The Sound of Music,* 20th Century-Fox
Actor: Lee Marvin, *Cat Ballou*
Actress: Julie Christie, *Darling*
Sup. Actor: Martin Balsam, *A Thousand Clowns*
Sup. Actress: Shelley Winters, *A Patch of Blue*
Director: Robert Wise, *The Sound of Music*

**1966**
Picture: *A Man for All Seasons,* Columbia
Actor: Paul Scofield, *A Man for All Seasons*
Actress: Elizabeth Taylor, *Who's Afraid of Virginia Woolf?*
Sup. Actor: Walter Matthau, *The Fortune Cookie*
Sup. Actress: Sandy Dennis, *Who's Afraid of Virginia Woolf?*
Director: Fred Zinnemann, *A Man for All Seasons*

**1967**
Picture: *In the Heat of the Night*
Actor: Rod Steiger, *In the Heat of the Night*
Actress: Katharine Hepburn, *Guess Who's Coming to Dinner*
Sup. Actor: George Kennedy, *Cool Hand Luke*
Sup. Actress: Estelle Parsons, *Bonnie and Clyde*
Director: Mike Nichols, *The Graduate*

**1968**
Picture: *Oliver!*
Actor: Cliff Robertson, *Charly*
Actress: Katharine Hepburn, *The Lion in Winter;* Barbra Streisand, *Funny Girl* (tie)
Sup. Actor: Jack Albertson, *The Subject Was Roses*
Sup. Actress: Ruth Gordon, *Rosemary's Baby*
Director: Sir Carol Reed, *Oliver!*

**1969**
Picture: *Midnight Cowboy*
Actor: John Wayne, *True Grit*
Actress: Maggie Smith, *The Prime of Miss Jean Brodie*
Sup. Actor: Gig Young, *They Shoot Horses, Don't They?*
Sup. Actress: Goldie Hawn, *Cactus Flower*
Director: John Schlesinger, *Midnight Cowboy*

**1970**
Picture: *Patton*
Actor: George C. Scott, *Patton* (refused)
Actress: Glenda Jackson, *Women in Love*
Sup. Actor: John Mills, *Ryan's Daughter*
Sup. Actress: Helen Hayes, *Airport*
Director: Franklin Schaffner, *Patton*

**1971**
Picture: *The French Connection*
Actor: Gene Hackman, *The French Connection*
Actress: Jane Fonda, *Klute*

*(continued)*

## Academy Awards *(continued)*

Sup. Actor: Ben Johnson, *The Last Picture Show*
Sup. Actress: Cloris Leachman, *The Last Picture Show*
Director: William Friedkin, *The French Connection*

**1972**
Picture: *The Godfather*
Actor: Marlon Brando, *The Godfather* (refused)
Actress: Liza Minnelli, *Cabaret*
Sup. Actor: Joel Grey, *Cabaret*
Sup. Actress: Eileen Heckart, *Butterflies Are Free*
Director: Bob Fosse, *Cabaret*

**1973**
Picture: *The Sting*
Actor: Jack Lemmon, *Save the Tiger*
Actress: Glenda Jackson, *A Touch of Class*
Sup. Actor: John Houseman, *The Paper Chase*
Sup. Actress: Tatum O'Neal, *Paper Moon*
Director: George Roy Hill, *The Sting*

**1974**
Picture: *The Godfather, Part II*
Actor: Art Carney, *Harry and Tonto*
Actress: Ellen Burstyn, *Alice Doesn't Live Here Anymore*
Sup. Actor: Robert DeNiro, *The Godfather, Part II*
Sup. Actress: Ingrid Bergman, *Murder on the Orient Express*
Director: Francis Ford Coppola, *The Godfather, Part II*

**1975**
Picture: *One Flew Over the Cuckoo's Nest*
Actor: Jack Nicholson, *One Flew Over the Cuckoo's Nest*
Actress: Louise Fletcher, *One Flew Over the Cuckoo's Nest*
Sup. Actor: George Burns, *The Sunshine Boys*
Sup. Actress: Lee Grant, *Shampoo*
Director: Milos Forman, *One Flew Over the Cuckoo's Nest*

**1976**
Picture: *Rocky*
Actor: Peter Finch, *Network*
Actress: Faye Dunaway, *Network*
Sup. Actor: Jason Robards, *All the President's Men*
Sup. Actress: Beatrice Straight, *Network*
Director: John G. Avildsen, *Rocky*

**1977**
Picture: *Annie Hall*
Actor: Richard Dreyfuss, *The Goodbye Girl*
Actress: Diane Keaton, *Annie Hall*
Sup. Actor: Jason Robards, *Julia*
Sup. Actress: Vanessa Redgrave, *Julia*
Director: Woody Allen, *Annie Hall*

**1978**
Picture: *The Deer Hunter*
Actor: Jon Voight, *Coming Home*
Actress: Jane Fonda, *Coming Home*
Sup. Actor: Christopher Walken, *The Deer Hunter*
Sup. Actress: Maggie Smith, *California Suite*
Director: Michael Cimino, *The Deer Hunter*

**1979**
Picture: *Kramer vs. Kramer*
Actor: Dustin Hoffman, *Kramer vs. Kramer*
Actress: Sally Field, *Norma Rae*
Sup. Actor: Melvyn Douglas, *Being There*
Sup. Actress: Meryl Streep, *Kramer vs. Kramer*
Director: Robert Benton, *Kramer vs. Kramer*

**1980**
Picture: *Ordinary People*
Actor: Robert DeNiro, *Raging Bull*
Actress: Sissy Spacek, *Coal Miner's Daughter*
Sup. Actor: Timothy Hutton, *Ordinary People*
Sup. Actress: Mary Steenburgen, *Melvin & Howard*
Director: Robert Redford, *Ordinary People*

**1981**
Picture: *Chariots of Fire*
Actor: Henry Fonda, *On Golden Pond*
Actress: Katharine Hepburn, *On Golden Pond*
Sup. Actor: John Gielgud, *Arthur*
Sup. Actress: Maureen Stapleton, *Reds*
Director: Warren Beatty, *Reds*

**1982**
Picture: *Gandhi*
Actor: Ben Kingsley, *Gandhi*
Actress: Meryl Streep, *Sophie's Choice*
Sup. Actor: Louis Gossett Jr., *An Officer and a Gentleman*
Sup. Actress: Jessica Lange, *Tootsie*
Director: Richard Attenborough, *Gandhi*

**1983**
Picture: *Terms of Endearment*
Actor: Robert Duvall, *Tender Mercies*
Actress: Shirley MacLaine, *Terms of Endearment*
Sup. Actor: Jack Nicholson, *Terms of Endearment*
Sup. Actress: Linda Hunt, *The Year of Living Dangerously*
Director: James L. Brooks, *Terms of Endearment*

**1984**
Picture: *Amadeus*
Actor: F. Murray Abraham, *Amadeus*
Actress: Sally Field, *Places in the Heart*
Sup. Actor: Haing S. Ngor, *The Killing Fields*
Sup. Actress: Peggy Ashcroft, *A Passage to India*
Director: Milos Forman, *Amadeus*

**1985**
Picture: *Out of Africa*
Actor: William Hurt, *Kiss of the Spider Woman*
Actress: Geraldine Page, *The Trip to Bountiful*
Sup. Actor: Don Ameche, *Cocoon*
Sup. Actress: Anjelica Huston, *Prizzi's Honor*
Director: Sydney Pollack, *Out of Africa*

**1986**
Picture: *Platoon*
Actor: Paul Newman, *The Color of Money*
Actress: Marlee Matlin, *Children of a Lesser God*
Sup. Actor: Michael Caine, *Hannah and Her Sisters*
Sup. Actress: Dianne Wiest, *Hannah and Her Sisters*
Director: Oliver Stone, *Platoon*

**1987**
Picture: *The Last Emperor*
Actor: Michael Douglas, *Wall Street*
Actress: Cher, *Moonstruck*
Sup. Actor: Sean Connery, *The Untouchables*
Sup. Actress: Olympia Dukakis, *Moonstruck*
Director: Bernardo Bertolucci, *The Last Emperor*

**1988**
Picture: *Rain Man*
Actor: Dustin Hoffman, *Rain Man*
Actress: Jodie Foster, *The Accused*
Sup. Actor: Kevin Kline, *A Fish Called Wanda*
Sup. Actress: Geena Davis, *The Accidental Tourist*
Director: Barry Levinson, *Rain Man*

**1989**
Picture: *Driving Miss Daisy*
Actor: Daniel Day-Lewis, *My Left Foot*
Actress: Jessica Tandy, *Driving Miss Daisy*
Sup. Actor: Denzel Washington, *Glory*
Sup. Actress: Brenda Fricker, *My Left Foot*
Director: Oliver Stone, *Born on the Fourth of July*

**1990**
Picture: *Dances With Wolves*
Actor: Jeremy Irons, *Reversal of Fortune*
Actress: Kathy Bates, *Misery*
Sup. Actor: Joe Pesci, *Goodfellas*
Sup. Actress: Whoopi Goldberg, *Ghost*
Director: Kevin Costner, *Dances With Wolves*

**1991**
Picture: *The Silence of the Lambs*
Actor: Anthony Hopkins, *The Silence of the Lambs*
Actress: Jodie Foster, *The Silence of the Lambs*
Sup. Actor: Jack Palance, *City Slickers*
Sup. Actress: Mercedes Ruehl, *The Fisher King*
Director: Jonathan Demme, *The Silence of the Lambs*

**1992**
Picture: *Unforgiven*
Actor: Al Pacino, *Scent of a Woman*
Actress: Emma Thompson, *Howards End*
Sup. Actor: Gene Hackman, *Unforgiven*
Sup. Actress: Marisa Tomei, *My Cousin Vinny*
Director: Clint Eastwood, *Unforgiven*

**1993**
Picture: *Schindler's List*
Actor: Tom Hanks, *Philadelphia*
Actress: Holly Hunter, *The Piano*
Sup. Actor: Tommy Lee Jones, *The Fugitive*
Sup. Actress: Anna Paquin, *The Piano*
Director: Steven Spielberg, *Schindler's List*

**1994**
Picture: *Forrest Gump*
Actor: Tom Hanks, *Forrest Gump*
Actress: Jessica Lange, *Blue Sky*
Sup. Actor: Martin Landau, *Ed Wood*
Sup. Actress: Dianne Wiest, *Bullets Over Broadway*
Director: Robert Zemeckis, *Forrest Gump*

**1995**
Picture: *Braveheart*
Actor: Nicolas Cage, *Leaving Las Vegas*
Actress: Susan Sarandon, *Dead Man Walking*
Sup. Actor: Kevin Spacey, *The Usual Suspects*
Sup. Actress: Mira Sorvino, *Mighty Aphrodite*
Director: Mel Gibson, *Braveheart*
Foreign Film: *Antonia's Line*
Original Screenplay: Christopher McQuarrie, *The Usual Suspects*
Adapted Screenplay: Emma Thompson, *Sense and Sensibility*
Cinematography: John Toll, *Braveheart*
Art Direction: Eugenio Zanetti, *Restoration*
Film Editing: Mike Hill, Dan Hanley, *Apollo 13*
Original Song: "Colors of the Wind," *Pocahontas*, Alan Menken, Stephen Schwartz
Original musical or comedy score: Alan Menken, Stephen Schwartz, *Pocahontas*
Original dramatic score: Luis Bacalov, *The Postman (Il Postino)*
Costume: James Acheson, *Restoration*
Makeup: Peter Frampton, Paul Pattison, Lois Burwell, *Braveheart*
Sound: Rick Dior, Steve Pederson, Scott Millan, David MacMillan, *Apollo 13*
Documentary Feature: *Anne Frank Remembered*
Documentary Short Subject: *One Survivor Remembers*
Short Film, Live: *Lieberman in Love*
Short Film, Animated: *A Close Shave*
Visual Effects: Scott E. Anderson, Charles Gibson, Neal Scanlan, John Cox, *Babe*
Honorary Award: Kirk Douglas, Chuck Jones
Gordon E. Sawyer Award: Donald C. Rogers
Special Achievement Award: John Lasseter, *Toy Story*

## Grammy Awards, 1958-94

**Source:** National Academy of Recording Arts & Sciences

(The first Grammys were awarded for records released in 1958.)

| Record | Year | Album |
|---|---|---|
| Domenico Modugno, "Nel Blu Dipinto Di Blu (Volare)" | 1958 | Henry Mancini, *The Music From Peter Gunn* |
| Bobby Darin, "Mack the Knife" | 1959 | Frank Sinatra, *Come Dance With Me* |
| Percy Faith, "Theme From a Summer Place" | 1960 | Bob Newhart, *Button Down Mind* |
| Henry Mancini, "Moon River" | 1961 | Judy Garland, *Judy at Carnegie Hall* |
| Tony Bennett, "I Left My Heart in San Francisco" | 1962 | Vaughn Meader, *The First Family* |
| Henry Mancini, "The Days of Wine and Roses" | 1963 | Barbra Streisand, *The Barbra Streisand Album* |
| Stan Getz, Astrud Gilberto, "The Girl From Ipanema" | 1964 | Stan Getz, Astrud Gilberto, *Getz/Gilberto* |
| Herb Alpert, "A Taste of Honey" | 1965 | Frank Sinatra, *September of My Years* |
| Frank Sinatra, "Strangers in the Night" | 1966 | Frank Sinatra, *A Man and His Music* |
| 5th Dimension, "Up, Up and Away" | 1967 | The Beatles, *Sgt. Pepper's Lonely Hearts Club Band* |
| Simon & Garfunkel, "Mrs. Robinson" | 1968 | Glen Campbell, *By the Time I Get to Phoenix* |
| 5th Dimension, "Aquarius/Let the Sunshine In" | 1969 | Blood Sweat and Tears, *Blood, Sweat and Tears* |
| Simon & Garfunkel, "Bridge Over Troubled Water" | 1970 | Simon & Garfunkel, *Bridge Over Troubled Water* |
| Carole King, "It's Too Late" | 1971 | Carole King, *Tapestry* |
| Roberta Flack, "The First Time Ever I Saw Your Face" | 1972 | George Harrison and friends, *The Concert for Bangla Desh* |
| Roberta Flack, "Killing Me Softly With His Song" | 1973 | Stevie Wonder, *Innervisions* |
| Olivia Newton-John, "I Honestly Love You" | 1974 | Stevie Wonder, *Fulfillingness' First Finale* |
| Captain & Tennille, "Love Will Keep Us Together" | 1975 | Paul Simon, *Still Crazy After All These Years* |
| George Benson, "This Masquerade" | 1976 | Stevie Wonder, *Songs in the Key of Life* |
| Eagles, "Hotel California" | 1977 | Fleetwood Mac, *Rumours* |
| Billy Joel, "Just the Way You Are" | 1978 | Bee Gees, *Saturday Night Fever* |
| The Doobie Brothers, "What a Fool Believes" | 1979 | Billy Joel, *52nd Street* |
| Christopher Cross, "Sailing" | 1980 | Christopher Cross, *Christopher Cross* |
| Kim Carnes, "Bette Davis Eyes" | 1981 | John Lennon, Yoko Ono, *Double Fantasy* |
| Toto, "Rosanna" | 1982 | Toto, *Toto IV* |
| Michael Jackson, "Beat It" | 1983 | Michael Jackson, *Thriller* |
| Tina Turner, "What's Love Got to Do With It" | 1984 | Lionel Richie, *Can't Slow Down* |
| USA for Africa, "We Are the World" | 1985 | Phil Collins, *No Jacket Required* |
| Steve Winwood, "Higher Love" | 1986 | Paul Simon, *Graceland* |
| Paul Simon, "Graceland" | 1987 | U2, *The Joshua Tree* |
| Bobby McFerrin, "Don't Worry, Be Happy" | 1988 | George Michael, *Faith* |
| Bette Midler, "Wind Beneath My Wings" | 1989 | Bonnie Raitt, *Nick of Time* |
| Phil Collins, "Another Day in Paradise" | 1990 | Quincy Jones, *Back on the Block* |
| Natalie Cole, with Nat "King" Cole, "Unforgettable" | 1991 | Natalie Cole, with Nat "King" Cole, *Unforgettable* |
| Eric Clapton, "Tears in Heaven" | 1992 | Eric Clapton, *Unplugged* |
| Whitney Houston, "I Will Always Love You" | 1993 | Whitney Houston, *The Bodyguard* |
| Sheryl Crow, "All I Wanna Do" | 1994 | Tony Bennett, *MTV Unplugged* |

### Selected 1995 Grammy Awards

(awarded in March 1996 for 1995 releases)

Record: "Kiss From a Rose," Seal
Album: *Jagged Little Pill*, Alanis Morissette
Song: "Kiss From a Rose," Seal
New artist: Hootie and the Blowfish
Female pop vocalist: Annie Lennox
Male pop vocalist: Seal
Pop album: *Turbulent Indigo*, Joni Mitchell
Traditional pop album: *Duets II*, Frank Sinatra
Rock vocalist, female: Alanis Morissette
Rock vocalist, male: Tom Petty
Rock song: "You Oughta Know," Alanis Morissette, Glen Ballard
Rock album: *Jagged Little Pill*, Alanis Morissette
R & B vocalist, female: Anita Baker
R & B vocalist, male: Stevie Wonder
R & B song: "For Your Love, " Stevie Wonder
R & B album: *CrazySexyCool*, T.L.C.
Rap solo: Coolio
Rap album: *Poverty's Paradise*, Naughty by Nature
Jazz vocalist: Lena Horne
Contemporary jazz album: *We Live Here*, Pat Metheny Group
Contemporary blues album: *Slippin In*, Buddy Guy
Traditional blues album: *Chill Out*, John Lee Hooker
Country vocalist, female: Alison Krauss
Country vocalist, male: Vince Gill
Country song: "Go Rest High on That Mountain," Vince Gill
Country album: *The Woman in Me*, Shania Twain
Traditional folk album: *South Coast*, Ramblin' Jack Elliott
Reggae Album: *Boombastic*, Shaggy
Polka album: *I Love to Polka*, Jimmy Sturr
Classical album: Debussy*: 'La Mer'; Nocturnes; 'Jeux,' etc.*, Pierre Boulez conducting the Cleveland Symphony

## Other Entertainment Awards

**Cannes Film Festival Awards**, Palme d'Or: *Secrets And Lies*, Mike Leigh, director; Grand Prix: Breaking the Waves, Lars Von Trier, director; best actress: Brenda Blethyn, *Secrets and Lies*; best actor: (dual) Daniel Auteuil and Pascal Duquenne, *Eighth Day*; best director: Joel Coen, *Fargo*; best screenplay: Jacques Audiard, *A Self-Made Hero*; Special jury prize: *Crash*, David Cronenberg, director; Short films: Palme d'Or: *Szel (The Wind)*, Marcell Ivanyl, director; Jury prize: *Small Deaths*, Lynne Ramsay, director; Camera d'Or: *Love Serenade*, Shirley Barrett, director; technical achievement: *Microcosmos*, Claude Nuridsany and Marie Perennou, directors.

**Christopher Awards**, by the Christophers: movies: *Apollo 13, Cry, The Beloved Country, Dead Man Walking*; television: *The Christmas Box, Discovering Women, If Someone Had Known, Living on the Edge, The More You Know, The Piano Lesson*

**Directors Guild of America Awards**, movie director: Ron Howard, *Apollo 13*; documentary: Terry Zwigoff, *Crumb*

**National Society of Film Critics Awards**, film: *Babe;* actor: Nicolas Cage, *Leaving Las Vegas;* actress: Elisabeth Shue, *Leaving Las Vegas;* director: Mike Figgis, *Leaving Las Vegas;* supporting actor: Don Cheadle, *Devil in a Blue Dress;* supporting actress: Joan Allen, *Nixon;* cinematography: Tak Fujimoto, *Devil in a Blue Dress;* screen writer: Amy Heckerling, *Clueless;* foreign language film: *Wild Reeds;* documentary: *Crumb*

**Rock and Roll Hall of Fame**, 1996 inductees: David Bowie, Gladys Knight and the Pips, Jefferson Airplane, Little Willie John, Pink Floyd, the Shirelles, and the Velvet Underground

**Sundance Film Festival Awards**, Grand Jury Prizes: (drama) *Welcome to the Dollhouse*, Todd Solondz; (documentary) *Troublesome Creek: A Mid-western*, Jeanne Jordan and Steven Ascher. Audience Awards: (drama) *Care of the Spitfire Girl*; (docu.) *Troublesome Creek: A Mid-western.* Filmmakers Trophies: (drama) *Girl's Town*, Jim Mckay; (docu.) *Cutting Loose*, Susan Todd and Andrew Young. Awards for cinematography: (drama) *Color of a Brisk and Leaping Day*, Rob Sweeney; (docu.) *Cutting Loose*, Andrew Young. Waldo Salt Screenwriting Award: *Big Night*, Stanley Tucci and Joseph Tropiano. Freedom of Expression Award: *The Celluloid Closet*, Rob Epstein and Jeffrey Friedman. Cinema 100/Sundance International Awards: Hirotaka Tahiro, Tang Danian, Chris Eyre, Walter Salles, and Ciro Cappellari

# NOTED PERSONALITIES

## Widely Known Americans of the Present

Government and political leaders, journalists, authors of nonfiction, and other widely known living persons. This list excludes categories listed elsewhere in Noted Personalities, such as Entertainers of the Present, or in the Sports section.

(as of mid-1996)

| Name (Birthplace) | Birthdate |
|---|---|
| Mortimer Adler (New York, NY) | 12/2/02 |
| Roger Ailes (Knoxville, TN) | 7/3/40 |
| Madeleine K. Albright (Prague, Czech.) | 5/15/37 |
| Lamar Alexander (Knoxville, TN) | 7/3/40 |
| Stephen E. Ambrose (Decatur, IL) | 1/10/36 |
| Jack Anderson (Long Beach, CA) | 10/19/22 |
| Walter H. Annenberg (Milwaukee, WI) | 3/13/08 |
| Roone Arledge (Forest Hills, NY) | 7/8/31 |
| Richard K. Armey (Cando, ND) | 7/7/40 |
| Neil Armstrong (Wapakoneta, OH) | 8/5/30 |
| Bruce Babbitt (Los Angeles, CA) | 6/27/38 |
| F. Lee Bailey (Waltham, MA) | 6/10/33 |
| Russell Baker (Loudoun Co., VA) | 8/14/25 |
| Dave Barry (Armonk, NY) | 7/3/47 |
| Marion Barry (Itta Bena, MS) | 3/6/36 |
| Sidney K. Barthelmy (New Orleans, LA) | 3/17/42 |
| William J. Bennett (Brooklyn, NY) | 7/31/43 |
| Lloyd Bentsen (Mission, TX) | 2/11/21 |
| Joseph R. Biden Jr. (Scranton, PA) | 11/20/42 |
| Harry Blackmun (Nashville, IL) | 11/12/08 |
| David Bonior (Detroit, MI) | 6/6/45 |
| Daniel Boorstin (Atlanta, GA) | 10/1/14 |
| Barbara Boxer (Brooklyn, NY) | 11/11/40 |
| Ben Bradlee (Boston, MA) | 8/26/21 |
| Bill Bradley (Crystal City, MO) | 7/28/43 |
| Ed Bradley (Philadelphia, PA) | 6/22/41 |
| James Brady (Grand Rapids, MI) | 9/17/44 |
| William J. Brennan Jr. (Newark, NJ) | 4/25/06 |
| Jimmy Breslin (Jamaica, NY) | 10/17/30 |
| Stephen Breyer (San Francisco, CA) | 8/15/38 |
| David Brinkley (Wilmington, NC) | 7/10/20 |
| David Broder (Chicago Heights, IL) | 9/11/29 |
| Jane Brody (Brooklyn, NY) | 5/19/41 |
| Tom Brokaw (Webster, SD) | 2/6/40 |
| Joyce Brothers (New York, NY) | 9/20/28 |
| Helen Gurley Brown (Green Forest, AR) | 2/18/22 |
| Jerry Brown (San Francisco, CA) | 4/7/38 |
| Pat Buchanan (Washington, DC) | 11/2/38 |
| Art Buchwald (Mt. Vernon, NY) | 10/20/25 |
| William F. Buckley Jr. (New York, NY) | 11/24/25 |
| Warren Buffett (Omaha, NE) | 8/30/30 |
| Leo Buscaglia (Los Angeles, CA) | 3/31/24 |
| Barbara Bush (Rye, NY) | 6/8/25 |
| George Bush (Milton, MA) | 6/12/24 |
| Robert Byrd (N. Wilkesboro, NC) | 11/20/17 |
| Jimmy Carter (Plains, GA) | 10/1/24 |
| Rosalynn Carter (Plains, GA) | 8/18/27 |
| James Carville Jr. (Fort Benning, GA) | 10/25/44 |
| Julia Child (Pasadena, CA) | 8/15/12 |
| Noam Chomsky (Philadelphia, PA) | 12/7/28 |
| Warren Christopher (Scranton, PA) | 10/27/25 |
| Connie Chung (Washington, DC) | 8/20/46 |
| Henry Cisneros (San Antonio, TX) | 6/11/47 |
| Liz Claiborne (Brussels, Belg.) | 3/31/29 |
| Marcia Clark (Berkeley, CA) | 8/31/53 |
| Bill Clinton (Hope, AR) | 8/19/46 |
| Chelsea Clinton (Little Rock, AR) | 2/27/80 |
| Hillary Rodham Clinton (Chicago, IL) | 10/26/47 |
| Johnnie L. Cochran Jr.(Shreveport, LA) | 10/2/37 |
| Henry Steele Commager (Pittsburgh, PA) | 10/25/02 |
| Joan Ganz Cooney (Phoenix, AZ) | 10/30/29 |
| Bob Costas (New York, NY) | 3/22/52 |
| Katie Couric (Washington, DC) | 1/7/57 |
| Walter Cronkite (St. Joseph, MO) | 11/4/16 |
| Mario Cuomo (Queens, NY) | 6/15/32 |
| Richard M. Daley (Chicago, IL) | 4/24/42 |
| Alfonse M. D'Amato (Brooklyn, NY) | 8/1/37 |
| Thomas Daschle (Aberdeen, SD) | 12/9/47 |
| Tom D. DeLay (Laredo, TX) | 4/8/47 |
| Ronald Dellums (Oakland, CA) | 11/24/35 |
| Alan Dershowitz (Brooklyn, NY) | 9/1/38 |
| Barry Diller (San Francisco, CA) | 2/2/42 |
| Christopher Dodd (Willimantic, CT) | 5/27/44 |
| Elizabeth Dole (Salisbury, NC) | 7/29/36 |
| Robert Dole (Russell, KS) | 7/22/23 |
| Pete Domenici (Albuquerque, NM) | 5/7/32 |
| Sam Donaldson (El Paso, TX) | 3/11/34 |
| Elizabeth Drew (Cincinnati, OH) | 11/16/35 |
| Michael S. Dukakis (Boston, MA) | 11/3/33 |
| Marian Wright Edelman (Bennettsville, SC) | 6/6/39 |
| Michael Eisner (New York, NY) | 3/7/42 |
| Nora Ephron (New York, NY) | 5/19/41 |
| Myrlie Evers-Williams (Vicksburg, MS) | 3/17/33 |
| James Fallows (Philadelphia, PA) | 8/2/49 |
| Jerry Falwell (Lynchburg, VA) | 8/11/33 |
| Louis Farrakhan (New York, NY) | 5/11/33 |
| Dianne Feinstein (San Francisco, CA) | 6/22/33 |
| Geraldine Ferraro (Newburgh, NY) | 8/26/35 |
| Shelby Foote (Greenville, MS) | 11/17/16 |
| Malcolm "Steve" Forbes Jr. (Morristown, NJ) | 7/18/47 |
| Betty Ford (Chicago, IL) | 4/8/18 |
| Gerald R. Ford (Omaha, NE) | 7/14/13 |
| Betty Friedan (Peoria, IL) | 2/4/21 |
| Milton Friedman (Brooklyn, NY) | 7/31/12 |
| John Kenneth Galbraith (Iona Station, Ont.) | 10/15/08 |
| Bill Gates (Seattle, WA) | 10/28/55 |
| Henry Louis Gates Jr. (Keyser, WV) | 9/16/50 |
| David Geffen (Brooklyn, NY) | 2/21/43 |
| Richard Gephardt (St. Louis, MO) | 1/31/41 |
| Charles Gibson (Evanston, IL) | 3/9/43 |
| Newt Gingrich (Harrisburg, PA) | 6/17/43 |
| Allen Ginsberg (Paterson, NJ) | 6/3/21 |
| Ruth Bader Ginsburg (Brooklyn, NY) | 3/15/33 |
| Rudolph Giuliani (New York, NY) | 5/28/44 |
| John Glenn (Cambridge, OH) | 7/18/21 |
| Barry M. Goldwater (Phoenix, AZ) | 1/1/09 |
| Ellen Goodman (Newton, MA) | 4/11/41 |
| Doris Kearns Goodwin (Rockville Center, NY) | 1/4/43 |
| Al Gore Jr. (Washington, DC) | 3/31/48 |
| Tipper Gore (Washington, DC) | 8/19/48 |
| Robert A. Gottlieb (New York, NY) | 4/29/31 |
| Stephen Jay Gould (New York, NY) | 9/10/41 |
| Billy Graham (Charlotte, NC) | 11/7/18 |
| Katharine Graham (New York, NY) | 6/16/17 |
| Phil Gramm (Ft. Benning, GA) | 7/8/42 |
| Jeff Greenfield (New York, NY) | 6/10/43 |
| Meg Greenfield (Seattle, WA) | 12/27/30 |
| Alan Greenspan (New York, NY) | 3/6/26 |
| Bryant Gumbel (New Orleans, LA) | 9/29/48 |
| David Halberstam (New York, NY) | 4/10/34 |
| Paul Harvey (Tulsa, OK) | 9/4/18 |
| Orrin Hatch (Homestead Park, PA) | 3/22/34 |
| Howell Heflin (Poulan, GA) | 6/19/21 |
| Jesse Helms (Monroe, NC) | 10/18/21 |
| Leona Helmsley (New York, NY) | c1920 |
| Heloise (Waco, TX) | 4/15/51 |
| H. Wayne Huizenga (Evergreen Park, IL) | 12/29/39 |
| Kay Bailey Hutchison (Galveston, TX) | 7/22/43 |
| Lee A. Iacocca (Allentown, PA) | 10/15/24 |
| Carl Icahn (Queens, NY) | 1936 |
| Patricia Ireland (Oak Park, IL) | 10/19/45 |
| Lance Ito (Los Angeles, CA) | 8/2/50 |
| Molly Ivins (Monterey, CA) | 8/30/44 |
| Jesse Jackson (Greenville, SC) | 10/8/41 |
| Peter Jennings (Toronto, Ont.) | 8/29/38 |
| Lady Bird Johnson (Karnack, TX) | 12/22/12 |
| John R. Kasich (McKees Rocks, PA) | 5/13/52 |
| Mickey Kantor (Nashville, TN) | 8/7/39 |
| Donna Karan (Forest Hills, NY) | 10/2/48 |
| Nancy Kassebaum (Topeka, KS) | 7/29/32 |
| Jeffrey Katzenberg (New York, NY) | 1950 |
| Jack Kemp (Los Angeles, CA) | 7/13/35 |
| Anthony Kennedy (Sacramento, CA) | 7/23/36 |
| Caroline Kennedy (Boston, MA) | 11/27/57 |
| Edward M. Kennedy (Brookline, MA) | 2/22/32 |
| John F. Kennedy Jr. (Washington, DC) | 11/25/60 |
| Alan Keyes (New York, NY) | 8/7/50 |
| Coretta Scott King (Marion, AL) | 4/27/27 |
| Larry King (Brooklyn, NY) | 11/19/34 |
| Michael Kinsley (Detroit, MI) | 3/9/51 |
| Lane Kirkland (Camden, SC) | 3/12/22 |
| Jeane Kirkpatrick (Duncan, OK) | 11/19/26 |
| Henry Kissinger (Fuerth, Germany) | 5/27/23 |
| Calvin Klein (New York, NY) | 11/19/42 |
| Edward I. Koch (New York, NY) | 12/12/24 |
| C. Everett Koop (Brooklyn, NY) | 10/14/16 |
| Ted Koppel (Lancashire, England) | 2/8/40 |
| William Kristol (New York, NY) | 12/23/52 |

| Name (Birthplace) | Birthdate |
|---|---|
| Charles Kuralt (Wilmington, NC) | 9/10/34 |
| Ann Landers (Sioux City, IA) | 7/4/18 |
| Estee Lauder (New York, NY) | 9/1/08 |
| Ralph Lauren (Bronx, NY) | 10/14/39 |
| Norman Lear (New Haven, CT) | 7/27/22 |
| Jim Lehrer (Wichita, KS) | 5/19/34 |
| Anthony Lewis (New York, NY) | 3/27/27 |
| Rush Limbaugh (Cape Girardeau MO) | 1/12/51 |
| Anne Morrow Lindbergh (Englewood, NJ) | 1906 |
| Frank Lorenzo (New York, NY) | 5/19/40 |
| Trent Lott (Grenada, MS) | 10/9/41 |
| Shannon Lucid (Shagnhai, China) | 1/14/43 |
| Richard G. Lugar (Indianapolis, IN) | 4/4/32 |
| Joan Lunden (Sacramento, CA) | 9/19/50 |
| Robert MacNeil (Montreal, Que.) | 1/19/31 |
| William Manchester (Attleboro, MA) | 4/1/22 |
| Janet Maslin (New York, NY) | 8/12/49 |
| Mary Matalin (Chicago, IL) | 8/19/53 |
| George McGovern (Avon, SD) | 7/19/22 |
| John McLaughlin (Providence, RI) | 3/29/27 |
| Robert McNamara (San Francisco, CA) | 6/9/16 |
| Howard Metzenbaum (Cleveland, OH) | 6/4/17 |
| Kweisi Mfume (Baltimore, MD) | 10/24/48 |
| Barbara Mikulski (Baltimore, MD) | 7/20/36 |
| Kate Millet (St. Paul, MN) | 9/14/34 |
| Walter Mondale (Ceylon, MN) | 1/5/28 |
| Carol Moseley-Braun (Chicago, IL) | 8/16/47 |
| Bill Moyers (Hugo, OK) | 6/5/34 |
| Daniel P. Moynihan (Tulsa, OK) | 3/16/27 |
| Rupert Murdoch (Melbourne, Australia) | 3/11/31 |
| Ralph Nader (Winsted, CT) | 2/27/34 |
| Oliver North (San Antonio, TX) | 10/7/43 |
| Eleanor Holmes Norton (Washington, DC) | 6/13/37 |
| Robert Novak (Joliet, IL) | 2/26/31 |
| Sam Nunn (Perry, GA) | 9/8/38 |
| Sandra Day O'Connor (nr. Duncan, AZ) | 3/26/30 |
| Charles Osgood (New York, NY) | 1/8/33 |
| Michael Ovitz (Encino, CA) | 12/4/46 |
| Bob Packwood (Portland, OR) | 9/11/32 |
| Camille Paglia (Endicott, NY) | 1947 |
| Leon F. Panetta (Monterey, CA) | 6/28/38 |
| Rosa Parks (Tuskegee, AL) | 2/4/13 |
| Jane Pauley (Indianapolis, IN) | 10/31/50 |
| H. Ross Perot (Texarkana, TX) | 6/27/30 |
| William J. Perry (Vandergrift, PA) | 10/11/27 |
| George Plimpton (New York, NY) | 3/18/27 |
| Norman Podhoretz (New York, NY) | 1/16/30 |
| Alvin F. Poussaint (New York, NY) | 5/15/34 |
| Colin Powell (New York, NY) | 4/5/37 |
| Lewis Powell Jr. (Suffolk, VA) | 9/19/07 |
| Dan Quayle (Indianapolis, IN) | 2/4/47 |
| Anna Quindlen (Philadelphia, PA) | 7/8/53 |
| Jane Bryant Quinn (Niagara Falls, NY) | 2/5/39 |
| Dan Rather (Wharton, TX) | 10/31/31 |
| Nancy Reagan (New York, NY) | 7/6/23 |
| Ronald Reagan (Tampico, IL) | 2/6/11 |
| Sumner M. Redstone (Boston, MA) | 5/27/23 |
| Ralph Reed (Portsmouth, VA) | 6/24/61 |
| William Rehnquist (Milwaukee, WI) | 10/1/24 |
| Robert B. Reich (Scranton, PA) | 6/24/46 |
| Janet Reno (Miami, FL) | 7/21/38 |
| Ann Richards (Waco, TX) | 9/3/33 |
| Sally K. Ride (Encino, CA) | 5/26/51 |
| Richard Riley (Greenville, SC) | 1/2/33 |
| Richard Riordan (Flushing, NY) | 1930 |
| Alice Rivlin (Philadelphia, PA) | 3/4/31 |
| Cokie Roberts (New Orleans, LA) | 12/27/43 |
| Oral Roberts (nr. Ada, OK) | 1/24/18 |
| Pat Robertson (Lexington, VA) | 3/22/30 |
| David Rockefeller (New York, NY) | 6/12/15 |
| John D. "Jay" Rockefeller, 4th (New York, NY) | 6/18/37 |
| Laurance S. Rockefeller (New York, NY) | 5/26/10 |
| Andy Rooney (Albany, NY) | 1/14/19 |
| Louis Rukeyser (New York, NY) | 1/30/33 |
| Mike Royko (Chicago, IL) | 9/19/32 |
| Morley Safer (Toronto, Ont.) | 11/8/31 |

| Name (Birthplace) | Birthdate |
|---|---|
| William Safire (New York, NY) | 12/17/29 |
| Carl Sagan (New York, NY) | 11/9/34 |
| Diane Sawyer (Glasgow, KY) | 12/22/45 |
| Antonin Scalia (Trenton, NJ) | 3/11/36 |
| Arthur Schlesinger Jr. (Columbus, OH) | 10/15/17 |
| Patricia Schroeder (Portland, OR) | 7/30/40 |
| Robert Schuller (Alton, IA) | 9/16/26 |
| H. Norman Schwarzkopf (Trenton, NJ) | 8/22/34 |
| Willard Scott (Alexandria, VA) | 3/7/34 |
| Brent Scowcroft (Ogden, UT) | 3/19/25 |
| Glenn T. Seaborg (Ishpeming, MI) | 4/19/12 |
| Donna E. Shalala (Cleveland, OH) | 2/14/41 |
| John Shalikashvili (Warsaw, Poland) | 6/27/36 |
| Albert Shanker (New York, NY) | 9/14/28 |
| Robert Shapiro (Plainfield, NJ) | 9/2/42 |
| Bernard Shaw (Chicago, IL) | 1940 |
| Maria Shriver (Chicago, IL) | 11/6/55 |
| George P. Shultz (New York, NY) | 12/13/20 |
| Alan K. Simpson (Cody, WY) | 9/2/31 |
| O. J. Simpson (San Francisco, CA) | 7/9/47 |
| Hedrick Smith (Kilmacolm, Scotland) | 7/9/33 |
| Liz Smith (Ft. Worth, TX) | 2/2/23 |
| David H. Souter (Melrose, MA) | 9/17/39 |
| Susan Sontag (New York, NY) | 1/28/33 |
| Arlen Specter (Wichita, KS) | 2/12/30 |
| Benjamin Spock (New Haven, CT) | 5/2/03 |
| Lesley Stahl (Lynn, MA) | 12/16/41 |
| George Steinbrenner (Rocky River, OH) | 7/4/30 |
| Gloria Steinem (Toledo, OH) | 3/25/34 |
| George Stephanopolous (Fall River, MA) | 2/10/61 |
| David J. Stern (New York, NY) | 9/22/42 |
| John Paul Stevens (Chicago, IL) | 4/20/20 |
| Martha Stewart (Nutley, NJ) | 8/3/41 |
| John J. Sweeney (New York, NY) | 5/5/34 |
| Arthur Ochs Sulzberger Sr. (New York, NY) | 2/5/26 |
| Arthur Ochs Sulzberger Jr. (Mt. Kisco, NY) | 9/22/51 |
| John H. Sununu (Havana, Cuba) | 7/2/39 |
| Paul Tagliabue (Jersey City, NJ) | 11/24/40 |
| Brandon Tartikoff (Long Island, NY) | 1/13/49 |
| Susan Taylor (New York, NY) | 1/23/46 |
| Studs Terkel (New York, NY) | 5/16/12 |
| Clarence Thomas (Savannah, GA) | 6/23/48 |
| R. David Thomas (Altantic City, NJ) | 7/2/32 |
| Hunter S. Thompson (Louisville, KY) | 7/18/37 |
| J. Strom Thurmond (Edgefield, SC) | 12/5/02 |
| Laurence Tisch (New York, NY) | 3/15/23 |
| Alvin Toffler (New York, NY) | 10/4/28 |
| John Toland (LaCrosse, WI) | 6/29/12 |
| Calvin Trillin (Kansas City, MO) | 12/5/35 |
| Margaret Truman (Independence, MO) | 2/17/24 |
| Donald Trump (New York, NY) | 1946 |
| Ted Turner (Cincinnati, OH) | 11/19/38 |
| Morris K. Udall (St. Johns, AZ) | 6/15/22 |
| Peter Ueberroth (Chicago, IL) | 9/2/37 |
| Jack Valenti (Houston, TX) | 9/5/21 |
| Abigail Van Buren (Sioux City, IA) | 7/4/18 |
| George Wallace (Clio, AL) | 8/25/19 |
| Mike Wallace (Brookline, MA) | 5/9/18 |
| Barbara Walters (Boston, MA) | 9/25/31 |
| Faye Wattleton (St. Louis, MO) | 7/8/43 |
| J. C. Watts (Eufoula, OK) | 11/18/57 |
| Jann Wenner (New York, NY) | 1/7/46 |
| Ruth Westheimer (Frankfurt, Germany) | 1928 |
| Bill White (Lakewood, FL) | 1/28/34 |
| Byron White (Ft. Collins, CO) | 6/8/17 |
| Christine Todd Whitman (New York) | 9/26/46 |
| Tom Wicker (Hamlet, NC) | 6/18/26 |
| Elie Wiesel (Sighet, Romania) | 9/30/28 |
| L. Douglas Wilder (Richmond, VA) | 1/17/31 |
| George Will (Champaign, IL) | 5/4/41 |
| Pete Wilson (Lake Forest, IL) | 8/23/33 |
| Molly Yard (Shanghai, China) | c1910 |
| Coleman Young (Tuscaloosa, AL) | 5/24/18 |
| Mortimer Zuckerman (Montreal, Que.) | 6/4/37 |

## Selected Architects and Some of Their Achievements

**Max Abramovitz,** b 1908, Avery Fisher Hall, NYC; U.S. Steel Building (now USX Towers), Pittsburgh, PA.

**Henry Bacon,** 1866-1924, Lincoln Memorial, Washington, DC.

**Pietro Belluschi,** 1899-1994, Juilliard School of Music, Lincoln Center, Pan Am Bldg. (now MetLife Bldg.) (with Walter Gropius), all NYC.

**Marcel Breuer,** 1902-81, Whitney Museum of American Art (with Hamilton Smith), NYC.

**Charles Bulfinch,** 1763-1844, State House, Boston; Capitol (part), Washington, DC.

**Gordon Bunshaft,** 1909-90, Lever House, Park Ave, NYC; Hirshhorn Museum, Washington, DC.

**Daniel H. Burnham,** 1846-1912, Union Station, Washington DC; Flatiron Bldg., NYC.

**Irwin Chanin,** 1892-1988, theaters, skyscrapers, NYC.

**Ralph Adams Cram,** 1863-1942, Cathedral of St. John the Divine, NYC; U.S. Military Academy (part), West Point, NY.

**R. Buckminster Fuller,** 1895-1983, U.S. Pavilion (geodesic domes), Expo 67, Montreal.
**Cass Gilbert,** 1859-1934, Custom House, Woolworth Bldg., NYC; Supreme Court Bldg., Washington, DC.
**Bertram G. Goodhue,** 1869-1924, Capitol, Lincoln, NE; St. Thomas's Church, St. Bartholomew's Church, NYC.
**Walter Gropius,** 1883-1969, Pan Am Building (now MetLife Bldg.) (with Pietro Belluschi), NYC.
**Peter Harrison,** 1716-75, Touro Synagogue, Redwood Library, Newport, RI.
**Wallace K. Harrison,** 1895-1981, Metropolitan Opera House, Lincoln Center, NYC.
**Thomas Hastings,** 1860-1929, NY Public Library (with John Carrère), Frick Mansion, NYC.
**James Hoban,** 1762-1831, White House, Washington, DC.
**Raymond Hood,** 1881-1934, Rockefeller Center (part), Daily News, NYC; Tribune, Chicago, IL.
**Richard M. Hunt,** 1827-95, Metropolitan Museum (part), NYC; National Observatory, Washington, DC.
**William Le Baron Jenney,** 1832-1907, Home Insurance (demolished 1931), Chicago, IL.
**Philip C. Johnson,** b 1906, AT&T headquarters (now 550 Madison Ave.), NYC; Transco Tower, Houston, TX.
**Albert Kahn,** 1869-1942, General Motors Bldg., Detroit, MI.
**Louis Kahn,** 1901-74, Salk Laboratory, La Jolla, CA; Yale Art Gallery, New Haven, CT.
**Christopher Grant LaFarge,** 1862-1938, Roman Catholic Chapel, West Point, NY.
**Benjamin H. Latrobe,** 1764-1820, Capitol (part), Washington, DC; State Capitol Building, Richmond, VA.
**William Lescaze,** 1896-1969, Philadelphia Savings Fund Society; Borg-Warner Bldg., Chicago.
**Maya Lin,** b 1959, Vietnam Veterans Memorial, Washington, DC.
**Bernard R. Maybeck,** 1862-1957, Hearst Hall, Univ. of CA, Berkeley; First Church of Christ Scientist, Berkeley, CA.
**Charles F. McKim,** 1847-1909, Public Library, Boston; Columbia Univ. (part), NYC.
**Charles M. McKim,** b 1920, KUHT-TV Transmitter Building, Lutheran Church of the Redeemer, Houston, TX.
**Ludwig Mies van der Rohe,** 1886-1969, Seagram Building, (with Philip C. Johnson), NYC; National Gallery, Berlin.
**Robert Mills,** 1781-1855, Washington Monument, Washington, DC.
**Charles Moore,** 1925-93, Sea Ranch, near San Francisco; Faculty Club, Santa Barbara, CA; Piazza d'Italia, New Orleans, LA.
**Richard J. Neutra,** 1892-1970, Mathematics Park, Princeton, NJ; Orange Co. Courthouse, Santa Ana, CA.
**Gyo Obata,** b 1923, Natl. Air & Space Museum, Smithsonian Inst., Washington, DC; Dallas-Ft. Worth Airport.
**Frederick L. Olmsted,** 1822-1903, Central Park, NYC; Fairmount Park, Philadelphia, PA.
**I(eoh) M(ing) Pei,** b 1917, East Wing, Natl. Gallery of Art, Washington, DC; Pyramid, The Louvre, Paris; Rock & Roll Hall of Fame and Museum, Cleveland, OH.
**Cesar Pelli,** b 1926, World Financial Center, Carnegie Hall Tower, NYC; Petronas Twin Towers, Malaysia.
**William Pereira,** 1909-85, Cape Canaveral; Transamerica Bldg., San Francisco, CA.
**John Russell Pope,** 1874-1937, National Gallery, Washington, DC.
**John Portman,** b 1924, Peachtree Center, Atlanta, GA.
**George Browne Post,** 1837-1913, NY Stock Exchange; Capitol, Madison, WI.
**James Renwick Jr.,** 1818-95, Grace Church, St. Patrick's Cathedral, NYC.; Corcoran Gallery (now Renwick Gallery), Washington, DC.
**Henry H. Richardson,** 1838-86, Trinity Church, Boston, MA.
**Kevin Roche,** b 1922, Oakland Museum, Oakland, CA; Fine Arts Center, University of Massachusetts, Amherst.
**James Gamble Rogers,** 1867-1947, Columbia-Presbyterian Medical Center, NYC; Northwestern Univ., Evanston, IL.
**John Wellborn Root,** 1887-1963, Palmolive Building, Chicago; Hotel Statler, Washington, DC.
**Paul Rudolph,** b 1918, Jewitt Art Center, Wellesley Colllege, MA; Art & Architecture Bldg., Yale Univ., New Haven, CT.
**Eero Saarinen,** 1910-61, Gateway to the West Arch, St. Louis, MO; Trans World Flight Center, NYC.
**Louis Skidmore,** 1897-1962, Atomic Energy Commission town site, Oak Ridge, TN; Terrace Plaza Hotel, Cincinnati, OH.
**Clarence S. Stein,** 1882-1975, Temple Emanu-El, NYC.
**Edward Durell Stone,** 1902-78, U.S. Embassy, New Delhi, India; (H. Hartford) Gallery of Modern Art, NYC.
**Louis H. Sullivan,** 1856-1924, Auditorium Building, Chicago, IL.
**Richard Upjohn,** 1802-78, Trinity Church, NYC.
**Max O. Urbahn,** 1912-95, Vehicle Assembly Bldg., Cape Canaveral, FL.
**Ralph T. Walker,** 1889-1973, NY Telephone Bldg. (now NYNEX); IBM Research Lab, Poughkeepsie, NY.
**Roland A. Wank,** 1898-1970, Cincinnati Union Terminal, OH; head architect (1933-44), Tennessee Valley Authority.
**Stanford White,** 1853-1906, Washington Arch in Washington Square Park, first Madison Square Garden, NYC.
**Frank Lloyd Wright,** 1867 (or 1869)-1959, Imperial Hotel, Tokyo; Guggenheim Museum, NYC; Unity Church, Oak Park, IL; Robie House, Chicago, IL; Taliesin, Spring Green, WI.
**William Wurster,** 1895-1973, Ghirardelli Sq., San Francisco; Cowell College, UC, Berkeley, CA.
**Minoru Yamasaki,** 1912-86, World Trade Center, NYC.

## Noted Artists, Photographers, and Sculptors of the Past

Artists are painters unless otherwise indicated.

**Berenice Abbot,** 1898-1991, (U.S.) photographer. Documentary of New York City, *Changing New York* (1939).
**Ansel Easton Adams,** 1902-84, (U.S.) photographer. Landscapes of the American Southwest.
**Washington Allston,** 1779-1843, (U.S.) landscapist. *Belshazzar's Feast.*
**Albrecht Altdorfer,** 1480-1538, (Ger.) landscapist.
**Andrea del Sarto,** 1486-1530, (It.) frescoes. *Madonna of the Harpies.*
**Fra Angelico,** c1400-55, (It.) Renaissance muralist. *Madonna of the Linen Drapers' Guild.*
**Diane Arbus,** 1923-71, (U.S.) photographer. Photographs of disturbing images of bizarre individuals.
**Alexsandr Archipenko,** 1887-1964, (U.S.) sculptor. *Boxing Match, Medranos.*
**Eugène Atget,** 1856-1927, (Fr.) photographer. Parisian life.
**John James Audubon,** 1785-1851, (U.S.) *Birds of America.*
**Hans Baldung-Grien,** 1484-1545, (Ger.) *Todentanz.*
**Ernst Barlach,** 1870-1938, (Ger.) Expressionist sculptor. *Man Drawing a Sword.*
**Frederic-Auguste Bartholdi,** 1834-1904, (Fr.) *Liberty Enlightening the World, Lion of Belfort.*
**Fra Bartolommeo,** 1472-1517, (It.) *Vision of St. Bernard.*
**Aubrey Beardsley,** 1872-98, (Br.) illustrator. *Salome, Lysistrata, Morte d'Arthur, Volpone.*
**Max Beckmann,** 1884-1950, (Ger.) Expressionist. *The Descent From the Cross.*
**Gentile Bellini,** 1426-1507, (It.) Renaissance. *Procession in St. Mark's Square.*
**Giovanni Bellini,** 1428-1516, (It.) *St. Francis in Ecstasy.*
**Jacopo Bellini,** 1400-70, (It.) *Crucifixion.*
**George Wesley Bellows,** 1882-1925, (U.S.) sports artist, portraitist, landscapist. *Stag at Sharkey's, Edith Clavell.*
**Thomas Hart Benton,** 1889-1975, (U.S.) American regionalist. *Threshing Wheat, Arts of the West.*
**Gianlorenzo Bernini,** 1598-1680, (It.) Baroque sculpture. *The Assumption.*
**Albert Bierstadt,** 1830-1902, (U.S.) landscapist. *The Rocky Mountains, Mount Corcoran.*
**George Caleb Bingham,** 1811-79, (U.S.) *Fur Traders Descending the Missouri.*
**William Blake,** 1752-1827, (Br.) engraver. *Book of Job, Songs of Innocence, Songs of Experience.*
**Rosa Bonheur,** 1822-99, (Fr.) *The Horse Fair.*
**Pierre Bonnard,** 1867-1947, (Fr.) Intimist. *The Breakfast Room, Girl in a Straw Hat.*
**Gutzon Borglum,** 1871-1941, (U.S.) sculptor. Mt. Rushmore Memorial.
**Hieronymus Bosch,** 1450-1516, (Flem.) religious allegories. *The Crowning With Thorns.*
**Sandro Botticelli,** 1444-1510, (It.) Renaissance. *Birth of Venus, Adoration of the Magi, Guiliano de'Medici.*
**Margaret Bourke-White,** 1906-71, (U.S.) photographer, photojournalist. WW2, USSR, rural South during the Depression.
**Mathew Brady,** c1823-96, (U.S.) photographer. Official photographer of the Civil War.
**Constantin Brancusi,** 1876-1957, (Rom.) Nonobjective sculptor. *Flying Turtle, The Kiss.*
**Georges Braque,** 1882-1963, (Fr.) Cubist. *Violin and Palette.*
**Pieter Bruegel the Elder,** c1525-69, (Flem.) *The Peasant Dance, Hunters in the Snow, Magpie on the Gallows.*
**Pieter Bruegel the Younger,** 1564-1638, (Flem.) *Village Fair, The Crucifixion.*
**Edward Burne-Jones,** 1833-98, (Br.) Pre-Raphaelite artist-craftsman. *The Mirror of Venus.*
**Alexander Calder,** 1898-1976, (U.S.) sculptor. *Lobster Trap and Fish Tail.*
**Julia Cameron,** 1815-79, (Br.) photographer. Considered one of the most important portraitists of the 19th cent.

**Robert Capa** (Andrei Friedmann), 1913-54, (Hung.-U.S.) photographer. War photojournalist; invasion of Normandy.
**Michelangelo Merisi da Caravaggio,** 1573-1610, (It.) Baroque. *The Supper at Emmaus.*
**Emily Carr,** 1871-1945, (Can.) landscapist. *Blunden Harbour, Big Raven, Rushing Sea of Undergrowth.*
**Carlo Carrà,** 1881-1966, (It.) Metaphysical school. *Lot's Daughters, The Enchanted Room.*
**Mary Cassatt,** 1844-1926, (U.S.) Impressionist. *The Cup of Tea, Woman Bathing, The Boating Party.*
**George Catlin,** 1796-1872, (U.S.) American Indian life. *Gallery of Indians, Buffalo Dance.*
**Benvenuto Cellini,** 1500-71, (It.) Mannerist sculptor, goldsmith. *Perseus and Medusa, Salt Cellar of Francis I.*
**Paul Cézanne,** 1839-1906, (Fr.) *Card Players, Mont-Sainte-Victoire With Large Pine Trees.*
**Marc Chagall,** 1887-1985, (Russ.) Jewish life and folklore. *I and the Village, The Praying Jew.*
**Jean Simeon Chardin,** 1699-1779, (Fr.) still lifes. *The Kiss, The Grace.*
**Frederick Church,** 1826-1900, (U.S.) Hudson River school. *Niagara, Andes of Ecuador.*
**Giovanni Cimabue,** 1240-1302, (It.) Byzantine mosaicist. *Madonna Enthroned With St. Francis.*
**Claude Lorrain** (Claude Gellé), 1600-82, (Fr.) ideal-landscapist. *The Enchanted Castle.*
**Thomas Cole,** 1801-48, (U.S.) Hudson River school. *The Ox-Bow, In the Catskills.*
**John Constable,** 1776-1837, (Br.) landscapist. *Salisbury Cathedral From the Bishop's Grounds.*
**John Singleton Copley,** 1738-1815, (U.S.) portraitist. *Samuel Adams, Watson and the Shark.*
**Lovis Corinth,** 1858-1925, (Ger.) Expressionist. *Apocalypse.*
**Jean-Baptiste-Camille Corot,** 1796-1875, (Fr.) landscapist. *Souvenir de Mortefontaine, Pastorale.*
**Correggio,** 1494-1534, (It.) Renaissance muralist. *Mystic Marriages of St. Catherine.*
**Gustave Courbet,** 1819-77, (Fr.) Realist. *The Artist's Studio.*
**Lucas Cranach the Elder,** 1472-1553, (Ger.) Protestant Reformation portraitist. *Luther.*
**Imogen Cunningham,** 1883-1976, (U.S.) photographer, portraitist. Plant photography.
**Nathaniel Currier,** 1813-88, and **James M. Ives,** 1824-95, (both U.S.) lithographers. *A Midnight Race on the Mississippi, American Forest Scene—Maple Sugaring.*
**John Steuart Curry,** 1897-1946, (U.S.) Americana, murals. *Baptism in Kansas.*
**Salvador Dalí,** 1904-89, (Sp.) Surrealist. *Persistence of Memory, The Crucifixion.*
**Honoré Daumier,** 1808-79, (Fr.) caricaturist. *The Third-Class Carriage.*
**Jacques-Louis David,** 1748-1825, (Fr.) Neoclassicist. *The Oath of the Horatii.*
**Arthur Davies,** 1862-1928, (U.S.) Romantic landscapist. *Unicorns, Leda and the Dioscuri.*
**Edgar Degas,** 1834-1917, (Fr.) *The Ballet Class.*
**Eugène Delacroix,** 1798-1863, (Fr.) Romantic. *Massacre at Chios, Liberty Leading the People.*
**Paul Delaroche,** 1797-1856, (Fr.) historical themes. *Children of Edward IV.*
**Luca Della Robbia,** 1400-82, (It.) Renaissance terracotta artist. *Cantoria* (singing gallery), Florence cathedral.
**Donatello,** 1386-1466, (It.) Renaissance sculptor. *David, Gattamelata.*
**Jean Dubuffet,** 1902-85, (Fr.) painter, sculptor, printmaker. *Group of Four Trees.*
**Marcel Duchamp,** 1887-1968, (Fr.) Dada artist. *Nude Descending a Staircase, No. 2.*
**Raoul Dufy,** 1877-1953, (Fr.) Fauvist. *Chateau and Horses.*
**Asher Brown Durand,** 1796-1886, (U.S.) Hudson River school. *Kindred Spirits.*
**Albrecht Dürer,** 1471-1528, (Ger.) Renaissance painter, engraver, woodcuts. *St. Jerome in His Study, Melencolia I.*
**Anthony van Dyck,** 1599-1641, (Flem.) Baroque portraitist. *Portrait of Charles I Hunting.*
**Thomas Eakins,** 1844-1916, (U.S.) Realist. *The Gross Clinic.*
**Alfred Eisenstaedt,** 1898-1995, (Ger.-U.S.) photographer, photojournalist. Famous for V-J Day, Aug. 14, 1945, photograph of sailor and nurse in Times Square, NYC.
**Peter Henry Emerson,** 1856-1936, (Br.) photographer. Promoted photography as an independent art form.
**Jacob Epstein,** 1880-1959, (Br.) religious and allegorical sculptor. *Genesis, Ecce Homo.*
**Jan van Eyck,** c1390-1441, (Flem.) naturalistic panels. *Adoration of the Lamb.*
**Roger Fenton,** 1819-68, (Br.) photographer. Crimean War photographer.
**Anselm Feuerbach,** 1829-80, (Ger.) Romantic Classicist. *Judgment of Paris, Iphigenia.*
**John Bernard Flannagan,** 1895-1942, (U.S.) animal sculptor. *Triumph of the Egg.*
**Jean-Honoré Fragonard,** 1732-1806, (Fr.) Rococo. *The Swing.*
**Daniel Chester French,** 1850-1931, (U.S.) *The Minute Man of Concord;* seated *Lincoln,* Lincoln Memorial, Washington, DC.
**Caspar David Friedrich,** 1774-1840, (Ger.) Romantic landscapes. *Man and Woman Gazing at the Moon.*
**Thomas Gainsborough,** 1727-88, (Br.) portraitist. *The Blue Boy, The Watering Place, Orpin the Parish Clerk.*
**Alexander Gardner,** 1821-82, (U.S.) photographer. Civil War; railroad construction; Great Plains Indians.
**Paul Gauguin,** 1848-1903, (Fr.) Post-impressionist. *The Tahitians, Spirit of the Dead Watching.*
**Lorenzo Ghiberti,** 1378-1455, (It.) Renaissance sculptor. Gates of Paradise baptistery doors, Florence.
**Alberto Giacometti,** 1901-66, (Swiss) attenuated sculptures of solitary figures. *Man Pointing.*
**Giorgione,** c1477-1510, (It.) Renaissance. *The Tempest.*
**Giotto di Bondone,** 1267-1337, (It.) Renaissance. *Presentation of Christ in the Temple.*
**François Girardon,** 1628-1715, (Fr.) Baroque sculptor of classical themes. *Apollo Tended by the Nymphs.*
**Vincent van Gogh,** 1853-90, (Dutch) *The Starry Night, L'Arlesienne, Bedroom at Arles, Self-Portrait.*
**Arshile Gorky,** 1905-48, (U.S.) Surrealist. *The Liver Is the Cock's Comb.*
**Francisco de Goya y Lucientes,** 1746-1828, (Sp.) *The Naked Maja, The Disasters of War* (etchings).
**El Greco,** 1541-1614, (Sp.) *View of Toledo, Assumption of the Virgin*
**Horatio Greenough,** 1805-52, (U.S.) Neo-classical sculptor. *George Washington.*
**Matthias Grünewald,** 1480-1528, (Ger.) mystical religious themes. *The Resurrection.*
**Frans Hals,** c1580-1666, (Dutch) portraitist. *Laughing Cavalier, Gypsy Girl.*
**Austin Hansen,** 1910-96, (U.S.) photographer. Chronicled life in Harlem, NY.
**Childe Hassam,** 1859-1935, (U.S.) Impressionist. *Southwest Wind, July 14 Rue Daunon.*
**Edward Hicks,** 1780-1849, (U.S.) folk painter. *The Peaceable Kingdom.*
**Lewis Wickes Hine,** 1874-1940, (U.S.) photographer. Studies of immigrants, children in industry.
**Hans Hofmann,** 1880-1966, (U.S.) early abstract Expressionist. *Spring, The Gate.*
**William Hogarth,** 1697-1764, (Br.) caricaturist. *The Rake's Progress.*
**Katsushika Hokusai,** 1760-1849, (Jpn.) printmaker. *Crabs.*
**Hans Holbein the Elder,** 1460-1524, (Ger.) late Gothic. *Presentation of Christ in the Temple.*
**Hans Holbein the Younger,** 1497-1543, (Ger.) portraitist. *Henry VIII, The French Ambassadors.*
**Winslow Homer,** 1836-1910, (U.S.) naturalist painter, marine themes. *Marine Coast, High Cliff.*
**Edward Hopper,** 1882-1967, (U.S.) realistic urban scenes. *Sunlight in a Cafeteria.*
**Jean-Auguste-Dominique Ingres,** 1780-1867, (Fr.) Classicist. *Valpincon Bather.*
**George Inness,** 1825-94, (U.S.) luminous landscapist. *Delaware Water Gap.*
**William Henry Jackson,** 1843-1942, (U.S.) photographer. American West, building of Union Pacific Railroad.
**Donald Judd,** 1928-94, (U.S.) sculptor, major Minimalist.
**Frida Kahlo,** 1907-54, (Mex.) painter; *Self-Portrait With Monkey.*
**Vasily Kandinsky,** 1866-1944, (Russ.) Abstractionist. *Capricious Forms, Improvisation 38 (second version).*
**Paul Klee,** 1879-1940, (Swiss) Abstractionist. *Twittering Machine, Pastoral, Death and Fire.*
**Gustav Klimt,** 1862-1918, (Austrian) cofounder of Vienna Secession Movement, *The Kiss*
**Oscar Kokoschka,** 1886-1980, (Austrian) Expressionist. *View of Prague, Harbor of Marseilles.*
**Kathe Kollwitz,** 1867-1945, (Ger.) printmaker, social justice themes. *The Peasant War.*
**Gaston Lachaise,** 1882-1935, (U.S.) figurative sculptor. *Standing Woman.*
**John La Farge,** 1835-1910, (U.S.) muralist. *Red and White Peonies, The Ascension.*
**Dorothea Lange,** 1895-1965, (U.S.), photographer. Depression photographs, migrant farm workers.
**Fernand Léger,** 1881-1955, (Fr.) machine art. *The Cyclists.*
**Leonardo da Vinci,** 1452-1519, (It.) *Mona Lisa, Last Supper, The Annunciation.*
**Emanuel Leutze,** 1816-68, (U.S.) historical themes. *Washington Crossing the Delaware.*
**Jacques Lipchitz,** 1891-1973, (Fr.) Cubist sculptor. *Harpist.*

**Filippino Lippi,** 1457-1504, (It.) Renaissance. *The Vision of St. Bernard.*
**Fra Filippo Lippi,** 1406-69, (It.) Renaissance. *Coronation of the Virgin, Madonna and Child With Angels.*
**Morris Louis,** 1912-62, (U.S.) abstract Expressionist. *Signa, Stripes, Alpha-Phi.*
**Aristide Maillol,** 1861-1944, (Fr.) sculptor. *L'Harmonie.*
**Édouard Manet,** 1832-83, (Fr.) forerunner of Impressionism. *Luncheon on the Grass, Olympia.*
**Andrea Mantegna,** 1431-1506, (It.) Renaissance frescoes. *Triumph of Caesar.*
**Franz Marc,** 1880-1916, (Ger.) Expressionist. *Blue Horses.*
**John Marin,** 1870-1953, (U.S.) Expressionist seascapes. *Maine Island.*
**Reginald Marsh,** 1898-1954, (U.S.) satirical artist. *Tattoo and Haircut.*
**Masaccio,** 1401-28, (It.) Renaissance. *The Tribute Money.*
**Henri Matisse,** 1869-1954, (Fr.) Fauvist. *Woman With the Hat.*
**Michelangelo Buonarroti,** 1475-1564, (It.) *Pietà, David, Moses, The Last Judgment,* Sistine Chapel ceiling.
**Jean-Francois Millet,** 1814-75, (Fr.) painter of peasant subjects. *The Gleaners, The Man With a Hoe.*
**Joan Miró,** 1893-1983, (Sp.) Exuberant colors, playful images. Catalan landscape, *Dutch Interior.*
**Amedeo Modigliani,** 1884-1920, (It.) *Reclining Nude.*
**Piet Mondrian,** 1872-1944, (Dutch) Abstractionist. *Composition With Red, Yellow and Blue.*
**Claude Monet,** 1840-1926, (Fr.) Impressionist. *The Bridge at Argenteuil, Haystacks.*
**Henry Moore,** 1898-1986, (Br.) sculptor of large-scale, abstract works. *Reclining Figure* (several).
**Gustave Moreau,** 1826-98, (Fr.) Symbolist. *The Apparition, Dance of Salome.*
**James Wilson Morrice,** 1865-1924, (Can.) landscapist. *The Ferry, Quebec, Venice, Looking Over the Lagoon.*
**William Morris,** 1834-1896 (Br.) decorative artist, leader of the Arts and Crafts movement.
**Grandma Moses,** 1860-1961, (U.S.) folk painter. *Out for the Christmas Trees, Thanksgiving Turkey.*
**Edvard Munch,** 1863-1944, (Nor.) Expressionist. *The Cry.*
**Bartolome Murillo,** 1618-82, (Sp.) Baroque religious artist. *Vision of St. Anthony, The Two Trinities.*
**Eadweard Muybridge,** 1830-1904, (Br.-U.S.) photographer. Studies of motion, *Animal Locomotion.*
**Nadar (Gaspar-Félix Tournachon)** 1820-1910, (Fr.) photographer, caricaturist, portraitist. Invented photo-essay.
**Barnett Newman,** 1905-70, (U.S.) abstract Expressionist. *Stations of the Cross.*
**Isamu Noguchi,** 1904-88, (U.S.) abstract sculptor, designer. *Kouros, BirdC(MU),* sculptural gardens.
**Georgia O'Keeffe,** 1887-1986, (U.S.) Southwest motifs. *Cow's Skull: Red, White, and Blue, The Shelton With Sunspots.*
**José Clemente Orozco,** 1883-1949, (Mex.) frescoes. *House of Tears, Pre-Columbian Golden Age.*
**Timothy H. O'Sullivan,** 1840-82, (U.S.) Civil War photographer.
**Charles Willson Peale,** 1741-1827, (U.S.) American Revolutionary portraitist. *The Staircase Group,* U.S. presidents.
**Rembrandt Peale,** 1778-1860, (U.S.) portraitist. Thomas Jefferson.
**Pietro Perugino,** 1446-1523, (It.) Renaissance. *Delivery of the Keys to St. Peter.*
**Pablo Picasso,** 1881-1973, (Sp.) painter, sculptor. *Guernica; Dove; Head of a Woman; Head of a Bull, Metamorphosis.*
**Piero della Francesca,** c1415-92, (It.) Renaissance. *Duke of Urbino, Flagellation of Christ.*
**Camille Pissarro,** 1830-1903, (Fr.) Impressionist. *Morning Sunlight, Bather in the Woods.*
**Jackson Pollock,** 1912-56, (U.S.) abstract Expressionist. *Autumn Rhythm.*
**Nicolas Poussin,** 1594-1665, (Fr.) Baroque pictorial classicism. *St. John on Patmos.*
**Maurice B. Prendergast,** c 1860-1924, (U.S.) Post-impressionist water colorist. *Umbrellas in the Rain.*
**Pierre-Paul Prud'hon,** 1758-1823, (Fr.) Romanticist. *Crime Pursued by Vengeance and Justice.*
**Pierre Cecile Puvis de Chavannes,** 1824-98, (Fr.) muralist. *The Poor Fisherman.*
**Raphael Sanzio,** 1483-1520, (It.) Renaissance. *Disputa, School of Athens, Sistine Madonna.*
**Man Ray,** 1890-1976, (U.S.) Dada artist. *Observing Time, The Lovers, Marquis de Sade.*
**Odilon Redon,** 1840-1916, (Fr.) Symbolist painter, lithographer. *In the Dream, Vase of Flowers.*
**Rembrandt van Rijn,** 1606-69, (Dutch) *The Bridal Couple, The Night Watch.*
**Frederic Remington,** 1861-1909, (U.S.) painter, sculptor. Portrayer of the American West, *Bronco Buster.*
**Pierre-Auguste Renoir,** 1841-1919, (Fr.) Impressionist. *The Luncheon of the Boating Party, Dance in the Country.*
**Joshua Reynolds,** 1723-92, (Br.) portraitist. *Mrs. Siddons As the Tragic Muse.*
**Diego Rivera,** 1886-1957, (Mex.) frescoes. *The Fecund Earth.*
**Henry Peach Robinson,** 1830-1901 (Br.) photographer. A leader of "high art" photography.
**Norman Rockwell,** 1894-1978, (U.S.) painter, illustrator. *Saturday Evening Post* covers.
**Auguste Rodin,** 1840-1917, (Fr.) sculptor. *The Thinker.*
**Mark Rothko,** 1903-70, (U.S.) abstract Expressionist. *Light, Earth and Blue.*
**Georges Rouault,** 1871-1958, (Fr.) Expressionist. *Three Judges.*
**Henri Rousseau,** 1844-1910, (Fr.) primitive exotic themes. *The Snake Charmer.*
**Theodore Rousseau,** 1812-67, (Swiss-Fr.) landscapist. *Under the Birches, Evening.*
**Peter Paul Rubens,** 1577-1640, (Flem.) Baroque. *Mystic Marriage of St. Catherine.*
**Jacob van Ruisdael,** c1628-82, (Dutch) landscapist. *Jewish Cemetery.*
**Charles M. Russell,** 1866-1926, (U.S.) Western life.
**Salomon van Ruysdael,** c1600-70, (Dutch) landscapist. *River with Ferry-Boat.*
**Albert Pinkham Ryder,** 1847-1917, (U.S.) seascapes and allegories. *Toilers of the Sea.*
**Augustus Saint-Gaudens,** 1848-1907, (U.S.) memorial statues. *Farragut, Mrs. Henry Adams (Grief).*
**Andrea Sansovino,** 1460-1529, (It.) Renaissance sculptor. *Baptism of Christ.*
**Jacopo Sansovino,** 1486-1570, (It.) Renaissance sculptor. *St. John the Baptist.*
**John Singer Sargent,** 1856-1925, (U.S.) Edwardian society portraitist. The Wyndham Sisters, Madam X.
**Georges Seurat,** 1859-91, (Fr.) Pointillist. *Sunday Afternoon on the Island of Grande Jatte.*
**Gino Severini,** 1883-1966, (It.) Futurist and Cubist. *Dynamic Hieroglyph of the Bal Tabarin.*
**Ben Shahn,** 1898-1969, (U.S.) social and political themes. Sacco and Vanzetti series, *Seurat's Lunch, Handball.*
**Charles Sheeler,** 1883-1965, (U.S.) abstractionist.
**David Alfaro Siqueiros,** 1896-1974, (Mex.) political muralist. *March of Humanity.*
**John F. Sloan,** 1871-1951, (U.S.) depictions of New York City.
**David Smith,** 1906-65, (U.S.) welded metal sculpture. *Hudson River Landscape, Zig, Cubi* series.
**Edward Steichen,** 1879-1973, (U.S.) photographer. Credited with the transformation of photography into an art form.
**Alfred Stieglitz,** 1864-1946, (U.S.) photographer, editor; helped create acceptance of phography as art.
**Paul Strand,** 1890-1976, (U.S.) photographer. People, nature, landscapes.
**Gilbert Stuart,** 1755-1828, (U.S.) portraitist. George Washington, Thomas Jefferson, James Madison.
**Thomas Sully,** 1783-1872, (U.S.) portraitist. *Col. Thomas Handasyd Perkins, The Passage of the Delaware.*
**William Henry Fox Talbot,** 1800-77, (Br.) photographer. *Pencil of Nature,* one of the first photographically illustrated books.
**George Tames,** 1919-94, (U.S.) photographer. Chronicled presidents, political leaders.
**Yves Tanguy,** 1900-55, (Fr.) Surrealist. *Rose of the Four Winds, Mama, Papa Is Wounded!*
**Giovanni Battista Tiepolo,** 1696-1770, (It.) Rococo frescoes. *The Crucifixion.*
**Jacopo Tintoretto,** 1518-94, (It.) Mannerist. *The Last Supper.*
**Titian,** c1485-1576, (It.) Renaissance. *Venus and the Lute Player, The Bacchanal.*
**Jose Rey Toledo,** 1916-94, (U.S.) Native American artist. Captured the essence of tribal dances on canvas.
**Henri de Toulouse-Lautrec,** 1864-1901, (Fr.) *At the Moulin Rouge.*
**John Trumbull,** 1756-1843, (U.S.) historical themes. *The Declaration of Independence.*
**J(oseph) M(allord) W(illiam) Turner,** 1775-1851, (Br.) Romantic landscapist. *Snow Storm.*
**Paolo Uccello,** 1397-1475, (It.) Gothic-Renaissance. *The Rout of San Romano.*
**Maurice Utrillo,** 1883-1955, (Fr.) Impressionist. *Sacre-Coeur de Montmartre.*
**John Vanderlyn,** 1775-1852, (U.S.) Neo-classicist. *Ariadne Asleep on the Island of Naxos.*
**Diego Velázquez,** 1599-1660, (Sp.) Baroque. *Las Meninas, Portrait of Juan de Pareja.*
**Jan Vermeer,** 1632-75, (Dutch) interior genre subjects. *Young Woman With a Water Jug.*
**Paolo Veronese,** 1528-88, (It.) devotional themes, vastly peopled canvases. *The Temptation of St. Anthony.*
**Andrea del Verrocchio,** 1435-88, (It.) Florentine sculptor. *Colleoni.*

**Maurice de Vlaminck,** 1876-1958, (Fr.) Fauvist landscapist.
**Andy Warhol,** 1928-87, (U.S.) Pop Art. *Campbell's Soup Cans, Marilyn Diptych.*
**Antoine Watteau,** 1684-1721, (Fr.) Rococo painter of "scenes of gallantry." *The Embarkation for Cythera.*
**George Frederic Watts,** 1817-1904, (Br.) painter and sculptor of grandiose allegorical themes. *Hope.*
**Benjamin West,** 1738-1820, (U.S.) realistic historical themes. *Death of General Wolfe.*
**Edward Weston,** 1886-1958, (U.S.) photographer. Landscapes of American West.
**James Abbott McNeill Whistler,** 1834-1903, (U.S.) *Arrangement in Grey and Black, No. 1: The Artist's Mother.*
**Archibald M. Willard,** 1836-1918, (U.S.) *The Spirit of '76.*
**Grant Wood,** 1891-1942, (U.S.) Midwestern regionalist. *American Gothic, Daughters of Revolution.*
**Ossip Zadkine,** 1890-1967, (Russ.) School of Paris sculptor. *The Destroyed City, Musicians, Christ.*

## Noted Black Americans of the Past

**Ralph David Abernathy,** 1926-90, organizer, 1957, president, 1968, Southern Christian Leadership Conference.
**Crispus Attucks,** c1723-70, agitator who led group that precipitated the "Boston Massacre," Mar. 5, 1770.
**James Baldwin,** 1924-87, author, playwright; *The Fire Next Time, Blues for Mister Charlie, Just Above My Head.*
**Benjamin Banneker,** 1731-1806, inventor, astronomer, mathematician, and gazetteer; served on commission that surveyed and planned Washington, DC.
**James P. Beckwourth,** 1798-c 1867, western fur trader, scout; Beckwourth Pass in N California named for him.
**Mary McCleod Bethune,** 1875-1955, adviser to presidents Franklin Roosevelt and Harry Truman; founder, president, Bethune-Cookman College.
**Henry Blair,** 19th century, obtained patents (believed among first issued to a black) for a corn-planter, 1834, and for a cotton-planter, 1836.
**Edward Bouchet,** 1852-1918, first black to earn a PhD at a U.S. university (Yale, 1876); first black elected to Phi Beta Kappa.
**Sterling A. Brown,** 1901-89, poet, literature professor; helped establish African-American literary criticism.
**William Wells Brown,** 1815-84, novelist, dramatist; first American black to publish a novel.
**Ralph Bunche,** 1904-71, first black to win the Nobel Peace Prize, 1950; undersecretary of the UN, 1950.
**George Washington Carver,** 1864-1943, botanist, chemist, and educator; his extensive experiments in soil building and plant diseases revolutionized the economy of the South.
**Charles Waddell Chesnutt,** 1858-1932, author known primarily for his short stories, including *The Conjure Woman.*
**James Cleveland,** 1931-91, composer, musician, singer; first black gospel artist to appear in Carnegie Hall.
**Countee Cullen,** 1903-46, poet, played a prominent role in the Harlem Renaissance of the 1920s; *The Black Christ.*
**Benjamin O. Davis Sr.,** 1877-1970, first black general, 1940, in U. S. Army.
**William L. Dawson,** 1886-1970, Illinois congressman, first black chairman of a major U.S. House committee.
**Aaron Douglas,** 1900-79, painter; called father of black American art.
**Frederick Douglass,** 1817-95, author, editor, orator, diplomat; edited the abolitionist weekly, *The North Star,* in Rochester, NY; U.S. minister and consul general to Haiti.
**St. Clair Drake,** 1911-90, black studies pioneer, *Black Metropolis* (1945, with Horace R. Cayton); first permanent director, African and African American Studies, Stanford Univ.
**Charles Richard Drew,** 1904-50, physician, pioneered in development of blood banks; director of American Red Cross blood donor project in WW2.
**William Edward Burghardt (W.E.B.) Du Bois,** 1868-1963, historian, sociologist; a founder of the National Association for the Advancement of Colored People (NAACP), 1909, and founder of its magazine *The Crisis.*
**Paul Laurence Dunbar,** 1872-1906, poet, novelist; won fame with *Lyrics of Lowly Life,* 1896.
**Jean Baptiste Point du Sable,** c1750-1818, pioneer trader and first settler of Chicago, 1779.
**Henry O. Flipper,** 1856-1940, first black to graduate, 1877, from West Point.
**Marcus Garvey,** 1887-1940, founded Universal Negro Improvement Assn., 1911.
**Ewart Guinier,** 1911-90, trade unionist; first chairman of Harvard Univ.'s Department of African American Studies.
**Jupiter Hammon,** c1720-1800, poet; the first black American to have his works published, 1761.
**Lorraine Hansberry,** 1930-65, playwright; won New York Drama Critics Circle Award, 1959; *A Raisin in the Sun.*
**William H. Hastie,** 1904-76, first black federal judge, appointed 1937; governor of Virgin Islands, 1946-49.
**Matthew A. Henson,** 1866-1955, member of Peary's 1909 expedition to the North Pole; placed U.S. flag at the pole.
**Chester Himes,** 1909-84, novelist. *Cotton Comes to Harlem.*
**William A. Hinton,** 1883-1959, physician, developed the Hinton and Davies-Hinton tests for detection of syphilis; first black professor, 1949, at Harvard Medical School.
**Charles Hamilton Houston,** 1895-1950, lawyer, Howard University instructor, and champion of minority rights,
**Langston Hughes,** 1902-67, poet, lyric writer, author; a major influence in the Harlem Renaissance of the 1920s.
**Daniel James Jr.,** 1920-78, first black 4-star general, 1975; Commander, North American Air Defense Command.
**Henry Johnson,** 1897-1929, the first American decorated by France in WW1 with the Croix de Guerre.
**James Weldon Johnson,** 1871-1938, poet, novelist, diplomat; lyricist for *Lift Every Voice and Sing.*
**Barbara Jordan,** 1936-96, congresswoman, orator, educator; first black woman to win a seat in the Texas senate (1966), served in U.S. House (D, TX) 1972-78.
**Ernest Everett Just,** 1883-1941, marine biologist; studied egg development; author, *Biology of Cell Surfaces,* 1941.
**Martin Luther King Jr.,** 1929-68, led 382-day Montgomery, AL, boycott that brought 1956 U.S. Supreme Court decision holding segregation on buses unconstitutional; founder, president, Southern Christian Leadership Conference, 1957.
**Lewis H. Latimer,** 1848-1928, associate of Edison; supervised installation of first electric street lighting in NYC.
**Mickey Leland,** 1944-89, U.S. representative from Texas, 1978 until death; chairman of Congressional Black Caucus.
**Henry Lewis,** 1932-1996, (U.S.) conductor; first black conductor and musical director of major American orchestra; first black to conduct at the Metropolitan Opera, NYC.
**Malcolm X** (Little), 1925-65, Black Muslim, black nationalist leader; promoted black pride.
**Thurgood Marshall,** 1908-93, first black U.S. solicitor general, 1965; first black justice of the U.S. Supreme Court, 1967-91; as a lawyer led the legal battery that won the Supreme Court decision *Brown* v. *Board of Education of Topeka,* 1954.
**Jan Matzeliger,** 1852-89, invented lasting machine, patented 1883, which revolutionized the shoe industry.
**Benjamin Mays,** 1895-1984, educator, civil rights leader; headed Morehouse College, 1940-67.
**Ronald McNair,** 1950-86, physicist, astronaut; killed in *Challenger* explosion.
**Dorie Miller,** 1919-43, Navy hero of Pearl Harbor attack; awarded the Navy Cross.
**Willard Motley,** 1912-65, novelist; *Knock on Any Door.*
**Elijah Muhammad,** 1897-1975, founded Black Muslims, 1931.
**Pedro Alonzo Niño,** navigator of the Niña, one of Columbus's 3 ships on his first voyage to the New World, 1492.
**Frederick D. Patterson,** 1901-88, founder of United Negro College Fund, 1944.
**Harold R. Perry,** 1916-91, first black American Roman Catholic bishop in the 20th century, 1966; first black clergyman to deliver the opening prayer in the U.S. Congress, 1964.
**Adam Clayton Powell Jr.,** 1908-72, early civil rights leader, congressman, 1945-69.
**Joseph H. Rainey,** 1832-87, first black elected to U.S. House of Representatives, 1869, from South Carolina.
**A. Philip Randolph,** 1889-1979, organized the Brotherhood of Sleeping Car Porters, 1925; an organizer of 1941 and 1963 March on Washington movements.
**Hiram R. Revels,** 1822-1901, first black U.S. senator, elected in Mississippi, served 1870-71.
**Norbert Rillieux,** 1806-94; invented a vacuum pan evaporator, 1846, revolutionizing the sugar-refining industry.
**Paul Robeson,** 1898-1976, actor, singer, civil rights activist; graduated first in class at Rutgers, 1918, Phi Beta Kappa.
**Max Robinson,** 1939-88, TV journalist, first black to anchor network news, 1978.
**John B. Russwurm,** 1799-1851, with **Samuel E. Cornish,** 1793-1858, founded, 1827, the nation's first black newspaper, *Freedom's Journal,* in NYC.
**Bayard Rustin,** 1910-87, an organizer of the 1963 March on Washington; executive director, A. Philip Randolph Institute.
**Peter Salem,** at the Battle of Bunker Hill, June 17, 1775, shot and killed British commander Maj. John Pitcairn.
**Stephen Spottswood,** 1897-1974, board chairman of NAACP, 1961-74.
**Carl Stokes,** 1927-1996, first black mayor of a major American city (Cleveland), (1967-72).

**Willard Townsend,** 1895-1957, organized the United Transport Service Employees (redcaps), 1935.

**Sojourner Truth,** 1797-1883, born Isabella Baumfree; preacher, abolitonist; worked for black educational opportunities.

**Harriet Tubman,** 1823-1913, Underground Railroad conductor, served as nurse and spy for Union Army in the Civil War.

**Nat Turner,** 1800-31, led the most significant of more than 200 slave revolts in U.S., in Southampton, VA; hanged.

**Booker T. Washington,** 1856-1915, founder, 1881, and first president of Tuskegee Institute; author, *Up From Slavery.*

**Harold Washington,** 1922-87, first black mayor of Chicago, from 1983 until death.

**Ida B. Wells (Barnett),** 1862-1931, journalist who waged anti-lynching crusade.

**Phillis Wheatley,** c1753-84, poet; second American woman and first black woman to have her works published, 1770.

**Walter White,** 1893-1955, exec. secretary, NAACP, 1931-55.

**Roy Wilkins,** 1901-81, exec. director, NAACP, 1955-77.

**Daniel Hale Williams,** 1858-1931, performed one of first two open-heart operations, 1893; first black elected a fellow of the American College of Surgeons.

**Granville T. Woods,** 1856-1910, invented the third-rail system now used in subways, and automatic air brake.

**Carter G. Woodson,** 1875-1950, historian; founded Assn. for the Study of Negro Life and History.

**Frank Yerby,** 1916-91, 1st best-selling American black novelist; *The Foxes of Harrow.*

## Noted Business Leaders, Industrialists, and Philanthropists of the Past

**Elizabeth Arden (F. N. Graham),** 1884-1966, (U.S.) Canadian-born founder of cosmetics empire.

**Philip D. Armour,** 1832-1901, (U.S.) industrialist; streamlined meatpacking.

**John Jacob Astor,** 1763-1848, (U.S.) German-born fur trader, banker, real estate magnate; at death, richest in U.S.

**Francis W. Ayer,** 1848-1923, (U.S.) ad industry pioneer.

**August Belmont,** 1816-90, (U.S.) German-born financier.

**James B. (Diamond Jim) Brady,** 1856-1917, (U.S.) financier, philanthropist, legendary bon vivant.

**Adolphus Busch,** 1839-1913, (U.S.) German-born businessman; established brewery empire.

**Asa Candler,** 1851-1929, (U.S.) founded Coca-Cola Co.

**Andrew Carnegie,** 1835-1919, (U.S.) Scottish-born industrialist; founded U.S. Steel; financed more than 2,800 libraries.

**Tom Carvel,** 1908-89, (Gr.-U.S.) founded ice cream chain.

**William Colgate,** 1783-1857, (Br.-U.S.) Br.-born businessman, philanthropist; founded soap-making empire.

**Jay Cooke,** 1821-1905, (U.S.) financier; sold $1 billion in Union bonds during Civil War.

**Peter Cooper,** 1791-1883, (U.S.) industrialist, inventor, philanthropist; founder Cooper Union (1859).

**Ezra Cornell,** 1807-74, (U.S.) businessman, philanthropist; headed Western Union, established university.

**Erastus Corning,** 1794-1872, (U.S.) financier; headed N.Y. Central.

**Charles Crocker,** 1822-88, (U.S.) railroad builder, financier.

**Samuel Cunard,** 1787-1865, (Can.) pioneered trans-Atlantic steam navigation.

**Marcus Daly,** 1841-1900, (U.S.) Irish-born copper magnate.

**George T. Delacorte,** 1893-1991, (U.S.) publisher; Central Park donations included Alice in Wonderland statue.

**W. Edwards Deming,** 1900-93, (U.S.) quality-control expert who revolutionized Japanese manufacturing.

**Walt Disney,** 1901-66, (U.S.) pioneer in cinema animation; built entertainment empire.

**Herbert H. Dow,** 1866-1930, (U.S.) founder of chemical co.

**James Duke,** 1856-1925, (U.S.) founded American Tobacco, Duke Univ.

**Eleuthere I. du Pont,** 1771-1834, (Fr.-U.S.) gunpowder manufacturer; founded one of the largest business empires.

**Thomas C. Durant,** 1820-85, (U.S.) railroad official, financier.

**William C. Durant,** 1861-1947, (U.S.) industrialist; formed General Motors.

**George Eastman,** 1854-1932, (U.S.) inventor; manufacturer of photographic equipment.

**Marshall Field,** 1834-1906, (U.S.) merchant; founded Chicago's largest department store.

**Harvey Firestone,** 1868-1938, (U.S.) founded tire company.

**Avery Fisher,** 1906-94, (U.S.) industrialist, philanthropist, founded Fisher electronics.

**Henry M. Flagler,** 1830-1913, (U.S.) financier; helped form Standard Oil; developed Florida as resort state.

**Malcolm Forbes,** 1919-90, (U.S.) magazine publisher.

**Henry Ford,** 1863-1947, (U.S.) auto maker; developed first popular low-priced car.

**Henry Ford 2d,** 1917-87, (U.S.) headed auto company founded by grandfather.

**Henry C. Frick,** 1849-1919, (U.S.) industrialist; helped organize U.S. Steel.

**Jakob Fugger (Jakob the Rich),** 1459-1525, (Ger.) headed leading banking, trading house, in 16th-century Europe.

**Alfred C. Fuller,** 1885-1973, (U.S.) Canadian-born businessman; founded brush co.

**Elbert H. Gary,** 1846-1927, (U.S.) one of the organizers of U.S. Steel; chairman of the board of directors, 1903-27.

**Jean Paul Getty,** 1892-1976, (U.S.) founded oil empire.

**Amadeo P. Giannini,** 1870-1949, (U.S.) founded Bank of America.

**Stephen Girard,** 1750-1831, (U.S.) French-born financier, philanthropist; richest man in U.S. at his death.

**Jay Gould,** 1836-92, (U.S.) railroad magnate, financier, speculator.

**Hetty Green,** 1834-1916, (U.S.) financier, the "witch of Wall St."; richest woman in U.S. in her day.

**William Gregg,** 1800-67, (U.S.) launched textile industry in the South.

**Meyer Guggenheim,** 1828-1905, (U.S.) Swiss-born merchant, philanthropist; built merchandising, mining empires.

**Armand Hammer,** 1898-1990, (U.S.) headed Occidental Petroleum; promoted U.S.-Soviet ties.

**Edward H. Harriman,** 1848-1909, (U.S.) railroad financier, administrator; headed Union Pacific.

**William Randolph Hearst,** 1863-1951, (U.S.) a dominant figure in American journalism; built vast publishing empire.

**Henry J. Heinz,** 1844-1919, (U.S.) founded food empire.

**James J. Hill,** 1838-1916, (U.S.) Canadian-born railroad magnate, financier; founded Great Northern Railway.

**Conrad N. Hilton,** 1888-1979, (U.S.) hotel chain founder.

**Howard Hughes,** 1905-76, (U.S.) industrialist, aviator, movie maker.

**H. L. Hunt,** 1889-1974, (U.S.) oil magnate.

**Collis P. Huntington,** 1821-1900, (U.S.) railroad magnate.

**Henry E. Huntington,** 1850-1927, (U.S.) railroad builder, philanthropist.

**Walter L. Jacobs,** 1898-1985, (U.S.) founder of the first rental car agency, which later became Hertz.

**Howard Johnson,** 1896-1972, (U.S.) founded restaurants.

**Henry J. Kaiser,** 1882-1967, (U.S.) industrialist; built empire in steel, aluminum.

**Minor C. Keith,** 1848-1929, (U.S.) railroad magnate; founded United Fruit Co.

**Will K. Kellogg,** 1860-1951, (U.S.) businessman, philanthropist; founded breakfast food co.

**Richard King,** 1825-85, (U.S.) cattleman; founded half-million-acre King Ranch in Texas.

**William S. Knudsen,** 1879-1948, (U.S.) Danish-born auto industry executive.

**Samuel H. Kress,** 1863-1955, (U.S.) businessman, art collector, philanthropist; founded "dime store" chain.

**Ray A. Kroc,** 1902-84, (U.S.) founded McDonald's fast food.

**Alfred Krupp,** 1812-87, (Ger.) armaments magnate.

**William Levitt,** 1907-94, (U.S.) industrialist, "suburb maker".

**Thomas Lipton,** 1850-1931, (Scot.) merchant, tea empire.

**James McGill,** 1744-1813, (Scot.-Can.) founded university.

**Andrew W. Mellon,** 1855-1937, (U.S.) financier, industrialist; benefactor of National Gallery of Art.

**Charles E. Merrill,** 1885-1956, (U.S.) financier; developed firm of Merrill Lynch.

**John Pierpont Morgan,** 1837-1913, (U.S.) most powerful figure in finance and industry at the turn of the century.

**Malcolm Muir,** 1885-1979, (U.S.) created *Business Week* magazine; headed *Newsweek,* 1937-61.

**Samuel Newhouse,** 1895-1979, (U.S.) publishing and broadcasting magnate; built communications empire.

**Aristotle Onassis,** 1906-75, (Gr.) shipping magnate.

**William S. Paley,** 1901-90, (U.S.) built CBS communications empire.

**George Peabody,** 1795-1869, (U.S.) merchant, financier, philanthropist.

**James C. Penney,** 1875-1971, (U.S.) businessman; developed department store chain.

**William C. Procter,** 1862-1934, (U.S.) headed soap company.

**John D. Rockefeller,** 1839-1937, (U.S.) industrialist; established Standard Oil.

**John D. Rockefeller Jr.,** 1874-1960, (U.S.) philanthropist; established foundation; provided land for United Nations.

**Meyer A. Rothschild,** 1743-1812, (Ger.) founded international banking house.

**Thomas Fortune Ryan,** 1851-1928, (U.S.) financier; a founder of American Tobacco.

**Russell Sage,** 1816-1906, (U.S.) financier.
**David Sarnoff,** 1891-1971, (U.S.) broadcasting pioneer; established first radio network, NBC.
**Richard Sears,** 1863-1914, (U.S.) founded mail-order co.
**(Ernst) Werner von Siemens,** 1816-92, (Ger.) industrialist; inventor.
**Alfred P. Sloan,** 1875-1966, (U.S.) industrialist, philanthropist; headed General Motors.
**A. Leland Stanford,** 1824-93, (U.S.) railroad official, philanthropist; founded university.
**Nathan Straus,** 1848-1931, (U.S.) German-born merchant, philanthropist; headed Macy's.
**Levi Strauss,** c1829-1902, (U.S.) pants manufacturer.
**Clement Studebaker,** 1831-1901, (U.S.) wagon, carriage manufacturer.
**Gustavus Swift,** 1839-1903, (U.S.) pioneer meatpacker.
**Gerard Swope,** 1872-1957, (U.S.) industrialist, economist; headed General Electric.
**James Walter Thompson,** 1847-1928, (U.S.) ad executive.
**Alice Tully,** 1902-93, (U.S.) philanthropist, arts patron.
**Theodore N. Vail,** 1845-1920, (U.S.) organized Bell Telephone system; headed AT&T.
**Cornelius Vanderbilt,** 1794-1877, (U.S.) financier; established steamship, railroad empires.
**Henry Villard,** 1835-1900, (U.S.) German-born railroad executive, financier.
**George Westinghouse,** 1846-1914, (U.S) inventor, manufacturer; organized Westinghouse Electric Co., 1886.
**Charles R. Walgreen,** 1873-1939, (U.S.) founded drugstore chain.
**DeWitt Wallace,** 1889-1981, (U.S.) and **Lila Wallace,** 1889-1984, (U.S.) cofounders of *Reader's Digest* magazine.
**Sam Walton,** 1918-92, (U.S.) founder of Wal-Mart stores.
**John Wanamaker,** 1838-1922, (U.S.) pioneered department-store merchandising.
**Aaron Montgomery Ward,** 1843-1913, (U.S.) established first mail-order firm.
**Thomas J. Watson,** 1874-1956, (U.S.) IBM head, 1924-49.
**John Hay Whitney,** 1905-82, (U.S.) publisher, sportsman, philanthropist.
**Charles E. Wilson,** 1890-1961, (U.S.) auto industry executive; public official.
**Frank W. Woolworth,** 1852-1919, (U.S.) created 5 & 10 chain.
**William Wrigley Jr.,** 1861-1932, (U.S.) founded chewing gum co.

# Noted American Cartoonists

**Scott Adams,** b 1957, Dilbert.
**Charles Addams,** 1912-88, macabre cartoons.
**Brad Anderson,** b 1924, Marmaduke.
**Peter Arno,** 1904-68, *New Yorker* urban characterizations.
**Tex Avery,** 1908-80, animator of Bugs Bunny, Porky Pig, and Daffy Duck.
**Arthur Babbitt,** 1907-92, Disney cartoonist.
**George Baker,** 1915-75, The Sad Sack.
**C. C. Beck,** 1910-89, Captain Marvel.
**Jim Berry,** b 1932, Berry's World.
**Herb Block (Herblock),** b 1909, political cartoonist.
**George Booth,** b 1926, *New Yorker* cartoonist.
**Berkeley Breathed,** b 1957, Bloom County.
**Clare Briggs,** 1875-1930, Mr. & Mrs.
**Dik Browne,** 1917-89, Hi & Lois, Hagar the Horrible.
**Marjorie Buell,** 1904-93, Little Lulu.
**Ernie Bushmiller,** 1905-82, Nancy.
**Milton Caniff,** 1907-88, Terry & the Pirates, Steve Canyon.
**Al Capp,** 1909-79, Li'l Abner.
**Roz Chast,** b 1954, *New Yorker* "bonfire of the banalities."
**Paul Conrad,** 1924, political cartoonist.
**Roy Crane,** 1901-77, Captain Easy, Buz Sawyer.
**Robert Crumb,** b 1943, "Underground" cartoonist.
**Shamus Culhane,** 1908-96, animator.
**Jay N. Darling (Ding),** 1876-1962, political cartoonist.
**Jack Davis,** b 1926, *Mad* magazine.
**Jim Davis,** b 1945, Garfield.
**Billy DeBeck,** 1890-1942, Barney Google.
**Rudolph Dirks,** 1877-1968, The Katzenjammer Kids.
**Walt Disney,** 1901-66, producer of animated cartoons, created Mickey Mouse and Donald Duck.
**Steve Ditko,** b 1927, Spider-Man.
**Mort Drucker,** b 1929, *Mad* magazine.
**Will Eisner,** b 1917, The Spirit.
**Jules Feiffer,** b 1929, satirical *Village Voice* cartoonist.
**Bud Fisher,** 1884-1954, Mutt & Jeff.
**Ham Fisher,** 1900-55, Joe Palooka.
**James Montgomery Flagg,** 1877-1960, illustrator, created the famous Uncle Sam recruiting poster during WWI.
**Max Fleischer,** 1883-1972, creator of Betty Boop, Popeye.
**Hal Foster,** 1892-1982, Tarzan, Prince Valiant.
**Fontaine Fox,** 1884-1964, Toonerville Folks.
**Isadore "Friz" Freleng,** 1905-95, animator, Yosemite Sam, Porky Pig, Sylvestor and Tweety.
**Al Frueh,** 1880-1968, *The New Yorker* cartoonist.
**Rube Goldberg,** 1883-1970, Boob McNutt.
**Chester Gould,** 1900-85, Dick Tracy.
**Harold Gray,** 1894-1968, Little Orphan Annie.
**Matt Groening,** b 1954, Life Is Hell, The Simpsons.
**Cathy Guisewite,** b 1950, Cathy.
**Bill Hanna,** b 1910, & **Joe Barbera,** b 1911, animators of Tom & Jerry, Huckleberry Hound, Yogi Bear, Flintstones.
**Johnny Hart,** b 1931, BC, Wizard of Id.
**Alfred Harvey,** 1913-94, created Casper the Friendly Ghost
**Jimmy Hatlo,** 1898-1963, Little Iodine.
**John Held Jr.,** 1889-1958, "Jazz Age" cartoonist.
**George Herriman,** 1881-1944, Krazy Kat.
**Harry Hershfield,** 1885-1974, Abie the Agent.
**Al Hirschfeld,** b 1903, *N.Y. Times* theater caricaturist.
**Burne Hogarth,** b 1911, Tarzan.
**Helen Hokinson,** 1900-49, satirized clubwomen.
**Nicole Hollander,** b 1939, Sylvia.
**Lynn Johnston,** b 1947, For Better or For Worse.
**Chuck Jones,** b 1912, animator, Bugs Bunny, Porky Pig, Daffy Duck
**Mike Judge,** Beavis and Butthead.
**Bob Kane,** b 1916, Batman.
**Bil Keane,** b 1922, The Family Circus.
**Walt Kelly,** 1913-73, Pogo.
**Hank Ketcham,** b 1920, Dennis the Menace.
**Ted Key,** b 1912, Hazel.
**Frank King,** 1883-1969, Gasoline Alley.
**Jack Kirby,** 1917-94, Fantastic Four, The Incredible Hulk.
**Rollin Kirby,** 1875-1952, political cartoonist.
**B(ernard) Kliban,** 1935-91, cat books.
**Edward Koren,** b 1935, *New Yorker* woolly characters.
**Harvey Kurtzman,** 1921-93, *Mad* magazine.
**Walter Lantz,** 1900-94, Woody Woodpecker.
**Gary Larson,** b 1950, The Far Side.
**Mell Lazarus,** b 1929, Momma, Miss Peach.
**Stan Lee,** b 1922, Marvel Comics.
**David Levine,** b 1926, *N.Y. Review of Books* caricatures.
**Doug Marlette,** b 1949, editorial cartoonist, Kudzu.
**Don Martin,** b 1931, *Mad* magazine.
**Bill Mauldin,** b 1921, depicted squalid life of the G.I. in WW2.
**Jeff MacNelly,** b 1947, political cartoonist, Shoe.
**Winsor McCay,** 1872-1934, Little Nemo.
**John T. McCutcheon,** 1870-1949, midwestern rural life.
**George McManus,** 1884-1954, Bringing Up Father.
**Dale Messick,** b 1906, Brenda Starr.
**Norman Mingo,** 1896-1980, Alfred E. Neuman.
**Bob Montana,** 1920-75, Archie.
**Dick Moores,** 1909-86, Gasoline Alley.
**Willard Mullin,** 1902-78, sports cartoonist, created Dodgers "Bum" and Mets "Kid."
**Russell Myers,** b 1938, Broom Hilda.
**Thomas Nast,** 1840-1902, political cartoonist, created the Democratic donkey and Republican elephant.
**Pat Oliphant,** b 1935, political cartoonist.
**Frederick Burr Opper,** 1857-1937, Happy Hooligan.
**Richard Outcault,** 1863-1928, Yellow Kid, Buster Brown.
**Mike Peters,** b 1943, editorial cartoons. Mother Goose & Grimm.
**George Price,** 1901-95, *New Yorker* lower-class life.
**Alex Raymond,** 1909-56, Flash Gordon, Jungle Jim.
**Forrest (Bud) Sagendorf,** 1915-94, Popeye
**Art Sansom,** 1920-91, The Born Loser.
**Charles Schulz,** b 1922, Peanuts.
**Elzie C. Segar,** 1894-1938, Popeye.
**Joe Shuster,** 1914-92, & **Jerry Siegel,** 1914-96, Superman.
**Sydney Smith,** 1887-1935, The Gumps.
**Otto Soglow,** 1900-75, Little King, Canyon Kiddies.
**Art Spiegelman,** b 1948, Raw, Maus.
**William Steig,** b 1907, *New Yorker* cartoonist.
**James Swinnerton,** 1875-1974, Little Jimmy.
**Paul Terry,** 1887-1971, animator of Mighty Mouse.
**Bob Thaves,** b 1924, Frank and Ernest.
**James Thurber,** 1894-61, *New Yorker* cartoonist.
**Garry Trudeau,** b 1948, Doonesbury.
**Mort Walker,** b 1923, Beetle Bailey.
**Bill Watterson,** b 1958, Calvin and Hobbes.
**Russ Westover,** 1887-1966, Tillie the Toiler.
**Frank Willard,** 1893-1958, Moon Mullins.
**J. R. Williams,** 1888-1957, The Willets Family, Out Our Way.
**Gahan Wilson,** b 1930, cartoonist of the macabre.
**Tom Wilson,** b 1931, Ziggy.
**Art Young,** 1866-1943, political radical and satirist.
**Chic Young,** 1901-73, Blondie.

# Noted Historians, Economists, and Social Scientists of the Past

**Brooks Adams,** 1848-1927, (U.S.) historian, political theoretician; *The Law of Civilization and Decay.*
**Henry Adams,** 1838-1918, (U.S.) historian; *History of the United States of America, The Education of Henry Adams.*
**Francis Bacon,** 1561-1626, (Eng.) philosopher, essayist, and statesman; applied scientific induction to philosophy.
**George Bancroft,** 1800-91, (U.S.) historian; wrote 10-volume *History of the United States.*
**Jack Barbash,** 1911-94, (U.S.) labor economist who helped create the AFL-CIO.
**Charles A. Beard,** 1874-1948, (U.S.) historian; *The Economic Basis of Politics.*
**Bede (the Venerable),** c673-735, (Eng.) scholar historian whose writings virtually constitute the learning of his time.
**Ruth Benedict,** 1887-1948, (U.S.) anthropologist; studied Indian tribes of the Southwest.
**Bruno Bettleheim,** 1903-90, (Aust.-U.S.) psychoanalyst specializing in autistic children; *The Uses of Enchantment.*
**Louis Blanc,** 1811-82, (Fr.) Socialist leader and historian whose ideas were a link between utopian and Marxist socialism.
**Leonard Bloomfield,** 1887-1949, (U.S.) linguist; *Language.*
**Franz Boas,** 1858-1942, (U.S.) German-born anthropologist; studied American Indians.
**Van Wyck Brooks,** 1886-1963, (U.S.) historian; critic of New England culture, especially literature.
**Edmund Burke,** 1729-97, (Ir.) British parliamentarian and political philosopher; influenced many Federalists.
**Joseph Campbell,** 1904-87, (U.S.) author, editor, teacher; wrote books on mythology, folklore.
**Thomas Carlyle,** 1795-1881, (Sc.) historian, critic; *Sartor Resartus, Past and Present, The French Revolution.*
**Edward Channing,** 1856-1931, (U.S.) historian; wrote 6-volume *History of the United States.*
**John R. Commons,** 1862-1945, (U.S.) economist, labor historian; *Legal Foundations of Capitalism.*
**Benedetto Croce,** 1866-1952, (It.) philosopher, statesman, and historian; *Philosophy of the Spirit.*
**Bernard A. De Voto,** 1897-1955, (U.S.) historian; wrote trilogy on American West; edited Mark Twain manuscripts.
**Ariel Durant,** 1898-1981, & **Will Durant,** 1885-1981, (U.S.) historians; *The Story of Civilization.*
**Emile Durkheim,** 1858-1917, (Fr.) a founder of modern sociology; *The Rules of Sociological Method.*
**Friedrich Engels,** 1820-95, (Ger.) political writer; with Marx wrote the *Communist Manifesto.*
**Erik Erikson,** 1902-94, (U.S.) psychoanalyst, author; theory of developmental stages of life, *Childhood and Society.*
**Irving Fisher,** 1867-1947, (U.S.) economist; contributed to the development of modern monetary theory.
**John Fiske,** 1842-1901, (U.S.) historian and lecturer; popularized Darwinian theory of evolution.
**Charles Fourier,** 1772-1837, (Fr.) utopian socialist.
**Sir James George Frazer,** 1854-1941, (Br.) anthropologist; studied myth in religion, *The Golden Bough.*
**Henry George,** 1839-97, (U.S.) economist, reformer; led single-tax movement.
**Edward Gibbon,** 1737-94, (Br.) historian; wrote *The History of the Decline and Fall of the Roman Empire.*
**Francesco Guicciardini,** 1483-1540, (It.) historian; wrote *Storia d'Italia,* principal historical work of the 16th cent.
**Thomas Hobbes,** 1588-1679, (Eng.) philosopher, political theorist; *Leviathan.*
**Richard Hofstadter,** 1916-70, (U.S.) historian; *The Age of Reform.*
**John Maynard Keynes,** 1883-1946, (Br.) economist; principal advocate of deficit spending.
**Russell Kirk,** 1918-94, (U.S.), social philosopher; *The Conservative Mind.*
**Alfred L. Kroeber,** 1876-1960, (U.S.) cultural anthropologist; studied Indians of North and South America.
**Christopher Lasch,** 1932-94, (U.S.) social critic, historian; *The Culture of Narcissism.*
**James L. Laughlin,** 1850-1933, (U.S.) economist; helped establish Federal Reserve System.
**Lucien Lévy-Bruhl,** 1857-1939, (Fr.) philosopher; studied the psychology of primitive societies; *Primitive Mentality.*
**Kurt Lewin,** 1890-1947, (U.S.) German-born psychologist, studied human motivation and group dynamics.
**John Locke,** 1632-1704, (Eng.) philosopher and political theorist; *Two Treatises of Government.*
**Konrad Lorenz,** 1904-89, (Austrian.) ethologist; pioneer in study of animal behavior.
**Thomas B. Macaulay,** 1800-59, (Br.) historian, statesman.
**Niccolò Machiavelli,** 1469-1527, (It.) writer, statesman. *The Prince, Discourses on Livy.*
**Bronislaw Malinowski,** 1884-1942, (Pol.) considered the father of social anthropology.
**Thomas R. Malthus,** 1766-1834, (Br.) economist; famed for *Essay on the Principle of Population.*
**Karl Mannheim,** 1893-1947, (Hung.) sociologist, historian; *Ideology and Utopia.*
**Karl Marx,** 1818-83, (Ger.) political philosopher, proponent of modern Communism; *Communist Manifesto, Das Kapital.*
**Giuseppe Mazzini,** 1805-72, (It.) political philosopher.
**George H. Mead,** 1863-1931, (U.S.) philosopher, social psychologist.
**Margaret Mead,** 1901-78, (U.S.) cultural anthropologist; popularized field, *Coming of Age in Samoa.*
**James Mill,** 1773-1836, (Sc.) philosopher, historian, economist; a proponent of utilitarianism.
**Perry G. Miller,** 1905-63, (U.S.) historian; interpreted 17th-century New England.
**Theodor Mommsen,** 1817-1903, (Ger.) historian; *The History of Rome.*
**Charles-Louis Montesquieu,** 1689-1755, (Fr.) social philosopher; *The Spirit of Laws.*
**Samuel Eliot Morison,** 1887-1976, (U.S.) historian; chronicled voyages of early explorers.
**Lewis Mumford,** 1895-1990, (U.S.) sociologist, critic; *The Culture of Cities.*
**Gunnar Myrdal,** 1898-1987, (Swed.) economist, social scientist; *Asian Drama: An Inquiry Into the Poverty of Nations.*
**Joseph Needham,** 1900-95, (Br.) scientific historian; *Science and Civilization in China.*
**Allan Nevins,** 1890-1971, (U.S.) historian, biographer; *The Ordeal of the Union.*
**José Ortega y Gasset,** 1883-1955, (Sp.) philosopher; advocated control by elite, *The Revolt of the Masses.*
**Robert Owen,** 1771-1858, (Br.) political philosopher, reformer; pioneer in cooperative movement.
**Thomas (Tom) Paine,** 1737-1809, (U.S.) political theorist, writer. *Common Sense.*
**Vilfredo Pareto,** 1848-1923, (It.) economist, sociologist.
**Francis Parkman,** 1823-93, (U.S.) historian; *France and England in North America, 1851-92.*
**William Prescott,** 1796-1859, (U.S.) early American historian; *The Conquest of Peru.*
**Pierre Joseph Proudhon,** 1809-65, (Fr.) social theorist; the father of anarchism, *The Philosophy of Property.*
**François Quesnay,** 1694-1774, (Fr.) economic theorist; demonstrated circular flow of economic activity through society.
**David Ricardo,** 1772-1823, (Br.) economic theorist; advocated free international trade.
**James H. Robinson,** 1863-1936, (U.S.) historian, educator.
**Carl Rogers,** 1902-87, (U.S.) psychotherapist, author.
**Jean-Jacques Rousseau,** 1712-78, (Fr.) social philosopher; the father of romantic sensibility; *Confessions.*
**Lee Salk,** 1926-92, (U.S.) child psychologist, author.
**Edward Sapir,** 1884-1939, (Ger.-U.S.) anthropologist; studied ethnology and linguistics of some U.S. Indian groups.
**Ferdinand de Saussure,** 1857-1913, (Swiss) a founder of modern linguistics.
**Hjalmar Schacht,** 1877-1970, (Ger.) economist.
**Joseph Schumpeter,** 1883-1950, (Czech.-U.S.) economist; championed big business, capitalism.
**George Simmel,** 1858-1918, (Ger.) sociologist, philosopher; helped establish German sociology.
**B. F. Skinner,** 1904-89, (U.S.) psychologist; behaviorism.
**Adam Smith,** 1723-90, (Br.) economist; advocated laissez-faire economy and free trade *The Wealth of Nations.*
**Jared Sparks,** 1789-1866, (U.S.) historian, educator, editor; *The Library of American Biography.*
**Oswald Spengler,** 1880-1936, (Ger.) philosopher and historian; *The Decline of the West.*
**William G. Sumner,** 1840-1910, (U.S.) social scientist, economist; laissez-faire economy, Social Darwinism.
**Hippolyte Taine,** 1828-93, (Fr.) historian; basis of naturalistic school; *The Origins of Contemporary France.*
**Frank W. Taussig,** 1859-1940, (U.S.) economist, educator.
**A(lan) J(ohn) P(ercivale) Taylor,** 1906-89, (Br.) historian; *The Origins of the Second World War.*
**Nikolaas Tinbergen,** 1907-88, (Dutch-Br.) ethologist; pioneer in study of animal behavior.
**Alexis de Tocqueville,** 1805-59, (Fr.) political scientist, historian; *Democracy in America.*
**Francis E. Townsend,** 1867-1960, (U.S.) led old-age pension movement, 1933.
**Arnold Toynbee,** 1889-1975, (Br.) historian; *A Study of History.*
**Heinrich von Treitschke,** 1834-96, (Ger.) historian, political writer; *A History of Germany in the 19th Century.*
**George Trevelyan,** 1838-1928, (Br.) historian, statesman; favored "literary" over "scientific" history; *History of England.*

**Barbara Tuchman,** 1912-89, (U.S.) author of popular history books, *The Guns of August, The March of Folly.*
**Frederick J. Turner,** 1861-1932, (U.S.) historian, educator; *The Frontier in American History.*
**Thorstein B. Veblen,** 1857-1929, (U.S.) economist, social philosopher; *The Theory of the Leisure Class.*
**Giovanni Vico,** 1668-1744, (It.) historian, philosopher; regarded by many as first modern historian; *New Science.*
**Izaak Walton,** 1593-1683, (Eng.) wrote biographies; political-philosophical study of fishing, *The Compleat Angler.*
**Sidney J.,** 1859-1947, and wife **Beatrice,** 1858-1943, **Webb,** (Br.) leading figures in Fabian Society and Br. Labour Party.
**Walter P. Webb,** 1888-1963, (U.S.) historian of the West.
**Max Weber,** 1864-1920, (Ger.) sociologist; *The Protestant Ethic and the Spirit of Capitalism.*

# Notable Military and Naval Leaders of the Past

**Creighton Abrams,** 1914-74, (U.S.) commanded forces in Vietnam, 1968-72.
**Harold Alexander,** 1891-1969, (Br.) led Allied invasion of Italy, 1943, WW2.
**Ethan Allen,** 1738-89, (U.S.) headed Green Mountain Boys; captured Ft. Ticonderoga, 1775, American Revolution.
**Edmund Allenby,** 1861-1936, (Br.) in Boer War, WW1; led Egyptian expeditionary force, 1917-18.
**Benedict Arnold,** 1741-1801, (U.S.) victorious at Saratoga; tried to betray West Point to British, American Revolution.
**Henry "Hap" Arnold,** 1886-1950, (U.S.) commanded Army Air Force in WW2.
**John Barry,** 1745-1803, (U.S.) won numerous sea battles during American Revolution.
**Pierre Beauregard,** 1818-93, (U.S.) Confederate general, ordered bombardment of Ft. Sumter that began the Civil War.
**Gebhard von Blücher,** 1742-1819, (Ger.) helped defeat Napoleon at Waterloo.
**Napoleon Bonaparte,** 1769-1821, (Fr.) defeated Russia and Austria at Austerlitz, 1805; invaded Russia, 1812; defeated at Waterloo, 1815.
**Edward Braddock,** 1695-1755, (Br.) commanded forces in French and Indian War.
**Omar N. Bradley,** 1893-1981, (U.S.) headed U.S. ground troops in Normandy invasion, 1944, WW2.
**John Burgoyne,** 1722-92, (Br.) defeated at Saratoga, American Revolution.
**Claire Chennault,** 1890-1958, (U.S.) headed Flying Tigers in WW2.
**Mark W. Clark,** 1896-1984, (U.S.) helped plan N. African invasion in WW2; commander of UN forces, Korean War.
**Karl von Clausewitz,** 1780-1831, (Prussian) wrote books on military theory.
**Lucius D. Clay,** 1897-1978, (U.S.) led Berlin airlift, 1948-49.
**Henry Clinton,** 1738-95, (Br.) commander of forces in American Revolution, 1778-81.
**Cochise,** c 1815-74, (Native American) chief of Chiricahua band of Apache Indians in Southwest.
**Charles Cornwallis,** 1738-1805, (Br.) victorious at Brandywine, 1777; surrendered at Yorktown, American Revolution.
**Crazy Horse,** 1849-77, (Native American) Sioux war chief victorious at the battle of Little Big Horn
**George Armstrong Custer,** 1839-76, (U.S.) U.S. army officer defeated and killed at the battle of Little Big Horn.
**Moshe Dayan,** 1915-81, (Isr.) directed campaigns in the 1967, 1973 Arab-Israeli wars.
**Stephen Decatur,** 1779-1820, (U.S.) naval hero of Barbary wars, War of 1812.
**Anton Denikin,** 1872-1947, (Russ.) led White forces in Russian civil war.
**George Dewey,** 1837-1917, (U.S.) destroyed Spanish fleet at Manila, 1898, Spanish-American War.
**Hugh C. Dowding,** 1883-1970, (Br.) headed RAF, 1936-40, WW2.
**Jubal Early,** 1816-94, (U.S.) Confederate general led raid on Washington, 1864, Civil War.
**Dwight D. Eisenhower,** 1890-1969, (U.S.) commanded Allied forces in Europe, WW2.
**David Farragut,** 1801-70, (U.S.) Union admiral, captured New Orleans, Mobile Bay, Civil War.
**Ferdinand Foch,** 1851-1929, (Fr.) headed victorious Allied armies, 1918, WW1.
**Nathan Bedford Forrest,** 1821-77, (U.S.) Confederate general, led raids against Union supply lines, Civil War.
**Frederick the Great,** 1712-86, (Prussian) led Prussia in The Seven Years War.
**Horatio Gates,** 1728-1806, (U.S.) commanded army at Saratoga, American Revolution.
**Geronimo,** 1829-1909 (Native American) leader of Chiricahua band of Apache Indians.
**Charles G. Gordon,** 1833-85, (Br.) led forces in China, Crimean War; killed at Khartoum.
**Ulysses S. Grant,** 1822-85, (U.S.) headed Union army, Civil War, 1864-65; forced Lee's surrender, 1865.
**Nathanael Greene,** 1742-86, (U.S.) defeated British in Southern campaign, 1780-81.
**Heinz Guderian,** 1888-1953, (Ger.) tank theorist, led panzer forces in Poland, France, Russia, WW2.
**Douglas Haig,** 1861-1928, (Br.) led British armies in France, 1915-18, WW1.
**William F. Halsey,** 1882-1959, (U.S.) defeated Japanese fleet at Leyte Gulf, 1944, WW2.
**Sir Arthur Travers Harris,** 1895-1984, (Br.) led Britain's WW2 bomber command.
**Richard Howe,** 1726-99, (Br.) commanded navy in American Revolution, 1776-78; June 1 victory against French, 1794.
**William Howe,** 1729-1814, (Br.) commanded forces in American Revolution, 1776-78.
**Isaac Hull,** 1773-1843, (U.S.) sunk British frigate *Guerriere,* War of 1812.
**Thomas (Stonewall) Jackson,** 1824-63, (U.S.) Confederate general led Shenandoah Valley campaign, Civil War.
**Joseph Joffre,** 1852-1931, (Fr.) headed Allied armies, won Battle of the Marne, 1914, WW1.
**Chief Joseph,** c 1840-1904, (Native American) chief of the Nez Percé, led his tribe across 3 states seeking refuge in Canada; surrendered about 30 mi from Canadian border.
**John Paul Jones,** 1747-92, (U.S.) commanded *Bonhomme Richard* in victory over Serapis, American Revolution, 1779.
**Stephen Kearny,** 1794-1848, (U.S.) headed Army of the West in Mexican War.
**Ernest J. King,** 1878-1956, (U.S.) chief naval strategist in WW2.
**Horatio H. Kitchener,** 1850-1916, (Br.) led forces in Boer War; victorious at Khartoum; organized army in WW1.
**Lavrenti Kornilov,** 1870-1918, (Russ.) commander-in-chief, 1917; led counter-revolutionary march on Petrograd.
**Thaddeus Kosciusko,** 1746-1817, (Pol.) aided American cause in American Revolution.
**Mikhail Kutuzov,** 1745-1813, (Russ.) fought French at Borodino, Napoleonic Wars, 1812; abandoned Moscow; forced French retreat.
**Marquis de Lafayette,** 1757-1834, (Fr.) aided American cause in American Revolution.
**T(homas) E. Lawrence (of Arabia),** 1888-1935, (Br.) organized revolt of Arabs against Turks in WW1.
**Henry (Light-Horse Harry) Lee,** 1756-1818, (U.S.) cavalry officer in American Revolution.
**Robert E. Lee,** 1807-70, (U.S.) Confederate general defeated at Gettysburg, Civil War; surrendered to Grant, 1865.
**Lyman Lemnitzer,** 1899-1988, (U.S.) WW2 hero, later general, chairman of Joint Chiefs of Staff.
**James Longstreet,** 1821-1904, (U.S.) aided Lee at Gettysburg, Civil War.
**Douglas MacArthur,** 1880-1964, (U.S.) commanded forces in SW Pacific in WW2; headed occupation forces in Japan, 1945-51; UN commander in Korean War.
**Carl Gustaf Mannerheim,** 1867-1951, (Finn.) army officer and president of Finland 1944-46.
**Francis Marion,** 1733-95, (U.S.) led guerrilla actions in South Carolina during American Revolution.
**Duke of Marlborough,** 1650-1722, (Br.) led forces against Louis XIV in War of the Spanish Succession.
**George C. Marshall,** 1880-1959, (U.S.) chief of staff in WW2; authored Marshall Plan.
**George B. McClellan,** 1826-85, (U.S.) Union general, commanded Army of the Potomac, 1861-62, Civil War.
**George Meade,** 1815-72; (U.S.) commanded Union forces at Gettysburg, Civil War.
**Billy Mitchell,** 1879-1936, (U.S.) WW1 air-power advocate; court-martialed for insubordination, later vindicated.
**Helmuth von Moltke,** 1800-91, (Ger.) victorious in Austro-Prussian, Franco-Prussian wars.
**Louis de Montcalm,** 1712-59, (Fr.) headed troops in Canada, French and Indian War; defeated at Quebec, 1759.
**Bernard Law Montgomery,** 1887-1976, (Br.) stopped German offensive at Alamein, 1942, WW2; helped plan Normandy invasion.
**Daniel Morgan,** 1736-1802, (U.S.) victorious at Cowpens, 1781, American Revolution.
**Louis Mountbatten,** 1900-79, (Br.) Supreme Allied Commander of SE Asia, 1943-46, WW2.
**Joachim Murat,** 1767-1815, (Fr.) leader of cavalry at Marengo, 1800; Austerlitz, 1805; and Jena, 1806, Napoleonic Wars.

**Horatio Nelson,** 1758-1805, (Br.) naval commander destroyed French fleet at Trafalgar.
**Michel Ney,** 1769-1815, (Fr.) commanded forces in Switz., Aust., Russ., Napoleonic Wars; defeated at Waterloo.
**Chester Nimitz,** 1885-1966, (U.S.) commander of naval forces in Pacific in WW2.
**George S. Patton,** 1885-1945, (U.S.) led assault on Sicily, 1943, Third Army invasion of Europe, WW2.
**Oliver Perry,** 1785-1819, (U.S.) won Battle of Lake Erie in War of 1812.
**John Pershing,** 1860-1948, (U.S.) commanded Mexican border campaign, 1916, American Expeditionary Force, WW1.
**Henri Philippe Pétain,** 1856-1951, (Fr.) defended Verdun, 1916; headed Vichy government in WW2.
**George E. Pickett,** 1825-75, (U.S.) Confederate general famed for "charge" at Gettysburg, Civil War.
**Hyman Rickover,** 1900-86, (U.S.) father of nuclear navy.
**Erwin Rommel,** 1891-1944, (Ger.) headed Afrika Korps, WW2.
**Gerd von Rundstedt,** 1875-1953, (Ger.) supreme commander in West, 1942-45, WW2.
**Aleksandr Samsonov,** 1859-1914, (Russ.) led invasion of E. Prussia, WW1, defeated at Tannenberg, 1914.
**Winfield Scott,** 1786-1866, (U.S.) hero of War of 1812; headed forces in Mexican war, took Mexico City.
**Philip Sheridan,** 1831-88, (U.S.) Union cavalry officer, headed Army of the Shenandoah, 1864-65, Civil War.
**William T. Sherman,** 1820-91, (U.S.) Union general, sacked Atlanta during "march to the sea," 1864, Civil War.
**Carl Spaatz,** 1891-1974, (U.S.) directed strategic bombing against Germany, later Japan, in WW2.
**Raymond Spruance,** 1886-1969, (U.S.) victorious at Midway Island, 1942, WW2.
**Joseph W. Stilwell,** 1883-1946, (U.S.) headed forces in the China, Burma, India theater in WW2.
**J.E.B. Stuart,** 1833-64, (U.S.) Confederate cavalry commander, Civil War.
**George H. Thomas,** 1816-70, (U.S.) saved Union army at Chattanooga, 1863; victorious at Nashville, 1864, Civil War.
**Semyon Timoshenko,** 1895-1970, (USSR) defended Moscow, Stalingrad, WW2; led winter offensive, 1942-43.
**Alfred von Tirpitz,** 1849-1930, (Ger.) responsible for submarine blockade in WW1.
**Jonathan M. Wainwright,** 1883-1953, (U.S.) forced to surrender on Corregidor, 1942, WW2.
**George Washington,** 1732-99, (U.S.) led Continental army, 1775-83, American Revolution.
**Archibald Wavell,** 1883-1950, (Br.) commanded forces in N. and E. Africa, and SE Asia in WW2.
**Anthony Wayne,** 1745-96, (U.S.) captured Stony Point, 1779, American Revolution.
**Duke of Wellington,** 1769-1852, (Br.) defeated Napoleon at Waterloo.
**James Wolfe,** 1727-59, (Br.) captured Quebec from French, 1759, French and Indian War.
**Isoroku Yamamoto,** 1884-1943 (Jpn.) commander in chief of Japanese fleet and naval planner before and during WW2.
**Georgi Zhukov,** 1895-1974, (Russ.) defended Moscow, 1941, led assault on Berlin, 1945, WW2.

# Noted Philosophers and Religious Figures of the Past

**Lyman Abbott,** 1835-1922, (U.S.) clergyman, reformer; advocate of Christian Socialism.
**Pierre Abelard,** 1079-1142, (Fr.) philosopher, theologian, teacher; used dialectic method to support Christian dogma.
**Felix Adler,** 1851-1933, (U.S.) German-born founder of the Ethical Culture Society.
**Thomas Aquinas,** 1225-74, (It.) preeminent medieval philosopher-theologian; saint; *Summa Theologica.*
**Aristotle,** 384-322 BC, (Gr.) pioneering wide-ranging realistic philosopher, logician, ethician, naturalist.
**Augustine,** 354-430, Latin philosopher, theologian, bishop; *Confessions, City of God.*
**J. L. Austin,** 1911-60, (Br.) leading ordinary-language philosopher.
**Averroes,** 1126-98, (Sp.) Islamic philosopher.
**Avicenna,** 980-1037, (Iran.) Islamic philosopher.
**A(lfred J(ules) Ayer,** 1910-89, (Br.) philosopher; logical positivist; *Language, Truth, and Logic.*
**Roger Bacon,** c1214-94, (Eng.) philosopher and scientist.
**Bahaullah** (Mirza Husayn Ali), 1817-92, (Pers.) founder of Bahá'í faith.
**Karl Barth,** 1886-1968, (Sw.) theologian; a leading force in 20th-century Protestantism.
**Thomas à Becket,** 1118-70, (Eng.) archbishop of Canterbury; opposed Henry II; murdered by King's men.
**St. Benedict,** c480-547, (It.) founded the Benedictines.
**Jeremy Bentham,** 1748-1832, (Br.) philosopher, reformer; enunciated utilitarianism.
**Henri Bergson,** 1859-1941, (Fr.) philosopher of evolution.
**George Berkeley,** 1685-1753, (Ir.) idealist philosopher, churchman.
**John Biddle,** 1615-62, (Eng.) founder of English Unitarianism.
**Jakob Boehme,** 1575-1624, (Ger.) theosophist and mystic.
**Dietrich Bonhoeffer,** 1906-1945 (Ger.) Lutheran theologian, pastor; executed as opponent of Nazis.
**William Brewster,** 1567-1644, (Eng.) headed Pilgrims.
**Emil Brunner,** 1889-1966, (Sw.) Protestant theologian.
**Giordano Bruno,** 1548-1600, (It.) philosopher; first to state the cosmic theory.
**Martin Buber,** 1878-1965, (Ger.) Jewish philosopher, theologian; *I and Thou.*
**Buddha** (Siddhartha Gautama), c563-c 483 BC, (Ind.) philosopher, founded Buddhism.
**Kenneth Burke,** 1897-1993 (U.S.), one of the founders of New Criticism literary philosophy, *A Grammar of Motives.*
**John Calvin,** 1509-64, (Fr.) theologian; a key figure in the Protestant Reformation.
**Rudolph Carnap,** 1891-1970, (U.S.) German-born philosopher; a founder of logical positivism.
**William Ellery Channing,** 1780-1842, (U.S.) clergyman; early spokesman for Unitarianism.
**Auguste Comte,** 1798-1857, (Fr.) philosopher; originated positivism.
**Confucius,** 551-479 BC, (Chin.) founder of Confucianism.
**John Cotton,** 1584-1652, (Eng.) Puritan theologian.
**Thomas Cranmer,** 1489-1556, (Eng.) churchman; wrote much of *Book of Common Prayer.*
**René Descartes,** 1596-1650, (Fr.) philosopher, mathematician; "father of modern philosophy." *Discourse on Method.*
**John Dewey,** 1859-1952, (U.S.) philosopher, educator; instrumentalist theory of knowledge; helped inaugurate progressive education movement.
**Denis Diderot,** 1713-84, (Fr.) philosopher, encyclopedist.
**John Duns Scotus,** c 1266-1308, (Sc.) Franciscan philosopher and theologian.
**Mary Baker Eddy,** 1821-1910, (U.S.) founder of Christian Science; *Science and Health.*
**Jonathan Edwards,** 1703-58, (U.S.) preacher, theologian.
**(Desiderius) Erasmus,** c1466-1536, (Du.) Renaissance humanist; *On the Freedom of the Will.*
**Johann Fichte,** 1762-1814, (Ger.) idealist philosopher.
**George Fox,** 1624-91, (Br.) founder of Society of Friends.
**St. Francis of Assisi,** 1182-1226, (It.) founded Franciscans.
**al-Ghazali,** 1058-1111, Islamic philosopher.
**Georg W. F. Hegel,** 1770-1831, (Ger.) idealist philosopher; *Phenomenology of Mind.*
**Martin Heidegger,** 1889-1976, (Ger.) existentialist philosopher; affected fields ranging from physics to literary criticism; *Being and Time.*
**Johann G. Herder,** 1744-1803, (Ger.) philosopher, cultural historian; a founder of German Romanticism.
**Thomas Hobbes,** 1588-1679, (Eng.) philosopher, political theorist; *Leviathan.*
**David Hume,** 1711-76, (Sc.) leading empiricist philosopher; *Enquiry Concerning Human Understanding.*
**Jan Hus,** 1369-1415, (Czech.) religious reformer.
**Edmund Husserl,** 1859-1938, (Ger.) philosopher; founded the phenomenological movement.
**Thomas Huxley,** 1825-95, (Br.) philosopher, educator.
**Ignatius of Loyola,** 1491-1556, (Sp.) founder of the Jesuits.
**William Inge,** 1860-1954, (Br.) theologian; explored the mystic aspects of Christianity.
**William James,** 1842-1910, (U.S.) philosopher, psychologist; advanced theory of the pragmatic nature of truth.
**Karl Jaspers,** 1883-1969, (Ger.) existentialist philosopher.
**Joan of Arc,** 1412-1431, (Fr.) national heroine and patron saint of France; key figure in the Hundred Years' War.
**Immanuel Kant,** 1724-1804, (Ger.) philosopher; preeminent founder of modern critical philosophy; *Critique of Pure Reason.*
**Thomas à Kempis,** c1380-1471, (Ger.) theologian; probably wrote *Imitation of Christ.*
**Soren Kierkegaard,** 1813-55, (Dan.) religious philosopher; a key precursor of existentialism.
**John Knox,** 1505-72, (Sc.) leader of the Protestant Reformation in Scotland.
**Lao-Tzu,** 604-531 BC, (Chin.) philosopher; considered the founder of the Taoist religion.
**Gottfried von Leibniz,** 1646-1716, (Ger.) rationalistic philosopher, logician, mathematician.
**John Locke,** 1632-1704, (Eng.) influential political theorist, empiricist philosopher; *Essay Concerning Human Understanding.*

**Martin Luther,** 1483-1546, (Ger.) leader of the Protestant Re formation, founded Lutheran church.
**Maimonides,** 1135-1204, (Sp.) Jewish philosopher.
**Gabriel Marcel,** 1889-1973, (Fr.) Roman Catholic existentialist philosopher, dramatist, and critic,
**Jacques Maritain,** 1882-1973, (Fr.) Neo-Thomist philosopher.
**Cotton Mather,** 1663-1728, (U.S.) defender of orthodox Puritanism; founded Yale, 1701.
**Philipp Melanchthon,** 1497-1560, (Ger.) theologian, humanist; an important voice in the Reformation.
**Maurice Merleau-Ponty,** 1908-61, (Fr.) existentialist philosopher.
**Thomas Merton,** 1915-68, (U.S.) Trappist monk, spiritual writer; *The Seven Storey Mountain.*
**John Stuart Mill,** 1806-73, (Br.) philosopher, economist; libertarian political theorist; *Utilitarianism.*
**Muhammad,** c570-632, (Arab) the prophet of Islam.
**Dwight Moody,** 1837-99, (U.S.) evangelist.
**G(eorge) E(dward) Moore,** 1873-1958, (Br.) philosopher; *Principia Ethica.*
**Elijah Muhammad,** 1897-1975, (U.S.) leader of the Black Muslim sect.
**Heinrich Muhlenberg,** 1711-87, (Ger.) organized the Lutheran Church in America.
**John H. Newman,** 1801-90, (Br.) Roman Catholic cardinal; led Oxford Movement; *Apologia pro Vita Sua.*
**Reinhold Niebuhr,** 1892-1971, (U.S.) Protestant theologian.
**Friedrich Nietzsche,** 1844-1900, (Ger.) philosopher; *The Birth of Tragedy, Beyond Good and Evil, Thus Spake Zarathustra.*
**Blaise Pascal,** 1623-62, (Fr.) philosopher, mathematician, *Pensées.*
**St. Patrick,** c389-c 461, brought Christianity to Ireland.
**St. Paul,** ?-c 67, a proponent of Christianity; his epistles are first Christian theological writing.
**Norman Vincent Peale,** 1898-1993, (U.S.) religious leader, author; *The Power of Positive Thinking.*
**C(harles) S. Peirce,** 1839-1914, (U.S.) philosopher, logician; originated concept of pragmatism, 1878.
**Plato,** c 428-347 BC, (Gr.) philosopher; wrote classic Socratic dialogues; argued for independent reality of ideas; *Republic.*
**Josiah Royce,** 1855-1916, (U.S.) idealist philosopher.
**Bertrand Russell,** 1872-1970, (Br.) philosopher, logician; one of the founders of modern logic and a prolific popular writer.
**Charles T. Russell,** 1852-1916, (U.S.) founder of Jehovah's Witnesses.
**Gilbert Ryle,** 1900-76, (Br.) analytic philosopher; *The Concept of Mind.*
**Jean-Paul Sartre,** 1905-80, (Fr.) philosopher, novelist, playwright. *Nausea, No Exit, Being and Nothingness.*
**Fredrich von Schelling,** 1775-1854, (Ger.) philosopher of romantic movement.
**Friedrich Schleiermacher,** 1768-1834, (Ger.) theologian; a founder of modern Protestant theology.
**Arthur Schopenhauer,** 1788-1860, (Ger.) philosopher; *The World as Will and Idea.*
**Albert Schweitzer,** 1875-1965, (Ger.) theologian, organist, social philosopher, medical missionary.
**Joseph Smith,** 1805-44, (U.S.) founded Latter-day Saints (Mormon) movement, 1830.
**Socrates,** 469-399 BC, (Gr.) influential philosopher immortalized by Plato.
**Herbert Spencer,** 1820-1903, (Br.) philosopher of evolution.
**Baruch Spinoza,** 1632-77, (Dutch) rationalist philosopher.
**Billy Sunday,** 1862-1935, (U.S.) evangelist.
**Pierre Teilhard de Chardin,** 1881-1955, (Fr.) Catholic priest, paleontologist, philosopher-theologian; *The Divine Milieu.*
**Daisetz Teitaro Suzuki,** 1870-1966, (Jpn.) Buddhist scholar.
**Emanuel Swedenborg,** 1688-1772, (Swed.) philosopher, mystic.
**Paul Tillich,** 1886-1965, (U.S.) German-born philosopher and theologian; brought depth psychology to Protestantism.
**John Wesley,** 1703-91, (Br.) theologian, evangelist; founded Methodism.
**Alfred North Whitehead,** 1861-1947, (Br.) philosopher, mathematician; *Process and Reality.*
**William of Occam,** c1285-c1349 (Eng.) medieval scholastic philosopher.
**Roger Williams,** c 1603-83, (U.S.) clergyman; championed religious freedom and separation of church and state.
**Ludwig Wittgenstein,** 1889-1951, (Austrian) philosopher; major influence on contemporary language philosophy; *Philosophical Investigations.*
**John Wycliffe,** 1320-84, (Eng.) theologian, reformer.
**Brigham Young,** 1801-77, (U.S.) Mormon leader after Smith's assassination, colonized Utah.
**Huldrych Zwingli,** 1484-1531, (Swed.) theologian; led Swiss Protestant Reformation.

# Noted Political Leaders of the Past

(Modern royalty; U.S. presidents, vice presidents, Supreme Court justices; signers of Decl. of Indep. listed elsewhere.)

**Abu Bakr,** 573-634, Muslim leader, first caliph, chosen successor to Muhammad.
**Dean Acheson,** 1893-1971, (U.S.) secretary of state; chief architect of cold war foreign policy.
**Samuel Adams,** 1722-1803, (U.S.) patriot, Boston Tea Party firebrand.
**Konrad Adenauer,** 1876-1967, (Ger.) W. German chancellor.
**Emilio Aguinaldo,** 1869-1964, (Philip.) revolutionary; fought against Spain and the U.S.
**Akbar,** 1542-1605, greatest Mogul emperor of India.
**Salvador Allende Gossens,** 1908-1973, (Chilean) president; advocate of democratic socialism.
**Herbert H. Asquith,** 1852-1928, (Br.) liberal prime minister; instituted an advanced program of social reform.
**Atahualpa,** ?-1533, Inca (ruling chief) of Peru.
**Kemal Ataturk,** 1881-1938, (Turk.) founded modern Turkey.
**Clement Attlee,** 1883-1967, (Br.) Labour party leader, prime minister; enacted natl. health, nationalized many industries.
**Stephen F. Austin,** 1793-1836, (U.S.) led Texas colonization.
**Mikhail Bakunin,** 1814-76, (Russ.) revolutionary; leading exponent of anarchism.
**Arthur J. Balfour,** 1848-1930, (Br.) foreign secretary under Lloyd George; issued Balfour Declaration expressing official British approval of Zionism.
**Bernard M. Baruch,** 1870-1965, (U.S.) financier, govt. adviser.
**Fulgencio Batista y Zaldívar,** 1901-73, (Cuban) Cuban president (1940-44, 1952-59) and dictator, overthrown by Castro.
**Lord Beaverbrook,** 1879-1964, (Br.) financier, statesman, newspaper owner.
**Menachem Begin,** 1913-92, (Isr.) Israeli prime minister, won 1978 Nobel Peace Prize.
**Eduard Benes,** 1884-1948, (Czech.) president during interwar and post-WW2 eras.
**David Ben-Gurion,** 1886-1973, (Isr.) first prime minister of Israel, 1948-53, 1955-63.
**Thomas Hart Benton,** 1782-1858, (U.S.) Missouri senator; championed agrarian interests and westward expansion.
**Lavrenti Beria,** 1899-1953, (USSR) Communist leader prominent in political purges under Stalin.
**Aneurin Bevan,** 1897-1960, (Br.) Labour party leader.
**Ernest Bevin,** 1881-1951, (Br.) Labour party leader, foreign minister; helped lay foundation for NATO.
**Otto von Bismarck,** 1815-98, (Ger.) statesman known as the Iron Chancellor; uniter of Germany, 1870.
**James G. Blaine,** 1830-93, (U.S.) Republican politician, diplomat; influential in launching Pan-American movement.
**Léon Blum,** 1872-1950, (Fr.) socialist leader, writer; headed first Popular Front government.
**Simón Bolívar,** 1783-1830, (Venez.) S. American revolutionary who liberated much of the continent from Spanish rule.
**William E. Borah,** 1865-1940, (U.S.) isolationist senator; helped block U.S. membership in League of Nations.
**Cesare Borgia,** 1476-1507, (It.) soldier, politician; an outstanding figure of the Italian Renaissance.
**Willy Brandt,** 1913-92, (Ger.) statesman, chancellor of West Germany, 1969-74; promoted East/West peace, *Ostpolitik.*
**Leonid Brezhnev,** 1906-82, (USSR) leader of the Soviet Union, 1964-82.
**Aristide Briand,** 1862-1932, (Fr.) foreign minister; chief architect of Locarno Pact and anti-war Kellogg-Briand Pact.
**William Jennings Bryan,** 1860-1925, (U.S.) Democratic, populist leader, orator; 3 times lost race for presidency.
**Nikolai Bukharin,** 1888-1938, (USSR) Communist leader.
**William C. Bullitt,** 1891-1967, (U.S.) diplomat; first ambassador to USSR, ambassador to France.
**Ralph Bunche,** 1904-71, (U.S.) a founder and key diplomat of United Nations for more than 20 years.
**John C. Calhoun,** 1782-1850, (U.S.) political leader; champion of states' rights and a symbol of the Old South.
**Robert Castlereagh,** 1769-1822, (Br.) foreign secretary; guided Grand Alliance against Napoleon.
**Camillo Benso Cavour,** 1810-61, (It.) statesman; largely responsible for uniting Italy under the House of Savoy.
**Nicolae Ceausescu,** 1918-89, (Rom.) Communist leader, head of state 1967-89.
**Austen Chamberlain,** 1863-1937, (Br.) Conservative party leader; largely responsible for Locarno Pact of 1925.
**Neville Chamberlain,** 1869-1940, (Br.) Conservative prime minister whose appeasement of Hitler led to Munich Pact.
**Salmon P. Chase,** 1808-73, (U.S.) public official, abolitionist, jurist; 6th chief justice of the U.S.
**Chiang Kai-shek,** 1887-1975, (Chin.) Nationalist Chinese president whose government was driven from mainland to Taiwan.

**Winston Churchill,** 1874-1965, (Br.) prime minister, soldier, author; guided Britain through WW2.
**Galeazzo Ciano,** 1903-44, (It.) fascist foreign minister; helped create Rome-Berlin Axis, executed by Mussolini.
**Henry Clay,** 1777-1852, (U.S.) "The Great Compromiser," one of the most influential pre-Civil War political leaders.
**Georges Clemenceau,** 1841-1929, (Fr.) twice premier, Wilson's antagonist at Paris Peace Conference after WW1.
**DeWitt Clinton,** 1769-1828, (U.S.) political leader; responsible for promoting idea of the Erie Canal.
**Robert Clive,** 1725-74, (Br.) first administrator of Bengal; laid foundation for British Empire in India.
**Jean Baptiste Colbert,** 1619-83, (Fr.) statesman; influential under Louis XIV, created the French navy.
**Oliver Cromwell,** 1599-1658, (Br.) Lord Protector of England, led parliamentary forces during Civil War.
**Curzon of Kedleston,** 1859-1925, (Br.) viceroy of India, foreign secretary; major force in dealing with post-WW1 problems in Europe and Far East.
**Édouard Daladier,** 1884-1970, (Fr.) radical socialist politician, arrested by Vichy, interned by Germans until 1945.
**Georges Danton,** 1759-94, (Fr.) a leading figure in the French Revolution.
**Jefferson Davis,** 1808-89, (U.S.) president of the Confederate States of America.
**Charles G. Dawes,** 1865-1951, (U.S.) statesman, banker; advanced Dawes Plan, 1924, to stabilize post-WW1 German finances.
**Alcide De Gasperi,** 1881-1954, (It.) prime minister; founder of the Christian Democratic party.
**Charles De Gaulle,** 1890-1970, (Fr.) general, statesman; first president of the Fifth Republic.
**Eamon De Valera,** 1882-1975, (Ir.-U.S.) statesman; led fight for Irish independence.
**Thomas E. Dewey,** 1902-71, (U.S.) New York governor; twice loser in try for presidency.
**Ngo Dinh Diem,** 1901-63, (Viet.) South Vietnamese president; assassinated in government takeover.
**Everett M. Dirksen,** 1896-1969, (U.S.) Senate Republican minority leader, orator.
**Benjamin Disraeli,** 1804-81, (Br.) prime minister; considered founder of modern Conservative party.
**Engelbert Dollfuss,** 1892-1934, (Aust.) chancellor; assassinated by Austrian Nazis.
**Andrea Doria,** 1466-1560, (It.) Genoese admiral, statesman; called "Father of Peace" and "Liberator of Genoa."
**Stephen A. Douglas,** 1813-61, (U.S.) Democratic leader, orator; opposed Lincoln for the presidency.
**Alexander Dubcek,** 1921-92, (Czech.) statesman whose attempted liberalization was crushed, 1968.
**John Foster Dulles,** 1888-1959, (U.S.) secretary of state under Eisenhower, cold war policy-maker.
**Friedrich Ebert,** 1871-1925, (Ger.) Social Democratic movement leader; 1st president of Weimar Republic, 1919-25.
**Sir Anthony Eden,** 1897-1977, (Br.) foreign secretary, prime minister during Suez invasion of 1956.
**Ludwig Erhard,** 1897-1977, (Ger.) economist, West German chancellor; led nation's economic rise after WW2.
**Hamilton Fish,** 1808-93, (U.S.) secretary of state, successfully mediated disputes with Great Britain, Latin America.
**James V. Forrestal,** 1892-1949, (U.S.) secretary of navy, first secretary of defense.
**Francisco Franco,** 1892-1975, (Sp.) leader of rebel forces during Spanish Civil War and dictator of Spain.
**Benjamin Franklin,** 1706-90, (U.S.) printer, publisher, author, inventor, scientist, diplomat.
**Louis de Frontenac,** 1620-98, (Fr.) governor of New France (Canada); encouraged explorations, fought Iroquois.
**J. William Fulbright,** 1905-95, (U.S.) U.S. senator; leading figure in U.S. foreign policy during cold war years.
**Hugh Gaitskell,** 1906-63, (Br.) Labour party leader; major force in reversing its stand for unilateral disarmament.
**Albert Gallatin,** 1761-1849, (U.S.) secretary of treasury who was instrumental in negotiating end of War of 1812.
**Léon Gambetta,** 1838-82, (Fr.) statesman, politician; one of the founders of the Third Republic.
**Indira Gandhi,** 1917-84, (In.) daughter of Jawaharlal Nehru, prime minister of India, 1966-77, 1980-84; assassinated.
**Mohandas K. Gandhi,** 1869-1948, (In.) political leader, ascetic; led nationalist movement against British rule.
**Giuseppe Garibaldi,** 1807-82, (It.) patriot, soldier; a leading figure in the Risorgimento, the Italian unification movement.
**Genghis Khan,** c1167-1227, Mongol conqueror, ruler of vast Asian empire.
**William E. Gladstone,** 1809-98, (Br.) prime minister 4 times; dominant force of Liberal party from 1868 to 1894.
**Paul Joseph Goebbels,** 1897-1945, (Ger.) Nazi propagandist, master of mass psychology.
**Klement Gottwald,** 1896-1953, (Czech.) Communist leader; ushered Communism into his country.
**Che (Ernesto) Guevara,** 1928-67, (Arg.) guerrilla leader; prominent in Cuban revolution, killed in Bolivia.
**Alexander Hamilton,** 1755-1804, (U.S.) first treasury secretary; champion of strong central government.
**Dag Hammarskjold,** 1905-61, (Swed.) statesman; UN secretary-general.
**John Hancock,** 1737-93, (U.S.) revolutionary leader; first signer of Declaration of Independence.
**John Hay,** 1838-1905, (U.S.) secretary of state; primarily associated with Open Door Policy toward China.
**Patrick Henry,** 1736-99, (U.S.) major revolutionary figure, remarkable orator.
**Édouard Herriot,** 1872-1957, (Fr.) Radical Socialist leader; twice premier, president of National Assembly.
**Theodor Herzl,** 1860-1904, (Hung.) founded modern Zionism.
**Heinrich Himmler,** 1900-45, (Ger.) notorious head of Nazi SS and Gestapo.
**Paul von Hindenburg,** 1847-1934, (Ger.) field marshal, WW1; 2d president of Weimar Republic, 1925-34.
**Adolf Hitler,** 1889-1945, (Ger.) dictator; founder of National Socialism; wrote *Mein Kampf*.
**Ho Chi Minh,** 1890-1969, (Viet.) N Vietnamese president, Vietnamese Communist leader.
**Harry L. Hopkins,** 1890-1946, (U.S.) New Deal administrator; closest adviser to FDR during WW2.
**Edward M. House,** 1858-1938, (U.S.) diplomat; confidential adviser to Woodrow Wilson.
**Samuel Houston,** 1793-1863, (U.S.) leader of struggle to win control of Texas from Mexico.
**Cordell Hull,** 1871-1955, (U.S.) secretary of state, 1933-44; initiated reciprocal trade to lower tariffs, helped organize UN.
**Hubert H. Humphrey,** 1911-78, (U.S.) Minnesota Democrat, senator, vice president; spent 32 years in public service.
**Jinnah, Muhammad Ali,** 1876-1948, (Pak.) founder, first governor-general of Pakistan.
**Benito Juarez,** 1806-72, (Mex.) rallied his country against foreign threats, sought to create democratic, federal republic.
**Frank B. Kellogg,** 1856-1937, (U.S.) secretary of state; negotiated Kellogg-Briand Pact to outlaw war.
**Robert F. Kennedy,** 1925-68, (U.S.) attorney general, senator; assassinated while seeking presidential nomination.
**Aleksandr Kerensky,** 1881-1970, (Russ.) headed provisional government after Feb. 1917 revolution.
**Ruhollah Khomeini,** 1900-89, (Iranian), religious leader with Islamic title "ayatollah," directed overthrow of shah, 1979.
**Nikita Khrushchev,** 1894-1971, (USSR) premier, first secretary of Communist party; initiated de-Stalinization.
**Kim Il Sung,** 1912-94, (Korean) N Korean dictator, 1948-94.
**Lajos Kossuth,** 1802-94, (Hung.) principal figure in 1848 Hungarian revolution.
**Pyotr Kropotkin,** 1842-1921, (Russ.) anarchist; championed the peasants but opposed Bolshevism.
**Kublai Khan,** c1215-94, Mongol emperor; founder of Yüan dynasty in China.
**Béla Kun,** 1886-c1939, (Hung.) member of 3d Communist Intl., tried to foment worldwide revolution.
**Robert M. LaFollette,** 1855-1925, (U.S.) Wisconsin public official; leader of progressive movement.
**Pierre Laval,** 1883-1945, (Fr.) politician, Vichy foreign minister; executed for treason.
**Andrew Bonar Law,** 1858-1923, (Br.) Conservative party politician; led opposition to Irish home rule.
**Vladimir Ilyich Lenin (Ulyanov),** 1870-1924, (Russ.) revolutionary; founder of Bolshevism, Soviet leader 1917-24.
**Ferdinand de Lesseps,** 1805-94, (Fr.) diplomat, engineer; conceived idea of Suez Canal.
**Rene Levesque,** 1922-87, (Can.) premier of Quebec, 1976-85; led unsuccessful fight to separate from Canada.
**Maxim Litvinov,** 1876-1951, (Pol.-Russ.) revolutionary, commissar of foreign affairs; favored cooperation with West.
**Liu Shaoqi,** c1898-1974, (Chin.) Communist leader; fell from grace during "cultural revolution."
**David Lloyd George,** 1863-1945, (Br.) Liberal party prime minister; laid foundations for modern welfare state.
**Henry Cabot Lodge,** 1850-1924, (U.S.) Republican senator; led opposition to participation in League of Nations.
**Huey P. Long,** 1893-1935, (U.S.) Louisiana political demagogue, governor; assassinated.
**Rosa Luxemburg,** 1871-1919, (Ger.) revolutionary; leader of the German Social Democratic party and Spartacus party.
**J. Ramsay MacDonald,** 1866-1937, (Br.) first Labour party prime minister of Great Britain.
**Harold Macmillan,** 1895-1986, (Br.) prime minister of Great Britain, 1957-63.
**Joseph R. McCarthy,** 1908-57, (U.S.) senator notorious for extremism in searching out alleged communists and Communist sympathizers.

**Makarios III,** 1913-77, (Cypriot) Greek Orthodox archbishop; first president of Cyprus.
**Mao Zedong,** 1893-1976, (Chin.) chief Chinese Marxist theorist, revolutionary, political leader; led Chinese revolution establishing his nation as Communist state.
**Jean Paul Marat,** 1743-93, (Fr.) revolutionary, politician; identified with radical Jacobins, assassinated.
**José Martí,** 1853-95, (Cub.) patriot, poet; leader of Cuban struggle for independence.
**Jan Masaryk,** 1886-1948, (Czech.) foreign minister; died by mysterious suicide following Communist coup.
**Thomas G. Masaryk,** 1850-1937, (Czech.) statesman, philosopher; first president of Czechoslovak Republic.
**Jules Mazarin,** 1602-61, (Fr.) cardinal, statesman; prime minister under Louis XIII and queen regent Anne of Austria.
**Giusseppe Mazzini,** 1805-72, (It.), reformer dedicated to Risorgimento movement for renewal of Italy.
**Tom Mboya,** 1930-69, (Kenyan) political leader; instrumental in securing independence for Kenya.
**Cosimo I de' Medici,** 1519-74, (It.) Duke of Florence, grand duke of Tuscany.
**Lorenzo de' Medici,** the Magnificent, 1449-92, (It.) merchant prince; a towering figure in Italian Renaissance.
**Catherine de Médicis,** 1519-89, (Fr.) queen consort of Henry II, regent of France; influential in Catholic-Huguenot wars.
**Golda Meir,** 1898-1978, (Isr.) a founder of the state of Israel and prime minister, 1969-74.
**Klemens W. N. L. Metternich,** 1773-1859, (Aust.) statesman; arbiter of post-Napoleonic Europe.
**François Mitterrand,** 1916-96, (Fr.) president of France, 1981-95; proponent of European unity.
**Guy Mollet,** 1905-75, (Fr.) social politician, resistance leader.
**Henry Morgenthau Jr.,** 1891-1967, (U.S.) secy. of treasury; fund-raiser for New Deal and U.S. WW2 activities.
**Gouverneur Morris,** 1752-1816, (U.S.) statesman, diplomat; financial expert who helped plan decimal coinage system.
**Benito Mussolini,** 1883-1945, (It.) dictator and leader of the Italian fascist state.
**Imre Nagy,** c1896-1958, (Hung.) Communist premier; assassinated after Soviets crushed 1956 uprising.
**Gamal Abdel Nasser,** 1918-70, (Egypt.) leader of Arab unification, 2d Egyptian president.
**Jawaharlal Nehru,** 1889-1964, (Indian) prime minister; guided India through its early years of independence.
**Kwame Nkrumah,** 1909-72, (Ghan.) 1st prime minister, 1957-60, and president, 1960-66, of Ghana.
**Frederick North,** 1732-92, (Br.) prime minister; his inept policies led to loss of American colonies.
**Daniel O'Connell,** 1775-1847, (Ir.) political leader; known as The Liberator.
**Omar,** c581-644, Muslim leader; 2d caliph, led Islam to become an imperial power.
**Thomas P. (Tip) O'Neill Jr.,** 1912-94, (U.S.) U.S. congressman, Speaker of the House, 1977-86.
**Ignace Paderewski,** 1860-1941, (Pol.) statesman, pianist; composer, briefly prime minister, an ardent patriot.
**Viscount Palmerston,** 1784-1865, (Br.) Whig-Liberal prime minister, foreign minister; embodied British nationalism.
**Andreas George Papandreou,** 1919-1996, (Gk.) leftist politician, served 2 times as premier, (1981-89, 1993-96).
**Georgios Papandreou,** 1888-1968, (Gk.) Republican politician; served 3 times as prime minister.
**Franz von Papen,** 1879-1969, (Ger.) politician; played major role in overthrow of Weimar Republic and rise of Hitler.
**Charles Stewart Parnell,** 1846-1891, (Ir.) nationalist leader; "uncrowned king of Ireland."
**Lester Pearson,** 1897-1972, (Can.) diplomat, Liberal party leader, prime minister.
**Robert Peel,** 1788-1850, (Br.) reformist prime minister, founder of Conservative party.
**Juan Perón,** 1895-1974, (Arg.) president of Argentina (1946-55 and 1973-74).
**Joseph Pilsudski,** 1867-1935, (Pol.) statesman; instrumental in reestablishing Polish state in the 20th century.
**Charles Pinckney,** 1757-1824, (U.S.) founding father; his Pinckney plan was largely incorporated into constitution.
**Christian Pineau,** 1905-95, (Fr.) leader of French Resistance during WW2; French foreign minister, 1956-58.
**William Pitt,** the Elder, 1708-78, (Br.) statesman; called the "Great Commoner," transformed Britain into imperial power.
**William Pitt,** the Younger, 1759-1806, (Br.) prime minister during French Revolutionary wars.
**Georgi Plekhanov,** 1857-1918, (Russ.) revolutionary, social philosopher; called "father of Russian Marxism."
**Raymond Poincaré,** 1860-1934, (Fr.) 9th president of the Republic; advocated harsh punishment of Germany after WW1.
**Georges Pompidou,** 1911-74, (Fr.) Gaullist political leader; president from 1969-74.
**Grigori Potemkin,** 1739-91, (Russ.) field marshal; favorite of Catherine II.
**Yitzhak Rabin,** 1922-95, (Isr.) military, political leader; prime minister of Israel, 1974-77, 1992-95; assassinated.
**Edmund Randolph,** 1753-1813, (U.S.) attorney; prominent in drafting, ratification of constitution.
**John Randolph,** 1773-1833, (U.S.) Southern planter; strong advocate of states' rights.
**Jeannette Rankin,** 1880-1973, (U.S.) pacifist; first woman member of U.S. Congress.
**Walter Rathenau,** 1867-1922, (Ger.) industrialist, statesman.
**Sam Rayburn,** 1882-1961, (U.S.) Democratic leader; representative for 47 years, House Speaker for 17.
**Paul Reynaud,** 1878-1966, (Fr.) statesman; premier in 1940 at the time of France's defeat by Germany.
**Syngman Rhee,** 1875-1965, (Korean) first pres. of S. Korea.
**Cecil Rhodes,** 1853-1902, (Br.) imperialist, industrial magnate; established Rhodes scholarships in his will
**Cardinal de Richelieu,** 1585-1642, (Fr.) statesman; known as "red eminence," chief minister to Louis XIII.
**Maximilien Robespierre,** 1758-94, (Fr.) leading figure of French Revolution, responsible for much of Reign of Terror.
**Nelson Rockefeller,** 1908-79, (U.S.) Republican governor of NY, 1959-73; U.S. vice president, 1974-77.
**George W. Romney,** 1907-95, (U.S.) president of American Motors; 3-term Republican governor of Michigan.
**Eleanor Roosevelt,** 1884-1962, (U.S.) First Lady, humanitarian, United Nations diplomat.
**Elihu Root,** 1845-1937, (U.S.) lawyer, statesman, diplomat; leading Republican supporter of the League of Nations.
**Dean Rusk,** 1909-95, (U.S.) statesman; secretary of state, 1961-69, during Vietnam War.
**John Russell,** 1792-1878, (Br.) Liberal prime minister during the Irish potato famine.
**Anwar al-Sadat,** 1918-81, (Egypt.) president, 1970-1981, promoted peace with Israel; assassinated.
**António de Salazar,** 1889-1970, (Port.) statesman; long-time dictator.
**José de San Martin,** 1778-1850, South American revolutionary; protector of Peru.
**Eisaku Sato,** 1901-75, (Jpn.) prime minister; presided over Japan's post-WW2 emergence as major world power.
**Philipp Scheidemann,** 1865-1939, (Ger.) Social Democratic leader; first chancellor of the German republic.
**Robert Schuman,** 1886-1963, (Fr.) statesman; founded European Coal and Steel Community.
**Carl Schurz,** 1829-1906, (U.S.) German-American political leader, journalist, orator, dedicated reformer.
**Kurt Schuschnigg,** 1897-1977, (Aust.) chancellor; unsuccessful in stopping his country's annexation by Germany.
**William H. Seward,** 1801-72, (U.S.) anti-slavery activist; as U.S. secretary of state purchased Alaska.
**Carlo Sforza,** 1872-1952, (It.) foreign minister, anti-fascist.
**Sitting Bull,** c1831-90, (Native American) Sioux leader in Battle of Little Bighorn over George A. Custer, 1876.
**Alfred E. Smith,** 1873-1944, (U.S.) New York Democratic governor; first Roman Catholic to run for presidency.
**Margaret Chase Smith,** 1897-1995, (U.S.) congresswoman, senator; 1st woman elected to both houses of Congress.
**Jan C. Smuts,** 1870-1950, (S. African) statesman, philosopher, soldier, prime minister.
**Paul Henri Spaak,** 1899-1972, (Belg.) statesman, socialist leader.
**Joseph Stalin,** 1879-1953, (USSR) Soviet dictator, 1924-53.
**Edwin M. Stanton,** 1814-69, (U.S.) secretary of war, 1862-68, during the Civil War.
**Edward R. Stettinius Jr.,** 1900-49, (U.S.) industrialist, secretary of state who coordinated aid to WW2 allies.
**Adlai E. Stevenson,** 1900-65, (U.S.) Democratic leader, diplomat, Illinois governor, presidential candidate.
**Henry L. Stimson,** 1867-1950, (U.S.) statesman; served in 5 administrations, foreign policy adviser in 1930s and 1940s.
**Gustav Stresemann,** 1878-1929, (Ger.) chancellor, foreign minister; strove to regain friendship for post-WW1 Germany.
**Sukarno,** 1901-70, (Indon.) dictatorial first president of the Indonesian republic.
**Sun Yat-sen,** 1866-1925, (Chin.) revolutionary; leader of Kuomintang, regarded as the father of modern China.
**Robert A. Taft,** 1889-1953, (U.S.) conservative Senate leader, called "Mr. Republican."
**Charles de Talleyrand,** 1754-1838, (Fr.) statesman, diplomat; the major force of the Congress of Vienna of 1814-15.
**U Thant,** 1909-74 (Bur.) statesman, UN secretary-general.
**Norman M. Thomas,** 1884-1968, (U.S.) social reformer; 6 times unsuccessful Socialist party presidential candidate.
**Josip Broz Tito,** 1892-1980, (Yug.) president of Yugoslavia from 1953, WW2 guerrilla chief, postwar rival of Stalin.

**Palmiro Togliatti,** 1893-1964, (It.) major leader of Italian Communist party.
**Hideki Tojo,** 1885-1948, (Jpn.) statesman, soldier; prime minister during most of WW2.
**François Toussaint L'Ouverture,** c1744-1803, (Haitian) patriot, martyr; thwarted French colonial aims.
**Leon Trotsky,** 1879-1940, (Russ.) revolutionary, founded Red Army, expelled from party in conflict with Stalin.
**Rafael L. Trujillo Molina,** 1891-1961, (Dom.) absolute dictator of Dominican Republic, 1930-61; assassinated.
**Moise K. Tshombe,** 1919-69, (Cong.) president of secessionist Katanga, premier of Republic of Congo (Zaire).
**William M. Tweed,** 1823-78, (U.S.) politician; absolute leader of Tammany Hall, NYC's Democratic political machine.
**Walter Ulbricht,** 1893-1973, (Ger.) Communist leader of German Democratic Republic.
**Arthur H. Vandenberg,** 1884-1951, (U.S.) senator; proponent of anti-communist bipartisan foreign policy after WW2.
**Eleutherios Venizelos,** 1864-1936, (Gk.) most prominent Greek statesman in early 20th century; expanded territory.
**Hendrik F. Verwoerd,** 1901-66, (S. African) prime minister; rigorously applied apartheid policy despite protest.
**Robert Walpole,** 1676-1745, (Br.) statesman; generally considered Britain's first prime minister.
**Daniel Webster,** 1782-1852, (U.S.) orator, politician; advocate of business interests during Jacksonian agrarianism.
**Chaim Weizmann,** 1874-1952, (Russ.-Isr.) Zionist leader, scientist; first Israeli president.
**Wendell L. Willkie,** 1892-1944, (U.S.) Republican who tried to unseat FDR when he ran for his 3d term.
**Harold Wilson,** 1916-95, (Br.) Labour party leader; prime minister, 1964-70, 1974-76.
**Emiliano Zapata,** c1879-1919, (Mex.) revolutionary; major influence on modern Mexico.
**Zhou Enlai,** 1898-1976, (Chin.) diplomat, prime minister; a leading figure of the Chinese Communist party.

# Noted Scientists of the Past

**Howard H. Aiken,** 1900-73, (U.S.) mathematician; credited with designing forerunner of digital computer.
**Albertus Magnus,** 1193-1280, (Ger.) theologian, philosopher; established medieval Christian study of natural science.
**Andre-Marie Ampère,** 1775-1836, (Fr.) scientist known for contributions to electrodynamics.
**Amedeo Avogadro,** 1776-1856, (It.) chemist, physicist; advanced important theories on properties of gases.
**John Bardeen,** 1908-91, (U.S.) co-inventor of the transistor that led to modern electronics.
**A. C. Becquerel,** 1788-1878, (Fr.) physicist; pioneer in electrochemical science.
**A. H. Becquerel,** 1852-1908, (Fr.) physicist; discovered radioactivity in uranium.
**Alexander Graham Bell,** 1847-1922, (U.S.) inventor; first to patent and commercially exploit the telephone, 1876.
**Daniel Bernoulli,** 1700-82, (Swiss) mathematician; advanced kinetic theory of gases and fluids.
**Jöns Jakob Berzelius,** 1779-1848, (Swed.) chemist; developed modern chemical symbols and formulas.
**Henry Bessemer,** 1813-98, (Br.) engineer; invented Bessemer steel-making process.
**Louis Blériot,** 1872-1936, (Fr.) engineer; pioneer aviator, invented and constructed monoplanes.
**Niels Bohr,** 1885-1962, (Dan.) physicist; leading figure in the development of quantum theory.
**Max Born,** 1882-1970, (Ger.) physicist known for research in quantum mechanics.
**Satyendranath Bose,** 1894-1974, (In.) physicist, chemist, mathematician; forerunner of modern quantum theory.
**Walter Brattain,** 1902-87, (U.S.) inventor; worked on invention of transistor.
**Louis de Broglie,** 1893-1987, (Fr.) physicist; best known for wave theory.
**Robert Bunsen,** 1811-99, (Ger.) chemist; invented Bunsen burner.
**Luther Burbank,** 1849-1926, (U.S.) plant breeder whose work developed plant breeding into a modern science.
**Vannevar Bush,** 1890-1974, (U.S.) electrical engineer; developed differential analyzer, 1st electronic analogue computer.
**Marvin Camras,** 1916-95, (U.S.) inventor, electrical engineer; invented magnetic tape recording.
**Alexis Carrel,** 1873-1944, (Fr.) surgeon, biologist; developed methods of suturing blood vessels and transplanting organs.
**George Washington Carver,** 1864-1943, (U.S.) botanist, chemist, and educator.
**Henry Cavendish,** 1731-1810, (Br.) chemist, physicist; discovered hydrogen.
**James Chadwick,** 1891-1974, (Br.) physicist; discovered the neutron.
**Darly Chapin,** 1906-95, (U.S.) physicist; co-developer of the solar energy cell.
**Jean M. Charcot,** 1825-93, (Fr.) neurologist known for work on hysteria, hypnotism, sclerosis.
**Albert Claude,** 1899-1983, (Belg.) a founder of modern cell biology.
**John D. Cockcroft,** 1897-1967, (Br.) nuclear physicist; constructed first atomic particle accelerator with E. T. S. Walton.
**Nicholas Copernicus,** 1473-1543, (Pol.) astronomer who first described solar system, with Earth as one of planets revolving around sun.
**Seymour Cray,** 1925-96, (U.S.) computer industry pioneer; developed supercomputers.
**William Crookes,** 1832-1919, (Br.) physicist, chemist; discovered thallium, invented a cathode-ray tube, radiometer.
**Marie Curie,** 1867-1934, (Pol.-Fr.) physical chemist known for work on radium and its compounds.
**Pierre Curie,** 1859-1906, (Fr.) physical chemist known for work, with his wife Marie, on radioactivity.
**Gottlieb Daimler,** 1834-1900, (Ger.) engineer, inventor; pioneer automobile manufacturer.
**John Dalton,** 1766-1844, (Br.) chemist, physicist; formulated atomic theory, made first table of atomic weights.
**Charles Darwin,** 1809-82, (Br.) naturalist; established theory of organic evolution; *Origin of Species.*
**Humphry Davy,** 1778-1829, (Br.) chemist; research in electrochemistry led to isolation of potassium, sodium, calcium, barium, boron, magnesium, and strontium.
**Lee De Forest,** 1873-1961, (U.S.) inventor; pioneer in development of wireless telegraphy, sound pictures, television.
**Max Delbruck,** 1907-81, (U.S.) pioneer in modern molecular genetics.
**Rudolf Diesel,** 1858-1913, (Ger.) mechanical engineer; patented Diesel engine.
**Christian Doppler,** 1803-53, (Aust.) physicist; showed change in energy wavelengths caused by motion, Doppler effect.
**J. Presper Eckert Jr.,** 1919-95, (U.S.) co-inventor with John W. Mauchly of the first electronic digital computer, the Eniac.
**Thomas A. Edison,** 1847-1931, (U.S.) inventor; held more than 1,000 patents, including incandescent electric lamp.
**Paul Ehrlich,** 1854-1915, (Ger.) bacteriologist; pioneer in modern immunology and bacteriology.
**Albert Einstein,** 1879-1955, (Ger.-U.S.) theoretical physicist; known for formulation of relativity theory.
**John F. Enders,** 1897-1985, (U.S.) virologist who helped discover vaccines against polio, measles, and mumps.
**Leonhard Euler,** 1707-83, (Swiss) mathematician, physicist; authored first calculus book.
**Gabriel Fahrenheit,** 1686-1736, (Ger.) physicist; introduced Fahrenheit scale for thermometers.
**Michael Faraday,** 1791-1867, (Br.) chemist, physicist; known for work in field of electricity.
**Pierre de Fermat,** 1601-65, (Fr.) mathematician; founded modern theory of numbers and calculus of probabilities.
**Enrico Fermi,** 1901-54, (It.-U.S.) physicist; one of primary architects of the nuclear age.
**Galileo Ferraris,** 1847-97, (It.) physicist; electrical engineer, discovered principle of rotary magnetic field.
**Richard Feynman,** 1918-88, (U.S.) a leading theoretical physicist; also a popular writer.
**Camille Flammarion,** 1842-1925, (Fr.) astronomer; popularized study of astronomy.
**Alexander Fleming,** 1881-1955, (Br.) bacteriologist; discovered penicillin.
**Jean B. J. Fourier,** 1768-1830, (Fr.) mathematician; discovered theorem governing periodic oscillation.
**James Franck,** 1882-1964, (Ger.) physicist; proved value of quantum theory.
**Sigmund Freud,** 1856-1939, (Austrian) psychiatrist; founder of psychoanalysis.
**Galileo Galilei,** 1564-1642, (It.) astronomer, physicist; a founder of the experimental method.
**Luigi Galvani,** 1737-98, (It.) physician, physicist; known as founder of galvanism.
**Carl Friedrich Gauss,** 1777-1855, (Ger.) mathematician, astronomer, physicist.
**Joseph Gay-Lussac,** 1778-1850, (Fr.) chemist, physicist; investigated behavior of gases, discovered law of combining volumes.
**Josiah W. Gibbs,** 1839-1903, (U.S.) theoretical physicist, chemist; founded chemical thermodynamics.
**Robert H. Goddard,** 1882-1945, (U.S.) physicist; father of modern rocketry.

**George W. Goethals,** 1858-1928, (U.S.) army engineer; built Panama Canal.
**William C. Gorgas,** 1854-1920, (U.S.) sanitarian, U.S. army surgeon-general; his work to prevent yellow fever, malaria helped ensure construction of Panama Canal.
**Ernest Haeckel,** 1834-1919, (Ger.) zoologist, evolutionist; a strong proponent of Darwin.
**Otto Hahn,** 1879-1968, (Ger.) chemist; worked on atomic fission.
**J. B. S. Haldane,** 1892-1964, (Br.) scientist; known for work as geneticist and application of mathematics to science.
**James Hall,** 1761-1832, (Br.) geologist, chemist; founded experimental geology, geochemistry.
**Edmund Halley,** 1656-1742, (Br.) astronomer; calculated the orbits of many planets.
**William Harvey,** 1578-1657, (Eng.) physician, anatomist; discovered circulation of the blood.
**Werner Heisenberg,** 1901-76, (Ger.) physicist; developed matrix mechanics and uncertainty principle.
**Hermann von Helmholtz,** 1821-94, (Ger.) physicist, anatomist, physiologist.
**William Herschel,** 1738-1822, (Br.) astronomer; discovered Uranus.
**Heinrich Hertz,** 1857-94, (Ger.) physicist; his discoveries led to wireless telegraphy.
**David Hilbert,** 1862-1943, (Ger.) mathematician; formulated 1st satisfactory set of axioms for modern Euclidean geometry.
**Edwin P. Hubble,** 1889-1953, (U.S.) astronomer; produced first observational evidence of expanding universe.
**Alexander von Humboldt,** 1769-1859, (Ger.) explorer, naturalist, earth scientist; originated ecology, geophysics.
**Julian Huxley,** 1887-1975, (Br.) biologist; a gifted exponent and philosopher of science.
**Edward Jenner,** 1749-1823, (Br.) physician; discovered vaccination.
**William Jenner,** 1815-98, (Br.) physician, pathological anatomist.
**Frederic Joliot-Curie,** 1900-58, (Fr.) physicist; with his wife continued work of Curies on radioactivity.
**Irene Joliot-Curie,** 1897-1956, (Fr.) physicist; continued work of Curies in radioactivity.
**James P. Joule,** 1818-89, (Br.) physicist; determined relationship between heat and mechanical energy (conservation of energy).
**Carl Jung,** 1875-1961, (Swiss) psychiatrist; founder of analytical psychology.
**William Thomson Kelvin,** 1824-1907, (Br.) mathematician, physicist; known for work on heat and electricity.
**Sister Elizabeth Kenny,** 1886-1952, (Austral.) nurse; developed method of treatment for polio.
**Johannes Kepler,** 1571-1630, (Ger.) astronomer; discovered important laws of planetary motion.
**Georges Köhler,** 1946-95, (Ger.) immunologist; co-inventor of monoclonal antibody technique.
**Joseph Lagrange,** 1736-1813, (Fr.) geometer, astronomer; number theorist, analytical and celestial mechanics.
**Jean B. Lamarck,** 1744-1829, (Fr.) naturalist; forerunner of Darwin in evolutionary theory.
**Edwin Land,** 1910-91, (U.S.) invented Polaroid camera.
**Irving Langmuir,** 1881-1957, (U.S.) physical chemist; colloid research and biochemistry.
**Pierre S. Laplace,** 1749-1827, (Fr.) astronomer, physicist; put forth nebular hypothesis of origin of solar system.
**Antoine Lavoisier,** 1743-94, (Fr.) chemist; founder of modern chemistry.
**Ernest O. Lawrence,** 1901-58, (U.S.) physicist; invented the cyclotron.
**Jerome Lejeune,** 1927-94, (Fr.) geneticist; discovered the cause of Down's syndrome.
**Louis Leakey,** 1903-72, (Br.) anthropologist; discovered important fossils, remains of early hominids.
**Anton van Leeuwenhoek,** 1632-1723, (Dutch) microscopist; father of microbiology.
**Justus von Liebig,** 1803-73, (Ger.) chemist; established quantitative organic chemical analysis.
**Joseph Lister,** 1827-1912, (Br.) pioneered antiseptic surgery.
**Percival Lowell,** 1855-1916, (U.S.) astronomer; predicted the existence of Pluto.
**Louis,** 1864-1984, and **Auguste Lumière,** 1862-1954, (Fr.) invented cinematograph.
**Guglielmo Marconi,** 1874-1937, (It.) physicist; known for his development of wireless telegraphy.
**John W. Mauchly,** 1908-80, (U.S.) co-inventor with J. Presper Eckert of the first electronic digital computer, the Eniac.
**James Clerk Maxwell,** 1831-79, (Br.) physicist; known especially for his work in electricity and magnetism.
**Maria Goeppert Mayer,** 1906-72, (Ger.-U.S.) physicist; independently developed theory of structure of atomic nuclei.
**Barbara McClintock,** 1902-92, (U.S.) geneticist; significant studies in the nature of mobile genetic elements.
**Lise Meitner,** 1878-1968, (Austrian) physicist whose work contributed to the development of the atomic bomb.
**Gregor J. Mendel,** 1822-84, (Austrian) botanist, monk; known for his experimental work on heredity.
**Franz Mesmer,** 1734-1815, (Ger.) physician; developed theory of animal magnetism.
**Albert A. Michelson,** 1852-1931, (U.S.) physicist; established speed of light as a fundamental constant.
**Robert A. Millikan,** 1868-1953, (U.S.) physicist; studied elementary electronic charge and photoelectric effect.
**Thomas Hunt Morgan,** 1866-1945, (U.S.) geneticist, embryologist; established chromosome theory of heredity.
**Isaac Newton,** 1642-1727, (Eng.) natural philosopher, mathematician; discovered law of gravitation, laws of motion.
**Robert N. Noyce,** 1927-89, (U.S.) inventor of the microchip, which revolutionized the electronics industry.
**J. Robert Oppenheimer,** 1904-67, (U.S.) physicist; director of Los Alamos during development of the atomic bomb.
**Wilhelm Ostwald,** 1853-1932, (Ger.) physical chemist, philosopher; primary founder of physical chemistry.
**Robert Morris Page,** 1903-92, (U.S.) physicist; a leading figure in development of radar technology.
**Louis Pasteur,** 1822-95, (Fr.) chemist; originated process of pasteurization.
**Clair C. Patterson,** 1922-95, (U.S.) geochemist; made first accurate determination of Earth's age, 4.6 bil years.
**Linus C. Pauling,** 1901-94, (U.S.) chemist; specializing in chemical bonds; political activist.
**Max Planck,** 1858-1947, (Ger.) physicist; originated and developed quantum theory.
**Roy J. Plunkett,** 1922-94, (U.S.) chemist; created Teflon ™.
**Henri Poincaré,** 1854-1912, (Fr.) mathematician, physicist; influenced cosmology, relativity, and topology.
**Joseph Priestley,** 1733-1804, (Br.) chemist; one of the discoverers of oxygen.
**Isidor Isaac Rabi,** 1899-1988, (U.S.) physicist; pioneered atom exploration.
**Walter S. Reed,** 1851-1902, (U.S.) army pathologist, bacteriologist; proved mosquitoes transmit yellow fever.
**Bernhard Riemann,** 1826-66, (Ger.) mathematician; contributed to development of calculus and mathematical physics.
**Wilhelm Roentgen,** 1845-1923, (Ger.) physicist; discovered the X ray.
**Ernest Rutherford,** 1871-1937, (Br.) physicist; discovered the atomic nucleus.
**Albert B. Sabin,** 1906-93, (Russ.-U.S.) In 1954, developed oral polio live-virus vaccine, which was licensed in 1961.
**Jonas Salk,** 1914-95, (U.S.) developed the first successful polio vaccine, which came into widespread use in 1950s.
**Giovanni Schiaparelli,** 1835-1910, (It.) astronomer; hypothesized canals on the surface of Mars.
**Angelo Secchi,** 1818-78, (It.) astronomer; pioneer in classifying stars by their spectra.
**Harlow Shapley,** 1885-1972, (U.S.) astronomer; noted for his studies of the galaxy.
**Roger Sperry,** 1913-94, (U.S.) brain expert; studied relationship between the right and left sides of the brain.
**Charles P. Steinmetz,** 1865-1923, (Ger.-U.S.) electrical engineer; developed basic ideas on alternating current systems.
**Frederick Stewart,** 1904-93, (Br.) botanist, cell biologist; studies considered foundations of molecular biology.
**George Stibitz,** 1904-95. (U.S.), invented first digital computer.
**Leo Szilard,** 1898-1964, (Hung.-U.S.) physicist; helped create first sustained nuclear reaction.
**Nikola Tesla,** 1856-1943, (Croatia-U.S.) electrical engineer; contributed to most developments in electronics.
**Rudolf Virchow,** 1821-1902, (Ger.) pathologist; a founder of cellular pathology.
**Alessandro Volta,** 1745-1827, (It.) physicist; pioneer in electricity.
**Werner von Braun,** 1912-77, (Ger.-U.S.) pioneered development of rockets for warfare and space exploration.
**Alfred Russell Wallace,** 1823-1913, (Br.) naturalist; proposed concept of evolution similar to Darwin's.
**August von Wasserman,** 1866-1925, (Ger.) bacteriologist; discovered reaction used as test for syphilis.
**James E. Watt,** 1736-1819, (Br.) mechanical engineer, inventor; invented modern steam-condensing engine.
**Alfred L. Wegener,** 1880-1930, (Ger.) meteorologist, geophysicist; postulated theory of continental drift.
**Norbert Wiener,** 1894-1964, (U.S.) mathematician; founder of the science of cybernetics.
**Eugene Wigner,** 1902-95, (U.S.) quantum theorist, nuclear physicist; helped perfect world's first nuclear reactor.
**Sewall Wright,** 1889-1988, (U.S.) evolutionary theorist.
**Ferdinand von Zeppelin,** 1838-1917, (Ger.) soldier, aeronaut, airship designer.

# Noted Social Reformers, Humanitarians, and Educators of the Past

**Jane Addams,** 1860-1935, (U.S.) cofounder of Hull House; won Nobel Peace Prize, 1931.
**Susan B. Anthony,** 1820-1906, (U.S.) a leader in temperance, anti-slavery, and woman suffrage movements.
**Henry Barnard,** 1811-1900, (U.S.) public school reformer.
**Thomas Barnardo,** 1845-1905, (Br.) social reformer; pioneered in the care of destitute children.
**Clara Barton,** 1821-1912, (U.S.) organizer of the American Red Cross.
**Henry Ward Beecher,** 1813-87, (U.S.) clergyman, abolitionist.
**Sarah G. Blanding,** 1899-1985, (U.S.) head of Vassar College, 1946-64.
**Amelia Bloomer,** 1818-94, (U.S.) social reformer.
**William Booth,** 1829-1912, (Br.) founded the Salvation Army.
**John Brown,** 1800-59, (U.S.) abolitionist who led murder of 5 pro-slavery men, was hanged.
**Nicholas Murray Butler,** 1862-1947, (U.S.) educator; headed Columbia Univ., 1902-45; Nobel Peace Prize, 1931.
**Frances X. (Mother) Cabrini,** 1850-1917, (It.-U.S.) Italian-born nun; founded charitable institutions; first American canonized as a Catholic saint, 1946.
**Carrie Chapman Catt,** 1859-1947, (U.S.) suffragette; helped win passage of the 19th amendment.
**Cesar Chavez,** 1927-93, (U.S.) labor leader; helped establish United Farm Workers of America.
**Clarence Darrow,** 1857-1938, (U.S.) lawyer; defender of "underdog," opponent of capital punishment.
**Dorothy Day,** 1897-1980, (U.S.) founder of Catholic Worker Movement.
**Eugene V. Debs,** 1855-1926, (U.S.) labor leader; led Pullman strike, 1894; 4-time Socialist presidential candidate.
**Melvil Dewey,** 1851-1931, (U.S.) devised decimal system of library-book classification.
**Dorothea Dix,** 1802-87, (U.S.) crusader for the mentally ill.
**Thomas Dooley,** 1927-61, (U.S.) "jungle doctor," noted for efforts to supply medical aid to developing countries.
**William Lloyd Garrison,** 1805-79, (U.S.) abolitionist.
**Giovanni Gentile,** 1875-1944, (It.) philosopher, educator; reformed Italian educational system.
**Emma Goldman,** 1869-1940, (Russ.-U.S.) published anarchist *Mother Earth,* birth-control advocate.
**Samuel Gompers,** 1850-1924, (U.S.) labor leader; a founder and president of AFL.
**William Green,** 1873-1952, (U.S.) president of AFL, 1924-52.
**Michael Harrington,** 1928-89, (U.S.) revealed poverty in affluent U.S. in *The Other America,* 1963.
**Sidney Hillman,** 1887-1946, (U.S.) labor leader; helped organize CIO.
**John Holt,** 1924-85, (U.S.) educator and author.
**Samuel G. Howe,** 1801-76, (U.S.) social reformer; changed public attitudes toward the handicapped.
**Helen Keller,** 1880-1968, (U.S.) crusader for better treatment for the handicapped.
**Maggie Kuhn,** 1905-95, (U.S.) founded Gray Panthers, 1970.
**William Kunstler,** 1919-95, (U.S.) civil liberties attorney.
**John L. Lewis,** 1880-1969, (U.S.) labor leader; headed United Mine Workers, 1920-60.
**Horace Mann,** 1796-1859, (U.S.) pioneered modern public school system.
**William H. McGuffey,** 1800-73, (U.S.) whose *Reader* was a mainstay of 19th-century U.S. public education.
**Alexander Meiklejohn,** 1872-1964, (U.S.) Br.-born educator; championed academic freedom and experimental curricula.
**Karl Menninger,** 1893-1990, (U.S.) with brother William found Menninger Clinic, and Menninger Foundation in Topeka, KS.
**Maria Montessori,** 1870-1952, (It.) educator, physician; originated Montessori method of student self-motivation.
**Lucretia Mott,** 1793-1880, (U.S.) reformer, pioneer feminist.
**Philip Murray,** 1886-1952, (U.S.) Scottish-born labor leader.
**Florence Nightingale,** 1820-1910, (Br.) founder of modern nursing.
**Emmeline Pankhurst,** 1858-1928, (Br.) woman suffragist.
**Elizabeth P. Peabody,** 1804-94, (U.S.) education pioneer; founded 1st kindergarten in U.S., 1860.
**Walter Reuther,** 1907-70, (U.S.) labor leader; headed UAW.
**Jacob Riis,** 1849-1914, (U.S.) crusader for urban reforms.
**Margaret Sanger,** 1883-1966, (U.S.) social reformer; pioneered the birth-control movement.
**Elizabeth Seton,** 1774-1821, (U.S.) nun; est. parochial school education in U.S.; first native-born American saint.
**Earl of Shaftesbury (A. A. Cooper),** 1801-85, (Br.) social reformer.
**Elizabeth Cady Stanton,** 1815-1902, (U.S.) woman suffrage pioneer.
**Lucy Stone,** 1818-93, (U.S.) feminist, abolitionist.
**Philip Vera Cruz,** 1905-94, (Filipino-U.S.) helped to found the United Farm Workers Union.
**William Wilberforce,** 1759-1833, (Br.) social reformer; prominent in struggle to abolish the slave trade.
**Emma Hart Willard,** 1787-1870, (U.S.) pioneered higher education for women.
**Frances E. Willard,** 1839-98, (U.S.) temperance, women's rights leader.
**Mary Wollstonecraft,** 1759-97, (Br.) wrote *Vindication of the Rights of Women.*

# Notable Writers of the Present

| Name (Birthplace) | Birthdate |
|---|---|
| Chinua Achebe (Ogidi, Nigeria) | 11/16/30 |
| Alice Adams (Fredericksburg, VA) | 8/14/26 |
| Edward Albee (Washington, DC) | 3/12/28 |
| Jorge Amado (Bahia, Brazil) | 8/1/12 |
| Martin Amis (Oxford, England) | 8/25/49 |
| Oscar Arias Sanchez (Heredia, Costa Rica) | 9/13/41 |
| Margaret Atwood (Ottawa, Ontario) | 11/18/39 |
| Louis Auchincloss (Lawrence, NY) | 9/27/17 |
| John Barth (Cambridge, MD) | 5/27/30 |
| Ann Beattie (Washington, DC) | 9/7/47 |
| Saul Bellow (Lachine, Quebec) | 7/10/15 |
| Peter Benchley (New York, NY) | 5/8/40 |
| Thomas Berger (Cincinnati, OH) | 7/20/24 |
| Judy Blume (Elizabeth, NJ) | 2/12/38 |
| Ray Bradbury (Waukegan, IL) | 8/22/20 |
| Barbara Taylor Bradford (Leeds, England) | 5/10/33 |
| Gwendolyn Brooks (Topeka, KS) | 6/7/17 |
| Hortense Calisher (New York, NY) | 12/20/11 |
| Tom Clancy (Baltimore, MD) | 1947 |
| Mary Higgins Clark (New York, NY) | 12/24/31 |
| Beverly Cleary (McMinnville, OR) | 1916 |
| Evan S. Connell (Kansas City, MO) | 8/17/24 |
| Pat Conroy (Atlanta, GA) | 10/26/45 |
| Robin Cook (New York, NY) | 5/4/40 |
| Harry Crews (Alma, GA) | 6/6/35 |
| Michael Crichton (Chicago, IL) | 10/23/42 |
| Janet Dailey (Storm Lake, IA) | 5/21/44 |
| Peter De Vries (Chicago, IL) | 2/27/10 |
| Joan Didion (Sacramento, CA) | 12/5/34 |
| E. L. Doctorow (New York, NY) | 1/6/31 |
| Takako Doi (Hyogo, Japan) | 11/30/28 |
| John Gregory Dunne (Hartford, CT) | 5/25/32 |
| Stanley Elkin (New York, NY) | 5/11/30 |
| Howard Fast (New York, NY) | 11/11/14 |
| Horton Foote (Wharton, TX) | 3/14/16 |
| Frederick Forsyth (Ashford, England) | 1938 |
| Paula Fox (New York, NY) | 4/22/23 |
| Marilyn French (New York, NY) | 11/21/29 |
| Carlos Fuentes (Mexico City, Mexico) | 11/11/28 |
| Charles Fuller (Philadelphia, PA) | 3/5/39 |
| William Gaddis (New York, NY) | 1922 |
| Gabriel Garcia Marquez (Aracata, Colombia) | 3/6/28 |
| Frank Gilroy (New York, NY) | 10/13/25 |
| Allen Ginsberg (Newark, NJ) | 6/3/26 |
| Gail Godwin (Birmingham, AL) | 6/18/37 |
| William Goldman (Chicago, IL) | 8/12/31 |
| Nadine Gordimer (Springs, S. Africa) | 11/20/23 |
| Mary Gordon (Long Island, NY) | 12/8/49 |
| Sue Grafton (Louisville, KY) | 4/24/40 |
| Günter Grass (Danzig, Germany) | 10/16/27 |
| Shirley Ann Grau (New Orleans, LA) | 7/8/29 |
| John Grisham (Jonesboro, AR) | 2/8/55 |
| John Guare (New York, NY) | 2/5/38 |
| Arthur Hailey (Luton, England) | 4/5/20 |
| John Hawkes (Stamford, CT) | 8/17/25 |
| Joseph Heller (Brooklyn, NY) | 5/1/23 |
| Mark Helprin (New York, NY) | 6/28/47 |
| S. E. Hinton (Tulsa, OK) | 1948 |
| Ted Hughes (Mytholmroyd, England) | 8/17/30 |
| John Irving (Exeter, NH) | 3/2/42 |
| John Jakes (Chicago, IL) | 3/31/32 |
| P. D. James (Oxford, England) | 8/3/20 |
| Erica Jong (New York, NY) | 3/26/42 |
| Garrison Keillor (Anoka, MN) | 8/7/42 |

| Name (Birthplace) | Birthdate |
|---|---|
| William Kennedy (Albany, NY) | 1/16/28 |
| Stephen King (Portland, ME) | 9/21/47 |
| Barbara Kingsolver (Annapolis, MD) | 4/8/55 |
| Maxine Hong Kingston (Stockton, CA) | 10/27/40 |
| Galway Kinnell (Providence, RI) | 2/1/27 |
| John Knowles (Fairmont, WV) | 9/16/26 |
| Kenneth Koch (Cincinnati, OH) | 2/27/25 |
| Dean Koontz (Everett, PA) | 7/9/45 |
| Judith Krantz (New York, NY) | 1/9/28 |
| Maxine Kumin (Philadelphia, PA) | 6/6/25 |
| John Le Carré (Poole, England) | 10/19/31 |
| Ursula LeGuin (Berkeley, CA) | 10/21/29 |
| Madeleine L'Engle (New York, NY) | 11/29/18 |
| Elmore Leonard (New Orleans, LA) | 10/11/25 |
| Doris Lessing (Kermanshah, Persia) | 10/22/19 |
| Ira Levin (New York, NY) | 8/27/29 |
| Robert Ludlum (New York, NY) | 5/25/27 |
| Alison Lurie (Chicago, IL) | 9/3/26 |
| Nagib Mahfuz (Cairo, Egypt) | 12/11/11 |
| Norman Mailer (Long Branch, NJ) | 1/31/23 |
| David Mamet (Chicago, IL) | 11/30/47 |
| Cormac McCarthy (Providence, RI) | 7/20/33 |
| Colleen McCullough (Wellington, N.S.W.) | 6/1/37 |
| Thomas McGuane (Wyandotte, MI) | 12/11/39 |
| Larry McMurtry (Wichita Falls, TX) | 6/3/36 |
| James A. Michener (New York, NY) | 2/3/07 |
| Arthur Miller (New York, NY) | 10/17/15 |
| Wright Morris (Central City, NE) | 1/6/10 |
| Toni Morrison (Lorain, OH) | 2/18/31 |
| Alice Munro (Wingham, Ontario) | 7/10/31 |
| Iris Murdoch (Dublin, Ire.) | 7/15/19 |
| V. S. Naipaul (Port-of-Spain, Trinidad) | 8/17/32 |
| Joyce Carol Oates (Lockport, NY) | 6/16/38 |
| Cynthia Ozick (New York, NY) | 4/17/28 |
| Grace Paley (New York, NY) | 12/11/22 |
| Octavio Paz (Mexico City, Mexico) | 3/31/14 |
| Marge Piercy (Detroit, MI) | 3/31/36 |
| Chaim Potok (New York, NY) | 2/17/29 |
| Reynolds Price (Macon, NC) | 2/1/33 |
| E. Annie Proulx (Norwich, CT) | 8/22/35 |
| Mario Puzo (New York, NY) | 10/15/20 |
| Thomas Pynchon (Glen Cove, NY) | 5/8/37 |
| David Rabe (Dubuque, IA) | 3/10/40 |

| Name (Birthplace) | Birthdate |
|---|---|
| Ishmael Reed (Chattanooga, TN) | 2/22/38 |
| Anne Rice (New Orleans, LA) | 10/14/41 |
| Adrienne Rich (Baltimore, MD) | 5/16/29 |
| Henry Roth (Austria-Hungary) | 2/8/06 |
| Philip Roth (Newark, NJ) | 3/19/33 |
| Salman Rushdie (Bombay, India) | 6/19/47 |
| J. D. Salinger (New York, NY) | 1/1/19 |
| Lawrence Sanders (New York, NY) | 1920 |
| Maurice Sendak (New York, NY) | 6/10/28 |
| Sidney Sheldon (Chicago, IL) | 2/11/17 |
| Sam Shepard (Ft. Sheridan, IL) | 11/5/43 |
| Carol Shields (Oak Park, IL) | 6/2/35 |
| Shel Silverstein (Chicago, IL) | 1932 |
| Neil Simon (New York, NY) | 7/4/27 |
| Aleksandr Solzhenitsyn (Kislovodsk, Russia) | 12/11/18 |
| Wole Soyinka (Abeokuta, Nigeria) | 7/13/34 |
| Mickey Spillane (Brooklyn, NY) | 3/9/18 |
| Danielle Steel (New York, NY) | 8/14/47 |
| Richard Stern, (New York, NY) | 2/25/28 |
| Mary Stewart (Sunderland, England) | 9/17/16 |
| Robert Stone (Brooklyn, NY) | 8/21/37 |
| Tom Stoppard (Zlin, Czechoslovakia) | 7/13/37 |
| William Styron (Newport News, VA) | 6/11/25 |
| Amy Tan (Oakland, CA) | 2/19/52 |
| Paul Theroux (Medford, MA) | 4/10/41 |
| Scott F. Turow (Chicago, IL) | 4/12/49 |
| Anne Tyler (Minneapolis, MN) | 10/25/41 |
| John Updike (Shillington, PA) | 3/18/32 |
| Leon Uris (Baltimore, MD) | 8/3/24 |
| Gore Vidal (West Point, NY) | 10/3/25 |
| Kurt Vonnegut Jr. (Indianapolis, IN) | 11/11/22 |
| Alice Walker (Eatonton, GA) | 2/9/44 |
| Robert James Waller (Rockford, IA) | 8/1/39 |
| Joseph Wambaugh (East Pittsburgh, PA) | 1/22/37 |
| Wendy Wasserstein (New York, NY) | 10/10/50 |
| Eudora Welty (Jackson, MS) | 4/13/09 |
| John Edgar Wideman (Pittsburgh, PA) | 6/14/41 |
| August Wilson (Pittsburgh, PA) | 4/27/45 |
| Lanford Wilson (Lebanon, MO) | 4/13/37 |
| Tom Wolfe (Richmond, VA) | 3/2/31 |
| Tobias Wolff (Birmingham, AL) | 6/19/45 |
| Herman Wouk (New York, NY) | 5/27/15 |

## Poets Laureate

There is no authentic record of the origin of the office of Poet Laureate of England. Henry III (1216-72) reportedly had a Versificator Regis, or King's Poet, who was paid 100 shillings a year. Other poets said to have filled the role and received payment include Geoffrey Chaucer (d 1400), Edmund Spenser (d 1599), and Ben Jonson (d 1637).

The first official English poet laureate was John Dryden, appointed in 1670, for life (as is customary). Robert Southey was appointed in 1813; followed by William Wordsworth, 1843; Alfred, Lord Tennyson, 1850; Alfred Austin, 1896; Robert Bridges, 1913; John Masefield, 1930; C. Day Lewis, 1967; Sir John Betjeman, 1972; Ted Hughes, 1984.

In the U.S., the appointment is made by the Librarian of Congress and is not for life. Robert Penn Warren was named the first official U.S. Poet Laureate, effective in Sept. 1986. Other appointments, all beginning in Sept., were 1987, Richard Wilbur; 1988, Howard Nemerov; 1990, Mark Strand; 1991, Joseph Brodsky; 1992, Mona Van Duyn, the first female poet laureate; 1993, Rita Dove, the first black poet laureate; 1995, Robert Hass.

## Noted Writers of the Past

Not including writers of ancient times, who are listed in Historical Figures section.

**Conrad Aiken,** 1889-1973, (U.S.) poet, critic. *Ushant.*
**Louisa May Alcott,** 1832-88, (U.S.) novelist. *Little Women.*
**Sholom Aleichem,** 1859-1916, (Russ.) Yiddish writer. *Tevye's Daughter, Adventures of Mottel, The Old Country.*
**Vicente Aleixandre,** 1898-1984, (Sp.) poet. *La destrucción o el amor, Dialogolos del conocimiento.*
**Horatio Alger,** 1832-1899, (U.S.) "rags-to-riches" books.
**Kingsley Amis,** 1922-95, (Br.) novelist, critic. *Lucky Jim.*
**Hans Christian Andersen,** 1805-75, (Dan.) author of fairy tales. *The Princess and the Pea, The Ugly Duckling.*
**Maxwell Anderson,** 1888-1959, (U.S.) playwright. *What Price Glory?, High Tor, Winterset, Key Largo.*
**Sherwood Anderson,** 1876-1941, (U.S.) short-story writer. "Death in the Woods"; *Winesburg, Ohio* (collection).
**Matthew Arnold,** 1822-88, (Br.) poet, critic. "Thrysis," "Dover Beach," "The Gypsy Scholar"; "Culture and Anarchy."
**Isaac Asimov,** 1920-92, (U.S.) science-fiction writer. *I Robot.*
**W(yston) H(ugh) Auden,** 1907-73, (Br.) poet, playwright, literary critic. "The Age of Anxiety."
**Jane Austen,** 1775-1817, (Br.) novelist. *Pride and Prejudice, Sense and Sensibility, Emma, Mansfield Park.*
**Isaac Babel,** 1894-1941, (Russ.) short-story writer, playwright. *Odessa Tales, Red Cavalry.*
**Honoré de Balzac,** 1799-1850, (Fr.) novelist. *Le Père Goriot, Cousine Bette, Eugénie Grandet.*
**James M. Barrie,** 1860-1937, (Br.) playwright, novelist. *Peter Pan, Dear Brutus, What Every Woman Knows.*
**Charles Baudelaire,** 1821-67, (Fr.) symbolist poet. *Les Fleurs du Mal.*
**L(yman) Frank Baum,** 1856-1919, (U.S.) writer. Wizard of Oz series.
**Simone de Beauvoir,** 1908-86, (Fr.) novelist, essayist. *The Second Sex, Memoirs of a Dutiful Daughter.*
**Samuel Beckett,** 1906-89, (Ir.) novelist, playwright. *Waiting for Godot, Endgame* (plays); *Murphy, Watt, Molloy* (novels).
**Brendan Behan,** 1923-64, (Ir.) playwright. *The Quare Fellow, The Hostage, Borstal Boy.*
**Robert Benchley,** 1889-1945, (U.S.) humorist.

**Stephen Vincent Benét,** 1898-1943, (U.S.) poet, novelist. *John Brown's Body.*
**John Berryman,** 1914-72, (U.S.) poet. *Homage to Mistress Bradstreet.*
**Ambrose Bierce,** 1842-1914, (U.S.) short-story writer, journalist. *In the Midst of Life, The Devil's Dictionary.*
**Elizabeth Bishop,** 1911-79, (U.S.) poet. *North and South—A Cold Spring.*
**William Blake,** 1757-1827, (Br.) poet, artist. *Songs of Innocence, Songs of Experience, The Marriage of Heaven and Hell.*
**Giovanni Boccaccio,** 1313-75, (It.) poet. *Decameron.*
**Heinrich Böll,** 1917-85, (Ger.) novelist, short-story writer. *Group Portrait With Lady.*
**Jorge Luis Borges,** 1900-86, (Arg.) short-story writer, poet, essayist. *Labyrinths.*
**James Boswell,** 1740-95, (Sc.) biographer. *The Life of Samuel Johnson.*
**Pierre Boulle,** (1913-94), (Fr.) novelist. *The Bridge Over the River Kwai, Planet of the Apes.*
**Anne Bradstreet,** c1612-72, (U.S.) poet. *The Tenth Muse Lately Sprung Up in America.*
**Bertolt Brecht,** 1898-1956, (Ger.) dramatist, poet. *The Threepenny Opera, Mother Courage and Her Children.*
**Charlotte Brontë,** 1816-55, (Br.) novelist. *Jane Eyre.*
**Emily Brontë,** 1818-48, (Br.) novelist. *Wuthering Heights.*
**Elizabeth Barrett Browning,** 1806-61, (Br.) poet. *Sonnets From the Portuguese, Aurora Leigh.*
**Joseph Brodsky,** 1940-96, (Russ.-U.S.) poet. *A Part of Speech, Less Than One, To Urania.*
**Robert Browning,** 1812-89, (Br.) poet. "My Last Duchess," "Fra Lippo Lippi," *The Ring and The Book.*
**Pearl S. Buck,** 1892-1973, (U.S.) novelist. *The Good Earth.*
**Mikhail Bulgakov,** 1891-1940, (Russ.) novelist, playwright. *The Heart of a Dog, The Master and Margarita.*
**John Bunyan,** 1628-88, (Br.) writer. *Pilgrim's Progress.*
**Anthony Burgess,** 1917-93, (Br.) author. *A Clockwork Orange.*
**Robert Burns,** 1759-96, (Sc.) poet. "Flow Gently, Sweet Afton," "My Heart's in the Highlands," "Auld Lang Syne."
**Virginia Lee Burton,** 1909-68, (U.S.), children's author. *Mike Mulligan and His Steam Shovel, The Little House.*
**Edgar Rice Burroughs,** 1875-1950, (U.S.) novelist. *Tarzan of the Apes.*
**George Gordon Byron, Lord Byron,** 1788-1824, (Br.) poet. *Don Juan, Childe Harold, Manfred, Cain.*
**Italo Calvino,** 1923-85, (It.) novelist, short-story writer. *If on a Winter's Night a Traveler.*
**Albert Camus,** 1913-60, (Fr.) writer. *The Stranger.*
**Karel Capek,** 1890-1938, (Czech.) playwright, novelist, essayist. *R.U.R. (Rossum's Universal Robots).*
**Truman Capote,** 1924-84, (U.S.) author. *Breakfast at Tiffany's.*
**Lewis Carroll (Charles Dodgson),** 1832-98, (Br.) writer, mathematician. *Alice's Adventures in Wonderland.*
**Rachel Carson,** 1907-64, (U.S.) marine biologist, author. *The Sea Around Us, Silent Spring.*
**Giacomo Casanova,** 1725-98, (It.) adventurer, memoirist.
**Willa Cather,** 1873-1947, (U.S.) novelist. *O Pioneers!, My Ántonia, Death Comes for the Archbishop.*
**Miguel de Cervantes Saavedra,** 1547-1616, (Sp.) novelist, dramatist, poet. *Don Quixote.*
**Raymond Chandler,** 1888-1959, (U.S.) writer of detective fiction. Philip Marlowe series.
**Geoffrey Chaucer,** c 1340-1400, (Br.) poet. *The Canterbury Tales, Troilus and Criseyde.*
**John Cheever,** 1912-82, (U.S.) short-story writer, novelist. *The Wapshot Scandal,* "The Country Husband."
**Anton Chekhov,** 1860-1904, (Russ.) short-story writer, dramatist. *Uncle Vanya, The Cherry Orchard, The Three Sisters.*
**G(ilbert) K(eith) Chesterton,** 1874-1936, (Br.) critic, novelist, relig. apologist. Father Brown series of mysteries.
**Kate Chopin,** 1851-1904, (U.S.) writer. *The Awakening.*
**Agatha Christie,** 1890-1976, (Br.) mystery writer. *And Then There Were None, Murder on the Orient Express.*
**James Clavell,** 1925-94, (Br.-U.S.) novelist. *Noble House, Shogun, King Rat.*
**Jean Cocteau,** 1889-1963, (Fr.) writer, visual artist, filmmaker. *The Beauty and the Beast, Les Enfants Terribles.*
**Samuel Taylor Coleridge,** 1772-1834, (Br.) poet, critic. "Kubla Khan," "The Rime of the Ancient Mariner."
**(Sidonie) Colette,** 1873-1954, (Fr.) novelist. *Claudine, Gigi.*
**Joseph Conrad,** 1857-1924, (Br.) novelist. *Lord Jim, Heart of Darkness, The Nigger of the Narcissus, Nostromo.*
**James Fenimore Cooper,** 1789-1851, (U.S.) novelist. Leatherstocking Tales.
**Pierre Corneille,** 1606-84, (Fr.) dramatist. *Medeé, Le Cid.*
**Hart Crane,** 1899-1932, (U.S.) poet. "The Bridge."
**Stephen Crane,** 1871-1900, (U.S.) novelist, short-story writer. *The Red Badge of Courage,* "The Open Boat."
**E. E. Cummings,** 1894-1962, (U.S.) poet. *Tulips and Chimneys.*
**Roald Dahl,** 1916-90, (Br.-U.S.) writer. *Charlie and the Chocolate Factory, James and the Giant Peach.*
**Gabriele D'Annunzio,** 1863-1938, (It.) poet, novelist, dramatist. *The Child of Pleasure, The Intruder, The Victim.*
**Dante Alighieri,** 1265-1321, (It.) poet. *The Divine Comedy.*
**Robertson Davies,** 1913-95, (Can.) novelist, playwright, essayist. Salterton Trilogy, Deptford Trilogy, Cornish Trilogy.
**Daniel Defoe,** 1660-1731, (Br.) writer. *Robinson Crusoe, Moll Flanders, Journal of the Plague Year.*
**Charles Dickens,** 1812-70, (Br.) novelist. *David Copperfield, Oliver Twist, Great Expectations, A Tale of Two Cities.*
**Emily Dickinson,** 1830-86, (U.S.) poet. "Because I could not stop for Death. . .", "Success is counted sweetest. . ."
**Isak Dinesen** (Karen Blixen), 1885-1962, (Dan.) author. *Out of Africa, Seven Gothic Tales, Winter's Tales.*
**John Donne,** 1573-1631, (Br.) poet. *Songs and Sonnets.*
**John Dos Passos,** 1896-1970, (U.S.) novelist. *U.S.A.*
**Fyodor Dostoyevsky,** 1821-81, (Russ.) novelist. *Crime and Punishment, The Brothers Karamazov, The Possessed.*
**Arthur Conan Doyle,** 1859-1930, (Br.) novelist. Sherlock Holmes mystery series.
**Theodore Dreiser,** 1871-1945, (U.S.) novelist. *An American Tragedy, Sister Carrie.*
**John Dryden,** 1631-1700, (Br.) poet, dramatist, critic. *All for Love, Mac Flecknoe, Absalom and Achitophel.*
**Alexandre Dumas,** 1802-70, (Fr.) novelist, dramatist. *The Three Musketeers, The Count of Monte Cristo.*
**Alexandre Dumas** (fils), 1824-95, (Fr.) dramatist, novelist. *La Dame aux Camélias, Le Demi-Monde.*
**Ilya G. Ehrenburg,** 1891-1967, (Russ.) writer. *The Thaw.*
**George Eliot** (Mary Ann Evans or Marian Evans), 1819-80, (Br.) novelist. *Silas Marner, Middlemarch.*
**T(homas) S(tearns) Eliot,** 1888-1965, (Br.) poet, critic. *The Waste Land,* "The Love Song of J. Alfred Prufrock."
**Ralph Ellison,** 1914-94, (U.S.), writer. *Invisible Man.*
**Ralph Waldo Emerson,** 1803-82, (U.S.) poet, essayist. "Brahma," "Nature," "The Over-Soul," "Self-Reliance."
**James T. Farrell,** 1904-79, (U.S.) novelist. *Studs Lonigan.*
**William Faulkner,** 1897-1962, (U.S.) novelist. *Sanctuary, Light in August, The Sound and the Fury, Absalom, Absalom!*
**Edna Ferber,** 1887-1968, (U.S.) novelist, short-story writer, playwright. *So Big, Cimarron, Show Boat.*
**Henry Fielding,** 1707-54, (Br.) novelist. *Tom Jones.*
**F(rancis) Scott Fitzgerald,** 1896-1940, (U.S.) short-story writer, novelist. *The Great Gatsby, Tender Is the Night.*
**Gustave Flaubert,** 1821-80, (Fr.) novelist. *Madame Bovary.*
**Ford Madox Ford,** 1873-1939, (Br.) novelist, critic, poet. *The Good Soldier.*
**C(ecil) S(cott) Forester,** 1899-1966, (Br.) writer. Horatio Hornblower books.
**E(dward) M(organ) Forster,** 1879-1970, (Br.) novelist. *A Passage to India.*
**Anatole France,** 1844-1924, (Fr.) writer. *Penguin Island, My Friend's Book, The Crime of Sylvestre Bonnard.*
**Robert Frost,** 1874-1963, (U.S.) poet. "Birches," "Fire and Ice," "Stopping by Woods on a Snowy Evening."
**John Galsworthy,** 1867-1933, (Br.) novelist, dramatist. *The Forsyte Saga, A Modern Comedy.*
**Erle Stanley Gardner,** 1889-1970, (U.S.) novelist. Perry Mason series of mysteries.
**Jean Genet,** 1911-86, (Fr.) playwright, novelist. *The Maids.*
**Kahlil Gibran,** 1883-1931, (Lebanese-U.S.) mystical novelist, essayist, poet. *The Prophet.*
**André Gide,** 1869-1951, (Fr.) writer. *The Immoralist, The Pastoral Symphony, Strait Is the Gate.*
**Jean Giraudoux,** 1882-1944, (Fr.) novelist, dramatist. *Electra, The Madwoman of Chaillot, Ondine, Tiger at the Gate.*
**Johann Wolfgang von Goethe,** 1749-1832, (Ger.) poet, dramatist, novelist. *Faust, The Sorrows of Young Werther.*
**Nikolai Gogol,** 1809-52, (Russ.) short-story writer, dramatist, novelist. *Dead Souls, The Inspector General.*
**William Golding,** 1911-93, (Br.) novelist. *Lord of the Flies.*
**Oliver Goldsmith,** 1730?-74, (Br.-Ir.) dramatist, novelist. *The Vicar of Wakefield, She Stoops to Conquer.*
**Maxim Gorky,** 1868-1936, (Russ.) dramatist, novelist. *The Lower Depths.*
**Robert Graves,** 1895-1985, (Br.) poet, classical scholar, novelist. *I, Claudius; The White Goddess.*
**Thomas Gray,** 1716-71, (Br.) poet. "Elegy Written in a Country Churchyard," "The Progress of Poesy."
**Graham Greene,** 1904-91, (Br.) novelist. *The Power and the Glory, The Heart of the Matter, The Ministry of Fear.*
**Zane Grey,** 1872-1939, (U.S.) writer of western stories.
**Jakob Grimm,** 1785-1863, (Ger.) philologist, folklorist. *German Methodology, Grimm's Fairy Tales.*
**Wilhelm Grimm,** 1786-1859, (Ger.) philologist, folklorist. *Grimm's Fairy Tales.*

**Alex Haley,** 1921-92, (U.S.) author. *Roots.*
**Dashiell Hammett,** 1894-1961, (U.S.) detective-story writer, created Sam Spade. *The Maltese Falcon, The Thin Man.*
**Knute Hamsun,** 1859-1952 (Nor.) novelist. *Hunger.*
**Thomas Hardy,** 1840-1928, (Br.) novelist, poet. *The Return of the Native, Tess of the D'Urbervilles, Jude the Obscure.*
**Joel Chandler Harris,** 1848-1908, (U.S.) short-story writer. Uncle Remus series.
**Moss Hart,** 1904-61, (U.S.) playwright. *Once in a Lifetime, You Can't Take It With You, The Man Who Came to Dinner.*
**Bret Harte,** 1836-1902, (U.S.) short-story writer, poet. *The Luck of Roaring Camp.*
**Jaroslav Hasek,** 1883-1923, (Czech.) writer. *The Good Soldier.*
**Nathaniel Hawthorne,** 1804-64, (U.S.) novelist, short-story writer. *The Scarlet Letter,* "Young Goodman Browne."
**Heinrich Heine,** 1797-1856, (Ger.) poet. *Book of Songs.*
**Lillian Hellman,** 1905-84, (U.S.) playwright, author of memoirs. *The Little Foxes, An Unfinished Woman, Pentimento.*
**Ernest Hemingway,** 1899-1961, (U.S.) novelist, short-story writer. *A Farewell to Arms, For Whom the Bell Tolls.*
**O. Henry** (W. S. Porter), 1862-1910, (U.S.) short-story writer. "The Gift of the Magi."
**James Herriot** (James Alfred Wight), 1916-95, (Br.) novelist, veterinarian. *All Creatures Great and Small.*
**John Hersey,** 1914-93, (U.S.) novelist, journalist. *Hiroshima, A Bell for Adano.*
**Hermann Hesse,** 1877-1962, (Ger.) novelist, poet. *Death and the Lover, Steppenwolf, Siddhartha.*
**Oliver Wendell Holmes,** 1809-94, (U.S.) poet, novelist. *The Autocrat of the Breakfast-Table.*
**A(lfred) E. Housman,** 1859-1936, (Br.) poet. *A Shropshire Lad.*
**William Dean Howells,** 1837-1920, (U.S.) novelist, critic. *The Rise of Silas Lapham.*
**Langston Hughes,** 1902-67, (U.S.) poet, playwright. *The Weary Blues, One-Way Ticket, Shakespeare in Harlem.*
**Victor Hugo,** 1802-85, (Fr.) poet, dramatist, novelist. *Notre Dame de Paris, Les Misérables.*
**Zora Neale Hurston,** 1903-60, (U.S.) novelist, folklorist. *Their Eyes Were Watching God, Mules and Men.*
**Aldous Huxley,** 1894-1963, (Br.) writer. *Brave New World.*
**Henrik Ibsen,** 1828-1906, (Nor.) dramatist, poet. *A Doll's House, Ghosts, The Wild Duck, Hedda Gabler.*
**William Inge,** 1913-73, (U.S.) playwright. *Picnic*; *Come Back, Little Sheba*; *Bus Stop.*
**Eugene Ionesco,** 1910-94, (Fr.) surrealist dramatist. *The Bald Soprano, The Chairs.*
**Washington Irving,** 1783-1859, (U.S.) writer. "Rip Van Winkle," "The Legend of Sleepy Hollow."
**Christopher Isherwood,** 1904-1986, (Br.) novelist, playwright. *The Berlin Stories.*
**Shirley Jackson,** 1919-65, (U.S.) writer. "The Lottery."
**Henry James,** 1843-1916, (U.S.) novelist, short-story writer, critic. *The Portrait of a Lady, The Ambassadors, Daisy Miller.*
**Robinson Jeffers,** 1887-1962, (U.S.) poet, dramatist. *Tamar and Other Poems, Medea.*
**Samuel Johnson,** 1709-84, (Br.) author, scholar, critic. *Dictionary of the English Language.*
**Ben Jonson,** 1572-1637, (Br.) dramatist, poet. *Volpone.*
**James Joyce,** 1882-1941, (Ir.) writer. *Ulysses, Dubliners, A Portrait of the Artist As a Young Man, Finnegans Wake.*
**Franz Kafka,** 1883-1924, (Ger.) novelist, short-story writer. *The Trial, Amerika, The Castle, The Metamorphosis.*
**George S. Kaufman,** 1889-1961, (U.S.) playwright. *The Man Who Came to Dinner, You Can't Take It With You, Stage Door.*
**Nikos Kazantzakis,** 1883?-1957, (Gk.) novelist. *Zorba the Greek, A Greek Passion.*
**John Keats,** 1795-1821, (Br.) poet. "Ode on a Grecian Urn," "Ode to a Nightingale," "La Belle Dame Sans Merci."
**Joyce Kilmer,** 1886-1918, (U.S.) poet, "Trees."
**Rudyard Kipling,** 1865-1936, (Br.) author, poet. "The White Man's Burden," "Gunga Din," *The Jungle Book.*
**Jean de la Fontaine,** 1621-95, (Fr.) poet. *Fables choisies.*
**Pär Lagerkvist,** 1891-1974, (Swed.) poet, dramatist, novelist. *Barabbas, The Sybil.*
**Selma Lagerlöf,** 1858-1940, (Swed.) novelist. *Jerusalem, The Ring of the Lowenskolds.*
**Alphonse de Lamartine,** 1790-1869, (Fr.) poet, novelist, statesman. *Méditations poétiques.*
**Charles Lamb,** 1775-1834, (Br.) essayist. *Specimens of English Dramatic Poets, Essays of Elia.*
**Giuseppe di Lampedusa,** 1896-1957, (It.) novelist. *The Leopard.*
**Ring Lardner,** 1885-1933, (U.S.) short-story writer, humorist.
**D(avid) H(erbert) Lawrence,** 1885-1930, (Br.) novelist. *Sons and Lovers, Women in Love, Lady Chatterley's Lover.*
**Mikhail Lermontov,** 1814-41, (Russ.) novelist, poet. "Demon," *Hero of Our Time.*
**Alain-René Lesage,** 1668-1747, (Fr.) novelist. *Gil Blas de Santillane.*
**Gotthold Lessing,** 1729-81, (Ger.) dramatist, philosopher, critic. *Miss Sara Sampson, Minna von Barnhelm.*
**C(live) S(taples) Lewis,** 1898-1963, (Br.) critic, novelist, religious writer. *Allegory of Love; The Lion, the Witch and the Wardrobe.*
**Sinclair Lewis,** 1885-1951, (U.S.) novelist. *Babbitt, Main Street, Arrowsmith, Dodsworth.*
**Vachel Lindsay,** 1879-1931, (U.S.) poet. *General William Booth Enters Into Heaven, The Congo.*
**Hugh Lofting,** 1886-1947, (Br.) writer. Dr. Doolittle series.
**Jack London,** 1876-1916, (U.S.) novelist, journalist. *Call of the Wild, The Sea-Wolf, White Fang.*
**Henry Wadsworth Longfellow,** 1807-82, (U.S.) poet. *Evangeline, The Song of Hiawatha.*
**Amy Lowell,** 1874-1925, (U.S.) poet, critic. "Lilacs."
**James Russell Lowell,** 1819-91, (U.S.) poet, editor. *Poems, The Biglow Papers.*
**Robert Lowell,** 1917-77, (U.S.) poet. "Lord Weary's Castle".
**Archibald MacLeish,** 1892-1982, (U.S.) poet. *Conquistador.*
**Bernard Malamud,** 1914-86, (U.S.) short-story writer, novelist. "The Magic Barrel," *The Assistant, The Fixer.*
**Stéphane Mallarmé,** 1842-98, (Fr.) poet. *Poésies.*
**Thomas Malory,** ?-1471, (Br.) writer. *Morte d'Arthur.*
**Andre Malraux,** 1901-76, (Fr.) novelist. *Man's Fate.*
**Osip Mandelstam,** 1891-1938, (Russ.) poet. *Stone, Tristia.*
**Thomas Mann,** 1875-1955, (Ger.) novelist, essayist. *Buddenbrooks, Death in Venice, The Magic Mountain.*
**Katherine Mansfield,** 1888-1923, (Br.) writer. "Bliss."
**Christopher Marlowe,** 1564-93, (Br.) dramatist, poet. *Tamburlaine the Great, Dr. Faustus, The Jew of Malta.*
**John Masefield,** 1878-1967, (Br.) poet. "Sea Fever," "Cargoes," *Salt Water Ballads.*
**Edgar Lee Masters,** 1869-1950, (U.S.) poet, biographer. *Spoon River Anthology.*
**W(illiam) Somerset Maugham,** 1874-1965, (Br.) author. *Of Human Bondage, The Moon and Sixpence.*
**Guy de Maupassant,** 1850-93, (Fr.) novelist, short-story writer. "A Life," "Bel-Ami," "The Necklace."
**François Mauriac,** 1885-1970, (Fr.) novelist, dramatist. *Viper's Tangle, The Kiss to the Leper.*
**Vladimir Mayakovsky,** 1893-1930, (Russ.) poet, dramatist. *The Cloud in Trousers.*
**Mary McCarthy,** 1912-89, (U.S.) critic, novelist, memoirist. *Memories of a Catholic Girlhood.*
**Carson McCullers,** 1917-67, (U.S.) novelist. *The Heart Is a Lonely Hunter, Member of the Wedding.*
**Herman Melville,** 1819-91, (U.S.) novelist, poet. *Moby Dick, Typee, Billy Budd, Omoo.*
**H(enry) L(ewis) Mencken,** 1880-1956, (U.S.) author, critic, editor. *Prejudices, The American Language.*
**George Meredith,** 1828-1909, (Br.) novelist, poet. *The Ordeal of Richard Feverel, The Egoist.*
**Prosper Mérimée,** 1803-70, (Fr.) author. *Carmen.*
**James Merrill,** 1926-95, (U.S.) poet. *Divine Comedies.*
**Edna St. Vincent Millay,** 1892-1950, (U.S.) poet. *The Harp Weaver and Other Poems, A Few Figs From Thistles.*
**Henry Miller,** 1891-1980, (U.S.), dramatist. *Tropic of Cancer.*
**A(lan) A(lexander) Milne,** 1882-1956, (Br.) author. *Winnie-the-Pooh.*
**John Milton,** 1608-74, (Br.) poet. *Paradise Lost.*
**Mishima Yukio** (Hiraoka Kimitake), 1925-70, (Jpn.) writer. *Confessions of a Mask.*
**Gabriela Mistral,** 1889-1957, (Chil.) poet. *Sonnets of Death.*
**Margaret Mitchell,** 1900-49, (U.S.) author. *Gone With the Wind.*
**Jean Baptiste Molière,** 1622-73, (Fr.) dramatist. *Le Tartuffe, Le Misanthrope, Le Bourgeois Gentilhomme.*
**Ferenc Molnár,** 1878-1952, (Hung.) dramatist, novelist. *Liliom, The Guardsman, The Swan.*
**Michel de Montaigne,** 1533-92, (Fr.) essayist. *Essais.*
**Eugenio Montale,** 1896-1981, (It.) poet.
**Clement C. Moore,** 1779-1863, (U.S.) poet, educator. "A Visit From Saint Nicholas."
**Marianne Moore,** 1887-1972, (U.S.) poet. *Collected Poems.*
**Sir Thomas More,** 1478-1535, (Br.) writer, statesman, saint. *Utopia.*
**Murasaki Shikibu,** c978-1031?, (Jpn.) novelist. *The Tale of Genji.*
**Alfred de Musset,** 1810-57, (Fr.) poet, dramatist. *La Confession d'un Enfant du Siècle.*
**Vladimir Nabokov,** 1899-1977, (Russ.-U.S.) novelist. *Lolita.*
**Ogden Nash,** 1902-71, (U.S.) poet of light verse.
**Pablo Neruda,** 1904-73, (Chil.) poet. *Twenty Love Poems and One Song of Despair, Toward the Splendid City.*
**Sean O'Casey,** 1884-1964, (Ir.) dramatist. *Juno and the Paycock, The Plough and the Stars.*
**Frank O'Connor** (Michael Donovan), 1903-66, (Ir.) short-story writer. "Guests of a Nation."

**Flannery O'Connor,** 1925-64, (U.S.) novelist, short-story writer. *Wise Blood,* "A Good Man Is Hard to Find."
**Clifford Odets,** 1906-63, (U.S.) playwright. *Waiting for Lefty, Awake and Sing, Golden Boy, The Country Girl.*
**John O'Hara,** 1905-70, (U.S.) novelist, short-story writer. *From the Terrace, Appointment in Samarra, Pal Joey.*
**Omar Khayyam,** c1028-1122, (Per.) poet. *Rubaiyat.*
**Eugene O'Neill,** 1888-1953, (U.S.) playwright. *Emperor Jones, Anna Christie, Long Day's Journey Into Night.*
**George Orwell,** 1903-50, (Br.) novelist, essayist. *Animal Farm, Nineteen Eighty-Four.*
**John Osborne,** 1929-95, (Br.) dramatist, novelist. *Look Back in Anger, The Entertainer.*
**Dorothy Parker,** 1893-1967, (U.S.) poet, short-story writer. *Enough Rope, Laments for the Living.*
**Boris Pasternak,** 1890-1960, (Russ.) poet, novelist. *Doctor Zhivago.*
**Samuel Pepys,** 1633-1703, (Br.) public official, diarist.
**S(idney) J(oseph) Perelman,** 1904-79, (U.S.) humorist. *The Road to Miltown, Under the Spreading Atrophy.*
**Charles Perrault,** 1628-1703, (Fr.) writer. *Tales From Mother Goose* (*Sleeping Beauty, Cinderella*).
**Petrarch** 1304-74, (It.) poet. *Africa, Trionfi, Canzoniere.*
**Luigi Pirandello,** 1867-1936, (It.) novelist, dramatist. *Six Characters in Search of an Author.*
**Sylvia Plath,** 1932-63, (U.S.) author, poet. *The Bell Jar.*
**Edgar Allan Poe,** 1809-49, (U.S.) poet, short-story writer, critic. "Annabel Lee," "The Raven," "The Purloined Letter."
**Alexander Pope,** 1688-1744, (Br.) poet. *The Rape of the Lock, An Essay on Man.*
**Katherine Anne Porter,** 1890-1980, (U.S.) novelist, short-story writer. *Ship of Fools.*
**Ezra Pound,** 1885-1972, (U.S.) poet. *Cantos.*
**Marcel Proust,** 1871-1922, (Fr.) novelist. *Remembrance of Things Past.*
**Aleksandr Pushkin,** 1799-1837, (Russ.) poet, prose writer. *Boris Godunov, Eugene Onegin, The Bronze Horseman.*
**François Rabelais,** 1495-1553, (Fr.) writer. *Gargantua.*
**Jean Racine,** 1639-99, (Fr.) dramatist. *Andromaque, Phèdre, Bérénice, Britannicus.*
**Ayn Rand,** 1905-82, (Russ.-U.S.) novelist, philosopher. *The Fountainhead, Atlas Shrugged.*
**Erich Maria Remarque,** 1898-1970, (Ger.-U.S.) novelist. *All Quiet on the Western Front.*
**Samuel Richardson,** 1689-1761, (Br.) novelist. *Pamela; or Virtue Rewarded.*
**Rainer Maria Rilke,** 1875-1926, (Ger.) poet. *Life and Songs, Duino Elegies, Poems From the Book of Hours.*
**Arthur Rimbaud,** 1854-91, (Fr.) poet. *A Season in Hell.*
**Edwin Arlington Robinson,** 1869-1935, (U.S.) poet. "Richard Cory," "Miniver Cheevy."
**Theodore Roethke,** 1908-63, (U.S.) poet. *Open House, The Waking, The Far Field.*
**Romain Rolland,** 1866-1944, (Fr.) novelist, biographer. *Jean-Christophe.*
**Pierre de Ronsard,** 1524-85, (Fr.) poet. *Sonnets pour Hélène, La Franciade.*
**Edmond Rostand,** 1868-1918, (Fr.) poet, dramatist. *Cyrano de Bergerac.*
**Damon Runyon,** 1880-1946, (U.S.) short-story writer, journalist. *Guys and Dolls, Blue Plate Special.*
**John Ruskin,** 1819-1900, (Br.) critic, social theorist. *Modern Painters, The Seven Lamps of Architecture.*
**Antoine de Saint-Exupéry,** 1900-44, (Fr.) writer. *Wind, Sand and Stars, The Little Prince.*
**Saki,** or H(erbert) H(ugh) Munro, 1870-1916, (Br.) writer. *The Chronicles of Clovis.*
**George Sand** (Amandine Lucie Aurore Dupin), 1804-76, (Fr.) novelist. *Consuelo, The Haunted Pool, The Master Bell-Ringer.*
**Carl Sandburg,** 1878-1967, (U.S.) poet. *The People, Yes; Chicago Poems, Smoke and Steel, Harvest Poems.*
**George Santayana,** 1863-1952, (U.S.) poet, essayist, philosopher. *The Sense of Beauty, The Realms of Being.*
**William Saroyan,** 1908-81, (U.S.) playwright, novelist. *The Time of Your Life, The Human Comedy.*
**May Sarton,** 1914-95, (Belg.-U.S.) poet, novelist. *Encounter in April, Anger.*
**Richard Scarry,** 1920-94, (U.S.) author of children's books. *Richard Scarry's Best Story Book Ever.*
**Friedrich von Schiller,** 1759-1805, (Ger.) dramatist, poet, historian. *Don Carlos, Maria Stuart, Wilhelm Tell.*
**Sir Walter Scott,** 1771-1832, (Sc.) novelist, poet. *Ivanhoe.*
**Jaroslav Seifert,** 1902-86, (Czech.) poet.
**Dr. Seuss** (Theodor Seuss Geisel), 1904-91, (U.S.) children's book author and illustrator. *The Cat in the Hat.*
**William Shakespeare,** 1564-1616, (Br.) dramatist, poet. *Romeo and Juliet, Hamlet, King Lear, Julius Caesar,* sonnets.
**George Bernard Shaw,** 1856-1950, (Ir.-Br.) playwright, critic. *St. Joan, Pygmalion, Major Barbara, Man and Superman.*
**Mary Wollstonecraft Shelley,** 1797-1851, (Br.) novelist, feminist. *Frankenstein, The Last Man.*
**Percy Bysshe Shelley,** 1792-1822, (Br.) poet. *Prometheus Unbound, Adonais,* "Ode to the West Wind," "To a Skylark."
**Richard B. Sheridan,** 1751-1816, (Br.) dramatist. *The Rivals, School for Scandal.*
**Robert Sherwood,** 1896-1955, (U.S.) playwright, biographer. *The Petrified Forest, Idiot's Delight, Abe Lincoln in Illinois.*
**Mikhail Sholokhov,** 1906-84, (Russ.) writer. *The Silent Don.*
**Upton Sinclair,** 1878-1968, (U.S.) novelist. *The Jungle.*
**Isaac Bashevis Singer,** 1904-91, (Pol.-U.S.) novelist, short story writer, in Yiddish. *The Magician of Lubin.*
**C(harles) P(ercy) Snow,** 1905-80, (Br.) novelist, scientist. *Strangers and Brothers, Corridors of Power.*
**Stephen Spender,** 1909-95, (Br.) poet, critic, novelist. *Twenty Poems,* "Elegy for Margaret."
**Edmund Spenser,** 1552-99, (Br.) poet. *The Faerie Queen.*
**Christina Stead,** 1903-83, (Austral.) novelist, short-story writer. *The Man Who Loved Children.*
**Richard Steele,** 1672-1729, (Br.) essayist, playwright, began the *Tatler* and *Spectator. The Conscious Lovers.*
**Lincoln Steffens,** 1866-1936, (U.S.) editor, writer. *The Shame of the Cities.*
**Gertrude Stein,** 1874-1946, (U.S.) writer. *Three Lives.*
**John Steinbeck,** 1902-68, (U.S.) novelist. *The Grapes of Wrath, Of Mice and Men, The Winter of Our Discontent.*
**Stendhal** (Marie Henri Beyle), 1783-1842, (Fr.) novelist. *The Red and the Black, The Charterhouse of Parma.*
**Laurence Sterne,** 1713-68, (Br.) novelist. *Tristram Shandy.*
**Wallace Stevens,** 1879-1955, (U.S.) poet. *Harmonium, The Man With the Blue Guitar, Notes Toward a Supreme Fiction.*
**Robert Louis Stevenson,** 1850-94, (Br.) novelist, poet, essayist. *Treasure Island, A Child's Garden of Verses.*
**Rex Stout,** 1886-1975, (U.S.) novelist, created Nero Wolfe.
**Harriet Beecher Stowe,** 1811-96, (U.S.) novelist. *Uncle Tom's Cabin.*
**Lytton Strachey,** 1880-1932, (Br.) biographer, critic. *Eminent Victorians, Queen Victoria, Elizabeth and Essex.*
**August Strindberg,** 1849-1912, (Swed.) dramatist, novelist. *The Father, Miss Julie, The Creditors.*
**Jonathan Swift,** 1667-1745, (Br.) satirist, poet. *Gulliver's Travels.*
**Algernon C. Swinburne,** 1837-1909, (Br.) writer. *Atalanta in Calydon.*
**John M. Synge,** 1871-1909, (Ir.) poet, dramatist. *Riders to the Sea, The Playboy of the Western World.*
**Rabindranath Tagore,** 1861-1941, (Ind.) author, poet. *Sadhana, The Realization of Life, Gitanjali.*
**Booth Tarkington,** 1869-1946, (U.S.) novelist. *Seventeen.*
**Peter Taylor,** 1917-94, (U.S.) novelist. *A Summons to Memphis.*
**Sara Teasdale,** 1884-1933, (U.S.) poet. *Helen of Troy and Other Poems, Rivers to the Sea, Flame and Shadow.*
**Alfred, Lord Tennyson,** 1809-92, (Br.) poet. *Idylls of the King, In Memoriam,* "The Charge of the Light Brigade."
**William Makepeace Thackeray,** 1811-63, (Br.) novelist. *Vanity Fair, Henry Esmond, Pendennis.*
**Dylan Thomas,** 1914-53, (Welsh) poet. *Under Milk Wood, A Child's Christmas in Wales.*
**Henry David Thoreau,** 1817-62, (U.S.) author. *Walden.*
**James Thurber,** 1894-1961, (U.S.) humorist, cartoonist. "The Secret Life of Walter Mitty," *My Life and Hard Times.*
**J(ohn) R(onald) R(euel) Tolkien,** 1892-1973, (Br.) writer. *The Hobbit, Lord of the Rings* trilogy.
**Leo Tolstoy,** 1828-1910, (Russ.) novelist, short-story writer. *War and Peace, Anna Karenina,* "The Death of Ivan Ilyich."
**Anthony Trollope,** 1815-82, (Br.) novelist. *The Warden, Barchester Towers,* The Palliser novels.
**Ivan Turgenev,** 1818-83, (Russ.) novelist, short-story writer. *Fathers and Sons, First Love, A Month in the Country.*
**Mark Twain** (Samuel Clemens), 1835-1910, (U.S.) novelist, humorist. *The Adventures of Huckleberry Finn, Tom Sawyer; Life on the Mississippi.*
**Sigrid Undset,** 1881-1949, (Nor.) novelist, poet. *Kristin Lavransdatter.*
**Paul Valéry,** 1871-1945, (Fr.) poet, critic. *La Jeune Parque, The Graveyard by the Sea.*
**Jules Verne,** 1828-1905, (Fr.) novelist. *Twenty Thousand Leagues Under the Sea.*
**François Villon,** 1431-63?, (Fr.) poet. *The Lays, The Grand Testament.*
**Voltaire** (F.M. Arouet), 1694-1778, (Fr.) writer of "philosophical romances"; philosopher, historian; *Candide.*
**Evelyn Waugh,** 1903-66, (Br.) novelist. *The Loved One; Brideshead Revisited; A Handful of Dust.*
**H(erbert) G(eorge) Wells,** 1866-1946, (Br.) novelist. *The Time Machine, The Invisible Man, The War of the Worlds.*

**Rebecca West,** 1893-1983, (Br.) novelist, critic, journalist. *Black Lamb and Grey Falcon.*
**Edith Wharton,** 1862-1937, (U.S.) novelist. *The Age of Innocence, The House of Mirth, Ethan Frome.*
**E(lwyn) B(rooks) White,** 1899-1985, (U.S.), essayist, novelist. *Here Is New York, Charlotte's Web, Stuart Little.*
**Patrick White,** 1912-90, (Austral.) novelist. *The Tree of Man.*
**T(erence) H(anbury) White,** 1906-64, (Br.) author. *The Once and Future King, A Book of Beasts.*
**Walt Whitman,** 1819-92, (U.S.) poet. *Leaves of Grass.*
**John Greenleaf Whittier,** 1807-92, (U.S.) poet, journalist. *Snow-Bound.*
**Oscar Wilde,** 1854-1900, (Ir.) novelist, playwright. *The Picture of Dorian Gray, The Importance of Being Earnest.*
**Laura Ingalls Wilder,** 1867-1957, (U.S.) novelist. Little House on the Prairie series of children's books.
**Thornton Wilder,** 1897-1975, (U.S.) playwright. *Our Town, The Skin of Our Teeth, The Matchmaker.*
**Tennessee Williams,** 1911-83, (U.S.) playwright. *A Streetcar Named Desire, Cat on a Hot Tin Roof, The Glass Menagerie.*
**William Carlos Williams,** 1883-1963, (U.S.) poet. *Tempers, Al Que Quiere! Paterson.*
**Edmund Wilson,** 1895-1972, (U.S.) critic, novelist. *Axel's Castle, To the Finland Station.*
**P(elham) G(renville) Wodehouse,** 1881-1975, (Br.-U.S.) humorist. The "Jeeves" novels, *Anything Goes.*
**Thomas Wolfe,** 1900-38, (U.S.) novelist. *Look Homeward, Angel; You Can't Go Home Again; Of Time and the River.*
**Virginia Woolf,** 1882-1941, (Br.) novelist, essayist. *Mrs. Dalloway, To the Lighthouse, The Waves, A Room of One's Own.*
**William Wordsworth,** 1770-1850, (Br.) poet. "Tintern Abbey," "Ode: Intimations of Immortality," *The Prelude.*
**Richard Wright,** 1908-60, novelist. *Native Son, Black Boy.*
**William Butler Yeats,** 1865-1939, (Ir.) poet, playwright. "The Second Coming," *The Wild Swans at Coole.*
**Émile Zola,** 1840-1902, (Fr.) novelist. *Nana, Thérèsè Raquin.*

# Composers of Classical and Avant Garde Music

**Carl Philipp Emanuel Bach,** 1714-88, (Ger.) Cantatas, passions, numerous keyboard and instrumental works.
**Johann Christian Bach,** 1735-82, (Ger.) Concertos, operas, sonatas.
**Johann Sebastian Bach,** 1685-1750, (Ger.) St. Matthew Passion, The Well-Tempered Clavier.
**Samuel Barber,** 1910-81, (U.S.) Adagio for Strings, Vanessa.
**Béla Bartók,** 1881-1945, (Hung.) Concerto for Orchestra, The Miraculous Mandarin.
**Ludwig van Beethoven,** 1770-1827, (Ger.) Concertos (Emperor), sonatas (Moonlight, Pathetique), 9 symphonies.
**Vincenzo Bellini,** 1801-35, (It.) I Puritani, La Sonnambula, Norma.
**Alban Berg,** 1885-1935, (Austrian) Wozzeck, Lulu.
**Hector Berlioz,** 1803-69, (Fr.) Damnation of Faust, Symphonie Fantastique, Requiem.
**Leonard Bernstein,** 1918-90, (U.S.) Chichester Psalms, Jeremiah Symphony, Mass.
**Georges Bizet,** 1838-75, (Fr.) Carmen, Pearl Fishers.
**Ernest Bloch,** 1880-1959, (Swiss-U.S.) Macbeth (opera), Schelomo, Voice in the Wilderness.
**Luigi Boccherini,** 1743-1805, (It.) Chamber music and guitar pieces.
**Alexander Borodin,** 1833-87, (Russ.) Prince Igor, In the Steppes of Central Asia, Polovtzian Dances.
**Johannes Brahms,** 1833-97, (Ger.) Liebeslieder Waltzes, Academic Festival Overture, chamber music, 4 symphonies.
**Benjamin Britten,** 1913-76, (Br.) Peter Grimes, Turn of the Screw, A Ceremony of Carols, War Requiem.
**Anton Bruckner,** 1824-96, (Aust.) 9 symphonies.
**Dietrich Buxtehude,** 1637-1707, (Dan.) Organ works, vocal music.
**William Byrd,** 1543-1623, (Br.) Masses, motets.
**John Cage,** b 1912, (U.S.) Winter Music, Fontana Mix.
**Emmanuel Chabrier,** 1841-94, (Fr.) Le Roi Malgré Lui, Espana.
**Gustave Charpentier,** 1860-1956, (Fr.) Louise.
**Frédéric Chopin,** 1810-49, (Pol.) Mazurkas, waltzes, etudes, nocturnes, polonaises (Polonaise No. 6 in A flat major [Heroic]), sonatas.
**Aaron Copland,** 1900-90, (U.S.) Appalachian Spring, Fanfare for the Common Man, Lincoln Portrait.
**Claude Debussy,** 1862-1918, (Fr.) Pelleas et Melisande, La Mer, Prelude to the Afternoon of a Faun.
**Gaetano Donizetti,** 1797-1848, (It.) Elixir of Love, Lucia di Lammermoor, Daughter of the Regiment.
**Paul Dukas,** 1865-1935, (Fr.) Sorcerer's Apprentice.
**Antonin Dvorak,** 1841-1904, (Czech.) Songs My Mother Taught Me, Symphony in E Minor (From the New World).
**Edward Elgar,** 1857-1934, (Br.) Enigma Variations, Pomp and Circumstance.
**Manuel de Falla,** 1876-1946, (Sp.) El Amor Brujo, La Vida Breve, The Three-Cornered Hat.
**Gabriel Faurè,** 1845-1924, (Fr.) Requiem, Elègie for Cello and Piano.
**Cesar Franck,** 1822-90, (Belg.) Symphony in D minor, Violin Sonata.
**George Gershwin,** 1898-1937, (U.S.) Rhapsody in Blue, An American in Paris, Porgy and Bess.
**Philip Glass,** b 1937, (U.S.) Einstein on the Beach, The Voyage.
**Mikhail Glinka,** 1804-57, (Russ.) A Life for the Tsar, Ruslan and Ludmilla.
**Christoph W. Gluck,** 1714-87, (Ger.) Alceste, Iphigènie en Tauride.
**Charles Gounod,** 1818-93, (Fr.) Faust, Romeo and Juliet.
**Edvard Grieg,** 1843-1907, (Nor.) Peer Gynt Suite, Concerto in A minor for piano.
**George Frideric Handel,** 1685-1759, (Ger.-Br.) Messiah, Water Music.
**Howard Hanson,** 1896-1981, (U.S.) Symphonies No. 1 (Nordic) and No. 2 (Romantic).
**Roy Harris,** 1898-1979, (U.S.) Symphonies.
**(Franz) Joseph Haydn,** 1732-1809, (Austrian) Symphonies (Clock, London Toy), chamber music, oratorios.
**Paul Hindemith,** 1895-1963, (U.S.) Mathis der Maler.
**Gustav Holst,** 1874-1934, (Br.) The Planets.
**Arthur Honegger,** 1892-1955, (Fr.) Judith, Le Roi David, Pacific 231.
**Alan Hovhaness,** b 1911, (U.S.) Symphonies, Magnificat.
**Engelbert Humperdinck,** 1854-1921, (Ger.) Hansel and Gretel.
**Charles Ives,** 1874-1954, (U.S.) Concord Sonata, symphonies.
**Aram Khachaturian,** 1903-78, (Russ.) Ballets, piano pieces, Sabre Dance.
**Zoltán Kodaly,** 1882-1967, (Hung.) Háry János, Psalmus Hungaricus.
**Fritz Kreisler,** 1875-1962, (Austrian) Caprice Viennois, Tambourin Chinois.
**Edouard Lalo,** 1823-92, (Fr.) Symphonie Espagnole.
**Ruggero Leoncavallo,** 1857-1919, (It.) Pagliacci.
**Franz Liszt,** 1811-86, (Hung.) 20 Hungarian rhapsodies, symphonic poems.
**Edward MacDowell,** 1861-1908, (U.S.) To a Wild Rose.
**Gustav Mahler,** 1860-1911, (Austrian) Das Lied von der Erde.
**Pietro Mascagni,** 1863-1945, (It.) Cavalleria Rusticana.
**Jules Massenet,** 1842-1912, (Fr.) Manon, Le Cid, Thaïs.
**Felix Mendelssohn,** 1809-47, (Ger.) A Midsummer Night's Dream, Songs Without Words, violin concerto.
**Gian-Carlo Menotti,** b 1911, (It.-U.S.) The Medium, The Consul, Amahl and the Night Visitors.
**Claudio Monteverdi,** 1567-1643, (It.) Opera, masses, madrigals.
**Modest Moussorgsky,** 1839-81, (Russ.) Boris Godunov, Pictures at an Exhibition.
**Wolfgang Amadeus Mozart,** 1756-91, (Austrian) Chamber music, concertos, operas (Magic Flute, Marriage of Figaro), 41 symphonies.
**Jacques Offenbach,** 1819-80, (Fr.) Tales of Hoffmann.
**Carl Orff,** 1895-1982, (Ger.) Carmina Burana.
**Johann Pachelbel,** 1653-1706, (Ger.) Canon and Gigue in D major.
**Ignacy Paderewski,** 1860-1941, (Pol.) Minuet in G.
**Niccolò Paganini,** 1782-1840, (It.) Caprices for violin solo.
**Palestrina,** c1525-94, (It.) Masses, madrigals.
**Francis Poulenc,** 1899-1963, (Fr.) Dialogues des Carmèlites.
**Sergei Prokofiev,** 1891-1953, (Russ.) Classical Symphony, Love for Three Oranges, Peter and the Wolf.
**Giacomo Puccini,** 1858-1924, (It.) La Boheme, Manon Lescaut, Tosca, Madama Butterfly.
**Henry Purcell,** 1659-95, (Eng.) Dido and Aeneas.
**Sergei Rachmaninov,** 1873-1943, (Russ.) Concertos, preludes (Prelude in c sharp minor), symphonies.
**Maurice Ravel,** 1875-1937, (Fr.) Bolèro, Daphnis et Chloè, Piano Concerto in D for Left Hand Alone.
**Nikolai Rimsky-Korsakov,** 1844-1908, (Russ.) Golden Cockerel, Capriccio Espagnol, Scheherazade, Russian Easter Overture, Flight of the Bumblebee.
**Gioacchino Rossini,** 1792-1868, (It.) Barber of Seville, Othello, William Tell.
**Camille Saint-Saëns,** 1835-1921, (Fr.) Carnival of Animals (The Swan), Samson and Delilah, Danse Macabre.
**Alessandro Scarlatti,** 1660-1725, (It.) Cantatas, oratorios, operas.
**Domenico Scarlatti,** 1685-1757, (It.) Harpsichord works.
**Arnold Schoenberg,** 1874-1951, (Austrian) Pelleas and Melisande, Pierrot Lunaire, Verklärte Nacht.
**Franz Schubert,** 1797-1828, (Austrian) Chamber music (Trout Quintet), lieder, symphonies (Unfinished).

**Robert Schumann,** 1810-56, (Ger.) Die Frauenliebe und Leben, Träumerei.
**Dimitri Shostakovich,** 1906-75, (Russ.) Symphonies, Lady Macbeth of the District Mzensk.
**Jean Sibelius,** 1865-1957, (Finn.) Finlandia.
**Bedrich Smetana,** 1824-84, (Czech.) The Bartered Bride.
**Karlheinz Stockhausen,** b 1928, (Ger.) KontraPunkte, Kontakte for Electronic Instruments.
**Richard Strauss,** 1864-1949, (Ger.) Salome, Elektra, Der Rosenkavalier, Thus Spake Zarathustra.
**Igor Stravinsky,** 1882-1971, (Russ.) Noah and the Flood, The Rake's Progress, The Rite of Spring.
**Toru Takemitsu,** 1930-96, (Jpn.) Requiem for Strings, Dorian Horizon.
**Peter I. Tchaikovsky,** 1840-93, (Russ.) Nutcracker, Swan Lake, The Sleeping Beauty.
**Virgil Thomson,** 1896-1989, (U.S.) Opera, film music, Four Saints in Three Acts.
**Ralph Vaughan Williams,** 1872-1958, (Eng.) Fantasiz on a Theme by Thomas Tallis, symphonies, vocal music.
**Giuseppe Verdi,** 1813-1901, (It.) Aida, Rigoletto, Don Carlo, Il Trovatore, La Traviata, Falstaff, Macbeth.
**Heitor Villa-Lobos,** 1887-1959, (Brazil) Bachianas Brasileiras.
**Antonio Vivaldi,** 1678-1741, (It.) Concerto grossos (The Four Seasons).
**Richard Wagner,** 1813-83, (Ger.) Rienzi, Tannhäuser, Lohengrin, Tristan und Isolde.
**Carl Maria von Weber,** 1786-1826, (Ger.) Der Freischutz.

## Composers of Operettas, Musicals, and Popular Music

**Richard Adler,** b 1921, (U.S.) *Pajama Game; Damn Yankees.*
**Milton Ager,** 1893-1979, (U.S.) I Wonder What's Become of Sally; Hard Hearted Hannah; Ain't She Sweet?
**Arthur Altman,** 1910-94, (U.S.) *All or Nothing at All.*
**Leroy Anderson,** 1908-75, (U.S.) Syncopated Clock.
**Paul Anka,** b 1941, (Can.) My Way; *Tonight Show* theme.
**Harold Arlen,** 1905-86, (U.S.) Stormy Weather; Over the Rainbow; Blues in the Night; That Old Black Magic.
**Burt Bacharach,** b 1928, (U.S.) Raindrops Keep Fallin' on My Head; Walk on By; What the World Needs Now Is Love.
**Ernest Ball,** 1878-1927, (U.S.) Mother Machree; When Irish Eyes Are Smiling.
**Irving Berlin,** 1888-1989, (U.S.) *Annie Get Your Gun; Call Me Madam;* God Bless America; White Christmas.
**Leonard Bernstein,** 1918-90, (U.S.) *On the Town; Wonderful Town; Candide; West Side Story.*
**Eubie Blake,** 1883-1983, (U.S.) *Shuffle Along;* I'm Just Wild About Harry.
**Jerry Bock,** b 1928, (U.S.) *Mr. Wonderful; Fiorello; Fiddler on the Roof; The Rothschilds.*
**Carrie Jacobs Bond,** 1862-1946, (U.S.) I Love You Truly.
**Nacio Herb Brown,** 1896-1964, (U.S.) Singing in the Rain; You Were Meant for Me; All I Do Is Dream of You.
**Hoagy Carmichael,** 1899-1981, (U.S.) Stardust; Georgia on My Mind; Old Buttermilk Sky.
**George M. Cohan,** 1878-1942, (U.S.) Give My Regards to Broadway; You're a Grand Old Flag; Over There.
**Cy Coleman,** b 1929, (U.S.) *Sweet Charity;* Witchcraft.
**Noel Coward,** 1899-1973, (Br.) *Bitter Sweet;* Mad Dogs and Englishmen; Mad About the Boy.
**Neil Diamond,** b 1941, (U.S.) I'm a Believer; Sweet Caroline.
**Walter Donaldson,** 1893-1947, (U.S.) My Buddy; Carolina in the Morning; You're Driving Me Crazy; Makin' Whoopee.
**Vernon Duke,** 1903-69, (U.S.) April in Paris.
**Bob Dylan,** b 1941, (U.S.) Blowin' in the Wind.
**Gus Edwards,** 1879-1945, (U.S.) School Days; By the Light of the Silvery Moon; In My Merry Oldsmobile.
**Sherman Edwards,** 1919-81, (U.S.) See You in September; Wonderful! Wonderful!
**Duke Ellington,** 1899-1974, (U.S.) Sophisticated Lady; Satin Doll; It Don't Mean a Thing; Solitude.
**Sammy Fain,** 1902-89, (U.S.) I'll Be Seeing You; Love Is a Many-Splendored Thing.
**Fred Fisher,** 1875-1942, (U.S.) Peg O' My Heart; Chicago.
**Stephen Collins Foster,** 1826-64, (U.S.) My Old Kentucky Home; Old Folks at Home.
**Rudolf Friml,** 1879-1972, (Czech-U.S.) *The Firefly; Rose Marie; Vagabond King; Bird of Paradise.*
**John Gay,** 1685-1732, (Br.) *The Beggar's Opera.*
**George Gershwin,** 1898-1937, (U.S.) Someone to Watch Over Me; I've Got a Crush on You; Embraceable You.
**Morton Gould,** 1913-96, (U.S.) Fall River Suite, Holocaust Suite, Spirituals for Orchestra, Stringmusic.
**Ferde Grofe,** 1892-1972, (U.S.) Grand Canyon Suite.
**Marvin Hamlisch,** b 1944, (U.S.) The Way We Were, Nobody Does It Better, *A Chorus Line.*
**Ray Henderson,** 1896-1970, (U.S.) *George White's Scandals;* That Old Gang of Mine; Five Foot Two, Eyes of Blue.
**Victor Herbert,** 1859-1924, (Ir.-U.S.) *Mlle. Modiste; Babes in Toyland; The Red Mill; Naughty Marietta; Sweethearts.*
**Jerry Herman,** b 1932, (U.S.) *Hello Dolly; Mame.*
**Brian Holland,** b 1941, **Lamont Dozier,** b 1941, **Eddie Holland,** b 1939, (all U.S.) Heat Wave; Stop! In the Name of Love; Baby, I Need Your Loving.
**Antonio Carlos Jobim,** 1927-94, (Brazil) *The Girl From Ipanema, Desafinado, One Note Samba.*
**Billy (William Martin) Joel,** b 1949, (U.S.) *Just the Way You Are, Honesty,* Piano Man.
**Scott Joplin,** 1868-1917, (U.S.) *Treemonisha.*
**John Kander,** b 1927, (U.S.) *Cabaret; Chicago; Funny Lady.*
**Jerome Kern,** 1885-1945, (U.S.) *Sally; Sunny; Show Boat.*
**Carole King,** b 1942, (U.S.) Will You Love Me Tomorrow?; Natural Woman; One Fine Day; Up on the Roof.
**Burton Lane,** b 1912, (U.S.) *Finian's Rainbow.*
**Franz Lehar,** 1870-1948, (Hung.) *Merry Widow.*
**Jerry Leiber,** & **Mike Stoller,** both b 1933, (both U.S.) Hound Dog; Searchin'; Yakety Yak; Love Me Tender.
**Mitch Leigh,** b 1928, (U.S.) *Man of La Mancha.*
**John Lennon,** 1940-80, & **Paul McCartney,** b 1942, (both Br.) I Want to Hold Your Hand; She Loves You.
**Frank Loesser,** 1910-69, (U.S.) *Guys and Dolls; Where's Charley?; The Most Happy Fella; How to Succeed ....*
**Frederick Loewe,** 1901-88, (Austrian-U.S.) *Brigadoon; Paint Your Wagon; My Fair Lady; Camelot.*
**Andrew Lloyd Webber,** b 1948, (Br.) *Jesus Christ Superstar, Evita, Cats, The Phantom of the Opera.*
**Henry Mancini,** 1924-94, (U.S.) Moon River; Days of Wine and Roses; Pink Panther Theme.
**Barry Mann,** b 1939, & **Cynthia Weil,** b 1937, (both U.S.) You've Lost That Loving Feeling.
**Jimmy McHugh,** 1894-1969, (U.S.) Don't Blame Me; I'm in the Mood for Love; I Feel a Song Coming On.
**Alan Menken,** b 1950, (U.S.) *Little Shop of Horrors.*
**Joseph Meyer,** 1894-1987, (U.S.) If You Knew Susie; California, Here I Come; Crazy Rhythm.
**Chauncey Olcott,** 1858-1932, (U.S.) Mother Machree.
**Jerome "Doc" Pomus,** 1925-91, (U.S.) Save the Last Dance for Me, A Teenager in Love.
**Cole Porter,** 1893-1964, (U.S.) *Anything Goes; Kiss Me Kate; Can Can; Silk Stockings.*
**Smokey Robinson,** b 1940, (U.S.) Shop Around; My Guy; My Girl; Get Ready.
**Richard Rodgers,** 1902-79, (U.S.) *Oklahoma!; Carousel; South Pacific; The King and I; The Sound of Music.*
**Sigmund Romberg,** 1887-1951, (Hung.) *Maytime; The Student Prince; Desert Song; Blossom Time.*
**Harold Rome,** 1908-93, (U.S.) *Pins and Needles; Call Me Mister; Wish You Were Here; Fanny; Destry Rides Again.*
**Vincent Rose,** b 1880-1944, (U.S.) Avalon; Whispering; Blueberry Hill.
**Harry Ruby,** 1895-1974, (U.S.) Three Little Words; Who's Sorry Now?
**Arthur Schwartz,** 1900-84, (U.S.) *The Band Wagon;* Dancing in the Dark; By Myself; That's Entertainment.
**Neil Sedaka,** b 1939, (U.S.) Breaking Up Is Hard to Do.
**Paul Simon,** b 1942, (U.S.) Sounds of Silence; I Am a Rock; Mrs. Robinson; Bridge Over Troubled Waters.
**Stephen Sondheim,** b 1930, (U.S.) *A Little Night Music; Company; Sweeney Todd; Sunday in the Park With George.*
**John Philip Sousa,** 1854-1932, (U.S.) *El Capitan;* Stars and Stripes Forever.
**Oskar Straus,** 1870-1954, (Austrian) *Chocolate Soldier.*
**Johann Strauss,** 1825-99, (Austrian) *Gypsy Baron; Die Fledermaus;* waltzes: Blue Danube, Artist's Life.
**Charles Strouse,** b 1928, (U.S.) *Bye Bye, Birdie; Annie.*
**Jule Styne,** 1905-94, (Br.-U.S.) *Gentlemen Prefer Blondes; Bells Are Ringing; Gypsy; Funny Girl.*
**Arthur S. Sullivan,** 1842-1900, (Br.) *H.M.S. Pinafore, Pirates of Penzance; The Mikado.*
**Deems Taylor,** 1885-1966, (U.S.) *Peter Ibbetson.*
**Harry Tobias,** 1905-94, (U.S.) *I'll Keep the Lovelight Burning.*
**Egbert van Alstyne,** 1882-1951, (U.S.) In the Shade of the Old Apple Tree; Memories; Pretty Baby.
**Jimmy Van Heusen,** 1913-90, (U.S.) Moonlight Becomes You; Swinging on a Star; All the Way; Love and Marriage.
**Albert von Tilzer,** 1878-1956, (U.S.) I'll Be With You in Apple Blossom Time; Take Me Out to the Ball Game.
**Harry von Tilzer,** 1872-1946, (U.S.) Only a Bird in a Gilded Cage; On a Sunday Afternoon.
**Fats Waller,** 1904-43, (U.S.) Honeysuckle Rose; Ain't Misbehavin'.
**Harry Warren,** 1893-1981, (U.S.) You're My Everything; We're in the Money; I Only Have Eyes for You.

**Jimmy Webb,** b 1946, (U.S.) Up, Up and Away; By the Time I Get to Phoenix; Didn't We?; Wichita Lineman.
**Kurt Weill,** 1900-50, (Ger.-U.S.) *Threepenny Opera; Lady in the Dark; Knickerbocker Holiday; One Touch of Venus.*
**Percy Wenrich,** 1887-1952, (U.S.) When You Wore a Tulip; Moonlight Bay; Put On Your Old Gray Bonnet.
**Richard A. Whiting,** 1891-1938, (U.S.) Till We Meet Again; Sleepytime Gal; Beyond the Blue Horizon; My Ideal.
**John Williams,** b 1932, (U.S.) *Jaws, E.T., Star Wars* series, *Raiders of the Lost Ark* series.
**Meredith Willson,** 1902-84, (U.S.) *The Music Man.*
**Stevie Wonder,** b 1950, (U.S.) You Are the Sunshine of My Life; Signed, Sealed, Delivered, I'm Yours.
**Vincent Youmans,** 1898-1946, (U.S.) *Two Little Girls in Blue; Wildflower; No, No, Nanette; Hit the Deck; Rainbow; Smiles.*

# Lyricists

**Howard Ashman,** 1950-91, (U.S.) Little Shop of Horrors, The Little Mermaid.
**Johnny Burke,** 1908-84, (U.S.) What's New?; Misty; Imagination; Polka Dots and Moonbeams.
**Sammy Cahn,** 1913-93, (U.S.) High Hopes; Love and Marriage; The Second Time Around; It's Magic.
**Betty Comden,** b 1919, (U.S.) and **Adolph Green,** b 1915, (U.S.) The Party's Over; Just in Time; New York, New York.
**Hal David,** b 1921, (U.S.) What the World Needs Now Is Love.
**Buddy De Sylva,** 1895-1950, (U.S.) When Day Is Done; Look for the Silver Lining; April Showers.
**Howard Dietz,** 1896-1983, (U.S.) Dancing in the Dark; You and the Night and the Music; That's Entertainment.
**Al Dubin,** 1891-1945, (U.S.) Tiptoe Through the Tulips; Anniversary Waltz; Lullaby of Broadway.
**Fred Ebb,** b 1936, (U.S.) Cabaret, Zorba, Woman of the Year.
**Dorothy Fields,** 1905-74, (U.S.) On the Sunny Side of the Street; Don't Blame Me; The Way You Look Tonight.
**Ira Gershwin,** 1896-1983, (U.S.) The Man I Love; Fascinating Rhythm; S'Wonderful; Embraceable You.
**William S. Gilbert,** 1836-1911, (Br.) The Mikado; H.M.S. Pinafore, Pirates of Penzance.
**Gerry Goffin,** b 1939, (U.S.) Will You Love Me Tomorrow, Take Good Care of My Baby, Up on the Roof.
**Mack Gordon,** 1905-59, (Pol.-U.S.) You'll Never Know; The More I See You; Chattanooga Choo-Choo.
**Oscar Hammerstein II,** 1895-1960, (U.S.) Ol' Man River; Oklahoma; Carousel.
**E. Y. (Yip) Harburg,** 1898-1981, (U.S.) Brother, Can You Spare a Dime; April in Paris; Over the Rainbow.
**Lorenz Hart,** 1895-1943, (U.S.) Isn't It Romantic; Blue Moon; Lover; Manhattan; My Funny Valentine.
**DuBose Heyward,** 1885-1940, (U.S.) Summertime; A Woman Is a Sometime Thing.
**Gus Kahn,** 1886-1941, (U.S.) Memories; Ain't We Got Fun.
**Alan J. Lerner,** 1918-86, (U.S.) Brigadoon; My Fair Lady; Camelot; Gigi; On a Clear Day You Can See Forever.
**Johnny Mercer,** 1909-76, (U.S.) Blues in the Night; Come Rain or Come Shine; Laura; That Old Black Magic.
**Bob Merrill,** b 1921, (U.S.) People; Don't Rain on My Parade.
**Jack Norworth,** 1879-1959, (U.S.) Take Me Out to the Ball Game; Shine On Harvest Moon.
**Mitchell Parish,** 1901-93, (U.S.) Stairway to the Stars; Stardust.
**Andy Razaf,** 1895-1973, (U.S.) Honeysuckle Rose, Ain't Misbehavin', S'posin'.
**Leo Robin,** 1900-84, (U.S.) Thanks for the Memory; Hooray for Love; Diamonds Are a Girl's Best Friend.
**Paul Francis Webster,** 1907-84, (U.S.) Secret Love, The Shadow of Your Smile, Love Is a Many-Splendored Thing.
**Jack Yellen,** 1892-1991, (U.S.) Down by the O-Hi-O; Ain't She Sweet; Happy Days Are Here Again.

# Some Notable Figures of the Past in Dance

**Source:** Reviewed by Gary Parks, Reviews editor, *Dance* magazine

**Alvin Ailey,** 1931-89, (U.S.) modern dancer, choreographer; melded modern dance and Afro-Caribbean techniques.
**Frederick Ashton,** 1904-88, (Br.) ballet choreographer; director of Great Britain's Royal Ballet, 1963-70.
**Fred Astaire,** 1899-1987, (U.S.) dancer, actor; teamed with dancer/actress **Ginger Rogers** (1911-95) in movie musicals.
**George Balanchine,** 1904-83, (Russ.-U.S.) ballet choreographer, teacher; most influential exponent of the neoclassical style, founded, with Lincoln Kirstein, School of American Ballet and New York City Ballet.
**Carlo Blasis,** 1803-78, (It.) ballet dancer, choreographer, writer; his teaching methods are standards of classical dance.
**August Bournonville,** 1805-79, (Dan.) ballet dancer, choreographer, teacher; developed a distinctly Danish style known for its exuberance and lightness.
**Enrico Cecchetti,** 1850-1928, (It.) ballet dancer, teacher of many leading dancers of Russia's Imperial Ballet; his technique is basis for Great Britain's Imperial Society of Teachers of Dancing.
**Gower Champion,** 1921-80, (U.S.) dancer, choreographer, director; with his wife **Marge,** b 1923, (U.S.), choreographed and danced in Broadway musicals and films.
**John Cranko,** 1927-73, (S. African) choreographer; created narrative ballets based on literary works.
**Agnes de Mille,** 1909-93, (U.S.) ballet dancer, choreographer; known for using American themes, she choreographed the ballet *Rodeo* and the musical *Oklahoma.*
**Sergei Diaghilev,** 1872-1929, (Russ.) impresario; founded Les Ballet Russes; saw ballet as an art unifying dance, drama, music, and decor.
**Isadora Duncan,** 1877-1927, (U.S.) expressive dancer who united free movement with serious music; one of the founders of modern dance.
**Fanny Elssler,** 1810-84, (Aust.) ballerina of the Romantic period; known for dramatic skill and sensual style.
**Michel Fokine,** 1880-1942, (Russ.) ballet dancer, choreographer, teacher; rejected strict classicism in favor of dramatically expressive style.
**Margot Fonteyn,** 1919-91, (Br.) prima ballerina, Royal Ballet of Great Britain; famed performance partner of Rudolf Nureyev.
**Bob Fosse,** 1927-87, (U.S.) jazz dancer, choreographer, director; Broadway musicals and film.
**Martha Graham,** 1893-1991, (U.S.) modern dancer, choreographer, created and codified her own dramatic technique.
**Martha Hill,** 1901-95, (U.S.) educator; leading figure in modern dance; founder American Dance Festival.
**Doris Humphrey,** 1895-1958, (U.S.) modern dancer, choreographer, writer, teacher; known for her intellect and choreographic range.
**Robert Joffrey,** 1930-88, (U.S.) ballet dancer, choreographer; cofounded with **Gerald Arpino,** b 1928, (U.S.), the Joffrey Ballet.
**Kurt Jooss,** 1901-79, (Ger.) choreographer, teacher; created expressionist works using modern and classical techniques.
**Tamara Karsavina,** 1885-1978, (Russ.) prima ballerina of Russia's Imperial Ballet and Diaghilev's Ballets Russes; partner of Nijinsky.
**Lincoln Kirstein,** 1907-96 (U.S.) brought ballet as an art form to U.S.; founded, with George Balanchine, School of American Ballet and New York City Ballet.
**Serge Lifar,** 1905-86, (Russ.-F.) premier danseur, choreographer; director of dance at Paris Opera, 1930-45, 1947-58.
**José Limón,** 1908-72, (Mex.-U.S.) modern dancer, choreographer, teacher; developed technique based on that of mentor Doris Humphrey.
**Catherine Littlefield,** 1908-51, (U.S.) ballet dancer, choreographer, teacher; pioneer of American ballet.
**Léonide Massine,** 1896-1979, (Russ.-U.S.) ballet dancer, choreographer; created "symphonic ballet" using concert music previously thought unsuitable for dance.
**Kenneth MacMillan,** 1929-92, (Br.) ballet dancer, choreographer; director of Royal Ballet of Great Britain 1970-77.
**Vaslav Nijinsky,** 1890-50, (Russ.) premier danseur, choreographer; leading member of Diaghilev's Ballets Russes; his ballets were revolutionary for their time.
**Alwin Nikolais,** 1910-93, (U.S.) modern choreographer; created dance theater utilizing mixed media effects.
**Jean-George Noverre,** 1727-1810, (Fr.) ballet choreographer, teacher, writer; his theories on dramatic ballet remain influential; called the "Shakespeare of the dance."
**Rudolf Nureyev,** 1938-93, (Russ.) premier danseur, choreographer; leading male dancer of his generation; director of dance at Paris Opera, 1983-89.
**Ruth Page,** 1903-91, (U.S.) ballet dancer, choreographer; danced and directed ballet at Chicago Lyric Opera.
**Anna Pavlova,** 1881-1931, (Russ.) prima ballerina; toured all over the world with her own company to great acclaim.
**Marius Petipa,** 1818-1910, (Fr.) ballet dancer, choreographer; as ballet master of the Imperial Ballet, he established Russian classicism as leading style of late 19th century.
**Pearl Primus,** 1919-95, (Trinidad-U.S.) modern dancer, choreographer, scholar; combined African, Caribbean, and African-American styles.
**Bill (Bojangles) Robinson,** 1878-1949, (U.S.) tap dancer; called the King of Tapology, he attained fame on stage and screen rare for an African-American of his era.
**Ruth St. Denis,** 1877-1968, (U.S.) interpretive dancer, choreographer, teacher; touring widely, she influenced many early modern dancers.

**Ted Shawn,** 1891-1972, (U.S.) modern dancer, choreographer; teamed with Ruth St. Denis to form Denishawn dance company and school.
**Marie Taglioni,** 1804-84, (It.) ballerina, teacher; in the title role of *La Sylphide* she established the image of the ethereal ballerina.
**Antony Tudor,** 1908-87, (Br.) choreographer, teacher; exponent of the "psychological ballet."
**Mary Wigman,** 1886-1973, (Ger.) modern dancer, choreographer, teacher; influential in European expressionist dance.
**Agrippina Vaganova,** 1879-1951, (Russ.) ballet teacher, director; codified Soviet ballet technique that developed virtuosity.

# Selected Notable Opera Singers of the Past

**Frances Alda,** 1883-1952, (NZ.) soprano
**Paul Althouse,** 1889-1954, (U.S.) tenor
**Pasquale Amato,** 1878-1942, (It.) baritone
**Marion Anderson,** 1902-93, (U.S.) contralto
**Jussi Björling,** 1911-60, (Swed.) tenor
**Lucrezia Bori,** 1887-1960, (It.) soprano
**Maria Callas,** 1923-77, (U.S.) soprano
**Emma Calvé,** 1858-1942, (Fr.) soprano
**Enrico Caruso,** 1873-1921, (It.) tenor
**Feodor Chaliapin,** 1873-1938, (Russ.) bass
**Richard Crooks,** 1900-72, (U.S.) tenor
**Giuseppe De Luca,** 1876-1950, (It.) baritone
**Edouard De Reszke,** 1853-1917, (Pol.) bass
**Jean De Reszke,** 1850-1925, (Pol.) tenor
**Emmy Destinn,** 1878-1930, (Czech.) soprano
**Emma Eames,** 1865-1952, (U.S.) soprano
**Geraldine Farrar,** 1882-1967, (U.S.) soprano
**Kirsten Flagstad,** 1895-1962, (Nor.) soprano.
**Olive Fremstad,** 1871-1951, (Swed.-U.S.) soprano
**Amelita Galli-Curci,** 1882-1963, (It.) soprano
**Mary Garden,** 1874-1967, (Br.) soprano
**Beniamino Gigli,** 1890-1957, (It.) tenor
**Tito Gobbi,** 1913-84, (It.) baritone
**Frieda Hempel,** 1885-1955, (Ger.) soprano
**Maria Jeritza,** 1887-1982, (Czech.) soprano
**Alexander Kipnis,** 1891-1978, (Russ.-U.S.) bass
**Lilli Lehmann,** 1848-1929, (Ger.) soprano
**Lotte Lehmann,** 1888-1976, (Ger.-U.S.) soprano
**Jenny Lind,** 1820-87, (Swed.) soprano
**John McCormack,** 1884-1945, (Ir.) tenor
**Blanche Marchesi,** 1863-1940, (Fr.) soprano
**Nellie Melba,** 1861-1931, (Austral.) soprano.
**Lauritz Melchior,** 1890-1973, (Dan.) tenor
**Zinka Milanov,** 1906-89, (Yugo.) soprano
**Lillian Nordica,** 1857-1914, (U.S.) soprano
**Adelina Patti,** 1843-1919, (It.) soprano
**Peter Pears,** 1910-86, (Eng.) tenor
**Jan Peerce,** 1904-84, (U.S.) tenor
**Ezio Pinza,** 1892-1957, (It.) bass
**Lily Pons,** 1898-1976, (Fr.) soprano
**Rosa Ponselle,** 1897-1981, (U.S.) soprano
**Marcella Sembrich,** 1858-1935, (Pol.) soprano
**Eleanor Steber,** 1916-90, (U.S.) soprano
**Luisa Tetrazzini,** 1871-1940, (It.) soprano
**Lawrence Tibbett,** 1896-1960, (U.S.) baritone
**Richard Tucker,** 1913-75, (U.S.) tenor
**Pauline Viardot,** 1821-1910, (Fr.) mezzo-soprano
**Leonard Warren,** 1911-60, (U.S.) baritone

# Some Notable Blues and Jazz Artists of the Past

**Julian "Cannonball" Adderley**, 1928-75, alto sax
**Louis "Satchmo" Armstrong**, 1900-71, trumpet, singer; originated the "scat" vocal
**Mildred Bailey**, 1907-51, blues singer
**Chet Baker**, 1929-88, trumpet
**Count Basie**, 1904-84, orchestra leader, piano
**Sidney Bechet**, 1897-1959, early innovator, soprano sax
**Bix Beiderbecke**, 1903-31, cornet, piano, composer
**Tommy Benford**, 1906-94, drummer
**Bunny Berigan**, 1909-42, trumpet, singer
**Barney Bigard**, 1906-80, clarinet
**Ed Blackwell**, 1929-92, drummer
**Jimmy Blanton**, 1921-42, bass
**Charles "Buddy" Bolden**, 1868-1931, cornet; formed the first jazz band in the 1890s
**Big Bill Broonzy**, 1893-1958, blues singer, guitar
**Don Byas**, 1912-72, tenor sax
**Cab Calloway**, 1907-94, band leader
**Harry Carney**, 1910-74, baritone sax
**Sidney Catlett**, 1910-51, drums
**Don Cherry**, 1937-95, lyrical jazz trumpeter
**Charlie Christian**, 1919-42, guitar
**Kenny Clarke**, 1914-85, pioneer of modern drums
**Buck Clayton**, 1911-91, trumpet, arranger
**James Cleveland**, 1931-91, gospel singer
**Al Cohn**, 1925-88, tenor sax, composer
**Cozy Cole**, 1909-81, drums
**John Coltrane**, 1926-67, tenor sax innovator
**Eddie Condon**, 1904-73, guitar, band leader; Dixieland
**Tadd Dameron**, 1917-65, piano, composer
**Eddie "Lockjaw" Davis**, 1921-86, tenor sax
**Miles Davis**, 1926-91, trumpet; pioneer of cool jazz
**Wild Bill Davison**, 1906-89, cornet, early Chicago jazz
**Paul Desmond**, 1924-77, alto sax
**Vic Dickenson**, 1906-84, trombone, composer
**Willy Dixon**, 1915-92, songwriter, blues, "You Shook Me"
**Warren "Baby" Dodds**, 1898-1959, Dixieland drummer
**Johnny Dodds**, 1892-1940, clarinet
**Jimmy Dorsey**, 1904-57, clarinet, alto sax; band leader
**Tommy Dorsey**, 1905-56, trombone; band leader
**Roy Eldridge**, 1911-89, trumpet, drums, singer
**Duke Ellington**, 1899-1974, piano, band leader, composer
**Bill Evans**, 1929-80, piano
**Gil Evans**, 1912-88, composer, arranger, piano
**Ella Fitzgerald**, 1918-1996, jazz vocalist, "first lady of song"
**"Red" Garland**, 1923-84; piano
**Erroll Garner**, 1921-77, piano, composer, "Misty"
**Stan Getz**, 1927-91, tenor sax
**Dizzy Gillespie**, 1917-93, trumpet, composer; bop developer
**Benny Goodman**, 1909-86, clarinet, band and combo leader
**Dexter Gordon**, 1923-90, tenor sax; bop-derived style
**Bobby Hackett**, 1915-76, trumpet, cornet
**W. C. Handy**, 1873-1958, composer, "St Louis Blues"
**Coleman Hawkins**, 1904-69, tenor sax; "Body and Soul," 1939
**Fletcher Henderson**, 1898-1952, orchestra leader, arranger
**Woody Herman**, 1913-87, clarinet, alto sax, band leader
**Jay C. Higginbotham**, 1906-73, trombone
**Earl "Fatha" Hines**, 1905-83, piano, songwriter
**Johnny Hodges**, 1906-70, alto sax
**Billie Holiday**, 1915-59, blues singer, "Strange Fruit"
**Sam "Lightnin'" Hopkins**, 1912-82, blues singer, guitarist
**Mahalia Jackson**, 1911-72, gospel singer
**Blind Lemon Jefferson**, 1897-1930, blues singer, guitar
**Little Willie John**, 1937-68, singer, songwriter
**Bunk Johnson**, 1879-1949, cornet, trumpet
**James P. Johnson**, 1891-1955, piano, composer
**Robert Johnson**, 1912-38, blues songwriter, singer,guitarist
**Jo Jones**, 1911-85, drums
**Philly Joe Jones**, 1923-85, drums
**Thad Jones**, 1923-86, trumpet, cornet
**Scott Joplin**, 1868-1917, composer, "Maple Leaf Rag"
**Louis Jordan**, 1908-75, singer, alto sax
**Stan Kenton**, 1912-79, orchestra leader, composer, piano
**Albert King**, 1923-92, blues guitarist
**Gene Krupa**, 1909-73, drums, band and combo leader
**Scott LaFaro**, 1936-61, bass
**Huddie Ledbetter** (Leadbelly), 1888-1949, blues singer, guitar
**Mel Lewis**, 1929-90, drummer, orchestra leader
**Jimmie Lunceford**, 1902-47, band leader, sax
**Jimmy McPartland**, 1907-91, trumpet
**Carmen McRae**, 1920-94, jazz singer
**Glenn Miller**, 1904-44, trombone, dance band leader
**Charles Mingus**, 1922-79, bass, composer, combo leader
**Thelonious Monk**, 1920-82, piano, composer, combo leader; a developer of bop
**Wes Montgomery**, 1925-68, guitar
**"Jelly Roll" Morton**, 1885-1941, composer, piano, singer
**Bennie Moten**, 1894-1935, piano
**Gerry Mulligan**, 1927-96, baritone sax, songwriter, "cool school"
**Turk Murphy**, 1915-87, trombone, band leader
**Theodore "Fats" Navarro**, 1923-50, trumpet
**Red Nichols**, 1905-65, cornet, combo leader
**King Oliver**, 1885-1938, cornet, band leader; teacher of Louis Armstrong
**Sy Oliver**, 1910-88, Swing Era arranger, composer, conductor
**Kid Ory**, 1886-1973, trombone, "Muskrat Ramble"
**Charlie "Bird" Parker**, 1920-55, alto sax, composer; rated by many as the greatest jazz improviser
**Joe Pass**, 1929-94, guitarist
**Art Pepper**, 1925-82, alto sax
**Oscar Pettiford**, 1922-60, a leading bassist in the bop era
**Bud Powell**, 1924-66, piano; modern jazz pioneer

**Don Pullen,** 1942-95, piano; percussive pianist
**Sun Ra**, 1915?-93, big band leader, pianist, composer
**Gertrude "Ma" Rainey**, 1886-1939, blues singer
**Don Redman**, 1900-64, composer, arranger
**Django Reinhardt**, 1910-53, guitar; Belgian gypsy, first European to influence American jazz
**Buddy Rich**, 1917-87, drums, band leader
**Red Rodney**, 1928-94, trumpeter
**Frank Rosollino**, 1926-78, trombone
**Jimmy Rowles,** 1918-96, jazz composer, accompanist
**Jimmy Rushing**, 1903-72, blues singer
**Pee Wee Russell**, 1906-69, clarinet
**Zoot Sims**, 1925-85, tenor, alto sax; clarinet
**Zutty Singleton**, 1898-1975, Dixieland drummer
**Bessie Smith**, 1894-1937, blues singer
**Clarence "Pinetop" Smith**, 1904-29, piano, singer; pioneer of boogie woogie
**Willie "The Lion" Smith**, 1897-1973, stride style pianist
**Muggsy Spanier**, 1906-67, cornet, band leader
**Billy Strayhorn**, 1915-67, composer, piano
**Sonny Stitt**, 1924-82, alto, tenor sax
**Art Tatum**, 1910-56, piano; technical virtuoso
**Art Taylor**, 1929-95, jazz drummer, bandleader
**Jack Teagarden**, 1905-64, trombone, singer
**Dave Tough**, 1908-48, drums
**Lennie Tristano**, 1919-78, piano, composer
**Joe Turner**, 1911-85, blues singer
**Sarah Vaughan**, 1924-90, singer
**Stevie Ray Vaughn**, 1954-90, virtuoso guitarist, singer
**Joe Venuti**, 1904-78, first great jazz violinist
**T-Bone Walker**, 1910-75, guitarist; pioneered electric blues guitar sound
**Thomas "Fats" Waller**, 1904-43, piano, singer, composer
**Dinah Washington**, 1924-63, singer
**Ethel Waters**, 1896-1977, jazz and blues singer
**Muddy Waters**, 1915-83, blues singer, songwriter
**Johnny Watson**, 1935-96, rhythm and blues guitarist
**Chick Webb**, 1902-39, band leader, drums
**Ben Webster**, 1909-73, tenor sax
**Paul Whiteman**, 1890-1967, jazz orchestra leader.
**Charles "Cootie" Williams**, 1908-85, trumpet, band leader
**Mary Lou Williams**, 1914-81, piano, composer
**Teddy Wilson**, 1912-86, piano, composer
**Kai Winding**, 1922-83, trombone, composer
**Jimmy Yancey**, 1894-1951, piano
**Lester "Pres" Young**, 1909-59, tenor sax, composer.

## Noted Country Music Artists of the Past

**Roy Acuff,** 1903-92, guitarist, singer, songwriter, "Precious Jewel"
**Boudleaux Bryant,** 1920-87, songwriter, singer, "Hey Joe"
**"Mother" Maybelle Carter,** 1909-78, singer
**Patsy Cline**, 1932-63, singer
**Vernon Dalhart,** 1883-1948, singer
**Lester Flatt,** 1914-79, singer
**Red Foley,** 1910-68, singer
**Tennessee Ernie Ford**, 1919-91, singer
**Lefty Frizzell,** 1928-75, singer, guitarist
**Kendall L. Hayes,** 1936-95, song writer, "Walk On By"
**Uncle Dave Macon,** 1870-1952, singer, banjo player
**J. D. Miller,** 1923-96, songwriter, "Honky-Tonk Angels"
**Roger Miller,** 1936-92, singer, songwriter, "King of the Road"
**Minnie Pearl,** 1912-96, comedienne, Grand Ole Opry star.
**Jim Reeves,** 1924-64, singer
**Charlie Rich (Silver Fox),** 1932-95, singer, songwriter, "The Most Beautiful Girl"
**Tex Ritter,** 1907-74, singer
**Marty Robbins,** 1925-82, singer, songwriter, "A White Sport Coat and a Pink Carnation"
**Jimmie Rodgers,** 1897-1933, singer
**Fred Rose,** 1898-1954, songwriter, singer, musician, "Blue Eyes Cryin' in the Rain"
**Original Sons of the Pioneers,** Len Slye (Roy Rogers), b 1912, Bob Nolan, 1908-80, singers, songwriters, "Tumbing Tumbleweed"; Tim Spencer, 1905-74, singer, songwriter, "Careless Kisses"; Hugh Farr, 1903-80, Karl Farr, 1909-61, Lloyd Perryman, 1917-77, singers
**Merle Travis,** 1917-83, singer, guitarist, songwriter, "16 Tons"
**Ernest Tubb,** 1914-84, singer
**Conway Twitty,** 1933-93, singer, songwriter
**Dottie West,** 1932-91, singer, songwriter, "Here Comes My Baby"
**Hank Williams Sr.**, 1923-53, singer, songwriter, "Your Cheatin' Heart"
**Bob Wills,** 1905-75, singer, bandleader, songwriter, "San Antonio Rose"

## Some Rock and Roll, Rhythm and Blues, and Rap Artists

**Paula Abdul:** "Forever Your Girl"
**AC/DC:** "Back in Black"
**Ace of Base:** "The Sign"
**Bryan Adams:** "Cuts Like A Knife"
**Aerosmith:** "Sweet Emotion"
**The Allman Brothers Band:** "Ramblin' Man"
**The Animals:** "House of the Rising Sun"
**Paul Anka:** "Lonely Boy"
**The Association:** "Cherish"
**Frankie Avalon:** "Venus"

**The Band:** "The Weight"
**The Beach Boys:** "Good Vibrations"
**Beastie Boys:** "(You Gotta) Fight for Your Right (to Party)"
**The Beatles:** *Sgt. Pepper's Lonely Hearts Club Band*
**The Bee Gees:** "Stayin' Alive"
**Pat Benatar:** "Hit Me With Your Best Shot"
**Chuck Berry:** "Johnny B. Goode"
**The Big Bopper:** "Chantilly Lace"
**Black Sabbath:** "Paranoid"
**Blind Faith:** "Can't Find My Way Home"
**Blondie:** "Heart of Glass"
**Blood, Sweat, and Tears:** "Spinning Wheel"
**Blues Traveler:** "Run Around"
**Gary "U.S." Bonds:** "Quarter to Three"
**Bon Jovi:** "Livin' on a Prayer"
**Booker T. and the MGs:** "Green Onions"
**Earl Bostic:** "Flamingo"
**David Bowie:** *Aladdin Sane*
**Boyz II Men:** "I'll Make Love to You"
**James Brown:** "Papa's Got a Brand New Bag"
**Jackson Browne:** "Doctor My Eyes"
**Buffalo Springfield:** "For What It's Worth"
**Bush:** *16 Stone*
**The Byrds:** "Turn! Turn! Turn!"

**Mariah Carey:** "Vision of Love"
**The Cars:** "Shake It Up"
**Ray Charles:** "Georgia on My Mind"
**Chubby Checker:** "The Twist"
**Chicago:** "Saturday in the Park"
**Eric Clapton:** "Lala"
**The Clash:** "Rock the Casbah"
**The Coasters:** "Yakety Yak"
**Eddie Cochran:** "Summertime Blues"
**Joe Cocker:** "With a Little Help From My Friends"
**Phil Collins:** "Against All Odds"
**Sam Cooke:** "You Send Me"
**Coolio:** "Gangsta's Paradise"
**Alice Cooper:** "School's Out"
**Elvis Costello:** "Alison"
**Cranberries:** "Zombie"
**Cream:** "Sunshine of Your Love"
**Creedence Clearwater Revival:** "Proud Mary"
**Crosby, Stills, Nash, and Young:** "Suite: Judy Blue Eyes"
**The Crystals:** "Da Doo Ron Ron"
**The Cure:** "Boys Don't Cry"

**Danny and the Juniors:** "At the Hop"
**Bobby Darin:** "Splish Splash"
**Spencer Davis Group:** "Gimme Some Lovin'"
**Def Leppard:** "Photograph"
**Depeche Mode:** "Strange Love"
**Bo Diddley:** "Who Do You Love?"
**Dion and the Belmonts:** "A Teenager in Love"
**Celine Dion:** "Because You Loved Me"
**Dire Straits:** "Money for Nothing"
**Fats Domino:** "Blueberry Hill"
**Donovan:** "Mellow Yellow"
**The Doobie Brothers:** "What a Fool Believes"
**The Doors:** "Light My Fire"
**The Drifters:** "Save the Last Dance for Me"
**Duran Duran:** "Hungry Like the Wolf"
**Bob Dylan:** "Like a Rolling Stone"
**The Eagles:** "Hotel California"
**Earth, Wind, and Fire:** "Shining Star"
**Emerson, Lake, and Palmer:** "From the Beginning"
**En Vogue:** "Hold On"
**The Eurythmics:** "Sweet Dreams (Are Made of This)"
**The Everly Brothers:** "Wake Up, Little Susie"
**The Five Satins:** "In the Still of the Night"
**Fleetwood Mac:** *Rumours*
**The Four Seasons:** "Sherry"
**The Four Tops:** "I Can't Help Myself (Sugar Pie, Honey Bunch)"
**Aretha Franklin:** "Respect"
**Peter Gabriel:** "Shock the Monkey"
**Marvin Gaye:** "I Heard It Through the Grapevine"
**Genesis:** "No Reply at All"
**Grand Funk Railroad:** "We're an American Band"
**The Grateful Dead:** "Uncle John's Band"
**Green Day:** *Dookie*
**Guns N' Roses:** "Sweet Child o' Mine"
**Bill Haley and His Comets:** "Rock Around the Clock"
**Hall and Oates:** "Kiss on My List"
**Heart:** "Barracuda"
**Jimi Hendrix:** "Purple Haze"

**Herman's Hermits:** "Mrs. Brown, You've Got a Lovely Daughter"
**Buddy Holly and the Crickets:** "That'll Be the Day"
**Hootie and the Blowfish:** *Cracked Rear View*
**Whitney Houston:** "I Will Always Love You"

**The Impressions:** "For Your Precious Love"
**INXS:** "Need You Tonight"
**The Isley Brothers:** "It's Your Thing"

**The Jackson 5/The Jacksons:** "ABC"
**Janet Jackson:** *Rhythm Nation*
**Michael Jackson:** *Thriller*
**Tommy James & The Shondells:** "Crimson and Clover"
**Jay and the Americans:** "This Magic Moment"
**The Jefferson Airplane/Jefferson Starship:** "White Rabbit"
**Jethro Tull:** *Aqualung*
**Joan Jett:** "I Love Rock 'n' Roll"
**Billy Joel:** "Piano Man"
**Elton John:** "Crocodile Rock"
**Janis Joplin:** "Me and Bobby McGee"

**K.C. and the Sunshine Band:** "Get Down Tonight"
**B. B. King:** "The Thrill Is Gone"
**Carole King:** *Tapestry*
**The Kinks:** "You Really Got Me"
**Kiss:** "Rock 'n' Roll All Night"
**Gladys Knight and the Pips:** "Midnight Train to Georgia"

**Led Zeppelin:** "Stairway to Heaven"
**Brenda Lee:** "I'm Sorry"
**John Lennon:** "Imagine"
**Jerry Lee Lewis:** "Whole Lotta Shakin' Going On"
**Little Anthony and the Imperials:** "Tears on My Pillow"
**Little Richard:** "Tutti Frutti"
**Live:** *Throwing Copper*
**L. L. Cool J:** "Mama Said Knock You Out"
**The Lovin' Spoonful:** "Summer in the City"
**Frankie Lymon and the Teenagers:** "Why Do Fools Fall in Love?"
**Lynyrd Skynyrd:** "Free Bird"

**Madonna:** "Material Girl"
**The Mamas and the Papas:** "Monday, Monday"
**Bob Marley:** "Jamming"
**Martha and the Vandellas:** "Dancin' in the Streets"
**The Marvelettes:** "Please, Mr. Postman"
**Paul McCartney:** "Band on the Run"
**Don McLean:** "American Pie"
**Meat Loaf:** "Paradise By the Dashboard Light"
**John Cougar Mellencamp:** "Jack and Diane"
**Men at Work:** "Who Can It Be Now?"
**Metallica:** "Enter Sandman"
**George Michael:** "Don't Let the Sun Go Down on Me"
**Joni Mitchell:** "Big Yellow Taxi"
**The Monkees:** "I'm a Believer"
**Moody Blues:** "Nights in White Satin"
**Alanis Morrissette:** *Jagged Little Pill*
**Van Morrison:** "Brown-Eyed Girl"

**Rick Nelson:** "Hello, Mary Lou"
**Nine Inch Nails:** "Closer"
**Nirvana:** *Nevermind*

**Oasis** "Wonderwall"
**Roy Orbison:** "Oh, Pretty Woman"
**Ozzy Osbourne:** "Crazy Train"

**Pearl Jam:** "Jeremy"
**Carl Perkins:** "Blue Suede Shoes"
**Peter, Paul, and Mary:** "Leavin' on a Jet Plane"
**Tom Petty and the Heartbreakers:** "Refugee"
**Wilson Pickett:** "Land of 1,000 Dances"
**Pink Floyd:** *The Wall*
**Poco:** *Deliverin'*
**The Police:** "Every Breath You Take"
**Iggy Pop:** "Lust for Life"
**Elvis Presley:** "Love Me Tender"
**The Pretenders:** "Brass in Pocket"
**Lloyd Price:** "Stagger Lee"
**Prince and the Revolution:** "Purple Rain"
**Procol Harum:** "A Whiter Shade of Pale"
**Public Enemy:** "Fight the Power"

**Queen:** "Bohemian Rhapsody"

**The Ramones:** "I Wanna be Sedated"
**Otis Redding:** "(Sittin' on) The Dock of the Bay"
**Red Hot Chili Peppers:** "Under the Bridge"
**Lou Reed:** "Walk on the Wild Side"
**R.E.M.:** "Losing My Religion"
**The Righteous Brothers:** "You've Lost That Lovin' Feelin' "
**Johnny Rivers:** "Poor Side of Town"
**Smokey Robinson and the Miracles:** "Shop Around"
**The Rolling Stones:** "Satisfaction"
**The Ronettes:** "Be My Baby"
**Linda Ronstadt:** "You're No Good"
**Run-D.M.C.:** "Raisin' Hell"
**Salt-N-Pepa:** "Shoop"
**Sam and Dave:** "Soul Man"
**Santana:** "Black Magic Woman"
**Seal:** "Kiss From A Rose"
**Neil Sedaka:** "Breaking Up Is Hard to Do"
**The Sex Pistols:** "Anarchy in the U.K."
**Del Shannon:** "Runaway"
**The Shirelles:** "Soldier Boy"
**Carly Simon:** "You're So Vain"
**Paul Simon:** "50 Ways to Leave Your Lover"
**Simon and Garfunkel:** "Bridge Over Troubled Water"
**Sly and the Family Stone:** "Everyday People"
**Smashing Pumpkins:** "Today"
**Patti Smith:** "Because the Night"
**Soundgarden:** "Black Hole Sun"
**Bruce Springsteen:** "Born to Run"
**Steely Dan:** "Rikki Don't Lose That Number"
**Steppenwolf:** "Born to Be Wild"
**Rod Stewart:** "Maggie Mae"
**Sting:** "If You Love Somebody, Set Them Free"
**Donna Summer:** "Bad Girls"
**The Supremes:** "Stop! In the Name of Love"

**Talking Heads:** "Once in a Lifetime"
**James Taylor:** "You've Got a Friend"
**The Temptations:** "My Girl"
**Three Dog Night:** "Joy to the World"
**TLC:** "Creep"
**Big Joe Turner:** "Shake, Rattle & Roll"
**Tina Turner:** "What's Love Got to Do With It?"

**U2:** "With or Without You"

**Ritchie Valens:** "La Bamba"
**Van Halen:** "Running With the Devil"
**The Velvet Underground:** "Sweet Jane"

**Dionne Warwick:** "I Say a Little Prayer"
**Mary Wells:** "My Guy"
**The Who:** "My Generation"
**Jackie Wilson:** "That's Why"
**Stevie Wonder:** "You Are the Sunshine of My Life"

**The Yardbirds:** "For Your Love"
**Yes:** "Owner of a Lonely Heart"
**Neil Young:** "Down by the River"
**The Young Rascals:** "Good Lovin'"

**Frank Zappa/Mothers of Invention:** *Sheik Yerbouti*

## Entertainment Personalities — Where and When Born

actors, dancers, musicians, producers, directors, radio-TV performers, singers
(as of mid-1996)

| Name | Birthplace | Birthdate | Name | Birthplace | Birthdate |
|---|---|---|---|---|---|
| Abbado, Claudio | Milan, Italy | 6/26/33 | Allen, Joan | Rochelle, IL | 8/20/56 |
| Abdul, Paula | San Fernando, CA | 6/19/62 | Allen, Karen | Carrollton, IL | 10/5/51 |
| Abraham, F. Murray | Pittsburgh, PA | 10/24/39 | Allen, Nancy | New York, NY | 6/24/49 |
| Adams, Bryan | Kingston, Ontario | 11/5/59 | Allen, Steve | New York, NY | 12/26/21 |
| Adams, Don | New York, NY | 4/19/26 | Allen, Tim | Denver, CO | 6/13/53 |
| Adams, Edie | Kingston, PA | 4/16/29 | Allen, Woody | Brooklyn, NY | 12/1/35 |
| Adams, Joey | New York, NY | 1/6/11 | Alley, Kirstie | Wichita, KS | 1/12/55 |
| Adams, Mason | New York, NY | 2/26/19 | Allman, Gregg | Nashville, TN | 12/7/47 |
| Adjani, Isabelle | Paris, France | 6/27/55 | Allyson, June | New York, NY | 10/7/17 |
| Agar, John | Chicago, IL | 1/31/21 | Alonso, Maria Conchita | Cuba | 6/29/57 |
| Agutter, Jenny | London, England | 12/20/52 | Alpert, Herb | Los Angeles, CA | 3/31/35 |
| Aiello, Danny | New York, NY | 6/20/33 | Altman, Robert | Kansas City, MO | 2/20/25 |
| Aimee, Anouk | Paris, France | 4/27/34 | Ames, Ed | Boston, MA | 7/9/27 |
| Albanese, Licia | Bari, Italy | 7/22/13 | Amos, John | Newark, NJ | 12/27/42 |
| Alberghetti, Anna Maria | Pesaro, Italy | 5/15/36 | Amos, Tori | North Carolina | 8/22/64 |
| Albert, Eddie | Rock Island, IL | 4/22/08 | Amsterdam, Morey | Chicago, IL | 12/14/14 |
| Albert, Marv | New York, NY | 6/12/43 | Anderson, Gillian | Chicago, IL | 8/9/68 |
| Alda, Alan | New York, NY | 1/28/36 | Anderson, Harry | Newport, RI | 10/14/49 |
| Alexander, Jane | Boston, MA | 10/28/39 | Anderson, Ian | Dunfermline, Scotland | 8/10/47 |
| Alexander, Jason | Newark, NJ | 9/23/59 | Anderson, Kevin | Illinois | 1/13/60 |
| Allen, Debbie | Houston, TX | 1/16/50 | Anderson, Loni | St. Paul, MN | 8/5/46 |

| Name | Birthplace | Birthdate |
|---|---|---|
| Anderson, Lynn | Grand Forks, ND | 9/26/47 |
| Anderson, Melissa Sue | Berkeley, CA | 9/26/62 |
| Anderson, Richard | Long Branch, NJ | 8/8/26 |
| Anderson, Richard Dean | Minneapolis, MN | 1/23/50 |
| Andersson, Bibi | Stockholm, Sweden | 11/11/35 |
| Andress, Ursula | Bern, Switzerland | 3/19/36 |
| Andrews, Anthony | London, England | 1/12/48 |
| Andrews, Julie | Walton, England | 10/1/35 |
| Andrews, Patty | Minneapolis, MN | 2/16/20 |
| Aniston, Jennifer | Sherman Oaks, CA | 2/11/69 |
| Anka, Paul | Ottawa, Ontario | 7/30/41 |
| Ann-Margret | Stockholm, Sweden | 4/28/41 |
| Applegate, Christina | Los Angeles, CA | 11/25/72 |
| Archer, Anne | Los Angeles, CA | 8/25/47 |
| Arkin, Adam | Brooklyn, NY | 8/19/56 |
| Arkin, Alan | New York, NY | 3/26/34 |
| Armstrong, Billie Joe | Rodeo, CA | 2/17/72 |
| Arnaz, Desi Jr. | Los Angeles, CA | 1/19/53 |
| Arnaz, Lucie | Los Angeles, CA | 7/17/51 |
| Arness, James | Minneapolis, MN | 5/26/23 |
| Arnold, Eddy | Henderson, TN | 5/15/18 |
| Arnold, Tom | Ottumwa, IA | 3/6/59 |
| Arquette, Patricia | New York, NY | 4/8/68 |
| Arquette, Rosanna | New York, NY | 8/10/59 |
| Arroyo, Martina | New York, NY | 2/2/37 |
| Arthur, Beatrice | New York, NY | 5/13/26 |
| Ashley, Elizabeth | Ocala, FL | 8/30/41 |
| Asner, Ed | Kansas City, MO | 11/15/29 |
| Assante, Armand | New York, NY | 10/4/49 |
| Astin, John | Baltimore, MD | 3/30/30 |
| Atkins, Chet | Luttrell, TN | 6/20/24 |
| Attenborough, Richard | Cambridge, England | 8/29/23 |
| Auberjonois, Rene | New York, NY | 6/1/40 |
| Aumont, Jean-Pierre | Paris, France | 1/5/09 |
| Austin, Patti | New York, NY | 8/10/48 |
| Autry, Alan | Shreveport, LA | 7/31/52 |
| Autry, Gene | Tioga, TX | 9/29/07 |
| Avalon, Frankie | Philadelphia, PA | 9/18/39 |
| Ax, Emmanuel | Lvov, Ukraine | 6/8/49 |
| Axton, Hoyt | Duncan, OK | 3/25/38 |
| Aykroyd, Dan | Ottawa, Ontario | 7/1/52 |
| Ayres, Lew | Minneapolis, MN | 12/28/08 |
| Aznavour, Charles | Paris, France | 5/22/24 |
| Bacall, Lauren | New York, NY | 9/16/24 |
| Bacon, Kevin | Philadelphia, PA | 7/8/58 |
| Baez, Joan | Staten Island, NY | 1/9/41 |
| Bain, Conrad | Lethbridge, Alberta | 2/4/23 |
| Baio, Scott | Brooklyn, NY | 9/22/61 |
| Baker, Anita | Toledo, OH | 1/26/58 |
| Baker, Carroll | Johnstown, PA | 5/28/31 |
| Baker, Joe Don | Groesbeck, TX | 2/12/36 |
| Baker, Kathy | Midland, TX | 6/8/50 |
| Bakula, Scott | St. Louis, MO | 10/9/55 |
| Baldwin, Alec | Massapequa, NY | 4/3/58 |
| Baldwin, Daniel | Massapequa, NY | — |
| Baldwin, Stephen | Massapequa, NY | 1966 |
| Baldwin, William | Massapequa, NY | 1963 |
| Ballard, Kaye | Cleveland, OH | 11/20/26 |
| Bancroft, Anne | New York, NY | 9/17/31 |
| Banderas, Antonio | Málaga, Spain | 8/10/60 |
| Bannon, Jack | Los Angeles, CA | 6/14/40 |
| Baranski, Christine | Buffalo, NY | 5/2/52 |
| Barbeau, Adrienne | Sacramento, CA | 6/11/45 |
| Bardot, Brigitte | Paris, France | 9/28/34 |
| Barker, Bob | Darrington, WA | 12/12/23 |
| Barkin, Ellen | New York, NY | 4/16/55 |
| Barrie, Barbara | Chicago, IL | 5/23/31 |
| Barry, Gene | New York, NY | 6/14/19 |
| Barty, Billy | Millsboro, PA | 10/25/24 |
| Barrymore, Drew | Los Angeles, CA | 2/22/75 |
| Bartoli, Cecilia | Rome, Italy | 6/4/66 |
| Bartolucci, Bernardo | Parma, Italy | 3/16/40 |
| Baryshnikov, Mikhail | Riga, Latvia | 1/28/48 |
| Basinger, Kim | Athens, GA | 12/8/53 |
| Bassett, Angela | New York, NY | 8/16/58 |
| Bassey, Shirley | Cardiff, Wales | 1/8/37 |
| Bateman, Jason | Rye, NY | 1/14/69 |
| Bateman, Justine | Rye, NY | 2/19/66 |
| Bates, Alan | Allestree, England | 2/17/34 |
| Bates, Kathy | Memphis, TN | 6/28/48 |
| Battle, Kathleen | Portsmouth, OH | 8/13/48 |
| Baxter, Meredith | Los Angeles, CA | 6/21/47 |
| Beal, John | Joplin, MO | 8/13/09 |
| Bean, Orson | Burlington, VT | 7/22/28 |
| Beasley, Allyce | New York, NY | 7/6/54 |
| Beatty, Ned | Louisville, KY | 7/6/37 |
| Beatty, Warren | Richmond, VA | 3/30/37 |
| Beck, John | Chicago, IL | 1/28/43 |

| Name | Birthplace | Birthdate |
|---|---|---|
| Bedelia, Bonnie | New York, NY | 3/25/48 |
| Begley, Ed Jr. | Los Angeles, CA | 9/16/49 |
| Belafonte, Harry | New York, NY | 3/1/27 |
| Bel Geddes, Barbara | New York, NY | 10/31/22 |
| Belmondo, Jean-Paul | Neuilly-sur-Seine, France | 4/9/33 |
| Belushi, Jim | Chicago, IL | 6/15/54 |
| Belzer, Richard | Bridgeport, CT | 8/4/— |
| Benatar, Pat | Brooklyn, NY | 1/10/53 |
| Benedict, Dirk | Helena, MT | 3/1/45 |
| Bening, Annette | Topeka, KS | 5/29/58 |
| Benjamin, Richard | New York, NY | 5/22/38 |
| Bennett, Tony | New York, NY | 8/3/26 |
| Benson, George | Pittsburgh, PA | 3/22/43 |
| Benson, Robby | Dallas, TX | 1/21/55 |
| Berenger, Tom | Chicago, IL | 5/31/50 |
| Bergen, Candice | Beverly Hills, CA | 5/9/46 |
| Bergen, Polly | Knoxville, TN | 7/14/30 |
| Bergman, Ingmar | Uppsala, Sweden | 7/14/18 |
| Berle, Milton | New York, NY | 7/12/08 |
| Berlinger, Warren | Brooklyn, NY | 8/31/37 |
| Berman, Lazar | Leningrad, Russia | 2/26/30 |
| Berman, Shelley | Chicago, IL | 2/3/26 |
| Bernard, Crystal | Dallas, TX | 9/30/64 |
| Bernhard, Sandra | Flint, MI | 6/6/55 |
| Bernsen, Corbin | N. Hollywood, CA | 9/7/54 |
| Berry, Chuck | St. Louis, MO | 10/18/26 |
| Berry, Halle | Cleveland, OH | 8/14/68 |
| Berry, Ken | Moline, IL | 11/3/33 |
| Bertinelli, Valerie | Wilmington, DE | 4/23/60 |
| Bialik, Mayim | San Diego, CA | 12/12/75 |
| Bikel, Theodore | Vienna, Austria | 5/2/24 |
| Billingsley, Barbara | Los Angeles, CA | 12/22/22 |
| Birney, David | Washington, DC | 4/23/39 |
| Bishop, Joey | Bronx, NY | 2/3/18 |
| Bisset, Jacqueline | Weybridge, England | 9/13/44 |
| Bissett, Josie | Seattle, WA | 10/5/69 |
| Black, Clint | Katy, TX | 2/4/62 |
| Black, Karen | Park Ridge, IL | 7/1/42 |
| Blackstone, Harry Jr. | Three Rivers, MI | 6/30/34 |
| Blades, Ruben | Panama City, Panama | 7/16/48 |
| Blair, Linda | St. Louis, MO | 1/22/59 |
| Blake, Robert | Nutley, NJ | 9/18/33 |
| Bledsoe, Tempestt | Chicago, IL | 8/1/73 |
| Bloom, Claire | London, England | 2/15/31 |
| Blyth, Ann | Mt. Kisco, NY | 8/16/28 |
| Bochco, Steven | New York, NY | 12/16/43 |
| Bogarde, Dirk | London, England | 3/28/20 |
| Bogosian, Eric | Boston, MA | 4/24/53 |
| Bogdanovich, Peter | Kingston, NY | 7/30/39 |
| Bologna, Joseph | Brooklyn, NY | 12/30/38 |
| Bolton, Michael | New Haven, CT | 2/26/53 |
| Bonet, Lisa | San Francisco, CA | 11/16/67 |
| Bonham-Carter, Helena | London, England | 5/26/66 |
| Bon Jovi, Jon | Sayreville, NJ | 3/2/62 |
| Bono (Vox) | Dublin, Ireland | 5/10/60 |
| Bono, Sonny | Detroit, MI | 2/16/35 |
| Boone, Debby | Hackensack, NJ | 9/22/56 |
| Boone, Pat | Jacksonville, FL | 6/1/34 |
| Borge, Victor | Copenhagen, Denmark | 1/3/09 |
| Borgnine, Ernest | Hamden, CT | 1/24/17 |
| Bosson, Barbara | Charleroi, PA | 11/1/39 |
| Bosco, Philip | Jersey City, NJ | 9/26/30 |
| Bosley, Tom | Chicago, IL | 10/1/27 |
| Bostwick, Barry | San Mateo, CA | 2/24/45 |
| Bottoms, Timothy | Santa Barbara, CA | 8/30/51 |
| Bowie, David | London, England | 1/8/47 |
| Boxleitner, Bruce | Elgin, IL | 5/12/50 |
| Boy George | London, England | 6/14/61 |
| Boyle, Peter | Philadelphia, PA | 10/18/33 |
| Bracco, Lorraine | Brooklyn, NY | 1955 |
| Bracken, Eddie | New York, NY | 2/7/20 |
| Branagh, Kenneth | Belfast, No. Ireland | 12/10/60 |
| Brando, Marlon | Omaha, NE | 4/3/24 |
| Brandy (Norwood) | Macomb, MS | 2/11/79 |
| Braugher, Andre | Chicago, Il | 7/1/— |
| Braxton, Toni | Severn, MD | 1968 |
| Brennan, Eileen | Los Angeles, CA | 9/3/35 |
| Brenner, David | Philadelphia, PA | 2/4/45 |
| Brewer, Teresa | Toledo, OH | 5/7/31 |
| Brickell, Edie | Oak Cliff, TX | 1966 |
| Bridges, Beau | Hollywood, CA | 12/9/41 |
| Bridges, Jeff | Los Angeles, CA | 12/4/49 |
| Bridges, Lloyd | San Leandro, CA | 1/15/13 |
| Brimley, Wilford | Salt Lake City, UT | 9/27/34 |
| Brinkley, Christie | Malibu, CA | 2/2/54 |
| Broderick, Matthew | New York, NY | 3/21/62 |
| Brolin, James | Los Angeles, CA | 7/18/40 |
| Bronson, Charles | Ehrenfeld, PA | 11/3/22 |

| Name | Birthplace | Birthdate |
|---|---|---|
| Brooks, Albert | Beverly Hills, CA | 7/22/47 |
| Brooks, Garth | Tulsa, OK | 2/7/62 |
| Brooks, James L | North Bergen, NJ | 5/9/40 |
| Brooks, Mel | New York, NY | 6/28/26 |
| Brosnan, Pierce | Co. Meath, Ireland | 5/16/53 |
| Brown, Blair | Washington, DC | 1948 |
| Brown, Bobby | Boston, MA | 2/5/69 |
| Brown, Bryan | Sydney, Australia | 6/23/47 |
| Brown, James | Pulaski, TN | 6/17/28 |
| Brown, Les | Reinerton, PA | 3/14/12 |
| Browne, Jackson | Heidelberg, Germany | 10/9/48 |
| Browne, Roscoe Lee | Woodbury, NJ | 5/2/25 |
| Brubeck, Dave | Concord, CA | 12/6/20 |
| Bryson, Peabo | Greenville, SC | 4/13/51 |
| Buckley, Betty | Ft. Worth, TX | 7/3/47 |
| Buffett, Jimmy | Pascagoula, MS | 12/25/46 |
| Bujold, Genevieve | Montreal, Quebec | 7/1/42 |
| Bullock, Sandra | Arlington, VA | 7/26/67 |
| Bumbry, Grace | St. Louis, MO | 1/4/37 |
| Burghoff, Gary | Bristol, CT | 5/24/40 |
| Burke, Delta | Orlando, FL | 7/30/56 |
| Burnett, Carol | San Antonio, TX | 4/26/33 |
| Burrows, Darren E. | Winfield, KS | 9/12/66 |
| Burstyn, Ellen | Detroit, MI | 12/7/32 |
| Burton, LeVar | Landstuhl, W Germany | 2/16/57 |
| Burton, Tim | Burbank, CA | 8/25/58 |
| Buscemi, Steve | Brooklyn, NY | 1958 |
| Busey, Gary | Goose Creek, TX | 6/29/44 |
| Busfield, Timothy | Lansing, MI | 6/12/57 |
| Butler, Brett | Montgomery, AL | 1/30/58 |
| Buttons, Red | New York, NY | 2/5/19 |
| Buzzi, Ruth | Westerly, RI | 7/24/36 |
| Byrne, David | Dumbarton, Scotland | 5/14/52 |
| Caan, James | New York, NY | 3/26/39 |
| Caballe, Montserrat | Barcelona, Spain | 4/12/33 |
| Caesar, Sid | Yonkers, NY | 9/8/22 |
| Cage, Nicolas | Long Beach, CA | 1/7/64 |
| Cain, Dean | Mt. Clemmons, MI | 7/31/66 |
| Caine, Michael | London, England | 3/14/33 |
| Caldwell, Sarah | Maryville, MO | 3/6/24 |
| Caldwell, Zoe | Melbourne, Australia | 9/14/33 |
| Calhoun, Rory | Los Angeles, CA | 8/8/23 |
| Cameron, Kirk | Panorama City, CA | 10/12/70 |
| Camp, Hamilton | London, England | 10/30/34 |
| Campanella, Joseph | New York, NY | 11/21/27 |
| Campbell, Glen | Billstown, AR | 4/22/36 |
| Campbell, Naomi | London, England | 5/22/70 |
| Campion, Jane | Wellington, New Zealand | 1955 |
| Cannell, Stephen J. | Los Angeles, CA | 2/5/42 |
| Cannon, Dyan | Tacoma, WA | 1/4/37 |
| Capshaw, Kate | Ft. Worth, TX | 1953 |
| Cara, Irene | New York, NY | 3/18/59 |
| Carey, Drew | Cleveland, OH | 5/23/— |
| Carey, Mariah | Huntington, NY | 3/27/70 |
| Cariou, Len | Winnipeg, Canada | 9/30/39 |
| Carlin, George | New York, NY | 5/12/37 |
| Carlisle, Kitty | New Orleans, LA | 9/3/15 |
| Carmen, Eric | Cleveland, OH | 8/11/49 |
| Carney, Art | Mt. Vernon, NY | 11/4/18 |
| Carpenter, Mary Chapin | Princeton, NJ | 2/21/58 |
| Caron, Leslie | Boulogne, France | 7/1/31 |
| Carr, Vikki | El Paso, TX | 7/19/41 |
| Carradine, David | Hollywood, CA | 10/8/36 |
| Carradine, Keith | San Mateo, CA | 8/8/49 |
| Carreras, Jose | Barcelona, Spain | 12/5/46 |
| Carroll, Diahann | Bronx, NY | 7/17/35 |
| Carroll, Pat | Shreveport, LA | 5/5/27 |
| Carrey, Jim | Jackson Point, Canada | 1/17/62 |
| Carson, Johnny | Corning, IA | 10/23/25 |
| Carter, Benny | New York, NY | 8/8/07 |
| Carter, Dixie | McLemoresville, TN | 5/25/39 |
| Carter, Jack | New York, NY | 6/24/23 |
| Carter, June | Maces Spring, VA | 6/23/29 |
| Carter, Lynda | Phoenix, AZ | 7/24/51 |
| Carter, Nell | Birmingham, AL | 9/13/48 |
| Carter, Ron | Royal Oak Twp, MI | 5/4/37 |
| Caruso, David | Forest Hills, NY | 1/17/56 |
| Carvey, Dana | Missoula, MT | 4/2/55 |
| Casadesus, Gaby | Marseilles, France | 8/9/01 |
| Cash, Johnny | Kingsland, AR | 2/26/32 |
| Cash, Rosanne | Memphis, TN | 5/24/55 |
| Cass, Peggy | Boston, MA | 5/21/24 |
| Cassidy, David | New York, NY | 4/12/50 |
| Cates, Phoebe | New York, NY | 7/16/63 |
| Cavett, Dick | Gibbon, NE | 11/19/36 |
| Chamberlain, Richard | Beverly Hills, CA | 3/31/35 |
| Chan, Jackie | Hong Kong | 4/7/54 |
| Channing, Carol | Seattle, WA | 1/31/23 |
| Channing, Stockard | New York, NY | 2/13/44 |
| Chaplin, Geraldine | Santa Monica, CA | 7/31/44 |
| Chapman, Tracy | Cleveland, OH | 3/30/64 |
| Charisse, Cyd | Amarillo, TX | 3/8/21 |
| Charles, Ray | Albany, GA | 9/23/30 |
| Charo | Murcia, Spain | 1/15/51 |
| Chase, Chevy | New York, NY | 10/8/43 |
| Cheadle, Don | Kansas City, MO | 11/29/96 |
| Checker, Chubby | Philadelphia, PA | 10/3/41 |
| Cher | El Centro, CA | 5/20/46 |
| Chiklis, Michael | Lowell, MA | 8/30/63 |
| Chong, Rae Dawn | Vancouver, Canada | 1962 |
| Chong, Thomas | Edmonton, Alberta | 5/24/38 |
| Christie, Julie | Assam, India | 4/14/40 |
| Christopher, William | Evanston, IL | 10/20/32 |
| Church, Thomas Hayden | El Paso, TX | 6/17/— |
| Clapton, Eric | Surrey, England | 3/30/45 |
| Clark, Dick | Mt. Vernon, NY | 11/30/29 |
| Clark, Petula | Ewell, Surrey, England | 11/15/32 |
| Clark, Roy | Meherrin, VA | 4/15/33 |
| Clark, Susan | Sarnia, Ontario | 3/8/40 |
| Clay, Andrew Dice | Brooklyn, NY | 1958 |
| Clayburgh, Jill | New York, NY | 4/30/44 |
| Cleese, John | Weston-Super-Mare, England | 10/27/39 |
| Cliburn, Van | Shreveport, LA | 7/12/34 |
| Clooney, George | Lexington, KY | 5/6/61 |
| Clooney, Rosemary | Maysville, KY | 5/23/28 |
| Close, Glenn | Greenwich, CT | 3/19/47 |
| Coburn, James | Laurel, NE | 8/31/28 |
| Coca, Imogene | Philadelphia, PA | 11/18/08 |
| Coen, Ethan | St. Louis Park, MN | 9/21/57 |
| Coen, Joel | St. Louis Park, MN | 11/29/54 |
| Cole, Gary | Park Ridge, IL | 9/20/57 |
| Cole, Natalie | Los Angeles, CA | 2/6/50 |
| Cole, Olivia | Memphis, TN | 11/26/42 |
| Coleman, Dabney | Austin, TX | 1/3/32 |
| Coleman, Gary | Zion, IL | 2/8/68 |
| Coleman, Ornette | Fort Worth, TX | 3/9/30 |
| Collins, Joan | London, England | 5/23/33 |
| Collins, Judy | Seattle, WA | 5/1/39 |
| Collins, Pauline | Exmouth, England | 9/3/40 |
| Collins, Phil | London, England | 1/30/51 |
| Comden, Betty | Brooklyn, NY | 5/3/19 |
| Como, Perry | Canonsburg, PA | 5/18/12 |
| Connery, Sean | Edinburgh, Scotland | 8/25/30 |
| Connick, Harry Jr. | New Orleans, LA | 9/11/67 |
| Conniff, Ray | Attleboro, MA | 11/6/16 |
| Connors, Mike | Fresno, CA | 8/15/25 |
| Conrad, Robert | Chicago, IL | 3/1/35 |
| Constantine, Michael | Reading, PA | 5/22/27 |
| Conti, Tom | Paisley, Scotland | 11/22/41 |
| Conway, Tim | Willoughby, OH | 12/15/33 |
| Cook, Barbara | Atlanta, GA | 10/25/27 |
| Cooke, Alistair | Manchester, England | 11/20/08 |
| Coolidge, Rita | Nashville, TN | 5/1/45 |
| Cooper, Alice | Detroit, MI | 2/4/48 |
| Cooper, Jackie | Los Angeles, CA | 9/15/21 |
| Copperfield, David | Metuchen, NJ | 9/16/56 |
| Coppola, Francis Ford | Detroit, MI | 4/7/39 |
| Corbin, Barry | Lamesa, TX | 10/16/40 |
| Corby, Ellen | Racine, WI | 6/3/13 |
| Cord, Alex | New York, NY | 8/3/31 |
| Corea, Chick | Chelsea, MA | 6/12/41 |
| Corelli, Franco | Ancona, Italy | 4/8/23 |
| Corey, Jeff | New York, NY | 8/10/14 |
| Corley, Pat | Dallas, TX | 6/1/30 |
| Cosby, Bill | Philadelphia, PA | 7/12/37 |
| Costas, Bob | New York, NY | 3/22/52 |
| Costello, Elvis | London, England | 8/25/54 |
| Costner, Kevin | Compton, CA | 1/18/55 |
| Courtenay, Tom | Hull, England | 2/25/37 |
| Cox, Courteney | Birmingham, AL | 6/15/64 |
| Coyote, Peter | New York, NY | 1942 |
| Cox, Ronny | Cloudcroft, NM | 8/23/38 |
| Crain, Jeanne | Barstow, CA | 5/25/25 |
| Crawford, Cindy | DeKalb, IL | 2/20/66 |
| Crawford, Michael | Salisbury, England | 1/19/42 |
| Crenna, Richard | Los Angeles, CA | 11/30/26 |
| Crespin, Regine | Marseilles, France | 2/23/26 |
| Cronyn, Hume | London, Ontario | 7/18/11 |
| Crosby, David | Los Angeles, CA | 8/14/41 |
| Cross, Ben | London, England | 12/16/47 |
| Crouse, Lindsay | New York, NY | 5/12/48 |
| Crow, Sheryl | Kennett, MO | 2/11/63 |
| Crowell, Rodney | Houston, TX | 8/17/50 |
| Cruise, Tom | Syracuse, NY | 7/3/62 |
| Crystal, Billy | Long Beach, NY | 3/14/47 |

| Name | Birthplace | Birthdate |
|---|---|---|
| Culkin, Macaulay | New York, NY | 8/26/80 |
| Cullum, John | Knoxville, TN | 3/2/30 |
| Culp, Robert | Oakland, CA | 8/16/30 |
| Cummings, Constance | Seattle, WA | 5/15/10 |
| Curry, Tim | Cheshire, England | 4/19/46 |
| Curtin, Jane | Cambridge, MA | 9/6/47 |
| Curtis, Jamie Lee | Los Angeles, CA | 11/22/58 |
| Curtis, Keene | Salt Lake City, UT | 2/15/23 |
| Curtis, Tony | New York, NY | 6/3/25 |
| Cusack, Joan | Evanston, IL | 10/11/62 |
| Cusack, John | Evanston, IL | 6/28/66 |
| Cyrus, Billy Ray | Flatwoods, KY | 8/25/61 |
| Dafoe, Willem | Appleton, WI | 7/22/55 |
| Dahl, Arlene | Minneapolis, MN | 8/11/28 |
| Dale, Jim | Rothwell, England | 8/15/35 |
| Dalton, Abby | Las Vegas, NV | 8/15/32 |
| Dalton, Timothy | Colwyn Bay, Wales | 3/21/44 |
| Daltrey, Roger | London, England | 3/1/44 |
| Daly, Timothy | Suffern, NY | 3/1/58 |
| Daly, Tyne | Madison, WI | 2/21/47 |
| Damone, Vic | Brooklyn, NY | 6/12/28 |
| Danes, Claire | New York, NY | 4/12/79 |
| D'Angelo, Beverly | Columbus, OH | 11/15/54 |
| Dangerfield, Rodney | Babylon, NY | 11/22/22 |
| Daniels, Charlie | Wilmington, NC | 10/28/36 |
| Daniels, Jeff | Georgia | 2/19/55 |
| Daniels, William | Brooklyn, NY | 3/31/27 |
| Danner, Blythe | Philadelphia, PA | 2/3/44 |
| Danson, Ted | San Diego, CA | 12/29/47 |
| Danza, Tony | New York, NY | 4/21/50 |
| Darby, Kim | Hollywood, CA | 7/8/48 |
| D'Arby, Terence Trent | New York, NY | 3/15/62 |
| Davidson, John | Pittsburgh, PA | 12/13/41 |
| Davis, Ann B. | Schenectady, NY | 5/5/26 |
| Davis, Clifton | Chicago, IL | 10/4/45 |
| Davis, Geena | Wareham, MA | 1/21/57 |
| Davis, Judy | Perth, Australia | 1955 |
| Davis, Mac | Lubbock, TX | 1/21/42 |
| Davis, Ossie | Cogdell, GA | 12/18/17 |
| Dawber, Pam | Farmington Hills, MI | 10/18/51 |
| Dawson, Richard | Hampshire, England | 11/20/32 |
| Day, Doris | Cincinnati, OH | 4/3/24 |
| Day-Lewis, Daniel | London, England | 4/29/57 |
| Dean, Jimmy | Plainview, TX | 8/10/28 |
| De Camp, Rosemary | Prescott, AZ | 11/14/10 |
| DeCarlo, Yvonne | Vancouver, BC | 9/1/22 |
| Dee, Frances | Los Angeles, CA | 11/26/07 |
| Dee, Ruby | Cleveland, OH | 10/27/23 |
| Dee, Sandra | Bayonne, NJ | 4/23/42 |
| DeFranco, Buddy | Camden, NJ | 2/17/23 |
| DeGeneres, Ellen | Metairie, LA | 1/26/58 |
| DeHaven, Gloria | Los Angeles, CA | 7/23/25 |
| De Havilland, Olivia | Tokyo, Japan | 7/1/16 |
| Delany, Dana | New York, NY | 3/11/56 |
| Delaney, Kim | Philadelphia, PA | 1964 |
| DeLaurentis, Dino | Torre Annunziata, Italy | 8/8/19 |
| Delon, Alain | Sceaux, France | 11/8/35 |
| DeLuise, Dom | Brooklyn, NY | 8/1/33 |
| Demme, Jonathan | Rockville Centre, NY | 2/22/44 |
| DeMornay, Rebecca | Santa Rosa, CA | 11/29/61 |
| Deneuve, Catherine | Paris, France | 10/22/43 |
| De Niro, Robert | New York, NY | 8/17/43 |
| Dennehy, Brian | Bridgeport, CT | 7/9/38 |
| Denver, Bob | New Rochelle, NY | 1/9/35 |
| Denver, John | Roswell, NM | 12/31/43 |
| DePalma, Brian | Newark, NJ | 9/11/40 |
| Depardieu, Gerard | Chateauroux, France | 12/27/48 |
| Depp, Johnny | Owensboro, KY | 6/9/63 |
| Derek, Bo | Long Beach, CA | 11/20/56 |
| Derek, John | Hollywood, CA | 8/12/26 |
| Dern, Bruce | Chicago, IL | 6/4/36 |
| Dern, Laura | Santa Monica, CA | 2/1/67 |
| Devane, William | Albany, NY | 9/5/37 |
| DeVito, Danny | Neptune, NJ | 11/17/44 |
| DeWitt, Joyce | Wheeling, WV | 4/23/49 |
| Dey, Susan | Pekin, IL | 12/10/52 |
| Diamond, Neil | Brooklyn, NY | 1/24/41 |
| DiCaprio, Leonardo | Los Angeles, CA | 11/11/74 |
| Dickinson, Angie | Kulm, ND | 9/30/31 |
| Diddley, Bo | McComb, MS | 12/20/28 |
| Diller, Phyllis | Lima, OH | 7/17/17 |
| Dillman, Bradford | San Francisco, CA | 4/14/30 |
| Dion, Celine | Charlemagne, Quebec | 3/30/68 |
| Dillon, Matt | New Rochelle, NY | 2/18/64 |
| Dobson, Kevin | New York, NY | 3/18/44 |
| Doherty, Shannen | Memphis, TN | 4/21/71 |
| Dolenz, Mickey | Los Angeles, CA | 3/8/45 |

| Name | Birthplace | Birthdate |
|---|---|---|
| Domingo, Placido | Madrid, Spain | 1/21/41 |
| Domino, Fats | New Orleans, LA | 2/26/28 |
| Donahue, Phil | Cleveland, OH | 12/21/35 |
| Donahue, Troy | New York, NY | 1/27/36 |
| Dotrice, Roy | Guernsey, England | 5/26/23 |
| Douglas, Kirk | Amsterdam, NY | 12/9/16 |
| Douglas, Michael | New Brunswick, NJ | 9/25/44 |
| Down, Leslie-Ann | London, England | 3/17/54 |
| Downey, Robert Jr. | New York, NY | 4/4/65 |
| Downs, Hugh | Akron, OH | 2/14/21 |
| Dragon, Daryl | Los Angeles, CA | 8/27/42 |
| Drescher, Fran | Queens, NY | 9/30/57 |
| Drew, Ellen | Kansas City, MO | 11/23/15 |
| Dreyfuss, Richard | Brooklyn, NY | 10/29/47 |
| Dryer, Fred | Hawthorne, CA | 7/6/46 |
| Duchovny, David | New York, NY | 3/7/60 |
| Duffy, Julia | Minneapolis, MN | 6/27/51 |
| Duffy, Patrick | Townsend, MT | 3/17/49 |
| Dukakis, Olympia | Lowell, MA | 6/20/31 |
| Duke, Patty | New York, NY | 12/14/46 |
| Dukes, David | San Francisco, CA | 6/6/45 |
| Dullea, Keir | Cleveland, OH | 5/30/36 |
| Dunaway, Faye | Bascom, FL | 1/14/41 |
| Duncan, Sandy | Henderson, TX | 2/20/46 |
| Dunham, Katherine | Joliet, IL | 6/22/10 |
| Dunne, Griffin | New York, NY | 6/8/55 |
| Durbin, Deanna | Winnipeg, Manitoba | 12/4/21 |
| Durning, Charles | Highland Falls, NY | 2/28/23 |
| Dussault, Nancy | Pensacola, FL | 6/30/36 |
| Dutton, Charles S. | Baltimore, MD | 1/30/51 |
| Duvall, Robert | San Diego, CA | 1/5/31 |
| Duvall, Shelley | Houston, TX | 7/7/49 |
| Dylan, Bob | Duluth, MN | 5/24/41 |
| Dysart, Richard | Augusta, ME | 3/30/29 |
| Easton, Sheena | Bellshill, Scotland | 4/27/59 |
| Eastwood, Clint | San Francisco, CA | 5/31/30 |
| Ebert, Roger | Urbana, IL | 6/18/42 |
| Ebsen, Buddy | Belleville, IL | 4/2/08 |
| Eden, Barbara | Tucson, AZ | 8/23/34 |
| Edwards, Anthony | Santa Barbara, CA | 7/19/63 |
| Edwards, Blake | Tulsa, OK | 7/26/22 |
| Edwards, Ralph | Merino, CO | 6/13/13 |
| Eichhorn, Lisa | Reading, PA | 2/4/52 |
| Eikenberry, Jill | New Haven, CT | 1/21/47 |
| Ekberg, Anita | Malmo, Sweden | 9/29/31 |
| Ekland, Britt | Stockholm, Sweden | 10/6/42 |
| Elam, Jack | Miami, AZ | 11/13/16 |
| Elizondo, Hector | New York, NY | 12/22/36 |
| Elliott, Bob | Boston, MA | 3/26/23 |
| Elliot, Chris | New York, NY | 1960 |
| Elliott, Sam | Sacramento, CA | 8/9/44 |
| Enberg, Dick | Auburn Hills, MI | 1/5/35 |
| Englund, Robert | Hollywood, CA | 6/6/48 |
| Elvira (Cassandra Peterson) | Manhattan, KS | 9/17/51 |
| Enya (Eithne Ni Bhraona) | Gweedore, Ireland | 1962 |
| Ephron, Nora | New York, NY | 5/19/41 |
| Estefan, Gloria | Havana, Cuba | 9/1/57 |
| Estevez, Emilio | New York, NY | 5/12/62 |
| Estrada, Erik | New York, NY | 3/16/49 |
| Etheridge, Melissa | Leavenworth, KS | 5/29/61 |
| Evans, Dale | Uvalde, TX | 10/31/12 |
| Evans, Linda | Hartford, CT | 11/18/42 |
| Evans, Robert | New York, NY | 6/29/30 |
| Everett, Chad | South Bend, IN | 6/11/36 |
| Everly, Don | Brownie, KY | 2/1/37 |
| Everly, Phil | Chicago, IL | 1/19/39 |
| Evigan, Greg | S. Amboy, NJ | 10/14/53 |
| Fabares, Shelley | Santa Monica, CA | 1/19/42 |
| Fabian (Forte) | Philadelphia, PA | 2/6/43 |
| Fabio | Milan, Italy | 3/15/61 |
| Fabray, Nanette | San Diego, CA | 10/27/20 |
| Fairbanks, Douglas Jr. | New York, NY | 12/9/09 |
| Fairchild, Morgan | Dallas, TX | 2/3/50 |
| Falana, Lola | Philadelphia, PA | 9/11/46 |
| Falk, Peter | New York, NY | 9/16/27 |
| Farentino, James | Brooklyn, NY | 2/24/38 |
| Fargo, Donna | Mt. Airy, NC | 11/10/45 |
| Farina, Dennis | Chicago, IL | 2/29/44 |
| Farley, Chris | Madison, WI | 2/15/64 |
| Farr, Jamie | Toledo, OH | 7/1/34 |
| Farrell, Eileen | Willimantic, CT | 2/13/20 |
| Farrell, Mike | St. Paul, MN | 2/6/39 |
| Farrow, Mia | Los Angeles, CA | 2/9/45 |
| Faustino, David | California | 3/3/74 |
| Fawcett, Farrah | Corpus Christi, TX | 2/2/47 |

| Name | Birthplace | Birthdate |
|---|---|---|
| Faye, Alice | New York, NY | 5/5/12 |
| Feinstein, Michael | Columbus, OH | 9/7/56 |
| Feldon, Barbara | Pittsburgh, PA. | 3/12/41 |
| Feliciano, Jose | Lares, Puerto Rico | 9/10/45 |
| Fell, Norman | Philadelphia, PA | 3/24/24 |
| Feldshuh, Tovah | New York, NY | 12/27/53 |
| Fenn, Sherilyn | Detroit, MI | 2/1/65 |
| Ferrell, Conchata | Charleston, WV | 3/28/43 |
| Ferrer, Mel | Elberon, NJ | 8/25/17 |
| Fiedler, John | Platville, WI | 2/3/25 |
| Field, Sally | Pasadena, CA | 11/6/46 |
| Fiennes, Ralph | Suffolk, England | 12/22/62 |
| Finney, Albert | Salford, England | 5/9/36 |
| Fiorentino, Linda | Philadelphia, PA | 3/9/60 |
| Firkusny, Rudolf | Napajedla, Czechoslovakia | 2/11/12 |
| Firth, Colin | Grayshott, England | 9/10/60 |
| Firth, Peter | Yorkshire, England | 10/27/53 |
| Fischer-Dieskau, Dietrich. | Berlin, Germany | 5/28/25 |
| Fishburne, Laurence | Augusta, GA | 7/30/61 |
| Fisher, Carrie | Beverly Hills, CA | 10/21/56 |
| Fisher, Eddie | Philadelphia, PA | 8/10/28 |
| Fitzgerald, Geraldine | Dublin, Ireland | 11/24/13 |
| Flack, Roberta | Black Mountain, NC | 2/10/39 |
| Flanagan, Fionnula | Dublin, Ireland | 12/10/41 |
| Fleming, Rhonda | Hollywood, CA | 8/10/23 |
| Fletcher, Louise | Birmingham, AL | 7/22/34 |
| Foch, Nina | Leyden, Netherlands | 4/20/24 |
| Fogelberg, Dan | Peoria, IL | 8/13/51 |
| Foley, Dave | Toronto, Canada | 1/4/— |
| Fonda, Bridget | Los Angeles, CA | 1/27/64 |
| Fonda, Jane | New York, NY | 12/21/37 |
| Fonda, Peter | New York, NY | 2/23/40 |
| Fontaine, Joan | Tokyo, Japan | 10/22/17 |
| Ford, Faith | Alexandria, LA | 9/14/64 |
| Ford, Glenn | Quebec, Canada | 5/1/16 |
| Ford, Harrison | Chicago, IL | 7/13/42 |
| Forsythe, John | Penns Grove, NJ | 1/29/18 |
| Foster, Jodie | New York, NY | 11/19/62 |
| Fox, James | London, England | 5/19/39 |
| Fox, Michael J. | Edmonton, Alberta | 6/9/61 |
| Foxworth, Robert | Houston, TX | 11/1/41 |
| Foxworthy, Jeff | Atlanta, GA | 9/6/57 |
| Frampton, Peter | Kent, England | 4/22/50 |
| Franciosa, Anthony | New York, NY | 10/25/28 |
| Francis, Anne | Ossining, NY | 9/16/30 |
| Francis, Arlene | Boston, MA | 10/20/08 |
| Francis, Connie | Newark, NJ | 12/12/38 |
| Franken, Al | New York, NY | 5/21/51 |
| Frankenheimer, John | Malba, NY | 2/19/30 |
| Franklin, Aretha | Memphis, TN | 3/25/42 |
| Franklin, Bonnie | Santa Monica, CA | 1/6/44 |
| Frann, Mary | St. Louis, MO | 2/27/43 |
| Franz, Dennis | Maywood, IL | 10/28/44 |
| Freeman, Al Jr. | San Antonio, TX | 3/21/34 |
| Freeman, Morgan | Memphis, TN | 6/1/37 |
| Fricker, Brenda | Dublin, Ireland | 2/17/45 |
| Friedkin, William | Chicago, IL | 8/29/39 |
| Frost, David | Tenterden, England | 4/7/39 |
| Funicello, Annette | Utica, NY | 10/22/42 |
| Funt, Allen | New York, NY | 9/16/14 |
| | | |
| Gabor, Zsa Zsa | Budapest, Hungary | 2/6/17 |
| Gabriel, John | Niagara Falls, NY | 5/25/31 |
| Gabriel, Peter | London, England | 2/13/50 |
| Gail, Max | Detroit, MI | 4/5/43 |
| Galway, James | Belfast, Ireland | 12/8/39 |
| Garagiola, Joe | St. Louis, MO | 2/12/26 |
| Garcia, Andy | Havana, Cuba | 4/12/56 |
| Garofalo, Janeane | New Jersey | 9/28/64 |
| Garfunkel, Art | New York, NY | 11/5/41 |
| Garland, Beverly | Santa Cruz, CA | 10/17/26 |
| Garner, James | Norman, OK | 4/7/28 |
| Garr, Teri | Lakewood, OH | 12/11/45 |
| Garrett, Betty | St. Joseph, MO | 5/23/19 |
| Garth, Jennie | Champaign, IL | 4/3/72 |
| Gatlin, Larry | Seminole, TX | 5/2/48 |
| Gayle, Crystal | Paintsville, KY | 1/9/51 |
| Gaynor, Mitzi | Chicago, IL | 9/4/30 |
| Gazzara, Ben | New York, NY | 8/28/30 |
| Geary, Anthony | Coalville, UT | 5/29/47 |
| Geary, Cynthia | Jackson, MS | 3/21/66 |
| Gedda, Nicolai | Stockholm, Sweden | 7/11/25 |
| Gere, Richard | Philadelphia, PA | 8/31/49 |
| Getty, Estelle | New York, NY | 7/25/24 |
| Ghostley, Alice | Eve, MO | 8/14/26 |
| Giannini, Giancarlo | Spezia, Italy | 8/1/42 |
| Gibbons, Leeza | South Carolina | 3/26/57 |
| Gibbs, Marla | Chicago, IL | 6/14/31 |
| Gibson, Debbie | New York, NY | 8/31/70 |
| Gibson, Henry | Germantown, PA | 9/21/35 |
| Gibson, Mel | Peekskill, NY | 1/3/56 |
| Gielgud, John | London, England | 4/14/04 |
| Gifford, Frank | Santa Monica, CA | 8/16/30 |
| Gifford, Kathy Lee | Paris, France | 8/16/53 |
| Gilbert, Sara | Santa Monica, CA | 1/29/75 |
| Gilbert, Melissa | Los Angeles, CA | 5/8/64 |
| Gilberto, Astrud | Salvador, Brazil | 3/30/40 |
| Gill, Vince | Norman, OK | 4/12/57 |
| Gillette, Anita | Baltimore, MD | 8/16/38 |
| Gilley, Mickey | Natchez, MS | 3/9/36 |
| Gilpin, Peri | Waco, TX | 5/27/— |
| Ginty, Robert | New York, NY | 11/14/48 |
| Givens, Robin | New York, NY | 11/27/64 |
| Glaser, Paul Michael | Cambridge, MA | 3/25/42 |
| Glenn, Scott | Pittsburgh, PA | 1/26/42 |
| Gless, Sharon | Los Angeles, CA | 5/31/43 |
| Glover, Crispin | New York, NY | 9/20/64 |
| Glover, Danny | San Francisco, CA | 7/22/47 |
| Glover, Savion | Newark, NJ | 1973 |
| Godard, Jean Luc | Paris, France | 12/3/30 |
| Goldberg, Whoopi | New York, NY | 11/13/49 |
| Goldblum, Jeff | Pittsburgh, PA | 10/22/52 |
| Goldsboro, Bobby | Marianna, FL | 1/18/42 |
| Goldthwait, Bobcat | Syracuse, NY | 5/1/62 |
| Goldwyn, Tony | Los Angeles, CA | 5/20/60 |
| Gooding Jr., Cuba | Bronx, NY | 1968 |
| Goodman, John | St. Louis, MO | 6/20/52 |
| Gorme, Eydie | Bronx, NY | 8/16/32 |
| Gorshin, Frank | Pittsburgh, PA | 4/5/34 |
| Gossett, Louis Jr. | Brooklyn, NY | 5/27/36 |
| Gould, Elliott | Brooklyn, NY | 8/29/38 |
| Gould, Harold | Schenectady, NY | 12/10/23 |
| Gould, Morton | Richmond Hill, NY | 12/10/13 |
| Goulet, Robert | Lawrence, MA | 11/26/33 |
| Gowdy, Curt | Green River, WY | 7/31/19 |
| Graham, Virginia | Chicago, IL | 7/4/12 |
| Grammer, Kelsey | St. Thomas, Virgin Islands | 2/20/55 |
| Granger, Farley | San Jose, CA | 7/1/25 |
| Grant, Amy | Augusta, GA | 12/25/60 |
| Grant, Hugh | London, England | 9/9/60 |
| Grant, Lee | New York, NY | 10/31/29 |
| Graves, Peter | Minneapolis, MN | 3/18/26 |
| Gray, Linda | Santa Monica, CA | 9/12/40 |
| Gray, Spaulding | Barrington, RI | 6/5/41 |
| Grayson, Kathryn | Winston-Salem, NC | 2/9/22 |
| Greco, Jose | Abruzzi, Italy | 12/23/18 |
| Green, Adolph | New York, NY | 12/2/15 |
| Green, Al | Forrest City, AR | 4/13/46 |
| Greene, Shecky | Chicago, IL | 4/8/26 |
| Greenwood, Bruce | Quebec, Canada | 1956 |
| Greer, Jane | Washington, DC | 9/9/24 |
| Gregory, Cynthia | Los Angeles, CA | 7/8/46 |
| Gregory, Dick | St. Louis, MO | 10/12/32 |
| Gregory, James | Bronx, NY | 12/23/11 |
| Grey, Jennifer | New York, NY | 3/22/60 |
| Grey, Joel | Cleveland, OH | 4/11/32 |
| Grier, David Alan | Detroit, MI | 6/30/55 |
| Griffin, Merv | San Mateo, CA | 7/6/25 |
| Griffith, Andy | Mount Airy, NC | 6/1/26 |
| Griffith, Melanie | New York, NY | 8/9/57 |
| Grimes, Tammy | Lynn, MA | 1/30/34 |
| Grizzard, George | Roanoke Rapids, NC | 4/1/28 |
| Grodin, Charles | Pittsburgh, PA | 4/21/35 |
| Groh, David | New York, NY | 5/21/41 |
| Grosbard, Ulu | Antwerp, Belgium | 1/19/29 |
| Gross, Michael | Chicago, IL | 6/21/47 |
| Guest, Christopher | New York, NY | 2/5/48 |
| Guillaume, Robert | St. Louis, MO | 11/30/37 |
| Guinness, Alec | London, England | 4/2/14 |
| Gumbel, Greg | New Orleans, LA | 5/3/46 |
| Guthrie, Arlo | New York, NY | 7/10/47 |
| Guttenberg, Steve | New York, NY | 8/24/58 |
| Guy, Buddy | Lettsworth, LA | 7/30/36 |
| Guy, Jasmine | Boston, MA | 3/10/64 |
| | | |
| Hackett, Buddy | Brooklyn, NY | 8/31/24 |
| Hackman, Gene | San Bernardino, CA | 1/30/30 |
| Hagen, Uta | Gottingen, Germany | 6/12/19 |
| Haggard, Merle | Bakersfield, CA | 4/6/37 |
| Hagman, Larry | Weatherford, TX | 9/21/31 |
| Haid, Charles | San Francisco, CA | 6/2/44 |
| Hale, Barbara | DeKalb, IL | 4/18/22 |
| Hall, Arsenio | Cleveland, OH | 2/12/55 |
| Hall, Daryl | Pottstown, PA | 10/11/48 |
| Hall, Deidre | Milwaukee, WI | 10/31/48 |
| Hall, Huntz | New York, NY | 8/15/19 |
| Hall, Monty | Winnipeg, Manitoba | 8/25/25 |

| Name | Birthplace | Birthdate |
|---|---|---|
| Hall, Tom T. | Olive Hill, KY | 5/25/36 |
| Hamel, Veronica | Philadelphia, PA | 11/20/43 |
| Hamill, Mark | Oakland, CA | 9/25/51 |
| Hamilton, George | Memphis, TN | 8/12/39 |
| Hamilton, Linda | Salisbury, MD | 9/26/56 |
| Hamlin, Harry | Pasadena, CA | 10/30/51 |
| Hammer | Oakland, CA | 3/29/63 |
| Hampton, Lionel | Birmingham, AL | 4/12/13 |
| Hancock, Herbie | Chicago, IL | 4/12/40 |
| Hanks, Tom | Oakland, CA | 7/9/56 |
| Hannah, Daryl | Chicago, IL | 12/3/60 |
| Hardison, Kadeem | New York, NY | 7/24/66 |
| Harewood, Dorian | Dayton, OH | 8/6/51 |
| Harmon, Mark | Burbank, CA | 9/2/51 |
| Harper, Jessica | Chicago, IL | 10/10/49 |
| Harper, Tess | Mammoth Springs, AR | 8/15/50 |
| Harper, Valerie | Suffern, NY | 8/22/40 |
| Harrelson, Woody | Midland, TX | 7/23/61 |
| Harrington, Pat | New York, NY | 8/13/29 |
| Harris, Barbara | Evanston, IL | 7/25/35 |
| Harris, Ed | Englewood, NJ | 11/28/50 |
| Harris, Emmylou | Birmingham, AL | 4/2/47 |
| Harris, Julie | Grosse Pte. Park, MI | 12/2/25 |
| Harris, Neil Patrick | Albuquerque, NM | 6/15/73 |
| Harris, Richard | Co. Limerick, Ireland | 10/1/33 |
| Harris, Rosemary | Ashby, England | 9/19/30 |
| Harrison, George | Liverpool, England | 2/25/43 |
| Harrison, Gregory | Avalon, CA | 5/31/50 |
| Harry, Deborah | Miami, FL | 7/1/45 |
| Hart, Mary | Madison, SD | 11/8/51 |
| Hartley, Mariette | New York, NY | 6/21/40 |
| Hartman, David | Pawtucket, RI | 5/19/35 |
| Hartman, Lisa | Houston, TX | 6/1/56 |
| Hartman, Phil | Ontario, Canada | 9/24/48 |
| Hasselhoff, David | Baltimore, MD | 7/17/52 |
| Hatcher, Teri | Sunnyvale, CA | 12/8/64 |
| Hauer, Rutger | Netherlands | 1/23/44 |
| Haver, June | Rock Island, IL | 6/10/26 |
| Havoc, June | Seattle, WA | 11/8/16 |
| Hawke, Ethan | Austin, TX | 11/6/70 |
| Hawn, Goldie | Washington, DC | 11/21/45 |
| Hayden, Melissa | Toronto, Ontario | 4/25/23 |
| Hayes, Isaac | Covington, TN | 8/20/42 |
| Hays, Robert | Bethesda, MD | 7/24/47 |
| Heard, John | Washington, DC | 3/7/45 |
| Hearn, George | Memphis, TN | 1935 |
| Heckart, Eileen | Columbus, OH | 3/29/19 |
| Helmond, Katherine | Galveston, TX | 7/5/34 |
| Hemingway, Mariel | Mill Valley, CA | 11/21/61 |
| Hemmings, David | Guildford, England | 11/18/41 |
| Hemsley, Sherman | Philadelphia, PA | 2/1/38 |
| Henderson, Florence | Dale, IN | 2/14/34 |
| Henderson, Skitch | Halstad, MN | 1/27/18 |
| Henley, Don | Gilmer, TX | 7/22/47 |
| Henner, Marilu | Chicago, IL | 4/6/52 |
| Henning, Doug | Ft. Garry, Manitoba | 5/3/47 |
| Henry, Buck | New York, NY | 12/9/30 |
| Hepburn, Katharine | Hartford, CT | 5/12/07 |
| Herman, Pee-Wee | Peekskill, NY | 8/27/52 |
| Herrmann, Edward | Washington, DC | 7/21/43 |
| Hershey, Barbara | Los Angeles, CA | 2/5/48 |
| Hesseman, Howard | Lebanon, OR | 2/27/40 |
| Heston, Charlton | Evanston, IL | 10/4/24 |
| Hewett, Christopher | Sussex, England | 4/5/— |
| Hewitt, Jennifer Love | Waco, TX | 2/21/— |
| Hildegarde | Adell, WI | 2/1/06 |
| Hill, Arthur | Melfort, Sask. | 8/1/22 |
| Hill, Steven | Seattle, WA | 2/24/22 |
| Hill, George Roy | Minneapolis, MN | 12/20/22 |
| Hiller, Wendy | Stockport, England | 8/15/12 |
| Hillerman, John | Denison, TX | 12/30/32 |
| Hindman, Earl | Bisbee, AZ | 10/20/— |
| Hines, Gregory | New York, NY | 2/14/46 |
| Hines, Roy | Boston, MA | 3/13/26 |
| Hines, Jerome | Hollywood, CA | 11/8/21 |
| Hingle, Pat | Miami, FL | 7/19/24 |
| Hirsch, Judd | New York, NY | 3/15/35 |
| Hirt, Al | New Orleans, LA | 11/7/22 |
| Ho, Don | Kakaako, Oahu, HI | 8/13/30 |
| Hoffman, Dustin | Los Angeles, CA | 8/8/37 |
| Hogan, Paul | New South Wales, Australia | 10/8/39 |
| Holbrook, Hal | Cleveland, OH | 2/17/25 |
| Holder, Geoffrey | Trinidad | 8/1/30 |
| Holliman, Earl | Delhi, LA | 9/11/28 |
| Holliday, Polly | Jasper, AL | 8/2/37 |
| Holly, Lauren | Bristol, PA | 10/28/63 |
| Holm, Celeste | New York, NY | 4/29/19 |
| Hooker, John Lee | Clarksdale, MS | 8/22/17 |
| Hooks, Jan | Decatur, GA | 4/23/57 |
| Hope, Bob | London, England | 5/29/03 |
| Hopkins, Anthony | Port Talbot, South Wales | 12/31/37 |
| Hopkins, Bo | Greenville, SC | 2/2/42 |
| Hopkins, Telma | Louisville, KY | 10/28/48 |
| Hopper, Dennis | Dodge City, KS | 5/17/36 |
| Horne, Lena | Brooklyn, NY | 6/30/17 |
| Horne, Marilyn | Bradford, PA | 1/16/34 |
| Hornsby, Bruce | Williamsburg, VA | 11/23/54 |
| Horsley, Lee | Muleshoe, TX | 5/15/55 |
| Hoskins, Bob | Suffolk, England | 10/26/42 |
| Houston, Whitney | E Orange, NJ | 8/9/63 |
| Howard, Ken | El Centro, CA | 3/28/44 |
| Howard, Ron | Duncan, OK | 3/1/53 |
| Howell, C. Thomas | Los Angeles, CA | 12/7/66 |
| Howes, Sally Ann | London, England | 7/20/30 |
| Hughes, Barnard | Bedford Hills, NY | 7/16/15 |
| Hulce, Tom | Whitewater, WI | 12/6/53 |
| Humperdinck, Engelbert | Madras, India | 5/3/36 |
| Hunt, Helen | Los Angeles, CA | 6/15/63 |
| Hunt, Linda | Morristown, NJ | 4/2/45 |
| Hunter, Holly | Conyers, GA | 3/20/58 |
| Hunter, Kim | Detroit, MI | 11/12/22 |
| Hunter, Tab | New York, NY | 7/11/31 |
| Hurley, Elizabeth | Hampshire, England | 6/10/65 |
| Hurt, John | Chesterfield, England | 1/22/40 |
| Hurt, Mary Beth | Marshalltown, IA | 9/26/46 |
| Hurt, William | Washington, DC | 3/20/50 |
| Hussey, Ruth | Providence, RI | 10/30/14 |
| Huston, Anjelica | Ireland | 7/8/51 |
| Hutton, Betty | Battle Creek, MI | 2/26/21 |
| Hutton, Lauren | Charleston, SC | 11/17/44 |
| Hutton, Timothy | Malibu, CA | 8/16/60 |
| Hyman, Earle | Rocky Mount, NC | 10/11/26 |
| Ian, Janis | New York, NY | 4/7/51 |
| Idle, Eric | Durham, England | 3/29/43 |
| Idol, Billy | London, England | 11/30/55 |
| Iman | Mogadishu, Somalia | 7/25/55 |
| Iglesias, Julio | Madrid, Spain | 9/23/43 |
| Imus, Don | Riverside, CA | 7/23/40 |
| Ireland, Kathy | Santa Barbara, CA | 3/8/63 |
| Ingram, James | Akron, OH | 2/16/56 |
| Irons, Jeremy | Cowes, England | 9/19/48 |
| Irving, Amy | Palo Alto, CA | 9/10/53 |
| Irving, George S. | Springfield, MA | 11/1/22 |
| Ivey, Judith | El Paso, TX | 9/4/51 |
| Ivory, James | Berkeley, CA | 6/7/28 |
| Jackee | Winston-Salem, NC | 8/14/56 |
| Jackson, Anne | Allegheny, PA | 9/3/25 |
| Jackson, Glenda | Liverpool, England | 5/9/36 |
| Jackson, Janet | Gary, IN | 5/16/66 |
| Jackson, Jermaine | Gary, IN | 12/11/54 |
| Jackson, La Toya | Gary, IN | 5/29/56 |
| Jackson, Kate | Birmingham, AL | 10/29/48 |
| Jackson, Michael | Gary, IN | 8/29/58 |
| Jackson, Milt | Detroit, MI | 1/1/22 |
| Jackson, Samuel L. | Chattanooga, TN | 1949 |
| Jacobi, Derek | London, England | 10/22/38 |
| Jaeckel, Richard | Long Beach, NY | 10/10/26 |
| Jagger, Mick | Dartford, England | 7/26/43 |
| James, Etta | Los Angeles, CA | 1938 |
| James, Dennis | Jersey City, NJ | 8/24/17 |
| Janis, Conrad | New York, NY | 2/11/28 |
| Jarmusch, Jim | Akron, OH | 1/22/53 |
| Jarreau, Al | Milwaukee, WI | 3/12/40 |
| Jarrette, Keith | Allentown, PA | 5/8/45 |
| Jeffreys, Anne | Goldsboro, NC | 1/26/23 |
| Jennings, Waylon | Littlefield, TX | 6/15/37 |
| Jeter, Michael | Lawrenceburg, TN | 8/20/52 |
| Jett, Joan | Philadelphia, PA | 9/22/60 |
| Jewison, Norman | Toronto, Ontario | 7/21/26 |
| Jillian, Ann | Cambridge, MA | 1/29/50 |
| Joel, Billy | Bronx, NY | 5/9/49 |
| John, Elton | Middlesex, England | 3/25/47 |
| Johns, Glynis | Durban, S Africa | 10/5/23 |
| Johnson, Arte | Benton Harbor, MI | 1/20/29 |
| Johnson, Beverly | Buffalo, NY | 10/13/52 |
| Johnson, Don | Flatt Creek, MO | 12/15/49 |
| Johnson, J. J. | Indianapolis, IN | 1/22/24 |
| Johnson, Kristen | Washington, DC | 9/20/— |
| Johnson, Van | Newport, RI | 8/25/16 |
| Jones, Charlie | Ft. Smith, AK | 11/9/30 |
| Jones, Davy | Manchester, England | 12/30/45 |
| Jones, Dean | Morgan City, AL | 1/25/35 |
| Jones, Elvin | Pontiac, MI | 9/9/27 |
| Jones, George | Saratoga, TX | 9/12/31 |

| Name | Birthplace | Birthdate |
|---|---|---|
| Jones, Grace | Spanishtown, Jamaica | 5/19/52 |
| Jones, Henry | Philadelphia, PA | 8/1/12 |
| Jones, Jack | Hollywood, CA | 1/14/38 |
| Jones, James Earl | Tate Co., MS | 1/17/31 |
| Jones, Jennifer | Tulsa, OK | 3/2/19 |
| Jones, Quincy | Chicago, IL | 3/14/33 |
| Jones, Shirley | Smithton, PA | 3/31/34 |
| Jones, Tom | Pontypridd, Wales | 6/7/40 |
| Jones, Tommy Lee | San Saba, TX | 9/15/46 |
| Jourdan, Louis | Marseilles, France | 6/19/19 |
| Judd, Naomi | Ashland, KY | 1/11/46 |
| Judd, Wynonna | Ashland, KY | 5/3/64 |
| Jump, Gordon | Dayton, OH | 4/1/32 |
| Kahn, Madeline | Boston, MA | 9/29/42 |
| Kanaly, Steve | Burbank, CA | 3/14/46 |
| Kane, Carol | Cleveland, OH | 6/18/52 |
| Karlen, John | New York, NY | 5/28/33 |
| Karn, Richard | Seattle, WA | 1956 |
| Karras, Alex | Gary, IN | 7/15/35 |
| Kasem, Casey | Detroit, MI | 1933 |
| Kavner, Julie | Los Angeles, CA | 9/7/51 |
| Kazan, Elia | Istanbul, Turkey | 9/7/09 |
| Kazan, Lainie | New York, NY | 5/15/42 |
| Keach, Stacy | Savannah, GA | 6/2/41 |
| Keaton, Diane | Santa Ana, CA | 1/5/46 |
| Keaton, Michael | Pittsburgh, PA | 9/9/51 |
| Keel, Howard | Gillespie, IL | 4/13/17 |
| Keeshan, Bob | Lynbrook, NY | 6/27/27 |
| Keitel, Harvey | Brooklyn, NY | 5/13/39 |
| Keith, Brian | Bayonne, NJ | 11/14/21 |
| Keith, David | Knoxville, TN | 5/8/54 |
| Kellerman, Sally | Long Beach, CA | 6/2/37 |
| Kelley, DeForest | Atlanta, GA | 1/20/20 |
| Kennedy, George | New York, NY | 2/18/25 |
| Kennedy, Jayne | Washington, DC | 11/27/51 |
| Kenny G | Seattle, WA | 6/5/56 |
| Kent, Allegrara | Los Angeles, CA | 8/11/37 |
| Kercheval, Ken | Wolcottville, IN | 7/15/35 |
| Kerns, Joanna | San Francisco, CA | 2/12/53 |
| Kerr, Deborah | Helensburgh, Scotland | 9/30/21 |
| Kessel, Barney | Muskogee, OK | 1923 |
| Khan, Chaka | Great Lakes, IL | 3/23/53 |
| Kidder, Margot | Yellowknife, N.W.T. | 10/17/48 |
| Kidman, Nicole | Hawaii | 6/20/67 |
| Kiley, Richard | Chicago, IL | 3/31/22 |
| Kilmer, Val | Los Angeles, CA | 12/31/59 |
| Kimbrough, Charles | St. Paul, MN | 5/23/— |
| King, Alan | Brooklyn, NY | 12/26/27 |
| King, B. B. | Itta Bena, MS | 9/16/25 |
| King, Carole | Brooklyn, NY | 2/9/42 |
| King, Larry | Brooklyn, NY | 11/19/33 |
| King, Perry | Alliance, OH | 4/30/48 |
| Kingsley, Ben | Yorkshire, England | 12/31/43 |
| Kinnear, Greg | Logansport, IN | 1964 |
| Kinski, Nastassja | Berlin, W. Germany | 1/24/60 |
| Kirby, Bruno | New York, NY | 4/28/49 |
| Kirby, Durward | Covington, KY | 8/24/12 |
| Kirkland, Gelsey | Bethlehem, PA | 12/29/53 |
| Kitt, Eartha | North, SC | 1/26/28 |
| Klein, Robert | New York, NY | 2/8/42 |
| Klemperer, Werner | Cologne, Germany | 3/22/19 |
| Kline, Kevin | St. Louis, MO | 10/24/47 |
| Klugman, Jack | Philadelphia, PA | 4/27/22 |
| Knight, Gladys | Atlanta, GA | 5/28/44 |
| Knotts, Don | Morgantown, WV | 7/21/24 |
| Konitz, Lee | Chicago, IL | 10/13/27 |
| Kopell, Bernie | New York, NY | 6/21/33 |
| Korman, Harvey | Chicago, IL | 2/15/27 |
| Kotto, Yaphet | New York, NY | 11/15/37 |
| Kramer, Stanley | New York, NY | 9/29/13 |
| Kristofferson, Kris | Brownsville, TX | 6/22/36 |
| Kubelik, Rafael | Bychori, Czechoslovakia | 6/29/14 |
| Kubrick, Stanley | Bronx, NY | 7/26/28 |
| Kudrow, Lisa | Encino, CA | 5/30/63 |
| Kurtz, Swoosie | Omaha, NE | 9/6/44 |
| LaBelle, Patti | Philadelphia, PA | 10/4/44 |
| Ladd, Cheryl | Huron, SD | 7/12/51 |
| Ladd, Diane | Meridian, MS | 11/29/32 |
| Lahti, Christine | Detroit, MI | 4/5/50 |
| Laine, Cleo | Middlesex, England | 10/28/27 |
| Laine, Frankie | Chicago, IL | 3/30/13 |
| Lake, Ricki | New York, NY | 9/21/68 |
| Lamarr, Hedy | Vienna, Austria | 11/9/13 |
| Lamas, Lorenzo | Santa Monica, CA | 1/20/58 |
| Lambert, Christopher | New York, NY | 3/29/57 |
| Landau, Martin | New York, NY | 6/20/34 |
| Landis, John | Chicago, IL | 8/3/50 |
| Lane, Diane | New York, NY | 1/22/63 |
| Lane, Nathan | Jersey City, NJ | 2/3/56 |
| lang, k.d. | Consort, Alberta | 11/2/61 |
| Lang, Stephen | New York, NY | 7/11/52 |
| Lange, Hope | Redding Ridge, CT | 11/28/31 |
| Lange, Jessica | Cloquet, MN | 4/20/49 |
| Langella, Frank | Bayonne, NJ | 1/1/40 |
| Langford, Frances | Lakeland, FL | 4/4/13 |
| Lansbury, Angela | London, England | 10/16/25 |
| Laredo, Ruth | Detroit, MI | 11/20/37 |
| Larroquette, John | New Orleans, LA | 11/25/47 |
| LaSalle, Eriq | Hartford, CT | 6/23/63 |
| Latifah, Queen | East Orange, NJ | 3/18/70 |
| Lauper, Cyndi | New York, NY | 6/20/53 |
| Laurie, Piper | Detroit, MI | 1/22/32 |
| Lavin, Linda | Portland, ME | 10/15/37 |
| Lawrence, Carol | Melrose Park, IL | 9/5/34 |
| Lawrence, Martin | Frankfurt, Germany | 4/16/55 |
| Lawrence, Joey | Montgomery, PA | 4/20/76 |
| Lawrence, Steve | Brooklyn, NY | 7/8/35 |
| Lawrence, Vicki | Inglewood, CA | 3/26/49 |
| Leach, Robin | London, England | 8/29/41 |
| Leachman, Cloris | Des Moines, IA | 4/4/26 |
| Lear, Norman | New Haven, CT | 7/27/22 |
| Learned, Michael | Washington, DC | 4/9/39 |
| LeBlanc, Matt | Newton, MA | 5/25/68 |
| LeBon, Simon | Bushey, England | 10/27/58 |
| Lee, Brenda | Atlanta, GA | 12/11/44 |
| Lee, Christopher | London, England | 5/27/22 |
| Lee, Michele | Los Angeles, CA | 6/24/42 |
| Lee, Pamela Anderson | Comox, Canada | 7/1/67 |
| Lee, Peggy | Jamestown, ND | 5/26/20 |
| Lee, Spike | Atlanta, GA | 3/20/57 |
| Leeves, Jane | East Grinstead, England | 4/13/63 |
| Legrand, Michel | Paris, France | 2/24/32 |
| Leibman, Ron | New York, NY | 10/11/37 |
| Leigh, Janet | Merced, CA | 7/6/27 |
| Leigh, Jennifer Jason | Los Angeles, CA | 2/5/62 |
| Leighton, Laura | Iowa City, IA | 3/14/69 |
| Lemmon, Jack | Boston, MA | 2/8/25 |
| Leno, Jay | New Rochelle, NY | 4/28/50 |
| Leonard, Robert Sean | Westwood, NJ | 2/28/69 |
| Leonard, Sheldon | New York, NY | 2/22/07 |
| Leslie, Joan | Detroit, MI | 1/26/25 |
| Letterman, David | Indianapolis, IN | 4/12/47 |
| Levine, James | Cincinnati, OH | 6/23/43 |
| Levinson, Barry | Baltimore, MD | 6/2/32 |
| Lewis, Huey | New York, NY | 7/5/51 |
| Lewis, Jerry | Newark, NJ | 3/16/26 |
| Lewis, Jerry Lee | Ferriday, LA | 9/29/35 |
| Lewis, John | La Grange, IL | 5/30/20 |
| Lewis, Juliette | San Fernando Valley, CA | 6/21/73 |
| Lewis, Richard | New York, NY | 6/29/47 |
| Lewis, Shari | New York, NY | 1/17/34 |
| Light, Judith | Trenton, NJ | 2/9/50 |
| Lightfoot, Gordon | Orillia, Ontario | 11/17/38 |
| Linden, Hal | New York, NY | 3/20/31 |
| Linkletter, Art | Saskatchewan, Canada | 7/17/12 |
| Linn-Baker, Mark | St. Louis, MO | 6/17/53 |
| Liotta, Ray | Newark, NJ | 12/18/55 |
| Lithgow, John | Rochester, NY | 10/19/45 |
| Little, Rich | Ottawa, Ontario | 11/26/38 |
| Little Richard | Macon, GA | 12/5/32 |
| L. L. Cool J | New York, NY | 1/14/68 |
| Lloyd, Christopher | Stamford, CT | 10/22/38 |
| Lloyd, Emily | England | 9/29/70 |
| Lloyd Webber, Andrew | London, England | 3/22/48 |
| Locke, Sondra | Shelbyville, TN | 5/28/47 |
| Lockhart, June | New York, NY | 6/25/25 |
| Locklear, Heather | Los Angeles, CA | 9/25/61 |
| Loggia, Robert | New York, NY | 1/3/30 |
| Loggins, Kenny | Everett, WA | 1/17/47 |
| Lollobrigida, Gina | Subiaco, Italy | 7/4/27 |
| Lom, Herbert | Prague, Czechoslovakia | 1/9/17 |
| Long, Shelley | Ft. Wayne, IN | 8/23/49 |
| Lord, Jack | New York, NY | 12/30/30 |
| Loren, Sophia | Rome, Italy | 9/20/34 |
| Loring, Gloria | New York, NY | 12/10/46 |
| Loudon, Dorothy | Boston, MA | 9/17/33 |
| Louis-Dreyfus, Julia | New York, NY | 1/13/61 |
| Love, Courtney | San Francisco, CA | 7/9/64 |
| Lovett, Lyle | Klein, TX | 11/1/57 |
| Lovitz, Jon | Tarzana, CA | 7/21/57 |
| Loveless, Patty | Pikeville, KY | 1/4/57 |
| Lowe, Rob | Charlottesville, VA | 3/17/64 |
| Lucas, George | Modesto, CA | 5/14/44 |
| Lucci, Susan | Scarsdale, NY | 12/23/50 |

| Name | Birthplace | Birthdate |
|---|---|---|
| Luckinbill, Laurence | Ft. Smith, AR | 11/21/34 |
| Ludwig, Christa | Berlin, Germany | 3/16/28 |
| Lumet, Sidney | Philadelphia, PA | 6/25/24 |
| LuPone, Patti | Northport, NY | 4/21/49 |
| Lynch, David | Missoula, MT | 1/20/46 |
| Lynley, Carol | New York, NY | 2/13/42 |
| Lynn, Jeffrey | Auburn, MA | 2/16/09 |
| Lynn, Loretta | Butcher Hollow, KY | 4/14/35 |
| Ma, Yo Yo | Paris, France | 10/7/55 |
| Maazel, Lorin | Paris, France | 3/6/30 |
| MacArthur, James | Los Angeles, CA | 12/8/37 |
| MacCorkindale, Simon | Cambridge, England | 2/12/52 |
| MacDowell, Andie | Gaffney, SC | 4/21/58 |
| MacGraw, Ali | Pound Ridge, NY | 4/1/38 |
| MacLachlan, Kyle | Yakima, WA | 2/22/59 |
| MacLaine, Shirley | Richmond, VA | 4/24/34 |
| MacLeod, Gavin | Mt. Kisco, NY | 2/28/30 |
| MacNee, Patrick | London, England | 2/6/22 |
| MacNeil, Cornell | Minneapolis, MN | 9/24/22 |
| MacPherson, Elle | Sydney, Australia | 3/29/64 |
| Macchio, Ralph | Long Island, NY | 11/4/62 |
| Macy, Bill | Revere, MA | 5/18/22 |
| Madden, John | Austin, MN | 4/10/36 |
| Madigan, Amy | Chicago, IL | 9/11/51 |
| Madonna (Ciccone) | Bay City, MI | 8/16/58 |
| Mahoney, John | Manchester, England | 6/20/40 |
| Majors, Lee | Wyandotte, MI | 4/23/40 |
| Malden, Karl | Chicago, IL | 3/22/13 |
| Malkovich, John | Christopher, IL | 12/9/53 |
| Malone, Dorothy | Chicago, IL | 1/30/25 |
| Manchester, Melissa | Bronx, NY | 2/15/51 |
| Mandel, Howie | Toronto, Ontario | 11/29/55 |
| Mandrell, Barbara | Houston, TX | 12/25/48 |
| Mangione, Chuck | Rochester, NY | 11/29/40 |
| Manilow, Barry | New York, NY | 6/17/46 |
| Mann, Herbie | New York, NY | 4/16/30 |
| Manoff, Dinah | New York, NY | 1/25/58 |
| Mantegna, Joe | Chicago, IL | 11/13/47 |
| Marceau, Marcel | Strasbourg, France | 3/22/23 |
| Marchand, Nancy | Buffalo, NY | 6/19/28 |
| Marin, Cheech | Los Angeles, CA | 7/13/46 |
| Marinaro, Ed | New York, NY | 3/31/50 |
| Markova, Alicia | London, England | 12/1/10 |
| Marriner, Neville | Lincoln, England | 4/15/24 |
| Marsalis, Branford | New Orleans, LA | 8/26/60 |
| Marsalis, Wynton | New Orleans, LA | 10/18/61 |
| Marsh, Jean | London, England | 7/1/34 |
| Marshall, E. G. | Owatonna, MN | 6/18/10 |
| Marshall, Garry | New York, NY | 11/13/34 |
| Marshall, Penny | New York, NY | 10/15/43 |
| Marshall, Peter | Huntington, WV | 3/30/27 |
| Martin, Dick | Detroit, MI | 1/30/23 |
| Martin, Steve | Waco, TX | 4/14/45 |
| Martin, Tony | San Francisco, CA | 12/25/13 |
| Martins, Peter | Copenhagen, Denmark | 10/27/46 |
| Mason, Jackie | Sheboygan, WI | 6/9/31 |
| Mason, Marsha | St. Louis, MO | 4/3/42 |
| Masterson, Mary Stuart | Los Angeles, CA | 6/28/66 |
| Mastrantonio, Mary Eliz. | Lombard, IL | 11/17/58 |
| Mastroianni, Marcello | Rome, Italy | 9/28/23 |
| Masur, Kurt | Brieg, Germany | 7/18/27 |
| Masur, Richard | New York, NY | 11/20/48 |
| Mathers, Jerry | Sioux City, IA | 6/2/48 |
| Matheson, Tim | Glendale, CA | 12/31/47 |
| Mathis, Johnny | San Francisco, CA | 9/30/35 |
| Matlin, Marlee | Morton Grove, IL | 8/24/65 |
| Mattea, Kathy | Cross Lanes, WV | — |
| Matthau, Walter | New York, NY | 10/1/20 |
| Mature, Victor | Louisville, KY | 1/29/16 |
| May, Elaine | Philadelphia, PA | 4/21/32 |
| Mayfield, Curtis | Chicago, IL | 6/3/42 |
| Mayo, Virginia | St. Louis, MO | 11/30/20 |
| Mazursky, Paul | Brooklyn, NY | 4/25/30 |
| McArdle, Andrea | Philadelphia, PA | 11/5/63 |
| McBride, Patricia | Teaneck, NJ | 8/23/42 |
| McCallum, David | Glasgow, Scotland | 9/19/33 |
| McCambridge, Mercedes | Joliet, IL | 3/17/18 |
| McCarthy, Andrew | Westfield, NJ | 11/29/62 |
| McCarthy, Jenny | Chicago, IL | 1973 |
| McCarthy, Kevin | Seattle, WA | 2/15/14 |
| McCartney, Paul | Liverpool, England | 6/18/42 |
| McCarver, Tim | Memphis, TN | 10/16/41 |
| McClanahan, Rue | Healdton, OK | 2/21/36 |
| McConaughey, Matthew | Uvalde, Texas | 1969 |
| McCoo, Marilyn | Jersey City, NJ | 9/30/43 |
| McDonnell, Mary | Wilkes-Barre, PA | 1952 |
| McDowall, Roddy | London, England | 9/28/28 |
| McDowell, Malcolm | Leeds, England | 6/13/43 |
| McEntire, Reba | McAlester, OK | 3/28/55 |
| McFerrin, Bobby | New York, NY | 3/11/50 |
| McGavin, Darren | Spokane, WA | 5/7/22 |
| McGillis, Kelly | Newport Beach, CA | 7/9/57 |
| McGoohan, Patrick | New York, NY | 3/19/28 |
| McGovern, Elizabeth | Evanston, IL | 7/18/61 |
| McGovern, Maureen | Youngstown, OH | 7/27/49 |
| McGuire, Al | New York, NY | 9/7/31 |
| McGuire, Dorothy | Omaha, NE | 6/14/19 |
| McKean, Michael | New York, NY | 10/17/47 |
| McKechnie, Donna | Pontiac, MI | 11/16/42 |
| McKellen, Ian | Burnley, England | 5/25/39 |
| McMahon, Ed | Detroit, MI | 3/6/23 |
| McNichol, Kristy | Los Angeles, CA | 9/11/62 |
| McParland, Marion | Stough, England | 3/20/20 |
| McRaney, Gerald | Collins, MS | 8/19/48 |
| Meadows, Jayne | Wu Chang, China | 9/27/20 |
| Meara, Anne | New York, NY | 9/20/29 |
| Meat Loaf | Dallas, TX | 9/27/47 |
| Mehta, Zubin | Bombay, India | 4/29/36 |
| Mellencamp, John | Seymour, IN | 10/7/51 |
| Mendes, Sergio | Niteroi, Brazil | 2/11/41 |
| Menuhin, Yehudi | New York, NY | 4/22/16 |
| Mercer, Marian | Akron, OH | 11/26/35 |
| Merchant, Natalie | Jamestown, NY | 10/26/63 |
| Meredith, Burgess | Cleveland, OH | 11/16/09 |
| Merrick, David | St. Louis, MO | 11/27/12 |
| Merrill, Dina | New York, NY | 12/9/25 |
| Merrill, Robert | Brooklyn, NY | 6/4/19 |
| Messina, Jim | Maywood, CA | 12/5/47 |
| Metcalf, Laurie | Carbondale, IL | 6/16/55 |
| Michael, George | Watford, England | 6/26/63 |
| Michaels, Al | New York, NY | 11/12/44 |
| Michaels, Lorne | Toronto, Canada | 11/17/44 |
| Midler, Bette | Paterson, NJ | 12/1/45 |
| Midori | Osaka, Japan | 10/25/71 |
| Milano, Alyssa | New York, NY | 12/19/72 |
| Miles, Sarah | Ingatestone, England | 12/31/41 |
| Miles, Vera | near Boise City, OK | 8/23/29 |
| Miller, Ann | Houston, TX | 4/12/19 |
| Miller, Dennis | Pittsburgh, PA | 11/3/53 |
| Miller, Mitch | Rochester, NY | 7/4/11 |
| Miller, Penelope Ann | Los Angeles, CA | 1/13/64 |
| Mills, Donna | Chicago, IL | 12/11/42 |
| Mills, John | Suffolk, England | 2/22/08 |
| Milner, Martin | Detroit, MI | 12/28/27 |
| Milnes, Sherrill | Downers Grove, IL | 1/10/35 |
| Milsap, Ronnie | Robinsville, NC | 1/16/44 |
| Minnelli, Liza | Los Angeles, CA | 3/12/46 |
| Mirren, Helen | London, England | 7/2/46 |
| Mitchell, Joni | McLeod, Alberta | 11/7/43 |
| Mitchum, Robert | Bridgeport, CT | 8/6/17 |
| Modine, Matthew | Loma Linda, CA | 3/22/59 |
| Moffat, Donald | Plymouth, England | 12/26/30 |
| Moffo, Anna | Wayne, PA | 6/27/27 |
| Molinaro, Al | Kenosha, WI | 6/24/19 |
| Moll, Richard | Pasadena, CA | 1/13/43 |
| Montalban, Ricardo | Mexico City, Mexico | 11/25/20 |
| Moody, Ron | London, England | 1/8/24 |
| Moore, Clayton | Chicago, IL | 9/14/08 |
| Moore, Demi | Roswell, NM | 11/11/62 |
| Moore, Dudley | London, England | 4/19/35 |
| Moore, Mary Tyler | Brooklyn, NY | 12/29/37 |
| Moore, Melba | New York, NY | 10/29/45 |
| Moore, Roger | London, England | 10/14/27 |
| Moore, Terry | Los Angeles, CA | 1/1/29 |
| Moranis, Rick | Toronto, Ontario | 4/18/53 |
| Moreno, Rita | Humacao, PR | 12/11/31 |
| Morgan, Harry | Detroit, MI | 4/10/15 |
| Moriarty, Michael | Detroit, MI | 4/5/41 |
| Morissette, Alanis | Ottawa, Ontario | 1975 |
| Morita, Pat | Isleton, CA | 6/28/32 |
| Morris, Howard | New York, NY | 9/4/25 |
| Morrison, Van | Belfast, Northern Ireland | 8/31/45 |
| Morrissey | Manchester, England | 5/22/59 |
| Morrow, Rob | New Rochelle, NY | 9/21/62 |
| Morse, Robert | Newton, MA | 5/18/31 |
| Morton, Joe | New York, NY | 10/18/47 |
| Moses, William | Los Angeles, CA | 11/17/59 |
| Moss, Kate | London, England | 1/16/74 |
| Muldaur, Diana | New York, NY | 8/19/38 |
| Mulgrew, Kate | Dubuque, IA | 4/29/55 |
| Mulhare, Edward | Ireland | 4/8/23 |
| Mull, Martin | Chicago, IL | 8/18/43 |
| Mulligan, Richard | New York, NY | 11/13/32 |
| Munsel, Patrice | Spokane, WA | 5/14/25 |
| Murphy, Ben | Jonesboro, AR | 3/6/42 |

| Name | Birthplace | Birthdate |
|---|---|---|
| Murphy, Eddie | Brooklyn, NY | 4/3/61 |
| Murphy, Michael | Los Angeles, CA | 5/5/38 |
| Murray, Anne | Springhill, Nova Scotia | 6/20/45 |
| Murray, Bill | Evanston, IL | 9/21/50 |
| Murray, Don | Hollywood, CA | 7/31/29 |
| Musburger, Brent | Portland, OR | 5/26/39 |
| Muti, Riccardo | Naples, Italy | 7/28/41 |
| Myers, Mike | Toronto, Ontario | 5/23/63 |
| Nabors, Jim | Sylacauga, AL | 6/12/33 |
| Nash, Graham | Blackpool, England | 2/2/42 |
| Naughton, James | Middletown, CT | 7/6/46 |
| Neal, Patricia | Packard, KY | 1/20/26 |
| Nealon, Kevin | Bridgeport, CT | 11/18/53 |
| Neeson, Liam | Ballymena, N. Ireland | 6/7/52 |
| Neill, Sam | New Zealand | 9/14/47 |
| Nelligan, Kate | London, Ontario | 3/16/51 |
| Nelson, Craig T. | Spokane, WA | 4/4/46 |
| Nelson, Ed | New Orleans, LA | 12/21/28 |
| Nelson, Judd | Portland, ME | 11/28/59 |
| Nelson, Tracy | Santa Monica, CA | 10/25/63 |
| Nelson, Willie | Abbott, TX | 4/30/33 |
| Nero, Peter | New York, NY | 5/22/34 |
| Nesmith, Mike | Dallas, TX | 12/30/42 |
| Neuwirth, Bebe | Princeton, NJ | 12/31/— |
| Neville, Aaron | New Orleans, LA | 1/24/41 |
| Newhart, Bob | Oak Park, IL | 9/29/29 |
| Newley, Anthony | Hackney, England | 9/24/31 |
| Newman, Paul | Cleveland, OH | 1/26/25 |
| Newman, Randy | Los Angeles, CA | 11/28/43 |
| Newton, Wayne | Norfolk, VA | 4/3/42 |
| Newton-John, Olivia | Cambridge, England | 9/26/47 |
| Nicholas, Denise | Detroit, MI | 7/12/44 |
| Nicholas, Fayard | Philadelphia, PA | 10/20/14 |
| Nicholas, Harold | Philadelphia, PA | 3/27/24 |
| Nichols, Mike | Berlin, Germany | 11/6/31 |
| Nicholson, Jack | Neptune, NJ | 4/28/37 |
| Nicks, Stevie | Phoenix, AZ | 5/26/48 |
| Nielsen, Leslie | Regina, Sask | 2/11/26 |
| Nilsson, Birgit | Karup, Sweden | 5/17/18 |
| Nimoy, Leonard | Boston, MA | 3/26/31 |
| Nolte, Nick | Omaha, NE | 2/8/40 |
| Norman, Jessye | Augusta, GA | 9/15/45 |
| Norris, Chuck | Ryan, OK | 3/10/40 |
| North, Sheree | Los Angeles, CA | 1/17/33 |
| Noth, Christopher | Madison, WI | 11/13/— |
| Novak, Kim | Chicago, IL | 2/13/33 |
| Oates, John | New York, NY | 4/7/48 |
| O'Brian, Hugh | Rochester, NY | 4/19/25 |
| O'Brien, Conan | Brookline, MA | 4/18/63 |
| O'Brien, Margaret | San Diego, CA | 1/15/37 |
| Ocean, Billy | Fyzabad, Trinidad | 1/21/50 |
| O'Connor, Carroll | New York, NY | 8/2/24 |
| O'Connor, Donald | Chicago, IL | 8/28/25 |
| O'Connor, Sinead | Dublin, Ireland | 12/8/66 |
| Odetta | Birmingham, AL | 12/31/30 |
| O'Donnell, Chris | Winnetka, IL | 6/26/70 |
| O'Donnell, Rosie | Commack, NY | 1962 |
| O'Hara, Maureen | Dublin, Ireland | 8/17/20 |
| O'Herlihy, Dan | Wexford, Ireland | 5/1/19 |
| Oldman, Gary | London, England | 3/21/58 |
| Olin, Ken | Chicago, IL | 7/30/54 |
| Olin, Lena | Stockholm, Sweden | 3/22/55 |
| Olmos, Edward James | E. Los Angeles, CA | 2/24/47 |
| Olsen, Ashley | California | 6/13/86 |
| Olsen, Mary-Kate | California | 6/13/86 |
| Olsen, Merlin | Logan, UT | 9/15/40 |
| O'Neal, Ryan | Los Angeles, CA | 4/20/41 |
| O'Neal, Tatum | Los Angeles, CA | 11/5/63 |
| O'Neill, Ed | Youngstown, OH | 4/12/46 |
| Ontkean, Michael | Vancouver, B.C. | 1/24/46 |
| Orbach, Jerry | New York, NY | 10/20/35 |
| Orlando, Tony | New York, NY | 4/3/44 |
| Ormond, Julia | Epsom, England | 1965 |
| Osbourne, Ozzy | Birmingham, England | 12/3/46 |
| O'Shea, Milo | Dublin, Ireland | 6/2/26 |
| Oslin, K.T. | Crosset, AR | 1942 |
| Osmond, Donny | Ogden, UT | 12/9/57 |
| Osmond, Marie | Ogden, UT | 10/13/59 |
| O'Sullivan, Maureen | Boyle, Ireland | 5/17/11 |
| O'Toole, Annette | Houston, TX | 4/1/53 |
| O'Toole, Peter | Connemara, Ireland | 8/2/32 |
| Owens, Buck | Sherman, TX | 8/12/29 |
| Oz, Frank | Herford, England | 5/25/44 |
| Ozawa, Seiji | Shenyang, China | 9/1/35 |
| Paar, Jack | Canton, OH | 5/1/18 |
| Pacino, Al | New York, NY | 4/25/40 |

| Name | Birthplace | Birthdate |
|---|---|---|
| Packer, Billy | Wellsville, NY | 2/25/40 |
| Page, Jimmy | Heston, England | 1/9/44 |
| Page, Patti | Claremore, OK | 11/8/27 |
| Paige, Janis | Tacoma, WA | 9/16/22 |
| Palance, Jack | Lattimer, PA | 2/18/20 |
| Palin, Michael | England | 5/5/43 |
| Palmer, Betsy | East Chicago, IN | 11/1/29 |
| Palmer, Robert | Bately, England | 1/19/49 |
| Palminteri, Chazz | Bronx, NY | 5/15/51 |
| Paltrow, Gwyneth | Los Angeles, CA | 9/28/73 |
| Papas, Irene | Chiliomedion, Greece | 3/9/26 |
| Paquin, Anna | Wellington, New Zealand | 1983 |
| Parker, Alan | London, England | 2/14/44 |
| Parker, Eleanor | Cedarville, OH | 6/26/22 |
| Parker, Fess | Ft. Worth, TX | 8/16/25 |
| Parker, Jameson | Baltimore, MD | 11/18/47 |
| Parker, Jean | Deer Lodge, MT | 8/11/12 |
| Parker, Mary-Louise | Fort Jackson, SC | 8/2/64 |
| Parker, Sarah Jessica | Nelsonville, OH | 3/25/65 |
| Parsons, Estelle | Lynn, MA | 11/20/27 |
| Parton, Dolly | Sevierville, TN | 1/19/46 |
| Patinkin, Mandy | Chicago, IL | 11/30/52 |
| Patric, Jason | Queens, NY | 6/17/66 |
| Pavarotti, Luciano | Modena, Italy | 10/12/35 |
| Paxton, Bill | Fort Worth, TX | — |
| Paycheck, Johnny | Greenfield, OH | 5/31/41 |
| Peck, Gregory | La Jolla, CA | 4/5/16 |
| Pendergrass, Teddy | Philadelphia, PA | 3/26/50 |
| Penn, Arthur | Philadelphia, PA | 9/27/22 |
| Penn, Sean | Burbank, CA | 8/17/60 |
| Penny, Joe | London, England | 9/14/56 |
| Perez, Rosie | Brooklyn, NY | 1963 |
| Perkins, Elizabeth | New York, NY | 11/18/60 |
| Perlman, Itzhak | Tel Aviv, Israel | 8/31/45 |
| Perlman, Rhea | Brooklyn, NY | 3/31/48 |
| Perlman, Ron | New York, NY | 4/13/50 |
| Perrine, Valerie | Galveston, TX | 9/3/43 |
| Perry, Luke | Fredericktown, OH | 10/11/66 |
| Perry, Mathew | Williamstown, MA | 8/19/70 |
| Persoff, Nehemiah | Jerusalem | 8/14/20 |
| Pesci, Joe | Newark, NJ | 2/9/43 |
| Peters, Bernadette | New York, NY | 2/28/48 |
| Peters, Brock | New York, NY | 7/2/27 |
| Peters, Roberta | New York, NY | 5/4/30 |
| Peterson, Oscar | Montreal, Quebec | 8/15/25 |
| Petty, Tom | Gainesville, FL | 10/20/53 |
| Pfeiffer, Michelle | Santa Ana, CA | 4/29/57 |
| Philbin, Regis | New York, NY | 8/25/34 |
| Phillips, Lou Diamond | Philippines | 2/17/62 |
| Phillips, Mackenzie | Alexandria, VA | 11/10/59 |
| Phillips, Michelle | Long Beach, CA | 6/4/44 |
| Pickett, Wilson | Prattville, AL | 3/18/41 |
| Pierce, David Hyde | Albany, NY | 4/3/59 |
| Pinchot, Bronson | New York, NY | 5/20/59 |
| Pirner, David | Green Bay, WI | 4/16/64 |
| Piscopo, Joe | Passaic, NJ | 6/17/51 |
| Pitt, Brad | Shawnee, OK | 12/18/64 |
| Plant, Robert | W. Bromwich, England | 8/20/48 |
| Pleshette, Suzanne | New York, NY | 1/31/37 |
| Plowright, Joan | Brigg, England | 10/28/29 |
| Plummer, Amanda | New York, NY | 3/23/57 |
| Plummer, Christopher | Toronto, Ontario | 12/13/27 |
| Poitier, Sidney | Miami, FL | 2/20/27 |
| Polanski, Roman | Paris, France | 8/18/33 |
| Pollack, Sydney | Lafayette, IN | 7/1/34 |
| Ponti, Carlo | Milan, Italy | 12/11/13 |
| Pop, Iggy | Ann Arbor, MI | 4/21/47 |
| Post, Markie | Palo Alto, CA | 11/4/50 |
| Poston, Tom | Columbus, OH | 10/17/27 |
| Potts, Annie | Nashville, TN | 10/28/52 |
| Povich, Maury | Washington, DC | 1/17/39 |
| Powell, Jane | Portland, OR | 4/1/28 |
| Powers, Stefanie | Hollywood, CA | 11/2/42 |
| Prentiss, Paula | San Antonio, TX | 3/4/39 |
| Presley, Priscilla | New York, NY | 5/24/46 |
| Preston, Billy | Houston, TX | 9/9/46 |
| Previn, Andre | Berlin, Germany | 4/6/29 |
| Price, Leontyne | Laurel, MS | 2/10/27 |
| Price, Ray | Perryville, TX | 1/12/26 |
| Pride, Charlie | Sledge, MS | 3/18/39 |
| Priestley, Jason | Vancouver, British Columbia | 8/28/69 |
| Prince (formerly) | Minneapolis, MN | 6/7/58 |
| Principal, Victoria | Fukuoka, Japan | 1/3/45 |
| Prosky, Robert | Philadelphia, PA | 12/13/30 |
| Pryce, Jonathan | Wales | 6/1/47 |
| Pryor, Richard | Peoria, IL | 12/1/40 |
| Puente, Tito | New York, NY | 4/20/23 |
| Pulliam, Keshia Knight | Newark, NJ | 4/9/79 |
| Pullman, Bill | Hornell, NY | 1954 |

| Name | Birthplace | Birthdate |
|---|---|---|
| Purcell, Sarah | Richmond, IN | 10/8/48 |
| Pyle, Denver | Bethune, CO | 5/11/20 |
| Quaid, Dennis | Houston, TX | 4/9/54 |
| Quaid, Randy | Houston, TX | 10/1/50 |
| Quinn, Aidan | Chicago, IL | 3/8/59 |
| Quinn, Anthony | Chihuahua, Mexico | 4/21/15 |
| Quinn, Martha | Albany, NY | 5/11/59 |
| Rabb, Ellis | Memphis, TN | 6/20/30 |
| Rabbitt, Eddie | Brooklyn, NY | 11/27/41 |
| Rachins, Alan | Cambridge, MA | 10/10/47 |
| Rae, Charlotte | Milwaukee, WI | 4/22/26 |
| Raffi | Cairo, Italy | 7/8/48 |
| Raitt, Bonnie | Burbank, CA | 11/8/49 |
| Ramey, Samuel | Colby, KS | 3/28/42 |
| Rampal, Jean-Pierre | Marseilles, France | 1/7/22 |
| Randall, Tony | Tulsa, OK | 2/26/20 |
| Randolph, John | New York, NY | 6/1/15 |
| Randolph, Joyce | Detroit, MI | 10/21/25 |
| Raphael, Sally Jessy | Easton, PA | 2/25/43 |
| Rashad, Phylicia | Houston, TX | 6/17/48 |
| Ratzenberger, John | Bridgeport, CT | 4/6/47 |
| Rawls, Lou | Chicago, IL | 12/1/36 |
| Raymond, Gene | New York, NY | 8/13/08 |
| Reddy, Helen | Melbourne, Australia | 10/25/41 |
| Redford, Robert | Santa Monica, CA | 8/18/37 |
| Redgrave, Lynn | London, England | 3/8/43 |
| Redgrave, Vanessa | London, England | 1/30/37 |
| Reed, Jerry | Atlanta, GA | 3/20/37 |
| Reed, Lou | Long Island, NY | 3/2/43 |
| Reed, Oliver | London, England | 2/13/38 |
| Reed, Rex | Ft. Worth, TX | 10/2/38 |
| Reese, Della | Detroit, MI | 7/6/31 |
| Reeve, Christopher | New York, NY | 9/25/52 |
| Reeves, Keanu | Beirut, Lebanon | 9/2/64 |
| Regalbuto, Joe | New York, NY | 8/24/— |
| Reagan, Ronald | Tampico, IL | 2/6/11 |
| Reid, Tim | Norfolk, VA | 12/19/44 |
| Reilly, Charles Nelson | New York, NY | 1/13/31 |
| Reiner, Carl | Bronx, NY | 3/20/22 |
| Reiner, Rob | Bronx, NY | 3/6/45 |
| Reinhold, Judge | Wilmington, DE | 5/21/56 |
| Reinking, Ann | Seattle, WA | 11/10/50 |
| Reiser, Paul | New York, NY | 3/30/57 |
| Resnik, Regina | New York, NY | 8/30/24 |
| Reynolds, Burt | Waycross, GA | 2/11/36 |
| Reynolds, Debbie | El Paso, TX | 4/1/32 |
| Richards, Keith | Kent, England | 12/18/43 |
| Richards, Michael | Culver City, CA | 7/21/49 |
| Richardson, Miranda | Lancashire, England | 1958 |
| Richardson, Natasha | London, England | 5/11/63 |
| Richardson, Patricia | Bethesda, MD | 2/23/51 |
| Richie, Lionel | Tuskegee, AL | 6/20/50 |
| Rickles, Don | New York, NY | 5/8/26 |
| Rickman, Alan | London, England | 1946 |
| Riegert, Peter | New York, NY | 4/11/47 |
| Rigg, Diana | Doncaster, England | 7/20/38 |
| Ringwald, Molly | Rosewood, CA | 2/14/68 |
| Ritter, John | Burbank, CA | 9/17/48 |
| Rivera, Chita | Washington, DC | 1/23/33 |
| Rivera, Geraldo | New York, NY | 7/4/43 |
| Rivers, Joan | Brooklyn, NY | 6/8/37 |
| Roach, Max | Elizabeth City, NC | 1/10/24 |
| Robards, Jason Jr. | Chicago, IL | 7/26/22 |
| Robbins, Jerome | New York, NY | 10/11/18 |
| Robbins, Tim | W. Covina, CA | 10/16/58 |
| Roberts, Doris | St. Louis, MO | 11/4/29 |
| Roberts, Eric | Biloxi, MS | 4/18/56 |
| Roberts, Julia | Smyrna, GA | 10/28/67 |
| Roberts, Pernell | Waycross, GA | 5/18/30 |
| Roberts, Tony | New York, NY | 10/22/39 |
| Robertson, Cliff | La Jolla, CA | 9/9/25 |
| Robertson, Dale | Harrah, OK | 7/14/23 |
| Robinson, Smokey | Detroit, MI | 2/19/40 |
| Roche, Eugene | Boston, MA | 9/22/28 |
| Rodgers, Jimmy | Camas, WA | 9/18/33 |
| Rodriquez, Johnny | Sabinal, TX | 12/10/51 |
| Rogers, Fred | Latrobe, PA | 3/20/28 |
| Rogers, Kenny | Houston, TX | 8/21/38 |
| Rogers, Mimi | Coral Gables, FL | 1/27/56 |
| Rogers, Roy | Cincinnati, OH | 11/5/12 |
| Rogers, Wayne | Birmingham, AL | 4/7/33 |
| Rolle, Esther | Pompano Beach, FL | 11/8/33 |
| Rollins, Howard | Baltimore, MD | 10/17/50 |
| Rollins, Sonny | New York, NY | 9/7/29 |
| Ronstadt, Linda | Tucson, AZ | 7/15/46 |
| Rooney, Mickey | Brooklyn, NY | 9/23/20 |
| Rose, Axl | Lafayette, IN | 2/6/62 |
| Rose Marie | New York, NY | 8/15/25 |
| Roseanne | Salt Lake City, UT | 11/3/52 |
| Ross, Diana | Detroit, MI | 3/26/44 |
| Ross, Katharine | Hollywood, CA | 1/29/42 |
| Ross, Marion | Albert Lea, MN | 10/25/28 |
| Rossellini, Isabella | Rome, Italy | 6/18/52 |
| Rostropovich, Mstislav | Baku, Azerbaijan | 3/12/27 |
| Roth, David Lee | Bloomington, IN | 10/10/55 |
| Roth, Tim | London, England | 1961 |
| Rotten, Johnny (John Lydon) | England | 1/31/56 |
| Rourke, Mickey | Schnectady, NY | 7/16/53 |
| Rowlands, Gena | Cambria, WI | 6/19/34 |
| Ruehl, Mercedes | Queens, NY | 2/28/48 |
| Rush, Barbara | Denver, CO | 1/4/30 |
| Russell, Jane | Bemidji, MN | 6/21/21 |
| Russell, Ken | Southampton, England | 7/3/27 |
| Russell, Kurt | Springfield, MA | 3/17/51 |
| Russell, Mark | Buffalo, NY | 8/23/32 |
| Russell, Leon | Lawton, OK | 4/2/41 |
| Russell, Nipsey | Atlanta, GA | 10/13/24 |
| Russell, Theresa | San Diego, CA | 3/20/57 |
| Russo, Rene | Los Angeles, CA | 1954 |
| Rutherford, Ann | Toronto, Ontario | 11/2/20 |
| Ruttan, Susan | Oregon City, OR | 9/16/50 |
| Ryan, Meg | Fairfield, CT | 11/19/61 |
| Ryan, Roz | Detroit, MI | 7/7/51 |
| Rydell, Bobby | Philadelphia, PA | 4/26/42 |
| Ryder, Winona | Winona, MN | 10/29/71 |
| Sade | Ibadan, Nigeria | 1/16/59 |
| Sagal, Katie | Los Angeles, CA | 1956 |
| Saget, Bob | Philadelphia, PA | 5/17/56 |
| Sahl, Mort | Montreal, Quebec | 5/11/27 |
| Saint, Eva Marie | Newark, NJ | 7/4/24 |
| Sandler, Adam | Brooklyn, NY | 9/9/66 |
| St. James, Susan | Los Angeles, CA | 8/14/46 |
| St. John, Jill | Los Angeles, CA | 8/19/40 |
| Sajak, Pat | Chicago, IL | 10/26/47 |
| Saks, Gene | New York, NY | 11/8/21 |
| Sales, Soupy | Franklinton, NC | 1/8/26 |
| Samms, Emma | London, England | 8/28/60 |
| Sanderson, William | Memphis, TN | 1/10/48 |
| Sands, Julian | Yorkshire, England | 1/15/58 |
| Sandy, Gary | Dayton, OH | 12/25/45 |
| Sanford, Isabel | New York, NY | 8/29/17 |
| Sarandon, Susan | New York, NY | 10/4/46 |
| Sarnoff, Dorothy | New York, NY | 5/25/17 |
| Sartain, Gailard | Tulsa, OK | 9/18/46 |
| Savage, Fred | Highland Park, IL | 7/9/76 |
| Saxon, John | Brooklyn, NY | 8/5/35 |
| Sayles, John | Schenectady, NY | 9/28/50 |
| Scaggs, Boz | Dallas, TX | 6/8/44 |
| Scalia, Jack | Brooklyn, NY | 11/10/51 |
| Schallert, William | Los Angeles, CA | 7/6/22 |
| Scheider, Roy | Orange, NJ | 11/10/32 |
| Schell, Maria | Vienna, Austria | 1/15/26 |
| Schell, Maximilian | Vienna, Austria | 12/8/30 |
| Schenkel, Chris | Bippus, IN | 8/21/23 |
| Schiffer, Claudia | Germany | 8/24/71 |
| Schneider, John | Mt. Kisco, NY | 4/8/54 |
| Schneider, Rob | San Francisco, CA | 10/31/— |
| Schroder, Rick | Staten Island, NY | 4/3/70 |
| Schwarzenegger, Arnold | Graz, Austria | 7/30/47 |
| Schwarzkopf, Elisabeth | Jarotschin, Poland | 12/9/15 |
| Schwimmer, David | Queens, NY | 11/1267 |
| Sciorra, Annabella | New York, NY | 1964 |
| Scofield, Paul | Hurst, Pierpont, England | 1/21/22 |
| Scolari, Peter | New Rochelle, IL | 9/12/54 |
| Scorsese, Martin | New York, NY | 11/17/42 |
| Scott, George C. | Wise, VA | 10/18/27 |
| Scott, Lizabeth | Scranton, PA | 9/29/22 |
| Scott, Martha | Jamesport, MO | 9/22/14 |
| Scotto, Renata | Savona, Italy | 2/24/35 |
| Scully, Vin | New York, NY | 11/29/27 |
| Seagal, Steven | Lansing, MI | 4/10/51 |
| Secor, Kyle | Tacoma, WA | 5/31/— |
| Sedaka, Neil | New York, NY | 3/13/39 |
| Seeger, Pete | New York, NY | 5/3/19 |
| Segal, George | Great Neck, NY | 2/13/34 |
| Seidelman, Susan | Philadelphia, PA | 12/11/52 |
| Seinfeld, Jerry | New York, NY | 4/29/55 |
| Sellecca, Connie | New York, NY | 5/25/55 |
| Selleck, Tom | Detroit, MI | 1/29/45 |
| Severinsen, Doc | Arlington, OR | 7/7/27 |
| Seymour, Jane | Middlesex, England | 2/15/51 |
| Shackelford, Ted | Oklahoma City, OK | 6/23/46 |

| Name | Birthplace | Birthdate |
|---|---|---|
| Shaffer, Paul | Thunder Bay, Ontario | 11/28/49 |
| Shandling, Garry | Chicago, IL | 11/29/49 |
| Shankar, Ravi | India | 4/7/20 |
| Sharif, Omar | Alexandria, Egypt | 4/10/32 |
| Shatner, William | Montreal, Quebec | 3/22/31 |
| Shaughnessy, Charles | London, England | 2/9/— |
| Shaver, Helen | St. Thomas, Ontario | 2/24/51 |
| Shaw, Artie | New York, NY | 5/23/10 |
| Shea, John | N. Conway, NH | 4/14/49 |
| Shearer, Harry | Los Angeles, CA | 12/23/43 |
| Shearer, Moira | Scotland | 1/17/26 |
| Shearing, George | London, England | 8/13/19 |
| Sheedy, Ally | New York, NY | 6/12/62 |
| Sheen, Charlie | Los Angeles, CA | 9/3/65 |
| Sheen, Martin | Dayton, OH | 8/3/40 |
| Shelley, Carole | London, England | 8/16/39 |
| Shepard, Sam | Ft. Sheridan, IL | 11/5/43 |
| Shepherd, Cybill | Memphis, TN | 2/18/49 |
| Sheridan, Nicollette | Northington, England | 11/21/63 |
| Shields, Brooke | New York, NY | 5/31/65 |
| Shire, Talia | New York, NY | 4/25/46 |
| Short, Bobby | Danville, IL | 9/15/24 |
| Short, Martin | Hamilton, Ontario | 3/26/50 |
| Show, Grant | Detroit, MI | 4/27/62 |
| Shue, Andrew | South Orange, NJ | 2/20/67 |
| Shue, Elisabeth | Wilmington, DE | 10/6/63 |
| Shull, Richard B. | Evanston, IL | 2/24/29 |
| Sidney, Sylvia | New York, NY | 8/8/10 |
| Siepi, Cesare | Milan, Italy | 2/10/23 |
| Sikking, James B. | Los Angeles, CA | 3/5/34 |
| Sills, Beverly | Brooklyn, NY | 5/25/29 |
| Silver, Ron | New York, NY | 7/2/46 |
| Silverman, Jonathan | Los Angeles, CA | 8/5/66 |
| Silverstone, Alicia | San Francisco, CA | 1976 |
| Simmons, Gene | Haifa, Israel | 8/25/49 |
| Simmons, Jean | London, England | 1/31/29 |
| Simmons, Richard | New Orleans, LA | 7/12/48 |
| Simon, Carly | New York, NY | 6/25/45 |
| Simon, Paul | Newark, NJ | 10/13/41 |
| Simone, Nina | Tyron, NC | 2/21/33 |
| Sinatra, Frank | Hoboken, NJ | 12/12/15 |
| Sinbad | Benton Harbor, MI | 11/10/56 |
| Sinclair, Madge | Kingston, Jamaica | 4/28/38 |
| Sinise, Gary | Blue Island, IL | 3/7/55 |
| Singleton, John | Los Angeles, CA | 1/6/68 |
| Siskel, Gene | Chicago, IL | 1/26/46 |
| Skelton, Red (Richard) | Vincennes, IN | 7/18/13 |
| Skerritt, Tom | Detroit, MI | 8/25/33 |
| Slater, Christian | New York, NY | 8/19/69 |
| Slater, Helen | Massapequa, NY | 12/14/63 |
| Slezak, Erika | Hollywood, CA | 8/5/46 |
| Slick, Grace | Chicago, IL | 10/30/39 |
| Smirnoff, Yakov | Odessa, Russia | 1/24/51 |
| Smith, Allison | New York, NY | 12/9/69 |
| Smith, Buffalo Bob | Buffalo, NY | 11/27/17 |
| Smith, Jaclyn | Houston, TX | 10/26/47 |
| Smith, Keely | Norfolk, VA | 3/9/35 |
| Smith, Maggie | Ilford, England | 12/28/34 |
| Smith, Will | Philadelphia, PA | 9/25/68 |
| Smits, Jimmy | New York, NY | 7/9/55 |
| Smothers, Dick | New York, NY | 11/20/39 |
| Smothers, Tom | New York, NY | 2/2/37 |
| Snipes, Wesley | Orlando, FL | 7/31/63 |
| Snow, Hank | Nova Scotia, Canada | 5/9/14 |
| Solti, Georg | Budapest, Hungary | 10/21/12 |
| Somers, Suzanne | San Bruno, CA | 10/16/46 |
| Sommer, Elke | Berlin, Germany | 11/5/41 |
| Sorvino, Mira | | 1969 |
| Sorvino, Paul | New York, NY | 1939 |
| Sothern, Ann | Valley City, ND | 1/22/09 |
| Soul, David | Chicago, IL | 8/28/43 |
| Spacek, Sissy | Quitman, TX | 12/25/49 |
| Spacey, Kevin | S. Orange, NJ | 7/26/59 |
| Spade, David | Scottsdale, AZ | — |
| Spader, James | Boston, MA | 2/7/60 |
| Spano, Joe | San Francisco, CA | 7/7/46 |
| Spelling, Aaron | Dallas, TX | 4/22/28 |
| Spelling, Tori | Los Angeles, CA | 5/16/73 |
| Spielberg, Steven | Cincinnati, OH | 12/18/47 |
| Springfield, Dusty | London, England | 4/16/39 |
| Springfield, Rick | Sydney, Australia | 8/23/49 |
| Springsteen, Bruce | Freehold, NJ | 9/23/49 |
| Stack, Robert | Los Angeles, CA | 1/13/19 |
| Stafford, Jo | Coalinga, CA | 11/12/18 |
| Stahl, Richard | Detroit, MI | 1/4/32 |
| Stallone, Sylvester | New York, NY | 7/6/46 |
| Stamos, John | Cypress, CA | 8/19/63 |
| Stamp, Terence | Stepney, England | 7/22/39 |

| Name | Birthplace | Birthdate |
|---|---|---|
| Stang, Arnold | New York, NY | 9/28/25 |
| Stanley, Kim | Tularosa, NM | 2/11/25 |
| Stanton, Harry Dean | West Irvine, Kentucky | 7/14/26 |
| Stapleton, Jean | New York, NY | 1/19/23 |
| Stapleton, Maureen | Troy, NY | 6/21/25 |
| Starr, Ringo | Liverpool, England | 7/7/40 |
| Steenburgen, Mary | Newport, AR | 2/8/53 |
| Steiger, Rod | W. Hampton, NY | 4/14/25 |
| Stephens, James | Mt. Kisco, NY | 5/18/51 |
| Stern, Daniel | Stamford, CT | 5/28/57 |
| Stern, Howard | New York, NY | 1/12/54 |
| Stern, Isaac | Kreminiecz, Russia | 7/21/20 |
| Sternhagen, Frances | Washington, DC | 1/13/30 |
| Stevens, Andrew | Memphis, TN | 6/10/55 |
| Stevens, Cat | London, England | 7/21/48 |
| Stevens, Connie | Brooklyn, NY | 8/8/38 |
| Stevens, Rise | New York, NY | 6/11/13 |
| Stevens, Stella | Yazoo City, MS | 10/1/36 |
| Stevenson, Parker | Philadelphia, PA | 6/4/52 |
| Stewart, James | Indiana, PA | 5/20/08 |
| Stewart, Jon | Lawrence, NJ | 1963 |
| Stewart, Patrick | Mirfield, England | 7/13/40 |
| Stewart, Rod | London, England | 1/10/45 |
| Stickney, Dorothy | Dickinson, ND | 6/21/1896 |
| Stiers, David Ogden | Peoria, IL | 10/31/42 |
| Stiller, Ben | New York, NY | 1966 |
| Stiller, Jerry | New York, NY | 6/8/29 |
| Stills, Stephen | Dallas, TX | 1/3/45 |
| Sting | Newcastle, England | 10/2/51 |
| Stipe, Michael | Decatur, GA | 1/4/60 |
| Stockwell, Dean | Hollywood, CA | 3/5/36 |
| Stoltz, Eric | American Samoa | 9/30/61 |
| Stone, Dee Wallace | Kansas City, KS | 12/14/48 |
| Stone, Oliver | New York, NY | 9/15/46 |
| Stone, Sharon | Meadville, PA | 3/10/58 |
| Stookey, Paul | Baltimore, MD | 12/30/37 |
| Storch, Larry | New York, NY | 1/8/23 |
| Storm, Gale | Bloomington, TX | 4/5/22 |
| Stowe, Madeleine | Los Angeles, CA | 8/18/58 |
| Straight, Beatrice | Old Westbury, NY | 8/2/18 |
| Strait, George | Pearsall, TX | 5/18/52 |
| Strasser, Robin | New York, NY | 5/7/45 |
| Stratas, Teresa | Toronto, Ontario | 5/26/38 |
| Strauss, Peter | New York, NY | 2/20/47 |
| Streep, Meryl | Summit, NJ | 6/22/49 |
| Streisand, Barbra | Brooklyn, NY | 4/24/42 |
| Stringfield, Sherry | Colorado Springs, CO | 6/24/— |
| Stritch, Elaine | Detroit, MI | 2/2/26 |
| Struthers, Sally | Portland, OR | 7/28/48 |
| Stuarti, Enzo | Rome, Italy | 3/3/25 |
| Sullivan, Susan | New York, NY | 11/18/44 |
| Sumac, Yma | Ichocan, Peru | 9/10/27 |
| Summer, Donna | Boston, MA | 12/31/48 |
| Sutherland, Donald | St. John, New Brunswick | 7/17/34 |
| Sutherland, Joan | Sydney, Australia | 11/7/26 |
| Sutherland, Kiefer | London, England | 12/20/66 |
| Swayze, Patrick | Houston, TX | 8/18/54 |
| Swit, Loretta | Passaic, NJ | 11/4/37 |
| | | |
| Mr. T (Lawrence Tero) | Chicago, IL | 5/21/52 |
| Takei, George | Los Angeles, CA | 4/20/39 |
| Tallchief, Maria | Fairfax, OK | 1/24/25 |
| Tarantino, Quentin | Knoxville, TN | 3/27/63 |
| Taylor, Billy | Greenville, SC | 7/24/21 |
| Taylor, Elizabeth | London, England | 2/27/32 |
| Taylor, James | Boston, MA | 3/12/48 |
| Taylor, Rip | Washington, DC | 1/13/30 |
| Taylor, Rod | Sydney, Australia | 1/11/29 |
| Te Kanawa, Kiri | Gisborne, New Zealand | 3/6/44 |
| Tebaldi, Renata | Pesaro, Italy | 2/1/22 |
| Temple, Shirley | Santa Monica, CA | 4/23/28 |
| Tennant, Victoria | London, England | 9/30/50 |
| Tennille, Toni | Montgomery, AL | 5/8/43 |
| Tesh, John | Garden City, NY | 7/9/52 |
| Tharp, Twyla | Portland, IN | 7/1/41 |
| Thicke, Alan | Kirkland Lake, Ontario | 3/1/47 |
| Thomas, Jay | New Orleans, LA | 7/12/48 |
| Thomas, Jonathan Taylor | Bethlehem, PA | 9/8/81 |
| Thomas, Marlo | Detroit, MI | 11/21/43 |
| Thomas, Philip Michael | Columbus, OH | 5/26/49 |
| Thomas, Richard | New York, NY | 6/13/51 |
| Thompson, Emma | London, England | 4/15/59 |
| Thompson, Jack | Sydney, Australia | 8/31/40 |
| Thompson, Lea | Rochester, MN | 5/31/61 |
| Thompson, Sada | Des Moines, IA | 9/27/29 |
| Thorne-Smith, Courtney | | 11/8/68 |
| Thurman, Uma | Boston, MA | 4/29/70 |
| Tiegs, Cheryl | Minnesota | 9/27/47 |

| Name | Birthplace | Birthdate |
|---|---|---|
| Tiffany | Norwalk, CA | 10/2/71 |
| Tillis, Mel | Tampa, FL | 8/8/32 |
| Tilly, Meg | Texada, B.C. | 2/14/60 |
| Tiny Tim | New York, NY | 4/12/23 |
| Todd, Richard | Dublin, Ireland | 6/11/19 |
| Tomei, Marisa | New York, NY | 12/4/64 |
| Tomlin, Lily | Detroit, MI | 9/1/39 |
| Tomlinson, David | Scotland | 5/7/17 |
| Torme, Mel | Chicago, IL | 9/13/25 |
| Tork, Peter | Washington, DC | 2/13/44 |
| Torn, Rip | Temple, TX | 2/6/31 |
| Townsend, Robert | Chicago, IL | 2/6/57 |
| Townshend, Peter | Chiswick, England | 5/19/45 |
| Travanti, Daniel J. | Kenosha, WI | 3/7/40 |
| Travers, Mary | Louisville, KY | 11/9/36 |
| Travis, Nancy | New York, NY | 9/21/61 |
| Travis, Randy | Marshville, NC | 5/4/59 |
| Travolta, John | Englewood, NJ | 2/18/54 |
| Trebek, Alex | Sudbury, Ontario | 7/22/40 |
| Trevor, Claire | New York, NY | 3/8/09 |
| Tritt, Travis | Marietta, GA | 2/9/63 |
| Tucker, Michael | Baltimore, MD | 2/6/44 |
| Tucker, Tanya | Seminole, TX | 10/10/58 |
| Tune, Tommy | Wichita Falls, TX | 2/28/39 |
| Turner, Janine | Lincoln, NE | 12/6/62 |
| Turner, Kathleen | Springfield, MO | 6/19/54 |
| Turner, Tina | Nutbush, TN | 11/26/39 |
| Turturro, John | Brooklyn, NY | 2/28/57 |
| Twain, Shania | Ontario, Canada | |
| Twiggy (Leslie Hornby) | London, England | 9/19/46 |
| Tyler, Liv | Portland, ME | 7/1/77 |
| Tyler, Steven | Boston, MA | 3/26/48 |
| Tyson, Cicely | New York, NY | 12/19/33 |
| | | |
| Uecker, Bob | Milwaukee, WI | 1/26/35 |
| Uggams, Leslie | New York, NY | 5/25/43 |
| Ullman, Tracey | Slough, England | 12/30/59 |
| Ullmann, Liv | Tokyo, Japan | 12/16/38 |
| Underwood, Blair | Tacoma, WA | 8/25/64 |
| Urich, Robert | Toronto, Ohio | 12/19/47 |
| Ustinov, Peter | London, England | 4/16/21 |
| | | |
| Vaccaro, Brenda | Brooklyn, NY | 11/18/39 |
| Vale, Jerry | New York, NY | 7/8/31 |
| Valente, Caterina | Paris, France | 1/14/31 |
| Valli, Frankie | Newark, NJ | 5/3/37 |
| Van Ark, Joan | New York, NY | 6/16/43 |
| Vandross, Luther | New York, NY | 4/20/51 |
| Van Damme, Jean-Claude | Brussels, Belgium | 1961 |
| Van Dyke, Dick | West Plains, MO | 12/13/25 |
| Van Dyke, Jerry | Danville, IL | 7/27/31 |
| Van Halen, Eddie | Nijmegen, Netherlands | 1/26/57 |
| Van Patten, Dick | New York, NY | 12/9/28 |
| Van Peebles, Mario | Mexico | 1/15/57 |
| Vaughn, Robert | New York, NY | 11/22/32 |
| Vedder, Eddie | Evanston, IL | 12/23/65 |
| Verdon, Gwen | Los Angeles, CA | 1/13/25 |
| Vereen, Ben | Miami, FL | 10/10/46 |
| Verrett, Shirley | New Orleans, LA | 5/31/31 |
| Vickers, Jon | Prince Albert, Sask. | 10/26/26 |
| Vincent, Jan-Michael | Denver, CO | 7/15/44 |
| Vinson, Helen | Beaumont, TX | 9/17/07 |
| Vinton, Bobby | Canonsburg, PA | 4/16/35 |
| Vitale, Dick | E Rutherford, NJ | 6/9/40 |
| Voight, Jon | Yonkers, NY | 12/29/38 |
| Von Stade, Frederica | Somerville, NJ | 6/1/45 |
| Von Sydow, Max | Lund, Sweden | 4/10/29 |
| | | |
| Wagner, Jack | Washington, MO | 10/3/59 |
| Wagner, Lindsay | Los Angeles, CA | 6/22/49 |
| Wagner, Robert | Detroit, MI | 2/10/30 |
| Wahl, Ken | Chicago, IL | 2/14/56 |
| Wain, Bea | Bronx, NY | 4/30/17 |
| Waite, Ralph | White Plains, NY | 6/22/29 |
| Waits, Tom | Pomona, CA | 12/7/49 |
| Walden, Robert | New York, NY | 9/25/43 |
| Walken, Christopher | New York, NY | 3/31/43 |
| Wallach, Eli | Brooklyn, NY | 12/7/15 |
| Walston, Ray | Laurel, MS | 11/2/24 |
| Walter, Jessica | New York, NY | 1/31/44 |
| Ward, Fred | San Diego, CA | 1943 |
| Ward, Sela | Meridian, MS | 8/11/56 |
| Ward, Simon | London, England | 10/19/41 |
| Warden, Jack | Newark, NJ | 9/18/20 |
| Warfield, William | W Helena, AR | 1/22/20 |
| Warner, Malcolm-Jamal | Jersey City, NJ | 8/18/70 |
| Warren, Lesley Ann | New York, NY | 8/16/46 |
| Warrick, Ruth | St. Joseph, MO | 6/29/16 |

| Name | Birthplace | Birthdate |
|---|---|---|
| Warwick, Dionne | E Orange, NJ | 12/12/41 |
| Washington, Denzel | Mt. Vernon, NY | 12/28/54 |
| Waters, John | Baltimore, MD | 4/22/46 |
| Waters, Roger | Great Bookham, England | 9/9/44 |
| Waterston, Sam | Cambridge, MA | 11/15/40 |
| Watts, Andre | Nuremberg, Germany | 6/20/46 |
| Wayans, Damon | New York, NY | 1960 |
| Wayans, Keenan Ivory | New York, NY | 6/8/58 |
| Waxman, Al | Toronto, Ontario | 3/2/35 |
| Weathers, Carl | New Orleans, LA | 1/14/48 |
| Weaver, Dennis | Joplin, MO | 6/4/24 |
| Weaver, Fritz | Pittsburgh, PA | 1/19/26 |
| Weaver, Sigourney | New York, NY | 10/8/49 |
| Weir, Peter | Sydney, Australia | 8/8/44 |
| Weitz, Bruce | Norwalk, CT | 5/27/43 |
| Welch, Raquel | Chicago, IL | 9/5/40 |
| Weld, Tuesday | New York, NY | 8/27/43 |
| Wells, Kitty | Nashville, TN | 8/30/19 |
| Wendt, George | Chicago, IL | 10/17/48 |
| West, Adam | Walla Walla, WA | 9/19/29 |
| Wettig, Patricia | Cincinnati, OH | 12/4/51 |
| Whalley-Kilme, Joanne | Manchester, England | 8/25/64 |
| Wheaton, Wil | Burbank, CA | 7/29/72 |
| Whitaker, Forest | Longview, TX | 7/15/61 |
| White, Barry | Galveston, TX | 9/12/44 |
| White, Betty | Oak Park, IL | 1/17/22 |
| White, Jaleel | Los Angeles, CA | 11/27/76 |
| White, Jesse | Buffalo, NY | 1/3/19 |
| White, Vanna | N Myrtle Beach, SC | 2/18/57 |
| Whiting, Margaret | Detroit, MI | 7/22/24 |
| Whitmore, James | White Plains, NY | 10/1/21 |
| Widmark, Richard | Sunrise, MN | 12/26/14 |
| Wiest, Dianne | Kansas City, MO | 3/28/48 |
| Wilder, Billy | Vienna, Austria | 6/22/06 |
| Wilder, Gene | Milwaukee, WI | 6/11/35 |
| Williams, Andy | Wall Lake, IA | 12/3/30 |
| Williams, Barry | Santa Monica, CA | 9/30/54 |
| Williams, Billy Dee | New York, NY | 4/6/37 |
| Williams, Cindy | Van Nuys, CA | 8/22/47 |
| Williams, Esther | Los Angeles, CA | 8/8/23 |
| Williams, Hal | Columbus, OH | 12/14/38 |
| Williams, Hank Jr. | Shreveport, LA | 5/26/49 |
| Williams, JoBeth | Houston, TX | 1953 |
| Williams, Montel | Baltimore, MD | 7/3/56 |
| Williams, Paul | Omaha, NE | 9/19/40 |
| Williams, Robin | Chicago, IL | 7/21/52 |
| Williams, Treat | Rowayton, CT | 12/1/51 |
| Williams, Vanessa | New York, NY | 3/18/63 |
| Williamson, Nicol | Hamilton, Scotland | 9/14/38 |
| Willis, Bruce | W Germany | 3/19/55 |
| Wilson, Demond | Valdosta, GA | 10/13/46 |
| Wilson, Elizabeth | Grand Rapids, MI | 4/4/25 |
| Wilson, Flip | Jersey City, NJ | 12/8/33 |
| Wilson, Nancy | Chillicothe, OH | 2/20/37 |
| Windom, William | New York, NY | 9/28/23 |
| Winfield, Paul | Los Angeles, CA | 5/22/41 |
| Winfrey, Oprah | Kosciusko, MS | 1/29/54 |
| Winger, Debra | Cleveland, OH | 5/16/55 |
| Winkler, Henry | New York, NY | 10/30/45 |
| Winningham, Mare | Phoenix, AZ | 5/6/59 |
| Winter, Johnny | Beaumont,TX | 2/23/44 |
| Winters, Jonathan | Dayton, OH | 11/11/25 |
| Winters, Shelley | St. Louis, MO | 8/18/22 |
| Winwood, Steve | Birmingham, England | 5/12/48 |
| Wiseman, Joseph | Montreal, Quebec | 5/15/18 |
| Withers, Jane | Atlanta, GA | 4/12/26 |
| Witt, Alicia | Worcester, MA | 1975 |
| Wonder, Stevie | Saginaw, MI | 5/13/50 |
| Wood, Elijah | Cedar Rapids, IA | 1/28/81 |
| Woodard, Alfre | Tulsa, OK | 11/2/53 |
| Woods, James | Vernal, NJ | 4/18/47 |
| Woodward, Edward | Croyden, England | 6/1/30 |
| Woodward, Joanne | Thomasville, GA | 2/27/30 |
| Wopat, Tom | Lodi, WI | 9/9/— |
| Worth, Irene | Nebraska | 6/23/16 |
| Wray, Fay | Alberta, Canada | 9/10/07 |
| Wright, Martha | Seattle, WA | 3/23/26 |
| Wright, Max | Detroit, MI | 8/2/43 |
| Wright, Steven | New York, NY | 12/6/55 |
| Wright, Teresa | New York, NY | 10/27/18 |
| Wyatt, Jane | Campgaw, NJ | 8/10/11 |
| Wyle, Noah | Hollywood, CA | 6/4/71 |
| Wyman, Jane | St. Joseph, MO | 1/4/14 |
| Wynette, Tammy | Red Bay, AL | 5/5/42 |
| | | |
| Yankovic, Weird Al | Los Angeles, CA | 10/23/59 |
| Yanni | Kalamata, Greece | 11/4/54 |

| Name | Birthplace | Birthdate | Name | Birthplace | Birthdate |
|---|---|---|---|---|---|
| Yarborough, Glenn | Milwaukee, WI | 1/12/30 | Young, Sean | Louisville, KY | 11/20/59 |
| Yarrow, Peter | New York, NY | 5/31/38 | Youngman, Henny | Liverpool, England | 1/12/06 |
| Yoakam, Dwight | Pikesville, KY | 10/23/56 | | | |
| York, Michael | Fulmer, England | 3/27/42 | Zeffirelli, Franco | Florence, Italy | 2/12/23 |
| York, Susannah | London, England | 1/9/42 | Zemeckis, Robert | Chicago, IL | 5/14/51 |
| Young, Alan | Northumberland, England | 11/19/19 | Zerbe, Anthony | Long Beach, CA | 5/20/36 |
| Young, Burt | New York, NY | 4/30/40 | Zimbalist, Efrem Jr. | New York, NY | 11/30/23 |
| Young, Loretta | Salt Lake City, UT | 1/6/13 | Zimbalist, Stephanie | Encino, CA | 10/8/56 |
| Young, Neil | Toronto, Ontario | 11/12/45 | Zukerman, Pinchas | Tel Aviv, Israel | 7/16/48 |
| Young, Robert | Chicago, IL | 2/22/07 | Zuniga, Daphne | Berkeley, CA | 1962 |

# Entertainment Personalities of the Past

(as of mid-1996)

| Born | Died | Name |
|---|---|---|
| 1895 | 1974 | Abbott, Bud |
| 1887 | 1995 | Abbott, George |
| 1903 | 1992 | Acuff, Roy |
| 1872 | 1953 | Adams, Maude |
| 1855 | 1926 | Adler, Jacob P |
| 1903 | 1984 | Adler, Luther |
| 1898 | 1933 | Adoree, Renee |
| 1902 | 1986 | Aherne, Brian |
| 1931 | 1989 | Ailey, Alvin |
| 1918 | 1994 | Akins, Claude |
| 1909 | 1964 | Albertson, Frank |
| 1907 | 1981 | Albertson, Jack |
| 1894 | 1956 | Allen, Fred |
| 1906 | 1964 | Allen, Gracie |
| 1913 | 1996 | Allen, Mel |
| 1883 | 1950 | Allgood, Sara |
| 1908 | 1993 | Ameche, Don |
| 1903 | 1993 | Ames, Leon |
| 1902 | 1993 | Anderson, Marian |
| 1909 | 1992 | Andrews, Dana |
| 1913 | 1967 | Andrews, Laverne |
| 1918 | 1995 | Andrews, Maxine |
| 1887 | 1933 | Arbuckle, Fatty (Roscoe) |
| 1908 | 1990 | Arden, Eve |
| 1900 | 1976 | Arlen, Richard |
| 1868 | 1946 | Arliss, George |
| 1888 | 1945 | Armetta, Henry |
| 1900 | 1971 | Armstrong, Louis |
| 1917 | 1986 | Arnaz, Desi |
| 1890 | 1956 | Arnold, Edward |
| 1905 | 1974 | Arquette, Cliff |
| 1900 | 1991 | Arthur, Jean |
| 1907 | 1991 | Ashcroft, Peggy |
| 1899 | 1987 | Astaire, Fred |
| 1906 | 1987 | Astor, Mary |
| 1885 | 1946 | Atwill, Lionel |
| 1905 | 1967 | Auer, Mischa |
| 1900 | 1972 | Austin, Gene |
| 1913 | 1989 | Backus, Jim |
| 1918 | 1990 | Bailey, Pearl |
| 1892 | 1968 | Bainter, Fay |
| 1906 | 1975 | Baker, Josephine |
| 1904 | 1983 | Balanchine, George |
| 1911 | 1989 | Ball, Lucille |
| 1919 | 1996 | Balsam, Martin |
| 1882 | 1956 | Bancroft, George |
| 1903 | 1968 | Bankhead, Tallulah |
| 1890 | 1952 | Banks, Leslie |
| 1890 | 1955 | Bara, Theda |
| 1810 | 1891 | Barnum, Phineas T. |
| 1879 | 1959 | Barrymore, Ethel |
| 1882 | 1942 | Barrymore, John |
| 1878 | 1954 | Barrymore, Lionel |
| 1848 | 1905 | Barrymore, Maurice |
| 1897 | 1963 | Barthelmess, Richard |
| 1914 | 1984 | Basehart, Richard |
| 1904 | 1984 | Basie, Count |
| 1923 | 1985 | Baxter, Anne |
| 1889 | 1951 | Baxter, Warner |
| 1904 | 1965 | Beatty, Clyde |
| 1902 | 1962 | Beavers, Louise |
| 1884 | 1946 | Beery, Noah, Sr. |
| 1913 | 1994 | Beery, Noah Jr. |
| 1889 | 1949 | Beery, Wallace |
| 1901 | 1970 | Begley, Ed |
| 1904 | 1991 | Bellamy, Ralph |
| 1949 | 1982 | Belushi, John |
| 1906 | 1968 | Benaderet, Bea |
| 1906 | 1964 | Bendix, William |
| 1904 | 1965 | Bennett, Constance |
| 1910 | 1990 | Bennett, Joan |
| 1943 | 1987 | Bennett, Michael |
| 1894 | 1974 | Benny, Jack |
| 1924 | 1970 | Benzell, Mimi |
| 1917 | 1996 | Beradino, John |

| Born | Died | Name |
|---|---|---|
| 1899 | 1966 | Berg, Gertrude |
| 1903 | 1978 | Bergen, Edgar |
| 1915 | 1982 | Bergman, Ingrid |
| 1895 | 1976 | Berkeley, Busby |
| 1923 | 1986 | Bernardi, Herschel |
| 1844 | 1923 | Bernhardt, Sarah |
| 1893 | 1943 | Bernie, Ben |
| 1939 | 1996 | Bessell, Ted |
| 1889 | 1967 | Bickford, Charles |
| 1934 | 1993 | Bixby, Bill |
| 1911 | 1960 | Bjoerling, Jussi |
| 1895 | 1973 | Blackmer, Sidney |
| 1931 | 1989 | Blake, Amanda |
| 1921 | 1995 | Blaine, Vivian |
| 1908 | 1989 | Blanc, Mel |
| 1928 | 1972 | Blocker, Dan |
| 1909 | 1979 | Blondell, Joan |
| 1888 | 1959 | Blore, Eric |
| 1901 | 1975 | Blue, Ben |
| 1899 | 1957 | Bogart, Humphrey |
| 1880 | 1965 | Boland, Mary |
| 1895 | 1969 | Boles, John |
| 1904 | 1987 | Bolger, Ray |
| 1903 | 1960 | Bond, Ward |
| 1892 | 1981 | Bondi, Beulah |
| 1917 | 1981 | Boone, Richard |
| 1833 | 1893 | Booth, Edwin |
| 1796 | 1852 | Booth, Junius Brutus |
| 1898 | 1992 | Booth, Shirley |
| 1905 | 1965 | Bow, Clara |
| 1874 | 1946 | Bowes, Maj. Edward |
| 1928 | 1977 | Boyd, Stephen |
| 1898 | 1972 | Boyd, William |
| 1899 | 1978 | Boyer, Charles |
| 1893 | 1939 | Brady, Alice |
| 1894 | 1974 | Brennan, Walter |
| 1904 | 1979 | Brent, George |
| 1891 | 1951 | Brice, Fanny |
| 1916 | 1994 | Brazzi, Rossano |
| 1891 | 1959 | Broderick, Helen |
| 1892 | 1973 | Brown, Joe E. |
| 1926 | 1966 | Bruce, Lenny |
| 1895 | 1953 | Bruce, Nigel |
| 1910 | 1982 | Bruce, Virginia |
| 1915 | 1985 | Brynner, Yul |
| 1903 | 1979 | Buchanan, Edgar |
| 1938 | 1982 | Buono, Victor |
| 1885 | 1970 | Burke, Billie |
| 1911 | 1967 | Burnette, Smiley |
| 1896 | 1996 | Burns, George |
| 1917 | 1993 | Burr, Raymond |
| 1925 | 1984 | Burton, Richard |
| 1897 | 1946 | Busch, Mae |
| 1883 | 1966 | Bushman, Francis X. |
| 1896 | 1946 | Butterworth, Charles |
| 1893 | 1971 | Byington, Spring |
| 1904 | 1972 | Cabot, Bruce |
| 1918 | 1977 | Cabot, Sebastian |
| 1899 | 1986 | Cagney, James |
| 1895 | 1956 | Calhern, Louis |
| 1923 | 1977 | Callas, Maria |
| 1907 | 1994 | Calloway, Cab |
| 1933 | 1976 | Cambridge, Godfrey |
| 1865 | 1940 | Campbell, Mrs. Patrick |
| 1950 | 1994 | Candy, John |
| 1892 | 1964 | Cantor, Eddie |
| 1897 | 1991 | Capra, Frank |
| 1878 | 1947 | Carey, Harry |
| 1913 | 1994 | Carey, Macdonald |
| 1950 | 1983 | Carpenter, Karen |
| 1906 | 1988 | Carradine, John |
| 1880 | 1961 | Carrillo, Leo |
| 1892 | 1972 | Carroll, Leo G. |
| 1905 | 1965 | Carroll, Nancy |
| 1910 | 1963 | Carson, Jack |

| Born | Died | Name |
|---|---|---|
| 1873 | 1921 | Caruso, Enrico |
| 1876 | 1973 | Casals, Pablo |
| 1929 | 1989 | Cassavetes, John |
| 1893 | 1969 | Castle, Irene |
| 1887 | 1918 | Castle, Vernon |
| 1873 | 1938 | Chaliapin, Feodor |
| 1919 | 1980 | Champion, Gower |
| 1918 | 1961 | Chandler, Jeff |
| 1883 | 1930 | Chaney, Lon |
| 1905 | 1973 | Chaney, Lon Jr. |
| 1942 | 1981 | Chapin, Harry |
| 1889 | 1977 | Chaplin, Charles |
| 1893 | 1961 | Chatterton, Ruth |
| 1888 | 1972 | Chevalier, Maurice |
| 1888 | 1960 | Clark, Bobby |
| 1914 | 1968 | Clark, Fred |
| 1920 | 1966 | Clift, Montgomery |
| 1932 | 1963 | Cline, Patsy |
| 1892 | 1967 | Clyde, Andy |
| 1967 | 1994 | Cobain, Kurt |
| 1911 | 1976 | Cobb, Lee J. |
| 1877 | 1961 | Coburn, Charles |
| 1878 | 1942 | Cohan, George M. |
| 1902 | 1986 | Cohen, Myron |
| 1903 | 1996 | Colbert, Claudette |
| 1919 | 1965 | Cole, Nat (King) |
| 1890 | 1965 | Collins, Ray |
| 1891 | 1958 | Colman, Ronald |
| 1908 | 1934 | Columbo, Russ |
| 1921 | 1992 | Connors, Chuck |
| 1920 | 1994 | Conrad, William |
| 1917 | 1982 | Conried, Hans |
| 1911 | 1975 | Conte, Richard |
| 1914 | 1984 | Coogan, Jackie |
| 1904 | 1995 | Cook, Elisha |
| 1935 | 1964 | Cooke, Sam |
| 1901 | 1961 | Cooper, Gary |
| 1888 | 1971 | Cooper, Gladys |
| 1896 | 1973 | Cooper, Melville |
| 1914 | 1968 | Corey, Wendell |
| 1893 | 1974 | Cornell, Katherine |
| 1890 | 1972 | Correll, Charles (Andy) |
| 1905 | 1979 | Costello, Dolores |
| 1906 | 1959 | Costello, Lou |
| 1905 | 1994 | Cotten, Joseph |
| 1899 | 1973 | Coward, Noel |
| 1924 | 1973 | Cox, Wally |
| 1908 | 1983 | Crabbe, Buster |
| 1928 | 1978 | Crane, Bob |
| 1911 | 1986 | Crawford, Broderick |
| 1908 | 1977 | Crawford, Joan |
| 1880 | 1942 | Crews, Laura Hope |
| 1880 | 1974 | Crisp, Donald |
| 1942 | 1973 | Croce, Jim |
| 1904 | 1977 | Crosby, Bing |
| 1910 | 1986 | Crothers, Scatman |
| 1908 | 1990 | Cummings, Robert |
| 1878 | 1968 | Currie, Finlay |
| 1914 | 1978 | Dailey, Dan |
| 1923 | 1965 | Dandridge, Dorothy |
| 1894 | 1963 | Daniell, Henry |
| 1901 | 1971 | Daniels, Bebe |
| 1936 | 1973 | Darin, Bobby |
| 1921 | 1965 | Darnell, Linda |
| 1879 | 1967 | Darwell, Jane |
| 1909 | 1986 | Da Silva, Howard |
| 1866 | 1949 | Davenport, Harry |
| 1908 | 1989 | Davis, Bette |
| 1907 | 1961 | Davis, Joan |
| 1925 | 1990 | Davis, Sammy Jr. |
| 1931 | 1955 | Dean, James |
| 1917 | 1993 | Defore, Don |
| 1905 | 1968 | Dekker, Albert |
| 1908 | 1983 | Del Rio, Dolores |
| 1892 | 1983 | Demarest, William |

| Born | Died | Name |
|---|---|---|
| 1905 | 1993 | DeMille, Agnes |
| 1881 | 1959 | DeMille, Cecil B. |
| 1937 | 1992 | Dennis, Sandy |
| 1891 | 1967 | Denny, Reginald |
| 1901 | 1974 | DeSica, Vittorio |
| 1905 | 1977 | Devine, Andy |
| 1924 | 1991 | Dewhurst, Colleen |
| 1942 | 1972 | De Wilde, Brandon |
| 1907 | 1974 | De Wolfe, Billy |
| 1920 | 1985 | Diamond, Selma |
| 1901 | 1992 | Dietrich, Marlene |
| 1879 | 1947 | Digges, Dudley |
| 1901 | 1966 | Disney, Walt |
| 1894 | 1949 | Dix, Richard |
| 1905 | 1958 | Donat, Robert |
| 1889 | 1972 | Donlevy, Brian |
| 1901 | 1981 | Douglas, Melvyn |
| 1907 | 1959 | Douglas, Paul |
| 1889 | 1956 | Draper, Ruth |
| 1881 | 1965 | Dresser, Louise |
| 1869 | 1934 | Dressler, Marie |
| 1820 | 1897 | Drew, Mrs. John |
| 1923 | 1996 | Dru, Joanne |
| 1909 | 1951 | Duchin, Eddy |
| 1917 | 1990 | Duff, Howard |
| 1890 | 1974 | Dumbrille, Douglass |
| 1889 | 1965 | Dumont, Margaret |
| 1878 | 1927 | Duncan, Isadora |
| 1905 | 1967 | Dunn, James |
| 1898 | 1990 | Dunne, Irene |
| 1893 | 1980 | Durante, Jimmy |
| 1907 | 1968 | Duryea, Dan |
| 1858 | 1924 | Duse, Eleanora |
| 1894 | 1929 | Eagels, Jeanne |
| 1914 | 1993 | Eckstine, Billy |
| 1901 | 1967 | Eddy, Nelson |
| 1933 | 1996 | Edelman, Herb |
| 1897 | 1971 | Edwards, Cliff |
| 1879 | 1945 | Edwards, Gus |
| 1928 | 1996 | Edwards, Vince |
| 1899 | 1974 | Ellington, Duke |
| 1941 | 1974 | Elliot, Cass |
| 1891 | 1967 | Elman, Mischa |
| 1881 | 1951 | Errol, Leon |
| 1888 | 1976 | Evans, Edith |
| 1901 | 1989 | Evans, Maurice |
| 1909 | 1994 | Ewell, Tom |
| 1883 | 1939 | Fairbanks, Douglas |
| 1914 | 1970 | Farmer, Frances |
| 1870 | 1929 | Farnum, Dustin |
| 1876 | 1953 | Farnum, William |
| 1882 | 1967 | Farrar, Geraldine |
| 1904 | 1971 | Farrell, Glenda |
| 1897 | 1961 | Fay, Frank |
| 1895 | 1962 | Fazenda, Louise |
| 1900 | 1993 | Feld, Fritz |
| 1933 | 1982 | Feldman, Marty |
| 1920 | 1993 | Fellini, Fedrico |
| 1912 | 1992 | Ferrer, Jose |
| 1898 | 1985 | Fetchit, Stepin |
| 1894 | 1979 | Fiedler, Arthur |
| 1918 | 1973 | Field, Betty |
| 1898 | 1979 | Fields, Gracie |
| 1879 | 1946 | Fields, W.C. |
| 1931 | 1978 | Fields, Totie |
| 1916 | 1977 | Finch, Peter |
| 1902 | 1975 | Fine, Larry |
| 1865 | 1932 | Fiske, Minnie Maddern |
| 1888 | 1961 | Fitzgerald, Barry |
| 1895 | 1962 | Flagstad, Kirsten |
| 1900 | 1971 | Flippen, Jay C. |
| 1909 | 1959 | Flynn, Errol |
| 1925 | 1974 | Flynn, Joe |
| 1910 | 1968 | Foley, Red |
| 1905 | 1982 | Fonda, Henry |
| 1920 | 1978 | Fontaine, Frank |
| 1887 | 1983 | Fontanne, Lynn |
| 1919 | 1991 | Fonteyn, Margot |
| 1895 | 1973 | Ford, John |
| 1901 | 1976 | Ford, Paul |
| 1919 | 1991 | Ford, Tennessee Ernie |
| 1899 | 1966 | Ford, Wallace |
| 1927 | 1987 | Fosse, Bob |
| 1901 | 1970 | Foster, Preston |
| 1922 | 1991 | Foxx, Redd |
| 1857 | 1928 | Foy, Eddie |
| 1903 | 1968 | Francis, Kay |
| 1893 | 1966 | Frawley, William |
| 1870 | 1955 | Friganza, Trixie |
| 1890 | 1958 | Frisco, Joe |
| 1916 | 1994 | Furness, Betty |
| 1901 | 1960 | Gable, Clark |
| 1920 | 1995 | Gabor, Eva |
| 1905 | 1990 | Garbo, Greta |
| 1942 | 1995 | Garcia, Jerry |
| 1922 | 1992 | Gardenia, Vincent |
| 1922 | 1990 | Gardner, Ava |
| 1913 | 1952 | Garfield, John |
| 1922 | 1969 | Garland, Judy |
| 1908 | 1996 | Garson, Greer |
| 1939 | 1984 | Gaye, Marvin |
| 1906 | 1984 | Gaynor, Janet |
| 1902 | 1978 | Geer, Will |
| 1900 | 1954 | George, Gladys |
| 1892 | 1962 | Gibson, Hoot |
| 1894 | 1971 | Gilbert, Billy |
| 1895 | 1936 | Gilbert, John |
| 1855 | 1937 | Gillette, William |
| 1897 | 1987 | Gingold, Hermione |
| 1898 | 1968 | Gish, Dorothy |
| 1893 | 1993 | Gish, Lillian |
| 1916 | 1987 | Gleason, Jackie |
| 1886 | 1959 | Gleason, James |
| 1884 | 1938 | Gluck, Alma |
| 1919 | 1991 | Gobel, George |
| 1905 | 1990 | Goddard, Paulette |
| 1903 | 1983 | Godfrey, Arthur |
| 1949 | 1995 | Godunov, Alexander |
| 1882 | 1974 | Goldwyn, Samuel |
| 1909 | 1986 | Goodman, Benny |
| 1915 | 1969 | Gorcey, Leo |
| 1906 | 1995 | Gordon, Gale |
| 1896 | 1985 | Gordon, Ruth |
| 1899 | 1982 | Gosden, Freeman (Amos) |
| 1869 | 1944 | Gottschalk, Ferdinand |
| 1829 | 1869 | Gottschalk, Louis |
| 1916 | 1973 | Grable, Betty |
| 1894 | 1991 | Graham, Martha |
| 1925 | 1981 | Grahame, Gloria |
| 1913 | 1993 | Granger, Stewart |
| 1904 | 1986 | Grant, Cary |
| 1915 | 1987 | Greene, Lorne |
| 1879 | 1954 | Greenstreet, Sydney |
| 1874 | 1948 | Griffith, David Wark |
| 1912 | 1980 | Griffith, Hugh |
| 1925 | 1995 | Guardino, Harry |
| 1912 | 1967 | Guthrie, Woody |
| 1875 | 1959 | Gwenn, Edmund |
| 1926 | 1993 | Gwynne, Fred |
| 1892 | 1950 | Hale, Alan |
| 1918 | 1990 | Hale, Alan Jr. |
| 1925 | 1981 | Haley, Bill |
| 1899 | 1979 | Haley, Jack |
| 1902 | 1985 | Hamilton, Margaret |
| 1847 | 1919 | Hammerstein, Oscar |
| 1893 | 1964 | Hardwicke, Cedric |
| 1892 | 1957 | Hardy, Oliver |
| 1911 | 1937 | Harlow, Jean |
| 1904 | 1995 | Harris, Phil |
| 1908 | 1990 | Harrison, Rex |
| 1870 | 1946 | Hart, William S. |
| 1928 | 1973 | Harvey, Laurence |
| 1910 | 1973 | Hawkins, Jack |
| 1890 | 1973 | Hayakawa, Sessue |
| 1885 | 1969 | Hayes, Gabby |
| 1900 | 1993 | Hayes, Helen |
| 1902 | 1971 | Hayward, Leland |
| 1917 | 1975 | Hayward, Susan |
| 1918 | 1987 | Hayworth, Rita |
| 1896 | 1937 | Healy, Ted |
| 1910 | 1971 | Heflin, Van |
| 1901 | 1987 | Heifetz, Jascha |
| 1873 | 1918 | Held, Anna |
| 1955 | 1996 | Hemingway, Margaux |
| 1942 | 1970 | Hendrix, Jimi |
| 1912 | 1969 | Henie, Sonja |
| 1908 | 1992 | Henreid, Paul |
| 1936 | 1990 | Henson, Jim |
| 1929 | 1993 | Hepburn, Audrey |
| 1886 | 1956 | Hersholt, Jean |
| 1925 | 1992 | Hill, Benny |
| 1899 | 1980 | Hitchcock, Alfred |
| 1914 | 1955 | Hodiak, John |
| 1894 | 1973 | Holden, Fay |
| 1918 | 1981 | Holden, William |
| 1922 | 1965 | Holliday, Judy |
| 1936 | 1959 | Holly, Buddy |
| 1888 | 1951 | Holt, Jack |
| 1918 | 1973 | Holt, Tim |
| 1898 | 1978 | Homolka, Oscar |
| 1967 | 1995 | Hoon, Shannon |
| 1902 | 1972 | Hopkins, Miriam |
| 1858 | 1935 | Hopper, DeWolf |
| 1915 | 1970 | Hopper, William |
| 1904 | 1989 | Horowitz, Vladimir |
| 1886 | 1970 | Horton, Edward Everett |
| 1874 | 1926 | Houdini, Harry |
| 1902 | 1988 | Houseman, John |
| 1906 | 1952 | Howard, Curly |
| 1881 | 1965 | Howard, Eugene |
| 1867 | 1961 | Howard, Joe |
| 1890 | 1943 | Howard, Leslie |
| 1897 | 1975 | Howard, Moe |
| 1891 | 1955 | Howard, Shemp |
| 1885 | 1955 | Howard, Tom |
| 1916 | 1988 | Howard, Trevor |
| 1885 | 1949 | Howard, Willie |
| 1925 | 1985 | Hudson, Rock |
| 1890 | 1977 | Hull, Henry |
| 1886 | 1957 | Hull, Josephine |
| 1895 | 1958 | Humphrey, Doris |
| 1925 | 1969 | Hunter, Jeffrey |
| 1921 | 1996 | Hunter, Ross |
| 1901 | 1962 | Husing, Ted |
| 1906 | 1987 | Huston, John |
| 1884 | 1950 | Huston, Walter |
| 1895 | 1969 | Ingram, Rex |
| 1895 | 1980 | Iturbi, Jose |
| 1936 | 1990 | Ireland, Jill |
| 1915 | 1992 | Ireland, John |
| 1838 | 1905 | Irving, Henry |
| 1909 | 1995 | Ives, Burl |
| 1875 | 1942 | Jackson, Joe |
| 1911 | 1972 | Jackson, Mahalia |
| 1891 | 1984 | Jaffe, Sam |
| 1903 | 1991 | Jagger, Dean |
| 1916 | 1983 | James, Harry |
| 1889 | 1956 | Janis, Elsie |
| 1886 | 1950 | Jannings, Emil |
| 1930 | 1980 | Janssen, David |
| 1900 | 1974 | Jenkins, Allen |
| 1898 | 1981 | Jessel, George |
| 1918 | 1996 | Johnson, Ben |
| 1892 | 1962 | Johnson, Chic |
| 1886 | 1950 | Jolson, Al |
| 1889 | 1942 | Jones, Buck |
| 1933 | 1983 | Jones, Carolyn |
| 1911 | 1965 | Jones, Spike |
| 1943 | 1970 | Joplin, Janis |
| 1902 | 1982 | Jory, Victor |
| 1905 | 1981 | Joslyn, Allyn |
| 1940 | 1994 | Julia, Raul |
| 1910 | 1966 | Kane, Helen |
| 1887 | 1969 | Karloff, Boris |
| 1893 | 1970 | Karns, Roscoe |
| 1913 | 1987 | Kaye, Danny |
| 1811 | 1868 | Kean, Charles |
| 1806 | 1880 | Kean, Mrs. Charles |
| 1787 | 1833 | Kean, Edmund |
| 1895 | 1966 | Keaton, Buster |
| 1910 | 1993 | Keeler, Ruby |
| 1894 | 1973 | Kellaway, Cecil |
| 1898 | 1979 | Kelly, Emmett |
| 1912 | 1996 | Kelly, Gene |
| 1929 | 1982 | Kelly, Grace |
| 1910 | 1981 | Kelly, Patsy |
| 1907 | 1968 | Kelton, Pert |
| 1926 | 1959 | Kendall, Kay |
| 1914 | 1990 | Kennedy, Arthur |
| 1890 | 1948 | Kennedy, Edgar |
| 1886 | 1956 | Kibbee, Guy |
| 1888 | 1964 | Kilbride, Percy |
| 1923 | 1986 | Knight, Ted |
| 1901 | 1980 | Kostelanetz, Andre |
| 1919 | 1962 | Kovacs, Ernie |
| 1885 | 1974 | Kruger, Otto |
| 1921 | 1991 | Kulp, Nancy |
| 1913 | 1964 | Ladd, Alan |
| 1895 | 1967 | Lahr, Bert |
| 1919 | 1973 | Lake, Veronica |
| 1915 | 1982 | Lamas, Fernando |
| 1914 | 1996 | Lamour, Dorothy |
| 1913 | 1994 | Lancaster, Burt |
| 1902 | 1986 | Lanchester, Elsa |
| 1917 | 1995 | Lane, Pricilla |
| 1919 | 1948 | Landis, Carole |
| 1904 | 1972 | Landis, Jessie Royce |
| 1936 | 1991 | Landon, Michael |
| 1884 | 1944 | Langdon, Harry |
| 1853 | 1929 | Langtry, Lillie |
| 1921 | 1959 | Lanza, Mario |
| 1870 | 1950 | Lauder, Harry |
| 1899 | 1962 | Laughton, Charles |
| 1890 | 1965 | Laurel, Stan |
| 1923 | 1984 | Lawford, Peter |

| Born | Died | Name |
|---|---|---|
| 1898 | 1952 | Lawrence, Gertrude |
| 1908 | 1991 | Lean, David |
| 1940 | 1973 | Lee, Bruce |
| 1907 | 1952 | Lee, Canada |
| 1914 | 1970 | Lee, Gypsy Rose |
| 1899 | 1991 | LeGallienne, Eva |
| 1888 | 1976 | Lehmann, Lotte |
| 1913 | 1967 | Leigh, Vivien |
| 1922 | 1976 | Leighton, Margaret |
| 1940 | 1980 | Lennon, John |
| 1898 | 1981 | Lenya, Lotte |
| 1870 | 1941 | Leonard, Eddie |
| 1900 | 1987 | LeRoy, Mervyn |
| 1906 | 1972 | Levant, Oscar |
| 1905 | 1980 | Levene, Sam |
| 1902 | 1971 | Lewis, Joe E. |
| 1892 | 1971 | Lewis, Ted |
| 1919 | 1987 | Liberace |
| 1820 | 1887 | Lind, Jenny |
| 1920 | 1995 | Lindfors, Viveca |
| 1894 | 1989 | Lillie, Beatrice |
| 1893 | 1971 | Lloyd, Harold |
| 1870 | 1922 | Lloyd, Marie |
| 1891 | 1957 | Lockhart, Gene |
| 1913 | 1969 | Logan, Ella |
| 1909 | 1942 | Lombard, Carole |
| 1902 | 1977 | Lombardo, Guy |
| 1927 | 1974 | Long, Richard |
| 1895 | 1975 | Lopez, Vincent |
| 1888 | 1968 | Lorne, Marion |
| 1904 | 1964 | Lorre, Peter |
| 1912 | 1962 | Lovejoy, Frank |
| 1890 | 1971 | Lowe, Edmund |
| 1905 | 1993 | Loy, Myrna |
| 1892 | 1947 | Lubitsch, Ernst |
| 1882 | 1956 | Lugosi, Bela |
| 1894 | 1971 | Lukas, Paul |
| 1892 | 1977 | Lunt, Alfred |
| 1914 | 1995 | Lupino, Ida |
| 1926 | 1982 | Lynde, Paul |
| 1926 | 1971 | Lynn, Diana |
| | | |
| 1903 | 1965 | MacDonald, Jeanette |
| 1902 | 1969 | MacLane, Barton |
| 1908 | 1991 | MacMurray, Fred |
| 1921 | 1986 | MacRae, Gordon |
| 1909 | 1973 | Macready, George |
| 1922 | 1996 | Madison, Guy |
| 1908 | 1973 | Magnani, Anna |
| 1924 | 1994 | Mancini, Henry |
| 1890 | 1975 | Main, Marjorie |
| 1932 | 1995 | Malle, Louis |
| 1932 | 1967 | Mansfield, Jayne |
| 1905 | 1980 | Mantovani, Annunzio |
| 1897 | 1975 | March, Fredric |
| 1945 | 1981 | Marley, Bob |
| 1890 | 1966 | Marshall, Herbert |
| 1917 | 1995 | Martin, Dean |
| 1913 | 1990 | Martin, Mary |
| 1920 | 1981 | Martin, Ross |
| 1924 | 1987 | Marvin, Lee |
| 1888 | 1964 | Marx, Arthur (Harpo) |
| 1901 | 1979 | Marx, Herbert (Zeppo) |
| 1890 | 1977 | Marx, Julius (Groucho) |
| 1886 | 1961 | Marx, Leonard (Chico) |
| 1893 | 1977 | Marx, Milton (Gummo) |
| 1909 | 1984 | Mason, James |
| 1896 | 1983 | Massey, Raymond |
| 1885 | 1957 | Mayer, Louis B. |
| 1895 | 1973 | Maynard, Ken |
| 1935 | 1995 | McClure, Doug |
| 1884 | 1945 | McCormack, John |
| 1905 | 1990 | McCrea, Joel |
| 1895 | 1952 | McDaniel, Hattie |
| 1899 | 1981 | McHugh, Frank |
| 1907 | 1991 | McIntire, John |
| 1883 | 1959 | McLaglen, Victor |
| 1907 | 1971 | McMahon, Horace |
| 1907 | 1979 | McNeill, Don |
| 1911 | 1995 | McQueen, Butterfly |
| 1930 | 1980 | McQueen, Steve |
| 1924 | 1996 | Meadows, Audrey |
| 1920 | 1980 | Medford, Kay |
| 1880 | 1946 | Meek, Donald |
| 1861 | 1931 | Melba, Nellie |
| 1890 | 1973 | Melchior, Lauritz |
| 1890 | 1963 | Menjou, Adolphe |
| 1902 | 1966 | Menken, Helen |
| 1925 | 1994 | Mercouri, Melina |
| 1908 | 1984 | Merman, Ethel |
| 1905 | 1986 | Milland, Ray |
| 1904 | 1944 | Miller, Glenn |
| 1898 | 1936 | Miller, Marilyn |
| 1913 | 1982 | Mills, Harry |
| 1903 | 1955 | Minnevitch, Borrah |
| 1939 | 1976 | Mineo, Sal |
| 1913 | 1955 | Miranda, Carmen |
| 1918 | 1994 | Mitchell, Cameron |
| 1892 | 1962 | Mitchell, Thomas |
| 1880 | 1940 | Mix, Tom |
| 1926 | 1962 | Monroe, Marilyn |
| 1911 | 1973 | Monroe, Vaughn |
| 1917 | 1951 | Montez, Maria |
| 1933 | 1995 | Montgomery, Elizabeth |
| 1904 | 1981 | Montgomery, Robert |
| 1901 | 1947 | Moore, Grace |
| 1914 | 1993 | Moore, Garry |
| 1876 | 1962 | Moore, Victor |
| 1906 | 1974 | Moorehead, Agnes |
| 1910 | 1994 | Morgan, Dennis |
| 1890 | 1949 | Morgan, Frank |
| 1900 | 1941 | Morgan, Helen |
| 1915 | 1994 | Morgan, Henry |
| 1901 | 1970 | Morris, Chester |
| 1934 | 1996 | Morris, Greg |
| 1914 | 1959 | Morris, Wayne |
| 1943 | 1971 | Morrison, Jim |
| 1932 | 1982 | Morrow, Vic |
| 1915 | 1977 | Mostel, Zero |
| 1897 | 1969 | Mowbray, Alan |
| 1927 | 1996 | Mulligan, Gerry |
| 1895 | 1967 | Muni, Paul |
| 1915 | 1970 | Munshin, Jules |
| 1924 | 1971 | Murphy, Audie |
| 1902 | 1992 | Murphy, George |
| 1885 | 1965 | Murray, Mae |
| | | |
| 1896 | 1970 | Nagel, Conrad |
| 1900 | 1973 | Naish, J. Carroll |
| 1898 | 1961 | Naldi, Nita |
| 1908 | 1994 | Natwick, Mildred |
| 1914 | 1994 | Nelson, Harriet (Hillard) |
| 1906 | 1975 | Nelson, Ozzie |
| 1940 | 1985 | Nelson, Rick |
| 1885 | 1967 | Nesbit, Evelyn |
| 1890 | 1950 | Nijinsky, Vaslav |
| 1893 | 1974 | Nilsson, Anna Q. |
| 1909 | 1983 | Niven, David |
| 1902 | 1985 | Nolan, Lloyd |
| 1894 | 1930 | Normand, Mabel |
| 1899 | 1968 | Novarro, Ramon |
| 1938 | 1993 | Nureyev, Rudolf |
| | | |
| 1903 | 1978 | Oakie, Jack |
| 1860 | 1926 | Oakley, Annie |
| 1928 | 1982 | Oates, Warren |
| 1911 | 1979 | Oberon, Merle |
| 1915 | 1985 | O'Brien, Edmond |
| 1899 | 1983 | O'Brien, Pat |
| 1908 | 1981 | O'Connell, Arthur |
| 1921 | 1993 | O'Connell, Helen |
| 1880 | 1959 | O'Connor, Una |
| 1908 | 1968 | O'Keefe, Dennis |
| 1880 | 1938 | Oland, Warner |
| 1860 | 1932 | Olcott, Chauncey |
| 1883 | 1942 | Oliver, Edna May |
| 1907 | 1989 | Olivier, Laurence |
| 1892 | 1963 | Olsen, Ole |
| 1927 | 1994 | O'Neal, Patrick |
| 1849 | 1920 | O'Neill, James |
| 1936 | 1988 | Orbison, Roy |
| 1899 | 1985 | Ormandy, Eugene |
| 1876 | 1949 | Ouspenskaya, Maria |
| 1887 | 1972 | Owen, Reginald |
| | | |
| 1860 | 1941 | Paderewski, Ignace |
| 1924 | 1987 | Page, Geraldine |
| 1889 | 1954 | Pallette, Eugene |
| 1914 | 1986 | Palmer, Lilli |
| 1894 | 1958 | Pangborn, Franklin |
| 1914 | 1992 | Parks, Bert |
| 1914 | 1975 | Parks, Larry |
| 1881 | 1940 | Pasternack, Josef A. |
| 1837 | 1908 | Pastor, Tony |
| 1843 | 1919 | Patti, Adelina |
| 1840 | 1889 | Patti, Carlotta |
| 1885 | 1931 | Pavlova, Anna |
| 1912 | 1989 | Payne, John |
| 1912 | 1996 | Pearl, Minnie |
| 1904 | 1984 | Peerce, Jan |
| 1899 | 1967 | Pendleton, Nat |
| 1905 | 1941 | Penner, Joe |
| 1928 | 1994 | Peppard, George |
| 1932 | 1992 | Perkins, Anthony |
| 1970 | 1993 | Phoenix, River |
| 1915 | 1963 | Piaf, Edith |
| 1893 | 1979 | Pickford, Mary |
| 1897 | 1984 | Pidgeon, Walter |
| 1892 | 1957 | Pinza, Ezio |
| 1898 | 1963 | Pitts, Zasu |
| 1904 | 1976 | Pons, Lily |
| 1897 | 1981 | Ponselle, Rosa |
| 1904 | 1963 | Powell, Dick |
| 1912 | 1982 | Powell, Eleanor |
| 1892 | 1984 | Powell, William |
| 1913 | 1958 | Power, Tyrone |
| 1905 | 1986 | Preminger, Otto |
| 1935 | 1977 | Presley, Elvis |
| 1918 | 1987 | Preston, Robert |
| 1911 | 1993 | Price, Vincent |
| 1911 | 1978 | Prima, Louis |
| 1954 | 1977 | Prinze, Freddie |
| 1936 | 1996 | Prowse, Juliet |
| | | |
| 1946 | 1989 | Radner, Gilda |
| 1895 | 1980 | Raft, George |
| 1890 | 1967 | Rains, Claude |
| 1902 | 1994 | Ralston, Esther |
| 1892 | 1967 | Rathbone, Basil |
| 1897 | 1960 | Ratoff, Gregory |
| 1926 | 1991 | Ray, Aldo |
| 1916 | 1994 | Raye, Martha |
| 1941 | 1967 | Redding, Otis |
| 1908 | 1985 | Redgrave, Michael |
| 1921 | 1986 | Reed, Donna |
| 1932 | 1992 | Reed, Robert |
| 1914 | 1959 | Reeves, George |
| 1873 | 1943 | Reinhardt, Max |
| 1935 | 1991 | Remick, Lee |
| 1909 | 1971 | Rennie, Michael |
| 1941 | 1996 | Rettig, Tommy |
| 1932 | 1995 | Rich, Charlie |
| 1902 | 1983 | Richardson, Ralph |
| 1921 | 1985 | Riddle, Nelson |
| 1898 | 1977 | Ritchard, Cyril |
| 1907 | 1974 | Ritter, Tex |
| 1905 | 1969 | Ritter, Thelma |
| 1901 | 1965 | Ritz, Al |
| 1906 | 1986 | Ritz, Harry |
| 1903 | 1985 | Ritz, Jimmy |
| 1925 | 1982 | Robbins, Marty |
| 1898 | 1976 | Robeson, Paul |
| 1878 | 1949 | Robinson, Bill |
| 1893 | 1973 | Robinson, Edward G. |
| 1905 | 1977 | Rochester (E. Anderson) |
| 1897 | 1933 | Rodgers, Jimmie |
| 1911 | 1995 | Rogers, Ginger |
| 1879 | 1935 | Rogers, Will |
| 1905 | 1994 | Roland, Gilbert |
| 1907 | 1994 | Romero, Cesar |
| 1880 | 1962 | Rooney, Pat |
| 1899 | 1966 | Rose, Billy |
| 1922 | 1987 | Rowan, Dan |
| 1887 | 1982 | Rubinstein, Artur |
| 1886 | 1970 | Ruggles, Charles |
| 1924 | 1961 | Russell, Gail |
| 1861 | 1922 | Russell, Lillian |
| 1911 | 1976 | Russell, Rosalind |
| 1892 | 1972 | Rutherford, Margaret |
| 1903 | 1973 | Ryan, Irene |
| 1909 | 1973 | Ryan, Robert |
| | | |
| 1933 | 1994 | Sargent, Dick |
| 1877 | 1968 | St. Denis, Ruth |
| 1884 | 1955 | Sakall, S.Z. |
| 1885 | 1936 | Sale (Chic), Charles |
| 1906 | 1972 | Sanders, George |
| 1924 | 1994 | Savalas, Telly |
| 1895 | 1964 | Schildkraut, Joseph |
| 1889 | 1965 | Schipa, Tito |
| 1882 | 1951 | Schnabel, Artur |
| 1920 | 1981 | Scott, Hazel |
| 1898 | 1987 | Scott, Randolph |
| 1914 | 1965 | Scott, Zachary |
| 1843 | 1896 | Scott-Siddons, Mrs. |
| 1938 | 1979 | Seberg, Jean |
| 1892 | 1974 | Seeley, Blossom |
| 1893 | 1987 | Segovia, Andres |
| 1971 | 1995 | Selena |
| 1925 | 1980 | Sellers, Peter |
| 1902 | 1965 | Selznick, David O. |
| 1884 | 1960 | Sennett, Mack |
| 1924 | 1975 | Serling, Rod |
| 1970 | 1996 | Shakur, Tupac |
| 1927 | 1978 | Shaw, Robert |
| 1891 | 1972 | Shawn, Ted |
| 1868 | 1949 | Shean, Al |
| 1902 | 1983 | Shearer, Norma |
| 1915 | 1967 | Sheridan, Ann |
| 1917 | 1994 | Shore, Dinah |
| 1875 | 1953 | Shubert, Lee |
| 1755 | 1831 | Siddons, Mrs. Sarah |

| Born | Died | Name |
|---|---|---|
| 1921 | 1985 | Signoret, Simone |
| 1912 | 1985 | Silvers, Phil |
| 1900 | 1976 | Sim, Alastair |
| 1858 | 1942 | Skinner, Otis |
| 1863 | 1948 | Smith, C. Aubrey |
| 1907 | 1986 | Smith, Kate |
| 1854 | 1932 | Sousa, John Philip |
| 1884 | 1957 | Sparks, Ned |
| 1908 | 1994 | Stander, Lionel |
| 1907 | 1990 | Stanwyck, Barbara |
| 1934 | 1970 | Stevens, Inger |
| 1929 | 1996 | Stevenson, McLean |
| 1882 | 1977 | Stokowski, Leopold |
| 1879 | 1953 | Stone, Lewis |
| 1904 | 1980 | Stone, Milburn |
| 1898 | 1959 | Sturges, Preston |
| 1911 | 1960 | Sullavan, Margaret |
| 1912 | 1994 | Sullivan, Barry |
| 1902 | 1974 | Sullivan, Ed |
| 1903 | 1956 | Sullivan, Francis L. |
| 1892 | 1946 | Summerville, Slim |
| 1899 | 1983 | Swanson, Gloria |
| 1904 | 1969 | Swarthout, Gladys |
| 1904 | 1996 | Talbot, Lyle |
| 1893 | 1957 | Talmadge, Norma |
| 1899 | 1972 | Tamiroff, Akim |
| 1909 | 1994 | Tandy, Jessica |
| 1878 | 1947 | Tanguay, Eva |
| 1885 | 1966 | Taylor, Deems |
| 1899 | 1958 | Taylor, Estelle |
| 1887 | 1946 | Taylor, Laurette |
| 1911 | 1969 | Taylor, Robert |
| 1847 | 1928 | Terry, Ellen |
| 1899 | 1936 | Thalberg, Irving |
| 1912 | 1991 | Thomas, Danny |
| 1882 | 1976 | Thorndike, Sybil |
| 1896 | 1960 | Tibbett, Lawrence |
| 1920 | 1991 | Tierney, Gene |
| 1909 | 1958 | Todd, Michael |
| 1903 | 1968 | Tone, Franchot |
| 1867 | 1957 | Toscanini, Arturo |
| 1898 | 1968 | Tracy, Lee |
| 1900 | 1967 | Tracy, Spencer |
| 1903 | 1972 | Traubel, Helen |
| 1894 | 1975 | Treacher, Arthur |
| 1853 | 1917 | Tree, Herbert Beerbohm |
| 1890 | 1973 | Truex, Ernest |
| 1932 | 1984 | Truffaut, Francois |
| 1919 | 1986 | Tucker, Forrest |
| 1913 | 1975 | Tucker, Richard |
| 1884 | 1966 | Tucker, Sophie |
| 1920 | 1995 | Turner, Lana |
| 1874 | 1940 | Turpin, Ben |
| 1908 | 1959 | Twelvetrees, Helen |
| 1933 | 1993 | Twitty, Conway |
| 1895 | 1926 | Valentino, Rudolph |
| 1901 | 1986 | Vallee, Rudy |
| 1912 | 1979 | Vance, Vivian |
| 1922 | 1996 | Van Fleet, Jo |
| 1924 | 1990 | Vaughan, Sarah |
| 1893 | 1943 | Veidt, Conrad |
| 1926 | 1981 | Vera-Ellen |
| 1958 | 1979 | Vicious, Sid |
| 1885 | 1957 | Von Stroheim, Erich |
| 1906 | 1981 | Von Zell, Harry |
| 1942 | 1995 | Walker, Junior |
| 1922 | 1992 | Walker, Nancy |
| 1914 | 1951 | Walker, Robert |
| 1887 | 1980 | Walsh, Raoul |
| 1876 | 1962 | Walter, Bruno |
| 1876 | 1958 | Warner, H. B. |
| 1924 | 1963 | Washington, Dinah |
| 1900 | 1977 | Waters, Ethel |
| 1914 | 1995 | Wayne, David |
| 1907 | 1979 | Wayne, John |
| 1891 | 1966 | Webb, Clifton |
| 1920 | 1982 | Webb, Jack |
| 1904 | 1984 | Weissmuller, Johnny |
| 1903 | 1992 | Welk, Lawrence |
| 1915 | 1985 | Welles, Orson |
| 1896 | 1975 | Wellman, William |
| 1892 | 1980 | West, Mae |
| 1924 | 1996 | Weston, Jack |
| 1895 | 1968 | Wheeler, Bert |
| 1889 | 1938 | White, Pearl |
| 1891 | 1967 | Whiteman, Paul |
| 1865 | 1948 | Whitty, May |
| 1910 | 1995 | Wickes, Mary |
| 1918 | 1989 | Wilde, Cornel |
| 1912 | 1979 | Wilding, Michael |
| 1877 | 1922 | Williams, Bert |
| 1923 | 1953 | Williams, Hank |
| 1905 | 1975 | Wills, Bob |
| 1903 | 1978 | Wills, Chill |
| 1917 | 1972 | Wilson, Marie |
| 1884 | 1969 | Winninger, Charles |
| 1904 | 1959 | Withers, Grant |
| 1907 | 1961 | Wong, Anna May |
| 1938 | 1981 | Wood, Natalie |
| 1892 | 1978 | Wood, Peggy |
| 1888 | 1963 | Woolley, Monty |
| 1902 | 1981 | Wyler, William |
| 1886 | 1966 | Wynn, Ed |
| 1916 | 1986 | Wynn, Keenan |
| 1929 | 1992 | York, Dick |
| 1890 | 1960 | Young, Clara Kimball |
| 1913 | 1978 | Young, Gig |
| 1887 | 1953 | Young, Roland |
| 1902 | 1979 | Zanuck, Darryl F. |
| 1940 | 1993 | Zappa, Frank |
| 1869 | 1932 | Ziegfeld, Florenz |
| 1873 | 1976 | Zukor, Adolph |

# Original Names of Selected Entertainers

**Edie Adams:** Elizabeth Edith Enke
**Eddie Albert:** Edward Albert Heimberger
**Alan Alda:** Alphonso D'Abruzzo
**Fred Allen:** John Sullivan
**Woody Allen:** Allen Konigsberg
**Greg Allman:** Gregory Lenoir
**June Allyson:** Ella Geisman
**Julie Andrews:** Julia Wells
**Eve Arden:** Eunice Quedens
**Beatrice Arthur:** Bernice Frankel
**Jean Arthur:** Gladys Greene
**Fred Astaire:** Frederick Austerlitz
**Alan Autry:** Carlos Brown
**Lauren Bacall:** Betty Joan Perske
**Anne Bancroft:** Anna Maria Italiano
**Brigitte Bardot:** Camille Javal
**Gene Barry:** Eugene Klass
**Drew Barrymore:** Andrew Barrymore
**Orson Bean:** Dallas Burrows
**Pat Benatar:** Patricia Andrejewski
**Robbie Benson:** Robert Segal
**Tony Bennett:** Anthony Benedetto
**Busby Berkeley:** William Berkeley Enos
**Irving Berlin:** Israel Baline
**Jack Benny:** Benjamin Kubelsky
**Joey Bishop:** Joseph Gottlieb
**Robert Blake:** Michael Gubitosi
**Bono (Vox):** Paul Hewson
**Victor Borge:** Borge Rosenbaum
**David Bowie:** David Robert Jones
**Boy George:** George Alan O'Dowd
**Fanny Brice:** Fanny Borach
**Charles Bronson:** Charles Buchinski
**Albert Brooks:** Albert Einstein
**Mel Brooks:** Melvin Kaminsky
**George Burns:** Nathan Birnbaum
**Ellen Burstyn:** Edna Gilhooley
**Richard Burton:** Richard Jenkins
**Red Buttons:** Aaron Chwatt
**Nicolas Cage:** Nicholas Coppola
**Michael Caine:** Maurice Micklewhite
**Maria Callas:** Maria Kalogeropoulos
**Vikki Carr:** Florencia Casillas
**Diahann Carroll:** Carol Diahann Johnson
**Cyd Charisse:** Tula Finklea
**Ray Charles:** Ray Charles Robinson
**Chubby Checker:** Ernest Evans
**Cher:** Cherilyn Sarkisian
**Patsy Cline:** Virginia Patterson Hensley
**Lee J. Cobb:** Leo Jacoby
**Claudette Colbert:** Lily Chauchoin
**Michael Connors:** Kreker Ohanian
**Robert Conrad:** Conrad Robert Falk
**Alice Cooper:** Vincent Furnier
**David Copperfield:** David Kotkin
**Howard Cosell:** Howard Cohen
**Elvis Costello:** Declan McManus
**Lou Costello:** Louis Cristillo
**Peter Coyote:** Peter Cohon
**Joan Crawford:** Lucille Le Sueur
**Michael Crawford:** Michael Dumble-Smith
**Tom Cruise:** Thomas Mapother IV
**Tony Curtis:** Bernard Schwartz
**Vic Damone:** Vito Farinola
**Rodney Dangerfield:** Jacob Cohen
**Bobby Darin:** Walden Robert Cassotto
**Doris Day:** Doris von Kappelhoff
**James Dean:** James Byron
**Yvonne De Carlo:** Peggy Middleton
**Sandra Dee:** Alexandra Zuck
**John Denver:** Henry John Deutschendorf Jr.
**Bo Derek:** Mary Cathleen Collins
**John Derek:** Derek Harris
**Danny DeVito:** Daniel Michaeli
**Angie Dickinson:** Angeline Brown
**Bo Diddley:** Elias Bates
**Phyllis Diller:** Phyllis Driver
**Diana Dors:** Diana Fluck
**Kirk Douglas:** Issur Danielovitch
**Melvyn Douglas:** Melvyn Hesselberg
**Bob Dylan:** Robert Zimmerman
**Sheena Easton:** Sheena Shirley Orr
**Barbara Eden:** Barbara Huffman
**Ron Ely:** Ronald Pierce
**Dale Evans:** Frances Smith
**Chad Everett:** Raymond Cramton
**Tom Ewell:** S. Yewell Tompkins
**Douglas Fairbanks:** Douglas Ullman
**Morgan Fairchild:** Patsy McClenny
**Jamie Farr:** Jameel Farah
**Alice Faye:** Ann Leppert
**Stepin Fetchit:** Lincoln Perry
**Sally Field:** Sally Mahoney
**W.C. Fields:** William Claude Dukenfield
**Peter Finch:** William Mitchell
**Barry Fitzgerald:** William Shields
**Joan Fontaine:** Joan de Havilland
**John Ford:** Sean O'Fearna
**John Forsythe:** John Freund
**Jodie Foster:** Alicia Christian Foster
**Redd Foxx :** John Sanford
**Anthony Franciosa:** Anthony Papaleo
**Arlene Francis:** Arlene Kazanjian
**Connie Francis:** Concetta Franconero
**Greta Garbo:** Greta Gustafsson
**Vincent Gardenia:** Vincent Scognamiglio
**John Garfield:** Julius Garfinkle
**Judy Garland:** Frances Gumm
**James Garner:** James Bumgarner
**Crystal Gayle:** Brenda Gayle Webb
**Kathy Lee Gifford:** Kathie Epstein
**Paulette Goddard:** Marion Levy
**Whoopi Goldberg:** Caryn Johnson
**Eydie Gorme:** Edith Gormezano
**Elle MacPherson:** Eleanor Gow
**Stewart Granger:** James Stewart
**Cary Grant:** Archibald Leach
**Lee Grant:** Lyova Rosenthal
**Joel Grey:** Joe Katz
**Robert Guillaume:** Robert Williams
**Buddy Hackett:** Leonard Hacker
**Hammer:** Stanley Kirk Burrell
**Jean Harlow:** Harlean Carpentier
**Rex Harrison:** Reginald Carey
**Laurence Harvey:** Larushka Skikne
**Helen Hayes:** Helen Brown
**Susan Hayward:** Edythe Marriner
**Rita Hayworth:** Margarita Cansino
**Pee-Wee Herman:** Paul Rubenfeld
**Barbara Hershey:** Barbara Herzstine
**William Holden:** William Beedle
**Billie Holliday:** Eleanora Fagan
**Judy Holliday:** Judith Tuvim
**Harry Houdini:** Ehrich Weiss
**Leslie Howard:** Leslie Stainer
**Moe Howard:** Moses Horowitz
**Rock Hudson:** Roy Scherer Jr. (later Fitzgerald)
**Engelbert Humperdinck:** Arnold Dorsey
**Kim Hunter:** Janet Cole
**Mary Beth Hurt:** Mary Supinger
**Betty Hutton:** Betty Thornberg
**Lauren Hutton:** Mary Laurence Hutton

**Billy Idol:** William Broad
**David Janssen:** David Meyer
**Anne Jillian:** Anne Nauseda
**Elton John:** Reginald Dwight
**Don Johnson:** Donald Wayne
**Al Jolson:** Asa Yoelson
**Jennifer Jones:** Phyllis Isley
**Tom Jones:** Thomas Woodward
**Louis Jourdan:** Louis Gendre
**Wynonna Judd:** Christina Judd
**Boris Karloff:** William Henry Pratt
**Danny Kaye:** David Kaminsky
**Diane Keaton:** Diane Hall
**Michael Keaton:** Michael Douglas
**Howard Keel:** Harold Leek
**Chaka Khan:** Yvette Stevens
**Carole King:** Carole Klein
**Larry King:** Larry Zeigler
**Ben Kingsley:** Krishna Banji
**Nastassja Kinski:** Nastassja Naksyznyski
**Ted Knight:** Tadeus Wladyslaw Konopka
**Cheryl Ladd:** Cheryl Stoppelmoor
**Veronica Lake:** Constance Ockleman
**Hedy Lamarr:** Hedwig Kiesler
**Dorothy Lamour:** Mary Kaumeyer
**Michael Landon:** Eugene Orowitz
**Mario Lanza:** Alfredo Cocozza
**Queen Latifah:** Dana Owens
**Stan Laurel:** Arthur Jefferson
**Steve Lawrence:** Sidney Leibowitz
**Brenda Lee:** Brenda Mae Tarpley
**Bruce Lee:** Lee Yuen Kam
**Gypsy Rose Lee:** Rose Louise Hovick
**Michelle Lee:** Michelle Dusiak
**Peggy Lee:** Norma Egstrom
**Janet Leigh:** Jeanette Morrison
**Vivien Leigh:** Vivian Hartley
**Huey Lewis:** Hugh Cregg
**Jerry Lewis:** Joseph Levitch
**Hal Linden:** Harold Lipshitz
**Carole Lombard:** Jane Peters
**Jack Lord:** John Joseph Ryan
**Sophia Loren:** Sophia Scicoloni
**Peter Lorre:** Laszio Lowenstein
**Myrna Loy:** Myrna Williams
**Bela Lugosi:** Bela Ferenc Blasko
**Moms Mabley:** Loretta Mary Aitken
**Shirley MacLaine:** Shirley Beaty
**Madonna:** Madonna Louise Ciccone
**Lee Majors:** Harvey Lee Yeary 2d
**Karl Malden:** Malden Sekulovich
**Barry Manilow:** Barry Alan Pincus
**Jayne Mansfield:** Vera Jane Palmer
**Fredric March:** Frederick Bickel
**Peter Marshall:** Pierre LaCock
**Walter Mathau:** Walter Matuschanskayasky
**Dean Martin:** Dino Crocetti
**Meat Loaf:** Marvin Lee Aday
**Ethel Merman:** Ethel Zimmerman
**George Michael:** Georgios Panayiotou
**Ray Milland:** Reginald Truscott-Jones
**Ann Miller:** Lucille Collier
**Joni Mitchell:** Roberta Joan Anderson
**Marilyn Monroe:** Norma Jean Mortenson, (later) Baker
**Yves Montand:** Ivo Levi
**Ron Moody:** Ronald Moodnick
**Demi Moore:** Demetria Guynes
**Garry Moore:** Thomas Garrison Morfit
**Rita Moreno:** Rosita Alverio
**Harry Morgan:** Harry Bratsburg
**Paul Muni:** Muni Weisenfreund
**Mike Nichols:** Michael Igor Peschowsky
**Chuck Norris:** Carlos Ray
**Sheree North:** Dawn Bethel
**Hugh O'Brian:** Hugh Krampke
**Maureen O'Hara:** Maureen Fitzsimons
**Patti Page:** Clara Ann Fowler
**Jack Palance:** Walter Palanuik
**Bert Parks:** Bert Jacobson
**Minnie Pearl:** Sarah Ophelia Cannon
**Bernadette Peters:** Bernadette Lazzaro
**Edith Piaf:** Edith Gassion
**Slim Pickens:** Louis Lindley
**Mary Pickford:** Gladys Smith
**Stephanie Powers:** Stefania Federkiewicz
**Paula Prentiss:** Paula Ragusa
**Robert Preston:** Robert Preston Meservey
**Prince:** Prince Rogers Nelson
**Tony Randall:** Leonard Rosenberg
**Johnnie Ray:** John Alvin
**Martha Raye:** Margaret O'Reed
**Donna Reed:** Donna Belle Mullenger
**Della Reese:** Delloreese Patricia Early
**Joan Rivers:** Joan Sandra Molinsky
**Edward G. Robinson:** Emmanuel Goldenberg
**Ginger Rogers:** Virginia McMath
**Roy Rogers:** Leonard Slye
**Mickey Rooney:** Joe Yule Jr.
**Johnnie Rotten:** John Lydon
**Lillian Russell:** Helen Leonard
**Theresa Russell:** Theresa Paup
**Winona Ryder:** Winona Horowitz
**Soupy Sales:** Milton Hines
**Susan Sarandon:** Susan Tomaling
**Randolph Scott:** George Randolph Crane
**Jane Seymour:** Joyce Frankenberg
**Omar Sharif:** Michael Shalhoub
**Charlie Sheen:** Carlos Irwin Estevez
**Martin Sheen:** Ramon Estevez
**Beverly Sills:** Belle Silverman
**Talia Shire:** Talia Coppola
**Phil Silvers:** Philip Silversmith
**Sinbad:** David Atkins
**Suzanne Somers:** Suzanne Mahoney
**Ann Sothern:** Harriette Lake
**Robert Stack:** Robert Modini
**Barbara Stanwyck:** Ruby Stevens
**Jean Stapleton:** Jeanne Murray
**Ringo Starr:** Richard Starkey
**Connie Stevens:** Concetta Ingolia
**Sting:** Gordon Sumner
**Donna Summer:** La Donna Gaines
**Rip Taylor:** Charles Elmer Jr.
**Robert Taylor:** Spangler Brugh
**Danny Thomas:** Muzyad Yakhoob, later Amos Jacobs
**Rip Torn:** Elmore Rual Torn Jr.
**Randy Travis:** Randy Traywick
**Sophie Tucker:** Sophia Kalish
**Tina Turner:** Annie Mae Bullock
**Conway Twitty:** Harold Lloyd Jenkins
**Rudolph Valentino:** Rudolpho D'Antonguolla
**Frankie Valli:** Frank Castelluccio
**Sid Vicious:** John Simon Ritchie
**David Wayne:** Wayne McMeekan
**John Wayne:** Marion Morrison
**Clifton Webb:** Webb Hollenbeck
**Raquel Welch:** Raquel Tejada
**Gene Wilder:** Jerome Silberman
**Shelley Winters:** Shirley Schrift
**Stevie Wonder:** Stevland Morris
**Natalie Wood:** Natasha Gurdin
**Jane Wyman:** Sarah Jane Fulks
**Gig Young:** Byron Barr

## Selected Royal Families of Europe

| Name (Birthplace) | Birthdate |
|---|---|
| **Belgium** | |
| King Albert II (Brussels) | 6/6/34 |
| Queen Paola (Calabria, Italy) | 9/11/37 |
| Prince Philippe (Brussels) | 4/15/60 |
| Princess Astrid (Brussels) | 6/5/62 |
| Prince Laurent (Brussels) | 10/19/63 |
| **United Kingdom** | |
| Queen Elizabeth II (London) | 4/21/26 |
| Prince Philip (Corfu, Greece) | 6/10/21 |
| Prince Charles (London) | 11/14/48 |
| Princess Diana[1] (Sandringham, England) | 7/1/61 |
| Prince William (London) | 6/21/82 |
| Prince Henry (London) | 9/15/84 |
| Princess Anne (London) | 8/15/50 |
| Prince Andrew (London) | 2/19/60 |
| Princess Beatrice (London) | 8/8/88 |
| Princess Eugenie (London) | 3/23/90 |
| Prince Edward (London) | 3/1/64 |
| Princess Margaret (Glamis, Scotland) | 8/21/30 |
| **Denmark** | |
| Queen Margrethe II (Copenhagen) | 4/16/40 |
| Prince Henrik (France) | — |
| Prince Frederik (Copenhagen) | 5/26/68 |
| Prince Joachim (Copenhagen) | 6/7/69 |
| **Liechtenstein** | |
| Prince Hans-Adam II (Liechtenstein) | 2/14/45 |
| Countess Marie | — |
| Crown Prince Alois (Liechtenstein) | 6/11/68 |
| Prince Maximilian (Liechtenstein) | 5/16/69 |
| Prince Constantin (Liechtenstein) | 3/15/72 |
| Princess Tatjana (Liechtenstein) | 4/10/73 |
| **Luxembourg** | |
| Grand Duke Jean (Berg Castle, Luxembourg) | 1/5/21 |
| Princess Joséphine-Charlotte (Belgium) | 10/11/27 |
| Princess Marie-Astrid (Luxembourg) | 2/17/54 |
| Prince Henri (Luxembourg) | 4/16/55 |
| Prince Jean (Luxembourg) | 5/15/57 |
| Princess Margaretha (Luxembourg) | 5/15/57 |
| Prince Guillaume (Luxembourg) | 5/1/63 |
| **Monaco** | |
| Prince Rainier III (Monaco) | 5/31/23 |
| Prince Albert (Monte Carlo) | 3/14/58 |
| Princess Caroline (Monte Carlo) | 1/23/57 |
| Princess Stephanie (Monaco-Ville, Monaco) | 2/1/65 |
| **Netherlands** | |
| Queen Beatrix (Baarn, Netherlands) | 1/31/38 |
| Prince Claus (Germany) | 6/9/26 |
| Prince Willem-Alexander (Netherlands) | 4/27/67 |
| Prince Johan Friso (Netherlands) | 9/25/68 |
| Prince Constantijn (Netherlands) | 10/11/69 |
| **Norway** | |
| King Harald V (Skaugum, Norway) | 2/21/37 |
| Queen Sonja (Oslo) | 7/4/37 |
| Princess Märtha Louise (Oslo) | 9/22/71 |
| Crown Prince Haakon (Oslo) | 7/20/73 |
| **Spain** | |
| King Juan Carlos I (Rome, Italy) | 1/5/38 |
| Princess Sofía (Athens, Greece) | 11/2/38 |
| Princess Elena (Madrid) | 12/20/63 |
| Princess Cristina (Madrid) | 6/13/65 |
| Crown Prince Felipe (Madrid) | 1/30/68 |
| **Sweden** | |
| King Carl XVI Gustav (Stockholm) | 4/30/46 |
| Queen Silvia | 12/23/43 |
| Princess Victoria (Stockholm) | 7/14/77 |
| Prince Carl Philip (Stockholm) | 5/13/79 |
| Princess Madeleine (Stockholm) | 6/10/82 |

(1) Divorced from Prince Charles, Aug. 28, 1996. Upon finalization of the divorce, relinquished the title "Her Royal Highness." Remained a member of the royal family and retained the title Diana, Princess of Wales.

# UNITED STATES POPULATION

## A Profile of America's Diversity—The View From the Census Bureau, 1996

by
Dr. Martha Farnsworth Riche
Director, Bureau of the Census
U.S. Department of Commerce

I'm often asked to describe the typical American. There is no such person! America's population is extraordinarily diverse, as Census Bureau data show. Here are some examples:

### Racial and Ethnic Composition

On Apr. 1, 1996, there were an estimated 264.6 million people living in the U.S., compared to Census Day, Apr. 1, 1990, 6 years earlier, when the nation's population stood at 248.7 mil. Of the 1996 population, 33.5 mil (13%) were black; the American Indian/Eskimo/Aleut populations made up 2.3 mil (1%); Asians and Pacific Islanders numbered 9.5 mil (4%). An estimated 27.7 mil (11%) were of Hispanic origin (persons of Hispanic origin may be of any race). About 194.1 mil (73%) considered themselves non-Hispanic white.

### Business Owners

This diversity reaches the ranks of the nation's business owners. There were 620,912 African-American owned firms in the U.S. in 1992, a total of 4% of all U.S. firms. Hispanic-owned firms numbered 862,605, a total of 5% of all firms in the U.S. About 6.4 mil, or one-third of all businesses in the nation—were owned by women.

### Age Structure

In the year 1996, 69.2 mil Americans (26%) were under 18 years old. At the other end of the continuum, 33.8 mil (13%) were age 65 or older. At the farthest tip were the centenarians—people 100 years old or more. About 56,000 fell into this exclusive group. The median age—with half of all Americans above and half below—was 34.5 years, the oldest it has ever been.

### Income Spectrum

The nation's families had a median income of $38,782 in 1994. But 8% had incomes of $100,000 and over, while 12% were below the official government poverty level ($15,141 for a family of four).

### Marriage and Families

In 1994, 56% of men and 52% of women aged 15 and older were married.

Of 97 mil households in 1994, 71% contained families. Married couples maintained 78% of all families, while women with no husband present maintained 18%.

About half of the nation's 68 mil families contained children. Most families with children (25 mil) included both a mother and a father; 8 mil had a mother only, and 1 mil contained only a father.

Of the 29 mil households without families, 83% consisted of a person living alone.

### Education

While 18% of Americans aged 25 and older lacked a high school diploma in 1995, 23% had a bachelor's degree or higher. These proportions differed greatly by age group. For example, 88% of 35- to 44-year-olds had a high school diploma and 27% had a bachelor's degree or more. But among those aged 75 or older, only 57% had a high school diploma and only 11% had a bachelor's degree or more.

### Elected Officials

Elected officials reflect the population's diversity. In 1992, there were 493,830 elected officials of U.S. local governments. More than 100,000 of these officials were women, more than 10,000 were blacks, more than 5,000 were Hispanics, and more than 2,000 were American Indians, Alaskan Natives, Asians, or Pacific Islanders. Fewer than one-fourth of the white elected local officials, but more than one-third of the minority officials, were women.

### The Foreign-Born Population

In 1995, an estimated 23 mil Americans, or 8.8% of the population, were foreign-born, the highest level since prior to World War II. More than one-fourth of these immigrants—6.7 mil—were born in Mexico. Other common immigrant homelands included: the Philippines (1.2 mil), China/Taiwan/Hong Kong (816,000), Cuba (797,000), Canada (695,000), El Salvador (650,000), Great Britain (617,000), Germany (598,000), Poland (538,000), Jamaica (531,000), and the Dominican Republic (509,000).

### The Lay of the Land

The nation's settlement landscape is just as disparate as the U.S. population. Urban areas were home to the majority of Americans in 1990 (75%). The most populous cities in 1994 were New York (7.3 mil), Los Angeles (3.4 mil), Chicago (2.7 mil), Houston (1.7 mil), and Philadelphia (1.5 mil). Among all cities with 1994 populations more than 100,000, the fastest-growing from 1990 to 1994 were Henderson, NV (whose population rose 57%), Palmdale, CA (47%), Chandler, AZ (33%), Las Vegas, NV (27%), and Plano, TX (23%).

On the other hand, about 25% of Americans lived in rural areas as of 1990. In 1992, the U.S. had 1.9 mil farms. These farms included an average of 491 acres; 166,000 were smaller than 10 acres and 71,000 were 2,000 acres or larger. As of 1990, 7% of rural residents lived on a farm, down from 53% in 1940.

### Businesses and Workers

In 1992, more than 87.6 mil persons worked for the nearly 4.7 mil employer businesses in the U.S. The majority of these businesses (more than 3.2 mil, or nearly 70%) had annual receipts of less than $500,000; these smaller firms employed a relatively small number of workers, around 10.5 mil persons—12% of the total. The remaining more than 1.4 mil employer businesses employed nearly 77.1 mil persons.

### International Trade

America's diversity also extends to the list of its leading trading partners. These include Canada ($70.5 bil in combined imports and exports during the first quarter of 1996), Japan ($45.8 bil), Mexico ($29.7 bil), Germany ($15.0 bil), the United Kingdom ($14.1 bil), China ($13.1 bil), South Korea ($12.5 bil), Taiwan ($11.2 bil), Singapore ($9.4 bil), and France ($8.1 bil).

### What the Future May Hold

The Census Bureau doesn't have a crystal ball, but the data we collect do give us an idea of what may happen—if current trends continue. According to our projections, the U.S. will have 393.9 mil people in the year 2050—49% more than the population today.

We expect the population then will be even more diverse than it is now. The non-Hispanic white share of the population is projected to fall from the current 73% to 53% by 2050. Meanwhile, persons of Hispanic origin should increase from 11% to 24% of the population. Asians and Pacific Islanders should see their population climb from 4% to 9%. Increases are expected to be smaller for the black (13% to 15%) and American Indian, Eskimo, and Aleut (from slightly under 1% to slightly more than 1%) populations.

Agewise, we anticipate that there will be relatively more persons aged 65 or older (a projected 20% of the population in 2050, compared to 13% now) and fewer children (24% in 2050, down from 26% currently).

We also expect the mix of families and households to change in the coming years. As the population continues to age, relatively fewer families would have children (a projected 41% in 2010, down from 50% in 1994). And it is projected that, among families with children, a lower proportion will include two married parents (72% in 2010, down from 74% in 1994). Meanwhile, households maintained by a person living alone should rise from 24% to 27% of all households.

# The Census Bureau on the Internet

**Source:** Bureau of the Census, U.S. Dept. of Commerce

The Internet is changing the way the Census Bureau disseminates information. At the Census Bureau's home page, **http://www.census.gov**, the Census Bureau displays many of the timely and relevant statistics about the people and economy of the U.S. that it gathers. Its censuses and surveys supply official statistics on a wide variety of key topics, including housing, health, crime, poverty, jobs, education, marriage and family, race and ethnicity, international trade, manufacturing, agricultural production, business growth, and retail sales.

The site represents the Census Bureau's latest effort to get more information to more people, more efficiently. Established in 1994, the site made the Census Bureau one of the pioneer federal agencies using the Internet to disseminate information. The site has been named one of the "hottest" on the World Wide Web. On average, the site gets about 145,000 "hits" per day—that's more than 6,000 per hour, 100 per minute! (A "hit" is anything from a casual stop to an extensive transfer of detailed files. Any time a user clicks on underlined text or a graphic, that's a hit.)

The Web site allows the Census Bureau to get its statistics out to a wider audience than ever before. Longtime, heavy users of Census Bureau data have benefited by getting statistics faster than they had in the past. Not long ago, users of Census Bureau information had to wait for a statistical report to be printed, then to come in the mail. Now, as soon as reports are composed, they can be loaded onto the Census Bureau's Web site. As a result, users have access to data weeks—even months—sooner.

The Internet also is getting users closer to the point where they will be able to access just the data they need for the specific geographic areas they need. The Census Bureau is already part of the way there. Interactive software at its site allows users to enter the name of any of the nation's states, counties, cities, or towns and, within moments, to receive online a variety of housing and population data pertaining to the specified geographic unit, based upon results from the decennial census. One also can get this same type of information for any 5-digit ZIP code or for a particular congressional district.

### The Future

By the time the Census Bureau is ready to release statistics collected in the census for the year 2000, the Data Access and Dissemination System (DADS) will be in place. DADS, which is to be located on the Census Bureau's Web site, will allow users to create customized data tabulations on demand. Presently, users must rely on data tables that the staff of the Census Bureau creates.

DADS will thus give users direct access to the Census Bureau's vast, largely untapped demographic and economic database. Of course, safeguards will be built into the system so that no information about an individual person or business establishment can be identified.

# Estimated Population of American Colonies, 1630-1780

**Source:** Bureau of the Census, U.S. Dept. of Commerce

(in thousands)

| Colony | 1780 | 1770 | 1750 | 1740 | 1720 | 1700 | 1690 | 1670 | 1650 | 1630 |
|---|---|---|---|---|---|---|---|---|---|---|
| **Total** | **2,780.4** | **2,148.1** | **1,170.8** | **905.6** | **466.2** | **250.9** | **210.4** | **111.9** | **50.4** | **4.6** |
| Maine (counties)[1] | 49.1 | 31.3 | ... | ... | ... | ... | ... | ... | 1.0 | 0.4 |
| New Hampshire[2] | 87.8 | 62.4 | 27.5 | 23.3 | 9.4 | 5.0 | 4.2 | 1.8 | 1.3 | 0.5 |
| Vermont[3] | 47.6 | 10.0 | ... | ... | ... | ... | ... | ... | ... | ... |
| Plymouth and Massachusetts[1,2,4] | 268.6 | 235.3 | 188.0 | 151.6 | 91.0 | 55.9 | 56.9 | 35.3 | 15.6 | 0.9 |
| Rhode Island[2] | 52.9 | 58.2 | 33.2 | 25.3 | 11.7 | 5.9 | 4.2 | 2.2 | 0.8 | ... |
| Connecticut[2] | 206.7 | 183.9 | 111.3 | 89.6 | 58.8 | 26.0 | 21.6 | 12.6 | 4.1 | ... |
| New York[2] | 210.5 | 162.9 | 76.7 | 63.7 | 36.9 | 19.1 | 13.9 | 5.8 | 4.1 | 0.4 |
| New Jersey[2] | 139.6 | 117.4 | 71.4 | 51.4 | 29.8 | 14.0 | 8.0 | 1.0 | ... | ... |
| Pennsylvania[2] | 327.3 | 240.1 | 119.7 | 85.6 | 31.0 | 18.0 | 11.4 | ... | ... | ... |
| Delaware[2] | 45.4 | 35.5 | 28.7 | 19.9 | 5.4 | 2.5 | 1.5 | 0.7 | 0.2 | ... |
| Maryland[2] | 245.5 | 202.6 | 141.1 | 116.1 | 66.1 | 29.6 | 24.0 | 13.2 | 4.5 | ... |
| Virginia[2] | 538.0 | 447.0 | 231.0 | 180.4 | 87.8 | 58.6 | 53.0 | 35.3 | 18.7 | 2.5 |
| North Carolina[2] | 270.1 | 197.2 | 73.0 | 51.8 | 21.3 | 10.7 | 7.6 | 3.8 | ... | ... |
| South Carolina[2] | 180.0 | 124.2 | 64.0 | 45.0 | 17.0 | 5.7 | 3.9 | 0.2 | ... | ... |
| Georgia[2] | 56.1 | 23.4 | 5.2 | 2.0 | ... | ... | ... | ... | ... | ... |
| Kentucky[5] | 45.0 | 15.7 | ... | ... | ... | ... | ... | ... | ... | ... |
| Tennessee[6] | 10.0 | 1.0 | ... | ... | ... | ... | ... | ... | ... | ... |

(1) For 1660-1750, Maine counties are included with Massachusetts. Maine was part of Massachusetts until it became a separate state in 1820. (2) One of the original 13 states. (3) Admitted to statehood in 1791. (4) Plymouth became a part of the Province of Massachusetts in 1691. (5) Admitted to statehood in 1792. (6) Admitted to statehood in 1796.

# Race and Hispanic Origin for the U.S., 1990 and 1980

**Source:** Bureau of the Census, U.S. Dept. of Commerce

| | 1990 Census | | 1980 Census | | Percentage change |
|---|---|---|---|---|---|
| | Number | Percent | Number | Percent | 1980-90 |
| **Race** | | | | | |
| **All persons** | **248,709,873[1]** | **100.0** | **226,545,805** | **100.0** | **9.8** |
| White | 199,686,070 | 80.3 | 188,371,622 | 83.1 | 6.0 |
| Black | 29,986,060 | 12.1 | 26,495,025 | 11.7 | 13.2 |
| American Indian, Eskimo, or Aleut | 1,959,234 | 0.8 | 1,420,400 | 0.6 | 37.9 |
| American Indian | 1,878,285 | 0.8 | 1,364,033 | 0.6 | 37.7 |
| Eskimo | 57,152 | 0.0 | 42,162 | 0.0 | 35.6 |
| Aleut | 23,797 | 0.0 | 14,205 | 0.0 | 67.5 |
| Asian-Pacific Islander | 7,273,662 | 2.9 | 3,500,439[2] | 1.5 | 107.8 |
| Chinese | 1,645,472 | 0.7 | 806,040 | 0.4 | 104.1 |
| Filipino | 1,406,770 | 0.6 | 774,652 | 0.3 | 81.6 |
| Japanese | 847,562 | 0.3 | 700,974 | 0.3 | 20.9 |
| Asian Indian | 815,447 | 0.3 | 361,531 | 0.2 | 125.6 |
| Korean | 798,849 | 0.3 | 354,593 | 0.2 | 125.3 |
| Vietnamese | 614,547 | 0.2 | 261,729 | 0.1 | 134.8 |
| Hawaiian | 211,014 | 0.1 | 166,814 | 0.1 | 26.5 |
| Samoan | 62,964 | 0.0 | 41,948 | 0.0 | 50.1 |
| Guamanian | 49,345 | 0.0 | 32,158 | 0.0 | 53.4 |
| Other Asian-Pacific Islander | 821,692 | 0.3 | NA | NA | NA |
| Other race | 9,804,847 | 3.9 | 6,758,319 | 3.0 | 45.1 |
| **Hispanic and non-Hispanic origin** | | | | | |
| Hispanic origin[3] | 22,354,059 | 9.0 | 14,608,673 | 6.4 | 53.0 |
| Mexican | 13,495,938 | 5.4 | 8,740,439 | 3.9 | 54.4 |
| Puerto Rican | 2,727,754 | 1.1 | 2,013,945 | 0.9 | 35.4 |
| Cuban | 1,043,932 | 0.4 | 803,226 | 0.4 | 30.0 |
| Other Hispanic | 5,086,435 | 2.0 | 3,051,063 | 1.3 | 66.7 |
| Not of Hispanic origin | 226,355,814 | 91.0 | 211,937,132 | 93.6 | 6.8 |

Percent totals may not add because of rounding. NA=Not available. (1) The race data shown here are based on the U.S. population as tabulated in the 1990 census. Figures do not reflect corrections to the 1990 population census; the corrected 1990 U.S. population is 248,718,301. (2) The 1980 count of 3,500,439 Asian-Pacific Islanders based on 100% tabulations includes only the 9 specific Asian-Pacific Islander groups listed separately in the 1980 race item. A figure of 3,726,440, from sample tabulations, is more comparable to the 1990 count since it includes groups not listed separately in the race item. (3) Persons of Hispanic origin may be of any race.

# U.S. Population, by Age, Sex, and Household, 1990

**Source:** Bureau of the Census, U.S. Dept. of Commerce; 1990 Census

| | |
|---|---|
| **Total population** | **248,709,873[1]** |
| **Age** | |
| Under 5 years | 18,354,443 |
| 5 to 17 years | 45,249,989 |
| 18 to 20 years | 11,726,868 |
| 21 to 24 years | 15,010,898 |
| 25 to 44 years | 80,754,835 |
| 45 to 54 years | 25,223,086 |
| 55 to 59 years | 10,531,756 |
| 60 to 64 years | 10,616,167 |
| 65 to 74 years | 18,106,558 |
| 75 to 84 years | 10,055,108 |
| 85 years and over | 3,080,165 |
| Median age | 32.9 |
| Under 18 years | 63,604,432 |
| Percentage of total population | 25.6 |
| 65 years and over | 31,241,831 |
| Percentage of total population | 12.6 |

| | |
|---|---|
| **Sex** | |
| Male | 121,239,418 |
| Female | 127,470,455 |
| **Households by type** | |
| **Total households** | **91,947,410** |
| Family households (families) | 64,517,947 |
| Married-couple families | 50,708,322 |
| Percentage of total households | 55.1 |
| Other family, male householder | 3,143,582 |
| Other family, female householder | 10,666,043 |
| Nonfamily households | 27,429,463 |
| Percentage of total households | 29.8 |
| Householder living alone | 22,580,420 |
| Householder 65 years and over | 8,824,845 |
| Persons living in households | 242,012,129 |
| Persons per household | 2.63 |
| Persons living in group quarters | 6,697,744 |
| Institutionalized persons | 3,334,018 |
| Other persons in group quarters | 3,363,726 |

(1) Data shown are based on the U.S. population as tabulated in the 1990 census, and do not reflect corrections to the 1990 population. The corrected 1990 U.S. population is 248,718,301.

# Definitions of Race and Hispanic Origin Groups

**Source:** Bureau of the Census, U.S. Dept. of Commerce

The concept of race as used by the Census Bureau does not reflect any clear-cut scientific definition of biological stock. The data for race represent self-classification by people according to the race with which they most closely identify. Persons could identify their race by classifying themselves in one of the categories listed on the census form, that is, white, black, American Indian, Eskimo, Aleut, Chinese, Filipino, Japanese, Asian Indian, Korean, Vietnamese, Hawaiian, Samoan, Guamanian, Other API (Asian-Pacific Islander), or Other race. Persons who identified themselves as "Other API" or "Other race" were directed to write in the name of their race in the space provided. Data for the Asian-Pacific Islander groups not listed on the census questionnaire but contained in Census Bureau tables—Cambodian, Hmong, Laotian, Thai, Bangladeshi, Burmese, Indonesian, Malayan, Okinawan, Pakistani, Sri Lankan, Tongan, Tahitian, Northern Mariana Islander, Palauan, and Fijian—were tabulated from write-in responses. The "Other race" category includes persons not included in the race categories described above. Persons reporting in the "Other race" category and providing write-in entries, such as the name of a Hispanic origin group, are included. In reality, no specific race can be determined from the classification "Hispanic." Persons of Spanish/Hispanic origin may be of any race.

Persons of Spanish/Hispanic origin or descent are those who classify themselves in one of the Hispanic origin categories listed on the census questionnaire—for example, Mexican, Puerto Rican, or Cuban—as well as those who indicated that they were of "other" Spanish/Hispanic origin. Persons reporting as "Other Spanish/Hispanic" are those whose origins are from other Spanish-speaking countries of the Caribbean, from Central or South America, or from Spain or are those identifying themselves generally as Spanish, Spanish-American, Hispano, Hispanic, Latino, etc.

## U.S. Population by Official

| State | 1790[1] | 1800[1] | 1810[1] | 1820 | 1830 | 1840 | 1850 | 1860 | 1870 | 1880 | 1890 |
|---|---|---|---|---|---|---|---|---|---|---|---|
| AL ...... | ....... | 1 | 9 | 127,901 | 309,527 | 590,756 | 771,623 | 964,201 | 996,992 | 1,262,505 | 1,513,401 |
| AK ...... | ....... | ....... | ....... | ....... | ....... | ....... | ....... | ....... | ....... | 33,426 | 32,052 |
| AZ ...... | ....... | ....... | ....... | ....... | ....... | ....... | ....... | ....... | 9,658 | 40,440 | 88,243 |
| AR ...... | ....... | ....... | 1 | 14,273 | 30,388 | 97,574 | 209,897 | 435,450 | 484,471 | 802,525 | 1,128,211 |
| CA ...... | ....... | ....... | ....... | ....... | ....... | ....... | 92,597 | 379,994 | 560,247 | 864,694 | 1,213,398 |
| CO ...... | ....... | ....... | ....... | ....... | ....... | ....... | ....... | 34,277 | 39,864 | 194,327 | 413,249 |
| CT ...... | 238 | 251 | 262 | 275,248 | 297,675 | 309,978 | 370,792 | 460,147 | 537,454 | 622,700 | 746,258 |
| DE ...... | 59 | 64 | 73 | 72,749 | 76,748 | 78,085 | 91,532 | 112,216 | 125,015 | 146,608 | 168,493 |
| DC ...... | ....... | 8 | 16 | 23,336 | 30,261 | 33,745 | 51,687 | 75,080 | 131,700 | 177,624 | 230,392 |
| FL ...... | ....... | ....... | ....... | ....... | 34,730 | 54,477 | 87,445 | 140,424 | 187,748 | 269,493 | 391,422 |
| GA ...... | 83 | 163 | 252 | 340,989 | 516,823 | 691,392 | 906,185 | 1,057,286 | 1,184,109 | 1,542,180 | 1,837,353 |
| HI ...... | ....... | ....... | ....... | ....... | ....... | ....... | ....... | ....... | ....... | ....... | ....... |
| ID ...... | ....... | ....... | ....... | ....... | ....... | ....... | ....... | ....... | 14,999 | 32,610 | 88,548 |
| IL ...... | ....... | ....... | 12 | 55,211 | 157,445 | 476,183 | 851,470 | 1,711,951 | 2,539,891 | 3,077,871 | 3,826,352 |
| IN ...... | ....... | 6 | 25 | 147,178 | 343,031 | 685,866 | 988,416 | 1,350,428 | 1,680,637 | 1,978,301 | 2,192,404 |
| IA ...... | ....... | ....... | ....... | ....... | ....... | 43,112 | 192,214 | 674,913 | 1,194,020 | 1,624,615 | 1,912,297 |
| KS ...... | ....... | ....... | ....... | ....... | ....... | ....... | ....... | 107,206 | 364,399 | 996,096 | 1,428,108 |
| KY ...... | 74 | 221 | 407 | 564,317 | 687,917 | 779,828 | 982,405 | 1,155,684 | 1,321,011 | 1,648,690 | 1,858,635 |
| LA ...... | ....... | ....... | 77 | 153,407 | 215,739 | 352,411 | 517,762 | 708,002 | 726,915 | 939,946 | 1,118,588 |
| ME ...... | 97 | 152 | 229 | 298,335 | 399,455 | 501,793 | 583,169 | 628,279 | 626,915 | 648,936 | 661,086 |
| MD ...... | 320 | 342 | 381 | 407,350 | 447,040 | 470,019 | 583,034 | 687,049 | 780,894 | 934,943 | 1,042,390 |
| MA ...... | 379 | 423 | 472 | 523,287 | 610,408 | 737,699 | 994,514 | 1,231,066 | 1,457,351 | 1,783,085 | 2,238,947 |
| MI ...... | ....... | ....... | 5 | 8,896 | 31,639 | 212,267 | 397,654 | 749,113 | 1,184,059 | 1,636,937 | 2,093,890 |
| MN ...... | ....... | ....... | ....... | ....... | ....... | ....... | 6,077 | 172,023 | 439,706 | 780,773 | 1,310,283 |
| MS ...... | ....... | 8 | 31 | 75,448 | 136,621 | 375,651 | 606,526 | 791,305 | 827,922 | 1,131,597 | 1,289,600 |
| MO ...... | ....... | ....... | 20 | 66,586 | 140,455 | 383,702 | 682,044 | 1,182,012 | 1,721,295 | 2,168,380 | 2,679,185 |
| MT ...... | ....... | ....... | ....... | ....... | ....... | ....... | ....... | ....... | 20,595 | 39,159 | 142,924 |
| NE ...... | ....... | ....... | ....... | ....... | ....... | ....... | ....... | 28,841 | 122,993 | 452,402 | 1,062,656 |
| NV ...... | ....... | ....... | ....... | ....... | ....... | ....... | ....... | 6,857 | 42,491 | 62,266 | 47,355 |
| NH ...... | 142 | 184 | 214 | 244,161 | 269,328 | 284,574 | 317,976 | 326,073 | 318,300 | 346,991 | 376,530 |
| NJ ...... | 184 | 211 | 246 | 277,575 | 320,823 | 373,306 | 489,555 | 672,035 | 906,096 | 1,131,116 | 1,444,933 |
| NM ...... | ....... | ....... | ....... | ....... | ....... | ....... | 61,547 | 93,516 | 91,874 | 119,565 | 160,282 |
| NY ...... | 340 | 589 | 959 | 1,372,812 | 1,918,608 | 2,428,921 | 3,097,394 | 3,880,735 | 4,382,759 | 5,082,871 | 6,003,174 |
| NC ...... | 394 | 478 | 556 | 638,829 | 737,987 | 753,419 | 869,039 | 992,622 | 1,071,361 | 1,399,750 | 1,617,949 |
| ND ...... | ....... | ....... | ....... | ....... | ....... | ....... | ....... | ....... | 2,405[2] | 36,909 | 190,983 |
| OH ...... | ....... | 45 | 231 | 581,434 | 937,903 | 1,519,467 | 1,980,329 | 2,339,511 | 2,665,260 | 3,198,062 | 3,672,329 |
| OK ...... | ....... | ....... | ....... | ....... | ....... | ....... | ....... | ....... | ....... | ....... | 258,657 |
| OR ...... | ....... | ....... | ....... | ....... | ....... | ....... | 12,093 | 52,465 | 90,923 | 174,768 | 317,704 |
| PA ...... | 434 | 602 | 810 | 1,049,458 | 1,348,233 | 1,724,033 | 2,311,786 | 2,906,215 | 3,521,951 | 4,282,891 | 5,258,113 |
| RI ...... | 69 | 69 | 77 | 83,059 | 97,199 | 108,830 | 147,545 | 174,620 | 217,353 | 276,531 | 345,506 |
| SC ...... | 249 | 346 | 415 | 502,741 | 581,185 | 594,398 | 668,507 | 703,708 | 705,606 | 995,577 | 1,151,149 |
| SD ...... | ....... | ....... | ....... | ....... | ....... | ....... | ....... | 4,8372 | 11,7762 | 98,268 | 348,600 |
| TN ...... | 36 | 106 | 262 | 422,823 | 681,904 | 829,210 | 1,002,717 | 1,109,801 | 1,258,520 | 1,542,359 | 1,767,518 |
| TX ...... | ....... | ....... | ....... | ....... | ....... | ....... | 212,592 | 604,215 | 818,579 | 1,591,749 | 2,235,527 |
| UT ...... | ....... | ....... | ....... | ....... | ....... | ....... | 11,380 | 40,273 | 86,786 | 143,963 | 210,779 |
| VT ...... | 85 | 154 | 218 | 235,981 | 280,652 | 291,948 | 314,120 | 315,098 | 330,551 | 332,286 | 332,422 |
| VA ...... | 692 | 808 | 878 | 938,261 | 1,044,054 | 1,025,227 | 1,119,348 | 1,219,630 | 1,225,163 | 1,512,565 | 1,655,980 |
| WA ...... | ....... | ....... | ....... | ....... | ....... | ....... | 1,201 | 11,594 | 23,955 | 75,116 | 357,232 |
| WV ...... | 56 | 79 | 105 | 136,808 | 176,924 | 224,537 | 302,313 | 376,688 | 442,014 | 618,457 | 762,794 |
| WI ...... | ....... | ....... | ....... | ....... | ....... | 30,945 | 305,391 | 775,881 | 1,054,670 | 1,315,497 | 1,693,330 |
| WY ...... | ....... | ....... | ....... | ....... | ....... | ....... | ....... | ....... | 9,118 | 20,789 | 62,555 |
| U.S. ..... | 3,929 | 5,308 | 7,240 | 9,638,453 | 12,866,020[3] | 17,068,953[3] | 23,191,876 | 31,443,321 | 38,558,371 | 50,189,209 | 62,979,766 |

**Note:** Where possible, population shown is that of the 1990 area of the state. Members of the Armed Forces overseas or other U.S. nationals abroad are not included. Totals have been revised to include corrections of initial tabulated counts.
(1) Totals for 1790, 1800, and 1810 are in thousands. (2) 1860 figure is for Dakota Territory; 1870 figures are for parts of Dakota Territory. (3) U.S. total includes persons (5,318 in 1830 and 6,100 in 1840) on public ships in the service of the U.S. not credited to any region, division, or state.

## Congressional Apportionment

**Source:** Bureau of the Census, U.S. Dept. of Commerce

| | 1990 | 1980 | | 1990 | 1980 | | 1990 | 1980 | | 1990 | 1980 | | 1990 | 1980 |
|---|---|---|---|---|---|---|---|---|---|---|---|---|---|---|
| AL ... | 7 | 7 | ID .... | 2 | 2 | MN ... | 8 | 8 | ND .... | 1 | 1 | VT ... | 1 | 1 |
| AK ... | 1 | 1 | IL .... | 20 | 22 | MS ... | 5 | 5 | OH ... | 19 | 21 | VA ... | 11 | 10 |
| AZ ... | 6 | 5 | IN .... | 10 | 10 | MO ... | 9 | 9 | OK .... | 6 | 6 | WA .. | 9 | 8 |
| AR ... | 4 | 4 | IA .... | 5 | 6 | MT ... | 1 | 2 | OR ... | 5 | 5 | WV .. | 3 | 4 |
| CA ... | 52 | 45 | KS ... | 4 | 5 | NE ... | 3 | 3 | PA .... | 21 | 23 | WI ... | 9 | 9 |
| CO ... | 6 | 6 | KY ... | 6 | 7 | NV ... | 2 | 2 | RI .... | 2 | 2 | WY .. | 1 | 1 |
| CT ... | 6 | 6 | LA .... | 7 | 8 | NH ... | 2 | 2 | SC .... | 6 | 6 | | | |
| DE ... | 1 | 1 | ME .... | 2 | 2 | NJ .... | 13 | 14 | SD .... | 1 | 1 | **Totals..** | **435** | **435** |
| FL ... | 23 | 19 | MD ... | 8 | 8 | NM ... | 3 | 3 | TN .... | 9 | 9 | | | |
| GA ... | 11 | 10 | MA ... | 10 | 11 | NY ... | 31 | 34 | TX .... | 30 | 27 | | | |
| HI .... | 2 | 2 | MI .... | 16 | 18 | NC ... | 12 | 11 | UT .... | 3 | 3 | | | |

The Constitution, in Article 1, Section 2, provided for a census of the population every 10 years to establish a basis for apportionment of representatives among the states. This apportionment largely determines the number of electoral votes allotted to each state.

The number of representatives of each state in Congress is determined by the state's population, but each state is entitled to one representative regardless of population. A congressional apportionment has been made after each decennial census except that of 1920.

Under provisions of a law that became effective Nov. 15, 1941, representatives are apportioned by the method of equal proportions. In the application of this method, the apportionment is made so that the average population per representative has the least possible variation between one state and any other. The first House of Representatives, in 1789, had 65 members, as provided by the Constitution. As the population grew, the number of representatives was increased, but the total membership has been fixed at 435 since the apportionment based on the 1910 census.

## Census, 1790-1990

| 1900 | 1910 | 1920 | 1930 | 1940 | 1950 | 1960 | 1970 | 1980 | 1990 |
|---|---|---|---|---|---|---|---|---|---|
| 1,828,697 | 2,138,093 | 2,348,174 | 2,646,248 | 2,832,961 | 3,061,743 | 3,266,740 | 3,444,354 | 3,894,025 | 4,040,389 |
| 63,592 | 64,356 | 55,036 | 59,278 | 72,524 | 128,643 | 226,167 | 302,583 | 401,851 | 550,043 |
| 122,931 | 204,354 | 334,162 | 435,573 | 499,261 | 749,587 | 1,302,161 | 1,775,399 | 2,716,546 | 3,665,339 |
| 1,311,564 | 1,574,449 | 1,752,204 | 1,854,482 | 1,949,387 | 1,909,511 | 1,786,272 | 1,923,322 | 2,286,357 | 2,350,624 |
| 1,485,053 | 2,377,549 | 3,426,861 | 5,677,251 | 6,907,387 | 10,586,223 | 15,717,204 | 19,971,069 | 23,667,764 | 29,758,213 |
| 539,700 | 799,024 | 939,629 | 1,035,791 | 1,123,296 | 1,325,089 | 1,753,947 | 2,209,596 | 2,889,735 | 3,294,473 |
| 908,420 | 1,114,756 | 1,380,631 | 1,606,903 | 1,709,242 | 2,007,280 | 2,535,234 | 3,032,217 | 3,107,564 | 3,287,116 |
| 184,735 | 202,322 | 223,003 | 238,380 | 266,505 | 318,085 | 446,292 | 548,104 | 594,338 | 666,168 |
| 278,718 | 331,069 | 437,571 | 486,869 | 663,091 | 802,178 | 763,956 | 756,668 | 638,432 | 606,900 |
| 528,542 | 752,619 | 968,470 | 1,468,211 | 1,897,414 | 2,771,305 | 4,951,560 | 6,791,418 | 9,746,961 | 12,938,071 |
| 2,216,331 | 2,609,121 | 2,895,832 | 2,908,506 | 3,123,723 | 3,444,578 | 3,943,116 | 4,587,930 | 5,462,982 | 6,478,149 |
| 154,001 | 191,874 | 255,881 | 368,300 | 422,770 | 499,794 | 632,772 | 769,913 | 964,691 | 1,108,229 |
| 161,772 | 325,594 | 431,866 | 445,032 | 524,873 | 588,637 | 667,191 | 713,015 | 944,127 | 1,006,734 |
| 4,821,550 | 5,638,591 | 6,485,280 | 7,630,654 | 7,897,241 | 8,712,176 | 10,081,158 | 11,110,285 | 11,427,409 | 11,430,602 |
| 2,516,462 | 2,700,876 | 2,930,390 | 3,238,503 | 3,427,796 | 3,934,224 | 4,662,498 | 5,195,392 | 5,490,214 | 5,544,156 |
| 2,231,853 | 2,224,771 | 2,404,021 | 2,470,939 | 2,538,268 | 2,621,073 | 2,757,537 | 2,825,368 | 2,913,808 | 2,776,831 |
| 1,470,495 | 1,690,949 | 1,769,257 | 1,880,999 | 1,801,028 | 1,905,299 | 2,178,611 | 2,249,071 | 2,364,236 | 2,477,588 |
| 2,147,174 | 2,289,905 | 2,416,630 | 2,614,589 | 2,845,627 | 2,944,806 | 3,038,156 | 3,220,711 | 3,660,324 | 3,686,891 |
| 1,381,625 | 1,656,388 | 1,798,509 | 2,101,593 | 2,363,880 | 2,683,516 | 3,257,022 | 3,644,637 | 4,206,116 | 4,220,164 |
| 694,466 | 742,371 | 768,014 | 797,423 | 847,226 | 913,774 | 969,265 | 993,722 | 1,125,043 | 1,227,928 |
| 1,188,044 | 1,295,346 | 1,449,661 | 1,631,526 | 1,821,244 | 2,343,001 | 3,100,689 | 3,923,897 | 4,216,933 | 4,780,753 |
| 2,805,346 | 3,366,416 | 3,852,356 | 4,249,614 | 4,316,721 | 4,690,514 | 5,148,578 | 5,689,170 | 5,737,093 | 6,016,425 |
| 2,420,982 | 2,810,173 | 3,668,412 | 4,842,325 | 5,256,106 | 6,371,766 | 7,823,194 | 8,881,826 | 9,262,044 | 9,295,287 |
| 1,751,394 | 2,075,708 | 2,387,125 | 2,563,953 | 2,792,300 | 2,982,483 | 3,413,864 | 3,806,103 | 4,075,970 | 4,375,665 |
| 1,551,270 | 1,797,114 | 1,790,618 | 2,009,821 | 2,183,796 | 2,178,914 | 2,178,141 | 2,216,994 | 2,520,770 | 2,575,475 |
| 3,106,665 | 3,293,335 | 3,404,055 | 3,629,367 | 3,784,664 | 3,954,653 | 4,319,813 | 4,677,623 | 4,916,766 | 5,116,901 |
| 243,329 | 376,053 | 548,889 | 537,606 | 559,456 | 591,024 | 674,767 | 694,409 | 786,690 | 799,065 |
| 1,066,300 | 1,192,214 | 1,296,372 | 1,377,963 | 1,315,834 | 1,325,510 | 1,411,330 | 1,485,333 | 1,569,825 | 1,578,417 |
| 42,335 | 81,875 | 77,407 | 91,058 | 110,247 | 160,083 | 285,278 | 488,738 | 800,508 | 1,201,675 |
| 411,588 | 430,572 | 443,083 | 465,293 | 491,524 | 533,242 | 606,921 | 737,681 | 920,610 | 1,109,252 |
| 1,883,669 | 2,537,167 | 3,155,900 | 4,041,334 | 4,160,165 | 4,835,329 | 6,066,782 | 7,171,112 | 7,365,011 | 7,730,188 |
| 195,310 | 327,301 | 360,350 | 423,317 | 531,818 | 681,187 | 951,023 | 1,017,055 | 1,303,302 | 1,515,069 |
| 7,268,894 | 9,113,614 | 10,385,227 | 12,588,066 | 13,479,142 | 14,830,192 | 16,782,304 | 18,241,391 | 17,558,165 | 17,990,778 |
| 1,893,810 | 2,206,287 | 2,559,123 | 3,170,276 | 3,571,623 | 4,061,929 | 4,556,155 | 5,084,411 | 5,880,095 | 6,632,448 |
| 319,146 | 577,056 | 646,872 | 680,845 | 641,935 | 619,636 | 632,446 | 617,792 | 652,717 | 638,800 |
| 4,157,545 | 4,767,121 | 5,759,394 | 6,646,697 | 6,907,612 | 7,946,627 | 9,706,397 | 10,657,423 | 10,797,603 | 10,847,115 |
| 790,391 | 1,657,155 | 2,028,283 | 2,396,040 | 2,336,434 | 2,233,351 | 2,328,284 | 2,559,463 | 3,025,487 | 3,145,576 |
| 413,536 | 672,765 | 783,389 | 953,786 | 1,089,684 | 1,521,341 | 1,768,687 | 2,091,533 | 2,633,156 | 2,842,337 |
| 6,302,115 | 7,665,111 | 8,720,017 | 9,631,350 | 9,900,180 | 10,498,012 | 11,319,366 | 11,800,766 | 11,864,720 | 11,882,842 |
| 428,556 | 542,610 | 604,397 | 687,497 | 713,346 | 791,896 | 859,488 | 949,723 | 947,154 | 1,003,464 |
| 1,340,316 | 1,515,400 | 1,683,724 | 1,738,765 | 1,899,804 | 2,117,027 | 2,382,594 | 2,590,713 | 3,120,729 | 3,486,310 |
| 401,570 | 583,888 | 636,547 | 692,849 | 642,961 | 652,740 | 680,514 | 666,257 | 690,768 | 696,004 |
| 2,020,616 | 2,184,789 | 2,337,885 | 2,616,556 | 2,915,841 | 3,291,718 | 3,567,089 | 3,926,018 | 4,591,023 | 4,877,203 |
| 3,048,710 | 3,896,542 | 4,663,228 | 5,824,715 | 6,414,824 | 7,711,194 | 9,579,677 | 11,198,655 | 14,225,513 | 16,986,335 |
| 276,749 | 373,351 | 449,396 | 507,847 | 550,310 | 688,862 | 890,627 | 1,059,273 | 1,461,037 | 1,722,850 |
| 343,641 | 355,956 | 352,428 | 359,611 | 359,231 | 377,747 | 389,881 | 444,732 | 511,456 | 562,758 |
| 1,854,184 | 2,061,612 | 2,309,187 | 2,421,851 | 2,677,773 | 3,318,680 | 3,966,949 | 4,651,448 | 5,346,797 | 6,189,197 |
| 518,103 | 1,141,990 | 1,356,621 | 1,563,396 | 1,736,191 | 2,378,963 | 2,853,214 | 3,413,244 | 4,132,353 | 4,866,669 |
| 958,800 | 1,221,119 | 1,463,701 | 1,729,205 | 1,901,974 | 2,005,552 | 1,860,421 | 1,744,237 | 1,950,186 | 1,793,477 |
| 2,069,042 | 2,333,860 | 2,632,067 | 2,939,006 | 3,137,587 | 3,434,575 | 3,951,777 | 4,417,821 | 4,705,642 | 4,891,769 |
| 92,531 | 145,965 | 194,402 | 225,565 | 250,742 | 290,529 | 330,066 | 332,416 | 469,557 | 453,589 |
| **76,212,168** | **92,228,496** | **106,021,537** | **123,202,624** | **132,164,569** | **151,325,798** | **179,323,175** | **203,302,031** | **226,542,203** | **248,718,301** |

## U.S. Center of Population, 1790-1990

**Source:** Bureau of the Census, U.S. Dept. of Commerce

**The U.S. Center of Population** is considered here as the center of population gravity, or that point upon which the U.S. would balance if it were a rigid plane without weight and the population distributed thereon, with each individual assumed to have equal weight and to exert an influence on a central point proportional to his or her distance from that point. The 1990 center is 818.6 miles from the 1790 center of population and is 39.5 miles SW of the 1980 center.

| Year | N Lat ° | ′ | ″ | W Long ° | ′ | ″ | Approximate location |
|---|---|---|---|---|---|---|---|
| 1790 | 39 | 16 | 30 | 76 | 11 | 12 | 23 miles east of Baltimore, MD |
| 1800 | 39 | 16 | 6 | 76 | 56 | 30 | 18 miles west of Baltimore, MD |
| 1810 | 39 | 11 | 30 | 77 | 37 | 12 | 40 miles northwest by west of Washington, DC (in VA) |
| 1820 | 39 | 5 | 42 | 78 | 33 | 0 | 16 miles east of Moorefield, WV[1] |
| 1830 | 38 | 57 | 54 | 79 | 16 | 54 | 19 miles west-southwest of Moorefield, WV[1] |
| 1840 | 39 | 2 | 0 | 80 | 18 | 0 | 16 miles south of Clarksburg, WV[1] |
| 1850 | 38 | 59 | 0 | 81 | 19 | 0 | 23 miles southeast of Parkersburg, WV[1] |
| 1860 | 39 | 0 | 24 | 82 | 48 | 48 | 20 miles south by east of Chillicothe, OH |
| 1870 | 39 | 12 | 0 | 83 | 35 | 42 | 48 miles east by north of Cincinnati, OH |
| 1880 | 39 | 4 | 8 | 84 | 39 | 40 | 8 miles west by south of Cincinnati, OH (in KY) |
| 1890 | 39 | 11 | 56 | 85 | 32 | 53 | 20 miles east of Columbus, IN |
| 1900 | 39 | 9 | 36 | 85 | 48 | 54 | 6 miles southeast of Columbus, IN |
| 1910 | 39 | 10 | 12 | 86 | 32 | 20 | In the city of Bloomington, IN |
| 1920 | 39 | 10 | 21 | 86 | 43 | 15 | 8 miles south-southeast of Spencer, Owen Co., IN |
| 1930 | 39 | 3 | 45 | 87 | 8 | 6 | 3 miles northeast of Linton, Greene Co., IN |
| 1940 | 38 | 56 | 54 | 87 | 22 | 35 | 2 miles southeast by east of Carlisle, Haddon township, Sullivan Co., IN |
| 1950 (inc. Alaska & Hawaii) | 38 | 48 | 15 | 88 | 22 | 8 | 3 miles northeast of Louisville, Clay Co., IL |
| 1960 | 38 | 35 | 58 | 89 | 12 | 35 | 6½ miles northwest of Centralia, Clinton Co., IL |
| 1970 | 38 | 27 | 47 | 89 | 42 | 22 | 5 miles east southeast of Mascoutah, St. Clair Co., IL |
| 1980 | 38 | 8 | 13 | 90 | 34 | 26 | ¼ mile west of De Soto, Jefferson Co., MO |
| 1990 | 37 | 52 | 20 | 91 | 12 | 55 | 9.7 miles northwest of Steelville, MO |

(1) West Virginia was set off from Virginia on Dec. 31, 1862, and was admitted as a state on June 20, 1863.

# U.S. Area and Population: 1790-1990

**Source:** Bureau of the Census, U.S. Dept. of Commerce

| Census date | Area (sq mi) Gross | Land | Water | Population Number | per sq mi of land | Increase over preceding census Number | % |
|---|---|---|---|---|---|---|---|
| 1990 (Apr. 1) | 3,787,319[1] | 3,536,278 | 251,041[1] | 248,718,301 | 70.3 | 22,176,098 | 9.8 |
| 1980 (Apr. 1) | 3,618,770 | 3,539,289 | 79,481 | 226,542,203 | 64.0 | 23,240,172 | 11.4 |
| 1970 (Apr. 1) | 3,618,770 | 3,536,855 | 81,915 | 203,302,031 | 57.5 | 23,978,856 | 13.4 |
| 1960 (Apr. 1) | 3,618,770 | 3,540,911 | 77,859 | 179,323,175 | 50.6 | 27,997,377 | 18.5 |
| 1950 (Apr. 1) | 3,618,770 | 3,552,206 | 66,564 | 151,325,798 | 42.6 | 19,161,229 | 14.5 |
| 1940 (Apr. 1) | 3,618,770 | 3,554,608 | 64,162 | 132,164,569 | 37.2 | 8,961,945 | 7.3 |
| 1930 (Apr. 1) | 3,618,770 | 3,551,608 | 67,162 | 123,202,624 | 34.7 | 17,181,087 | 16.2 |
| 1920 (Jan. 1) | 3,618,770 | 3,546,931 | 71,839 | 106,021,537 | 29.9 | 13,793,041 | 15.0 |
| 1910 (Apr. 15) | 3,618,770 | 3,547,045 | 71,725 | 92,228,496 | 26.0 | 16,016,328 | 21.0 |
| 1900 (June 1) | 3,618,770 | 3,547,314 | 71,456 | 76,212,168 | 21.5 | 13,232,402 | 21.0 |
| 1890 (June 1) | 3,612,299 | 3,540,705 | 71,594 | 62,979,766 | 17.8 | 12,790,557 | 25.5 |
| 1880 (June 1) | 3,612,299 | 3,540,705 | 71,594 | 50,189,209 | 14.2 | 11,630,838 | 30.2 |
| 1870 (June 1) | 3,612,299 | 3,540,705 | 71,594 | 38,558,371 | 10.9 | 7,115,050 | 22.6 |
| 1860 (June 1) | 3,021,295 | 2,969,640 | 51,655 | 31,443,321 | 10.6 | 8,251,445 | 35.6 |
| 1850 (June 1) | 2,991,655 | 2,940,042 | 51,613 | 23,191,876 | 7.9 | 6,122,423 | 35.9 |
| 1840 (June 1) | 1,792,552 | 1,749,462 | 43,090 | 17,068,953[2] | 9.8 | 4,203,433 | 32.7 |
| 1830 (June 1) | 1,792,552 | 1,749,462 | 43,090 | 12,866,020[2] | 7.4 | 3,227,567 | 33.5 |
| 1820 (June 1) | 1,792,552 | 1,749,462 | 43,090 | 9,638,453 | 5.5 | 2,398,572 | 33.1 |
| 1810 (Aug. 6) | 1,722,685 | 1,681,828 | 40,857 | 7,239,881 | 4.3 | 1,931,398 | 36.4 |
| 1800 (Aug. 4) | 891,364 | 864,746 | 26,618 | 5,308,483 | 6.1 | 1,379,269 | 35.1 |
| 1790 (Aug. 2) | 891,364 | 864,746 | 26,618 | 3,929,214 | 4.5 | — | — |

(1) Includes inland, coastal, Great Lakes, and territorial water. Data for prior years cover inland water only. (2) U.S. total includes persons (5,318 in 1830 and 6,100 in 1840) on public ships in the service of the U.S. not credited to any region, division, or state.

**Note**: Percent changes are computed on the basis of change in population since the preceding census date, and the period covered therefore is not always exactly 10 years.

Population density figures given for various years represent the area within the boundaries of the U.S. that was under the jurisdiction on the date in question, including in some cases considerable areas not organized or settled and not actually covered by the census. In 1870, for example, Alaska was not covered by the census.

Population figures shown here may reflect corrections made to the initial tabulated census counts.

# Population, by Sex, Race, Residence, and Median Age, 1790-1996

**Source:** Bureau of the Census, U.S. Dept. of Commerce

(in thousands, except as indicated)

| Date | Sex Male | Female | Race White | Black Number | Black Percent | Other | Residence Urban | Rural | Median Age (years) All races | White | Black |
|---|---|---|---|---|---|---|---|---|---|---|---|
| **Conterminous U.S.[1]** | | | | | | | | | | | |
| 1790 (Aug. 2) | NA | NA | 3,172 | 757 | 19.3 | NA | 202 | 3,728 | NA | NA | NA |
| 1810 (Aug. 6) | NA | NA | 5,862 | 1,378 | 19.0 | NA | 525 | 6,714 | NA | 16.0 | NA |
| 1820 (Aug. 7) | 4,897 | 4,742 | 7,867 | 1,772 | 18.4 | NA | 693 | 8,945 | 16.7 | 16.6 | 17.2 |
| 1840 (June 1) | 8,689 | 8,381 | 14,196 | 2,874 | 16.8 | NA | 1,845 | 15,224 | 17.8 | 17.9 | 17.6 |
| 1860 (June 1) | 16,085 | 15,358 | 26,923 | 4,442 | 14.1 | 79 | 6,217 | 25,227 | 19.4 | 19.7 | 17.5 |
| 1870 (June 1) | 19,494 | 19,065 | 33,589 | 4,880 | 12.7 | 89 | 9,902 | 28,656 | 20.2 | 20.4 | 18.5 |
| 1880 (June 1) | 25,519 | 24,637 | 43,403 | 6,581 | 13.1 | 172 | 14,130 | 36,026 | 20.9 | 21.4 | 18.0 |
| 1890 (June 1) | 32,237 | 30,711 | 55,101 | 7,489 | 11.9 | 358 | 22,106 | 40,841 | 22.0 | 22.5 | 17.8 |
| 1900 (June 1) | 38,816 | 37,178 | 66,809 | 8,834 | 11.6 | 351 | 30,160 | 45,835 | 22.9 | 23.4 | 19.4 |
| 1920 (Jan. 1) | 53,900 | 51,810 | 94,821 | 10,463 | 9.9 | 427 | 54,158 | 51,553 | 25.3 | 25.5 | 22.3 |
| 1930 (Apr. 1) | 62,137 | 60,638 | 110,287 | 11,891 | 9.7 | 597 | 68,955 | 53,820 | 26.5 | 26.9 | 23.5 |
| 1940 (Apr. 1) | 66,062 | 65,608 | 118,215 | 12,866 | 9.8 | 589 | 74,424 | 57,246 | 29.0 | 29.5 | 25.3 |
| **United States** | | | | | | | | | | | |
| 1950 (Apr. 1) | 74,833 | 75,864 | 135,150 | 15,045 | 9.9 | 1,131 | 96,467 | 54,230 | 30.2 | 30.7 | 26.2 |
| 1960 (Apr. 1) | 88,331 | 90,992 | 158,832 | 18,872 | 10.5 | 1,620 | 125,269 | 54,054 | 29.5 | 30.3 | 23.5 |
| 1970 (Apr. 1)[2] | 98,912 | 104,300 | 177,749 | 22,580 | 11.1 | 2,883 | 149,647 | 53,565 | 28.1 | 28.9 | 22.4 |
| 1980 (Apr. 1)[3] | 110,053 | 116,493 | 194,713 | 26,683 | 11.8 | 5,150 | 167,051 | 59,495 | 30.0 | 30.9 | 24.9 |
| 1983 (July 1, est) | 113,647 | 120,145 | 199,420 | 27,867 | 11.9 | 6,505 | NA | NA | 30.8 | 31.7 | 25.9 |
| 1985 (July 1, est) | 115,730 | 122,194 | 202,031 | 28,569 | 12.0 | 7,324 | NA | NA | 31.4 | 32.3 | 26.6 |
| 1990 (Apr. 1)[4] | 121,239 | 127,470 | 199,686 | 29,986 | 12.1 | 19,038 | 187,053 | 61,656 | 32.9 | 34.4 | 28.1 |
| 1993 (July 1, est) | 125,812 | 131,988 | 214,805 | 32,174 | 12.5 | 10,821 | NA | NA | 33.7 | 34.7 | 28.7 |
| 1994 (July 1, est) | 127,085 | 133,265 | 216,496 | 32,669 | 12.5 | 11,185 | NA | NA | 34.0 | 35.0 | 29.0 |
| 1995 (July 1, est) | 128,314 | 134,441 | 218,085 | 33,141 | 12.6 | 11,529 | NA | NA | 34.3 | 35.3 | 29.2 |
| 1996 (May 1, est) | 129,325 | 135,430 | 219,377 | 33,536 | 12.7 | 11,841 | NA | NA | 34.5 | 35.6 | 29.3 |

NA=Not available. **Note:** Urban and rural definitions may change from census to census. The figures in this table have been adjusted to be consistent with the 1990 urban and rural definitions. (1) Excludes Alaska and Hawaii. (2) The revised 1970 resident population count is 203,302,031, which incorporates changes due to errors found after tabulations were completed. The race and sex data shown here reflect the official 1970 census count; the residence data come from the tabulated count. (3) The race data shown for Apr. 1, 1980, have been modified. (4) The data shown are based on the U.S. population as tabulated in the 1990 census. Figures do not reflect corrections to the 1990 population. The corrected 1990 U.S. population is 248,718,301.

# Immigrants Admitted, by Top 30 Metropolitan Areas of Intended Residence, 1995

**Source:** Immigration and Naturalization Service, U.S. Dept. of Justice

(fiscal year 1995)

| Metropolitan Statistical Area | Number | Percentage |
|---|---|---|
| New York, NY | 111,687 | 15.5 |
| Los Angeles–Long Beach, CA | 54,669 | 7.6 |
| Chicago, IL | 31,730 | 4.4 |
| Miami, FL | 30,935 | 4.3 |
| Washington, DC–MD–VA | 25,717 | 3.6 |
| Orange County, CA | 18,187 | 2.5 |
| Boston–Lawrence–Lowell–Brockton, MA | 16,750 | 2.3 |
| San Francisco, CA | 15,773 | 2.2 |
| Houston, TX | 14,379 | 2.0 |
| San Jose, CA | 12,855 | 1.8 |
| San Diego, CA | 12,077 | 1.7 |
| Oakland, CA | 12,011 | 1.7 |
| Philadelphia, PA–NJ | 11,440 | 1.6 |
| Newark, NJ | 11,162 | 1.6 |
| Detroit, MI | 9,899 | 1.4 |
| Dallas, TX | 9,843 | 1.4 |
| Seattle–Bellevue–Everett, WA | 9,652 | 1.3 |
| Atlanta, GA | 9,494 | 1.3 |
| Bergen–Passaic, NJ | 9,385 | 1.3 |
| Fort Lauderdale, FL | 8,373 | 1.2 |
| Nassau–Suffolk, NY | 8,039 | 1.1 |
| Riverside–San Bernardino, CA | 7,568 | 1.1 |
| Jersey City, NJ | 7,032 | 1.0 |
| Minneapolis–St. Paul, MN–WI | 7,027 | 1.0 |
| Honolulu, HI | 6,063 | 0.8 |
| Middlesex–Somerset–Hunterdon, NJ | 5,596 | 0.8 |
| El Paso, TX | 4,996 | 0.7 |
| West Palm Beach, FL | 4,942 | 0.7 |
| Denver, CO | 4,823 | 0.7 |
| Orlando, FL | 4,806 | 0.7 |
| **Total U.S. Metro. Area Pop.[1]** | **720,461** | **100.0** |

(1) Includes metropolitan areas not listed.

# Immigrants Admitted, by State of Intended Residence, 1995

**Source:** Immigration and Naturalization Service, U.S. Dept. of Justice

(fiscal year 1995)

| State | Number of immigrants |
|---|---|
| AL | 1,900 |
| AK | 1,049 |
| AZ | 7,700 |
| AR | 934 |
| CA | 166,482 |
| CO | 7,713 |
| CT | 9,240 |
| DE | 1,051 |
| DC | 3,047 |
| FL | 62,023 |
| GA | 12,381 |
| HI | 7,537 |
| ID | 1,612 |
| IL | 33,898 |
| IN | 3,590 |
| IA | 2,260 |
| KS | 2,434 |
| KY | 1,857 |
| LA | 3,000 |
| ME | 814 |
| MD | 15,055 |
| MA | 20,523 |
| MI | 14,135 |
| MN | 8,111 |
| MS | 757 |
| MO | 3,990 |
| MT | 409 |
| NE | 1,831 |
| NV | 4,306 |
| NH | 1,186 |
| NJ | 39,729 |
| NM | 2,758 |
| NY | 128,406 |
| NC | 5,617 |
| ND | 483 |
| OH | 8,585 |
| OK | 2,792 |
| OR | 4,923 |
| PA | 15,065 |
| RI | 2,609 |
| SC | 2,165 |
| SD | 495 |
| TN | 3,392 |
| TX | 49,963 |
| UT | 2,831 |
| VT | 535 |
| VA | 16,319 |
| WA | 15,862 |
| WV | 540 |
| WI | 4,919 |
| WY | 252 |
| Other: | |
| Guam | 2,419 |
| N Mariana Isls. | 171 |
| Puerto Rico | 7,160 |
| Virgin Isls. | 1,511 |
| Armed Service Posts | 122 |
| Other or unknown | 13 |
| **Total** | **720,461** |

# U.S. Foreign-Born Population, 1995

**Source:** Bureau of the Census, U.S. Dept. of Commerce

## Percentage of U.S. Population That Is Foreign-Born, 1900-95

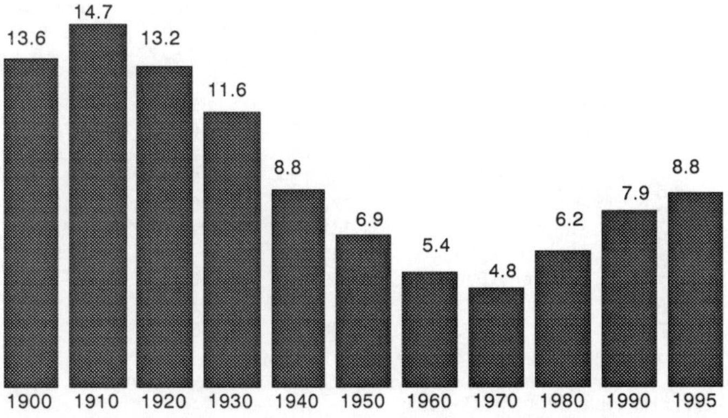


## Highest-Ranking Countries of Birth of U.S. Foreign-Born Population, 1995

| Country | Number (in thousands) |
|---|---|
| Mexico | 6,719 |
| Philippines | 1,200 |
| China/Taiwan/Hong Kong | 816 |
| Cuba | 797 |
| Canada | 695 |
| El Salvador | 650 |
| Great Britain | 617 |
| Germany | 598 |
| Poland | 538 |
| Jamaica | 531 |
| Dominican Republic | 509 |

## Population by State, 1990-95

**Source:** Bureau of the Census, U.S. Dept. of Commerce

| Rank | State | 1995 population | 1990 population | Percentage change 1990-95 |
|---|---|---|---|---|
| | **U.S.** . . . | **262,755,270** | **248,718,301** | **5.6** |
| 1. | CA . . . . | 31,589,153 | 29,758,213 | 6.2 |
| 2. | TX . . . . | 18,723,991 | 16,986,335 | 10.2 |
| 3. | NY . . . . | 18,136,081 | 17,990,778 | 0.8 |
| 4. | FL. . . . . | 14,165,570 | 12,938,071 | 9.5 |
| 5. | PA . . . . | 12,071,842 | 11,882,842 | 1.6 |
| 6. | IL . . . . . | 11,829,940 | 11,430,602 | 3.5 |
| 7. | OH . . . . | 11,150,506 | 10,847,115 | 2.8 |
| 8. | MI. . . . . | 9,549,353 | 9,295,287 | 2.7 |
| 9. | NJ. . . . . | 7,945,298 | 7,730,188 | 2.8 |
| 10. | GA . . . . | 7,200,882 | 6,478,149 | 11.2 |
| 11. | NC . . . . | 7,195,138 | 6,632,448 | 8.5 |
| 12. | VA . . . . | 6,618,358 | 6,189,197 | 6.9 |
| 13. | MA . . . . | 6,073,550 | 6,016,425 | 0.9 |
| 14. | IN . . . . . | 5,803,471 | 5,544,156 | 4.7 |
| 15. | WA . . . . | 5,430,940 | 4,866,669 | 11.6 |
| 16. | MO . . . . | 5,323,523 | 5,116,901 | 4.0 |
| 17. | TN . . . . | 5,256,051 | 4,877,203 | 7.8 |
| 18. | WI. . . . . | 5,122,871 | 4,891,769 | 4.7 |
| 19. | MD . . . . | 5,042,438 | 4,780,753 | 5.5 |
| 20. | MN . . . . | 4,609,548 | 4,375,665 | 5.3 |
| 21. | LA. . . . . | 4,342,334 | 4,220,164 | 2.9 |
| 22. | AL. . . . . | 4,252,982 | 4,040,389 | 5.3 |
| 23. | AZ . . . . | 4,217,940 | 3,665,339 | 15.1 |
| 24. | KY . . . . | 3,860,219 | 3,686,891 | 4.7 |
| 25. | CO . . . . | 3,746,585 | 3,294,473 | 13.7 |
| 26. | SC . . . . | 3,673,287 | 3,486,310 | 5.4 |
| 27. | OK . . . . | 3,277,687 | 3,145,576 | 4.2 |
| 28. | CT. . . . . | 3,274,662 | 3,287,116 | –0.4 |
| 29. | OR . . . . | 3,140,585 | 2,842,337 | 10.5 |
| 30. | IA . . . . . | 2,841,764 | 2,776,831 | 2.3 |
| 31. | MS . . . . | 2,697,243 | 2,575,475 | 4.7 |
| 32. | KS. . . . . | 2,565,328 | 2,477,588 | 3.5 |
| 33. | AR . . . . | 2,483,769 | 2,350,624 | 5.7 |
| 34. | UT. . . . . | 1,951,408 | 1,722,850 | 13.3 |
| 35. | WV . . . . | 1,828,140 | 1,793,477 | 1.9 |
| 36. | NM . . . . | 1,685,401 | 1,515,069 | 11.2 |
| 37. | NE . . . . | 1,637,112 | 1,578,417 | 3.7 |
| 38. | NV . . . . | 1,530,108 | 1,201,675 | 27.3 |
| 39. | ME . . . . | 1,241,382 | 1,227,928 | 1.1 |
| 40. | HI . . . . . | 1,186,815 | 1,108,229 | 7.1 |
| 41. | ID . . . . . | 1,163,261 | 1,006,734 | 15.5 |
| 42. | NH . . . . | 1,148,253 | 1,109,252 | 3.5 |
| 43. | RI . . . . . | 989,794 | 1,003,464 | –1.4 |
| 44. | MT . . . . | 870,281 | 799,065 | 8.9 |
| 45. | SD . . . . | 729,034 | 696,004 | 4.7 |
| 46. | DE . . . . | 717,197 | 666,168 | 7.7 |
| 47. | ND . . . . | 641,367 | 638,800 | 0.4 |
| 48. | AK. . . . . | 603,617 | 550,043 | 9.7 |
| 49. | VT. . . . . | 584,771 | 562,758 | 3.9 |
| 50. | DC . . . . | 554,256 | 606,900 | –8.7 |
| 51. | WY . . . . | 480,184 | 453,589 | 5.9 |

**Note:** Population figures for 1990 include corrections to the original tabulated population.

## Density of Population by State, 1920-90

**Source:** Bureau of the Census, U.S. Dept. of Commerce

(per square mile, land area only)

| State | 1920 | 1960 | 1980 | 1990 |
|---|---|---|---|---|
| AL. . . . | 45.8 | 64.2 | 76.6 | 79.6 |
| AK* . . . | 0.1 | 0.4 | 0.7 | 1.0 |
| AZ. . . . | 2.9 | 11.5 | 23.9 | 32.3 |
| AR. . . . | 33.4 | 34.2 | 43.9 | 45.1 |
| CA. . . . | 22.0 | 100.4 | 151.4 | 190.8 |
| CO. . . . | 9.1 | 16.9 | 27.9 | 31.8 |
| CT. . . . | 286.4 | 520.6 | 637.8 | 678.4 |
| DE. . . . | 113.5 | 225.2 | 307.6 | 340.8 |
| DC. . . . | 7,292.9 | 12,523.9 | 10,132.3 | 9,882.8 |
| FL. . . . | 17.7 | 91.5 | 180.0 | 239.6 |
| GA. . . . | 49.3 | 67.8 | 94.1 | 111.9 |
| HI*. . . . | 39.9 | 98.5 | 150.1 | 172.5 |
| ID . . . . | 5.2 | 8.1 | 11.5 | 12.2 |
| IL. . . . . | 115.7 | 180.4 | 205.3 | 205.6 |
| IN . . . . | 81.3 | 128.8 | 152.8 | 154.6 |
| IA . . . . | 43.2 | 49.2 | 52.1 | 49.7 |
| KS. . . . | 21.6 | 26.6 | 28.9 | 30.3 |
| KY. . . . | 60.1 | 76.2 | 92.3 | 92.8 |
| LA. . . . | 39.6 | 72.2 | 94.5 | 96.9 |
| ME. . . . | 25.7 | 31.3 | 36.3 | 39.8 |
| MD . . . | 145.8 | 313.5 | 428.7 | 489.2 |
| MA. . . . | 479.2 | 657.3 | 733.3 | 767.6 |
| MI . . . . | 63.8 | 137.7 | 162.6 | 163.6 |
| MN . . . | 29.5 | 43.1 | 51.2 | 55.0 |
| MS. . . . | 38.6 | 46.0 | 53.4 | 54.9 |
| MO . . . | 49.5 | 62.6 | 71.3 | 74.3 |
| MT. . . . | 3.8 | 4.6 | 5.4 | 5.5 |
| NE. . . . | 16.9 | 18.4 | 20.5 | 20.5 |
| NV. . . . | 0.7 | 2.6 | 7.3 | 10.9 |
| NH. . . . | 49.1 | 67.2 | 102.4 | 123.7 |
| NJ . . . . | 420.0 | 805.5 | 986.2 | 1,042.0 |
| NM . . . | 2.9 | 7.8 | 10.7 | 12.5 |
| NY. . . . | 217.9 | 350.6 | 370.6 | 381.0 |
| NC. . . . | 52.5 | 93.2 | 120.4 | 136.1 |
| ND. . . . | 9.2 | 9.1 | 9.4 | 9.3 |
| OH. . . . | 141.4 | 236.6 | 263.3 | 264.9 |
| OK. . . . | 29.2 | 33.8 | 44.1 | 45.8 |
| OR. . . . | 8.2 | 18.4 | 27.4 | 29.6 |
| PA. . . . | 194.5 | 251.4 | 264.3 | 265.1 |
| RI . . . . | 566.4 | 819.3 | 897.8 | 960.3 |
| SC. . . . | 55.2 | 78.7 | 103.4 | 115.8 |
| SD. . . . | 8.3 | 9.0 | 9.1 | 9.2 |
| TN. . . . | 56.1 | 86.2 | 111.6 | 118.3 |
| TX . . . . | 17.8 | 36.4 | 54.3 | 64.9 |
| UT. . . . | 5.5 | 10.8 | 17.8 | 21.0 |
| VT. . . . | 38.6 | 42.0 | 55.2 | 60.8 |
| VA. . . . | 57.4 | 99.6 | 134.7 | 156.3 |
| WA . . . | 20.3 | 42.8 | 62.1 | 73.1 |
| WV . . . | 60.9 | 77.2 | 80.8 | 74.5 |
| WI . . . . | 47.6 | 72.6 | 86.5 | 90.1 |
| WY . . . | 2.0 | 3.4 | 4.9 | 4.7 |
| **U.S.** . . . | **29.9*** | **50.6** | **64.0** | **70.3** |

(*) For purposes of comparison, Alaska and Hawaii are included in above tabulation for 1920, even though not states then.

## 25 Largest Counties, by Population, 1990-95

**Source:** Bureau of the Census, U.S. Dept of Commerce

| County | 1995 population | 1990 population | Percentage change, 1990-95 |
|---|---|---|---|
| Los Angeles, CA. . . . | 9,138,789 | 8,863,052 | 3.1 |
| Cook, IL . . . . . . . . . . | 5,136,877 | 5,105,044 | 0.6 |
| Harris, TX. . . . . . . . . | 3,076,867 | 2,818,101 | 9.2 |
| San Diego, CA . . . . . | 2,644,132 | 2,498,016 | 5.8 |
| Orange, CA . . . . . . . | 2,563,971 | 2,410,668 | 6.4 |
| Maricopa, AZ . . . . . . | 2,432,372 | 2,122,101 | 14.6 |
| Kings, NY . . . . . . . . . | 2,244,021 | 2,300,664 | –2.5 |
| Wayne, MI . . . . . . . . | 2,055,500 | 2,111,687 | –2.7 |
| Dade, FL . . . . . . . . . | 2,031,336 | 1,937,194 | 4.9 |
| Queens, NY . . . . . . . | 1,963,628 | 1,951,598 | 0.6 |
| Dallas, TX. . . . . . . . . | 1,959,281 | 1,852,810 | 5.7 |
| King, WA . . . . . . . . . | 1,595,243 | 1,507,305 | 5.8 |
| San Bernardino, CA . | 1,569,586 | 1,418,380 | 10.7 |
| Santa Clara, CA. . . . . | 1,565,253 | 1,497,577 | 4.5 |
| New York, NY . . . . . . | 1,518,910 | 1,487,536 | 2.1 |
| Philadelphia, PA. . . . . | 1,498,971 | 1,585,577 | –5.5 |
| Broward, FL. . . . . . . . | 1,412,165 | 1,255,531 | 12.5 |
| Middlesex, MA . . . . . . | 1,408,450 | 1,398,468 | 0.7 |
| Cuyahoga, OH . . . . . . | 1,398,169 | 1,412,140 | –1.0 |
| Riverside, CA. . . . . . . | 1,379,801 | 1,170,413 | 17.9 |
| Suffolk, NY . . . . . . . . | 1,353,704 | 1,321,768 | 2.4 |
| Alameda, CA . . . . . . . | 1,323,312 | 1,276,702 | 3.7 |
| Allegheny, PA . . . . . . | 1,309,821 | 1,336,449 | –2.0 |
| Nassau, NY. . . . . . . . | 1,305,772 | 1,287,444 | 1.4 |
| Bexar, TX . . . . . . . . . | 1,296,731 | 1,185,394 | 9.4 |

**Note:** The following are the **smallest counties**, by 1995 population: Kalawao County, HI (91); Loving County, TX (140); King County, TX (316); Arthur County, NE (440); Kenedy County, TX (442); Petroleum County, MT (527); McPherson County, NE (544); San Juan County, CO (546); Mineral County, CO (634); and Hinsdale County, CO (648).

# Metropolitan Areas, 1990-94

**Source:** Bureau of the Census, U.S. Dept. of Commerce

(CMSAs and MSAs of more than 600,000 persons listed by 1994 population estimates)

Metropolitan statistical areas (MSAs) are defined for federal statistical use by the Office of Management and Budget (OMB), with technical asistance from the Bureau of the Census. Most individual metropolitan areas with populations over 1 mil may, under specified circumstances, be subdivided into component Primary Metropolitan Statistical Areas (PMSAs), in which case the area as a whole is designated a Consolidated Metropolitan Statistical Area (CMSA).

Effective June 30, 1995, the Office of Management and Budget designated 253 MSAs, 76 PMSAs, and 19 CMSAs for the U.S. and Puerto Rico based on standards published in the Federal Register on Mar. 30, 1990, as applied to 1990 census data.

| CMSAs and MSAs | Population 1990 | Population 1994 | Percentage change 1990-94 |
|---|---|---|---|
| New York–Northern New Jersey–Long Island, NY–NJ–CT–PA CMSA | 19,549,649 | 19,796,430 | 1.3 |
| Los Angeles–Riverside–Orange County, CA CMSA | 14,531,529 | 15,302,275 | 5.3 |
| Chicago–Gary–Kenosha, IL–IN–WI CMSA | 8,239,820 | 8,526,804 | 3.5 |
| Washington–Baltimore, DC–MD–VA–WV CMSA | 6,726,395 | 7,051,495 | 4.8 |
| San Francisco–Oakland–San Jose, CA CMSA | 6,249,881 | 6,513,322 | 4.2 |
| Philadelphia–Wilmington–Atlantic City, PA–NJ–DE–MD CMSA | 5,893,019 | 5,959,301 | 1.1 |
| Boston–Worcester–Lawrence, MA–NH–ME–CT CMSA | 5,455,403 | 5,497,284 | 0.8 |
| Detroit–Ann Arbor–Flint, MI CMSA | 5,187,171 | 5,255,700 | 1.3 |
| Dallas–Fort Worth, TX CMSA | 4,037,282 | 4,362,483 | 8.1 |
| Houston–Galveston–Brazoria, TX CMSA | 3,731,029 | 4,098,776 | 9.9 |
| Miami–Fort Lauderdale, FL CMSA | 3,192,725 | 3,408,038 | 6.7 |
| Atlanta, GA | 2,959,500 | 3,330,997 | 12.6 |
| Seattle–Tacoma–Bremerton, WA CMSA | 2,970,300 | 3,225,517 | 8.6 |
| Cleveland, Akron, OH CMSA | 2,859,644 | 2,898,855 | 1.4 |
| Minneapolis–St. Paul | 2,538,766 | 2,688,455 | 5.9 |
| San Diego, CA | 2,498,016 | 2,632,078 | 5.4 |
| St. Louis, MO–IL | 2,492,348 | 2,536,080 | 1.8 |
| Phoenix–Mesa, AZ | 2,238,498 | 2,473,384 | 10.5 |
| Pittsburgh, PA | 2,394,811 | 2,402,012 | 0.3 |
| Denver–Boulder–Greeley, CO CMSA | 1,980,140 | 2,189,994 | 10.6 |
| Tampa–St. Petersburgh–Clearwater, FL | 2,067,959 | 2,156,546 | 4.3 |
| Portland–Salem, OR–WA CMSA | 1,793,476 | 1,982,238 | 10.5 |
| Cincinnati–Hamilton, OH–KY–IN, CMSA | 1,817,569 | 1,894,071 | 4.2 |
| Kansas City, MO | 1,582,874 | 1,647,241 | 4.1 |
| Milwaukee–Racine, WI CMSA | 1,607,183 | 1,637,278 | 1.9 |
| Sacramento–Yolo, CA . CMSA | 1,481,220 | 1,587,898 | 7.2 |
| Norfolk–Virginia Beach–Newport News, VA–NC | 1,444,710 | 1,529,207 | 5.8 |
| Indianapolis, IN | 1,380,491 | 1,461,693 | 5.9 |
| San Antonio, TX | 1,324,749 | 1,437,306 | 8.5 |
| Columbus, OH | 1,345,450 | 1,422,875 | 5.8 |
| Orlando, FL | 1,224,844 | 1,361,489 | 11.2 |
| New Orleans, LA | 1,285,262 | 1,308,904 | 1.8 |
| Charlotte–Gastonia–Rock Hill, NC–SC | 1,162,140 | 1,260,390 | 8.5 |
| Buffalo–Niagara Falls, NY | 1,189,340 | 1,189,237 | 0.0 |
| Salt Lake City–Odgen, UT | 1,072,227 | 1,178,338 | 9.9 |
| Hartford, CT | 1,157,585 | 1,151,413 | –0.5 |
| Providence–Fall River–Warwick, RI–MA | 1,134,350 | 1,129,172 | –0.5 |
| Greensboro–Winston–Salem–High Point, NC | 1,050,304 | 1,107,051 | 5.4 |
| Rochester, NY | 1,062,470 | 1,090,596 | 2.6 |
| Las Vegas, NV–AZ | 852,646 | 1,076,267 | 26.2 |
| Nashville, TN | 985,026 | 1,069,648 | 8.6 |
| Memphis, TN–AR–MS | 1,007,306 | 1,056,096 | 4.8 |
| Oklahoma City, OK | 958,839 | 1,007,302 | 5.1 |
| Grand Rapids–Muskegon–Holland, MI | 937,891 | 984,990 | 5.0 |
| Louisville, KY–IN | 949,012 | 980,855 | 3.4 |
| Jacksonville, FL | 906,727 | 971,829 | 7.2 |
| Raleigh–Durham–Chapel Hill, NC | 858,485 | 965,127 | 12.4 |
| Austin–San Marcos, TX | 846,227 | 963,981 | 13.9 |
| Dayton–Springfield, OH | 951,270 | 956,382 | 0.5 |
| West Palm Beach–Boca Raton, FL | 863,503 | 954,539 | 10.5 |
| Richmond–Petersburg, VA | 865,640 | 916,674 | 5.9 |
| Albany–Schenectady–Troy, NY | 861,623 | 875,240 | 1.6 |
| Honolulu, HI | 836,231 | 874,330 | 4.6 |
| Greenville–Spartanburg–Anderson, SC | 830,539 | 873,356 | 5.2 |
| Birmingham, AL | 839,942 | 872,222 | 3.8 |
| Fresno, CA | 755,580 | 834,663 | 10.5 |
| Syracuse, NY | 742,237 | 753,980 | 1.6 |
| Tulsa, OK | 708,954 | 743,107 | 4.8 |
| Tucson, AZ | 666,957 | 731,523 | 9.7 |
| El Paso, TX | 591,610 | 664,813 | 12.4 |
| Omaha, NE–IA | 639,580 | 662,811 | 3.6 |
| Albuquerque, NM | 589,131 | 645,533 | 9.6 |
| Scranton–Wilkes-Barre–Hazleton, PA | 638,524 | 636,993 | –0.2 |
| Knoxville, TN | 585,960 | 631,107 | 7.7 |
| Toledo, OH | 614,128 | 613,945 | 0.0 |
| Allentown–Bethlehem–Easton, PA | 595,208 | 611,765 | 2.8 |
| Harrisburg–Lebanon–Carlisle, PA | 587,986 | 609,715 | 3.7 |
| Bakersfield, CA | 544,981 | 609,332 | 11.8 |
| Youngstown–Warren, OH | 600,895 | 604,123 | 0.5 |

Final 1990 census figures showed that the nation in that year had 40 metropolitan areas of at least 1 mil population, including 5 that had reached that size since 1980. The 40 areas had 128.2 mil people, or 51.5% of the U.S. population, in 1990. It is estimated that since the 1990 census, the populations of 3 additional metropolitan areas (Las Vegas, NV–AZ; Nashville, TN; and Oklahoma City, OK) have increased to more than 1 mil. By 1994, 54.5% of the population lived in metropolitan areas that had a total of at least 1 mil inhabitants.

Some 260.3 mil people resided in metropolitan areas in 1994, an increase of more than 11.6 mil (4.7%) since 1990. The population outside metropolitan areas totaled 52.7 mil in 1994, up 2.0 mil (3.9%) from 1990. The metropolitan population in 1994 was 79.8% of the U.S. total, compared with 79.4% in 1990 and 76.2% in 1980.

# Population of 100 Largest U.S. Cities, 1850-1994

**Source:** Bureau of the Census, U.S. Dept. of Commerce (100 most populous cities ranked by July 1, 1994, population estimates)

| Rank | City | 1994 | 1990 | 1980 | 1970 | 1950 | 1900 | 1850 |
|---|---|---|---|---|---|---|---|---|
| 1. | New York, NY | 7,333,253 | 7,322,564 | 7,071,639 | 7,895,563 | 7,891,957 | 3,437,202 | 696,115 |
| 2. | Los Angeles, CA | 3,448,613 | 3,485,557 | 2,968,528 | 2,811,801 | 1,970,358 | 102,479 | 1,610 |
| 3. | Chicago, IL | 2,731,743 | 2,783,726 | 3,005,072 | 3,369,357 | 3,620,962 | 1,698,575 | 29,963 |
| 4. | Houston, TX | 1,702,086 | 1,629,902 | 1,595,138 | 1,233,535 | 596,163 | 44,633 | 2,396 |
| 5. | Philadelphia, PA | 1,524,249 | 1,585,577 | 1,688,210 | 1,949,996 | 2,071,605 | 1,293,697 | 121,376 |
| 6. | San Diego, CA | 1,151,977 | 1,110,623 | 875,538 | 697,471 | 334,387 | 17,700 | ... |
| 7. | Phoenix, AZ | 1,048,949 | 983,403 | 789,704 | 584,303 | 106,818 | 5,544 | ... |
| 8. | Dallas, TX | 1,022,830 | 1,007,618 | 904,599 | 844,401 | 434,462 | 42,638 | ... |
| 9. | San Antonio, TX | 998,905 | 935,393 | 785,940 | 654,153 | 408,442 | 53,321 | 3,488 |
| 10. | Detroit, MI | 992,038 | 1,027,974 | 1,203,368 | 1,514,063 | 1,849,568 | 285,704 | 21,019 |
| 11. | San Jose, CA | 816,884 | 782,224 | 629,400 | 459,913 | 95,280 | 21,500 | ... |
| 12. | Indianapolis, IN[1] | 752,279 | 731,327 | 700,807 | 736,856 | 427,173 | 169,164 | 8,091 |
| 13. | San Francisco, CA | 734,676 | 723,959 | 678,974 | 715,674 | 775,357 | 342,782 | 34,776 |
| 14. | Baltimore, MD | 702,979 | 736,014 | 786,741 | 905,787 | 949,708 | 508,957 | 169,054 |
| 15. | Jacksonville, FL[1] | 665,070 | 635,230 | 540,920 | 504,265 | 204,517 | 28,429 | 1,045 |
| 16. | Columbus, OH | 635,913 | 632,945 | 565,021 | 540,025 | 375,901 | 125,560 | 17,882 |
| 17. | Milwaukee, WI | 617,044 | 628,088 | 636,297 | 717,372 | 637,392 | 285,315 | 20,061 |
| 18. | Memphis, TN | 614,289 | 610,337 | 646,174 | 623,988 | 396,000 | 102,320 | 8,841 |
| 19. | El Paso, TX | 579,307 | 515,342 | 425,259 | 322,261 | 130,485 | 15,906 | ... |
| 20. | Washington, DC | 567,094 | 606,900 | 638,432 | 756,668 | 802,178 | 278,718 | 40,001 |
| 21. | Boston, MA | 547,725 | 574,283 | 562,994 | 641,071 | 801,444 | 560,892 | 136,881 |
| 22. | Seattle, WA | 520,947 | 516,259 | 493,846 | 530,831 | 467,591 | 80,671 | ... |
| 23. | Austin, TX | 514,013 | 465,648 | 345,890 | 253,539 | 132,459 | 22,258 | 629 |
| 24. | Nashville, TN[1] | 504,505 | 488,374 | 455,651 | 426,029 | 174,307 | 80,865 | 10,165 |
| 25. | Denver, CO | 493,559 | 467,610 | 492,686 | 514,678 | 415,786 | 133,859 | ... |
| 26. | Cleveland, OH | 492,901 | 505,616 | 573,822 | 750,879 | 914,808 | 381,768 | 17,034 |
| 27. | New Orleans, LA | 484,149 | 496,938 | 557,927 | 593,471 | 570,445 | 287,104 | 116,375 |
| 28. | Oklahoma City, OK | 463,201 | 444,724 | 404,014 | 368,164 | 243,504 | 10,037 | ... |
| 29. | Fort Worth, TX | 451,814 | 447,619 | 385,164 | 393,455 | 278,778 | 26,688 | ... |
| 30. | Portland, OR | 450,777 | 438,802 | 368,148 | 379,967 | 373,628 | 90,426 | ... |
| 31. | Kansas City, MO | 443,878 | 434,829 | 448,028 | 507,330 | 456,622 | 163,752 | ... |
| 32. | Charlotte, NC | 437,797 | 395,925 | 315,474 | 241,420 | 134,042 | 18,091 | 1,065 |
| 33. | Tucson, AZ | 434,726 | 405,323 | 330,537 | 262,933 | 45,454 | 7,531 | ... |
| 34. | Long Beach, CA | 433,852 | 429,321 | 361,498 | 358,879 | 250,767 | 2,252 | ... |
| 35. | Virginia Beach, VA | 430,295 | 393,089 | 262,199 | 172,106 | 5,390 | ... | ... |
| 36. | Albuquerque, NM | 411,994 | 384,619 | 332,920 | 244,501 | 96,815 | 6,238 | ... |
| 37. | Atlanta, GA | 396,052 | 393,929 | 425,022 | 495,039 | 331,314 | 89,872 | 2,572 |
| 38. | Fresno, CA | 386,551 | 354,091 | 217,491 | 165,655 | 91,669 | 12,470 | ... |
| 39. | Honolulu, HI[2] | 385,881 | 365,272 | 365,048 | 324,871 | 248,034 | 39,306 | ... |
| 40. | Tulsa, OK | 374,851 | 367,302 | 360,919 | 330,350 | 182,740 | 1,390 | ... |
| 41. | Sacramento, CA | 373,964 | 369,365 | 275,741 | 257,105 | 137,572 | 29,282 | 6,820 |
| 42. | Miami, FL | 373,024 | 358,648 | 346,681 | 334,859 | 249,276 | 1,681 | ... |
| 43. | St. Louis, MO | 368,215 | 396,685 | 452,801 | 622,236 | 856,796 | 575,238 | 77,860 |
| 44. | Oakland, CA | 366,926 | 372,242 | 339,337 | 361,561 | 384,575 | 66,960 | ... |
| 45. | Pittsburgh, PA | 358,883 | 369,879 | 423,959 | 520,089 | 676,806 | 321,616 | 46,601 |
| 46. | Cincinnati, OH | 358,170 | 364,114 | 385,409 | 453,514 | 503,998 | 325,902 | 115,435 |
| 47. | Minneapolis, MN | 354,590 | 368,383 | 370,951 | 434,400 | 521,718 | 202,718 | ... |
| 48. | Omaha, NE | 345,033 | 335,719 | 313,939 | 346,929 | 251,117 | 102,555 | ... |
| 49. | Las Vegas, NV | 327,878 | 258,204 | 164,674 | 125,787 | 24,624 | ... | ... |
| 50. | Toledo, OH | 322,550 | 332,943 | 354,635 | 383,062 | 303,616 | 131,822 | 3,829 |
| 51. | Colorado Springs, CO | 316,480 | 280,430 | 215,105 | 135,517 | 45,472 | 21,085 | ... |
| 52. | Mesa, AZ | 313,649 | 288,104 | 152,404 | 63,049 | 16,790 | 722 | ... |
| 53. | Buffalo, NY | 312,965 | 328,175 | 357,870 | 462,768 | 580,132 | 352,387 | 42,261 |
| 54. | Wichita, KS | 310,236 | 304,017 | 279,838 | 276,554 | 168,279 | 24,671 | ... |
| 55. | Santa Ana, CA | 290,827 | 293,827 | 204,023 | 155,710 | 45,533 | 4,933 | ... |
| 56. | Arlington, TX | 286,922 | 261,717 | 160,113 | 90,229 | 7,692 | 1,079 | ... |
| 57. | Tampa, FL | 285,523 | 280,015 | 271,577 | 277,714 | 124,681 | 15,839 | ... |
| 58. | Anaheim, CA | 282,133 | 266,406 | 219,494 | 166,408 | 14,556 | 1,456 | ... |
| 59. | Corpus Christi, TX | 275,419 | 257,428 | 232,134 | 204,525 | 108,287 | 4,703 | ... |
| 60. | Louisville, KY | 270,308 | 269,555 | 298,694 | 361,706 | 369,129 | 204,731 | 43,194 |
| 61. | Birmingham, AL | 264,527 | 265,347 | 284,413 | 300,910 | 326,037 | 38,415 | ... |
| 62. | St. Paul, MN | 262,071 | 272,235 | 270,230 | 309,866 | 311,349 | 163,065 | 1,112 |
| 63. | Newark, NJ | 258,751 | 275,221 | 329,248 | 381,930 | 438,776 | 246,070 | 38,894 |
| 64. | Anchorage, AK | 253,649 | 226,338 | 174,431 | 48,081 | 11,254 | ... | ... |
| 65. | Aurora, CO | 250,717 | 222,103 | 158,588 | 74,974 | 11,421 | 202 | ... |
| 66. | Riverside, CA | 241,644 | 226,546 | 170,591 | 140,089 | 46,764 | 7,973 | ... |
| 67. | Norfolk, VA | 241,426 | 261,250 | 266,979 | 307,951 | 213,513 | 46,624 | 14,326 |
| 68. | St. Petersburg, FL | 238,585 | 240,318 | 238,647 | 216,159 | 96,738 | 1,575 | ... |
| 69. | Lexington, KY | 237,612 | 225,366 | 204,165 | 108,137 | 55,534 | 26,369 | 8,159 |
| 70. | Raleigh, NC | 236,707 | 212,092 | 150,255 | 122,830 | 65,679 | 13,643 | 4,518 |
| 71. | Rochester, NY | 231,170 | 230,356 | 241,741 | 295,011 | 332,488 | 162,608 | 36,403 |
| 72. | Baton Rouge, LA | 227,482 | 219,531 | 220,394 | 165,921 | 125,629 | 11,269 | 3,905 |
| 73. | Jersey City, NJ | 226,022 | 228,517 | 223,532 | 260,350 | 299,017 | 206,433 | 6,856 |
| 74. | Stockton, CA | 222,633 | 210,943 | 148,283 | 109,963 | 70,853 | 17,506 | ... |
| 75. | Akron, OH | 221,886 | 223,019 | 237,177 | 275,425 | 274,605 | 42,728 | 3,266 |
| 76. | Mobile, AL | 204,490 | 196,263 | 200,452 | 190,026 | 129,009 | 38,469 | 20,515 |
| 77. | Lincoln, NE | 203,076 | 191,972 | 171,932 | 149,518 | 98,884 | 40,169 | ... |
| 78. | Richmond, VA | 201,108 | 202,798 | 219,214 | 249,332 | 230,310 | 85,050 | 27,570 |
| 79. | Shreveport, LA | 196,982 | 198,518 | 206,989 | 182,064 | 127,206 | 16,013 | 1,728 |
| 80. | Greensboro, NC | 196,167 | 183,894 | 155,642 | 144,076 | 74,389 | 10,035 | ... |
| 81. | Montgomery, AL | 195,471 | 187,543 | 177,857 | 133,386 | 106,525 | 30,346 | 8,728 |
| 82. | Madison, WI | 194,586 | 190,766 | 170,616 | 171,809 | 96,056 | 19,164 | 1,525 |
| 83. | Lubbock, TX | 194,467 | 186,206 | 174,361 | 149,101 | 71,747 | ... | ... |
| 84. | Garland, TX | 194,218 | 180,635 | 138,857 | 81,437 | 10,571 | 819 | ... |
| 85. | Hialeah, FL | 194,120 | 188,008 | 145,254 | 102,452 | 19,676 | ... | ... |

| Rank | City | 1994 | 1990 | 1980 | 1970 | 1950 | 1900 | 1850 |
|---|---|---|---|---|---|---|---|---|
| 86. | Des Moines, IA | 193,965 | 193,189 | 191,003 | 201,404 | 177,965 | 62,139 | ... |
| 87. | Jackson, MS | 193,097 | 196,637 | 202,895 | 153,968 | 98,271 | 7,816 | 1,881 |
| 88. | Spokane, WA | 192,781 | 177,165 | 171,300 | 170,516 | 161,721 | 36,848 | ... |
| 89. | Bakersfield, CA | 191,060 | 174,978 | 105,611 | 69,515 | 34,784 | 4,836 | ... |
| 90. | Grand Rapids, MI | 190,395 | 189,126 | 181,843 | 197,649 | 176,515 | 87,565 | 2,686 |
| 91. | Huntington Beach, CA | 189,220 | 181,519 | 170,505 | 115,960 | 5,237 | ... | ... |
| 92. | Columbus, GA[1] | 186,470 | 178,681 | 169,441 | 155,028 | 79,611 | 17,614 | 9,621 |
| 93. | Fremont, CA | 183,575 | 173,339 | 131,945 | 100,869 | ... | ... | ... |
| 94. | Yonkers, NY | 183,490 | 188,082 | 195,351 | 204,297 | 152,798 | 47,931 | ... |
| 95. | Fort Wayne, IN | 183,359 | 172,971 | 172,391 | 178,269 | 133,607 | 45,115 | 4,282 |
| 96. | Tacoma, WA | 183,060 | 176,664 | 158,501 | 154,407 | 143,673 | 37,714 | ... |
| 97. | San Bernardino, CA | 181,718 | 164,164 | 118,794 | 104,251 | 63,058 | 6,150 | ... |
| 98. | Chesapeake, VA | 180,577 | 151,982 | 114,486 | 89,580 | ... | ... | ... |
| 99. | Newport News, VA | 179,127 | 171,439 | 144,903 | 138,177 | 42,358 | 19,635 | ... |
| 100. | Dayton, OH | 178,540 | 182,005 | 193,536 | 243,023 | 243,872 | 85,333 | 10,977 |

**Note:** The Apr. 1, 1990, census counts include count resolution corrections and geographic changes. (1) Indianapolis, IN; Jacksonville, FL; Nashville-Davidson, TN; and Columbus, GA, are parts of consolidated city-county governments. Populations of other incorporated places in the county have been excluded from the population totals shown here. For years that predate the establishment of a consolidated city-county government, city population is shown. (2) Locations in Hawaii are called "census designated places (CDPs)." Although these areas are not incorporated, they are recognized for census purposes as large urban places. Honolulu CDP is coextensive with Honolulu Judicial District within the city and county of Honolulu.

# Geographic Mobility Rates, by Type of Movement, 1960-94

**Source:** Bureau of the Census, U.S. Dept. of Commerce

(in thousands)

| | | | Residing in the U.S. at the beginning of the period | | | | | |
|---|---|---|---|---|---|---|---|---|
| | | | | | Different county | | | |
| Mobility period | Total, 1 yr. old and older | Total movers | Total | Different house, same county | Total | Different house, same state | Different house, different state | Movers from abroad[1] |
| 1993-94 | 255,774 | 42,835 | 41,590 | 26,638 | 14,952 | 8,226 | 6,726 | 1,245 |
| 1992-93 | 250,210 | 42,048 | 40,743 | 26,212 | 14,532 | 7,735 | 6,797 | 1,305 |
| 1991-92 | 247,380 | 42,800 | 41,545 | 26,587 | 14,957 | 7,853 | 7,105 | 1,255 |
| 1990-91 | 244,884 | 41,539 | 40,154 | 25,151 | 15,003 | 7,881 | 7,122 | 1,385 |
| 1989-90 | 242,208 | 43,381 | 41,821 | 25,726 | 16,094 | 8,061 | 8,033 | 1,560 |
| 1988-89 | 239,793 | 42,620 | 41,153 | 26,123 | 15,030 | 7,949 | 7,081 | 1,467 |
| 1987-88 | 237,431 | 42,174 | 40,974 | 26,201 | 14,772 | 7,727 | 7,046 | 1,200 |
| 1986-87 | 235,089 | 43,693 | 42,551 | 27,196 | 15,355 | 8,762 | 6,593 | 1,142 |
| 1985-86 | 232,998 | 43,237 | 42,037 | 26,401 | 15,636 | 8,665 | 6,971 | 1,200 |
| 1984-85 | 230,333 | 46,470 | 45,043 | 30,126 | 14,917 | 7,995 | 6,921 | 1,427 |
| 1983-84 | 228,232 | 39,379 | 38,300 | 23,659 | 14,641 | 8,198 | 6,444 | 1,079 |
| 1982-83 | 225,874 | 37,408 | 36,430 | 22,858 | 13,572 | 7,403 | 6,169 | 978 |
| 1981-82 | 223,719 | 38,127 | 37,039 | 23,081 | 13,959 | 7,330 | 6,628 | 1,088 |
| 1980-81 | 221,641 | 38,200 | 36,887 | 23,097 | 13,789 | 7,614 | 6,175 | 1,313 |
| 1970-71 | 201,506 | 37,705 | 36,161 | 23,018 | 13,143 | 6,197 | 6,946 | 1,544 |
| 1960-61 | 177,354 | 36,533 | 35,535 | 24,289 | 11,246 | 5,493 | 5,753 | 998 |

(1) Movers from abroad include immigrants and U.S. citizens returning from other countries, including members of the military and their dependents.

# Projections of Total Population, by Age, 1995-2050

**Source:** Bureau of the Census, U.S. Dept. of Commerce

| | 1995 | | 2000 | | 2010 | | 2050 | |
|---|---|---|---|---|---|---|---|---|
| Age | Population[1] | Percentage distribution | Population[1] | Percentage distribution | Population[1] | Percentage distribution | Population[1] | Percentage distribution |
| Total | 262,820 | 100.0 | 274,634 | 100.0 | 297,716 | 100.0 | 393,931 | 100.0 |
| Under 5 years | 19,591 | 7.5 | 18,987 | 6.9 | 20,012 | 6.7 | 27,106 | 6.9 |
| 5-13 years | 34,378 | 13.1 | 36,043 | 13.1 | 35,605 | 12.0 | 47,804 | 12.1 |
| 14-17 years | 14,773 | 5.6 | 15,752 | 5.7 | 16,894 | 5.7 | 21,207 | 5.4 |
| 18-24 years | 24,926 | 9.5 | 26,258 | 9.6 | 30,138 | 10.1 | 36,333 | 9.2 |
| 25-34 years | 40,863 | 15.5 | 37,233 | 13.6 | 38,292 | 12.9 | 49,365 | 12.5 |
| 35-44 years | 42,514 | 16.2 | 44,659 | 16.3 | 38,521 | 12.9 | 47,393 | 12.0 |
| 45-54 years | 31,092 | 11.8 | 37,030 | 13.5 | 43,564 | 14.6 | 43,494 | 11.0 |
| 55-64 years | 21,139 | 8.0 | 23,961 | 8.7 | 35,283 | 11.9 | 42,368 | 10.8 |
| 65 years and over | 33,543 | 12.8 | 34,709 | 12.6 | 39,408 | 13.2 | 78,859 | 20.0 |
| 85 years and over | 3,634 | 1.4 | 4,259 | 1.6 | 5,671 | 1.9 | 18,223 | 4.6 |
| 100 years and over | 54 | 0.0 | 72 | 0.0 | 131 | 0.0 | 834 | 0.2 |

**Note:** All figures shown are for July 1 of the given year, exclude Armed Forces overseas, and are middle series population projections. For the series shown, different assumptions were made regarding fertility rates (lifetime births per woman), life expectancy, and immigration in the coming decades. Assumptions were based on a July 1, 1994, estimate of U.S. population consistent with the 1990 decennial census, as enumerated. Yearly net immigration was assumed to be 820,000. Percentage distribution may not equal 100, because of overlapping categories shown and rounding. (1) In thousands.

# Poverty Level by Family Size, 1993-95

**Source:** Bureau of the Census, U.S. Dept. of Commerce

| | 1993 | 1994 | 1995 |
|---|---|---|---|
| 1 person | $ 7,363 | $ 7,547 | $ 7,763 |
| Under 65 years | 7,518 | 7,710 | 7,929 |
| 65 years and over | 6,930 | 7,108 | 7,309 |
| 2 persons | 9,414 | 9,661 | 9,933 |
| Householder under 65 years | 9,728 | 9,979 | 10,259 |
| Householder 65 years and over | 8,740 | 8,967 | 9,219 |
| 3 persons | $ 11,522 | $ 11,821 | $ 12,158 |
| 4 persons | 14,763 | 15,141 | 15,569 |
| 5 persons | 17,449 | 17,900 | 18,408 |
| 6 persons | 19,718 | 20,235 | 20,804 |
| 7 persons | 22,383 | 22,923 | 23,552 |
| 8 persons | 24,838 | 25,427 | 26,237 |
| 9 persons or more | 29,529 | 30,300 | 31,280 |

# Poverty Rate

**Source:** Bureau of the Census, U.S. Dept. of Commerce

The poverty rate is the proportion of the population whose income falls below the government's official poverty level, which is adjusted each year for inflation. The national poverty rate was 13.8% in 1995. Children remained overrepresented among the poor, with a poverty rate of 20.8%. As a group the elderly were slightly underrepresented.

# Poverty by Family Status, Sex, and Race, 1978-95

**Source:** Bureau of the Census, U.S. Dept. of Commerce

(numbers in thousands)

| | 1995 | | 1994 | | 1990 | | 1986 | | 1978 | |
|---|---|---|---|---|---|---|---|---|---|---|
| | No. | %[1] | No. | %[1] | No. | %[1] | No. | %[1] | No. | %[1] |
| **Total poor** | **36,425** | **13.8** | **38,059** | **14.5** | **33,585** | **13.5** | **32,370** | **13.6** | **24,497** | **11.4** |
| **In families** | **27,501** | **12.3** | **28,965** | **13.1** | **25,232** | **12.0** | **24,754** | **12.0** | **19,062** | **10.0** |
| Head of household | 7,532 | 10.8 | 8,053 | 11.6 | 7,098 | 10.7 | 7,023 | 10.9 | 5,280 | 9.1 |
| Related children | 13,999 | 20.2 | 14,610 | 21.2 | 12,715 | 19.9 | 12,257 | 19.8 | 9,722 | 15.7 |
| **Unrelated individuals** | **8,247** | **20.9** | **8,287** | **21.5** | **7,446** | **20.7** | **6,846** | **21.6** | **5,435** | **22.1** |
| **In families, female householder, no husband present** | **14,205** | **36.5** | **14,380** | **38.6** | **12,578** | **37.2** | **11,944** | **38.3** | **9,269** | **35.6** |
| Head of household | 4,057 | 32.4 | 4,232 | 34.6 | 3,768 | 33.4 | 3,613 | 34.6 | 2,654 | 31.4 |
| Related children | 8,364 | 50.3 | 8,427 | 52.9 | 7,363 | 53.4 | 6,943 | 54.4 | 5,687 | 50.6 |
| **Unrelated female individuals** | **4,865** | **23.5** | **5,012** | **24.9** | **4,589** | **24.0** | **4,311** | **25.1** | **3,611** | **26.0** |
| **All other families** | **13,296** | **7.2** | **14,605** | **7.9** | **12,654** | **7.1** | **12,811** | **7.3** | **9,793** | **5.9** |
| Head of household | 3,475 | 6.1 | 3,821 | 6.7 | 3,330 | 6.0 | 3,410 | 6.3 | 2,626 | 5.3 |
| Related children | 5,635 | 10.7 | 6,183 | 11.7 | 5,352 | 10.7 | 5,313 | 10.8 | 4,035 | 7.9 |
| **Unrelated male individuals** | **3,382** | **18.0** | **3,276** | **17.8** | **2,857** | **16.9** | **2,536** | **17.5** | **1,824** | **17.1** |
| **Total white poor** | **24,423** | **11.2** | **25,379** | **11.7** | **22,326** | **10.7** | **22,183** | **11.0** | **16,259** | **8.7** |
| **In families** | **17,593** | **9.6** | **18,474** | **10.1** | **15,916** | **9.0** | **16,393** | **9.4** | **12,050** | **7.3** |
| Head of household | 4,994 | 8.5 | 5,312 | 9.1 | 4,622 | 8.1 | 4,811 | 8.6 | 3,523 | 6.9 |
| Related children | 8,474 | 15.5 | 8,826 | 16.3 | 7,696 | 15.1 | 7,714 | 15.3 | 5,674 | 11.0 |
| **Female householder, no spouse present** | **2,200** | **26.6** | **2,329** | **29.0** | **2,010** | **26.8** | **2,041** | **28.2** | **1,391** | **23.5** |
| **Unrelated individuals** | **6,336** | **19.0** | **6,292** | **19.3** | **5,739** | **18.6** | **5,198** | **19.2** | **4,209** | **19.8** |
| **Total black poor** | **9,872** | **29.3** | **10,196** | **30.6** | **9,837** | **31.9** | **8,983** | **31.1** | **7,625** | **30.6** |
| **In families** | **8,189** | **28.5** | **8,447** | **29.6** | **8,160** | **31.0** | **7,410** | **29.7** | **6,493** | **29.5** |
| Head of household | 2,127 | 26.4 | 2,212 | 27.3 | 2,193 | 29.3 | 1,987 | 28.0 | 1,622 | 27.5 |
| Related children | 4,644 | 41.5 | 4,787 | 43.3 | 4,412 | 44.2 | 4,039 | 42.7 | 3,781 | 41.2 |
| **Female householder, no spouse present** | **1,701** | **45.1** | **1,715** | **46.1** | **1,648** | **48.1** | **1,488** | **50.1** | **1,208** | **50.6** |
| **Unrelated individuals** | **1,551** | **32.6** | **1,617** | **34.8** | **1,491** | **35.1** | **1,431** | **38.5** | **1,132** | **38.6** |

(1) Percentage of total U.S. population in that general category who fell below poverty level and are enumerated here. For example, of all black female heads of households in 1995, 45.1%, or 1,701,000, were poor.

# Persons Below Poverty Level, 1960-95

**Source:** Bureau of the Census, U.S. Dept. of Commerce

| Year | Number below poverty level (in millions) | | | | Percentage below poverty level | | | | Avg. income cutoffs for family of 4 at poverty level[3] |
|---|---|---|---|---|---|---|---|---|---|
| | All races[1] | White | Black | Hispanic origin[2] | All races[1] | White | Black | Hispanic origin[2] | |
| 1960 | 39.9 | 28.3 | NA | NA | 22.2 | 17.8 | NA | NA | $3,022 |
| 1970 | 25.4 | 17.5 | 7.5 | NA | 12.6 | 9.9 | 33.5 | NA | 3,968 |
| 1980 | 29.3 | 19.7 | 8.6 | 3.5 | 13.0 | 10.2 | 32.5 | 25.7 | 8,414 |
| 1990 | 33.6 | 22.3 | 9.8 | 6.0 | 13.5 | 10.7 | 31.9 | 28.1 | 13,359 |
| 1991 | 35.7 | 23.7 | 10.2 | 6.3 | 14.2 | 11.3 | 32.7 | 28.7 | 13,924 |
| 1992 | 38.0 | 25.3 | 10.8 | 7.6 | 14.8 | 11.9 | 33.4 | 29.6 | 14,335 |
| 1993 | 39.3 | 26.2 | 10.9 | 8.1 | 15.1 | 12.2 | 33.1 | 30.6 | 14,763 |
| 1994 | 38.1 | 25.4 | 10.2 | 8.4 | 14.5 | 11.7 | 30.6 | 30.7 | 15,141 |
| 1995 | 36.4 | 24.4 | 9.9 | 8.6 | 13.8 | 11.2 | 29.3 | 30.3 | 15,569 |

NA = Not available. **Note:** Because of a change in the definition of poverty, data prior to 1980 are not directly comparable to data since 1980. (1) Includes other races not shown separately. (2) Persons of Hispanic origin may be of any race. (3) Figures for 1960-80 represent only nonfarm families.

# Persons in Poverty, by State, 1994-95

**Source:** Bureau of the Census, U.S. Dept. of Commerce

| State | 1995 Percentage | 1994 Percentage |
|---|---|---|
| AL | 20.1 | 16.4 |
| AK | 7.1 | 10.2 |
| AZ | 16.1 | 15.9 |
| AR | 14.9 | 15.3 |
| CA | 16.7 | 17.9 |
| CO | 8.8 | 9.0 |
| CT | 9.7 | 10.8 |
| DE | 10.3 | 8.3 |
| DC | 22.2 | 21.2 |
| FL | 16.2 | 14.9 |
| GA | 12.1 | 14.0 |
| HI | 10.3 | 8.7 |
| ID | 14.5 | 12.0 |
| IL | 12.4 | 12.4 |
| IN | 9.6 | 13.7 |
| IA | 12.2 | 10.7 |
| KS | 10.8 | 14.9 |
| KY | 14.7 | 18.5 |
| LA | 19.7 | 25.7 |
| ME | 11.2 | 9.4 |
| MD | 10.1 | 10.7 |
| MA | 11.0 | 9.7 |
| MI | 12.2 | 14.1 |
| MN | 9.2 | 11.7 |
| MS | 23.5 | 19.9 |
| MO | 9.4 | 15.6 |
| MT | 15.3 | 11.5 |
| NE | 9.6 | 8.8 |
| NV | 11.1 | 11.1 |
| NH | 5.3 | 7.7 |
| NJ | 7.8 | 9.2 |
| NM | 25.3 | 21.1 |
| NY | 16.5 | 17.0 |
| NC | 12.6 | 14.2 |
| ND | 12.0 | 10.4 |
| OH | 11.5 | 14.1 |
| OK | 17.1 | 16.7 |
| OR | 11.2 | 11.8 |
| PA | 12.2 | 12.5 |
| RI | 10.6 | 10.3 |
| SC | 19.9 | 13.8 |
| SD | 14.5 | 14.5 |
| TN | 15.5 | 14.6 |
| TX | 17.4 | 19.1 |
| UT | 8.4 | 8.0 |
| VT | 10.3 | 7.6 |
| VA | 10.2 | 10.7 |
| WA | 12.5 | 11.7 |
| WV | 16.7 | 18.6 |
| WI | 8.5 | 9.0 |
| WY | 12.2 | 9.3 |

## Aid to Families With Dependent Children, Fiscal Year 1995

**Source:** Admin. for Children and Families, Office of Family Assistance, U.S Dept. of Health and Human Services

| State | Total assistance payments[1] | Average monthly caseload | Average monthly recipients | Average monthly children | Average monthly payment per Family | Person |
|---|---|---|---|---|---|---|
| Alabama | $ 82,580 | 46,030 | 117,734 | 86,952 | $149.51 | $58.45 |
| Alaska | 107,335 | 12,426 | 36,856 | 23,530 | 719.81 | 242.69 |
| Arizona | 251,184 | 69,609 | 190,199 | 129,829 | 300.71 | 110.05 |
| Arkansas | 48,795 | 24,296 | 63,278 | 45,469 | 167.37 | 64.26 |
| California | 6,125,351 | 919,471 | 2,679,653 | 1,833,203 | 555.15 | 190.49 |
| Colorado | 142,796 | 38,557 | 108,871 | 74,095 | 308.62 | 109.30 |
| Connecticut | 383,084 | 60,985 | 170,568 | 114,057 | 523.47 | 187.16 |
| Delaware | 36,385 | 10,775 | 24,920 | 16,899 | 281.39 | 121.67 |
| Dist. of Col. | 124,051 | 26,789 | 72,881 | 50,609 | 385.90 | 141.84 |
| Florida | 763,835 | 230,807 | 621,950 | 432,078 | 275.78 | 102.34 |
| Georgia | 414,423 | 139,135 | 382,634 | 268,623 | 248.21 | 90.26 |
| Guam | 13,658 | 2,099 | 7,573 | 5,300 | 542.30 | 150.29 |
| Hawaii | 172,780 | 21,674 | 65,606 | 43,397 | 664.30 | 219.47 |
| Idaho | 31,631 | 9,071 | 23,910 | 16,267 | 290.59 | 110.24 |
| Illinois | 882,099 | 236,205 | 696,157 | 477,662 | 311.21 | 105.59 |
| Indiana | 196,620 | 65,618 | 188,961 | 129,410 | 249.70 | 86.71 |
| Iowa | 149,372 | 36,483 | 100,541 | 66,018 | 341.19 | 123.81 |
| Kansas | 113,597 | 28,232 | 79,515 | 54,609 | 335.30 | 119.05 |
| Kentucky | 182,572 | 75,384 | 189,447 | 127,638 | 201.82 | 80.31 |
| Louisiana | 151,133 | 79,825 | 251,161 | 173,336 | 157.78 | 50.14 |
| Maine | 101,087 | 21,694 | 59,934 | 37,591 | 388.30 | 140.55 |
| Maryland | 307,871 | 80,383 | 223,258 | 152,062 | 319.17 | 114.92 |
| Massachusetts | 646,081 | 100,852 | 273,561 | 176,370 | 533.85 | 196.81 |
| Michigan | 999,834 | 201,696 | 597,652 | 397,540 | 413.09 | 139.41 |
| Minnesota | 356,022 | 57,061 | 167,227 | 112,277 | 519.94 | 177.41 |
| Mississippi | 75,068 | 52,528 | 144,148 | 105,835 | 119.09 | 43.40 |
| Missouri | 275,569 | 89,299 | 253,909 | 175,225 | 257.16 | 90.44 |
| Montana | 48,308 | 11,508 | 33,781 | 22,096 | 349.82 | 119.17 |
| Nebraska | 56,688 | 14,828 | 41,382 | 28,604 | 318.58 | 114.15 |
| Nevada | 51,640 | 15,708 | 40,893 | 28,822 | 273.96 | 105.24 |
| New Hampshire | 56,919 | 10,800 | 27,945 | 18,048 | 439.19 | 169.73 |
| New Jersey | 509,787 | 118,883 | 316,068 | 213,209 | 357.34 | 134.41 |
| New Mexico | 154,128 | 34,444 | 103,743 | 67,147 | 372.90 | 123.81 |
| New York | 3,042,437 | 456,929 | 1,255,561 | 811,468 | 554.87 | 201.93 |
| North Carolina | 334,445 | 125,503 | 313,269 | 211,118 | 222.07 | 88.97 |
| North Dakota | 22,636 | 5,215 | 14,459 | 9,663 | 361.74 | 130.46 |
| Ohio | 849,137 | 228,171 | 612,019 | 415,462 | 310.12 | 115.62 |
| Oklahoma | 151,959 | 44,790 | 123,701 | 85,600 | 282.72 | 102.37 |
| Oregon | 180,804 | 39,264 | 104,007 | 70,538 | 383.74 | 144.86 |
| Pennsylvania | 904,739 | 204,771 | 596,288 | 402,787 | 368.19 | 126.44 |
| Puerto Rico | 68,330 | 54,799 | 168,250 | 114,242 | 103.91 | 33.84 |
| Rhode Island | 133,642 | 22,194 | 61,318 | 40,674 | 501.80 | 181.62 |
| South Carolina | 107,055 | 48,981 | 128,935 | 95,704 | 182.14 | 69.19 |
| South Dakota | 22,667 | 6,286 | 17,116 | 12,397 | 300.50 | 110.36 |
| Tennessee | 198,664 | 104,009 | 276,113 | 189,739 | 159.17 | 59.96 |
| Texas | 519,795 | 274,505 | 749,538 | 525,949 | 157.80 | 57.79 |
| Utah | 69,661 | 16,648 | 45,664 | 30,583 | 348.70 | 127.13 |
| Vermont | 61,947 | 9,648 | 27,225 | 16,817 | 535.08 | 189.61 |
| Virgin Islands | 4,269 | 1,308 | 4,558 | 3,363 | 271.98 | 78.05 |
| Virginia | 222,373 | 72,147 | 183,975 | 127,869 | 256.85 | 100.73 |
| Washington | 605,693 | 101,949 | 286,323 | 184,069 | 495.10 | 176.28 |
| West Virginia | 108,910 | 38,404 | 104,748 | 66,889 | 236.33 | 86.64 |
| Wisconsin | 389,358 | 72,366 | 208,660 | 145,739 | 448.37 | 155.50 |
| Wyoming | 20,780 | 5,200 | 14,589 | 10,059 | 333.02 | 118.70 |
| **U.S. Total** | **$22,031,584** | **4,876,240** | **13,652,232** | **9,274,536** | **$376.51** | **$134.48** |

**Note:** Under the Personal Responsibility and Work Opportunity Reconciliation Act of 1996, the AFDC program is converted to a state block-grant program, effective July 1, 1997. (1) Total assistance payments given in thousands. These include federal, state, and local payments for AFDC-Basic and AFDC-Unemployed Parent, Title IV-A Payments under JOBS, Home Repair, and payments to Indian tribes.

## Income Distribution by Population Fifths, 1994

**Source:** Bureau of the Census, U.S. Dept. of Commerce

| Families | Upper limit of each fifth[1] Lowest | Second | Third | Fourth | Top 5%[2] | Percentage distribution of total income Lowest fifth | Second fifth | Third fifth | Fourth fifth | Top fifth | Top 5% |
|---|---|---|---|---|---|---|---|---|---|---|---|
| All races | $17,940 | $31,300 | $47,000 | $69,998 | $120,043 | 4.2 | 10.0 | 15.7 | 23.3 | 46.9 | 20.1 |
| White | 19,946 | 33,406 | 49,228 | 72,200 | 124,090 | 4.6 | 10.3 | 15.8 | 23.0 | 46.3 | 20.0 |
| Black | 9,453 | 18,674 | 31,120 | 51,120 | 86,865 | 3.2 | 8.5 | 15.1 | 24.7 | 48.7 | 18.9 |

(1) The highest fifth does not have an upper limit. (2) Lower limit for top 5%.

## Mean Income Received by Population Fifths, 1967-94

**Source:** Bureau of the Census, U.S. Dept. of Commerce

| Year | Lowest fifth | Second fifth | Third fifth | Fourth fifth | Fifth fifth | Top 5% |
|---|---|---|---|---|---|---|
| 1994 | $7,762 | $19,224 | $32,385 | $50,395 | $105,945 | $183,044 |
| 1993 | 7,602 | 19,134 | 32,073 | 49,843 | 103,846 | 178,234 |
| 1992 | 7,698 | 19,205 | 32,356 | 49,669 | 96,240 | 152,751 |
| 1991 | 7,903 | 19,748 | 32,803 | 50,006 | 95,895 | 149,649 |
| 1990 | 8,158 | 20,444 | 33,768 | 50,913 | 98,804 | 157,335 |
| 1985 | $7,984 | $19,595 | $32,525 | $48,925 | $91,390 | $140,975 |
| 1980 | 8,073 | 19,316 | 31,875 | 46,959 | 83,728 | 125,122 |
| 1975 | 8,001 | 18,844 | 30,916 | 44,924 | 79,316 | 120,364 |
| 1970 | 7,281 | 19,359 | 31,176 | 43,947 | 77,810 | 119,432 |
| 1967 | 6,638 | 18,098 | 28,897 | 40,430 | 73,267 | 116,784 |

**Note:** Average incomes were adjusted for inflation. A change in survey methodology occurred in 1992. As a result, data prior to 1992 are not directly comparable to later data. Restrictions are placed on the level of income reported. Actual income reported may exceed the amount recorded in the Census Bureau's survey. In 1993, the restrictions were changed; as a result, earlier data are not directly comparable to data since 1993.

# U.S. Places of 5,000 or More Population—With ZIP and Area Codes

**Source:** U.S. Bureau of the Census, Dept. of Commerce

The following is a list of places of 5,000 or more inhabitants recognized by the Bureau of the Census, U.S. Dept. of Commerce, based on data collected in the 1990 Decennial Census. More recent estimates were not available for all cities as of late 1996. This list includes places that are incorporated under the laws of their respective states as cities, boroughs, towns, and villages, with the following exceptions: boroughs in Alaska and towns in the 6 New England states (Connecticut, Maine, Massachusetts, New Hampshire, Rhode Island, and Vermont), New York, and Wisconsin. Unincorporated places that the Census Bureau designates as "census designated places (CDPs)" are also included. These unincorporated communities, marked (u), are statistically compatible with incorporated communities because of their population density. CDP boundaries can change from one census to another. Hawaii is the only state that has no incorporated places recognized by the Census Bureau; all places shown for Hawaii are CDPs.

This list also includes, in *italics*, minor civil divisions (MCDs) for the following states: Connecticut, Maine, Massachusetts, New Hampshire, New Jersey, Rhode Island, Vermont, and Wisconsin. MCDs are areas that are not incorporated under the laws of the state and that are not recognized by the Census Bureau as CDPs, but are often the primary political or administrative divisions of a county. These areas may also serve as general-purpose local governments.

The geographical boundaries for places marked with a dagger (†) changed from the 1980 census to the 1990 census.

An asterisk (*) denotes that the ZIP code given is for general delivery; named streets and/or post office boxes within the community may differ. Consult the local postmaster for the correct ZIP code for specific addresses within the community.

Area codes, given in parentheses, refer only to home and business telephone numbers. Overlay area codes are excluded. When 2 area codes are listed for one locale, consult local operators for further assistance.

## Alabama

| ZIP | Place | | 1990 | 1980 |
|---|---|---|---|---|
| 35007 | Alabaster | (205) | 14,619 | 7,079 |
| 35950 | Albertville | (205) | 14,507 | 12,039 |
| 35010 | Alexander City | (205) | 14,917 | 13,807 |
| 36420 | Andalusia | (334) | 9,269 | 10,415 |
| *36201 | Anniston | (205) | 26,638 | 29,135 |
| 35016 | Arab | (205) | 6,321 | 6,053 |
| 35611 | Athens | (205) | 16,901 | 14,558 |
| *36502 | Atmore | (334) | 8,046 | 8,789 |
| 35954 | Attalla | (205) | 6,859 | 7,737 |
| *36830 | Auburn | (334) | 33,830 | 28,471 |
| 36507 | Bay Minette | (334) | 7,168 | 7,455 |
| *35020 | Bessemer | (205) | 33,581 | 31,729 |
| *35203 | Birmingham | (205) | 265,347 | 284,413 |
| 35957 | Boaz | (205) | 6,928 | 7,151 |
| *36426 | Brewton | (334) | 5,885 | 6,680 |
| 35215 | Center Point(u) | (205) | 22,658 | 23,317 |
| 36611 | Chickasaw | (205) | 6,649 | 7,402 |
| 35045 | Clanton | (205) | 7,669 | 5,832 |
| *35055 | Cullman | (205) | 13,367 | 13,084 |
| 36322 | Daleville | (334) | 5,117 | 4,250 |
| 36526 | Daphne | (205) | 11,291 | 3,406 |
| *35601 | Decatur | (205) | 48,778 | 42,002 |
| 36732 | Demopolis | (334) | 7,512 | 7,678 |
| *36302 | Dothan | (334) | 53,721 | 48,750 |
| *36330 | Enterprise | (334) | 20,119 | 18,033 |
| *36027 | Eufaula | (334) | 13,220 | 12,097 |
| 35064 | Fairfield | (205) | 12,200 | 13,242 |
| 36532 | Fairhope | (334) | 8,490 | 7,286 |
| *35630 | Florence | (205) | 36,426 | 37,029 |
| 35214 | Forestdale(u) | (205) | 10,395 | 10,814 |
| 35967 | Fort Payne | (205) | 11,838 | 11,485 |
| 36362 | Fort Rucker(u) | (205) | 7,593 | 8,932 |
| 35068 | Fultondale | (205) | 6,400 | 6,217 |
| *35901 | Gadsden | (205) | 42,523 | 47,565 |
| 35071 | Gardendale | (205) | 9,251 | 8,005 |
| 36037 | Greenville | (334) | 7,494 | 7,807 |
| 35976 | Guntersville | (205) | 7,038 | 7,041 |
| 35570 | Hamilton | (205) | 5,787 | 5,093 |
| 35640 | Hartselle | (205) | 10,867 | 8,858 |
| 35209 | Homewood | (205) | 23,644 | 21,412 |
| *35244 | Hoover | (205) | 40,000 | 18,996 |
| 35023 | Hueytown | (205) | 15,280 | 13,452 |
| *35801 | Huntsville | (205) | 159,880 | 142,513 |
| 35210 | Irondale | (205) | 9,458 | 6,510 |
| 36545 | Jackson | (334) | 5,819 | 6,073 |
| 36265 | Jacksonville | (205) | 10,283 | 9,735 |
| *35501 | Jasper | (205) | 13,553 | 11,894 |
| 36863 | Lanett | (205) | 8,985 | 8,922 |
| 35094 | Leeds | (205) | 10,009 | 8,638 |
| 35758 | Madison | (205) | 14,792 | 4,057 |
| 35228 | Midfield | (205) | 5,559 | 6,182 |
| 36054 | Millbrook | (205) | 6,046 | 3,101 |
| *36601 | Mobile | (334) | 196,263 | 200,452 |
| *36460 | Monroeville | (334) | 6,993 | 5,674 |
| *36104 | Montgomery | (334) | 187,543 | 177,857 |
| *35223 | Mountain Brook | (205) | 19,810 | 19,718 |
| 35667 | Muscle Shoals | (205) | 9,611 | 8,911 |
| 35476 | Northport | (205) | 17,297 | 14,291 |
| *36801 | Opelika | (334) | 22,122 | 21,896 |
| 36467 | Opp | (334) | 7,011 | 7,204 |
| 36203 | Oxford | (205) | 9,537 | 8,939 |
| *36360 | Ozark | (334) | 13,030 | 13,188 |
| 35124 | Pelham | (205) | 9,356 | 6,759 |
| *35125 | Pell City | (205) | 7,945 | 6,616 |
| 36867 | Phenix City | (334) | 25,311 | 26,928 |
| 36272 | Piedmont | (205) | 5,347 | 5,544 |
| 35126 | Pinson-Clay-Chalkville(u) | (205) | 10,987 | .... |
| 35127 | Pleasant Grove | (205) | 8,458 | 7,102 |
| *36067 | Prattville | (334) | 19,816 | 18,647 |
| 36610 | Prichard | (205) | 34,320 | 39,541 |
| 35906 | Rainbow City | (205) | 7,667 | 6,299 |
| 36274 | Roanoke | (334) | 6,362 | 5,809 |
| 35653 | Russellville | (205) | 7,812 | 8,195 |
| 36201 | Saks(u) | (205) | 11,138 | 11,118 |
| 36571 | Saraland | (205) | 11,760 | 9,833 |
| 36572 | Satsuma | (205) | 5,194 | 3,822 |
| 35768 | Scottsboro | (205) | 13,786 | 14,758 |
| *36701 | Selma | (334) | 23,755 | 26,684 |
| 35660 | Sheffield | (205) | 10,380 | 11,903 |
| 35901 | Southside | (205) | 5,580 | 5,141 |
| 35150 | Sylacauga | (205) | 12,520 | 12,708 |
| 35160 | Talladega | (205) | 18,175 | 19,128 |
| 36078 | Tallassee | (334) | 5,112 | 4,763 |
| 35217 | Tarrant City | (205) | 8,046 | 8,148 |
| *36582 | Theodore(u) | (205) | 6,509 | 6,392 |
| 36619 | Tillman's Corner(u) | (205) | 17,988 | 15,941 |
| 36081 | Troy | (334) | 13,051 | 13,124 |
| 35173 | Trussville | (205) | 8,283 | 3,507 |
| *35401 | Tuscaloosa | (205) | 77,866 | 75,211 |
| 35674 | Tuscumbia | (205) | 8,413 | 9,137 |
| 36083 | Tuskegee | (334) | 12,257 | 13,327 |
| *36854 | Valley† | (205) | 8,215 | 8,946 |
| 35216 | Vestavia Hills | (205) | 19,550 | 15,722 |

## Alaska (907)

| ZIP | Place | 1990 | 1980 |
|---|---|---|---|
| *99501 | Anchorage | 226,338 | 174,431 |
| *99708 | College(u) | 11,249 | 4,043 |
| 99702 | Eielson AFB(u) | 5,251 | 5,232 |
| *99701 | Fairbanks | 30,843 | 22,645 |
| *99801 | Juneau | 26,751 | 19,528 |
| 99611 | Kenai | 6,327 | 4,324 |
| *99901 | Ketchikan | 8,263 | 7,198 |
| *99615 | Kodiak | 6,365 | 4,756 |
| 99639 | Ninilchik(u) | 10,523 | 341 |
| 99835 | Sitka | 8,588 | 7,803 |

## Arizona

| ZIP | Place | | 1990 | 1980 |
|---|---|---|---|---|
| *85220 | Apache Junction | (602) | 18,092 | 9,935 |
| 85323 | Avondale | (602) | 16,182 | 8,168 |
| 85603 | Bisbee | (520) | 6,288 | 7,154 |
| 85326 | Buckeye | (602) | 4,436 | 3,434 |
| *86430 | Bullhead City† | (520) | 21,951 | 10,719 |
| 86322 | Camp Verde† | (520) | 6,243 | 3,824 |
| *85222 | Casa Grande | (520) | 19,076 | 14,971 |
| *85225 | Chandler | (602) | 89,862 | 29,673 |
| 86503 | Chinle(u) | (520) | 5,059 | 2,815 |
| 85228 | Coolidge | (520) | 6,934 | 6,851 |
| 86326 | Cottonwood | (520) | 5,918 | 4,550 |
| 86326 | Cottonwood-Verde Village(u) | (520) | 7,037 | .... |
| *85607 | Douglas | (520) | 13,137 | 13,058 |
| 85335 | El Mirage | (602) | 5,001 | 4,307 |
| 85231 | Eloy | (520) | 7,211 | 6,240 |
| *86004 | Flagstaff | (520) | 45,857 | 34,743 |
| 85232 | Florence | (520) | 7,321 | 3,391 |
| 85726 | Flowing Wells(u) | (520) | 14,013 | .... |
| ..... | Fortuna Foothills(u) | (520) | 7,737 | .... |
| *85269 | Fountain Hills† | (602) | 10,030 | 2,771 |
| *85234 | Gilbert | (602) | 29,122 | 5,717 |
| *85301 | Glendale | (602) | 147,864 | 97,172 |
| *85501 | Globe | (520) | 6,062 | 6,886 |
| 85338 | Goodyear | (602) | 6,258 | 2,747 |

| ZIP | Place | | 1990 | 1980 |
|---|---|---|---|---|
| *85622 | Green Valley(u) | (520) | 13,231 | 7,999 |
| 85283 | Guadalupe | (602) | 5,458 | 4,506 |
| 86401 | Kingman | (520) | 12,722 | 9,257 |
| *86403 | Lake Havasu City | (520) | 24,363 | 15,909 |
| *85201 | Mesa | (602) | 288,104 | 152,404 |
| 86440 | Mohave Valley(u) | (520) | 6,962 | .... |
| ..... | New Kingman-Butler(u) | (520) | 11,627 | .... |
| *85621 | Nogales | (520) | 19,489 | 15,683 |
| 85737 | Oro Valley | (520) | 6,670 | 1,489 |
| 86040 | Page | (520) | 6,598 | 4,907 |
| 85253 | Paradise Valley | (602) | 11,773 | 11,085 |
| *85541 | Payson | (520) | 8,377 | 5,068 |
| *85345 | Peoria | (602) | 50,675 | 12,171 |
| *85026 | Phoenix | (602) | 983,403 | 789,704 |
| *86301 | Prescott | (520) | 26,592 | 19,865 |
| *86301 | Prescott Valley | (520) | 8,904 | 2,284 |
| *85546 | Safford | (520) | 7,359 | 7,010 |
| *85251 | Scottsdale | (602) | 130,075 | 88,622 |
| *86336 | Sedona† | (520) | 7,720 | 5,319 |
| 85901 | Show Low | (520) | 5,020 | 4,298 |
| *85635 | Sierra Vista | (520) | 32,983 | 24,937 |
| 85635 | Sierra Vista Southeast(u) | (520) | 9,237 | .... |
| 85350 | Somerton | (520) | 5,282 | 3,969 |
| 85713 | South Tucson | (520) | 5,171 | 6,554 |
| *85351 | Sun City(u) | (602) | 38,126 | 40,505 |
| 85375 | Sun City West(u) | (602) | 15,997 | 3,772 |
| 85248 | Sun Lakes(u) | (602) | 6,578 | 1,925 |
| 85374 | Surprise | (602) | 7,122 | 3,723 |
| *85282 | Tempe | (602) | 141,993 | 106,919 |
| 86045 | Tuba City(u) | (520) | 7,323 | 5,045 |
| *85726 | Tucson | (520) | 405,323 | 330,537 |
| 86047 | Winslow | (520) | 9,279 | 7,921 |
| *85364 | Yuma | (520) | 56,966 | 42,481 |

## Arkansas (501)

| ZIP | Place | 1990 | 1980 |
|---|---|---|---|
| 71923 | Arkadelphia | 10,014 | 10,005 |
| 71822 | Ashdown | 5,150 | 4,218 |
| *72501 | Batesville | 9,187 | 8,447 |
| 72714 | Bella Vista(u) | 9,083 | 2,589 |
| *72015 | Benton | 18,177 | 17,717 |
| 72712 | Bentonville | 11,257 | 8,756 |
| 72315 | Blytheville | 22,523 | 23,844 |
| 72022 | Bryant | 5,269 | 2,682 |
| 72023 | Cabot | 8,319 | 4,806 |
| 71701 | Camden | 14,701 | 15,356 |
| 72830 | Clarksville | 5,833 | 5,237 |
| *72032 | Conway | 26,481 | 20,375 |
| 71635 | Crossett | 6,282 | 6,706 |
| 71639 | Dumas | 5,520 | 6,091 |
| *71730 | El Dorado | 23,146 | 25,270 |
| *72701 | Fayetteville | 42,247 | 36,608 |
| 72335 | Forrest City | 13,364 | 13,803 |
| *72901 | Fort Smith | 72,798 | 71,626 |
| *72601 | Harrison | 9,936 | 9,567 |
| 72543 | Heber Springs | 5,628 | 4,589 |
| 72342 | Helena | 7,491 | 9,598 |
| 71801 | Hope | 9,768 | 10,290 |
| *71901 | Hot Springs | 32,462 | 35,781 |
| 71909 | Hot Springs Village(u) | 6,361 | 2,083 |
| *72076 | Jacksonville | 29,101 | 27,589 |
| 72401 | Jonesboro | 46,535 | 31,530 |
| *72201 | Little Rock | 175,727 | 159,151 |
| 71753 | Magnolia | 11,151 | 11,909 |
| 72104 | Malvern | 9,236 | 10,163 |
| 72360 | Marianna | 6,033 | 6,220 |
| 72113 | Maumelle† | 6,714 | 1,368 |
| 71953 | Mena | 5,475 | 5,154 |
| 71655 | Monticello | 8,119 | 8,259 |
| 72110 | Morrilton | 6,551 | 7,355 |
| 72653 | Mountain Home | 9,027 | 8,066 |
| 72112 | Newport | 7,459 | 8,339 |
| *72114 | North Little Rock | 61,829 | 64,388 |
| 72370 | Osceola | 8,930 | 8,881 |
| *72450 | Paragould | 18,540 | 15,248 |
| *71601 | Pine Bluff | 57,140 | 56,636 |
| 72455 | Pocahontas | 6,151 | 5,995 |
| *72756 | Rogers | 24,692 | 17,429 |
| *72801 | Russellville | 21,260 | 14,518 |
| *72143 | Searcy | 15,180 | 13,612 |
| 72120 | Sherwood | 18,878 | 10,423 |
| 72761 | Siloam Springs | 8,151 | 7,940 |
| *72764 | Springdale | 29,945 | 23,458 |
| 72160 | Stuttgart | 10,420 | 10,941 |
| 75502 | Texarkana | 22,631 | 21,459 |
| 72472 | Trumann | 6,346 | 6,395 |
| 72956 | Van Buren | 14,899 | 12,020 |
| 71671 | Warren | 6,455 | 7,646 |
| 72390 | West Helena | 10,137 | 11,367 |
| *72301 | West Memphis | 28,259 | 28,138 |
| 72396 | Wynne | 8,817 | 7,927 |

## California

*Area code (562) goes into effect on Jan. 25, 1997. Before then, use (310).*
*Area code (760) goes into effect on Mar. 22, 1997. Before then, use (619).*

| ZIP | Place | | 1990 | 1980 |
|---|---|---|---|---|
| 94301 | Adelanto | (805) | 6,791 | 2,164 |
| *91376 | Agoura Hills† | (818) | 20,391 | 11,399 |
| *94501 | Alameda | (510) | 73,979 | 63,852 |
| 94507 | Alamo(u) | (510) | 12,277 | 8,505 |
| 94706 | Albany | (510) | 16,327 | 15,130 |
| *91802 | Alhambra | (818) | 82,087 | 64,767 |
| 92656 | Aliso Viejo(u) | | 7,612 | .... |
| 90249 | Alondra Park(u) | (310) | 12,215 | 12,189 |
| *91901 | Alpine(u) (San Diego) | (619) | 9,695 | 5,368 |
| *91001 | Altadena(u) | (818) | 42,658 | 40,983 |
| 95945 | Alta Sierra(u) | (916) | 5,709 | 2,168 |
| 94589 | American Canyon(u) | (707) | 7,706 | 5,712 |
| *92803 | Anaheim | (714) | 266,406 | 219,494 |
| 96007 | Anderson | (916) | 8,299 | 7,381 |
| *94509 | Antioch | (510) | 62,195 | 42,683 |
| *92307 | Apple Valley† | (760) | 46,079 | 16,748 |
| *95003 | Aptos(u) | (408) | 9,061 | 7,039 |
| *91006 | Arcadia | (818) | 48,284 | 45,993 |
| 95521 | Arcata | (707) | 15,211 | 12,849 |
| 95825 | Arden-Arcade(u) | (916) | 92,040 | 87,570 |
| *93420 | Arroyo Grande | (805) | 14,432 | 11,290 |
| *90701 | Artesia | (562) | 15,464 | 14,301 |
| 93203 | Arvin | (805) | 9,286 | 6,863 |
| 94577 | Ashland(u) | (510) | 16,590 | 13,893 |
| 93422 | Atascadero | (805) | 23,138 | 16,232 |
| 94025 | Atherton | (415) | 7,163 | 7,797 |
| 95301 | Atwater | (209) | 22,282 | 17,530 |
| *95603 | Auburn | (916) | 10,653 | 7,540 |
| 92505 | August(u) | (714) | 6,376 | 6,350 |
| 93204 | Avenal | (209) | 9,770 | 4,137 |
| 91746 | Avocado Heights(u) | (818) | 14,232 | 11,733 |
| 91702 | Azusa | (818) | 41,203 | 29,380 |
| *93302 | Bakersfield | (805) | 174,978 | 105,611 |
| 91706 | Baldwin Park | (818) | 69,330 | 50,554 |
| 92220 | Banning | (909) | 20,572 | 14,020 |
| *92312 | Barstow | (760) | 21,472 | 17,690 |
| 94565 | Bay Point(u) | (510) | 17,453 | 10,244 |
| 93402 | Baywood-Los Osos(u) | (805) | 14,377 | 10,933 |
| 95903 | Beale AFB(u) | (916) | 6,912 | 6,329 |
| 92223 | Beaumont | (714) | 9,685 | 6,818 |
| 90201 | Bell | (213) | 34,365 | 25,450 |
| *90706 | Bellflower | (213) | 61,815 | 53,441 |
| 90201 | Bell Gardens | (213)/(562) | 42,315 | 34,117 |
| 94002 | Belmont | (415) | 24,165 | 24,505 |
| 94510 | Benicia | (707) | 24,437 | 15,376 |
| 95005 | Ben Lomond(u) | (408) | 7,884 | 7,238 |
| *94704 | Berkeley | (510) | 102,724 | 103,328 |
| *90210 | Beverly Hills | (213)/(310) | 31,971 | 32,646 |
| 92315 | Big Bear Lake† | (909) | 5,351 | 4,896 |
| 94506 | Black Hawk(u) | (510) | 6,199 | .... |
| 92316 | Bloomington(u) | (909) | 15,116 | 12,781 |
| *92225 | Blythe | (760) | 8,448 | 6,805 |
| 93637 | Bonadella Ranchos-Madera Ranchos(u) | (209) | 5,705 | 3,272 |
| 91902 | Bonita(u) | (619) | 12,542 | 6,257 |
| 92021 | Bostonia(u) | (619) | 13,670 | .... |
| 95006 | Boulder Creek(u) | (408) | 6,725 | 5,662 |
| 95416 | Boyes Hot Springs(u) | (707) | 5,973 | 4,177 |
| 92227 | Brawley | (760) | 18,923 | 14,946 |
| *92622 | Brea | (714) | 32,873 | 27,913 |
| 94513 | Brentwood | (510) | 7,563 | 4,434 |
| *90622 | Buena Park | (714) | 68,784 | 64,165 |
| *91510 | Burbank | (818) | 93,649 | 84,625 |
| *94010 | Burlingame | (415) | 26,666 | 26,173 |
| *92231 | Calexico | (760) | 18,633 | 14,412 |
| *93504 | California City | (805) | 5,955 | 2,743 |
| *93010 | Camarillo | (805) | 52,297 | 37,797 |
| 93428 | Cambria(u) | (805) | 5,382 | 3,061 |
| 95682 | Cameron Park(u) | (916) | 11,897 | 5,607 |
| 95008 | Campbell | (408) | 36,048 | 26,843 |
| 92055 | Camp Pendleton North(u) | (714) | 10,373 | 2,065 |
| 92055 | Camp Pendleton South(u) | (714) | 11,299 | 7,952 |
| 92587 | Canyon Lake(u) | (909) | 7,938 | 2,039 |
| 95010 | Capitola | (408) | 10,171 | 9,095 |
| *92008 | Carlsbad | (760) | 63,292 | 35,490 |
| *95608 | Carmichael(u) | (916) | 48,702 | 43,108 |
| *93013 | Carpinteria | (805) | 13,747 | 10,835 |
| *90745 | Carson | (310) | 83,995 | 81,221 |
| 92077 | Casa de Oro-Mt. Helix(u) | (619) | 30,727 | 19,651 |
| *94544 | Castro Valley(u) | (510) | 48,619 | 43,810 |
| 95012 | Castroville | (408) | 5,272 | 4,396 |
| *92235 | Cathedral City† | (760) | 30,085 | 11,096 |
| 95307 | Ceres | (209) | 26,413 | 13,281 |
| 90703 | Cerritos | (562) | 53,244 | 53,020 |
| 91724 | Charter Oak(u) | (818) | 8,858 | 6,840 |
| 94541 | Cherryland(u) | (415) | 11,088 | 9,425 |
| 92223 | Cherry Valley(u) | (714) | 5,945 | 5,012 |
| *95926 | Chico | (916) | 39,970 | 26,716 |
| *91708 | Chino | (909) | 59,682 | 40,165 |
| 91709 | Chino Hills(u) | (909) | 27,608 | .... |
| 93610 | Chowchilla | (209) | 5,930 | 5,122 |
| *91910 | Chula Vista | (619) | 135,160 | 83,927 |
| 95610 | Citrus(u) | (916) | 9,481 | 12,450 |
| *95621 | Citrus Heights(u) | (916) | 107,439 | 85,911 |
| 91711 | Claremont | (909) | 32,610 | 31,028 |
| 94517 | Clayton | (510) | 7,317 | 4,325 |
| 95422 | Clearlake† | | 11,804 | 8,343 |
| *93612 | Clovis | (209) | 50,323 | 33,021 |
| 92236 | Coachella | (760) | 16,896 | 9,129 |
| 93210 | Coalinga | (209) | 8,212 | 6,593 |
| 92324 | Colton | (714) | 40,213 | 21,310 |
| 90022 | Commerce | (213)/(562) | 12,135 | 10,509 |

| ZIP | Place | 1990 | 1980 |
|---|---|---|---|
| *90221 | Compton (310) | 90,454 | 81,350 |
| *94520 | Concord (510) | 111,308 | 103,763 |
| 93212 | Corcoran (209) | 13,360 | 6,454 |
| 96021 | Corning (916) | 5,870 | 4,745 |
| *91718 | Corona (909) | 75,943 | 37,791 |
| *92118 | Coronado (619) | 26,540 | 18,790 |
| *94925 | Corte Madera (415) | 8,272 | 8,074 |
| *92628 | Costa Mesa (714) | 96,357 | 82,562 |
| 94931 | Cotati (707) | 5,714 | 3,346 |
| 94556 | Country Club(u) (209) | 9,325 | 9,585 |
| *91722 | Covina (818) | 43,332 | 32,746 |
| 92325 | Crestline(u) (714) | 8,594 | 6,715 |
| 90201 | Cudahy (213) | 22,817 | 18,275 |
| *90230 | Culver City (230)/(310) | 38,793 | 38,139 |
| *95014 | Cupertino (408) | 39,967 | 34,297 |
| 90630 | Cypress (714) | 42,655 | 40,738 |
| *94015 | Daly City (415) | 92,088 | 78,519 |
| 92629 | Dana Point† (714) | 31,896 | 21,271 |
| *94526 | Danville† (510) | 31,306 | 26,143 |
| 95616 | Davis (916) | 46,322 | 36,640 |
| 90250 | Del Aire(u) (310) | 8,040 | 8,487 |
| *93215 | Delano (805) | 22,762 | 16,491 |
| 93953 | Del Monte Forest(u) (408) | 5,069 | .... |
| *92240 | Desert Hot Springs (760) | 11,668 | 5,941 |
| *91765 | Diamond Bar (909) | 53,672 | .... |
| 93618 | Dinuba (209) | 12,743 | 9,907 |
| 94514 | Discovery Bay(u) (510) | 5,351 | 1,326 |
| 95620 | Dixon (916) | 10,417 | 7,541 |
| *90241 | Downey (562) | 91,444 | 82,602 |
| *91009 | Duarte (818) | 20,716 | 16,766 |
| 94568 | Dublin† (510) | 23,229 | 13,496 |
| 93219 | Earlimart(u) (805) | 5,881 | 4,578 |
| 90220 | East Compton(u) (310) | 7,967 | 6,435 |
| ..... | East Foothills(u) | 14,898 | 16,890 |
| 92343 | East Hemet(u) (909) | 17,611 | 14,712 |
| 90638 | East La Mirada(u) (562) | 9,367 | 9,688 |
| 90022 | East Los Angeles(u) (213)/(562) | 126,379 | 110,017 |
| 94303 | East Palo Alto† (415) | 23,451 | 18,106 |
| 91117 | East Pasadena(u) | 5,910 | .... |
| 93257 | East Porterville(u) (209) | 5,790 | 5,218 |
| ..... | East San Gabriel(u) (818) | 12,736 | .... |
| *93523 | Edwards AFB(u) (805) | 7,423 | 8,554 |
| *92020 | El Cajon (619) | 88,693 | 73,892 |
| *92244 | El Centro (760) | 31,405 | 23,996 |
| 94530 | El Cerrito (510) | 22,869 | 22,731 |
| 95762 | El Dorado Hills(u) (916) | 6,395 | 3,453 |
| *95624 | Elk Grove(u) (916) | 17,483 | 10,959 |
| *91734 | El Monte (818) | 106,162 | 79,494 |
| *93446 | El de Paso Robles (805) | 18,583 | 9,163 |
| 93030 | El Rio(u) (805) | 6,419 | 5,674 |
| 90245 | El Segundo (310) | 15,223 | 13,752 |
| *94802 | El Sobrante(u) (510) | 9,852 | 10,535 |
| 92630 | El Toro(u) (714) | 62,685 | 38,153 |
| 92709 | El Toro Station(u) (714) | 6,869 | 7,632 |
| *94612 | Emeryville (510) | 5,740 | 3,714 |
| *92024 | Encinitas† (760) | 55,406 | 36,550 |
| *92025 | Escondido (760) | 108,648 | 64,355 |
| *95501 | Eureka (707) | 27,025 | 24,153 |
| 93221 | Exeter (209) | 7,276 | 5,606 |
| *94930 | Fairfax (415) | 6,931 | 7,391 |
| 94533 | Fairfield (707) | 78,650 | 58,099 |
| 95628 | Fair Oaks(u) (Sacramento) (916) | 26,867 | 22,602 |
| 96052 | Fairview(u) (Trinity) | 9,045 | .... |
| *92028 | Fallbrook(u) (760) | 22,095 | 14,041 |
| 93223 | Farmersville (209) | 6,235 | 5,544 |
| 95018 | Felton(u) (408) | 5,350 | 4,564 |
| *93015 | Fillmore (805) | 11,992 | 9,602 |
| 90001 | Florence-Graham(u) (213) | 57,147 | 48,662 |
| 95828 | Florin(u) (916) | 24,330 | 16,523 |
| *95630 | Folsom (916) | 29,802 | 11,003 |
| *92334 | Fontana (909) | 87,535 | 36,804 |
| 95841 | Foothill Farms(u) (916) | 17,135 | 13,700 |
| 95437 | Fort Bragg (707) | 6,078 | 5,019 |
| 95540 | Fortuna (707) | 8,788 | 7,591 |
| 94404 | Foster City (415) | 28,176 | 23,287 |
| 92728 | Fountain Valley (714) | 53,691 | 55,080 |
| 95019 | Freedom(u) (408) | 8,361 | 6,416 |
| *94537 | Fremont (510) | 173,339 | 131,945 |
| *93706 | Fresno (209) | 354,091 | 217,491 |
| *92634 | Fullerton (714) | 114,144 | 102,246 |
| 95632 | Galt (209) | 8,889 | 5,514 |
| *90247 | Gardena (310) | 49,841 | 45,165 |
| 95205 | Garden Acres(u) (213) | 8,547 | 7,361 |
| *92642 | Garden Grove (714) | 143,965 | 123,307 |
| 92394 | George AFB(u) (760) | 5,085 | 7,061 |
| *95020 | Gilroy (408) | 31,487 | 21,641 |
| 92509 | Glen Avon(u) (714) | 12,663 | 8,444 |
| *91209 | Glendale (818) | 180,038 | 139,060 |
| 91741 | Glendora (818) | 47,832 | 38,500 |
| 93561 | Golden Hills(u) | 5,423 | .... |
| 92313 | Grand Terrace (714) | 10,946 | 8,498 |
| *95945 | Grass Valley (916) | 9,048 | 6,697 |
| 93308 | Greenacres(u) (805) | 7,379 | 5,381 |
| 93927 | Greenfield (Monterey) (408) | 7,464 | 4,181 |
| 93433 | Grover City (805) | 11,602 | 8,827 |
| 93434 | Guadalupe (805) | 5,479 | 3,629 |
| 91745 | Hacienda Heights(u) (818) | 52,354 | 49,422 |
| 94019 | Half Moon Bay (415) | 8,886 | 7,282 |
| *93230 | Hanford (209) | 30,463 | 20,958 |
| 90716 | Hawaiian Gardens (213) | 13,639 | 10,548 |

| ZIP | Place | 1990 | 1980 |
|---|---|---|---|
| *90250 | Hawthorne (213)/(310) | 71,349 | 56,437 |
| *94544 | Hayward (510) | 111,343 | 93,585 |
| 95448 | Healdsburg (707) | 9,469 | 7,217 |
| 92546 | Hemet (909) | 36,094 | 22,531 |
| 94547 | Hercules (415) | 16,829 | 5,963 |
| 90254 | Hermosa Beach (310) | 18,219 | 18,070 |
| *92340 | Hesperia† (760) | 50,418 | 20,612 |
| 92346 | Highland† (909) | 34,439 | 21,720 |
| 94010 | Hillsborough (415) | 10,667 | 10,372 |
| *95023 | Hollister (408) | 19,318 | 11,488 |
| 91720 | Home Gardens(u) (714) | 7,780 | 5,783 |
| *92647 | Huntington Beach (714) | 181,519 | 170,505 |
| 90255 | Huntington Park (213) | 56,129 | 45,932 |
| *91932 | Imperial Beach (619) | 26,512 | 22,689 |
| *92201 | Indio (760) | 36,850 | 21,611 |
| *90301 | Inglewood (213)/(310) | 109,602 | 94,162 |
| ..... | Interlaken(u) | 6,404 | .... |
| 95640 | Ione (916) | 6,516 | 2,207 |
| *92719 | Irvine (714) | 110,330 | 62,134 |
| 93117 | Isla Vista(u) (805) | 20,395 | .... |
| 94914 | Kentfield(u) (415) | 6,030 | .... |
| 93630 | Kerman (209) | 5,448 | 4,002 |
| 93930 | King City (408) | 7,634 | 5,495 |
| 93631 | Kingsburg (209) | 7,245 | 5,115 |
| *91011 | La Canada Flintridge (818) | 19,378 | 20,153 |
| *91224 | La Crescenta-Montrose(u) (818) | 16,968 | 16,531 |
| 90045 | Ladera Heights(u) (310) | 6,316 | 6,647 |
| 94549 | Lafayette (510) | 23,366 | 20,837 |
| ..... | Laguna(u) | 9,828 | .... |
| *92607 | Laguna Beach (714) | 23,170 | 17,858 |
| *92654 | Laguna Hills(u) (714) | 46,731 | 33,600 |
| 92607 | Laguna Niguel† (714) | 44,723 | 12,237 |
| *90631 | La Habra (562) | 51,263 | 45,232 |
| 90631 | La Habra Heights (562) | 6,226 | 4,786 |
| 92352 | Lake Arrowhead(u) (714) | 6,539 | 6,272 |
| *92531 | Lake Elsinore† (714) | 18,316 | 5,982 |
| 92530 | Lakeland Village(u) (714) | 5,159 | 2,796 |
| 93535 | Lake Los Angeles(u) (805) | 7,977 | .... |
| 92040 | Lakeside(u) (619) | 39,412 | 23,921 |
| *90714 | Lakewood (562) | 73,553 | 74,511 |
| *91941 | La Mesa (619) | 52,911 | 50,308 |
| *90638 | La Mirada (714) | 40,452 | 40,986 |
| 93241 | Lamont(u) (805) | 11,517 | 9,616 |
| *93539 | Lancaster (805) | 97,300 | 48,027 |
| 90623 | La Palma (714) | 15,392 | 15,399 |
| *91747 | La Puente (818) | 36,955 | 30,882 |
| 92253 | La Quinta† (909) | 11,215 | 4,027 |
| 95401 | La Riviera(u) (916) | 10,986 | 10,906 |
| 95403 | Larkfield-Wikiup(u) (707) | 6,779 | .... |
| *94939 | Larkspur (415) | 11,068 | 11,064 |
| 95330 | Lathrop† (209) | 6,841 | 4,112 |
| 91750 | La Verne (909) | 30,843 | 23,508 |
| *90260 | Lawndale (310) | 27,331 | 23,460 |
| *91945 | Lemon Grove (619) | 23,984 | 20,780 |
| 93245 | Lemoore (209) | 13,622 | 8,832 |
| 90304 | Lennox(u) (310) | 22,757 | 18,445 |
| 95648 | Lincoln (916) | 7,248 | 4,132 |
| 95901 | Linda(u) (916) | 13,033 | 10,225 |
| 93247 | Lindsay (209) | 8,338 | 6,936 |
| 95953 | Live Oak(u) (Santa Cruz) (916) | 15,212 | 11,482 |
| *94550 | Livermore (510) | 56,741 | 48,349 |
| 95334 | Livingston (209) | 7,317 | 5,326 |
| *95240 | Lodi (209) | 51,874 | 35,221 |
| 92354 | Loma Linda (714) | 18,470 | 10,694 |
| 90717 | Lomita (213) | 19,442 | 18,807 |
| *93436 | Lompoc (805) | 37,649 | 26,267 |
| *90801 | Long Beach (310)/(562) | 429,321 | 361,498 |
| 95650 | Loomis† (916) | 5,705 | 3,663 |
| *90720 | Los Alamitos (562) | 11,788 | 11,529 |
| *94022 | Los Altos (415) | 26,599 | 25,769 |
| 94022 | Los Altos Hills (415) | 7,514 | 7,421 |
| *90086 | Los Angeles (818)/(213)/(310) | 3,485,557 | 2,968,528 |
| 93635 | Los Banos (209) | 14,519 | 10,341 |
| *95030 | Los Gatos (408) | 27,357 | 26,906 |
| 91709 | Los Serranos(u) (909) | 7,099 | .... |
| 94903 | Lucas Valley-Marinwood(u) (415) | 5,982 | 6,409 |
| 90262 | Lynwood (213)/(310) | 61,945 | 48,289 |
| 93250 | Mc Farland (805) | 7,005 | 5,151 |
| 95521 | McKinleyville(u) (707) | 10,749 | 7,772 |
| *93638 | Madera (209) | 29,282 | 21,732 |
| 93637 | Madera Acres(u) (209) | 5,245 | 2,173 |
| 95954 | Magalia(u) (916) | 8,987 | .... |
| *90266 | Manhattan Beach (310) | 32,063 | 31,542 |
| *95336 | Manteca (209) | 40,773 | 24,925 |
| 92518 | March AFB(u) (714) | 5,523 | 3,607 |
| 93933 | Marina (408) | 26,512 | 20,647 |
| *90291 | Marina Del Rey(u) (310) | 7,431 | 6,336 |
| 94553 | Martinez (510) | 31,808 | 22,582 |
| 95901 | Marysville (916) | 12,324 | 9,898 |
| 90270 | Maywood (213) | 27,893 | 21,810 |
| 93640 | Mendota (209) | 6,821 | 5,038 |
| *94025 | Menlo Park (415) | 28,403 | 26,438 |
| 92359 | Mentone(u) (909) | 5,675 | .... |
| *95340 | Merced (209) | 56,155 | 36,423 |
| 94030 | Millbrae (415) | 20,414 | 20,058 |
| *94941 | Mill Valley (415) | 13,038 | 12,967 |
| *95035 | Milpitas (408) | 50,690 | 37,820 |
| 91752 | Mira Loma(u) (909) | 15,786 | 7,394 |
| 93641 | Mira Monte(u) (805) | 7,744 | .... |
| *92691 | Mission Viejo† (714) | 72,820 | 48,503 |

| ZIP | Place | | 1990 | 1980 |
|---|---|---|---|---|
| *95350 | Modesto | (209) | 164,746 | 106,963 |
| *91017 | Monrovia | (818) | 35,733 | 30,531 |
| 91763 | Montclair | (909) | 28,434 | 22,628 |
| 90640 | Montebello | (213) | 59,564 | 52,929 |
| 93940 | Monterey | (408) | 31,954 | 27,558 |
| *91754 | Monterey Park | (818) | 60,738 | 54,338 |
| *93021 | Moorpark† | (805) | 25,494 | 7,798 |
| *94556 | Moraga | (510) | 15,987 | 15,014 |
| *92552 | Moreno Valley† | (909) | 118,779 | 28,139 |
| *95037 | Morgan Hill | (408) | 23,928 | 17,060 |
| *93442 | Morro Bay | (805) | 9,664 | 9,064 |
| *94041 | Mountain View | (415) | 67,365 | 58,655 |
| 92405 | Muscoy(u) | (714) | 7,541 | 6,188 |
| *94558 | Napa | (707) | 61,865 | 50,879 |
| *91950 | National City | (619) | 54,249 | 48,772 |
| 92363 | Needles | (760) | 5,191 | 4,120 |
| 94560 | Newark | (510) | 37,861 | 32,126 |
| *92658 | Newport Beach | (714) | 66,643 | 62,556 |
| 93444 | Nipomo(u) | (805) | 7,109 | 5,247 |
| 91760 | Norco | (909) | 23,302 | 19,732 |
| 95603 | North Auburn(u) | (916) | 10,301 | 7,619 |
| 94025 | North Fair Oaks(u) | (415) | 13,912 | 10,308 |
| 95660 | North Highlands(u) | (916) | 42,105 | 37,825 |
| 90650 | Norwalk | (562) | 94,279 | 84,901 |
| *94947 | Novato | (415) | 47,585 | 43,916 |
| 95361 | Oakdale | (209) | 11,978 | 8,474 |
| *94617 | Oakland | (510) | 372,242 | 339,337 |
| 94561 | Oakley(u) | (510) | 18,374 | 2,816 |
| 93445 | Oceano(u) | (805) | 6,169 | 4,478 |
| *92054 | Oceanside | (760) | 128,090 | 76,698 |
| 93308 | Oildale(u) | (805) | 26,553 | 23,382 |
| *93023 | Ojai | (805) | 7,613 | 6,816 |
| 95961 | Olivehurst(u) | (916) | 9,738 | 8,929 |
| *91761 | Ontario | (909) | 133,179 | 88,820 |
| 95060 | Opal Cliffs(u) | (408) | 5,940 | 5,041 |
| *92613 | Orange | (714) | 110,658 | 91,450 |
| 93646 | Orange Cove | (209) | 5,604 | 4,026 |
| 95662 | Orangevale(u) | (916) | 26,266 | 20,585 |
| 94563 | Orinda† | (510) | 16,642 | 17,030 |
| 95963 | Orland | (916) | 5,052 | 4,031 |
| 93647 | Orosi(u) | (209) | 5,486 | 4,076 |
| *95965 | Oroville | (916) | 11,885 | 8,683 |
| 95965 | Oroville East(u) | (916) | 8,462 | .... |
| *93030 | Oxnard | (805) | 142,560 | 108,195 |
| 94044 | Pacifica | (415) | 37,670 | 36,866 |
| 93950 | Pacific Grove | (408) | 16,117 | 15,755 |
| 95968 | Palermo(u) | (916) | 5,260 | 2,572 |
| 93590 | Palmdale | (805) | 68,946 | 12,277 |
| 92260 | Palm Desert | (760) | 23,252 | 11,801 |
| ..... | Palm Desert Country(u) | | 5,626 | .... |
| *92262 | Palm Springs | (760) | 40,144 | 32,359 |
| *94303 | Palo Alto | (415) | 55,900 | 55,225 |
| 90274 | Palos Verdes Estates | (310) | 13,512 | 14,376 |
| *95969 | Paradise | (916) | 25,401 | 22,571 |
| 90723 | Paramount | (562) | 47,669 | 36,407 |
| 95823 | Parkway-So. Sacramento(u) | (916) | 31,903 | 26,815 |
| 93648 | Parlier | (209) | 7,938 | 2,902 |
| *91109 | Pasadena | (818) | 131,586 | 118,072 |
| | Paso Robles. *See El de Paso Robles* | | | |
| 95363 | Patterson | (209) | 8,626 | 3,908 |
| 92509 | Pedley(u) | | 8,869 | .... |
| *92572 | Perris | (909) | 21,500 | 6,827 |
| *94952 | Petaluma | (707) | 43,166 | 33,834 |
| *90660 | Pico Rivera | (562) | 59,177 | 53,387 |
| *94612 | Piedmont | (510) | 10,602 | 10,498 |
| 94564 | Pinole | (510) | 17,460 | 14,253 |
| *93449 | Pismo Beach | (805) | 7,669 | 5,364 |
| 94565 | Pittsburg | (510) | 47,607 | 33,465 |
| 92670 | Placentia | (714) | 41,259 | 35,041 |
| 95667 | Placerville | (916) | 8,286 | 6,739 |
| 94523 | Pleasant Hill | (510) | 31,583 | 25,547 |
| *94566 | Pleasanton | (510) | 50,570 | 35,160 |
| *91769 | Pomona | (909) | 131,700 | 92,742 |
| *93257 | Porterville | (209) | 29,521 | 19,707 |
| *93041 | Port Hueneme | (805) | 20,322 | 17,803 |
| 92064 | Poway† | (619) | 43,396 | 33,439 |
| 93907 | Prunedale(u) | (408) | 7,393 | .... |
| *93551 | Quartz Hill(u) | (805) | 9,626 | 7,421 |
| 92065 | Ramona(u) | (760) | 13,040 | 8,173 |
| *95670 | Rancho Cordova(u) | (916) | 48,731 | 42,881 |
| *91729 | Rancho Cucamonga | (714) | 101,409 | 55,250 |
| 92270 | Rancho Mirage | (760) | 9,778 | 6,281 |
| *90275 | Rancho Palos Verdes | (310) | 41,667 | 36,577 |
| 91941 | Rancho San Diego(u) | (619) | 6,977 | .... |
| 92688 | Rancho Santa Margarita(u) | (714) | 11,390 | .... |
| 96080 | Red Bluff | (916) | 12,363 | 9,490 |
| *96049 | Redding | (916) | 66,462 | 42,103 |
| *92373 | Redlands | (909) | 60,395 | 43,619 |
| *90277 | Redondo Beach | (310) | 60,167 | 57,102 |
| *94063 | Redwood City | (415) | 66,072 | 54,951 |
| 93654 | Reedley | (209) | 15,791 | 11,071 |
| *92377 | Rialto | (909) | 72,395 | 37,862 |
| *94802 | Richmond | (510) | 86,019 | 74,676 |
| *93555 | Ridgecrest | (760) | 28,295 | 15,929 |
| 95003 | Rio Del Mar(u) | (408) | 8,919 | 7,067 |
| 95673 | Rio Linda(u) | (916) | 9,481 | 7,359 |
| 95366 | Ripon | (209) | 7,455 | 3,509 |
| 95367 | Riverbank | (209) | 8,591 | 5,695 |
| *92502 | Riverside | (909) | 226,546 | 170,591 |
| *95677 | Rocklin | (916) | 18,806 | 7,344 |
| 94572 | Rodeo(u) | (415) | 7,589 | 8,286 |
| *94928 | Rohnert Park | (707) | 36,326 | 22,965 |
| 90274 | Rolling Hills Estates | (310) | 7,789 | 7,701 |
| 93560 | Rosamond(u) | (805) | 7,430 | 2,869 |
| 95401 | Roseland(u) | (707) | 8,779 | 7,915 |
| 91770 | Rosemead | (818) | 51,638 | 42,604 |
| 95826 | Rosemont(u) | (916) | 22,851 | 18,888 |
| *95678 | Roseville | (916) | 44,685 | 24,347 |
| 90720 | Rossmoor(u) | (562) | 9,893 | 10,457 |
| 91748 | Rowland Heights(u) | (818) | 42,647 | 28,258 |
| 92509 | Rubidoux(u) | (909) | 24,367 | 17,048 |
| *95814 | Sacramento | (916) | 369,365 | 275,741 |
| *93907 | Salinas | (408) | 108,777 | 80,479 |
| *94960 | San Anselmo | (415) | 11,735 | 12,067 |
| *92401 | San Bernardino | (909) | 164,676 | 118,794 |
| *94066 | San Bruno | (415) | 38,961 | 35,417 |
| *93001 | San Buenaventura (Ventura) | (805) | 92,557 | 73,774 |
| 94070 | San Carlos | (415) | 26,382 | 24,710 |
| *92674 | San Clemente | (714) | 41,100 | 27,325 |
| *92138 | San Diego | (619) | 1,110,623 | 875,538 |
| 92065 | San Diego Country Estates(u) | (760) | 6,874 | .... |
| 91773 | San Dimas | (909) | 32,398 | 24,014 |
| *91341 | San Fernando | (818) | 22,580 | 17,731 |
| *94142 | San Francisco | (415) | 723,959 | 678,974 |
| *91778 | San Gabriel | (818) | 37,120 | 30,072 |
| 93657 | Sanger | (209) | 16,839 | 12,542 |
| *92581 | San Jacinto | (909) | 16,210 | 7,098 |
| *95113 | San Jose | (408) | 782,224 | 629,400 |
| *92675 | San Juan Capistrano | (714) | 26,183 | 18,959 |
| *94577 | San Leandro | (510) | 68,223 | 63,952 |
| 94580 | San Lorenzo(u) | (510) | 19,987 | 20,545 |
| *93401 | San Luis Obispo | (805) | 41,958 | 34,252 |
| *92069 | San Marcos | (760) | 38,974 | 17,479 |
| *91118 | San Marino | (818) | 12,959 | 13,307 |
| *94402 | San Mateo | (415) | 85,619 | 77,640 |
| 94806 | San Pablo | (510) | 25,158 | 19,750 |
| *94915 | San Rafael | (415) | 48,410 | 44,700 |
| 94583 | San Ramon† | (510) | 35,303 | 20,511 |
| *92711 | Santa Ana | (714) | 293,827 | 204,023 |
| *93102 | Santa Barbara | (805) | 85,571 | 74,414 |
| *95050 | Santa Clara | (408) | 93,613 | 87,700 |
| *91380 | Santa Clarita | (805) | 110,690 | .... |
| *95060 | Santa Cruz | (408) | 49,711 | 41,483 |
| 90670 | Santa Fe Springs | (562) | 15,520 | 14,520 |
| 93454 | Santa Maria | (805) | 61,552 | 39,685 |
| *90401 | Santa Monica | (310) | 86,905 | 88,314 |
| *93060 | Santa Paula | (805) | 25,062 | 20,658 |
| *95402 | Santa Rosa | (707) | 113,261 | 82,658 |
| 92071 | Santee† | (619) | 52,902 | 40,298 |
| *95070 | Saratoga | (408) | 28,061 | 29,261 |
| *94965 | Sausalito | (415) | 7,152 | 7,338 |
| *95066 | Scotts Valley | (408) | 8,667 | 6,891 |
| 90740 | Seal Beach | (562) | 25,098 | 25,975 |
| 93955 | Seaside | (408) | 38,826 | 36,567 |
| *95472 | Sebastopol | (707) | 7,008 | 5,595 |
| 93662 | Selma | (209) | 14,757 | 10,942 |
| 93263 | Shafter | (805) | 8,409 | 7,010 |
| *91025 | Sierra Madre | (818) | 10,762 | 10,837 |
| 90806 | Signal Hill | (562) | 8,371 | 5,734 |
| *93065 | Simi Valley | (805) | 100,218 | 77,500 |
| 92075 | Solana Beach† | (619) | 12,956 | 12,250 |
| 93960 | Soledad | (408) | 7,161 | 5,928 |
| 95476 | Sonoma | (707) | 8,168 | 6,054 |
| 95073 | Soquel(u) | (408) | 9,188 | 6,212 |
| 91733 | South El Monte | (213) | 20,850 | 16,623 |
| 90280 | South Gate | (213)/(562) | 86,284 | 66,784 |
| *96151 | South Lake Tahoe | (916) | 21,586 | 20,681 |
| 95965 | South Oroville(u) | (916) | 7,463 | 7,246 |
| *91030 | South Pasadena | (818) | 23,936 | 22,681 |
| *94080 | South San Francisco | (415) | 54,312 | 49,393 |
| 91770 | South San Gabriel(u) | (213) | 7,700 | 5,421 |
| 91744 | South San Jose Hills(u) | (408) | 17,814 | 16,076 |
| 90605 | South Whittier(u) | (562) | 49,514 | 43,815 |
| 95991 | South Yuba(u) | (916) | 8,816 | 7,530 |
| *91977 | Spring Valley(u) | (619) | 55,331 | 40,191 |
| 94305 | Stanford(u) | (415) | 18,097 | 11,045 |
| 90680 | Stanton | (714) | 30,491 | 23,723 |
| *95208 | Stockton | (209) | 210,943 | 148,283 |
| 94585 | Suisun City | (707) | 22,704 | 11,087 |
| *92586 | Sun City(u) | (714) | 14,930 | 8,460 |
| *94086 | Sunnyvale | (408) | 117,324 | 106,618 |
| 96130 | Susanville | (916) | 7,279 | 6,520 |
| 93268 | Taft | (805) | 5,902 | 5,316 |
| 94941 | Tamalpais-Homestead Valley(u) | (415) | 9,601 | 8,511 |
| *93581 | Tehachapi | (805) | 6,182 | 4,126 |
| *92589 | Temecula† | (909) | 27,177 | 4,289 |
| 91780 | Temple City | (818) | 31,153 | 28,972 |
| 95965 | Thermalito(u) | (916) | 5,646 | 4,961 |
| *91359 | Thousand Oaks | (805) | 104,381 | 77,072 |
| 94920 | Tiburon | (415) | 7,554 | 6,685 |
| *90503 | Torrance | (310) | 133,107 | 129,881 |
| *95376 | Tracy | (209) | 33,558 | 18,428 |
| *93274 | Tulare | (209) | 33,249 | 22,530 |
| *95380 | Turlock | (209) | 42,224 | 26,287 |
| *92681 | Tustin | (714) | 50,689 | 32,248 |
| 92705 | Tustin Foothills(u) | (714) | 24,358 | 26,174 |
| *92277 | Twentynine Palms† | (760) | 11,821 | 8,802 |
| 92278 | Twentynine Palms Base(u) | (760) | 10,606 | 7,079 |
| 95060 | Twin Lakes(u) | (408) | 5,379 | 4,502 |

| ZIP | Place | | 1990 | 1980 |
|---|---|---|---|---|
| 95482 | Ukiah | (707) | 14,632 | 12,035 |
| 94587 | Union City | (510) | 53,762 | 39,406 |
| *91785 | Upland | (909) | 63,374 | 47,647 |
| *95687 | Vacaville | (707) | 71,476 | 43,367 |
| 91744 | Valinda(u) | (818) | 18,735 | 18,712 |
| *94590 | Vallejo | (707) | 109,199 | 80,303 |
| 92343 | Valle Vista(u) | (714) | 8,751 | 5,474 |
| 93437 | Vandenberg AFB(u) | (805) | 9,846 | 8,136 |
| 93436 | Vandenberg Village(u) | (805) | 5,971 | 5,839 |
| | Ventura. *See San Buenaventura* | | | |
| *92393 | Victorville | (760) | 40,674 | 14,220 |
| 90043 | View Park-Windsor Hills(u) | (310) | 11,769 | 12,101 |
| 92667 | Villa Park | (714) | 6,299 | 7,137 |
| ..... | Vincent(u) | | 13,713 | .... |
| *93277 | Visalia | (209) | 75,659 | 49,729 |
| *92083 | Vista | (760) | 71,865 | 35,834 |
| *91788 | Walnut | (909) | 29,105 | 12,478 |
| *94596 | Walnut Creek | (510) | 60,569 | 54,033 |
| 90255 | Walnut Park(u) | (213) | 14,722 | 11,811 |
| 93280 | Wasco | (805) | 12,412 | 9,613 |
| *95076 | Watsonville | (408) | 31,099 | 23,662 |
| 90044 | West Athens(u) | (310) | 8,859 | 8,531 |
| 90502 | West Carson(u) | (213) | 20,143 | 17,997 |
| 90247 | West Compton(u) | (310) | 5,451 | 5,907 |
| *91793 | West Covina | (818) | 96,226 | 80,292 |
| 90069 | West Hollywood† | (213/(310) | 36,118 | 35,754 |
| 91359 | Westlake Village† | (805) | 7,455 | 6,130 |
| 92684 | Westminster | (714) | 78,293 | 71,133 |
| 90047 | Westmont(u) | (213) | 31,044 | 27,916 |
| 91746 | West Puente Valley(u) | (818) | 20,254 | 20,445 |
| 95691 | West Sacramento† | (916) | 28,898 | 24,482 |
| *90606 | West Whittier-Los Nietos(u) | (562) | 24,164 | 21,001 |
| *90605 | Whittier | (562) | 77,671 | 68,558 |
| 92595 | Wildomar(u) | (907) | 10,411 | .... |
| 95490 | Willits | (707) | 5,027 | 4,008 |
| 90222 | Willowbrook(u) | (213) | 32,772 | 30,962 |
| 95988 | Willows | (916) | 5,988 | 4,777 |
| 95492 | Windsor(u) | (707) | 13,371 | .... |
| 95388 | Winton(u) | (209) | 7,559 | 4,995 |
| 92502 | Woodcrest(u) | (909) | 7,796 | .... |
| 93286 | Woodlake | (209) | 5,678 | 4,343 |
| *95695 | Woodland | (916) | 40,230 | 30,235 |
| 94062 | Woodside | (415) | 5,034 | 5,291 |
| *92686 | Yorba Linda | (714) | 52,422 | 28,254 |
| 96097 | Yreka | (916) | 6,948 | 5,916 |
| *95991 | Yuba City | (916) | 27,385 | 18,736 |
| 92399 | Yucaipa† | (909) | 32,824 | 27,654 |
| *92286 | Yucca Valley(u) | (760) | 13,701 | 8,294 |

## Colorado

| ZIP | Place | | 1990 | 1980 |
|---|---|---|---|---|
| *80840 | Air Force Academy | (719) | 9,062 | 8,655 |
| 81101 | Alamosa | (719) | 7,579 | 6,830 |
| 80401 | Applewood(u) | (303) | 11,069 | 12,040 |
| *80004 | Arvada | (303) | 89,218 | 84,576 |
| *81611 | Aspen | (970) | 5,049 | 3,678 |
| *80017 | Aurora | (303) | 222,103 | 158,588 |
| 80908 | Black Forest(u) | (719) | 8,143 | 3,372 |
| *80302 | Boulder | (303) | 83,295 | 76,685 |
| 80601 | Brighton | (303) | 14,203 | 12,773 |
| *80020 | Broomfield | (303) | 24,638 | 20,730 |
| *81212 | Canon City | (719) | 12,687 | 13,037 |
| 80104 | Castle Rock | (303) | 8,710 | 3,921 |
| 80120 | Castlewood(u) | (303) | 24,392 | 16,413 |
| 80110 | Cherry Hills Village | (303) | 5,245 | 5,127 |
| 81220 | Cimarron Hills(u) | (719) | 11,160 | 6,597 |
| 81520 | Clifton(u) | (970) | 12,671 | 5,223 |
| *80903 | Colorado Springs | (719) | 280,430 | 215,105 |
| 80120 | Columbine(u) | (303) | 23,969 | 23,523 |
| *80022 | Commerce City | (303) | 16,466 | 16,234 |
| 81321 | Cortez | (970) | 7,284 | 7,095 |
| *81625 | Craig | (970) | 8,091 | 8,133 |
| *80202 | Denver | (303) | 467,610 | 492,686 |
| 80022 | Derby(u) | (303) | 6,043 | 8,578 |
| *81301 | Durango | (970) | 12,439 | 11,649 |
| *80110 | Englewood | (303) | 29,396 | 30,021 |
| 80620 | Evans | (970) | 5,876 | 5,063 |
| 80439 | Evergreen(u) | (303) | 7,582 | 6,376 |
| 80221 | Federal Heights | (303) | 9,342 | 7,838 |
| 80913 | Fort Carson(u) | (719) | 11,309 | 13,219 |
| *80525 | Fort Collins | (970) | 87,491 | 65,092 |
| 80621 | Fort Lupton | (970) | 5,159 | 4,251 |
| 80701 | Fort Morgan | (970) | 9,068 | 8,768 |
| 80817 | Fountain | (719) | 10,175 | 8,324 |
| 81504 | Fruitvale(u) | (303) | 5,222 | .... |
| 81522 | Gateway(u) | (970) | 7,510 | .... |
| *81601 | Glenwood Springs | (970) | 6,561 | 4,637 |
| *80401 | Golden | (303) | 13,127 | 12,237 |
| *81501 | Grand Junction | (970) | 29,255 | 27,956 |
| *80631 | Greeley | (970) | 60,454 | 53,006 |
| *80111 | Greenwood Village | (303) | 7,589 | 5,729 |
| 80501 | Gunbarrel(u) | (303) | 9,388 | 5,172 |
| 80126 | Highlands Ranch(u) | (303) | 10,181 | .... |
| 80127 | Ken Caryl(u) | (303) | 24,391 | 10,661 |
| 80026 | Lafayette | (303) | 14,708 | 8,985 |
| 81050 | La Junta | (719) | 7,678 | 8,338 |
| *80226 | Lakewood | (303) | 126,475 | 113,808 |
| 81052 | Lamar | (719) | 8,343 | 7,713 |
| *80126 | Littleton | (303) | 33,711 | 28,631 |
| *80501 | Longmont | (303) | 51,529 | 42,942 |
| 80027 | Louisville | (303) | 12,363 | 5,593 |
| *80538 | Loveland | (970) | 37,357 | 30,215 |
| *81401 | Montrose | (970) | 8,854 | 8,722 |
| 80233 | Northglenn | (303) | 27,195 | 29,847 |
| 80649 | Orchard Mesa(u) | (303) | 5,977 | 4,876 |
| 80134 | Parker† | (303) | 5,450 | 290 |
| *81003 | Pueblo | (719) | 98,640 | 101,686 |
| 81503 | Redlands(u) | (970) | 9,355 | .... |
| 80911 | Security-Widefield(u) | (719) | 23,822 | 18,768 |
| 80221 | Sherrelwood(u) | (303) | 16,636 | 17,629 |
| 80122 | Southglenn(u) | (303) | 43,087 | 37,787 |
| *80477 | Steamboat Springs | (970) | 6,695 | 5,098 |
| 80751 | Sterling | (970) | 10,362 | 11,385 |
| 80906 | Stratmoor(u) | (719) | 5,854 | 5,519 |
| 80229 | Thornton | (303) | 55,031 | 42,054 |
| 81082 | Trinidad | (719) | 8,580 | 9,663 |
| 80229 | Welby(u) | (303) | 10,218 | 9,668 |
| 80030 | Westminster | (303) | 74,619 | 50,211 |
| 80221 | Westminster East(u) | (303) | 5,197 | 6,002 |
| *80033 | Wheat Ridge | (303) | 29,419 | 30,293 |
| 80550 | Windsor | (970) | 5,062 | 4,277 |

## Connecticut

*See note on page 390*

| ZIP | Place | | 1990 | 1980 |
|---|---|---|---|---|
| 06401 | Ansonia | (203) | 18,403 | 19,039 |
| 06001 | *Avon* | (860) | 13,937 | 11,201 |
| 06403 | *Beacon Falls* | (203) | 5,083 | 3,995 |
| 06037 | *Berlin* | (860) | 16,787 | 15,121 |
| 06801 | *Bethel* | (203) | 17,541 | 16,004 |
| 06002 | *Bloomfield* | (860) | 19,483 | 18,608 |
| 06405 | *Branford* | (203) | 27,603 | 23,363 |
| *06602 | Bridgeport | (203) | 141,686 | 142,546 |
| *06010 | Bristol | (860) | 60,640 | 57,370 |
| 06804 | *Brookfield* | (203) | 14,113 | 12,872 |
| 06234 | *Brooklyn* | (860) | 6,681 | 5,691 |
| 06013 | *Burlington* | (860) | 7,026 | 5,660 |
| 06019 | *Canton* | (860) | 8,268 | 7,635 |
| 06040 | Central Manchester(u) | (860) | 30,934 | 31,058 |
| 06410 | *Cheshire* | (203) | 25,684 | 21,788 |
| 06413 | *Clinton* | (860) | 12,767 | 11,195 |
| 06415 | *Colchester* | (860) | 10,980 | 7,761 |
| 06340 | Conning Towers-Nautilus Park(u) | (860) | 10,013 | 9,665 |
| 06238 | *Coventry* | (860) | 10,063 | 8,895 |
| 06416 | *Cromwell* | (860) | 12,286 | 10,265 |
| *06810 | Danbury | (203) | 65,585 | 60,470 |
| 06820 | Darien | (203) | 18,130 | 18,892 |
| 06418 | Derby | (203) | 12,199 | 12,346 |
| 06422 | *Durham* | (860) | 5,732 | 5,143 |
| 06423 | *East Haddam* | (860) | 6,676 | 5,621 |
| 06424 | *East Hampton* | (860) | 10,428 | 8,572 |
| *06101 | East Hartford(u) | (860) | 50,452 | 52,563 |
| 06512 | East Haven(u) | (203) | 26,144 | 25,036 |
| 06333 | *East Lyme* | (860) | 15,340 | 13,870 |
| 06016 | *East Windsor* | (860) | 10,081 | 8,925 |
| 06425 | *Easton* | (203) | 6,303 | 5,962 |
| 06029 | *Ellington* | (860) | 11,197 | 9,711 |
| *06082 | *Enfield* | (860) | 45,532 | 42,695 |
| 06426 | *Essex* | (860) | 5,904 | 5,078 |
| 06430 | *Fairfield* | (203) | 53,418 | 54,849 |
| *06032 | *Farmington* | (860) | 20,608 | 16,407 |
| 06033 | Glastonbury Center(u) | (860) | 7,082 | 7,049 |
| 06035 | *Granby* | (860) | 9,369 | 7,956 |
| *06830 | *Greenwich* | (203) | 58,441 | 59,565 |
| 06351 | *Griswold* | (860) | 10,384 | 8,967 |
| 06340 | *Groton* | (860) | 45,144 | 41,062 |
| 06340 | Groton Borough | (860) | 9,837 | 10,086 |
| 06437 | *Guilford* | (203) | 19,848 | 17,375 |
| 06438 | *Haddam* | (860) | 6,769 | 6,383 |
| *06514 | *Hamden* | (203) | 52,434 | 51,071 |
| *06101 | Hartford | (860) | 139,739 | 136,392 |
| 06791 | *Harwinton* | (860) | 5,228 | 4,889 |
| 06082 | Hazardville(u) | (860) | 5,179 | 5,436 |
| 06248 | Hebron | (860) | 7,079 | 5,453 |
| 06037 | Kensington(u) | (860) | 8,306 | 7,502 |
| 06239 | *Killingly* | (860) | 15,889 | 14,519 |
| 06249 | Lebanon | (860) | 6,041 | 4,762 |
| 06339 | *Ledyard* | (860) | 14,913 | 13,735 |
| 06759 | *Litchfield* | (860) | 8,365 | 7,605 |
| 06443 | *Madison* | (203) | 15,485 | 14,031 |
| 06040 | *Manchester* | (860) | 51,618 | 49,761 |
| 06250 | *Mansfield* | (860) | 21,103 | 20,634 |
| 06447 | *Marlborough* | (860) | 5,535 | 4,746 |
| *06450 | Meriden | (203) | 59,479 | 57,118 |
| 06762 | *Middlebury* | (203) | 6,145 | 5,995 |
| 06457 | Middletown | (860) | 42,762 | 39,040 |
| 06460 | Milford | (203) | 49,938 | 48,168 |
| 06468 | *Monroe* | (203) | 16,896 | 14,010 |
| 06353 | *Montville* | (860) | 16,673 | 16,455 |
| 06770 | Naugatuck | (203) | 30,625 | 26,456 |
| *06050 | New Britain | (860) | 75,491 | 73,840 |
| 06840 | *New Canaan* | (203) | 17,864 | 17,931 |
| 06810 | *New Fairfield* | (203) | 12,911 | 11,260 |
| 06057 | *New Hartford* | (860) | 5,769 | 4,884 |
| *06511 | New Haven | (203) | 130,474 | 126,089 |
| *06111 | Newington(u) | (860) | 29,208 | 28,841 |

| ZIP | Place | Area code | 1990 | 1980 |
|---|---|---|---|---|
| 06320 | New London | (860) | 28,540 | 28,842 |
| 06776 | *New Milford* | (860) | 23,629 | 19,420 |
| 06470 | *Newtown* | (203) | 20,779 | 19,107 |
| 06471 | *North Branford* | (203) | 12,996 | 11,554 |
| 06473 | North Haven(u) | (203) | 22,249 | 22,080 |
| *06856 | Norwalk | (203) | 78,331 | 77,767 |
| 06360 | Norwich | (860) | 37,391 | 38,074 |
| 06779 | Oakville(u) | (860) | 8,741 | 8,737 |
| 06371 | *Old Lyme* | (860) | 6,535 | 6,159 |
| 06475 | *Old Saybrook* | (860) | 9,552 | 9,287 |
| 06477 | *Orange* | (203) | 12,830 | 13,237 |
| 06478 | *Oxford* | (203) | 8,685 | 6,634 |
| 02891 | Pawcatuck(u) | (860) | 5,289 | 5,216 |
| 06374 | *Plainfield* | (860) | 14,363 | 12,774 |
| 06062 | *Plainville* | (860) | 17,392 | 16,401 |
| 06782 | *Plymouth* | (860) | 11,822 | 10,732 |
| 06480 | *Portland* | (860) | 8,418 | 8,383 |
| 06365 | *Preston* | (860) | 5,006 | 4,644 |
| 06712 | *Prospect* | (203) | 7,775 | 6,807 |
| 06260 | Putnam | (860) | 6,835 | 6,855 |
| 06260 | *Putnam*† | (860) | 9,031 | 8,580 |
| 06898 | *Redding* | (203) | 7,927 | 7,272 |
| 06877 | Ridgefield Center(u) | (203) | 6,363 | 6,066 |
| 06877 | *Ridgefield* | (203) | 20,919 | 20,120 |
| 06067 | *Rocky Hill* | (860) | 16,554 | 14,559 |
| 06483 | *Seymour* | (203) | 14,288 | 13,434 |
| 06484 | Shelton | (203) | 35,418 | 31,314 |
| 06082 | Sherwood Manor(u) | (860) | 6,357 | 6,303 |
| 06070 | *Simsbury* | (860) | 22,023 | 21,161 |
| 06071 | *Somers* | (860) | 9,108 | 8,473 |
| 06488 | *Southbury* | (203) | 15,818 | 14,156 |
| 06489 | *Southington* | (860) | 38,518 | 36,879 |
| 06074 | *South Windsor* | (860) | 22,090 | 17,198 |
| 06082 | Southwood Acres(u) | (860) | 8,963 | 9,779 |
| 06075 | *Stafford* | (860) | 11,091 | 9,268 |
| *06904 | Stamford | (203) | 108,056 | 102,466 |
| 06378 | *Stonington* | (860) | 16,919 | 16,220 |
| 06268 | Storrs(u) | (860) | 12,198 | 11,394 |
| 06497 | Stratford(u) | (203) | 49,389 | 50,541 |
| 06078 | *Suffield* | (860) | 11,427 | 9,294 |
| 06786 | Terryville(u) | (860) | 5,426 | 5,234 |
| 06787 | *Thomaston* | (860) | 6,947 | 6,272 |
| 06277 | *Thompson* | (860) | 8,668 | 8,141 |
| 06082 | Thompsonville(u) | (860) | 8,458 | 8,151 |
| 06084 | *Tolland* | (860) | 11,001 | 9,694 |
| 06790 | Torrington | (860) | 33,687 | 30,987 |
| 06611 | Trumbull(u) | (203) | 32,000 | 32,989 |
| 06066 | *Vernon* | (860) | 29,841 | 27,974 |
| 06492 | *Wallingford* | (203) | 40,822 | 37,274 |
| *06701 | Waterbury | (203) | 108,961 | 103,266 |
| 06385 | *Waterford* | (860) | 17,930 | 17,843 |
| 06795 | *Watertown* | (860) | 20,456 | 19,489 |
| 06107 | West Hartford(u) | (860) | 60,110 | 61,301 |
| 06516 | West Haven | (203) | 54,021 | 53,184 |
| 06498 | *Westbrook* | (860) | 5,414 | 5,216 |
| 06883 | *Weston* | (203) | 8,648 | 8,284 |
| *06880 | Westport(u) | (203) | 24,407 | 25,290 |
| 06109 | Wethersfield(u) | (860) | 25,651 | 26,013 |
| 06226 | Willimantic(u)† | (860) | 14,746 | 14,652 |
| 06279 | *Willington* | (860) | 5,979 | 4,694 |
| 06897 | *Wilton* | (203) | 15,989 | 15,351 |
| 06094 | *Winchester* | (860) | 11,524 | 10,841 |
| 06280 | *Windham* | (860) | 22,039 | 21,062 |
| 06095 | *Windsor* | (860) | 27,817 | 25,204 |
| 06096 | Windsor Locks(u) | (860) | 12,358 | 12,190 |
| 06098 | Winsted | (860) | 8,254 | 8,092 |
| 06716 | *Wolcott* | (203) | 13,700 | 13,008 |
| 06525 | *Woodbridge* | (203) | 7,924 | 7,761 |
| 06798 | *Woodbury* | (203) | 8,131 | 6,942 |
| 06281 | *Woodstock* | (860) | 6,008 | 5,117 |

## Delaware (302)

| ZIP | Place | 1990 | 1980 |
|---|---|---|---|
| 19713 | Brookside(u) | 15,307 | 15,255 |
| 19703 | Claymont(u) | 9,800 | 10,022 |
| *19901 | Dover | 27,630 | 23,507 |
| 19809 | Edgemoor(u) | 5,853 | 7,397 |
| 19805 | Elsmere | 5,935 | 6,493 |
| 19963 | Milford | 6,032 | 5,366 |
| *19711 | Newark | 26,463 | 25,247 |
| 19800 | Pike Creek(u) | 10,163 | .... |
| 19973 | Seaford | 5,689 | 5,256 |
| 19977 | Smyrna | 5,231 | 4,750 |
| 19804 | Stanton(u) | 5,028 | 5,495 |
| 19803 | Talleyville(u) | 6,346 | 6,880 |
| *19899 | Wilmington | 71,529 | 70,195 |
| 19720 | Wilmington Manor | 8,568 | 9,233 |

## District of Columbia (202)

| ZIP | Place | 1990 | 1980 |
|---|---|---|---|
| *20090 | Washington | 606,900 | 638,432 |

## Florida

| ZIP | Place | Area code | 1990 | 1980 |
|---|---|---|---|---|
| *32714 | Altamonte Springs | (407) | 35,167 | 21,105 |
| ..... | Andover(u) | | 6,251 | .... |
| 33572 | Apollo Beach(u) | (813) | 6,025 | 4,014 |
| *32712 | Apopka | (407) | 13,611 | 6,019 |
| 33821 | Arcadia | (941) | 6,488 | 6,002 |
| 32233 | Atlantic Beach | (904) | 11,636 | 7,847 |
| 33823 | Auburndale | (941) | 8,846 | 6,501 |
| 33280 | Aventura(u) | (305) | 14,914 | 9,698 |
| 33825 | Avon Park | (941) | 8,078 | 8,026 |
| 32857 | Azalea Park(u) | (407) | 8,926 | 8,301 |
| *33830 | Bartow | (941) | 14,716 | 14,780 |
| ..... | Bay Hill(u) | | 5,346 | .... |
| 34667 | Bayonet Point(u) | (813) | 21,860 | 16,455 |
| 33505 | Bayshore Gardens(u) | (813) | 17,062 | 14,945 |
| 33589 | Beacon Square(u) | (813) | 6,265 | 6,513 |
| 34233 | Bee Ridge | (941) | 6,406 | 3,313 |
| 32073 | Bellair-Meadowbrook Terrace(u) | (813) | 15,606 | 12,144 |
| 33430 | Belle Glade | (561) | 16,177 | 16,535 |
| *32802 | Belle Isle | (407) | 5,272 | 2,848 |
| 34420 | Belleview(u) | (352) | 19,386 | 15,439 |
| *34464 | Beverly Hills(u) | (352) | 6,163 | 5,024 |
| *33509 | Bloomingdale(u) | (813) | 13,912 | .... |
| ..... | Boca Del Mar(u) | | 17,754 | .... |
| *33431 | Boca Raton | (561) | 61,486 | 49,447 |
| *33923 | Bonita Springs(u) | (941) | 13,600 | 5,435 |
| *33436 | Boynton Beach | (561) | 46,284 | 35,624 |
| *34206 | Bradenton | (941) | 43,769 | 30,228 |
| *33509 | Brandon(u) | (813) | 57,985 | 41,826 |
| 32503 | Brent(u) | (904) | 21,624 | 21,872 |
| 33317 | Broadview Park(u) | (954) | 6,109 | 6,022 |
| 33313 | Broadview-Pompano Park(u) | (954) | 5,230 | 5,223 |
| *34601 | Brooksville | (352) | 7,589 | 5,582 |
| 33311 | Browardale(u) | (954) | 6,257 | 7,409 |
| 33142 | Brownsville(u) | (813) | 15,607 | 18,058 |
| 34743 | Buena Ventura Lakes(u) | | 14,148 | .... |
| 32404 | Callaway | (904) | 12,253 | 7,154 |
| 32920 | Cape Canaveral | (407) | 8,014 | 5,733 |
| *33990 | Cape Coral | (941) | 74,991 | 32,103 |
| 33055 | Carol City(u) | (305) | 53,331 | 47,349 |
| *33688 | Carrollwood(u) | (813) | 7,195 | .... |
| *33601 | Carrollwood Village(u) | (813) | 15,051 | .... |
| *32707 | Casselberry | (407) | 18,849 | 15,037 |
| 33401 | Century Village(u) | (305) | 8,363 | 10,619 |
| *34618 | Clearwater | (813) | 98,699 | 85,170 |
| *34711 | Clermont | (352) | 6,910 | 5,461 |
| 33440 | Clewiston | (941) | 6,085 | 5,219 |
| *32922 | Cocoa | (407) | 17,710 | 16,096 |
| *32931 | Cocoa Beach | (407) | 12,123 | 10,926 |
| 32922 | Cocoa West(u) | (407) | 6,160 | 6,432 |
| *33063 | Coconut Creek | (954) | 27,269 | 6,288 |
| 33064 | Collier Manor-Cresthaven(u) | (954) | 7,322 | 7,045 |
| 33801 | Combee Settlement(u) | (813) | 5,463 | 5,400 |
| 32809 | Conway(u) | (407) | 13,159 | 24,027 |
| 33328 | Cooper City | (954) | 21,335 | 10,140 |
| 33114 | Coral Gables | (305) | 40,091 | 43,241 |
| *33060 | Coral Springs | (954) | 78,864 | 37,349 |
| 33157 | Coral Terrace(u) | (305) | 23,255 | 22,702 |
| *32536 | Crestview | (904) | 9,886 | 7,617 |
| 33803 | Crystal Lake(u) | (813) | 5,300 | 6,827 |
| 33157 | Cutler(u) | (305) | 16,201 | 15,608 |
| 33157 | Cutler Ridge(u) | (305) | 21,268 | 20,886 |
| 33884 | Cypress Gardens(u) | (941) | 9,188 | 8,043 |
| 33919 | Cypress Lake(u) | (941) | 10,491 | 8,721 |
| *33525 | Dade City | (352) | 5,633 | 4,923 |
| 33004 | Dania | (954) | 13,183 | 11,796 |
| 33314 | Davie | (954) | 47,143 | 20,500 |
| *32114 | Daytona Beach | (904) | 61,991 | 54,176 |
| 32713 | De Bary | (407) | 7,176 | 4,980 |
| *33441 | Deerfield Beach | (954) | 46,997 | 39,193 |
| 32433 | DeFuniak Springs | (904) | 5,200 | 5,563 |
| *32720 | De Land | (904) | 16,622 | 15,354 |
| *33444 | Delray Beach | (561) | 47,184 | 34,329 |
| 33617 | Del Rio(u) | (813) | 8,248 | 7,409 |
| *32763 | Deltona(u) | (407) | 50,828 | 15,710 |
| *32541 | Destin† | (904) | 8,090 | 3,913 |
| ..... | Doctor Phillips(u) | | 7,963 | .... |
| *34698 | Dunedin | (813) | 34,427 | 30,203 |
| 33610 | East Lake-Orient Park(u) | (813) | 6,171 | 5,612 |
| 33940 | East Naples(u) | (941) | 22,951 | 12,127 |
| *32132 | Edgewater | (904) | 15,351 | 6,726 |
| 32542 | Eglin AFB(u) | (904) | 8,347 | 7,574 |
| 33614 | Egypt Lake(u) | (813) | 14,580 | 11,932 |
| 34680 | Elfers(u) | (813) | 12,356 | 11,396 |
| *34223 | Englewood(u) | (941) | 15,025 | 10,229 |
| 32534 | Ensley(u) | (904) | 16,362 | 14,422 |
| *32726 | Eustis | (352) | 12,856 | 9,453 |
| 32804 | Fairview Shores(u) | (305) | 13,192 | 10,174 |
| *32034 | Fernandina Beach | (904) | 8,765 | 7,224 |
| 32730 | Fern Park(u) | (407) | 8,294 | 8,904 |
| 32514 | Ferry Pass(u) | (904) | 26,301 | 16,910 |
| 33034 | Florida City | (305) | 5,978 | 6,174 |
| 32960 | Florida Ridge(u) | (561) | 12,218 | 4,988 |
| 32714 | Forest City(u) | (407) | 10,638 | 6,819 |
| ..... | Forest Island Park(u) | | 5,988 | .... |
| *33310 | Fort Lauderdale | (954) | 149,238 | 153,279 |
| *33902 | Fort Myers | (941) | 44,947 | 36,638 |
| *33931 | Fort Myers Beach(u) | (941) | 9,284 | 5,753 |
| *33922 | Fort Myers Shores(u) | (941) | 5,460 | 4,426 |
| *34981 | Fort Pierce | (561) | 36,830 | 33,802 |
| 33452 | Fort Pierce North(u) | (561) | 5,833 | 5,929 |
| 34982 | Fort Pierce South(u) | (561) | 5,320 | 3,324 |

| ZIP | Place | | 1990 | 1980 |
|---|---|---|---|---|
| *32548 | Fort Walton Beach | (904) | 21,407 | 20,829 |
| *32043 | Fruit Cove(u) | (904) | 5,904 | 3,906 |
| 34230 | Fruitville(u) | (941) | 9,808 | 2,551 |
| *32602 | Gainesville | (352) | 85,075 | 81,371 |
| 33801 | Gibsonia(u) | (813) | 5,168 | 5,011 |
| 33534 | Gibsonton(u) | (813) | 7,706 | .... |
| 32960 | Gifford(u) | (561) | 6,278 | 6,240 |
| 33138 | Gladeview(u) | (954) | 15,637 | 18,919 |
| 33143 | Glenvar Heights(u) | (305) | 14,823 | 13,216 |
| 33999 | Golden Gate(u) | (941) | 14,148 | 4,327 |
| 33055 | Golden Glades(u) | (305) | 25,474 | 23,154 |
| 32733 | Goldenrod(u) | (407) | 12,362 | 13,677 |
| 32560 | Gonzalez(u) | (904) | 7,669 | 6,084 |
| 33170 | Goulds(u) | (305) | 7,284 | 7,078 |
| ..... | Greater Northdale(u) | | 16,318 | .... |
| 33463 | Greenacres City | (561) | 18,683 | 8,870 |
| *32561 | Gulf Breeze | (904) | 5,530 | 5,478 |
| 33581 | Gulf Gate Estates(u) | (813) | 11,622 | 9,248 |
| 33707 | Gulfport | (941) | 11,709 | 11,180 |
| *33844 | Haines City | (941) | 11,683 | 10,799 |
| *33009 | Hallandale | (305)/(954) | 30,997 | 36,517 |
| ..... | Hammocks(u) | | 10,897 | .... |
| ..... | Hamptons at Boca Raton(u) | | 11,686 | .... |
| *33010 | Hialeah | (305) | 188,008 | 145,254 |
| 33016 | Hialeah Gardens | (305) | 7,727 | 2,700 |
| ..... | Highpoint | | 13,818 | .... |
| *33455 | Hobe Sound(u) | (561) | 11,507 | 6,822 |
| *34689 | Holiday(u) | (813) | 19,360 | 18,392 |
| 32117 | Holly Hill | (904) | 11,141 | 9,953 |
| *33022 | Hollywood | (954) | 121,720 | 121,323 |
| *33030 | Homestead | (305) | 26,694 | 20,668 |
| 33039 | Homestead AFB(u) | (305) | 5,153 | 7,594 |
| 34447 | Homosassa Springs(u)† | (352) | 6,271 | 1,426 |
| *34667 | Hudson(u) | (813) | 7,344 | 5,799 |
| 33934 | Immokalee(u) | (941) | 14,120 | 11,038 |
| 32937 | Indian Harbour Beach | (407) | 6,933 | 5,967 |
| *34450 | Inverness | (352) | 5,797 | 4,095 |
| 33880 | Inwood(u) | (941) | 6,824 | 6,668 |
| ..... | Iona(u) | | 9,565 | .... |
| 33162 | Ives Estates(u) | (305) | 13,531 | 10,613 |
| *32203 | Jacksonville | (904) | 635,230 | 540,920 |
| 32250 | Jacksonville Beach | (904) | 17,839 | 15,462 |
| 33880 | Jan Phyl Village(u) | (941) | 5,308 | 2,785 |
| 33568 | Jasmine Estates(u) | (813) | 17,136 | 11,995 |
| *34957 | Jensen Beach(u) | (561) | 9,884 | 6,642 |
| *33458 | Jupiter | (561) | 24,907 | 9,868 |
| 33183 | Kendale Lakes(u) | (305) | 48,524 | 32,769 |
| 33256 | Kendall(u) | (305) | 87,271 | 73,758 |
| ..... | Kendall Lakes West(u) | (305) | 6,038 | .... |
| 33149 | Key Biscayne(u) | (305) | 8,854 | 6,313 |
| 33037 | Key Largo(u) | (305) | 11,336 | 7,447 |
| *33040 | Key West | (305) | 24,832 | 24,382 |
| *33573 | Kings Point(u) | (305) | 12,422 | 8,724 |
| *34744 | Kissimmee | (407) | 30,337 | 15,487 |
| *32159 | Lady Lake | (352) | 8,071 | 1,193 |
| *32055 | Lake City | (904) | 9,626 | 9,257 |
| *33804 | Lakeland | (941) | 70,576 | 47,406 |
| 33801 | Lakeland Highlands(u) | (941) | 9,972 | 10,426 |
| 32569 | Lake Lorraine(u) | (904) | 6,779 | 5,427 |
| 33054 | Lake Lucerne(u) | (305) | 9,478 | 9,762 |
| 33612 | Lake Magdalene(u) | (813) | 15,973 | 13,256 |
| *32746 | Lake Mary | (407) | 5,929 | 2,853 |
| 33403 | Lake Park | (561) | 6,704 | 6,909 |
| ..... | Lakes by the Bay(u) | | 5,615 | .... |
| 32073 | Lakeside(u) | (904) | 29,137 | 10,534 |
| *33853 | Lake Wales | (941) | 9,670 | 8,466 |
| 34951 | Lakewood Park(u) | (561) | 7,211 | 3,411 |
| *33461 | Lake Worth | (561) | 28,564 | 27,048 |
| 34639 | Land O'Lakes(u) | (813) | 7,892 | 4,515 |
| 33462 | Lantana | (561) | 8,392 | 8,048 |
| *34640 | Largo | (813) | 65,910 | 57,958 |
| 33313 | Lauderdale Lakes | (954) | 27,341 | 25,426 |
| 33313 | Lauderhill | (954) | 49,015 | 37,271 |
| 34272 | Laurel(u) | (941) | 8,245 | 6,368 |
| 33714 | Lealman(u) | (813) | 21,748 | 19,873 |
| *34748 | Leesburg | (352) | 14,783 | 13,191 |
| *33936 | Lehigh Acres(u) | (813) | 13,611 | 9,604 |
| 33033 | Leisure City(u) | (305) | 19,379 | 17,905 |
| 33074 | Lighthouse Point | (954) | 10,378 | 11,488 |
| 33177 | Lindgren Acres(u) | (305) | 22,290 | 11,986 |
| 32060 | Live Oak | (904) | 6,332 | 6,732 |
| 32860 | Lockhart(u) | (407) | 11,636 | 10,569 |
| 34228 | Longboat Key | (941) | 5,937 | 4,843 |
| *32750 | Longwood | (407) | 13,316 | 10,029 |
| 33549 | Lutz(u) | (813) | 10,552 | 5,555 |
| 32444 | Lynn Haven | (904) | 9,270 | 6,239 |
| ..... | McGregor(u) | | 6,504 | .... |
| *32751 | Maitland | (407) | 8,932 | 8,763 |
| 33550 | Mango(u) † | (813) | 8,700 | 6,493 |
| 33050 | Marathon(u) | (305) | 8,857 | 7,568 |
| *33937 | Marco(u) | (941) | 9,493 | 4,694 |
| 33063 | Margate | (954) | 42,985 | 35,900 |
| *32446 | Marianna | (904) | 6,292 | 7,006 |
| *32901 | Melbourne | (407) | 60,034 | 46,536 |
| 32666 | Melrose Park(u) | (954) | 6,477 | 5,672 |
| 33561 | Memphis(u) | (941) | 6,760 | 5,501 |
| *32953 | Merritt Island(u) | (407) | 32,886 | 30,708 |
| *33101 | Miami | (305) | 358,648 | 346,681 |
| *33152 | Miami Beach | (305) | 92,639 | 96,298 |
| 33023 | Miami Gardens-Utopia-Carver(u) | (954) | 7,448 | 8,482 |
| 33014 | Miami Lakes(u) | (305) | 12,750 | 9,809 |
| 33153 | Miami Shores | (305) | 10,084 | 9,244 |
| 33166 | Miami Springs | (305) | 13,268 | 12,350 |
| 32976 | Micco(u) | (561) | 8,757 | 3,585 |
| *32068 | Middleburg(u) | (904) | 6,223 | .... |
| *32570 | Milton | (904) | 7,216 | 7,206 |
| 32754 | Mims(u) | (407) | 9,412 | 7,583 |
| 33023 | Miramar | (954) | 40,663 | 32,813 |
| 32757 | Mount Dora | (352) | 7,316 | 5,883 |
| 32526 | Myrtle Grove(u) | (904) | 17,402 | 14,238 |
| *33940 | Naples | (941) | 19,505 | 17,581 |
| 33940 | Naples Park(u) | (941) | 8,002 | 5,438 |
| 33092 | Naranja(u)† | (305) | 5,790 | 10,381 |
| 32266 | Neptune Beach | (904) | 6,816 | 5,248 |
| *34653 | New Port Richey | (813) | 14,044 | 11,196 |
| 33552 | New Port Richey East(u) | (813) | 9,683 | 6,147 |
| *32168 | New Smyrna Beach | (904) | 16,549 | 13,557 |
| *32578 | Niceville | (904) | 10,509 | 8,543 |
| 33269 | Norland(u) | (305) | 22,109 | 19,471 |
| 33308 | North Andrews Gardens(u) | (954) | 9,002 | 8,994 |
| 33141 | North Bay Village | (305) | 5,383 | 4,920 |
| 33918 | North Fort Myers(u) | (941) | 30,027 | 22,808 |
| 33068 | North Lauderdale | (954) | 26,473 | 18,653 |
| 33961 | North Miami | (305) | 50,001 | 42,566 |
| 33160 | North Miami Beach | (305) | 35,361 | 36,553 |
| 33940 | North Naples(u) | (941) | 13,422 | 7,950 |
| 33408 | North Palm Beach | (561) | 11,284 | 11,344 |
| 34287 | North Port | (941) | 11,973 | 6,205 |
| 34234 | North Sarasota(u) | (941) | 6,702 | 4,997 |
| 33334 | Oakland Park | (305) | 26,326 | 22,944 |
| 33860 | Oak Ridge(u) | (813) | 15,388 | 15,477 |
| *34478 | Ocala | (352) | 42,045 | 37,170 |
| 32548 | Ocean City(u) | (904) | 5,422 | 5,582 |
| 32761 | Ocoee | (407) | 12,778 | 7,803 |
| 33163 | Ojus(u) | (305) | 15,519 | 17,344 |
| 34677 | Oldsmar | (813) | 8,361 | 2,608 |
| 33265 | Olympia Heights(u) | (305) | 37,792 | 33,112 |
| *33054 | Opa-Locka | (305) | 15,283 | 14,460 |
| 33054 | Opa-Locka North(u) | (305) | 6,568 | 5,721 |
| *32763 | Orange City | (904) | 5,347 | 2,795 |
| *32073 | Orange Park | (904) | 9,488 | 8,766 |
| *32802 | Orlando | (407) | 164,674 | 128,291 |
| 32861 | Orlo Vista(u) | (407) | 5,990 | 6,474 |
| *32174 | Ormond Beach | (904) | 29,721 | 21,436 |
| 32074 | Ormond By-The-Sea(u) | (904) | 8,157 | 7,665 |
| *32765 | Oviedo | (407) | 11,114 | 3,074 |
| 32571 | Pace(u) | (904) | 6,277 | 5,006 |
| ..... | Page Park-Pine Manor(u) | | 5,116 | .... |
| 33476 | Pahokee | (561) | 6,822 | 6,346 |
| *32177 | Palatka | (904) | 10,447 | 10,175 |
| *32906 | Palm Bay | (407) | 62,543 | 18,560 |
| 33480 | Palm Beach | (561) | 9,814 | 9,729 |
| 33403 | Palm Beach Gardens | (561) | 22,990 | 14,407 |
| 32136 | Palm Coast(u) | (904) | 14,287 | 2,837 |
| *34221 | Palmetto | (941) | 9,268 | 8,637 |
| 33157 | Palmetto Estates(u) | (305) | 12,293 | 11,116 |
| *34683 | Palm Harbor(u) | (813) | 50,256 | 5,215 |
| *33601 | Palm River-Clair Mel(u) | (813) | 13,691 | 14,447 |
| 33460 | Palm Springs | (561) | 9,763 | 8,166 |
| 33012 | Palm Springs North(u) | (305) | 5,300 | 5,838 |
| 32082 | Palm Valley | (904) | 9,960 | .... |
| *32401 | Panama City | (904) | 34,396 | 33,346 |
| 33029 | Pembroke Pines | (954) | 65,566 | 35,776 |
| *32502 | Pensacola | (904) | 59,198 | 57,619 |
| 33257 | Perrine(u) | (305) | 15,576 | 16,129 |
| 32347 | Perry | (904) | 7,151 | 8,254 |
| 32859 | Pine Castle(u) | (407) | 8,276 | 9,992 |
| 32858 | Pine Hills(u) | (407) | 35,322 | 31,029 |
| ..... | Pine Island Ridge | | 5,244 | .... |
| *34665 | Pinellas Park | (813) | 43,571 | 32,811 |
| 33168 | Pinewood(u) | (305) | 15,518 | 14,346 |
| 33318 | Plantation | (954) | 66,814 | 48,653 |
| *33566 | Plant City | (813) | 22,754 | 17,064 |
| *33060 | Pompano Beach | (954) | 72,411 | 52,618 |
| 33064 | Pompano Beach Highlands(u) | (954) | 17,915 | 16,154 |
| *33952 | Port Charlotte(u) | (941) | 41,535 | 25,770 |
| 32124 | Port Orange | (904) | 35,399 | 18,756 |
| 32927 | Port St. John(u) | (407) | 8,933 | 1,837 |
| *34981 | Port St. Lucie | (561) | 55,761 | 14,690 |
| 34992 | Port Salerno(u) | (561) | 7,786 | 4,511 |
| 33032 | Princeton(u) | (305) | 7,073 | .... |
| *33950 | Punta Gorda | (941) | 10,637 | 6,797 |
| *32351 | Quincy | (904) | 7,452 | 8,591 |
| 33156 | Richmond Heights(u) | (305) | 8,583 | 8,577 |
| 33312 | Riverland(u) | (954) | 5,376 | 5,919 |
| 33569 | Riverview(u) | (813) | 6,478 | .... |
| 33419 | Riviera Beach | (561) | 27,646 | 26,489 |
| *32955 | Rockledge | (407) | 16,023 | 11,877 |
| 33411 | Royal Palm Beach | (561) | 15,532 | 3,423 |
| *33570 | Ruskin(u) | (813) | 6,046 | 5,117 |
| 34695 | Safety Harbor | (813) | 15,120 | 6,461 |
| *32084 | Saint Augustine | (904) | 11,695 | 11,985 |
| *34769 | Saint Cloud | (407) | 12,684 | 7,840 |
| *33733 | Saint Petersburg | (813) | 240,318 | 238,647 |
| 33736 | Saint Petersburg Beach | (813) | 9,200 | 9,354 |
| 33912 | San Carlos Park(u) | (941) | 11,785 | 3,590 |
| 33432 | Sandalfoot Cove(u) | (305) | 14,214 | 5,299 |
| *32771 | Sanford | (407) | 32,387 | 23,176 |
| 33957 | Sanibel | (941) | 5,468 | 3,363 |

| ZIP | Place | | 1990 | 1980 |
|---|---|---|---|---|
| *34230 | Sarasota | (941) | 50,897 | 48,868 |
| 33577 | Sarasota Springs(u) | (941) | 16,088 | 13,860 |
| 32937 | Satellite Beach | (407) | 9,889 | 9,163 |
| 33055 | Scott Lake(u) | (305) | 14,588 | 14,154 |
| *32958 | Sebastian | (561) | 10,248 | 2,831 |
| *33870 | Sebring | (941) | 8,841 | 8,736 |
| 33584 | Seffner(u) | (813) | 5,371 | .... |
| *34640 | Seminole | (813) | 9,251 | 4,856 |
| *34242 | Siesta Key(u) | (941) | 7,772 | 7,010 |
| 34472 | Silver Springs Shores(u) | (352) | 6,421 | 3,983 |
| 32809 | Sky Lake(u) | (407) | 6,202 | 6,692 |
| 32703 | South Apopka(u) | (407) | 6,360 | 5,687 |
| 33505 | South Bradenton(u) | (941) | 20,398 | 14,297 |
| 32121 | South Daytona | (904) | 12,488 | 11,252 |
| 34277 | Southgate(u) | (813) | 7,324 | 7,322 |
| 34233 | South Gate Ridge(u) | (941) | 5,924 | 4,259 |
| 33243 | South Miami | (305) | 10,404 | 10,895 |
| 33157 | South Miami Heights(u) | (305) | 30,030 | 23,559 |
| 33707 | South Pasadena | (813) | 5,644 | 4,188 |
| 32937 | South Patrick Shores(u) | (407) | 10,249 | 9,816 |
| 34230 | South Sarasota(u) | (941) | 5,298 | 4,267 |
| 33595 | South Venice(u) | (813) | 11,951 | 8,075 |
| 32401 | Springfield | (904) | 8,719 | 7,220 |
| *34601 | Spring Hill(u) | (352) | 31,117 | 6,468 |
| 32091 | Starke | (904) | 5,226 | 5,306 |
| *34994 | Stuart | (561) | 11,936 | 9,467 |
| 33573 | Sun City Center(u) | (813) | 8,326 | 5,605 |
| 33160 | Sunny Isles(u) | (305) | 11,772 | 12,564 |
| *33322 | Sunrise | (954) | 65,683 | 39,681 |
| 33283 | Sunset(u) | (305) | 15,810 | 13,531 |
| 33144 | Sweetwater | (305) | 13,909 | 8,067 |
| *32301 | Tallahassee | (904) | 124,773 | 81,548 |
| 33320 | Tamarac | (954) | 44,822 | 29,376 |
| 33144 | Tamiami(u) | (305) | 33,845 | 17,607 |
| *33602 | Tampa | (813) | 280,015 | 271,577 |
| *34689 | Tarpon Springs | (813) | 17,874 | 13,251 |
| 32778 | Tavares | (352) | 7,383 | 4,398 |
| *33601 | Temple Terrace | (813) | 16,444 | 11,097 |
| *32780 | Titusville | (407) | 39,394 | 31,910 |
| 32601 | Town 'n' Country(u) | (813) | 60,946 | 37,834 |
| 33706 | Treasure Island | (813) | 7,266 | 6,316 |
| 32867 | Union Park(u) | (407) | 6,890 | 19,175 |
| 33620 | University West(u)† | (813) | 23,760 | 24,514 |
| 32401 | Upper Grand Lagoon(u) | (904) | 7,855 | 3,314 |
| 32580 | Valparaiso | (904) | 6,316 | 6,142 |
| *34285 | Venice | (941) | 17,052 | 12,153 |
| 33595 | Venice Gardens(u) | (813) | 7,701 | 6,568 |
| *32960 | Vero Beach | (561) | 17,350 | 16,176 |
| 32960 | Vero Beach South(u) | (561) | 16,973 | 12,636 |
| ..... | Villages of Oriole(u) | | 5,698 | .... |
| 33901 | Villas(u) | (813) | 9,898 | 8,724 |
| 32507 | Warrington(u) | (904) | 16,040 | 15,792 |
| 33314 | Washington Park(u) | (954) | 6,930 | 7,240 |
| 32703 | Wekiva Springs(u) | (407) | 23,026 | 13,386 |
| 33414 | Wellington(u) | (561) | 20,670 | 4,622 |
| 33155 | Westchester(u) | (305) | 29,883 | 29,272 |
| ..... | Westgate-Belvedere Homes(u) | | 6,880 | .... |
| 33138 | West Little River(u) | (305) | 33,575 | 32,492 |
| 32904 | West Melbourne | (407) | 8,398 | 5,078 |
| 33144 | West Miami | (305) | 5,727 | 6,076 |
| *33406 | West Palm Beach | (561) | 67,764 | 63,305 |
| ..... | West Park(u) | | 10,347 | 9,003 |
| 32505 | West Pensacola(u) | (904) | 22,107 | 24,371 |
| 33168 | Westview(u) | (305) | 9,668 | 9,102 |
| 33165 | Westwood Lakes(u) | (305) | 11,522 | 11,478 |
| ..... | Whiskey Creek(u) | | 5,061 | .... |
| 33305 | Wilton Manors | (954) | 11,804 | 12,742 |
| 33803 | Winston(u) | (813) | 9,118 | 9,315 |
| *34787 | Winter Garden | (407) | 9,863 | 6,789 |
| *33880 | Winter Haven | (941) | 24,725 | 21,119 |
| *32789 | Winter Park | (407) | 22,623 | 22,339 |
| *32707 | Winter Springs | (407) | 22,151 | 10,475 |
| 32547 | Wright(u) | (904) | 18,945 | 13,011 |
| 32097 | Yulee(u) | (904) | 6,915 | 3,168 |
| *33540 | Zephyrhills | (813) | 8,220 | 5,742 |

## Georgia

| ZIP | Place | | 1990 | 1980 |
|---|---|---|---|---|
| 31620 | Adel | (912) | 5,093 | 5,592 |
| *31706 | Albany | (912) | 78,804 | 74,425 |
| *30201 | Alpharetta | (770) | 13,002 | 3,128 |
| 31709 | Americus | (912) | 16,516 | 16,120 |
| *30603 | Athens | (706) | 45,734 | 42,549 |
| *30301 | Atlanta | (404) | 393,929 | 425,022 |
| *30903 | Augusta | (706) | 44,707 | 47,532 |
| 31717 | Bainbridge | (912) | 10,803 | 10,553 |
| 30032 | Belvedere Park(u) | (404) | 18,089 | 17,766 |
| 31723 | Blakely | (912) | 5,595 | 5,880 |
| *31520 | Brunswick | (912) | 16,433 | 17,605 |
| *30518 | Buford | (404) | 8,771 | 6,578 |
| 31728 | Cairo | (912) | 9,035 | 8,777 |
| *30701 | Calhoun | (706) | 7,135 | 5,563 |
| 31730 | Camilla | (912) | 5,124 | 5,414 |
| 30032 | Candler-McAfee(u) | (404) | 29,491 | 27,306 |
| *30117 | Carrollton | (770) | 16,029 | 14,078 |
| 30120 | Cartersville | (770) | 12,037 | 9,247 |
| 30125 | Cedartown | (770) | 7,976 | 8,619 |
| 30366 | Chamblee | (404) | 7,668 | 7,137 |
| 30021 | Clarkston | (404) | 5,385 | 4,539 |
| 30337 | College Park | (404) | 20,645 | 24,632 |
| *31908 | Columbus | (706) | 178,681 | 169,441 |
| 30027 | Conley(u) | (404) | 5,528 | 6,033 |
| *30208 | Conyers | (404) | 7,380 | 6,567 |
| 31015 | Cordele | (912) | 10,833 | 11,184 |
| ..... | Country Club Estates(u) | | 7,500 | .... |
| 30209 | Covington | (770) | 9,860 | 10,586 |
| *30720 | Dalton | (706) | 22,218 | 20,581 |
| 31742 | Dawson | (912) | 5,295 | 5,699 |
| *30030 | Decatur (DeKalb) | (404) | 17,304 | 18,404 |
| 31520 | Dock Junction(u) | (912) | 7,094 | 6,189 |
| 30362 | Doraville | (404) | 7,626 | 7,414 |
| 31533 | Douglas | (912) | 10,464 | 10,980 |
| *30134 | Douglasville | (404) | 11,635 | 7,641 |
| 30333 | Druid Hills(u) | (404) | 12,174 | 12,700 |
| *31021 | Dublin | (912) | 16,312 | 16,083 |
| 30136 | Duluth | (404) | 9,821 | 2,956 |
| 30356 | Dunwoody(u) | (404) | 26,302 | 17,768 |
| 31023 | Eastman | (912) | 5,241 | 5,330 |
| 30364 | East Point | (404) | 34,595 | 37,486 |
| 30635 | Elberton | (706) | 5,682 | 5,686 |
| 30809 | Evans(u) | (706) | 13,713 | .... |
| 30060 | Fair Oaks(u) | (404) | 6,996 | 8,486 |
| 30535 | Fairview(u) | (706) | 6,444 | 6,558 |
| 30214 | Fayetteville | (404) | 5,827 | 2,715 |
| 31750 | Fitzgerald | (912) | 8,901 | 10,187 |
| *30050 | Forest Park | (404) | 16,958 | 18,782 |
| 31905 | Fort Benning South(u) | (706) | 14,617 | 15,074 |
| 30905 | Fort Gordon(u) | (706) | 9,140 | 14,069 |
| 30742 | Fort Oglethorpe | (706) | 5,880 | 5,443 |
| 31314 | Fort Stewart(u) | (912) | 13,774 | 15,031 |
| 31030 | Fort Valley | (912) | 8,198 | 9,000 |
| 30605 | Gaines School(u) | (706) | 11,354 | .... |
| *30501 | Gainesville | (770) | 17,885 | 15,280 |
| 31408 | Garden City | (912) | 7,410 | 6,895 |
| 31754 | Georgetown(u) | (912) | 5,554 | 2,785 |
| 30316 | Gresham Park(u) | (404) | 9,000 | 6,232 |
| *30223 | Griffin | (770) | 21,325 | 20,728 |
| 30354 | Hapeville | (404) | 5,483 | 6,166 |
| 31313 | Hinesville | (912) | 21,596 | 11,309 |
| 31545 | Jesup | (912) | 8,958 | 9,418 |
| 30144 | Kennesaw | (404) | 8,936 | 5,095 |
| 31548 | Kingsland | (912) | 5,474 | 2,008 |
| 30728 | La Fayette | (706) | 6,313 | 6,517 |
| *30240 | La Grange | (706) | 25,574 | 24,204 |
| 30741 | Lakeview(u) | (706) | 5,237 | 5,403 |
| *30245 | Lawrenceville | (404) | 17,250 | 8,928 |
| *30247 | Lilburn | (404) | 9,295 | 3,765 |
| 30057 | Lithia Springs(u) | (404) | 11,403 | 9,145 |
| 30059 | Mableton(u) | (404) | 25,725 | 25,111 |
| *31201 | Macon | (912) | 107,365 | 116,896 |
| *30060 | Marietta | (404) | 44,129 | 30,821 |
| 30917 | Martinez(u) | (706) | 33,731 | 16,472 |
| 31061 | Milledgeville | (912) | 17,727 | 12,176 |
| *30655 | Monroe | (770) | 9,759 | 8,854 |
| *30260 | Morrow | (404) | 5,168 | 3,791 |
| *31768 | Moultrie | (912) | 14,865 | 15,105 |
| 30087 | Mountain Park(u) | (404) | 11,025 | 9,425 |
| *30263 | Newnan | (770) | 12,497 | 11,449 |
| *30071 | Norcross | (404) | 5,947 | 3,363 |
| 30319 | North Atlanta(u) | (404) | 27,812 | 30,521 |
| 30033 | North Decatur(u) | (404) | 13,936 | 11,830 |
| 30033 | North Druid Hills(u) | (404) | 14,170 | 12,438 |
| 30032 | Panthersville(u) | (404) | 9,874 | 11,366 |
| 30269 | Peachtree City | (404) | 19,027 | 6,429 |
| 31069 | Perry | (912) | 9,452 | 9,453 |
| 30073 | Powder Springs | (404) | 6,862 | 3,381 |
| 31643 | Quitman | (912) | 5,292 | 5,188 |
| 30074 | Redan(u) | (404) | 24,376 | .... |
| *30274 | Riverdale | (404) | 9,455 | 7,121 |
| *30161 | Rome | (706) | 30,325 | 28,915 |
| *30077 | Roswell | (404) | 47,986 | 23,337 |
| 31558 | Saint Marys | (912) | 8,204 | 3,596 |
| 31522 | Saint Simons Island(u) | (912) | 12,026 | 6,566 |
| 31082 | Sandersville | (912) | 6,290 | 6,137 |
| 30358 | Sandy Springs(u) | (404) | 67,842 | 46,877 |
| *31402 | Savannah | (912) | 137,812 | 141,654 |
| 30079 | Scottdale(u) | (404) | 8,636 | 8,770 |
| *30080 | Smyrna | (404) | 30,981 | 20,312 |
| 30278 | Snellville | (404) | 12,084 | 8,514 |
| 30901 | South Augusta(u) | (706) | 55,998 | 51,072 |
| *30458 | Statesboro | (912) | 15,854 | 14,866 |
| *30086 | Stone Mountain | (404) | 6,544 | 4,867 |
| 30747 | Summerville | (706) | 5,025 | 4,878 |
| 30401 | Swainsboro | (912) | 7,361 | 7,602 |
| 31791 | Sylvester | (912) | 6,023 | 5,860 |
| 30286 | Thomaston | (706) | 9,127 | 9,682 |
| *31792 | Thomasville | (912) | 17,554 | 18,463 |
| 30824 | Thomson | (706) | 6,862 | 7,001 |
| *31794 | Tifton | (912) | 14,215 | 13,749 |
| 30577 | Toccoa | (706) | 8,720 | 8,869 |
| *30084 | Tucker(u) | (404) | 25,781 | 25,399 |
| 30291 | Union City | (404) | 8,887 | 4,780 |
| *31603 | Valdosta | (912) | 40,038 | 37,596 |
| 30474 | Vidalia | (912) | 11,118 | 10,393 |
| 30180 | Villa Rica | (770) | 6,542 | 3,420 |
| 30339 | Vinings(u) | (404) | 7,417 | .... |
| *31088 | Warner Robins | (912) | 43,861 | 39,893 |
| *31501 | Waycross | (912) | 16,410 | 19,371 |

| ZIP | Place | | 1990 | 1980 |
|---|---|---|---|---|
| 30830 | Waynesboro | (706) | 5,669 | 5,760 |
| 30901 | West Augusta(u) | (706) | 27,637 | 24,242 |
| 31410 | Wilmington Island(u) | (912) | 11,230 | 7,546 |
| 30680 | Winder | (770) | 7,373 | 6,705 |

## Hawaii (808)

*See note on page 390*

| ZIP | Place | 1990 | 1980 |
|---|---|---|---|
| 96701 | Aiea(u) | 8,906 | 32,879 |
| 96818 | Aliamanu(u) | 8,835 | .... |
| 96706 | Ewa Beach(u) | 14,315 | 14,369 |
| ..... | Halawa(u) | 13,408 | .... |
| 96744 | Heeia(u) | 5,010 | 5,432 |
| 96853 | Hickam Housing(u) | 6,553 | 4,425 |
| *96720 | Hilo(u) | 37,808 | 35,269 |
| *96820 | Honolulu(u) | 365,272 | 365,048 |
| 96732 | Kahului(u) | 16,889 | 12,978 |
| 96734 | Kailua(u) | 9,126 | 4,751 |
| 96863 | Kailua(u) | 36,818 | 35,812 |
| 96744 | Kaneohe(u) | 35,448 | 29,919 |
| ..... | Kaneohe Station(u) | 11,662 | 11,615 |
| 96746 | Kapaa(u) | 8,149 | 4,467 |
| 96753 | Kihei(u) | 11,107 | 5,644 |
| *96761 | Lahaina(u) | 9,073 | 6,095 |
| 96762 | Laie(u) | 5,577 | 4,643 |
| 96766 | Lihue(u) | 5,536 | 4,000 |
| 96792 | Maili(u) | 6,059 | 5,026 |
| 96792 | Makaha(u) | 7,990 | 6,582 |
| 96706 | Makakilo(u) | 9,828 | 7,691 |
| 96768 | Makawao(u) | 5,405 | 2,900 |
| 96789 | Mililani Town(u) | 29,359 | 21,365 |
| 96792 | Nanakuli(u) | 9,575 | 8,185 |
| 96782 | Pearl City(u) | 30,993 | 42,575 |
| 96788 | Pukalani(u) | 5,879 | 3,950 |
| 96786 | Schofield Barracks(u) | 19,597 | 18,851 |
| ..... | Village Park(u) | 7,407 | .... |
| 96786 | Wahiawa(u) | 17,386 | 16,911 |
| 96792 | Waianae(u) | 8,758 | 7,941 |
| 96793 | Wailuku(u) | 10,688 | 10,260 |
| ..... | Waimalu(u) | 29,967 | .... |
| 96796 | Waimea(u) | 5,972 | 1,179 |
| 96797 | Waipahu(u) | 31,435 | 29,139 |
| 96797 | Waipio(u) | 11,812 | .... |
| 96786 | Waipio Acres(u) | 5,304 | 4,091 |

## Idaho (208)

| ZIP | Place | 1990 | 1980 |
|---|---|---|---|
| 83401 | Ammon | 5,002 | 4,669 |
| 83221 | Blackfoot | 9,646 | 10,065 |
| *83707 | Boise City | 125,551 | 102,249 |
| 83318 | Burley | 8,702 | 8,761 |
| *83605 | Caldwell | 18,400 | 17,699 |
| 83202 | Chubbuck | 7,794 | 7,052 |
| *83814 | Coeur D'Alene | 24,561 | 19,913 |
| 83714 | Garden City | 6,369 | 4,571 |
| *83402 | Idaho Falls | 43,973 | 39,739 |
| 83338 | Jerome | 6,529 | 6,891 |
| 83501 | Lewiston | 28,082 | 27,986 |
| *83642 | Meridian | 9,596 | 6,658 |
| 83843 | Moscow | 18,398 | 16,513 |
| 83647 | Mountain Home | 7,913 | 7,540 |
| 83648 | Mountain Home AFB(u) | 5,936 | 6,403 |
| *83651 | Nampa | 28,365 | 25,112 |
| 83661 | Payette | 5,672 | 5,448 |
| *83201 | Pocatello | 46,117 | 46,340 |
| 83854 | Post Falls | 7,349 | 5,736 |
| 83440 | Rexburg | 14,298 | 11,559 |
| 83350 | Rupert | 5,455 | 5,476 |
| 83864 | Sandpoint | 5,203 | 4,460 |
| *83301 | Twin Falls | 27,634 | 26,209 |

## Illinois

| ZIP | Place | | 1990 | 1980 |
|---|---|---|---|---|
| 60101 | Addison | (630) | 32,053 | 29,826 |
| 60102 | Algonquin | (847) | 11,693 | 5,834 |
| 60658 | Alsip | (708) | 18,227 | 17,134 |
| 62002 | Alton | (618) | 33,064 | 34,171 |
| 60002 | Antioch | (847) | 6,105 | 4,419 |
| *60005 | Arlington Heights | (847) | 75,463 | 66,116 |
| *60505 | Aurora | (630) | 99,556 | 81,293 |
| *60010 | Barrington | (847) | 9,538 | 9,029 |
| 60103 | Bartlett | (630) | 19,395 | 13,254 |
| 61607 | Bartonville | (309) | 5,671 | 6,137 |
| 60510 | Batavia | (630) | 17,076 | 12,574 |
| 60085 | Beach Park† | (847) | 9,492 | 8,468 |
| 62618 | Beardstown | (217) | 5,270 | 6,338 |
| *62220 | Belleville | (618) | 42,806 | 41,580 |
| 60104 | Bellwood | (708) | 20,241 | 19,811 |
| 61008 | Belvidere | (815) | 15,962 | 15,176 |
| 60106 | Bensenville | (630) | 17,767 | 16,106 |
| 62812 | Benton | (618) | 7,216 | 7,778 |
| 60163 | Berkeley | (708) | 5,137 | 5,467 |
| 60402 | Berwyn | (708) | 45,426 | 46,849 |
| 62010 | Bethalto | (618) | 9,507 | 8,630 |
| 60108 | Bloomingdale | (630) | 16,614 | 12,656 |
| *61701 | Bloomington | (309) | 51,889 | 44,189 |
| 60406 | Blue Island | (708) | 21,203 | 21,855 |
| 60440 | Bolingbrook | (630) | 40,843 | 37,261 |
| 60538 | Boulder Hill(u) | (630) | 8,894 | 9,333 |
| 60914 | Bourbonnais | (815) | 13,929 | 13,280 |
| 60915 | Bradley | (815) | 10,918 | 11,015 |
| 60455 | Bridgeview | (708) | 14,402 | 14,155 |
| 60153 | Broadview | (708) | 8,538 | 8,618 |
| 60513 | Brookfield | (708) | 18,876 | 19,395 |
| 60089 | Buffalo Grove | (847) | 36,417 | 22,230 |
| 60459 | Burbank | (708) | 27,600 | 28,462 |
| 60521 | Burr Ridge | (630) | 7,684 | 3,838 |
| 62206 | Cahokia | (618) | 17,550 | 18,904 |
| 60409 | Calumet City | (708) | 37,840 | 39,697 |
| 60643 | Calumet Park | (708) | 8,418 | 8,788 |
| 61520 | Canton | (309) | 13,959 | 14,626 |
| *62901 | Carbondale | (618) | 27,033 | 26,414 |
| 62626 | Carlinville | (217) | 5,416 | 5,439 |
| 62821 | Carmi | (618) | 5,626 | 6,107 |
| *60188 | Carol Stream | (630) | 31,759 | 15,472 |
| 60110 | Carpentersville | (847) | 23,049 | 23,272 |
| 60013 | Cary | (847) | 10,043 | 6,640 |
| 62801 | Centralia | (618) | 14,274 | 15,126 |
| 62206 | Centreville | (618) | 7,489 | 9,747 |
| *61821 | Champaign | (217) | 63,502 | 58,267 |
| 61920 | Charleston | (217) | 20,398 | 19,355 |
| 62629 | Chatham | (217) | 6,074 | 5,597 |
| 62233 | Chester | (618) | 8,204 | 8,401 |
| *60607 | Chicago | (312)/(773) | 2,783,726 | 3,005,072 |
| 60411 | Chicago Heights | (708) | 32,966 | 37,026 |
| 60415 | Chicago Ridge | (708) | 13,643 | 13,473 |
| 61523 | Chillicothe | (309) | 5,959 | 6,176 |
| 60650 | Cicero | (708) | 67,436 | 61,232 |
| 60514 | Clarendon Hills | (630) | 6,994 | 6,870 |
| 61727 | Clinton | (217) | 7,437 | 8,014 |
| 62234 | Collinsville | (618) | 22,424 | 19,475 |
| 62236 | Columbia | (618) | 5,524 | 4,269 |
| 60478 | Country Club Hills | (708) | 15,431 | 14,676 |
| 60525 | Countryside | (708) | 5,961 | 6,242 |
| 60435 | Crest Hill | (815) | 10,999 | 9,252 |
| 60445 | Crestwood | (708) | 10,823 | 10,852 |
| 60417 | Crete | (708) | 6,773 | 5,417 |
| 61610 | Creve Coeur | (309) | 5,938 | 6,851 |
| *60014 | Crystal Lake | (815) | 24,696 | 18,590 |
| *61832 | Danville | (217) | 33,828 | 38,985 |
| 60561 | Darien | (630) | 18,148 | 14,956 |
| *62525 | Decatur | (217) | 83,900 | 93,939 |
| 60015 | Deerfield | (847) | 17,327 | 17,432 |
| 60115 | De Kalb | (815) | 35,076 | 33,157 |
| *60018 | Des Plaines | (847) | 53,414 | 53,568 |
| 61021 | Dixon | (815) | 15,134 | 15,710 |
| 60419 | Dolton | (708) | 23,956 | 24,766 |
| *60515 | Downers Grove | (630) | 46,845 | 42,259 |
| 62832 | Du Quoin | (618) | 6,697 | 6,594 |
| 62024 | East Alton | (618) | 7,063 | 7,096 |
| 61244 | East Moline | (309) | 20,147 | 20,907 |
| 61611 | East Peoria | (309) | 21,378 | 22,385 |
| *62201 | East St. Louis | (618) | 40,944 | 55,200 |
| 62025 | Edwardsville | (618) | 14,582 | 12,480 |
| 62401 | Effingham | (217) | 11,927 | 11,270 |
| *60120 | Elgin | (847) | 77,010 | 63,668 |
| *60009 | Elk Grove Village | (847) | 33,429 | 28,679 |
| 60126 | Elmhurst | (630) | 42,029 | 44,276 |
| 60635 | Elmwood Park | (708) | 23,206 | 24,016 |
| *60201 | Evanston | (847) | 73,233 | 73,706 |
| 60642 | Evergreen Park | (708) | 20,874 | 22,260 |
| 62837 | Fairfield | (618) | 5,442 | 5,944 |
| 62208 | Fairview Heights | (618) | 14,351 | 12,111 |
| 62839 | Flora | (618) | 5,093 | 5,379 |
| 60422 | Flossmoor | (708) | 8,651 | 8,423 |
| 60130 | Forest Park | (708) | 14,918 | 15,177 |
| 60020 | Fox Lake | (847) | 7,539 | 6,831 |
| 60423 | Frankfort | (815) | 7,180 | 4,357 |
| ..... | Frankfort Square(u) | (815) | 6,227 | .... |
| 60131 | Franklin Park | (847) | 18,485 | 17,507 |
| 61032 | Freeport | (815) | 25,840 | 26,266 |
| 60030 | Gages Lake(u) | (847) | 8,349 | 3,814 |
| *61401 | Galesburg | (309) | 33,530 | 35,305 |
| 61254 | Geneseo | (309) | 5,990 | 6,373 |
| 60134 | Geneva | (630) | 12,625 | 9,881 |
| 62034 | Glen Carbon | (618) | 7,774 | 5,197 |
| 60022 | Glencoe | (847) | 8,499 | 9,200 |
| 60139 | Glendale Heights | (630) | 27,915 | 23,251 |
| *60137 | Glen Ellyn | (630) | 24,919 | 23,691 |
| 60025 | Glenview | (847) | 37,052 | 32,060 |
| 60425 | Glenwood | (708) | 9,289 | 10,538 |
| 62035 | Godfrey(u) | (618) | 5,436 | .... |
| ..... | Goodings Grove(u) | (815) | 14,054 | .... |
| 62040 | Granite City | (618) | 32,766 | 36,815 |
| 60030 | Grayslake | (847) | 7,388 | 5,260 |
| 62246 | Greenville | (618) | 5,108 | 5,271 |
| 60031 | Gurnee | (847) | 13,715 | 7,179 |
| *60103 | Hanover Park | (630) | 32,918 | 28,719 |
| 62946 | Harrisburg | (618) | 9,318 | 10,410 |
| 60033 | Harvard | (815) | 5,975 | 5,126 |
| 60426 | Harvey | (708) | 29,771 | 35,810 |
| 60656 | Harwood Heights | (708) | 7,680 | 8,228 |
| 60429 | Hazel Crest | (708) | 13,334 | 13,973 |
| 62948 | Herrin | (618) | 10,857 | 10,708 |

| ZIP | Place | | 1990 | 1980 |
|---|---|---|---|---|
| 60457 | Hickory Hills | (708) | 13,021 | 13,778 |
| 62249 | Highland | (618) | 7,546 | 7,122 |
| *60035 | Highland Park | (847) | 30,575 | 30,599 |
| 60040 | Highwood | (847) | 5,331 | 5,455 |
| 60162 | Hillside | (708) | 7,672 | 8,279 |
| *60521 | Hinsdale | (630) | 16,029 | 16,726 |
| *60195 | Hoffman Estates | (847) | 46,363 | 37,272 |
| 60430 | Homewood | (708) | 19,278 | 19,724 |
| 60942 | Hoopeston | (217) | 5,871 | 6,411 |
| 60067 | Inverness | (847) | 6,516 | 4,046 |
| 60143 | Itasca | (630) | 6,947 | 7,129 |
| *62650 | Jacksonville | (217) | 19,327 | 20,284 |
| 62052 | Jerseyville | (618) | 7,382 | 7,506 |
| *60436 | Joliet | (815) | 77,217 | 77,956 |
| 60458 | Justice | (708) | 11,137 | 10,552 |
| 60901 | Kankakee | (815) | 27,541 | 29,633 |
| 61443 | Kewanee | (309) | 12,969 | 14,508 |
| 60525 | La Grange | (708) | 15,362 | 15,693 |
| 60525 | La Grange Park | (708) | 12,861 | 13,359 |
| 60044 | Lake Bluff | (847) | 5,486 | 4,434 |
| 60045 | Lake Forest | (847) | 17,836 | 15,245 |
| 60102 | Lake in the Hills | (847) | 5,900 | 5,651 |
| 60047 | Lake Zurich | (847) | 14,927 | 8,225 |
| 60438 | Lansing | (708) | 28,131 | 29,039 |
| 61301 | La Salle | (815) | 9,717 | 10,347 |
| 60439 | Lemont | (630) | 7,359 | 5,640 |
| *60048 | Libertyville | (847) | 19,174 | 16,520 |
| 62656 | Lincoln | (217) | 15,418 | 16,327 |
| 60645 | Lincolnwood | (847) | 11,365 | 11,921 |
| 60046 | Lindenhurst | (847) | 8,044 | 6,220 |
| 60532 | Lisle | (630) | 19,584 | 13,638 |
| 62056 | Litchfield | (217) | 6,883 | 7,204 |
| 60441 | Lockport | (815) | 9,401 | 9,192 |
| 60148 | Lombard | (630) | 39,408 | 36,879 |
| *61130 | Loves Park | (815) | 15,457 | 13,192 |
| 60411 | Lynwood | (708) | 6,535 | 4,195 |
| 60534 | Lyons (Cook) | (708) | 9,828 | 9,925 |
| *60050 | McHenry | (815) | 16,343 | 10,737 |
| 61115 | Machesney Park† | (815) | 19,042 | 19,514 |
| 61455 | Macomb | (309) | 19,952 | 19,863 |
| 62959 | Marion | (618) | 14,545 | 14,031 |
| 60426 | Markham (Cook) | (708) | 13,136 | 15,172 |
| 62258 | Mascoutah | (618) | 5,511 | 4,962 |
| 60443 | Matteson | (708) | 11,378 | 10,223 |
| 61938 | Mattoon | (217) | 18,441 | 19,293 |
| *60153 | Maywood | (708) | 27,139 | 27,998 |
| *60160 | Melrose Park | (708) | 20,859 | 20,735 |
| 61342 | Mendota | (815) | 7,017 | 7,134 |
| 62960 | Metropolis | (618) | 6,734 | 7,171 |
| 60445 | Midlothian | (708) | 14,372 | 14,274 |
| 61264 | Milan | (309) | 5,753 | 6,371 |
| 60448 | Mokena | (708) | 6,128 | 4,578 |
| *61265 | Moline | (309) | 43,080 | 46,407 |
| 61462 | Monmouth | (309) | 9,489 | 10,706 |
| 60450 | Morris | (815) | 10,274 | 8,833 |
| 61550 | Morton | (309) | 13,799 | 14,178 |
| 60053 | Morton Grove | (847) | 22,373 | 23,747 |
| 62863 | Mount Carmel | (618) | 8,287 | 8,908 |
| 60056 | Mount Prospect | (847) | 53,168 | 52,634 |
| 62864 | Mount Vernon | (618) | 17,082 | 17,193 |
| 60060 | Mundelein | (847) | 21,224 | 17,053 |
| 62966 | Murphysboro | (618) | 9,176 | 9,866 |
| *60540 | Naperville | (630) | 85,806 | 42,601 |
| 60451 | New Lenox | (815) | 9,698 | 5,792 |
| 60714 | Niles | (847) | 28,375 | 30,363 |
| 61761 | Normal | (309) | 40,023 | 35,672 |
| 60634 | Norridge | (708) | 14,459 | 16,483 |
| 60542 | North Aurora | (630) | 6,010 | 5,205 |
| *60062 | Northbrook | (708) | 32,572 | 30,778 |
| 60064 | North Chicago | (847) | 34,978 | 38,774 |
| 60164 | Northlake | (708) | 12,505 | 12,166 |
| 60546 | North Riverside | (708) | 6,180 | 6,764 |
| 60521 | Oak Brook | (630) | 9,087 | 6,676 |
| 60452 | Oak Forest | (708) | 26,202 | 25,040 |
| *60455 | Oak Lawn | (708) | 56,182 | 60,590 |
| *60303 | Oak Park | (708) | 53,648 | 54,887 |
| 62269 | O'Fallon | (618) | 16,064 | 12,173 |
| 62450 | Olney | (618) | 8,661 | 9,026 |
| 60477 | Orland Hills | (708) | 5,510 | 2,784 |
| 60462 | Orland Park | (708) | 35,720 | 23,045 |
| 61350 | Ottawa | (815) | 17,528 | 18,166 |
| *60067 | Palatine | (847) | 38,894 | 32,171 |
| 60463 | Palos Heights | (708) | 11,478 | 11,096 |
| 60465 | Palos Hills | (708) | 17,803 | 16,654 |
| 62557 | Pana | (217) | 5,796 | 6,040 |
| 61944 | Paris | (217) | 9,016 | 9,885 |
| 60466 | Park Forest | (708) | 24,656 | 26,222 |
| 60068 | Park Ridge | (847) | 36,175 | 38,704 |
| *61554 | Pekin | (309) | 32,254 | 33,967 |
| *61601 | Peoria | (309) | 113,504 | 124,160 |
| 61603 | Peoria Heights | (309) | 6,930 | 7,453 |
| 61354 | Peru | (815) | 9,302 | 10,886 |
| 60545 | Plano | (630) | 5,104 | 4,875 |
| 61764 | Pontiac | (815) | 11,428 | 11,227 |
| 61356 | Princeton | (815) | 7,197 | 7,342 |
| 60070 | Prospect Heights | (847) | 15,236 | 11,823 |
| *62301 | Quincy | (217) | 39,682 | 42,554 |
| 61866 | Rantoul | (217) | 17,212 | 20,161 |
| 60471 | Richton Park | (708) | 10,523 | 9,403 |
| 60627 | Riverdale | (708) | 13,671 | 13,233 |
| 60305 | River Forest | (708) | 11,669 | 12,392 |
| 60171 | River Grove | (708) | 9,961 | 10,368 |
| 60546 | Riverside | (708) | 8,774 | 9,236 |
| 60472 | Robbins | (708) | 7,498 | 8,853 |
| 62454 | Robinson | (618) | 6,740 | 7,285 |
| 61068 | Rochelle | (815) | 8,769 | 8,982 |
| 61071 | Rock Falls | (815) | 9,669 | 10,633 |
| *61125 | Rockford | (815) | 139,704 | 139,712 |
| *61201 | Rock Island | (309) | 40,630 | 46,821 |
| 60008 | Rolling Meadows | (847) | 22,598 | 20,167 |
| 60446 | Romeoville | (815) | 14,101 | 15,519 |
| *60172 | Roselle | (630) | 20,803 | 17,034 |
| 60073 | Round Lake Beach | (847) | 16,406 | 12,921 |
| *60174 | Saint Charles | (630) | 22,620 | 17,492 |
| 62881 | Salem | (618) | 7,470 | 7,813 |
| 60548 | Sandwich | (815) | 5,607 | 5,356 |
| 60411 | Sauk Village | (708) | 9,926 | 10,906 |
| *60194 | Schaumburg | (847) | 68,586 | 53,355 |
| 60176 | Schiller Park | (847) | 11,189 | 11,458 |
| 62225 | Scott AFB(u) | (618) | 7,245 | 8,648 |
| 60436 | Shorewood | (815) | 6,264 | 4,714 |
| 61282 | Silvis | (309) | 6,926 | 7,130 |
| *60077 | Skokie | (847) | 59,432 | 60,278 |
| 60177 | South Elgin | (847) | 7,474 | 5,970 |
| 60473 | South Holland | (708) | 22,105 | 24,977 |
| *62703 | Springfield | (217) | 105,417 | 100,054 |
| 61362 | Spring Valley | (815) | 5,246 | 5,822 |
| 60475 | Steger | (708) | 8,592 | 9,269 |
| 61081 | Sterling | (815) | 15,142 | 16,281 |
| 60402 | Stickney | (708) | 5,678 | 5,893 |
| 60107 | Streamwood | (630) | 31,197 | 23,456 |
| 61364 | Streator | (815) | 14,121 | 14,795 |
| 60501 | Summit | (708) | 9,971 | 10,110 |
| 62221 | Swansea | (618) | 8,201 | 5,529 |
| 60178 | Sycamore | (815) | 9,896 | 9,219 |
| 62568 | Taylorville | (217) | 11,133 | 11,386 |
| 60477 | Tinley Park | (708) | 37,115 | 26,178 |
| 62294 | Troy | (618) | 6,019 | 3,772 |
| 60466 | University Park | (708) | 6,204 | 6,245 |
| 61801 | Urbana | (217) | 36,383 | 35,978 |
| 62471 | Vandalia | (618) | 6,114 | 5,338 |
| 60061 | Vernon Hills | (847) | 15,319 | 9,827 |
| 60181 | Villa Park | (630) | 22,279 | 23,155 |
| 60555 | Warrenville | (630) | 11,389 | 7,519 |
| 61571 | Washington | (309) | 10,136 | 10,364 |
| 62204 | Washington Park | (618) | 7,431 | 8,223 |
| 62298 | Waterloo | (618) | 5,030 | 4,646 |
| 60970 | Watseka | (815) | 5,424 | 5,543 |
| 60084 | Wauconda | (847) | 6,294 | 5,688 |
| *60085 | Waukegan | (847) | 69,481 | 67,653 |
| 60154 | Westchester | (708) | 17,301 | 17,730 |
| *60185 | West Chicago | (630) | 14,808 | 12,550 |
| 60558 | Western Springs | (708) | 11,956 | 12,876 |
| 62896 | West Frankfort | (618) | 8,526 | 9,437 |
| 60559 | Westmont | (630) | 21,402 | 17,353 |
| 61604 | West Peoria(u) | (309) | 5,314 | 5,219 |
| *60187 | Wheaton | (630) | 51,441 | 43,043 |
| *60090 | Wheeling | (847) | 29,911 | 23,266 |
| 60514 | Willowbrook | (630) | 8,701 | 4,953 |
| 60091 | Wilmette | (847) | 26,694 | 28,221 |
| 60190 | Winfield | (630) | 7,096 | 4,422 |
| 60093 | Winnetka | (847) | 12,210 | 12,772 |
| 60096 | Winthrop Harbor | (847) | 6,240 | 5,427 |
| 60097 | Wonder Lake(u) | (815) | 6,664 | 5,917 |
| 60191 | Wood Dale | (630) | 12,394 | 11,251 |
| *60517 | Woodridge | (630) | 26,359 | 21,763 |
| 62095 | Wood River | (618) | 11,490 | 12,446 |
| 60098 | Woodstock | (815) | 14,368 | 11,725 |
| 60482 | Worth | (708) | 11,208 | 11,592 |
| 60099 | Zion | (847) | 19,783 | 17,865 |

## Indiana

| ZIP | Place | | 1990 | 1980 |
|---|---|---|---|---|
| 46001 | Alexandria | (317) | 5,709 | 6,028 |
| *46011 | Anderson | (317) | 59,459 | 64,695 |
| 46703 | Angola | (219) | 5,851 | 5,486 |
| 46706 | Auburn | (219) | 9,386 | 8,122 |
| 47421 | Bedford | (812) | 13,817 | 14,410 |
| 46107 | Beech Grove | (317) | 13,383 | 13,196 |
| *47408 | Bloomington | (812) | 60,633 | 52,663 |
| 46714 | Bluffton | (219) | 9,104 | 8,705 |
| 47601 | Boonville | (812) | 6,686 | 6,300 |
| 47834 | Brazil | (812) | 7,640 | 7,852 |
| 46112 | Brownsburg | (317) | 7,628 | 6,242 |
| *46032 | Carmel | (317) | 25,380 | 18,272 |
| 46303 | Cedar Lake | (219) | 8,885 | 8,754 |
| 47111 | Charlestown | (812) | 5,889 | 5,596 |
| 46304 | Chesterton | (219) | 9,118 | 8,531 |
| 47129 | Clarksville (Clark Co.) | (812) | 19,838 | 15,164 |
| 47842 | Clinton | (317) | 5,040 | 5,267 |
| 46725 | Columbia City | (219) | 5,700 | 5,091 |
| *47201 | Columbus | (812) | 31,802 | 30,614 |
| 47331 | Connersville | (317) | 15,550 | 17,023 |
| 47933 | Crawfordsville | (317) | 13,584 | 13,325 |
| 46307 | Crown Point | (219) | 17,728 | 16,455 |
| 46733 | Decatur | (219) | 8,642 | 8,649 |

| ZIP | Place | | 1990 | 1980 |
|---|---|---|---|---|
| 46514 | Dunlap(u) | (219) | 5,705 | 5,397 |
| 46311 | Dyer | (219) | 10,923 | 9,555 |
| 46312 | East Chicago | (219) | 33,892 | 39,786 |
| *46515 | Elkhart | (219) | 43,627 | 41,305 |
| 46036 | Elwood | (317) | 9,494 | 10,867 |
| *47708 | Evansville | (812) | 126,272 | 130,496 |
| 46038 | Fishers | (317) | 7,189 | 2,008 |
| *46802 | Fort Wayne | (219) | 172,971 | 172,391 |
| 46041 | Frankfort | (317) | 14,754 | 15,168 |
| 46131 | Franklin | (317) | 12,932 | 11,563 |
| 46738 | Garrett | (219) | 5,349 | 4,751 |
| *46401 | Gary | (219) | 116,646 | 151,968 |
| 46933 | Gas City | (317) | 6,296 | 6,370 |
| *46526 | Goshen | (219) | 23,794 | 19,665 |
| 46530 | Granger(u) | (219) | 20,241 | .... |
| 46135 | Greencastle | (317) | 8,984 | 8,403 |
| 46140 | Greenfield | (317) | 11,657 | 11,288 |
| 47240 | Greensburg | (812) | 9,286 | 9,254 |
| *46142 | Greenwood | (317) | 26,507 | 19,327 |
| 46319 | Griffith | (219) | 17,914 | 17,026 |
| *46320 | Hammond | (219) | 84,236 | 93,714 |
| 47348 | Hartford City | (317) | 6,960 | 7,622 |
| 46322 | Highland | (219) | 23,696 | 25,935 |
| 46342 | Hobart | (219) | 21,822 | 22,987 |
| 47542 | Huntingburg | (812) | 5,236 | 5,376 |
| 46750 | Huntington | (219) | 16,389 | 16,202 |
| *46206 | Indianapolis | (317) | 731,327 | 700,807 |
| *47546 | Jasper | (812) | 10,030 | 9,097 |
| *47130 | Jeffersonville | (812) | 21,968 | 21,220 |
| 46755 | Kendallville | (219) | 7,773 | 7,299 |
| *46902 | Kokomo | (317) | 44,996 | 47,808 |
| *47901 | Lafayette | (317) | 43,758 | 43,011 |
| ..... | Lakes of the Four Seasons(u) | (219) | 6,556 | .... |
| 46405 | Lake Station | (219) | 13,899 | 15,087 |
| *46350 | La Porte | (219) | 21,507 | 21,796 |
| 46226 | Lawrence | (317) | 26,779 | 25,591 |
| 46052 | Lebanon | (317) | 12,059 | 11,456 |
| 47441 | Linton | (812) | 5,814 | 6,315 |
| 46947 | Logansport | (219) | 16,865 | 17,731 |
| 46356 | Lowell | (219) | 6,430 | 5,827 |
| 47250 | Madison | (812) | 12,006 | 12,472 |
| *46952 | Marion | (317) | 32,607 | 35,874 |
| 46151 | Martinsville | (317) | 11,677 | 11,311 |
| 46410 | Merrillville | (219) | 27,257 | 27,677 |
| *46360 | Michigan City | (219) | 33,822 | 36,850 |
| *46544 | Mishawaka | (219) | 42,635 | 40,201 |
| 47960 | Monticello | (219) | 5,237 | 5,162 |
| 46158 | Mooresville | (317) | 5,541 | 5,349 |
| 47620 | Mount Vernon | (812) | 7,217 | 7,656 |
| *47302 | Muncie | (317) | 71,170 | 77,216 |
| 46321 | Munster | (219) | 19,949 | 20,671 |
| 46550 | Nappanee | (219) | 5,474 | 4,694 |
| *47150 | New Albany | (812) | 36,322 | 37,103 |
| 47362 | New Castle | (317) | 17,753 | 20,056 |
| 46774 | New Haven | (219) | 9,338 | 6,714 |
| 46060 | Noblesville | (317) | 17,655 | 12,253 |
| 46962 | North Manchester | (219) | 6,383 | 5,998 |
| 47265 | North Vernon | (812) | 5,129 | 5,768 |
| 47130 | Oak Park(u) | (812) | 5,630 | 5,871 |
| 46970 | Peru | (317) | 12,843 | 13,764 |
| 46168 | Plainfield | (317) | 10,438 | 9,191 |
| 46563 | Plymouth | (219) | 8,291 | 7,693 |
| 46368 | Portage | (219) | 29,062 | 27,409 |
| 47371 | Portland | (219) | 6,483 | 7,074 |
| 47670 | Princeton | (812) | 8,127 | 8,976 |
| 47978 | Rensselaer | (219) | 5,045 | 4,944 |
| *47374 | Richmond | (317) | 38,705 | 41,349 |
| 46975 | Rochester | (219) | 5,969 | 5,050 |
| 46173 | Rushville | (317) | 5,533 | 6,113 |
| 47167 | Salem | (812) | 5,619 | 5,290 |
| 46375 | Schererville | (219) | 20,155 | 13,209 |
| 47170 | Scottsburg | (812) | 5,334 | 5,068 |
| 47172 | Sellersburg | (812) | 5,914 | 3,211 |
| 47274 | Seymour | (812) | 15,579 | 15,050 |
| 46176 | Shelbyville | (317) | 15,347 | 14,989 |
| *46624 | South Bend | (219) | 105,511 | 109,727 |
| 46383 | South Haven(u) | (219) | 6,112 | 6,679 |
| 46224 | Speedway | (317) | 13,092 | 12,641 |
| 47586 | Tell City | (812) | 8,088 | 8,704 |
| *47808 | Terre Haute | (812) | 55,430 | 61,125 |
| *46383 | Valparaiso | (219) | 24,414 | 22,247 |
| 47591 | Vincennes | (812) | 19,867 | 20,857 |
| 46992 | Wabash | (219) | 12,127 | 12,985 |
| *46580 | Warsaw | (219) | 10,968 | 10,647 |
| 47501 | Washington | (812) | 10,864 | 11,325 |
| *47901 | West Lafayette | (317) | 26,144 | 21,247 |
| 46391 | Westville | (219) | 5,255 | 2,887 |
| 46394 | Whiting | (219) | 5,155 | 5,630 |
| 47394 | Winchester | (317) | 5,095 | 5,659 |
| 46077 | Zionsville | (317) | 5,281 | 3,948 |

## Iowa

| ZIP | Place | | 1990 | 1980 |
|---|---|---|---|---|
| 50511 | Algona | (515) | 6,015 | 6,289 |
| 50009 | Altoona | (515) | 7,242 | 5,764 |
| *50010 | Ames | (515) | 47,198 | 45,775 |
| 52205 | Anamosa | (319) | 5,100 | 4,958 |
| 50021 | Ankeny | (515) | 18,482 | 15,429 |
| 50022 | Atlantic | (712) | 7,432 | 7,789 |
| 52722 | Bettendorf | (319) | 28,139 | 27,381 |
| 50036 | Boone | (515) | 12,392 | 12,602 |
| 52601 | Burlington | (319) | 27,208 | 29,529 |
| 51401 | Carroll | (712) | 9,579 | 9,705 |
| 50613 | Cedar Falls | (319) | 34,298 | 36,322 |
| *52401 | Cedar Rapids | (319) | 108,772 | 110,243 |
| 52544 | Centerville | (515) | 5,936 | 6,558 |
| 50616 | Charles City | (515) | 7,878 | 8,778 |
| 51012 | Cherokee | (712) | 6,026 | 7,004 |
| 51632 | Clarinda | (712) | 5,104 | 5,458 |
| 50428 | Clear Lake | (515) | 8,183 | 7,458 |
| *52732 | Clinton | (319) | 29,201 | 32,828 |
| 50325 | Clive | (515) | 7,462 | 6,064 |
| 52241 | Coralville | (319) | 10,347 | 7,687 |
| *51501 | Council Bluffs | (712) | 54,315 | 56,449 |
| 50801 | Creston | (515) | 7,911 | 8,429 |
| *52802 | Davenport | (319) | 95,333 | 103,264 |
| 52101 | Decorah | (319) | 8,063 | 7,991 |
| 51442 | Denison | (712) | 6,604 | 6,675 |
| *50318 | Des Moines | (515) | 193,189 | 191,003 |
| *52001 | Dubuque | (319) | 57,538 | 62,374 |
| 51334 | Estherville | (712) | 6,720 | 7,518 |
| 52556 | Fairfield | (515) | 9,768 | 9,428 |
| 50501 | Fort Dodge | (515) | 25,894 | 29,423 |
| 52627 | Fort Madison | (319) | 11,614 | 13,520 |
| 50112 | Grinnell | (515) | 8,902 | 8,868 |
| *51537 | Harlan | (712) | 5,148 | 5,357 |
| 50644 | Independence | (319) | 5,972 | 6,392 |
| 50125 | Indianola | (515) | 11,340 | 10,843 |
| *52240 | Iowa City | (319) | 59,735 | 50,508 |
| 50126 | Iowa Falls | (515) | 5,435 | 6,174 |
| 52632 | Keokuk | (319) | 12,451 | 13,536 |
| 50138 | Knoxville | (515) | 8,232 | 8,143 |
| 51031 | Le Mars | (712) | 8,454 | 8,276 |
| 52057 | Manchester | (319) | 5,137 | 4,942 |
| 52060 | Maquoketa | (319) | 6,130 | 6,313 |
| 52302 | Marion | (319) | 20,442 | 19,474 |
| 50158 | Marshalltown | (515) | 25,178 | 26,938 |
| *50401 | Mason City | (515) | 29,040 | 30,144 |
| 52641 | Mount Pleasant | (319) | 7,959 | 7,322 |
| 52761 | Muscatine | (319) | 22,881 | 23,467 |
| 50201 | Nevada | (515) | 6,009 | 5,912 |
| 50208 | Newton | (515) | 14,799 | 15,292 |
| 50211 | Norwalk | (515) | 5,726 | 2,676 |
| 50662 | Oelwein | (319) | 6,493 | 7,564 |
| 52577 | Oskaloosa | (515) | 10,600 | 10,989 |
| 52501 | Ottumwa | (515) | 24,488 | 27,381 |
| 50219 | Pella | (515) | 9,270 | 8,349 |
| 50220 | Perry | (515) | 6,652 | 7,053 |
| *51566 | Red Oak | (712) | 6,264 | 6,810 |
| 51601 | Shenandoah | (712) | 5,572 | 6,274 |
| 51250 | Sioux Center | (712) | 5,074 | 4,588 |
| *51101 | Sioux City | (712) | 80,505 | 82,003 |
| 51301 | Spencer | (712) | 11,066 | 11,726 |
| 50588 | Storm Lake | (712) | 8,769 | 8,814 |
| 50322 | Urbandale | (515) | 23,500 | 17,869 |
| 52349 | Vinton | (319) | 5,103 | 5,040 |
| 52353 | Washington | (319) | 7,074 | 6,584 |
| *50701 | Waterloo | (319) | 66,467 | 75,985 |
| 50677 | Waverly | (319) | 8,539 | 8,444 |
| 50595 | Webster City | (515) | 7,894 | 8,572 |
| *50265 | West Des Moines | (515) | 31,702 | 21,894 |
| 50311 | Windsor Heights | (515) | 5,190 | 5,474 |

## Kansas

| ZIP | Place | | 1990 | 1980 |
|---|---|---|---|---|
| 67410 | Abilene | (913) | 6,242 | 6,572 |
| 67005 | Arkansas City | (316) | 12,762 | 13,201 |
| 66002 | Atchison | (913) | 10,656 | 11,407 |
| 67010 | Augusta | (316) | 7,848 | 6,968 |
| 66012 | Bonner Springs | (913) | 6,413 | 6,266 |
| 66720 | Chanute | (316) | 9,488 | 10,506 |
| 67337 | Coffeyville | (316) | 12,917 | 15,185 |
| 67701 | Colby | (913) | 5,510 | 5,544 |
| 66901 | Concordia | (913) | 6,152 | 6,847 |
| 67037 | Derby | (316) | 14,691 | 9,786 |
| 67801 | Dodge City | (316) | 21,129 | 18,001 |
| 67042 | El Dorado | (316) | 11,495 | 11,551 |
| 66801 | Emporia | (316) | 25,512 | 25,287 |
| 66442 | Fort Riley North(u) | (913) | 12,848 | 16,086 |
| 66701 | Fort Scott | (316) | 8,362 | 8,893 |
| 67846 | Garden City | (316) | 24,097 | 18,256 |
| 67530 | Great Bend | (316) | 15,427 | 16,608 |
| 67601 | Hays | (913) | 17,814 | 16,301 |
| 67060 | Haysville | (316) | 8,364 | 8,006 |
| *67501 | Hutchinson | (316) | 39,308 | 40,284 |
| 67301 | Independence | (316) | 10,030 | 10,598 |
| 66749 | Iola | (316) | 6,351 | 6,938 |
| 66441 | Junction City | (913) | 20,642 | 19,305 |
| *66102 | Kansas City | (913) | 149,800 | 161,148 |
| 66043 | Lansing | (913) | 7,120 | 5,307 |
| *66044 | Lawrence | (913) | 65,608 | 52,738 |
| 66048 | Leavenworth | (913) | 38,495 | 33,656 |
| 66209 | Leawood | (913) | 19,693 | 13,360 |
| 66210 | Lenexa | (913) | 34,110 | 18,639 |
| *67901 | Liberal | (316) | 16,573 | 14,911 |

| ZIP | Place | | 1990 | 1980 |
|---|---|---|---|---|
| 67460 | McPherson | (316) | 12,422 | 11,753 |
| *66502 | Manhattan | (913) | 37,737 | 32,644 |
| 66202 | Merriam | (913) | 11,819 | 10,794 |
| 66202 | Mission | (913) | 9,504 | 8,643 |
| 67114 | Newton | (316) | 16,700 | 16,332 |
| *66061 | Olathe | (913) | 63,402 | 37,258 |
| 66067 | Ottawa | (913) | 10,667 | 11,016 |
| 66202 | Overland Park | (913) | 111,790 | 81,784 |
| 67219 | Park City† | (316) | 5,054 | 4,056 |
| 67357 | Parsons | (316) | 11,919 | 12,898 |
| 66762 | Pittsburg | (316) | 17,789 | 18,770 |
| 66202 | Prairie Village | (913) | 23,186 | 24,657 |
| 67124 | Pratt | (316) | 6,687 | 6,885 |
| 66205 | Roeland Park | (913) | 7,706 | 7,962 |
| *67401 | Salina | (913) | 42,299 | 41,843 |
| 66203 | Shawnee | (913) | 37,962 | 29,653 |
| *66601 | Topeka | (913) | 119,883 | 118,690 |
| 67880 | Ulysses | (316) | 5,474 | 4,653 |
| 67152 | Wellington | (316) | 8,517 | 8,212 |
| *67209 | Wichita | (316) | 304,017 | 279,838 |
| 67156 | Winfield | (316) | 11,931 | 10,736 |

## Kentucky

| ZIP | Place | | 1990 | 1980 |
|---|---|---|---|---|
| 41001 | Alexandria | (606) | 5,592 | 4,735 |
| *41101 | Ashland | (606) | 23,622 | 27,064 |
| 40004 | Bardstown | (502) | 6,712 | 6,155 |
| 41073 | Bellevue | (606) | 6,997 | 7,678 |
| 40403 | Berea | (606) | 9,129 | 8,226 |
| *42101 | Bowling Green | (502) | 41,688 | 40,450 |
| 40261 | Buechel(u) | (502) | 7,081 | 6,855 |
| 41005 | Burlington(u) | (606) | 6,070 | .... |
| *42718 | Campbellsville | (502) | 9,592 | 8,715 |
| 42330 | Central City | (502) | 5,015 | 5,214 |
| *40701 | Corbin | (606) | 7,644 | 8,075 |
| *41011 | Covington | (606) | 43,646 | 49,585 |
| 41031 | Cynthiana | (606) | 6,497 | 5,881 |
| *40422 | Danville | (606) | 12,559 | 12,942 |
| 41074 | Dayton | (606) | 6,576 | 6,979 |
| ..... | Douglass Hills | (502) | 5,431 | 4,384 |
| 41017 | Edgewood | (606) | 8,143 | 7,243 |
| *42701 | Elizabethtown | (502) | 18,167 | 15,380 |
| 41018 | Elsmere | (606) | 6,847 | 7,203 |
| 41018 | Erlanger | (606) | 15,979 | 14,466 |
| 40118 | Fairdale(u) | (502) | 6,563 | 7,315 |
| 40291 | Fern Creek(u) | (502) | 16,406 | 16,866 |
| 41139 | Flatwoods | (606) | 7,799 | 8,354 |
| *41042 | Florence | (606) | 18,586 | 15,586 |
| 42223 | Fort Campbell North(u) | (502) | 18,861 | 17,211 |
| 40121 | Fort Knox(u) | (502) | 21,495 | 31,055 |
| 41017 | Fort Mitchell | (606) | 7,438 | 7,294 |
| 41075 | Fort Thomas | (606) | 16,032 | 16,012 |
| 41011 | Fort Wright | (606) | 6,404 | 4,481 |
| *40601 | Frankfort | (502) | 26,535 | 25,973 |
| *42134 | Franklin | (502) | 7,607 | 7,738 |
| 40324 | Georgetown | (502) | 11,414 | 10,972 |
| *42141 | Glasgow | (502) | 12,351 | 12,958 |
| 40330 | Harrodsburg | (606) | 7,335 | 7,265 |
| *41701 | Hazard | (606) | 5,416 | 5,371 |
| 42420 | Henderson | (502) | 25,945 | 24,834 |
| 40228 | Highview(u) | (502) | 14,814 | 13,286 |
| 40229 | Hillview | (502) | 6,119 | 5,196 |
| *42240 | Hopkinsville | (502) | 29,809 | 27,318 |
| 41051 | Independence | (606) | 10,444 | 7,998 |
| 40269 | Jeffersontown | (502) | 23,223 | 15,795 |
| 40342 | Lawrenceburg | (502) | 5,911 | 5,167 |
| 40033 | Lebanon | (502) | 5,695 | 6,590 |
| *40507 | Lexington | (606) | 225,366 | 204,165 |
| *40741 | London | (606) | 5,757 | 4,002 |
| *40232 | Louisville | (502) | 269,555 | 298,694 |
| 40252 | Lyndon | (502) | 8,037 | 1,553 |
| 42431 | Madisonville | (502) | 16,203 | 16,979 |
| 42066 | Mayfield | (502) | 9,935 | 10,705 |
| 41056 | Maysville | (606) | 7,169 | 7,983 |
| 40965 | Middlesboro | (606) | 11,328 | 12,251 |
| 40253 | Middletown | (502) | 5,016 | 414 |
| 42633 | Monticello | (606) | 5,357 | 5,677 |
| 40351 | Morehead | (606) | 8,357 | 7,789 |
| 40353 | Mount Sterling | (606) | 5,362 | 5,820 |
| 40047 | Mount Washington | (502) | 5,256 | 3,997 |
| 42071 | Murray | (502) | 14,442 | 14,248 |
| 40218 | Newburg(u) | (502) | 21,647 | 24,612 |
| *41071 | Newport | (606) | 18,871 | 21,587 |
| *40356 | Nicholasville | (606) | 13,603 | 10,400 |
| 40259 | Okolona(u) | (502) | 18,902 | 20,039 |
| *42301 | Owensboro | (502) | 53,577 | 54,450 |
| *42003 | Paducah | (502) | 27,256 | 29,315 |
| *40361 | Paris | (606) | 8,730 | 7,935 |
| *41501 | Pikeville | (606) | 6,324 | 4,756 |
| 40268 | Pleasure Ridge Park(u) | (502) | 25,131 | 27,332 |
| 42445 | Princeton | (502) | 6,940 | 7,073 |
| *40160 | Radcliff | (502) | 19,778 | 14,656 |
| *40475 | Richmond | (606) | 21,183 | 21,705 |
| 42276 | Russellville | (502) | 7,454 | 7,520 |
| 40216 | Saint Dennis(u) | (502) | 10,326 | .... |
| 40206 | Saint Matthews | (502) | 15,691 | 13,519 |
| *40066 | Shelbyville | (502) | 6,155 | 5,329 |
| 40256 | Shively | (502) | 15,535 | 16,645 |
| *42501 | Somerset | (606) | 10,735 | 10,649 |
| 41015 | Taylor Mill | (606) | 5,530 | 4,509 |
| 40272 | Valley Station(u) | (502) | 22,840 | 24,474 |
| 40383 | Versailles | (606) | 7,269 | 6,427 |
| 41016 | Villa Hills | (606) | 7,370 | 4,384 |
| 41101 | Westwoods(u) | (606) | 5,300 | 5,973 |
| 40769 | Williamsburg | (606) | 5,493 | 5,560 |
| *40391 | Winchester | (606) | 15,799 | 15,216 |

## Louisiana

| ZIP | Place | | 1990 | 1980 |
|---|---|---|---|---|
| *70510 | Abbeville | (318) | 11,184 | 12,391 |
| *71301 | Alexandria | (318) | 49,049 | 51,648 |
| 70032 | Arabi(u) | (504) | 8,787 | 10,248 |
| 70094 | Avondale(u) | (504) | 5,813 | 6,699 |
| *70714 | Baker | (504) | 13,087 | 12,865 |
| *71220 | Bastrop | (318) | 13,916 | 15,527 |
| *70821 | Baton Rouge | (504) | 219,531 | 220,394 |
| 70360 | Bayou Cane(u) | (504) | 15,876 | 15,723 |
| 70037 | Belle Chasse(u) | (504) | 8,512 | 5,412 |
| *70427 | Bogalusa | (504) | 14,280 | 16,976 |
| *71111 | Bossier City | (318) | 52,721 | 50,817 |
| 70517 | Breaux Bridge | (318) | 6,694 | 5,922 |
| 70094 | Bridge City(u) | (504) | 8,327 | .... |
| 70811 | Brownfields(u) | (504) | 5,229 | .... |
| 71291 | Brownsville-Bawcomville(u) | (318) | 7,397 | 7,252 |
| 71322 | Bunkie | (318) | 5,044 | 5,364 |
| 70520 | Carencro | (318) | 5,518 | 3,712 |
| *70043 | Chalmette(u) † | (504) | 31,860 | 33,847 |
| 71291 | Claiborne(u) | (318) | 8,300 | 6,278 |
| *70433 | Covington | (504) | 7,691 | 7,892 |
| *70526 | Crowley | (318) | 13,983 | 16,036 |
| 70345 | Cut Off(u) | (504) | 5,325 | 5,049 |
| *70726 | Denham Springs | (504) | 8,381 | 8,563 |
| 70634 | De Ridder | (318) | 9,868 | 10,337 |
| 70047 | Destrehan | (504) | 8,031 | 2,382 |
| 70346 | Donaldsonville | (504) | 7,949 | 7,901 |
| 70072 | Estelle(u) | (504) | 14,091 | 12,724 |
| 70535 | Eunice | (318) | 11,162 | 12,479 |
| 71459 | Fort Polk South | (318) | 10,911 | 12,498 |
| 70538 | Franklin | (318) | 9,004 | 9,584 |
| 70820 | Gardere | | 7,209 | .... |
| *70737 | Gonzales | (504) | 7,208 | 7,287 |
| 71245 | Grambling | (318) | 5,512 | 4,226 |
| *70053 | Gretna | (504) | 17,208 | 20,615 |
| *70401 | Hammond | (504) | 15,871 | 15,226 |
| 70123 | Harahan | (504) | 9,927 | 11,384 |
| *70058 | Harvey(u) | (504) | 21,222 | 22,709 |
| *70360 | Houma | (504) | 30,495 | 32,602 |
| 70544 | Jeanerette | (318) | 6,205 | 6,511 |
| 70502 | Jefferson(u) | (504) | 14,521 | 15,550 |
| 70546 | Jennings | (318) | 11,305 | 12,401 |
| *70062 | Kenner | (504) | 72,033 | 66,382 |
| 70445 | Lacombe(u) | (504) | 6,523 | 5,146 |
| *70501 | Lafayette | (318) | 94,438 | 80,584 |
| *70601 | Lake Charles | (318) | 70,580 | 75,226 |
| 71254 | Lake Providence | (318) | 5,380 | 6,361 |
| *70068 | La Place(u) | (504) | 24,194 | 16,112 |
| 70373 | Larose(u) | (504) | 5,772 | 5,234 |
| *71446 | Leesville | (318) | 7,638 | 9,054 |
| *70448 | Mandeville | (504) | 7,474 | 6,076 |
| 71052 | Mansfield | (318) | 5,389 | 6,485 |
| 71351 | Marksville | (318) | 5,526 | 5,113 |
| *70072 | Marrero(u) | (504) | 36,671 | 36,548 |
| 70075 | Meraux(u) | (504) | 8,849 | .... |
| 70812 | Merrydale(u) | (318) | 10,395 | .... |
| *70009 | Metairie(u) | (504) | 149,428 | 164,160 |
| *71055 | Minden | (318) | 13,661 | 15,084 |
| *71203 | Monroe | (318) | 54,909 | 57,597 |
| *70380 | Morgan City | (504) | 14,531 | 16,114 |
| 70612 | Moss Bluff(u) | (318) | 8,039 | 7,004 |
| *71457 | Natchitoches | (318) | 16,609 | 16,664 |
| *70560 | New Iberia | (318) | 31,828 | 32,766 |
| *70140 | New Orleans | (504) | 496,938 | 557,927 |
| 70760 | New Roads | (504) | 5,303 | 3,924 |
| 71463 | Oakdale | (318) | 6,837 | 7,155 |
| 70808 | Oak Hills Place | | 5,479 | .... |
| *70570 | Opelousas | (318) | 19,091 | 18,903 |
| 70392 | Patterson | (504) | 5,166 | 4,693 |
| *71360 | Pineville | (318) | 12,255 | 12,034 |
| *70764 | Plaquemine | (504) | 7,101 | 7,521 |
| 70454 | Ponchatoula | (504) | 5,425 | 5,469 |
| 70767 | Port Allen | (504) | 6,277 | 6,114 |
| 70601 | Prien(u) | (318) | 6,448 | 6,224 |
| 70394 | Raceland(u) | (504) | 5,564 | 6,302 |
| 70578 | Rayne | (318) | 8,502 | 9,066 |
| 71037 | Red Chute(u) | | 5,431 | .... |
| 70084 | Reserve(u) | (504) | 8,847 | 7,288 |
| 70123 | River Ridge(u) | (504) | 14,800 | 17,146 |
| *71270 | Ruston | (318) | 20,071 | 20,585 |
| 70582 | Saint Martinville | (318) | 7,226 | 7,965 |
| 70087 | Saint Rose(u) | (504) | 6,259 | .... |
| 70817 | Shenandoah(u) | | 13,429 | .... |
| *71102 | Shreveport | (318) | 198,518 | 206,989 |
| *70458 | Slidell | (504) | 24,124 | 26,718 |
| 71075 | Springhill | (318)/(504) | 5,668 | 6,516 |
| *70663 | Sulphur | (318) | 20,125 | 19,709 |

| ZIP | Place | | 1990 | 1980 |
|---|---|---|---|---|
| *71282 | Tallulah | (318) | 8,526 | 11,341 |
| 70056 | Terrytown(u) | (504) | 23,787 | 23,548 |
| *70301 | Thibodaux | (504) | 14,125 | 15,810 |
| 70053 | Timberlane(u) | (504) | 12,614 | 11,579 |
| 70809 | Village Saint George(u) | (504) | 6,242 | .... |
| 70586 | Ville Platte | (318) | 9,037 | 9,201 |
| 70092 | Violet(u) | (504) | 8,574 | 11,678 |
| 70094 | Waggaman(u) | (504) | 9,405 | 9,004 |
| 70669 | Westlake | (318) | 5,007 | 5,246 |
| *71291 | West Monroe | (318) | 14,096 | 14,993 |
| *70094 | Westwego | (504) | 11,218 | 12,663 |
| 71483 | Winnfield | (318) | 6,138 | 7,311 |
| 71295 | Winnsboro | (318) | 5,755 | 5,921 |
| 70791 | Zachary | (504) | 9,036 | 7,297 |

## Maine (207)

*See note on page 390*

| ZIP | Place | 1990 | 1980 |
|---|---|---|---|
| *04210 | Auburn | 24,309 | 23,128 |
| *04330 | Augusta | 21,325 | 21,819 |
| *04401 | Bangor | 33,181 | 31,643 |
| 04530 | Bath | 9,799 | 10,246 |
| 04915 | Belfast | 6,355 | 6,243 |
| 03901 | *Berwick* | 5,995 | 4,149 |
| *04005 | Biddeford | 20,710 | 19,638 |
| 04412 | Brewer | 9,021 | 9,017 |
| 04011 | Brunswick Center(u) | 14,683 | 10,990 |
| 04011 | *Brunswick* | 20,906 | 17,366 |
| 04093 | *Buxton* | 6,494 | 5,775 |
| 04843 | *Camden* | 5,060 | 4,584 |
| 04107 | *Cape Elizabeth* | 8,854 | 7,838 |
| 04736 | Caribou | 9,415 | 9,916 |
| 04021 | *Cumberland* | 5,836 | 5,284 |
| 03903 | *Eliot* | 5,329 | 4,948 |
| 04605 | Ellsworth | 5,975 | 5,179 |
| 04937 | *Fairfield* | 6,718 | 6,113 |
| 04105 | *Falmouth* | 7,610 | 6,853 |
| 04938 | *Farmington* | 7,436 | 6,730 |
| 04032 | *Freeport* | 6,905 | 5,863 |
| 04345 | Gardiner | 6,746 | 6,485 |
| 04038 | *Gorham* | 11,856 | 10,101 |
| 04039 | Gray | 5,904 | 4,344 |
| 04444 | *Hampden* | 5,974 | 5,250 |
| *04079 | *Harpswell* | 5,012 | 3,796 |
| 04730 | Houlton Center(u) | 5,627 | 5,730 |
| 04730 | *Houlton* | 6,613 | 6,766 |
| 04239 | *Jay* | 5,080 | 5,080 |
| 04043 | *Kennebunk* | 8,004 | 6,621 |
| 03904 | Kittery Center(u) | 5,151 | 5,465 |
| 03904 | *Kittery* | 9,372 | 9,314 |
| *04240 | Lewiston | 39,757 | 40,481 |
| 04750 | *Limestone* | 9,922 | 8,719 |
| 04457 | *Lincoln* | 5,587 | 5,066 |
| 04250 | *Lisbon* | 9,457 | 8,769 |
| 04751 | Loring AFB(u) | 7,829 | 6,572 |
| 04462 | Millinocket Center(u) | 6,922 | 7,567 |
| 04462 | *Millinocket* | 6,956 | 7,567 |
| 04963 | *Oakland* | 5,595 | 5,162 |
| 04064 | Old Orchard Beach Ctr.(u) | 7,789 | 6,023 |
| 04064 | *Old Orchard Beach* | 7,789 | 6,291 |
| 04468 | Old Town | 8,317 | 8,422 |
| 04473 | Orono Center(u) | 9,789 | 9,891 |
| 04473 | *Orono* | 10,573 | 10,578 |
| *04101 | Portland | 64,358 | 61,572 |
| 04769 | Presque Isle | 10,550 | 11,172 |
| 04841 | Rockland | 7,972 | 7,919 |
| 04276 | Rumford Compact(u) | 5,419 | 6,256 |
| 04276 | *Rumford* | 7,078 | 8,240 |
| 04072 | Saco | 15,181 | 12,921 |
| 04073 | Sanford Center(u) | 10,296 | 10,268 |
| 04073 | *Sanford* | 20,463 | 18,020 |
| *04074 | *Scarborough* | 12,518 | 11,347 |
| 04976 | Skowhegan Center(u) | 6,990 | 6,517 |
| 04976 | *Skowhegan* | 8,725 | 8,098 |
| 03908 | *South Berwick* | 5877 | 4,046 |
| *04101 | South Portland | 23,163 | 22,712 |
| 04084 | *Standish* | 7,678 | 5,946 |
| 04086 | *Topsham* | 8,746 | 6,431 |
| *04901 | Waterville | 17,173 | 17,779 |
| 04090 | *Wells* | 7,778 | 8,211 |
| *04092 | Westbrook | 16,121 | 14,976 |
| 04062 | *Windham* | 13,020 | 11,282 |
| 04901 | Winslow Center(u) | 5,436 | 5,903 |
| 04901 | *Winslow* | 7,997 | 8,057 |
| 04364 | *Winthrop* | 5,986 | 5,889 |
| 04096 | *Yarmouth* | 7,862 | 6,585 |
| 03909 | *York* | 9,818 | 8,465 |

## Maryland

| ZIP | Place | | 1990 | 1980 |
|---|---|---|---|---|
| 21001 | Aberdeen | (410) | 13,087 | 11,533 |
| 21005 | Aberdeen Proving Ground(u) | (410) | 5,267 | 5,722 |
| 20783 | Adelphi(u) | (301) | 13,524 | 12,530 |
| 20335 | Andrews AFB(u) | (410) | 10,228 | 10,064 |
| *21401 | Annapolis | (410) | 33,195 | 31,740 |
| 21227 | Arbutus(u) | (410) | 19,750 | 20,163 |
| 21012 | Arnold(u) | (410) | 20,261 | 12,285 |
| 20916 | Aspen Hill(u) | (301) | 45,494 | 47,455 |
| 21220 | Ballenger Creek† | (410) | 5,546 | 2,659 |
| *21203 | Baltimore | (410) | 736,014 | 786,741 |
| *21014 | Bel Air | (410) | 8,942 | 7,814 |
| 21050 | Bel Air North(u) | (410) | 14,880 | 5,043 |
| 21014 | Bel Air South(u) | (410) | 26,421 | 9,140 |
| *20705 | Beltsville(u) | (301) | 14,476 | 12,760 |
| *20814 | Bethesda(u) | (301) | 62,936 | 63,022 |
| 20710 | Bladensburg | (301) | 8,064 | 7,691 |
| *20715 | Bowie | (301) | 37,642 | 33,695 |
| ..... | Bowleys Quarters(u) | (410) | 5,595 | .... |
| 21225 | Brooklyn Park(u) | (410) | 10,987 | 11,508 |
| 21716 | Brunswick | (301) | 5,117 | 4,572 |
| 20866 | Burtonsville(u) | (410) | 5,853 | 2,046 |
| 20818 | Cabin John(u) | (301) | 5,341 | 5,135 |
| 20619 | California(u) | (410) | 7,626 | 5,770 |
| 20705 | Calverton(u) | (301) | 12,046 | 7,649 |
| 21613 | Cambridge | (410) | 11,514 | 11,703 |
| 20748 | Camp Springs(u) | (301) | 16,392 | 16,118 |
| 21401 | Cape St. Clair(u) | (410) | 7,878 | 6,022 |
| 21234 | Carney(u) | (410) | 25,578 | 21,488 |
| 21228 | Catonsville(u) | (410) | 35,233 | 33,208 |
| 20657 | Chesapeake Ranch Estates(u) | (301) | 5,423 | .... |
| 20784 | Cheverly | (301) | 6,023 | 5,751 |
| *20815 | Chevy Chase(u) | (301) | 8,559 | 12,232 |
| 20783 | Chillum(u) | (301) | 31,309 | 32,775 |
| 20735 | Clinton(u) | (301) | 19,987 | 16,438 |
| 20904 | Cloverly(u) | (301) | 7,904 | 5,153 |
| *21030 | Cockeysville(u) | (410) | 18,668 | 17,013 |
| 20914 | Colesville(u) | (301) | 18,819 | 14,359 |
| *20740 | College Park | (301) | 23,714 | 23,614 |
| *21045 | Columbia(u) | (410)/(301) | 75,883 | 52,518 |
| 20743 | Coral Hills(u) | (410) | 11,032 | 11,602 |
| 21114 | Crofton(u) | (410) | 12,781 | 12,009 |
| *21502 | Cumberland | (301) | 23,712 | 25,933 |
| 20872 | Damascus(u) | (301) | 9,817 | 4,129 |
| *20747 | District Heights | (301) | 6,711 | 6,799 |
| 21222 | Dundalk(u) | (410) | 65,800 | 71,293 |
| 21601 | Easton | (410) | 9,372 | 7,536 |
| 20737 | East Riverdale(u) | (301) | 14,187 | 14,104 |
| 21219 | Edgemere(u) | (410) | 9,226 | 9,078 |
| 21040 | Edgewood(u) | (410) | 23,903 | 19,455 |
| 21784 | Eldersburg(u) | (410) | 9,720 | 4,959 |
| 21227 | Elkridge(u) | (410) | 12,953 | .... |
| *21921 | Elkton | (410) | 9,073 | 6,468 |
| *21043 | Ellicott City(u) | (410) | 41,396 | 21,784 |
| 21221 | Essex(u) | (410) | 40,872 | 39,614 |
| 20904 | Fairland(u) | (301) | 19,828 | 5,154 |
| 21047 | Fallston(u) | (410) | 5,730 | 5,572 |
| 21061 | Ferndale(u) | (410) | 16,355 | 14,314 |
| 20747 | Forestville(u) | (301) | 16,731 | 16,401 |
| 20755 | Fort Meade(u) | (301) | 12,509 | 14,083 |
| 20744 | Fort Washington(u) | (301) | 24,032 | .... |
| *21701 | Frederick | (301) | 40,186 | 28,086 |
| 20744 | Friendly(u) | (301) | 9,028 | 8,848 |
| 21532 | Frostburg | (301) | 8,069 | 7,715 |
| *20877 | Gaithersburg | (301) | 39,676 | 26,424 |
| 21055 | Garrison(u) | (410) | 5,045 | .... |
| *20874 | Germantown(u) | (301) | 41,145 | 9,721 |
| 20706 | Glenarden | (301) | 5,025 | 4,993 |
| *21061 | Glen Burnie(u) | (410) | 37,305 | 37,263 |
| 20769 | Glenn Dale(u) | (301) | 9,689 | 4,829 |
| 20772 | Greater Upper Marlboro | | 11,528 | .... |
| *20770 | Greenbelt | (301) | 20,561 | 17,332 |
| 21122 | Green Haven(u) | (410) | 14,416 | 6,577 |
| 21771 | Green Valley(u) | (301) | 9,424 | 4,504 |
| *21740 | Hagerstown | (301) | 35,306 | 34,132 |
| 21740 | Halfway(u) | (301) | 8,873 | 8,659 |
| 21078 | Havre de Grace | (410) | 8,952 | 8,763 |
| 20903 | Hillandale(u) | (301) | 10,318 | 9,686 |
| 20748 | Hillcrest Heights(u) | (301) | 17,136 | 17,021 |
| *20780 | Hyattsville | (301) | 13,864 | 12,709 |
| 20794 | Jessup(u) | (410) | 6,537 | 4,288 |
| 21085 | Joppatowne(u) | (410) | 11,084 | 11,348 |
| 20785 | Kentland(u) | (301) | 7,967 | 8,596 |
| 20772 | Kettering(u) | (301) | 9,901 | 6,972 |
| 21122 | Lake Shore(u) | (410) | 13,269 | 10,181 |
| 20785 | Landover(u) | (301) | 5,052 | 5,374 |
| 20787 | Langley Park(u) | (301) | 17,474 | 14,038 |
| 20706 | Lanham-Seabrook(u) | (301) | 16,792 | 15,814 |
| 21227 | Lansdowne-Baltimore Highlands(u) | | 15,509 | 16,759 |
| 20646 | La Plata | (301) | 5,841 | 2,484 |
| 20772 | Largo(u) | (301) | 9,475 | 5,557 |
| *20707 | Laurel | (301) | 19,086 | 12,103 |
| 20653 | Lexington Park(u) | (410) | 9,943 | 10,361 |
| 21090 | Linthicum(u) | (410) | 7,547 | 7,457 |
| 21207 | Lochearn(u) | (410) | 25,240 | 26,908 |
| 21037 | Londontowne(u) | (410) | 6,992 | 6,052 |
| 21784 | Long Meadow(u)† | (410) | 5,594 | 1,203 |
| *21093 | Lutherville-Timonium(u) | (410) | 16,442 | 16,871 |
| 20748 | Marlow Heights(u) | (301) | 5,885 | 5,824 |
| 20772 | Marlton | (301) | 5,523 | .... |
| 20707 | Maryland City(u) | (301) | 6,813 | 6,949 |
| 21093 | Mays Chapel(u) | (410) | 10,132 | 5,213 |
| 21220 | Middle River(u) | (410) | 24,616 | 26,756 |
| 21207 | Milford Mill(u) | (410) | 22,547 | 20,354 |
| 20717 | Mitchellville | (301) | 12,593 | .... |

| ZIP | Place | | 1990 | 1980 |
|---|---|---|---|---|
| 20879 | Montgomery Village(u) | (301) | 32,315 | 18,725 |
| 20712 | Mount Rainier | (301) | 7,954 | 7,361 |
| 21402 | Naval Academy(u) | (410) | 5,420 | 5,367 |
| 20784 | New Carrollton | (301) | 12,002 | 12,632 |
| 20815 | North Bethesda(u) | (301) | 29,656 | 22,671 |
| 20895 | North Kensington(u) | (301) | 8,607 | 9,039 |
| 20707 | North Laurel(u) | (301) | 15,008 | 6,093 |
| 20878 | North Potomac(u) | (301) | 18,456 | .... |
| 21842 | Ocean City | (410) | 5,146 | 4,946 |
| 21113 | Odenton(u) | (410) | 12,833 | 13,270 |
| *20832 | Olney(u) | (301) | 23,019 | 13,026 |
| 21206 | Overlea(u) | (410) | 12,137 | 12,965 |
| 21117 | Owings Mills(u) | (410) | 9,474 | 9,526 |
| *20745 | Oxon Hill-Glassmanor(u)† | (301) | 35,794 | 36,267 |
| 20785 | Palmer Park(u) | (301) | 7,019 | 7,986 |
| 21234 | Parkville(u) | (410) | 31,617 | 35,159 |
| 21401 | Parole(u) | (410) | 10,054 | 3,377 |
| 21122 | Pasadena(u) | (410) | 10,012 | 7,439 |
| 21128 | Perry Hall(u) | (410) | 22,723 | 13,455 |
| 21208 | Pikesville(u) | (410) | 24,815 | 22,555 |
| *20850 | Potomac(u) | (301) | 45,634 | 40,313 |
| 21227 | Pumphrey(u) | (410) | 5,483 | 5,666 |
| 21133 | Randallstown(u) | (301) | 26,277 | 25,927 |
| ..... | Redland(u) | (301) | 16,145 | 10,528 |
| 21136 | Reisterstown(u) | (410) | 19,314 | 19,385 |
| 21122 | Riviera Beach(u) | (410) | 11,376 | 8,812 |
| *20850 | Rockville | (301) | 44,830 | 43,811 |
| 20772 | Rosaryville(u) | (301) | 8,976 | .... |
| 21237 | Rosedale(u) | (410) | 18,703 | 19,956 |
| ..... | Rossmoor(u) | | 6,182 | .... |
| 21221 | Rossville(u) | (410) | 9,492 | 8,646 |
| 20602 | Saint Charles(u) | (301) | 28,717 | 13,921 |
| *21801 | Salisbury | (410) | 20,592 | 16,429 |
| 20763 | Savage-Guilford(u) | (410) | 9,669 | 2,928 |
| 20743 | Seat Pleasant | (301) | 5,359 | 5,217 |
| 21144 | Severn(u) | (410) | 24,499 | 20,147 |
| 21146 | Severna Park(u) | (410) | 25,879 | 21,253 |
| *20907 | Silver Spring(u) | (301) | 76,046 | 72,893 |
| 21061 | South Gate(u) | (410) | 27,564 | 24,185 |
| 20895 | South Kensington(u) | (301) | 8,777 | 9,344 |
| 20707 | South Laurel(u) | (301) | 18,591 | 18,034 |
| *20746 | Suitland-Silver Hills(u) | (301) | 35,111 | 32,164 |
| *20907 | Takoma Park | (301) | 16,724 | 16,231 |
| *20748 | Temple Hills(u) | (301) | 6,865 | 6,630 |
| 21285 | Towson(u) | (410) | 49,445 | 51,083 |
| *20602 | Waldorf(u) | (301) | 15,058 | 9,782 |
| 20743 | Walker Mill(u) | (301) | 10,920 | 10,651 |
| *21157 | Westminster | (410) | 13,060 | 8,808 |
| 20902 | Wheaton-Glenmont(u) | (301) | 53,720 | 48,598 |
| 21162 | White Marsh(u) | (410) | 8,183 | .... |
| 20903 | White Oak(u) | (301) | 18,671 | 13,700 |
| 21207 | Woodlawn(u) (Baltimore) | (410) | 32,907 | 29,453 |
| 21284 | Woodlawn(u) (Prince George's) | (410) | 5,329 | 5,306 |

## Massachusetts

*See note on page 390*

| ZIP | Place | | 1990 | 1980 |
|---|---|---|---|---|
| 02351 | Abington(u) | (617) | 13,817 | 13,887 |
| 01720 | *Acton* | (508) | 17,872 | 17,544 |
| 02743 | *Acushnet* | (508) | 9,554 | 8,704 |
| 01220 | Adams Center(u) | (413) | 6,356 | 6,857 |
| 01220 | *Adams* | (413) | 9,445 | 10,381 |
| 01001 | *Agawam* | (413) | 27,323 | 26,271 |
| 01913 | Amesbury Center(u) | (508) | 12,109 | 12,236 |
| 01913 | *Amesbury* | (508) | 14,997 | 13,971 |
| *01002 | Amherst Center(u) | (413) | 17,824 | 17,773 |
| *01002 | *Amherst* | (413) | 35,228 | 33,229 |
| *01810 | Andover(u) | (508) | 8,242 | 8,445 |
| *01810 | *Andover* | (508) | 29,151 | 26,370 |
| 02174 | Arlington(u) | (617) | 44,630 | 48,219 |
| 01430 | *Ashburnham* | (508) | 5,433 | 4,075 |
| 01721 | *Ashland* | (508) | 12,066 | 9,165 |
| 01331 | Athol Center(u) | (508) | 8,732 | 8,708 |
| 01331 | *Athol* | (508) | 11,451 | 10,634 |
| 02703 | Attleboro | (508) | 38,383 | 34,196 |
| 01501 | *Auburn* | (508) | 15,005 | 14,845 |
| 01432 | *Ayer* | (508) | 6,871 | 6,993 |
| 02630 | *Barnstable* | (508) | 40,949 | 30,898 |
| 01730 | *Bedford* | (617) | 12,996 | 13,067 |
| 01007 | *Belchertown* | (413) | 10,579 | 8,339 |
| 02019 | *Bellingham* | (508) | 14,877 | 14,300 |
| 02178 | Belmont(u) | (617) | 24,720 | 26,100 |
| 01915 | Beverly | (508) | 38,195 | 37,655 |
| *01821 | *Billerica* | (508) | 37,609 | 36,727 |
| 01504 | *Blackstone* | (508) | 8,023 | 6,570 |
| *02205 | Boston | (617) | 574,283 | 562,994 |
| 02532 | *Bourne* | (508) | 16,064 | 13,874 |
| 01921 | *Boxford* | (508) | 6,266 | 5,374 |
| *02205 | Braintree(u) | (617) | 33,836 | 36,337 |
| 02631 | *Brewster* | (508) | 8,440 | 5,226 |
| 02324 | *Bridgewater* | (508) | 21,249 | 17,202 |
| *02403 | Brockton | (508) | 92,788 | 95,172 |
| 02146 | Brookline(u) | (617) | 54,718 | 55,062 |
| 01803 | *Burlington* | (617) | 23,302 | 23,486 |
| *02139 | Cambridge | (617) | 95,802 | 95,322 |
| 02021 | *Canton* | (617) | 18,530 | 18,182 |
| 02330 | *Carver* | (508) | 10,590 | 6,988 |
| *02632 | Centerville | (508) | 9,190 | 3,640 |
| 01507 | *Charlton* | (508) | 9,576 | 6,719 |
| 02633 | *Chatham* | (508) | 6,579 | 6,071 |
| 01824 | Chelmsford(u) | (508) | 32,383 | 31,174 |
| 02150 | Chelsea | (617) | 28,710 | 25,431 |
| *01020 | Chicopee | (413) | 56,632 | 55,112 |
| 01510 | *Clinton* | (508) | 13,222 | 12,771 |
| 01778 | Cochituate(u) | (508) | 6,046 | 6,126 |
| 02025 | *Cohasset* | (617) | 7,075 | 7,174 |
| 01742 | *Concord* | (508) | 17,076 | 16,293 |
| *01226 | *Dalton* | (413) | 7,155 | 6,797 |
| 01923 | Danvers(u) | (508) | 24,174 | 24,100 |
| 02714 | *Dartmouth* | (508) | 27,244 | 23,966 |
| *02026 | Dedham(u) | (617) | 23,782 | 25,298 |
| 01342 | *Deerfield* | (413) | 5,018 | 4,517 |
| 02638 | *Dennis* | (508) | 13,864 | 12,360 |
| 02715 | *Dighton* | (508) | 5,631 | 5,352 |
| 01516 | *Douglas* | (508) | 5,438 | 3,730 |
| 01826 | *Dracut* | (508) | 25,594 | 21,249 |
| 01571 | *Dudley* | (508) | 9,540 | 8,717 |
| *02332 | *Duxbury* | (617) | 13,895 | 11,807 |
| 02333 | *East Bridgewater* | (508) | 11,104 | 9,945 |
| 02536 | East Falmouth(u) | (508) | 5,577 | 5,181 |
| 01027 | *Easthampton* | (413) | 15,537 | 15,580 |
| 01028 | *East Longmeadow* | (413) | 13,367 | 12,905 |
| 02334 | *Easton* | (508) | 19,807 | 16,623 |
| 02149 | Everett | (617) | 35,701 | 37,195 |
| 02719 | *Fairhaven* | (508) | 16,132 | 15,759 |
| *02722 | Fall River | (508) | 92,703 | 92,574 |
| *02540 | *Falmouth* | (508) | 27,960 | 23,640 |
| 01420 | Fitchburg | (508) | 41,194 | 39,580 |
| 01433 | Fort Devens(u) | (508) | 8,973 | 9,546 |
| 02035 | Foxborough(u) | (508) | 5,706 | 5,697 |
| 01701 | *Framingham* | (508) | 64,989 | 65,113 |
| 02038 | Franklin Center(u) | (508) | 9,965 | 9,296 |
| 02038 | *Franklin* | (508) | 22,095 | 18,217 |
| 02702 | *Freetown* | (508) | 8,522 | 7,058 |
| 01440 | Gardner | (508) | 20,125 | 17,900 |
| 01833 | *Georgetown* | (508) | 6,384 | 5,687 |
| *01930 | Gloucester | (508) | 28,716 | 27,768 |
| 01519 | *Grafton* | (508) | 13,035 | 11,238 |
| 01033 | *Granby* | (413) | 5,565 | 5,380 |
| 01230 | *Great Barrington* | (413) | 7,725 | 7,405 |
| *01301 | Greenfield Center(u) | (413) | 14,016 | 14,198 |
| 01302 | *Greenfield* | (413) | 18,666 | 18,436 |
| 01450 | *Groton* | (508) | 7,511 | 6,154 |
| 01834 | *Groveland* | (508) | 5,214 | 5,040 |
| 02338 | *Halifax* | (617) | 6,526 | 5,513 |
| 01936 | *Hamilton* | (508) | 7,280 | 6,960 |
| 02339 | *Hanover* | (617) | 11,912 | 11,358 |
| 02341 | *Hanson* | (617) | 9,028 | 8,617 |
| 01451 | *Harvard* | (508) | 12,329 | 12,170 |
| 02645 | *Harwich* | (508) | 10,275 | 8,971 |
| *01830 | Haverhill | (508) | 51,418 | 46,865 |
| 02043 | *Hingham* | (617) | 19,821 | 20,339 |
| 02343 | Holbrook(u) | (617) | 11,041 | 11,140 |
| 01520 | *Holden* | (508) | 14,628 | 13,336 |
| 01746 | *Holliston* | (508) | 12,926 | 12,622 |
| *01040 | Holyoke | (413) | 43,704 | 44,678 |
| 01747 | *Hopedale* | (508) | 5,666 | 3,905 |
| 01748 | *Hopkinton* | (508) | 9,191 | 7,114 |
| 01749 | Hudson Center(u) | (508) | 14,267 | 14,156 |
| 01749 | *Hudson* | (508) | 17,233 | 16,408 |
| 02045 | Hull(u) | (617) | 10,466 | 9,714 |
| 02601 | Hyannis(u) | (508) | 14,120 | 9,118 |
| 01938 | *Ipswich* | (508) | 11,873 | 11,158 |
| 02364 | *Kingston* | (617) | 9,045 | 7,362 |
| 02347 | *Lakeville* | (508) | 7,785 | 5,931 |
| 01523 | *Lancaster* | (508) | 6,661 | 6,334 |
| *01842 | Lawrence | (508) | 70,207 | 63,175 |
| 01238 | *Lee* | (413) | 5,849 | 6,247 |
| 01524 | *Leicester* | (508) | 10,191 | 9,446 |
| 01240 | *Lenox* | (413) | 5,069 | 6,523 |
| 01453 | Leominster | (508) | 38,145 | 34,508 |
| 02173 | Lexington(u) | (617) | 28,974 | 29,479 |
| 01773 | *Lincoln* | (617) | 7,666 | 7,098 |
| 01460 | *Littleton* | (508) | 7,051 | 6,970 |
| *01028 | Longmeadow(u) | (413) | 15,467 | 16,301 |
| *01853 | Lowell | (508) | 103,439 | 92,418 |
| 01056 | *Ludlow* | (413) | 18,820 | 18,150 |
| 01462 | *Lunenburg* | (508) | 9,117 | 8,405 |
| *01901 | Lynn | (617) | 81,245 | 78,471 |
| 01940 | Lynnfield(u) | (617) | 11,274 | 11,267 |
| 02148 | Malden | (617) | 53,884 | 53,386 |
| 01944 | *Manchester* | (508) | 5,286 | 5,424 |
| 02048 | *Mansfield* | (508) | 16,568 | 13,453 |
| 01945 | Marblehead(u) | (617) | 19,971 | 20,126 |
| 01752 | Marlborough | (508) | 31,813 | 30,617 |
| 02050 | *Marshfield* | (617) | 21,531 | 20,916 |
| 02648 | Marstons Mills(u) | (508) | 8,017 | .... |
| 02649 | *Mashpee* | (508) | 7,884 | 3,700 |
| 02739 | *Mattapoisett* | (508) | 5,850 | 5,597 |
| 01754 | Maynard(u) | (508) | 10,325 | 9,590 |
| 02052 | *Medfield* | (508) | 10,531 | 10,220 |
| 02155 | Medford | (617) | 57,407 | 58,076 |
| 02053 | *Medway* | (508) | 9,931 | 8,447 |
| *02176 | Melrose | (617) | 28,150 | 30,055 |
| 01860 | Merrimac | (508) | 5,166 | 4,451 |
| 01844 | *Methuen* | (508) | 39,990 | 36,701 |

| ZIP | Place | | 1990 | 1980 |
|---|---|---|---|---|
| 02346 | Middleborough Center(u) | (508) | 6,837 | 7,012 |
| 02346 | *Middleborough* | (508) | 17,867 | 16,404 |
| 01757 | Milford Center(u) | (508) | 23,339 | 21,730 |
| 01757 | *Milford* | (508) | 25,355 | 23,390 |
| 01527 | *Millbury* | (508) | 12,228 | 11,808 |
| 02054 | *Millis* | (508) | 7,613 | 6,908 |
| 02186 | Milton(u) | (617) | 25,725 | 25,860 |
| 01057 | *Monson* | (413) | 7,776 | 7,315 |
| 01351 | *Montague* | (413) | 8,316 | 8,011 |
| *02554 | *Nantucket* | (508) | 6,012 | 5,087 |
| 01760 | *Natick* | (508) | 30,510 | 29,461 |
| *02205 | Needham(u) | (617) | 27,557 | 27,901 |
| *02740 | New Bedford | (508) | 99,922 | 98,478 |
| 01951 | *Newbury* | (508) | 5,623 | 4,529 |
| 01950 | Newburyport | (508) | 16,317 | 15,900 |
| *02205 | Newton | (617) | 82,585 | 83,622 |
| 02056 | *Norfolk* | (508) | 9,270 | 6,363 |
| 01247 | North Adams | (413) | 16,797 | 18,063 |
| 01002 | North Amherst(u) | (413) | 6,239 | 5,616 |
| *01060 | Northampton | (413) | 29,289 | 29,286 |
| 01845 | *North Andover* | (508) | 22,792 | 20,129 |
| *02760 | *North Attleborough* | (508) | 25,038 | 21,095 |
| 01532 | *Northborough* | (508) | 11,929 | 10,568 |
| 01534 | *Northbridge* | (508) | 13,371 | 12,246 |
| 01864 | *North Reading* | (508) | 12,002 | 11,455 |
| 02766 | *Norton* | (508) | 14,265 | 12,690 |
| 02061 | *Norwell* | (617) | 9,279 | 9,182 |
| 02062 | Norwood(u) | (617) | 28,700 | 29,711 |
| 01364 | *Orange* | (508) | 7,312 | 6,844 |
| 02653 | *Orleans* | (508) | 5,838 | 5,306 |
| 01540 | Oxford Center(u) | (508) | 5,969 | 6,369 |
| 01540 | *Oxford* | (508) | 12,588 | 11,680 |
| 01069 | *Palmer* | (413) | 12,054 | 11,389 |
| *01960 | Peabody | (508) | 47,264 | 45,976 |
| 02359 | *Pembroke* | (617) | 14,544 | 13,487 |
| 01463 | *Pepperell* | (508) | 10,098 | 8,061 |
| 01866 | Pinehurst(u) | (508) | 6,614 | 6,588 |
| *01201 | Pittsfield | (413) | 48,622 | 51,974 |
| 02762 | *Plainville* | (508) | 6,871 | 5,857 |
| *02360 | Plymouth Center(u) | (508) | 7,258 | 7,232 |
| *02360 | *Plymouth* | (508) | 45,608 | 35,913 |
| *02205 | Quincy | (617) | 84,985 | 84,743 |
| 02368 | Randolph(u) | (617) | 30,093 | 28,218 |
| 02767 | *Raynham* | (508) | 9,867 | 9,085 |
| 01867 | Reading(u) | (617) | 22,539 | 22,678 |
| 02769 | *Rehoboth* | (508) | 8,656 | 7,570 |
| 02151 | Revere | (617) | 42,786 | 42,423 |
| 02370 | *Rockland* | (617) | 16,123 | 15,695 |
| 01966 | *Rockport* | (508) | 7,482 | 6,345 |
| *01970 | Salem | (508) | 38,091 | 38,276 |
| 01952 | *Salisbury* | (508) | 6,882 | 5,973 |
| 02563 | *Sandwich* | (508) | 15,489 | 8,727 |
| 01906 | Saugus(u) | (617) | 25,549 | 24,746 |
| 02066 | *Scituate* | (617) | 16,786 | 17,317 |
| 02771 | *Seekonk* | (508) | 13,046 | 12,269 |
| 02067 | *Sharon* | (617) | 15,517 | 13,601 |
| 01464 | *Shirley* | (508) | 6,118 | 5,124 |
| 01545 | *Shrewsbury* | (508) | 24,146 | 22,674 |
| *02722 | Somerset(u) | (508) | 17,655 | 18,813 |
| *02205 | Somerville(u) | (617) | 76,210 | 77,372 |
| 01002 | South Amherst | (413) | 5,053 | 4,861 |
| 01772 | *Southborough* | (508) | 6,628 | 6,193 |
| 01550 | Southbridge Center(u) | (508) | 13,631 | 12,882 |
| 01550 | *Southbridge* | (508) | 17,816 | 16,665 |
| 01075 | *South Hadley* | (413) | 16,685 | 16,399 |
| 01077 | *Southwick* | (413) | 7,667 | 7,382 |
| 02664 | South Yarmouth(u) | (508) | 10,358 | 7,525 |
| 01562 | Spencer Center(u) | (508) | 6,306 | 6,350 |
| 01562 | *Spencer* | (508) | 11,645 | 10,774 |
| *01101 | Springfield | (413) | 156,983 | 152,319 |
| 01564 | *Sterling* | (508) | 6,481 | 5,440 |
| 02180 | *Stoneham* | (617) | 22,203 | 21,424 |
| 02072 | *Stoughton* | (617) | 26,777 | 26,710 |
| 01775 | *Stow* | (508) | 5,328 | 5,144 |
| 01566 | *Sturbridge* | (508) | 7,775 | 5,976 |
| 01776 | *Sudbury* | (508) | 14,358 | 14,027 |
| 01590 | *Sutton* | (508) | 6,824 | 5,855 |
| 01907 | Swampscott(u) | (617) | 13,650 | 13,837 |
| 02777 | *Swansea* | (508) | 15,411 | 15,461 |
| 02780 | Taunton | (508) | 49,832 | 45,001 |
| 01468 | *Templeton* | (508) | 6,438 | 6,070 |
| 01876 | *Tewksbury* | (508) | 27,266 | 24,635 |
| 01983 | *Topsfield* | (508) | 5,754 | 5,709 |
| 01469 | *Townsend* | (508) | 8,496 | 7,201 |
| 01879 | *Tyngsborough* | (508) | 8,642 | 5,683 |
| 01569 | *Uxbridge* | (508) | 10,415 | 8,374 |
| 01880 | Wakefield(u) | (617) | 24,825 | 24,895 |
| 02081 | *Walpole* | (508) | 20,223 | 18,859 |
| *02205 | Waltham | (617) | 57,878 | 58,200 |
| 01082 | Ware Center(u) | (413) | 6,533 | 6,806 |
| 01082 | *Ware* | (413) | 9,808 | 8,953 |
| 02571 | *Wareham* | (508) | 19,232 | 18,457 |
| *02205 | Watertown(u) | (617) | 33,284 | 34,384 |
| 01778 | *Wayland* | (508) | 11,874 | 12,170 |
| 01570 | Webster Center(u) | (508) | 11,849 | 11,175 |
| 01570 | *Webster* | (508) | 16,196 | 14,480 |
| 02181 | *Wellesley* | (617) | 26,615 | 27,209 |
| 01581 | *Westborough* | (508) | 14,133 | 13,619 |
| 01583 | *West Boylston* | (508) | 6,611 | 6,204 |
| 02379 | *West Bridgewater* | (508) | 6,389 | 6,359 |

| ZIP | Place | | 1990 | 1980 |
|---|---|---|---|---|
| 01742 | West Concord(u) | (508) | 5,761 | 5,331 |
| *01085 | Westfield | (413) | 38,372 | 36,465 |
| 01886 | *Westford* | (508) | 16,392 | 13,434 |
| 01473 | *Westminster* | (508) | 6,191 | 5,139 |
| 02193 | *Weston* | (617) | 10,200 | 11,169 |
| 02790 | *Westport* | (508) | 13,852 | 13,763 |
| *01089 | West Springfield(u) | (413) | 27,537 | 27,042 |
| 02090 | *Westwood* | (617) | 12,557 | 13,212 |
| 02673 | West Yarmouth | (508) | 5,409 | 3,852 |
| *02205 | Weymouth(u) | (617) | 54,063 | 55,601 |
| 01588 | Whitinsville(u) | (508) | 5,639 | 5,379 |
| 02382 | *Whitman* | (617) | 13,240 | 13,534 |
| 01095 | *Wilbraham* | (413) | 12,635 | 12,053 |
| 01267 | *Williamstown* | (413) | 8,220 | 8,741 |
| 01887 | Wilmington(u) | (508) | 17,651 | 17,471 |
| 01475 | *Winchendon* | (508) | 8,805 | 7,019 |
| 01890 | Winchester(u) | (617) | 20,267 | 20,701 |
| 02152 | Winthrop(u) | (617) | 18,127 | 19,294 |
| *01801 | Woburn | (617) | 35,943 | 36,626 |
| *01613 | Worcester | (508) | 169,759 | 161,799 |
| 02093 | *Wrentham* | (508) | 9,006 | 7,580 |
| 02675 | *Yarmouth* | (508) | 21,174 | 18,449 |

## Michigan

| ZIP | Place | | 1990 | 1980 |
|---|---|---|---|---|
| 49221 | Adrian | (517) | 22,097 | 21,276 |
| 49224 | Albion | (517) | 10,066 | 11,059 |
| 49401 | Allendale(u) | (616) | 6,950 | .... |
| 48101 | Allen Park | (313) | 31,092 | 34,196 |
| 48801 | Alma | (517) | 9,034 | 9,652 |
| 49707 | Alpena | (517) | 11,354 | 12,214 |
| *48106 | Ann Arbor | (313) | 109,608 | 107,969 |
| *48321 | Auburn Hills† | (810) | 17,076 | 15,388 |
| *49016 | Battle Creek | (616) | 53,516 | 35,724 |
| *48707 | Bay City | (517) | 38,936 | 41,593 |
| 48505 | Beecher(u) | (313) | 14,465 | 17,178 |
| 48809 | Belding | (616) | 5,969 | 5,634 |
| *49022 | Benton Harbor | (616) | 12,818 | 14,707 |
| 49022 | Benton Heights(u) | (616) | 5,465 | 6,787 |
| 48072 | Berkley | (810) | 16,960 | 18,637 |
| 48025 | Beverly Hills | (810) | 10,610 | 11,598 |
| 49307 | Big Rapids | (616) | 12,603 | 14,361 |
| *48012 | Birmingham | (810) | 19,997 | 21,689 |
| 48301 | Bloomfield(u) | (810) | 42,137 | 42,876 |
| 48722 | Bridgeport(u) | (517) | 8,569 | .... |
| 48116 | Brighton | (810) | 5,686 | 4,268 |
| 48601 | Buena Vista(u) | | 8,196 | .... |
| *48501 | Burton | (810) | 27,437 | 29,976 |
| 49601 | Cadillac | (616) | 10,104 | 10,199 |
| *48187 | Canton(u) | (313) | 57,047 | .... |
| 48724 | Carrollton(u) | (517) | 6,521 | 7,482 |
| 48015 | Center Line | (810) | 9,026 | 9,293 |
| 48813 | Charlotte | (517) | 8,083 | 8,251 |
| 48017 | Clawson | (810) | 13,874 | 15,103 |
| *48046 | Clinton(u) | (517) | 85,866 | 72,400 |
| 49036 | Coldwater | (517) | 9,607 | 9,461 |
| 49321 | Comstock Park(u) | (616) | 6,530 | 5,506 |
| 49508 | Cutlerville(u) | (616) | 11,228 | 8,256 |
| 48423 | Davison | (810) | 5,693 | 6,087 |
| *48120 | Dearborn | (313) | 89,286 | 90,660 |
| *48127 | Dearborn Heights | (313) | 60,838 | 67,706 |
| *48231 | Detroit | (313) | 1,027,974 | 1,203,368 |
| 49047 | Dowagiac | (616) | 6,418 | 6,307 |
| 49506 | East Grand Rapids | (616) | 10,807 | 10,914 |
| *48826 | East Lansing | (517) | 50,677 | 51,392 |
| 48021 | Eastpointe | (810) | 35,283 | 38,280 |
| 49001 | Eastwood(u) | (616) | 6,340 | 7,186 |
| 48229 | Ecorse | (313) | 12,180 | 14,447 |
| 49829 | Escanaba | (906) | 13,659 | 14,355 |
| 49022 | Fair Plain(u) | (616) | 8,051 | 8,289 |
| *48333 | Farmington | (810) | 10,170 | 11,022 |
| 48333 | Farmington Hills | (810) | 74,614 | 58,056 |
| 48430 | Fenton | (313) | 8,434 | 8,098 |
| 48220 | Ferndale | (810) | 25,084 | 26,227 |
| 48134 | Flat Rock | (313) | 7,290 | 6,853 |
| *48501 | Flint | (810) | 140,925 | 140,925 |
| 48433 | Flushing | (810) | 8,542 | 8,624 |
| 49506 | Forest Hills(u) | (616) | 16,690 | .... |
| 48026 | Fraser | (810) | 13,899 | 14,560 |
| *48135 | Garden City | (313) | 31,846 | 35,640 |
| 48439 | Grand Blanc | (810) | 7,760 | 6,848 |
| 49417 | Grand Haven | (616) | 11,951 | 11,763 |
| 48837 | Grand Ledge | (517) | 7,562 | 6,920 |
| *49501 | Grand Rapids | (616) | 189,126 | 181,843 |
| *49418 | Grandville | (616) | 15,624 | 12,412 |
| 48838 | Greenville | (616) | 8,101 | 8,019 |
| 48138 | Grosse Ile(u) | (313) | 9,781 | 9,320 |
| *48231 | Grosse Pointe | (313) | 5,681 | 5,901 |
| 48230 | Grosse Pointe Farms | (313) | 10,092 | 10,551 |
| 48230 | Grosse Pointe Park | (313) | 12,857 | 13,562 |
| 48230 | Grosse Pointe Woods | (313) | 17,715 | 18,886 |
| 48212 | Hamtramck | (313) | 18,372 | 21,300 |
| 48225 | Harper Woods | (313) | 14,903 | 16,361 |
| 48625 | Harrison(u) | (517) | 24,685 | 23,649 |
| 48840 | Haslett(u) | (517) | 10,230 | 7,025 |
| 49058 | Hastings | (616) | 6,549 | 6,418 |
| 48030 | Hazel Park | (810) | 20,051 | 20,914 |
| 48203 | Highland Park | (313) | 20,121 | 27,909 |

| ZIP | Place | | 1990 | 1980 |
|---|---|---|---|---|
| 49242 | Hillsdale | (517) | 8,175 | 7,432 |
| *49423 | Holland | (616) | 30,745 | 26,281 |
| 48442 | Holly | (810) | 5,595 | 4,874 |
| 48842 | Holt(u) | (517) | 11,744 | 10,097 |
| 49931 | Houghton | (906) | 7,498 | 7,512 |
| *48843 | Howell | (517) | 8,147 | 6,976 |
| 49426 | Hudsonville | (616) | 6,170 | 4,844 |
| 48070 | Huntington Woods | (810) | 6,419 | 6,937 |
| 48141 | Inkster | (313) | 30,772 | 35,190 |
| 48846 | Ionia | (616) | 5,990 | 5,920 |
| *49801 | Iron Mountain | (906) | 8,525 | 8,341 |
| 49938 | Ironwood | (906) | 6,849 | 7,741 |
| 49849 | Ishpeming | (906) | 7,200 | 7,538 |
| *49204 | Jackson | (517) | 37,425 | 39,739 |
| *49428 | Jenison(u) | (616) | 17,882 | 16,330 |
| *49001 | Kalamazoo | (616) | 80,277 | 79,722 |
| 49518 | Kentwood | (616) | 37,826 | 30,438 |
| 49801 | Kingsford | (906) | 5,480 | 5,290 |
| 49843 | K.I. Sawyer AFB(u) | (906) | 6,577 | 7,345 |
| 48144 | Lambertville(u) | (313) | 7,860 | 6,341 |
| *48901 | Lansing | (517) | 127,321 | 130,414 |
| 48446 | Lapeer | (810) | 7,759 | 6,198 |
| 48146 | Lincoln Park | (313) | 41,832 | 45,105 |
| *48150 | Livonia | (313) | 100,850 | 104,814 |
| 49431 | Ludington | (616) | 8,507 | 8,937 |
| 48071 | Madison Heights | (810) | 32,196 | 35,375 |
| 49660 | Manistee | (616) | 6,734 | 7,665 |
| 49855 | Marquette | (906) | 21,977 | 23,288 |
| 49068 | Marshall | (616) | 6,941 | 7,201 |
| 48040 | Marysville | (810) | 8,515 | 7,345 |
| 48854 | Mason | (517) | 6,768 | 6,019 |
| 48122 | Melvindale | (313) | 11,216 | 12,322 |
| 49858 | Menominee | (906) | 9,398 | 10,099 |
| *48640 | Midland | (517) | 38,053 | 37,269 |
| *48381 | Milford | (810) | 5,500 | 5,041 |
| 48161 | Monroe | (313) | 22,902 | 23,531 |
| *48046 | Mount Clemens | (810) | 18,405 | 18,991 |
| *48804 | Mount Pleasant | (517) | 23,299 | 23,746 |
| *49440 | Muskegon | (616) | 39,809 | 40,823 |
| 49444 | Muskegon Heights | (616) | 13,176 | 14,611 |
| *48047 | New Baltimore | (810) | 5,798 | 5,439 |
| 49120 | Niles | (616) | 12,458 | 13,115 |
| 49505 | Northview(u) | (616) | 13,712 | 11,662 |
| 48167 | Northville | (313) | 6,226 | 5,698 |
| 49441 | Norton Shores | (616) | 21,755 | 22,025 |
| *48376 | Novi | (810) | 32,998 | 22,525 |
| 48237 | Oak Park | (810) | 30,468 | 31,537 |
| *48805 | Okemos(u) | (517) | 20,216 | 8,882 |
| 48867 | Owosso | (517) | 16,322 | 16,455 |
| 49770 | Petoskey | (616) | 6,056 | 6,097 |
| 48170 | Plymouth | (313) | 9,560 | 9,986 |
| 48170 | Plymouth Township(u) | (313) | 23,646 | .... |
| *48343 | Pontiac | (810) | 71,136 | 76,715 |
| 49081 | Portage | (616) | 41,042 | 38,157 |
| *48061 | Port Huron | (810) | 33,694 | 33,981 |
| *48231 | Redford(u) | (313) | 54,387 | 58,441 |
| 48218 | River Rouge | (313) | 11,314 | 12,912 |
| 48192 | Riverview | (313) | 13,894 | 14,569 |
| *48308 | Rochester | (810) | 7,130 | 7,203 |
| 48306 | Rochester Hills† | (810) | 61,766 | 40,704 |
| 48174 | Romulus | (313) | 22,897 | 24,857 |
| 48066 | Roseville | (810) | 51,412 | 54,311 |
| *48068 | Royal Oak | (810) | 65,410 | 70,893 |
| *48605 | Saginaw | (517) | 69,512 | 77,508 |
| 48604 | Saginaw Township North(u) | (517) | 23,018 | .... |
| 48603 | Saginaw Township South(u) | (517) | 13,987 | .... |
| 48079 | Saint Clair | (810) | 5,116 | 4,780 |
| *48080 | Saint Clair Shores | (810) | 68,107 | 76,210 |
| 48879 | Saint Johns | (517) | 7,392 | 7,376 |
| 49085 | Saint Joseph | (616) | 9,214 | 9,622 |
| 48176 | Saline | (313) | 6,663 | 6,483 |
| 49783 | Sault Sainte Marie | (906) | 14,689 | 14,448 |
| 49455 | Shelby(u) | (616) | 48,655 | .... |
| 48609 | Shields(u) | (517) | 6,634 | .... |
| *48037 | Southfield | (810) | 75,727 | 75,568 |
| 48195 | Southgate | (313) | 30,771 | 32,058 |
| 49090 | South Haven | (616) | 5,563 | 5,943 |
| 48178 | South Lyon | (810) | 6,479 | 5,214 |
| 48161 | South Monroe(u) | (313) | 5,266 | 4,232 |
| 49015 | Springfield | (616) | 5,582 | 5,917 |
| *48311 | Sterling Heights | (810) | 117,810 | 108,999 |
| 49091 | Sturgis | (616) | 10,130 | 9,468 |
| 48180 | Taylor | (313) | 70,811 | 77,568 |
| 49286 | Tecumseh | (517) | 7,462 | 7,320 |
| 48182 | Temperance(u) | (313) | 6,542 | .... |
| 49093 | Three Rivers | (616) | 7,464 | 7,015 |
| *49685 | Traverse City | (616) | 15,155 | 15,516 |
| 48183 | Trenton | (313) | 20,586 | 22,762 |
| *48099 | Troy | (810) | 72,884 | 67,102 |
| *48318 | Utica | (810) | 5,081 | 5,282 |
| 49504 | Walker | (616) | 17,279 | 15,088 |
| *48390 | Walled Lake | (810) | 6,278 | 4,748 |
| *48090 | Warren | (810) | 144,864 | 161,134 |
| 48329 | Waterford(u) | (810) | 66,692 | 64,250 |
| 48917 | Waverly(u) | | 15,614 | .... |
| 48184 | Wayne | (313) | 19,899 | 21,159 |
| *48325 | West Bloomfield(u) | (810) | 54,843 | 41,962 |
| 48185 | Westland | (313) | 84,724 | 84,603 |
| 49019 | Westwood(u) | (616) | 8,957 | 8,519 |
| 48393 | Wixom | (313) | 8,550 | 6,705 |
| 48183 | Woodhaven | (313) | 11,631 | 10,902 |
| 48753 | Wurtsmith AFB(u) | (517) | 5,080 | 5,166 |
| *48192 | Wyandotte | (313) | 30,938 | 34,006 |
| 49509 | Wyoming | (616) | 63,891 | 59,616 |
| *48197 | Ypsilanti | (313) | 24,846 | 24,031 |
| 49464 | Zeeland | (616) | 5,417 | 4,764 |

## Minnesota

| ZIP | Place | | 1990 | 1980 |
|---|---|---|---|---|
| 56007 | Albert Lea | (507) | 18,310 | 19,200 |
| 56308 | Alexandria | (320) | 8,029 | 7,608 |
| 55304 | Andover | (612) | 15,216 | 9,387 |
| *55303 | Anoka | (612) | 17,192 | 15,634 |
| 55124 | Apple Valley | (612) | 34,598 | 21,818 |
| 55112 | Arden Hills | (612) | 9,199 | 8,012 |
| 55912 | Austin | (507) | 21,926 | 23,020 |
| 56601 | Bemidji | (218) | 11,165 | 10,949 |
| 55449 | Blaine | (612) | 38,975 | 28,558 |
| *55420 | Bloomington | (612) | 86,335 | 81,831 |
| 56401 | Brainerd | (218) | 12,353 | 11,489 |
| 55429 | Brooklyn Center | (612) | 28,887 | 31,230 |
| 55443 | Brooklyn Park | (612) | 56,381 | 43,332 |
| 55313 | Buffalo | (612) | 6,856 | 4,560 |
| *55337 | Burnsville | (612) | 51,288 | 35,674 |
| 55008 | Cambridge | (612) | 5,094 | 3,287 |
| 55316 | Champlin | (612) | 16,849 | 9,006 |
| 55317 | Chanhassen | (612) | 11,732 | 6,359 |
| 55318 | Chaska | (612) | 11,339 | 8,346 |
| 55719 | Chisholm | (218) | 5,290 | 5,930 |
| 55720 | Cloquet | (218) | 10,885 | 11,142 |
| 55421 | Columbia Heights | (612) | 18,910 | 20,029 |
| 55433 | Coon Rapids | (612) | 52,978 | 35,826 |
| 55340 | Corcoran | (612) | 5,199 | 4,252 |
| 55016 | Cottage Grove | (612) | 22,935 | 18,994 |
| 56716 | Crookston | (218) | 8,119 | 8,628 |
| 55428 | Crystal | (612) | 23,788 | 25,543 |
| *56501 | Detroit Lakes | (218) | 6,635 | 7,106 |
| *55806 | Duluth | (218) | 85,493 | 92,811 |
| 55121 | Eagan | (612) | 47,409 | 20,700 |
| 55005 | East Bethel | (612) | 8,050 | 6,626 |
| 56721 | East Grand Forks | (218) | 8,658 | 8,537 |
| *55344 | Eden Prairie | (612) | 39,311 | 16,263 |
| 55424 | Edina | (612) | 46,075 | 46,073 |
| 55330 | Elk River | (612) | 11,143 | 6,785 |
| 56031 | Fairmont | (507) | 11,265 | 11,506 |
| 55113 | Falcon Heights | (612) | 5,380 | 5,291 |
| 55021 | Faribault | (507) | 17,085 | 16,241 |
| 55024 | Farmington | (612) | 5,940 | 4,370 |
| *56537 | Fergus Falls | (218) | 12,362 | 12,519 |
| 55025 | Forest Lake | (612) | 5,833 | 4,596 |
| 55432 | Fridley | (612) | 28,335 | 30,228 |
| 55427 | Golden Valley | (612) | 20,971 | 22,775 |
| *55744 | Grand Rapids | (218) | 7,976 | 7,934 |
| *55304 | Ham Lake | (612) | 8,924 | 7,832 |
| 55033 | Hastings | (612) | 15,478 | 12,827 |
| 55810 | Hermantown | (218) | 6,761 | 6,759 |
| *55746 | Hibbing | (218) | 18,046 | 21,193 |
| *55343 | Hopkins | (612) | 16,529 | 15,336 |
| 55350 | Hutchinson | (320) | 11,459 | 9,244 |
| 56649 | International Falls | (218) | 8,301 | 5,611 |
| *55075 | Inver Grove Heights | (612) | 22,477 | 17,171 |
| 55042 | Lake Elmo | (612) | 5,900 | 5,296 |
| 55044 | Lakeville | (612) | 24,854 | 14,790 |
| 55014 | Lino Lakes | (612) | 8,807 | 4,966 |
| 55355 | Litchfield | (320) | 6,041 | 5,904 |
| 55117 | Little Canada | (612) | 8,971 | 7,102 |
| 56345 | Little Falls | (320) | 7,371 | 7,250 |
| 55115 | Mahtomedi | (612) | 5,633 | 3,851 |
| *56001 | Mankato | (507) | 31,405 | 28,646 |
| 55311 | Maple Grove | (612) | 38,736 | 20,525 |
| 55109 | Maplewood | (612) | 30,954 | 26,990 |
| 56258 | Marshall | (507) | 12,023 | 11,161 |
| 55118 | Mendota Heights | (612) | 9,388 | 7,288 |
| *55440 | Minneapolis | (612) | 368,383 | 370,951 |
| 55345 | Minnetonka | (612) | 48,370 | 38,683 |
| 56265 | Montevideo | (320) | 5,499 | 5,845 |
| *55362 | Monticello | (612) | 5,045 | 4,693 |
| *56560 | Moorhead | (218) | 32,295 | 29,998 |
| 56267 | Morris | (320) | 5,613 | 5,367 |
| 55364 | Mound | (612) | 9,634 | 9,280 |
| 55112 | Mounds View | (612) | 12,541 | 12,593 |
| 55112 | New Brighton | (612) | 22,207 | 23,269 |
| 54427 | New Hope | (612) | 21,853 | 23,087 |
| 56073 | New Ulm | (507) | 13,132 | 13,755 |
| 55057 | Northfield | (507) | 14,684 | 12,562 |
| 56001 | North Mankato | (507) | 10,662 | 9,145 |
| 55109 | North Saint Paul | (612) | 12,376 | 11,921 |
| 55128 | Oakdale | (612) | 18,377 | 12,123 |
| 55323 | Orono | (612) | 7,285 | 6,845 |
| 55060 | Owatonna | (507) | 19,386 | 18,632 |
| 55421 | Plymouth | (612) | 50,889 | 31,615 |
| 55372 | Prior Lake | (612) | 11,482 | 7,284 |
| 55303 | Ramsey | (612) | 12,408 | 10,093 |
| 55066 | Red Wing | (612) | 15,134 | 13,736 |
| 55423 | Richfield | (612) | 35,710 | 37,851 |
| 55422 | Robbinsdale | (612) | 14,396 | 14,422 |
| *55901 | Rochester | (507) | 70,729 | 57,906 |
| 55068 | Rosemount | (612) | 8,622 | 5,083 |
| 55113 | Roseville | (612) | 33,485 | 35,820 |

| ZIP | Place | | 1990 | 1980 |
|---|---|---|---|---|
| 55418 | Saint Anthony | (612) | 7,727 | 7,981 |
| *56301 | Saint Cloud | (320) | 48,812 | 42,566 |
| 55426 | Saint Louis Park | (612) | 43,787 | 42,931 |
| *55101 | Saint Paul | (612) | 272,235 | 270,230 |
| 56082 | Saint Peter | (507) | 9,481 | 9,056 |
| 56377 | Sartell | (320) | 5,409 | 3,427 |
| 56379 | Sauk Rapids | (320) | 7,823 | 5,793 |
| 56378 | Savage | (612) | 9,906 | 3,954 |
| 55379 | Shakopee | (612) | 11,739 | 9,941 |
| 55126 | Shoreview | (612) | 24,587 | 17,300 |
| 55331 | Shorewood | (612) | 5,917 | 4,646 |
| 55075 | South Saint Paul | (612) | 20,197 | 21,235 |
| 55432 | Spring Lake Park | (612) | 6,532 | 6,477 |
| *55082 | Stillwater | (612) | 13,882 | 12,290 |
| 56701 | Thief River Falls | (218) | 8,010 | 9,105 |
| 55127 | Vadnais Heights | (612) | 11,041 | 5,111 |
| *55792 | Virginia | (218) | 9,410 | 11,056 |
| 56387 | Waite Park | (320) | 5,020 | 3,496 |
| 56093 | Waseca | (507) | 8,385 | 8,219 |
| 55118 | West Saint Paul | (612) | 19,248 | 18,527 |
| 55110 | White Bear Lake | (612) | 24,622 | 22,538 |
| 56201 | Willmar | (320) | 17,531 | 15,895 |
| 55987 | Winona | (507) | 25,435 | 25,075 |
| 55125 | Woodbury | (612) | 20,075 | 10,297 |
| 56187 | Worthington | (507) | 9,977 | 10,243 |

## Mississippi (601)

| ZIP | Place | 1990 | 1980 |
|---|---|---|---|
| 39730 | Aberdeen | 6,837 | 7,184 |
| 38821 | Amory | 7,093 | 7,307 |
| 38606 | Batesville | 6,403 | 5,162 |
| *39520 | Bay Saint Louis | 8,063 | 7,850 |
| *39530 | Biloxi | 46,319 | 49,311 |
| 38829 | Booneville | 7,955 | 6,199 |
| *39042 | Brandon | 11,077 | 9,626 |
| 39601 | Brookhaven | 10,243 | 10,800 |
| 39046 | Canton | 10,062 | 11,116 |
| 38614 | Clarksdale | 19,717 | 21,137 |
| 38732 | Cleveland | 15,384 | 14,524 |
| *39056 | Clinton | 21,847 | 14,660 |
| 39429 | Columbia | 6,815 | 7,733 |
| *39701 | Columbus | 23,799 | 27,503 |
| 38834 | Corinth | 11,820 | 13,180 |
| 39059 | Crystal Springs | 5,643 | 4,902 |
| 39532 | D'Iberville† | 6,566 | 6,236 |
| 39074 | Forest | 5,062 | 5,229 |
| 39553 | Gautier† | 10,088 | 10,392 |
| *38701 | Greenville | 45,226 | 40,613 |
| *38930 | Greenwood | 18,906 | 20,115 |
| *38901 | Grenada | 10,864 | 11,508 |
| 39564 | Gulf Hills(u) | 5,004 | 4,512 |
| *39501 | Gulfport | 40,775 | 39,676 |
| *39401 | Hattiesburg | 41,906 | 40,829 |
| *38635 | Holly Springs | 7,261 | 7,285 |
| 38637 | Horn Lake | 9,069 | 4,326 |
| 38751 | Indianola | 11,809 | 8,050 |
| *39205 | Jackson | 196,637 | 202,895 |
| 39090 | Kosciusko | 6,986 | 7,415 |
| *39440 | Laurel | 18,827 | 21,897 |
| 38756 | Leland | 6,366 | 6,667 |
| 39560 | Long Beach | 15,804 | 14,199 |
| 39339 | Louisville | 7,165 | 7,323 |
| 39648 | McComb | 11,797 | 12,331 |
| *39110 | Madison | 7,471 | 2,241 |
| *39302 | Meridian | 41,036 | 46,577 |
| *39567 | Moss Point | 17,837 | 18,998 |
| *39120 | Natchez | 19,460 | 22,209 |
| 38652 | New Albany | 6,775 | 7,072 |
| *39564 | Ocean Springs | 14,673 | 14,504 |
| 39567 | Orange Grove(u) | 15,676 | 13,476 |
| 38655 | Oxford | 10,026 | 9,882 |
| *39567 | Pascagoula | 25,899 | 29,318 |
| 39571 | Pass Christian | 5,557 | 5,014 |
| 39288 | Pearl | 19,588 | 18,602 |
| 39465 | Petal | 7,883 | 8,476 |
| 39350 | Philadelphia | 6,758 | 6,434 |
| 39466 | Picayune | 10,633 | 10,361 |
| *39157 | Ridgeland | 11,714 | 5,461 |
| 38663 | Ripley | 5,371 | 4,271 |
| 39533 | Saint Martin(u) | 6,349 | .... |
| 38671 | Southaven† | 17,949 | 16,441 |
| 39759 | Starkville | 18,458 | 16,139 |
| *38801 | Tupelo | 30,685 | 23,905 |
| *39180 | Vicksburg | 20,909 | 25,434 |
| 39576 | Waveland | 5,369 | 4,186 |
| 39367 | Waynesboro | 5,143 | 5,349 |
| ..... | West Hattiesburg(u) | 5,450 | .... |
| 39773 | West Point | 8,489 | 8,811 |
| 38967 | Winona | 5,724 | 6,177 |
| 39194 | Yazoo City | 12,427 | 12,092 |

## Missouri

| ZIP | Place | | 1990 | 1980 |
|---|---|---|---|---|
| 63123 | Affton(u) | (314) | 21,106 | 23,181 |
| 63010 | Arnold | (314) | 18,828 | 19,141 |
| 65605 | Aurora | (417) | 6,459 | 6,437 |
| *63011 | Ballwin | (314) | 21,406 | 12,656 |
| 63137 | Bellefontaine Neighbors | (314) | 10,918 | 12,082 |
| 64012 | Belton | (816) | 18,145 | 12,708 |
| 63134 | Berkeley | (314) | 12,250 | 15,922 |
| 63031 | Black Jack | (314) | 6,131 | 5,293 |
| *64015 | Blue Springs | (816) | 40,103 | 25,936 |
| 65613 | Bolivar | (417) | 6,845 | 5,919 |
| 65233 | Boonville | (816) | 7,095 | 6,959 |
| 63114 | Breckenridge Hills | (314) | 5,181 | 5,666 |
| 63144 | Brentwood | (314) | 8,150 | 8,209 |
| 63044 | Bridgeton | (314) | 17,732 | 18,445 |
| *63701 | Cape Girardeau | (573) | 34,475 | 34,361 |
| 64836 | Carthage | (417) | 10,747 | 11,104 |
| 63830 | Caruthersville | (573) | 7,389 | 7,958 |
| 63834 | Charleston | (573) | 5,085 | 5,230 |
| 63017 | Chesterfield† | (314) | 38,630 | 28,384 |
| 64601 | Chillicothe | (816) | 8,799 | 9,089 |
| 63105 | Clayton | (314) | 13,926 | 14,306 |
| 64735 | Clinton | (816) | 8,703 | 8,366 |
| *65201 | Columbia | (573) | 69,133 | 62,061 |
| 63128 | Concord(u) | (314) | 19,859 | 20,896 |
| 63126 | Crestwood | (314) | 11,229 | 12,815 |
| 63141 | Creve Coeur | (314) | 12,289 | 11,743 |
| 63136 | Dellwood | (314) | 5,245 | 6,200 |
| 63020 | De Soto | (314) | 5,993 | 5,993 |
| 63131 | Des Peres | (314) | 8,388 | 7,953 |
| 63841 | Dexter | (573) | 7,506 | 7,043 |
| 63011 | Ellisville | (314) | 7,183 | 6,233 |
| 64024 | Excelsior Springs | (816) | 10,373 | 10,424 |
| 63640 | Farmington | (573) | 11,596 | 8,270 |
| 63135 | Ferguson | (314) | 22,290 | 24,549 |
| 63028 | Festus | (314) | 8,105 | 7,574 |
| *63033 | Florissant | (314) | 51,038 | 55,721 |
| 65473 | Fort Leonard Wood(u) | (573) | 15,863 | 21,262 |
| 65251 | Fulton | (573) | 10,033 | 11,046 |
| 64118 | Gladstone | (816) | 26,243 | 24,990 |
| 65254 | Glasgow Village(u) | (573) | 5,199 | .... |
| 63122 | Glendale | (314) | 5,945 | 6,035 |
| 64030 | Grandview | (816) | 24,973 | 24,561 |
| 63401 | Hannibal | (573) | 18,004 | 18,811 |
| 64701 | Harrisonville | (816) | 7,696 | 6,372 |
| 63042 | Hazelwood | (314) | 15,512 | 13,098 |
| *64050 | Independence | (816) | 112,301 | 111,797 |
| 63755 | Jackson | (573) | 9,256 | 7,827 |
| *65101 | Jefferson City | (573) | 35,517 | 33,619 |
| 63136 | Jennings | (314) | 15,841 | 16,934 |
| *64801 | Joplin | (417) | 40,866 | 39,126 |
| *64108 | Kansas City | (816) | 434,829 | 448,028 |
| 63857 | Kennett | (573) | 10,941 | 10,145 |
| 63501 | Kirksville | (816) | 17,152 | 17,167 |
| 63122 | Kirkwood | (314) | 27,291 | 27,739 |
| 63124 | Ladue (St. Louis Co.) | (314) | 8,795 | 9,369 |
| 63367 | Lake Saint Louis | (314) | 7,536 | 3,843 |
| 65536 | Lebanon | (417) | 9,983 | 9,507 |
| *64063 | Lee's Summit | (816) | 46,418 | 28,741 |
| 63125 | Lemay(u) | (314) | 18,005 | 35,424 |
| 64068 | Liberty | (816) | 20,459 | 16,251 |
| 63552 | Macon | (816) | 5,571 | 5,680 |
| 63863 | Malden | (573) | 5,123 | 6,096 |
| 63011 | Manchester | (314) | 6,447 | 6,351 |
| 63143 | Maplewood | (314) | 9,962 | 10,960 |
| 65340 | Marshall | (816) | 12,711 | 12,781 |
| 63043 | Maryland Heights† | (314) | 25,440 | 26,413 |
| 64468 | Maryville | (816) | 10,663 | 9,558 |
| 63129 | Mehlville(u) | (314) | 27,557 | .... |
| 65265 | Mexico | (573) | 11,290 | 12,276 |
| 65270 | Moberly | (816) | 12,839 | 13,418 |
| 65708 | Monett | (417) | 6,529 | 6,148 |
| 63026 | Murphy(u) | (314) | 9,342 | 8,121 |
| 64850 | Neosho | (417) | 9,254 | 9,493 |
| 64772 | Nevada | (417) | 8,597 | 9,044 |
| 63121 | Normandy | (314) | 5,063 | 5,174 |
| 63121 | Northwoods | (314) | 5,106 | 5,831 |
| 63129 | Oakville(u) | (314) | 31,750 | .... |
| 63366 | O'Fallon | (314) | 17,427 | 8,677 |
| 63132 | Olivette | (314) | 7,573 | 7,952 |
| 63114 | Overland | (314) | 17,987 | 19,620 |
| 63775 | Perryville | (573) | 6,933 | 7,343 |
| 63120 | Pine Lawn | (314) | 5,083 | 6,570 |
| *63901 | Poplar Bluff | (573) | 16,841 | 17,139 |
| 64083 | Raymore | (816) | 5,592 | 3,154 |
| 64133 | Raytown | (816) | 30,601 | 31,831 |
| 65738 | Republic | (417) | 6,290 | 4,485 |
| 64085 | Richmond | (816) | 5,738 | 5,499 |
| 63117 | Richmond Heights | (314) | 10,448 | 11,516 |
| 63124 | Rock Hill | (314) | 5,217 | 5,702 |
| 65401 | Rolla | (573) | 14,090 | 13,303 |
| 63074 | Saint Ann | (314) | 14,449 | 15,523 |
| *63301 | Saint Charles | (314) | 50,634 | 37,379 |
| 63114 | Saint John | (314) | 7,502 | 7,854 |
| *64501 | Saint Joseph | (816) | 71,852 | 76,691 |
| *63166 | Saint Louis | (314) | 396,685 | 452,801 |
| 63376 | Saint Peters | (314) | 40,660 | 15,700 |
| 63126 | Sappington(u) | (314) | 10,917 | 11,388 |
| *65301 | Sedalia | (816) | 19,800 | 20,927 |
| 63119 | Shrewsbury | (314) | 6,416 | 5,077 |
| 63801 | Sikeston | (573) | 17,641 | 17,431 |
| 63138 | Spanish Lake(u) | (314) | 20,322 | 20,632 |
| *65801 | Springfield | (417) | 140,494 | 133,116 |
| 63080 | Sullivan | (573) | 5,661 | 5,461 |
| 63006 | Town and Country | (314) | 9,503 | 3,187 |
| 64683 | Trenton | (816) | 6,129 | 6,811 |
| 63084 | Union | (314) | 6,048 | 5,506 |

| ZIP | Place | Area code | 1990 | 1980 |
|---|---|---|---|---|
| 63130 | University City | (314) | 40,087 | 42,690 |
| 64093 | Warrensburg | (816) | 15,244 | 13,807 |
| 63090 | Washington | (314) | 10,704 | 9,251 |
| 64870 | Webb City | (417) | 7,449 | 7,309 |
| 63119 | Webster Groves | (314) | 22,992 | 23,097 |
| 65775 | West Plains | (417) | 8,913 | 7,741 |

## Montana (406)

| ZIP | Place | 1990 | 1980 |
|---|---|---|---|
| 59711 | Anaconda | 10,356 | 12,518 |
| *59101 | Billings | 81,125 | 66,818 |
| *59715 | Bozeman | 22,660 | 21,645 |
| *59701 | Butte | 33,336 | 37,205 |
| *59401 | Great Falls | 55,125 | 56,884 |
| 59501 | Havre | 10,201 | 10,891 |
| *59601 | Helena | 24,609 | 23,938 |
| ..... | Helena Valley West Central(u) | 6,327 | .... |
| *59901 | Kalispell | 11,917 | 10,689 |
| 59044 | Laurel | 5,686 | 5,481 |
| 59457 | Lewistown | 6,097 | 7,104 |
| 59047 | Livingston | 6,701 | 6,994 |
| 59402 | Malmstrom AFB(u) | 5,938 | 6,675 |
| 59301 | Miles City | 8,461 | 9,602 |
| *59801 | Missoula | 42,918 | 33,351 |
| 59801 | Orchard Homes(u) | 10,317 | 10,837 |
| 59270 | Sidney | 5,217 | 5,726 |

## Nebraska

| ZIP | Place | Area code | 1990 | 1980 |
|---|---|---|---|---|
| 69301 | Alliance | (308) | 9,765 | 9,920 |
| 68310 | Beatrice | (402) | 12,352 | 12,891 |
| *68005 | Bellevue | (402) | 30,948 | 21,813 |
| *68008 | Blair | (402) | 6,860 | 6,418 |
| 69337 | Chadron | (308) | 5,588 | 5,933 |
| 68108 | Chalco(u) | (402) | 7,337 | .... |
| *68601 | Columbus | (402) | 19,480 | 17,328 |
| 68025 | Fremont | (402) | 23,680 | 23,979 |
| 69341 | Gering | (308) | 7,946 | 7,760 |
| *68802 | Grand Island | (308) | 39,487 | 33,180 |
| *68901 | Hastings | (402) | 22,837 | 23,045 |
| 68949 | Holdrege | (308) | 5,671 | 5,624 |
| *68847 | Kearney | (308) | 24,396 | 21,158 |
| 68128 | La Vista | (402) | 9,840 | 9,588 |
| 68850 | Lexington | (308) | 6,600 | 7,040 |
| *68501 | Lincoln | (402) | 191,972 | 171,932 |
| 69001 | McCook | (308) | 8,112 | 8,404 |
| 68410 | Nebraska City | (402) | 6,547 | 7,127 |
| *68701 | Norfolk | (402) | 21,476 | 19,449 |
| *69101 | North Platte | (308) | 22,605 | 24,509 |
| 68113 | Offutt AFB West(u) | (402) | 10,883 | 8,787 |
| 69153 | Ogallala | (308) | 5,095 | 5,638 |
| *68108 | Omaha | (402) | 335,719 | 313,939 |
| *68046 | Papillion | (402) | 10,378 | 6,399 |
| 68048 | Plattsmouth | (402) | 6,415 | 6,295 |
| 68127 | Ralston | (402) | 6,236 | 5,143 |
| *69361 | Scottsbluff | (308) | 13,711 | 14,156 |
| 68434 | Seward | (402) | 5,641 | 5,713 |
| 69162 | Sidney | (308) | 5,959 | 6,010 |
| 68776 | South Sioux City | (402) | 9,677 | 9,339 |
| 68787 | Wayne | (402) | 5,142 | 5,240 |
| 68467 | York | (402) | 7,940 | 7,723 |

## Nevada (702)

| ZIP | Place | 1990 | 1980 |
|---|---|---|---|
| *89005 | Boulder City | 12,567 | 9,590 |
| *89701 | Carson City | 40,443 | 32,022 |
| 89112 | East Las Vegas(u) | 11,087 | 6,449 |
| *89801 | Elko | 14,836 | 8,758 |
| ..... | Enterprise(u) | 6,412 | .... |
| *89406 | Fallon | 6,430 | 4,262 |
| 89408 | Fernley(u) | 5,164 | .... |
| 89410 | Gardnerville Ranchos(u) | 7,455 | 3,542 |
| *89015 | Henderson | 64,948 | 24,363 |
| *89450 | Incline Village-Crystal Bay(u) | 7,119 | 6,225 |
| *89125 | Las Vegas | 258,204 | 164,674 |
| 89191 | Nellis AFB(u) | 8,377 | 7,476 |
| *89030 | North Las Vegas | 47,849 | 42,739 |
| 89041 | Pahrump(u) | 7,424 | .... |
| 89109 | Paradise(u) | 124,682 | 84,818 |
| *89501 | Reno | 133,850 | 100,756 |
| *89431 | Sparks | 53,367 | 40,780 |
| *89801 | Spring Creek(u)† | 5,866 | 4,155 |
| ..... | Spring Valley(u) | 51,726 | .... |
| 89110 | Sunrise Manor(u) | 95,362 | 44,155 |
| 89433 | Sun Valley(u) | 11,391 | 8,822 |
| 89101 | Winchester(u) | 23,365 | 19,728 |
| *89445 | Winnemucca | 6,102 | 4,140 |

## New Hampshire (603)

*See note on page 390*

| ZIP | Place | 1990 | 1980 |
|---|---|---|---|
| 03031 | *Amherst* | 9,068 | 8,243 |
| 03811 | *Atkinson* | 5,188 | 4,397 |
| 03825 | *Barrington* | 6,164 | 4,404 |
| 03102 | *Bedford* | 12,563 | 9,481 |
| 03220 | *Belmont* | 5,796 | 4,026 |
| 03570 | Berlin | 11,824 | 13,084 |
| 03304 | *Bow* | 5,500 | 4,015 |
| 03743 | Claremont | 13,902 | 14,557 |
| *03301 | Concord | 36,006 | 30,400 |
| 03818 | *Conway* | 7,940 | 7,158 |
| 03038 | Derry Compact(u) | 20,446 | 12,248 |
| 03038 | *Derry* | 29,603 | 18,875 |
| *03820 | Dover | 25,042 | 22,377 |
| 03824 | Durham Compact(u) | 9,236 | 8,448 |
| 03824 | *Durham* | 11,818 | 10,652 |
| 03042 | *Epping* | 5,162 | 3,460 |
| 03833 | Exeter Compact(u) | 9,556 | 8,947 |
| 03833 | *Exeter* | 12,481 | 11,024 |
| 03835 | *Farmington* | 5,739 | 4,630 |
| 03235 | Franklin | 8,304 | 7,901 |
| 03246 | *Gilford* | 5,867 | 4,841 |
| 03045 | *Goffstown* | 14,621 | 11,315 |
| 03841 | *Hampstead* | 6,732 | 3,785 |
| *03842 | Hampton Compact(u) | 7,989 | 6,779 |
| *03842 | *Hampton* | 12,278 | 10,493 |
| 03755 | Hanover Compact(u) | 6,538 | 6,861 |
| 03755 | *Hanover* | 9,212 | 9,119 |
| 03049 | *Hollis* | 5,705 | 4,679 |
| 03106 | *Hooksett* | 9,002 | 7,303 |
| 03051 | *Hudson* | 19,530 | 14,022 |
| 03452 | *Jaffrey* | 5,361 | 4,349 |
| 03431 | Keene | 22,430 | 21,449 |
| 03848 | *Kingston* | 5,591 | 4,111 |
| *03246 | Laconia | 15,743 | 15,575 |
| *03766 | Lebanon | 12,183 | 11,134 |
| 03501 | *Litchfield* | 5,516 | 4,150 |
| 03561 | *Littleton* | 5,827 | 5,558 |
| 03053 | Londonderry Compact(u) | 10,114 | .... |
| 03053 | *Londonderry* | 19,781 | 13,598 |
| *03103 | Manchester | 99,332 | 90,936 |
| 03054 | *Merrimack* | 22,156 | 15,406 |
| 03055 | Milford Compact(u) | 8,015 | 6,269 |
| 03055 | *Milford* | 11,795 | 8,685 |
| *03060 | Nashua | 79,662 | 67,865 |
| 03857 | *Newmarket* | 7,157 | 4,290 |
| 03773 | *Newport* | 6,110 | 6,229 |
| 03076 | *Pelham* | 9,408 | 8,090 |
| 03275 | *Pembroke* | 6,561 | 6,561 |
| 03458 | *Peterborough* | 5,239 | 4,895 |
| 03865 | *Plaistow* | 7,316 | 5,609 |
| 03264 | *Plymouth* | 5,811 | 5,094 |
| *03801 | Portsmouth | 25,925 | 26,254 |
| 03077 | *Raymond* | 8,713 | 5,453 |
| *03867 | Rochester | 26,630 | 21,560 |
| 03079 | *Salem* | 25,746 | 24,124 |
| 03874 | *Seabrook* | 6,503 | 5,917 |
| 03878 | Somersworth | 11,249 | 10,350 |
| 03275 | Suncook(u) | 5,214 | 4,698 |
| *03431 | *Swanzey* | 6,236 | 5,183 |
| 03281 | *Weare* | 6,193 | 3,232 |
| 03087 | *Windham* | 9,000 | 5,664 |

## New Jersey

*See note on page 390*

| ZIP | Place | Area code | 1990 | 1980 |
|---|---|---|---|---|
| 08201 | Absecon | (609) | 7,298 | 6,859 |
| 07401 | Allendale | (201) | 5,900 | 5,901 |
| 07712 | Asbury Park | (908) | 16,799 | 17,015 |
| *08401 | Atlantic City | (609) | 37,986 | 40,199 |
| 08106 | Audubon | (609) | 9,205 | 9,533 |
| 07001 | Avenel(u) | (908) | 15,504 | .... |
| 08007 | Barrington | (609) | 6,792 | 7,418 |
| 07002 | Bayonne | (201) | 61,464 | 65,047 |
| 08722 | Beachwood | (908) | 9,324 | 7,687 |
| 07109 | Belleville(u)† | (201) | 34,213 | 35,367 |
| *08031 | Bellmawr | (609) | 12,603 | 13,721 |
| 07719 | Belmar | (908) | 5,877 | 6,771 |
| 07621 | Bergenfield | (201) | 24,458 | 25,568 |
| 07922 | Berkeley Heights Twp.(u) | (908) | 11,980 | 12,549 |
| 08009 | Berlin | (609) | 5,672 | 5,786 |
| 07924 | Bernardsville | (908) | 6,597 | 6,715 |
| 08012 | Blackwood(u) | (609) | 5,120 | 5,219 |
| 07003 | Bloomfield(u)† | (201) | 45,061 | 47,792 |
| 07403 | Bloomingdale | (201) | 7,530 | 7,867 |
| 07603 | Bogota | (201) | 7,824 | 8,344 |
| 07005 | Boonton | (201) | 8,343 | 8,620 |
| 08805 | Bound Brook | (908) | 9,487 | 9,710 |
| *08723 | Brick Twp.(u) | (201) | 66,473 | 53,629 |
| 08302 | Bridgeton | (609) | 18,942 | 18,795 |
| 08807 | Bridgewater Twp.(u) | (908) | 32,509 | 29,175 |
| 08203 | Brigantine | (609) | 11,354 | 8,318 |
| 08015 | Browns Mills(u) | (609) | 11,429 | 10,568 |
| 07828 | Budd Lake(u) | (201) | 7,272 | 6,523 |
| 08016 | Burlington | (609) | 9,835 | 10,246 |
| 07405 | Butler | (201) | 7,392 | 7,616 |
| *07006 | Caldwell(u)† | (201) | 7,549 | 7,624 |
| *08101 | Camden | (609) | 87,492 | 84,910 |
| 07072 | Carlstadt | (201) | 5,510 | 6,166 |
| 08069 | Carney's Point Twp. (u) | (609) | 8,443 | 8,396 |
| 07008 | Carteret | (908) | 19,025 | 20,598 |

| ZIP | Place | | 1990 | 1980 |
|---|---|---|---|---|
| 07009 | Cedar Grove Twp.(u)(Essex) | (201) | 12,053 | 12,600 |
| 07928 | Chatham | (201) | 8,007 | 8,537 |
| *08034 | Cherry Hill Twp.(u) | (609) | 69,319 | 68,785 |
| 08077 | Cinnaminson Twp.(u) | (609) | 14,583 | 16,072 |
| 07066 | Clark Twp.(u) | (908) | 14,629 | 16,699 |
| 08312 | Clayton | (609) | 6,155 | 6,013 |
| 08021 | Clementon | (609) | 5,601 | 5,764 |
| 07010 | Cliffside Park | (201) | 20,393 | 21,464 |
| *07015 | Clifton | (201) | 71,984 | 74,388 |
| 07624 | Closter | (201) | 8,094 | 8,164 |
| 08108 | Collingswood | (609) | 15,289 | 15,838 |
| 07067 | Colonia(u) | (908) | 18,238 | .... |
| 07016 | Cranford Twp.(u) | (908) | 22,633 | 24,573 |
| 07626 | Cresskill | (201) | 7,558 | 7,609 |
| 08759 | Crestwood Village(u) | (201) | 8,030 | 7,965 |
| *07801 | Dover | (201) | 15,115 | 14,681 |
| 07628 | Dumont | (201) | 17,187 | 18,334 |
| 08812 | Dunellen | (908) | 6,528 | 6,593 |
| 08816 | East Brunswick Twp.(u) | (908) | 43,548 | 37,711 |
| 07936 | East Hanover Twp.(u) | (201) | 9,926 | 9,319 |
| *07019 | East Orange | (201) | 73,552 | 77,878 |
| 07073 | East Rutherford | (201) | 7,902 | 7,849 |
| 07724 | Eatontown | (908) | 13,800 | 12,703 |
| 07020 | Edgewater | (201) | 5,001 | 4,628 |
| 08010 | Edgewater Park Twp.(u) | (609) | 8,388 | 9,273 |
| *08818 | Edison Twp.(u) | (908) | 88,680 | 70,193 |
| *07207 | Elizabeth | (908) | 110,002 | 106,201 |
| 07407 | Elmwood Park | (201) | 17,623 | 18,377 |
| 07630 | Emerson | (201) | 6,930 | 7,793 |
| 07631 | Englewood | (201) | 24,850 | 23,701 |
| 07632 | Englewood Cliffs | (201) | 5,634 | 5,698 |
| 08618 | Ewing Twp.(u) | (609) | 34,185 | 34,842 |
| 07004 | Fairfield(u) | (201) | 7,615 | 7,987 |
| 07704 | Fair Haven | (908) | 5,270 | 5,679 |
| 07410 | Fair Lawn | (201) | 30,548 | 32,229 |
| 07022 | Fairview (Bergen) | (201) | 10,733 | 10,519 |
| 07023 | Fanwood | (908) | 7,115 | 7,767 |
| 08518 | Florence-Roebling(u) | (609) | 8,564 | 7,677 |
| 07932 | Florham Park | (201) | 8,521 | 9,359 |
| 08863 | Fords(u) | (908) | 14,392 | .... |
| 08640 | Fort Dix(u) | (609) | 10,205 | 14,297 |
| 07024 | Fort Lee | (201) | 31,997 | 32,449 |
| 07417 | Franklin Lakes | (201) | 9,873 | 8,769 |
| *08873 | Franklin Twp. (Somerset)(u) | (201) | 42,780 | 31,358 |
| 07728 | Freehold | (908) | 10,742 | 10,020 |
| 07026 | Garfield | (201) | 26,727 | 26,803 |
| 08753 | Gilford Park(u) | (908) | 8,668 | 6,528 |
| 08028 | Glassboro | (609) | 15,614 | 14,574 |
| 08029 | Glendora(u) | (609) | 5,201 | 5,632 |
| 07028 | Glen Ridge(u)† | (201) | 7,076 | 7,855 |
| 07452 | Glen Rock | (201) | 10,883 | 11,497 |
| 08030 | Gloucester City | (609) | 12,649 | 13,121 |
| 07093 | Guttenberg | (201) | 8,268 | 7,340 |
| *07602 | Hackensack | (201) | 37,049 | 36,039 |
| 07840 | Hackettstown | (908) | 8,120 | 8,850 |
| 08033 | Haddonfield | (609) | 11,633 | 12,337 |
| 08035 | Haddon Heights | (609) | 7,860 | 8,361 |
| *07510 | Haledon | (201) | 6,951 | 6,607 |
| *08609 | Hamilton Twp. (Mercer)(u) | (609) | 86,553 | 82,801 |
| 08037 | Hammonton | (609) | 12,208 | 12,298 |
| 07981 | Hanover Twp.(u) | (201) | 11,538 | 11,846 |
| 07029 | Harrison | (201) | 13,425 | 12,242 |
| 07604 | Hasbrouck Heights | (201) | 11,488 | 12,166 |
| *07510 | Hawthorne | (201) | 17,084 | 18,200 |
| 07730 | Hazlet Twp.(u) | (908) | 21,976 | 23,013 |
| 08904 | Highland Park (Middlesex) | (908) | 13,279 | 13,396 |
| 08520 | Hightstown | (609) | 5,126 | 4,581 |
| 07642 | Hillsdale | (201) | 9,750 | 10,495 |
| 07205 | Hillside Twp.(u) | (908) | 21,044 | 21,440 |
| 07030 | Hoboken | (201) | 33,397 | 42,460 |
| 08753 | Holiday City-Berkeley(u) | (908) | 14,293 | 9,019 |
| ..... | Holiday City South(u) | (908) | 5,452 | .... |
| 07843 | Hopatcong | (201) | 15,586 | 15,531 |
| 08525 | Hopewell Twp. (Mercer)(u) | (609) | 11,590 | 10,893 |
| 07111 | Irvington(u)† | (201) | 59,774 | 61,473 |
| 08830 | Iselin(u) | (908) | 16,141 | .... |
| *08527 | Jackson Twp.(u) | (908) | 33,283 | 25,644 |
| 08831 | Jamesburg | (908) | 5,294 | 4,114 |
| *07303 | Jersey City | (201) | 228,517 | 223,532 |
| 07734 | Keansburg | (908) | 11,069 | 10,613 |
| 07032 | Kearny | (201) | 34,874 | 35,735 |
| 08824 | Kendall Park(u) | (908) | 7,127 | 7,419 |
| 07033 | Kenilworth | (908) | 7,574 | 8,221 |
| 07735 | Keyport | (908) | 7,586 | 7,413 |
| 07405 | Kinnelon | (201) | 8,470 | 7,770 |
| 07871 | Lake Mohawk(u) | (201) | 8,930 | 8,498 |
| 08701 | Lakewood(u) | (908) | 26,095 | 22,863 |
| 08879 | Laurence Harbor(u) | (908) | 6,361 | 6,737 |
| 08648 | Lawrenceville(u) | (609) | 6,446 | .... |
| *08733 | Leisure Village West-Pine Lake Park(u) | (908) | 10,139 | .... |
| 07605 | Leonia | (201) | 8,365 | 8,027 |
| 07035 | Lincoln Park | (201) | 10,978 | 8,806 |
| 07738 | Lincroft(u) | (908) | 6,193 | .... |
| 07036 | Linden | (908) | 36,701 | 37,836 |
| 08021 | Lindenwold | (609) | 18,734 | 18,196 |
| 08221 | Linwood | (609) | 6,866 | 6,144 |
| 07424 | Little Falls Twp.(u) | (201) | 11,294 | 11,496 |
| 07643 | Little Ferry | (201) | 9,989 | 9,399 |
| 07739 | Little Silver | (908) | 5,721 | 5,548 |
| 07039 | Livingston Twp.(u) | (201) | 26,609 | 28,040 |
| 07644 | Lodi | (201) | 22,355 | 23,956 |
| 07740 | Long Branch | (908) | 28,658 | 29,819 |
| *07946 | Long Hill Twp.(u) | (908) | 7,826 | 7,275 |
| 07071 | Lyndhurst Twp.(u) | (201) | 18,262 | 20,326 |
| 08641 | McGuire AFB(u) | (609) | 7,580 | 7,853 |
| 07940 | Madison | (201) | 15,850 | 15,357 |
| 08859 | Madison Park(u) | (201) | 7,490 | 7,447 |
| *07430 | Mahwah Twp.(u) | (201) | 17,905 | 12,127 |
| 08736 | Manasquan | (908) | 5,369 | 5,354 |
| 08835 | Manville | (908) | 10,567 | 11,278 |
| 08052 | Maple Shade Twp.(u) | (609) | 19,211 | 20,525 |
| 07040 | Maplewood Twp.(u) | (201) | 21,756 | 22,950 |
| 08402 | Margate City | (609) | 8,431 | 9,179 |
| 07746 | Marlboro Twp.(u) | (908) | 27,974 | 17,560 |
| 08053 | Marlton(u) | (609) | 10,228 | 9,411 |
| 07747 | Matawan | (908) | 9,239 | 8,837 |
| 07607 | Maywood | (201) | 9,536 | 9,895 |
| 08619 | Mercerville-Hamilton Sq.(u) | (609) | 26,873 | 25,446 |
| 08840 | Metuchen | (908) | 12,804 | 13,762 |
| 08846 | Middlesex | (908) | 13,055 | 13,480 |
| 07748 | Middletown Twp.(u) | (908) | 68,183 | 62,574 |
| 07432 | Midland Park | (201) | 7,047 | 7,381 |
| 07041 | Millburn Twp.(u) | (201) | 18,630 | 19,543 |
| 08850 | Milltown (Middlesex) | (908) | 6,968 | 7,136 |
| 08332 | Millville | (609) | 25,992 | 24,815 |
| 08094 | Monroe Twp. (Gloucester)(u) | (609) | 26,703 | 21,639 |
| *07042 | Montclair(u) | (201) | 37,729 | 38,321 |
| 07645 | Montvale | (201) | 6,946 | 7,318 |
| 07045 | Montville Twp.(u) | (201) | 15,600 | 14,290 |
| 08057 | Moorestown-Lenola(u) | (609) | 13,242 | 13,695 |
| 07950 | Morris Plains | (201) | 5,219 | 5,305 |
| *07960 | Morristown | (201) | 16,189 | 16,614 |
| 07092 | Mountainside | (908) | 6,657 | 7,118 |
| 08060 | Mount Holly Twp.(u) | (609) | 10,639 | 10,818 |
| 08087 | Mystic Island(u) | (609) | 7,400 | 4,929 |
| *07753 | Neptune Twp.(u) | (609) | 28,148 | 28,366 |
| *07102 | Newark | (201) | 275,221 | 329,248 |
| *08901 | New Brunswick | (908) | 41,711 | 41,442 |
| 07646 | New Milford | (201) | 15,990 | 16,876 |
| 07974 | New Providence | (908) | 11,439 | 12,426 |
| 07860 | Newton | (201) | 7,521 | 7,748 |
| 07031 | North Arlington | (201) | 13,790 | 16,587 |
| 07047 | North Bergen Twp.(u) | (201) | 48,414 | 47,019 |
| 08902 | North Brunswick Twp.(u)† | (908) | 31,287 | 22,220 |
| 07006 | North Caldwell(u)† | (201) | 6,706 | 5,832 |
| 08225 | Northfield | (609) | 7,305 | 7,795 |
| 07508 | North Haledon | (201) | 7,987 | 8,177 |
| 07060 | North Plainfield | (908) | 18,820 | 19,108 |
| 08260 | North Wildwood | (609) | 5,017 | 4,714 |
| 07110 | Nutley(u)† | (201) | 27,099 | 28,998 |
| 07436 | Oakland | (201) | 11,997 | 13,443 |
| *08758 | Ocean Twp. (Ocean)(u) | (908) | 5,416 | 3,731 |
| *08050 | Ocean Acres(u) | (609) | 5,587 | 4,850 |
| 08226 | Ocean City | (609) | 15,512 | 13,949 |
| 07757 | Oceanport | (908) | 6,146 | 5,888 |
| 08857 | Old Bridge(u) | (908) | 22,151 | 21,815 |
| 08857 | Old Bridge Twp.(u) | (908) | 56,493 | 51,515 |
| 07649 | Oradell | (201) | 8,024 | 8,658 |
| *07051 | Orange(u)† | (201) | 29,925 | 31,136 |
| 07650 | Palisades Park | (201) | 14,536 | 13,732 |
| 08065 | Palmyra | (609) | 7,056 | 7,085 |
| 07652 | Paramus | (201) | 25,004 | 26,474 |
| 07656 | Park Ridge | (201) | 8,102 | 8,515 |
| 07054 | Parsippany-Troy Hills Twp.(u) | (201) | 48,478 | 49,868 |
| 07055 | Passaic | (201) | 58,041 | 52,463 |
| *07510 | Paterson | (201) | 140,891 | 137,970 |
| 08066 | Paulsboro | (609) | 6,577 | 6,944 |
| 08110 | Pennsauken Twp.(u) | (609) | 34,738 | 33,775 |
| 08069 | Penns Grove | (609) | 5,228 | 5,760 |
| 08070 | Pennsville Center(u) | (609) | 12,218 | 12,467 |
| 07440 | Pequannock Twp.(u) | (201) | 12,844 | 13,776 |
| *08861 | Perth Amboy | (908) | 41,967 | 38,951 |
| 08865 | Phillipsburg | (908) | 15,757 | 16,647 |
| 08021 | Pine Hill | (609) | 9,854 | 8,684 |
| *08854 | Piscataway Twp.(u) | (908) | 47,089 | 42,223 |
| 08071 | Pitman | (609) | 9,365 | 9,744 |
| *07061 | Plainfield | (908) | 46,577 | 45,555 |
| 08232 | Pleasantville | (609) | 16,027 | 13,435 |
| 08742 | Point Pleasant | (908) | 18,177 | 17,747 |
| 08742 | Point Pleasant Beach | (908) | 5,112 | 5,415 |
| 07442 | Pompton Lakes | (201) | 10,539 | 10,660 |
| *08540 | Princeton | (609) | 12,016 | 12,035 |
| 07508 | Prospect Park | (201) | 5,053 | 5,142 |
| 07065 | Rahway | (908) | 25,325 | 26,723 |
| 08057 | Ramblewood(u) | (609) | 6,181 | 6,475 |
| 07446 | Ramsey | (201) | 13,228 | 12,899 |
| 07869 | Randolph Twp.(u) | (201) | 19,974 | 17,828 |
| 08869 | Raritan | (908) | 5,798 | 6,128 |
| 07701 | Red Bank | (908) | 10,636 | 12,031 |
| 07657 | Ridgefield | (201) | 9,996 | 10,294 |
| 07660 | Ridgefield Park | (201) | 12,454 | 12,738 |
| *07451 | Ridgewood | (201) | 24,152 | 25,208 |
| 07456 | Ringwood | (201) | 12,623 | 12,625 |
| 07661 | River Edge | (201) | 10,603 | 11,111 |
| 08075 | Riverside Twp.(u) | (609) | 7,974 | 7,941 |
| 07675 | River Vale(u) | (201) | 9,410 | 9,489 |
| 07726 | Robertsville(u) | (908) | 9,841 | 8,461 |
| 07662 | Rochelle Park Twp. | (201) | 5,587 | 5,603 |
| 07866 | Rockaway | (201) | 6,243 | 6,852 |

| ZIP | Place | 1990 | 1980 |
|---|---|---|---|
| 07203 | Roselle (908) | 20,314 | 20,641 |
| 07204 | Roselle Park (201) | 12,805 | 13,377 |
| 07760 | Rumson (908) | 6,701 | 7,623 |
| 08078 | Runnemede (609) | 9,042 | 9,461 |
| *07070 | Rutherford (201) | 17,790 | 19,068 |
| 07663 | Saddle Brook Twp.(u) (201) | 13,296 | 14,084 |
| 08079 | Salem (609) | 6,883 | 6,959 |
| 08872 | Sayreville (908) | 34,998 | 29,969 |
| 07076 | Scotch Plains Twp.(u) (908) | 21,150 | 20,774 |
| *07094 | Secaucus (201) | 14,061 | 13,719 |
| 08753 | Silverton (908) | 9,175 | 7,236 |
| 08083 | Somerdale (609) | 5,440 | 5,900 |
| *08873 | Somerset(u) (908) | 22,070 | 21,731 |
| 08244 | Somers Point (609) | 11,216 | 10,330 |
| 08876 | Somerville (908) | 11,632 | 11,973 |
| 08879 | South Amboy (908) | 7,851 | 8,322 |
| 07079 | South Orange Twp.(u) (201) | 16,390 | 15,864 |
| 07080 | South Plainfield (908) | 20,489 | 20,521 |
| 08882 | South River (908) | 13,692 | 14,361 |
| 07871 | Sparta Twp.(u) (201) | 15,157 | 13,333 |
| 08884 | Spotswood (908) | 7,983 | 7,840 |
| 07081 | Springfield Twp.(u) (201) | 13,420 | 13,955 |
| 07762 | Spring Lake Heights (908) | 5,341 | 5,424 |
| 08084 | Stratford (609) | 7,614 | 8,005 |
| 07747 | Strathmore(u) (201) | 7,060 | .... |
| 07876 | Succasunna-Kenvil(u) (201) | 11,781 | 10,931 |
| *07901 | Summit (908) | 19,757 | 21,071 |
| 07666 | Teaneck Twp.(u) (201) | 37,825 | 39,007 |
| 07670 | Tenafly (201) | 13,326 | 13,552 |
| 07724 | Tinton Falls (908) | 12,361 | 7,740 |
| *08753 | Toms River(u) (908) | 7,524 | 7,465 |
| *07512 | Totowa (201) | 10,177 | 11,448 |
| *08650 | Trenton (609) | 88,675 | 92,124 |
| 08520 | Twin Rivers(u) (609) | 7,715 | 7,742 |
| 07083 | Union Twp. (Union)(u) (908) | 50,024 | 50,184 |
| 07735 | Union Beach (908) | 6,156 | 6,354 |
| 07087 | Union City (201) | 58,012 | 55,593 |
| 07458 | Upper Saddle River (201) | 7,198 | 7,958 |
| 08406 | Ventnor City (609) | 11,005 | 11,704 |
| 07044 | Verona(u)† (201) | 13,597 | 14,166 |
| 08251 | Villas(u) (609) | 8,136 | 5,909 |
| 08360 | Vineland (609) | 54,780 | 53,753 |
| 07463 | Waldwick (201) | 9,757 | 10,802 |
| 07057 | Wallington (201) | 10,828 | 10,741 |
| 07465 | Wanaque (201) | 9,711 | 10,025 |
| 07882 | Washington (908) | 6,474 | 6,429 |
| 07675 | Washington Twp.(Bergen)(u) (201) | 9,245 | 9,550 |
| 07060 | Watchung (908) | 5,110 | 5,290 |
| *07470 | Wayne Twp.(u) (201) | 47,025 | 46,474 |
| 07087 | Weehawken Twp.(u) (201) | 12,385 | 13,168 |
| 07006 | West Caldwell(u)† (201) | 10,422 | 11,407 |
| *07091 | Westfield (908) | 28,870 | 30,447 |
| 07728 | West Freehold(u) (908) | 11,166 | 9,929 |
| 07764 | West Long Branch (908) | 7,690 | 7,380 |
| 07480 | West Milford Twp.(u)† (201) | 25,430 | 22,750 |
| 07093 | West New York (201) | 38,125 | 39,194 |
| 07052 | West Orange(u)† (201) | 39,103 | 39,510 |
| 07424 | West Paterson (201) | 10,982 | 11,293 |
| 07675 | Westwood (201) | 10,446 | 10,714 |
| 07885 | Wharton (201) | 5,405 | 5,485 |
| 08610 | White Horse(u) (609) | 9,397 | 10,098 |
| 07886 | White Meadow Lake(u) (201) | 8,002 | 8,429 |
| 08094 | Williamstown (609) | 10,891 | 5,768 |
| 08046 | Willingboro Twp.(u) (609) | 36,291 | 39,912 |
| 08095 | Winslow Twp.(u) (609) | 30,087 | 20,034 |
| 07095 | Woodbridge(u) (908) | 17,434 | .... |
| *07095 | Woodbridge Twp.(u) (908) | 93,092 | 90,074 |
| 08096 | Woodbury (609) | 10,904 | 10,353 |
| 07675 | Woodcliff Lake (201) | 5,303 | 5,644 |
| 07075 | Wood-Ridge (201) | 7,506 | 7,929 |
| 07481 | Wyckoff Twp.(u) (201) | 15,372 | 15,500 |
| 08620 | Yardville-Groveville(u) (609) | 9,248 | 9,414 |
| 07726 | Yorketown(u) (609) | 6,313 | 5,330 |

## New Mexico (505)

| ZIP | Place | 1990 | 1980 |
|---|---|---|---|
| *88310 | Alamogordo | 27,596 | 24,024 |
| *87101 | Albuquerque | 384,619 | 332,920 |
| 88021 | Anthony(u) | 5,160 | 3,285 |
| *88210 | Artesia | 10,610 | 10,385 |
| 87410 | Aztec | 5,480 | 5,512 |
| 87002 | Belen | 6,547 | 5,617 |
| 87004 | Bernalillo | 5,960 | 2,988 |
| 87413 | Bloomfield | 5,214 | 4,881 |
| *88220 | Carlsbad | 24,952 | 25,496 |
| *88101 | Clovis | 30,954 | 31,194 |
| 87048 | Corrales | 5,453 | 2,791 |
| *88030 | Deming | 10,970 | 9,964 |
| *87532 | Espanola | 8,389 | 6,803 |
| *87401 | Farmington | 33,997 | 31,222 |
| *87301 | Gallup | 19,157 | 18,167 |
| 87020 | Grants | 8,626 | 11,439 |
| *88240 | Hobbs | 29,121 | 29,153 |
| 88330 | Holloman AFB(u) | 5,891 | 7,245 |
| *88001 | Las Cruces | 62,360 | 45,086 |
| 87701 | Las Vegas | 14,753 | 14,322 |
| 87544 | Los Alamos(u) | 11,455 | 11,039 |
| 87031 | Los Lunas | 6,013 | 3,525 |
| 88260 | Lovington | 9,322 | 9,727 |
| 87107 | North Valley(u) | 12,507 | 12,984 |
| 87114 | Paradise Hills(u) | 5,513 | 5,096 |
| 88130 | Portales | 10,690 | 9,940 |
| 87740 | Raton | 7,372 | 8,225 |
| *87124 | Rio Rancho† | 32,512 | 9,985 |
| *88201 | Roswell | 44,260 | 39,676 |
| 87115 | Sandia(u) | 6,742 | 5,288 |
| *87501 | Santa Fe | 56,537 | 49,160 |
| 87420 | Shiprock(u) | 7,687 | 7,237 |
| *88061 | Silver City | 10,683 | 9,887 |
| 87801 | Socorro | 8,159 | 7,173 |
| 87105 | South Valley(u) | 35,701 | 38,898 |
| 88063 | Sunland Park† | 8,179 | 4,313 |
| 87901 | Truth or Consequences | 6,221 | 5,219 |
| 88401 | Tucumcari | 6,827 | 6,765 |
| 87544 | White Rock(u) | 6,192 | 6,560 |
| 87327 | Zuni Pueblo(u) | 5,857 | 5,551 |

## New York

*See note on page 390*

| ZIP | Place | 1990 | 1980 |
|---|---|---|---|
| 10901 | Airmont(u) (914) | 7,835 | .... |
| *12201 | Albany (518) | 100,031 | 101,727 |
| 11507 | Albertson(u) (516) | 5,166 | 5,561 |
| 14411 | Albion (716) | 5,863 | 4,897 |
| 14226 | Amherst (716) | 111,711 | 108,706 |
| 11701 | Amityville (516) | 9,286 | 9,076 |
| 12010 | Amsterdam (518) | 20,714 | 21,872 |
| 12603 | Arlington(u) (914) | 11,948 | 11,305 |
| *13021 | Auburn (315) | 31,258 | 32,548 |
| *11702 | Babylon (516) | 12,249 | 12,388 |
| 11510 | Baldwin(u) (516) | 22,719 | 31,630 |
| 11510 | Baldwin Harbor(u) (516) | 7,899 | .... |
| 13027 | Baldwinsville (315) | 6,591 | 6,446 |
| 12020 | Ballston Spa (518) | 5,194 | 4,711 |
| 14020 | Batavia (716) | 16,310 | 16,703 |
| 14810 | Bath (607) | 5,801 | 6,042 |
| 11705 | Bayport(u) (516) | 7,702 | 9,282 |
| 11706 | Bay Shore(u) (516) | 21,279 | 10,784 |
| 11709 | Bayville (516) | 7,193 | 7,034 |
| 11751 | Baywood(u) (516) | 7,351 | .... |
| 12508 | Beacon (914) | 13,243 | 12,937 |
| 11710 | Bellmore(u) (516) | 16,438 | 18,106 |
| 11714 | Bethpage(u) (516) | 15,761 | 16,840 |
| *13902 | Binghamton (607) | 53,008 | 55,860 |
| 11716 | Bohemia(u) (516) | 9,556 | 9,308 |
| 11717 | Brentwood(u) (516) | 45,218 | 44,321 |
| 10510 | Briarcliff Manor (914) | 7,070 | 7,115 |
| 14610 | Brighton (u) (716) | 34,455 | 35,776 |
| 14420 | Brockport (716) | 8,749 | 9,776 |
| 10708 | Bronxville (914) | 6,028 | 6,267 |
| *14205 | Buffalo (716) | 328,175 | 357,870 |
| *14424 | Canandaigua (716) | 10,725 | 10,419 |
| 13617 | Canton (315) | 6,379 | 7,055 |
| 11514 | Carle Place(u) (516) | 5,107 | 5,470 |
| 11516 | Cedarhurst (516) | 5,716 | 6,162 |
| 11720 | Centereach(u) (516) | 26,720 | 30,136 |
| 11934 | Center Moriches(u) (516) | 5,987 | 5,703 |
| 11721 | Centerport(Suffolk)(u) (516) | 5,333 | 6,576 |
| 11722 | Central Islip(u) (516) | 26,028 | 19,734 |
| *14225 | Cheektowaga(u) (716) | 84,387 | 92,145 |
| 10977 | Chestnut Ridge† (914) | 7,517 | 8,217 |
| 12065 | CliftonPark (518) | 30,117 | |
| 12043 | Cobleskill (518) | 5,268 | 5,272 |
| 12047 | Cohoes (518) | 16,825 | 18,144 |
| 12205 | Colonie (518) | 8,019 | 8,869 |
| 11725 | Commack(u) (516) | 36,124 | 34,719 |
| 10920 | Congers(u) (914) | 8,003 | 7,123 |
| 11726 | Copiague(u) (516) | 20,769 | 20,132 |
| 11727 | Coram(u) (516) | 30,111 | 24,752 |
| 14830 | Corning (607) | 11,938 | 12,953 |
| 13045 | Cortland (607) | 19,801 | 20,138 |
| *10520 | Croton-on-Hudson (914) | 7,018 | 6,889 |
| 14437 | Dansville (716) | 5,002 | 4,979 |
| 11729 | Deer Park(u) (516) | 28,840 | 30,394 |
| 12054 | Delmar(u) (518) | 8,360 | 8,423 |
| 14043 | Depew (716) | 17,673 | 19,819 |
| 13214 | DeWitt(u) (315) | 8,244 | 9,024 |
| 11746 | Dix Hills(u) (516) | 25,849 | 26,693 |
| 10522 | Dobbs Ferry (914) | 9,940 | 10,053 |
| 14048 | Dunkirk (716) | 13,989 | 15,310 |
| 14052 | East Aurora (716) | 6,647 | 6,803 |
| 10709 | Eastchester(u) (914) | 18,537 | 20,305 |
| 12302 | East Glenville(u) (518) | 6,518 | 6,537 |
| 11576 | East Hills (516) | 6,746 | 7,160 |
| 11730 | East Islip(u) (516) | 14,325 | 13,852 |
| 11758 | East Massapequa(u) (516) | 19,550 | 13,987 |
| 11554 | East Meadow(u) (516) | 36,909 | 39,317 |
| 11731 | East Northport(u) (516) | 20,411 | 20,187 |
| 11772 | East Patchogue(u) (516) | 20,195 | 18,139 |
| 14445 | East Rochester (716) | 6,932 | 7,596 |
| 11518 | East Rockaway (516) | 10,152 | 10,917 |
| 11786 | East Shoreham(u) (516) | 5,461 | .... |
| *14901 | Elmira (607) | 33,724 | 35,327 |
| 11003 | Elmont(u) (516) | 28,612 | 27,592 |
| 11731 | Elwood(u) (516) | 10,916 | 11,847 |
| *13760 | Endicott (607) | 13,531 | 14,457 |
| 13762 | Endwell(u) (607) | 12,602 | 13,745 |

| ZIP | Place | | 1990 | 1980 |
|---|---|---|---|---|
| 13219 | Fairmount(u) | (315) | 12,266 | 13,415 |
| 14450 | Fairport | (716) | 5,943 | 5,970 |
| 11735 | Farmingdale | (516) | 8,022 | 7,946 |
| 11738 | Farmingville(u) | (516) | 14,842 | 13,398 |
| *11001 | Floral Park | (516) | 15,947 | 16,805 |
| 13603 | Fort Drum(u) | (315) | 11,578 | .... |
| 11768 | Fort Salonga(u) | (516) | 9,176 | 9,550 |
| 11010 | Franklin Square(Nassau)(u) | (516) | 28,205 | 29,051 |
| 14063 | Fredonia | (716) | 10,436 | 11,126 |
| 11520 | Freeport | (516) | 39,894 | 38,272 |
| 13069 | Fulton | (315) | 12,929 | 13,312 |
| *11530 | Garden City | (516) | 21,675 | 22,927 |
| 11040 | Garden City Park(u) | (516) | 7,437 | 7,712 |
| 14624 | Gates-North Gates(u) | (716) | 14,995 | 15,244 |
| 14454 | Geneseo | (716) | 7,187 | 6,746 |
| 14456 | Geneva | (315) | 14,143 | 15,133 |
| 11542 | Glen Cove | (516) | 24,149 | 24,618 |
| 12801 | Glens Falls | (518) | 15,023 | 15,897 |
| 12801 | Glens Falls North(u) | (518) | 7,978 | 6,956 |
| 12078 | Gloversville | (518) | 16,656 | 17,836 |
| 10924 | Goshen | (914) | 5,255 | 4,874 |
| *11022 | Great Neck | (516) | 8,745 | 9,168 |
| 11020 | Great Neck Plaza | (516) | 5,897 | 5,604 |
| 14616 | Greece(u) | (716) | 15,632 | 16,177 |
| 11740 | Greenlawn(u) | (516) | 13,208 | 13,869 |
| *10583 | Greenville(Westchester)(u) | (914) | 9,528 | 8,706 |
| 14075 | Hamburg | (716) | 10,442 | 10,582 |
| 11946 | Hampton Bays(u) | (516) | 7,893 | 7,256 |
| 10528 | Harrison | (914) | 23,308 | 23,046 |
| 10530 | Hartsdale(u) | (914) | 9,587 | 10,216 |
| 10706 | Hastings-on-Hudson | (914) | 8,000 | 8,573 |
| *11787 | Hauppauge(u) | (516) | 19,750 | 20,960 |
| 10927 | Haverstraw | (914) | 9,438 | 8,800 |
| *11551 | Hempstead | (516) | 47,982 | 40,404 |
| 13350 | Herkimer | (315) | 7,945 | 8,383 |
| 11557 | Hewlett(u) | (516) | 6,620 | 6,986 |
| *11802 | Hicksville(u) | (516) | 40,174 | 43,245 |
| 10977 | Hillcrest(u) | (914) | 6,447 | 5,733 |
| 14468 | Hilton | (716) | 5,216 | 4,151 |
| 11741 | Holbrook(u) | (516) | 25,273 | 24,382 |
| 11742 | Holtsville(u) | (516) | 14,972 | 13,515 |
| 14843 | Hornell | (607) | 9,877 | 10,234 |
| *14845 | Horseheads | (607) | 6,802 | 7,348 |
| 12534 | Hudson | (518) | 8,034 | 7,986 |
| 12839 | Hudson Falls | (518) | 7,651 | 7,419 |
| 11743 | Huntington(u) | (516) | 18,243 | 21,727 |
| 11746 | Huntington Station(u) | (516) | 28,247 | 28,769 |
| 13357 | Ilion | (315) | 8,888 | 9,450 |
| 11696 | Inwood(u) | (516) | 7,767 | 8,228 |
| 14617 | Irondequoit(u) | (716) | 52,322 | 57,648 |
| 10533 | Irvington | (914) | 6,348 | 5,774 |
| 11751 | Islip(u) | (516) | 18,924 | 13,438 |
| 11752 | Islip Terrace(u) | (516) | 5,530 | 5,588 |
| *14850 | Ithaca | (607) | 29,541 | 28,732 |
| *14702 | Jamestown | (716) | 34,681 | 35,775 |
| 10535 | Jefferson Valley-Yorktown(u) | (914) | 14,118 | 13,380 |
| 11753 | Jericho(Nassau)(u) | (516) | 13,141 | 12,739 |
| 13790 | Johnson City | (607) | 16,578 | 17,126 |
| 12095 | Johnstown | (518) | 9,058 | 9,360 |
| 14217 | Kenmore | (716) | 17,180 | 18,474 |
| 11754 | Kings Park(u) | (516) | 17,773 | 16,131 |
| 12401 | Kingston | (914) | 23,095 | 24,481 |
| 10950 | Kiryas Joel | (914) | 7,437 | 2,088 |
| 14218 | Lackawanna | (716) | 20,585 | 22,701 |
| 10512 | Lake Carmel(u) | (914) | 8,489 | 7,295 |
| 11755 | Lake Grove | (516) | 9,612 | 9,692 |
| 11779 | Lake Ronkonkoma(u) | (516) | 18,997 | 38,336 |
| 11552 | Lakeview(u) | (516) | 5,476 | 5,276 |
| 14086 | Lancaster | (716) | 11,940 | 13,056 |
| 10538 | Larchmont | (914) | 6,181 | 6,308 |
| 12110 | Latham(u) | (518) | 10,131 | 11,182 |
| 11559 | Lawrence | (516) | 6,513 | 6,175 |
| 11756 | Levittown(u) | (516) | 53,286 | 57,045 |
| 11757 | Lindenhurst | (516) | 26,879 | 26,919 |
| 13365 | Little Falls | (315) | 5,829 | 6,156 |
| *14094 | Lockport | (716) | 24,426 | 24,844 |
| 11561 | Long Beach | (516) | 33,510 | 34,073 |
| 12211 | Loudonville(u) | (518) | 10,822 | 11,480 |
| 11563 | Lynbrook | (516) | 19,208 | 20,424 |
| 10541 | Mahopac(u) | (914) | 7,755 | 7,681 |
| 12953 | Malone | (518) | 6,777 | 7,668 |
| 11565 | Malverne | (516) | 9,054 | 9,262 |
| 10543 | Mamaroneck | (914) | 17,325 | 17,616 |
| 11030 | Manhasset(u) | (516) | 7,718 | 8,485 |
| 11050 | Manorhaven | (516) | 5,672 | 5,384 |
| 11949 | Manorville(u) | (516) | 6,198 | .... |
| 11758 | Massapequa(u) | (516) | 22,018 | 24,454 |
| 11762 | Massapequa Park | (516) | 18,044 | 19,779 |
| 13662 | Massena | (315) | 11,716 | 12,851 |
| 11950 | Mastic(u) | (516) | 13,778 | 10,413 |
| 11951 | Mastic Beach(u) | (516) | 10,293 | 8,318 |
| 13211 | Mattydale(u) | (315) | 6,418 | 7,511 |
| 12118 | Mechanicville | (518) | 5,249 | 5,500 |
| 11763 | Medford(u) | (516) | 21,274 | 20,418 |
| 14103 | Medina | (716) | 6,686 | 6,392 |
| 11746 | Melville(u) | (516) | 12,586 | 8,139 |
| 11566 | Merrick(u) | (516) | 23,042 | 24,478 |
| 11953 | Middle Island(u) | (516) | 7,848 | 5,703 |
| *10940 | Middletown | (914) | 24,160 | 21,454 |
| 11764 | Miller Place(u) | (516) | 9,315 | 7,877 |
| 11501 | Mineola | (516) | 19,005 | 20,757 |
| 10950 | Monroe | (914) | 6,672 | 5,996 |
| 10952 | Monsey(u) | (914) | 13,986 | 12,380 |
| 12701 | Monticello | (914) | 6,597 | 6,306 |
| 10970 | Mount Ivy(u) | (914) | 6,013 | .... |
| 10549 | Mount Kisco | (914) | 9,108 | 8,025 |
| 11766 | Mount Sinai(u) | (516) | 8,023 | 6,591 |
| *10551 | Mount Vernon | (914) | 67,153 | 66,713 |
| 12590 | Myers Corner(u) | (914) | 5,599 | 5,180 |
| 10954 | Nanuet(u) | (914) | 14,065 | 12,578 |
| 11767 | Nesconset(u) | (516) | 10,712 | 10,706 |
| 14513 | Newark | (315) | 9,849 | 10,017 |
| *12550 | Newburgh | (914) | 26,454 | 23,438 |
| 11590 | New Cassel(u) | (516) | 10,257 | 9,635 |
| 10956 | New City(u) | (914) | 33,673 | 35,859 |
| *11040 | New Hyde Park | (516) | 9,728 | 9,801 |
| 12561 | New Paltz | (914) | 5,470 | 4,938 |
| *10802 | New Rochelle | (914) | 67,265 | 70,794 |
| *12550 | New Windsor Center(u) | (914) | 8,898 | 7,812 |
| *10001 | New York | (212)/(718) | 7,322,564 | 7,071,639 |
| *14302 | Niagara Falls | (716) | 61,840 | 71,384 |
| 11701 | North Amityville(u) | (516) | 13,849 | 13,140 |
| 11703 | North Babylon(u) | (516) | 18,081 | 19,019 |
| 11706 | North Bay Shore(u) | (516) | 12,799 | 35,020 |
| 11710 | North Bellmore(u) | (516) | 19,707 | 20,630 |
| 11713 | North Bellport(u) | (516) | 8,182 | 7,432 |
| 11757 | North Lindenhurst(u) | (516) | 10,563 | 11,511 |
| 11758 | North Massapequa(u) | (516) | 19,365 | 21,385 |
| 11566 | North Merrick(u) | (516) | 12,113 | 12,848 |
| 11040 | North New Hyde Park(u) | (516) | 14,359 | 15,114 |
| 11772 | North Patchogue(u) | (516) | 7,374 | 7,126 |
| 11768 | Northport | (516) | 7,572 | 7,651 |
| 13212 | North Syracuse | (315) | 7,363 | 7,970 |
| 10591 | North Tarrytown | (914) | 8,152 | 7,994 |
| 14120 | North Tonawanda | (716) | 34,989 | 35,760 |
| 11580 | North Valley Stream(u) | (516) | 14,574 | 14,530 |
| 11793 | North Wantagh(u) | (516) | 12,276 | 12,677 |
| 13815 | Norwich | (607) | 7,613 | 8,082 |
| 10960 | Nyack | (914) | 6,558 | 6,428 |
| 11769 | Oakdale(u) | (516) | 7,875 | 8,090 |
| 11572 | Oceanside(u) | (516) | 32,423 | 33,639 |
| 13669 | Ogdensburg | (315) | 13,521 | 12,375 |
| 11804 | Old Bethpage(u) | (516) | 5,610 | 6,215 |
| 14760 | Olean | (716) | 16,946 | 18,207 |
| 13421 | Oneida | (315) | 10,850 | 10,810 |
| 13820 | Oneonta | (607) | 13,954 | 14,933 |
| 12550 | Orange Lake(u) | (914) | 5,196 | 5,120 |
| 10562 | Ossining | (914) | 22,582 | 20,196 |
| 13126 | Oswego | (315) | 19,195 | 19,793 |
| 11771 | Oyster Bay(u) | (516) | 6,687 | 6,497 |
| 11772 | Patchogue | (516) | 11,060 | 11,291 |
| 10965 | Pearl River(u) | (914) | 15,314 | 15,893 |
| 10566 | Peekskill | (914) | 19,536 | 18,236 |
| 10803 | Pelham | (914) | 6,413 | 6,848 |
| 10803 | Pelham Manor | (914) | 5,443 | 6,130 |
| 14527 | Penn Yan | (315) | 5,257 | 5,242 |
| 11714 | Plainedge(u) | (516) | 8,739 | 9,629 |
| 11803 | Plainview(u) | (516) | 26,207 | 28,037 |
| *12901 | Plattsburgh | (518) | 21,255 | 21,057 |
| 12903 | Plattsburgh AFB(u) | (518) | 5,483 | 5,905 |
| 10570 | Pleasantville | (914) | 6,592 | 6,749 |
| 10573 | Port Chester | (914) | 24,728 | 23,565 |
| 11777 | Port Jefferson | (516) | 7,455 | 6,731 |
| 11776 | Port Jefferson Station(u) | (516) | 7,232 | 17,009 |
| 12771 | Port Jervis | (914) | 9,060 | 8,699 |
| 11050 | Port Washington(u) | (516) | 15,387 | 14,521 |
| 13676 | Potsdam | (315) | 10,251 | 10,635 |
| *12601 | Poughkeepsie | (914) | 28,844 | 29,757 |
| 12144 | Rensselaer | (518) | 8,255 | 9,047 |
| 11961 | Ridge(u) | (516) | 11,734 | 8,977 |
| 11901 | Riverhead(u) | (516) | 8,814 | 6,339 |
| *14692 | Rochester | (716) | 230,356 | 241,741 |
| *11571 | Rockville Centre | (516) | 24,727 | 25,412 |
| 11778 | Rocky Point(u) | (516) | 8,596 | 7,012 |
| 12205 | Roessleville(u) | (518) | 10,753 | 11,685 |
| *13440 | Rome | (315) | 44,350 | 43,826 |
| 11779 | Ronkonkoma(u) | (516) | 20,391 | .... |
| 11575 | Roosevelt(u) | (516) | 15,030 | 14,109 |
| 11577 | Roslyn Heights(u) | (516) | 6,405 | 6,546 |
| 12303 | Rotterdam(u) | (518) | 21,228 | 22,933 |
| 10580 | Rye | (914) | 14,936 | 15,083 |
| 10573 | Rye Brook† | (914) | 7,765 | 7,996 |
| 11780 | Saint James(u) | (516) | 12,703 | 12,122 |
| 14779 | Salamanca | (716) | 6,566 | 6,890 |
| 13454 | Salisbury(u) | (315) | 12,226 | 9,732 |
| 12983 | Saranac Lake | (518) | 5,377 | 5,578 |
| 12866 | Saratoga Springs | (518) | 25,001 | 23,906 |
| 11782 | Sayville(u) | (516) | 16,550 | 12,013 |
| 10583 | Scarsdale | (914) | 16,987 | 17,650 |
| *12301 | Schenectady | (518) | 65,566 | 67,972 |
| 10940 | Scotchtown(u) | (914) | 8,765 | 7,352 |
| 12302 | Scotia | (518) | 7,359 | 7,280 |
| 11579 | Sea Cliff | (516) | 5,054 | 5,364 |
| 11783 | Seaford(u) | (516) | 15,597 | 16,117 |
| 11507 | Searingtown(u) | (516) | 5,020 | .... |
| 11784 | Selden(u) | (516) | 20,608 | 17,259 |
| 13148 | Seneca Falls | (315) | 7,370 | 7,466 |
| 11733 | Setauket-East Setauket(u) | (516) | 13,634 | 10,176 |
| 11967 | Shirley(Suffolk)(u) | (516) | 22,936 | 18,072 |

| ZIP | Place | | 1990 | 1980 |
|---|---|---|---|---|
| 11787 | Smithtown(u) | (516) | 25,638 | 30,906 |
| 13209 | Solvay | (315) | 6,717 | 7,140 |
| 11789 | Sound Beach(u) | (516) | 9,102 | 8,071 |
| 11735 | South Farmingdale(u) | (516) | 15,377 | 16,439 |
| 14850 | South Hill(u) | (607) | 5,423 | 5,276 |
| 11746 | South Huntington(u) | (516) | 9,624 | 14,854 |
| 14094 | South Lockport(u) | (716) | 7,112 | 3,366 |
| 11971 | Southold(u) | (516) | 5,192 | 4,770 |
| 14904 | Southport(u) | (607) | 7,753 | 8,329 |
| 11581 | South Valley Stream(u) | (516) | 5,328 | 5,462 |
| 10977 | Spring Valley | (914) | 21,802 | 20,537 |
| 11790 | Stony Brook(u) | (516) | 13,726 | 16,155 |
| 10980 | Stony Point(u) (Rockland) | (914) | 10,587 | 8,686 |
| 10901 | Suffern | (914) | 11,055 | 10,794 |
| 11791 | Syosset(u) | (516) | 18,967 | 9,818 |
| *13220 | Syracuse | (315) | 163,860 | 170,105 |
| 10983 | Tappan(u) | (914) | 6,867 | 8,267 |
| 10591 | Tarrytown | (914) | 10,739 | 10,648 |
| 11776 | Terryville | (516) | 10,275 | .... |
| 10984 | Thiells | (914) | 5,204 | .... |
| 10594 | Thornwood(u) | (914) | 7,025 | 7,197 |
| *14150 | Tonawanda | (716) | 17,284 | 18,693 |
| *14150 | Tonawanda(u) | (716) | 65,284 | 72,795 |
| *12180 | Troy | (518) | 54,269 | 56,638 |
| 10707 | Tuckahoe | (914) | 6,302 | 6,076 |
| 11553 | Uniondale(u) | (516) | 20,328 | 20,016 |
| *13504 | Utica | (315) | 68,637 | 75,632 |
| 10989 | Valley Cottage(u) | (914) | 9,007 | 8,214 |
| *11582 | Valley Stream | (516) | 33,946 | 35,769 |
| 11792 | Wading River(u) | (516) | 5,317 | .... |
| 12586 | Walden | (914) | 5,836 | 5,659 |
| 11793 | Wantagh(u) | (516) | 18,567 | 19,817 |
| 10990 | Warwick | (914) | 5,984 | 4,320 |
| 13165 | Waterloo | (315) | 5,116 | 5,303 |
| *13601 | Watertown | (315) | 29,429 | 27,861 |
| 12189 | Watervliet | (518) | 11,061 | 11,354 |
| 14580 | Webster | (716) | 5,464 | 5,499 |
| 14895 | Wellsville | (716) | 5,241 | 5,769 |
| *11702 | West Babylon(u) | (516) | 42,410 | 41,699 |
| 11590 | Westbury (Nassau) | (516) | 13,060 | 13,871 |
| 14905 | West Elmira(u) | (607) | 5,218 | 5,485 |
| 12801 | West Glens Falls(u) | (518) | 5,964 | 5,331 |
| 10993 | West Haverstraw | (914) | 9,183 | 9,181 |
| 11552 | West Hempstead(u) | (516) | 17,689 | 18,536 |
| 11743 | West Hills(u) | (516) | 5,849 | 6,071 |
| 11795 | West Islip(u) | (516) | 28,419 | 29,533 |
| 12203 | Westmere(u) | (518) | 6,750 | 6,881 |
| *10996 | West Point(u) | (914) | 8,024 | 8,105 |
| 14224 | West Seneca(u) | (716) | 47,866 | 51,210 |
| 13219 | Westvale(u) | (315) | 5,952 | 6,169 |
| 11798 | Wheatley Heights(u) | (516) | 5,027 | .... |
| *10602 | White Plains | (914) | 48,718 | 46,999 |
| 14221 | Williamsville | (716) | 5,583 | 6,017 |
| 11596 | Williston Park | (516) | 7,516 | 8,216 |
| 11797 | Woodbury(u) | (516) | 8,008 | 7,043 |
| 11598 | Woodmere(u) | (516) | 15,578 | 17,205 |
| 11798 | Wyandach(u) | (516) | 8,950 | 13,215 |
| *10702 | Yonkers | (914) | 188,082 | 195,351 |
| 10598 | Yorktown Heights(u) | (914) | 7,690 | 7,696 |

## North Carolina

| ZIP | Place | | 1990 | 1980 |
|---|---|---|---|---|
| *28001 | Albemarle | (704) | 14,940 | 15,110 |
| 27263 | Archdale | (919) | 6,975 | 5,326 |
| *27203 | Asheboro | (910) | 16,362 | 15,252 |
| *28801 | Asheville | (704) | 61,855 | 54,022 |
| 28012 | Belmont | (704) | 8,434 | 4,607 |
| 28711 | Black Mountain | (704) | 5,533 | 4,083 |
| 28607 | Boone | (704) | 12,949 | 10,191 |
| 28712 | Brevard | (704) | 5,388 | 5,323 |
| *27215 | Burlington | (910) | 39,498 | 37,266 |
| 28547 | Camp Lejeune(u) | (919) | 36,716 | 30,764 |
| 27510 | Carrboro | (919) | 12,134 | 7,336 |
| *27511 | Cary | (919) | 44,397 | 21,763 |
| *27514 | Chapel Hill | (919) | 38,711 | 32,421 |
| *28204 | Charlotte | (704) | 395,925 | 315,474 |
| 27012 | Clemmons† | (919) | 5,982 | 4,842 |
| 28328 | Clinton | (910) | 8,385 | 7,552 |
| *28025 | Concord | (704) | 27,601 | 16,942 |
| 28613 | Conover | (704) | 5,311 | 4,245 |
| *28334 | Dunn | (910) | 8,556 | 8,962 |
| *27701 | Durham | (919) | 136,612 | 101,149 |
| *27288 | Eden | (910) | 15,238 | 15,672 |
| 27932 | Edenton | (919) | 5,268 | 5,357 |
| *27909 | Elizabeth City | (919) | 14,292 | 14,004 |
| *28302 | Fayetteville | (910) | 75,850 | 59,507 |
| 28043 | Forest City | (704) | 7,475 | 7,688 |
| 28307 | Fort Bragg(u) | (919) | 34,744 | 37,834 |
| 27529 | Garner | (919) | 14,716 | 10,073 |
| *28052 | Gastonia | (704) | 54,725 | 47,218 |
| *27530 | Goldsboro | (919) | 40,709 | 31,871 |
| 27253 | Graham | (919) | 10,368 | 8,674 |
| *27420 | Greensboro | (919) | 183,894 | 155,642 |
| *27834 | Greenville | (919) | 46,305 | 35,740 |
| 28540 | Half Moon(u) | (910) | 6,306 | 3,592 |
| 28345 | Hamlet | (919) | 6,324 | 4,720 |
| 28532 | Havelock | (919) | 20,300 | 17,718 |
| 27536 | Henderson | (919) | 15,655 | 13,522 |
| *28739 | Hendersonville | (704) | 7,284 | 6,862 |
| *28603 | Hickory | (704) | 28,474 | 20,757 |
| *27260 | High Point | (910) | 69,428 | 63,479 |
| 28348 | Hope Mills | (919) | 8,272 | 5,412 |
| *28540 | Jacksonville | (910) | 30,398 | 18,237 |
| *28081 | Kannapolis† | (704) | 29,709 | 30,303 |
| *27284 | Kernersville | (910) | 10,899 | 5,875 |
| 28086 | Kings Mountain | (704) | 8,768 | 9,080 |
| *28502 | Kinston | (919) | 25,295 | 25,234 |
| *28352 | Laurinburg | (919) | 11,643 | 11,480 |
| 28645 | Lenoir | (704) | 14,223 | 13,748 |
| *27292 | Lexington | (704) | 16,583 | 15,711 |
| *28092 | Lincolnton | (704) | 6,955 | 4,879 |
| *28358 | Lumberton | (910) | 18,656 | 18,241 |
| 28403 | Masonboro(u) | (910) | 7,010 | 3,729 |
| *28105 | Matthews | (704) | 13,651 | 1,648 |
| 28227 | Mint Hill | (704) | 11,615 | 7,915 |
| *28110 | Monroe | (704) | 16,385 | 12,639 |
| 28115 | Mooresville | (704) | 9,317 | 8,575 |
| 28557 | Morehead | (919) | 6,046 | 4,359 |
| *28655 | Morganton | (704) | 15,085 | 13,763 |
| 27030 | Mount Airy | (910) | 7,156 | 6,862 |
| 28120 | Mount Holly | (704) | 7,710 | 4,530 |
| *28562 | New Bern | (919) | 17,363 | 14,557 |
| 27604 | New Hope (Wake)(u) | (704) | 5,694 | 6,745 |
| 28540 | New River Station(u) | (919) | 9,732 | 5,401 |
| 28658 | Newton | (704) | 9,077 | 7,624 |
| 27565 | Oxford | (919) | 7,965 | 7,709 |
| 28374 | Pinehurst† | (919) | 5,091 | 1,746 |
| 28399 | Piney Green(u) | (919) | 8,999 | 6,058 |
| *27611 | Raleigh | (919) | 212,092 | 150,255 |
| *27320 | Reidsville | (910) | 12,183 | 12,492 |
| 27870 | Roanoke Rapids | (919) | 15,722 | 14,702 |
| 28379 | Rockingham | (910) | 9,399 | 8,300 |
| *27801 | Rocky Mount | (919) | 49,438 | 41,526 |
| 27573 | Roxboro | (910) | 7,332 | 7,532 |
| 28601 | Saint Stephens(u) | (704) | 8,734 | 10,797 |
| *28144 | Salisbury | (704) | 23,626 | 22,677 |
| *27330 | Sanford | (919) | 14,755 | 14,773 |
| 28403 | Seagate(u) | (910) | 5,444 | 3,421 |
| *28150 | Shelby | (704) | 14,669 | 15,310 |
| ..... | Smith Creek(u) | | 7,461 | 6,562 |
| 27577 | Smithfield | (919) | 7,540 | 7,288 |
| *28387 | Southern Pines | (910) | 9,213 | 8,620 |
| 28052 | South Gastonia(u) | (704) | 5,487 | 4,767 |
| 28390 | Spring Lake | (919) | 7,552 | 6,273 |
| *28677 | Statesville | (704) | 17,567 | 18,622 |
| 27886 | Tarboro | (919) | 11,037 | 8,741 |
| *27360 | Thomasville | (910) | 15,915 | 14,144 |
| 27370 | Trinity(u) | (919) | 5,469 | 6,887 |
| *27587 | Wake Forest | (919) | 5,832 | 3,780 |
| 27889 | Washington | (919) | 9,160 | 8,418 |
| 28786 | Waynesville | (704) | 6,760 | 6,765 |
| 28472 | Whiteville | (910) | 5,078 | 5,565 |
| 27892 | Williamston | (919) | 5,503 | 6,159 |
| *28402 | Wilmington | (910) | 55,530 | 44,000 |
| *27893 | Wilson | (919) | 36,930 | 34,424 |
| *27102 | Winston-Salem | (910) | 143,532 | 131,885 |

## North Dakota (701)

| ZIP | Place | 1990 | 1980 |
|---|---|---|---|
| *58501 | Bismarck | 49,272 | 44,485 |
| 58301 | Devils Lake | 7,782 | 7,442 |
| *58601 | Dickinson | 16,097 | 15,924 |
| *58102 | Fargo | 74,084 | 61,383 |
| *58201 | Grand Forks | 49,417 | 43,765 |
| 58204 | Grand Forks AFB(u) | 9,343 | 9,390 |
| *58401 | Jamestown | 15,571 | 16,280 |
| 58554 | Mandan | 15,177 | 15,513 |
| *58701 | Minot | 34,544 | 32,843 |
| *58704 | Minot AFB(u) | 9,095 | 9,880 |
| 58072 | Valley City | 7,163 | 7,774 |
| *58075 | Wahpeton | 8,751 | 9,064 |
| 58078 | West Fargo | 12,287 | 10,099 |
| *58801 | Williston | 13,136 | 13,336 |

## Ohio

| ZIP | Place | | 1990 | 1980 |
|---|---|---|---|---|
| 45810 | Ada | (419) | 5,428 | 5,669 |
| *44309 | Akron | (330) | 223,019 | 237,177 |
| 44601 | Alliance | (330) | 23,376 | 24,315 |
| 44001 | Amherst | (216) | 10,332 | 10,638 |
| 44805 | Ashland | (419) | 20,079 | 20,326 |
| *44004 | Ashtabula | (216) | 21,633 | 23,449 |
| 45701 | Athens | (614) | 21,265 | 19,743 |
| 44202 | Aurora | (216) | 9,192 | 8,177 |
| 44515 | Austintown(u) | (330) | 32,371 | 33,636 |
| 44011 | Avon | (216) | 7,337 | 7,241 |
| 44012 | Avon Lake | (216) | 15,066 | 13,222 |
| 44203 | Barberton | (330) | 27,623 | 29,751 |
| 44140 | Bay Village | (216) | 17,000 | 17,846 |
| 44122 | Beachwood | (216) | 10,644 | 9,983 |
| 45434 | Beavercreek | (937) | 33,626 | 31,589 |
| 44146 | Bedford | (216) | 14,822 | 15,056 |
| 44146 | Bedford Heights | (216) | 12,131 | 13,214 |
| 43906 | Bellaire | (614) | 6,028 | 8,241 |

| ZIP | Place | | 1990 | 1980 |
|---|---|---|---|---|
| 45305 | Bellbrook | (937) | 6,511 | 5,174 |
| 43311 | Bellefontaine | (937) | 12,126 | 11,888 |
| 44811 | Bellevue | (419) | 8,157 | 8,187 |
| 45714 | Belpre | (614) | 6,796 | 7,193 |
| 44017 | Berea | (216) | 19,051 | 19,567 |
| 43209 | Bexley | (614) | 13,088 | 13,405 |
| 43004 | Blacklick Estates(u) | (614) | 10,080 | 11,223 |
| 45242 | Blue Ash | (513) | 11,923 | 9,510 |
| 44513 | Boardman(u) | (330) | 38,596 | 39,086 |
| 43402 | Bowling Green | (419) | 28,303 | 25,728 |
| 44141 | Brecksville | (216) | 11,818 | 10,132 |
| 45211 | Bridgetown North(u) | (513) | 11,748 | 11,460 |
| 44147 | Broadview Heights | (216) | 12,219 | 10,920 |
| 44144 | Brooklyn | (216) | 11,706 | 12,342 |
| 44142 | Brook Park | (216) | 22,865 | 26,195 |
| 44212 | Brunswick | (330) | 28,218 | 28,104 |
| 43506 | Bryan | (419) | 8,348 | 7,879 |
| 44820 | Bucyrus | (419) | 13,496 | 13,433 |
| 43725 | Cambridge | (614) | 11,748 | 13,573 |
| 44405 | Campbell | (330) | 10,038 | 11,619 |
| 44406 | Canfield | (330) | 5,409 | 5,535 |
| *44711 | Canton | (330) | 84,161 | 93,077 |
| 45822 | Celina | (419) | 9,923 | 9,137 |
| 45459 | Centerville (Montgomery) | (937) | 21,082 | 18,886 |
| 45211 | Cheviot | (513) | 9,616 | 9,888 |
| 45601 | Chillicothe | (614) | 21,923 | 23,420 |
| *45202 | Cincinnati | (513) | 364,114 | 385,409 |
| 43113 | Circleville | (614) | 11,666 | 11,700 |
| *44101 | Cleveland | (216) | 505,616 | 573,822 |
| 44118 | Cleveland Heights | (216) | 54,052 | 56,438 |
| 43410 | Clyde | (419) | 5,776 | 5,489 |
| *43216 | Columbus | (614) | 632,945 | 565,021 |
| 44030 | Conneaut | (216) | 13,241 | 13,835 |
| 44410 | Cortland | (330) | 5,652 | 5,011 |
| 43812 | Coshocton | (614) | 12,193 | 13,405 |
| 45238 | Covedale(u) | (513) | 6,669 | 5,830 |
| *44222 | Cuyahoga Falls | (330) | 48,950 | 43,890 |
| *45401 | Dayton | (937) | 182,005 | 193,536 |
| 45236 | Deer Park | (513) | 6,181 | 6,745 |
| 43512 | Defiance | (419) | 16,787 | 16,810 |
| 43015 | Delaware | (614) | 19,966 | 18,780 |
| 45833 | Delphos | (419) | 7,093 | 7,314 |
| 45247 | Dent(u) | (513) | 6,416 | .... |
| 44622 | Dover (Tuscarawas) | (330) | 11,329 | 11,782 |
| 45427 | Drexel(u) | (937) | 5,143 | .... |
| 45663 | Dry Run(u) | (614) | 5,389 | .... |
| 43016 | Dublin | (614) | 16,366 | 3,855 |
| 44112 | East Cleveland | (216) | 33,096 | 36,957 |
| 44095 | Eastlake | (216) | 21,161 | 22,104 |
| 43920 | East Liverpool | (330) | 13,654 | 16,687 |
| 44413 | East Palestine | (330) | 5,168 | 5,306 |
| 45320 | Eaton | (937) | 7,396 | 6,839 |
| 44004 | Edgewood(u) | (216) | 5,189 | 3,099 |
| *44035 | Elyria | (216) | 56,746 | 57,538 |
| 45322 | Englewood | (937) | 11,402 | 11,329 |
| *44101 | Euclid | (216) | 54,875 | 59,999 |
| 45324 | Fairborn | (937) | 31,300 | 29,702 |
| 45014 | Fairfield | (513) | 39,709 | 30,777 |
| 44313 | Fairlawn | (330) | 5,779 | 6,100 |
| 44126 | Fairview Park | (216) | 18,028 | 19,311 |
| *45839 | Findlay | (419) | 35,703 | 35,594 |
| 45224 | Finneytown(u) | (513) | 13,096 | .... |
| 45405 | Forest Park | (513) | 18,621 | 18,566 |
| 45230 | Forestville(u) | (513) | 9,185 | .... |
| 45426 | Fort McKinley(u) | (937) | 9,740 | 10,161 |
| 44830 | Fostoria | (419) | 14,971 | 15,743 |
| 45005 | Franklin | (513) | 11,026 | 10,711 |
| 43420 | Fremont | (419) | 17,619 | 17,834 |
| 43230 | Gahanna | (614) | 23,898 | 18,001 |
| 44833 | Galion | (419) | 11,859 | 12,391 |
| 44125 | Garfield Heights | (216) | 31,739 | 34,938 |
| 44041 | Geneva | (216) | 6,597 | 6,655 |
| 44420 | Girard | (330) | 11,304 | 12,517 |
| 43212 | Grandview Heights | (614) | 7,010 | 7,420 |
| 45123 | Greenfield | (937) | 5,172 | 5,150 |
| 45331 | Greenville | (937) | 12,863 | 12,999 |
| 45239 | Groesbeck(u) | (513) | 6,684 | 9,594 |
| 43123 | Grove City | (614) | 19,661 | 16,816 |
| *45011 | Hamilton | (513) | 61,436 | 63,189 |
| 45030 | Harrison | (513) | 7,520 | 5,855 |
| 43056 | Heath | (614) | 7,231 | 6,969 |
| 44134 | Highland Heights | (216) | 6,249 | 5,739 |
| 43026 | Hilliard | (614) | 11,794 | 8,131 |
| 45133 | Hillsboro | (937) | 6,235 | 6,356 |
| 44484 | Howland Center(u) | (330) | 6,732 | 7,441 |
| 44425 | Hubbard | (330) | 8,248 | 9,245 |
| 45424 | Huber Heights | (937) | 38,696 | 35,480 |
| 43081 | Huber Ridge(u) | (614) | 5,255 | 5,835 |
| 44236 | Hudson | (216) | 5,159 | 4,615 |
| 44839 | Huron | (419) | 7,067 | 7,123 |
| 44131 | Independence (Cuyahoga) | (216) | 6,500 | 6,607 |
| 45638 | Ironton | (614) | 12,751 | 14,290 |
| 45640 | Jackson | (614) | 6,167 | 6,675 |
| *44240 | Kent | (330) | 28,835 | 26,164 |
| 43326 | Kenton | (419) | 8,356 | 8,605 |
| 43606 | Kenwood(u) | (513) | 7,469 | 9,943 |
| 45429 | Kettering | (937) | 60,569 | 61,186 |
| 44094 | Kirtland | (216) | 5,881 | 5,969 |
| 44107 | Lakewood | (216) | 59,718 | 61,963 |
| 43130 | Lancaster | (614) | 34,507 | 34,953 |
| 45039 | Landen(u) | (513) | 9,263 | 2,870 |
| 45036 | Lebanon (Warren) | (513) | 10,461 | 9,636 |
| *45802 | Lima | (419) | 45,553 | 47,827 |
| 43228 | Lincoln Village(u) | (614) | 9,958 | 10,548 |
| 43138 | Logan | (614) | 6,725 | 6,557 |
| 43140 | London | (614) | 7,807 | 6,958 |
| *44052 | Lorain | (216) | 71,245 | 75,416 |
| 44641 | Louisville | (330) | 8,087 | 7,996 |
| 45140 | Loveland | (513) | 10,122 | 9,106 |
| 44124 | Lyndhurst | (216) | 15,982 | 18,092 |
| 44056 | Macedonia | (216) | 7,509 | 6,571 |
| ..... | Mack South(u) | | 5,767 | .... |
| 45243 | Madeira | (513) | 9,141 | 9,341 |
| *44901 | Mansfield | (419) | 50,627 | 53,927 |
| 44137 | Maple Heights | (216) | 27,089 | 29,735 |
| 45750 | Marietta | (614) | 15,026 | 16,467 |
| *43302 | Marion | (614) | 34,075 | 37,040 |
| 43935 | Martins Ferry | (614) | 8,003 | 9,331 |
| 43040 | Marysville | (937) | 9,656 | 7,414 |
| 45040 | Mason | (513) | 11,450 | 8,692 |
| *44646 | Massillon | (330) | 30,969 | 30,557 |
| 43537 | Maumee | (419) | 15,561 | 15,747 |
| 44124 | Mayfield Heights | (216) | 19,847 | 21,550 |
| *44256 | Medina | (330) | 19,231 | 15,268 |
| *44060 | Mentor | (216) | 47,491 | 42,065 |
| 44060 | Mentor-on-the-Lake | (216) | 8,271 | 7,919 |
| *45343 | Miamisburg | (937) | 17,834 | 15,304 |
| 44130 | Middleburg Heights | (216) | 14,702 | 16,218 |
| *45042 | Middletown | (513) | 46,022 | 43,719 |
| 45150 | Milford | (513) | 5,660 | 5,232 |
| 45242 | Montgomery | (513) | 9,733 | 10,084 |
| 45439 | Moraine | (937) | 5,989 | 5,325 |
| 45231 | Mount Healthy | (513) | 7,580 | 7,562 |
| 43050 | Mount Vernon | (614) | 14,550 | 14,323 |
| 44262 | Munroe Falls | (330) | 5,359 | 4,731 |
| 43545 | Napoleon | (419) | 8,884 | 8,614 |
| *43055 | Newark | (614) | 44,396 | 41,200 |
| 45344 | New Carlisle | (937) | 6,049 | 6,498 |
| 43764 | New Lexington | (614) | 5,117 | 5,179 |
| 44663 | New Philadelphia | (330) | 15,698 | 16,883 |
| 44446 | Niles | (330) | 21,128 | 23,088 |
| 45239 | Northbrook(u) | (513) | 11,471 | 8,357 |
| 44720 | North Canton | (330) | 14,904 | 14,228 |
| 45239 | North College Hill | (513) | 11,002 | 11,114 |
| 45251 | Northgate(u) | (513) | 7,864 | .... |
| 44057 | North Madison(u) | (216) | 8,699 | 8,741 |
| 44070 | North Olmsted | (216) | 34,204 | 36,486 |
| 45502 | Northridge(u) (Clark) | (937) | 5,939 | 5,559 |
| 45414 | Northridge(u) (Montgomery) | (937) | 9,448 | 9,720 |
| 44039 | North Ridgeville | (216) | 21,564 | 21,522 |
| 44133 | North Royalton | (216) | 23,197 | 17,671 |
| 45322 | Northview(u) | (937) | 10,337 | 9,973 |
| 43619 | Northwood | (419) | 5,506 | 5,495 |
| 44203 | Norton | (330) | 11,477 | 12,242 |
| 44857 | Norwalk | (419) | 14,731 | 14,358 |
| 45212 | Norwood | (513) | 23,674 | 26,342 |
| 44146 | Oakwood (Cuyahoga) | (216) | 8,957 | 9,372 |
| 44074 | Oberlin | (216) | 8,191 | 8,660 |
| 44138 | Olmsted Falls | (216) | 6,741 | 5,868 |
| *43601 | Oregon | (419) | 18,334 | 18,675 |
| 44667 | Orrville | (330) | 7,712 | 7,511 |
| 45431 | Overlook-Page Manor(u) | (937) | 13,242 | 14,825 |
| 45056 | Oxford | (513) | 18,937 | 17,655 |
| 44077 | Painesville | (216) | 15,769 | 16,391 |
| 44129 | Parma | (216) | 87,876 | 92,548 |
| 44130 | Parma Heights | (216) | 21,448 | 23,112 |
| 44124 | Pepper Pike | (216) | 6,185 | 6,177 |
| 44646 | Perry Heights(u) | (330) | 9,055 | 9,206 |
| *43551 | Perrysburg | (419) | 12,551 | 10,215 |
| 43147 | Pickerington | (614) | 5,668 | 3,917 |
| 45356 | Piqua | (937) | 20,612 | 20,480 |
| 44319 | Portage Lakes(u) | (330) | 13,373 | 11,310 |
| 43452 | Port Clinton | (419) | 7,106 | 7,223 |
| 45662 | Portsmouth | (614) | 22,676 | 25,943 |
| 44266 | Ravenna | (330) | 12,069 | 11,987 |
| 45215 | Reading | (513) | 12,038 | 12,843 |
| 43068 | Reynoldsburg | (614) | 25,748 | 20,661 |
| 44143 | Richmond Heights | (216) | 9,611 | 10,095 |
| 44270 | Rittman | (330) | 6,147 | 6,063 |
| 44116 | Rocky River | (216) | 20,410 | 21,084 |
| 43460 | Rossford | (419) | 5,861 | 5,978 |
| 45217 | Saint Bernard | (513) | 5,344 | 5,396 |
| 43950 | Saint Clairsville | (614) | 5,136 | 5,452 |
| 45885 | Saint Marys | (419) | 8,441 | 8,414 |
| 44460 | Salem | (330) | 12,233 | 12,869 |
| *44870 | Sandusky | (419) | 29,764 | 31,360 |
| 44870 | Sandusky South(u) | (419) | 6,336 | 6,548 |
| 44131 | Seven Hills | (216) | 12,339 | 13,650 |
| 44120 | Shaker Heights | (216) | 30,955 | 32,487 |
| 45241 | Sharonville | (513) | 13,121 | 10,108 |
| 44054 | Sheffield Lake | (216) | 9,825 | 10,484 |
| 44875 | Shelby | (419) | 9,610 | 9,703 |
| 44878 | Shiloh(u) | (419) | 11,607 | 11,735 |
| 45365 | Sidney | (937) | 18,710 | 17,657 |
| 45236 | Silverton | (513) | 5,859 | 6,172 |
| 44139 | Solon | (216) | 18,548 | 14,341 |
| 44121 | South Euclid | (216) | 23,866 | 25,713 |

| ZIP | Place | | 1990 | 1980 |
|---|---|---|---|---|
| 45066 | Springboro | (937) | 6,574 | 4,962 |
| 45246 | Springdale | (513) | 10,621 | 10,111 |
| *45501 | Springfield | (937) | 70,487 | 72,563 |
| 43952 | Steubenville | (614) | 22,125 | 26,400 |
| 44224 | Stow | (330) | 27,998 | 25,303 |
| 44241 | Streetsboro | (330) | 9,932 | 9,055 |
| 44136 | Strongsville | (216) | 35,308 | 28,577 |
| 44471 | Struthers | (330) | 12,284 | 13,624 |
| 43560 | Sylvania | (419) | 17,489 | 15,527 |
| 44278 | Tallmadge | (330) | 14,870 | 15,269 |
| 45243 | The Village of Indian Hill | (513) | 5,383 | 5,521 |
| 44883 | Tiffin | (419) | 18,604 | 19,549 |
| 45371 | Tipp City | (937) | 6,027 | 5,595 |
| *43601 | Toledo | (419) | 332,943 | 354,635 |
| 43964 | Toronto | (614) | 6,127 | 6,934 |
| 45067 | Trenton | (513) | 6,189 | 6,401 |
| 45426 | Trotwood | (937) | 8,816 | 7,802 |
| 45373 | Troy | (937) | 19,478 | 19,086 |
| 44087 | Twinsburg | (216) | 9,606 | 7,632 |
| 44683 | Uhrichsville | (614) | 5,604 | 6,130 |
| 45322 | Union | (937) | 5,531 | 5,219 |
| 44118 | University Heights | (216) | 14,787 | 15,401 |
| 43221 | Upper Arlington | (614) | 34,128 | 35,648 |
| 43351 | Upper Sandusky | (419) | 5,906 | 5,967 |
| 43078 | Urbana | (937) | 11,353 | 10,762 |
| 45377 | Vandalia | (937) | 13,872 | 13,161 |
| 45891 | Van Wert | (419) | 10,922 | 11,035 |
| 44089 | Vermilion | (216) | 11,127 | 11,012 |
| 44281 | Wadsworth | (330) | 15,718 | 15,166 |
| 45895 | Wapakoneta | (419) | 9,214 | 8,402 |
| *44481 | Warren | (330) | 50,793 | 56,629 |
| 44122 | Warrensville Heights | (216) | 15,745 | 16,565 |
| 43160 | Washington Court House | (614) | 13,080 | 12,682 |
| 43567 | Wauseon | (419) | 6,322 | 6,173 |
| 45692 | Wellston | (614) | 6,049 | 6,016 |
| 45449 | West Carrollton City | (937) | 14,403 | 13,148 |
| *43081 | Westerville | (614) | 30,269 | 23,414 |
| 44145 | Westlake | (216) | 27,018 | 19,483 |
| 45694 | Wheelersburg(u) | (614) | 5,113 | 4,796 |
| 43213 | Whitehall | (614) | 20,572 | 21,299 |
| 45239 | White Oak(u) | (513) | 12,430 | 9,563 |
| 44092 | Wickliffe | (216) | 14,558 | 16,790 |
| 44890 | Willard | (419) | 6,210 | 5,720 |
| *44094 | Willoughby | (216) | 20,510 | 19,329 |
| 44094 | Willoughby Hills | (216) | 8,427 | 8,612 |
| 44095 | Willowick | (216) | 15,269 | 17,834 |
| 45177 | Wilmington | (937) | 11,199 | 10,431 |
| 45459 | Woodbourne-Hyde Park(u) | (937) | 7,837 | 8,826 |
| 44691 | Wooster | (330) | 22,427 | 19,289 |
| 43085 | Worthington | (614) | 14,869 | 15,016 |
| 45431 | Wright-Patterson AFB(u) | (937) | 8,579 | 9,155 |
| 45215 | Wyoming | (513) | 8,128 | 8,282 |
| 45385 | Xenia | (937) | 24,836 | 24,653 |
| *44501 | Youngstown | (330) | 95,732 | 115,511 |
| *43701 | Zanesville | (614) | 26,778 | 28,655 |

## Oklahoma

| ZIP | Place | | 1990 | 1980 |
|---|---|---|---|---|
| *74820 | Ada | (405) | 15,765 | 15,902 |
| *73521 | Altus | (405) | 21,910 | 23,101 |
| 73717 | Alva | (405) | 5,495 | 6,416 |
| 73005 | Anadarko | (405) | 6,586 | 6,378 |
| *73401 | Ardmore | (405) | 23,079 | 23,689 |
| *74003 | Bartlesville | (918) | 34,256 | 34,568 |
| 73008 | Bethany | (405) | 20,075 | 22,038 |
| 74008 | Bixby | (918) | 9,502 | 6,969 |
| 74631 | Blackwell | (405) | 7,538 | 8,400 |
| *74012 | Broken Arrow | (918) | 58,082 | 35,761 |
| *73018 | Chickasha | (405) | 14,988 | 15,828 |
| *73020 | Choctaw | (405) | 8,545 | 7,520 |
| *74017 | Claremore | (918) | 13,280 | 12,085 |
| 73601 | Clinton | (405) | 9,298 | 8,796 |
| 74429 | Coweta | (918) | 6,159 | 4,554 |
| 74023 | Cushing | (918) | 7,218 | 7,720 |
| 73115 | Del City | (405) | 23,928 | 28,523 |
| *73533 | Duncan | (405) | 21,732 | 22,517 |
| *74701 | Durant | (405) | 12,929 | 11,972 |
| *73034 | Edmond | (405) | 52,310 | 34,637 |
| *73644 | Elk City | (405) | 10,428 | 9,579 |
| 73036 | El Reno | (405) | 15,414 | 15,486 |
| *73701 | Enid | (405) | 45,309 | 50,363 |
| 73503 | Fort Sill(u) | (405) | 12,107 | 15,924 |
| 73542 | Frederick | (405) | 5,221 | 6,153 |
| 74033 | Glenpool | (918) | 6,688 | 2,706 |
| 73044 | Guthrie | (405) | 10,440 | 10,312 |
| 73942 | Guymon | (405) | 7,803 | 8,492 |
| 74437 | Henryetta | (918) | 5,872 | 6,432 |
| 74743 | Hugo | (405) | 5,978 | 7,172 |
| 74745 | Idabel | (405) | 6,957 | 7,622 |
| 74037 | Jenks | (918) | 7,484 | 5,876 |
| *73501 | Lawton | (405) | 80,561 | 80,054 |
| *74501 | McAlester | (918) | 16,739 | 17,255 |
| *74354 | Miami | (918) | 13,142 | 14,237 |
| 73140 | Midwest City | (405) | 52,267 | 49,559 |
| 73153 | Moore | (405) | 40,318 | 35,063 |
| *74401 | Muskogee | (918) | 37,708 | 40,011 |
| 73064 | Mustang | (405) | 10,434 | 7,496 |
| *73069 | Norman | (405) | 80,071 | 68,020 |
| *73125 | Oklahoma City | (405) | 444,724 | 404,014 |
| 74447 | Okmulgee | (918) | 13,441 | 16,263 |
| 74055 | Owasso | (918) | 11,151 | 6,149 |
| 73075 | Pauls Valley | (405) | 6,150 | 5,664 |
| *74601 | Ponca City | (405) | 26,359 | 26,238 |
| 74953 | Poteau | (918) | 7,210 | 7,089 |
| 74361 | Pryor Creek | (918) | 8,327 | 8,483 |
| 74955 | Sallisaw | (918) | 7,122 | 6,403 |
| 74063 | Sand Springs | (918) | 15,339 | 13,121 |
| *74066 | Sapulpa | (918) | 18,074 | 15,853 |
| *74868 | Seminole | (405) | 7,071 | 8,590 |
| *74801 | Shawnee | (405) | 26,017 | 26,506 |
| *74074 | Stillwater | (405) | 36,676 | 38,268 |
| *74464 | Tahlequah | (918) | 10,586 | 9,708 |
| 74873 | Tecumseh | (405) | 5,570 | 5,123 |
| *74103 | Tulsa | (918) | 367,302 | 360,919 |
| 73156 | Village | (405) | 10,353 | 11,114 |
| 74301 | Vinita | (918) | 5,804 | 6,740 |
| *74467 | Wagoner | (918) | 6,894 | 6,191 |
| 73132 | Warr Acres | (405) | 9,288 | 9,940 |
| 73096 | Weatherford | (405) | 10,124 | 9,640 |
| *73801 | Woodward | (405) | 12,340 | 13,781 |
| *73099 | Yukon | (405) | 20,935 | 17,112 |

## Oregon

| ZIP | Place | | 1990 | 1980 |
|---|---|---|---|---|
| 97321 | Albany | (541) | 29,540 | 26,511 |
| 97006 | Aloha(u) | (503) | 34,284 | 28,353 |
| 97601 | Altamont(u) | (541) | 18,591 | 19,805 |
| 97520 | Ashland | (541) | 16,252 | 14,943 |
| 97103 | Astoria | (503) | 10,069 | 9,998 |
| 97814 | Baker City | (541) | 9,140 | 9,471 |
| *97005 | Beaverton | (503) | 53,307 | 31,962 |
| *97701 | Bend | (541) | 20,447 | 17,263 |
| 97013 | Canby | (503) | 8,990 | 7,659 |
| 97225 | Cedar Hills(u) | (503) | 9,294 | 9,619 |
| 97291 | Cedar Mill(u)† | (503) | 9,697 | 22,118 |
| 97502 | Central Point | (541) | 7,512 | 6,357 |
| 97420 | Coos Bay | (541) | 15,076 | 14,424 |
| 97113 | Cornelius | (503) | 6,148 | 4,462 |
| *97333 | Corvallis | (541) | 44,757 | 40,960 |
| 97424 | Cottage Grove | (541) | 7,403 | 7,148 |
| 97338 | Dallas | (503) | 9,422 | 8,530 |
| *97401 | Eugene | (541) | 112,773 | 105,664 |
| 97439 | Florence | (541) | 5,171 | 4,411 |
| 97116 | Forest Grove | (503) | 13,559 | 11,499 |
| 97301 | Four Corners(u) | (503) | 12,156 | 11,316 |
| 97223 | Garden Home-Whitford(u) | (503) | 6,652 | 6,911 |
| 97027 | Gladstone | (503) | 10,152 | 9,500 |
| *97526 | Grants Pass | (541) | 17,503 | 15,032 |
| 97470 | Green(u) | (541) | 5,076 | 3,897 |
| *97030 | Gresham | (503) | 68,249 | 33,005 |
| 97303 | Hayesville(u) | (503) | 14,318 | 9,413 |
| 97230 | Hazelwood(u) | (503) | 11,480 | 25,541 |
| 97838 | Hermiston | (541) | 10,047 | 9,408 |
| *97123 | Hillsboro | (503) | 37,598 | 27,664 |
| 97222 | Jennings Lodge(u) | (503) | 6,530 | .... |
| 97303 | Keizer† | (503) | 21,884 | 19,785 |
| *97601 | Klamath Falls | (541) | 17,737 | 16,661 |
| 97850 | La Grande | (541) | 11,766 | 11,354 |
| *97034 | Lake Oswego | (503) | 30,576 | 22,527 |
| 97355 | Lebanon | (541) | 10,950 | 10,413 |
| 97367 | Lincoln City | (541) | 5,903 | 5,469 |
| 97128 | McMinnville | (503) | 17,894 | 14,080 |
| *97501 | Medford | (541) | 47,021 | 39,746 |
| 97862 | Milton-Freewater | (541) | 5,533 | 5,086 |
| 97222 | Milwaukie | (503) | 18,670 | 17,931 |
| 97361 | Monmouth | (503) | 6,288 | 5,594 |
| 97132 | Newberg | (503) | 13,086 | 10,394 |
| 97365 | Newport | (541) | 8,437 | 7,519 |
| 97459 | North Bend | (541) | 9,614 | 9,779 |
| 97477 | North Springfield(u) | (541) | 5,451 | 6,140 |
| 97268 | Oak Grove(u) | (503) | 12,576 | 11,640 |
| ..... | Oak Hills(u) | | 6,450 | .... |
| ..... | Oatfield(u) | | 15,348 | .... |
| 97914 | Ontario | (541) | 9,394 | 8,814 |
| 97045 | Oregon City | (503) | 14,698 | 14,673 |
| 97801 | Pendleton | (541) | 15,142 | 14,521 |
| *97208 | Portland | (503) | 438,802 | 368,148 |
| 97236 | Powellhurst-Centennial(u) | (503) | 28,756 | 20,122 |
| 97754 | Prineville | (541) | 5,355 | 5,276 |
| 97225 | Raleigh Hills(u) | (503) | 6,066 | 6,517 |
| 97756 | Redmond | (541) | 7,165 | 6,452 |
| 97404 | River Road(u) | (541) | 9,443 | 10,370 |
| ..... | Rockcreek(u) | | 8,282 | .... |
| 97470 | Roseburg | (541) | 17,069 | 16,644 |
| 97470 | Roseburg North(u) | (541) | 6,831 | .... |
| 97051 | Saint Helens | (503) | 7,535 | 7,064 |
| *97301 | Salem | (503) | 107,793 | 89,091 |
| 97401 | Santa Clara(u) | (541) | 12,834 | 14,288 |
| 97138 | Seaside | (503) | 5,359 | 5,193 |
| 97381 | Silverton | (503) | 5,635 | 5,168 |
| *97477 | Springfield | (541) | 44,664 | 41,621 |
| 97383 | Stayton | (503) | 5,011 | 4,396 |
| 97479 | Sutherlin | (541) | 5,020 | 4,560 |

| ZIP | Place | Area code | 1990 | 1980 |
|---|---|---|---|---|
| 97386 | Sweet Home | (541) | 6,850 | 6,921 |
| 97058 | The Dalles, City of | (541) | 11,021 | 10,820 |
| 97223 | Tigard | (503) | 29,435 | 14,799 |
| 97060 | Troutdale | (503) | 7,852 | 5,908 |
| 97062 | Tualatin | (503) | 14,664 | 7,483 |
| 97225 | West Haven-Sylvan(u) | (503) | 6,009 | .... |
| 97068 | West Linn | (503) | 16,389 | 11,358 |
| 97225 | West Slope(u) | (503) | 7,959 | 5,364 |
| 97503 | White City(u) | (541) | 5,891 | 5,445 |
| 97070 | Wilsonville | (503) | 7,106 | 2,920 |
| 97071 | Woodburn | (503) | 13,404 | 11,196 |

## Pennsylvania

| ZIP | Place | Area code | 1990 | 1980 |
|---|---|---|---|---|
| 15001 | Aliquippa | (412) | 13,374 | 17,094 |
| *18105 | Allentown (Lehigh) | (610) | 105,301 | 103,758 |
| *16603 | Altoona | (814) | 51,881 | 57,078 |
| 19002 | Ambler | (215)/(610) | 6,609 | 6,628 |
| 15003 | Ambridge | (412) | 8,133 | 9,575 |
| 18403 | Archbald | (717) | 6,291 | 6,295 |
| 19003 | Ardmore(u) | (610) | 12,646 | .... |
| 15068 | Arnold | (412) | 6,113 | 6,853 |
| 19407 | Audubon(u)† | (610) | 6,328 | 6,853 |
| 15202 | Avalon | (412) | 5,784 | 6,240 |
| 15005 | Baden | (412) | 5,074 | 5,318 |
| 15234 | Baldwin | (412) | 21,923 | 24,714 |
| 18013 | Bangor | (610) | 5,383 | 5,006 |
| 15009 | Beaver | (412) | 5,028 | 5,441 |
| 15010 | Beaver Falls | (412) | 10,687 | 12,525 |
| 16823 | Bellefonte | (814) | 6,358 | 6,300 |
| 15202 | Bellevue | (412) | 9,126 | 10,128 |
| 18603 | Berwick | (717) | 10,976 | 11,850 |
| 15102 | Bethel Park | (412) | 33,823 | 34,755 |
| *18016 | Bethlehem | (610) | 71,427 | 70,419 |
| 18447 | Blakely | (717) | 7,222 | 7,438 |
| 17815 | Bloomsburg | (717) | 12,439 | 11,717 |
| 19422 | Blue Bell(u) | (215)/(610) | 6,091 | .... |
| 19061 | Boothwyn(u) | (610) | 5,069 | .... |
| 16701 | Bradford | (814) | 9,625 | 11,211 |
| 15227 | Brentwood | (412) | 10,823 | 11,859 |
| 15017 | Bridgeville | (412) | 5,445 | 6,154 |
| 19007 | Bristol | (215) | 10,405 | 10,867 |
| 19015 | Brookhaven | (610) | 8,567 | 7,912 |
| 19008 | Broomall(u) | (610) | 10,930 | .... |
| *16001 | Butler | (412) | 15,714 | 17,026 |
| 15419 | California | (412) | 5,748 | 5,703 |
| *17011 | Camp Hill | (717) | 7,831 | 8,422 |
| 15317 | Canonsburg | (412) | 9,200 | 10,459 |
| 18407 | Carbondale | (717) | 10,664 | 11,255 |
| 17013 | Carlisle | (717) | 18,419 | 18,314 |
| 15106 | Carnegie | (412) | 9,278 | 10,099 |
| 15108 | Carnot-Moon(u) | (412) | 10,187 | 11,102 |
| 15234 | Castle Shannon | (412) | 9,135 | 10,164 |
| 18032 | Catasauqua | (610) | 6,662 | 6,711 |
| 17201 | Chambersburg | (717) | 16,647 | 16,174 |
| 15022 | Charleroi | (412) | 5,014 | 5,717 |
| *19013 | Chester | (610) | 41,856 | 45,794 |
| 19013 | Chester Twp.(u) | (610) | 5,399 | 5,687 |
| 15025 | Clairton | (412) | 9,656 | 12,188 |
| 16214 | Clarion | (814) | 6,457 | 6,198 |
| 18411 | Clarks Summit | (717) | 5,433 | 5,272 |
| 16830 | Clearfield | (814) | 6,633 | 7,580 |
| 19018 | Clifton Heights | (610) | 7,111 | 7,320 |
| 19320 | Coatesville | (610) | 11,038 | 10,698 |
| 19023 | Collingdale | (610) | 9,175 | 9,539 |
| 17109 | Colonial Park(u) (Dauphin) | (717) | 13,777 | .... |
| 17512 | Columbia | (717) | 10,701 | 10,466 |
| 15425 | Connellsville | (412) | 9,229 | 10,319 |
| 19428 | Conshohocken | (215)/(610) | 8,064 | 8,591 |
| 15108 | Coraopolis | (412) | 6,747 | 7,308 |
| 16407 | Corry | (814) | 7,216 | 7,149 |
| 15205 | Crafton | (412) | 7,188 | 7,623 |
| 19021 | Croydon(u) | (215) | 9,967 | .... |
| 17821 | Danville | (717) | 5,165 | 5,239 |
| 19023 | Darby | (610) | 11,140 | 11,513 |
| 19036 | Darby Twp.(u) | (610) | 10,955 | 12,264 |
| 19333 | Devon-Berwyn(u) | (610) | 5,019 | 5,246 |
| 18519 | Dickson City | (717) | 6,276 | 6,699 |
| 15033 | Donora | (412) | 5,928 | 7,524 |
| 15216 | Dormont | (412) | 9,772 | 11,275 |
| 19335 | Downingtown | (610) | 7,749 | 7,650 |
| 18901 | Doylestown | (215) | 8,575 | 8,717 |
| 19026 | Drexel Hill(u) | (610) | 29,744 | .... |
| 15801 | Du Bois | (814) | 8,286 | 9,290 |
| 18512 | Dunmore | (717) | 15,403 | 16,781 |
| 15110 | Duquesne | (412) | 8,525 | 10,094 |
| 19401 | East Norriton(u) | (215)/(610) | 13,324 | 12,711 |
| *18042 | Easton | (610) | 26,276 | 26,027 |
| 18301 | East Stroudsburg | (717) | 8,781 | 8,039 |
| 17405 | East York(u) | (717) | 8,487 | .... |
| 15005 | Economy | (412) | 9,305 | 9,538 |
| 16412 | Edinboro | (814) | 7,736 | 6,324 |
| 18704 | Edwardsville | (717) | 5,399 | 5,729 |
| 17022 | Elizabethtown | (717) | 9,952 | 8,233 |
| 16117 | Ellwood City | (412) | 8,894 | 9,998 |
| 18049 | Emmaus | (610) | 11,157 | 11,001 |
| 17025 | Enola(u) | (717) | 5,961 | .... |
| 17522 | Ephrata | (717) | 12,133 | 11,095 |
| *16501 | Erie | (814) | 108,718 | 119,123 |
| 18643 | Exeter | (717) | 5,691 | 5,493 |
| 19030 | Fairless Hills(u) | (215) | 9,026 | .... |
| 16121 | Farrell | (412) | 6,835 | 8,645 |
| 19053 | Feasterville-Trevose(u) | (215) | 6,696 | .... |
| 16063 | Fernway(u) | (412) | 9,072 | 3,843 |
| 19032 | Folcroft | (610) | 7,506 | 8,231 |
| 19033 | Folsom(u) | (610) | 8,173 | .... |
| 15221 | Forest Hills | (412) | 8,173 | 8,198 |
| 18704 | Forty Fort | (717) | 5,049 | 5,590 |
| 15238 | Fox Chapel | (412) | 5,319 | 5,049 |
| 16323 | Franklin | (814) | 7,329 | 8,146 |
| 15143 | Franklin Park | (412) | 10,109 | 6,135 |
| 18052 | Fullerton(u) | (610) | 13,127 | 8,055 |
| 17325 | Gettysburg | (717) | 7,025 | 7,194 |
| 15045 | Glassport | (412) | 5,582 | 6,242 |
| 19036 | Glenolden | (610) | 7,260 | 7,633 |
| 19038 | Glenside(u) | (215) | 8,704 | .... |
| 15601 | Greensburg | (412) | 16,318 | 17,558 |
| 16125 | Greenville | (412) | 6,734 | 7,730 |
| 16127 | Grove City | (412) | 8,240 | 8,162 |
| 15101 | Hampton Twp.(u) (Allegheny) | (412) | 15,568 | .... |
| 17331 | Hanover | (717) | 14,399 | 14,890 |
| 19438 | Harleysville(u) | (215)/(610) | 7,405 | 3,673 |
| *17105 | Harrisburg | (717) | 52,376 | 53,264 |
| 15065 | Harrison Twp.(u) (Allegheny) | (412) | 11,763 | .... |
| 19040 | Hatboro | (215) | 7,382 | 7,579 |
| 18201 | Hazleton | (717) | 24,730 | 27,318 |
| 18055 | Hellertown | (610) | 5,662 | 6,025 |
| 16148 | Hermitage† | (412) | 15,260 | 16,365 |
| 17033 | Hershey(u) | (717) | 11,860 | 13,249 |
| 16648 | Hollidaysburg | (814) | 5,624 | 5, 892 |
| 16001 | Homeacre-Lyndora(u) | (412) | 7,511 | 8,333 |
| 19044 | Horsham(u) | (215) | 15,051 | 9,900 |
| 16652 | Huntingdon | (814) | 6,843 | 7,042 |
| 15701 | Indiana | (412) | 15,174 | 16,051 |
| 15644 | Jeannette | (412) | 11,221 | 13,106 |
| 15344 | Jefferson | (412) | 9,533 | 8,643 |
| 18229 | Jim Thorpe | (717) | 5,048 | 5,263 |
| *15907 | Johnstown | (814) | 28,124 | 35,496 |
| 15108 | Kennedy Twp.(u) | (412) | 7,152 | 7,159 |
| 19348 | Kennett Square | (610) | 5,218 | 4,715 |
| 19406 | King of Prussia(u) | (215)/(610) | 18,406 | .... |
| 18704 | Kingston | (717) | 14,507 | 15,681 |
| 16201 | Kittanning | (412) | 5,120 | 5,432 |
| 19443 | Kulpsville(u) | (215) | 5,183 | .... |
| *17604 | Lancaster | (717) | 55,551 | 54,725 |
| 19446 | Lansdale | (215) | 16,362 | 16,526 |
| 19050 | Lansdowne | (610) | 11,712 | 11,891 |
| 15650 | Latrobe | (412) | 9,265 | 10,799 |
| 17540 | Leacock-Leola-Bareville(u) | (717) | 5,685 | .... |
| *17042 | Lebanon | (717) | 24,800 | 25,711 |
| 18235 | Lehighton | (610) | 5,914 | 5,826 |
| *19055 | Levittown(u) | (215) | 55,362 | .... |
| 17837 | Lewisburg | (717) | 5,785 | 5,407 |
| 17044 | Lewistown (Mifflin) | (717) | 9,341 | 9,830 |
| 17112 | Linglestown(u) | (717) | 5,862 | .... |
| 19353 | Lionville-Marchwood(u) | (610) | 6,468 | .... |
| 17543 | Lititz | (717) | 8,280 | 7,590 |
| 17745 | Lock Haven | (717) | 9,230 | 9,617 |
| 17011 | Lower Allen(u) | (717) | 6,329 | .... |
| 15068 | Lower Burrell | (412) | 12,251 | 13,200 |
| 15237 | McCandless Twp.(u) | (412) | 28,781 | 26,191 |
| *15134 | McKeesport | (412) | 26,016 | 31,012 |
| 15136 | McKees Rocks | (412) | 7,691 | 8,742 |
| 17948 | Mahanoy City | (717) | 5,209 | 6,167 |
| 17545 | Manheim | (717) | 5,011 | 5,015 |
| 19002 | Maple Glen(u) | (215) | 5,881 | .... |
| 16335 | Meadville | (814) | 14,318 | 15,544 |
| 17055 | Mechanicsburg | (717) | 9,452 | 9,487 |
| *19063 | Media | (610) | 5,957 | 6,119 |
| 17057 | Middletown (Dauphin) | (717) | 9,254 | 10,122 |
| 18017 | Middletown (u) (Northampton) | (610) | 6,866 | 5,801 |
| 17551 | Millersville | (717) | 8,099 | 7,668 |
| 17847 | Milton | (717) | 6,746 | 6,730 |
| 15061 | Monaca | (412) | 6,739 | 7,661 |
| 15062 | Monessen | (412) | 9,901 | 11,928 |
| 15146 | Monroeville | (412) | 29,169 | 30,977 |
| 18936 | Montgomeryville(u) | (215) | 9,114 | .... |
| 18507 | Moosic | (717) | 5,397 | 6,068 |
| 19067 | Morrisville (Bucks) | (215) | 9,765 | 9,845 |
| 17851 | Mount Carmel | (717) | 7,196 | 8,190 |
| 17552 | Mount Joy | (717) | 6,398 | 5,680 |
| 15228 | Mount Lebanon(u) | (412) | 33,362 | 34,414 |
| 15120 | Munhall | (412) | 13,158 | 14,535 |
| 15668 | Murrysville | (412) | 17,240 | 16,036 |
| 18634 | Nanticoke | (717) | 12,267 | 13,044 |
| 18064 | Nazareth | (610) | 5,713 | 5,443 |
| ..... | Nether Providence Twp.(u) | (610) | 13,229 | 12,730 |
| 15066 | New Brighton | (412) | 6,854 | 7,364 |
| *16108 | New Castle | (412) | 28,334 | 33,621 |
| 17070 | New Cumberland | (717) | 7,665 | 8,051 |
| 15068 | New Kensington | (412) | 15,894 | 17,660 |
| *19401 | Norristown | (610) | 30,754 | 34,684 |
| 18067 | Northampton | (610) | 8,717 | 8,240 |
| 15104 | North Braddock | (412) | 7,036 | 8,711 |
| 15137 | North Versailles(u) | (412) | 12,302 | 13,294 |
| 16421 | Northwest Harborcreek(u) | (814) | 6,662 | 7,485 |

| ZIP | Place | | 1990 | 1980 |
|---|---|---|---|---|
| 19074 | Norwood (Delaware) | (610) | 6,162 | 6,647 |
| 15139 | Oakmont (Allegheny) | (412) | 6,961 | 7,039 |
| 15238 | O'Hara(u) | (412) | 9,096 | .... |
| 16301 | Oil City | (814) | 11,949 | 13,881 |
| 18518 | Old Forge | (717) | 8,834 | 9,304 |
| 18447 | Olyphant | (717) | 5,222 | 5,204 |
| 19075 | Oreland(u) | (215) | 5,695 | .... |
| 18071 | Palmerton | (610) | 5,394 | 5,455 |
| 17078 | Palmyra | (717) | 6,910 | 7,228 |
| 19301 | Paoli(u) | (610) | 5,603 | 5,277 |
| 16801 | Park Forest Village(u) | (814) | 6,703 | .... |
| 17331 | Parkville(u) | (717) | 6,014 | 5,009 |
| 15235 | Penn Hills(u) | (717) | 51,430 | 57,632 |
| 19151 | Penn Wynne(u) | (215) | 5,807 | .... |
| 18944 | Perkasie | (215) | 7,787 | 5,241 |
| *19104 | Philadelphia | (215) | 1,585,577 | 1,688,210 |
| 19460 | Phoenixville | (610) | 15,066 | 14,165 |
| *15233 | Pittsburgh | (412) | 369,879 | 423,959 |
| *18640 | Pittston | (717) | 9,389 | 9,903 |
| 15236 | Pleasant Hills | (412) | 8,884 | 9,604 |
| 15239 | Plum | (412) | 25,609 | 25,309 |
| 18651 | Plymouth | (717) | 7,134 | 7,605 |
| 19462 | Plymouth Meeting(u) | (215)/(610) | 6,241 | .... |
| *19464 | Pottstown | (610) | 21,831 | 22,729 |
| 17901 | Pottsville | (717) | 16,603 | 18,195 |
| 17109 | Progress(u) | (717) | 9,654 | .... |
| 19076 | Prospect Park | (610) | 6,764 | 6,593 |
| 15767 | Punxsutawney | (814) | 6,782 | 7,479 |
| 18951 | Quakertown | (215) | 8,982 | 8,867 |
| 19087 | Radnor Twp.(u) | (610) | 28,705 | 27,676 |
| *19612 | Reading | (610) | 78,380 | 78,686 |
| 17356 | Red Lion | (717) | 6,130 | 5,824 |
| 18954 | Richboro(u) | (215) | 5,332 | 5,141 |
| 19078 | Ridley Park | (610) | 7,592 | 7,889 |
| 15136 | Robinson (Allegheny)(u) | (412) | 10,830 | .... |
| 15237 | Ross Twp.(u) | (412) | 33,482 | 35,102 |
| 15857 | Saint Marys | (814) | 5,511 | 6,417 |
| 19464 | Sanatoga(u) | (610) | 5,534 | 3,723 |
| 18840 | Sayre | (717) | 5,791 | 6,951 |
| 17972 | Schuylkill Haven | (717) | 5,610 | 5,977 |
| 15683 | Scottdale | (412) | 5,184 | 5,833 |
| 15106 | Scott Twp.(u) | (412) | 17,118 | 20,413 |
| *18505 | Scranton | (717) | 81,805 | 88,117 |
| 17870 | Selinsgrove | (717) | 5,384 | 5,227 |
| 15116 | Shaler Twp.(u) | (412) | 30,533 | 33,694 |
| 17872 | Shamokin | (717) | 9,184 | 10,357 |
| 16146 | Sharon | (412) | 17,533 | 19,057 |
| 19079 | Sharon Hill | (610) | 5,771 | 6,221 |
| 17976 | Shenandoah | (717) | 6,221 | 7,589 |
| 19607 | Shillington | (610) | 5,062 | 5,601 |
| 17404 | Shiloh(u) | (717) | 8,245 | 5,315 |
| 17257 | Shippensburg | (717) | 5,331 | 5,261 |
| 15501 | Somerset | (814) | 6,454 | 6,474 |
| 18964 | Souderton | (215) | 5,957 | 6,657 |
| 15129 | South Park Twp.(u) | (814) | 14,292 | .... |
| 17701 | South Williamsport | (717) | 6,496 | 6,581 |
| 19064 | Springfield (u) (Delaware) | (610) | 24,160 | 25,326 |
| *16804 | State College | (814) | 38,981 | 36,130 |
| 17113 | Steelton | (717) | 5,152 | 6,484 |
| 15136 | Stowe Twp.(u) | (412) | 7,681 | 9,202 |
| 18360 | Stroudsburg | (717) | 5,312 | 5,148 |
| 16323 | Sugar Creek | (717) | 5,532 | 5,954 |
| 17801 | Sunbury | (717) | 11,591 | 12,292 |
| 19081 | Swarthmore | (610) | 6,157 | 5,950 |
| 15218 | Swissvale | (412) | 10,637 | 11,345 |
| 18704 | Swoyersville | (717) | 5,630 | 5,795 |
| 18252 | Tamaqua | (717) | 7,943 | 8,843 |
| 15084 | Tarentum | (412) | 5,674 | 6,419 |
| 18517 | Taylor | (717) | 6,941 | 7,246 |
| 16354 | Titusville | (814) | 6,434 | 6,884 |
| 19401 | Trooper(u) | (610) | 5,137 | 7,370 |
| 15145 | Turtle Creek | (412) | 6,556 | 6,959 |
| 16686 | Tyrone | (814) | 5,743 | 6,346 |
| 15401 | Uniontown (Fayette) | (412) | 12,034 | 14,510 |
| 19063 | Upper Providence Twp.(u) | (610) | 9,727 | 9,477 |
| 15241 | Upper Saint Clair(u) | (412) | 19,692 | 19,023 |
| 15690 | Vandergrift | (412) | 5,904 | 6,823 |
| 19013 | Village Green-Green Ridge(u) | (610) | 9,026 | .... |
| 16365 | Warren | (814) | 11,122 | 12,146 |
| 15301 | Washington | (412) | 15,864 | 18,363 |
| 17268 | Waynesboro | (717) | 9,578 | 9,726 |
| 17315 | Weigelstown(u) | (717) | 8,665 | 5,213 |
| *19380 | West Chester | (610) | 18,041 | 17,435 |
| 19380 | West Goshen(u) | (610) | 8,948 | 7,998 |
| *15122 | West Mifflin | (412) | 23,644 | 26,322 |
| 15905 | Westmont | (814) | 5,789 | 6,113 |
| 19401 | West Norriton(u) | (610) | 15,209 | 14,034 |
| 18643 | West Pittston | (717) | 5,590 | 5,980 |
| 15229 | West View | (412) | 7,734 | 7,648 |
| 15227 | Whitehall (Allegheny) | (412) | 14,451 | 15,143 |
| 15131 | White Oak | (717) | 8,761 | 9,480 |
| *18703 | Wilkes-Barre | (717) | 47,523 | 51,551 |
| 15221 | Wilkinsburg | (412) | 21,080 | 23,669 |
| 15145 | Wilkins Twp.(u) | (412) | 7,487 | 8,472 |
| *17701 | Williamsport | (717) | 31,933 | 33,401 |
| 19090 | Willow Grove(u) (Montgomery) | (610) | 16,325 | .... |
| 17584 | Willow Street(u) | (717) | 5,817 | .... |
| 15025 | Wilson | (412) | 7,830 | 7,564 |

| ZIP | Place | | 1990 | 1980 |
|---|---|---|---|---|
| 19094 | Woodlyn(u) | (610) | 10,151 | .... |
| 19118 | Wyndmoor(u) | (215) | 5,682 | .... |
| 19610 | Wyomissing | (610) | 7,332 | 6,551 |
| 19050 | Yeadon | (610) | 11,980 | 11,727 |
| *17405 | York | (717) | 42,192 | 44,619 |

## Rhode Island (401)

*See note on page 390*

| ZIP | Place | 1990 | 1980 |
|---|---|---|---|
| 02806 | Barrington(u) | 15,849 | 16,174 |
| 02809 | Bristol(u) | 21,625 | 20,128 |
| 02830 | *Burrillville* | 16,230 | 13,164 |
| 02863 | Central Falls | 17,638 | 16,995 |
| 02813 | *Charlestown* | 6,478 | 4,800 |
| 02816 | *Coventry* | 31,083 | 27,065 |
| *02910 | Cranston | 76,060 | 71,992 |
| 02864 | *Cumberland* | 29,038 | 27,069 |
| 02864 | Cumberland Hill(u) | 6,379 | 5,421 |
| 02818 | *East Greenwich* | 11,865 | 10,211 |
| 02914 | East Providence | 50,380 | 50,980 |
| 02822 | Exeter | 5,461 | 4,453 |
| 02814 | *Glocester* | 9,227 | 7,550 |
| 02828 | Greenville(u) | 8,303 | 7,576 |
| 02833 | *Hopkinton* | 6,873 | 6,406 |
| 02919 | *Johnston* | 26,542 | 24,907 |
| 02881 | Kingston(u) | 6,504 | 5,479 |
| 02865 | *Lincoln* | 18,045 | 16,949 |
| 02840 | *Middletown* | 19,460 | 17,216 |
| 02882 | *Narragansett* | 15,004 | 12,088 |
| 02840 | Newport | 28,227 | 29,259 |
| 02843 | Newport East(u) | 11,080 | 11,030 |
| *02852 | *North Kingstown* | 23,786 | 21,938 |
| 02908 | North Providence(u) | 32,090 | 29,188 |
| 02876 | *North Smithfield* | 10,497 | 9,972 |
| 02859 | Pascoag(u) | 5,011 | 3,807 |
| *02860 | Pawtucket | 72,644 | 71,204 |
| 02871 | *Portsmouth* | 16,857 | 14,257 |
| *02904 | Providence | 160,728 | 156,804 |
| 02812 | Richmond | 5,351 | 4,018 |
| 02857 | *Scituate* | 9,796 | 8,405 |
| 02917 | *Smithfield* | 19,163 | 16,886 |
| 02879 | *South Kingstown* | 24,631 | 20,414 |
| 02878 | Tiverton(u) | 7,259 | 7,653 |
| 02878 | *Tiverton* | 14,312 | 13,526 |
| 02864 | Valley Falls(u) | 11,175 | 10,892 |
| *02879 | Wakefield-Peacedale(u) | 7,134 | 6,474 |
| 02885 | *Warren* | 11,385 | 10,640 |
| *02886 | Warwick | 85,427 | 87,123 |
| 02891 | *Westerly* | 21,605 | 18,580 |
| 02891 | Westerly Center(u) | 16,477 | 14,093 |
| 02893 | West Warwick (u) | 29,268 | 27,026 |
| 02895 | Woonsocket | 43,877 | 45,914 |

## South Carolina

| ZIP | Place | | 1990 | 1980 |
|---|---|---|---|---|
| 29620 | Abbeville | (864) | 5,778 | 5,833 |
| *29801 | Aiken | (803) | 20,386 | 14,978 |
| *29621 | Anderson | (864) | 26,385 | 27,546 |
| 29812 | Barnwell | (803) | 5,255 | 5,572 |
| *29902 | Beaufort | (803) | 9,576 | 8,634 |
| 29841 | Belvedere(u) | (803) | 6,133 | 6,859 |
| 29512 | Bennettsville | (803) | 10,095 | 8,774 |
| 29611 | Berea(u) | (864) | 13,535 | 13,164 |
| 29115 | Brookdale(u) | (803) | 5,339 | 6,123 |
| 29902 | Burton(u) | (803) | 6,917 | 3,619 |
| 29020 | Camden | (803) | 6,696 | 7,462 |
| 29033 | Cayce | (803) | 10,824 | 11,701 |
| *29402 | Charleston | (803) | 79,925 | 69,779 |
| 29520 | Cheraw | (803) | 5,553 | 5,654 |
| 29706 | Chester | (803) | 7,158 | 6,820 |
| *29631 | Clemson | (864) | 11,145 | 8,118 |
| 29325 | Clinton | (864) | 9,603 | 8,596 |
| *29201 | Columbia | (803) | 103,477 | 101,229 |
| *29526 | Conway | (803) | 9,819 | 10,240 |
| *29532 | Darlington | (803) | 7,310 | 7,989 |
| 29204 | Dentsville(u) | (803) | 11,839 | 13,579 |
| 29536 | Dillon | (803) | 6,829 | 7,060 |
| *29640 | Easley | (864) | 15,179 | 14,264 |
| *29501 | Florence | (803) | 29,913 | 29,842 |
| 29206 | Forest Acres | (803) | 7,181 | 6,062 |
| *29341 | Gaffney | (864) | 13,149 | 13,453 |
| 29605 | Gantt(u) | (864) | 13,891 | 13,719 |
| ..... | Garden City(u) | | 6,305 | .... |
| *29440 | Georgetown | (803) | 9,517 | 10,144 |
| 29445 | Goose Creek | (803) | 24,692 | 17,811 |
| *29602 | Greenville | (864) | 58,256 | 58,242 |
| *29646 | Greenwood | (864) | 20,807 | 21,613 |
| *29650 | Greer | (864) | 10,322 | 10,525 |
| 29406 | Hanahan | (803) | 13,176 | 13,224 |
| *29550 | Hartsville | (803) | 8,372 | 7,631 |
| *29928 | Hilton Head Island† | (803) | 23,694 | 11,239 |
| 29621 | Homeland Park(u) | (864) | 6,569 | 6,720 |
| 29063 | Irmo | (803) | 11,277 | 3,957 |
| 29456 | Ladson(u) | (803) | 13,540 | 13,246 |
| 29560 | Lake City | (803) | 7,153 | 6,731 |
| *29720 | Lancaster | (803) | 8,914 | 9,703 |

| ZIP | Place | | 1990 | 1980 |
|---|---|---|---|---|
| 29360 | Laurens | (864) | 9,694 | 10,587 |
| 29571 | Marion | (803) | 7,658 | 7,700 |
| 29662 | Mauldin | (864) | 11,662 | 8,143 |
| 29461 | Moncks Corner | (803) | 5,599 | 4,179 |
| *29464 | Mount Pleasant | (803) | 30,108 | 14,464 |
| 29574 | Mullins | (803) | 5,910 | 6,068 |
| *29577 | Myrtle Beach | (803) | 24,848 | 18,446 |
| 29108 | Newberry | (803) | 10,543 | 9,866 |
| 29841 | North Augusta | (803) | 15,684 | 13,593 |
| 29405 | North Charleston | (803) | 70,304 | 62,479 |
| *29582 | North Myrtle Beach | (803) | 8,731 | 3,960 |
| 29565 | Oak Grove(u) | (803) | 7,173 | 7,092 |
| *29115 | Orangeburg | (803) | 13,772 | 14,933 |
| ..... | Parker(u) | | 11,072 | .... |
| 29905 | Parris Island(u) | (803) | 7,172 | 7,752 |
| ..... | Red Bank(u) | | 5,950 | .... |
| ..... | Red Hill(u) | | 6,112 | .... |
| *29730 | Rock Hill | (803) | 41,610 | 35,327 |
| 29417 | Saint Andrews(u) | (803) | 25,692 | 20,245 |
| 29609 | Sans Souci(u) | (864) | 7,612 | 8,393 |
| *29678 | Seneca | (864) | 7,726 | 7,436 |
| 29210 | Seven Oaks(u) | (803) | 15,722 | 16,604 |
| *29681 | Simpsonville | (864) | 11,744 | 9,037 |
| 29577 | Socastee(u) | (803) | 10,426 | 1,082 |
| *29306 | Spartanburg | (864) | 43,479 | 43,826 |
| *29483 | Summerville | (803) | 22,519 | 6,492 |
| *29150 | Sumter | (803) | 40,977 | 24,921 |
| 29687 | Taylors(u) | (864) | 19,619 | 15,801 |
| 29379 | Union | (864) | 9,840 | 10,523 |
| 29607 | Wade Hampton(u) | (864) | 20,014 | 20,180 |
| 29488 | Walterboro | (803) | 5,595 | 6,209 |
| 29611 | Welcome(u) | (864) | 6,560 | 6,922 |
| *29169 | West Columbia | (803) | 10,974 | 10,409 |
| 29206 | Woodfield(u) | (803) | 8,862 | 9,588 |
| 29745 | York | (803) | 6,709 | 6,412 |

## South Dakota (605)

| ZIP | Place | 1990 | 1980 |
|---|---|---|---|
| *57401 | Aberdeen | 24,995 | 25,851 |
| 57006 | Brookings | 16,270 | 14,951 |
| 57706 | Ellsworth AFB(u) | 7,017 | 4,766 |
| 57350 | Huron | 12,448 | 13,000 |
| 57042 | Madison | 6,257 | 6,210 |
| 57301 | Mitchell | 13,798 | 13,916 |
| 57501 | Pierre | 12,906 | 11,973 |
| *57701 | Rapid City | 54,523 | 46,492 |
| 57701 | Rapid Valley(u) | 5,968 | 3,265 |
| *57101 | Sioux Falls | 100,836 | 81,343 |
| 57754 | Spearfish Canyon | 6,966 | 5,251 |
| 57785 | Sturgis | 5,330 | 5,184 |
| 57069 | Vermillion | 10,034 | 10,136 |
| 57201 | Watertown | 17,632 | 15,49 |
| 57078 | Yankton | 12,703 | 12,011 |

## Tennessee

| ZIP | Place | | 1990 | 1980 |
|---|---|---|---|---|
| 37701 | Alcoa | (423) | 6,400 | 6,870 |
| *37303 | Athens | (423) | 12,054 | 12,080 |
| 38134 | Bartlett | (901) | 26,989 | 17,170 |
| 37660 | Bloomingdale(u) | (423) | 10,953 | 12,088 |
| 38008 | Bolivar | (901) | 5,969 | 6,597 |
| *37027 | Brentwood | (615) | 16,392 | 9,431 |
| *37621 | Bristol | (423) | 23,421 | 23,986 |
| 38012 | Brownsville | (901) | 10,017 | 9,307 |
| *37401 | Chattanooga | (423) | 152,393 | 169,514 |
| *37040 | Clarksville | (615) | 75,542 | 54,777 |
| *37311 | Cleveland | (423) | 30,354 | 26,415 |
| *37716 | Clinton | (423) | 8,960 | 5,245 |
| 37315 | Collegedale | (423) | 5,048 | 4,607 |
| *38017 | Collierville | (901) | 14,501 | 7,839 |
| 37663 | Colonial Heights(u) | (423) | 6,716 | 6,744 |
| *38401 | Columbia | (615) | 28,583 | 26,571 |
| *38501 | Cookeville | (615) | 21,744 | 20,535 |
| 38019 | Covington | (901) | 7,487 | 6,065 |
| *38555 | Crossville | (615) | 6,930 | 6,394 |
| 37321 | Dayton | (423) | 5,671 | 5,233 |
| *37055 | Dickson | (615) | 8,783 | 7,040 |
| *38024 | Dyersburg | (901) | 16,321 | 15,856 |
| 37801 | Eagleton Village(u) | (423) | 5,169 | 5,331 |
| 37411 | East Brainerd(u) | (423) | 11,594 | .... |
| 37412 | East Ridge | (423) | 21,101 | 21,236 |
| *37643 | Elizabethton | (423) | 11,931 | 12,431 |
| 37650 | Erwin | (423) | 5,017 | 4,739 |
| 37922 | Farragut† | (423) | 12,802 | 5,992 |
| 37334 | Fayetteville | (615) | 7,158 | 7,559 |
| *37064 | Franklin | (615) | 20,098 | 12,407 |
| 37066 | Gallatin | (615) | 18,794 | 17,191 |
| *38138 | Germantown | (901) | 33,016 | 21,467 |
| *37072 | Goodlettsville | (615) | 11,219 | 8,327 |
| *37743 | Greeneville | (423) | 13,532 | 14,097 |
| 37215 | Green Hills(u) | (615) | 6,763 | .... |
| 38040 | Halls(u) | (901) | 6,450 | 10,363 |
| 37748 | Harriman | (423) | 7,119 | 8,303 |
| 37341 | Harrison(u) | (423) | 7,191 | 6,206 |
| *37075 | Hendersonville | (615) | 32,188 | 26,561 |
| 38343 | Humboldt | (901) | 9,651 | 10,209 |
| *38301 | Jackson | (901) | 49,145 | 49,258 |
| 37760 | Jefferson City | (423) | 5,522 | 5,612 |
| *37601 | Johnson City | (423) | 49,479 | 39,753 |
| *37662 | Kingsport | (423) | 36,353 | 32,027 |
| *37950 | Knoxville | (423) | 165,039 | 175,045 |
| 37766 | La Follette | (423) | 7,201 | 8,198 |
| 37086 | La Vergne | (615) | 7,499 | 5,495 |
| 38464 | Lawrenceburg | (615) | 10,397 | 10,184 |
| *37087 | Lebanon | (615) | 15,208 | 11,872 |
| *37771 | Lenoir City | (423) | 6,147 | 5,180 |
| 37091 | Lewisburg | (615) | 9,879 | 8,760 |
| 38351 | Lexington | (901) | 5,810 | 5,934 |
| 38201 | McKenzie | (901) | 5,168 | 5,405 |
| 37110 | McMinnville | (423) | 11,194 | 10,683 |
| 37355 | Manchester | (615) | 7,709 | 7,250 |
| 38237 | Martin | (901) | 8,588 | 8,898 |
| *37804 | Maryville | (423) | 19,208 | 17,480 |
| *38101 | Memphis | (901) | 610,337 | 646,174 |
| 37343 | Middle Valley(u) | (423) | 12,255 | 11,420 |
| 38358 | Milan | (901) | 7,512 | 8,083 |
| *38053 | Millington | (901) | 17,866 | 20,236 |
| *37813 | Morristown | (423) | 21,316 | 19,570 |
| 37122 | Mount Juliet | (615) | 5,389 | 2,879 |
| *37130 | Murfreesboro | (615) | 44,922 | 32,845 |
| *37202 | Nashville | (615) | 488,374 | 455,651 |
| 37821 | Newport | (423) | 7,123 | 7,580 |
| *37830 | Oak Ridge | (423) | 27,310 | 27,662 |
| 38242 | Paris | (901) | 9,332 | 10,728 |
| 37148 | Portland | (615) | 5,165 | 4,030 |
| 37849 | Powell(u) | (423) | 7,534 | 7,220 |
| 38478 | Pulaski | (615) | 7,916 | 7,184 |
| 37415 | Red Bank | (423) | 12,320 | 13,129 |
| 38063 | Ripley | (901) | 6,188 | 6,366 |
| 37854 | Rockwood | (423) | 5,348 | 5,687 |
| 38372 | Savannah | (901) | 6,547 | 6,992 |
| *37862 | Sevierville | (423) | 7,178 | 4,556 |
| 37865 | Seymour(u) | (423) | 7,026 | .... |
| 37160 | Shelbyville | (615) | 14,042 | 13,530 |
| 37377 | Signal Mountain | (423) | 7,034 | 5,818 |
| 37167 | Smyrna | (615) | 13,647 | 8,839 |
| 37379 | Soddy-Daisy | (423) | 8,240 | 8,388 |
| 37311 | South Cleveland(u) | (423) | 5,372 | 4,360 |
| 37172 | Springfield | (615) | 11,227 | 10,814 |
| 37874 | Sweetwater | (423) | 5,066 | 4,725 |
| 37388 | Tullahoma | (423) | 16,761 | 15,800 |
| *38261 | Union City | (901) | 10,513 | 10,436 |
| 37398 | Winchester | (615) | 6,305 | 5,821 |

## Texas

| ZIP | Place | | 1990 | 1980 |
|---|---|---|---|---|
| *79604 | Abilene | (915) | 106,707 | 98,315 |
| 75001 | Addison | (972) | 8,783 | 5,553 |
| 78516 | Alamo | (210) | 8,352 | 5,831 |
| 78209 | Alamo Heights | (210) | 6,502 | 6,252 |
| 77039 | Aldine(u) | (713) | 11,133 | 12,623 |
| *78332 | Alice | (512) | 19,788 | 20,961 |
| 75002 | Allen | (972) | 19,315 | 8,314 |
| *79830 | Alpine | (915) | 5,622 | 5,465 |
| *77511 | Alvin | (713) | 19,220 | 16,515 |
| *79105 | Amarillo | (806) | 157,571 | 149,230 |
| 78750 | Anderson Mill(u) | | 9,468 | .... |
| 79714 | Andrews | (915) | 10,678 | 11,061 |
| *77515 | Angleton | (409) | 17,140 | 13,929 |
| *78336 | Aransas Pass | (512) | 7,180 | 7,173 |
| *76004 | Arlington | (817) | 261,717 | 160,113 |
| 75751 | Athens | (903) | 10,982 | 10,197 |
| 75551 | Atlanta | (972) | 6,118 | 6,272 |
| *78767 | Austin | (512) | 465,648 | 345,890 |
| *76020 | Azle | (817) | 8,868 | 5,822 |
| 77518 | Bacliff(u) | (409) | 5,549 | 4,851 |
| 75180 | Balch Springs | (972) | 17,406 | 13,746 |
| *77414 | Bay City | (409) | 18,170 | 17,837 |
| *77520 | Baytown | (713) | 63,843 | 56,923 |
| *77707 | Beaumont | (409) | 114,323 | 118,102 |
| *76021 | Bedford | (817) | 43,762 | 20,821 |
| *78102 | Beeville | (512) | 13,547 | 14,574 |
| *77401 | Bellaire | (713) | 13,844 | 14,950 |
| 76704 | Bellmead | (817) | 8,336 | 7,569 |
| 76513 | Belton | (817) | 12,463 | 10,660 |
| 76126 | Benbrook | (817) | 19,564 | 13,579 |
| *79720 | Big Spring | (915) | 23,093 | 24,804 |
| 75418 | Bonham | (903) | 6,688 | 7,338 |
| *79007 | Borger | (806) | 15,675 | 15,837 |
| 76825 | Brady | (915) | 5,946 | 5,969 |
| 76424 | Breckenridge | (817) | 5,665 | 6,921 |
| *77833 | Brenham | (409) | 11,952 | 10,966 |
| 77611 | Bridge City | (409) | 8,010 | 7,667 |
| 79316 | Brownfield | (806) | 9,560 | 10,387 |
| *78520 | Brownsville | (210) | 98,962 | 84,997 |
| *76801 | Brownwood | (915) | 18,387 | 19,396 |
| 78717 | Brushy Creek(u) | (903) | 5,833 | .... |
| *77801 | Bryan | (409) | 55,002 | 44,337 |
| 76354 | Burkburnett | (817) | 10,145 | 10,668 |
| *76028 | Burleson | (817) | 16,113 | 11,734 |
| 76520 | Cameron | (817) | 5,635 | 5,721 |
| 79015 | Canyon | (806) | 11,365 | 10,724 |
| 78130 | Canyon Lake(u) | (210) | 9,975 | .... |
| 78834 | Carrizo Springs | (210) | 5,745 | 6,886 |
| *75006 | Carrolton | (972) | 82,169 | 40,595 |

| ZIP | Place | | 1990 | 1980 |
|---|---|---|---|---|
| 75633 | Carthage | (903) | 6,496 | 6,447 |
| *75104 | Cedar Hill | (972) | 19,988 | 6,849 |
| *78613 | Cedar Park | (512) | 5,121 | 3,474 |
| 77530 | Channelview(u) | (713) | 25,564 | 17,471 |
| 79201 | Childress | (817) | 5,055 | 5,817 |
| *76031 | Cleburne | (817) | 22,205 | 19,218 |
| *77327 | Cleveland | (713) | 7,124 | 5,977 |
| 77015 | Cloverleaf(u) | (713) | 18,230 | 17,317 |
| 77531 | Clute | (409) | 9,467 | 9,577 |
| 76834 | Coleman | (915) | 5,410 | 5,960 |
| *77840 | College Station | (409) | 52,443 | 37,272 |
| 76034 | Colleyville | (817) | 12,724 | 6,700 |
| *75428 | Commerce | (903) | 6,825 | 8,136 |
| *77301 | Conroe | (409) | 27,675 | 18,034 |
| 78109 | Converse | (512) | 8,887 | 5,150 |
| 75019 | Coppell | (972) | 16,881 | 3,826 |
| 76522 | Copperas Cove | (817) | 24,079 | 19,469 |
| *78469 | Corpus Christi | (512) | 257,428 | 232,134 |
| *75110 | Corsicana | (903) | 22,911 | 21,712 |
| 75835 | Crockett | (409) | 7,024 | 7,405 |
| 76036 | Crowley | (817) | 6,974 | 5,852 |
| 78839 | Crystal City | (512) | 8,263 | 8,334 |
| 77954 | Cuero | (512) | 6,700 | 7,124 |
| 79022 | Dalhart | (806) | 6,246 | 6,854 |
| *75221 | Dallas | (214)/(972) | 1,007,618 | 904,599 |
| 77535 | Dayton | (409) | 5,042 | 4,908 |
| 77536 | Deer Park | (713) | 27,424 | 22,648 |
| *78840 | Del Rio | (210) | 30,705 | 30,034 |
| *75020 | Denison | (903) | 21,505 | 23,884 |
| *76201 | Denton | (817) | 66,270 | 48,063 |
| 79323 | Denver City | (512) | 5,156 | 4,704 |
| *75115 | De Soto | (972) | 30,544 | 15,538 |
| 77539 | Dickinson | (713) | 9,497 | 7,505 |
| 78537 | Donna | (210) | 12,652 | 9,952 |
| 79029 | Dumas | (806) | 12,871 | 12,194 |
| *75138 | Duncanville | (972) | 35,008 | 27,781 |
| 76135 | Eagle Mountain(u) | (817) | 5,847 | .... |
| *78852 | Eagle Pass | (210) | 20,651 | 21,407 |
| *78539 | Edinburg | (210) | 29,885 | 24,075 |
| 77957 | Edna | (512) | 5,343 | 5,650 |
| 77437 | El Campo | (409) | 10,511 | 10,462 |
| *79910 | El Paso | (915) | 515,342 | 425,259 |
| 78543 | Elsa | (210) | 5,242 | 5,061 |
| *75119 | Ennis | (972) | 13,869 | 12,110 |
| *76039 | Euless | (817) | 38,149 | 24,002 |
| 76140 | Everman | (817) | 5,672 | 5,387 |
| 79838 | Fabens(u) | (915) | 5,599 | 4,285 |
| 78355 | Falfurrias | (512) | 5,788 | 6,103 |
| 75234 | Farmers Branch | (972) | 24,250 | 24,863 |
| ..... | First Colony(u) | | 18,327 | .... |
| 78114 | Floresville | (210) | 5,247 | 4,381 |
| 75028 | Flower Mound | (972) | 15,527 | 4,402 |
| 76119 | Forest Hill | (817) | 11,482 | 11,684 |
| 79906 | Fort Bliss(u) | (915) | 13,915 | 12,687 |
| 76544 | Fort Hood(u) | (817) | 35,580 | 31,250 |
| 79735 | Fort Stockton | (915) | 8,524 | 8,688 |
| *76161 | Fort Worth | (817) | 447,619 | 385,164 |
| 78624 | Fredericksburg | (210) | 6,934 | 6,412 |
| 77541 | Freeport | (409) | 11,389 | 13,444 |
| 77546 | Friendswood | (713) | 22,814 | 10,719 |
| 75034 | Frisco | (972) | 6,138 | 3,499 |
| *76240 | Gainesville | (817) | 14,256 | 14,081 |
| 77547 | Galena Park | (713) | 10,033 | 9,879 |
| *77550 | Galveston | (409) | 59,067 | 61,902 |
| *75040 | Garland | (972) | 180,635 | 138,857 |
| *76528 | Gatesville | (817) | 11,492 | 6,078 |
| *78626 | Georgetown | (512) | 14,840 | 9,468 |
| 75647 | Gladewater | (903) | 6,027 | 6,548 |
| 78629 | Gonzales | (210) | 6,527 | 7,152 |
| 76450 | Graham | (817) | 8,986 | 9,170 |
| *75051 | Grand Prairie | (972) | 99,606 | 71,462 |
| *76051 | Grapevine | (817) | 29,198 | 11,801 |
| *75401 | Greenville | (903) | 23,071 | 22,161 |
| 77619 | Groves | (409) | 16,744 | 17,090 |
| 76117 | Haltom City | (817) | 32,856 | 29,014 |
| 76543 | Harker Heights | (817) | 12,932 | 7,345 |
| *78550 | Harlingen | (210) | 48,746 | 43,543 |
| 77859 | Hearne | (409) | 5,132 | 5,418 |
| *75652 | Henderson | (903) | 11,139 | 11,473 |
| 79045 | Hereford | (806) | 14,745 | 15,853 |
| 76643 | Hewitt | (817) | 8,983 | 5,247 |
| 75205 | Highland Park | (972) | 8,739 | 8,909 |
| *77562 | Highlands(u) | (713) | 6,632 | 6,467 |
| 75067 | Highland Village | (972) | 7,027 | 3,246 |
| 76645 | Hillsboro | (817) | 7,072 | 7,397 |
| 77563 | Hitchcock | (409) | 5,868 | 6,103 |
| 78861 | Hondo | (210) | 6,018 | 6,057 |
| *77052 | Houston | (713) | 1,629,902 | 1,595,138 |
| *77338 | Humble | (713) | 12,060 | 6,729 |
| *77340 | Huntsville | (409) | 27,925 | 23,936 |
| *76053 | Hurst | (817) | 33,574 | 31,420 |
| 78362 | Ingleside | (512) | 5,696 | 5,436 |
| 76367 | Iowa Park | (817) | 6,072 | 6,184 |
| *75015 | Irving | (972) | 155,037 | 109,943 |
| 77029 | Jacinto City | (713) | 9,343 | 8,953 |
| 75766 | Jacksonville | (972) | 12,765 | 12,264 |
| 75951 | Jasper | (409) | 7,160 | 6,959 |
| 78729 | Jollyville(u) | (512) | 15,206 | .... |
| *77449 | Katy | (713) | 8,004 | 5,660 |
| 75142 | Kaufman | (972) | 5,251 | 4,658 |
| *76248 | Keller | (817) | 13,683 | 4,156 |
| 79745 | Kermit | (915) | 6,875 | 8,015 |
| *78028 | Kerrville | (210) | 17,384 | 15,276 |
| *75662 | Kilgore | (903) | 11,066 | 11,331 |
| *76540 | Killeen | (817) | 63,535 | 46,296 |
| *78363 | Kingsville | (512) | 25,276 | 28,808 |
| 77325 | Kingwood(u) | (713) | 37,397 | 16,261 |
| 78219 | Kirby | (210) | 8,326 | 6,435 |
| 78236 | Lackland AFB(u) | (210) | 9,352 | 14,459 |
| 77566 | Lake Jackson | (409) | 22,771 | 19,102 |
| 77568 | La Marque | (409) | 14,120 | 15,372 |
| 79331 | Lamesa | (806) | 10,809 | 11,790 |
| 76550 | Lampasas | (512) | 6,382 | 6,165 |
| *75146 | Lancaster | (972) | 22,117 | 14,807 |
| *77571 | La Porte | (713) | 27,910 | 14,062 |
| *78041 | Laredo | (210) | 122,893 | 91,449 |
| *77573 | League City | (713) | 30,159 | 16,578 |
| 78268 | Leon Valley | (210) | 9,581 | 9,088 |
| *79336 | Levelland | (806) | 13,986 | 13,809 |
| *75067 | Lewisville | (972) | 46,521 | 24,273 |
| 77575 | Liberty | (713) | 7,690 | 7,945 |
| 79339 | Littlefield | (806) | 6,489 | 7,409 |
| 78233 | Live Oak | (210) | 10,023 | 8,183 |
| 77351 | Livingston | (409) | 5,019 | 4,928 |
| 78644 | Lockhart | (512) | 9,205 | 7,953 |
| *75606 | Longview | (903) | 70,311 | 62,762 |
| *79408 | Lubbock | (806) | 186,206 | 174,361 |
| *75904 | Lufkin | (409) | 30,210 | 28,562 |
| 77657 | Lumberton | (409) | 6,640 | 2,480 |
| *78501 | McAllen | (210) | 84,021 | 66,281 |
| *75070 | McKinney | (972) | 21,283 | 16,256 |
| 76063 | Mansfield | (817) | 15,615 | 8,102 |
| 76661 | Marlin | (817) | 6,386 | 7,099 |
| *75670 | Marshall | (903) | 23,682 | 24,921 |
| 78368 | Mathis | (512) | 5,423 | 5,667 |
| 78570 | Mercedes | (210) | 12,694 | 11,851 |
| *75149 | Mesquite | (972) | 101,484 | 67,053 |
| 76667 | Mexia | (817) | 6,933 | 7,094 |
| *79701 | Midland | (915) | 89,343 | 70,525 |
| 76065 | Midlothian | (972) | 5,040 | 3,219 |
| *76067 | Mineral Wells | (817) | 14,935 | 14,468 |
| *78572 | Mission | (210) | 28,653 | 22,653 |
| ..... | Mission Bend(u) | | 24,945 | .... |
| *77489 | Missouri City | (713) | 36,178 | 24,423 |
| 79756 | Monahans | (915) | 8,101 | 8,397 |
| *75455 | Mount Pleasant | (903) | 12,291 | 11,003 |
| *75961 | Nacogdoches | (409) | 30,872 | 27,149 |
| 77868 | Navasota | (409) | 6,296 | 5,971 |
| 77627 | Nederland | (409) | 16,192 | 16,855 |
| 75570 | New Boston | (903) | 5,057 | 4,628 |
| *78130 | New Braunfels | (210) | 27,334 | 22,402 |
| 76118 | North Richland Hills | (817) | 45,895 | 30,592 |
| *79761 | Odessa | (915) | 89,699 | 90,027 |
| *77630 | Orange | (409) | 19,370 | 23,628 |
| *75801 | Palestine | (903) | 18,042 | 15,948 |
| *79065 | Pampa | (806) | 19,959 | 21,396 |
| *75460 | Paris | (903) | 24,799 | 25,498 |
| *77501 | Pasadena | (713) | 119,604 | 112,560 |
| *77581 | Pearland | (713) | 18,927 | 13,248 |
| 78061 | Pearsall | (210) | 6,924 | 7,383 |
| 78721 | Pecan Grove(u) | | 9,502 | .... |
| 79772 | Pecos | (915) | 12,069 | 12,855 |
| 79070 | Perryton | (806) | 7,619 | 7,991 |
| 78577 | Pharr | (210) | 32,921 | 21,381 |
| *79072 | Plainview | (806) | 21,698 | 22,187 |
| *75074 | Plano | (972) | 127,885 | 72,331 |
| 78064 | Pleasanton | (210) | 7,678 | 6,346 |
| *77640 | Port Arthur | (409) | 58,551 | 61,251 |
| 78374 | Portland | (512) | 12,224 | 12,023 |
| 77979 | Port Lavaca | (512) | 10,886 | 10,911 |
| 77651 | Port Neches | (409) | 12,908 | 13,944 |
| 78580 | Raymondville | (210) | 8,880 | 9,493 |
| 76028 | Rendon(u) | (817) | 7,658 | .... |
| *75080 | Richardson | (972) | 74,840 | 72,496 |
| 76118 | Richland Hills | (817) | 7,978 | 7,977 |
| *77469 | Richmond | (713) | 10,042 | 9,692 |
| 78582 | Rio Grande City(u) | (210) | 9,891 | 8,930 |
| 77019 | River Oaks | (817) | 6,580 | 6,890 |
| 76701 | Robinson | (817) | 7,111 | 6,074 |
| 78380 | Robstown | (512) | 12,849 | 12,100 |
| 76567 | Rockdale | (512) | 5,235 | 5,611 |
| 75087 | Rockwall | (972) | 10,486 | 5,939 |
| 78584 | Roma | (210) | 8,059 | 3,384 |
| 77471 | Rosenberg | (713) | 20,183 | 17,840 |
| *78681 | Round Rock | (512) | 30,923 | 12,740 |
| *75088 | Rowlett | (972) | 23,260 | 7,522 |
| 75048 | Sachse | (972) | 5,346 | 1,640 |
| 76179 | Saginaw | (817) | 8,551 | 5,736 |
| *76902 | San Angelo | (915) | 84,462 | 73,240 |
| *78265 | San Antonio | (210) | 935,393 | 785,940 |
| 78586 | San Benito | (210) | 20,125 | 17,988 |
| 78589 | San Juan | (210) | 10,815 | 7,608 |
| *78666 | San Marcos | (512) | 28,738 | 23,420 |
| *77510 | Santa Fe | (713) | 8,429 | 6,172 |
| 78154 | Schertz | (210) | 10,597 | 7,262 |
| 77586 | Seabrook | (713) | 6,685 | 4,670 |
| 75159 | Seagoville | (972) | 8,969 | 7,304 |
| *78155 | Seguin | (210) | 18,692 | 17,854 |
| 79360 | Seminole | (915) | 6,342 | 6,080 |
| *75090 | Sherman | (903) | 31,584 | 30,413 |

| ZIP | Place | | 1990 | 1980 |
|---|---|---|---|---|
| 77656 | Silsbee | (409) | 6,368 | 7,684 |
| 78387 | Sinton | (512) | 5,549 | 6,044 |
| 79364 | Slaton | (806) | 6,078 | 6,804 |
| *79549 | Snyder | (915) | 12,195 | 12,705 |
| 79910 | Socorro | (915) | 22,995 | 12,341† |
| 77587 | South Houston | (713) | 14,207 | 13,293 |
| 76092 | Southlake | (817) | 7,082 | 2,808 |
| *77373 | Spring(u) | (713) | 33,111 | .... |
| *77477 | Stafford | (713) | 8,395 | 4,755 |
| 76401 | Stephenville | (817) | 13,502 | 11,881 |
| *77478 | Sugar Land | (713) | 24,549 | 8,826 |
| *75482 | Sulphur Springs | (903) | 14,062 | 12,804 |
| 79556 | Sweetwater | (915) | 11,967 | 12,242 |
| 76574 | Taylor | (512) | 11,472 | 10,619 |
| *76501 | Temple | (817) | 46,150 | 42,354 |
| 75160 | Terrell | (972) | 12,490 | 13,269 |
| *75501 | Texarkana | (903) | 31,658 | 31,271 |
| *77590 | Texas City | (409) | 40,822 | 41,201 |
| 75056 | The Colony | (972) | 22,113 | 11,586 |
| 77387 | The Woodlands(u) | (713) | 29,205 | 8,443 |
| *77335 | Tomball | (713) | 6,370 | 3,996 |
| ..... | Town West(u) | | 6,166 | .... |
| *75702 | Tyler | (903) | 75,450 | 70,508 |
| *78148 | Universal City | (512) | 13,057 | 10,720 |
| 76308 | University Park | (972) | 22,259 | 22,254 |
| *78801 | Uvalde | (210) | 14,729 | 14,178 |
| *76384 | Vernon | (817) | 12,001 | 12,695 |
| *77901 | Victoria | (512) | 55,076 | 50,695 |
| *77662 | Vidor | (409) | 10,935 | 11,834 |
| *76702 | Waco | (817) | 103,590 | 101,261 |
| 76148 | Watauga | (817) | 20,009 | 10,284 |
| 75165 | Waxahachie | (972) | 17,984 | 14,624 |
| *76086 | Weatherford | (817) | 14,804 | 12,049 |
| 78728 | Wells Branch(u) | | 7,094 | .... |
| *78596 | Weslaco | (210) | 21,877 | 19,331 |
| 79764 | West Odessa(u) | (915) | 16,568 | .... |
| 77005 | West University Place | (713) | 12,920 | 12,010 |
| 77488 | Wharton | (409) | 9,011 | 9,033 |
| 75693 | White Oak | (903) | 5,136 | 4,415 |
| 76108 | White Settlement | (817) | 15,472 | 13,508 |
| *76307 | Wichita Falls | (817) | 96,259 | 94,201 |
| 78239 | Windcrest | (210) | 5,331 | 5,332 |
| 76712 | Woodway | (817) | 8,695 | 7,091 |
| 75098 | Wylie | (972) | 8,716 | 3,152 |
| 77995 | Yoakum | (512) | 5,611 | 6,148 |
| 78076 | Zapata(u) | (512) | 7,119 | 3,831 |

## Utah (801)

| ZIP | Place | 1990 | 1980 |
|---|---|---|---|
| 84003 | American Fork | 15,722 | 12,564 |
| *84010 | Bountiful | 36,147 | 32,877 |
| 84302 | Brigham City | 15,644 | 15,596 |
| 84109 | Canyon Rim(u) | 10,527 | .... |
| *84720 | Cedar City | 13,443 | 10,972 |
| 84014 | Centerville | 11,500 | 8,069 |
| *84015 | Clearfield | 21,435 | 17,982 |
| 84015 | Clinton | 7,945 | 5,777 |
| 84121 | Cottonwood Heights(u) | 28,766 | 22,665 |
| 84121 | Cottonwood West(u) | 17,476 | 11,117 |
| 84020 | Draper | 7,143 | 5,521 |
| 84109 | East Millcreek(u) | 21,184 | 24,150 |
| 84025 | Farmington | 9,049 | 4,691 |
| 84003 | Highland | 5,007 | 2,435 |
| 84117 | Holladay-Cottonwood(u)† | 14,095 | 22,189 |
| 84037 | Kaysville | 13,961 | 9,811 |
| 84118 | Kearns(u) | 28,374 | 21,353 |
| *84041 | Layton | 41,784 | 22,862 |
| 84043 | Lehi | 8,475 | 6,848 |
| ..... | Little Cottonwood Creek Valley(u) | 5,042 | .... |
| *84321 | Logan | 32,771 | 26,844 |
| 84044 | Magna(u) | 17,829 | 13,138 |
| 84047 | Midvale | 11,886 | 10,146 |
| 84109 | Millcreek(u) | 32,230 | .... |
| 84117 | Mount Olympus(u) | 7,413 | 6,068 |
| 84107 | Murray | 31,274 | 25,750 |
| 84404 | North Ogden | 11,593 | 9,309 |
| 84054 | North Salt Lake | 6,464 | 5,548 |
| *84401 | Ogden | 63,943 | 64,407 |
| ..... | Oquirrh(u) | 7,593 | .... |
| *84057 | Orem | 67,561 | 52,399 |
| 84651 | Payson | 9,510 | 8,246 |
| 84062 | Pleasant Grove | 13,476 | 10,833 |
| 84501 | Price | 8,712 | 9,086 |
| *84601 | Provo | 86,835 | 74,111 |
| 84701 | Richfield | 5,593 | 5,482 |
| 84403 | Riverdale | 6,419 | 6,031 |
| 84065 | Riverton | 11,261 | 7,032 |
| 84067 | Roy | 24,595 | 19,694 |
| *84770 | Saint George | 28,572 | 11,350 |
| *84101 | Salt Lake City | 159,928 | 163,034 |
| *84070 | Sandy | 75,240 | 52,210 |
| 84335 | Smithfield | 5,566 | 4,993 |
| 84095 | South Jordan | 12,215 | 7,492 |
| 84403 | South Ogden | 12,105 | 11,366 |
| 84165 | South Salt Lake | 10,129 | 10,413 |
| 84660 | Spanish Fork | 11,272 | 9,825 |
| 84663 | Springville | 13,950 | 12,101 |
| 84015 | Sunset | 5,128 | 5,733 |
| 84107 | Taylorsville-Bennion(u)† | 52,351 | 17,448 |
| 84074 | Tooele | 13,887 | 14,335 |
| 84047 | Union(u) | 13,684 | 9,665 |
| *84078 | Vernal | 6,640 | 6,600 |
| 84403 | Washington Terrace | 8,189 | 8,212 |
| *84084 | West Jordan | 42,915 | 27,325 |
| *84119 | West Valley City† | 86,969 | 72,509 |
| 84070 | White City(u) | 6,506 | 7,267 |
| 84087 | Woods Cross | 5,384 | 4,263 |

## Vermont (802)

*See note on page 390*

| ZIP | Place | 1990 | 1980 |
|---|---|---|---|
| 05641 | Barre | 9,482 | 9,824 |
| 05641 | *Barre* | 7,411 | 7,090 |
| 05201 | *Bennington* | 16,451 | 15,815 |
| 05201 | Bennington(u) | 9,532 | 9,349 |
| *05301 | Brattleboro Center(u) | 8,612 | 8,596 |
| *05301 | *Brattleboro* | 12,241 | 11,886 |
| *05401 | Burlington | 39,127 | 37,712 |
| *05446 | *Colchester* | 14,731 | 12,629 |
| 05451 | *Essex* | 16,498 | 14,392 |
| *05452 | Essex Junction | 8,396 | 7,033 |
| 05047 | *Hartford* | 9,404 | 7,963 |
| 05849 | *Lyndon* | 5,371 | 5,371 |
| *05753 | Middlebury | 8,034 | 7,574 |
| 05468 | *Milton* | 8,404 | 6,829 |
| *05602 | Montpelier | 8,247 | 8,241 |
| 05663 | *Northfield* | 5,610 | 5,435 |
| 05101 | *Rockingham* | 5,484 | 5,538 |
| *05701 | Rutland | 18,230 | 18,436 |
| 05478 | Saint Albans | 7,339 | 7,308 |
| 05819 | Saint Johnsbury(u) | 7,608 | 6,424 |
| 05482 | *Shelburne* | 5,871 | 5,000 |
| *05403 | South Burlington | 12,809 | 10,679 |
| 05156 | *Springfield* | 9,579 | 10,190 |
| 05488 | Swanton | 5,636 | 5,141 |
| 05404 | Winooski | 6,649 | 6,318 |

## Virginia

| ZIP | Place | | 1990 | 1980 |
|---|---|---|---|---|
| *24210 | Abingdon | (540) | 7,003 | 4,318 |
| *22313 | Alexandria | (703) | 111,182 | 103,217 |
| 22003 | Annandale(u) | (540) | 50,975 | 49,524 |
| 22554 | Aquia Harbour(u) | (703) | 6,308 | 2,870 |
| *22210 | Arlington(u) | (703) | 170,936 | 152,599 |
| 23005 | Ashland | (804) | 5,864 | 4,640 |
| 22041 | Bailey's Crossroads(u) | (703) | 19,507 | 12,564 |
| 24523 | Bedford | (540) | 6,073 | 5,991 |
| 22306 | Belle Haven(u) | (757) | 6,427 | 6,520 |
| 23234 | Bellwood(u) | (804) | 6,178 | 6,439 |
| 23234 | Bensley(u) | (804) | 5,093 | 5,299 |
| *24060 | Blacksburg | (540) | 34,590 | 30,638 |
| 24605 | Bluefield | (540) | 5,363 | 5,946 |
| 23235 | Bon Air(u) | (804) | 16,413 | 16,224 |
| *24203 | Bristol | (540) | 18,426 | 19,042 |
| 24416 | Buena Vista | (540) | 6,406 | 6,717 |
| ..... | Bull Run(u) | | 5,525 | .... |
| *22015 | Burke(u) | (703) | 57,734 | 33,835 |
| 24018 | Cave Spring(u) | (540) | 24,053 | 21,682 |
| 22020 | Centreville(u) | (703) | 26,585 | 7,473 |
| *22021 | Chantilly(u) | (703) | 29,337 | 12,259 |
| *22906 | Charlottesville | (804) | 40,475 | 39,916 |
| *23320 | Chesapeake | (757) | 151,982 | 114,486 |
| 23831 | Chester(u) | (804) | 14,986 | 11,728 |
| *24073 | Christiansburg | (540) | 15,004 | 10,345 |
| 24078 | Collinsville(u) | (540) | 7,280 | 7,517 |
| 23834 | Colonial Heights | (804) | 16,064 | 16,509 |
| 22901 | Commonwealth(u) | (804) | 5,538 | 3,505 |
| ..... | Countryside(u) | | 8,349 | .... |
| 24426 | Covington | (540) | 6,991 | 9,063 |
| 22701 | Culpeper | (540) | 8,581 | 6,621 |
| 22193 | Dale City(u) | (540) | 47,170 | 33,127 |
| *24541 | Danville | (804) | 53,056 | 45,642 |
| 23228 | Dumbarton(u) | (804) | 8,526 | 8,149 |
| 22027 | Dunn Loring(u) | (703) | 6,509 | 6,077 |
| 23222 | East Highland Park(u) | (804) | 11,850 | 11,797 |
| 23847 | Emporia | (804) | 5,479 | 4,840 |
| 23803 | Ettrick(u) | (804) | 5,290 | 4,890 |
| *22030 | Fairfax | (703) | 19,629 | 19,390 |
| *22046 | Falls Church | (703) | 9,522 | 9,515 |
| 23901 | Farmville | (804) | 6,046 | 6,067 |
| 24551 | Forest(u) | (804) | 5,624 | .... |
| 22060 | Fort Belvoir(u) | (703) | 8,590 | 7,726 |
| 22308 | Fort Hunt(u) | (703) | 12,989 | 14,294 |
| 23801 | Fort Lee(u) | (804) | 6,895 | 9,784 |
| 22310 | Franconia(u) | (703) | 19,882 | 8,476 |
| 23851 | Franklin | (757) | 7,864 | 7,308 |
| *22404 | Fredericksburg | (540) | 19,027 | 15,322 |
| *22630 | Front Royal | (540) | 11,880 | 11,126 |
| 24333 | Galax | (540) | 6,670 | 6,524 |
| *23060 | Glen Allen(u) | (804) | 9,010 | 6,202 |
| 23062 | Gloucester Point(u) | (804) | 8,509 | 5,841 |
| 22066 | Great Falls(u) | (703) | 6,945 | 2,419 |
| 22306 | Groveton(u) | (703) | 19,997 | 18,860 |
| *23670 | Hampton | (757) | 133,811 | 122,617 |
| 22801 | Harrisonburg | (540) | 30,707 | 19,671 |

| ZIP | Place | | 1990 | 1980 |
|---|---|---|---|---|
| *22070 | Herndon | (703) | 16,139 | 11,449 |
| 23075 | Highland Springs(u) | (804) | 13,823 | 12,146 |
| 24019 | Hollins(u) | (540) | 13,305 | 12,295 |
| 23860 | Hopewell | (804) | 23,101 | 23,397 |
| 22303 | Huntington(u) | (703) | 7,489 | 5,813 |
| 22306 | Hybla Valley(u) | (703) | 15,491 | 15,533 |
| 22043 | Idylwood(u) | (703) | 14,710 | 11,982 |
| 22042 | Jefferson(u) | (703) | 25,782 | 24,342 |
| 22041 | Lake Barcroft(u) | (703) | 8,686 | 8,725 |
| 22191 | Lake Ridge(u) | (540) | 23,862 | 11,072 |
| 23228 | Lakeside(u) | (804) | 12,081 | 12,289 |
| 23060 | Laurel(u) | (804) | 13,011 | 10,569 |
| 22075 | Leesburg | (703) | 16,202 | 8,357 |
| 24450 | Lexington | (540) | 6,959 | 7,292 |
| 22312 | Lincolnia(u) | (703) | 13,041 | 10,350 |
| *22079 | Lorton(u) | (703) | 15,385 | 5,813 |
| *24506 | Lynchburg | (804) | 66,049 | 66,743 |
| *22101 | McLean(u) | (703) | 38,168 | 35,664 |
| 24572 | Madison Heights(u) | (804) | 11,700 | 14,146 |
| *22110 | Manassas | (703) | 27,957 | 15,438 |
| 22110 | Manassas Park | (703) | 6,734 | 6,524 |
| 22030 | Mantua(u) | (703) | 6,804 | 6,523 |
| 24354 | Marion | (540) | 6,630 | 7,287 |
| *24112 | Martinsville | (540) | 16,162 | 18,149 |
| 23111 | Mechanicsville(u) | (804) | 22,027 | 9,269 |
| *22116 | Merrifield(u) | (703) | 8,399 | 7,525 |
| ..... | Montclair(u) | | 11,399 | 4,098 |
| 23231 | Montrose(u) | (804) | 6,405 | 5,349 |
| 22121 | Mount Vernon(u) | (703) | 27,485 | 24,058 |
| 22122 | Newington(u) | (703) | 17,965 | 8,313 |
| *23607 | Newport News | (757) | 171,439 | 144,903 |
| *23501 | Norfolk | (757) | 261,250 | 266,979 |
| 22151 | North Springfield(u) | (703) | 8,996 | 9,538 |
| 22124 | Oakton(u) | (703) | 24,610 | 19,150 |
| *23804 | Petersburg | (804) | 37,027 | 41,055 |
| 22043 | Pimmit Hills(u) | (703) | 6,019 | 6,658 |
| 23662 | Poquoson | (757) | 11,005 | 8,726 |
| *23705 | Portsmouth | (757) | 103,910 | 104,577 |
| 24301 | Pulaski | (540) | 9,985 | 10,106 |
| 22134 | Quantico Station(u) | (703) | 7,425 | 7,121 |
| *24141 | Radford | (540) | 15,940 | 13,225 |
| *22090 | Reston(u) | (703) | 48,556 | 36,407 |
| *23232 | Richmond | (804) | 202,798 | 219,214 |
| 22901 | Rio | (804) | 5,133 | 2,851 |
| *24022 | Roanoke | (540) | 96,509 | 100,220 |
| 24281 | Rose Hill(u) | (540) | 12,675 | 11,926 |
| 24153 | Salem | (540) | 23,797 | 23,958 |
| 22044 | Seven Corners(u) | (703) | 7,280 | 6,058 |
| 24592 | South Boston | (804) | 6,997 | 7,093 |
| *22150 | Springfield(u) | (703) | 23,706 | 21,435 |
| *24402 | Staunton | (540) | 24,461 | 21,857 |
| *20164 | Sterling(u) | (703) | 20,512 | 16,080 |
| 24477 | Stuarts Draft(u) | (804) | 5,087 | 1,776 |
| 23162 | Sudley(u) | (540) | 7,321 | 4,674 |
| *23434 | Suffolk | (757) | 52,143 | 47,621 |
| 22170 | Sugarland Run(u) | (703) | 9,357 | 6,258 |
| 24502 | Timberlake(u) | (804) | 10,314 | 9,697 |
| 23229 | Tuckahoe(u) | (804) | 42,629 | 39,868 |
| 22101 | Tysons Corner(u) | (703) | 13,124 | 10,065 |
| 22901 | University Heights(u) | (804) | 6,900 | 6,736 |
| *22180 | Vienna | (703) | 14,852 | 15,469 |
| 24179 | Vinton | (540) | 7,643 | 8,027 |
| *23458 | Virginia Beach | (757) | 393,089 | 262,199 |
| 22980 | Waynesboro | (540) | 18,549 | 15,329 |
| 22110 | West Gate(u) | (703) | 6,565 | 7,119 |
| 22152 | West Springfield(u) | (703) | 28,126 | 25,012 |
| *23185 | Williamsburg | (757) | 11,409 | 9,870 |
| *22601 | Winchester | (540) | 21,947 | 20,217 |
| 24592 | Wolf Trap(u) | (703) | 13,133 | 9,875 |
| *22191 | Woodbridge(u) | (540) | 26,401 | 24,004 |
| 24382 | Wytheville | (540) | 8,036 | 7,135 |
| 22110 | Yorkshire(u) | (703) | 5,699 | 4,940 |

## Washington

| ZIP | Place | | 1990 | 1980 |
|---|---|---|---|---|
| 98520 | Aberdeen | (360) | 16,565 | 18,739 |
| 98036 | Alderwood Manor-Bothell North(u) | (206) | 22,945 | 16,524 |
| 98221 | Anacortes | (360) | 11,451 | 9,013 |
| 98335 | Artondale(u) | (206) | 7,141 | .... |
| *98002 | Auburn | (206) | 33,650 | 26,417 |
| *98009 | Bellevue | (206) | 86,872 | 73,903 |
| *98225 | Bellingham | (360) | 52,179 | 45,794 |
| 98390 | Bonney Lake | (206) | 7,494 | 5,328 |
| *98011 | Bothell | (206) | 12,345 | 7,943 |
| *98337 | Bremerton | (206) | 38,142 | 36,208 |
| 98036 | Brier | (206) | 5,633 | 2,915 |
| 98178 | Bryn Mawr-Skyway(u) | (206) | 12,514 | 11,754 |
| 98166 | Burien(u) | (206) | 25,089 | 23,189 |
| 98607 | Camas | (360) | 6,442 | 5,681 |
| 98055 | Cascade-Fairwood(u) | (206) | 30,107 | 16,939 |
| 98684 | Cascade Park East(u) | (206) | 6,996 | .... |
| 98684 | Cascade Park West(u) | (206) | 6,656 | .... |
| 98531 | Centralia | (360) | 12,101 | 11,555 |
| 98532 | Chehalis | (360) | 6,527 | 6,100 |
| 99004 | Cheney | (509) | 7,723 | 7,630 |
| 99403 | Clarkston | (509) | 6,753 | 6,903 |
| 99324 | College Place | (509) | 6,308 | 5,771 |
| 99218 | Country Homes(u) | (509) | 5,126 | .... |
| 98042 | Covington-Sawyer-Wilderness(u) | | 24,321 | .... |
| 98198 | Des Moines | (206) | 17,283 | 7,378 |
| 99213 | Dishman(u) | (509) | 9,671 | 10,169 |
| ..... | East Hill-Meridian(u) | | 42,696 | .... |
| 98366 | East Port Orchard(u) | | 5,409 | 4,631 |
| 98056 | East Renton Highlands(u) | (206) | 13,218 | 11,695 |
| 98801 | East Wenatchee Bench(u) | (509) | 12,539 | 11,410 |
| ..... | Edgewood-North Hill(u) | | 9,120 | .... |
| *98020 | Edmonds | (206) | 30,743 | 27,679 |
| 98387 | Elk Plain(u) | | 12,197 | .... |
| 98926 | Ellensburg | (509) | 12,360 | 11,752 |
| ..... | Ellsworth North(u) | | 5,796 | .... |
| 98022 | Enumclaw | (360) | 7,227 | 5,427 |
| 98823 | Ephrata | (509) | 5,349 | 5,359 |
| 99210 | Esperance(u) | (509) | 11,236 | 11,120 |
| *98201 | Everett | (360) | 69,974 | 54,413 |
| 98411 | Evergreen(u) | | 11,249 | .... |
| 98055 | Fairwood(u) | (206) | 5,807 | 5,337 |
| *98002 | Federal Way | (206) | 67,554 | .... |
| 98248 | Ferndale | (360) | 5,398 | 3,855 |
| 98466 | Fircrest | (206) | 5,258 | 5,477 |
| 98597 | Five Corners(u) | | 6,776 | .... |
| 98433 | Fort Lewis(u) | (206) | 22,224 | 23,761 |
| 98930 | Grandview | (509) | 7,169 | 5,615 |
| ..... | Harbour Pointe(u) | | 9,107 | .... |
| 98660 | Hazel Dell North(u)† | (206) | 6,924 | 15,386 |
| 98665 | Hazel Dell South(u) | (206) | 5,796 | .... |
| 98550 | Hoquiam | (206) | 8,972 | 9,719 |
| 98011 | Inglewood-Finn Hill(u)† | (206) | 29,132 | 12,467 |
| 98027 | Issaquah | (206) | 7,786 | 5,536 |
| 98626 | Kelso | (360) | 11,767 | 11,129 |
| 98028 | Kenmore(u) | (206) | 8,917 | 7,281 |
| *99336 | Kennewick | (509) | 42,148 | 34,397 |
| *98031 | Kent | (206) | 37,960 | 22,961 |
| 98033 | Kingsgate(u) | (206) | 14,259 | 12,652 |
| *98033 | Kirkland | (206) | 40,059 | 18,785 |
| 98503 | Lacey | (360) | 19,279 | 13,940 |
| 98155 | Lake Forest North(u) | (206) | 8,002 | 7,995 |
| 98002 | Lakeland North(u) | (206) | 14,402 | 11,648 |
| 98002 | Lakeland South(u) | (206) | 9,027 | 5,225 |
| 98036 | Lake Serene-North Lynnwood(u) | | 14,290 | .... |
| 98665 | Lake Shore(u) | (360) | 6,268 | .... |
| 98259 | Lakewood(u) | (206) | 58,412 | 54,533 |
| ..... | Lea Hill(u) | | 6,876 | .... |
| 98632 | Longview | (360) | 31,499 | 31,052 |
| 98264 | Lynden | (360) | 5,709 | 4,022 |
| *98046 | Lynnwood | (206) | 28,637 | 22,641 |
| 98012 | Martha Lake(u) | (206) | 10,155 | 7,022 |
| *98270 | Marysville | (360) | 10,328 | 5,080 |
| 98040 | Mercer Island | (206) | 20,816 | 21,522 |
| ..... | Midland(u) | | 5,587 | .... |
| 98082 | Mill Creek† | (206) | 7,180 | 1,803 |
| ..... | Minnehaha(u) | | 9,661 | .... |
| 98837 | Moses Lake | (509) | 11,235 | 10,629 |
| 98043 | Mountlake Terrace | (206) | 19,320 | 16,534 |
| 98273 | Mount Vernon | (360) | 17,647 | 13,009 |
| 98275 | Mukilteo | (206) | 6,982 | 1,426 |
| 98006 | Newport Hills(u) | (206) | 14,736 | 12,245 |
| 98166 | Normandy Park | (206) | 6,709 | 4,268 |
| 98155 | North City-Ridgecrest(u) | (206) | 13,832 | 13,551 |
| ..... | North Creek-Canyon Park(u) | | 23,236 | .... |
| 98166 | North Hill(u) | (206) | 5,706 | 10,170 |
| 98270 | North Marysville(u) | (206) | 18,711 | 15,159 |
| 98277 | Oak Harbor | (360) | 17,176 | 12,271 |
| *98501 | Olympia | (360) | 33,729 | 27,447 |
| 99214 | Opportunity(u) | (509) | 22,326 | 21,241 |
| 98662 | Orchards North(u)† | (360) | 6,479 | 8,828 |
| 98662 | Orchards South(u) | (360) | 12,956 | .... |
| 99027 | Otis Orchards-East Farms(u) | (360) | 5,811 | 4,597 |
| ..... | Paine Field-Lake Stickney(u) | | 18,670 | .... |
| 98444 | Parkland(u) | (206) | 20,882 | 23,355 |
| 98366 | Parkwood(u) | | 6,853 | 4,599 |
| *99301 | Pasco | (509) | 20,337 | 18,428 |
| 98027 | Pine Lake(u) | | 13,940 | .... |
| 98362 | Port Angeles | (360) | 17,710 | 17,311 |
| 98368 | Port Townsend | (360) | 7,001 | 6,067 |
| 98390 | Prairie Ridge(u) | | 8,278 | .... |
| *99163 | Pullman | (509) | 23,478 | 23,579 |
| *98371 | Puyallup | (206) | 23,878 | 18,251 |
| *98052 | Redmond | (206) | 35,800 | 23,318 |
| *98058 | Renton | (206) | 41,688 | 31,031 |
| 99352 | Richland | (509) | 32,315 | 33,578 |
| 98160 | Richmond Beach-Innis Arden(u) | (206) | 7,242 | 6,700 |
| 98113 | Richmond Highlands(u) | (206) | 26,037 | 24,463 |
| 98188 | Riverton-Boulevard Park(u)† | (206) | 15,337 | 14,182 |
| ..... | Sahalee(u) | | 13,951 | .... |
| 98686 | Salmon Creek(u) | | 11,989 | .... |
| *98148 | Seatac | (206) | 22,694 | .... |
| *98101 | Seattle | (206) | 516,259 | 493,846 |
| 98284 | Sedro Woolley | (360) | 6,333 | 6,110 |
| 98942 | Selah | (509) | 5,113 | 4,500 |
| 98584 | Shelton | (360) | 7,241 | 7,629 |
| 98155 | Sheridan Beach(u) | (206) | 6,518 | 6,873 |
| *98383 | Silverdale(u) | (360) | 7,660 | .... |
| 98201 | Silver Lake-Fircrest(u) | (360) | 24,474 | 10,299 |
| *98290 | Snohomish | (360) | 6,499 | 5,294 |
| 98373 | South Hill(u) | | 12,963 | .... |

| ZIP | Place | Area code | 1990 | 1980 |
|---|---|---|---|---|
| 98387 | Spanaway(u) | (206) | 15,001 | 8,868 |
| *99210 | Spokane | (509) | 177,165 | 171,300 |
| 98388 | Steilacoom | (206) | 5,728 | 4,886 |
| *98371 | Summit(u) | (206) | 6,312 | .... |
| 98390 | Sumner | (206) | 6,459 | 4,936 |
| 98944 | Sunnyside | (509) | 11,238 | 9,225 |
| *98402 | Tacoma | (206) | 176,664 | 158,501 |
| 98501 | Tanglewilde-Thompson Place(u) | (360) | 6,061 | 5,910 |
| 98948 | Toppenish | (509) | 7,419 | 6,517 |
| 98138 | Tukwila | (206) | 11,874 | 3,578 |
| 98501 | Tumwater | (360) | 9,976 | 6,705 |
| 98464 | University Place(u) | (206) | 27,701 | 20,381 |
| *98661 | Vancouver | (360) | 46,380 | 42,834 |
| 98662 | Vancouver Mall(u) | (360) | 6,938 | .... |
| 99037 | Veradale(u) | (509) | 7,836 | 7,256 |
| 99362 | Walla Walla | (509) | 26,482 | 25,618 |
| ..... | Waller(u) | | 6,415 | .... |
| *98801 | Wenatchee | (509) | 21,746 | 17,257 |
| ..... | West Lake Sammamish(u) | | 6,087 | .... |
| 98258 | West Lake Stevens(u) | (206) | 12,453 | .... |
| 99301 | West Pasco(u) | (509) | 7,312 | 5,726 |
| 99181 | West Valley(u) | | 6,594 | .... |
| 98166 | White Center-Shorewood(u) | (206) | 20,531 | 19,362 |
| 98072 | Woodinville(u) | (206) | 23,654 | .... |
| 98032 | Woodmont Beach(u) | (206) | 7,493 | .... |
| *98903 | Yakima | (509) | 54,843 | 49,826 |

## West Virginia (304)

| ZIP | Place | 1990 | 1980 |
|---|---|---|---|
| *25801 | Beckley | 18,274 | 20,492 |
| 24701 | Bluefield | 12,756 | 16,060 |
| 26330 | Bridgeport | 6,695 | 6,604 |
| 26201 | Buckhannon | 5,909 | 6,820 |
| *25301 | Charleston | 57,287 | 63,968 |
| *26301 | Clarksburg | 17,970 | 22,371 |
| 25301 | Cross Lanes(u) | 10,878 | .... |
| 25064 | Dunbar | 8,697 | 9,285 |
| 26241 | Elkins | 7,494 | 8,536 |
| *26554 | Fairmont | 20,210 | 23,863 |
| 26354 | Grafton | 5,524 | 6,845 |
| *25704 | Huntington | 54,844 | 63,684 |
| 26726 | Keyser | 5,870 | 6,569 |
| 25401 | Martinsburg | 14,073 | 13,063 |
| *26505 | Morgantown | 25,879 | 27,605 |
| 26041 | Moundsville | 10,753 | 12,419 |
| 26155 | New Martinsville | 6,705 | 7,109 |
| 25143 | Nitro | 6,851 | 8,074 |
| 25901 | Oak Hill | 6,812 | 7,120 |
| *26101 | Parkersburg | 33,862 | 39,946 |
| ..... | Pea Ridge(u) | 6,535 | .... |
| 24740 | Princeton | 7,043 | 7,538 |
| 25177 | Saint Albans | 11,257 | 12,402 |
| *25301 | South Charleston | 13,645 | 15,968 |
| 25569 | Teays Valley(u) | 8,436 | .... |
| 26105 | Vienna | 10,862 | 11,618 |
| 26062 | Weirton | 22,124 | 25,371 |
| 26003 | Wheeling | 34,882 | 43,070 |

## Wisconsin

*See note on page 390*

| ZIP | Place | Area code | 1990 | 1980 |
|---|---|---|---|---|
| 54301 | Allouez† | (414) | 14,431 | 14,882 |
| 54720 | Altoona | (715) | 5,889 | 4,393 |
| 54409 | Antigo | (715) | 8,284 | 8,653 |
| *59411 | Appleton | (414) | 65,695 | 58,913 |
| 54806 | Ashland | (715) | 8,695 | 9,115 |
| 54304 | Ashwaubenon | (414) | 16,376 | 14,486 |
| 53913 | Baraboo | (608) | 9,203 | 8,081 |
| 53916 | Beaver Dam | (414) | 14,196 | 14,149 |
| 54311 | Bellevue Town(u) | (414) | 7,541 | .... |
| *53511 | Beloit | (608) | 35,571 | 35,207 |
| 54923 | Berlin | (414) | 5,371 | 5,478 |
| *53045 | Brookfield | (414) | 35,184 | 34,035 |
| 53209 | Brown Deer | (414) | 12,236 | 12,921 |
| 53105 | Burlington | (414) | 8,855 | 8,385 |
| 53012 | Cedarburg | (414) | 10,086 | 9,005 |
| 54729 | Chippewa Falls | (715) | 12,727 | 12,270 |
| 53110 | Cudahy | (414) | 18,659 | 19,547 |
| 53018 | Delafield | (414) | 5,347 | 4,083 |
| 53115 | Delavan | (414) | 6,073 | 5,684 |
| 54115 | De Pere | (414) | 16,569 | 14,892 |
| *54703 | Eau Claire | (715) | 56,806 | 51,509 |
| 53121 | Elkhorn | (414) | 5,337 | 4,605 |
| 53122 | Elm Grove | (414) | 6,261 | 6,735 |
| 53714 | Fitchburg† | (608) | 15,648 | 11,965 |
| *54935 | Fond Du Lac | (414) | 37,757 | 35,863 |
| 53538 | Fort Atkinson | (414) | 10,213 | 9,785 |
| 53217 | Fox Point | (414) | 7,238 | 7,649 |
| 53132 | Franklin | (414) | 21,855 | 16,871 |
| 53022 | Germantown | (414) | 13,658 | 10,729 |
| 53209 | Glendale | (414) | 14,088 | 13,882 |
| 53024 | Grafton | (414) | 9,340 | 8,381 |
| *54303 | Green Bay | (414) | 96,466 | 87,899 |
| 53129 | Greendale | (414) | 15,128 | 16,928 |
| 53220 | Greenfield | (414) | 33,403 | 31,353 |
| 53130 | Hales Corners | (414) | 7,623 | 7,110 |
| 53027 | Hartford | (414) | 8,188 | 7,159 |
| 53029 | Hartland | (414) | 6,906 | 5,559 |
| 54303 | Howard | (414) | 9,874 | 8,240 |
| 54016 | Hudson | (715) | 6,378 | 5,434 |
| *53545 | Janesville | (608) | 52,210 | 51,071 |
| 53549 | Jefferson | (414) | 6,078 | 5,647 |
| 54130 | Kaukauna | (414) | 11,982 | 11,310 |
| *53140 | Kenosha | (414) | 80,426 | 77,685 |
| 54136 | Kimberly | (414) | 5,406 | 5,881 |
| *54601 | La Crosse | (608) | 51,120 | 48,347 |
| 53147 | Lake Geneva | (414) | 5,979 | 5,612 |
| 54140 | Little Chute | (414) | 9,207 | 7,907 |
| 53558 | McFarland | (608) | 5,232 | 3,783 |
| *53714 | Madison | (608) | 190,766 | 170,616 |
| *54220 | Manitowoc | (414) | 32,521 | 32,547 |
| 54143 | Marinette | (715) | 11,843 | 11,965 |
| 54449 | Marshfield | (715) | 19,291 | 18,290 |
| 54952 | Menasha | (414) | 14,711 | 14,728 |
| *53051 | Menomonee Falls | (414) | 26,840 | 27,845 |
| 54751 | Menomonie | (715) | 13,547 | 12,769 |
| 53097 | Mequon | (414) | 18,885 | 16,193 |
| 54452 | Merrill | (715) | 9,860 | 9,578 |
| 53562 | Middleton | (608) | 13,785 | 11,851 |
| *53201 | Milwaukee | (414) | 628,088 | 636,297 |
| 53716 | Monona | (608) | 8,637 | 8,809 |
| 53566 | Monroe | (608) | 10,241 | 10,027 |
| 53150 | Muskego | (414) | 16,813 | 15,277 |
| *54956 | Neenah | (414) | 23,219 | 22,432 |
| *53151 | New Berlin | (414) | 33,592 | 30,529 |
| 54961 | New London | (414) | 6,658 | 6,210 |
| 54017 | New Richmond | (715) | 5,106 | 4,306 |
| 53154 | Oak Creek | (414) | 19,513 | 16,932 |
| 53066 | Oconomowoc | (414) | 10,993 | 9,909 |
| 54650 | Onalaska | (608) | 11,414 | 9,249 |
| *54901 | Oshkosh | (414) | 55,006 | 49,620 |
| 53072 | Pewaukee | (414) | 5,287 | 4,637 |
| 53818 | Platteville | (608) | 9,862 | 9,580 |
| 53158 | Pleasant Prairie† | (414) | 12,037 | 12,176 |
| 54467 | Plover | (715) | 8,176 | 5,310 |
| 53073 | Plymouth | (414) | 6,769 | 6,027 |
| 53901 | Portage | (608) | 8,640 | 7,896 |
| 53074 | Port Washington | (414) | 9,338 | 8,612 |
| 53821 | Prairie du Chien | (608) | 5,657 | 5,859 |
| *53401 | Racine | (414) | 84,298 | 85,725 |
| 53959 | Reedsburg | (608) | 5,834 | 5,038 |
| 54501 | Rhinelander | (715) | 7,382 | 7,873 |
| 54868 | Rice Lake | (715) | 7,998 | 7,691 |
| 53581 | Richland Center | (608) | 5,018 | 4,997 |
| 54971 | Ripon | (414) | 7,241 | 7,111 |
| 54022 | River Falls | (715) | 10,610 | 9,019 |
| 53207 | Saint Francis | (414) | 9,245 | 10,095 |
| 54166 | Shawano | (715) | 7,598 | 7,013 |
| *53081 | Sheboygan | (414) | 49,587 | 48,085 |
| 53085 | Sheboygan Falls | (414) | 5,823 | 5,253 |
| 53211 | Shorewood | (414) | 14,116 | 14,327 |
| 53172 | South Milwaukee | (414) | 20,958 | 21,069 |
| 54656 | Sparta | (608) | 7,788 | 6,934 |
| 54481 | Stevens Point | (715) | 23,006 | 22,970 |
| 53589 | Stoughton | (608) | 8,786 | 7,589 |
| 54235 | Sturgeon Bay | (414) | 9,176 | 8,847 |
| 53590 | Sun Prairie | (608) | 15,333 | 12,931 |
| 54880 | Superior | (715) | 27,134 | 29,571 |
| 53089 | Sussex | (414) | 5,039 | 3,482 |
| 54660 | Tomah | (608) | 7,570 | 7,204 |
| 54241 | Two Rivers | (414) | 13,030 | 13,354 |
| 53593 | Verona | (608) | 5,374 | 3,336 |
| *53094 | Watertown | (414) | 19,142 | 18,113 |
| *53186 | Waukesha | (414) | 56,958 | 50,365 |
| 53597 | Waunakee | (608) | 5,897 | 3,866 |
| 53963 | Waupun | (414) | 8,844 | 8,132 |
| *54403 | Wausau | (715) | 37,060 | 32,426 |
| 53213 | Wauwatosa | (414) | 49,366 | 51,308 |
| 53214 | West Allis | (414) | 63,221 | 63,982 |
| 53095 | West Bend | (414) | 24,470 | 21,484 |
| 54476 | Weston(u) | (715) | 9,714 | 8,775 |
| 53217 | Whitefish Bay | (414) | 14,272 | 14,930 |
| 53190 | Whitewater | (414) | 12,636 | 11,520 |
| *54494 | Wisconsin Rapids | (715) | 18,245 | 17,995 |

## Wyoming (307)

| ZIP | Place | 1990 | 1980 |
|---|---|---|---|
| *82601 | Casper | 46,765 | 51,016 |
| *82001 | Cheyenne | 50,008 | 47,283 |
| 82414 | Cody | 7,897 | 6,599 |
| 82633 | Douglas | 5,076 | 6,030 |
| *82930 | Evanston | 10,904 | 6,265 |
| *82716 | Gillette | 17,545 | 12,134 |
| 82935 | Green River | 12,711 | 12,807 |
| 82520 | Lander | 7,023 | 7,867 |
| *82070 | Laramie | 26,687 | 24,410 |
| 82435 | Powell | 5,292 | 5,310 |
| 82301 | Rawlins | 9,380 | 11,547 |
| 82501 | Riverton | 9,202 | 9,562 |
| *82901 | Rock Springs | 19,050 | 19,458 |
| 82801 | Sheridan | 13,904 | 15,146 |
| 82240 | Torrington | 5,651 | 5,441 |
| 82401 | Worland | 5,742 | 6,391 |

# Populations and Areas of Counties and States

**Source:** U.S. Bureau of the Census, Dept. of Commerce; World Almanac research

State population figures below are estimates for July 1, 1995. For counties, July 1, 1995, population estimates and Apr. 1, 1990, decennial census figures are given.

## Alabama

(67 counties, 50,750 sq mi land; pop. 4,252,982)

| County | County seat or courthouse | 1995 Pop. | 1990 Pop. | Land area sq mi |
|---|---|---|---|---|
| Autauga | Prattville | 39,381 | 34,222 | 596 |
| Baldwin | Bay Minette | 120,198 | 98,280 | 1,597 |
| Barbour | Clayton | 26,469 | 25,417 | 885 |
| Bibb | Centreville | 17,942 | 16,576 | 622 |
| Blount | Oneonta | 42,721 | 39,248 | 646 |
| Bullock | Union Springs | 11,149 | 11,042 | 625 |
| Butler | Greenville | 21,798 | 21,892 | 777 |
| Calhoun | Anniston | 117,263 | 116,032 | 609 |
| Chambers | Lafayette | 37,262 | 36,876 | 597 |
| Cherokee | Centre | 21,038 | 19,543 | 553 |
| Chilton | Clanton | 34,912 | 32,458 | 694 |
| Choctaw | Butler | 16,079 | 16,018 | 914 |
| Clarke | Grove Hill | 27,993 | 27,240 | 1,239 |
| Clay | Ashland | 13,551 | 13,252 | 605 |
| Cleburne | Heflin | 13,272 | 12,730 | 560 |
| Coffee | Elba | 42,359 | 40,240 | 679 |
| Colbert | Tuscumbia | 52,586 | 51,666 | 595 |
| Conecuh | Evergreen | 14,022 | 14,054 | 851 |
| Coosa | Rockford | 11,680 | 11,063 | 653 |
| Covington | Andalusia | 37,459 | 36,478 | 1,035 |
| Crenshaw | Luverne | 13,624 | 13,635 | 610 |
| Cullman | Cullman | 72,489 | 67,613 | 739 |
| Dale | Ozark | 50,001 | 49,633 | 561 |
| Dallas | Selma | 48,022 | 48,130 | 981 |
| De Kalb | Fort Payne | 57,271 | 54,651 | 778 |
| Elmore | Wetumpka | 57,071 | 49,210 | 622 |
| Escambia | Brewton | 36,541 | 35,518 | 948 |
| Etowah | Gadsden | 100,259 | 99,840 | 535 |
| Fayette | Fayette | 18,019 | 17,962 | 628 |
| Franklin | Russellville | 29,313 | 27,814 | 636 |
| Geneva | Geneva | 24,727 | 23,647 | 576 |
| Greene | Eutaw | 10,076 | 10,153 | 646 |
| Hale | Greensboro | 16,212 | 15,498 | 644 |
| Henry | Abbeville | 15,752 | 15,374 | 562 |
| Houston | Dothan | 84,367 | 81,331 | 580 |
| Jackson | Scottsboro | 50,128 | 47,796 | 1,079 |
| Jefferson | Birmingham | 657,827 | 651,520 | 1,113 |
| Lamar | Vernon | 15,754 | 15,715 | 605 |
| Lauderdale | Florence | 83,598 | 79,661 | 670 |
| Lawrence | Moulton | 32,803 | 31,513 | 693 |
| Lee | Opelika | 94,029 | 87,146 | 609 |
| Limestone | Athens | 59,344 | 54,135 | 568 |
| Lowndes | Hayneville | 12,946 | 12,658 | 718 |
| Macon | Tuskegee | 23,959 | 24,928 | 611 |
| Madison | Huntsville | 258,340 | 238,912 | 805 |
| Marengo | Linden | 23,662 | 23,084 | 977 |
| Marion | Hamilton | 30,382 | 29,830 | 742 |
| Marshall | Guntersville | 78,195 | 70,832 | 567 |
| Mobile | Mobile | 397,413 | 378,643 | 1,233 |
| Monroe | Monroeville | 24,550 | 23,968 | 1,026 |
| Montgomery | Montgomery | 218,880 | 209,085 | 790 |
| Morgan | Decatur | 107,034 | 100,043 | 582 |
| Perry | Marion | 12,708 | 12,759 | 720 |
| Pickens | Carrollton | 20,956 | 20,699 | 882 |
| Pike | Troy | 28,848 | 27,595 | 671 |
| Randolph | Wedowee | 20,323 | 19,881 | 581 |
| Russell | Phenix City | 51,436 | 46,860 | 641 |
| Saint Clair | Ashville & Pell City | 57,713 | 49,811 | 634 |
| Shelby | Columbiana | 123,500 | 99,363 | 795 |
| Sumter | Livingston | 16,390 | 16,174 | 905 |
| Talladega | Talladega | 76,737 | 74,109 | 740 |
| Tallapoosa | Dadeville | 39,737 | 38,826 | 718 |
| Tuscaloosa | Tuscaloosa | 158,732 | 150,522 | 1,325 |
| Walker | Jasper | 69,678 | 67,670 | 795 |
| Washington | Chatom | 17,385 | 16,694 | 1,081 |
| Wilcox | Camden | 13,628 | 13,568 | 889 |
| Winston | Double Springs | 23,489 | 22,053 | 615 |

## Alaska

(27 divisions, 570,374 sq mi land; pop. 603,617)

| Census Division | 1995 Pop. | 1990 Pop. | Land area sq mi |
|---|---|---|---|
| Aleutians East Borough | 2,305 | 2,464 | 6,985 |
| Aleutians West Census Area | 5,259 | 9,478 | 4,402 |
| Anchorage Borough | 251,335 | 226,338 | 1,698 |
| Bethel Census Area | 15,525 | 13,656 | 41,087 |
| Bristol Bay Borough | 1,023 | 1,410 | 519 |
| Denali Borough | 1,878 | 1,764 | 12,719 |
| Dillingham Census Area | 4,360 | 4,012 | 18,467 |
| Fairbanks North Star Borough | 83,374 | 77,720 | 7,362 |
| Haines Borough | 2,181 | 2,117 | 2,357 |
| Juneau Borough | 29,378 | 26,751 | 2,594 |
| Kenai Peninsula Borough | 46,151 | 40,802 | 16,079 |
| Ketchikan Gateway Borough | 14,422 | 13,828 | 1,220 |
| Kodiak Island Borough | 14,987 | 13,309 | 6,463 |
| Lake and Peninsula Borough | 1,787 | 1,668 | 23,632 |
| Matanuska-Susitna Borough | 50,686 | 39,683 | 24,694 |
| Nome Census Area | 8,754 | 8,288 | 23,013 |
| North Slope Borough | 7,024 | 5,979 | 87,861 |
| Northwest Arctic Borough | 6,501 | 6,113 | 35,863 |
| Prince of Wales-Outer Ketchikan Census Area | 7,109 | 6,278 | 7,325 |
| Sitka Borough | 8,710 | 8,588 | 2,882 |
| Skagway-Hoonah-Angoon Census Area | 3,867 | 3,680 | 8,012 |
| Southeast Fairbanks Census Area | 6,018 | 5,913 | 25,110 |
| Valdez-Cordova Census Area | 10,475 | 9,952 | 36,945 |
| Wade Hampton Census Area | 6,574 | 5,791 | 17,124 |
| Wrangell-Petersburg Census Area | 7,089 | 7,042 | 5,809 |
| Yakutat Borough | 788 | 705 | 4,865 |
| Yukon-Koyukuk Census Area | 6,057 | 6,714 | 145,287 |

## Arizona

(15 counties, 113,642 sq mi land; pop. 4,217,940)

| County | County seat or courthouse | 1995 Pop. | 1990 Pop. | Land area sq mi |
|---|---|---|---|---|
| Apache | Saint Johns | 67,803 | 61,591 | 11,206 |
| Cochise | Bisbee | 110,062 | 97,624 | 6,170 |
| Coconino | Flagstaff | 110,498 | 96,591 | 18,619 |
| Gila | Globe | 46,039 | 40,216 | 4,768 |
| Graham | Safford | 29,589 | 26,554 | 4,630 |
| Greenlee | Clifton | 9,232 | 8,008 | 1,847 |
| La Paz | Parker | 14,310 | 13,844 | 4,500 |
| Maricopa | Phoenix | 2,432,372 | 2,122,101 | 9,204 |
| Mohave | Kingman | 121,602 | 93,497 | 13,312 |
| Navajo | Holbrook | 89,253 | 77,674 | 9,954 |
| Pima | Tucson | 752,428 | 666,957 | 9,187 |
| Pinal | Florence | 131,210 | 116,397 | 5,370 |
| Santa Cruz | Nogales | 36,078 | 29,676 | 1,238 |
| Yavapai | Prescott | 134,595 | 107,714 | 8,124 |
| Yuma | Yuma | 132,869 | 106,895 | 5,514 |

## Arkansas

(75 counties, 52,075 sq mi land; pop. 2,483,769)

| County | County seat or courthouse | 1995 Pop. | 1990 Pop. | Land area sq mi |
|---|---|---|---|---|
| Arkansas | DeWitt & Stuttgart | 21,032 | 21,653 | 989 |
| Ashley | Hamburg | 24,651 | 24,319 | 921 |
| Baxter | Mountain Home | 35,666 | 31,186 | 554 |
| Benton | Bentonville | 120,932 | 97,499 | 843 |
| Boone | Harrison | 31,364 | 28,297 | 591 |
| Bradley | Warren | 11,650 | 11,793 | 651 |
| Calhoun | Hampton | 5,801 | 5,826 | 628 |
| Carroll | Berryville & Eureka Springs | 21,933 | 18,654 | 634 |
| Chicot | Lake Village | 15,289 | 15,713 | 644 |
| Clark | Arkadelphia | 22,101 | 21,437 | 866 |
| Clay | Corning & Piggott | 17,601 | 18,107 | 639 |
| Cleburne | Heber Springs | 21,865 | 19,411 | 553 |
| Cleveland | Rison | 8,084 | 7,781 | 598 |
| Columbia | Magnolia | 25,670 | 25,691 | 766 |
| Conway | Morrilton | 19,671 | 19,151 | 566 |
| Craighead | Jonesboro & Lake City | 74,794 | 68,956 | 711 |
| Crawford | Van Buren | 48,100 | 42,493 | 611 |
| Crittenden | Marion | 49,889 | 49,939 | 616 |
| Cross | Wynne | 19,370 | 19,225 | 616 |
| Dallas | Fordyce | 9,493 | 9,614 | 668 |
| Desha | Arkansas City | 15,487 | 16,798 | 765 |
| Drew | Monticello | 17,853 | 17,369 | 828 |
| Faulkner | Conway | 71,758 | 60,006 | 647 |
| Franklin | Charleston & Ozark | 16,122 | 14,897 | 610 |
| Fulton | Salem | 10,732 | 10,037 | 618 |
| Garland | Hot Springs | 81,049 | 73,397 | 678 |
| Grant | Sheridan | 15,022 | 13,948 | 632 |
| Greene | Paragould | 34,620 | 31,804 | 578 |
| Hempstead | Hope | 22,194 | 21,621 | 729 |
| Hot Spring | Malvern | 27,876 | 26,115 | 615 |
| Howard | Nashville | 13,655 | 13,569 | 588 |
| Independence | Batesville | 32,752 | 31,192 | 764 |
| Izard | Melbourne | 12,619 | 11,364 | 581 |
| Jackson | Newport | 18,622 | 18,944 | 634 |
| Jefferson | Pine Bluff | 84,042 | 85,487 | 885 |
| Johnson | Clarksville | 20,508 | 18,221 | 662 |
| Lafayette | Lewisville | 9,213 | 9,643 | 527 |
| Lawrence | Walnut Ridge | 17,468 | 17,455 | 587 |
| Lee | Marianna | 12,962 | 13,053 | 620 |
| Lincoln | Star City | 14,119 | 13,690 | 561 |
| Little River | Ashdown | 13,413 | 13,966 | 532 |
| Logan | Booneville & Paris | 21,050 | 20,557 | 710 |
| Lonoke | Lonoke | 45,966 | 39,268 | 766 |
| Madison | Huntsville | 12,943 | 11,618 | 837 |

| County | County seat or courthouse | 1995 Pop. | 1990 Pop. | Land area sq mi |
|---|---|---|---|---|
| Marion | Yellville | 13,855 | 12,001 | 598 |
| Miller | Texarkana | 39,082 | 38,467 | 624 |
| Mississippi | Blytheville & Osceola | 50,811 | 57,525 | 898 |
| Monroe | Clarendon | 10,374 | 11,333 | 607 |
| Montgomery | Mount Ida | 8,356 | 7,841 | 781 |
| Nevada | Prescott | 9,996 | 10,101 | 620 |
| Newton | Jasper | 7,989 | 7,666 | 823 |
| Ouachita | Camden | 28,580 | 30,574 | 733 |
| Perry | Perryville | 8,823 | 7,969 | 551 |
| Phillips | Helena | 27,386 | 28,830 | 693 |
| Pike | Murfreesboro | 10,332 | 10,086 | 603 |
| Poinsett | Harrisburg | 24,640 | 24,664 | 758 |
| Polk | Mena | 18,832 | 17,347 | 860 |
| Pope | Russellville | 51,181 | 45,883 | 812 |
| Prairie | Des Arc & De Valls Bluff | 9,312 | 9,518 | 646 |
| Pulaski | Little Rock | 352,240 | 349,569 | 771 |
| Randolph | Pocahontas | 17,430 | 16,558 | 652 |
| Saint Francis | Forrest City | 27,859 | 28,497 | 634 |
| Saline | Benton | 73,604 | 64,183 | 725 |
| Scott | Waldron | 10,628 | 10,205 | 894 |
| Searcy | Marshall | 7,626 | 7,841 | 667 |
| Sebastian | Fort Smith & Greenwood | 104,402 | 99,590 | 536 |
| Sevier | De Queen | 14,501 | 13,637 | 564 |
| Sharp | Ash Flat | 16,172 | 14,109 | 604 |
| Stone | Mountain View | 10,784 | 9,775 | 607 |
| Union | El Dorado | 46,191 | 46,719 | 1,039 |
| Van Buren | Clinton | 15,198 | 14,008 | 712 |
| Washington | Fayetteville | 131,708 | 113,409 | 950 |
| White | Searcy | 61,016 | 54,676 | 1,034 |
| Woodruff | Augusta | 9,121 | 9,520 | 587 |
| Yell | Danville & Dardanelle | 18,739 | 17,759 | 928 |

## California

(58 counties, 155,973 sq mi land; pop. 31,589,153)

| County | County seat or courthouse | 1995 Pop. | 1990 Pop. | Land area sq mi |
|---|---|---|---|---|
| Alameda | Oakland | 1,323,312 | 1,276,702 | 738 |
| Alpine | Markleeville | 1,229 | 1,113 | 739 |
| Amador | Jackson | 33,162 | 30,039 | 593 |
| Butte | Oroville | 192,880 | 182,120 | 1,640 |
| Calaveras | San Andreas | 37,694 | 31,998 | 1,020 |
| Colusa | Colusa | 17,596 | 16,275 | 1,151 |
| Contra Costa | Martinez | 872,099 | 803,732 | 720 |
| Del Norte | Crescent City | 26,956 | 23,460 | 1,008 |
| El Dorado | Placerville | 148,217 | 125,995 | 1,712 |
| Fresno | Fresno | 737,289 | 667,490 | 5,963 |
| Glenn | Willows | 26,028 | 24,798 | 1,315 |
| Humboldt | Eureka | 122,747 | 119,118 | 3,573 |
| Imperial | El Centro | 138,072 | 109,303 | 4,175 |
| Inyo | Independence | 18,435 | 18,281 | 10,192 |
| Kern | Bakersfield | 617,528 | 544,981 | 8,142 |
| Kings | Hanford | 113,089 | 101,469 | 1,390 |
| Lake | Lakeport | 55,783 | 50,631 | 1,259 |
| Lassen | Susanville | 28,279 | 27,598 | 4,558 |
| Los Angeles | Los Angeles | 9,138,789 | 8,863,052 | 4,060 |
| Madera | Madera | 107,004 | 88,090 | 2,138 |
| Marin | San Rafael | 233,883 | 230,096 | 520 |
| Mariposa | Mariposa | 15,772 | 14,302 | 1,451 |
| Mendocino | Ukiah | 82,499 | 80,345 | 3,509 |
| Merced | Merced | 194,407 | 178,403 | 1,929 |
| Modoc | Alturas | 9,559 | 9,678 | 3,944 |
| Mono | Bridgeport | 10,433 | 9,956 | 3,045 |
| Monterey | Salinas | 348,841 | 355,660 | 3,322 |
| Napa | Napa | 115,751 | 110,765 | 754 |
| Nevada | Nevada City | 87,318 | 78,510 | 958 |
| Orange | Santa Ana | 2,563,971 | 2,410,668 | 790 |
| Placer | Auburn | 205,239 | 172,796 | 1,404 |
| Plumas | Quincy | 20,451 | 19,739 | 2,554 |
| Riverside | Riverside | 1,379,801 | 1,170,413 | 7,208 |
| Sacramento | Sacramento | 1,103,499 | 1,041,219 | 966 |
| San Benito | Hollister | 42,625 | 36,697 | 1,389 |
| San Bernardino | San Bernardino | 1,569,586 | 1,418,380 | 20,062 |
| San Diego | San Diego | 2,644,132 | 2,498,016 | 4,205 |
| San Francisco | San Francisco | 730,570 | 723,959 | 47 |
| San Joaquin | Stockton | 523,969 | 480,628 | 1,399 |
| San Luis Obispo | San Luis Obispo | 226,071 | 217,162 | 3,305 |
| San Mateo | Redwood City | 681,362 | 649,623 | 449 |
| Santa Barbara | Santa Barbara | 381,401 | 369,608 | 2,739 |
| Santa Clara | San Jose | 1,565,253 | 1,497,577 | 1,291 |
| Santa Cruz | Santa Cruz | 236,669 | 229,734 | 446 |
| Shasta | Redding | 160,940 | 147,036 | 3,786 |
| Sierra | Downieville | 3,399 | 3,318 | 953 |
| Siskiyou | Yreka | 44,253 | 43,531 | 6,287 |
| Solano | Fairfield | 366,134 | 339,471 | 828 |
| Sonoma | Santa Rosa | 414,569 | 388,222 | 1,576 |
| Stanislaus | Modesto | 410,870 | 370,522 | 1,495 |
| Sutter | Yuba City | 74,963 | 64,415 | 603 |
| Tehama | Red Bluff | 53,798 | 49,625 | 2,951 |
| Trinity | Weaverville | 13,429 | 13,063 | 3,179 |
| Tulare | Visalia | 346,843 | 311,921 | 4,824 |
| Tuolumne | Sonora | 51,777 | 48,456 | 2,236 |
| Ventura | Ventura | 710,018 | 669,016 | 1,846 |
| Yolo | Woodland | 147,769 | 141,210 | 1,012 |
| Yuba | Marysville | 61,141 | 58,228 | 631 |

## Colorado

(63 counties, 103,973 sq mi land; pop. 3,746,585)

| County | County seat or courthouse | 1995 Pop. | 1990 Pop. | Land area sq mi |
|---|---|---|---|---|
| Adams | Brighton | 303,297 | 265,038 | 1,192 |
| Alamosa | Alamosa | 14,215 | 13,617 | 723 |
| Arapahoe | Littleton | 449,103 | 391,511 | 803 |
| Archuleta | Pagosa Springs | 7,100 | 5,345 | 1,349 |
| Baca | Springfield | 4,384 | 4,556 | 2,556 |
| Bent | Las Animas | 5,518 | 5,048 | 1,514 |
| Boulder | Boulder | 253,850 | 225,339 | 743 |
| Chaffee | Salida | 14,413 | 12,684 | 1,014 |
| Cheyenne | Cheyenne Wells | 2,312 | 2,397 | 1,782 |
| Clear Creek | Georgetown | 8,745 | 7,619 | 396 |
| Conejos | Conejos | 7,807 | 7,453 | 1,287 |
| Costilla | San Luis | 3,384 | 3,190 | 1,227 |
| Crowley | Ordway | 4,303 | 3,946 | 789 |
| Custer | Westcliffe | 2,702 | 1,926 | 739 |
| Delta | Delta | 25,077 | 20,980 | 1,142 |
| Denver | Denver | 494,462 | 467,610 | 153 |
| Dolores | Dove Creek | 1,588 | 1,504 | 1,067 |
| Douglas | Castle Rock | 99,577 | 60,391 | 840 |
| Eagle | Eagle | 28,844 | 21,928 | 1,688 |
| Elbert | Kiowa | 14,565 | 9,646 | 1,851 |
| El Paso | Colorado Springs | 465,800 | 397,014 | 2,127 |
| Fremont | Canon City | 39,794 | 32,273 | 1,533 |
| Garfield | Glenwood Springs | 35,338 | 29,974 | 2,948 |
| Gilpin | Central City | 3,576 | 3,070 | 150 |
| Grand | Hot Sulphur Springs | 9,188 | 7,966 | 1,850 |
| Gunnison | Gunnison | 11,931 | 10,273 | 3,239 |
| Hinsdale | Lake City | 648 | 467 | 1,118 |
| Huerfano | Walsenburg | 6,356 | 6,009 | 1,591 |
| Jackson | Walden | 1,537 | 1,605 | 1,613 |
| Jefferson | Golden | 484,869 | 438,430 | 772 |
| Kiowa | Eads | 1,627 | 1,688 | 1,771 |
| Kit Carson | Burlington | 7,301 | 7,140 | 2,161 |
| Lake | Leadville | 6,296 | 6,007 | 377 |
| La Plata | Durango | 38,314 | 32,284 | 1,692 |
| Larimer | Fort Collins | 217,215 | 186,136 | 2,601 |
| Las Animas | Trinidad | 14,268 | 13,765 | 4,773 |
| Lincoln | Hugo | 5,602 | 4,529 | 2,586 |
| Logan | Sterling | 17,869 | 17,567 | 1,839 |
| Mesa | Grand Junction | 106,548 | 93,145 | 3,328 |
| Mineral | Creede | 634 | 558 | 876 |
| Moffat | Craig | 12,136 | 11,357 | 4,743 |
| Montezuma | Cortez | 21,591 | 18,672 | 2,037 |
| Montrose | Montrose | 28,829 | 24,423 | 2,241 |
| Morgan | Fort Morgan | 23,729 | 21,939 | 1,286 |
| Otero | La Junta | 20,788 | 20,185 | 1,263 |
| Ouray | Ouray | 3,033 | 2,295 | 542 |
| Park | Fairplay | 10,589 | 7,174 | 2,201 |
| Phillips | Holyoke | 4,309 | 4,189 | 688 |
| Pitkin | Aspen | 13,589 | 12,661 | 970 |
| Prowers | Lamar | 13,591 | 13,347 | 1,641 |
| Pueblo | Pueblo | 129,759 | 123,051 | 2,389 |
| Rio Blanco | Meeker | 6,472 | 6,051 | 3,221 |
| Rio Grande | Del Norte | 11,262 | 10,770 | 913 |
| Routt | Steamboat Springs | 16,709 | 14,088 | 2,362 |
| Saguache | Saguache | 5,514 | 4,619 | 3,169 |
| San Juan | Silverton | 546 | 745 | 388 |
| San Miguel | Telluride | 4,929 | 3,653 | 1,287 |
| Sedgwick | Julesburg | 2,606 | 2,690 | 548 |
| Summit | Breckenridge | 17,204 | 12,881 | 608 |
| Teller | Cripple Creek | 17,478 | 12,468 | 557 |
| Washington | Akron | 4,687 | 4,812 | 2,521 |
| Weld | Greeley | 148,014 | 131,821 | 3,993 |
| Yuma | Wray | 9,264 | 8,954 | 2,366 |

## Connecticut

(8 counties, 4,845 sq mi land; pop. 3,274,662)

| County | County seat or courthouse | 1995 Pop. | 1990 Pop. | Land area sq mi |
|---|---|---|---|---|
| Fairfield | Bridgeport | 830,728 | 827,645 | 626 |
| Hartford | Hartford | 835,589 | 851,783 | 736 |
| Litchfield | Litchfield | 179,316 | 174,092 | 920 |
| Middlesex | Middletown | 148,030 | 143,196 | 369 |
| New Haven | New Haven | 794,785 | 804,219 | 606 |
| New London | Norwich | 250,404 | 254,957 | 666 |
| Tolland | Rockville | 131,604 | 128,699 | 410 |
| Windham | Putnam | 104,206 | 102,525 | 513 |

## Delaware

(3 counties, 1,955 sq mi land; pop. 717,197)

| County | County seat or courthouse | 1995 Pop. | 1990 Pop. | Land area sq mi |
|---|---|---|---|---|
| Kent | Dover | 121,725 | 110,993 | 591 |
| New Castle | Wilmington | 467,889 | 441,946 | 426 |
| Sussex | Georgetown | 127,583 | 113,229 | 938 |

## District of Columbia

(68 sq mi land; pop. 554,256)

# Florida

(67 counties, 53,937 sq mi land; pop. 14,165,570)

| County | County seat or courthouse | 1995 Pop. | 1990 Pop. | Land area sq mi |
|---|---|---|---|---|
| Alachua | Gainesville | 196,106 | 181,596 | 874 |
| Baker | Macclenny | 20,153 | 18,486 | 585 |
| Bay | Panama City | 142,690 | 126,994 | 764 |
| Bradford | Starke | 24,182 | 22,515 | 293 |
| Brevard | Titusville | 450,646 | 398,978 | 1,019 |
| Broward | Fort Lauderdale | 1,412,165 | 1,255,531 | 1,209 |
| Calhoun | Blountstown | 11,858 | 11,011 | 567 |
| Charlotte | Punta Gorda | 129,381 | 110,975 | 694 |
| Citrus | Inverness | 107,333 | 93,513 | 584 |
| Clay | Green Cove Springs | 124,431 | 105,986 | 601 |
| Collier | Naples | 181,381 | 152,099 | 2,026 |
| Columbia | Lake City | 48,376 | 42,613 | 797 |
| Dade | Miami | 2,031,336 | 1,937,194 | 1,945 |
| De Soto | Arcadia | 25,048 | 23,865 | 637 |
| Dixie | Cross City | 12,159 | 10,585 | 704 |
| Duval | Jacksonville | 701,673 | 672,971 | 774 |
| Escambia | Pensacola | 273,804 | 262,798 | 664 |
| Flagler | Bunnell | 40,643 | 28,701 | 485 |
| Franklin | Apalachicola | 10,301 | 8,967 | 534 |
| Gadsden | Quincy | 43,378 | 41,116 | 516 |
| Gilchrist | Trenton | 12,332 | 9,667 | 349 |
| Glades | Moore Haven | 7,665 | 7,591 | 774 |
| Gulf | Port Saint Joe | 13,390 | 11,504 | 565 |
| Hamilton | Jasper | 11,773 | 10,930 | 515 |
| Hardee | Wauchula | 19,952 | 19,499 | 637 |
| Hendry | La Belle | 28,114 | 25,773 | 1,153 |
| Hernando | Brooksville | 120,054 | 101,115 | 478 |
| Highlands | Sebring | 74,507 | 68,432 | 1,029 |
| Hillsborough | Tampa | 884,608 | 834,054 | 1,051 |
| Holmes | Bonifay | 17,520 | 15,778 | 483 |
| Indian River | Vero Beach | 97,144 | 90,208 | 503 |
| Jackson | Marianna | 43,891 | 41,375 | 916 |
| Jefferson | Monticello | 12,950 | 11,296 | 598 |
| Lafayette | Mayo | 6,043 | 5,578 | 543 |
| Lake | Tavares | 180,160 | 152,104 | 953 |
| Lee | Fort Myers | 375,381 | 335,113 | 804 |
| Leon | Tallahassee | 213,917 | 192,493 | 667 |
| Levy | Bronson | 29,738 | 25,912 | 1,118 |
| Liberty | Bristol | 6,400 | 5,569 | 836 |
| Madison | Madison | 17,231 | 16,569 | 692 |
| Manatee | Bradenton | 229,864 | 211,707 | 741 |
| Marion | Ocala | 226,678 | 194,835 | 1,579 |
| Martin | Stuart | 111,069 | 100,900 | 556 |
| Monroe | Key West | 81,850 | 78,024 | 997 |
| Nassau | Fernandina Beach | 50,767 | 43,941 | 652 |
| Okaloosa | Crestview | 163,707 | 143,777 | 936 |
| Okeechobee | Okeechobee | 30,222 | 29,627 | 774 |
| Orange | Orlando | 749,631 | 677,491 | 908 |
| Osceola | Kissimmee | 130,771 | 107,728 | 1,322 |
| Palm Beach | West Palm Beach | 972,093 | 863,503 | 1,974 |
| Pasco | New Port Richey | 304,938 | 281,131 | 745 |
| Pinellas | Clearwater | 870,884 | 851,659 | 280 |
| Polk | Bartow | 436,701 | 405,382 | 1,875 |
| Putnam | Palatka | 69,481 | 65,070 | 722 |
| Saint Johns | Saint Augustine | 102,174 | 83,829 | 609 |
| Saint Lucie | Fort Pierce | 172,483 | 150,171 | 573 |
| Santa Rosa | Milton | 104,110 | 81,608 | 1,016 |
| Sarasota | Sarasota | 295,942 | 277,776 | 572 |
| Seminole | Sanford | 330,012 | 287,521 | 308 |
| Sumter | Bushnell | 34,788 | 31,577 | 546 |
| Suwannee | Live Oak | 30,103 | 26,780 | 688 |
| Taylor | Perry | 17,445 | 17,111 | 1,042 |
| Union | Lake Butler | 12,433 | 10,252 | 240 |
| Volusia | De Land | 408,261 | 370,737 | 1,106 |
| Wakulla | Crawfordville | 17,111 | 14,202 | 607 |
| Walton | De Funiak Springs | 33,615 | 27,759 | 1,058 |
| Washington | Chipley | 18,623 | 16,919 | 580 |

# Georgia

(159 counties, 57,919 sq mi land; pop. 7,200,882)

| County | County seat or courthouse | 1995 Pop. | 1990 Pop. | Land area sq mi |
|---|---|---|---|---|
| Appling | Baxley | 16,359 | 15,744 | 509 |
| Atkinson | Pearson | 6,749 | 6,213 | 338 |
| Bacon | Alma | 10,438 | 9,566 | 285 |
| Baker | Newton | 3,766 | 3,615 | 343 |
| Baldwin | Milledgeville | 41,854 | 39,530 | 259 |
| Banks | Homer | 11,616 | 10,308 | 234 |
| Barrow | Winder | 35,699 | 29,721 | 162 |
| Bartow | Cartersville | 63,732 | 55,915 | 460 |
| Ben Hill | Fitzgerald | 17,258 | 16,245 | 252 |
| Berrien | Nashville | 15,466 | 14,153 | 453 |
| Bibb | Macon | 155,066 | 150,137 | 250 |
| Bleckley | Cochran | 10,958 | 10,430 | 217 |
| Brantley | Nahunta | 12,698 | 11,077 | 444 |
| Brooks | Quitman | 15,837 | 15,398 | 494 |
| Bryan | Pembroke | 21,190 | 15,438 | 442 |
| Bulloch | Statesboro | 48,642 | 43,125 | 683 |
| Burke | Waynesboro | 21,742 | 20,579 | 831 |
| Butts | Jackson | 16,025 | 15,326 | 187 |
| Calhoun | Morgan | 4,851 | 5,013 | 280 |
| Camden | Woodbine | 40,714 | 30,167 | 630 |
| Candler | Metter | 8,637 | 7,744 | 247 |
| Carroll | Carrollton | 77,977 | 71,422 | 499 |
| Catoosa | Ringgold | 48,008 | 42,464 | 162 |
| Charlton | Folkston | 9,296 | 8,496 | 781 |
| Chatham | Savannah | 226,160 | 216,774 | 440 |
| Chattahoochee | Cusseta | 15,871 | 16,934 | 249 |
| Chattooga | Summerville | 22,884 | 22,242 | 314 |
| Cherokee | Canton | 114,751 | 90,204 | 424 |
| Clarke | Athens | 90,207 | 87,594 | 121 |
| Clay | Fort Gaines | 3,473 | 3,364 | 195 |
| Clayton | Jonesboro | 198,551 | 181,436 | 143 |
| Clinch | Homerville | 6,438 | 6,160 | 809 |
| Cobb | Marietta | 525,453 | 447,745 | 340 |
| Coffee | Douglas | 32,697 | 29,592 | 599 |
| Colquitt | Moultrie | 38,072 | 36,645 | 552 |
| Columbia | Appling | 83,674 | 66,031 | 290 |
| Cook | Adel | 13,950 | 13,456 | 229 |
| Coweta | Newnan | 72,021 | 53,853 | 443 |
| Crawford | Knoxville | 10,166 | 8,991 | 325 |
| Crisp | Cordele | 20,716 | 20,011 | 274 |
| Dade | Trenton | 14,158 | 13,147 | 174 |
| Dawson | Dawsonville | 12,237 | 9,429 | 211 |
| Decatur | Bainbridge | 26,390 | 25,517 | 597 |
| De Kalb | Decatur | 582,095 | 546,171 | 268 |
| Dodge | Eastman | 17,956 | 17,607 | 501 |
| Dooly | Vienna | 10,314 | 9,901 | 393 |
| Dougherty | Albany | 97,511 | 96,321 | 330 |
| Douglas | Douglasville | 82,297 | 71,120 | 199 |
| Early | Blakely | 12,198 | 11,854 | 511 |
| Echols | Statenville | 2,325 | 2,334 | 404 |
| Effingham | Springfield | 32,118 | 25,687 | 480 |
| Elbert | Elberton | 19,173 | 18,949 | 369 |
| Emanuel | Swainsboro | 20,954 | 20,546 | 686 |
| Evans | Claxton | 9,438 | 8,724 | 185 |
| Fannin | Blue Ridge | 17,480 | 15,992 | 386 |
| Fayette | Fayetteville | 78,879 | 62,415 | 197 |
| Floyd | Rome | 83,935 | 81,251 | 513 |
| Forsyth | Cumming | 62,335 | 44,083 | 226 |
| Franklin | Carnesville | 17,701 | 16,650 | 263 |
| Fulton | Atlanta | 700,689 | 648,779 | 529 |
| Gilmer | Ellijay | 15,916 | 13,368 | 427 |
| Glascock | Gibson | 2,456 | 2,357 | 144 |
| Glynn | Brunswick | 65,565 | 62,496 | 422 |
| Gordon | Calhoun | 38,442 | 35,067 | 355 |
| Grady | Cairo | 21,312 | 20,279 | 458 |
| Greene | Greensboro | 12,781 | 11,793 | 388 |
| Gwinnett | Lawrenceville | 457,058 | 352,910 | 433 |
| Habersham | Clarkesville | 30,146 | 27,622 | 278 |
| Hall | Gainesville | 108,238 | 95,434 | 394 |
| Hancock | Sparta | 9,100 | 8,908 | 473 |
| Haralson | Buchanan | 23,378 | 21,966 | 282 |
| Harris | Hamilton | 20,479 | 17,788 | 464 |
| Hart | Hartwell | 20,848 | 19,712 | 232 |
| Heard | Franklin | 9,573 | 8,628 | 296 |
| Henry | McDonough | 84,553 | 58,741 | 323 |
| Houston | Perry | 99,647 | 89,208 | 377 |
| Irwin | Ocilla | 8,725 | 8,649 | 357 |
| Jackson | Jefferson | 33,921 | 30,005 | 342 |
| Jasper | Monticello | 9,168 | 8,453 | 371 |
| Jeff Davis | Hazlehurst | 12,366 | 12,032 | 333 |
| Jefferson | Louisville | 17,872 | 17,408 | 528 |
| Jenkins | Millen | 8,658 | 8,247 | 350 |
| Johnson | Wrightsville | 8,436 | 8,329 | 304 |
| Jones | Gray | 22,077 | 20,739 | 394 |
| Lamar | Barnesville | 13,797 | 13,038 | 185 |
| Lanier | Lakeland | 6,312 | 5,531 | 187 |
| Laurens | Dublin | 42,852 | 39,988 | 813 |
| Lee | Leesburg | 19,922 | 16,250 | 356 |
| Liberty | Hinesville | 58,749 | 52,745 | 519 |
| Lincoln | Lincolnton | 8,055 | 7,442 | 211 |
| Long | Ludowici | 7,885 | 6,202 | 401 |
| Lowndes | Valdosta | 82,952 | 75,981 | 504 |
| Lumpkin | Dahlonega | 16,822 | 14,573 | 285 |
| McDuffie | Thomson | 21,627 | 20,119 | 260 |
| McIntosh | Darien | 9,456 | 8,634 | 434 |
| Macon | Oglethorpe | 13,249 | 13,114 | 403 |
| Madison | Danielsville | 23,396 | 21,050 | 284 |
| Marion | Buena Vista | 6,370 | 5,590 | 367 |
| Meriwether | Greenville | 23,041 | 22,411 | 503 |
| Miller | Colquitt | 6,161 | 6,280 | 283 |
| Mitchell | Camilla | 20,859 | 20,275 | 512 |
| Monroe | Forsyth | 18,950 | 17,113 | 396 |
| Montgomery | Mount Vernon | 7,635 | 7,379 | 245 |
| Morgan | Madison | 14,006 | 12,883 | 350 |
| Murray | Chatsworth | 30,032 | 26,147 | 344 |
| Muscogee | Columbus | 184,594 | 179,280 | 216 |
| Newton | Covington | 50,644 | 41,808 | 276 |
| Oconee | Watkinsville | 21,190 | 17,618 | 186 |
| Oglethorpe | Lexington | 10,911 | 9,763 | 441 |
| Paulding | Dallas | 59,920 | 41,611 | 314 |
| Peach | Fort Valley | 22,906 | 21,189 | 151 |
| Pickens | Jasper | 16,881 | 14,432 | 232 |
| Pierce | Blackshear | 14,821 | 13,328 | 343 |
| Pike | Zebulon | 11,441 | 10,224 | 218 |
| Polk | Cedartown | 34,771 | 33,815 | 311 |

| County | County seat or courthouse | 1995 Pop. | 1990 Pop. | Land area sq mi |
|---|---|---|---|---|
| Pulaski | Hawkinsville | 8,245 | 8,108 | 247 |
| Putnam | Eatonton | 15,991 | 14,137 | 345 |
| Quitman | Georgetown | 2,420 | 2,210 | 152 |
| Rabun | Clayton | 12,738 | 11,648 | 371 |
| Randolph | Cuthbert | 8,092 | 8,023 | 429 |
| Richmond | Augusta | 195,508 | 189,719 | 324 |
| Rockdale | Conyers | 64,448 | 54,091 | 131 |
| Schley | Ellaville | 3,783 | 3,590 | 168 |
| Screven | Sylvania | 14,336 | 13,842 | 649 |
| Seminole | Donalsonville | 9,097 | 9,010 | 238 |
| Spalding | Griffin | 57,306 | 54,457 | 198 |
| Stephens | Toccoa | 25,000 | 23,436 | 179 |
| Stewart | Lumpkin | 5,438 | 5,654 | 459 |
| Sumter | Americus | 31,245 | 30,232 | 485 |
| Talbot | Talbotton | 6,741 | 6,524 | 393 |
| Taliaferro | Crawfordville | 1,883 | 1,915 | 195 |
| Tattnall | Reidsville | 18,588 | 17,722 | 484 |
| Taylor | Butler | 8,048 | 7,642 | 378 |
| Telfair | MacRae | 11,623 | 11,000 | 441 |
| Terrell | Dawson | 11,007 | 10,653 | 336 |
| Thomas | Thomasville | 41,419 | 38,943 | 548 |
| Tift | Tifton | 35,932 | 34,998 | 265 |
| Toombs | Lyons | 25,276 | 24,072 | 367 |
| Towns | Hiawassee | 7,559 | 6,754 | 167 |
| Treutlen | Soperton | 5,943 | 5,994 | 201 |
| Troup | La Grange | 57,882 | 55,532 | 414 |
| Turner | Ashburn | 8,916 | 8,703 | 286 |
| Twiggs | Jeffersonville | 10,060 | 9,806 | 360 |
| Union | Blairsville | 14,427 | 11,993 | 323 |
| Upson | Thomaston | 26,961 | 26,300 | 326 |
| Walker | La Fayette | 60,654 | 58,340 | 446 |
| Walton | Monroe | 46,694 | 38,586 | 329 |
| Ware | Waycross | 35,589 | 35,471 | 903 |
| Warren | Warrenton | 6,057 | 6,078 | 286 |
| Washington | Sandersville | 19,953 | 19,112 | 681 |
| Wayne | Jesup | 24,818 | 22,356 | 645 |
| Webster | Preston | 2,260 | 2,263 | 210 |
| Wheeler | Alamo | 4,830 | 4,903 | 298 |
| White | Cleveland | 15,330 | 13,006 | 242 |
| Whitfield | Dalton | 78,033 | 72,462 | 290 |
| Wilcox | Abbeville | 7,100 | 7,008 | 380 |
| Wilkes | Washington | 10,615 | 10,597 | 471 |
| Wilkinson | Irwinton | 10,627 | 10,228 | 447 |
| Worth | Sylvester | 21,643 | 19,744 | 570 |

# Hawaii

(5 counties, 6,423 sq mi land; pop. 1,186,815)

| County | County seat or courthouse | 1995 Pop. | 1990 Pop. | Land area sq mi |
|---|---|---|---|---|
| Hawaii | Hilo | 137,531 | 120,317 | 4,028 |
| Honolulu | Honolulu | 877,198 | 836,231 | 600 |
| Kalawao[1] | | 91 | 130 | 13 |
| Kauai | Lihue | 56,131 | 51,177 | 623 |
| Maui | Wailuku | 115,864 | 100,374 | 1,159 |

(1) Administered by state government.

# Idaho

(44 counties, 82,751 sq mi land; pop. 1,163,261)

| County | County seat or courthouse | 1995 Pop. | 1990 Pop. | Land area sq mi |
|---|---|---|---|---|
| Ada | Boise | 251,831 | 205,775 | 1,055 |
| Adams | Council | 3,877 | 3,254 | 1,365 |
| Bannock | Pocatello | 72,115 | 66,026 | 1,113 |
| Bear Lake | Paris | 6,600 | 6,084 | 971 |
| Benewah | Saint Maries | 8,780 | 7,937 | 776 |
| Bingham | Blackfoot | 41,188 | 37,583 | 2,095 |
| Blaine | Hailey | 16,471 | 13,552 | 2,645 |
| Boise | Idaho City | 4,768 | 3,509 | 1,903 |
| Bonner | Sandpoint | 33,080 | 26,622 | 1,738 |
| Bonneville | Idaho Falls | 79,531 | 72,207 | 1,869 |
| Boundary | Bonners Ferry | 9,548 | 8,332 | 1,269 |
| Butte | Arco | 3,008 | 2,918 | 2,233 |
| Camas | Fairfield | 848 | 727 | 1,075 |
| Canyon | Caldwell | 108,510 | 90,076 | 590 |
| Caribou | Soda Springs | 7,280 | 6,963 | 1,766 |
| Cassia | Burley | 21,095 | 19,532 | 2,567 |
| Clark | Dubois | 822 | 762 | 1,765 |
| Clearwater | Orofino | 9,115 | 8,505 | 2,462 |
| Custer | Challis | 4,316 | 4,133 | 4,926 |
| Elmore | Mountain Home | 23,181 | 21,205 | 3,078 |
| Franklin | Preston | 10,286 | 9,232 | 666 |
| Fremont | Saint Anthony | 11,532 | 10,937 | 1,867 |
| Gem | Emmett | 13,856 | 11,844 | 563 |
| Gooding | Gooding | 12,980 | 11,633 | 731 |
| Idaho | Grangeville | 14,789 | 13,768 | 8,485 |
| Jefferson | Rigby | 18,786 | 16,543 | 1,095 |
| Jerome | Jerome | 17,017 | 15,138 | 600 |
| Kootenai | Coeur d'Alene | 91,678 | 69,795 | 1,245 |
| Latah | Moscow | 32,860 | 30,617 | 1,077 |
| Lemhi | Salmon | 7,973 | 6,899 | 4,564 |
| Lewis | Nez Perce | 3,937 | 3,516 | 479 |
| Lincoln | Shoshone | 3,729 | 3,308 | 1,206 |
| Madison | Rexberg | 23,811 | 23,674 | 472 |
| Minidoka | Rupert | 21,065 | 19,361 | 760 |
| Nez Perce | Lewiston | 36,549 | 33,754 | 849 |
| Oneida | Malad City | 3,843 | 3,492 | 1,200 |
| Owyhee | Murphy | 9,520 | 8,392 | 7,678 |
| Payette | Payette | 19,532 | 16,434 | 408 |
| Power | American Falls | 7,986 | 7,086 | 1,406 |
| Shoshone | Wallace | 14,042 | 13,931 | 2,634 |
| Teton | Driggs | 4,706 | 3,439 | 450 |
| Twin Falls | Twin Falls | 59,480 | 53,580 | 1,925 |
| Valley | Cascade | 7,877 | 6,109 | 3,678 |
| Washington | Weiser | 9,463 | 8,550 | 1,456 |

# Illinois

(102 counties, 55,593 sq mi land; pop. 11,829,940)

| County | County seat or courthouse | 1995 Pop. | 1990 Pop. | Land area sq mi |
|---|---|---|---|---|
| Adams | Quincy | 68,043 | 66,090 | 857 |
| Alexander | Cairo | 10,180 | 10,626 | 236 |
| Bond | Greenville | 15,738 | 14,991 | 380 |
| Boone | Belvidere | 36,180 | 30,806 | 281 |
| Brown | Mount Sterling | 6,247 | 5,836 | 306 |
| Bureau | Princeton | 36,049 | 35,688 | 869 |
| Calhoun | Hardin | 4,948 | 5,322 | 254 |
| Carroll | Mount Carroll | 16,872 | 16,805 | 444 |
| Cass | Virginia | 13,330 | 13,437 | 376 |
| Champaign | Urbana | 169,096 | 173,025 | 997 |
| Christian | Taylorville | 34,920 | 34,418 | 709 |
| Clark | Marshall | 16,284 | 15,921 | 502 |
| Clay | Louisville | 14,435 | 14,460 | 469 |
| Clinton | Carlyle | 35,285 | 33,944 | 474 |
| Coles | Charleston | 52,357 | 51,644 | 508 |
| Cook | Chicago | 5,136,877 | 5,105,044 | 946 |
| Crawford | Robinson | 19,911 | 19,464 | 444 |
| Cumberland | Toledo | 11,110 | 10,670 | 346 |
| DeKalb | Sycamore | 83,441 | 77,932 | 634 |
| De Witt | Clinton | 16,824 | 16,516 | 398 |
| Douglas | Tuscola | 19,799 | 19,464 | 417 |
| Du Page | Wheaton | 853,458 | 781,689 | 334 |
| Edgar | Paris | 19,984 | 19,595 | 624 |
| Edwards | Albion | 7,262 | 7,440 | 222 |
| Effingham | Effingham | 33,009 | 31,704 | 479 |
| Fayette | Vandalia | 21,235 | 20,893 | 717 |
| Ford | Paxton | 14,127 | 14,275 | 486 |
| Franklin | Benton | 40,809 | 40,319 | 412 |
| Fulton | Lewiston | 38,788 | 38,080 | 866 |
| Gallatin | Shawneetown | 6,779 | 6,909 | 324 |
| Greene | Carrollton | 15,643 | 15,317 | 543 |
| Grundy | Morris | 35,159 | 32,337 | 420 |
| Hamilton | McLeansboro | 8,525 | 8,499 | 435 |
| Hancock | Carthage | 21,292 | 21,373 | 795 |
| Hardin | Elizabethtown | 5,184 | 5,189 | 178 |
| Henderson | Oquawka | 8,432 | 8,096 | 379 |
| Henry | Cambridge | 51,719 | 51,159 | 823 |
| Iroquois | Watseka | 31,411 | 30,787 | 1,117 |
| Jackson | Murphysboro | 61,502 | 61,067 | 588 |
| Jasper | Newton | 10,591 | 10,609 | 494 |
| Jefferson | Mount Vernon | 38,998 | 37,020 | 571 |
| Jersey | Jerseyville | 21,188 | 20,539 | 369 |
| Jo Daviess | Galena | 21,931 | 21,821 | 601 |
| Johnson | Vienna | 12,426 | 11,347 | 346 |
| Kane | Geneva | 359,950 | 317,471 | 521 |
| Kankakee | Kankakee | 102,046 | 96,255 | 678 |
| Kendall | Yorkville | 45,398 | 39,413 | 321 |
| Knox | Galesburg | 56,070 | 56,393 | 716 |
| Lake | Waukegan | 572,431 | 516,418 | 448 |
| La Salle | Ottawa | 109,955 | 106,913 | 1,135 |
| Lawrence | Lawrenceville | 15,918 | 15,972 | 372 |
| Lee | Dixon | 35,798 | 34,392 | 725 |
| Livingston | Pontiac | 40,404 | 39,301 | 1,044 |
| Logan | Lincoln | 31,267 | 30,798 | 618 |
| McDonough | Macomb | 35,519 | 35,244 | 589 |
| McHenry | Woodstock | 224,677 | 183,241 | 604 |
| McLean | Bloomington | 139,274 | 129,180 | 1,184 |
| Macon | Decatur | 116,414 | 117,206 | 581 |
| Macoupin | Carlinville | 48,729 | 47,679 | 864 |
| Madison | Edwardsville | 256,458 | 249,238 | 725 |
| Marion | Salem | 41,997 | 41,561 | 572 |
| Marshall | Lacon | 12,791 | 12,846 | 386 |
| Mason | Havana | 16,691 | 16,269 | 539 |
| Massac | Metropolis | 15,370 | 14,752 | 239 |
| Menard | Petersburg | 12,284 | 11,164 | 314 |
| Mercer | Aledo | 17,444 | 17,290 | 561 |
| Monroe | Waterloo | 24,719 | 22,422 | 388 |
| Montgomery | Hillsboro | 30,994 | 30,728 | 704 |
| Morgan | Jacksonville | 36,171 | 36,397 | 569 |
| Moultrie | Sullivan | 14,168 | 13,930 | 336 |
| Ogle | Oregon | 49,406 | 45,957 | 759 |
| Peoria | Peoria | 183,377 | 182,827 | 620 |
| Perry | Pinckneyville | 21,295 | 21,412 | 441 |
| Piatt | Monticello | 16,158 | 15,548 | 440 |
| Pike | Pittsfield | 17,338 | 17,577 | 830 |
| Pope | Golconda | 4,691 | 4,373 | 371 |
| Pulaski | Mound City | 7,464 | 7,523 | 201 |
| Putnam | Hennepin | 5,718 | 5,730 | 160 |

| County | County seat or courthouse | 1995 Pop. | 1990 Pop. | Land area sq mi |
|---|---|---|---|---|
| Randolph | Chester | 34,296 | 34,583 | 578 |
| Richland | Olney | 16,788 | 16,545 | 360 |
| Rock Island | Rock Island | 149,830 | 148,723 | 427 |
| Saint Clair | Belleville | 265,424 | 262,852 | 664 |
| Saline | Harrisburg | 26,521 | 26,551 | 383 |
| Sangamon | Springfield | 184,731 | 178,386 | 868 |
| Schuyler | Rushville | 7,798 | 7,498 | 437 |
| Scott | Winchester | 5,629 | 5,644 | 251 |
| Shelby | Shelbyville | 22,561 | 22,261 | 759 |
| Stark | Toulon | 6,396 | 6,534 | 288 |
| Stephenson | Freeport | 48,844 | 48,052 | 564 |
| Tazewell | Pekin | 127,602 | 123,692 | 649 |
| Union | Jonesboro | 18,114 | 17,619 | 416 |
| Vermilion | Danville | 86,541 | 88,257 | 899 |
| Wabash | Mount Carmel | 12,929 | 13,111 | 224 |
| Warren | Monmouth | 18,816 | 19,181 | 543 |
| Washington | Nashville | 15,238 | 14,965 | 563 |
| Wayne | Fairfield | 17,208 | 17,241 | 714 |
| White | Carmi | 15,903 | 16,522 | 495 |
| Whiteside | Morrison | 60,352 | 60,186 | 685 |
| Will | Joliet | 413,379 | 357,313 | 837 |
| Williamson | Marion | 59,750 | 57,733 | 424 |
| Winnebago | Rockford | 264,952 | 252,913 | 514 |
| Woodford | Eureka | 34,576 | 32,653 | 528 |

## Indiana

(92 counties, 35,870 sq mi land; pop. 5,803,471)

| County | County seat or courthouse | 1995 Pop. | 1990 Pop. | Land area sq mi |
|---|---|---|---|---|
| Adams | Decatur | 32,311 | 31,095 | 339 |
| Allen | Fort Wayne | 308,503 | 300,836 | 657 |
| Bartholomew | Columbus | 68,065 | 63,657 | 407 |
| Benton | Fowler | 9,703 | 9,441 | 406 |
| Blackford | Hartford City | 14,162 | 14,067 | 165 |
| Boone | Lebanon | 41,813 | 38,147 | 423 |
| Brown | Nashville | 15,098 | 14,080 | 312 |
| Carroll | Delphi | 19,505 | 18,809 | 372 |
| Cass | Logansport | 38,584 | 38,413 | 413 |
| Clark | Jeffersonville | 91,826 | 87,774 | 375 |
| Clay | Brazil | 26,306 | 24,705 | 358 |
| Clinton | Frankfort | 32,594 | 30,974 | 405 |
| Crawford | English | 10,442 | 9,914 | 306 |
| Daviess | Washington | 28,603 | 27,533 | 431 |
| Dearborn | Lawrenceburg | 44,367 | 38,835 | 305 |
| Decatur | Greensburg | 24,998 | 23,645 | 373 |
| DeKalb | Auburn | 37,955 | 35,324 | 363 |
| Delaware | Muncie | 118,577 | 119,659 | 393 |
| Dubois | Jasper | 38,732 | 36,616 | 430 |
| Elkhart | Goshen | 166,994 | 156,198 | 464 |
| Fayette | Connersville | 26,430 | 26,015 | 215 |
| Floyd | New Albany | 70,058 | 64,404 | 148 |
| Fountain | Covington | 18,060 | 17,808 | 396 |
| Franklin | Brookville | 20,957 | 19,580 | 386 |
| Fulton | Rochester | 19,922 | 18,840 | 369 |
| Gibson | Princeton | 32,165 | 31,913 | 489 |
| Grant | Marion | 73,720 | 74,169 | 414 |
| Greene | Bloomfield | 32,696 | 30,410 | 542 |
| Hamilton | Noblesville | 140,650 | 108,936 | 398 |
| Hancock | Greenfield | 50,768 | 45,527 | 306 |
| Harrison | Corydon | 32,594 | 29,890 | 485 |
| Hendricks | Danville | 86,620 | 75,717 | 408 |
| Henry | New Castle | 49,275 | 48,139 | 393 |
| Howard | Kokomo | 83,763 | 80,827 | 293 |
| Huntington | Huntington | 36,807 | 35,427 | 383 |
| Jackson | Brownstown | 40,403 | 37,730 | 509 |
| Jasper | Rensselaer | 27,895 | 24,960 | 560 |
| Jay | Portland | 21,901 | 21,512 | 384 |
| Jefferson | Madison | 30,813 | 29,797 | 361 |
| Jennings | Vernon | 26,168 | 23,661 | 377 |
| Johnson | Franklin | 101,690 | 88,109 | 320 |
| Knox | Vincennes | 40,194 | 39,884 | 516 |
| Kosciusko | Warsaw | 69,210 | 65,294 | 538 |
| Lagrange | Lagrange | 31,653 | 29,477 | 380 |
| Lake | Crown Point | 482,672 | 475,594 | 497 |
| La Porte | La Porte | 110,384 | 107,066 | 598 |
| Lawrence | Bedford | 45,097 | 42,836 | 449 |
| Madison | Anderson | 132,796 | 130,669 | 452 |
| Marion | Indianapolis | 817,604 | 797,159 | 396 |
| Marshall | Plymouth | 44,879 | 42,182 | 444 |
| Martin | Shoals | 10,545 | 10,369 | 336 |
| Miami | Peru | 32,611 | 36,897 | 376 |
| Monroe | Bloomington | 115,208 | 108,978 | 394 |
| Montgomery | Crawfordsville | 36,090 | 34,436 | 505 |
| Morgan | Martinsville | 62,115 | 55,920 | 407 |
| Newton | Kentland | 14,413 | 13,551 | 402 |
| Noble | Albion | 40,884 | 37,877 | 411 |
| Ohio | Rising Sun | 5,395 | 5,315 | 87 |
| Orange | Paoli | 19,011 | 18,409 | 400 |
| Owen | Spencer | 19,663 | 17,281 | 385 |
| Parke | Rockville | 16,094 | 15,410 | 445 |
| Perry | Cannelton | 19,129 | 19,107 | 381 |
| Pike | Petersburg | 12,610 | 12,509 | 336 |
| Porter | Valparaiso | 140,487 | 128,932 | 418 |
| Posey | Mount Vernon | 26,493 | 25,968 | 409 |

| County | County seat or courthouse | 1995 Pop. | 1990 Pop. | Land area sq mi |
|---|---|---|---|---|
| Pulaski | Winamac | 12,960 | 12,643 | 434 |
| Putnam | Greencastle | 32,939 | 30,315 | 480 |
| Randolph | Winchester | 27,377 | 27,148 | 453 |
| Ripley | Versailles | 26,829 | 24,616 | 446 |
| Rush | Rushville | 18,456 | 18,129 | 408 |
| Saint Joseph | South Bend | 258,083 | 247,052 | 457 |
| Scott | Scottsburg | 22,568 | 20,991 | 190 |
| Shelby | Shelbyville | 42,809 | 40,307 | 413 |
| Spencer | Rockport | 20,374 | 19,490 | 399 |
| Starke | Knox | 22,620 | 22,747 | 309 |
| Steuben | Angola | 30,060 | 27,446 | 309 |
| Sullivan | Sullivan | 19,879 | 18,993 | 447 |
| Switzerland | Vevay | 8,222 | 7,738 | 221 |
| Tippecanoe | Lafayette | 135,285 | 130,598 | 500 |
| Tipton | Tipton | 16,463 | 16,119 | 260 |
| Union | Liberty | 7,292 | 6,976 | 162 |
| Vanderburgh | Evansville | 168,065 | 165,058 | 235 |
| Vermillion | Newport | 16,841 | 16,773 | 257 |
| Vigo | Terre Haute | 106,622 | 106,107 | 403 |
| Wabash | Wabash | 34,896 | 35,069 | 413 |
| Warren | Williamsport | 8,394 | 8,176 | 365 |
| Warrick | Boonville | 49,380 | 44,920 | 384 |
| Washington | Salem | 26,088 | 23,717 | 515 |
| Wayne | Richmond | 72,802 | 71,951 | 404 |
| Wells | Bluffton | 26,506 | 25,948 | 370 |
| White | Monticello | 24,505 | 23,265 | 505 |
| Whitley | Columbia City | 29,426 | 27,651 | 336 |

## Iowa

(99 counties, 55,875 sq mi land; pop. 2,841,764)

| County | County seat or courthouse | 1995 Pop. | 1990 Pop. | Land area sq mi |
|---|---|---|---|---|
| Adair | Greenfield | 8,286 | 8,409 | 569 |
| Adams | Corning | 4,500 | 4,866 | 424 |
| Allamakee | Waukon | 14,079 | 13,855 | 640 |
| Appanoose | Centerville | 13,674 | 13,743 | 496 |
| Audubon | Audubon | 6,875 | 7,334 | 443 |
| Benton | Vinton | 24,137 | 22,429 | 717 |
| Black Hawk | Waterloo | 123,077 | 123,798 | 567 |
| Boone | Boone | 25,502 | 25,186 | 572 |
| Bremer | Waverly | 23,218 | 22,813 | 438 |
| Buchanan | Independence | 21,294 | 20,844 | 571 |
| Buena Vista | Storm Lake | 20,065 | 19,965 | 575 |
| Butler | Allison | 15,745 | 15,731 | 580 |
| Calhoun | Rockwell City | 11,430 | 11,508 | 570 |
| Carroll | Carroll | 21,603 | 21,423 | 569 |
| Cass | Atlantic | 15,047 | 15,128 | 564 |
| Cedar | Tipton | 17,682 | 17,444 | 580 |
| Cerro Gordo | Mason City | 46,633 | 46,733 | 568 |
| Cherokee | Cherokee | 13,591 | 14,098 | 577 |
| Chickasaw | New Hampton | 13,429 | 13,295 | 505 |
| Clarke | Osceola | 8,136 | 8,287 | 431 |
| Clay | Spencer | 17,412 | 17,585 | 569 |
| Clayton | Elkader | 18,833 | 19,054 | 779 |
| Clinton | Clinton | 50,889 | 51,040 | 695 |
| Crawford | Denison | 16,461 | 16,775 | 714 |
| Dallas | Adel | 32,947 | 29,755 | 587 |
| Davis | Bloomfield | 8,539 | 8,312 | 503 |
| Decatur | Leon | 8,177 | 8,338 | 532 |
| Delaware | Manchester | 18,394 | 18,035 | 578 |
| Des Moines | Burlington | 42,679 | 42,614 | 416 |
| Dickinson | Spirit Lake | 15,664 | 14,909 | 381 |
| Dubuque | Dubuque | 88,566 | 86,403 | 608 |
| Emmet | Estherville | 11,153 | 11,569 | 396 |
| Fayette | West Union | 21,799 | 21,843 | 731 |
| Floyd | Charles City | 16,603 | 17,058 | 501 |
| Franklin | Hampton | 11,106 | 11,364 | 583 |
| Fremont | Sidney | 8,097 | 8,226 | 511 |
| Greene | Jefferson | 10,080 | 10,045 | 568 |
| Grundy | Grundy Center | 12,303 | 12,029 | 503 |
| Guthrie | Guthrie Center | 11,406 | 10,935 | 591 |
| Hamilton | Webster City | 16,193 | 16,071 | 577 |
| Hancock | Garner | 12,184 | 12,638 | 571 |
| Hardin | Eldora | 18,685 | 19,094 | 569 |
| Harrison | Logan | 15,115 | 14,730 | 697 |
| Henry | Mount Pleasant | 19,826 | 19,226 | 435 |
| Howard | Cresco | 9,887 | 9,809 | 473 |
| Humboldt | Dakota City | 10,284 | 10,756 | 434 |
| Ida | Ida Grove | 8,193 | 8,365 | 432 |
| Iowa | Marengo | 15,193 | 14,630 | 587 |
| Jackson | Maquoketa | 20,120 | 19,950 | 636 |
| Jasper | Newton | 35,163 | 34,795 | 730 |
| Jefferson | Fairfield | 16,829 | 16,310 | 435 |
| Johnson | Iowa City | 101,291 | 96,119 | 615 |
| Jones | Anamosa | 20,273 | 19,444 | 575 |
| Keokuk | Sigourney | 11,564 | 11,624 | 579 |
| Kossuth | Algona | 18,147 | 18,591 | 973 |
| Lee | Fort Madison & Keokuk | 39,130 | 38,687 | 517 |
| Linn | Cedar Rapids | 178,559 | 168,767 | 718 |
| Louisa | Wapello | 11,793 | 11,592 | 402 |
| Lucas | Chariton | 9,015 | 9,070 | 431 |
| Lyon | Rock Rapids | 11,890 | 11,952 | 588 |
| Madison | Winterset | 13,490 | 12,483 | 561 |
| Mahaska | Oskaloosa | 21,927 | 21,532 | 571 |

| County | County seat or courthouse | 1995 Pop. | 1990 Pop. | Land area sq mi |
|---|---|---|---|---|
| Marion | Knoxville | 31,102 | 30,001 | 554 |
| Marshall | Marshalltown | 38,627 | 38,276 | 572 |
| Mills | Glenwood | 13,802 | 13,202 | 437 |
| Mitchell | Osage | 11,129 | 10,928 | 469 |
| Monona | Onawa | 9,968 | 10,034 | 693 |
| Monroe | Albia | 8,177 | 8,114 | 433 |
| Montgomery | Red Oak | 11,939 | 12,076 | 424 |
| Muscatine | Muscatine | 41,435 | 39,907 | 439 |
| O'Brien | Primghar | 15,349 | 15,444 | 573 |
| Osceola | Sibley | 7,077 | 7,267 | 399 |
| Page | Clarinda | 16,676 | 16,870 | 535 |
| Palo Alto | Emmetsburg | 10,200 | 10,669 | 564 |
| Plymouth | Le Mars | 24,220 | 23,388 | 864 |
| Pocahontas | Pocahontas | 9,119 | 9,525 | 578 |
| Polk | Des Moines | 349,560 | 327,140 | 570 |
| Pottawattamie | Council Bluffs | 83,701 | 82,628 | 954 |
| Poweshiek | Montezuma | 19,014 | 19,033 | 585 |
| Ringgold | Mount Ayr | 5,373 | 5,420 | 538 |
| Sac | Sac City | 12,087 | 12,324 | 576 |
| Scott | Davenport | 156,694 | 150,973 | 458 |
| Shelby | Harlan | 13,089 | 13,230 | 591 |
| Sioux | Orange City | 31,398 | 29,903 | 768 |
| Story | Nevada | 74,638 | 74,252 | 573 |
| Tama | Toledo | 17,878 | 17,419 | 721 |
| Taylor | Bedford | 7,152 | 7,114 | 534 |
| Union | Creston | 12,416 | 12,750 | 424 |
| Van Buren | Keosauqua | 7,767 | 7,676 | 485 |
| Wapello | Ottumwa | 35,770 | 35,696 | 432 |
| Warren | Indianola | 38,940 | 36,033 | 572 |
| Washington | Washington | 20,508 | 19,612 | 569 |
| Wayne | Corydon | 6,866 | 7,067 | 526 |
| Webster | Fort Dodge | 39,206 | 40,342 | 715 |
| Winnebago | Forest City | 11,900 | 12,122 | 401 |
| Winneshiek | Decorah | 21,058 | 20,847 | 690 |
| Woodbury | Sioux City | 101,827 | 98,276 | 873 |
| Worth | Northwood | 7,926 | 7,991 | 400 |
| Wright | Clarion | 14,314 | 14,269 | 581 |

## Kansas

(105 counties, 81,823 sq mi land; pop. 2,565,328)

| County | County seat or courthouse | 1995 Pop. | 1990 Pop. | Land area sq mi |
|---|---|---|---|---|
| Allen | Iola | 14,739 | 14,638 | 503 |
| Anderson | Garnett | 8,000 | 7,803 | 583 |
| Atchison | Atchison | 16,258 | 16,932 | 432 |
| Barber | Medicine Lodge | 5,603 | 5,874 | 1,134 |
| Barton | Great Bend | 28,614 | 29,382 | 894 |
| Bourbon | Fort Scott | 15,013 | 14,966 | 637 |
| Brown | Hiawatha | 11,075 | 11,128 | 571 |
| Butler | El Dorado | 57,746 | 50,580 | 1,428 |
| Chase | Cottonwood Falls | 2,885 | 3,021 | 776 |
| Chautauqua | Sedan | 4,439 | 4,407 | 642 |
| Cherokee | Columbus | 22,437 | 21,374 | 587 |
| Cheyenne | Saint Francis | 3,230 | 3,243 | 1,020 |
| Clark | Ashland | 2,379 | 2,418 | 975 |
| Clay | Clay Center | 9,317 | 9,158 | 644 |
| Cloud | Concordia | 10,488 | 11,023 | 716 |
| Coffey | Burlington | 8,691 | 8,404 | 630 |
| Comanche | Coldwater | 2,099 | 2,313 | 788 |
| Cowley | Winfield | 37,107 | 36,915 | 1,126 |
| Crawford | Girard | 36,488 | 35,582 | 593 |
| Decatur | Oberlin | 3,547 | 4,021 | 894 |
| Dickinson | Abilene | 19,911 | 18,958 | 848 |
| Doniphan | Troy | 7,608 | 8,134 | 392 |
| Douglas | Lawrence | 88,206 | 81,798 | 457 |
| Edwards | Kinsley | 3,564 | 3,787 | 622 |
| Elk | Howard | 3,356 | 3,327 | 648 |
| Ellis | Hays | 26,145 | 26,004 | 900 |
| Ellsworth | Ellsworth | 6,445 | 6,586 | 716 |
| Finney | Garden City | 34,913 | 33,070 | 1,300 |
| Ford | Dodge City | 28,909 | 27,463 | 1,099 |
| Franklin | Ottawa | 23,164 | 21,994 | 574 |
| Geary | Junction City | 29,638 | 30,453 | 384 |
| Gove | Gove | 3,091 | 3,231 | 1,072 |
| Graham | Hill City | 3,336 | 3,543 | 898 |
| Grant | Ulysses | 7,837 | 7,159 | 575 |
| Gray | Cimarron | 5,367 | 5,396 | 869 |
| Greeley | Tribune | 1,834 | 1,774 | 778 |
| Greenwood | Eureka | 8,032 | 7,847 | 1,140 |
| Hamilton | Syracuse | 2,343 | 2,388 | 997 |
| Harper | Anthony | 6,651 | 7,124 | 802 |
| Harvey | Newton | 31,145 | 31,028 | 539 |
| Haskell | Sublette | 4,027 | 3,886 | 577 |
| Hodgeman | Jetmore | 2,268 | 2,177 | 860 |
| Jackson | Holton | 11,809 | 11,525 | 657 |
| Jefferson | Oskaloosa | 17,133 | 15,905 | 536 |
| Jewell | Mankato | 3,952 | 4,251 | 909 |
| Johnson | Olathe | 401,054 | 355,021 | 477 |
| Kearny | Lakin | 4,182 | 4,027 | 870 |
| Kingman | Kingman | 8,566 | 8,292 | 864 |
| Kiowa | Greensburg | 3,605 | 3,660 | 722 |
| Labette | Oswego | 22,862 | 23,693 | 649 |
| Lane | Dighton | 2,275 | 2,375 | 717 |
| Leavenworth | Leavenworth | 69,323 | 64,371 | 463 |
| Lincoln | Lincoln | 3,431 | 3,653 | 719 |

| County | County seat or courthouse | 1995 Pop. | 1990 Pop. | Land area sq mi |
|---|---|---|---|---|
| Linn | Mound City | 8,698 | 8,254 | 599 |
| Logan | Oakley | 3,178 | 3,081 | 1,073 |
| Lyon | Emporia | 34,650 | 34,732 | 851 |
| McPherson | McPherson | 27,267 | 27,268 | 900 |
| Marion | Marion | 12,961 | 12,888 | 943 |
| Marshall | Marysville | 11,261 | 11,705 | 903 |
| Meade | Meade | 4,355 | 4,247 | 979 |
| Miami | Paola | 25,187 | 23,466 | 577 |
| Mitchell | Beloit | 7,092 | 7,203 | 700 |
| Montgomery | Independence | 37,694 | 38,816 | 645 |
| Morris | Council Grove | 6,327 | 6,198 | 697 |
| Morton | Elkhart | 3,303 | 3,480 | 730 |
| Nemaha | Seneca | 10,443 | 10,446 | 719 |
| Neosho | Erie | 16,994 | 17,035 | 572 |
| Ness | Ness City | 3,752 | 4,033 | 1,075 |
| Norton | Norton | 5,735 | 5,947 | 878 |
| Osage | Lyndon | 16,729 | 15,248 | 704 |
| Osborne | Osborne | 4,696 | 4,867 | 893 |
| Ottawa | Minneapolis | 5,749 | 5,634 | 721 |
| Pawnee | Larned | 7,615 | 7,555 | 754 |
| Phillips | Phillipsburg | 6,270 | 6,590 | 886 |
| Pottawatomie | Westmoreland | 17,548 | 16,128 | 844 |
| Pratt | Pratt | 9,696 | 9,702 | 735 |
| Rawlins | Atwood | 3,234 | 3,404 | 1,070 |
| Reno | Hutchinson | 63,263 | 62,389 | 1,255 |
| Republic | Belleville | 6,215 | 6,482 | 717 |
| Rice | Lyons | 10,086 | 10,610 | 727 |
| Riley | Manhattan | 69,784 | 67,139 | 610 |
| Rooks | Stockton | 5,884 | 6,039 | 888 |
| Rush | LaCrosse | 3,541 | 3,842 | 718 |
| Russell | Russell | 7,701 | 7,835 | 885 |
| Saline | Salina | 51,831 | 49,301 | 720 |
| Scott | Scott City | 5,074 | 5,289 | 718 |
| Sedgwick | Wichita | 419,333 | 403,662 | 1,000 |
| Seward | Liberal | 19,370 | 18,743 | 640 |
| Shawnee | Topeka | 165,062 | 160,976 | 550 |
| Sheridan | Hoxie | 2,824 | 3,043 | 896 |
| Sherman | Goodland | 6,706 | 6,926 | 1,056 |
| Smith | Smith Center | 4,782 | 5,078 | 896 |
| Stafford | Saint John | 5,193 | 5,365 | 792 |
| Stanton | Johnson | 2,331 | 2,333 | 680 |
| Stevens | Hugoton | 5,257 | 5,048 | 728 |
| Sumner | Wellington | 26,519 | 25,841 | 1,182 |
| Thomas | Colby | 8,331 | 8,258 | 1,075 |
| Trego | WaKeeney | 3,449 | 3,694 | 888 |
| Wabaunsee | Alma | 6,603 | 6,603 | 798 |
| Wallace | Sharon Springs | 1,798 | 1,821 | 914 |
| Washington | Washington | 6,833 | 7,073 | 899 |
| Wichita | Leoti | 2,841 | 2,758 | 719 |
| Wilson | Fredonia | 10,321 | 10,289 | 574 |
| Woodson | Yates Center | 3,999 | 4,116 | 501 |
| Wyandotte | Kansas City | 153,826 | 162,026 | 151 |

## Kentucky

(120 counties, 39,732 sq mi land; pop. 3,860,219)

| County | County seat or courthouse | 1995 Pop. | 1990 Pop. | Land area sq mi |
|---|---|---|---|---|
| Adair | Columbia | 16,292 | 15,360 | 407 |
| Allen | Scottsville | 15,706 | 14,628 | 346 |
| Anderson | Lawrenceburg | 17,152 | 14,571 | 203 |
| Ballard | Wickliffe | 8,232 | 7,902 | 251 |
| Barren | Glasgow | 35,768 | 34,001 | 491 |
| Bath | Owingsville | 10,159 | 9,692 | 279 |
| Bell | Pineville | 30,490 | 31,506 | 361 |
| Boone | Burlington | 70,097 | 57,589 | 246 |
| Bourbon | Paris | 19,257 | 19,236 | 291 |
| Boyd | Catlettsburg | 50,613 | 51,150 | 160 |
| Boyle | Danville | 26,699 | 25,641 | 182 |
| Bracken | Brooksville | 8,209 | 7,766 | 203 |
| Breathitt | Jackson | 15,539 | 15,703 | 495 |
| Breckinridge | Hardinsburg | 16,722 | 16,312 | 572 |
| Bullitt | Shepherdsville | 56,127 | 47,567 | 299 |
| Butler | Morgantown | 11,634 | 11,245 | 428 |
| Caldwell | Princeton | 13,207 | 13,232 | 347 |
| Calloway | Murray | 32,506 | 30,735 | 386 |
| Campbell | Newport | 87,111 | 83,866 | 152 |
| Carlisle | Bardwell | 5,443 | 5,238 | 193 |
| Carroll | Carrollton | 9,668 | 9,292 | 130 |
| Carter | Grayson | 26,172 | 24,340 | 411 |
| Casey | Liberty | 14,508 | 14,211 | 446 |
| Christian | Hopkinsville | 65,666 | 68,941 | 721 |
| Clark | Winchester | 30,822 | 29,496 | 254 |
| Clay | Manchester | 22,835 | 21,746 | 471 |
| Clinton | Albany | 9,309 | 9,135 | 198 |
| Crittenden | Marion | 9,470 | 9,196 | 362 |
| Cumberland | Burkesville | 6,957 | 6,784 | 306 |
| Daviess | Owensboro | 90,662 | 87,189 | 462 |
| Edmonson | Brownsville | 10,758 | 10,357 | 303 |
| Elliott | Sandy Hook | 6,543 | 6,455 | 234 |
| Estill | Irvine | 15,646 | 14,614 | 254 |
| Fayette | Lexington | 238,885 | 225,366 | 285 |
| Fleming | Flemingsburg | 13,054 | 12,292 | 351 |
| Floyd | Prestonsburg | 44,100 | 43,586 | 394 |
| Franklin | Frankfort | 46,136 | 44,143 | 211 |

| County | County seat or courthouse | 1995 Pop. | 1990 Pop. | Land area sq mi |
|---|---|---|---|---|
| Fulton | Hickman | 7,317 | 8,271 | 209 |
| Gallatin | Warsaw | 6,175 | 5,393 | 99 |
| Garrard | Lancaster | 12,994 | 11,579 | 231 |
| Grant | Williamstown | 18,763 | 15,737 | 260 |
| Graves | Mayfield | 35,139 | 33,550 | 556 |
| Grayson | Leitchfield | 22,744 | 21,050 | 504 |
| Green | Greensburg | 10,416 | 10,371 | 289 |
| Greenup | Greenup | 36,992 | 36,742 | 346 |
| Hancock | Hawesville | 8,483 | 7,864 | 189 |
| Hardin | Elizabethtown | 90,345 | 89,240 | 628 |
| Harlan | Harlan | 36,237 | 36,574 | 467 |
| Harrison | Cynthiana | 16,978 | 16,248 | 310 |
| Hart | Munfordville | 16,209 | 14,890 | 416 |
| Henderson | Henderson | 44,431 | 43,044 | 440 |
| Henry | New Castle | 14,208 | 12,823 | 289 |
| Hickman | Clinton | 5,346 | 5,566 | 245 |
| Hopkins | Madisonville | 46,640 | 46,126 | 551 |
| Jackson | McKee | 12,702 | 11,955 | 346 |
| Jefferson | Louisville | 672,918 | 665,123 | 385 |
| Jessamine | Nicholasville | 34,218 | 30,508 | 173 |
| Johnson | Paintsville | 24,063 | 23,248 | 262 |
| Kenton | Covington | 145,474 | 142,031 | 163 |
| Knott | Hindman | 18,414 | 17,906 | 352 |
| Knox | Barbourville | 31,371 | 29,676 | 388 |
| Larue | Hodgenville | 12,641 | 11,679 | 263 |
| Laurel | London | 48,076 | 43,438 | 436 |
| Lawrence | Louisa | 15,339 | 13,998 | 419 |
| Lee | Beattyville | 7,858 | 7,422 | 210 |
| Leslie | Hyden | 13,616 | 13,642 | 404 |
| Letcher | Whitesburg | 26,957 | 27,000 | 339 |
| Lewis | Vanceburg | 13,365 | 13,029 | 485 |
| Lincoln | Stanford | 21,485 | 20,045 | 337 |
| Livingston | Smithland | 9,365 | 9,062 | 316 |
| Logan | Russellville | 25,774 | 24,416 | 556 |
| Lyon | Eddyville | 7,752 | 6,624 | 216 |
| McCracken | Paducah | 64,577 | 62,879 | 251 |
| McCreary | Whitley City | 16,612 | 15,603 | 428 |
| McLean | Calhoun | 9,705 | 9,628 | 254 |
| Madison | Richmond | 63,112 | 57,508 | 441 |
| Magoffin | Salyersville | 13,743 | 13,077 | 310 |
| Marion | Lebanon | 16,755 | 16,499 | 347 |
| Marshall | Benton | 29,329 | 27,205 | 305 |
| Martin | Inez | 12,897 | 12,526 | 231 |
| Mason | Maysville | 17,214 | 16,666 | 241 |
| Meade | Brandenburg | 27,371 | 24,170 | 309 |
| Menifee | Frenchburg | 5,387 | 5,092 | 204 |
| Mercer | Harrodsburg | 20,045 | 19,148 | 251 |
| Metcalfe | Edmonton | 9,318 | 8,963 | 291 |
| Monroe | Tompkinsville | 11,677 | 11,401 | 331 |
| Montgomery | Mount Sterling | 20,582 | 19,561 | 199 |
| Morgan | West Liberty | 13,344 | 11,648 | 381 |
| Muhlenberg | Greenville | 31,709 | 31,318 | 475 |
| Nelson | Bardstown | 33,422 | 29,710 | 423 |
| Nicholas | Carlisle | 6,999 | 6,725 | 197 |
| Ohio | Hartford | 21,555 | 21,105 | 594 |
| Oldham | La Grange | 41,011 | 33,263 | 189 |
| Owen | Owenton | 9,589 | 9,035 | 352 |
| Owsley | Booneville | 5,384 | 5,036 | 198 |
| Pendleton | Falmouth | 13,461 | 12,036 | 280 |
| Perry | Hazard | 31,286 | 30,283 | 342 |
| Pike | Pikeville | 73,710 | 72,583 | 788 |
| Powell | Stanton | 12,211 | 11,686 | 180 |
| Pulaski | Somerset | 54,570 | 49,489 | 662 |
| Robertson | Mount Olivet | 2,226 | 2,124 | 100 |
| Rockcastle | Mount Vernon | 15,417 | 14,803 | 318 |
| Rowan | Morehead | 21,541 | 20,353 | 281 |
| Russell | Jamestown | 15,856 | 14,716 | 254 |
| Scott | Georgetown | 27,813 | 23,867 | 285 |
| Shelby | Shelbyville | 27,696 | 24,824 | 384 |
| Simpson | Franklin | 16,084 | 15,145 | 236 |
| Spencer | Taylorsville | 8,178 | 6,801 | 186 |
| Taylor | Campbellsville | 22,677 | 21,146 | 270 |
| Todd | Elkton | 11,182 | 10,940 | 376 |
| Trigg | Cadiz | 11,497 | 10,361 | 443 |
| Trimble | Bedford | 6,912 | 6,090 | 149 |
| Union | Morganfield | 16,499 | 16,557 | 345 |
| Warren | Bowling Green | 84,448 | 77,720 | 545 |
| Washington | Springfield | 10,704 | 10,441 | 301 |
| Wayne | Monticello | 18,411 | 17,468 | 459 |
| Webster | Dixon | 13,469 | 13,955 | 335 |
| Whitley | Williamsburg | 35,216 | 33,326 | 440 |
| Wolfe | Campton | 7,230 | 6,503 | 223 |
| Woodford | Versailles | 21,629 | 19,955 | 191 |

# Louisiana

(64 parishes, 43,566 sq mi land; pop. 4,342,334)

| Parish | Parish seat or courthouse | 1995 Pop. | 1990 Pop. | Land area sq mi |
|---|---|---|---|---|
| Acadia | Crowley | 57,380 | 55,882 | 655 |
| Allen | Oberlin | 23,615 | 21,226 | 765 |
| Ascension | Donaldsonville | 65,847 | 58,214 | 292 |
| Assumption | Napoleonville | 22,859 | 22,753 | 339 |
| Avoyelles | Marksville | 40,115 | 39,159 | 833 |
| Beauregard | De Ridder | 31,788 | 30,083 | 1,160 |
| Bienville | Arcadia | 15,812 | 15,979 | 811 |
| Bossier | Benton | 90,886 | 86,088 | 839 |
| Caddo | Shreveport | 246,697 | 248,253 | 882 |
| Calcasieu | Lake Charles | 175,868 | 168,134 | 1,071 |
| Caldwell | Columbia | 10,198 | 9,806 | 530 |
| Cameron | Cameron | 8,801 | 9,260 | 1,313 |
| Catahoula | Harrisonburg | 11,175 | 11,065 | 704 |
| Claiborne | Homer | 17,261 | 17,405 | 755 |
| Concordia | Vidalia | 21,055 | 20,828 | 696 |
| De Soto | Mansfield | 25,174 | 25,346 | 877 |
| East Baton Rouge | Baton Rouge | 397,364 | 380,105 | 456 |
| East Carroll | Lake Providence | 9,506 | 9,709 | 422 |
| East Feliciana | Clinton | 20,554 | 19,211 | 453 |
| Evangeline | Ville Platte | 33,843 | 33,274 | 664 |
| Franklin | Winnsboro | 22,270 | 22,387 | 623 |
| Grant | Colfax | 18,270 | 17,526 | 645 |
| Iberia | New Iberia | 71,291 | 68,297 | 575 |
| Iberville | Plaquemine | 31,073 | 31,049 | 619 |
| Jackson | Jonesboro | 15,722 | 15,705 | 570 |
| Jefferson | Gretna | 457,333 | 448,306 | 306 |
| Jefferson Davis | Jennings | 31,725 | 30,722 | 652 |
| Lafayette | Lafayette | 179,689 | 164,762 | 270 |
| Lafourche | Thibodaux | 87,577 | 85,860 | 1,085 |
| La Salle | Jena | 13,894 | 13,662 | 624 |
| Lincoln | Ruston | 43,140 | 41,745 | 471 |
| Livingston | Livingston | 80,572 | 70,523 | 648 |
| Madison | Tallulah | 12,688 | 12,463 | 624 |
| Morehouse | Bastrop | 32,052 | 31,938 | 794 |
| Natchitoches | Natchitoches | 37,861 | 36,689 | 1,256 |
| Orleans | New Orleans | 481,913 | 496,938 | 181 |
| Ouachita | Monroe | 146,826 | 142,191 | 611 |
| Plaquemines | Pointe a la Hache | 25,693 | 25,575 | 845 |
| Pointe Coupee | New Roads | 23,265 | 22,540 | 557 |
| Rapides | Alexandria | 127,167 | 131,556 | 1,323 |
| Red River | Coushatta | 9,430 | 9,387 | 389 |
| Richland | Rayville | 20,763 | 20,629 | 559 |
| Sabine | Many | 23,659 | 22,646 | 865 |
| Saint Bernard | Chalmette | 67,297 | 66,631 | 465 |
| Saint Charles | Hahnville | 46,515 | 42,437 | 284 |
| Saint Helena | Greensburg | 9,817 | 9,874 | 408 |
| Saint James | Convent | 21,038 | 20,879 | 246 |
| Saint John the Baptist | Edgard | 42,092 | 39,996 | 219 |
| Saint Landry | Opelousas | 82,791 | 80,312 | 929 |
| Saint Martin | Saint Martinville | 45,997 | 44,097 | 740 |
| Saint Mary | Franklin | 57,443 | 58,086 | 613 |
| Saint Tammany | Covington | 173,413 | 144,500 | 854 |
| Tangipahoa | Amite | 93,229 | 85,709 | 790 |
| Tensas | Saint Joseph | 6,899 | 7,103 | 603 |
| Terrebonne | Houma | 101,180 | 96,982 | 1,255 |
| Union | Farmerville | 21,541 | 20,796 | 878 |
| Vermilion | Abbeville | 50,746 | 50,055 | 1,174 |
| Vernon | Leesville | 55,260 | 61,961 | 1,329 |
| Washington | Franklinton | 43,154 | 43,185 | 670 |
| Webster | Minden | 42,195 | 41,989 | 596 |
| West Baton Rouge | Port Allen | 20,211 | 19,419 | 191 |
| West Carroll | Oak Grove | 12,138 | 12,093 | 359 |
| West Feliciana | Saint Francisville | 12,679 | 12,915 | 406 |
| Winn | Winnfield | 17,028 | 16,269 | 951 |

# Maine

(16 counties, 30,865 sq mi land; pop. 1,241,382)

| County | County seat or courthouse | 1995 Pop. | 1990 Pop. | Land area sq mi |
|---|---|---|---|---|
| Androscoggin | Auburn | 103,751 | 105,259 | 470 |
| Aroostook | Houlton | 78,633 | 86,936 | 6,672 |
| Cumberland | Portland | 248,526 | 243,135 | 836 |
| Franklin | Farmington | 29,511 | 29,008 | 1,698 |
| Hancock | Ellsworth | 49,272 | 46,948 | 1,589 |
| Kennebec | Augusta | 117,000 | 115,904 | 868 |
| Knox | Rockland | 37,372 | 36,310 | 366 |
| Lincoln | Wiscasset | 31,334 | 30,357 | 456 |
| Oxford | South Paris | 53,440 | 52,602 | 2,078 |
| Penobscot | Bangor | 145,905 | 146,601 | 3,396 |
| Piscataquis | Dover-Foxcroft | 18,486 | 18,653 | 3,967 |
| Sagadahoc | Bath | 33,959 | 33,535 | 254 |
| Somerset | Skowhegan | 51,346 | 49,767 | 3,927 |
| Waldo | Belfast | 35,707 | 33,018 | 730 |
| Washington | Machias | 36,156 | 35,308 | 2,569 |
| York | Alfred | 170,984 | 164,587 | 991 |

# Maryland

(23 counties, 1 ind. city, 9,775 sq mi land; pop. 5,042,438)

| County | County seat or courthouse | 1995 Pop. | 1990 Pop. | Land area sq mi |
|---|---|---|---|---|
| Allegany | Cumberland | 73,954 | 74,946 | 425 |
| Anne Arundel | Annapolis | 461,807 | 427,239 | 416 |
| Baltimore | Towson | 715,360 | 692,134 | 599 |
| Calvert | Prince Frederick | 64,598 | 51,372 | 215 |
| Caroline | Denton | 29,072 | 27,035 | 320 |
| Carroll | Westminster | 140,203 | 123,372 | 449 |

| County | County seat or courthouse | 1995 Pop. | 1990 Pop. | Land area sq mi |
|---|---|---|---|---|
| Cecil | Elkton | 78,174 | 71,347 | 348 |
| Charles | La Plata | 111,633 | 101,154 | 461 |
| Dorchester | Cambridge | 30,170 | 30,236 | 558 |
| Frederick | Frederick | 175,399 | 150,208 | 663 |
| Garrett | Oakland | 29,461 | 28,138 | 648 |
| Harford | Bel Air | 205,367 | 182,132 | 440 |
| Howard | Ellicott City | 219,125 | 187,328 | 252 |
| Kent | Chestertown | 18,736 | 17,842 | 279 |
| Montgomery | Rockville | 809,569 | 757,027 | 495 |
| Prince George's | Upper Marlboro | 767,413 | 728,553 | 486 |
| Queen Anne's | Centreville | 36,992 | 33,953 | 372 |
| Saint Mary's | Leonardtown | 81,037 | 75,974 | 361 |
| Somerset | Princess Anne | 24,431 | 23,440 | 327 |
| Talbot | Easton | 32,405 | 30,549 | 269 |
| Washington | Hagerstown | 127,199 | 121,393 | 458 |
| Wicomico | Salisbury | 79,256 | 74,339 | 377 |
| Worcester | Snow Hill | 39,946 | 35,028 | 473 |
| Independent City | | | | |
| Baltimore | | 691,131 | 736,014 | 81 |

# Massachusetts

(14 counties, 7,838 sq mi land; pop. 6,073,550)

| County | County seat or courthouse | 1995 Pop. | 1990 Pop. | Land area sq mi |
|---|---|---|---|---|
| Barnstable | Barnstable | 199,804 | 186,605 | 396 |
| Berkshire | Pittsfield | 135,743 | 139,352 | 931 |
| Bristol | Taunton | 512,637 | 506,325 | 556 |
| Dukes | Edgartown | 12,808 | 11,639 | 104 |
| Essex | Salem | 683,723 | 670,080 | 498 |
| Franklin | Greenfield | 70,903 | 70,092 | 702 |
| Hampden | Springfield | 443,463 | 456,310 | 619 |
| Hampshire | Northampton | 149,124 | 146,568 | 529 |
| Middlesex | East Cambridge | 1,408,450 | 1,398,468 | 824 |
| Nantucket | Nantucket | 7,153 | 6,012 | 48 |
| Norfolk | Dedham | 635,578 | 616,087 | 400 |
| Plymouth | Plymouth | 454,151 | 435,276 | 661 |
| Suffolk | Boston | 641,155 | 663,906 | 59 |
| Worcester | Worcester | 718,858 | 709,705 | 1,513 |

# Michigan

(83 counties, 56,809 sq mi land; pop. 9,549,353)

| County | County seat or courthouse | 1995 Pop. | 1990 Pop. | Land area sq mi |
|---|---|---|---|---|
| Alcona | Harrisville | 10,587 | 10,145 | 675 |
| Alger | Munising | 9,846 | 8,972 | 918 |
| Allegan | Allegan | 97,692 | 90,509 | 828 |
| Alpena | Alpena | 30,841 | 30,605 | 574 |
| Antrim | Bellaire | 20,257 | 18,185 | 477 |
| Arenac | Standish | 16,151 | 14,906 | 367 |
| Baraga | L'Anse | 8,493 | 7,954 | 904 |
| Barry | Hastings | 52,643 | 50,057 | 556 |
| Bay | Bay City | 111,529 | 111,723 | 444 |
| Benzie | Beulah | 13,660 | 12,200 | 321 |
| Berrien | Saint Joseph | 162,623 | 161,378 | 571 |
| Branch | Coldwater | 42,738 | 41,502 | 507 |
| Calhoun | Marshall | 140,689 | 135,982 | 709 |
| Cass | Cassopolis | 49,603 | 49,477 | 492 |
| Charlevoix | Charlevoix | 23,052 | 21,468 | 417 |
| Cheboygan | Cheboygan | 22,854 | 21,398 | 716 |
| Chippewa | Sault Sainte Marie | 36,859 | 34,604 | 1,561 |
| Clare | Harrison | 28,078 | 24,952 | 567 |
| Clinton | Saint Johns | 61,657 | 57,893 | 572 |
| Crawford | Grayling | 13,523 | 12,260 | 558 |
| Delta | Escanaba | 38,655 | 37,780 | 1,170 |
| Dickinson | Iron Mountain | 27,176 | 26,831 | 766 |
| Eaton | Charlotte | 98,087 | 92,879 | 577 |
| Emmet | Petoskey | 27,352 | 25,040 | 468 |
| Genesee | Flint | 436,381 | 430,459 | 640 |
| Gladwin | Gladwin | 24,304 | 21,896 | 507 |
| Gogebic | Bessemer | 17,894 | 18,052 | 1,102 |
| Grand Traverse | Traverse City | 70,869 | 64,273 | 465 |
| Gratiot | Ithaca | 39,973 | 38,982 | 570 |
| Hillsdale | Hillsdale | 45,224 | 43,431 | 599 |
| Houghton | Houghton | 36,140 | 35,446 | 1,012 |
| Huron | Bad Axe | 35,224 | 34,951 | 837 |
| Ingham | Mason | 277,889 | 281,912 | 559 |
| Ionia | Ionia | 59,846 | 57,024 | 573 |
| Iosco | Tawas City | 24,482 | 30,209 | 549 |
| Iron | Crystal Falls | 13,177 | 13,175 | 1,167 |
| Isabella | Mount Pleasant | 56,213 | 54,624 | 574 |
| Jackson | Jackson | 154,010 | 149,756 | 707 |
| Kalamazoo | Kalamazoo | 227,973 | 223,411 | 562 |
| Kalkaska | Kalkaska | 14,696 | 13,497 | 561 |
| Kent | Grand Rapids | 525,355 | 500,631 | 856 |
| Keweenaw | Eagle River | 1,967 | 1,701 | 541 |
| Lake | Baldwin | 9,664 | 8,583 | 568 |
| Lapeer | Lapeer | 83,854 | 74,768 | 654 |
| Leelanau | Leland | 18,502 | 16,527 | 349 |
| Lenawee | Adrian | 96,706 | 91,476 | 751 |
| Livingston | Howell | 133,601 | 115,645 | 568 |
| Luce | Newberry | 5,599 | 5,763 | 903 |
| Mackinac | Saint Ignace | 10,978 | 10,674 | 1,022 |
| Macomb | Mount Clemens | 733,607 | 717,400 | 480 |
| Manistee | Manistee | 22,915 | 21,265 | 544 |
| Marquette | Marquette | 65,442 | 70,887 | 1,821 |
| Mason | Ludington | 27,487 | 25,537 | 495 |
| Mecosta | Big Rapids | 37,725 | 37,308 | 556 |
| Menominee | Menominee | 24,569 | 24,920 | 1,044 |
| Midland | Midland | 79,748 | 75,651 | 521 |
| Missaukee | Lake City | 13,522 | 12,147 | 567 |
| Monroe | Monroe | 139,550 | 133,600 | 551 |
| Montcalm | Stanton | 57,866 | 53,059 | 708 |
| Montmorency | Atlanta | 9,683 | 8,936 | 548 |
| Muskegon | Muskegon | 164,459 | 158,983 | 509 |
| Newaygo | White Cloud | 43,587 | 38,206 | 842 |
| Oakland | Pontiac | 1,153,461 | 1,083,592 | 873 |
| Oceana | Hart | 23,875 | 22,455 | 541 |
| Ogemaw | West Branch | 20,559 | 18,681 | 564 |
| Ontonagon | Ontonagon | 8,639 | 8,854 | 1,312 |
| Osceola | Reed City | 21,756 | 20,146 | 566 |
| Oscoda | Mio | 8,682 | 7,842 | 565 |
| Otsego | Gaylord | 20,762 | 17,957 | 515 |
| Ottawa | Grand Haven | 210,389 | 187,768 | 566 |
| Presque Isle | Rogers City | 14,242 | 13,743 | 660 |
| Roscommon | Roscommon | 22,593 | 19,776 | 521 |
| Saginaw | Saginaw | 212,295 | 211,946 | 809 |
| Saint Clair | Port Huron | 154,231 | 145,607 | 725 |
| Saint Joseph | Centreville | 60,684 | 58,913 | 504 |
| Sanilac | Sandusky | 42,203 | 39,928 | 964 |
| Schoolcraft | Manistique | 8,700 | 8,302 | 1,178 |
| Shiawassee | Corunna | 72,079 | 69,770 | 539 |
| Tuscola | Caro | 57,491 | 55,498 | 813 |
| Van Buren | Paw Paw | 74,591 | 70,060 | 611 |
| Washtenaw | Ann Arbor | 292,609 | 282,937 | 710 |
| Wayne | Detroit | 2,055,500 | 2,111,687 | 614 |
| Wexford | Cadillac | 28,686 | 26,360 | 566 |

# Minnesota

(87 counties, 79,617 sq mi land; pop. 4,609,548)

| County | County seat or courthouse | 1995 Pop. | 1990 Pop. | Land area sq mi |
|---|---|---|---|---|
| Aitkin | Aitkin | 13,444 | 12,425 | 1,819 |
| Anoka | Anoka | 275,760 | 243,641 | 424 |
| Becker | Detroit Lakes | 29,119 | 27,881 | 1,311 |
| Beltrami | Bemidji | 37,932 | 34,384 | 2,505 |
| Benton | Foley | 32,950 | 30,185 | 408 |
| Big Stone | Ortonville | 5,898 | 6,285 | 497 |
| Blue Earth | Mankato | 54,134 | 54,044 | 752 |
| Brown | New Ulm | 27,128 | 26,984 | 611 |
| Carlton | Carlton | 30,421 | 29,259 | 860 |
| Carver | Chaska | 59,220 | 47,915 | 357 |
| Cass | Walker | 24,738 | 21,791 | 2,018 |
| Chippewa | Montevideo | 13,114 | 13,228 | 583 |
| Chisago | Center City | 37,024 | 30,521 | 418 |
| Clay | Moorhead | 52,178 | 50,422 | 1,045 |
| Clearwater | Bagley | 8,366 | 8,309 | 995 |
| Cook | Grand Marais | 4,479 | 3,868 | 1,451 |
| Cottonwood | Windom | 12,371 | 12,694 | 640 |
| Crow Wing | Brainerd | 49,779 | 44,249 | 997 |
| Dakota | Hastings | 316,466 | 275,189 | 570 |
| Dodge | Mantorville | 16,701 | 15,731 | 440 |
| Douglas | Alexandria | 30,397 | 28,674 | 634 |
| Faribault | Blue Earth | 16,434 | 16,937 | 714 |
| Fillmore | Preston | 20,751 | 20,777 | 861 |
| Freeborn | Albert Lea | 31,934 | 33,060 | 708 |
| Goodhue | Red Wing | 42,297 | 40,690 | 759 |
| Grant | Elbow Lake | 6,221 | 6,246 | 547 |
| Hennepin | Minneapolis | 1,053,467 | 1,032,431 | 557 |
| Houston | Caledonia | 19,296 | 18,497 | 558 |
| Hubbard | Park Rapids | 16,116 | 14,939 | 923 |
| Isanti | Cambridge | 28,286 | 25,921 | 439 |
| Itasca | Grand Rapids | 43,047 | 40,863 | 2,665 |
| Jackson | Jackson | 11,777 | 11,677 | 702 |
| Kanabec | Mora | 13,580 | 12,802 | 525 |
| Kandiyohi | Willmar | 40,793 | 38,761 | 796 |
| Kittson | Hallock | 5,459 | 5,767 | 1,097 |
| Koochiching | International Falls | 15,983 | 16,299 | 3,102 |
| Lac qui Parle | Madison | 8,398 | 8,924 | 765 |
| Lake | Two Harbors | 10,570 | 10,415 | 2,099 |
| Lake of the Woods | Baudette | 4,491 | 4,076 | 1,297 |
| Le Sueur | Le Center | 24,361 | 23,239 | 449 |
| Lincoln | Ivanhoe | 6,697 | 6,890 | 537 |
| Lyon | Marshall | 24,995 | 24,789 | 714 |
| McLeod | Glencoe | 33,254 | 32,030 | 492 |
| Mahnomen | Mahnomen | 5,145 | 5,044 | 556 |
| Marshall | Warren | 10,596 | 10,993 | 1,772 |
| Martin | Fairmont | 22,493 | 22,914 | 709 |
| Meeker | Litchfield | 21,293 | 20,846 | 609 |
| Mille Lacs | Milaca | 20,083 | 18,670 | 575 |
| Morrison | Little Falls | 30,178 | 29,604 | 1,125 |
| Mower | Austin | 37,312 | 37,385 | 712 |
| Murray | Slayton | 9,511 | 9,660 | 705 |
| Nicollet | Saint Peter | 29,722 | 28,076 | 452 |
| Nobles | Worthington | 20,166 | 20,098 | 716 |
| Norman | Ada | 7,724 | 7,975 | 876 |
| Olmsted | Rochester | 112,619 | 106,470 | 653 |
| Otter Tail | Fergus Falls | 53,207 | 50,714 | 1,980 |

| County | County seat or courthouse | 1995 Pop. | 1990 Pop. | Land area sq mi |
|---|---|---|---|---|
| Pennington | Thief River Falls | 13,372 | 13,306 | 617 |
| Pine | Pine City | 22,878 | 21,264 | 1,411 |
| Pipestone | Pipestone | 10,339 | 10,491 | 466 |
| Polk | Crookston | 32,692 | 32,589 | 1,971 |
| Pope | Glenwood | 10,940 | 10,745 | 670 |
| Ramsey | Saint Paul | 482,115 | 485,783 | 156 |
| Red Lake | Red Lake Falls | 4,418 | 4,525 | 432 |
| Redwood | Redwood Falls | 16,947 | 17,254 | 880 |
| Renville | Olivia | 17,280 | 17,673 | 983 |
| Rice | Faribault | 51,931 | 49,183 | 498 |
| Rock | Luverne | 9,837 | 9,806 | 483 |
| Roseau | Roseau | 15,997 | 15,026 | 1,663 |
| Saint Louis | Duluth | 197,144 | 198,213 | 6,226 |
| Scott | Shakopee | 69,916 | 57,846 | 357 |
| Sherburne | Elk River | 52,861 | 41,945 | 437 |
| Sibley | Gaylord | 14,720 | 14,366 | 589 |
| Stearns | Saint Cloud | 125,852 | 119,324 | 1,345 |
| Steele | Owatonna | 31,503 | 30,729 | 430 |
| Stevens | Morris | 10,416 | 10,634 | 562 |
| Swift | Benson | 10,784 | 10,724 | 744 |
| Todd | Long Prairie | 23,994 | 23,363 | 942 |
| Traverse | Wheaton | 4,290 | 4,463 | 574 |
| Wabasha | Wabasha | 20,502 | 19,744 | 525 |
| Wadena | Wadena | 13,173 | 13,154 | 536 |
| Waseca | Waseca | 18,002 | 18,079 | 423 |
| Washington | Stillwater | 179,824 | 145,858 | 392 |
| Watonwan | Saint James | 11,616 | 11,682 | 435 |
| Wilkin | Breckenridge | 7,404 | 7,516 | 752 |
| Winona | Winona | 48,558 | 47,828 | 626 |
| Wright | Buffalo | 78,623 | 68,710 | 661 |
| Yellow Medicine | Granite Falls | 11,745 | 11,684 | 758 |

# Mississippi

(82 counties, 46,914 sq mi land; pop. 2,697,243)

| County | County seat or courthouse | 1995 Pop. | 1990 Pop. | Land area sq mi |
|---|---|---|---|---|
| Adams | Natchez | 34,645 | 35,356 | 460 |
| Alcorn | Corinth | 32,781 | 31,722 | 400 |
| Amite | Liberty | 13,581 | 13,328 | 730 |
| Attala | Kosciusko | 18,433 | 18,481 | 735 |
| Benton | Ashland | 7,937 | 8,046 | 407 |
| Bolivar | Cleveland & Rosedale | 41,434 | 41,875 | 876 |
| Calhoun | Pittsboro | 14,862 | 14,908 | 587 |
| Carroll | Carrollton & Vaiden | 9,900 | 9,237 | 628 |
| Chickasaw | Houston & Okolona | 18,355 | 18,085 | 502 |
| Choctaw | Ackerman | 9,123 | 9,071 | 419 |
| Claiborne | Port Gibson | 11,567 | 11,370 | 487 |
| Clarke | Quitman | 17,741 | 17,313 | 691 |
| Clay | West Point | 21,765 | 21,120 | 409 |
| Coahoma | Clarksdale | 31,558 | 31,665 | 554 |
| Copiah | Hazlehurst | 28,639 | 27,592 | 777 |
| Covington | Collins | 17,239 | 16,527 | 414 |
| De Soto | Hernando | 83,567 | 67,910 | 478 |
| Forrest | Hattiesburg | 72,553 | 68,314 | 467 |
| Franklin | Meadville | 8,260 | 8,377 | 565 |
| George | Lucedale | 18,230 | 16,673 | 478 |
| Greene | Leakesville | 11,476 | 10,220 | 713 |
| Grenada | Grenada | 22,211 | 21,555 | 422 |
| Hancock | Bay Saint Louis | 37,814 | 31,760 | 477 |
| Harrison | Gulfport | 175,240 | 165,365 | 581 |
| Hinds | Jackson & Raymond | 251,031 | 254,441 | 869 |
| Holmes | Lexington | 21,325 | 21,604 | 756 |
| Humphreys | Belzoni | 11,533 | 12,134 | 418 |
| Issaquena | Mayersville | 1,676 | 1,909 | 413 |
| Itawamba | Fulton | 20,902 | 20,017 | 532 |
| Jackson | Pascagoula | 128,494 | 115,243 | 727 |
| Jasper | Bay Springs & Paulding | 17,433 | 17,114 | 676 |
| Jefferson | Fayette | 8,549 | 8,653 | 519 |
| Jefferson Davis | Prentiss | 14,073 | 14,051 | 408 |
| Jones | Ellisville & Laurel | 63,001 | 62,031 | 694 |
| Kemper | De Kalb | 10,429 | 10,356 | 766 |
| Lafayette | Oxford | 33,463 | 31,826 | 631 |
| Lamar | Purvis | 33,642 | 30,424 | 497 |
| Lauderdale | Meridian | 76,910 | 75,555 | 704 |
| Lawrence | Monticello | 12,780 | 12,458 | 431 |
| Leake | Carthage | 19,056 | 18,436 | 583 |
| Lee | Tupelo | 72,272 | 65,579 | 450 |
| Leflore | Greenwood | 37,410 | 37,341 | 592 |
| Lincoln | Brookhaven | 31,417 | 30,278 | 586 |
| Lowndes | Columbus | 60,823 | 59,308 | 502 |
| Madison | Canton | 66,282 | 53,794 | 719 |
| Marion | Columbia | 26,258 | 25,544 | 542 |
| Marshall | Holly Springs | 32,078 | 30,361 | 706 |
| Monroe | Aberdeen | 37,771 | 36,582 | 764 |
| Montgomery | Winona | 12,428 | 12,387 | 407 |
| Neshoba | Philadelphia | 26,747 | 24,800 | 570 |
| Newton | Decatur | 21,256 | 20,291 | 578 |
| Noxubee | Macon | 12,407 | 12,604 | 695 |
| Oktibbeha | Starkville | 38,653 | 38,375 | 458 |
| Panola | Batesville & Sardis | 32,407 | 29,996 | 684 |
| Pearl River | Poplarville | 43,466 | 38,714 | 812 |
| Perry | New Augusta | 11,542 | 10,865 | 647 |
| Pike | Magnolia | 38,067 | 36,882 | 409 |
| Pontotoc | Pontotoc | 24,236 | 22,237 | 497 |
| Prentiss | Booneville | 23,842 | 23,278 | 415 |
| Quitman | Marks | 10,100 | 10,490 | 405 |
| Rankin | Brandon | 98,984 | 87,161 | 775 |
| Scott | Forest | 25,042 | 24,137 | 609 |
| Sharkey | Rolling Fork | 6,917 | 7,066 | 428 |
| Simpson | Mendenhall | 25,144 | 23,953 | 589 |
| Smith | Raleigh | 15,093 | 14,798 | 636 |
| Stone | Wiggins | 12,382 | 10,750 | 445 |
| Sunflower | Indianola | 35,752 | 35,129 | 694 |
| Tallahatchie | Charleston & Sumner | 15,052 | 15,210 | 644 |
| Tate | Senatobia | 22,737 | 21,432 | 405 |
| Tippah | Ripley | 20,649 | 19,523 | 458 |
| Tishomingo | Iuka | 18,235 | 17,683 | 424 |
| Tunica | Tunica | 8,132 | 8,164 | 455 |
| Union | New Albany | 22,875 | 22,085 | 416 |
| Walthall | Tylertown | 14,304 | 14,352 | 404 |
| Warren | Vicksburg | 49,176 | 47,880 | 587 |
| Washington | Greenville | 66,451 | 67,935 | 724 |
| Wayne | Waynesboro | 19,864 | 19,517 | 810 |
| Webster | Walthall | 10,500 | 10,222 | 423 |
| Wilkinson | Woodville | 9,710 | 9,678 | 677 |
| Winston | Louisville | 19,723 | 19,433 | 607 |
| Yalobusha | Coffeeville & Water Valley | 12,362 | 12,033 | 467 |
| Yazoo | Yazoo City | 25,489 | 25,506 | 920 |

# Missouri

(114 cos., 1 ind. city, 68,898 sq mi land; pop. 5,323,523)

| County | County seat or courthouse | 1995 Pop. | 1990 Pop. | Land area sq mi |
|---|---|---|---|---|
| Adair | Kirksville | 24,755 | 24,577 | 568 |
| Andrew | Savannah | 15,202 | 14,632 | 435 |
| Atchison | Rockport | 7,137 | 7,457 | 545 |
| Audrain | Mexico | 23,588 | 23,599 | 693 |
| Barry | Cassville | 31,382 | 27,547 | 779 |
| Barton | Lamar | 11,736 | 11,312 | 594 |
| Bates | Butler | 15,425 | 15,025 | 849 |
| Benton | Warsaw | 15,489 | 13,859 | 706 |
| Bollinger | Marble Hill | 11,253 | 10,619 | 621 |
| Boone | Columbia | 123,742 | 112,379 | 685 |
| Buchanan | Saint Joseph | 82,477 | 83,083 | 410 |
| Butler | Poplar Buff | 40,267 | 38,765 | 698 |
| Caldwell | Kingston | 8,569 | 8,380 | 429 |
| Callaway | Fulton | 34,870 | 32,809 | 839 |
| Camden | Camdenton | 31,611 | 27,495 | 655 |
| Cape Girardeau | Jackson | 65,313 | 61,633 | 579 |
| Carroll | Carrollton | 10,378 | 10,748 | 695 |
| Carter | Van Buren | 6,024 | 5,515 | 508 |
| Cass | Harrisonville | 73,547 | 63,808 | 699 |
| Cedar | Stockton | 12,892 | 12,093 | 476 |
| Chariton | Keytesville | 8,829 | 9,202 | 756 |
| Christian | Ozark | 42,740 | 32,644 | 563 |
| Clark | Kahoka | 7,449 | 7,547 | 507 |
| Clay | Liberty | 165,981 | 153,411 | 397 |
| Clinton | Plattsburg | 17,810 | 16,595 | 419 |
| Cole | Jefferson City | 67,641 | 63,579 | 392 |
| Cooper | Boonville | 15,989 | 14,835 | 565 |
| Crawford | Steelville | 21,329 | 19,173 | 743 |
| Dade | Greenfield | 8,010 | 7,449 | 490 |
| Dallas | Buffalo | 14,637 | 12,646 | 542 |
| Daviess | Gallatin | 7,896 | 7,865 | 567 |
| De Kalb | Maysville | 10,553 | 9,967 | 424 |
| Dent | Salem | 14,164 | 13,702 | 754 |
| Douglas | Ava | 12,120 | 11,876 | 815 |
| Dunklin | Kennett | 32,965 | 33,112 | 546 |
| Franklin | Union | 87,769 | 80,603 | 922 |
| Gasconade | Hermann | 14,529 | 14,006 | 520 |
| Gentry | Albany | 6,800 | 6,854 | 492 |
| Greene | Springfield | 224,976 | 207,949 | 675 |
| Grundy | Trenton | 10,417 | 10,536 | 436 |
| Harrison | Bethany | 8,270 | 8,469 | 725 |
| Henry | Clinton | 20,960 | 20,044 | 703 |
| Hickory | Hermitage | 8,312 | 7,335 | 399 |
| Holt | Oregon | 5,662 | 6,034 | 462 |
| Howard | Fayette | 9,661 | 9,631 | 466 |
| Howell | West Plains | 34,507 | 31,447 | 928 |
| Iron | Ironton | 10,886 | 10,726 | 551 |
| Jackson | Kansas City | 635,637 | 633,234 | 605 |
| Jasper | Carthage | 96,275 | 90,465 | 640 |
| Jefferson | Hillsboro | 186,435 | 171,380 | 657 |
| Johnson | Warrensburg | 46,603 | 42,514 | 831 |
| Knox | Edina | 4,347 | 4,482 | 506 |
| Laclede | Lebanon | 29,111 | 27,158 | 766 |
| Lafayette | Lexington | 32,191 | 31,107 | 629 |
| Lawrence | Mount Vernon | 31,698 | 30,236 | 613 |
| Lewis | Monticello | 10,219 | 10,233 | 505 |
| Lincoln | Troy | 32,969 | 28,892 | 631 |
| Linn | Linneus | 14,004 | 13,885 | 620 |
| Livingston | Chillicothe | 14,349 | 14,592 | 535 |
| McDonald | Pineville | 18,553 | 16,938 | 540 |
| Macon | Macon | 15,213 | 15,345 | 804 |
| Madison | Fredericktown | 11,211 | 11,127 | 497 |
| Maries | Vienna | 8,293 | 7,976 | 528 |
| Marion | Palmyra | 27,891 | 27,682 | 438 |

| County | County seat or courthouse | 1995 Pop. | 1990 Pop. | Land area sq mi |
|---|---|---|---|---|
| Mercer | Princeton | 4,087 | 3,723 | 455 |
| Miller | Tuscumbia | 21,974 | 20,700 | 592 |
| Mississippi | Charleston | 13,817 | 14,442 | 413 |
| Moniteau | California | 12,985 | 12,298 | 417 |
| Monroe | Paris | 8,821 | 9,104 | 646 |
| Montgomery | Montgomery City | 11,609 | 11,355 | 539 |
| Morgan | Versailles | 17,180 | 15,574 | 598 |
| New Madrid | New Madrid | 20,711 | 20,928 | 678 |
| Newton | Neosho | 47,529 | 44,445 | 627 |
| Nodaway | Maryville | 21,097 | 21,709 | 877 |
| Oregon | Alton | 10,029 | 9,470 | 792 |
| Osage | Linn | 12,374 | 12,018 | 606 |
| Ozark | Gainesville | 9,517 | 8,598 | 747 |
| Pemiscot | Caruthersville | 21,700 | 21,921 | 493 |
| Perry | Perryville | 17,318 | 16,648 | 475 |
| Pettis | Sedalia | 36,641 | 35,437 | 685 |
| Phelps | Rolla | 37,477 | 35,248 | 673 |
| Pike | Bowling Green | 16,200 | 15,969 | 673 |
| Platte | Platte City | 66,529 | 57,867 | 420 |
| Polk | Bolivar | 24,501 | 21,826 | 637 |
| Pulaski | Waynesville | 38,516 | 41,307 | 547 |
| Putnam | Unionville | 5,094 | 5,079 | 518 |
| Ralls | New London | 8,789 | 8,476 | 471 |
| Randolph | Huntsville | 23,924 | 24,370 | 482 |
| Ray | Richmond | 22,368 | 21,968 | 570 |
| Reynolds | Centerville | 6,733 | 6,661 | 811 |
| Ripley | Doniphan | 13,450 | 12,303 | 630 |
| Saint Charles | Saint Charles | 248,327 | 212,751 | 561 |
| Saint Clair | Osceola | 8,880 | 8,457 | 677 |
| Saint Francois | Farmington | 53,254 | 48,904 | 502 |
| Saint Louis | Clayton | 1,007,834 | 993,508 | 450 |
| Sainte Genevieve | Sainte Genevieve | 16,643 | 16,037 | 508 |
| Saline | Marshall | 23,022 | 23,523 | 756 |
| Schuyler | Lancaster | 4,333 | 4,236 | 308 |
| Scotland | Memphis | 4,846 | 4,822 | 439 |
| Scott | Benton | 40,303 | 39,376 | 421 |
| Shannon | Eminence | 8,070 | 7,613 | 1,004 |
| Shelby | Shelbyville | 6,884 | 6,942 | 501 |
| Stoddard | Bloomfield | 29,573 | 28,895 | 827 |
| Stone | Galena | 25,079 | 19,078 | 463 |
| Sullivan | Milan | 6,553 | 6,326 | 651 |
| Taney | Forsyth | 32,260 | 25,561 | 632 |
| Texas | Houston | 22,186 | 21,476 | 1,179 |
| Vernon | Nevada | 19,299 | 19,041 | 834 |
| Warren | Warrenton | 22,574 | 19,534 | 432 |
| Washington | Potosi | 21,907 | 20,380 | 760 |
| Wayne | Greenville | 12,646 | 11,543 | 761 |
| Webster | Marshfield | 26,810 | 23,753 | 593 |
| Worth | Grant City | 2,346 | 2,440 | 267 |
| Wright | Hartville | 18,702 | 16,758 | 682 |
| Independent City | | | | |
| Saint Louis | | 358,704 | 396,685 | 62 |

# Montana

(56 counties, 145,556 sq mi land; pop. 870,281)

| County | County seat or courthouse | 1995 Pop. | 1990 Pop. | Land area sq mi |
|---|---|---|---|---|
| Beaverhead | Dillon | 9,008 | 8,424 | 5,543 |
| Big Horn | Hardin | 12,215 | 11,337 | 4,995 |
| Blaine | Chinook | 7,032 | 6,728 | 4,226 |
| Broadwater | Townsend | 3,885 | 3,318 | 1,192 |
| Carbon | Red Lodge | 9,029 | 8,080 | 2,048 |
| Carter | Ekalaka | 1,464 | 1,503 | 3,340 |
| Cascade | Great Falls | 81,091 | 77,691 | 2,698 |
| Chouteau | Fort Benton | 5,492 | 5,452 | 3,973 |
| Custer | Miles City | 12,193 | 11,697 | 3,783 |
| Daniels | Scobey | 2,140 | 2,266 | 1,426 |
| Dawson | Glendive | 9,095 | 9,505 | 2,373 |
| Deer Lodge | Anaconda | 10,149 | 10,356 | 737 |
| Fallon | Baker | 3,003 | 3,103 | 1,620 |
| Fergus | Lewistown | 12,689 | 12,083 | 4,339 |
| Flathead | Kalispell | 69,512 | 59,218 | 5,099 |
| Gallatin | Bozeman | 59,406 | 50,463 | 2,507 |
| Garfield | Jordan | 1,419 | 1,589 | 4,668 |
| Glacier | Cut Bank | 12,677 | 12,121 | 2,995 |
| Golden Valley | Ryegete | 980 | 912 | 1,175 |
| Granite | Philipsburg | 2,619 | 2,548 | 1,728 |
| Hill | Havre | 17,668 | 17,654 | 2,896 |
| Jefferson | Boulder | 9,233 | 7,939 | 1,657 |
| Judith Basin | Stanford | 2,281 | 2,282 | 1,870 |
| Lake | Polson | 24,479 | 21,041 | 1,494 |
| Lewis & Clark | Helena | 52,785 | 47,495 | 3,461 |
| Liberty | Chester | 2,246 | 2,295 | 1,430 |
| Lincoln | Libby | 18,678 | 17,481 | 3,613 |
| McCone | Circle | 2,121 | 2,276 | 2,643 |
| Madison | Virginia City | 6,662 | 5,989 | 3,587 |
| Meagher | White Sulphur Springs | 1,826 | 1,819 | 2,392 |
| Mineral | Superior | 3,626 | 3,315 | 1,220 |
| Missoula | Missoula | 87,130 | 78,687 | 2,598 |
| Musselshell | Roundup | 4,491 | 4,106 | 1,867 |
| Park | Livingston | 15,856 | 14,484 | 2,656 |
| Petroleum | Winnett | 527 | 519 | 1,654 |
| Phillips | Malta | 5,151 | 5,163 | 5,140 |
| Pondera | Conrad | 6,274 | 6,433 | 1,625 |
| Powder River | Broadus | 2,011 | 2,090 | 3,297 |
| Powell | Deer Lodge | 6,859 | 6,620 | 2,326 |
| Prairie | Terry | 1,342 | 1,383 | 1,737 |
| Ravalli | Hamilton | 32,230 | 25,010 | 2,394 |
| Richland | Sidney | 10,351 | 10,716 | 2,084 |
| Roosevelt | Wolf Point | 11,243 | 10,999 | 2,356 |
| Rosebud | Forsyth | 10,881 | 10,505 | 5,012 |
| Sanders | Thompson Falls | 10,089 | 8,669 | 2,762 |
| Sheridan | Plentywood | 4,431 | 4,732 | 1,677 |
| Silver Bow | Butte | 34,795 | 33,941 | 718 |
| Stillwater | Columbus | 7,466 | 6,536 | 1,795 |
| Sweet Grass | Big Timber | 3,374 | 3,154 | 1,855 |
| Teton | Choteau | 6,371 | 6,271 | 2,273 |
| Toole | Shelby | 5,103 | 5,046 | 1,911 |
| Treasure | Hysham | 837 | 874 | 979 |
| Valley | Glasgow | 8,462 | 8,239 | 4,921 |
| Wheatland | Harlowton | 2,425 | 2,246 | 1,423 |
| Wibaux | Wibaux | 1,170 | 1,191 | 889 |
| Yellowstone | Billings | 124,655 | 113,419 | 2,635 |

# Nebraska

(93 counties, 76,878 sq mi land; pop. 1,637,112)

| County | County seat or courthouse | 1995 Pop. | 1990 Pop. | Land area sq mi |
|---|---|---|---|---|
| Adams | Hastings | 29,728 | 29,625 | 563 |
| Antelope | Neligh | 7,502 | 7,965 | 857 |
| Arthur | Arthur | 440 | 462 | 715 |
| Banner | Harrisburg | 848 | 852 | 746 |
| Blaine | Brewster | 667 | 675 | 711 |
| Boone | Albion | 6,517 | 6,667 | 687 |
| Box Butte | Alliance | 13,006 | 13,130 | 1,075 |
| Boyd | Butte | 2,763 | 2,835 | 540 |
| Brown | Ainsworth | 3,652 | 3,657 | 1,221 |
| Buffalo | Kearney | 39,516 | 37,447 | 968 |
| Burt | Tekamah | 7,970 | 7,868 | 493 |
| Butler | David City | 8,591 | 8,601 | 584 |
| Cass | Plattsmouth | 22,913 | 21,318 | 559 |
| Cedar | Hartington | 10,071 | 10,131 | 740 |
| Chase | Imperial | 4,287 | 4,381 | 895 |
| Cherry | Valentine | 6,374 | 6,307 | 5,961 |
| Cheyenne | Sidney | 9,573 | 9,494 | 1,196 |
| Clay | Clay Center | 7,132 | 7,123 | 573 |
| Colfax | Schuyler | 10,140 | 9,139 | 413 |
| Cuming | West Point | 10,147 | 10,117 | 572 |
| Custer | Broken Bow | 12,258 | 12,270 | 2,576 |
| Dakota | Dakota City | 18,206 | 16,742 | 264 |
| Dawes | Chadron | 9,140 | 9,021 | 1,396 |
| Dawson | Lexington | 22,688 | 19,940 | 1,013 |
| Deuel | Chappell | 2,119 | 2,237 | 440 |
| Dixon | Ponca | 6,282 | 6,143 | 476 |
| Dodge | Fremont | 34,722 | 34,500 | 535 |
| Douglas | Omaha | 434,147 | 416,444 | 331 |
| Dundy | Benkelman | 2,441 | 2,582 | 920 |
| Fillmore | Geneva | 6,966 | 7,103 | 577 |
| Franklin | Franklin | 3,715 | 3,938 | 576 |
| Frontier | Stockville | 3,168 | 3,101 | 975 |
| Furnas | Beaver City | 5,658 | 5,553 | 718 |
| Gage | Beatrice | 22,848 | 22,794 | 855 |
| Garden | Oshkosh | 2,240 | 2,460 | 1,705 |
| Garfield | Burwell | 2,066 | 2,141 | 570 |
| Gosper | Elwood | 2,150 | 1,928 | 458 |
| Grant | Hyannis | 777 | 769 | 776 |
| Greeley | Greeley | 2,958 | 3,006 | 570 |
| Hall | Grand Island | 51,178 | 48,925 | 546 |
| Hamilton | Aurora | 9,305 | 8,862 | 544 |
| Harlan | Alma | 3,689 | 3,810 | 553 |
| Hayes | Hayes Center | 1,140 | 1,222 | 713 |
| Hitchcock | Trenton | 3,427 | 3,750 | 710 |
| Holt | O'Neill | 12,387 | 12,599 | 2,413 |
| Hooker | Mullen | 733 | 793 | 721 |
| Howard | Saint Paul | 6,339 | 6,057 | 570 |
| Jefferson | Fairbury | 8,445 | 8,759 | 573 |
| Johnson | Tecumseh | 4,583 | 4,673 | 376 |
| Kearney | Minden | 6,638 | 6,629 | 516 |
| Keith | Ogallala | 8,622 | 8,584 | 1,061 |
| Keya Paha | Springview | 1,020 | 1,029 | 773 |
| Kimball | Kimball | 4,143 | 4,108 | 952 |
| Knox | Center | 9,409 | 9,564 | 1,108 |
| Lancaster | Lincoln | 228,638 | 213,641 | 839 |
| Lincoln | North Platte | 33,468 | 32,508 | 2,564 |
| Logan | Stapleton | 853 | 878 | 571 |
| Loup | Taylor | 695 | 683 | 570 |
| McPherson | Tryon | 544 | 546 | 859 |
| Madison | Madison | 34,341 | 32,655 | 573 |
| Merrick | Central City | 8,156 | 8,049 | 485 |
| Morrill | Bridgeport | 5,347 | 5,423 | 1,424 |
| Nance | Fullerton | 4,241 | 4,275 | 441 |
| Nemaha | Auburn | 8,033 | 7,980 | 409 |
| Nuckolls | Nelson | 5,569 | 5,786 | 575 |
| Otoe | Nebraska City | 14,346 | 14,252 | 616 |
| Pawnee | Pawnee City | 3,322 | 3,317 | 432 |
| Perkins | Grant | 3,265 | 3,367 | 883 |
| Phelps | Holdrege | 9,982 | 9,715 | 540 |
| Pierce | Pierce | 7,874 | 7,827 | 574 |

| County | County seat or courthouse | 1995 Pop. | 1990 Pop. | Land area sq mi |
|---|---|---|---|---|
| Platte | Columbus | 30,651 | 29,820 | 678 |
| Polk | Osceola | 5,659 | 5,668 | 439 |
| Red Willow | McCook | 11,416 | 11,705 | 717 |
| Richardson | Falls City | 9,696 | 9,937 | 554 |
| Rock | Bassett | 1,870 | 2,019 | 1,009 |
| Saline | Wilber | 12,938 | 12,715 | 575 |
| Sarpy | Papillion | 111,806 | 102,583 | 241 |
| Saunders | Wahoo | 19,010 | 18,285 | 754 |
| Scotts Bluff | Gering | 37,161 | 36,025 | 739 |
| Seward | Seward | 16,267 | 15,450 | 575 |
| Sheridan | Rushville | 6,704 | 6,750 | 2,441 |
| Sherman | Loup City | 3,584 | 3,718 | 566 |
| Sioux | Harrison | 1,619 | 1,549 | 2,067 |
| Stanton | Stanton | 6,229 | 6,244 | 430 |
| Thayer | Hebron | 6,393 | 6,635 | 575 |
| Thomas | Thedford | 848 | 851 | 713 |
| Thurston | Pender | 7,199 | 6,936 | 394 |
| Valley | Ord | 4,914 | 5,169 | 568 |
| Washington | Blair | 17,755 | 16,607 | 391 |
| Wayne | Wayne | 9,561 | 9,364 | 444 |
| Webster | Red Cloud | 4,137 | 4,279 | 575 |
| Wheeler | Bartlett | 953 | 948 | 575 |
| York | York | 14,624 | 14,428 | 576 |

## Nevada

(16 counties, 1 ind. city, 109,806 sq mi land; pop. 1,530,108)

| County | County seat or courthouse | 1995 Pop. | 1990 Pop. | Land area sq mi |
|---|---|---|---|---|
| Churchill | Fallon | 21,096 | 17,938 | 4,929 |
| Clark | Las Vegas | 992,593 | 741,368 | 7,911 |
| Douglas | Minden | 34,695 | 27,637 | 710 |
| Elko | Elko | 41,732 | 33,463 | 17,182 |
| Esmeralda | Goldfield | 1,185 | 1,344 | 3,589 |
| Eureka | Eureka | 1,413 | 1,547 | 4,176 |
| Humboldt | Winnemucca | 16,038 | 12,844 | 9,648 |
| Lander | Battle Mountain | 6,473 | 6,266 | 5,494 |
| Lincoln | Pioche | 3,837 | 3,775 | 10,635 |
| Lyon | Yerington | 25,867 | 20,001 | 1,994 |
| Mineral | Hawthorne | 6,182 | 6,475 | 3,757 |
| Nye | Tonopah | 24,563 | 17,781 | 18,147 |
| Pershing | Lovelock | 4,526 | 4,336 | 6,009 |
| Storey | Virginia City | 2,835 | 2,526 | 264 |
| Washoe | Reno | 290,833 | 254,667 | 6,343 |
| White Pine | Ely | 9,957 | 9,264 | 8,877 |
| Independent City | | | | |
| Carson City | Carson City | 46,283 | 40,443 | 144 |

## New Hampshire

(10 counties, 8,969 sq mi land; pop. 1,148,253)

| County | County seat or courthouse | 1995 Pop. | 1990 Pop. | Land area sq mi |
|---|---|---|---|---|
| Belknap | Laconia | 50,940 | 49,216 | 401 |
| Carroll | Ossipee | 37,583 | 35,410 | 934 |
| Cheshire | Keene | 71,158 | 70,121 | 708 |
| Coos | Lancaster | 33,580 | 34,828 | 1,801 |
| Grafton | Woodsville | 77,736 | 74,929 | 1,714 |
| Hillsborough | Nashua | 349,572 | 335,838 | 877 |
| Merrimack | Concord | 123,348 | 120,240 | 935 |
| Rockingham | Exeter | 257,579 | 245,845 | 695 |
| Strafford | Dover | 107,265 | 104,233 | 369 |
| Sullivan | Newport | 39,492 | 38,592 | 537 |

## New Jersey

(21 counties, 7,419 sq mi land; pop. 7,945,298)

| County | County seat or courthouse | 1995 Pop. | 1990 Pop. | Land area sq mi |
|---|---|---|---|---|
| Atlantic | Mays Landing | 233,996 | 224,327 | 561 |
| Bergen | Hackensack | 845,189 | 825,380 | 234 |
| Burlington | Mount Holly | 403,337 | 395,066 | 805 |
| Camden | Camden | 507,157 | 502,824 | 222 |
| Cape May | Cape May Courthouse | 98,340 | 95,089 | 255 |
| Cumberland | Bridgeton | 138,058 | 138,053 | 489 |
| Essex | Newark | 758,626 | 777,964 | 126 |
| Gloucester | Woodbury | 243,748 | 230,082 | 325 |
| Hudson | Jersey City | 550,183 | 553,099 | 47 |
| Hunterdon | Flemington | 116,516 | 107,802 | 430 |
| Mercer | Trenton | 330,305 | 325,824 | 226 |
| Middlesex | New Brunswick | 698,494 | 671,811 | 311 |
| Monmouth | Freehold | 585,230 | 553,093 | 472 |
| Morris | Morristown | 444,354 | 421,361 | 469 |
| Ocean | Toms River | 464,822 | 433,203 | 636 |
| Passaic | Paterson | 463,466 | 453,302 | 185 |
| Salem | Salem | 64,921 | 65,294 | 338 |
| Somerset | Somerville | 265,440 | 240,245 | 305 |
| Sussex | Newton | 140,198 | 130,943 | 521 |
| Union | Elizabeth | 496,310 | 493,819 | 103 |
| Warren | Belvidere | 96,608 | 91,607 | 358 |

## New Mexico

(33 counties, 121,364 sq mi land; pop. 1,685,401)

| County | County seat or courthouse | 1995 Pop. | 1990 Pop. | Land area sq mi |
|---|---|---|---|---|
| Bernalillo | Albuquerque | 522,328 | 480,577 | 1,166 |
| Catron | Reserve | 2,719 | 2,563 | 6,928 |
| Chaves | Roswell | 61,770 | 57,849 | 6,071 |
| Cibola | Grants | 25,166 | 23,794 | 4,540 |
| Colfax | Raton | 13,860 | 12,925 | 3,757 |
| Curry | Clovis | 47,464 | 42,207 | 1,406 |
| DeBaca | Fort Sumner | 2,373 | 2,252 | 2,325 |
| Dona Ana | Las Cruces | 158,849 | 135,510 | 3,807 |
| Eddy | Carlsbad | 52,758 | 48,605 | 4,182 |
| Grant | Silver City | 30,076 | 27,676 | 3,966 |
| Guadalupe | Santa Rosa | 4,075 | 4,156 | 3,031 |
| Harding | Mosquero | 913 | 987 | 2,126 |
| Hidalgo | Lordsburg | 6,259 | 5,958 | 3,446 |
| Lea | Lovington | 56,793 | 55,765 | 4,393 |
| Lincoln | Carrizozo | 14,853 | 12,219 | 4,831 |
| Los Alamos | Los Alamos | 18,604 | 18,115 | 109 |
| Luna | Deming | 22,121 | 18,110 | 2,965 |
| McKinley | Gallup | 66,991 | 60,686 | 5,449 |
| Mora | Mora | 4,581 | 4,264 | 1,931 |
| Otero | Alamogordo | 55,027 | 51,928 | 6,627 |
| Quay | Tucumcari | 10,488 | 10,823 | 2,875 |
| Rio Arriba | Tierra Amarilla | 36,959 | 34,365 | 5,858 |
| Roosevelt | Portales | 18,465 | 16,702 | 2,449 |
| Sandoval | Bernalillo | 79,781 | 63,319 | 3,710 |
| San Juan | Aztec | 100,470 | 91,605 | 5,514 |
| San Miguel | Las Vegas | 28,490 | 25,743 | 4,717 |
| Santa Fe | Santa Fe | 116,414 | 98,928 | 1,909 |
| Sierra | Truth or Consequences | 10,600 | 9,912 | 4,181 |
| Socorro | Socorro | 15,853 | 14,764 | 6,647 |
| Taos | Taos | 25,581 | 23,118 | 2,203 |
| Torrance | Estancia | 12,835 | 10,285 | 3,345 |
| Union | Clayton | 4,139 | 4,124 | 3,830 |
| Valencia | Los Lunas | 57,746 | 45,235 | 1,068 |

## New York

(62 counties, 47,224 sq mi land; pop. 18,136,081)

| County | County seat or courthouse | 1995 Pop. | 1990 Pop. | Land area sq mi |
|---|---|---|---|---|
| Albany | Albany | 289,549 | 292,793 | 524 |
| Allegany | Belmont | 51,390 | 50,470 | 1,030 |
| Bronx[1] | Bronx | 1,187,798 | 1,203,789 | 42 |
| Broome | Binghamton | 204,436 | 212,160 | 707 |
| Cattaraugus | Little Valley | 85,596 | 84,234 | 1,310 |
| Cayuga | Auburn | 82,988 | 82,313 | 693 |
| Chautauqua | Mayville | 141,677 | 141,895 | 1,062 |
| Chemung | Elmira | 94,082 | 95,195 | 408 |
| Chenango | Norwich | 51,977 | 51,768 | 894 |
| Clinton | Plattsburgh | 83,370 | 85,969 | 1,039 |
| Columbia | Hudson | 63,703 | 62,982 | 636 |
| Cortland | Cortland | 49,052 | 48,963 | 500 |
| Delaware | Delhi | 47,584 | 47,225 | 1,446 |
| Dutchess | Poughkeepsie | 262,062 | 259,462 | 802 |
| Erie | Buffalo | 962,046 | 968,584 | 1,045 |
| Essex | Elizabethtown | 37,887 | 37,152 | 1,797 |
| Franklin | Malone | 49,400 | 46,540 | 1,632 |
| Fulton | Johnstown | 54,106 | 54,191 | 496 |
| Genesee | Batavia | 61,316 | 60,060 | 494 |
| Greene | Catskill | 47,660 | 44,739 | 648 |
| Hamilton | Lake Pleasant | 5,208 | 5,279 | 1,721 |
| Herkimer | Herkimer | 66,354 | 65,809 | 1,412 |
| Jefferson | Watertown | 114,712 | 110,943 | 1,272 |
| Kings[1] | Brooklyn | 2,244,021 | 2,300,664 | 71 |
| Lewis | Lowville | 27,711 | 26,796 | 1,276 |
| Livingston | Geneseo | 65,770 | 62,372 | 632 |
| Madison | Wampsville | 71,490 | 69,166 | 656 |
| Monroe | Rochester | 723,177 | 713,968 | 659 |
| Montgomery | Fonda | 52,068 | 51,981 | 405 |
| Nassau | Mineola | 1,305,772 | 1,287,444 | 287 |
| New York[1] | New York | 1,518,910 | 1,487,536 | 28 |
| Niagara | Lockport | 222,006 | 220,756 | 523 |
| Oneida | Utica | 242,208 | 250,836 | 1,213 |
| Onondaga | Syracuse | 469,818 | 468,973 | 780 |
| Ontario | Canandaigua | 99,138 | 95,101 | 644 |
| Orange | Goshen | 322,892 | 307,647 | 816 |
| Orleans | Albion | 45,144 | 41,846 | 391 |
| Oswego | Oswego | 125,794 | 121,785 | 953 |
| Otsego | Cooperstown | 61,575 | 60,517 | 1,003 |
| Putnam | Carmel | 90,320 | 83,941 | 232 |
| Queens[1] | Jamaica | 1,963,628 | 1,951,598 | 109 |
| Rensselaer | Troy | 155,684 | 154,429 | 654 |
| Richmond[1] | Saint George | 397,719 | 378,977 | 59 |
| Rockland | New City | 276,898 | 265,475 | 174 |
| Saint Lawrence | Canton | 115,482 | 111,974 | 2,686 |
| Saratoga | Ballston Spa | 194,332 | 181,276 | 812 |
| Schenectady | Schenectady | 148,888 | 149,285 | 206 |
| Schoharie | Schoharie | 32,840 | 31,859 | 622 |
| Schuyler | Watkins Glen | 19,247 | 18,662 | 329 |
| Seneca | Ovid & Waterloo | 32,593 | 33,683 | 325 |
| Steuben | Bath | 99,949 | 99,088 | 1,393 |

| County | County seat or courthouse | 1995 Pop. | 1990 Pop. | Land area sq mi |
|---|---|---|---|---|
| Suffolk | Riverhead | 1,353,704 | 1,321,768 | 911 |
| Sullivan | Monticello | 70,452 | 69,277 | 970 |
| Tioga | Owego | 52,967 | 52,337 | 519 |
| Tompkins | Ithaca | 96,384 | 94,097 | 476 |
| Ulster | Kingston | 167,862 | 165,304 | 1,127 |
| Warren | Queensbury | 61,544 | 59,209 | 870 |
| Washington | Hudson Falls | 61,015 | 59,330 | 836 |
| Wayne | Lyons | 93,971 | 89,123 | 604 |
| Westchester | White Plains | 890,918 | 874,866 | 433 |
| Wyoming | Warsaw | 44,083 | 42,507 | 593 |
| Yates | Penn Yan | 24,154 | 22,810 | 338 |

(1) New York City consists of five counties: Bronx, Kings (Brooklyn), New York (Manhattan), Queens, and Richmond (Staten Island).

## North Carolina

(100 counties, 48,718 sq mi land; pop. 7,195,138)

| County | County seat or courthouse | 1995 Pop. | 1990 Pop. | Land area sq mi |
|---|---|---|---|---|
| Alamance | Graham | 115,062 | 108,213 | 431 |
| Alexander | Taylorsville | 29,892 | 27,544 | 260 |
| Alleghany | Sparta | 9,893 | 9,590 | 235 |
| Anson | Wadesboro | 24,177 | 23,474 | 532 |
| Ashe | Jefferson | 23,371 | 22,209 | 426 |
| Avery | Newland | 15,323 | 14,867 | 247 |
| Beaufort | Washington | 44,123 | 42,283 | 828 |
| Bertie | Windsor | 20,847 | 20,388 | 699 |
| Bladen | Elizabethtown | 29,963 | 28,663 | 875 |
| Brunswick | Bolivia | 60,795 | 50,985 | 855 |
| Buncombe | Asheville | 189,506 | 174,819 | 656 |
| Burke | Morganton | 79,859 | 75,740 | 507 |
| Cabarrus | Concord | 110,030 | 98,935 | 364 |
| Caldwell | Lenoir | 74,060 | 70,709 | 472 |
| Camden | Camden | 6,453 | 5,904 | 241 |
| Carteret | Beaufort | 57,880 | 52,553 | 531 |
| Caswell | Yanceyville | 21,324 | 20,693 | 426 |
| Catawba | Newton | 126,425 | 118,412 | 400 |
| Chatham | Pittsboro | 42,536 | 38,759 | 683 |
| Cherokee | Murphy | 21,602 | 20,170 | 455 |
| Chowan | Edenton | 14,013 | 13,506 | 173 |
| Clay | Hayesville | 7,858 | 7,155 | 215 |
| Cleveland | Shelby | 89,772 | 84,713 | 464 |
| Columbus | Whiteville | 51,400 | 49,587 | 937 |
| Craven | New Bern | 85,518 | 81,613 | 696 |
| Cumberland | Fayetteville | 285,869 | 274,713 | 653 |
| Currituck | Currituck | 16,274 | 13,736 | 262 |
| Dare | Manteo | 26,047 | 22,746 | 382 |
| Davidson | Lexington | 135,373 | 126,677 | 552 |
| Davie | Mocksville | 29,610 | 27,859 | 265 |
| Duplin | Kenansville | 41,987 | 39,995 | 818 |
| Durham | Durham | 195,261 | 181,854 | 291 |
| Edgecombe | Tarboro | 56,371 | 56,692 | 505 |
| Forsyth | Winston-Salem | 281,052 | 265,878 | 410 |
| Franklin | Louisburg | 41,395 | 36,414 | 492 |
| Gaston | Gastonia | 181,466 | 175,093 | 357 |
| Gates | Gatesville | 9,854 | 9,305 | 341 |
| Graham | Robbinsville | 7,622 | 7,196 | 292 |
| Granville | Oxford | 40,911 | 38,341 | 531 |
| Greene | Snow Hill | 16,942 | 15,384 | 265 |
| Guilford | Greensboro | 374,438 | 347,420 | 650 |
| Halifax | Halifax | 57,497 | 55,516 | 725 |
| Harnett | Lillington | 76,310 | 67,833 | 595 |
| Haywood | Waynesville | 49,737 | 46,942 | 554 |
| Henderson | Hendersonville | 76,704 | 69,285 | 374 |
| Hertford | Winton | 22,587 | 22,523 | 354 |
| Hoke | Raeford | 27,627 | 22,856 | 391 |
| Hyde | Swan Quarter | 5,366 | 5,411 | 613 |
| Iredell | Statesville | 103,412 | 92,935 | 574 |
| Jackson | Sylva | 29,029 | 26,846 | 491 |
| Johnston | Smithfield | 94,777 | 81,306 | 792 |
| Jones | Trenton | 9,797 | 9,414 | 473 |
| Lee | Sanford | 45,945 | 41,370 | 257 |
| Lenoir | Kinston | 59,257 | 57,274 | 400 |
| Lincoln | Lincolnton | 56,017 | 50,319 | 299 |
| McDowell | Marion | 37,471 | 35,681 | 442 |
| Macon | Franklin | 26,180 | 23,499 | 517 |
| Madison | Marshall | 17,942 | 16,953 | 449 |
| Martin | Williamston | 26,396 | 25,078 | 463 |
| Mecklenburg | Charlotte | 579,473 | 511,481 | 527 |
| Mitchell | Bakersville | 14,699 | 14,433 | 222 |
| Montgomery | Troy | 23,487 | 23,352 | 491 |
| Moore | Carthage | 67,174 | 59,000 | 699 |
| Nash | Nashville | 85,561 | 76,677 | 540 |
| New Hanover | Wilmington | 139,815 | 120,284 | 199 |
| Northampton | Jackson | 20,905 | 20,798 | 536 |
| Onslow | Jacksonville | 143,324 | 149,838 | 767 |
| Orange | Hillsborough | 107,648 | 93,851 | 400 |
| Pamlico | Bayboro | 12,066 | 11,368 | 337 |
| Pasquotank | Elizabeth City | 33,866 | 31,298 | 227 |
| Pender | Burgaw | 35,080 | 28,855 | 871 |
| Perquimans | Hertford | 10,798 | 10,447 | 247 |
| Person | Roxboro | 32,376 | 30,180 | 392 |
| Pitt | Greenville | 117,740 | 108,480 | 652 |
| Polk | Columbus | 15,800 | 14,416 | 238 |
| Randolph | Asheboro | 114,624 | 106,546 | 788 |
| Richmond | Rockingham | 45,660 | 44,518 | 474 |
| Robeson | Lumberton | 112,038 | 105,170 | 949 |
| Rockingham | Wentworth | 88,414 | 86,064 | 567 |
| Rowan | Salisbury | 119,211 | 110,605 | 511 |
| Rutherford | Rutherfordton | 59,210 | 56,919 | 564 |
| Sampson | Clinton | 50,485 | 47,297 | 946 |
| Scotland | Laurinburg | 35,304 | 33,763 | 319 |
| Stanly | Albemarle | 54,172 | 51,765 | 395 |
| Stokes | Danbury | 40,723 | 37,223 | 452 |
| Surry | Dobson | 65,159 | 61,704 | 537 |
| Swain | Bryson City | 11,815 | 11,268 | 528 |
| Transylvania | Brevard | 27,339 | 25,520 | 378 |
| Tyrrell | Columbia | 3,894 | 3,856 | 390 |
| Union | Monroe | 99,155 | 84,210 | 637 |
| Vance | Henderson | 40,720 | 38,892 | 254 |
| Wake | Raleigh | 513,639 | 426,301 | 834 |
| Warren | Warrenton | 17,984 | 17,265 | 429 |
| Washington | Plymouth | 14,119 | 13,997 | 348 |
| Watauga | Boone | 39,799 | 36,952 | 313 |
| Wayne | Goldsboro | 110,174 | 104,666 | 553 |
| Wilkes | Wilkesboro | 60,922 | 59,393 | 757 |
| Wilson | Wilson | 67,362 | 66,061 | 371 |
| Yadkin | Yadkinville | 32,958 | 30,488 | 336 |
| Yancey | Burnsville | 16,241 | 15,419 | 312 |

## North Dakota

(53 counties, 68,994 sq mi land; pop. 641,367)

| County | County seat or courthouse | 1995 Pop. | 1990 Pop. | Land area sq mi |
|---|---|---|---|---|
| Adams | Hettinger | 2,593 | 3,174 | 988 |
| Barnes | Valley City | 12,042 | 12,545 | 1,492 |
| Benson | Minnewaukan | 6,990 | 7,198 | 1,389 |
| Billings | Medora | 1,157 | 1,108 | 1,152 |
| Bottineau | Bottineau | 7,706 | 8,011 | 1,669 |
| Bowman | Bowman | 3,229 | 3,596 | 1,162 |
| Burke | Bowbells | 2,501 | 3,002 | 1,104 |
| Burleigh | Bismarck | 64,807 | 60,131 | 1,633 |
| Cass | Fargo | 111,440 | 102,874 | 1,766 |
| Cavalier | Langdon | 5,474 | 6,064 | 1,489 |
| Dickey | Ellendale | 5,775 | 6,107 | 1,131 |
| Divide | Crosby | 2,558 | 2,899 | 1,259 |
| Dunn | Manning | 3,790 | 4,005 | 2,010 |
| Eddy | New Rockford | 2,851 | 2,951 | 632 |
| Emmons | Linton | 4,564 | 4,830 | 1,510 |
| Foster | Carrington | 3,892 | 3,983 | 635 |
| Golden Valley | Beach | 1,962 | 2,108 | 1,002 |
| Grand Forks | Grand Forks | 71,879 | 70,683 | 1,438 |
| Grant | Carson | 3,235 | 3,549 | 1,660 |
| Griggs | Cooperstown | 3,036 | 3,303 | 709 |
| Hettinger | Mott | 3,020 | 3,445 | 1,132 |
| Kidder | Steele | 3,036 | 3,332 | 1,352 |
| La Moure | La Moure | 5,026 | 5,383 | 1,147 |
| Logan | Napoleon | 2,477 | 2,847 | 993 |
| McHenry | Towner | 6,322 | 6,528 | 1,874 |
| McIntosh | Ashley | 3,649 | 4,021 | 975 |
| McKenzie | Watford City | 5,779 | 6,383 | 2,742 |
| McLean | Washburn | 9,847 | 10,457 | 2,110 |
| Mercer | Stanton | 9,466 | 9,808 | 1,045 |
| Morton | Mandan | 24,633 | 23,700 | 1,926 |
| Mountrail | Stanley | 6,797 | 7,021 | 1,824 |
| Nelson | Lakota | 4,065 | 4,410 | 982 |
| Oliver | Center | 2,186 | 2,381 | 724 |
| Pembina | Cavalier | 8,791 | 9,238 | 1,119 |
| Pierce | Rugby | 4,675 | 5,052 | 1,018 |
| Ramsey | Devils Lake | 12,680 | 12,681 | 1,186 |
| Ransom | Lisbon | 5,887 | 5,921 | 863 |
| Renville | Mohall | 2,843 | 3,160 | 875 |
| Richland | Wahpeton | 18,177 | 18,148 | 1,437 |
| Rolette | Rolla | 13,779 | 12,772 | 903 |
| Sargent | Forman | 4,564 | 4,549 | 859 |
| Sheridan | McClusky | 1,895 | 2,148 | 972 |
| Sioux | Fort Yates | 3,994 | 3,761 | 1,094 |
| Slope | Amidon | 821 | 907 | 1,218 |
| Stark | Dickinson | 22,434 | 22,832 | 1,338 |
| Steele | Finley | 2,312 | 2,420 | 712 |
| Stutsman | Jamestown | 21,457 | 22,241 | 2,222 |
| Towner | Cando | 3,212 | 3,627 | 1,025 |
| Traill | Hillsboro | 8,695 | 8,752 | 862 |
| Walsh | Grafton | 12,789 | 13,840 | 1,282 |
| Ward | Minot | 58,778 | 57,921 | 2,013 |
| Wells | Fessenden | 5,254 | 5,864 | 1,271 |
| Williams | Williston | 20,546 | 21,129 | 2,071 |

## Ohio

(88 counties, 40,953 sq mi land; pop. 11,150,506)

| County | County seat or courthouse | 1995 Pop. | 1990 Pop. | Land area sq mi |
|---|---|---|---|---|
| Adams | West Union | 27,670 | 25,371 | 584 |
| Allen | Lima | 109,399 | 109,755 | 405 |
| Ashland | Ashland | 51,240 | 47,507 | 424 |
| Ashtabula | Jefferson | 102,360 | 99,821 | 703 |
| Athens | Athens | 60,687 | 59,549 | 507 |
| Auglaize | Wapakoneta | 46,877 | 44,585 | 401 |

| County | County seat or courthouse | 1995 Pop. | 1990 Pop. | Land area sq mi |
|---|---|---|---|---|
| Belmont | Saint Clairsville | 70,379 | 71,074 | 537 |
| Brown | Georgetown | 38,850 | 34,966 | 492 |
| Butler | Hamilton | 315,601 | 291,479 | 467 |
| Carroll | Carrollton | 28,142 | 26,521 | 395 |
| Champaign | Urbana | 37,686 | 36,019 | 429 |
| Clark | Springfield | 147,731 | 147,548 | 400 |
| Clermont | Batavia | 166,941 | 150,167 | 452 |
| Clinton | Wilmington | 38,019 | 35,417 | 411 |
| Columbiana | Lisbon | 111,853 | 108,276 | 533 |
| Coshocton | Coshocton | 36,244 | 35,427 | 564 |
| Crawford | Bucyrus | 47,733 | 47,870 | 402 |
| Cuyahoga | Cleveland | 1,398,169 | 1,412,140 | 458 |
| Darke | Greenville | 54,318 | 53,619 | 600 |
| Defiance | Defiance | 40,115 | 39,350 | 411 |
| Delaware | Delaware | 78,956 | 66,929 | 443 |
| Erie | Sandusky | 78,805 | 76,779 | 255 |
| Fairfield | Lancaster | 117,556 | 103,472 | 506 |
| Fayette | Washington Courthouse | 28,431 | 27,466 | 407 |
| Franklin | Columbus | 1,011,019 | 961,437 | 540 |
| Fulton | Wauseon | 40,846 | 38,498 | 407 |
| Gallia | Gallipolis | 32,582 | 30,954 | 469 |
| Geauga | Chardon | 84,260 | 81,129 | 404 |
| Greene | Xenia | 141,181 | 136,731 | 415 |
| Guernsey | Cambridge | 40,246 | 39,024 | 522 |
| Hamilton | Cincinnati | 863,908 | 866,228 | 407 |
| Hancock | Findlay | 68,239 | 65,536 | 531 |
| Hardin | Kenton | 31,558 | 31,111 | 470 |
| Harrison | Cadiz | 16,100 | 16,085 | 404 |
| Henry | Napoleon | 29,814 | 29,108 | 417 |
| Highland | Hillsboro | 39,245 | 35,728 | 553 |
| Hocking | Logan | 27,997 | 25,533 | 423 |
| Holmes | Millersburg | 36,160 | 32,849 | 423 |
| Huron | Norwalk | 58,613 | 56,240 | 493 |
| Jackson | Jackson | 31,927 | 30,230 | 420 |
| Jefferson | Steubenville | 78,262 | 80,298 | 410 |
| Knox | Mount Vernon | 51,009 | 47,473 | 527 |
| Lake | Painesville | 223,003 | 215,499 | 228 |
| Lawrence | Ironton | 64,206 | 61,834 | 455 |
| Licking | Newark | 136,593 | 128,300 | 687 |
| Logan | Bellefontaine | 45,204 | 42,310 | 459 |
| Lorain | Elyria | 281,447 | 271,126 | 493 |
| Lucas | Toledo | 455,018 | 462,361 | 340 |
| Madison | London | 40,878 | 37,068 | 465 |
| Mahoning | Youngstown | 262,338 | 264,806 | 415 |
| Marion | Marion | 65,781 | 64,274 | 404 |
| Medina | Medina | 135,735 | 122,354 | 422 |
| Meigs | Pomeroy | 24,066 | 22,987 | 430 |
| Mercer | Celina | 40,906 | 39,443 | 463 |
| Miami | Troy | 97,010 | 93,182 | 407 |
| Monroe | Woodsfield | 15,388 | 15,497 | 456 |
| Montgomery | Dayton | 570,490 | 573,809 | 462 |
| Morgan | McConnelsville | 14,602 | 14,194 | 418 |
| Morrow | Mount Gilead | 30,136 | 27,749 | 406 |
| Muskingum | Zanesville | 84,169 | 82,068 | 665 |
| Noble | Caldwell | 12,096 | 11,336 | 399 |
| Ottawa | Port Clinton | 40,591 | 40,029 | 255 |
| Paulding | Paulding | 20,443 | 20,488 | 416 |
| Perry | New Lexington | 33,550 | 31,557 | 410 |
| Pickaway | Circleville | 52,510 | 48,244 | 502 |
| Pike | Waverly | 26,775 | 24,249 | 442 |
| Portage | Ravenna | 148,699 | 142,585 | 492 |
| Preble | Eaton | 42,174 | 40,113 | 425 |
| Putnam | Ottawa | 35,089 | 33,819 | 484 |
| Richland | Mansfield | 128,421 | 126,137 | 497 |
| Ross | Chillicothe | 73,941 | 69,330 | 689 |
| Sandusky | Fremont | 62,997 | 61,963 | 409 |
| Scioto | Portsmouth | 81,414 | 80,327 | 612 |
| Seneca | Tiffin | 60,369 | 59,733 | 551 |
| Shelby | Sidney | 47,079 | 44,915 | 409 |
| Stark | Canton | 375,553 | 367,585 | 576 |
| Summit | Akron | 530,135 | 514,990 | 413 |
| Trumbull | Warren | 228,417 | 227,813 | 616 |
| Tuscarawas | New Philadelphia | 87,323 | 84,090 | 568 |
| Union | Marysville | 36,528 | 31,969 | 437 |
| Van Wert | Van Wert | 30,463 | 30,464 | 410 |
| Vinton | McArthur | 12,072 | 11,098 | 414 |
| Warren | Lebanon | 131,295 | 113,927 | 400 |
| Washington | Marietta | 63,836 | 62,254 | 635 |
| Wayne | Wooster | 107,526 | 101,461 | 555 |
| Williams | Bryan | 37,846 | 36,956 | 422 |
| Wood | Bowling Green | 116,934 | 113,269 | 617 |
| Wyandot | Upper Sandusky | 22,732 | 22,254 | 406 |

# Oklahoma

(77 counties, 68,679 sq mi land; pop. 3,277,687)

| County | County seat or courthouse | 1995 Pop. | 1990 Pop. | Land area sq mi |
|---|---|---|---|---|
| Adair | Stillwell | 19,904 | 18,421 | 576 |
| Alfalfa | Cherokee | 6,110 | 6,416 | 867 |
| Atoka | Atoka | 13,263 | 12,778 | 978 |
| Beaver | Beaver | 5,883 | 6,023 | 1,815 |
| Beckham | Sayre | 18,568 | 18,812 | 902 |
| Blaine | Watonga | 10,896 | 11,470 | 929 |
| Bryan | Durant | 33,720 | 32,089 | 909 |
| Caddo | Anadarko | 30,625 | 29,550 | 1,278 |
| Canadian | El Reno | 81,593 | 74,409 | 900 |
| Carter | Ardmore | 44,137 | 42,919 | 824 |
| Cherokee | Tahlequah | 37,098 | 34,049 | 751 |
| Choctaw | Hugo | 15,263 | 15,302 | 774 |
| Cimarron | Boise City | 3,018 | 3,301 | 1,835 |
| Cleveland | Norman | 191,059 | 174,253 | 536 |
| Coal | Coalgate | 6,014 | 5,780 | 518 |
| Comanche | Lawton | 115,672 | 111,486 | 1,069 |
| Cotton | Walters | 6,891 | 6,651 | 637 |
| Craig | Vinita | 14,211 | 14,104 | 761 |
| Creek | Sapulpa | 64,299 | 60,915 | 956 |
| Custer | Arapaho | 26,320 | 26,897 | 987 |
| Delaware | Jay | 32,401 | 28,070 | 741 |
| Dewey | Taloga | 5,126 | 5,551 | 1,000 |
| Ellis | Arnett | 4,251 | 4,497 | 1,229 |
| Garfield | Enid | 57,330 | 56,735 | 1,059 |
| Garvin | Pauls Valley | 26,849 | 26,605 | 809 |
| Grady | Chickasha | 43,817 | 41,747 | 1,101 |
| Grant | Medford | 5,503 | 5,689 | 1,001 |
| Greer | Mangum | 6,556 | 6,559 | 639 |
| Harmon | Hollis | 3,669 | 3,793 | 538 |
| Harper | Buffalo | 3,814 | 4,063 | 1,039 |
| Haskell | Stigler | 11,125 | 10,940 | 577 |
| Hughes | Holdenville | 12,932 | 13,014 | 807 |
| Jackson | Altus | 29,754 | 28,764 | 803 |
| Jefferson | Waurika | 6,877 | 7,010 | 759 |
| Johnston | Tishomingo | 10,283 | 10,032 | 645 |
| Kay | Newkirk | 47,676 | 48,056 | 919 |
| Kingfisher | Kingfisher | 13,377 | 13,212 | 903 |
| Kiowa | Hobart | 11,105 | 11,347 | 1,015 |
| Latimer | Wilburton | 10,416 | 10,333 | 722 |
| Le Flore | Poteau | 45,641 | 43,270 | 1,586 |
| Lincoln | Chandler | 30,528 | 29,216 | 959 |
| Logan | Guthrie | 31,189 | 29,011 | 745 |
| Love | Marietta | 8,735 | 8,157 | 515 |
| McClain | Purcell | 25,162 | 22,795 | 570 |
| McCurtain | Idabel | 34,477 | 33,433 | 1,852 |
| McIntosh | Eufaula | 18,407 | 16,779 | 620 |
| Major | Fairview | 7,703 | 8,055 | 957 |
| Marshall | Madill | 11,718 | 10,829 | 371 |
| Mayes | Pryor | 36,047 | 33,366 | 656 |
| Murray | Sulphur | 12,213 | 12,042 | 418 |
| Muskogee | Muskogee | 69,297 | 68,078 | 814 |
| Noble | Perry | 11,333 | 11,045 | 732 |
| Nowata | Nowata | 9,966 | 9,992 | 565 |
| Okfuskee | Okemah | 11,339 | 11,551 | 625 |
| Oklahoma | Oklahoma City | 625,337 | 599,611 | 709 |
| Okmulgee | Okmulgee | 37,760 | 36,490 | 697 |
| Osage | Pawhuska | 42,577 | 41,645 | 2,251 |
| Ottawa | Miami | 30,649 | 30,561 | 471 |
| Pawnee | Pawnee | 15,918 | 15,575 | 570 |
| Payne | Stillwater | 63,577 | 61,507 | 686 |
| Pittsburg | McAlester | 42,819 | 40,581 | 1,306 |
| Pontotoc | Ada | 34,689 | 34,119 | 720 |
| Pottawatomie | Shawnee | 60,834 | 58,760 | 788 |
| Pushmataha | Antlers | 11,481 | 10,997 | 1,397 |
| Roger Mills | Cheyenne | 3,880 | 4,147 | 1,142 |
| Rogers | Claremore | 62,095 | 55,170 | 675 |
| Seminole | Wewoka | 25,000 | 25,412 | 633 |
| Sequoyah | Sallisaw | 36,070 | 33,828 | 674 |
| Stephens | Duncan | 42,929 | 42,299 | 877 |
| Texas | Guymon | 16,759 | 16,419 | 2,037 |
| Tillman | Frederick | 9,775 | 10,384 | 872 |
| Tulsa | Tulsa | 525,115 | 503,341 | 570 |
| Wagoner | Wagoner | 52,414 | 47,883 | 563 |
| Washington | Bartlesville | 47,594 | 48,066 | 417 |
| Washita | Cordell | 11,779 | 11,441 | 1,004 |
| Woods | Alva | 8,611 | 9,103 | 1,287 |
| Woodward | Woodward | 18,865 | 18,976 | 1,242 |

# Oregon

(36 counties, 96,002 sq mi land; pop. 3,140,585)

| County | County seat or courthouse | 1995 Pop. | 1990 Pop. | Land area sq mi |
|---|---|---|---|---|
| Baker | Baker City | 16,471 | 15,317 | 3,068 |
| Benton | Corvallis | 75,235 | 70,811 | 677 |
| Clackamas | Oregon City | 316,428 | 278,850 | 1,868 |
| Clatsop | Astoria | 35,372 | 33,301 | 827 |
| Columbia | Saint Helens | 41,816 | 37,557 | 657 |
| Coos | Coquille | 62,822 | 60,273 | 1,601 |
| Crook | Prineville | 16,386 | 14,111 | 2,980 |
| Curry | Gold Beach | 21,243 | 19,327 | 1,627 |
| Deschutes | Bend | 94,974 | 74,976 | 3,018 |
| Douglas | Roseburg | 99,906 | 94,649 | 5,037 |
| Gilliam | Condon | 1,861 | 1,717 | 1,204 |
| Grant | Canyon City | 7,976 | 7,853 | 4,529 |
| Harney | Burns | 7,075 | 7,060 | 10,135 |
| Hood River | Hood River | 18,589 | 16,903 | 522 |
| Jackson | Medford | 166,060 | 146,387 | 2,785 |
| Jefferson | Madras | 15,969 | 13,676 | 1,781 |
| Josephine | Grants Pass | 71,335 | 62,649 | 1,640 |

| County | County seat or courthouse | 1995 Pop. | 1990 Pop. | Land area sq mi |
|---|---|---|---|---|
| Klamath | Klamath Falls | 61,043 | 57,702 | 5,945 |
| Lake | Lakeview | 7,421 | 7,186 | 8,136 |
| Lane | Eugene | 303,426 | 282,912 | 4,554 |
| Lincoln | Newport | 44,347 | 38,889 | 980 |
| Linn | Albany | 100,130 | 91,227 | 2,291 |
| Malheur | Vale | 27,860 | 26,038 | 9,888 |
| Marion | Salem | 255,044 | 228,483 | 1,185 |
| Morrow | Heppner | 8,922 | 7,625 | 2,033 |
| Multnomah | Portland | 614,104 | 583,887 | 435 |
| Polk | Dallas | 56,678 | 49,541 | 741 |
| Sherman | Moro | 1,886 | 1,918 | 823 |
| Tillamook | Tillamook | 23,767 | 21,570 | 1,102 |
| Umatilla | Pendleton | 64,040 | 59,249 | 3,215 |
| Union | La Grande | 24,948 | 23,598 | 2,037 |
| Wallowa | Enterprise | 7,535 | 6,911 | 3,145 |
| Wasco | The Dalles | 22,737 | 21,683 | 2,381 |
| Washington | Hillsboro | 370,197 | 311,554 | 724 |
| Wheeler | Fossil | 1,539 | 1,396 | 1,715 |
| Yamhill | McMinnville | 75,443 | 65,551 | 716 |

# Pennsylvania

(67 counties, 44,820 sq mi land; pop. 12,071,842)

| County | County seat or courthouse | 1995 Pop. | 1990 Pop. | Land area sq mi |
|---|---|---|---|---|
| Adams | Gettysburg | 83,998 | 78,274 | 520 |
| Allegheny | Pittsburgh | 1,309,821 | 1,336,449 | 730 |
| Armstrong | Kittanning | 74,569 | 73,478 | 654 |
| Beaver | Beaver | 187,979 | 186,093 | 435 |
| Bedford | Bedford | 49,192 | 47,919 | 1,015 |
| Berks | Reading | 349,583 | 336,523 | 859 |
| Blair | Hollidaysburg | 131,647 | 130,542 | 526 |
| Bradford | Towanda | 62,260 | 60,967 | 1,151 |
| Bucks | Doylestown | 573,901 | 541,174 | 608 |
| Butler | Butler | 165,557 | 152,013 | 789 |
| Cambria | Ebensburg | 160,531 | 163,062 | 688 |
| Cameron | Emporium | 5,707 | 5,913 | 397 |
| Carbon | Jim Thorpe | 58,832 | 56,973 | 383 |
| Centre | Bellefonte | 131,968 | 124,812 | 1,108 |
| Chester | West Chester | 404,945 | 376,396 | 756 |
| Clarion | Clarion | 42,338 | 41,699 | 603 |
| Clearfield | Clearfield | 79,724 | 78,097 | 1,147 |
| Clinton | Lock Haven | 37,215 | 37,182 | 891 |
| Columbia | Bloomsburg | 64,492 | 63,202 | 486 |
| Crawford | Meadville | 89,173 | 86,170 | 1,013 |
| Cumberland | Carlisle | 205,959 | 195,257 | 550 |
| Dauphin | Harrisburg | 246,338 | 237,813 | 525 |
| Delaware | Media | 548,708 | 547,651 | 184 |
| Elk | Ridgway | 35,125 | 34,878 | 829 |
| Erie | Erie | 280,460 | 275,572 | 802 |
| Fayette | Uniontown | 146,827 | 145,351 | 790 |
| Forest | Tionesta | 5,001 | 4,802 | 428 |
| Franklin | Chambersburg | 126,444 | 121,082 | 772 |
| Fulton | McConnellsburg | 14,362 | 13,837 | 438 |
| Greene | Waynesburg | 41,114 | 39,550 | 576 |
| Huntingdon | Huntingdon | 44,933 | 44,164 | 875 |
| Indiana | Indiana | 90,604 | 89,994 | 830 |
| Jefferson | Brookville | 46,620 | 46,083 | 656 |
| Juniata | Mifflintown | 21,701 | 20,625 | 392 |
| Lackawanna | Scranton | 215,688 | 219,097 | 459 |
| Lancaster | Lancaster | 447,521 | 422,822 | 949 |
| Lawrence | New Castle | 96,604 | 96,246 | 361 |
| Lebanon | Lebanon | 116,789 | 113,744 | 362 |
| Lehigh | Allentown | 297,838 | 291,130 | 347 |
| Luzerne | Wilkes-Barre | 326,063 | 328,149 | 891 |
| Lycoming | Williamsport | 120,194 | 118,710 | 1,235 |
| McKean | Smethport | 48,503 | 47,131 | 982 |
| Mercer | Mercer | 122,254 | 121,003 | 672 |
| Mifflin | Lewistown | 47,066 | 46,197 | 411 |
| Monroe | Stroudsburg | 116,091 | 95,582 | 607 |
| Montgomery | Norristown | 705,178 | 678,193 | 483 |
| Montour | Danville | 18,223 | 17,735 | 131 |
| Northampton | Easton | 256,796 | 247,105 | 374 |
| Northumberland | Sunbury | 96,260 | 96,771 | 460 |
| Perry | New Bloomfield | 43,531 | 41,172 | 554 |
| Philadelphia | Philadelphia | 1,498,971 | 1,585,577 | 135 |
| Pike | Milford | 36,852 | 27,966 | 547 |
| Potter | Coudersport | 17,090 | 16,717 | 1,081 |
| Schuylkill | Pottsville | 153,616 | 152,585 | 779 |
| Snyder | Middleburg | 37,845 | 36,680 | 331 |
| Somerset | Somerset | 80,113 | 78,218 | 1,075 |
| Sullivan | Laporte | 6,184 | 6,104 | 450 |
| Susquehanna | Montrose | 41,800 | 40,380 | 823 |
| Tioga | Wellsboro | 41,534 | 41,126 | 1,134 |
| Union | Lewisburg | 40,928 | 36,176 | 317 |
| Venango | Franklin | 59,057 | 59,381 | 675 |
| Warren | Warren | 44,928 | 45,049 | 884 |
| Washington | Washington | 208,017 | 204,584 | 857 |
| Wayne | Honesdale | 44,070 | 39,944 | 729 |
| Westmoreland | Greensburg | 376,501 | 370,321 | 1,023 |
| Wyoming | Tunkhannock | 29,316 | 28,076 | 397 |
| York | York | 362,793 | 339,574 | 905 |

# Rhode Island

(5 counties, 1,045 sq mi land; pop. 989,794)

| County | County seat or courthouse | 1995 Pop. | 1990 Pop. | Land area sq mi |
|---|---|---|---|---|
| Bristol | Bristol | 48,781 | 48,859 | 25 |
| Kent | East Greenwich | 162,143 | 161,135 | 170 |
| Newport | Newport | 81,993 | 87,194 | 104 |
| Providence | Providence | 580,015 | 596,270 | 413 |
| Washington | West Kingston | 116,862 | 110,006 | 333 |

# South Carolina

(46 counties, 30,111 sq mi land; pop. 3,673,287)

| County | County seat or courthouse | 1995 Pop. | 1990 Pop. | Land area sq mi |
|---|---|---|---|---|
| Abbeville | Abbeville | 24,258 | 23,862 | 508 |
| Aiken | Aiken | 133,059 | 120,991 | 1,073 |
| Allendale | Allendale | 11,580 | 11,722 | 408 |
| Anderson | Anderson | 154,478 | 145,177 | 718 |
| Bamberg | Bamberg | 16,698 | 16,902 | 393 |
| Barnwell | Barnwell | 21,478 | 20,293 | 549 |
| Beaufort | Beaufort | 99,841 | 86,425 | 587 |
| Berkeley | Moncks Corner | 135,337 | 128,776 | 1,100 |
| Calhoun | Saint Matthews | 13,369 | 12,753 | 380 |
| Charleston | Charleston | 281,983 | 295,041 | 917 |
| Cherokee | Gaffney | 47,184 | 44,506 | 393 |
| Chester | Chester | 33,050 | 32,170 | 581 |
| Chesterfield | Chesterfield | 39,365 | 38,575 | 799 |
| Clarendon | Manning | 29,415 | 28,450 | 607 |
| Colleton | Walterboro | 36,738 | 34,377 | 1,057 |
| Darlington | Darlington | 64,997 | 61,851 | 562 |
| Dillon | Dillon | 29,759 | 29,114 | 405 |
| Dorchester | Saint George | 89,100 | 83,060 | 575 |
| Edgefield | Edgefield | 19,341 | 18,360 | 502 |
| Fairfield | Winnsboro | 22,504 | 22,295 | 687 |
| Florence | Florence | 122,769 | 114,344 | 799 |
| Georgetown | Georgetown | 50,890 | 46,302 | 815 |
| Greenville | Greenville | 339,908 | 320,167 | 792 |
| Greenwood | Greenwood | 61,954 | 59,567 | 456 |
| Hampton | Hampton | 19,120 | 18,191 | 560 |
| Horry | Conway | 157,902 | 144,053 | 1,134 |
| Jasper | Ridgeland | 16,404 | 15,487 | 654 |
| Kershaw | Camden | 46,768 | 43,599 | 726 |
| Lancaster | Lancaster | 56,325 | 54,516 | 549 |
| Laurens | Laurens | 60,804 | 58,092 | 713 |
| Lee | Bishopville | 18,672 | 18,437 | 410 |
| Lexington | Lexington | 191,879 | 167,611 | 701 |
| McCormick | McCormick | 9,224 | 8,868 | 360 |
| Marion | Marion | 35,203 | 33,899 | 489 |
| Marlboro | Bennettsville | 29,963 | 29,716 | 480 |
| Newberry | Newberry | 34,215 | 33,172 | 631 |
| Oconee | Walhalla | 61,605 | 57,494 | 625 |
| Orangeburg | Orangeburg | 87,719 | 84,803 | 1,106 |
| Pickens | Pickens | 102,407 | 93,896 | 497 |
| Richland | Columbia | 289,839 | 286,321 | 757 |
| Saluda | Saluda | 16,903 | 16,357 | 451 |
| Spartanburg | Spartanburg | 240,329 | 226,793 | 811 |
| Sumter | Sumter | 106,823 | 101,276 | 666 |
| Union | Union | 30,836 | 30,337 | 514 |
| Williamsburg | Kingstree | 37,467 | 36,815 | 934 |
| York | York | 143,825 | 131,497 | 683 |

# South Dakota

(66 counties, 75,896 sq mi land; pop. 729,034)

| County | County seat or courthouse | 1995 Pop. | 1990 Pop. | Land area sq mi |
|---|---|---|---|---|
| Aurora | Plankinton | 3,091 | 3,135 | 708 |
| Beadle | Huron | 18,143 | 18,253 | 1,259 |
| Bennett | Martin | 3,313 | 3,206 | 1,185 |
| Bon Homme | Tyndall | 7,008 | 7,089 | 563 |
| Brookings | Brookings | 26,450 | 25,207 | 795 |
| Brown | Aberdeen | 35,734 | 35,580 | 1,713 |
| Brule | Chamberlain | 5,633 | 5,485 | 819 |
| Buffalo | Gannvalley | 1,832 | 1,759 | 471 |
| Butte | Belle Fourche | 8,896 | 7,914 | 2,249 |
| Campbell | Mound City | 1,881 | 1,965 | 736 |
| Charles Mix | Lake Andes | 9,479 | 9,131 | 1,098 |
| Clark | Clark | 4,382 | 4,403 | 958 |
| Clay | Vermillion | 13,606 | 13,186 | 412 |
| Codington | Watertown | 24,829 | 22,698 | 688 |
| Corson | McIntosh | 4,258 | 4,195 | 2,473 |
| Custer | Custer | 6,675 | 6,179 | 1,558 |
| Davison | Mitchell | 17,823 | 17,503 | 436 |
| Day | Webster | 6,713 | 6,978 | 1,029 |
| Deuel | Clear Lake | 4,449 | 4,522 | 624 |
| Dewey | Timber Lake | 5,783 | 5,523 | 2,303 |
| Douglas | Armour | 3,615 | 3,746 | 434 |
| Edmunds | Ipswich | 4,344 | 4,356 | 1,146 |
| Fall River | Hot Springs | 7,089 | 7,353 | 1,740 |
| Faulk | Faulkton | 2,592 | 2,744 | 1,000 |
| Grant | Milbank | 8,237 | 8,372 | 683 |
| Gregory | Burke | 5,112 | 5,359 | 1,016 |
| Haakon | Philip | 2,548 | 2,624 | 1,813 |
| Hamlin | Hayti | 5,372 | 4,974 | 511 |

| County | County seat or courthouse | 1995 Pop. | 1990 Pop. | Land area sq mi |
|---|---|---|---|---|
| Hand | Miller | 4,202 | 4,272 | 1,437 |
| Hanson | Alexandria | 2,935 | 2,994 | 435 |
| Harding | Buffalo | 1,542 | 1,669 | 2,671 |
| Hughes | Pierre | 15,537 | 14,817 | 741 |
| Hutchinson | Olivet | 8,016 | 8,262 | 813 |
| Hyde | Highmore | 1,675 | 1,696 | 861 |
| Jackson | Kadoka | 2,867 | 2,811 | 1,869 |
| Jerauld | Wessington Springs | 2,338 | 2,425 | 530 |
| Jones | Murdo | 1,318 | 1,324 | 971 |
| Kingsbury | De Smet | 5,745 | 5,925 | 838 |
| Lake | Madison | 10,797 | 10,550 | 563 |
| Lawrence | Deadwood | 22,452 | 20,655 | 800 |
| Lincoln | Canton | 17,666 | 15,427 | 578 |
| Lyman | Kennebec | 3,779 | 3,638 | 1,640 |
| McCook | Salem | 5,824 | 5,688 | 575 |
| McPherson | Leola | 3,036 | 3,228 | 1,137 |
| Marshall | Britton | 4,714 | 4,844 | 839 |
| Meade | Sturgis | 23,084 | 21,878 | 3,471 |
| Mellette | White River | 2,002 | 2,137 | 1,307 |
| Miner | Howard | 3,064 | 3,272 | 570 |
| Minnehaha | Sioux Falls | 135,641 | 123,809 | 809 |
| Moody | Flandreau | 6,616 | 6,507 | 520 |
| Pennington | Rapid City | 87,304 | 81,343 | 2,776 |
| Perkins | Bison | 3,703 | 3,932 | 2,872 |
| Potter | Gettysburg | 2,990 | 3,190 | 867 |
| Roberts | Sisseton | 9,949 | 9,914 | 1,101 |
| Sanborn | Woonsocket | 2,798 | 2,833 | 569 |
| Shannon | (Attached to Fall River) | 11,675 | 9,902 | 2,094 |
| Spink | Redfield | 7,844 | 7,981 | 1,504 |
| Stanley | Fort Pierre | 2,823 | 2,453 | 1,443 |
| Sully | Onida | 1,573 | 1,589 | 1,007 |
| Todd | (Attached to Tripp) | 9,105 | 8,352 | 1,388 |
| Tripp | Winner | 6,902 | 6,924 | 1,614 |
| Turner | Parker | 8,603 | 8,576 | 617 |
| Union | Elk Point | 11,225 | 10,189 | 460 |
| Walworth | Selby | 5,834 | 6,087 | 708 |
| Yankton | Yankton | 20,754 | 19,252 | 522 |
| Ziebach | Dupree | 2,215 | 2,220 | 1,963 |

## Tennessee

(95 counties, 41,219 sq mi land; pop. 5,256,051)

| County | County seat or courthouse | 1995 Pop. | 1990 Pop. | Land area sq mi |
|---|---|---|---|---|
| Anderson | Clinton | 71,663 | 68,250 | 338 |
| Bedford | Shelbyville | 33,126 | 30,411 | 474 |
| Benton | Camden | 15,770 | 14,524 | 395 |
| Bledsoe | Pikeville | 10,173 | 9,669 | 406 |
| Blount | Maryville | 97,014 | 85,969 | 559 |
| Bradley | Cleveland | 78,830 | 73,712 | 329 |
| Campbell | Jacksboro | 37,033 | 35,079 | 480 |
| Cannon | Woodbury | 11,399 | 10,467 | 266 |
| Carroll | Huntingdon | 28,617 | 27,514 | 599 |
| Carter | Elizabethton | 52,791 | 51,505 | 341 |
| Cheatham | Ashland City | 32,248 | 27,140 | 303 |
| Chester | Henderson | 13,703 | 12,819 | 289 |
| Claiborne | Tazewell | 28,542 | 26,137 | 434 |
| Clay | Celina | 7,230 | 7,238 | 236 |
| Cocke | Newport | 31,110 | 29,141 | 434 |
| Coffee | Manchester | 43,696 | 40,339 | 429 |
| Crockett | Alamo | 13,589 | 13,378 | 265 |
| Cumberland | Crossville | 40,445 | 34,736 | 682 |
| Davidson | Nashville | 530,796 | 510,786 | 502 |
| Decatur | Decaturville | 10,788 | 10,472 | 334 |
| De Kalb | Smithville | 15,290 | 14,360 | 305 |
| Dickson | Charlotte | 38,740 | 35,061 | 490 |
| Dyer | Dyersburg | 35,900 | 34,854 | 511 |
| Fayette | Somerville | 26,954 | 25,559 | 705 |
| Fentress | Jamestown | 15,565 | 14,669 | 499 |
| Franklin | Winchester | 36,442 | 34,725 | 553 |
| Gibson | Trenton | 47,728 | 46,315 | 603 |
| Giles | Pulaski | 28,168 | 25,741 | 611 |
| Grainger | Rutledge | 18,667 | 17,095 | 280 |
| Greene | Greeneville | 58,095 | 55,853 | 622 |
| Grundy | Altamont | 13,695 | 13,362 | 361 |
| Hamblen | Morristown | 52,763 | 50,480 | 161 |
| Hamilton | Chattanooga | 293,771 | 285,536 | 543 |
| Hancock | Sneedville | 6,844 | 6,739 | 222 |
| Hardeman | Bolivar | 24,184 | 23,377 | 668 |
| Hardin | Savannah | 24,399 | 22,633 | 578 |
| Hawkins | Rogersville | 47,724 | 44,565 | 487 |
| Haywood | Brownsville | 19,608 | 19,437 | 533 |
| Henderson | Lexington | 23,245 | 21,844 | 520 |
| Henry | Paris | 29,429 | 27,888 | 562 |
| Hickman | Centerville | 19,068 | 16,754 | 613 |
| Houston | Erin | 7,579 | 7,018 | 200 |
| Humphreys | Waverly | 16,532 | 15,813 | 532 |
| Jackson | Gainesboro | 9,326 | 9,297 | 309 |
| Jefferson | Dandridge | 38,838 | 33,016 | 274 |
| Johnson | Mountain City | 16,341 | 13,766 | 299 |
| Knox | Knoxville | 361,407 | 335,749 | 509 |
| Lake | Tiptonville | 8,539 | 7,129 | 163 |
| Lauderdale | Ripley | 24,103 | 23,491 | 471 |
| Lawrence | Lawrenceburg | 38,292 | 35,303 | 617 |
| Lewis | Hohenwald | 10,292 | 9,247 | 282 |
| Lincoln | Fayetteville | 28,785 | 28,157 | 570 |
| Loudon | Loudon | 35,927 | 31,255 | 229 |
| McMinn | Athens | 45,001 | 42,383 | 430 |
| McNairy | Selmer | 23,410 | 22,422 | 560 |
| Macon | Lafayette | 16,927 | 15,906 | 307 |
| Madison | Jackson | 83,715 | 77,982 | 557 |
| Marion | Jasper | 26,469 | 24,860 | 500 |
| Marshall | Lewisburg | 24,900 | 21,539 | 375 |
| Maury | Columbia | 65,207 | 54,812 | 613 |
| Meigs | Decatur | 9,198 | 8,033 | 195 |
| Monroe | Madisonville | 32,867 | 30,541 | 635 |
| Montgomery | Clarksville | 123,811 | 100,498 | 539 |
| Moore | Lynchburg | 5,189 | 4,721 | 129 |
| Morgan | Wartburg | 18,280 | 17,300 | 522 |
| Obion | Union City | 32,413 | 31,717 | 545 |
| Overton | Livingston | 18,309 | 17,636 | 433 |
| Perry | Linden | 7,055 | 6,612 | 415 |
| Pickett | Byrdstown | 4,583 | 4,548 | 163 |
| Polk | Benton | 14,263 | 13,643 | 435 |
| Putnam | Cookeville | 57,319 | 51,373 | 401 |
| Rhea | Dayton | 26,833 | 24,344 | 316 |
| Roane | Kingston | 48,607 | 47,227 | 361 |
| Robertson | Springfield | 47,955 | 41,492 | 477 |
| Rutherford | Murfreesboro | 148,041 | 118,570 | 619 |
| Scott | Huntsville | 19,550 | 18,358 | 532 |
| Sequatchie | Dunlap | 9,648 | 8,863 | 266 |
| Sevier | Sevierville | 59,542 | 51,043 | 592 |
| Shelby | Memphis | 865,058 | 826,330 | 755 |
| Smith | Carthage | 15,356 | 14,143 | 314 |
| Stewart | Dover | 10,586 | 9,479 | 458 |
| Sullivan | Blountville | 148,783 | 143,596 | 413 |
| Sumner | Gallatin | 116,845 | 103,281 | 529 |
| Tipton | Covington | 43,423 | 37,568 | 459 |
| Trousdale | Hartsville | 6,449 | 5,920 | 114 |
| Unicoi | Erwin | 16,819 | 16,549 | 186 |
| Union | Maynardville | 15,147 | 13,694 | 224 |
| Van Buren | Spencer | 5,095 | 4,846 | 274 |
| Warren | McMinnville | 35,225 | 32,992 | 433 |
| Washington | Jonesboro | 98,477 | 92,315 | 326 |
| Wayne | Waynesboro | 16,032 | 13,935 | 734 |
| Weakley | Dresden | 32,346 | 31,972 | 580 |
| White | Sparta | 21,304 | 20,090 | 377 |
| Williamson | Franklin | 102,061 | 81,021 | 583 |
| Wilson | Lebanon | 77,150 | 67,675 | 571 |

## Texas

(254 counties, 261,914 sq mi land; pop. 18,723,991)

| County | County seat or courthouse | 1995 Pop. | 1990 Pop. | Land area sq mi |
|---|---|---|---|---|
| Anderson | Palestine | 50,708 | 48,024 | 1,071 |
| Andrews | Andrews | 14,228 | 14,338 | 1,501 |
| Angelina | Lufkin | 75,488 | 69,884 | 802 |
| Aransas | Rockport | 21,179 | 17,892 | 252 |
| Archer | Archer City | 8,147 | 7,973 | 910 |
| Armstrong | Claude | 2,111 | 2,021 | 914 |
| Atascosa | Jourdanton | 33,808 | 30,533 | 1,232 |
| Austin | Bellville | 22,373 | 19,832 | 653 |
| Bailey | Muleshoe | 6,891 | 7,064 | 827 |
| Bandera | Bandera | 13,482 | 10,562 | 792 |
| Bastrop | Bastrop | 44,487 | 38,263 | 889 |
| Baylor | Seymour | 4,250 | 4,385 | 871 |
| Bee | Beeville | 26,874 | 25,135 | 880 |
| Bell | Belton | 217,891 | 191,073 | 1,059 |
| Bexar | San Antonio | 1,296,731 | 1,185,394 | 1,247 |
| Blanco | Johnson City | 7,651 | 5,972 | 711 |
| Borden | Gail | 799 | 799 | 899 |
| Bosque | Meridian | 16,502 | 15,125 | 989 |
| Bowie | Boston | 83,909 | 81,665 | 888 |
| Brazoria | Angleton | 216,016 | 191,707 | 1,387 |
| Brazos | Bryan | 130,486 | 121,862 | 586 |
| Brewster | Alpine | 9,120 | 8,653 | 6,193 |
| Briscoe | Silverton | 1,849 | 1,971 | 900 |
| Brooks | Falfurrias | 8,412 | 8,204 | 943 |
| Brown | Brownwood | 35,960 | 34,371 | 944 |
| Burleson | Caldwell | 15,011 | 13,625 | 666 |
| Burnet | Burnet | 27,257 | 22,677 | 995 |
| Caldwell | Lockhart | 29,091 | 26,392 | 546 |
| Calhoun | Port Lavaca | 20,469 | 19,053 | 512 |
| Callahan | Baird | 12,308 | 11,859 | 899 |
| Cameron | Brownsville | 309,578 | 260,120 | 906 |
| Camp | Pittsburg | 10,518 | 9,904 | 198 |
| Carson | Panhandle | 6,639 | 6,576 | 923 |
| Cass | Linden | 30,654 | 29,982 | 938 |
| Castro | Dimmitt | 8,616 | 9,070 | 898 |
| Chambers | Anahuac | 22,042 | 20,088 | 599 |
| Cherokee | Rusk | 41,155 | 41,049 | 1,052 |
| Childress | Childress | 6,529 | 5,953 | 710 |
| Clay | Henrietta | 10,157 | 10,024 | 1,098 |
| Cochran | Morton | 4,188 | 4,377 | 775 |
| Coke | Robert Lee | 3,473 | 3,424 | 899 |
| Coleman | Coleman | 9,623 | 9,710 | 1,273 |
| Collin | McKinney | 346,232 | 264,036 | 848 |
| Collingsworth | Wellington | 3,371 | 3,573 | 919 |
| Colorado | Columbus | 18,799 | 18,383 | 963 |
| Comal | New Braunfels | 64,155 | 51,832 | 562 |
| Comanche | Comanche | 13,532 | 13,381 | 938 |
| Concho | Paint Rock | 2,993 | 3,044 | 992 |

| County | County seat or courthouse | 1995 Pop. | 1990 Pop. | Land area sq mi |
|---|---|---|---|---|
| Cooke | Gainesville | 31,733 | 30,777 | 874 |
| Coryell | Gatesville | 72,012 | 64,226 | 1,052 |
| Cottle | Paducah | 2,048 | 2,247 | 901 |
| Crane | Crane | 4,515 | 4,652 | 786 |
| Crockett | Ozona | 4,403 | 4,078 | 2,808 |
| Crosby | Crosbyton | 7,269 | 7,304 | 900 |
| Culberson | Van Horn | 3,245 | 3,407 | 3,813 |
| Dallam | Dalhart | 6,379 | 5,461 | 1,505 |
| Dallas | Dallas | 1,959,281 | 1,852,810 | 880 |
| Dawson | Lamesa | 15,051 | 14,349 | 902 |
| Deaf Smith | Hereford | 19,422 | 19,153 | 1,497 |
| Delta | Cooper | 4,877 | 4,857 | 277 |
| Denton | Denton | 334,070 | 273,525 | 889 |
| DeWitt | Cuero | 18,481 | 18,840 | 909 |
| Dickens | Dickens | 2,419 | 2,571 | 904 |
| Dimmit | Carrizo Springs | 10,508 | 10,433 | 1,331 |
| Donley | Clarendon | 3,743 | 3,696 | 930 |
| Duval | San Diego | 12,994 | 12,918 | 1,793 |
| Eastland | Eastland | 17,873 | 18,488 | 926 |
| Ector | Odessa | 123,450 | 118,934 | 901 |
| Edwards | Rocksprings | 3,110 | 2,266 | 2,120 |
| Ellis | Waxahachie | 94,223 | 85,167 | 940 |
| El Paso | El Paso | 678,313 | 591,610 | 1,013 |
| Erath | Stephenville | 30,352 | 27,991 | 1,086 |
| Falls | Marlin | 17,950 | 17,712 | 769 |
| Fannin | Bonham | 25,638 | 24,804 | 892 |
| Fayette | La Grange | 21,113 | 20,095 | 950 |
| Fisher | Roby | 4,539 | 4,842 | 901 |
| Floyd | Floydada | 8,392 | 8,497 | 992 |
| Foard | Crowell | 1,662 | 1,794 | 707 |
| Fort Bend | Richmond | 292,765 | 225,421 | 875 |
| Franklin | Mount Vernon | 8,934 | 7,802 | 286 |
| Freestone | Fairfield | 17,035 | 15,818 | 885 |
| Frio | Pearsall | 15,250 | 13,472 | 1,133 |
| Gaines | Seminole | 14,479 | 14,123 | 1,502 |
| Galveston | Galveston | 237,533 | 217,396 | 399 |
| Garza | Post | 4,742 | 5,143 | 896 |
| Gillespie | Fredericksburg | 19,408 | 17,204 | 1,061 |
| Glasscock | Garden City | 1,390 | 1,447 | 901 |
| Goliad | Goliad | 6,363 | 5,980 | 854 |
| Gonzales | Gonzales | 17,378 | 17,205 | 1,068 |
| Gray | Pampa | 23,155 | 23,967 | 928 |
| Grayson | Sherman | 98,336 | 95,019 | 934 |
| Gregg | Longview | 110,725 | 104,948 | 274 |
| Grimes | Anderson | 21,624 | 18,828 | 794 |
| Guadalupe | Seguin | 72,632 | 64,873 | 711 |
| Hale | Plainview | 36,223 | 34,671 | 1,005 |
| Hall | Memphis | 3,632 | 3,905 | 903 |
| Hamilton | Hamilton | 7,662 | 7,733 | 836 |
| Hansford | Spearman | 5,264 | 5,848 | 920 |
| Hardeman | Quanah | 4,872 | 5,283 | 695 |
| Hardin | Kountze | 46,607 | 41,320 | 894 |
| Harris | Houston | 3,076,867 | 2,818,101 | 1,729 |
| Harrison | Marshall | 58,703 | 57,483 | 899 |
| Hartley | Channing | 3,815 | 3,634 | 1,462 |
| Haskell | Haskell | 6,358 | 6,820 | 903 |
| Hays | San Marcos | 77,522 | 65,614 | 678 |
| Hemphill | Canadian | 3,594 | 3,720 | 910 |
| Henderson | Athens | 64,293 | 58,543 | 874 |
| Hidalgo | Edinburg | 479,783 | 383,545 | 1,569 |
| Hill | Hillsboro | 28,759 | 27,146 | 962 |
| Hockley | Levelland | 24,245 | 24,199 | 908 |
| Hood | Granbury | 33,384 | 28,981 | 422 |
| Hopkins | Sulphur Springs | 29,738 | 28,833 | 785 |
| Houston | Crockett | 21,917 | 21,375 | 1,231 |
| Howard | Big Spring | 32,450 | 32,343 | 903 |
| Hudspeth | Sierra Blanca | 3,194 | 2,915 | 4,571 |
| Hunt | Greenville | 66,972 | 64,343 | 841 |
| Hutchinson | Stinnett | 24,522 | 25,689 | 887 |
| Irion | Mertzon | 1,631 | 1,629 | 1,052 |
| Jack | Jacksboro | 6,953 | 6,981 | 917 |
| Jackson | Edna | 13,649 | 13,039 | 830 |
| Jasper | Jasper | 32,825 | 31,102 | 938 |
| Jeff Davis | Fort Davis | 2,122 | 1,946 | 2,265 |
| Jefferson | Beaumont | 243,339 | 239,389 | 904 |
| Jim Hogg | Hebbronville | 5,096 | 5,109 | 1,136 |
| Jim Wells | Alice | 39,923 | 37,679 | 865 |
| Johnson | Cleburne | 106,181 | 97,165 | 729 |
| Jones | Anson | 18,058 | 16,490 | 931 |
| Karnes | Karnes City | 12,477 | 12,455 | 750 |
| Kaufman | Kaufman | 60,114 | 52,220 | 786 |
| Kendall | Boerne | 19,413 | 14,589 | 663 |
| Kenedy | Sarita | 442 | 460 | 1,457 |
| Kent | Jayton | 912 | 1,010 | 902 |
| Kerr | Kerrville | 40,264 | 36,304 | 1,106 |
| Kimble | Junction | 4,104 | 4,122 | 1,251 |
| King | Guthrie | 316 | 354 | 912 |
| Kinney | Brackettville | 3,289 | 3,119 | 1,364 |
| Kleberg | Kingsville | 30,629 | 30,274 | 871 |
| Knox | Benjamin | 4,620 | 4,837 | 854 |
| Lamar | Paris | 45,214 | 43,949 | 917 |
| Lamb | Littlefield | 14,796 | 15,072 | 1,016 |
| Lampasas | Lampasas | 16,606 | 13,521 | 712 |
| La Salle | Cotulla | 6,055 | 5,254 | 1,489 |
| Lavaca | Hallettsville | 18,614 | 18,690 | 970 |
| Lee | Giddings | 13,934 | 12,854 | 629 |
| Leon | Centerville | 13,738 | 12,665 | 1,072 |
| Liberty | Liberty | 59,054 | 52,726 | 1,160 |
| Limestone | Groesbeck | 20,896 | 20,946 | 909 |
| Lipscomb | Lipscomb | 3,054 | 3,143 | 932 |
| Live Oak | George West | 10,254 | 9,556 | 1,036 |
| Llano | Llano | 12,698 | 11,631 | 935 |
| Loving | Mentone | 140 | 107 | 673 |
| Lubbock | Lubbock | 232,276 | 222,636 | 900 |
| Lynn | Tahoka | 6,448 | 6,758 | 892 |
| McCulloch | Brady | 8,589 | 8,778 | 1,069 |
| McLennan | Waco | 200,111 | 189,123 | 1,042 |
| McMullen | Tilden | 794 | 817 | 1,113 |
| Madison | Madisonville | 11,911 | 10,931 | 470 |
| Marion | Jefferson | 10,370 | 9,984 | 381 |
| Martin | Stanton | 4,956 | 4,956 | 915 |
| Mason | Mason | 3,590 | 3,423 | 932 |
| Matagorda | Bay City | 38,297 | 36,928 | 1,115 |
| Maverick | Eagle Pass | 45,766 | 36,378 | 1,280 |
| Medina | Hondo | 32,918 | 27,312 | 1,328 |
| Menard | Menard | 2,382 | 2,252 | 902 |
| Midland | Midland | 115,795 | 106,611 | 900 |
| Milam | Cameron | 23,644 | 22,946 | 1,017 |
| Mills | Goldthwaite | 4,730 | 4,531 | 748 |
| Mitchell | Colorado City | 8,713 | 8,016 | 910 |
| Montague | Montague | 17,844 | 17,274 | 931 |
| Montgomery | Conroe | 233,684 | 182,201 | 1,044 |
| Moore | Dumas | 19,157 | 17,865 | 900 |
| Morris | Daingerfield | 13,169 | 13,200 | 255 |
| Motley | Matador | 1,308 | 1,532 | 989 |
| Nacogdoches | Nacogdoches | 56,380 | 54,753 | 947 |
| Navarro | Corsicana | 40,849 | 39,926 | 1,071 |
| Newton | Newton | 14,358 | 13,569 | 933 |
| Nolan | Sweetwater | 16,251 | 16,594 | 912 |
| Nueces | Corpus Christi | 312,708 | 291,145 | 836 |
| Ochiltree | Perryton | 8,652 | 9,128 | 918 |
| Oldham | Vega | 2,218 | 2,278 | 1,501 |
| Orange | Orange | 84,691 | 80,509 | 356 |
| Palo Pinto | Palo Pinto | 25,051 | 25,055 | 953 |
| Panola | Carthage | 22,969 | 22,035 | 801 |
| Parker | Weatherford | 73,794 | 64,785 | 904 |
| Parmer | Farwell | 10,242 | 9,863 | 882 |
| Pecos | Fort Stockton | 15,427 | 14,675 | 4,764 |
| Polk | Livingston | 39,756 | 30,687 | 1,057 |
| Potter | Amarillo | 104,574 | 97,841 | 909 |
| Presidio | Marfa | 7,656 | 6,637 | 3,856 |
| Rains | Emory | 7,634 | 6,715 | 232 |
| Randall | Canyon | 96,438 | 89,673 | 915 |
| Reagan | Big Lake | 4,364 | 4,514 | 1,175 |
| Real | Leakey | 2,590 | 2,412 | 700 |
| Red River | Clarksville | 14,036 | 14,317 | 1,050 |
| Reeves | Pecos | 15,373 | 15,852 | 2,636 |
| Refugio | Refugio | 7,834 | 7,976 | 770 |
| Roberts | Miami | 977 | 1,025 | 924 |
| Robertson | Franklin | 15,535 | 15,511 | 855 |
| Rockwall | Rockwall | 32,725 | 25,604 | 129 |
| Runnels | Ballinger | 11,271 | 11,294 | 1,055 |
| Rusk | Henderson | 44,670 | 43,735 | 924 |
| Sabine | Hemphill | 10,487 | 9,586 | 490 |
| San Augustine | San Augustine | 8,016 | 7,999 | 528 |
| San Jacinto | Coldspring | 19,236 | 16,372 | 571 |
| San Patricio | Sinton | 66,228 | 58,749 | 692 |
| San Saba | San Saba | 6,031 | 5,401 | 1,135 |
| Schleicher | Eldorado | 3,057 | 2,990 | 1,311 |
| Scurry | Snyder | 18,105 | 18,634 | 903 |
| Shackelford | Albany | 3,221 | 3,316 | 914 |
| Shelby | Center | 22,436 | 22,034 | 794 |
| Sherman | Stratford | 2,857 | 2,858 | 923 |
| Smith | Tyler | 161,986 | 151,309 | 929 |
| Somervell | Glen Rose | 5,952 | 5,360 | 187 |
| Starr | Rio Grande City | 51,482 | 40,518 | 1,223 |
| Stephens | Breckenridge | 9,166 | 9,010 | 895 |
| Sterling | Sterling City | 1,460 | 1,438 | 923 |
| Stonewall | Aspermont | 1,892 | 2,013 | 919 |
| Sutton | Sonora | 4,414 | 4,135 | 1,454 |
| Swisher | Tulia | 8,597 | 8,133 | 901 |
| Tarrant | Fort Worth | 1,278,606 | 1,170,103 | 864 |
| Taylor | Abilene | 122,791 | 119,655 | 916 |
| Terrell | Sanderson | 1,299 | 1,410 | 2,358 |
| Terry | Brownfield | 12,796 | 13,218 | 890 |
| Throckmorton | Throckmorton | 1,836 | 1,880 | 912 |
| Titus | Mount Pleasant | 24,782 | 24,009 | 411 |
| Tom Green | San Angelo | 101,555 | 98,458 | 1,522 |
| Travis | Austin | 664,802 | 576,407 | 989 |
| Trinity | Groveton | 12,294 | 11,445 | 693 |
| Tyler | Woodville | 18,933 | 16,646 | 923 |
| Upshur | Gilmer | 34,521 | 31,370 | 588 |
| Upton | Rankin | 4,054 | 4,447 | 1,242 |
| Uvalde | Uvalde | 25,331 | 23,340 | 1,557 |
| Val Verde | Del Rio | 43,690 | 38,721 | 3,171 |
| Van Zandt | Canton | 41,494 | 37,944 | 849 |
| Victoria | Victoria | 79,992 | 74,361 | 883 |
| Walker | Huntsville | 54,666 | 50,917 | 788 |
| Waller | Hempstead | 26,432 | 23,389 | 514 |
| Ward | Monahans | 12,152 | 13,115 | 836 |
| Washington | Brenham | 28,020 | 26,154 | 609 |
| Webb | Laredo | 170,863 | 133,239 | 3,357 |
| Wharton | Wharton | 40,376 | 39,955 | 1,090 |
| Wheeler | Wheeler | 5,462 | 5,879 | 914 |

| County | County seat or courthouse | 1995 Pop. | 1990 Pop. | Land area sq mi |
|---|---|---|---|---|
| Wichita | Wichita Falls | 125,239 | 122,378 | 628 |
| Wilbarger | Vernon | 14,356 | 15,121 | 971 |
| Willacy | Raymondville | 19,500 | 17,705 | 597 |
| Williamson | Georgetown | 184,034 | 139,551 | 1,124 |
| Wilson | Floresville | 27,291 | 22,650 | 807 |
| Winkler | Kermit | 7,981 | 8,626 | 841 |
| Wise | Decatur | 38,594 | 34,679 | 905 |
| Wood | Quitman | 32,305 | 29,380 | 650 |
| Yoakum | Plains | 8,235 | 8,786 | 800 |
| Young | Graham | 17,781 | 18,126 | 922 |
| Zapata | Zapata | 11,075 | 9,279 | 997 |
| Zavala | Crystal City | 12,413 | 12,162 | 1,299 |

## Utah

(29 counties, 82,168 sq mi land; pop. 1,951,408)

| County | County seat or courthouse | 1995 Pop. | 1990 Pop. | Land area sq mi |
|---|---|---|---|---|
| Beaver | Beaver | 5,383 | 4,765 | 2,590 |
| Box Elder | Brigham City | 39,590 | 36,485 | 5,724 |
| Cache | Logan | 77,298 | 70,183 | 1,165 |
| Carbon | Price | 20,653 | 20,228 | 1,479 |
| Daggett | Manila | 770 | 690 | 698 |
| Davis | Farmington | 215,382 | 187,941 | 305 |
| Duchesne | Duchesne | 13,799 | 12,645 | 3,238 |
| Emery | Castle Dale | 10,638 | 10,332 | 4,452 |
| Garfield | Panguitch | 4,092 | 3,980 | 5,175 |
| Grand | Moab | 7,824 | 6,620 | 3,682 |
| Iron | Parowan | 25,921 | 20,789 | 3,299 |
| Juab | Nephi | 6,675 | 5,817 | 3,392 |
| Kane | Kanab | 6,000 | 5,169 | 3,992 |
| Millard | Fillmore | 12,157 | 11,333 | 6,590 |
| Morgan | Morgan | 6,592 | 5,528 | 609 |
| Piute | Junction | 1,419 | 1,277 | 758 |
| Rich | Randolph | 1,831 | 1,725 | 1,029 |
| Salt Lake | Salt Lake City | 808,383 | 725,956 | 737 |
| San Juan | Monticello | 13,917 | 12,621 | 7,821 |
| Sanpete | Manti | 19,340 | 16,259 | 1,588 |
| Sevier | Richfield | 17,166 | 15,431 | 1,910 |
| Summit | Coalville | 23,292 | 15,518 | 1,871 |
| Tooele | Tooele | 29,263 | 26,601 | 6,946 |
| Uintah | Vernal | 25,004 | 22,211 | 4,477 |
| Utah | Provo | 298,789 | 263,590 | 1,998 |
| Wasatch | Heber City | 11,757 | 10,089 | 1,181 |
| Washington | Saint George | 70,610 | 48,560 | 2,427 |
| Wayne | Loa | 2,305 | 2,177 | 2,461 |
| Weber | Ogden | 175,558 | 158,330 | 576 |

## Vermont

(14 counties, 9,249 sq mi land; pop. 584,771)

| County | County seat or courthouse | 1995 Pop. | 1990 Pop. | Land area sq mi |
|---|---|---|---|---|
| Addison | Middlebury | 34,811 | 32,953 | 770 |
| Bennington | Bennington | 36,276 | 35,845 | 676 |
| Caledonia | Saint Johnsbury | 28,564 | 27,846 | 651 |
| Chittenden | Burlington | 139,041 | 131,761 | 539 |
| Essex | Guildhall | 6,570 | 6,405 | 665 |
| Franklin | Saint Albans | 43,250 | 39,980 | 637 |
| Grand Isle | North Hero | 5,884 | 5,318 | 83 |
| Lamoille | Hyde Park | 21,150 | 19,735 | 461 |
| Orange | Chelsea | 27,361 | 26,149 | 689 |
| Orleans | Newport | 24,970 | 24,053 | 697 |
| Rutland | Rutland | 62,732 | 62,142 | 932 |
| Washington | Montpelier | 56,367 | 54,928 | 690 |
| Windham | Newfane | 42,757 | 41,588 | 789 |
| Windsor | Woodstock | 55,038 | 54,055 | 971 |

## Virginia

(95 cos., 40 ind. cities, 39,598 sq mi land; pop. 6,618,358)

| County | County seat or courthouse | 1995 Pop. | 1990 Pop. | Land area sq mi |
|---|---|---|---|---|
| Accomack | Accomac | 32,266 | 31,703 | 455 |
| Albemarle | Charlottesville | 73,203 | 68,172 | 723 |
| Alleghany | Covington | 12,604 | 13,176 | 446 |
| Amelia | Amelia Courthouse | 9,670 | 8,787 | 357 |
| Amherst | Amherst | 29,770 | 28,578 | 475 |
| Appomattox | Appomattox | 12,777 | 12,298 | 334 |
| Arlington | Arlington | 172,660 | 170,897 | 26 |
| Augusta | Staunton | 59,510 | 54,677 | 972 |
| Bath | Warm Springs | 4,870 | 4,799 | 532 |
| Bedford | Bedford | 52,335 | 45,656 | 755 |
| Bland | Bland | 6,783 | 6,514 | 359 |
| Botetourt | Fincastle | 27,279 | 24,992 | 543 |
| Brunswick | Lawrenceville | 16,465 | 15,987 | 566 |
| Buchanan | Grundy | 30,430 | 31,333 | 504 |
| Buckingham | Buckingham | 13,316 | 12,873 | 581 |
| Campbell | Rustburg | 48,918 | 47,572 | 505 |
| Caroline | Bowling Green | 21,079 | 19,217 | 533 |
| Carroll | Hillsville | 27,634 | 26,594 | 477 |
| Charles City | Charles City | 6,733 | 6,282 | 183 |
| Charlotte | Charlotte Courthouse | 12,188 | 11,688 | 475 |
| Chesterfield | Chesterfield | 239,659 | 209,564 | 426 |
| Clarke | Berryville | 12,390 | 12,101 | 177 |

| County | County seat or courthouse | 1995 Pop. | 1990 Pop. | Land area sq mi |
|---|---|---|---|---|
| Craig | New Castle | 4,821 | 4,372 | 330 |
| Culpeper | Culpeper | 30,528 | 27,791 | 381 |
| Cumberland | Cumberland | 7,737 | 7,825 | 299 |
| Dickenson | Clintwood | 17,586 | 17,620 | 333 |
| Dinwiddie | Dinwiddie | 22,944 | 22,319 | 504 |
| Essex | Tappahannock | 9,251 | 8,689 | 258 |
| Fairfax | Fairfax | 887,205 | 818,623 | 396 |
| Fauquier | Warrenton | 51,473 | 48,860 | 650 |
| Floyd | Floyd | 12,642 | 11,965 | 382 |
| Fluvanna | Palmyra | 16,058 | 12,429 | 287 |
| Franklin | Rocky Mount | 42,856 | 39,549 | 692 |
| Frederick | Winchester | 51,549 | 45,723 | 415 |
| Giles | Pearisburg | 16,374 | 16,366 | 358 |
| Gloucester | Gloucester | 33,421 | 30,131 | 217 |
| Goochland | Goochland | 16,138 | 14,163 | 285 |
| Grayson | Independence | 16,380 | 16,278 | 443 |
| Greene | Stanardsville | 12,660 | 10,297 | 157 |
| Greensville | Emporia | 10,967 | 8,630 | 296 |
| Halifax | Halifax | 37,474 | 36,030 | 475 |
| Hanover | Hanover | 74,641 | 63,306 | 473 |
| Henrico | Henrico | 232,799 | 217,849 | 238 |
| Henry | Martinsville | 56,585 | 56,942 | 382 |
| Highland | Monterey | 2,575 | 2,635 | 416 |
| Isle of Wight | Isle of Wight | 27,769 | 25,053 | 316 |
| James City | Williamsburg | 40,489 | 34,970 | 143 |
| King and Queen | King and Queen Courthouse | 6,441 | 6,289 | 316 |
| King George | King George | 16,463 | 13,527 | 180 |
| King William | King William | 12,244 | 10,913 | 275 |
| Lancaster | Lancaster | 11,161 | 10,896 | 133 |
| Lee | Jonesville | 24,411 | 24,496 | 437 |
| Loudoun | Leesburg | 115,870 | 86,129 | 520 |
| Louisa | Louisa | 22,887 | 20,325 | 498 |
| Lunenburg | Lunenburg | 11,155 | 11,419 | 432 |
| Madison | Madison | 12,252 | 11,949 | 322 |
| Mathews | Mathews | 8,947 | 8,348 | 86 |
| Mecklenburg | Boydton | 30,760 | 29,241 | 624 |
| Middlesex | Saluda | 9,327 | 8,653 | 130 |
| Montgomery | Christiansburg | 75,756 | 73,913 | 388 |
| Nelson | Lovingston | 13,357 | 12,778 | 472 |
| New Kent | New Kent | 11,679 | 10,445 | 210 |
| Northampton | Eastville | 13,013 | 13,061 | 207 |
| Northumberland | Heathsville | 11,122 | 10,524 | 192 |
| Nottoway | Nottoway | 15,160 | 14,993 | 315 |
| Orange | Orange | 23,763 | 21,421 | 342 |
| Page | Luray | 22,718 | 21,690 | 311 |
| Patrick | Stuart | 17,762 | 17,473 | 483 |
| Pittsylvania | Chatham | 56,101 | 55,672 | 971 |
| Powhatan | Powhatan | 18,905 | 15,328 | 261 |
| Prince Edward | Farmville | 18,752 | 17,320 | 353 |
| Prince George | Prince George | 28,383 | 27,394 | 266 |
| Prince William | Manassas | 245,184 | 215,677 | 338 |
| Pulaski | Pulaski | 34,426 | 34,496 | 321 |
| Rappahannock | Washington | 7,117 | 6,622 | 267 |
| Richmond | Warsaw | 8,247 | 7,273 | 192 |
| Roanoke | Salem | 81,717 | 79,294 | 251 |
| Rockbridge | Lexington | 19,116 | 18,350 | 600 |
| Rockingham | Harrisonburg | 61,894 | 57,482 | 851 |
| Russell | Lebanon | 29,261 | 28,667 | 475 |
| Scott | Gate City | 23,197 | 23,204 | 537 |
| Shenandoah | Woodstock | 33,423 | 31,636 | 512 |
| Smyth | Marion | 33,231 | 32,370 | 452 |
| Southampton | Courtland | 17,313 | 17,550 | 600 |
| Spotsylvania | Spotsylvania | 71,981 | 57,403 | 401 |
| Stafford | Stafford | 80,107 | 61,236 | 270 |
| Surry | Surry | 6,388 | 6,145 | 279 |
| Sussex | Sussex | 10,078 | 10,248 | 491 |
| Tazewell | Tazewell | 47,146 | 45,960 | 520 |
| Warren | Front Royal | 29,264 | 26,142 | 214 |
| Washington | Abingdon | 48,347 | 45,887 | 564 |
| Westmoreland | Montross | 16,464 | 15,480 | 229 |
| Wise | Wise | 39,925 | 39,573 | 403 |
| Wythe | Wytheville | 26,350 | 25,471 | 463 |
| York | Yorktown | 54,108 | 42,434 | 106 |
| Independent Cities | | | | |
| Alexandria | | 115,609 | 111,182 | 15 |
| Bedford | | 6,479 | 6,073 | 7 |
| Bristol | | 17,918 | 18,426 | 12 |
| Buena Vista | | 6,405 | 6,406 | 7 |
| Charlottesville | | 40,227 | 40,475 | 10 |
| Chesapeake | | 187,998 | 151,982 | 341 |
| Clifton Forge | | 4,460 | 4,679 | 3 |
| Colonial Heights | | 16,951 | 16,064 | 8 |
| Covington | | 6,787 | 6,991 | 4 |
| Danville | | 53,789 | 53,056 | 43 |
| Emporia | | 5,835 | 5,479 | 7 |
| Fairfax | | 20,637 | 19,629 | 6 |
| Falls Church | | 9,617 | 9,522 | 2 |
| Franklin | | 8,407 | 7,864 | 8 |
| Fredericksburg | | 21,953 | 19,027 | 11 |
| Galax | | 6,632 | 6,670 | 8 |
| Hampton | | 139,181 | 133,811 | 52 |
| Harrisonburg | | 33,158 | 30,707 | 18 |
| Hopewell | | 22,548 | 23,101 | 10 |
| Lexington | | 7,206 | 6,959 | 3 |
| Lynchburg | | 66,710 | 66,049 | 49 |

| County | County seat or courthouse | 1995 Pop. | 1990 Pop. | Land area sq mi |
|---|---|---|---|---|
| Independent Cities | | | | |
| Manassas | | 32,657 | 27,957 | 10 |
| Manassas Park | | 7,417 | 6,734 | 2 |
| Martinsville | | 15,924 | 16,162 | 11 |
| Newport News | | 179,794 | 171,439 | 68 |
| Norfolk | | 237,570 | 261,250 | 54 |
| Norton | | 4,335 | 4,247 | 7 |
| Petersburg | | 37,782 | 37,027 | 23 |
| Poquoson | | 11,727 | 11,005 | 16 |
| Portsmouth | | 102,735 | 103,910 | 33 |
| Radford | | 16,212 | 15,940 | 10 |
| Richmond | | 198,273 | 202,798 | 60 |
| Roanoke | | 95,701 | 96,509 | 43 |
| Salem | | 24,198 | 23,797 | 15 |
| Staunton | | 24,796 | 24,461 | 20 |
| Suffolk | | 56,787 | 52,143 | 400 |
| Virginia Beach | | 431,000 | 393,089 | 248 |
| Waynesboro | | 18,926 | 18,549 | 14 |
| Williamsburg | | 12,646 | 11,409 | 9 |
| Winchester | | 23,237 | 21,947 | 9 |

## Washington

(39 counties, 66,581 sq mi land; pop. 5,430,940)

| County | County seat or courthouse | 1995 Pop. | 1990 Pop. | Land area sq mi |
|---|---|---|---|---|
| Adams | Ritzville | 15,150 | 13,603 | 1,925 |
| Asotin | Asotin | 20,252 | 17,605 | 636 |
| Benton | Prosser | 133,070 | 112,560 | 1,703 |
| Chelan | Wenatchee | 57,854 | 52,250 | 2,922 |
| Clallam | Port Angeles | 62,504 | 56,210 | 1,745 |
| Clark | Vancouver | 292,272 | 238,053 | 628 |
| Columbia | Dayton | 4,219 | 4,024 | 869 |
| Cowlitz | Kelso | 88,904 | 82,119 | 1,139 |
| Douglas | Waterville | 31,054 | 26,205 | 1,821 |
| Ferry | Republic | 7,140 | 6,295 | 2,204 |
| Franklin | Pasco | 44,459 | 37,473 | 1,242 |
| Garfield | Pomeroy | 2,297 | 2,248 | 711 |
| Grant | Ephrata | 64,493 | 54,798 | 2,676 |
| Grays Harbor | Montesano | 67,221 | 64,175 | 1,917 |
| Island | Coupeville | 68,682 | 60,195 | 209 |
| Jefferson | Port Townsend | 25,028 | 20,406 | 1,809 |
| King | Seattle | 1,595,243 | 1,507,305 | 2,126 |
| Kitsap | Port Orchard | 226,720 | 189,731 | 396 |
| Kittitas | Ellensburg | 30,158 | 26,725 | 2,297 |
| Klickitat | Goldendale | 18,231 | 16,616 | 1,873 |
| Lewis | Chehalis | 65,921 | 59,358 | 2,408 |
| Lincoln | Davenport | 9,510 | 8,864 | 2,311 |
| Mason | Shelton | 47,127 | 38,341 | 961 |
| Okanogan | Okanogan | 36,628 | 33,350 | 5,268 |
| Pacific | South Bend | 20,807 | 18,882 | 975 |
| Pend Oreille | Newport | 10,749 | 8,915 | 1,401 |
| Pierce | Tacoma | 648,994 | 586,203 | 1,676 |
| San Juan | Friday Harbor | 11,783 | 10,035 | 175 |
| Skagit | Mount Vernon | 94,023 | 79,545 | 1,735 |
| Skamania | Stevenson | 9,098 | 8,289 | 1,657 |
| Snohomish | Everett | 533,526 | 465,628 | 2,090 |
| Spokane | Spokane | 401,205 | 361,333 | 1,764 |
| Stevens | Colville | 37,608 | 30,948 | 2,478 |
| Thurston | Olympia | 191,974 | 161,238 | 727 |
| Wahkiakum | Cathlamet | 3,710 | 3,327 | 264 |
| Walla Walla | Walla Walla | 52,982 | 48,439 | 1,271 |
| Whatcom | Bellingham | 148,929 | 127,780 | 2,120 |
| Whitman | Colfax | 39,380 | 38,775 | 2,159 |
| Yakima | Yakima | 212,035 | 188,823 | 4,296 |

## West Virginia

(55 counties, 24,087 sq mi land; pop. 1,828,140)

| County | County seat or courthouse | 1995 Pop. | 1990 Pop. | Land area sq mi |
|---|---|---|---|---|
| Barbour | Philippi | 16,229 | 15,699 | 341 |
| Berkeley | Martinsburg | 66,572 | 59,253 | 321 |
| Boone | Madison | 26,291 | 25,870 | 503 |
| Braxton | Sutton | 13,401 | 12,998 | 514 |
| Brooke | Wellsburg | 26,866 | 26,992 | 89 |
| Cabell | Huntington | 96,837 | 96,827 | 282 |
| Calhoun | Grantsville | 7,918 | 7,885 | 281 |
| Clay | Clay | 10,380 | 9,983 | 342 |
| Doddridge | West Union | 7,409 | 6,994 | 321 |
| Fayette | Fayetteville | 48,655 | 47,952 | 664 |
| Gilmer | Glenville | 7,359 | 7,669 | 340 |
| Grant | Petersburg | 11,059 | 10,428 | 477 |
| Greenbrier | Lewisburg | 35,556 | 34,693 | 1,021 |
| Hampshire | Romney | 18,381 | 16,498 | 642 |
| Hancock | New Cumberland | 34,734 | 35,233 | 83 |
| Hardy | Moorefield | 11,642 | 10,977 | 583 |
| Harrison | Clarksburg | 70,931 | 69,371 | 416 |
| Jackson | Ripley | 27,200 | 25,938 | 466 |
| Jefferson | Charles Town | 39,477 | 35,926 | 210 |
| Kanawha | Charleston | 206,195 | 207,619 | 903 |
| Lewis | Weston | 17,629 | 17,223 | 389 |
| Lincoln | Hamlin | 22,167 | 21,382 | 438 |
| Logan | Logan | 42,451 | 43,032 | 454 |
| McDowell | Welch | 32,662 | 35,233 | 535 |
| Marion | Fairmont | 58,063 | 57,249 | 310 |
| Marshall | Moundsville | 37,105 | 37,356 | 307 |
| Mason | Point Pleasant | 25,638 | 25,178 | 432 |
| Mercer | Princeton | 64,889 | 64,980 | 421 |
| Mineral | Keyser | 27,321 | 26,697 | 328 |
| Mingo | Williamson | 33,646 | 33,739 | 423 |
| Monongalia | Morgantown | 78,060 | 75,509 | 361 |
| Monroe | Union | 12,977 | 12,406 | 473 |
| Morgan | Berkeley Springs | 13,182 | 12,128 | 229 |
| Nicholas | Summersville | 27,622 | 26,775 | 649 |
| Ohio | Wheeling | 49,865 | 50,871 | 106 |
| Pendleton | Franklin | 8,128 | 8,054 | 698 |
| Pleasants | St. Marys | 7,525 | 7,546 | 131 |
| Pocahontas | Marlinton | 8,962 | 9,008 | 940 |
| Preston | Kingwood | 29,847 | 29,037 | 648 |
| Putnam | Winfield | 48,944 | 42,835 | 346 |
| Raleigh | Beckley | 78,656 | 76,819 | 607 |
| Randolph | Elkins | 28,939 | 27,803 | 1,040 |
| Ritchie | Harrisville | 10,154 | 10,233 | 454 |
| Roane | Spencer | 15,389 | 15,120 | 484 |
| Summers | Hinton | 14,050 | 14,204 | 361 |
| Taylor | Grafton | 15,335 | 15,144 | 173 |
| Tucker | Parsons | 7,783 | 7,728 | 419 |
| Tyler | Middlebourne | 10,160 | 9,796 | 258 |
| Upshur | Buckhannon | 23,891 | 22,867 | 355 |
| Wayne | Wayne | 42,669 | 41,636 | 506 |
| Webster | Webster Springs | 10,409 | 10,729 | 556 |
| Wetzel | New Martinsville | 18,909 | 19,258 | 359 |
| Wirt | Elizabeth | 5,513 | 5,192 | 233 |
| Wood | Parkersburg | 88,295 | 86,915 | 367 |
| Wyoming | Pineville | 28,213 | 28,990 | 501 |

## Wisconsin

(72 counties, 54,314 sq mi land; pop. 5,122,871)

| County | County seat or courthouse | 1995 Pop. | 1990 Pop. | Land area sq mi |
|---|---|---|---|---|
| Adams | Friendship | 17,422 | 15,682 | 648 |
| Ashland | Ashland | 16,446 | 16,307 | 1,044 |
| Barron | Barron | 42,785 | 40,750 | 863 |
| Bayfield | Washburn | 14,955 | 14,008 | 1,476 |
| Brown | Green Bay | 210,303 | 194,594 | 529 |
| Buffalo | Alma | 13,980 | 13,584 | 685 |
| Burnett | Meenon | 14,164 | 13,084 | 822 |
| Calumet | Chilton | 37,369 | 34,291 | 320 |
| Chippewa | Chippewa Falls | 54,175 | 52,360 | 1,011 |
| Clark | Neillsville | 32,660 | 31,647 | 1,216 |
| Columbia | Portage | 49,113 | 45,088 | 774 |
| Crawford | Prairie du Chien | 16,552 | 15,940 | 573 |
| Dane | Madison | 393,296 | 367,085 | 1,202 |
| Dodge | Juneau | 79,375 | 76,559 | 882 |
| Door | Sturgeon Bay | 26,836 | 25,690 | 483 |
| Douglas | Superior | 42,777 | 41,758 | 1,309 |
| Dunn | Menomonie | 38,392 | 35,909 | 852 |
| Eau Claire | Eau Claire | 88,488 | 85,183 | 638 |
| Florence | Florence | 5,256 | 4,590 | 488 |
| Fond du Lac | Fond du Lac | 93,347 | 90,083 | 723 |
| Forest | Crandon | 9,361 | 8,776 | 1,014 |
| Grant | Lancaster | 49,432 | 49,266 | 1,148 |
| Green | Monroe | 32,492 | 30,339 | 584 |
| Green Lake | Green Lake | 19,326 | 18,651 | 354 |
| Iowa | Dodgeville | 21,701 | 20,150 | 763 |
| Iron | Hurley | 6,443 | 6,153 | 757 |
| Jackson | Black River Falls | 17,233 | 16,588 | 987 |
| Jefferson | Jefferson | 73,001 | 67,783 | 557 |
| Juneau | Mauston | 23,528 | 21,650 | 768 |
| Kenosha | Kenosha | 139,938 | 128,181 | 273 |
| Kewaunee | Kewaunee | 19,448 | 18,878 | 343 |
| La Crosse | La Crosse | 101,709 | 97,904 | 453 |
| Lafayette | Darlington | 16,544 | 16,074 | 634 |
| Langlade | Antigo | 20,478 | 19,505 | 873 |
| Lincoln | Merrill | 28,921 | 26,993 | 883 |
| Manitowoc | Manitowoc | 82,507 | 80,421 | 592 |
| Marathon | Wausau | 120,776 | 115,400 | 1,545 |
| Marinette | Marinette | 42,273 | 40,548 | 1,402 |
| Marquette | Montello | 14,045 | 12,321 | 456 |
| Menominee | Keshena | 4,601 | 3,890 | 358 |
| Milwaukee | Milwaukee | 931,242 | 959,275 | 242 |
| Monroe | Sparta | 38,776 | 36,633 | 901 |
| Oconto | Oconto | 32,298 | 30,226 | 998 |
| Oneida | Rhinelander | 34,816 | 31,679 | 1,125 |
| Outagamie | Appleton | 149,313 | 140,510 | 640 |
| Ozaukee | Port Washington | 79,111 | 72,831 | 232 |
| Pepin | Durand | 7,151 | 7,107 | 232 |
| Pierce | Ellsworth | 34,724 | 32,765 | 577 |
| Polk | Balsam Lake | 37,289 | 34,773 | 917 |
| Portage | Stevens Point | 64,704 | 61,405 | 806 |
| Price | Phillips | 15,950 | 15,600 | 1,253 |
| Racine | Racine | 182,892 | 175,034 | 333 |
| Richland | Richland Center | 17,895 | 17,521 | 586 |
| Rock | Janesville | 148,349 | 139,510 | 721 |
| Rusk | Ladysmith | 15,345 | 15,079 | 913 |
| Saint Croix | Hudson | 54,851 | 50,251 | 722 |
| Sauk | Baraboo | 51,310 | 46,975 | 838 |
| Sawyer | Hayward | 15,664 | 14,181 | 1,257 |
| Shawano | Shawano | 38,442 | 37,157 | 893 |
| Sheboygan | Sheboygan | 108,326 | 103,877 | 514 |
| Taylor | Medford | 19,234 | 18,901 | 975 |

| County | County seat or courthouse | 1995 Pop. | 1990 Pop. | Land area sq mi |
|---|---|---|---|---|
| Trempealeau | Whitehall | 25,835 | 25,263 | 734 |
| Vernon | Viroqua | 27,116 | 25,617 | 795 |
| Vilas | Eagle River | 20,416 | 17,707 | 873 |
| Walworth | Elkhorn | 82,045 | 75,000 | 555 |
| Washburn | Shell Lake | 14,982 | 13,772 | 810 |
| Washington | West Bend | 109,632 | 95,328 | 431 |
| Waukesha | Waukesha | 337,954 | 304,715 | 556 |
| Waupaca | Waupaca | 49,156 | 46,104 | 751 |
| Waushara | Wautoma | 21,018 | 19,385 | 626 |
| Winnebago | Oshkosh | 149,391 | 140,320 | 439 |
| Wood | Wisconsin Rapids | 76,196 | 73,605 | 793 |

## Wyoming

(23 counties, 97,105 sq mi land; pop. 480,184)

| County | County seat or courthouse | 1995 Pop. | 1990 Pop. | Land area sq mi |
|---|---|---|---|---|
| Albany | Laramie | 30,980 | 30,797 | 4,274 |
| Big Horn | Basin | 11,110 | 10,525 | 3,137 |
| Campbell | Gillette | 31,668 | 29,370 | 4,797 |
| Carbon | Rawlins | 16,110 | 16,659 | 7,897 |
| Converse | Douglas | 11,965 | 11,128 | 4,255 |
| Crook | Sundance | 5,656 | 5,294 | 2,859 |
| Fremont | Lander | 35,710 | 33,662 | 9,183 |
| Goshen | Torrington | 12,627 | 12,373 | 2,226 |
| Hot Springs | Thermopolis | 4,567 | 4,809 | 2,004 |
| Johnson | Buffalo | 6,644 | 6,145 | 4,166 |
| Laramie | Cheyenne | 78,444 | 73,142 | 2,686 |
| Lincoln | Kemmerer | 13,918 | 12,625 | 4,069 |
| Natrona | Casper | 64,025 | 61,226 | 5,340 |
| Niobrara | Lusk | 2,618 | 2,499 | 2,626 |
| Park | Cody | 25,534 | 23,178 | 6,943 |
| Platte | Wheatland | 8,343 | 8,145 | 2,085 |
| Sheridan | Sheridan | 25,088 | 23,562 | 2,523 |
| Sublette | Pinedale | 5,507 | 4,843 | 4,882 |
| Sweetwater | Green River | 40,976 | 38,823 | 10,426 |
| Teton | Jackson | 13,444 | 11,173 | 4,008 |
| Unita | Evanston | 20,087 | 18,705 | 2,082 |
| Washakie | Worland | 8,657 | 8,388 | 2,240 |
| Weston | Newcastle | 6,506 | 6,518 | 2,398 |

# Population of Outlying Areas

**Source:** Bureau of the Census, U.S. Dept. of Commerce; World Almanac research

Population estimates for July 1, 1993, are given for Puerto Rican municipios; all other population counts and all land area figures are from the U.S. census conducted on Apr. 1, 1990. Because only selected areas are shown, the population and land area figures may not equal the total reported. ZIP codes with an asterisk (*) are general delivery ZIP codes. Consult the local postmaster for more specific delivery information. Wake Atoll, Johnston Atoll, and Midway Atoll receive mail through APO and FPO addresses. U.S. outlying areas that are not listed in this table may not receive U.S. mail delivery.

## Commonwealth of Puerto Rico

| ZIP code | Municipio | 1993 Pop. | Land area sq mi |
|---|---|---|---|
| *00601 | Adjuntas | 19,579 | 67 |
| 00602 | Aguada | 37,175 | 31 |
| *00605 | Aguadilla | 64,176 | 37 |
| 00703 | Aguas Buenas | 26,281 | 31 |
| 00705 | Aibonito | 25,469 | 31 |
| 00610 | Añasco | 26,806 | 39 |
| *00612 | Arecibo | 94,513 | 126 |
| 00714 | Arroyo | 19,230 | 15 |
| 00617 | Barceloneta | 21,940 | 23 |
| 00794 | Barranquitas | 26,713 | 34 |
| *00958 | Bayamón | 225,338 | 44 |
| 00623 | Cabo Rojo | 40,559 | 70 |
| *00726 | Caguas | 139,228 | 59 |
| 00627 | Camuy | 30,725 | 46 |
| 00729 | Canóvanas | 39,653 | 33 |
| *00984 | Carolina | 185,732 | 45 |
| *00962 | Cataño | 33,485 | 5 |
| *00737 | Cayey | 46,993 | 52 |
| 00735 | Ceiba | 17,521 | 29 |
| 00638 | Ciales | 18,855 | 67 |
| 00739 | Cidra | 36,055 | 36 |
| 00769 | Coamo | 33,402 | 78 |
| 00782 | Comerío | 19,659 | 28 |
| 00783 | Corozal | 33,754 | 43 |
| 00775 | Culebra | 1,724 | 12 |
| 00646 | Dorado | 32,198 | 23 |
| 00738 | Fajardo | 37,107 | 30 |
| 00650 | Florida | 9,008 | 10 |
| 00653 | Guánica | 21,251 | 37 |
| *00784 | Guayama | 41,336 | 65 |
| 00656 | Guayanilla | 21,554 | 42 |
| *00970 | Guaynabo | 97,879 | 27 |
| 00778 | Gurabo | 30,948 | 28 |
| 00659 | Hatillo | 33,575 | 42 |
| 00660 | Hormigüeros | 15,992 | 11 |
| *00792 | Humacao | 55,954 | 45 |
| 00662 | Isabela | 39,836 | 55 |
| 00664 | Jayuya | 16,061 | 45 |
| 00795 | Juana Díaz | 46,951 | 60 |
| 00777 | Juncos | 32,272 | 27 |
| 00667 | Lajas | 25,433 | 60 |
| 00669 | Lares | 29,014 | 62 |
| 00670 | Las Marías | 10,096 | 46 |
| 00771 | Las Piedras | 29,088 | 34 |
| 00772 | Loíza | 30,110 | 19 |
| 00773 | Luquillo | 18,799 | 26 |
| 00674 | Manatí | 39,409 | 45 |
| 00606 | Maricao | 5,887 | 37 |
| 00707 | Maunabo | 12,809 | 21 |
| *00681 | Mayagüez | 102,390 | 78 |
| 00676 | Moca | 33,456 | 50 |
| 00687 | Morovis | 26,926 | 39 |
| 00718 | Naguabo | 23,079 | 52 |
| 00719 | Naranjito | 28,359 | 27 |
| 00720 | Orocovis | 22,635 | 64 |
| 00723 | Patillas | 20,218 | 47 |
| 00624 | Peñuelas | 21,879 | 45 |
| *00732 | Ponce | 189,734 | 116 |
| 00678 | Quebradillas | 21,653 | 23 |
| 00677 | Rincón | 12,311 | 14 |
| 00721 | Río Grande | 46,329 | 61 |
| 00637 | Sabana Grande | 24,196 | 36 |
| 00751 | Salinas | 29,266 | 69 |
| 00683 | San Germán | 36,622 | 55 |
| *00936 | San Juan | 443,372 | 48 |
| 00754 | San Lorenzo | 35,988 | 53 |
| 00685 | San Sebastián | 39,081 | 70 |
| 00757 | Santa Isabel | 19,482 | 34 |
| *00953 | Toa Alta | 46,274 | 27 |
| *00951 | Toa Baja | 94,633 | 23 |
| *00976 | Trujillo Alto | 66,992 | 21 |
| 00641 | Utuado | 35,666 | 114 |
| 00692 | Vega Alta | 35,550 | 28 |
| *00693 | Vega Baja | 56,914 | 46 |
| 00765 | Vieques | 8,582 | 51 |
| 00766 | Villalba | 24,115 | 36 |
| 00767 | Yabucoa | 37,667 | 55 |
| 00698 | Yauco | 41,642 | 68 |
| **Total** | | **3,622,063** | **3,427** |

## Commonwealth of the Northern Mariana Islands

| ZIP code | Municipality | 1990 Pop. | Land area sq mi |
|---|---|---|---|
| 96950 | Northern Islands | 36 | 60 |
| 96951 | Rota | 2,295 | 33 |
| 96950 | Saipan | 38,896 | 47 |
| 96952 | Tinian | 2,118 | 39 |
| **Total** | | **43,345** | **179** |

## Other U.S. External Territories

### American Samoa

| ZIP code | Location | 1990 Pop. | Land area sq mi |
|---|---|---|---|
| 96799 | American Samoa | 46,773 | 77 |

### Guam

| ZIP code | Location | 1990 Pop. | Land area sq mi |
|---|---|---|---|
| 96910 | Agaña | 1,139 | 1 |
| 96919 | Agaña Hts. | 3,646 | 1 |
| *96928 | Agat | 4,960 | 10 |
| 96922 | Asan | 2,070 | 6 |
| *96921 | Barrigada | 8,846 | 9 |
| 96924 | Chalan-Pago-Ordot | 4,451 | 6 |
| 96912 | Dededo | 31,728 | 30 |
| 96917 | Inarajan | 2,469 | 19 |
| 96923 | Mangilao | 10,483 | 10 |
| 96916 | Merizo | 1,742 | 6 |
| 96927 | Mongmong-Toto-Maite | 5,845 | 2 |
| 96925 | Piti | 1,827 | 7 |
| 96915 | Santa Rita | 11,857 | 17 |
| 96926 | Sinajana | 2,658 | 1 |
| 96930 | Talofofo | 2,310 | 17 |
| *96931 | Tamuning | 16,673 | 6 |
| 96918 | Umatac | 897 | 6 |
| 96929 | Yigo | 14,213 | 35 |
| 96914 | Yona | 5,338 | 20 |
| **Total** | | **133,152** | **210** |

### Virgin Islands

| ZIP code | Location | 1990 Pop. | Land area sq mi |
|---|---|---|---|
| *00820 | Saint Croix | 50,139 | 83 |
| *00820 | Christiansted | 2,555 | |
| *00840 | Frederiksted | 1,064 | |
| *00830 | Saint John | 3,504 | 20 |
| *00801 | Saint Thomas | 48,166 | 31 |
| 00801 | Charlotte Amalie | 12,331 | |
| **Total** | | **101,809** | **134** |

# ASTRONOMY AND CALENDAR

**Edited by Dr. Lee T. Shapiro, Planetarium Director**
**Morehead Planetarium, University of North Carolina at Chapel Hill**

## Celestial Events Summary, 1997

(Greenwich Mean Time, or GMT)

At the start of the year, only Mars and Saturn are prominent in the sky. On Feb. 6, Mercury, Venus, Jupiter, Uranus, and Neptune are all within 5° of the Moon. The grouping, however, is low in the morning sky and will be difficult to observe. Venus passes Neptune, Jupiter, and Uranus in the space of about a week from Feb. 1-7, with Mercury matching the performance a week later (Feb. 7-13). The Moon continues a series of monthly occultations of Aldebaran, starting on Jan. 19, that will last throughout the year.

By Mar., Saturn is lost in the Sun's glare; but once returning to view in late Apr., Saturn progressively brightens through most of the remainder of the year. Jupiter, after starting the year hiding near the Sun, emerges in Feb. to remain visible for the balance of the year.

In 1996, the world was surprised to learn of a comet that would pass slightly more than 9 mil mi from the Earth on Mar. 25, 1996, less than 2 months after its discovery by Japanese amateur astronomer Yuji Hyakutake. There has been more warning for Comet Hale-Bopp, which was discovered in the summer of 1995 by amateur astronomers Alan Hale and Thomas Bopp and will be nearest to the Earth on Mar. 23, 1997—almost exactly one year after Comet Hyakutake. Oddly, the 3 most recent bright comets (Comet West 1976, Comet Halley 1986, Comet Hyakutake 1996) reached their peak brightness and best visibility near the beginning of spring, as will Comet Hale-Bopp. In late Mar. and early Apr. plan to view what may be the last bright comet of this century.

On May 4, the Moon occults Saturn, with several more Saturn occultations to follow in the 2d half of the year. In Aug., Mercury nearly catches Venus, but falls short and reaches greatest eastern elongation on Aug. 4.

Mars never appears in conjunction with the Sun during 1997, and is visible all year long. Watch for some pretty red object doubling when it catches its rival, Antares, on Oct. 12. After a nearly yearlong chase, Venus passes Mars on Oct. 26, but then slows in Dec. and is passed by Mars on Dec. 22.

## Celestial Events Highlights, 1997

(GMT, or as indicated)

### January

**Mercury** begins the year already in retrograde motion, passing through inferior conjunction on the first day of the year; it passes north of Venus on the 12th and reaches greatest western elongation on the 24th.

**Venus**, low in the southeast in the glare of sunrise, passes Mercury on the 12th.

**Mars**, in Virgo, is brightening and is farthest away from the Sun on the 29th.

**Jupiter**, in conjunction this month, is lost in the glare of the Sun and leaves Sagittarius to enter Capricornus on the 18th.

**Saturn** starts the year at its dimmest in Pisces.

**Moon** passes Mars on the 1st, Pluto on the 6th, Venus on the 7th, Mercury and Jupiter on the 8th, Uranus on the 10th, Saturn on the 14th, continues a series of occultations of Aldebaran on the 19th, and passes Mars on the 28th.

**Jan. 1**—Earth at perihelion, 91.4 mil mi from the Sun; Mercury at inferior conjunction, between the Earth and the Sun; Mars 3° north of Moon.

**Jan. 6**—Pluto 8° north of Moon.

**Jan. 7**—Venus 4° south of Moon.

**Jan. 8**—Jupiter 0.8° south of Neptune; Mercury 1° and Jupiter 4° south of Moon.

**Jan. 10**—Uranus 4° south of Moon.

**Jan. 12**—Mercury 2.7° north of Venus.

**Jan. 14**—Saturn 2° south of Moon.

**Jan. 15**—Mercury stationary, resumes direct motion.

**Jan. 17**—Neptune in conjunction with the Sun.

**Jan. 18**—Jupiter enters Capricornus.

**Jan. 19**—Jupiter in conjunction with the Sun; Moon is 0.8° north of Aldebaran, occulting it.

**Jan. 20**—Sun enters Capricornus.

**Jan. 24**—Uranus in conjunction with the Sun; Mercury at greatest western elongation of 24.5° (west of the Sun and rising before the Sun).

**Jan. 28**—Mars 3° north of Moon.

**Jan. 29**—Mars at aphelion, 154 mil mi from the Sun.

### February

**Mercury**, in direct eastward motion chasing the Sun, passes to the south of 3 planets in a week, going past Neptune on the 7th, Jupiter on the 12th, and Uranus on the 13th.

**Venus**, beating Mercury to the punch, also passes the same three planets about a week earlier, past Neptune on the 1st, Jupiter on the 5th, and Uranus on the 7th.

**Mars**, brighter than Spica, is in Virgo; begins its retrograde motion on the 7th.

**Jupiter**, on the 7th, is bookended between the Mercury-Neptune and Venus-Uranus conjunctions, as it emerges as a bright morning object preceding the glare of the rising Sun.

**Saturn**, getting lower in the west, is still visible for a few hours after sunset.

**Moon** passes Pluto on the 2d; Mercury, Venus, Jupiter, Uranus, and Neptune all on the 6th; Saturn on the 10th; and Mars on the 24th.

**Feb. 1**—Venus 1° south of Neptune.

**Feb. 2**—Pluto 8° north of Moon.

**Feb. 5**—Venus 0.3° south of Jupiter.

**Feb. 6**—Mercury 5°, Venus 4°, Jupiter 4°, Uranus 4°, and Neptune 4° south of Moon.

**Feb. 7**—Mars stationary, beginning retrograde motion. Mercury 1.4° south of Neptune; Venus 0.2° south of Uranus.

**Feb. 10**—Saturn 1° south of Moon.

**Feb. 12**—Mercury 1° south of Jupiter.

**Feb. 13**—Mercury 0.9° south of Uranus.

**Feb. 16**—Jupiter 0.2° north of Uranus; Sun enters Aquarius.

**Feb. 24**—Mars 4° north of Moon.

### March

**Mercury** passes Venus on the 2d and Saturn on the 21st, emerging into the evening sky.

**Venus**, lost in the glare of the Sun, passes Saturn on the 31st.

**Mars**, at opposition on the 17th and at its nearest to the Earth on the 20th, enters Leo on the 27th.

**Jupiter**, the conspicuous bright object in the southeast before sunrise, makes a prominent pairing with the Moon on the 6th.

**Saturn** passes through conjunction late in the month and is lost to view.

**Moon** passes Pluto on the 1st, Neptune on the 5th, Jupiter and Uranus on the 6th, Mercury and Venus on the 8th, Saturn on the 10th, occults Aldebaran on the 14th, passes Mars on the 23d, and passes Pluto again on the 29th.

**Mar. 1**—Pluto 8° north of Moon.

**Mar. 2**—Mercury 0.8° south of Venus.

**Mar. 5**—Neptune 3° south of Moon.

**Mar. 6**—Jupiter 4° and Uranus 4° south of Moon.

**Mar. 8**—Mercury 2° and Venus 2° south of Moon.

**Mar. 10**—Saturn 1° south of Moon; Pluto stationary, beginning retrograde motion.

**Mar. 11**—Mercury at superior conjunction with the Sun, on the far side of its orbit from the Earth.

**Mar. 12**—Sun enters Pisces.

**Mar. 14**—Moon is 0.6° north of Aldebaran, occulting it.

**Mar. 17**—Mars at opposition.

**Mar. 20**—Vernal Equinox at 13:56 GMT (8:56 AM EST); spring begins in the northern hemisphere, autumn in the southern hemisphere; Mars at its nearest to the Earth for this year.

**Mar. 21**—Mercury 2.1° north of Saturn.

**Mar. 23**—Mars 5° north of Moon.

**Mar. 27**—Mars enters Leo.

**Mar. 29**—Pluto 8° north of Moon.

**Mar. 30**—Saturn in conjunction with the Sun.

**Mar. 31**—Venus 1° north of Saturn.

## April

**Mercury,** at greatest elongation on the 6th, with the best evening views of this planet during the 1st week of this month.

**Venus**, still in the glare of the Sun, passes superior conjunction on the 2d.

**Mars**, though still very bright, has begun to fade.

**Jupiter**, gradually getting brighter and higher, is the prominent bright object in the southeast before sunrise, again pairing with a waning crescent Moon on the 3d.

**Saturn**, still hidden in the Sun's glare, rises before the Sun only by about one hour at the end of the month.

**Moon** passes Uranus and Neptune on the 2d, Jupiter on the 3d, Mercury on the 8th, occults Aldebaran on the 11th, passes Mars on the 19th, Neptune again on the 29th, Jupiter and Uranus again on the 30th.

**Apr. 2**—Venus at superior conjunction with the Sun, on the far side of its orbit from the Earth; Uranus and Neptune 4° south of Moon.

**Apr. 3**—Jupiter 4° south of Moon.

**Apr. 6**—Mercury at greatest eastern elongation of 19.2° (east of the Sun and setting after the Sun).

**Apr. 8**—Mercury 7° north of Moon.

**Apr. 11**—Moon is 0.5° north of Aldebaran, occulting it.

**Apr. 15**—Mercury stationary, beginning retrograde motion.

**Apr. 18**—Sun enters Aries.

**Apr. 19**—Mars 4° north of Moon.

**Apr. 21**—Mercury 3.1° north of Venus.

**Apr. 25**—Mercury at inferior conjunction with the Sun; Pluto 9° north of Moon.

**Apr. 29**—Neptune 3° south of Moon; Mars stationary, resuming direct motion.

**Apr. 30**—Jupiter 3° and Uranus 4° south of Moon.

## May

**Mercury** at greatest western elongation before sunrise on the 22d, but very low in the sky.

**Venus** still close to the Sun in the early evening sky.

**Mars** in Leo is much brighter than Regulus.

**Jupiter** is the prominent bright object in the south before sunrise.

**Saturn** is a 1st magnitude star in Pisces, seen in the early morning sky in the east.

**Moon** initiates a series of occultations of Saturn on the 4th; passes Mercury on the 5th, Venus on the 7th, Mars on the 16th, Pluto on the 22d, Neptune on the 26th, Uranus on the 27th, and Jupiter on the 28th.

**May 4**—Moon is 0.8° north of Saturn, occulting it; Saturn is 1° south of Moon.

**May 5**—Mercury 2° north of Moon.

**May 7**—Venus 5° north of Moon.

**May 8**—Moon is 0.6° north of Aldebaran, occulting it; Mercury stationary, resumes direct motion.

**May 13**—Sun enters Taurus; Uranus stationary, beginning retrograde motion.

**May 16**—Mars 3° north of Moon.

**May 20**—Neptune stationary, beginning retrograde motion.

**May 22**—Mercury at greatest western elongation of 25.4°; Pluto 9° north of Moon.

**May 25**—Pluto at opposition.

**May 26**—Neptune 3° south of Moon.

**May 27**—Uranus 4° south of Moon.

**May 28**—Jupiter 3° south of Moon.

## June

**Mercury**, diving into the glare of the Sun, is at superior conjunction on the 25th.

**Venus**, gradually getting higher in the early evening sky, is near the Gemini twins, Castor and Pollux, about the 23d.

**Mars** reenters Virgo, still fading in brightness.

**Jupiter** is the prominent bright object in the southeast at the middle of the night.

**Saturn** is a 1st magnitude star in Pisces, brightening very slightly.

**Moon** passes Saturn on the 1st, Mercury on the 3d, occults Aldebaran on the 4th, then passes Venus on the 6th, Mars on the 13th, Pluto on the 18th, Neptune on the 22d, Uranus on the 23d, Jupiter on the 24th, and Saturn once more on the 28th.

**June 1**—Saturn 1° north of Moon; Mars enters Virgo.

**June 3**—Mercury 2° north of Moon.

**June 4**—Moon is 0.7° north of Aldebaran, occulting it.

**June 6**—Venus 6° north of Moon.

**June 10**—Jupiter stationary, beginning retrograde motion.

**June 13**—Mars 1° north of Moon.

**June 18**—Pluto 9° north of Moon.

**June 21**—Northern solstice at 8:21 GMT (4:21 AM EDT); summer begins in the northern hemisphere, winter begins in the southern hemisphere; Sun enters Gemini.

**June 22**—Neptune 3° south of Moon.

**June 23**—Uranus 4° south of Moon.

**June 24**—Jupiter 3° south of Moon.

**June 25**—Mercury at superior conjunction with the Sun.

**June 28**—Saturn 1° north of Moon.

## July

**Mercury**, low in the west at sunset, passes Regulus on the 27th.

**Venus** makes a bright pair with the Moon on the 7th and passes Regulus on the 23d.

**Mars**, in Virgo, is now only slightly brighter than Spica.

**Jupiter** is the prominent bright object rising in the southeast an hour after sunset.

**Saturn** is a 1st magnitude star in Pisces, rising an hour or 2 before the middle of the night.

**Moon** passes Mercury on the 5th, Venus on the 7th, Mars on the 12th, Pluto on the 16th, Uranus and Neptune on the 20th, Jupiter on the 21st, Saturn on the 25th, and occults Aldebaran on the 29th.

**July 4**—Earth at aphelion, 94.5 mil mi from the Sun.

**July 5**—Mercury 6° north of Moon.

**July 7**—Venus 5° north of Moon.

**July 12**—Mars 1° south of Moon.

**July 16**—Pluto 9° north of Moon.

**July 20**—Sun enters Cancer; Uranus 4° and Neptune 3° south of Moon.

**July 21**—Neptune at opposition; Jupiter 3° south of Moon.

**July 25**—Saturn 1° north of Moon.

**July 28**—Uranus nearest to the Earth this year.

**July 29**—Uranus at opposition; Moon is 0.4° north of Aldebaran, occulting it.

### August

**Mercury** at greatest elongation on the 4th, begins retrograde motion on the 17th.

**Venus** paired with the waxing crescent Moon on the 6th.

**Mars,** still fading, enters Libra, passing Spica on the 3d.

**Jupiter**, at its brightest, is the prominent bright object rising in the southeast at sunset.

**Saturn** is stationary early in the month on the 3d, beginning its retrograde motion.

**Moon** passes Mercury on the 5th, Venus on the 6th, Mars on the 9th, Pluto on the 12th, Neptune on the 16th, Jupiter and Uranus on the 17th, Saturn on the 22d, and occults Aldebaran on the 25th.

**Aug. 3**—Saturn stationary, beginning its retrograde motion.

**Aug. 4**—Mercury at greatest eastern elongation of 27.3°

**Aug. 5**—Mercury 1° south of Moon.

**Aug. 6**—Venus 2° north of Moon.

**Aug. 9**—Jupiter at opposition; Mars 3° south of Moon.

**Aug. 10**—Jupiter nearest to the Earth this year; Sun enters Leo.

**Aug. 12**—Pluto 8° north of Moon.

**Aug. 16**—Neptune 3° south of Moon; Pluto stationary, resuming direct motion.

**Aug. 17**—Jupiter 4° and Uranus 3° south of Moon; Mercury stationary, beginning retrograde motion.

**Aug. 22**—Saturn 1° north of Moon.

**Aug. 25**—Moon 0.3° north of Aldebaran, occulting it.

**Aug. 26**—Mars enters Libra.

**Aug. 31**—Mercury at inferior conjunction with the Sun.

### September

**Mercury**, stationary on the 9th, resumes direct motion and is at greatest western elongation on the 16th.

**Venus** pairs with the crescent Moon on the 5th, and passes Spica on the 6th.

**Mars** continues to fade as it enters Scorpius near the end of the month, approaching the star known as its rival, Antares.

**Jupiter**, fading slightly, dominates the southeast after sunset.

**Saturn** is nearly a zero magnitude star in Pisces at 0.3 magnitude.

**Moon** passes Venus on the 5th, Mars on the 7th, Pluto on the 8th, Neptune on the 12th, Uranus on the 13th, Jupiter on the 14th, occults Saturn on the 18th, and passes Mercury on the 30th.

**Sept. 5**—Venus 3° south of Moon.

**Sept. 7**—Mars 5° south of Moon.

**Sept. 8**—Pluto 8° north of Moon.

**Sept. 9**—Mercury stationary, resumes direct motion.

**Sept. 12**—Neptune 3° south of Moon.

**Sept. 13**—Uranus 4° south of Moon.

**Sept. 14**—Jupiter 3° south of Moon.

**Sept. 16**—Mercury at greatest western elongation of 17.9°; Sun enters Virgo.

**Sept. 18**—Moon is 0.2° north of Saturn, occulting it.

**Sept. 23**—Autumnal Equinox at 23:57 GMT (7:57 PM EDT); autumn begins in the northern hemisphere; spring begins in the southern hemisphere.

**Sept. 29**—Mars enter Scorpius.

**Sept. 30**—Mercury 2° north of Moon.

### October

**Mercury** at superior conjunction on the 13th.

**Venus** passes Antares on the 17th and Mars on the 26th.

**Mars** is about 1st magnitude as it enters the 13th constellation of the ecliptic, Ophiuchus; passes its look-alike star, Antares, on the 12th.

**Jupiter** is the brilliant object in the southeast after sunset.

**Saturn** is at its brightest this month, 0.2 magnitude, as it goes through opposition on the 10th.

**Moon** passes Venus on the 5th, Mars and Pluto on the 6th, Uranus and Neptune on the 10th, Jupiter on the 11th, Saturn on the 15th, and occults Aldebaran on the 19th.

**Oct. 5**—Venus 7° south of Moon.

**Oct. 6**—Mars 6° south and Pluto 8° north of Moon.

**Oct. 8**—Jupiter stationary, resuming direct motion.

**Oct. 9**—Neptune stationary, resuming direct motion; Mars enters Ophiuchus.

**Oct. 10**—Saturn at opposition; Uranus 4° and Neptune 3° south of Moon.

**Oct. 11**—Jupiter 4° south of Moon.

**Oct. 12**—Mars in 3.5° north of Antares.

**Oct. 13**—Mercury at superior conjunction with the Sun.

**Oct. 14**—Uranus stationary, resuming direct motion.

**Oct. 15**—Saturn 1° north of Moon.

**Oct. 19**—Moon is 0.4° north of Aldebaran, occulting it.

**Oct. 26**—Venus 2.1° south of Mars.

**Oct. 31**—Sun enters Libra.

### November

**Mercury** passes Antares on the 14th.

**Venus**, still low in the southwest at sunset, reaches greatest eastern elongation on the 6th.

**Mars**, at 1st magnitude, enters Sagittarius, grouped nicely with Venus and Moon on the 4th.

**Jupiter** is the brilliant object in the south after sunset.

**Saturn** begins to fade again, low in the east after sunset.

**Moon** passes Mercury on the 1st, Pluto on the 2d, Venus and Mars on the 4th, Neptune on the 6th, Jupiter and Uranus on the 7th, occults Saturn on the 12th, and passes Pluto again on the 29th.

**Nov. 1**—Mercury 5° south of Moon.

**Nov. 2**—Pluto 7° north of Moon.

**Nov. 3**—Mars enters Sagittarius.

**Nov. 4**—Venus 8° and Mars 6° south of Moon.

**Nov. 6**—Venus at greatest eastern elongation of 47.1°; Neptune 3° south of Moon.

**Nov. 7**—Jupiter 3° and Uranus 4° south of Moon.

**Nov. 12**—Moon is 0.4° north of Saturn, occulting it.

**Nov. 22**—Sun enters Scorpius.

**Nov. 27**—Pluto in conjunction with the Sun.

**Nov. 28**—Mercury at greatest western elongation of 21.6°.

**Nov. 29**—Sun enters Ophiuchus; Pluto 8° north of Moon.

### December

**Mercury** begins retrograde motion on the 8th, but resumes direct motion on the 28th.

**Venus**, Mars, and the crescent Moon make a striking sight on the 3d. Venus begins retrograde motion on the 26th.

**Mars**, at its faintest for the year, enters Capricornus and passes both Neptune and Uranus.

**Jupiter** is the 2d brightest starlike object in the south after sunset.

**Saturn** resumes its direct motion on the 17th, having spent the whole year in the constellation of Pisces.

**Moon** passes Mercury on the 1st; Venus, Mars, and Neptune on the 3d; Uranus on the 4th; Jupiter on the 5th; occults Saturn on the 9th; occults Aldebaran on the 13th; passes Pluto on the 27th; and passes Mercury again on the 28th.

**Dec. 1**—Mercury 6° south of Moon.

**Dec. 3**—Venus 6°, Mars 5°, and Neptune 2° south of Moon.

**Dec. 4**—Uranus 3° south of Moon.

**Dec. 5**—Jupiter 3° south of Moon.

**Dec. 8**—Mercury stationary, beginning retrograde motion.

**Dec. 9**—Moon is 0.2° north of Saturn, occulting it.

**Dec. 13**—Moon 0.5° north of Aldebaran, occulting it.

**Dec. 15**—Mars 1.6° south of Neptune.

**Dec. 17**—Mercury at inferior conjunction with the Sun; Sun enters Sagittarius; Saturn stationary, resuming its direct motion; Mars enters Capricornus.

**Dec. 21**—Southern solstice at 20:09 GMT (3:09 PM EST); winter begins in the northern hemisphere, summer begins in the southern hemisphere; Mercury at inferior conjunction with the Sun.

**Dec. 22**—Venus 1.1° north of Mars.

**Dec. 26**—Mars 0.6° south of Uranus; Venus stationary, beginning retrograde motion.

**Dec. 27**—Pluto 8° north of Moon.

**Dec. 28**—Mercury 2° south of Moon; Mercury stationary, resumes direct motion.

# Comet Hale-Bopp and Comet Hyakutake

On July 23, 1995, 2 amateur astronomers, Alan Hale in New Mexico and Thomas Bopp in Arizona, independently discovered a new comet. Since comets are the one type of astronomical phenomenon named after the discoverers, it became known as Comet Hale-Bopp. Shortly after its discovery, observations indicated that when Comet Hale-Bopp reaches its brightest as viewed from Earth in 1997, it could well be the brightest comet to appear in our skies in 2 decades (since Comet West in 1976). This was the first comet discovered by either man. At the time of its discovery, the comet was beyond the orbit of Jupiter and was located farther away from the Earth than any comet previously discovered by amateur astronomers.

Just as cautious excitement was building over the anticipation of Comet Hale-Bopp, 1996 brought another comet discovery, with the detection of Comet Hyakutake on Jan. 31, 1996, less than 2 months before its closest approach to the Earth on Mar. 25. On the latter date it passed at a distance of 0.102 AU (about 9.5 mil mi) and reached approximately 0 (zero) magnitude (rivaling bright stars Capella, Vega, or Arcturus, but more diffuse) with a tail reportedly stretching tens of degrees across dark skies. The brightness of a comet, particularly one for which astronomers have no records, is particularly hard to predict. However, the current estimates are that Comet Hale-Bopp may also reach a magnitude of 0 (zero). It may end up even brighter than Jupiter.

Bouncing radio signals off of Comet Hyakutake, astronomers were able to estimate the nucleus of the comet as being 1-2 mi in diameter. The head of a comet, which includes the cloud of gas, dust, and debris around it, is often 100,000 mi in diameter. Much cruder estimates of the nucleus of Comet Hale-Bopp place its diameter at about 25 mi.

Nearly a year to the day after the closest approach of Comet Hyakutake, Comet Hale-Bopp will make its closest approach to the Earth on Mar. 23, 1997, coming within 1.3 AU (120 mil mi). Though it will be more than 12 times farther away than Comet Hyakutake, it is expected to put on at least as good an appearance. Starting a couple of days after closest approach—as the Moon, with its interfering light gets out of the way—there should be about 2 weeks of excellent viewing in the northwest after sunset.

The table below indicates where to look for Comet Hale-Bopp during much of 1997. Binoculars are recommended over telescopes, because they have a wider field of view.

## Comet Hale-Bopp Predicted Location & Brightness

| Date | | Right Ascension h | m | Declination ° | ′ | Constellation | Estimated Magnitude |
|---|---|---|---|---|---|---|---|
| Jan. | 5 | 18 | 48.6 | + 05 | 46 | Serpens Cauda | 3.7 |
| Jan. | 20 | 19 | 14.6 | + 10 | 26 | Aquila | 3.1 |
| Feb. | 9 | 20 | 01.8 | + 19 | 40 | Sagitta | 2.1 |
| Feb. | 24 | 20 | 56.7 | + 29 | 31 | Cygnus | 1.3 |
| Mar. | 11 | 22 | 28.4 | + 40 | 35 | Lacerta | 0.6 |
| Mar. | 26 | 00 | 49.2 | + 45 | 49 | Andromeda | 0.3 |
| Apr. | 10 | 02 | 59.8 | + 39 | 56 | Perseus | 0.6 |
| Apr. | 25 | 04 | 19.1 | + 29 | 53 | Taurus | 1.1 |
| May | 10 | 05 | 07.3 | + 20 | 45 | Taurus | 1.8 |
| May | 25 | 05 | 41.2 | + 13 | 12 | Orion | 2.5 |
| June | 9 | 06 | 08.2 | + 06 | 46 | Orion | 3.2 |
| June | 24 | 06 | 31.4 | + 00 | 59 | Monoceros | 3.7 |
| July | 9 | 06 | 52.0 | − 04 | 32 | Monoceros | 4.2 |
| July | 24 | 07 | 10.7 | − 10 | 00 | Monoceros | 4.6 |
| Aug. | 8 | 07 | 27.5 | − 15 | 36 | Puppis | 4.9 |
| Aug. | 23 | 07 | 42.3 | − 21 | 24 | Puppis | 5.3 |

# Astronomical Positions

Two celestial bodies are in **conjunction** when they are due north and south of each other, either in **Right Ascension** (with respect to the north celestial pole) or in **Celestial Longitude** (with respect to the north ecliptic pole). If the bodies are seen near each other, they will rise and set at nearly the same time. They are in **opposition** when their Right Ascensions differ by exactly 12 hours, or when their Celestial Longitudes differ by 180°. One of the 2 objects in opposition will rise while the other is setting. **Quadrature** refers to the arrangement where the coordinates of 2 bodies differ by exactly 90°. These terms may refer to the relative positions of any 2 bodies as seen from the Earth, but one of the bodies is so frequently the Sun, that mention of the Sun is omitted; otherwise, both bodies are named. The geocentric angular separation between the Sun and an object is termed **elongation**. Elongation is limited only for Mercury and Venus; the greatest elongation for each of these bodies is noted in the appropriate table and is approximately the time for longest observation. The term **perihelion** means nearest to the Sun, and **aphelion**, farthest from the Sun. An **occultation** of a planet or a star is an **eclipse** of it by some other body, usually the Moon.

# Planets and the Sun

The planets of the solar system, in order of their mean distance from the Sun, are Mercury, Venus, Earth, Mars, Jupiter, Saturn, Uranus, Neptune, and Pluto. Both Uranus and Neptune are visible through good binoculars, but Pluto is so distant and so small that only large telescopes or long-exposure photographs can make it visible.

Because Mercury and Venus are nearer to the Sun than is the Earth, their motions about the Sun are seen from the Earth as wide swings first to one side of the Sun and then to the other, although both planets are passing continuously around the Sun in orbits that are almost circular. When their passage takes them either between the Earth and the Sun or beyond the Sun as seen from the Earth, they are invisible to us. Because of the laws that govern the motions of planets about the Sun, both Mercury and Venus require much less time to pass between the Earth and the Sun than around the far side of the Sun; so their periods of visibility and invisibility are unequal.

The planets that lie farther from the Sun than does the Earth may be seen for longer periods of time and are invisible only when they are so located in our sky that they rise and set at about the same time as the Sun—and thus become overwhelmed by the Sun's great brilliance. Although several of the giant planets seem to generate and emit their own energy, they are observed from the Earth as a result of sunlight reflecting from their surfaces or cloud layers. Mercury and Venus, because they are between the Earth and the Sun, show phases very much as the Moon does. The planets farther from the Sun are always seen as full, although Mars does occasionally present a slightly gibbous phase—like the Moon when not quite full.

The planets appear to move rapidly among the stars because the planets are very much nearer to the Earth. The stars are also in motion, some of them at tremendous speeds, but they are so far away that their motion does not change their apparent positions in the heavens sufficiently for anyone to perceive that change in a single lifetime. The very nearest star is about 7,000 times as far away as the most distant planet in our solar system.

# Planets of the Solar System

## Mercury

Mercury, the nearest planet to the Sun, is the 2d smallest of the 9 planets known to be orbiting the Sun. Its diameter is 3,031 mi, and its mean distance from the Sun is 36,000,000 mi.

Mercury moves with great speed in its journey about the Sun, averaging about 30 mi a second to complete its circuit in about 88 Earth days. Mercury rotates upon its axis over a period of nearly 59 days, thus exposing all its surface periodically to the Sun. Because its orbital period is only about 50% longer than its sidereal rotation, the solar (synodic) day on Mercury, or the time from one sunrise to the next, takes about 176 days, resulting in a solar day on Mercury that is twice as long as a Mercurian year. It is believed that the surface passing before the Sun may have a temperature of about 800° F, while the temperature on the nighttime side may fall as low as –300° F. Although Mercury is the closest planet to the Sun, it has the largest range of temperature change from day to night—no other planet even comes close.

Uncertainty about conditions on Mercury and its motion arises from its shorter angular distance from the Sun as seen from the Earth. Mercury is always too much in line with the Sun to be observed against a dark sky, but is always seen during either morning or evening twilight.

*Mariner 10* passed Mercury 3 times in 1974 and 1975. A large fraction of the surface was photographed from varying distances, revealing a degree of cratering similar to that of the Moon. An atmosphere of hydrogen and helium may be made up of gases of the solar wind temporarily concentrated by the presence of Mercury. The discovery of a weak but permanent magnetic field was a surprise to scientists. It has been held that both a fluid core and rapid rotation were necessary for the generation of a planetary magnetic field. Mercury may demonstrate these conditions to be unnecessary, or the field may reveal something about the history of Mercury.

## Venus

Venus, slightly smaller than the Earth, moves about the Sun at a mean distance of 67,000,000 mi in 225 Earth days. Its synodical revolution—its return to the same relationship with the Earth and the Sun, which is a result of the combination of its own motion with that of the Earth—is 584 days. As a result, every 19 months, Venus is nearer to the Earth than any other planet in the solar system. The planet is covered with a dense, white, cloudy atmosphere that conceals whatever is below it. This same cloud reflects sunlight efficiently so that when Venus is favorably situated, it is the 3d brightest object in the sky, exceeded only by the Sun and the Moon.

Spectral analysis of sunlight reflected from Venus's cloud tops has shown features that can best be explained by identifying material of the clouds as sulfuric acid. Infrared spectroscopy from a balloon-borne telescope nearly 20 mi above the Earth's surface gave indications of a small amount of water vapor present in the same region of the atmosphere of Venus. In 1956, radio astronomers at the Naval Research Laboratories in Washington, DC, found a temperature for Venus of about 600° F, in marked contrast to –125° F previously found at the cloud tops. Subsequent radio work confirmed a high temperature and produced evidence associating this temperature with the solid body of Venus. With this peculiarity in mind, space scientists devised experiments for the U.S. space probe *Mariner 2* to perform when it flew by in 1962. *Mariner 2* confirmed the high temperature and the fact that it pertained to the ground rather than to some special activity of the atmosphere. In addition, *Mariner 2* was unable to detect the existence of a magnetic field even as weak as 1/100,000 of the Earth's magnetic field.

In 1967, a Russian space probe, *Venera 4*, and the American *Mariner 5* arrived at Venus within a few hours of each other. *Venera 4* was designed to allow an instrument package to land gently on the surface via parachute. It ceased to transmit information in about 75 minutes when its temperature reading went above 500° F. After considerable controversy, it was agreed that the instrument package still had 20 mi to go to reach the surface. *Mariner 5* went around the night side of Venus at a distance of about 6,000 mi. Again, it detected no significant field, but its radio signals passed to Earth through Venus's atmosphere twice (once on the night side and once on the day side). The results were startling. Venus's atmosphere is nearly all carbon dioxide and must exert a pressure at the planet's surface of as much as 100 times the Earth's normal sea-level pressure of one atmosphere. Because Earth and Venus are about the same size and were presumably formed at the same time by the same general process and from the same mixture of chemical elements, one is faced with the question: Which is the planet with the unusual history—Earth or Venus? Recent measurements indicate that Venus has a surface temperature of about 900° F as a result of an extreme greenhouse effect. Because of the thick atmosphere, the temperature is essentially the same both day and night.

Radar astronomers using powerful transmitters as well as sensitive receivers and computers succeeded in determining the rotation period of Venus. It turns out to be 243 days clockwise—in other words, contrary to the spin of the other planets and to its own motion around the Sun. If it were exactly 243.16 days, Venus would present the same face toward the Earth at every inferior conjunction. This rate and sense of rotation allows a solar day (sunrise to sunrise) on Venus of 117.4 Earth days. Any part of Venus will receive sunlight on its clouds for more than 58 days and then return to darkness for 58 days. Earth-based radar observations have shown surface features below the clouds. Large craters, continent-sized highlands, and extensive, dry "ocean" basins were identified.

*Mariner 10* passed Venus before traveling on to Mercury in 1974. The carbon dioxide molecule found in such abundance in the atmosphere is rather opaque to certain ultraviolet wavelengths, enabling sensitive television cameras to photograph the Venusian cloud cover. Photos radioed to Earth showed a spiral pattern in the clouds from the equator to the poles.

In Dec. 1978, two U.S. *Pioneer* probes arrived at Venus. One went into orbit around Venus; the other split into 5 separate probes targeted for widely spaced entry points to sample different conditions. The instrument ensemble was selected on the basis of previous missions that had shown the range of conditions to be studied. The probes confirmed expected high surface temperatures and high winds aloft. Winds of about 200 mi per hour there may account for the transfer of heat into the night side despite the low rotation speed of the planet. However, surface winds were light at the time. Atmosphere and cloud chemistries were examined in detail, providing much data for continued analysis. The probes detected 4 layers of clouds and more light on the surface than expected solely from sunlight. This light allowed Soviet scientists to obtain, in 1975 and later in 1982, 4 photos of rocks on the surface. Sulfur seems to play a large role in the chemistry of Venus, and reactions involving sulfur may be responsible for the glow. To learn more about the weather and atmospheric circulation on Venus, the orbiter took daily photos of the daylight-side cloud cover. It confirmed the cloud pattern and its circulation shown by *Mariner 10*. The ionosphere showed large variability. The orbiter's radar operated in 2 modes: one for ground elevation variability, the other for ground reflectivity in 2 dimensions, thus "imaging" the surface. Radar maps of the entire planet showing the large features mentioned above were produced.

The Venus orbiter *Magellan* was launched May 4, 1989. It was equipped to observe Venus by a side-scanning radar system, together with one to gather data on the variations in elevations directly beneath the craft. *Magellan* mapped all but a small fraction of the planet. The side-looking radar illuminated the surface and its features with radio waves and recorded the strength and distance of the returning echoes. Computer processing produced a view of the landscape as if it had been seen through a clear atmosphere from above, near sunset, with a visibility better than about 500 feet on Venus. Information on vertical relief had a resolution of about 30 feet.

Craters more than 20 mi wide are believed to have been caused by impacting bodies. Theia Mons, a huge shield volcano, has a diameter of over 500 mi and a height of over 3 mi. (Compare this to the largest Hawaiian volcano, which is only about 125 mi in diameter, but with a height of nearly 5.5 mi from the ocean floor.) Many lava flows have been seen, and some old craters and plains seem to be filled with lava.

Most of the surface is believed to be younger than 1 bil to 500 mil years old. Modifications of previously existing surface features have been caused by weathering and by tectonic actions such as faulting. Tectonic actions on Venus in general are distinctly different from such actions on Earth. The intense heat at the surface of Venus can prevent the surface materials from cooling to the same brittle condition as on Earth. The same actions may produce somewhat different results on Earth than they would on Venus. No activity on Venus seems to be similar to the Earth's moving tectonic plates, but local stretching and compressing may produce rift valleys and higher plains and mountains. Although no weathering is due to water on Venus, the action of the winds is in evidence. Extensive sand dunes have been seen, and windblown deposits indicate stable wind patterns for very long periods of time. Although there are deep regions, somewhat similar to Earth's ocean basins, there is no water to fill them. The orbit of *Magellan* was adjusted to a nearly circular shape about 300 mi from the planet's surface in 1993. In this mode, variation in *Magellan*'s orbital speed revealed information on irregularities in the gravitational field, presumably due to details in the internal structure of the planet. Although *Magellan* ceased operating in Oct. 1994, the tremendous amount of information about the topography of Venus's surface obtained by the probe will keep teams of analysts and theoreticians busy for years.

## Mars

Mars is the first planet beyond the Earth, away from the Sun. Mars's diameter is about 4,200 mi, although a determination of the radius and mass of Mars by the space probe *Mariner 4*, which flew by Mars at a distance of less than 6,000 mi on July 14, 1965, indicated that these dimensions were slightly larger than had been previously estimated. Although Mars's orbit is nearly circular, it is somewhat more eccentric than the orbits of many of the other planets, and Mars is more than 30 mil mi farther from the Sun in some parts of its year than it is at others. Mars takes 687 Earth days to make one circuit of the Sun, traveling at about 15 mi a second. Mars rotates upon its axis in almost the same period of time that the Earth does—24 hours and 37 minutes. Mars's mean distance from the Sun is 141 mil mi; so the temperature on Mars would be lower than that on the Earth even if Mars's atmosphere were about the same as Earth's. The atmosphere is not, however, for *Mariner 4* reported that atmospheric pressure on Mars is between 1% and 2% of the Earth's atmospheric pressure. As is the case with Venus, Mars's thin atmosphere appears to be composed largely of carbon dioxide. No evidence of free water was found.

There appears to be no magnetic field around Mars. If that is the case, the previous conception of a dangerous radiation belt around the planet is erroneous. The lack of a magnetic field would expose the surface of Mars to an influx of cosmic radiation about 100 times as intense as that on Earth.

Deductions from years of telescopic observation indicate that about 5/8 of the surface of Mars is a desert of reddish rock, sand, and soil. The rest of Mars is covered by irregular patches that appear generally green, in hues that change through the Martian year. These were formerly held to be some sort of primitive vegetation, but with the findings of *Mariner 4* of a complete lack of water and oxygen, it appeared that such growth would not be possible. The nature of the green areas is now unknown. They may be regions covered with volcanic salts whose color changes with changing temperatures and atmospheric conditions, or they may be gray rather than green. When large gray areas are placed beside large red areas, the gray areas appear green to the eye.

Mars's axis of rotation is inclined from a vertical to the plane of its orbit about the Sun by about 25°, and therefore Mars has seasons as does the Earth, except that the Martian seasons are longer because the Martian year is longer. White caps form about the winter pole of Mars, growing in the winter and shrinking in the summer. These polar caps are now believed to be both water ice and carbon dioxide ice. It is the carbon dioxide that is seen to come and go with the seasons. The water ice is apparently in many layers with dust between them, indicating climatic cycles.

The canals of Mars have become more of a mystery than they were before the voyage of *Mariner 4*. Markings forming a network of fine lines crossing much of the surface of Mars have been seen by diligent observers, but no canals have shown clearly enough in previous photographs to be universally accepted. A few of the 21 photographs sent back to Earth by *Mariner 4* covered areas crossed by canals. The pictures show faint, ill-defined, broad, dark markings, the nature of which could not be positively determined.

*Mariners 6* and *7* in 1969 sent back many more photographs of higher quality than those of the pioneering *Mariner 4*. These pictures showed cratering similar to the earlier views, but in addition showed 2 other types of terrain. Some regions seemed featureless over large areas, but others were chaotic, showing high relief without apparent organization into mountain chains or craters. *Mariner 9*, the first artificial body to be placed in an orbit about Mars, transmitted more than 10,000 photographs covering 100% of the planet's surface. Although study of these photos and other data shows that Mars resembles no other planet we know, scientists using terrestrial terms describe features that seem to be clearly of volcanic origin. One of these features is Olympus Mons, apparently a shield volcano whose caldera is more than 50 mi wide, whose outer slopes are more than 300 mi in diameter, and which stands more than 15 mi above the surrounding plain. Some features may have been produced by cracking (faulting) of the surface and the sliding of one region over or past another. Many craters seem to have been produced by impacting bodies that may have come from the nearby asteroid belt. Features near the south pole may have been produced by glaciers no longer present. Valles Marineris, a huge series of interrelated canyons, stretches more than 3,000 mi.

Although the Russians landed a probe on the Martian surface, it transmitted for only 20 seconds. In 1976, the U.S. landed 2 *Viking* spacecraft on the Martian surface. The landers had devices aboard to perform chemical analyses of the soil in search of evidence of life; results were inconclusive. The 2 *Viking* orbiters returned the best pictures yet of Martian topographic features. Scientists believe many features can be explained only if Mars once had large quantities of flowing water.

Mars's position in its orbit and its speed around that orbit in relation to the Earth's position and speed bring Mars fairly close to the Earth on occasions about 2 years apart and then move Mars and the Earth too far apart for accurate observation and photography. Every 15-17 years, the close approaches are especially favorable for observation.

Mars has 2 satellites, discovered in 1877 by Asaph Hall. The outer satellite, Deimos, revolves around the planet in about 31 hours. The inner satellite, Phobos, whips around Mars in a little more than 7 hours, making 3 trips around the planet each Martian day. Since it orbits Mars faster than the planet rotates, Phobos rises in the west and sets in the east, opposite to what everything else appears to do in the Martian sky. *Mariner* and *Viking* photos show these bodies to be irregularly shaped and pitted with numerous craters. Phobos also shows a system of linear grooves, each about 1/3 mi across and roughly parallel. Phobos measures about 8 by 12 mi and Deimos about 5 by 7.5 mi.

In 1996, a NASA research team concluded that a meteorite found in 1984 on an Antarctic ice field not only might be a rock blasted from the surface of Mars but also might contain evidence that life existed on Mars more than 3.5 bil years ago. The meteorite has been age-dated to about 4.5 bil years. The scientists theorize that 3.5 bil years ago, Mars may have been warmer and wetter, and microscopic life may have formed and left evidence in the rock, including possible fossilized microscopic organisms. Then 16 mil years ago, it is believed that a huge asteroid or comet struck Mars, blasting material, including this rock, into space. The rock may have entered the Earth's atmosphere about 13,000 years ago, landing in Antarctica. The evidence is intriguing, but definitely not conclusive; and even if the above conclusions are correct they indicate the presence only of microscopic life, at a time far in the Martian past.

## Jupiter

Jupiter is the largest of the planets. Its equatorial diameter is 88,000 mi, 11 times the diameter of the Earth. Its polar diameter is about 6,000 mi shorter. As a result of an equilibrium condition resulting from the liquidity of the planet and its extremely rapid rate of rotation, a day is less than 10 Earth hours long. For a planet this size, this rotational speed is amazing. A point on Jupiter's equator moves at a speed of 22,000 mi per hour, as compared with a speed of 1,000 mi for a point on the Earth's equator. Jupiter is at an average distance of 480 mil mi from the Sun and takes almost 12 Earth years to make one complete circuit of the Sun.

The major observable chemical constituents of Jupiter's atmosphere are methane ($CH_4$) and ammonia ($NH_3$), but it is reasonable to assume the same mixture of elements were available to make Jupiter as to make the Sun. This would mean a large amount of hydrogen and helium must be present also, as well as water ($H_2O$). The temperature at the tops of the clouds may be about –280° F. The clouds are probably ammonia ice crystals, becoming ammonia droplets lower down. There may be a space before water ice crystals show up as clouds: in turn, these become water droplets near the bottom of the entire cloud layer. The total atmosphere may be only a few hundred mi in depth, pulled down by the surface gravity (the equivalent of 2.64 times Earth's gravity) to a relatively thin layer. Of course, the gases become denser with depth, until they may turn into a slush or slurry. Perhaps there is no real interface between the gaseous atmosphere and the hydrogen ocean that accounts for most of Jupiter's volume. *Pioneers 10* and *11* provided evidence for considering Jupiter almost entirely liquid hydrogen. Long before a rocky core about the size of the Earth is reached, scientists believe hydrogen mixed with helium becomes a liquid metal at very high temperature and pressure. Jupiter's cloudy atmosphere is a fairly good reflector of sunlight and makes it appear far brighter than any of the stars.

Fourteen of Jupiter's nearly dozen-and-a-half known satellites have been found through Earth-based observations. Four of the moons are large and bright, rivaling the Earth's Moon and the planet Mercury in diameter, and may be seen through binoculars. They move rapidly around Jupiter, and their change of position from night to night is extremely interesting to watch. The other satellites are much smaller, and in all but one instance much farther from Jupiter, and cannot be seen except through powerful telescopes. The 4 outermost satellites are revolving around Jupiter clockwise as seen from the north, contrary to the motions of the great majority of the satellites in the solar system and to the direction of revolution of the planets around the Sun. The reason for this retrograde motion is not known; one theory is that Jupiter's tremendous gravitational power may have captured 4 of the minor planets or asteroids that move about the Sun between Mars and Jupiter and that these would necessarily revolve backward. (At the great distance of these bodies from Jupiter—some 14 mil mi—direct motion would result in decay of the orbits, while retrograde orbits would be stable.) Jupiter's mass is more than twice the mass of all the other planets put together; this accounts for Jupiter's tremendous gravitational field, and so, probably, for its numerous satellites and its dense atmosphere.

In Dec. 1973, *Pioneer 10* passed about 80,000 mi from the equator of Jupiter and was whipped into a path that would take it beyond the system of planets on June 13, 1983, and out of the Earth's solar system in about 50 years. In Dec. 1974, *Pioneer 11* passed within 30,000 mi of Jupiter, moving roughly from south to north, over the poles.

Photographs from both encounters were useful at the time but were far surpassed by those of *Voyagers I* and *II*, both of which were launched in 1977 and rendezvoused with Jupiter in 1979. Thousands of high-resolution multicolor pictures show rapid variations of features both large and small. The Great Red Spot exhibited internal counterclockwise rotation. Much turbulence was seen in adjacent material passing north or south of it. The satellites Amalthea, Io, Europa, Ganymede, and Callisto were photographed, some in great detail. Each is individual and unique, with no similarities to other known planets or satellites. Io has active volcanoes that probably have ejected material into a doughnut-shaped ring enveloping its orbit about Jupiter. This is not to be confused with the thin, flat disklike ring closer to Jupiter's surface.

Beginning July 16, 1994, the 21 large fragments of Comet Shoemaker-Levy 9 collided with Jupiter in a dramatic 6-day barrage. Moving at 134,000 mph, stretched out like a 21-car freight train, the fragments impacted one after another against the side of Jupiter facing away from the Earth. The high speed of the planet's rotation, allowing the impact sites to rotate quickly into view, along with the sheer scope of the reactions, provided a show unprecedented in astronomy. Massive plumes of gas erupted from the impact sites, forming brilliant fireballs and leaving dark blotches and smears behind. One of the largest chunks, labeled the G fragment, impacted with the force of 6 mil megatons of TNT, 100,000 times the power of the largest nuclear bomb ever detonated. It produced a plume 1,200-1,600 mi high and 5,000 mi wide and left a dark discoloration larger than the Earth. These impacts, predicted a year in advance, were closely observed and produced a massive amount of data for scientists and astronomers to analyze, even as they continued to observe Jupiter for the event's aftermath.

Scientists produced their own impact, when the *Galileo* spacecraft went into orbit around Jupiter and released an atmospheric probe into the Jovian atmosphere on Dec. 7, 1995. The cone-shaped probe, traveling at a speed of more than 106,000 mph, survived deceleration forces of 228 times Earth's gravity as it plunged 400 mi, relaying information about Jupiter's atmosphere for 57 minutes before expiring. Initial findings revealed a relatively dry atmosphere for the planet with about 1/5 the atmosphere for the amount of water expected from studies of the Comet Shoemaker-Levy 9 impacts. There were also higher-than-expected concentrations of helium. The probe gave evidence of wind speeds of more than 4,000 mph and a relative absence of lightning. These findings, together with data transmitted from the *Galileo* spacecraft still orbiting the planet, have raised many questions about Jupiter and its satellites that still need to be unraveled by scientists.

## Saturn

Saturn, last of the planets visible to the unaided eye, is almost twice as far from the Sun as Jupiter, almost 900 mil mi. It is second in size to Jupiter, but its mass is much smaller. Saturn's specific gravity is less than that of water. Its diameter is about 71,000 mi at the equator; its rotational speed spins it completely around in a little more than 10 hours, and its atmosphere is much like that of Jupiter, except that its temperature at the top of its cloud layer is at least 100° F lower. At about 300° F below zero, the ammonia would be frozen out of Saturn's clouds. The theoretical construction of Saturn resembles that of Jupiter; it likely has a small dense center surrounded by a layer of liquid and a deep atmosphere.

Detecting the precise number of satellites surrounding Saturn is complicated by the fact that the clearest observations can be made only at those times when the planet's rings are edge-on and virtually invisible. Until *Pioneer 11* passed Saturn in Sept. 1979, only 10 satellites of the planet were known from ground-based observation. Since that time, the *Voyager I* and *II* fly-bys and improved scientific equipment have yielded more information about Saturn's icy satellites. In 1995, astronomers using the Hubble Space Telescope detected at least 2 previously unknown moons of Saturn, perhaps bringing the total to 20 or more, with some sharing orbits.

Saturn's ring system begins about 7,000 mi above the visible disk of Saturn, lying above its equator and extending about 35,000 mi into space. The diameter of the ring system visible from Earth is about 170,000 mi; the rings are estimated to be no thicker than 10 mi. In 1973, radar observation showed the ring particles to be large chunks of material averaging a meter on a side.

*Voyager I* and *II* observations showed the rings to be considerably more complex than had been believed, so much so that interpretation will take much time. To the untrained eye, the *Voyager* photographs could be mistaken for pictures of a colorful phonograph record.

## Uranus

*Voyager II*, after passing Saturn in Aug. 1981, headed for a rendezvous with Uranus, culminating in a fly-by Jan. 24, 1986. This encounter answered many questions and raised others.

Uranus, discovered by Sir William Herschel on Mar. 13, 1781, lies at a distance of 1.8 bil mi from the Sun, taking 84 years to make its circuit around our star. Uranus has a diameter of about 32,000 mi and spins once in some 16.8 hours, according to fly-by data. One of the most fascinating features of Uranus is how far over it is tipped. Its north pole lies 98° from being directly up and down to its orbit plane.

Thus, its seasons are extreme. When the Sun rises at the north pole, it stays up for 42 Earth years; then it sets, and the north pole is in darkness (and winter) for 42 Earth years.

The satellite system of Uranus consists of at least 15 moons (the 5 largest having been known before the fly-by), which have orbits lying in the plane of the planet's equator. In that plane there is also a complex of rings, 9 of which were discovered in 1978. Invisible from Earth, the 9 original rings were found by observers watching Uranus pass before a star. As they waited, they saw their photoelectric equipment register several short eclipses of the star; then the planet occulted the star as expected. After the star came out from behind Uranus, the star winked out several more times. Subsequent observations and analyses indicated the 9 narrow, nearly opaque rings circling Uranus. Evidence from the *Voyager II* fly-by has shown the ring particles to be predominantly a yard or so in diameter.

In addition to photos of the 10 new, very small satellites, *Voyager II* returned detailed photos of the 5 large satellites. As in the case of other satellites newly observed in the *Voyager* program, these bodies proved to be entirely different from one another and from any others. Miranda has grooved markings, reminiscent of Jupiter's Ganymede, but often arranged in a chevron pattern. Ariel shows rifts and channels. Umbriel is extremely dark, prompting some observers to regard its surface as among the oldest in the system. Titania has rifts and fractures, but not the evidence of flow found on Ariel. Oberon's main feature is its surface saturated with craters, unrelieved by other formations.

The structure of Uranus is subject to some debate. Basically, however, it is likely to have a rocky core surrounded by a thick, icy mantle or perhaps a liquid mantle of water, methane, and ammonia on top of which is a slushy layer of hydrogen and helium that gradually becomes an atmosphere. Perhaps continued analysis of the wealth of data returned by *Voyager II* will shed some light on this problem.

## Neptune

Neptune, currently the most distant planet from the Sun (until 1999), lies at an average distance of 2.8 bil mi. It was the last planet visited in *Voyager II*'s epic 12-year trek (1977-89) from Earth. Although much new information was immediately perceived, much more must await analysis of the tremendous amount of data returned from the spacecraft.

As with the other giant planets, Neptune may have no solid surface to give real meaning to a measure of a diameter. However, a mean value of 30,600 mi may be assigned to a diameter between atmosphere levels where the pressure is about the same as sea level on Earth, as determined by radio experimentalists. Without a solid surface, it is challenging to determine a "true" rotation rate for a giant planet. Astronomers use a determination of the rotation rate of the planet's magnet field to indicate the internal rotation rate, which in the case of Neptune is 16.1 hours. Neptune orbits the Sun in 164 years in a nearly circular orbit. Neptune was not discovered until 1846; it will not be until 2010 that Neptune will have completed one full trip around the Sun since its discovery.

*Voyager II*, which passed 3,000 mi from Neptune's north pole, found a magnetic field that is considerably asymmetric to the planet's structure, similar to, but not so extreme as, that found at Uranus.

Neptune's atmosphere was seen to be quite blue, with quickly changing white clouds often suspended high above an apparent surface. In that apparent surface were found features, one of which, called the Great Dark Spot, was reminiscent of the Great Red Spot of Jupiter, even to the counterclockwise rotation expected in a high-pressure system in the southern hemisphere. Interestingly, observations with the Hubble Space Telescope have recently shown that the Great Dark Spot has apparently dissipated. Atmospheric constituents are mostly hydrocarbon compounds. Although lightning and auroras have been found on other giant planets, only the aurora phenomenon has been seen on Neptune.

Six new satellites were definitively discerned around Neptune, one confirming a 1981 sighting that was then difficult to recover for proper identification. Five of these satellites orbit Neptune in a half day or less. Of the 8 satellites of Neptune, the largest, Triton, is in a retrograde orbit suggesting that it was captured rather than being coeval with Neptune. Triton's large size, sufficient to raise significant tides on the planet, will one day, say 100 mil years from now, cause Triton to come close enough to Neptune for it to be torn apart. Nereid was found in 1949 and has the highest orbital eccentricity (0.75) of any moon. Its long looping orbit suggests that it, too, was captured. Each of the satellites that has been photographed by the 2 *Voyagers* in the planetary encounters has been different from any of the other satellites, and certainly different from any of the planets. Only about half of Triton has been observed, but its terrain shows cratering and a strange regional feature described as resembling the skin of a cantaloupe. Triton has a tenuous atmosphere of nitrogen with a trace of hydrocarbons and evidence of active geysers injecting material into it. At –238° Celsius, Triton is one of the coldest objects in the solar system observed by *Voyager II*.

In addition to the satellite system, *Voyager II* confirmed the existence of at least 3 rings composed of very fine particles. There may be some clumpiness in the rings structure. It is not known whether Neptune's satellites influence the formation or maintenance of the rings, as they have in other systems.

As with the other giant planets, Neptune is emitting more energy than it receives from the Sun. *Voyager* found the excess to be 2.7 times the solar contribution. Cooling from internal heat sources and from the heat of formation of the planets is thought to be responsible for the excess energy emission.

## Pluto

Although Pluto on the average stays about 3.6 bil mi from the Sun, its orbit is so eccentric that its minimum distance of 2.7 bil mi is less than the current distance of Neptune. Thus, Pluto, until 1999, is temporarily the 8th planet from the Sun. At its mean distance, Pluto takes 247.7 years to circumnavigate the Sun, a 3/2 resonance with Neptune. Until recently, this was about all that was known of Pluto.

About a century ago, a hypothetical planet was believed to lie beyond Neptune and Uranus because neither planet followed the paths predicted by astronomers even when all known gravitational influences were considered. In what was little more than a guess, a mass of one Earth was assigned to the mysterious body, and mathematical searches were begun. Amid some controversy about the validity of the predictive process, Pluto was discovered nearly where it had been predicted to lie. It was found by Clyde Tombaugh at the Lowell Observatory in Flagstaff, AZ, in 1930.

At the U.S. Naval Observatory, also in Flagstaff, on July 2, 1978, James Christy obtained a photograph of Pluto that was distinctly elongated. Repeated observations of this shape and its variation were convincing evidence of the discovery of a satellite of Pluto, now named Charon. Subsequent observations show it to be 750 mi across, at a distance of more than 12,000 mi from Pluto, and taking 6.4 days to move around Pluto. In this same length of time, Pluto and Charon both rotate once around their individual axes. The Pluto-Charon system thus appears to rotate as virtually a ridged body. Gravitational laws allow these interactions to give the mass of Pluto as 0.0020 of the Earth. This mass, together with a new diameter for Pluto of 1,430 mi, make the density about twice that of water. Theorists predict that Pluto has a rocky core, surrounded by a thick mantle of ice.

It is now clear that Pluto, the body found by Tombaugh, could not have influenced Neptune and Uranus to go astray. Theorists are again looking for a new planet X.

Because the rotational axis of the system is tipped from the reference plane of the solar system by about 98.3°, similar to that of Uranus, there is only a short interval every half solar period when Pluto and Charon alternately eclipse each other. Analysis of the variations in light in and out of the recent eclipses has led to determination of the diameters given above and to knowledge of other interesting aspects of the system. Both components are approximately spherical, but they are otherwise different. Pluto is red, Charon gray. Charon's surface is identified as water ice; Pluto's surface is frozen methane. Large regions on Pluto are dark, others light; Pluto has spots and, perhaps, polar caps. Although extremely cold, Pluto's methane surface produces a tenuous atmosphere that may be slowly escaping into space, perhaps going to Charon. When Pluto occulted a star, the star's light faded in such a way as to have passed through a haze layer lying above the planet's surface, indicating an inversion of temperatures—110 K above and 50 K below—suggesting Pluto has primitive weather.

There are tentative plans for a spacecraft reconnaissance of the Pluto system, to complete direct, close-up observation of each planet of the solar system.

## Morning and Evening Stars, 1997

(Greenwich Mean Time)

| | Morning | Evening |
|---|---|---|
| **Jan.** | Mercury, from Jan. 1<br>Venus<br>Mars<br>Jupiter, from Jan. 19<br>Uranus, from Jan. 24<br>Neptune, from Jan. 17<br>Pluto | Mercury, to Jan. 1<br>Jupiter, to Jan. 19<br>Saturn<br>Uranus, to Jan. 24<br>Neptune, to Jan. 17 |
| **Feb.** | Mercury<br>Venus<br>Mars<br>Jupiter<br>Uranus<br>Neptune<br>Pluto | Saturn |
| **Mar.** | Mercury, to Mar. 11<br>Venus<br>Mars, to Mar. 17<br>Jupiter<br>Saturn, from Mar. 30<br>Uranus<br>Neptune<br>Pluto | Mercury, from Mar. 11<br>Mars, from Mar. 17<br>Saturn, to Mar. 30 |
| **Apr.** | Mercury, from Apr. 25<br>Venus, to Apr. 2<br>Jupiter<br>Saturn<br>Uranus<br>Neptune<br>Pluto | Mercury, to Apr. 25<br>Venus, from Apr. 2<br>Mars |
| **May** | Mercury<br>Jupiter<br>Saturn<br>Uranus<br>Neptune<br>Pluto, to May 25 | Venus<br>Mars<br>Pluto, from May 25 |
| **June** | Mercury, to June 25<br>Jupiter<br>Saturn<br>Uranus<br>Neptune | Mercury, from June 25<br>Venus<br>Mars<br>Pluto |
| **July** | Jupiter<br>Saturn<br>Uranus, to July 29<br>Neptune, to July 21 | Mercury<br>Venus<br>Mars<br>Uranus, from July 29<br>Neptune, from July 21<br>Pluto |
| **Aug.** | Mercury, from Aug. 31<br>Jupiter, to Aug. 9<br>Saturn | Mercury, to Aug. 31<br>Venus<br>Mars<br>Jupiter, from Aug. 9<br>Uranus<br>Neptune<br>Pluto |
| **Sept.** | Mercury<br>Saturn | Venus<br>Mars<br>Jupiter<br>Uranus<br>Neptune<br>Pluto |
| **Oct.** | Mercury, to Oct. 13<br>Saturn, to Oct. 10 | Mercury, from Oct. 13<br>Venus<br>Mars<br>Jupiter<br>Saturn, from Oct. 10<br>Uranus<br>Neptune<br>Pluto |
| **Nov.** | Pluto, from Nov. 27 | Mercury<br>Venus<br>Mars<br>Jupiter<br>Saturn<br>Uranus<br>Neptune<br>Pluto, to Nov. 27 |
| **Dec.** | Mercury, from Dec. 17<br>Pluto | Mercury, to Dec. 17<br>Venus<br>Mars<br>Jupiter<br>Saturn<br>Uranus<br>Neptune |

## Greenwich Sidereal Time for 0h GMT, 1997

(Add 12 hours to obtain Right Ascension of Mean Sun)

| Date | d | h | m | Date | d | h | m | Date | d | h | m |
|---|---|---|---|---|---|---|---|---|---|---|---|
| Jan. | 1 | 6 | 42.7 | May | 1 | 14 | 35.8 | Sept. | 8 | 23 | 08.4 |
| | 11 | 7 | 22.2 | | 11 | 15 | 15.3 | | 18 | 23 | 47.8 |
| | 21 | 8 | 01.6 | | 21 | 15 | 54.7 | | 28 | 0 | 27.2 |
| | 31 | 8 | 41.0 | | 31 | 16 | 34.1 | Oct. | 8 | 1 | 06.7 |
| Feb. | 10 | 9 | 20.4 | June | 10 | 17 | 13.5 | | 18 | 1 | 46.1 |
| | 20 | 9 | 59.9 | | 20 | 17 | 53.0 | | 28 | 2 | 25.5 |
| Mar. | 2 | 10 | 39.3 | | 30 | 18 | 32.4 | Nov. | 7 | 3 | 04.9 |
| | 12 | 11 | 18.7 | July | 10 | 19 | 11.8 | | 17 | 3 | 44.4 |
| | 22 | 11 | 58.1 | | 20 | 19 | 51.3 | | 27 | 4 | 23.8 |
| Apr. | 1 | 12 | 37.6 | | 30 | 20 | 30.9 | Dec. | 7 | 5 | 03.2 |
| | 11 | 13 | 17.0 | Aug. | 9 | 21 | 10.1 | | 17 | 5 | 42.6 |
| | 21 | 13 | 56.4 | | 19 | 21 | 49.5 | | 27 | 6 | 22.1 |
| | | | | | 29 | 22 | 29.0 | | | | |

## Star Tables

These tables include stars of visual magnitude 2.4 and brighter (the lower the number, the brighter the star). Stars of variable magnitude are designated by v. Coordinates are for mid-1997. If no parallax figures are given, the trigonometric parallax figure is smaller than the margin for error and the distance given is obtained by indirect methods. Greek letters in the star names were adopted to indicate perceived degree of relative brightness within the constellation, alpha being the brightest.

To find the time when the star is on the meridian, subtract Right Ascension of Mean Sun (from sidereal timetable above) from the star's Right Ascension, first adding 24h to the latter, if necessary. Mark this result PM, if less than 12h, but if greater than 12, subtract 12h and mark the remainder AM.

| Star | Magnitude | Parallax ″ | Light yrs. | Right ascen. h | Right ascen. m | Declination ° ′ |
|---|---|---|---|---|---|---|
| α Andromedae (Alpheratz) | 2.06 | 0.02 | 90 | 0 | 08.3 | +29 04 |
| β Cassiopeiae (Caph) | 2.27v | 0.07 | 45 | 0 | 09.1 | +59 08 |
| α Phoenicia (Ankaa) | 2.39 | 0.04 | 93 | 0 | 26.2 | –42 19 |
| α Cassiopeiae (Schedar) | 2.23 | 0.01 | 150 | 0 | 40.4 | +56 31 |
| β Ceti (Deneb Kaitos) | 2.04 | 0.06 | 57 | 0 | 43.5 | –18 00 |
| β Andromedae (Mirach) | 2.06 | 0.04 | 76 | 1 | 09.5 | +35 36 |
| α Eridani (Achnerar) | 0.46 | 0.02 | 118 | 1 | 37.5 | –57 16 |
| γ Andromedae (Almaak) | 2.26 | | 260 | 2 | 03.6 | +42 18 |
| α Arietis (Hamal) | 2.06 | 0.04 | 76 | 2 | 06.9 | +23 26 |
| o Ceti (Mira) | 2.00 | 0.01 | 103 | 2 | 19.2 | – 3 00 |
| α Ursae Minoris (Polaris) | 2.02v | | 680 | 2 | 31.8 | +89 16 |
| β Persei (Algol) | 2.12v | 0.03 | 105 | 3 | 08.2 | +40 57 |
| α Persei (Mirphak) | 1.80 | 0.03 | 150 | 3 | 24.1 | +49 51 |
| α Tauri (Aldebaran) | 0.85v | 0.05 | 68 | 4 | 35.8 | +16 30 |
| β Orionis (Rigel) | 0.12v | | 900 | 5 | 14.4 | – 8 12 |
| α Aurigae (Capella) | 0.08 | 0.07 | 45 | 5 | 16.5 | +46 00 |
| γ Orionis (Bellatrix) | 1.64 | 0.03 | 470 | 5 | 25.0 | + 6 21 |
| β Tauri (Elnath) | 1.65 | 0.02 | 300 | 5 | 26.1 | +28 36 |
| δ Orionis (Mintaka) | 2.23v | | 1500 | 5 | 31.9 | – 0 18 |
| ε Orionis (Alnilam) | 1.70 | | 1600 | 5 | 36.1 | – 1 12 |
| ζ Orionis (Alnitak) | 2.05 | 0.02 | 1600 | 5 | 40.5 | – 1 57 |
| κ Orionis (Saiph) | 2.06 | 0.01 | 2100 | 5 | 47.6 | – 9 40 |
| α Orionis (Betelgeuse) | 0.50 | | 520 | 5 | 55.0 | + 7 24 |
| β Aurigae (Menkalinan) | 1.90 | 0.04 | 88 | 5 | 59.3 | +44 57 |
| β Canis Majoris (Mirzam) | 1.98 | 0.01 | 750 | 6 | 22.6 | –17 57 |
| α Carinae (Canopus) | –0.72 | 0.02 | 98 | 6 | 23.9 | –52 42 |
| γ Geminorum (Alhena) | 1.93 | 0.03 | 105 | 6 | 37.5 | +16 24 |
| α Canis Majoris (Sirius) | –1.46 | 0.38 | 8.7 | 6 | 45.0 | –16 43 |
| ε Canis Majoris (Adhara) | 1.50 | | 680 | 6 | 58.5 | –28 58 |
| δ Canis Majoris (Wezen) | 1.86 | | 2100 | 7 | 08.3 | –26 24 |
| α Geminorum (Castor) | 1.99 | 0.07 | 45 | 7 | 34.4 | +31 54 |
| α Canis Minoris (Procyon) | 0.38 | 0.29 | 11.3 | 7 | 39.1 | + 5 14 |
| β Procyon (Pollux) | 1.14 | 0.09 | 35 | 7 | 45.1 | +28 02 |
| ζ Puppis (Naos) | 2.25 | | 2400 | 8 | 03.5 | –40 00 |
| γ Velorum (Al Suhail) | 1.82 | | 520 | 8 | 09.4 | –47 20 |
| ε Carinae (Avior) | 1.86 | | 340 | 8 | 22.4 | –59 30 |
| δ Velorum | 1.96 | 0.04 | 76 | 8 | 44.6 | –54 42 |
| λ Velorum (Suhail) | 2.21 | 0.02 | 750 | 9 | 07.9 | –43 26 |
| β Carinae (Miaplacidus) | 1.68 | 0.04 | 86 | 9 | 13.1 | –69 43 |
| ι Carinae (Tureis) | 2.25 | | 750 | 9 | 17.0 | –59 16 |
| α Hydrae (Alphard) | 1.98 | 0.02 | 94 | 9 | 27.4 | – 8 39 |
| α Leonis (Regulus) | 1.35 | 0.04 | 84 | 10 | 08.2 | +11 59 |
| γ Leonis (Algieba) | 1.90 | 0.02 | 90 | 10 | 19.8 | +19 54 |
| β Ursae Majoris (Merak) | 2.37 | 0.04 | 78 | 11 | 01.7 | +56 24 |
| α Ursae Majoris (Dubhe) | 1.79 | 0.03 | 105 | 11 | 03.5 | +61 46 |
| β Leonis (Denebola) | 2.14 | 0.08 | 43 | 11 | 48.9 | +14 35 |
| α Crucis (Acrux) | 1.58 | | 370 | 12 | 26.5 | –63 05 |
| γ Crucis (Gacrux) | 1.63 | | 220 | 12 | 31.0 | –57 06 |
| γ Centauri | 2.17 | | 160 | 12 | 41.3 | –48 56 |
| β Crucis (Becrux) | 1.25v | | 490 | 12 | 47.6 | –59 41 |
| ε Ursae Majoris (Alioth) | 1.77v | 0.01 | 68 | 12 | 53.9 | +55 59 |
| ζ Ursae Majoris (Mizar) | 2.27 | 0.04 | 88 | 13 | 23.8 | +54 57 |
| α Virginis (Pica) | 0.97v | 0.02 | 220 | 13 | 25.1 | –11 09 |
| ε Centauri | 2.30v | | 570 | 13 | 39.7 | –53 27 |
| ε Ursae Majoris (Alkaid) | 1.86 | | 210 | 13 | 47.4 | +49 20 |
| β Centauri (Hadar) | 0.61v | 0.02 | 490 | 14 | 03.7 | –60 22 |
| τ Centauri (Menkent) | 2.06 | 0.06 | 55 | 14 | 06.6 | –36 22 |
| α Bootis (Arcturus) | 0.04 | 0.09 | 36 | 14 | 15.6 | +19 12 |
| ε Centauri | 2.31v | | 390 | 14 | 35.4 | –42 09 |
| α Centauri (Rigel Kentaurus) | 0.01 | 0.75 | 4.3 | 14 | 39.5 | –60 50 |
| α Lupi | 2.30v | | 430 | 14 | 41.8 | –47 23 |
| ε Bootis (Izar) | 2.40 | 0.01 | 103 | 14 | 44.8 | +27 06 |
| β Ursae Minoris (Kochab) | 2.08 | 0.03 | 105 | 14 | 50.7 | +74 10 |
| α Coronae Borealis (Gemma) | 2.23v | 0.04 | 76 | 15 | 34.5 | +26 44 |
| δ Scorpii (Dschubba) | 2.32 | | 590 | 16 | 00.2 | –22 37 |
| α Scorpii (Antares) | 0.96v | 0.02 | 520 | 16 | 29.3 | –26 25 |
| α Trianguli Australis (Atria) | 1.92 | 0.02 | 82 | 16 | 48.5 | –69 01 |
| ε Scorpii | 2.29 | 0.05 | 66 | 16 | 50.0 | –34 17 |
| λ Scorpii (Shaula) | 1.63v | | 310 | 17 | 33.5 | –37 06 |
| α Ophiuchi (Rasalhague) | 2.08 | 0.06 | 58 | 17 | 34.8 | +12 34 |
| τ Scorpii | 1.87 | 0.02 | 650 | 17 | 37.2 | –43 00 |
| γ Draconis (Eltanin) | 2.23 | 0.02 | 108 | 17 | 56.6 | +51 30 |
| ε Sagittarii (Kaus Australis) | .85 | 0.02 | 124 | 18 | 24.0 | –34 23 |
| α Lyrae (Vega) | 0.03 | 0.12 | 26.5 | 18 | 36.9 | +38 47 |
| o Sagittarii (Nunki) | 2.02 | | 300 | 18 | 55.1 | –26 18 |
| α Aquilae (Altair) | 0.77 | 0.20 | 16.5 | 19 | 50.7 | + 8 52 |
| γ Cygni (Sadr) | 2.20 | | 750 | 20 | 22.2 | +40 15 |
| α Pavonis (Peacock) | 1.94 | | 310 | 20 | 25.5 | –56 44 |
| α Cygni (Deneb) | 1.25 | | 1600 | 20 | 41.4 | +45 16 |
| ε Pegasi (Enif) | 2.39 | | 780 | 21 | 44.1 | + 9 52 |
| α Gruis (Al Nair) | 1.74 | 0.05 | 64 | 22 | 08.1 | –46 58 |
| β Gruis | 2.11v | | 280 | 22 | 42.5 | –46 54 |
| α Piscis Austrinis (Fomalhaut) | 1.16 | 0.14 | 22.6 | 22 | 57.5 | –29 38 |

## Astronomical Constants; Speed of Light

The following were adopted as part of the International Astronomical Union System of Astronomical Constants (1976): **Speed of light**, 299,792.458 kilometers per second, or about 186,282 statute mi per second; **solar parallax**, 8″.794148; **Astronomical Unit**, 149,597,870 kilometers, or about 92,976,000 mi; **constant of nutation**, 9″.2025; and **constant of aberration**, 20″.49552.

# Constellations

Culturally, constellations are imagined patterns among the stars that, in some cases, have been recognized through millennia of tradition. In the early days of astronomy, knowledge of the constellations was necessary in order to function as an astronomer. For today's astronomers, constellations are simply areas on the entire sky in which interesting objects await observation and interpretation.

Because Western culture has prevailed in establishing modern science, equally viable and interesting constellations and celestial traditions of other cultures (of Asia or Africa, for example) are not well-known outside their regions of origin. Even the patterns with which we are most familiar today have undergone considerable change over the centuries, because the Western heritage embraces teachings of cultures disparate in time as well as place.

Today more than 88 constellations are recognized. Although many of these have their origins in ancient days, some are "modern," contrived out of unformed stars by astronomers a few centuries ago. Unformed stars were those usually too faint or inconveniently placed to be included in depicting the more prominent constellations.

When astronomers began to travel to South Africa in the 16th and 17th centuries, they found a sky that itself was unformed and showed numerous brilliant stars. Thus, we find constellations in the southern hemisphere that depict technological marvels of the time, as well as some arguably traditional forms, such as the "fly."

Many of the commonly recognized constellations had their origins in ancient Asia Minor—Syria, Babylonia, etc. These were adopted by the Greeks and Romans, who translated their names and stories into their own languages, modifying some details in the process. After the declines of these cultures, most such knowledge entered oral tradition or remained hidden in monastic libraries. Beginning in the 8th cent., the Muslim explosion spread through the Mediterranean world. Wherever possible, everything was translated into Arabic to be taught in the universities the Muslims established all over their new-found world.

In the 13th cent., Alphonsus XX of Spain, an avid student of astronomy, succeeded in having Ptolemy's *Almagest,* as its Arabian title was known, translated into Latin. It thus became widely available to European scholars. In the process, the constellation names were translated, but the star names were retained in their Arabic forms. Transliterating Arabic into the Roman alphabet has never been an exact art, so many of the star names we use today only "seem" Arabic to those who are not scholars.

Names of stars often indicated what parts of the traditional figures they represented: Deneb, the tail of the swan; Betelgeuse, the armpit of the giant. Thus, the names were an indication of the position in the sky of a particular star, provided one recognized the traditional form of the mythic figure.

In English, usage of the Latin names for the constellations couples often inconceivable creatures, represented in unimaginable configurations, with names that often seem unintelligible. Avoiding traditional names, astronomers may designate the brighter stars in a constellation with Greek letters, usually in order of brightness. Thus, the "alpha star" is often the brightest star of that constellation. The "of" implies possession, so the genitive (possessive) form of the constellation name is used, as in Alpha Orionis, the first star of Orion (Betelgeuse). Astronomers usually use a 3-letter form for the constellation name, as indicated here.

Until the 1920s, astronomers used curved boundaries for the constellation areas. As these were rather arbitrary at best, the International Astronomical Union adopted new constellation boundaries that ran due north-south and east-west, filling the sky much as the contiguous states fill up the area of the "lower 48" United States.

Within these boundaries, and occasionally crossing them, popular "asterisms" are recognized: the so-called Big Dipper is a small part of the constellation Ursa Major, the big bear; the Sickle is the traditional head and mane of Leo, the lion; one of the horntips of Taurus, the bull, properly belongs to Auriga, the charioteer; the northeast star of the Great Square of Pegasus is Alpha Andromedae.

It is unlikely that further change will occur in the realm of the celestial constellations.

| Name | Genitive | Abbrev. | Meaning |
|---|---|---|---|
| Andromeda | Andromedae | And | Chained Maiden |
| Antlia | Antliae | Ant | Air Pump |
| Apus | Apodis | Aps | Bird of Paradise |
| Aquarius | Aquarii | Aqr | Water Bearer |
| Aquila | Aquilae | Aql | Eagle |
| Ara | Arae | Ara | Altar |
| Aries | Arietis | Ari | Ram |
| Auriga | Aurigae | Aur | Charioteer |
| Bootes | Bootis | Boo | Herdsmen |
| Caelum | Caeli | Cae | Chisel |
| Camelopardalis | Camelopardalis | Cam | Giraffe |
| Cancer | Cancri | Cnc | Crab |
| Canes Venatici | Canum Venaticorum | CVn | Hunting Dogs |
| Canis Major | Canis Majoris | CMa | Great Dog |
| Canis Minor | Canis Minoris | CMi | Little Dog |
| Capricornus | Capricorni | Cap | Sea-goat |
| Carina | Carinae | Car | Keel |
| Cassiopeia | Cassiopeiae | Cas | Queen |
| Centaurus | Centauri | Cen | Centaur |
| Cepheus | Cephei | Cep | King |
| Cetus | Ceti | Cet | Whale |
| Chamaeleon | Chamaeleontis | Cha | Chameleon |
| Circinus | Circini | Cir | Compasses (art) |
| Columba | Columbae | Col | Dove |
| Coma Berenices | Comae Berenices | Com | Berenice's Hair |
| Corona Australis | Coronae Australis | CrA | Southern Crown |
| Corona Borealis | Coronae Borealis | CrB | Northern Crown |
| Corvus | Corvi | Crv | Crow |
| Crater | Crateris | Crt | Cup |
| Crux | Crucis | Cru | Cross (southern) |
| Cygnus | Cygni | Cyg | Swan |
| Delphinus | Delphini | Del | Dolphin |
| Dorado | Doradus | Dor | Goldfish |
| Draco | Draconis | Dra | Dragon |
| Equuleus | Equulei | Equ | Little Horse |
| Eridanus | Eridani | Eri | River |
| Fornax | Fornacis | For | Furnace |
| Gemini | Geminorum | Gem | Twins |
| Grus | Gruis | Gru | Crane (bird) |
| Hercules | Herculis | Her | Hercules |
| Horologium | Horologii | Hor | Clock |
| Hydra | Hydrae | Hya | Water Snake (female) |
| Hydrus | Hydri | Hyi | Water Snake (male) |
| Indus | Indi | Ind | Indian |
| Lacerta | Lacertae | Lac | Lizard |
| Leo | Leonis | Leo | Lion |
| Leo Minor | Leonis Minoris | LMi | Little Lion |
| Lepus | Leporis | Lep | Hare |
| Libra | Librae | Lib | Balance |
| Lupus | Lupi | Lup | Wolf |
| Lynx | Lyncis | Lyn | Lynx |
| Lyra | Lyrae | Lyr | Lyre |
| Mensa | Mensae | Men | Table Mountain |
| Microscopium | Microscopii | Mic | Microscope |
| Monoceros | Monocerotis | Mon | Unicorn |
| Musca | Muscae | Mus | Fly |
| Norma | Normae | Nor | Square (rule) |
| Octans | Octantis | Oct | Octant |
| Ophiuchus | Ophiuchi | Oph | Serpent Bearer |
| Orion | Orionis | Ori | Hunter |
| Pavo | Pavonis | Pav | Peacock |
| Pegasus | Pegasi | Peg | Flying Horse |
| Perseus | Persei | Per | Hero |
| Phoenix | Phoenicis | Phe | Phoenix |
| Pictor | Pictoris | Pic | Painter |
| Pisces | Piscium | Psc | Fishes |
| Piscis Austrinius | Piscis Austrini | PsA | Southern Fish |
| Puppis | Puppis | Pup | Stern (deck) |
| Pyxis | Pyxidis | Pyx | Compass (sea) |
| Reticulum | Reticuli | Ret | Reticle |
| Sagitta | Sagittae | Sge | Arrow |
| Sagittarius | Sagittarii | Sgr | Archer |
| Scorpius | Scorpii | Sco | Scorpion |
| Sculptor | Sculptoris | Scl | Sculptor |
| Scutum | Scuti | Sct | Shield |
| Serpens | Serpentis | Ser | Serpent |
| Sextans | Sextantis | Sex | Sextant |
| Taurus | Tauri | Tau | Bull |
| Telescopium | Telescopii | Tel | Telescope |
| Triangulum | Trianguli | Tri | Triangle |
| Triangulum Australe | Trianguli Australis | TrA | Southern Triangle |
| Tucana | Tucanae | Tuc | Toucan |
| Ursa Major | Ursae Majoris | UMa | Great Bear |
| Ursa Minor | Ursae Minoris | UMi | Little Bear |
| Vela | Velorum | Vel | Sail |
| Virgo | Virginis | Vir | Maiden |
| Volans | Volantis | Vol | Flying Fish |
| Vulpecula | Vulpeculae | Vul | Fox |

# Rising and Setting of Planets, 1997

Greenwich Mean Time (0 designates midnight)

## Venus, 1997

| Date | 20° N Latitude | | 30° N Latitude | | 40° N Latitude | | 50° N Latitude | | 60° N Latitude | |
|---|---|---|---|---|---|---|---|---|---|---|
| | Rise | Set | Rise | Set | Rise | Set | Rise | Set | Rise | Set |
| | h m | h m | h m | h m | h m | h m | h m | h m | h m | h m |
| Jan. 1 | 4 59 | 15 57 | 5 19 | 15 36 | 5 44 | 15 11 | 6 20 | 14 36 | 7 21 | 13 35 |
| 11 | 5 15 | 16 10 | 5 36 | 15 49 | 6 03 | 15 23 | 6 40 | 14 45 | 7 46 | 13 40 |
| 21 | 5 30 | 16 26 | 5 51 | 16 05 | 6 17 | 15 39 | 6 53 | 15 02 | 7 57 | 13 58 |
| 31 | 5 42 | 16 42 | 6 01 | 16 23 | 6 25 | 15 59 | 6 59 | 15 26 | 7 56 | 14 29 |
| Feb. 10 | 5 51 | 16 59 | 6 07 | 16 43 | 6 28 | 16 22 | 6 57 | 15 54 | 7 44 | 15 07 |
| 20 | 5 56 | 17 16 | 6 10 | 17 02 | 6 26 | 16 46 | 6 49 | 16 24 | 7 25 | 15 48 |
| Mar. 2 | 5 59 | 17 31 | 6 09 | 17 22 | 6 20 | 17 10 | 6 36 | 16 54 | 7 01 | 16 30 |
| 12 | 6 00 | 17 46 | 6 05 | 17 40 | 6 12 | 17 34 | 6 21 | 17 25 | 6 35 | 17 12 |
| 22 | 5 59 | 17 59 | 6 00 | 17 58 | 6 02 | 17 57 | 6 04 | 17 55 | 6 07 | 17 53 |
| Apr. 1 | 5 58 | 18 13 | 5 55 | 18 16 | 5 51 | 18 20 | 5 46 | 18 25 | 5 38 | 18 34 |
| 11 | 5 57 | 18 26 | 5 49 | 18 34 | 5 40 | 18 43 | 5 28 | 18 56 | 5 09 | 19 16 |
| 21 | 5 57 | 18 41 | 5 46 | 18 52 | 5 31 | 19 07 | 5 12 | 19 27 | 4 41 | 19 58 |
| May 1 | 5 59 | 18 56 | 5 44 | 19 11 | 5 25 | 19 31 | 4 59 | 19 58 | 4 15 | 20 42 |
| 11 | 6 04 | 19 12 | 5 46 | 19 31 | 5 22 | 19 55 | 4 49 | 20 28 | 3 53 | 21 26 |
| 21 | 6 12 | 19 29 | 5 51 | 19 50 | 5 24 | 20 17 | 4 46 | 20 56 | 3 37 | 22 06 |
| 31 | 6 24 | 19 45 | 6 01 | 20 08 | 5 32 | 20 37 | 4 50 | 21 19 | 3 33 | 22 37 |
| June 10 | 6 38 | 19 59 | 6 15 | 20 22 | 5 45 | 20 52 | 5 03 | 21 34 | 3 44 | 22 53 |
| 20 | 6 53 | 20 11 | 6 31 | 20 33 | 6 03 | 21 01 | 5 23 | 21 41 | 4 10 | 22 53 |
| 30 | 7 09 | 20 20 | 6 49 | 20 39 | 6 25 | 21 04 | 5 49 | 21 39 | 4 48 | 22 39 |
| July 10 | 7 25 | 20 25 | 7 08 | 20 41 | 6 47 | 21 02 | 6 18 | 21 30 | 5 30 | 22 18 |
| 20 | 7 39 | 20 27 | 7 26 | 20 40 | 7 10 | 20 55 | 6 48 | 21 17 | 6 13 | 21 52 |
| 30 | 7 52 | 20 26 | 7 44 | 20 35 | 7 33 | 20 45 | 7 18 | 21 00 | 6 55 | 21 22 |
| Aug. 9 | 8 04 | 20 24 | 8 00 | 20 28 | 7 55 | 20 33 | 7 47 | 20 40 | 7 35 | 20 51 |
| 19 | 8 16 | 20 20 | 8 16 | 20 20 | 8 15 | 20 19 | 8 15 | 20 19 | 8 15 | 20 19 |
| 29 | 8 26 | 20 15 | 8 31 | 20 11 | 8 36 | 20 05 | 8 43 | 19 58 | 8 54 | 19 47 |
| Sept. 8 | 8 37 | 20 12 | 8 46 | 20 03 | 8 57 | 19 52 | 9 11 | 19 37 | 9 34 | 19 14 |
| 18 | 8 49 | 20 09 | 9 02 | 19 56 | 9 18 | 19 40 | 9 40 | 19 18 | 10 14 | 18 42 |
| 28 | 9 01 | 20 08 | 9 18 | 19 51 | 9 39 | 19 30 | 10 08 | 19 00 | 10 56 | 18 12 |
| Oct. 8 | 9 13 | 20 09 | 9 34 | 19 49 | 9 59 | 19 23 | 10 35 | 18 47 | 11 38 | 17 44 |
| 18 | 9 25 | 20 12 | 9 48 | 19 49 | 10 17 | 19 20 | 10 59 | 18 38 | 12 17 | 17 21 |
| 28 | 9 35 | 20 17 | 10 00 | 19 52 | 10 32 | 19 21 | 11 18 | 18 35 | 12 46 | 17 06 |
| Nov. 7 | 9 43 | 20 23 | 10 08 | 19 57 | 10 40 | 19 25 | 11 27 | 18 38 | 13 00 | 17 05 |
| 17 | 9 45 | 20 27 | 10 10 | 20 02 | 10 41 | 19 31 | 11 27 | 18 45 | 12 54 | 17 18 |
| 27 | 9 41 | 20 27 | 10 04 | 20 04 | 10 33 | 19 35 | 11 15 | 18 53 | 12 32 | 17 37 |
| 7 | 9 28 | 20 21 | 9 49 | 20 00 | 10 15 | 19 34 | 10 52 | 18 57 | 11 57 | 17 53 |
| Dec. 17 | 9 04 | 20 05 | 9 22 | 19 46 | 9 45 | 19 23 | 10 17 | 18 51 | 11 11 | 17 58 |
| 27 | 8 26 | 19 34 | 8 42 | 19 18 | 9 02 | 18 58 | 9 30 | 18 30 | 10 15 | 17 45 |

## Mars, 1997

| Date | 20° N Latitude | | 30° N Latitude | | 40° N Latitude | | 50° N Latitude | | 60° N Latitude | |
|---|---|---|---|---|---|---|---|---|---|---|
| | Rise | Set | Rise | Set | Rise | Set | Rise | Set | Rise | Set |
| | h m | h m | h m | h m | h m | h m | h m | h m | h m | h m |
| Jan. 1 | 23 10 | 11 24 | 23 07 | 11 26 | 23 04 | 11 29 | 23 00 | 11 34 | 22 53 | 11 40 |
| 11 | 22 43 | 10 54 | 22 41 | 10 56 | 22 39 | 10 58 | 22 36 | 11 01 | 22 32 | 11 05 |
| 21 | 22 13 | 10 22 | 22 12 | 10 23 | 22 10 | 10 25 | 22 08 | 10 27 | 22 05 | 10 30 |
| 31 | 21 38 | 9 47 | 21 37 | 9 48 | 21 36 | 9 49 | 21 35 | 9 51 | 21 32 | 9 54 |
| Feb. 10 | 20 59 | 9 09 | 20 58 | 9 10 | 20 57 | 9 11 | 20 55 | 9 13 | 20 52 | 9 16 |
| 20 | 20 15 | 8 26 | 20 13 | 8 28 | 20 11 | 8 30 | 20 08 | 8 33 | 20 04 | 8 37 |
| Mar. 2 | 19 25 | 7 40 | 19 22 | 7 42 | 19 19 | 7 45 | 19 15 | 7 49 | 19 08 | 7 56 |
| 12 | 18 31 | 6 50 | 18 27 | 6 53 | 18 22 | 6 58 | 18 16 | 7 04 | 18 06 | 7 14 |
| 22 | 17 35 | 5 58 | 17 30 | 6 03 | 17 24 | 6 09 | 17 16 | 6 17 | 17 03 | 6 29 |
| Apr. 1 | 16 40 | 5 06 | 16 34 | 5 12 | 16 27 | 5 19 | 16 17 | 5 29 | 16 02 | 5 44 |
| 11 | 15 49 | 4 18 | 15 43 | 4 24 | 15 35 | 4 32 | 15 24 | 4 43 | 15 07 | 4 59 |
| 21 | 15 04 | 3 32 | 14 57 | 3 39 | 14 49 | 3 47 | 14 38 | 3 58 | 14 21 | 4 15 |
| May 1 | 14 24 | 2 51 | 14 17 | 2 57 | 14 10 | 3 05 | 13 59 | 3 16 | 13 43 | 3 32 |
| 11 | 13 49 | 2 14 | 13 43 | 2 19 | 13 36 | 2 26 | 13 27 | 2 36 | 13 12 | 2 51 |
| 21 | 13 18 | 1 39 | 13 13 | 1 44 | 13 08 | 1 50 | 13 00 | 1 58 | 12 48 | 2 10 |
| 31 | 12 51 | 1 08 | 12 48 | 1 11 | 12 43 | 1 16 | 12 38 | 1 22 | 12 28 | 1 31 |
| June 10 | 12 27 | 0 39 | 12 25 | 0 41 | 12 22 | 0 43 | 12 19 | 0 47 | 12 13 | 0 52 |
| 20 | 12 05 | 0 11 | 12 05 | 0 12 | 12 04 | 0 12 | 12 03 | 0 13 | 12 02 | 0 15 |
| 30 | 11 45 | 23 43 | 11 46 | 23 42 | 11 48 | 23 40 | 11 50 | 23 38 | 11 53 | 23 34 |
| July 10 | 11 27 | 23 19 | 11 30 | 23 15 | 11 34 | 23 11 | 11 39 | 23 06 | 11 47 | 22 58 |
| 20 | 11 10 | 22 56 | 11 16 | 22 50 | 11 22 | 22 44 | 11 30 | 22 35 | 11 43 | 22 22 |
| 30 | 10 55 | 22 34 | 11 02 | 22 26 | 11 11 | 22 18 | 11 23 | 22 06 | 11 41 | 21 47 |
| Aug. 9 | 10 41 | 22 13 | 10 50 | 22 04 | 11 02 | 21 52 | 11 17 | 21 37 | 11 41 | 21 13 |
| 19 | 10 29 | 21 54 | 10 40 | 21 42 | 10 54 | 21 28 | 11 13 | 21 09 | 11 42 | 20 39 |
| 29 | 10 17 | 21 35 | 10 30 | 21 22 | 10 47 | 21 05 | 11 09 | 20 43 | 11 45 | 20 07 |
| Sept. 8 | 10 07 | 21 19 | 10 22 | 21 03 | 10 41 | 20 44 | 11 07 | 20 18 | 11 50 | 19 35 |
| 18 | 9 58 | 21 03 | 10 15 | 20 46 | 10 36 | 20 25 | 11 06 | 19 55 | 11 55 | 19 05 |
| 28 | 9 50 | 20 50 | 10 09 | 20 31 | 10 32 | 20 07 | 11 05 | 19 34 | 12 01 | 18 38 |
| Oct. 8 | 9 42 | 20 38 | 10 03 | 20 17 | 10 28 | 19 52 | 11 04 | 19 15 | 12 07 | 18 13 |
| 18 | 9 36 | 20 27 | 9 57 | 20 06 | 10 24 | 19 39 | 11 03 | 19 00 | 12 11 | 17 51 |
| 28 | 9 29 | 20 19 | 9 52 | 19 56 | 10 20 | 19 28 | 11 00 | 18 48 | 12 13 | 17 35 |
| Nov. 7 | 9 23 | 20 11 | 9 46 | 19 49 | 10 15 | 19 20 | 10 56 | 18 39 | 12 10 | 17 24 |
| 17 | 9 17 | 20 05 | 9 39 | 19 43 | 10 08 | 19 14 | 10 48 | 18 34 | 12 02 | 17 20 |
| 27 | 9 10 | 20 00 | 9 32 | 19 38 | 9 59 | 19 11 | 10 39 | 18 32 | 11 49 | 17 21 |
| Dec. 7 | 9 02 | 19 56 | 9 23 | 19 35 | 9 49 | 19 09 | 10 26 | 18 32 | 11 31 | 17 28 |
| 17 | 8 53 | 19 52 | 9 12 | 19 33 | 9 37 | 19 09 | 10 10 | 18 35 | 11 08 | 17 38 |
| 27 | 8 43 | 19 48 | 9 01 | 19 31 | 9 22 | 19 09 | 9 52 | 18 39 | 10 42 | 17 50 |

## Jupiter, 1997

| Date | 20° N Latitude Rise h m | 20° N Latitude Set h m | 30° N Latitude Rise h m | 30° N Latitude Set h m | 40° N Latitude Rise h m | 40° N Latitude Set h m | 50° N Latitude Rise h m | 50° N Latitude Set h m | 60° N Latitude Rise h m | 60° N Latitude Set h m |
|---|---|---|---|---|---|---|---|---|---|---|
| Jan. 1 | 7 35 | 18 34 | 7 54 | 18 14 | 8 18 | 17 50 | 8 52 | 17 17 | 9 49 | 16 20 |
| 11 | 7 05 | 18 05 | 7 24 | 17 46 | 7 47 | 17 23 | 8 20 | 16 50 | 9 15 | 15 55 |
| 21 | 6 35 | 17 36 | 6 53 | 17 18 | 7 16 | 16 55 | 7 48 | 16 23 | 8 41 | 15 30 |
| 31 | 6 04 | 17 07 | 6 22 | 16 49 | 6 44 | 16 27 | 7 15 | 15 57 | 8 06 | 15 05 |
| Feb. 10 | 5 34 | 16 38 | 5 51 | 16 21 | 6 12 | 16 00 | 6 42 | 15 30 | 7 32 | 14 41 |
| 20 | 5 03 | 16 09 | 5 20 | 15 53 | 5 40 | 15 32 | 6 09 | 15 03 | 6 57 | 14 16 |
| Mar. 2 | 4 32 | 15 40 | 4 48 | 15 24 | 5 08 | 15 04 | 5 36 | 14 36 | 6 21 | 13 50 |
| 12 | 4 00 | 15 10 | 4 16 | 14 54 | 4 35 | 14 35 | 5 02 | 14 08 | 5 45 | 13 25 |
| 22 | 3 28 | 14 39 | 3 43 | 14 24 | 4 02 | 14 06 | 4 28 | 13 40 | 5 09 | 12 58 |
| Apr. 1 | 2 55 | 14 08 | 3 10 | 13 54 | 3 28 | 13 36 | 3 53 | 13 11 | 4 33 | 12 31 |
| 11 | 2 22 | 13 37 | 2 36 | 13 22 | 2 54 | 13 05 | 3 18 | 12 41 | 3 56 | 12 02 |
| 21 | 1 48 | 13 04 | 2 02 | 12 50 | 2 19 | 12 33 | 2 42 | 12 10 | 3 19 | 11 33 |
| May 1 | 1 13 | 12 30 | 1 27 | 12 17 | 1 43 | 12 00 | 2 06 | 11 37 | 2 42 | 11 01 |
| 11 | 0 37 | 11 55 | 0 51 | 11 42 | 1 07 | 11 26 | 1 29 | 11 04 | 2 04 | 10 29 |
| 21 | 0 01 | 11 19 | 0 14 | 11 06 | 0 30 | 10 50 | 0 52 | 10 29 | 1 26 | 9 54 |
| 31 | 23 19 | 10 42 | 23 32 | 10 29 | 23 48 | 10 13 | 0 14 | 9 52 | 0 48 | 9 17 |
| June 10 | 22 41 | 10 03 | 22 54 | 9 50 | 23 09 | 9 35 | 23 31 | 9 13 | 0 09 | 8 39 |
| 20 | 22 01 | 9 23 | 22 14 | 9 10 | 22 30 | 8 54 | 22 52 | 8 33 | 23 26 | 7 58 |
| 30 | 21 20 | 8 42 | 21 33 | 8 29 | 21 49 | 8 13 | 22 11 | 7 50 | 22 47 | 7 15 |
| July 10 | 20 38 | 7 59 | 20 51 | 7 46 | 21 08 | 7 29 | 21 31 | 7 07 | 22 07 | 6 31 |
| 20 | 19 55 | 7 15 | 20 09 | 7 02 | 20 26 | 6 45 | 20 49 | 6 22 | 21 26 | 5 44 |
| 30 | 19 12 | 6 31 | 19 26 | 6 17 | 19 44 | 5 59 | 20 07 | 5 35 | 20 46 | 4 57 |
| Aug. 9 | 18 28 | 5 46 | 18 43 | 5 31 | 19 01 | 5 13 | 19 25 | 4 49 | 20 05 | 4 09 |
| 19 | 17 44 | 5 01 | 17 59 | 4 46 | 18 18 | 4 27 | 18 43 | 4 02 | 19 24 | 3 21 |
| 29 | 17 01 | 4 16 | 17 16 | 4 01 | 17 35 | 3 42 | 18 01 | 3 16 | 18 43 | 2 34 |
| Sept. 8 | 16 18 | 3 32 | 16 34 | 3 17 | 16 53 | 2 57 | 17 19 | 2 31 | 18 02 | 1 48 |
| 18 | 15 36 | 2 49 | 15 52 | 2 34 | 16 11 | 2 14 | 16 38 | 1 47 | 17 22 | 1 03 |
| 28 | 14 55 | 2 08 | 15 11 | 1 52 | 15 30 | 1 32 | 15 58 | 1 05 | 16 42 | 0 21 |
| Oct. 8 | 14 15 | 1 28 | 14 31 | 1 12 | 14 51 | 0 52 | 15 18 | 0 25 | 16 02 | 23 37 |
| 18 | 13 36 | 0 49 | 13 52 | 0 33 | 14 12 | 0 14 | 14 39 | 23 43 | 15 23 | 22 59 |
| 28 | 12 59 | 0 12 | 13 14 | 23 53 | 13 34 | 23 33 | 14 01 | 23 07 | 14 44 | 22 23 |
| Nov. 7 | 12 22 | 23 33 | 12 38 | 23 17 | 12 57 | 22 58 | 13 23 | 22 32 | 14 06 | 21 49 |
| 17 | 11 47 | 22 58 | 12 02 | 22 43 | 12 21 | 22 25 | 12 46 | 21 59 | 13 28 | 21 17 |
| 27 | 11 12 | 22 25 | 11 27 | 22 10 | 11 45 | 21 52 | 12 10 | 21 27 | 12 51 | 20 47 |
| Dec. 7 | 10 38 | 21 53 | 10 53 | 21 39 | 11 10 | 21 21 | 11 34 | 20 57 | 12 13 | 20 18 |
| 17 | 10 05 | 21 21 | 10 19 | 21 08 | 10 36 | 20 51 | 10 59 | 20 28 | 11 36 | 19 51 |
| 27 | 9 32 | 20 51 | 9 46 | 20 37 | 10 02 | 20 21 | 10 24 | 19 59 | 10 59 | 19 24 |

## Saturn, 1997

| Date | 20° N Latitude Rise h m | 20° N Latitude Set h m | 30° N Latitude Rise h m | 30° N Latitude Set h m | 40° N Latitude Rise h m | 40° N Latitude Set h m | 50° N Latitude Rise h m | 50° N Latitude Set h m | 60° N Latitude Rise h m | 60° N Latitude Set h m |
|---|---|---|---|---|---|---|---|---|---|---|
| Jan. 1 | 11 24 | 23 22 | 11 25 | 23 21 | 11 27 | 23 20 | 11 28 | 23 18 | 11 31 | 23 16 |
| 11 | 10 46 | 22 46 | 10 47 | 22 45 | 10 48 | 22 44 | 10 50 | 22 42 | 10 52 | 22 40 |
| 21 | 10 09 | 22 09 | 10 10 | 22 09 | 10 11 | 22 08 | 10 12 | 22 07 | 10 13 | 22 06 |
| 31 | 9 33 | 21 34 | 9 33 | 21 33 | 9 33 | 21 33 | 9 34 | 21 33 | 9 34 | 21 32 |
| Feb. 10 | 8 56 | 20 59 | 8 56 | 20 59 | 8 56 | 20 59 | 8 56 | 20 59 | 8 55 | 20 59 |
| 20 | 8 20 | 20 24 | 8 20 | 20 24 | 8 19 | 20 25 | 8 18 | 20 26 | 8 17 | 20 27 |
| Mar. 2 | 7 44 | 19 49 | 7 44 | 19 50 | 7 42 | 19 51 | 7 41 | 19 53 | 7 39 | 19 55 |
| 12 | 7 09 | 19 15 | 7 07 | 19 16 | 7 06 | 19 18 | 7 04 | 19 20 | 7 00 | 19 23 |
| 22 | 6 33 | 18 41 | 6 32 | 18 43 | 6 29 | 18 45 | 6 27 | 18 48 | 6 22 | 18 52 |
| Apr. 1 | 5 58 | 18 07 | 5 56 | 18 09 | 5 53 | 18 12 | 5 50 | 18 15 | 5 44 | 18 21 |
| 11 | 5 22 | 17 33 | 5 20 | 17 35 | 5 17 | 17 38 | 5 13 | 17 43 | 5 06 | 17 49 |
| 21 | 4 47 | 16 59 | 4 44 | 17 02 | 4 40 | 17 05 | 4 36 | 17 10 | 4 28 | 17 18 |
| May 1 | 4 11 | 16 25 | 4 08 | 16 28 | 4 04 | 16 32 | 3 58 | 16 37 | 3 50 | 16 46 |
| 11 | 3 35 | 15 50 | 3 32 | 15 54 | 3 27 | 15 58 | 3 21 | 16 04 | 3 12 | 16 14 |
| 21 | 3 00 | 15 15 | 2 56 | 15 19 | 2 51 | 15 24 | 2 44 | 15 31 | 2 34 | 15 41 |
| 31 | 2 23 | 14 40 | 2 19 | 14 44 | 2 14 | 14 49 | 2 07 | 14 57 | 1 56 | 15 08 |
| June 10 | 1 47 | 14 04 | 1 42 | 14 09 | 1 37 | 14 14 | 1 29 | 14 22 | 1 17 | 14 34 |
| 20 | 1 10 | 13 28 | 1 05 | 13 33 | 1 00 | 13 39 | 0 52 | 13 47 | 0 39 | 13 59 |
| 30 | 0 33 | 12 51 | 0 28 | 12 56 | 0 22 | 13 02 | 0 14 | 13 10 | 0 01 | 13 23 |
| July 10 | 23 51 | 12 14 | 23 46 | 12 19 | 23 40 | 12 25 | 23 32 | 12 34 | 23 19 | 12 47 |
| 20 | 23 13 | 11 36 | 23 08 | 11 41 | 23 02 | 11 47 | 22 53 | 11 56 | 22 40 | 12 09 |
| 30 | 22 34 | 10 57 | 22 29 | 11 02 | 22 23 | 11 08 | 22 14 | 11 17 | 22 01 | 11 30 |
| Aug. 9 | 21 55 | 10 18 | 21 50 | 10 23 | 21 44 | 10 29 | 21 35 | 10 37 | 21 22 | 10 50 |
| 19 | 21 15 | 9 37 | 21 10 | 9 42 | 21 04 | 9 48 | 20 56 | 9 57 | 20 43 | 10 09 |
| 29 | 20 34 | 8 57 | 20 30 | 9 01 | 20 24 | 9 07 | 20 16 | 9 15 | 20 03 | 9 28 |
| Sept. 8 | 19 54 | 8 15 | 19 49 | 8 19 | 19 43 | 8 25 | 19 36 | 8 33 | 19 24 | 8 45 |
| 18 | 19 12 | 7 33 | 19 08 | 7 37 | 19 03 | 7 43 | 18 55 | 7 50 | 18 44 | 8 01 |
| 28 | 18 31 | 6 51 | 18 27 | 6 55 | 18 22 | 7 00 | 18 15 | 7 06 | 18 04 | 7 17 |
| Oct. 8 | 17 49 | 6 08 | 17 45 | 6 12 | 17 41 | 6 16 | 17 34 | 6 23 | 17 24 | 6 33 |
| 18 | 17 07 | 5 25 | 17 04 | 5 29 | 16 59 | 5 33 | 16 53 | 5 39 | 16 44 | 5 49 |
| 28 | 16 25 | 4 43 | 16 22 | 4 46 | 16 18 | 4 50 | 16 13 | 4 56 | 16 04 | 5 05 |
| Nov. 7 | 15 44 | 4 01 | 15 41 | 4 04 | 15 37 | 4 08 | 15 32 | 4 13 | 15 24 | 4 21 |
| 17 | 15 03 | 3 19 | 15 00 | 3 22 | 14 56 | 3 25 | 14 51 | 3 30 | 14 44 | 3 38 |
| 27 | 14 22 | 2 38 | 14 19 | 2 41 | 14 16 | 2 44 | 14 11 | 2 49 | 14 04 | 2 56 |
| Dec. 7 | 13 42 | 1 57 | 13 39 | 2 00 | 13 36 | 2 04 | 13 31 | 2 08 | 13 24 | 2 16 |
| 17 | 13 02 | 1 18 | 13 00 | 1 20 | 12 56 | 1 24 | 12 51 | 1 29 | 12 44 | 1 36 |
| 27 | 12 23 | 0 39 | 12 20 | 0 42 | 12 17 | 0 45 | 12 12 | 0 50 | 12 04 | 0 58 |

## Aurora Borealis and Aurora Australis

The Aurora Borealis, also called the Northern Lights, is a broad display of rather faint light in the northern skies at night. The Aurora Australis, a similar phenomenon, appears at the same time in southern skies. The aurora appears in a wide variety of forms. Sometimes it is seen as a quiet glow, almost foglike in character; sometimes as vertical streamers in which there may be considerable motion; sometimes as a series of luminous expanding arcs. There are many colors, with white, yellow, and red predominating.

The auroras are most vivid and most frequently seen at about 20 degrees from the magnetic poles, along the northern coast of the North American continent and the eastern part of the northern coast of Europe. The Aurora Borealis has been seen as far south as Key West, and the Aurora Australis has been seen as far north as Australia and New Zealand. Such occurrences are rare, however.

Although the cause of the auroras is not known beyond question, there does seem to be a definite correlation between auroral displays and Sunspot activity. It is thought that atomic particles expelled from the Sun by the forces that cause solar flares speed through space at velocities of 400 to 600 mi per second. These particles are entrapped by the Earth's magnetic field, forming what are termed the Van Allen belts. The encounter of these clouds of the solar wind with the Earth's magnetic field weakens the field so that previously trapped particles are allowed to impact the upper atmosphere. The collisions between solar and terrestrial atoms result in the glow in the upper atmosphere called the aurora. The glow may be vivid where the lines of magnetic force converge near the magnetic poles.

The auroral displays appear at heights ranging from 50 to about 600 mi and have given us a means of estimating the extent of the Earth's atmosphere.

The auroras are often accompanied by magnetic storms whose forces, also guided by the lines of force of the Earth's magnetic field, disrupt electrical communication.

## Eclipses, 1997

(Greenwich Mean Time)

There are 4 eclipses in 1997, 2 of the Sun and 2 of the Moon.

### I. Total Solar Eclipse, Mar. 9

Totality will be visible from parts of eastern Asia. The path of the totality begins at Sunrise in eastern Kazakstan, moving through Mongolia to eastern Siberia, and concluding at Sunset over the Arctic Ocean. The partial eclipse is visible over a much wider area, including eastern Asia, the northern Pacific, and the far northwest corner of North America.

**Circumstances of the Eclipse**

| Event | Date | h | m |
|---|---|---|---|
| Partial eclipse begins | Mar. 8 | 23 | 17.6 |
| Total eclipse begins | 9 | 0 | 42.1 |
| Instant of greatest eclipse | 9 | 1 | 24.8 |
| Total eclipse ends | 9 | 2 | 7.2 |
| Partial eclipse ends | 9 | 3 | 31.8 |

### II. Partial Lunar Eclipse, Mar. 24

The beginning of the umbral phase of this eclipse is visible in all of the continental United States except Alaska, all the western part of Canada, Central America, South America, all but the extreme east of Africa and Europe. The end of the umbral phase is visible in North America, Central America, South America, and extreme western parts of Africa and Europe.

**Circumstances of the Eclipse**

| Event | Date | h | m |
|---|---|---|---|
| Moon enters penumbra | Mar. 24 | 1 | 40.5 |
| Moon enters umbra | 24 | 2 | 57.6 |
| Middle of eclipse | 24 | 4 | 39.4 |
| Moon leaves umbra | 24 | 6 | 21.5 |
| Moon leaves penumbra | 24 | 7 | 38.4 |

Magnitude of eclipse: 0.92

### III. Partial Solar Eclipse, Sept. 2

This partial solar eclipse is visible from Australia, New Zealand, the southwest Pacific Ocean, and part of Antarctica.

**Circumstances of the Eclipse**

| Event | Date | h | m |
|---|---|---|---|
| Eclipse begins | Sept. 1 | 21 | 44.1 |
| Greatest eclipse | 2 | 0 | 3.7 |
| Eclipse ends | 2 | 2 | 23.1 |

Magnitude of greatest eclipse: 0.90

### IV. Total Lunar Eclipse, Sept. 16

The beginning of the umbral phase of this eclipse is visible in Asia, Australia, the eastern half of Africa, and the eastern portions of Europe. The end of the umbral phase is visible in Europe, Africa, all but extreme eastern portions of Asia, and all but the eastern region of Australia.

**Circumstances of the Eclipse**

| Event | Date | h | m |
|---|---|---|---|
| Moon enters penumbra | Sept. 16 | 16 | 11.0 |
| Moom enters umbra | 16 | 17 | 8.0 |
| Moon enters totality | 16 | 18 | 15.6 |
| Middle of eclipse | 16 | 18 | 46.6 |
| Moon leaves totality | 16 | 19 | 18.0 |
| Moon leaves umbra | 16 | 20 | 25.4 |
| Moon leaves penumbra | 16 | 21 | 22.4 |

Magnitude of eclipse: 1.20

# The Planets: Motion, Distance, and Brightness

| Planet | Mean daily motion ″ | Orbital velocity mi per sec. | Sidereal revolution days | Synodic revolution days | Distance from Sun in millions of mi Max. | Min. | Distance from Earth in millions of mi Max. | Min. | Light at[1] perihelion | aphelion |
|---|---|---|---|---|---|---|---|---|---|---|
| Mercury | 14,732 | 29.75 | 88.0 | 115.9 | 43.4 | 28.6 | 136 | 50 | 10.58 | 4.59 |
| Venus | 5,768 | 21.76 | 224.7 | 583.9 | 67.7 | 66.8 | 161 | 25 | 1.94 | 1.89 |
| Earth | 3,548 | 18.51 | 365.3 | ------- | 94.6 | 91.4 | ----- | --- | 1.03 | 0.97 |
| Mars | 1,886 | 14.99 | 687.0 | 779.9 | 155.0 | 128.5 | 248 | 35 | 0.524 | 0.360 |
| Jupiter | 299 | 8.12 | 4,331.8 | 398.9 | 507.0 | 460.6 | 600 | 368 | 0.0408 | 0.0333 |
| Saturn | 120 | 5.99 | 10,760.0 | 378.1 | 937.5 | 838.4 | 1,031 | 745 | 0.01230 | 0.00984 |
| Uranus | 42 | 4.23 | 30,684.0 | 369.7 | 1,859.7 | 1,669.3 | 1,953 | 1,606 | 0.00300 | 0.00250 |
| Neptune | 21 | 3.38 | 60,188.3 | 367.5 | 2,821.7 | 2,760.4 | 2,915 | 2,667 | 0.00114 | 0.00109 |
| Pluto | 14 | 2.95 | 90,466.8 | 366.7 | 4,551.4 | 2,756.4 | 4,644 | 2,663 | 0.00114 | 0.00042 |

(1) Light at perihelion and aphelion is solar illumination in units of mean illumination at Earth.

# Orbital Elements of the Planets, 1997

| Planet | Mean longitude of:[1] ascending node ° | ′ | ″ | perihelion ° | ′ | ″ | Inclination[1] of orbit to ecliptic ° | ′ | ″ | Mean[1] dist. AUs[2] | Eccentricity[1] of orbit | Mean longitude at the epoch[1] ° | ′ | ″ |
|---|---|---|---|---|---|---|---|---|---|---|---|---|---|---|
| Mercury | 48 | 17 | 49 | 77 | 24 | 43 | 7 | 0 | 18 | 0.387097 | 0.205638 | 215 | 54 | 59 |
| Venus | 76 | 39 | 18 | 131 | 45 | 36 | 3 | 23 | 41 | 0.723332 | 0.006792 | 276 | 28 | 22 |
| Earth | 0 | 0 | 0 | 102 | 50 | 2 | 0 | 0 | 0 | 1.000002 | 0.016740 | 131 | 14 | 33 |
| Mars | 49 | 32 | 10 | 336 | 2 | 28 | 1 | 50 | 59 | 1.523705 | 0.093338 | 157 | 34 | 18 |
| Jupiter | 100 | 26 | 46 | 15 | 41 | 35 | 1 | 18 | 17 | 5.20237 | 0.048432 | 305 | 53 | 51 |
| Saturn | 113 | 36 | 11 | 89 | 19 | 52 | 2 | 29 | 7 | 9.56627 | 0.052749 | 14 | 13 | 29 |
| Uranus | 74 | 5 | 17 | 176 | 17 | 42 | 0 | 46 | 24 | 19.3045 | 0.043329 | 300 | 44 | 57 |
| Neptune | 131 | 45 | 22 | 3 | 49 | 12 | 1 | 46 | 8 | 30.2760 | 0.009733 | 298 | 33 | 15 |
| Pluto | 110 | 21 | 7 | 224 | 47 | 2 | 17 | 7 | 9 | 39.6595 | 0.251642 | 234 | 54 | 21 |

(1) Consistent for the epoch: Feb. 1, 1997, 12:00 Ephemeris Time. (2) Astronomical units.

# Planets and the Sun, by Selected Characteristics

| Sun and planets | Semi-diameter at unit distance ′ ″ | at mean least distance ′ ″ | in mi mean s.d. | Volume[1] | Mass[1] | Density[1] | Sidereal period of rotation d | h | m | s | Gravity at surface[1] | Reflecting power Pct° | Probable temp. °F |
|---|---|---|---|---|---|---|---|---|---|---|---|---|---|
| Sun | 959.62 | --- | 432,449 | 1,299,370 | 332,946 | 0.26 | 24 | 16 | 48 | | 27.90 | — | +10,000 |
| Mercury | 3.37 | 5.5 | 1,516 | 0.0559 | 0.0553 | 1.00 | 58 | 15 | 30 | | 0.37 | 0.11 | +620 |
| Venus | 8.34 | 30.1 | 3,761 | 0.8541 | 0.8150 | 0.97 | 243 | R | | | 0.88 | 0.65 | +900 |
| Earth | --- | --- | 3,964 | 1.000 | 1.000 | 1.00 | | 23 | 56 | 6.7 | 1.00 | 0.37 | +72 |
| Moon | 2.40 | 932.4 | 1,080 | 0.020 | 0.0123 | 0.62 | 27 | 7 | 43 | | 0.17 | 0.12 | –10 |
| Mars | 4.69 | 8.95 | 2,109 | 0.1506 | 0.1074 | 0.73 | | 24 | 37 | 26 | 0.38 | 0.15 | –10 |
| Jupiter | 98.35 | 23.4 | 44,375 | 1,403 | 317.89 | 0.25 | | 9 | 3 | 30 | 2.64 | 0.52 | –240 |
| Saturn | 82.83 | 9.7 | 37,495 | 832 | 95.18 | 0.13 | | 10 | 39 | 22 | 1.15 | 0.47 | –300 |
| Uranus | 35.4 | 1.9 | 15,885 | 63 | 14.54 | 0.23 | | 17 | 14 | R | 1.15 | 0.40 | –340 |
| Neptune | 33.4 | 1.2 | 15,391 | 55 | 17.15 | 0.30 | | 16 | 6 | | 1.12 | 0.35 | –370 |
| Pluto | 1.9 | 0.05 | 715 | 0.006 | 0.0020 | 0.37 | 6 | 9 | 17 | | 0.04 | 0.5 | ? |

(1) Earth = 1. R = Retrograde rotation of Venus and Uranus.

# The Sun

The Sun, the controlling body of the Earth's solar system, is a star often described as average. Yet, the Sun's mass and luminosity are greater than that of 80% of the stars in the Earth's galaxy. On the other hand, most of the stars that can be easily seen on any clear night are bigger and brighter than the Sun. It is the Sun's proximity to the Earth that makes it appear tremendously large and bright. The Sun is 400,000 times as bright as the full moon and gives the Earth 6 million times as much light as do all the other stars put together. A series of thermonuclear reactions involving the atoms of the elements of which it is composed produces the heat and light that make life possible on Earth.

The Sun has a diameter of 864,000 mi and, on average, is 92,900,000 mi from the Earth. It is 1.41 times as dense as water. The light of the Sun reaches the Earth in 499.012 seconds, or in slightly more than 8 minutes. The average solar surface temperature has been measured at a value of 5,800 K, or about 10,000° F. The interior temperature of the Sun is theorized to be about 27,000,000° F.

When Sunlight is analyzed with a spectroscope, it is found to consist of a continuous spectrum composed of all the colors of the rainbow in order, crossed by many dark lines. The "absorption lines" are produced by gaseous materials in the atmosphere of the Sun. More than 60 of the natural terrestrial elements have been identified in the Sun, all in gaseous form because of the Sun's intense heat.

### Spheres and Corona

The radiating surface of the Sun is called the **photosphere**, and just above it is the **chromosphere**. The chromosphere is visible to the naked eye only at times of total solar eclipses, appearing then to be a pinkish-violet layer with occasional great prominences projecting above its general level. With proper instruments, the chromosphere can be seen or photographed whenever the Sun is visible without waiting for a total eclipse. Above the chromosphere is the **corona**, also visible to the naked eye only at times of total eclipse. Instruments also permit the brighter portions of the corona to be studied whenever conditions are favorable. The pearly light of the corona surges millions of mi from the Sun. Iron, nickel, and calcium are believed to be principal contributors to the composition of the corona, all in a state of extreme attenuation and high ionization that indicates temperatures on the order of a million degrees Fahrenheit.

### Sunspots

There is an intimate connection between Sunspots and the corona. At times of low Sunspot activity, the fine streamers of the corona are longer above the Sun's equator than over the polar regions of the Sun; during periods of high Sunspot activity, the corona extends fairly evenly outward from all regions of the Sun, but to a much greater distance in space. Sunspots are dark, irregularly shaped regions whose diameters may reach lengths of tens of thousands of mi. The average life of a Sunspot group is from 2 to 3 weeks, but some Sunspot groups have lasted for more than a year by being carried repeatedly around as the Sun rotated upon its axis.

The record for the duration of a Sunspot is 18 months. Sunspots reach a low point every 11.3 years, with a peak of activity occurring irregularly between 2 successive minima.

## The Zodiac

The Sun's apparent yearly path among the stars is known as the ecliptic. The zone, 18° wide, 9° on each side of the **ecliptic**, is known as the **zodiac**. Inside this zone are the apparent paths of the Sun, Moon, Earth, and the other planets. Only Pluto regularly strays outside this band on the celestial sphere. The zodiac is used both astrologically and astronomically. Though the two had a common beginning, they are no longer the same.

Beginning at the point on the ecliptic that marks the position of the Sun at the vernal equinox and proceeding eastward, the astrological zodiac is divided into 12 signs of 30° each, shown below. These signs are named from the 12 constellations of the zodiac with which the signs coincided in the time of the astronomer Hipparchus, about 2,000 years ago. Owing to the precession of the equinoxes, that is to say, to the retrograde motion of the equinoxes along the ecliptic, each sign in the zodiac has, in the course of 2,000 years, moved backward about 30° into the constellation west of it; the sign Aries is now in the constellation Pisces, for example, and so on. The vernal equinox will move from Pisces into Aquarius about the middle of the 26th century.

The astronomical constellations of the zodiac, unlike the astrological signs, are no longer equal in size. The ecliptic actually moves through parts of 13, not 12, astronomical constellations, the 13th being Ophiuchus. Also, the constellation of the scorpion is called Scorpius, while the sign is called Scorpio. Because of the width of the zodiac, it actually cuts through parts of 26 different constellations, not just 12.

The signs of the zodiac, with their Latin and English names, are as follows:

| | | | | |
|---|---|---|---|---|
| **Spring** | 1. | ♈ | Aries | The Ram |
| | 2. | ♉ | Taurus | The Bull |
| | 3. | ♊ | Gemini | The Twins |
| **Summer** | 4. | ♋ | Cancer | The Crab |
| | 5. | ♌ | Leo | The Lion |
| | 6. | ♍ | Virgo | The Virgin |
| **Autumn** | 7. | ♎ | Libra | The Balance |
| | 8. | ♏ | Scorpio | The Scorpion |
| | 9. | ♐ | Sagittarius | The Archer |
| **Winter** | 10. | ♑ | Capricorn | The Goat |
| | 11. | ♒ | Aquarius | The Water Bearer |
| | 12. | ♓ | Pisces | The Fishes |

Although the ecliptic does not pass through the constellation of Cetus, it comes so close that on Mar. 27, 1997, the disk of the Sun will clip a corner of Cetus. The constellations of the zodiac with the approximate dates that the Sun is in each constellation in 1997, are as follows:

| | |
|---|---|
| Jan. 1 - Jan. 19 | Sagittarius |
| Jan. 20 - Feb. 15 | Capricornus |
| Feb. 16 - Mar. 11 | Aquarius |
| Mar. 12 - Apr. 18 | Pisces |
| Apr. 19 - May 13 | Aries |
| May 14 - June 20 | Taurus |
| June 21 - July 20 | Gemini |
| July 21 - Aug. 10 | Cancer |
| Aug. 11 - Sept. 16 | Leo |
| Sept. 17 - Oct. 30 | Virgo |
| Oct. 31 - Nov. 22 | Libra |
| Nov. 23 - Nov. 29 | Scorpius |
| Nov. 30 - Dec. 17 | Ophiuchus |
| Dec. 18 - Dec. 31 | Sagittarius |

## The Moon

The Moon completes a circuit around the Earth in a period whose mean or average duration is 27 days, 7 hours, 43.2 minutes. This is the Moon's **sidereal period**. Because of the motion of the Moon in common with the Earth around the Sun, the mean duration of the lunar month—the period from one New Moon to the next New Moon—is 29 days, 12 hours, 44.05 minutes. This is the Moon's **synodical period**.

The mean distance of the Moon from the Earth is 238,857 mi. Because the orbit of the Moon about the Earth is not circular but elliptical, however, the maximum distance from the Earth that the Moon may reach is 252,710 mi and the least distance is 221,463 mi. (All distances are from the center of one body to the center of the other.)

The Moon's diameter is 2,160 mi. If we deduct the radius of the Moon, 1,080 mi, and the radius of the Earth, 3,963 mi, from the minimum distance, or **perigee**, the figure for the nearest approach of the bodies' surfaces comes to 216,420 mi.

The Moon rotates on its axis in a period of time that is exactly equal to its sidereal revolution about the Earth: 27.321666 days. Thus the backside or farside of the Moon always faces away from the Earth. This does not mean that the backside is always dark, since the Sun is the main source of light in the Solar System. The farside of the Moon gets just as much direct Sunlight as the nearside. At New Moon phase, the farside of the Moon is fully lit. In 1997, there is no Last Quarter Moon in February.

The Moon's revolution about the Earth is irregular because of its elliptical orbit. The Moon's rotation, however, is regular, and this, together with the irregular revolution, produces what is called "libration in longitude," which permits the observer on Earth to see first farther around the east side and then farther around the west side of the Moon. The Moon's variation north or south of the ecliptic permits one to see farther over first one pole and then the other of the Moon; this is called "libration in latitude." These two libration effects permit observers on Earth to see a total of about 60% of the Moon's surface over a period of time. The hidden side of the Moon was first photographed in 1959 by the Soviet space vehicle *Lunik III*. Since then, many excellent pictures of nearly all of the Moon's surface have been transmitted to Earth by Lunar Orbiters launched by the U.S. However, the farside does appear noticeably different from the nearside, in that the farside has practically none of the large lava plains, called maria, which are so prominent on the nearside of the Moon.

Tides on the Earth are caused mainly by the Moon, because of its proximity to the Earth. The ratio of the tide-raising power of the Moon to that of the Sun is 11 to 5.

### Harvest Moon and Hunter's Moon

The Harvest Moon, the full Moon nearest the autumnal equinox, ushers in a period of several successive days when the Moon rises soon after sunset. This phenomenon gives farmers in temperate latitudes extra hours of light in which to harvest their crops before frost and winter come. The 1997 Harvest Moon falls on Sept. 16 GMT. Harvest Moon in the southern hemisphere temperate latitudes falls on Mar. 23.

The next full Moon after Harvest Moon is called the Hunter's Moon; it is accompanied by a similar but less marked phenomenon. In 1997, the Hunter's Moon occurs on Oct. 15, northern hemisphere; Apr. 22, southern hemisphere.

## Moon's Perigee and Apogee, 1997

(Greenwich Mean Time)

| Perigee | | | | Apogee | | | |
|---|---|---|---|---|---|---|---|
| Date | Hour | Date | Hour | Date | Hour | Date | Hour |
| Jan. 10 | 9 | July 21 | 23 | Jan. 25 | 17 | Aug. 6 | 14 |
| Feb. 7 | 21 | Aug. 19 | 5 | Feb. 21 | 17 | Sept. 2 | 21 |
| Mar. 8 | 9 | Sept. 16 | 15 | Mar. 21 | 20 | Sept. 29 | 23 |
| Apr. 5 | 17 | Oct. 15 | 2 | Apr. 17 | 15 | Oct. 27 | 9 |
| May 3 | 11 | Nov. 12 | 8 | May 15 | 10 | Nov. 24 | 2 |
| May 29 | 7 | Dec. 9 | 17 | June 12 | 5 | Dec. 21 | 23 |
| June 24 | 5 | | | July 9 | 23 | | |

## Moon Phases, 1997

(Greenwich Mean Time)

| New Moon | | | | First Quarter | | | | Full Moon | | | | Last Quarter | | | |
|---|---|---|---|---|---|---|---|---|---|---|---|---|---|---|---|
| Month | d | h | m | Month | d | h | m | Month | d | h | m | Month | d | h | m |
| | | | | | | | | | | | | Jan. | 2 | 1 | 46 |
| Jan. | 9 | 4 | 27 | Jan. | 15 | 20 | 03 | Jan. | 23 | 15 | 12 | Jan. | 31 | 19 | 41 |
| Feb. | 7 | 15 | 07 | Feb. | 14 | 8 | 59 | Feb. | 22 | 10 | 28 | Mar. | 2 | 9 | 39 |
| Mar. | 9 | 1 | 16 | Mar. | 16 | 0 | 07 | Mar. | 24 | 4 | 46 | Mar. | 31 | 19 | 39 |
| Apr. | 7 | 11 | 03 | Apr. | 14 | 17 | 01 | Apr. | 22 | 20 | 35 | Apr. | 30 | 2 | 38 |
| May | 6 | 20 | 48 | May | 14 | 10 | 56 | May | 22 | 9 | 14 | May | 29 | 7 | 52 |
| June | 5 | 7 | 05 | June | 13 | 4 | 53 | June | 20 | 19 | 10 | June | 27 | 12 | 43 |
| July | 4 | 18 | 41 | July | 12 | 21 | 45 | July | 20 | 3 | 21 | July | 26 | 18 | 29 |
| Aug. | 3 | 8 | 15 | Aug. | 11 | 12 | 43 | Aug. | 18 | 10 | 56 | Aug. | 25 | 2 | 25 |
| Sept. | 1 | 23 | 53 | Sept. | 10 | 1 | 32 | Sept. | 16 | 18 | 52 | Sept. | 23 | 13 | 36 |
| Oct. | 1 | 16 | 53 | Oct. | 9 | 12 | 23 | Oct. | 16 | 3 | 47 | Oct. | 23 | 4 | 49 |
| Oct. | 31 | 10 | 2 | Nov. | 7 | 21 | 44 | Nov. | 14 | 14 | 13 | Nov. | 21 | 23 | 59 |
| Nov. | 30 | 2 | 15 | Dec. | 7 | 6 | 10 | Dec. | 14 | 2 | 38 | Dec. | 21 | 21 | 44 |
| Dec. | 29 | 16 | 58 | | | | | | | | | | | | |

## The Earth: Size, Computation of Time, Seasons

### Size and Dimensions

The Earth is the 5th largest planet and the 3d from the Sun. Its mass is 6 sextillion, 588 quintillion short tons. Using the parameters of an ellipsoid adopted by the International Astronomical Union in 1964 and recognized by the International Union of Geodesy and Geophysics in 1967, the length of the equator is 24,901.55 mi, the length of a meridian is 24,859.82 mi, the equatorial diameter is 7,926.41 mi, and the area of this reference ellipsoid is approximately 196,938,800 sq. mi.

The Earth is considered a solid, rigid mass with a dense core of magnetic, probably metallic material. The outer part of the core is probably liquid. Around the core is a thick shell or mantle of heavy crystalline rock that in turn is covered by a thin crust forming the solid granite and basalt base of the continents and ocean basins. Over broad areas of the Earth's surface, the crust has a thin cover of sedimentary rock such as sandstone, shale, and limestone formed by weathering of the Earth's surface and deposition of sands, clays, and plant and animal remains.

The temperature in the Earth increases about 1° F with every 100 to 200 feet in depth, in the upper 100 kilometers of the Earth, and the temperature near the core is believed to be near the melting point of the core materials under the conditions at that depth. The heat of the Earth is believed to be derived from radioactivity in the rocks, pressures developed within the Earth, and the original heat of formation.

## Atmosphere of the Earth

The Earth's atmosphere is a blanket composed of nitrogen, oxygen, and argon, in amounts of about 77%, 21%, and 1% by volume. Also present in minute quantities are carbon dioxide, hydrogen, neon, helium, krypton, and xenon. Water vapor displaces other gases and varies from nearly zero to about 4% by volume. The atmosphere rests on the Earth's surface with the weight equivalent to a layer of water 34 ft deep. For about 300,000 ft upward, the gases remain in the proportions stated. Gravity holds the gases to the Earth. The weight of the air compresses it at the bottom so that the greatest density is at the Earth's surface. Pressure, as well as density, decreases as height increases because the weight pressing upon any layer is always less than that pressing upon the layers below.

The temperature of the air drops with increased height until the **tropopause** is reached. Altitude of the tropopause may vary from 25,000 to 60,000 ft. The atmosphere below the tropopause is the **troposphere,** which contains 90% of the air and the tallest mountains. This is also where most weather phenomena occur. The atmosphere for about 20 mi above the tropopause is the **stratosphere,** where the temperature generally increases with height except at high latitudes in winter. The stratophere also contains ozone, which prevents ultraviolet rays from reaching the Earth's surface. The height of the **ozone** layer varies from approximately 12 to 21 mi above the Earth. Traces exist as low as 6 mi and as high as 35 mi. A temperature maximum near the 30-mi level is called the **stratopause.**

Above this boundary is the **mesosphere,** where the temperature decreases with height to a minimum, the **mesopause,** at a height of 50 mi. Extending above the mesosphere to the outer fringes of the atmosphere is the **thermosphere,** a region where temperature increases with height to a value measured in thousands of degrees Fahrenheit. The lower portion of this region, extending from 50 to about 400 mi in altitude, is characterized by a high ion density and is thus called the **ionosphere.** The outer region is called the **exosphere;** this is the region where gas molecules traveling at high speed may escape into outer space, above 600 mi.

## Latitude, Longitude

Position on the globe is measured by means of meridians and parallels. Meridians, which are imaginary lines drawn around the Earth through the poles, determine **longitude.** The meridian running through Greenwich, England, is the **prime meridian of longitude,** and all others are either east or west. Parallels, which are imaginary circles parallel with the equator, determine **latitude.** The length of a degree of longitude varies as the cosine of the latitude. At the equator a degree is 69.171 statute mi; this is gradually reduced toward the poles. Value of a longitude degree at the poles is zero.

**Latitude** is reckoned by the number of degrees north or south of the equator, an imaginary circle on the Earth's surface everywhere equidistant between the two poles. According to the International Astronomical Union ellipsoid of 1964, the length of a degree of latitude is 68.708 statute mi at the equator and varies slightly north and south because of the oblate form of the globe; at the poles it is 69.403 statute mi.

## Definitions of Time

The Earth rotates on its axis and follows an elliptical orbit around the Sun. The rotation makes the Sun appear to move across the sky from east to west. This rotation determines day and night, and the complete rotation, in relation to the Sun, is called the **apparent** or **true solar day.** This length of time varies, but an average determines the **mean solar day** of 24 hours.

The mean solar day is in universal use for civil purposes. It may be obtained from apparent solar time by correcting observations of the Sun for the **equation of time**, but when high precision is required, the mean solar time is calculated from its relation to sidereal time. These relations are extremely complicated, but for most practical uses, they may be considered as follows:

**Sidereal time** is the measure of time defined by the diurnal motion of the vernal equinox and is determined from observation of the meridian transits of stars. One complete rotation of the Earth relative to the equinox is called the **sidereal day.** The **mean sidereal day** is 23 hours, 56 minutes, 4.091 seconds of mean solar time.

The interval required for the Earth to make one absolute revolution around the Sun is a **sidereal year;** it consisted of 365 days, 6 hours, 9 minutes, and 9.5 seconds of mean solar time (approximately 24 hours per day) in 1900 and has been increasing at the rate of 0.0001 second annually.

The **Tropical Year,** upon which our calendar is based, is the interval between 2 consecutive returns of the Sun to the vernal equinox. The tropical year consisted of 365 days, 5 hours, 48 minutes, and 46 seconds in 1900. It has been decreasing at the rate of 0.530 second per century. The **Calendar Year** begins at 12 o'clock midnight precisely, local clock time, on the night of Dec. 31-Jan. 1. The day and the calendar month also begin at midnight by the clock.

In 1956 the unit of time interval was defined to be identical with the second of **Ephemeris Time,** 1/31,556,925.9747 of the tropical year for 1900 January 0d 12th hour E.T. A physical definition of the second based on a quantum transition of cesium (atomic second) was adopted in 1964. The atomic second is equal to 9,192,631,770 cycles of the emitted radiation. In 1967 this atomic second was adopted as the unit of time interval for the International System of Units.

## The Zones and Seasons

The 5 zones of the Earth's surface are the Torrid, lying between the Tropics of Cancer and Capricorn; the North Temperate, between Cancer and the Arctic Circle; the South Temperate, between Capricorn and the Antarctic Circle; and the 2 Frigid Zones, between the Polar Circles and the Poles.

The inclination or tilt of the Earth's axis with respect to the Sun determines the seasons. These are commonly marked in the North Temperate Zone, where spring begins at the vernal equinox, summer at the summer solstice, autumn at the autumnal equinox, and winter at the winter solstice.

In the South Temperate Zone, the seasons are reversed. Spring begins at the autumnal equinox, summer at the winter solstice, etc.

If the Earth's axis were perpendicular to the plane of the Earth's orbit around the Sun, there would be no change of seasons. Day and night would be of nearly constant length, and there would be equable conditions of temperature. But the axis is tilted 23° 27′ away from a perpendicular to the orbit, and only in Mar. and Sept. is the axis at right angles to the Sun.

The points at which the Sun crosses the equator are the equinoxes, when day and night are most nearly equal. The points at which the Sun is at a maximum distance from the equator are the solstices. Days and nights are then most unequal. However, at the equator, day and night are equal throughout the year.

In June, the North Pole is tilted 23° 27′ toward the Sun, and the days in the northern hemisphere are longer than the nights, while the days in the southern hemisphere are shorter than the nights. In December, the North Pole is tilted 23° 27′ away from the Sun, and the situation is reversed.

## The Seasons in 1997

In 1997 the 4 seasons will begin as shown below. (Add one hour to Eastern Standard Time for Atlantic Time; subtract one hour for Central, 2 hours for Mountain, 3 hours for Pacific, 4 hours for Alaska, 5 hours for Hawaii-Aleutian. Also shown is Greenwich Mean Time.)

| Seasons | Date | GMT | EST |
|---|---|---|---|
| Vernal Equinox | Mar. 20 | 13:56 | 8:56 |
| Summer Solstice | June 21 | 8:21 | 3:21 |
| Autumnal Equinox | Sept. 22 | 23:57 | 18:57 |
| Winter Solstice | Dec. 21 | 20:09 | 15:09 |

## Poles of the Earth

The geographic (rotation) poles, or points where the Earth's axis of rotation cuts the surface, are not absolutely fixed in the body of the Earth. The pole of rotation describes an irregular curve about its mean position.

Two periods have been detected in this motion: (1) an annual period due to seasonal changes in barometric pressure, to load of ice and snow on the surface, and to other phenomena of seasonal character; (2) a period of about 14 months due to the shape and constitution of the Earth.

In addition, there are small but as yet unpredictable irregularities. The whole motion is so small that the actual pole at any time remains within a circle of 30 or 40 feet in radius centered at the mean position of the pole.

The pole of rotation for the time being is of course the pole having a latitude of 90° and an indeterminate longitude.

## Magnetic Poles

The **north magnetic pole** of the Earth is that region where the magnetic force is vertically downward, and the **south magnetic pole** is that region where the magnetic force is vertically upward. A compass placed at the magnetic poles experiences no directive force in azimuth.

There are slow changes in the distribution of the Earth's magnetic field. These changes were at one time attributed in part to a periodic movement of the magnetic poles around the geographical poles, but later evidence refutes this theory and points, rather, to a slow migration of "disturbance" foci over the Earth.

There appear shifts in position of the magnetic poles due to the changes in the Earth's magnetic field. The center of the area designated as the north magnetic pole was estimated to be in about latitude 70.5° N and longitude 96° W in 1905; from recent nearby measurements and studies of the secular changes, the position in 1970 was estimated as latitude 76.2° N and longitude 101° W. Improved data rather than actual motion account for at least part of the change.

The position of the south magnetic pole in 1912 was near 71° S and longitude 150° E. In 1970 it was estimated at latitude 66° S and longitude 139.1° E.

The direction of the horizontal components of the magnetic field at any point is known as magnetic north at that point, and the angle by which it deviates east or west of true north is known as the magnetic declination or, in the mariner's terminology, the **variation of the compass.**

A compass without error points in the direction of magnetic north. (In general, this is not the direction of the magnetic north pole.) If one follows the direction indicated by the north end of the compass, he or she will travel along a rather irregular curve that eventually reaches the north magnetic pole (though not usually by a great-circle route). However, the action of the compass should not be thought of as due to any influence of the distant pole, but simply as an indication of the distribution of the Earth's magnetism at the place of observation.

## Rotation of the Earth

The **speed of rotation** of the Earth about its axis has been found to be slightly variable. The variations may be classified as:

(A) **Secular.** Tidal friction acts as a brake on the rotation and causes a slow secular increase in the length of the day, about 1 millisecond per century.

(B) **Irregular.** The speed of rotation may increase for a number of years, about 5 to 10, and then start decreasing. The maximum difference from the mean in the length of the day during a century is about 5 milliseconds. The accumulated difference in time has amounted to approximately 44 seconds since 1900. The cause is probably motion in the interior of the Earth.

(C) **Periodic.** Seasonal variations exist with periods of 1 year and 6 months. The cumulative effect is such that each year, the Earth is late about 30 milliseconds near June 1 and is ahead about 30 milliseconds near Oct. 1. The maximum seasonal variation in the length of the day is about 0.5 millisecond. It is believed that the principal cause of the annual variation is the seasonal change in the wind patterns of the northern and southern hemispheres. The semiannual variation is due chiefly to tidal action of the Sun, which distorts the shape of the Earth slightly.

The secular and irregular variations were discovered by comparing time based on the rotation of the Earth with time based on the orbital motion of the Moon about the Earth and of the planets about the Sun. The periodic variation was determined largely with the aid of quartz-crystal clocks. The introduction of the cesium-beam atomic clock in 1955 made it possible to determine in greater detail than before the nature of the irregular and periodic variations.

## Chronological Eras, 1997

The year 1997 of the Christian Era comprises the latter part of the 221st and the beginning of the 222d year of the independence of the U.S.

| Era | Year | Begins in 1997 | Era | Year | Begins in 1997 |
|---|---|---|---|---|---|
| Byzantine | 7506 | Sept. 14 | Grecian (Seleucidae) | 2309 | Sept. 14 or Oct. 14 |
| Jewish | 5758 | Oct. 1[1] | | | |
| Roman (Ab Urbe Condita) | 2750 | Jan. 14 | Diocletian | 1714 | Sept. 11 |
| Nabonassar (Babylonian) | 2746 | Apr. 24 | Indian (Saka) | 1919 | Mar. 22 |
| Japanese | 2657 | Jan. 1 | Islamic/Muslim (Hegira) | 1418 | May 7[1] |

(1) Year begins at sunset.

## Chronological Cycles, 1997

| | | | | | |
|---|---|---|---|---|---|
| Dominical Letter | E | Golden Number (Lunar Cycle) | III | Roman Indiction | 5 |
| Epact | 21 | Solar Cycle | 18 | Julian Period (year of) | 6710 |

## Twilight

**Twilight** is that evening period of waning light from the time of sunset to dark, often termed dusk. Morning twilight, a time of increasing light, is called **dawn**. The source of this light is the Sun shining on the atmosphere above the observer. Twilight is a time of very slowly changing sky illumination with no abrupt variations. Nevertheless, there are 3 commonly accepted divisions in this smooth continuum defined by the distance the Sun lies below the astronomical horizon: civil twilight, nautical twilight, and astronomical twilight. The **astronomical horizon** is that great circle lying 90° from the zenith, the point directly over the observer's head. Twilight ends in the evening or begins in the morning at a particular time. Nominally, evening events are repeated in reverse order in the morning. **Civil twilight** is the time from the moment of sunset, when the Sun's apparent upper edge is just at the horizon, until the center of the Sun is 6° directly below the horizon. In many states, this is the time in the evening when automobile headlights must be turned on, not to see better, but to be seen by other drivers. After this time, a newspaper becomes increasingly difficult to read in the absence of artificial light. **Nautical twilight** ends when the Sun's center is 12° below the horizon. By this time in the evening, the bright stars used by navigators have appeared, and the horizon may still be seen. After this time, the horizon is more difficult to perceive, preventing navigators from sighting stars. **Astronomical twilight** ends in the evening when the Sun is 18° below the horizon and the sky is dark enough, at least away from the Sun's location, to allow astronomical work to proceed. Sunlight, however, is still shining on the higher levels of the atmosphere from the observer's zenith to the horizon toward the Sun. Although not named as a period of twilight, when the Sun is 24° below the horizon, no part of the observer's atmosphere, even toward the Sun, receives any sunlight. In the tropics, the Sun moves nearly vertically, accomplishing its 6°, 12°, or 18° depression very quickly. In the polar regions, the Sun's diurnal motion may actually be nearly along the horizon, prolonging the twilight period or even not permitting darkness to fall at all. In mid-latitudes, civil twilight may last about a half hour; nautical, an hour; and astronomers can go to work in about 90 minutes. The twilight tables given in *The World Almanac* are for the beginning of morning twilight and the end of evening astronomical twilight, and are presented for reference only. Although the instant of the Sun's horizontal depression may be calculated precisely, the phenomena associated with the event are sufficiently imprecise that the table is not recalculated each year.

## Astronomical Twilight—Meridian of Greenwich, 1997

| Date | 20° Morn. h m | 20° Even. h m | 30° Morn. h m | 30° Even. h m | 40° Morn. h m | 40° Even. h m | 50° Morn. h m | 50° Even. h m | 60° Morn. h m | 60° Even. h m |
|---|---|---|---|---|---|---|---|---|---|---|
| Jan. 1 | 5 17 | **6 51** | 5 31 | **6 37** | 5 45 | **6 23** | 6 00 | **6 08** | 6 18 | **5 49** |
| 11 | 5 20 | **6 56** | 5 33 | **6 44** | 5 45 | **6 31** | 5 58 | **6 18** | 6 14 | **6 03** |
| 21 | 5 21 | **7 02** | 5 32 | **6 51** | 5 42 | **6 41** | 5 53 | **6 30** | 6 04 | **6 19** |
| Feb. 1 | 5 20 | **7 08** | 5 28 | **6 59** | 5 36 | **6 52** | 5 42 | **6 46** | 5 47 | **6 41** |
| 11 | 5 17 | **7 12** | 5 23 | **7 06** | 5 27 | **7 03** | 5 29 | **7 01** | 5 27 | **7 03** |
| 21 | 5 12 | **7 16** | 5 14 | **7 13** | 5 15 | **7 13** | 5 12 | **7 17** | 5 02 | **7 26** |
| Mar. 1 | 5 07 | **7 18** | 5 07 | **7 19** | 5 04 | **7 22** | 4 56 | **7 30** | 4 40 | **7 47** |
| 11 | 4 59 | **7 22** | 4 55 | **7 25** | 4 48 | **7 33** | 4 35 | **7 47** | 4 08 | **8 14** |
| 21 | 4 50 | **7 25** | 4 43 | **7 32** | 4 31 | **7 44** | 4 11 | **8 05** | 3 33 | **8 44** |
| Apr. 1 | 4 40 | **7 28** | 4 29 | **7 40** | 4 11 | **7 57** | 3 43 | **8 26** | 2 47 | **9 24** |
| 11 | 4 30 | **7 32** | 4 15 | **7 47** | 3 53 | **8 10** | 3 16 | **8 48** | 1 56 | **10 11** |
| 21 | 4 21 | **7 36** | 4 02 | **7 56** | 3 35 | **8 24** | 2 48 | **9 12** | | |

| Date | 20° | | 30° | | 40° | | 50° | | 60° | |
|---|---|---|---|---|---|---|---|---|---|---|
| | Morn. | Even. | Morn. | Even. | Morn. | Even. | Morn. | Even. | Morn. | Even. |
| | h m | h m | h m | h m | h m | h m | h m | h m | h m | h m |
| May 1 | 4 13 | **7 42** | 3 50 | **8 04** | 3 17 | **8 38** | 2 17 | **9 39** | | |
| 11 | 4 06 | **7 47** | 3 40 | **8 14** | 3 00 | **8 53** | 1 45 | **10 10** | | |
| 21 | 4 01 | **7 53** | 3 31 | **8 22** | 2 46 | **9 08** | 1 10 | **10 47** | | |
| June 1 | 3 57 | **7 59** | 3 25 | **8 31** | 2 35 | **9 22** | | | | |
| 11 | 3 56 | **8 03** | 3 22 | **8 37** | 2 29 | **9 31** | | | | |
| 21 | 3 57 | **8 06** | 3 23 | **8 41** | 2 28 | **9 36** | | | | |
| July 1 | 4 00 | **8 07** | 3 26 | **8 41** | 2 32 | **9 35** | | | | |
| 11 | 4 05 | **8 06** | 3 32 | **8 38** | 2 42 | **9 28** | | | | |
| 21 | 4 10 | **8 03** | 3 40 | **8 32** | 2 54 | **9 18** | 1 12 | **10 57** | | |
| Aug. 1 | 4 16 | **7 56** | 3 49 | **8 23** | 3 09 | **9 02** | 1 53 | **10 17** | | |
| 11 | 4 21 | **7 49** | 3 58 | **8 12** | 3 24 | **8 45** | 2 23 | **9 45** | | |
| 21 | 4 25 | **7 41** | 4 06 | **7 59** | 3 38 | **8 27** | 2 50 | **9 15** | | |
| Sept. 1 | 4 29 | **7 30** | 4 14 | **7 45** | 3 52 | **8 07** | 3 15 | **8 43** | 1 55 | **10 01** |
| 11 | 4 33 | **7 20** | 4 21 | **7 31** | 4 04 | **7 48** | 3 36 | **8 16** | 2 39 | **9 11** |
| 21 | 4 35 | **7 10** | 4 28 | **7 18** | 4 15 | **7 30** | 3 54 | **7 50** | 3 14 | **8 30** |
| Oct. 1 | 4 38 | **7 01** | 4 34 | **7 05** | 4 26 | **7 12** | 4 12 | **7 26** | 3 44 | **7 54** |
| 11 | 4 40 | **6 53** | 4 40 | **6 53** | 4 36 | **6 56** | 4 28 | **7 04** | 4 10 | **7 22** |
| 21 | 4 43 | **6 46** | 4 46 | **6 43** | 4 46 | **6 42** | 4 43 | **6 45** | 4 34 | **6 53** |
| Nov. 1 | 4 47 | **6 40** | 4 53 | **6 34** | 4 57 | **6 29** | 5 00 | **6 26** | 4 59 | **6 27** |
| 11 | 4 51 | **6 37** | 5 00 | **6 28** | 5 07 | **6 20** | 5 14 | **6 13** | 5 20 | **6 07** |
| 21 | 4 55 | **6 36** | 5 07 | **6 25** | 5 17 | **6 14** | 5 28 | **6 04** | 5 39 | **5 52** |
| Dec. 1 | 5 01 | **6 37** | 5 14 | **6 24** | 5 26 | **6 12** | 5 40 | **5 58** | 5 55 | **5 42** |
| 11 | 5 06 | **6 40** | 5 20 | **6 26** | 5 34 | **6 12** | 5 49 | **5 57** | 6 08 | **5 38** |
| 21 | 5 12 | **6 45** | 5 26 | **6 30** | 5 41 | **6 16** | 5 56 | **6 00** | 6 16 | **5 41** |
| 31 | 5 16 | **6 50** | 5 30 | **6 36** | 5 44 | **6 22** | 6 00 | **6 07** | 6 18 | **5 48** |

# Total Solar Eclipses, 1950-2010

Total solar eclipses actually take place nearly as often as total lunar eclipses; they occur at a rate of about 3 every 4 years, while total lunar eclipses come at a rate of about 5 every 6 years. The major difference in the likelihood of seeing one type over the other is that total lunar eclipses are visible over at least half the Earth, while total solar eclipse can be seen only along a very narrow path up to a few hundred mi wide and a few thousand mi long. Total solar eclipses are thus a rarity for most people. Unlike lunar eclipses, solar eclipses can be dangerous to observe. This is not because the Sun emits more potent rays during an eclipse than at other times, but because the Sun is always dangerous to observe directly and people are particularly likely to stare at it during a solar eclipse.

| Date | Duration[1] m | s | Width (miles) | Path of Totality |
|---|---|---|---|---|
| 1950, Sept. 12 | 1 | 13 | 83 | Arctic Ocean, Siberia, Pacific Ocean |
| 1952, Feb. 25 | 3 | 09 | 85 | Africa, Middle East, Soviet Union |
| 1954, June 30 | 2 | 35 | 95 | U.S., Canada, Iceland, Europe, Middle East |
| 1955, June 20 | 7 | 07 | 157 | SE Asia, Philippines, Pacific Ocean |
| 1956, June 8 | 4 | 44 | 266 | South Pacific Ocean |
| 1958, Oct. 12 | 5 | 10 | 129 | Pacific Ocean, Chile, Argentina |
| 1959, Oct. 2 | 3 | 01 | 75 | New England, Atlantic Ocean, Africa |
| 1961, Feb. 15 | 2 | 45 | 160 | Europe, Soviet Union |
| 1962, Feb. 5 | 4 | 08 | 91 | Borneo, New Guinea, Pacific Ocean |
| 1963, July 20 | 1 | 39 | 63 | Pacific Ocean, Alaska, Canada, Maine |
| 1965, May 30 | 5 | 15 | 123 | New Zealand, Pacific Ocean |
| 1966, Nov. 12 | 1 | 57 | 52 | Pacific Ocean, South America, Atlantic Ocean |
| 1968, Sept. 22 | 0 | 39 | 64 | Soviet Union, China |
| 1970, Mar. 7 | 3 | 27 | 95 | Pacific Ocean, Mexico, Eastern U.S., Canada |
| 1972, July 10 | 2 | 35 | 109 | Siberia, Alaska, Canada |
| 1973, June 30 | 7 | 03 | 159 | Atlantic Ocean, Central Africa, Indian Ocean |
| 1974, June 20 | 5 | 08 | 214 | Indian Ocean, Australia |
| 1976, Oct. 23 | 4 | 46 | 123 | Africa, Indian Ocean, Australia |
| 1977, Oct. 12 | 2 | 37 | 61 | Pacific Ocean, Colombia, Venezuela |
| 1979, Feb. 26 | 2 | 49 | 185 | NW U.S., Canada, Greenland |
| 1980, Feb. 16 | 4 | 08 | 92 | Africa, Indian Ocean, India, Burma, China |
| 1981, July 31 | 2 | 02 | 67 | Soviet Union, Pacific Ocean |
| 1983, June 11 | 5 | 10 | 123 | Indian Ocean, Indonesia, New Guinea |
| 1984, Nov. 22 | 1 | 59 | 53 | New Guinea, Pacific Ocean |
| 1985, Nov. 12 | 1 | 58 | 430 | Antarctica |
| 1986, Oct. 3h | 0 | 01 | 1 | North Atlantic Ocean |
| 1987, Mar. 29h | 0 | 07 | 3 | South Atlantic Ocean, Africa |
| 1988, Mar. 18 | 3 | 46 | 104 | Sumatra, Borneo, Philippines, Pacific Ocean |
| 1990, July 22 | 2 | 32 | 125 | Finland, Soviet Union, Aleutian Islands |
| 1991, July 11 | 6 | 53 | 160 | Hawaii, Mexico, Central America, Colombia, Brazil |
| 1992, June 30 | 5 | 20 | 182 | South Atlantic Ocean |
| 1994, Nov. 3 | 4 | 23 | 117 | Peru, Bolivia, Paraguay, Brazil |
| 1995, Oct. 24 | 2 | 09 | 48 | Iran, India, SE Asia |
| 1997, Mar. 9 | 2 | 50 | 221 | Mongolia, Siberia |
| 1998, Feb. 26 | 4 | 08 | 94 | Galapagos Islands, Panama, Colombia, Venezuela |
| 1999, Aug. 11 | 2 | 22 | 69 | Europe, Middle East, India |
| 2001, June 21 | 4 | 56 | 125 | Atlantic Ocean, Africa, Madagascar |
| 2002, Dec. 4 | 2 | 04 | 54 | South Africa, Indian Ocean, Australia |
| 2003, Nov. 23 | 1 | 57 | 338 | Antarctica |
| 2005, Apr. 8h | 0 | 42 | 17 | Pacific Ocean, NW South America |

*(continued)*

## Total Solar Eclipses *(continued)*

| Date | Duration m | Duration s | Width (miles) | Path of Totality |
|---|---|---|---|---|
| 2006, Mar. 29 | 4 | 07 | 114 | Atlantic Ocean, Africa, Asia |
| 2008, Aug. 1 | 2 | 27 | 144 | Arctic Ocean, Asia |
| 2009, July 22 | 6 | 39 | 160 | Asia, Pacific Ocean |
| 2010, July 11 | 5 | 20 | 160 | Atlantic Ocean |

h = indicates annular-total hybrid eclipse. (1) Duration refers to length of time at optimal viewing area.

## Calculation of Rise Times

The Daily Calendar pages contain rise and set times for the Sun and Moon for the Greenwich Meridian at north latitudes 20°, 30°, 40°, 50°, and 60°. You probably live somewhere west of the Greenwich meridian, 0° longitude, and within the range of latitudes in the table. Notice that from day to day, the values for the Sun at any particular latitude do not change very much. This slow variation for the Sun means that no important correction needs to be made from one day to the next, once a proper correction for your latitude has been made. Thus, whenever the Sun rises or sets at the 0° meridian, that will also be the time of that phenomenon at your Standard Time meridian. Any correction necessary for you to be able to observe that phenomenon from your location will be to account for your distance from the Standard Time meridian and for your latitude.

The Moon, however, moves its own diameter, about one-half degree, in an hour, or about 12.5° in one complete turn of the Earth—one day. Most of this is eastward against the background stars of the sky, but some is also north or south of the equator. If there is little change on the same day of the times over the range of latitudes, the Moon is near the celestial equator. All this motion considerably affects the times of rise or set, as you can see from the adjacent entries in the table. Thus, it is necessary to take your longitude into account in addition to your latitude. If you have no need for total accuracy, simply note that the time will be between the 4 values you find surrounding your location and the dates of interest.

The process of finding more accurate corrections is called interpolation. In the example, linear interpolation involving simple differences is used. In extreme cases, higher order interpolation should be used. If such cases are important to you, it is suggested that you plot the times, draw smooth curves through the plots, and interpolate by eye between the relevant curves. Some people find this exercise fun.

Let's find the time of the moonrise for the June Full Moon at Lima, OH.

First, where is Lima, OH? Find Lima's latitude and longitude in the "Latitude, Longitude, and Altitude of U.S. and Canadian Cities" table found in the World Exploration and Geography section of *The World Almanac.* You must also know the time zone in which the city is located, which you can estimate from the "International Time Zones" map in the map section of *The World Almanac.*

**I.** Lima, OH: 40° 44′ 35′′ N
84° 06′ 20′′ W

**IA.** Convert these values to decimals:

35/60 = 0.58
44 + 0.58 = 44.58
44.58/60 = 0.74
40 + 0.74 = 40.74 N
20/60 = 0.33
6 + 0.33 = 6.33
6.33/60 = 0.11
84 + 0.11 = 84.11 W

**IB.** Fraction Lima lies between 40° and 50°:

40.58 – 40 = 0.58; 0.58/10 = 0.058

**IC.** Fraction world must turn between Greenwich and Rapid City:

84.11/360 = 0.234

**ID.** Lima is in the Eastern Standard Time zone and the EST meridian is 75°, thus 84.11 is 84.11 – 75 = 9.11° west of the East Standard Meridian. In 24 hours, there are 24 × 60 = 1,440 minutes; 1,440/360 = 4 minutes for every degree around the Earth. So events happen 4 × 9.11 = 36.4 minutes later in Lima than at the 75° meridian. (If the location is east of the Standard Meridian, events happen earlier.)

**IE.** The values IB and IC are interpolates for Lima; ID is the time correction from local to Standard time for Lima. These values need never be calculated again for Lima.

**IIA.** From the table of Moon Phases, 1997, we see that June's Full Moon occurs on June 20. We need the Greenwich times for moonrise at latitudes 40° and 50°, and for June 20 and 21, the day of the Full Moon and the next day. These values are found in the Astronomy Daily Calendar 1997: we then compute the difference between the two latitudes.

| | 40° | Diff. | 50° |
|---|---|---|---|
| June 20 | 19:07 | 0:31 | 19:38 |
| June 21 | 20:04 | 0:29 | 20:33 |

**IIB.** We want IB and the June 20 time difference:

0.074 × 31 = 2.3

Add this to the June 20, 40° rise time:

19:07 + 2.3 = 19:09.3

And for June 21:

0.074 × 29 = 2.1

Add this to the June 21, 40° rise time:

20:04 + 2.1 = 20:06.1

These 2 times are for the latitude of Lima, but for the Greenwich meridian.

**IIC.** To get the time for Lima meridian, take the difference between these 2 times just determined,

20:06.1 – 19:09.3 = 56.8 minutes,

and find what fraction of this 24-hour change took place while the Earth turned between Greenwich and Lima, 0.234 (See IC)

56.9 × 0.234 = 13.3 minutes after 19:09.3

Thus 19:09.3 + 13.3 = 19:22.6 is the time the Full Moon will rise in the local time of Lima.

**IID.** But this happens 36.4 minutes (See ID) later than EST clock time at Lima, thus

19:22.6 + 36.4 = 19:59 EST.

But this is summer, and daylight time is in effect;

19:59 + 1:00 = 20:59 EDT is the rise time for the Full Moon at Lima the evening of June 20, 1997. Can you confirm that sunset will be at 21:12?

**1st Month** **January 1997** **31 days**

Greenwich Mean Time

**NOTE**: For each day, times on first line are for Sun. *Italic* times on second line are for *Moon*. Degrees are North Latitude.

Moon Phases: FM = full moon; LQ = last quarter; NM = new moon; FQ = first quarter. Sun's declination is in degrees; Sun's distance is in Astronomical Units.

**CAUTION**: Must be converted to local time. For instructions see page 462.

| Day of month, of week, *of year* | Sun on Meridian *Moon Phase* h m s | Sun's Declination ° ′ *Distance* | 20° Rise Sun *Moon* h m | 20° Set Sun *Moon* h m | 30° Rise Sun *Moon* h m | 30° Set Sun *Moon* h m | 40° Rise Sun *Moon* h m | 40° Set Sun *Moon* h m | 50° Rise Sun *Moon* h m | 50° Set Sun *Moon* h m | 60° Rise Sun *Moon* h m | 60° Set Sun *Moon* h m |
|---|---|---|---|---|---|---|---|---|---|---|---|---|
| 1 WE | 12 03 39 | -23 01 | 6 35 | 17 32 | 6 56 | 17 11 | 7 22 | 16 46 | 7 59 | 16 09 | 9 02 | 15 05 |
| *1* | | *.9832* | *24 00* | *11 29* | *none* | *11 28* | *none* | *11 26* | *none* | *11 24* | *none* | *11 20* |
| 2 TH | 12 04 07 | -22 56 | 6 35 | 17 33 | 6 56 | 17 12 | 7 22 | 16 46 | 7 58 | 16 10 | 9 02 | 15 07 |
| *2* | *1 46 LQ* | *.9832* | *none* | *12 07* | *0 03* | *12 03* | *0 07* | *11 57* | *0 13* | *11 49* | *0 21* | *11 36* |
| 3 FR | 12 04 34 | -22 50 | 6 36 | 17 33 | 6 56 | 17 13 | 7 22 | 16 47 | 7 58 | 16 11 | 9 01 | 15 08 |
| *3* | | *.9832* | *0 51* | *12 48* | *0 57* | *12 39* | *1 06* | *12 29* | *1 17* | *12 16* | *1 35* | *11 54* |
| 4 SA | 12 05 02 | -22 44 | 6 36 | 17 34 | 6 57 | 17 14 | 7 22 | 16 48 | 7 58 | 16 12 | 9 00 | 15 10 |
| *4* | | *.9832* | *1 44* | *13 31* | *1 54* | *13 20* | *2 06* | *13 05* | *2 23* | *12 46* | *2 51* | *12 16* |
| 5 SU | 12 05 29 | -22 38 | 6 36 | 17 35 | 6 57 | 17 14 | 7 22 | 16 49 | 7 58 | 16 13 | 9 00 | 15 12 |
| *5* | | *.9832* | *2 39* | *14 18* | *2 52* | *14 04* | *3 08* | *13 47* | *3 31* | *13 23* | *4 07* | *12 44* |
| 6 MO | 12 05 55 | -22 31 | 6 37 | 17 35 | 6 57 | 17 15 | 7 22 | 16 50 | 7 58 | 16 15 | 8 59 | 15 13 |
| *6* | | *.9833* | *3 37* | *15 10* | *3 53* | *14 54* | *4 12* | *14 34* | *4 39* | *14 06* | *5 23* | *13 21* |
| 7 TU | 12 06 21 | -22 23 | 6 37 | 17 36 | 6 57 | 17 16 | 7 22 | 16 51 | 7 57 | 16 16 | 8 58 | 15 15 |
| *7* | | *.9833* | *4 37* | *16 08* | *4 54* | *15 50* | *5 15* | *15 29* | *5 45* | *14 59* | *6 34* | *14 09* |
| 8 WE | 12 06 47 | -22 16 | 6 37 | 17 37 | 6 57 | 17 17 | 7 22 | 16 52 | 7 57 | 16 17 | 8 57 | 15 17 |
| *8* | | *.9833* | *5 37* | *17 09* | *5 54* | *16 52* | *6 16* | *16 31* | *6 45* | *16 01* | *7 35* | *15 13* |
| 9 TH | 12 07 12 | -22 07 | 6 37 | 17 37 | 6 57 | 17 18 | 7 22 | 16 53 | 7 56 | 16 18 | 8 56 | 15 19 |
| *9* | *4 27 NM* | *.9833* | *6 36* | *18 13* | *6 52* | *17 58* | *7 12* | *17 39* | *7 39* | *17 13* | *8 24* | *16 30* |
| 10 FR | 12 07 37 | -21 59 | 6 37 | 17 38 | 6 57 | 17 18 | 7 22 | 16 54 | 7 56 | 16 20 | 8 54 | 15 21 |
| *10* | | *.9834* | *7 33* | *19 17* | *7 46* | *19 05* | *8 03* | *18 50* | *8 26* | *18 29* | *9 02* | *17 55* |
| 11 SA | 12 08 00 | -21 50 | 6 38 | 17 39 | 6 57 | 17 19 | 7 21 | 16 55 | 7 55 | 16 21 | 8 53 | 15 23 |
| *11* | | *.9834* | *8 26* | *20 21* | *8 36* | *20 13* | *8 48* | *20 02* | *9 05* | *19 48* | *9 32* | *19 25* |
| 12 SU | 12 08 24 | -21 40 | 6 38 | 17 39 | 6 57 | 17 20 | 7 21 | 16 56 | 7 55 | 16 22 | 8 52 | 15 25 |
| *12* | | *.9834* | *9 15* | *21 23* | *9 21* | *21 19* | *9 29* | *21 13* | *9 40* | *21 06* | *9 55* | *20 54* |
| 13 MO | 12 08 46 | -21 30 | 6 38 | 17 40 | 6 57 | 17 21 | 7 21 | 16 57 | 7 54 | 16 24 | 8 51 | 15 27 |
| *13* | | *.9835* | *10 02* | *22 23* | *10 04* | *22 23* | *10 07* | *22 23* | *10 11* | *22 22* | *10 16* | *22 22* |
| 14 TU | 12 09 08 | -21 20 | 6 38 | 17 41 | 6 57 | 17 22 | 7 20 | 16 58 | 7 53 | 16 25 | 8 49 | 15 30 |
| *14* | | *.9835* | *10 47* | *23 21* | *10 45* | *23 25* | *10 43* | *23 30* | *10 40* | *23 36* | *10 35* | *23 47* |
| 15 WE | 12 09 30 | -21 09 | 6 38 | 17 41 | 6 57 | 17 23 | 7 20 | 16 59 | 7 53 | 16 27 | 8 48 | 15 32 |
| *15* | *20 03 FQ* | *.9836* | *11 31* | *none* | *11 25* | *none* | *11 18* | *none* | *11 09* | *none* | *10 55* | *none* |
| 16 TH | 12 09 50 | -20 58 | 6 38 | 17 42 | 6 57 | 17 23 | 7 20 | 17 00 | 7 52 | 16 28 | 8 46 | 15 34 |
| *16* | | *.9836* | *12 15* | *0 18* | *12 06* | *0 26* | *11 54* | *0 35* | *11 39* | *0 48* | *11 16* | *1 08* |
| 17 FR | 12 10 10 | -20 46 | 6 38 | 17 43 | 6 56 | 17 24 | 7 19 | 17 01 | 7 51 | 16 30 | 8 44 | 15 37 |
| *17* | | *.9837* | *13 00* | *1 13* | *12 47* | *1 25* | *12 32* | *1 38* | *12 12* | *1 57* | *11 40* | *2 27* |
| 18 SA | 12 10 30 | -20 34 | 6 38 | 17 43 | 6 56 | 17 25 | 7 19 | 17 03 | 7 50 | 16 31 | 8 43 | 15 39 |
| *18* | | *.9838* | *13 46* | *2 08* | *13 31* | *2 22* | *13 13* | *2 39* | *12 48* | *3 02* | *12 08* | *3 40* |
| 19 SU | 12 10 48 | -20 22 | 6 38 | 17 44 | 6 56 | 17 26 | 7 18 | 17 04 | 7 49 | 16 33 | 8 41 | 15 41 |
| *19* | | *.9838* | *14 33* | *3 01* | *14 17* | *3 17* | *13 56* | *3 36* | *13 29* | *4 04* | *12 43* | *4 48* |
| 20 MO | 12 11 06 | -20 09 | 6 38 | 17 45 | 6 56 | 17 27 | 7 18 | 17 05 | 7 48 | 16 34 | 8 39 | 15 44 |
| *20* | | *.9839* | *15 21* | *3 53* | *15 05* | *4 10* | *14 43* | *4 31* | *14 14* | *5 00* | *13 26* | *5 48* |
| 21 TU | 12 11 23 | -19 56 | 6 38 | 17 45 | 6 55 | 17 28 | 7 17 | 17 06 | 7 47 | 16 36 | 8 37 | 15 46 |
| *21* | | *.9840* | *16 11* | *4 43* | *15 54* | *4 59* | *15 34* | *5 20* | *15 05* | *5 50* | *14 17* | *6 38* |
| 22 WE | 12 11 39 | -19 43 | 6 38 | 17 46 | 6 55 | 17 29 | 7 16 | 17 07 | 7 46 | 16 38 | 8 35 | 15 49 |
| *22* | | *.9841* | *17 01* | *5 30* | *16 45* | *5 46* | *16 26* | *6 06* | *15 59* | *6 33* | *15 15* | *7 18* |
| 23 TH | 12 11 54 | -19 29 | 6 38 | 17 46 | 6 55 | 17 29 | 7 16 | 17 08 | 7 45 | 16 39 | 8 33 | 15 51 |
| *23* | *15 12 FM* | *.9842* | *17 51* | *6 15* | *17 37* | *6 29* | *17 20* | *6 47* | *16 57* | *7 12* | *16 19* | *7 51* |
| 24 FR | 12 12 09 | -19 15 | 6 37 | 17 47 | 6 54 | 17 30 | 7 15 | 17 10 | 7 44 | 16 41 | 8 31 | 15 54 |
| *24* | | *.9843* | *18 40* | *6 57* | *18 29* | *7 09* | *18 15* | *7 24* | *17 57* | *7 45* | *17 27* | *8 17* |
| 25 SA | 12 12 23 | -19 00 | 6 37 | 17 48 | 6 54 | 17 31 | 7 14 | 17 11 | 7 43 | 16 42 | 8 29 | 15 56 |
| *25* | | *.9844* | *19 29* | *7 37* | *19 21* | *7 46* | *19 11* | *7 58* | *18 57* | *8 14* | *18 35* | *8 38* |
| 26 SU | 12 12 36 | -18 45 | 6 37 | 17 48 | 6 53 | 17 32 | 7 14 | 17 12 | 7 42 | 16 44 | 8 27 | 15 59 |
| *26* | | *.9845* | *20 18* | *8 15* | *20 13* | *8 22* | *20 06* | *8 30* | *19 58* | *8 40* | *19 45* | *8 57* |
| 27 MO | 12 12 48 | -18 30 | 6 37 | 17 49 | 6 53 | 17 33 | 7 13 | 17 13 | 7 40 | 16 46 | 8 25 | 16 01 |
| *27* | | *.9846* | *21 06* | *8 52* | *21 04* | *8 56* | *21 02* | *9 00* | *20 59* | *9 05* | *20 55* | *9 13* |
| 28 TU | 12 12 59 | -18 14 | 6 37 | 17 50 | 6 53 | 17 34 | 7 12 | 17 14 | 7 39 | 16 47 | 8 23 | 16 04 |
| *28* | | *.9847* | *21 54* | *9 29* | *21 56* | *9 29* | *21 58* | *9 29* | *22 01* | *9 29* | *22 06* | *9 29* |
| 29 WE | 12 13 10 | -17 58 | 6 36 | 17 50 | 6 52 | 17 35 | 7 11 | 17 16 | 7 38 | 16 49 | 8 21 | 16 06 |
| *29* | | *.9849* | *22 44* | *10 06* | *22 49* | *10 03* | *22 55* | *9 59* | *23 04* | *9 53* | *23 18* | *9 44* |
| 30 TH | 12 13 20 | -17 42 | 6 36 | 17 51 | 6 51 | 17 36 | 7 10 | 17 17 | 7 36 | 16 51 | 8 18 | 16 09 |
| *30* | | *.9850* | *23 34* | *10 45* | *23 43* | *10 38* | *23 53* | *10 30* | *none* | *10 19* | *none* | *10 02* |
| 31 FR | 12 13 29 | -17 26 | 6 36 | 17 51 | 6 51 | 17 36 | 7 10 | 17 18 | 7 35 | 16 53 | 8 16 | 16 12 |
| *31* | *19 41 LQ* | *.9851* | *none* | *11 26* | *none* | *11 16* | *none* | *11 03* | *0 08* | *10 47* | *0 31* | *10 21* |

## 2d Month — February 1997 — 28 days

Greenwich Mean Time

**NOTE**: For each day, times on first line are for Sun. *Italic* times on second line are for *Moon*.
Degrees are North Latitude.

Moon Phases: FM = full moon; LQ = last quarter; NM = new moon; FQ = first quarter.
Sun's declination is in degrees; Sun's distance is in Astronomical Units.

**CAUTION**: Must be converted to local time. For instructions see page 462.

| Day of month, of week, *of year* | Sun on Meridian *Moon Phase* h m s | Sun's Declination ° ′ *Distance* | 20° Rise Sun *Moon* h m | 20° Set Sun *Moon* h m | 30° Rise Sun *Moon* h m | 30° Set Sun *Moon* h m | 40° Rise Sun *Moon* h m | 40° Set Sun *Moon* h m | 50° Rise Sun *Moon* h m | 50° Set Sun *Moon* h m | 60° Rise Sun *Moon* h m | 60° Set Sun *Moon* h m |
|---|---|---|---|---|---|---|---|---|---|---|---|---|
| 1 SA | 12 13 37 | -17 09 | 6 36 | 17 52 | 6 50 | 17 37 | 7 09 | 17 19 | 7 34 | 16 54 | 8 14 | 16 14 |
| *32* | | *.9853* | *0 27* | *12 09* | *0 39* | *11 57* | *0 53* | *11 41* | *1 13* | *11 19* | *1 45* | *10 45* |
| 2 SU | 12 13 45 | -16 52 | 6 35 | 17 53 | 6 50 | 17 38 | 7 08 | 17 20 | 7 32 | 16 56 | 8 11 | 16 17 |
| *33* | | *.9854* | *1 22* | *12 58* | *1 36* | *12 42* | *1 54* | *12 24* | *2 18* | *11 58* | *2 58* | *11 16* |
| 3 MO | 12 13 51 | -16 34 | 6 35 | 17 53 | 6 49 | 17 39 | 7 07 | 17 22 | 7 31 | 16 58 | 8 09 | 16 20 |
| *34* | | *.9856* | *2 19* | *13 50* | *2 35* | *13 34* | *2 55* | *13 13* | *3 23* | *12 44* | *4 10* | *11 57* |
| 4 TU | 12 13 57 | -16 16 | 6 34 | 17 54 | 6 48 | 17 40 | 7 06 | 17 23 | 7 29 | 16 59 | 8 07 | 16 22 |
| *35* | | *.9858* | *3 17* | *14 48* | *3 34* | *14 31* | *3 56* | *14 09* | *4 25* | *13 40* | *5 15* | *12 50* |
| 5 WE | 12 14 02 | -15 58 | 6 34 | 17 54 | 6 48 | 17 41 | 7 05 | 17 24 | 7 28 | 17 01 | 8 04 | 16 25 |
| *36* | | *.9859* | *4 16* | *15 49* | *4 33* | *15 33* | *4 53* | *15 13* | *5 22* | *14 45* | *6 10* | *13 59* |
| 6 TH | 12 14 06 | -15 40 | 6 34 | 17 55 | 6 47 | 17 41 | 7 04 | 17 25 | 7 26 | 17 03 | 8 02 | 16 27 |
| *37* | | *.9861* | *5 14* | *16 54* | *5 29* | *16 40* | *5 47* | *16 22* | *6 13* | *15 58* | *6 54* | *15 19* |
| 7 FR | 12 14 10 | -15 21 | 6 33 | 17 55 | 6 46 | 17 42 | 7 02 | 17 26 | 7 24 | 17 05 | 7 59 | 16 30 |
| *38* | *15 07 NM* | *.9862* | *6 09* | *17 59* | *6 21* | *17 48* | *6 36* | *17 35* | *6 56* | *17 17* | *7 28* | *16 48* |
| 8 SA | 12 14 12 | -15 03 | 6 33 | 17 56 | 6 46 | 17 43 | 7 01 | 17 28 | 7 23 | 17 06 | 7 57 | 16 33 |
| *39* | | *.9864* | *7 02* | *19 04* | *7 10* | *18 57* | *7 21* | *18 49* | *7 35* | *18 38* | *7 56* | *18 20* |
| 9 SU | 12 14 14 | -14 44 | 6 32 | 17 56 | 6 45 | 17 44 | 7 00 | 17 29 | 7 21 | 17 08 | 7 54 | 16 35 |
| *40* | | *.9866* | *7 52* | *20 07* | *7 56* | *20 05* | *8 01* | *20 02* | *8 08* | *19 58* | *8 19* | *19 52* |
| 10 MO | 12 14 15 | -14 24 | 6 32 | 17 57 | 6 44 | 17 45 | 6 59 | 17 30 | 7 19 | 17 10 | 7 51 | 16 38 |
| *41* | | *.9868* | *8 39* | *21 08* | *8 39* | *21 10* | *8 40* | *21 13* | *8 40* | *21 16* | *8 40* | *21 21* |
| 11 TU | 12 14 16 | -14 05 | 6 31 | 17 57 | 6 43 | 17 46 | 6 58 | 17 31 | 7 18 | 17 12 | 7 49 | 16 41 |
| *42* | | *.9869* | *9 26* | *22 08* | *9 22* | *22 14* | *9 17* | *22 21* | *9 10* | *22 32* | *9 01* | *22 47* |
| 12 WE | 12 14 15 | -13 45 | 6 31 | 17 58 | 6 43 | 17 46 | 6 57 | 17 32 | 7 16 | 17 13 | 7 46 | 16 43 |
| *43* | | *.9871* | *10 11* | *23 06* | *10 04* | *23 16* | *9 54* | *23 28* | *9 41* | *23 44* | *9 22* | *none* |
| 13 TH | 12 14 14 | -13 25 | 6 30 | 17 58 | 6 42 | 17 47 | 6 56 | 17 34 | 7 14 | 17 15 | 7 43 | 16 46 |
| *44* | | *.9873* | *10 57* | *none* | *10 46* | *none* | *10 32* | *none* | *10 14* | *none* | *9 45* | *0 10* |
| 14 FR | 12 14 12 | -13 04 | 6 30 | 17 59 | 6 41 | 17 48 | 6 54 | 17 35 | 7 12 | 17 17 | 7 41 | 16 49 |
| *45* | *8 59 FQ* | *.9875* | *11 44* | *0 02* | *11 30* | *0 15* | *11 13* | *0 31* | *10 49* | *0 52* | *10 13* | *1 27* |
| 15 SA | 12 14 09 | -12 44 | 6 29 | 17 59 | 6 40 | 17 49 | 6 53 | 17 36 | 7 11 | 17 18 | 7 38 | 16 51 |
| *46* | | *.9877* | *12 31* | *0 57* | *12 15* | *1 12* | *11 56* | *1 30* | *11 29* | *1 56* | *10 46* | *2 38* |
| 16 SU | 12 14 06 | -12 23 | 6 29 | 18 00 | 6 39 | 17 50 | 6 52 | 17 37 | 7 09 | 17 20 | 7 35 | 16 54 |
| *47* | | *.9879* | *13 19* | *1 49* | *13 02* | *2 06* | *12 42* | *2 26* | *12 13* | *2 54* | *11 26* | *3 41* |
| 17 MO | 12 14 01 | -12 02 | 6 28 | 18 00 | 6 38 | 17 50 | 6 50 | 17 38 | 7 07 | 17 22 | 7 33 | 16 56 |
| *48* | | *.9881* | *14 08* | *2 40* | *13 51* | *2 56* | *13 31* | *3 17* | *13 02* | *3 46* | *12 14* | *4 34* |
| 18 TU | 12 13 56 | -11 41 | 6 27 | 18 01 | 6 37 | 17 51 | 6 49 | 17 39 | 7 05 | 17 24 | 7 30 | 16 59 |
| *49* | | *.9883* | *14 58* | *3 27* | *14 42* | *3 44* | *14 22* | *4 04* | *13 54* | *4 32* | *13 09* | *5 18* |
| 19 WE | 12 13 51 | -11 20 | 6 27 | 18 01 | 6 36 | 17 52 | 6 48 | 17 41 | 7 03 | 17 25 | 7 27 | 17 02 |
| *50* | | *.9885* | *15 47* | *4 13* | *15 33* | *4 28* | *15 15* | *4 46* | *14 51* | *5 12* | *14 11* | *5 53* |
| 20 TH | 12 13 44 | -10 59 | 6 26 | 18 02 | 6 35 | 17 53 | 6 46 | 17 42 | 7 01 | 17 27 | 7 24 | 17 04 |
| *51* | | *.9887* | *16 37* | *4 56* | *16 25* | *5 09* | *16 10* | *5 25* | *15 49* | *5 46* | *15 17* | *6 21* |
| 21 FR | 12 13 38 | -10 37 | 6 26 | 18 02 | 6 34 | 17 53 | 6 45 | 17 43 | 6 59 | 17 29 | 7 21 | 17 07 |
| *52* | | *.9889* | *17 25* | *5 36* | *17 16* | *5 47* | *17 05* | *6 00* | *16 49* | *6 17* | *16 25* | *6 44* |
| 22 SA | 12 13 30 | -10 15 | 6 25 | 18 02 | 6 33 | 17 54 | 6 44 | 17 44 | 6 57 | 17 30 | 7 19 | 17 09 |
| *53* | *10 28 FM* | *.9891* | *18 14* | *6 15* | *18 08* | *6 23* | *18 00* | *6 32* | *17 50* | *6 44* | *17 34* | *7 03* |
| 23 SU | 12 13 22 | - 9 53 | 6 24 | 18 03 | 6 32 | 17 55 | 6 42 | 17 45 | 6 55 | 17 32 | 7 16 | 17 12 |
| *54* | | *.9893* | *19 02* | *6 53* | *19 00* | *6 57* | *18 56* | *7 03* | *18 51* | *7 10* | *18 44* | *7 21* |
| 24 MO | 12 13 13 | - 9 31 | 6 24 | 18 03 | 6 31 | 17 56 | 6 41 | 17 46 | 6 54 | 17 34 | 7 13 | 17 15 |
| *55* | | *.9896* | *19 51* | *7 30* | *19 52* | *7 31* | *19 52* | *7 32* | *19 53* | *7 34* | *19 55* | *7 37* |
| 25 TU | 12 13 03 | - 9 09 | 6 23 | 18 04 | 6 30 | 17 56 | 6 39 | 17 47 | 6 52 | 17 35 | 7 10 | 17 17 |
| *56* | | *.9898* | *20 40* | *8 07* | *20 44* | *8 05* | *20 49* | *8 02* | *20 56* | *7 58* | *21 06* | *7 53* |
| 26 WE | 12 12 53 | - 8 47 | 6 22 | 18 04 | 6 29 | 17 57 | 6 38 | 17 48 | 6 50 | 17 37 | 7 07 | 17 20 |
| *57* | | *.9900* | *21 30* | *8 45* | *21 37* | *8 39* | *21 46* | *8 33* | *21 59* | *8 24* | *22 18* | *8 09* |
| 27 TH | 12 12 43 | - 8 24 | 6 21 | 18 04 | 6 28 | 17 58 | 6 36 | 17 50 | 6 47 | 17 39 | 7 04 | 17 22 |
| *58* | | *.9903* | *22 21* | *9 25* | *22 32* | *9 16* | *22 45* | *9 05* | *23 02* | *8 51* | *23 31* | *8 28* |
| 28 FR | 12 12 32 | - 8 02 | 6 21 | 18 05 | 6 27 | 17 58 | 6 35 | 17 51 | 6 45 | 17 40 | 7 01 | 17 25 |
| *59* | | *.9905* | *23 14* | *10 07* | *23 27* | *9 55* | *23 44* | *9 41* | *none* | *9 21* | *none* | *8 50* |

**3d Month** **March 1997** **31 days**

Greenwich Mean Time

**NOTE**: For each day, times on first line are for Sun. *Italic* times on second line are for *Moon*. Degrees are North Latitude.

Moon Phases: FM = full moon; LQ = last quarter; NM = new moon; FQ = first quarter. Sun's declination is in degrees; Sun's distance is in Astronomical Units.

**CAUTION**: Must be converted to local time. For instructions see page 462.

| Day of month, of week, *of year* | Sun on Meridian *Moon Phase* h m s | Sun's Declination ° ′ *Distance* | 20° Rise Sun *Moon* h m | 20° Set Sun *Moon* h m | 30° Rise Sun *Moon* h m | 30° Set Sun *Moon* h m | 40° Rise Sun *Moon* h m | 40° Set Sun *Moon* h m | 50° Rise Sun *Moon* h m | 50° Set Sun *Moon* h m | 60° Rise Sun *Moon* h m | 60° Set Sun *Moon* h m |
|---|---|---|---|---|---|---|---|---|---|---|---|---|
| 1 SA | 12 12 20 | - 7 39 | 6 20 | 18 05 | 6 26 | 17 59 | 6 34 | 17 52 | 6 43 | 17 42 | 6 59 | 17 27 |
| *60* | | *.9908* | *none* | *10 52* | *none* | *10 38* | *none* | *10 20* | *0 06* | *9 56* | *0 43* | *9 17* |
| 2 SU | 12 12 08 | - 7 16 | 6 19 | 18 05 | 6 25 | 18 00 | 6 32 | 17 53 | 6 41 | 17 44 | 6 56 | 17 30 |
| *61* | *9 39 LQ* | *.9910* | *0 09* | *11 41* | *0 24* | *11 25* | *0 43* | *11 05* | *1 10* | *10 38* | *1 53* | *9 53* |
| 3 MO | 12 11 56 | - 6 53 | 6 18 | 18 06 | 6 24 | 18 00 | 6 31 | 17 54 | 6 39 | 17 45 | 6 53 | 17 32 |
| *62* | | *.9913* | *1 04* | *12 34* | *1 21* | *12 18* | *1 42* | *11 56* | *2 11* | *11 27* | *2 59* | *10 39* |
| 4 TU | 12 11 43 | - 6 30 | 6 18 | 18 06 | 6 23 | 18 01 | 6 29 | 17 55 | 6 37 | 17 47 | 6 50 | 17 35 |
| *63* | | *.9915* | *2 01* | *13 32* | *2 18* | *13 15* | *2 39* | *12 54* | *3 08* | *12 26* | *3 56* | *11 38* |
| 5 WE | 12 11 30 | - 6 07 | 6 17 | 18 06 | 6 22 | 18 02 | 6 27 | 17 56 | 6 35 | 17 49 | 6 47 | 17 37 |
| *64* | | *.9918* | *2 57* | *14 33* | *3 13* | *14 18* | *3 33* | *13 59* | *4 00* | *13 33* | *4 44* | *12 50* |
| 6 TH | 12 11 16 | - 5 44 | 6 16 | 18 07 | 6 21 | 18 02 | 6 26 | 17 57 | 6 33 | 17 50 | 6 44 | 17 40 |
| *65* | | *.9921* | *3 52* | *15 36* | *4 06* | *15 23* | *4 23* | *15 08* | *4 46* | *14 47* | *5 22* | *14 12* |
| 7 FR | 12 11 02 | - 5 21 | 6 15 | 18 07 | 6 19 | 18 03 | 6 24 | 17 58 | 6 31 | 17 52 | 6 41 | 17 42 |
| *66* | | *.9923* | *4 45* | *16 40* | *4 56* | *16 31* | *5 08* | *16 20* | *5 26* | *16 05* | *5 53* | *15 41* |
| 8 SA | 12 10 47 | - 4 57 | 6 14 | 18 07 | 6 18 | 18 04 | 6 23 | 17 59 | 6 29 | 17 54 | 6 38 | 17 45 |
| *67* | | *.9926* | *5 36* | *17 44* | *5 43* | *17 39* | *5 51* | *17 33* | *6 02* | *17 25* | *6 19* | *17 13* |
| 9 SU | 12 10 32 | - 4 34 | 6 14 | 18 08 | 6 17 | 18 04 | 6 21 | 18 00 | 6 27 | 17 55 | 6 35 | 17 47 |
| *68* | *1 16 NM* | *.9928* | *6 25* | *18 47* | *6 28* | *18 47* | *6 31* | *18 47* | *6 35* | *18 46* | *6 41* | *18 45* |
| 10 MO | 12 10 17 | - 4 10 | 6 13 | 18 08 | 6 16 | 18 05 | 6 20 | 18 02 | 6 25 | 17 57 | 6 32 | 17 50 |
| *69* | | *.9931* | *7 13* | *19 49* | *7 12* | *19 53* | *7 09* | *19 58* | *7 07* | *20 05* | *7 02* | *20 15* |
| 11 TU | 12 10 01 | - 3 47 | 6 12 | 18 08 | 6 15 | 18 06 | 6 18 | 18 03 | 6 22 | 17 58 | 6 29 | 17 52 |
| *70* | | *.9934* | *8 01* | *20 50* | *7 55* | *20 58* | *7 48* | *21 08* | *7 38* | *21 21* | *7 24* | *21 42* |
| 12 WE | 12 09 45 | - 3 23 | 6 11 | 18 09 | 6 14 | 18 06 | 6 17 | 18 04 | 6 20 | 18 00 | 6 26 | 17 55 |
| *71* | | *.9936* | *8 48* | *21 49* | *8 39* | *22 01* | *8 27* | *22 15* | *8 11* | *22 34* | *7 47* | *23 05* |
| 13 TH | 12 09 29 | - 3 00 | 6 10 | 18 09 | 6 12 | 18 07 | 6 15 | 18 05 | 6 18 | 18 02 | 6 23 | 17 57 |
| *72* | | *.9939* | *9 36* | *22 47* | *9 24* | *23 01* | *9 08* | *23 18* | *8 47* | *23 43* | *8 13* | *none* |
| 14 FR | 12 09 12 | - 2 36 | 6 09 | 18 09 | 6 11 | 18 08 | 6 13 | 18 06 | 6 16 | 18 03 | 6 20 | 18 00 |
| *73* | | *.9942* | *10 25* | *23 42* | *10 10* | *23 58* | *9 51* | *none* | *9 26* | *none* | *8 45* | *0 22* |
| 15 SA | 12 08 56 | - 2 12 | 6 09 | 18 10 | 6 10 | 18 08 | 6 12 | 18 07 | 6 14 | 18 05 | 6 17 | 18 02 |
| *74* | | *.9944* | *11 14* | *none* | *10 58* | *none* | *10 37* | *0 17* | *10 09* | *0 45* | *9 23* | *1 30* |
| 16 SU | 12 08 39 | - 1 49 | 6 08 | 18 10 | 6 09 | 18 09 | 6 10 | 18 08 | 6 12 | 18 07 | 6 14 | 18 05 |
| *75* | *0 07 FQ* | *.9947* | *12 04* | *0 34* | *11 47* | *0 51* | *11 26* | *1 12* | *10 57* | *1 40* | *10 09* | *2 28* |
| 17 MO | 12 08 22 | - 1 25 | 6 07 | 18 10 | 6 08 | 18 10 | 6 08 | 18 09 | 6 10 | 18 08 | 6 11 | 18 07 |
| *76* | | *.9950* | *12 53* | *1 24* | *12 37* | *1 40* | *12 17* | *2 01* | *11 49* | *2 29* | *11 03* | *3 16* |
| 18 TU | 12 08 04 | - 1 01 | 6 06 | 18 10 | 6 06 | 18 10 | 6 07 | 18 10 | 6 07 | 18 10 | 6 08 | 18 10 |
| *77* | | *.9952* | *13 43* | *2 10* | *13 28* | *2 26* | *13 10* | *2 45* | *12 44* | *3 11* | *12 03* | *3 54* |
| 19 WE | 12 07 46 | - 0 37 | 6 05 | 18 11 | 6 05 | 18 11 | 6 05 | 18 11 | 6 05 | 18 11 | 6 05 | 18 12 |
| *78* | | *.9955* | *14 32* | *2 54* | *14 20* | *3 08* | *14 04* | *3 24* | *13 42* | *3 48* | *13 07* | *4 24* |
| 20 TH | 12 07 29 | - 0 14 | 6 04 | 18 11 | 6 04 | 18 11 | 6 04 | 18 12 | 6 03 | 18 13 | 6 02 | 18 15 |
| *79* | | *.9958* | *15 21* | *3 35* | *15 11* | *3 46* | *14 59* | *4 00* | *14 42* | *4 19* | *14 14* | *4 49* |
| 21 FR | 12 07 11 | + 0 10 | 6 03 | 18 11 | 6 03 | 18 12 | 6 02 | 18 13 | 6 01 | 18 14 | 5 59 | 18 17 |
| *80* | | *.9961* | *16 10* | *4 15* | *16 03* | *4 23* | *15 54* | *4 34* | *15 42* | *4 48* | *15 23* | *5 09* |
| 22 SA | 12 06 53 | + 0 34 | 6 02 | 18 12 | 6 02 | 18 13 | 6 00 | 18 14 | 5 59 | 18 16 | 5 56 | 18 19 |
| *81* | | *.9963* | *16 59* | *4 53* | *16 55* | *4 58* | *16 50* | *5 05* | *16 43* | *5 14* | *16 33* | *5 27* |
| 23 SU | 12 06 34 | + 0 57 | 6 02 | 18 12 | 6 00 | 18 13 | 5 59 | 18 15 | 5 56 | 18 18 | 5 53 | 18 22 |
| *82* | | *.9966* | *17 47* | *5 30* | *17 47* | *5 32* | *17 46* | *5 35* | *17 45* | *5 38* | *17 44* | *5 44* |
| 24 MO | 12 06 16 | + 1 21 | 6 01 | 18 12 | 5 59 | 18 14 | 5 57 | 18 16 | 5 54 | 18 19 | 5 50 | 18 24 |
| *83* | *4 46 FM* | *.9969* | *18 36* | *6 07* | *18 39* | *6 06* | *18 43* | *6 05* | *18 48* | *6 03* | *18 55* | *6 00* |
| 25 TU | 12 05 58 | + 1 45 | 6 00 | 18 12 | 5 58 | 18 14 | 5 56 | 18 17 | 5 52 | 18 21 | 5 47 | 18 27 |
| *84* | | *.9972* | *19 27* | *6 45* | *19 33* | *6 41* | *19 41* | *6 35* | *19 51* | *6 28* | *20 08* | *6 17* |
| 26 WE | 12 05 40 | + 2 08 | 5 59 | 18 13 | 5 57 | 18 15 | 5 54 | 18 18 | 5 50 | 18 22 | 5 44 | 18 29 |
| *85* | | *.9975* | *20 18* | *7 25* | *20 27* | *7 17* | *20 39* | *7 07* | *20 55* | *6 54* | *21 21* | *6 35* |
| 27 TH | 12 05 22 | + 2 32 | 5 58 | 18 13 | 5 56 | 18 16 | 5 52 | 18 19 | 5 48 | 18 24 | 5 41 | 18 32 |
| *86* | | *.9978* | *21 10* | *8 06* | *21 23* | *7 55* | *21 38* | *7 42* | *21 59* | *7 24* | *22 33* | *6 56* |
| 28 FR | 12 05 03 | + 2 55 | 5 57 | 18 13 | 5 54 | 18 16 | 5 51 | 18 20 | 5 46 | 18 26 | 5 38 | 18 34 |
| *87* | | *.9981* | *22 04* | *8 50* | *22 19* | *8 37* | *22 37* | *8 20* | *23 03* | *7 57* | *23 44* | *7 21* |
| 29 SA | 12 04 45 | + 3 18 | 5 56 | 18 13 | 5 53 | 18 17 | 5 49 | 18 21 | 5 43 | 18 27 | 5 35 | 18 36 |
| *88* | | *.9983* | *22 59* | *9 38* | *23 15* | *9 22* | *23 36* | *9 03* | *none* | *8 36* | *none* | *7 53* |
| 30 SU | 12 04 27 | + 3 42 | 5 55 | 18 14 | 5 52 | 18 17 | 5 47 | 18 22 | 5 41 | 18 29 | 5 31 | 18 39 |
| *89* | | *.9986* | *23 54* | *10 29* | *none* | *10 12* | *none* | *9 51* | *0 04* | *9 22* | *0 51* | *8 35* |
| 31 MO | 12 04 09 | + 4 05 | 5 55 | 18 14 | 5 51 | 18 18 | 5 46 | 18 23 | 5 39 | 18 30 | 5 28 | 18 41 |
| *90* | *19 39 LQ* | *.9989* | *none* | *11 23* | *0 11* | *11 07* | *0 32* | *10 46* | *1 01* | *10 16* | *1 50* | *9 28* |

**4th Month** **April 1997** **30 days**

Greenwich Mean Time

**NOTE**: For each day, times on first line are for Sun. *Italic* times on second line are for *Moon*. Degrees are North Latitude.

Moon Phases: FM = full moon; LQ = last quarter; NM = new moon; FQ = first quarter. Sun's declination is in degrees; Sun's distance is in Astronomical Units.

**CAUTION**: Must be converted to local time. For instructions see page 462.

| Day of month, of week, *of year* | Sun on Meridian *Moon Phase* h m s | Sun's Decli-nation ° ′ *Distance* | 20° Rise Sun *Moon* h m | 20° Set Sun *Moon* h m | 30° Rise Sun *Moon* h m | 30° Set Sun *Moon* h m | 40° Rise Sun *Moon* h m | 40° Set Sun *Moon* h m | 50° Rise Sun *Moon* h m | 50° Set Sun *Moon* h m | 60° Rise Sun *Moon* h m | 60° Set Sun *Moon* h m |
|---|---|---|---|---|---|---|---|---|---|---|---|---|
| 1 TU | 12 03 51 | + 4 28 | 5 54 | 18 14 | 5 50 | 18 19 | 5 44 | 18 24 | 5 37 | 18 32 | 5 25 | 18 44 |
| *91* | | *.9992* | *0 48* | *12 21* | *1 05* | *12 05* | *1 25* | *11 46* | *1 53* | *11 18* | *2 40* | *10 33* |
| 2 WE | 12 03 33 | + 4 51 | 5 53 | 18 15 | 5 48 | 18 19 | 5 43 | 18 25 | 5 35 | 18 33 | 5 22 | 18 46 |
| *92* | | *.9995* | *1 42* | *13 21* | *1 57* | *13 07* | *2 15* | *12 50* | *2 40* | *12 27* | *3 20* | *11 49* |
| 3 TH | 12 03 16 | + 5 14 | 5 52 | 18 15 | 5 47 | 18 20 | 5 41 | 18 26 | 5 33 | 18 35 | 5 19 | 18 49 |
| *93* | | *.9998* | *2 34* | *14 22* | *2 46* | *14 12* | *3 01* | *13 59* | *3 21* | *13 41* | *3 52* | *13 12* |
| 4 FR | 12 02 58 | + 5 37 | 5 51 | 18 15 | 5 46 | 18 20 | 5 39 | 18 27 | 5 30 | 18 37 | 5 16 | 18 51 |
| *94* | | *1.0001* | *3 24* | *15 24* | *3 32* | *15 18* | *3 43* | *15 09* | *3 57* | *14 58* | *4 19* | *14 40* |
| 5 SA | 12 02 41 | + 6 00 | 5 50 | 18 15 | 5 45 | 18 21 | 5 38 | 18 28 | 5 28 | 18 38 | 5 13 | 18 54 |
| *95* | | *1.0004* | *4 13* | *16 27* | *4 17* | *16 24* | *4 23* | *16 21* | *4 30* | *16 16* | *4 42* | *16 09* |
| 6 SU | 12 02 24 | + 6 23 | 5 49 | 18 16 | 5 44 | 18 22 | 5 36 | 18 29 | 5 26 | 18 40 | 5 10 | 18 56 |
| *96* | | *1.0007* | *5 00* | *17 29* | *5 01* | *17 30* | *5 01* | *17 32* | *5 02* | *17 35* | *5 03* | *17 40* |
| 7 MO | 12 02 07 | + 6 46 | 5 49 | 18 16 | 5 42 | 18 22 | 5 35 | 18 30 | 5 24 | 18 41 | 5 07 | 18 58 |
| *97* | *11 03 NM* | *1.0010* | *5 48* | *18 30* | *5 44* | *18 36* | *5 39* | *18 43* | *5 33* | *18 53* | *5 24* | *19 09* |
| 8 TU | 12 01 51 | + 7 08 | 5 48 | 18 16 | 5 41 | 18 23 | 5 33 | 18 31 | 5 22 | 18 43 | 5 04 | 19 01 |
| *98* | | *1.0013* | *6 35* | *19 31* | *6 28* | *19 41* | *6 18* | *19 53* | *6 05* | *20 09* | *5 46* | *20 35* |
| 9 WE | 12 01 34 | + 7 31 | 5 47 | 18 16 | 5 40 | 18 24 | 5 32 | 18 32 | 5 20 | 18 44 | 5 01 | 19 03 |
| *99* | | *1.0016* | *7 24* | *20 31* | *7 13* | *20 44* | *6 59* | *21 00* | *6 40* | *21 22* | *6 11* | *21 57* |
| 10 TH | 12 01 18 | + 7 53 | 5 46 | 18 17 | 5 39 | 18 24 | 5 30 | 18 33 | 5 18 | 18 46 | 4 58 | 19 06 |
| *100* | | *1.0018* | *8 13* | *21 29* | *7 59* | *21 44* | *7 42* | *22 03* | *7 18* | *22 29* | *6 41* | *23 12* |
| 11 FR | 12 01 02 | + 8 15 | 5 45 | 18 17 | 5 38 | 18 25 | 5 28 | 18 34 | 5 16 | 18 48 | 4 55 | 19 08 |
| *101* | | *1.0021* | *9 04* | *22 24* | *8 48* | *22 40* | *8 28* | *23 01* | *8 01* | *23 29* | *7 17* | *none* |
| 12 SA | 12 00 47 | + 8 37 | 5 44 | 18 17 | 5 37 | 18 25 | 5 27 | 18 35 | 5 14 | 18 49 | 4 52 | 19 11 |
| *102* | | *1.0024* | *9 55* | *23 16* | *9 38* | *23 33* | *9 17* | *23 54* | *8 48* | *none* | *8 01* | *0 16* |
| 13 SU | 12 00 31 | + 8 59 | 5 44 | 18 18 | 5 36 | 18 26 | 5 25 | 18 36 | 5 11 | 18 51 | 4 49 | 19 13 |
| *103* | | *1.0027* | *10 46* | *none* | *10 29* | *none* | *10 08* | *none* | *9 40* | *0 22* | *8 52* | *1 10* |
| 14 MO | 12 00 16 | + 9 21 | 5 43 | 18 18 | 5 34 | 18 27 | 5 24 | 18 37 | 5 09 | 18 52 | 4 47 | 19 16 |
| *104* | *17 01 FQ* | *1.0030* | *11 36* | *0 05* | *11 21* | *0 21* | *11 02* | *0 41* | *10 35* | *1 08* | *9 51* | *1 53* |
| 15 TU | 12 00 02 | + 9 42 | 5 42 | 18 18 | 5 33 | 18 27 | 5 22 | 18 38 | 5 07 | 18 54 | 4 44 | 19 18 |
| *105* | | *1.0032* | *12 26* | *0 50* | *12 13* | *1 05* | *11 56* | *1 23* | *11 33* | *1 47* | *10 55* | *2 26* |
| 16 WE | 11 59 47 | +10 04 | 5 41 | 18 19 | 5 32 | 18 28 | 5 21 | 18 39 | 5 05 | 18 55 | 4 41 | 19 21 |
| *106* | | *1.0035* | *13 16* | *1 33* | *13 05* | *1 45* | *12 51* | *2 00* | *12 32* | *2 21* | *12 02* | *2 53* |
| 17 TH | 11 59 33 | +10 25 | 5 41 | 18 19 | 5 31 | 18 28 | 5 19 | 18 40 | 5 03 | 18 57 | 4 38 | 19 23 |
| *107* | | *1.0038* | *14 05* | *2 13* | *13 56* | *2 22* | *13 46* | *2 34* | *13 32* | *2 50* | *13 10* | *3 15* |
| 18 FR | 11 59 20 | +10 46 | 5 40 | 18 19 | 5 30 | 18 29 | 5 18 | 18 41 | 5 01 | 18 58 | 4 35 | 19 26 |
| *108* | | *1.0041* | *14 53* | *2 51* | *14 48* | *2 58* | *14 42* | *3 06* | *14 33* | *3 17* | *14 19* | *3 34* |
| 19 SA | 11 59 07 | +11 07 | 5 39 | 18 19 | 5 29 | 18 30 | 5 16 | 18 42 | 4 59 | 19 00 | 4 32 | 19 28 |
| *109* | | *1.0043* | *15 42* | *3 29* | *15 40* | *3 32* | *15 38* | *3 36* | *15 35* | *3 42* | *15 30* | *3 51* |
| 20 SU | 11 58 54 | +11 27 | 5 38 | 18 20 | 5 28 | 18 30 | 5 15 | 18 43 | 4 57 | 19 02 | 4 29 | 19 30 |
| *110* | | *1.0046* | *16 31* | *4 06* | *16 32* | *4 06* | *16 34* | *4 06* | *16 37* | *4 06* | *16 41* | *4 07* |
| 21 MO | 11 58 41 | +11 48 | 5 38 | 18 20 | 5 27 | 18 31 | 5 14 | 18 44 | 4 55 | 19 03 | 4 26 | 19 33 |
| *111* | | *1.0049* | *17 21* | *4 44* | *17 26* | *4 40* | *17 32* | *4 36* | *17 41* | *4 31* | *17 54* | *4 23* |
| 22 TU | 11 58 29 | +12 08 | 5 37 | 18 20 | 5 26 | 18 32 | 5 12 | 18 45 | 4 53 | 19 05 | 4 23 | 19 35 |
| *112* | *20 35 FM* | *1.0051* | *18 12* | *5 23* | *18 21* | *5 16* | *18 31* | *5 08* | *18 45* | *4 57* | *19 08* | *4 40* |
| 23 WE | 11 58 18 | +12 28 | 5 36 | 18 21 | 5 25 | 18 32 | 5 11 | 18 46 | 4 51 | 19 06 | 4 20 | 19 38 |
| *113* | | *1.0054* | *19 05* | *6 04* | *19 17* | *5 54* | *19 31* | *5 42* | *19 51* | *5 26* | *20 22* | *5 00* |
| 24 TH | 11 58 07 | +12 48 | 5 35 | 18 21 | 5 24 | 18 33 | 5 09 | 18 47 | 4 49 | 19 08 | 4 18 | 19 40 |
| *114* | | *1.0057* | *19 59* | *6 48* | *20 13* | *6 35* | *20 31* | *6 19* | *20 56* | *5 58* | *21 35* | *5 24* |
| 25 FR | 11 57 56 | +13 08 | 5 35 | 18 21 | 5 23 | 18 33 | 5 08 | 18 49 | 4 48 | 19 09 | 4 15 | 19 43 |
| *115* | | *1.0060* | *20 55* | *7 35* | *21 11* | *7 20* | *21 31* | *7 01* | *21 59* | *6 35* | *22 44* | *5 54* |
| 26 SA | 11 57 46 | +13 27 | 5 34 | 18 22 | 5 22 | 18 34 | 5 07 | 18 50 | 4 46 | 19 11 | 4 12 | 19 45 |
| *116* | | *1.0062* | *21 50* | *8 25* | *22 07* | *8 09* | *22 28* | *7 48* | *22 58* | *7 20* | *23 47* | *6 33* |
| 27 SU | 11 57 37 | +13 47 | 5 33 | 18 22 | 5 21 | 18 35 | 5 05 | 18 51 | 4 44 | 19 12 | 4 09 | 19 48 |
| *117* | | *1.0065* | *22 45* | *9 19* | *23 02* | *9 02* | *23 23* | *8 41* | *23 52* | *8 11* | *none* | *7 22* |
| 28 MO | 11 57 28 | +14 06 | 5 33 | 18 22 | 5 20 | 18 35 | 5 04 | 18 52 | 4 42 | 19 14 | 4 06 | 19 50 |
| *118* | | *1.0068* | *23 38* | *10 16* | *23 54* | *9 59* | *none* | *9 39* | *none* | *9 10* | *0 39* | *8 23* |
| 29 TU | 11 57 19 | +14 24 | 5 32 | 18 23 | 5 19 | 18 36 | 5 03 | 18 53 | 4 40 | 19 16 | 4 04 | 19 53 |
| *119* | | *1.0070* | *none* | *11 14* | *none* | *11 00* | *0 13* | *10 41* | *0 39* | *10 16* | *1 22* | *9 35* |
| 30 WE | 11 57 11 | +14 43 | 5 31 | 18 23 | 5 18 | 18 37 | 5 01 | 18 54 | 4 38 | 19 17 | 4 01 | 19 55 |
| *120* | *2 38 LQ* | *1.0073* | *0 30* | *12 14* | *0 43* | *12 02* | *0 59* | *11 47* | *1 21* | *11 27* | *1 56* | *10 55* |

**5th Month** **May 1997** **31 days**

Greenwich Mean Time

**NOTE**: For each day, times on first line are for Sun. *Italic* times on second line are for *Moon*.
Degrees are North Latitude.

Moon Phases: FM = full moon; LQ = last quarter; NM = new moon; FQ = first quarter.
Sun's declination is in degrees; Sun's distance is in Astronomical Units.

**CAUTION**: Must be converted to local time. For instructions see page 462.

| Day of month, of week, *of year* | Sun on Meridian *Moon Phase* h m s | Sun's Declination ° ′ *Distance* | 20° Rise Sun *Moon* h m | 20° Set Sun *Moon* h m | 30° Rise Sun *Moon* h m | 30° Set Sun *Moon* h m | 40° Rise Sun *Moon* h m | 40° Set Sun *Moon* h m | 50° Rise Sun *Moon* h m | 50° Set Sun *Moon* h m | 60° Rise Sun *Moon* h m | 60° Set Sun *Moon* h m |
|---|---|---|---|---|---|---|---|---|---|---|---|---|
| 1 TH | 11 57 04 | +15 01 | 5 31 | 18 23 | 5 17 | 18 37 | 5 00 | 18 55 | 4 37 | 19 19 | 3 58 | 19 58 |
| *121* | | *1.0076* | *1 19* | *13 14* | *1 29* | *13 05* | *1 41* | *12 55* | *1 58* | *12 41* | *2 23* | *12 19* |
| 2 FR | 11 56 57 | +15 19 | 5 30 | 18 24 | 5 16 | 18 38 | 4 59 | 18 56 | 4 35 | 19 20 | 3 55 | 20 00 |
| *122* | | *1.0078* | *2 06* | *14 14* | *2 13* | *14 09* | *2 20* | *14 04* | *2 30* | *13 56* | *2 46* | *13 45* |
| 3 SA | 11 56 51 | +15 37 | 5 30 | 18 24 | 5 16 | 18 39 | 4 58 | 18 57 | 4 33 | 19 22 | 3 53 | 20 03 |
| *123* | | *1.0081* | *2 53* | *15 14* | *2 55* | *15 14* | *2 58* | *15 13* | *3 01* | *15 13* | *3 07* | *15 12* |
| 4 SU | 11 56 45 | +15 55 | 5 29 | 18 25 | 5 15 | 18 39 | 4 57 | 18 58 | 4 31 | 19 23 | 3 50 | 20 05 |
| *124* | | *1.0083* | *3 38* | *16 14* | *3 37* | *16 18* | *3 34* | *16 23* | *3 31* | *16 29* | *3 27* | *16 40* |
| 5 MO | 11 56 40 | +16 12 | 5 29 | 18 25 | 5 14 | 18 40 | 4 55 | 18 59 | 4 30 | 19 25 | 3 47 | 20 08 |
| *125* | | *1.0086* | *4 25* | *17 14* | *4 19* | *17 22* | *4 12* | *17 32* | *4 02* | *17 45* | *3 48* | *18 06* |
| 6 TU | 11 56 35 | +16 29 | 5 28 | 18 25 | 5 13 | 18 41 | 4 54 | 19 00 | 4 28 | 19 26 | 3 45 | 20 10 |
| *126* | *20 48 NM* | *1.0088* | *5 12* | *18 14* | *5 02* | *18 25* | *4 51* | *18 39* | *4 35* | *18 59* | *4 10* | *19 30* |
| 7 WE | 11 56 31 | +16 46 | 5 28 | 18 26 | 5 12 | 18 41 | 4 53 | 19 01 | 4 26 | 19 28 | 3 42 | 20 13 |
| *127* | | *1.0091* | *6 01* | *19 13* | *5 48* | *19 27* | *5 32* | *19 45* | *5 11* | *20 09* | *4 37* | *20 49* |
| 8 TH | 11 56 28 | +17 02 | 5 27 | 18 26 | 5 11 | 18 42 | 4 52 | 19 02 | 4 25 | 19 29 | 3 40 | 20 15 |
| *128* | | *1.0093* | *6 51* | *20 10* | *6 36* | *20 26* | *6 17* | *20 46* | *5 51* | *21 14* | *5 10* | *22 00* |
| 9 FR | 11 56 25 | +17 18 | 5 27 | 18 27 | 5 11 | 18 42 | 4 51 | 19 03 | 4 23 | 19 31 | 3 37 | 20 17 |
| *129* | | *1.0095* | *7 42* | *21 05* | *7 26* | *21 21* | *7 05* | *21 43* | *6 37* | *22 12* | *5 50* | *23 00* |
| 10 SA | 11 56 23 | +17 34 | 5 26 | 18 27 | 5 10 | 18 43 | 4 50 | 19 04 | 4 22 | 19 32 | 3 35 | 20 20 |
| *130* | | *1.0098* | *8 34* | *21 56* | *8 18* | *22 13* | *7 56* | *22 33* | *7 27* | *23 02* | *6 39* | *23 49* |
| 11 SU | 11 56 21 | +17 50 | 5 26 | 18 27 | 5 09 | 18 44 | 4 49 | 19 05 | 4 20 | 19 34 | 3 32 | 20 22 |
| *131* | | *1.0100* | *9 26* | *22 44* | *9 10* | *22 59* | *8 50* | *23 18* | *8 22* | *23 45* | *7 36* | *none* |
| 12 MO | 11 56 20 | +18 05 | 5 25 | 18 28 | 5 09 | 18 44 | 4 48 | 19 05 | 4 19 | 19 35 | 3 30 | 20 25 |
| *132* | | *1.0102* | *10 18* | *23 28* | *10 03* | *23 42* | *9 45* | *23 58* | *9 20* | *none* | *8 39* | *0 27* |
| 13 TU | 11 56 19 | +18 20 | 5 25 | 18 28 | 5 08 | 18 45 | 4 47 | 19 06 | 4 17 | 19 37 | 3 27 | 20 27 |
| *133* | | *1.0104* | *11 08* | *none* | *10 56* | *none* | *10 40* | *none* | *10 19* | *0 21* | *9 45* | *0 57* |
| 14 WE | 11 56 19 | +18 35 | 5 24 | 18 28 | 5 07 | 18 46 | 4 46 | 19 07 | 4 16 | 19 38 | 3 25 | 20 30 |
| *134* | *10 56 FQ* | *1.0106* | *11 58* | *0 10* | *11 48* | *0 21* | *11 36* | *0 34* | *11 20* | *0 52* | *10 54* | *1 21* |
| 15 TH | 11 56 20 | +18 49 | 5 24 | 18 29 | 5 07 | 18 46 | 4 45 | 19 08 | 4 14 | 19 39 | 3 22 | 20 32 |
| *135* | | *1.0109* | *12 46* | *0 49* | *12 40* | *0 57* | *12 32* | *1 07* | *12 20* | *1 20* | *12 03* | *1 40* |
| 16 FR | 11 56 20 | +19 03 | 5 24 | 18 29 | 5 06 | 18 47 | 4 44 | 19 09 | 4 13 | 19 41 | 3 20 | 20 34 |
| *136* | | *1.0111* | *13 35* | *1 27* | *13 31* | *1 32* | *13 27* | *1 38* | *13 22* | *1 46* | *13 13* | *1 58* |
| 17 SA | 11 56 22 | +19 17 | 5 23 | 18 30 | 5 05 | 18 48 | 4 43 | 19 10 | 4 11 | 19 42 | 3 18 | 20 37 |
| *137* | | *1.0113* | *14 23* | *2 04* | *14 23* | *2 05* | *14 24* | *2 07* | *14 24* | *2 10* | *14 24* | *2 14* |
| 18 SU | 11 56 24 | +19 31 | 5 23 | 18 30 | 5 05 | 18 48 | 4 42 | 19 11 | 4 10 | 19 43 | 3 16 | 20 39 |
| *138* | | *1.0115* | *15 13* | *2 41* | *15 16* | *2 39* | *15 21* | *2 37* | *15 27* | *2 34* | *15 36* | *2 29* |
| 19 MO | 11 56 27 | +19 44 | 5 23 | 18 31 | 5 04 | 18 49 | 4 41 | 19 12 | 4 09 | 19 45 | 3 13 | 20 41 |
| *139* | | *1.0117* | *16 04* | *3 19* | *16 11* | *3 14* | *16 19* | *3 08* | *16 31* | *2 59* | *16 50* | *2 46* |
| 20 TU | 11 56 30 | +19 56 | 5 22 | 18 31 | 5 04 | 18 49 | 4 41 | 19 13 | 4 08 | 19 46 | 3 11 | 20 43 |
| *140* | | *1.0119* | *16 56* | *3 59* | *17 06* | *3 51* | *17 19* | *3 40* | *17 37* | *3 26* | *18 05* | *3 04* |
| 21 WE | 11 56 34 | +20 09 | 5 22 | 18 31 | 5 03 | 18 50 | 4 40 | 19 14 | 4 06 | 19 47 | 3 09 | 20 46 |
| *141* | | *1.0121* | *17 51* | *4 42* | *18 04* | *4 31* | *18 20* | *4 16* | *18 43* | *3 57* | *19 20* | *3 26* |
| 22 TH | 11 56 38 | +20 21 | 5 22 | 18 32 | 5 03 | 18 51 | 4 39 | 19 15 | 4 05 | 19 49 | 3 07 | 20 48 |
| *142* | *9 14 FM* | *1.0123* | *18 46* | *5 29* | *19 02* | *5 14* | *19 21* | *4 57* | *19 48* | *4 33* | *20 33* | *3 54* |
| 23 FR | 11 56 43 | +20 33 | 5 21 | 18 32 | 5 02 | 18 51 | 4 38 | 19 16 | 4 04 | 19 50 | 3 05 | 20 50 |
| *143* | | *1.0124* | *19 43* | *6 19* | *20 00* | *6 03* | *20 21* | *5 42* | *20 51* | *5 15* | *21 40* | *4 29* |
| 24 SA | 11 56 48 | +20 44 | 5 21 | 18 33 | 5 02 | 18 52 | 4 38 | 19 16 | 4 03 | 19 51 | 3 03 | 20 52 |
| *144* | | *1.0126* | *20 40* | *7 13* | *20 57* | *6 56* | *21 18* | *6 34* | *21 48* | *6 04* | *22 37* | *5 15* |
| 25 SU | 11 56 54 | +20 55 | 5 21 | 18 33 | 5 02 | 18 52 | 4 37 | 19 17 | 4 02 | 19 52 | 3 01 | 20 54 |
| *145* | | *1.0128* | *21 35* | *8 10* | *21 51* | *7 53* | *22 11* | *7 32* | *22 39* | *7 02* | *23 24* | *6 13* |
| 26 MO | 11 57 00 | +21 06 | 5 21 | 18 33 | 5 01 | 18 53 | 4 36 | 19 18 | 4 01 | 19 54 | 2 59 | 20 56 |
| *146* | | *1.0130* | *22 28* | *9 09* | *22 42* | *8 53* | *22 59* | *8 34* | *23 23* | *8 07* | *none* | *7 23* |
| 27 TU | 11 57 07 | +21 16 | 5 21 | 18 34 | 5 01 | 18 54 | 4 36 | 19 19 | 4 00 | 19 55 | 2 58 | 20 58 |
| *147* | | *1.0132* | *23 18* | *10 08* | *23 29* | *9 56* | *23 42* | *9 39* | *none* | *9 17* | *0 01* | *8 41* |
| 28 WE | 11 57 14 | +21 26 | 5 20 | 18 34 | 5 00 | 18 54 | 4 35 | 19 20 | 3 59 | 19 56 | 2 56 | 21 00 |
| *148* | | *1.0134* | *none* | *11 08* | *none* | *10 59* | *none* | *10 47* | *0 01* | *10 30* | *0 30* | *10 04* |
| 29 TH | 11 57 22 | +21 35 | 5 20 | 18 35 | 5 00 | 18 55 | 4 35 | 19 20 | 3 58 | 19 57 | 2 54 | 21 02 |
| *149* | *7 52 LQ* | *1.0135* | *0 05* | *12 08* | *0 13* | *12 02* | *0 22* | *11 55* | *0 35* | *11 45* | *0 54* | *11 29* |
| 30 FR | 11 57 30 | +21 44 | 5 20 | 18 35 | 5 00 | 18 55 | 4 34 | 19 21 | 3 57 | 19 58 | 2 52 | 21 04 |
| *150* | | *1.0137* | *0 51* | *13 07* | *0 55* | *13 05* | *0 59* | *13 03* | *1 05* | *13 00* | *1 15* | *12 55* |
| 31 SA | 11 57 38 | +21 53 | 5 20 | 18 35 | 5 00 | 18 56 | 4 34 | 19 22 | 3 57 | 19 59 | 2 51 | 21 06 |
| *151* | | *1.0139* | *1 36* | *14 05* | *1 35* | *14 07* | *1 35* | *14 10* | *1 35* | *14 14* | *1 34* | *14 20* |

**6th Month** **June 1997** **30 days**

Greenwich Mean Time

**NOTE**: For each day, times on first line are for Sun. *Italic* times on second line are for *Moon*. Degrees are North Latitude.

Moon Phases: FM = full moon; LQ = last quarter; NM = new moon; FQ = first quarter. Sun's declination is in degrees; Sun's distance is in Astronomical Units.

**CAUTION**: Must be converted to local time. For instructions see page 462.

| Day of month, of week, of year | Sun on Meridian, Moon Phase (h m s) | Sun's Declination (° ′), Distance | 20° Rise Sun/Moon (h m) | 20° Set Sun/Moon (h m) | 30° Rise Sun/Moon (h m) | 30° Set Sun/Moon (h m) | 40° Rise Sun/Moon (h m) | 40° Set Sun/Moon (h m) | 50° Rise Sun/Moon (h m) | 50° Set Sun/Moon (h m) | 60° Rise Sun/Moon (h m) | 60° Set Sun/Moon (h m) |
|---|---|---|---|---|---|---|---|---|---|---|---|---|
| 1 SU | 11 57 48 | +22 02 | 5 20 | 18 36 | 4 59 | 18 56 | 4 33 | 19 23 | 3 56 | 20 00 | 2 49 | 21 07 |
| 152 | | 1.0140 | 2 20 | 15 03 | 2 16 | 15 10 | 2 11 | 15 18 | 2 04 | 15 28 | 1 53 | 15 45 |
| 2 MO | 11 57 57 | +22 10 | 5 20 | 18 36 | 4 59 | 18 57 | 4 33 | 19 23 | 3 55 | 20 01 | 2 48 | 21 09 |
| 153 | | 1.0142 | 3 06 | 16 02 | 2 58 | 16 12 | 2 48 | 16 24 | 2 34 | 16 41 | 2 14 | 17 08 |
| 3 TU | 11 58 07 | +22 17 | 5 20 | 18 36 | 4 59 | 18 57 | 4 33 | 19 24 | 3 55 | 20 02 | 2 47 | 21 11 |
| 154 | | 1.0143 | 3 53 | 17 00 | 3 41 | 17 13 | 3 27 | 17 29 | 3 08 | 17 52 | 2 38 | 18 28 |
| 4 WE | 11 58 17 | +22 24 | 5 20 | 18 37 | 4 59 | 18 58 | 4 32 | 19 25 | 3 54 | 20 03 | 2 45 | 21 12 |
| 155 | | 1.0145 | 4 41 | 17 57 | 4 27 | 18 13 | 4 09 | 18 32 | 3 45 | 18 59 | 3 07 | 19 42 |
| 5 TH | 11 58 28 | +22 31 | 5 20 | 18 37 | 4 59 | 18 58 | 4 32 | 19 25 | 3 53 | 20 04 | 2 44 | 21 14 |
| 156 | 7 05 NM | 1.0146 | 5 32 | 18 53 | 5 15 | 19 10 | 4 55 | 19 31 | 4 28 | 20 00 | 3 43 | 20 48 |
| 6 FR | 11 58 39 | +22 38 | 5 20 | 18 38 | 4 59 | 18 59 | 4 32 | 19 26 | 3 53 | 20 05 | 2 43 | 21 15 |
| 157 | | 1.0148 | 6 23 | 19 46 | 6 06 | 20 03 | 5 45 | 20 24 | 5 16 | 20 54 | 4 27 | 21 42 |
| 7 SA | 11 58 50 | +22 44 | 5 20 | 18 38 | 4 58 | 18 59 | 4 31 | 19 27 | 3 52 | 20 06 | 2 42 | 21 17 |
| 158 | | 1.0149 | 7 16 | 20 36 | 6 59 | 20 52 | 6 38 | 21 12 | 6 09 | 21 40 | 5 21 | 22 25 |
| 8 SU | 11 59 01 | +22 50 | 5 20 | 18 38 | 4 58 | 19 00 | 4 31 | 19 27 | 3 52 | 20 07 | 2 41 | 21 18 |
| 159 | | 1.0150 | 8 08 | 21 22 | 7 52 | 21 37 | 7 33 | 21 55 | 7 06 | 22 20 | 6 22 | 22 59 |
| 9 MO | 11 59 13 | +22 55 | 5 20 | 18 39 | 4 58 | 19 00 | 4 31 | 19 28 | 3 52 | 20 07 | 2 40 | 21 19 |
| 160 | | 1.0151 | 8 59 | 22 06 | 8 46 | 22 18 | 8 29 | 22 33 | 8 05 | 22 53 | 7 28 | 23 26 |
| 10 TU | 11 59 25 | +23 00 | 5 20 | 18 39 | 4 58 | 19 01 | 4 31 | 19 28 | 3 51 | 20 08 | 2 39 | 21 20 |
| 161 | | 1.0152 | 9 50 | 22 46 | 9 38 | 22 55 | 9 25 | 23 07 | 9 06 | 23 23 | 8 36 | 23 47 |
| 11 WE | 11 59 37 | +23 04 | 5 20 | 18 39 | 4 58 | 19 01 | 4 31 | 19 29 | 3 51 | 20 09 | 2 38 | 21 22 |
| 162 | | 1.0154 | 10 39 | 23 24 | 10 31 | 23 31 | 10 21 | 23 39 | 10 07 | 23 49 | 9 46 | none |
| 12 TH | 11 59 49 | +23 08 | 5 20 | 18 40 | 4 58 | 19 01 | 4 31 | 19 29 | 3 51 | 20 09 | 2 38 | 21 23 |
| 163 | | 1.0155 | 11 27 | none | 11 22 | none | 11 16 | none | 11 08 | none | 10 56 | 0 05 |
| 13 FR | 12 00 02 | +23 12 | 5 20 | 18 40 | 4 58 | 19 02 | 4 31 | 19 30 | 3 50 | 20 10 | 2 37 | 21 23 |
| 164 | 4 53 FQ | 1.0156 | 12 15 | 0 02 | 12 14 | 0 05 | 12 12 | 0 09 | 12 10 | 0 14 | 12 06 | 0 21 |
| 14 SA | 12 00 14 | +23 15 | 5 20 | 18 40 | 4 58 | 19 02 | 4 31 | 19 30 | 3 50 | 20 10 | 2 37 | 21 24 |
| 165 | | 1.0156 | 13 04 | 0 38 | 13 06 | 0 38 | 13 08 | 0 38 | 13 12 | 0 37 | 13 17 | 0 37 |
| 15 SU | 12 00 27 | +23 18 | 5 20 | 18 41 | 4 58 | 19 02 | 4 31 | 19 30 | 3 50 | 20 11 | 2 36 | 21 25 |
| 166 | | 1.0157 | 13 54 | 1 16 | 13 59 | 1 12 | 14 06 | 1 08 | 14 15 | 1 02 | 14 29 | 0 53 |
| 16 MO | 12 00 40 | +23 20 | 5 21 | 18 41 | 4 59 | 19 03 | 4 31 | 19 31 | 3 50 | 20 11 | 2 36 | 21 26 |
| 167 | | 1.0158 | 14 45 | 1 54 | 14 54 | 1 47 | 15 05 | 1 39 | 15 20 | 1 27 | 15 43 | 1 10 |
| 17 TU | 12 00 53 | +23 22 | 5 21 | 18 41 | 4 59 | 19 03 | 4 31 | 19 31 | 3 50 | 20 12 | 2 36 | 21 26 |
| 168 | | 1.0159 | 15 38 | 2 36 | 15 50 | 2 25 | 16 05 | 2 13 | 16 25 | 1 56 | 16 58 | 1 29 |
| 18 WE | 12 01 06 | +23 24 | 5 21 | 18 41 | 4 59 | 19 03 | 4 31 | 19 31 | 3 50 | 20 12 | 2 36 | 21 27 |
| 169 | | 1.0160 | 16 34 | 3 20 | 16 48 | 3 07 | 17 06 | 2 51 | 17 32 | 2 29 | 18 13 | 1 54 |
| 19 TH | 12 01 19 | +23 25 | 5 21 | 18 42 | 4 59 | 19 04 | 4 31 | 19 32 | 3 50 | 20 12 | 2 36 | 21 27 |
| 170 | | 1.0161 | 17 31 | 4 09 | 17 47 | 3 53 | 18 08 | 3 34 | 18 36 | 3 08 | 19 24 | 2 25 |
| 20 FR | 12 01 32 | +23 26 | 5 21 | 18 42 | 4 59 | 19 04 | 4 31 | 19 32 | 3 50 | 20 13 | 2 36 | 21 27 |
| 171 | 19 10 FM | 1.0161 | 18 29 | 5 01 | 18 46 | 4 44 | 19 07 | 4 23 | 19 38 | 3 54 | 20 27 | 3 06 |
| 21 SA | 12 01 45 | +23 26 | 5 21 | 18 42 | 4 59 | 19 04 | 4 31 | 19 32 | 3 51 | 20 13 | 2 36 | 21 28 |
| 172 | | 1.0162 | 19 26 | 5 58 | 19 43 | 5 41 | 20 04 | 5 19 | 20 33 | 4 49 | 21 21 | 3 59 |
| 22 SU | 12 01 58 | +23 26 | 5 22 | 18 42 | 5 00 | 19 04 | 4 32 | 19 32 | 3 51 | 20 13 | 2 36 | 21 28 |
| 173 | | 1.0163 | 20 21 | 6 58 | 20 36 | 6 42 | 20 55 | 6 21 | 21 21 | 5 53 | 22 03 | 5 06 |
| 23 MO | 12 02 10 | +23 26 | 5 22 | 18 42 | 5 00 | 19 04 | 4 32 | 19 33 | 3 51 | 20 13 | 2 36 | 21 28 |
| 174 | | 1.0163 | 21 14 | 7 59 | 21 26 | 7 45 | 21 42 | 7 28 | 22 02 | 7 03 | 22 35 | 6 24 |
| 24 TU | 12 02 23 | +23 25 | 5 22 | 18 43 | 5 00 | 19 05 | 4 32 | 19 33 | 3 51 | 20 13 | 2 37 | 21 28 |
| 175 | | 1.0164 | 22 04 | 9 01 | 22 12 | 8 50 | 22 24 | 8 36 | 22 38 | 8 18 | 23 01 | 7 48 |
| 25 WE | 12 02 36 | +23 23 | 5 22 | 18 43 | 5 00 | 19 05 | 4 32 | 19 33 | 3 52 | 20 13 | 2 37 | 21 28 |
| 176 | | 1.0164 | 22 51 | 10 02 | 22 56 | 9 55 | 23 02 | 9 46 | 23 10 | 9 33 | 23 23 | 9 14 |
| 26 TH | 12 02 49 | +23 22 | 5 23 | 18 43 | 5 01 | 19 05 | 4 33 | 19 33 | 3 52 | 20 13 | 2 38 | 21 27 |
| 177 | | 1.0165 | 23 36 | 11 02 | 23 37 | 10 58 | 23 38 | 10 55 | 23 40 | 10 49 | 23 43 | 10 41 |
| 27 FR | 12 03 01 | +23 20 | 5 23 | 18 43 | 5 01 | 19 05 | 4 33 | 19 33 | 3 53 | 20 13 | 2 39 | 21 27 |
| 178 | 12 43 LQ | 1.0165 | none | 12 00 | none | 12 01 | none | 12 03 | none | 12 04 | none | 12 06 |
| 28 SA | 12 03 13 | +23 17 | 5 23 | 18 43 | 5 01 | 19 05 | 4 33 | 19 33 | 3 53 | 20 13 | 2 39 | 21 27 |
| 179 | | 1.0166 | 0 20 | 12 58 | 0 17 | 13 03 | 0 14 | 13 09 | 0 09 | 13 18 | 0 02 | 13 31 |
| 29 SU | 12 03 26 | +23 14 | 5 24 | 18 43 | 5 02 | 19 05 | 4 34 | 19 33 | 3 54 | 20 13 | 2 40 | 21 26 |
| 180 | | 1.0166 | 1 05 | 13 56 | 0 58 | 14 05 | 0 50 | 14 15 | 0 39 | 14 30 | 0 22 | 14 53 |
| 30 MO | 12 03 37 | +23 11 | 5 24 | 18 43 | 5 02 | 19 05 | 4 34 | 19 33 | 3 54 | 20 13 | 2 41 | 21 25 |
| 181 | | 1.0166 | 1 50 | 14 53 | 1 40 | 15 05 | 1 27 | 15 20 | 1 10 | 15 40 | 0 44 | 16 13 |

**7th Month** **July 1997** **31 days**

Greenwich Mean Time

**NOTE**: For each day, times on first line are for Sun. *Italic* times on second line are for *Moon*.
Degrees are North Latitude.

Moon Phases: FM = full moon; LQ = last quarter; NM = new moon; FQ = first quarter.
Sun's declination is in degrees; Sun's distance is in Astronomical Units.

**CAUTION**: Must be converted to local time. For instructions see page 462.

| Day of month, of week, *of year* | Sun on Meridian *Moon Phase* h m s | Sun's Decli- nation ° ′ *Distance* | 20° Rise Sun *Moon* h m | 20° Set Sun *Moon* h m | 30° Rise Sun *Moon* h m | 30° Set Sun *Moon* h m | 40° Rise Sun *Moon* h m | 40° Set Sun *Moon* h m | 50° Rise Sun *Moon* h m | 50° Set Sun *Moon* h m | 60° Rise Sun *Moon* h m | 60° Set Sun *Moon* h m |
|---|---|---|---|---|---|---|---|---|---|---|---|---|
| 1 TU | 12 03 49 | +23 07 | 5 24 | 18 43 | 5 02 | 19 05 | 4 35 | 19 33 | 3 55 | 20 12 | 2 42 | 21 25 |
| *182* | | *1.0167* | *2 37* | *15 49* | *2 24* | *16 04* | *2 07* | *16 22* | *1 45* | *16 47* | *1 10* | *17 28* |
| 2 WE | 12 04 01 | +23 03 | 5 24 | 18 43 | 5 03 | 19 05 | 4 35 | 19 33 | 3 56 | 20 12 | 2 43 | 21 24 |
| *183* | | *1.0167* | *3 26* | *16 45* | *3 10* | *17 01* | *2 51* | *17 21* | *2 24* | *17 50* | *1 42* | *18 37* |
| 3 TH | 12 04 12 | +22 58 | 5 25 | 18 44 | 5 03 | 19 05 | 4 36 | 19 32 | 3 56 | 20 12 | 2 44 | 21 23 |
| *184* | | *1.0167* | *4 16* | *17 38* | *3 59* | *17 55* | *3 38* | *18 16* | *3 09* | *18 46* | *2 22* | *19 35* |
| 4 FR | 12 04 23 | +22 53 | 5 25 | 18 44 | 5 04 | 19 05 | 4 36 | 19 32 | 3 57 | 20 11 | 2 46 | 21 22 |
| *185* | *18 41 NM* | *1.0167* | *5 07* | *18 29* | *4 50* | *18 46* | *4 29* | *19 06* | *4 00* | *19 35* | *3 11* | *20 22* |
| 5 SA | 12 04 33 | +22 48 | 5 25 | 18 44 | 5 04 | 19 05 | 4 37 | 19 32 | 3 58 | 20 11 | 2 47 | 21 21 |
| *186* | | *1.0167* | *5 59* | *19 17* | *5 43* | *19 32* | *5 23* | *19 51* | *4 55* | *20 18* | *4 08* | *21 00* |
| 6 SU | 12 04 44 | +22 42 | 5 26 | 18 44 | 5 05 | 19 05 | 4 38 | 19 32 | 3 59 | 20 10 | 2 48 | 21 20 |
| *187* | | *1.0167* | *6 51* | *20 01* | *6 36* | *20 15* | *6 18* | *20 31* | *5 53* | *20 54* | *5 12* | *21 29* |
| 7 MO | 12 04 53 | +22 36 | 5 26 | 18 44 | 5 05 | 19 05 | 4 38 | 19 31 | 4 00 | 20 10 | 2 50 | 21 19 |
| *188* | | *1.0167* | *7 42* | *20 43* | *7 30* | *20 54* | *7 14* | *21 07* | *6 53* | *21 25* | *6 20* | *21 53* |
| 8 TU | 12 05 03 | +22 30 | 5 27 | 18 43 | 5 05 | 19 04 | 4 39 | 19 31 | 4 00 | 20 09 | 2 51 | 21 18 |
| *189* | | *1.0167* | *8 32* | *21 22* | *8 22* | *21 30* | *8 11* | *21 40* | *7 55* | *21 53* | *7 29* | *22 12* |
| 9 WE | 12 05 12 | +22 23 | 5 27 | 18 43 | 5 06 | 19 04 | 4 39 | 19 31 | 4 01 | 20 09 | 2 53 | 21 16 |
| *190* | | *1.0167* | *9 21* | *22 00* | *9 14* | *22 05* | *9 06* | *22 10* | *8 56* | *22 18* | *8 39* | *22 29* |
| 10 TH | 12 05 20 | +22 15 | 5 27 | 18 43 | 5 06 | 19 04 | 4 40 | 19 30 | 4 02 | 20 08 | 2 55 | 21 15 |
| *191* | | *1.0166* | *10 09* | *22 37* | *10 06* | *22 38* | *10 02* | *22 40* | *9 57* | *22 42* | *9 49* | *22 45* |
| 11 FR | 12 05 29 | +22 08 | 5 28 | 18 43 | 5 07 | 19 04 | 4 41 | 19 30 | 4 03 | 20 07 | 2 56 | 21 13 |
| *192* | | *1.0166* | *10 57* | *23 13* | *10 57* | *23 11* | *10 58* | *23 09* | *10 58* | *23 06* | *10 59* | *23 00* |
| 12 SA | 12 05 36 | +22 00 | 5 28 | 18 43 | 5 07 | 19 04 | 4 41 | 19 29 | 4 04 | 20 06 | 2 58 | 21 12 |
| *193* | *21 45 FQ* | *1.0166* | *11 45* | *23 51* | *11 49* | *23 45* | *11 54* | *23 39* | *12 00* | *23 30* | *12 10* | *23 16* |
| 13 SU | 12 05 44 | +21 51 | 5 28 | 18 43 | 5 08 | 19 03 | 4 42 | 19 29 | 4 05 | 20 06 | 3 00 | 21 10 |
| *194* | | *1.0165* | *12 35* | *none* | *12 42* | *none* | *12 51* | *none* | *13 03* | *23 57* | *13 22* | *23 34* |
| 14 MO | 12 05 50 | +21 42 | 5 29 | 18 43 | 5 09 | 19 03 | 4 43 | 19 28 | 4 06 | 20 05 | 3 02 | 21 09 |
| *195* | | *1.0165* | *13 26* | *0 30* | *13 37* | *0 22* | *13 50* | *0 11* | *14 07* | *none* | *14 35* | *23 56* |
| 15 TU | 12 05 56 | +21 33 | 5 29 | 18 43 | 5 09 | 19 03 | 4 44 | 19 28 | 4 07 | 20 04 | 3 04 | 21 07 |
| *196* | | *1.0164* | *14 20* | *1 12* | *14 33* | *1 00* | *14 50* | *0 46* | *15 12* | *0 27* | *15 49* | *none* |
| 16 WE | 12 06 02 | +21 23 | 5 29 | 18 42 | 5 10 | 19 02 | 4 44 | 19 27 | 4 09 | 20 03 | 3 05 | 21 05 |
| *197* | | *1.0164* | *15 15* | *1 58* | *15 31* | *1 44* | *15 50* | *1 26* | *16 17* | *1 02* | *17 01* | *0 23* |
| 17 TH | 12 06 07 | +21 14 | 5 30 | 18 42 | 5 10 | 19 02 | 4 45 | 19 27 | 4 10 | 20 02 | 3 07 | 21 03 |
| *198* | | *1.0163* | *16 13* | *2 48* | *16 30* | *2 32* | *16 51* | *2 11* | *17 20* | *1 44* | *18 09* | *0 58* |
| 18 FR | 12 06 12 | +21 03 | 5 30 | 18 42 | 5 11 | 19 01 | 4 46 | 19 26 | 4 11 | 20 01 | 3 09 | 21 01 |
| *199* | | *1.0162* | *17 11* | *3 43* | *17 28* | *3 25* | *17 49* | *3 04* | *18 19* | *2 34* | *19 08* | *1 45* |
| 19 SA | 12 06 16 | +20 53 | 5 31 | 18 42 | 5 11 | 19 01 | 4 47 | 19 25 | 4 12 | 20 00 | 3 12 | 21 00 |
| *200* | | *1.0162* | *18 08* | *4 41* | *18 24* | *4 24* | *18 44* | *4 03* | *19 12* | *3 34* | *19 57* | *2 45* |
| 20 SU | 12 06 19 | +20 42 | 5 31 | 18 41 | 5 12 | 19 01 | 4 48 | 19 25 | 4 13 | 19 59 | 3 14 | 20 58 |
| *201* | *3 21 FM* | *1.0161* | *19 03* | *5 43* | *19 17* | *5 28* | *19 34* | *5 09* | *19 58* | *4 42* | *20 35* | *3 59* |
| 21 MO | 12 06 22 | +20 30 | 5 31 | 18 41 | 5 12 | 19 00 | 4 48 | 19 24 | 4 15 | 19 57 | 3 16 | 20 55 |
| *202* | | *1.0160* | *19 56* | *6 46* | *20 06* | *6 34* | *20 19* | *6 18* | *20 37* | *5 57* | *21 05* | *5 22* |
| 22 TU | 12 06 25 | +20 19 | 5 32 | 18 41 | 5 13 | 19 00 | 4 49 | 19 23 | 4 16 | 19 56 | 3 18 | 20 53 |
| *203* | | *1.0159* | *20 46* | *7 50* | *20 52* | *7 41* | *21 01* | *7 30* | *21 12* | *7 14* | *21 29* | *6 50* |
| 23 WE | 12 06 26 | +20 07 | 5 32 | 18 41 | 5 14 | 18 59 | 4 50 | 19 22 | 4 17 | 19 55 | 3 20 | 20 51 |
| *204* | | *1.0159* | *21 33* | *8 52* | *21 36* | *8 47* | *21 39* | *8 41* | *21 44* | *8 33* | *21 50* | *8 20* |
| 24 TH | 12 06 28 | +19 54 | 5 32 | 18 40 | 5 14 | 18 58 | 4 51 | 19 21 | 4 18 | 19 54 | 3 22 | 20 49 |
| *205* | | *1.0158* | *22 19* | *9 53* | *22 18* | *9 52* | *22 16* | *9 52* | *22 13* | *9 50* | *22 10* | *9 49* |
| 25 FR | 12 06 28 | +19 41 | 5 33 | 18 40 | 5 15 | 18 58 | 4 52 | 19 20 | 4 20 | 19 52 | 3 24 | 20 47 |
| *206* | | *1.0157* | *23 04* | *10 53* | *22 59* | *10 56* | *22 52* | *11 00* | *22 43* | *11 06* | *22 30* | *11 15* |
| 26 SA | 12 06 28 | +19 28 | 5 33 | 18 40 | 5 15 | 18 57 | 4 53 | 19 20 | 4 21 | 19 51 | 3 27 | 20 45 |
| *207* | *18 29 LQ* | *1.0156* | *23 50* | *11 51* | *23 41* | *11 58* | *23 29* | *12 08* | *23 14* | *12 20* | *22 51* | *12 40* |
| 27 SU | 12 06 28 | +19 15 | 5 34 | 18 39 | 5 16 | 18 57 | 4 54 | 19 19 | 4 22 | 19 50 | 3 29 | 20 42 |
| *208* | | *1.0155* | *none* | *12 48* | *none* | *12 59* | *none* | *13 13* | *23 48* | *13 32* | *23 16* | *14 01* |
| 28 MO | 12 06 27 | +19 01 | 5 34 | 18 39 | 5 17 | 18 56 | 4 55 | 19 18 | 4 24 | 19 48 | 3 31 | 20 40 |
| *209* | | *1.0154* | *0 36* | *13 45* | *0 24* | *13 59* | *0 09* | *14 16* | *none* | *14 39* | *23 46* | *15 18* |
| 29 TU | 12 06 25 | +18 47 | 5 34 | 18 38 | 5 17 | 18 55 | 4 55 | 19 17 | 4 25 | 19 47 | 3 34 | 20 38 |
| *210* | | *1.0153* | *1 24* | *14 40* | *1 09* | *14 56* | *0 51* | *15 16* | *0 26* | *15 43* | *none* | *16 28* |
| 30 WE | 12 06 23 | +18 33 | 5 35 | 18 38 | 5 18 | 18 55 | 4 56 | 19 16 | 4 26 | 19 45 | 3 36 | 20 35 |
| *211* | | *1.0152* | *2 13* | *15 34* | *1 56* | *15 50* | *1 36* | *16 11* | *1 08* | *16 41* | *0 22* | *17 29* |
| 31 TH | 12 06 20 | +18 19 | 5 35 | 18 37 | 5 18 | 18 54 | 4 57 | 19 15 | 4 28 | 19 44 | 3 38 | 20 33 |
| *212* | | *1.0151* | *3 03* | *16 25* | *2 46* | *16 41* | *2 25* | *17 02* | *1 55* | *17 32* | *1 07* | *18 19* |

**8th Month** **August 1997** **31 days**

Greenwich Mean Time

**NOTE**: For each day, times on first line are for Sun. *Italic* times on second line are for *Moon*. Degrees are North Latitude.

Moon Phases: FM = full moon; LQ = last quarter; NM = new moon; FQ = first quarter. Sun's declination is in degrees; Sun's distance is in Astronomical Units.

**CAUTION**: Must be converted to local time. For instructions see page 462.

| Day of month, of week, *of year* | Sun on Meridian *Moon Phase* h m s | Sun's Declination ° ′ *Distance* | 20° Rise Sun *Moon* h m | 20° Set Sun *Moon* h m | 30° Rise Sun *Moon* h m | 30° Set Sun *Moon* h m | 40° Rise Sun *Moon* h m | 40° Set Sun *Moon* h m | 50° Rise Sun *Moon* h m | 50° Set Sun *Moon* h m | 60° Rise Sun *Moon* h m | 60° Set Sun *Moon* h m |
|---|---|---|---|---|---|---|---|---|---|---|---|---|
| 1 FR | 12 06 17 | +18 04 | 5 35 | 18 37 | 5 19 | 18 53 | 4 58 | 19 14 | 4 29 | 19 42 | 3 41 | 20 30 |
| *213* | | *1.0150* | *3 54* | *17 13* | *3 37* | *17 29* | *3 17* | *17 49* | *2 48* | *18 16* | *2 01* | *19 00* |
| 2 SA | 12 06 13 | +17 48 | 5 36 | 18 36 | 5 20 | 18 52 | 4 59 | 19 13 | 4 31 | 19 41 | 3 43 | 20 28 |
| *214* | | *1.0148* | *4 45* | *17 58* | *4 30* | *18 13* | *4 11* | *18 30* | *3 45* | *18 54* | *3 01* | *19 32* |
| 3 SU | 12 06 08 | +17 33 | 5 36 | 18 36 | 5 20 | 18 52 | 5 00 | 19 12 | 4 32 | 19 39 | 3 45 | 20 25 |
| *215* | *8 15 NM* | *1.0147* | *5 36* | *18 41* | *5 23* | *18 53* | *5 07* | *19 07* | *4 44* | *19 27* | *4 07* | *19 58* |
| 4 MO | 12 06 03 | +17 17 | 5 36 | 18 35 | 5 21 | 18 51 | 5 01 | 19 10 | 4 33 | 19 38 | 3 48 | 20 23 |
| *216* | | *1.0146* | *6 26* | *19 21* | *6 16* | *19 30* | *6 03* | *19 41* | *5 45* | *19 56* | *5 16* | *20 19* |
| 5 TU | 12 05 57 | +17 01 | 5 37 | 18 35 | 5 21 | 18 50 | 5 02 | 19 09 | 4 35 | 19 36 | 3 50 | 20 20 |
| *217* | | *1.0144* | *7 15* | *19 59* | *7 08* | *20 05* | *6 58* | *20 13* | *6 46* | *20 22* | *6 26* | *20 37* |
| 6 WE | 12 05 50 | +16 45 | 5 37 | 18 34 | 5 22 | 18 49 | 5 03 | 19 08 | 4 36 | 19 34 | 3 52 | 20 18 |
| *218* | | *1.0143* | *8 04* | *20 36* | *7 59* | *20 39* | *7 54* | *20 42* | *7 47* | *20 47* | *7 36* | *20 53* |
| 7 TH | 12 05 44 | +16 28 | 5 37 | 18 34 | 5 23 | 18 48 | 5 04 | 19 07 | 4 38 | 19 33 | 3 55 | 20 15 |
| *219* | | *1.0141* | *8 52* | *21 13* | *8 51* | *21 12* | *8 50* | *21 11* | *8 48* | *21 10* | *8 45* | *21 09* |
| 8 FR | 12 05 36 | +16 11 | 5 38 | 18 33 | 5 23 | 18 48 | 5 05 | 19 06 | 4 39 | 19 31 | 3 57 | 20 12 |
| *220* | | *1.0140* | *9 40* | *21 50* | *9 42* | *21 46* | *9 45* | *21 41* | *9 49* | *21 34* | *9 55* | *21 24* |
| 9 SA | 12 05 28 | +15 54 | 5 38 | 18 33 | 5 24 | 18 47 | 5 06 | 19 05 | 4 41 | 19 29 | 4 00 | 20 10 |
| *221* | | *1.0138* | *10 28* | *22 28* | *10 34* | *22 20* | *10 41* | *22 12* | *10 51* | *22 00* | *11 06* | *21 41* |
| 10 SU | 12 05 19 | +15 37 | 5 38 | 18 32 | 5 24 | 18 46 | 5 07 | 19 03 | 4 42 | 19 27 | 4 02 | 20 07 |
| *222* | | *1.0136* | *11 18* | *23 08* | *11 27* | *22 57* | *11 38* | *22 45* | *11 53* | *22 27* | *12 17* | *22 01* |
| 11 MO | 12 05 09 | +15 19 | 5 39 | 18 31 | 5 25 | 18 45 | 5 08 | 19 02 | 4 44 | 19 26 | 4 04 | 20 04 |
| *223* | *12 43 FQ* | *1.0135* | *12 09* | *23 50* | *12 21* | *23 37* | *12 36* | *23 21* | *12 57* | *22 59* | *13 29* | *22 24* |
| 12 TU | 12 04 59 | +15 01 | 5 39 | 18 31 | 5 26 | 18 44 | 5 09 | 19 01 | 4 45 | 19 24 | 4 07 | 20 01 |
| *224* | | *1.0133* | *13 03* | *none* | *13 17* | *none* | *13 35* | *none* | *14 00* | *23 37* | *14 40* | *22 55* |
| 13 WE | 12 04 49 | +14 43 | 5 39 | 18 30 | 5 26 | 18 43 | 5 10 | 18 59 | 4 47 | 19 22 | 4 09 | 19 59 |
| *225* | | *1.0131* | *13 58* | *0 37* | *14 14* | *0 22* | *14 34* | *0 03* | *15 02* | *none* | *15 49* | *23 34* |
| 14 TH | 12 04 38 | +14 25 | 5 40 | 18 29 | 5 27 | 18 42 | 5 11 | 18 58 | 4 48 | 19 20 | 4 12 | 19 56 |
| *226* | | *1.0129* | *14 54* | *1 28* | *15 11* | *1 11* | *15 32* | *0 51* | *16 02* | *0 22* | *16 51* | *none* |
| 15 FR | 12 04 26 | +14 06 | 5 40 | 18 29 | 5 27 | 18 41 | 5 11 | 18 57 | 4 50 | 19 18 | 4 14 | 19 53 |
| *227* | | *1.0127* | *15 51* | *2 24* | *16 08* | *2 07* | *16 28* | *1 45* | *16 57* | *1 16* | *17 45* | *0 26* |
| 16 SA | 12 04 14 | +13 48 | 5 40 | 18 28 | 5 28 | 18 40 | 5 12 | 18 55 | 4 51 | 19 16 | 4 17 | 19 50 |
| *228* | | *1.0126* | *16 47* | *3 23* | *17 02* | *3 07* | *17 21* | *2 47* | *17 46* | *2 19* | *18 28* | *1 32* |
| 17 SU | 12 04 01 | +13 29 | 5 41 | 18 27 | 5 28 | 18 39 | 5 13 | 18 54 | 4 53 | 19 15 | 4 19 | 19 47 |
| *229* | | *1.0124* | *17 41* | *4 26* | *17 54* | *4 12* | *18 09* | *3 54* | *18 30* | *3 30* | *19 02* | *2 50* |
| 18 MO | 12 03 48 | +13 09 | 5 41 | 18 26 | 5 29 | 18 38 | 5 14 | 18 53 | 4 54 | 19 13 | 4 21 | 19 45 |
| *230* | *10 56 FM* | *1.0122* | *18 34* | *5 30* | *18 42* | *5 19* | *18 53* | *5 06* | *19 08* | *4 47* | *19 30* | *4 17* |
| 19 TU | 12 03 34 | +12 50 | 5 41 | 18 26 | 5 30 | 18 37 | 5 15 | 18 51 | 4 55 | 19 11 | 4 24 | 19 42 |
| *231* | | *1.0120* | *19 24* | *6 34* | *19 28* | *6 27* | *19 34* | *6 19* | *19 42* | *6 07* | *19 54* | *5 48* |
| 20 WE | 12 03 20 | +12 30 | 5 41 | 18 25 | 5 30 | 18 36 | 5 16 | 18 50 | 4 57 | 19 09 | 4 26 | 19 39 |
| *232* | | *1.0118* | *20 12* | *7 38* | *20 12* | *7 35* | *20 13* | *7 32* | *20 13* | *7 27* | *20 15* | *7 20* |
| 21 TH | 12 03 05 | +12 10 | 5 42 | 18 24 | 5 31 | 18 35 | 5 17 | 18 48 | 4 58 | 19 07 | 4 29 | 19 36 |
| *233* | | *1.0116* | *20 59* | *8 40* | *20 55* | *8 42* | *20 51* | *8 44* | *20 44* | *8 47* | *20 35* | *8 51* |
| 22 FR | 12 02 50 | +11 50 | 5 42 | 18 23 | 5 31 | 18 34 | 5 18 | 18 47 | 5 00 | 19 05 | 4 31 | 19 33 |
| *234* | | *1.0114* | *21 46* | *9 41* | *21 38* | *9 47* | *21 29* | *9 54* | *21 16* | *10 04* | *20 57* | *10 20* |
| 23 SA | 12 02 34 | +11 30 | 5 42 | 18 23 | 5 32 | 18 33 | 5 19 | 18 45 | 5 01 | 19 03 | 4 33 | 19 30 |
| *235* | | *1.0112* | *22 33* | *10 41* | *22 22* | *10 51* | *22 08* | *11 02* | *21 50* | *11 19* | *21 21* | *11 45* |
| 24 SU | 12 02 18 | +11 10 | 5 42 | 18 22 | 5 32 | 18 32 | 5 20 | 18 44 | 5 03 | 19 01 | 4 36 | 19 27 |
| *236* | | *1.0110* | *23 21* | *11 39* | *23 07* | *11 52* | *22 50* | *12 08* | *22 27* | *12 30* | *21 49* | *13 05* |
| 25 MO | 12 02 02 | +10 49 | 5 43 | 18 21 | 5 33 | 18 31 | 5 21 | 18 42 | 5 04 | 18 59 | 4 38 | 19 24 |
| *237* | *2 25 LQ* | *1.0108* | *none* | *12 36* | *23 54* | *12 51* | *23 35* | *13 09* | *23 08* | *13 36* | *22 24* | *14 18* |
| 26 TU | 12 01 45 | +10 29 | 5 43 | 18 20 | 5 34 | 18 29 | 5 22 | 18 41 | 5 06 | 18 57 | 4 40 | 19 21 |
| *238* | | *1.0105* | *0 10* | *13 30* | *none* | *13 46* | *none* | *14 07* | *23 54* | *14 36* | *23 06* | *15 23* |
| 27 WE | 12 01 28 | +10 08 | 5 43 | 18 19 | 5 34 | 18 28 | 5 23 | 18 39 | 5 07 | 18 55 | 4 43 | 19 18 |
| *239* | | *1.0103* | *1 00* | *14 22* | *0 44* | *14 39* | *0 23* | *15 00* | *none* | *15 29* | *23 57* | *16 17* |
| 28 TH | 12 01 10 | + 9 47 | 5 43 | 18 19 | 5 35 | 18 27 | 5 24 | 18 38 | 5 09 | 18 52 | 4 45 | 19 15 |
| *240* | | *1.0101* | *1 51* | *15 11* | *1 34* | *15 27* | *1 13* | *15 47* | *0 44* | *16 15* | *none* | *17 00* |
| 29 FR | 12 00 52 | + 9 25 | 5 44 | 18 18 | 5 35 | 18 26 | 5 25 | 18 36 | 5 10 | 18 50 | 4 48 | 19 12 |
| *241* | | *1.0099* | *2 42* | *15 57* | *2 26* | *16 11* | *2 07* | *16 30* | *1 39* | *16 55* | *0 55* | *17 35* |
| 30 SA | 12 00 34 | + 9 04 | 5 44 | 18 17 | 5 36 | 18 25 | 5 26 | 18 35 | 5 12 | 18 48 | 4 50 | 19 10 |
| *242* | | *1.0097* | *3 32* | *16 40* | *3 19* | *16 52* | *3 01* | *17 08* | *2 37* | *17 29* | *1 59* | *18 02* |
| 31 SU | 12 00 16 | + 8 42 | 5 44 | 18 16 | 5 36 | 18 24 | 5 27 | 18 33 | 5 13 | 18 46 | 4 52 | 19 07 |
| *243* | | *1.0094* | *4 22* | *17 21* | *4 11* | *17 31* | *3 57* | *17 43* | *3 37* | *17 59* | *3 06* | *18 25* |

**9th Month** | **September 1997** | **30 days**

Greenwich Mean Time

**NOTE**: For each day, times on first line are for Sun. *Italic* times on second line are for *Moon.* Degrees are North Latitude.

Moon Phases: FM = full moon; LQ = last quarter; NM = new moon; FQ = first quarter. Sun's declination is in degrees; Sun's distance is in Astronomical Units.

**CAUTION**: Must be converted to local time. For instructions see page 462.

| Day of month, of week, *of year* | Sun on Meridian *Moon Phase* h m s | Sun's Decli- nation ° ′ *Distance* | 20° Rise Sun *Moon* h m | 20° Set Sun *Moon* h m | 30° Rise Sun *Moon* h m | 30° Set Sun *Moon* h m | 40° Rise Sun *Moon* h m | 40° Set Sun *Moon* h m | 50° Rise Sun *Moon* h m | 50° Set Sun *Moon* h m | 60° Rise Sun *Moon* h m | 60° Set Sun *Moon* h m |
|---|---|---|---|---|---|---|---|---|---|---|---|---|
| 1 MO | 11 59 57 | + 8 21 | 5 44 | 18 15 | 5 37 | 18 23 | 5 28 | 18 32 | 5 15 | 18 44 | 4 55 | 19 04 |
| *244* | *23 53 NM* | *1.0092* | *5 12* | *17 59* | *5 03* | *18 06* | *4 52* | *18 15* | *4 38* | *18 26* | *4 15* | *18 44* |
| 2 TU | 11 59 38 | + 7 59 | 5 45 | 18 14 | 5 37 | 18 21 | 5 29 | 18 30 | 5 16 | 18 42 | 4 57 | 19 01 |
| *245* | | *1.0090* | *6 00* | *18 37* | *5 55* | *18 41* | *5 48* | *18 45* | *5 39* | *18 51* | *5 25* | *19 01* |
| 3 WE | 11 59 18 | + 7 37 | 5 45 | 18 14 | 5 38 | 18 20 | 5 30 | 18 28 | 5 18 | 18 40 | 4 59 | 18 58 |
| *246* | | *1.0087* | *6 48* | *19 13* | *6 46* | *19 14* | *6 44* | *19 14* | *6 40* | *19 15* | *6 34* | *19 16* |
| 4 TH | 11 58 59 | + 7 15 | 5 45 | 18 13 | 5 39 | 18 19 | 5 30 | 18 27 | 5 19 | 18 38 | 5 02 | 18 55 |
| *247* | | *1.0085* | *7 36* | *19 50* | *7 38* | *19 47* | *7 39* | *19 44* | *7 41* | *19 39* | *7 44* | *19 32* |
| 5 FR | 11 58 39 | + 6 53 | 5 45 | 18 12 | 5 39 | 18 18 | 5 31 | 18 25 | 5 21 | 18 35 | 5 04 | 18 52 |
| *248* | | *1.0082* | *8 25* | *20 27* | *8 29* | *20 21* | *8 35* | *20 14* | *8 43* | *20 04* | *8 55* | *19 48* |
| 6 SA | 11 58 18 | + 6 30 | 5 45 | 18 11 | 5 40 | 18 17 | 5 32 | 18 24 | 5 22 | 18 33 | 5 07 | 18 49 |
| *249* | | *1.0080* | *9 14* | *21 06* | *9 21* | *20 57* | *9 31* | *20 46* | *9 44* | *20 30* | *10 05* | *20 07* |
| 7 SU | 11 57 58 | + 6 08 | 5 46 | 18 10 | 5 40 | 18 15 | 5 33 | 18 22 | 5 24 | 18 31 | 5 09 | 18 45 |
| *250* | | *1.0077* | *10 04* | *21 47* | *10 15* | *21 35* | *10 28* | *21 21* | *10 46* | *21 00* | *11 16* | *20 28* |
| 8 MO | 11 57 38 | + 5 46 | 5 46 | 18 09 | 5 41 | 18 14 | 5 34 | 18 20 | 5 25 | 18 29 | 5 11 | 18 42 |
| *251* | | *1.0075* | *10 55* | *22 31* | *11 09* | *22 17* | *11 25* | *21 59* | *11 49* | *21 35* | *12 26* | *20 55* |
| 9 TU | 11 57 17 | + 5 23 | 5 46 | 18 08 | 5 41 | 18 13 | 5 35 | 18 19 | 5 27 | 18 27 | 5 14 | 18 39 |
| *252* | | *1.0072* | *11 48* | *23 19* | *12 04* | *23 03* | *12 23* | *22 43* | *12 50* | *22 15* | *13 34* | *21 30* |
| 10 WE | 11 56 56 | + 5 00 | 5 46 | 18 07 | 5 42 | 18 12 | 5 36 | 18 17 | 5 28 | 18 25 | 5 16 | 18 36 |
| *253* | *1 32 FQ* | *1.0069* | *12 42* | *none* | *12 59* | *23 54* | *13 20* | *23 33* | *13 49* | *23 04* | *14 37* | *22 15* |
| 11 TH | 11 56 35 | + 4 38 | 5 47 | 18 06 | 5 42 | 18 10 | 5 37 | 18 15 | 5 30 | 18 22 | 5 18 | 18 33 |
| *254* | | *1.0067* | *13 37* | *0 11* | *13 54* | *none* | *14 15* | *none* | *14 44* | *none* | *15 33* | *23 12* |
| 12 FR | 11 56 14 | + 4 15 | 5 47 | 18 05 | 5 43 | 18 09 | 5 38 | 18 14 | 5 31 | 18 20 | 5 21 | 18 30 |
| *255* | | *1.0064* | *14 32* | *1 07* | *14 48* | *0 50* | *15 07* | *0 29* | *15 35* | *0 00* | *16 20* | *none* |
| 13 SA | 11 55 52 | + 3 52 | 5 47 | 18 05 | 5 43 | 18 08 | 5 39 | 18 12 | 5 33 | 18 18 | 5 23 | 18 27 |
| *256* | | *1.0061* | *15 26* | *2 06* | *15 39* | *1 51* | *15 56* | *1 32* | *16 20* | *1 06* | *16 57* | *0 23* |
| 14 SU | 11 55 31 | + 3 29 | 5 47 | 18 04 | 5 44 | 18 07 | 5 40 | 18 10 | 5 34 | 18 16 | 5 25 | 18 24 |
| *257* | | *1.0059* | *16 18* | *3 08* | *16 29* | *2 56* | *16 42* | *2 40* | *17 00* | *2 18* | *17 28* | *1 43* |
| 15 MO | 11 55 10 | + 3 06 | 5 47 | 18 03 | 5 44 | 18 05 | 5 41 | 18 09 | 5 36 | 18 14 | 5 28 | 18 21 |
| *258* | | *1.0056* | *17 09* | *4 12* | *17 16* | *4 03* | *17 24* | *3 51* | *17 36* | *3 36* | *17 53* | *3 11* |
| 16 TU | 11 54 48 | + 2 43 | 5 48 | 18 02 | 5 45 | 18 04 | 5 42 | 18 07 | 5 37 | 18 11 | 5 30 | 18 18 |
| *259* | *18 52 FM* | *1.0053* | *17 58* | *5 16* | *18 01* | *5 11* | *18 04* | *5 05* | *18 09* | *4 56* | *18 16* | *4 43* |
| 17 WE | 11 54 27 | + 2 20 | 5 48 | 18 01 | 5 46 | 18 03 | 5 43 | 18 06 | 5 39 | 18 09 | 5 32 | 18 15 |
| *260* | | *1.0050* | *18 47* | *6 20* | *18 45* | *6 19* | *18 43* | *6 19* | *18 41* | *6 18* | *18 37* | *6 16* |
| 18 TH | 11 54 05 | + 1 56 | 5 48 | 18 00 | 5 46 | 18 02 | 5 44 | 18 04 | 5 40 | 18 07 | 5 35 | 18 12 |
| *261* | | *1.0048* | *19 35* | *7 23* | *19 30* | *7 27* | *19 22* | *7 32* | *19 13* | *7 38* | *18 59* | *7 48* |
| 19 FR | 11 53 44 | + 1 33 | 5 48 | 17 59 | 5 47 | 18 00 | 5 45 | 18 02 | 5 42 | 18 05 | 5 37 | 18 09 |
| *262* | | *1.0045* | *20 24* | *8 25* | *20 15* | *8 33* | *20 03* | *8 43* | *19 47* | *8 57* | *19 22* | *9 18* |
| 20 SA | 11 53 22 | + 1 10 | 5 48 | 17 58 | 5 47 | 17 59 | 5 46 | 18 01 | 5 43 | 18 03 | 5 39 | 18 06 |
| *263* | | *1.0042* | *21 14* | *9 27* | *21 01* | *9 38* | *20 45* | *9 52* | *20 24* | *10 12* | *19 50* | *10 43* |
| 21 SU | 11 53 01 | + 0 47 | 5 49 | 17 57 | 5 48 | 17 58 | 5 46 | 17 59 | 5 45 | 18 00 | 5 42 | 18 03 |
| *264* | | *1.0039* | *22 04* | *10 26* | *21 49* | *10 40* | *21 30* | *10 58* | *21 04* | *11 23* | *20 23* | *12 03* |
| 22 MO | 11 52 40 | + 0 23 | 5 49 | 17 56 | 5 48 | 17 57 | 5 47 | 17 57 | 5 46 | 17 58 | 5 44 | 18 00 |
| *265* | | *1.0037* | *22 55* | *11 23* | *22 39* | *11 39* | *22 18* | *11 59* | *21 50* | *12 27* | *21 03* | *13 13* |
| 23 TU | 11 52 19 | - 0 00 | 5 49 | 17 55 | 5 49 | 17 55 | 5 48 | 17 56 | 5 48 | 17 56 | 5 46 | 17 57 |
| *266* | *13 36 LQ* | *1.0034* | *23 47* | *12 17* | *23 30* | *12 34* | *23 09* | *12 55* | *22 40* | *13 24* | *21 52* | *14 12* |
| 24 WE | 11 51 58 | - 0 23 | 5 49 | 17 54 | 5 49 | 17 54 | 5 49 | 17 54 | 5 49 | 17 54 | 5 49 | 17 54 |
| *267* | | *1.0031* | *none* | *13 07* | *none* | *13 24* | *none* | *13 45* | *23 34* | *14 13* | *22 48* | *15 00* |
| 25 TH | 11 51 37 | - 0 47 | 5 49 | 17 54 | 5 50 | 17 53 | 5 50 | 17 52 | 5 51 | 17 52 | 5 51 | 17 51 |
| *268* | | *1.0029* | *0 38* | *13 55* | *0 22* | *14 10* | *0 02* | *14 29* | *none* | *14 55* | *23 50* | *15 37* |
| 26 FR | 11 51 17 | - 1 10 | 5 50 | 17 53 | 5 50 | 17 52 | 5 51 | 17 51 | 5 52 | 17 49 | 5 53 | 17 48 |
| *269* | | *1.0026* | *1 29* | *14 39* | *1 14* | *14 52* | *0 56* | *15 09* | *0 31* | *15 31* | *none* | *16 07* |
| 27 SA | 11 50 56 | - 1 34 | 5 50 | 17 52 | 5 51 | 17 50 | 5 52 | 17 49 | 5 54 | 17 47 | 5 56 | 17 45 |
| *270* | | *1.0023* | *2 19* | *15 20* | *2 07* | *15 31* | *1 51* | *15 44* | *1 30* | *16 02* | *0 57* | *16 31* |
| 28 SU | 11 50 36 | - 1 57 | 5 50 | 17 51 | 5 52 | 17 49 | 5 53 | 17 47 | 5 55 | 17 45 | 5 58 | 17 42 |
| *271* | | *1.0020* | *3 08* | *15 59* | *2 59* | *16 07* | *2 47* | *16 17* | *2 31* | *16 30* | *2 05* | *16 50* |
| 29 MO | 11 50 16 | - 2 20 | 5 50 | 17 50 | 5 52 | 17 48 | 5 54 | 17 46 | 5 57 | 17 43 | 6 01 | 17 39 |
| *272* | | *1.0017* | *3 57* | *16 37* | *3 50* | *16 42* | *3 42* | *16 48* | *3 31* | *16 56* | *3 14* | *17 08* |
| 30 TU | 11 49 57 | - 2 44 | 5 51 | 17 49 | 5 53 | 17 47 | 5 55 | 17 44 | 5 58 | 17 41 | 6 03 | 17 36 |
| *273* | | *1.0015* | *4 45* | *17 14* | *4 42* | *17 16* | *4 38* | *17 17* | *4 32* | *17 20* | *4 24* | *17 24* |

## 10th Month — October 1997 — 31 days

Greenwich Mean Time

**NOTE**: For each day, times on first line are for Sun. *Italic* times on second line are for *Moon*. Degrees are North Latitude.

Moon Phases: FM = full moon; LQ = last quarter; NM = new moon; FQ = first quarter. Sun's declination is in degrees; Sun's distance is in Astronomical Units.

**CAUTION**: Must be converted to local time. For instructions see page 462.

| Day of month, of week, *of year* | Sun on Meridian *Moon Phase* h m s | Sun's Decli-nation ° ′ *Distance* | 20° Rise Sun *Moon* h m | 20° Set Sun *Moon* h m | 30° Rise Sun *Moon* h m | 30° Set Sun *Moon* h m | 40° Rise Sun *Moon* h m | 40° Set Sun *Moon* h m | 50° Rise Sun *Moon* h m | 50° Set Sun *Moon* h m | 60° Rise Sun *Moon* h m | 60° Set Sun *Moon* h m |
|---|---|---|---|---|---|---|---|---|---|---|---|---|
| 1 WE | 11 49 38 | - 3 07 | 5 51 | 17 48 | 5 53 | 17 46 | 5 56 | 17 42 | 6 00 | 17 38 | 6 05 | 17 33 |
| *274* | *16 53 NM* | *1.0012* | *5 33* | *17 51* | *5 33* | *17 49* | *5 34* | *17 47* | *5 34* | *17 44* | *5 34* | *17 39* |
| 2 TH | 11 49 18 | - 3 30 | 5 51 | 17 47 | 5 54 | 17 44 | 5 57 | 17 41 | 6 01 | 17 36 | 6 08 | 17 30 |
| *275* | | *1.0009* | *6 22* | *18 28* | *6 25* | *18 23* | *6 29* | *18 17* | *6 35* | *18 08* | *6 45* | *17 55* |
| 3 FR | 11 49 00 | - 3 53 | 5 51 | 17 46 | 5 54 | 17 43 | 5 58 | 17 39 | 6 03 | 17 34 | 6 10 | 17 27 |
| *276* | | *1.0006* | *7 11* | *19 06* | *7 17* | *18 58* | *7 26* | *18 48* | *7 37* | *18 34* | *7 55* | *18 13* |
| 4 SA | 11 48 41 | - 4 17 | 5 52 | 17 46 | 5 55 | 17 42 | 5 59 | 17 38 | 6 04 | 17 32 | 6 13 | 17 24 |
| *277* | | *1.0003* | *8 00* | *19 47* | *8 10* | *19 36* | *8 23* | *19 22* | *8 40* | *19 03* | *9 07* | *18 34* |
| 5 SU | 11 48 23 | - 4 40 | 5 52 | 17 45 | 5 56 | 17 41 | 6 00 | 17 36 | 6 06 | 17 30 | 6 15 | 17 21 |
| *278* | | *1.0000* | *8 51* | *20 30* | *9 04* | *20 16* | *9 20* | *19 59* | *9 42* | *19 36* | *10 17* | *18 58* |
| 6 MO | 11 48 06 | - 5 03 | 5 52 | 17 44 | 5 56 | 17 40 | 6 01 | 17 34 | 6 08 | 17 28 | 6 17 | 17 18 |
| *279* | | *.9997* | *9 44* | *21 16* | *9 59* | *21 00* | *10 17* | *20 41* | *10 43* | *20 14* | *11 26* | *19 30* |
| 7 TU | 11 47 48 | - 5 26 | 5 52 | 17 43 | 5 57 | 17 38 | 6 02 | 17 33 | 6 09 | 17 26 | 6 20 | 17 15 |
| *280* | | *.9994* | *10 37* | *22 05* | *10 53* | *21 48* | *11 14* | *21 27* | *11 42* | *20 58* | *12 30* | *20 10* |
| 8 WE | 11 47 31 | - 5 49 | 5 53 | 17 42 | 5 57 | 17 37 | 6 03 | 17 31 | 6 11 | 17 23 | 6 22 | 17 12 |
| *281* | | *.9991* | *11 30* | *22 58* | *11 47* | *22 41* | *12 08* | *22 20* | *12 38* | *21 50* | *13 27* | *21 02* |
| 9 TH | 11 47 15 | - 6 12 | 5 53 | 17 41 | 5 58 | 17 36 | 6 04 | 17 30 | 6 12 | 17 21 | 6 25 | 17 09 |
| *282* | *12 23 FQ* | *.9988* | *12 23* | *23 54* | *12 39* | *23 38* | *13 00* | *23 18* | *13 29* | *22 51* | *14 15* | *22 05* |
| 10 FR | 11 46 59 | - 6 34 | 5 53 | 17 40 | 5 59 | 17 35 | 6 05 | 17 28 | 6 14 | 17 19 | 6 27 | 17 06 |
| *283* | | *.9986* | *13 15* | *none* | *13 30* | *none* | *13 49* | *none* | *14 14* | *23 58* | *14 55* | *23 19* |
| 11 SA | 11 46 43 | - 6 57 | 5 54 | 17 40 | 5 59 | 17 34 | 6 06 | 17 27 | 6 15 | 17 17 | 6 29 | 17 03 |
| *284* | | *.9983* | *14 06* | *0 53* | *14 19* | *0 39* | *14 34* | *0 22* | *14 54* | *none* | *15 27* | *none* |
| 12 SU | 11 46 28 | - 7 20 | 5 54 | 17 39 | 6 00 | 17 33 | 6 07 | 17 25 | 6 17 | 17 15 | 6 32 | 17 00 |
| *285* | | *.9980* | *14 56* | *1 54* | *15 05* | *1 43* | *15 16* | *1 29* | *15 30* | *1 11* | *15 53* | *0 41* |
| 13 MO | 11 46 13 | - 7 42 | 5 54 | 17 38 | 6 01 | 17 31 | 6 08 | 17 24 | 6 19 | 17 13 | 6 34 | 16 57 |
| *286* | | *.9977* | *15 45* | *2 55* | *15 50* | *2 48* | *15 56* | *2 39* | *16 04* | *2 27* | *16 16* | *2 08* |
| 14 TU | 11 45 59 | - 8 05 | 5 54 | 17 37 | 6 01 | 17 30 | 6 09 | 17 22 | 6 20 | 17 11 | 6 37 | 16 54 |
| *287* | | *.9974* | *16 33* | *3 58* | *16 34* | *3 55* | *16 34* | *3 51* | *16 36* | *3 46* | *16 37* | *3 39* |
| 15 WE | 11 45 46 | - 8 27 | 5 55 | 17 36 | 6 02 | 17 29 | 6 10 | 17 21 | 6 22 | 17 09 | 6 39 | 16 51 |
| *288* | | *.9971* | *17 21* | *5 01* | *17 17* | *5 02* | *17 13* | *5 04* | *17 07* | *5 07* | *16 58* | *5 11* |
| 16 TH | 11 45 33 | - 8 49 | 5 55 | 17 36 | 6 02 | 17 28 | 6 11 | 17 19 | 6 23 | 17 07 | 6 42 | 16 48 |
| *289* | *3 47 FM* | *.9968* | *18 10* | *6 04* | *18 02* | *6 10* | *17 53* | *6 17* | *17 40* | *6 27* | *17 21* | *6 42* |
| 17 FR | 11 45 20 | - 9 11 | 5 55 | 17 35 | 6 03 | 17 27 | 6 12 | 17 18 | 6 25 | 17 05 | 6 44 | 16 45 |
| *290* | | *.9965* | *19 00* | *7 07* | *18 49* | *7 17* | *18 35* | *7 29* | *18 16* | *7 46* | *17 47* | *8 12* |
| 18 SA | 11 45 08 | - 9 33 | 5 56 | 17 34 | 6 04 | 17 26 | 6 14 | 17 16 | 6 27 | 17 03 | 6 47 | 16 43 |
| *291* | | *.9963* | *19 52* | *8 09* | *19 37* | *8 22* | *19 20* | *8 38* | *18 56* | *9 01* | *18 17* | *9 37* |
| 19 SU | 11 44 57 | - 9 55 | 5 56 | 17 34 | 6 04 | 17 25 | 6 15 | 17 15 | 6 28 | 17 01 | 6 49 | 16 40 |
| *292* | | *.9960* | *20 44* | *9 09* | *20 28* | *9 24* | *20 08* | *9 44* | *19 40* | *10 11* | *18 55* | *10 54* |
| 20 MO | 11 44 46 | -10 16 | 5 56 | 17 33 | 6 05 | 17 24 | 6 16 | 17 13 | 6 30 | 16 59 | 6 52 | 16 37 |
| *293* | | *.9957* | *21 37* | *10 06* | *21 20* | *10 23* | *20 59* | *10 44* | *20 30* | *11 13* | *19 42* | *12 01* |
| 21 TU | 11 44 36 | -10 38 | 5 57 | 17 32 | 6 06 | 17 23 | 6 17 | 17 12 | 6 31 | 16 57 | 6 54 | 16 34 |
| *294* | | *.9954* | *22 30* | *11 00* | *22 14* | *11 17* | *21 53* | *11 38* | *21 24* | *12 07* | *20 36* | *12 55* |
| 22 WE | 11 44 27 | -10 59 | 5 57 | 17 31 | 6 07 | 17 22 | 6 18 | 17 11 | 6 33 | 16 55 | 6 57 | 16 31 |
| *295* | | *.9952* | *23 23* | *11 50* | *23 07* | *12 06* | *22 48* | *12 26* | *22 22* | *12 53* | *21 38* | *13 38* |
| 23 TH | 11 44 19 | -11 20 | 5 58 | 17 31 | 6 07 | 17 21 | 6 19 | 17 09 | 6 35 | 16 53 | 6 59 | 16 28 |
| *296* | *4 49 LQ* | *.9949* | *none* | *12 36* | *none* | *12 50* | *23 44* | *13 08* | *23 21* | *13 32* | *22 45* | *14 10* |
| 24 FR | 11 44 11 | -11 41 | 5 58 | 17 30 | 6 08 | 17 20 | 6 20 | 17 08 | 6 36 | 16 51 | 7 02 | 16 26 |
| *297* | | *.9946* | *0 14* | *13 19* | *0 00* | *13 31* | *none* | *13 45* | *none* | *14 05* | *23 53* | *14 36* |
| 25 SA | 11 44 04 | -12 02 | 5 58 | 17 29 | 6 09 | 17 19 | 6 21 | 17 06 | 6 38 | 16 49 | 7 04 | 16 23 |
| *298* | | *.9944* | *1 04* | *13 59* | *0 53* | *14 08* | *0 40* | *14 19* | *0 22* | *14 34* | *none* | *14 57* |
| 26 SU | 11 43 58 | -12 23 | 5 59 | 17 29 | 6 09 | 17 18 | 6 22 | 17 05 | 6 40 | 16 48 | 7 07 | 16 20 |
| *299* | | *.9941* | *1 53* | *14 37* | *1 45* | *14 43* | *1 36* | *14 50* | *1 23* | *15 00* | *1 02* | *15 15* |
| 27 MO | 11 43 52 | -12 43 | 5 59 | 17 28 | 6 10 | 17 17 | 6 23 | 17 04 | 6 41 | 16 46 | 7 09 | 16 17 |
| *300* | | *.9938* | *2 41* | *15 14* | *2 37* | *15 17* | *2 31* | *15 20* | *2 24* | *15 24* | *2 12* | *15 31* |
| 28 TU | 11 43 47 | -13 03 | 6 00 | 17 28 | 6 11 | 17 16 | 6 24 | 17 03 | 6 43 | 16 44 | 7 12 | 16 15 |
| *301* | | *.9936* | *3 29* | *15 50* | *3 28* | *15 50* | *3 27* | *15 49* | *3 25* | *15 48* | *3 22* | *15 47* |
| 29 WE | 11 43 43 | -13 23 | 6 00 | 17 27 | 6 12 | 17 16 | 6 26 | 17 01 | 6 45 | 16 42 | 7 14 | 16 12 |
| *302* | | *.9933* | *4 17* | *16 27* | *4 20* | *16 24* | *4 23* | *16 19* | *4 26* | *16 12* | *4 33* | *16 02* |
| 30 TH | 11 43 40 | -13 43 | 6 01 | 17 27 | 6 12 | 17 15 | 6 27 | 17 00 | 6 46 | 16 40 | 7 17 | 16 09 |
| *303* | | *.9930* | *5 06* | *17 06* | *5 12* | *16 58* | *5 19* | *16 49* | *5 29* | *16 38* | *5 44* | *16 19* |
| 31 FR | 11 43 37 | -14 03 | 6 01 | 17 26 | 6 13 | 17 14 | 6 28 | 16 59 | 6 48 | 16 39 | 7 20 | 16 07 |
| *304* | *10 02 NM* | *.9928* | *5 56* | *17 46* | *6 05* | *17 35* | *6 16* | *17 23* | *6 32* | *17 05* | *6 56* | *16 38* |

**11th Month** **November 1997** **30 days**

Greenwich Mean Time

**NOTE**: For each day, times on first line are for Sun. *Italic* times on second line are for *Moon*. Degrees are North Latitude.

Moon Phases: FM = full moon; LQ = last quarter; NM = new moon; FQ = first quarter. Sun's declination is in degrees; Sun's distance is in Astronomical Units.

**CAUTION**: Must be converted to local time. For instructions see page 462.

| Day of month, of week, *of year* | Sun on Meridian *Moon Phase* h m s | Sun's Decli- nation ° ′ *Distance* | 20° Rise Sun *Moon* h m | 20° Set Sun *Moon* h m | 30° Rise Sun *Moon* h m | 30° Set Sun *Moon* h m | 40° Rise Sun *Moon* h m | 40° Set Sun *Moon* h m | 50° Rise Sun *Moon* h m | 50° Set Sun *Moon* h m | 60° Rise Sun *Moon* h m | 60° Set Sun *Moon* h m |
|---|---|---|---|---|---|---|---|---|---|---|---|---|
| 1 SA | 11 43 35 | -14 22 | 6 01 | 17 26 | 6 14 | 17 13 | 6 29 | 16 58 | 6 50 | 16 37 | 7 22 | 16 04 |
| *305* | | .9925 | *6 47* | *18 28* | *6 59* | *18 15* | *7 14* | *17 59* | *7 35* | *17 37* | *8 08* | *17 02* |
| 2 SU | 11 43 34 | -14 41 | 6 02 | 17 25 | 6 15 | 17 12 | 6 30 | 16 57 | 6 51 | 16 35 | 7 25 | 16 02 |
| *306* | | .9923 | *7 40* | *19 14* | *7 54* | *18 58* | *8 12* | *18 39* | *8 37* | *18 13* | *9 18* | *17 31* |
| 3 MO | 11 43 34 | -15 00 | 6 02 | 17 25 | 6 15 | 17 11 | 6 31 | 16 55 | 6 53 | 16 34 | 7 27 | 15 59 |
| *307* | | .9920 | *8 33* | *20 02* | *8 49* | *19 46* | *9 10* | *19 25* | *9 38* | *18 56* | *10 25* | *18 08* |
| 4 TU | 11 43 35 | -15 19 | 6 03 | 17 24 | 6 16 | 17 11 | 6 32 | 16 54 | 6 55 | 16 32 | 7 30 | 15 56 |
| *308* | | .9917 | *9 27* | *20 54* | *9 44* | *20 37* | *10 05* | *20 16* | *10 35* | *19 46* | *11 25* | *18 56* |
| 5 WE | 11 43 36 | -15 37 | 6 03 | 17 24 | 6 17 | 17 10 | 6 34 | 16 53 | 6 56 | 16 30 | 7 32 | 15 54 |
| *309* | | .9915 | *10 20* | *21 49* | *10 37* | *21 32* | *10 58* | *21 12* | *11 27* | *20 43* | *12 16* | *19 55* |
| 6 TH | 11 43 39 | -15 55 | 6 04 | 17 23 | 6 18 | 17 09 | 6 35 | 16 52 | 6 58 | 16 29 | 7 35 | 15 51 |
| *310* | | .9912 | *11 12* | *22 46* | *11 27* | *22 31* | *11 47* | *22 12* | *12 14* | *21 47* | *12 57* | *21 04* |
| 7 FR | 11 43 42 | -16 13 | 6 04 | 17 23 | 6 18 | 17 09 | 6 36 | 16 51 | 7 00 | 16 27 | 7 38 | 15 49 |
| *311* | *21 44 FQ* | .9910 | *12 02* | *23 44* | *12 15* | *23 32* | *12 32* | *23 17* | *12 54* | *22 56* | *13 31* | *22 22* |
| 8 SA | 11 43 46 | -16 31 | 6 05 | 17 22 | 6 19 | 17 08 | 6 37 | 16 50 | 7 01 | 16 26 | 7 40 | 15 47 |
| *312* | | .9907 | *12 50* | *none* | *13 01* | *none* | *13 13* | *none* | *13 31* | *none* | *13 58* | *23 45* |
| 9 SU | 11 43 50 | -16 48 | 6 05 | 17 22 | 6 20 | 17 07 | 6 38 | 16 49 | 7 03 | 16 24 | 7 43 | 15 44 |
| *313* | | .9905 | *13 37* | *0 43* | *13 44* | *0 34* | *13 52* | *0 24* | *14 03* | *0 09* | *14 20* | *none* |
| 10 MO | 11 43 56 | -17 05 | 6 06 | 17 22 | 6 21 | 17 07 | 6 39 | 16 48 | 7 05 | 16 23 | 7 45 | 15 42 |
| *314* | | .9902 | *14 24* | *1 43* | *14 26* | *1 38* | *14 30* | *1 32* | *14 34* | *1 24* | *14 41* | *1 11* |
| 11 TU | 11 44 02 | -17 22 | 6 07 | 17 21 | 6 22 | 17 06 | 6 40 | 16 47 | 7 06 | 16 21 | 7 48 | 15 39 |
| *315* | | .9900 | *15 10* | *2 44* | *15 09* | *2 43* | *15 07* | *2 42* | *15 04* | *2 41* | *15 01* | *2 39* |
| 12 WE | 11 44 10 | -17 38 | 6 07 | 17 21 | 6 23 | 17 05 | 6 42 | 16 46 | 7 08 | 16 20 | 7 50 | 15 37 |
| *316* | | .9898 | *15 57* | *3 45* | *15 51* | *3 48* | *15 45* | *3 53* | *15 35* | *3 59* | *15 21* | *4 09* |
| 13 TH | 11 44 18 | -17 55 | 6 08 | 17 21 | 6 23 | 17 05 | 6 43 | 16 45 | 7 09 | 16 19 | 7 53 | 15 35 |
| *317* | | .9895 | *16 46* | *4 46* | *16 36* | *4 54* | *16 24* | *5 04* | *16 09* | *5 17* | *15 44* | *5 38* |
| 14 FR | 11 44 27 | -18 10 | 6 08 | 17 20 | 6 24 | 17 04 | 6 44 | 16 45 | 7 11 | 16 17 | 7 55 | 15 33 |
| *318* | *14 13 FM* | .9893 | *17 36* | *5 49* | *17 23* | *6 00* | *17 07* | *6 14* | *16 46* | *6 34* | *16 12* | *7 05* |
| 15 SA | 11 44 36 | -18 26 | 6 09 | 17 20 | 6 25 | 17 04 | 6 45 | 16 44 | 7 13 | 16 16 | 7 58 | 15 31 |
| *319* | | .9891 | *18 29* | *6 50* | *18 13* | *7 05* | *17 54* | *7 23* | *17 28* | *7 48* | *16 46* | *8 28* |
| 16 SU | 11 44 47 | -18 41 | 6 09 | 17 20 | 6 26 | 17 03 | 6 46 | 16 43 | 7 14 | 16 15 | 8 00 | 15 28 |
| *320* | | .9889 | *19 23* | *7 50* | *19 06* | *8 06* | *18 45* | *8 27* | *18 16* | *8 55* | *17 28* | *9 42* |
| 17 MO | 11 44 59 | -18 56 | 6 10 | 17 20 | 6 27 | 17 03 | 6 47 | 16 42 | 7 16 | 16 14 | 8 03 | 15 26 |
| *321* | | .9886 | *20 17* | *8 47* | *20 00* | *9 04* | *19 39* | *9 25* | *19 09* | *9 55* | *18 20* | *10 44* |
| 18 TU | 11 45 11 | -19 11 | 6 11 | 17 20 | 6 27 | 17 03 | 6 48 | 16 42 | 7 18 | 16 12 | 8 05 | 15 24 |
| *322* | | .9884 | *21 11* | *9 40* | *20 55* | *9 57* | *20 35* | *10 18* | *20 07* | *10 47* | *19 20* | *11 34* |
| 19 WE | 11 45 24 | -19 25 | 6 11 | 17 19 | 6 28 | 17 02 | 6 50 | 16 41 | 7 19 | 16 11 | 8 08 | 15 22 |
| *323* | | .9882 | *22 04* | *10 29* | *21 50* | *10 45* | *21 32* | *11 04* | *21 07* | *11 30* | *20 27* | *12 12* |
| 20 TH | 11 45 38 | -19 39 | 6 12 | 17 19 | 6 29 | 17 02 | 6 51 | 16 40 | 7 21 | 16 10 | 8 10 | 15 20 |
| *324* | | .9880 | *22 56* | *11 14* | *22 44* | *11 28* | *22 29* | *11 44* | *22 09* | *12 06* | *21 36* | *12 41* |
| 21 FR | 11 45 53 | -19 52 | 6 12 | 17 19 | 6 30 | 17 02 | 6 52 | 16 40 | 7 22 | 16 09 | 8 13 | 15 19 |
| *325* | *23 59 LQ* | .9878 | *23 46* | *11 56* | *23 37* | *12 07* | *23 26* | *12 19* | *23 10* | *12 37* | *22 46* | *13 04* |
| 22 SA | 11 46 08 | -20 05 | 6 13 | 17 19 | 6 31 | 17 01 | 6 53 | 16 39 | 7 24 | 16 08 | 8 15 | 15 17 |
| *326* | | .9876 | *none* | *12 35* | *none* | *12 43* | *none* | *12 52* | *none* | *13 04* | *23 56* | *13 23* |
| 23 SU | 11 46 25 | -20 18 | 6 14 | 17 19 | 6 32 | 17 01 | 6 54 | 16 38 | 7 25 | 16 07 | 8 17 | 15 15 |
| *327* | | .9875 | *0 35* | *13 13* | *0 29* | *13 17* | *0 22* | *13 22* | *0 12* | *13 29* | *none* | *13 39* |
| 24 MO | 11 46 42 | -20 30 | 6 14 | 17 19 | 6 32 | 17 01 | 6 55 | 16 38 | 7 27 | 16 06 | 8 20 | 15 13 |
| *328* | | .9873 | *1 23* | *13 49* | *1 20* | *13 50* | *1 17* | *13 51* | *1 13* | *13 52* | *1 07* | *13 54* |
| 25 TU | 11 47 00 | -20 42 | 6 15 | 17 19 | 6 33 | 17 00 | 6 56 | 16 37 | 7 28 | 16 05 | 8 22 | 15 11 |
| *329* | | .9871 | *2 11* | *14 26* | *2 12* | *14 23* | *2 13* | *14 20* | *2 15* | *14 16* | *2 17* | *14 10* |
| 26 WE | 11 47 19 | -20 54 | 6 15 | 17 19 | 6 34 | 17 00 | 6 57 | 16 37 | 7 30 | 16 05 | 8 24 | 15 10 |
| *330* | | .9869 | *3 00* | *15 03* | *3 04* | *14 57* | *3 09* | *14 50* | *3 17* | *14 40* | *3 28* | *14 26* |
| 27 TH | 11 47 38 | -21 05 | 6 16 | 17 19 | 6 35 | 17 00 | 6 58 | 16 37 | 7 31 | 16 04 | 8 26 | 15 08 |
| *331* | | .9867 | *3 49* | *15 42* | *3 57* | *15 33* | *4 06* | *15 22* | *4 19* | *15 07* | *4 40* | *14 43* |
| 28 FR | 11 47 59 | -21 16 | 6 17 | 17 19 | 6 36 | 17 00 | 6 59 | 16 36 | 7 33 | 16 03 | 8 29 | 15 07 |
| *332* | | .9866 | *4 40* | *16 24* | *4 51* | *16 12* | *5 05* | *15 57* | *5 23* | *15 37* | *5 52* | *15 05* |
| 29 SA | 11 48 20 | -21 27 | 6 17 | 17 19 | 6 37 | 17 00 | 7 00 | 16 36 | 7 34 | 16 02 | 8 31 | 15 05 |
| *333* | | .9864 | *5 33* | *17 09* | *5 46* | *16 54* | *6 03* | *16 36* | *6 27* | *16 11* | *7 05* | *15 31* |
| 30 SU | 11 48 41 | -21 37 | 6 18 | 17 19 | 6 37 | 17 00 | 7 02 | 16 36 | 7 35 | 16 02 | 8 33 | 15 04 |
| *334* | *2 15 NM* | .9862 | *6 27* | *17 57* | *6 42* | *17 41* | *7 02* | *17 20* | *7 30* | *16 52* | *8 15* | *16 06* |

**12th Month** **December 1997** **31 days**

Greenwich Mean Time

**NOTE**: For each day, times on first line are for Sun. *Italic* times on second line are for *Moon*. Degrees are North Latitude.

Moon Phases: FM = full moon; LQ = last quarter;„NM = new moon; FQ = first quarter. Sun's declination is in degrees; Sun's distance is in Astronomical Units.

**CAUTION**: Must be converted to local time. For instructions see page 462.

| Day of month, of week, *of year* | Sun on Meridian *Moon Phase* h m s | Sun's Declination ° ′ *Distance* | 20° Rise Sun *Moon* h m | 20° Set Sun *Moon* h m | 30° Rise Sun *Moon* h m | 30° Set Sun *Moon* h m | 40° Rise Sun *Moon* h m | 40° Set Sun *Moon* h m | 50° Rise Sun *Moon* h m | 50° Set Sun *Moon* h m | 60° Rise Sun *Moon* h m | 60° Set Sun *Moon* h m |
|---|---|---|---|---|---|---|---|---|---|---|---|---|
| 1 MO | 11 49 04 | -21 46 | 6 19 | 17 19 | 6 38 | 17 00 | 7 03 | 16 35 | 7 37 | 16 01 | 8 35 | 15 03 |
| *335* | | *.9861* | *7 21* | *18 49* | *7 38* | *18 32* | *8 00* | *18 10* | *8 30* | *17 40* | *9 19* | *16 50* |
| 2 TU | 11 49 27 | -21 55 | 6 19 | 17 20 | 6 39 | 17 00 | 7 04 | 16 35 | 7 38 | 16 01 | 8 37 | 15 02 |
| *336* | | *.9859* | *8 16* | *19 44* | *8 33* | *19 27* | *8 55* | *19 05* | *9 25* | *18 36* | *10 15* | *17 46* |
| 3 WE | 11 49 50 | -22 04 | 6 20 | 17 20 | 6 40 | 17 00 | 7 05 | 16 35 | 7 39 | 16 00 | 8 39 | 15 00 |
| *337* | | *.9857* | *9 09* | *20 41* | *9 25* | *20 25* | *9 46* | *20 06* | *10 14* | *19 38* | *11 00* | *18 53* |
| 4 TH | 11 50 14 | -22 13 | 6 21 | 17 20 | 6 41 | 17 00 | 7 05 | 16 35 | 7 41 | 16 00 | 8 41 | 14 59 |
| *338* | | *.9856* | *10 00* | *21 39* | *10 15* | *21 26* | *10 33* | *21 09* | *10 57* | *20 46* | *11 36* | *20 09* |
| 5 FR | 11 50 39 | -22 20 | 6 21 | 17 20 | 6 41 | 17 00 | 7 06 | 16 35 | 7 42 | 15 59 | 8 43 | 14 58 |
| *339* | | *.9854* | *10 49* | *22 38* | *11 01* | *22 28* | *11 15* | *22 15* | *11 35* | *21 58* | *12 05* | *21 30* |
| 6 SA | 11 51 04 | -22 28 | 6 22 | 17 20 | 6 42 | 17 00 | 7 07 | 16 35 | 7 43 | 15 59 | 8 44 | 14 57 |
| *340* | | *.9853* | *11 36* | *23 37* | *11 44* | *23 30* | *11 54* | *23 22* | *12 08* | *23 12* | *12 28* | *22 55* |
| 7 SU | 11 51 30 | -22 35 | 6 22 | 17 21 | 6 43 | 17 00 | 7 08 | 16 35 | 7 44 | 15 59 | 8 46 | 14 57 |
| *341* | *6 10 FQ* | *.9851* | *12 22* | *none* | *12 26* | *none* | *12 31* | *none* | *12 38* | *none* | *12 49* | *none* |
| 8 MO | 11 51 56 | -22 42 | 6 23 | 17 21 | 6 44 | 17 00 | 7 09 | 16 35 | 7 45 | 15 58 | 8 48 | 14 56 |
| *342* | | *.9850* | *13 06* | *0 35* | *13 07* | *0 33* | *13 07* | *0 30* | *13 07* | *0 26* | *13 08* | *0 20* |
| 9 TU | 11 52 23 | -22 48 | 6 24 | 17 21 | 6 44 | 17 00 | 7 10 | 16 35 | 7 46 | 15 58 | 8 49 | 14 55 |
| *343* | | *.9849* | *13 51* | *1 34* | *13 47* | *1 36* | *13 43* | *1 38* | *13 36* | *1 42* | *13 27* | *1 46* |
| 10 WE | 11 52 50 | -22 54 | 6 24 | 17 21 | 6 45 | 17 01 | 7 11 | 16 35 | 7 47 | 15 58 | 8 51 | 14 55 |
| *344* | | *.9847* | *14 37* | *2 33* | *14 30* | *2 40* | *14 20* | *2 47* | *14 07* | *2 57* | *13 48* | *3 13* |
| 11 TH | 11 53 17 | -22 59 | 6 25 | 17 22 | 6 46 | 17 01 | 7 12 | 16 35 | 7 48 | 15 58 | 8 52 | 14 54 |
| *345* | | *.9846* | *15 25* | *3 33* | *15 14* | *3 43* | *15 00* | *3 56* | *14 41* | *4 12* | *14 11* | *4 39* |
| 12 FR | 11 53 45 | -23 04 | 6 25 | 17 22 | 6 46 | 17 01 | 7 12 | 16 35 | 7 49 | 15 58 | 8 54 | 14 54 |
| *346* | | *.9845* | *16 16* | *4 34* | *16 01* | *4 47* | *15 44* | *5 03* | *15 19* | *5 26* | *14 41* | *6 02* |
| 13 SA | 11 54 13 | -23 08 | 6 26 | 17 22 | 6 47 | 17 01 | 7 13 | 16 35 | 7 50 | 15 58 | 8 55 | 14 53 |
| *347* | | *.9844* | *17 08* | *5 33* | *16 52* | *5 49* | *16 32* | *6 09* | *16 03* | *6 36* | *15 18* | *7 20* |
| 14 SU | 11 54 42 | -23 12 | 6 27 | 17 23 | 6 48 | 17 02 | 7 14 | 16 35 | 7 51 | 15 58 | 8 56 | 14 53 |
| *348* | *2 38 FM* | *.9843* | *18 02* | *6 32* | *17 45* | *6 49* | *17 24* | *7 10* | *16 54* | *7 40* | *16 04* | *8 29* |
| 15 MO | 11 55 10 | -23 15 | 6 27 | 17 23 | 6 48 | 17 02 | 7 15 | 16 36 | 7 52 | 15 58 | 8 57 | 14 53 |
| *349* | | *.9842* | *18 57* | *7 27* | *18 40* | *7 44* | *18 19* | *8 06* | *17 50* | *8 36* | *17 01* | *9 25* |
| 16 TU | 11 55 39 | -23 18 | 6 28 | 17 24 | 6 49 | 17 02 | 7 15 | 16 36 | 7 53 | 15 59 | 8 58 | 14 53 |
| *350* | | *.9841* | *19 52* | *8 19* | *19 36* | *8 35* | *19 17* | *8 55* | *18 50* | *9 23* | *18 06* | *10 09* |
| 17 WE | 11 56 08 | -23 21 | 6 28 | 17 24 | 6 49 | 17 03 | 7 16 | 16 36 | 7 53 | 15 59 | 8 59 | 14 53 |
| *351* | | *.9840* | *20 45* | *9 07* | *20 32* | *9 21* | *20 15* | *9 39* | *19 52* | *10 04* | *19 15* | *10 43* |
| 18 TH | 11 56 38 | -23 23 | 6 29 | 17 24 | 6 50 | 17 03 | 7 17 | 16 37 | 7 54 | 15 59 | 9 00 | 14 53 |
| *352* | | *.9839* | *21 37* | *9 51* | *21 26* | *10 03* | *21 13* | *10 18* | *20 55* | *10 37* | *20 26* | *11 09* |
| 19 FR | 11 57 07 | -23 24 | 6 29 | 17 25 | 6 51 | 17 04 | 7 17 | 16 37 | 7 55 | 15 59 | 9 01 | 14 53 |
| *353* | | *.9838* | *22 27* | *10 32* | *22 19* | *10 41* | *22 10* | *10 52* | *21 57* | *11 07* | *21 38* | *11 29* |
| 20 SA | 11 57 37 | -23 25 | 6 30 | 17 25 | 6 51 | 17 04 | 7 18 | 16 37 | 7 55 | 16 00 | 9 01 | 14 54 |
| *354* | | *.9838* | *23 15* | *11 10* | *23 11* | *11 16* | *23 06* | *11 23* | *22 59* | *11 33* | *22 48* | *11 47* |
| 21 SU | 11 58 07 | -23 26 | 6 30 | 17 26 | 6 52 | 17 05 | 7 18 | 16 38 | 7 56 | 16 00 | 9 02 | 14 54 |
| *355* | *21 44 LQ* | *.9837* | *none* | *11 47* | *none* | *11 50* | *none* | *11 53* | *none* | *11 57* | *23 59* | *12 03* |
| 22 MO | 11 58 37 | -23 26 | 6 31 | 17 26 | 6 52 | 17 05 | 7 19 | 16 38 | 7 56 | 16 01 | 9 02 | 14 55 |
| *356* | | *.9836* | *0 04* | *12 24* | *0 03* | *12 23* | *0 02* | *12 22* | *0 01* | *12 20* | *none* | *12 18* |
| 23 TU | 11 59 07 | -23 26 | 6 31 | 17 27 | 6 53 | 17 06 | 7 19 | 16 39 | 7 57 | 16 01 | 9 03 | 14 55 |
| *357* | | *.9836* | *0 52* | *13 00* | *0 54* | *12 56* | *0 58* | *12 51* | *1 02* | *12 44* | *1 09* | *12 33* |
| 24 WE | 11 59 37 | -23 25 | 6 32 | 17 27 | 6 53 | 17 06 | 7 20 | 16 40 | 7 57 | 16 02 | 9 03 | 14 56 |
| *358* | | *.9835* | *1 40* | *13 38* | *1 46* | *13 31* | *1 54* | *13 21* | *2 04* | *13 09* | *2 20* | *12 49* |
| 25 TH | 12 00 06 | -23 24 | 6 32 | 17 28 | 6 54 | 17 07 | 7 20 | 16 40 | 7 58 | 16 03 | 9 03 | 14 57 |
| *359* | | *.9835* | *2 30* | *14 18* | *2 40* | *14 08* | *2 51* | *13 54* | *3 07* | *13 37* | *3 32* | *13 09* |
| 26 FR | 12 00 36 | -23 22 | 6 33 | 17 28 | 6 54 | 17 07 | 7 20 | 16 41 | 7 58 | 16 03 | 9 04 | 14 58 |
| *360* | | *.9834* | *3 22* | *15 01* | *3 34* | *14 48* | *3 50* | *14 31* | *4 11* | *14 08* | *4 45* | *13 32* |
| 27 SA | 12 01 06 | -23 20 | 6 33 | 17 29 | 6 54 | 17 08 | 7 21 | 16 42 | 7 58 | 16 04 | 9 04 | 14 59 |
| *361* | | *.9834* | *4 15* | *15 48* | *4 30* | *15 32* | *4 49* | *15 13* | *5 14* | *14 46* | *5 56* | *14 02* |
| 28 SU | 12 01 35 | -23 17 | 6 34 | 17 30 | 6 55 | 17 09 | 7 21 | 16 42 | 7 58 | 16 05 | 9 03 | 15 00 |
| *362* | | *.9834* | *5 10* | *16 39* | *5 27* | *16 22* | *5 48* | *16 01* | *6 17* | *15 31* | *7 05* | *14 42* |
| 29 MO | 12 02 05 | -23 14 | 6 34 | 17 30 | 6 55 | 17 09 | 7 21 | 16 43 | 7 58 | 16 06 | 9 03 | 15 01 |
| *363* | *16 58 NM* | *.9833* | *6 06* | *17 34* | *6 23* | *17 16* | *6 45* | *16 54* | *7 15* | *16 24* | *8 06* | *15 33* |
| 30 TU | 12 02 34 | -23 11 | 6 34 | 17 31 | 6 55 | 17 10 | 7 22 | 16 44 | 7 59 | 16 07 | 9 03 | 15 02 |
| *364* | | *.9833* | *7 01* | *18 31* | *7 18* | *18 15* | *7 39* | *17 54* | *8 09* | *17 25* | *8 57* | *16 38* |
| 31 WE | 12 03 03 | -23 06 | 6 35 | 17 31 | 6 56 | 17 11 | 7 22 | 16 44 | 7 59 | 16 08 | 9 03 | 15 04 |
| *365* | | *.9833* | *7 55* | *19 31* | *8 10* | *19 16* | *8 29* | *18 58* | *8 56* | *18 33* | *9 38* | *17 52* |

# Julian and Gregorian Calendars; Leap Year; Century

Calendars based on the movements of the sun and moon have been used since ancient times, but none has been perfect. The **Julian calendar**, under which Western nations measured time until AD 1582, was authorized by Julius Caesar in 46 BC, the year 709 of Rome. His expert was a Greek, Sosigenes. The Julian calendar, on the assumption that the length of the true year was 365 1/4 days, gave every 4th year 366 days. St. Bede the Venerable, an Anglo-Saxon monk, announced in AD 730 that the 365 1/4-day Julian year was 11 min, 14 sec too long, a cumulative error of about a day every 128 years, but nothing was done about it for more than 800 years.

By 1582 the accumulated error was estimated to amount to 10 days. In that year Pope Gregory XIII decreed that the day following Oct. 4, 1582, should be called Oct. 15, thus dropping 10 days and initiating what became known as the **Gregorian calendar.**

However, with common years 365 days and a 366-day leap year every 4th year, the error in the length of the year would have recurred at the rate of a little more than 3 days every 400 years. Therefore, 3 of every 4 centesimal years (years ending in 00) were made common years, not leap years. Thus, 1600 was a leap year; 1700, 1800, and 1900 were not, but 2000 will be. **Leap years** are those years divisible by 4, except centesimal years, which are common unless divisible by 400.

The Gregorian calendar was adopted at once by France, Italy, Spain, Portugal, and Luxembourg. Within 2 years most German Catholic states, Belgium, and parts of Switzerland and the Netherlands were brought under the new calendar, and Hungary followed in 1587. The rest of the Netherlands, along with Denmark and the German Protestant states, made the change in 1699-1700 (German Protestants retained the old reckoning of Easter until 1776).

The British government imposed the Gregorian calendar on all its possessions, including the American colonies, in 1752. The British decreed that the day following Sept. 2, 1752, should be called Sept. 14, a loss of 11 days. All dates preceding were marked OS, for Old Style. In addition, New Year's Day was moved to Jan. 1 from Mar. 25 (e.g., under the old reckoning, Mar. 24, 1700, had been followed by Mar. 25, 1701). George Washington's birthdate, which was Feb. 11, 1731, OS, became Feb. 22, 1732, NS (New Style). In 1753 Sweden too went Gregorian, retaining the old Easter rules until 1844.

In 1793 the French revolutionary government adopted a calendar of 12 months of 30 days each, with 5 extra days in September of each common year and a 6th extra day every 4th year. Napoleon reinstated the Gregorian calendar in 1806.

The Gregorian system later spread to non-European regions, first in the European colonies and then in the independent countries, replacing traditional calendars at least for official purposes. Japan in 1873, Egypt in 1875, China in 1912, and Turkey in 1925 made the change, usually in conjunction with political upheavals. In China, the republican government began reckoning years from its 1911 founding — e.g., 1948 was designated the year 37. After 1949, the Communists adopted the Common, or Christian Era, year count, even for the traditional lunar calendar.

In 1918 the revolutionary government in the Soviet Union decreed that the day after Jan. 31, 1918, OS, would become Feb. 14, 1918, NS. Greece followed in 1923. (The Russian Orthodox Church has retained the Julian calendar, as have various Middle Eastern Christian sects.) For the first time in history, all major cultures have one calendar.

To convert from the Julian to the Gregorian calendar, add 10 days to dates Oct. 5, 1582, through Feb. 28, 1700; after that date add 11 days through Feb. 28, 1800; 12 days through Feb. 28, 1900; and 13 days through Feb. 28, 2100.

A **century** consists of 100 consecutive calendar years. The 1st century AD consisted of the years 1 through 100. The 20th century consists of the years 1901 through 2000 and will end Dec. 31, 2000. The 21st century will begin Jan. 1, 2001.

# Julian Calendar

To find which of the 14 calendars printed on pages 476-77 applies to any year, starting Jan. 1, under the Julian system, find the century for the desired year in the 3 leftmost columns below; read across. Then find the year in the 4 top rows; read down. The number in the intersection is the calendar designation for that year.

**Year (last 2 figures of desired year)**

| | | | | 01 | 02 | 03 | 04 | 05 | 06 | 07 | 08 | 09 | 10 | 11 | 12 | 13 | 14 | 15 | 16 | 17 | 18 | 19 | 20 | 21 | 22 | 23 | 24 | 25 | 26 | 27 | 28 |
|---|---|---|---|---|---|---|---|---|---|---|---|---|---|---|---|---|---|---|---|---|---|---|---|---|---|---|---|---|---|---|---|
| | | | | 29 | 30 | 31 | 32 | 33 | 34 | 35 | 36 | 37 | 38 | 39 | 40 | 41 | 42 | 43 | 44 | 45 | 46 | 47 | 48 | 49 | 50 | 51 | 52 | 53 | 54 | 55 | 56 |
| | | | | 57 | 58 | 59 | 60 | 61 | 62 | 63 | 64 | 65 | 66 | 67 | 68 | 69 | 70 | 71 | 72 | 73 | 74 | 75 | 76 | 77 | 78 | 79 | 80 | 81 | 82 | 83 | 84 |
| Century | | | 00 | 85 | 86 | 87 | 88 | 89 | 90 | 91 | 92 | 93 | 94 | 95 | 96 | 97 | 98 | 99 | | | | | | | | | | | | | |
| 0 | 700 | 1400 | 12 | 7 | 1 | 2 | 10 | 5 | 6 | 7 | 8 | 3 | 4 | 5 | 13 | 1 | 2 | 3 | 11 | 6 | 7 | 1 | 9 | 4 | 5 | 6 | 14 | 2 | 3 | 4 | 12 |
| 100 | 800 | 1500 | 11 | 6 | 7 | 1 | 9 | 4 | 5 | 6 | 14 | 2 | 3 | 4 | 12 | 7 | 1 | 2 | 10 | 5 | 6 | 7 | 8 | 3 | 4 | 5 | 13 | 1 | 2 | 3 | 11 |
| 200 | 900 | 1600 | 10 | 5 | 6 | 7 | 8 | 3 | 4 | 5 | 13 | 1 | 2 | 3 | 11 | 6 | 7 | 1 | 9 | 4 | 5 | 6 | 14 | 2 | 3 | 4 | 12 | 7 | 1 | 2 | 10 |
| 300 | 1000 | 1700 | 9 | 4 | 5 | 6 | 14 | 2 | 3 | 4 | 12 | 7 | 1 | 2 | 10 | 5 | 6 | 7 | 8 | 3 | 4 | 5 | 13 | 1 | 2 | 3 | 11 | 6 | 7 | 1 | 9 |
| 400 | 1100 | 1800 | 8 | 3 | 4 | 5 | 13 | 1 | 2 | 3 | 11 | 6 | 7 | 1 | 9 | 4 | 5 | 6 | 14 | 2 | 3 | 4 | 12 | 7 | 1 | 2 | 10 | 5 | 6 | 7 | 8 |
| 500 | 1200 | 1900 | 14 | 2 | 3 | 4 | 12 | 7 | 1 | 2 | 10 | 5 | 6 | 7 | 8 | 3 | 4 | 5 | 13 | 1 | 2 | 3 | 11 | 6 | 7 | 1 | 9 | 4 | 5 | 6 | 14 |
| 600 | 1300 | 2000 | 13 | 1 | 2 | 3 | 11 | 6 | 7 | 1 | 9 | 4 | 5 | 6 | 14 | 2 | 3 | 4 | 12 | 7 | 1 | 2 | 10 | 5 | 6 | 7 | 8 | 3 | 4 | 5 | 13 |

# Gregorian Calendar

Choose the desired year from the table below or from page 476 (for years 1803 to 2080). The number shown with each year designates which calendar to use for that year, as shown on pages 476-77. (The Gregorian calendar was inaugurated Oct. 15, 1582. From that date to Dec. 31, 1582, use calendar 6.)

## 1583-1802

| | | | | | | | | | | | | | | | | | | | |
|---|---|---|---|---|---|---|---|---|---|---|---|---|---|---|---|---|---|---|---|
| 1583 | 7 | 1603 | 4 | 1623 | 1 | 1643 | 5 | 1663 | 2 | 1683 | 6 | 1703 | 2 | 1723 | 6 | 1743 | 3 | 1763 | 7 | 1783 | 4 |
| 1584 | 8 | 1604 | 12 | 1624 | 9 | 1644 | 13 | 1664 | 10 | 1684 | 14 | 1704 | 10 | 1724 | 14 | 1744 | 11 | 1764 | 8 | 1784 | 12 |
| 1585 | 3 | 1605 | 7 | 1625 | 4 | 1645 | 1 | 1665 | 5 | 1685 | 2 | 1705 | 5 | 1725 | 2 | 1745 | 6 | 1765 | 3 | 1785 | 7 |
| 1586 | 4 | 1606 | 1 | 1626 | 5 | 1646 | 2 | 1666 | 6 | 1686 | 3 | 1706 | 6 | 1726 | 3 | 1746 | 7 | 1766 | 4 | 1786 | 1 |
| 1587 | 5 | 1607 | 2 | 1627 | 6 | 1647 | 3 | 1667 | 7 | 1687 | 4 | 1707 | 7 | 1727 | 4 | 1747 | 1 | 1767 | 5 | 1787 | 2 |
| 1588 | 13 | 1608 | 10 | 1628 | 14 | 1648 | 11 | 1668 | 8 | 1688 | 12 | 1708 | 8 | 1728 | 12 | 1748 | 9 | 1768 | 13 | 1788 | 10 |
| 1589 | 1 | 1609 | 5 | 1629 | 2 | 1649 | 6 | 1669 | 3 | 1689 | 7 | 1709 | 3 | 1729 | 7 | 1749 | 4 | 1769 | 1 | 1789 | 5 |
| 1590 | 2 | 1610 | 6 | 1630 | 3 | 1650 | 7 | 1670 | 4 | 1690 | 1 | 1710 | 4 | 1730 | 1 | 1750 | 5 | 1770 | 2 | 1790 | 6 |
| 1591 | 3 | 1611 | 7 | 1631 | 4 | 1651 | 1 | 1671 | 5 | 1691 | 2 | 1711 | 5 | 1731 | 2 | 1751 | 6 | 1771 | 3 | 1791 | 7 |
| 1592 | 11 | 1612 | 8 | 1632 | 12 | 1652 | 9 | 1672 | 13 | 1692 | 10 | 1712 | 13 | 1732 | 10 | 1752 | 14 | 1772 | 11 | 1792 | 8 |
| 1593 | 6 | 1613 | 3 | 1633 | 7 | 1653 | 4 | 1673 | 1 | 1693 | 5 | 1713 | 1 | 1733 | 5 | 1753 | 2 | 1773 | 6 | 1793 | 3 |
| 1594 | 7 | 1614 | 4 | 1634 | 1 | 1654 | 5 | 1674 | 2 | 1694 | 6 | 1714 | 2 | 1734 | 6 | 1754 | 3 | 1774 | 7 | 1794 | 4 |
| 1595 | 1 | 1615 | 5 | 1635 | 2 | 1655 | 6 | 1675 | 3 | 1695 | 7 | 1715 | 3 | 1735 | 7 | 1755 | 4 | 1775 | 1 | 1795 | 5 |
| 1596 | 9 | 1616 | 13 | 1636 | 10 | 1656 | 14 | 1676 | 11 | 1696 | 8 | 1716 | 11 | 1736 | 8 | 1756 | 12 | 1776 | 9 | 1796 | 13 |
| 1597 | 4 | 1617 | 1 | 1637 | 5 | 1657 | 2 | 1677 | 6 | 1697 | 3 | 1717 | 6 | 1737 | 3 | 1757 | 7 | 1777 | 4 | 1797 | 1 |
| 1598 | 5 | 1618 | 2 | 1638 | 6 | 1658 | 3 | 1678 | 7 | 1698 | 4 | 1718 | 7 | 1738 | 4 | 1758 | 1 | 1778 | 5 | 1798 | 2 |
| 1599 | 6 | 1619 | 3 | 1639 | 7 | 1659 | 4 | 1679 | 1 | 1699 | 5 | 1719 | 1 | 1739 | 5 | 1759 | 2 | 1779 | 6 | 1799 | 3 |
| 1600 | 14 | 1620 | 11 | 1640 | 8 | 1660 | 12 | 1680 | 9 | 1700 | 6 | 1720 | 9 | 1740 | 13 | 1760 | 10 | 1780 | 14 | 1800 | 4 |
| 1601 | 2 | 1621 | 6 | 1641 | 3 | 1661 | 7 | 1681 | 4 | 1701 | 7 | 1721 | 4 | 1741 | 1 | 1761 | 5 | 1781 | 2 | 1801 | 5 |
| 1602 | 3 | 1622 | 7 | 1642 | 4 | 1662 | 1 | 1682 | 5 | 1702 | 1 | 1722 | 5 | 1742 | 2 | 1762 | 6 | 1782 | 3 | 1802 | 6 |

# Perpetual Calendar

The number shown for each year indicates which Gregorian calendar to use. For 1583-1802, see "Gregorian Calendar" on page 475. For 1803-20, use numbers for 1983-2000, respectively. For Julian Calendar, see "Julian Calendar" on page 475.

| | | | | | | | | | |
|---|---|---|---|---|---|---|---|---|---|
| 1821 ... 2 | 1847 ... 6 | 1873 ... 4 | 1899 ... 1 | 1925 ... 5 | 1951 ... 2 | 1977 ... 7 | 2003 ... 4 | 2029 ... 2 | 2055 ... 6 |
| 1822 ... 3 | 1848 ... 14 | 1874 ... 5 | 1900 ... 2 | 1926 ... 6 | 1952 ... 10 | 1978 ... 1 | 2004 ... 12 | 2030 ... 3 | 2056 ... 14 |
| 1823 ... 4 | 1849 ... 2 | 1875 ... 6 | 1901 ... 3 | 1927 ... 7 | 1953 ... 5 | 1979 ... 2 | 2005 ... 7 | 2031 ... 4 | 2057 ... 2 |
| 1824 ... 12 | 1850 ... 3 | 1876 ... 14 | 1902 ... 4 | 1928 ... 8 | 1954 ... 6 | 1980 ... 10 | 2006 ... 1 | 2032 ... 12 | 2058 ... 3 |
| 1825 ... 7 | 1851 ... 4 | 1877 ... 2 | 1903 ... 5 | 1929 ... 3 | 1955 ... 7 | 1981 ... 5 | 2007 ... 2 | 2033 ... 7 | 2059 ... 4 |
| 1826 ... 1 | 1852 ... 12 | 1878 ... 3 | 1904 ... 13 | 1930 ... 4 | 1956 ... 8 | 1982 ... 6 | 2008 ... 10 | 2034 ... 1 | 2060 ... 12 |
| 1827 ... 2 | 1853 ... 7 | 1879 ... 4 | 1905 ... 1 | 1931 ... 5 | 1957 ... 3 | 1983 ... 7 | 2009 ... 5 | 2035 ... 2 | 2061 ... 7 |
| 1828 ... 10 | 1854 ... 1 | 1880 ... 12 | 1906 ... 2 | 1932 ... 13 | 1958 ... 4 | 1984 ... 8 | 2010 ... 6 | 2036 ... 10 | 2062 ... 1 |
| 1829 ... 5 | 1855 ... 2 | 1881 ... 7 | 1907 ... 3 | 1933 ... 1 | 1959 ... 5 | 1985 ... 3 | 2011 ... 7 | 2037 ... 5 | 2063 ... 2 |
| 1830 ... 6 | 1856 ... 10 | 1882 ... 1 | 1908 ... 11 | 1934 ... 2 | 1960 ... 13 | 1986 ... 4 | 2012 ... 8 | 2038 ... 6 | 2064 ... 10 |
| 1831 ... 7 | 1857 ... 5 | 1883 ... 2 | 1909 ... 6 | 1935 ... 3 | 1961 ... 1 | 1987 ... 5 | 2013 ... 3 | 2039 ... 7 | 2065 ... 5 |
| 1832 ... 8 | 1858 ... 6 | 1884 ... 10 | 1910 ... 7 | 1936 ... 11 | 1962 ... 2 | 1988 ... 13 | 2014 ... 4 | 2040 ... 8 | 2066 ... 6 |
| 1833 ... 3 | 1859 ... 7 | 1885 ... 5 | 1911 ... 1 | 1937 ... 6 | 1963 ... 3 | 1989 ... 1 | 2015 ... 5 | 2041 ... 3 | 2067 ... 7 |
| 1834 ... 4 | 1860 ... 8 | 1886 ... 6 | 1912 ... 9 | 1938 ... 7 | 1964 ... 11 | 1990 ... 2 | 2016 ... 13 | 2042 ... 4 | 2068 ... 8 |
| 1835 ... 5 | 1861 ... 3 | 1887 ... 7 | 1913 ... 4 | 1939 ... 1 | 1965 ... 6 | 1991 ... 3 | 2017 ... 1 | 2043 ... 5 | 2069 ... 3 |
| 1836 ... 13 | 1862 ... 4 | 1888 ... 8 | 1914 ... 5 | 1940 ... 9 | 1966 ... 7 | 1992 ... 11 | 2018 ... 2 | 2044 ... 13 | 2070 ... 4 |
| 1837 ... 1 | 1863 ... 5 | 1889 ... 3 | 1915 ... 6 | 1941 ... 4 | 1967 ... 1 | 1993 ... 6 | 2019 ... 3 | 2045 ... 1 | 2071 ... 5 |
| 1838 ... 2 | 1864 ... 13 | 1890 ... 4 | 1916 ... 14 | 1942 ... 5 | 1968 ... 9 | 1994 ... 7 | 2020 ... 11 | 2046 ... 2 | 2072 ... 13 |
| 1839 ... 3 | 1865 ... 1 | 1891 ... 5 | 1917 ... 2 | 1943 ... 6 | 1969 ... 4 | 1995 ... 1 | 2021 ... 6 | 2047 ... 3 | 2073 ... 1 |
| 1840 ... 11 | 1866 ... 2 | 1892 ... 13 | 1918 ... 3 | 1944 ... 14 | 1970 ... 5 | 1996 ... 9 | 2022 ... 7 | 2048 ... 11 | 2074 ... 2 |
| 1841 ... 6 | 1867 ... 3 | 1893 ... 1 | 1919 ... 4 | 1945 ... 2 | 1971 ... 6 | 1997 ... 4 | 2023 ... 1 | 2049 ... 6 | 2075 ... 3 |
| 1842 ... 7 | 1868 ... 11 | 1894 ... 2 | 1920 ... 12 | 1946 ... 3 | 1972 ... 14 | 1998 ... 5 | 2024 ... 9 | 2050 ... 7 | 2076 ... 11 |
| 1843 ... 1 | 1869 ... 6 | 1895 ... 3 | 1921 ... 7 | 1947 ... 4 | 1973 ... 2 | 1999 ... 6 | 2025 ... 4 | 2051 ... 1 | 2077 ... 6 |
| 1844 ... 9 | 1870 ... 7 | 1896 ... 11 | 1922 ... 1 | 1948 ... 12 | 1974 ... 3 | 2000 ... 14 | 2026 ... 5 | 2052 ... 9 | 2078 ... 7 |
| 1845 ... 4 | 1871 ... 1 | 1897 ... 6 | 1923 ... 2 | 1949 ... 7 | 1975 ... 4 | 2001 ... 2 | 2027 ... 6 | 2053 ... 4 | 2079 ... 1 |
| 1846 ... 5 | 1872 ... 9 | 1898 ... 7 | 1924 ... 10 | 1950 ... 1 | 1976 ... 12 | 2002 ... 3 | 2028 ... 14 | 2054 ... 5 | 2080 ... 9 |

## 1

**JANUARY**

| S | M | T | W | T | F | S |
|---|---|---|---|---|---|---|
|1|2|3|4|5|6|7|
|8|9|10|11|12|13|14|
|15|16|17|18|19|20|21|
|22|23|24|25|26|27|28|
|29|30|31| | | | |

**MAY**

| S | M | T | W | T | F | S |
|---|---|---|---|---|---|---|
| |1|2|3|4|5|6|
|7|8|9|10|11|12|13|
|14|15|16|17|18|19|20|
|21|22|23|24|25|26|27|
|28|29|30|31| | | |

**SEPTEMBER**

| S | M | T | W | T | F | S |
|---|---|---|---|---|---|---|
| | | | | |1|2|
|3|4|5|6|7|8|9|
|10|11|12|13|14|15|16|
|17|18|19|20|21|22|23|
|24|25|26|27|28|29|30|

**FEBRUARY**

| S | M | T | W | T | F | S |
|---|---|---|---|---|---|---|
| | | |1|2|3|4|
|5|6|7|8|9|10|11|
|12|13|14|15|16|17|18|
|19|20|21|22|23|24|25|
|26|27|28| | | | |

**JUNE**

| S | M | T | W | T | F | S |
|---|---|---|---|---|---|---|
| | | | |1|2|3|
|4|5|6|7|8|9|10|
|11|12|13|14|15|16|17|
|18|19|20|21|22|23|24|
|25|26|27|28|29|30| |

**OCTOBER**

| S | M | T | W | T | F | S |
|---|---|---|---|---|---|---|
|1|2|3|4|5|6|7|
|8|9|10|11|12|13|14|
|15|16|17|18|19|20|21|
|22|23|24|25|26|27|28|
|29|30|31| | | | |

**MARCH**

| S | M | T | W | T | F | S |
|---|---|---|---|---|---|---|
| | | |1|2|3|4|
|5|6|7|8|9|10|11|
|12|13|14|15|16|17|18|
|19|20|21|22|23|24|25|
|26|27|28|29|30|31| |

**JULY**

| S | M | T | W | T | F | S |
|---|---|---|---|---|---|---|
| | | | | | |1|
|2|3|4|5|6|7|8|
|9|10|11|12|13|14|15|
|16|17|18|19|20|21|22|
|23|24|25|26|27|28|29|
|30|31| | | | | |

**NOVEMBER**

| S | M | T | W | T | F | S |
|---|---|---|---|---|---|---|
| | | |1|2|3|4|
|5|6|7|8|9|10|11|
|12|13|14|15|16|17|18|
|19|20|21|22|23|24|25|
|26|27|28|29|30| | |

**APRIL**

| S | M | T | W | T | F | S |
|---|---|---|---|---|---|---|
| | | | | | |1|
|2|3|4|5|6|7|8|
|9|10|11|12|13|14|15|
|16|17|18|19|20|21|22|
|23|24|25|26|27|28|29|
|30| | | | | | |

**AUGUST**

| S | M | T | W | T | F | S |
|---|---|---|---|---|---|---|
| | |1|2|3|4|5|
|6|7|8|9|10|11|12|
|13|14|15|16|17|18|19|
|20|21|22|23|24|25|26|
|27|28|29|30|31| | |

**DECEMBER**

| S | M | T | W | T | F | S |
|---|---|---|---|---|---|---|
| | | | | |1|2|
|3|4|5|6|7|8|9|
|10|11|12|13|14|15|16|
|17|18|19|20|21|22|23|
|24|25|26|27|28|29|30|
|31| | | | | | |

## 2

**JANUARY**

| S | M | T | W | T | F | S |
|---|---|---|---|---|---|---|
| |1|2|3|4|5|6|
|7|8|9|10|11|12|13|
|14|15|16|17|18|19|20|
|21|22|23|24|25|26|27|
|28|29|30|31| | | |

**MAY**

| S | M | T | W | T | F | S |
|---|---|---|---|---|---|---|
| | |1|2|3|4|5|
|6|7|8|9|10|11|12|
|13|14|15|16|17|18|19|
|20|21|22|23|24|25|26|
|27|28|29|30|31| | |

**SEPTEMBER**

| S | M | T | W | T | F | S |
|---|---|---|---|---|---|---|
| | | | | | |1|
|2|3|4|5|6|7|8|
|9|10|11|12|13|14|15|
|16|17|18|19|20|21|22|
|23|24|25|26|27|28|29|
|30| | | | | | |

**FEBRUARY**

| S | M | T | W | T | F | S |
|---|---|---|---|---|---|---|
| | | | |1|2|3|
|4|5|6|7|8|9|10|
|11|12|13|14|15|16|17|
|18|19|20|21|22|23|24|
|25|26|27|28| | | |

**JUNE**

| S | M | T | W | T | F | S |
|---|---|---|---|---|---|---|
| | | | | |1|2|
|3|4|5|6|7|8|9|
|10|11|12|13|14|15|16|
|17|18|19|20|21|22|23|
|24|25|26|27|28|29|30|

**OCTOBER**

| S | M | T | W | T | F | S |
|---|---|---|---|---|---|---|
| |1|2|3|4|5|6|
|7|8|9|10|11|12|13|
|14|15|16|17|18|19|20|
|21|22|23|24|25|26|27|
|28|29|30|31| | | |

**MARCH**

| S | M | T | W | T | F | S |
|---|---|---|---|---|---|---|
| | | | |1|2|3|
|4|5|6|7|8|9|10|
|11|12|13|14|15|16|17|
|18|19|20|21|22|23|24|
|25|26|27|28|29|30|31|

**JULY**

| S | M | T | W | T | F | S |
|---|---|---|---|---|---|---|
|1|2|3|4|5|6|7|
|8|9|10|11|12|13|14|
|15|16|17|18|19|20|21|
|22|23|24|25|26|27|28|
|29|30|31| | | | |

**NOVEMBER**

| S | M | T | W | T | F | S |
|---|---|---|---|---|---|---|
| | | | |1|2|3|
|4|5|6|7|8|9|10|
|11|12|13|14|15|16|17|
|18|19|20|21|22|23|24|
|25|26|27|28|29|30| |

**APRIL**

| S | M | T | W | T | F | S |
|---|---|---|---|---|---|---|
|1|2|3|4|5|6|7|
|8|9|10|11|12|13|14|
|15|16|17|18|19|20|21|
|22|23|24|25|26|27|28|
|29|30| | | | | |

**AUGUST**

| S | M | T | W | T | F | S |
|---|---|---|---|---|---|---|
| | | |1|2|3|4|
|5|6|7|8|9|10|11|
|12|13|14|15|16|17|18|
|19|20|21|22|23|24|25|
|26|27|28|29|30|31| |

**DECEMBER**

| S | M | T | W | T | F | S |
|---|---|---|---|---|---|---|
| | | | | | |1|
|2|3|4|5|6|7|8|
|9|10|11|12|13|14|15|
|16|17|18|19|20|21|22|
|23|24|25|26|27|28|29|
|30|31| | | | | |

## 3

**JANUARY**

| S | M | T | W | T | F | S |
|---|---|---|---|---|---|---|
| | |1|2|3|4|5|
|6|7|8|9|10|11|12|
|13|14|15|16|17|18|19|
|20|21|22|23|24|25|26|
|27|28|29|30|31| | |

**MAY**

| S | M | T | W | T | F | S |
|---|---|---|---|---|---|---|
| | | |1|2|3|4|
|5|6|7|8|9|10|11|
|12|13|14|15|16|17|18|
|19|20|21|22|23|24|25|
|26|27|28|29|30|31| |

**SEPTEMBER**

| S | M | T | W | T | F | S |
|---|---|---|---|---|---|---|
|1|2|3|4|5|6|7|
|8|9|10|11|12|13|14|
|15|16|17|18|19|20|21|
|22|23|24|25|26|27|28|
|29|30| | | | | |

**FEBRUARY**

| S | M | T | W | T | F | S |
|---|---|---|---|---|---|---|
| | | | | |1|2|
|3|4|5|6|7|8|9|
|10|11|12|13|14|15|16|
|17|18|19|20|21|22|23|
|24|25|26|27|28| | |

**JUNE**

| S | M | T | W | T | F | S |
|---|---|---|---|---|---|---|
| | | | | | |1|
|2|3|4|5|6|7|8|
|9|10|11|12|13|14|15|
|16|17|18|19|20|21|22|
|23|24|25|26|27|28|29|
|30| | | | | | |

**OCTOBER**

| S | M | T | W | T | F | S |
|---|---|---|---|---|---|---|
| | |1|2|3|4|5|
|6|7|8|9|10|11|12|
|13|14|15|16|17|18|19|
|20|21|22|23|24|25|26|
|27|28|29|30|31| | |

**MARCH**

| S | M | T | W | T | F | S |
|---|---|---|---|---|---|---|
| | | | | |1|2|
|3|4|5|6|7|8|9|
|10|11|12|13|14|15|16|
|17|18|19|20|21|22|23|
|24|25|26|27|28|29|30|
|31| | | | | | |

**JULY**

| S | M | T | W | T | F | S |
|---|---|---|---|---|---|---|
| |1|2|3|4|5|6|
|7|8|9|10|11|12|13|
|14|15|16|17|18|19|20|
|21|22|23|24|25|26|27|
|28|29|30|31| | | |

**NOVEMBER**

| S | M | T | W | T | F | S |
|---|---|---|---|---|---|---|
| | | | | |1|2|
|3|4|5|6|7|8|9|
|10|11|12|13|14|15|16|
|17|18|19|20|21|22|23|
|24|25|26|27|28|29|30|

**APRIL**

| S | M | T | W | T | F | S |
|---|---|---|---|---|---|---|
| |1|2|3|4|5|6|
|7|8|9|10|11|12|13|
|14|15|16|17|18|19|20|
|21|22|23|24|25|26|27|
|28|29|30| | | | |

**AUGUST**

| S | M | T | W | T | F | S |
|---|---|---|---|---|---|---|
| | | | |1|2|3|
|4|5|6|7|8|9|10|
|11|12|13|14|15|16|17|
|18|19|20|21|22|23|24|
|25|26|27|28|29|30|31|

**DECEMBER**

| S | M | T | W | T | F | S |
|---|---|---|---|---|---|---|
|1|2|3|4|5|6|7|
|8|9|10|11|12|13|14|
|15|16|17|18|19|20|21|
|22|23|24|25|26|27|28|
|29|30|31| | | | |

## 4 1997

**JANUARY**

| S | M | T | W | T | F | S |
|---|---|---|---|---|---|---|
| | | |1|2|3|4|
|5|6|7|8|9|10|11|
|12|13|14|15|16|17|18|
|19|20|21|22|23|24|25|
|26|27|28|29|30|31| |

**MAY**

| S | M | T | W | T | F | S |
|---|---|---|---|---|---|---|
| | | | |1|2|3|
|4|5|6|7|8|9|10|
|11|12|13|14|15|16|17|
|18|19|20|21|22|23|24|
|25|26|27|28|29|30|31|

**SEPTEMBER**

| S | M | T | W | T | F | S |
|---|---|---|---|---|---|---|
| |1|2|3|4|5|6|
|7|8|9|10|11|12|13|
|14|15|16|17|18|19|20|
|21|22|23|24|25|26|27|
|28|29|30| | | | |

**FEBRUARY**

| S | M | T | W | T | F | S |
|---|---|---|---|---|---|---|
| | | | | | |1|
|2|3|4|5|6|7|8|
|9|10|11|12|13|14|15|
|16|17|18|19|20|21|22|
|23|24|25|26|27|28| |

**JUNE**

| S | M | T | W | T | F | S |
|---|---|---|---|---|---|---|
|1|2|3|4|5|6|7|
|8|9|10|11|12|13|14|
|15|16|17|18|19|20|21|
|22|23|24|25|26|27|28|
|29|30| | | | | |

**OCTOBER**

| S | M | T | W | T | F | S |
|---|---|---|---|---|---|---|
| | | |1|2|3|4|
|5|6|7|8|9|10|11|
|12|13|14|15|16|17|18|
|19|20|21|22|23|24|25|
|26|27|28|29|30|31| |

**MARCH**

| S | M | T | W | T | F | S |
|---|---|---|---|---|---|---|
| | | | | | |1|
|2|3|4|5|6|7|8|
|9|10|11|12|13|14|15|
|16|17|18|19|20|21|22|
|23|24|25|26|27|28|29|
|30|31| | | | | |

**JULY**

| S | M | T | W | T | F | S |
|---|---|---|---|---|---|---|
| | |1|2|3|4|5|
|6|7|8|9|10|11|12|
|13|14|15|16|17|18|19|
|20|21|22|23|24|25|26|
|27|28|29|30|31| | |

**NOVEMBER**

| S | M | T | W | T | F | S |
|---|---|---|---|---|---|---|
| | | | | | |1|
|2|3|4|5|6|7|8|
|9|10|11|12|13|14|15|
|16|17|18|19|20|21|22|
|23|24|25|26|27|28|29|
|30| | | | | | |

**APRIL**

| S | M | T | W | T | F | S |
|---|---|---|---|---|---|---|
| | |1|2|3|4|5|
|6|7|8|9|10|11|12|
|13|14|15|16|17|18|19|
|20|21|22|23|24|25|26|
|27|28|29|30| | | |

**AUGUST**

| S | M | T | W | T | F | S |
|---|---|---|---|---|---|---|
| | | | | |1|2|
|3|4|5|6|7|8|9|
|10|11|12|13|14|15|16|
|17|18|19|20|21|22|23|
|24|25|26|27|28|29|30|
|31| | | | | | |

**DECEMBER**

| S | M | T | W | T | F | S |
|---|---|---|---|---|---|---|
| |1|2|3|4|5|6|
|7|8|9|10|11|12|13|
|14|15|16|17|18|19|20|
|21|22|23|24|25|26|27|
|28|29|30|31| | | |

## 5 1998

**JANUARY**

| S | M | T | W | T | F | S |
|---|---|---|---|---|---|---|
| | | | |1|2|3|
|4|5|6|7|8|9|10|
|11|12|13|14|15|16|17|
|18|19|20|21|22|23|24|
|25|26|27|28|29|30|31|

**MAY**

| S | M | T | W | T | F | S |
|---|---|---|---|---|---|---|
| | | | | |1|2|
|3|4|5|6|7|8|9|
|10|11|12|13|14|15|16|
|17|18|19|20|21|22|23|
|24|25|26|27|28|29|30|
|31| | | | | | |

**SEPTEMBER**

| S | M | T | W | T | F | S |
|---|---|---|---|---|---|---|
| | |1|2|3|4|5|
|6|7|8|9|10|11|12|
|13|14|15|16|17|18|19|
|20|21|22|23|24|25|26|
|27|28|29|30| | | |

**FEBRUARY**

| S | M | T | W | T | F | S |
|---|---|---|---|---|---|---|
|1|2|3|4|5|6|7|
|8|9|10|11|12|13|14|
|15|16|17|18|19|20|21|
|22|23|24|25|26|27|28|

**JUNE**

| S | M | T | W | T | F | S |
|---|---|---|---|---|---|---|
| |1|2|3|4|5|6|
|7|8|9|10|11|12|13|
|14|15|16|17|18|19|20|
|21|22|23|24|25|26|27|
|28|29|30| | | | |

**OCTOBER**

| S | M | T | W | T | F | S |
|---|---|---|---|---|---|---|
| | | | |1|2|3|
|4|5|6|7|8|9|10|
|11|12|13|14|15|16|17|
|18|19|20|21|22|23|24|
|25|26|27|28|29|30|31|

**MARCH**

| S | M | T | W | T | F | S |
|---|---|---|---|---|---|---|
|1|2|3|4|5|6|7|
|8|9|10|11|12|13|14|
|15|16|17|18|19|20|21|
|22|23|24|25|26|27|28|
|29|30|31| | | | |

**JULY**

| S | M | T | W | T | F | S |
|---|---|---|---|---|---|---|
| | | |1|2|3|4|
|5|6|7|8|9|10|11|
|12|13|14|15|16|17|18|
|19|20|21|22|23|24|25|
|26|27|28|29|30|31| |

**NOVEMBER**

| S | M | T | W | T | F | S |
|---|---|---|---|---|---|---|
|1|2|3|4|5|6|7|
|8|9|10|11|12|13|14|
|15|16|17|18|19|20|21|
|22|23|24|25|26|27|28|
|29|30| | | | | |

**APRIL**

| S | M | T | W | T | F | S |
|---|---|---|---|---|---|---|
| | | |1|2|3|4|
|5|6|7|8|9|10|11|
|12|13|14|15|16|17|18|
|19|20|21|22|23|24|25|
|26|27|28|29|30| | |

**AUGUST**

| S | M | T | W | T | F | S |
|---|---|---|---|---|---|---|
| | | | | | |1|
|2|3|4|5|6|7|8|
|9|10|11|12|13|14|15|
|16|17|18|19|20|21|22|
|23|24|25|26|27|28|29|
|30|31| | | | | |

**DECEMBER**

| S | M | T | W | T | F | S |
|---|---|---|---|---|---|---|
| | |1|2|3|4|5|
|6|7|8|9|10|11|12|
|13|14|15|16|17|18|19|
|20|21|22|23|24|25|26|
|27|28|29|30|31| | |

## 6

**JANUARY**

| S | M | T | W | T | F | S |
|---|---|---|---|---|---|---|
| | | | | |1|2|
|3|4|5|6|7|8|9|
|10|11|12|13|14|15|16|
|17|18|19|20|21|22|23|
|24|25|26|27|28|29|30|
|31| | | | | | |

**MAY**

| S | M | T | W | T | F | S |
|---|---|---|---|---|---|---|
| | | | | | |1|
|2|3|4|5|6|7|8|
|9|10|11|12|13|14|15|
|16|17|18|19|20|21|22|
|23|24|25|26|27|28|29|
|30|31| | | | | |

**SEPTEMBER**

| S | M | T | W | T | F | S |
|---|---|---|---|---|---|---|
| | | |1|2|3|4|
|5|6|7|8|9|10|11|
|12|13|14|15|16|17|18|
|19|20|21|22|23|24|25|
|26|27|28|29|30| | |

**FEBRUARY**

| S | M | T | W | T | F | S |
|---|---|---|---|---|---|---|
| |1|2|3|4|5|6|
|7|8|9|10|11|12|13|
|14|15|16|17|18|19|20|
|21|22|23|24|25|26|27|
|28| | | | | | |

**JUNE**

| S | M | T | W | T | F | S |
|---|---|---|---|---|---|---|
| | |1|2|3|4|5|
|6|7|8|9|10|11|12|
|13|14|15|16|17|18|19|
|20|21|22|23|24|25|26|
|27|28|29|30| | | |

**OCTOBER**

| S | M | T | W | T | F | S |
|---|---|---|---|---|---|---|
| | | | | |1|2|
|3|4|5|6|7|8|9|
|10|11|12|13|14|15|16|
|17|18|19|20|21|22|23|
|24|25|26|27|28|29|30|
|31| | | | | | |

**MARCH**

| S | M | T | W | T | F | S |
|---|---|---|---|---|---|---|
| |1|2|3|4|5|6|
|7|8|9|10|11|12|13|
|14|15|16|17|18|19|20|
|21|22|23|24|25|26|27|
|28|29|30|31| | | |

**JULY**

| S | M | T | W | T | F | S |
|---|---|---|---|---|---|---|
| | | | |1|2|3|
|4|5|6|7|8|9|10|
|11|12|13|14|15|16|17|
|18|19|20|21|22|23|24|
|25|26|27|28|29|30|31|

**NOVEMBER**

| S | M | T | W | T | F | S |
|---|---|---|---|---|---|---|
| |1|2|3|4|5|6|
|7|8|9|10|11|12|13|
|14|15|16|17|18|19|20|
|21|22|23|24|25|26|27|
|28|29|30| | | | |

**APRIL**

| S | M | T | W | T | F | S |
|---|---|---|---|---|---|---|
| | | | |1|2|3|
|4|5|6|7|8|9|10|
|11|12|13|14|15|16|17|
|18|19|20|21|22|23|24|
|25|26|27|28|29|30| |

**AUGUST**

| S | M | T | W | T | F | S |
|---|---|---|---|---|---|---|
|1|2|3|4|5|6|7|
|8|9|10|11|12|13|14|
|15|16|17|18|19|20|21|
|22|23|24|25|26|27|28|
|29|30|31| | | | |

**DECEMBER**

| S | M | T | W | T | F | S |
|---|---|---|---|---|---|---|
| | | |1|2|3|4|
|5|6|7|8|9|10|11|
|12|13|14|15|16|17|18|
|19|20|21|22|23|24|25|
|26|27|28|29|30|31| |

## 7

**JANUARY**

| S | M | T | W | T | F | S |
|---|---|---|---|---|---|---|
| | | | | | | 1 |
| 2 | 3 | 4 | 5 | 6 | 7 | 8 |
| 9 | 10 | 11 | 12 | 13 | 14 | 15 |
| 16 | 17 | 18 | 19 | 20 | 21 | 22 |
| 23 | 24 | 25 | 26 | 27 | 28 | 29 |
| 30 | 31 | | | | | |

**FEBRUARY**

| S | M | T | W | T | F | S |
|---|---|---|---|---|---|---|
| | | 1 | 2 | 3 | 4 | 5 |
| 6 | 7 | 8 | 9 | 10 | 11 | 12 |
| 13 | 14 | 15 | 16 | 17 | 18 | 19 |
| 20 | 21 | 22 | 23 | 24 | 25 | 26 |
| 27 | 28 | | | | | |

**MARCH**

| S | M | T | W | T | F | S |
|---|---|---|---|---|---|---|
| | | 1 | 2 | 3 | 4 | 5 |
| 6 | 7 | 8 | 9 | 10 | 11 | 12 |
| 13 | 14 | 15 | 16 | 17 | 18 | 19 |
| 20 | 21 | 22 | 23 | 24 | 25 | 26 |
| 27 | 28 | 29 | 30 | 31 | | |

**APRIL**

| S | M | T | W | T | F | S |
|---|---|---|---|---|---|---|
| | | | | | 1 | 2 |
| 3 | 4 | 5 | 6 | 7 | 8 | 9 |
| 10 | 11 | 12 | 13 | 14 | 15 | 16 |
| 17 | 18 | 19 | 20 | 21 | 22 | 23 |
| 24 | 25 | 26 | 27 | 28 | 29 | 30 |

**MAY**

| S | M | T | W | T | F | S |
|---|---|---|---|---|---|---|
| 1 | 2 | 3 | 4 | 5 | 6 | 7 |
| 8 | 9 | 10 | 11 | 12 | 13 | 14 |
| 15 | 16 | 17 | 18 | 19 | 20 | 21 |
| 22 | 23 | 24 | 25 | 26 | 27 | 28 |
| 29 | 30 | 31 | | | | |

**JUNE**

| S | M | T | W | T | F | S |
|---|---|---|---|---|---|---|
| | | | 1 | 2 | 3 | 4 |
| 5 | 6 | 7 | 8 | 9 | 10 | 11 |
| 12 | 13 | 14 | 15 | 16 | 17 | 18 |
| 19 | 20 | 21 | 22 | 23 | 24 | 25 |
| 26 | 27 | 28 | 29 | 30 | | |

**JULY**

| S | M | T | W | T | F | S |
|---|---|---|---|---|---|---|
| | | | | | 1 | 2 |
| 3 | 4 | 5 | 6 | 7 | 8 | 9 |
| 10 | 11 | 12 | 13 | 14 | 15 | 16 |
| 17 | 18 | 19 | 20 | 21 | 22 | 23 |
| 24 | 25 | 26 | 27 | 28 | 29 | 30 |
| 31 | | | | | | |

**AUGUST**

| S | M | T | W | T | F | S |
|---|---|---|---|---|---|---|
| | 1 | 2 | 3 | 4 | 5 | 6 |
| 7 | 8 | 9 | 10 | 11 | 12 | 13 |
| 14 | 15 | 16 | 17 | 18 | 19 | 20 |
| 21 | 22 | 23 | 24 | 25 | 26 | 27 |
| 28 | 29 | 30 | 31 | | | |

**SEPTEMBER**

| S | M | T | W | T | F | S |
|---|---|---|---|---|---|---|
| | | | | 1 | 2 | 3 |
| 4 | 5 | 6 | 7 | 8 | 9 | 10 |
| 11 | 12 | 13 | 14 | 15 | 16 | 17 |
| 18 | 19 | 20 | 21 | 22 | 23 | 24 |
| 25 | 26 | 27 | 28 | 29 | 30 | |

**OCTOBER**

| S | M | T | W | T | F | S |
|---|---|---|---|---|---|---|
| | | | | | | 1 |
| 2 | 3 | 4 | 5 | 6 | 7 | 8 |
| 9 | 10 | 11 | 12 | 13 | 14 | 15 |
| 16 | 17 | 18 | 19 | 20 | 21 | 22 |
| 23 | 24 | 25 | 26 | 27 | 28 | 29 |
| 30 | 31 | | | | | |

**NOVEMBER**

| S | M | T | W | T | F | S |
|---|---|---|---|---|---|---|
| | | 1 | 2 | 3 | 4 | 5 |
| 6 | 7 | 8 | 9 | 10 | 11 | 12 |
| 13 | 14 | 15 | 16 | 17 | 18 | 19 |
| 20 | 21 | 22 | 23 | 24 | 25 | 26 |
| 27 | 28 | 29 | 30 | | | |

**DECEMBER**

| S | M | T | W | T | F | S |
|---|---|---|---|---|---|---|
| | | | | 1 | 2 | 3 |
| 4 | 5 | 6 | 7 | 8 | 9 | 10 |
| 11 | 12 | 13 | 14 | 15 | 16 | 17 |
| 18 | 19 | 20 | 21 | 22 | 23 | 24 |
| 25 | 26 | 27 | 28 | 29 | 30 | 31 |

## 8

**JANUARY**

| S | M | T | W | T | F | S |
|---|---|---|---|---|---|---|
| 1 | 2 | 3 | 4 | 5 | 6 | 7 |
| 8 | 9 | 10 | 11 | 12 | 13 | 14 |
| 15 | 16 | 17 | 18 | 19 | 20 | 21 |
| 22 | 23 | 24 | 25 | 26 | 27 | 28 |
| 29 | 30 | 31 | | | | |

**FEBRUARY**

| S | M | T | W | T | F | S |
|---|---|---|---|---|---|---|
| | | | 1 | 2 | 3 | 4 |
| 5 | 6 | 7 | 8 | 9 | 10 | 11 |
| 12 | 13 | 14 | 15 | 16 | 17 | 18 |
| 19 | 20 | 21 | 22 | 23 | 24 | 25 |
| 26 | 27 | 28 | 29 | | | |

**MARCH**

| S | M | T | W | T | F | S |
|---|---|---|---|---|---|---|
| | | | | 1 | 2 | 3 |
| 4 | 5 | 6 | 7 | 8 | 9 | 10 |
| 11 | 12 | 13 | 14 | 15 | 16 | 17 |
| 18 | 19 | 20 | 21 | 22 | 23 | 24 |
| 25 | 26 | 27 | 28 | 29 | 30 | 31 |

**APRIL**

| S | M | T | W | T | F | S |
|---|---|---|---|---|---|---|
| 1 | 2 | 3 | 4 | 5 | 6 | 7 |
| 8 | 9 | 10 | 11 | 12 | 13 | 14 |
| 15 | 16 | 17 | 18 | 19 | 20 | 21 |
| 22 | 23 | 24 | 25 | 26 | 27 | 28 |
| 29 | 30 | | | | | |

**MAY**

| S | M | T | W | T | F | S |
|---|---|---|---|---|---|---|
| | | 1 | 2 | 3 | 4 | 5 |
| 6 | 7 | 8 | 9 | 10 | 11 | 12 |
| 13 | 14 | 15 | 16 | 17 | 18 | 19 |
| 20 | 21 | 22 | 23 | 24 | 25 | 26 |
| 27 | 28 | 29 | 30 | 31 | | |

**JUNE**

| S | M | T | W | T | F | S |
|---|---|---|---|---|---|---|
| | | | | | 1 | 2 |
| 3 | 4 | 5 | 6 | 7 | 8 | 9 |
| 10 | 11 | 12 | 13 | 14 | 15 | 16 |
| 17 | 18 | 19 | 20 | 21 | 22 | 23 |
| 24 | 25 | 26 | 27 | 28 | 29 | 30 |

**JULY**

| S | M | T | W | T | F | S |
|---|---|---|---|---|---|---|
| 1 | 2 | 3 | 4 | 5 | 6 | 7 |
| 8 | 9 | 10 | 11 | 12 | 13 | 14 |
| 15 | 16 | 17 | 18 | 19 | 20 | 21 |
| 22 | 23 | 24 | 25 | 26 | 27 | 28 |
| 29 | 30 | 31 | | | | |

**AUGUST**

| S | M | T | W | T | F | S |
|---|---|---|---|---|---|---|
| | | | 1 | 2 | 3 | 4 |
| 5 | 6 | 7 | 8 | 9 | 10 | 11 |
| 12 | 13 | 14 | 15 | 16 | 17 | 18 |
| 19 | 20 | 21 | 22 | 23 | 24 | 25 |
| 26 | 27 | 28 | 29 | 30 | 31 | |

**SEPTEMBER**

| S | M | T | W | T | F | S |
|---|---|---|---|---|---|---|
| | | | | | | 1 |
| 2 | 3 | 4 | 5 | 6 | 7 | 8 |
| 9 | 10 | 11 | 12 | 13 | 14 | 15 |
| 16 | 17 | 18 | 19 | 20 | 21 | 22 |
| 23 | 24 | 25 | 26 | 27 | 28 | 29 |
| 30 | | | | | | |

**OCTOBER**

| S | M | T | W | T | F | S |
|---|---|---|---|---|---|---|
| | 1 | 2 | 3 | 4 | 5 | 6 |
| 7 | 8 | 9 | 10 | 11 | 12 | 13 |
| 14 | 15 | 16 | 17 | 18 | 19 | 20 |
| 21 | 22 | 23 | 24 | 25 | 26 | 27 |
| 28 | 29 | 30 | 31 | | | |

**NOVEMBER**

| S | M | T | W | T | F | S |
|---|---|---|---|---|---|---|
| | | | | 1 | 2 | 3 |
| 4 | 5 | 6 | 7 | 8 | 9 | 10 |
| 11 | 12 | 13 | 14 | 15 | 16 | 17 |
| 18 | 19 | 20 | 21 | 22 | 23 | 24 |
| 25 | 26 | 27 | 28 | 29 | 30 | |

**DECEMBER**

| S | M | T | W | T | F | S |
|---|---|---|---|---|---|---|
| | | | | | | 1 |
| 2 | 3 | 4 | 5 | 6 | 7 | 8 |
| 9 | 10 | 11 | 12 | 13 | 14 | 15 |
| 16 | 17 | 18 | 19 | 20 | 21 | 22 |
| 23 | 24 | 25 | 26 | 27 | 28 | 29 |
| 30 | 31 | | | | | |

## 9 1996

**JANUARY**

| S | M | T | W | T | F | S |
|---|---|---|---|---|---|---|
| | 1 | 2 | 3 | 4 | 5 | 6 |
| 7 | 8 | 9 | 10 | 11 | 12 | 13 |
| 14 | 15 | 16 | 17 | 18 | 19 | 20 |
| 21 | 22 | 23 | 24 | 25 | 26 | 27 |
| 28 | 29 | 30 | 31 | | | |

**FEBRUARY**

| S | M | T | W | T | F | S |
|---|---|---|---|---|---|---|
| | | | | 1 | 2 | 3 |
| 4 | 5 | 6 | 7 | 8 | 9 | 10 |
| 11 | 12 | 13 | 14 | 15 | 16 | 17 |
| 18 | 19 | 20 | 21 | 22 | 23 | 24 |
| 25 | 26 | 27 | 28 | 29 | | |

**MARCH**

| S | M | T | W | T | F | S |
|---|---|---|---|---|---|---|
| | | | | | 1 | 2 |
| 3 | 4 | 5 | 6 | 7 | 8 | 9 |
| 10 | 11 | 12 | 13 | 14 | 15 | 16 |
| 17 | 18 | 19 | 20 | 21 | 22 | 23 |
| 24 | 25 | 26 | 27 | 28 | 29 | 30 |
| 31 | | | | | | |

**APRIL**

| S | M | T | W | T | F | S |
|---|---|---|---|---|---|---|
| | 1 | 2 | 3 | 4 | 5 | 6 |
| 7 | 8 | 9 | 10 | 11 | 12 | 13 |
| 14 | 15 | 16 | 17 | 18 | 19 | 20 |
| 21 | 22 | 23 | 24 | 25 | 26 | 27 |
| 28 | 29 | 30 | | | | |

**MAY**

| S | M | T | W | T | F | S |
|---|---|---|---|---|---|---|
| | | | 1 | 2 | 3 | 4 |
| 5 | 6 | 7 | 8 | 9 | 10 | 11 |
| 12 | 13 | 14 | 15 | 16 | 17 | 18 |
| 19 | 20 | 21 | 22 | 23 | 24 | 25 |
| 26 | 27 | 28 | 29 | 30 | 31 | |

**JUNE**

| S | M | T | W | T | F | S |
|---|---|---|---|---|---|---|
| | | | | | | 1 |
| 2 | 3 | 4 | 5 | 6 | 7 | 8 |
| 9 | 10 | 11 | 12 | 13 | 14 | 15 |
| 16 | 17 | 18 | 19 | 20 | 21 | 22 |
| 23 | 24 | 25 | 26 | 27 | 28 | 29 |
| 30 | | | | | | |

**JULY**

| S | M | T | W | T | F | S |
|---|---|---|---|---|---|---|
| | 1 | 2 | 3 | 4 | 5 | 6 |
| 7 | 8 | 9 | 10 | 11 | 12 | 13 |
| 14 | 15 | 16 | 17 | 18 | 19 | 20 |
| 21 | 22 | 23 | 24 | 25 | 26 | 27 |
| 28 | 29 | 30 | 31 | | | |

**AUGUST**

| S | M | T | W | T | F | S |
|---|---|---|---|---|---|---|
| | | | | 1 | 2 | 3 |
| 4 | 5 | 6 | 7 | 8 | 9 | 10 |
| 11 | 12 | 13 | 14 | 15 | 16 | 17 |
| 18 | 19 | 20 | 21 | 22 | 23 | 24 |
| 25 | 26 | 27 | 28 | 29 | 30 | 31 |

**SEPTEMBER**

| S | M | T | W | T | F | S |
|---|---|---|---|---|---|---|
| 1 | 2 | 3 | 4 | 5 | 6 | 7 |
| 8 | 9 | 10 | 11 | 12 | 13 | 14 |
| 15 | 16 | 17 | 18 | 19 | 20 | 21 |
| 22 | 23 | 24 | 25 | 26 | 27 | 28 |
| 29 | 30 | | | | | |

**OCTOBER**

| S | M | T | W | T | F | S |
|---|---|---|---|---|---|---|
| | | 1 | 2 | 3 | 4 | 5 |
| 6 | 7 | 8 | 9 | 10 | 11 | 12 |
| 13 | 14 | 15 | 16 | 17 | 18 | 19 |
| 20 | 21 | 22 | 23 | 24 | 25 | 26 |
| 27 | 28 | 29 | 30 | 31 | | |

**NOVEMBER**

| S | M | T | W | T | F | S |
|---|---|---|---|---|---|---|
| | | | | | 1 | 2 |
| 3 | 4 | 5 | 6 | 7 | 8 | 9 |
| 10 | 11 | 12 | 13 | 14 | 15 | 16 |
| 17 | 18 | 19 | 20 | 21 | 22 | 23 |
| 24 | 25 | 26 | 27 | 28 | 29 | 30 |

**DECEMBER**

| S | M | T | W | T | F | S |
|---|---|---|---|---|---|---|
| 1 | 2 | 3 | 4 | 5 | 6 | 7 |
| 8 | 9 | 10 | 11 | 12 | 13 | 14 |
| 15 | 16 | 17 | 18 | 19 | 20 | 21 |
| 22 | 23 | 24 | 25 | 26 | 27 | 28 |
| 29 | 30 | 31 | | | | |

## 10

**JANUARY**

| S | M | T | W | T | F | S |
|---|---|---|---|---|---|---|
| | | 1 | 2 | 3 | 4 | 5 |
| 6 | 7 | 8 | 9 | 10 | 11 | 12 |
| 13 | 14 | 15 | 16 | 17 | 18 | 19 |
| 20 | 21 | 22 | 23 | 24 | 25 | 26 |
| 27 | 28 | 29 | 30 | 31 | | |

**FEBRUARY**

| S | M | T | W | T | F | S |
|---|---|---|---|---|---|---|
| | | | | | 1 | 2 |
| 3 | 4 | 5 | 6 | 7 | 8 | 9 |
| 10 | 11 | 12 | 13 | 14 | 15 | 16 |
| 17 | 18 | 19 | 20 | 21 | 22 | 23 |
| 24 | 25 | 26 | 27 | 28 | 29 | |

**MARCH**

| S | M | T | W | T | F | S |
|---|---|---|---|---|---|---|
| | | | | | | 1 |
| 2 | 3 | 4 | 5 | 6 | 7 | 8 |
| 9 | 10 | 11 | 12 | 13 | 14 | 15 |
| 16 | 17 | 18 | 19 | 20 | 21 | 22 |
| 23 | 24 | 25 | 26 | 27 | 28 | 29 |
| 30 | 31 | | | | | |

**APRIL**

| S | M | T | W | T | F | S |
|---|---|---|---|---|---|---|
| | | 1 | 2 | 3 | 4 | 5 |
| 6 | 7 | 8 | 9 | 10 | 11 | 12 |
| 13 | 14 | 15 | 16 | 17 | 18 | 19 |
| 20 | 21 | 22 | 23 | 24 | 25 | 26 |
| 27 | 28 | 29 | 30 | | | |

**MAY**

| S | M | T | W | T | F | S |
|---|---|---|---|---|---|---|
| | | | | 1 | 2 | 3 |
| 4 | 5 | 6 | 7 | 8 | 9 | 10 |
| 11 | 12 | 13 | 14 | 15 | 16 | 17 |
| 18 | 19 | 20 | 21 | 22 | 23 | 24 |
| 25 | 26 | 27 | 28 | 29 | 30 | 31 |

**JUNE**

| S | M | T | W | T | F | S |
|---|---|---|---|---|---|---|
| 1 | 2 | 3 | 4 | 5 | 6 | 7 |
| 8 | 9 | 10 | 11 | 12 | 13 | 14 |
| 15 | 16 | 17 | 18 | 19 | 20 | 21 |
| 22 | 23 | 24 | 25 | 26 | 27 | 28 |
| 29 | 30 | | | | | |

**JULY**

| S | M | T | W | T | F | S |
|---|---|---|---|---|---|---|
| | | 1 | 2 | 3 | 4 | 5 |
| 6 | 7 | 8 | 9 | 10 | 11 | 12 |
| 13 | 14 | 15 | 16 | 17 | 18 | 19 |
| 20 | 21 | 22 | 23 | 24 | 25 | 26 |
| 27 | 28 | 29 | 30 | 31 | | |

**AUGUST**

| S | M | T | W | T | F | S |
|---|---|---|---|---|---|---|
| | | | | | 1 | 2 |
| 3 | 4 | 5 | 6 | 7 | 8 | 9 |
| 10 | 11 | 12 | 13 | 14 | 15 | 16 |
| 17 | 18 | 19 | 20 | 21 | 22 | 23 |
| 24 | 25 | 26 | 27 | 28 | 29 | 30 |
| 31 | | | | | | |

**SEPTEMBER**

| S | M | T | W | T | F | S |
|---|---|---|---|---|---|---|
| | 1 | 2 | 3 | 4 | 5 | 6 |
| 7 | 8 | 9 | 10 | 11 | 12 | 13 |
| 14 | 15 | 16 | 17 | 18 | 19 | 20 |
| 21 | 22 | 23 | 24 | 25 | 26 | 27 |
| 28 | 29 | 30 | | | | |

**OCTOBER**

| S | M | T | W | T | F | S |
|---|---|---|---|---|---|---|
| | | | 1 | 2 | 3 | 4 |
| 5 | 6 | 7 | 8 | 9 | 10 | 11 |
| 12 | 13 | 14 | 15 | 16 | 17 | 18 |
| 19 | 20 | 21 | 22 | 23 | 24 | 25 |
| 26 | 27 | 28 | 29 | 30 | 31 | |

**NOVEMBER**

| S | M | T | W | T | F | S |
|---|---|---|---|---|---|---|
| | | | | | | 1 |
| 2 | 3 | 4 | 5 | 6 | 7 | 8 |
| 9 | 10 | 11 | 12 | 13 | 14 | 15 |
| 16 | 17 | 18 | 19 | 20 | 21 | 22 |
| 23 | 24 | 25 | 26 | 27 | 28 | 29 |
| 30 | | | | | | |

**DECEMBER**

| S | M | T | W | T | F | S |
|---|---|---|---|---|---|---|
| | 1 | 2 | 3 | 4 | 5 | 6 |
| 7 | 8 | 9 | 10 | 11 | 12 | 13 |
| 14 | 15 | 16 | 17 | 18 | 19 | 20 |
| 21 | 22 | 23 | 24 | 25 | 26 | 27 |
| 28 | 29 | 30 | 31 | | | |

## 11

**JANUARY**

| S | M | T | W | T | F | S |
|---|---|---|---|---|---|---|
| | | | 1 | 2 | 3 | 4 |
| 5 | 6 | 7 | 8 | 9 | 10 | 11 |
| 12 | 13 | 14 | 15 | 16 | 17 | 18 |
| 19 | 20 | 21 | 22 | 23 | 24 | 25 |
| 26 | 27 | 28 | 29 | 30 | 31 | |

**FEBRUARY**

| S | M | T | W | T | F | S |
|---|---|---|---|---|---|---|
| | | | | | | 1 |
| 2 | 3 | 4 | 5 | 6 | 7 | 8 |
| 9 | 10 | 11 | 12 | 13 | 14 | 15 |
| 16 | 17 | 18 | 19 | 20 | 21 | 22 |
| 23 | 24 | 25 | 26 | 27 | 28 | 29 |

**MARCH**

| S | M | T | W | T | F | S |
|---|---|---|---|---|---|---|
| 1 | 2 | 3 | 4 | 5 | 6 | 7 |
| 8 | 9 | 10 | 11 | 12 | 13 | 14 |
| 15 | 16 | 17 | 18 | 19 | 20 | 21 |
| 22 | 23 | 24 | 25 | 26 | 27 | 28 |
| 29 | 30 | 31 | | | | |

**APRIL**

| S | M | T | W | T | F | S |
|---|---|---|---|---|---|---|
| | | | 1 | 2 | 3 | 4 |
| 5 | 6 | 7 | 8 | 9 | 10 | 11 |
| 12 | 13 | 14 | 15 | 16 | 17 | 18 |
| 19 | 20 | 21 | 22 | 23 | 24 | 25 |
| 26 | 27 | 28 | 29 | 30 | | |

**MAY**

| S | M | T | W | T | F | S |
|---|---|---|---|---|---|---|
| | | | | | 1 | 2 |
| 3 | 4 | 5 | 6 | 7 | 8 | 9 |
| 10 | 11 | 12 | 13 | 14 | 15 | 16 |
| 17 | 18 | 19 | 20 | 21 | 22 | 23 |
| 24 | 25 | 26 | 27 | 28 | 29 | 30 |
| 31 | | | | | | |

**JUNE**

| S | M | T | W | T | F | S |
|---|---|---|---|---|---|---|
| | 1 | 2 | 3 | 4 | 5 | 6 |
| 7 | 8 | 9 | 10 | 11 | 12 | 13 |
| 14 | 15 | 16 | 17 | 18 | 19 | 20 |
| 21 | 22 | 23 | 24 | 25 | 26 | 27 |
| 28 | 29 | 30 | | | | |

**JULY**

| S | M | T | W | T | F | S |
|---|---|---|---|---|---|---|
| | | | 1 | 2 | 3 | 4 |
| 5 | 6 | 7 | 8 | 9 | 10 | 11 |
| 12 | 13 | 14 | 15 | 16 | 17 | 18 |
| 19 | 20 | 21 | 22 | 23 | 24 | 25 |
| 26 | 27 | 28 | 29 | 30 | 31 | |

**AUGUST**

| S | M | T | W | T | F | S |
|---|---|---|---|---|---|---|
| | | | | | | 1 |
| 2 | 3 | 4 | 5 | 6 | 7 | 8 |
| 9 | 10 | 11 | 12 | 13 | 14 | 15 |
| 16 | 17 | 18 | 19 | 20 | 21 | 22 |
| 23 | 24 | 25 | 26 | 27 | 28 | 29 |
| 30 | 31 | | | | | |

**SEPTEMBER**

| S | M | T | W | T | F | S |
|---|---|---|---|---|---|---|
| | | 1 | 2 | 3 | 4 | 5 |
| 6 | 7 | 8 | 9 | 10 | 11 | 12 |
| 13 | 14 | 15 | 16 | 17 | 18 | 19 |
| 20 | 21 | 22 | 23 | 24 | 25 | 26 |
| 27 | 28 | 29 | 30 | | | |

**OCTOBER**

| S | M | T | W | T | F | S |
|---|---|---|---|---|---|---|
| | | | | 1 | 2 | 3 |
| 4 | 5 | 6 | 7 | 8 | 9 | 10 |
| 11 | 12 | 13 | 14 | 15 | 16 | 17 |
| 18 | 19 | 20 | 21 | 22 | 23 | 24 |
| 25 | 26 | 27 | 28 | 29 | 30 | 31 |

**NOVEMBER**

| S | M | T | W | T | F | S |
|---|---|---|---|---|---|---|
| 1 | 2 | 3 | 4 | 5 | 6 | 7 |
| 8 | 9 | 10 | 11 | 12 | 13 | 14 |
| 15 | 16 | 17 | 18 | 19 | 20 | 21 |
| 22 | 23 | 24 | 25 | 26 | 27 | 28 |
| 29 | 30 | | | | | |

**DECEMBER**

| S | M | T | W | T | F | S |
|---|---|---|---|---|---|---|
| | | 1 | 2 | 3 | 4 | 5 |
| 6 | 7 | 8 | 9 | 10 | 11 | 12 |
| 13 | 14 | 15 | 16 | 17 | 18 | 19 |
| 20 | 21 | 22 | 23 | 24 | 25 | 26 |
| 27 | 28 | 29 | 30 | 31 | | |

## 12

**JANUARY**

| S | M | T | W | T | F | S |
|---|---|---|---|---|---|---|
| | | | | 1 | 2 | 3 |
| 4 | 5 | 6 | 7 | 8 | 9 | 10 |
| 11 | 12 | 13 | 14 | 15 | 16 | 17 |
| 18 | 19 | 20 | 21 | 22 | 23 | 24 |
| 25 | 26 | 27 | 28 | 29 | 30 | 31 |

**FEBRUARY**

| S | M | T | W | T | F | S |
|---|---|---|---|---|---|---|
| 1 | 2 | 3 | 4 | 5 | 6 | 7 |
| 8 | 9 | 10 | 11 | 12 | 13 | 14 |
| 15 | 16 | 17 | 18 | 19 | 20 | 21 |
| 22 | 23 | 24 | 25 | 26 | 27 | 28 |
| 29 | | | | | | |

**MARCH**

| S | M | T | W | T | F | S |
|---|---|---|---|---|---|---|
| | 1 | 2 | 3 | 4 | 5 | 6 |
| 7 | 8 | 9 | 10 | 11 | 12 | 13 |
| 14 | 15 | 16 | 17 | 18 | 19 | 20 |
| 21 | 22 | 23 | 24 | 25 | 26 | 27 |
| 28 | 29 | 30 | 31 | | | |

**APRIL**

| S | M | T | W | T | F | S |
|---|---|---|---|---|---|---|
| | | | | 1 | 2 | 3 |
| 4 | 5 | 6 | 7 | 8 | 9 | 10 |
| 11 | 12 | 13 | 14 | 15 | 16 | 17 |
| 18 | 19 | 20 | 21 | 22 | 23 | 24 |
| 25 | 26 | 27 | 28 | 29 | 30 | |

**MAY**

| S | M | T | W | T | F | S |
|---|---|---|---|---|---|---|
| | | | | | | 1 |
| 2 | 3 | 4 | 5 | 6 | 7 | 8 |
| 9 | 10 | 11 | 12 | 13 | 14 | 15 |
| 16 | 17 | 18 | 19 | 20 | 21 | 22 |
| 23 | 24 | 25 | 26 | 27 | 28 | 29 |
| 30 | 31 | | | | | |

**JUNE**

| S | M | T | W | T | F | S |
|---|---|---|---|---|---|---|
| | | 1 | 2 | 3 | 4 | 5 |
| 6 | 7 | 8 | 9 | 10 | 11 | 12 |
| 13 | 14 | 15 | 16 | 17 | 18 | 19 |
| 20 | 21 | 22 | 23 | 24 | 25 | 26 |
| 27 | 28 | 29 | 30 | | | |

**JULY**

| S | M | T | W | T | F | S |
|---|---|---|---|---|---|---|
| | | | | 1 | 2 | 3 |
| 4 | 5 | 6 | 7 | 8 | 9 | 10 |
| 11 | 12 | 13 | 14 | 15 | 16 | 17 |
| 18 | 19 | 20 | 21 | 22 | 23 | 24 |
| 25 | 26 | 27 | 28 | 29 | 30 | 31 |

**AUGUST**

| S | M | T | W | T | F | S |
|---|---|---|---|---|---|---|
| 1 | 2 | 3 | 4 | 5 | 6 | 7 |
| 8 | 9 | 10 | 11 | 12 | 13 | 14 |
| 15 | 16 | 17 | 18 | 19 | 20 | 21 |
| 22 | 23 | 24 | 25 | 26 | 27 | 28 |
| 29 | 30 | 31 | | | | |

**SEPTEMBER**

| S | M | T | W | T | F | S |
|---|---|---|---|---|---|---|
| | | | 1 | 2 | 3 | 4 |
| 5 | 6 | 7 | 8 | 9 | 10 | 11 |
| 12 | 13 | 14 | 15 | 16 | 17 | 18 |
| 19 | 20 | 21 | 22 | 23 | 24 | 25 |
| 26 | 27 | 28 | 29 | 30 | | |

**OCTOBER**

| S | M | T | W | T | F | S |
|---|---|---|---|---|---|---|
| | | | | | 1 | 2 |
| 3 | 4 | 5 | 6 | 7 | 8 | 9 |
| 10 | 11 | 12 | 13 | 14 | 15 | 16 |
| 17 | 18 | 19 | 20 | 21 | 22 | 23 |
| 24 | 25 | 26 | 27 | 28 | 29 | 30 |
| 31 | | | | | | |

**NOVEMBER**

| S | M | T | W | T | F | S |
|---|---|---|---|---|---|---|
| | 1 | 2 | 3 | 4 | 5 | 6 |
| 7 | 8 | 9 | 10 | 11 | 12 | 13 |
| 14 | 15 | 16 | 17 | 18 | 19 | 20 |
| 21 | 22 | 23 | 24 | 25 | 26 | 27 |
| 28 | 29 | 30 | | | | |

**DECEMBER**

| S | M | T | W | T | F | S |
|---|---|---|---|---|---|---|
| | | | 1 | 2 | 3 | 4 |
| 5 | 6 | 7 | 8 | 9 | 10 | 11 |
| 12 | 13 | 14 | 15 | 16 | 17 | 18 |
| 19 | 20 | 21 | 22 | 23 | 24 | 25 |
| 26 | 27 | 28 | 29 | 30 | 31 | |

## 13

**JANUARY**

| S | M | T | W | T | F | S |
|---|---|---|---|---|---|---|
| | | | | | 1 | 2 |
| 3 | 4 | 5 | 6 | 7 | 8 | 9 |
| 10 | 11 | 12 | 13 | 14 | 15 | 16 |
| 17 | 18 | 19 | 20 | 21 | 22 | 23 |
| 24 | 25 | 26 | 27 | 28 | 29 | 30 |
| 31 | | | | | | |

**FEBRUARY**

| S | M | T | W | T | F | S |
|---|---|---|---|---|---|---|
| | 1 | 2 | 3 | 4 | 5 | 6 |
| 7 | 8 | 9 | 10 | 11 | 12 | 13 |
| 14 | 15 | 16 | 17 | 18 | 19 | 20 |
| 21 | 22 | 23 | 24 | 25 | 26 | 27 |
| 28 | 29 | | | | | |

**MARCH**

| S | M | T | W | T | F | S |
|---|---|---|---|---|---|---|
| | | 1 | 2 | 3 | 4 | 5 |
| 6 | 7 | 8 | 9 | 10 | 11 | 12 |
| 13 | 14 | 15 | 16 | 17 | 18 | 19 |
| 20 | 21 | 22 | 23 | 24 | 25 | 26 |
| 27 | 28 | 29 | 30 | 31 | | |

**APRIL**

| S | M | T | W | T | F | S |
|---|---|---|---|---|---|---|
| | | | | | 1 | 2 |
| 3 | 4 | 5 | 6 | 7 | 8 | 9 |
| 10 | 11 | 12 | 13 | 14 | 15 | 16 |
| 17 | 18 | 19 | 20 | 21 | 22 | 23 |
| 24 | 25 | 26 | 27 | 28 | 29 | 30 |

**MAY**

| S | M | T | W | T | F | S |
|---|---|---|---|---|---|---|
| 1 | 2 | 3 | 4 | 5 | 6 | 7 |
| 8 | 9 | 10 | 11 | 12 | 13 | 14 |
| 15 | 16 | 17 | 18 | 19 | 20 | 21 |
| 22 | 23 | 24 | 25 | 26 | 27 | 28 |
| 29 | 30 | 31 | | | | |

**JUNE**

| S | M | T | W | T | F | S |
|---|---|---|---|---|---|---|
| | | | 1 | 2 | 3 | 4 |
| 5 | 6 | 7 | 8 | 9 | 10 | 11 |
| 12 | 13 | 14 | 15 | 16 | 17 | 18 |
| 19 | 20 | 21 | 22 | 23 | 24 | 25 |
| 26 | 27 | 28 | 29 | 30 | | |

**JULY**

| S | M | T | W | T | F | S |
|---|---|---|---|---|---|---|
| | | | | | 1 | 2 |
| 3 | 4 | 5 | 6 | 7 | 8 | 9 |
| 10 | 11 | 12 | 13 | 14 | 15 | 16 |
| 17 | 18 | 19 | 20 | 21 | 22 | 23 |
| 24 | 25 | 26 | 27 | 28 | 29 | 30 |
| 31 | | | | | | |

**AUGUST**

| S | M | T | W | T | F | S |
|---|---|---|---|---|---|---|
| | 1 | 2 | 3 | 4 | 5 | 6 |
| 7 | 8 | 9 | 10 | 11 | 12 | 13 |
| 14 | 15 | 16 | 17 | 18 | 19 | 20 |
| 21 | 22 | 23 | 24 | 25 | 26 | 27 |
| 28 | 29 | 30 | 31 | | | |

**SEPTEMBER**

| S | M | T | W | T | F | S |
|---|---|---|---|---|---|---|
| | | | | 1 | 2 | 3 |
| 4 | 5 | 6 | 7 | 8 | 9 | 10 |
| 11 | 12 | 13 | 14 | 15 | 16 | 17 |
| 18 | 19 | 20 | 21 | 22 | 23 | 24 |
| 25 | 26 | 27 | 28 | 29 | 30 | |

**OCTOBER**

| S | M | T | W | T | F | S |
|---|---|---|---|---|---|---|
| | | | | | | 1 |
| 2 | 3 | 4 | 5 | 6 | 7 | 8 |
| 9 | 10 | 11 | 12 | 13 | 14 | 15 |
| 16 | 17 | 18 | 19 | 20 | 21 | 22 |
| 23 | 24 | 25 | 26 | 27 | 28 | 29 |
| 30 | 31 | | | | | |

**NOVEMBER**

| S | M | T | W | T | F | S |
|---|---|---|---|---|---|---|
| | | 1 | 2 | 3 | 4 | 5 |
| 6 | 7 | 8 | 9 | 10 | 11 | 12 |
| 13 | 14 | 15 | 16 | 17 | 18 | 19 |
| 20 | 21 | 22 | 23 | 24 | 25 | 26 |
| 27 | 28 | 29 | 30 | | | |

**DECEMBER**

| S | M | T | W | T | F | S |
|---|---|---|---|---|---|---|
| | | | | 1 | 2 | 3 |
| 4 | 5 | 6 | 7 | 8 | 9 | 10 |
| 11 | 12 | 13 | 14 | 15 | 16 | 17 |
| 18 | 19 | 20 | 21 | 22 | 23 | 24 |
| 25 | 26 | 27 | 28 | 29 | 30 | 31 |

## 14

**JANUARY**

| S | M | T | W | T | F | S |
|---|---|---|---|---|---|---|
| | | | | | | 1 |
| 2 | 3 | 4 | 5 | 6 | 7 | 8 |
| 9 | 10 | 11 | 12 | 13 | 14 | 15 |
| 16 | 17 | 18 | 19 | 20 | 21 | 22 |
| 23 | 24 | 25 | 26 | 27 | 28 | 29 |
| 30 | 31 | | | | | |

**FEBRUARY**

| S | M | T | W | T | F | S |
|---|---|---|---|---|---|---|
| | | 1 | 2 | 3 | 4 | 5 |
| 6 | 7 | 8 | 9 | 10 | 11 | 12 |
| 13 | 14 | 15 | 16 | 17 | 18 | 19 |
| 20 | 21 | 22 | 23 | 24 | 25 | 26 |
| 27 | 28 | 29 | | | | |

**MARCH**

| S | M | T | W | T | F | S |
|---|---|---|---|---|---|---|
| | | | 1 | 2 | 3 | 4 |
| 5 | 6 | 7 | 8 | 9 | 10 | 11 |
| 12 | 13 | 14 | 15 | 16 | 17 | 18 |
| 19 | 20 | 21 | 22 | 23 | 24 | 25 |
| 26 | 27 | 28 | 29 | 30 | 31 | |

**APRIL**

| S | M | T | W | T | F | S |
|---|---|---|---|---|---|---|
| | | | | | | 1 |
| 2 | 3 | 4 | 5 | 6 | 7 | 8 |
| 9 | 10 | 11 | 12 | 13 | 14 | 15 |
| 16 | 17 | 18 | 19 | 20 | 21 | 22 |
| 23 | 24 | 25 | 26 | 27 | 28 | 29 |
| 30 | | | | | | |

**MAY**

| S | M | T | W | T | F | S |
|---|---|---|---|---|---|---|
| | 1 | 2 | 3 | 4 | 5 | 6 |
| 7 | 8 | 9 | 10 | 11 | 12 | 13 |
| 14 | 15 | 16 | 17 | 18 | 19 | 20 |
| 21 | 22 | 23 | 24 | 25 | 26 | 27 |
| 28 | 29 | 30 | 31 | | | |

**JUNE**

| S | M | T | W | T | F | S |
|---|---|---|---|---|---|---|
| | | | | 1 | 2 | 3 |
| 4 | 5 | 6 | 7 | 8 | 9 | 10 |
| 11 | 12 | 13 | 14 | 15 | 16 | 17 |
| 18 | 19 | 20 | 21 | 22 | 23 | 24 |
| 25 | 26 | 27 | 28 | 29 | 30 | |

**JULY**

| S | M | T | W | T | F | S |
|---|---|---|---|---|---|---|
| | | | | | | 1 |
| 2 | 3 | 4 | 5 | 6 | 7 | 8 |
| 9 | 10 | 11 | 12 | 13 | 14 | 15 |
| 16 | 17 | 18 | 19 | 20 | 21 | 22 |
| 23 | 24 | 25 | 26 | 27 | 28 | 29 |
| 30 | 31 | | | | | |

**AUGUST**

| S | M | T | W | T | F | S |
|---|---|---|---|---|---|---|
| | | 1 | 2 | 3 | 4 | 5 |
| 6 | 7 | 8 | 9 | 10 | 11 | 12 |
| 13 | 14 | 15 | 16 | 17 | 18 | 19 |
| 20 | 21 | 22 | 23 | 24 | 25 | 26 |
| 27 | 28 | 29 | 30 | 31 | | |

**SEPTEMBER**

| S | M | T | W | T | F | S |
|---|---|---|---|---|---|---|
| | | | | | 1 | 2 |
| 3 | 4 | 5 | 6 | 7 | 8 | 9 |
| 10 | 11 | 12 | 13 | 14 | 15 | 16 |
| 17 | 18 | 19 | 20 | 21 | 22 | 23 |
| 24 | 25 | 26 | 27 | 28 | 29 | 30 |

**OCTOBER**

| S | M | T | W | T | F | S |
|---|---|---|---|---|---|---|
| 1 | 2 | 3 | 4 | 5 | 6 | 7 |
| 8 | 9 | 10 | 11 | 12 | 13 | 14 |
| 15 | 16 | 17 | 18 | 19 | 20 | 21 |
| 22 | 23 | 24 | 25 | 26 | 27 | 28 |
| 29 | 30 | 31 | | | | |

**NOVEMBER**

| S | M | T | W | T | F | S |
|---|---|---|---|---|---|---|
| | | | 1 | 2 | 3 | 4 |
| 5 | 6 | 7 | 8 | 9 | 10 | 11 |
| 12 | 13 | 14 | 15 | 16 | 17 | 18 |
| 19 | 20 | 21 | 22 | 23 | 24 | 25 |
| 26 | 27 | 28 | 29 | 30 | | |

**DECEMBER**

| S | M | T | W | T | F | S |
|---|---|---|---|---|---|---|
| | | | | | 1 | 2 |
| 3 | 4 | 5 | 6 | 7 | 8 | 9 |
| 10 | 11 | 12 | 13 | 14 | 15 | 16 |
| 17 | 18 | 19 | 20 | 21 | 22 | 23 |
| 24 | 25 | 26 | 27 | 28 | 29 | 30 |
| 31 | | | | | | |

# The Julian Period

How many days have you lived? To determine this, multiply your age by 365, add the number of days since your last birthday, and account for all leap years. Chances are your calculations will go wrong somewhere. Astronomers, however, find it convenient to express dates and time intervals in days rather than in years, months, and days. This is done by placing events within the Julian period.

The Julian period was devised in 1582 by the French classical scholar Joseph Scaliger (1540-1609) and named after his father, Julius Caesar Scaliger (1484-1558), not after the Julian calendar. Joseph Scaliger began Julian Day (JD) #1 at noon, Jan. 1, 4713 BC, the most recent time that 3 major chronological cycles began on the same day—(1) the 28-year solar cycle, after which dates in the Julian calendar (e.g., Feb. 11) return to the same days of the week (e.g., Monday); (2) the 19-year lunar cycle, after which the phases of the moon return to the same dates of the year; and (3) the 15-year indiction cycle, used in ancient Rome to regulate taxes. It will take 7,980 years to complete the period, the product of 28, 19, and 15.

Noon of Dec. 31, 1996, marks the beginning of JD 2,450,449; that many days will have passed since the start of the Julian period. The JD at noon of any date in 1997 may be found by adding to this figure the day of the year for that date, which can be obtained from the left half of the "Days Between Two Dates" chart.

# Days Between Two Dates

This table covers a period of 2 ordinary years. To use the table, find the **boldface number** for each date and subtract the smaller from the larger. Example—For days between Feb. 10, 1994, and Dec. 15, 1995, subtract 41 from 714; answer is 673 days. For leap year, such as 1996, one day must be added: answer for days between Feb. 10, 1995, and Dec. 15, 1996, would be 674.

**First Year**

| Date | Jan. | Feb. | Mar. | April | May | June | July | Aug. | Sept. | Oct. | Nov. | Dec. |
|---|---|---|---|---|---|---|---|---|---|---|---|---|
| 1 | 1 | 32 | 60 | 91 | 121 | 152 | 182 | 213 | 244 | 274 | 305 | 335 |
| 2 | 2 | 33 | 61 | 92 | 122 | 153 | 183 | 214 | 245 | 275 | 306 | 336 |
| 3 | 3 | 34 | 62 | 93 | 123 | 154 | 184 | 215 | 246 | 276 | 307 | 337 |
| 4 | 4 | 35 | 63 | 94 | 124 | 155 | 185 | 216 | 247 | 277 | 308 | 338 |
| 5 | 5 | 36 | 64 | 95 | 125 | 156 | 186 | 217 | 248 | 278 | 309 | 339 |
| 6 | 6 | 37 | 65 | 96 | 126 | 157 | 187 | 218 | 249 | 279 | 310 | 340 |
| 7 | 7 | 38 | 66 | 97 | 127 | 158 | 188 | 219 | 250 | 280 | 311 | 341 |
| 8 | 8 | 39 | 67 | 98 | 128 | 159 | 189 | 220 | 251 | 281 | 312 | 342 |
| 9 | 9 | 40 | 68 | 99 | 129 | 160 | 190 | 221 | 252 | 282 | 313 | 343 |
| 10 | 10 | 41 | 69 | 100 | 130 | 161 | 191 | 222 | 253 | 283 | 314 | 344 |
| 11 | 11 | 42 | 70 | 101 | 131 | 162 | 192 | 223 | 254 | 284 | 315 | 345 |
| 12 | 12 | 43 | 71 | 102 | 132 | 163 | 193 | 224 | 255 | 285 | 316 | 346 |
| 13 | 13 | 44 | 72 | 103 | 133 | 164 | 194 | 225 | 256 | 286 | 317 | 347 |
| 14 | 14 | 45 | 73 | 104 | 134 | 165 | 195 | 226 | 257 | 287 | 318 | 348 |
| 15 | 15 | 46 | 74 | 105 | 135 | 166 | 196 | 227 | 258 | 288 | 319 | 349 |
| 16 | 16 | 47 | 75 | 106 | 136 | 167 | 197 | 228 | 259 | 289 | 320 | 350 |
| 17 | 17 | 48 | 76 | 107 | 137 | 168 | 198 | 229 | 260 | 290 | 321 | 351 |
| 18 | 18 | 49 | 77 | 108 | 138 | 169 | 199 | 230 | 261 | 291 | 322 | 352 |
| 19 | 19 | 50 | 78 | 109 | 139 | 170 | 200 | 231 | 262 | 292 | 323 | 353 |
| 20 | 20 | 51 | 79 | 110 | 140 | 171 | 201 | 232 | 263 | 293 | 324 | 354 |
| 21 | 21 | 52 | 80 | 111 | 141 | 172 | 202 | 233 | 264 | 294 | 325 | 355 |
| 22 | 22 | 53 | 81 | 112 | 142 | 173 | 203 | 234 | 265 | 295 | 326 | 356 |
| 23 | 23 | 54 | 82 | 113 | 143 | 174 | 204 | 235 | 266 | 296 | 327 | 357 |
| 24 | 24 | 55 | 83 | 114 | 144 | 175 | 205 | 236 | 267 | 297 | 328 | 358 |
| 25 | 25 | 56 | 84 | 115 | 145 | 176 | 206 | 237 | 268 | 298 | 329 | 359 |
| 26 | 26 | 57 | 85 | 116 | 146 | 177 | 207 | 238 | 269 | 299 | 330 | 360 |
| 27 | 27 | 58 | 86 | 117 | 147 | 178 | 208 | 239 | 270 | 300 | 331 | 361 |
| 28 | 28 | 59 | 87 | 118 | 148 | 179 | 209 | 240 | 271 | 301 | 332 | 362 |
| 29 | 29 | — | 88 | 119 | 149 | 180 | 210 | 241 | 272 | 302 | 333 | 363 |
| 30 | 30 | — | 89 | 120 | 150 | 181 | 211 | 242 | 273 | 303 | 334 | 364 |
| 31 | 31 | — | 90 | — | 151 | — | 212 | 243 | — | 304 | — | 365 |

**Second Year**

| Date | Jan. | Feb. | Mar. | April | May | June | July | Aug. | Sept. | Oct. | Nov. | Dec. |
|---|---|---|---|---|---|---|---|---|---|---|---|---|
| 1 | 366 | 397 | 425 | 456 | 486 | 517 | 547 | 578 | 609 | 639 | 670 | 700 |
| 2 | 367 | 398 | 426 | 457 | 487 | 518 | 548 | 579 | 610 | 640 | 671 | 701 |
| 3 | 368 | 399 | 427 | 458 | 488 | 519 | 549 | 580 | 611 | 641 | 672 | 702 |
| 4 | 369 | 400 | 428 | 459 | 489 | 520 | 550 | 581 | 612 | 642 | 673 | 703 |
| 5 | 370 | 401 | 429 | 460 | 490 | 521 | 551 | 582 | 613 | 643 | 674 | 704 |
| 6 | 371 | 402 | 430 | 461 | 491 | 522 | 552 | 583 | 614 | 644 | 675 | 705 |
| 7 | 372 | 403 | 431 | 462 | 492 | 523 | 553 | 584 | 615 | 645 | 676 | 706 |
| 8 | 373 | 404 | 432 | 463 | 493 | 524 | 554 | 585 | 616 | 646 | 677 | 707 |
| 9 | 374 | 405 | 433 | 464 | 494 | 525 | 555 | 586 | 617 | 647 | 678 | 708 |
| 10 | 375 | 406 | 434 | 465 | 495 | 526 | 556 | 587 | 618 | 648 | 679 | 709 |
| 11 | 376 | 407 | 435 | 466 | 496 | 527 | 557 | 588 | 619 | 649 | 680 | 710 |
| 12 | 377 | 408 | 436 | 467 | 497 | 528 | 558 | 589 | 620 | 650 | 681 | 711 |
| 13 | 378 | 409 | 437 | 468 | 498 | 529 | 559 | 590 | 621 | 651 | 682 | 712 |
| 14 | 379 | 410 | 438 | 469 | 499 | 530 | 560 | 591 | 622 | 652 | 683 | 713 |
| 15 | 380 | 411 | 439 | 470 | 500 | 531 | 561 | 592 | 623 | 653 | 684 | 714 |
| 16 | 381 | 412 | 440 | 471 | 501 | 532 | 562 | 593 | 624 | 654 | 685 | 715 |
| 17 | 382 | 413 | 441 | 472 | 502 | 533 | 563 | 594 | 625 | 655 | 686 | 716 |
| 18 | 383 | 414 | 442 | 473 | 503 | 534 | 564 | 595 | 626 | 656 | 687 | 717 |
| 19 | 384 | 415 | 443 | 474 | 504 | 535 | 565 | 596 | 627 | 657 | 688 | 718 |
| 20 | 385 | 416 | 444 | 475 | 505 | 536 | 566 | 597 | 628 | 658 | 689 | 719 |
| 21 | 386 | 417 | 445 | 476 | 506 | 537 | 567 | 598 | 629 | 659 | 690 | 720 |
| 22 | 387 | 418 | 446 | 477 | 507 | 538 | 568 | 599 | 630 | 660 | 691 | 721 |
| 23 | 388 | 419 | 447 | 478 | 508 | 539 | 569 | 600 | 631 | 661 | 692 | 722 |
| 24 | 389 | 420 | 448 | 479 | 509 | 540 | 570 | 601 | 632 | 662 | 693 | 723 |
| 25 | 390 | 421 | 449 | 480 | 510 | 541 | 571 | 602 | 633 | 663 | 694 | 724 |
| 26 | 391 | 422 | 450 | 481 | 511 | 542 | 572 | 603 | 634 | 664 | 695 | 725 |
| 27 | 392 | 423 | 451 | 482 | 512 | 543 | 573 | 604 | 635 | 665 | 696 | 726 |
| 28 | 393 | 424 | 452 | 483 | 513 | 544 | 574 | 605 | 636 | 666 | 697 | 727 |
| 29 | 394 | — | 453 | 484 | 514 | 545 | 575 | 606 | 637 | 667 | 698 | 728 |
| 30 | 395 | — | 454 | 485 | 515 | 546 | 576 | 607 | 638 | 668 | 699 | 729 |
| 31 | 396 | — | 455 | — | 516 | — | 577 | 608 | — | 669 | — | 730 |

# Lunar Calendar, Chinese New Year, Vietnamese Tet

**Source:** Chinese Information and Culture Center, New York, NY

The Chinese lunar calendar is divided into 12 months of either 29 or 30 days (compensating for the lunar month's mean duration of 29 days, 12 hr, 44.05 min). The calendar is synchronized with the solar year by the addition of extra months at fixed intervals.

The Chinese calendar runs on a 60-year cycle. The cycles 1876-1935 and 1936-95, with the years grouped under their 12 animal designations, are printed below, along with the first 24 years of the current cycle. It began in 1996 and will last until 2055. The year 1997 (Lunar Year 4695) is found in the 2d column, under Ox, and is known as a Year of the Ox. Readers can find the animal name for the year of their birth, marriage, etc., in the same chart. (Note: The first 3-7 weeks of each Western year belong to the previous Chinese year and animal designation.)

Both the Western (Gregorian) and traditional lunar calendars are used publicly in China and in North and South Korea, and 2 New Year's celebrations are held. In Taiwan, in overseas Chinese communities, and in Vietnam, the lunar calendar is used only to set the dates for traditional festivals, with the Gregorian system in general use.

The 4-day Chinese New Year, Hsin Nien, the 3-day Vietnamese New Year festival, Tet, and the 3-to-4-day Korean festival, Suhl, begin at the second new moon after the winter solstice. Because the date is fixed according to the date of the new moon in the Far East, which is west of the International Date Line, the date may be one day later than that of the new moon in the U.S. The day may fall, therefore, between Jan. 21 and Feb. 19 of the Gregorian calendar. Feb. 7 marks the start of the new Chinese year in 1997.

| Rat | Ox | Tiger | Hare (Rabbit) | Dragon | Snake | Horse | Sheep (Goat) | Monkey | Rooster | Dog | Pig |
|---|---|---|---|---|---|---|---|---|---|---|---|
| 1876 | 1877 | 1878 | 1879 | 1880 | 1881 | 1882 | 1883 | 1884 | 1885 | 1886 | 1887 |
| 1888 | 1889 | 1890 | 1891 | 1892 | 1893 | 1894 | 1895 | 1896 | 1897 | 1898 | 1899 |
| 1900 | 1901 | 1902 | 1903 | 1904 | 1905 | 1906 | 1907 | 1908 | 1909 | 1910 | 1911 |
| 1912 | 1913 | 1914 | 1915 | 1916 | 1917 | 1918 | 1919 | 1920 | 1921 | 1922 | 1923 |
| 1924 | 1925 | 1926 | 1927 | 1928 | 1929 | 1930 | 1931 | 1932 | 1933 | 1934 | 1935 |
| 1936 | 1937 | 1938 | 1939 | 1940 | 1941 | 1942 | 1943 | 1944 | 1945 | 1946 | 1947 |
| 1948 | 1949 | 1950 | 1951 | 1952 | 1953 | 1954 | 1955 | 1956 | 1957 | 1958 | 1959 |
| 1960 | 1961 | 1962 | 1963 | 1964 | 1965 | 1966 | 1967 | 1968 | 1969 | 1970 | 1971 |
| 1972 | 1973 | 1974 | 1975 | 1976 | 1977 | 1978 | 1979 | 1980 | 1981 | 1982 | 1983 |
| 1984 | 1985 | 1986 | 1987 | 1988 | 1989 | 1990 | 1991 | 1992 | 1993 | 1994 | 1995 |
| 1996 | 1997 | 1998 | 1999 | 2000 | 2001 | 2002 | 2003 | 2004 | 2005 | 2006 | 2007 |
| 2008 | 2009 | 2010 | 2011 | 2012 | 2013 | 2014 | 2015 | 2016 | 2017 | 2018 | 2019 |

# Standard Time, Daylight Saving Time, and Others

**Source:** Defense Mapping Agency Hydrographic/Topographic Center; U.S. Dept. of Transportation

## Standard Time

Standard Time is reckoned from Greenwich, England, recognized as the Prime Meridian of Longitude. The world is divided into 24 zones, each 15° of arc, or one hour in time apart. The Greenwich meridian (0°) extends through the center of the initial zone, and the zones to the east are numbered from 1 to 12, with the prefix "minus" indicating the number of hours to be subtracted to obtain Greenwich Time. Each zone extends 7.5° on either side of its central meridian.

Westward zones are similarly numbered, but prefixed "plus" showing the number of hours that must be added to get Greenwich Time. Although these zones apply generally to sea areas, the Standard Time maintained in many countries does not coincide with zone time. A graphical representation of the zones is shown on the Standard Time Zone Chart of the World published by the Defense Mapping Agency, Distribution Division, National Ocean Service, Riverdale, MD 20737; telephone: (301) 436-6990.

The U.S. and possessions are divided into 10 Standard Time zones. Each zone is approximately 15° of longitude in width. All places in each zone use, instead of their own local time, the time counted from the transit of the "mean sun" across the Standard Time meridian that passes near the middle of that zone. These time zones are designated as Atlantic, Eastern, Central, Mountain, Pacific, Alaska, Hawaii-Aleutian, Samoa, Wake Island, and Guam, and the time in these zones is basically reckoned from the 60th, 75th, 90th, 105th, 120th, 135th, 150th, and 165th meridians west of Greenwich and the 165th and 150th meridians east of Greenwich. The time zone line wanders to conform to local geographical regions. The time in the various zones in the U.S. and U.S. territories is earlier than Greenwich Time by 4, 5, 6, 7, 8, 9, 10, and 11 hours, respectively. However, Wake Island and Guam cross the International Date Line and are 12 and 10 hours later than Greenwich Time, respectively.

## 24-Hour Time

Twenty-four-hour time is widely used in scientific work throughout the world. In the U.S. it is used also in operations of the armed forces. In Europe it is frequently used by the transportation networks in preference to the 12-hour AM and PM system. With the 24-hour system, the day begins at midnight and is designated 0000 through 2359.

## International Date Line

The Date Line is a zig-zag line that approximately coincides with the 180th meridian, and it separates the calendar dates. The date must be advanced one day when crossing in a westerly direction and set back one day when crossing in an easterly direction. The line is deflected eastward through the Bering Strait and westward of the Aleutians to prevent separating these areas by date. The line is again deflected eastward of the Tonga and New Zealand Islands in the South Pacific for the same reason. The line is established by international custom and not prescribed by any international rule or law. Some Pacific Island nations have supported or opposed further changes in the line that could alter its traditional observance.

## Daylight Saving Time

Daylight Saving Time is achieved by advancing the clock one hour. Since 1987, Daylight Saving Time in the U.S. has begun at 2 AM on the first Sunday in Apr. and ended at 2 AM on the last Sunday in Oct.

Daylight Saving Time was first observed in the U.S. during World War I, and then again during World War II. In the intervening years, some states and communities observed Daylight Saving Time using whatever beginning and ending dates they chose. In 1966, Congress passed the Uniform Time Act, which provided that any state or territory that chooses to observe Daylight Saving Time must begin and end on the federal dates. Any state could, by law, exempt itself; a 1972 amendment to the act authorized states split by time zones to observe Daylight Saving Time in one time zone and standard time in the other time zone. Currently, Arizona, Hawaii, the eastern time zone portion of Indiana, Puerto Rico, the U.S. Virgin Islands, and American Samoa do not observe Daylight Saving Time.

Congress and the secretary of transportation both have authority to change time zone boundaries. Since 1966 there have been a number of changes to U.S. time zone boundaries. Efforts to conserve energy have also prompted various changes to the times that Daylight Saving Time was observed in the past.

## International Usage

Adjusting clock time to be able to use the added daylight on summer evenings is common throughout the world.

Canada, which lies over 6 time zones, observes Daylight Saving Time from the first Sunday of Apr. until the last Sunday of Oct. Saskatchewan remains on standard time throughout the year. Communities elsewhere in Canada also may choose to exempt themselves from Daylight Saving Time.

Beginning in 1996, member nations of the European Union (EU) observed a "summer-time period," the EU's version of Daylight Saving Time, from the last Sunday of March until the last Sunday in Oct.

Russia, which lies over 11 time zones, maintains its Standard Time 1 hour fast for its zone designation. Additionally, it proclaims Daylight Saving Time from the 4th Sunday in March until the 4th Sunday in Sept.

China, which lies across 5 time zones, has decreed that the entire country be placed on Greenwich Time plus 8 hours. Daylight Saving Time is not observed. Japan, which lies in one time zone, and Mexico, which occupies 3 times zones, also do not modify their legal time during the summer months.

Many countries in the Southern Hemisphere maintain Daylight Saving Time, generally from Oct. to Mar.; however, most countries near the equator do not deviate from Standard Time.

For more information, see "International Time Zones" in the map section.

# Standard Time Differences—World Cities

The time indicated in the table is fixed by law and is called the legal time or, more generally, Standard Time. Use of Daylight Saving Time varies widely. * Indicates morning of the following day. At 12:00 noon, Eastern Standard Time, the Standard Time (in 24-hour time) in selected cities is as follows:

| | | | | | | | |
|---|---|---|---|---|---|---|---|
| Addis Ababa | 20 00 | Cape Town | 19 00 | Lima | 12 00 | Santiago (Chile) | 13 00 |
| Alexandria | 19 00 | Caracas | 13 00 | Lisbon | 17 00 | Seoul | 2 00* |
| Amsterdam | 18 00 | Casablanca | 17 00 | Liverpool | 17 00 | Shanghai | 1 00* |
| Athens | 19 00 | Copenhagen | 18 00 | London | 17 00 | Singapore | 1 00* |
| Auckland | 5 00* | Delhi | 22 30 | Madrid | 18 00 | Stockholm | 18 00 |
| Baghdad | 20 00 | Dhaka | 23 00 | Manila | 1 00* | Sydney (Australia) | 3 00* |
| Bangkok | 0 00* | Dublin | 17 00 | Mecca (Saudi Arabia) | 20 00 | Tashkent | 23 00 |
| Beijing | 1 00* | Gdánsk | 18 00 | Melbourne | 3 00* | Tehran | 20 30 |
| Belfast | 17 00 | Geneva | 18 00 | Mexico City | 11 00 | Tel Aviv | 19 00 |
| Berlin | 18 00 | Havana | 12 00 | Montevideo | 14 00 | Tokyo | 2 00* |
| Bogotá | 12 00 | Helsinki | 19 00 | Moscow | 20 00 | Valparaíso | 13 00 |
| Bombay | 22 30 | Ho Chi Minh City | 0 00* | Nagasaki | 2 00* | Vladivostok | 3 00* |
| Bremen | 18 00 | Hong Kong | 1 00* | Oslo | 18 00 | Vienna | 18 00 |
| Brussels | 18 00 | Istanbul | 19 00 | Paris | 18 00 | Warsaw | 18 00 |
| Bucharest | 19 00 | Jakarta | 0 00* | Prague | 18 00 | Wellington (NZ) | 5 00* |
| Budapest | 18 00 | Jerusalem | 19 00 | Rio de Janeiro | 14 00 | Yangon (Rangoon) | 23 30 |
| Buenos Aires | 14 00 | Johannesburg | 19 00 | Rome | 18 00 | Yokohama | 2 00* |
| Cairo | 19 00 | Karachi | 22 00 | St. Petersburg | 20 00 | Zürich | 18 00 |
| Calcutta | 22 30 | Le Havre | 18 00 | | | | |

## Standard Time Differences — North American Cities

At 12:00 noon, Eastern Standard Time, the Standard Time in North American cities is as follows:

| City | Hour | Min. | |
|---|---|---|---|
| Akron, OH | 12 | 00 | Noon |
| Albuquerque, NM | 10 | 00 | AM |
| Atlanta, GA | 12 | 00 | Noon |
| Austin, TX | 11 | 00 | AM |
| Baltimore, MD | 12 | 00 | Noon |
| Birmingham, AL | 11 | 00 | AM |
| Bismarck, ND | 11 | 00 | AM |
| Boise, ID | 10 | 00 | AM |
| Boston, MA | 12 | 00 | Noon |
| Buffalo, NY | 12 | 00 | Noon |
| Butte, MT | 10 | 00 | AM |
| Calgary, Alta. | 10 | 00 | AM |
| Charleston, SC | 12 | 00 | Noon |
| Charleston, WV | 12 | 00 | Noon |
| Charlotte, NC | 12 | 00 | Noon |
| Charlottetown, PEI | 1 | 00 | PM |
| Chattanooga, TN | 12 | 00 | Noon |
| Cheyenne, WY | 10 | 00 | AM |
| Chicago, IL | 11 | 00 | AM |
| Cleveland, OH | 12 | 00 | Noon |
| Colorado Spr., CO | 10 | 00 | AM |
| Columbus, OH | 12 | 00 | Noon |
| Dallas, TX | 11 | 00 | AM |
| *Dawson, Yuk. | 9 | 00 | AM |
| Dayton, OH | 12 | 00 | Noon |
| Denver, CO | 10 | 00 | AM |
| Des Moines, IA | 11 | 00 | AM |
| Detroit, MI | 12 | 00 | Noon |
| Duluth, MN | 11 | 00 | AM |
| El Paso, TX | 10 | 00 | AM |
| Erie, PA | 12 | 00 | Noon |
| Evansville, IN | 11 | 00 | AM |
| Fairbanks, AK | 8 | 00 | AM |
| Flint, MI | 12 | 00 | Noon |
| *Fort Wayne, IN | 12 | 00 | Noon |
| Fort Worth, TX | 11 | 00 | AM |
| Frankfort, KY | 12 | 00 | Noon |
| Galveston, TX | 11 | 00 | AM |
| Grand Rapids, MI | 12 | 00 | Noon |
| Halifax, NS | 1 | 00 | PM |
| Hartford, CT | 12 | 00 | Noon |
| Helena, MT | 10 | 00 | AM |
| *Honolulu, HI | 7 | 00 | AM |
| Houston, TX | 11 | 00 | AM |
| *Indianapolis, IN | 12 | 00 | Noon |
| Jacksonville, FL | 12 | 00 | Noon |
| Juneau, AK | 8 | 00 | AM |
| Kansas City, MO | 11 | 00 | AM |
| Knoxville, TN | 12 | 00 | Noon |
| Lexington, KY | 12 | 00 | Noon |
| Lincoln, NE | 11 | 00 | AM |
| Little Rock, AR | 11 | 00 | AM |
| Los Angeles, CA | 9 | 00 | AM |
| Louisville, KY | 12 | 00 | Noon |
| *Mexico City | 11 | 00 | AM |
| Memphis, TN | 11 | 00 | AM |
| Miami, FL | 12 | 00 | Noon |
| Milwaukee, WI | 11 | 00 | AM |
| Minneapolis, MN | 11 | 00 | AM |
| Mobile, AL | 11 | 00 | AM |
| Montreal, Que | 12 | 00 | Noon |
| Nashville, TN | 11 | 00 | AM |
| New Haven, CT | 12 | 00 | Noon |
| New Orleans, LA | 11 | 00 | AM |
| New York, NY | 12 | 00 | Noon |
| Nome, AK | 8 | 00 | AM |
| Norfolk, VA | 12 | 00 | Noon |
| Oklahoma City, OK | 11 | 00 | AM |
| Omaha, NE | 11 | 00 | AM |
| Peoria, IL | 11 | 00 | AM |
| Philadelphia, PA | 12 | 00 | Noon |
| *Phoenix, AZ | 10 | 00 | AM |
| Pierre, SD | 11 | 00 | AM |
| Pittsburgh, PA | 12 | 00 | Noon |
| Portland, ME | 12 | 00 | Noon |
| Portland, OR | 9 | 00 | AM |
| Providence, RI | 12 | 00 | Noon |
| *Regina, Sask. | 11 | 00 | AM |
| Reno, NV | 9 | 00 | AM |
| Richmond, VA | 12 | 00 | Noon |
| Rochester, NY | 12 | 00 | Noon |
| Sacramento, CA | 9 | 00 | AM |
| St. John's, Nfld. | 1 | 30 | PM |
| St. Louis, MO | 11 | 00 | AM |
| St. Paul, MN | 11 | 00 | AM |
| Salt Lake City, UT | 10 | 00 | AM |
| San Antonio, TX | 11 | 00 | AM |
| San Diego, CA | 9 | 00 | AM |
| San Francisco, CA | 9 | 00 | AM |
| Santa Fe, NM | 10 | 00 | AM |
| Savannah, GA | 12 | 00 | Noon |
| Seattle, WA | 9 | 00 | AM |
| Shreveport, LA | 11 | 00 | AM |
| Sioux Falls, SD | 11 | 00 | AM |
| Spokane, WA | 9 | 00 | AM |
| Tampa, FL | 12 | 00 | Noon |
| Toledo, OH | 12 | 00 | Noon |
| Topeka, KS | 11 | 00 | AM |
| Toronto, Ont. | 12 | 00 | Noon |
| *Tucson, AZ | 10 | 00 | AM |
| Tulsa, OK | 11 | 00 | AM |
| Vancouver, BC | 9 | 00 | AM |
| Washington, DC | 12 | 00 | Noon |
| Wichita, KS | 11 | 00 | AM |
| Wilmington, DE | 12 | 00 | Noon |
| Winnipeg, Man. | 11 | 00 | AM |

**Note:** This same table can be used for Daylight Saving Time when it is in effect, but allowance must be made for cities that do not observe it; they are marked with an asterisk. Daylight Saving Time is one hour later than Standard Time.

## U.S. Legal or Public Holidays, 1997

Technically, the U.S. observes no national holidays; each state has jurisdiction over its holidays, which are designated by legislative enactment or executive proclamation. In practice, however, most states observe the federal legal public holidays, even though the president and the U.S. Congress can legally designate holidays only for the District of Columbia and for federal employees. Federal legal public holidays are New Year's Day, Martin Luther King Jr. Day, Presidents' Day, Memorial Day, Independence Day, Labor Day, Columbus Day, Veterans Day, Thanksgiving, and Christmas.

### Chief Legal or Public Holidays

When a holiday falls on a Sunday or a Saturday, it is usually observed on the following Monday or the preceding Friday. For some holidays, government and business closing practices vary. In most states, the office of the secretary of state can provide details for holiday closings. The following will be legal or public holidays in most states in 1997:

**Jan. 1 (Wed.)** — New Year's Day

**Jan. 20 (3d Mon. in Jan.)** — Martin Luther King Jr. Day

**Feb. 12 (Wed.)** — Lincoln's Birthday

**Feb. 17 (3d Mon. in Feb.)** — Washington's Birthday, or Presidents' Day, or Washington-Lincoln Day

**May 26 (last Mon. in May)** — Memorial Day, or Decoration Day

**July 4 (Fri.)** — Independence Day

**Sept. 1 (1st Mon. in Sept.)** — Labor Day

**Nov. 11 (Tues.)** — Veterans Day

**Nov. 27 (4th Thurs. in Nov.)** — Thanksgiving

**Dec. 25 (Thur.)** — Christmas Day

In some states, the following will be legal or public holidays in 1997:

**Mar. 28 (Fri.)** — Good Friday. (In some states, observed for half or part of day.)

**Oct. 13 (2d Mon. in Oct.)** — Columbus Day, or Discoverers' Day, or Pioneers' Day

**Nov. 4 (1st Tues. after 1st Mon. in Nov.)** — Election Day

## Selected International Holidays, 1997

**Jan. 27** — Australia Day obsvd., Australia
**Feb. 5** — Constitution Day, Mexico
**Feb. 8-11** — Carnival, Brazil
**Mar. 10** — Commonwealth Day, Canada, Great Britain
**Mar. 17** — St. Patrick's Day, Ireland
**Mar. 21** — Benito Juarez's Birthday, Mexico
**Apr. 8** — Buddha's Birthday, Korea, Japan
**Apr. 23** — Children's Day, Turkey
**May 5** — Cinco de Mayo (Battle of Puebla Day), Mexico
**May 17** — Constitution Day, Norway
**May 19** — Victoria Day, Canada
**June 9** — Dragon Boat Festival, China
**June 23** — Midsummer Eve, Baltics, Scandinavia
**July 1** — Canada Day, Canada
**July 14** — Bastille Day, France
**Aug. 30** — St. Rose of Lima, Peru
**Sept. 1** — Labor Day, Canada
**Sept. 16** — Independence Day, Mexico
**Sept. 19** — St. Gennaro, Italy
**Oct. 12** — Dia de la Raza, Mexico
**Oct. 13** — Thanksgiving Day, Canada
**Nov. 1-2** — Day of the Dead, Mexico
**Nov. 5** — Guy Fawkes Day, Great Britain
**Nov. 11** — Remembrance Day, Canada
**Dec. 12** — Jamhuri Day, Kenya; Guadalupe Day, Mexico
**Dec. 26** — Boxing Day, Australia, Canada, Great Britain, New Zealand

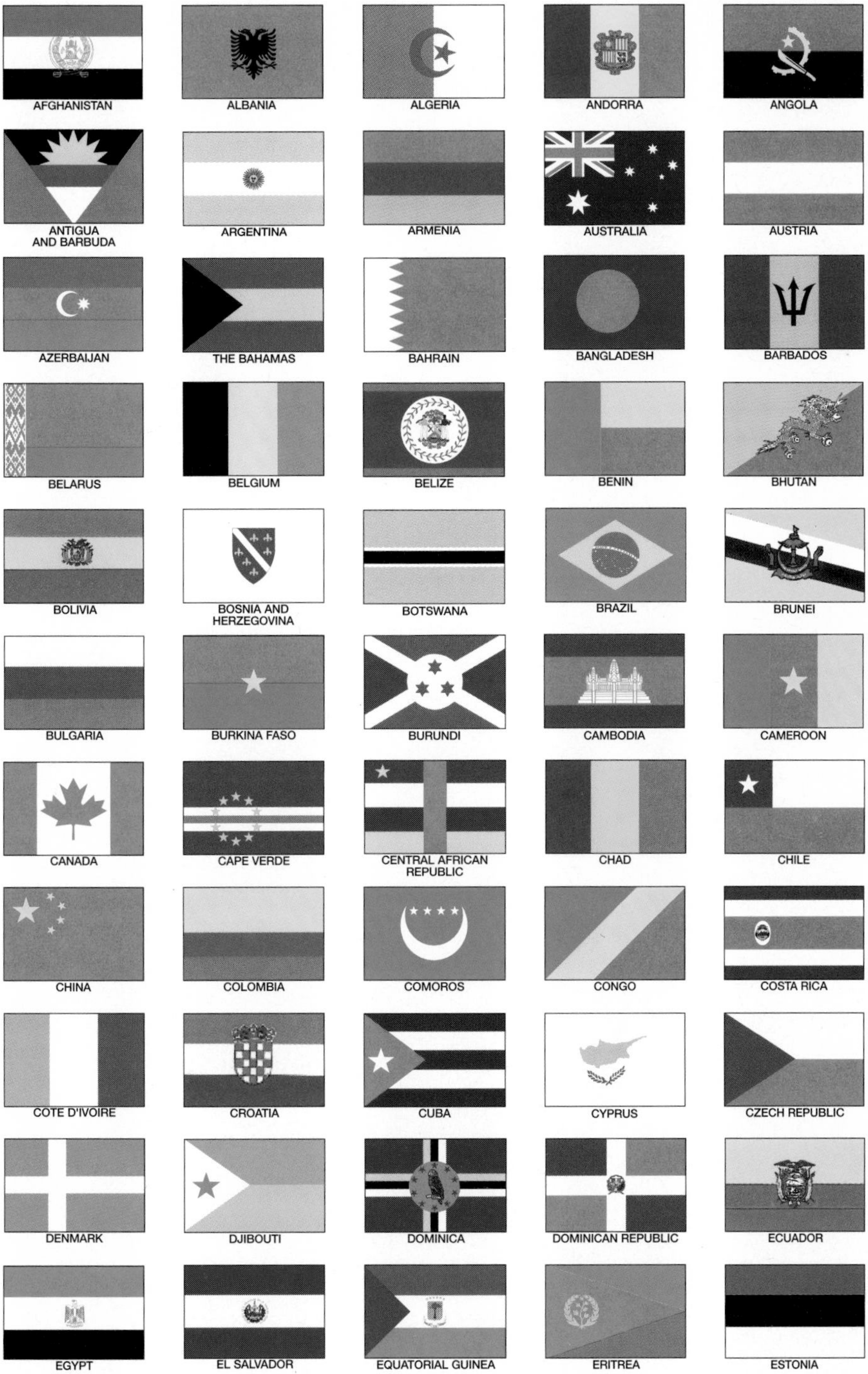
AFGHANISTAN
ALBANIA
ALGERIA
ANDORRA
ANGOLA
ANTIGUA AND BARBUDA
ARGENTINA
ARMENIA
AUSTRALIA
AUSTRIA
AZERBAIJAN
THE BAHAMAS
BAHRAIN
BANGLADESH
BARBADOS
BELARUS
BELGIUM
BELIZE
BENIN
BHUTAN
BOLIVIA
BOSNIA AND HERZEGOVINA
BOTSWANA
BRAZIL
BRUNEI
BULGARIA
BURKINA FASO
BURUNDI
CAMBODIA
CAMEROON
CANADA
CAPE VERDE
CENTRAL AFRICAN REPUBLIC
CHAD
CHILE
CHINA
COLOMBIA
COMOROS
CONGO
COSTA RICA
COTE D'IVOIRE
CROATIA
CUBA
CYPRUS
CZECH REPUBLIC
DENMARK
DJIBOUTI
DOMINICA
DOMINICAN REPUBLIC
ECUADOR
EGYPT
EL SALVADOR
EQUATORIAL GUINEA
ERITREA
ESTONIA

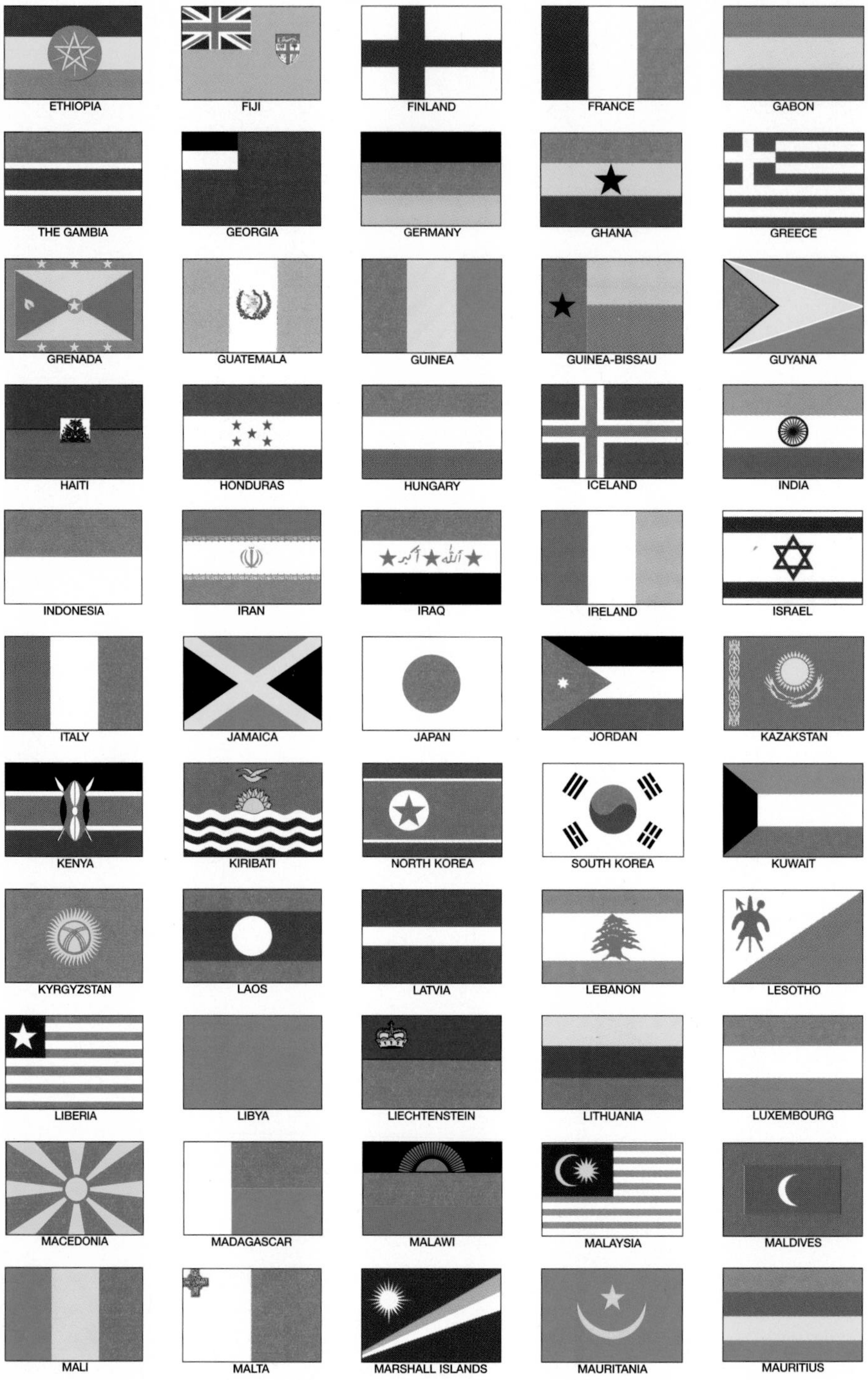
ETHIOPIA
FIJI
FINLAND
FRANCE
GABON
THE GAMBIA
GEORGIA
GERMANY
GHANA
GREECE
GRENADA
GUATEMALA
GUINEA
GUINEA-BISSAU
GUYANA
HAITI
HONDURAS
HUNGARY
ICELAND
INDIA
INDONESIA
IRAN
IRAQ
IRELAND
ISRAEL
ITALY
JAMAICA
JAPAN
JORDAN
KAZAKSTAN
KENYA
KIRIBATI
NORTH KOREA
SOUTH KOREA
KUWAIT
KYRGYZSTAN
LAOS
LATVIA
LEBANON
LESOTHO
LIBERIA
LIBYA
LIECHTENSTEIN
LITHUANIA
LUXEMBOURG
MACEDONIA
MADAGASCAR
MALAWI
MALAYSIA
MALDIVES
MALI
MALTA
MARSHALL ISLANDS
MAURITANIA
MAURITIUS

MEXICO
MICRONESIA, FEDERATED STATES OF
MOLDOVA
MONACO
MONGOLIA
MOROCCO
MOZAMBIQUE
MYANMAR (BURMA)
NAMIBIA
NAURU
NEPAL
NETHERLANDS
NEW ZEALAND
NICARAGUA
NIGER
NIGERIA
NORWAY
OMAN
PAKISTAN
PALAU
PANAMA
PAPUA NEW GUINEA
PARAGUAY
PERU
PHILIPPINES
POLAND
PORTUGAL
QATAR
ROMANIA
RUSSIA
RWANDA
ST. KITTS AND NEVIS
ST. LUCIA
ST. VINCENT AND THE GRENADINES
SAN MARINO
SAO TOME AND PRINCIPE
SAUDI ARABIA
SENEGAL
SEYCHELLES
SIERRA LEONE
SINGAPORE
SLOVAKIA
SLOVENIA
SOLOMON ISLANDS
SOMALIA
SOUTH AFRICA
SPAIN
SRI LANKA
SUDAN
SURINAME
SWAZILAND
SWEDEN
SWITZERLAND
SYRIA
TAIWAN

TAJIKISTAN

TANZANIA

THAILAND

TOGO

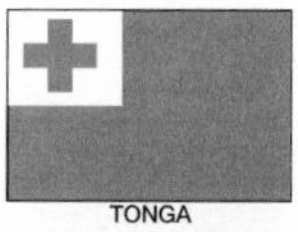
TONGA

TRINIDAD AND TOBAGO

TUNISIA

TURKEY

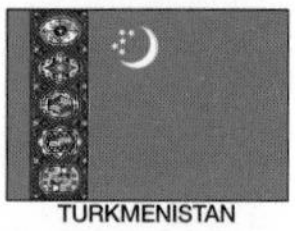
TURKMENISTAN

TUVALU

UGANDA

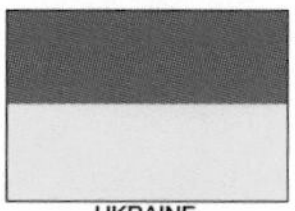
UKRAINE

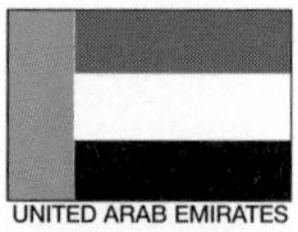
UNITED ARAB EMIRATES

UNITED KINGDOM

UNITED STATES

URUGUAY

UZBEKISTAN

VANUATU

VATICAN CITY

VENEZUELA

VIETNAM

WESTERN SAMOA

YEMEN

YUGOSLAVIA

ZAIRE

ZAMBIA

ZIMBABWE

## INTERNATIONAL TIME ZONES

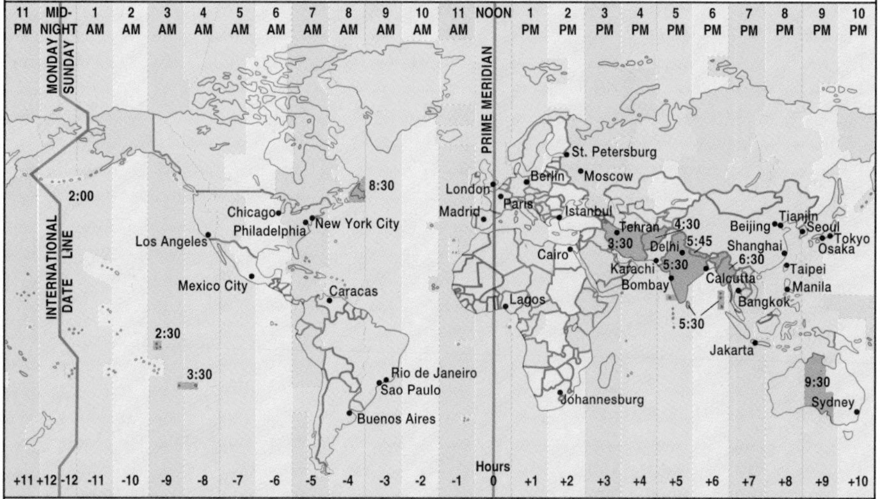


The world is divided into 24 time zones, each 15° longitude wide. The longitudinal meridian passing through Greenwich, England, is the starting point, and is called the *prime meridian.* The 12th zone is divided by the 180th meridian (International Date Line). When the line is crossed going west, the date is advanced one day; when crossed going east, the date becomes a day earlier.

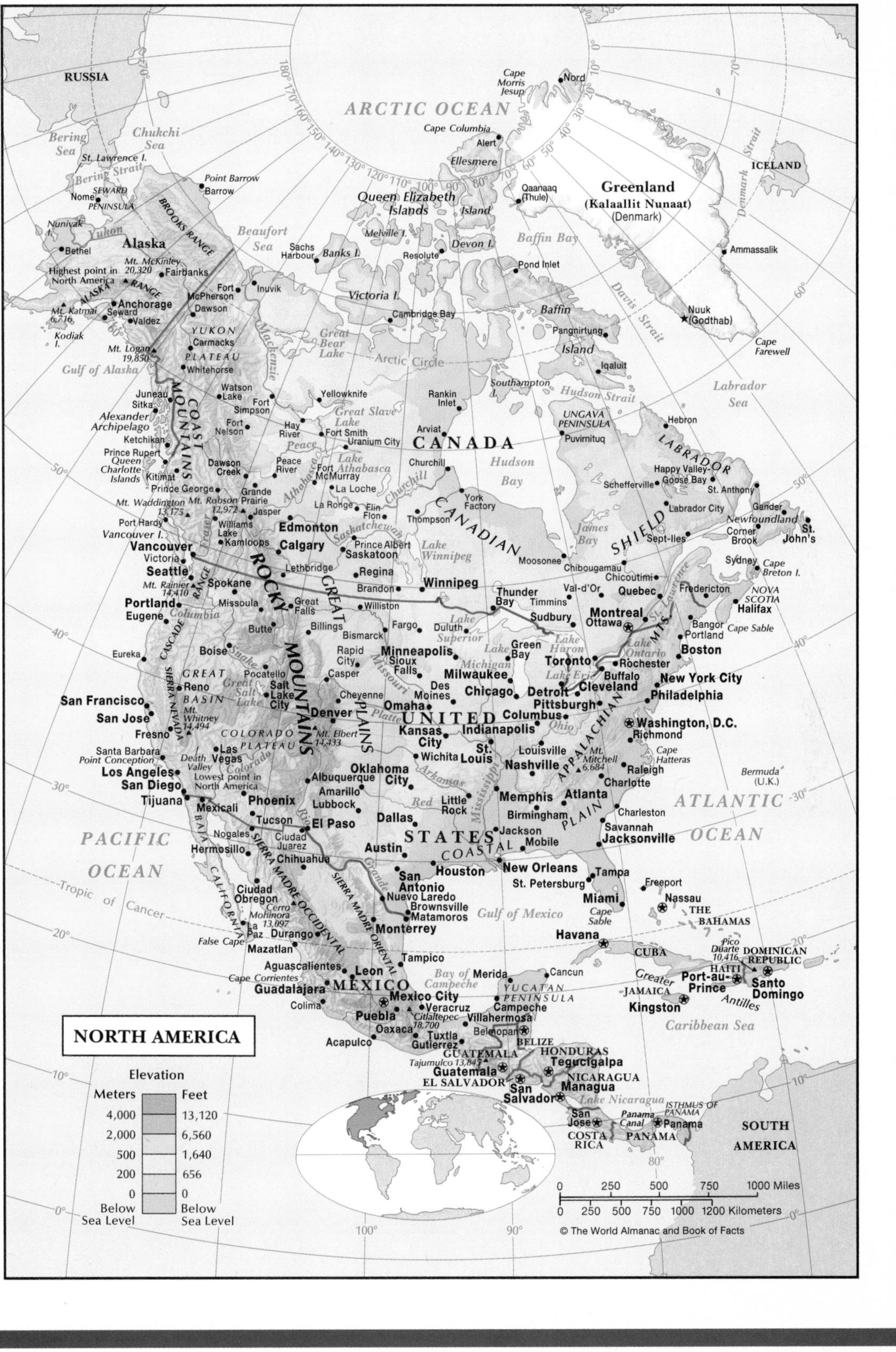

NORTH AMERICA
RUSSIA
ARCTIC OCEAN
Cape Morris Jesup
Nord
Cape Columbia
Alert
Ellesmere
Island
Bering Sea
Chukchi Sea
St. Lawrence I.
Bering Strait
Point Barrow
Barrow
SEWARD PENINSULA
Nome
BROOKS RANGE
Beaufort Sea
Queen Elizabeth Islands
Qaanaaq (Thule)
Greenland
(Kalaallit Nunaat)
(Denmark)
ICELAND
Denmark Strait
Nunivak I.
Yukon
Alaska
Bethel
Mt. McKinley 20,320
Highest point in North America
Fairbanks
ALASKA RANGE
Sachs Harbour
Banks I.
Melville I.
Resolute
Devon I.
Baffin Bay
Pond Inlet
Ammassalik
Inuvik
Fort McPherson
Dawson
Anchorage
Seward
Valdez
Mt. Katmai 6,716
Kodiak I.
Victoria I.
Cambridge Bay
Baffin
Island
Davis Strait
Nuuk (Godthab)
Pangnirtung
YUKON PLATEAU
Carmacks
Whitehorse
Mt. Logan 19,850
Gulf of Alaska
Mackenzie
Great Bear Lake
Arctic Circle
Iqaluit
Cape Farewell
Juneau
Sitka
Alexander Archipelago
COAST MOUNTAINS
Watson Lake
Fort Simpson
Fort Nelson
Yellowknife
Great Slave Lake
Hay River
Fort Smith
Uranium City
Rankin Inlet
Southampton I.
Hudson Strait
Labrador Sea
UNGAVA PENINSULA
Puvirnituq
Hebron
Arviat
CANADA
Ketchikan
Prince Rupert
Queen Charlotte Islands
Kitimat
Dawson Creek
Peace River
Peace
Fort McMurray
Lake Athabasca
Athabasca
Churchill
Hudson Bay
LABRADOR
Happy Valley-Goose Bay
Schefferville
St. Anthony
Prince George
Grande Prairie
La Loche
Mt. Waddington 13,175
Mt. Robson 12,972
Jasper
La Ronge
Flin Flon
York Factory
Thompson
CANADIAN SHIELD
Labrador City
Gander
Newfoundland
St. John's
Port Hardy
Vancouver I.
Williams Lake
Kamloops
Fraser
Edmonton
Calgary
Saskatchewan
Prince Albert
Saskatoon
Lake Winnipeg
James Bay
Corner Brook
Sept-Iles
Vancouver
Victoria
Seattle
Mt. Rainier 14,410
CASCADE RANGE
Spokane
ROCKY MOUNTAINS
Lethbridge
Regina
Moosonee
Chibougamau
Chicoutimi
Sydney
Cape Breton I.
Brandon
Winnipeg
Thunder Bay
Timmins
Val-d'Or
Quebec
Fredericton
NOVA SCOTIA
Halifax
Portland
Eugene
Columbia
Missoula
Great Falls
GREAT PLAINS
Williston
Lake Superior
Sudbury
Montreal
Ottawa
St. Lawrence
Bangor
Portland
Cape Sable
Butte
Billings
Bismarck
Fargo
Duluth
Lake Huron
Green Bay
MTS.
Boston
Eureka
Boise
Snake
Rapid City
Minneapolis
Sioux Falls
Lake Michigan
Toronto
Lake Ontario
Rochester
Pocatello
Casper
Missouri
Milwaukee
Buffalo
Lake Erie
New York City
GREAT BASIN
Reno
Great Salt Lake
Salt Lake City
Cheyenne
Des Moines
Chicago
Detroit
Cleveland
Philadelphia
San Francisco
San Jose
SIERRA NEVADA
Mt. Whitney 14,494
Denver
Platte
Omaha
UNITED STATES
Columbus
Pittsburgh
Ohio
Washington, D.C.
Richmond
Fresno
COLORADO PLATEAU
Mt. Elbert 14,433
Kansas City
Indianapolis
St. Louis
Louisville
Santa Barbara
Point Conception
Las Vegas
Death Valley
Lowest point in North America
Colorado
Wichita
Nashville
APPALACHIAN
Mt. Mitchell 6,684
Cape Hatteras
Raleigh
Bermuda (U.K.)
Los Angeles
San Diego
Tijuana
Oklahoma City
Albuquerque
Amarillo
Arkansas
Charlotte
Mexicali
Phoenix
Lubbock
Red
Little Rock
Memphis
Mississippi
Atlanta
Birmingham
ATLANTIC OCEAN
BAJA CALIFORNIA
Tucson
El Paso
Dallas
Jackson
PLAIN
Charleston
Savannah
Jacksonville
PACIFIC OCEAN
Nogales
Ciudad Juarez
Rio Grande
Austin
COASTAL
Mobile
Hermosillo
Chihuahua
SIERRA MADRE OCCIDENTAL
San Antonio
Houston
New Orleans
Tampa
St. Petersburg
Freeport
Tropic of Cancer
Ciudad Obregon
SIERRA MADRE ORIENTAL
Nuevo Laredo
Brownsville
Matamoros
Gulf of Mexico
Miami
Nassau
THE BAHAMAS
Cerro Mohinora 13,097
La Paz
Durango
Monterrey
Cape Sable
Havana
False Cape
Mazatlan
Tampico
CUBA
Pico Duarte 10,416
HAITI
DOMINICAN REPUBLIC
Aguascalientes
Leon
Cape Corrientes
Guadalajara
MEXICO
Bay of Campeche
Merida
Cancun
YUCATAN PENINSULA
Greater Antilles
JAMAICA
Port-au-Prince
Santo Domingo
Kingston
Mexico City
Colima
Veracruz
Campeche
Puebla
Citlaltepec 18,700
Villahermosa
Oaxaca
Belmopan
BELIZE
Caribbean Sea
Acapulco
Tuxtla Gutierrez
GUATEMALA
HONDURAS
Tajumulco 13,845
Guatemala
Tegucigalpa
NICARAGUA
EL SALVADOR
San Salvador
Managua
Lake Nicaragua
ISTHMUS OF PANAMA
San Jose
COSTA RICA
Panama Canal
Panama
PANAMA
SOUTH AMERICA
Elevation
Meters
Feet
4,000
13,120
2,000
6,560
500
1,640
200
656
0
0
Below Sea Level
Below Sea Level
0
250
500
750
1000 Miles
0
250
500
750
1000
1200 Kilometers
© The World Almanac and Book of Facts

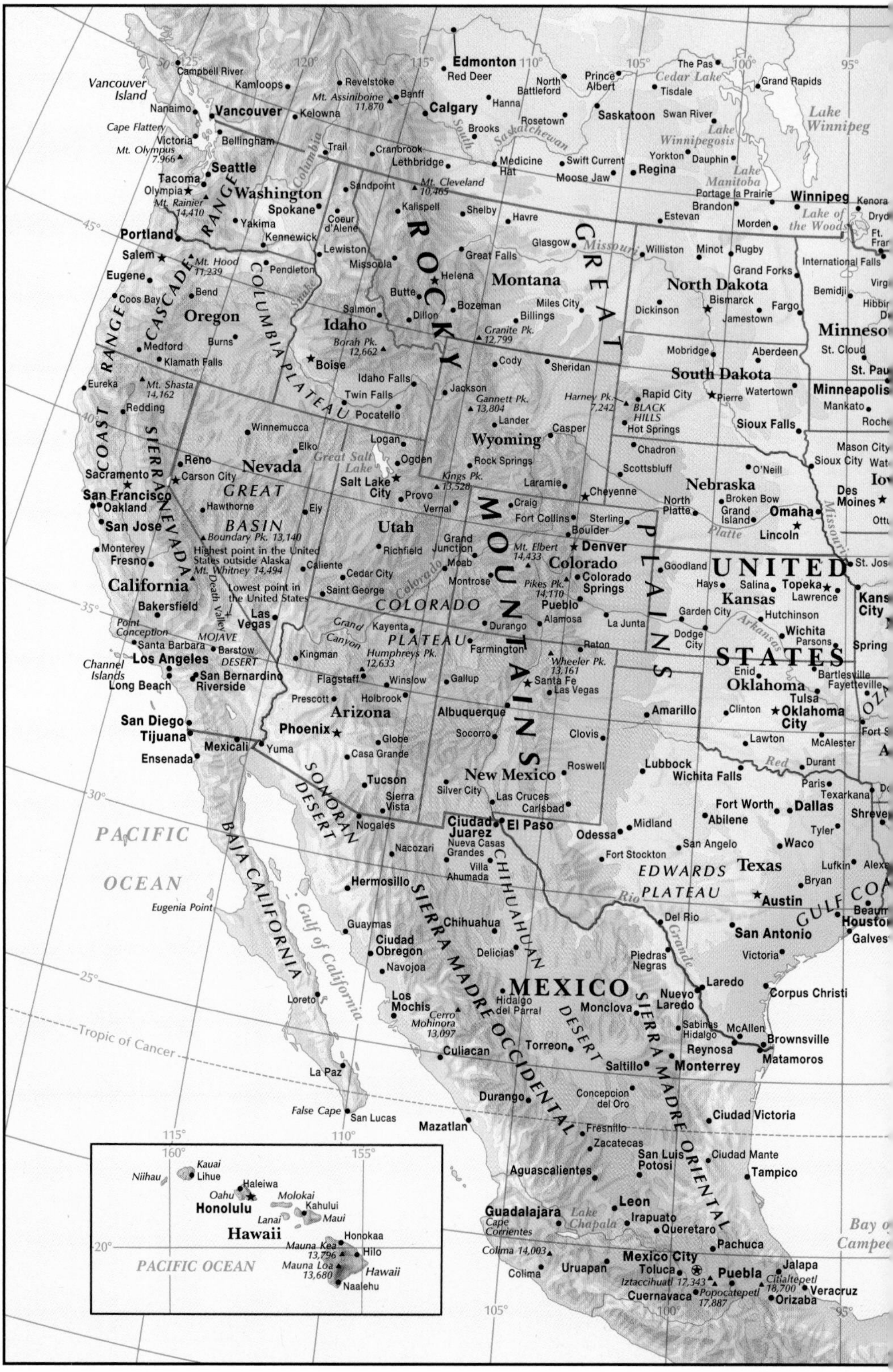

Edmonton
Red Deer
Campbell River
Kamloops
Revelstoke
Mt. Assiniboine 11,870
Banff
Calgary
Vancouver Island
Nanaimo
Vancouver
Kelowna
Cape Flattery
Victoria
Bellingham
Mt. Olympus 7,966
Trail
Cranbrook
Lethbridge
Seattle
Tacoma
Olympia
Mt. Rainier 14,410
Washington
Spokane
Yakima
Coeur d'Alene
Kennewick
Portland
Salem
Mt. Hood 11,239
Eugene
Coos Bay
Bend
Pendleton
Oregon
Medford
Klamath Falls
Burns
CASCADE RANGE
COAST RANGE
COLUMBIA PLATEAU
Lewiston
Missoula
Sandpoint
Kalispell
Mt. Cleveland 10,465
Shelby
Havre
Great Falls
Helena
Butte
Bozeman
Salmon
Dillon
Idaho
Borah Pk. 12,662
Boise
Idaho Falls
Twin Falls
Pocatello
Montana
Miles City
Billings
Granite Pk. 12,799
Cody
Sheridan
Jackson
Gannett Pk. 13,804
Lander
Casper
Wyoming
Rock Springs
Laramie
Cheyenne
ROCKY MOUNTAINS
GREAT PLAINS
Hanna
Brooks
Medicine Hat
North Battleford
Prince Albert
Saskatoon
Rosetown
Swift Current
Moose Jaw
Regina
Yorkton
The Pas
Cedar Lake
Tisdale
Swan River
Lake Winnipegosis
Dauphin
Lake Manitoba
Portage la Prairie
Brandon
Estevan
Grand Rapids
Lake Winnipeg
Winnipeg
Kenora
Lake of the Woods
Morden
Glasgow
Missouri
Williston
Minot
Rugby
Grand Forks
International Falls
North Dakota
Bismarck
Fargo
Dickinson
Jamestown
Bemidji
Minnesota
Mobridge
Aberdeen
St. Cloud
South Dakota
St. Paul
Minneapolis
Rapid City
Pierre
Watertown
Mankato
Harney Pk. 7,242
BLACK HILLS
Hot Springs
Sioux Falls
Chadron
Scottsbluff
O'Neill
Mason City
Sioux City
Nebraska
Broken Bow
Des Moines
North Platte
Grand Island
Omaha
Lincoln
Sterling
Boulder
Denver
Colorado
Colorado Springs
Pikes Pk. 14,110
Pueblo
Mt. Elbert 14,433
Grand Junction
Moab
Montrose
Alamosa
La Junta
Goodland
Hays
Salina
Topeka
Lawrence
Kansas
Kansas City
St. Joseph
UNITED STATES
Garden City
Hutchinson
Wichita
Parsons
Dodge City
Arkansas
Springfield
Enid
Bartlesville
Fayetteville
Oklahoma
Tulsa
Oklahoma City
Clinton
Lawton
McAlester
Red
Durant
Paris
Texarkana
Amarillo
Lubbock
Wichita Falls
Fort Worth
Dallas
Abilene
Shreveport
Tyler
Waco
Midland
Odessa
San Angelo
Texas
Lufkin
Bryan
Austin
Fort Stockton
EDWARDS PLATEAU
Rio Grande
Del Rio
San Antonio
Houston
Galveston
GULF COAST
Victoria
Laredo
Corpus Christi
McAllen
Brownsville
Matamoros
Piedras Negras
Nuevo Laredo
Sabinas Hidalgo
Monclova
Reynosa
Monterrey
Saltillo
Torreon
MEXICO
SIERRA MADRE ORIENTAL
Winnemucca
Elko
Great Salt Lake
Logan
Ogden
Salt Lake City
Provo
Kings Pk. 13,528
Vernal
Craig
Fort Collins
Utah
Richfield
Nevada
GREAT BASIN
Reno
Carson City
Hawthorne
Ely
Boundary Pk. 13,140
Highest point in the United States outside Alaska
Mt. Whitney 14,494
Lowest point in the United States
Death Valley
Caliente
Cedar City
Saint George
Las Vegas
COLORADO PLATEAU
Grand Canyon
Kayenta
Durango
Farmington
Raton
Wheeler Pk. 13,161
Santa Fe
Las Vegas
Humphreys Pk. 12,633
Kingman
Flagstaff
Winslow
Gallup
Prescott
Holbrook
Arizona
Phoenix
Albuquerque
Socorro
Clovis
Globe
Casa Grande
Roswell
Tucson
Sierra Vista
New Mexico
Silver City
Las Cruces
Carlsbad
Nogales
Ciudad Juarez
El Paso
Eureka
Mt. Shasta 14,162
Redding
SIERRA NEVADA
Sacramento
San Francisco
Oakland
San Jose
Monterey
Fresno
California
Bakersfield
Point Conception
Santa Barbara
MOJAVE DESERT
Barstow
Channel Islands
Los Angeles
Long Beach
San Bernardino
Riverside
San Diego
Tijuana
Ensenada
Mexicali
Yuma
SONORAN DESERT
PACIFIC OCEAN
Eugenia Point
BAJA CALIFORNIA
Gulf of California
Nacozari
Nueva Casas Grandes
Villa Ahumada
CHIHUAHUAN DESERT
Hermosillo
SIERRA MADRE OCCIDENTAL
Guaymas
Chihuahua
Ciudad Obregon
Navojoa
Delicias
Hidalgo del Parral
Los Mochis
Cerro Mohinora 13,097
Loreto
Tropic of Cancer
Culiacan
La Paz
Durango
Concepcion del Oro
False Cape
San Lucas
Mazatlan
Fresnillo
Zacatecas
Ciudad Victoria
San Luis Potosi
Ciudad Mante
Aguascalientes
Tampico
Leon
Guadalajara
Lake Chapala
Irapuato
Queretaro
Cape Corrientes
Pachuca
Colima 14,003
Mexico City
Toluca
Puebla
Jalapa
Uruapan
Iztaccihuatl 17,343
Citlaltepetl 18,700
Colima
Cuernavaca
Popocatepetl 17,887
Orizaba
Veracruz
Bay of Campeche
Kauai
Niihau
Lihue
Haleiwa
Oahu
Molokai
Honolulu
Kahului
Lanai
Maui
Hawaii
Honokaa
Mauna Kea 13,796
Hilo
Mauna Loa 13,680
Hawaii
Naalehu
PACIFIC OCEAN

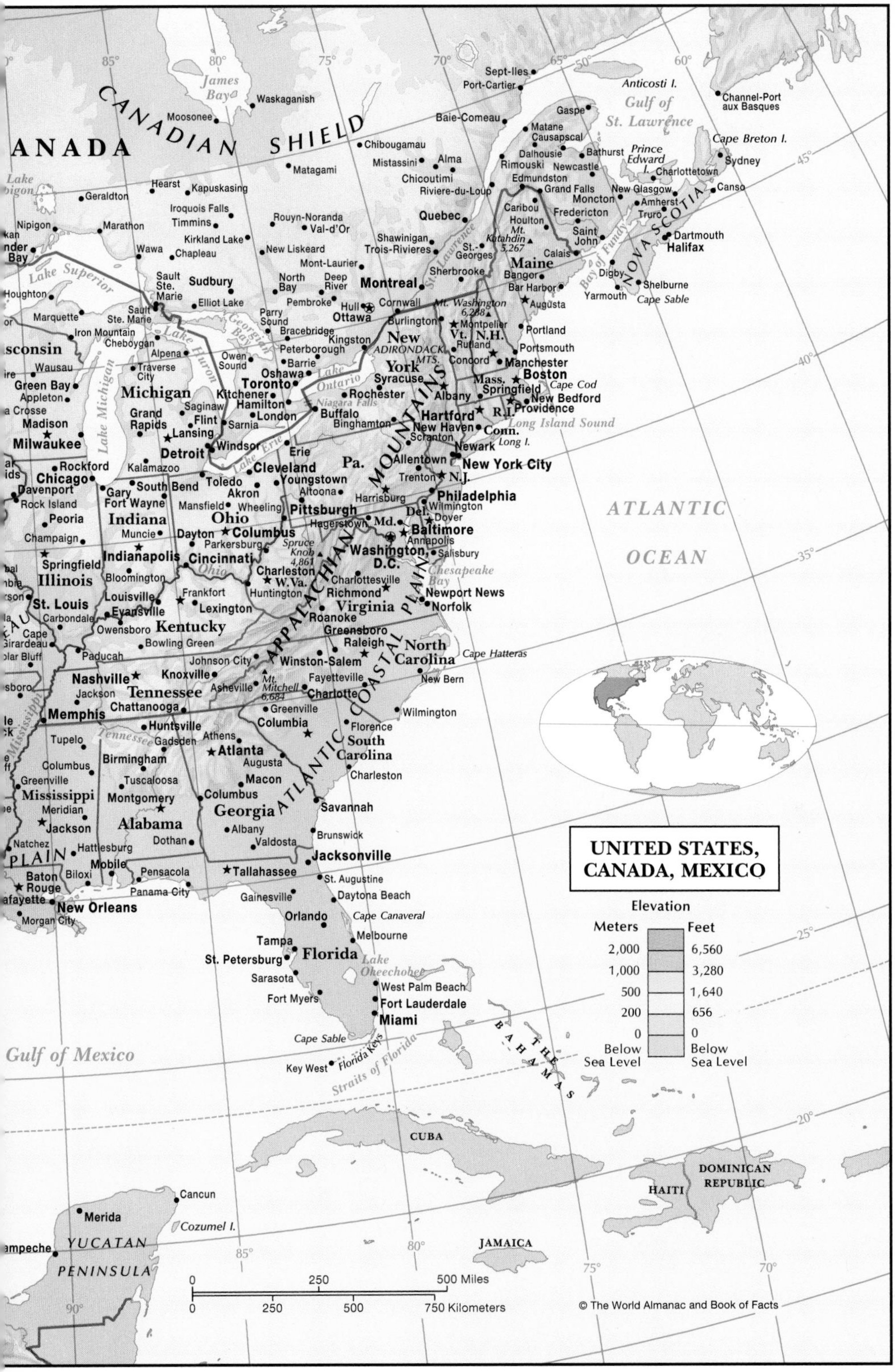

UNITED STATES, CANADA, MEXICO
Elevation
Meters
Feet
2,000
6,560
1,000
3,280
500
1,640
200
656
0
0
Below Sea Level
Below Sea Level
CANADIAN SHIELD
ANADA
ATLANTIC OCEAN
APPALACHIAN MOUNTAINS
ATLANTIC COASTAL PLAIN
NOVA SCOTIA
Gulf of St. Lawrence
Gulf of Mexico
James Bay
Lake Superior
Lake Michigan
Lake Huron
Georgian Bay
Lake Ontario
Lake Erie
Niagara Falls
Long Island Sound
Chesapeake Bay
Bay of Fundy
Anticosti I.
Prince Edward I.
Cape Breton I.
Cape Sable
Cape Cod
Long I.
Cape Hatteras
Cape Canaveral
Lake Okeechobee
Florida Keys
Straits of Florida
THE BAHAMAS
CUBA
HAITI
DOMINICAN REPUBLIC
JAMAICA
YUCATAN PENINSULA
Cozumel I.
Merida
Cancun
ampeche
Quebec
Montreal
Ottawa
Toronto
Hamilton
London
Windsor
Sudbury
Kingston
Halifax
Dartmouth
Fredericton
Saint John
Moncton
Charlottetown
Sydney
Canso
Sept-Iles
Port-Cartier
Baie-Comeau
Gaspe
Chicoutimi
Alma
Sherbrooke
Trois-Rivieres
Shawinigan
Waskaganish
Moosonee
Chibougamau
Matagami
Kapuskasing
Timmins
Geraldton
Marathon
Wawa
Sault Ste. Marie
Sarnia
Maine
Augusta
Bangor
Bar Harbor
Portland
Vt.
N.H.
Mass.
Boston
R.I.
Providence
Conn.
Hartford
New Haven
New York
Albany
Syracuse
Rochester
Buffalo
New York City
N.J.
Trenton
Newark
Philadelphia
Pa.
Pittsburgh
Harrisburg
Del.
Dover
Md.
Baltimore
Annapolis
Washington, D.C.
Virginia
Richmond
Norfolk
Newport News
W.Va.
Charleston
North Carolina
Raleigh
Charlotte
South Carolina
Columbia
Georgia
Atlanta
Savannah
Florida
Tallahassee
Jacksonville
Orlando
Tampa
Miami
Fort Lauderdale
West Palm Beach
Key West
Alabama
Montgomery
Birmingham
Mobile
Mississippi
Jackson
Tennessee
Nashville
Memphis
Knoxville
Kentucky
Frankfort
Louisville
Lexington
Ohio
Columbus
Cleveland
Cincinnati
Indiana
Indianapolis
Illinois
Springfield
Chicago
St. Louis
Michigan
Lansing
Detroit
Wisconsin
Madison
Milwaukee
New Orleans
Baton Rouge
Mt. Washington 6,288
Mt. Katahdin 5,267
Mt. Mitchell 6,684
Spruce Knob 4,861
© The World Almanac and Book of Facts
0
250
500 Miles
0
250
500
750 Kilometers

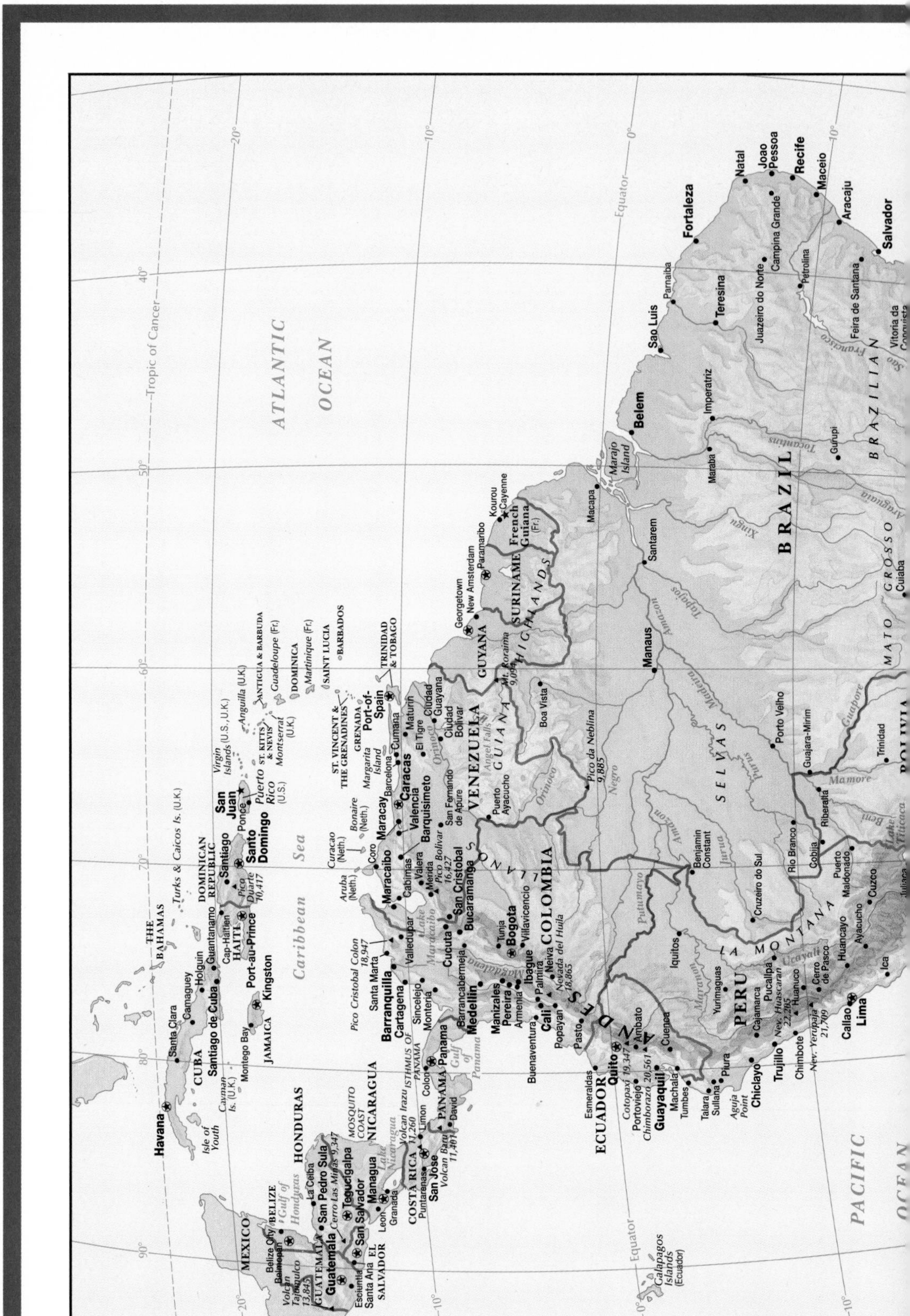
ATLANTIC
OCEAN
Caribbean
Sea
PACIFIC
Tropic of Cancer
Equator
THE BAHAMAS
Turks & Caicos Is. (U.K.)
CUBA
Havana
Santa Clara
Camaguey
Holguin
Santiago de Cuba
Guantanamo
Isle of Youth
Cayman Is. (U.K.)
JAMAICA
Montego Bay
Kingston
HAITI
Cap-Haitien
Port-au-Prince
DOMINICAN REPUBLIC
Santiago
Santo Domingo
Pico Duarte 10,417
San Juan
Ponce
Puerto Rico (U.S.)
Virgin Islands (U.S., U.K.)
Anguilla (U.K.)
ST. KITTS & NEVIS
ANTIGUA & BARBUDA
Montserrat (U.K.)
Guadeloupe (Fr.)
DOMINICA
Martinique (Fr.)
SAINT LUCIA
BARBADOS
ST. VINCENT & THE GRENADINES
GRENADA
TRINIDAD & TOBAGO
Port-of-Spain
Aruba (Neth.)
Curacao (Neth.)
Bonaire (Neth.)
MEXICO
BELIZE
Belize City
Belmopan
Gulf of Honduras
GUATEMALA
Guatemala
Volcan Tajumulco 13,845
Escuintla
Santa Ana
EL SALVADOR
San Salvador
HONDURAS
San Pedro Sula
La Ceiba
Tegucigalpa
Cerro Las Minas 9,347
NICARAGUA
Managua
Leon
Granada
Lake Nicaragua
MOSQUITO COAST
COSTA RICA
San Jose
Puntarenas
Limon
Volcan Irazu 11,260
Volcan Baru 11,401
PANAMA
Panama
Colon
David
ISTHMUS OF PANAMA
Gulf of Panama
COLOMBIA
Barranquilla
Cartagena
Santa Marta
Pico Cristobal Colon 18,947
Valledupar
Sincelejo
Monteria
Medellin
Barrancabermeja
Bucaramanga
Cucuta
Manizales
Pereira
Armenia
Ibague
Bogota
Tunja
Villavicencio
Cali
Palmira
Neiva
Nevada del Huila 18,865
Popayan
Pasto
Buenaventura
VENEZUELA
Maracaibo
Lake Maracaibo
Cabimas
Coro
Maracay
Valencia
Caracas
Barquisimeto
Valera
Merida
Pico Bolivar 16,427
San Cristobal
Barcelona
Cumana
Maturin
El Tigre
Ciudad Guayana
Ciudad Bolivar
San Fernando de Apure
Puerto Ayacucho
Margarita Island
Angel Falls
Orinoco
GUYANA
Georgetown
New Amsterdam
SURINAME
Paramaribo
French Guiana (Fr.)
Kourou
Cayenne
Mt. Roraima 9,094
GUIANA HIGHLANDS
LLANOS
ECUADOR
Quito
Esmeraldas
Portoviejo
Guayaquil
Cotopaxi 19,347
Chimborazo 20,561
Ambato
Cuenca
Machala
Galapagos Islands (Ecuador)
PERU
Tumbes
Talara
Sullana
Piura
Aguja Point
Chiclayo
Cajamarca
Trujillo
Chimbote
New Huascaran 22,205
Huanuco
Cerro de Pasco
Nev. Yerupaja 21,709
Callao
Lima
Ica
Huancayo
Ayacucho
Cuzco
Juliaca
Puerto Maldonado
Iquitos
Yurimaguas
Pucallpa
LA MONTANA
ANDES
Putumayo
Maranon
Ucayali
Negro
Pico da Neblina 9,885
BRAZIL
Boa Vista
Manaus
Santarem
Macapa
Marajo Island
Belem
Sao Luis
Parnaiba
Teresina
Fortaleza
Natal
Joao Pessoa
Recife
Campina Grande
Maceio
Aracaju
Salvador
Juazeiro do Norte
Petrolina
Feira de Santana
Vitoria da Conquista
Imperatriz
Maraba
Gurupi
Porto Velho
Guajara-Mirim
Riberalta
Rio Branco
Cobija
Cruzeiro do Sul
Benjamin Constant
Trinidad
Cuiaba
SELVAS
MATO GROSSO
BRAZILIAN
BOLIVIA
Amazon
Madeira
Tapajos
Xingu
Tocantins
Araguaia
Sao Francisco
Jurua
Purus
Mamore
Guapore
Beni
Lake Titicaca
20°
10°
0°
90°
80°
70°
60°
50°
40°

SOUTH AMERICA
CENTRAL AMERICA
& THE CARIBBEAN
Elevation
Meters
Feet
4,000
13,120
2,000
6,560
500
1,640
200
656
0
0
Below Sea Level
Below Sea Level
0
250
500
750 Miles
0
250
500
750
1,000 Kilometers
© The World Almanac and Book of Facts
Tropic of Capricorn
ANDES
CHILE
ARGENTINA
PARAGUAY
URUGUAY
GRAN CHACO
PAMPAS
PATAGONIA
ATACAMA DESERT
Arica
Tacna
Iquique
Antofagasta
Calama
Copiapo
La Serena
Vina del Mar
Valparaiso
Santiago
San Bernardo
Rancagua
Talca
Chillan
Talcahuano
Concepcion
Temuco
Valdivia
Osorno
Puerto Montt
Chiloe Island
Chonos Archipelago
Taitao Peninsula
Punta Arenas
Cerro Ojos del Salado 22,572
Cerro Bonete 22,546
Highest point in South America Cerro Aconcagua 22,834
Cerro Tupungato 22,310
San Felix Island (Chile)
San Ambrosio Island (Chile)
Juan Fernandez Islands (Chile)
Lake Poopo
Sucre
Potosi
Tarija
San Salvador de Jujuy
Salta
San Miguel de Tucuman
Catamarca
La Rioja
Santiago del Estero
Cordoba
San Juan
Mendoza
Rio Cuarto
San Rafael
Neuquen
San Carlos de Bariloche
Esquel
Comodoro Rivadavia
Trelew
Rawson
Viedma
Santa Rosa
Bahia Blanca
Punta Alta
Mar del Plata
La Plata
Avellaneda
Buenos Aires
Junin
Rosario
Santa Fe
Parana
Concordia
Cruzu Cuatia
Santo Tome
Resistencia
Corrientes
Formosa
Asuncion
Concepcion
Encarnacion
Posadas
Coronel Oviedo
Iguazu Falls
Foz do Iguacu
Corumba
Pilcomayo
Paraguay
Parana
Uruguay
Rio de la Plata
Montevideo
Minas
Melo
Paysandu
Salto
Rivera
Pelotas
Santa Maria
Porto Alegre
Caxias do Sul
Passo Fundo
Florianopolis
Joinvile
Curitiba
Ponta Grossa
Campo Grande
Presidente Prudente
Londrina
Sorocaba
Sao Paulo
Santos
Jundiai
Campinas
Bauru
Sao Jose do Rio Preto
Ribeirao Preto
Uberlandia
Belo Horizonte
Governador Valadares
Vitoria
Juiz de Fora
Pico da Bandeira 9,482
Volta Redonda
Niteroi
Rio de Janeiro
San Matias Gulf
Valdes Peninsula
Lowest point in South America
Gulf of San Jorge
Cape Tres Puntas
Bahia Grande
Rio Gallegos
Str. of Magellan
Tierra del Fuego
Ushuaia
Cape Horn
Stanley
Falkland Islands (U.K.) (Islas Malvinas)
South Georgia (U.K.)

EUROPE
Elevation
Meters
Feet
4,000
13,120
2,000
6,560
500
1,640
200
656
0
0
Below Sea Level
Below Sea Level
Greenland (Kalaallit Nunaat) (Denmark)
Arctic Circle
North Cape
Hammerfest
Tromso
Murmansk
Ivalo
LAPLAND
Kiruna
Bodo
Keflavik
Reykjavik
Akureyri
ICELAND
Hekla 4,892
Norwegian Sea
Rovaniemi
Arkhangelsk
Lulea
Oulu
Belomorsk
NORWAY
Gulf of Bothnia
FINLAND
Trondheim
Umea
Kuopio
Faeroe Is. (Den.)
Alesund
Ostersund
Vaasa
Lake Onega
SWEDEN
Petrozavodsk
Galdhopiggen 8,098
Tampere
Lake Ladoga
Shetland Is. (U.K.)
Bergen
Gavle
Aland Is. (Fin.)
Turku
Helsinki
Orkney Is.
Oslo
Gulf of Finland
St. Petersburg
Stavanger
Skien
Uppsala
Tallinn
ATLANTIC OCEAN
Hebrides
Inverness
Stockholm
ESTONIA
Novgorod
Aberdeen
Kristiansand
Linkoping
Tartu
RUSSIA
Glasgow
Dundee
Jonkoping
Edinburgh
Goteborg
Gotland (Swe.)
Baltic Sea
Belfast
UNITED KINGDOM
North Sea
Alborg
Jutland
Riga
LATVIA
IRELAND
Newcastle
Arhus
Helsingborg
Daugavpils
Dublin
Liverpool
Leeds
Copenhagen
Malmo
Klaipeda
Smolensk
Cork
Limerick
DENMARK
Odense
LITHUANIA
Vitsyebsk
Manchester
Sheffield
Bornholm (Den.)
(RUSSIA)
Kaunas
Vilnius
Birmingham
Hamburg
Rostock
Gdansk
Kaliningrad
Mahilyow
Bryansk
NETHERLANDS
Bremen
Szczecin
Bialystok
Minsk
Cardiff
Amsterdam
BELARUS
Bristol
London
Thames
Hague
Hannover
Berlin
POLAND
Homyel
Land's End
Plymouth
Portsmouth
Rotterdam
Essen
Magdeburg
Poznan
Warsaw
Brest
English Channel
Antwerp
Cologne
Leipzig
Wisla
Channel Is. (U.K.)
Brussels
Dresden
Lodz
Dnieper
Le Havre
Rouen
BELGIUM
Bonn
GERMANY
Wroclaw
Brest
Luxembourg
Frankfurt
Katowice
Lublin
Kiev
Paris
LUX.
Prague
Ostrava
Kracow
Lviv
UKRAINE
Nurnberg
CZECH REP.
Nantes
Orleans
Mannheim
Stuttgart
Brno
CARPATHIAN MOUNTAINS
Dniester
Vynnytsya
Strasbourg
SLOVAKIA
Kosice
Loire
Tours
Dijon
Basel
Munich
Linz
Danube
Miskolc
MOLDOVA
Bay of Biscay
FRANCE
Bern
Zurich
Salzburg
Vienna
Bratislava
Iasi
Chisinau
Limoges
SWITZ.
LIECH.
AUSTRIA
Debrecen
Odesa
A Coruna
Geneva
ALPS
Graz
Budapest
Cluj-Napoca
Gijon
Bordeaux
Lyon
Matterhorn 14,690
HUNGARY
ROMANIA
Vigo
Garonne
Mt. Blanc 15,771
Milan
SLOVE.
Ljubljana
Pecs
Brasov
Bilbao
Grenoble
Verona
Trieste
CROATIA
Timisoara
Porto
Donostia-San Sebastian
Toulouse
Turin
Venice
Zagreb
Valladolid
PYRENEES
Rhone
Genoa
Bologna
DINARIC ALPS
Belgrade
Bucharest
Constanta
Coimbra
Ebro
Pico de Aneto 11,168
Marseille
Nice
MONACO
APENNINES
SAN MARINO
BOS. & HERZ.
SERBIA
Danube
PORTUGAL
IBERIAN
Madrid
Zaragoza
ANDORRA
Florence
Split
Sarajevo
Ruse
Varna
Tagus
Corsica (Fr.)
Elba
Adriatic Sea
Dubrovnik
YUGO.
BALKAN
Burgas
Black Sea
Lisbon
SPAIN
Barcelona
Ajaccio
MONT.
Skopje
Sofia
BULGARIA
PENINSULA
Rome
ITALY
Tirane
MACE.
Plovdiv
Cape St. Vincent
Cordoba
Valencia
Naples
Bari
ALBANIA
Thessaloniki
Palma de Mallorca
Vesuvius 4,202
Vlore
Olympus 9,570
TURKEY
Seville
Balearic Is. (Sp.)
Sardinia (It.)
Alicante
Cagliari
Tyrrhenian Sea
Corfu
Larisa
Volos
Aegean Sea
Cadiz
Granada
Malaga
Euboea
Strait of Gibraltar
Gibraltar (U.K.)
Mediterranean Sea
Palermo
Messina
Ionian Sea
GREECE
Athens
Etna 11,053
Catania
Patras
Peloponnesus
Sicily
Rhodes
MALTA
Iraklion
AFRICA
Crete
0
250
500 Miles
0
250
500
750 Kilometers
© The World Almanac and Book of Facts

# RUSSIA, UKRAINE & CENTRAL ASIA

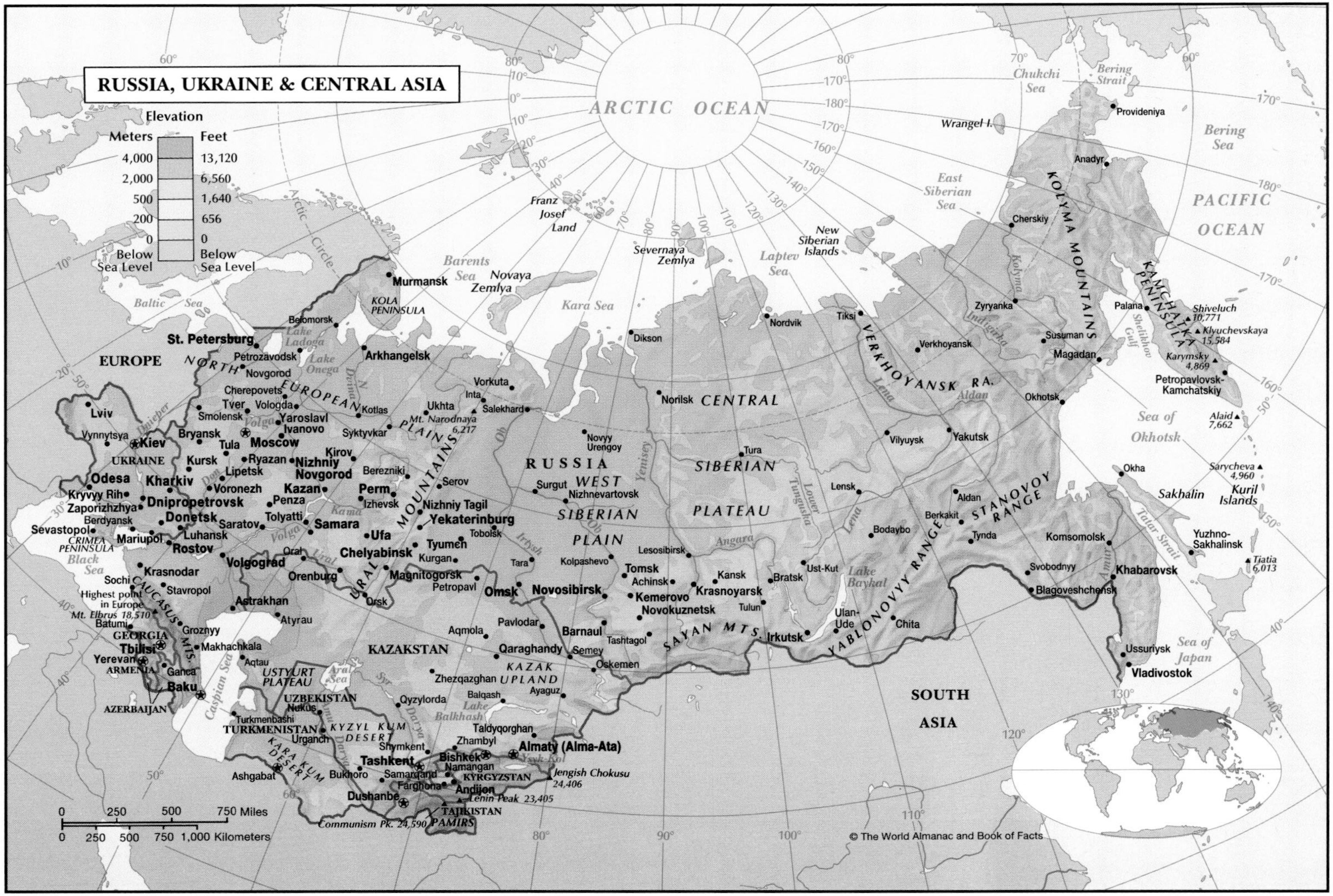

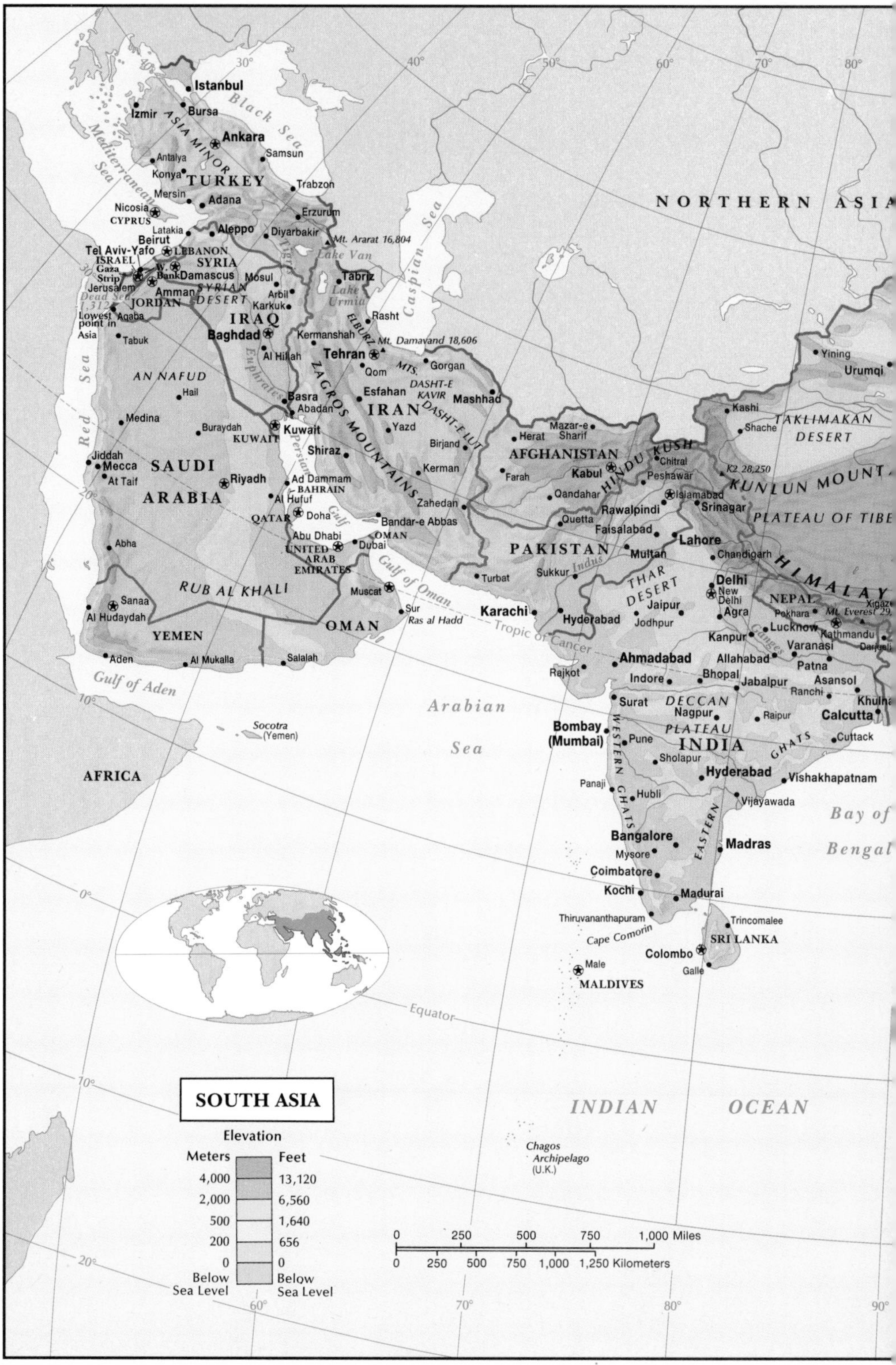
SOUTH ASIA
Elevation
Meters
Feet
4,000
13,120
2,000
6,560
500
1,640
200
656
0
0
Below Sea Level
Below Sea Level
0
250
500
750
1,000 Miles
0
250
500
750
1,000
1,250 Kilometers
NORTHERN ASIA
Istanbul
Bursa
Izmir
Ankara
Samsun
Antalya
Konya
TURKEY
ASIA MINOR
Black Sea
Mediterranean Sea
Trabzon
Mersin
Adana
Nicosia
CYPRUS
Erzurum
Latakia
Aleppo
Diyarbakir
Mt. Ararat 16,804
Beirut
LEBANON
Tel Aviv-Yafo
ISRAEL
SYRIA
Gaza Strip
W. Bank
Damascus
Jerusalem
Amman
JORDAN
SYRIAN DESERT
Mosul
Arbil
Karkuk
Dead Sea -1,312 Lowest point in Asia
Aqaba
Tabuk
IRAQ
Baghdad
Al Hillah
Lake Van
Tabriz
Lake Urmia
Caspian Sea
Rasht
Kermanshah
ELBURZ MTS.
Mt. Damavand 18,606
Tehran
Qom
Gorgan
DASHT-E KAVIR
DASHT-E-LUT
Mashhad
Esfahan
IRAN
ZAGROS MOUNTAINS
Yazd
Birjand
Kerman
Zahedan
Bandar-e Abbas
AN NAFUD
Hail
Medina
Buraydah
Euphrates
Tigris
Basra
Abadan
Kuwait
KUWAIT
Shiraz
Persian Gulf
Red Sea
Jiddah
Mecca
At Taif
SAUDI ARABIA
Riyadh
Ad Dammam
BAHRAIN
Al Hufuf
QATAR
Doha
Abu Dhabi
UNITED ARAB EMIRATES
Dubai
OMAN
Gulf of Oman
Muscat
Sur
Ras al Hadd
Abha
RUB AL KHALI
Sanaa
Al Hudaydah
YEMEN
OMAN
Aden
Al Mukalla
Salalah
Gulf of Aden
Socotra (Yemen)
AFRICA
Arabian Sea
Mazar-e Sharif
Herat
AFGHANISTAN
HINDU KUSH
Chitral
Kabul
Farah
Peshawar
Qandahar
Islamabad
Rawalpindi
Quetta
Faisalabad
Lahore
PAKISTAN
Multan
Sukkur
Indus
Turbat
Karachi
Hyderabad
THAR DESERT
Jaipur
Jodhpur
Chandigarh
Delhi
New Delhi
Agra
Srinagar
K2 28,250
Yining
Urumqi
Kashi
Shache
TAKLIMAKAN DESERT
KUNLUN MOUNT
PLATEAU OF TIBE
HIMALAY
NEPAL
Pokhara
Kathmandu
Mt. Everest 29,
Lucknow
Kanpur
Ganges
Varanasi
Allahabad
Patna
Asansol
Ranchi
Khulna
Calcutta
Tropic of Cancer
Rajkot
Ahmadabad
Bhopal
Indore
Jabalpur
Surat
DECCAN PLATEAU
Nagpur
Raipur
Cuttack
Bombay (Mumbai)
Pune
WESTERN GHATS
INDIA
EASTERN GHATS
Sholapur
Hyderabad
Vishakhapatnam
Panaji
Hubli
Vijayawada
Bay of Bengal
Bangalore
Mysore
Madras
Coimbatore
Kochi
Madurai
Thiruvananthapuram
Cape Comorin
Trincomalee
SRI LANKA
Colombo
Galle
Male
MALDIVES
Equator
INDIAN OCEAN
Chagos Archipelago (U.K.)
30°
40°
50°
60°
70°
80°
90°
20°
10°
0°

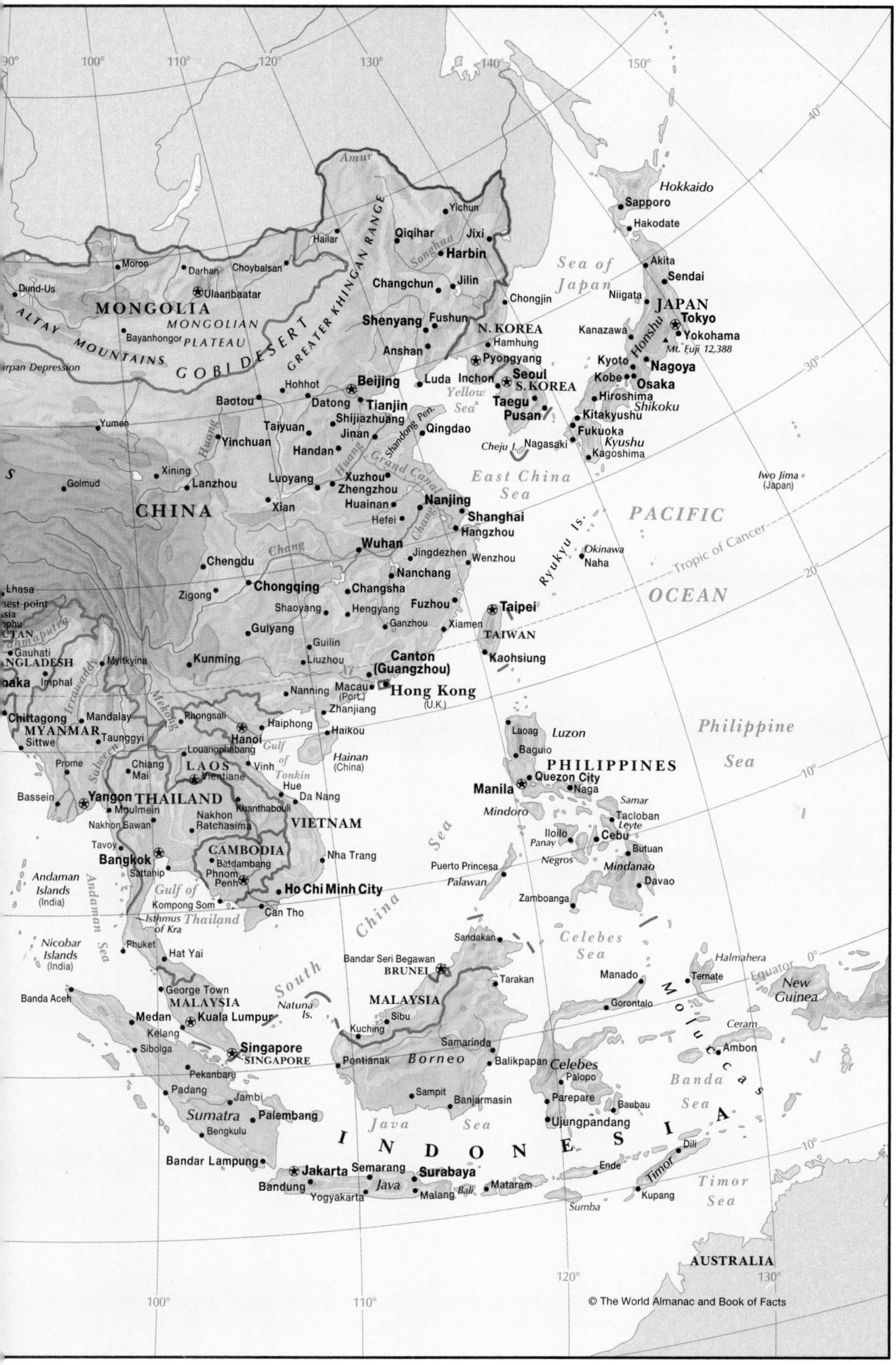

MONGOLIA
MONGOLIAN PLATEAU
ALTAY MOUNTAINS
GOBI DESERT
GREATER KHINGAN RANGE
Amur
Songhua
Yichun
Hailar
Qiqihar
Jixi
Harbin
Moron
Darhan
Choybalsan
Dund-Us
Ulaanbaatar
Jilin
Changchun
Chongjin
Bayanhongor
Shenyang
Fushun
Anshan
N. KOREA
Hamhung
Pyongyang
Seoul
S. KOREA
Inchon
Taegu
Pusan
Luda
Yellow Sea
Beijing
Hohhot
Tianjin
Datong
Baotou
Shijiazhuang
Taiyuan
Jinan
Qingdao
Shandong Pen.
Handan
Yinchuan
Yumen
Huang
Grand Canal
Xining
Golmud
Lanzhou
Luoyang
Xuzhou
Zhengzhou
Xian
Huainan
Nanjing
Hefei
Shanghai
Hangzhou
CHINA
Chang
Wuhan
Jingdezhen
Wenzhou
Chengdu
Chongqing
Nanchang
Changsha
Zigong
Shaoyang
Hengyang
Fuzhou
Ganzhou
Xiamen
Guiyang
Guilin
Liuzhou
Kunming
Canton (Guangzhou)
Nanning
Macau (Port.)
Hong Kong (U.K.)
Zhanjiang
Haikou
Hainan (China)
Taipei
TAIWAN
Kaohsiung
Lhasa
Gauhati
Myitkyina
Imphal
Chittagong
Mandalay
MYANMAR
Taunggyi
Sittwe
Prome
Bassein
Yangon
Moulmein
Irrawaddy
Salween
Mekong
Phongsali
Hanoi
Haiphong
Louangphrabang
Gulf of Tonkin
Vinh
LAOS
Vientiane
Hue
Da Nang
Chiang Mai
THAILAND
Khanthabouli
Nakhon Ratchasima
Nakhon Sawan
VIETNAM
Tavoy
Bangkok
Sattahip
CAMBODIA
Batdambang
Phnom Penh
Nha Trang
Ho Chi Minh City
Can Tho
Kompong Som
Gulf of Thailand
Isthmus of Kra
Andaman Islands (India)
Andaman Sea
Nicobar Islands (India)
Phuket
Hat Yai
Banda Aceh
George Town
MALAYSIA
Medan
Kuala Lumpur
Kelang
Sibolga
Singapore
SINGAPORE
Pekanbaru
Padang
Jambi
Sumatra
Palembang
Bengkulu
Bandar Lampung
Jakarta
Bandung
Semarang
Yogyakarta
Java
Surabaya
Malang
Bali
Mataram
Natuna Is.
South China Sea
Bandar Seri Begawan
BRUNEI
Sandakan
Tarakan
MALAYSIA
Sibu
Kuching
Samarinda
Pontianak
Borneo
Balikpapan
Sampit
Banjarmasin
Java Sea
INDONESIA
Celebes
Palopo
Parepare
Baubau
Ujungpandang
Celebes Sea
Manado
Gorontalo
Ternate
Halmahera
Moluccas
Ceram
Ambon
Banda Sea
Ende
Dili
Timor
Kupang
Sumba
Timor Sea
AUSTRALIA
New Guinea
Equator
Luzon
Laoag
Baguio
PHILIPPINES
Quezon City
Manila
Naga
Mindoro
Samar
Tacloban
Leyte
Iloilo
Panay
Cebu
Negros
Butuan
Mindanao
Davao
Puerto Princesa
Palawan
Zamboanga
Philippine Sea
Sea of Japan
Hokkaido
Sapporo
Hakodate
Akita
Sendai
Niigata
JAPAN
Tokyo
Kanazawa
Honshu
Yokohama
Mt. Fuji 12,388
Kyoto
Nagoya
Kobe
Osaka
Hiroshima
Shikoku
Kitakyushu
Fukuoka
Nagasaki
Kyushu
Kagoshima
Cheju I.
East China Sea
Ryukyu Is.
Okinawa
Naha
Iwo Jima (Japan)
PACIFIC OCEAN
Tropic of Cancer
90°
100°
110°
120°
130°
140°
150°
40°
30°
20°
10°
0°
© The World Almanac and Book of Facts

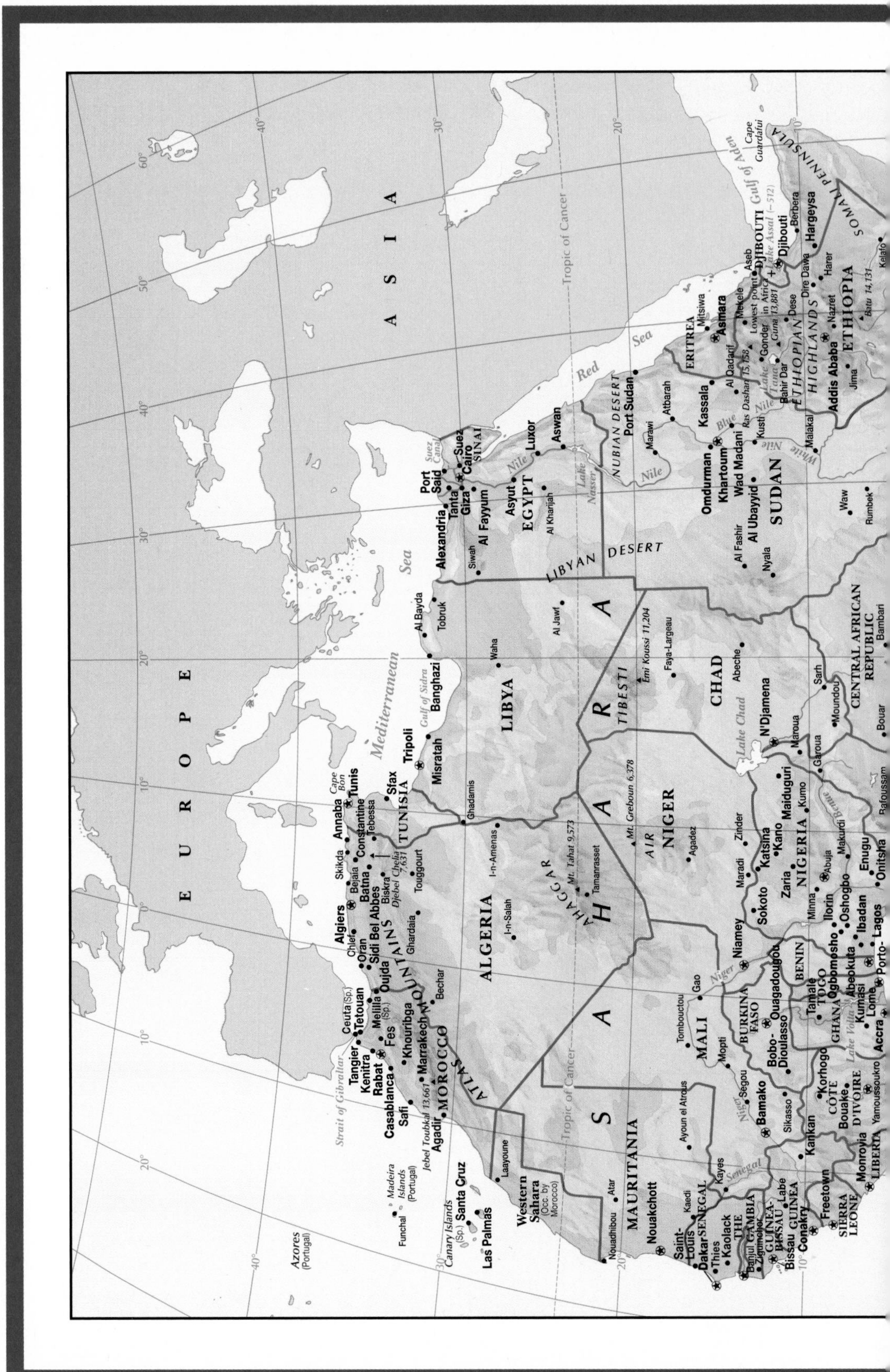

E U R O P E
A S I A
S A H A R A
Mediterranean Sea
Red Sea
Gulf of Aden
Tropic of Cancer
Azores (Portugal)
Madeira Islands (Portugal)
Funchal
Canary Islands (Sp.)
Santa Cruz
Las Palmas
Strait of Gibraltar
Tangier
Ceuta (Sp.)
Tetouan
Melilla (Sp.)
Kenitra
Rabat
Fes
Casablanca
Khouribga
Safi
Marrakech
Jebel Toubkal 13,661
Agadir
MOROCCO
ATLAS MOUNTAINS
Oujda
Oran
Chlef
Sidi Bel Abbes
Algiers
Bejaia
Batna
Skikda
Constantine
Annaba
Tebessa
Biskra
Djebel Chelia 7,631
Touggourt
Ghardaia
Bechar
ALGERIA
I-n-Salah
I-n-Amenas
AHAGGAR
Mt. Tahat 9,573
Tamanrasset
Cape Bon
Tunis
Sfax
TUNISIA
Ghadamis
Tripoli
Misratah
Gulf of Sidra
Banghazi
Al Bayda
Tobruk
LIBYA
Waha
Al Jawf
TIBESTI
Emi Koussi 11,204
Alexandria
Tanta
Port Said
Suez Canal
Suez
Cairo
Giza
SINAI
Al Fayyum
Asyut
Siwah
EGYPT
Al Kharijah
Luxor
Aswan
Lake Nasser
Nile
LIBYAN DESERT
NUBIAN DESERT
Port Sudan
Marawi
Atbarah
Omdurman
Khartoum
Kassala
Wad Madani
Al Fashir
Al Ubayyid
Kusti
Nyala
SUDAN
Blue Nile
White Nile
Malakal
Waw
Rumbek
ERITREA
Mitsiwa
Asmara
Aseb
DJIBOUTI
Djibouti
Lake Assal (–512)
Lowest point in Africa
Mekele
Al Qadarif
Ras Dashan 15,158
Gonder
Lake Tana
Guna 13,881
Bahir Dar
Dese
ETHIOPIAN HIGHLANDS
ETHIOPIA
Addis Ababa
Nazret
Dire Dawa
Harer
Jima
Batu 14,131
Berbera
Hargeysa
Kelafo
SOMALI PENINSULA
Cape Guardafui
CHAD
Faya-Largeau
Abeche
Lake Chad
N'Djamena
Sarh
Moundou
CENTRAL AFRICAN REPUBLIC
Bambari
Bouar
NIGER
AIR
Mt. Greboun 6,378
Agadez
Zinder
Maradi
Niamey
Garoua
Maroua
Maiduguri
Kumo
Kano
Katsina
Zaria
Sokoto
NIGERIA
Abuja
Makurdi
Benue
Minna
Ilorin
Oshogbo
Ogbomosho
Abeokuta
Ibadan
Lagos
Porto-Novo
Enugu
Onitsha
Bafoussam
BENIN
TOGO
Lome
GHANA
Tamale
Kumasi
Accra
Lake Volta
BURKINA FASO
Ouagadougou
Bobo-Dioulasso
MALI
Gao
Tombouctou
Mopti
Segou
Bamako
Niger
Sikasso
Korhogo
COTE D'IVOIRE
Bouake
Yamoussoukro
LIBERIA
Monrovia
Kankan
SIERRA LEONE
Freetown
GUINEA
Conakry
Labe
GUINEA-BISSAU
Bissau
THE GAMBIA
Banjul
Ziguinchor
SENEGAL
Dakar
Thies
Kaolack
Saint-Louis
Kaedi
Kayes
Senegal
MAURITANIA
Nouakchott
Nouadhibou
Atar
Ayoun el Atrous
Western Sahara (Occ. by Morocco)
Laayoune

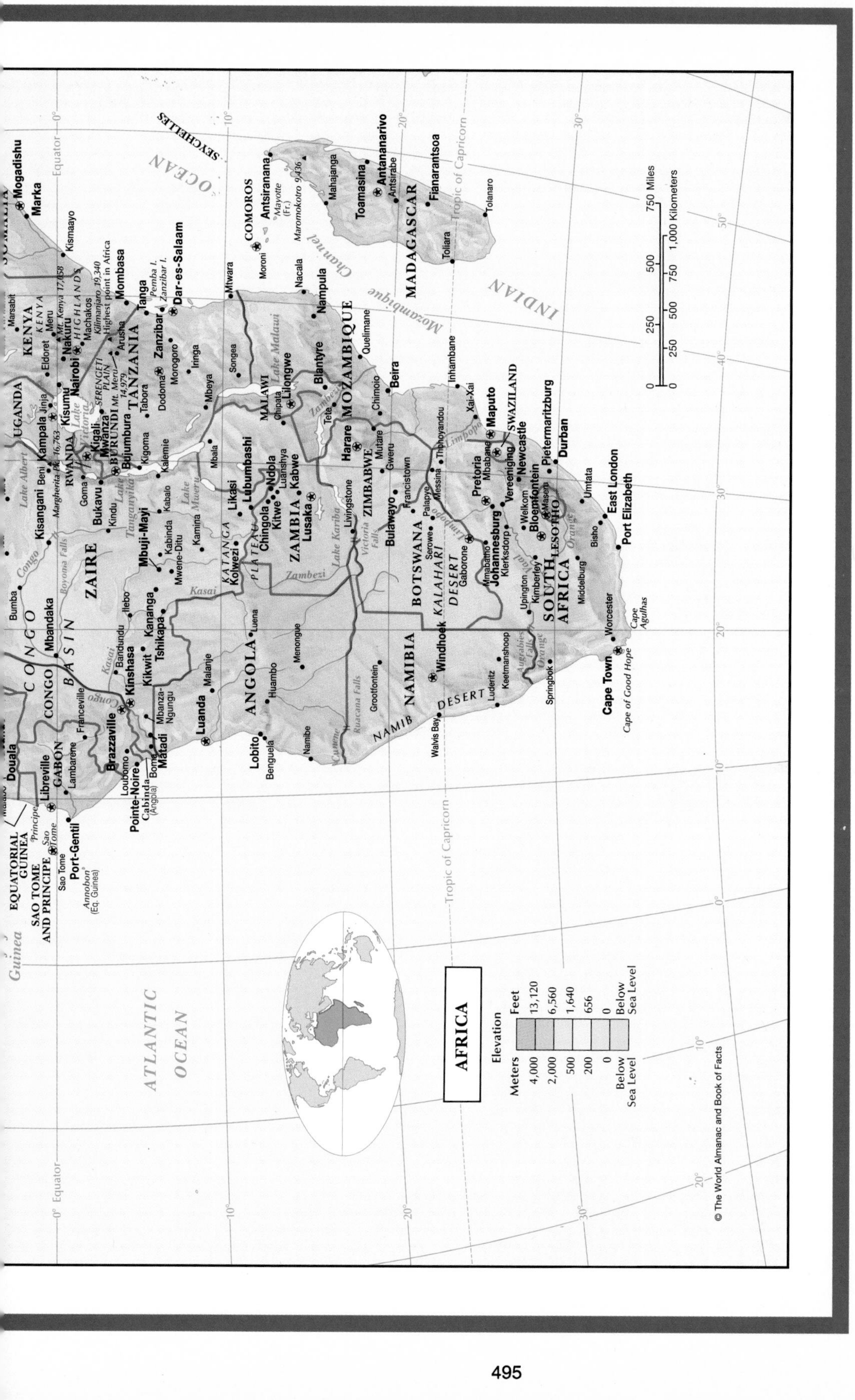
AFRICA
Elevation
Meters
Feet
4,000
13,120
2,000
6,560
500
1,640
200
656
0
0
Below Sea Level
Below Sea Level
0 250 500 750 Miles
0 250 500 750 1,000 Kilometers
ATLANTIC OCEAN
INDIAN OCEAN
Equator
Tropic of Capricorn
Mozambique Channel
EQUATORIAL GUINEA
SAO TOME AND PRINCIPE
Sao Tome
Port-Gentil
Annobon (Eq. Guinea)
Libreville
GABON
Lambarene
Douala
CONGO
Brazzaville
Pointe-Noire
Loubomo
Franceville
Cabinda (Angola)
Boma
Matadi
Kinshasa
Mbandaka
CONGO BASIN
ZAIRE
Kisangani
Bumba
Kikwit
Bandundu
Ilebo
Kananga
Tshikapa
Mbuji-Mayi
Kabinda
Mwene-Ditu
Kamina
Kolwezi
Likasi
Lubumbashi
KATANGA PLATEAU
Kindu
Bukavu
Goma
Kalemie
Kabalo
ANGOLA
Luanda
Lobito
Benguela
Huambo
Malanje
Luena
Menongue
Namibe
NAMIBIA
Windhoek
Walvis Bay
Luderitz
Keetmanshoop
Grootfontein
NAMIB DESERT
BOTSWANA
KALAHARI DESERT
Gaborone
Francistown
Serowe
Palapye
ZAMBIA
Lusaka
Kabwe
Ndola
Kitwe
Chingola
Luanshya
Livingstone
Victoria Falls
Lake Kariba
ZIMBABWE
Harare
Bulawayo
Gweru
Mutare
MALAWI
Lilongwe
Blantyre
Chipata
Lake Malawi
MOZAMBIQUE
Beira
Maputo
Nampula
Quelimane
Chimoio
Tete
Inhambane
Xai-Xai
Nacala
Mtwara
SOUTH AFRICA
Cape Town
Cape of Good Hope
Cape Agulhas
Worcester
Port Elizabeth
East London
Bisho
Umtata
Durban
Pietermaritzburg
Newcastle
Pretoria
Johannesburg
Vereeniging
Bloemfontein
Welkom
Kimberley
Klerksdorp
Mmabatho
Upington
Springbok
Middelburg
LESOTHO
Maseru
SWAZILAND
Mbabane
Messina
Thohoyandou
UGANDA
Kampala
Jinja
Lake Albert
Lake Victoria
KENYA
Nairobi
Nakuru
Kisumu
Eldoret
Marsabit
Meru
Machakos
Mombasa
KENYA HIGHLANDS
Mt. Kenya 17,058
Kilimanjaro 19,340 Highest point in Africa
TANZANIA
Dar-es-Salaam
Dodoma
Tanga
Zanzibar
Morogoro
Iringa
Mbeya
Songea
Tabora
Kigoma
Arusha
Mwanza
Mt. Meru 14,979
SERENGETI PLAIN
Pemba I.
Zanzibar I.
RWANDA
Kigali
BURUNDI
Bujumbura
Lake Tanganyika
Lake Mweru
Margherita Pk. 16,763
Mogadishu
Marka
Kismaayo
SEYCHELLES
COMOROS
Moroni
Mayotte (Fr.)
MADAGASCAR
Antananarivo
Antsirabe
Antsiranana
Mahajanga
Toamasina
Fianarantsoa
Toliara
Tolanaro
Maromokotro 9,436
Congo
Kasai
Zambezi
Limpopo
Orange
Cunene
© The World Almanac and Book of Facts

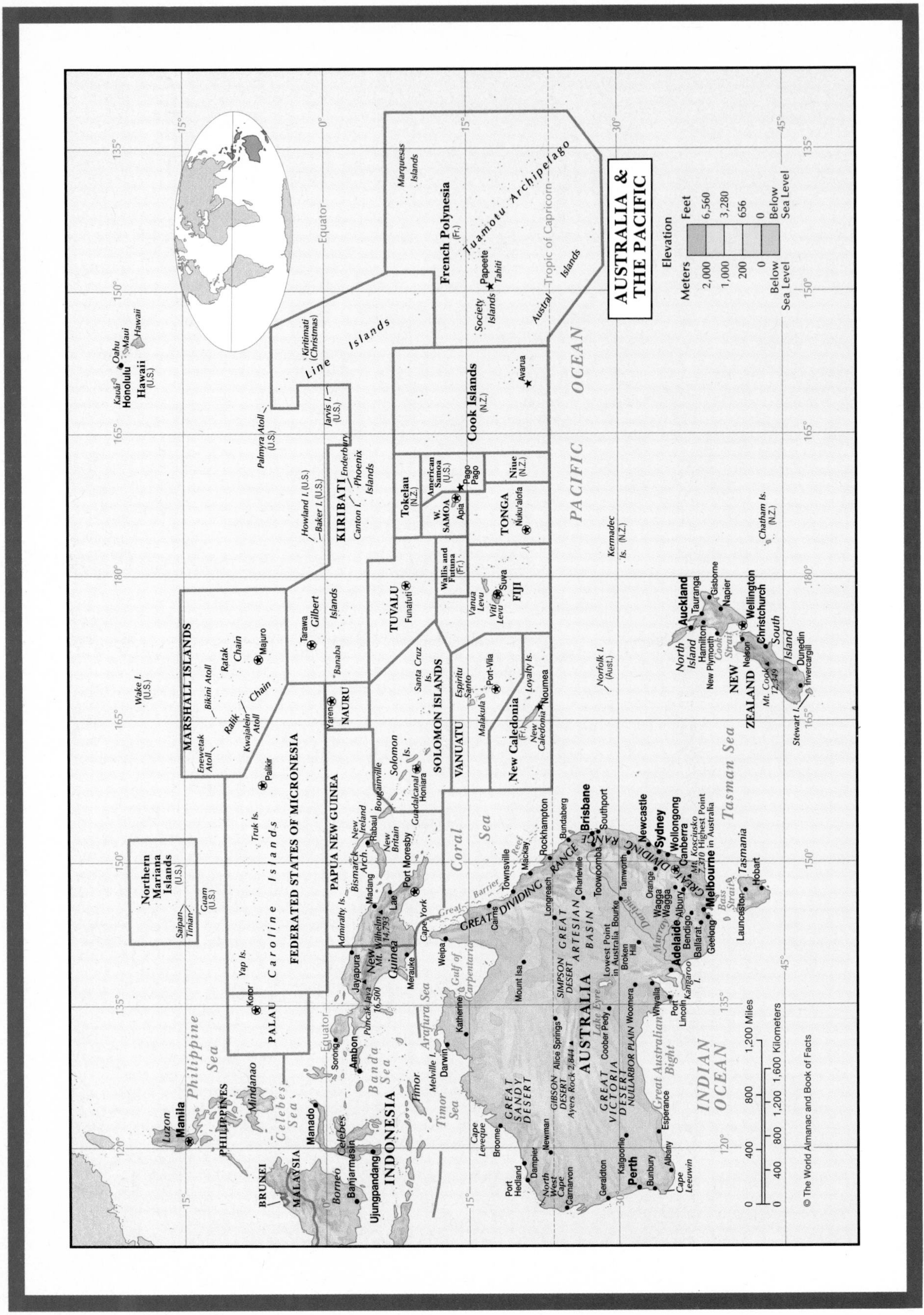
AUSTRALIA & THE PACIFIC
Elevation
Meters
Feet
2,000
6,560
1,000
3,280
200
656
0
0
Below Sea Level
Below Sea Level
0
400
800
1,200 Miles
0
400
800
1,200
1,600 Kilometers
© The World Almanac and Book of Facts
PACIFIC OCEAN
INDIAN OCEAN
AUSTRALIA
NEW ZEALAND
INDONESIA
PHILIPPINES
MALAYSIA
BRUNEI
PAPUA NEW GUINEA
FEDERATED STATES OF MICRONESIA
PALAU
MARSHALL ISLANDS
NAURU
KIRIBATI
TUVALU
SOLOMON ISLANDS
VANUATU
FIJI
TONGA
W. SAMOA
Northern Mariana Islands (U.S.)
Guam (U.S.)
Saipan
Tinian
Hawaii (U.S.)
Honolulu
Kauai
Oahu
Maui
Hawaii
Wake I. (U.S.)
Palmyra Atoll (U.S.)
Jarvis I. (U.S.)
Howland I. (U.S.)
Baker I. (U.S.)
Kiritimati (Christmas)
Line Islands
Phoenix Islands
Canton I.
Enderbury
Gilbert Islands
Tarawa
Banaba
Yaren
Funafuti
Tokelau (N.Z.)
American Samoa (U.S.)
Pago Pago
Apia
Cook Islands (N.Z.)
Avarua
Niue (N.Z.)
Nuku'alofa
Wallis and Futuna (Fr.)
Vanua Levu
Viti Levu
Suva
French Polynesia (Fr.)
Marquesas Islands
Tuamotu Archipelago
Society Islands
Papeete
Tahiti
Austral Islands
Tropic of Capricorn
Equator
Kermadec Is. (N.Z.)
Chatham Is. (N.Z.)
Norfolk I. (Aust.)
New Caledonia (Fr.)
Noumea
Loyalty Is.
Port-Vila
Espiritu Santo
Malakula
Santa Cruz Is.
Solomon Is.
Guadalcanal
Honiara
Bougainville
Bikini Atoll
Enewetak Atoll
Kwajalein Atoll
Ralik Chain
Ratak Chain
Majuro
Palikir
Caroline Islands
Truk Is.
Yap Is.
Koror
Admiralty Is.
Bismarck Arch.
New Ireland
New Britain
Rabaul
Madang
Lae
Port Moresby
Mt. Wilhelm 14,793
New Guinea
Jayapura
Puncak Jaya 16,500
Merauke
Sorong
Ambon
Banda Sea
Arafura Sea
Timor Sea
Timor
Celebes Sea
Celebes
Manado
Mindanao
Luzon
Manila
Philippine Sea
Borneo
Banjarmasin
Ujungpandang
Coral Sea
Great Barrier Reef
Cape York
Gulf of Carpentaria
Weipa
Melville I.
Darwin
Katherine
Mount Isa
Cairns
Townsville
Mackay
Rockhampton
Bundaberg
Brisbane
Southport
Toowoomba
Charleville
Longreach
GREAT DIVIDING RANGE
GREAT ARTESIAN BASIN
SIMPSON DESERT
GIBSON DESERT
GREAT SANDY DESERT
GREAT VICTORIA DESERT
NULLARBOR PLAIN
Alice Springs
Ayers Rock 2,844
Lake Eyre
Lowest Point in Australia
Coober Pedy
Woomera
Whyalla
Port Lincoln
Kangaroo I.
Adelaide
Broken Hill
Bourke
Darling
Murray
Tamworth
Newcastle
Sydney
Wollongong
Canberra
Orange
Wagga Wagga
Albury
Mt. Kosciusko 7,310 Highest Point in Australia
Bendigo
Ballarat
Geelong
Melbourne
Bass Strait
Launceston
Tasmania
Hobart
Tasman Sea
Great Australian Bight
Esperance
Albany
Cape Leeuwin
Bunbury
Perth
Kalgoorlie
Geraldton
Carnarvon
North West Cape
Dampier
Port Hedland
Newman
Broome
Cape Leveque
North Island
South Island
Auckland
Tauranga
Gisborne
Hamilton
New Plymouth
Napier
Cook Strait
Wellington
Nelson
Christchurch
Mt. Cook 12,349
Dunedin
Invercargill
Stewart I.

# UNITED STATES HISTORY

**1492**

**Christopher Columbus** and crew sighted land **Oct. 12** in the present-day Bahamas.

**1497**

**John Cabot** explored northeast coast to Delaware.

**1513**

**Juan Ponce de León** explored Florida coast.

**1524**

**Giovanni da Verrazano** led French expedition along coast from Carolina north to Nova Scotia; entered New York harbor.

**1539**

**Hernando de Soto** landed in Florida **May 28;** crossed Mississippi River, **1541.**

**1540**

**Francisco Vásquez de Coronado** explored Southwest north of Rio Grande. Hernando de Alarcón reached Colorado River, Don Garcia Lopez de Cardenas reached Grand Canyon. Others explored California coast.

**1565**

**St. Augustine, FL,** founded by Pedro Menéndez. Razed by Francis Drake **1586.**

**1579**

**Francis Drake** entered San Francisco Bay and claimed region for Britain.

**1607**

**Capt. John Smith** and 105 cavaliers in 3 ships landed on Virginia coast, started first permanent English settlement in New World at **Jamestown** in May.

**1609**

**Henry Hudson,** English explorer of Northwest Passage, employed by Dutch, sailed into New York harbor in **Sept.,** and up Hudson to Albany. The same year, **Samuel de Champlain** explored Lake Champlain just to the north.

Spaniards settled **Santa Fe, NM.**

**1619**

**House of Burgesses,** first representative assembly in New World, elected **July 30** at Jamestown, VA.

**First black laborers**—indentured servants—in English N. American colonies, landed by Dutch at Jamestown in **Aug.** Chattel slavery legally recognized, **1650.**

**1620**

**Plymouth Pilgrims,** Puritan separatists from Church of England, some living in Holland, left Plymouth, England, **Sept. 16** on *Mayflower*. Original destination Virginia, they reached Cape Cod **Nov. 19,** explored coast; 103 passengers landed **Dec. 26** at Plymouth. Mayflower Compact was agreement to form a government and abide by its laws. Half of colony died during harsh winter.

**1624**

Dutch colonies started in Albany and in New York area, where New Netherland was established in May.

**1626**

Peter Minuit bought Manhattan for Dutch from Man-a-hat-a Indians during summer for goods valued at $24; named island New Amsterdam.

**1630**

Settlement of **Boston** established by Massachusetts colonists led by John Winthrop.

**1634**

**Maryland** founded as Catholic colony with religious tolerance.

**1636**

**Roger Williams** founded Providence, RI, **June,** as a democratically ruled colony with separation of church and state. Charter was granted, **1644.**

**Harvard College** founded **Oct. 28,** now oldest in U.S.; grammar school, compulsory education established at Boston.

**1660**

British Parliament passed **Navigation Act,** regulating colonial commerce to suit English needs.

**1664**

Three hundred **British troops Sept. 8 seized New Netherland** from Dutch, who yield peacefully. Charles II granted province of New Netherland and city of New Amsterdam to brother, Duke of York; both renamed New York. The Dutch recaptured the colony **Aug. 9, 1673,** but ceded it to Britain **Nov. 10, 1674.**

**1676**

**Nathaniel Bacon** led planters against autocratic British Gov. Berkeley, burned Jamestown, VA. Bacon died, 23 followers executed.

Bloody **Indian war** in New England ended **Aug. 12.** King Philip, Wampanoag chief, and many Narragansett Indians killed.

**1682**

**Robert Cavelier, Sieur de La Salle,** claimed lower Mississippi River country for France, called it Louisiana **Apr. 9.** Had French outposts built in Illinois and Texas, **1684.** Killed during mutiny **Mar. 19, 1687.**

**1683**

**William Penn** signed treaty with Delaware Indians and made payment for Pennsylvania lands.

**1692**

Witchcraft delusion at Salem, MA; 20 alleged witches executed by special court.

**1696**

**Capt. William Kidd,** who was born in Scotland and settled in America, was hired by British to fight pirates and take booty, but himself became a pirate. Arrested and sent to England, he was hanged **1701.**

**1699**

**French settlements** made in Mississippi, Louisiana.

**1704**

**Indians attacked Deerfield,** MA, **Feb. 28-29;** killed 40, carried off 100.

*Boston News Letter,* first regular newspaper, started by John Campbell, postmaster. (An earlier paper, *Publick Occurences,* was suppressed after one issue **1690.**)

**1709**

British-Colonial troops captured French fort, Port Royal, Nova Scotia, in **Queen Anne's War 1701-13.** France yielded Nova Scotia by treaty **1713.**

**1712**

**Slaves revolted** in New York **Apr. 6.** Six committed suicide, 21 were executed. Second rising, **1741;** 13 slaves hanged, 13 burned, 71 deported.

**1716**

**First theater** in colonies opened in Williamsburg, VA.

**1732**

Benjamin Franklin published first *Poor Richard's Almanac;* published annually to 1757.

**1735**

**Freedom of the press** recognized in New York by acquittal of John Peter Zenger, editor of *Weekly Journal,* on charge of libeling British Gov. Cosby by criticizing his conduct in office.

**1740-41**

**Capt. Vitus Bering,** Dane employed by Russians, reached Alaska.

**1744**

**King George's War** pitted British and colonials vs. French. Colonials captured Louisburg, Cape Breton Is. **June 17, 1745.** Returned to France **1748** by Treaty of Aix-la-Chapelle.

**1752**

**Benjamin Franklin,** flying kite in thunderstorm, proved lightning is electricity **June 15;** invented lightning rod.

**1754**

**French and Indian War** (in Europe called 7 Years War, started 1756) began when French occupied Ft. Duquesne (Pittsburgh). British moved Acadian French from Nova Scotia to Louisiana **Oct. 8, 1755.** British captured Québec **Sept. 18, 1759,** in battles in which French Gen. Montcalm and British Gen. Wolfe were killed. Peace signed **Feb. 10, 1763.** French lost Canada and American Midwest. British tightened colonial administration in North America.

**1764**

**Sugar Act** placed duties on lumber, foodstuffs, molasses, and rum in colonies, to pay French and Indian War debts.

**1765**

**Stamp Act** required revenue stamps to help defray cost of royal troops. Nine colonies, led by New York and Massachusetts at Stamp Act Congress in New York **Oct. 7-25, 1765,** adopted Declaration of Rights opposing taxation without representation in Parliament and trial without jury by admiralty courts. Stamp Act **repealed Mar. 17, 1766.**

**1767**

**Townshend Acts** levied taxes on glass, painter's lead, paper, and tea. In **1770** all duties except on tea were repealed.

**1770**

British troops fired **Mar. 5** into Boston mob, killed 5 including **Crispus Attucks,** a black man, reportedly leader of group; later called **Boston Massacre.**

**1773**

**East India Co. tea ships** turned back at Boston, New York, Philadelphia in **May.** Cargo ship burned at Annapolis **Oct. 14,** cargo thrown overboard at **Boston Tea Party Dec. 16,** to protest the tea tax.

**1774**

**"Intolerable Acts"** of Parliament curtailed Massachusetts self-rule; barred use of Boston harbor till tea was paid for.

**First Continental Congress** held in Philadelphia **Sept. 5-Oct. 26;** protested British measures, called for civil disobedience.

**Rhode Island** abolished slavery.

**1775**

**Patrick Henry** addressed Virginia convention, **Mar. 23,** said "Give me liberty or give me death."

**Paul Revere** and William Dawes on night of **Apr. 18** rode to alert patriots that British were on way to Concord to destroy arms. At Lexington, MA, **Apr. 19** Minutemen lost 8. On return from Concord, British took 273 casualties.

Col. Ethan Allen (joined by Col. Benedict Arnold) captured Ft. **Ticonderoga, NY, May 10;** also Crown Point. Colonials headed for **Bunker Hill,** fortified Breed's Hill, Charlestown, MA, repulsed British under Gen. William Howe twice before retreating **June 17;** British casualties 1,000; called Battle of Bunker Hill. Continental Congress **June 15** named **George Washington** commander in chief.

**1776**

**France and Spain** each agreed **May 2** to provide one million livres in arms to Americans.

In Continental Congress **June 7,** Richard Henry Lee (VA) moved "that these united colonies are and of right ought to be free and independent states." Resolution adopted July 2. **Declaration of Independence** approved **July 4.**

Col. Moultrie's batteries at **Charleston, SC,** repulsed British sea attack **June 28.**

Washington, with 10,000 men, lost **Battle of Long Island Aug. 27,** evacuated New York.

**Nathan Hale executed** as spy by British **Sept. 22.**

Brig. Gen. Arnold's **Lake Champlain** fleet was defeated at Valcour **Oct. 11,** but British returned to Canada. Howe failed to destroy Washington's army at **White Plains Oct. 28.** Hessians captured Ft. Washington, Manhattan, and 3,000 men **Nov. 16;** captured Ft. Lee, NJ, **Nov. 18.**

Washington in Pennsylvania, recrossed **Delaware River Dec. 25-26,** defeated 1,400 Hessians at Trenton, NJ, **Dec. 26.**

**1777**

Washington defeated Lord Cornwallis at **Princeton Jan. 3.** Continental Congress adopted Stars and Stripes.

Maj. Gen. John Burgoyne, force of 8,000 from Canada, captured **Ft. Ticonderoga July 6.** Americans beat back Burgoyne at Bemis Heights **Oct. 7** and cut off British escape route. Burgoyne surrendered 5,000 men at **Saratoga, NY, Oct. 17.**

**Marquis de Lafayette,** aged 20, made major general.

**Articles of Confederation** and Perpetual Union adopted by Continental Congress **Nov. 15.**

**France** recognized independence of 13 colonies **Dec. 17.**

**1778**

**France signed treaty** of aid with U.S. **Feb. 6.** Sent fleet; British evacuated Philadelphia in consequence **June 18.**

**1779**

**John Paul Jones** on the *Bonhomme Richard* defeated *Serapis* in British North Sea waters **Sept. 23.**

**1780**

**Charleston, SC,** fell to the British **May 12,** but a British force was defeated near **Kings Mountain, NC, Oct. 7** by militiamen.

**Benedict Arnold** found to be a traitor **Sept. 23.** Arnold escaped, made brigadier general in British army.

**1781**

**Bank of North America** incorporated in Philadelphia **May 26.**

Cornwallis, sapped by patriot victories, retired to **Yorktown, VA.** Adm. De Grasse landed 3,000 French and stopped British fleet in Hampton Roads. Washington and Rochambeau joined forces, arrived near Williamsburg **Sept. 26.** When siege of Cornwallis began **Oct. 6,** British had 6,000, Americans 8,846, French 7,800. **Cornwallis surrendered Oct. 19.**

**1782**

New **British** cabinet agreed **in March** to **recognize U.S.** independence. Preliminary agreement signed in Paris **Nov. 30.**

**1783**

Massachusetts Supreme Court **outlawed slavery** in that state, noting the words in the state Bill of Rights "all men are born free and equal."

Britain, U.S. signed **peace treaty Sept. 3** (Congress ratified it **Jan. 14, 1784).**

**Washington ordered army disbanded Nov. 3,** bade farewell to his officers at Fraunces Tavern, New York City, **Dec. 4.**

Noah Webster published *American Spelling Book,* great best-seller.

**1784**

Jefferson's proposal to **ban slavery** in new territory after 1802 was narrowly defeated **Mar. 1.**

First successful daily newspaper, ***Pennsylvania Packet & General Advertiser,*** published **Sept. 21.**

**1786**

Delegates from 5 states at **Annapolis, MD, Sept. 11-14** asked Congress to call convention in Philadelphia to write practical constitution for the 13 states.

**1787**

**Shays's Rebellion,** of debt-ridden farmers in Massachusetts, failed **Jan. 25.**

**Northwest Ordinance** adopted **July 13** by Continental Congress. Determined government of Northwest Territory north of Ohio River, west of New York; 60,000 inhabitants could get statehood. Guaranteed freedom of religion, support for schools, no slavery.

**Constitutional convention** opened at Philadelphia **May 25** with George Washington presiding. Constitution adopted by delegates **Sept. 17;** ratification by 9th state, New Hampshire, **June 21, 1788,** meant adoption; declared in effect **Mar. 4, 1789.**

**1789**

**George Washington chosen president** by all electors voting (73 eligible, 69 voting, 4 absent); John Adams, vice president, 34 votes. **Feb. 4.** First Congress met at Federal Hall, New York City; regular sessions began **Apr. 6.** Washington inaugurated there **Apr. 30.** Supreme Court created by Federal Judiciary Act **Sept. 24.** Congress submitted Bill of Rights to states **Sept. 25.**

**1790**

Congress passed **Census Act Mar. 1; Naturalization Act** (2-year residency) **Mar. 26.**

**Congress met** in Philadelphia **Dec. 6,** new temporary capital.

**1791**

**Bill of Rights** went into effect **Dec. 15.**

**1792**

Coinage Act established **U.S. Mint** in Philadelphia **Apr. 2.**

Gen. **"Mad" Anthony Wayne** made commander in Ohio-Indiana area, trained "American Legion," established string of forts. Routed Indians at Fallen Timbers on Maumee River **Aug. 20, 1794,** checked British at Fort Miami, OH.

**White House** cornerstone laid **Oct. 13.**

**1793**

Eli Whitney invented **cotton gin,** reviving southern slavery.

**1794**

**Whiskey Rebellion,** west Pennsylvania farmers protesting liquor tax of **1791,** was suppressed by 15,000 militiamen **Sept. 1794.** Alexander Hamilton used incident to establish authority of the new federal government in enforcing its laws.

**1795**

U.S. bought peace from **Algerian pirates** by paying $1 million ransom for 115 seamen **Sept. 5,** followed by annual tributes.

**Gen. Wayne** signed peace with Indians at Fort Greenville.

**University of North Carolina** became first operating state university.

**1796**

**Washington's Farewell Address** as president delivered **Sept. 19.** Gave strong warnings against permanent alliances with foreign powers, big public debt, large military establishment, and devices of "small, artful, enterprising minority" to control or change government.

**1797**

U.S. **frigate *United States*** launched at Philadelphia **July 10;** Constellation at Baltimore **Sept. 7;** Constitution (Old Ironsides) at Boston **Sept. 20.**

**1798**

**Alien & Sedition Acts** passed by Federalists **June-July**; intended to silence political opposition.

**War with France threatened** over French raids on U.S. shipping and rejection of U.S. diplomats. Congress voided all treaties with France, ordered Navy to capture French armed ships. Navy (45 ships) and 365 privateers captured 84 French ships. *USS Constellation* took French warship *Insurgente* **1799.** Napoleon stopped French raids after becoming First Consul.

**1800**

Federal government moved from Philadelphia to **Washington, DC.**

**1801**

**Tripoli declared war June 10** against U.S., which refused added tribute to commerce-raiding Arab corsairs. Land and naval campaigns forced Tripoli to negotiate **peace June 4, 1805.**

**1803**

Supreme Court, in **Marbury *v* Madison** case, for the first time overturned a U.S. law **Feb. 24.**

Napoleon, who had recovered Louisiana from Spain by secret treaty, sold all of **Louisiana,** stretching to Canadian border, to U.S., for $11,250,000 in bonds, plus $3,750,000 indemnities to American citizens with claims against France. U.S. took title **Dec. 20.** Purchases doubled U.S. area.

**1804**

**Lewis and Clark** expedition ordered by Pres. Thomas Jefferson to explore what is now northwest U.S. Started from St. Louis **May 14;** ended **Sept. 23, 1806.** Sacagawea, an Indian woman, served as guide.

Vice Pres. **Aaron Burr,** after long political rivalry, **shot Alexander Hamilton** in a duel **July 11** in Weehawken, NJ; Hamilton died the next day.

**1807**

**Robert Fulton** made first practical steamboat trip; left New York City **Aug. 17,** reached Albany, 150 mi, in 32 hr.

**Embargo Act** banned all trade with foreign countries, forbidding ships to set sail for foreign ports **Dec. 22.**

**1808**

**Slave importation** outlawed. Some 250,000 slaves were illegally imported **1808-60.**

**1811**

**William Henry Harrison,** governor of Indiana, defeated Indians under the Prophet, in battle of Tippecanoe **Nov. 7.**

**Cumberland Road** begun at Cumberland, MD; became important route to West.

**1812**

**War of 1812** had 3 main causes: Britain seized U.S. ships trading with France; Britain seized 4,000 naturalized U.S. sailors by **1810;** Britain armed Indians who raided western border. U.S. stopped trade with Europe **1807** and **1809.** Trade with Britain only was stopped, **1810.**

Unaware that Britain had raised the blockade against France 2 days before, **Congress declared war June 18** by a small majority. The West favored war; New England opposed it. The British were handicapped by war with France.

**U.S. naval victories** in **1812** included: *USS Essex* captured *Alert* **Aug. 13;** *USS Constitution* destroyed *Guerriere* **Aug. 19;** *USS Wasp* took *Frolic* **Oct. 18;** *USS United States* defeated *Macedonian* off Azores **Oct. 25;** *Constitution* beat *Java* **Dec. 29.** British captured Detroit **Aug. 16.**

**1813**

**Oliver H. Perry** defeated British fleet at Battle of Lake Erie, **Sept. 10.** U.S. victory at Battle of the Thames, Ontario, **Oct. 5,** broke Indian allies of Britain, and made Detroit frontier safe for U.S. But Americans failed in Canadian invasion attempts. York (Toronto) and Buffalo were burned.

**1814**

**British** landed in Maryland in August, defeated U.S. force **Aug. 24, burned Capitol and White House.** Maryland militia stopped British advance **Sept. 12.** Bombardment of Ft. McHenry, Baltimore, for 25 hours, **Sept. 13-14,** by British fleet failed; Francis Scott Key wrote words to **"Star Spangled Banner."**

U.S. won naval Battle of **Lake Champlain Sept. 11.** Peace treaty signed at Ghent **Dec. 24.**

**1815**

Some 5,300 British, unaware of peace treaty, attacked U.S. entrenchments near **New Orleans, Jan. 8.** British had more than 2,000 casualties; Americans lost 71.

U.S. flotilla finally ended piracy by **Algiers, Tunis, Tripoli** by **Aug. 6.**

**1816**

Second **Bank of the U.S.** chartered.

**1817**

**Rush-Bagot treaty** signed **Apr. 28-29;** limited U.S., British armaments on the Great Lakes.

**1819**

Spain cedes **Florida** to U.S. **Feb. 22.**

**American steamship *Savannah*** made first part steam-powered, part sail-powered crossing of Atlantic, Savannah, GA, to Liverpool, England, 29 days.

**1820**

First organized **immigration of blacks to Africa** from U.S. began with 86 free blacks sailing **Feb.** to Sierra Leone, Brit. colony.

Henry Clay's **Missouri Compromise** bill passed by Congress **March 3.** Slavery was allowed in Missouri, but not elsewhere west of the Mississippi River north of 36° 30′ latitude (the southern line of Missouri). Repealed **1854.**

**1821**

**Emma Willard** founded Troy Female Seminary, first U.S. women's college.

**1823**

**Monroe Doctrine** enunciated **Dec. 2,** opposing European intervention in the Americas.

**1824**

Pawtucket, RI, **weavers strike** marked the first such action by women.

**1825**

**Erie Canal opened;** first boat left Buffalo **Oct. 26,** reached NYC **Nov. 4.** Canal cost $7 million but opened Great Lakes area, made NYC chief Atlantic port.

John Stevens, of Hoboken, NJ, built and operated first experimental **steam locomotive** in U.S.

**1828**

South Carolina **Dec. 19** declared the right of state **nullification of federal laws,** opposing the "Tariff of Abominations."

**Noah Webster** published his *American Dictionary of the English Language.*

**Baltimore & Ohio,** 1st U.S. passenger railroad, was begun **July 4.**

**1830**

**Mormon church** organized by Joseph Smith in Fayette, NY, **Apr. 6.**

**1831**

William Lloyd Garrison began abolitionist newspaper *The Liberator* **Jan. 1.**

**Nat Turner,** black slave in Virginia, led local slave rebellion, killed 57 whites in **Aug.** Troops called in, 100 slaves killed, Turner captured, tried, and hanged.

**1832**

**Black Hawk War** (IL-WI) **Apr.-Sept.** pushed Sauk and Fox Indians west across Mississippi.

South Carolina convention passed **Ordinance of Nullification in Nov.** against permanent tariff, threatening to withdraw from the Union. Congress **Feb. 1833** passed a compromise tariff act, whereupon South Carolina repealed its act.

**1833**

**Oberlin College,** first in U.S. to adopt coeducation; refused to bar students on account of race, **1835.**

**1835**

**Seminole Indians** in Florida under Osceola began attacks **Nov. 1,** protesting forced removal. The unpopular 8-year war ended **Aug. 14, 1842;** Indians were sent to Oklahoma. War cost the U.S. 1,500 soldiers.

**Texas proclaimed** right to secede from Mexico; Sam Houston put in command of Texas army, **Nov. 2-4.**

Gold discovered on **Cherokee land** in Georgia. Indians forced to cede lands **Dec. 20** and to cross Mississippi.

**1836**

**Texans besieged in Alamo** in San Antonio by Mexicans under Santa Anna **Feb. 23-Mar. 6;** entire garrison killed. Texas independence declared, **Mar. 2.** At San Jacinto **Apr. 21,** Sam Houston and Texans defeated Mexicans.

Marcus Whitman, H. H. Spaulding, and wives reached Fort Walla Walla on Columbia River, OR. **First white women to cross plains.**

**1838**

Cherokee Indians made **"Trail of Tears,"** removed from Georgia to Oklahoma starting **Oct.**

**1841**

First emigrant **wagon train for California,** 47 persons, left Independence, MO, **May 1,** reached California **Nov. 4.**

**Brook Farm** commune set up by New England Transcendentalist intellectuals. Lasts to **1846.**

**1842**

**Webster-Ashburton Treaty** signed **Aug. 9,** fixing the U.S.-Canada border in Maine and Minnesota.

First use of **anesthetic** (sulphuric ether gas).

Settlement of Oregon began via **Oregon Trail.**

**1843**

More than 1,000 settlers left Independence, MO, for Oregon **May 22,** arrived **Oct.**

**1844**

First message over first **telegraph line** sent **May 24** by inventor Samuel F.B. Morse from Washington to Baltimore: "What hath God wrought!"

**1845**

**Texas** Congress **voted for annexation** by U.S. **July 4.** U.S. Congress admits Texas to Union **Dec. 29.**

**1846**

**Mexican War.** Pres. James K. Polk ordered Gen. Zachary Taylor to seize disputed Texan land settled by Mexicans. After border clash, U.S. declared war **May 13;** Mexico **May 23.** Northern Whigs opposed war, southerners backed it.

Bear flag of Republic of California raised by American settlers at Sonoma **June 14.**

About 12,000 U.S. troops took Vera Cruz Mar. 27, 1847, Mexico City Sept. 14, 1847. By **treaty, Feb. 1848,** Mexico ceded claims to Texas, California, Arizona, New Mexico, Nevada, Utah, part of Colorado. U.S. assumed $3 million American claims and paid Mexico $15 million.

Treaty with Great Britain **June 15** set **boundary in Oregon** territory at 49th parallel (extension of existing line). Expansionists had used slogan "54° 40′ or fight."

**Mormons,** after violent clashes with settlers over polygamy, left Nauvoo, IL, for West under Brigham Young; settled **July 1847 at Salt Lake City, UT.**

Elias Howe invented **sewing machine.**

**1847**

First **adhesive U.S. postage stamps** on sale **July 1;** Benjamin Franklin 5¢, Washington 10¢.

**Ralph Waldo Emerson** published first book of poems; **Henry Wadsworth Longfellow** published *Evangeline.*

**1848**

**Gold discovered Jan. 24** in California; 80,000 prospectors emigrate in **1849.**

Lucretia Mott and Elizabeth Cady Stanton led **Seneca Falls, NY, Women's Rights Convention July 19-20.**

**1850**

Sen. Henry Clay's **Compromise of 1850** admitted California as 31st state **Sept. 9,** with slavery forbidden; made Utah and New Mexico territories without decision on slavery; made Fugitive Slave Law more harsh; ended District of Columbia slave trade.

**1851**

**Herman Melville's** *Moby Dick,* **Nathaniel Hawthorne's** *House of the Seven Gables* published.

**1852**

*Uncle Tom's Cabin,* by **Harriet Beecher Stowe,** published.

**1853**

**Commodore Matthew C. Perry,** U.S.N., received by Lord of Toda, Japan **July 14; negotiated treaty to open Japan** to U.S. ships.

**1854**

**Republican Party** formed at Ripon, WI, **Feb. 28.** Opposed Kansas-Nebraska Act (became law **May 30**), which left issue of slavery to vote of settlers.

**Henry David Thoreau** published *Walden.*

**1855**

**Walt Whitman** published *Leaves of Grass.*

First railroad train crossed Mississippi on the river's first bridge, Rock Island, IL, Davenport, IA, **Apr. 21.**

**1856**

Republican Party's first nominee for president, **John C. Fremont,** defeated. Abraham Lincoln made 50 speeches for him.

**Lawrence, KS,** sacked **May 21** by proslavery group; abolitionist **John Brown** led antislavery men against Missourians at **Osawatomie, KS, Aug. 30.**

**1857**

**Dred Scott decision** by U.S. Supreme Court **Mar. 6** held, 6-3, that a slave did not become free when taken into a free state, Congress could not bar slavery from a territory, and blacks could not be citizens.

**1858**

First **Atlantic cable** completed by Cyrus W. Field **Aug. 5;** cable failed **Sept. 1.**

**Lincoln-Douglas debates** in Illinois **Aug. 21-Oct. 15.**

**1859**

First commercially productive **oil well,** drilled near Titusville, PA, by Edwin L. Drake **Aug. 27.**

Abolitionist **John Brown,** with 21 men, seized U.S. Armory at **Harpers Ferry (then Virginia) Oct. 16.** U.S. Marines captured raiders, killing several. Brown was hanged for treason by Virginia **Dec. 2.**

**1860**

Approximately 20,000 **New England shoe workers** went on strike **Feb. 22** and won higher wages.

**Abraham Lincoln,** Republican, elected president in 4-way race.

First **Pony Express** between Sacramento, CA, and St. Joseph, MO, started **Apr. 3;** service ended **Oct. 24, 1861,** when first transcontinental telegraph line was completed.

**1861**

Seven southern states set up **Confederate States of America Feb. 8,** with Jefferson Davis as president, captured federal arsenals and forts. **Civil War** began as Confederates fired on **Ft. Sumter** in Charleston, SC, **Apr. 12;** they captured it **Apr. 14.**

President **Lincoln called for 75,000 volunteers Apr. 15.** By **May,** 11 states had seceded. Lincoln blockaded southern ports **Apr. 19,** cutting off vital exports, aid.

Confederates repelled Union forces at first **Battle of Bull Run July 21.**

First **transcontinental telegraph** was put in operation.

**1862**

**Homestead Act** was approved **May 20;** it granted free family farms to settlers.

**Land Grant Act** approved **July 7,** providing for public land sale to benefit agricultural education; eventually led to establishment of state university systems.

Union forces were victorious in western campaigns, took **New Orleans.** Battles in East were inconclusive.

**1863**

Lincoln issued **Emancipation Proclamation Jan. 1,** freeing "all slaves in areas still in rebellion."

The entire **Mississippi River** was in Union hands by **July 4.** Union forces won a major victory at **Gettysburg, PA, July 1-3.** Lincoln read his **Gettysburg Address Nov. 19.**

In **draft riots** in New York City about 1,000 were killed or wounded; some blacks were hanged by mobs **July 13-16.** Rioters protested provision allowing money payment in place of service. Such payments were ended **1864.**

**1864**

**Gen. Sherman marched through Georgia,** taking Atlanta **Sept. 1,** Savannah **Dec. 22.**

**Sand Creek massacre** of Cheyenne and Arapaho Indians **Nov. 29.** Cavalry attacked Indians who were awaiting surrender terms.

**1865**

**Gen. Robert E. Lee surrendered** 27,800 Confederate troops to Gen. Ulysses S. Grant at Appomattox Court House, VA, **Apr. 9.** J. E. Johnston surrendered 31,200 to Sherman at Durham Station, NC, **Apr. 18.** Last rebel troops surrendered **May 26.**

President **Lincoln was shot Apr. 14** by John Wilkes Booth in Ford's Theater, Washington, DC; died the following morning. Booth was reported dead **Apr. 26.** Four co-conspirators were hanged **July 7.**

**Thirteenth Amendment,** abolishing slavery, was ratified **Dec. 6.**

**1866**

**Ku Klux Klan** formed secretly in South to terrorize blacks who voted. Disbanded **1869-71.** A second Klan was organized **1915.**

Congress took control of southern Reconstruction, backed freedmen's rights.

**1867**

**Alaska** sold to U.S. by Russia for $7.2 million **Mar. 30** through efforts of Sec. of State William H. Seward.

**Horatio Alger** published first book, *Ragged Dick.*

The **Grange** was organized **Dec. 4,** to protect farmer interests.

**1868**

***The World Almanac,*** a publication of the *New York World,* appeared for the first time.

Pres. **Andrew Johnson** tried to remove Edwin M. Stanton, secretary of war; was impeached by House **Feb. 24** for violation of Tenure of Office Act; acquitted by Senate **March-May.** Stanton resigned.

**1869**

Financial **"Black Friday"** in New York **Sept. 24;** caused by attempt to "corner" gold.

**Transcontinental railroad** completed; golden spike driven at Promontory, UT, **May 10,** marking the junction of Central Pacific and Union Pacific.

**Knights of Labor** formed in Philadelphia. By **1886,** this labor union had 700,000 members nationally.

**Woman suffrage** law passed in Territory of Wyoming on **Dec. 10.**

**1871**

**Great fire destroyed Chicago Oct. 8-11;** loss estimated at $196 million.

**1872**

**Amnesty Act** restored civil rights to citizens of the South **May 22** except for 500 Confederate leaders.

Congress founded first national park—**Yellowstone** in Wyoming.

**1873**

First U.S. **postal card** issued **May 1.**

**Banks failed,** panic began in **Sept.** Depression lasted 5 years.

**"Boss" William Tweed** of New York City convicted of stealing public funds. He died in jail in **1878.**

Bellevue Hospital in New York City started the first **school of nursing.**

**1875**

Congress passed **Civil Rights Act Mar. 1,** giving equal rights to blacks in public accommodations and jury duty. Act invalidated in **1883** by Supreme Court.

First **Kentucky Derby** held **May 17** at Churchill Downs, Louisville, KY.

**1876**

**Samuel J. Tilden,** Democrat, received majority of popular votes for president over **Rutherford B. Hayes,** Republican, but 22 electoral votes were in dispute; issue left to Congress. Hayes given presidency **in Feb. 1877** after Republicans agree to end Reconstruction of South.

Col. **George A. Custer** and 264 soldiers of the 7th Cavalry killed **June 25** in "last stand," Battle of the Little Big Horn, MT, in Sioux Indian War.

**Mark Twain** published *Tom Sawyer.*

**1877**

**Molly Maguires,** Irish terrorist society in Scranton, PA, mining areas, broken up by hanging of 11 leaders for murders of mine officials and police.

Pres. Rutherford B. Hayes sent troops in violent national **railroad strike.**

**1878**

First commercial **telephone** exchange opened, New Haven, CT, **Jan. 28.**

Thomas A. Edison founded **Edison Electric Light Co.** on **Oct. 15.**

**1879**

**F. W. Woolworth** opened his first five-and-ten store in Utica, NY, **Feb. 22.**

**Henry George** published *Progress & Poverty,* advocating single tax on land.

**1881**

Pres. **James A. Garfield shot** in Washington, DC, **July 2;** died **Sept. 19.**

**Booker T. Washington** founded Tuskegee Institute for blacks.

**Helen Hunt Jackson** published *A Century of Dishonor,* about mistreatment of Indians.

**1883**

**Pendleton Act,** passed **Jan. 16,** reformed federal civil service.

**Brooklyn Bridge** opened **May 24.**

**1884**

**Mark Twain**'s masterpiece, *The Adventures of Huckleberry Finn,* appeared.

**1886**

**Haymarket riot** and bombing, evening of **May 4,** followed bitter labor battles for 8-hour day in Chicago; 7 police and 4 workers died, 66 wounded. Eight anarchists found guilty. Gov. John P. Altgeld denounced trial as unfair.

**Geronimo,** Apache Indian, finally surrendered **Sept. 4.**

The **Statue of Liberty** was dedicated **Oct. 28.**

**American Federation of Labor** (AFL) formed **Dec. 8** by 25 craft unions.

**1888**

**Great blizzard** struck eastern U.S. **Mar. 11-14,** causing about 400 deaths.

**1889**

U.S. declared Oklahoma open to white settlement **Apr. 22;** within 24 hours **claims for 2 million acres** were staked by 50,000 settlers.

**Johnstown, PA, flood May 31;** 2,200 lives lost.

**1890**

First execution by **electrocution:** William Kemmler **Aug. 6** at Auburn Prison, Auburn, NY, for murder.

Battle of **Wounded Knee, SD, Dec. 29,** the last major conflict between Indians and U.S. troops. About 200 Indian men, women, and children and 29 soldiers were killed.

**Sherman Antitrust Act** began federal effort to curb monopolies.

**Jacob Riis** published *How the Other Half Lives,* about city slums.

**1891**

**Forest Reserve Act Mar. 3** let president close public forest land to settlement for establishment of national parks.

**1892**

**Homestead, PA,** strike at Carnegie steel mills; 7 guards and 11 strikers and spectators shot to death **July 6;** setback for unions.

**Ellis Island** opened as New York immigration depot.

**1893**

**Financial panic** began, led to 4-year depression.

**1894**

Thomas A. **Edison's kinetoscope** (motion pictures) (invented **1887**) given first public showing **Apr. 14.**

**Jacob S. Coxey** led 500 unemployed from the Midwest into Washington, DC, **Apr. 30.** Coxey was arrested for trespassing on Capitol grounds.

**1896**

**William Jennings Bryan** delivered "Cross of Gold" speech **July 8;** won Democratic Party nomination.

Supreme Court, in **Plessy *v* Ferguson,** approved racial segregation under the "separate but equal" doctrine.

**1898**

U.S. **battleship *Maine*** blown up **Feb. 15** at Havana; 260 killed.

**U.S. blockaded Cuba Apr. 22** in aid of independence forces. U.S. declared war on Spain, **Apr. 24,** destroyed Spanish fleet in Philippines **May 1,** took Guam **June 20.**

**Puerto Rico** taken by U.S. **July 25-Aug. 12.** Spain agreed **Dec. 10** to cede Philippines, Puerto Rico, and Guam, and approved independence for Cuba.

U.S. annexed independent republic of **Hawaii.**

**1899**

**Filipino insurgents,** unable to get recognition of independence from U.S., started guerrilla war **Feb. 4.** Their leader, Emilio Aguinaldo, captured **May 23, 1901.** Philippine Insurrection ended 1902.

U.S. declared **Open Door Policy** to make China an open international market and to preserve its integrity as a nation.

**John Dewey** published *School and Society,* backing "progressive education."

**1900**

**Carry Nation,** Kansas antisaloon agitator, began raiding with hatchet.

U.S. helped suppress **"Boxers"** in Beijing.

**International Ladies' Garment Workers Union** was founded in New York City in **November.**

1901

**Texas** had first significant **oil strike, Jan. 10.**

Pres. William **McKinley was shot Sept. 6** by an anarchist, Leon Czolgosz; died **Sept. 14.**

1903

Treaty between U.S. and Colombia to have U.S. dig **Panama Canal** signed **Jan. 22,** rejected by Colombia. Panama declared independence with U.S. support **Nov. 3;** recognized by Pres. Theodore Roosevelt **Nov. 6.** U.S., Panama signed canal treaty **Nov. 18.**

Wisconsin set first **direct primary** voting system **May 23.**

First **automobile trip** across U.S. from San Francisco to New York **May 23-Aug. 1.**

First successful flight in heavier-than-air mechanically propelled airplane by **Orville Wright Dec. 17** near Kitty Hawk, NC, 120 ft in 12 seconds. Fourth flight same day by **Wilbur Wright,** 852 ft in 59 seconds. Improved plane patented **May 22, 1906.**

**Jack London** published *Call of the Wild.*

*Great Train Robbery,* pioneering film, produced.

1904

**Ida Tarbell** published muckraking *History of Standard Oil.*

1905

First **Rotary Club** founded in Chicago **December.**

1906

**San Francisco earthquake** and fire **Apr. 18-19** left 503 dead, $350 million damages.

**Pure Food and Drug Act** and Meat Inspection Act both passed **June 30.**

1907

**Financial panic** and depression started **Mar. 13.**

First round-world cruise of U.S. **"Great White Fleet";** 16 battleships, 12,000 men.

1908

**Henry Ford** introduced **Model T** car, priced at $850 **Oct. 1.**

1909

Adm. Robert E. Peary reached **North Pole Apr. 6** on 6th attempt, accompanied by Matthew Henson, a black man, and 4 Eskimos.

**National Conference on the Negro** convened **May 30,** leading to founding of the National Association for the Advancement of Colored People.

1910

**Boy Scouts** of America founded **Feb. 8.**

1911

Supreme Court dissolved **Standard Oil Co. May 15.**

Building holding NYC's **Triangle Shirtwaist Co.** sweatshop caught fire **Mar. 25;** 146 died, mostly young women; some were trapped and killed, others jumped to their deaths.

First **transcontinental airplane flight** (with numerous stops) by C. P. Rodgers, New York to Pasadena, **Sept. 17-Nov. 5;** time in air 82 hr, 4 min.

1912

American Girl Guides founded **Mar. 12;** name changed in 1913 to **Girl Scouts.**

U.S. sent Marines **Aug. 14** to **Nicaragua,** which was in default of loans to U.S. and Europe.

1913

**NY Armory Show** brought modern art to U.S. **Feb. 17.**

**U.S. blockaded Mexico** in support of revolutionaries.

**Charles Beard** published his *Economic Interpretation of the Constitution.*

**Federal Reserve System** was authorized **Dec. 23,** in a major reform of U.S. banking and finance.

1914

**Ford Motor Co.** raised basic wage rates from $2.40 for 9-hr day to $5 for 8-hr day **Jan. 5.**

When U.S. sailors were arrested at Tampico, Mexico, **Apr. 9,** Atlantic fleet was sent to **Veracruz,** occupied city.

Pres. Wilson proclaimed **U.S. neutrality** in the European war **Aug. 4.**

**Panama Canal** was officially opened **Aug. 15.**

The **Clayton Antitrust Act** was passed **Oct. 15,** strengthening federal antimonopoly powers.

1915

First **telephone talk,** New York to San Francisco, **Jan. 25** by Alexander Graham Bell and Thomas A. Watson.

British ship ***Lusitania*** sunk **May 7** by German submarine; 128 American passengers lost (Germany had warned passengers in advance). As a result of U.S. campaign, Germany issued apology and promise of payments **Oct. 5.** Pres. Wilson asked for a military fund increase **Dec. 7.**

U.S. troops landed in **Haiti July 28.** Haiti became a virtual U.S. protectorate under **Sept. 16** treaty.

1916

Gen. John J. **Pershing entered Mexico** to pursue Francisco (Pancho) Villa, who had raided U.S. border areas. Forces withdrawn **Feb. 5, 1917.**

**Rural Credits** Act passed **July 17,** followed by Warehouse Act **Aug. 11;** both provided financial aid to farmers.

**Bomb exploded** during **San Francisco** Preparedness Day parade **July 22,** killed 10. Thomas J. Mooney, labor organizer, and Warren K. Billings, shoe worker, were convicted; both pardoned in **1939.**

U.S. bought **Virgin Islands** from Denmark **Aug. 4.**

**Jeannette Rankin,** 1st U.S. congresswoman (R, MT), elected.

U.S. established military government in the **Dominican Republic Nov. 29.**

Trade and loans to **European allies** soared during the year.

**John Dewey** published *Democracy and Education.*

**Carl Sandburg** published *Chicago Poems.*

1917

Germany, suffering from British blockade, declared almost unrestricted **submarine warfare Jan. 31.** U.S. cut diplomatic ties with Germany **Feb. 3,** and formally declared war **Apr. 6.**

**Conscription** law was passed **May 18.** First U.S. troops arrived in Europe **June 26.**

The 18th **(Prohibition)** Amendment to the Constitution was submitted to the states by Congress **Dec. 18.** On **Jan. 16, 1919,** the 36th state (Nevada) ratified it. Franklin D. Roosevelt, as 1932 presidential candidate, endorsed repeal; ratification of 21st Amendment, which repealed it, completed **Dec. 5, 1933.**

1918

Pres. Woodrow Wilson set out his **14 Points** as basis for peace **Jan. 8.**

More than 1 million **American troops** were in Europe by **July.** War ended **Nov. 11.**

**Influenza** epidemic killed an estimated 20 million worldwide, 548,000 in U.S.

1919

First **transatlantic flight,** by U.S. Navy seaplane, left Rockaway, NY, **May 8,** stopped at Newfoundland, Azores, Lisbon **May 27.**

**Boston police strike Sept. 9;** National Guard breaks strike.

**Sherwood Anderson** published *Winesburg, Ohio.*

About 250 **alien radicals** were deported **Dec. 22.**

1920

In national **Red Scare,** some 2,700 Communists, anarchists, and other radicals were arrested **Jan.-May.**

Senate refused **Mar. 19** to ratify the **League of Nations Covenant.**

**Nicola Sacco,** 29, shoe factory employee and radical agitator, and **Bartolomeo Vanzetti,** 32, fish peddler and anarchist, accused of killing 2 men in Massachusetts payroll holdup **Apr. 15.** Found guilty **1921.** A 6-year campaign for release on grounds of alleged inconclusive evidence and prejudice failed. Both executed **Aug. 23, 1927.** Controversial verdict in effect reversed **July 19, 1977,** by proclamation of Massachusetts Gov. Michael Dukakis.

First regular licensed **radio broadcasting** begun **Aug. 20.**

**19th Amendment** ratified **Aug. 18,** giving women right to vote.

**League of Women Voters** founded.

**Wall St.,** New York City, **bomb** explosion killed 30, injured 100, did $2 million damage **Sept. 16.**

**Sinclair Lewis's** *Main Street,* **F. Scott Fitzgerald's** *This Side of Paradise* published.

1921

Congress sharply curbed **immigration,** set national quota system **May 19.**

Joint congressional resolution declaring **peace with Germany, Austria, and Hungary** signed **July 2** by Pres. Warren G. Harding; treaties were signed in **August.**

**Limitation of Armaments** Conference met in Washington **Nov. 12-Feb. 6, 1922.** Major powers agreed to curtail naval construction, outlaw poison gas, restrict submarine attacks on merchant vessels, respect integrity of China.

**Ku Klux Klan** began revival with violence against Catholics in North, South, and Midwest.

1922

Violence during **coal-mine strike** at Herrin, IL, **June 22-23** cost 36 lives, 21 of them nonunion miners.

*Reader's Digest* founded.

1923

First **sound-on-film motion picture,** *Phonofilm,* was shown by Lee de Forest at Rivoli Theater, New York City, beginning in **April.**

1924

Law approved by Congress **June 15** making all **Indians citizens.**

**Nellie Tayloe Ross** elected governor of Wyoming **Nov. 9** after death of her husband **Oct. 2;** installed **Jan. 5, 1925,** first woman governor. **Miriam (Ma) Ferguson** elected governor of Texas **Nov. 9;** installed **Jan. 20, 1925.**

**George Gershwin** wrote *Rhapsody in Blue.*

1925

**John T. Scopes** found guilty of having taught evolution in Dayton, TN, high school, fined $100 and costs **July 24.**

1926

Dr. Robert H. Goddard demonstrated practicality of **rockets Mar. 16** at Auburn, MA, with first liquid fuel rocket; rocket traveled 184 ft in 2.5 seconds.

Congress established **Army Air Corps July 2.**

**Air Commerce Act** passed **Nov. 2,** providing federal aid for airlines and airports.

1927

About 1,000 **marines landed in China Mar. 5** to protect property in civil war.

Capt. **Charles A. Lindbergh** left Roosevelt Field, NY, **May 20** alone in plane Spirit of St. Louis on first New York-Paris nonstop flight. Reached Le Bourget airfield **May 21,** 3,610 mi in 33 ½ hours.

*The Jazz Singer,* with **Al Jolson,** demonstrated part-talking pictures in New York City **Oct. 6.**

*Show Boat* opened in New York **Dec. 27.**

**O. E. Rolvaag** published *Giants in the Earth.*

1928

**Herbert Hoover** elected president, defeating **Alfred E. Smith,** the Catholic governor of New York.

**Amelia Earhart** became first woman to fly the Atlantic, **June 17.**

1929

**"St. Valentine's Day massacre"** in Chicago **Feb. 14;** gangsters killed 7 rivals.

Farm price stability aided by **Agricultural Marketing Act,** passed **June 15.**

Albert B. Fall, former secretary of the interior, was convicted of accepting a bribe of $100,000 in the leasing of the **Elk Hills (Teapot Dome)** naval oil reserve; sentenced **Nov. 1** to a year in prison and fined $100,000.

**Stock market crash Oct. 29** marked end of postwar prosperity as stock prices plummeted. Stock losses for 1929-31 estimated at $50 billion; worst American depression began.

**Thomas Wolfe** published *Look Homeward, Angel.* **William Faulkner** published *The Sound and the Fury.*

1930

London **Naval Reduction Treaty** signed by U.S., Britain, Italy, France, and Japan **Apr. 22;** in effect **Jan. 1, 1931;** expired **Dec. 31, 1936.**

**Hawley-Smoot Tariff** signed; rate hikes slash world trade.

1931

**Empire State Building** opened in New York City **May 1.**

**Al Capone** was convicted of tax evasion **Oct. 17.**

**Pearl Buck** published *The Good Earth.*

1932

**Reconstruction Finance Corp.** established **Jan. 22** to stimulate banking and business. Unemployment at 12 million.

**Charles Lindbergh Jr. kidnapped Mar. 1;** found dead **May 12.**

**Bonus March** on Washington, DC, **May 29** by World War I veterans demanding Congress pay their bonus in full.

1933

**Franklin D. Roosevelt** elected president for the first time.

Pres. Roosevelt named **Frances Perkins** U.S. secretary of labor; first woman in U.S. cabinet.

All **banks in the U.S. were ordered closed** by Pres. Roosevelt **Mar. 6.**

In the "100 days" special session, **Mar. 9-June 16,** Congress passed **New Deal** social and economic measures, including measures to regulate banks, distribute funds to the jobless, create jobs, raise agricultural prices, and set wage and production standards for industry.

**Tennessee Valley Authority** created.

**Gold standard dropped** by U.S.; announced by Pres. Roosevelt **Apr. 19,** ratified by Congress **June 5.**

**Prohibition ended** in the U.S. as 36th state ratified 21st Amendment **Dec. 5.**

U.S. foreswore armed intervention in **western hemisphere** nations **Dec. 26.**

1934

U.S. troops pull out of **Haiti Aug. 6.**

1935

Comedian **Will Rogers** and aviator Wiley Post **killed Aug. 15** in Alaska plane crash.

**Social Security** Act passed by Congress **Aug. 14.**

**Huey Long,** senator from Louisiana and national political leader, was **assassinated Sept. 8.**

*Porgy and Bess,* **George Gershwin** opera on American theme, opened **Oct. 10** in New York City.

**Committee for Industrial Organization** (CIO; later Congress of Industrial Organizations) formed to expand industrial unionism **Nov. 9.**

1936

**Boulder Dam** completed.

**Margaret Mitchell** published *Gone With the Wind.*

1937

**Joe Louis** knocked out James J. Braddock, became world heavyweight champ **June 22.**

**Amelia Earhart,** aviator, and copilot Fred Noonan lost **July 2** near Howland Island, in the Pacific.

Pres. Roosevelt asked for 6 additional Supreme Court justices; **"packing" plan** defeated.

**Auto, steel labor unions** won first big contracts.

1938

**Naval Expansion** Act passed **May 17.**

**National minimum wage** enacted **June 25.**

Orson Welles radio dramatization of Martian invasion *War of the Worlds* caused nationwide scare **Oct. 30.**

1939

Pres. Roosevelt asked for **defense budget hike Jan. 5, 12.**

**NY World's Fair** opened **Apr. 30,** closed **Oct. 31;** reopened **May 11, 1940,** and finally closed **Oct. 21.**

Einstein alerted Roosevelt to **A-bomb** opportunity in **Aug. 2** letter.

**U.S. declared its neutrality** in European war **Sept. 5.**

Roosevelt proclaimed a limited **national emergency Sept. 8,** an unlimited emergency **May 27, 1941.** Both ended by Pres. Harry Truman **Apr. 28, 1952.**

**John Steinbeck** published *Grapes of Wrath.*

1940

U.S. okayed sale of **surplus war material** to Britain **June 3;** announced transfer of 50 overaged destroyers **Sept. 3.**

First **peacetime draft** approved **Sept. 14.**

**Richard Wright** published *Native Son.*

1941

The **Four Freedoms** termed essential by Pres. Roosevelt in speech to Congress **Jan. 6:** freedom of speech and religion, freedom from want and fear.

Lend-Lease Act signed **Mar. 11,** providing $7 billion in military credits for Britain. Lend-Lease for USSR approved in **November.**

U.S. occupied **Iceland July 7.**

The **Atlantic Charter,** 8-point declaration of principles, issued by Roosevelt and Winston Churchill **Aug. 14.**

Japan attacked **Pearl Harbor,** Hawaii, 7:55 AM Hawaiian time, **Dec. 7;** 19 ships sunk or damaged, 2,300 dead. U.S. declared war on Japan **Dec. 8,** on Germany and Italy **Dec. 11** after those countries declared war.

1942

Federal government forcibly moved 110,000 **Japanese-Americans** (including 75,000 U.S. citizens) from West Coast to detention camps. Exclusion lasted 3 years.

Battle of **Midway June 4-7** was Japan's first major defeat.

Marines landed on **Guadalcanal Aug. 7;** last Japanese not expelled until **Feb. 9, 1943.**

U.S., Britain invaded North Africa **Nov. 8.**

First **nuclear chain reaction** (fission of uranium isotope U-235) produced at University of Chicago, under physicists Arthur Compton, Enrico Fermi, others **Dec. 2.**

1943

All war contractors barred from **racial discrimination** on **May 27.**

Pres. Roosevelt signed **June 10** the pay-as-you-go income tax bill. Starting **July 1** wage and salary earners were subject to a **paycheck withholding** tax.

**Race riot in Detroit June 21;** 34 dead, 700 injured. Riot in Harlem section of New York City; 6 killed.

U.S. troops invaded Italy **Sept. 9.**

Marines advanced on **Gilbert Island in Nov.**

1944

U.S., Allied forces invaded Europe at **Normandy June 6.**

**G.I. Bill of Rights** signed **June 22,** providing veterans benefits.

U.S. forces landed on **Leyte,** Philippines, **Oct. 20.**

1945

**Yalta Conference** met in the Crimea, USSR, **Feb. 4-11.** Roosevelt, Churchill, and Stalin agreed that their 3 countries, plus France, would occupy Germany and that the Soviet Union would enter war against Japan.

Marines landed on **Iwo Jima Feb. 19;** U.S. forces invaded **Okinawa Apr. 1.**

**Pres. Roosevelt, 63, died** of cerebral hemorrhage in Warm Springs, GA, **Apr. 12;** Vice President **Harry S. Truman** became president.

**Germany surrendered May 7.**

First **atomic bomb,** produced at Los Alamos, NM, exploded at Alamogordo, NM, **July 16.** Bomb dropped on **Hiroshima Aug. 6,** on **Nagasaki Aug. 9.** Japan agreed to surrender, **Aug. 14**; formally surrendered, Sept. 2.

At **Potsdam Conference, July 17-Aug. 2,** leaders of U.S., USSR, and Britain agreed on disarmament of Germany, occupation zones, war crimes trials.

U.S. forces entered **Korea** south of 38th parallel to displace Japanese **Sept. 8.**

**Gen. Douglas MacArthur** took over supervision of Japan **Sept. 9.**

1946

Strike by 400,000 **mine workers** began **Apr. 1;** other industries followed.

**Philippines** given independence by U.S. **July 4.**

1947

**Truman Doctrine:** Pres. Truman asked Congress to aid Greece and Turkey to combat Communist terrorism **Mar. 12.** Approved **May 15.**

United Nations Security Council voted unanimously **Apr. 2** to place under **U.S. trusteeship** the Pacific islands formerly mandated to Japan.

**Jackie Robinson** joined the Brooklyn Dodgers **Apr. 11,** breaking the color barrier in major league baseball.

**Taft-Hartley** Labor Act curbing strikes was vetoed by Truman **June 20;** Congress overrode the veto.

Proposals known as the **Marshall Plan,** under which the U.S. would extend aid to European countries, were made by Secretary of State George C. Marshall **June 5.** Congress authorized some $12 billion in next 4 years.

1948

The USSR began a land **blockade of Berlin's** Allied sectors **Apr. 1.** This blockade and Western counterblockade were lifted **Sept. 30, 1949,** after British and U.S. planes had lifted 2,343,315 tons of food and coal into the city.

**Organization of American States** founded **Apr. 30.**

**Alger Hiss,** former State Department official, indicted **Dec. 15** for perjury, after denying he had passed secret documents to Whittaker Chambers for transmission to a Communist spy ring. His second trial ended in conviction **Jan. 21, 1950,** and a sentence of 5 years in prison.

**Kinsey Report** on sexuality in the human male published.

1949

U.S. troops withdrawn from **Korea June 29.**

North Atlantic Treaty Organization **(NATO)** established **Aug. 24** by U.S., Canada, and 10 Western European nations, agreeing that an armed attack against one or more of them would be considered an attack against all.

Mrs. I. Toguri D'Aquino **(Tokyo Rose** of Japanese wartime broadcasts) was sentenced **Oct. 7** to 10 years in prison for treason. Paroled **1956,** pardoned **1977.**

Eleven leaders of **U.S. Communist Party** convicted **Oct. 14,** after 9-month trial in New York City, of advocating violent overthrow of U.S. government. Ten defendants sentenced to 5 years in prison each, and the 11th to 3 years. Supreme Court upheld the convictions **June 4, 1951.**

1950

U.S. **Jan. 14** recalled all consular officials from **China** after the latter seized the American consulate general in Beijing.

Masked bandits robbed **Brink's, Inc.,** Boston express office, **Jan. 17** of $2.8 million, of which $1.2 million was in cash. Case solved **1956;** 8 sentenced to life.

Pres. Truman authorized production of **H-bomb Jan. 31.**

United Nations asked for troops to restore Korea peace **June 25.**

Truman ordered Air Force and Navy to Korea **June 27** after North Korea invaded South. Truman approved ground forces, air strikes against North **June 30.**

U.S. sent 35 military advisers to **South Vietnam June 27,** and agreed to provide military and economic aid to anti-Communist government.

**Army seized all railroads Aug. 27** on Truman's order to prevent a general strike; RR returned to owners in **1952.**

**U.S. forces landed at Inchon Sept. 15;** UN force took Pyongyang **Oct. 20,** reached China border **Nov. 20,** China sent troops across border **Nov. 26.**

Two members of a **Puerto Rican nationalist** movement tried to kill Pres. Truman **Nov. 1.**

U.S. **Dec. 8** banned shipments to **Communist China** and to Asiatic ports trading with it.

1951

**Sen. Estes Kefauver** led Senate investigation into organized crime. Preliminary report **Feb. 28** said gambling take was more than $20 billion a year.

**Julius Rosenberg,** his wife, Ethel, and Morton Sobell, all U.S. citizens, were found guilty **Mar. 29** of conspiracy to commit wartime espionage. Rosenbergs sentenced to death, Sobell to 30 years. Rosenbergs **executed June 19, 1953.** Sobell released **Jan. 14, 1969.**

**Gen. Douglas MacArthur** was removed from his Korea command **Apr. 11** by Pres. Truman for unauthorized policy statements.

Korea cease-fire talks began in July; lasted 2 years. **Fighting ended July 27, 1953.**

**Tariff concessions** by the U.S. to the Soviet Union, Communist China, and all Communist-dominated lands were suspended **Aug. 1.**

The **U.S., Australia,** and **New Zealand** signed a mutual security pact **Sept. 1.**

**Transcontinental television** inaugurated **Sept. 4** with Pres. Truman's address at the Japanese Peace Treaty Conference in San Francisco.

**Japanese Peace Treaty** signed in San Francisco **Sept. 8** by U.S., Japan, and 47 other nations.

**J. D. Salinger** published *Catcher in the Rye.*

1952

U.S. **seizure of nation's steel mills** was ordered by Pres. Truman **Apr. 8** to avert a strike. Ruled illegal by Supreme Court **June 2.**

**Peace contract** between West Germany, U.S., Great Britain, and France was signed **May 26.**

The last racial and ethnic barriers to naturalization were removed, **June 26-27,** with the passage of the **Immigration and Naturalization Act of 1952.**

First **hydrogen device** explosion **Nov. 1** at Eniwetok Atoll in Pacific.

1953

Pres. Dwight D. Eisenhower announced **May 8** that the U.S. had given France $60 million for **Indochina War.** More aid was announced in **September.** In **1954** it was reported that three fourths of the war's costs were met by the U.S.

1954

***Nautilus,*** first atomic-powered submarine, was launched at Groton, CT, **Jan. 21.**

Five members of Congress were wounded in the House **Mar. 1** by 4 **Puerto Rican independence supporters** who fired at random from a spectators' gallery.

**Sen. Joseph McCarthy** (R, WI) led televised hearings **Apr. 22-June 17** into alleged Communist influence in the Army.

**Racial segregation** in public schools was unanimously ruled unconstitutional by the Supreme Court **May 17,** as a violation of the 14th Amendment clause guaranteeing equal protection of the laws.

Southeast Asia Treaty Organization **(SEATO)** formed by collective defense pact signed in Manila **Sept. 8** by the U.S., Britain, France, Australia, New Zealand, Philippines, Pakistan, and Thailand.

Condemnation of **Sen. McCarthy** voted by Senate, 67-22, **Dec. 2** for contempt of a Senate elections subcommittee, abuse of its members, and insults to the Senate during his Army investigation hearings.

**1955**

U.S. agreed **Feb. 12** to help train **South Vietnamese** army.

Supreme Court ordered **"all deliberate speed"** in integration of public schools **May 31.**

A **summit meeting** of leaders of U.S., Britain, France, and USSR took place **July 18-23** in Geneva, Switzerland.

**Rosa Parks** refused **Dec. 1** to give her seat to a white man on a bus in Montgomery, AL. Bus segregation ordinance declared unconstitutional by a federal court following boycott and NAACP protest.

Merger of America's 2 largest labor organizations was effected **Dec. 5** under the name American Federation of Labor and Congress of Industrial Organizations. The merged **AFL-CIO** had a membership estimated at 15 million.

**1956**

**Massive resistance** to Supreme Court desegregation rulings was called for **Mar. 12** by 101 Southern congressmen.

Federal-Aid **Highway Act** signed **June 29,** inaugurating interstate highway system.

First transatlantic **telephone cable** went into operation **Sept. 25.**

**1957**

Congress approved first **civil rights bill** for blacks since Reconstruction **Apr. 29,** to protect voting rights.

National Guardsmen, called out by Arkansas Gov. Orval Faubus **Sept. 4,** barred 9 black students from entering previously all-white Central High School in **Little Rock.** Faubus complied **Sept. 21** with a federal court order to remove the National Guardsmen. The blacks entered school **Sept. 23** but were ordered to withdraw by local authorities because of fear of mob violence. Pres. Eisenhower sent federal troops **Sept. 24** to enforce the court's order.

**Jack Kerouac** published *On the Road.*

**1958**

First U.S. earth satellite to go into orbit, **Explorer I,** launched by Army **Jan. 31** at Cape Canaveral, FL; discovered Van Allen radiation belt.

Five thousand U.S. Marines sent to **Lebanon** to protect elected government from threatened overthrow **July-October.**

First domestic **jet airline** passenger service in U.S. opened by National Airlines **Dec. 10** between New York and Miami.

**1959**

**Alaska** admitted as 49th state **Jan. 3; Hawaii** admitted **Aug. 21.**

**St. Lawrence Seaway** opened **Apr. 25.**

Soviet **Premier Nikita Khrushchev** paid unprecedented visit to U.S. **Sept. 15-27,** made transcontinental tour.

**1960**

**Sit-ins** began **Feb. 1** when 4 black college students in Greensboro, NC, refused to move from a Woolworth lunch counter when denied service. By **Sept. 1961** more than 70,000 students, whites and blacks, had participated in sit-ins.

Congress approved a strong **voting rights act Apr. 21.**

A **U-2 reconnaisance plane** of the U.S. was shot down in the Soviet Union **May 1.** The incident led to cancellation of an imminent Paris summit conference.

U.S. announced **Dec. 15** it backed rightist group in **Laos,** which took power the next day.

**1961**

The U.S. severed diplomatic and consular relations with **Cuba Jan. 3,** after disputes over nationalizations of U.S. firms, U.S. military presence at Guantanamo base.

Invasion of Cuba's **"Bay of Pigs" Apr. 17** by Cuban exiles trained, armed, and directed by the U.S., attempting to overthrow the regime of Premier Fidel Castro, failed.

**Peace Corps** created by executive order, **Mar. 1.**

**Commander Alan B. Shepard Jr.** was rocketed from Cape Canaveral, FL, 116.5 mi above the earth in a Mercury capsule **May 5** in the first U.S.-crewed suborbital space flight.

**"Freedom Rides"** from Washington, DC, across deep South launched in May **to protest segregation** in interstate transportation.

**1962**

**Lt. Col. John H. Glenn Jr.** became the first American in orbit **Feb. 20** when he circled the earth 3 times in the Mercury capsule ***Friendship 7.***

Pres. Kennedy said **Feb. 14** U.S. military advisers in Vietnam would fire if fired upon.

Supreme Court **Mar. 26** backed **"one-man one-vote"** apportionment of seats in state legislatures.

First U.S. **communications satellite** launched in **July.**

**James Meredith** became first black student at University of Mississippi **Oct. 1** after 3,000 troops put down riots.

A Soviet **offensive missile buildup in Cuba** was revealed **Oct. 22** by Pres. Kennedy, who ordered a naval and air quarantine on shipment of offensive military equipment to the island. Kennedy and Soviet Premier Khrushchev reached agreement **Oct. 28** on a formula to end the crisis. Kennedy announced **Nov. 2** that Soviet missile bases in Cuba were being dismantled.

**Rachel Carson's** *Silent Spring* launched environmentalist movement.

**1963**

Supreme Court ruled **Mar. 18** that all **criminal defendants** must have counsel and that illegally acquired evidence was inadmissible in state as well as federal courts.

Supreme Court ruled, 8-1, **June 17** that laws requiring **recitation of the Lord's Prayer** or Bible verses in public schools were unconstitutional.

A limited **nuclear test-ban treaty** was agreed upon **July 25** by the U.S., the Soviet Union, and Britain barring all above ground nuclear tests.

**March on Washington** by 200,000 persons **Aug. 28** in support of **black demands** for equal rights. Highlight was speech in which **Dr. Martin Luther King Jr.** said: "I have a dream that this nation will rise up and live out the true meaning of its creed, 'We hold these truths to be self-evident: that all men are created equal.'"

South Vietnam Pres. **Ngo Dinh Diem assassinated Nov. 2;** U.S. had earlier withdrawn support.

**Pres. John F. Kennedy was shot** and fatally wounded by an assassin **Nov. 22** as he rode in a motorcade through downtown Dallas, TX. Vice Pres. Lyndon B. Johnson was sworn in as president shortly after in Dallas. Lee Harvey Oswald arrested and charged with the murder. He was shot and fatally wounded **Nov. 24** by Jack Ruby, 52, a Dallas nightclub owner, who was convicted of murder **Mar. 14, 1964,** and sentenced to death. Ruby died of natural causes **Jan. 3, 1967,** while awaiting retrial.

U.S. troops in **Vietnam** totaled more than 15,000 by year's end; U.S. aid to South Vietnam came to more than $500 million in **1963.**

**Betty Friedan's** *Feminine Mystique* ignites the women's movement.

**1964**

**Panama** suspended relations with U.S. **Jan. 9** after riots. U.S. offered **Dec. 18** to negotiate a new canal treaty.

Supreme Court ordered **Feb. 17** that **congressional districts** have equal populations.

U.S. reported **May 27** it was sending military planes to **Laos.**

Omnibus **civil rights bill** cleared by Congress **July 2,** signed same day by Pres. Johnson, banning discrimination in voting, jobs, public accommodations.

Three **civil rights workers** were reported missing in Mississippi **June 22;** found buried **Aug. 4.** Twenty-one white men were arrested. On **Oct. 20, 1967,** an all-white federal jury convicted 7 of conspiracy in the slayings.

Bill establishing **Medicare,** government health insurance program for persons over 65, signed **July 30.**

U.S. Congress **Aug. 7** passed **Tonkin Gulf Resolution,** authorizing presidential action in Vietnam, after N Vietnamese boats reportedly attacked 2 U.S. destroyers **Aug. 2.**

Congress approved **War on Poverty bill Aug. 11,** providing for a domestic Peace Corps **(VISTA),** a **Job Corps,** and antipoverty funding.

The **Warren Commission** released **Sept. 27** a report concluding that Lee Harvey Oswald was solely responsible for the Kennedy assassination.

**Pres. Johnson was elected** to a full term, **Nov. 3,** defeating conservative Republican **Sen. Barry Goldwater** (AZ) in a landslide.

**1965**

Pres. Johnson in **Feb.** ordered continuous **bombing of North Vietnam** below 20th parallel.

Some 14,000 U.S. troops sent to **Dominican Republic** during civil war **Apr. 28.** All troops withdrawn by next year.

**March from Selina to Montgomery,** AL, led by Martin Luther King Jr. to demand federal protection of **blacks' voting rights.** New **Voting Rights Act** signed **Aug. 6.**

Los Angeles riot by blacks living in **Watts** area resulted in death of 34 persons and property damage estimated at $200 million **Aug. 11-16.**

National origins quota system of **immigration** abolished **Oct. 3.**

**Electric power failure** blacked out most of northeastern U.S., parts of 2 Canadian provinces the night of **Nov. 9-10.**

U.S. forces in **S. Vietnam** reached 184,300 by year-end.

**1966**

U.S. forces began firing into **Cambodia May 1.**

**Bombing of Hanoi** area of N Vietnam by U.S. planes began **June 29.** By **Dec. 31,** 385,300 U.S. troops were stationed in S Vietnam, plus 60,000 offshore and 33,000 in Thailand.

**Medicare** began **July 1.**

**Edward Brooke** (R, MA) elected **Nov. 8** as first black U.S. senator in 85 years.

**1967**

Black representative **Adam Clayton Powell** (D, NY) was denied **Mar. 1** his seat in Congress because of charges he misused government funds. Reelected in 1968, he was seated, but fined $25,000 and stripped of his 22 years' seniority.

Pres. Johnson and Soviet Premier Aleksei Kosygin met **June 23 and 25** at **Glassboro State College** in NJ; agreed not to let any crisis push them into war.

The **25th Amendment,** providing for **presidential succession,** was ratified **Feb. 10.**

Riots by blacks in **Newark, NJ, July 12-17** killed 26, injured 1,500; more than 1,000 arrested. In Detroit, MI, **July 23-30,** more than 40 died; 2,000 injured, 5,000 left homeless by rioting, looting, burning in city's black ghetto.

**Thurgood Marshall** sworn in **Oct. 2** as first black U.S. Supreme Court Justice. Carl B. Stokes (D, Cleveland) and Richard G. Hatcher (D, Gary, IN) were elected first black mayors of major U.S. cities **Nov. 7.**

By **December** 475,000 U.S. troops were in **South Vietnam.**

**1968**

***USS Pueblo*** and 83-man crew seized in Sea of Japan **Jan. 23** by North Koreans; 82 men released **Dec. 22.**

**"Tet offensive":** Communist troops attacked Saigon, 30 province capitals **Jan. 30,** suffer heavy casualties.

Pres. Johnson **curbed bombing** of North Vietnam **Mar. 31.** Peace talks began in Paris **May 10.** All bombing of North halted **Oct. 31.**

**Martin Luther King Jr., 39, assassinated Apr. 4** in Memphis, TN. James Earl Ray, an escaped convict, pleaded guilty to the slaying, was sentenced to 99 years.

**Sen. Robert F. Kennedy** (D, NY), 42, **shot June 5** in Hotel Ambassador, Los Angeles, after celebrating presidential primary victories. Died **June 6.** Sirhan Bishara Sirhan, Jordanian, convicted of murder.

Vice Pres. **Hubert Humphrey nominated** for president by Democrats **at national convention in Chicago,** marked by clash between police and **antiwar protesting, Aug. 26-29.**

The Republican nominee, **Richard Nixon, won the presidency,** defeating Hubert Humphrey in a close race **Nov. 5.**

**Rep. Shirley Chisholm** (D, NY) became the first black woman elected to Congress.

**1969**

Expanded 4-party **Vietnam peace talks** began **Jan. 18.** U.S. force peaked at 543,400 in April. Withdrawal started **July 8.** Pres. Nixon set Vietnamization policy **Nov. 3.**

U.S. astronaut **Neil A. Armstrong,** 38, commander of the Apollo 11 mission, became the first person to **set foot on the moon, July 20.**

**Woodstock music festival** near Bethel, NY, drew 300,000-500,000 people, **Aug. 15-17.**

Anti-Vietnam War **demonstrations reached peak** in U.S.; some 250,000 marched in Washington, DC, **Nov. 15.**

Massacre of hundreds of civilians at **Mylai, South Vietnam,** in 1968 incident reported **Nov. 16.**

**1970**

United Mine Workers official **Joseph A. Yablonski,** his wife, and their daughter were found shot **Jan. 5** in their Clarksville, PA, home. UMW chief W. A. (Tony) Boyle was later convicted of the killing.

A federal jury **Feb. 18** found the **"Chicago 7"** antiwar activists innocent of conspiring to incite riots during the 1968 Democratic National Convention. However, 5 were convicted of crossing state lines with intent to incite riots.

Millions of Americans participated in antipollution demonstrations **Apr. 22** to mark the first **Earth Day.**

U.S. and South Vietnamese forces crossed **Cambodian** borders **Apr. 30** to get at enemy bases. Four students were killed **May 4** at **Kent State** University in Ohio by National Guardsmen during a protest against the war.

Two **women generals,** the first in U.S. history, were named by Pres. Nixon **May 15.**

A **postal reform** measure was signed **Aug. 12,** creating an independent U.S. Postal Service, ending governmental control of the U.S. mails after almost 2 centuries.

**1971**

**Charles Manson,** 36, and 3 of his cult followers were found guilty **Jan. 26** of first-degree murder in the 1969 slaying of actress Sharon Tate and 6 others.

The 26th Amendment, lowering the **voting age to 18** in all elections, was ratified **June 20.**

A court-martial jury Mar. 29, convicted **Lt. William L. Calley Jr.** of premeditated murder of 22 South Vietnamese at Mylai on **Mar. 16, 1968.** He was sentenced to life imprisonment **Mar. 31.** Sentence was reduced to 20 years **Aug. 20.**

Publication of classified **Pentagon papers** on the U.S. involvement in Vietnam was begun **June 13** by the *New York Times.* In a 6-3 vote, the U.S. Supreme Court **June 30** upheld the right of the *Times* and the *Washington Post* to publish the documents under the protection of the First Amendment.

U.S. bombers struck massively in North Vietnam for 5 days starting **Dec. 26,** in retaliation for alleged violations of agreements reached prior to the 1968 bombing halt. U.S. forces at year-end were down to 140,000.

**1972**

Pres. Nixon arrived in **Beijing Feb. 21** for an 8-day visit to China, which he called a "journey for peace." The unprecedented visit ended with a joint communiqué pledging that both powers would work for "a normalization of relations."

By a vote of 84 to 8, the Senate approved **Mar. 22** a constitutional amendment banning **discrimination** on the basis of sex and sent the measure to the states for ratification.

**North Vietnamese** forces launched the biggest attacks in 4 years across the demilitarized zone **Mar. 30.** The U.S. responded **Apr. 15** by resumption of bombing of Hanoi and Haiphong after a 4-year lull.

Nixon announced **May 8** the mining of **North Vietnam ports.** Last U.S. combat troops left **Aug. 11.**

**Alabama Gov. George C. Wallace,** campaigning for the presidency at a Laurel, MD, shopping center **May 15, was shot** and seriously wounded. Arthur H. Bremer, 21, was sentenced to 63 years for shooting Wallace and 3 bystanders.

In the first visit of a U.S. president to Moscow, Nixon arrived **May 22** for a week of summit talks with Kremlin leaders that culminated in a landmark **strategic arms pact.**

Five men were arrested **June 17** for breaking into the offices of the Democratic National Committee in the **Watergate** office complex in Washington, DC.

Full-scale bombing of North Vietnam resumed after Paris peace negotiations reached an impasse **Dec. 18.**

**1973**

Five of seven defendants in the **Watergate** break-in trial pleaded guilty **Jan. 11 and 15,** and the other 2 were convicted **Jan. 30.**

In **Roe *v* Wade,** the Supreme Court ruled, 7-2, **Jan. 22,** that a state may not prevent a woman from having an **abortion** during the **first 3 months of pregnancy** and that a state may regulate but may not prohibit abortions during the 2d trimester.

Four-party **Vietnam peace pacts** were signed in Paris **Jan. 27,** and North Vietnam released some 590 U.S. prisoners by **Apr. 1.** Last U.S. troops left **Mar. 29.**

The **end of the military draft** was announced **Jan. 27.**

Top **Nixon aides** H. R. Haldeman, John D. Ehrlichman, and John W. Dean and Attorney General Richard Kleindienst **resigned Apr. 30** amid charges of White House efforts to obstruct justice in the Watergate case.

**John Dean,** former Nixon counsel, told Senate hearings **June 25** that Nixon, his staff and campaign aides, and the Justice Department had conspired to cover up Watergate facts.

The U.S. officially ceased bombing in **Cambodia** at midnight **Aug. 14** in accord with a June congressional action.

**Vice President Spiro T. Agnew Oct. 10 resigned** and pleaded nolo contendere (no contest) to charges of tax evasion on payments made to him by Maryland contractors when he was governor of that state. Gerald R. Ford **Oct. 12** became first appointed vice president under the 25th Amendment; sworn in **Dec. 6.**

A total ban on **oil exports** to the U.S. was imposed by Arab oil-producing nations **Oct. 19-21** after the outbreak of an Arab-Israeli war. The ban was lifted **Mar. 18, 1974.**

**Attorney General Elliot Richardson** resigned, and his deputy William D. Ruckelshaus and Watergate Special Prosecutor Archibald Cox were fired by Pres. Nixon **Oct. 20,** when Cox threatened to secure a judicial ruling that Nixon was violating a court order to turn tapes over to Watergate case Judge John Sirica.

**Leon Jaworski,** conservative Texas Democrat, was named **Nov. 1** by the Nixon administration to be special prosecutor to succeed Archibald Cox.

Congress overrode **Nov. 7** Nixon's veto of the **war powers** bill, which curbed the president's power to commit armed forces to hostilities abroad without congressional approval.

### 1974

**Impeachment** hearings were opened **May 9** against Pres. Nixon by the House Judiciary Committee.

John D. Ehrlichman and 3 **White House "plumbers"** were found guilty **July 12** of conspiring to violate the civil rights of a former psychiatrist to Pentagon Papers leaker Daniel Ellsberg, by breaking into his Beverly Hills, CA, office.

The U.S. Supreme Court ruled, 8-0, **July 24** that Nixon had to turn over **64 tapes** of White House conversations sought by Watergate Special Prosecutor Jaworski.

The House Judiciary Committee, in televised hearings **July 24-30,** recommended 3 **articles of impeachment** against Nixon. The first, voted 27-11 **July 27,** charged Nixon with taking part in a criminal conspiracy to obstruct justice in the Watergate cover-up. The 2d, voted 28-10 **July 29,** charged a series of alleged abuses of power. The 3d, voted 21-17 **July 30,** accused him of unconstitutional defiance of committee subpoenas. The House of Representatives voted without debate **Aug. 20,** by 412-3, to accept the committee report, which included the recommended impeachment articles.

**Nixon resigned Aug. 9. Vice President Gerald R. Ford** was sworn in as the 38th U.S. president on the same day.

An **unconditional pardon** to ex-Pres. Nixon for all federal crimes that he "committed or may have committed" while president was issued by Pres. Gerald Ford **Sept. 8.**

### 1975

Found guilty of **Watergate** cover-up charges **Jan. 1** were ex-Atty. Gen. John N. Mitchell, ex-presidential advisers H. R. Haldeman and John D. Ehrlichman.

The U.S. launched an **evacuation of American and some South Vietnamese from Saigon Apr. 29** as Communist forces completed takeover of South Vietnam; the **South Vietnamese** government officially **surrendered Apr. 30.**

U.S. merchant ship ***Mayaguez*** and its crew of 39 were seized by Cambodian forces in Gulf of Siam **May 12.** In rescue operation, U.S. Marines attacked Tang Island, planes bombed air base; Cambodia surrendered ship and crew.

Congress voted $405 million for **South Vietnam refugees May 16;** 140,000 were flown to the U.S.

Illegal **CIA operations,** including records on 300,000 persons and groups, and infiltration of agents into black, antiwar, and political movements, were described by a "blue-ribbon" panel headed by Vice Pres. Nelson Rockefeller **June 10.**

FBI agents captured publishing heiress **Patricia (Patty) Hearst,** kidnapped **Feb. 4, 1974,** by militants of the "Symbionese Liberation Army" in San Francisco **Sept. 18** with others. A San Francisco jury convicted her **Mar. 20, 1976,** of bank robbery.

### 1976

The U.S. celebrated its **bicentennial July 4,** marking the 200th anniversary of its independence with festivals, parades, and New York City's Operation Sail, a gathering of tall ships from around the world viewed by 6 million persons.

A mysterious ailment named **"legionnaire's disease"** killed 29 persons who attended an American Legion convention **July 21-24** in Philadelphia. The cause was later found to be a bacterium.

**The *Viking II*** set down on **Mars'** Utopia Plains **Sept. 3,** following the successful landing by *Viking I* **July 20.**

### 1977

Pres. Jimmy Carter **Jan. 21** pardoned most Vietnam War **draft evaders,** who numbered some 10,000.

Convicted murderer **Gary Gilmore** was executed by a Utah firing squad **Jan. 17,** in the first exercise of capital punishment anywhere in the U.S. since **1967.** Gilmore had opposed all attempts to delay the execution.

Pres. Carter signed an act **Aug. 4** creating a new cabinet-level **Energy Department.**

### 1978

U.S. Senate voted **Apr. 18** to turn over the **Panama Canal** to Panama on Dec. 31, 1999; **Mar. 16** vote had given approval to a treaty guaranteeing the area's neutrality after the year 2000.

### 1979

A major accident occurred, **Mar. 28,** at a nuclear reactor on **Three Mile Island** near Middletown, PA, when a partial meltdown released radioactive material.

The federal government announced, **Nov. 1,** a $1.5 billion loan-guarantee plan to aid the nation's 3d largest automaker, **Chrysler Corp.,** which had reported a loss of $460.6 million for the 3d quarter of 1979.

Some 90 people, including 63 Americans, were taken hostage, **Nov. 4,** at the **American embassy in Tehran,** Iran, by militant student followers of Iranian leader Ayatollah Khomeini. He demanded the return of former Shah Muhammad Reza Pahlavi, who was undergoing medical treatment in New York City.

### 1980

Pres. Carter announced, **Jan. 4, punitive measures against the USSR,** including an embargo on the sale of grain and high technology, in retaliation for the Soviet invasion of Afghanistan. At Carter's request, the **U.S. Olympic Committee** voted, **Apr. 12,** against U.S. participation in the Moscow Summer Olympics.

Eight Americans were killed and 5 wounded, **Apr. 24,** in an ill-fated attempt to **rescue the hostages** held by Iranian **militants** at the U.S. Embassy in Tehran.

In the state of Washington, **Mt. St. Helens erupted, May 18,** in a violent blast estimated to be 500 times as powerful as the Hiroshima atomic bomb. The blast, followed by others on **May 25** and **June 12,** left about 60 dead and economic losses estimated at nearly $3 billion.

In a sweeping victory, **Nov. 4, Ronald Wilson Reagan** was elected 40th president of the U.S., defeating incumbent Jimmy Carter. Republicans also gained control of the Senate.

Former Beatle **John Lennon** was shot and killed, **Dec. 8,** outside his apartment building in New York City.

### 1981

Minutes after the **inauguration of Pres. Ronald Reagan, Jan. 20,** the **52 Americans** who had been held **hostage in Iran** for 444 days were flown to freedom following an arrangement in which the U.S. agreed to return to Iran $8 billion in frozen assets.

**Pres. Reagan** was **shot in the chest** by a would-be assassin, **Mar. 30,** in Washington, DC, as he walked to his limousine following an address.

The world's first reusable spacecraft, the **space shuttle** *Columbia,* was sent into space, **Apr. 12.**

Congress passed, **July 29,** Pres. Reagan's **tax-cut legislation.** The largest tax cut in the nation's history was expected to save taxpayers $750 billion over the next 5 years.

**Federal air traffic controllers, Aug. 3,** began an **illegal nationwide strike.** Most defied a back-to-work order and were dismissed by Reagan **Aug. 5.**

In a 99-0 vote, the Senate confirmed, **Sept. 21,** the appointment of **Sandra Day O'Connor** as an **associate justice of the U.S. Supreme Court.** She was the first woman appointed to that body.

### 1982

The 13-year-old lawsuit against **AT&T** by the **Justice Dept.** was settled **Jan. 8.** AT&T agreed to give up the 22 Bell System companies; in return it was allowed to expand into such areas as data processing, telephone and computer equipment sales, and computer communication devices.

**The Equal Rights Amendment was defeated** after a 10-year struggle for ratification.

In December, the **unemployment rate** rose to 10.8%, the highest since 1940.

The **space shuttle** *Columbia* completed its first operational flight **Nov. 16.**

A retired dentist, **Dr. Barney B. Clark,** 61, became the first recipient of a **permanent artificial heart** during a 7½ hour operation in Salt Lake City **Dec. 2.**

**1983**

On **Apr. 20, Pres. Reagan** signed a compromise, bipartisan bill designed to rescue the **Social Security System** from bankruptcy.

In an 8-1 decision, **the U.S. Supreme Court** held, **May 24,** that the **Internal Revenue Service** could deny **tax exemptions** to **private schools** that practiced **racial discrimination.**

**Sally Ride** became the first American **woman** to travel in **space, June 18,** when the **space shuttle** *Challenger* was launched from Cape Canaveral, FL.

On **Sept. 1, a South Korean passenger jet** infringing on Soviet air space was **shot down;** 269 people killed.

On **Oct. 23,** 241 **U.S. Marines and sailors,** members of the multinational **peacekeeping force** in **Lebanon,** were killed when a TNT-laden suicide bomb blew up Marine headquarters at **Beirut** International Airport.

**U.S. Marines and Rangers** and a small force from 6 **Caribbean** nations invaded the island of **Grenada** on **Oct. 25,** in response to a request from the **Organization of Eastern Caribbean States.** After a few days, Grenadian militia and Cuban "construction workers" were overcome, hundreds of U.S. citizens evacuated safely, and the Marxist regime deposed. The U.S. Congress applied the War Powers Resolution, requiring U.S. troops to leave Grenada by **Dec. 24.**

**1984**

The space shuttle *Challenger* was launched on its 4th trip into space, **Feb. 3.** On **Feb. 7,** Navy Capt. Bruce McCandless, followed by Army Lt. Colonel Robert Stewart, **became the first humans to fly free of a spacecraft.**

On **May 7,** American **Vietnam war** veterans reached an **out-of-court settlement with 7 chemical companies** in their class-action suit regarding the herbicide **Agent Orange.**

On **June 6,** former vice president **Walter Mondale** won the **Democratic presidental nomination.** In a historic move, **July 12, Mondale chose a woman, Rep. Geraldine Ferraro (D, NY)** as candidate for **vice president.**

**Ronald Reagan** was reelected U.S. president **Nov. 6** in the greatest Republican **landslide** in history, carrying 49 states against Walter F. Mondale.

**1985**

**"Live Aid,"** a 17-hour rock concert broadcast **July 13** on radio and TV from London and Philadelphia to 152 countries, raised $70 million for the starving peoples of Africa.

On **June 14** a TWA jet was seized by terrorists after takeoff from Athens; 153 passengers and crew held hostage for 17 days; 1 U.S. serviceman killed.

On **Oct. 7, 4 Palestinian hijackers seized an Italian cruise ship, the** ***Achille Lauro,*** in the open sea as it approached Port Said, Egypt. More than 400 passengers and crew were held hostage for 2 days; one American, Leon Klinghoffer, was killed.

For the first time in 6 years, the leaders of the U.S. and the Soviet Union met at a **summit conference, Nov. 19-20,** in Geneva, Switzerland.

**1986**

On **Jan. 20,** for the first time, the U.S. officially observed **Martin Luther King Jr. Day.**

Moments after liftoff, **Jan. 28,** the **space shuttle** ***Challenger*** **exploded, killing 6 astronauts and Christa McAuliffe, a New Hampshire teacher on board.** Subsequent investigations found that NASA had not taken adequate safety precautions.

U.S. officials predicted, **June 12, that AIDS cases and deaths would increase tenfold in the next 5 years.** At that time, the government had recorded 21,517 cases, 11,713 deaths. An antiviral drug, azidothymidine (AZT), was found to improve the health of some AIDS patients.

The U.S., **via Congress's Sept. override of Pres. Reagan's veto,** joined other nations in imposing **economic sanctions on South Africa,** pressuring the government to end apartheid.

The U.S. Senate confirmed, **Sept. 17,** Pres. Reagan's nomination of **William Rehnquist as chief justice and Antonin Scalia as associate justice of the Supreme Court.**

Congress passed, in late **September,** a comprehensive **tax reform law.** It simplified the system, drastically changing tax brackets, deductions, and more.

In the **congressional races, Nov. 4, Democrats won a 55-45 Senate majority,** after 6 years of Republican majority, and **enlarged their House majority by 5, to 258-177.**

Press reports **Nov. 6** broke first news of the **Iran-contra scandal,** involving secret U.S. sale of arms to Iran.

The most scandalous year in Wall Street history ended with **Ivan Boesky's agreeing, Nov. 14,** to **plead guilty** to an unspecified criminal count, pay a $100 million fine, and return profits; he was barred for life from trading securities.

**1987**

Pres. Reagan produced the nation's first **trillion-dollar budget, Jan. 5.**

The stock market continued its phenomenal rise. The **Dow closed at 2002.25, Jan. 8,** its first finish above 2000.

An **Iraqi warplane missile killed 37 sailors** on the frigate U.S.S. *Stark* in the Persian Gulf, **May 17.** Iraq called it an accident. The *Stark's* officers were found negligent.

**Public hearings** by the Senate and House committees investigating the **Iran-contra affair** were held **May-Aug.** Lt. Col. Oliver North said he had believed all his activities were authorized by his superiors. Pres. Reagan, **Aug. 12,** denied knowing of the funds' diversion to the contras.

**Wall Street crashed, Oct. 19,** with the Dow plummeting a record 508 points.

**Pres. Reagan** and **Soviet leader Gorbachev** met in Wash., **Dec. 8,** and signed **an unprecedented agreement** calling for the **dismantling of all 1,752 U.S. and 859 Soviet missiles with a 300- to 3,400-mile range.**

**1988**

Nearly **1.4 million illegal aliens** met the **May 4** deadline for applying for **amnesty** under a U.S. Immigration and Naturalization Service policy.

Much of the U.S. suffered the worst **drought** in more than 50 years. By June 23, half the nation's agricultural counties had been designated disaster areas.

A missile, fired from the **U.S. Navy warship** ***Vincennes,*** in the Persian Gulf, **mistakenly struck and destroyed a commercial Iranian airliner, July 3, killing all 290 persons** on the plane.

**George Bush,** vice president under Reagan, **was elected 41st U.S. president, Nov. 8.** Bush decisively defeated the Democratic nominee, Gov. Michael Dukakis (MA).

**Drexel Burnham Lambert** agreed, **Dec. 21, to plead guilty to 6 violations of federal law,** including insider trading, stock manipulation, and falsified records; and **to pay penalties of $650 million,** by far the largest such settlement.

**1989**

One of the **largest oil spills in U.S. history** occurred after the *Exxon Valdez* struck Bligh Reef in **Alaska's Prince William Sound, Mar. 24.**

Former National Security Council staff member **Oliver North** became the first person, **May 4, convicted in a jury trial** in connection with the **Iran-contra** scandal.

Legislation passed by Congress to **rescue the savings and loan industry** was signed into law, **Aug. 9,** by Pres. Bush.

**Army Gen. Colin Powell** was nominated by Pres. Bush, **Aug. 10,** to serve as **chairman of the Joint Chiefs of Staff;** he became the first black to hold the post.

Minutes before the start of a World Series game, **Oct. 17,** an **earthquake struck the San Francisco Bay area,** causing more than 60 deaths.

**Democrats** won most of the **top offices** at stake in off-year elections, **Nov. 7.** Lt. Gov. L. Douglas Wilder, a Democrat, was elected governor of Virginia, the nation's first black governor since Reconstruction.

Pres. Bush signed into law, **Nov. 19,** an increase in the **minimum wage** to $4.25 an hour by 1991, with a training wage of $3.35 for 16- to 19-year-olds.

**U.S. troops invaded Panama, Dec. 20,** overthrowing the government of **Manuel Noriega.** Noriega, wanted by U.S. authorities on drug charges, took refuge in the Vatican mission; he surrendered to the U.S. Jan. 3, 1990.

### 1990

Pres. Bush signed the **Americans With Disabilities Act** on **July 26,** barring discrimination against such individuals.

**Justice William Brennan** announced, **July 20,** his immediate resignation from the U.S. Supreme Court, due to illness. Pres. Bush nominated **Judge David Souter,** and the Senate voted to confirm him, **Sept. 27.**

**Operation Desert Shield** forces left for **Saudi Arabia, Aug. 7,** to defend that country following the **invasion** of its neighbor **Kuwait by Iraq,** Aug. 2.

Pres. Bush **vetoed, Oct. 22,** a **civil rights bill** that sought in effect to reverse 6 recent Supreme Court decisions.

Pres. Bush signed, **Nov. 5,** a bill designed to **reduce budget deficits** by nearly $500 billion over 5 years, through spending curbs and tax hikes. The top personal income tax rate rose from 28 to 31%.

### 1991

The **U.S. and its allies defeated Iraq** in the **Persian Gulf War** and liberated Kuwait, which Iraq had overrun in Aug. 1990. On **Jan. 17,** the allies launched a devasting **attack on Iraq from the air**. In a **ground war** starting **Feb. 24,** that lasted just 100 hours, the U.S.-led attackers killed or captured many thousands of Iraqi soldiers and sent the rest into retreat before Pres. Bush ordered a cease-fire **Feb. 27.**

The **Dow Jones Industrial Average** finished above 3000 for the first time, **Apr. 17,** closing at 3004.46.

The **Iran-contra case against Oliver North was "terminated,"** with all charges dropped, **Sept. 16.**

The **U.S. Senate approved, Oct. 15, the nomination of Clarence Thomas** as an **associate justice of the Supreme Court,** after investigating an allegation of sexual harassment leveled against him by **Anita Hill, a law professor at the University of Oklahoma.** He became the 2d African-American to serve on the Court, replacing retiring Justice **Thurgood Marshall,** the 1st black to serve on the Court.

**Charles Keating was convicted of 17 counts of securities fraud, Dec. 4.** The prosecution asserted that as chairman of an S&L, Keating had induced some 17,000 investors to buy $250 million in bonds that were not insured.

### 1992

**Rioting, looting, and arson** swept **South-Central Los Angeles** starting **Apr. 29,** after a jury that included no blacks acquitted 4 policemen on all but one count in the Mar. 1991 beating of a black motorist, **Rodney King.** The attack on King had been videotaped and shown on TV newcasts. The death toll in the L.A. violence was put at 52.

A **27th Amendment, regarding congressional pay raises,** became part of the **Constitution** in **May,** almost 200 years after it was first approved by Congress.

The **Democratic Party** nominated **Gov. Bill Clinton (AR)** as its **candidate for president, July 15,** and **Sen. Al Gore Jr. (TN)** as its **candidate for vice president, July 16,** in New York City. **Texan H. Ross Perot,** an independent, announced, **July 16,** that he would **not seek the presidency**, but he returned to the race **Oct. 1.** The **Republican Party** renominated **Pres. George Bush** and **Vice Pres. Dan Quayle** at a convention in Houston, TX, in **early August**.

**Gov. Bill Clinton** was **elected 42d president of the U.S.** on **Nov. 3,** and his running mate, **Sen. Al Gore Jr.,** was **elected vice president**. Clinton won 43% of the popular vote, with Bush taking 38% and Perot 19%. **Democrats** retained control of both houses of Congress.

### 1993

Bill Clinton was inaugurated **Jan. 20** as the 42d president of the U.S. On **Jan. 25,** he appointed his wife, **Hillary Rodham Clinton, head of a task force on health-care reform.**

A powerful bomb exploded in a parking garage beneath the **World Trade Center** in New York City, **Feb. 26,** killing 6 people. More than 1,000 people suffered injuries.

**Janet Reno** became the first woman to serve as attorney general of the U.S., **Mar. 12.**

**Four agents of the U.S. Bureau of Alcohol, Tobacco, and Firearms were killed, Feb. 28,** during an unsuccessful raid on the **Branch Davidian compound in Waco, TX.** A 51-day siege of the compound by federal agents ended **Apr. 19,** when armored vehicles pumped tear gas into it. Those inside responded with gunfire. Shortly after noon, the compound was leveled by fire, leaving about 80 cult members dead.

A federal jury, **Apr. 17, found 2 Los Angeles police officers, Sgt. Stacey Koon and Officer Laurence Powell, guilty** and 2 officers not guilty of violating the civil rights of motorist **Rodney King,** in 1991. The two officers convicted were sentenced, **Aug. 4,** to 2½ years in prison.

The **"motor-voter" bill** was signed by Pres. Clinton, **May 20,** allowing citizens to register to vote when applying for a driver's license.

**"The Great Flood of 1993"** inundated 8 million acres of land in 9 Midwestern states; the flooding of the Mississippi and its tributaries left 50 people dead and some 70,000 homeless. Officials put total damage estimates at $12 billion.

Pres. Clinton, **July 19,** announced a "don't ask, don't tell, don't pursue" policy for **homosexuals** in the U.S. military.

**Vincent Foster,** deputy White House counsel and long time friend of Bill and Hillary Clinton, was found shot to death in a park in northern Virginia **July 20.** An autopsy indicated that he had committed suicide.

**Judge Ruth Bader Ginsburg was sworn in, Aug. 10, as the 107th justice of the U.S. Supreme Court,** replacing Associate Justice Byron White, who retired.

After a long and acrimonious debate, **Congress narrowly approved a bill designed to reduce federal budget deficits by $496 billion over 5 years,** through $255 billion in spending cuts and $241 billion in new taxes. Pres. Clinton signed the bill **Aug. 10.**

The **"Brady Bill,"** a major gun-control measure, was signed into law by Pres. Clinton **Nov. 30.**

The space shuttle *Endeavour* was launched **Dec. 2.** The mission to repair the Hubble telescope was successful.

### 1994

The North American Free Trade Agreement took effect **Jan. 1.**

A predawn **earthquake struck the Los Angeles area, Jan. 17,** claiming 61 lives and causing heavy damage.

Attorney Gen. Janet Reno on **Jan. 20** appointed Robert Fiske independent counsel to investigate the so-called **Whitewater affair,** named for the Whitewater real estate venture in Arkansas in which the Clintons were partners with banker **James McDougal.** In a report **June 30,** Fiske said he had not found sufficient evidence that officials had "acted with the intent to corruptly influence" an investigation by the Resolution Trust Corp. into the collapse of McDougal's Madison Guaranty Savings and Loan. The House Banking Committee, **July 26,** and the Senate Banking Committee, **July 29,** began hearings into the Whitewater affair. A panel of 3 federal judges, **Aug. 5,** named a new Whitewater prosecutor to succeed Fiske.

Pres. Bill Clinton announced, **Feb. 3,** that **the U.S. was lifting its trade embargo against Vietnam.**

**Byron De La Beckwith, a white supremacist, was convicted Feb. 5** of the 1963 murder of **civil rights leader Medgar Evers**. Beckwith was sentenced to life in prison.

On **Feb. 21, Aldrich Ames,** a long-time counterintelligence officer in the CIA, and his wife **were arrested and charged with selling information to the Soviet Union and Russia**. Under a plea bargain, he received a life sentence in prison, while she was sentenced to 63 months.

Eleven members of **the Branch Davidian religious cult** were found not guilty, **Feb. 26,** of murder and conspiracy charges in the deaths of 4 federal agents in a 1993 shootout at the cult's compound near Waco, TX.

**Four men were found guilty, Mar. 4,** of a total of 38 charges related to **the 1993 bombing at the World Trade Center in New York City.**

**A former Arkansas state employee, Paula Jones, filed a suit, May 6,** that accused Pres. Clinton of sexual harassment while governor of Arkansas.

**O. J. Simpson**, one of the most successful running backs in football history, **was charged, June 17, with the murders of his former wife, Nicole Brown Simpson, and** a friend of hers, **Ronald Goldman.** After midnight on **June 13,** the 2 victims had been found stabbed to death outside Nicole Simpson's condominium in Los Angeles. The trial got underway officially **Sept. 26** in Los Angeles.

**Major league baseball players went on strike,** following the conclusion of the **Aug. 11** games; the playoffs and **World Series** were ultimately canceled.

Congress on **Aug. 25** approved **the $30.2 billion 1994 Omnibus Violent Crime Control and Preventions Act;** it was signed by Pres. Bill Clinton on **Sept. 13.**

Clinton's **health-care reform proposal gradually lost support.** On **Sept. 26** Senate Majority Leader George Mitchell (D, ME) abandoned his effort to pass it.

The regular 1994 session of the **103d Congress ended, Oct. 8**, as bills failed in the face of Republican filibusters. Barely surviving was the California Desert Protection Bill, **the largest land-conservation bill ever enacted** for the U.S. outside Alaska.

On **Nov. 3**, **Susan Smith**, a South Carolina mother, was **charged with murdering her 2 young sons,** by allowing her car to roll into a lake with them inside.

**The Republican Party captured control of both houses of Congress** in the **Nov. 8** elections.

Congress approved the tariff-cutting provisions of the Uruguay Round of the General Agreement on Tariffs and Trade (GATT; new name, **World Trade Organization** [WTO]); Pres. Clinton signed the legislation **Dec. 8**.

**1995**

When the **Republican-controlled 104th Congress opened, Jan. 4, Sen. Bob Dole (R, KS) became Senate majority leader, and Rep. Newt Gingrich (R, GA) was formally elected Speaker of the House.** A measure to end Congress's exemption from federal labor laws, the **first in a series of measures championed by Republicans in a so-called Contract With America, cleared Congress Jan. 17** and was signed **Jan. 23** by Pres. Bill Clinton.

Pres. Clinton invoked emergency powers, **Jan. 31**, to extend a **$20 billion loan to help Mexico** avert financial collapse.

Sen. Phil Gramm (TX) announced his **candidacy for the GOP presidential nomination, Feb. 24.** Former Tennessee Gov. Lamar Alexander officially entered the race **Feb. 28,** and political commentator Pat Buchanan entered **Mar. 20.** Sen. Dole formally announced his candidacy **Apr. 10;** California Gov. Pete Wilson announced **June 15** (he withdrew **Sept. 29**). Sen. Arlen Specter (PA) announced **Mar. 30** (he quit **Nov. 21**).

A bill making it more difficult for Congress to approve any **"unfunded mandate"**—or measure requiring but not funding certain actions by the states—cleared Congress **Mar. 15-16** and was signed by Pres. Clinton **Mar. 22.** A **proposed constitutional amendment mandating a balanced budget** passed the House **Jan. 26** but, on **Mar. 2,** failed in the Senate. Both measures were part of the GOP Contract With America. A number of other bills championed in the Contract passed in the House but stalled in the Senate, and a **proposed constitutional amendment limiting terms of members of Congress,** also part of the Contract, failed in the House, **Mar. 29,** amid opposition from longer-serving members.

The last UN peacekeeping troops withdrew from **Somalia Feb. 28-Mar. 3,** with the aid of U.S. Marines. In **Haiti,** peacekeeping responsibilities were transferred from U.S. to UN forces **Mar. 31,** with the U.S. providing 2,400 soldiers as part of the UN operation.

**A bomb exploded outside a federal office building in Oklahoma City on the morning of Apr. 19, killing 169 people** (including one rescue worker). The bomb had been left in a truck parked in front; Timothy McVeigh was charged in the crime, **Apr. 21.** A 2d suspect, Terry Nichols, was charged **May 10;** Nichols's brother James was charged as an accessory.

On **Apr. 24 a package bomb attributed to the so-called Unabomber** killed the president of a forestry association in Sacramento, CA.

In baseball, regular-season play got underway **Apr. 25, ending the longest strike in sports history.**

The Senate, **May 9**, by a vote of 98-0, confirmed John Deutch as **Director of Central Intelligence.**

**Pres. Bill Clinton and Pres. Boris Yeltsin of Russia held a summit meeting in Moscow, May 10.**

Pres. Clinton's **nominee for surgeon general, Dr. Henry Foster**, failed to win Senate approval **June 21-22.**

**Webster Hubbell**, a close friend of the Clintons and former associate U.S. attorney general, was **sentenced June 28 to 21 months in prison** for tax evasion and mail fraud.

The U.S. space shuttle ***Atlantis* docked with the Russian space station *Mir*, June 29-July 4,** in the first in a series of planned dockings preparatory to construction of an international space station.

A U.S. **F-16 fighter jet piloted by Air Force Capt. Scott O'Grady was shot down** by a surface-to-air missile **over Bosnia and Herzegovina June 2**; O'Grady survived in the woods and **was rescued by U.S. Marines** 6 days later.

**At least 800 people died** in the Middle West and Northeast **from a heat wave July 12-17;** in Chicago, where the temperature hit a record 106 degrees on **July 13**, 536 deaths were blamed on the heat.

**In his first such action, Pres. Bill Clinton, June 7, vetoed a so-called rescissions bill** which cut $16.4 billion from spending previously appropriated by Congress. On **July 27,** however, he signed a revised version that cut about $16.3 billion while restoring some funds for education and environmental programs.

**Arkansas Gov. Jim Guy Tucker was indicted June 7** on felony charges that grew out of the Whitewater investigation but were unrelated to the Whitewater venture itself.

The U.S. announced on **July 11** that it was **reestablishing diplomatic relations with Vietnam**

**Hearings begun in the Senate July 18 and the House Aug. 7** focused on such issues as White House handling of documents following the apparent 1993 suicide of deputy counsel Vincent Foster and ties between the **Whitewater venture** and an Arkansas S&L owned by the Clintons' Whitewater partner James McDougal. **McDougal and his ex-wife, Susan, were indicted** by a grand jury **Aug. 17** on charges of arranging fraudulent loans.

**Shannon Faulkner won her long legal fight to gain admission** to the previously all-male cadet corps of **The Citadel, Aug. 11,** though she dropped out after a few days of training.

**Sen. Bob Packwood (R, OR) announced Sept. 7 that he would resign** from the Senate, after the Senate Ethics Committee voted, 6-0, to recommend his expulsion for sexual misconduct and other charges.

Publisher **Malcolm (Steve) Forbes announced his candidacy** for the GOP presidential nomination **Sept. 22.**

Ten Muslim militants were **convicted in New York, Oct. 1,** on conspiracy charges stemming from a failed **plot to blow up UN Headquarters** and other buildings and assassinate political leaders.

After a televised trial that galvanized national attention, former star running back **O. J. Simpson was found not guilty Oct. 3** of the murders of his former wife, Nicole Brown Simpson, and a friend of hers, Ronald Goldman.

Hundreds of thousands of African-American men participated in **a "Million Man March" and rally in Washington, DC, Oct. 16,** organized by the controversial Rev. Louis Farrakhan, leader of the Nation of Islam.

Results of widely scattered **elections held on Nov. 7** indicated no further surge in Republican fortunes. After some suspense, **Gen. Colin Powell (ret.) announced, Nov. 8,** that he was a Republican but **that he would not seek the GOP nomination** for president in 1996.

**Billy Dale,** discharged as head of the White House travel office by the Clinton administration, **was acquitted of embezzlement** by a federal jury **Nov. 16.**

The **federal 55-mile-an-hour speed limit was repealed** by a measure signed **Nov. 28.**

After talks opening **Nov. 1,** at Wright-Patterson Air Force Base outside Dayton, OH, the **warring parties in Bosnia and Herzegovina reached an agreement Nov. 21** to end their conflict; a **treaty was signed Dec. 14,** after which the first of some 20,000 **U.S. peacekeeping troops arrived in Bosnia.**

**Five Americans** were among 7 people **killed, Nov. 13,** when **2 bombs exploded** at a military training and communications center **in Riyadh, Saudi Arabia.**

An impasse between Congress and Pres. Clinton over the federal budget led to a **partial government shutdown, Nov. 14.** Operations resumed **Nov. 20** under continuing resolutions. On **Dec. 6, Clinton vetoed a budget reconciliation bill** including tax cuts and cuts in projected spending for Medicare and other programs, aimed at achieving a balanced federal budget in 7 years; on **Dec. 16** the continuing resolution expired and a longer shutdown began.

The House Ethics Committee **voted unanimously Dec. 6 to have an independent counsel probe charges that Speaker Newt Gingrich had violated tax laws**; the committee also found that a book deal by Gingrich with HarperCollins created "the impression of exploiting one's office for personal gain."

After lengthy negotiations the **White House Dec. 22 yielded to the Senate Whitewater Committee notes from a Nov. 1993 meeting**; these provided no clear evidence that the White House had improperly pressed for information about the Whitewater probe but opened what Republicans called avenues for further inquiry.

The **Dow Jones Industrial Average** closed **Dec. 13** at an all-time high of 5216.47 and **closed Dec. 29 at 5117.12, up an impressive 33.5% for the year.**

## The Mayflower Compact

The threat of James I to "harry them out of the land" sent a little band of religious dissenters from England to Holland in 1608. They were known as Separatists because they wished to cut all ties with the established church. In 1620, some of them, known now as the Pilgrims, joined with a larger group in England to set sail on the *Mayflower* for the New World. A joint stock company financed their venture.

In November, they sighted Cape Cod and decided to land an exploring party at Plymouth Harbor. A rebellious group picked up at Southampton and London troubled the Pilgrim leaders, however, and to control their actions 41 Pilgrims drew up the Mayflower Compact and signed it before going ashore. The voluntary agreement to govern themselves was America's first written constitution.

In the name of God, Amen. We, whose names are underwritten, the Loyal Subjects of our dread Sovereign Lord, King *James,* by the Grace of God, of *Great Britain, France and Ireland,* King, *Defender of the Faith,* etc.

Having undertaken for the Glory of God, and Advancement of the Christian Faith, and the Honour of our King and Country, a voyage to plant the first colony in the northern Parts of Virginia; do by these Presents, solemnly and mutually in the Presence of God and one of another, convenant and combine ourselves together into a civil Body Politick, for our better Ordering and Preservation, and Furtherance of the Ends aforesaid; And by Virtue hereof to enact, constitute, and frame, such just and equal Laws, Ordinances, Acts, Constitutions and Offices, from time to time, as shall be thought most meet and convenient for the General good of the Colony; unto which we promise all due Submission and Obedience.

In Witness whereof we have hereunto subscribed our names at *Cape Cod* the eleventh of *November,* in the Reign of our Sovereign Lord, King *James* of *England, France* and *Ireland,* the eighteenth, and of *Scotland* the fifty-fourth. *Anno Domini, 1620.*

## The Continental Congress: Meetings, Presidents

| Meeting places | Dates of meetings | Congress presidents | Date elected |
|---|---|---|---|
| Philadelphia, PA | Sept. 5 to Oct. 26, 1774 | Peyton Randolph, VA (1) | Sept. 5, 1774 |
| " | " | Henry Middleton, SC | Oct. 22, 1774 |
| Philadelphia, PA | May 10, 1775 to Dec. 12, 1776 | Peyton Randolph, VA | May 10, 1775 |
| " | " | John Hancock, MA | May 24, 1775 |
| Baltimore, MD | Dec. 20, 1776 to Mar. 4, 1777 | " | |
| Philadelphia, PA | Mar. 5 to Sept. 18, 1777 | " | |
| Lancaster, PA | Sept. 27, 1777 (one day) | " | |
| York, PA | Sept. 30, 1777 to June 27, 1778 | Henry Laurens, SC | Nov. 1, 1777(4) |
| Philadelphia, PA | July 2, 1778 to June 21, 1783 | John Jay, NY | Dec. 10, 1778 |
| " | " | Samuel Huntington, CT | Sept. 28, 1779 |
| " | " | Thomas McKean, DE | July 10, 1781 |
| " | " | John Hanson, MD (2) | Nov. 5, 1781 |
| " | " | Elias Boudinot, NJ | Nov. 4, 1782 |
| Princeton, NJ | June 30 to Nov. 4, 1783 | Thomas Mifflin, PA | Nov. 3, 1783 |
| Annapolis, MD | Nov. 26, 1783 to June 3, 1784 | " | |
| Trenton, NJ | Nov. 1 to Dec. 24, 1784 | Richard Henry Lee, VA | Nov. 30, 1784 |
| New York City, NY | Jan. 11 to Nov. 4, 1785 | " | |
| " | Nov. 7, 1785 to Nov. 3, 1786 | John Hancock, MA (3) | Nov. 23, 1785 |
| " | " | Nathaniel Gorham, MA | June 6, 1786 |
| " | Nov. 6, 1786 to Oct. 30, 1787 | Arthur St. Clair, PA | Feb. 2, 1787 |
| " | Nov. 5, 1787 to Oct. 21, 1788 | Cyrus Griffin, VA | Jan. 22, 1788 |
| " | Nov. 3, 1788 to Mar. 2, 1789 | " | |

(1) Resigned Oct. 22, 1774. (2) Titled "President of the United States in Congress Assembled," John Hanson is considered by some the first U.S. president because he was the first to serve under the Articles of Confederation. He was, however, little more than presiding officer of the Congress, which retained full executive power. He could be considered the head of government, but not head of state. (3) Resigned May 29, 1786, without serving, because of illness. (4) Articles of Confederation agreed upon, Nov. 15, 1777; last ratification from Maryland, Mar. 1, 1781.

## Patrick Henry's Speech to the Virginia Convention

The following is an excerpt from Patrick Henry's speech to the Virginia Convention on Mar. 23, 1775:

Gentlemen may cry, peace, peace—but there is no peace. The war is actually begun! The next gale that sweeps from the north will bring to our ears the clash of resounding arms! Our brethren are already in the field! Why stand we here idle? What is it that gentlemen wish? What would they have? Is life so dear, or peace so sweet, as to be purchased at the price of chains and slavery? Forbid it, Almighty God! I know not what course others may take; but as for me, give me liberty, or give me death!

## *Common Sense*

The following is an excerpt from Thomas Paine's *Common Sense.* Paine adopted the doctrine of separation from Britain after the battles of Lexington and Concord and published his pamphlet in Jan. 1776.

The cause of America is in great measure the cause of all mankind. Many circumstances hath, and will arise, which are not local, but universal, and through which principles of all Lovers of Mankind are affected, and in the Event of which, their Affections are interested. The laying a Country desolate with Fire and Sword, declaring war against natural rights of all Mankind, and extirpating the Defenders thereof from the Face of the Earth, is the Concern of every Man to whom Nature hath given the Power of feeling; . . . It is repugnant to reason, to the universal order of things, to all examples from former ages, to suppose, that this continent can longer remain subject to any external power . . .

The last cord is now broken, the people of England are presenting addresses against us. There are injuries which nature cannot forgive; she would cease to be nature if she did . . .

O ye that love mankind! Ye that dare oppose, not only the tyranny, but the tyrant, stand forth! Every spot of the old world is overrun with oppression. Freedom hath been hunted round the globe. Asia, and Africa, have long expelled her—Europe regards her like a stranger, and England hath given her warning to depart. O! Receive the fugitive, and prepare in time an asylum for mankind.

## How the Declaration of Independence Was Adopted

On June 7, 1776, Richard Henry Lee, who had issued the first call for a congress of the colonies, introduced in the Continental Congress at Philadelphia a resolution declaring "that these United Colonies are, and of right ought to be, free and independent states, that they are absolved from all allegiance to the British Crown, and that all political connection between them and the state of Great Britain is, and ought to be, totally dissolved."

The resolution, seconded by John Adams on behalf of the Massachusetts delegation, came up again on June 10 when a committee of 5, headed by Thomas Jefferson, was appointed to express the purpose of the resolution in a declaration of independence. The others on the committee were John Adams, Benjamin Franklin, Robert R. Livingston, and Roger Sherman.

Drafting the Declaration was assigned to Jefferson, who worked on a portable desk of his own construction in a room at Market and 7th Sts. The committee reported the result on June 28, 1776. The members of the Congress suggested a number of changes, which Jefferson called "deplorable." They didn't approve Jefferson's arraignment of the British people and King George III for encouraging and fostering the slave trade, which Jefferson called "an execrable commerce." They made 86 changes, eliminating 480 words and leaving 1,337. In the final form, capitalization was erratic. Jefferson had written that men were endowed with "inalienable" rights; in the final copy it came out as "unalienable" and has been thus ever since.

The Lee-Adams resolution of independence was adopted by 12 yeas on July 2—the actual date of the act of independence. The Declaration, which explains the act, was adopted July 4, in the evening.

After the Declaration was adopted, July 4, 1776, it was turned over to John Dunlap, printer, to be printed on broadsides. The original copy was lost and one of his broadsides was attached to a page in the journal of the Congress. It was read aloud July 8 in Philadelphia, PA, Easton, PA, and Trenton, NJ. On July 9 at 6 PM it was read by order of Gen. George Washington to the troops assembled on the Common in New York City (City Hall Park).

The Continental Congress of July 19, 1776, adopted the following resolution:

"Resolved, That the Declaration passed on the 4th, be fairly engrossed on parchment with the title and stile of 'The Unanimous Declaration of the thirteen United States of America' and that the same, when engrossed, be signed by every member of Congress."

Not all delegates who signed the engrossed Declaration were present on July 4. Robert Morris (PA), William Williams (CT), and Samuel Chase (MD) signed on Aug. 2; Oliver Wolcott (CT), George Wythe (VA), Richard Henry Lee (VA), and Elbridge Gerry (MA) signed in August and September; Matthew Thornton (NH) joined the Congress Nov. 4 and signed later. Thomas McKean (DE) rejoined Washington's army before signing and said later that he signed in 1781.

Charles Carroll of Carrollton was appointed a delegate by Maryland on July 4, 1776, presented his credentials July 18, and signed the engrossed Declaration on Aug. 2. Born Sept. 19, 1737, he was 95 years old and the last surviving signer when he died on Nov. 14, 1832.

Two Pennsylvania delegates who did not support the Declaration on July 4 were replaced.

The 4 New York delegates did not have authority from their state to vote on July 4. On July 9, the New York state convention authorized its delegates to approve the Declaration, and the Congress was so notified on July 15, 1776. The 4 signed the Declaration on Aug. 2.

The original engrossed Declaration is preserved in the National Archives Building in Washington.

## Declaration of Independence

The Declaration of Independence was adopted by the Continental Congress in Philadelphia on July 4, 1776. John Hancock was president of the Congress, and Charles Thomson was secretary. A copy of the Declaration, engrossed on parchment, was signed by members of Congress on and after Aug. 2, 1776. On Jan. 18, 1777, Congress ordered that "an authenticated copy, with the names of the members of Congress subscribing the same, be sent to each of the United States, and that they be desired to have the same put upon record." Authenticated copies were printed in broadside form in Baltimore, where the Continental Congress was then in session. The following text is that of the original printed by John Dunlap at Philadelphia for the Continental Congress.

# IN CONGRESS, July 4, 1776.

# A DECLARATION

### By the REPRESENTATIVES of the

# UNITED STATES OF AMERICA,

### In GENERAL CONGRESS assembled

When in the Course of human Events, it becomes necessary for one People to dissolve the Political Bands which have connected them with another, and to assume among the Powers of the Earth, the separate and equal Station to which the Laws of Nature and of Nature's God entitle them, a decent Respect to the Opinions of Mankind requires that they should declare the causes which impel them to the Separation.

We hold these Truths to be self-evident, that all Men are created equal, that they are endowed by their Creator with certain unalienable Rights, that among these are Life, Liberty, and the Pursuit of Happiness—That to secure these Rights, Governments are instituted among Men, deriving their just Powers from the Consent of the Governed, that whenever any Form of Government becomes destructive of these Ends, it is the Right of the People to alter or to abolish it, and to institute new Government, laying its Foundation on such Principles, and organizing its Powers in such Form, as to them shall seem most likely to effect their Safety and Happiness. Prudence, indeed, will dictate that Governments long established should not be changed for light and transient Causes; and accordingly all Experience hath shewn, that Mankind are more disposed to suffer, while Evils are sufferable, than to right themselves by abolishing the Forms to which they are accustomed. But when a long Train of Abuses and Usurpations, pursuing invariably the same Object, evinces a Design to reduce them under absolute Despotism, it is their Right, it is their Duty, to throw off such Government, and to provide new Guards for their future Security. Such has been the patient Sufferance of these Colonies; and such is now the Necessity which constrains them to alter their former Systems of Government. The History of the present King of Great-Britain is a History of repeated Injuries and Usurpations, all having in direct Object the Establishment of an absolute Tyranny over these States. To prove this, let Facts be submitted to a candid World.

He has refused his Assent to Laws, the most wholesome and necessary for the public Good.

He has forbidden his Governors to pass Laws of immediate and pressing Importance, unless suspended in their Operation till his Assent should be obtained; and when so suspended, he has utterly neglected to attend to them.

He has refused to pass other Laws for the Accommodation of large Districts of People, unless those People would relinquish the Right of Representation in the Legislature, a Right inestimable to them, and formidable to Tyrants only.

He has called together Legislative Bodies at Places unusual, uncomfortable, and distant from the Depository of their Public Records, for the sole Purpose of fatiguing them into Compliance with his Measures.

He has dissolved Representative Houses repeatedly, for opposing with manly Firmness his Invasions on the Rights of the People.

He has refused for a long Time, after such Dissolutions, to cause others to be elected; whereby the Legislative Powers, incapable of Annihilation, have returned to the People at large for their exercise; the State remaining in the mean time exposed to all the Dangers of Invasion from without, and Convulsions within.

He has endeavoured to prevent the Population of these States; for that Purpose obstructing the Laws for Naturalization of Foreigners; refusing to pass others to encourage their Migrations hither, and raising the Conditions of new Appropriations of Lands.

He has obstructed the Administration of Justice, by refusing his Assent to Laws for establishing Judiciary Powers.

He has made Judges dependent on his Will alone, for the Tenure of their Offices, and the Amount and payment of their Salaries.

He has erected a Multitude of new Offices, and sent hither Swarms of Officers to harrass our People, and eat out their Substance.

He has kept among us, in Times of Peace, Standing Armies, without the consent of our Legislatures.

He has affected to render the Military independent of, and superior to the Civil Power.

He has combined with others to subject us to a Jurisdiction foreign to our Constitution, and unacknowledged by our Laws; giving his Assent to their Acts of pretended Legislation:

For quartering large Bodies of Armed Troops among us:

For protecting them, by a mock Trial, from Punishment for any Murders which they should commit on the Inhabitants of these States:

For cutting off our Trade with all Parts of the World:

For imposing Taxes on us without our Consent:

For depriving us, in many Cases, of the Benefits of Trial by Jury:

For transporting us beyond Seas to be tried for pretended Offences:

For abolishing the free System of English Laws in a neighbouring Province, establishing therein an arbitrary Government, and enlarging its Boundaries, so as to render it at once an Example and fit Instrument for introducing the same absolute Rule into these Colonies:

For taking away our Charters, abolishing our most valuable Laws, and altering fundamentally the Forms of our Governments:

For suspending our own Legislatures, and declaring themselves invested with Power to legislate for us in all Cases whatsoever.

He has abdicated Government here, by declaring us out of his Protection and waging War against us.

He has plundered our Seas, ravaged our Coasts, burnt our towns, and destroyed the Lives of our People.

He is, at this Time, transporting large Armies of foreign Mercenaries to complete the works of Death, Desolation, and Tyranny, already begun with circumstances of Cruelty and Perfidy, scarcely paralleled in the most barbarous Ages, and totally unworthy the Head of a civilized Nation.

He has constrained our fellow Citizens taken Captive on the high Seas to bear Arms against their Country, to become the Executioners of their Friends and Brethren, or to fall themselves by their Hands.

He has excited domestic Insurrections amongst us, and has endeavoured to bring on the Inhabitants of our Frontiers, the merciless Indian Savages, whose known Rule of Warfare, is an undistinguished Destruction, of all Ages, Sexes and Conditions.

In every stage of these Oppressions we have Petitioned for Redress in the most humble Terms: Our repeated Petitions have been answered only by repeated Injury. A Prince, whose Character is thus marked by every act which may define a Tyrant, is unfit to be the Ruler of a free People.

Nor have we been wanting in Attentions to our British Brethren. We have warned them from Time to Time of Attempts by their Legislature to extend an unwarrantable Jurisdiction over us. We have reminded them of the Circumstances of our Emigration and Settlement here. We have appealed to their native Justice and Magnanimity, and we have conjured them by the Ties of our common Kindred to disavow these Usurpations, which, would inevitably interrupt our Connections and Correspondence. They too have been deaf to the Voice of Justice and of Consanguinity. We must, therefore, acquiesce in the Necessity, which denounces our Separation, and hold them, as we hold the rest of Mankind, Enemies in War, in Peace, Friends.

We, therefore, the Representatives of the UNITED STATES OF AMERICA, in General Congress, Assembled, appealing to the Supreme Judge of the World for the Rectitude of our Intentions, do, in the Name, and by Authority of the good People of these Colonies, solemnly Publish and Declare, That these United Colonies are, and of Right ought to be, Free and Independent States; that they are absolved from all Allegiance to the British Crown, and that all political Connection between them and the State of Great-Britain, is and ought to be totally dissolved; and that as Free and Independent States, they have full Power to levy War, conclude Peace, contract Alliances, establish Commerce, and to do all other Acts and Things which Independent States may of right do. And for the support of this declaration, with a firm Reliance on the Protection of Divine Providence, we mutually pledge to each other our lives, our Fortunes, and our sacred Honor.

**JOHN HANCOCK, President**

Attest.
**CHARLES THOMSON, Secretary.**

# Signers of the Declaration of Independence

| Delegate (state) | Occupation | Birthplace | Born | Died |
|---|---|---|---|---|
| Adams, John (MA) | Lawyer | Braintree (Quincy), MA | Oct. 30, 1735 | July 4, 1826 |
| Adams, Samuel (MA) | Political leader | Boston, MA | Sept. 27, 1722 | Oct. 2, 1803 |
| Bartlett, Josiah (NH) | Physician, judge | Amesbury, MA | Nov. 21, 1729 | May 19, 1795 |
| Braxton, Carter (VA) | Farmer | Newington Plantation, VA | Sept. 10, 1736 | Oct. 10, 1797 |
| Carroll, Chas. of Carrollton (MD) | Lawyer | Annapolis, MD | Sept. 19, 1737 | Nov. 14, 1832 |
| Chase, Samuel (MD) | Judge | Princess Anne, MD | Apr. 17, 1741 | June 19, 1811 |
| Clark, Abraham (NJ) | Surveyor | Roselle, NJ | Feb. 15, 1726 | Sept. 15, 1794 |
| Clymer, George (PA) | Merchant | Philadelphia, PA | Mar. 16, 1739 | Jan. 23, 1813 |
| Ellery, William (RI) | Lawyer | Newport, RI | Dec. 22, 1727 | Feb. 15, 1820 |
| Floyd, William (NY) | Soldier | Brookhaven, NY | Dec. 17, 1734 | Aug. 4, 1821 |
| Franklin, Benjamin (PA) | Printer, publisher | Boston, MA | Jan. 17, 1706 | Apr. 17, 1790 |
| Gerry, Elbridge (MA) | Merchant | Marblehead, MA | July 17, 1744 | Nov. 23, 1814 |
| Gwinnett, Button (GA) | Merchant | Down Hatherly, England | c. 1735 | May 19, 1777 |
| Hall, Lyman (GA) | Physician | Wallingford, CT | Apr. 12, 1724 | Oct. 19, 1790 |
| Hancock, John (MA) | Merchant | Braintree (Quincy), MA | Jan. 12, 1737 | Oct. 8, 1793 |

| Delegate (state) | Occupation | Birthplace | Born | Died |
|---|---|---|---|---|
| Harrison, Benjamin (VA) | Farmer | Berkeley, VA | Apr. 5, 1726 | Apr. 24, 1791 |
| Hart, John (NJ) | Farmer | Stonington, CT | c. 1711 | May 11, 1779 |
| Hewes, Joseph (NC) | Merchant | Princeton, NJ | Jan. 23, 1730 | Nov. 10, 1779 |
| Heyward, Thos. Jr. (SC) | Lawyer, farmer | St. Luke's Parish, SC | July 28, 1746 | Mar. 6, 1809 |
| Hooper, William (NC) | Lawyer | Boston, MA | June 28, 1742 | Oct. 14, 1790 |
| Hopkins, Stephen (RI) | Judge, educator | Providence, RI | Mar. 7, 1707 | July 13, 1785 |
| Hopkinson, Francis (NJ) | Judge, author | Philadelphia, PA | Sept. 21, 1737 | May 9, 1791 |
| Huntington, Samuel (CT) | Judge | Windham County, CT | July 3, 1731 | Jan. 5, 1796 |
| Jefferson, Thomas (VA) | Lawyer | Shadwell, VA | Apr. 13, 1743 | July 4, 1826 |
| Lee, Francis Lightfoot (VA) | Farmer | Westmoreland County, VA | Oct. 14, 1734 | Jan. 11, 1797 |
| Lee, Richard Henry (VA) | Farmer | Westmoreland County, VA | Jan. 20, 1732 | June 19, 1794 |
| Lewis, Francis (NY) | Merchant | Llandaff, Wales | Mar., 1713 | Dec. 31, 1802 |
| Livingston, Philip (NY) | Merchant | Albany, NY | Jan. 15, 1716 | June 12, 1778 |
| Lynch, Thomas Jr. (SC) | Farmer | Winyah, SC | Aug. 5, 1749 | (at sea) 1779 |
| McKean, Thomas (DE) | Lawyer | New London, PA | Mar. 19, 1734 | June 24, 1817 |
| Middleton, Arthur (SC) | Farmer | Charleston, SC | June 26, 1742 | Jan. 1, 1787 |
| Morris, Lewis (NY) | Farmer | Morrisania (Bronx County), NY | Apr. 8, 1726 | Jan. 22, 1798 |
| Morris, Robert (PA) | Merchant | Liverpool, England | Jan. 20, 1734 | May 9, 1806 |
| Morton, John (PA) | Judge | Ridley, PA | 1724 | Apr., 1777 |
| Nelson, Thos. Jr. (VA) | Farmer | Yorktown, VA | Dec. 26, 1738 | Jan. 4, 1789 |
| Paca, William (MD) | Judge | Abingdon, MD | Oct. 31, 1740 | Oct. 23, 1799 |
| Paine, Robert Treat (MA) | Judge | Boston, MA | Mar. 11, 1731 | May 12, 1814 |
| Penn, John (NC) | Lawyer | Near Port Royal, VA | May 17, 1741 | Sept. 14, 1788 |
| Read, George (DE) | Judge | Near North East, MD | Sept. 18, 1733 | Sept. 21, 1798 |
| Rodney, Caesar (DE) | Judge | Dover, DE | Oct. 7, 1728 | June 29, 1784 |
| Ross, George (PA) | Judge | New Castle, DE | May 10, 1730 | July 14, 1779 |
| Rush, Benjamin (PA) | Physician | Byberry, PA (Philadelphia) | Dec. 24, 1745 | Apr. 19, 1813 |
| Rutledge, Edward (SC) | Lawyer | Charleston, SC | Nov. 23, 1749 | Jan. 23, 1800 |
| Sherman, Roger (CT) | Lawyer | Newton, MA | Apr. 19, 1721 | July 23, 1793 |
| Smith, James (PA) | Lawyer | Dublin, Ireland | c. 1719 | July 11, 1806 |
| Stockton, Richard (NJ) | Lawyer | Near Princeton, NJ | Oct. 1, 1730 | Feb. 28, 1781 |
| Stone, Thomas (MD) | Lawyer | Charles County, MD | 1743 | Oct. 5, 1787 |
| Taylor, George (PA) | Ironmaster | Ireland | 1716 | Feb. 23, 1781 |
| Thornton, Matthew (NH) | Physician | Ireland | 1714 | June 24, 1803 |
| Walton, George (GA) | Judge | Prince Edward County, VA | 1741 | Feb. 2, 1804 |
| Whipple, William (NH) | Merchant, judge | Kittery, ME. | Jan. 14, 1730 | Nov. 28, 1785 |
| Williams, William (CT) | Merchant | Lebanon, CT | Apr. 23, 1731 | Aug. 2, 1811 |
| Wilson, James (PA) | Judge | Carskerdo, Scotland | Sept. 14, 1742 | Aug. 28, 1798 |
| Witherspoon, John (NJ) | Clergyman, educator | Gifford, Scotland | Feb. 5, 1723 | Nov. 15, 1794 |
| Wolcott, Oliver (CT) | Judge | Windsor, CT | Dec. 1, 1726 | Dec. 1, 1797 |
| Wythe, George (VA) | Lawyer | Elizabeth City Co. (Hampton), VA | 1726 | June 8, 1806 |

# Origin of the Constitution

The War of Independence was conducted by delegates from the original 13 states, called the Congress of the United States of America and known as the Continental Congress. In 1777 the Congress submitted to the legislatures of the states the Articles of Confederation and Perpetual Union, which were ratified by New Hampshire, Massachusetts, Rhode Island, Connecticut, New York, New Jersey, Pennsylvania, Delaware, Virginia, North Carolina, South Carolina, and Georgia and finally, in 1781, by Maryland.

The first article of the instrument read: "The stile of this confederacy shall be the United States of America." This did not signify a sovereign nation, because the states delegated only those powers they could not handle individually. Taxes for the payment of such debts were levied by the individual states. The president under the Articles signed himself "President of the United States in Congress assembled," but here the United States were considered in the plural, a cooperating group. Canada was invited to join the union on equal terms but did not act.

When the war was won, it became evident that a stronger federal union was needed. The Congress left the initiative to the legislatures. Virginia in Jan. 1786 appointed commissioners to meet with representatives of other states; delegates from Virginia, Delaware, New York, New Jersey, and Pennsylvania met at Annapolis. Alexander Hamilton prepared for their call, asking delegates from all states to meet in Philadelphia in May 1787 "to render the Constitution of the Federal government adequate to the exigencies of the union." Congress endorsed the plan on Feb. 21, 1787. Delegates were appointed by all states except Rhode Island.

The convention met on May 14, 1787. George Washington was chosen president (presiding officer). The states certified 65 delegates, but 10 did not attend. The work was done by 55, not all of whom were present at all sessions. Of the 55 attending delegates, 16 failed to sign, and 39 actually signed Sept. 17, 1787, some with reservations. Some historians have said 74 delegates (9 more than the 65 actually certified) were named and 19 failed to attend. These 9 additional persons refused the appointment, were never delegates, and never counted as absentees. Washington sent the Constitution to Congress, and that body, Sept. 28, 1787, ordered it sent to the legislatures, "in order to be submitted to a convention of delegates chosen in each state by the people thereof."

The Constitution was ratified by votes of state conventions as follows: Delaware, Dec. 7, 1787, unanimous; Pennsylvania, Dec. 12, 1787, 43 to 23; New Jersey, Dec. 18, 1787, unanimous; Georgia, Jan. 2, 1788, unanimous; Connecticut, Jan. 9, 1788, 128 to 40; Massachusetts, Feb. 6, 1788, 187 to 168; Maryland, Apr. 28, 1788, 63 to 11; South Carolina, May 23, 1788, 149 to 73; New Hampshire, June 21, 1788, 57 to 46; Virginia, June 25, 1788, 89 to 79; New York, July 26, 1788, 30 to 27. Nine states were needed to establish the operation of the Constitution "between the states so ratifying the same," and New Hampshire was the 9th state. The government did not declare the Constitution in effect until the first Wednesday in Mar. 1789, which was Mar. 4. After that, North Carolina ratified it on Nov. 21, 1789, 194 to 77; and Rhode Island, May 29, 1790, 34 to 32. Vermont in convention ratified it on Jan. 10, 1791, and by act of Congress approved on Feb. 18, 1791, was admitted into the Union as the 14th state, Mar. 4, 1791.

# Constitution of the United States

## The Original 7 Articles

The text of the Constitution below (with the exception of Amendment XXVII) is taken from the pocket-size edition of the Constitution published by the U.S. Government Printing Office as a result of a U.S. House and Senate resolution to print the Constitution in its original form as amended through July 5, 1971. Text in **boldface** summarizes an article or amendment and was added by *The World Almanac*. Text in *italic* indicates that an item has been superseded or amended, or provides background information on amendments.

PREAMBLE

We, the People of the United States, in Order to form a more perfect Union, establish Justice, insure domestic Tranquility, provide for the common defence, promote the general Welfare, and secure the Blessings of Liberty to ourselves and our Posterity, do ordain and establish this Constitution for the United States of America.

ARTICLE I.

**Section 1—Legislative powers; in whom vested:**

All legislative Powers herein granted shall be vested in a Congress of the United States, which shall consist of a Senate and House of Representatives.

**Section 2—House of Representatives, how and by whom chosen. Qualifications of a Representative. Representatives and direct taxes, how apportioned. Enumeration. Vacancies to be filled. Power of choosing officers, and of impeachment.**

The House of Representatives shall be composed of Members chosen every second Year by the People of the several States, and the Electors in each State shall have the Qualifications requisite for Electors of the most numerous Branch of the State Legislature.

No person shall be a Representative who shall not have attained to the Age of twenty-five Years, and been seven Years a Citizen of the United States, and who shall not, when elected, be an Inhabitant of that State in which he shall be chosen.

*(Representatives and direct taxes shall be apportioned among the several States which may be included within this Union, according to their respective Numbers, which shall be determined by adding to the whole Number of free Persons, including those bound to Service for a Term of Years, and excluding Indians not taxed, three-fifths of all other persons.) (The previous sentence was superseded by Amendment XIV, section 2.)* The actual Enumeration shall be made within three Years after the first Meeting of the Congress of the United States, and within every subsequent Term of ten Years, in such Manner as they shall by Law direct. The Number of Representatives shall not exceed one for every thirty Thousand, but each State shall have at Least one Representative; and until such enumeration shall be made, the State of New Hampshire shall be entitled to chuse three, Massachusetts eight, Rhode-Island and Providence Plantations one, Connecticut five, New-York six, New Jersey four, Pennsylvania eight, Delaware one, Maryland six, Virginia ten, North Carolina five, South Carolina five, and Georgia three.

When vacancies happen in the Representation from any State, the Executive Authority thereof shall issue Writs of Election to fill such Vacancies.

The House of Representatives shall chuse their Speaker and other Officers; and shall have the sole Power of Impeachment.

**Section 3—Senators, how and by whom chosen. How classified. Qualifications of a Senator. President of the Senate, his right to vote. President pro tem., and other officers of the Senate, how chosen. Power to try impeachments. When President is tried, Chief Justice to preside. Sentence.**

The Senate of the United States shall be composed of two Senators from each State, *(chosen by the Legislature thereof), (The preceding five words were superseded by Amendment XVII, section 1.)* for six Years; and each Senator shall have one Vote.

Immediately after they shall be assembled in Consequence of the first Election, they shall be divided as equally as may be into three Classes. The Seats of the Senators of the first Class shall be vacated at the Expiration of the second Year, of the second Class at the Expiration of the fourth Year, and of the third Class at the Expiration of the Sixth year, so that one-third may be chosen every second Year; *(and if Vacancies happen by Resignation, or otherwise, during the Recess of the Legislature of any State, the Executive thereof may make temporary Appointments until the next Meeting of the Legislature, which shall then fill such Vacancies.) (The words in parentheses were superseded by Amendment XVII, section 2.)*

No person shall be a Senator who shall not have attained to the Age of thirty Years, and been nine Years a Citizen of the United States, and who shall not, when elected, be an Inhabitant of that State for which he shall be chosen.

The Vice President of the United States shall be President of the Senate, but shall have no Vote, unless they be equally divided.

The Senate shall chuse their other Officers, and also a President pro tempore, in the absence of the Vice President, or when he shall exercise the Office of President of the United States.

The Senate shall have the sole Power to try all Impeachments. When sitting for that Purpose, they shall be on Oath or Affirmation. When the President of the United States is tried, the Chief Justice shall preside: And no Person shall be convicted without the Concurrence of two thirds of the Members present.

Judgment in Cases of Impeachment shall not extend further than to removal from Office, and disqualification to hold and enjoy any Office of honor, Trust or Profit under the United States: but the Party convicted shall nevertheless be liable and subject to Indictment, Trial, Judgment and Punishment, according to Law.

**Section 4—Times, etc., of holding elections, how prescribed. One session each year.**

The Times, Places and Manner of holding Elections for Senators and Representatives, shall be prescribed in each State by the Legislature thereof; but the Congress may at any time by Law make or alter such Regulations, except as to the Place of Chusing Senators.

The Congress shall assemble at least once in every Year, and such Meeting shall *(be on the first Monday in December,) (The words in parentheses were superseded by Amendment XX, section 2.)* unless they shall by Law appoint a different Day.

**Section 5—Membership, quorum, adjournments, rules. Power to punish or expel. Journal. Time of adjournments, how limited, etc.**

Each House shall be the Judge of the Elections, Returns and Qualifications of its own Members, and a Majority of each shall constitute a Quorum to do Business; but a smaller number may adjourn from day to day, and may be authorized to compel the Attendance of absent Members, in such manner, and under such Penalties as each House may provide.

Each House may determine the Rules of its Proceedings, punish its members for disorderly Behavior, and, with the Concurrence of two thirds, expel a Member.

Each House shall keep a Journal of its Proceedings, and from time to time publish the same, excepting such Parts as may in their Judgment require Secrecy; and the Yeas and Nays of the Members of either House on any question shall, at the Desire of one fifth of those Present, be entered on the Journal.

Neither House, during the Session of Congress, shall, without the Consent of the other, adjourn for more than three days, nor to any other Place than that in which the two Houses shall be sitting.

**Section 6—Compensation, privileges, disqualifications in certain cases.**

The Senators and Representatives shall receive a Compensation for their Services, to be ascertained by Law, and paid out of the Treasury of the United States. They shall in all Cases, except Treason, Felony and Breach of the Peace, be privileged from Arrest during their Attendance at the Session of their respective Houses, and in going to and returning from the same; and for any Speech or Debate in either House, they shall not be questioned in any other Place.

No Senator or Representative shall, during the Time for which he was elected, be appointed to any civil Office under the Authority of the United States, which shall have been created, or the Emoluments whereof shall have been encreased during such time; and no Person holding any Office under the United States, shall be a Member of either House during his Continuance in Office.

**Section 7—House to originate all revenue bills. Veto. Bill may be passed by two-thirds of each House, notwithstanding, etc. Bill, not returned in ten days, to become a law. Provisions as to orders, concurrent resolutions, etc.**

All bills for raising Revenue shall originate in the House of Representatives; but the Senate may propose or concur with Amendments as on other Bills.

Every Bill which shall have passed the House of Representatives and the Senate, shall, before it become a Law, be presented to the President of the United States; If he approve he shall sign it, but if not he shall return it, with his Objections to that House in which it shall have originated, who shall enter the Objections at large on their Journal, and proceed to reconsider it. If after such Reconsideration two thirds of that House shall agree to pass the Bill, it shall be sent, together with the Objections, to the other House, by which it shall likewise be reconsidered, and if approved by two thirds of that House, it shall become a Law. But in all such Cases the Votes of both Houses shall be determined by Yeas and Nays, and the Names of the Persons voting for and against the Bill shall be entered on the Journal of each House respectively. If any Bill shall not be returned by the President within ten Days (Sundays excepted) after it shall have been presented to him, the Same shall be a Law, in like Manner as if he had signed it, unless the Congress by their Adjournment prevent its Return, in which Case it shall not be a Law.

Every order, Resolution, or Vote to which the Concurrence of the Senate and House of Representatives may be necessary (except on a question of Adjournment) shall be presented to the President of the United States; and before the Same shall take Effect, shall be approved by him, or being disapproved by him, shall be repassed by two thirds of the Senate and House of Representatives, according to the Rules and Limitations prescribed in the Case of a Bill.

**Section 8—Powers of Congress.**

The Congress shall have Power To lay and collect Taxes, Duties, Imposts and Excises, to pay the Debts and provide for the common Defence and general Welfare of the United States; but all Duties, Imposts and Excises shall be uniform throughout the United States;

To borrow money on the credit of the United States;

To regulate Commerce with foreign Nations, and among the several States, and with the Indian Tribes;

To establish an uniform Rule of Naturalization, and uniform Laws on the subject of Bankruptcies throughout the United States;

To coin Money, regulate the Value thereof, and of foreign Coin, and fix the Standard of Weights and Measures;

To provide for the Punishment of counterfeiting the Securities and current Coin of the United States;

To establish Post Offices and post Roads;

To promote the Progress of Science and useful Arts, by securing for limited Times to Authors and Inventors the exclusive Right to their respective Writings and Discoveries;

To constitute Tribunals inferior to the supreme Court;

To define and punish Piracies and Felonies committed on the high Seas, and Offenses against the Law of Nations;

To declare War, grant Letters of Marque and Reprisal, and make Rules concerning Captures on Land and Water;

To raise and support Armies, but no Appropriation of Money to that Use shall be for a longer Term than two Years;

To provide and maintain a Navy;

To make Rules for the Government and Regulation of the land and naval Forces;

To provide for calling forth the Militia to execute the Laws of the Union, suppress Insurrections and repel Invasions;

To provide for organizing, arming, and disciplining the Militia, and for governing such Part of them as may be employed in the Service of the United States, reserving to the States respectively, the Appointment of the Officers, and the Authority of training the Militia according to the discipline prescribed by Congress;

To exercise exclusive Legislation in all Cases whatsoever, over such District (not exceeding ten Miles square) as may, by Cession of particular States, and the acceptance of Congress, become the Seat of the Government of the United States, and to exercise like Authority over all Places purchased by the Consent of the Legislature of the State in which the Same shall be, for the Erection of Forts, Magazines, Arsenals, dock-Yards, and other needful Buildings;—And

To make all Laws which shall be necessary and proper for carrying into Execution the foregoing Powers, and all other Powers vested by this Constitution in the Government of the United States, or in any Department or Officer thereof.

**Section 9—Provision as to migration or importation of certain persons. Habeas corpus, bills of attainder, etc. Taxes, how apportioned. No export duty. No commercial preference. Money, how drawn from Treasury, etc. No titular nobility. Officers not to receive presents, etc.**

The Migration or Importation of such Persons as any of the States now existing shall think proper to admit, shall not be prohibited by the Congress prior to the Year one thousand eight hundred and eight, but a tax or duty may be imposed on such Importation, not exceeding ten dollars for each Person.

The privilege of the Writ of Habeas Corpus shall not be suspended, unless when in Cases of Rebellion or Invasion the public Safety may require it.

No Bill of Attainder or ex post facto Law shall be passed.

No capitation, or other direct, Tax shall be laid, unless in Proportion to the Census or Enumeration herein before directed to be taken. *(Modified by Amendment XVI.)*

No Tax or Duty shall be laid on Articles exported from any State.

No Preference shall be given by any Regulation of Commerce or Revenue to the Ports of one State over those of another: nor shall Vessels bound to, or from, one State, be obliged to enter, clear, or pay Duties in another.

No Money shall be drawn from the Treasury, but in Consequence of Appropriations made by Law; and a regular Statement and Account of the Receipts and Expenditures of all public Money shall be published from time to time.

No Title of Nobility shall be granted by the United States: and no Person holding any Office of Profit or Trust under them, shall, without the Consent of the Congress, accept of any present, Emolument, Office, or Title, of any kind whatever, from any King, Prince, or foreign State.

**Section 10—States prohibited from the exercise of certain powers.**

No State shall enter into any Treaty, Alliance, or Confederation; grant Letters of Marque and Reprisal; coin Money; emit Bills of Credit; make any Thing but gold and silver Coin a Tender in Payment of Debts; pass any Bill of Attainder, ex post facto Law, or Law impairing the Obligation of Contracts, or grant any Title of Nobility.

No State shall, without the Consent of the Congress, lay any Imposts or Duties on Imports or Exports, except what may be absolutely necessary for executing its inspection Laws: and the net Produce of all Duties and Imposts, laid by any State on Imports or Exports, shall be for the Use of the Treasury of the United States; and all such Laws shall be subject to the Revision and Control of the Congress.

No State shall, without the Consent of Congress, lay any duty of Tonnage, keep Troops, or Ships of War in time of Peace, enter into any Agreement or Compact with another State, or with a foreign Power, or engage in War, unless actually invaded, or in such imminent Danger as will not admit of delay.

ARTICLE II.

**Section 1—President: his term of office. Electors of President; number and how appointed. Electors to vote on same day. Qualification of President. On whom his duties devolve in case of his removal, death, etc. President's compensation. His oath of office.**

The executive Power shall be vested in a President of the United States of America. He shall hold his Office during the Term of four Years, and, together with the Vice President, chosen for the same Term, be elected, as follows.

Each State shall appoint, in such Manner as the Legislature thereof may direct, a Number of Electors, equal to the whole Number of Senators and Representatives to which the State may be entitled in the Congress: but no Senator or Representative, or Person holding an Office of Trust or Profit under the United States, shall be appointed an Elector.

*(The Electors shall meet in their respective States, and vote by Ballot for two persons, of whom one at least shall not be an Inhabitant of the same State with themselves. And they shall make a List of all the Persons voted for, and of the Number of Votes for each; which List they shall sign and certify, and transmit sealed to the Seat of the Government of the United States, directed to the President of the Senate. The President of the Senate shall, in the Presence of the Senate and House of Representatives, open all the Certificates, and the Votes shall then be counted. The Person having the greatest Number of Votes shall be the President, if such Number be a Majority of the whole Number of Electors appointed; and if there be more than one who have such Majority, and have an equal Number of Votes, then the House of Representatives shall immediately chuse by Ballot one of them for President; and if no Person have a Majority, then from the five highest on the List the said House shall in like Manner chuse the President. But in chusing the President, the Votes shall be taken by States, the Representation from each State having one Vote; a quorum for this Purpose shall consist of a Member or Members from two thirds of the States, and a Majority of all the States shall be necessary to a Choice. In every Case, after the Choice of the President, the Person having the greatest Number of Votes of the Electors shall be the Vice President. But if there should remain two or more who have equal Votes, the Senate shall chuse from them by Ballot the Vice-President.)*

*(This clause was superseded by Amendment XII.)*

The Congress may detemine the Time of chusing the Electors, and the Day on which they shall give their Votes; which Day shall be the same throughout the United States.

No person except a natural born Citizen, or a Citizen of the United States, at the time of the Adoption of this Constitution, shall be eligible to the Office of President; neither shall any Person be eligible to that Office who shall not have attained to the Age of thirty-five Years, and been fourteen Years a Resident within the United States.

*(For qualification of the Vice President, see Amendment XII.)*

In Case of the Removal of the President from Office, or of his Death, Resignation, or Inability to discharge the Powers and Duties of the said Office, the same shall devolve on the Vice President, and the Congress may by Law, provide for the Case of Removal, Death, Resignation or Inability, both of the President and Vice President, declaring what Officer shall then act as President, and such Officer shall act accordingly, until the Disability be removed, or a President shall be elected.

*(This clause has been modified by Amendments XX and XXV.)*

The President shall, at stated Times, receive for his Services, a Compensation, which shall neither be encreased nor diminished during the Period for which he shall have been elected, and he shall not receive within that Period any other Emolument from the United States, or any of them.

Before he enter on the Execution of his Office, he shall take the following Oath or Affirmation:–"I do solemnly swear (or affirm) that I will faithfully execute the Office of President of the United States, and will to the best of my Ability, preserve, protect and defend the Constitution of the United States."

**Section 2—President to be Commander-in-Chief. He may require opinions of cabinet officers, etc., may pardon. Treaty-making power. Nomination of certain officers. When President may fill vacancies.**

The President shall be Commander in Chief of the Army and Navy of the United States, and of the Militia of the several States, when called into the actual Service of the United States; he may require the Opinion in writing, of the principal Officer in each of the executive Departments, upon any subject relating to the Duties of their respective Offices, and he shall have Power to Grant Reprieves and Pardons for Offenses against the United States, except in Cases of Impeachment.

He shall have Power, by and with the Advice and Consent of the Senate, to make Treaties, provided two-thirds of the Senators present concur; and he shall nominate, and by and with the Advice and Consent of the Senate, shall appoint Ambassadors, other public Ministers and Consuls, Judges of the supreme Court, and all other Officers of the United States, whose Appointments are not herein otherwise provided for, and which shall be established by Law: but the Congress may by Law vest the Appointment of such inferior Officers, as they think proper, in the President alone, in the Courts of Law, or in the Heads of Departments.

The President shall have Power to fill up all Vacancies that may happen during the Recess of the Senate, by granting Commissions which shall expire at the End of their next Session.

**Section 3—President shall communicate to Congress. He may convene and adjourn Congress, in case of disagreement, etc. Shall receive ambassadors, execute laws, and commission officers.**

He shall from time to time give to the Congress Information of the State of the Union, and recommend to their Consideration such Measures as he shall judge necessary and expedient; he may, on extraordinary Occasions, convene both Houses, or either of them, and in Case of Disagreement between them, with Respect to the Time of Adjournment, he may adjourn them to such Time as he shall think proper; he shall receive Ambassadors and other public Ministers; he shall take Care that the Laws be faithfully executed, and shall Commission all the Officers of the United States.

**Section 4—All civil offices forfeited for certain crimes.**

The President, Vice President and all civil Officers of the United States, shall be removed from Office on Impeachment for, and Conviction of, Treason, Bribery, or other high Crimes and Misdemeanors.

ARTICLE III.

**Section 1—Judicial powers, Tenure. Compensation.**

The judicial Power of the United States, shall be vested in one supreme Court, and in such inferior Courts as the Congress may from time to time ordain and establish. The Judges, both of the supreme and inferior Courts, shall hold their Offices during good Behaviour, and shall, at stated Times, receive for their Services, a Compensation, which shall not be diminished during their Continuance in Office.

**Section 2—Judicial power; to what cases it extends. Original jurisdiction of Supreme Court; appellate jurisdiction. Trial by jury, etc. Trial, where.**

The judicial Power shall extend to all Cases, in Law and Equity, arising under this Constitution, the Laws of the United States, and Treaties made, or which shall be made, under their Authority;–to all Cases affecting Ambassadors, other public Ministers and Consuls;–to all Cases of admiralty and maritime Jurisdiction;–to Controversies to which the United States shall be a Party;–to Controversies between two or more States;–between a State and Citizens of another State;–between Citizens of different States;–between Citizens of the same State claiming Lands under Grants of different States, and between a State, or the Citizens thereof, and foreign States, Citizens or Subjects.

*(This section is modified by Amendment XI.)*

In all Cases affecting Ambassadors, other public Ministers and Consuls, and those in which a State shall be Party, the supreme Court shall have original Jurisdiction. In all the other Cases before mentioned, the supreme Court shall have appellate Jurisdiction, both as to Law and Fact, with such Exceptions, and under such Regulations as the Congress shall make.

The trial of all Crimes, except in Cases of Impeachment, shall be by Jury; and such Trial shall be held in the State where the said Crimes shall have been committed; but when not committed within any State, the Trial shall be at such Place or Places as the Congress may by Law have directed.

**Section 3—Treason Defined, Proof of, Punishment of.**

Treason against the United States, shall consist only in levying War against them, or in adhering to their Enemies, giving them Aid and Comfort. No Person shall be convicted of Treason unless on the Testimony of two Witnesses to the same overt Act, or on Confession in open Court.

The Congress shall have Power to declare the Punishment of Treason, but no Attainder of Treason shall work Corruption of Blood, or Forfeiture except during the Life of the Person attainted.

ARTICLE IV.

**Section 1—Each State to give credit to the public acts, etc., of every other State.**

Full Faith and Credit shall be given in each State to the public Acts, Records, and judicial Proceedings of every other State. And the Congress may by general Laws prescribe the Manner in which such Acts, Records and Proceedings shall be proved, and the Effect thereof.

**Section 2—Privileges of citizens of each State. Fugitives from justice to be delivered up. Persons held to service having escaped, to be delivered up.**

The Citizens of each State shall be entitled to all Privileges and Immunities of Citizens in the several States.

A Person charged in any State with Treason, Felony, or other Crime, who shall flee from Justice, and be found in another State, shall on demand of the executive Authority of the State from which he fled, be delivered up, to be removed to the State having Jurisdiction of the Crime.

*(No Person held to Service or Labour in one State, under the Laws thereof, escaping into another, shall, in Consequence of any Law or Regulation therein, be discharged from such Service or Labour, but shall be delivered up on Claim of the Party to whom such Service or Labour may be due.) (This clause was superseded by Amendment XIII.)*

**Section 3—Admission of new States. Power of Congress over territory and other property.**

New States may be admitted by the Congress into this Union; but no new State shall be formed or erected within the Jurisdiction of any other State; nor any State be formed by the Junction of two or more States, or parts of States, without the Consent of the Legislatures of the States concerned as well as of the Congress.

The Congress shall have Power to dispose of and make all needful Rules and Regulations respecting the Territory or other Property belonging to the United States; and nothing in this Constitution shall be so construed as to Prejudice any Claims of the United States, or of any particular State.

**Section 4—Republican form of government guaranteed. Each state to be protected.**

The United States shall guarantee to every State in this Union a Republican Form of Government, and shall protect each of them against Invasion; and on Application of the Legislature, or of the Executive (when the Legislature cannot be convened) against domestic Violence.

ARTICLE V.

**Constitution: how amended; proviso.**

The Congress, whenever two-thirds of both Houses shall deem it necessary, shall propose Amendments to this Constitution, or, on the Application of the Legislatures of two-thirds of the several States, shall call a Convention for proposing Amendments, which, in either Case, shall be valid to all Intents and Purposes, as part of this Constitution, when ratified by the Legislatures of three-fourths of the several States, or by Conventions in three-fourths thereof, as the one or the other Mode of Ratification may be proposed by the Congress: Provided that no Amendment which may be made prior to the Year One thousand eight hundred and eight shall in any Manner affect the first and fourth Clauses in the Ninth Section of the first Article; and that no State, without its Consent, shall be deprived of its equal Suffrage in the Senate.

ARTICLE VI.

**Certain debts, etc., declared valid. Supremacy of Constitution, treaties, and laws of the United States. Oath to support Constitution, by whom taken. No religious test.**

All Debts contracted and Engagements entered into, before the Adoption of this Constitution, shall be as valid against the United States under this Constitution, as under the Confederation.

This Constitution, and the Laws of the United States which shall be made in Pursuance thereof; and all Treaties made, or which shall be made, under the Authority of the United States, shall be the supreme Law of the Land; and the Judges in every State shall be bound thereby, any Thing in the Constitution or Laws of any State to the Contrary notwithstanding.

The Senators and Representatives before mentioned, and the Members of the several State Legislatures, and all executive and judicial Officers, both of the United States and of the several States, shall be bound by Oath or Affirmation, to support this Constitution; but no religious Test shall ever be required as a Qualification to any Office or public Trust under the United States.

ARTICLE VII.

**What ratification shall establish Constitution.**

The Ratification of the Conventions of nine States shall be sufficient for the Establishment of this Constitution between the States so ratifying the Same.

Done in Convention by the Unanimous Consent of the States present the Seventeenth Day of September in the Year of our Lord one thousand seven hundred and Eighty seven and of the Independence of the United States of America the Twelfth.

In Witness whereof We have hereunto subscribed our Names.

Go WASHINGTON, Presidt and deputy from Virginia
New Hampshire—John Langdon, Nicholas Gilman
Massachusetts—Nathaniel Gorham, Rufus King
Connecticut—Wm Saml Johnson, Roger Sherman
New York—Alexander Hamilton
New Jersey—Wil: Livingston, David Brearley, Wm Paterson, Jona: Dayton
Pennsylvania—B Franklin, Thomas Mifflin, Robt. Morris, Geo. Clymer, Thos. FitzSimons, Jared Ingersoll, James Wilson, Gouv Morris
Delaware—Geo: Read, Gunning Bedford jun, John Dickinson, Richard Bassett, Jaco: Broom
Maryland—James McHenry, Dan: of St Thos Jenifer, Danl Carrol
Virginia—John Blair, James Madison Jr.
North Carolina—Wm Blount, Richd. Dobbs Spaight, Hu Williamson
South Carolina—J. Rutledge, Charles Cotesworth Pinckney, Charles Pinckney, Pierce Butler
Georgia—William Few, Abr Baldwin
Attest: William Jackson, Secretary.

# Ten Original Amendments: The Bill of Rights

In force Dec. 15, 1791

*(The First Congress, at its first session in the City of New York, Sept. 25, 1789, submitted to the states 12 amendments to clarify certain individual and state rights not named in the Constitution. They are generally called the Bill of Rights.*

*(Influential in framing these amendments was the Declaration of Rights of Virginia, written by George Mason (1725-1792) in 1776. Mason, a Virginia delegate to the Constitutional Convention, did not sign the Constitution and opposed its ratification on the ground that it did not sufficiently oppose slavery or safeguard individual rights.*

*(In the preamble to the resolution offering the proposed amendments, Congress said: "The conventions of a number of the States having at the time of their adopting the Constitution, expressed a desire, in order to prevent misconstruction or abuse of its powers, that further declaratory and restrictive clauses should be added, and as extending the ground of public confidence in the government will best insure the beneficent ends of its institution, be it resolved," etc.*

*(Ten of these amendments, now commonly known as 1one to 10 inclusive, but originally 3 to 12 inclusive, were ratified by the states as follows: New Jersey, Nov. 20, 1789; Maryland, Dec. 19, 1789; North Carolina, Dec. 22, 1789; South Carolina, Jan. 19, 1790; New Hampshire, Jan. 25, 1790; Delaware, Jan. 28, 1790; New York, Feb. 27, 1790; Pennsylvania, Mar. 10, 1790; Rhode Island, June 7, 1790; Vermont, Nov. 3, 1791; Virginia, Dec. 15, 1791; Massachusetts, Mar. 2, 1939; Georgia, Mar. 18, 1939; Connecticut, Apr. 19, 1939. These original 10 ratified amendments follow as Amendments I to X inclusive.*

*(Of the 2two original proposed amendments that were not ratified promptly by the necessary number of states, the first related to apportionment of Representatives; the second, relating to compensation of members of Congress, was ratified in 1992 and became Amendment 27.)*

AMENDMENT I.

**Religious establishment prohibited. Freedom of speech, of the press, and right to petition.**

Congress shall make no law respecting an establishment of religion, or prohibiting the free exercise thereof; or abridging the freedom of speech, or of the press; or the right of the people peaceably to assemble, and to petition the Government for a redress of grievances.

AMENDMENT II.

**Right to keep and bear arms.**

A well regulated Militia, being necessary to the security of a free State, the right of the people to keep and bear Arms, shall not be infringed.

AMENDMENT III.

**Conditions for quarters for soldiers.**

No Soldier shall, in time of peace be quartered in any house, without the consent of the Owner, nor in time of war, but in a manner to be prescribed by law.

AMENDMENT IV.

**Right of search and seizure regulated.**

The right of the people to be secure in their persons, houses, papers, and effects, against unreasonable searches and seizures, shall not be violated, and no Warrants shall issue, but upon probable cause, supported by Oath or affirmation, and particularly describing the place to be searched, and the persons or things to be seized.

AMENDMENT V.

**Provisions concerning prosecution. Trial and punishment—private property not to be taken for public use without compensation.**

No person shall be held to answer for a capital, or otherwise infamous crime, unless on a presentment or indictment of a Grand Jury, except in cases arising in the land or naval forces, or in the Militia, when in actual service in time of War or public danger; nor shall any person be subject for the same offence to be twice put in jeopardy of life or limb; nor shall be compelled in any criminal case to be a witness against himself, nor be deprived of life, liberty, or property, without due process of law; nor shall private property be taken for public use, without just compensation.

AMENDMENT VI.

**Right to speedy trial, witnesses, etc.**

In all criminal prosecutions, the accused shall enjoy the right to a speedy and public trial, by an impartial jury of the State and district wherein the crime shall have been committed, which district shall have been previously ascertained by law, and to be informed of the nature and cause of the accusation; to be confronted with the witnesses against him; to have compulsory process for obtaining witnesses in his favor, and to have the Assistance of Counsel for his defence.

AMENDMENT VII.

**Right of trial by jury.**

In suits at common law, where the value in controversy shall exceed twenty dollars, the right of trial by jury shall be preserved, and no fact tried by a jury, shall be otherwise reexamined in any Court of the United States, than according to the rules of the common law.

AMENDMENT VIII.

**Excessive bail or fines and cruel punishment prohibited.**

Excessive bail shall not be required, nor excessive fines imposed, nor cruel and unusual punishments inflicted.

AMENDMENT IX.

**Rule of construction of Constitution.**

The enumeration in the Constitution, of certain rights, shall not be construed to deny or disparage others retained by the people.

AMENDMENT X.

**Rights of States under Constitution.**

The powers not delegated to the United States by the Constitution, nor prohibited by it to the States, are reserved to the States respectively, or to the people.

# Amendments Since the Bill of Rights

AMENDMENT XI.

**Judicial powers construed.**

The Judicial power of the United States shall not be construed to extend to any suit in law or equity, commenced or prosecuted against one of the United States by Citizens of another State, or by Citizens or Subjects of any Foreign State.

*(This amendment was proposed to the Legislatures of the several States by the Third Congress on Marrch. 4, 1794, and was declared to have been ratified in a message from the President to Congress, dated Jan. 8, 1798.*

*(It was on Jan. 5, 1798, that Secretary of State Pickering received from 12 of the States authenticated ratifications, and informed President John Adams of that fact.*

*(As a result of later research in the Department of State, it is now established that Amendment XI became part of the Constitution on Feb. 7, 1795, for on that date it had been ratified by 12 States as follows:*

*(1. New York, Mar. 27, 1794. 2. Rhode Island, Mar. 31, 1794. 3. Connecticut, May 8, 1794. 4. New Hampshire, June 16, 1794. 5. Massachusetts, June 26, 1794. 6. Vermont, between Oct. 9, 1794, and Nov. 9, 1794. 7. Virginia, Nov. 18,*

*1794. 8. Georgia, Nov. 29, 1794. 9. Kentucky, Dec. 7, 1794. 10. Maryland, Dec. 26, 1794. 11. Delaware, Jan. 23, 1795. 12. North Carolina, Feb. 7, 1795.*

*(On June 1, 1796, more than a year after Amendment XI had become a part of the Constitution—but before anyone was officially aware of this—Tennessee had been admitted as a State; but not until Oct. 16, 1797, was a certified copy of the resolution of Congress proposing the amendment sent to the Governor of Tennessee, John Sevier, by Secretary of State Pickering, whose office was then at Trenton, New Jersey, because of the epidemic of yellow fever at Philadelphia; it seems, however, that the Legislature of Tennessee took no action on Amendment XI, owing doubtless to the fact that public announcement of its adoption was made soon thereafter.*

*(Besides the necessary 12 States, one other, South Carolina, ratified Amendment XI, but this action was not taken until Dec. 4, 1797; the two remaining States, New Jersey and Pennsylvania, failed to ratify.)*

AMENDMENT XII.

**Manner of choosing President and Vice-President.**

*(Proposed by Congress Dec. 9, 1803; ratified June 15, 1804.)*

The Electors shall meet in their respective states and vote by ballot for President and Vice-President, one of whom, at least, shall not be an inhabitant of the same state with themselves; they shall name in their ballots the person voted for as President, and in distinct ballots the person voted for as Vice-President, and they shall make distinct lists of all persons voted for as President, and of all persons voted for as Vice-President, and of the number of votes for each, which lists they shall sign and certify, and transmit sealed to the seat of the government of the United States, directed to the President of the Senate;–The President of the Senate shall, in presence of the Senate and House of Representatives, open all the certificates and the votes shall then be counted;—The person having the greatest number of votes for President, shall be the President, if such number be a majority of the whole number of Electors appointed; and if no person have such majority, then from the persons having the highest numbers not exceeding three on the list of those voted for as President, the House of Representatives shall choose immediately, by ballot, the President. But in choosing the President, the votes shall be taken by states, the representation from each state having one vote; a quorum for this purpose shall consist of a member or members from two-thirds of the states, and a majority of all the states shall be necessary to a choice. *(And if the House of Representatives shall not choose a President whenever the right of choice shall devolve upon them, before the fourth day of March next following, then the Vice-President shall act as President, as in the case of the death or other constitutional disability of the President.) (The words in parentheses were superseded by Amendment XX, section 3.)* The person having the greatest number of votes as Vice-President, shall be the Vice-President, if such number be a majority of the whole number of Electors appointed, and if no person have a majority, then from the two highest numbers on the list, the Senate shall choose the Vice-President; a quorum for the purpose shall consist of two-thirds of the whole number of Senators, and a majority of the whole number shall be necessary to a choice. But no person constitutionally ineligible to the office of President shall be eligible to that of Vice-President of the United States.

## THE RECONSTRUCTION AMENDMENTS

***(Amendments XIII, XIV, and XV are commonly known as the Reconstruction Amendments, inasmuch as they followed the Civil War, and were drafted by Republicans who were bent on imposing their own policy of reconstruction on the South. Post-bellum legislatures there—Mississippi, South Carolina, Georgia, for example—had set up laws which, it was charged, were contrived to perpetuate Negro slavery under other names.)***

AMENDMENT XIII.

**Slavery abolished.**

*(Proposed by Congress Jan. 31, 1865; ratified Dec. 6, 1865. The amendment, when first proposed by a resolution in Congress, was passed by the Senate, 38 to 6, on Apr. 8, 1864, but was defeated in the House, 95 to 66 on June 15, 1864. On reconsideration by the House, on Jan. 31, 1865, the resolution passed, 119 to 56. It was approved by President Lincoln on Feb. 1, 1865, although the Supreme Court had decided in 1798 that the President has nothing to do with the proposing of amendments to the Constitution or their adoption.)*

1. Neither slavery nor involuntary servitude, except as a punishment for crime whereof the party shall have been duly convicted, shall exist within the United States, or any place subject to their jurisdiction.

2. Congress shall have power to enforce this article by appropriate legislation.

AMENDMENT XIV.

**Citizenship rights not to be abridged.**

*(The following amendment was proposed to the Legislatures of the several states by the 39th Congress, June 13, 1866, ratified July 9, 1868, and declared to have been ratified in a proclamation by the Secretary of State, July 28, 1868.*

*(The 14th amendment was adopted only by virtue of ratification subsequent to earlier rejections. Newly constituted legislatures in both North Carolina and South Carolina (respectively July 4 and 9, 1868), ratified the proposed amendment, although earlier legislatures had rejected the proposal. The Secretary of State issued a proclamation, which, though doubtful as to the effect of attempted withdrawals by Ohio and New Jersey, entertained no doubt as to the validity of the ratification by North and South Carolina. The following day (July 21, 1868), Congress passed a resolution which declared the 14th Amendment to be a part of the Constitution and directed the Secretary of State so to promulgate it. The Secretary waited, however, until the newly constituted Legislature of Georgia had ratified the amendment, subsequent to an earlier rejection, before the promulgation of the ratification of the new amendment.)*

1. All persons born or naturalized in the United States, and subject to the jurisdiction thereof, are citizens of the United States and of the State wherein they reside. No State shall make or enforce any law which shall abridge the privileges or immunities of citizens of the United States; nor shall any State deprive any person of life, liberty, or property, without due process of law; nor deny to any person within its jurisdiction the equal protection of the laws.

2. Representatives shall be apportioned among the several States according to their respective numbers, counting the whole number of persons in each State, excluding Indians not taxed. But when the right to vote at any election for the choice of electors for President and Vice-President of the United States, Representatives in Congress, the Executive and Judicial officers of a State, or the members of the Legislature thereof, is denied to any of the male inhabitants of such State, being twenty-one years of age, and citizens of the United States, or in any way abridged, except for participation in rebellion, or other crime, the basis of representation therein shall be reduced in the proportion which the number of such male citizens shall bear to the whole number of male citizens twenty-one years of age in such State.

3. No person shall be a Senator or Representative in Congress, or elector of President and Vice-President, or hold any office, civil or military, under the United States, or under any State, who, having previously taken an oath, as a member of Congress, or as an officer of the United States, or as a member of any State legislature, or as an executive or judicial officer of any State, to support the Constitution of the United States, shall have engaged in insurrection or rebellion against the same, or given aid or comfort to the enemies thereof. But Congress may by a vote of two-thirds of each House, remove such disability.

4. The validity of the public debt of the United States, authorized by law, including debts incurred for payment of pensions and bounties for services in suppressing insurrection or rebellion, shall not be questioned. But neither the United States nor any State shall assume or pay any debt or obligation incurred in aid of insurrection or rebellion against the United

States, or any claim for the loss or emancipation of any slave; but all such debts, obligations and claims shall be held illegal and void.

The Congress shall have power to enforce, by appropriate legislation, the provisions of this article.

AMENDMENT XV.

**Race no bar to voting rights.**

*(The following amendment was proposed to the legislatures of the several States by the 40th Congress, Feb. 26, 1869, and ratified Feb. 8, 1870.)*

1. The right of citizens of the United States to vote shall not be denied or abridged by the United States or by any State on account of race, color, or previous condition of servitude–

2. The Congress shall have power to enforce this article by appropriate legislation.

AMENDMENT XVI.

**Income taxes authorized.**

*(Proposed by Congress July 12, 1909; ratified Feb. 3, 1913.)*

The Congress shall have power to lay and collect taxes on incomes, from whatever source derived, without apportionment among the several States, and without regard to any census or enumeration.

AMENDMENT XVII.

**United States Senators to be elected by direct popular vote.**

*(Proposed by Congress May 13, 1912; ratified Apr. 8, 1913.)*

The Senate of the United States shall be composed of two Senators from each State, elected by the people thereof, for six years; and each Senator shall have one vote. The electors in each State shall have the qualifications requisite for electors of the most numerous branch of the State legislatures.

When vacancies happen in the representation of any State in the Senate, the executive authority of such State shall issue writs of election to fill such vacancies: *Provided,* That the legislature of any State may empower the executive thereof to make temporary appointments until the people fill the vacancies by election as the legislature may direct.

This amendment shall not be so construed as to affect the election or term of any Senator chosen before it becomes valid as part of the Constitution.

AMENDMENT XVIII.

**Liquor prohibition amendment.**

*(Proposed by Congress Dec. 18, 1917; ratified Jan. 16, 1919. Repealed by Amendment XXI, effective Dec. 5, 1933.)*

1. After one year from the ratification of this article the manufacture, sale, or transportation of intoxicating liquors within, the importation thereof into, or the exportation thereof from the United States and all territory subject to the jurisdiction thereof for beverage purposes is hereby prohibited.

2. The Congress and the several States shall have concurrent power to enforce this article by appropriate legislation.

3. This article shall be inoperative unless it shall have been ratified as an amendment to the Constitution by the legislatures of the several States as provided in the Constitution, within seven years from the date of the submission hereof to the States by the Congress.

*(The total vote in the Senates of the various States was 1,310 for, 237 against—84.6% dry. In the lower houses of the States the vote was 3,782 for, 1,035 against—78.5% dry.*

*(The amendment ultimately was adopted by all the States except Connecticut and Rhode Island.)*

AMENDMENT XIX.

**Giving nationwide suffrage to women.**

*(Proposed by Congress June 4, 1919; ratified Aug. 18, 1920.)*

The right of citizens of the United States to vote shall not be denied or abridged by the United States or by any State on account of sex.

Congress shall have power to enforce this Article by appropriate legislation.

AMENDMENT XX.

**Terms of President and Vice President to begin on Jan. 20; those of Senators, Representatives, Jan. 3.**

*(Proposed by Congress Mar. 2, 1932; ratified Jan. 23, 1933.)*

1. The terms of the President and Vice President shall end at noon on the 20th day of January, and the terms of Senators and Representatives at noon on the 3d day of January, of the years in which such terms would have ended if this article had not been ratified; and the terms of their successors shall then begin.

2. The Congress shall assemble at least once in every year, and such meeting shall begin at noon on the 3d day of January, unless they shall by law appoint a different day.

3. If, at the time fixed for the beginning of the term of the President, the President elect shall have died, the Vice President elect shall become President. If a President shall not have been chosen before the time fixed for the beginning of his term, or if the President elect shall have failed to qualify, then the Vice President elect shall act as President until a President shall have qualified; and the Congress may by law provide for the case wherein neither a President elect nor a Vice President elect shall have qualified, declaring who shall then act as President, or the manner in which one who is to act shall be selected, and such person shall act accordingly until a President or Vice President shall have qualified.

4. The Congress may by law provide for the case of the death of any of the persons from whom the House of Representatives may choose a President whenever the right of choice shall have devolved upon them, and for the case of the death of any of the persons from whom the Senate may choose a Vice President whenever the right of choice shall have devolved upon them.

5. Sections 1 and 2 shall take effect on the 15th day of October following the ratification of this article (Oct. 1933).

6. This article shall be inoperative unless it shall have been ratified as an amendment to the Constitution by the legislatures of three-fourths of the several States within seven years from the date of its submission.

AMENDMENT XXI.

**Repeal of Amendment XVIII.**

*(Proposed by Congress Feb. 20, 1933; ratified Dec. 5, 1933.)*

1. The eighteenth article of amendment to the Constitution of the United States is hereby repealed.

2. The transportation or importation into any State, Territory, or possession of the United States for delivery or use therein of intoxicating liquors, in violation of the laws thereof, is hereby prohibited.

3. This article shall be inoperative unless it shall have been ratified as an amendment to the Constitution by conventions in the several States, as provided in the Constitution, within seven years from the date of the submission hereof to the States by the Congress.

AMENDMENT XXII.

**Limiting Presidential terms of office.**

*(Proposed by Congress Mar. 24, 1947; ratified Feb. 27, 1951.)*

1. No person shall be elected to the office of the President more than twice, and no person who has held the office of President, or acted as President, for more than two years of a term to which some other person was elected President shall be elected to the office of the President more than once. But this Article shall not apply to any person holding the office of

President when this Article was proposed by the Congress, and shall not prevent any person who may be holding the office of President, or acting as President, during the term within which this Article becomes operative from holding the office of President or acting as President during the remainder of such term.

2. This article shall be inoperative unless it shall have been ratified as an amendment to the Constitution by the legislatures of three-fourths of the several States within seven years from the date of its submission to the States by the Congress.

AMENDMENT XXIII.

**Presidential vote for District of Columbia.**

*(Proposed by Congress June 16, 1960; ratified Mar. 29, 1961.)*

1. The District constituting the seat of Government of the United States shall appoint in such manner as the Congress may direct:

A number of electors of President and Vice President equal to the whole number of Senators and Representatives in Congress to which the District would be entitled if it were a State, but in no event more than the least populous State; they shall be in addition to those appointed by the States, but they shall be considered, for the purposes of the election of President and Vice President, to be electors appointed by a State; and they shall meet in the District and perform such duties as provided by the twelfth article of amendment.

2. The Congress shall have power to enforce this article by appropriate legislation.

AMENDMENT XXIV.

**Barring poll tax in federal elections.**

*(Proposed by Congress Aug. 27, 1962; ratified Jan. 23, 1964.)*

1. The right of citizens of the United States to vote in any primary or other election for President or Vice President, for electors for President or Vice President, or for Senator or Representative in Congress, shall not be denied or abridged by the United States or any State by reason of failure to pay any poll tax or other tax.

2. The Congress shall have power to enforce this article by appropriate legislation.

AMENDMENT XXV.

**Presidential disability and succession.**

*(Proposed by Congress July 6, 1965; ratified Feb. 10, 1967.)*

1. In case of the removal of the President from office or of his death or resignation, the Vice President shall become President.

2. Whenever there is a vacancy in the office of the Vice President, the President shall nominate a Vice President who shall take office upon confirmation by a majority vote of both houses of Congress.

3. Whenever the President transmits to the President pro tempore of the Senate and the Speaker of the House of Representatives his written declaration that he is unable to discharge the powers and duties of his office, and until he transmits to them a written declaration to the contrary, such powers and duties shall be discharged by the Vice President as Acting President.

4. Whenever the Vice President and a majority of either the principal officers of the executive departments or of such other body as Congress may by law provide, transmit to the President pro tempore of the Senate and the Speaker of the House of Representatives their written declaration that the President is unable to discharge the powers and duties of his office, the Vice President shall immediately assume the powers and duties of the office as Acting President.

Thereafter, when the President transmits to the President pro tempore of the Senate and the Speaker of the House of Representatives his written declaration that no inability exists, he shall resume the powers and duties of his office unless the Vice President and a majority of either the principal officers of the executive department or of such other body as Congress may by law provide, transmit within four days to the President pro tempore of the Senate and the Speaker of the House of Representatives their written declaration that the President is unable to discharge the powers and duties of his office. Thereupon Congress shall decide the issue, assembling within forty-eight hours for that purpose if not in session. If the Congress, within twenty-one days after receipt of the latter written declaration, or, if Congress is not in session, within twenty-one days after Congress is required to assemble, determines by two-thirds vote of both Houses that the President is unable to discharge the powers and duties of his office, the Vice President shall continue to discharge the same as Acting President; otherwise, the President shall resume the powers and duties of his office.

AMENDMENT XXVI.

**Lowering voting age to 18 years.**

*(Proposed by Congress Mar. 23, 1971; ratified July 1, 1971.)*

1. The right of citizens of the United States, who are eighteen years of age or older, to vote shall not be denied or abridged by the United States or by any State on account of age.

2. The Congress shall have the power to enforce this article by appropriate legislation.

AMENDMENT XXVII.

**Congressional pay.**

*(Proposed by Congress Sept. 25, 1789; ratified May 7, 1992.)*

No law, varying the compensation for the services of the Senators and Representatives, shall take effect, until an election of Representatives shall have intervened.

# How a Bill Becomes a Law

1. A senator or representative introduces a bill by sending it to the clerk of the House or the Senate, who assigns it a number and title. This procedure is termed the first reading. The clerk then refers the bill to the appropriate Senate or House committee.
2. If the committee opposes the bill, it will table, or kill, it. Otherwise, the committee holds hearings to listen to opinions and facts offered by members and other interested people. The committee then debates the bill and possibly offers amendments. A vote is taken, and if favorable, the bill is sent back to the clerk of the House or Senate.
3. The clerk reads the bill to the house—the second reading. Members may then debate the bill and suggest amendments.
4. After debate and possibly amendment, the bill is given a third reading, simply of the title, and put to a voice or roll-call vote.
5. If passed, the bill goes to the other house, where it may be defeated or passed, with or without amendments. If defeated, the bill dies. If passed with amendments, a conference committee made up of members of both houses works out the differences and arrives at a compromise.
6. After passage of the final version by both houses, the bill is sent to the president. If the president signs it, the bill becomes a law. The president may, however, veto the bill by refusing to sign it and sending it back to the house where it originated, with reasons for the veto.
7. The president's objections are then read and debated, and a roll-call vote is taken. If the bill receives less than a two-thirds majority, it is defeated. If it receives at least two-thirds, it is sent to the other house. If that house also passes it by at least a two-thirds majority, the veto is overridden, and the bill becomes a law.
8. If the president neither signs nor vetoes the bill within 10 days—not including Sundays—it automatically becomes a law even without the president's signature. However, if Congress has adjourned within those 10 days, the bill is automatically killed; this indirect rejection is termed a pocket veto.

*Note:* Under "line-item veto" legislation effective Jan. 1, 1997, the president could also, under certain circumstances, eliminate a tax cut or expenditure (not including entitlements such as Medicare or Social Security) in a bill without vetoing the whole bill.

# Confederate States and Secession

The American Civil War (1861-65) grew out of sectional disputes over the continued existence of slavery in the South and the contention of Southern legislators that the states retained many sovereign rights, including the right to secede from the Union.

The war was not fought by state against state but by one federal regime against another, the Confederate government in Richmond assuming control over the economic, political, and military life of the South, under protest from Georgia and South Carolina.

South Carolina voted an ordinance of secession from the Union, repealing its 1788 ratification of the U.S. Constitution on Dec. 20, 1860, to take effect on Dec. 24. Other states seceded in 1861. Their votes in conventions were:

Mississippi, Jan. 9, 84-15; Florida, Jan. 10, 62-7; Alabama, Jan. 11, 61-39; Georgia, Jan. 19, 208-89; Louisiana, Jan. 26, 113-17; Texas, Feb. 1, 166-7, ratified by popular vote on Feb. 23 (for 34,794, against 11,325); Virginia, Apr. 17, 88-55, ratified by popular vote on May 23 (for 128,884; against 32,134); Arkansas, May 6, 69-1; Tennessee, May 7, ratified by popular vote on June 8 (for 104,019, against 47,238); North Carolina, May 21.

Missouri Unionists stopped secession in conventions Feb. 28 and Mar. 9. The legislature condemned secession Mar. 7. Under the protection of Confederate troops, secessionist members of the legislature adopted a resolution of secession at Neosho, Oct. 31. The Confederate Congress seated the secessionists' representatives.

Kentucky did not secede, and its government remained Unionist. In a part of the state occupied by Confederate troops, Kentuckians approved secession, and the Confederate Congress admitted their representatives.

The Maryland legislature voted against secession Apr. 27, 53-13. Delaware did not secede. Western Virginia held conventions at Wheeling, named a pro-Union governor on June 11, 1861; and was admitted to the Union as West Virginia on June 20, 1863. Its constitution provided for gradual abolition of slavery.

## Confederate Government

Forty-two delegates from South Carolina, Georgia, Alabama, Mississippi, Louisiana, and Florida met in convention at Montgomery, AL, on Feb. 4, 1861. They adopted a provisional constitution of the Confederate States of America and elected Jefferson Davis (MS) as provisional president and Alexander H. Stephens (GA) as provisional vice president.

A permanent constitution was adopted on Mar. 11; it abolished the African slave trade. The Congress moved to Richmond, VA, on July 20. Davis was elected president in October and was inaugurated on Feb. 22, 1862.

The Congress adopted a flag, consisting of a red field with a white stripe, and a blue jack with a circle of white stars. Later the more popular flag was the red field with blue diagonal crossbars that held 13 white stars. The stars represented the 11 states actually in the Confederacy plus Kentucky and Missouri.

# Lincoln's Address at Gettysburg, 1863

Fourscore and seven years ago our fathers brought forth on this continent a new nation, conceived in liberty and dedicated to the proposition that all men are created equal.

Now we are engaged in a great civil war, testing whether that nation or any nation so conceived and so dedicated can long endure. We are met on a great battle field of that war. We have come to dedicate a portion of that field, as a final resting-place for those who here gave their lives that that nation might live. It is altogether fitting and proper that we should do this.

But, in a larger sense, we can not dedicate—we can not consecrate—we can not hallow—this ground. The brave men, living and dead, who struggled here, have consecrated it, far above our poor power to add or detract. The world will little note, nor long remember, what we say here, but it can never forget what they did here. It is for us the living, rather, to be dedicated here to the unfinished work which they who fought here have thus far so nobly advanced. It is rather for us to be here dedicated to the great task remaining before us—that from these honored dead we take increased devotion to that cause for which they gave the last full measure of devotion—that we here highly resolve that these dead shall not have died in vain—that this nation, under God, shall have a new birth of freedom—and that government of the people, by the people, for the people, shall not perish from the earth.

# Selected Landmark Decisions of the U.S. Supreme Court

**1803: Marbury v. Madison.** The Court ruled that Congress exceeded its power in the Judiciary Act of 1789; thus, the Court established its power to review acts of Congress and declare invalid those it found in conflict with the Constitution.

**1819: McCulloch v. Maryland.** The Court ruled that Congress had the authority to charter a national bank, under the Constitution's granting of the power to enact all laws "necessary and proper" to exact the responsibilities of government. The Court also held that the national bank was immune to state taxation.

**1819: Trustees of Dartmouth College v. Woodward.** The Court ruled that a state could not arbitrarily alter the terms of a college's contract. (In later years the Court widened the implications by using the same principle to limit the states' ability to interfere with business contracts.)

**1857: Dred Scott v. Sanford.** The Court declared unconstitutional the already-repealed Missouri Compromise of 1820 because it deprived a person of his or her property—a slave—without due process of law. The Court also ruled that slaves were not citizens of any state nor of the U.S. (The latter part of the decision was overturned by ratification of the 14th Amendment in 1868.)

**1896: Plessy v. Ferguson.** The Court ruled that a state law requiring federal railroad trains to provide separate but equal facilities for black and white passengers neither infringed upon federal authority to regulate interstate commerce nor violated the 13th and 14th Amendments. (The "separate but equal" doctrine remained effective until the 1954 Brown v. Board of Education decision.)

**1904: Northern Securities Co. v. U.S.** The Court ruled that a holding company formed solely to eliminate competition between two railroad lines was a combination in restraint of trade, violating the federal antitrust act.

**1908: Muller v. Oregon.** The Court upheld a state law limiting the working hours of women. (Instead of presenting legal arguments, Louis D. Brandeis, counsel for the state, brought forth evidence from social workers, physicians, and factory inspectors that the number of hours women worked affected their health and morals.)

**1911: Standard Oil Co. of New Jersey et al. v. U.S.** The Court ruled that the Standard Oil Trust must be dissolved because of its unreasonable restraint of trade, not because of its size.

**1919: Schenck v. U.S.** In its first decision regarding the extent of protection afforded by the First Amendment, the Court sustained the Espionage Act of 1917, maintaining that freedom of speech and press could be constrained if "the words used are in such circumstances and are of such a nature as to create a clear and present danger. . ."

**1925: Gitlow v. New York.** The Court ruled that the First Amendment prohibition against government abridgement of the freedom of speech applied to the states as well as to the federal government. The decision was the first of a number of rulings holding that the 14th Amendment extended the guarantees of the Bill of Rights to state action.

**1935: Schechter Poultry Corp. v. U.S.** The Court ruled that Congress exceeded its authority to delegate legislative powers and to regulate interstate commerce when it enacted the National Industrial Recovery Act, which afforded the U.S. president too much discretionary power.

**1951: Dennis et al. v. U.S.** The Court upheld convictions under the Smith Act of 1940 for speaking about Communist theory that advocated the forcible overthrow of the government. (In the 1957 **Yates** v. **U.S.** decision, the Court moderated this ruling by allowing such advocacy in the abstract, if not connected to action to achieve the goal.)

**1954: Brown v. Board of Education of Topeka.** The Court ruled that separate public schools for black and white students were inherently unequal, thus state-sanctioned segregation in public schools violated the equal protection guarantee of the 14th Amendment. And in **Bolling v. Sharpe** the Court ruled that the congressionally mandated segregated public school system in the District of Columbia violated the Fifth Amendment's due process guarantee of personal liberty. (The Brown ruling also led to the abolition of state-sponsored segregation in other public facilities.)

**1957: Roth v. U.S., Alberts v. California.** The Court ruled that obscene material was not protected by the First Amendment guarantees of freedom of speech and press, defining obscene as "utterly without redeeming social value" and appealing to "prurient interests" in the view of the average person. (This definition, the first offered by the Court, was modified in several subsequent decisions, and the "average person" standard was replaced by the "local community" standard in the **1973 Miller v. California** case.)

**1961: Mapp v. Ohio.** The Court ruled that evidence obtained in violation of the 4th Amendment guarantee against unreasonable search and seizure must be excluded from use at state as well as federal trials.

**1962: Engel v. Vitale.** The Court ruled that public school officials could not require pupils to recite a state-composed prayer at the start of each school day, even if the prayer was nondenominational and pupils who so desired could be excused from reciting it, because such official state sanction of religious utterances was an unconstitutional attempt to establish religion.

**1962: Baker v. Carr.** The Court held that the constitutional challenges to the unequal distribution of voters among legislative districts could be resolved by federal courts, rejecting the doctrine set out in **Colegrove v. Green** in 1946 that such apportionment challenges were "political questions."

**1963: Gideon v. Wainwright.** The Court ruled that the due process clause of the 14th Amendment extended to state as well as federal defendants, thus all persons charged with serious crimes must be provided with an attorney, and states were required to appoint counsel for defendants unable to pay their own attorneys' fees.

**1964: New York Times Co. v. Sullivan.** The Court ruled that the First Amendment guarantee of freedom of the press protected the press from libel suits for defamatory reports on public officials unless the officials proved that the reports were made from actual malice. The Court defined malice as "with knowledge that (the defamatory statement) was false or with reckless disregard of whether it was false or not."

**1965: Griswold v. Conn.** The Court ruled that a state unconstitutionally interfered with personal privacy in the marriage relationship when it prohibited anyone, including married couples, from using contraceptives.

**1966: Miranda v. Arizona.** The Court ruled that the guarantee of due process required that before any questioning of suspects in police custody, the suspects must be informed of their right to remain silent, that anything they say may be used against them, and that they have the right to counsel.

**1973: Roe v. Wade, Doe v. Bolton.** The Court ruled that the fetus was not a "person" with constitutional rights and that a right to privacy inherent in the 14th Amendment's due process guarantee of personal liberty protected a woman's decision whether or not to bear a child. During the first trimester of pregnancy, the Court maintained, the decision to have an abortion should be left entirely to a woman and her physician. Some regulation of abortion procedures was allowed in the 2d trimester, and some restriction of abortion in the 3d.

**1974: U.S. v. Nixon.** The Court ruled that neither the separation of powers nor the need to preserve the confidentiality of presidential communications could alone justify an absolute executive privilege of immunity from judicial demands for evidence to be used in a criminal trial.

**1976: Gregg v. Georgia, Profitt v. Fla., Jurek v. Texas.** The Court held that death, as a punishment for persons convicted of first degree murder, was not in and of itself cruel and unusual punishment in violation of the 8th Amendment. The Court also ruled that the amendment required the sentencing judge and jury to consider the individual character of the offender and the circumstances of the particular crime before deciding whether to impose the death sentence. In the associated **Woodson v. N.C., Roberts v. La.,** the Court ruled that states could not make death the mandatory penalty for first-degree murder, since that would fail to meet the constitutional requirement for the consideration of the individual offender and offense.

**1978: Regents of Univ. of Calif. v. Bakke.** The Court ruled that a special admissions program for a state medical school under which a set number of places were set aside for minority group members, with white applicants denied the opportunity to compete for those seats, violated Title XIV of the 1964 Civil Rights Act, which forbids the exclusion of anyone, because of race, from participation in a federally funded program. The Court also ruled that admissions programs that considered race as one of a complex of factors involved in the decision to admit or reject an applicant were not unconstitutional.

**1986: Bowers v. Hardwick.** The Court refused to extend any constitutional right of privacy to homosexual activity, upholding a Georgia law that in effect made such activity a crime. (Although the Georgia law specifically prohibited sodomy, whether heterosexual or homosexual, enforcement had been confined to homosexual sodomy.) In **Romer v. Evans (1996),** however, in a decision more favorable to gay rights, the Court struck down a Colorado constitutional provision that barred legislation protecting homosexuals from discrimination.

**1990: Cruzan v. Missouri.** The Court ruled that a person had the right to refuse life-sustaining medical treatment. However, the Court also ruled that, for a comatose patient, a state could require "clear and convincing evidence" that the patient would not have wanted to live under those conditions before treatment could be withheld.

**1995: Adarand Constructors v. Peña.** The Court held that federal programs that classify people by race, unless "narrowly tailored" to accomplish a "compelling governmental interest," may deny individuals the right to equal protection. Such federal programs, the Court maintained, must adhere to the same strict standards required of state-run affirmative action programs.

**1995: U.S. Term Limits Inc. v. Thorton.** The Court ruled that it is unconstitutional for either the states or Congress to limit the terms of members of Congress, since the Constitution reserves the right to choose federal lawmakers to the people. (This ruling invalidated 23 congressional term-limit laws that had been passed since 1990.)

## Presidential Oath of Office

The Constitution (Article II) directs that the president shall take the following oath or affirmation: "I do solemnly swear (affirm) that I will faithfully execute the office of President of the United States, and will, to the best of my ability, preserve, protect, and defend the Constitution of the United States." (Custom decrees the use of the words "So help me God" at the end of the oath when taken by the president-elect, his or her left hand on the Bible for the duration of the oath, with his or her right hand slightly raised.)

## Law on Succession to the Presidency

If by reason of death, resignation, removal from office, inability, or failure to qualify there is neither a president nor vice president to discharge the powers and duties of the office of president, then the speaker of the House of Representatives shall upon his resignation as speaker and as representative, act as president. The same rule shall apply in the case of the death, resignation, removal from office, or inability of an individual acting as president.

If at the time when a speaker is to begin the discharge of the powers and duties of the office of president there is no speaker, or the speaker fails to qualify as acting president, then the president pro tempore of the Senate, upon his resignation as president pro tempore and as senator, shall act as president.

An individual acting as president shall continue to act until the expiration of the then current presidential term, except that (1) if his discharge of the powers and duties of the office is founded in whole or in part in the failure of both the president-elect and the vice president-elect to qualify, then he shall act only until a president or vice president qualifies, and (2) if his discharge of the powers and duties of the office is founded in whole or in part on the inability of the president or vice president, then he shall act only until the removal of the disability of one of such individuals.

If, by reason of death, resignation, removal from office, or failure to qualify, there is no president pro tempore to act as president, then the officer of the United States who is highest on the following list, and who is not under any disability to discharge the powers and duties of president shall act as president; the secretaries of state, treasury, defense, attorney general; secretaries of interior, agriculture, commerce, labor, health and human services, housing and urban development, transportation, energy, education, veterans affairs.

*(Legislation approved July 18, 1947; amended Sept. 9, 1965, Oct. 15, 1966, Aug. 4, 1977, and Sept. 27, 1979. See also Constitutional Amendment XXV.)*

## Origin of the United States National Motto

*In God We Trust,* designated as the U.S. National Motto by Congress in 1956, originated during the Civil War as an inscription for U. S. coins, although it was used by Francis Scott Key in a slightly different form when he wrote "The Star-Spangled Banner" in 1814. On Nov. 13, 1861, when Union morale had been shaken by battlefield defeats, the Rev. M. R. Watkinson, of Ridleyville, PA, wrote to Secy. of the Treasury Salmon P. Chase. "From my heart I have felt our national shame in disowning God as not the least of our present national disasters," the minister wrote, suggesting "recognition of the Almighty God in some form on our coins." Secy. Chase ordered designs prepared with the inscription *In God We Trust* and backed coinage legislation that authorized use of this slogan. It first appeared on some U.S. coins in 1864, disappeared and reappeared on various coins until 1955, when Congress ordered it placed on all paper money and all coins.

## The Great Seal of the U.S.

On July 4, 1776, the Continental Congress appointed a committee consisting of Benjamin Franklin, John Adams, and Thomas Jefferson "to bring in a device for a seal of the United States of America." The designs submitted by this and a subsequent committee were considered unacceptable. After many delays, a third committee, appointed early in 1782, presented a design prepared by William Barton. Charles Thomson, the secretary of Congress, suggested certain changes, and Congress finally approved the design on June 20, 1782. The obverse side of the seal shows an American bald eagle. In its mouth is a ribbon bearing the motto *e pluribus unum* (one out of many). In the eagle's talons are the arrows of war and an olive branch of peace. The reverse side shows an unfinished pyramid with an eye (the eye of Providence) above it.

## The American's Creed

**William Tyler Page, Clerk of the U.S. House of Representatives, wrote "The American's Creed" in 1917. It was accepted by the House on behalf of the American people on April 3, 1918.**

"I believe in the United States of America as a government of the people, by the people, for the people; whose just powers are derived from the consent of the governed; a democracy in a republic; a sovereign Nation of many sovereign States; a perfect union, one and inseparable; established upon those principles of freedom, equality, justice, and humanity for which American patriots sacrificed their lives and fortunes.

"I therefore believe it is my duty to my country to love it, to support its Constitution, to obey its laws, to respect its flag, and to defend it against all enemies."

## The Flag of the U.S.—The Stars and Stripes

The 50-star flag of the United States was raised for the first time officially at 12:01 AM on July 4, 1960, at Fort McHenry National Monument in Baltimore, MD. The 50th star had been added for Hawaii; a year earlier the 49th, for Alaska. Before that, no star had been added since 1912, when New Mexico and Arizona were admitted to the Union.

The true history of the Stars and Stripes has become so cluttered by myth and tradition that the facts are difficult, and in some cases impossible, to establish. For example, it is not certain who designed the Stars and Stripes, who made the first such flag, or even whether it ever flew in any sea fight or land battle of the American Revolution.

All agree, however, that the Stars and Stripes originated as the result of a resolution offered by the Marine Committee of the Second Continental Congress at Philadelphia and adopted on June 14, 1777. It read:

*Resolved: that the flag of the United States be thirteen stripes, alternate red and white; that the union be thirteen stars, white in a blue field, representing a new constellation.*

Congress gave no hint as to the designer of the flag, no instructions as to the arrangement of the stars, and no information on its appropriate uses. Historians have been unable to find the original flag law.

The resolution establishing the flag was not even published until Sept. 2, 1777. Despite repeated requests, Washington did not get the flags until 1783, after the American Revolution was over. And there is no certainty that they were the Stars and Stripes.

## Early Flags

Many historians consider the first flag of the U.S. to have been the Grand Union (sometimes called Great Union) flag, although the Continental Congress never officially adopted it. This flag was a modification of the British Meteor flag, which had the red cross of St. George and the white cross of St. Andrew combined in the blue canton. For the Grand Union flag, 6 horizontal stripes were imposed on the red field, dividing it into 13 alternating red and white stripes. On Jan. 1, 1776, when the Continental Army came into formal existence, this flag was unfurled on Prospect Hill, Somerville, MA. Washington wrote that "we hoisted the Union Flag in compliment to the United Colonies."

One of several flags about which controversy has raged for years is at Easton, PA. Containing the devices of the national flag in reversed order, this flag has been in the public library at Easton for more than 150 years. Some contend that this flag was actually the first Stars and Stripes, first displayed on July 8, 1776. This flag has 13 red and white stripes in the canton, 13 white stars centered in a blue field.

A flag was hastily improvised from garments by the defenders of Fort Schuyler at Rome, NY, Aug. 3-22, 1777. Historians believe it was the Grand Union Flag.

The Sons of Liberty had a flag of 9 red and white stripes, to signify 9 colonies, when they met in New York in 1765 to oppose the Stamp Tax. By 1775, the flag had grown to 13 red and white stripes, with a rattlesnake on it.

At Concord, Apr. 19, 1775, the minutemen from Bedford, MA, are said to have carried a flag having a silver arm with sword on a red field.

At Cambridge, MA, the Sons of Liberty used a plain red flag with a green pine tree on it.

In June 1775, Washington went from Philadelphia to Boston to take command of the army, escorted to New York by the Philadelphia Light Horse Troop. It carried a yellow flag that had an elaborate coat of arms—the shield charged with 13 knots, the motto "For These We Strive"—and a canton of 13 blue and silver stripes.

In Feb. 1776, Col. Christopher Gadsden, a member of the Continental Congress, gave the South Carolina Provincial Congress a flag "such as is to be used by the commander-in-chief of the American Navy." It had a yellow field, with a rattlesnake about to strike and the words "Don't Tread on Me."

At the Battle of Bennington, Aug. 16, 1777, patriots used a flag of 7 white and 6 red stripes with a blue canton extending down 9 stripes and showing an arch of 11 white stars over the figure 76 and a star in each of the upper corners. The stars are 7-pointed. This flag is preserved in the Historical Museum at Bennington, VT.

At the Battle of Cowpens, Jan. 17, 1781, the 3d Maryland Regiment is said to have carried a flag of 13 red and white stripes, with a blue canton containing 12 stars in a circle around one star.

**Who Designed the Flag?** No one knows for certain. Francis Hopkinson, designer of a naval flag, declared he also had designed the flag and in 1781 asked Congress to reimburse him for his services. Congress did not do so. Dumas Malone of Columbia University wrote: "This talented man . . . designed the American flag."

**Who Called the Flag "Old Glory"?** The flag is said to have been named Old Glory by William Driver, a sea captain of Salem, MA. One legend has it that when he raised the flag on his brig, the *Charles Doggett*, in 1824, he said: "I name thee Old Glory." But his daughter, who presented the flag to the Smithsonian Institution, said he named it at his 21st birthday celebration on Mar. 17, 1824, when his mother presented the homemade flag to him.

**The Betsy Ross Legend.** The widely publicized legend that Mrs. Betsy Ross made the first Stars and Stripes in June 1776, at the request of a committee composed of George Washington, Robert Morris, and George Ross, an uncle, was first made public in 1870, by a grandson of Mrs. Ross. Historians have been unable to find a historical record of such a meeting or committee.

## Adding New Stars

The flag of 1777 was used until 1795. Then, on the admission of Vermont and Kentucky to the Union, Congress passed and Pres. Washington signed an act that after May 1, 1795, the flag should have 15 stripes, alternating red and white, and 15 white stars on a blue field.

When new states were admitted, it became evident that the flag would become burdened with stripes. Congress thereupon ordered that after July 4, 1818, the flag should have 13 stripes, symbolizing the 13 original states; that the union have 20 stars, and that whenever a new state was admitted a new star should be added on the July 4 following admission. No law designates the permanent arrangement of the stars. However, since 1912, when a new state has been admitted, the new design has been announced by executive order. No star is specifically identified with any state.

# Code of Etiquette for Display and Use of the U.S. Flag

Although the Stars and Stripes originated in 1777, it was not until 146 years later that there was a serious attempt to establish a uniform code of etiquette for the U.S. flag. On Feb. 15, 1923, the War Department issued a circular on the rules of flag usage. These rules were adopted almost in their entirety June 14, 1923, by a conference of 68 patriotic organizations in Washington. Finally, on June 22, 1942, a joint resolution of Congress, amended by Public Law 94-344 July 7, 1976, codified "existing rules and customs pertaining to the display and use of the flag . . ."

**When to Display the Flag**—The flag should be displayed on all days, especially on legal holidays and other special occasions, on official buildings when in use, in or near polling places on election days, and in or near schools when in session. Citizens may fly the flag at any time. It is customary to display the flag only from sunrise to sunset on buildings and on stationary flagstaffs in the open. It may be displayed at night, however, on special occasions, preferably lighted. In Washington, the flag now flies over the White House both day and night. It flies over the Senate wing of the Capitol when the Senate is in session and over the House wing when that body is in session. It flies day and night over the east and west fronts of the Capitol, without floodlights at night but receiving light from the illuminated Capitol Dome. It flies 24 hours a day at several other places, including the Fort McHenry National Monument in Baltimore, where it inspired Francis Scott Key to write "The Star Spangled Banner." The flag also flies 24 hours a day, properly illuminated, at U.S. Customs ports of entry.

**Flying the Flag at Half-Staff**—Flying the flag at half-staff, that is, halfway up the staff, is a signal of mourning. The flag should be hoisted to the top of the staff for an instant before being lowered to half-staff. It should be hoisted to the peak again before being lowered for the day or night.

As provided by presidential proclamation, the flag should fly at half-staff for 30 days from the day of death of a president or former president; for 10 days from the day of death of a vice president, chief justice or retired chief justice of the U.S., or speaker of the House of Representatives; from day of death until burial of an associate justice of the Supreme Court, cabinet member, former vice president, Senate president pro tempore, or majority or minority Senate or House leader; for a U.S. senator, representative, territorial delegate, or the resident commissioner of Puerto Rico, on day of death and the following day within the metropolitan area of the District of Columbia and from day of death until burial within the decedent's state, congressional district, territory or commonwealth; and for the death of the governor of a state, territory, or possession of the U.S., from day of death until burial.

On Memorial Day, the flag should fly at half-staff until noon and then be raised to the peak. The flag should also fly at half-staff on Korean War Veterans Armistice Day (July 27), National Pearl Harbor Remembrance Day (Dec. 7), and Peace Officers Memorial Day (May 15).

**How to Fly the Flag**—The flag should be hoisted briskly and lowered ceremoniously and should never be allowed to touch the ground or the floor. When the flag is hung over a sidewalk from a rope extending from a building to a pole, the union should be away from the building. When the flag is hung over the center of a street the union should be to the north in an east-west street and to the east in a north-south street. No other flag may be flown above or, if on the same level, to the right of the U.S. flag, except that at the United Nations Headquarters the UN flag may be placed above flags of all member nations and other national flags may be flown with equal prominence or honor with the flag of the U.S. At services by Navy chaplains at sea, the church pennant may be flown above the flag.

When 2 flags are placed against a wall with crossed staffs, the U.S. flag should be at right—its own right, and its staff should be in front of the staff of the other flag; when a number of flags are grouped and displayed from staffs, it should be at the center and highest point of the group.

**Church and Platform Use**—In an auditorium, the flag may be displayed flat, above and behind the speaker. When displayed from a staff in a church or in a public auditorium, the flag should hold the position of superior prominence, in advance of the audience, and in the position of honor at the speaker's right as she or he faces the audience. Any other flag so displayed should be placed on the left of the speaker or to the right of the audience.

When the flag is displayed horizontally or vertically against a wall, the stars should be uppermost and at the observer's left.

When used to cover a casket, the flag should be placed so that the union is at the head and over the left shoulder. It should not be lowered into the grave nor touch the ground.

**How to Dispose of Worn Flags**—When the flag is in such condition that it is no longer a fitting emblem for display, it should be destroyed in a dignified way, preferably by burning.

**When to Salute the Flag**—All persons present should face the flag, stand at attention, and salute on the following occasions: (1) when the flag is passing in a parade or in a review, (2) during the ceremony of hoisting or lowering, (3) when the national anthem is played, and (4) during the Pledge of Allegiance. Those present in uniform should render the military salute. Those not in uniform should place the right hand over the heart. A man wearing a hat should remove it with his right hand and hold it to his left shoulder during the salute.

**Prohibited Uses of the Flag**—The flag should not be dipped to any person or thing. (An exception—customarily, ships salute by dipping their colors.) It should never be displayed with the union down save as a distress signal. It should never be carried flat or horizontally, but always aloft and free.

It should not be displayed on a float, an automobile, or a boat except from a staff. It should never be used as a covering for a ceiling, nor have placed on it any word, design, or drawing. It should never be used as a receptacle for carrying anything. It should not be used to cover a statue or a monument.

The flag should never be used for advertising purposes, nor be embroidered on such articles as cushions or handkerchiefs, printed or otherwise impressed on boxes or anything that is designed for temporary use and discard; or used as a costume or athletic uniform. Advertising signs should not be fastened to its staff or halyard.

The flag should never be used as drapery of any sort, never festooned, drawn back, nor up, in folds, but always allowed to fall free. Bunting of blue, white, and red, always arranged with the blue above and the white in the middle, should be used for covering a speaker's desk, draping the front of a platform, and for decoration in general.

An act of Congress approved on Feb. 8, 1917, provided certain penalties for the desecration, mutilation, or improper use of the flag within the District of Columbia. A 1968 federal law provided penalties of as much as a year's imprisonment or a $1,000 fine or both for publicly burning or otherwise desecrating any U.S. flag. In addition, many states have laws against flag desecration. In 1989, the Supreme Court ruled that no laws could prohibit political protesters from burning the flag. The decision had the effect of declaring unconstitutional the flag desecration laws of 48 states, as well as a similar federal statute, in cases of peaceful political expression.

The Supreme Court, June 1990, declared that a new federal law making it a crime to burn or deface the American flag violates the free-speech guarantee of the First Amendment. The 5-4 decision led to renewed calls in Congress for a constitutional amendment to make it possible to prosecute flag burners.

### Pledge of Allegiance to the Flag

*I pledge allegiance to the flag of the United States of America and to the republic for which it stands, one nation under God, indivisible, with liberty and justice for all.*

This, the current official version of the Pledge of Allegiance, has developed from the original pledge, which was first published in the Sept. 8, 1892, issue of *Youth's Companion*, a weekly magazine then published in Boston. The original pledge contained the phrase "my flag," which was changed more than 30 years later to "flag of the United States of America." A 1954 act of Congress added the words "under God."

The authorship of the pledge had been in dispute for many years. The *Youth's Companion* stated in 1917 that the original draft was written by James B. Upham, an executive of the magazine who died in 1910. A leaflet circulated by the magazine later named Upham as the originator of the draft "afterwards condensed and perfected by him and his associates of the Companion force."

Francis Bellamy, a former member of *Youth's Companion* editorial staff, publicly claimed authorship of the pledge in 1923. The United States Flag Association, acting on the advice of a committee named to study the controversy, upheld in 1939 the claim of Bellamy, who had died 8 years earlier. The Library of Congress issued in 1957 a report attributing the authorship to Bellamy.

## The History of the National Anthem

"The Star-Spangled Banner" was ordered played by the military and naval services by President Woodrow Wilson in 1916. It was designated the national anthem by Act of Congress, Mar. 3, 1931. It was written by Francis Scott Key, of Georgetown, MD, during the bombardment of Fort McHenry, Baltimore, MD, Sept. 13-14, 1814. Key was a lawyer, a graduate of St. John's College, Annapolis, and a volunteer in a light artillery company. When a friend, Dr. Beanes, a physician of Upper Marlborough, MD, was taken aboard Admiral Cockburn's British squadron for interfering with ground troops, Key and J. S. Skinner, carrying a note from President Madison, went to the fleet under a flag of truce on a cartel ship to ask Beanes's release. Cockburn consented, but as the fleet was about to sail up the Patapsco to bombard Fort McHenry, he detained them, first on HMS *Surprise* and then on a supply ship.

Key witnessed the bombardment from his own vessel. It began at 7 AM, Sept. 13, 1814, and lasted, with intermissions, for 25 hr. The British fired more than 1,500 shells, each weighing as much as 220 lb. They were unable to approach closely because the U.S. had sunk 22 vessels. Only 4 Americans were killed and 24 wounded. A British bomb-ship was disabled.

During the bombardment, Key wrote a stanza on the back of an envelope. Next day at Indian Queen Inn, Baltimore, he wrote out the poem and gave it to his brother-in-law, Judge J. H. Nicholson. Nicholson suggested the tune, Anacreon in Heaven, and had the poem printed on broadsides, of which 2 survive. On Sept. 20 it appeared in the *Baltimore American*. Later Key made 3 copies; one is in the Library of Congress, and one is in the Pennsylvania Historical Society.

The copy that Key wrote in his hotel on Sept. 14, 1814, remained in the Nicholson family for 93 years. In 1907 it was sold to Henry Walters of Baltimore. In 1934 it was bought at auction in New York from the Walters estate by the Walters Art Gallery, Baltimore, for $26,400. The Walters Gallery in 1953 sold the manuscript to the Maryland Historical Society for the same price.

The flag that Key saw during the bombardment is preserved in the Smithsonian Institution, Washington, DC. It is 30 by 42 ft and has 15 alternating red and white stripes and 15 stars, for the original 13 states plus Kentucky and Vermont. It was made by Mary Young Pickersgill. The Baltimore Flag House, a museum, occupies her premises, which were restored in 1953.

## The Star-Spangled Banner

I

Oh, say can you see by the dawn's early light
What so proudly we hailed at the twilight's last gleaming?
Whose broad stripes and bright stars thru the perilous fight,
O'er the ramparts we watched were so gallantly streaming?
And the rocket's red glare, the bombs bursting in air,
Gave proof through the night that our flag was still there.
Oh, say does that star-spangled banner yet wave
O'er the land of the free and the home of the brave?

II

On the shore, dimly seen through the mists of the deep,
Where the foe's haughty host in dread silence reposes,
What is that which the breeze, o'er the towering steep,
As it fitfully blows, half conceals, half discloses?
Now it catches the gleam of the morning's first beam,
In full glory reflected now shines in the stream:
'Tis the star-spangled banner! Oh long may it wave
O'er the land of the free and the home of the brave!

III

And where is that band who so vauntingly swore
That the havoc of war and the battle's confusion,
A home and a country should leave us no more!
Their blood has washed out their foul footsteps' pollution.
No refuge could save the hireling and slave
From the terror of flight, or the gloom of the grave:
And the star-spangled banner in triumph doth wave
O'er the land of the free and the home of the brave!

IV

Oh! thus be it ever, when freemen shall stand
Between their loved home and the war's desolation!
Blest with victory and peace, may the heav'n rescued land
Praise the Power that hath made and preserved us a nation.
Then conquer we must, when our cause it is just,
And this be our motto: "In God is our trust."
And the star-spangled banner in triumph shall wave
O'er the land of the free and the home of the brave!

## America
## (My Country 'Tis of Thee)

First sung in public on July 4, 1831, at a service in the Park Street Church, Boston, the words were written by Rev. Samuel Francis Smith, a Baptist clergyman, who set them to a melody he found in a German songbook, unaware that it was the tune for the British anthem, "God Save the King/Queen."

My country, 'tis of thee,
Sweet land of liberty, Of thee I sing.
Land where my fathers died!
Land of the Pilgrims' pride!
From ev'ry mountainside,
Let freedom ring!

My native country, thee,
Land of the noble free,
Thy name I love.
I love thy rocks and rills,
Thy woods and templed hills;
My heart with rapture thrills
Like that above.

Let music swell the breeze,
And ring from all the trees
Sweet freedom's song.
Let mortal tongues awake;
Let all that breathe partake;
Let rocks their silence break,
The sound prolong.

Our fathers' God, to Thee,
Author of liberty,
To Thee we sing.
Long may our land be bright
With freedom's holy light;
Protect us by Thy might,
Great God, our King!

## America, the Beautiful

Composed by Katharine Lee Bates, a Massachusetts educator and author, in 1893. It was inspired by the view Bates experienced atop Pikes Peak. Its final form was established in 1911 and is set to the music of Samuel A. Ward's "Materna."

O beautiful for spacious skies,
For amber waves of grain,
For purple mountain majesties
Above the fruited plain.
America! America!
God shed His grace on thee,
And crown thy good with brotherhood
From sea to shining sea.
O beautiful for pilgrim feet
Whose stern impassion'd stress
A thorough-fare for freedom beat
Across the wilderness.
America! America!
God mend thine ev'ry flaw,
Confirm thy soul in self control,
Thy liberty in law.

O beautiful for heroes prov'd
In liberating strife,
Who more than self their country lov'd
And mercy more than life.
America! America!
May God thy gold refine
Till all success be nobleness,
And ev'ry gain divine.
O beautiful for patriot dream
That sees beyond the years,
Thine alabaster cities gleam,
Undimmed by human tears.
America! America!
God shed His grace on thee,
And crown thy good with brotherhood
From sea to shining sea.

## The Liberty Bell: Its History and Significance

The Liberty Bell, in Independence National Historical Park, Philadelphia, is an object of great reverence to Americans because of its association with the historic events of the American Revolution.

The original Province bell was ordered by Assembly Speaker and Chairman of the State House Superintendents Isaac Norris and was ordered from Thomas Lester, Whitechapel Foundry, London. It reached Philadelphia at the end of August 1752. It bore an inscription from Leviticus 25:10: "PROCLAIM LIBERTY THROUGHOUT ALL THE LAND UNTO ALL THE INHABITANTS THEREOF."

The bell was cracked by a stroke of its clapper in Sept. 1752 while it hung on a truss in the State House yard for testing. Pass & Stow, Philadelphia founders, recast the bell, adding 1½ ounces of copper to a pound of the original "Whitechapel" metal to reduce its high tone and brittleness. It was found that the bell contained too much copper, injuring its tone, so Pass & Stow recast it again, this time successfully.

In June 1753 the bell was hung in the old wooden steeple of the State House, erected on top of the brick tower. In use while the Continental Congress was in session in the State House, it rang out in defiance of British tax and trade restrictions, and it proclaimed the Boston Tea Party and the first public reading of the Declaration of Independence.

On Sept. 18, 1777, when the British Army was about to occupy Philadelphia, the bell was moved in a baggage train of the American Army to Allentown, PA, where it was hidden in the Zion Reformed Church until June 27, 1778. It was moved back to Philadelphia after the British left.

In July 1781 the wooden steeple became insecure and had to be taken down. The bell was lowered into the brick section of the tower, where it remained until 1828. Between 1828 and 1844 the old State House bell continued to ring during special occasions. It rang for the last time on Feb. 23, 1846. In 1852 it was placed on exhibition in the Declaration Chamber of Independence Hall.

In 1876, when many thousands of Americans visited Philadelphia for the Centennial Exposition, the bell was placed in its old wooden support in the tower hallway. In 1877 it was hung from the ceiling of the tower by a chain of 13 links. It was returned again to the Declaration Chamber and in 1896 taken back to the tower hall, where it occupied a glass case. In 1915 the case was removed so that the public might touch it. On Jan. 1, 1976, just after midnight to mark the opening of the Bicentennial Year, the bell was moved to a new glass and steel pavilion behind Independence Hall for easier viewing by the larger number of visitors expected during the year.

The measurements of the bell are: circumference around the lip, 12 ft ½ in; circumference around the crown, 6 ft 11¼ in; lip to the crown, 3 ft; height over the crown, 2 ft 3 in; thickness at lip, 3 in; thickness at crown, 1¼ in; weight, 2,080 lb; length of clapper, 3 ft 2 in; cost, £60 14s 5d.

The specific source of the crack in the bell is unknown.

# Statue of Liberty National Monument

Since 1886, the Statue of Liberty Enlightening the World has stood as a symbol of freedom in New York harbor. It also commemorates French-American friendship, for it was given by the people of France and designed by French sculptor Frederic Auguste Bartholdi (1834-1904).

Edouard de Laboulaye, French historian and admirer of American political institutions, suggested that the French present a monument to the U.S., the latter to provide pedestal and site. Bartholdi visualized a colossal statue at the entrance of New York harbor, welcoming the peoples of the world with the torch of liberty.

On Washington's Birthday, Feb. 22, 1877, Congress approved the use of a site on Bedloe's Island suggested by Bartholdi. This island of 12 acres had been owned in the 17th century by a Walloon named Isaac Bedloe. It was called Bedloe's until Aug. 3, 1956, when Pres. Eisenhower approved a resolution of Congress changing the name to Liberty Island.

The statue was finished on May 21, 1884, and formally presented to the U.S. minister to France, Levi Parsons Morton, July 4, 1884, by Ferdinand de Lesseps, head of the Franco-American Union, promoter of the Panama Canal, and builder of the Suez Canal.

On Aug. 5, 1884, the Americans laid the cornerstone for the pedestal. This was to be built on the foundations of Fort Wood, which had been erected by the government in 1811. The American committee had raised $125,000, but this was found to be inadequate. Joseph Pulitzer, owner of the *New York World,* appealed on Mar. 16, 1885, for general donations. By Aug. 11, 1885, he had raised $100,000.

The statue arrived dismantled, in 214 packing cases, from Rouen, France, in June 1885. The last rivet of the statue was driven on Oct. 28, 1886, when Pres. Grover Cleveland dedicated the monument.

The statue weighs 450,000 lb, or 225 tons. The copper sheeting weighs 200,000 lb. There are 167 steps from the land level to the top of the pedestal, 168 steps inside the statue to the head, and 54 rungs on the ladder leading to the arm that holds the torch.

A $2.5 million building housing the American Museum of Immigration was opened by Pres. Richard Nixon on Sept. 26, 1972, at the base of the statue. It houses a permanent exhibition of photos, posters, and artifacts tracing the history of American immigration. The Statue of Liberty National Monument is administered by the National Park Service.

Two years of restoration work was completed before the statue's centennial celebration on July 4, 1986. Among other repairs, the multimillion dollar project included replacing the 1,600 wrought iron bands that hold the statue's copper skin to its frame, replacing its torch, and installing an elevator.

A 4-day extravaganza of concerts, tall ships, ethnic festivals, and fireworks celebrated the 100th anniversary. The festivities included Chief Justice Warren E. Burger's swearing-in of 5,000 new citizens on Ellis Island, while 20,000 others across the country were simultaneously sworn in through a satellite telecast.

The ceremonies were followed by others on Oct. 28, 1986, the statue's 100th birthday.

| Dimensions of the Statue | Ft. | In. |
|---|---|---|
| Height from base to torch (45.3 meters) | 151 | 1 |
| Foundation of pedestal to torch (91.5 meters) | 305 | 1 |
| Heel to top of head | 111 | 1 |
| Length of hand | 16 | 5 |
| Index finger | 8 | 0 |
| Circumference at second joint | 3 | 6 |
| Size of finger nail 13x10 in. | | |
| Head from chin to cranium | 17 | 3 |
| Head thickness from ear to ear | 10 | 0 |
| Distance across the eye | 2 | 6 |
| Length of nose | 4 | 6 |
| Right arm, length | 42 | 0 |
| Right arm, greatest thickness | 12 | 0 |
| Thickness of waist | 35 | 0 |
| Width of mouth | 3 | 0 |
| Tablet, length | 23 | 7 |
| Tablet, width | 13 | 7 |
| Tablet, thickness | 2 | 0 |

## Emma Lazarus's Famous Poem

A poem by Emma Lazarus is graven on a tablet within the pedestal on which the Statue of Liberty stands.

*The New Colossus*

*Not like the brazen giant of Greek fame,*
*With conquering limbs astride from land to land;*
*Here at our sea-washed, sunset gates shall stand*
*A mighty woman with a torch, whose flame*
*Is the imprisoned lightning, and her name*
*Mother of Exiles. From her beacon-hand*
*Glows world-wide welcome; her mild eyes command*
*The air-bridged harbor that twin cities frame.*
*"Keep ancient lands, your storied pomp!" cries she*
*With silent lips. "Give me your tired, your poor,*
*Your huddled masses yearning to breathe free,*
*The wretched refuse of your teeming shore.*
*Send these, the homeless, tempest-tost to me,*
*I lift my lamp beside the golden door!"*

## Ellis Island

Ellis Island was the gateway to America for more than 12 million immigrants between 1892 and 1924. In the late 18th century, Samuel Ellis, a New York City merchant, purchased the island and gave it his name. From Ellis, it passed to New York State, and the U.S. government bought it in 1808. In 1892 the government opened an immigration center on the island. The 27½-acre site eventually supported more than 35 buildings, including the Main Building with its Great Hall, in which as many as 5,000 people a day were processed during peak periods. Closed as an immigration station in 1954, Ellis Island was proclaimed part of the National Monument in 1965 by Pres. Lyndon B. Johnson. After an 8-year privately funded $156 million restoration project, Ellis Island was reopened as a museum in 1990. Artifacts, historic photographs and documents, oral histories, and ethnic music depicting 400 years of American immigration are housed in the museum. The museum also includes the American Immigrant Wall of Honor, inscribed with some 520,000 names.

# BIOGRAPHIES OF U.S. PRESIDENTS

## George Washington (1789-97)

George Washington, first president, Federalist, was born on Feb. 22, 1732, in Wakefield on Pope's Creek, Westmoreland Co., VA, the son of Augustine and Mary Ball Washington. He spent his early childhood on a farm near Fredericksburg. His father died when George was 11. He studied mathematics and surveying, and when he was 16, he went to live with his elder half brother, Lawrence, who built and named Mount Vernon. George surveyed the lands of Thomas Fairfax in the Shenandoah Valley, keeping a diary. He accompanied Lawrence to Barbados, West Indies, where he contracted smallpox and was deeply scarred. Lawrence died in 1752, and George inherited his property. He valued land, and when he died, he owned 70,000 acres in Virginia and 40,000 acres in what is now West Virginia.

Washington's military service began in 1753, when Lt. Gov. Robert Dinwiddie of Virginia sent him on missions deep into Ohio country. He clashed with the French and had to surrender Fort Necessity on July 3, 1754. He was an aide to the British general Edward Braddock and was at his side when the army was ambushed and defeated (July 9, 1755) on a march to Fort Duquesne. He helped take Fort Duquesne from the French in 1758.

After Washington's marriage to Martha Dandridge Custis, a widow, in 1759, he managed his family estate at Mount Vernon. Although not at first for independence, he opposed the repressive measures of the British crown and took charge of the Virginia troops before war broke out. He was made commander of the newly created Continental Army by the Continental Congress on June 15, 1775.

The American victory was due largely to Washington's leadership. He was resourceful, a stern disciplinarian, and the one strong, dependable force for unity. Washington favored a federal government. He became chairman of the Constitutional Convention of 1787 and helped get the Constitution ratified. Unanimously elected president by the Electoral College, he was inaugurated Apr. 30, 1789, on the balcony of New York's Federal Hall.

He was reelected in 1792. Washington made an effort to avoid partisan politics as president.

Refusing to consider a 3d term, he retired to Mount Vernon in March 1797. He suffered acute laryngitis after a ride in snow and rain around his estate, was bled profusely, and died Dec. 14, 1799.

## John Adams (1797-1801)

John Adams, 2d president, Federalist, was born on Oct. 30, 1735, in Braintree (now Quincy), MA, the son of John and Susanna Boylston Adams. He was a great-grandson of Henry Adams, who came from England in 1636. He graduated from Harvard in 1755 and then taught school and studied law. He married Abigail Smith in 1764. In 1765 he argued against taxation without representation before the royal governor. In 1770 he successfully defended in court the British soldiers who fired on civilians in the Boston Massacre. He was a delegate to the Continental Congress and a signer of the Declaration of Independence. In 1778, Congress sent Adams and John Jay to join Benjamin Franklin as diplomatic respresentatives in Europe. Because he ran second to Washington in Electoral College balloting in February 1789, Adams became the nation's first vice president; he was reelected in 1792.

In 1796 Adams was chosen president by the electors. His administration was marked by rivalry with Alexander Hamilton and a crisis in U.S.-French relations. He was extraordinarily unpopular for securing passage of the Alien and Sedition Acts in 1798. His foreign policy contributed significantly to the election of Thomas Jefferson in 1800.

Adams lived for a quarter century after he left office, during which time he wrote extensively. He died July 4, 1826, on the same day as Thomas Jefferson (the 50th anniversary of the Declaration of Independence).

## Thomas Jefferson (1801-9)

Thomas Jefferson, 3d president, Democratic-Republican, was born on Apr. 13, 1743, in Shadwell in Goochland (now Albemarle) Co., VA, the son of Peter and Jane Randolph Jefferson. Peter died when Thomas was 14, leaving him 2,750 acres and his slaves. Jefferson attended (1760-62) the College of William and Mary, read Greek and Latin classics, and played the violin. In 1769 he was elected to the Virginia House of Burgesses. In 1770 he began building his home, Monticello, and in 1772 he married Martha Wayles Skelton, a wealthy widow. Jefferson helped establish the Virginia Committee of Correspondence. As a member of the Second Continental Congress he drafted the Declaration of Independence in late June 1776. He also was a member of the Virginia House of Delegates (1776-79) and was first elected governor of Virginia in 1779, succeeding Patrick Henry. He was reelected governor in 1780 but resigned in June 1781 after British troops invaded Virginia. During his term he wrote the statute on religious freedom. After his wife's death in 1782, Jefferson again became a delegate to the Congress, and in 1784 he drafted the report that was the basis for the Ordinances of 1784, 1785, and 1787. He was minister to France from 1785 to 1789, when George Washington appointed him secretary of state.

Jefferson's strong faith in the consent of the governed conflicted with the emphasis on executive control, favored by Alexander Hamilton, secretary of the Treasury, and Jefferson resigned on Dec. 31, 1793. In the 1796 election Jefferson was the Democratic-Republican candidate for president; John Adams won the election, and Jefferson became vice president. In 1800, Jefferson and Aaron Burr received equal Electoral College votes. The House of Representatives elected Jefferson president. Major events of his first term were the Louisiana Purchase (1803) and the Lewis and Clark Expedition. An important development during his second term was passage of the Embargo Act, barring U.S. ships from setting sail to foreign ports. Jefferson established the University of Virginia and designed its buildings. He died July 4, 1826, on the same day as John Adams (the 50th anniversary of the Declaration of Independence).

## James Madison (1809-17)

James Madison, 4th president, Democratic-Republican, was born on Mar. 16, 1751, in Port Conway, King George Co., VA, the son of James and Eleanor Rose Conway Madison. Madison graduated from Princeton in 1771. He served in the Virginia Constitutional Convention (1776), and, in 1780, became a delegate to the Second Continental Congress. He was chief recorder at the Constitutional Convention in 1787 and supported ratification in the *Federalist Papers*, written with Alexander Hamilton and John Jay. In 1789, Madison was elected to the House of Representatives, where he helped frame the Bill of Rights and fought against passage of the Alien and Sedition Acts. In the 1790s, he helped found the Democratic-Republican Party, which ultimately became the Democratic Party. He became Jefferson's secretary of state in 1801.

Madison was elected president in 1808. His first term was marked by tensions with Great Britain, and his conduct of foreign policy was criticized by the Federalists and by his own party. Nevertheless, he was reelected in 1812, the year war was declared on Great Britain. The war that many considered a second American revolution ended with a treaty that settled none of the issues. Madison's most important action after the war was demilitarizing the U.S.-Canadian border.

In 1817, Madison retired to his estate, Montpelier, where he served as an elder statesman, "the last of the fathers." He edited his famous papers on the Constitutional Convention and helped found the University of Virginia, of which he became rector in 1826. He died June 28, 1836.

## James Monroe (1817-25)

James Monroe, 5th president, Democratic-Republican, was born on Apr. 28, 1758, in Westmoreland Co., VA, the son of Spence and Eliza Jones Monroe. He entered the College of William and Mary in 1774 but left to serve in the 3d Virginia Regiment during the American Revolution. After the war, he studied law with Thomas Jefferson. In 1782 he was elected to the Virginia House of Delegates, and he served (1783-86) as a delegate to the Confederation Congress. He opposed ratification of the Constitution because it lacked a bill of rights. Monroe was elected to the U.S. Senate in 1790. In 1794 President George Washington appointed Monroe minister to France. He served twice as governor of Virginia (1799-1802, 1811). President Jefferson also sent him to France as minister (1803), and from 1803 to 1807 he served as minister to Great Britain.

In 1816 Monroe was elected president; he was reelected in 1820 with all but one Electoral College vote. His administration became known as the Era of Good Feeling. He obtained Florida from Spain, settled boundary disputes with Britain over Canada, and eliminated border forts. He supported the antislavery position that led to the Missouri Compromise. His most significant contribution was the Monroe Doctrine, which opposed European intervention in the Western Hemisphere and became a cornerstone of U.S. foreign policy.

Although Monroe retired to Oak Hill, VA, financial problems forced him to sell his property and move to New York City. He died there on July 4, 1831.

## John Quincy Adams (1825-29)

John Quincy Adams, 6th president, independent Federalist, later Democratic-Republican, was born on July 11, 1767, in Braintree (now Quincy), MA, the son of John and Abigail Adams. His father was the 2d president. He studied abroad and at Harvard Univeristy from which he graduated in 1787. In 1803, he was elected to the U.S. Senate. President Monroe chose him as his secretary of state in 1817. In this capacity he negotiated the cession of the Floridas from Spain, supported exclusion of slavery in the Missouri Compromise, and helped formulate the Monroe Doctrine.

In 1824 Adams was elected president by the House of Representatives after he failed to win an Electoral College majority. His expansion of executive powers was strongly opposed, and in the 1828 election he lost to Andrew Jackson. In 1831 he entered the House of Representatives and served 17 years with distinction. He opposed slavery, the annexation of Texas, and the Mexican War. He helped establish the Smithsonian Institution. He suffered a stroke in the House and died in the Speaker's Room on Feb. 23, 1848.

## Andrew Jackson (1829-37)

Andrew Jackson, 7th president, Democratic-Republican, later a Democrat, was born on Mar. 15, 1767, in the Waxhaw district, on the border of North Carolina and South Carolina, the son of Andrew and Elizabeth Hutchinson Jackson. At the age of 13, he joined the militia to fight in the American Revolution and was captured. Orphaned at the age of 14, Jackson was brought up by a well-to-do uncle. By age 20, he was practicing law, and he later served as prosecuting attorney in Nashville, TN. In 1796 he helped draft the constitution of Tennessee, and for a year he occupied its one seat in the House of Representatives. The next year he served in the U.S. Senate.

In the War of 1812, Jackson crushed (1814) the Creek Indians at Horseshoe Bend, AL, and, with an army consisting chiefly of backwoodsmen, defeated (1815) General Edward Pakenham's British troops at the Battle of New Orleans. In 1818 he briefly invaded Spanish Florida to quell Seminoles and outlaws who harassed frontier settlements. In 1824 he ran for president against John Quincy Adams. Although he won the most popular and electoral votes, he did not have a majority. The House of Representatives decided the election and chose Adams. In the 1828 election, however, Jackson defeated Adams, carrying the West and the South.

As president, Jackson introduced what became known as the spoils system—rewarding party members with government posts. Perhaps his most controversial act, however, was depositing federal funds in so-called pet banks, those directed by Democratic bankers, rather than in the Bank of the United States. "Let the people rule" was his slogan. In 1832, Jackson killed the congressional caucus for nominating presidential candidates and substituted the national convention. When South Carolina refused to collect imports under his protective tariff, he ordered army and naval forces to Charleston. After leaving office in 1837, he retired to the Hermitage, outside Nashville, where he died on June 8, 1845.

## Martin Van Buren (1837-41)

Martin Van Buren, 8th president, Democrat, was born on Dec. 5, 1782, in Kinderhook, NY, the son of Abraham and Maria Hoes Van Buren. After attending local schools, he studied law and became a lawyer at the age of 20. A consummate politician, Van Buren began his career in the New York state senate and then served as state attorney general from 1816 to 1819. He was elected to the U.S. Senate in 1821. He helped swing eastern support to Andrew Jackson in the 1828 election and then served as Jackson's secretary of state from 1829 to 1831. In 1832 he was elected vice president. Known as the Little Magician, Van Buren was extremely influential in Jackson's administration. In the election of 1836 he defeated William Henry Harrison for president and took office as the financial panic of 1837 initiated a nationwide depression. Although he instituted the independent treasury system, his refusal to spend land revenues led to his defeat by William Henry Harrison in the election of 1840. In 1844 he lost the Democratic nomination to James Knox Polk. In 1848 he again ran for president on the Free Soil ticket but lost. He died in Kinderhook on July 24, 1862.

## William Henry Harrison (1841)

William Henry Harrison, 9th president, Whig, who served only 31 days, was born on Feb. 9, 1773, in Berkeley, Charles City Co., VA, the son of Benjamin Harrison, a signer of the Declaration of Independence, and of Elizabeth Bassett Harrison. He attended Hampden-Sidney College. Harrison served as secretary of the Northwest Territory in 1798 and was its delegate to the House of Representatives in 1799. He was the first governor of the Indiana Territory and served as superintendent of Indian affairs. With 900 men he put down a Shawnee uprising at Tippecanoe, IN, on Nov. 7, 1811. A generation later, in 1840, he waged a rousing presidential campaign, using the slogan "Tippecanoe and Tyler too." The Tyler of the slogan was his running mate, John Tyler. Although born to one of the wealthiest, most prestigious, and most influential families in Virginia, Harrison was elected president with a "log cabin and hard cider" slogan. He caught pneumonia during the inauguration and died Apr. 4, 1841.

## John Tyler (1841-45)

John Tyler, 10th president, independent Whig, was born on Mar. 29, 1790, in Greenway, Charles City Co., VA, the son of John and Mary Armistead Tyler. His father was governor of Virginia (1808-11). Tyler graduated from the College of William and Mary in 1807 and in 1811 was elected to the Virginia legislature. In 1816 he was chosen for the U.S. House of Representatives. He served in the Virginia legislature again from 1823 to 1825, when he was elected governor of Virginia. After a stint in the U.S. Senate (1827-36), he was elected vice president (1840). When William Henry Harrison died only a month after taking office, Tyler succeeded him. Because he was the first person to occupy the presidency without having been elected to that office, he was referred to as "His Accidency." Tyler gained passage of the Preemption Act of 1841, which gave squatters on government land the right to buy 160 acres at the minimum auction price. His last act as president was to sign the resolution annexing Texas. Tyler accepted renomination in 1844 from some Democrats but withdrew in favor of the official party candidate, James K. Polk. He died in Richmond, VA, on Jan. 18, 1862.

## James Knox Polk (1845-49)

James Knox Polk, 11th president, Democrat, was born on Nov. 2, 1795, in Mecklenburg Co., NC, the son of Samuel and Jane Knox Polk. He graduated from the University of North Carolina in 1818 and served in the Tennessee state legislature from 1823 to 1825. He served in the U.S. House of Representatives from 1825 to 1839, the last 4 years as Speaker. He was governor of Tennessee from 1839 to 1841. In 1844, after the Democratic National Convention became deadlocked, it nominated Polk, who thus became the nation's first "dark horse" candidate for president. He was nominated primarily because he was known to favor annexation of Texas. As president, Polk reestablished the independent treasury system originated by Van Buren. He was so intent on acquiring California from Mexico that he sent troops under Zachary Taylor to the Mexican border and, when Mexicans attacked, declared that a state of war existed. The Mexican War ended with the annexation of California and much of the Southwest as part of America's "manifest destiny." Polk compromised on the Oregon boundary ("54-40 or fight!") by accepting the 49th parallel and yielding Vancouver Island to the British. A few weeks after leaving office, Polk died in Nashville, TN, on June 15, 1849.

## Zachary Taylor (1849-50)

Zachary Taylor, 12th president, Whig, who served only 16 months, was born on Nov. 24, 1784, in Orange Co., VA, the son of Richard and Sarah Strother Taylor. He grew up on his father's plantation near Louisville, KY, where he was educated by private tutors. In 1808 Taylor joined the regular army and was commissioned first lieutenant. He fought in the War of 1812, the Black Hawk War (1832), and the second Seminole War (beginning in 1837). He was called "Old Rough and Ready." In 1846 President Polk sent him with an army to the Rio Grande. When the Mexicans attacked him, Polk declared war. Outnumbered 4-1, Taylor defeated (1847) Santa Anna at Buena Vista. A national hero, he received the Whig nomination in 1848 and was elected president, even though he had never bothered to vote. He resumed the spoils system and, though a slaveholder, worked to admit California as a free state. He fell ill and died in office on July 9, 1850.

## Millard Fillmore (1850-53)

Millard Fillmore, 13th president, Whig, was born on Jan. 7, 1800, in Cayuga Co., NY, the son of Nathaniel and Phoebe Millard Fillmore. Although he had little schooling, he became a law clerk at the age of 22 and a year later was admitted to the bar. He was elected to the New York state assembly in 1828 and served until 1831. From 1833 until 1835 and again from 1837 to 1843, he represented his district in the U.S. House of Representatives. He opposed the entrance of Texas as a slave territory and voted for a protective tariff. In 1844 he was defeated for governor of New York. In 1848 he was elected vice president, and he succeeded as president after Taylor's death. Fillmore favored the Compromise of 1850 and signed the Fugitive Slave Law. His policies pleased neither expansionists nor slaveholders, and he was not renominated in 1852. In 1856 he was nominated by the American (Know-Nothing) Party, but despite the support of the Whigs, he was defeated by James Buchanan. He died in Buffalo, NY, on Mar. 8, 1874.

## Franklin Pierce (1853-57)

Franklin Pierce, 14th president, Democrat, was born on Nov. 23, 1804, in Hillsboro, NH, the son of Benjamin Pierce, an American Revolutionary War general and governor of New Hampshire, and Anna Kendrick. He graduated from Bowdoin College in 1824 and was admitted to the bar in 1827. He was elected to the New Hampshire state legislature in 1829 and was chosen Speaker in 1831. He went to the U.S. House of Representatives in 1833 and was elected a U.S. senator in 1837. He enlisted in the Mexican War and became brigadier general under Gen. Winfield Scott. In 1852 Pierce was nominated as the Democratic presidential candidate on the 49th ballot. He decisively defeated Gen. Scott, his Whig opponent, in the election. Although against slavery, Pierce was influenced by pro-slavery Southerners. He supported the controversial Kansas-Nebraska Act, which left the question of slavery in the new territories of Kansas and Nebraska to popular vote. Pierce signed a reciprocity treaty with Canada and approved the Gadsden Purchase, a border area on a proposed railroad route, from Mexico. Denied renomination by the Democrats, he spent most of his remaining years in Concord, NH, where he died on Oct. 8, 1869.

## James Buchanan (1857-61)

James Buchanan, 15th president, Federalist, later Democrat, was born on Apr. 23, 1791, near Mercersburg, PA, the son of James and Elizabeth Speer Buchanan. He graduated from Dickinson College in 1809 and was admitted to the bar in 1812. He fought in the War of 1812 as a volunteer. He was twice elected to the Pennsylvania general assembly, and in 1821 he entered the U.S. House of Representatives. After briefly serving (1832-33) as minister to Russia, he was elected U.S. senator from Pennsylvania. As Polk's secretary of state (1845-49), he ended the Oregon dispute with Britain and supported the Mexican War and annexation of Texas. As minister to Great Britain, he signed the Ostend Manifesto (1854), declaring a U.S. right to take Cuba by force should efforts to purchase it fail. Nominated by Democrats, Buchanan was elected president in 1856. On slavery he favored popular sovereignty and choice by state constitutions but did not consistently uphold this position. He denied the right of states to secede but opposed coercion and attempted to keep peace by not provoking secessionists. Buchanan left office having failed to deal decisively with the situation. He died at Wheatland, his estate, near Lancaster, PA, on June 1, 1868.

## Abraham Lincoln (1861-65)

Abraham Lincoln, 16th president, Republican, was born on Feb. 12, 1809, in a log cabin on a farm then in Hardin Co., KY, now in Larue, the son of Thomas and Nancy Hanks Lincoln. The Lincolns moved to Spencer Co., IN, near Gentryville, when Abe was 7. After Abe's mother died, his father married (1819) Mrs. Sarah Bush Johnston. In 1830 the family moved to Macon Co., IL.

Defeated in 1832 in a race for the state legislature, Lincoln was elected on the Whig ticket 2 years later and served in the lower house from 1834 to 1842. In 1837 Lincoln was admitted to the bar and became partner in a Springfield, IL, law office. He soon won recognition as an effective and resourceful attorney. In 1846, he was elected to the House of Representatives, where he attracted attention during a single term for his opposition to the Mexican War and his position on slavery. In 1856 he campaigned for the newly founded Republican Party, and in 1858 he became its senatorial candidate against Stephen A. Douglas. Although he lost the election, Lincoln gained national recognition from his debates with Douglas.

In 1860, Lincoln was nominated for president by the Republican Party on a platform of restricting slavery. He ran against Douglas, a northern Democrat; John C. Breckinridge, a Southern proslavery Democrat; and John Bell, of the Constitutional Union Party. As a result of Lincoln's winning the election, South Carolina seceded from the Union on Dec. 20, 1860, followed in 1861 by 10 other Southern states.

The Civil War erupted when Fort Sumter, which Lincoln decided to resupply, was attacked by Confederate forces on Apr. 12, 1861. Lincoln called successfully for recruits from the North. On Sept. 22, 1862, 5 days after the Battle of Antietam, Lincoln announced that slaves in territory then in rebellion would be free Jan. 1, 1863, the date of the Emancipation Proclamation. His speeches, including his Gettysburg and Inaugural addresses, are remembered for their eloquence.

Lincoln was reelected, in 1864, over Gen. George B. McClellan, Democrat. Lee surrendered on Apr. 9, 1865. On Apr. 14, Lincoln was shot by actor John Wilkes Booth in Ford's Theater, in Washington, DC. He died the next day.

## Andrew Johnson (1865-69)

Andrew Johnson, 17th president, Democrat, was born on Dec. 29, 1808, in Raleigh, NC, the son of Jacob and Mary McDonough Johnson. He was apprenticed to a tailor as a youth, but ran away after two years and eventually settled in Greeneville, TN. He became popular with the townspeople and in 1829 was elected councilman and later mayor. In 1835 he was sent to the state general assembly. In 1843 he was elected to the U.S. House of Representatives, where he served for 10 years. Johnson was governor of Tennessee from 1853 to 1857, when he was elected to the U.S. Senate. He supported John C. Breckinridge against Lincoln in the 1860 election. Although Johnson had held slaves, he opposed secession and tried to prevent Tennessee from seceding. In Mar. 1862, Lincoln appointed him military governor of occupied Tennessee.

In 1864, in order to balance Lincoln's ticket with a Southern Democrat, the Republicans nominated Johnson for vice president. He was elected vice president with Lincoln and then succeeded to the presidency upon Lincoln's death. Soon afterward, in a controversy with Congress over the president's power over the South, he proclaimed an amnesty to all Confederates, except certain leaders, if they would ratify the 13th Amendment abolishing slavery. States doing so added anti-

Negro provisions that enraged Congress, which restored military control over the South. When Johnson removed Edwin M. Stanton, secretary of war, without notifying the Senate, the House, in Feb. 1868, impeached him. Ostensibly charging him with thereby having violated the Tenure of Office Act, the House was actually responding to his opposition to harsh congressional Reconstruction, expressed in repeated vetoes. He was tried by the Senate, and in May, in two separate votes on different counts, was acquitted, both times by only one vote. Johnson was denied renomination but remained politically active. He was re-elected to the Senate in 1874. Johnson died July 31, 1875, at Carter Station, TN.

## Ulysses Simpson Grant (1869-77)

Ulysses S. Grant, 18th president, Republican, was born on Apr. 27, 1822, in Point Pleasant, OH, the son of Jesse R. and Hannah Simpson Grant. The next year the family moved to Georgetown, OH. Grant was named Hiram Ulysses, but on entering West Point in 1839, his name was put down as Ulysses Simpson, and he adopted it. He graduated in 1843. During the Mexican War, Grant served under both Gen. Zachary Taylor and Gen. Winfield Scott. In 1854, he resigned his commission because of loneliness and drinking problems, and in the following years he engaged in generally unsuccessful farming and business ventures. With the start of the Civil War, he was named colonel and then brigadier general of the Illinois Volunteers. He took Forts Henry and Donelson and fought at Shiloh. His brilliant campaign against Vicksburg and his victory at Chattanooga made him so prominent that Lincoln placed him in command of all Union armies. Grant accepted Lee's surrender at Appomattox Court House on Apr. 9, 1865. President Johnson appointed Grant secretary of war when he suspended Stanton, but Grant was not confirmed. He was nominated for president by the Republicans in 1868 and elected over Horatio Seymour, Democrat. The 15th Amendment, amnesty bill, and the peaceful settlement of disputes with Great Britain were events of his administration. The Liberal Republicans and Democrats opposed him with Horace Greeley in the 1872 election, but Grant was reelected. His second administration was marked by many scandals, including widespread corruption in the Treasury Department and the Indian Service. An attempt by the Stalwarts (Old Guard Republicans) to nominate him in 1880 failed. In 1884 the collapse of Grant & Ward, an investment firm in which he was a partner, left him penniless. He wrote his personal memoirs while ill with cancer and completed them shortly before his death at Mt. McGregor, NY, on July 23, 1885.

## Rutherford Birchard Hayes (1877-81)

Rutherford B. Hayes, 19th president, Republican, was born on Oct. 4, 1822, in Delaware, OH, the son of Rutherford and Sophia Birchard Hayes. He was reared by his uncle, Sardis Birchard. Hayes graduated from Kenyon College in 1842 and from Harvard Law School in 1845. He practiced law in Lower Sandusky (now Fremont), OH, and was city solicitor of Cincinnati from 1858 to 1861. During the Civil War, he was major of the 23d Ohio Volunteers. He was wounded several times, and by the end of the war he had risen to the rank of brevet major general. While serving (1865-67) in the U.S. House of Representatives, Hayes supported Reconstruction and Johnson's impeachment. He was twice elected governor of Ohio (1867, 1869). After losing a race for the U.S. House in 1872, he was reelected governor of Ohio in 1875. In 1876 he was nominated for president and believed he had lost the election to Samuel J. Tilden, Democrat. But a few Southern states submitted 2 sets of electoral votes, and the result was in dispute. An electoral commission, appointed by Congress and consisting of 8 Republicans and 7 Democrats, awarded all disputed votes to Hayes, allowing him to become president by one electoral vote. Hayes, keeping a promise to southerners, withdrew troops from areas still occupied in the South, ending the era of Reconstruction. He proposed civil service reforms, alienating those favoring the spoils system, and advocated repeal of the Tenure of Office Act restricting presidential power to dismiss officials. He supported sound money and specie payments. Hayes died in Fremont, OH, on Jan. 17, 1893.

## James Abram Garfield (1881)

James A. Garfield, 20th president, Republican, was born on Nov. 19, 1831, in Orange, Cuyahoga Co., OH, the son of Abram and Eliza Ballou Garfield. His father died in 1833, and he was reared in poverty by his mother. He worked as a canal bargeman, a farmer, and a carpenter and managed to secure a college education. He taught at Hiram College and later became principal. In 1859 he was elected to the Ohio legislature. Antislavery and antisecession, he volunteered for military service in the Civil War, becoming colonel of the 42d Ohio Infantry and brigadier in 1862. He fought at Shiloh, was chief of staff for Gen. William Starke Rosecrans, and was made major general for gallantry at Chickamauga. He entered Congress as a radical Republican in 1863, calling for execution or exile of Confederate leaders, but he moderated his views after the Civil War. On the electoral commission in 1877 he voted for Hayes against Tilden on strict party lines. He was a senator-elect in 1880 when he became the Republican nominee for president. He was chosen as a compromise over Gen. Grant, James G. Blaine, and John Sherman, and won election despite some bitterness among Grant's supporters. On July 2, 1881, Garfield was shot and seriously wounded by a mentally disturbed office-seeker, Charles J. Guiteau, while entering a railroad station in Washington, DC. He died on Sept. 19, 1881, in Elberon, NJ.

## Chester Alan Arthur (1881-85)

Chester A. Arthur, 21st president, Republican, was born on Oct. 5, 1829, in Fairfield, VT, the son of William and Malvina Stone Arthur. He graduated from Union College in 1848, taught school in Vermont, then studied law and opened a practice in New York City. In 1853 he argued in a fugitive slave case that slaves transported through New York state were thereby freed. In 1871, he was appointed to the lucrative post of collector of the Port of New York. President Hayes, an opponent of the spoils system, forced Arthur to resign in 1878. This made the New York machine strong enemies of Hayes. Arthur and the Stalwarts (Old Guard Republicans) tried to nominate Grant for a 3d term in 1880. When Garfield was nominated, Arthur received 2d place in the interests of harmony. Upon Garfield's assassination, Arthur became president. Despite his past connections, he signed civil service reform legislation. Arthur tried to dissuade Congress from enacting the high protective tariff of 1883. He was defeated for renomination in 1884 by James G. Blaine. He died in New York City on Nov. 18, 1886.

## Grover Cleveland (1885-89; 1893-97)

*(According to a ruling of the State Dept., Grover Cleveland should be counted as both the 22d and the 24th president, because his 2 terms were not consecutive.)*

Grover Cleveland, Democrat, was born Stephen Grover Cleveland on Mar. 18, 1837, in Caldwell, NJ, the son of Richard F. and Ann Neal Cleveland. When he was a small boy, his family moved to New York. Prevented by his father's death from attending college, he studied by himself and was admitted to the bar in Buffalo, NY, in 1859. In succesion he became assistant district attorney (1863), sheriff (1871), mayor (1881), and governor of New York (1882). He was an independent, honest administrator who hated corruption. He was nominated for president over Tammany Hall opposition in 1884 and defeated Republican James G. Blaine. As president, he enlarged the civil service and vetoed many pension raids on the Treasury. In the 1888 election he was defeated by Benjamin Harrison, although his popular vote was larger. Reelected over Harrison in 1892, he faced a money crisis brought about by a lowered gold reserve, circulation of paper, and exorbitant silver purchases under the Sherman Silver Purchase Act. He obtained a repeal of the Sherman Act, but was unable to secure effective tariff reform. A severe economic depression and labor troubles racked his administration, but he refused to interfere in business matters and rejected Jacob Coxey's demand for unemployment relief. In 1894, he broke the Pullman strike. In 1896, the Democrats repudiated his administration and chose silverite William Jennings Bryan as their candidate. Cleveland died in Princeton, NJ, on June 24, 1908.

## Benjamin Harrison (1889-93)

Benjamin Harrison, 23d president, Republican, was born on Aug. 20, 1833, in North Bend, OH, the son of John Scott and Elizabeth Irwin Harrison. His great-grandfather, Benjamin Harrison, was a signer of the Declaration of Independence; his grandfather, William Henry Harrison, was 9th president; his father was a member of Congress. He attended school on his father's farm and graduated from Miami University in Oxford, OH, in 1852. He was admitted to the bar in 1854 and practiced in Indianapolis. During the Civil War, he rose to the rank of brevet brigadier general and fought at Kennesaw Mountain, at Peachtree Creek, at Nashville, and in the Atlanta campaign. He lost the 1876 gubernatorial election in Indiana but succeeded in becoming a U.S. senator in 1881. In 1888 he defeated Cleveland for president despite receiving fewer popular votes. As president, he expanded the pension list and signed the McKinley high tariff bill, the Sherman Antitrust Act, and the Sherman Silver Purchase Act. During his administration, 6 states were admitted to the Union. He was defeated for reelection in 1892. He died in Indianapolis on Mar. 13, 1901.

## William McKinley (1897-1901)

William McKinley, 25th president, Republican, was born on Jan. 29, 1843, in Niles, OH, the son of William and Nancy Allison McKinley. McKinley briefly attended Allegheny College. When the Civil War broke out in 1861, he enlisted and served for the duration. He rose to captain and in 1865 was made brevet major. After studying law in Albany, NY, he opened (1867) a law office in Canton, OH. He served twice in the U.S. House of Representatives (1877-83; 1885-91) and led the fight there for the McKinley Tariff, which was passed in 1890. However, he was not reelected to the House as a result. He served two terms (1892-96) as governor of Ohio. In 1896 he was elected president as a proponent of a protective tariff and sound money (gold standard), over William Jennings Bryan, the Democrat and a proponent of free silver. McKinley was reluctant to intervene in Cuba, but the loss of the battleship *Maine* at Havana crystallized opinion. He demanded Spain's withdrawal from Cuba; Spain made some concessions, but Congress announced a state of war as of Apr. 21, 1898. He was reelected in the 1900 campaign, defeating Bryan's anti-imperialist arguments with the promise of a "full dinner pail." McKinley was respected for his conciliatory nature and for his conservative stance on business issues. On Sept. 6, 1901, while welcoming citizens at the Pan-American Exposition, in Buffalo, NY, he was shot by Leon Czolgosz, an anarchist. He died Sept. 14.

## Theodore Roosevelt (1901-9)

Theodore Roosevelt, 26th president, Republican, was born on Oct. 27, 1858, in New York City, the son of Theodore and Martha Bulloch Roosevelt. He was a 5th cousin of Franklin D. Roosevelt and an uncle of Eleanor Roosevelt. Roosevelt graduated from Harvard University in 1880. He attended Columbia Law School briefly but abandoned the study of law to enter politics. He was elected to the New York state assembly in 1881 and served until 1884. He spent the next 2 years ranching and hunting in the Dakota Territory. Back in politics in 1886, he ran unsuccessfully for mayor of New York City. He was Civil Service commissioner in Washington, DC, from 1889 to 1895. From 1895 to 1897, he served as New York City's police commissioner. He was assistant secretary of the navy under McKinley. The Spanish-American War made Roosevelt a nationally known figure. He organized the 1st U.S. Volunteer Cavalry (Rough Riders) and, as lieutenant colonel, led the charge up Kettle Hill in San Juan. Elected New York governor in 1898, he fought the spoils system and achieved taxation of corporation franchises.

Nominated for vice president in 1900, he became the nation's youngest president when McKinley was assassinated. He was reelected in 1904. As president he fought corruption of politics by big business, dissolved the Northern Securities Co. and others for violating antitrust laws, intervened in the 1902 coal strike on behalf of the public, obtained the Elkins Law (1903) forbidding rebates to favored corporations, and helped pass the Hepburn Railway Rate Act of 1906 (extending Jurisdiction of the Interstate Commerce Commission). He helped obtain passage of the Pure Food and Drug Act (1906), and employers' liability laws. Roosevelt vigorously organized conservation efforts. He mediated (1905) the peace between Japan and Russia, for which he won the Nobel Peace Prize. He abetted the 1903 revolution in Panama that led to U.S. acquisition of territory for the Panama Canal.

In 1908 Roosevelt obtained the nomination of William H. Taft, who was elected. Feeling that Taft had abandoned his policies, Roosevelt unsuccessfully sought the nomination in 1912. He bolted the party and ran on the Progressive "Bull Moose" ticket against Taft and Woodrow Wilson, splitting the Republicans and ensuring Wilson's election. He was shot during the campaign but recovered. In 1916, after unsuccessfully seeking the presidential nomination for himself, Roosevelt supported the Republican candidate, Charles E. Hughes. A strong friend of Britain, he fought for American intervention in World War I. He wrote some 40 books on many topics; his book *The Winning of the West* is perhaps best known. He died Jan. 6, 1919, at Sagamore Hill, Oyster Bay, NY.

## William Howard Taft (1909-13)

William Howard Taft, 27th president, Republican, and 10th chief justice of the U.S., was born on Sept. 15, 1857, in Cincinnati, OH, the son of Alphonso and Louisa Maria Torrey Taft. His father was secretary of war and attorney general in Grant's cabinet and minister to Austria and Russia under Arthur. Taft graduated from Yale in 1878 and from Cincinnati Law School in 1880. After working as a law reporter for Cincinnati newspapers, he served as assistant prosecuting attorney (1881-82), assistant county solicitor (1885), judge, superior court (1887), U.S. solicitor-general (1890), and federal circuit judge (1892). In 1900 he became head of the U.S. Philippines Commission and was the first civil governor of the Philippines (1901-4). In 1904 he served as secretary of war, and in 1906 he was sent to Cuba to help avert a threatened revolution. He was groomed for the presidency by Theodore Roosevelt and elected over William Jennings Bryan in 1908. Taft vigorously continued Roosevelt's trust-busting, instituted the Department of Labor, and drafted the amendments calling for direct election of senators and the income tax. His tariff and conservation policies angered progressives. Although renominated in 1912, he was opposed by Roosevelt, who ran on the Progressive Party ticket; the result was Democrat Woodrow Wilson's election. Taft, with some reservations, supported the League of Nations. After leaving office, he was professor of constitutional law at Yale (1913-21) and chief justice of the U.S. (1921-30). Taft was the only person in U.S. history to have headed 2 branches of the federal government. Illness forced him to resign from the Court in Feb. 1930, and he died in Washington, DC, on Mar. 8, 1930.

## Woodrow Wilson (1913-21)

Thomas Woodrow Wilson, 28th president, Democrat, was born on Dec. 28, 1856, in Staunton, VA, the son of Joseph Ruggles and Janet (Jessie) Woodrow Wilson. He grew up in Georgia and South Carolina. He attended Davidson College in North Carolina before graduating from Princeton University in 1879. He studied law at the University of Virginia and then studied political science at Johns Hopkins University, where he received his PhD in 1886. He taught at Bryn Mawr (1885-88) and then at Wesleyan (1888-90) before joining the faculty at Princeton. He was president of Princeton from 1902 until 1910, when he was elected governor of New Jersey. In 1912 he was nominated for president with the aid of William Jennings Bryan, who sought to block James "Champ" Clark and Tammany Hall. Wilson won the election because the Republican vote for Taft was split by the Progressives.

As president, Wilson protected American interests in revolutionary Mexico and fought for American rights on the high seas. He oversaw the creation of the Federal Reserve system, cut the tariff, and developed a reputation as a reformer. His sharp warnings to Germany led to the resignation of his secretary of state, Bryan, a pacifist. In 1916 he was reelected by a slim margin with the slogan, "He kept us out of war," although his attempts to mediate in the war failed. After several American ships had been sunk by the Germans, he secured a declaration of war against Germany on Apr. 6, 1917.

Wilson outlined his peace program on Jan. 8, 1918, in the Fourteen Points, a state paper that had worldwide influence. He enunciated a doctrine of self-determination for the settlement of territorial disputes. The Germans accepted his terms and an armistice on Nov. 11, 1918.

Wilson went to Paris to help negotiate the peace treaty, the crux of which he considered the League of Nations. The Senate demanded reservations that would not make the U.S. subordinate to the votes of other nations in case of war. Wilson refused to consider any reservations and toured the country to get support. He suffered a stroke in Oct. 1919. An invalid for months, he clung to his executive powers while his wife and doctors effectively functioned as president.

Wilson was awarded the 1919 Nobel Peace Prize, but the treaty embodying the League of Nations was ultimately rejected by the Senate in 1920. He left the White House in Mar. 1921. He died in Washington, DC, on Feb. 3, 1924.

## Warren Gamaliel Harding (1921-23)

Warren Gamaliel Harding, 29th president, Republican, was born on Nov. 2, 1865, near Corsica (now Blooming Grove), OH, the son of George Tyron and Phoebe Elizabeth Dickerson Harding. He attended Ohio Central College, studied law, and became editor and publisher of a county newspaper. He entered the political arena as state senator (1901-4) and then served as lieutenant governor (1904-6). In 1910 he ran unsuccessfully for governor of Ohio; then in 1914 he was elected to the U.S. Senate. In the Senate he voted for antistrike legislation, woman suffrage, and the Volstead Prohibition Enforcement Act over President Wilson's veto. He opposed the League of Nations. In 1920 he was nominated for president and defeated James M. Cox in the election. The Republicans capitalized on war weariness and fear that Wilson's League of Nations would curtail U.S. sovereignty. Harding stressed a return to "normalcy" and worked for tariff revision and the repeal of excess profits law and high income taxes. Two Harding appointees, Albert B. Fall (secretary of the interior) and Harry Daugherty (attorney general), became involved in the Teapot Dome scandal. As rumors began to circulate about the corruption in his administration, Harding became ill while returning from a trip to Alaska, and he died in San Francisco on Aug. 2, 1923.

## Calvin Coolidge (1923-29)

John Calvin Coolidge, 30th president, Republican, was born on July 4, 1872, in Plymouth, VT, the son of John Calvin and Victoria J. Moor Coolidge. Coolidge graduated from Amherst College in 1895. He entered Republican state politics and served as mayor of Northampton, MA, as state senator, as lieutenant governor, and, in 1919, as governor. In Sept. 1919, Coolidge attained national prominence by calling out the state guard in the Boston police strike. He declared: "There is no right to strike against the public safety by anybody, anywhere, anytime." This brought his name before the Republican convention of 1920, where he was nominated for vice president. He succeeded to the presidency on Harding's death. As president, he opposed the League of Nations and the soldiers' bonus bill, which was passed over his veto. In 1924 he was elected by a huge majority. He substantially reduced the national debt. He twice vetoed the McNary-Haugen farm bill, which would have provided relief to financially hard-pressed farmers. With Republicans eager to renominate him, Coolidge simply announced, Aug. 2, 1927: "I do not choose to run for president in 1928." He died in Northampton, MA, on Jan. 5, 1933.

## Herbert Clark Hoover (1929-33)

Herbert Hoover, 31st president, Republican, was born on Aug. 10, 1874, in West Branch, IA, the son of Jesse Clark and Hulda Randall Minthorn Hoover. Hoover grew up in Indian Territory (now Oklahoma) and Oregon and graduated from Stanford University with a degree in engineering in 1895. He worked briefly with the U.S. Geological Survey and then managed mines in Australia, Asia, Europe, and Africa. While chief engineer of imperial mines in China, he directed food relief for victims of the Boxer Rebellion. He gained a reputation not only as an engineer but as a humanitarian as he directed the American Relief Committee, London (1914-15) and the U.S. Commission for Relief in Belgium (1915-19). He was U.S. Food Administrator (1917-19), American Relief Administrator (1918-23), and in charge of Russian Relief (1918-23). He served as secretary of commerce under both Harding and Coolidge. Some historians believe that he was the most effective secretary of commerce ever to hold that office. In 1928 he was elected president over Alfred E. Smith. In 1929 the stock market crashed, and the economy collapsed. During the depression, Hoover inaugurated some government assistance programs, but he was opposed to administration of aid through a federal bureaucracy. As the effects of the depression continued, he was defeated in the 1932 election by Franklin D. Roosevelt. President Truman named him coordinator of the European Food Program (1946) and chairman of the Commission on Organization of the Executive Branch (1947-49; 1953-55). Hoover died in New York City on Oct. 20, 1964.

## Franklin Delano Roosevelt (1933-45)

Franklin D. Roosevelt, 32d president, Democrat, was born on Jan. 30, 1882, near Hyde Park, NY, the son of James and Sara Delano Roosevelt. He graduated from Harvard University in 1904. He attended Columbia University Law School without taking a degree and was admitted to the New York state bar in 1907. His political career began when he was elected to the New York state senate in 1910. In 1913 President Wilson appointed him assistant secretary of the navy, a post he held during World War I.

In 1920 Roosevelt ran for vice president with James Cox and was defeated. From 1921 to 1928 he worked in his New York law office and was also vice president of Fidelity & Deposit Co. of Maryland. In Aug. 1921, he was stricken with poliomyelitis, which left his legs paralyzed. As a result of therapy he was able to stand, or walk a few steps, with the aid of leg braces.

Roosevelt served 2 terms as governor of New York (1929-33). In 1932, W. G. McAdoo, pledged to John N. Garner, threw his votes to Roosevelt, who was nominated for president. The depression and the promise to repeal Prohibition ensured his election. He asked for emergency powers, proclaimed the New Deal, and put into effect a vast number of administrative changes. Foremost was the use of public funds for relief and public works, resulting in deficit financing. He greatly expanded the federal government's regulation of business and by an excess profits tax and progressive income taxes produced a redistribution of earnings on an unprecedented scale. The Wagner Act gave labor many advantages in organizing and collective bargaining. He promoted legislation establishing the Social Security system. He was the last president inaugurated on Mar. 4 (1933) and the first inaugurated on Jan. 20 (1937).

Roosevelt was the first president to use radio for "fireside chats." When the Supreme Court nullified some New Deal laws, he sought power to "pack" the court with additional justices, but Congress refused to give him the authority. He was the first president to break the "no 3d term" tradition (1940) and was elected to a 4th term in 1944, despite failing health. He was openly hostile to fascist governments before World War II and launched a lend-lease program on behalf of the Allies. He wrote the principles of fair dealing into the Atlantic Charter, Aug. 14, 1941 (with Winston Churchill), and urged the Four Freedoms (freedom of speech, of worship, from want, from fear) Jan. 6, 1941. When Japan attacked Pearl Harbor on Dec. 7, 1941, the U.S. entered the war. Roosevelt conferred with allied heads of state at Casablanca (Jan. 1943), Quebec (Aug. 1943), Teheran (Nov.-Dec. 1943), Cairo (Nov. and Dec. 1943), and Yalta (Feb. 1945). He did not, however, see the end of the war. He died of a cerebral hemorrhage in Warm Springs, GA, on Apr. 12, 1945.

## Harry S. Truman (1945-53)

Harry S. Truman, 33d president, Democrat, was born on May 8, 1884, in Lamar, MO, the son of John Anderson and Martha Ellen Young Truman. A family disagreement on whether his middle name should be Shippe or Solomon, after names of 2 grandfathers, resulted in his using only the middle initial S. After graduating from high school in Independence, MO, he worked (1901) for the *Kansas City Star,* as a railroad timekeeper, and as a clerk in Kansas City banks until about 1905. He ran his family's farm from 1906 to 1917. He served in France during World War I. After the war he opened a haberdashery shop, was a judge on the Jackson Co. Court (1922-24), and attended Kansas City School of Law (1923-25).

Truman was elected to the U.S. Senate in 1934 and re-elected in 1940. In 1944, with Roosevelt's backing, he was nominated for vice president and elected. On Roosevelt's death in 1945, Truman became president. In 1948, in a famous upset victory, he defeated Republican Thomas E. Dewey to win election to a new term.

Truman authorized the first uses of the atomic bomb (Hiroshima and Nagasaki, Aug. 6 and 9, 1945), bringing World War II to a rapid end. He was responsible for what came to be called the Truman Doctrine (to aid nations such as Greece and Turkey, threatened by Communist takeover), and his strong commitment to NATO and to the Marshall Plan helped bring them about. In 1948-49, he broke a Soviet blockade of West Berlin with a massive airlift. When Communist North Korea invaded South Korea (June 1950), he won UN approval for a "police action" and sent in forces under Gen. Douglas MacArthur. When MacArthur opposed his policy of limited objectives, Truman removed him.

Truman was responsible for a higher minimum-wage, increased Social Security, and aid-for-housing laws. He died in Kansas City, MO, on Dec. 26, 1972.

## Dwight David Eisenhower (1953-61)

Dwight D. Eisenhower, 34th president, Republican, was born on Oct. 14, 1890, in Denison, TX, the son of David Jacob and Ida Elizabeth Stover Eisenhower. He grew up on a small farm in Abilene, KS, and graduated from West Point in 1915. He was on the staff of Gen. Douglas MacArthur in the Philippines from 1935 to 1939. In 1942, he was made commander of Allied forces landing in North Africa; the next year he was made full general. He became supreme Allied commander in Europe that same year and as such led the Normandy invasion (June 6, 1944). He was given the rank of general of the army on Dec. 20, 1944, which was made permanent in 1946. On May 7, 1945, he received the surrender of Germany at Rheims. He returned to the U.S. to serve as chief of staff (1945-48). In 1948, Eisenhower published *Crusade in Europe,* his war memoirs, which quickly became a best-seller. In 1948 he became president of Columbia University; in 1950 he became Commander of NATO forces.

Eisenhower resigned from the army and was nominated for president by the Republicans in 1952. He defeated Adlai E. Stevenson in the 1952 election and then again in 1956. He called himself a moderate; favored the "free market system" vs. government price and wage controls; kept government out of labor disputes; reorganized the defense establishment; and promoted missile programs. He continued foreign aid; sped the end of the Korean War; endorsed Taiwan and SE Asia defense treaties; backed the UN in condemning the Anglo-French raid on Egypt; and advocated the "open skies" policy of mutual inspection with the USSR. He sent U.S. troops into Little Rock, AR, in Sept. 1957, during the segregation crisis.

Eisenhower died on Mar. 28, 1969, in Washington, DC.

## John Fitzgerald Kennedy (1961-63)

John F. Kennedy, 35th president, Democrat, was born on May 29, 1917, in Brookline, MA, the son of Joseph P. and Rose Fitzgerald Kennedy. He graduated from Harvard University in 1940. While serving in the navy (1941-45), he commanded a PT boat in the Solomons and won the Navy and Marine Corps Medal. In 1956, while recovering from spinal surgery, he wrote *Profiles in Courage,* which won a Pulitzer Prize in 1957. He served in the House of Representatives from 1947 to 1953 and was elected to the Senate in 1952 and again in 1958. In 1960, Kennedy won the Democratic nomination for president and defeated Richard M. Nixon, Republican. He was the youngest president ever elected and the first Roman Catholic. In Apr. 1961, Kennedy's new administration suffered a severe setback when an invasion force of anti-Castro Cubans, trained and directed by the U.S. Central Intelligence Agency, failed to establish a beachhead at the Bay of Pigs in Cuba.

One of Kennedy's most important acts was his successful demand on Oct. 22, 1962, that the Soviet Union dismantle its missile bases in Cuba. He established a quarantine of arms shipments to Cuba and continued surveillance by air. Kennedy also defied Soviet attempts to force the Allies out of Berlin. He backed civil rights and expanded medical care for the aged. Space exploration was greatly developed during his administration.

On Nov. 22, 1963, Kennedy was assassinated in Dallas, TX.

## Lyndon Baines Johnson (1963-69)

Lyndon B. Johnson, 36th president, Democrat, was born on Aug. 27, 1908, near Stonewall, TX, the son of Sam Ealy and Rebekah Baines Johnson. He graduated from Southwest Texas State Teachers College in 1930 and attended Georgetown University Law School. He taught public speaking in Houston (1930-31) and then served as secretary to Rep. R. M. Kleberg (1931-35). In 1937 Johnson won an election to fill the vacancy caused by the death of a representative and in 1938 was elected to the full term, after which he returned for 4 terms. He was elected U.S. senator in 1948 and reelected in 1954. He became Democratic leader of the Senate in 1953. Johnson had strong support for the Democratic presidential nomination at the 1960 convention, where the nominee, John F. Kennedy, asked him to run for vice president. His campaigning helped overcome religious bias against Kennedy in the South.

Johnson became president when Kennedy was assassinated. He was elected to a full term in 1964. Johnson won passage of major civil rights, anti-poverty, aid to education, and health-care (Medicare, Medicaid) legislation—the "Great Society" program. However, his escalation of the war in Vietnam came to overshadow the achievements of his administration. In the face of increasing division in the nation and in his own party over his handling of the war, Johnson did not seek another term.

Johnson died on Jan. 22, 1973, in San Antonio, TX.

## Richard Milhous Nixon (1969-74)

Richard M. Nixon, 37th president, Republican, was born on Jan. 9, 1913, in Yorba Linda, CA, the son of Francis Anthony and Hannah Milhous Nixon. He graduated from Whittier College in 1934 and from Duke University Law School in 1937. After practicing law in Whittier and serving briefly in the Office of Price Administration in 1942, he entered the navy and served in the South Pacific. Nixon was elected to the House of Representatives in 1946 and 1948. He achieved prominence as the House Un-American Activities Committee member who forced the showdown that resulted in the Alger Hiss perjury conviction. In 1950 he was elected to the Senate.

Nixon was elected vice president in the Eisenhower landslides of 1952 and 1956. He won the Republican nomination for president in 1960 but was defeated by Democrat John F. Kennedy. Returning to California, he ran unsuccessfully for governor in 1962. In 1968, he won the Republican presidential nomination and went on to defeat Democrat Hubert H. Humphrey for the presidency.

Nixon was the first U.S. president to visit China (1972). He and his foreign affairs adviser, Henry A. Kissinger, achieved détente with the Soviet Union. Nixon appointed 4 Supreme Court justices, including the chief justice, altering the court's balance in a conservative direction.

Reelected in 1972, Nixon secured a cease-fire agreement in Vietnam. But his 2d term was cut short by a series of scandals, beginning with disclosures relating to the burglary of Democratic Party national headquarters in the Watergate office complex on June 17, 1972. On July 16, 1973, a White House aide, under questioning by a Senate committee, revealed that most of Nixon's office conversations and phone calls had been recorded. The courts and Congress sought the tapes for criminal proceedings against former White House aides and for a House inquiry into possible impeachment. Nixon claimed executive privilege to keep the tapes secret, but on July 24, 1974, the Supreme Court ruled against him. That same day, the House Judiciary Committee opened debate on impeachment. In late July, the committee recommended House adoption of 3 articles of impeachment charging Nixon with obstruction of justice, abuse of power, and contempt of Congress.

On Aug. 5, Nixon released transcripts of conversations held 6 days after the Watergate break-in showing that he had known of, approved, and directed cover-up activities. He resigned from office on Aug. 9, becoming the first president ever to do so. In later years, Nixon emerged as an elder statesman. He died Apr. 22, 1994, in New York City.

## Gerald Rudolph Ford (1974-77)

Gerald R. Ford, 38th president, Republican, was born on July 14, 1913, in Omaha, NE, the son of Leslie and Dorothy Gardner King, and was named Leslie Jr. When he was 2, his parents were divorced, and his mother moved with the boy to Grand Rapids, MI. There she met and married Gerald R. Ford, who formally adopted him and gave him his own name. Ford graduated from the University of Michigan in 1935 and from Yale Law School in 1941. He began practicing law in Grand Rapids, but in 1942 joined the navy and served in the Pacific, leaving the service in 1946 as a lieutenant commander. He entered the House of Representatives in 1949 and spent 25 years in the House, 8 of them as Republican leader.

On Oct. 12, 1973, after Vice President Spiro T. Agnew resigned, Ford was nominated by President Nixon to replace him. It was the first use of the procedures set out in the 25th Amendment. When Nixon resigned, Aug. 9, 1974, Ford became president; he was the only president who was never elected either to the presidency or to the vice presidency. On Sept. 8, in a controversial move, he pardoned Nixon for any federal crimes he might have committed as president. Ford vetoed 48 bills in his first 21 months in office, saying most would prove too costly. He visited China. He was defeated in the 1976 election by Democrat Jimmy Carter.

## Jimmy (James Earl) Carter (1977-81)

Jimmy (James Earl) Carter, 39th president, Democrat, was the first president from the Deep South since before the Civil War. He was born on Oct. 1, 1924, in Plains, GA, the son of James and Lillian Gordy Carter.

Carter graduated from the U.S. Naval Academy in 1946 and in 1952 entered the navy's nuclear submarine program as an aide to Capt. (later Adm.) Hyman Rickover. He studied nuclear physics at Union College. Carter's father died in 1953, and he left the navy to take over the family businesses. He served in the Georgia state senate (1963-67) and as governor of Georgia (1971-75). In 1976, Carter won the Democratic nomination and defeated President Gerald R. Ford.

On his first full day in office, Carter pardoned all Vietnam draft evaders. He played a major role in the peace negotiations between Israel and Egypt. However, Carter was widely criticized for the poor state of the economy and was viewed by many as weak in his handling of foreign policy. In Nov. 1979, Iranian student militants attacked the U.S. embassy in Tehran and held members of the embassy staff hostage. Efforts to obtain release of the hostages were a major preoccupation during the rest of his term. He reacted to the Soviet invasion of Afghanistan by imposing a grain embargo and boycotting the Moscow Olympic Games.

Carter was defeated by Ronald Reagan in the 1980 election. Carter administration efforts finally resulted in the release of the hostages on Inauguration Day, 1981, just after Reagan officially became president. After leaving office, Carter was hailed for his humanitarian efforts and took a prominent role in mediating international disputes.

## Ronald Wilson Reagan (1981-89)

Ronald Wilson Reagan, 40th president, Republican, was born on Feb. 6, 1911, in Tampico, IL, the son of John Edward and Nellie Wilson Reagan. Reagan graduated from Eureka College in 1932, after which he worked as a sports announcer in Des Moines, IA. He began a successful career as an actor in 1937, starring in numerous movies, and later in television, until the 1960s. He served as president of the Screen Actors Guild from 1947 to 1952 and in 1959-60. Reagan was elected governor of California in 1966 and reelected in 1970.

In 1980, Reagan gained the Republican presidential nomination and won a landslide victory over Jimmy Carter. He was easily reelected in 1984. Reagan successfully forged a bipartisan coalition in Congress, which led to enactment of his program of large-scale tax cuts, cutbacks in many government programs, and a major defense buildup. He signed a Social Security reform bill designed to provide for the long-term solvency of the system. In 1986, he signed into law a major tax-reform bill. He was shot in an assassination attempt in 1981.

In 1982, the U.S. joined France and Italy in maintaining a peacekeeping force in Beirut, Lebanon, and the next year Reagan sent a task force to lead the invasion of Grenada. Reagan's opposition to international terrorism led to the U.S. bombing of Libyan military installations in 1986. He strongly supported El Salvador, the Nicaraguan contras, and other anti-communist governments and forces throughout the world. He also held 4 summit meetings with Soviet leader Mikhail Gorbachev. At the 1987 meeting in Washington, DC, a historic treaty eliminating short- and medium-range missiles from Europe was signed.

Reagan faced a crisis in 1986-87, when it was revealed that the U.S. had sold weapons to Iran in exchange for release of U.S. hostages being held in Lebanon and that subsequently some of the money was diverted to the Nicaraguan contras (Congress had barred aid to the contras). The scandal led to the resignation of leading White House aides. As Reagan left office in Jan. 1989, the nation was experiencing its 6th consecutive year of economic prosperity. Reagan, however, was unable to control the high budget deficits that plagued him throughout his administration.

In 1994, in a handwritten, personal letter to the American people, Reagan revealed that he was suffering from Alzheimer's disease.

## George Herbert Walker Bush (1989-93)

George Herbert Walker Bush, 41st president, Republican, was born on June 12, 1924, in Milton, MA, the son of Prescott and Dorothy Walker Bush. He served as a U.S. Navy pilot in World War II. After graduating from Yale University in 1948, he settled in Texas, where, in 1953, he helped found an oil company. After losing a bid for a U.S. Senate seat in Texas in 1964, he was elected to the House of Representatives in 1966 and 1968. He lost a 2d U.S. Senate race in 1970. Subsequently he served as U.S. ambassador to the United Nations (1971-73), headed the U.S. Liaison Office in Beijing (1974-75), and was director of central intelligence (1976-77).

Following an unsuccessful bid for the 1980 Republican presidential nomination, Bush was chosen by Ronald Reagan as his vice presidential running mate. He served as U.S. vice president from 1981 to 1989.

In 1988, Bush gained the Republican presidential nomination and defeated Democrat Michael Dukakis in the November elections. Bush took office faced with the ongoing U.S. budget and trade deficits as well as the rescue of insolvent U.S. savings and loan institutions. He annually faced a severe budget deficit, struggled with military cutbacks in light of reduced cold war tensions, and vetoed abortion-rights legislation, a minimum-wage law, and an anti-discrimination bill that did not reflect his own views.

Bush supported Soviet reforms and Eastern Europe democratization. He was criticized, however, for keeping U.S. policy tied closely to Mikhail Gorbachev as the Soviet leader lost power, and for underreaction to the Chinese government's violent repression of pro-democracy demonstrators in 1989. In Dec. 1989, Bush sent military forces to Panama; these forces overthrew the government and captured military strongman Gen. Manuel Noriega.

Bush reacted to Iraq's Aug. 1990 invasion of Kuwait by sending U.S. forces to the Persian Gulf area and assembling a UN-backed coalition, including NATO and Arab League members. After a month-long air war, in Feb. 1991, Allied forces retook Kuwait in a 4-day ground assault. The quick victory gave Bush one of the highest presidential approval ratings in history. His popularity plummeted by the end of 1991, however, as the economy struggled through a prolonged recession. He was defeated by his Democratic opponent, Bill Clinton, in the 1992 election.

### Bill (William Jefferson) Clinton (1993- )

Bill Clinton, 42d president, Democrat, was born on Aug. 19, 1946, in Hope, AR, the son of William Blythe and Virginia Cassidy Blythe, and was named William Jefferson Blythe IV. Blythe died in an auto accident before his son was born. His widow married Roger Clinton, and at age 16, William Jefferson Blythe IV changed his name to Bill Clinton. Clinton attended Georgetown University, Oxford University in England as a Rhodes scholar, and Yale Law School.

Clinton worked on George McGovern's 1972 presidential campaign. He taught at the University of Arkansas from 1973 to 1976, when he was elected state attorney general. In 1978, he was elected governor, becoming the nation's youngest governor. Defeated for reelection in 1980, he was returned to office in 1982, 1984, 1986, and 1990. He married Hillary Rodham in 1975.

Despite personal attacks on his character, Clinton won most of the 1992 presidential primaries, moving the Democratic Party toward the center as he tried to broaden his appeal, and became the Democratic presidential nominee. He defeated Pres. George Bush in the November election.

In 1993, Clinton narrowly won congressional passage of some $500 billion in taxes and spending cuts to reduce the federal budget deficit. He proposed major health-care reform legislation, but his plan died in Congress. He achieved a measure of success with congressional approval of the North American Free Trade Agreement.

Following the 1994 midterm elections, Clinton faced Republican majorities in both houses of Congress, which clashed with him over the scope of federal spending. He pursued a centrist course on most domestic issues, winning passage of a major anti-crime bill in 1995 and supporting, in 1996 (with reservations), a measure to overhaul the welfare system and end federal guarantees of support. Among other measures, he approved an increase in the minimum wage. Clinton sustained limited political damage over his involvement while governor in an Arkansas real estate venture (Whitewater) and over the White House's obtaining of FBI files of Republicans.

In foreign policy, Clinton pursued peace efforts in the Middle East, where he also was involved in confrontations with Iraqi leader Saddam Hussein. He sent U.S. troops to Bosnia to help implement a peace settlement there.

## Wives and Children of the Presidents

(listed in order of presidential administrations)

| Name (Born–died, married) | State | Sons/ daughters |
|---|---|---|
| Martha Dandridge Custis Washington (1731-1802, 1759) | VA | None |
| Abigail Smith Adams (1744-1818, 1764) | MA | 3/2 |
| Martha Wayles Skelton Jefferson (1748-82, 1772) | VA | 1/5 |
| Dorothea "Dolley" Payne Todd Madison (1768-1849, 1794) | NC | None |
| Elizabeth Kortright Monroe (1768-1830, 1786) | NY | . . ./2 (A) |
| Louisa Catherine Johnson Adams (1775-1852, 1797) | MD(B) | 3/1 |
| Rachel Donelson Robards Jackson (1767-1828, 1791) | VA | None |
| Hannah Hoes Van Buren (1783-1819, 1807) | NY | 4/. . . |
| Anna Tuthill Symmes Harrison (1775-1864, 1795) | NJ | 6/4 |
| Letitia Christian Tyler (1790-1842, 1813) | VA | 3/4 (A) |
| Julia Gardiner Tyler (1820-89, 1844) | NY | 5/2 |
| Sarah Childress Polk (1803-91, 1824) | TN | None |
| Margaret Mackall Smith Taylor (1788-1852, 1810) | MD | 1/5 |
| Abigail Powers Fillmore (1798-1853, 1826) | NY | 1/1 |
| Caroline Carmichael McIntosh Fillmore (1813-81, 1858) | NJ | None |
| Jane Means Appleton Pierce (1806-63, 1834) | NH | 3/. . . |
| Mary Todd Lincoln (1818-82, 1842) | KY | 4/. . . |
| Eliza McCardle Johnson (1810-76, 1827) | TN | 3/2 |
| Julia Boggs Dent Grant (1826-1902, 1848) | MO | 3/1 |
| Lucy Ware Webb Hayes (1831-89, 1852) | OH | 7/1 |
| Lucretia Rudolph Garfield (1832-1918, 1858) | OH | 4/1 |
| Ellen Lewis Herndon Arthur (1837-80, 1859) | VA | 2/1 |
| Frances Folsom Cleveland (1864-1947, 1886) | NY | 2/3 |
| Caroline Lavinia Scott Harrison (1832-92, 1853) | OH | 1/1 |
| Mary Scott Lord Dimmick Harrison (1858-1948, 1896) | PA | . . ./1 |
| Ida Saxton McKinley (1847-1907, 1871) | OH | . . ./2 |
| Alice Hathaway Lee Roosevelt (1861-84, 1880) | MA | . . ./1 |
| Edith Kermit Carow Roosevelt (1861-1948, 1886) | CT | 4/1 |
| Helen Herron Taft (1861-1943, 1886) | OH | 2/1 |
| Ellen Louise Axson Wilson (1860-1914, 1885) | GA | . . ./3 |
| Edith Bolling Galt Wilson (1872-1961, 1915) | VA | None |
| Florence Kling De Wolfe Harding (1860-1924, 1891) | OH | None |
| Grace Anna Goodhue Coolidge (1879-1957, 1905) | VT | 2/. . . |
| Lou Henry Hoover (1875-1944, 1899) | IA | 2/. . . |
| Anna Eleanor Roosevelt Roosevelt (1884-1962, 1905) | NY | 4/1 (A) |
| Elizabeth Virginia "Bess" Wallace Truman (1885-1982, 1919) | MO | . . ./1 |
| Mamie Geneva Doud Eisenhower (1896-1979, 1916) | IA | 1/. . . (A) |
| Jacqueline Lee Bouvier Kennedy (1929-94, 1953) | NY | 1/1 (A) |
| Claudia "Lady Bird" Alta Taylor Johnson (b 1912, 1934) | TX | . . ./2 |
| Thelma Catherine Patricia Ryan Nixon (1912-1993, 1940) | NV | . . ./2 |
| Elizabeth Bloomer Warren Ford (b 1918, 1948) | IL | 3/1 |
| Rosalynn Smith Carter (b 1927, 1946) | GA | 3/1 |
| Anne Frances "Nancy" Robbins Davis Reagan (b 1921, 1952) | NY | 1/1 (C) |
| Barbara Pierce Bush (b 1925, 1945) | NY | 4/2 |
| Hillary Rodham Clinton (b 1947, 1975) | IL | . . ./1 |

James Buchanan, 15th president, was unmarried. (A) plus one infant, deceased. (B) Born London, father a MD citizen. (C) President Reagan married and divorced Jane Wyman. They had a son and a daughter.

## First Lady Hillary Rodham Clinton

Hilary Rodham Clinton was born in Chicago, Ill., Oct. 26, 1947, the daughter of Hugh and Dorothy Rodham. She graduated from Wellesley College and Yale Law School. She married Bill Clinton in 1975, and a daughter, Chelsea, was born in 1980. From 1977 to 1992, she was a partner in the Rose law firm in Little Rock, AR, and in 1988 and 1991, she was voted one of the "100 Most Influential Lawyers in America" by the *National Law Journal.*

As first lady she played a leading role in an unsuccessful effort to reform the U.S. health-care system. In 1995 her book *It Takes a Village*, about the needs of children, was published. Public reaction to the first lady tended to polarize along party lines, with her past involvement with the failed Whitewater real-estate venture in Arkansas a matter of controversy.

## Presidential Facts

- **Youngest president**: Theodore Roosevelt, who was 42 when sworn in after McKinley's death
- **Oldest president**: Ronald Reagan, who was 77 when he left office
- **Only president to serve more than 2 terms**: Franklin D. Roosevelt
- **Only president to resign:** Richard Nixon, after a House committee recommended impeachment for Watergate scandal
- **Only president to serve 2 terms that were not back to back**: Grover Cleveland, who was both the 22d and the 24th president
- **President who served the shortest term**: William Henry Harrison, who died of pneumonia 31 days after being inaugurated
- **Only president to also serve as chief justice of the U.S.:** William Howard Taft
- **First president to live in the White House:** John Adams
- **State that has produced the greatest number of presidents**: Virginia
- **Only president who was never married**: James Buchanan. His niece acted as White House hostess.
- **Only president to serve without having been elected vice president or president in a national election**: Gerald Ford
- **Presidents who died on July 4**: John Adams, Thomas Jefferson, and James Monroe
- **Presidents who died in office**: Eight presidents have died in office. Four of them were assassinated: Abraham Lincoln, James Garfield, William McKinley, and John F. Kennedy. The other four were William Henry Harrison, Zachary Taylor, Warren G. Harding, and Franklin Delano Roosevelt.

## Burial Places of the Presidents

| President | Burial Place | President | Burial Place | President | Burial Place |
|---|---|---|---|---|---|
| Washington | Mt. Vernon, VA | Fillmore | Buffalo, NY | T. Roosevelt | Oyster Bay, NY |
| J. Adams | Quincy, MA | Pierce | Concord, NH | Taft | Arlington Natl. Cem. |
| Jefferson | Charlottesville, VA | Buchanan | Lancaster, PA | Wilson | Wash. Natl. Cathedral |
| Madison | Montpelier Station, VA | Lincoln | Springfield, IL | Harding | Marion, OH |
| Monroe | Richmond, VA | A. Johnson | Greeneville, TN | Coolidge | Plymouth, VT |
| J. Q. Adams | Quincy, MA | Grant | New York, NY | Hoover | West Branch, IA |
| Jackson | Nashville, TN | Hayes | Fremont, OH | F. Roosevelt | Hyde Park, NY |
| Van Buren | Kinderhook, NY | Garfield | Cleveland, OH | Truman | Independence, MO |
| W. H. Harrison | North Bend, OH | Arthur | Albany, NY | Eisenhower | Abilene, KS |
| Tyler | Richmond, VA | Cleveland | Princeton, NJ | Kennedy | Arlington Natl. Cem. |
| Polk | Nashville, TN | B. Harrison | Indianapolis, IN | L. B. Johnson | Johnson City, TX |
| Taylor | Louisville, KY | McKinley | Canton, OH | Nixon | Yorba Linda, CA |

## Presidential Libraries

The libraries listed below, except for that of Richard Nixon (which is a private institution), are coordinated by the National Archives and Records Administration in Washington, DC.; further information is available at the NARA Web site (http://www.nara.gov). It also has custody of the Nixon presidential historical materials and those of George Bush. The Bush presidential library was under construction in 1996 in College Station, TX, at Texas A&M University; completion was expected in 1997. Materials for presidents prior to Herbert Hoover are held by private institutions.

**Herbert Hoover Library**
210 Parkside Dr., PO Box 488
West Branch, IA 52358
PHONE: 319-643-5301
FAX: 319-643-5825
E-MAIL: library@hoover.nara.gov

**Franklin D. Roosevelt Library**
511 Albany Post Rd.
Hyde Park, NY 12538
PHONE: 914-229-8114
FAX: 914-229-0872
E-MAIL: library@roosevelt.nara.gov

**Harry S. Truman Library**
U.S. Hwy. 24 & Delaware St.
Independence, MO 64050-1798
PHONE: 816-833-1400
FAX: 816-833-4368
E-MAIL: library@truman.nara.gov

**Dwight D. Eisenhower Library**
Southeast Fourth St.
Abilene, KS 67410
PHONE: 913-263-4751
FAX: 913-263-4218
E-MAIL: library@eisenhower.nara.gov

**John Fitzgerald Kennedy Library**
Columbia Pt.,
Boston, MA 02125
PHONE: 617-929-4500
FAX: 617-929-4538
E-MAIL: library@kennedy.nara.gov

**Lyndon Baines Johnson Library**
2313 Red River St.
Austin, TX 78705
PHONE: 512-916-5137
FAX: 512-478-9104
E-MAIL: library@johnson.nara.gov

**Richard Nixon Library & Birthplace**
18001 Yorba Linda Blvd.
Yorba Linda, CA 92686
PHONE: 714-993-3393
FAX: 714-528-0544
WEB SITE: http://www.chapman.edu/nixon
E-MAIL: stedman@chapman.edu

**Gerald R. Ford Library**
1000 Beal Ave.
Ann Arbor, MI 48109
PHONE: 313-741-2218
FAX: 313-741-2341
E-MAIL: library@fordlib.nara.gov.

**Jimmy Carter Library**
441 Freedom Pkwy. & One Copenhill Ave.
Atlanta, GA 30307
PHONE: 404-331-3942
FAX: 404-730-2215
E-MAIL: library@carter.nara.gov

**Ronald Reagan Library**
40 Presidential Dr.
Simi Valley, CA 93065
PHONE: 805-522-8444
FAX: 805-522-9621
E-MAIL: library@reagan.nara.gov

# UNITED STATES FACTS

## Superlative U.S. Statistics

**Source:** U.S. Geological Survey, Dept. of the Interior; U.S. Bureau of the Census, Dept. of Commerce; World Almanac research

| | | |
|---|---|---|
| Area for 50 states and Washington, DC | Total | 3,787,319 sq mi |
| | Land, 3,536,278 sq mi; Water, 251,041 sq mi | |
| Largest state | Alaska | 656,424 sq mi |
| Smallest state | Rhode Island | 1,545 sq mi |
| Largest county (excludes Alaska) | San Bernardino County, CA | 20,064 sq mi |
| Smallest county | Kalawao, HI | 14 sq mi |
| Largest incorporated city | Sitka, AK | 2,881 sq mi |
| Northernmost city | Barrow, AK | 71°17′ N |
| Northernmost point | Point Barrow, AK | 71°23′ N |
| Southernmost city | Hilo, HI | 19°43′ N |
| Southernmost settlement | Naalehu, HI | 19°03′ N |
| Southernmost point | Ka Lae (South Cape), Island of Hawaii | 18°55′ N(155°41′ W) |
| Easternmost city | Eastport, ME | 66°59′ 02″ W |
| Easternmost settlement[1] | Amchitka Isl., AK | 179°15′ E |
| Easternmost point[1] | Semisopochnoi Isl., AK | 179°52′ E |
| Westernmost city | Atka, AK | 174°20′ W |
| Westernmost settlement | Adak Station, AK | 176°39′ W |
| Westernmost point | Amatignak Isl., AK | 179°06′ W |
| Highest settlement | Climax, CO | 11,560 ft |
| Lowest settlement | Calipatria, CA | –185 ft |
| Highest point on Atlantic coast | Cadillac Mountain, Mount Desert Isl., ME | 1,530 ft |
| Oldest national park | Yellowstone National Park (1872), WY, MT, ID | 2,219,791 acres |
| Largest national park | Wrangell-St. Elias, AK | 8,323,618 acres |
| Highest waterfall | Yosemite Falls—Total in 3 sections | 2,425 ft |
| | Upper Yosemite Fall | 1,430 ft |
| | Cascades in middle section | 675 ft |
| | Lower Yosemite Fall | 320 ft |
| Longest river | Mississippi-Missouri-Red Rock | 3,710 mi |
| Highest mountain | Mount McKinley, AK | 20,320 ft |
| Lowest point | Death Valley, CA | –282 ft |
| Deepest lake | Crater Lake, OR | 1,932 ft |
| Rainiest spot | Mount Waialeale, HI | Annual avg rainfall 460 in |
| Largest gorge | Grand Canyon, Colorado River, AZ | 277 mi long, 600 ft to 18 mi wide, 1 mi deep |
| Deepest gorge | Hells Canyon, Snake River, OR-ID | 7,900 ft |
| Strongest surface wind | Mount Washington, NH recorded 1934 | 231 mph |
| Largest dam | New Cornelia Tailings, Ten Mile Wash, AZ[2] | 274,026,000 cu yds material used |
| Tallest building | Sears Tower, Chicago, IL | 1,454 ft |
| Largest building | Boeing 747 Manufacturing Plant, Everett, WA | 205,600,000 cu ft; covers 47 acres |
| Tallest structure | TV tower, Blanchard, ND | 2,063 ft |
| Longest bridge span | Verrazano-Narrows, NY | 4,260 ft |
| Highest bridge | Royal Gorge, CO | 1,053 ft above water |
| Deepest well | Gas well, Washita County, OK | 31,441 ft |

### The 48 Contiguous States

| | | |
|---|---|---|
| Area for 48 states and Washington, DC | Total | 3,119,963 sq mi |
| | Land, 2,959,481 sq mi; Water, 160,483 sq mi | |
| Largest state | Texas | 268,601 sq mi |
| Northernmost city | Bellingham, WA | 48°46′ N |
| Northernmost settlement | Angle Inlet, MN | 49°21′ N |
| Northernmost point | Northwest Angle, MN | 49°23′ N |
| Southernmost city | Key West, FL | 24°32′ N |
| Southernmost mainland city | Florida City, FL | 25°27′ N |
| Southernmost point | Key West, FL | 24°32′ N |
| Easternmost settlement | Lubec, ME | 66°58′49″ W |
| Easternmost point | West Quoddy Head, ME | 66°57′ W |
| Westernmost town | La Push, WA | 124°38′ W |
| Westernmost point | Cape Alava, WA | 124°44′ W |
| Highest mountain | Mount Whitney, CA | 14,494 ft |

(1) Alaska's Aleutian Islands extend into the eastern hemisphere and therefore technically contain the easternmost point and settlement in the U.S. (2) The New Cornelia Tailings Dam is a privately owned industrial dam composed of tailings, which are remnants of a mining process that once occurred on this site.

## Geodetic Datum of North America

In July 1986, the National Oceanic and Atmospheric Administration's National Geodetic Survey (NGS), in cooperation with Canada and Mexico, completed the readjustment and redefinition of the system of latitudes and longitudes. Known as the North American Datum of 1983 (NAD 83), it replaces the North American Datum of 1927, as well as local reference systems for the Hawaiian Islands (the Old Hawaiian Datum) and Puerto Rico and the Virgin Islands (the Puerto Rico Datum). The change was prompted by an increased need for accurate coordinate information. To facilitate the use of satellite surveying and navigation systems, such as the Global Positioning System (GPS), the new datum was redefined using the Geodetic Reference System 1980 as the reference ellipsoid because this model more closely approximates the true size and shape of the earth. In addition, the origin of the coordinate system is referenced to the mass center of the earth to coincide with the orbital orientation of the GPS satellites. Positional changes resulting from the datum redefinition can be as much as 330 ft in the continental U.S., Can., and Mex. Changes that exceed 660 ft can be expected in AK, PR, and the Virgin Islands. Hawaii's coordinates changed approximately 1,300 ft.

## Additional Statistical Information About the U.S.

In the *Statistical Abstract of the United States,* the Bureau of the Census, U.S. Dept. of Commerce, annually publishes a summary of social, political, and economic information. A book of more than 1,000 pages, it is prepared under the direction of Glenn W. King, Chief, Statistical Compendia Staff. Information concerning these and other publications may be obtained by writing New Orders, Supt. of Documents, PO Box 371954, Pittsburgh, PA 15250-7954, or by phoning the Census Customer Services Dept. at (301) 457-4100.

# Highest and Lowest Altitudes in the U.S. and Territories

**Source:** U.S. Geological Survey, Dept. of the Interior

(Minus sign means below sea level.)

| State/Terr. | Highest Point | | | Lowest Point | | |
|---|---|---|---|---|---|---|
| | Name | County | Elev. (ft) | Name | County | Elev. (ft) |
| Alabama | Cheaha Mountain | Cleburne | 2,405 | Gulf of Mexico | | Sea level |
| Alaska | Mount McKinley | | 20,320 | Pacific Ocean | | Sea level |
| Arizona | Humphreys Peak | Coconino | 12,633 | Colorado R | Yuma | 70 |
| Arkansas | Magazine Mountain | Logan | 2,753 | Ouachita R | Ashley-Union | 55 |
| California | Mount Whitney | Inyo-Tulare | 14,494 | Death Valley | Inyo | –282 |
| Colorado | Mount Elbert | Lake | 14,433 | Arkansas R | Prowers | 3,350 |
| Connecticut | Mount Frissell | Litchfield | 2,380 | Long Island Sound | | Sea level |
| Delaware | On Ebright Road | New Castle | 442 | Atlantic Ocean | | Sea level |
| Dist. of Col. | Tenleytown | N W part | 410 | Potomac R | | 1 |
| Florida | Sec. 30, T6N, R20W[1] | Walton | 345 | Atlantic Ocean | | Sea level |
| Georgia | Brasstown Bald | Towns-Union | 4,784 | Atlantic Ocean | | Sea level |
| Guam | Mount Lamlam | Agat District | 1,332 | Pacific Ocean | | Sea level |
| Hawaii | Mauna Kea | Hawaii | 13,796 | Pacific Ocean | | Sea level |
| Idaho | Borah Peak | Custer | 12,662 | Snake R | Nez Perce | 710 |
| Illinois | Charles Mound | Jo Daviess | 1,235 | Mississippi R | Alexander | 279 |
| Indiana | Franklin Township | Wayne | 1,257 | Ohio R | Posey | 320 |
| Iowa | Sec. 29, T100N, R41W[1] | Osceola | 1,670 | Mississippi R | Lee | 480 |
| Kansas | Mount Sunflower | Wallace | 4,039 | Verdigris R | Montgomery | 679 |
| Kentucky | Black Mountain | Harlan | 4,139 | Mississippi R | Fulton | 257 |
| Louisiana | Driskill Mountain | Bienville | 535 | New Orleans | Orleans | –8 |
| Maine | Mount Katahdin | Piscataquis | 5,267 | Atlantic Ocean | | Sea level |
| Maryland | Backbone Mountain | Garrett | 3,360 | Atlantic Ocean | | Sea level |
| Massachusetts | Mount Greylock | Berkshire | 3,487 | Atlantic Ocean | | Sea level |
| Michigan | Mount Arvon | Baraga | 1,979 | Lake Erie | Monroe | 571 |
| Minnesota | Eagle Mountain | Cook | 2,301 | Lake Superior | | 600 |
| Mississippi | Woodall Mountain | Tishomingo | 806 | Gulf of Mexico | | Sea level |
| Missouri | Taum Sauk Mt. | Iron | 1,772 | St. Francis R | Dunklin | 230 |
| Montana | Granite Peak | Park | 12,799 | Kootenai R | Lincoln | 1,800 |
| Nebraska | Johnson Township | Kimball | 5,426 | Missouri R | Richardson | 840 |
| Nevada | Boundary Peak | Esmeralda | 13,140 | Colorado R | Clark | 479 |
| New Hamp. | Mt. Washington | Coos | 6,288 | Atlantic Ocean | Rockingham | Sea level |
| New Jersey | High Point | Sussex | 1,803 | Atlantic Ocean | | Sea level |
| New Mexico | Wheeler Peak | Taos | 13,161 | Red Bluff Res. | Eddy | 2,842 |
| New York | Mount Marcy | Essex | 5,344 | Atlantic Ocean | | Sea level |
| North Carolina | Mount Mitchell | Yancey | 6,684 | Atlantic Ocean | | Sea level |
| North Dakota | White Butte | Slope | 3,506 | Red R | Pembina | 750 |
| Ohio | Campbell Hill | Logan | 1,549 | Ohio R | Hamilton | 455 |
| Oklahoma | Black Mesa | Cimarron | 4,973 | Little R | McCurtain | 289 |
| Oregon | Mount Hood | Clackamas-Hood R. | 11,239 | Pacific Ocean | | Sea level |
| Pennsylvania | Mt. Davis | Somerset | 3,213 | Delaware R | Delaware | Sea level |
| Puerto Rico | Cerro de Punta | Ponce District | 4,390 | Atlantic Ocean | | Sea level |
| Rhode Island | Jerimoth Hill | Providence | 812 | Atlantic Ocean | | Sea level |
| Samoa | Lata Mountain | Tau Island | 3,160 | Pacific Ocean | | Sea level |
| South Carolina | Sassafras Mountain | Pickens | 3,560 | Atlantic Ocean | | Sea level |
| South Dakota | Harney Peak | Pennington | 7,242 | Big Stone Lake | Roberts | 966 |
| Tennessee | Clingmans Dome | Sevier | 6,643 | Mississippi R | Shelby | 178 |
| Texas | Guadalupe Peak | Culberson | 8,749 | Gulf of Mexico | | Sea level |
| Utah | Kings Peak | Duchesne | 13,528 | Beaverdam Wash | Washington | 2,000 |
| Vermont | Mount Mansfield | Lamoille | 4,393 | Lake Champlain | | 95 |
| Virginia | Mount Rogers | Grayson-Smyth | 5,729 | Atlantic Ocean | | Sea level |
| Virgin Islands | Crown Mountain | St. Thomas Island | 1,556 | Atlantic Ocean | | Sea level |
| Washington | Mount Rainier | Pierce | 14,410 | Pacific Ocean | | Sea level |
| West Virginia | Spruce Knob | Pendleton | 4,861 | Potomac R | Jefferson | 240 |
| Wisconsin | Timms Hill | Price | 1,951 | Lake Michigan | | 579 |
| Wyoming | Gannett Peak | Fremont | 13,804 | Belle Fourche R | Crook | 3,099 |

(1) Sec.=section; T=township; R=range; N=north; W=west.

# U.S. Coastline by States

**Source:** National Oceanic and Atmospheric Administration, U.S. Dept. of Commerce

(in statute miles)

| State | Coastline[1] | Shoreline[2] |
|---|---|---|
| **Atlantic coast** | **2,069** | **28,673** |
| Connecticut | 0 | 618 |
| Delaware | 28 | 381 |
| Florida | 580 | 3,331 |
| Georgia | 100 | 2,344 |
| Maine | 228 | 3,478 |
| Maryland | 31 | 3,190 |
| Massachusetts | 192 | 1,519 |
| New Hampshire | 13 | 131 |
| New Jersey | 130 | 1,792 |
| New York | 127 | 1,850 |
| North Carolina | 301 | 3,375 |
| Pennsylvania | 0 | 89 |
| Rhode Island | 40 | 384 |
| South Carolina | 187 | 2,876 |
| Virginia | 112 | 3,315 |

| State | Coastline[1] | Shoreline[2] |
|---|---|---|
| **Gulf coast** | **1,631** | **17,141** |
| Alabama | 53 | 607 |
| Florida | 770 | 5,095 |
| Louisiana | 397 | 7,721 |
| Mississippi | 44 | 359 |
| Texas | 367 | 3,359 |
| **Pacific coast** | **7,623** | **40,298** |
| Alaska | 5,580 | 31,383 |
| California | 840 | 3,427 |
| Hawaii | 750 | 1,052 |
| Oregon | 296 | 1,410 |
| Washington | 157 | 3,026 |
| **Arctic coast, Alaska** | **1,060** | **2,521** |
| **United States** | **12,383** | **88,633** |

(1) Figures are lengths of general outline of seacoast. Measurements were made with a unit measure of 30 minutes of latitude on charts as near the scale of 1:1,200,000 as possible. Coastline of sounds and bays is included to a point where they narrow to width of unit measure, and includes the distance across at such point. (2) Figures obtained in 1939-40 with a recording instrument on the largest-scale charts and maps then available. Shoreline of outer coast, offshore islands, sounds, bays, rivers, and creeks is included to the head of tidewater or to a point where tidal waters narrow to a width of 100 ft.

# States: Settled, Capitals, Entry Into Union, Area, Rank

The 13 colonies that seceded from Great Britain and fought the War of Independence (American Revolution) became the 13 original states. They were (in the order in which they ratified the Constitution): Delaware, Pennsylvania, New Jersey, Georgia, Connecticut, Massachusetts, Maryland, South Carolina, New Hampshire, Virginia, New York, North Carolina, and Rhode Island.

| State | Settled[1] | Capital | Entered Union Date | Entered Union Order | Extent in miles Long (approx.) | Extent in miles Wide (mean) | Area in sq. mi Land | Area in sq. mi Inland Water | Area in sq. mi Total | Rank in area[2] |
|---|---|---|---|---|---|---|---|---|---|---|
| AL | 1702 | Montgomery | Dec. 14, 1819 | 22 | 330 | 190 | 50,750 | 1,673 | 52,423 | 30 |
| AK | 1784 | Juneau | Jan. 3, 1959 | 49 | 1,480[3] | 810[3] | 570,374 | 86,050 | 656,424 | 1 |
| AZ | 1776 | Phoenix | Feb. 14, 1912 | 48 | 400 | 310 | 113,642 | 364 | 114,006 | 6 |
| AR | 1686 | Little Rock | June 15, 1836 | 25 | 260 | 240 | 52,075 | 1,107 | 53,182 | 29 |
| CA | 1769 | Sacramento | Sept. 9, 1850 | 31 | 770 | 250 | 155,973 | 7,734 | 163,707 | 3 |
| CO | 1858 | Denver | Aug. 1, 1876 | 38 | 380 | 280 | 103,729 | 371 | 104,100 | 8 |
| CT | 1634 | Hartford | Jan. 9, 1788 | 5 | 110 | 70 | 4,845 | 698 | 5,544 | 48 |
| DE | 1638 | Dover | Dec. 7, 1787 | 1 | 100 | 30 | 1,955 | 535 | 2,489 | 49 |
| DC | NA | Washington | NA | NA | ... | ... | 61 | 7 | 68 | 51 |
| FL | 1565 | Tallahassee | Mar. 3, 1845 | 27 | 500 | 160 | 53,937 | 11,821 | 65,756 | 22 |
| GA | 1733 | Atlanta | Jan. 2, 1788 | 4 | 300 | 230 | 57,919 | 1,522 | 59,441 | 24 |
| HI | 1820 | Honolulu | Aug. 21, 1959 | 50 | ... | ... | 6,423 | 4,508 | 10,932 | 43 |
| ID | 1842 | Boise | July 3, 1890 | 43 | 570 | 300 | 82,751 | 823 | 83,574 | 14 |
| IL | 1720 | Springfield | Dec. 3, 1818 | 21 | 390 | 210 | 55,593 | 2,325 | 57,918 | 25 |
| IN | 1733 | Indianapolis | Dec. 11, 1816 | 19 | 270 | 140 | 35,870 | 550 | 36,420 | 38 |
| IA | 1788 | Des Moines | Dec. 28, 1846 | 29 | 310 | 200 | 55,875 | 401 | 56,276 | 26 |
| KS | 1727 | Topeka | Jan. 29, 1861 | 34 | 400 | 210 | 81,823 | 459 | 82,282 | 15 |
| KY | 1774 | Frankfort | June 1, 1792 | 15 | 380 | 140 | 39,732 | 679 | 40,411 | 37 |
| LA | 1699 | Baton Rouge | Apr. 30, 1812 | 18 | 380 | 130 | 43,566 | 8,277 | 51,843 | 31 |
| ME | 1624 | Augusta | Mar. 15, 1820 | 23 | 320 | 190 | 30,865 | 4,523 | 35,387 | 39 |
| MD | 1634 | Annapolis | Apr. 28, 1788 | 7 | 250 | 90 | 9,775 | 2,632 | 12,407 | 42 |
| MA | 1620 | Boston | Feb. 6, 1788 | 6 | 190 | 50 | 7,838 | 2,717 | 10,555 | 44 |
| MI | 1668 | Lansing | Jan. 26, 1837 | 26 | 490 | 240 | 56,809 | 39,896 | 96,705 | 11 |
| MN | 1805 | St. Paul | May 11, 1858 | 32 | 400 | 250 | 79,617 | 7,326 | 86,943 | 12 |
| MS | 1699 | Jackson | Dec. 10, 1817 | 20 | 340 | 170 | 46,914 | 1,520 | 48,434 | 32 |
| MO | 1735 | Jefferson City | Aug. 10, 1821 | 24 | 300 | 240 | 68,898 | 811 | 69,709 | 21 |
| MT | 1809 | Helena | Nov. 8, 1889 | 41 | 630 | 280 | 145,556 | 1,490 | 147,046 | 4 |
| NE | 1823 | Lincoln | Mar. 1, 1867 | 37 | 430 | 210 | 76,878 | 481 | 77,358 | 16 |
| NV | 1849 | Carson City | Oct. 31, 1864 | 36 | 490 | 320 | 109,806 | 761 | 110,567 | 7 |
| NH | 1623 | Concord | June 21, 1788 | 9 | 190 | 70 | 8,969 | 382 | 9,351 | 46 |
| NJ | 1660 | Trenton | Dec. 18, 1787 | 3 | 150 | 70 | 7,419 | 1,303 | 8,722 | 47 |
| NM | 1610 | Santa Fe | Jan. 6, 1912 | 47 | 370 | 343 | 121,364 | 234 | 121,598 | 5 |
| NY | 1614 | Albany | July 26, 1788 | 11 | 330 | 283 | 47,224 | 7,247 | 54,471 | 27 |
| NC | 1660 | Raleigh | Nov. 21, 1789 | 12 | 500 | 150 | 48,718 | 5,103 | 53,821 | 28 |
| ND | 1812 | Bismarck | Nov. 2, 1889 | 39 | 340 | 211 | 68,994 | 1,710 | 70,704 | 19 |
| OH | 1788 | Columbus | Mar. 1, 1803 | 17 | 220 | 220 | 40,953 | 3,875 | 44,828 | 34 |
| OK | 1889 | Oklahoma City | Nov. 16, 1907 | 46 | 400 | 220 | 68,679 | 1,224 | 69,903 | 20 |
| OR | 1811 | Salem | Feb. 14, 1859 | 33 | 360 | 261 | 96,002 | 2,383 | 98,386 | 9 |
| PA | 1682 | Harrisburg | Dec. 12, 1787 | 2 | 283 | 160 | 44,820 | 1,239 | 46,058 | 33 |
| RI | 1636 | Providence | May 29, 1790 | 13 | 40 | 30 | 1,045 | 500 | 1,545 | 50 |
| SC | 1670 | Columbia | May 23, 1788 | 8 | 260 | 200 | 30,111 | 1,897 | 32,008 | 40 |
| SD | 1859 | Pierre | Nov. 2, 1889 | 40 | 380 | 210 | 75,896 | 1,225 | 77,121 | 17 |
| TN | 1769 | Nashville | June 1, 1796 | 16 | 440 | 120 | 41,219 | 926 | 42,146 | 36 |
| TX | 1682 | Austin | Dec. 29, 1845 | 28 | 790 | 660 | 261,914 | 6,687 | 268,601 | 2 |
| UT | 1847 | Salt Lake City | Jan. 4, 1896 | 45 | 350 | 270 | 82,168 | 2,736 | 84,904 | 13 |
| VT | 1724 | Montpelier | Mar. 4, 1791 | 14 | 160 | 80 | 9,249 | 366 | 9,615 | 45 |
| VA | 1607 | Richmond | June 25, 1788 | 10 | 430 | 200 | 39,598 | 3,179 | 42,777 | 35 |
| WA | 1811 | Olympia | Nov. 11, 1889 | 42 | 360 | 240 | 66,581 | 4,721 | 71,302 | 18 |
| WV | 1727 | Charleston | June 20, 1863 | 35 | 240 | 130 | 24,087 | 145 | 24,231 | 41 |
| WI | 1766 | Madison | May 29, 1848 | 30 | 310 | 260 | 54,314 | 11,186 | 65,499 | 23 |
| WY | 1834 | Cheyenne | July 10, 1890 | 44 | 360 | 280 | 97,105 | 714 | 97,818 | 10 |

NA=Not applicable. (1) First permanent European settlement. (2) Rank is based on total area, including inland and coastal waters. (3) Aleutian Islands and Alexander Archipelago are not considered in these measurements.

# The Continental Divide of the U.S.

The Continental Divide of the U.S., also known as the Great Divide, is located at the watershed that is created by the mountain ranges, or tablelands, of the Rocky Mountains. This watershed separates the waters that drain easterly into the Atlantic Ocean and its marginal seas, such as the Gulf of Mexico, from those waters that drain westerly into the Pacific Ocean. The majority of easterly flowing water drains into the Gulf of Mexico before reaching the Atlantic Ocean. The majority of westerly flowing water, before reaching the Pacific Ocean, either drains through the Columbia R. or through the Colorado R., which flows into the Gulf of California before reaching the Pacific Ocean.

The location and route of the Continental Divide across the U.S. can briefly be described as follows:

Beginning at point of crossing the U.S.-Mexican boundary, near long. 108°45′ W, the Divide, in a northerly direction, crosses New Mexico along the western edge of the Rio Grande drainage basin, entering Colorado near long. 106°41′ W.

From there by a very irregular route north across Colorado along the W summits of the Rio Grande and of the Arkansas, the South Platte, and the North Platte river basins, and across Rocky Mountain National Park, entering Wyoming near long. 106°52′ W.

From there in a northwesterly direction, forming the W rims of the North Platte, the Big Horn, and the Yellowstone river basins, crossing the SW portion of Yellowstone National Park.

From there in a westerly and then a northerly direction forming the common boundary of Idaho and Montana, to a point on said boundary near long. 114°00′ W.

From there northeasterly and northwesterly through Montana and the Glacier National Park, entering Canada near long. 114°04′ W.

# Chronological List of Territories, With State Admissions to Union

**Source:** National Archives and Records Service

| Name of territory | Date of Organic Act creating territory | Organic Act effective | Admission as state | Yrs. terr. |
|---|---|---|---|---|
| Northwest Territory[1] | July 13, 1787 | No fixed date | Mar. 1, 1803[2] | 16 |
| Territory southwest of River Ohio | May 26, 1790 | No fixed date | June 1, 1796[3] | 6 |
| Mississippi | Apr. 7, 1798 | When president acted | Dec. 10, 1817 | 19 |
| Indiana | May 7, 1800 | July 4, 1800 | Dec. 11, 1816 | 16 |
| Orleans | Mar. 26, 1804 | Oct. 1, 1804 | Apr. 30, 1812[4] | 7 |
| Michigan | Jan. 11, 1805 | June 30, 1805 | Jan. 26, 1837 | 31 |
| Louisiana-Missouri[5] | Mar. 3, 1805 | July 4, 1805 | Aug. 10, 1821 | 16 |
| Illinois | Feb. 3, 1809 | Mar. 1, 1809 | Dec. 3, 1818 | 9 |
| Alabama | Mar. 3, 1817 | When MS became a state | Dec. 14, 1819 | 2 |
| Arkansas | Mar. 2, 1819 | July 4, 1819 | June 15, 1836 | 17 |
| Florida | Mar. 30, 1822 | No fixed date | Mar. 3, 1845 | 23 |
| Wisconsin | Apr. 20, 1836 | July 3, 1836 | May 29, 1848 | 12 |
| Iowa | June 12, 1838 | July 3, 1838 | Dec. 28, 1846 | 8 |
| Oregon | Aug. 14, 1848 | Date of act | Feb. 14, 1859 | 10 |
| Minnesota | Mar. 3, 1849 | Date of act | May 11, 1858 | 9 |
| New Mexico | Sept. 9, 1850 | On president's proclamation | Jan. 6, 1912 | 61 |
| Utah | Sept. 9, 1850 | Date of act | Jan. 4, 1896 | 46 |
| Washington | Mar. 2, 1853 | Date of act | Nov. 11, 1889 | 36 |
| Nebraska | May 30, 1854 | Date of act | Mar. 1, 1867 | 12 |
| Kansas | May 30, 1854 | Date of act | Jan. 29, 1861 | 6 |
| Colorado | Feb. 28, 1861 | Date of act | Aug. 1, 1876 | 15 |
| Nevada | Mar. 2, 1861 | Date of act | Oct. 31, 1864 | 3 |
| Dakota | Mar. 2, 1861 | Date of act | Nov. 2, 1889 | 28 |
| Arizona | Feb. 24, 1863 | Date of act | Feb. 14, 1912 | 49 |
| Idaho | Mar. 3, 1863 | Date of act | July 3, 1890 | 27 |
| Montana | May 26, 1864 | Date of act | Nov. 8, 1889 | 25 |
| Wyoming | July 25, 1868 | When officers were qualified | July 10, 1890 | 22 |
| Alaska[6] | May 17, 1884 | No fixed date | Jan. 3, 1959 | 75 |
| Oklahoma | May 2, 1890 | Date of act | Nov. 16, 1907 | 17 |
| Hawaii | Apr. 30, 1900 | June 14, 1900 | Aug. 21, 1959 | 59 |

(1) Included what is now Ohio, Indiana, Illinois, Michigan, Wisconsin, eastern Minnesota. (2) Whole territory admitted as the state of Ohio. (3) Admitted as the state of Tennessee. (4) Admitted as the state of Louisiana. (5) The organic act for Missouri Territory of June 4, 1812, became effective Dec. 7, 1812. (6) Although the May 17, 1884, act actually constituted Alaska as a district, it was often referred to as a territory, and unofficially administered as such. The Territory of Alaska was legally and formally organized by an act of Aug. 24, 1912.

# Geographic Centers, U.S. and Each State

**Source:** U.S. Geological Survey, Dept. of the Interior

There is no generally accepted definition of geographic center and no uniform method for determining it. Following the U.S. Geological Survey, the geographic center of an area is defined here as the center of gravity of the surface, or that point on which the surface would balance if it were a plane of uniform thickness. All localities in the following list, therefore, are approximate.

No marked or monumented point has been established by any government agency as the geographic center of either the 50 states, the conterminous U.S., or the North American continent. A monument was erected in Lebanon, KS, the conterminous U.S. center, by a group of citizens. A cairn in Rugby, ND, marks the center of the North American continent.

**United States, including Alaska and Hawaii**—W of Castle Rock, Butte County, South Dakota; lat. 44°58′N, long. 103°46′W
**Conterminous U.S. (48 states)**—Near Lebanon, Smith Co., Kansas, lat. 39°50′N, long. 98°35′W
**North American continent**—6 mi W of Balta, Pierce County, North Dakota; lat. 48°10′N, long. 100°10′W

**State—county, locality**

**Alabama**—Chilton, 12 mi SW of Clanton
**Alaska**—lat. 63°50′N, long. 152°W; approx. 60 mi NW of Mt. McKinley
**Arizona**—Yavapai, 55 mi E-SE of Prescott
**Arkansas**—Pulaski, 12 mi NW of Little Rock
**California**—Madera, 38 mi E of Madera
**Colorado**—Park, 30 mi NW of Pikes Peak
**Connecticut**—Hartford, at East Berlin
**Delaware**—Kent, 11 mi S of Dover
**District of Columbia**—Near 4th and L Sts. NW
**Florida**—Hernando, 12 mi N-NW of Brooksville
**Georgia**—Twiggs, 18 mi SE of Macon
**Hawaii**—Hawaii, lat. 20°15′N, long. 156°20′W, off Maui Isl.
**Idaho**—Custer, at Custer, SW of Challis
**Illinois**—Logan, 28 mi NE of Springfield
**Indiana**—Boone, 14 mi N-NW of Indianapolis
**Iowa**—Story, 5 mi NE of Ames
**Kansas**—Barton, 15 mi NE of Great Bend
**Kentucky**—Marion, 3 mi N-NW of Lebanon
**Louisiana**—Avoyelles, 3 mi SE of Marksville
**Maine**—Piscataquis, 18 mi N of Dover
**Maryland**—Prince Georges, 4.5 mi NW of Davidsonville
**Massachusetts**—Worcester, north part of city
**Michigan**—Wexford, 5 mi N-NW of Cadillac
**Minnesota**—Crow Wing, 10 mi SW of Brainerd
**Mississippi**—Leake, 9 mi W-NW of Carthage
**Missouri**—Miller, 20 mi SW of Jefferson City
**Montana**—Fergus, 11 mi W of Lewistown
**Nebraska**—Custer, 10 mi NW of Broken Bow
**Nevada**—Lander, 26 mi SE of Austin
**New Hampshire**—Belknap, 3 mi E of Ashland
**New Jersey**—Mercer, 5 mi SE of Trenton
**New Mexico**—Torrance, 12 mi S-SW of Willard
**New York**—Madison, 12 mi S of Oneida and 26 mi SW of Utica
**North Carolina**—Chatham, 10 mi NW of Sanford
**North Dakota**—Sheridan, 5 mi SW of McClusky
**Ohio**—Delaware, 25 mi N-NE of Columbus
**Oklahoma**—Oklahoma, 8 mi N of Oklahoma City
**Oregon**—Crook, 25 mi S-SE of Prineville
**Pennsylvania**—Centre, 2.5 mi SW of Bellefonte
**Rhode Island**—Kent, 1 mi S-SW of Crompton
**South Carolina**—Richland, 13 mi SE of Columbia
**South Dakota**—Hughes, 8 mi NE of Pierre
**Tennessee**—Rutherford, 5 mi NE of Murfreesboro
**Texas**—McCulloch, 15 mi NE of Brady
**Utah**—Sanpete, 3 mi N of Manti
**Vermont**—Washington, 3 mi E of Roxbury
**Virginia**—Buckingham, 5 mi SW of Buckingham
**Washington**—Chelan, 10 mi W-SW of Wenatchee
**West Virginia**—Braxton, 4 mi E of Sutton
**Wisconsin**—Wood, 9 mi SE of Marshfield
**Wyoming**—Fremont, 58 mi E-NE of Lander

# International Boundary Lines of the U.S.

The length of the N boundary of the conterminous U.S.—the U.S.-Canadian border, excluding Alaska—is 3,987 mi according to the U.S. Geological Survey, Dept. of the Interior. The length of the Alaskan-Canadian border is 1,538 mi. The length of the U.S.-Mexican border, from the Gulf of Mexico to the Pacific Ocean, is approximately 1,933 mi (1963 boundary agreement).

# Origins of the Names of U.S. States

**Source:** State officials, Smithsonian Institution, and Topographic Division, U.S. Geological Survey, Dept. of the Interior

**Alabama**—Indian for tribal town, later a tribe (Alabamas or Alibamons) of the Creek confederacy.

**Alaska**—Russian version of Aleutian (Eskimo) word, *alakshak*, for "peninsula," "great lands," or "land that is not an island."

**Arizona**—Spanish version of Pima Indian word for "little spring place," or Aztec *arizuma*, meaning "silver-bearing."

**Arkansas**—French name for Quapaw ("downstream people"), a Siouan people.

**California**—Bestowed by the Spanish conquistadors (possibly by Cortez). It was the name of an imaginary island, an earthly paradise, in "Las Serges de Esplandian," a Spanish romance written by Montalvo in 1510. *Baja California* (Lower California, in Mexico) was first visited by Spanish in 1533. The present U.S. state was called *Alta* (Upper) *California*.

**Colorado**—From Spanish for "red", first applied to Colorado River.

**Connecticut**—From Mohican and other Algonquin words meaning "long river place."

**Delaware**—Named for Lord De La Warr, early governor of Virginia; first applied to river, then to Indian tribe (Lenni-Lenape), and the state.

**District of Columbia**—For Christopher Columbus, 1791.

**Florida**—Named by Ponce de Leon on *Pascua Florida*, "Flowery Easter," on Easter Sunday, 1513.

**Georgia**—For King George II of England, by James Oglethorpe, colonial administrator, 1732.

**Hawaii**—Possibly derived from native word for homeland, *Hawaiki* or *Owhyhee*.

**Idaho**—Said to be a coined name with an invented meaning: "gem of the mountains"; originally suggested for the Pikes Peak mining territory (Colorado), then applied to the new mining territory of the Pacific Northwest. Another theory suggests Idaho may be a Kiowa Apache term for the Comanche.

**Illinois**—French for *Illini* or "land of *Illini*," Algonquin word meaning "men" or "warriors."

**Indiana**—Means "land of the Indians."

**Iowa**— Indian word variously translated as "here I rest" or "beautiful land." Named for the Iowa R., which was named for the Iowa Indians.

**Kansas**—Sioux word for "south wind people."

**Kentucky**—Indian word that is variously translated as "dark and bloody ground," "meadowland," and "land of tomorrow."

**Louisiana**—Part of territory called Louisiana by Sieur de La Salle for French King Louis XIV.

**Maine**—From Maine, ancient French province. Also: descriptive, referring to the mainland as distinct from the many coastal islands.

**Maryland**—For Queen Henrietta Maria, wife of Charles I of England.

**Massachusetts**—From Indian tribe named after "large hill place" identified by Capt. John Smith as being near Milton, MA.

**Michigan**—From Chippewa words, *mici gama*, meaning "great water," after the lake of the same name.

**Minnesota**—From Dakota Sioux word meaning "cloudy water" or "sky-tinted water" of the Minnesota River.

**Mississippi**—Probably Chippewa; *mici zibi*, "great river" or "gathering-in of all the waters." Also: Algonquin word, *messipi*.

**Missouri**—An Algonquin Indian term meaning "river of the big canoes."

**Montana**—Latin or Spanish for "mountainous."

**Nebraska**—From Omaha or Otos Indian word meaning "broad water" or "flat river," describing the Platte River.

**Nevada**—Spanish, meaning "snow-clad."

**New Hampshire**—Named, 1629, by Capt. John Mason of Plymouth Council for his home county in England.

**New Jersey**—The Duke of York, 1664, gave a patent to John Berkeley and Sir George Carteret to be called Nova Caesaria, or New Jersey, after England's Isle of Jersey.

**New Mexico**—Spaniards in Mexico applied term to land north and west of Rio Grande in the 16th century.

**New York**—For Duke of York and Albany, who received patent to New Netherland from his brother Charles II and sent an expedition to capture it, 1664.

**North Carolina**—In 1619 Charles I gave a large patent to Sir Robert Heath to be called Province of Carolana, from *Carolus*, Latin name for Charles. A new patent was granted by Charles II to Earl of Clarendon and others. Divided into North and South Carolina, 1710.

**North Dakota**—*Dakota* is Sioux for "friend" or "ally."

**Ohio**—Iroquois word for "fine or good river."

**Oklahoma**—Choctaw word meaning "red man," proposed by Rev. Allen Wright, Choctaw-speaking Indian.

**Oregon**—Origin unknown. One theory holds that the name may have been derived from that of the Wisconsin River, shown on a 1715 French map as "Ouaricon-sint."

**Pennsylvania**—William Penn, the Quaker who was made full proprietor of this area by King Charles II in 1681, suggested "Sylvania," or "woodland," for his tract. The king's government owed Penn's father, Admiral William Penn, £16,000, and the land was granted as partial settlement. Charles II added the "Penn" to Sylvania, against the desires of the modest proprietor, in honor of the admiral.

**Puerto Rico**—Spanish for "rich port."

**Rhode Island**—Exact origin is unknown. One theory notes that Giovanni de Verrazano recorded an island about the size of Rhodes in the Mediterranean in 1524, but others believe the state was named Roode Eylandt by Adriaen Block, Dutch explorer, because of its red clay.

**South Carolina**—See North Carolina.

**South Dakota**—See North Dakota.

**Tennessee**—*Tanasi* was the name of Cherokee villages on the Little Tennessee River. From 1784 to 1788 this was the State of Franklin, or Frankland.

**Texas**—Variant of word used by Caddo and other Indians meaning "friends" or "allies," and applied to them by the Spanish in eastern Texas. Also written *texias, tejas, teysas*.

**Utah**—From a Navajo word meaning "upper," or "higher up," as applied to a Shoshone tribe called Ute. Spanish form is *Yutta*. The English is *Uta* or *Utah*. Proposed name *Deseret*, "land of honeybees," from Book of Mormon, was rejected by Congress.

**Vermont**—From French words *vert* (green) and *mont* (mountain). The Green Mountains were said to have been named by Samuel de Champlain. When the state was formed, 1777, Dr. Thomas Young suggested combining *vert* and *mont* into Vermont.

**Virginia**—Named by Sir Walter Raleigh, who fitted out the expedition of 1584, in honor of Queen Elizabeth, the Virgin Queen of England.

**Washington**—Named after George Washington. When the bill creating the Territory of Columbia was introduced in the 32d Congress, the name was changed to Washington because of the existence of the District of Columbia.

**West Virginia**—So named when western counties of Virginia refused to secede from the U.S. in 1863.

**Wisconsin**—An Indian name, spelled *Ouisconsin* and *Mesconsing* by early chroniclers. Believed to mean "grassy place" in Chippewa. Congress made it *Wisconsin*.

**Wyoming**—From the Algonquin words for "large prairie place," "at the big plains," or "on the great plain."

# Territorial Sea of the U.S.

According to a Dec. 27, 1988, proclamation by Pres. Ronald Reagan: "The territorial sea of the United States henceforth extends to 12 nautical miles from the baselines of the United States determined in accordance with international law. In accordance with international law, as reflected in the applicable provisions of the 1982 United Nations Convention on the Law of the Sea, within the territorial sea of the United States, the ships of all countries enjoy the right of innocent passage and the ships and aircraft of all countries enjoy the right of transit passage through international straits."

# Accession of Territory by the U.S.

**Source:** U.S. Dept. of the Interior; Bureau of the Census, U.S. Dept. of Commerce

| | Acquisition date | Land area (sq mi)[1] |
|---|---|---|
| **Total U.S.**[2] | **NA** | **3,540,305** |
| 50 states and Washington, DC | NA | 3,536,278 |
| Territory in 1790[3] | NA | 895,415 |
| Louisiana Purchase[4] | 1803 | 909,380 |
| Purchase of Florida | 1819 | 58,666 |
| Texas | 1845 | 388,687 |
| Oregon Territory | 1846 | 286,541 |
| Mexican Cession | 1848 | 529,189 |
| Gadsden Purchase | 1853 | 29,670 |
| Alaska | 1867 | 570,374 |
| Hawaii | 1898 | 6,423 |
| Other areas: | | |
| Puerto Rico[5] | 1899 | 3,427 |
| Guam[6] | 1899 | 210 |
| American Samoa[7] | 1900 | 77 |
| U.S. Virgin Islands | 1917 | 134 |
| N Mariana Islands[8] | 1986 | 179 |
| All other[9] | NA | 16 |

NA=not applicable. (1) Area figures from the Bureau of the Census, Apr. 1, 1990. As a result of independent rounding, the sum of these figures do not equal the total. (2) Includes outlying areas. (3) Includes that part of a drainage basin of Red River of the North, S of 49th parallel, sometimes considered part of Louisiana Purchase. (4) Also acquired areas west of the Mississippi River amounting to 22,834 sq mi, but relinquished to Spain 97,150 sq mi, or a net loss of 15,650 sq mi. (5) Ceded by Spain in 1898, ratified in 1899, and became the Commonwealth of Puerto Rico by Act of Congress on July 25, 1952. (6) Acquired 1898; ratified 1899. (7) Acquired 1899; ratified 1900. (8) Acquired 1986. (9) Comprises the following islands with gross areas as indicated in sq mi: Midway (2), Wake (3), Palmyra (2), Navassa (3), Baker, Howland, and Jarvis (combined area, 3), Johnson Atoll (combined area, less than 1), and Kingman Reef (less than 0.5).

# Federally Owned Land, by State, 1994

**Source:** Bureau of Land Management, U.S. Dept. of the Interior; as of Sept. 30, 1994

| State | Federal acreage[1] | Total acreage of state[2] | Percentage of federally-owned acreage[1] |
|---|---|---|---|
| AL | 1,081,371.5 | 32,678,400 | 3.309 |
| AK | 242,795,760.9 | 365,481,600 | 66.432 |
| AZ | 32,488,417.9 | 72,688,000 | 44.696 |
| AR | 2,932,563.1 | 33,599,360 | 8.728 |
| CA | 46,956,437.6 | 100,206,720 | 46.860 |
| CO | 24,140,220.4 | 66,485,760 | 36.309 |
| CT | 12,358.7 | 3,135,360 | 0.394 |
| DE | 241,642.0 | 1,265,920 | 19.088 |
| DC | 9,151.9 | 39,040 | 23.442 |
| FL | 2,719,390.1 | 34,721,280 | 7.832 |
| GA | 1,676,945.3 | 37,295,360 | 4.496 |
| HI | 688,129.5 | 4,105,600 | 16.761 |
| ID | 32,946,170.9 | 52,933,120 | 62.241 |
| IL | 1,078,210.7 | 35,795,200 | 3.012 |
| IN | 470,098.6 | 23,158,400 | 2.030 |
| IA | 417,634.0 | 35,860,480 | 1.165 |
| KS | 376,699.5 | 52,510,720 | 0.717 |
| KY | 1,073,672.8 | 25,512,320 | 4.208 |
| LA | 1,011,232.7 | 28,867,840 | 3.503 |
| ME | 329,478.8 | 19,847,680 | 1.660 |
| MD | 529,977.7 | 6,319,360 | 8.387 |
| MA | 201,947.6 | 5,034,880 | 4.011 |
| MI | 4,713,346.4 | 36,492,160 | 12.916 |
| MN | 7,303,590.6 | 51,205,760 | 14.263 |
| MS | 1,358,177.9 | 30,222,720 | 4.494 |
| MO | 2,107,879.7 | 44,248,320 | 4.764 |
| MT | 25,959,402.6 | 93,271,040 | 27.832 |
| NE | 700,446.8 | 49,031,680 | 1.429 |
| NV | 58,295,285.5 | 70,264,320 | 82.966 |
| NH | 762,667.3 | 5,768,960 | 13.220 |
| NJ | 638,192.0 | 4,813,440 | 13.259 |
| NM | 26,549,504.6 | 77,766,400 | 34.140 |
| NY | 423,120.7 | 30,680,960 | 1.379 |
| NC | 2,447,946.7 | 31,402,880 | 7.795 |
| ND | 1,848,925.6 | 44,452,480 | 4.159 |
| OH | 349,725.6 | 26,222,080 | 1.334 |
| OK | 769,790.8 | 44,087,680 | 1.746 |
| OR | 36,939,181.5 | 61,598,720 | 59.967 |
| PA | 725,499.2 | 28,804,480 | 2.519 |
| RI | 17,658.9 | 677,120 | 2.608 |
| SC | 791,436.9 | 19,374,080 | 4.085 |
| SD | 2,697,618.3 | 48,881,920 | 5.519 |
| TN | 1,563,946.3 | 26,727,680 | 5.851 |
| TX | 2,356,223.0 | 168,217,600 | 1.401 |
| UT | 33,838,181.9 | 52,696,960 | 64.213 |
| VT | 432,370.5 | 5,936,640 | 7.283 |
| VA | 3,018,081.6 | 25,496,320 | 11.837 |
| WA | 11,456,307.1 | 42,693,760 | 26.834 |
| WV | 1,092,265.2 | 15,410,560 | 7.088 |
| WI | 2,929,170.8 | 35,011,200 | 8.366 |
| WY | 31,024,073.9 | 62,343,040 | 49.764 |
| **Total** | **676,615,420.3** | **2,271,343,360** | **29.789** |

**Note:** Totals do not include inland water. (1) Excludes trust properties. (2) Bureau of the Census, U.S. Dept. of Commerce figures.

# National Recreation Areas Administered by the U.S. Forest Service, 1996

**Source:** U.S. Forest Service, Dept. of Agriculture

| Area name | Location | Estab. | Acres |
|---|---|---|---|
| Admiralty Island | AK | 1980 | 978,881 |
| Allegheny | PA | 1984 | 23,063 |
| Arapaho | CO | 1978 | 30,690 |
| Beech Creek | OK | 1988 | 7,500 |
| Cascade Head | OR | 1974 | 6,630 |
| Columbia River Gorge | OR-WA | 1986 | 63,150 |
| Coosa Bald | GA | 1991 | 7,100 |
| Ed Jenkins | GA | 1991 | 23,166 |
| Flaming Gorge | WY-UT | 1968 | 189,825 |
| Grand Island | MI | 1990 | 12,961 |
| Hells Canyon | ID-OR | 1975 | 536,648 |
| Indian Nations | OK | 1988 | 40,051 |
| Jemez | NM | 1993 | 57,000 |
| Misty Fiords | AK | 1980 | 2,293,428 |
| Mono Basin | CA | 1984 | 115,600 |
| Mount Baker | WA | 1984 | 8,473 |
| Mount Pleasant | VA | 1994 | 7,580 |
| Mount Rogers | VA | 1966 | 114,520 |
| Mount St. Helens | WA | 1989 | 112,593 |
| Newberry | OR | 1990 | 54,822 |
| North Cascades | WA | 1984 | 87,600 |
| Oregon Dunes | OR | 1972 | 27,212 |
| Pine Ridge | NE | 1986 | 6,600 |
| Rattlesnake | MT | 1980 | 59,119 |
| Sawtooth | ID | 1972 | 729,322 |
| Smith River | CA | 1990 | 305,169 |
| Spring Mt. | NV | 1993 | 312,683 |
| Spruce Knob-Seneca Rocks | WV | 1965 | 57,237 |
| Whiskeytown-Shasta-Trinity | CA | 1965 | 176,367 |
| White Rocks | VT | 1984 | 36,400 |
| Winding Stair Mt. | OK | 1988 | 25,890 |

# National Parks, Other Areas Administered by National Park Service

Dates that the sites were authorized for initial protection by Congress or by presidential proclamation are given in parenthesis. If different, the date the area was given its current designation, or was transferred to the National Park Service, follows. Gross area in acres, as of Dec. 31, 1995, follows date(s). Approximately 83 mil acres of federal land are administered by the National Park Service.

## National Parks

**Acadia,** ME (1916/1929) 46,996. Includes Mount Desert Island, half of Isle au Haut, Schoodic Peninsula on mainland. Highest elevation on Eastern seaboard.

**American Samoa,** AS (1988) 9,000. Features a paleotropical rain forest and a coral reef. No federal facilities.

**Arches,** UT (1929/1971) 73,379. Contains giant red sandstone arches and other products of erosion.

**Badlands,** SD (1929/1978) 242,756; prairie with bison, bighorn, and antelope. Contains animal fossils from 26 to 37 mil years ago.

**Big Bend,** TX (1935) 801,163. Rio Grande, Chisos Mts.

**Biscayne,** FL (1968/1980) 172,924. Aquatic park encompassing chain of islands south of Miami.

**Bryce Canyon,** UT (1923/1928) 35,835. Spectacularly colorful and unusual display of erosion effects.

**Canyonlands,** UT (1964) 337,570. At junction of Colorado and Green rivers; extensive evidence of prehistoric Indians.

**Capitol Reef,** UT (1937/1971) 241,904. A 70-mi uplift of sandstone cliffs dissected by high-walled gorges.

**Carlsbad Caverns,** NM (1923/1930) 46,766. Largest known caverns; not yet fully explored.

**Channel Islands,** CA (1938/1980) 249,354. Sea lion breeding place, nesting sea birds, unique plants.

**Crater Lake,** OR (1902) 183,224. Extraordinary blue lake in the crater of Mt. Mazama, a volcano that erupted about 7,700 years ago; deepest U.S. lake.

**Death Valley,** CA-NV (1933/1994) 3,367,628. Large desert area. Includes the lowest point in the Western Hemisphere; also includes Scottys Castle.

**Denali,** AK (1917/1980) 4,741,910. Name changed from Mt. McKinley NP. Contains highest mountain in U.S.; wildlife.

**Dry Tortugas,** FL (1935/1992) 64,700. Formerly Ft. Jefferson National Monument.

**Everglades,** FL (1934) 1,507,850. Largest remaining subtropical wilderness in continental U.S.

**Gates of the Arctic,** AK (1978/1984) 7,523,888. Vast wilderness in north central region. Limited federal facilities.

**Glacier,** MT (1910) 1,013,572. Superb Rocky Mt. scenery, numerous glaciers and glacial lakes. Part of Waterton-Glacier Intl. Peace Park established by U.S. and Canada in 1932.

**Glacier Bay,** AK (1925/1986) 3,224,794. Great tidewater glaciers that move down mountainsides and break up into the sea; much wildlife.

**Grand Canyon,** AZ (1893/1919) 1,217,158. Most spectacular part of Colorado River's greatest canyon.

**Grand Teton,** WY (1929) 309,994. Most impressive part of the Teton Mountains, winter feeding ground of largest American elk herd.

**Great Basin,** NV (1922/1986) 77,180. Includes Wheeler Pk., Lexington Arch, and Lehman Caves.

**Great Smoky Mountains,** NC-TN (1926/1934) 521,053. Largest Eastern mountain range, magnificent forests.

**Guadalupe Mountains,** TX (1966) 86,416. Extensive Permian limestone fossil reef; tremendous earth fault.

**Haleakala,** HI (1916/1960) 28,091. Dormant volcano on Maui with large colorful craters.

**Hawaii Volcanoes,** HI (1916/1961) 209,695. Contains Kilauea and Mauna Loa, active volcanoes.

**Hot Springs,** AR (1832/1921) 5,550. Bathhouses are furnished with thermal waters from the park's 47 hot springs; these waters are used for bathing and drinking.

**Isle Royale,** MI (1931) 571,790. Largest island in Lake Superior, noted for its wilderness area and wildlife.

**Joshua Tree,** CA (1936/1994) 792,750. Desert region includes Joshua trees and other plant and animal life.

**Katmai,** AK (1918/1980) 3,674,541. "Valley of Ten Thousand Smokes," scene of 1912 volcanic eruption.

**Kenai Fjords,** AK (1978/1980) 670,643. Abundant marine mammals, birdlife; the Harding Icefield, one of the 4 major icecaps in U.S.

**Kings Canyon,** CA (1890/1940) 461,901. Mountain wilderness, dominated by Kings River Canyons and High Sierra; contains giant sequoias.

**Kobuk Valley,** AK (1978/1980) 1,750,737. Contains geological and recreational sites. Limited federal facilities.

**Lake Clark,** AK (1978/1980) 2,619,859. Across Cook Inlet from Anchorage. A scenic wilderness rich in fish and wildlife. Limited federal facilities.

**Lassen Volcanic,** CA (1907/1916) 106,372. Contains Lassen Peak, recently active volcano, and other volcanic phenomena.

**Mammoth Cave,** KY (1926/1941) 52,830. 144 mi of surveyed underground passages, beautiful natural formations, river 300 ft below surface.

**Mesa Verde,** CO (1906) 52,122. Most notable and best preserved prehistoric cliff dwellings in the U.S.

**Mount Rainier,** WA (1899) 235,613. Greatest single-peak glacial system in the U.S.

**North Cascades,** WA (1968) 504,781. Spectacular mountainous region with many glaciers, lakes.

**Olympic,** WA (1909/1938) 922,651. Mountain wilderness containing finest remnant of Pacific Northwest rain forest, active glaciers, Pacific shoreline, rare elk.

**Petrified Forest,** AZ (1906/1962) 93,533. Extensive petrified wood and Indian artifacts. Contains part of Painted Desert.

**Redwood,** CA (1968) 110,232. 40 mi of Pacific coastline, groves of ancient redwoods and world's tallest trees.

**Rocky Mountain,** CO (1915) 265,727. On the Continental Divide; includes peaks over 14,000 ft.

**Saguaro,** AZ (1933/1994) 91,571. Part of the Sonoran Desert; includes the giant saguaro cacti, unique to the region.

**Sequoia,** CA (1890) 402,482. Groves of giant sequoias, highest mountain in conterminous U.S.—Mt. Whitney (14,494 ft). World's largest tree.

**Shenandoah,** VA (1926) 196,559. Portion of the Blue Ridge Mts.; overlooks Shenandoah Valley; Skyline Drive.

**Theodore Roosevelt,** ND (1947/1978) 70,447. Contains part of T.R.'s ranch and scenic badlands.

**Virgin Islands,** VI (1956) 14,689. Authorized to cover 75% of St. John Isl. and Hassel Isl.; lush growth, lovely beaches, Carib Indian petroglyphs, evidence of colonial Danes.

**Voyageurs,** MN (1971) 218,035. Abundant lakes, forests, wildlife, canoeing, boating.

**Wind Cave,** SD (1903) 28,295. Limestone caverns in Black Hills. Extensive wildlife includes a herd of bison.

**Wrangell-St. Elias,** AK (1978/1980) 8,323,618. Largest area in park system, most peaks over 16,000 ft, abundant wildlife; day's drive east of Anchorage. Limited federal facilities.

**Yellowstone,** ID-MT-WY, (1872) 2,219,791. World's first national park. World's greatest geyser area has about 10,000 geysers and hot springs; spectacular falls and impressive canyons of the Yellowstone River; grizzly bear, moose, and bison.

**Yosemite,** CA (1890) 761,236. Yosemite Valley, the nation's highest waterfall, grove of sequoias, and mountains.

**Zion,** UT (1909/1919) 146,598. Unusual shapes and landscapes have resulted from erosion and faulting; evidence of past volcanic acitivity; Zion Canyon, with sheer walls ranging up to 2,640 ft, is readily accessible.

## National Historical Parks

**Appomattox Court House,** VA (1930/1954) 1,775. Where Lee surrendered to Grant.

**Boston,** MA (1974) 41. Includes Faneuil Hall, Old North Church, Bunker Hill, Paul Revere House.

**Cane River Creole,** LA (1994) 206. Preserves the Creole culture as it developed along the Cane R.

**Chaco Culture,** NM (1907/1980) 33,974. Ruins of pueblos built by prehistoric Indians.

**Chesapeake and Ohio Canal,** MD-DC-WV (1938/1971) 19,237. 184-mi historic canal; DC to Cumberland, MD.

**Colonial,** VA (1930/1936) 9,330. Includes most of Jamestown Island, site of first successful English colony; Yorktown, site of Cornwallis's surrender to George Washington; and the Colonial Parkway.

**Cumberland Gap,** KY-TN-VA (1940) 20,444. Mountain pass of the Wilderness Road, which carried the first great migration of pioneers into America's interior.

**Dayton Aviation,** OH (1992) 86. Commemorates the area's aviation heritage.

**George Rogers Clark,** Vincennes, IN (1966) 26. Commemorates American defeat of British in West during Revolution.

**Harpers Ferry,** MD-VA-WV (1944/1963) 2,287. At the confluence of the Shenandoah and Potomac rivers, the site of John Brown's 1859 raid on the Army arsenal.

**Hopewell Culture,** OH (1923/1992) 1,130. Formerly Mound City Group National Monument.

**Independence,** PA (1948) 45. Contains several properties in Philadelphia associated with the American Revolution and the founding of the U.S. Includes Independence Hall.

**Jean Laffite** (and preserve), LA (1907/1978) 20,020. Includes Chalmette, site of 1815 Battle of New Orleans; French Quarter.

**Kalaupapa,** HI (1980) 10,779. Molokai's former leper colony site and other historic areas.

**Kaloko-Honokohau,** HI (1978) 1,161. Preserves the native culture of Hawaii. No federal facilities.

**Keweenaw,** MI (1992) 1,870. Site of first significant copper mine in U.S. Federal facilities are under development.

**Klondike Gold Rush,** AK-WA (1976) 13,191. Alaskan Trails in 1898 Gold Rush. Museum in Seattle.

**Lowell,** MA (1978) 137. Textile mills, canal, 19th-cent. structures; park shows planned city of Industrial Revolution.

**Lyndon B. Johnson,** TX (1969/1980) 1,570. President's birthplace, boyhood home, ranch.

**Marsh-Billings,** VT (1992) 643. Boyhood home of pioneer conservationist George Perkins Marsh. No federal facilities.

**Minute Man,** MA (1959) 935. Where the colonial Minute Men battled the British, Apr. 19, 1775. Also contains Nathaniel Hawthorne's home.

**Morristown,** NJ (1933) 1,684. Sites of important military encampments during the American Revolution; Washington's headquarters, 1777, 1779-80.

**Natchez,** MS (1988) 108. Mansions, townhouses, and villas related to history of Natchez, MS.

**New Orleans Jazz,** LA (1994) Acreage undetermined. Preserves, educates, and interprets jazz as it has evolved in New Orleans.

**Nez Perce,** ID (1965) 2,110. Illustrates the history and culture of the Nez Perce Indian country (38 separate sites).

**Pecos,** NM (1965/1990) 6,671. Ruins of ancient Pueblo of Pecos, archaeological sites, and 2 associated Spanish colonial missions from the 17th and 18th centuries.

**Pu'uhonua o Honaunau,** HI (1955/1978) 182. Until 1819, a sanctuary for Hawaiians vanquished in battle and for those guilty of crimes or breaking taboos.

**Salt River Bay** (ecological preserve), St. Croix, VI (1992) 945. The only site known where, 500 years ago, members of a Columbus party landed on what is now territory of the U.S.

**San Antonio Missions,** TX (1978) 819. Four of finest Spanish missions in U.S., 18th-cent. irrigation system.

**San Francisco Maritime,** CA (1988) 31. Artifacts, photographs, and historic vessels related to the development of the Pacific Coast.

**San Juan Island,** WA (1966) 1,752. Commemorates peaceful relations between the U.S., Canada, and Great Britain since the 1872 boundary disputes.

**Saratoga,** NY (1938) 3,393. Scene of a major battle that became a turning point in the American Revolution.

**Sitka,** AK (1910/1972) 107. Scene of last major resistance of the Tlingit Indians to the Russians, 1804.

**Tumacacori,** AZ (1908/1990) 47. Historic Spanish Catholic mission building stands near the site first visited by Jesuit Father Kino in 1691.

**Valley Forge,** PA (1976) 3,466. Continental Army campsite in 1777-78 winter.

**War in the Pacific,** GU (1978) 1,960. Seven distinct units illustrating the Pacific theater of WWII. Limited federal facilities.

**Women's Rights,** NY (1980) 7. Seneca Falls site where Susan B. Anthony, Elizabeth Cady Stanton began rights movement in 1848.

## National Battlefields

**Antietam,** MD (1890/1978) 3,256. Battle here ended first Confederate invasion of North, Sept. 17, 1862.

**Big Hole,** MT (1910/1963) 656. Site of major battle with Nez Perce Indians.

**Cowpens,** SC (1929/1972) 842. American Revolution battlefield.

**Fort Donelson,** TN (1928/1985) 552. Site of first major Union victory.

**Fort Necessity,** PA (1931/1961) 903. Some of first battle of French and Indian War.

**Monocacy,** MD (1934/1976) 1,647. Civil War battle in defense of Washington, DC, fought here, July 9, 1864.

**Moores Creek,** NC (1926/1980) 87. 1776 battle between Patriots and Loyalists commemorated here.

**Petersburg,** VA (1926/1962) 2,744. Scene of 10-month Union campaigns 1864-65.

**Stones River,** TN (1927/1960) 709. Scene of battle that began federal offensive to trisect the Confederacy.

**Tupelo,** MS (1929/1961) 1. Site of crucial battle over Sherman's supply line.

**Wilson's Creek,** MO (1960/1970) 1,750. Scene of Civil War battle for control of Missouri.

## National Battlefield Parks

**Kennesaw Mountain,** GA (1917/1935) 2,884. Site of two major battles of Atlanta campaign in Civil War.

**Manassas,** VA (1940) 5,072. Scene of two battles in Civil War, 1861 and 1862.

**Richmond,** VA (1936) 772. Site of battles defending Confederate capital.

## National Battlefield Site

**Brices Cross Roads,** MS (1929) 1. Civil War battlefield.

## National Military Parks

**Chickamauga and Chattanooga,** GA-TN (1890) 8,119. Site of major Confederate victory, 1863.

**Fredericksburg and Spotsylvania County,** VA (1927/1933) 7,782. Sites of several major Civil War battles and campaigns.

**Gettysburg,** PA (1895/1933) 5,907. Site of decisive Confederate defeat in North and Gettysburg Address.

**Guilford Courthouse,** NC (1917/1933) 220. American Revolution battle site.

**Horseshoe Bend,** AL (1956) 2,040. On Tallapoosa River, where Gen. Andrew Jackson's forces broke the power of the Upper Creek Indian Confederacy.

**Kings Mountain,** SC (1931/1933) 3,945. Site of American Revolution battle.

**Pea Ridge,** AR (1956) 4,300. Scene of Civil War battle.

**Shiloh,** TN (1894/1933) 3,973. Major Civil War battlesite; includes some well-preserved Indian burial mounds.

**Vicksburg,** MS-LA (1899/1933) 1,736. Union victory gave North control of the Mississippi and split the Confederate forces.

## National Memorials

**Arkansas Post,** AR (1960) 389. First permanent French settlement in the lower Mississippi River valley.

**Arlington House, the Robert E. Lee Memorial,** VA (1925/1972) 28. Lee's home overlooking the Potomac.

**Chamizal,** El Paso, TX (1966/1974) 55. Commemorates 1963 settlement of 99-year border dispute with Mexico.

**Coronado,** AZ (1941/1952) 4,750. Commemorates first European exploration of the Southwest.

**DeSoto,** FL (1948) 27. Commemorates 16th-cent. Spanish explorations.

**Federal Hall,** NY (1939/1955) 0.45. First seat of U.S. government under the Constitution.

**Fort Caroline,** FL (1950) 138. On St. Johns River, overlooks site of a French Huguenot colony.

**Fort Clatsop,** OR (1958) 125. Lewis and Clark encampment, 1805-6.

**General Grant,** NY (1958) 0.76. Tomb of Grant and wife.

**Hamilton Grange,** NY (1962) 0.11. Home of Alexander Hamilton.

**Jefferson National Expansion Memorial,** St. Louis, MO (1935) 91. Commemorates westward expansion.

**Johnstown Flood,** PA (1964) 164. Commemorates tragic flood of 1889.

**Korean War Veterans,** DC (1986) 2.2. Dedicated in 1995; honors those who served in the Korean War.

**Lincoln Boyhood,** IN (1962) 200. Lincoln grew up here.

**Lincoln Memorial,** DC (1911/1933) 107. Marble statue of the 16th U.S. president.

**Lyndon B. Johnson Grove on the Potomac,** DC (1973) 17. Overlooks the Potomac R.; vista of the Capital.

**Mount Rushmore,** SD (1925) 1,278. World-famous sculpture of 4 presidents.

**Perry's Victory and International Peace Memorial,** Put-in-Bay, OH (1936/1972) 25. The world's most massive Doric column, constructed 1912-15, promotes pursuit of international peace through arbitration and disarmament.

**Roger Williams,** Providence, RI (1965) 5. Memorial to founder of Rhode Island.

**Thaddeus Kosciuszko,** PA (1972) 0.02. Memorial to Polish hero of American Revolution.

**Theodore Roosevelt Island,** DC (1932/1933) 89. Statue of Roosevelt in wooded island sanctuary.

**Thomas Jefferson Memorial,** DC (1934) 18. Statue of Jefferson in an inscribed circular, colonnaded structure.

**USS *Arizona*,** HI (1980). Less than 1 acre. Memorializes American losses at Pearl Harbor.

**Vietnam Veterans,** DC (1980) 2. Black granite wall inscribed with names of those killed in action and missing in the Vietnam War.

**Washington Monument,** DC (1848/1933) 106. Obelisk honoring the first U.S. president.

**Wright Brothers,** NC (1927/1953) 428. Site of first powered flight.

## National Historic Sites

**Abraham Lincoln Birthplace,** Hodgenville, KY (1916/1959) 117. Early 17th-cent. cabin.

**Adams,** Quincy, MA (1946/1952) 14. Home of Presidents John Adams, John Quincy Adams, and celebrated descendants.

**Allegheny Portage Railroad,** PA (1964) 1,247. Linked the Pennsylvania Canal system and the West.

**Andersonville,** Andersonville, GA (1970) 495. Noted Civil War prisoner-of-war camp.

**Andrew Johnson,** Greeneville, TN (1935/1963) 17. Two homes and the tailor shop of the 17th U.S. president.

**Bent's Old Fort,** CO (1960) 800. Reconstruction of S Plains outpost.

**Boston African American,** MA (1980) Acreage undetermined. Pre-Civil War black history structures.

**Brown v. Board of Education,** KS (1992) 2. Commemorates the landmark 1954 U.S. Supreme Court decision.

**Carl Sandburg Home,** Flat Rock, NC (1968) 264. Poet's home.

**Charles Pinckney,** SC (1988) 28. Statesman's farm.

**Christiansted,** St. Croix, VI (1952/1961) 27. Commemorates Danish colony.

**Clara Barton,** MD (1974) 9. Home of founder of American Red Cross.

**Edgar Allan Poe,** PA (1978/1980) 0.52. U.S. writer's home.

**Edison,** West Orange, NJ (1955/1962) 21. Inventor's home and laboratory.

**Eisenhower,** Gettysburg, PA (1967) 690. Home of 34th president.

**Eleanor Roosevelt,** Hyde Park, NY (1977) 181. Personal retreat.

**Eugene O'Neill,** Danville, CA (1976) 13. Playwright's home.

**Ford's Theatre,** DC (1866/1970) 0.29. Includes theater, now restored, where Lincoln was assassinated, house where he died, and Lincoln Museum.

**Fort Bowie,** AZ (1964) 1,000. Focal point of operations against Geronimo and the Apaches.

**Fort Davis,** TX (1961) 460. Key frontier outpost in West Texas.

**Fort Laramie,** WY (1938/1960) 833. Military post on Oregon Trail.

**Fort Larned,** KS (1964/1966) 718. Military post on Santa Fe Trail.

**Fort Point,** San Francisco, CA (1970) 29. West Coast fortification.

**Fort Raleigh,** NC (1941) 513. First attempted English settlement in North America.

**Fort Scott,** KS (1965/1978) 17. Commemorates U.S. frontier of 1840s and '50s.

**Fort Smith,** AR-OK (1961) 75. Active post during 1817-90.

**Fort Union Trading Post,** MT-ND (1966) 442. Principal fur-trading post on upper Missouri, 1829-67.

**Fort Vancouver,** WA (1948/1961) 209. Headquarters for Hudson's Bay Company in 1825. Early political seat.

**Frederick Douglass,** DC (1962/1988) 9. Home of nation's leading black spokesman.

**Frederick Law Olmsted,** MA (1979) 2. Home of famous city planner.

**Friendship Hill,** PA (1978) 675. Home of Albert Gallatin, Jefferson's and Madison's secretary of treasury.

**Golden Spike,** UT (1957) 2,735. Commemorates completion of first transcontinental railroad in 1869.

**Grant-Kohrs Ranch,** MT (1972) 1,498. Ranch house and part of 19th-cent. ranch.

**Hampton,** MD (1948) 62. 18th-cent. Georgian mansion.

**Harry S. Truman,** MO (1983) 7. Home of Pres. Truman after 1919.

**Herbert Hoover,** West Branch, IA (1965) 187. Birthplace and boyhood home of 31st president.

**Home of Franklin D. Roosevelt,** Hyde Park, NY (1944) 290. Birthplace, home, and "Summer White House" of 32d president.

**Hopewell Furnace,** PA (1938/1985) 848. 19th-cent. iron-making village.

**Hubbell Trading Post,** AZ (1965) 160. Still-active trading post.

**James A. Garfield,** Mentor, OH (1980) 8. Home of 20th president.

**Jimmy Carter,** GA (1987) 71. Birthplace and home of 39th president.

**John Fitzgerald Kennedy,** Brookline, MA (1967) 0.09. Birthplace and childhood home of 35th president.

**John Muir,** Martinez, CA (1964) 345. Home of early conservationist and writer.

**Knife River Indian Villages,** ND (1974) 1,758. Remnants of villages last occupied by Hidatsa and Mandan Indians.

**Lincoln Home,** Springfield, IL (1971) 12. Lincoln's residence at the time he was elected 16th president, 1860.

**Longfellow,** Cambridge, MA (1972) 2. Longfellow's home, 1837-82, and Washington's headquarters during Boston Siege, 1775-76.

**Maggie L. Walker,** VA (1978) 1. Richmond home of black leader and bank president; daughter of an ex-slave.

**Manzanar,** Lone Pine, CA (1992) 500. Commemorates Manzanar War Relocation Ctr., a Japanese-American internment camp during WWII. No federal facilities.

**Martin Luther King, Jr.,** Atlanta, GA (1980) 37. Birthplace, grave, and church of the civil rights leader. Limited federal facilities.

**Martin Van Buren,** NY (1974) 40. Lindenwald, home of 8th president, near Kinderhook.

**Mary McLeod Bethune Council House,** DC (1982/1991) 0.07. Commemorates Bethune's leadership in the black women's movement.

**Ninety Six,** SC (1976) 989. Colonial trading village.

**Palo Alto Battlefield,** TX (1978) 3,357. Scene of first battle of the Mexican War.

**Pennsylvania Avenue,** DC (1965) Acreage undetermined. Also includes area adjacent to the road between Capitol and White House, encompassing Ford's Theatre and a number of other federal structures.

**Puukohola Heiau,** HI (1972) 80. Ruins of temple built by King Kamehameha.

**Sagamore Hill,** Oyster Bay, NY (1962) 83. Home of President Theodore Roosevelt from 1885 until his death in 1919.

**Saint-Gaudens,** Cornish, NH (1964) 148. Home, studio, and gardens of American sculptor Augustus Saint-Gaudens.

**Saint Paul's Church,** NY (1943) 6. 18th-cent. site associated with John Peter Zenger's "freedom of press" trial.

**Salem Maritime,** MA (1938) 9. Only port never seized from the patriots by the British. Major fishing and whaling port.

**San Juan,** PR (1949) 75. 16th-cent. Span. fortifications.

**Saugus Iron Works,** MA (1974) 9. Reconstructed 17th-cent. colonial ironworks.

**Springfield Armory,** MA (1974) 55. Small-arms manufacturing center for nearly 200 years.

**Steamtown,** PA (1986) 62. Railyard, roadhouse, and repair shops of former Delaware, Lackawanna, and Western Railroad.

**Theodore Roosevelt Birthplace,** New York, NY (1962) 0.11. Reconstructed brownstone.

**Theodore Roosevelt Inaugural,** Buffalo, NY (1966) 1. Wilcox House where he took oath of office, 1901.

**Thomas Stone,** MD (1978) 328. Home of signer of Declaration of Independence, built in 1771.

**Tuskegee Institute,** AL (1974) 58. College founded by Booker T. Washington in 1881 for blacks.

**Ulysses S. Grant,** St. Louis Co., MO (1989) 10. Home of Grant during pre-Civil War years.

**Vanderbilt Mansion,** Hyde Park, NY (1940) 212. Mansion of 19th-cent. financier.

**Weir Farm,** Wilton, CT (1990) 60. Home and studio of American impressionist painter J. Alden Weir.

**Whitman Mission,** WA (1936/1963) 98. Site where Dr. and Mrs. Marcus Whitman ministered to the Indians until slain by them in 1847.

**William Howard Taft,** Cincinnati, OH (1969) 3. Birthplace and early home of the 27th president.

## National Monuments

| Name | State | Year[1] | Acreage |
|---|---|---|---|
| Agate Fossil Beds | NE | 1965 | 3,055 |
| Alibates Flint Quarries | NM-TX | 1965 | 1,371 |
| Aniakchak** | AK | 1978 | 137,176 |
| Aztec Ruins | NM | 1923 | 320 |
| Bandelier | NM | 1916 | 32,737 |
| Black Canyon of the Gunnison | CO | 1933 | 20,766 |
| Booker T. Washington | VA | 1956 | 224 |
| Buck Island Reef | VI | 1961 | 880 |
| Cabrillo | CA | 1913 | 137 |
| Canyon de Chelly | AZ | 1931 | 83,840 |
| Cape Krusenstern† | AK | 1978 | 649,712 |
| Capulin Volcano | NM | 1916 | 793 |
| Casa Grande Ruins | AZ | 1889 | 473 |
| Castillo de San Marcos | FL | 1924 | 21 |
| Castle Clinton | NY | 1946 | 1 |
| Cedar Breaks | UT | 1933 | 6,155 |
| Chiricahua | AZ | 1924 | 11,985 |
| Colorado | CO | 1911 | 20,454 |
| Congaree Swamp | SC | 1976 | 22,200 |
| Craters of the Moon | ID | 1924 | 53,545 |
| Devils Postpile | CA | 1911 | 798 |
| Devils Tower | WY | 1906 | 1,347 |
| Dinosaur | CO-UT | 1915 | 210,844 |
| Effigy Mounds | IA | 1949 | 1,481 |
| El Malpais | NM | 1987 | 114,277 |
| El Morro | NM | 1906 | 1,279 |
| Florissant Fossil Beds | CO | 1969 | 5,998 |
| Fort Frederica | GA | 1936 | 241 |
| Fort Matanzas | FL | 1924 | 228 |
| Fort McHenry National Monument and Historic Shrine | MD | 1925 | 43 |
| Fort Pulaski | GA | 1924 | 5,623 |
| Fort Stanwix | NY | 1935 | 16 |
| Fort Sumter | SC | 1948 | 195 |
| Fort Union | NM | 1954 | 721 |
| Fossil Butte | WY | 1972 | 8,198 |
| G. Washington Birthplace | VA | 1930 | 550 |
| George Washington Carver | MO | 1943 | 210 |
| Gila Cliff Dwellings | NM | 1907 | 533 |
| Grand Portage | MN | 1951 | 710 |
| Grand Staircase-Escalante[2] | UT | 1996 | 1,700,000 |
| Great Sand Dunes | CO | 1932 | 38,662 |
| Hagerman Fossil Beds† | ID | 1988 | 4,281 |
| Hohokam Pima* | AZ | 1972 | 1,690 |
| Homestead Natl. Monument of America | NE | 1936 | 195 |
| Hovenweep | CO-UT | 1923 | 785 |
| Jewel Cave | SD | 1908 | 1,274 |
| John Day Fossil Beds | OR | 1974 | 14,014 |
| Lava Beds | CA | 1925 | 46,560 |
| Little Big Horn Battlefield | MT | 1879 | 765 |
| Montezuma Castle | AZ | 1906 | 858 |
| Muir Woods | CA | 1908 | 554 |

| Name | State | Year[1] | Acreage |
|---|---|---|---|
| Natural Bridges | UT | 1908 | 7,636 |
| Navajo | AZ | 1909 | 360 |
| Ocmulgee | GA | 1934 | 702 |
| Oregon Caves | OR | 1909 | 488 |
| Organ Pipe Cactus | AZ | 1937 | 330,689 |
| Petroglyph | NM | 1990 | 7,240 |
| Pinnacles | CA | 1908 | 16,265 |
| Pipe Spring | AZ | 1923 | 40 |
| Pipestone | MN | 1937 | 282 |
| Poverty Point** | LA | 1988 | 911 |
| Rainbow Bridge† | UT | 1910 | 160 |
| Russell Cave | AL | 1961 | 310 |
| Salinas Pueblo Missions | NM | 1909 | 1,071 |
| Scotts Bluff | NE | 1919 | 3,003 |
| Statue of Liberty | NJ-NY | 1924 | 58 |
| Sunset Crater | AZ | 1930 | 3,040 |
| Timpanogos Cave | UT | 1922 | 250 |
| Tonto | AZ | 1907 | 1,120 |
| Tuzigoot | AZ | 1939 | 801 |
| Walnut Canyon | AZ | 1915 | 2,249 |
| White Sands | NM | 1933 | 143,733 |
| Wupatki | AZ | 1924 | 35,253 |
| Yucca House* | CO | 1919 | 10 |

## National Preserves

| Name | State | Year[1] | Acreage |
|---|---|---|---|
| Aniakchak | AK | 1978 | 465,603 |
| Bering Land Bridge† | AK | 1978 | 2,698,406 |
| Big Cypress | FL | 1974 | 716,000 |
| Big Thicket | TX | 1974 | 96,678 |
| Denali | AK | 1917 | 1,334,618 |
| Gates of the Arctic | AK | 1978 | 948,629 |
| Glacier Bay | AK | 1925 | 58,406 |
| Katmai | AK | 1918 | 418,699 |
| Lake Clark | AK | 1978 | 1,410,641 |
| Little River Canyon** | AL | 1992 | 13,669 |
| Mojave | CA | 1994 | 1,450,000 |
| Noatak† | AK | 1978 | 6,569,904 |
| Timucuan Ecological & Historic Preserve† | FL | 1988 | 46,000 |
| Wrangell-St. Elias | AK | 1978 | 4,852,773 |
| Yukon-Charley Rivers† | AK | 1978 | 2,526,509 |

## National Seashores

| Name | State | Year[1] | Acreage |
|---|---|---|---|
| Assateague Island | MD-VA | 1965 | 39,733 |
| Canaveral | FL | 1975 | 57,662 |
| Cape Cod | MA | 1961 | 43,569 |
| Cape Hatteras | NC | 1937 | 30,319 |
| Cape Lookout | NC | 1966 | 28,243 |
| Cumberland Island | GA | 1972 | 36,415 |
| Fire Island | NY | 1964 | 19,579 |
| Gulf Islands | FL-MS | 1971 | 135,607 |
| Padre Island | TX | 1962 | 130,434 |
| Point Reyes | CA | 1962 | 71,049 |

## National Parkways

| Name | State | Year[1] | Acreage |
|---|---|---|---|
| Blue Ridge | NC-VA | 1933 | 87,925 |
| George Washington Memorial | VA-MD-DC | 1930 | 7,248 |
| John D. Rockefeller Jr. Mem. | WY | 1972 | 23,777 |
| Natchez Trace | MS-AL-TN | 1938 | 51,748 |

## National Lakeshores

| Name | State | Year[1] | Acreage |
|---|---|---|---|
| Apostle Islands | WI | 1970 | 69,372 |
| Indiana Dunes | IN | 1966 | 15,058 |
| Pictured Rocks | MI | 1966 | 73,228 |
| Sleeping Bear Dunes | MI | 1970 | 71,189 |

## National Reserves

| Name | State | Year[1] | Acreage |
|---|---|---|---|
| City of Rocks† | ID | 1988 | 14,407 |
| Ebey's Landing† | WA | 1978 | 19,000 |

## National Rivers

| Name | State | Year[1] | Acreage |
|---|---|---|---|
| Big South Fork Natl. R and Recreation Area | KY-TN | 1976 | 125,000 |
| Buffalo | AR | 1972 | 94,309 |
| Mississippi Natl. R and Recreation Area | MN | 1988 | 53,775 |
| Niobrara | NE-SD | 1991 | NA |
| Ozark | MO | 1964 | 80,790 |

## National Wild and Scenic Rivers

| Name | State | Year[1] | Acreage |
|---|---|---|---|
| Alagnak | AK | 1980 | 30,745 |
| Bluestone** | WV | 1978 | 4,268 |
| Delaware | NY-NJ-PA | 1978 | 1,973 |
| Great Egg Harbor | NJ | 1992 | NA |
| Missouri | NE-SD | 1991 | NA |
| Obed | TN | 1976 | 5,056 |
| Rio Grande** | TX | 1978 | 9,600 |
| Saint Croix | MN-WI | 1968 | 67,456 |
| Upper Delaware | NY-PA | 1978 | 75,000 |

## National Recreation Areas

| Name | State | Year[1] | Acreage |
|---|---|---|---|
| Amistad | TX | 1965 | 58,500 |
| Bighorn Canyon | MT-WY | 1966 | 120,296 |
| Chattahoochee R. | GA | 1978 | 9,260 |
| Chickasaw | OK | 1902 | 9,889 |
| Coulee Dam | WA | 1946 | 100,390 |
| Curecanti | CO | 1965 | 41,972 |
| Cuyahoga Valley | OH | 1974 | 32,525 |
| Delaware Water Gap | NJ-PA | 1965 | 67,192 |
| Gateway | NJ-NY | 1972 | 26,629 |
| Gauley R.† | WV | 1988 | 11,150 |
| Glen Canyon | AZ-UT | 1958 | 1,236,880 |
| Golden Gate | CA | 1972 | 74,451 |
| Lake Chelan | WA | 1968 | 61,887 |
| Lake Mead | AZ-NV | 1936 | 1,495,666 |
| Lake Meredith | TX | 1965 | 44,978 |
| Ross Lake | WA | 1968 | 117,575 |
| Santa Monica Mts.† | CA | 1978 | 150,050 |
| Whiskeytown | CA | 1965 | 42,503 |

## National Scenic Trails

| Name | State | Year[1] | Acreage |
|---|---|---|---|
| Appalachian | ME to GA | 1968 | 170,811 |
| Natchez Trace | MS-AL-TN | 1983 | 10,995 |
| Potomac Heritage | MD-DC-VA-PA | 1983 | NA |

## Parks (no other classification)

| Name | State | Year[1] | Acreage |
|---|---|---|---|
| Catoctin Mountain | MD | 1954 | 5,770 |
| Constitution Gardens | DC | 1974 | 52 |
| Fort Washington | MD | 1930 | 341 |
| Greenbelt | MD | 1950 | 1,176 |
| National Capital | DC | 1933 | 6,547 |
| National Mall | DC | 1933 | 146 |
| Piscataway | MD | 1961 | 4,441 |
| Prince William Forest | VA | 1948 | 18,572 |
| Rock Creek | DC | 1890 | 1,754 |
| White House | DC | 1933 | 18 |
| Wolf Trap Farm Park for the Performing Arts | VA | 1966 | 130 |

## International Historic Sites

| Name | State | Year[1] | Acreage |
|---|---|---|---|
| Saint Croix Island** | ME | 1949 | 35 |

NA=Not available. *Not open to the public. **No federal facilities. † Limited federal facilities. (1) First designated. (2) Administered by Bureau of Land Management; acreage is estimated.

# Most-Visited Sites in the National Park System, 1995

**Source:** National Park Service, Dept. of the Interior

Attendance at all areas administered by the National Park Service in 1995 was 269,564,307 recreation visits.

| Site (location) | Recreation visits |
|---|---|
| Blue Ridge Parkway (NC, VA) | 17,415,519 |
| Golden Gate National Recreation Area (CA) | 14,695,771 |
| Lake Mead National Recreation Area (AZ, NV) | 9,838,702 |
| Great Smoky Mountains National Park (TN, NC) | 9,080,420 |
| George Washington Memorial National Parkway (VA, MD) | 6,546,803 |
| Gateway National Recreation Area (NY, NJ) | 6,064,254 |
| Natchez Trace National Parkway (MS, AL, TN) | 5,849,061 |
| National Capital Parks (DC) | 5,513,009 |
| Cape Cod National Seashore (MA) | 5,141,039 |
| Delaware Water Gap National Recreation Area (PA, NJ) | 4,726,251 |
| Grand Canyon National Park (AZ) | 4,557,645 |
| Gulf Islands National Seashore (FL, MS) | 4,520,356 |
| Statue of Liberty National Monument (NY, NJ) | 4,244,725 |
| Yosemite National Park (CA) | 3,958,406 |
| Castle Clinton National Monument (NY) | 3,672,620 |
| Olympic National Park (WA) | 3,658,615 |
| San Francisco Maritime National Historical Park (CA) | 3,631,994 |
| Chattahoochee River National Recreation Area (GA) | 3,475,002 |
| Colonial National Historical Park (VA) | 3,303,324 |
| Jefferson National Expansion Memorial (MO) | 3,234,977 |

# Federal Indian Reservations and Trust Lands[1]

**Source:** Tiller Research, Inc., Albuquerque, NM

| State | No. of reser. | Tribally owned acreage[2] | Individually owned acreage[2] | No. of persons[3] | Major tribes and/or nations |
|---|---|---|---|---|---|
| Alabama | 1 | 230 | 0 | 16,506 | Poarch Creek |
| Alaska | 1[4] | 86,773 | 1,265,432 | 85,698 | Aleut, Eskimo, Athapascan,[5] Haida, Tlingit, Tsimpshian |
| Arizona | 23 | 19,775,959 | 311,579 | 203,527 | Navajo, Apache, Papago, Hopi, Yavapai, Pima |
| California | 96 | 520,049 | 66,769 | 242,164 | Hoopa, Paiute, Yurok, Karok, Cherokee |
| Colorado | 2 | 764,120 | 2,805 | 27,776 | Ute |
| Connecticut | 1 | 1,638 | 0 | 6,654 | Mashantucket Pequot |
| Florida | 4 | 153,874 | 0 | 36,335 | Seminole, Miccosukee, Cherokee |
| Idaho | 4 | 609,622 | 327,301 | 13,780 | Shoshone, Bannock, Nez Perce |
| Iowa | 1 | 3,550 | 0 | 7,349 | Sac and Fox |
| Kansas | 4 | 7,219 | 23,763 | 21,965 | Potawatomi, Kickapoo, Iowa |
| Louisiana | 3 | 415 | 0 | 18,541 | Chitimacha, Coushatta, Tunica-Biloxi |
| Maine | 3 | 191,511 | 0 | 5,998 | Passamaquoddy, Penobscot, Maliseet |
| Massachusetts | 1 | 157 | 0 | 12,241 | Wampanoag |
| Michigan | 8 | 14,411 | 9,276 | 55,638 | Chippewa, Potawatomi, Ottawa, Cherokee |
| Minnesota | 14 | 779,138 | 50,338 | 49,909 | Chippewa, Sioux |
| Mississippi | 1 | 20,486 | 0 | 8,525 | Choctaw |
| Montana | 7 | 2,663,385 | 2,911,450 | 47,679 | Blackfeet, Crow, Sioux, Assiniboine, Cheyenne |
| Nebraska | 3 | 23,792 | 43,208 | 12,410 | Omaha, Winnebago, Santee Sioux |
| Nevada | 19 | 1,147,088 | 78,529 | 19,637 | Paiute, Shoshone, Washoe |
| New Mexico | 25 | 7,252,326 | 630,293 | 134,355 | Apache, Navajo, Pueblo |
| New York | 8 | 118,199 | 0 | 62,651 | Seneca, Mohawk, Onondaga, Oneida |
| North Carolina | 1 | 56,509 | 0 | 80,155 | Cherokee, Lumbee |
| North Dakota | 3 | 214,006 | 627,289 | 25,917 | Sioux, Chippewa, Mandan, Arikara, Hidatsa |
| Oklahoma | 36[6] | 96,839 | 1,000,165 | 252,420 | Cherokee, Creek, Choctaw, Chickasaw, Osage, Cheyenne, Arapahoe, Kiowa, Comanche |
| Oregon | 7 | 660,367 | 135,053 | 38,496 | Warm Springs, Wasco, Paiute, Umatilla, Siletz |
| Rhode Island | 1 | 1,800 | 0 | 4,071 | Narragansett |
| South Carolina | 1 | 639 | 0 | 8,246 | Catawba |
| South Dakota | 9 | 2,399,531 | 2,121,188 | 50,575 | Sioux |
| Texas | 3 | 4,726 | 0 | 65,877 | Alabama-Coushatta, Tiwa, Kickapoo |
| Utah | 4 | 2,286,448 | 32,838 | 24,283 | Ute, Goshute, Southern Paiute, Navajo |
| Washington | 27 | 2,250,731 | 467,785 | 81,483 | Yakama, Lummi, Quinault |
| Wisconsin | 11 | 338,097 | 80,345 | 39,387 | Chippewa, Oneida, Winnebago |
| Wyoming | 1 | 1,958,095 | 101,537 | 9,479 | Shoshone, Arapahoe |

(1) In Oct. 1993, the Bureau of Indian Affairs of the U.S. Dept. of the Interior published in the *Federal Register* (vol. 58, no. 202, pp. 54364-69) a comprehensive listing of 552 "Indian Entities Recognized and Eligible To Receive Services From the United States Bureau of Indian Affairs" (328 in the conterminous 48 states, 224 in Alaska). The term *Indian entities* includes Indian tribes, bands, villages, groups, and pueblos; also included are Eskimo and Aleut villages and tribes. All such entities have a government-to-government relationship with the U.S. Some reservation boundaries transcend state boundaries (e.g., Navajo, which is in Arizona, New Mexico, and Utah). For the purpose of "Number of Reservations," such reservations are counted in the state where their population is predominant and/or tribal headquarters are located. (2) Information provided by the Bureau of Indian Affairs; data current as of 1990. Acreages refer only to lands that are either owned by the tribes and individual members or that are held in trust by the U.S. government. Many of these parcels are located off reservations. Not all lands within reservation boundaries are necessarily trust lands. Many are privately owned by tribes, tribal members, or non-Indians. Others are the property of various governmental agencies. (3) Total Native American (Indian, Eskimo, or Aleut) population in each state with reservation/trust lands, including those persons living outside the Bureau of Indian Affairs service area. Populations as of 1990. (4) The only federally recognized reservation in Alaska is the Annette Island Reserve. In all other cases, the U.S. government's relationship to Native Americans in Alaska is set out by the Alaska Native Claims Settlement Act of 1971. The act provided for the establishment of regional and village corporations to conduct business for profit and nonprofit purposes; these corporations are also landowners. There are 12 regional corporations, each with organized village corporations, plus one regional corporation for Alaska Natives outside the state. (5) Aleuts and Eskimos are racially and linguistically related. Athapascans are related to the Navajo and Apache Indians. (6) There are 36 tribal entities in Oklahoma, each of which owns land in the state. Because of the way in which the state of Oklahoma was formed out of the Oklahoma and Indian territories, the reservation status of land in the state is frequently disputed in both civil and criminal proceedings.

# American Indian Population

**Source:** Bureau of the Census, U.S. Dept. of Commerce, 1990 Census

The Bureau of the Census figures reflect personal self-identification and are not based on any designation by a federal or state government.

| State | Total | State | Total | State | Total | State | Total | State | Total | State | Total |
|---|---|---|---|---|---|---|---|---|---|---|---|
| AL | 16,312 | FL | 35,461 | LA | 18,361 | NE | 12,344 | OK | 252,089 | VT | 1,650 |
| AK | 31,245 | GA | 12,926 | ME | 5,945 | NV | 19,377 | OR | 37,443 | VA | 14,893 |
| AZ | 203,009 | HI | 4,738 | MD | 12,601 | NH | 2,075 | PA | 14,210 | WA | 77,627 |
| AR | 12,641 | ID | 13,594 | MA | 11,857 | NJ | 14,500 | RI | 3,987 | WV | 2,365 |
| CA | 236,078 | IL | 20,970 | MI | 56,131 | NM | 134,097 | SC | 8,049 | WI | 38,986 |
| CO | 27,271 | IN | 12,453 | MN | 49,392 | NY | 60,855 | SD | 50,501 | WY | 9,426 |
| CT | 6,472 | IA | 7,217 | MS | 8,435 | NC | 79,825 | TN | 9,859 | | |
| DE | 1,982 | KS | 21,767 | MO | 19,508 | ND | 25,870 | TX | 64,349 | **Total** | |
| DC | 1,432 | KY | 5,614 | MT | 47,524 | OH | 19,859 | UT | 24,093 | **U.S.** | **1,878,285** |

# WORLD HISTORY

## Prehistory: Our Ancestors Take Over

*Homo sapiens.* The precise origins of *Homo sapiens,* the species to which all humans belong, are subject to broad speculation based on a small number of fossils, on genetic and anatomical studies, and on the geological record. Most scientists agree, however, that humans evolved from apelike primate ancestors in a process that began millions of years ago.

Current theories trace the first hominid (humanlike primate) to Africa, where 2 lines of hominids appeared 5 to 7 million years ago. One was *Australopithecus,* a social animal that lived from perhaps 4 million to 3 million years ago, and then apparently died out. The other was a human line, *Homo habilis,* a large-brained specimen that walked upright and had a dextrous hand. *Homo habilis* appeared some 2.5 million years ago, lived in semipermanent camps, and had a food-gathering and sharing economy.

*Homo erectus,* the nearest ancestor to humans, appeared in Africa perhaps 1.75 million years ago and began spreading into Asia and Europe soon after. It had a fairly large brain and a skeletal structure similar to that of modern humans. *Homo erectus* learned to control fire and probably had primitive language skills. The final brain development to *Homo sapiens,* and then to the subspecies of *Homo sapiens sapiens,* occurred between 500,000 and 50,000 years ago, either in one place—probably Africa—or virtually simultaneously and independently in parts of Africa, Europe, and Asia. All modern races are members of the subspecies *Homo sapiens sapiens.*

The spread of humankind into the remaining habitable continents probably took place near the end of the last Ice Age: from Asia to the Americas; from Asia across a land bridge to Australia across the Timor Straits.

**Earliest cultures.** A variety of cultural modes—in toolmaking, diet, shelter, and possibly social arrangements and spiritual expression—arose as early humankind adapted to different geographic and climatic zones.

Archaeologists recognize 3 basic toolmaking traditions as arising and often coexisting from one million years ago to the near past: the *chopper tradition,* found largely in E Asia, producing crude chopping tools and simple flake tools; the *flake tradition,* found in Africa and W Europe, producing a variety of small cutting and flaking tools; and the *biface* tradition, found in all of Africa, W and S Europe, and S Asia, producing pointed hand axes chipped on both faces. Later biface sites yield more refined axes and a variety of other tools, weapons, and ornaments using bone, antler, and wood as well as stone.

Only sketchy evidence remains for the stages in increasing control over the environment. Traces of 400,000-year-old covered wood shelters have been found at Nice, France. Scraping tools found at certain sites (200,000-30,000 BC in Europe, N Africa, the Middle East, and Central Asia) suggest the treatment of skins for clothing. Sites from all over the world show seasonal migration patterns and exploitation of a wide range of plant and animal food sources.

Painting and decoration, for which there is evidence at the Nice site, flourished, along with stone and ivory sculpture, from 25,000 years ago: more than 200 caves in Europe, mainly in S France (Lascaux) and N Spain (Altamira), show remarkable examples of wall painting. Other examples have been found in Africa. Proto-religious rites are suggested by these works, by evidence of ritual cannibalism by Peking Man (500,000 BC), and by evidence of ritual burial with medicinal plants and flowers at Shanidar in Iraq.

**The Neolithic Revolution.** Some time after 10,000 BC, among widely separated human communities, a series of dramatic technological and social changes occurred that are summed up as the Neolithic Revolution. The cultivation of previously wild plants encouraged the growth of permanent settlements. Animals were domesticated as a work force and a food source. The manufacture of pottery and cloth began. These techniques permitted a huge increase in world population and in human control over the earth.

No region can claim priority as "inventor" of these techniques. Sites in Cen. and S America, SE Europe, and the Middle East show roughly contemporaneous (10,000-8000 BC) evidence of one or other "neolithic" trait. Dates near 6000-3000 BC have been given for E and S Asian, W European, and sub-Saharan African neolithic remains. The variety of crops—field grains, rice, maize, and roots—and the varying mix of other characteristics suggest that the revolution occurred independently in all these regions.

## History Begins: 4000-1000 BC

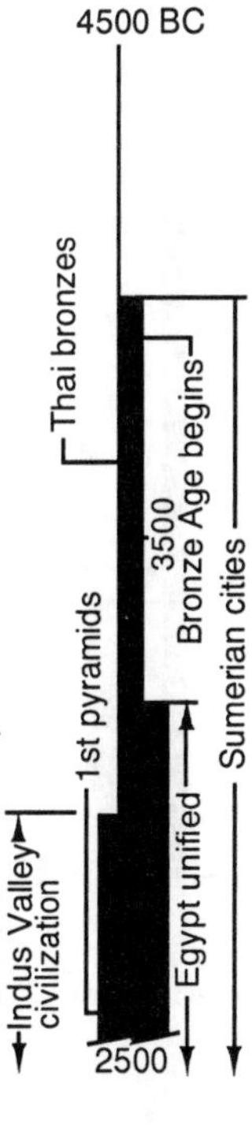


**Near Eastern cradle.** If history began with writing, the first chapter opened in Mesopotamia, the Tigris-Euphrates river valley. The Sumerians used clay tablets with pictographs to keep records after 4000 BC. A **cuneiform** (wedge-shaped) script evolved by 3000 BC as a full syllabic alphabet. Neighboring peoples adapted the script to their own language.

**Sumerian** life centered, from 4000 BC, on large cities (Eridu, Ur, Uruk, Nippur, Kish, and Lagash) organized around temples and priestly bureaucracies, with surrounding plains watered by vast irrigation works and worked with traction plows. Sailboats, wheeled vehicles, potter's wheels, and kilns were used. Copper was smelted and tempered from c 4000 BC; bronze was produced not long after. Ores, as well as precious stones and metals, were obtained through long-distance ship and caravan trade. Iron was used from c 2000 BC. Improved ironworking, developed partly by the Hittites, became widespread by 1200 BC.

Sumerian political primacy passed among cities and their kingly dynasties. Semitic-speaking peoples, with cultures derived from the Sumerian, founded a succession of dynasties that ruled in Mesopotamia and neighboring areas for most of 1800 years; among them were the **Akkadians** (first under Sargon I c 2350 BC), the Amorites (whose laws, codified by **Hammurabi,** c 1792-1750 BC, have biblical parallels), and the Assyrians, with interludes of rule by the Hittites, Kassites, and Mitanni, all possibly Indo-Europeans. The political and cultural center of gravity shifted NW with each successive empire.

Mesopotamian learning, maintained by scribes and preserved by successive rulers in vast libraries, was not abstract or theoretical. Advances in mathematics were related to construction, commerce, and administration. Systematic lists of astronomical phenomena, plants, animals, and stones were kept; medical texts listed ailments and their herbal cures.

The Sumerians worshiped anthropomorphic gods representing natural forces, such as Anu, god of heaven, and Enlil (Ea), god of water. Sacrifices were made at **ziggurats**—huge stepped temples. Gods were thought to control all events, which could be foretold using oracular materials. This religious pattern persisted into the 1st millennium BC.

The Syria-Palestine area, site of some of the earliest urban remains (Jericho, 7000 BC), and of the recently uncovered **Ebla** civilization (fl 2500 BC), experienced Egyptian cultural and political influence along with Mesopotamian. The **Phoenician** coast was an active commercial center. A phonetic alphabet was invented here before 1600 BC. It became the ancestor of all European, Middle Eastern, Indian, SE Asian, Ethiopian, and many other alphabets.

**Egypt.** Agricultural villages along the Nile were united by 3300 BC into 2 kingdoms, Upper and Lower Egypt, which were unified (c 3100 BC) under the pharaoh Menes. A bureaucracy supervised construction of canals and monuments (**pyramids** starting 2700 BC). Control over Nubia to the S was asserted from 2600 BC. Brilliant Old Kingdom Period achievements in architecture, sculpture, and painting, which reached their height during the 3d and 4th Dynasties, set the standards for subsequent Egyptian civilization. **Hieroglyphic writing** appeared by 3200 BC, recording a sophisticated literature that included religious writings, philosophies, history, and science.

An ordered hierarchy of gods, including totemistic animal elements, was served by a powerful priesthood in Memphis. The pharaoh was identified with the falcon god Horus. Other trends included belief in an afterlife and short-lived quasi-monotheistic reforms introduced by the pharaoh **Akhenaton** (c 1379-1362 BC).

After a period of dominance by Semitic Hyksos from Asia (c 1700-1550 BC), the New Kingdom established an empire in Syria. Egypt became increasingly embroiled in Asiatic wars and diplomacy. Conquered by Persia in 525 BC, it eventually faded away as an independent culture.

**India.** An urban civilization with a so-far-undeciphered writing system stretched across the Indus Valley and along the Arabian Sea c 3000-1500 BC. Major sites are Harappa and **Mohenjo-Daro** in Pakistan, well-planned geometric cities with underground sewers and vast granaries. The entire region (600,000 sq mi) may have been ruled as a single state. Bronze was used, and arts and crafts were well developed. Religious life apparently took the form of fertility cults. Indus civilization was probably in decline when it was destroyed by **Aryan invaders** from the NW, speaking an Indo-European language from which most languages of Pakistan, N India, and Bangladesh descend. Led by a warrior aristocracy whose legendary deeds are in the **Rig Veda**, the Aryans spread E and S, bringing their sky gods, elaborate priestly (Brahman) ritual, and the beginnings of the caste system; local customs and beliefs were assimilated by the conquerors.

**Europe.** On Crete, the Bronze Age **Minoan civilization** emerged c 2500 BC. A prosperous economy and richly decorative art was supported by seaborne commerce. Mycenae and other cities in mainland Greece and in Asia Minor (e.g., **Troy**) preserved elements of the culture until c 1200 BC. Cretan Linear A script (c 2000-1700 BC) remains undeciphered; Linear B script (c 1300-1200 BC) records an early Greek dialect. Unclear is the possible connection between Mycenaean monumental stonework and the great megalithic monuments and tombs of W Europe, Iberia, and Malta (c 4000-1500 BC).

**China.** Proto-Chinese neolithic cultures had long covered N and SE China when the first large political state was organized in the north by the **Shang dynasty** (c 1523 BC). Shang kings called themselves Sons of Heaven, and they presided over a cult of human and animal sacrifice to ancestors and nature gods. The Chou dynasty, starting c 1027 BC, expanded the area of the Son of Heaven's dominion, but feudal states exercised most temporal power.

A writing system with 2,000 characters was already in use under the Shang, with **pictographs** later supplemented by phonetic characters. Many of its principles and symbols, despite changes in spoken Chinese, were preserved in later writing systems. Technical advances allowed urban specialists to create fine ceramic and jade products, and bronze casting after 1500 BC was the most advanced in the world. Bronze artifacts have recently been discovered in northern Thailand dating from 3600 BC, hundreds of years before similar Middle Eastern finds.

**Americas. Olmecs** settled (1500 BC) on the Gulf coast of Mexico and soon developed the first civilization in the western hemisphere. Temple cities and huge stone sculpture date from 1200 BC. A rudimentary calendar and writing system existed. Olmec religion, centering on a jaguar god, and Olmec art forms influenced all later Meso-American cultures.

## Classical Era of Old World Civilizations: 1000 BC - 400 BC

**Greece.** After a period of decline during the Dorian Greek invasions (1200-1000 BC), Greece and the Aegean area developed a unique civilization. Drawing upon Mycenaean traditions, Mesopotamian learning (weights and measures, lunisolar calendar, astronomy, musical scales), the Phoenician alphabet (modified for Greek), and Egyptian art, the revived **Greek city-states** saw a rich elaboration of intellectual life. Homer's epics, the *Iliad* and the *Odyssey,* were probably composed around the 8th cent. BC. Long-range commerce was aided by metal coinage (introduced by the Lydians in Asia Minor before 700 BC); colonies were founded around the Mediterranean (Cumae in Italy in 760 BC; Massalia in France c 600 BC) and Black Sea shores.

**Philosophy,** starting with Ionian speculation on the nature of matter (Thales, c 634-546 BC), continued by other "Pre-Socratics" (e.g., Heraditus, c 535-415 BC) reached a high point in Athens in the rationalist idealism of the classic dialogues of **Plato** (c 428-347 BC), a disciple of **Socrates** (c 469-399 BC; sentenced to death for alleged impiety), and in the teachings of **Aristotle** (384-322 BC), who made key contributions in many fields, from natural sciences to logic, ethics, and metaphysics. The **arts** were highly valued by the Greeks. Architecture culminated in the **Parthenon** (438 BC) by Phidias (fl 490-430 BC). Poetry (Sappho, c 610-580 BC; Pindar, c 518-438 BC) and drama (Aeschylus, 525-456 BC; Sophocles, c 496-406 BC; Euripides, c 484-406 BC) thrived. Male beauty and strength, a chief artistic theme, were enhanced at the gymnasium and celebrated at the national games at Olympia. Ruled by local tyrants or oligarchies, the Greeks were not politically united, but managed to resist inclusion in the Persian Empire (the Persian king Darius was defeated at Marathon in 490 BC, his son Xerxes at Salamis in 480 BC, and the Persian army at Plataea in 479 BC). Local warfare was common; the **Peloponnesian Wars** (431-404 BC) ended in Sparta's victory over Athens. Greek political power waned, but Greek cultural forms spread throughout the ancient world from the Atlantic to India.

**Hebrews.** Nomadic Hebrew tribes entered Canaan before 1200 BC, settling among other Semitic peoples speaking the same language. They brought from the desert a **monotheistic** faith said to have been revealed to Abraham in Canaan c 1800 BC and to Moses at Mt. Sinai c 1250 BC, after the Hebrews' escape from bondage in Egypt. David (r 1000-961 BC) and Solomon (r 961-922 BC) united them in a kingdom that briefly dominated the area. Phoenicians to the N established colonies around the E and W Mediterranean (Carthage, c 814 BC) and sailed into the Atlantic.

*(continues on p. 554)*

# Paleontology: The History of Life

All dates are approximate, and are subject to change based on new fossil finds or new dating techniques; but the sequence of events is generally accepted. Dates are in years before the present.

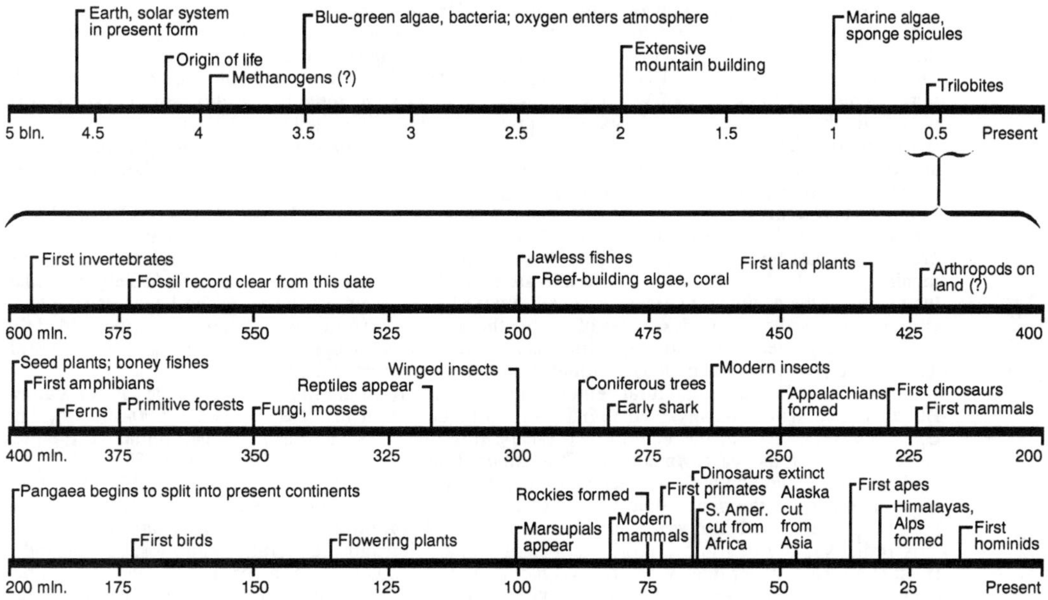


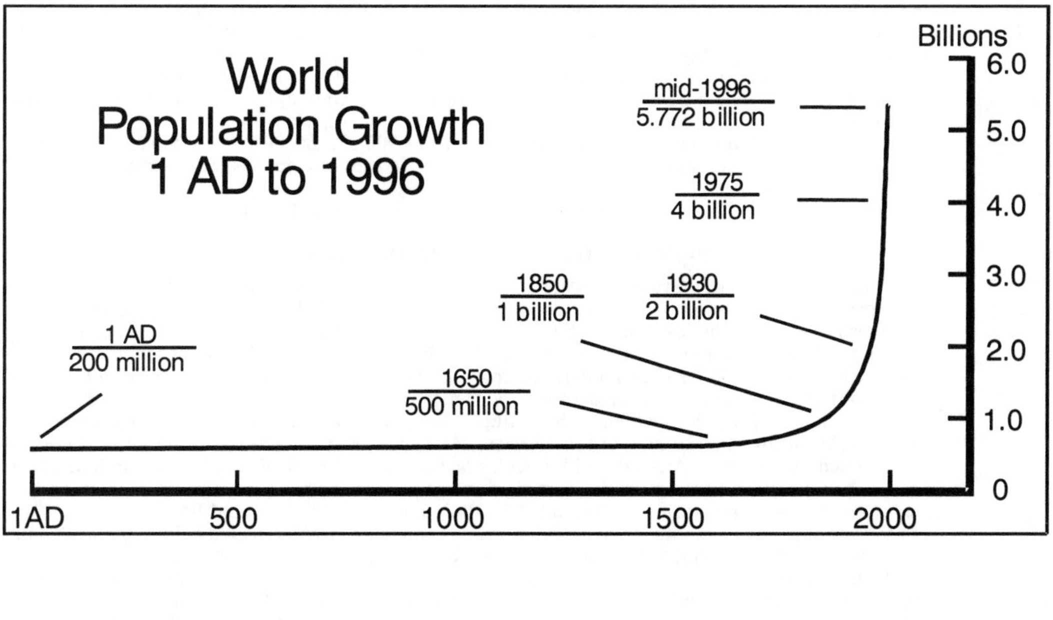

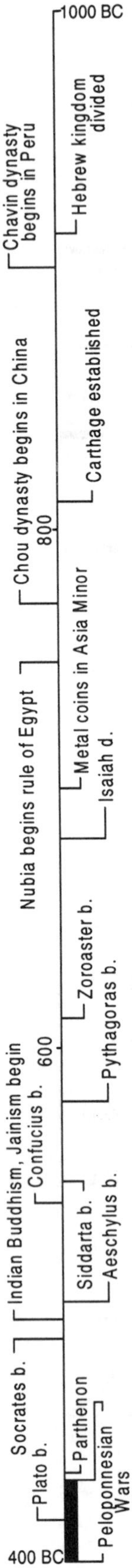


A temple in Jerusalem became the national religious center, with sacrifices performed by a hereditary priesthood. Polytheistic influences, especially of the fertility cult of Baal, were opposed by **prophets** (Elijah, Amos, Isaiah).

Divided into **two kingdoms** after Solomon, the Hebrews were unable to resist the revived Assyrian empire, which conquered Israel, the N kingdom, in 722 BC. Judah, the S kingdom, was conquered in 586 BC by the Babylonians under Nebuchadnezzar II. But with the fixing of most of the biblical canon by the mid-4th cent. BC and the emergence of rabbis, Judaism successfully survived the loss of Hebrew autonomy. A Jewish kingdom was revived under the Hasmoneans (168-42 BC).

**China.** During the **Eastern Chou** dynasty (770-256 BC), Chinese culture spread E to the sea and S to the Yangtze R. Large feudal states on the periphery of the empire contended for preeminence, but continued to recognize the Son of Heaven (king), who retained a purely ritual role enriched with courtly music and dance. In the Age of Warring States (403-221 BC), when the first sections of the **Great Wall** were built, the Ch'in state in the W gained supremacy and finally united all of China.

Iron tools entered China c 500 BC, and casting techniques were advanced, aiding agriculture. Peasants owned their land and owed civil and military service to nobles. Cities grew in number and size, although barter remained the chief trade medium.

Intellectual ferment among noble scribes and officials produced the Classical Age of Chinese literature and philosophy. **Confucius** (551-479 BC) urged a restoration of a supposedly harmonious social order of the past through proper conduct in accordance with one's station and through filial and ceremonial piety. The *Analects* attributed to him are revered throughout E Asia. **Mencius** (d 289 BC) added the view that the Mandate of Heaven can be removed from an unjust dynasty. The Legalists sought to curb the supposed natural wickedness of people through new institutions and harsh laws; they aided the Ch'in rise to power. The Naturalists emphasized the balance of opposites—yin, yang—in the world. **Taoists** sought mystical knowledge through meditation and disengagement.

**India**. The political and cultural center of India shifted from the Indus to the Ganges River Valley. Buddhism, Jainism, and mystical revisions of orthodox Vedism all developed c 500-300 BC. The *Upanishads,* last part of the *Veda*, urged escape from the physical world. Vedism remained the preserve of the Brahman caste. In contrast, **Buddhism**, founded by Siddarta Gautama (c 563-c 483 BC)—Buddha ("Enlightened One")—appealed to merchants in the urban centers and took hold at first (and most lastingly) on the geographic fringes of Indian civilization. The classic Indian epics were composed in this era: the **Ramayana** perhaps c 300 BC, the **Mahabharata** over a period starting 400 BC.

N India was divided into a large number of monarchies and aristocratic republics, probably derived from tribal groupings, when the Magadha kingdom was formed in Bihar c 542 BC. It soon became the dominant power. The **Maurya dynasty**, founded by Chandragupta c 321 BC, expanded the kingdom, uniting most of N India in a centralized bureaucratic empire. The third Mauryan king, **Asoka** (reigned c 274-236 BC), conquered most of the subcontinent. He converted to Buddhism and inscribed its tenets on pillars throughout India. He downplayed the caste system and tried to end expensive sacrificial rites.

Before its final decline in India, Buddhism developed into a popular worship of heavenly Bodhisattvas ("enlightened beings"); and produced a refined architecture (the Great Stupa [shrine] at Sanchi, 100 AD) and sculpture (Gandhara reliefs, AD 1-400).

**Persia.** Aryan peoples (Persians, Medes) dominated the area of present Iran by the beginning of the 1st millennium BC. The prophet **Zoroaster** (born c 628 BC) introduced a dualistic religion in which the forces of good (Ahura Mazda, "Lord of Wisdom") and evil (Ahriam) battle for dominance; individuals are judged by their actions and earn damnation or salvation. Zoroaster's hymns (*Gathas*) are included in the *Avesta*, the Zoroastrian scriptures. A version of this faith became the established religion of the Persian Empire and probably influenced later monotheistic religions.

**Africa**. Nubia, periodically occupied by Egypt since about 2600 BC, ruled Egypt c 750-661 BC and survived as an independent Egyptianized kingdom (**Kush;** capital Meroe) for 1,000 years. The Iron Age Nok culture flourished c 500 BC-200 AD on the Benue Plateau of **Nigeria**.

**Americas**. The Chavin culture controlled N Peru from 900 BC to 200 BC. Its ceremonial centers, featuring the jaguar god, survived long after. Chavin architecture, ceramics, and textiles influenced other Peruvian cultures.

**Mayan civilization** began to develop in Central America as early as 1500 BC.

## Great Empires Unite the Civilized World: 400 BC - AD 400

**Persia and Alexander the Great. Cyrus,** ruler of a small kingdom in Persia from 559 BC, united the Persians and Medes within 10 years and conquered Asia Minor and Babylonia in another 10. His son Cambyses followed by **Darius** (r 522-486 BC) added vast lands to the E and N as far as the Indus Valley and Central Asia, as well as Egypt and Thrace. The whole empire was ruled by an international bureaucracy and army, with Persians holding the chief positions. The resources and styles of all the subject civilizations were exploited to create a rich syncretic art.

The kingdom of Macedon, which under Philip II dominated the Greek world and Egypt, passed to his son **Alexander** in 336 BC. Within 13 years, Alexander had conquered all the Persian dominions. Imbued by his tutor Aristotle with Greek ideals, Alexander encouraged Greek colonization, and Greek-style cities were founded. After his death in 323 BC, wars of succession divided the empire into 3 parts—**Macedon,** Egypt (ruled by the **Ptolemies**), and the **Seleucid** Empire.

In the ensuing 300 years (the **Hellenistic Era**), a cosmopolitan Greek-oriented culture permeated the ancient world from W Europe to the borders of India, absorbing native elites everywhere.

**Hellenistic philosophy** stressed the private individual's search for happiness. The Cynics followed Diogenes (c 372-287 BC), who stressed self-sufficiency and restriction of desires and expressed contempt for luxury and social convention. Zeno (c 335-c 263 BC) and the **Stoics** exalted reason, identified it with virtue, and counseled an ascetic disregard for misfortune. The **Epicureans** tried to build lives of moderate pleasure without political or emotional involvement. Hellenistic arts imitated life realistically, especially in sculpture and literature (comedies of Menander, 342-292 BC).

*(continues on p. 556)*

## The Seven Wonders of the Ancient World

These ancient works of art and architecture were considered awe-inspiring in splendor and/or size by the Greek and Roman world of the Alexandrian epoch. Later classical writers disagreed as to which works made up the list of Wonders, but the following were usually included:

**The Pyramids of Egypt:** The only surviving ancient Wonder, these monumental structures of masonry, located at Giza on the W bank of the Nile R above Cairo, were built from c 2700 to 2500 BC as royal tombs. Three—Khufu (Cheops), Khafra (Chephren), and Menkaura (Mycerimus)—were often grouped as the first Wonder of the World. The largest, the Great Pyramid of Khufu, is a solid mass of limestone blocks covering 13 acres. It is estimated to contain 2.3 million blocks of stone, the stones themselves averaging 2½ tons and some weighing 30 tons. Its construction reputedly took 100,000 laborers 20 years.

**The Hanging Gardens of Babylon:** These gardens were laid out on a brick terrace about 400 ft square and 75 ft above the ground. To irrigate the trees, shrubs, and flowers, screws were turned to lift water from the Euphrates R. The gardens were probably built by King Nebuchadnezzar II about 600 BC. The Walls of Babylon, long, thick, and made of colorfully glazed brick, were considered by some among the Seven Wonders.

**The Statue of Zeus (Jupiter) at Olympia:** This statue of the king of the gods showed him seated on a throne. His flesh was made of ivory, his robe and ornaments of gold. Reputedly 40 ft high, the statue was made by Phidias and was placed in the great temple of Zeus in the sacred grove of Olympia about 457 BC.

**The Colossus of Rhodes:** A bronze statue of the sun god Helios, the Colossus was worked on for 12 years in the third century BC by the sculptor Chares. It was probably 120 ft high. A symbol of the city of Rhodes at its height, the statue stood on a promontory overlooking the harbor.

**The Temple of Artemis (Diana) at Ephesus:** This largest and most complex temple of ancient times was built about 550 BC and was made of marble except for its tile-covered wooden roof. It was begun in honor of a non-Hellenic goddess who later became identified with the Greek goddess of the same name. Ephesus was one of the greatest of the Ionian cities.

**The Mausoleum at Halicarnassus:** The source of our word *mausoleum*, this marble tomb was built in what is now SE Turkey by Artemisia for her husband Mausolus, king of Caria in Asia Minor, who died in 353 BC. About 135 ft high, the tomb was adorned with the works of 4 sculptors.

**The Pharos (Lighthouse) of Alexandria:** This structure was designed about 270 BC, during the reign of Ptolemy II, by the Greek architect Sostratos. Estimates of its height range from 200 to 600 ft.

## The Seven Wonders of the Middle Ages

These sites and structures were considered significant by the people of the Middle Ages (from c 5th cent. to c 15th cent.).

**The Colosseum of Rome:** Erected by the Roman emperor Vespasian, this amphitheater was dedicated by his son and successor, Titus, in AD 80. It could seat about 50,000 persons and was used for Roman spectacles and contests. It is now in ruins.

**The Catacombs of Alexandria, Egypt:** This network of subterranean chambers and galleries was used for burial purposes by peoples of the ancient world and as refuge for early Christians.

**The Great Wall of China:** Begun c 221 BC and completed c 204 BC, this fortification finally reached a length of about 1500 mi. It is built of earth and stone and is faced with brick in the E parts. On average, it is about 20 ft thick at the base and tapers to some 12 ft at the top. The height averages 25 ft, exclusive of the crenellated parapets. Several hundred miles of the Great Wall in the E reaches still are intact.

**Stonehenge:** This prehistoric ritual monument is situated on Salisbury Plain, N of Salisbury, England, and dates from the late Stone and early Bronze ages (c. 3000-1000 BC). The monument itself consists of 4 concentric ranges of stones. Grouped around the main structure are a number of barrows, some of which contain chips of a blue stone similar to that found in the concentric ranges. In 1964, an American astronomer, Gerald S. Hawkins, concluded that Stonehenge functioned as a means of predicting the positions of the sun and moon relative to the earth, and thereby the seasons, and perhaps also as a simple daily calendar.

**The Leaning Tower of Pisa (Italy):** Construction on this bell tower began in 1174 but was suspended when the builders became aware that the shallow foundation would be inadequate in the soft soil. The structure was nevertheless complete by the late 14th cent. The Leaning Tower is cylindrical in shape, with 8 arcaded stories, and today slants more than 14 ft from the perpendicular.

**The Porcelain Tower of Nanking:** This tower in China was built to a height of 260 ft during the 15th cent. and was destroyed in 1853.

**The Mosque of Hagia Sophia:** Built in the 6th cent., this imposing structure was originally a church (Holy Wisdom). It was converted to a mosque in the 15th cent. and is now a museum.

## The Seven Natural Wonders of the World

This list names features of significance noted by world travelers during recent centuries.

**Mt. Everest:** The highest peak in the world, Mt. Everest is in S central Asia, in the Himalaya range, on the frontier of Nepal and Tibet. Controversy surrounds its actual elevation. A 1954 Indian government survey placed it at 29,028 ft above sea level; however, more recent surveys cast some doubt on this figure. The summit was first scaled in 1953.

**Victoria Falls:** This 400-ft waterfall is on the Zambezi R in S central Africa on the border between Zimbabwe and Zambia. The river here is about 1 mi wide. A railroad bridge, completed in 1905, spans the gorge below the falls.

**The Grand Canyon:** This exceptionally deep (more than 1 mi) and extremely beautiful steep-walled chasm in NW Arizona is about 217 mi long and up to 18 mi wide. Excavated by the Colorado R, it is of relatively recent origin; apparently, erosion began a little more than a million years ago. The canyon contains towering buttes, mesas, and valleys within its main gorge.

**The Great Barrier Reef:** This chain of coral reefs is in the Coral Sea, off the E coast of Queensland, Australia. It is the largest known deposit of coral and extends in a NW direction more than 1200 mi. The reef serves as a barrier to disturbances in the Coral Sea, thus affording a sheltered passage for ships.

**The Northern Lights:** Also known as aurora borealis, the Northern Lights consists of rapidly shifting patches and dancing columns of light of various hues. The aurora assumes an endless variety of forms, including the arch, the band, filaments and streamers at right angles to the arch or band, the corona, clouds, the glow, and curtains, fans, flames, or streamers of various shapes.

**Paricutin:** This volcano is one of the world's youngest. It was discovered in 1943 west of Mexico City.

**The Harbor at Rio de Janeiro, Brazil (as seen from the sea):** One of the world's most beautiful natural harbors, the harbor at Rio is surrounded by low mountain ranges whose spurs extend almost to the waterside, and thus divide the city.

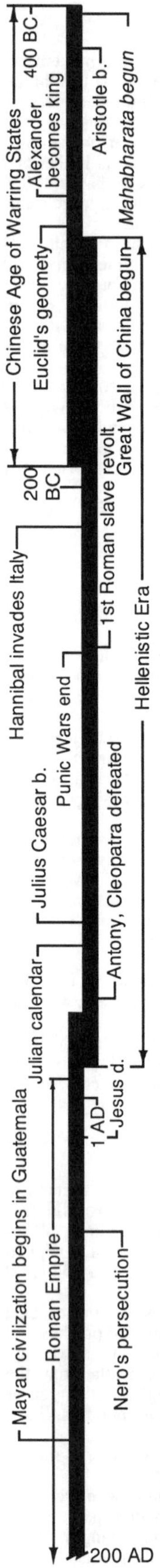


The sciences thrived, especially at Alexandria, where the Ptolemies financed a great library and museum. Fields of study included mathematics (**Euclid's** geometry, c 300 BC); astronomy (heliocentric theory of Aristarchus, 310-230 BC; Julian calendar, 45 BC; Ptolemy's *Almagest*, c 150 AD); geography (world map of Eratosthenes, 276-194 BC); hydraulics (**Archimedes,** 287-212 BC); medicine (Galen, 130-200 AD); and chemistry. Inventors refined uses for siphons, valves, gears, springs, screws, levers, cams, and pulleys.

A restored Persian empire under the **Parthians** (N Iranian tribesmen) controlled the eastern Hellenistic world from 250 BC to 229 AD. The Parthians and the succeeding Sassanian dynasty (c 224-651 AD) fought with Rome periodically. The **Sassanians** revived Zoroastrianism as a state religion and patronized a nationalistic artistic and scholarly renaissance.

**Rome**. The city of Rome was founded, according to legend, by Romulus in 753 BC. Through military expansion and colonization, and by granting citizenship to conquered tribes, the city annexed all of Italy south of the Po in the 100-year period before 268 BC. The Latin and other Italic tribes were annexed first, followed by the **Etruscans** (founders of a great civilization, N of Rome) and the Greek colonies in the S. With a large standing army and reserve forces of several hundred thousand, Rome was able to defeat **Carthage** in the 3 **Punic Wars** (264-241, 218-201, 149-146 BC), despite the invasion of Italy (218 BC) by **Hannibal,** thus gaining Sicily and territory in Spain and North Africa.

New provinces were added in the E, as Rome exploited local disputes to conquer Greece and Asia Minor in the 2d century BC, and Egypt in the 1st (after the defeat and suicide of **Antony and Cleopatra**, 30 BC). All the Mediterranean civilized world up to the disputed Parthian border was now Roman and remained so for 500 years. Less civilized regions were added to the Empire: Gaul (conquered by **Julius Caesar**, 58-51 BC), Britain (43 AD), and Dacia NE of the Danube (107 AD).

The original aristocratic republican government, with democratic features added in the 5th and 4th centuries BC, deteriorated under the pressures of empire and class conflict (**Gracchus** brothers, social reformers, murdered in 133 BC and 121 BC; slave revolts in 135 BC and 73 BC). After a series of civil wars (Marius vs. Sulla 88-82 BC, Caesar vs. Pompey 49-45 BC, triumvirate vs. Caesar's assassins 44-43 BC, Antony vs. Octavian 32-30 BC), the empire came under the rule of a deified monarch (first emperor, **Augustus**, 27 BC-14 AD). Provincials (nearly all granted citizenship by Caracalla, 212 AD) came to dominate the army and civil service. Traditional Roman law, systematized and interpreted by independent jurists, and local self-rule in provincial cities were supplanted by a vast tax-collecting bureaucracy in the 3d and 4th centuries. The legal rights of women, children, and slaves were strengthened.

Roman innovations in **civil engineering** included water mills, windmills, and rotary mills and the use of cement that hardened under water. Monumental architecture (baths, theaters, temples) relied on the arch and the dome. The network of roads (some still standing) stretched 53,000 mi, passing through mountain tunnels as long as 3.5 mi. Aqueducts brought water to cities; underground sewers removed waste.

Roman art and literature were to a large extent derivative of Greek models. Innovations were made in sculpture (naturalistic busts and equestrian statues), decorative wall painting (as at Pompeii), satire (Juvenal, 60-127 AD), history (Tacitus, 56-120 AD), prose romance (Petronius, d 66 AD). Gladiatorial contests dominated mass public amusements, which were supported by the state.

**India**. The **Gupta** monarchs reunited N India c 320 AD. Their peaceful and prosperous reign saw a revival of Hindu religious thought and Brahman power. The old Vedic traditions were combined with devotion to a plethora of indigenous deities (who were seen as manifestations of Vedic gods). **Caste lines** were reinforced, and Buddhism gradually disappeared. The art (often erotic), architecture, and literature of the period, patronized by the Gupta court, are considered among India's finest achievements (Kalidasa, poet and dramatist, fl. c 400 AD). Mathematical innovations included the use of the zero and decimal numbers. Invasions by White Huns from the NW destroyed the empire c 550.

Rich cultures also developed in S India in this era. Emotional Tamil religious poetry aided the Hindu revival. The Pallava kingdom controlled much of S India c 350-880 and helped spread Indian civilization to SE Asia.

**China**. The Ch'in ruler Shih Huang Ti (r 221-210 BC), known as the First Emperor, centralized political authority in China, standardized the written language, laws, weights, measures, and coinage, and conducted a census, but tried to destroy most philosophical texts. The **Han dynasty** (202 BC-220 AD) instituted the Mandarin bureaucracy, which lasted for 2,000 years. Local officials were selected by examination in the Confucian classics and trained at the imperial university and at provincial schools. The invention of **paper** facilitated this bureaucratic system. Agriculture was promoted, but the peasants bore most of the tax burden. Irrigation was improved, water clocks and sundials were used, astronomy and mathematics thrived, and landscape painting was perfected.

With the expansion S and W (to nearly the present borders of today's China), trade was opened with India, SE Asia, and the Middle East, over sea and caravan routes. Indian missionaries brought Mahayana Buddhism to China by the 1st century AD and spawned a variety of sects. Taoism was revived and merged with popular superstitions. Taoist and Buddhist monasteries and convents multiplied in the turbulent centuries after the collapse of the Han dynasty.

## Monotheism Emerges: AD 1-750

**Christianity**. In the Roman Empire polytheism was practiced, and religions indigenous to particular Middle Eastern nations became international in the first 3 centuries of the Roman Empire. Roman citizens worshiped **Isis** of Egypt, **Mithras** of Persia, **Demeter** of Greece, and the great mother **Cybele** of Phrygia. Their cults centered on mysteries (secret ceremonies) and the promise of an afterlife, symbolized by the death and rebirth of the god. The Jews living in the empire preserved their monotheistic religion—Judaism, the world's oldest (c 1200 BC) continuous religion. Its teachings are contained in the Bible (the Old Testament). First-century Judaism embraced several sects, including the **Sadducees**, mostly drawn from the Temple priesthood, who were culturally Hellenized; the **Pharisees**, who upheld the full range of traditional customs and practices as of equal weight to literal scriptural law and elaborated synagogue worship; and the **Essenes**, an ascetic, millennarian sect. Messianic fervor led to repeated, unsuccessful rebellions against Rome (66-70, 135). As a result, the Temple in Jerusalem was destroyed and the population decimated; this event marked the beginning of the Diaspora (living in exile).

To avoid the dissolution of the faith, a program of codification of law was begun at the academy of Yavneh. The work continued for some 500 years in Palestine and in Babylonia, ending in the final redaction (c 600) of the **Talmud**, a huge collection of legal and moral debates, rulings, liturgy, biblical exegesis, and legendary materials.

Christianity, which emerged as a distinct sect in the second half of the 1st cent. AD, is based on the teachings of **Jesus**, whom believers considered the Savior (Messiah or Christ) and the son of God. The missionary activities of the Apostles and such early leaders as **Paul of Tarsus** spread the faith. Intermittent persecution, as in Rome under Nero in 64 AD, on grounds of suspected disloyalty, failed to disrupt the Christian communities. Each congregation, generally urban and of plebeian character, was tightly organized under a leader (bishop), elders (presbyters or priests), and assistants (deacons). The four Gospels (accounts of the life and teachings of Jesus) and the Acts of the Apostles were written down in the late 1st and early 2d centuries and circulated along with letters of Paul and other Christian leaders. An authoritative canon of these writings was not fixed until the 4th century.

A school for priests was established at Alexandria in the 2d century. Its teachers (**Origen** c 182-251) helped define Christian doctrine and promote the faith in Greek-style philosophical works. Pagan Neoplatonism was given Christian coloration in the works of Church Fathers such as **Augustine** (354-430). Christian hermits, often drawn from the lower classes, began to associate in monasteries, first in Egypt (St. Pachomius c 290-345), then in other E lands, then in the W (**St. Benedict's rule**, 529). Popular devotion to saints, especially Mary, mother of Jesus, spread.

Under **Constantine** (r 306-37), Christianity became in effect the established religion of the Empire. Pagan temples were expropriated, state funds were used to build huge churches and support the hierarchy, and laws were adjusted in accordance with Christian ideas. Pagan worship was banned by the end of the 4th century, and severe restrictions were placed on Judaism.

The newly established church was rocked by doctrinal disputes, often exacerbated by regional rivalries both within and outside the Empire. Chief heresies (as defined by church councils backed by imperial authority) were **Arianism**, which denied the divinity of Jesus; the **Monophysite** position denying the dual nature of Christ; **Donatism**, which denied the validity of sacraments performed by sinful clergy; and **Pelagianism,** which denied the necessity of unmerited grace for salvation.

**Islam**. The earliest Arab civilization emerged by the end of the 2d millennium BC in the watered highlands of Yemen. Seaborne and caravan trade in frankincense and myrrh connected the area with the Nile and the Fertile Crescent. The Minaean, Sabean (Sheba), and Himyarite states successively held sway. By Muhammad's time (7th cent. AD), the region was a province of Sassanian Persia. In the N, the **Nabataean kingdom** at Petra and the kingdom of Palmyra were first Aramaicized, then Romanized, and finally absorbed, as neighboring Judea had been, into the Roman Empire. Nomads shared the central region with a few trading towns and oases. Wars between tribes and raids on settled communities were common and were celebrated in a poetic tradition that by the 6th century helped establish a classic literary Arabic.

In 611 **Muhammad**, a 40-year-old Arab of Mecca, announced a revelation from the one true God, calling on him to repudiate pagan idolatry. Drawing on elements of Judaism and Christianity, and eventually incorporating some Arab pagan traditions (such as reverence for the black stone at the Kaaba shrine in Mecca), Muhammad's teachings, recorded in the **Koran**, forged a new religion, Islam (submission to Allah). Opposed by the leaders of Mecca, Muhammad made a *hejira* (migration) to Medina to the N in 622, the beginning of the Muslim lunar calendar. He and his followers defeated the Meccans in 624 in the first *jihad* (holy war), and by his death (632) nearly all the Arabian peninsula accepted his religious and secular leadership.

Under the first two **caliphs** (successors), Abu Bakr (632-34) and Omar (634-44), Muslim rule over Arabia was confirmed. Raiding parties into Byzantine and Persian border areas developed into campaigns of conquest against the 2 empires, which had been weakened by wars and by disaffection among subject peoples (including Coptic and Syriac Christians opposed to the Byzantine Orthodox church). Syria, Palestine, Egypt, Iraq, and Persia all fell to the Arab armies. The Arabs at first remained a distinct minority, using non-Muslims in the new administrative system and tolerating Christians, Jews, and Zoroastrians as self-governing "Peoples of the Book," whose taxes supported the empire.

Disputes over the succession, and puritan reaction to the wealth and refinement that empire brought to the ruling strata, led to the growth of schismatic movements. The followers of Muhammad's son-in-law Ali (assassinated 661) and his descendants became the founders of the more mystical **Shi'ite** sect, still the largest non-orthodox Muslim sect. The Karijites, puritanical, militant, and egalitarian, persist as a minor sect to the present.

Under the **Omayyad** caliphs (661-750), the boundaries of Islam were extended across N Africa and into Spain (711). Arab armies in the W were stopped at Tours (France) in 732 by the Frankish King **Charles Martel**. Asia Minor, the Indus Valley, and Transoxiana were conquered in the E. The vast majority of the subject population gradually converted to Islam, encouraged by tax and career privileges. The Arab language supplanted the local tongues in the central and W areas, but Arab soldiers and rulers in the E eventually became assimilated to the indigenous languages.

## New Peoples Enter World History: 400-900

**Barbarian invasions**. Germanic tribes infiltrated S and E from their Baltic homeland during the 1st millennium BC, reaching S Germany by 100 BC and the Black Sea by 214 AD. Organized into large federated tribes under elected kings, most resisted Roman domination and raided the empire in time of civil war (Goths took Dacia in 214 and raided Thrace in 251-69). Germanic troops and commanders came to dominate the Roman armies by the end of the 4th century. **Huns**, invaders from Asia, entered Europe in 372, driving more Germans into the W empire. Emperor Valens allowed Visigoths to cross the Danube in 376. Huns under Attila (d 453) raided Gaul, Italy, and the Balkans. The W empire, weakened by overtaxation and social stagnation, was overrun in the 5th cent. Gaul was effectively lost in 406-7, Spain in 409, Britain in 410, and Africa in 429-39. Rome was sacked in 410 by Visigoths under Alaric and in

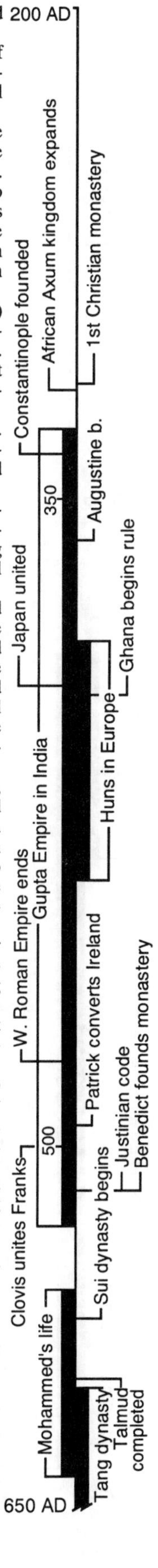

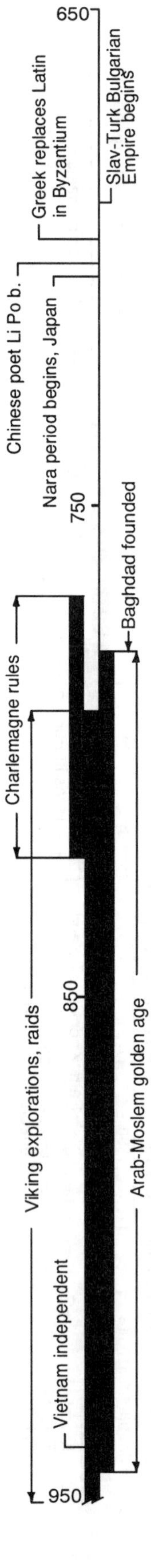


455 by Vandals. The last western emperor, Romulus Augustulus, was deposed in 476 by the Germanic chief Odovacar.

**Celts**. Celtic cultures, which in pre-Roman times covered most of W Europe, were confined almost entirely to the British Isles after the Germanic invasions. **St. Patrick** completed (c 457-92) the conversion of Ireland. A strong monastic tradition took hold. Irish monastic missionaries in Scotland, England, and the continent (Columba c 521-97; Columban c 543-615) helped restore Christianity after the Germanic invasions. The monasteries became renowned centers of classic and Christian learning and presided over the recording of a Christianized Celtic mythology, elaborated by secular writers and bards. An intricate decorative art style developed, especially in book illumination (Lindisfarne Gospels, c 700; Book of Kells, 8th cent.).

**Successor states**. The Visigothic kingdom in Spain (from 419) and much of France (to 507) saw a continuation of much Roman administration, language, and law (Breviary of Alaric, 506) until its destruction by the Muslims in 711. The Vandal kingdom in Africa, from 429, was conquered by the Byzantines in 533. Italy was ruled in succession by an Ostrogothic kingdom under Byzantine suzerainty (489-554), direct Byzantine government, and the German Lombards (568-774). The latter divided the peninsula with the Byzantines and the papacy under the dynamic reformer **Pope Gregory the Great** (590-604) and his successors.

King Clovis (r 481-511) united the Franks on both sides of the Rhine and, after his conversion to Christianity, defeated the Arian heretics, the Burgundians (after 500), and the Visigoths (507) with the support of the native clergy and the papacy. Under the **Merovingian** kings, a feudal system emerged: Power was fragmented among hierarchies of military landowners. Social stratification, which in late Roman times had acquired legal, hereditary sanction, was reinforced. The Carolingians (747-987) expanded the kingdom and restored central power. **Charlemagne** (r 768-814) conquered nearly all the Germanic lands, including Lombard Italy, and was crowned Emperor by Pope Leo III in Rome in 800. A centuries-long decline in commerce and the arts was reversed under Charlemagne's patronage. He welcomed Jews to his kingdom, which became a center of Jewish learning (Rashi, 1040-1105). He sponsored the Carolingian Renaissance of learning under the Anglo-Latin scholar Alcuin (c 732-804), who reformed church liturgy.

**Byzantine Empire**. Under **Diocletian** (r 284-305) the empire had been divided into 2 parts to facilitate administration and defense. **Constantine** founded (330) **Constantinople** (at old Byzantium) as a fully Christian city. Commerce and taxation financed a sumptuous, orientalized court, a class of hereditary bureaucratic families, and magnificent urban construction (Hagia Sophia, 532-37). The city's fortifications and naval innovations (Greek fire) repelled assaults by Goths, Huns, Slavs, Bulgars, Avars, Arabs, and Scandinavians. Greek replaced Latin as the official language by c 700. Byzantine art, a solemn, sacral, and stylized variation of late classical styles (mosaics at the Church of San Vitale, Ravenna, Italy 526-48), was a starting point for medieval art in E and W Europe.

**Justinian** (r 527-65) reconquered parts of Spain, N Africa, and Italy, codified Roman law (Codex Justinianus [529] was medieval Europe's chief legal text), closed the Platonic Academy at Athens, and ordered all pagans to convert. Lombards in Italy and Arabs in Africa retook most of his conquests. The Isaurian dynasty from Anatolia (from 717) and the Macedonian dynasty (867-1054) restored military and commercial power. The Iconoclast controversy (726-843) over the permissibility of images helped alienate the Eastern Church from the papacy.

**Arab Empire. Baghdad** (est 762) became the seat of the **Abbasid** Caliphate (est 750), while Ummayads continued to rule in Spain. A brilliant cosmopolitan civilization emerged, inaugurating an Arab-Muslim golden age. Arab lyric poetry revived; Greek, Syriac, Persian, and Sanskrit books were translated into Arabic, often by Syriac Christians and Jews, whose theology and Talmudic law, respectively, influenced Islam. The arts and music flourished at the court of **Harun al-Rashid** (786-809), celebrated in *The Arabian Nights*. The sciences, medicine, and mathematics were pursued at Baghdad, Cordova, and Cairo (est 969). Science and Aristotelian philosophy culminated in the systems of Avicenna (980-1037), Averroes (1126-98), and Maimonides (1135-1204), a Jew; all influenced later Christian scholarship and theology. The Islamic ban on images encouraged a sinuous, geometric decorative tradition, applied to architecture and illumination. A gradual loss of Arab control in Persia (from 874) led to the capture (945) of Baghdad by Persians. By the next century, Spain and N Africa were ruled by Berbers, while Turks prevailed in Asia Minor and the Levant. The loss of political power by the caliphs allowed for the growth of nonorthodox trends, especially the mystical **Sufi** tradition (theologian Ghazali, 1058-1111).

**Africa**. Immigrants from Saba in S Arabia helped set up the **Axum** kingdom in Ethiopia in the 1st century (their language, Ge'ez, is preserved by the Ethiopian Church). In the 3d century, when the kingdom became Christianized, it defeated Kushite Meroe and expanded its influence into Yemen. Axum was the center of a vast ivory trade and controlled the Red Sea coast until c 1100. Arab conquest in Egypt cut Axum's political and economic ties with Byzantium.

The Iron Age entered W Africa by the end of the 1st millennium BC. **Ghana**, the first known sub-Saharan state, ruled in the upper Senegal-Niger region c 400-1240, controlling the trade of gold from mines in the S to trans-Sahara caravan routes to the N. The **Bantu** peoples, probably of W African origin, began to spread E and S perhaps 2,000 years ago, displacing the Pygmies and Bushmen of central and S Africa during a 1,500-year period.

**Japan**. The advanced Neolithic Yayoi period, when irrigation, rice farming, and iron and bronze casting techniques were introduced from China or Korea, persisted to c 400 AD. The myriad Japanese states were then united by the **Yamato** clan, under an emperor who acted as the chief priest of the animistic Shinto cult. Japanese political and military intervention by the 6th century in Korea, which was then under strong Chinese influence, quickened a Chinese cultural invasion of Japan, bringing Buddhism, the Chinese language (which long remained a literary and governmental medium), Chinese ideographs, and Buddhist styles in painting, sculpture, literature, and architecture (7th century, Horyu-ji temple at Nara). The Taika Reforms (646) tried to centralize Japan according to Chinese bureaucratic and Buddhist philosophical values, but failed to curb traditional Japanese decentralization. A nativist reaction against the Buddhist **Nara period** (710-94) ushered in the **Heian period** (794-1185) centered at the new capital, Kyoto. Japanese elegance and simplicity modified Chinese styles in architecture, scroll painting, and literature; the writing system was also simplified. The courtly novel *Tale of Genji* (1010-20) testifies to the enhanced role of women.

**Southeast Asia**. The historic peoples of Southeast Asia began arriving some 2,500 years ago from China and Tibet, displacing scattered aborigines. Their agriculture relied on rice and tubers (yams), which they may have introduced to Africa. Indian cultural influences were strongest; literacy and Hindu and Buddhist ideas followed the southern India-China trade route. From the southern tip of Indochina, the kingdom of **Funan** (1st-7th century) traded as far W as Persia. It was absorbed by Chenla, itself conquered by the **Khmer Empire** (600-1300). The Khmers, under Hindu god-kings (Suryavarman II, 1113-c 1150) built the monumental Angkor Wat temple center for the royal phallic cult. The **Nam-Viet** kingdom in Annam, dominated by China and Chinese culture for 1,000 years, emerged in the 10th century, growing at the expense of the Khmers, who also lost ground in the NW to the new, highly organized **Thai** kingdom. On Sumatra, the **Srivijaya** Empire at Palembang controlled vital sea lanes (7th to 10th century). A Buddhist dynasty, the Sailendras, ruled central **Java** (8th-9th century), building at Borobudur one of the largest stupas in the world.

**China**. The short-lived Sui dynasty (581-618) ushered in a period of commercial, artistic, and scientific achievement in China, continuing under the **Tang** dynasty (618-906). Such inventions as the magnetic compass, gunpowder, the abacus, and printing were introduced or perfected. Medical innovations included cataract surgery. The state, from the cosmopolitan capital, Chang-an, supervised foreign trade, which exchanged Chinese silks, porcelains, and artworks for spices, ivory, etc. over Central Asian caravan routes and sea routes reaching Africa. A golden age of poetry bequeathed tens of thousands of works to later generations (Tu Fu, 712-70; Li Po, 701-62). Landscape painting flourished. Commercial and industrial expansion continued under the **Northern Sung** dynasty (960-1126), facilitated by paper money and credit notes. But commerce never achieved respectability; government monopolies expropriated successful merchants. The population, long stable at 50 million, doubled in 200 years with the introduction of early-ripening rice and the double harvest. In art, native Chinese styles were revived.

**Americas**. From 300 to 600 a Native American empire stretched from the Valley of Mexico to Guatemala, centering on the huge city **Teotihuacán** (founded 100 BC). To the S, in Guatemala, a high **Mayan** civilization developed (150-900) around hundreds of rural ceremonial centers. The Mayans improved on Olmec writing and the calendar and pursued astronomy and mathematics (using the idea of zero). In South America, a widespread pre-Inca culture grew from **Tiahuanacu,** Bolivia, near Lake Titicaca (Gateway of the Sun, c 700).

## Christian Europe Regroups and Expands: 900-1300

**Scandinavians**. Pagan Danish and Norse (Viking) adventurers, traders, and pirates raided the coasts of the British Isles (Dublin, founded c 831), France, and even the Mediterranean for more than 200 years beginning in the late 8th century. Inland settlement in the W was limited to Great Britain (King Canute, 994-1035) and Normandy, settled (911) under Rollo, as a fief of France. Other Vikings reached Iceland (874), Greenland (c 986), and North America (**Leif Eriksson,** c 1000). Norse traders (**Varangians**) developed Russian river commerce from the 8th to the 11th century and helped set up a state at Kiev in the late 9th century. Conversion to Christianity occurred during the 10th century, reaching Sweden 100 years later. Eleventh-century Norman bands conquered S Italy and Sicily. Duke **William of Normandy** conquered (1066) England, bringing continental feudalism and the French language, essential elements in later English civilization.

**Central and East Europe**. Slavs began to expand from about 150 AD in all directions in Europe, and by the 7th cent. they reached as far S as the Adriatic and Aegean seas. In the Balkan Peninsula they dislocated Romanized local populations or assimilated newcomers (Bulgarians, a Turkic people). The first Slavic states were Moravia (628) in Central Europe and the Bulgarian state (680) in the Balkans. Missions of St. Methodius and Cyril (whose Greek-based cyrillic alphabet is still used by some S and E Slavs) converted (863) Moravia. The Eastern Slavs, part-civilized under the overlordship of the Turkish-Jewish **Khazar** trading empire (7th-10th century), gravitated toward Constantinople by the 9th century. The **Kievan state** adopted (989) Eastern Christianity under Prince Vladimir. King Boleslav I (992-1025) began **Poland's** long history of eastern conquest. The Magyars (**Hungarians**), in present-day Hungary since 896, accepted (1001) Latin Christianity.

**Germany**. The German kingdom that emerged after the breakup of Charlemagne's W Empire remained a confederation of largely autonomous states. Otto I, a Saxon who was king from 936, established the **Holy Roman Empire**—a union of Germany and N Italy—in alliance with Pope John XII, who crowned (962) him emperor; he defeated (955) the Magyars. Imperial power was greatest under the **Hohenstaufens** (1138-1254), despite the growing opposition of the papacy, which ruled central Italy, and the Lombard League cities. Frederick II (1194-1250) improved administration and patronized the arts; after his death, German influence was removed from Italy.

**Christian Spain**. From its N mountain redoubts, Christian rule slowly migrated S through the 11th century, when Muslim unity collapsed. After the capture (1085) of **Toledo**, the kingdoms of Portugal, Castile, and Aragon undertook repeated crusades of reconquest, finally completed in 1492. Elements of Islamic civilization persisted in recaptured areas, influencing all Western Europe.

**Crusades**. Pope Urban II called (1095) for a crusade to restore Asia Minor to Byzantium and to regain the Holy Land from the Turks. Some 10 crusades (to 1291) succeeded only in founding 4 temporary Frankish states in the Levant. The 4th crusade sacked (1204) Constantinople. In Rhineland (1096), England (1290), and France (1306), Jews were massacred or expelled, and wars were launched against Christian heretics (**Albigensian** crusade in France, 1229). Trade in eastern luxuries expanded, led by the Venetian naval empire.

**Economy**. The agricultural base of European life benefited from improvements in **plow design** (c 1000) and by draining of lowlands and clearing of forests, leading to a rural population increase. Towns grew in N Italy, Flanders, and N Germany (Hanseatic League). Improvements in **loom design** permitted factory textile production. **Guilds** dominated urban trades from the 12th century. Banking (centered in Italy, 12th-15th century) facilitated long-distance trade.

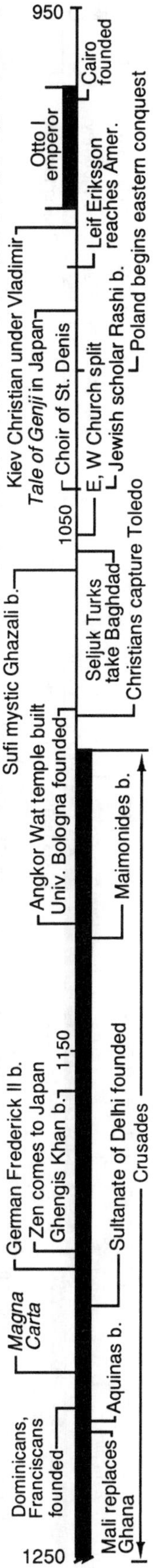

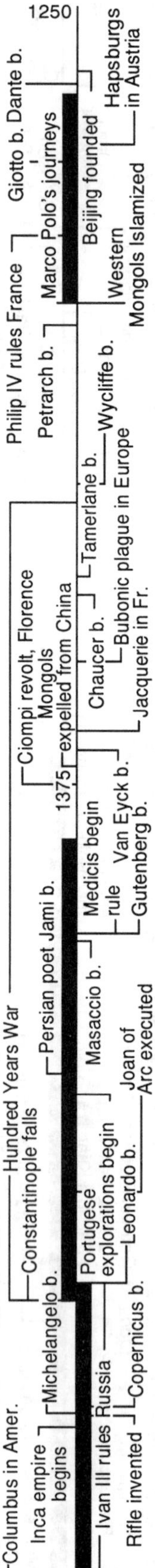


**The Church**. The split between the Eastern and Western churches was formalized in 1054. Western and Central Europe was divided into 500 bishoprics under one united hierarchy, but conflicts between secular and church authorities were frequent (German **Investiture Controversy**, 1075-1122). Clerical power was first strengthened through the international monastic reform begun at Cluny in 910. Popular religious enthusiasm often expressed itself in heretical movements (Waldensians from 1173), but was channelled by the **Dominican** (1215) and **Franciscan** (1223) friars into the religious mainstream.

**Arts**. **Romanesque** architecture (11th-12th century) expanded on late Roman models, using the rounded arch and massed stone to support enlarged basilicas. Painting and sculpture followed Byzantine models. The literature of **chivalry** was exemplified by the epic (*Chanson de Roland*, c 1100) and by courtly love poems of the troubadours of Provence and minnesingers of Germany. **Gothic** architecture emerged in France (choir of St. Denis, c 1040) and spread as French cultural influence predominated in Europe. Rib vaulting and pointed arches were used to combine soaring heights with delicacy, and they freed walls for display of stained glass. Exteriors were covered with painted relief sculpture and elaborate architectural detail.

**Learning**. Law, medicine, and philosophy were advanced at independent **universities** (Bologna, late 11th century), originally corporations of students and masters. Twelfth-century translations of Greek classics, especially Aristotle, encouraged an analytic approach. Scholastic philosophy, from Anselm (1033-1109) to **Aquinas** (1225-74), attempted to understand revelation through reason.

## Apogee of Central Asian Power; Islam Grows: 1250-1500

**Turks**. Turkic peoples, of Central Asian ancestry, were a military threat to the Byzantine and Persian Empires from the 6th century. After several waves of invasions, during which most of the Turks adopted Islam, the **Seljuk Turks** took (1055) Baghdad. They ruled Persia, Iraq and, after 1071, Asia Minor, where massive numbers of Turks settled. The empire was divided in the 12th century into smaller states ruled by Seljuks, Kurds (**Saladin,** c 1137-93), and Mamluks (a military caste of former Turk, Kurd, and Circassian slaves), which governed Egypt and the Middle East until the Ottoman era (c 1290-1922).

Osman I (r c 1290-1326) and succeeding sultans united Anatolian Turkish warriors in a militaristic state that waged holy war against Byzantium and Balkan Christians. Most of the Balkans had been subdued, and Anatolia united, when Constantinople fell (1453). By the mid-16th century, Hungary, the Middle East, and North Africa had been conquered. The Turkish advance was stopped at Vienna (1529) and at the naval battle of Lepanto (1571) by Spain, Venice, and the papacy.

**The Ottoman state** was governed in accordance with orthodox Muslim law. Greek, Armenian, and Jewish communities were segregated and were ruled by religious leaders responsible for taxation; they dominated trade. State offices and most army ranks were filled by slaves through a system of child conscription among Christians.

**India**. Mahmud of Ghazni (971-1030) led repeated Turkish raids into N India. Turkish power was consolidated in 1206 with the start of the **Sultanate at Delhi**. Centralization of state power under the early Delhi sultans went far beyond traditional Indian practice. Muslim rule of most of the subcontinent lasted until the British conquest some 600 years later.

**Mongols**. **Genghis Khan** (c 1167-1227) first united the feuding Mongol tribes, and built their armies into an effective offensive force around a core of highly mobile cavalry. He and his immediate successors created the largest land empire in history; by 1279 it stretched from the E coast of Asia to the Danube, from the Siberian steppes to the Arabian Sea. East-West trade and contacts were facilitated (Marco Polo, c 1254-1324). The W Mongols were Islamized by 1295; successor states soon lost their Mongol character by assimilation. They were briefly reunited under the Turk Tamerlane (1336-1405).

**Kublai Khan** ruled China from his new capital Beijing (est c 1264). Naval campaigns against Japan (1274, 1281) and Java (1293) were defeated, the latter by the Hindu-Buddhist maritime kingdom of Majapahit. The **Yuan** dynasty used Mongols and other foreigners (including Europeans) in official posts and tolerated the return of Nestorian Christianity (suppressed 841-45) and the spread of Islam in the S and W. A native reaction expelled the Mongols in 1367-68.

**Russia**. The Kievan state in Russia, weakened by the decline of Byzantium and the rise of the Catholic Polish-Lithuanian state, was overrun (1238-40) by the Mongols. Only the N trading republic of Novgorod remained independent. The grand dukes of Moscow emerged as leaders of a coalition of princes that eventually (by 1481) defeated the Mongols. With the fall of Constantinople, the **Tsars** (Caesars) at Moscow (from Ivan III, r 1462-1505) set up an independent Russian Orthodox Church. Commerce failed to revive. The isolated Russian state remained agrarian, with the peasant class falling into serfdom.

**Persia**. A revival of Persian literature, using the Arab alphabet and literary forms, began in the 10th cent. (epic of Firdausi, 935-1020). An art revival, influenced by Chinese styles introduced after the Mongols came to power in Iran, began in the 13th. Persian cultural and political forms, and often the Persian language, were used for centuries by Turkish and Mongol elites from the Balkans to India. Persian mystics from Rumi (1207-73) to Jami (1414-92) promoted **Sufism** in their poetry.

**Africa**. Two militant Islamic Berber dynasties emerged from the Sahara to carve out empires from the Sahel to central Spain—the **Almoravids** (c 1050-1140) and the fanatical **Almohads** (c 1125-1269). The Ghanaian empire was replaced in the upper Niger by Mali (c 1230-c 1340), whose Muslim rulers imported Egyptians to help make **Timbuktu** a center of commerce (in gold, leather, and slaves) and learning. The Songhay empire (to 1590) replaced Mali. To the S, forest kingdoms produced refined artworks (Ife terra cotta, **Benin** bronzes). Other Muslim states in Nigeria (Hausas) and Chad originated in the 11th cent. and continued in some form until the 19th-cent. European conquest. Less-developed Bantu kingdoms existed across central Africa.

Some 40 Muslim Arab-Persian trading colonies and city-states were established all along the E African coast from the 10th cent. (Kilwa, Mogadishu). The interchange with Bantu peoples produced the **Swahili** language and culture. Gold, palm oil, and slaves were brought from the interior, stimulating the growth of the Monamatapa kingdom of the Zambezi (15th cent.). The Christian Ethiopian empire (from 13th cent.) continued the traditions of Axum.

**Southeast Asia**. Islam was introduced into Malaya and the Indonesian islands by Arab, Persian, and Indian traders. Coastal Muslim cities and states (starting before 1300), enriched by trade, soon dominated the interior. Chief among these was the **Malacca** state (c 1400-1511), on the Malay peninsula.

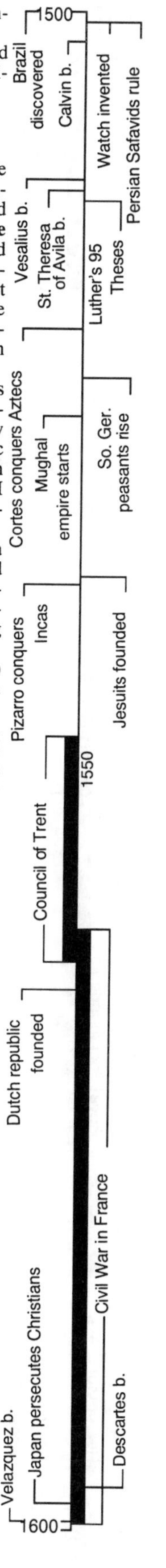


## Arts and Statecraft Thrive in Europe: 1350-1600

**Italian Renaissance & Humanism.** Distinctive Italian achievements in the arts in the late Middle Ages (**Dante,** 1265-1321; Giotto, 1276-1337) led to the vigorous new styles of the Renaissance (14th-16th century). Patronized by the rulers of the quarreling petty states of Italy (Medicis in Florence and the papacy, c 1400-1737), the plastic arts perfected realistic techniques, including **perspective** (Masaccio, 1401-28, Leonardo, 1452-1519). Classical motifs were used in architecture, and increased talent and expense were put into secular buildings. The Florentine dialect was refined as a national literary language (Petrarch, 1304-74). Greek refugees from the E strengthened the respect of humanist scholars for the classic sources (Bruni, 1370-1444). Soon an international movement aided by the spread of **printing** (Gutenberg, c 1400-68), **humanism** was optimistic about the power of human reason (Erasmus of Rotterdam, 1466-1536, Thomas More's *Utopia*, 1516) and valued individual effort in the arts and in politics (Machiavelli, 1469-1527).

**France**. The French monarchy, strengthened in its repeated struggles with powerful nobles (Burgundy, Flanders, Aquitaine) by alliances with the growing commercial towns, consolidated bureaucratic control under Philip IV (r 1285-1314) and extended French influence into Germany and Italy (popes at Avignon, France, 1309-1417). The **Hundred Years War** (1337-1453) ended English dynastic claims in France (battles of Crécy, 1346, and Poitiers, 1356; Joan of Arc executed, 1431). A French Renaissance, dating from royal invasions (1494, 1499) of Italy, was encouraged at the court of Francis I (r 1515-47), who centralized taxation and law. French vernacular literature consciously asserted its independence (La Pléiade, 1549).

**England**. The evolution of England's unique political institutions began with the **Magna Carta** (1215), by which King John guaranteed the privileges of nobles and church against the monarchy and assured jury trial. After the Wars of the Roses (1455-85), the **Tudor dynasty** reasserted royal prerogatives (Henry VIII, r 1509-47), but the trend toward independent departments and ministerial government also continued. English trade (wool exports from c 1340) was protected by the nation's growing maritime power (**Spanish Armada** destroyed, 1588).

English replaced French and Latin in the late 14th cent. in law and literature (Chaucer, c 1340-1400) and English translation of the Bible began (Wycliffe, 1380s). Elizabeth I (r 1558-1603) presided over a confident flowering of poetry (Spenser, 1552-99), drama (**Shakespeare**, 1564-1616), and music.

**German Empire**. From among a welter of minor feudal states, church lands, and independent cities, the **Hapsburgs** assembled a far-flung territorial domain, based in Austria from 1276. The family held the title Holy Roman Emperor from 1438 to the Empire's dissolution in 1806, but failed to centralize its domains, leaving Germany disunited for centuries. Resistance to Turkish expansion brought Hungary under Austrian control from the 16th cent. The Netherlands, Luxembourg, and Burgundy were added in 1477, curbing French expansion.

The Flemish painting tradition of naturalism, technical proficiency, and bourgeois subject matter began in the 15th cent. (Jan Van Eyck, c 1390-1441), the earliest northern manifestation of the Renaissance. **Dürer** (1471-1528) typified the merging of late Gothic and Italian trends in 16th-cent. German art. Imposing civic architecture flourished in the prosperous commercial cities.

**Spain**. Despite the unification of Castile and Aragon in 1479, the 2 countries retained separate governments, and the nobility, especially in Aragon and Catalonia, retained many privileges. Spanish lands in Italy (Naples, Sicily) and the Netherlands entangled the country in European wars through the mid-17th cent., while explorers, traders, and conquerors built up a Spanish empire in the Americas and the Philippines.

From the late 15th century, a **golden age** of literature and art produced works of social satire (plays of Lope de Vega, 1562-1635; Cervantes, 1547-1616), as well as spiritual intensity (El Greco, 1541-1614; Velazquez, 1599-1660).

**Black Death**. The bubonic plague reached Europe from the E in 1348, killing as much as half the population by 1350. Labor scarcity forced a rise in wages and brought greater freedom to the peasantry, making possible **peasant uprisings** (Jacquerie in France, 1358; Wat Tyler's rebellion in England, 1381). In the *ciompi* revolt (1378), Florentine wage earners demanded a say in economic and political power.

**Explorations**. Organized European maritime exploration began, seeking to evade the Venice-Ottoman monopoly of E trade and to promote Christianity. Beginning in 1418, expeditions from Portugal explored the W coast of Africa, until **Vasco da Gama** rounded the Cape of Good Hope in 1497 and reached India. A Portuguese trading empire was consolidated by the seizure of Goa (1510) and Malacca (1551). Japan was reached in 1542. The voyages of **Columbus** (1492-1504) uncovered a new world, which Spain hastened to subdue. Navigation schools in Spain and Portugal, the development of large sailing ships (carracks), and the invention (c 1475) of the rifle aided European penetration.

**Mughals and Safavids**. East of the Ottoman Empire, 2 Muslim dynasties ruled unchallenged in the 16th and 17th centuries. The Mughal dynasty of India, founded by Persianized Turkish invaders from the NW under Babur, dates from their 1526 conquest of the Delhi Sultanate. The dynasty ruled most of India for more than 200 years, surviving nominally until 1857. **Akbar** (r 1556-1605) consolidated administration at his glorious court, where the Urdu language (Persian-influenced Hindi) developed. Trade relations with Europe increased. Under Shah Jahan (1629-58), a secularized art fusing Hindu and Muslim element flourished in miniature painting and in architecture (Taj Mahal). Sikhism (founded c 1519) combined elements of both faiths. Suppression of Hindus and Shi'ite Muslims in S India in the late 17th cent. weakened the empire.

Fanatical devotion to the Shi'ite sect characterized the Safavids (1502-1736) of Persia and led to hostilities with the Sunni Ottomans for more than a century. The prosperity and the strength of the empire are evidenced by the mosques at its capital, **Isfahan**. The Safavids enhanced Iranian national consciousness.

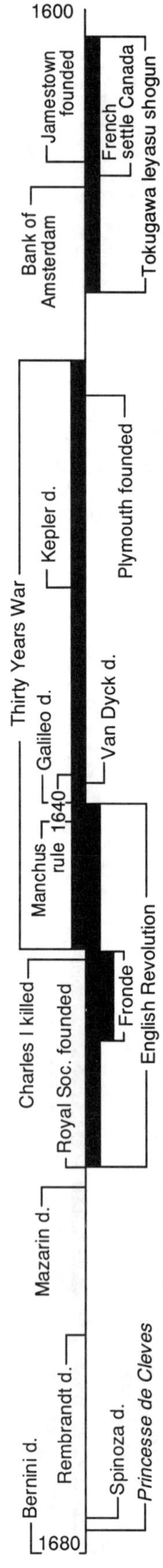


**China**. The **Ming** emperors (1368-1644), the last native dynasty in China, wielded unprecedented personal power, while the Confucian bureaucracy began to suffer from inertia. European trade (Portuguese monopoly through **Macao** from 1557) was strictly controlled. Jesuit scholars and scientists (Matteo Ricci, 1552-1610) introduced some Western science; their writings familiarized the West with China. Chinese technological inventiveness declined from this era, but the arts thrived, especially painting and ceramics.

**Japan**. After the decline of the first hereditary shogunate (chief generalship) at **Kamakura** (1185-1333), fragmentation of power accelerated, as did the consequent social mobility. Under Kamakura and the Ashikaga shogunate (1338-1573), the daimyos (lords) and samurai (warriors) grew more powerful and promoted a martial ideology. Japanese pirates and traders plied the China coast. Popular Buddhist movements included the nationalist Nichiren sect (from c 1250) and **Zen** (brought from China, 1191), which stressed meditation and a disciplined esthetic (tea ceremony, gardening, martial arts, No drama).

## Reformed Europe Expands Overseas: 1500-1700

**Reformation begun**. Theological debate and protests against real and perceived clerical corruption existed in the medieval Christian world, expressed by such dissenters as **Wycliffe** (c 1320-84) and his followers, the Lollards, in England, and **Huss** (burned as a heretic, 1415) in Bohemia.

**Luther** (1483-1546) preached that faith alone leads to salvation, without the mediation of clergy or good works. He attacked the authority of the pope, rejected priestly celibacy, and recommended individual study of the Bible (which he translated c 1525). His 95 Theses (1517) led to his excommunication (1521). **Calvin** (1509-64) said that God's elect were predestined for salvation and that good conduct and success were signs of election. Calvin in Geneva and Knox (1505-72) in Scotland established theocratic states.

Henry VIII asserted English national authority and secular power by breaking away (1534) from the Catholic Church. Monastic property was confiscated, and some Protestant doctrines given official sanction.

**Religious wars**. A century and a half of religious wars began with a South German peasant uprising (1524), repressed with Luther's support. Radical sects—democratic, pacifist, millennarian—arose (Anabaptists ruled Münster in 1534-35) and were suppressed violently. Civil war in France from 1562 between **Huguenots** (Protestant nobles and merchants) and Catholics ended with the 1598 Edict of Nantes tolerating Protestants (revoked 1685). Hapsburg attempts to restore Catholicism in Germany were resisted in 25 years of fighting; the 1555 Peace of Augsburg guarantee of religious independence to local princes and cities was confirmed only after the **Thirty Years War** (1618-48), when much of Germany was devastated by local and foreign armies (Sweden, France).

A Catholic Reformation, or **Counter Reformation**, met the Protestant challenge, clearly defining an official theology at the Council of Trent (1545-63). The **Jesuit** order (Society of Jesus), founded in 1534 by Loyola (1491-1556), helped reconvert large areas of Poland, Hungary, and S Germany and sent missionaries to the New World, India, and China, while the Inquisition helped suppress heresy in Catholic countries. A revival of piety appeared in the devotional literature (Theresa of Avila, 1515-82) and the grandiose Baroque art (Bernini, 1598-1680) of Roman Catholic countries.

**Scientific Revolution**. The late nominalist thinkers (Ockham, c 1300-49) of Paris and Oxford challenged Aristotelian orthodoxy, allowing for a freer scientific approach. But metaphysical values, such as the Neoplatonic faith in an orderly, mathematical cosmos, still motivated and directed subsequent inquiry. **Copernicus** (1473-1543) promoted the heliocentric theory, which was confirmed when Kepler (1571-1630) discovered the mathematical laws describing the orbits of the planets. The traditional Christian-Aristotelian belief that heavens and earth were fundamentally different collapsed when **Galileo** (1564-1642) discovered moving sunspots, irregular moon topography, and moons around Jupiter. He and **Newton** (1642-1727) developed a mechanics that unified cosmic and earthly phenomena. To meet the needs of the new physics, Newton and Leibnitz (1646-1716) invented calculus, and Descartes (1596-1650) invented analytic geometry.

An explosion of **observational science** included the discovery of blood circulation (Harvey, 1578-1657) and microscopic life (Leeuwenhoek, 1632-1723) and advances in anatomy (Vesalius, 1514-64, dissected corpses) and chemistry (Boyle, 1627-91). Scientific research institutes were founded: Florence (1657), London (**Royal Society**, 1660), Paris (1666). Inventions proliferated (Savery's steam engine, 1696).

**Arts**. Mannerist trends of the High Renaissance (**Michelangelo**, 1475-1564) exploited virtuosity, grace, novelty, and exotic subjects and poses. The notion of artistic genius was promoted, in contrast to the anonymous medieval artisan. Private connoisseurs entered the art market. These trends were elaborated in the 17th cent. **Baroque** era on a grander scale. Dynamic movement in painting and sculpture was emphasized by sharp lighting effects, use of rich materials (colored marble, gilt), and realistic details. Curved facades, broken lines, rich, deep-cut detail, and ceiling decoration characterized Baroque architecture, especially in Germany. Monarchs, princes, and prelates, usually Catholic, used Baroque art to enhance and embellish their authority, as in royal portraits by Velazquez (1599-1660) and Van Dyck (1599-1641).

National styles emerged. In France, a taste for rectilinear order and serenity (Poussin, 1594-1665), linked to the new rational philosophy, was expressed in classical forms. The influence of **classical values** in French literature (tragedies of **Racine**, 1639-99) gave rise to the "battle of the Ancients and Moderns." New forms included the essay (**Montaigne**, 1533-92) and novel (*Princesse de Cleves*, La Fayette, 1678).

Dutch painting of the 17th cent. was unique in its wide social distribution. The Flemish tradition of undemonstrative realism reached its peak in **Rembrandt** (1606-69) and Vermeer (1632-75).

**Economy**. European economic expansion was stimulated by the new trade with the East, by New World gold and silver, and by a doubling of population (50 million in 1450, 100 million in 1600). New business and financial techniques were developed and refined, such as joint-stock companies, insurance, and letters of credit and exchange. The Bank of Amsterdam (1609) and the Bank of England (1694) broke the old monopoly of private banking families. The rise of a business mentality was typified by the spread of clock towers in cities in the 14th cent. By the mid-15th cent., portable clocks were available; the first watch was invented in 1502.

By 1650, most governments had adopted the **mercantile system**, in which they sought to amass metallic wealth by protecting their merchants' foreign and colonial trade monopolies. The rise in prices and the new coin-based economy undermined the craft guild and feudal manorial systems. Expanding industries, such as clothweaving and mining, benefited from technical advances. Coal replaced disappearing wood as the chief fuel; it was used to fuel new 16th-cent. blast furnaces making cast iron.

**New World**. The **Aztecs** united much of the Meso-American culture area in a militarist empire by 1519, from their capital, Tenochtitlán (pop. 300,000), which was the center of a cult requiring enormous levels of ritual human sacrifice. Most of the civilized areas of South America were ruled by the centralized Inca Empire (1476-1534), stretching 2,000 mi from Ecuador to NW Argentina. Lavish and sophisticated traditions in pottery, weaving, sculpture, and architecture were maintained in both regions.

These empires, beset by revolts, fell in 2 short campaigns to gold-seeking Spanish forces based in the Antilles and Panama. **Cortes** took Mexico (1519-21); **Pizarro,** Peru (1532-35). From these centers, land and sea expeditions claimed most of North and South America for Spain. The Indian high cultures did not survive the impact of Christian missionaries and the new upper class of whites and mestizos. In turn, New World silver and such Indian products as potatoes, tobacco, corn, peanuts, chocolate, and rubber exercised a major economic influence on Europe. Although the Spanish administration intermittently concerned itself with the welfare of Indians, the population remained impoverished at most levels, despite the growth of a distinct South American civilization. European diseases reduced the native population.

Brazil, which the Portuguese reached in 1500 and settled after 1530, and the Caribbean colonies of several European nations developed a plantation economy where sugarcane, tobacco, cotton, coffee, rice, indigo, and lumber were grown commercially by slaves. From the early 16th to the late 19th century, some 10 million Africans were transported to **slavery** in the New World.

**Netherlands**. The urban, Calvinist N provinces of the Netherlands rebelled (1568) against Hapsburg Spain and founded an oligarchic mercantile republic. Their strategic control of the Baltic grain market enabled them to exploit Mediterranean food shortages. Religious refugees—French and Belgian Protestants, Iberian Jews—added to the cosmopolitan commercial talent pool. After Spain absorbed Portugal in 1580, the Dutch seized Portuguese possessions and created a vast, though generally short-lived commercial empire in Brazil, the Antilles, Africa, India, Ceylon, Malacca, Indonesia, and Taiwan and challenged or supplanted Portuguese traders in China and Japan. Revolution in 1640 restored Portuguese independence.

**England**. Anglicanism became firmly established under Elizabeth I after a brief Catholic interlude under "Bloody Mary" (1553-58). But religious and political conflicts led to a rebellion (1642) by Parliament. Roundheads (Puritans) defeated Cavaliers (Royalists); Charles I was beheaded (1649). The new **Commonwealth** was ruled as a military dictatorship by Cromwell, who also brutally crushed (1649-51) an Irish rebellion. Conflicts within the Puritan camp (democratic Levelers defeated 1649) aided the Stuart restoration (1660), but Parliament was permanently strengthened and the peaceful **"Glorious Revolution"** (1688) advanced political and religious liberties (writings of **Locke,** 1632-1704). British privateers (Drake, 1540-96) challenged Spanish control of the New World and penetrated Asian trade routes (Madras taken, 1639). North American colonies (Jamestown, 1607; Plymouth, 1620) provided an outlet for religious dissenters from Europe.

**France**. Emerging from the religious civil wars in 1628, France regained military and commercial great power status under the ministries of **Richelieu** (1624-42), Mazarin (1643-61), and Colbert (1662-83). Under **Louis XIV** (reigned 1643-1715) royal absolutism triumphed over nobles and local *parlements* (defeat of Fronde, 1648-53). Permanent colonies were founded in Canada (1608), the Caribbean (1626), and India (1674).

**Sweden**. Sweden seceded from the Scandinavian Union in 1523. The thinly populated agrarian state (with copper, iron, and timber exports) was united by the Vasa kings, whose conquests by the mid-17th cent. made Sweden the dominant Baltic power. The empire collapsed in the Great Northern War (1700-21).

**Poland**. After the union with Lithuania in 1447, Poland ruled vast territories from the Baltic to the Black Sea, resisting German and Turkish incursions. Catholic nobles failed to gain the loyalty of their Orthodox Christian subjects in the E; commerce and trades were practiced by German and Jewish immigrants. The bloody 1648-49 Cossack uprising began the kingdom's dismemberment.

**China**. A new dynasty, the Manchus, invaded from the NE, seized power in 1644, and expanded Chinese control to its greatest extent in Central and Southeast Asia. Trade and diplomatic contact with Europe grew, carefully controlled by China. New crops (sweet potato, maize, peanut) allowed an economic and population growth (pop. 300 million, in 1800). Traditional arts and literature were pursued with increased sophistication (*Dream of the Red Chamber*, novel, mid-18th cent.).

**Japan**. Tokugawa Ieyasu, shogun from 1603, finally unified and pacified feudal Japan. Hereditary daimyos and samurai monopolized government office and the professions. An urban merchant class grew, literacy spread, and a cultural renaissance occurred (haiku, a verse innovation of the poet Basho, 1644-94). Fear of European domination led to persecution of Christian converts from 1597 and to stringent isolation from outside contact from 1640.

## Philosophy, Industry, and Revolution: 1700-1800

**Science and Reason**. Greater faith in human reason and empirical observation as a source of truth and a means to improve the physical and social environment, espoused since the Renaissance (Francis Bacon, 1561-1626), was bolstered by scientific discoveries in spite of theological opposition (Galileo's forced retraction, 1633). **Descartes** used a rationalistic approach modeled on geometry to discover "self-evident" truths as a foundation of knowledge. **Newton** emphasized induction from experimental observation. **Spinoza** (1632-77), who called for political and intellectual freedom, developed a systematic rationalistic philosophy in his classic work *Ethics*.

French philosophers assumed leadership of the **Enlightenment** in the 18th cent. Montesquieu (1689-1755) used British history to support his notions of limited government. **Voltaire**'s (1694-1778) diaries and novels of exotic travel illustrated the intellectual trends toward secular ethics and relativism. Rousseau's (1712-1778) radical concepts of the **social contract** and of the inherent goodness of the common

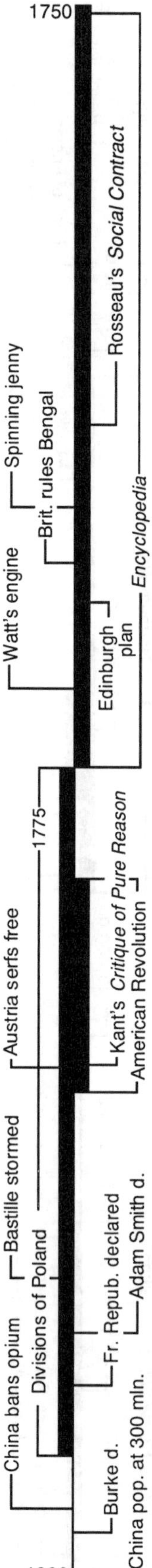


man gave impetus to antimonarchical republicanism. The *Encyclopedia* (1751-72), edited by Diderot and d'Alembert and designed as a monument to reason, was largely devoted to practical technology.

In England, ideals of political and religious liberty were connected with empiricist philosophy and science in the followers of Locke. But British empiricism, especially as developed by the skeptical **Hume** (1711-76), radically reduced the role of reason in philosophy, as did the evolutionary approach to law and politics of Burke (1729-97) and the utilitarian ethics of Bentham (1748-1832). Adam Smith (1723-90) and other **physiocrats** called for a rationalization of economic activity by removing artificial barriers to a supposedly natural free exchange of goods.

Despite the political disunity and backwardness of most of Germany, German writers participated in the new philosophical trends popularized by Wolff (1679-1754). **Kant's** (1724-1804) transcendental idealism, unifying an empirical epistemology with a priori moral and logical concepts, directed German thought away from skepticism. Italian contributions included work on electricity by Galvani (1737-98) and Volta (1745-1827), the pioneer **historiography of Vico** (1668-1744), and writings on penal reform by Beccaria (1738-94). Benjamin Franklin (1706-90) was celebrated in Europe for his varied achievements.

The growth of the **press** (*Spectator*, 1711-12) and the wide distribution of realistic but sentimental **novels** attested to the increase of a large bourgeois public.

**Arts**. **Rococo** art, characterized by extravagant decorative effects, asymmetries copied from organic models, and artificial pastoral subjects, was favored by the continental aristocracy for most of the century (Watteau, 1684-1721) and had musical analogies in the ornamentalized polyphony of late Baroque. The **Neoclassical** art after 1750, associated with the new scientific archaeology, was more streamlined and was infused with the supposed moral and geometric rectitude of the Roman Republic (David, 1748-1825). In England, **town planning** on a grand scale began.

**Industrial Revolution in England**. Agricultural improvements, such as the sowing drill (1701) and livestock breeding, were implemented on the large fields provided by enclosure of common lands by private owners. Profits from agriculture and from colonial and foreign trade (1800 volume, £54 million) were chaneled through hundreds of banks and the **Stock Exchange** (est 1773) into new industrial processes.

The Newcomen steam pump (1712) aided coal mining. Coal fueled the new efficient steam engines patented by Watt in 1769, and coke-smelting produced cheap, sturdy iron for machinery by the 1730s. The **flying shuttle** (1733) and **spinning jenny** (c 1764) were used in the large new cotton textile factories, where women and children were much of the work force. Goods were transported cheaply over **canals** (2,000 mi; built 1760-1800).

**American Revolution**. The British colonies in North America attracted a mass immigration of religious dissenters and poor people throughout the 17th and 18th centuries, coming from the British Isles, Germany, the Netherlands, and other countries. The population reached 3 million non-natives by the 1770s. The small native population was greatly reduced by European diseases and by wars with and between the various colonies. British attempts to control colonial trade and to tax the colonists to pay for the costs of colonial administration and defense clashed with traditions of local self-government and eventually provoked the colonies to rebellion.

**Central and East Europe**. The monarchs of the three states that dominated E Europe—Austria, Prussia, and Russia—accepted the advice and legitimation of philosophes in creating more modern, centralized institutions in their kingdoms, enlarged by the division (1772-95) of Poland.

Under **Frederick II** (r 1740-86) Prussia, with its efficient modern army, doubled in size. State monopolies and tariff protection fostered industry, and some legal reforms were introduced. Austria's heterogeneous realms were unified under **Maria Theresa** (r 1740-80) and **Joseph II** (r 1780-90). Reforms in education, law, and religion were enacted, and the Austrian serfs were freed (1781). With its defeat in the Seven Years' War in 1763, Austria failed to regain Silesia, which had been seized by Prussia, but was compensated by expansion to the E and S (Hungary, Slavonia, 1699; Galicia, 1772).

Russia, whose borders continued to expand in all directions, adopted some Western bureaucratic and economic policies under **Peter I** (r 1682-1725) and Catherine II (r 1762-96). Trade and cultural contacts with the West multiplied from the new Baltic Sea capital, **St. Petersburg** (est 1703).

**French Revolution**. The growing French middle class lacked political power and resented aristocratic tax privileges, especially in light of the successful American Revolution. Peasants lacked adequate land and were burdened with feudal obligations to nobles. Wars with Britain drained the treasury, finally forcing the king to call the **Estates-General** in 1789 (first time since 1614), in an atmosphere of food riots (poor crop in 1788).

Aristocratic resistance to absolutism was soon overshadowed by the reformist Third Estate (middle class), which proclaimed itself the **National Constituent Assembly** June 17 and took the "Tennis Court oath" on June 20 to secure a constitution. The storming of the **Bastille** on July 14 by Parisian artisans was followed by looting and seizure of aristocratic property throughout France. Assembly reforms included abolition of class and regional privileges, a Declaration of Rights, suffrage by taxpayers (75% of males), and the **Civil Constitution of the Clergy** providing for election and loyalty oaths for priests. A republic was declared Sept. 22, 1792, in spite of royalist pressure from Austria and Prussia, which had declared war in April (joined by Britain the next year). Louis XVI was beheaded Jan. 21, 1793, Queen Marie Antoinette was beheaded Oct. 16, 1793.

Royalist uprisings in La Vendée and military reverses led to a **reign of terror** in which tens of thousands of opponents of the Revolution and criminals were executed. Radical reforms in the **Convention** period (Sept. 1793-Oct. 1795) included the abolition of colonial slavery, economic measures to aid the poor, support of public education, and a short-lived de-Christianization.

Division among radicals (execution of Hebert, Danton, and Robespierre, 1794) aided the ascendance of a moderate **Directory**, which consolidated military victories. **Napoleon Bonaparte** (1769-1821), a popular young general, exploited political divisions and participated in a coup Nov. 9, 1799, making himself first consul (dictator).

**India**. Sikh and Hindu rebels (Rajputs, Marathas) and Afghans destroyed the power of the Mughals during the 18th cent. After France's defeat (1763) in the Seven Years' War, Britain was the primary European trade power in India. Its control of inland **Bengal and Bihar** was recognized (1765) by the

Mughal shah, who granted the **British East India Co.** (under Clive, 1725-74) the right to collect land revenue there. Despite objections from Parliament (1784 India Act), the company's involvement in local wars and politics led to repeated acquisitions of new territory. The company exported Indian textiles, sugar, and indigo.

## Change Gathers Steam: 1800-40

**French ideals and empire spread**. Inspired by the ideals of the French Revolution, and supported by the expanding French armies, new republican regimes arose near France: the **Batavian** Republic in the Netherlands (1795-1806), the **Helvetic** Republic in Switzerland (1798-1803), the **Cisalpine** Republic in N Italy (1797-1805), the **Ligurian** Republic in Genoa (1797-1805), and the **Parthenopean** Republic in S Italy (1799). A Roman Republic existed briefly in 1798 after Pope Pius VI was arrested by French troops. In Italy and Germany, new nationalist sentiments were stimulated both in imitation of and in reaction to developments in France (anti-French and anti-Jacobin peasant uprisings in Italy, 1796-99).

From 1804, when Napoleon declared himself emperor, to 1812, a succession of military victories (Austerlitz, 1805; Jena, 1806) extended his control over most of Europe, through puppet states (**Confederation of the Rhine** united W German states for the first time and **Grand Duchy of Warsaw** revived Polish national hopes), expansion of the empire, and alliances.

Among the lasting reforms initiated under Napoleon's absolutist reign were: establishment of the Bank of France, centralization of tax collection, codification of law along Roman models (Code Napoléon), and reform and extension of secondary and university education. In an 1801 concordat, the papacy recognized the effective autonomy of the French Catholic Church. Some 400,000 French soldiers were killed in the Napoleonic Wars, along with 600,000 foreign troops.

**Last gasp of old regime**. France's coastal blockade of Europe (**Continental System**) failed to neutralize Britain. The disastrous 1812 invasion of Russia exposed Napoleon's overextension. After Napoleon's 1814 exile at Elba, his armies were defeated (1815) at **Waterloo**, by British and Prussian troops.

At the **Congress of Vienna**, the monarchs and princes of Europe redrew their boundaries, to the advantage of Prussia (in Saxony and the Ruhr), Austria (in Illyria and Venetia), and Russia (in Poland and Finland). British conquest of Dutch and French colonies (S Africa, Ceylon, Mauritius) was recognized, and France, under the restored Bourbons, retained its expanded 1792 borders. The settlement brought 50 years of international peace to Europe.

But the Congress was unable to check the advance of liberal ideals and of nationalism among the smaller European nations. The 1825 **Decembrist uprising** by liberal officers in Russia was easily suppressed. But an independence movement in **Greece**, stirred by commercial prosperity and a cultural revival, succeeded in expelling Ottoman rule by 1831, with the aid of Britain, France, and Russia.

A constitutional monarchy was secured in France by the **1830 Revolution**; Louis Philippe became king. The revolutionary contagion spread to **Belgium**, which gained its independence (1830) from the Dutch monarchy, to **Poland**, whose rebellion was defeated (1830-31) by Russia, and to Germany.

**Romanticism**. A new style in intellectual and artistic life began to replace Neoclassicism and Rococo after the mid-18th cent. By the early 19th cent., this style, Romanticism, had prevailed in the European world.

**Rousseau** had begun the reaction against rationalism; in education (*Émile*, 1762) he stressed subjective spontaneity over regularized instruction. In Germany, Lessing (1729-81) and Herder (1744-1803) favorably compared the German folk song to classical forms and began a cult of Shakespeare, whose passion and "natural" wisdom was a model for the romantic *Sturm und Drang* (Storm and Stress) movement. **Goethe's** *Sorrows of Young Werther* (1774) set the model for the tragic, passionate genius.

A new interest in **Gothic architecture** in England after 1760 (Walpole, 1717-97) spread through Europe, associated with an aesthetic Christian and mystic revival (Blake, 1757-1827). Celtic, Norse, and German mythology and folk tales were revived or imitated (Macpherson's Ossian translation, 1762; Grimm's Fairy Tales, 1812-22). The medieval revival (Scott's *Ivanhoe*, 1819) led to a new interest in history, stressing national differences and organic growth (Carlyle, 1795-1881; Michelet, 1798-1874), corresponding to theories of natural evolution (Lamarck's *Philosophie Zoologique*, 1809; Lyell's *Geology*, 1830-33). A reaction against classicism characterized the English **romantic poets,** beginning with **Wordsworth** (1770-1850). Revolution and war fed an obsession with freedom and conflict, expressed by both poets (**Byron**, 1788-1824; **Hugo**, 1802-85) and philosophers (**Hegel**, 1770-1831).

Wild gardens replaced the formal French variety, and painters favored rural, stormy, and mountainous landscapes (**Turner**, 1775-1851; **Constable**, 1776-1837). Clothing became freer, with wigs, hoops, and ruffles discarded. Originality and genius were expected in the life as well as the work of inspired artists (Murger's *Scenes from Bohemian Life*, 1847-49). Exotic locales and themes (as in Gothic horror stories) were used in art and literature (Delacroix, 1798-1863; **Poe**, 1809-49).

Music exhibited the new dramatic style and a breakdown of classical forms (Beethoven, 1770-1827). The use of folk melodies and modes aided the growth of distinct national traditions (Glinka in Russia, 1804-57).

**Latin America**. Haiti, under the former slave **Toussaint L'Ouverture**, was the first Latin American independent state (1804). All the mainland Spanish colonies won their independence (1810-24), under such leaders as **Bolivar** (1783-1830). Brazil became an independent empire (1822) under the Portuguese prince regent. A new class of military officers divided power with large landholders and the church.

**United States**. Heavy immigration and exploitation of ample natural resources fueled rapid economic growth. The spread of the franchise, public education, and antislavery sentiment were signs of a widespread democratic ethic.

**China**. Failure to keep pace with Western arms technology exposed China to greater European influence and hampered efforts to bar imports of opium, which had damaged Chinese society and drained wealth overseas. In the **Opium War** (1839-42), Britain forced China to expand trade opportunities and to cede Hong Kong.

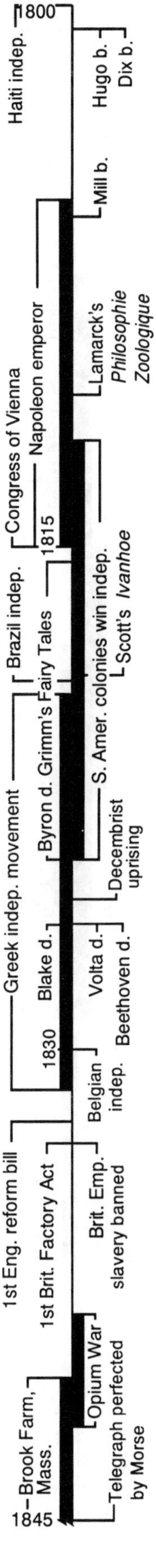

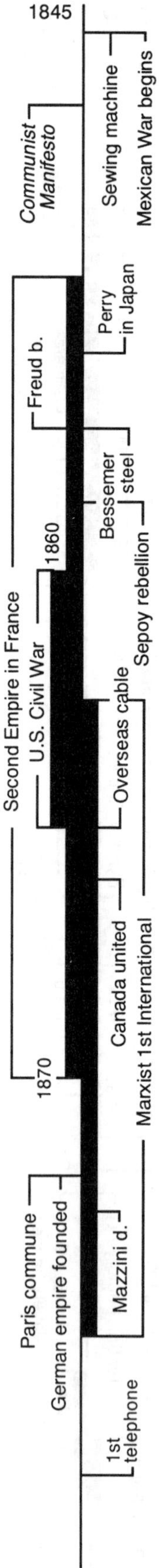


# Triumph of Progress: 1840-80

**Idea of Progress**. As a result of the cumulative scientific, economic, and political changes of the preceding eras, the idea took hold among literate people in the West that continuing growth and improvement was the usual state of human and natural life.

Darwin's statement of the **theory of evolution** and survival of the fittest (*Origin of Species*, 1859), defended by intellectuals and scientists against theological objections, was taken as confirmation that progress was the natural direction of life. The controversy helped define popular ideas of the dedicated scientist and ever-expanding human knowledge of and control over the world (Foucault's demonstration of earth's rotation, 1851; Pasteur's germ theory, 1861).

**Liberals** following Ricardo (1772-1823) in their faith that unrestrained competition would bring continuous economic expansion sought to adjust political life to the new social realities and believed that unregulated competition of ideas would yield truth (Mill, 1806-73). In England, successive reform bills (1832, 1867, 1884) gave representation to the new industrial towns and extended the franchise to the middle and lower classes and to Catholics, Dissenters, and Jews. On both sides of the Atlantic, reformists tried to improve conditions for the mentally ill (Dix, 1802-87), women (Anthony, 1820-1906), and prisoners. Slavery was barred in the British Empire (1833); the U.S. (1865); and Brazil (1888).

**Socialist theories** based on ideas of human perfectibility or historical progress were widely disseminated. Utopian socialists such as Saint-Simon (1760-1825) envisaged an orderly, just society directed by a technocratic elite. A model factory town, New Lanark, Scotland, was set up by utopian Robert Owen (1771-1858), and utopian communal experiments were tried in the U.S. (Brook Farm, Mass., 1841-47). Bakunin's (1814-76) anarchism represented the opposite utopian extreme of total freedom. **Marx** (1818-83) posited the inevitable triumph of socialism in the industrial countries through a historical process of class conflict.

**Spread of industry**. The technical processes and managerial innovations of the English industrial revolution spread to Europe (especially Germany) and the U.S., causing an explosion of industrial production, demand for raw materials, and competition for markets. Inventors, both trained and self-educated, provided the means for larger-scale production (Bessemer steel, 1856; sewing machine, 1846). Many inventions were shown at the 1851 London Great Exhibition at the **Crystal Palace,** the theme of which was universal prosperity.

Local specialization and long-distance trade were aided by a revolution in transportation and communication. Railroads were first introduced in the 1820s in England and the U.S. More than 150,000 mi of track had been laid worldwide by 1880, with another 100,000 mi laid in the next decade. Steamships were improved (*Savannah* crossed Atlantic, 1819). The telegraph, perfected by 1844 (Morse), connected the Old and New Worlds by cable in 1866 and quickened the pace of international commerce and politics. The first commercial telephone exchange went into operation in the U.S. in 1878.

The new class of industrial workers, uprooted from their rural homes, lacked job security and suffered from dangerous overcrowded conditions at work and at home. Many responded by organizing **trade unions** (legalized in England, 1824; France, 1884). The U.S. Knights of Labor had 700,000 members by 1886. The First International (1864-76) tried to unite workers internationally around a Marxist program. The quasi-Socialist Paris Commune uprising (1871) was violently suppressed. Factory Acts to reduce child labor and regulate conditions were passed (1833-50 in England). Social security measures were introduced by the Bismarck regime (1883-89) in Germany.

**Revolutions of 1848**. Among the causes of the continent-wide revolutions were an international collapse of credit and resulting unemployment, bad harvests in 1845-47, and a cholera epidemic. The new urban proletariat and expanding bourgeoisie demanded a greater political role. Republics were proclaimed in France, Rome, and Venice. Nationalist feelings reached fever pitch in the Hapsburg empire, as Hungary declared independence under Kossuth, as a Slav Congress demanded equality, and as Piedmont tried to drive Austria from Lombardy. A national liberal assembly at Frankfurt called for German unification.

But riots fueled bourgeois fears of socialism (**Marx and Engels**, *Communist Manifesto*, 1848), and peasants remained conservative. The old establishment—the Papacy, the Hapsburgs with the help of the Czarist Russian army —was able to rout the revolutionaries by 1849. The French Republic succumbed to a renewed monarchy by 1852 (Emperor Napoleon III).

**Great nations unified**. Using the "blood and iron" tactics of Bismarck from 1862, Prussia controlled N Germany by 1867 (war with Denmark, 1864; Austria, 1866). After defeating France in 1870 (annexation of Alsace-Lorraine), it won the allegiance of S German states. A new **German Empire** was proclaimed (1871). **Italy**, inspired by Mazzini (1805-72) and Garibaldi (1807-82), was unified by the reformed Piedmont kingdom through uprisings, plebiscites, and war.

The **U.S.**, its area expanded after the 1846-48 Mexican War, defeated (1861-65) a secession attempt by slave states. The Canadian provinces were united in an autonomous **Dominion of Canada** (1867). Control in **India** was removed from the East India Co. and centralized under British administration after the 1857-58 Sepoy rebellion, laying the groundwork for the modern Indian State. Queen Victoria was named Empress of India (1876).

**Europe dominates Asia**. The Ottoman Empire began to collapse in the face of Balkan nationalisms and European imperial incursions in N Africa (Suez Canal, 1869). The Turks had lost control of most of both regions by 1882. Russia completed its expansion S by 1884 (despite the temporary setback of the Crimean War with Turkey, Britain, and France, 1853-56), taking Turkestan, all the Caucasus, and Chinese areas in the E and sponsoring Balkan Slavs against the Turks. A succession of reformist and reactionary regimes presided over a slow modernization (serfs freed, 1861). Persian independence suffered as Russia and British India competed for influence.

**China** was forced to sign a series of unequal treaties with European powers and Japan. Overpopulation and an inefficient dynasty brought misery and caused rebellions (Taiping, Muslims) leaving tens of millions dead. Japan was forced by the U.S. (Commodore Perry's visits, 1853-54) and Europe to end its isolation. The Meiji restoration (1868) gave power to a Westernizing oligarchy. Intensified empire-building gave Burma to Britain (1824-85) and Indochina to France (1862-95). Christian missionary activity followed imperial and trade expansion in Asia.

**Respectability**. The fine arts were expected to reflect and encourage the progress of morals and manners among the Victorians. Prudery, exaggerated delicacy, and familial piety were heralded by **Bowdler's** expurgated edition (1818) of Shakespeare. Government-supported mass education inculcated a work ethic as a means to escape poverty (Horatio Alger, 1832-99).

The official **Beaux Arts** school in Paris set an international style of imposing public buildings (Paris Opera, 1861-74; Vienna Opera, 1861-69) and uplifting statues (Bartholdi's *Statue of Liberty*, 1884). Realist painting, influenced by photography (Daguerre, 1837), appealed to a new mass audience with social or historical narrative (Wilkie, 1785-1841; Poynter, 1836-1919) or with serious religious, moral, or social messages (pre-Raphaelites, Millet's *Angelus*, 1858) often drawn from ordinary life. The **Impressionists** (Monet, 1840-1926; Pissarro, 1830-1903; Renoir, 1841-1919) rejected the formalism, sentimentality, and precise techniques of academic art in favor of a spontaneous, undetailed rendering of the world through careful representation of the effect of natural light on objects.

Realistic **novelists** presented the full panorama of social classes and personalities, but retained sentimentality and moral judgment (Dickens, 1812-70; Eliot, 1819-80; Tolstoy, 1828-1910; Balzac, 1799-1850).

## Veneer of Stability: 1880-1900

**Imperialism triumphant.** The vast **African** interior, visited by European explorers (Barth, 1821-65; Livingstone, 1813-73), was conquered by the European powers in rapid, competitive thrusts from their coastal bases after 1880, mostly for domestic political and international strategic reasons. W African Muslim kingdoms (Fulani), Arab slave traders (Zanzibar), and Bantu military confederations (Zulu) were alike subdued. Only Christian Ethiopia (defeat of Italy, 1896) and Liberia resisted successfully. France (W Africa) and Britain ("Cape to Cairo," Boer War, 1899-1902) were the major beneficiaries. The ideology of "the white man's burden" (Kipling, *Barrack Room Ballads*, 1892) or of a "civilizing mission" (France) justified the conquests.

W European foreign capital investment soared to nearly $40 billion by 1914, but most was in E Europe (France, Germany), the Americas (Britain), and the Europeans' colonies. The foundation of the modern interdependent world economy was laid, with cartels dominating raw material trade.

**An industrious world**. Industrial and technological proficiency characterized the 2 new great powers—Germany and the **U.S.** Coal and iron deposits enabled Germany to reach 2d or 3d place status in iron, steel, and shipbuilding by the 1900s. German electrical and chemical industries were world leaders. The U.S. post-Civil War boom (interrupted by "panics"—1884, 1893, 1896) was shaped by massive immigration from S and E Europe from 1880, government subsidy of railroads, and huge private monopolies (Standard Oil, 1870; U.S. Steel, 1901). The **Spanish-American War**, 1898 (Philippine Insurrection, 1899-1902), and the Open Door policy in China (1899) made the U.S. a world power.

England led in **urbanization** (72% by 1890), with **London** the world capital of finance, insurance, and shipping. Sewer systems (Paris, 1850s), electric subways (London, 1890), parks, and bargain department stores helped improve living standards for most of the urban population of the industrial world.

**Westernization of Asia**. Asian reaction to European economic, military, and religious incursions took the form of imitation of Western techniques and adoption of Western ideas of progress and freedom. The Chinese "self-strengthening" movement of the 1860s and '70s included rail, port, and arsenal improvements and metal and textile mills. Reformers such as **K'ang Yu-wei** (1858-1927) won liberalizing reforms in 1898, right after the European and Japanese "scramble for concessions."

A universal education system in Japan and importation of foreign industrial, scientific, and military experts aided Japan's unprecedented rapid modernization after 1868, under the authoritarian Meiji regime. Japan's victory in the **Sino-Japanese War** (1894-95) put Formosa and Korea in its power.

In India, the British alliance with the remaining princely states masked reform sentiment among the Westernized urban elite; higher education had been conducted largely in English for 50 years. The **Indian National Congress**, founded in 1885, demanded a larger government role for Indians.

***Fin-de-siècle* sophistication**. **Naturalist** writers pushed realism to its extreme limits, adopting a quasi-scientific attitude and writing about formerly taboo subjects such as sex, crime, extreme poverty, and corruption (Flaubert, 1821-80; Zola, 1840-1902; Hardy, 1840-1928). Unseen or repressed psychological motivations were explored in the clinical and theoretical works of **Freud** (1856-1939) and in the fiction of **Dostoyevsky** (1821-81), James (1843-1916), Schnitzler (1862-1931), and others.

A contempt for bourgeois life or a desire to shock a complacent audience was shared by the French **symbolist** poets (Verlaine, 1844-96; Rimbaud, 1854-91), by neopagan English writers (Swinburne, 1837-1909), by continental dramatists (Ibsen, 1828-1906), and by satirists (Wilde, 1854-1900). **Nietzsche** (1844-1900) was influential in his elitism and pessimism.

Postimpressionist art neglected long-cherished conventions of representation (Cezanne, 1839-1906) and showed a willingness to learn from primitive and non-European art (Gauguin, 1848-1903; Japanese prints).

**Racism**. Gobineau (1816-82) gave a pseudobiological foundation to modern racist theories, which spread in the latter 19th cent., along with **Social Darwinism**, the belief that societies are and should be organized as a struggle for survival of the fittest. The medieval period was interpreted as an era of natural Germanic rule (Chamberlain, 1855-1927), and notions of superiority were associated with German national aspirations (Treitschke, 1834-96). **Anti-Semitism**, with a new racist rationale, became a significant political force in Germany (Anti-Semitic Petition, 1880), Austria (Lueger, 1844-1910), and France (Dreyfus case, 1894-1906).

## Last Respite: 1900-9

**Alliances.** While the peace of Europe (and its dependencies) continued to hold (1907 **Hague Conference** extended the rules of war and international arbitration procedures), imperial rivalries, protectionist trade practices (in Germany and France), and the escalating arms race (British *Dreadnought* battleship launched; Germany widens Kiel canal, 1906) exacerbated minor disputes (German-French Moroccan "crises," 1905, 1911).

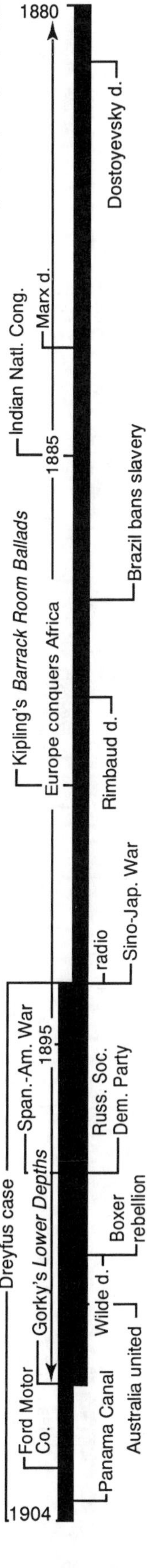

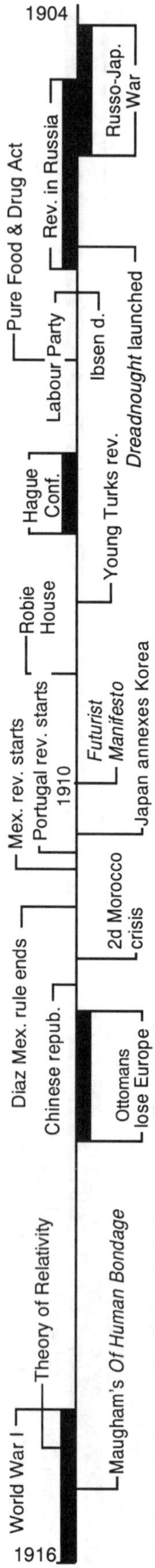


Security was sought through alliances: **Triple Alliance** (Germany, Austria-Hungary, Italy; renewed in 1902 and 1907); Anglo-Japanese Alliance (1902), Franco-Russian Alliance (1899), **Entente Cordiale** (Britain, France, 1904), Anglo-Russian Treaty (1907), German-Ottoman friendship.

**Ottomans decline**. The inefficient, corrupt Ottoman government was unable to resist further loss of territory. Nearly all European lands were lost in 1912 to Serbia, Greece, Montenegro, and Bulgaria. Italy took Libya and the Dodecanese islands the same year, and Britain took Kuwait (1899) and the Sinai (1906). The **Young Turk** revolution in 1908 forced the sultan to restore a constitution, and it introduced some social reform, industrialization, and secularization.

**British Empire**. British trade and cultural influence remained dominant in the empire, but constitutional reforms presaged its eventual dissolution: The colonies of **Australia** were united in 1901 under a self-governing commonwealth. **New Zealand** acquired dominion status in 1907. The old Boer republics joined Cape Colony and Natal in the self-governing **Union of South Africa** in 1910.

The 1909 Indian Councils Act enhanced the role of elected province legislatures in **India**. The Muslim League (founded 1906) sought separate communal representation.

**East Asia**. Japan exploited its growing industrial power to expand its empire. Victory in the 1904-5 war against Russia (naval battle of Tsushima, 1905) assured Japan's domination of **Korea** (annexed 1910) and Manchuria (Port Arthur taken, 1905).

In China, central authority began to crumble (empress died, 1908). Reforms (Confucian exam system ended 1905, modernization of the army, building of railroads) were inadequate, and secret societies of reformers and nationalists, inspired by the Westernized **Sun Yat-sen** (1866-1925) fomented periodic uprisings in the S.

**Siam**, whose independence had been guaranteed by Britain and France in 1896, was split into spheres of influence by those countries in 1907.

**Russia**. The population of the Russian Empire approached 150 million in 1900. Reforms in education, in law, and in local institutions (*zemstvos*) and an industrial boom starting in the 1880s (oil, railroads) created the beginnings of a modern state, despite the autocratic tsarist regime. Liberals (1903 Union of Liberation), Socialists (Social Democrats founded 1898, Bolsheviks split off 1903), and populists (Social Revolutionaries founded 1901) were periodically repressed, and national minorities were persecuted (anti-Jewish pogroms, 1903, 1905-6).

An industrial crisis after 1900 and harvest failures aggravated poverty among urban workers, and the 1904-5 defeat by Japan (which checked Russia's Asian expansion) sparked the Revolution of 1905-6. A **Duma** (parliament) was created, and an agricultural reform (under Stolypin, prime minister 1906-11) created a large class of landowning peasants (kulaks).

**The world shrinks**. Developments in transportation and communication and mass population movements helped create an awareness of an interdependent world. Early **automobiles** (Daimler, Benz, 1885) were experimental or were designed as luxuries. Assembly-line mass production (Ford Motor Co., 1903) made the invention practicable, and by 1910 nearly 500,000 motor vehicles were registered in the U.S. alone. **Heavier-than-air flights** began in 1903 in the U.S. (Wright brothers), preceded by glider, balloon, and model plane advances in several countries. Trade was advanced by improvements in **ship design** (gyrocompass, 1910), speed (*Lusitania* crossed Atlantic in 5 days, 1907), and reach (Panama Canal begun, 1904).

The first transatlantic **radio** telegraphic transmission occurred in 1901, 6 years after Marconi discovered radio. Radio transmission of human speech had been made in 1900. Telegraphic transmission of photos was achieved in 1904, lending immediacy to news reports. **Phonographs**, popularized by Caruso's recordings (starting 1902), made for quick international spread of musical styles (ragtime). **Motion pictures**, perfected in the 1890s (Dickson, Lumière brothers), became a popular and artistic medium after 1900; newsreels appeared in 1909.

**Emigration** from crowded European centers soared in the decade: 9 million migrated to the U.S., and millions more went to Siberia, Canada, Argentina, Australia, South Africa, and Algeria. Some 70 million Europeans emigrated in the century before 1914. Several million Chinese, Indians, and Japanese migrated to Southeast Asia, where their urban skills often enabled them to take a predominant economic role.

**Social reform**. The social and economic problems of the poor were kept in the public eye by realist fiction writers (Dreiser's *Sister Carrie*, 1900; Gorky's *Lower Depths*, 1902; Sinclair's *Jungle*, 1906), journalists (U.S. **muckrakers**—Steffens, Tarbell), and artists (Ashcan school). Frequent labor strikes and occasional assassinations by anarchists or radicals (Empress Elizabeth of Austria, 1898; King Umberto I of Italy, 1900; U.S. Pres. McKinley, 1901; Russian Interior Minister Plehve, 1904; Portugal's King Carlos, 1908) added to social tension and fear of revolution.

But democratic reformism prevailed. In Germany, Bernstein's (1850-1932) **revisionist Marxism**, downgrading revolution, was accepted by the powerful Social Democrats and trade unions. The British Fabian Society (the Webbs, Shaw) and the Labour Party (founded 1906) worked for reforms such as Social Security and union rights (1906), while woman suffragists grew more militant. U.S. **progressives** fought big business (Pure Food and Drug Act, 1906). In France, the 10-hour work day (1904) and separation of church and state (1905) were reform victories, as was universal suffrage in Austria (1907).

**Arts**. An unprecedented period of experimentation, centered in France, produced several new **painting** styles: Fauvism exploited bold color areas (Matisse, *Woman with Hat*, 1905); expressionism reflected powerful inner emotions (the Brücke group, 1905); cubism combined several views of an object on one flat surface (Picasso's *Demoiselles*, 1906-7); futurism tried to depict speed and motion (Italian Futurist Manifesto, 1910). **Architects** explored new uses of steel structures, with facades either neoclassical (Adler and Sullivan in U.S.); curvilinear Art Nouveau (Gaudi's Casa Mila, 1905-10); or functionally streamlined (Wright's Robie House, 1909).

**Music and dance** shared the experimental spirit. Ruth St. Denis (1877-1968) and Isadora Duncan (1878-1927) pioneered modern dance, while Diaghilev in Paris revitalized classic ballet from 1909. Composers explored atonal music (Debussy, 1862-1918) and dissonance (Schoenberg, 1874-1951) or revolutionized classical forms (Stravinsky, 1882-1971), often showing jazz or folk music influences.

## War and Revolution: 1910-19

**War threatens**. Germany under Wilhelm II sought a political and imperial role consonant with its industrial strength, challenging Britain's world supremacy and threatening France, which was still resenting the loss (1871) of Alsace-Lorraine. Austria wanted to curb an expanded Serbia (after 1912) and the threat it posed to its own Slav lands. Russia feared Austrian and German political and economic aims in the Balkans and Turkey. An accelerated arms race resulted: The German standing army rose to more than 2 million men by 1914. Russia and France had more than a million each, and Austria and the British Empire nearly a million each. Dozens of enormous battleships were built by the powers after 1906.

The **assassination of Austrian Archduke Franz Ferdinand** by a Serbian, June 28, 1914, was the pretext for war. The system of alliances made the conflict Europe-wide; Germany's invasion of Belgium to outflank France forced Britain to enter the war. Patriotic fervor was nearly unanimous among all classes in most countries.

**World War I**. German forces were stopped in France in one month. The rival armies dug **trench networks**. Artillery and improved machine guns prevented either side from any lasting advance despite repeated assaults (600,000 dead at **Verdun**, Feb.-July 1916). Poison gas, used by Germany in 1915, proved ineffective. More than 1 million U.S. troops tipped the balance after mid-1917, forcing Germany to sue for peace the next year. The formal armistice was signed at 5 AM, Nov. 11, 1918.

In the E, the Russian armies were thrown back (battle of **Tannenberg**, Aug. 20, 1914), and the war grew unpopular in Russia. An allied attempt to relieve Russia through Turkey failed (**Gallipoli,** 1915). The **Russian Revolution** (1917) abolished the monarchy. The new Bolshevik regime signed the capitulatory Brest-Litovsk peace in March 1918. Italy entered the war on the allied side in May 1915 but was pushed back by Oct. 1917. A renewed offensive with Allied aid in Oct.-Nov. 1918 forced Austria to surrender.

The British Navy successfully blockaded Germany, which responded with submarine U-boat attacks; **unrestricted submarine warfare** against neutrals after Jan. 1917 helped bring the U.S. into the war. Other battlefields included Palestine and Mesopotamia, both of which Britain wrested from the Turks in 1917, and the African and Pacific colonies of Germany, most of which fell to Britain, France, Australia, Japan, and South Africa.

From 1916, the civilian populations and economies of both sides were mobilized to an unprecedented degree. Hardships intensified among fighting nations in 1917 (French mutiny crushed in May). More than 10 million soldiers died in the war.

**Settlement**. At the **Paris Peace Conference** (Jan.-June 1919), concluded by the **Treaty of Versailles**, and in subsequent negotiations and local wars (Russian-Polish War, 1920), the map of Europe was redrawn with a nod to U.S. Pres. Wilson's principle of self-determination. Austria and Hungary were separated, and much of their land was given to Yugoslavia (formerly Serbia), Romania, Italy, and the newly independent Poland and Czechoslovakia. Germany lost territory in the W, N, and E, while Finland and the Baltic states were detached from Russia. Turkey lost nearly all its Arab lands to British-sponsored Arab states or to direct French and British rule. Belgium's sovereignty was recognized.

A huge **reparations** burden and partial demilitarization were imposed on Germany. Pres. Wilson obtained approval for a League of Nations, but the U.S. Senate refused to allow the U.S. to join.

**Russian revolution**. Military defeats and high casualties caused a contagious lack of confidence in Tsar Nicholas, who was forced to abdicate Mar. 1917. A liberal provisional government failed to end the war, and massive desertions, riots, and fighting between factions followed. A moderate socialist government under Kerensky was overthrown in a violent coup by the **Bolsheviks** in Petrograd under **Lenin,** who disbanded the elected Constituent Assembly in Nov. 1917.

The Bolsheviks brutally suppressed all opposition and ended the war with Germany in Mar. 1918. **Civil war** broke out in the summer between the Red Army, including the Bolsheviks and their supporters, and monarchists, anarchists, nationalities (Ukrainians, Georgians, Poles), and others. Small U.S., British, French, and Japanese units also opposed the Bolsheviks (1918-19; Japan in Vladivostok to 1922). The civil war, anarchy, and pogroms devastated the country until the 1920 Red Army victory. The wartime total monopoly of political, economic, and police power by the Communist Party leadership was retained.

**Other European revolutions**. An unpopular monarchy in **Portugal** was overthrown in 1910. The new republic took severe anticlerical measures in 1911.

After a century of Home Rule agitation, during which **Ireland** was devastated by famine (1 million dead, 1846-47) and emigration, republican militants staged an unsuccessful uprising in Dublin during Easter 1916. The execution of the leaders and mass arrests by the British won popular support for the rebels. The Irish Free State, comprising all but the 6 N counties, achieved dominion status in 1922.

In the aftermath of the world war, radical revolutions were attempted in Germany (**Spartacist** uprising, Jan. 1919), **Hungary** (Kun regime, 1919), and elsewhere. All were suppressed or failed for lack of support.

**Chinese revolution**. The Manchu Dynasty was overthrown and a republic proclaimed in Oct. 1911. First president Sun Yat-sen resigned in favor of strongman Yuan Shih-k'ai. Sun organized the parliamentarian **Kuomintang** party.

Students launched protests on May 4, 1919, against League of Nations concessions in China to Japan. Nationalist, liberal, and socialist ideas and political groups spread. The **Communist Party** was founded in 1921. A Communist regime took power in Mongolia with Soviet support in 1921.

**India restive**. Indian objections to British rule erupted in nationalist riots as well as in the nonviolent tactics of Gandhi (1869-1948). Nearly 400 unarmed demonstrators were shot at **Amritsar** in Apr. 1919. Britain approved limited self-rule that year.

**Mexican revolution**. Under the long Diaz dictatorship (1877-1911) the economy advanced, but Indian and mestizo lands were confiscated, and concessions to foreigners (mostly U.S.) damaged the middle class. A **revolution in 1910** led to civil wars and U.S. intervention (1914, 1916-17). Land reform and a more democratic constitution (1917) were achieved.

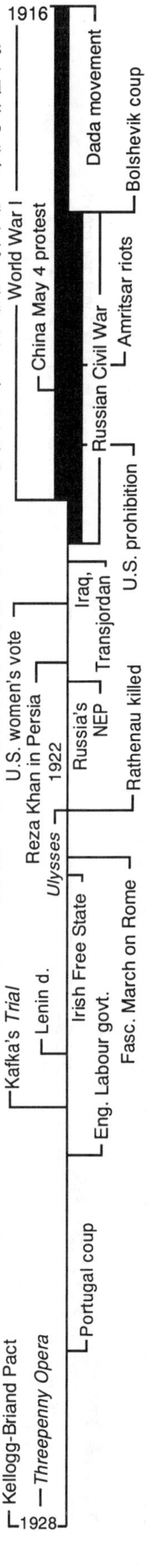

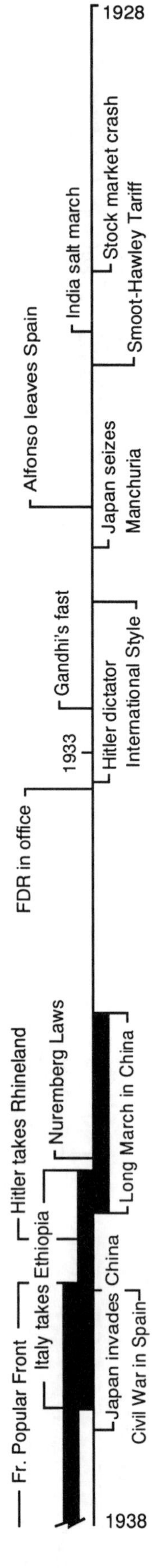


## The Aftermath of War: 1920-29

**U.S.** Easy credit, technological ingenuity, and war-related industrial decline in Europe caused a long economic boom, in which ownership of the new products—autos, phones, radios—became democratized. Prosperity, an increase in women workers, woman suffrage (1920), and drastic change in fashion (flappers, mannish bob for women, clean-shaven men) created a wide perception of social change, despite prohibition of alcoholic beverages (1919-33). Union membership and strikes increased. Fear of radicals led to Palmer raids (1919-20) and the Sacco/Vanzetti case (1921-27).

**Europe sorts itself out.** Germany's liberal **Weimar constitution** (1919) could not guarantee a stable government in the face of rightist violence (Rathenau assassinated, 1922) and Communist refusal to cooperate with Socialists. Reparations and Allied occupation of the Rhineland caused staggering inflation that destroyed middle-class savings, but economic expansion resumed after mid-decade, aided by U.S. loans. A sophisticated, innovative culture developed in architecture and design (Bauhaus, 1919-28), film (Lang, *M*, 1931), painting (Grosz), music (Weill, *Threepenny Opera*, 1928), theater (Brecht, *A Man's a Man*, 1926), criticism (Benjamin), philosophy (Jung), and fashion. This culture was considered decadent and socially disruptive by rightists.

**England** elected its first Labour governments (Jan. 1924, June 1929). A 10-day general strike in support of coal miners failed in May 1926. In **Italy**, strikes, political chaos, and violence by small Fascist bands culminated in the Oct. 1922 Fascist March on Rome, which established Mussolini's dictatorship. Strikes were outlawed (1926), and Italian influence was pressed in the Balkans (Albania a protectorate, 1926). A conservative dictatorship was also established in **Portugal** in a 1926 military coup.

**Czechoslovakia**, the only stable democracy to emerge from the war in Central or East Europe, faced opposition from Germans (in the Sudetenland), Ruthenians, and some Slovaks. As the industrial heartland of the old Hapsburg empire, it remained fairly prosperous. With French backing, it formed the Little Entente with Yugoslavia (1920) and **Romania** (1921) to block Austrian or Hungarian irredentism. Hungary remained dominated by the landholding classes and expansionist feeling. Croats and Slovenes in **Yugoslavia** demanded a federal state until King Alexander I proclaimed (1929) a royal dictatorship. Poland faced nationality problems as well (Germans, Ukrainians, Jews); Pilsudski ruled as dictator from 1926. The Baltic states were threatened by traditionally dominant ethnic Germans and by Soviet-supported Communists.

An economic collapse and famine in **Russia** (1921-22) claimed 5 million lives. The New Economic Policy (1921) allowed landownership by peasants and some private commerce and industry. Stalin was absolute ruler within 4 years of Lenin's death (1924). He inaugurated a brutal collectivization program (1929-32) and used foreign Communist parties for Soviet state advantage.

**Internationalism.** Revulsion against World War I led to pacifist agitation, to the Kellogg-Briand Pact renouncing aggressive war (1928), and to **naval disarmament** pacts (Washington, 1922; London, 1930). But the League of Nations was able to arbitrate only minor disputes (Greece-Bulgaria, 1925).

**Middle East.** Mustafa Kemal (Ataturk) led **Turkish** nationalists in resisting Italian, French, and Greek military advances (1919-23). The sultanate was abolished (1922), and elaborate reforms were passed, including secularization of law and adoption of the Latin alphabet. Ethnic conflict led to persecution of **Armenians** (more than 1 million dead in 1915, 1 million expelled), Greeks (forced Greek-Turk population exchange, 1923), and Kurds (1925 uprising).

With evacuation of the Turks from **Arab** lands, the puritanical Wahabi dynasty of E Arabia conquered (1919-25) what is now Saudi Arabia. British, French, and Arab dynastic and nationalist maneuvering resulted in the creation of 2 more Arab monarchies in 1921—Iraq and Transjordan (both under British control)—and 2 French mandates—Syria and Lebanon. Jewish immigration into British-mandated **Palestine**, inspired by the Zionist movement, was resisted by Arabs, at times violently (1921, 1929 massacres).

Reza Khan ruled **Persia** after his 1921 coup (shah from 1925), centralized control, and created the trappings of a modern state.

**China.** The Kuomintang under **Chiang Kai-shek** (1887-1975) subdued the warlords by 1928. The Communists were brutally suppressed after their alliance with the Kuomintang was broken in 1927. Relative peace thereafter allowed for industrial and financial improvements, with some Russian, British, and U.S. cooperation.

**Arts.** Nearly all bounds of subject matter, style, and attitude were broken in the arts of the period. **Abstract** art first took inspiration from natural forms or narrative themes (Kandinsky from 1911) and then worked free of any representational aims (Malevich's suprematism, 1915-19; Mondrian's geometric style from 1917). The **Dada** movement (from 1916) mocked artistic pretension with absurd collages and constructions (Arp, Tzara, from 1916). Paradox, illusion, and psychological taboos were exploited by **surrealists** by the latter 1920s (Dali, Magritte). Architectural schools celebrated industrial values, whether vigorous abstract constructivism (Tatlin, *Monument to 3rd International*, 1919) or the machined, streamlined **Bauhaus** style, which was extended to many design fields (Helvetica typeface).

Prose writers explored revolutionary narrative modes related to dreams (Kafka's *Trial*, 1925), internal monologue (Joyce's **Ulysses**, 1922), and word play (Stein's *Making of Americans*, 1925). Poets and novelists wrote of modern alienation (Eliot's *Waste Land*, 1922) and aimlessness (Lost Generation).

**Sciences.** Scientific specialization prevailed by the 20th cent. Advances in knowledge and technological aptitude increased with the geometric rise in the number of practitioners. Physicists challenged common-sense views of causality, observation, and a mechanistic universe, putting science further beyond popular grasp (**Einstein's** general theory of relativity, 1915; Bohr's quantum mechanics, 1913; Heisenberg's uncertainty principle, 1927).

## Rise of Totalitarians: 1930-39

**Depression.** A worldwide financial panic and economic depression began with the Oct. 1929 U.S. stock market crash and the May 1931 failure of the Austrian Credit-Anstalt. A credit crunch caused international bankruptcies and **unemployment**: 12 million jobless by 1932 in the U.S., 5.6 million in Germany, 2.7 million in England. Governments responded with **tariff restrictions** (Smoot-Hawley Act,

1930; Ottawa Imperial Conference, 1932), which dried up world trade. Government public works programs were vitiated by deflationary budget balancing.

**Germany**. Years of agitation by violent extremists were brought to a head by the Depression. Nazi leader **Hitler** was named chancellor by Pres. Hindenburg in Jan. 1933 and given dictatorial power by the Reichstag in March. Opposition parties were disbanded, strikes banned, and all aspects of economic, cultural, and religious life were brought under central government and Nazi party control and manipulated by sophisticated propaganda. Severe persecution of Jews began (**Nuremberg Laws,** Sept. 1935). Many Jews, political opponents, and others were sent to concentration camps (Dachau, 1933), where thousands died or were killed. Public works, renewed conscription (1935), arms production, and a 4-year plan (1936) all but ended unemployment.

Hitler's expansionism started with reincorporation of the Saar (1935), occupation of the **Rhineland** (Mar. 1936), and annexation of Austria (Mar. 1938). At **Munich** (Sept. 1938) an indecisive Britain and France sanctioned German dismemberment of Czechoslovakia.

**Russia**. Urbanization and education advanced. Rapid industrialization was achieved through successive **5-year-plans** starting in 1928, using severe labor discipline and mass forced labor. Industry was financed by a decline in living standards and exploitation of agriculture, which was almost totally collectivized by the early 1930s (*kolkhoz*, collective farm; *sovkhoz*, state farm, often in newly worked lands). Successive **purges** increased the role of professionals and management at the expense of workers. Millions perished in a series of manufactured disasters: elimination (1929-34) of kulaks (peasant landowners), severe famine (1932-33), party purges and show trials (Great Purge, 1936-38), suppression of nationalities, and poor conditions in labor camps.

**Spain**. An industrial revolution during World War I created an urban proletariat, which was attracted to socialism and anarchism; Catalan nationalists challenged central authority. The 5 years after King Alfonso left Spain in Apr. 1931 were dominated by tension between intermittent leftist and anticlerical governments and clericals, monarchists, and other rightists. Anarchist and Communist rebellions were crushed, but a July 1936 extreme right rebellion led by Gen. Francisco Franco and aided by Nazi Germany and Fascist Italy succeeded, after a 3-year **civil war** (more than 1 million dead in battles and atrocities). The war polarized international public opinion.

**Italy**. Despite propaganda for the ideal of the Corporate State, few domestic reforms were attempted. An entente with Hungary and Austria (Mar. 1934), a pact with Germany and Japan (Nov. 1937), and intervention by 50,000-75,000 troops in Spain (1936-39) sealed Italy's identification with the fascist bloc (anti-Semitic laws after Mar. 1938). Ethiopia was conquered (1935-36), and **Albania** annexed (Jan. 1939) in conscious imitation of ancient Rome.

**East Europe**. Repressive regimes fought for power against an active opposition (liberals, socialists, Communists, peasants, Nazis). Minority groups and Jews were restricted within national boundaries that did not coincide with ethnic population patterns. In the destruction of **Czechoslovakia**, **Hungary** occupied S Slovakia (Nov. 1938) and Ruthenia (Mar. 1939), and a pro-Nazi regime took power in the rest of Slovakia. Other boundary disputes (e.g., Poland-Lithuania, Yugoslavia-Bulgaria, Romania-Hungary) doomed attempts to build joint fronts against Germany or Russia. Economic depression was severe.

**East Asia**. After a period of liberalism in **Japan**, nativist militarists dominated the government with peasant support. Manchuria was seized (Sept. 1931-Feb. 1932), and a puppet state was set up (Manchukuo). Adjacent Jehol (Inner Mongolia) was occupied in 1933. China proper was invaded in July 1937; large areas were conquered by Oct. 1938.

In **China** Communist forces left Kuomintang-besieged strongholds in the S in a Long March (1934-35) to the N. The Kuomintang-Communist civil war was suspended in Jan. 1937 in the face of threatening Japan.

**The democracies**. The Roosevelt Administration, in office Mar. 1933, embarked on an extensive program of **New Deal** social reform and economic stimulation, including protection for labor unions (heavy industries organized), Social Security, public works, wage-and-hour laws, and assistance to farmers. Isolationist sentiment (1937 Neutrality Act) prevented U.S. intervention in Europe, but military expenditures were increased in 1939.

French political instability and polarization prevented resolution of economic and international security questions. The **Popular Front** government under Blum (June 1936-Apr. 1938) passed social reforms (40-hour week) and raised arms spending. National coalition governments, which ruled Britain from Aug. 1931, brought some economic recovery but failed to define a consistent international policy until Chamberlain's government (from May 1937), which practiced deliberate **appeasement** of Germany and Italy.

**India**. Twenty years of agitation for autonomy and then for independence (Gandhi's **salt march**, 1930) achieved some constitutional reform (extended provincial powers, 1935) despite Muslim-Hindu strife. Social issues assumed prominence with peasant uprisings (1921), strikes (1928), Gandhi's efforts for untouchables (1932 "fast unto death"), and social and agrarian reform by the provinces after 1937.

**Arts**. The streamlined, geometric design motifs of Art Deco (from 1925) prevailed through the 1930s. **Abstract art** flourished (Moore sculptures from 1931) alongside a new **realism** related to social and political concerns (Socialist Realism, the official Soviet style from 1934; Mexican muralist Rivera, 1886-1957; and Orozco, 1883-1949), which were also expressed in fiction and poetry (Steinbeck's *Grapes of Wrath*, 1939; Sandburg's *The People, Yes*, 1936). Modern architecture (International Style, 1932) was unchallenged in its use of artificial materials (concrete, glass), lack of decoration, and monumentality (Rockefeller Center, 1929-40). U.S.-made films captured a worldwide audience with their larger-than-life fantasies (*Gone With the Wind*, 1939).

## War, Hot and Cold: 1940-49

**War in Europe**. The Nazi-Soviet nonaggression pact (Aug. 1939) freed Germany to attack Poland (Sept.). Britain and France, who had guaranteed Polish independence, declared war on Germany. Russia seized E Poland (Sept.), attacked Finland (Nov.), and took the Baltic states (July 1940). Mobile German forces staged *blitzkrieg* attacks during Apr.-June 1940, conquering neutral Denmark, Norway, and the Low Countries and defeating France; 350,000 British and French troops were evacuated at **Dunkirk**

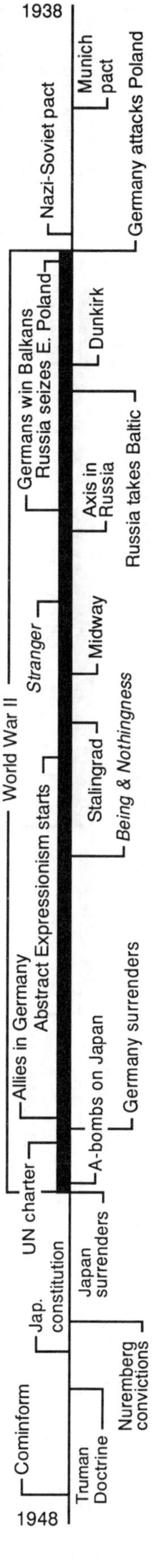

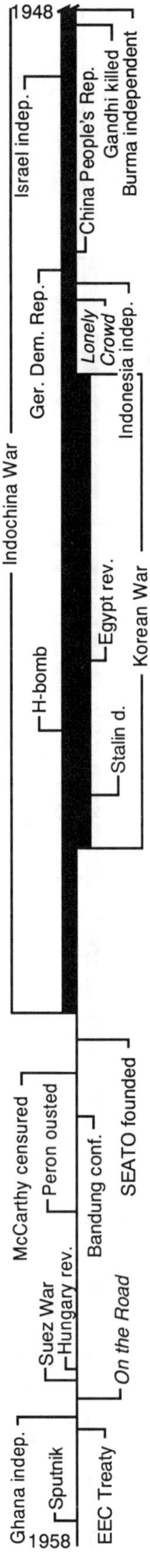


(May). The Battle of Britain (June-Dec. 1940) denied Germany air superiority. German-Italian campaigns won the Balkans by Apr. 1941. Three million Axis troops **invaded Russia** in June 1941, marching through Ukraine to the Caucasus, and through White Russia and the Baltic republics to Moscow and Leningrad.

Russian winter counterthrusts (1941-42 and 1942-43) stopped the German advance (Stalingrad, Sept. 1942-Feb. 1943). With British and U.S. Lend-Lease aid and sustaining great casualties, the Russians drove the Axis from all E Europe and the Balkans in the next 2 years. Invasions of N Africa (Nov. 1942), Italy (Sept. 1943), and **Normandy** (June 1944) brought U.S., British, Free French, and allied troops to Germany by spring 1945. Germany surrendered May 7, 1945.

**War in Asia-Pacific**. Japan occupied Indochina in Sept. 1940, dominated Thailand in Dec. 1941, and attacked Hawaii, the Philippines, Hong Kong, Malaya on Dec. 7, 1941. Indonesia was attacked in Jan. 1942, and Burma was conquered in Mar. 1942. The Battle of **Midway** (June 1942) turned back the Japanese advance. "Island-hopping" battles (Guadalcanal, Aug. 1942-Jan. 1943; **Leyte Gulf,** Oct. 1944; Iwo Jima, Feb.-Mar. 1945; Okinawa, Apr. 1945) and massive bombing raids on Japan from June 1944 wore out Japanese defenses. U.S. atom bombs, dropped Aug. 6 and 9 on **Hiroshima** and Nagasaki, forced Japan to agree, on Aug. 14, to surrender; formal surrender was on Sept. 2, 1945.

**Atrocities**. The war brought 20th-cent. cruelty to its peak. The Nazi regime systematically killed 5-6 million Jews, including some 3 million who died in death camps (e.g., **Auschwitz**). Gypsies, political opponents, sick and retarded people, and others deemed undesirable were also murdered by the Nazis, as were vast numbers of Slavs, especially leaders.

**Civilian deaths**. German bombs killed 70,000 British civilians. Some 100,000 Chinese civilians were killed by Japanese forces in the capture of Nanking. Severe retaliation by the Soviet army, E European partisans, Free French, and others took a heavy toll. U.S. and British bombing of Germany killed hundreds of thousands, as did U.S. bombing of Japan (80,000-200,000 at Hiroshima alone). Some 45 million people lost their lives in the war.

**Settlement**. The **United Nations** charter was signed in San Francisco on June 26, 1945, by 50 nations. The International Tribunal at **Nuremberg** convicted 22 German leaders for war crimes in Sept. 1946; 23 Japanese leaders were convicted in Nov. 1948. Postwar border changes included large gains in territory for the USSR, losses for Germany, a shift to the west in Polish borders, and minor losses for Italy. Communist regimes, supported by Soviet troops, took power in most of E Europe, including Soviet-occupied Germany (GDR proclaimed Oct. 1949). Japan lost all overseas lands.

**Recovery**. Basic political and social changes were imposed on Japan and W Germany by the western allies (Japan constitution adopted, Nov. 1946; W German basic law, May 1949). U.S. Marshall Plan aid ($12 billion, 1947-51) spurred W European economic recovery after a period of severe inflation and strikes in Europe and the U.S. The British Labour Party introduced a national health service and nationalized basic industries in 1946.

**Cold War**. Western fears of further Soviet advances (Cominform formed in Oct. 1947; Czechoslovakia coup, Feb. 1948; Berlin blockade, Apr. 1948-Sept. 1949) led to the formation of **NATO**. Civil War in Greece and Soviet pressure on Turkey led to U.S. aid under the Truman Doctrine (Mar. 1947). Other anti-Communist security pacts were the Organization of American States (Apr. 1948) and the Southeast Asia Treaty Organization (Sept. 1954). A new wave of Soviet purges and repression intensified in the last years of Stalin's rule, extending to E Europe (Slansky trial in Czechoslovakia, 1951). Only Yugoslavia resisted Soviet control (expelled by Cominform, June 1948; U.S. aid, June 1949).

**China, Korea**. Communist forces emerged from World War II strengthened by the Soviet takeover of industrial Manchuria. In 4 years of fighting, the Kuomintang was driven from the mainland; the People's Republic was proclaimed Oct. 1, 1949. Korea was divided by USSR and U.S. occupation forces. Separate republics were proclaimed in the 2 zones in Aug.-Sept. 1948.

**India**. India and Pakistan became independent dominions on Aug. 15, 1947. Millions of Hindu and Muslim refugees were created by the partition; riots (1946-47) took hundreds of thousands of lives; Gandhi was assassinated in Jan. 1948. Burma became completely independent in Jan. 1948; Ceylon took dominion status in Feb.

**Middle East**. The UN approved partition of Palestine into Jewish and Arab states. Israel was proclaimed on May 14, 1948. Arabs rejected partition, but failed to defeat Israel in war (May 1948-July 1949). Immigration from Europe and the Middle East swelled Israel's Jewish population. British and French forces left Lebanon and Syria in 1946. Transjordan occupied most of Arab Palestine.

**Southeast Asia**. Communists and others fought against restoration of French rule in Indochina from 1946; a non-Communist government was recognized by France in Mar. 1949, but fighting continued. Both Indonesia and the Philippines became independent; the former in 1949 after 4 years of war with Netherlands, the latter in 1946. Philippine economic and military ties with the U.S. remained strong; a Communist-led peasant rising was checked in 1948.

**Arts**. New York became the center of the world art market; **abstract expressionism** was the chief mode (Pollock from 1943, de Kooning from 1947). Literature and philosophy explored **existentialism** (Camus's *Stranger*, 1942; Sartre's *Being and Nothingness*, 1943). Non-Western attempts to revive or create regional styles (Senghor's Négritude, Mishima's novels) only confirmed the emergence of a universal culture. Radio and phonograph records spread American popular music (swing, bebop) around the world.

## The American Decade: 1950-59

**Polite decolonization**. The peaceful decline of European political and military power in Asia and Africa accelerated in the 1950s. Nearly all of **N Africa** was freed by 1956, but France fought a bitter war to retain Algeria, with its large European minority, until 1962. **Ghana**, independent in 1957, led a parade of new black African nations (more than 2 dozen by 1962), which altered the political character of the UN. Ethnic disputes often exploded in the new nations after decolonization (UN troops in Cyprus, 1964; **Nigeria** civil war, 1967-70). Leaders of the new states, mostly sharing socialist ideologies, tried to create an Afro-Asian bloc (Bandung Conference, 1955), but Western economic influence and U.S. political ties remained strong (Baghdad Pact, 1955).

**Trade**. World trade volume soared, in an atmosphere of monetary stability assured by international accords (**Bretton Woods,** 1944). In Europe, economic integration advanced (**European Economic Community,** 1957; European Free Trade Association, 1960). Comecon (1949) coordinated the economies of Soviet-bloc countries.

**U.S**. Economic growth produced an abundance of consumer goods (9.3 million motor vehicles sold, 1955). Suburban housing tracts changed life patterns for middle and working classes (Levittown, 1946-51). **Eisenhower's** landslide election victories (1952, 1956) reflected consensus politics. Senate condemnation of **McCarthy** (Dec. 1954) curbed the political abuse of anti-Communism. A system of alliances and military bases bolstered U.S. influence on all continents. Trade and payments surpluses were balanced by overseas investments and foreign aid ($50 billion, 1950-59).

**USSR**. In the "thaw" after Stalin's death in 1953, relations with the West improved (evacuation of Vienna, Geneva summit conference, both 1955). Repression of scientific and cultural life eased, and many prisoners were freed or rehabilitated culminating in **de-Stalinization** (1956). **Khrushchev's** leadership aimed at consumer sector growth, but farm production lagged, despite the virgin lands program (from 1954). Soviet crushing of the 1956 Hungarian revolution, the 1960 U-2 spy plane episode, and other incidents renewed East-West tension and domestic curbs.

**East Europe**. Resentment of Russian domination and Stalinist repression combined with nationalist, economic, and religious factors to produce periodic violence. East Berlin workers rioted (1953), Polish workers rioted in Poznan (June 1956), and a broad-based revolution broke out in Hungary (Oct. 1956). All were suppressed by Soviet force or threats (at least 7,000 dead in Hungary). But Poland was allowed to restore private ownership of farms, and a degree of personal and economic freedom returned to Hungary. Yugoslavia experimented with worker self-management and a market economy.

**Korea**. The 1945 division of Korea along the 38th parallel left industry in the N, which was organized into a militant regime and armed by the USSR. The S was politically disunited. More than 60,000 North Korean troops invaded the S on June 25, 1950. The U.S., backed by the UN Security Council, sent troops. UN troops reached the Chinese border in Nov. Some 200,000 Chinese troops crossed the Yalu R. and drove back UN forces. By spring 1951 battle lines had become stabilized near the original 38th parallel border, but heavy fighting continued. Finally, an armistice was signed on July 27, 1953. U.S. troops remained in the S, and U.S. economic and military aid continued. The war stimulated rapid economic recovery in Japan.

**China**. Starting in 1952, industry, agriculture, and social institutions were forcibly collectivized. In a massive purge, as many as several million people were executed as Kuomintang supporters or as class and political enemies. The Great Leap Forward (1958-60) unsuccessfully tried to force the pace of development by substituting labor for investment.

**Indochina**. Ho Chi Minh's forces, aided by the USSR and the new Chinese Communist government, fought French and pro-French Vietnamese forces to a standstill and captured the strategic Dienbienphu camp in May 1954. The Geneva Agreements divided Vietnam in half pending elections (never held) and recognized Laos and Cambodia as independent. The U.S. aided the anti-Communist Republic of Vietnam in the S.

**Middle East**. Arab revolutions placed leftist, militantly nationalist regimes in power in Egypt (1952) and Iraq (1958). But Arab unity attempts failed (United Arab Republic joined Egypt, Syria, Yemen, 1958-61). Arab refusal to recognize Israel (Arab League economic blockade began Sept. 1951) led to a permanent state of war, with repeated incidents (Gaza, 1955). Israel occupied Sinai, and Britain and France took (Oct. 1956) the Suez Canal, but were replaced by the UN Emergency Force. The Mossadegh government in Iran nationalized (May 1951) the British-owned oil industry May, but was overthrown (Aug. 1953) in a U.S.-aided coup.

**Latin America**. Argentinian Dictator Juan Perón, in office 1946, enforced land reform, some nationalization, welfare state measures, and curbs on the Roman Catholic Church, and crushed opposition. A Sept. 1955 coup deposed Perón. The 1952 revolution in Bolivia brought land reform, nationalization of tin mines, and improvement in the status of Indians, who nevertheless remained poor. The Batista regime in Cuba was overthrown (Jan. 1959) by Fidel Castro, who imposed a Communist dictatorship, aligned Cuba with the USSR, and improved education and health care. A U.S.-backed anti-Castro invasion (Bay of Pigs, Apr. 1961) was crushed. Self-government advanced in the British Caribbean.

**Technology**. Large outlays on research and development in the U.S. and the USSR focused on military applications (H-bomb in U.S., 1952; USSR, 1953; Britain, 1957; intercontinental missiles, late 1950s). Soviet launching of the Sputnik satellite (Oct. 1957) spurred increases in U.S. science education funds (National Defense Education Act).

**Literature and film**. Alienation from social and literary conventions reached an extreme in the theater of the absurd (Beckett's *Waiting for Godot,* 1952), the "new novel" (Robbe-Grillet's *Voyeur,* 1955), and avant-garde film (Antonioni's *L'Avventura,* 1960). U.S. beatniks (Kerouac's *On the Road,* 1957) and others rejected the supposed conformism of Americans (Riesman's *The Lonely Crowd,* 1950).

## Rising Expectations: 1960-69

**Economic boom**. The longest sustained economic boom on record spanned almost the entire decade in the capitalist world; the closely watched GNP figure doubled (1960-70) in the U.S., fueled by Vietnam War–related budget deficits. The **General Agreement on Tariffs and Trade** (1967) stimulated W European prosperity, which spread to peripheral areas (Spain, Italy, E Germany). Japan became a top economic power. Foreign investment aided the industrialization of Brazil. There were limited Soviet economic reform attempts.

**Reform and radicalization**. Pres. John F. Kennedy, inaugurated 1961, emphasized youthful idealism and vigor; he was assassinated Nov. 22, 1963. A series of political and social reform movements took root in the U.S., later spreading to other countries. Blacks demonstrated nonviolently and with partial success against segregation and poverty (1963 March on Washington; 1964 **Civil Rights Act**), but some urban ghettos erupted in extensive riots (Watts, 1965; Detroit, 1967; King assassination, Apr. 4, 1968). New concern for the poor (Harrington's *Other America,* 1963) helped lead to Pres. Johnson's **"Great Society"** programs (Medicare, Water Quality Act, Higher Education Act, all 1965). Concern

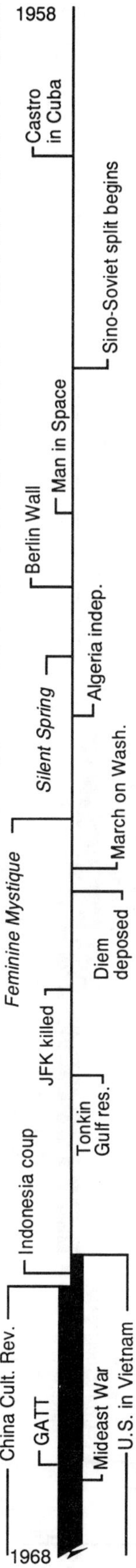

with the **environment** surged (Carson's *Silent Spring*, 1962). **Feminism** revived as a cultural and political movement (Friedan's *Feminine Mystique*, 1963; National Organization for Women founded 1966), and a movement for homosexual rights emerged (Stonewall riot in NYC, 1969). Pope John XXIII called the Second Vatican Council (1962-65), which liberalized Roman Catholic liturgy and some other aspects of Catholicism.

Opposition to U.S. involvement in Vietnam, especially among university students (**Moratorium** protest, Nov. 1969), turned violent (Weatherman Chicago riots, Oct. 1969). **New Left** and Marxist theories became popular, and membership in radical groups (Students for a Democratic Society, Black Panthers) increased. Maoist groups, especially in Europe, called for total transformation of society. In France, students sparked a nationwide strike affecting 10 million workers in May-June 1968, but an electoral reaction barred revolutionary change.

**Arts and styles**. The boundary between fine and popular arts was blurred in the 1960s by Pop Art (Warhol) and rock musicals (*Hair*, 1968). Informality and exaggeration prevailed in fashion (beards, miniskirts). A nonpolitical "counterculture" developed, rejecting traditional bourgeois life goals and personal habits, and use of marijuana and hallucinogens spread (Woodstock festival, Aug. 1969). Indian influence was felt in religion (Ram Dass) and fashion, and The Beatles, who brought unprecedented sophistication to rock music, became for many a symbol of the decade.

**Science**. Achievements in space (**humans on the moon,** July 1969) and electronics (lasers, integrated circuits) encouraged a faith in scientific solutions to problems in agriculture ("green revolution"), medicine (heart transplants, 1967), and other areas. Harmful effects of science, it was believed, could be controlled (1963 nuclear weapon test ban treaty, 1968 nonproliferation treaty).

**China**. Mao's revolutionary militancy caused disputes with the USSR under "revisionist" Khrushchev, starting in 1960. The 2 powers exchanged fire in 1969 border disputes. China used force to capture (1962) areas disputed with India. The **"Great Proletarian Cultural Revolution"** tried to impose a utopian egalitarian program in China and spread revolution abroad; political struggle, often violent, convulsed China in 1965-68.

**Indochina**. Communist-led guerrillas aided by N Vietnam fought from 1960 against the S Vietnam government of Ngo Dinh Diem (killed 1963). The U.S. military role increased after the 1964 Tonkin Gulf incident. U.S. forces peaked at 543,400 in Apr. 1969. Massive numbers of N Vietnamese troops also fought. Laotian and Cambodian neutrality were threatened by Communist insurgencies, with N Vietnamese aid, and U.S. intrigues.

**Third World**. A bloc of authoritarian leftist regimes among the newly independent nations emerged in political opposition to the U.S.-led Western alliance and came to dominate the conference of nonaligned nations (Belgrade, 1961; Cairo, 1964; Lusaka, 1970). Soviet political ties and military bases were established in Cuba, Egypt, Algeria, Guinea, and other countries, whose leaders were regarded as revolutionary heroes by opposition groups in pro-Western or colonial countries. Some leaders were ousted in coups by pro-Western groups—Zaire's Lumumba (killed 1961), Ghana's Nkrumah (exiled 1966), and Indonesia's Sukarno (effectively ousted in 1965 after a Communist coup failed).

**Middle East**. Arab-Israeli tension erupted into a brief war June 1967. Israel emerged as a major regional power. Military shipments before and after the war brought much of the Arab world into the Soviet political sphere. Most Arab states broke U.S. diplomatic ties, while Communist countries cut their ties to Israel. Intra-Arab disputes continued: Egypt and Saudi Arabia supported rival factions in a bloody Yemen civil war 1962-70; Lebanese troops fought Palestinian commandos 1969.

**East Europe**. To stop the large-scale exodus of citizens, E German authorities built (Aug. 1961) a **fortified wall across Berlin.** Soviet sway in the Balkans was weakened by Albania's support of China (USSR broke ties in Dec. 1961) and Romania's assertion (1964) of industrial and foreign policy autonomy. Liberalization (spring 1968) in Czechoslovakia was crushed with massive force by troops of 5 Warsaw Pact countries. W German treaties (1970) with the USSR and Poland facilitated the transfer of German technology and confirmed postwar boundaries.

## Disillusionment: 1970-79

**U.S.: Caution and neoconservatism**. A relatively sluggish economy, energy and resource shortages (natural gas crunch, 1975; gasoline shortage, 1979), and environmental problems contributed to a **"limits of growth"** philosophy. Suspicion of science and technology killed or delayed major projects (supersonic transport dropped, 1971; Seabrook nuclear power plant protests, 1977-78) and was fed by the Three Mile Island nuclear reactor accident (Mar. 1979).

Mistrust of big government weakened support for government reform plans among liberals. School busing and racial quotas were opposed (Bakke decision, June 1978); the Equal Rights Amendment for women languished; civil rights for homosexuals were opposed (Dade County referendum, June 1977).

Completion of Communist forces' takeover of **S Vietnam** (evacuation of U.S. civilians, Apr. 1975), revelations of Central Intelligence Agency misdeeds (Rockefeller Commission report, June 1975), and **Watergate** scandals (Nixon resigned in Aug. 1974) reduced faith in U.S. moral and material capacity to influence world affairs. Revelations of Soviet crimes (Solzhenitsyn's *Gulag Archipelago,* 1974) and Russian intervention in Africa aided a revival of anti-Communist sentiment.

**Economy sluggish**. The 1960s boom faltered in the 1970s; a severe recession in the U.S. and Europe (1974-75) followed a huge oil price hike (Dec. 1973). Monetary instability (U.S. cut ties to gold in Aug. 1971), the decline of the dollar, and **protectionist** moves by industrial countries (1977-78) threatened trade. Business investment and spending for research declined. Severe inflation plagued many countries (25% in Britain, 1975; 18% in U.S., 1979).

**China picks up pieces**. After the 1976 deaths of Mao and Zhou, a power struggle for the leadership succession was won by pragmatists. A nationwide purge of orthodox Maoists was carried out, and the **Gang of Four** led by Mao's widow, Chiang Ching, were arrested.

The new leaders freed more than 100,000 political prisoners and reduced public adulation of Mao. Political and trade ties were expanded with Japan, Europe, and the U.S. in the late 1970s, as relations worsened with the USSR, Cuba, and Vietnam (4-week invasion by China, 1979). Ideological guidelines in industry, science, education, and the armed forces, which the ruling faction said had caused chaos and decline, were reversed (bonuses to workers, Dec. 1977; exams for college entrance, Oct. 1977). Severe restrictions on cultural expression were eased (Beethoven ban lifted, Mar. 1977).

**Europe**. European unity moves (EEC-EFTA trade accord, 1972) faltered as economic problems appeared (Britain floated pound, 1972; France floated franc, 1974). Germany and Switzerland curbed guest workers from S Europe. Greece and Turkey quarreled over Cyprus and Aegean oil rights.

All non-Communist Europe was under democratic rule after free elections were held (June 1976) in **Spain** 7 months after the death of Franco. The conservative, colonialist regime in **Portugal** was overthrown in Apr. 1974. In **Greece** the 7-year-old military dictatorship yielded power in 1974. N Europe, though ruled mostly by Socialists (**Swedish** Socialists unseated in 1976 after 44 years in power), turned conservative. The **British** Labour government imposed (1975) wage curbs and suspended nationalization schemes. Terrorism in **Germany** (1972 Munich Olympics killings) led to laws curbing some civil liberties. **French** "new philosophers" rejected leftist ideologies, and the shaky Socialist-Communist coalition lost a 1978 election bid.

**Religion back in politics**. The improvement in Muslim countries' political fortunes by the 1950s (with the exception of Central Asia under Soviet and Chinese rule) and the growth of Arab oil wealth were followed by a resurgence of traditional piety. Libyan dictator Qaddafi mixed Islamic laws with socialism and called for Muslim return to Spain and Sicily. The illegal Muslim Brotherhood in **Egypt** was accused of violence, while extreme groups bombed (1977) theaters to protest secular values.

In **Turkey**, the National Salvation Party was the first Islamic group to share (1974) power since secularization in the 1920s. Religious authorities, such as Ayatollah Ruhollah Khomeini, led the **Iranian** revolution, and religiously motivated Muslims took part in the insurrection in Saudi Arabia that briefly seized (1979) the Grand Mosque in Mecca. Muslim puritan opposition to **Pakistan** Pres. Bhutto helped lead to his overthrow in July 1977. Muslim solidarity, however, could not prevent Pakistan's E province (**Bangladesh**) from declaring (Dec. 1971) independence after a bloody civil war.

Muslim and Hindu resentment of coerced sterilization in **India** helped defeat the Gandhi government, which was replaced (Mar. 1977) by a coalition including religious Hindu parties and led by devout Hindu Desai. Muslims in the S **Philippines**, aided by Libya, rebelled against central rule from 1973.

Evangelical Protestant groups grew in numbers and prosperity in the U.S. A revival of interest in Orthodox Christianity occurred among **Russian** intellectuals (Solzhenitsyn). The secularist **Israeli** Labor party, after decades of rule, was ousted in 1977 by conservatives led by Begin, an observant Jew; religious militants founded settlements on the disputed West Bank, part of biblically promised Israel. U.S. Reform Judaism revived many previously discarded traditional practices.

The Buddhist Soka Gakkai movement launched (1964) the Komeito party in Japan, which became a major opposition party in 1972 and 1976 elections.

Old-fashioned religious wars raged intermittently in **N Ireland** (Catholic vs. Protestant, 1969- ) and **Lebanon** (Christian vs. Muslim, 1975- ) while religious militancy complicated the Israel-Arab dispute (1973 Israel-Arab war). Despite a **1979 peace treaty between Egypt and Israel,** increased religious militancy on the West Bank prevented a quick resolution.

**Latin America**. Repressive conservative regimes strengthened their hold on most of the continent, with the violent coup against the elected (Sept. 1973) Allende government in **Chile**, the 1976 military coup in **Argentina**, and coups against reformist regimes in **Bolivia** (1971, 1979) and **Peru** (1976). In Central America increasing liberal and leftist militancy led to the ouster (1979) of the Somoza regime of Nicaragua and civil conflict in El Salvador.

**Indochina**. Communist victories in Vietnam, Cambodia, and Laos by May 1975 did not bring peace. The Pol Pot regime ordered millions of city-dwellers to resettle in rural areas, in a program of forced labor, combined with terrorism, that cost as many as 2 million lives (1975-79) and caused hundreds of thousands of ethnic Chinese and others to flee Vietnam ("boat people," 1979). The Vietnamese invasion of Cambodia swelled the refugee population and contributed to widespread starvation in that devastated country.

**Russian expansion**. Soviet influence, checked in some countries (troops ousted by Egypt, 1972) was projected further afield, often with the use of Cuban troops (Angola, 1975-89; Ethiopia, 1977-88) and aided by a growing navy, a merchant fleet, and international banking ability. Détente with the West — 1972 Berlin pact, 1972 strategic arms pact (**SALT**)—gave way to a more antagonistic relationship in the late 1970s, exacerbated by the Soviet invasion (1979) of Afghanistan.

**Africa**. The last remaining European colonies were granted independence (**Spanish Sahara**, 1976; **Djibouti,** 1977) and, after 10 years of civil war and many negotiation sessions, a black government took over (1979) in Zimbabwe (Rhodesia); white domination remained in **S Africa**. Great power involvement in local wars (Russia in **Angola, Ethiopia**; France in **Chad, Zaire, Mauritania**) and the use of tens of thousands of Cuban troops were denounced by some African leaders as neocolonialism. Ethnic or tribal clashes made Africa the chief world locus of sustained warfare in the late 1970s.

**Arts**. Traditional modes in painting, architecture, and music, pursued in relative obscurity for much of the 20th cent., returned to popular and critical attention in the 1970s. The pictorial emphasis in neorealist and photorealist painting, the return of many architects to detail, decoration, and natural materials, and the concern with ordered structure in musical composition were, ironically, novel experiences for artistic consumers after the exhaustion of experimental possibilities. These more conservative styles, however, coexisted with modernist works in an atmosphere of variety and tolerance.

## Revitalization of Capitalism, Demand for Democracy: 1980-89

**USSR, Eastern Europe.** A troublesome 1980-85 for the USSR was followed by 5 years of astonishing change: the surrender of the Communist monopoly, remaking of the Soviet state, and disintegration of the Soviet empire. After the deaths of **Brezhnev** (1982), Andropov (1984), and Chernenko (1985); the harsh treatment of dissent and restriction of emigration; and the invasion (Dec. 1979) of Afghanistan, Gen. Secy. Mikhail **Gorbachev** (in office 1985-1991) promoted *glasnost* and *perestroika*—economic, political, and social reform. Supported by the Communist Party (July 1988), he signed (Dec. 1987) the INF treaty, and he pledged (1988) to cut the military budget. Military withdrawal from Afghanistan was completed in Feb. 1989, democratization was not hindered in Poland and Hungary, and

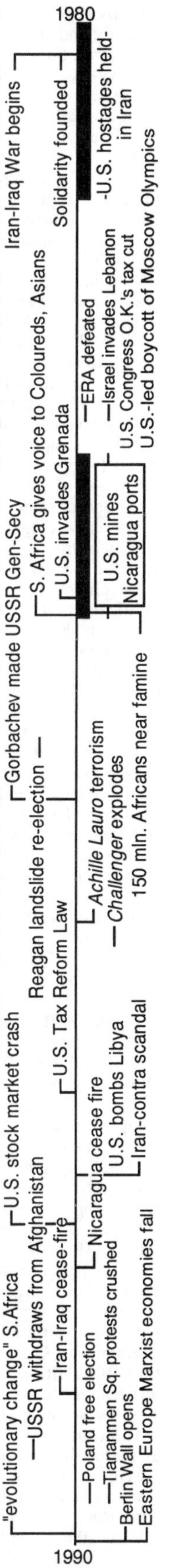

the Soviet people chose (Mar. 1989) part of the new Congress from competing candidates. By 1989 the **Cold War** had apparently ended, with much of the credit given to Gorbachev.

**Poland. Solidarity**, the labor union founded (1980) by **Lech Walesa**, was outlawed in 1982 and then legalized in 1988, after years of unrest. Poland's first free election since the Communist takeover brought Solidarity victory (June 1989); Tadeusz Mazowiecki, a Walesa adviser, became (Aug. 1989) prime minister in a government with the Communists.

In the fall of 1989 the failure of Marxist economies in **Hungary, E Germany, Czechoslovakia, Bulgaria, and Romania** brought the fall of the Communist monopoly and a demand for democracy. The **Berlin Wall** was opened in Nov. 1989.

**U.S. "The Reagan Years"** (1981-88) brought the **longest economic boom** in U.S. history via budget and tax cuts, deregulation, "junk bond" financing, leveraged buyouts, and mergers and takeovers, as well as a **strong anti-Communist stance**, via increased defense spending, aid to anti-Communists in Central America, invasion of Cuba-threatened Grenada, and championing of the MX missile system and "Star Wars." The Republican Party, and conservatism, appeared to strengthen. Four Reagan-Gorbachev summits (1985-88) climaxed in the INF treaty (1987). The Iran-contra affair (North's TV testimony, July 1987) was a major political scandal. There were also significant financial scandals (E. F. Hutton, 1985; Ivan Boesky, 1986). The stock market crashed (Oct. 1987), the U.S. trade imbalance grew (especially with Japan), and the federal budget deficit soared. Homelessness and drug abuse (esp. "crack") were growing social problems. In 1988, Vice Pres. Bush was elected to succeed Reagan as president.

**Middle East**. This area remained militarily unstable, with sharp divisions along economic, political, racial, and religious lines. In **Iran**, an Islamic revolution (1979-80) and violent political upheavals after, brought a strong anti-U.S. stance. In Sept. 1980, **Iraq** repudiated its border agreement with Iran and began major hostilities that led to an 8-year war in which millions were killed.

**Libya's** support for international terrorism induced the U.S. to close (May 1981) its diplomatic mission there and embargo (Mar. 1982) Libyan oil. The U.S. accused Libyan leader Muammar al-Qaddafi of aiding (Dec. 1985) terrorists in Rome and of Vienna airport attacks, and retaliated by bombing (Apr. 1986) Libya.

**Israel** affirmed (July 1980) all Jerusalem as its capital, destroyed (1981) an Iraqi atomic reactor, and invaded (1982) Lebanon, forcing the PLO to agree to withdraw. A **Palestinian uprising**, including women and children hurling rocks and bottles at troops, began (Dec. 1987) in Israeli-occupied Gaza and spread to the West Bank; troops responded with force, killing 300 by the end of 1988, with 6,000 more in detention camps.

Israeli withdrawal from **Lebanon** began in Feb. 1985 and ended in June 1985, as Lebanon continued torn by military and political conflict. Premier Karami was assassinated in June 1987. Artillery duels (Mar.-Apr. 1989) between Christian East Beirut and Muslim West Beirut left 200 dead and 700 wounded. At decade's end, violence still dominated.

**Central America**. In **Nicaragua**, the leftist Sandinista National Liberation Front, in power after the 1979 civil war, faced problems as a result of Nicaragua's military aid to leftist guerrillas in El Salvador and U.S. backing of antigovernment contras. The U.S. CIA admitted (1984) having directed the mining of Nicaraguan ports, and the U.S. sent humanitarian (1985) and military (1986) aid. Profits from secret arms sales to Iran were found (1987) diverted to contras. Cease-fire talks between the Sandinista government and contras came in 1988, and elections were held in Feb. 1990.

In **El Salvador**, a military coup (Oct. 1979) failed to halt extreme right-wing violence and left-wing insurrection. Archbishop Oscar Romero was assassinated in Mar. 1980; from Jan. to June some 4,000 civilians reportedly were killed. In 1984, newly elected Pres. Duarte worked to stem human rights abuses. Leftist guerrillas continued their offensive in 1989.

**Africa**. 1980-85 marked a rapid decline in the economies of virtually all African countries, a result of accelerating desertification, the world economic recession, heavy indebtedness to overseas creditors, rapid population growth, and political instability. Some 60 million Africans faced prolonged hunger in 1981; much of Africa had one of the worst droughts ever in 1983, and by year's end **150 million faced near-famine**. "Live Aid," a marathon rock concert, was presented in July 1985, and the U.S. and Western nations sent aid in Sept. 1985. Economic hardship fueled political unrest and coups. Wars in Ethiopia and Sudan and military strife in several other nations continued through 1989. AIDS took a heavy toll.

**South Africa. Antiapartheid sentiment gathered force**; demonstrations and violent police response grew. South African white voters approved (Nov. 1983) the first constitution to give Coloureds and Asians a voice, while still excluding blacks—70% of the population. The U.S. imposed economic sanctions in Aug. 1985, and 11 Western nations followed in Sept. **P. W. Botha**, 1980s president, was succeeded by **F. W. de Klerk**, in Sept. 1989, on a platform of "evolutionary" change via negotiation with the black population.

**China**. From 1980 through mid-1989 the Communist Party, under **Chairman Deng Xiaoping**, pursued **far-reaching changes**, expanding commercial and technical ties to the industrialized world and increasing the role of market forces in stimulating urban economic development. Apr. 1989 brought new demands for democratization: student demonstrators camped out in Tiananmen Sq., Beijing, in a massive peaceful protest. Some 100,000 students and workers marched, and at least 20 other cities saw protests. In response, martial law was imposed; army troops crushed the demonstration in Tiananmen Sq. on June 3-4, with death toll estimates at 500-7,000, as many as 10,000 injured, as many as 10,000 dissidents arrested, and 31 people tried and executed. The conciliatory Communist Party chief was ousted; the Politburo adopted (July) reforms against official corruption.

**Japan**. Relations with other nations, especially the U.S., were dominated (1980-89) by **trade imbalances favoring Japan**. In 1985 the U.S. trade deficit with Japan was $49.7 billion, one-third of the total U.S. trade deficit. After Japan was found (Apr. 1986) to sell semiconductors and computer memory chips below cost, the U.S. was assured a "fair share" of the market, but charged (Mar. 1987) Japan with failing to live up to the agreement. The **Omnibus Trade Bill** (Aug. 1988) provided for retaliation; Pres. Bush called Japan's practices "unjustifiable," and the law gave Japan 18 months to stop or face trade restrictions.

**European Community**. With the addition of Greece, Portugal, and Spain, the EC became a **common market of more than 300 million people**, the West's largest trading entity. **Margaret Thatcher** became the first British prime minister in this century to win 3 consecutive terms (1987). France elected (1981) its first socialist president, **François Mitterrand**, who was reelected in 1988. Italy elected (1983) its first socialist premier, **Bettino Craxi**.

**International Terrorism**. With the 1979 overthrow of the Shah of Iran, terrorism became a prominent political tactic that increased through the '80s, but with fewer high-profile attacks after 1985. In 1979-81, Iranian militants held 52 Americans hostage in Iran for 444 days; in 1983 a TNT-laden suicide terrorist blew up U.S. Marine headquarters in Beirut, killing 241 Americans, and a truck bomb blew up a French paratroop barracks, killing 58. The *Achille Lauro* was hijacked (1985), an American passenger killed, and the U.S. subsequently intercepted the Egyptian plane flying the terrorists to safety. Incidents rose to 700 in 1985, and to 1,000 in 1988. **Assassinated leaders** included Egypt's Pres. **Anwar al-Sadat** (1981), India's Prime Minister **Indira Gandhi** (1984), and Lebanese Premier **Rashid Karami** (1987).

# HISTORICAL FIGURES

## Ancient Greeks and Latins

### Greeks

**Aeschines,** orator, 389-314BC.
**Aeschylus,** dramatist, 525-456BC.
**Aesop,** fableist, c620-c560BC.
**Alcibiades,** politician, 450-404BC.
**Anacreon,** poet, c582-c485BC.
**Anaxagoras,** philosopher, c500-428BC.
**Anaximander,** philosopher, 611-546BC.
**Antiphon,** speechwriter, c480-411BC.
**Apollonius,** mathematician, c265-170BC.
**Archimedes,** math. 287-212BC.
**Aristophanes,** dramatist, c448-380BC.
**Aristotle,** philosopher, 384-322BC.
**Athenaeus,** scholar, fl. c200.
**Callicrates,** architect, fl. 5th cent.BC.
**Callimachus,** poet, c305-240BC.
**Cratinus,** comic dramatist, 520-421BC.
**Democritus,** philosopher, c460-370BC.
**Demosthenes,** orator, 384-322BC.
**Diodorus,** historian, fl. 20BC.
**Diogenes,** philosopher, 372-c287BC.
**Dionysius,** historian, d. c7BC.
**Empedocles,** philosopher, c490-430BC.
**Epicharmus,** dramatist, c530-440BC.
**Epictetus,** philosopher, c55-c135.
**Epicurus,** philosopher, 341-270BC.
**Eratosthenes,** scientist, 276-194BC.
**Euclid,** mathematician, fl. c300BC.
**Euripides,** dramatist, c484-406BC.
**Galen,** physician, 130-200.
**Heraclitus,** philosopher, c535-c475BC.
**Herodotus,** historian, c484-420BC.
**Hesiod,** poet, 8th cent. BC.
**Hippocrates,** physician, c460-377BC.
**Homer,** poet, fl. c700BC(?).
**Isocrates,** orator, 436-338BC.
**Menander,** dramatist, 342-292BC.
**Phidias,** sculptor, c500-435BC.
**Pindar,** poet, c518-c438BC.
**Plato,** philosopher, c428-347BC.
**Plutarch,** biographer, c46-120.
**Polybius,** historian, c200-c118BC.
**Praxiteles,** sculptor, 400-330BC.
**Pythagoras,** phil., math., c580-c500BC.
**Sappho,** poet, c610-c580BC.
**Simonides,** poet, 556-c468BC.
**Socrates,** philosopher, 469-399BC.
**Solon,** statesman, 640-560BC.
**Sophocles,** dramatist, c496-406BC.
**Strabo,** geographer, c63BC-AD24.
**Thales,** philosopher, c634-546BC.
**Themistocles,** politician, c524-c460BC.
**Theocritus,** poet, c310-250BC.
**Theophrastus,** phil., c372-c287BC.
**Thucydides,** historian, fl. 5th cent.BC.
**Timon,** philosopher, c320-c230BC.
**Xenophon,** historian, c434-c355BC.
**Zeno,** philosopher, c495-c430BC.

### Latins

**Ammianus,** historian, c330-395.
**Apuleius,** satirist, c124-c170.
**Boethius,** scholar, c480-524.
**Caesar, Julius,** leader, 100-44BC.
**Catilina,** politician, c108-62BC.
**Cato** (Elder), statesman, 234-149BC.
**Catullus,** poet, c84-54BC.
**Cicero,** orator, 106-43BC.
**Claudian,** poet, c370-c404.
**Ennius,** poet, 239-170BC.
**Gellius,** author, c130-c165.
**Horace,** poet, 65-8BC.
**Juvenal,** satirist, 60-127.
**Livy,** historian, 59BC-AD17.
**Lucan,** poet, 39-65.
**Lucilius,** poet, c180-c102BC.
**Lucretius,** poet, c99-c55BC.
**Martial,** epigrammatist, c38-c103.
**Nepos,** historian, c100-c25BC.
**Ovid,** poet, 43BC-AD17.
**Persius,** satirist, 34-62.
**Plautus,** dramatist, c254-c184BC.
**Pliny,** scholar, 23-79.
**Pliny** (Younger), author, 62-113.
**Quintilian,** rhetorician, c35-c97.
**Sallust,** historian, 86-34BC.
**Seneca,** philosopher, 4BC-AD65.
**Silius,** poet, c25-101.
**Statius,** poet, c45-c96.
**Suetonius,** biographer, c69-c122.
**Tacitus,** historian, 56-120.
**Terence,** dramatist, 185-c159BC.
**Tibullus,** poet, c55-c19BC.
**Virgil,** poet, 70-19BC.
**Vitruvius,** architect, fl. 1st cent.BC.

## Rulers of England and Great Britain

### England

| Name | | Began | Died | Age | Rgd |
|---|---|---|---|---|---|
| | **Saxons and Danes** | | | | |
| **Egbert** | King of Wessex, won allegiance of all English | **829** | **839** | — | 10 |
| **Ethelwulf** | Son, King of Wessex, Sussex, Kent, Essex | **839** | **858** | — | 19 |
| **Ethelbald** | Son of Ethelwulf, displaced father in Wessex | **858** | **860** | — | 2 |
| **Ethelbert** | 2d son of Ethelwulf, united Kent and Wessex | **860** | **866** | — | 6 |
| **Ethelred I** | 3d son, King of Wessex, fought Danes | **866** | **871** | — | 5 |
| **Alfred** | The Great, 4th son, defeated Danes, fortified London | **871** | **899** | 52 | 28 |
| **Edward** | The Elder, Alfred's son, united English, claimed Scotland | **899** | **924** | 55 | 25 |
| **Athelstan** | The Glorious, Edward's son, King of Mercia, Wessex | **924** | **940** | 45 | 16 |
| **Edmund** | 3d son of Edward, King of Wessex, Mercia | **940** | **946** | 25 | 6 |
| **Edred** | 4th son of Edward | **946** | **955** | 32 | 9 |
| **Edwy** | The Fair, eldest son of Edmund, King of Wessex | **955** | **959** | 18 | 3 |
| **Edgar** | The Peaceful, 2d son of Edmund, ruled all English | **959** | **975** | 32 | 17 |
| **Edward** | The Martyr, eldest son of Edgar, murdered by stepmother | **975** | **978** | 17 | 4 |
| **Ethelred II** | The Unready, 2d son of Edgar, married Emma of Normandy | **978** | **1016** | 48 | 37 |
| **Edmund II** | Ironside, son of Ethelred II, King of London | **1016** | **1016** | 27 | 0 |
| **Canute** | The Dane, gave Wessex to Edmund, married Emma | **1016** | **1035** | 40 | 19 |
| **Harold I** | Harefoot, natural son of Canute | **1035** | **1040** | — | 5 |
| **Hardecanute** | Son of Canute by Emma, Danish King | **1040** | **1042** | 24 | 2 |
| **Edward** | The Confessor, son of Ethelred II (canonized 1161) | **1042** | **1066** | 62 | 24 |
| **Harold II** | Edward's brother-in-law, last Saxon King | **1066** | **1066** | 44 | 0 |
| | **House of Normandy** | | | | |
| **William I** | The Conqueror, defeated Harold at Hastings | **1066** | **1087** | 60 | 21 |
| **William II** | Rufus, 3d son of William I, killed by arrow | **1087** | **1100** | 43 | 13 |
| **Henry I** | Beauclerc, youngest son of William I | **1100** | **1135** | 67 | 35 |
| | **House of Blois** | | | | |
| **Stephen** | Son of Adela, daughter of William I, and Count of Blois | **1135** | **1154** | 50 | 19 |
| | **House of Plantagenet** | | | | |
| **Henry II** | Son of Geoffrey Plantagenet (Angevin) by Matilda, daughter of Henry I | **1154** | **1189** | 56 | 35 |
| **Richard I** | Coeur de Lion, son of Henry II, crusader | **1189** | **1199** | 42 | 10 |
| **John** | Lackland, son of Henry II, signed Magna Carta, 1215 | **1199** | **1216** | 50 | 17 |
| **Henry III** | Son of John, acceded at 9, under regency until 1227 | **1216** | **1272** | 65 | 56 |
| **Edward I** | Longshanks, son of Henry III | **1272** | **1307** | 68 | 35 |
| **Edward II** | Son of Edward I, deposed by Parliament, 1327 | **1307** | **1327** | 43 | 20 |
| **Edward III** | Of Windsor, son of Edward II | **1327** | **1377** | 65 | 50 |
| **Richard II** | Grandson of Edward III, minor until 1389, deposed 1399 | **1377** | **1400** | 33 | 22 |
| | **House of Lancaster** | | | | |
| **Henry IV** | Son of John of Gaunt, Duke of Lancaster, son of Edward III | **1399** | **1413** | 47 | 13 |
| **Henry V** | Son of Henry IV, victor of Agincourt | **1413** | **1422** | 34 | 9 |
| **Henry VI** | Son of Henry V, deposed 1461, died in Tower | **1422** | **1471** | 49 | 39 |

| Name | | Began | Died | Age | Rgd |
|---|---|---|---|---|---|
| | **House of York** | | | | |
| **Edward IV** | Great-great-grandson of Edward III, son of Duke of York | **1461** | **1483** | 40 | 22 |
| **Edward V** | Son of Edward IV, murdered in Tower of London | **1483** | **1483** | 13 | 0 |
| **Richard III** | Crookback, brother of Edward IV, fell at Bosworth Field | **1483** | **1485** | 32 | 2 |
| | **House of Tudor** | | | | |
| **Henry VII** | Son of Edmund Tudor, Earl of Richmond, whose father had married the widow of Henry V; descended from Edward III through his mother, Margaret Beaufort via John of Gaunt. By marriage with daughter of Edward IV he united Lancaster and York | **1485** | **1509** | 53 | 24 |
| **Henry VIII** | Son of Henry VII by Elizabeth, dau. of Edward IV | **1509** | **1547** | 56 | 38 |
| **Edward VI** | Son of Henry VIII, by Jane Seymour, his 3d queen. Ruled under regents. Was forced to name Lady Jane Grey his successor. Council of State proclaimed her queen July 10, 1553. Mary Tudor won Council, was proclaimed queen July 19, 1553. Mary had Lady Jane Grey beheaded for treason, Feb., 1554 | **1547** | **1553** | 16 | 6 |
| **Mary I** | Daughter of Henry VIII, by Catherine of Aragon | **1553** | **1558** | 43 | 5 |
| **Elizabeth I** | Daughter of Henry VIII, by Anne Boleyn | **1558** | **1603** | 69 | 44 |

## Great Britain

| Name | | Began | Died | Age | Rgd |
|---|---|---|---|---|---|
| | **House of Stuart** | | | | |
| **James I** | James VI of Scotland, son of Mary, Queen of Scots. *First to call himself King of Great Britain. This became official with the Act of Union, 1707.* | **1603** | **1625** | 59 | 22 |
| **Charles I** | Only surviving son of James I; beheaded Jan. 30, 1649 | **1625** | **1649** | 48 | 24 |
| | **Commonwealth, 1649-1660** | | | | |
| | Council of State, 1649; Protectorate, 1653 | | | | |
| **The Cromwells** | Oliver Cromwell, Lord Protector | **1653** | **1658** | 59 | — |
| | Richard Cromwell, son, Lord Protector, resigned May 25, 1659 | **1658** | **1712** | 86 | — |
| | **House of Stuart (Restored)** | | | | |
| **Charles II** | Eldest son of Charles I, died without issue | **1660** | **1685** | 55 | 25 |
| **James II** | 2d son of Charles I. Deposed 1688. Interregnum Dec. 11, 1688, to Feb. 13, 1689 | **1685** | **1701** | 68 | 3 |
| **William III** | Son of William, Prince of Orange, by Mary, daughter of Charles I | **1689** | **1702** | 51 | 13 |
| **and Mary II** | Eldest daughter of James II and wife of William III | | **1694** | 33 | 6 |
| **Anne** | 2d daughter of James II | **1702** | **1714** | 49 | 12 |
| | **House of Hanover** | | | | |
| **George I** | Son of Elector of Hanover, by Sophia, granddaughter of James I | **1714** | **1727** | 67 | 13 |
| **George II** | Only son of George I, married Caroline of Brandenburg | **1727** | **1760** | 77 | 33 |
| **George III** | Grandson of George II, married Charlotte of Mecklenburg | **1760** | **1820** | 81 | 59 |
| **George IV** | Eldest son of George III, Prince Regent, from Feb. 1811 | **1820** | **1830** | 67 | 10 |
| **William IV** | 3d son of George III, married Adelaide of Saxe-Meiningen | **1830** | **1837** | 71 | 7 |
| **Victoria** | Daughter of Edward, 4th son of George III; married (1840) Prince Albert of Saxe-Coburg and Gotha, who became Prince Consort | **1837** | **1901** | 81 | 63 |
| | **House of Saxe-Coburg and Gotha** | | | | |
| **Edward VII** | Eldest son of Victoria, married Alexandra, Princess of Denmark | **1901** | **1910** | 68 | 9 |
| | **House of Windsor** | | | | |
| | *Name Adopted July 17, 1917* | | | | |
| **George V** | 2d son of Edward VII, married Princess Mary of Teck | **1910** | **1936** | 70 | 25 |
| **Edward VIII** | Eldest son of George V; acceded Jan. 20, 1936, abdicated Dec. 11 | **1936** | **1972** | 77 | 1 |
| **George VI** | 2d son of George V; married Lady Elizabeth Bowes-Lyon | **1936** | **1952** | 56 | 15 |
| **Elizabeth II** | Elder daughter of George VI, acceded Feb. 6, 1952 | **1952** | **—** | — | — |

## Rulers of Scotland

Kenneth I MacAlpin was the first Scot to rule both Scots and Picts, AD 846.

Duncan I was the first general ruler, 1034. Macbeth seized the kingdom 1040, was slain by Duncan's son, Malcolm III MacDuncan (Canmore), 1057.

Malcolm married Margaret, Saxon princess who had fled from the Normans. Queen Margaret introduced English language and English monastic customs. She was canonized, 1250. Her son Edgar, 1097, moved the court to Edinburgh. His brothers Alexander I and David I succeeded. Malcolm IV, the Maiden, 1153, grandson of David I, was followed by his brother, William the Lion, 1165, whose son was Alexander II, 1214. The latter's son, Alexander III, 1249, defeated the Norse and regained the Hebrides. When he died, 1286, his granddaughter, Margaret, child of Eric of Norway and grandniece of Edward I of England, known as the Maid of Norway, was chosen ruler, but died 1290, aged 8.

John Baliol, 1292-1296. (Interregnum, 10 years.)

Robert Bruce (The Bruce), 1306-1329, victor at Bannockburn, 1314.

David II, only son of Robert Bruce, ruled 1329-1371.

Robert II, 1371-1390, grandson of Robert Bruce, son of Walter, the Steward of Scotland, was called The Steward, first of the so-called Stuart line.

Robert III, son of Robert II, 1390-1406.

James I, son of Robert III, 1406-1437.

James II, son of James I, 1437-1460.

James III, eldest son of James II, 1460-1488.

James IV, eldest son of James III, 1488-1513.

James V, eldest son of James IV, 1513-1542.

Mary, daughter of James V, born 1542, became queen when one week old; was crowned 1543. Married, 1558, Francis, son of Henry II of France, who became king 1559, died 1560. Mary ruled Scots 1561 until abdication, 1567. She also married Henry Stewart, Lord Darnley (1565), and James, Earl of Bothwell (1567). Imprisoned by Elizabeth I, Mary was beheaded 1587.

James VI, 1566-1625, son of Mary and Lord Darnley, became King of England on death of Elizabeth in 1603. Although the thrones were thus united, the legislative union of Scotland and England was not effected until the Act of Union, May 1, 1707.

## Prime Ministers of Great Britain

Designations in parentheses describe each government;
W=Whig; T=Tory; Cl=Coalition; P=Peelite; L=Liberal; C=Conservative; La=Labour.

| | |
|---|---|
| Sir Robert Walpole (W) | 1721-1742 |
| Earl of Wilmington (W) | 1742-1743 |
| Henry Pelham (W) | 1743-1754 |
| Duke of Newcastle (W) | 1754-1756 |
| Duke of Devonshire (W) | 1756-1757 |
| Duke of Newcastle (W) | 1757-1762 |
| Earl of Bute (T) | 1762-1763 |
| George Grenville (W) | 1763-1765 |
| Marquess of Rockingham (W) | 1765-1766 |
| William Pitt the Elder(Earl of Chatham) (W) | 1766-1768 |
| Duke of Grafton (W) | 1768-1770 |
| Frederick North (Lord North) (T) | 1770-1782 |
| Marquess of Rockingham (W) | 1782 |
| Earl of Shelburne (W) | 1782-1783 |
| Duke of Portland (Cl) | 1783 |
| William Pitt the Younger (T) | 1783-1801 |
| Henry Addington (T) | 1801-1804 |
| William Pitt the Younger (T) | 1804-1806 |
| William Wyndham Grenville, Baron Grenville (W) | 1806-1807 |
| Duke of Portland (T) | 1807-1809 |
| Spencer Perceval (T) | 1809-1812 |
| Earl of Liverpool (T) | 1812-1827 |
| George Canning (T) | 1827 |
| Viscount Goderich (T) | 1827-1828 |
| Duke of Wellington (T) | 1828-1830 |
| Earl Grey (W) | 1830-1834 |
| Viscount Melbourne (W) | 1834 |
| Sir Robert Peel (T) | 1834-1835 |
| Viscount Melbourne (W) | 1835-1841 |
| Sir Robert Peel (T) | 1841-1846 |
| Lord John Russell (later Earl) (W) | 1846-1852 |
| Earl of Derby (T) | 1852 |
| Earl of Aberdeen (P) | 1852-1855 |
| Viscount Palmerston (L) | 1855-1858 |
| Earl of Derby (C) | 1858-1859 |
| Viscount Palmerston (L) | 1859-1865 |
| Earl Russell (L) | 1865-1866 |
| Earl of Derby (C) | 1866-1868 |
| Benjamin Disraeli (C) | 1868 |
| William E. Gladstone (L) | 1868-1874 |
| Benjamin Disraeli (C) | 1874-1880 |
| William E. Gladstone (L) | 1880-1885 |
| Marquess of Salisbury (C) | 1885-1886 |
| William E. Gladstone (L) | 1886 |
| Marquess of Salisbury (C) | 1886-1892 |
| William E. Gladstone (L) | 1892-1894 |
| Earl of Rosebery (L) | 1894-1895 |
| Marquess of Salisbury (C) | 1895-1902 |
| Arthur J. Balfour (C) | 1902-1905 |
| Sir Henry Campbell-Bannerman (L) | 1905-1908 |
| Herbert H. Asquith (L) | 1908-1915 |
| Herbert H. Asquith (Cl) | 1915-1916 |
| David Lloyd George (Cl) | 1916-1922 |
| Andrew Bonar Law (C) | 1922-1923 |
| Stanley Baldwin (C) | 1923-1924 |
| James Ramsay MacDonald (La) | 1924 |
| Stanley Baldwin (C) | 1924-1929 |
| James Ramsay MacDonald (La) | 1929-1931 |
| James Ramsay MacDonald (Cl) | 1931-1935 |
| Stanley Baldwin (Cl) | 1935-1937 |
| Neville Chamberlain (Cl) | 1937-1940 |
| Winston Churchill (Cl) | 1940-1945 |
| Winston Churchill (C) | 1945 |
| Clement Attlee (La) | 1945-1951 |
| Sir Winston Churchill (C) | 1951-1955 |
| Sir Anthony Eden (C) | 1955-1957 |
| Harold Macmillan (C) | 1957-1963 |
| Sir Alec Douglas-Home (C) | 1963-1964 |
| Harold Wilson (La) | 1964-1970 |
| Edward Heath (C) | 1970-1974 |
| Harold Wilson (La) | 1974-1976 |
| James Callaghan (La) | 1976-1979 |
| Margaret Thatcher (C) | 1979-1990 |
| John Major (C) | 1990- |

## Historical Periods of Japan

| | | |
|---|---|---|
| **Yamato** | c. 300-592 | Conquest of Yamato plain c. AD 300. |
| **Asuka** | 592-710 | Accession of Empress Suiko, 592. |
| **Nara** | 710-794 | Completion of Heijo (Nara), 710; capital moves to Nagaoka, 784. |
| **Heian** | 794-1185 | Completion of Heian (Kyoto), 794. |
| **Fujiwara** | 858-1160 | Fujiwara-no-Yoshifusa becomes regent, 858. |
| **Taira** | 1160-1185 | Taira-no-Kiyomori assumes control, 1160; Minamoto-no-Yoritomo victor over Taira, 1185. |
| **Kamakura** | 1192-1333 | Yoritomo becomes shogun, 1192. |
| **Namboku** | 1334-1392 | Restoration of Emperor Godaigo, 1334; Southern Court established by Godaigo at Yoshino, 1336. |
| **Ashikaga** | 1338-1573 | Ashikaga Takauji becomes shogun, 1338. |
| **Muromachi** | 1392-1573 | Unification of Southern and Northern Courts, 1392. |
| **Sengoku** | 1467-1600 | Beginning of the Onin war, 1467. |
| **Momoyama** | 1573-1603 | Oda Nobunaga enters Kyoto, 1568; Nobunaga deposes last Ashikaga shogun, 1573; Tokugawa Ieyasu victor at Sekigahara, 1600. |
| **Edo** | 1603-1867 | Ieyasu becomes shogun, 1603. |
| **Meiji** | 1868-1912 | Enthronement of Emperor Mutsuhito (Meiji), 1867; Meiji Restoration and Charter Oath, 1868. |
| **Taisho** | 1912-1926 | Accession of Emperor Yoshihito, 1912. |
| **Showa** | 1926-1989 | Accession of Emperor Hirohito, 1926. |
| **Heisei** | 1989- | Accession of Emperor Akihito, 1989. |

## Rulers of France: Kings, Queens, Presidents

### Caesar to Charlemagne

Julius Caesar subdued the Gauls, native tribes of Gaul (France) 58 to 51 BC. The Romans ruled 500 years. The Franks, a Teutonic tribe, reached the Somme from the East c. AD 250. By the 5th century the Merovingian Franks ousted the Romans. In 451, with the help of Visigoths, Burgundians and others, they defeated Attila and the Huns at Chalons-sur-Marne.

Childeric I became leader of the Merovingians 458. His son Clovis I (Chlodwig, Ludwig, Louis), crowned 481, founded the dynasty. After defeating the Alemanni (Germans) 496, he was baptized a Christian and made Paris his capital. His line ruled until Childeric III was deposed, 751.

The West Merovingians were called Neustrians, the eastern Austrasians. Pepin of Herstal (687-714), major domus, or head of the palace, of Austrasia, took over Neustria as dux (leader) of the Franks. Pepin's son, Charles, called Martel (the Hammer), defeated the Saracens at Tours-Poitiers, 732; was succeeded by his son, Pepin the Short, 741, who deposed Childeric III and ruled as king until 768.

His son, Charlemagne, or Charles the Great (742-814), became king of the Franks, 768, with his brother Carloman, who died 771. Charlemagne ruled France, Germany, parts of Italy, Spain, Austria, and enforced Christianity. Crowned Emperor of the Romans by Pope Leo III in St. Peter's, Rome, Dec. 25, 800. Succeeded by son, Louis I the Pious, 814. At death, 840, Louis left empire to sons, Lothair (Roman emperor); Pepin I (king of Aquitaine); Louis II (of Germany); Charles the Bald (France). They quarreled and by the peace of Verdun, 843, divided the empire.

**Date in bold is year of accession.**

### The Carolingians

**843** Charles I (the Bald); Roman Emperor, 875
**877** Louis II (the Stammerer), son
**879** Louis III (died 882) and Carloman, brothers
**885** Charles II (the Fat); Roman Emperor, 881
**888** Eudes (Odo), elected by nobles
**898** Charles III (the Simple), son of Louis II, defeated by
**922** Robert, brother of Eudes, killed in war
**923** Rudolph (Raoul), Duke of Burgundy
**936** Louis IV, son of Charles III
**954** Lothair, son, aged 13, defeated by Capet
**986** Louis V (the Sluggard), left no heirs

### The Capets

**987** Hugh Capet, son of Hugh the Great
**996** Robert II (the Wise), his son
**1031** Henry I, his son
**1060** Philip I (the Fair), son
**1108** Louis VI (the Fat), son
**1137** Louis VII (the Younger), son
**1180** Philip II (Augustus), son, crowned at Reims
**1223** Louis VIII (the Lion), son
**1226** Louis IX, son, crusader; Louis IX (1214-1270) reigned 44 years, arbitrated disputes with English King Henry III; led crusades, 1248 (captured in Egypt 1250) and 1270, when he died of plague in Tunis. Canonized 1297 as St. Louis.
**1270** Philip III (the Hardy), son
**1285** Philip IV (the Fair), son, king at 17
**1314** Louis X (the Headstrong), son. His posthumous son, John I, lived only 7 days
**1316** Philip V (the Tall), brother of Louis X
**1322** Charles IV (the Fair), brother of Louis X

### House of Valois

**1328** Philip VI (of Valois), grandson of Philip III
**1350** John II (the Good), his son, retired to England
**1364** Charles V (the Wise), son
**1380** Charles VI (the Beloved), son
**1422** Charles VII (the Victorious), son. In 1429 Joan of Arc (Jeanne d'Arc) promised Charles to oust the English, who occupied northern France. Joan won at Orleans and Patay and had Charles crowned at Reims, July 17, 1429. Joan was captured May 24, 1430, and executed May 30, 1431, at Rouen for heresy. Charles ordered her rehabilitation, effected 1455.
**1461** Louis XI (the Cruel), son, civil reformer
**1483** Charles VIII (the Affable), son
**1498** Louis XII, great-grandson of Charles V
**1515** Francis I, of Angouleme, nephew, son-in-law. Francis I (1494-1547) reigned 32 years, fought 4 big wars, was patron of the arts, aided Cellini, del Sarto, Leonardo da Vinci, Rabelais, embellished Fontainebleau.
**1547** Henry II, son, killed at a joust in a tournament. He was the husband of Catherine de Medicis (1519-1589) and the lover of Diane de Poitiers (1499-1566). Catherine was born in Florence, daughter of Lorenzo de Medici. By her marriage to Henry II she became the mother of Francis II, Charles IX, Henry III and Queen Margaret (Reine Margot), wife of Henry IV. She persuaded Charles IX to order the massacre of Huguenots on the Feast of St. Bartholomew, Aug. 24, 1572, the day her daughter was married to Henry of Navarre.
**1559** Francis II, son. In 1548, Mary, Queen of Scots since infancy, was betrothed when 6 to Francis, aged 4. They were married 1558. Francis died 1560, aged 16; Mary ruled Scotland, abdicated 1567.
**1560** Charles IX, brother
**1574** Henry III, brother, assassinated

### House of Bourbon

**1589** Henry IV, of Navarre, assassinated. Henry IV made enemies when he gave tolerance to Protestants by Edict of Nantes, 1598. He was grandson of Queen Margaret of Navarre, literary patron. He married Margaret of Valois, daughter of Henry II and Catherine de Medicis; was divorced; in 1600 married Marie de Medicis, who became Regent of France, 1610-1617, for her son, Louis XIII, but was exiled by Richelieu, 1631.
**1610** Louis XIII (the Just), son. Louis XIII (1601-1643) married Anne of Austria. His ministers were Cardinals Richelieu and Mazarin.
**1643** Louis XIV (The Grand Monarch), son. Louis XIV was king 72 years. He exhausted a prosperous country in wars for thrones and territory. By revoking the Edict of Nantes (1685) he caused the emigration of the Huguenots. He said: "I am the state."
**1715** Louis XV, great-grandson. Louis XV married a Polish princess; lost Canada to the English. His favorites, Mme. Pompadour and Mme. Du Barry, influenced policies. Noted for saying "After me, the deluge."
**1774** Louis XVI, grandson; married Marie Antoinette, daughter of Empress Maria Therese of Austria. King and queen beheaded by Revolution, 1793. Their son, called Louis XVII, died in prison, never ruled.

### First Republic

**1792** National Convention of the French Revolution
**1795** Directory, under Barras and others
**1799** Consulate, Napoleon Bonaparte, first consul. Elected consul for life, 1802.

### First Empire

**1804** Napoleon I (Napoleon Bonaparte), emperor. Josephine (de Beauharnais), empress, 1804-1809; Marie Louise, empress, 1810-1814. Her son, Francois (1811-1832), titular King of Rome, later Duke de Reichstadt and "Napoleon II," never ruled. Napoleon abdicated 1814, died 1821.

### Bourbons Restored

**1814** Louis XVIII, king; brother of Louis XVI
**1824** Charles X, brother; reactionary; deposed by the July Revolution, 1830

### House of Orleans

**1830** Louis-Philippe, the "citizen king"

### Second Republic

**1848** Louis Napoleon Bonaparte, president, nephew of Napoleon I.

### Second Empire

**1852** Napoleon III (Louis Napoleon Bonaparte), emperor; Eugenie (de Montijo), empress. Lost Franco-Prussian war, deposed 1870. Son, Prince Imperial (1856-1879), died in Zulu War. Eugenie died 1920.

### Third Republic—Presidents

**1871** Thiers, Louis Adolphe (1797-1877)
**1873** MacMahon, Marshal Patrice M. de (1808-1893)
**1879** Grevy, Paul J. (1807-1891)
**1887** Sadi-Carnot, M. (1837-1894), assassinated
**1894** Casimir-Perier, Jean P. P. (1847-1907)
**1895** Faure, François Felix (1841-1899)
**1899** Loubet, Emile (1838-1929)
**1906** Fallieres, C. Armand (1841-1931)
**1913** Poincare, Raymond (1860-1934)
**1920** Deschanel, Paul (1856-1922)
**1920** Millerand, Alexandre (1859-1943)
**1924** Doumergue, Gaston (1863-1937)
**1931** Doumer, Paul (1857-1932), assassinated
**1932** Lebrun, Albert (1871-1950), resigned 1940
**1940** Vichy govt. under German armistice: Henri Philippe Petain (1856-1951), Chief of State, 1940-1944. Provisional govt. after liberation: Charles de Gaulle (1890-1970), Oct. 1944-Jan. 21, 1946; Felix Gouin (1884-1977), Jan. 23, 1946; Georges Bidault (1899-1983), June 24, 1946.

### Fourth Republic—Presidents

**1947** Auriol, Vincent (1884-1966)
**1954** Coty, Rene (1882-1962)

### Fifth Republic—Presidents

**1959** De Gaulle, Charles Andre J. M. (1890-1970)
**1969** Pompidou, Georges (1911-1974)
**1974** Giscard d'Estaing, Valery (1926- )
**1981** Mitterrand, François (1916-1996)
**1995** Chirac, Jacques (1932- )

# Rulers of Middle Europe; Rise and Fall of Dynasties; Rulers of Germany

## Carolingian Dynasty

Charles the Great, or Charlemagne, ruled France, Italy, and Middle Europe; established Ostmark (later Austria); crowned Roman emperor by pope in Rome, AD 800; died 814.

Louis I (Ludwig) the Pious, son; crowned by Charlemagne 814; died 840.

Louis II, the German, son; succeeded to East Francia (Germany) 843-876.

Charles the Fat, son; inherited East Francia and West Francia (France) 876, reunited empire, crowned emperor by pope 881, deposed 887.

Arnulf, nephew, 887-899. Partition of empire.

Louis the Child, 899-911, last direct descendant of Charlemagne.

Conrad I, duke of Franconia, first elected German king, 911-918, founded House of Franconia.

## Saxon Dynasty; First Reich

Henry I, the Fowler, duke of Saxony, 919-936.

Otto I, the Great, 936-973, son; crowned Holy Roman Emperor by pope, 962.

Otto II, 973-983, son; failed to oust Greeks and Arabs from Sicily.

Otto III, 983-1002, son; crowned emperor at 16.

Henry II, the Saint, duke of Bavaria, 1002-1024, great-grandson of Otto the Great.

## House of Franconia

Conrad II, 1024-1039, elected king of Germany.

Henry III, the Black, 1039-1056, son; deposed 3 popes; annexed Burgundy.

Henry IV, 1056-1106, son; regency by his mother, Agnes of Poitou. Banned by Pope Gregory VII, he did penance at Canossa.

Henry V, 1106-1125, son; last of Salic House.

Lothair, duke of Saxony, 1125-1137. Crowned emperor in Rome, 1134.

## House of Hohenstaufen

Conrad III, duke of Swabia, 1138-1152. In 2d Crusade.

Frederick I, Barbarossa, 1152-1190; Conrad's nephew.

Henry VI, 1190-1196, took lower Italy from Normans. Son became king of Sicily.

Philip of Swabia, 1197-1208, brother.

Otto IV, of House of Welf, 1198-1215; deposed.

Frederick II, 1215-1250, son of Henry VI; king of Sicily; crowned king of Jerusalem in 5th Crusade.

Conrad IV, 1250-1254, son; lost lower Italy to Charles of Anjou.

Conradin, 1252-1268, son, king of Jerusalem and Sicily, beheaded. Last Hohenstaufen.

Interregnum, 1254-1273, Rise of the Electors.

## Transition

Rudolph I of Hapsburg, 1273-1291, defeated King Ottocar II of Bohemia. Bequeathed duchy of Austria to eldest son, Albert.

Adolph of Nassau, 1292-1298, killed in war with Albert of Austria.

Albert I, king of Germany, 1298-1308, son of Rudolph.

Henry VII, of Luxemburg, 1308-1313, crowned emperor in Rome. Seized Bohemia, 1310.

Louis IV of Bavaria (Wittelsbach), 1314-1347. Also elected was Frederick of Austria, 1314-1330 (Hapsburg). Abolition of papal sanction for election of Holy Roman Emperor.

Charles IV, of Luxemburg, 1347-1378, grandson of Henry VII, German emperor and king of Bohemia, Lombardy, Burgundy; took Mark of Brandenburg.

Wenceslaus, 1378-1400, deposed.

Rupert, Duke of Palatine, 1400-1410.

Sigismund, 1411-1437.

## Hungary

Stephen I, house of Arpad, 997-1038. Crowned king 1000; converted Magyars; canonized 1083. After several centuries of feuds Charles Robert of Anjou became Charles I, 1308-1342.

Louis I, the Great, son, 1342-1382; joint ruler of Poland with Casimir III, 1370. Defeated Turks.

Mary, daughter, 1382-1395, ruled with husband. Sigismund of Luxemburg, 1387-1437, also king of Bohemia. As bro. of Wenceslaus he succeeded Rupert as Holy Roman Emperor, 1410.

Albert, 1438-1439, son-in-law of Sigismund; also Roman emperor as Albert II *(see under Hapsburg)*.

Ulaszlo I of Poland, 1440-1444.

Ladislaus V, posthumous son of Albert II, 1444-1457. John Hunyadi (Hunyadi Janos), governor (1446-1452), fought Turks, Czechs; died 1456.

Matthias I (Corvinus), son of Hunyadi, 1458-1490. Shared rule of Bohemia, captured Vienna, 1485, annexed Austria, Styria, Carinthia.

Ulaszlo II (king of Bohemia), 1490-1516.

Louis II, son, aged 10, 1516-1526. Wars with Suleiman, Turk. In 1527 Hungary split between Ferdinand I, Archduke of Austria, bro.-in-law of Louis II, and John Zapolya of Transylvania. After Turkish invasion, 1547, Hungary split between Ferdinand, Prince John Sigismund (Transylvania), and the Turks.

## House of Hapsburg

Albert V of Austria, Hapsburg, crowned king of Hungary, Jan. 1438, Roman emperor, March 1438, as Albert II; died 1439.

Frederick III, cousin, 1440-1493. Fought Turks.

Maximilian I, son, 1493-1519. Assumed title of Holy Roman Emperor (German), 1493.

Charles V, grandson, 1519-1556. King of Spain with mother co-regent; crowned Roman emperor at Aix, 1520. Confronted Luther at Worms; attempted church reform and religious conciliation; abdicated 1556.

Ferdinand I, king of Bohemia, 1526, of Hungary, 1527; disputed. German king, 1531. Crowned Roman emperor on abdication of brother Charles V, 1556.

Maximilian II, son, 1564-1576.

Rudolph II, son, 1576-1612.

Matthias, brother, 1612-1619, king of Bohemia and Hungary.

Ferdinand II of Styria, king of Bohemia, 1617, of Hungary, 1618, Roman emperor, 1619. Bohemian Protestants deposed him, elected Frederick V of Palatine, starting Thirty Years War.

Ferdinand III, son, king of Hungary, 1625, Bohemia, 1627, Roman emperor, 1637. Peace of Westphalia, 1648, ended war. Leopold I, 1658-1705; Joseph I, 1705-1711; Charles VI, 1711-1740.

Maria Theresa, daughter, 1740-1780, Archduchess of Austria, queen of Hungary; ousted pretender, Charles VII, crowned 1742; in 1745 obtained election of her husband Francis I as Roman emperor and co-regent (d. 1765). Fought Seven Years' War with Frederick II of Prussia. Mother of Marie Antoinette.

Joseph II, son, 1765-1790, Roman emperor, reformer; powers restricted by Empress Maria Theresa until her death, 1780. First partition of Poland. Leopold II, 1790-1792.

Francis II, son, 1792-1835. Fought Napoleon. Proclaimed first hereditary emperor of Austria, 1804. Forced to abdicate as Roman emperor, 1806; last use of title. Ferdinand I, son, 1835-1848, abdicated during revolution.

## Austro-Hungarian Monarchy

Francis Joseph I, nephew, 1848-1916, emperor of Austria, king of Hungary. Dual monarchy of Austria-Hungary formed, 1867. After assassination of heir, Archduke Francis Ferdinand, June 28, 1914, Austrian diplomacy precipitated World War I.

Charles I, grand-nephew, 1916-1918, last emperor of Austria and king of Hungary. Abdicated Nov. 11-13, 1918, died 1922.

## Rulers of Prussia

Nucleus of Prussia was the Mark of Brandenburg. First margrave Albert the Bear (Albrecht), 1134-1170. First Hohenzollern margrave was Frederick, burgrave of Nuremberg, 1417-1440.

Frederick William, 1640-1688, the Great Elector. Son, Frederick III, 1688-1713, crowned King Frederick of Prussia, 1701.

Frederick William I, son, 1713-1740.

Frederick II, the Great, son, 1740-1786, annexed Silesia, part of Austria.

Frederick William II, nephew, 1786-1797.

Frederick William III, son, 1797-1840. Napoleonic wars.

Frederick William IV, son, 1840-1861. Uprising of 1848 and first parliament and constitution.

## Second and Third Reich

William I, 1861-1888, brother. Annexation of Schleswig and Hanover; Franco-Prussian war, 1870-1871, proclamation of German Reich, Jan. 18, 1871, at Versailles; William, German emperor (Deutscher Kaiser), Bismarck, chancellor.

Frederick III, son, 1888.

William II, son, 1888-1918. Led Germany in World War I, abdicated as German emperor and king of Prussia, Nov. 9, 1918. Died in exile in Netherlands, June 4, 1941. Minor rulers of Bavaria, Saxony, Wurttemberg also abdicated.

Germany proclaimed republic at Weimar, July 1, 1919. Presidents: Frederick Ebert, 1919-1925; Paul von Hindenburg-Beneckendorff, 1925, reelected 1932, d. Aug. 2, 1934. Adolf Hitler, chancellor, chosen successor as Leader-Chancellor (Fuehrer-Reichskanzler) of Third Reich. Annexed Austria, Mar., 1938. Precipitated World War II, 1939-1945. Suicide Apr. 30, 1945.

## Germany After 1945

Following World War II, Germany was split between democratic West and Soviet-dominated East. West German chancellors: Konrad Adenauer, 1949-1963; Ludwig Erhard, 1963-1966; Kurt Georg Kiesinger, 1966-1969; Willy Brandt, 1969-1974; Helmut Schmidt, 1974-1982; Helmut Kohl, 1982-1990. East German Communist party leaders: Walter Ulbricht, 1946-1971; Erich Honecker, 1971-1989; Egon Krenz, 1989-1990.

Germany was reunited Oct. 3, 1990. First post-reunification chancellor: Helmut Kohl, 1990- .

# Rulers of Poland

### House of Piasts

Miesko I, 962?-992; Poland Christianized 966. Expansion under 3 Boleslavs: I, 992-1025, son, crowned king 1024; II, 1058-1079, great-grandson, exiled after killing bishop Stanislav who became chief patron saint of Poland; III, 1106-1138, nephew, divided Poland among 4 sons, eldest suzerain.

1138-1306, feudal division. 1226 founding in Prussia of military order Teutonic Knights. 1226 invasion by Tartars/Mongols.

Vladislav I, 1306-1333, reunited most Polish territories, crowned king 1320. Casimir III the Great, 1333-1370, son, developed economic, cultural life, foreign policy.

### House of Anjou

Louis I, 1370-1382, nephew/was also Louis I of Hungary.

Jadwiga, 1384-1399, daughter, married 1386 Jagiello, Grand Duke of Lithuania.

### House of Jagiellonians

Vladislav II, 1386-1434, Christianized Lithuania, founded personal union between Poland & Lithuania. Defeated 1410 Teutonic Knights at Grunwald.

Vladislav III, 1434-1444, son, simultaneously king of Hungary. Fought Turks, killed 1444 in battle of Varna.

Casimir IV, 1446-1492, brother, competed with Hapsburgs, put son Vladislav on throne of Bohemia, later also of Hungary (Ulaszlo II).

Sigismund I, 1506-1548, son, patronized science and arts, his and son's reign "Golden Age."

Sigismund II, 1548-1572, son, established 1569 real union of Poland and Lithuania (lasted until 1795).

### Elective Kings

Polish nobles in 1572 proclaimed Poland a republic headed by king to be elected by whole nobility.

Stephen Batory, 1576-1586, duke of Transylvania, married Ann, sister of Sigismund II August. Fought Russians.

Sigismund III Vasa, 1587-1632, nephew of Sigismund II. 1592-1598 also king of Sweden. His generals fought Russians, Turks.

Vladislav II Vasa, 1632-1648, son. Fought Russians.

John II Casimir Vasa, 1648-1668, brother. Fought Cossacks, Swedes, Russians, Turks, Tatars (the "Deluge"). Abdicated 1668.

John III Sobieski, 1674-1696. Won Vienna from besieging Turks, 1683.

Stanislav II, 1764-1795, last king. Encouraged reforms; 1791 1st modern Constitution in Europe. 1772, 1793, 1795 Poland partitioned among Russia, Prussia, Austria. Unsuccessful insurrection against foreign invasion 1794 under Kosciuszko, American-Polish general.

### 1795-1918: Poland Under Foreign Rule

1807-1815 Grand Duchy of Warsaw created by Napoleon I, Frederick August of Saxony grand duke.

1815 Congress of Vienna proclaimed part of Poland "Kingdom" in personal union with Russia.

Polish uprisings: 1830 against Russia; 1846, 1848 against Austria; 1863 against Russia—all repressed.

### 1918-1939: Second Republic

1918-1922 Head of State Jozef Pilsudski. Presidents: Gabriel Narutowicz 1922, assassinated; Stanislav Wojciechowski 1922-1926, had to abdicate after Pilsudski's coup d'état; Ignacy Moscicki, 1926-1939, ruled (with Pilsudski until his death, 1935) as virtual dictator.

### 1939-1945: Poland Under Foreign Occupation

Nazi aggression Sept. 1939. Polish government-in-exile, first in France, then in England. Vladislav Raczkiewicz president; Gen. Vladislav Sikorski, then Stanislav Mikolajczyk, prime ministers. Soviet-sponsored Polish Committee of National Liberation proclaimed at Lublin July 1944, transformed into government Jan. 1, 1945.

### Poland After 1945

In the late 1940s, Poland came increasingly under Soviet-control. Communist party ruled in Poland until Aug. 1989, when democratic Solidarity party gained control of government. Solidarity leader Lech Walesa was elected president, Nov. 1990; succeeded by former Communist Aleksander Kwasniewski, Nov. 1995.

# Rulers of Denmark, Sweden, Norway

### Denmark

Earliest rulers invaded Britain; King Canute, who ruled in London 1016-1035, was most famous. The Valdemars furnished kings until the 15th century. In 1282 the Danes won the first national assembly, Danehof, from King Erik V.

Most redoubtable medieval character was Margaret, daughter of Valdemar IV, born 1353, married at 10 to King Haakon VI of Norway. In 1376 she had her first infant son Olaf made king of Denmark. After his death, 1387, she was regent of Denmark and Norway. In 1388 Sweden accepted her as sovereign. In 1389 she made her grand-nephew, Duke Erik of Pomerania, titular king of Denmark, Sweden, and Norway, with herself as regent. In 1397 she effected the Union of Kalmar of the three kingdoms and had Erik VII crowned. In 1439 the three kingdoms deposed him and elected, 1440, Christopher of Bavaria king (Christopher III). On his death, 1448, the union broke up.

Succeeding rulers were unable to enforce their claims as rulers of Sweden until 1520, when Christian II conquered Sweden. He was thrown out 1522, and in 1523 Gustavus Vasa united Sweden. Denmark continued to dominate Norway until the Napoleonic wars, when Frederick VI, 1808-1839, joined the Napoleonic cause after Britain had destroyed the Danish fleet, 1807. In 1814 he was forced to cede Norway to Sweden and Helgoland to Britain, receiving Lauenburg. Successors Christian VIII, 1839; Frederick VII, 1848; Christian IX, 1863; Frederick VIII, 1906; Christian X, 1912; Frederick IX, 1947; Margrethe II, 1972.

### Sweden

Early kings ruled at Uppsala, but did not dominate the country. Sverker, c1130-c1156, united the Swedes and Goths. In 1435 Sweden obtained the Riksdag, or parliament. After the Union of Kalmar, 1397, the Danes either ruled or harried the country until Christian II of Denmark conquered it anew, 1520. This led to a rising under Gustavus Vasa, who ruled Sweden 1523-1560, and established an independent kingdom. Charles IX, 1599-1611, crowned 1604, conquered Moscow. Gustavus II Adolphus, 1611-1632, was called the Lion of the North. Later rulers: Christina, 1632; Charles X Gustavus, 1654; Charles XI, 1660; Charles XII (invader of Russia and Poland, defeated at Poltava, June 28, 1709), 1697; Ulrika Eleanora, sister, elected queen 1718; Frederick I (of Hesse), her husband, 1720; Adolphus Frederick, 1751; Gustavus III, 1771; Gustavus IV Adolphus, 1792; Charles XIII, 1809. (Union with Norway began 1814.) Charles XIV John, 1818 (he was Jean Bernadotte, Napoleon's Prince of Ponte Corvo, elected 1810 to succeed Charles XIII); he founded the present dynasty: Oscar I, 1844; Charles XV, 1859; Oscar II, 1872; Gustavus V, 1907; Gustav VI Adolf, 1950; Carl XVI Gustaf, 1973.

### Norway

Overcoming many rivals, Harald Haarfager, 872-930, conquered Norway, Orkneys, and Shetlands; Olaf I, great-grandson, 995-1000, brought Christianity into Norway, Iceland, and Greenland. In 1035 Magnus the Good also became king of Denmark. Haakon V, 1299-1319, had married his daughter to Erik of Sweden. Their son, Magnus, became ruler of Norway and Sweden at 6. His son, Haakon VI, married Margaret of Denmark; their son Olaf IV became king of Norway and Denmark, followed by Margaret's regency and the Union of Kalmar, 1397.

In 1450 Norway became subservient to Denmark. Christian IV, 1588-1648, founded Christiania, now Oslo. After Napoleonic wars, when Denmark ceded Norway to Sweden, a strong nationalist movement forced recognition of Norway as an independent kingdom united with Sweden under the Swedish kings, 1814-1905. In 1905 the union was dissolved and Prince Charles of Denmark became Haakon VII. He died Sept. 21, 1957; succeeded by son, Olav V. Olav V died Jan. 17, 1991; succeeded by son, Harald V.

# Rulers of the Netherlands and Belgium

### The Netherlands (Holland)

William Frederick, Prince of Orange, led a revolt against French rule, 1813, and was crowned King of the Netherlands, 1815. Belgium seceded Oct. 4, 1830, after a revolt. The secession was ratified by the two kingdoms by treaty Apr. 19, 1839.

Succession: William II, son, 1840; William III, son, 1849; Wilhelmina, daughter of William III and his 2d wife Princess Emma of Waldeck, 1890; Wilhelmina abdicated, Sept. 4, 1948, in favor of daughter, Juliana. Juliana abdicated, Apr. 30, 1980, in favor of daughter, Beatrix.

### Belgium

A national congress elected Prince Leopold of Saxe-Coburg as king; he took the throne July 21, 1831, as Leopold I. Succession: Leopold II, son, 1865; Albert I, nephew of Leopold II, 1909; Leopold III, son of Albert, 1934; Prince Charles, Regent 1944; Leopold returned 1950, yielded powers to son Baudouin, Prince Royal, Aug. 6, 1950, abdicated July 16, 1951. Baudouin I took throne July 17, 1951, died July 31, 1993; succeeded by brother, Albert II.

# Roman Rulers

From Romulus to the end of the Empire in the West. Rulers of the Roman Empire in the East sat in Constantinople and for a brief period in Nicaea, until the capture of Constantinople by the Turks in 1453, when Byzantium was succeeded by the Ottoman Empire.

| BC | Name |
|---|---|
| | **The Kingdom** |
| 753 | Romulus (Quirinus) |
| 716 | Numa Pompilius |
| 673 | Tullus Hostilius |
| 640 | Ancus Marcius |
| 616 | L. Tarquinius Priscus |
| 578 | Servius Tullius |
| 534 | L. Tarquinius Superbus |
| | **The Republic** |
| 509 | Consulate established |
| 509 | Quaestorship instituted |
| 498 | Dictatorship introduced |
| 494 | Plebeian Tribunate created |
| 494 | Plebeian Aedileship created |
| 444 | Consular Tribunate organized |
| 435 | Censorship instituted |
| 366 | Praetorship established |
| 366 | Curule Aedileship created |
| 362 | Military Tribunate elected |
| 326 | Proconsulate introduced |
| 311 | Naval Duumvirate elected |
| 217 | Dictatorship of Fabius Maximus |
| 133 | Tribunate of Tiberius Gracchus |
| 123 | Tribunate of Gaius Gracchus |
| 82 | Dictatorship of Sulla |
| 60 | First Triumvirate formed (Caesar, Pompeius, Crassus) |
| 46 | Dictatorship of Caesar |
| 43 | Second Triumvirate formed (Octavianus, Antonius, Lepidus) |
| | **The Empire** |
| 27 | Augustus (Gaius Julius Caesar Octavianus) |
| AD | |
| 14 | Tiberius I |
| 37 | Gaius Caesar (Caligula) |
| 41 | Claudius I |
| 54 | Nero |
| 68 | Galba |
| 69 | Galba; Otho, Vitellius |
| 69 | Vespasianus |
| 79 | Titus |
| 81 | Domitianus |
| 96 | Nerva |

| AD | Name |
|---|---|
| 98 | Trajanus |
| 117 | Hadrianus |
| 138 | Antoninus Pius |
| 161 | Marcus Aurelius and Lucius Verus |
| 169 | Marcus Aurelius (alone) |
| 180 | Commodus |
| 193 | Pertinax; Julianus I |
| 193 | Septimius Severus |
| 211 | Caracalla and Geta |
| 212 | Caracalla (alone) |
| 217 | Macrinus |
| 218 | Elagabalus (Heliogabalus) |
| 222 | Alexander Severus |
| 235 | Maximinus I (the Thracian) |
| 238 | Gordianus I and Gordianus II; Pupienus and Balbinus |
| 238 | Gordianus III |
| 244 | Philippus (the Arabian) |
| 249 | Decius |
| 251 | Gallus and Volusianus |
| 253 | Aemilianus |
| 253 | Valerianus and Gallienus |
| 258 | Gallienus (alone) |
| 268 | Claudius Gothicus |
| 270 | Quintillus |
| 270 | Aurelianus |
| 275 | Tacitus |
| 276 | Florianus |
| 276 | Probus |
| 282 | Carus |
| 283 | Carinus and Numerianus |
| 284 | Diocletianus |
| 286 | Diocletianus and Maximianus |
| 305 | Galerius and Constantius I |
| 306 | Galerius, Maximinus II, Severus I |
| 307 | Galerius, Maximinus II, Constantinus I, Licinius, Maxentius |
| 311 | Maximinus II, Constantinus I, Licinius, Maxentius |
| 314 | Maximinus II, Constantinus I, Licinius |
| 314 | Constantinus I and Licinius |
| 324 | Constantinus I (the Great) |

| AD | Name |
|---|---|
| 337 | Constantinus II, Constans I, Constantius II |
| 340 | Constantius II and Constans I |
| 350 | Constantius II |
| 361 | Julianus II (the Apostate) |
| 363 | Jovianus |
| | **West (Rome) and East (Constantinople)** |
| 364 | Valentinianus I (West) and Valens (East) |
| 367 | Valentinianus I with Gratianus (West) and Valens (East) |
| 375 | Gratianus with Valentinianus II (West) and Valens (East) |
| 378 | Gratianus with Valentinianus II (West), Theodosius I (East) |
| 383 | Valentinianus II (West) and Theodosius I (East) |
| 394 | Theodosius I (the Great) |
| 395 | Honorius (West) and Arcadius (East) |
| 408 | Honorius (West) and Theodosius II (East) |
| 423 | Valentinianus III (West) and Theodosius II (East) |
| 450 | Valentinianus III (West) and Marcianus (East) |
| 455 | Maximus (West), Avitus (West); Marcianus (East) |
| 456 | Avitus (West), Marcianus (East) |
| 457 | Majorianus (West), Leo I (East) |
| 461 | Severus II (West), Leo I (East) |
| 467 | Anthemius (West), Leo I (East) |
| 472 | Olybrius (West), Leo I (East) |
| 473 | Glycerius (West), Leo I (East) |
| 474 | Julius Nepos (West), Leo II (East) |
| 475 | Romulus Augustulus (West) and Zeno (East) |
| 476 | End of Empire in West; Odovacar, King, drops title of Emperor; murdered by King Theodoric of Ostrogoths, 493 |

# Rulers of Modern Italy

After the fall of Napoleon in 1814, the Congress of Vienna, 1815, restored Italy as a political patchwork, comprising the Kingdom of Naples and Sicily, the Papal States, and smaller units. Piedmont and Genoa were awarded to Sardinia, ruled by King Victor Emmanuel I of Savoy.

United Italy emerged under the leadership of Camillo, Count di Cavour (1810-1861), Sardinian prime minister. Agitation was led by Giuseppe Mazzini (1805-1872) and Giuseppe Garibaldi (1807-1882), soldier; Victor Emmanuel I abdicated 1821. After a brief regency for a brother, Charles Albert was King 1831-1849, abdicating when defeated by the Austrians at Novara. Succeeded by Victor Emmanuel II, 1849-1861.

In 1859 France forced Austria to cede Lombardy to Sardinia, which gave rights to Savoy and Nice to France. In 1860 Garibaldi led 1,000 volunteers in a spectacular campaign, took Sicily and expelled the King of Naples. In 1860 the House of Savoy annexed Tuscany, Parma,

Modena, Romagna, the Two Sicilies, the Marches, and Umbria. Victor Emmanuel assumed the title of King of Italy at Turin Mar. 17, 1861. In 1866 he allied with Prussia in the Austro-Prussian War, with Prussia's victory received Venetia. On Sept. 20, 1870, his troops under Gen. Raffaele entered Rome and took over the Papal States, ending the temporal power of the Roman Catholic Church.

Succession: Umberto I, 1878, assassinated 1900; Victor Emmanuel III, 1900, abdicated 1946, died 1947; Humbert II, 1946, ruled a month. In 1921 Benito Mussolini (1883-1945) formed the Fascist party; he became prime minister Oct. 31, 1922. He entered World War II as an ally of Hitler. He was deposed July 25, 1943.

At a plebiscite June 2, 1946, Italy voted for a republic; Premier Alcide de Gasperi became chief of state June 13, 1946. On June 28, 1946, the Constituent Assembly elected Enrico de Nicola, Liberal, provisional president. Successive presidents: Luigi Einaudi, elected May 11, 1948; Giovanni Gronchi, Apr. 29, 1955; Antonio Segni, May 6, 1962; Giuseppe Saragat, Dec. 28, 1964; Giovanni Leone, Dec. 29, 1971; Alessandro Pertini, July 9, 1978; Francesco Cossiga, July 9, 1985; Oscar Luigi Scalfaro, May 28, 1992.

## Rulers of Spain

From 8th to 11th centuries Spain was dominated by the Moors (Arabs and Berbers). The Christian reconquest established small kingdoms (Asturias, Aragon, Castile, Catalonia, Leon, Navarre, and Valencia). In 1474 Isabella, b. 1451, became Queen of Castile & Leon. Her husband, Ferdinand, b. 1452, inherited Aragon 1479, with Catalonia, Valencia, and the Balearic Islands, became Ferdinand V of Castile. By Isabella's request Pope Sixtus IV established the Inquisition, 1478. Last Moorish kingdom, Granada, fell 1492. Columbus opened New World of colonies, 1492. Isabella died 1504, succeeded by her daughter, Juana "the Mad," but Ferdinand ruled until his death 1516.

Charles I, b. 1500, son of Juana and grandson of Ferdinand and Isabella, and of Maximilian I of Hapsburg; succeeded later as Holy Roman Emperor, Charles V, 1520; abdicated 1556. Philip II, son, 1556-1598, inherited only Spanish throne; conquered Portugal, fought Turks, persecuted non-Catholics, sent Armada against England. Was married to Mary I of England, 1554-1558. Succession: Philip III, 1598-1621; Philip IV, 1621-1665; Charles II, 1665-1700, left Spain to Philip of Anjou, grandson of Louis XIV, who as Philip V, 1700-1746, founded Bourbon dynasty; Ferdinand VI, 1746-1759; Charles III, 1759-1788; Charles IV, 1788-1808, abdicated.

Napoleon now dominated politics and made his brother Joseph King of Spain 1808, but the Spanish ousted him in 1813. Ferdinand VII, 1808, 1814-1833, lost American colonies; succeeded by daughter Isabella II, aged 3, with wife Maria Christina of Naples regent until 1843. Isabella deposed by revolution 1868. Elected king by the Cortes, Amadeo of Savoy, 1870; abdicated 1873. First republic, 1873-74. Alphonso XII, son of Isabella, 1875-85. His posthumous son was Alphonso XIII, with his mother, Queen Maria Christina regent; Spanish-American war, Spain lost Cuba, gave up Puerto Rico, Philippines, Sulu Is., Marianas. Alphonso took throne 1902, aged 16, married British Princess Victoria Eugenia of Battenberg. The dictatorship of Primo de Rivera, 1923-30, precipitated the revolution of 1931. Alphonso agreed to leave without formal abdication. The monarchy was abolished and the second republic established, with socialist backing. Niceto Alcala Zamora was president until 1936, when Manuel Azaña was chosen.

In July 1936, the army in Morocco revolted against the government and General Francisco Franco led the troops into Spain. The revolution succeeded by Feb. 1939, when Azaña resigned. Franco became chief of state, with provisions that if he was incapacitated the Regency Council by two-thirds vote could propose a king to the Cortes, which needed to have a two-thirds majority to elect him.

Alphonso XIII died in Rome Feb. 28, 1941, aged 54. His property and citizenship had been restored.

A succession law restoring the monarchy was approved in a 1947 referendum. Prince Juan Carlos, b. 1938, grandson of Alphonso XIII, was designated by Franco and the Cortes in 1969 as the future king and chief of state. Franco died Nov. 20, 1975; Juan Carlos was proclaimed king, Nov. 22, 1975.

## Leaders in the South American Wars of Liberation

Simon Bolivar (1783-1830), Jose Francisco de San Martin (1778-1850), and Francisco Antonio Gabriel Miranda (1750-1816) are among the heroes of the early 19th century struggles of South American nations to free themselves from Spain. All three, and their contemporaries, operated in periods of factional strife, during which soldiers and civilians suffered.

Miranda, a Venezuelan, who had served with the French in the American Revolution and commanded parts of the French Revolutionary armies in the Netherlands, attempted to start a revolt in Venezuela in 1806 and failed. In 1810, with British and American backing, he returned and was briefly a dictator, until the British withdrew their support. In 1812 he was overcome by the royalists in Venezuela and taken prisoner, dying in a Spanish prison in 1816.

San Martin was born in Argentina and during 1789-1811 served in campaigns of the Spanish armies in Europe and Africa. He first joined the independence movement in Argentina in 1812 and in 1817 invaded Chile with 4,000 men over the mountain passes. Here he and Gen. Bernardo O'Higgins (1778-1842) defeated the Spaniards at Chacabuco, 1817, and O'Higgins was named Liberator and became first director of Chile, 1817-23. In 1821 San Martin occupied Lima and Callao, Peru, and became protector of Peru.

Bolivar, the greatest leader of South American liberation from Spain, was born in Venezuela, the son of an aristocratic family. He first served under Miranda in 1812 and in 1813 captured Caracas, where he was named Liberator. Forced out next year by civil strife, he led a campaign that captured Bogota in 1814. In 1817 he was again in control of Venezuela and was named dictator. He organized Nueva Granada with the help of General Francisco de Paula Santander (1792-1840). By joining Nueva Granada, Venezuela, and the area that is now Panama and Ecuador, the republic of Colombia was formed, with Bolivar president. After numerous setbacks he decisively defeated the Spaniards in the second battle of Carabobo, Venezuela, June 24, 1821.

In May, 1822, Gen. Antonio Jose de Sucre, Bolivar's lieutenant, took Quito. Bolivar went to Guayaquil to confer with San Martin, who resigned as protector of Peru and withdrew from politics. With a new army of Colombians and Peruvians Bolivar defeated the Spaniards in a battle at Junín in 1824 and cleared Peru.

De Sucre organized Charcas (Upper Peru) as Republica Bolivar (now Bolivia) and acted as president in place of Bolivar, who wrote its constitution. De Sucre defeated the Spanish faction of Peru at Ayacucho, Dec. 19, 1824.

Continued civil strife finally caused the Colombian federation to break apart. Santander turned against Bolivar, but the latter defeated him and banished him. In 1828 Bolivar gave up the presidency he had held precariously for 14 years. He became ill from tuberculosis and died Dec. 17, 1830. He is buried in the national pantheon in Caracas.

# Rulers of Russia; Leaders of the USSR and Russian Federation

First ruler to consolidate Slavic tribes was Rurik, leader of the Russians who established himself at Novgorod, AD 862. He and his immediate successors had Scandinavian affiliations. They moved to Kiev after 972 and ruled as Dukes of Kiev. In 988 Vladimir was converted and adopted the Byzantine Greek Orthodox service, later modified by Slav influences. Important as organizer and lawgiver was Yaroslav, 1019-1054, whose daughters married kings of Norway, Hungary, and France. His grandson, Vladimir II (Monomakh), 1113-1125, was progenitor of several rulers, but in 1169 Andrew Bogolubski overthrew Kiev and began the line known as Grand Dukes of Vladimir.

Of the Grand Dukes of Vladimir, Alexander Nevsky, 1246-1263, had a son, Daniel, first to be called Duke of Muscovy (Moscow), who ruled 1294-1303. His successors became Grand Dukes of Muscovy. After Dmitri III Donskoi defeated the Tatars in 1380, they also became Grand Dukes of all Russia. Independence of the Tatars and considerable territorial expansion were achieved under Ivan III, 1462-1505.

Tsars of Muscovy—Ivan III was referred to in church ritual as Tsar. He married Sofia, niece of the last Byzantine emperor. His successor, Basil III, died in 1533 when Basil's son Ivan was only 3. He became Ivan IV, "the Terrible"; crowned 1547 as Tsar of all the Russias, ruled until 1584. Under the weak rule of his son, Feodor I, 1584-1598, Boris Godunov had control. The dynasty died, and after years of tribal strife and intervention by Polish and Swedish armies, the Russians united under 17-year-old Michael Romanov, distantly related to the first wife of Ivan IV. He ruled 1613-1645 and established the Romanov line. Fourth ruler after Michael was Peter I.

Tsars, or Emperors, of Russia (Romanovs)—Peter I, 1682-1725, known as Peter the Great, took title of Emperor in 1721. His successors and dates of accession were: Catherine, his widow, 1725; Peter II, his grandson, 1727; Anne, Duchess of Courland, 1730, daughter of Peter the Great's brother, Tsar Ivan V; Ivan VI, 1740, great-grandson of Ivan V, child, kept in prison and murdered 1764; Elizabeth, daughter of Peter I, 1741; Peter III, grandson of Peter I, 1761, deposed 1762 for his consort, Catherine II, former princess of Anhalt Zerbst (Germany) who is known as Catherine the Great; Paul I, her son, 1796, killed 1801; Alexander I, son of Paul, 1801, defeated Napoleon; Nicholas I, his brother, 1825; Alexander II, son of Nicholas, 1855, assassinated 1881 by terrorists; Alexander III, son, 1881.

Nicholas II, son, 1894-1917, last Tsar of Russia, was forced to abdicate by the Revolution that followed losses to Germany in WWI. The Tsar, the Empress, the Tsarevich (Crown Prince), and the Tsar's 4 daughters were murdered by the Bolsheviks in Yekaterinburg, July 16, 1918.

Provisional Government—Prince Georgi Lvov and Alexander Kerensky, premiers, 1917.

### Union of Soviet Socialist Republics

Bolshevik Revolution, Nov. 7, 1917, displaced Kerensky; council of People's Commissars formed, Lenin (Vladimir Ilyich Ulyanov), premier. Lenin died Jan. 21, 1924. Aleksei Rykov (executed 1938) and V. M. Molotov held the office, but actual ruler was Joseph Stalin (Joseph Vissarionovich Djugashvili), general secretary of the Central Committee of the Communist Party. Stalin became president of the Council of Ministers (premier) May 7, 1941, died Mar. 5, 1953. Succeeded by Georgi M. Malenkov, as head of the Council and premier, and Nikita S. Khrushchev, first secretary of the Central Committee. Malenkov resigned Feb. 8, 1955, became deputy premier, was dropped July 3, 1957. Marshal Nikolai A. Bulganin became premier Feb. 8, 1955; was demoted and Khrushchev became premier Mar. 27, 1958. Khrushchev was ousted Oct. 14-15, 1964, replaced by Leonid I. Brezhnev as first secretary of the party and by Aleksei N. Kosygin as premier. On June 16, 1977, Brezhnev took office as president. Brezhnev died Nov. 10, 1982; 2 days later the Central Committee elected former KGB head Yuri V. Andropov president. Andropov died Feb. 9, 1984; on Feb. 13, Konstantin U. Chernenko chosen by Central Committee as its general secretary. Chernenko died Mar. 10, 1985; on Mar. 11, he was succeeded as general secretary by Mikhail Gorbachev, who replaced Andrei Gromyko as president on Oct. 1, 1988. Gorbachev resigned Dec. 25, 1991, and the Soviet Union officially disbanded the next day. A loose Commonwealth of Independent States, made up of most of the 15 former Soviet constituent republics, was created.

### Post-Soviet Russia

After adopting a degree of sovereignty, the Russian Republic had held elections in June 1991. Boris Yeltsin was sworn in, July 10, 1991, as Russia's first elected president. With the Dec. 1991 dissolution of the Soviet Union, Russia (officially Russian Federation) became a founding member of the Commonwealth of Independent States.

# Governments of China

(Until 221 BC and frequently thereafter, China was not a unified state. Where dynastic dates overlap, the rulers or events referred to appeared in different areas of China.)

| | | | |
|---|---|---|---|
| Hsia | c1994 BC | - | c1523 BC |
| Shang | c1523 | - | c1028 |
| Western Chou | c1027 | - | 770 |
| Eastern Chou | 770 | - | 256 |
| Warring States | 403 | - | 222 |
| Ch'in (first unified empire) | 221 | - | 206 |
| Han | 202 BC | - | AD 220 |
| Western Han (expanded Chinese state beyond the Yellow and Yangtze River valleys) | 202 BC | - | AD 9 |
| Hsin (Wang Mang, usurper) | AD 9 | - | AD 23 |
| Eastern Han (expanded Chinese state into Indochina and Turkestan) | 25 | - | 220 |
| Three Kingdoms (Wei, Shu, Wu) | 220 | - | 265 |
| Chin (western) | 265 | - | 317 |
| (eastern) | 317 | - | 420 |
| Northern Dynasties (followed several short-lived governments by Turks, Mongols, etc.) | 386 | - | 581 |
| Southern Dynasties (capital: Nanjing) | 420 | - | 589 |
| Sui (reunified China) | 581 | - | 618 |
| Tang (a golden age of Chinese culture; capital: Xian) | 618 | - | 906 |
| Five Dynasties (Yellow River basin) | 902 | - | 960 |
| Ten Kingdoms (southern China) | 907 | - | 979 |
| Liao (Khitan Mongols; capital at site of Beijing) | 947 | - | 1125 |
| Sung | 960 | - | 1279 |
| Northern Sung (reunified central and southern China) | 960 | - | 1126 |
| Western Hsai (non-Chinese rulers in northwest) | 990 | - | 1227 |
| Chin (Tatars; drove Sung out of central China) | 1115 | - | 1234 |
| Yuan (Mongols; Kublai Khan est. capital at site of Beijing, c. 1264) | 1271 | - | 1368 |
| Ming (China reunified under Chinese rule; capital: Nanjing, then Beijing in 1420) | 1368 | - | 1644 |
| Ch'ing (Manchus, descendents of Tatars) | 1644 | - | 1911 |
| Republic (disunity; provincial rulers, warlords) | 1912 | - | 1949 |
| People's Republic of China | 1949 | - | — |

## Leaders of China Since 1949

| | |
|---|---|
| Mao Zedong | Chairman, Central People's Administrative Council, Communist Party (CPC), 1949-1976 |
| Zhou Enlai | Premier, foreign minister, 1949-1976 |
| Deng Xiaoping | Vice Premier, 1949-1976; 1977-1987 |
| Liu Shaoqi | President, 1959-1969 |
| Hua Guofeng | Premier, 1976-1980; CPC Chairman, 1976-1981 |
| Zhao Ziyang | Premier, 1980-1988; CPC General Secretary, 1987-1989 |
| Hu Yaobang | CPC Chairman, 1981-1982; CPC General Secretary 1982-1987 |
| Li Xiannian | President, 1983-1988 |
| Yang Shangkun | President, 1988-1993 |
| Li Peng | Premier, 1988- |
| Jiang Zemin | CPC General Secretary, 1989- ; President, 1993- |

# WORLD EXPLORATION AND GEOGRAPHY

## Early Explorers of the Western Hemisphere

The first people to discover the New World, or Western Hemisphere, are believed to have walked across a "land bridge" from Siberia to Alaska, an isthmus since broken by the Bering Strait. From Alaska, these ancestors of the Native Americans spread through what became known as North, Central, and South America. Anthropologists have placed these crossings at between 18,000 and 14,000 BC, but evidence found in 1967 near Puebla, Mex., indicates people may have reached there as early as 35,000-40,000 years ago.

At first, these people were hunters, using flint weapons and tools. In Mexico, about 7000-6000 BC, they founded farming cultures and developed crops, such as corn and squash. Eventually they created complex civilizations—the Olmec, Toltec, Aztec, Maya, and, in South America, the Inca. Carbon-14 tests show that humans lived about 8000 BC near what are now Front Royal, VA, Kanawha, WV, and Dutchess Quarry, NY. The Hopewell Culture, based on farming, flourished about 1000 BC; remains of it are seen today in large mounds in Ohio and other states.

Norsemen (Norwegian Vikings sailing out of Iceland and Greenland) are credited by most scholars with being the first Europeans to discover America, with at least 5 voyages occurring about AD 1000 to areas they called Helluland, Markland, and Vinland—possibly what are known today as Labrador, Nova Scotia or Newfoundland, and New England.

Christopher Columbus, the most famous explorer, was born Cristoforo Colombo (c 1451) in or near Genoa, Italy, but made his voyages of exploration for the Spanish rulers Ferdinand and Isabella. Details of his voyages follow:

**1492—First voyage.** Left Palos, Spain, Aug. 3 with 88 (est.) men. His fleet consisted of 3 vessels—the *Niña,* the *Pinta,* and the *Santa María.* Landed at San Salvador (Guanahani or Watling Isl., Bahamas) Oct. 12; also reached Cuba and Hispaniola (Haiti-Dominican Republic); built Fort La Navidad on Hispaniola.

**1493—Second voyage, first part.** Left Cadiz, Spain, Sept. 25, with 17 ships, 1,500 men. Traveled to Dominica (Lesser Antilles) Nov. 3. Landed at Guadeloupe, Montserrat, Antigua, San Martin, Santa Cruz, Puerto Rico, Virgin Islands. Settled at Isabela on Hispaniola. **Second part.** Columbus remained in Western Hemisphere. Reached Jamaica, Isle of Pines, La Mona Isl.

**1498—Third voyage.** Left Sanlucar, Spain, May 30, with 6 ships. Landed at Trinidad. Saw South American continent, Aug. 1, 1498; called it Isla Sancta (Holy Island). Entered Gulf of Paria and landed, first time on continental soil. At mouth of Orinoco, Aug. 14, he decided this was the mainland.

**1502—Fourth voyage.** Left Cadiz, Spain, May 9, with 4 caravels, 150 men. Reached St. Lucia, Guanaja off Honduras; Cape Gracias a Dios, Honduras; San Juan River, Costa Rica; Almirante, Portobelo, and Laguna de Chiriquí, Panama.

| Year | Explorer | Nationality (employer, if different) | Area reached or explored |
|---|---|---|---|
| 1497 | John Cabot | Italian (English) | Newfoundland or Nova Scotia |
| 1498 | John and Sebastian Cabot | Italian (English) | Labrador to Hatteras |
| 1499 | Alonso de Ojeda | Spanish | N South American coast, Venezuela |
| 1500, Feb. | Vicente Yáñez Pinzón | Spanish | South American coast, Amazon R. |
| 1500, Apr. | Pedro Alvarez Cabral | Portuguese | Brazil |
| 1500-02 | Gaspar Corte-Real | Portuguese | Labrador |
| 1501 | Rodrigo de Bastidas | Spanish | Central America |
| 1513 | Vasco Núñez de Balboa | Spanish | Panama, Pacific Ocean |
| 1513 | Juan Ponce de León | Spanish | Florida, Yucatán Peninsula |
| 1515 | Juan de Solis | Spanish | Río de la Plata |
| 1519 | Alonso de Pineda | Spanish | Mouth of Mississippi R. |
| 1519 | Hernando Cortés | Spanish | Mexico |
| 1519-20 | Ferdinand Magellan | Portuguese (Spanish) | Straits of Magellan, Tierra del Fuego |
| 1524 | Giovanni da Verrazano | Italian (French) | Atlantic coast, inc. New York harbor |
| 1528 | Cabeza de Vaca | Spanish | Texas coast and interior |
| 1532 | Francisco Pizarro | Spanish | Peru |
| 1534 | Jacques Cartier | French | Canada, Gulf of St. Lawrence |
| 1536 | Pedro de Mendoza | Spanish | Buenos Aires |
| 1539 | Francisco de Ulloa | Spanish | California coast |
| 1539-41 | Hernando de Soto | Spanish | Mississippi R., near Memphis |
| 1539 | Marcos de Niza | Italian (Spanish) | SW United States |
| 1540 | Francisco de Coronado | Spanish | SW United States |
| 1540 | Hernando Alarcón | Spanish | Colorado R. |
| 1540 | Garcia de L. Cardenas | Spanish | Colorado, Grand Canyon |
| 1541 | Francisco de Orellana | Spanish | Amazon R. |
| 1542 | Juan Rodriguez Cabrillo | Portuguese (Spanish) | W Mexico, San Diego harbor |
| 1565 | Pedro Menéndez de Aviles | Spanish | St. Augustine, FL |
| 1576 | Sir Martin Frobisher | English | Frobisher's Bay, Canada |
| 1577-80 | Sir Francis Drake | English | California coast |
| 1582 | Antonio de Espejo | Spanish | SW U.S. (New Mexico) |
| 1584 | Amadas & Barlow (for Raleigh) | English | Virginia |
| 1585-87 | Sir Walter Raleigh's men | English | Roanoke Isl., NC |
| 1595 | Sir Walter Raleigh | English | Orinoco R. |
| 1603-09 | Samuel de Champlain | French | Canadian interior, Lake Champlain |
| 1607 | Capt. John Smith | English | Atlantic coast |
| 1609-10 | Henry Hudson | English (Dutch) | Hudson R., Hudson Bay |
| 1634 | Jean Nicolet | French | Lake Michigan, Wisconsin |
| 1673 | Jacques Marquette, Louis Jolliet | French | Mississippi R., S to Arkansas |
| 1682 | Robert Cavelier, sieur de La Salle | French | Mississippi R., S to Gulf of Mexico |
| 1789 | Sir Alexander Mackenzie | Canadian | NW Canada |

## Arctic Exploration

### Early Explorers

**1587** — John Davis (Eng.). Davis Strait to Sanderson's Hope, 72°12´ N.

**1596** — Willem Barents and Jacob van Heemskerck (Holland). Discovered Bear Isl., touched NW tip of Spitsbergen, 79°49´ N, rounded Novaya Zemlya, wintered at Ice Haven.

**1607** — Henry Hudson (Eng.). North along Greenland's E coast to Cape Hold-with-Hope, 73°30´, then N of Spitsbergen to 80°23´. Returning he explored Hudson's Touches (Jan Mayen).

**1616** — William Baffin and Robert Bylot (Eng.). Baffin Bay to Smith Sound.

**1728** — Vitus Bering (Russ.). Proved Asia and America were separated by sailing through strait now bearing his name.

**1733-40** — Great Northern Expedition (Russ.). Surveyed Siberian Arctic coast.

**1741** — Vitus Bering (Russ.). Sighted Alaska from sea, named Mount St. Elias. His lieutenant, Chirikof, explored coast.

**1771** — Samuel Hearne (Hudson's Bay Co.). Overland from Prince of Wales Fort (Churchill) on Hudson Bay to mouth of Coppermine R.

**1778** — James Cook (Brit.). Through Bering Strait to Icy Cape, AK, and North Cape, Siberia.

**1789** — Alexander Mackenzie (North West Co., Brit.). Montreal to mouth of Mackenzie River.

**1806** — William Scoresby (Brit.). N of Spitsbergen to 81°30′.

**1820-23** — Ferdinand von Wrangel (Russ.). Completed a survey of Siberian Arctic coast. His exploration joined that of James Cook at North Cape, confirming separation of the continents.

**1878-79** — (Nils) Adolf Erik Nordenskjöld (Swed.). The first to navigate the Northeast Passage—an ocean route connecting Europe's North Sea, along the Arctic coast of Asia and through the Bering Sea, to the Pacific Ocean.

**1881** — The U.S. steamer *Jeannette*, led by Lt. Cmdr. George W. DeLong, was trapped in ice and crushed, June 1881. DeLong and 11 others died; 12 survived.

**1888** — Fridtjof Nansen (Nor.) crossed Greenland's ice-cap.

**1893-96** — Nansen in *Fram* drifted from New Siberian Isls. to Spitsbergen; tried polar dash in 1895, reached Franz Josef Land, 86°14′ N.

**1897** — Salomon A. Andrée (Switz.) and 2 others started in balloon from Spitsbergen, July 11, to drift across pole to U.S., and disappeared. More than 33 yrs. later, Aug. 6, 1930, their frozen bodies were found on White Isl., 82°57′ N, 29°52′ E.

**1903-6** — Roald Amundsen (Nor.) first sailed the Northwest Passage—an ocean route linking the Atlantic Ocean to the Pacific via Canada's marine waterways.

## North Pole Exploration

Robert E. Peary explored Greenland's coast, 1891-92; tried for North Pole, 1893. In 1900 he reached N limit of Greenland and 83°50′ N; in 1902 he reached 84°06′ N; in 1906 he went from Ellesmere Isl. to 87°06′ N. He sailed in the *Roosevelt,* July 1908, to winter off Cape Sheridan, Grant Land. The dash for the North Pole began Mar. 1 from Cape Columbia, Ellesmere Isl. Peary reportedly reached the pole, 90° N, Apr. 6, 1909; however, subsequent research suggests that he may have miscalculated and fallen short of his goal by c. 30-60 mi. Peary had several supporting groups carrying supplies until the last group turned back at 87°47′ N. Peary, Matthew Henson, and 4 Eskimos proceeded with dog teams and sleds. They were said to have crossed the pole several times, then built an igloo there and remained 36 hours. Started south, Apr. 7 at 4 PM, for Cape Columbia.

**1914** — Donald MacMillan (U.S.). Northwest, 200 mi, from Axel Heiberg Isl. to seek Peary's Crocker Land.

**1915-17** — Vihjalmur Stefansson (Can.). Discovered Borden, Brock, Meighen, and Lougheed Isls.

**1918-20** — Amundsen sailed the Northeast Passage.

**1925** — Amundsen and Lincoln Ellsworth (U.S.) reached 87°44′ N in attempt to fly to North Pole from Spitsbergen.

**1926** — Richard E. Byrd and Floyd Bennett (U.S.) reputedly flew over North Pole, May 9. (Claim to have reached the Pole is in dispute, however.)

**1926** — Amundsen, Ellsworth, and Umberto Nobile (It.) flew from Spitsbergen over North Pole May 12, to Teller, AK, in dirigible *Norge.*

**1928** — Nobile crossed North Pole in airship, May 24; crashed, May 25. Amundsen died attempting a rescue.

## North Pole Exploration Records

On Aug. 3, 1958, the *Nautilus,* under Comdr. William R. Anderson, became the first ship to cross the North Pole beneath the Arctic ice.

In Aug. 1960, the nuclear-powered U.S. submarine *Seadragon* (Comdr. George P. Steele 2d) made the first E-W underwater transit through the Northwest Passage. Traveling submerged for the most part, it took 6 days to make the 850-mi trek from Baffin Bay to the Beaufort Sea.

On Aug. 16, 1977, the Soviet nuclear icebreaker *Arktika* reached the North Pole, becoming the first surface ship to break through the Arctic ice pack.

On Apr. 30, 1978, Naomi Uemura (Jap.) became the first person to reach the North Pole alone. Traveling by dog sled during the 54-day, 600-mi trek over the frozen Arctic, Uemura survived attacks by a marauding polar bear.

In Apr. 1982, Sir Ranulph Fiennes and Charles Burton, Brit. explorers, reached the North Pole and became the first to circle the earth from pole to pole. They had reached the South Pole 16 months earlier. The 52,000-mi trek took 3 years, involved 23 people, and cost an estimated $18 mil. The expedition was also the first to travel down the Scott Glacier and the first to journey up the Yukon and through the Northwest Passage in a single season.

On May 2, 1986, 6 Amer. and Can. explorers reached the North Pole assisted only by dogs. They became the first to reach the pole without aerial logistics support since Robert E. Peary planted a flag there in 1909. The explorers, Amer. Will Steger, Paul Schurke, Anne Bancroft, and Geoff Carroll, and Can. Brent Boddy and Richard Weber, completed the 500-mi journey in 56 days.

On June 15, 1995, Weber and Russ. Mikhail Malakhov became the first pair to make it to the pole and back without any mechanical assistance. The 940-mi trip, made entirely on skis, took 121 days.

# Antarctic Exploration

## Early History

Antarctica has been approached since 1773-75, when Capt. James Cook (Brit.) reached 71° 10′ S. Many sea and landmarks bear names of early explorers. Fabian von Bellingshausen (Russ.) discovered Peter I and Alexander I Isls., 1819-21. Nathaniel Palmer (U.S.) traveled throughout Palmer Peninsula, 60° W, 1820, without realizing that this was a continent. Capt. John Davis (U.S.) made the first known landing on the continent on Feb. 7, 1821. Later, in 1823, James Weddell (Brit.) found Weddell Sea, 74° 15′ S, the southernmost point that had been reached.

First to announce existence of the continent of Antarctica was Charles Wilkes (U.S.), who followed the coast for 1,500 mi, 1840. Adelie Coast, 140° E, was found by Dumont d'Urville (Fr.), 1840. Ross Ice Shelf was found by James Clark Ross (Brit.), 1841-42.

**1895** — Leonard Kristensen (Nor.) landed a party on the coast of Victoria Land. They were the first ashore on the main continental mass. C. E. Borchgrevink, a member of that party, returned in 1899 with a Brit. expedition, first to winter on Antarctica.

**1902-4** — Robert F. Scott (Brit.) explored Edward VII Peninsula. He reached 82° 17′ S, 146° 33′ E from McMurdo Sound.

**1908-9** — Ernest Shackleton (Brit.) introduced the use of Manchurian ponies in Antarctic sledging. He reached 88° 23′ S, discovering a route on to the plateau by way of the Beardmore Glacier and pioneering the way to the pole.

## South Pole Exploration

**1911** — Roald Amundsen (Nor.) with 4 men and dog teams reached the pole, Dec. 14.

**1912** — Scott reached the pole from Ross Isl., Jan. 18, with 4 companions. None of Scott's party survived. Their bodies and expedition notes were found, Nov. 12.

**1928** — First person to use an airplane over Antarctica was Sir George Hubert Wilkins (Austral.).

**1929** — Richard E. Byrd (U.S.) established Little America on Bay of Whales. On 1,600-mi airplane flight begun Nov. 28, he crossed South Pole, Nov. 29, with 3 others.

**1934-35** — Byrd led 2d expedition to Little America, explored 450,000 sq mi, wintered alone at weather station, 80°08′ S.

**1934-37** — John Rymill led British Graham Land expedition; discovered that Palmer Penin. is part of Antarctic mainland.

**1935** — Lincoln Ellsworth (U.S.) flew S along E Coast of Palmer Penin., then crossed continent to Little America, making 4 landings on unprepared terrain in bad weather.

**1939-41** — U.S. Antarctic Service Expedition built West Base on Ross Ice Shelf under Paul Siple, and East Base on Palmer Peninsula under Richard Black. U.S. Navy plane flights discovered about 150,000 sq mi of new land.

**1940** — Byrd charted most of coast between Ross Sea and Palmer Penin.

**1946-47** — U.S. Navy undertook Operation Highjump, commanded by Byrd, included 13 ships and 4,000 men. Airplanes photomapped coastline and penetrated beyond pole.

**1946-48** — Ronne Antarctic Research Expedition Comdr., Finn Ronne, USNR, determined the Antarctic to be only one continent with no strait between Weddell Sea and Ross Sea; explored 250,000 sq mi of land by flights to 79° S. Mrs. Ronne and Mrs. H. Darlington were the first women to winter on Antarctica.

**1955-57** — U.S. Navy's Operation Deep Freeze led by Adm. Byrd. Supporting U.S. scientific efforts for the International Geophysical Year (IGY), the operation was commanded by Rear Adm. George Dufek. It established 5 coastal stations fronting the Indian, Pacific, and Atlantic oceans and also 3 interior stations; explored more than 1,000,000 sq mi in Wilkes Land.

**1957-58** — During the IGY, July 1957 through Dec. 1958, scientists from 12 countries conducted ambitious programs of Antarctic research at a network of some 60 stations on the continent.

Dr. Vivian E. Fuchs led a 12-person Trans-Antarctic Expedition on the first land crossing of Antarctica. Starting from the Weddell Sea, they reached Scott Station, Mar. 2, 1958, after traveling 2,158 mi in 98 days.

**1958** — A group of 5 U.S. scientists led by Edward C. Thiel, seismologist, moving by tractor from Ellsworth Station on Weddell Sea, identified a huge mountain range, 5,000 ft above the ice sheet and 9,000 ft above sea level. The range, originally seen by a Navy plane, was named the Dufek Massif, for Rear Adm. George Dufek.

**1959** — 12 nations — Argentina, Australia, Belgium, Chile, France, Japan, New Zealand, Norway, South Africa, the Soviet Union, the United Kingdom, and the U.S. — signed a treaty suspending any territorial claims for 30 yrs. and reserving the continent, S of 60° S, for research.

**1961-62** — Scientists discovered the Bentley Trench, running from Ross Ice Shelf into Marie Byrd Land, near the end of the Ellsworth Mts., toward the Weddell Sea.

**1962** — First nuclear power plant began operation at McMurdo Sound.

**1963** — On Feb. 22, a U.S. plane made the longest nonstop flight ever in the S Pole area, covering 3,600 mi in 10 hr. The flight was from McMurdo Station S past the geographical S Pole to Shackleton Mts., SE to the "Area of Inaccessibility," and back to McMurdo Station.

**1964** — A Brit. survey team was landed by helicopter on Cook Island, the first recorded visit since 1775.

**1964** — New Zealanders mapped the mountain area from Cape Adare W some 400 mi to Pennell Glacier.

**1985** — Igor A. Zotikov, a Moscow Institute of Geography researcher, discovered sediments in the Ross Ice Shelf that seem to support the continental drift theory. Research by the Ocean Drilling Project off the Queen Maud Land coast indicated the ice sheets of E Antarctica are 37 million yrs. old.

**1989** — Victoria Murden and Shirley Metz became both the first women and the first Americans to reach the South Pole overland when they arrived with 9 others on Jan. 17, 1989. The 51-day trek on skis covered 740 mi.

**1991** — 24 nations approved a protocol to the 1959 Antarctia Treaty, Oct. 4. Amendments called for various conservation provisions, including banning oil and other mineral exploration for 50 yrs.

**1995** — On Dec. 22, a Norwegian, Borge Ousland, reached the South Pole in the fastest time on skis: 44 days.

# Volcanoes

**Sources:** *Volcanoes of the World*, Geoscience Press; Global Volcanism Network, Smithsonian Institution; as of June 1996

Nearly 75% of the world's approximately 540 historically active volcanoes—those that were active and could become active again—lie within the Ring of Fire, a zone running along the W coast of the Americas from Chile to Alaska, down the E coast of Asia from Siberia to New Guinea, and continuing to New Zealand. About 20% of these volcanoes are in Indonesia. Other prominent groupings are in Japan, the Aleutian Islands, and Central America. Almost all active regions are at the boundaries of the large moving plates that constitute the earth's surface. The Ring of Fire marks the boundary between the plates underlying the Pacific Ocean and those underlying the surrounding continents. Other active regions, such as the Mediterranean and Iceland, are on plate boundaries.

## Notable Volcanic Eruptions of the Past

Approximately 7,000 years ago, Mazama, a 9,900-ft volcano in S Oregon, erupted violently, ejecting ash and lava. The ash spread over the entire northwestern U.S. and as far away as Saskatchewan, Can. During the eruption, the top of the mountain collapsed, leaving a caldera 6 mi across and about a half mile deep, which filled with rainwater to form what is now called Crater Lake.

In AD 79, Vesuvio, or Vesuvius, a 4,190-ft volcano overlooking Naples Bay, became active after several centuries of quiescence. On Aug. 24 of that year, a heated mud and ash flow swept down the mountain, engulfing the cities of Pompeii, Herculaneum, and Stabiae with debris more than 60 ft deep. About 10% of the population of the 3 towns were killed.

Some of the largest eruptions in recent centuries have been in Indonesia. In 1883, an eruption similar to the Mazama eruption occurred on the island of Krakatau. At least 2,000 people died in pyroclastic flows on Aug. 26. The next day, the 2,640-ft peak of the volcano collapsed to 1,000 ft below sea level, leaving only a small portion of the island standing above the sea and killing more than 3,000 people. A tsunami (tidal wave) generated by the collapse then killed more than 31,000 people in nearby Java and Sumatra and eventually reached England. Ash from the eruption colored sunsets around the world for 2 years. A similar, but even more powerful, eruption had taken place 68 years earlier at Mt. Tambora on the Indonesian island of Sumbawa.

| Date | Volcano | Estimated Deaths |
|---|---|---|
| Aug. 24, AD 79 | Mt. Vesuvius, Italy | 16,000 |
| 1586 | Kelut, Java, Indon. | 10,000 |
| Dec. 15, 1631 | Mt. Vesuvius, Italy | 4,000 |
| Aug. 12, 1772 | Mt. Papandayan, Java, Indon. | 3,000 |
| June 8, 1783 | Laki, Iceland | 9,350 |
| May 21, 1792 | Mt. Unzen, Japan | 14,500 |
| Apr. 10-12, 1815 | Mt. Tambora, Sumbawa, Indon. | 92,000(1) |
| Aug. 26-28, 1883 | Krakatau, Indon. | 36,000 |
| Apr. 24, 1902 | Santa María, Guatemala | 1,000(2) |
| May 8, 1902 | Mt. Pelée, Martinique | 28,000 |
| Jan. 30, 1911 | Mt. Taal, Phil. | 1,400 |
| May 19, 1919 | Mt. Kelud, Java, Indon. | 5,000 |
| Jan. 17-21, 1951 | Mt. Lamington, New Guinea | 3,000 |
| May 18, 1980 | Mt. St. Helens, U.S. | 57 |
| Mar. 28, 1982 | El Chichon, Mex. | 1,880 |
| Nov. 13, 1985 | Nevado del Ruiz, Colombia | 23,000 |
| Aug. 21, 1986 | Lake Nyos, Cameroon | 1,700 |
| June 15, 1991 | Mt. Pinatubo, Luzon, Phil. | 800 |

(1) Of these, 10,000 were directly related to the eruption; an additional 82,000 were the result of starvation and disease brought on by the event. (2) An additional 3,000 deaths due to a malaria outbreak are sometimes attributed to the eruption.

# Notable Active Volcanoes

Active volcanoes display a wide range of activity. In this table, years are given for the last display of eruptive activity, as of May 1996. Eruptions are defined as the explosive ejection of new or old fragmental material, the escape of liquid lava, or both.

| Name (latest eruption) | Location | Height (ft) |
|---|---|---|
| **Africa** | | |
| Cameroon (1982) | Cameroon | 13,354 |
| Nyiragogo (1994) | Zaire | 11,400 |
| Nyamuragira (1994) | Zaire | 10,028 |
| Ol Doinyo Lengai (1996) | Tanzania | 9,469 |
| Karthala (1991) | Comoros | 8,000 |
| Piton de la Fournaise (1992) | Réunion Isl. | 5,981 |
| Lake Nyos (1986) | Cameroon | 3,011 |
| Erta-Ale (1995) | Ethiopia | 1,650 |
| **Antarctica** | | |
| Erebus (1995) | Ross Isl. | 12,450 |
| Deception Island (1970) | S. Shetland Isl. | 1,890 |
| **Asia-Oceania** | | |
| Kliuchevskoi (1995) | Russia | 15,584 |
| Kerinci (1970) | Sumatra, Indon. | 12,467 |
| Fuji (1708) | Honshu, Japan | 12,388 |
| Tolbachik (1876) | Russia | 12,080 |
| Semeru (1995) | Java, Indon. | 12,060 |
| Slamet (1989) | Java, Indon. | 11,247 |
| Raung (1993) | Java, Indon. | 10,932 |
| On-take (1980) | Honshu, Japan | 10,049 |
| Mayon (1993) | Luzon, Phil. | 9,991 |
| Merapi (1995) | Java, Indon. | 9,551 |
| Marapi (1993) | Sumatra, Indon. | 9,485 |
| Bezymianny (1995) | Russia | 9,455 |
| Ruapehu (1995) | New Zealand | 9,175 |
| Baitoushan (1702) | China/Korea | 9,003 |
| Asama (1990) | Honshu, Japan | 8,300 |
| Niigata Yake-yama (1989) | Honshu, Japan | 8,111 |
| Canlaon (1993) | Negros, Phil. | 8,070 |
| Alaid (1986) | Kuril Isl., Russia | 7,662 |
| Ulawun (1993) | Papua New Guinea | 7,532 |
| Ngauruhoe (1977) | New Zealand | 7,515 |
| Chokai (1974) | Honshu, Japan | 7,300 |
| Galunggung (1984) | Java, Indon. | 7,113 |
| Azuma (1977) | Honshu, Japan | 6,700 |
| Bagana (1993) | Papua New Guinea | 6,558 |
| Sangeang Api (1988) | Lesser Sunda Isl., Indon. | 6,351 |
| Nasu (1963) | Honshu, Japan | 6,210 |
| Tiatia (1981) | Kuril Isl., Russia | 6,013 |
| Manam (1996) | Papua New Guinea | 6,000 |
| Soputan (1996) | Celebes, Indon. | 5,994 |
| Bandai (1888) | Honshu, Japan | 5,968 |
| Karangetang (1995) | Sangihe, Indon. | 5,853 |
| Kelud (1990) | Java, Indon. | 5,679 |
| Gamalama (1993) | Halmahera, Indon. | 5,627 |
| Kirishima (1992) | Kyushu, Japan | 5,577 |
| Pinatubo (1995) | Luzon, Phil. | 5,770 |
| Akita Komaga-take (1996) | Honshu, Japan | 5,449 |
| Gamkonora (1987) | Halmahera, Indon. | 5,364 |
| Aso (1995) | Kyushu, Japan | 5,223 |
| Lokon-Empung (1992) | Celebes, Indon. | 5,187 |
| Bulusan (1995) | Luzon, Phil. | 5,115 |
| Sarychev Peak (1989) | Kuril Isl., Russia | 4,960 |
| Karkar (1979) | Papua New Guinea | 4,920 |
| Karymsky (1996) | Russia | 4,869 |
| Lopevi (1982) | Vanuatu | 4,755 |
| Unzen (1996) | Kyushu, Japan | 4,462 |
| Ambrym (1991) | Vanuatu | 4,376 |
| Awu (1992) | Sangihe Isl., Indon. | 4,350 |
| Sakura-jima (1996) | Kyushu, Japan | 3,668 |
| Langila (1996) | Papua New Guinea | 3,586 |
| Krakatau (1995) | Indonesia | 2,667 |
| Suwanose-jima (1996) | Kyushu, Japan | 2,640 |
| Oshima (1990) | Izu Isl., Japan | 2,550 |
| Usu (1982) | Hokkaido, Japan | 2,400 |
| Rabaul (1996) | Papua New Guinea | 2,257 |
| Pagan (1993) | N. Mariana Isl. | 1,870 |
| White Island (1995) | New Zealand | 1,075 |
| Taal (1977) | Luzon, Phil. | 984 |

| Name (latest eruption) | Location | Height (ft) |
|---|---|---|
| **Central America—Caribbean** | | |
| Acatenango (1972) | Guatemala | 12,992 |
| Fuego (1987) | Guatemala | 12,582 |
| Tacana (1986) | Guatemala | 12,400 |
| Santa María (1993) | Guatemala | 12,362 |
| Irazú (1965) | Costa Rica | 11,260 |
| Turrialba (1866) | Costa Rica | 10,650 |
| Póas (1994) | Costa Rica | 8,930 |
| Pacaya (1995) | Guatemala | 8,346 |
| San Miguel (1986) | El Salvador | 6,994 |
| Rincón de la Vieja (1995) | Costa Rica | 6,234 |
| San Cristobal (1977) | Nicaragua | 5,840 |
| Concepción (1986) | Nicaragua | 5,106 |
| Arenal (1996) | Costa Rica | 5,092 |
| Pelee (1932) | Martinique | 4,583 |
| Momotombo (1905) | Nicaragua | 4,199 |
| Soufrière St. Vincent (1979) | St. Vincent | 4,048 |
| Masaya (1994) | Nicaragua | 2,083 |
| **South America** | | |
| Llullaillaco (1877) | Chile | 22,057 |
| Guallatiri (1960) | Chile | 19,882 |
| Láscar (1995) | Chile | 19,652 |
| Cotopaxi (1940) | Ecuador | 19,347 |
| El Misti (1870?) | Peru | 19,101 |
| Tupungatito (1986) | Chile | 18,504 |
| Ruiz (1991) | Colombia | 17,716 |
| Sangay (1996) | Ecuador | 17,159 |
| Guagua Pichincha (1993) | Ecuador | 15,696 |
| Purace (1977) | Colombia | 15,601 |
| Galeras (1993) | Colombia | 13,996 |
| Llaima (1995) | Chile | 10,239 |
| Villarrica (1992) | Chile | 9,318 |
| Cerro Hudson (1991) | Chile | 8,580 |
| Fernandina (1995) | Galapagos Isls., Ecuador | 4,905 |
| **Mid-Pacific** | | |
| Mauna Loa (1984) | Hawaii, HI | 13,680 |
| Kilauea (1996) | Hawaii, HI | 4,077 |
| **Mid-Atlantic Ridge** | | |
| Beerenberg (1985) | Jan Mayen Isl., Norway | 7,470 |
| Hekla (1991) | Iceland | 4,892 |
| Krafla (1984) | Iceland | 2,145 |
| **Europe** | | |
| Etna (1996) | Italy | 11,053 |
| Stromboli (1996) | Italy | 3,038 |
| Santorini (1950) | Greece | 1,850 |
| **North America** | | |
| Citlaltepetl (Orizaba) (1687) | Mexico | 18,700 |
| Popocatépetl (1996) | Mexico | 17,930 |
| Rainier (1894?) | Washington | 14,410 |
| Wrangell (1907?) | Alaska | 14,163 |
| Shasta (1786) | California | 14,162 |
| Colima (1994) | Mexico | 14,003 |
| Redoubt (1990) | Alaska | 10,197 |
| Iliamna (1953) | Alaska | 10,016 |
| Shishaldin (1995) | Aleutian Isl., AK | 9,387 |
| St. Helens (1991) | Washington | 8,363 |
| Pavlof (1988) | Alaska | 8,261 |
| Veniaminof (1995) | Alaska | 8,225 |
| El Chichon (1982) | Mexico | 7,300 |
| Novarupta (Katmai) (1912) | Alaska | 6,715 |
| Makushin (1987) | Aleutian Isl., AK | 6,680 |
| Great Sitkin (1974) | Aleutian Isl., AK | 5,710 |
| Cleveland (1994) | Aleutian Isl., AK | 5,675 |
| Gareloi (1989) | Aleutian Isl., AK | 5,334 |
| Korovin (1987) | Aleutian Isl., AK | 4,852 |
| Akutan (1992) | Aleutian Isl., AK | 4,275 |
| Kiska (1990) | Aleutian Isl., AK | 4,275 |
| Augustine (1986) | Alaska | 3,999 |
| Okmok (1988) | Aleutian Isl., AK | 3,519 |
| Seguam (1993) | Aleutian Isl., AK | 3,458 |

# Mountains

## Height of Mount Everest

Mt. Everest was considered 29,002 ft when Edmund Hillary and Tenzing Norgay scaled it in 1953. This triangulation figure had been accepted since 1850. In 1954 the Surveyor General of the Republic of India set the height at 29,028 ft, plus or minus 10 ft because of snow; this figure is used below. The National Geographic Society accepts it, but many mountaineering groups still use 29,002 ft.

In 1987, new calculations based on satellite measurements suggested that the Himalayan peak K-2 rose 29,064 ft above sea level and that Mt. Everest is 800 ft higher. The National Geographic Society has not accepted the revised figure.

## United States, Canada, Mexico

| Name | Place | Height (ft) |
|---|---|---|
| McKinley | AK | 20,320 |
| Logan | Yukon | 19,850 |
| Citlaltepetl (Orizaba) | Mexico | 18,700 |
| St. Elias | AK-Yukon | 18,008 |
| Popocatépetl | Mexico | 17,930 |
| Foraker | AK | 17,400 |
| Iztaccihuatl | Mexico | 17,343 |
| Lucania | Yukon | 17,147 |
| King | Yukon | 16,971 |
| Steele | Yukon | 16,644 |
| Bona | AK | 16,550 |
| Blackburn | AK | 16,390 |
| Kennedy | AK | 16,286 |
| Sanford | AK | 16,237 |
| Vancouver | AK-Yukon | 15,979 |
| South Buttress | AK | 15,885 |
| Wood | Yukon | 15,885 |
| Churchill | AK | 15,638 |
| Fairweather | AK-BC | 15,300 |
| Zinantecatl (Toluca) | Mexico | 15,016 |
| Hubbard | AK-Yukon | 15,015 |
| Bear | AK | 14,831 |
| Walsh | Yukon | 14,780 |
| East Buttress | AK | 14,730 |
| Matlalcueyetl | Mexico | 14,636 |
| Hunter | AK | 14,573 |

| Name | Place | Height (ft) |
|---|---|---|
| Alverstone | AK-Yukon | 14,565 |
| Browne Tower | AK | 14,530 |
| Whitney | CA | 14,494 |
| Elbert | CO | 14,433 |
| Massive | CO | 14,421 |
| Harvard | CO | 14,420 |
| Rainier | WA | 14,410 |
| University Peak | AK | 14,410 |
| Williamson | CA | 14,375 |
| La Plata Peak | CO | 14,361 |
| Blanca Peak | CO | 14,345 |
| Uncompahgre Peak | CO | 14,309 |
| Crestone Peak | CO | 14,294 |
| Lincoln | CO | 14,286 |
| Grays Peak | CO | 14,270 |
| Antero | CO | 14,269 |
| Torreys Peak | CO | 14,267 |
| Castle Peak | CO | 14,265 |
| Quandary Peak | CO | 14,265 |
| Evans | CO | 14,264 |
| Longs Peak | CO | 14,255 |
| McArthur | Yukon | 14,253 |
| Wilson | CO | 14,246 |
| White Mt. Peak | CA | 14,246 |
| North Palisade | CA | 14,242 |
| Cameron | CO | 14,238 |

| Name | Place | Height (ft) |
|---|---|---|
| Shavano | CO | 14,229 |
| Belford | CO | 14,197 |
| Princeton | CO | 14,197 |
| Crestone Needle | CO | 14,197 |
| Yale | CO | 14,196 |
| Bross | CO | 14,172 |
| Kit Carson | CO | 14,165 |
| Wrangell | AK | 14,163 |
| Shasta | CA | 14,162 |
| El Diente Peak | CO | 14,159 |
| Point Success | WA | 14,158 |
| Maroon Peak | CO | 14,156 |
| Tabeguache | CO | 14,155 |
| Oxford | CO | 14,153 |
| Sill | CA | 14,153 |
| Sneffels | CO | 14,150 |
| Democrat | CO | 14,148 |
| Capitol Peak | CO | 14,130 |
| Liberty Cap | WA | 14,112 |
| Pikes Peak | CO | 14,110 |
| Snowmass | CO | 14,092 |
| Russell | CA | 14,088 |
| Eolus | CO | 14,083 |
| Windom | CO | 14,082 |
| Columbia | CO | 14,073 |
| Augusta | AK | 14,070 |

## South America

| Peak, country | Height (ft) |
|---|---|
| Aconcagua, Argentina | 22,834 |
| Ojos del Salado, Arg.-Chile | 22,572 |
| Bonete, Argentina | 22,546 |
| Tupungato, Argentina-Chile | 22,310 |
| Pissis, Argentina | 22,241 |
| Mercedario, Argentina | 22,211 |
| Huascaran, Peru | 22,205 |
| Llullaillaco, Argentina-Chile | 22,057 |
| El Libertador, Argentina | 22,047 |
| Cachi, Argentina | 22,047 |
| Incahuasi, Argentina-Chile | 21,720 |
| Yerupaja, Peru | 21,709 |
| Galan, Argentina | 21,654 |
| El Muerto, Argentina-Chile | 21,457 |
| Sajama, Bolivia | 21,391 |
| Nacimiento, Argentina | 21,302 |
| Illimani, Bolivia | 21,201 |

| Peak, country | Height (ft) |
|---|---|
| Coropuna, Peru | 21,083 |
| Laudo, Argentina | 20,997 |
| Ancohuma, Bolivia | 20,958 |
| Ausangate, Peru | 20,945 |
| Toro, Argentina-Chile | 20,932 |
| Illampu, Bolivia | 20,873 |
| Tres Cruces, Argentina-Chile | 20,853 |
| Huandoy, Peru | 20,852 |
| Parinacota, Bolivia-Chile | 20,768 |
| Tortolas, Argentina-Chile | 20,745 |
| Ampato, Peru | 20,702 |
| El Condor, Argentina | 20,669 |
| Salcantay, Peru | 20,574 |
| Chimborazo, Ecuador | 20,561 |
| Huancarhuas, Peru | 20,531 |
| Famatina, Argentina | 20,505 |
| Pumasillo, Peru | 20,492 |

| Peak, country | Height (ft) |
|---|---|
| Solo, Argentina | 20,492 |
| Polleras, Argentina | 20,456 |
| Pular, Chile | 20,423 |
| Chani, Argentina | 20,341 |
| Aucanquilcha, Chile | 20,295 |
| Juncal, Argentina-Chile | 20,276 |
| Negro, Argentina | 20,184 |
| Quela, Argentina | 20,128 |
| Condoriri, Bolivia | 20,095 |
| Palermo, Argentina | 20,079 |
| Solimana, Peru | 20,068 |
| San Juan, Argentina-Chile | 20,049 |
| Sierra Nevada, Arg.-Chile | 20,023 |
| Antofalla, Argentina | 20,013 |
| Marmolejo, Argentina-Chile | 20,013 |
| Chachani, Peru | 19,931 |

The highest point in the West Indies is in the Dominican Republic, Pico Duarte (10,417 ft).

## Africa, SE Asian Islands, Australia, New Zealand

| Peak, country/island | Height (ft) |
|---|---|
| Kilimanjaro, Tanzania | 19,340 |
| Kenya, Kenya | 17,058 |
| Margherita Pk., Uganda-Zaire | 16,763 |
| Jaya, New Guinea | 16,500 |
| Trikora, New Guinea | 15,585 |
| Mandala, New Guinea | 15,420 |
| Ras Dashan, Ethiopia | 15,158 |
| Meru, Tanzania | 14,979 |

| Peak, country/island | Height (ft) |
|---|---|
| Wilhelm, New Guinea | 14,793 |
| Karisimbi, Zaire-Rwanda | 14,787 |
| Elgon, Kenya-Uganda | 14,178 |
| Batu, Ethiopia | 14,131 |
| Guna, Ethiopia | 13,881 |
| Gughe, Ethiopia | 13,780 |
| Toubkal, Morocco | 13,661 |

| Peak, country/island | Height (ft) |
|---|---|
| Kinabalu, Malaysia | 13,455 |
| Cameroon, Cameroon | 13,353 |
| Kerinci, Sumatra, Indon. | 12,467 |
| Cook, New Zealand | 12,349 |
| Teide, Canary Isls. | 12,198 |
| Semeru, Java, Indon. | 12,060 |
| Kosciusko, Australia | 7,310 |

## Europe

| Peak, country | Height (ft) |
|---|---|
| **Alps** | |
| Mont Blanc, Fr.-It. | 15,771 |
| Monte Rosa (highest peak of group), Switz. | 15,203 |
| Dom, Switz. | 14,911 |
| Liskamm, It., Switz. | 14,852 |
| Weisshom, Switz. | 14,780 |
| Taschhorn, Switz. | 14,733 |
| Matterhorn, It., Switz. | 14,690 |

| Peak, country | Height (ft) |
|---|---|
| Dent Blanche, Switz. | 14,293 |
| Nadelhorn, Switz. | 14,196 |
| Grand Combin, Switz. | 14,154 |
| Lenzpitze, Switz. | 14,088 |
| Finsteraarhorn, Switz. | 14,022 |
| Castor, Switz. | 13,865 |
| Zinalrothorn, Switz. | 13,849 |
| Hohberghom, Switz. | 13,842 |
| Alphubel, Switz. | 13,799 |
| Rimpfischhom, Switz. | 13,776 |

| Peak, country | Height (ft) |
|---|---|
| Aletschorn, Switz. | 13,763 |
| Strahlhorn, Switz. | 13,747 |
| Dent D'Herens, Switz. | 13,686 |
| Breithorn, It., Switz. | 13,665 |
| Bishorn, Switz. | 13,645 |
| Jungfrau, Switz. | 13,642 |
| Ecrins, Fr. | 13,461 |
| Monch, Switz. | 13,448 |
| Pollux, Switz. | 13,422 |
| Schreckhorn, Switz. | 13,379 |

| Peak, country | Height (ft) |
|---|---|
| Ober Gabelhorn, Switz. | 13,330 |
| Gran Paradiso, It. | 13,323 |
| Bernina, It., Switz. | 13,284 |
| Fiescherhorn, Switz. | 13,283 |
| Grunhorn, Switz. | 13,266 |
| Lauteraarhorn, Switz. | 13,261 |
| Durrenhorn, Switz. | 13,238 |
| Allalinhorn, Switz. | 13,213 |
| Weissmies, Switz. | 13,199 |
| Lagginhorn, Switz. | 13,156 |
| Zupo, Switz. | 13,120 |
| Fletschhorn, Switz. | 13,110 |

| Peak, country | Height (ft) |
|---|---|
| Adlerhorn, Switz. | 13,081 |
| Gletscherhorn, Switz. | 13,068 |
| Schalihorn, Switz. | 13,040 |
| Scerscen, Switz. | 13,028 |
| Eiger, Switz. | 13,025 |
| Jagerhorn, Switz. | 13,024 |
| Rottalhorn, Switz. | 13,022 |

### Pyrenees

| Peak, country | Height (ft) |
|---|---|
| Aneto, Sp. | 11,168 |
| Posets, Sp. | 11,073 |
| Perdido, Sp. | 11,007 |

| Peak, country | Height (ft) |
|---|---|
| Vignemale, Fr.-Sp. | 10,820 |
| Long, Sp. | 10,479 |
| Estats, Sp. | 10,304 |
| Montcalm, Sp. | 10,105 |

### Caucasus (Europe-Asia)

| Peak, country | Height (ft) |
|---|---|
| Elbrus, Russia | 18,510 |
| Shkara, Russia | 17,064 |
| Dykh Tau, Russia | 17,054 |
| Kashtan Tau, Russia | 16,877 |
| Dzhangi Tau, Russia | 16,565 |
| Kazbek, Russia | 16,558 |

## Asia (Mainland)

| Peak | Place | Height (ft) |
|---|---|---|
| Everest | Nepal-Tibet | 29,028 |
| K2 (Godwin Austen) | Kashmir | 28,250 |
| Kanchenjunga | India-Nepal | 28,208 |
| Lhotse I (Everest) | Nepal-Tibet | 27,923 |
| Makalu I | Nepal-Tibet | 27,824 |
| Lhotse II (Everest) | Nepal-Tibet | 27,560 |
| Dhaulagiri | Nepal | 26,810 |
| Manaslu I | Nepal | 26,760 |
| Cho Oyu | Nepal-Tibet | 26,750 |
| Nanga Parbat | Kashmir | 26,660 |
| Annapurna I | Nepal | 26,504 |
| Gasherbrum | Kashmir | 26,470 |
| Broad | Kashmir | 26,400 |
| Gosainthan | Tibet | 26,287 |
| Annapurna II | Nepal | 26,041 |
| Gyachung Kang | Nepal-Tibet | 25,910 |
| Disteghil Sar | Kashmir | 25,868 |
| Himalchuli | Nepal | 25,801 |
| Nuptse (Everest) | Nepal-Tibet | 25,726 |
| Masherbrum | Kashmir | 25,660 |
| Nanda Devi | India | 25,645 |
| Rakaposhi | Kashmir | 25,550 |
| Kamet | India-Tibet | 25,447 |
| Namcha Barwa | Tibet | 25,445 |
| Gurla Mandhata | Tibet | 25,355 |
| Ulugh Muz Tagh | Xinjiang-Tibet | 25,340 |
| Kungur | Xinjiang | 25,325 |

| Peak | Place | Height (ft) |
|---|---|---|
| Tirich Mir | Pakistan | 25,230 |
| Makalu II | Nepal-Tibet | 25,120 |
| Minya Konka | China | 24,900 |
| Kula Gangri | Bhutan-Tibet | 24,784 |
| Changtzu (Everest) | Nepal-Tibet | 24,780 |
| Muz Tagh Ata | Xinjiang | 24,757 |
| Skyang Kangri | Kashmir | 24,750 |
| Communism Peak | Tajikistan | 24,590 |
| Jongsang Peak | India-Nepal | 24,472 |
| Jengish Chokusu | Xinjiang-Kyrgyzstan | 24,406 |
| Sia Kangri | Kashmir | 24,350 |
| Haramosh Peak | Pakistan | 24,270 |
| Istoro Nal | Pakistan | 24,240 |
| Tent Peak | India-Nepal | 24,165 |
| Chomo Lhari | Bhutan-Tibet | 24,040 |
| Chamlang | Nepal | 24,012 |
| Kabru | India-Nepal | 24,002 |
| Alung Gangri | Tibet | 24,000 |
| Baltoro Kangri | Kashmir | 23,990 |
| Mussu Shan | Xinjiang | 23,890 |
| Mana | India | 23,860 |
| Baruntse | Nepal | 23,688 |
| Nepal Peak | India-Nepal | 23,500 |
| Amne Machin | China | 23,490 |
| Gauri Sankar | Nepal-Tibet | 23,440 |

| Peak | Place | Height (ft) |
|---|---|---|
| Badrinath | India | 23,420 |
| Nunkun | Kashmir | 23,410 |
| Lenin Peak | Tajikistan | 23,405 |
| Pyramid | India-Nepal | 23,400 |
| Api | Nepal | 23,399 |
| Pauhunri | India-Tibet | 23,385 |
| Trisul | India | 23,360 |
| Kangto | India-Tibet | 23,260 |
| Nyenchhe Thanglha | Tibet | 23,255 |
| Trisuli | India | 23,210 |
| Pumori | Nepal-Tibet | 23,190 |
| Dunagiri | India | 23,184 |
| Lombo Kangra | Tibet | 23,165 |
| Saipal | Nepal | 23,100 |
| Macha Pucchare | Nepal | 22,958 |
| Numbar | Nepal | 22,817 |
| Kanjiroba | Nepal | 22,580 |
| Ama Dablam | Nepal | 22,350 |
| Cho Polu | Nepal | 22,093 |
| Lingtren | Nepal-Tibet | 21,972 |
| Khumbutse | Nepal-Tibet | 21,785 |
| Hlako Gangri | Tibet | 21,266 |
| Mt. Grosvenor | China | 21,190 |
| Thagchhab Gangri | Tibet | 20,970 |
| Damavand | Iran | 18,606 |
| Ararat | Turkey | 16,804 |

## Antarctica

| Peak | Height (ft) |
|---|---|
| Vinson Massif | 16,864 |
| Tyree | 16,290 |
| Shinn | 15,750 |
| Gardner | 15,375 |
| Epperly | 15,100 |
| Kirkpatrick | 14,855 |
| Elizabeth | 14,698 |
| Markham | 14,290 |
| Bell | 14,117 |
| Mackellar | 14,098 |
| Anderson | 13,957 |
| Bentley | 13,934 |
| Kaplan | 13,878 |

| Peak | Height (ft) |
|---|---|
| Andrew Jackson | 13,750 |
| Sidley | 13,720 |
| Ostenso | 13,710 |
| Minto | 13,668 |
| Miller | 13,650 |
| Long Gables | 13,620 |
| Dickerson | 13,517 |
| Giovinetto | 13,412 |
| Wade | 13,400 |
| Fisher | 13,386 |
| Fridtjof Nansen | 13,350 |
| Wexler | 13,202 |
| Lister | 13,200 |

| Peak | Height (ft) |
|---|---|
| Shear | 13,100 |
| Odishaw | 13,008 |
| Donaldson | 12,894 |
| Ray | 12,808 |
| Sellery | 12,779 |
| Waterman | 12,730 |
| Anne | 12,703 |
| Press | 12,566 |
| Falla | 12,549 |
| Rucker | 12,520 |
| Goldthwait | 12,510 |
| Morris | 12,500 |
| Erebus | 12,450 |

| Peak | Height (ft) |
|---|---|
| Campbell | 12,434 |
| Don Pedro Christophersen | 12,355 |
| Lysaght | 12,326 |
| Huggins | 12,247 |
| Sabine | 12,200 |
| Astor | 12,175 |
| Mohl | 12,172 |
| Frankes | 12,064 |
| Jones | 12,040 |
| Gjelsvik | 12,008 |
| Coman | 12,000 |

## Some Notable U.S. Mountains

| Name | Place | Height (ft) |
|---|---|---|
| Gannett Peak | WY | 13,804 |
| Grand Teton | WY | 13,766 |
| Kings | UT | 13,528 |
| Cloud | WY | 13,175 |
| Wheeler | NM | 13,161 |
| Boundary | NV | 13,140 |
| Granite | MT | 12,799 |
| Borah | ID | 12,662 |
| Humphreys | AZ | 12,633 |

| Name | Place | Height (ft) |
|---|---|---|
| Adams | WA | 12,307 |
| San Gorgonio | CA | 11,502 |
| Hood | OR | 11,239 |
| Lassen | CA | 10,457 |
| Granite | CA | 10,321 |
| Guadalupe | TX | 8,749 |
| Olympus | WA | 7,965 |
| Harney | SD | 7,242 |
| Mitchell | NC | 6,684 |

| Name | Place | Height (ft) |
|---|---|---|
| Clingmans Dome | NC-TN | 6,643 |
| Washington | NH | 6,288 |
| Rogers | VA | 5,729 |
| Marcy | NY | 5,344 |
| Katahdin | ME | 5,268 |
| Spruce Knob | WV | 4,862 |
| Mansfield | VT | 4,393 |
| Black Mountain | KY | 4,145 |

# Important Islands and Their Areas

**Source:** Bureau of the Census, U.S. Dept. of Commerce; National Atlas Information Services, Natural Resources Canada; World Almanac research

Figure in parentheses shows rank among the world's 10 largest individual islands. Because some islands have not been surveyed accurately, some areas shown are estimates. Figures are for total land area in square miles. Some "islands" listed are island groups.

## Arctic Ocean

### Canadian

| | |
|---|---|
| Axel Heiberg | 16,671 |
| Baffin (5) | 195,928 |
| Banks | 27,038 |
| Bathurst | 6,194 |
| Devon | 21,331 |
| Ellesmere (10) | 75,767 |
| Melville | 16,274 |
| Prince of Wales | 12,872 |
| Somerset | 9,570 |
| Southampton | 15,913 |
| Victoria (9) | 83,897 |

### Norwegian

| | |
|---|---|
| Svalbard | 23,957 |
| Nordaustlandet | 5,410 |
| Spitsbergen | 15,060 |

### Russian

| | |
|---|---|
| Franz Josef Land | 8,000 |
| Novaya Zemlya (2 isls.) | 31,730 |
| Wrangel | 2,800 |

## Atlantic Ocean

| | |
|---|---|
| Anticosti, Canada | 3,066 |
| Ascension, UK | 34 |
| Azores, Portugal | 868 |
| Faial | 67 |
| Sao Miguel | 291 |
| Bahamas | 5,382 |
| Bermuda Isls., UK | 20 |
| Bioko Isl., Equatorial Guinea | 785 |
| Block Isl., RI | 10 |
| Canary Isls., Spain | 2,807 |
| Fuerteventura | 668 |
| Gran Canaria | 592 |
| Tenerife | 795 |
| Cape Breton, Canada | 3,981 |
| Cape Verde Isls. | 1,557 |
| Faeroe Isls., Denmark | 540 |
| Falkland Isls., UK | 4,700 |
| Fernando de Noronha Archipelago, Brazil | 7 |
| Greenland, Denmark (1) | 840,000 |
| Iceland | 39,699 |
| Long Island, NY | 1,320 |
| Madeira Isls., Portugal | 306 |
| Marajo, Brazil | 15,444 |
| Martha's Vineyard, MA | 89 |
| Mount Desert, ME | 104 |
| Nantucket, MA | 45 |
| Newfoundland, Canada | 42,031 |
| Prince Edward, Canada | 2,185 |
| St. Helena, UK | 47 |
| South Georgia, UK | 1,450 |
| Tierra del Fuego, Chile and Argentina | 18,800 |
| Tristan da Cunha, UK | 40 |

### British Isles

| | |
|---|---|
| Great Britain, mainland (8) | 84,200 |
| Channel Isls. | 75 |
| Guernsey | 24 |
| Jersey | 45 |
| Sark | 2 |
| Hebrides | 2,744 |
| Ireland | 32,589 |
| Irish Republic | 27,137 |
| Northern Ireland | 5,452 |
| Isle of Man | 227 |
| Orkney Isls. | 390 |
| Scilly Isls. | 6 |
| Shetland Isls. | 567 |
| Skye | 670 |
| Wight | 147 |

## Baltic Sea

| | |
|---|---|
| Aland Isls., Finland | 590 |
| Bornholm, Denmark | 227 |
| Gotland, Sweden | 1,159 |

## Caribbean Sea

| | |
|---|---|
| Antigua | 108 |
| Aruba, Netherlands | 75 |
| Barbados | 166 |
| Cuba | 42,804 |
| Isle of Youth | 926 |
| Curaçao, Netherlands | 171 |
| Dominica | 290 |
| Guadeloupe, France | 687 |
| Hispaniola, Haiti and Dominican Republic | 29,389 |
| Jamaica | 4,244 |
| Martinique, France | 436 |
| Puerto Rico, U.S. | 3,339 |
| Tobago | 116 |
| Trinidad | 1,864 |
| Virgin Isls., UK | 59 |
| Virgin Isls., U.S. | 134 |

## Indian Ocean

| | |
|---|---|
| Andaman Isls., India | 2,500 |
| Madagascar (4) | 226,658 |
| Mauritius | 720 |
| Pemba, Tanzania | 380 |
| Réunion, France | 970 |
| Seychelles | 176 |
| Sri Lanka | 25,332 |
| Zanzibar, Tanzania | 640 |

### Persian Gulf

| | |
|---|---|
| Bahrain | 217 |

## Mediterranean Sea

| | |
|---|---|
| Balearic Isls., Spain | 1,927 |
| Corfu, Greece | 229 |
| Corsica, France | 3,369 |
| Crete, Greece | 3,189 |
| Cyprus | 3,572 |
| Elba, Italy | 86 |
| Euboea, Greece | 1,411 |
| Malta | 95 |
| Rhodes, Greece | 540 |
| Sardinia, Italy | 9,301 |
| Sicily, Italy | 9,926 |

## Pacific Ocean

| | |
|---|---|
| Aleutian Isls., AK. | 6,912 |
| Adak | 275 |
| Amchitka | 116 |
| Attu | 350 |
| Kanaga | 142 |
| Kiska | 106 |
| Tanaga | 195 |
| Umnak | 686 |
| Unalaska | 1,051 |
| Unimak | 1,571 |
| Canton, Kiribati* | 4 |
| Christmas, Kiribati* | 94 |
| Clipperton, France | 2 |
| Diomede, Big, Russia | 11 |
| Diomede, Little, U.S. | 3 |
| Easter Isl., Chile | 69 |
| Fiji | 7,056 |
| Vanua Levu | 2,242 |
| Viti Levu | 4,109 |
| Funafuti, Tuvalu* | 2 |
| Galapagos Isls., Ecuador | 3,043 |
| Guadalcanal, Solomon Isls. | 2,180 |
| Guam, U.S. | 210 |
| Hainan, China | 13,000 |
| Hawaiian Isls., HI | 6,423 |
| Hawaii | 4,028 |
| Oahu | 600 |
| Hong Kong | 31 |
| Japan | 145,850 |
| Hokkaido | 30,144 |
| Honshu (7) | 87,805 |
| Iwo Jima | 8 |
| Kyushu | 14,114 |
| Okinawa | 459 |
| Shikoku | 7,049 |
| Kodiak, AK | 3,465 |
| Marquesas Isls., France | 492 |
| Marshall Isls. | 70 |
| Bikini* | 2 |
| Micronesia | 271 |
| Nauru | 8 |
| New Caledonia, France | 6,530 |
| New Zealand | 104,454 |
| Chatham Isls. | 372 |
| North | 44,702 |
| South | 58,384 |
| Stewart | 674 |
| Northern Mariana Isls., U.S. | 179 |
| Palau | 188 |
| Philippines | 115,860 |
| Leyte | 2,787 |
| Luzon | 40,880 |
| Mindanao | 36,775 |
| Mindoro | 3,790 |
| Negros | 4,907 |
| Palawan | 4,554 |
| Panay | 4,446 |
| Samar | 5,050 |
| Sakhalin, Russia | 29,500 |
| Samoa Isls. | 1,177 |
| American Samoa, U.S. | 84 |
| Tutuila | 55 |
| Samoa (Western) | 1,093 |
| Savaii | 659 |
| Upolu | 432 |
| Santa Catalina, CA | 75 |
| Tahiti, France | 402 |
| Taiwan | 13,969 |
| Quemoy | 56 |
| Tasmania, Australia | 26,178 |
| Tonga Isls. | 290 |
| Vancouver, Canada | 12,079 |
| Vanuatu | 4,707 |

### East Indies

| | |
|---|---|
| Bali, Indonesia | 2,171 |
| Borneo, Indonesia-Malaysia-Brunei (3) | 280,100 |
| Celebes, Indonesia | 69,000 |
| Java, Indonesia | 48,900 |
| Madura, Indonesia | 2,113 |
| Moluccas, Indonesia | 32,307 |
| New Britain, Papua New Guinea | 14,093 |
| New Guinea, Indonesia-Papua New Guinea (2) | 306,000 |
| New Ireland, Papua New Guinea | 3,707 |
| Sumatra, Indonesia (6) | 165,000 |
| Timor, Indonesia | 13,094 |

*** Atolls:** Bikini (lagoon area, 230 sq mi; land area, 2 sq mi); Canton (lagoon, 20 sq mi; land, 4 sq mi), Kiribati; Christmas (lagoon, 140 sq mi; land, 94 sq mi), Kiribati; Funafuti (lagoon, 84 sq mi; land, 2 sq mi), Tuvalu.

**Australia,** sometimes called an island, is classified as a continent.

**Islands in minor waters:** Manhattan (22 sq mi), Staten (59 sq mi), and Governors (173 acres), all in New York Harbor, U.S.; Isle Royale (209 sq mi), Lake Superior, U.S.; Manitoulin (1,068 sq mi), Lake Huron, Canada; Pinang (110 sq mi), Strait of Malacca, Malaysia; Singapore (239 sq mi), Singapore Strait, Singapore.

## Areas and Average Depths of Oceans, Seas, and Gulfs

Geographers and mapmakers recognize four major bodies of water: the Pacific, the Atlantic, the Indian, and the Arctic oceans. The Atlantic and Pacific oceans are considered divided at the equator into the N and S Atlantic and the N and S Pacific. The Arctic Ocean is the name for waters N of the continental landmasses in the region of the Arctic Circle.

| | Area (sq mi) | Avg. depth (ft) |
|---|---|---|
| Pacific Ocean | 64,186,300 | 12,925 |
| Atlantic Ocean | 33,420,000 | 11,730 |
| Indian Ocean | 28,350,500 | 12,598 |
| Arctic Ocean | 5,105,700 | 3,407 |
| South China Sea | 1,148,500 | 4,802 |
| Caribbean Sea | 971,400 | 8,448 |
| Mediterranean Sea | 969,100 | 4,926 |
| Bering Sea | 873,000 | 4,893 |
| Gulf of Mexico | 582,100 | 5,297 |
| Sea of Okhotsk | 537,500 | 3,192 |
| Sea of Japan | 391,100 | 5,468 |

| | Area (sq mi) | Avg. depth (ft) |
|---|---|---|
| Hudson Bay | 281,900 | 305 |
| East China Sea | 256,600 | 620 |
| Andaman Sea | 218,100 | 3,667 |
| Black Sea | 196,100 | 3,906 |
| Red Sea | 174,900 | 1,764 |
| North Sea | 164,900 | 308 |
| Baltic Sea | 147,500 | 180 |
| Yellow Sea | 113,500 | 121 |
| Persian Gulf | 88,800 | 328 |
| Gulf of California | 59,100 | 2,375 |

## Principal Ocean Depths

**Source:** Defense Mapping Agency, Hydrographic/Topographic Center, U.S. Dept. of Defense

| Name of area | Location (lat.) | Location (long.) | Depth (meters) | Depth (fathoms) | Depth (ft) |
|---|---|---|---|---|---|
| **Pacific Ocean** | | | | | |
| Mariana Trench | 11°22′ N | 142°36′ E | 10,924 | 5,973 | 35,840 |
| Tonga Trench | 23°16′ S | 174°44′ W | 10,800 | 5,906 | 35,433 |
| Philippine Trench | 10°38′ N | 126°36′ E | 10,057 | 5,499 | 32,995 |
| Kermadec Trench | 31°53′ S | 177°21′ W | 10,047 | 5,494 | 32,963 |
| Bonin Trench | 24°30′ N | 143°24′ E | 9,994 | 5,464 | 32,788 |
| Kuril Trench | 44°15′ N | 150°34′ E | 9,750 | 5,331 | 31,988 |
| Izu Trench | 31°05′ N | 142°10′ E | 9,695 | 5,301 | 31,808 |
| New Britain Trench | 06°19′ S | 153°45′ E | 8,940 | 4,888 | 29,331 |
| Yap Trench | 08°33′ N | 138°02′ E | 8,527 | 4,663 | 27,976 |
| Japan Trench | 36°08′ N | 142°43′ E | 8,412 | 4,600 | 27,599 |
| Peru-Chile Trench | 23°18′ S | 71°14′ W | 8,064 | 4,409 | 26,457 |
| Palau Trench | 07°52′ N | 134°56′ E | 8,054 | 4,404 | 26,424 |
| Aleutian Trench | 50°51′ N | 177°11′ E | 7,679 | 4,199 | 25,194 |
| New Hebrides Trench | 20°36′ S | 168°37′ E | 7,570 | 4,139 | 24,836 |
| North Ryukyu Trench | 24°00′ N | 126°48′ E | 7,181 | 3,927 | 23,560 |
| Mid. America Trench | 14°02′ N | 93°39′ W | 6,662 | 3,643 | 21,857 |
| **Atlantic Ocean** | | | | | |
| Puerto Rico Trench | 19°55′ N | 65°27′ W | 8,605 | 4,705 | 28,232 |
| S Sandwich Trench | 55°42′ S | 25°56′ E | 8,325 | 4,552 | 27,313 |
| Romanche Gap | 0°13′ S | 18°26′ W | 7,728 | 4,226 | 25,354 |
| Cayman Trench | 19°12′ N | 80°00′ W | 7,535 | 4,120 | 24,721 |
| Brazil Basin | 09°10′ S | 23°02′ W | 6,119 | 3,346 | 20,076 |
| **Indian Ocean** | | | | | |
| Java Trench | 10°19′ S | 109°58′ E | 7,125 | 3,896 | 23,376 |
| Ob' Trench | 09°45′ S | 67°18′ E | 6,874 | 3,759 | 22,553 |
| Diamantina Trench | 35°50′ S | 105°14′ E | 6,602 | 3,610 | 21,660 |
| Vema Trench | 09°08′ S | 67°15′ E | 6,402 | 3,501 | 21,004 |
| Agulhas Basin | 45°20′ S | 26°50′ E | 6,195 | 3,387 | 20,325 |
| **Arctic Ocean** | | | | | |
| Eurasia Basin | 82°23′ N | 19°31′ E | 5,450 | 2,980 | 17,881 |
| **Mediterranean Sea** | | | | | |
| Ionian Basin | 36°32′ N | 21°06′ E | 5,150 | 2,816 | 16,896 |

**Note:** Greater depths have been reported in some of the above areas. They are not official, however, unless confirmed by research vessels.

## Latitude, Longitude, and Altitude of World Cities

**Source:** Defense Mapping Agency, Hydrographic/Topographic Center, U.S. Dept. of Defense

| City | Lat. ° | Lat. ′ | Long. ° | Long. ′ | Alt. (ft) |
|---|---|---|---|---|---|
| Athens, Greece | 37 | 59 N | 23 | 44 E | 300 |
| Bangkok, Thailand | 13 | 45 N | 100 | 31 E | 0 |
| Beijing, China | 39 | | 116 | 24 E | 600 |
| Berlin, Germany | 52 | 31 N | 13 | 25 E | 110 |
| Bogotá, Colombia | 04 | 36 N | 74 | 05 W | 8,660 |
| Bombay (Mumbai), India | 18 | 58 N | 72 | 50 E | 27 |
| Buenos Aires, Argentina | 34 | 36 S | 58 | 28 W | 0 |
| Cairo, Egypt | 30 | 03 N | 31 | 15 E | 381 |
| Jakarta, Indonesia | 06 | 10 S | 106 | 48 E | 26 |
| Jerusalem, Israel | 31 | 46 N | 35 | 14 E | 2,500 |
| Johannesburg, So. Afr. | 26 | 12 S | 28 | 05 E | 5,740 |
| Kathmandu, Nepal | 27 | 43 N | 85 | 19 E | 4,500 |
| Kiev, Ukraine | 50 | 26 N | 30 | 31 E | 0 |
| London, UK (Greenwich) | 51 | 30 N | 00 | 00 | 245 |
| Manila, Philippines | 14 | 35 N | 120 | 00 E | 0 |
| Mecca, Saudi Arabia | 21 | 27 N | 39 | 49 E | 6,562 |
| Mexico City, Mexico | 19 | 24 N | 99 | 09 W | 7,347 |
| Moscow, Russia | 55 | 45 N | 37 | 35 E | 394 |
| New Delhi, India | 28 | 36 N | 77 | 12 E | 770 |
| Panama City, Panama | 08 | 58 N | 79 | 32 W | 0 |
| Paris, France | 48 | 52 N | 02 | 20 E | 300 |
| Quito, Ecuador | 00 | 13 S | 78 | 30 W | 9,222 |
| Rio de Janeiro, Brazil | 22 | 43 S | 43 | 13 W | 30 |
| Rome, Italy | 41 | 53 N | 12 | 30 E | 95 |
| Santiago, Chile | 33 | 27 S | 70 | 40 W | 4,921 |
| Seoul, South Korea | 37 | 34 N | 127 | 00 E | 34 |
| Sydney, Australia | 33 | 53 S | 151 | 12 E | 25 |
| Tehran, Iran | 35 | 40 N | 51 | 26 E | 3,937 |
| Tokyo, Japan | 35 | 42 N | 139 | 46 E | 30 |
| Tripoli, Libya | 32 | 54 N | 13 | 11 E | 0 |
| Warsaw, Poland | 52 | 15 N | 21 | 00 E | 360 |
| Wellington, New Zealand | 41 | 18 S | 174 | 47 E | 0 |

# Latitude, Longitude, and Altitude of U.S. and Canadian Cities

**Source:** U.S. geographic positions were provided by National Oceanic Atmospheric Administration, U.S. Dept. of Commerce. U.S. altitudes were provided by Geological Survey, U.S. Dept. of the Interior. Canadian geographic positions were provided by the Geodetic Survey of Canada, Natural Resources Canada. Canadian altitudes were provided by National Atlas Information Service, Natural Resources Canada.

Altitudes are measured in feet at the downtown business areas of U.S. cities or at the city hall of Canadian cities, except where (a) indicates that measurements were made at the tower of a major airport located within the city.

| City | Lat. N ° | ′ | ″ | Long. W ° | ′ | ″ | Alt. (ft) |
|---|---|---|---|---|---|---|---|
| Abilene, TX | 32 | 27 | 05 | 99 | 43 | 51 | 1,710 |
| Akron, OH | 41 | 05 | 00 | 81 | 30 | 44 | 874 |
| Albany, NY | 42 | 39 | 01 | 73 | 45 | 01 | 20 |
| Albuquerque, NM | 35 | 05 | 01 | 106 | 39 | 05 | 4,945 |
| Alert, N.W.T. | 82 | 29 | 50 | 62 | 21 | 15 | 95 |
| Allentown, PA | 40 | 36 | 11 | 75 | 28 | 06 | 255 |
| Amarillo, TX | 35 | 12 | 27 | 101 | 50 | 04 | 3,685 |
| Anchorage, AK | 61 | 10 | 00 | 149 | 59 | 00 | 118 |
| Ann Arbor, MI | 42 | 16 | 59 | 83 | 44 | 52 | 880 |
| Asheville, NC | 35 | 35 | 42 | 82 | 33 | 26 | 1,985 |
| Ashland, KY | 38 | 28 | 36 | 82 | 38 | 23 | 536 |
| Atlanta, GA | 33 | 45 | 10 | 84 | 23 | 37 | 1,050 |
| Atlantic City, NJ | 39 | 21 | 32 | 74 | 25 | 53 | 10 |
| Augusta, GA | 33 | 28 | 20 | 81 | 58 | 00 | 143 |
| Augusta, ME | 44 | 18 | 53 | 69 | 46 | 29 | 45 |
| Austin, TX | 30 | 16 | 09 | 97 | 44 | 37 | 505 |
| Bakersfield, CA | 35 | 22 | 31 | 119 | 01 | 18 | 400 |
| Baltimore, MD | 39 | 17 | 26 | 76 | 36 | 45 | 20 |
| Bangor, ME | 44 | 48 | 13 | 68 | 46 | 18 | 20 |
| Baton Rouge, LA | 30 | 26 | 58 | 91 | 11 | 00 | 57 |
| Battle Creek, MI | 42 | 18 | 58 | 85 | 10 | 48 | 820 |
| Bay City, MI | 43 | 36 | 04 | 83 | 53 | 15 | 595 |
| Beaumont, TX | 30 | 05 | 20 | 94 | 06 | 09 | 20 |
| Belleville, Ont. | 44 | 09 | 42 | 77 | 23 | 11 | 257 |
| Bellingham, WA | 48 | 45 | 34 | 122 | 28 | 36 | 60 |
| Berkeley, CA | 37 | 52 | 10 | 122 | 16 | 17 | 40 |
| Billings, MT | 45 | 47 | 00 | 108 | 30 | 04 | 3,120 |
| Biloxi, MS | 30 | 23 | 48 | 88 | 53 | 00 | 20 |
| Binghamton, NY | 42 | 06 | 03 | 75 | 54 | 47 | 865 |
| Birmingham, AL | 33 | 31 | 01 | 86 | 48 | 36 | 600 |
| Bismarck, ND | 46 | 48 | 23 | 100 | 47 | 17 | 1,674 |
| Bloomington, IL | 40 | 28 | 58 | 88 | 59 | 36 | 800 |
| Boise, ID | 43 | 37 | 07 | 116 | 11 | 58 | 2,704 |
| Boston, MA | 42 | 21 | 24 | 71 | 03 | 25 | 21 |
| Bowling Green, KY | 36 | 59 | 41 | 86 | 26 | 33 | 510 |
| Brandon, Man. | 49 | 51 | 00 | 99 | 57 | 00 | 1,343(a) |
| Brantford, Ont. | 43 | 08 | 34 | 80 | 15 | 39 | 705(a) |
| Brattleboro, VT | 42 | 51 | 06 | 72 | 33 | 48 | 300 |
| Bridgeport, CT | 41 | 10 | 49 | 73 | 11 | 22 | 10 |
| Brockton, MA | 42 | 05 | 02 | 71 | 01 | 25 | 130 |
| Buffalo, NY | 42 | 52 | 52 | 78 | 52 | 21 | 585 |
| Burlington, Ont. | 43 | 19 | 33 | 79 | 47 | 57 | 284 |
| Burlington, VT | 44 | 28 | 34 | 73 | 12 | 46 | 110 |
| Butte, MT | 46 | 01 | 06 | 112 | 32 | 11 | 5,765 |
| Calgary, Alta. | 51 | 02 | 46 | 114 | 03 | 24 | 3,427 |
| Cambridge, MA | 42 | 22 | 01 | 71 | 06 | 22 | 20 |
| Canton, OH | 40 | 47 | 50 | 81 | 22 | 37 | 1,030 |
| Carson City, NV | 39 | 10 | 00 | 119 | 46 | 00 | 4,680 |
| Cedar Rapids, IA | 41 | 58 | 01 | 91 | 39 | 53 | 730 |
| Central Islip, NY | 40 | 47 | 24 | 73 | 12 | 00 | 80 |
| Champaign, IL | 40 | 07 | 05 | 88 | 14 | 48 | 740 |
| Charleston, SC | 32 | 46 | 35 | 79 | 55 | 53 | 9 |
| Charleston, WV | 38 | 21 | 01 | 81 | 37 | 52 | 601 |
| Charlotte, NC | 35 | 13 | 44 | 80 | 50 | 45 | 720 |
| Charlottetown, P.E.I. | 46 | 14 | 07 | 63 | 07 | 49 | 31 |
| Chattanooga, TN | 35 | 02 | 41 | 85 | 18 | 32 | 675 |
| Cheyenne, WY | 41 | 08 | 09 | 104 | 49 | 07 | 6,100 |
| Chicago, IL | 41 | 52 | 28 | 87 | 38 | 22 | 595 |
| Churchill, Man. | 58 | 45 | 15 | 94 | 10 | 00 | 94(a) |
| Cincinnati, OH | 39 | 06 | 07 | 84 | 30 | 35 | 550 |
| Cleveland, OH | 41 | 29 | 51 | 81 | 41 | 50 | 660 |
| Colorado Springs, CO | 38 | 50 | 07 | 104 | 49 | 16 | 5,980 |
| Columbia, MO | 38 | 57 | 03 | 92 | 19 | 46 | 730 |
| Columbia, SC | 34 | 00 | 02 | 81 | 02 | 00 | 190 |
| Columbus, GA | 32 | 28 | 07 | 84 | 59 | 24 | 265 |
| Columbus, OH | 39 | 57 | 47 | 83 | 00 | 17 | 780 |
| Concord, NH | 43 | 12 | 22 | 71 | 32 | 25 | 290 |
| Corpus Christi, TX | 27 | 47 | 51 | 97 | 23 | 45 | 35 |
| Dallas, TX | 32 | 47 | 09 | 96 | 47 | 37 | 435 |
| Dartmouth, N.S. | 44 | 39 | 50 | 63 | 34 | 08 | 24 |
| Dawson, Yukon | 64 | 03 | 30 | 139 | 26 | 00 | 1,050 |
| Dayton, OH | 39 | 45 | 32 | 84 | 11 | 43 | 574 |
| Daytona Beach, FL | 29 | 12 | 44 | 81 | 01 | 10 | 7 |
| Decatur, IL | 39 | 50 | 42 | 88 | 56 | 47 | 682 |
| Denver, CO | 39 | 44 | 58 | 104 | 59 | 22 | 5,280 |
| Des Moines, IA | 41 | 35 | 14 | 93 | 37 | 00 | 803 |
| Detroit, MI | 42 | 19 | 48 | 83 | 02 | 57 | 585 |
| Dodge City, KS | 37 | 45 | 17 | 100 | 01 | 09 | 2,480 |
| Dubuque, IA | 42 | 29 | 55 | 90 | 40 | 08 | 620 |
| Duluth, MN | 46 | 46 | 56 | 92 | 06 | 24 | 610 |
| Durham, NC | 36 | 00 | 00 | 78 | 54 | 45 | 405 |
| Eau Claire, WI | 44 | 48 | 31 | 91 | 29 | 49 | 790 |
| Edmonton, Alta. | 53 | 32 | 43 | 113 | 29 | 21 | 2,186 |
| Elizabeth, NJ | 40 | 39 | 43 | 74 | 12 | 59 | 21 |
| El Paso, TX | 31 | 45 | 36 | 106 | 29 | 11 | 3,695 |
| Enid, OK | 36 | 23 | 40 | 97 | 52 | 35 | 1,240 |
| Erie, PA | 42 | 07 | 15 | 80 | 04 | 57 | 685 |
| Eugene, OR | 44 | 03 | 16 | 123 | 05 | 30 | 422 |
| Eureka, CA | 40 | 48 | 08 | 124 | 09 | 46 | 45 |
| Evansville, IN | 37 | 58 | 20 | 87 | 34 | 21 | 385 |
| Fairbanks, AK | 64 | 48 | 00 | 147 | 51 | 00 | 448 |
| Fall River, MA | 41 | 42 | 06 | 71 | 09 | 18 | 40 |
| Fargo, ND | 46 | 52 | 30 | 96 | 47 | 18 | 900 |
| Flagstaff, AZ | 35 | 11 | 36 | 111 | 39 | 06 | 6,900 |
| Flint, MI | 43 | 00 | 50 | 83 | 41 | 33 | 750 |
| Ft. Smith, AR | 35 | 23 | 10 | 94 | 25 | 36 | 440 |
| Ft. Wayne, IN | 41 | 04 | 21 | 85 | 08 | 26 | 790 |
| Ft. Worth, TX | 32 | 44 | 55 | 97 | 19 | 44 | 670 |
| Fredericton, N.B. | 45 | 57 | 47 | 66 | 38 | 38 | 29 |
| Fresno, CA | 36 | 44 | 12 | 119 | 47 | 11 | 285 |
| Gadsden, AL | 34 | 00 | 57 | 86 | 00 | 41 | 555 |
| Gainesville, FL | 29 | 38 | 56 | 82 | 19 | 19 | 175 |
| Gallup, NM | 35 | 31 | 30 | 108 | 44 | 30 | 6,540 |
| Galveston, TX | 29 | 18 | 10 | 94 | 47 | 43 | 5 |
| Gary, IN | 41 | 36 | 12 | 87 | 20 | 19 | 590 |
| Grand Junction, CO | 39 | 04 | 06 | 108 | 33 | 54 | 4,590 |
| Grand Rapids, MI | 42 | 58 | 03 | 85 | 40 | 13 | 610 |
| Great Falls, MT | 47 | 29 | 33 | 111 | 18 | 23 | 3,340 |
| Green Bay, WI | 44 | 30 | 48 | 88 | 00 | 50 | 590 |
| Greensboro, NC | 36 | 04 | 17 | 79 | 47 | 25 | 839 |
| Greenville, SC | 34 | 50 | 50 | 82 | 24 | 01 | 966 |
| Guelph, Ont. | 43 | 32 | 35 | 80 | 14 | 54 | 1,065 |
| Gulfport, MS | 30 | 22 | 04 | 89 | 05 | 36 | 20 |
| Halifax, N.S. | 44 | 38 | 54 | 63 | 34 | 30 | 60 |
| Hamilton, OH | 39 | 23 | 59 | 84 | 33 | 47 | 600 |
| Hamilton, Ont. | 43 | 15 | 20 | 79 | 52 | 30 | 329 |
| Harrisburg, PA | 40 | 15 | 43 | 76 | 52 | 59 | 365 |
| Hartford, CT | 41 | 46 | 12 | 72 | 40 | 49 | 40 |
| Helena, MT | 46 | 35 | 33 | 112 | 02 | 24 | 4,155 |
| Hilo, HI | 19 | 43 | 30 | 155 | 05 | 24 | 40 |
| Honolulu, HI | 21 | 18 | 22 | 157 | 51 | 35 | 21 |
| Houston, TX | 29 | 45 | 26 | 95 | 21 | 37 | 40 |
| Hull, Que. | 45 | 25 | 42 | 75 | 42 | 41 | 185 |
| Huntsville, AL | 34 | 44 | 18 | 86 | 35 | 19 | 640 |
| Indianapolis, IN | 39 | 46 | 07 | 86 | 09 | 46 | 710 |
| Iowa City, IA | 41 | 39 | 37 | 91 | 31 | 53 | 685 |
| Jackson, MI | 42 | 14 | 43 | 84 | 24 | 22 | 940 |
| Jackson, MS | 32 | 17 | 56 | 90 | 11 | 06 | 298 |
| Jacksonville, FL | 30 | 19 | 44 | 81 | 39 | 42 | 20 |
| Jersey City, NJ | 40 | 43 | 50 | 74 | 03 | 56 | 20 |
| Johnstown, PA | 40 | 19 | 35 | 78 | 55 | 03 | 1,185 |
| Joplin, MO | 37 | 05 | 26 | 94 | 30 | 00 | 990 |
| Juneau, AK | 58 | 18 | 12 | 134 | 24 | 30 | 50 |
| Kalamazoo, MI | 42 | 17 | 29 | 85 | 35 | 14 | 755 |
| Kansas City, KS | 39 | 07 | 04 | 94 | 38 | 24 | 750 |
| Kansas City, MO | 39 | 04 | 56 | 94 | 35 | 20 | 750 |
| Kenosha, WI | 42 | 35 | 43 | 87 | 50 | 11 | 610 |
| Key West, FL | 24 | 33 | 30 | 81 | 48 | 12 | 5 |
| Kingston, Ont. | 44 | 13 | 53 | 76 | 28 | 48 | 264 |
| Kitchener, Ont. | 43 | 26 | 58 | 80 | 29 | 12 | 1,100 |
| Knoxville, TN | 35 | 57 | 39 | 83 | 55 | 07 | 890 |
| Lafayette, IN | 40 | 25 | 11 | 86 | 53 | 39 | 550 |
| Lancaster, PA | 40 | 02 | 25 | 76 | 18 | 29 | 355 |
| Lansing, MI | 42 | 44 | 01 | 84 | 33 | 15 | 830 |
| Laredo, TX | 27 | 30 | 22 | 99 | 30 | 30 | 440 |
| La Salle, Que. | 45 | 25 | 30 | 73 | 39 | 30 | 110 |
| Las Vegas, NV | 36 | 10 | 20 | 115 | 08 | 37 | 2,030 |
| Laval, Que. | 45 | 33 | 05 | 73 | 44 | 42 | 142 |
| Lawrence, MA | 42 | 42 | 16 | 71 | 10 | 08 | 65 |
| Lethbridge, Alta. | 49 | 41 | 38 | 112 | 49 | 58 | 2,985 |
| Lexington, KY | 38 | 02 | 50 | 84 | 29 | 46 | 955 |
| Lihue, HI | 21 | 58 | 48 | 159 | 22 | 30 | 210 |
| Lima, OH | 40 | 44 | 35 | 84 | 06 | 20 | 865 |

| City | Lat. N ° | ′ | ″ | Long. W ° | ′ | ″ | Alt. (ft) |
|---|---|---|---|---|---|---|---|
| Lincoln, NE | 40 | 48 | 59 | 96 | 42 | 15 | 1,150 |
| Little Rock, AR | 34 | 44 | 42 | 92 | 16 | 37 | 286 |
| London, Ont. | 42 | 59 | 17 | 81 | 14 | 03 | 822 |
| Los Angeles, CA | 34 | 03 | 15 | 118 | 14 | 28 | 340 |
| Louisville, KY | 38 | 14 | 47 | 85 | 45 | 49 | 450 |
| Lowell, MA | 42 | 38 | 25 | 71 | 19 | 14 | 100 |
| Lubbock, TX | 33 | 35 | 05 | 101 | 50 | 33 | 3,195 |
| Macon, GA | 32 | 50 | 12 | 83 | 37 | 36 | 335 |
| Madison, WI | 43 | 04 | 23 | 89 | 22 | 55 | 860 |
| Manchester, NH | 42 | 59 | 28 | 71 | 27 | 41 | 175 |
| Marshall, TX | 32 | 33 | 00 | 94 | 23 | 00 | 410 |
| Memphis, TN | 35 | 08 | 46 | 90 | 03 | 13 | 275 |
| Meriden, CT | 41 | 32 | 06 | 72 | 47 | 30 | 190 |
| Miami, FL | 25 | 46 | 37 | 80 | 11 | 32 | 10 |
| Milwaukee, WI | 43 | 02 | 19 | 87 | 54 | 15 | 635 |
| Minneapolis, MN | 44 | 58 | 57 | 93 | 15 | 43 | 815 |
| Minot, ND | 48 | 14 | 09 | 101 | 17 | 38 | 1,550 |
| Mississauga, Ont. | 43 | 33 | 00 | 79 | 35 | 00 | 510 |
| Mobile, AL | 30 | 41 | 36 | 88 | 02 | 33 | 5 |
| Moncton, N.B. | 46 | 05 | 18 | 64 | 46 | 41 | 38 |
| Montgomery, AL | 32 | 22 | 33 | 86 | 18 | 31 | 160 |
| Montpelier, VT | 44 | 15 | 36 | 72 | 34 | 41 | 485 |
| Montréal, Que. | 45 | 30 | 33 | 73 | 33 | 14 | 90 |
| Moose Jaw, Sask. | 50 | 23 | 34 | 105 | 32 | 04 | 1,784 |
| Muncie, IN | 40 | 11 | 28 | 85 | 23 | 16 | 950 |
| Nashville, TN | 36 | 09 | 33 | 86 | 46 | 55 | 450 |
| Natchez, MS | 31 | 33 | 48 | 91 | 23 | 30 | 210 |
| Newark, NJ | 40 | 44 | 14 | 74 | 10 | 19 | 55 |
| New Britain, CT | 41 | 40 | 08 | 72 | 46 | 59 | 200 |
| New Haven, CT | 41 | 18 | 25 | 72 | 55 | 30 | 40 |
| New Orleans, LA | 29 | 56 | 53 | 90 | 04 | 10 | 5 |
| New York, NY | 40 | 45 | 06 | 73 | 59 | 39 | 55 |
| Niagara Falls, Ont. | 43 | 06 | 22 | 79 | 03 | 51 | 590 |
| Nome, AK | 64 | 30 | 00 | 165 | 25 | 00 | 25 |
| Norfolk, VA | 36 | 51 | 10 | 76 | 17 | 21 | 10 |
| North Bay, Ont. | 46 | 18 | 35 | 79 | 27 | 45 | 670 |
| Oakland, CA | 37 | 48 | 03 | 122 | 15 | 54 | 25 |
| Ogden, UT | 41 | 13 | 31 | 111 | 58 | 21 | 4,295 |
| Oklahoma City, OK | 35 | 28 | 26 | 97 | 31 | 04 | 1,195 |
| Omaha, NE | 41 | 15 | 42 | 95 | 56 | 14 | 1,040 |
| Orlando, FL | 28 | 32 | 42 | 81 | 22 | 38 | 70 |
| Ottawa, Ont. | 45 | 26 | 24 | 75 | 41 | 42 | 185 |
| Paducah, KY | 37 | 05 | 13 | 88 | 35 | 56 | 345 |
| Pasadena, CA | 34 | 08 | 44 | 118 | 08 | 41 | 830 |
| Paterson, NJ | 40 | 55 | 01 | 74 | 10 | 21 | 100 |
| Pensacola, FL | 30 | 24 | 51 | 87 | 12 | 56 | 15 |
| Peoria, IL | 40 | 41 | 42 | 89 | 35 | 33 | 470 |
| Peterborough, Ont. | 44 | 18 | 32 | 78 | 19 | 13 | 673 |
| Philadelphia, PA | 39 | 56 | 58 | 75 | 09 | 21 | 100 |
| Phoenix, AZ | 33 | 27 | 12 | 112 | 04 | 28 | 1,090 |
| Pierre, SD | 44 | 22 | 18 | 100 | 20 | 54 | 1,480 |
| Pittsburgh, PA | 40 | 26 | 19 | 80 | 00 | 00 | 745 |
| Pittsfield, MA | 42 | 26 | 53 | 73 | 15 | 14 | 1,015 |
| Pocatello, ID | 42 | 51 | 38 | 112 | 27 | 01 | 4,460 |
| Pt. Arthur, TX | 29 | 52 | 30 | 93 | 56 | 15 | 10 |
| Portland, ME | 43 | 39 | 33 | 70 | 15 | 19 | 25 |
| Portland, OR | 45 | 31 | 06 | 122 | 40 | 35 | 77 |
| Portsmouth, NH | 43 | 04 | 30 | 70 | 45 | 24 | 20 |
| Portsmouth, VA | 36 | 50 | 07 | 76 | 18 | 14 | 10 |
| Prince Rupert, B.C. | 54 | 19 | 00 | 130 | 19 | 00 | 125(a) |
| Providence, RI | 41 | 49 | 32 | 71 | 24 | 41 | 80 |
| Provo, UT | 40 | 14 | 06 | 111 | 39 | 24 | 4,550 |
| Pueblo, CO | 38 | 16 | 17 | 104 | 36 | 33 | 4,690 |
| Québec City, Que. | 46 | 48 | 51 | 71 | 12 | 30 | 163 |
| Racine, WI | 42 | 43 | 49 | 87 | 47 | 12 | 630 |
| Raleigh, NC | 35 | 46 | 38 | 78 | 38 | 21 | 365 |
| Rapid City, SD | 44 | 04 | 52 | 103 | 13 | 11 | 3,230 |
| Reading, PA | 40 | 20 | 09 | 75 | 55 | 40 | 265 |
| Regina, Sask. | 50 | 26 | 55 | 104 | 36 | 50 | 1,894(a) |
| Reno, NV | 39 | 31 | 27 | 119 | 48 | 40 | 4,490 |
| Richmond, VA | 37 | 32 | 15 | 77 | 26 | 09 | 160 |
| Roanoke, VA | 37 | 16 | 13 | 79 | 56 | 44 | 905 |
| Rochester, MN | 44 | 01 | 21 | 92 | 28 | 03 | 990 |
| Rochester, NY | 43 | 09 | 41 | 77 | 36 | 21 | 515 |
| Rockford, IL | 42 | 16 | 07 | 89 | 05 | 48 | 715 |
| Sacramento, CA | 38 | 34 | 57 | 121 | 29 | 41 | 30 |
| Saginaw, MI | 43 | 25 | 52 | 83 | 56 | 05 | 595 |
| St. Catharines, Ont. | 43 | 09 | 33 | 79 | 14 | 50 | 362(a) |
| St. Cloud, MN | 45 | 34 | 00 | 94 | 10 | 24 | 1,040 |
| St. John, N.B. | 45 | 16 | 22 | 66 | 03 | 48 | 27 |
| St. John's, Nfld. | 47 | 33 | 42 | 52 | 42 | 48 | 200(a) |

| City | Lat. N ° | ′ | ″ | Long. W ° | ′ | ″ | Alt. (ft) |
|---|---|---|---|---|---|---|---|
| St. Joseph, MO | 39 | 45 | 57 | 94 | 51 | 02 | 850 |
| St. Louis, MO | 38 | 37 | 45 | 90 | 12 | 22 | 455 |
| St. Paul, MN | 44 | 57 | 19 | 93 | 06 | 07 | 780 |
| St. Petersburg, FL | 27 | 46 | 18 | 82 | 38 | 19 | 20 |
| Salem, OR | 44 | 56 | 24 | 123 | 01 | 59 | 155 |
| Salina, KS | 38 | 50 | 36 | 97 | 36 | 46 | 1,229 |
| Salt Lake City, UT | 40 | 45 | 23 | 111 | 53 | 26 | 4,390 |
| San Antonio, TX | 29 | 25 | 37 | 98 | 29 | 06 | 650 |
| San Bernardino, CA | 34 | 06 | 30 | 117 | 17 | 28 | 1,080 |
| San Diego, CA | 32 | 42 | 53 | 117 | 09 | 21 | 20 |
| San Francisco, CA | 37 | 46 | 39 | 122 | 24 | 40 | 65 |
| San Jose, CA | 37 | 20 | 16 | 121 | 53 | 24 | 90 |
| San Juan, P.R. | 18 | 27 | 00 | 66 | 04 | 15 | 35 |
| Santa Barbara, CA | 34 | 25 | 18 | 119 | 41 | 55 | 100 |
| Santa Cruz, CA | 36 | 58 | 18 | 122 | 01 | 18 | 20 |
| Santa Fe, NM | 35 | 41 | 11 | 105 | 56 | 10 | 6,950 |
| Sarasota, FL | 27 | 20 | 05 | 82 | 32 | 30 | 20 |
| Saskatoon, Sask. | 52 | 07 | 49 | 106 | 39 | 35 | 1,587 |
| Sault Ste. Marie, Ont. | 46 | 30 | 24 | 84 | 20 | 04 | 589 |
| Savannah, GA | 32 | 04 | 42 | 81 | 05 | 37 | 20 |
| Schenectady, NY | 42 | 48 | 42 | 73 | 55 | 42 | 245 |
| Seattle, WA | 47 | 36 | 32 | 122 | 20 | 12 | 10 |
| Sheboygan, WI | 43 | 45 | 03 | 87 | 42 | 52 | 630 |
| Sherbrooke, Que. | 45 | 24 | 27 | 71 | 51 | 07 | 627 |
| Sheridan, WY | 44 | 47 | 55 | 106 | 57 | 10 | 3,740 |
| Shreveport, LA | 32 | 30 | 46 | 93 | 44 | 58 | 204 |
| Sioux City, IA | 42 | 29 | 46 | 96 | 24 | 30 | 1,110 |
| Sioux Falls, SD | 43 | 32 | 35 | 96 | 43 | 35 | 1,395 |
| South Bend, IN | 41 | 40 | 33 | 86 | 15 | 01 | 710 |
| Spartanburg, SC | 34 | 57 | 03 | 81 | 56 | 06 | 875 |
| Spokane, WA | 47 | 39 | 32 | 117 | 25 | 33 | 1,890 |
| Springfield, IL | 39 | 47 | 58 | 89 | 38 | 51 | 610 |
| Springfield, MA | 42 | 06 | 21 | 72 | 35 | 32 | 85 |
| Springfield, MO | 37 | 13 | 03 | 93 | 17 | 32 | 1,300 |
| Springfield, OH | 39 | 55 | 38 | 83 | 48 | 29 | 980 |
| Stamford, CT | 41 | 03 | 09 | 73 | 32 | 24 | 35 |
| Steubenville, OH | 40 | 21 | 42 | 80 | 36 | 53 | 660 |
| Stockton, CA | 37 | 57 | 30 | 121 | 17 | 16 | 20 |
| Sudbury, Ont. | 46 | 29 | 24 | 80 | 59 | 24 | 879 |
| Superior, WI | 46 | 43 | 14 | 92 | 06 | 07 | 630 |
| Sydney, N.S. | 46 | 08 | 15 | 60 | 11 | 48 | 25 |
| Syracuse, NY | 43 | 03 | 04 | 76 | 09 | 14 | 400 |
| Tacoma, WA | 47 | 14 | 59 | 122 | 26 | 15 | 110 |
| Tallahassee, FL | 30 | 26 | 30 | 84 | 16 | 56 | 150 |
| Tampa, FL | 27 | 56 | 58 | 82 | 27 | 25 | 15 |
| Terre Haute, IN | 39 | 28 | 03 | 87 | 24 | 26 | 496 |
| Texarkana, TX | 33 | 25 | 48 | 94 | 02 | 30 | 324 |
| Thunder Bay, Ont. | 48 | 22 | 54 | 89 | 14 | 42 | 616 |
| Toledo, OH | 41 | 39 | 14 | 83 | 32 | 39 | 585 |
| Topeka, KS | 39 | 03 | 16 | 95 | 40 | 23 | 930 |
| Toronto, Ont. | 43 | 39 | 10 | 79 | 23 | 00 | 300 |
| Trenton, NJ | 40 | 13 | 14 | 74 | 46 | 13 | 35 |
| Trois-Rivières, Que. | 46 | 20 | 36 | 72 | 32 | 37 | 115(a) |
| Troy, NY | 42 | 43 | 45 | 73 | 40 | 58 | 35 |
| Tucson, AZ | 32 | 13 | 15 | 110 | 58 | 08 | 2,390 |
| Tulsa, OK | 36 | 09 | 12 | 95 | 59 | 34 | 804 |
| Urbana, IL | 40 | 06 | 42 | 88 | 12 | 06 | 725 |
| Utica, NY | 43 | 06 | 12 | 75 | 13 | 33 | 415 |
| Vancouver, B.C. | 49 | 18 | 56 | 123 | 04 | 44 | 141 |
| Victoria, B.C. | 48 | 25 | 43 | 123 | 21 | 49 | 57 |
| Waco, TX | 31 | 33 | 12 | 97 | 08 | 00 | 405 |
| Walla Walla, WA | 46 | 04 | 08 | 118 | 20 | 24 | 936 |
| Washington, DC | 38 | 53 | 51 | 77 | 00 | 33 | 25 |
| Waterloo, IA | 42 | 29 | 40 | 92 | 20 | 20 | 850 |
| West Palm Beach, FL | 26 | 42 | 36 | 80 | 03 | 07 | 15 |
| Wheeling, WV | 40 | 04 | 03 | 80 | 43 | 20 | 650 |
| Whitehorse, Yukon | 60 | 43 | 17 | 135 | 03 | 03 | 2,050 |
| White Plains, NY | 41 | 02 | 00 | 73 | 45 | 48 | 220 |
| Wichita, KS | 37 | 41 | 30 | 97 | 20 | 16 | 1,290 |
| Wilkes-Barre, PA | 41 | 14 | 32 | 75 | 53 | 17 | 640 |
| Wilmington, DE | 39 | 44 | 46 | 75 | 32 | 51 | 135 |
| Wilmington, NC | 34 | 14 | 14 | 77 | 56 | 58 | 35 |
| Windsor, Ont. | 42 | 18 | 56 | 83 | 02 | 10 | 603 |
| Winnipeg, Man. | 49 | 53 | 56 | 97 | 08 | 23 | 762 |
| Winston-Salem, NC | 36 | 05 | 52 | 80 | 14 | 42 | 860 |
| Worcester, MA | 42 | 15 | 37 | 71 | 48 | 17 | 475 |
| Yakima, WA | 46 | 36 | 09 | 120 | 30 | 39 | 1,060 |
| Yellowknife, N.W.T. | 62 | 27 | 16 | 114 | 22 | 33 | 674 |
| Youngstown, OH | 41 | 05 | 57 | 80 | 39 | 02 | 840 |
| Yuma, AZ | 32 | 42 | 54 | 114 | 37 | 24 | 160 |
| Zanesville, OH | 39 | 56 | 18 | 82 | 00 | 30 | 720 |

## Principal World Rivers

**Source:** Geological Survey, U.S. Dept. of the Interior

| River | Outflow | Length (mi) |
|---|---|---|
| Albany | James Bay | 610 |
| Amazon | Atlantic Ocean | 4,000 |
| Amu | Aral Sea | 1,578 |
| Amur | Tatar Strait | 2,744 |
| Angara | Yenisey River | 1,151 |
| Arkansas | Mississippi R. | 1,459 |
| Back, N.W.T. | Arctic Ocean | 605 |
| Brahmaputra | Bay of Bengal | 1,800 |
| Bug, Southern | Dnieper River | 532 |
| Bug, Western | Wisla River | 481 |
| Canadian | Arkansas River | 906 |
| Chang | E China Sea | 3,964 |
| Churchill, Man. | Hudson Bay | 1,000 |
| Churchill, Que. | Atlantic Ocean | 532 |
| Colorado, AZ | Gulf of Calif. | 1,450 |
| Columbia | Pacific Ocean | 1,243 |
| Congo | Atlantic Ocean | 2,718 |
| Danube | Black Sea | 1,776 |
| Dnieper | Black Sea | 1,420 |
| Dniester | Black Sea | 877 |
| Don | Sea of Azov | 1,224 |
| Drava | Danube River | 447 |
| Dvina, North | White Sea | 824 |
| Dvina, West. | Gulf of Riga | 634 |
| Ebro | Mediterranean. | 565 |
| Elbe | North Sea | 724 |
| Euphrates | Shatt al-Arab. | 1,700 |
| Fraser | Str. of Georgia | 850 |
| Gambia | Atlantic Ocean | 700 |
| Ganges | Bay of Bengal | 1,560 |
| Garonne | Bay of Biscay | 357 |
| Huang | Yellow Sea | 3,395 |
| Indus | Arabian Sea | 1,800 |
| Irrawaddy | Bay of Bengal | 1,337 |
| Japura | Amazon River | 1,750 |
| Jordan | Dead Sea | 200 |
| Kootenay | Columbia R. | 485 |
| Lena | Laptev Sea | 2,734 |
| Loire | Bay of Biscay | 634 |
| Mackenzie | Arctic Ocean | 1,025 |
| Madeira | Amazon River | 2,013 |
| Magdalena | Caribbean Sea | 956 |
| Marne | Seine River | 326 |
| Mekong | S China Sea | 2,600 |
| Meuse | North Sea | 580 |
| Mississippi | Southwest Pass | 2,340 |
| Missouri | Mississippi R. | 2,315 |
| Murray-Darling | Indian Ocean | 2,310 |
| Negro | Amazon | 1,400 |
| Nelson | Hudson Bay | 410 |
| Niger | Gulf of Guinea. | 2,590 |
| Nile | Mediterranean. | 4,160 |
| Ob-Irtysh | Gulf of Ob | 3,362 |
| Oder | Baltic Sea | 567 |
| Ohio | Mississippi | 981 |
| Orange | Atlantic Ocean | 1,300 |
| Orinoco | Atantic Ocean | 1,600 |
| Ottawa | St. Lawrence R. | 790 |
| Paraguay | Parana River | 1,584 |
| Parana | Rio de la Plata | 2,485 |
| Peace | Slave River | 1,210 |
| Pilcomayo | Paraguay River | 1,000 |
| Po | Adriatic Sea | 405 |
| Purus | Amazon River | 2,100 |
| Red | Atchafalaya R. | 1,290 |
| Red River of N. | Lake Winnipeg | 545 |
| Rhine | North Sea | 820 |
| Rhone | Gulf of Lions | 505 |
| Rio de la Plata | Atlantic Ocean | 150 |
| Rio Grande | Gulf of Mexico | 1,900 |
| Rio Roosevelt | Aripuana | 400 |
| Saguenay | St. Lawrence R. | 434 |
| St. John | Bay of Fundy | 418 |
| St. Lawrence | Gulf of St. Law. | 800 |
| Salween | Andaman Sea | 1,500 |
| Sao Francisco | Atlantic Ocean | 1,988 |
| Seine | English Chan. | 496 |
| Shannon | Atlantic Ocean | 230 |
| Snake | Columbia River | 1,038 |
| Songhua | Amur River | 1,150 |
| Syr | Aral Sea | 1,370 |
| Tajo, Tagus | Atlantic Ocean | 626 |
| Tennessee | Ohio River | 652 |
| Thames | North Sea | 236 |
| Tiber | Tyrrhenian Sea | 252 |
| Tigris | Shatt al-Arab | 1,180 |
| Tisza | Danube River | 600 |
| Tocantins | Para River | 1,677 |
| Ural | Caspian Sea | 1,575 |
| Uruguay | Rio de la Plata | 1,000 |
| Volga | Caspian Sea | 2,290 |
| Weser | North Sea | 454 |
| Wisla | Bay of Danzig | 675 |
| Xi | S. China Sea | 1,200 |
| Yangtze. See Chang | | |
| Yellow. See Huang | | |
| Yenisey | Kara Sea | 2,543 |
| Yukon | Bering Sea | 1,979 |
| Zambezi | Indian Ocean | 1,700 |

## Major Rivers in North America

**Source:** Geological Survey, U.S. Dept. of the Interior

| River | Source or upper limit of length | Outflow | Length (mi) |
|---|---|---|---|
| Alabama | Gilmer County, GA | Mobile River | 729 |
| Albany | Lake St. Joseph, Ontario | James Bay | 610 |
| Allegheny | Potter County, PA | Ohio River | 325 |
| Altamaha-Ocmulgee | Junction of Yellow and South Rivers, Newton County, GA | Atlantic Ocean | 392 |
| Apalachicola-Chattahoochee | Towns County, GA | Gulf of Mexico | 524 |
| Arkansas | Lake County, CO | Mississippi River | 1,459 |
| Assiniboine | Eastern Saskatchewan | Red River | 450 |
| Attawapiskat | Attawapiskat, Ontario | James Bay | 465 |
| Back (N.W.T.) | Contwoyto Lake | Chantrey Inlet, Arctic Ocean | 605 |
| Big Black (MS) | Webster County, MS | Mississippi River | 330 |
| Brazos | Junction of Salt and Double Mountain Forks, Stonewall County, TX | Gulf of Mexico | 923 |
| Canadian | Las Animas County, CO | Arkansas River | 906 |
| Cedar (IA) | Dodge County, MN | Iowa River | 329 |
| Cheyenne | Junction of Antelope Creek and Dry Fork, Converse County, WY | Missouri River | 290 |
| Churchill, Man. | Methy Lake, Saskatchewan | Hudson Bay | 1,000 |
| Cimarron | Colfax County, NM | Arkansas River | 600 |
| Colorado (AZ) | Rocky Mountain Natl. Park, CO (90 mi in Mexico) | Gulf of California | 1,450 |
| Colorado (TX) | West Texas | Matagorda Bay | 862 |
| Columbia | Columbia Lake, British Columbia | Pacific Ocean, bet. OR and WA | 1,243 |
| Columbia, Upper | Columbia Lake, British Columbia | To mouth of Snake River | 890 |
| Connecticut | Third Connecticut Lake, NH | Long Island Sound, CT | 407 |
| Coppermine (N.W.T.) | Lac de Gras | Coronation Gulf (Arctic Ocean) | 525 |
| Cumberland | Letcher County, KY | Ohio River | 720 |
| Delaware | Schoharie County, NY | Liston Point, Delaware Bay | 390 |
| Fraser | Near Mount Robson (on Continental Divide) | Strait of Georgia | 850 |
| Gila | Catron County, NM | Colorado River | 649 |
| Green (UT-WY) | Junction of Wells and Trail Creeks, Sublette County, WY | Colorado River | 730 |
| Hamilton (Lab.) | Lake Ashuanipi | Atlantic Ocean | 532 |
| Hudson | Henderson Lake, Essex County, NY | Upper NY Bay | 306 |
| Illinois | St. Joseph County, IN | Mississippi River | 420 |
| James (ND-SD) | Wells County, ND | Missouri River | 710 |
| James (VA) | Junction of Jackson and Cowpasture Rivers, Botetourt County, VA | Hampton Roads | 340 |
| Kanawha-New | Junction of North and South Forks of New River, NC | Ohio River | 352 |
| Kentucky | Junction of North and Middle Forks, Lee County, KY | Ohio River | 259 |
| Klamath | Lake Ewauna, Klamath Falls, OR | Pacific Ocean | 250 |
| Koyukuk | Endicott Mountains, AK | Yukon River | 470 |
| Kuskokwim | Alaska Range | Kuskokwim Bay | 724 |
| Liard | Southern Yukon, Alaska | Mackenzie River | 693 |
| Little Missouri | Crook County, WY | Missouri River | 560 |

| River | Source or upper limit of length | Outflow | Length (mi) |
|---|---|---|---|
| Mackenzie | Great Slave Lake, N.W.T. | Arctic Ocean | 1,025 |
| Milk | Junction of North and South Forks, Alberta | Missouri River | 625 |
| Minnesota | Big Stone Lake, MN | Mississippi River | 332 |
| Mississippi | Lake Itasca, MN | Mouth of Southwest Pass | 2,340 |
| Mississippi, Upper | Lake Itasca, MN | To mouth of Missouri River | 1,171 |
| Mississippi-Missouri-Red Rock | Source of Red Rock, Beaverhead Co., MT | Mouth of Southwest Pass | 3,710 |
| Missouri | Junction of Jefferson, Madison, and Gallatin rivers, Madison County, MT | Mississippi River | 2,315 |
| Missouri-Red Rock | Source of Red Rock, Beaverhead Co., MT | Mississippi River | 2,540 |
| Mobile-Alabama-Coosa | Gilmer County, GA | Mobile Bay | 774 |
| Nelson (Man.) | Lake Winnipeg | Hudson Bay | 410 |
| Neosho | Morris County, KS | Arkansas River, OK | 460 |
| Niobrara | Niobrara County, WY | Missouri River, NE | 431 |
| North Canadian | Union County, NM | Canadian River, OK | 800 |
| North Platte | Junction of Grizzly and Little Grizzly creeks, Jackson County, CO | Platte River, NE | 618 |
| Ohio | Junction of Allegheny and Monongahela rivers, Pittsburgh, PA | Mississippi River | 981 |
| Ohio-Allegheny | Potter County, PA | Mississippi River | 1,310 |
| Osage | East-central Kansas | Missouri River | 500 |
| Ottawa | Lake Capimitchigama | St. Lawrence River | 790 |
| Ouachita | Polk County, AR | Black River | 605 |
| Peace | Stikine Mountains, B.C. | Slave River | 1,210 |
| Pearl | Neshoba County, MS | Gulf of Mexico | 411 |
| Pecos | Mora County, NM | Rio Grande | 926 |
| Pee Dee-Yadkin | Watauga County, NC | Winyah Bay | 435 |
| Pend Oreille-Clark Fork | Near Butte, MT | Columbia River | 531 |
| Platte | Junction of North and South Platte Rivers, NE | Missouri River | 310 |
| Porcupine | Ogilvie Mountains, AK | Yukon River, Alaska | 569 |
| Potomac | Garrett County, MD | Chesapeake Bay | 383 |
| Powder | Junction of South and Middle Forks, WY | Yellowstone River | 375 |
| Red (OK-TX-LA) | Curry County, NM | Atchafalaya River | 1,290 |
| Red River of the North | Junction of Otter Tail and Bois de Sioux Rivers, Wilkin County, MN | Lake Winnipeg | 545 |
| Republican | Junction of North Fork and Arikaree River, NE | Kansas River | 445 |
| Rio Grande | San Juan County, CO | Gulf of Mexico | 1,900 |
| Roanoke | Junction of North and South Forks, Montgomery County, VA | Albemarle Sound | 380 |
| Rock (IL-WI) | Dodge County, WI | Mississippi River | 300 |
| Sabine | Junction of South and Caddo Forks, Hunt County, TX | Sabine Lake | 380 |
| Sacramento | Siskiyou County, CA | Suisun Bay | 377 |
| St. Francis | Iron County, MO | Mississippi River | 425 |
| St. Lawrence | Lake Ontario | Gulf of St. Lawrence (Atlantic Ocean) | 800 |
| Salmon (ID) | Custer County, ID | Snake River | 420 |
| San Joaquin | Junction of South and Middle Forks, Madera County, CA | Suisun Bay | 350 |
| San Juan | Silver Lake, Archuleta County, CO | Colorado River | 360 |
| Santee-Wateree-Catawba | McDowell County, NC | Atlantic Ocean | 538 |
| Saskatchewan, North | Rocky Mountains | Saskatchewan R. | 800 |
| Saskatchewan, South | Rocky Mountains | Saskatchewan R. | 865 |
| Savannah | Junction of Seneca and Tugaloo rivers, Anderson County, SC | Atlantic Ocean, GA-SC | 314 |
| Severn (Ont.) | Sandy Lake | Hudson Bay | 610 |
| Smoky Hill | Cheyenne County, CO | Kansas River, KS | 540 |
| Snake | Teton County, WY | Columbia River, WA | 1,038 |
| South Platte | Junction of South and Middle Forks, Park County, CO | Platte River | 424 |
| Susitna | Alaska Range | Cook Inlet | 313 |
| Susquehanna | Huyden Creek, Otsego County, NY | Chesapeake Bay | 447 |
| Tallahatchie | Tippah County, MS | Yazoo River | 301 |
| Tanana | Wrangell Mountains, AK | Yukon River | 659 |
| Tennessee | Junction of French Broad and Holston Rivers | Ohio River | 652 |
| Tennessee-French Broad | Courthouse Creek, Transylvania County, NC | Ohio River | 886 |
| Tombigbee | Prentiss County, MS | Mobile River | 525 |
| Trinity | North of Dallas, TX | Galveston Bay | 360 |
| Wabash | Darke County, OH | Ohio River | 512 |
| Washita | Hemphill County, TX | Red River, OK | 500 |
| White (AR-MO) | Madison County, AR | Mississippi River | 722 |
| Willamette | Douglas County, OR | Columbia River | 309 |
| Wind-Bighorn | Junction of Wind and Little Wind Rivers, Fremont Co., WY (Source of Wind R. is Togwotee Pass, Teton Co., WY) | Yellowstone River | 336 |
| Wisconsin | Lac Vieux Desert, Vilas County, WI | Mississippi River | 430 |
| Yellowstone | Park County, WY | Missouri River | 692 |
| Yukon | McNeil R., Yukon Territory | Bering Sea | 1,979 |

## Highest and Lowest Continental Altitudes

**Source:** National Geographic Society

| Continent | Highest point | Elevation (ft) | Lowest point | ft below sea level |
|---|---|---|---|---|
| Asia | Mount Everest, Nepal-Tibet | 29,028 | Dead Sea, Israel-Jordan | 1,312 |
| South America | Mount Aconcagua, Argentina | 22,834 | Valdes Peninsula, Argentina | 131 |
| North America | Mount McKinley, AK | 20,320 | Death Valley, California | 282 |
| Africa | Kilimanjaro, Tanzania | 19,340 | Lake Assal, Djibouti | 512 |
| Europe | Mount Elbrus, Russia | 18,510 | Caspian Sea, Russia, Azerbaijan | 92 |
| Antarctica | Vinson Massif | 16,864 | Bentley Subglacial Trench | 8,327[1] |
| Australia | Mount Kosciusko, New South Wales | 7,310 | Lake Eyre, South Australia | 52 |

(1) Estimated. Lower points that have yet to be discovered may exist beneath the ice.

# Major Natural Lakes of the World

**Source:** Geological Survey, U.S. Dept. of the Interior

A lake is generally defined as a body of water surrounded by land. By this definition some bodies of water that are called seas, such as the Caspian Sea and the Aral Sea, are really lakes. The word *lake* is omitted when part of name.

| Name | Continent | Area (sq mi) | Length (mi) | Maximum depth (ft) | Elevation (ft) |
|---|---|---|---|---|---|
| Caspian Sea | Asia-Europe | 143,244 | 760 | 3,363 | –92 |
| Superior | North America | 31,700 | 350 | 1,330 | 600 |
| Victoria | Africa | 26,828 | 250 | 270 | 3,720 |
| Aral Sea | Asia | 24,904[1] | 280 | 220 | 174 |
| Huron | North America | 23,000 | 206 | 750 | 579 |
| Michigan | North America | 22,300 | 307 | 923 | 579 |
| Tanganyika | Africa | 12,700 | 420 | 4,823 | 2,534 |
| Baykal | Asia | 12,162 | 395 | 5,315 | 1,493 |
| Great Bear | North America | 12,096 | 192 | 1,463 | 512 |
| Nyasa (Malawi) | Africa | 11,150 | 360 | 2,280 | 1,550 |
| Great Slave | North America | 11,031 | 298 | 2,015 | 513 |
| Erie | North America | 9,910 | 241 | 210 | 570 |
| Winnipeg | North America | 9,417 | 266 | 60 | 713 |
| Ontario | North America | 7,340 | 193 | 802 | 245 |
| Balkhash | Asia | 7,115 | 376 | 85 | 1,115 |
| Ladoga | Europe | 6,835 | 124 | 738 | 13 |
| Chad | Africa | 6,300 | 175 | 24 | 787 |
| Maracaibo | South America | 5,217 | 133 | 115 | sea level |
| Onega | Europe | 3,710 | 145 | 328 | 108 |
| Eyre | Australia | 3,600[2] | 90 | 4 | –52 |
| Volta | Africa | 3,276 | 250 | .... | .... |
| Titicaca | South America | 3,200 | 122 | 922 | 12,500 |
| Nicaragua | Central America | 3,100 | 102 | 230 | 102 |
| Athabasca | North America | 3,064 | 208 | 407 | 700 |
| Reindeer | North America | 2,568 | 143 | 720 | 1,106 |
| Turkana (Rudolf) | Africa | 2,473 | 154 | 240 | 1,230 |
| Issyk Kul | Asia | 2,355 | 115 | 2,303 | 5,279 |
| Torrens | Australia | 2,230 | 130 | .... | 92 |
| Vanern | Europe | 2,156 | 91 | 328 | 144 |
| Nettilling | North America | 2,140 | 67 | .... | 95 |
| Winnipegosis | North America | 2,075 | 141 | 38 | 830 |
| Albert | Africa | 2,075 | 100 | 168 | 2,030 |
| Kariba | Africa | 2,050 | 175 | 390 | 1,590 |
| Nipigon | North America | 1,872 | 72 | 540 | 1,050 |
| Gairdner | Australia | 1,840 | 90 | .... | 112 |
| Urmia | Asia | 1,815 | 90 | 49 | 4,180 |
| Manitoba | North America | 1,799 | 140 | 12 | 813 |

(1) Probably less because of the diversion of feeder rivers. (2) Approximate figure, subject to great seasonal variation.

# The Great Lakes

**Source:** National Ocean Service, U.S. Dept. of Commerce

The Great Lakes form the largest body of fresh water in the world and with their connecting waterways are the largest inland water transportation unit. Draining the great North Central basin of the U.S., they enable shipping to reach the Atlantic via their outlet, the St. Lawrence R., and also the Gulf of Mexico via the Illinois Waterway, from Lake Michigan to the Mississippi R. A third outlet connects with the Hudson R. and then the Atlantic via the New York State Barge Canal System. Traffic on the Illinois Waterway and the New York State Barge Canal System is limited to recreational boating and small shipping vessels.

Only one of the lakes, Lake Michigan, is wholly in the U.S.; the others are shared with Canada. Ships move from the shores of Lake Superior to Whitefish Bay at the E end of the lake, then through the Soo (Sault Ste. Marie) locks, through the St. Mary's R. and into Lake Huron. To reach Gary and the Port of Indiana and South Chicago, IL, ships move W from Lake Huron to Lake Michigan through the Straits of Mackinac.

Lake Superior is 600 ft above mean water level at Point-au-Pere, Quebec, on the International Great Lakes Datum (1955). From Duluth, MN, to the E end of Lake Ontario is 1,156 mi.

| | Superior | Michigan | Huron | Erie | Ontario |
|---|---|---|---|---|---|
| Length in mi | 350 | 307 | 206 | 241 | 193 |
| Breadth in mi | 160 | 118 | 183 | 57 | 53 |
| Deepest soundings in ft | 1,333 | 923 | 750 | 210 | 802 |
| Volume of water in cu mi | 2,935 | 1,180 | 850 | 116 | 393 |
| Area (sq mi) water surface—U.S. | 20,600 | 22,300 | 9,100 | 4,980 | 3,460 |
| Canada | 11,100 | ..... | 13,900 | 4,930 | 3,880 |
| Area (sq mi) entire drainage basin—U.S. | 16,900 | 45,600 | 16,200 | 18,000 | 15,200 |
| Canada | 32,400 | ..... | 35,500 | 4,720 | 12,100 |
| **Total area (sq mi) U.S. and Canada** | **81,000** | **67,900** | **74,700** | **32,630** | **34,850** |
| Mean surface above mean water level at Point-au-Pere, Quebec, avg. level in ft (1900-88) | 600.61 | 578.34 | 578.34 | 570.53 | 244.74 |
| Latitude, North | 46° 25′ | 41° 37′ | 43° 00′ | 41° 23′ | 43° 11′ |
| | 49° 00′ | 46° 06′ | 46° 17′ | 42° 52′ | 44° 15′ |
| Longitude, West | 84° 22′ | 84° 45′ | 79° 43′ | 78° 51′ | 76° 03′ |
| | 92° 06′ | 88° 02′ | 84° 45′ | 83° 29′ | 79° 53′ |
| National boundary line in mi | 282.8 | None | 260.8 | 251.5 | 174.6 |
| United States shoreline (mainland only) mi | 863 | 1,400 | 580 | 431 | 300 |

# Famous Waterfalls

**Source:** National Geographic Society

The earth has thousands of waterfalls, some of considerable magnitude. Their importance is determined not only by height but by volume of flow, steadiness of flow, crest width, whether the water drops sheerly or over a sloping surface, and whether it descends in one leap or a succession of leaps. A series of low falls flowing over a considerable distance is known as a cascade.

Estimated mean annual flow, in cubic feet per second, of major waterfalls are as follows: Niagara, 212,200; Paulo Afonso, 100,000; Urubupunga, 97,000; Iguazu, 61,000; Patos-Maribondo, 53,000; Victoria, 35,400; and Kaieteur, 23,400.

Height = total drop in feet in one or more leaps. †= falls of more than one leap; *= falls that diminish greatly seasonally; **= falls that reduce to a trickle or are dry for part of each year. If river names not shown, they are same as the falls. R. = river; L. = lake; (C) = cascade type.

## Africa

| Name and location | Elevation (ft) |
|---|---|
| **Angola** | |
| Ruacana, Cuene R. | 406 |
| **Ethiopia** | |
| Fincha | 508 |
| **Lesotho** | |
| Maletsunyane* | 630 |
| **Zimbabwe-Zambia** | |
| Victoria, Zambezi R.* | 343 |
| **South Africa** | |
| Augrabies, Orange R.* | 480 |
| Tugela† | 2,014 |
| **Tanzania-Zambia** | |
| Kalambo* | 726 |

## Asia

| Name and location | Elevation (ft) |
|---|---|
| **India**—Cauvery* | 330 |
| Jog (Gersoppa), Sharavathi R.* | 830 |
| **Japan** | |
| Kegon, Daiya R.* | 330 |

## Australasia

| Name and location | Elevation (ft) |
|---|---|
| **Australia** | |
| New South Wales | |
| Wentworth | 614 |
| Wollomombi | 1,100 |
| Queensland | |
| Tully | 885 |
| Wallaman, Stony Cr.† | 1,137 |
| **New Zealand** | |
| Helena | 890 |
| Sutherland, Arthur R.† | 1,904 |

## Europe

| Name and location | Elevation (ft) |
|---|---|
| **Austria**—Gasteint† | 492 |
| Krimml† | 1,312 |
| **France**—Gavarnie* | 1,385 |
| **Great Britain** | |
| Scotland | |
| Glomach | 370 |
| Wales | |
| Rhaiadr | 240 |
| **Italy**—Frua, Toce R. (C) | 470 |
| **Norway** | |
| Mardalsfossen (Northern) | 1,535 |
| Mardalsfossen (Southern)† | 2,149 |
| Skjeggedal, Nybuai R.†** | 1,378 |
| Skykje** | 984 |
| Vetti, Morka-Koldedola R. | 900 |
| **Sweden** | |
| Handol† | 427 |
| **Switzerland** | |
| Giessbach (C) | 984 |
| Reichenbach† | 656 |
| Simmen† | 459 |
| Staubbach | 984 |
| Trummelbach† | 1,312 |

## North America

| Name and location | Elevation (ft) |
|---|---|
| **Canada** | |
| Alberta | |
| Panther, Nigel Cr. | 600 |
| British Columbia | |
| Della† | 1,443 |
| Takakkaw, Daly Glacier† | 1,200 |
| Quebec | |
| Montmorency | 274 |
| **Canada—United States** | |
| Niagara: American | 182 |
| Horseshoe | 173 |
| **United States** | |
| California | |
| Feather, Fall R. * | 640 |
| Yosemite National Park | |
| Bridalveil* | 620 |
| Illilouette* | 370 |
| Nevada, Merced R.* | 594 |
| Ribbon** | 1,612 |
| Silver Strand, Meadow Br.** | 1,170 |
| Vernal, Merced R. * | 317 |
| Yosemite†** | 2,425 |
| Colorado | |
| Seven, South Cheyenne Cr.† | 300 |
| Hawaii | |
| Akaka, Kolekole Str. | 442 |
| Idaho | |
| Shoshone, Snake R.** | 212 |
| Kentucky | |
| Cumberland | 68 |
| Maryland | |
| Great, Potomac R. (C) * | 71 |
| Minnesota | |
| Minnehaha** | 53 |
| New Jersey | |
| Passaic | 70 |
| New York | |
| Taughannock* | 215 |
| Oregon | |
| Multnomah† | 620 |
| Tennessee | |
| Fall Creek | 256 |
| Washington | |
| Mt. Rainier Natl. Park | |
| Sluiskin, Paradise R. | 300 |
| Snoqualmie** | 268 |
| Wisconsin | |
| Big Manitou, Black R. (C)* | 165 |
| Wyoming | |
| Yellowstone Natl. Pk. Tower | 132 |
| Yellowstone (upper)* | 109 |
| Yellowstone (lower)* | 308 |
| **Mexico** | |
| El Salto | 218 |

## South America

| Name and location | Elevation (ft) |
|---|---|
| **Argentina-Brazil** | |
| Iguazu | 230 |
| **Brazil** | |
| Glass | 1,325 |
| Patos-Maribondo, Grande R. | 115 |
| Paulo Afonso, Sao Francisco R. | 275 |
| Urubupunga, Parana R. | 39 |
| **Colombia** | |
| Catarata de Candelas, Cusiana R. | 984 |
| Tequendama, Bogota R. * | 427 |
| **Ecuador** | |
| Agoyan, Pastaza R. * | 200 |
| **Guyana** | |
| Kaieteur, Potaro R. | 741 |
| Great, Kamarang R. | 1,600 |
| Marina, Ipobe R. † | 500 |
| **Venezuela** | |
| Angel†* | 3,212 |
| Cuquenan | 2,000 |

# Notable Deserts of the World

**Arabian (Eastern),** 70,000 sq mi in Egypt between the Nile river and Red Sea, extending southward into Sudan
**Atacama,** 600-mi-long area rich in nitrate and copper deposits in N Chile
**Chihuahuan,** 140,000 sq mi in TX, NM, AZ, and Mexico
**Dasht-e Kauir,** approx. 300 mi long by approx. 100 mi wide in N central Iran
**Dasht-e Lut,** 20,000 sq mi in E Iran
**Death Valley,** 3,300 sq mi in CA and NV
**Gibson,** 120,000 sq mi in the interior of W Australia
**Gobi,** 500,000 sq mi in Mongolia and China
**Great Sandy,** 150,000 sq mi in W Australia
**Great Victoria,** 150,000 sq mi in SW Australia
**Kalahari,** 225,000 sq mi in S Africa
**Kara Kum,** 120,000 sq mi in Turkmenistan
**Kyzyl Kum,** 100,000 sq mi in Kazakstan and Uzbekistan
**Libyan,** 450,000 sq mi in the Sahara, extending from Libya through SW Egypt into Sudan
**Mojave,** 15,000 sq mi in southern CA
**Namib,** long narrow area (varies from 30-100 mi wide) extending 800 mi along SW coast of Africa
**Nubian,** 100,000 sq mi in the Sahara in NE Sudan
**Patagonia,** 300,000 sq mi in S Argentina
**Painted Desert,** section of high plateau in northern AZ extending 150 mi
**Rub al-Khali (Empty Quarter),** 250,000 sq mi in the S Arabian Peninsula
**Sahara,** 3,500,000 sq mi in N Africa extending westward to the Atlantic. Largest desert in the world
**Sonoran,** 70,000 sq mi in southwestern AZ and southeastern CA extending into NW Mexico
**Syrian,** 100,000-sq-mi arid wasteland extending over much of N Saudi Arabia, E Jordan, S Syria, and W Iraq
**Taklimakan,** 140,000 sq mi in Xinjiang Prov., China
**Thar (Great Indian),** 100,000-sq-mi arid area extending 400 mi along India-Pakistan border

# WEIGHTS AND MEASURES

**Source:** National Institute of Standards and Technology, U.S. Dept. of Commerce

## The International System of Units (SI)

Two systems of weights and measures coexist in the U.S. today: the U.S. Customary System and the International System of Units (SI, after the initials of Système International). SI, commonly identified with the metric system, is actually a more complete, coherent version of it. Throughout U.S. history, the Customary System (inherited from, but now different from, the British Imperial System) has been generally used; federal and state legislation has given it, through implication, standing as the primary weights and measures system. The metric system, however, is the only system that Congress has ever specifically sanctioned. An 1866 law reads:

> It shall be lawful throughout the United States of America to employ the weights and measures of the metric system; and no contract or dealing, or pleading in any court, shall be deemed invalid or liable to objection because the weights or measures expressed or referred to therein are weights or measures of the metric system.

Since that time, use of the metric system in the U.S. has slowly and steadily increased, particularly in the scientific community, in the pharmaceutical industry, and in the manufacturing sector—the last motivated by the practice in international commerce, in which the metric system is now predominantly used.

On Feb. 10, 1964, the National Bureau of Standards (now known as the National Institute of Standards and Technology) issued the following statement:

> Henceforth it shall be the policy of the National Bureau of Standards to use the units of the International System (SI), as adopted by the 11th General Conference on Weights and Measures (October 1960), except when the use of these units would obviously impair communication or reduce the usefulness of a report.

On Dec. 23, 1975, Pres. Gerald R. Ford signed the Metric Conversion Act of 1975. It defines the metric system as being the International System of Units as interpreted in the U.S. by the secretary of commerce. The Trade Act of 1988 and other legislation declare the metric system the preferred system of weights and measures for U.S. trade and commerce, call for the federal government to adopt metric specifications, and mandate the Commerce Dept. to oversee the program. However, the metric system has still not become the system of choice for most Americans' daily use.

The following 7 units serve as the base units for the International System: **length**—meter; **mass**—kilogram; **time**—second; **electric current**—ampere; **thermodynamic temperature**—kelvin; **amount of substance**—mole; and **luminous intensity**—candela.

### Prefixes

The following prefixes, in combination with the basic unit names, provide the multiples and submultiples in the International System. For example, the unit name *meter*, with the prefix *kilo* added, produces *kilometer*, meaning "1,000 meters."

| Prefix | Symbol | Multiples | Equivalent |
|---|---|---|---|
| yotta | Y | $10^{24}$ | septillionfold |
| zetta | Z | $10^{21}$ | sextillionfold |
| exa | E | $10^{18}$ | quintillionfold |
| peta | P | $10^{15}$ | quadrillionfold |
| tera | T | $10^{12}$ | trillionfold |
| giga | G | $10^{9}$ | billionfold |
| mega | M | $10^{6}$ | millionfold |
| kilo | k | $10^{3}$ | thousandfold |
| hecto | h | $10^{2}$ | hundredfold |
| deka | da | 10 | tenfold |

| Prefix | Symbol | Submultiples | Equivalent |
|---|---|---|---|
| deci | d | $10^{-1}$ | tenth part |
| centi | c | $10^{-2}$ | hundredth part |
| milli | m | $10^{-3}$ | thousandth part |
| micro | m | $10^{-6}$ | millionth part |
| nano | n | $10^{-9}$ | billionth part |
| pico | p | $10^{-12}$ | trillionth part |
| femto | f | $10^{-15}$ | quadrillionth part |
| atto | a | $10^{-18}$ | quintillionth part |
| zepto | z | $10^{-21}$ | sextillionth part |
| yocto | y | $10^{-24}$ | septillionth part |

## Tables of Metric Weights and Measures

(**Note:** The SI generally uses the term *mass* instead of *weight.* Mass is a measure of an object's inertial property, or the amount of matter it contains. Weight is a measure of the force exerted on an object by gravity or the force needed to support it. Also, the SI does not make a distinction between "dry volume" and "liquid volume.")

### Length

| | |
|---|---|
| 10 millimeters (mm) | = 1 centimeter (cm) |
| 10 centimeters | = 1 decimeter (dm) = 100 millimeters |
| 10 decimeters | = 1 meter (m) = 1,000 millimeters |
| 10 meters | = 1 dekameter (dam) |
| 10 dekameters | = 1 hectometer (hm) = 100 meters |
| 10 hectometers | = 1 kilometer (km) = 1,000 meters |

### Area

| | |
|---|---|
| 100 square millimeters ($mm^2$) | = 1 square centimeter ($cm^2$) |
| 10,000 square centimeters | = 1 square meter ($m^2$) = 1,000,000 square millimeters |
| 100 square meters | = 1 are (a) |
| 100 ares | = 1 hectare (ha) = 10,000 square meters |
| 100 hectares | = 1 square kilometer ($km^2$) = 1,000,000 square meters |

### Volume

| | |
|---|---|
| 10 milliliters (mL) | = 1 centiliter (cL) |
| 10 centiliters | = 1 deciliter (dL) = 100 milliliters |
| 10 deciliters | = 1 liter (L) = 1,000 milliliters |
| 10 liters | = 1 dekaliter (daL) |
| 10 dekaliters | = 1 hectoliter (hL) = 100 liters |
| 10 hectoliters | = 1 kiloliter (kL) = 1,000 liters |

### Volume (Cubic Measure)

| | |
|---|---|
| 1,000 cubic millimeters ($mm^3$) | = 1 cubic centimeter ($cm^3$) |
| 1,000 cubic centimeters | = 1 cubic decimeter ($dm^3$) = 1,000,000 cubic millimeters |
| 1,000 cubic decimeters | = 1 cubic meter ($m^3$) = 1 stere = 1,000,000 cubic centimeters = 1,000,000,000 cubic millimeters |

### Weight (Mass)

| | |
|---|---|
| 10 milligrams (mg) | = 1 centigram (cg) |
| 10 centigrams | = 1 decigram (dg) = 100 milligrams |
| 10 decigrams | = 1 gram (g) = 1,000 milligrams |
| 10 grams | = 1 dekagram (dag) |
| 10 dekagrams | = 1 hectogram (hg) = 100 grams |
| 10 hectograms | = 1 kilogram (kg) = 1,000 grams |
| 1,000 kilograms | = 1 metric ton (t) |

## Table of U.S. Customary Weights and Measures

### Length

| | |
|---|---|
| 12 inches (in) | = 1 foot (ft) |
| 3 feet | = 1 yard (yd) |
| 5 ½ yards | = 1 rod (rd), pole, or perch (16 ½ feet) |
| 40 rods | = 1 furlong (fur)=220 yards= 660 feet |
| 8 furlongs | = 1 statute mile (mi) = 1,760 yards = 5,280 feet |
| 3 miles | = 1 league = 5,280 yards = 15,840 feet |
| 6076.11549 feet | = 1 international nautical mile |

### Volume (Liquid Measure)

When necessary to distinguish the liquid pint or quart from the dry pint or quart, the word *liquid* or the abbreviation *liq* is used in combination with the name or abbreviation of the liquid unit.

| | |
|---|---|
| 4 gills (gi) | = 1 pint (pt) = 28.875 cubic inches |
| 2 pints | = 1 quart (qt) = 57.75 cubic inches |
| 4 quarts | = 1 gallon (gal) = 231 cubic inches = 8 pints = 32 gills |

### Volume (Dry Measure)

When necessary to distinguish the dry pint or quart from the liquid pint or quart, the word *dry* is used in combination with the name or abbreviation of the dry unit.

| | |
|---|---|
| 2 pints (pt) | = 1 quart (qt) = 67.2006 cubic inches |
| 8 quarts | = 1 peck (pk) = 537.605 cubic inches = 16 pints |
| 4 pecks | = 1 bushel (bu) = 2,150.42 cubic inches = 32 quarts |

### Area

Squares and cubes of units are sometimes abbreviated by using superscripts. For example, $ft^2$ means square foot, and $ft^3$ means cubic foot.

| | |
|---|---|
| 144 square inches | = 1 square foot ($ft^2$) |
| 9 square feet | = 1 square yard ($yd^2$) = 1,296 square inches |
| 30 ¼ square yards | = 1 square rod ($rd^2$) = 272 ¼ square feet |
| 160 square rods | = 1 acre = 4,840 square yards = 43,560 square feet |
| 640 acres | = 1 square mile ($mi^2$) |
| 1 mile square | = 1 section (of land) |
| 6 miles square | = 1 township = 36 sections = 36 square miles |

### Cubic Measure

| | |
|---|---|
| 1 cubic foot ($ft^3$) | = 1,728 cubic inches ($in^3$) |
| 27 cubic feet | = 1 cubic yard ($yd^3$) |

### Gunter's, or Surveyor's, Chain Measure

| | |
|---|---|
| 7.92 inches (in) | = 1 link |
| 100 links | = 1 chain (ch) = 4 rods = 66 feet |
| 80 chains | = 1 statute mile (mi) = 320 rods = 5,280 feet |

### Avoirdupois Weight

When necessary to distinguish the avoirdupois ounce or pound from the troy ounce or pound, the word *avoirdupois* or the abbreviation *avdp* is used in combination with the name or abbreviation of the avoirdupois unit. The *grain* is the same in avoirdupois and troy weight.

| | |
|---|---|
| 27 11/32 grains | = 1 dram (dr) |
| 16 drams | = 1 ounce (oz) = 437 ½ grains |
| 16 ounces | = 1 pound (lb) = 256 drams = 7,000 grains |
| 100 pounds | = 1 hundredweight (cwt)° |
| 20 hundredweights | = 1 ton = 2,000 pounds° |

In *gross* or *long* measure, the following values are recognized.

| | |
|---|---|
| 112 pounds | = 1 gross or long hundredweight° |
| 20 gross or long hundredweights | = 1 gross or long ton = 2,240 pounds° |

°When the terms *hundredweight* and *ton* are used unmodified, they are commonly understood to mean the 100-pound hundredweight and the 2,000-pound ton, respectively; these units may be designated *net* or *short* when necessary to distinguish them from the corresponding units in gross or long measure.

### Troy Weight

| | |
|---|---|
| 24 grains | = 1 pennyweight (dwt) |
| 20 pennyweights | = 1 ounce troy (oz t) = 480 grains |
| 12 ounces troy | = 1 pound troy (lb t) = 240 pennyweights = 5,760 grains |

# Tables of Equivalents

In this table it is necessary to distinguish between the *international* and the *survey* foot. The international foot, defined in 1959 as exactly equal to 0.3048 meter, is shorter than the old survey foot by exactly 2 parts in one million. The survey foot is still used in data expressed in feet in geodetic surveys within the U.S. In this table the survey foot is italicized.

When the name of a unit is enclosed in brackets thus, [1 hand], either (1) the unit is not in general current use in the U.S. or (2) the unit is believed to be based on custom and usage rather than on formal definition.

Equivalents involving decimals are, in most instances, rounded to the third decimal place; exact equivalents are so designated.

### Lengths

| | |
|---|---|
| 1 angstrom (Å) | = 0.1 nanometer (exactly) = 0.000 1 micrometer (exactly) = 0.000 000 1 millimeter (exactly) = 0.000 000 004 inch |
| 1 cable's length | = 120 fathoms (exactly) = 720 *feet* (exactly) = 219 meters |
| 1 centimeter (cm) | = 0.3937 inch |
| 1 chain (ch) (Gunter's or surveyor's) | = 66 *feet* (exactly) = 20.1168 meters |
| 1 chain (engineer's) | = 100 feet = 30.48 meters (exactly) |
| 1 decimeter (dm) | = 3.937 inches |
| 1 degree (geographical) | = 364,566.929 feet = 69.047 miles (avg.) = 111.123 kilometers (avg.) |
| -of latitude | = 68.708 miles at equator = 69.403 miles at poles |
| -of longitude | = 69.171 miles at equator |
| 1 dekameter (dam) | = 32.808 feet |
| 1 fathom | = 6 *feet* (exactly) = 1.8288 meters |
| 1 foot (ft) | = 0.3048 meters (exactly) |
| 1 furlong (fur) | = 10 chains (surveyors) (exactly) = 660 *feet* (exactly) = 1/8 statute mile (exactly) = 201.168 meters |
| [1 hand] (height measure for horses from ground to top of shoulders) | = 4 inches |
| 1 inch (in) | = 2.54 centimeters (exactly) |
| 1 kilometer (km) | = 0.621 mile = 3,280.8 feet |
| 1 league (land) | = 3 statute miles (exactly) = 4.828 kilometers |
| 1 link (Gunter's or surveyor's) | = 7.92 inches (exactly) = 0.201 meter |
| 1 link (engineer's) | = 1 foot = 0.305 meter |
| 1 meter (m) | = 39.37 inches = 1.094 yards |
| 1 micrometer ($\mu$m) [the Greek letter mu] | = 0.001 millimeter (exactly) = 0.000 039 37 inch |
| 1 mil | = 0.001 inch (exactly) = 0.025 4 millimeter (exactly) |
| 1 mile (mi) (statute or land) | = 5,280 *feet* (exactly) = 1.609 kilometers |
| 1 international nautical mile (nmi) | = 1.852 kilometers (exactly) = 1.150779 statute miles = 6,076.11549 feet |
| 1 millimeter (mm) | = 0.039 37 inch |
| 1 nanometer (nm) | = 0.001 micrometer (exactly) = 0.000 000 039 37 inch |
| 1 pica (typography) | = 12 points |
| 1 point (typography) | = 0.013 837 inch (exactly) = 0.351 millimeter |
| 1 rod (rd), pole, or perch | = 16½ *feet* (exactly) = 5.029 meters |
| 1 yard (yd) | = 0.9144 meter (exactly) |

### Areas or Surfaces

| | |
|---|---|
| 1 acre | = 43,560 square *feet* (exactly) = 4,840 square yards = 0.405 hectare |
| 1 are (a) | = 119.599 square yards = 0.025 acre |

| | |
|---|---|
| 1 bolt (cloth measure): | |
| length | = 100 yards (on modern looms) |
| width | = 45 or 60 inches |
| 1 hectare (ha) | = 2.471 acres |
| [1 square (building)] | = 100 square feet |
| 1 square centimeter ($cm^2$) | = 0.155 square inch |
| 1 square decimeter ($dm^2$) | = 15.500 square inches |
| 1 square foot ($ft^2$) | = 929.030 square centimeters |
| 1 square inch ($in^2$) | = 6.4516 square centimeters (exactly) |
| 1 square kilometer ($km^2$) | = 247.104 acres |
| | = 0.386 square mile |
| 1 square meter ($m^2$) | = 1.196 square yards |
| | = 10.764 square feet |
| 1 square mile ($mi^2$) | = 258.999 hectares |
| 1 square millimeter ($mm^2$) | = 0.002 square inch |
| 1 square rod ($rd^2$), sq. pole, or sq. perch | = 25.293 square meters |
| 1 square yard ($yd^2$) | = 0.836 square meter |

## Capacities or Volumes

| | |
|---|---|
| 1 barrel (bbl), liquid | = 31 to 42 gallons° |

°There are a variety of "barrels" established by law or usage. For example: federal taxes on fermented liquors are based on a barrel of 31 gallons; many state laws fix the "barrel for liquids" as 31½ gallons; one state fixes a 36-gallon barrel for cistern measurement; federal law recognizes a 40-gallon barrel for "proof spirits"; by custom, 42 gallons constitute a barrel of crude oil or petroleum products for statistical purposes, and this equivalent is recognized "for liquids" by 4 states.

| | |
|---|---|
| 1 barrel (bbl), standard for fruits, vegetables, and other dry commodities except dry cranberries | = 7,056 cubic inches |
| | = 105 dry quarts |
| | = 3.281 bushels, struck measure |
| 1 barrel (bbl), standard, cranberry | = 5,826 cubic inches |
| | = 86 45/64 dry quarts |
| | = 2.709 bushels, struck measure |
| 1 board foot (lumber measure) | = a foot-square board 1 inch thick |
| 1 bushel (bu) (U.S.) (struck measure) | = 2,150.42 cubic inches (exactly) |
| | = 35.239 liters |
| [1 bushel, heaped (U.S.)] | = 2,747.715 cubic inches |
| | = 1.278 bushels, struck measure° |

°Frequently recognized as 1¼ bushels, struck measure.

| | |
|---|---|
| [1 bushel (bu) (British Imperial) (struck measure)] | = 1.032 U.S. bushels, struck measure |
| | = 2,219.36 cubic inches |
| 1 cord (cd) firewood | = 128 cubic feet (exactly) |
| 1 cubic centimeter ($cm^3$) | = 0.061 cubic inch |
| 1 cubic decimeter ($dm^3$) | = 61.024 cubic inches |
| 1 cubic inch ($in^3$) | = 0.554 fluid ounce |
| | = 4.433 fluid drams |
| | = 16.387 cubic centimeters |
| 1 cubic foot ($ft^3$) | = 7.481 gallons |
| | = 28.317 cubic decimeters |
| 1 cubic meter ($m^3$) | = 1.308 cubic yards |
| 1 cubic yard ($yd^3$) | = 0.765 cubic meter |
| 1 cup, measuring | = 8 fluid ounces (exactly) |
| | = ½ liquid pint (exactly) |
| [1 drachm, fluid (fl dr) (British)] | = 0.961 U.S. fluid dram |
| | = 0.217 cubic inch |
| | = 3.552 milliliters |
| 1 dekaliter (daL) | = 2.642 gallons |
| | = 1.135 pecks |
| 1 gallon (gal) (U.S.) | = 231 cubic inches (exactly) |
| | = 3.785 liters |
| | = 0.833 British gallon |
| | = 128 U.S. fluid ounces (exactly) |
| [1 gallon (gal) British Imperial] | = 277.42 cubic inches |
| | = 1.201 U.S. gallons |
| | = 4.546 liters |
| | = 160 British fluid ounces (exactly) |
| 1 gill (gi) | = 7.219 cubic inches |
| | = 4 fluid ounces (exactly) |
| | = 0.118 liter |
| 1 hectoliter (hL) | = 26.418 gallons |
| | = 2.838 bushels |
| 1 liter (L) (1 cubic decimeter exactly) | = 1.057 liquid quarts |
| | = 0.908 dry quart |
| | = 61.025 cubic inches |
| 1 milliliter (mL) (1 cu cm exactly) | = 0.271 fluid dram |
| | = 16.231 minims |
| | = 0.061 cubic inch |
| 1 ounce, liquid (U.S.) | = 1.805 cubic inches |
| | = 29.574 milliliters |
| | = 1.041 British fluid ounces |
| [1 ounce, fluid (fl oz) (British)] | = 0.961 U.S. fluid ounce |
| | = 1.734 cubic inches |
| | = 28.412 milliliters |
| 1 peck (pk) | = 8.810 liters |
| 1 pint (pt), dry | = 33.600 cubic inches |
| | = 0.551 liter |
| 1 pint (pt), liquid | = 28.875 cubic inches (exactly) |
| | = 0.473 liter |
| 1 quart (qt), dry (U.S.) | = 67.201 cubic inches |
| | = 1.101 liters |
| | = 0.969 British quart |
| 1 quart (qt), liquid (U.S.) | = 57.75 cubic in (exactly) |
| | = 0.946 liter |
| | = 0.833 British quart |
| [1 quart (qt) (British)] | = 69.354 cubic inches |
| | = 1.032 U.S. dry quarts |
| | = 1.201 U.S. liquid quarts |
| 1 tablespoon | = 3 teaspoons°(exactly) |
| | = 4 fluid drams |
| | = ½ fluid ounce (exactly) |
| 1 teaspoon | = ⅓ tablespoon°(exactly) |
| | = 1⅓ fluid drams° |

°The equivalent "1 teaspoon=1⅓ fluid drams" has been found by the bureau to correspond more closely with the actual capacities of "measuring" and silver teaspoons than the equivalent "1 teaspoon=1 fluid dram" which is given by many dictionaries.

## Weights or Masses

| | |
|---|---|
| 1 assay ton°° (AT) | = 29.167 grams |

°°Used in assaying. The assay ton bears the same relation to the milligram that a ton of 2,000 pounds avoirdupois bears to the ounce troy; hence, the weight in milligrams of precious metal obtained from one assay ton of ore gives directly the number of troy ounces to the net ton.

| | |
|---|---|
| 1 bale (cotton measure) | = 500 pounds in U.S. |
| | = 750 pounds in Egypt |
| 1 carat (c) | = 200 milligrams (exactly) |
| | = 3.086 grains |
| 1 dram avoirdupois (dr avdp) | = 27 11/32 (=27.344) grains |
| | = 1.772 grams |
| 1 gamma (γ) | = 1 microgram (exactly), see below |
| 1 grain | = 64.799 milligrams |
| 1 gram | = 15.432 grains |
| | = 0.035 ounce, avoirdupois |
| 1 hundredweight, gross or long°°° (gross cwt) | = 112 pounds (exactly) |
| | = 50.802 kilograms |
| 1 hundredweight, net or short (cwt or net cwt) | = 100 pounds (exactly) |
| | = 45.359 kilograms |
| 1 kilogram (kg) | = 2.205 pounds |
| 1 microgram ($\mu g$ [the Greek letter mu in combination with the letter g]) | = 0.000001 gram (exactly) |
| 1 milligram (mg) | = 0.015 grain |
| 1 ounce, avoirdupois (oz avdp) | = 437.5 grains (exactly) |
| | = 0.911 troy ounce |
| | = 28.350 grams |
| 1 ounce, troy (oz t) | = 480 grains (exactly) |
| | = 1.097 avoirdupois ounces |
| | = 31.103 grams |
| 1 pennyweight (dwt) | = 1.555 grams |
| 1 pound, avoirdupois (lb avdp) | = 7,000 grains (exactly) |
| | = 1.215 troy pounds |
| | = 453.592 37 grams (exactly) |
| 1 pound, troy (lb t) | = 5,760 grains (exactly) |
| | = 0.823 avoirdupois pound |
| | = 373.242 grams |
| 1 ton, gross or long°°° (gross ton) | = 2,240 pounds (exactly) |
| | = 1.12 net tons (exactly) |
| | = 1.016 metric tons |

°°°The gross or long ton and hundredweight are used commercially in the U.S. to only a limited extent, usually in restricted industrial fields. These units are the same as the British ton and hundredweight.

| | |
|---|---|
| 1 ton, metric (t) | = 2,204.623 pounds |
| | = 0.984 gross ton |
| | = 1.102 net tons |
| | = 2,000 pounds (exactly) |
| 1 ton, net or short (sh ton) | = 0.893 gross ton |
| | = 0.907 metric ton |

# Tables of Interrelation of Units of Measurement

Units of length and area of the international and survey measures are included in the following tables. Units unique to the survey measure are *italicized*. See Tables of Equivalents, 1st paragraph.

| | |
|---|---|
| 1 international foot | = 0.999 998 survey foot (exactly) |
| 1 survey foot | = 1200/3937 meter (exactly) |
| 1 international foot | = 12 × 0.0254 meter (exactly) |

**Boldface** type indicates exact values.

## Units of Length

| Units | Inches | *Links* | Feet | Yards | *Rods* | *Chains* | Miles | Cm | Meters |
|---|---|---|---|---|---|---|---|---|---|
| 1 inch= | **1** | 0.126 263 | 0.083 333 | 0.027 778 | 0.005 051 | 0.001 263 | 0.000 016 | **2.54** | **0.025 4** |
| 1 *link*= | **7.92** | 1 | **0.66** | **0.22** | **0.04** | 0.01 | 0.000 125 | 20.117 | 0.201 168 |
| 1 foot= | **12** | 1.515 152 | **1** | 0.333 333 | 0.060 606 | 0.015 152 | 0.000 189 | **30.48** | **0.304 8** |
| 1 yard= | **36** | 4.545 45 | **3** | **1** | 0.181 818 | 0.045 455 | 0.000 568 | **91.44** | **0.914 4** |
| 1 *rod*= | **198** | **25** | **16.5** | **5.5** | **1** | **0.25** | **0.003 125** | 502.92 | 5.029 2 |
| 1 *chain*= | **792** | **100** | **66** | **22** | **4** | **1** | **0.012 5** | 2011.68 | 20.116 8 |
| 1 mile= | **63 360** | **8000** | **5280** | **1760** | **320** | **80** | **1** | **160 934.4** | **1609.344** |
| 1 cm= | 0.3937 | 0.049 710 | 0.032 808 | 0.010 936 | 0.001 988 | 0.000 497 | 0.000 006 | **1** | **0.01** |
| 1 meter= | 39.37 | 4.970 960 | 3.280 840 | 1.093 613 | 0.198 838 | 0.049 710 | 0.000 621 | **100** | **1** |

## Units of Area

| Units | Sq. inches | *Sq. links* | Sq. feet | Sq. yards | *Sq. rods* | *Sq. chains* |
|---|---|---|---|---|---|---|
| 1 sq. inch= | 1 | 0.015 942 3 | 0.006 944 | 0.000 771 605 | 0.000 025 5 | 0.000 001 594 |
| 1 sq. *link*= | 62.726 4 | 1 | **0.435 6** | **0.0484** | **0.0016** | 0.000 1 |
| 1 sq. foot= | **144** | 2.295 684 | **1** | 0.111 111 1 | 0.003 673 09 | 0.000 229 568 |
| 1 sq. yard= | **1296** | 20.661 16 | **9** | **1** | 0.033 057 85 | 0.002 066 12 |
| 1 sq. *rod*= | **39 204** | **625** | **272.25** | **30.25** | **1** | 0.062 5 |
| 1 sq. *chain*= | **627 264** | **10 000** | **4 356** | **484** | **16** | **1** |
| 1 *acre*= | **6 272 640** | **100 000** | **43 560** | **4 840** | **160** | **10** |
| 1 sq. mile= | **4 014 489 600** | **64 000 000** | **27 878 400** | **3 097 600** | **102 400** | **6400** |
| 1 sq. cm= | 0.155 000 3 | 0.002 471 05 | 0.001 076 | 0.000 119 599 | 0.000 003 954 | 0.000 000 247 |
| 1 sq. meter= | 1550.003 | 24.710 44 | 10.763 91 | 1.195 990 | 0.039 536 70 | 0.002 471 044 |
| 1 *hectare*= | 15 500 031 | 247 104 | 107 639.1 | 11 959.90 | 395.367 0 | **24.710 44** |

| Units | *Acres* | Sq. miles | Sq. cm | Sq. meters | *Hectares* |
|---|---|---|---|---|---|
| 1 sq. inch= | 0.000 000 159 423 | 0.000 000 000 249 10 | **6.451 6** | **0.000 645 16** | 0.000 000 065 |
| 1 sq. *link*= | **0.000 01** | **0.000 000 015 625** | 404.685 642 24 | 0.040 468 56 | 0.000 004 047 |
| 1 sq. foot= | 0.000 022 956 84 | 0.000 000 035 870 06 | 929.034 1 | 0.092 903 41 | 0.000 009 290 |
| 1 sq. yard= | 0.000 206 611 6 | 0.000 000 322 830 6 | **8 361.273 6** | 0.836 127 36 | 0.000 083 613 |
| 1 sq. *rod*= | **0.006 25** | **0.000 009 765 625** | 252 929.5 | 25.292 95 | 0.002 529 295 |
| 1 sq. *chain*= | **0.1** | **0.000 156 25** | 4 046 873 | 404.687 3 | 0.040 468 73 |
| 1 *acre*= | **1** | **0.001 562 5** | 40 468 730 | 4 046.873 | 0.404 687 3 |
| 1 sq. mile= | **640** | **1** | 25 899 881 103 | 2 589 988.11 | 258.998 811 034 |
| 1 sq. cm= | 0.000 000 024 711 | 0.000 000 000 038 610 | **1** | **0.000 1** | **0.000 000 01** |
| 1 sq. meter= | 0.000 247 104 4 | 0.000 000 386 102 2 | **10 000** | **1** | **0.0001** |
| 1 *hectare*= | 2.471 044 | 0.003 861 006 | **100 000 000** | **10 000** | **1** |

## Units of Weight or Mass Not Greater Than Pounds and Kilograms

| Units | Grains | Pennyweights | Avdp drams | Avdp ounces |
|---|---|---|---|---|
| 1 grain= | **1** | 0.041 666 67 | 0.036 571 43 | 0.002 285 71 |
| 1 pennyweight= | **24** | **1** | 0.877 714 3 | 0.054 857 14 |
| 1 dram avdp= | **27.343 75** | 1.139 323 | **1** | **0.062 5** |
| 1 ounce avdp= | **437.5** | 18.229 17 | **16** | **1** |
| 1 ounce troy= | **480** | **20** | 17.554 29 | 1.097 143 |
| 1 pound troy= | **5760** | **240** | 210.651 4 | 13.165 71 |
| 1 pound avdp= | **7000** | 291.666 7 | **256** | **16** |
| 1 milligram= | 0.015 432 | 0.000 643 015 | 0.000 564 383 | 0.000 035 274 |
| 1 gram= | 15.432 36 | 0.643 014 9 | 0.564 383 4 | 0.035 273 96 |
| 1 kilogram= | 15 432.36 | 643.014 9 | 564.383 4 | 35.273 96 |

| Units | Troy ounces | Troy pounds | Avdp pounds | Milligrams | Grams | Kilograms |
|---|---|---|---|---|---|---|
| 1 grain= | 0.002 083 33 | 0.000 173 611 | 0.000 142 857 | **64.798 91** | **0.064 798 91** | 0.000 064 799 |
| 1 pennywt.= | **0.05** | 0.004 166 667 | 0.003 428 571 | **1555.173 84** | **1.555 173 84** | 0.001 555 174 |
| 1 dram avdp= | 0.056 966 15 | 0.004 747 179 | 0.003 906 25 | 1771.845 195 | 1.771 845 195 | 0.001 771 845 |
| 1 oz avdp= | 0.911 458 3 | 0.075 954 86 | 0.062 5 | **28 349.523 125** | **28.349 523 125** | 0.028 349 52 |
| 1 oz troy= | **1** | 0.083 333 333 | 0.068 571 43 | **31 103.476 8** | **31.103 476 8** | 0.031 103 48 |
| 1 lb troy= | **12** | **1** | 0.822 857 1 | **373 241.721 6** | **373.241 721 6** | 0.373 241 722 |
| 1 lb avdp= | 14.583 33 | 1.215 278 | **1** | **453 592.37** | **453.592 37** | **0.453 592 37** |
| 1 milligram= | 0.000 032 151 | 0.000 002 679 | 0.000 002 205 | **1** | **0.001** | **0.000 001** |
| 1 gram= | 0.032 150 75 | 0.002 679 229 | 0.002 204 623 | **1000** | **1** | **0.001** |
| 1 kilogram= | 32.150 75 | 2.679 229 | 2.204 623 | **1 000 000** | **1000** | **1** |

## Units of Weight or Mass Not Less Than Avoirdupois Ounces

| Units | Avdp oz | Avdp lb | Short cwt | Short tons | Long tons | Kilograms | Metric tons |
|---|---|---|---|---|---|---|---|
| 1 oz avdp= | **1** | **0.0625** | **0.000 625** | **0.000 031 25** | 0.000 027 902 | 0.028 349 523 | 0.000 028 350 |
| 1 lb avdp= | **16** | **1** | **0.01** | **0.000 5** | 0.000 446 429 | **0.453 592 37** | 0.000 453 592 |
| 1 sh cwt= | **1 600** | **100** | **1** | **0.05** | 0.044 642 86 | **45.359 237** | **0.045 359 237** |
| 1 sh ton= | **32 000** | **2000** | **20** | **1** | 0.892 857 1 | **907.184 74** | **0.907 184 74** |
| 1 long ton= | **35 840** | **2240** | **22.4** | **1.12** | **1** | **1 016.046 908 8** | 1.016 046 909 |
| 1 kg= | 35.273 96 | 2.204 623 | 0.022 046 23 | 0.001 102 311 | 0.000 984 207 | **1** | **0.001** |
| 1 metric ton= | 35 273.96 | 2 204.623 | 22.046 23 | 1.102 311 | 0.984 206 5 | **1000** | **1** |

## Units of Volume

| Units | Cubic inches | Cubic feet | Cubic yards | Cubic cm | Cubic dm | Cubic meters |
|---|---|---|---|---|---|---|
| 1 cubic inch= | 1 | 0.000 578 704 | 0.000 021 433 | 16.387 064 | 0.016 387 | 0.000 016 387 |
| 1 cubic foot= | 1728 | 1 | 0.037 037 04 | 28 316.846 592 | 28.316 847 | 0.028 316 847 |
| 1 cubic yard= | 46 656 | 27 | 1 | 764 554.857 984 | 764.554 858 | 0.764 554 858 |
| 1 cubic cm= | 0.061 023 74 | 0.000 035 315 | 0.000 001 308 | 1 | 0.001 | 0.000 001 |
| 1 cubic dm= | 61.023 74 | 0.035 314 67 | 0.001 307 951 | 1 000 | 1 | 0.001 |
| 1 cubic meter= | 61 023.74 | 35.314 67 | 1.307 951 | 1 000 000 | 1000 | 1 |

## Units of Capacity (Liquid Measure)

| Units | Minims | Fluid drams | Fluid ounces | Gills | Liquid pint |
|---|---|---|---|---|---|
| 1 minim= | 1 | 0.016 666 7 | 0.002 083 33 | 0.000 520 833 | 0.000 130 208 |
| 1 fluid dram= | 60 | 1 | 0.125 | 0.031 25 | 0.007 812 5 |
| 1 fluid ounce= | 480 | 8 | 1 | 0.25 | 0.062 5 |
| 1 gill= | 1920 | 32 | 4 | 1 | 0.25 |
| 1 liquid pint= | 7680 | 128 | 16 | 4 | 1 |
| 1 liquid quart= | 15 360 | 256 | 32 | 8 | 2 |
| 1 gallon= | 61 440 | 1024 | 128 | 32 | 8 |
| 1 cubic inch= | 265.974 | 4.432 900 | 0.554 112 6 | 0.138 528 1 | 0.034 632 03 |
| 1 cubic foot= | 459 603.1 | 7 660.052 | 957.506 5 | 239.376 6 | 59.844 16 |
| 1 liter= | 16 230.73 | 270.512 18 | 33.814 02 | 8.453 506 | 2.113 376 |

| Units | Liquid quarts | Gallons | Cubic inches | Cubic feet | Liters |
|---|---|---|---|---|---|
| 1 minim= | 0.000 065 104 17 | 0.000 016 276 04 | 0.003 759 766 | 0.000 002 175 790 | 0.000 061 611 52 |
| 1 flu. dram= | 0.003 906 25 | 0.000 976 562 5 | 0.225 585 9 | 0.000 130 547 4 | 0.003 696 691 |
| 1 fluid oz= | 0.031 25 | 0.007 812 5 | 1.804 687 5 | 0.001 044 379 | 0.029 573 53 |
| 1 gill= | 0.125 | 0.031 25 | 7.218 75 | 0.004 177 517 | 0.118 294 118 |
| 1 liquid pt= | 0.5 | 0.125 | 28.875 | 0.016 710 07 | 0.473 176 473 |
| 1 liquid qt= | 1 | 0.25 | 57.75 | 0.033 420 14 | 0.946 352 946 |
| 1 gallon= | 4 | 1 | 231 | 0.133 680 6 | 3.785 411 784 |
| 1 cubic inch= | 0.017 316 02 | 0.004 329 004 | 1 | 0.000 578 703 7 | 0.016 387 064 |
| 1 cubic foot= | 29.922 08 | 7.480 519 | 1728 | 1 | 28.316 846 592 |
| 1 liter= | 1.056 688 | 0.264 172 05 | 61.023 74 | 0.035 314 67 | 1 |

## Units of Capacity (Dry Measure)

| Units | Dry pints | Dry quarts | Pecks | Bushels | Cubic in. | Liters |
|---|---|---|---|---|---|---|
| 1 dry pint= | 1 | 0.5 | 0.062 5 | 0.015 625 | 33.600 312 5 | 0.550 610 47 |
| 1 dry quart= | 2 | 1 | 0.125 | 0.031 25 | 67.200 625 | 1.101 220 9 |
| 1 peck= | 16 | 8 | 1 | 0.25 | 537.605 | 8.809 767 5 |
| 1 bushel= | 64 | 32 | 4 | 1 | 2 150.42 | 35.239 07 |
| 1 cubic inch= | 0.029 761 6 | 0.014 880 8 | 0.001 860 10 | 0.000 465 025 | 1 | 0.016 387 06 |
| 1 liter= | 1.816 166 | 0.908 083 | 0.113 510 37 | 0.028 377 59 | 61.023 74 | 1 |

# Miscellaneous Measures

**Caliber**—the diameter of a gun bore. In the U.S., caliber is traditionally expressed in hundredths of inches, e.g. .22 or .30. In Britain, caliber is often expressed in thousandths of inches, e.g. .270 or .465. Now, it is commonly expressed in millimeters, e.g. the 5.56 mm M16 rifle. Heavier weapons' caliber has long been expressed in millimeters, e.g. the 81 mm mortar, the 105 mm howitzer (light), the 155 mm howitzer (medium or heavy).

Naval guns' caliber refers to the barrel length as a multiple of the bore diameter. A 5-inch, 50-caliber naval gun has a 5-inch bore and a barrel length of 250 inches.

**Carat**—a measure of the amount of alloy per 24 parts in gold. Thus 24-carat gold is pure; 18-carat gold is one-fourth alloy.

**Decibel** (dB)—a measure of the relative loudness or intensity of sound. A 20-decibel sound is 10 times louder than a 10-decibel sound; 30 decibels is 100 times louder; 40 decibels is 1,000 times louder, etc. One decibel is the smallest difference between sounds detectable by the human ear. A 120-decibel sound is painful.

| | |
|---|---|
| 10 decibels | – a light whisper |
| 20 | – quiet conversation |
| 30 | – normal conversation |
| 40 | – light traffic |
| 50 | – typewriter, loud conversation |
| 60 | – noisy office |
| 70 | – normal traffic, quiet train |
| 80 | – rock music, subway |
| 90 | – heavy traffic, thunder |
| 100 | – jet plane at takeoff |

**Em**—a printer's measure designating the square width of any given type size. Thus, an em of 10-point type is 10 points. An en is half an em.

**Gauge**—a measure of shotgun bore diameter. Gauge numbers originally referred to the number of lead balls of the gun barrel diameter in a pound. Thus, a 16-gauge shotgun's bore was smaller than a 12-gauge shotgun's. Today, an international agreement assigns millimeter measures to each gauge, e.g.:

| Gauge | Bore diameter in mm |
|---|---|
| 6 | 23.34 |
| 10 | 19.67 |
| 12 | 18.52 |
| 14 | 17.60 |
| 16 | 16.81 |
| 20 | 15.90 |

**Horsepower**—the power needed to lift 550 pounds 1 foot in 1 second or to lift 33,000 pounds 1 foot in 1 minute. Equivalent to 746 watts or 2,546.0756 Btu/h.

**Knot**—a measure of the speed of ships. A knot equals 1 nautical mile per hour.

**Quire**—25 sheets of paper

**Ream**—500 sheets of paper

# Electrical Units

The **watt** is the unit of power (electrical, mechanical, thermal, etc.). Electrical power is given by the product of the voltage and the current.

Energy is sold by the **joule,** but in common practice the billing of electrical energy is expressed in terms of the **kilowatt-hour,** which is 3,600,000 joules or 3.6 megajoules.

The **horsepower** is a nonmetric unit sometimes used in mechanics. It is equal to 746 watts.

The **ohm** is the unit of electrical resistance and represents the physical property of a conductor that offers a resistance to the flow of electricity, permitting just 1 ampere to flow at 1 volt of pressure.

# Compound Interest

### Compounded Annually

| Principal | Period | 4% | 5% | 6% | 7% | 8% | 9% | 10% | 12% | 14% | 16% |
|---|---|---|---|---|---|---|---|---|---|---|---|
| $100 | 1 day | 0.011 | 0.014 | 0.016 | 0.019 | 0.022 | 0.025 | 0.027 | 0.033 | 0.038 | 0.044 |
| | 1 week | 0.077 | 0.096 | 0.115 | 0.134 | 0.153 | 0.173 | 0.192 | 0.230 | 0.268 | 0.307 |
| | 6 mos. | 2.00 | 2.50 | 3.00 | 3.50 | 4.00 | 4.50 | 5.00 | 6.00 | 7.00 | 8.00 |
| | 1 year | 4.00 | 5.00 | 6.00 | 7.00 | 8.00 | 9.00 | 10.00 | 12.00 | 14.00 | 16.00 |
| | 2 years | 8.16 | 10.25 | 12.36 | 14.49 | 16.64 | 18.81 | 21.00 | 25.44 | 29.96 | 34.56 |
| | 3 years | 12.49 | 15.76 | 19.10 | 22.50 | 25.97 | 29.50 | 33.10 | 40.49 | 48.15 | 56.09 |
| | 4 years | 16.99 | 21.55 | 26.25 | 31.08 | 36.05 | 41.16 | 46.41 | 57.35 | 68.90 | 81.06 |
| | 5 years | 21.67 | 27.63 | 33.82 | 40.26 | 46.93 | 53.86 | 61.05 | 76.23 | 92.54 | 110.03 |
| | 6 years | 26.53 | 34.01 | 41.85 | 50.07 | 58.69 | 67.71 | 77.16 | 97.38 | 119.50 | 143.64 |
| | 7 years | 31.59 | 40.71 | 50.36 | 60.58 | 71.38 | 82.80 | 94.87 | 121.07 | 150.23 | 182.62 |
| | 8 years | 36.86 | 47.75 | 59.38 | 71.82 | 85.09 | 99.26 | 114.36 | 147.60 | 185.26 | 227.84 |
| | 9 years | 42.33 | 55.13 | 68.95 | 83.85 | 99.90 | 117.19 | 135.79 | 177.31 | 225.19 | 280.30 |
| | 10 years | 48.02 | 62.89 | 79.08 | 96.72 | 115.89 | 136.74 | 159.37 | 210.58 | 270.72 | 341.14 |
| | 12 years | 60.10 | 79.59 | 101.22 | 125.22 | 151.82 | 181.27 | 213.84 | 289.60 | 381.79 | 493.60 |
| | 15 years | 80.09 | 107.89 | 139.66 | 175.90 | 217.22 | 264.25 | 317.72 | 447.36 | 613.79 | 826.55 |
| | 20 years | 119.11 | 165.33 | 220.71 | 286.97 | 366.10 | 460.44 | 572.75 | 864.63 | 1,274.35 | 1,846.08 |

# Ancient Measures

**Biblical**

| | | |
|---|---|---|
| Cubit | = | 21.8 inches |
| Omer | = | 0.45 peck |
| | = | 3.964 liters |
| Ephah | = | 10 omers |
| Shekel | = | 0.497 ounce |
| | = | 14.1 grams |

**Greek**

| | | |
|---|---|---|
| Cubit | = | 18.3 inches |
| Stadion | = | 607.2 or 622 feet |
| Obolos | = | 715.38 milligrams |
| Drachma | = | 4.2923 grams |
| Mina | = | 0.9463 pound |
| Talent | = | 60 mina |

**Roman**

| | |
|---|---|
| Cubit | = 17.5 inches |
| Stadium | = 202 yards |
| As, libra, pondus | = 325.971 grams |
| | = 0.71864 pound |

# Weight or Mass of Water

**Weight, at 20°C**

| | | |
|---|---|---|
| 1 | cubic inch | 0.0360 pound |
| 12 | cubic inches | 0.433 pound |
| 1 | cubic foot | 62.4 pounds |
| 1 | cubic foot | 7.48052 U.S. gal |
| 1.8 | cubic feet | 112.0 pounds |
| 35.96 | cubic feet | 2240.0 pounds |

| | | |
|---|---|---|
| 1 | U.S. gallon | 8.33 pounds |
| 13.45 | U.S. gallons | 112.0 pounds |
| 269.0 | U.S. gallons | 2240.0 pounds |

**Mass, at 4°C (Maximum Density)**

| | | |
|---|---|---|
| 1 | cubic centimeter | 1 gram |
| 1 | liter | 1 kilogram |
| 1 | cubic meter | 1 metric ton |

# Density of Gases and Vapors

at 0°C and 760 mmHg; kilograms per cubic meter

| Gas | Mass | Gas | Mass | Gas | Mass |
|---|---|---|---|---|---|
| Acetylene | 1.171 | Ethylene | 1.260 | Methyl fluoride | 1.545 |
| Air | 1.293 | Fluorine | 1.696 | Mono methylamine | 1.38 |
| Ammonia | 0.759 | Helium | 0.178 | Neon | 0.900 |
| Argon | 1.784 | Hydrogen | 0.090 | Nitric oxide | 1.341 |
| Arsine | 3.48 | Hydrogen bromide | 3.50 | Nitrogen | 1.250 |
| Butane-iso | 2.60 | Hydrogen chloride | 1.639 | Nitrosyl chloride | 2.99 |
| Butane-n | 2.519 | Hydrogen iodide | 5.724 | Nitrous oxide | 1.997 |
| Carbon dioxide | 1.977 | Hydrogen selenide | 3.66 | Oxygen | 1.429 |
| Carbon monoxide | 1.250 | Hydrogen sulfide | 1.539 | Phosphine | 1.48 |
| Carbon oxysulfide | 2.72 | Krypton | 3.745 | Propane | 2.020 |
| Chlorine | 3.214 | Methane | 0.717 | Silicon tetrafluoride | 4.67 |
| Chlorine monoxide | 3.89 | Methyl chloride | 2.25 | Sulfur dioxide | 2.927 |
| Ethane | 1.356 | Methyl ether | 2.091 | Xenon | 5.897 |

# Temperature Conversion Table

The numbers in **boldface type** refer to the temperatures either in degrees Celsius or Fahrenheit that are to be converted. If converting from degrees Fahrenheit to Celsius, refer to the column on the left; if converting from degrees Celsius to Fahrenheit, consult the column on the right.

**For temperatures not shown.** To convert Fahrenheit to Celsius by formula, subtract 32 degrees and divide by 1.8; to convert Celsius to Fahrenheit, multiply by 1.8 and add 32 degrees.

Note: Although the term *centigrade* is still frequently used, the International Committee on Weights and Measures and the National Institute of Standards and Technology have recommended since 1948 that this scale be called Celsius.

| Celsius | | Fahrenheit | Celsius | | Fahrenheit | Celsius | | Fahrenheit |
|---|---|---|---|---|---|---|---|---|
| −273.2 | **−459.7** | ...... | −17.8 | **0** | 32 | 35.0 | **95** | 203 |
| −184 | **−300** | ...... | −12.2 | **10** | 50 | 36.7 | **98** | 208.4 |
| −169 | **−273** | − 459.4 | − 6.67 | **20** | 68 | 37.8 | **100** | 212 |
| −157 | **−250** | − 418 | − 1.11 | **30** | 86 | 43 | **110** | 230 |
| −129 | **−200** | − 328 | 4.44 | **40** | 104 | 49 | **120** | 248 |
| −101 | **−150** | − 238 | 10.0 | **50** | 122 | 54 | **130** | 266 |
| − 73.3 | **−100** | − 148 | 15.6 | **60** | 140 | 60 | **140** | 284 |
| − 45.6 | **− 50** | − 58 | 21.1 | **70** | 158 | 66 | **150** | 302 |
| − 40.0 | **− 40** | − 40 | 23.9 | **75** | 167 | 93 | **200** | 392 |
| − 34.4 | **− 30** | − 22 | 26.7 | **80** | 176 | 121 | **250** | 482 |
| − 28.9 | **− 20** | − 4 | 29.4 | **85** | 185 | 149 | **300** | 572 |
| − 23.3 | **− 10** | 14 | 32.2 | **90** | 194 | | | |

# Boiling and Freezing Points

Water boils at 212°F at sea level. For every 550 feet above sea level, boiling point of water is lower by about 1°F. Methyl alcohol boils at 148°F. Average human oral temperature, 98.6°F. Water freezes at 32°F.

## Breaking the Sound Barrier; Speed of Sound

The prefix Mach is used to describe supersonic speed. It was named for Ernst Mach (1838-1916), a Czech-born Austrian physicist, who contributed to the study of sound. When a plane moves at the speed of sound, it is Mach 1. When moving at twice the speed of sound, it is Mach 2. When it is below the speed of sound, the speed can be designated accordingly—for example, Mach 0.90. Mach is defined as "the ratio of the velocity of a rocket or a jet to the velocity of sound in the medium being considered."

When a plane passes the sound barrier—flying faster than sound travels—listeners in the area hear thunderclaps, but the pilot of the plane does not hear them.

Sound is produced by vibrations of an object and is transmitted by alternate increase and decrease in pressures that radiate outward through a material media of molecules —somewhat like waves spreading out on a pond after a rock has been tossed into it.

The frequency of sound is determined by the number of times the vibrating waves undulate per second and is measured in cycles per second. The slower the cycle of waves, the lower the frequency. As frequencies increase, the sound is higher in pitch.

Sound is audible to human beings only if the frequency falls within a certain range. The human ear is usually not sensitive to frequencies of fewer than 20 vibrations per second or greater than about 20,000 vibrations per second—although this range varies among individuals. Any sound at a pitch higher than the human ear can hear is termed ultrasonic.

Intensity, or loudness, is the strength of the pressure of these radiating waves and is measured in decibels. The human ear responds to intensity in a range from zero to 120 decibels. Any sound with a pressure of more than 120 decibels is painful to the human ear.

The speed of sound is generally defined as 1,088 feet per second at sea level at 32°F. It varies in other temperatures and in different media. Sound travels faster in water than in air, and even faster in iron and steel. It takes 5 seconds to travel a mile in air, and 1 second to move a mile under water, and sound travels through iron in 1/3 second. It travels through ice-cold vapor at approximately 4,708 feet per second; ice-cold water, 4,938; granite, 12,960; hardwood, 12,620; brick, 11,960; glass, 16,410 to 19,690; silver, 8,658; gold, 5,717.

## Colors of the Spectrum

Color, an electromagnetic wave phenomenon, is a sensation produced through the excitation of the retina of the eye by rays of light. The colors of the spectrum may be produced by viewing a light beam refracted by passage through a prism, which breaks the light into its wavelengths.

Customarily, the primary colors of the spectrum are those 6 monochromatic colors that occupy relatively large areas of the spectrum: red, orange, yellow, green, blue, and violet. However, Sir Isaac Newton named a 7th, indigo, situated between blue and violet on the spectrum. Aubert estimated (1865) the solar spectrum to contain approximately 1,000 distinguishable hues, of which, according to Rood (1881), 2 million tints and shades can be distinguished; Luckiesh stated (1915) that 55 distinctly different hues have been seen in a single spectrum.

Many physicists recognize only 3 primary colors: red, yellow, and blue (Mayer, 1775); red, green, and violet (Thomas Young, 1801); red, green, and blue (Clerk Maxwell, 1860).

The color sensation of black is due to complete lack of stimulation of the retina, that of white to complete stimulation. The infrared and ultraviolet rays, below the red (long) end of the spectrum and above the violet (short) end respectively, are invisible to the naked eye. Heat is the principal effect of the infrared rays, and chemical action that of the ultraviolet rays.

## Common Fractions Reduced to Decimals

| 8ths | 16ths | 32ds | 64ths | |
|---|---|---|---|---|
| | | | 1 | = 0.015625 |
| | | 1 | 2 | = 0.03125 |
| | | | 3 | = 0.046875 |
| | 1 | 2 | 4 | = 0.0625 |
| | | | 5 | = 0.078125 |
| | | 3 | 6 | = 0.09375 |
| | | | 7 | = 0.109375 |
| 1 | 2 | 4 | 8 | = 0.125 |
| | | | 9 | = 0.140625 |
| | | 5 | 10 | = 0.15625 |
| | | | 11 | = 0.171875 |
| | 3 | 6 | 12 | = 0.1875 |
| | | | 13 | = 0.203125 |
| | | 7 | 14 | = 0.21875 |
| | | | 15 | = 0.234375 |
| 2 | 4 | 8 | 16 | = 0.25 |
| | | | 17 | = 0.265625 |
| | | 9 | 18 | = 0.28125 |
| | | | 19 | = 0.296875 |
| | 5 | 10 | 20 | = 0.3125 |
| | | | 21 | = 0.328125 |
| | | 11 | 22 | = 0.34375 |

| 8ths | 16ths | 32ds | 64ths | |
|---|---|---|---|---|
| | | | 23 | = 0.359375 |
| 3 | 6 | 12 | 24 | = 0.375 |
| | | | 25 | = 0.390625 |
| | | 13 | 26 | = 0.40625 |
| | | | 27 | = 0.421875 |
| | 7 | 14 | 28 | = 0.4375 |
| | | | 29 | = 0.453125 |
| | | 15 | 30 | = 0.46875 |
| | | | 31 | = 0.484375 |
| 4 | 8 | 16 | 32 | = 0.5 |
| | | | 33 | = 0.515625 |
| | | 17 | 34 | = 0.53125 |
| | | | 35 | = 0.546875 |
| | | 18 | 36 | = 0.5625 |
| | | | 37 | = 0.578125 |
| | | 19 | 38 | = 0.59375 |
| | | | 39 | = 0.609375 |
| 5 | 10 | 20 | 40 | = 0.625 |
| | | | 41 | = 0.640625 |
| | | 21 | 42 | = 0.65625 |
| | | | 43 | = 0.671875 |

| 8ths | 16ths | 32ds | 64ths | |
|---|---|---|---|---|
| | 11 | 22 | 44 | = 0.6875 |
| | | | 45 | = 0.703125 |
| | | 23 | 46 | = 0.71875 |
| | | | 47 | = 0.734375 |
| 6 | 12 | 24 | 48 | = 0.75 |
| | | | 49 | = 0.765625 |
| | | 25 | 50 | = 0.78125 |
| | | | 51 | = 0.796875 |
| | 13 | 26 | 52 | = 0.8125 |
| | | | 53 | = 0.828125 |
| | | 27 | 54 | = 0.84375 |
| | | | 55 | = 0.859375 |
| 7 | 14 | 28 | 56 | = 0.875 |
| | | | 57 | = 0.890625 |
| | | 29 | 58 | = 0.90625 |
| | | | 59 | = 0.921875 |
| | 15 | 30 | 60 | = 0.9375 |
| | | | 61 | = 0.953125 |
| | | 31 | 62 | = 0.96875 |
| | | | 63 | = 0.984375 |
| 8 | 16 | 32 | 64 | = 1.0 |

## Spirits Measures

| | |
|---|---|
| Pony | = 0.5 jigger |
| Shot | = 0.666 jigger |
| | = 1.0 ounce |
| Jigger | = 1.5 shots |
| Pint | = 16 shots |
| | = 0.625 fifth |
| Fifth | = 25.6 shots |
| | = 1.6 pints |
| | = 0.8 quart |
| | = 0.75706 liter |

| | |
|---|---|
| Quart | = 32 shots |
| | = 1.25 fifths |
| Magnum | = 2 quarts |
| | = 2.49797 bottles (wine) |

For champagne and brandy only:

| | |
|---|---|
| Jeroboam | = 6.4 pints |
| | = 1.6 magnum |
| | = 0.8 gallon |

For champagne only:

| | |
|---|---|
| Rehoboam | = 3 magnums |
| Methuselah | = 4 magnums |
| Salmanazar | = 6 magnums |
| Balthazar | = 8 magnums |
| Nebuchadnezzar | = 10 magnums |

| | |
|---|---|
| Wine bottle (standard) | = 0.800633 quart |
| | = 0.7576778 liter |

# Mathematical Formulas

*Note*: The value of $\pi$ (a number representing the ratio of the circumference of a circle to the diameter) is approximately 3.14159625, often rounded further to 3.1416 or 3.14.

### To find the CIRCUMFERENCE of a:

**Circle** — Multiply the diameter by $\pi$.

### To find the AREA of a:

**Circle** — Multiply the square of the radius by $\pi$.
**Rectangle** — Multiply the length of the base by the height.
**Sphere (surface)** — Multiply the square of the radius by $\pi$ and multiply by 4.
**Square** — Square the length of one side.
**Trapezoid** — Add the two parallel sides, multiply by the height, and divide by 2.
**Triangle** — Multiply the base by the height, divide by 2.

### To find the VOLUME of a:

**Cone** — Multiply the square of the radius of the base by $\pi$, multiply by the height, and divide by 3.

**Cube** — Cube the length of one edge.

**Cylinder**— Multiply the square of the radius of the base by $\pi$ and multiply by the height.

**Pyramid** — Multiply the area of the base by the height and divide by 3.
**Rectangular Prism** — Multiply the length by the width by the height.
**Sphere** —Multiply the cube of the radius by $\pi$, multiply by 4, and divide by 3.

# Playing Cards and Dice Chances

**5-Card Poker Hands**

| Hand | Number possible | Odds against |
|---|---|---|
| Royal flush | 4 | 649,739 to 1 |
| Other straight flush | 36 | 72,192 to 1 |
| Four of a kind | 624 | 4,164 to 1 |
| Full house | 3,744 | 693 to 1 |
| Flush | 5,108 | 508 to 1 |
| Straight | 10,200 | 254 to 1 |
| Three of a kind | 54,912 | 46 to 1 |
| Two pairs | 123,552 | 20 to 1 |
| One pair | 1,098,240 | 4 to 3 (1.37 to 1) |
| Nothing | 1,302,540 | 1 to 1 |
| **Total** | **2,598,960** | |

**Dice**

(probabilities on 2 dice)

| Total | Odds against (single toss) | Total | Odds against (single toss) |
|---|---|---|---|
| 2 | 35 to 1 | 8 | 31 to 5 |
| 3 | 17 to 1 | 9 | 8 to 1 |
| 4 | 11 to 1 | 10 | 11 to 1 |
| 5 | 8 to 1 | 11 | 17 to 1 |
| 6 | 31 to 5 | 12 | 35 to 1 |
| 7 | 5 to 1 | | |

**Dice**

(probabilities of consecutive winning plays)

| No. consecutive wins | By 7,11, or point | No. consecutive wins | By 7, 11, or point |
|---|---|---|---|
| 1 | 244 in 495 | 6 | 1 in 70 |
| 2 | 6 in 25 | 7 | 1 in 141 |
| 3 | 3 in 25 | 8 | 1 in 287 |
| 4 | 1 in 17 | 9 | 1 in 582 |
| 5 | 1 in 34 | | |

**Pinochle Auction**

(odds against finding in "widow" of 3 cards)

| Open places | Odds | Open places | Odds |
|---|---|---|---|
| 1 | 5 to 1 against | 4 | 1½ to 1 for |
| 2 | 2 to 1 against | 5 | 2 to 1 for |
| 3 | Even | 6 | 3 to 1 for |

**Bridge**

**The odds**—against suit distribution in a hand of 4-4-3-2 are about 4 to 1, against 5-4-2-2 about 8 to 1, against 6-4-2-1 about 20 to 1, against 7-4-1-1 about 254 to 1, against 8-4-1-0 about 2,211 to 1, and against 13-0-0-0 about 158,753,389,899 to 1.

# Measures of Force and Pressure

**Dyne** = force necessary to accelerate a 1-gram mass 1 centimeter per second squared = 0.000072 poundal
**Poundal** = force necessary to accelerate a 1-pound mass 1 foot per second squared = 13,825.5 dynes = 0.138255 newtons
**Newton** = force needed to accelerate a 1-kilogram mass 1 meter per second squared
**Pascal** (pressure) = 1 newton per square meter = 0.020885 pound per square foot
**Atmosphere** (air pressure at sea level) = 2,116.102 pounds per square foot = 14.6952 pounds per square inch = 1.0332 kilograms per square centimeter = 101,323 newtons per square meter.

# Large Numbers

| U.S. | Number of zeros | French, British, German |
|---|---|---|
| million | 6 | million |
| billion | 9 | milliard |
| trillion | 12 | billion |
| quadrillion | 15 | 1,000 billion |
| quintillion | 18 | trillion |
| sextillion | 21 | 1,000 trillion |
| septillion | 24 | quadrillion |
| octillion | 27 | 1,000 quadrillion |
| nonillion | 30 | quintillion |
| decillion | 33 | 1,000 quintillion |

# Roman Numerals

| | | | | | | | | | | | |
|---|---|---|---|---|---|---|---|---|---|---|---|
| I | 1 | VI | 6 | XI | 11 | L | 50 | CD | 400 | $\overline{X}$ | 10,000 |
| II | 2 | VII | 7 | XIX | 19 | LX | 60 | D | 500 | $\overline{L}$ | 50,000 |
| III | 3 | VIII | 8 | XX | 20 | XC | 90 | CM | 900 | $\overline{C}$ | 100,000 |
| IV | 4 | IX | 9 | XXX | 30 | C | 100 | M | 1,000 | $\overline{D}$ | 500,000 |
| V | 5 | X | 10 | XL | 40 | CC | 200 | $\overline{V}$ | 5,000 | $\overline{M}$ | 1,000,000 |

# HEALTH

## Basic First Aid

First aid experts stress that knowing what to do for an injured person until a doctor or trained person gets to an accident scene can save a life, especially in cases of stoppage of breathing, severe bleeding, and shock.

People with special medical problems, such as diabetes, cardiovascular disease, epilepsy, or allergy, are urged to wear some sort of emblem identifying the problem, as a safeguard against use of medication in an emergency that might be injurious or fatal. Emblems may be obtained from Medic Alert Foundation, Turlock, CA 95380.

Most accidents occur in homes, as shown by National Safety Council figures.

In all cases, get medical assistance as soon as possible.

**Animal bite** — Wound should be washed with soap under running water and antibiotic ointment and dressing applied. When possible, the animal should be caught alive for rabies testing.

**Asphyxiation** — Start rescue breathing immediately after getting patient to fresh air.

**Bleeding** — Elevate the wound above the heart if possible. Press hard on wound with sterile compress until bleeding stops. Send for doctor if it is severe.

**Burn** — If mild, with skin unbroken and no blisters, put into ice water until pain subsides. Apply a dry dressing if necessary. Send for physician if burn is severe. Apply sterile compresses and keep patient comfortably warm until doctor's arrival. Do not try to clean burn or to break blisters.

**Chemical in eye** — With patient lying down, pour cupsful of water immediately into corner of eye, letting it run to other side to remove chemicals thoroughly. Cover with sterile compress. Get medical attention immediately.

**Choking** — See **Abdominal Thrust**.

**Convulsions** — Place person on back on bed or rug. Loosen clothing. Turn head to side. Do not place a blunt object between the victim's teeth. If convulsions do not stop, get medical attention immediately.

**Cut (minor)** — Apply mild antiseptic and sterile compress after washing with soap under warm running water.

**Fainting** — If victim feels faint, lower head to knees. Lay victim down on back with head turned to side if he or she becomes unconscious. Elevate the legs 8 to 10 inches. Loosen clothing and open windows. Keep patient lying quietly for at least 15 minutes after he or she regains consciousness. Call doctor if faint lasts for more than a few minutes.

**Foreign body in eye** — Touch object with moistened corner of handkerchief if it can be seen. If it cannot be seen or does not come out after a few attempts, take patient to doctor. Do not rub eye.

**Frostbite**— Handle frostbitten area gently. Do not rub. Soak the affected area in water no warmer than 105°F. Do not allow frostbitten area to touch the container. Soak until frostbitten part looks red and feels warm. Loosely bandage. If fingers or toes are frostbitten, place gauze between them.

**Heat Stroke and Heat Exhaustion** — Remove the victim from the heat. Loosen any tight clothing and apply cool, wet cloths to the skin. Give the victim cool water, to drink slowly. Call an ambulance if the victim refuses water, vomits, or experiences changes in consciousness.

**Hypothermia** — Move victim to a warm place. Remove wet clothing and dry victim, if necessary. Warm victim gradually by wrapping the person in warm blankets or clothing. If available, apply heat pads or other heat sources, but not directly to the body. Give the victim warm liquids. Call an ambulance if breathing is slowed or stopped or if the pulse is slow or irregular.

**Loss of Limb** — If a limb is severed, it is important to properly protect the limb so that it can possibly be reattached to the victim. After the victim is cared for, the limb should be wrapped in a sterile gauze or clean material and placed in a clean plastic bag, garbage can, or other suitable container. Pack ice around the limb on the OUTSIDE of the bag to keep the limb cold. Call ahead to the hospital to alert staff there of the situation.

**Poisoning** — Call doctor. Use antidote listed on label if container is found. Call local Poison Control Center if possible. Do not give the victim any food or drink or induce vomiting, unless specified on the label or by a medical professional.

**Shock (injury-related)** — Keep the victim lying down; if uncertain as to his or her injuries, keep the victim flat on the back. Maintain the victim's normal body temperature; if the weather is cold or damp, place blankets or extra clothing over and under the victim; if weather is hot, provide shade.

**Snakebite** —Wash the injury. Keep the area still and at a lower level than the heart. Keep the victim quiet. If available, use a snakebite kit.

**Sprains and fractures** — Apply ice to reduce swelling and pain. Do not try to straighten or move broken limbs. Apply a splint to immobilize the injured area if the victim must be transported.

**Sting from insect** — If possible, remove stinger. Wash the area with soap and water; cover it to keep it clean. Apply a cold pack to reduce pain and swelling. Call physician immediately if body swells or patient collapses.

**Unconsciousness** — Send for doctor and place person on his or her back. Start rescue breathing if victim stops breathing. Never give food or liquids.

### Abdominal Thrust

The American Red Cross and the American Heart Association both agree that the recommended first aid for choking victims is the abdominal thrust, also known as the Heimlich maneuver, after its creator, Dr. Henry Heimlich. Slaps on the back are no longer advised and may even prove detrimental in an attempt to assist a choking victim.

- Get behind the victim and wrap your arms around him or her above the waist.
- Make a fist with one hand and place it, with the thumb knuckle pressing inward, just below the point of the "v" of the rib cage.
- Grasp the wrist with the other hand and give one or more upward thrusts or hugs.
- Start rescue breathing if breathing stops.

### Rescue Breathing

Stressing that your breath can save a life, the American Red Cross gives the following directions for rescue breathing if the victim is not breathing:

- Determine consciousness by tapping the victim on the shoulder and asking loudly, "Are you okay?"
- Tilt the victim's head back so that the chin is pointing upward. Do not press on the soft tissue under the chin, as this might obstruct the airway. If you suspect that an accident victim might have neck or back injuries, open the airway by placing the tips of your index and middle fingers on the corners of the victim's jaw to lift it forward without tilting the head.
- Place your cheek and ear close to the victim's mouth and nose. Look at the victim's chest to see if it rises and falls. Listen and feel for air to be exhaled for about 5 seconds.
- If there is no breathing, pinch the victim's nostrils shut with the thumb and index finger of your hand that is pressing on the victim's forehead. Another way to prevent leakage of air when the lungs are inflated is to press your cheek against the victim's nose.
- Blow air into victim's mouth by taking a deep breath and then sealing your mouth tightly around the victim's mouth. Initially, give 2, quick (approx. 1.5 seconds each), full breaths without allowing the lungs to deflate completely between each breath.
- Watch the victim's chest to see if it rises.
- Stop when victim's chest is expanded. Raise your mouth; turn your head to the side and listen for exhalation.
- Watch the chest to see if it falls.
- Repeat the blowing cycle until the victim starts breathing.

**Note:** Infants (up to 1 year) and children (1 to 8 years) should be administered rescue breathing as described above, except for the following:

- Do not tilt the head as far back as an adult's head.
- Both the mouth and nose of an infant should be sealed by the mouth.
- Give breaths to a child once every three seconds.
- Blow into the infant's mouth and nose once every three seconds with less pressure and volume than for a child.

## Finding Your Target Heart Rate

**Source:** Carole Casten, EdD, and Peg Jordan, RN, *Aerobics Today*, Aerobic Fitness Association of America

The target heart rate is the heartbeat rate a person should have during aerobic exercise (such as running, fast walking, cycling, or cross-country skiing) to get the full benefit of the exercise for cardiovascular conditioning.

First, determine the intensity level at which one would like to exercise. A sedentary person may want to begin an exercise regimen at the 60% level and work up gradually to the 70% level. Athletes and highly fit individuals must work at the 85-95% level to receive the benefits of exercise.

Second, calculate the target heart rate. One common way of doing this is by using the American College of Sports Medicine Method.

To obtain cardiovascular fitness benefits from aerobic exercise, it is recommended that an individual participate in an aerobic activity at least 3-5 times a week for 20-30 minutes per session, although cardiac patients and very sedentary individuals can obtain benefits with shorter periods (15-20 minutes). Generally, training changes occur in 4-6 weeks but can occur in as little as 2 weeks.

### The American College of Sports Medicine Method

Using the American College of Sports Medicine Method to calculate one's target heart rate, an individual should subtract his or her age from 220, then multiply by the desired intensity level of the workout. Then divide the answer by 6 for a 10-second pulse count. (The 10-second pulse count is useful for checking whether the target heart rate is being achieved during the workout. One can easily check one's pulse—at the wrist or side of the neck—counting the number of beats in 10 seconds.)

For example, a 20-year-old wishing to exercise at 70% intensity, would employ the following steps:

| | |
|---|---|
| Maximum Heart Rate | 220 - 20 = 200 |
| Target Heart Rate | 200 × .70 =140 |
| 10-second Pulse Count | 140 ÷ 6 =23 |

To work at the desired level of intensity, this 20-year old would strive for a target heart rate of 140 beats per minute, or a 10-second pulse count of 23.

## Food and Nutrition

Food contains proteins, carbohydrates, fats, water, vitamins, and minerals. Nutrition is the way your body takes in and uses these ingredients to maintain proper functioning.

The U.S. Dept. of Health and Human Services and the Dept. of Agriculture reissued dietary guidelines Jan. 2, 1996, that offered dietary and exercise advice for children age 2 and over, as well as adults. Recommended were: (1) no more than 30 percent of calories from fat, or about 65 grams of fat in a 2,000-calorie daily diet; and no more than 10 percent of calories, or 20 grams of fat, from saturated fats; (2) maximum alcohol consumption of about 1 drink a day for women, 2 for men; (3) daily consumption of vegetables of 3-5 servings; fruits, 2-4; pastas, cereals, or breads, 6-11; milk, 2-3; meat, poultry, fish, beans, and eggs, 2-3. (For vegetables, 1 serving equals about 1 cup raw leafy greens or one-half cup other kinds; fruit, 1 medium apple, banana, or orange; grains, 1 slice of bread, ½ cup of pasta, or 1 oz. cereal; milk, 1 cup or 1.5 oz. of cheese; meat and poultry, 2-3 oz. cooked lean beef or chicken without skin; cooked dry beans, ½ cup.)

### Protein

Proteins, composed of amino acids, are indispensable in the diet. They build, maintain, and repair the body. Best sources: eggs, milk, fish, meat, poultry, soybeans, nuts. High-quality proteins such as eggs, meat, or fish supply all 8 amino acids needed in the diet. Plant foods can be combined to meet protein needs as well: whole grain breads and cereals, rice, oats, soybeans, other beans, split peas, and nuts.

### Fats

Fats provide energy by furnishing calories to the body, and they also carry vitamins A, D, E, and K. They are the most concentrated source of energy in the diet. Best sources of polyunsaturated and monounsaturated fats: margarine, vegetable/plant oils, nuts. Meats, cheeses, butter, cream, egg yolks, lard are concentrated sources of saturated fats.

### Carbohydrates

Carbohydrates provide energy for body function and activity by supplying immediate calories. The carbohydrate group includes sugars, starches, fiber, and starchy vegetables. Best sources: grains, legumes, potatoes, vegetables, fruits.

### Water

Water dissolves and transports other nutrients throughout the body, aiding the processes of digestion, absorption, circulation, and excretion. It helps regulate body temperature.

### Vitamins

Vitamin A—promotes good eyesight and helps keep the skin and mucous membranes resistant to infection. Best sources: liver, sweet potatoes, carrots, kale, cantaloupe, turnip greens, collard greens, broccoli, fortified milk.

Vitamin $B_1$ (thiamine)—prevents beriberi. Essential to carbohydrate metabolism and health of nervous system. Best sources: pork, enriched cereals, grains, soybeans, and nuts.

Vitamin $B_2$ (riboflavin)—protects skin, mouth, eyes, eyelids, and mucous membranes. Essential to protein and energy metabolism. Best sources: milk, meat, poultry, cheese, broccoli, spinach.

Vitamin $B_6$ (pyridoxine)—important in the regulation of the central nervous system and in protein metabolism. Best sources: whole grains, meats, fish, poultry, nuts, brewers' yeast.

Vitamin $B_{12}$ (cobalamin)—needed to form red blood cells. Best sources: meat, fish, poultry, eggs, dairy products.

Niacin—maintains the health of skin, tongue, and digestive system. Best sources: poultry, peanuts, fish, enriched flour and bread.

Folic acid (folacin)—required for normal blood cell formation, growth, and reproduction and for important chemical reactions in body cells. Best sources: yeast, orange juice, green leafy vegetables, wheat germ, asparagus, broccoli, nuts.

Other B vitamins—biotin, pantothenic acid.

Vitamin C (ascorbic acid)—maintains collagen, a protein necessary for the formation of skin, ligaments, and bones. It helps heal wounds and mend fractures and aids in resisting some types of viral and bacterial infections. Best sources: citrus fruits and juices, cantaloupe, broccoli, brussels sprouts, potatoes and sweet potatoes, tomatoes, cabbage.

Vitamin D—important for bone development. Best sources: sunlight, fortified milk and milk products, fish-liver oils, egg yolks.

Vitamin E (tocopherol)—helps protect red blood cells. Best sources: vegetable oils, wheat germ, whole grains, eggs, peanuts, margarine, green leafy vegetables.

Vitamin K—necessary for formation of prothrombin, which helps blood to clot. Also made by intestinal bacteria. Best dietary sources: green leafy vegetables, tomatoes.

### Minerals

Calcium—the most abundant mineral in the body, works with phosphorus in building and maintaining bones and teeth. Best sources: milk and milk products, cheese, blackstrap molasses, tofu.

Phosphorus—the 2d most abundant mineral, performs more functions than any other mineral, and plays a part in nearly every chemical reaction in the body. Best sources: cheese, milk, meats, poultry, fish, tofu.

Iron—Necessary for the formation of myoglobin, which is a reservoir of oxygen for muscle tissue, and hemoglobin, which transports oxygen in the blood. Best sources: lean meats, beans, green leafy vegetables, shellfish, enriched breads and cereals, whole grains.

Other minerals—chromium, cobalt, copper, fluorine, iodine, magnesium, manganese, molybdenum, potassium, selenium, sodium, sulfur, and zinc.

# Nutritive Value of Food (Calories, Proteins, etc.)

**Source:** *Home and Garden Bulletin No. 72*; available from Supt. of Documents, U.S. Government Printing Office, Washington, DC 20402

| Food | Measure | Grams | Food Energy (calories) | Protein (grams) | Fat (grams) | Saturated fats (grams) | Carbohydrate (grams) | Calcium (milligrams) | Iron (milligrams) | Sodium (milligrams) | Vitamin A (I.U.) | Ascorbic Acid (milligrams) |
|---|---|---|---|---|---|---|---|---|---|---|---|---|
| **Dairy products** | | | | | | | | | | | | |
| Cheese, cheddar, cut pieces | 1 oz. | 28 | 115 | 7 | 9 | 6.0 | T | 204 | 0.2 | 176 | 300 | 0 |
| Cheese, cottage, small curd | 1 cup | 210 | 215 | 26 | 9 | 6.0 | 6 | 126 | 0.3 | 850 | 340 | T |
| Cheese, cream | 1 oz. | 28 | 100 | 2 | 10 | 6.2 | 1 | 23 | 0.3 | 84 | 400 | 0 |
| Cheese, Swiss | 1 oz. | 28 | 95 | 7 | 7 | 4.5 | 1 | 219 | 0.2 | 388 | 230 | 0 |
| Half-and-half | 1 tbsp. | 15 | 20 | T | 2 | 1.1 | 1 | 16 | T | 6 | 70 | T |
| Cream, sour | 1 tbsp. | 12 | 25 | T | 3 | 1.6 | 1 | 14 | T | 6 | 90 | T |
| Milk, whole | 1 cup | 244 | 150 | 8 | 8 | 5.1 | 11 | 291 | 0.1 | 120 | 310 | 2 |
| Milk, nonfat (skim) | 1 cup | 245 | 85 | 8 | T | 0.3 | 12 | 302 | 0.1 | 126 | 500 | 2 |
| Milkshake, chocolate | 10 oz. | 283 | 355 | 9 | 8 | 4.8 | 60 | 374 | 0.9 | 314 | 240 | 0 |
| Ice cream, hardened | 1 cup | 133 | 270 | 5 | 14 | 8.9 | 32 | 176 | 0.1 | 116 | 540 | 1 |
| Sherbet | 1 cup | 193 | 270 | 2 | 4 | 2.4 | 59 | 103 | 0.3 | 88 | 190 | 4 |
| Yogurt, fruit-flavored | 8 oz. | 227 | 230 | 10 | 2 | 1.6 | 43 | 345 | 0.2 | 133 | 100 | 1 |
| **Eggs** | | | | | | | | | | | | |
| Fried in margarine | 1 | 46 | 90 | 6 | 7 | 1.9 | 1 | 25 | 0.7 | 162 | 390 | 0 |
| Hard-cooked | 1 | 50 | 75 | 6 | 5 | 1.6 | 1 | 25 | 0.6 | 62 | 280 | 0 |
| Scrambled (milk added) in margarine | 1 | 61 | 100 | 7 | 7 | 2.2 | 1 | 44 | 0.7 | 171 | 420 | T |
| **Fats & oils** | | | | | | | | | | | | |
| Butter, salted | 1 tbsp. | 14 | 100 | T | 11 | 7.1 | T | 3 | T | 116 | 430 | 0 |
| Margarine, salted | 1 tbsp. | 14 | 100 | T | 11 | 2.2 | T | 4 | T | 132 | 460 | T |
| Olive oil | 1 tbsp. | 14 | 125 | 0 | 14 | 1.9 | 0 | 0 | 0 | 0 | 0 | 0 |
| Salad dressing, blue cheese | 1 tbsp. | 15 | 75 | 1 | 8 | 1.5 | 1 | 12 | T | 164 | 30 | T |
| Salad dressing, French, regular | 1 tbsp. | 16 | 85 | T | 9 | 1.4 | 1 | 2 | T | 188 | T | T |
| Salad dressing, French, low calorie | 1 tbsp. | 16 | 25 | T | 2 | 0.2 | 2 | 6 | T | 306 | T | T |
| Salad dressing, Italian | 1 tbsp. | 15 | 80 | T | 9 | 1.3 | 1 | 1 | T | 162 | 30 | T |
| Mayonnaise | 1 tbsp. | 14 | 100 | T | 11 | 1.7 | T | 3 | 0.1 | 80 | 40 | 0 |
| **Fish, meat, poultry** | | | | | | | | | | | | |
| Clams, raw, meat only | 3 oz. | 85 | 65 | 11 | 1 | 0.3 | 2 | 59 | 2.6 | 102 | 90 | 9 |
| Crabmeat, canned | 1 cup | 135 | 135 | 23 | 3 | 0.5 | 1 | 61 | 1.1 | 1,350 | 50 | 0 |
| Fish sticks, frozen, reheated | 1 fish stick | 28 | 70 | 6 | 3 | 0.8 | 4 | 11 | 0.3 | 53 | 20 | 0 |
| Salmon canned (pink), solids and liquid | 3 oz. | 85 | 120 | 17 | 5 | 0.9 | 0 | 167 | 0.7 | 443 | 60 | 0 |
| Sardines, Atlantic, canned in oil, drained solids | 3 oz. | 85 | 175 | 20 | 9 | 2.1 | 0 | 371 | 2.6 | 425 | 190 | 0 |
| Shrimp, French fried | 3 oz. | 85 | 200 | 16 | 10 | 2.5 | 11 | 61 | 2.0 | 384 | 90 | 0 |
| Trout, broiled, with butter and lemon juice | 3 oz. | 85 | 175 | 21 | 9 | 4.1 | T | 26 | 1.0 | 122 | 230 | 1 |
| Tuna, canned in oil | 3 oz. | 85 | 165 | 24 | 7 | 1.4 | 0 | 7 | 1.6 | 303 | 70 | 0 |
| Bacon, broiled or fried crisp | 3 slices | 19 | 110 | 6 | 9 | 3.3 | T | 2 | 0.3 | 303 | 0 | 6 |
| Ground beef, broiled, regular | 3 oz. | 85 | 245 | 20 | 18 | 6.9 | 0 | 9 | 2.1 | 70 | T | 0 |
| Roast beef, relatively lean (lean only) | 2.6 oz. | 75 | 135 | 22 | 5 | 1.9 | 0 | 3 | 1.5 | 46 | T | 0 |
| Beef steak, lean and fat | 3 oz. | 85 | 240 | 23 | 15 | 6.4 | 0 | 9 | 2.6 | 53 | T | 0 |
| Beef & vegetable stew | 1 cup | 245 | 220 | 16 | 11 | 4.4 | 15 | 29 | 2.9 | 292 | 5,690 | 17 |
| Lamb, chop, broiled loin, lean and fat | 2.8 oz. | 80 | 235 | 22 | 16 | 7.3 | 0 | 16 | 1.4 | 62 | T | 0 |
| Liver, beef, fried | 3 oz. | 85 | 185 | 23 | 7 | 2.5 | 7 | 9 | 5.3 | 90 | 30,690 | 23 |
| Ham, light cure, roasted, lean and fat | 3 oz. | 85 | 205 | 18 | 14 | 5.1 | 0 | 6 | 0.7 | 1,009 | 0 | 0 |
| Pork, chop, broiled, lean and fat | 3.1 oz. | 87 | 275 | 24 | 19 | 7.0 | 0 | 3 | 0.7 | 61 | 10 | T |
| Bologna | 2 slices | 57 | 180 | 7 | 16 | 6.1 | 2 | 7 | 0.9 | 581 | 0 | 12 |
| Frankfurter, pork, cooked | 1 | 45 | 145 | 5 | 13 | 4.8 | 1 | 5 | 0.5 | 504 | 0 | 12 |
| Sausage, pork link, cooked | 1 link | 13 | 50 | 3 | 4 | 1.4 | T | 4 | 0.2 | 168 | 0 | T |
| Veal, cutlet, braised or broiled | 3 oz. | 85 | 185 | 23 | 9 | 4.1 | 0 | 9 | 0.8 | 56 | T | 0 |
| Chicken, drumstick, fried, bones removed | 2.5 oz. | 72 | 195 | 16 | 11 | 3.0 | 6 | 12 | 1.0 | 194 | 60 | 0 |
| Chicken, roasted, half breast, without skin | 3 oz. | 86 | 140 | 27 | 3 | 0.9 | 0 | 13 | 0.9 | 64 | 20 | 0 |
| Turkey, roasted, chopped light and dark meat | 1 cup | 140 | 240 | 41 | 7 | 2.3 | 0 | 35 | 2.5 | 98 | 0 | 0 |
| Frankfurter, chicken, cooked | 1 | 45 | 115 | 6 | 9 | 2.5 | 3 | 43 | 0.9 | 616 | 60 | 0 |
| **Fruits & fruit products** | | | | | | | | | | | | |
| Apple, raw, 2-3/4 in. diam. | 1 | 138 | 80 | T | T | 0.1 | 21 | 10 | 0.2 | T | 70 | 8 |
| Apple juice | 1 cup | 248 | 115 | T | T | T | 29 | 17 | 0.9 | 7 | T | 2 |
| Apricots, raw | 3 | 106 | 50 | 1 | T | T | 12 | 15 | 0.6 | 1 | 2,770 | 11 |
| Banana, raw | 1 | 114 | 105 | 1 | 1 | 0.2 | 27 | 7 | 0.4 | 1 | 90 | 10 |
| Cherries, sweet, raw | 10 | 68 | 50 | 1 | 1 | 0.1 | 11 | 10 | 0.3 | T | 150 | 5 |
| Cranberry juice cocktail, sweetened | 1 cup | 253 | 145 | T | T | T | 38 | 8 | 0.4 | 10 | 10 | 108 |
| Fruit cocktail, canned, in heavy syrup | 1 cup | 255 | 185 | 1 | T | T | 48 | 15 | 0.7 | 15 | 520 | 5 |
| Grapefruit, raw, medium, white | 1/2 | 120 | 40 | 1 | T | T | 10 | 14 | 0.1 | T | 10 | 41 |
| Grapes, Thompson seedless | 10 | 50 | 35 | T | T | 0.1 | 9 | 6 | 0.1 | 1 | 40 | 5 |
| Lemonade, frozen, unsweetened | 6 oz. | 244 | 55 | 1 | 1 | 0.1 | 16 | 20 | 0.3 | 2 | 30 | 77 |
| Cantaloupe, 5-in. diam. | 1/2 | 267 | 95 | 2 | 1 | 0.1 | 22 | 29 | 0.6 | 24 | 8,610 | 113 |
| Orange, 2-5/8 in. diam. | 1 | 131 | 60 | 1 | T | T | 15 | 52 | 0.1 | T | 270 | 70 |
| Orange juice, frozen, diluted | 1 cup | 249 | 110 | 2 | T | T | 27 | 22 | 0.2 | 2 | 190 | 97 |
| Peach, raw, 2-1/2 in. diam. | 1 | 87 | 35 | 1 | T | T | 10 | 4 | 0.1 | T | 470 | 6 |
| Raisins, seedless | 1 cup | 145 | 435 | 5 | 1 | 0.2 | 115 | 71 | 3.0 | 17 | 10 | 5 |
| Strawberries, whole | 1 cup | 149 | 45 | 1 | 1 | T | 10 | 21 | 0.6 | 1 | 40 | 84 |
| Watermelon, 4 by 8 in. wedge | 1piece | 482 | 155 | 3 | 2 | 0.3 | 35 | 39 | 0.8 | 10 | 1,760 | 46 |
| **Grain products** | | | | | | | | | | | | |
| Bagel, plain | 1 | 68 | 200 | 7 | 2 | 0.3 | 38 | 29 | 1.8 | 245 | 0 | 0 |
| Biscuit, 2 in. diam., from home recipe | 1 | 28 | 100 | 2 | 5 | 1.2 | 13 | 47 | 0.7 | 195 | 10 | T |
| Bread, pita, enriched, white, 6-1/2 in. diam | 1 pita | 60 | 165 | 6 | 1 | 0.1 | 12 | 15 | 0.7 | 124 | 0 | 0 |
| Bread, white, enriched | 1 slice | 25 | 65 | 2 | 1 | 0.3 | 12 | 32 | 0.7 | 129 | T | T |
| Bread, whole-wheat | 1 slice | 28 | 70 | 3 | 1 | 0.4 | 13 | 20 | 1.0 | 180 | T | T |
| Oatmeal or rolled oats, without added salt | 1 cup | 234 | 145 | 6 | 2 | 0.4 | 25 | 19 | 1.6 | 2 | 40 | 0 |
| Bran flakes (40% bran), added sugar, salt, iron, vitamins | 1 oz. | 28 | 90 | 4 | 1 | 0.1 | 22 | 14 | 8.1 | 264 | 1,250 | 0 |
| Corn flakes, added sugar, salt, iron, vitamins | 1 oz. | 28 | 110 | 2 | T | T | 24 | 1 | 1.8 | 351 | 1,250 | 15 |
| Rice, puffed, added iron, thiamine, niacin | 1 oz. | 28 | 110 | 2 | T | T | 25 | 4 | 1.8 | 340 | 1,250 | 15 |
| Wheat, shredded, plain, 1 biscuit or 2/3 cup | 1 oz. | 28 | 100 | 3 | 1 | 0.1 | 23 | 11 | 1.2 | 3 | 0 | 0 |
| Bulgur, uncooked | 1 cup | 170 | 600 | 19 | 3 | 1.2 | 129 | 49 | 9.5 | 7 | 0 | 0 |
| Cake, angel food, 1/12 of cake | 1 | 53 | 125 | 3 | T | T | 29 | 44 | 0.2 | 269 | 0 | 0 |
| Cupcake, 2-1/2 in. diam., with chocolate icing | 1 | 35 | 120 | 2 | 4 | 1.8 | 20 | 21 | 0.7 | 92 | 50 | T |

| Food | Measure | Grams | Food Energy (calories) | Protein (grams) | Fat (grams) | Saturated fats (grams) | Carbohydrate (grams) | Calcium (miligrams) | Iron (miligrams) | Sodium (miligrams) | Vitamin A (I.U.) | Ascorbic Acid (miligrams) |
|---|---|---|---|---|---|---|---|---|---|---|---|---|
| Plain sheet cake with white, uncooked frosting, 1/9 of cake | 1 | 121 | 445 | 4 | 14 | 4.6 | 77 | 61 | 1.2 | 275 | 240 | T |
| Fruitcake, dark, 1/32 of loaf | 1 | 43 | 165 | 2 | 7 | 1.5 | 25 | 41 | 1.2 | 67 | 50 | 16 |
| Cake, pound, 1/17 of loaf | 1 | 29 | 110 | 2 | 5 | 3.0 | 15 | 8 | 0.5 | 108 | 160 | 0 |
| Cheesecake, 1/12 of 9-in. diam. cake | 1 | 92 | 280 | 5 | 18 | 9.9 | 26 | 52 | 0.4 | 204 | 230 | 5 |
| Brownies, with nuts, from commercial recipe | 1 | 25 | 100 | 1 | 4 | 1.6 | 16 | 13 | 0.6 | 59 | 70 | T |
| Cookies, chocolate chip, from home recipe | 4 | 40 | 185 | 2 | 11 | 3.9 | 26 | 13 | 1.0 | 82 | 20 | 0 |
| Crackers, graham, 2-1/2 in. squares | 2 | 14 | 60 | 1 | 1 | 0.4 | 11 | 6 | 0.4 | 86 | 0 | 0 |
| Crackers, saltines | 4 | 12 | 50 | 1 | 1 | 0.5 | 9 | 3 | 0.5 | 165 | 0 | 0 |
| Danish pastry, round piece | 1 | 57 | 220 | 4 | 12 | 3.6 | 26 | 60 | 1.1 | 218 | 60 | T |
| Doughnut, cake type | 1 | 50 | 210 | 3 | 12 | 2.8 | 24 | 22 | 1.0 | 192 | 20 | T |
| Macaroni, firm stage (hot) | 1 cup | 130 | 190 | 7 | 1 | 0.1 | 39 | 14 | 2.1 | 1 | 0 | 0 |
| Muffin, bran, commercial mix | 1 | 45 | 140 | 3 | 4 | 1.3 | 24 | 27 | 1.7 | 385 | 100 | 0 |
| Muffin, corn, from home recipe | 1 | 45 | 145 | 3 | 5 | 1.5 | 21 | 66 | 0.9 | 169 | 80 | T |
| Noodles, enriched, cooked | 1 cup | 160 | 200 | 7 | 2 | 0.5 | 37 | 16 | 2.6 | 3 | 110 | 0 |
| Pie, apple, 1/6 of pie | 1 | 158 | 405 | 3 | 18 | 4.6 | 60 | 13 | 1.6 | 476 | 50 | 2 |
| Pie, cherry, 1/6 of pie | 1 | 158 | 410 | 4 | 18 | 4.7 | 61 | 22 | 1.6 | 480 | 700 | 0 |
| Pie, lemon meringue, 1/6 of pie | 1 | 140 | 355 | 5 | 14 | 4.3 | 53 | 20 | 1.4 | 395 | 240 | 4 |
| Pie, pecan, 1/6 of pie | 1 | 138 | 575 | 7 | 32 | 4.7 | 71 | 65 | 4.6 | 305 | 220 | 0 |
| Popcorn, air-popped, plain | 1 cup | 8 | 30 | 1 | T | T | 6 | 1 | 0.2 | T | 10 | 0 |
| Pretzels, stick | 10 | 3 | 10 | T | T | T | 2 | 1 | 0.1 | 48 | 0 | 0 |
| Rolls, enriched, brown & serve | 1 | 28 | 85 | 2 | 2 | 0.5 | 14 | 33 | 0.8 | 155 | T | T |
| Rolls, frankfurter & hamburger | 1 | 40 | 115 | 3 | 2 | 0.5 | 20 | 54 | 1.2 | 241 | T | T |
| Tortillas, corn | 1 | 30 | 65 | 2 | 1 | 0.1 | 13 | 42 | 0.6 | 1 | 80 | 0 |
| **Legumes, nuts, seeds** | | | | | | | | | | | | |
| Beans, Black | 1 cup | 171 | 225 | 15 | 1 | 0.1 | 41 | 47 | 2.9 | 1 | T | 0 |
| Beans, Great Northern, cooked | 1 cup | 180 | 210 | 14 | 1 | 0.1 | 38 | 90 | 4.9 | 13 | 0 | 0 |
| Peanuts, roasted in oil, salted | 1 cup | 145 | 840 | 39 | 71 | 9.9 | 27 | 125 | 2.8 | 626 | 0 | 0 |
| Peanut butter | 1 tbsp. | 16 | 95 | 5 | 8 | 1.4 | 3 | 5 | 0.3 | 75 | 0 | 0 |
| Refried beans, canned | 1 cup | 290 | 295 | 18 | 3 | 0.4 | 51 | 141 | 5.1 | 1,228 | 0 | 17 |
| Tofu | 1 piece | 120 | 85 | 9 | 5 | 0.7 | 3 | 108 | 2.3 | 8 | 0 | 0 |
| Sunflower seeds, hulled | 1 oz. | 28 | 160 | 6 | 14 | 1.5 | 5 | 33 | 1.9 | 1 | 10 | T |
| Mixed foods | | | | | | | | | | | | |
| Chop suey with beef and pork, home recipe | 1 cup | 250 | 300 | 26 | 17 | 4.3 | 13 | 60 | 4.8 | 1,053 | 600 | 33 |
| Enchilada | 1 | 230 | 235 | 20 | 16 | 7.7 | 24 | 97 | 3.3 | 1,332 | 2,720 | T |
| Pizza, cheese, 1/8 of 15 in.-diam. pie | 1 | 120 | 290 | 15 | 9 | 4.1 | 39 | 220 | 1.6 | 699 | 750 | 2 |
| Spaghetti with meatballs & tomato sauce | 1 cup | 248 | 330 | 19 | 12 | 3.9 | 39 | 124 | 3.7 | 1,009 | 1,590 | 22 |
| **Sugars & sweets** | | | | | | | | | | | | |
| Candy, caramels | 1 oz. | 28 | 115 | 1 | 3 | 2.2 | 22 | 42 | 0.4 | 64 | T | T |
| Candy, milk chocolate | 1 oz. | 28 | 145 | 2 | 9 | 5.4 | 16 | 50 | 0.4 | 23 | 30 | T |
| Fudge, chocolate | 1 oz. | 28 | 115 | 1 | 3 | 2.1 | 21 | 22 | 0.3 | 54 | T | T |
| Gelatin dessert, from prepared powder | 1/2 cup | 120 | 70 | 2 | 0 | 0.0 | 17 | 2 | T | 55 | 0 | 0 |
| Candy, hard | 1 oz. | 28 | 110 | 0 | 0 | 0.0 | 28 | T | 0.1 | 7 | 0 | 0 |
| Honey | 1 tbsp. | 21 | 65 | T | 0 | 0.0 | 17 | 1 | 0.1 | 1 | 0 | T |
| Jams & Preserves | 1 tbsp. | 20 | 55 | T | T | 0.0 | 14 | 4 | 0.2 | 2 | T | T |
| Popsicle, 3 fl. oz. | 1 | 95 | 70 | 0 | 0 | 0.0 | 18 | 0 | T | 11 | 0 | 0 |
| Sugar, white, granulated | 1 tbsp. | 12 | 45 | 0 | 0 | 0.0 | 12 | T | T | T | 0 | 0 |
| **Vegetables** | | | | | | | | | | | | |
| Asparagus, spears, cooked from raw | 4 spears | 60 | 15 | 2 | T | T | 3 | 14 | 0.4 | 2 | 500 | 16 |
| Beans, green, from frozen, cuts | 1 cup | 135 | 35 | 2 | T | T | 8 | 61 | 1.1 | 18 | 710 | 11 |
| Broccoli, cooked from raw | 1 spear | 180 | 50 | 5 | 1 | 0.1 | 10 | 82 | 2.1 | 20 | 2,540 | 113 |
| Cabbage, raw, coarsely shredded or sliced | 1 cup | 70 | 15 | 1 | T | T | 4 | 33 | 0.4 | 13 | 90 | 33 |
| Carrots, raw, 7-1/2 by 1-1/8 in. | 1 | 72 | 30 | 1 | T | T | 7 | 19 | 0.4 | 25 | 20,250 | 7 |
| Cauliflower, cooked, drained, from raw | 1 cup | 125 | 30 | 2 | T | T | 6 | 34 | 0.5 | 8 | 20 | 69 |
| Celery, raw | 1 stalk | 40 | 5 | T | T | T | 1 | 14 | 0.2 | 35 | 50 | 3 |
| Collards, cooked from raw | 1 cup | 190 | 25 | 2 | T | 0.1 | 5 | 148 | 0.8 | 36 | 4,220 | 19 |
| Corn, sweet, yellow, cooked from raw | 1 ear | 77 | 85 | 3 | 1 | 0.2 | 19 | 2 | 0.5 | 13 | 170 | 5 |
| Eggplant, cooked, steamed | 1 cup | 96 | 25 | 1 | T | T | 6 | 6 | 0.3 | 3 | 60 | 1 |
| Lettuce, iceberg, chopped | 1 cup | 55 | 5 | 1 | T | T | 1 | 10 | 0.3 | 5 | 180 | 2 |
| Lettuce, looseleaf (such as romaine) | 1 cup | 56 | 10 | 1 | T | T | 2 | 38 | 0.8 | 5 | 1,060 | 10 |
| Mushrooms, raw | 1 cup | 70 | 20 | 1 | T | T | 3 | 4 | 0.9 | 3 | 0 | 2 |
| Onions, raw, chopped | 1 cup | 160 | 55 | 2 | T | 0.1 | 12 | 40 | 0.6 | 3 | 0 | 13 |
| Peas, green, frozen, cooked | 1 cup | 160 | 125 | 8 | T | 0.1 | 23 | 38 | 2.5 | 139 | 1,070 | 16 |
| Potatoes, baked, peeled | 1 | 156 | 145 | 3 | T | T | 34 | 8 | 0.5 | 8 | 0 | 20 |
| Potatoes, frozen, French fried (oven-heated) | 10 | 50 | 110 | 2 | 4 | 2.1 | 17 | 5 | 0.7 | 16 | 0 | 5 |
| Potatoes, mashed, milk added | 1 cup | 210 | 160 | 4 | 1 | 0.7 | 37 | 55 | 0.6 | 636 | 40 | 14 |
| Potato chips | 10 | 20 | 105 | 1 | 7 | 1.8 | 10 | 5 | 0.2 | 94 | 0 | 8 |
| Potato salad | 1 cup | 250 | 360 | 7 | 21 | 3.6 | 28 | 48 | 1.6 | 1,323 | 520 | 25 |
| Spinach, drained, cooked from raw | 1 cup | 180 | 40 | 5 | T | 0.1 | 7 | 245 | 6.4 | 126 | 14,740 | 18 |
| Sweet potatoes, baked in skin, peeled | 1 | 114 | 115 | 2 | T | T | 28 | 32 | 0.5 | 11 | 24,880 | 28 |
| Tomatoes, raw | 1 | 123 | 25 | 1 | T | T | 5 | 9 | 0.6 | 10 | 1,390 | 22 |
| Vegetable juice cocktail, canned | 1 cup | 242 | 45 | 2 | T | T | 11 | 27 | 1.0 | 883 | 2,830 | 67 |
| **Miscellaneous** | | | | | | | | | | | | |
| Beer, regular | 12 fl. oz. | 360 | 150 | 1 | 0 | 0.0 | 13 | 14 | 0.1 | 18 | 0 | 0 |
| Gin, rum, vodka, whisky, 86 proof | 1-1/2 fl. oz. | 42 | 105 | 0 | 0 | 0.0 | T | T | T | T | 0 | 0 |
| Wine, table, white | 3-1/2 fl. oz. | 102 | 80 | T | 0 | 0.0 | 3 | 9 | 0.3 | 5 | (1) | 0 |
| Cola-type beverage | 12 fl. oz. | 369 | 160 | 0 | 0 | 0.0 | 41 | 11 | 0.2 | 18 | 0 | 0 |
| Ginger ale | 12 fl. oz | 366 | 125 | 0 | 0 | 0.0 | 32 | 11 | 0.1 | 29 | 0 | 0 |
| Coffee, brewed | 6 fl. oz. | 180 | T | T | T | T | T | 4 | T | 2 | 0 | 0 |
| Tea, brewed | 8 fl. oz. | 240 | T | T | T | T | T | 0 | T | 1 | 0 | 0 |
| Catsup | 1 tbsp. | 15 | 15 | T | T | T | 4 | 3 | 0.1 | 156 | 210 | 2 |
| Mustard, prepared, yellow | 1 tsp. | 5 | 5 | T | T | T | T | 4 | 0.1 | 63 | 0 | T |
| Olives, canned, green | 4 medium | 13 | 15 | T | 2 | 0.2 | T | 8 | 0.2 | 312 | 40 | 0 |
| Pickles, dill, whole | 1 | 65 | 5 | T | T | T | 1 | 17 | 0.7 | 928 | 70 | 4 |
| Relish, finely chopped, sweet | 1 tbsp. | 15 | 20 | T | T | T | 5 | 3 | 0.1 | 107 | 20 | 1 |
| Soup, tomato, prepared with milk | 1 cup | 248 | 160 | 6 | 6 | 2.9 | 22 | 159 | 1.8 | 932 | 850 | 68 |
| Soup, chicken noodle, prepared with water | 1 cup | 241 | 75 | 4 | 2 | 0.7 | 9 | 17 | 0.8 | 1,106 | 710 | T |
| Soup, green pea, prepared with water | 1 cup | 250 | 165 | 9 | 3 | 1.4 | 27 | 28 | 2.0 | 988 | 200 | 2 |
| Soup, vegetarian, prepared with water | 1 cup | 241 | 70 | 2 | 2 | 0.3 | 12 | 22 | 1.1 | 822 | 3,010 | 1 |

T — Indicates trace (1) — Value not determined. **Note:** Values shown here for these foods may be from several different manufacturers and, therefore, may differ somewhat from the values provided by one source.

# Recommended Daily Dietary Allowances

**Source:** Food and Nutrition Board, Natl. Academy of Sciences—Natl. Research Council; 1989

| | | | | Fat soluble vitamins | | | | Water soluble vitamins | | | | | | | Minerals | | | | | | |
|---|---|---|---|---|---|---|---|---|---|---|---|---|---|---|---|---|---|---|---|---|---|
| | Age (years) and sex group | Weight (lbs.) | Protein (grams) | Vitamin A* | Vitamin D** | Vitamin E† | Vitamin K (micrograms) | Vitamin C (mg.) | Thiamine (mg.) | Riboflavin (mg.) | Niacin (mg.)‡ | Vitamin B6 (mg.) | Folate (micrograms) | Vitamin B12 (micrograms) | Calcium (mg.) | Phosphorus (mg.) | Magnesium (mg.) | Iron (mg.) | Zinc (mg.) | Iodine (micrograms) | Selenium (micrograms) |
| Infants . . . | to 5 mos. | 13 | 13 | 375 | 7.5 | 3 | 5 | 30 | 0.3 | 0.4 | 5 | 0.3 | 25 | 0.3 | 400 | 300 | 40 | 6 | 5 | 40 | 10 |
| | to 1 yr. | 20 | 14 | 375 | 10 | 4 | 10 | 35 | 0.4 | 0.5 | 6 | 0.6 | 35 | 0.5 | 600 | 500 | 60 | 10 | 5 | 50 | 15 |
| Children . . | 1-3 | 29 | 16 | 400 | 10 | 6 | 15 | 40 | 0.7 | 0.8 | 9 | 1.0 | 50 | 0.7 | 800 | 800 | 80 | 10 | 10 | 70 | 20 |
| | 4-6 | 44 | 24 | 500 | 10 | 7 | 20 | 45 | 0.9 | 1.1 | 12 | 1.1 | 75 | 1.0 | 800 | 800 | 120 | 10 | 10 | 90 | 20 |
| | 7-10 | 62 | 28 | 700 | 10 | 7 | 30 | 45 | 1.0 | 1.2 | 13 | 1.4 | 100 | 1.4 | 800 | 800 | 170 | 10 | 10 | 120 | 30 |
| Males . . . . | 11-14 | 99 | 45 | 1000 | 10 | 10 | 45 | 50 | 1.3 | 1.5 | 17 | 1.7 | 150 | 2.0 | 1200 | 1200 | 270 | 12 | 15 | 150 | 40 |
| | 15-18 | 145 | 59 | 1000 | 10 | 10 | 65 | 60 | 1.5 | 1.8 | 20 | 2.0 | 200 | 2.0 | 1200 | 1200 | 400 | 12 | 15 | 150 | 50 |
| | 19-24 | 160 | 58 | 1000 | 10 | 10 | 70 | 60 | 1.5 | 1.7 | 19 | 2.0 | 200 | 2.0 | 1200 | 1200 | 350 | 10 | 15 | 150 | 70 |
| | 25-50 | 174 | 63 | 1000 | 5 | 10 | 80 | 60 | 1.5 | 1.7 | 19 | 2.0 | 200 | 2.0 | 800 | 800 | 350 | 10 | 15 | 150 | 70 |
| | 51+ | 170 | 63 | 1000 | 5 | 10 | 80 | 60 | 1.2 | 1.4 | 15 | 2.0 | 200 | 2.0 | 800 | 800 | 350 | 10 | 15 | 150 | 70 |
| Females . . | 11-14 | 101 | 46 | 800 | 10 | 8 | 45 | 50 | 1.1 | 1.3 | 15 | 1.4 | 150 | 2.0 | 1200 | 1200 | 280 | 15 | 12 | 150 | 45 |
| | 15-18 | 120 | 44 | 800 | 10 | 8 | 55 | 60 | 1.1 | 1.3 | 15 | 1.5 | 180 | 2.0 | 1200 | 1200 | 300 | 15 | 12 | 150 | 50 |
| | 19-24 | 128 | 46 | 800 | 10 | 8 | 60 | 60 | 1.1 | 1.3 | 15 | 1.6 | 180 | 2.0 | 1200 | 1200 | 280 | 15 | 12 | 150 | 55 |
| | 25-50 | 138 | 50 | 800 | 5 | 8 | 65 | 60 | 1.1 | 1.3 | 15 | 1.6 | 180 | 2.0 | 800 | 800 | 280 | 15 | 12 | 150 | 55 |
| | 51+ | 143 | 50 | 800 | 5 | 8 | 65 | 60 | 1.0 | 1.2 | 13 | 1.6 | 180 | 2.0 | 800 | 800 | 280 | 10 | 12 | 150 | 55 |

* Retinol equivalents. ** Micrograms of cholecalciferol. † Milligrams alpha-tocopherol equivalents. ‡ Niacin equivalents.

# Weight Ranges for Adults

**Source:** U.S. Department of Agriculture; U.S. Department of Health and Human Services, 1995

Weight in lbs., without clothes. Height without shoes.

| Height | Healthy weight | Moderately overweight | Severely overweight[1] | Height | Healthy weight | Moderately overweight | Severely overweight[1] |
|---|---|---|---|---|---|---|---|
| 4'10" | 91-118 | 119-137 | 138 | 5'9" | 129-168 | 169-195 | 196 |
| 4'11" | 94-123 | 124-143 | 144 | 5'10" | 132-173 | 174-201 | 202 |
| 5'0" | 97-127 | 128-147 | 148 | 5'11" | 136-178 | 179-206 | 207 |
| 5'1" | 101-131 | 132-152 | 153 | 6'0" | 140-183 | 184-212 | 213 |
| 5'2" | 104-136 | 137-157 | 158 | 6'1" | 144-188 | 189-218 | 219 |
| 5'3" | 107-140 | 141-162 | 163 | 6'2" | 148-194 | 195-224 | 225 |
| 5'4" | 111-145 | 146-168 | 169 | 6'3" | 152-199 | 200-231 | 232 |
| 5'5" | 114-149 | 150-173 | 174 | 6'4" | 156-204 | 205-237 | 238 |
| 5'6" | 118-154 | 155-178 | 179 | 6'5" | 160-210 | 211-243 | 244 |
| 5'7" | 121-159 | 160-184 | 185 | 6'6" | 164-215 | 216-249 | 250 |
| 5'8" | 125-163 | 164-189 | 190 | | | | |

**Note:** The higher weights apply to people with more muscle and bone, such as many men. You ordinarily do not need to lose weight if you have gained less than 10 lb. since reaching your adult height, are within the "healthy" weight range for your height and volume of muscle and bone, and are otherwise healthy. (1) Number given is low end of range.

# Understanding Food Label Claims

**Source:** Food Labeling Education Information Center, Beltville, Md.

The federal Nutrition Labeling and Education Act of 1990 requires that manufacturers can make certain claims on processed food labels only if they meet the following definitions:

### Sugar

**Sugar free:** less than 0.5 g per serving

**No added sugar; Without added sugar; No sugar added:**

- No sugars added during processing or packing, including ingredients that contain sugars (for example, fruit juices, applesauce, or dried fruit).
- Processing does not increase the sugar content above the amount naturally present in the ingredients. (A functionally insignificant increase in sugars is acceptable from the processes used for purposes other than increasing sugar content.)
- The compared food normally contains added sugars.

**Reduced sugar:** at least 25% less sugar than a compared food

### Calories

**Calorie free:** fewer than 5 calories per serving

**Low calorie:** 40 calories or less per serving; if the serving is 30 g or less or 2 tablespoons or less, 40 calories or less per 50 g of food

**Reduced or Fewer calories:** at least 25% fewer calories than a compared food

### Fat

**Fat free:** less than 0.5 g of fat per serving

**Saturated fat free:** less than 0.5 g of saturated fat per serving, and the level of trans fatty acids does not exceed 1% of total fat

**Low fat:** 3 g or less per serving and, if the serving is 30 g or less or 2 tbs or less, per 50 g of the food

**Low saturated fat:** 1 g or less per serving and not more than 15% of calories from saturated fatty acids

**Reduced or Less fat:** at least 25% less per serving than compared food

### Cholesterol

**Cholesterol free:** less than 2 mg of cholesterol and 2 g or less of saturated fat per serving

**Low cholesterol:** 20 mg or less and 2 g or less of saturated fat per serving and, if the serving is 30 g or less or 2 tbs or less, per 50 g of the food

**Reduced or Less cholesterol:** at least 25% less than compared food

### Sodium

**Sodium free:** less than 5 mg per serving

**Low sodium:** 140 mg or less per serving and, if the serving is 30 g or less or 2 tbs or less, per 50 g of the food

**Very low sodium:** 35 mg or less per serving and, if the serving is 30 g or less or 2 tbs or less, per 50 g of the food

**Reduced or Less sodium:** at least 25% less per serving than compared food

### Fiber

**High fiber:** 5 g or more per serving. (Also, must meet low-fat definition, or state level of total fat.)

**Good source of fiber:** 2.5 g to 4.9 g per serving

**More or Added fiber:** at least 2.5 g more per serving than reference food

# Immunization Schedule for Infants and Children

**Source:** American Academy of Pediatrics, Aug. 1996

By ensuring that your child gets immunized on schedule, you can provide the best defense against dangerous childhood diseases. Childhood immunization means protection from 10 major diseases: hepatitis B, polio, measles, mumps, rubella (German measles), pertussis (whooping cough), diphtheria, tetanus (lockjaw), chickenpox, and *Haemophilus influenzae* type b (a bacterium that can cause such serious infections as meningitis and pneumonia). In 1995 the Food and Drug Administration approved the chickenpox vaccine for use in the U.S. to vaccinate persons against what is currently one of the most common childhood viral infections.

If you do not have a pediatrician, call your local public health department. It usually has supplies of vaccine and may give immunizations free.

| | DTP[1] | Polio[2] | Hepatitis B[3] | Measles[4] | Mumps[4] | Rubella[4] | Chicken-pox[5] | Hib[6] | Tetanus-Diphtheria[7] |
|---|---|---|---|---|---|---|---|---|---|
| Birth-2 months | | | X | | | | | | |
| 1-4 months | | | X | | | | | | |
| 2 months | X | X | | | | | | X | |
| 4 months | X | X | | | | | | X | |
| 6 months | X | | | | | | | X | |
| 6-18 months | | X | X | | | | | | |
| 12-15 months | | | | X | X | X | | X | |
| 12-18 months | X | | | | | | X | | |
| 4-6 years | X | X | | X or | X or | X or | | | |
| 11-12 years | | | X | X | X | X | X | | X |
| 14-16 years | | | | | | | | | X |

(1) For the best possible protection against diphtheria, tetanus, and pertussis, your child needs a series of 5 shots of the combination diphtheria-tetanus-pertussis (DTP) vaccine. The first 3 doses should be given at 2, 4, and 6 months of age. The 4th dose may be given at 12 to 18 months of age, provided the child has received the 3d dose of DTP 6 months prior to receiving the 4th dose. A 5th booster dose should be given before school entry (4 to 6 years). After the child has reached 15 months of age, the acellular (DTaP) vaccine may be substituted for the DTP vaccine.

(2) For protection against polio, your child needs a series of 4 oral polio vaccine doses, the first 3 at 2, 4, and 6 to 18 months and the final dose before school entry (4 to 6 years). Inactivated poliovirus vaccine (IPV) is recommended for persons with a congenital or acquired immune deficiency disease or an altered immune status as a result of disease or immunosuppressive therapy. The primary 3-dose series for IPV should be given with a minimum interval of 4 weeks between the 1st and 2d doses and 6 months between the 2d and 3d dose.

(3) Infants of mothers with positive blood tests for hepatitis B must receive both the hepatitis B immune globulin (HBIG) and either the Recombivax or the Engerix-B vaccine within 12 hours of birth. In these infants, the 2d dose is recommended at 1 month and a 3d hepatitis B vaccine injection at 6 months of age. To be completely protected against hepatitis B, infants born to hepatitis B-negative mothers also need to be vaccinated with a series of 3 hepatitis B virus (HBV) vaccine shots. The American Academy of Pediatrics recommends that these immunizations be given at birth to 2 months, at 2 to 4 months, and at 6 to 18 months of age (with at least a one-month lapse between doses). Adolescents who have not previously received 3 doses of the vaccine should initiate or complete the 3-dose series at 11-12 years of age.

(4) At 12 to 15 months, your child should have an immunization for measles, mumps, and rubella (the combined MMR vaccine). A 2d MMR vaccination, primarily to boost measles and mumps immunity, should be given to children either at 4 to 6 years or at 11 to 12 years, consistent with state school or public health authority immunization requirements.

(5) The varicella zoster virus vaccine (VZV) is routinely recommended at 12 to 18 months of age to prevent chickenpox. Children who have not been vaccinated previously and who lack a reliable history of chickenpox should be vaccinated at the 11-12 year-old visit. VZV can be adminstered to susceptible children any time after 12 months of age. Persons 13 years of age and older should receive 2 doses of the vaccine 4 to 8 weeks apart.

(6) Several vaccines are available for protection against *Haemophilus influenzae* type b (Hib). However, only 3 vaccines—HbOC, PRP-T, and PRP-OMP—are approved for children under 15 months of age. The Academy recommends that your child receive either the HbOC or the PRP-T vaccine at 2, 4, and 6 months of age or the PRP-OMP vaccine at 2 and 4 months. Any licensed Hib conjugate vaccine may be used as a booster dose at 12-15 months.

(7) The tetanus and diptheria toxoids (Td) vaccine is recommended at 11-12 years and 14-16 years (must be 5 years from last booster dose of DTP). Repeat every 10 years throughout life.

# Some Benefits of Quitting Smoking

**Source:** American Cancer Society, phone: (800) 227-2345; U.S. Centers for Disease Control and Prevention

**Within 20 Minutes**
- Blood pressure drops to normal
- Pulse rate drops to normal
- Body temperature of hands and feet increases to normal

**Within 8 Hours**
- Carbon monoxide level in blood drops to normal
- Oxygen level in blood increases to normal

**Within 24 Hours**
- Chance of heart attack decreases

**Within 48 Hours**
- Nerve endings start regrowing
- Ability to smell and taste is enhanced

**Within 2 Weeks to 3 Months**
- Circulation improves
- Walking becomes easier
- Lung function increases up to 30 percent

**Within 1 to 9 Months**
- Coughing, sinus congestion, fatigue, shortness of breath decrease
- Cilia regrow in lungs, increasing ability to handle mucus, clean the lungs, reduce infection
- Body's overall energy increases

**Within 1 Year**
- Excess risk of coronary heart disease is cut by half.

**Within 5 Years**
- Lung cancer death rate for average former smoker (one pack a day) decreases by almost half
- Stroke risk is reduced to that of a nonsmoker 5-15 years after quitting
- Risk of cancer of the mouth, throat, and esophagus is half that of a smoker's

**Within 10 Years**
- Lung cancer death rate similar to that of nonsmokers
- Precancerous cells are replaced
- Risk of cancer of the mouth, throat, esophagus, bladder, kidney, and pancreas decreases

**Within 15 Years**
- Risk of coronary heart disease is that of a nonsmoker

## Cancer's 7 Warning Signals*

**Source:** American Cancer Society, 1599 Clifton Road NE, Atlanta, GA 30329-4251; phone: (800) 227-2345

1. A change in bowel or bladder habits.
2. A sore that does not heal.
3. Unusual bleeding or discharge.
4. Thickening or lump in breast or elsewhere.
5. Indigestion or difficulty in swallowing.
6. Obvious change in wart or mole.
7. Nagging cough or hoarseness.

*If you have a warning signal, see your doctor.

## Cancer Prevention

**Source:** American Cancer Society, 1599 Clifton Road NE, Atlanta, GA 30329-4251; phone: (800) 227-2345

**PRIMARY PREVENTION:** steps that can be taken to avoid those factors that might lead to the development of cancer.

**Smoking** — Cigarette smoking is responsible for 90% of lung cancer cases among men, 79% among women—about 87% overall. Smoking accounts for about 30% of all cancer deaths. Those who smoke two or more packs of cigarettes a day have lung cancer mortality rates 12-25 times greater than nonsmokers.

**Nutrition** — Risk for colon, breast, gallbladder, ovarian, prostate, and uterine cancers increases in obese people. High-fat diets may contribute to the development of certain cancers, particularly those of the breast, colon, and prostate. High-fiber foods may help reduce risk of colon cancer. A varied diet containing plenty of vegetables and fruits rich in vitamins A and C may reduce risk for many cancers. Salt-cured, smoked, and nitrite-cured foods have been linked to esophageal and stomach cancer.

**Sunlight** — Almost all of the more than 800,000 cases of non-melanoma skin cancer diagnosed each year in the U.S. are sun-related. Epidemiological evidence shows that sun exposure is a major factor in the development of melanoma, and the incidence increases for those living near the equator.

**Alcohol** — Oral cancer and cancers of the larynx, throat, esophagus, and liver occur more frequently among heavy drinkers of alcohol, especially when accompanied by cigarette smoking or use of chewing tobacco.

**Smokeless Tobacco** — Use of chewing tobacco or snuff increases risk of cancers of the mouth, larynx, throat, and esophagus.

**Estrogen** — Estrogen treatment to control menopausal symptoms can increase risk of endometrial cancer. However, including progesterone in estrogen replacement therapy helps to minimize this risk. Use of estrogen by menopausal women needs careful discussion by the woman and her physician, while research continues.

**Radiation** — Excessive exposure to ionizing radiation can increase cancer risk. Most medical and dental X rays are adjusted to deliver the lowest dose possible without sacrificing image quality. Excessive radon exposure in the home may increase lung cancer risk, especially in cigarette smokers. If levels are found to be too high, remedial actions should be taken.

**Occupational Hazards** — Exposure to several different industrial agents (including nickel, chromate, asbestos, and vinyl chloride) increases risk of various cancers. Risk of lung cancer from asbestos is greatly increased when combined with smoking.

**SECONDARY PREVENTION:** steps to diagnose a cancer or precursor as early as possible after it has developed.

**Colorectal Tests** — The ACS recommends 3 tests for the early detection of colon and rectum cancer in people without symptoms: A digital rectal examination should be performed by a physician during an office visit every year after the age of 40; a stool blood test, every year after 50; and a sigmoidoscopy examination, preferably flexible, every 3 to 5 years after age 50, based on the advice of a physician.

**Pap Test** — For cervical cancer, women who are or have been sexually active, or have reached 18 years, should have an annual Pap test and pelvic examination. After a woman has had 3 or more consecutive satisfactory normal exams, the Pap test may be performed less frequently at the discretion of her physician.

**Breast Cancer Detection** — The ACS recommends monthly breast self-examination by women 20 years and older. Examination of the breast by a health-care professional should be done every 3 years from ages 20-40, and then every year for women over 40. A mammogram is recommended every year for asymptomatic women age 50 and over. Women age 40-49 should have mammography every 1-2 years, depending on physical and mammographic findings. It is also recommended that women have at least one mammogram prior to age 40.

**Prostate Cancer Detection** — For early detection of prostate cancer, the ACS recommends that men over age 40 should have an annual digital rectal examination. After age 50, men should have an annual prostate-specific antigen blood test.

## Diabetes

**Source:** American Diabetes Association, 1660 Duke St., Alexandria, VA 22314; phone: (800) 232-3472

Diabetes is a chronic disease in which the body does not produce or properly use insulin, a hormone that is needed in order to convert sugar, starches, and other foods into energy that is needed for daily life. Both genetics and environment appear to play roles in the onset of diabetes. This disease, which has no cure, is the 4th-leading cause of death by disease in the U.S. In 1996, more than 178,000 Americans were expected to die from the disease and its related complications.

There are two major types of diabetes:

**Insulin dependent (type I)**—The body produces very little or no insulin; disease most often begins in childhood or early adulthood. People with type I diabetes must take daily insulin injections to stay alive.

**Non-insulin dependent (type II)**—The body does not produce enough or cannot properly use insulin. It is the most common form of the disease (90-95% of cases in people over age 20) and often begins later in life.

### Warning Signs of Diabetes

**Type I Diabetes** (usually occur suddenly):

- frequent urination
- unusual thirst
- extreme hunger
- unusual weight loss
- extreme fatigue
- irritability

**Type II Diabetes** (occur less suddenly):

- any type I symptoms
- frequent infections
- blurred vision
- cuts/bruises slow to heal
- tingling/numbness in hands or feet
- recurring skin, gum, or bladder infections

### Complications of Diabetes

More than half of all individuals with diabetes do not know that they have the disease until one of its life-threatening complications occurs. Potential complications include:

**Blindness.** Diabetes is the leading cause of blindness in people ages 20-74. Each year, from 12,000 to 24,000 people lose their sight because of diabetes.

**Kidney disease.** 10% to 21% of all people with diabetes develop kidney disease. In 1992, more than 19,800 people initiated treatment for end-stage renal disease (kidney failure) because of diabetes.

**Amputations.** Diabetes is the most frequent cause of nontraumatic lower limb amputations. The risk of a leg amputation is 15 to 40 times greater for a person with diabetes than for the average American. Each year, 54,000 people lose a foot or leg to complications brought on by diabetes.

**Heart disease and stroke.** People with diabetes are 2 to 4 times more likely to have heart disease (more than 77,000 deaths due to heart disease annually). And they are 2 to 4 times more likely to suffer a stroke (more than 11,000 diabetes-related stroke deaths each year).

Health-care and related costs for the treatment of the disease, as well as the cost of lost productivity, total nearly $92 billion annually in the U.S.

## Alzheimer's Disease

**Source:** Alzheimer's Association, 919 N Michigan Ave., Suite 1000, Chicago, IL 60611-1676; phone: (800) 272-3900

Alzheimer's disease is a progressive, degenerative disease of the brain in which brain cells die and are not replaced. It results in impaired memory, thinking, and behavior, and is the most common form of dementing illness. The debilitating nature of the disease renders patients susceptible to infections (such as pneumonia and urinary tract infections) as they become emaciated, incontinent, immobile, or enter a persistent vegetative state.

Alzheimer's disease afflicts an estimated 4 million Americans, striking equally among men and women of all races. Although most people diagnosed with Alzheimer's are older than age 60, the disease can occur in people in their 40s and 50s. Ten percent of those 65 years of age or older, and almost half of those over age 85, have the disease. It is estimated that the cost of diagnosis, treatment, and long-term care for patients with the disease costs American society $100 billion per year.

The rate of the progression of Alzheimer's disease from the onset of symptoms until death ranges from 3 to 20 years; the average is 8 years. Eventually, patients become totally incapable of caring for themselves.

Diagnosis is complicated by the lack of a single, simple test to identify the disease. Through a series of diagnostic tests by a qualified physician, possible causes of symptoms, such as depression, drug interactions, nutrient imblances, or other forms of dementia, such as those associated with stroke, Huntington's disease, Parkinson's disease, Pick's disease, and infections (AIDS, meningitis, syphilis) are ruled out, yielding a diagnosis (by process of elimination) that is 80-90% accurate. A definitive diagnosis is possible only with a brain biopsy or an autopsy.

No treatment has proven successful in reversing the course of the disease, and providing care for patients with Alzheimer's disease is very physically and psychologically demanding. Nearly 70% of those afflicted with Alzheimer's disease live at home and are cared for by family and friends. In the last stages of the disease, it is often necessary for those afflicted to be cared for in a nursing home. Nearly half of all nursing home patients in the United States suffer from Alzheimer's disease.

People with Alzheimer's disease need a safe, stable environment and should maintain a regular daily schedule. Physical exercise and social activity are important, as is proper nutrition. A medical bracelet identifying the person's name and his or her condition may be helpful in case the person wanders away.

The causes of Alzheimer's disease are unknown.

### Warning Signs

- Recent memory loss that affects job performance
- Inability to learn new information
- Difficulty with everyday tasks such as cooking or dressing
- Inability to remember simple words
- Use of inappropriate words when communicating
- Disorientation of time and place
- Poor or decreased judgment
- Problems with abstract thinking
- Misplacing objects in inappropriate places
- Rapid changes in mood or behavior
- Increased irritability, anxiety, depression, confusion, and restlessness
- Prolonged loss of initiative

## State Laws Regarding the Care of the Critically Ill

**Source:** Choice In Dying, Inc., 200 Varick Street, 10th Floor, New York, NY 10014-4810; phone: (800) 989-9455; Copyright © 1996

(The specifics of each state's legislation vary)

**Living wills authorized**—Washington, DC, and all states, except MA, MI, and NY.

**Appointment of a health care agent authorized**—Washington, DC, and all states except AL and AK.

**Surrogate decision-making in the absence of advance directive allowed**—AZ, AR, CO, CT, DE, FL, IL, IN, IA, KY, LA, ME, MD, MT, NV, NM, NC, OH, OR, SC, TX, UT, VA, WV, WY, and Washington, DC.

**Nonhospital do-not-resuscitate orders authorized**—AK, AZ, AR, CA, CO, CT, FL, GA, HI, ID, IL, KS, KY, MD, MI, MT, NM, NY, PA, RI, SC, TN, TX, UT, VA, WA, WV, WI, and WY.

**Individuals permitted to refuse artificial nutrition and hydration in their living wills**—AK, AZ(1), CA, CO, CT, GA, HI, ID, IL(2), IN, IA, KY, LA, ME, MD, MN, NV, NJ, NH, NM, NC, ND, OH, OK, OR, PA, RI, SC, SD, TN, UT, VA, WA, WI, and WY

**Artificial nutrition and hydration required except in very limited circumstances**—MO(3)

**Health care agents permitted to order the withholding or withdrawal of artificial nutrition and hydration**—AZ, CO, CT, GA, HI, ID, IL, IN, IA, KY, LA, ME, MD, MN, MO, NE, NV, NH, NJ, NM, NY, NC, OH, OK, OR, PA, SC, SD, TN, UT, VA, VT, WA, and WI.

**Statutes recognize living will documents executed in other states**—AK, AZ, AR, CA, FL, HI, IL, IA, LA, ME, MD, MN, MT, NE, NV, NH, NJ, NM, ND, OH, OK, OR, RI, SC, SD, TN, UT, VA, WA, and WV

**Statutes recognize health care agents appointed in documents executed in other states**—AZ, AR, CA, CO, FL, IN, IA, KS, ME, MD, MA, MN, NE, NH, NJ, NM, NY, ND, OH, OK, OR, RI, SC, TN, TX, UT, VT, VA, WA, and WV.

**Statutes define death to include brain death**—Washington, DC, and all states except MA, NY, and WA(4).

(1) The authority to withhold or withdraw artificial nutrition and hydration is explicitly mentioned only in the sample document, not in the text of the Arizona statute. (2) Artificial nutrition and hydration cannot be withheld or withdrawn if the resulting death is due to starvation or dehydration. (3) The medical power of attorney statute in Missouri permits appointed agents to refuse artificial nutrition and hydration on behalf of the principal. (4) Massachusetts and Washington have case law that defines death to include brain death. New York has state regulations that define death to include brain death.

# Heart and Blood Vessel Disease

**Source:** American Heart Association, 7272 Greenville Ave., Dallas, TX 75231-4596; phone: (800) 242-8721

## Warning Signs

**Of Heart Attack**
- Uncomfortable pressure, fullness, squeezing, or pain in the center of the chest lasting two minutes or longer
- Pain may radiate to the shoulder, arm, neck, or jaw
- Sweating may accompany pain or discomfort
- Nausea and vomiting may also occur
- Shortness of breath, dizziness, or fainting may accompany other signs

The American Heart Association advises immediate action at the onset of these symptoms. The association points out that more than half of heart attack victims die within 1 hour of the onset of symptoms and before they have reached the hospital.

**Of Stroke**
- Sudden temporary weakness or numbness of face or limbs on one side of the body
- Temporary loss of speech, or trouble speaking or understanding speech
- Temporary dim or lost vision, especially in one eye
- Unexplained dizziness, unsteadiness, or sudden falls

## Some Major Risk Factors

**Blood pressure**—High blood pressure increases the risk of stroke, heart attack, kidney failure, and congestive heart failure.

**Cholesterol**—A blood cholesterol level over 240 mg/dl (milligrams of cholesterol per deciliter of blood) approximately doubles the risk of coronary heart disease; about 20% of the U.S. adult population (38.3 mil) falls into this category. Blood cholesterol levels between 200 and 240 mg/dl are in a zone of moderate and increasing risk. An estimated 27.4 mil (37% of) youths age 19 and under have levels of 170 mg/dl or higher, comparable to a level of 200 mg/dl in adults.

**Cigarettes**—Cigarette smokers have more than twice the risk of heart attack and 2-4 times the risk of sudden cardiac death as nonsmokers. Young smokers have a higher risk for early death from stroke.

**Obesity**—More than 60 mil adults are 20% or more over their desirable weight.

# Understanding Blood Pressure

**Source:** American Heart Association, 7272 Greenville Ave., Dallas TX 75231-4596; phone: (800) 242-8721

High blood pressure, or hypertension, affects people of all races, sexes, ethnic origins, and ages. There are a variety of causes that can trigger this often symptomless disease. Since hypertension can increase one's risk for stroke, heart attack, kidney failure, and congestive heart failure, it is recommended that individuals have a blood pressure reading at least once every 2 years (more often if advised by a physician).

A blood pressure reading is really two measurements in one, with one written over the other, such as 122/78. The **upper number (systolic pressure)** represents the amount of pressure in the blood vessels when the heart contracts (beats) and pushes blood through the circulatory system. The **lower number (diastolic pressure)** represents the pressure in the blood vessels between beats, when the heart is resting. According to National Institutes of Health guidelines, normal blood pressure is below 130/85 and "high normal" is between 130/85 and 139/89. High blood pressure is divided into 4 stages, based on severity:

- **Stage 1 (mild)** high blood pressure ranges from 140/90 to 159/99
- **Stage 2 (moderate)** is from 160/100 to 179/109
- **Stage 3 (severe)** is from 180/110 to 209/119
- **Stage 4 (very severe)** is 210/120 and up

As these numbers climb higher, the condition becomes more serious. The diagnosis of hypertension can be based on either the systolic or the diastolic reading.

High blood pressure is a chronic disorder, which means it usually cannot be cured, but it can be controlled in a variety of ways, including lifestyle modifications and medication. Treatment should be at the direction and under the supervision of a physician.

# Allergies and Asthma

**Source:** Asthma and Allergy Foundation of America, Washington, DC

One out of every five Americans suffers from allergies. People with allergies have extra-sensitive immune systems which react to normally harmless substances. *Allergens* that sometimes produce this reaction include plant pollen, dust mites, or animal dander; plants such as poison ivy; certain drugs, such as penicillin; and certain foods such as eggs, milk, nuts, or seafood.

The tendency to develop a particular kind of allergy is inherited, and allergies usually begin to appear in childhood, but they can show up at any age. Common allergies for infants include food allergies and eczema (patches of dry skin). Older children and adults may often develop allergic rhinitis (hay fever), a reaction to an inhaled allergen; common symptoms include nasal congestion, runny nose, and sneezing.

The best course of action is to avoid contact with the allergen, but this is not always feasible. In some cases, drugs such as antihistamines are used to decrease the reaction, and there are treatments aimed at gradually desensitizing the patient. Other effective allergy treatments include decongestants, eye drops, and ointments.

Some people with allergies also have asthma, and allergens are a common asthma trigger. Asthma is a complex disease involving constriction of the passages that carry air into and out of the lungs. It is most often seen in children, but can develop at any age.

People with asthma have inflamed, supersensitive airways that tighten and become filled with mucus during an asthma episode. Wheezing, difficulty in breathing, painless tightening of the chest, and coughing are common symptoms. Asthma can progress through stages to become life-threatening if not controlled. Emergency symptoms of asthma include a bluish cast to the face and lips, severe anxiety, increased pulse rate, and sweating.

Besides common allergens, tobacco smoke, cold air, and air pollutants can trigger an asthma attack, as can respiratory infections or physical exercise that taxes the breathing. Of course, an accurate diagnosis by a physician is important. Besides avoidance of triggers, treatment for asthma includes preventive drugs and allergy immunotherapy, as well as bronchodilators and anti-inflammatory agents to better control the breathing.

# Where to Get Help

**Source:** Reprinted from Health & Medical Year Book 1996, "Where to Get Help," pp. 279-285.


Listed below are some of the major U.S. and Canadian organizations providing information about good health practices generally or about specific conditions and how to deal with them. (Canadian sources are identified as such.) Where a toll-free number is not available, an address is given when possible.

Some entries conclude with an address for the organization's Internet site, where you can also obtain useful information. When inputting an address, be certain to type it exactly as it appears, including capital and lowercase letters, nonalphanumeric characters, and spaces (generally none). In addition to these selected sites, there is a vast array of medical information on the Internet; however, it is very important to be certain that the source of information is reliable and accurate. Remember, always check with a physician before embarking on any new health-related ventures.

### General Sources

**Centers for Disease Control and Prevention Voice Information System**
404-332-4555
Tape-recorded information about public health topics, such as AIDS and Lyme disease. Also, you can request to talk with a CDC expert.
http://www.cdc.gov

**National Health Information Center**
800-336-4797; in Maryland, 301-565-4167
Phone numbers for more than 1,000 health-related organizations in the United States and offers printed materials.

**National Institutes of Health**
Bethesda, MD 20892
301-496-4000
Free information, including the latest research findings, on a wide range of diseases.
http://www.nih.gov

**Tel-Med**
Check the phone book for local listings or call Tel-Med headquarters at 909-825-6034
Tape-recorded information on over 600 health topics. Sponsored by local medical societies, health organizations, or hospitals.

### Aging

**National Association of Area Agencies on Aging's Eldercare Locator**
800-677-1116
Information and assistance on a wide range of services and programs including adult daycare and respite services, consumer fraud, hospital and nursing home information, legal services, elder abuse/protective services, Medicaid/Medigap information, tax assistance, and transportation.

**National Institute on Aging**
800-222-2225
Information and publications about disabling conditions, support groups, and community resources.

### AIDS

**AIDS Clinical Trials Information Service**
800-874-2572;
for the hearing impaired, 800-243-7012
Information on federally and privately sponsored clinical trials for patients with AIDS or HIV.

**Canadian AIDS Society**
800-499-1986
Written materials and referrals in the Toronto area.

**Centers for Disease Control and Prevention National AIDS Hotline**
800-342-AIDS 24 hours;
in Spanish, 800-344-SIDA;
for the hearing impaired, 800-AIDS-TTY
Information on the prevention and spread of AIDS, along with referrals.

**HIV-AIDS Treatment Information Service**
800-HIV-0440; to receive directions for accessing the service's computer data base, 800-272-4787.
Treatment information to people with AIDS, their families, and health care providers.

### Alcoholism and Drug Abuse

**Alcohol and Drug Helpline**
800-821-4357
Referrals to local facilities (24 hours).

**American Council on Alcoholism**
800-527-5344
Treatment referrals and counseling for recovering alcoholics.

**National Clearinghouse for Alcohol and Drug Information**
800-729-6686
Provides written materials on alcohol and drug-related subjects.
http://www.health.org

**National Cocaine Hotline**
800-COCAINE
Answers questions about cocaine and other drugs and provides referrals to treatment centers. Operates 24 hours.

**National Council on Alcoholism and Drug Dependence Hopeline**
800-622-2255
Information on alcoholism and drug dependence and counseling referrals (24 hours).

**National Drug Information, Treatment, and Referral Hotline**
800-662-HELP
Information on drug/alcohol abuse and on HIV/AIDS as they relate to substance abuse. Makes referrals to support groups and treatment programs.

### Alzheimer's Disease

**Alzheimer's Association**
800-621-0379
Referrals to local chapters and support groups; offers information on publications available from the association.
http://www.alz.org

**Alzheimer's Society of Canada**
1320 Yonge Street, Suite 201
Toronto, ON M4T 1X2
416-925-3552
Phone numbers for local support chapters. Publishes support materials.

### Amyotrophic Lateral Sclerosis

**ALS Association**
800-782-4747; in the San Fernando Valley, 818-340-7500
Information and educational materials about ALS (Lou Gehrig's Disease) and referrals to ALS specialists; also provides referrals to local chapters and support groups.

### Arthritis

**Arthritis Foundation**
800-283-7800
Information, publications, and referrals to local groups.
http://www.arthritis.org

**Arthritis Society (Canada)**
250 Bloor Street East, Suite 901
Toronto, ON M4W 3P2
416-967-1414; in Ontario only, 800-361-1112
Phone numbers for local chapters.

**National Arthritis and Musculoskeletal and Skin Diseases Information Clearinghouse**
301-495-4484
Subject searches and resource referrals.

### Asthma and Allergies
### See also *Lung Diseases*

**Allergy Foundation of Canada**
Box 1904, Saskatoon, SK S7K 3S5
306-373-7591
Information.

**Asthma and Allergy Foundation Information Clearinghouse**
800-7-ASTHMA
A free packet of information, on request.

**American Academy of Allergy and Immunology Referral Line**
800-822-ASMA
Written information on asthma and allergies. Operates 24 hours.

### Blindness and Eye Care

**Canadian National Institute for the Blind**
1929 Bayview Avenue
Toronto, ON M4G 3E8
416-480-7594 or contact your local chapter
The national office offers training and a library with braille books and audiotapes. Local chapters provide core services: orientation in mobility, sight enhancement, counseling, referrals, and career development.

**Foundation Fighting Blindness**
800-683-5555; in Maryland, 410-225-9400; for the hearing impaired, 800-683-5551
Answers questions; written materials.
http://blindness.org

**Library of Congress National Service for the Blind and Physically Handicapped**
800-424-9100; in Washington, DC, 202-707-5100
Information on libraries that offer talking books and books in braille.
http://lcweb.loc.gov/nls/nls.html

**National Association for Parents of the Visually Impaired**
800-562-6265
Support and information for parents of individuals who are visually impaired.

### Blood Disorders

**Cooley's Anemia Foundation**
800-522-7222
Information on patient care and support groups; makes referrals to local chapters.

**Sickle Cell Disease Association of America**
800-421-8453; in California, 310-216-6363
Genetic counseling and information packet.

### Burns

**Phoenix Society**
800-888-2876
Counseling for burn victims and information on self-help services for burn victims and their families.

### Cancer

**American Cancer Society**
800-ACS-2345
Publications and information about cancer and coping with cancer; makes referrals to local chapters for support services.
http://www.cancer.org

**Canadian Cancer Information Service**
800-263-6750
Written materials, videos, support services, and referrals.

**National Cancer Institute's Cancer Information Service**
800-4-CANCER
Information about clinical trials, treatments, and success rates for any type of cancer.
http://wwwicic.nci.nih.gov/occdocs/cis/cis.html

**Y-Me Breast Cancer Support Program**
800-221-2141; in Illinois, 312-986-8228, 24 hours
Information and literature on breast cancer, counseling, and referrals.
http://www.y-me.org

### Cerebral Palsy

**Ontario Federation for Cerebral Palsy**
1630 Lawrence Avenue West
Toronto, ON M6L 1C5
416-244-8003
Canada does not have a national cerebral palsy organization, but the provincial organizations (which provide information on housing, services, and coping with life) network and provide contact numbers for the others.

**United Cerebral Palsy Associations**
800-USA-5UCP;
in Washington, DC, 202-776-0406
Written materials.

### Child Abuse

**Childhelp's USA National Child Abuse Hotline**
800-4-A-CHILD
Crisis intervention, professional counseling, referrals to local groups offering counseling and to shelters for runaways, and literature in English and Spanish. Operates 24 hours.

**National Center for Missing and Exploited Children**
800-843-5678; for the hearing impaired, 800-826-7653
Hotline for reporting missing children and sightings of missing children.

### Chronic Fatigue Syndrome

**CFIDS Association of America**
800-442-3437
Literature and a list of support groups.

### Crisis

**National Runaway Switchboard**
800-621-4000
Crisis intervention and referrals for runaways. Runaways can leave messages for parents, and vice versa. Operates 24 hours.
**National Youth Crisis Hotline**
800-HIT-HOME
Counseling for youths dealing with drug abuse, pregnancy, molestation, suicide, and child abuse; makes referrals to local drug treatment centers, shelters, and counseling services. Operates 24 hours.

### Cystic Fibrosis

**Canadian Cystic Fibrosis Foundation**
416-485-9149; for long distance in Canada, 800-378-2233
Information and brochures, makes referrals to local chapters.
**Cystic Fibrosis Foundation**
800-FIGHT-CF
Answers questions and offers literature and referrals to local clinics.

### Diabetes

**American Diabetes Association**
800-ADA-DISC; in Virginia and Washington, DC, 703-549-1500
Information about diabetes, nutrition, exercise, and treatment and offers referrals to diabetes specialists.
http://www.diabetes.org
**Canadian Diabetes Association**
15 Toronto Street, Suite 800, Toronto, ON M5C 2E3
416-363-3373; in Ontario only, 800-361-1306
Information and publications.
http://www.diabetes.ca/cda
**Juvenile Diabetes Foundation Hotline**
800-223-1138 or 800-533-2873; in New York City, 212-889-7575
Answers questions, provides literature (some in Spanish), and offers referrals to local chapters, physicians, and clinics.

### Digestive Diseases

**Crohn's and Colitis Foundation of America**
800-343-3637; in New York, 212-685-3440
Educational materials; offer referrals to local chapters which then provide referrals to support groups and physicians.
**Crohn's Colitis Foundation of Canada**
21 St. Clair Avenue E, Suite 301, Toronto, ON M4T 1L9
416-920-5035; in Canada only, 800-387-1479
Educational materials.

### Disabilities

**National Association for the Craniofacially Handicapped**
800-332-2373; in Tennessee, 423-266-1632
Information on treatment centers, support groups, and financial assistance for individuals with severe facial deformities.
**National Information Center for Children and Youth With Disabilities**
800-695-0285
Information on how to improve the lives of children and youths with disabilities; referrals.
**National Information Clearinghouse for Infants With Life-Threatening Conditions and Severe Disabilities**
800-922-9234
Referrals to support groups and to sources of financial, medical, and legal assistance for developmentally disabled and chronically ill children, aged up to three.

### Domestic Violence

**National Council on Child Abuse and Family Violence**
800-222-2000; in Washington, DC, 202-429-6695
A recording provides 800 numbers to call for information or referrals.

### Down Syndrome

**National Down Syndrome Congress**
800-232-6372; in Georgia, 404-633-1555
Answers questions on all aspects of Down syndrome; referrals to local organizations.
**National Down Syndrome Society Hotline**
800-221-4602; in New York City, 212-460-9330
Information; referrals for local programs for newborns.
http://www.pcsltd.com/ndss

### Dyslexia

**Orton Dyslexia Society**
800-ABCD-123; in Maryland, 410-296-0232
Information on testing, tutoring, and computers used to aid people with dyslexia and related disorders.

### Eating Disorders

**National Association of Anorexia Nervosa and Associated Disorders**
Box 7, Highland Park, IL 60035
847-831-3438
Written materials, referrals, and telephone counseling.

### Endometriosis

**Endometriosis Association**
800-992-ENDO; in Canada, 800-426-2END
A packet of information (24 hours).

### Epilepsy

**Epilepsy Foundation of America**
800-332-1000
Information and referrals to local chapters.

### Food Safety and Nutrition

**Meat and Poultry Hotline of the U.S. Department of Agriculture's Food, Safety, and Inspection Service**
800-535-4555
Information on proper handling, preparation, storage, and cooking of meat, poultry, and eggs.
**Nutrition Hotline of the American Dietetic Association**
800-366-1655
General information on nutrition, answers questions, and provides literature.
**Seafood Hotline of the U.S.Food and Drug Administration (Department of Health and Human Services)**
800-FDA-4010; in Washington, DC, 202-205-4314
Information on how to buy and use seafood products and on their proper handling and storage. Callers may speak to food specialists, Mon. through Fri., 12 noon to 4 PM (EST).

### Grief

**Grief Recovery Helpline**
800-445-4808
Counseling services on coping with loss.

### Headaches

**National Headache Foundation**
800-843-2256
Literature on headaches and treatment.

### Head Injuries

**National Head Injury Foundation Family Helpline**
800-444-NHIF
Information on living with head injuries.

### Heart Disease and Stroke

**American Heart Association**
800-242-8721
Information, publications, and referrals to organizations.
http://www.amhrt.org
**Heart and Stroke Foundation of Canada**
477 Mount Pleasant Road, 4th Floor Toronto, ON M4S 2L9
416-489-7100 in Toronto; elsewhere contact your local chapter.
Written material and referrals.
**National Institute of Neurological Disorders and Stroke**
800-352-9424
Literature, information, and referrals.
**National Stroke Association**
800-787-6537
Information on support networks for stroke victims and their families; referrals.
http://www.stroke.org

### Hospices

**Children's Hospice International**
800-242-4453; in Virginia, 703-684-0330
Information; referrals to children's hospices.
**Hospice Education Institute Hospicelink**
800-331-1620
General information about hospice care and makes referrals to local programs.

### Huntington's Disease

**Huntington's Disease Society of America**
800-345-4372; in New York, 212-242-1968
Information and referrals to physicians and support groups.
**Huntington Society of Canada**
P.O. Box 1269,13 Water Street North, Suite 3, Cambridge, ON N1R 7G6
519-622-1002
Information, including telephone numbers of local services, and publications and referrals.

### Hysterectomy

**Hysterectomy Educational Resources/Services Foundation**
422 Bryn Mawr Avenue, Bala Cynwyd, PA 19004
610-667-7757
Peer support, referrals, telephone counseling, and written materials.

### Impotence

**Impotence Information Center**
800-843-4315
Information on the causes and treatment of impotence.
**Impotence Institute of America Hotline**
800-669-1603
Written materials, physician referrals, and telephone phone numbers of local Impotents Anonymous chapters.

### Kidney Diseases

**Kidney Foundation of Canada**
800-361-7494; in Ontario, 514-369-4806
Educational materials and general information.
**National Kidney and Urologic Diseases Information Clearinghouse**
3 Information Way
Bethesda, MD 20892-3580
301-654-4415
Information about kidney and urologic diseases and referrals to organizations.
http://www.niddk.nih.gov
**National Kidney Foundation**
800-622-9010
Information and referrals.

### Lead Exposure

**National Lead Information Center Hotline**
800-LEAD-FYI
Recommendations (in English and Spanish) for reducing a child's exposure to lead. Referrals to state and local agencies.
http://www.nsc.org/nsc/ehc/lead.html

### Liver Diseases

**American Liver Foundation**
800-223-0179; in New Jersey, 201-256-2550
Information and physician and support group referrals.
http://sadieo.ucsf.edu/alf/alffinal/homepagealf.html

### Lung Diseases

**See also *Asthma and Allergies***

**American Lung Association**
Check the phone book for local listings or call the national office at 800-LUNG-USA for automatic connection to the office nearest you. Answers questions about asthma and lung diseases; publications and referrals.
**National Jewish Center for Immunology and Respiratory Medicine Information Service**
800-222-LUNG; in Denver, 303-355-LUNG
Answers questions on asthma, emphysema, allergies, smoking, and other respiratory and immune system disorders.
http://www.njc.org/markethtml/NJCmore.html

### Lupus

**American Lupus Society Information Line**
800-331-1802
A packet of information. Operates 24 hours.

**Lupus Foundation of America**
800-558-0121;
in Rockville, MD, 301-670-9292
Answers questions; offers literature about lupus; refers to local affiliates.
http://internet-plaza.net/lupus/index.html

### Lyme Disease

**Lyme Disease Foundation**
800-886-LYME
Written information; referrals (24 hours).

### Mental Health

**Canadian Mental Health Association**
800-260-0999
Information; referrals to regional branches.
**D/ART (Depression awareness, recognition, and treatment)**
800-421-4211
Information on seasonal affective disorder and other depressive illnesses. Sponsored by the U.S. National Institute of Mental Health. Operates 24 hours.
http://www.nimh.nih.gov/publicat/eduprogs/dart.htm
**National Clearinghouse on Family Support and Children's Mental Health**
800-628-1696
Publications, computerized databank, and state-by-state resource file ( 24 hours).
**National Depressive and Manic Depressive Association**
800-826-3632
Support for patients and families, answers questions, provides publications, and makes referrals to affiliated organizations.
**National Foundation for Depressive Illness**
800-248-4344
Recorded message describing the symptoms of depression and offering an address for more information and physician referral (24 hours).
**National Institute of Mental Health**
5600 Fisher's Lane, Room 7C02
Rockville, MD 20857
301-443-4513
Information on a range of topics, from children's mental disorders to schizophrenia, depression, eating disorders, and others.
http://www.nimh.nih.gov
**National Mental Health Association**
800-969-6642
Referrals to mental health groups.

### Multiple Sclerosis

**Multiple Sclerosis Society of Canada**
800-268-7582
Counseling, literature, and referrals to local chapters.
**National Multiple Sclerosis Society**
800-344-4867
A 24-hour recording allows you to request information.
http://www.nmss.org

### Muscular Dystrophy

**Muscular Dystrophy Association**
800-572-1717
Written materials on 40 neuro-muscular diseases, including muscular dystrophy. Will give information over the phone about such matters as MDA clinics, support groups, summer camps, and wheelchair purchase assistance.

### Nutrition

See *Food Safety and Nutrition*

### Organ Donation

**Living Bank**
800-528-2971
A registry and referral service for people wanting to commit organs to transplantation or research. Operates 24 hours.
**Organ Donor Hotline**
800-24-DONOR
Information and referrals for organ donation and transplantation; handles requests for organ donor cards. Operates 24 hours.

### Osteoporosis

**National Osteoporosis Foundation**
800-223-9994
Free information packet available on request.
http://www.nof.org

### Pain

**National Chronic Pain Outreach Association**
7979 Old Georgetown Road, Suite 100
Bethesda, MD 20814-2429
301-652-4948
Information clearinghouse, makes referrals, and publishes newsletters.

### Parkinson's Disease

**National Parkinson Foundation**
800-327-4545; in Florida, 800-433-7022; in Miami, 305-547-6666
Answers questions, makes physician referrals, and provides written information in English and Spanish.
http://www.parkinson.org
**Parkinson's Educational Program**
800-344-7872
Written materials, information on support groups, and physician referrals (24 hours).
**Parkinson Foundation of Canada**
800-565-3000
Information; referrals to support groups.

### Plastic Surgery

**Plastic Surgery Information Service**
800-635-0635
Referrals to board-certified plastic surgeons in the U.S. and Canada; written materials on procedures and operations.

### Polio

**International Polio Network**
427 Lindell Blvd., #110
St. Louis, MO 63108
314-534-0475
Information on coping with the late effects of polio; referrals to other organizations.

### Prostate Problems

**Prostate Information Line**
800-543-9632
Advice on treatment.

### Rare Disorders

**National Organization for Rare Disorders**
800-999-6673
Information on diseases and networking programs; referrals to organizations for specific disorders.

### Rehabilitation

**National Rehabilitation Information Center**
800-34-NARIC; in Maryland, 301-588-9284
Information on rehabilitation and research on disabilities.
http://www.cais.net/naric

### Scleroderma

**United Scleroderma Foundation**
800-722-4673; in California, 408-728-2202
Referrals to local support groups and treatment centers, as well as information on scleroderma and related skin disorders.

### Sexually Transmitted Diseases

**American Social Health Association's National STD Hotline**
800-227-8922
Information; confidential referrals.

### Sjogren's Syndrome

**Sjogren's Syndrome Foundation**
800-4-SJOGREN
Provides an answering machine for callers to request treatment literature.

### Skin Problems

**National Psoriasis Foundation**
800-723-9166
Information and referrals.
http://www.psoriasis.org

### Speech and Hearing

**American Speech-Language-Hearing Association Helpline**
800-638-8255 (also TTY); in Maryland, 301-897-0039
Materials on speech and language disorders and hearing impairment; referrals.
**Canadian Hard of Hearing Association**
2435 Holly Lane, Suite 205
Ottawa, ON K1V 7P2
613-526-1584; TTY 613-526-2692; fax 613-526-4718
Publications; answers general questions.
**Dial a Hearing Screening Test**
800-222-EARS;
in Pennsylvania, 800-345-EARS
Answers questions on hearing problems and makes referrals to local telephone numbers for a two-minute hearing test. Also makes referrals to ear, nose, and throat specialists and to organizations that can provide specialized ear and hearing aid information.
**National Center for Stuttering**
800-221-2483
in New York State, 212-532-1460
Information on stuttering in all age groups.
**National Hearing Aid Helpline**
800-521-5247
Information and distributes a directory of hearing aid specialists certified by the International Hearing Society.
**Stuttering Foundation of America**
800-992-9392
Referrals to speech pathologists, resource lists, and other publications (24 hours).

### Spina Bifida

Spina Bifida Association of America
800-621-3141
Offers a package of information on spina bifida, a list of SBAA chapters, and a list of SBAA publications.

### Spinal Injuries

**American Paralysis Association**
800-526-3456
Written materials on spinal cord injuries; referrals to organizations and support groups.
http://teri.bio.uci.edu:80/apa
**National Spinal Cord Injury Association**
800-962-9629;
in Massachusetts, 617-441-8500
Peer counseling; referrals to local chapters and other organizations.

### Stroke

***see Heart Disease and Stroke***

### Sudden Infant Death Syndrome

**American Sudden Infant Death Syndrome Institute**
800-232-SIDS; in Georgia, 800-847-7437
Answers questions; literature; referrals to other organizations (24 hours).
**National SIDS Foundation**
800-221-SIDS; in Maryland, 410-653-8226
Literature on medical information, referrals, and support groups.

### Tourette Syndrome

**Tourette Syndrome Association**
800-237-0717; in New York, 718-224-2999
Printed information in either English or Spanish (24 hours).

### Urinary Incontinence

**Help for Incontinent People**
800-BLADDER
Information on bladder control, services available for incontinence, and assistive devices.
**Simon Foundation**
800-23-SIMON
Support and literature on incontinence.

### Women's Health

**National Women's Health Network**
514 10th Street NW, Suite 400
Washington, DC 20004
202-347-1140
Information and referrals on more than 70 women's health topics.
**National Women's Health Resource Center**
2425 L Street NW, Third Floor
Washington, DC 20037
202-293-6045
Information, primarily written materials.

# ASSOCIATIONS AND SOCIETIES

**Source:** World Almanac questionnaire

Selected list; arranged according to first important word in each title. Founding year of organization in parentheses; last figure after ZIP code indicates membership, as reported by the organization. See also Directory of Sports Organizations, under Sports; Where to Get Help directory, under Health; Labor Union Directory, under Employment.

**Aaron Burr Assn.** (1946), 4520 King Edward Ct., Annandale, VA 22003; 200.
**Abortion Federation, Natl.** (1977), 1436 U St. NW, Ste. 103, Wash., DC 20009; 350 organizations.
**Accountants, Amer. Institute of Certified Public** (1887), 1211 Ave. of the Americas, New York, NY 10036; 330,000.
**Accountants, Institute of Management** (1919), 10 Paragon Dr., Box 433, Montvale, NJ 07645; 85,000.
**Accountants, Natl. Assn. of Enrolled Federal Tax** (1960), PO Box 59-009, Chicago, IL 60659; 450.
**Accountants for Cooperatives, Natl. Soc. of** (1936), 6320 Augusta Dr., Ste. 800, Springfield, VA 22150; 2,000.
**Acoustical Society of America** (1929), 500 Sunnyside Blvd., Woodbury, NY 11797; 7,000.
**Actors' Equity Assn.** (1913), 165 W. 46th St., New York, NY 10036.
**Actors Guild, Screen** (1933), 5757 Wilshire Blvd., Los Angeles, CA 90036; 82,000.
**Actuaries, Society of** (1949), 475 N. Martingale Rd., Ste. 800, Schaumburg, IL 60173; 16,500.
**Advertisers, Assn. of Natl.** (1910), 155 E. 44th St., New York, NY 10017; 5,300.
**Advertising Agencies, Amer. Assn. of** (1917), 405 Lexington Ave., New York, New York 10174; 600 agencies.
**Aeronautic Assn., Natl.** (1905), 1815 N. Fort Myer Dr., Ste. 700, Arlington, VA 22209; 350,000.
**Aerospace Industries Assn. of America** (1919), 1250 Eye St. NW, Wash., DC 20005; 50 cos.
**African Violet Soc. of America** (1946), 2375 North, Beaumont, TX 77702; 12,000.
**Afro-American Life and History, Assn. for the Study of** (1915), 1407 14th St. NW, Wash., DC 20005; 2,000.
**Aging Assn., Amer.** (1970), 2129 Providence Ave., Chester, PA 19013; 400.
**Agricultural Economics Assn., Amer.** (1910), 1110 Buckeye Ave., Ames, IA 50010; 3,068.
**Agricultural History Society** (1919), Ste. 932, 1301 New York Ave. NW, Wash., DC 20005; 1,400.
**Agronomy, Amer. Society of** (1907), 677 S. Segoe Rd., Madison, WI 53711; 12,500.
**Aircraft Assn., Experimental** (1953), 3000 Poberezny Rd., PO Box 3086, Oshkosh, WI 54902; 152,000+.
**Aircraft Owners and Pilots Assn.** (1939), 421 Aviation Way, Frederick, MD 21701; 340,000.
**Air Force Assn.** (1946), 1501 Lee Hwy., Arlington, VA 22209.
**Air Force Gunners Assn.** (1986), 453 Plaza Circle, Bossier City, LA 71111; 1,700.
**Airline Pilots Assn.** (1931), 1625 Massachusetts Ave. NW, Wash., DC 20036; 41,000.
**Airmen, Assn. of Independent** (1989), 1625 Massachusetts Ave. NW, Wash., DC 20036; 3,000.
**Air & Waste Management Assn.** (1907), One Gateway Center, Pittsburgh, PA 15222; 17,000.
**Al-Anon Family Groups** (1951), 1600 Corporate Landing Parkway, Virginia Beach, VA 23454; 500,000 worldwide.
**Alcoholics Anonymous** (1935), 475 Riverside Dr., New York, NY 10115; 2 mil+.
**Alcoholism and Drug Dependence, Natl. Council on** (1944), 12 W. 21st St., New York, NY 10010.
**Alcohol Problems, Amer. Council on** (1895), 3426 Bridgeland Dr., Bridgeton, MO 63044; 36 state affiliates.
**Allergy, Asthma, and Immunology, Amer. Academy of** (1943), 611 E. Wells St., Milwaukee, WI 53202; 5,000.
**Alpha Delta Kappa Intl.** (1947), 1615 West 92d St., Kansas City, MO 64114; 60,000.
**Alpine Club, Amer.** (1902), 710 Tenth St., Ste. 100, Golden, CO 80401; 2,000+.
**Alzheimer's Assn.** (1980), 919 Michigan Ave., Chicago, IL 60611.
**Americares Foundation** (1982), 161 Cherry St., New Canaan, CT 06840.
**Amnesty Intl. USA** (1961), 322 8th Ave., New York, NY 10001.
**Amputation Foundation, Natl.** (1919), 73 Church St., Malverne, NY 11565; 1,500.
**Amusement Parks and Attractions, Intl. Assn. of** (1918), 1448 Duke St., Alexandria, VA 22314; 5,000.
**Animals, Amer. Society for Prevention of Cruelty to (ASPCA)** (1866), 424 E. 92d St., New York, NY 10128; 299,000.
**Animals, People for the Ethical Treatment of (PETA)** (1980), 501 Front St., Norfolk, VA 23510; 500,000.
**Animal Protection Institute of America** (1968), 2831 Fruitridge Rd., Sacramento, CA 95822; 65,000.
**Animal Welfare Institute** (1951), PO Box 3650, Wash., DC 20007; 15,000.
**Anthropological Assn., Amer.** (1902), 4350 N. Fairfax Dr., Ste. 640, Arlington, VA 22203; 10,505.
**Antiquarian Society, Amer.** (1812), 185 Salisbury St., Worcester, MA 01609; 558.
**Appalachian Mountain Club** (1907), 5 Joy St., Boston, MA 02108; 68,000.
**Appalachian Trail Conference** (1925), Washington & Jackson Sts., Harpers Ferry, WV 25425; 23,000.
**Appraisers, Amer. Society of** (1936), 555 Herndon Pkwy., Ste. 125, Herndon, VA 22070; 6,500.
**Arab Americans, Natl. Assn. of** (1972), 1212 New York Ave. NW, Wash., DC 20005.
**Arbitration Assn., Amer.** (1926), 140 W. 51st St., New York, NY 10020-1203; 13,000.
**Arc, The** (1950), 500 E. Border St., Ste. 300, Arlington, TX 76010; 140,000.
**Archaeological Institute of America** (1879), 656 Beacon St., 4th floor, Boston, MA 02215; 10,500.
**Archaeology, Institute of Nautical** (1972), PO Drawer HG, College Station, TX 77841; 1,300.
**Archery Assn., Natl.** (1879), One Olympic Plaza, Colorado Springs, CO 80909; 5,000.
**Architects, Amer. Institute of** (1857), 1735 New York Ave. NW, Wash., DC 20006; 55,000.
**Architectural Historians, Society of** (1940), 1365 North Astor St., Chicago, IL 60610; 4,000.
**Armed Forces Communications and Electronics Assn.** (1946), 4400 Fair Lakes Ct., Fairfax, VA 22033; 40,000.
**Army, Assn. of the United States** (1950), 2425 Wilson Blvd., Arlington, VA 22201; 117,000.
**Art Glass Suppliers Assn. Int'l,** (1986), 1100-H Brandywine Blvd., PO Box 2188, Zanesville, OH 43702; 383.
**Arthritis Foundation** (1948), 1314 Spring St. NW, Atlanta, GA 30309; 300,000.
**Arts, Amer. Council for the** (1960), One E. 53d St., New York, NY 10022; 1,500.
**Arts, Amer. Federation of** (1909), 41 E. 65th St., New York, NY 10021; 520+ museums/inst.
**Arts and Letters, American Academy of** (1898), 633 W. 155 St., New York, NY 10032; 250.
**Arts and Letters, Natl. Society of** (1944), 655 15th St. NW, Wash., DC 20005; 1,600.
**Arts and Sciences, Amer. Academy of** (1780), Norton's Woods, 136 Irving St., Cambridge, MA 02138; 633.
**Association Executives, Amer. Society of** (1920), 1575 I St. NW, Wash., DC 20005; 18,000.
**Astrologers, Inc., Amer. Federation of** (1938), PO Box 22040, Tempe, AZ 85285; 4,000.
**Astronautical Society, Amer.** (1954), 6352 Rolling Mill Pl., Ste. 102, Springfield, VA 22152; 1,400.
**Astronomical Society, Amer.** (1899), 2000 Florida Ave. NW, Ste. 400, Wash., DC 20009; 6,500.
**Ataxia Foundation, Natl.** (1957), 15500 Wayzata Blvd., Ste. 750, Wayzata, MN 55391; 8,000.
**Atheists, Amer.** (1963), PO Box 140195, Austin, TX 78714.
**Athletic Assn., Natl. Junior College** (1938), PO Box 7305, Colorado Springs, CO 80918; 520+.
**Athletic Associations, Natl. Federation of State H. S.** (1920), 11724 Plaza Circle, Box 20626, Kansas City, MO 64195.
**Athletics, Natl. Assn. of Intercollegiate** (1940), 6120 S. Yale Ave., Ste. 1450, Tulsa, OK 74136; 392 schools.
**Athletic Union of the U.S., Amateur** (1888), 3600 W. 86th St., Indianapolis, IN 46268; 300,000.
**Auctioneers Assn., Natl.** (1949), 8880 Ballentine, Overland Park, KS 66214; 5,600.
**Audubon Society, Natl.** (1905), 700 Broadway, New York, NY 10003; 550,000.
**Authors Guild, Inc., The** (1913), 330 W. 42d St., 29th Fl., New York, NY 10036; 6,500.
**Authors League of America** (1912), 234 W. 44th St., New York, NY 10036; 15,000.
**Authors Registry, The** (1995), 330 W. 42d St., 29th Floor, New York, NY 10036; 50,000.
**Autism Society of America** (1965), 7910 Woodmont Ave., Ste. 650, Bethesda, MD 20814; 19,000.
**Autograph Collectors Club, Universal** (1965), PO Box 6181, Wash., DC 20044; 2,100.
**Automobile Assn., Amer.** (1902), 1000 AAA Dr., Heathrow, FL 32746; 38 mil.
**Automobile Club of America, Antique** (1935), 501 W. Governor Rd., Hershey, PA 17033; 53,000.
**Automobile Dealers Assn., Natl.** (1917), 8400 Westpark Dr., McLean, VA 22102; 19,500.

**Automobile License Plate Collectors Assn.** (1954), PO Box 77, Horner, WV 26372; 2,500.
**Automotive Hall of Fame** (1939), 3225 Cook Rd., PO Box 1727, Midland, MI 48641; 1,500.

**Badminton Assn., U.S.** (1936), One Olympic Plaza, Colorado Springs, CO 80909; 2,500+.
**Baker Street Irregulars** (1934), 34 Pierson Ave., Norwood, NJ 07648; 300.
**Bald-Headed Men of America** (1973), 102 Bald Dr., Morehead City, NC 28557; 30,000.
**Ball Players of Amer., Assn. of Professional** (1924), 12062 Valley View St., Ste. 211, Garden Grove, CA 92645; 15,000+.
**Band & Choral Directors Hall of Fame, Natl.** (1985), 519 N. Halifax Ave., Daytona Beach, FL 32118.
**Bankers Assn., Amer.** (1875), 1120 Connecticut Ave. NW, Wash., DC 20036.
**Bankers Assn. of Amer., Independent** (1930), One Thomas Circle NW, Ste. 950, Wash., DC 20005; 5,800 banks.
**Bar Assn., Federal** (1920), 1815 H St. NW, Wash., DC 20006; 15,200.
**Barber Shop Quartet Singing in Amer., Inc., Soc. for the Preservation & Encouragement of** (1938), 6315 Third Ave., Kenosha, WI 53143; 34,000.
**Baseball Congress, Amer. Amateur** (1935), 118-119 Redfield Plaza, Marshall, MI 49068; 1,300 leagues.
**Baseball Congress, Natl.** (1931), PO Box 1420, Wichita, KS 67201; 1,000.
**Baseball Research, Society for Amer.** (1971), PO Box 93183, Cleveland, OH 44101; 6,500.
**Basketball Assn., Natl.** (1946), 645 Fifth Ave., New York, NY 10022.
**Battleship Assn., Amer.** (1964), PO Box 711247, San Diego, CA 92171; 1,350.
**Beer Can Collectors of America** (1970), 747 Merus Ct., Fenton, MO 63026; 4,100.
**Beta Gamma Sigma** (1913), 11701 Borman Dr., Ste. 320, St. Louis, MO 63146; 360,000.
**Beta Sigma Phi** (1931), 1800 W. 91st Pl., Kansas City, MO 64114; 210,000.
**Bible Society, Amer.** (1816), 1865 Broadway, New York, NY 10023; 280,000.
**Biblical Literature, Society of** (1880), 1549 Clairmont Rd., Ste. 204, Decatur, GA 30033; 6,000+.
**Bibliographical Society of America** (1904), PO Box 397, Grand Central Station, New York, NY 10163; 1,200.
**Big Brothers/Big Sisters of America** (1902), 230 N. 13th St., Philadelphia, PA 19107; 494 agencies.
**Biochemistry and Molecular Biology, Amer. Society for** (1906), 9650 Rockville Pike, Bethesda, MD 20814; 9,300.
**Biological Sciences, American Institute of** (1947), 730 11th St. NW, Wash., DC 20001; 5,000.
**Biology, Society for Integrative and Comparative** (1890), 401 N. Michigan Ave. Chicago, IL 60611; 2300.
**Black History Honors & Awards, Contemporary &** (1990), 6514 Georgia Rd., Birmingham, AL 35212; 152.
**Blind, Amer. Council of the** (1961), 1155 15th St. NW, Ste. 720, Wash., DC 20005; 40,000.
**Blind, Natl. Federation of the** (1940), 1800 Johnson St., Baltimore, MD 21230; 50,000.
**Blindness, Natl. Society to Prevent** (1908), 500 E. Remington Rd., Schaumburg, IL 60173; 26 affiliates.
**Blueberry Council, North Amer.** (1965), 4995 Golden Foothill Pkwy., Ste. 2, El Dorado Hills, CA 95762.
**B'nai B'rith Intl.** (1853), 1640 Rhode Island Ave. NW, Wash., DC 20036; 150,000.
**Boat Club, Chris Craft Antique** (1973), 217 S. Adams St., Tallahassee, FL 32301; 3,400.
**Boat Owners Assn. of the U.S.** (1966), 880 S. Pickett St., Alexandria, VA 22304; 500,000.
**Bookplate Collectors and Designers, Amer. Soc. of** (1922), 605 N. Stoneman Ave., #F, Alhambra, CA 91801; 200.
**Booksellers Assn., Amer.** (1900), 828 South Broadway, Tarrytown, NY 10591; 8,500.
**Bowling Congress, Amer.** (1895), 5301 S. 76th St., Greendale, WI 53129; 2.4 mil.
**Boy Scouts of America** (1910), 1325 Walnut Hill Lane, Irving, TX 75015; 3,471,043.
**Boys & Girls Clubs of America** (1906), 1230 W. Peachtree St. NW, Atlanta, GA 30309; 2 million+.
**Bread for the World, Inc.** (1974), 1100 Wayne Ave., Ste. 1000, Silver Spring, MD 20910; 44,000.
**Bridge, Tunnel & Turnpike Assn., Intl.** (1932), 2120 L St. NW, Ste. 305, Wash., DC 20037; 250 organizations.
**Broadcasters, Natl. Assn. of** (1922-23), 1771 N St. NW, Wash., DC 20036.
**Burroughs Bibliophiles, The** (1960), 454 Elaine Dr., Pittsburgh, PA 15236; 663.
**Business Bureaus, Council of Better** (1970), 4200 Wilson Blvd., Ste. 800, Arlington, VA 22203; 138 bureaus.
**Business Clubs, Amer. (AMBUCS)** (1922), 3315 N. Main St., High Point, NC 27265; 6,500.
**Business Communicators, Intl. Assn. of** (1970), One Hallidie Plaza, Ste. 600, San Francisco, CA 94102; 12,500.
**Business Education Assn., Natl.** (1946), 1906 Association Dr., Reston, VA 22091; 18,000.
**Business Women's Assn., American** (1949), 9100 Ward Pkwy., PO Box 8728, Kansas City, MO 64114; 80,000.
**Button Society, Natl.** (1938), 2733 Juno Pl., Akron, OH 44333; 4,400.
**Byron Society, The** (1971 in Eng., 1973 in U.S.), Dept. of English, Univ. of Delaware, Newark, DE 19716; 110 institutions.

**Campers and RVers, Family** (1949), 4804 Transit Rd., Bldg. 2, Depew, NY 14043; 56,000 families.
**Camp Fire Boys & Girls** (1910), 4601 Madison, Kansas City, MO 64112; 700,000.
**Camping Assn., Amer.** (1910), 5000 State Rd. 67 N., Martinsville, IN 46131; 5,400.
**Cancer Society, Amer.** (1913), 1599 Clifton Rd. NE, Atlanta, GA 30329.
**Carnegie Hero Fund Commission** (1904), 2307 Oliver Bldg., Pittsburgh, PA 15222; 21 members.
**Cartoonists Society, Natl.** (1946), Columbus Circle Station, PO Box 20267, New York, NY 10023; 630.
**Cat Fanciers' Assn.** (1906), PO Box 1005., Manasquan, NJ 08736; 664 clubs.
**Catholic Bishops, Natl. Conference of U.S.** (1966), 3211 4th St. NE, Wash., DC 20015.
**Catholic Church Extension Society** (1905), 35 E. Wacker Dr., #400, Chicago, IL 60601; 90,000.
**Catholic Daughters of the Americas** (1903), 10 W. 71st St., New York, NY 10023; 125,000.
**Catholic Educational Assn., Natl.** (1904), 1077 30th St. NW, Ste. 100, Wash., DC 20007; 18,353.
**Catholic Historical Soc., Amer.** (1884), 263 S. Fourth St., PO Box 84, Philadelphia, PA 19105; 750.
**Catholic Rural Life Conference, Natl.** (1923), 4625 Beaver Ave., Des Moines, IA 50310-2199; 4,000.
**Cemetery Assn., Amer.** (1887), 1895 Preston White Dr., #220, Reston, VA 22091; 2,200.
**Ceramic Society, Amer.** (1898), 735 Ceramic Place, Westerville, OH 43081; 13,000.
**Cerebral Palsy Assns., United** (1948), 1522 K St. NW, Ste. 1112, Wash., DC 20005; 155 affiliates.
**Chamber of Commerce of the U.S.A.** (1912), 1615 H St. NW, Wash., DC 20062; 215,000.
**Chamber Music Players, Inc., Amateur** (1969), 1123 Broadway, Rm. 304, New York, NY 10010; 4,200.
**Checker Federation, Amer.** (1948), 220 Lynn Ray Rd., PO Box 365, Petal, MS 39465; 1,000.
**Chemical Manufacturers Assn.** (1872), 1300 Wilson Blvd., Arlington, VA 22202; 185 cos.
**Chemical Society, Amer.** (1876), 1155 16th St. NW, Wash., DC 20036; 151,000.
**Chemists, Amer. Assn. of Cereal** (1914), 3340 Pilot Knob Rd., St. Paul, MN 55121; 4,000.
**Chemists, Amer. Society of Brewing** (1939), 3340 Pilot Knob Rd., St. Paul MN 55121; 840.
**Chess Federation, U.S.** (1949), 186 Rt. 9W, New Windsor, NY 12553; 84,327.
**Chess League of Amer., Correspondence** (1897), PO Box 3481, Barrington, IL 60011; 1,200.
**Childhood Education, Intl. Assn. for** (1892), 11501 Georgia Ave., Ste. 315, Wheaton, MD 20902; 11,194.
**Children, Natl. Center for Missing and Exploited** (1984), 2101 Wilson Blvd., #550, Arlington, VA 22201.
**Children and Adults, Natl. Assn. for Creative** (1974), 8080 Springvalley Dr., Cincinnati, OH 45236; 6,000.
**Children of the Amer. Revolution, Natl. Society of the** (1895), 1776 D St. NW, Wash., DC 20006.
**Children's Aid Society** (1853), 105 E. 22d St., New York, NY 10010; 1,207.
**Children's Book Council** (1945), 568 Broadway, Ste. 404, New York, NY 10012; 80 publishing houses.
**Child Welfare League of America** (1920), 440 First St. NW, Wash., DC 20001; 800+ agencies.
**Chiropractic Assn., Amer.** (1930), 1701 Clarendon Blvd., Arlington, VA 22209; 21,000.
**Christian Endeavor Union, The World's** (1895), 3575 Valley Rd., PO Box 820, Liberty Corner, NJ 07938.
**Christian Laity Counseling Board** (1970), 5901 Plainfield Dr., Charlotte, NC 28215; 38 mil.
**Christians and Jews, Natl. Conference of** (1927), 71 Fifth Ave., Ste. 1100, New York, NY 10003.

**Churches, U.S. Conference for the World Council of** (1948), 475 Riverside Dr., New York, NY 10115; 317 denominations.
**Church Federation, Ecumenical** (1982), 13014-270 N. Dalemabry, Tampa, FL 33618.
**Church Women United** (1941), 475 Riverside Dr., Rm. 812, New York, NY 10115.
**Cincinnati, Society of the** (1783), 2118 Massachusetts Ave. NW, Wash., DC 20008; 3,300.
**Circulation Managers Assn., Intl.** (1889), 11600 Sunrise Valley Dr., Reston, VA 22091; 1,705.
**Cities, Natl. League of** (1924), 1301 Pennsylvania Ave. NW, Wash., DC 20004; 1,449 cities.
**City/County Management Assn., Intl.** (1914), 777 N. Capitol St. NE, Ste. 500, Wash., DC 20002-4201.
**Civic League, Natl.** (1894), 1445 Market St., Ste. 300, Denver, CO 80202; 1,500.
**Civil Air Patrol** (1941), HQ CAP-USAF, Maxwell AFB, AL 36112; 63,000.
**Civil Liberties Union, Amer. (ACLU)** (1920), 132 W. 43d St., New York, NY 10036; 250,000.
**Civitan International** (1917), One Civitan Pl., Birmingham, AL 35213; 57,000.
**Classical League, Amer.** (1919), Miami Univ., Oxford, OH 45056; 3,604.
**CLU & CHFC, Amer. Soc. of** (1928), 270 S. Bryn Mawr Ave., Bryn Mawr, PA 19010; 36,000.
**Coal Association, Natl.** (1917), 1130 17th St. NW, Wash., DC 20036; 150 corporate members.
**Coaster Enthusiasts, American** (1978), PO Box 8226, Chicago, IL 60680; 4,700+.
**Codependents Anonymous** (1986), 5150 N. 16th St., Phoenix, AZ 85016.
**College Admission Counseling, Natl. Assn. for** (1937), 1631 Prince St., Alexandria, VA 22314; 5,926.
**College Board, The** (1900), 45 Columbus Ave., New York, NY 10023; 2,900 institutions.
**College Music Society** (1958), 202 W. Spruce St., Missoula, MT 59802; 4,000.
**Colleges, Amer. Assn. of Community and Jr.** (1921), One Dupont Circle NW, Ste. 410, Wash., DC 20036.
**Colleges and Employers, Natl. Assn. of** (1956), 62 Highland Ave., Bethlehem, PA 18017; 2,920.
**Colleges and Universities, Assn. of Amer.** (1915), 1818 R St. NW, Wash., DC 20009; 650 institutions.
**Colleges and Universities, Assn. of Intl.** (1973), 1301 S. Noland Rd., Independence, MO 64055; 8,729 ind., 26 inst.
**Collegiate Athletic Assn., Natl.** (1906), 6201 College Blvd., Overland Park, KS 66211; 1,200 institutions.
**Collegiate Schools of Business, Amer. Assembly of** (1916), 600 Emerson Rd. Ste. 300, St. Louis, MO 63141; 850 inst..
**Colonial Dames XVII Century, Natl. Society of** (1915), 1300 New Hampshire Ave. NW, Wash., DC 20036; 14,000.
**Colonial Wars, General Society of** (1892), 840 Woodbine Ave., Glendale, OH 45246; 4,300.
**Commerce, U.S. Junior Chamber of** (1915), 4 W. 21st St., Tulsa, OK 74114; 200,000.
**Commercial Collectors Assn., Amer.** (1970), 4040 W. 70th St., Minneapolis, MN 55431; 325.
**Commercial Law League of America** (1895), 150 N. Michigan, #600, Chicago, IL 60601; 4,500.
**Common Cause** (1970), 2030 M St. NW, Wash., DC 20036.
**Communication, Intl. Training in** (1938), 2519 Woodland Dr., Anaheim, CA 92801; 15,000.
**Communication Industry Assn., Personal** (1949), 500 Montgomery St., Ste. 700, Alexandria, VA 22314; 1,400.
**Communities, Federation of Egalitarian** (1976), E. Wind, Rt. 3, Box 6B2, Tecumseh, MO 65760; 250+.
**Community Cultural Center Assn., Amer.** (1978), 149 Cannongate III, Nashua, NH 03063.
**Composers, Authors & Publishers, Amer. Soc. of (ASCAP)** (1914), One Lincoln Plaza, New York, NY 10023; 24,000.
**Composers/USA, Natl. Assn. of (NACUSA)** (1932), PO Box 49256, Barrington Sta., Los Angeles, CA 90049; 600.
**Computer Professionals, Inst. for Certification of** (1973), 2200 E. Devon Ave., Ste. 247, Des Plaines, IL 60018; 6,000.
**Computing Machinery, Assn. for** (1947), 1515 Broadway, 17th Fl., New York, NY 10036; 85,000.
**Concrete Institute, Amer.** (1904), 22400 W. Seven Mile Rd., Detroit, MI 48219; 20,000.
**Conscientious Objectors, Central Committee for** (1948), 1515 Cherry St., Philadelphia, PA 19102.
**Constantian Society, The** (1970), 123 Orr Rd., Pittsburgh, PA 15241; 558.
**Construction Industry Manufacturers Assn.** (1911), 111 E. Wisconsin Ave., Milwaukee, WI 53202; 460 cos.
**Construction Specifications Institute** (1948), 601 Madison St., Alexandria, VA 22314; 17,298.
**Consulting Organizations, Council of** (1989), 521 5th Ave., New York, NY 10175.
**Consumer Credit Assn., Intl.** (1912), 243 N. Lindbergh Blvd., St. Louis, MO 63141; 20,000.
**Consumer Federation of America** (1968), 1424 16th St. NW, #604, Wash., DC 20036; 240 organizations.
**Consumer Interests, Amer. Council on** (1953), 240 Stanley Hall, Univ. of Missouri, Columbia, MO 65211; 1,300.
**Consumer Protection Institute** (1970), 5901 Plainfield Dr., Charlotte, NC 28215.
**Consumers Union of the U.S.** (1936), 101 Truman Ave., Yonkers, NY 10703; 405,990.
**Contract Bridge League, Amer.** (1938), 2990 Airways Blvd., Memphis, TN 38116; 180,000.
**Contractors of Amer., General** (1919), 1957 E St. NW, Wash., DC 20006; 32,000.
**Cooperative Business Assn., Natl.** (1916), 1401 New York Ave. NW, Ste. 1100, Wash., DC 20005; 540.
**Cooperative League of the U.S.A.** (1916), 1401 New York Ave. NW, Ste. 1100, Wash., DC 20005; 285 co-ops.
**Correctional Assn., Amer.** (1870), 4380 Forbes Blvd., Lanham, MD 20706; 20,000+.
**Correctional Officers, Intl. Assn. of** (1977), 8600 Glenarden Pkwy., Glenarden, MD 20706.
**Cosmetology Assn., Natl.** (1921), 3510 Olive St., St. Louis, MO 63103; 33,000.
**Cotton Council of America, Natl.** (1938), 1918 N. Parkway, Memphis, TN 38112.
**Counseling Assn., Amer.** (1952), 5999 Stevenson Ave., Alexandria, VA 22304; 55,738.
**Country Music Assn.** (1958), One Music Circle S, Nashville, TN 37203; 6,588.
**Crafts & Creative Industries, Assn. of (ACCI)** (1976), 1100-H Brandywine Blvd., PO Box 2188, Zanesville, OH 43702; 5,759.
**Credit Assn., Intl.** (1912), 243 N. Lindbergh Blvd., St. Louis, MO 63141; 7,100.
**Credit Union Natl. Assn. & Affiliates** (1934), 5710 Mineral Point Rd., Madison, WI 53705; 51 credit union leagues.
**Cribbage Congress, American** (1979), PO Box 10486, Napa, CA 94581; 6,800.
**Crime and Delinquency, Natl. Council on** (1907), 685 Market St., Ste. 620, San Francisco, CA 94105; 500.
**Criminology, Amer. Society of** (1941), 1314 Kinnear Rd., Ste. 212, Columbus, OH 43212; 2,600.
**Crop Protection Assn., American** (1933), 1156 15th St. NW, Ste. 900, Wash., DC 20005; 80 cos.
**Crop Science Society of America** (1955), 677 S. Segoe Rd., Madison, WI 53711; 4,450.
**Cryogenic Soc. of Amer.** (1964), 1033 South Blvd., Ste. 13, Oak Park, IL 60302; 2,550.
**Customs Brokers & Forwarders Assn. of America, Natl.** (1897), One W T C, Ste. 1153, New York, NY 10048; 612.
**Cystic Fibrosis Foundation** (1955), 6931 Arlington Rd., Bethesda, MD 20814.

**Dairy Council, Natl.** (1915), 6300 N. River Rd., Rosemont, IL 60018.
**Dairy and Food Industries Supply Assn.** (1917), 6245 Executive Blvd., Rockville, MD 20852; 800 cos.
**Dairy Goat Assn., American** (1904), 209 W. Main St., Spindale, NC 28160; 13,000.
**Danish Brotherhood in America** (1882), 3717 Harney St., Omaha, NE 68131; 8,600.
**Daughters of the American Revolution, Natl. Society** (1890), 1776 D St. NW, Wash., DC 20006; 190,000.
**Daughters of the British Empire in the U.S.A., Inc.** (1909), 800 Carrington Dr., Raleigh, NC 27615; 5,018.
**Daughters of the Confederacy, United** (1894), 328 North Blvd., Richmond, VA 23220; 24,000.
**Daughters of the Republic of Texas** (1891), 510 E. Anderson Ln., Austin, TX 78752; 7,400.
**Daughters of Union Veterans of the Civil War** (1885), 503 S. Walnut St., Springfield, IL 62704; 3,700.
**Deaf, Alexander Graham Bell Assn. for the** (1890), 3417 Volta Pl. NW, Wash., DC 20007.
**Deaf, Natl. Assn. of the** (1880), 814 Thayer Ave., Silver Spring, MD 20910; 22,000.
**Defense Preparedness Assn., Amer.** (1919), 2101 Wilson Blvd., Ste. 400, Arlington, VA 22201; 23,000.
**Delta Kappa Gamma Society Intl.** (1929), 416 W. 12th St., Austin, TX 78701; 165,000.
**Delta Mu Delta** (1913), PO Box 46935, St. Louis, MO 63146; 70,000.
**Deltiologists of America** (1960), PO Box 8, Norwood, PA 19074; 725.
**Democratic Natl. Committee** (1792), 430 S. Capitol St. SE, Wash., DC 20003; 432.
**DeMolay International** (1919), 10200 N. Executive Hills Blvd., Kansas City, MO 64153; 30,000.

**Dental Assn., Amer.** (1859), 211 E. Chicago Ave., Chicago, IL 60611; 140,000.
**Descendants of the Colonial Clergy, Society of the** (1933), 30 Leewood Rd., Wellesley, MA 02181; 1,024.
**Descendants of the Signers of the Declaration of Independence** (1907), 1986 Towhee La., Richmond, VA 23231; 990
**Descendants of Washington's Army at Valley Forge, Society of** (1976), PO Box 915, Valley Forge, PA 19482; 900.
**Desert Protective Council** (1954), PO Box 2312, Valley Center, CA 92082; 400.
**Diabetes Assn., Amer.** (1940), 1660 Duke St., Alexandria, VA 22314; 300,000.
**Dialect Society, Amer.** (1889), c/o Allan Metcalf, English Dept., MacMurray College, Jacksonville, IL 62650; 550.
**Digital Printing & Imaging Assn**. (1992), 10015 Main St., Fairfax, VA 22031; 600 cos.
**Directors Guild of America** (1936), 7920 Sunset Blvd., Los Angeles, CA 90046; 9,700.
**Disabled Collectors' Correspondence Club** (1991), PO Box 3113, Fremont, CA 94539.
**Disabled Sports USA** (1967), 451 Hungerford Dr., Ste. 100, Rockville, MD 20850; 20,000.
**Dogs International, Inc., Therapy** (1976), 6 Hilltop Rd., Mendham, NJ 07945; 4,000+
**Dogs on Stamps Study Unit** (1979), 3208 Hana Rd., Edison, NJ 08817; 400.
**Dollhouse Museum of the Southwest** (1981), 2208 Routh St., Dallas, TX 75201; 250.
**Dozenal Society of America** (1944), Math Dept., Nassau Community College, Garden City, NY 11530; 144.
**Dracula Society, Count** (1962), 334 W. 54th St., Los Angeles, CA 90037; 400.
**Drug, Chemical and Allied Trades Assn.** (1890), 2 Roosevelt Ave., Syosset, NY 11791; 2,018.
**Ducks Unlimited** (1937), One Waterfowl Way, Memphis, TN 38120; 500,000+.
**Dutch Settlers Soc. of Albany** (1924), 203 Holmes Dale, Albany, NY 12208; 300.

**Eaglehunters Intl.** (1994), PO Box 1539, Hernando, FL 34442; 500.
**Eagles, Fraternal Order of** (1898), 12660 W. Capitol Dr., Brookfield, WI 53055; 1.1 mil.
**Easter Seal Society, Natl.** (1938), 230 W. Monroe, Chicago, IL 60606.
**Eastern Star, General Grand Chapter, Order of the** (1876), 1618 New Hampshire Ave. NW, Wash., DC 20009; 1.5 mil.
**Economic Assn., Amer.** (1885), 2014 Broadway, Ste. 305, Nashville, TN 37203; 20,000.
**Edsel Club, Intl.** (1969), PO Box 371, Sully, IA 50251-0379; 1,090.
**Education, Amer. Council on** (1918), One Dupont Circle NW, #800, Wash., DC 20036; 1,800.
**Education, Council for Advancement & Support of** (1974), 11 Dupont Circle NW, Wash., DC 20036; 2,950 schools.
**Education, Institute of Intl.** (1919), 809 United Nations Plaza, New York, NY 10017; 650 U.S. colleges and universities.
**Education, Natl. Assn. for Family and Community** (1936), 5963 Jefferson St., Burlington, KY 41005; 45,000.
**Education Assn., National** (1857), 1201 16th St. NW, Wash., DC 20036; 2.2 mil.
**Educational Exchange, Council on Intl.** (1947), 205 E. 42d St., New York, NY 10017; 240 organizations.
**Educational Research Assn., Amer.** (1916), 1230 17th St. NW, Wash., DC 20036; 22,400.
**Education of Young Children, Natl. Assn. for the** (1926), 1509 16th St. NW, Wash., DC 20036; 95,000.
**Educators, Assn. of Intl. (NAFSA)** (1948), 1875 Connecticut Ave., Ste. 1000, Wash., DC 20009; 8,100.
**Educators for World Peace, International Assn. of** (1969), PO Box 3282, Mastin Lake Station, Huntsville, AL 35810; 25,000.
**8th Air Force Historical Society** (1975), PO Box 7215, St. Paul, MN 55107; 18,000.
**88th Infantry Division Assn., Inc.** (1948), PO Box 925, Havertown, PA 19083; 5,300.
**82d Airborne Division Assn., Inc.** (1946), NFCS, PO Box 9308, Fayetteville, NC 28311; 23,000 +.
**Electrical Manufacturers Assn., Natl.** (1926), 2101 L St. NW, Wash., DC 20037; 560 cos.
**Electrochemical Society** (1902), 10 S. Main St., Pennington, NJ 08534; 6,500.
**Electronic Circuits, The Institute for Interconnecting & Packaging** (1957), 7380 N. Lincoln, Lincolnwood, IL 60646; 1,900 cos.
**Electronic Industries Assn.** (1924), 2001 Pennsylvania Ave., Wash., DC 20006; 1,058 cos.
**Electronics Technicians, Intl. Society of Certified** (1970), 2708 W. Berry, Ft. Worth, TX 76109; 2,000.
**Electroplaters' and Surface Finishers' Society, Amer.** (1909), 12644 Research Pkwy., Orlando, FL 32826; 8,500.
**Elks of the U.S.A., Benevolent and Protective Order of** (1868), 2750 N. Lakeview Ave., Chicago, IL 60614; 1.5 mil.
**Elvis Presley Burning Love Fan Club** (1983), 1904 Williamsburg Dr., Streamwood, IL 60107; 1,500+.
**Energy Research Institute, Clean** (1974), Univ. of Miami, Coral Gables, FL, 33124; 120.
**Engineering, Natl. Academy of** (1964), 2101 Constitution Ave. NW, Wash., DC 20418; 1,800.
**Engineering, Soc. for the Advancement of Material & Process** (1944), P. O. Box 2459, Covina, CA 91722; 6,000.
**Engineering in Agricultural, Food, and Biological Systems, Society for** (1907), 2950 Niles Rd., St. Joseph, MI 49085; 8,000.
**Engineering Society of N. America, Illuminating** (1906), 120 Wall St., 17th Floor, New York, NY 10005; 10,000.
**Engineers, Amer. Inst. of Chemical** (1908), 345 E. 47th St., New York, NY 10017; 56,800.
**Engineers, Amer. Institute of Mining, Metallurgical and Petroleum** (1871), 345 E. 47th St., New York, NY 10017.
**Engineers, Amer. Soc. of Agricultural (ASAE)** (1907), 2950 Niles Rd., St. Joseph, MI 49085; 7,500.
**Engineers, Amer. Society of Civil** (1852), 345 E. 47th St., New York, NY 10017; 104,000.
**Engineers, Inc., Amer. Soc. of Heating, Refrigerating & Air Conditioning** (1894), 1791 Tullie Cir. NE, Atlanta, GA 30329; 50,000.
**Engineers, American Soc. of Mechanical** (1881), 345 E. 47th St., New York, NY 10017; 120,000.
**Engineers, Amer. Soc. of Safety** (1911), 1800 E. Oakton St., Des Plaines, IL 60018; 32,000.
**Engineers, Assn. of Conservation** (1961), 64 N. Union St., Rm. 479, Montgomery, AL 36104; 295
**Engineers, Assn. of Energy** (1977), 4025 Pleasantdale Rd., Ste. 420, Atlanta, GA 30340; 8,500.
**Engineers, Assn. of Iron and Steel** (1907), Three Gateway Center, Ste. 2350, Pittsburgh, PA 15222; 10,000.
**Engineers, Institute of Electrical and Electronics** (1884), 345 E. 47th St., New York, NY 10017; 320,000.
**Engineers, Institute of Industrial** (1948), 25 Technology Park, Norcross, GA 30092; 27,000.
**Engineers, Inst. of Transportation** (1930), 525 School St. SW, Ste. 410, Wash., DC 20024; 12,800.
**Engineers, Natl. Society of Professional** (1934), 1420 King St., Alexandria, VA 22314; 65,000.
**Engineers, Soc. of Fire Protection** (1950), One Liberty Sq., Boston, MA 02109; 4,150.
**Engineers, Soc. of Logistics** (1966), 8100 Professional Place, Ste. 211, New Carrollton, MD 20785; 5,200.
**Engineers, Soc. of Manufacturing** (1932), One SME Drive, Dearborn, MI 48121; 70,000.
**Engineers, Society of Mining** (1871), 8307 Shaffer Pkwy., Littleton, CO 80127; 23,058.
**Engineers, Soc. of Motion Picture & Television** (1916), 595 W. Hartsdale Ave., White Plains, NY 10607; 9,000+.
**Engineers, Society of Plastics** (1942), 14 Fairfield Dr., Brookfield, CT 06804; 37,500.
**Engineers, Society of Women** (1950), 120 Wall St., 11th Fl., New York, NY 10005; 16,500.
**English, U.S.** (1983), 818 Connecticut Ave. NW, Ste. 200, Wash., DC 20006; 611,000.
**English Assn., Inc., The College** (1938), English Dept., Winthrop Univ., Rock Hill, SC 29732; 741.
**English-Speaking Union of the U.S.** (1920), 16 E. 69th St., New York, NY 10021; 18,000.
**Entomological Society of America** (1950), 9301 Annapolis Rd., Lanham, MD 20706; 8,500.
**Environmental Health Assn., Natl.** (1937), 720 S. Colorado Blvd., Ste. 970, Denver, CO 80222; 5,500.
**Environmental Information Assn.** (1983), 1777 N.E. Expressway, Ste. 150, Atlanta, GA 30329; 2,000.
**Environmental Medicine, American Academy of** (1965), 4510 W. 89th St., Ste. 110, Prairie Village, KS 66207; 570.
**Epigraphic Society, Inc., The** (1974),8216 Labbe La., Vienna, VA 22182; 700.
**Esperanto League for North America** (1953), PO Box 1129, El Cerrito, CA 94530; 1,000+.
**Evangelism Crusades, Intl.** (1959), 14617 Victory Blvd., Van Nuys, CA 91411; 6,000.
**Exchange Club, Natl.** (1911), 3050 Central Ave., Toledo, OH 43606-1700; 35,500.

**Fairs & Expositions, Intl. Assn. of** (1919), PO Box 985, Springfield, MO 65801; 2,800.
**Family Relations, Natl. Council on** (1938), 3989 Central Ave. NE, Ste. 550, Minneapolis, MN 55421; 3,800.
**Family Service America** (1911), 11700 W. Lake Park Dr., Milwaukee, WI 53224; 290 agencies.

**Farm Bureau Federation, Amer.** (1919), 225 Touhy Ave., Park Ridge, IL 60068; 4 mil.
**Farmers of America Org., Natl. Future** (1928), 5632 Mt. Vernon Memorial Hwy., Alexandria, VA 22309; 443,428.
**Farmers Educational & Co-operative Union of Amer.** (1902), 10065 E. Harvard Ave., Denver, CO 80231; 250,000.
**Farmers Union, Natl.** (1902), Denver, CO 80251; 250,000.
**Fat Acceptance, Natl. Assn. to Advance (NAAFA)** (1969), PO Box 188620, Sacramento, CA 95818; 5,000.
**Federal Employees, Natl. Fed. of** (1917), 1016 16th St. NW, Wash., DC 20036; 150,000.
**Feminists for Life of America** (1972), 733 15th St. NW, Wash., DC 20005; 5,000.
**Financial Analysts Federation** (1945), 5 Boar's Head Lane, Charlottesville, VA 22903; 22,700.
**Financial Executives Institute** (1938), 10 Madison Ave., PO Box 1938, Morristown, NJ 07962; 14,000.
**Financial Women Intl.,** (1921), 200 North Globe Rd., Ste. 814, Arlington, VA 22203; 10,000.
**Financiers, Intl. Society of** (1979), PO Box 18508, Asheville, NC 28814; 300.
**Fire Chiefs, Intl. Assn. of** (1873), 4025 Fair Ridge Dr., Fairfax, VA 22033; 10,000+.
**Fire Protection Assn., Natl.** (1896), One Batterymarch Park, Quincy, MA 02269; 65,000.
**First Amendment Studies, Institute for** (1984), 187 Main St., Great Barrington, MA 01230.
**Fish Assn., Intl. Game** (1939), 1301 E. Atlantic Blvd., Pompano Beach, FL 33060; 20,000.
**Fisheries Soc., American** (1870), 5410 Grosvenor Lane, Ste. 110, Bethesda, MD 20814; 10,000.
**Fishes, Soc. for the Protection of Old** (1967), School of Fisheries, 357980, Univ. of Washington, Seattle, WA 98195.
**Flag Research Center, The** (1962), Box 580, Winchester, MA 01890; 1,300.
**Flight Attendants, Assn. of** (1973), 1625 Massachusetts Ave. NW, Wash., DC 20036; 28,000.
**Fly Fishers, Fed. of** (1965), 502 S. 19th, Ste. 1, Bozeman, MT 59715; 11,000.
**Flying Disc Federation, World** (1985), Gnejsvägen 24, 85357, Sundsvall, Sweden; 15,000.
**Food Institute, Amer. Frozen** (1942), 2000 Corporate Ridge, Ste. 1000, McLean, VA 22102; 540 firms.
**Food Technologists, Institute of** (1939), 221 N. LaSalle, Ste. 300, Chicago, IL 60601; 28,000.
**Footwear Industries Assn., Amer.** (1869), 1420 K St. NW, Wash., DC 20005; 156 cos.
**Foreign Student Affairs, Natl. Assn. for** (1948), 1875 Connecticut Ave., Ste. 1000, Wash., DC 20009; 6,800.
**Foreign Study, Amer. Institute for** (1964), 102 Greenwich Ave., Greenwich, CT 06830; 300,000.
**Foreign Trade Council, Inc., Natl.** (1914), 1625 K St. NW, Wash., DC 20006; 500 cos.
**Forensic Sciences, Amer. Academy of** (1948), 410 N. 21st St., Ste. 203, Colorado Springs, CO 80901; 4,500.
**Foresters, Society of Amer.** (1900), 5400 Grosvenor La., Bethesda, MD 20814; 18,800.
**Forest History Society** (1946), 701 Vickers Ave., Durham, NC 27701; 1,200.
**Forest & Paper Assn., Amer.** (1993), 1111 19th St. NW, Wash., DC 20036; 400 cos.
**Forest Products Society** (1947), 2801 Marshall Ct., Madison, WI 53705; 3,300.
**Forestry Assn., Amer.** (1875), 1516 P St. NW, Wash., DC 20005; 150,000.
**Forests, Amer.** (1875), 1516 P St. NW, Wash., DC 20005; 60,000.
***Forrestal* CVA/CV/AVT-59 Assn., Inc., USS** (1991), 300 Cassady Ave., Virginia Beach, VA 23452; 1,106.
**Fortean Organization, Intl.** (1965), PO Box 367, Arlington, VA 22210; 60.
**Founders and Patriots of Amer., The Order of the** (1896), 3892 College Ave., Ellicott City, MD 21043; 1,250.
**Foundrymen's Society, Amer.** (1896), 505 State St., Des Plaines, IL 60016; 14,000.
**4-H Clubs** (1901-1905), Extension Service, U.S. Dept of Agriculture, Wash., DC 20250; 5.8 mil.
**458th Service Squadron Assn.-WWII** (1991) 2114 W. 29th St., Erie, PA 16508; 83.
**Frederick A. Cook Society, The** (1940), PO Box 11421, Pittsburgh, PA 15238; 238.
**Freedom of Information Center** (1958), 127 Neff Annex, Univ. of Missouri, Columbia, MO 65211.
**Freedom, Inc., Legion for the Survival of** (1952), PO Box 2739, Newport Beach, CA 92659.
**Freedoms Foundation at Valley Forge** (1949), Rt. 23, PO Box 706, Valley Forge, PA 19482; 4,800.
**French Institute/Alliance Française** (1898), 22 E. 60th St., New York, NY 10022; 7,000.
**Friendship and Good Will, Intl. Soc. of** (1978), 9538 Summerville St., Spring Valley, CA 91977; 4,218.
**Funeral & Memorial Societies of America** (1963), P. O. Box 10, Hinesburg, VT 05461; 600,000.

**Gamblers Anonymous** (1957), PO Box 17173, Los Angeles, CA 90017.
**Garden Club of Amer.** (1913), 598 Madison Ave., New York, NY 10022; 15,000.
**Garden Clubs, Natl. Council of State** (1929), 4401 Magnolia Ave., St. Louis, MO 63110; 308,623.
**Gas Appliance Manufacturers Assn.** (1935), 1901 N. Moore St., Arlington, VA 22209; 205 cos.
**Gas Assn., Amer.** (1918), 1515 Wilson Blvd., Arlington, VA 22209; 229 cos.; 3,000 individuals.
**Gay and Lesbian Task Force, Natl.** (1973), 2320 17th St. NW, Wash., DC 20009; 35,000.
**Genealogical Society, Natl.** (1903), 4527 17th St. N, Arlington, VA 22207; 15,000.
**Genetic Assn., Amer.** (1905), PO Box 39, Buckeystown, MD 21717; 750.
**Geographers, Assn. of Amer.** (1904), 1710 16th St. NW, Wash., DC 20009; 7,400.
**Geographical Society, Amer.** (1851), 156 Fifth Ave., Ste. 600, New York, NY 10010; 1,400+.
**Geographic Education, Natl. Council for** (1915), 16A Leonard Hall, IUP, Indiana, PA 15705; 2,400.
**Geographic Society, Natl.** (1888), 1145 17th St. NW, Wash., DC 20036; 9.7 mil.
**Geological Society of America** (1888), 3300 Penrose Pl., PO Box 9140, Boulder, CO 80301; 14,400.
**Geologists, Amer. Assn. of Petroleum** (1917), 1444 S. Boulder, Tulsa, OK 74119; 31,961.
**Geophysicists, Society of Exploration** (1930), PO Box 702740, Tulsa, OK 74170; 14,500.
**George S. Patton, Jr. Historical Society, The** (1970), 3116 Thorn St., San Diego, CA 92104; 25.
**Geriatrics Society, Amer.** (1942), 770 Lexington Ave., Ste. 300, New York, NY 10021; 6,000.
**Gideons Intl.** (1899), 2900 Lebanon Rd., Nashville, TN 37214; 131,000.
**Gifted Children, Natl. Assn. for** (1954), 1707 L St. NW, Ste. 550, Wash., DC 20005; 7,000.
**Girl Scouts of the U.S.A.** (1912), 420 5th Ave., New York, NY 10018; 3.5 mil.
**Girls Incorporated** (1945), 30 E. 33d St., New York, NY 10016; 250,000.
**Golf Association, U.S.** (1894), Golf House, PO Box 708, Far Hills, NJ 07931; 8,631 clubs.
**Gospel Music Assn.** (1964), 1205 Division St., Nashville, TN 37203; 5,500.
**Government Finance Officers Assn.** (1906), 180 N. Michigan Ave., Ste. 800, Chicago, IL 60601; 13,600.
**Graduate Schools, Council of** (1960), One Dupont Circle NW, #430 Wash., DC 20036; 415 institutions.
**Grandmothers Clubs of America, Natl. Federation of** (1938), 313 E. Liberty St., Wauconda, IL 60084; 6000.
**Graphic Arts, Amer. Institute of** (1914), 1059 Third Ave., New York, NY 10021; 6,000.
**Gray Panthers** (1970), PO Box 21477, Wash., DC 20009; 40,000.
**Green Mountain Club, The** (1910), RR1, Box 650, Rt. 100 Waterbury Ctr., VT 05677; 6,500.
**Grocers Association, Nat'l.** (1984), 1825 Samuel Morse Dr., Reston, VA 22090; 2,500.
**Grocery Manufacturers of America** (1908), 1010 Wisconsin Ave., Ste. 800, Wash., DC 20007; 140 cos.
**Guide Dog Foundation for the Blind** (1946), 371 E. Jericho Tpk., Smithtown, NY 11787-2976.
**Gyro Intl.** (1912), 1096 Mentor Ave., Painesville, OH 44077.

**Hadassah, the Women's Zionist Organization of America** (1912), 50 W. 58th St., New York, NY 10019; 385,000.
**Hairdressers and Cosmetologists Assn., Natl.** (1921), 3510 Olive St., St. Louis, MO 63103; 50,406.
**Handball Assn., U.S.** (1951), 2333 N. Tucson Blvd., Tucson, AZ 85716; 9,200.
**Handicapped, Federation of the** (1935), 211 W. 14th St., New York, NY 10011; 650.
**Handicapped, Natl. Assn. of the Physically** (1958), NAPH Business Office, Bethesda Scarlet Oaks, 440 Lafayette Ave., #GA4, Cincinnati, OH 45220; 800.
**Health, Physical Education, Recreation and Dance, Amer. Alliance for** (1885), 1900 Association Dr., Reston, VA 22091.
**Health Council, Natl.** (1920), 1730 M St. NW, Ste. 500, Wash., DC 20036.
**Health Info. Management Assn., American** (1928), 919 N. Michigan Ave., #1400, Chicago, IL 60611; 35,000.

**Healthcare Planning and Marketing, Soc. for** (1978), One N. Franklin, Chicago, IL 60606; 4,000.
**Hearing Society, Intl.** (1951), 20361 Middlebelt Rd., Livonia, MI 48152; 3,000.
**Hearing and Speech Action, Natl. Assn. for** (1910), 10801 Rockville Pike, Rockville, MD 20852.
**Heart Assn., Amer.** (1924), 7272 Greenville Ave., Dallas, TX 75231.
**Hearts, Mended** (1951), 7320 Greenville Ave., Dallas, TX 75231; 20,000.
**Hebrew Immigrant Aid Society (HIAS)** (1880), 333 7th Ave., 17th Floor, New York, NY 10001.
**Helicopter Assn. Intl.** (1948), 1635 Prince St., Alexandria, VA 22314; 1,800.
**Helicopter Society, Amer.** (1943), 217 N. Washington St., Alexandria, VA 22314; 6,140.
**Hemispheric Affairs, Council on** (1975), 724 9th St. NW, Wash., DC 20001; 2,200.
**Highpointers Club** (1987), PO Box 70, Arcadia, MO 63621; 1,150.
**High School Assns., Natl. Federation of State** (1920), PO Box 20626, Kansas City, MO 64195; 51 state assns.
**High Twelve International.** (1921), 11155 B2 South Towne Square, St. Louis, MO 63123; 25,000.
**Hiking Society, Amer.** (1976), PO Box 20160, Wash., DC 20041; 5,500.
**Historians, Organization of Amer.** (1907), 112 N. Bryan St., Bloomington, IN 47408; 9,200.
**Historical Assn., Amer.** (1884), 400 A St. SE, Wash., DC 20003; 16,000.
**Historic Preservation, Natl. Trust for** (1949), 1785 Massachusetts Ave. NW, Wash., DC 20036; 250,000.
**History, Amer. Assn. for State & Local** (1940), 530 Church St., Ste. 600, Nashville, TN 37219; 5,000.
**Hockey, U.S.A.** (1937), 4965 N. 30th St., Colorado Springs, CO 80919; 300,000.
**Home Builders, Natl. Assn. of** (1942), 1201 15th St. NW, Wash., DC 20005; 157,000.
**Home Economics Assn., Amer.** (1909), 1555 King St., Alexandria, VA 22314; 20,000.
**Homemakers of America, Future** (1945), 1910 Association Dr., Reston, VA 22091; 281,000+.
**Honor Society, Natl.** (1921), 1904 Association Dr., Reston, VA 22091; 21,000.
**Horatio Alger Soc.** (1961), 585 St. Andrews Dr., Media, PA 19063; 250.
**Horse Council, Inc., American** (1969), 1700 K St. NW, #300, Wash., DC 20006; 2,000 members, 200 org.
**Horse Protection Assn., Amer.** (1966), 1000 29th St. NW, Ste. T-100, Wash., DC 20007; 8,000.
**Horse Shows Assn., Amer.** (1917), 220 E. 42d St., New York, NY 10017; 63,000.
**Hospital Association, Amer.** (1899), 1 N. Franklin, Chicago, IL 60606; 5,100 hospitals.
**Hospital Marketing and Public Relations, Amer. Society for** (1964), 840 N. Lake Shore Dr., Chicago, IL 60611; 3,167.
**Hostelling Intl., American Youth Hostels** (1934), 733 15th Street NW, Ste. 840, Wash., DC 20005; 125,000.
**Hotel & Motel Assn., Amer.** (1910), 1201 New York Ave. NW, Wash., DC 20005; 10,000+.
**Hot Rod Assn., Natl.** (1951), 2035 Financial Way, Glendora, CA 91741; 85,000.
**Humane Society of the U.S.** (1954), 2100 L St. NW, Wash., DC 20037; 650,000.
**Human Resource Management, Society for** (1948), 606 N. Washington St., Alexandria, VA 22314.
**Husbandry, Natl. Grange of the Order of Patrons of** (1867), 1616 H St. NW, Wash., DC 20006; 28,000.
**Hybrid & Alternative Vehicle Society** (1994), 3301 N. Belaire Dr., Altadena, CA 91001; 5,000.
**Hydrogen Energy, Intl. Assn. for** (1975), PO Box 248266, Coral Gables, FL 33124; 2,500.

***Idaho* Assn., U.S.S. (BB-42)** (1957), PO Box 711247, San Diego, CA 92171; 528.
**Identification, Intl. Assn. for** (1915), PO Box 2423, Alameda, CA 94501; 4,100.
**Illustrators, Inc., Society of** (1901), 128 E. 63d St., New York, NY 10021; 850.
**Impotence Inst. of Amer.** (1983), 2020 Pennsylvania Ave. NW, Ste. 292, Wash., DC 20006.
**Industrial Designers Society of America** (1965), 1142-E Walker Rd., Great Falls, VA 22066; 2,350.
**Industrial Health Foundation** (1935), 34 Penn Circle W, Pittsburgh, PA 15206; 170 cos.
**Industrial Security, Amer. Soc. for** (1955), 1655 N. Ft. Myer Dr., Ste. 1200, Arlington, VA 22209; 24,000.
**Information and Image Management, Assn. for** (1943), 1100 Wayne Ave., Ste. 1100, Silver Spring, MD 20910; 11,000.
**Information Industry Assn.** (1968), 1625 Massachusetts Ave. NW, Ste. 700, Wash., DC 20036; 550 cos.
**Inner Network, The** (1991), 300 Darby Hill Rd., RD #1, Delanson, NY 12053; 452.
**Insurance Assn., Amer.** (1964), 1130 Connecticut Ave. NW, Ste. 1000, Wash., DC 20036; 250+ cos.
**Insurance Society, Inc., Intl.** (1965), Univ. of Alabama, Rm. 445, Alston Hall, Tuscaloosa, AL 35487; 1,200.
**Intellectual Property Owners** (1972), 1255 23d St. NW, #850, Wash., DC 20037; 725.
**Intelligence Officers, Assn. of Former** (1975), 6723 Whittier Ave., Ste. 303A, McLean, VA 22101; 2,700.
**Intercultural Programs, Intl.** (1947), 220 E. 42d St., New York, NY 10017; 475,000.
**Interior Designers, Amer. Society of** (1975), 608 Massachusetts Ave. NE, Wash., DC 20002; 30,500.
**Inventors, Amer. Assn. of** (1891), 2020 Pennsylvania Ave. NW, Wash., DC 20006; 5,727.
**Investment Clubs, Natl. Assn. of** (1951), 1515 E. Eleven Mile Rd., Royal Oak, MI 48067; 140,000.
**Investment Management and Research, Assn. for** (1990), 5 Boar's Head La., Charlottesville, VA 22901; 27,400.
**Investors Corp., Natl. Assn. of** (1951), 711 W. Thirteen Mile Rd., Madison Heights, MI 48068 410,000.
**Irish-American Cultural Inst.** (1962), 1 Lackawanna Pl., Morristown, NJ 07960; 4,000.
**Irish Historical Society, American-** (1897), 991 5th Ave., New York, NY 10028; 750.
**Iron Castings Society** (1897), 455 State St., Des Plaines, IL 60016; 200 firms.
**Iron and Steel Institute, Amer.** (1855), 1101 17th St. NW, Ste. 1300, Wash., DC 20036; 1,100.
**Italian Historical Society of America** (1949), 111 Columbia Heights, Brooklyn, NY 11201.
**Izaak Walton League of America, The** (1922), 1401 Wilson Blvd., Level B, Arlington, VA 22209; 53,000.

**Jail Assn., Amer.** (1982), 2053 Day Rd., Ste. 100, Hagerstown, MD 21740; 5,000.
**Jane Austen Society of North Amer.** (1979), 207 Pinecroft Dr., Raleigh, NC 27609; 3,100.
**Japanese Amer. Citizens League** (1929), 1765 Sutter St., San Francisco, CA 94115; 22,295.
**Jewish Book Council** (1946), 15 E. 26th St., New York, NY 10010.
**Jewish Committee, Amer.** (1906), 165 E. 56th St., New York, NY 10022; 50,000.
**Jewish Community Centers Assn.** (1917), 15 E. 26th St., New York, NY 10010.
**Jewish Congress, Amer.** (1918), 15 E. 84th St., New York, NY 10028; 50,000.
**Jewish Federations, Council of** (1932), 730 Broadway, New York, NY 10003; 200 agencies.
**Jewish Historical Society, Amer.** (1892), 2 Thornton Rd., Waltham, MA 02154; 4,000.
**Jewish Women, Natl. Council of** (1893), 53 W. 23d St., 6th Floor, New York, NY 10010; 90,000.
**Job's Daughters, Intl. Order of** (1920), 233 W. 6th St., Papillion, NE 68046; 21,000.
**Jockey Club** (1894), 40 E. 52d St., New York, NY 10022; 90.
**John Birch Society** (1958), 770 Westhill Blvd, PO Box 8040, Appleton, WI 54913; about 50,000.
**Joseph Diseases Foundation, Intl.** (1977), 4047 First St., Ste. 107, Livermore, CA 94550; 1,800.
**Journalists, Society of Professional** (1909), 16 South Jackson St., Greencastle, IN 46135; 14,000.
**Journalists and Authors, Amer. Society of** (1948), 1501 Broadway, Ste. 302, New York, NY 10036; 900.
**Judaism, Amer. Council for** (1943), PO Box 9009, Alexandria, VA 22304.
**Judicature Society, Amer.** (1913), 25 E. Washington, Chicago, IL 60602; 20,000.
**Jugglers Assn., Intl.** (1947), 11 School St., PO Box 218, Montague, MA 01351; 3,500.
**Junior Achievement** (1919), One Education Way, Colorado Springs, CO 80906; 300,000.
**Junior Auxiliaries, Natl. Assn. of** (1941), 845 S. Main St., Greenville, MS 38701; 11,500.
**Junior Leagues, Assn. of** (1921), 660 First Ave., New York, NY 10016; 190,000.

**Kennel Club, Amer.** (1884), 51 Madison Ave., New York, NY 10010; 500+ clubs.
**Kidney Fund, Amer.** (1971), 6110 Executive Blvd., Ste. 1010, Rockville, MD 20852.
**Kiwanis International** (1915), 3636 Woodview Trace, Indianapolis, IN 46268; 325,000.
**Knights of Columbus** (1882), One Columbus Plaza, New Haven, CT 06510; 1,560,633.

**Knights of Pythias** (1864), 2785 E. Desert Inn Rd., Ste. 150, Las Vegas, NV 89121; 70,000.
**Knights Templar U.S.A., Grand Encampment** (1816), 5097 N. Elston, Ste. 101, Chicago, IL 60630.
**Krishna Consciousness, Intl. Soc. for (ISKON)** (1966), 3764 Watseka Ave., Los Angeles, CA 92109.

**La Leche League Intl.** (1956), 1400 N. Meacham Rd., Schaumburg, IL 60173; 50,000+
**Labor Party of America** (1996), 295 Auburn Pkwy., Athens, GA 30606; 51.
**Lambs, The** (1874), 3 W. 51st St., New York, NY 10019; 200.
**Landscape Architects, Amer. Society of** (1899), 4401 Connecticut Ave. NW, Wash., DC 20008; 11,500.
**Language Assn. of America, Modern** (1883), 10 Astor Pl., New York, NY 10003; 32,000.
**Language Teachers Assns., Natl. Federation of Modern** (1916), Gannon Univ., Erie, PA 16541; 7,200.
**Laurel & Hardy Appreciation Soc., Sons of the Desert** (1965), PO Box 8341, Universal City, CA 91608; 10,000.
**Law, Amer. Society of Intl.** (1906), 2223 Massachusetts Ave. NW, Wash., DC 20008; 4,400.
**Law Libraries, Amer. Assn. of** (1906), 53 W. Jackson Blvd., #940, Chicago, IL 60604; 5,000.
***LCI* National Assn., U.S.S.** (1991), 134 Lancaster Ave., Columbia, PA 17512; 2,880.
**Learned Societies, Amer. Council of** (1919), 228 E. 45th St., New York, NY 10017; 56 societies.
**Lefthanders Intl.** (1975), PO Box 8249, Topeka, KS 66608.
**Legal Administrators, Assn. of** (1971), 175 E. Hawthorn Pkwy., #325, Vernon Hills, IL 60061; 8,000.
**Legion, The American** (1919), PO Box 1055, Indianapolis, IN 46206; 2.9 mil.
**Legion Auxiliary, The American** (1919), 777 N. Meridian St., Indianapolis, IN 46204; 1 mil.
**Legion of Valor of the U.S.A.** (1890), 92 Oak Leaf Lane, Chapel Hill, NC 27516; 800.
**Leif Ericson Society** (1926), 128 Asbury Ave., Ste. 103, Evanston, IL 60202; 999.
**Leprosy Missions, Amer.** (1906), One Alm Way, Greenville, SC 29601.
**Leukemia Society of America** (1949), 600 Third Ave., New York, NY 10016.
**Lewis and Clark Trail Heritage Foundation, Inc.** (1969), PO Box 3434, Great Falls, MT 59403; 1,600.
**Lewis Carroll Society of N. America** (1974), 1655 34th St. NW, Wash., DC 20007; 370.
**Libertarian Party, The** (1971), 2600 Virginia Ave. NW, Ste. 100, Wash., DC 20037; 123,000.
**Liberty Library** (1955), 300 Independence Ave. SE, Wash., DC 20003; 20,000.
**Libraries Assn., Special** (1909), 1700 18th St. NW, Wash., DC 20009; 15,000.
**Library Assn., American** (1876), 50 E. Huron St., Chicago, IL 60611; 57,000.
**Library Assn., American Theological** (1947), 820 Church St., Ste. 300, Evanston, IL 60201; 188 libraries.
**Library Assn., Medical** (1898), 6 N. Michigan Ave., Ste. 300, Chicago, IL 60602; 5,000.
**Life Insurance, Amer. Council of** (1976), 1001 Pennsylvania Ave. NW, Wash., DC 20004; 616 firms.
**Lighter Than Air Society** (1952), 1436 Triplett Blvd., Akron, OH 44306; 1,600.
**Lions Clubs, Intl Assn. of** (1917), 300 22d St., Oak Brook, IL 60521-8842; 1,425,000.
**Liquid Crystal Soc., Intl.** (1965), Liquid Crystal Institute, Kent State Univ., Kent, OH 44242; 1,000.
**Linguistic Society of America**, (1924), 1325 18th St. NW, Ste. 211, Wash., DC 20036; 6,500.
**Literacy Volunteers of America** (1962), 5795 Widewaters Pkwy., Syracuse, NY 13214.
**Little League Baseball, Inc.** (1939), PO Box 3485, Rt. 15, S. Williamsport, PA 17701; 3 mil. players.
**Little People of America** (1957), PO Box 9897, Wash., DC 20016; 3,000.
**London Club** (1975), Rt. 1, Lecompton, KS 66050; 100+.
**Lung Assn., Amer.** (1904), 1740 Broadway, New York, NY 10019.
**Lutheran Education Assn.** (1942), 7400 Augusta St., River Forest, IL 60305; 3,800.

**Magazine Publishers of America** (1919), 919 Third Ave., New York, NY 10022; 1,200 titles.
**Magicians, Intl. Brotherhood of** (1922), PO Box 192090, Saint Louis, MO 63119; 14,000.
**Magicians, Society of Amer.** (1902), PO Box 510260, St. Louis, MO 63151; 5,500.
**Management Assn., Amer.** (1923), 135 W. 50th St., New York, NY 10020; 70,000.
**Management Consulting Firms, The Assn. of** (1929), 521 5th Ave., 35th Fl., New York, NY 10175; 50 firms.
**Manufacturers, Natl. Assn. of** (1895), 1331 Pennsylvania Ave. NW, Ste. 1500 N. Tower, Wash., DC 20004; 14,000 cos.
**Manufacturers' Agents Natl. Assn.** (1947), 23016 Mill Creek Rd., Laguna Hills, CA 92654; 7,000.
**March of Dimes Birth Defects Foundation** (1938), 1275 Mamaroneck Ave., White Plains, NY 10605; 2 mil+.
**Marine Corps League** (1937), PO Box 3070, Merrifield, VA 22116; 42,000.
**Marine Manufacturers Assn., Natl.** (1904), 401 N. Michigan Ave., Chicago, IL 60611; 1,650 cos.
**Marketing Assn., Amer.** (1934), 250 S. Wacker Dr., Chicago, IL 60606; 40,000.
**Marketing Assn., Inc., Direct** (1917), 1120 Ave. of the Americas, New York, NY 10036; 3,500.
**Masonic Relief Assn. of U.S. and Canada** (1889), 3827 Canal St., New Orleans, LA 70119.
**Masons, Royal Arch, General Grand Chapter** (1798), PO Box 589, 451 Main St., Danville, KY 40422; 250,000.
**Masons, Supreme Council 33°, Ancient and Accepted Scottish Rite, Northern Masonic Jurisdiction** (1813), PO Box 519, 33 Marrett Rd., Lexington, MA 02173; 345,257; **Southern Jurisdiction** (1801), PO Box 3467, 1733 16th St. NW, Wash., DC 20009; 478,747.
**Mathematical Society, Amer.** (1888), 201 Charles St., Providence, RI 02904; 30,000.
**Mathematical Statistics, Institute of** (1935), 3401 Investment Blvd., Ste. 7, Hayward, CA 94545; 4,000.
**Mathematics, Society for Industrial and Applied** (1952), 3600 Univ. Science Ctr., Philadelphia, PA 19104; 9,300.
**Mayflower Descendants, General Society of** (1897), 4 Winslow St., PO Box 3297, Plymouth, MA 02361; 30,000+.
**Mayors, U.S. Conference of** (1932), 1620 I St. NW, Wash., DC 20006.
**Mechanics, Amer. Academy of** (1969), Dept. of Civil Engineering, Northwestern Univ., Evanston, IL 60201; 1,200.
**Medical Assn., Aerospace** (1929), 320 S. Henry St., Alexandria, VA 22314; 3,600.
**Medical Assn., American** (1847), 515 N. State St., Chicago, IL 60610; 300,000.
**Medical Assn., Natl.** (1895), 1012 Tenth St. NW, Wash., DC 20001; 22,000.
**Medical Record Assn., Amer.** (1928), 919 N. Michigan Ave., Chicago, IL 60611; 31,000.
**Medieval Academy of America** (1925), 1430 Massachusetts Ave., Cambridge, MA 02138; 4,400.
**Men, Natl. Coalition of Free** (1977), PO Box 129, Manhasset, NY 11030.
**Mensa, Ltd., Amer.**, (1960), 201 Main St., Ste. 1101, Fort Worth, TX 76102.
**Mental Health Assn., Natl.** (1909), 1021 Prince St., Alexandria, VA 22314; 325 affiliates.
**Mental Health Program Directors, Natl. Assn. of State** (1959), 66 Canal Ctr. Plaza, Ste. 302, Alexandria, VA 22314; 55.
**Mentally Ill, Natl. Alliance for the** (1980), 200 North Glebe Rd., Arlington, VA 22203; 140,000.
**Merrill's Marauders Assn.** (1946), 11244 N. 33d St., Phoenix, AZ 85028; 1,689.
**Metallurgy Institute Intl., Amer. Powder** (1959), 105 College Rd. East, Princeton, NJ 08540; 2,831.
**Metal Powder Industries Federation** (1944), 105 College Rd. East, Princeton, NJ 08540; 235 cos.
**Metals International (ASM), Amer. Society for** (1913), 9639 Kinsman Rd., Materials Park, OH 44073; 47,000.
**Meteorological Society, Amer.** (1920), 45 Beacon St., Boston, MA 02108; 11,000.
**Metric Assn., U.S.** (1916), 10245 Andasol Ave., Northridge, CA 91325; 1,200.
**Microbiology, Amer. Society for** (1899), 1325 Massachusetts Ave. NW, Wash., DC 20005; 43,000.
**Mideast Educational & Training Services, Amer.** (1951), 1730 M St. NW, Ste. 1100, Wash., DC 20036; 190 institutions.
**Military Order of the Loyal Legion of the U.S.** (1865), 1805 Pine St., Philadelphia, PA 19103; 930.
**Military Order of the Purple Heart of the USA** (1932), 5413-B Backlick Rd., Springfield, VA 22151; 30,000.
**Military Order of the World Wars** (1920), 435 N. Lee St., Alexandria, VA 22314; 13,000.
**Miniatures Industry Association of America (MIAA)** (1979), 1100-H Brandywine Blvd., PO Box 2188, Zanesville, OH 43702; 365.
**Mining, Metallurgy and Exploration, Inc., Society for** (1871), PO Box 625002, Littleton, CO 80162; 17,000.
**Ministerial Assn., Amer.** (1929), 2210 Wilshire Blvd., Ste. 582, Santa Monica, CA 90403; 1,000+.

**Model Railroad Assn., Natl.** (1935), 4121 Cromwell Rd., Chattanooga, TN 37421; 25,000.
**Molecular Plant-Microbe Interactions, Int'l. Society for** (1990), 3340 Pilot Knob Rd., St. Paul, MN 55121; 538.
**Moose Intl., Inc.** (1988), Mooseheart, IL 60539; 1.8 mil.
**Mothers, Amer., Gold Star** (1928), 2128 Leroy Pl. NW, Wash., DC 20008; 2,500.
**Mothers, Amer. War** (1925), 2615 Woodley Pl. NW, Wash., DC 20008; 1,200.
**Mothers, Inc.®, American** (1935), 301 Park Ave., New York, NY 10022; 9,000.
**Mothers of Twins Clubs, Natl. Organization of** (1960), PO Box 23188, Albuquerque, NM 87192; 14,000.
**Motion Picture Arts & Sciences, Academy of** (1927), 8949 Wilshire Blvd., Beverly Hills, CA 90211; 5,900.
**Motion Pictures, Natl. Board of Review of** (1909), PO Box 589, Lenox Hill Sta., New York, NY 10021.
**Motorcyclist Assn., American** (1924), 33 Collegeview Rd., Westerville, OH 43081; 200,000.
**Motor Fire Apparatus in Amer., Soc. for the Preservation & Appreciation of Antique** (1958), PO Box 2005, Syracuse, NY 13220; 3,000.
**Motor Vehicle Manufacturers Assn.** (1903), 7430 2d Ave., Ste. 300, Detroit, MI 48202; 7 cos.
**Multiple Sclerosis Society, Natl.** (1945), 733 Third Ave., New York, NY 10017; 400,000.
**Muscular Dystrophy Assn.** (1950), 3300 E. Sunrise Dr., Tucson, AZ 85718.
**Museums, Amer. Assn. of** (1906), 1225 I St. NW, Ste. 200, Wash., DC 20005; 12,000.
**Music Center, Amer.** (1939), 30 W. 26th St., New York, NY 10010.
**Music Educators Natl. Conference** (1907), 1806 Robert Fulton Dr., Reston, VA 22091; 65,000+.
**Musicological Society, Amer.** (1934), 201 S. 34th St., Philadelphia, PA 19104; 5,000.
**Music Scholarship Assn., Amer.** (1956), The Carew Tower, 441 Vine St., Ste. 1030, Cincinnati, OH 45202.
**Music Teachers Natl. Assn.** (1876), The Carew Tower, 441 Vine St., Ste. 505, Cincinnati, OH 45202; 24,000.
**Muzzle Loading Rifle Assn., Natl.** (1933), PO Box 67, Friendship, IN 47021; 25,000.
**Myasthenia Gravis Foundation of America, The** (1952), 222 S. Riverside Plaza, Ste. 1540, Chicago, IL 60606; 30,000.
**Mystery Writers of Amer.** (1945), 17 E. 47th St., 6th Fl., New York, NY 10017; 2,600.

**NA'AMAT USA** (1925), 200 Madison Ave., New York, NY 10016; 50,000.
**Narcotics Anonymous** (1953), PO Box 9999, Van Nuys, CA 91409; 270,000.
**Natl. Assn. for the Advancement of Colored People (NAACP)** (1909), 4805 Mt. Hope Dr., Baltimore, MD 21215.
**National Guard Assn. of the U.S.** (1878), One Massachusetts Ave. NW, Wash., DC 20001; 56,000.
**Nature Conservancy** (1951), 1815 N. Lynn St., Arlington, VA 22209; 692,000.
**Naturist Society, The** (1980), 454 Main St., Oshkosh, WI 54901; 20,000.
**Naval Architects & Marine Engineers, The Society of** (1893), 601 Pavonia Ave., Ste. 400, Jersey City, NJ 07306; 10,000.
**Naval Beach Group One Assn., Inc.** (1993) 804 N. Main, Washburn, Il 61570; 560.
**Naval Engineers, Soc. of** (1888), 1452 Duke St., Alexandria, VA 22314; 6,200.
**Naval Institute, U.S.** (1873), 118 Maryland Ave., Annapolis, MD 21402; 85,000.
**Naval Reserve Assn.** (1954), 1619 King St., Alexandria, VA 22314; 25,000.
**Navigation, Institute of** (1945), 1800 Diagonal Rd., Ste. 480, Alexandria, VA 22314; 3,000.
**Navy League of the U.S.** (1902), 2300 Wilson Blvd., Arlington, VA 22201; 71,308.
**Needlework Guild of America** (1885), 1007-B Street Rd., Southampton, PA 18966; 75,000.
**Negro College Fund, United** (1944), 500 E. 62d St., New York, NY 10021; 41 institutions.
**New Age Walkers** (1982), 3301 Bellaire Dr., Altadena, CA 91001; 4,700.
**Newspaper Assn. of Amer. (NAA)** (1992), The Newspaper Center, 11600 Sunrise Valley Dr., Reston, VA 22091; 1,800.
**Newspaper Marketing Assn., Intl.** (1930), 11600 Sunrise Valley Dr., Reston, VA 22071; 1,532.
**Newswomen's Club of New York, Inc.** (1922), 15 Gramercy Park S., New York, NY 10011; 230.
**Nikola Tesla Walkers** (1982), 10799 Sherman Grove Ave., #18, Sunland, CA 91040; 5,000.
**Ninety-Nines (Intl. Organization of Women Pilots)** (1929), Box 965, Will Rogers Airport, Oklahoma City, OK 73159; 6,400.
**Nobel Center, Amer.** (1941), 1 Morningside Dr. N., Westport, CT 06880; 195.
**Non-Commissioned Officers Assn.** (1960), 10635 IH 35 North, San Antonio, TX 78233; 160,000.
**Northern Cross Society** (1986), Rt. One, Big Springs, KS 66050; 100+.
**Notaries, Amer. Society of** (1965), PO Box 5707, Tallahassee, FL 32314; 19,200.
**Nuclear Society, Amer.** (1954), 555 N. Kensington Ave., La Grange Park, IL 60525; 16,000.
**Nude Recreation, Amer. Assn. for** (1931), 1703 N. Main St., Kissimmee, FL 34744; 45,000.
**Numismatic Assn., Amer.** (1891), 818 N. Cascade Ave., Colorado Springs, CO 80903; 25,000.
**Numismatic Society, Amer.** (1858), Broadway at 155th St., New York, NY 10032; 2,000.
**Nurses Assn., Amer.** (1896), 600 Maryland Ave. SW, Ste. 100, Wash., DC 20024; 200,000.
**Nursing, Natl. League for** (1952), 350 Hudson St., New York, NY 10014; 16,000.
**Nutrition, Amer. Institute of** (1928), 9650 Rockville Pike, Bethesda, MD 20814; 3,500.

**Odd Fellows, Independent Order of** (1819), 422 Trade St., Winston-Salem, NC 27101; 350,000.
**Old Crows, Assn. of** (1964), 1000 N. Payne St., Alexandria, VA 22314; 25,000.
**Olympic Committee, U.S.** (1921), One Olympic Plaza, Colorado Springs, CO 80909.
**Opthalmology, Amer. Academy of** (1979), 655 Beach St., San Francisco, CA 94109; 21,000.
**Optical Society of America** (1917), 2010 Massachusetts Ave. NW, Wash., DC 20036; 11,000.
**Optimist Intl.** (1919), 4494 Lindell Blvd., St. Louis, MO 63108; 150,000.
**Optometric Assn., Amer.** (1898), 243 N. Lindbergh Blvd., St. Louis, MO 63141; 31,000+.
**Organists, Amer. Guild of** (1896), 475 Riverside Dr., Ste. 1260, New York, NY 10115; 20,200.
**Oriental Society, Amer.** (1842), 329 Sterling Memorial Library, Yale Sta., New Haven, CT 06520; 1,500.
**ORT Federation, Amer. (Org. for Rehabilitation through Training)** (1924), 817 Broadway, 10th Fl., New York, NY 10003; 20,000.
**Ornithologists' Union, Amer.** (1883), c/o Division of Birds, MRC-116, Smithsonian Institution, Wash., DC 20560; 4,500.
**Osteopathic Assn., Amer.** (1887), 212 E. Ohio St., Chicago, IL 60611; 23,292.
**Ostomy Assn., United** (1962), 36 Executive Park, Ste. 120, Irving, CA 92714, 35,500.
**Outlaw and Lawman History, Natl. Association for** (1974), 1201 Holly Ct., Harker Heights, TX 76548; 475.

**Paper Industry, Technical Assn. of the Pulp and** (1915), 15 Technology Pkwy. S/Atlanta, Norcross, GA 30092; 33,000.
**Parametric Analysts, Intl. Soc. of** (1979), PO Box 1056, Germantown, MD 20878; 600.
**Parents Without Partners** (1957), 401 N. Michigan Ave., Chicago, IL 60611; 70,000.
**Parkinson's Disease Foundation, Inc.** (1957), 710 W. 168th St., New York, NY 10032; 95,000.
**Parliamentarians, Natl. Assn. of** (1930), 213 S. Main St., Independence, MO 64050; 4,292.
**Parliamentary Law, Intl. Organization of Professionals in** (1975), 3611 Victoria Ave., Los Angeles, CA 90016; 250.
**Pasta Assn., Natl.** (1904), 2101 Wilson Blvd., Ste. 920, Arlington, VA 22201; 82 cos.
**Pathologists, Amer. Assn. of** (1976), 9650 Rockville Pike, Bethesda, MD 20814; 2,000.
**Pathologists, Amer. Society of Clinical** (1922), 2100 W. Harrison St., Chicago, IL 60612; 70,000.
**Pathology, Inc., Amer. Soc. for Investigative** (1900), 9650 Rockville Pike, Bethesda, MD 20814; 2,300.
**Pearl Harbor History Associates, Inc.** (1983), PO Box 25432, Seattle, WA 98125; 385.
**PEN American Center** (1922), 568 Broadway, New York, NY 10012; 2,800.
**Pen Friends, Intl.** (1967), PO Box 65, Brooklyn, NY 11229; 300,000.
**PEN Women, Natl. League of American** (1897), 1300 17th St. NW, Wash., DC 20036; 5,000.
**P.E.O. (Philanthropic Educational Organization) Sisterhood** (1869), 3700 Grand Ave., Des Moines, IA 50312; 242,000.
**Personnel Administration, Amer. Society for** (1948), 606 N. Washington St., Alexandria, VA 22314; 40,000.
**Petroleum Equipment Inst.** (1951), 6514 E. 69 St., Tulsa, OK 74133; 1,755 cos.
**Petroleum Institute, Amer.** (1919), 1220 L St. NW, Wash., DC 20005; 250 corporations.

**Pharmaceutical Assn., Amer.** (1852), 2215 Constitution Ave. NW, Wash., DC 20037; 48,000.
**Phi Delta Kappa** (1906), 408 N. Union, PO Box 789, Bloomington, IN 47402; 172,000.
**Philatelic Pages & Panels, Amer. Soc. for** (1984), 4116 Kilmer Ave., Allentown, PA 18104; 950.
**Philatelic Society, Amer.** (1886), 100 Oakwood Ave., PO Box 8000, State College, PA 16803; 56,000.
**Philological Assn., Amer.** (1869), Dept. of Classics, College of the Holy Cross, Worcester, MA 01610; 3,300.
**Philosophical Assn., Amer.** (1900), 31 Amstell Ave., Univ. of Delaware, Newark, DE 19716; 10,000.
**Philosophical Enquiry, Intl. Soc. For** (1974), 5409 Pipers Gap Dr., Memphis, TN 38134; 700+.
**Philosophical Society, Amer.** (1743), 104 S. 5th St., Philadelphia, PA 19106; 690.
**Photogrammetry and Remote Sensing, Amer. Society of** (1934), 5410 Grosvenor Ln., Ste. 210, Bethesda, MD 20814.
**Photographers of America, Professional** (1880), 57 Forsyth St. NW, Ste. 1600, Atlanta, GA 30303; 14,000.
**Photographic Society of Amer.** (1934), 3000 United Founders Blvd., #103, Oklahoma City, OK 73112.
**Physical Therapy Assn., Amer.** (1921), 1111 N. Fairfax St., Alexandria, VA 22314; 70,000.
**Physicians, Amer. Academy of Family** (1947), 8880 Ward Pkwy., Kansas City, MO 64114; 81,964.
**Physics, Amer. Inst. of** (1931), One Physics Ellipse, College Park, MD 20740; 100,000.
**Physiological Society, Amer.** (1887), 9650 Rockville Pike, Bethesda, MD 20814; 8,300.
**Phytopathological Society, Amer.**, (1909), 3340 Pilot Knob Rd., St. Paul, MN 55121; 5,500.
**Pilgrim Society** (1820), 75 Court St., Plymouth, MA 02360-3891; 900.
**Pilot Intl. & Pilot Intl. Foundation** (1921, 1975), PO Box 4844, Macon, GA 31208; 17,172.
**Planetary Society** (1980), 65 N. Catalina Ave., Pasadena, CA 91106; 100,000.
**Planned Parenthood Federation of America** (1916), 810 Seventh Ave., New York, NY 10019; 187 affiliates.
**Plastic Modelers Society, Intl.** (1963), PO Box 6138, Warner Robins, GA 31095; 4,750.
**Plastics Industry, Inc., Society of the** (1937), 1275 K St. NW, Ste. 400, Wash., DC 20005; 2,000.
**Platform Assn., Intl.** (1830), Box 250, Winnetka, IL 60093; 5,000.
**Poetry Day Committee, Natl.** (1947), 1110 N. Venetian Dr., Miami, FL 33139; 17,500.
**Poetry Society of America** (1910), 15 Gramercy Park, New York, NY 10003; 3,000.
**Poets, Academy of Amer.** (1934), 584 Broadway, Ste. 1208, New York, NY 10012; 4,220.
**Police, International Assn. of Chiefs of** (1893), 515 N. Washington St., #400, Alexandria, VA 22314; 13,920.
**Polish Cultural Society of America** (1940), PO Box 31, Wall St., New York, NY 10005; 116,911.
**Political Items Collectors, Amer.** (1945), PO Box 340339, San Antonio, TX 78234; 3,200.
**Political Science, Academy of** (1880), 475 Riverside Dr., Ste. 1274, New York, NY 10115; 7,000.
**Political Science Assn., Amer.** (1903), 1527 New Hampshire Ave. NW, Wash., DC 20036; 16,200.
**Political Science Assn., Southern** (1939), Dept. of Political Science, Univ. of Mississippi, University, MS 38677; 1,200.
**Political & Social Science, Amer. Academy of** (1889), 3937 Chestnut St., Philadelphia, PA 19104; 5,000.
**Polo Assn., U.S.** (1890), 4059 Iron Works Pike, Lexington, KY, 40511; 3,000.
**Population Assn. of America** (1931), 721 Ellsworth Dr., Ste. 303, Silver Spring, MD 20910.
**Portuguese-American Federation, Inc.** (1974), PO Box 694, Bristol, RI 02809; 220.
**Portuguese Continental Union of the U.S.A.** (1925), 899 Boylston St., Boston, MA 02115; 6,584.
**Postmasters of the U.S., Natl. Assn. of** (1898), 8 Herbert St., Arlington, VA 22305; 43,000.
**Postmasters, Natl. League of** (1904), 1023 N. Royal St., Alexandria, VA 22314; 28,000.
**Poultry Science Assn.** (1908), 1111 N. Dunlap Ave. Savoy, IL 61874; 1,780.
**Power Boat Assn., Amer.** (1903), 17640 E. Nine Mile Rd., PO Box 377, Eastpointe, MI 48021; 6,000.
**Precancel Collectors, Natl. Assn. of** (1951), 5121 Park Blvd., Wildwood, NJ 08260; 7,600.
**Press, Associated** (1848), 50 Rockefeller Plaza, New York, NY 10020; 1,554 newspapers & 6,000 broadcast stations.
**Press Club, Natl.** (1908), 529 14th St. NW, Wash., DC 20045.
**Press Intl., United** (1907), 1400 I St. NW, Wash., DC 20005.
**Press and Radio Club** (1948), 29 Bradley Dr., Montgomery, AL 36109; 772.
**Printing Industries of America** (1887), 100 Dangerfield Rd., Alexandria, VA 22314; 14,000.
**Prisoners of War, Amer. Ex-** (1942), 3201 E. Pioneer Pkwy., #40, Arlington, TX 76010; 32,000.
**Procrastinators Club of America** (1956), Box 712, Bryn Athyn, PA 19009; 6,600.
**Production and Inventory Control Soc., American,** (1957), 500 W. Annandale Rd., Falls Church, VA 22046; 69,114.
**Psoriasis Foundation, Natl.** (1968), 6600 SW 92d Ave., Ste. 300, Portland, OR 97223; 35,000.
**Psychiatric Assn., Amer.** (1844), 1400 K St. NW, Wash., DC 20005; 40,453.
**Psychical Research, Amer. Society for** (1907), 5 W. 73d St., New York, NY 10023; 2,000.
**Psychoanalytic Assn., Amer.** (1911), 309 E. 49th St., New York, NY 10017; 3,000.
**Psychological Assn., Amer.** (1892), 750 1st St. NE, Wash., DC 20002; 142,000.
**Psychological Assn. for Psychoanalysis, Inc., Natl.** (1948), 150 W. 13th St., New York, NY 10011; 355.
**PTA, Natl., (Natl. Congress of Parents and Teachers)** (1897), 330 N. Wabash, Chicago, IL 60611; 7 mil.
**Public Administration, Amer. Soc. for** (1939), 1120 G St. NW, Wash., DC 20005; 14,800.
**Public Health Assn., World Fed. of** (1967), 1015 15th St. NW, Wash., DC 20005; 48 natl. assn.
**Public Relations Soc. of Amer., Inc.** (1947), 33 Irving Pl., 3d Floor, New York, NY 10003; 17,383.
**Publishers, Inc., Assn. of Amer.** (1970), 71 5th Ave., New York, NY 10003; 200 cos.
**Puppeteers of Amer.** (1936), 5 Cricklewood Path, Pasadena, CA 91107; 2,400.
**Puzzle Buffs Intl.** (1979), 1772 State Rd., Cuyahoga Falls, OH 44223; 65,000.

**Quality Control, Amer. Society for (ASQC),** (1946), 611 E. Wisconsin Ave., Milwaukee, WI 53201; 140,000.
**Quota International, Inc.** (1919), 1420 21st St. NW, Wash., DC 20036; 11,000+.

**Rabbis, Central Conference of Amer.** (1889), 192 Lexington Ave., New York, NY 10016; 1,540.
**Racial Equality, Congress of, (CORE)** (1942), 2111 Nostrand Ave., Brooklyn, NY 11210; 100,000.
**Racquetball Assn., American Amateur** (1968), 815 N. Weber, Colorado Springs, CO 80903.
**Radio, Natl. Assn. of Business and Educational** (1965), 1501 Duke St., Alexandria, VA 22314; 2,400.
**Radio Relay League, Amer.** (1914), 225 Main St., Newington, CT 06111; 172,000.
**Radio and Television Society Foundation, Intl.** (1939), 420 Lexington Ave., Ste. 1714, New York, NY 10170; 1,500.
**Radio and TV, Inc., Amer. Women in** (1950), 1650 Tyson's Blvd., Ste. 200, McLean, VA 22102.
**Radio Union, Intl. Amateur** (1925), PO Box 310905, Newington, CT 06131; 148 organizations.
**Railsplitter Society, Inc., 84th Infantry Div.** (1945), PO Box 827, Sioux Falls, SD 57101; 3,000.
**Railway Historical Society, Natl.** (1935), PO Box 58153, Philadelphia, PA 19102; 21,000+.
**Railway Progress Institute** (1908), 700 N. Fairfax St., Ste. 601, Alexandria, VA 22314; 100 cos.
**Range Management, Society for** (1948), 1839 York St., Denver, CO 80206; 5,000.
**Reading Assn., Intl.** (1955), 800 Barksdale Rd., Newark, DE 19714; 92,000.
**Real Estate Institute, Intl.** (1975), 8383 E. Evans Rd., Scottsdale, AZ 85260; 3,000+.
**Rebekah Assemblies, Intl. Assn. of** (1922), 422 N. Trade St., Winston-Salem, NC 27101; 147,238.
**Reconciliation, Fellowship of** (1915), 523 N. Broadway, Nyack, NY 10960; 10,000.
**Records Managers & Administrators, Assn. of** (1975), 4200 Somerset Dr., Ste. 215, Prairie Village, KS 66208; 10,600.
**Recreation and Park Assn., Natl.** (1965), 2775 S. Quincy St., Ste. 300, Arlington, VA 22206; 23,533.
**Recycling Coalition, Natl.,** (1979), 1727 King St., Ste. 105, Alexandria, VA 22514; 3,500.
**Red Cross, American** (1881), 8111 Gatehouse Rd., Falls Church, VA 22042; 1.44 mil volunteers.
**Red Men, Improved Order of** (1765), 4521 Speight Ave., Waco, TX 76711; 28,000.
**Redwoods League, Save-the-** (1918), 114 Sansome St., Rm. 605, San Francisco, CA 94104; 43,000.
**Rehabilitation Assn., Natl.** (1925), 633 S. Washington St., Alexandria, VA 22314; 14,000.

**Religion, Amer. Academy of** (1909), 1703 Clifton Rd. NE, Ste. 6-5, Atlanta, GA 30329; 7,500.
**Religion Foundation, Freedom From** (1978), PO Box 750, Madison, WI 53701; 3,469.
**Renaissance Society of America** (1954), 24 W. 12th St., 3d Floor, New York, NY 10011; 3,700.
**Republican National Committee** (1856), 310 1st St. SE, Wash., DC 20003-1801.
**Reserve Officers Assn. of the U.S.** (1922), One Constitution Ave. NE, Wash., DC 20003; 95,000.
**Restaurant Assn., Natl.** (1919), 1200 17th St. NW, Wash., DC 20036; 20,000.
**Retail Federation, Natl.** (1918), 100 W. 31st St., New York, NY 10001; 50,000.
**Retired Credit Union People, Natl. Assn. for** (1978), PO Box 391, 5910 Mineral Pt. Rd., Madison, WI 53705; 81,180.
**Retired Federal Employees, Natl. Assn. of** (1921), 1533 New Hampshire Ave. NW, Wash., DC 20036; 500,000.
**Retired Officers Assn.** (1929), 201 N. Washington St., Alexandria, VA 22314; 400,000.
**Retired Persons, Amer. Assn. of** (1958), 601 E St. NW, Wash., DC 20049; 32 mil.
**Retired Teachers Assn., Natl.** (1947), 1909 K St. NW, Wash., DC 20049; 540,000.
**Revolver Assn., U.S.** (1900), 40 Larchmont Ave., Taunton, MA 02780; 1,450.
**Reye's Syndrome Foundation, Natl.** (1974), 426 N. Lewis, Box 829, Bryan, OH 43506; 5,000+.
**Richard III Society** (1969), PO Box 13786, New Orleans, LA 70185; 700.
**Rifle Assn., Natl.** (1871), 11250 Waples Mill Rd., Fairfax, VA 22030; 3.4 mil.
**Road & Transportation Builders' Assn., Amer.** (1902), 1010 Massachusetts Ave. NW, Wash., DC 20001; 3,985.
**Rodeo Cowboys Assn., Professional** (1936), 101 Pro Rodeo Dr., Colorado Springs, CO 80919; 11,135.
**Roller Skating, U.S. Amateur Confederation of** (1937), 4730 South St., PO Box 6579, Lincoln, NE 68506; 34,000.
**Rose Society, Amer.** (1892), PO Box 30,000, Shreveport, LA 71130; 23,000.
**Rotary Intl.** (1905), 1560 Sherman Ave., Evanston, IL 60201; 1,203,726.
**Running and Fitness Assn., Amer.** (1968), 4405 East West Highway Ste. 405, Bethesda, MD 20877; 15,000.
**Ruritan Natl.** (1928), PO Box 487, Dublin, VA 24084; 36,000.

**Safety Council, Natl.** (1913), 1121 Spring Lake Dr., Itasca, IL 60143; 17,400.
**Safety and Fairness Everywhere, Nat'l. Organization Taunting (NOT-SAFE)** (1981), PO Box 5743-WA96, Montecito, CA 93150; 987.
**Sailors, Tin Can** (1976), PO Box 100, Somerset, MA 02726; 17,000.
**Sailors Assn., Destroyer-Escort** (1975), PO Box 680085, Orlando, FL 32868-0085; 11,760.
**St. Andrew, The Brotherhood of** (1883), 1109 Merchant St., PO Box 632, Ambridge, PA 15003; 5,000.
**St. Paul, Natl. Guild of** (1937), 601 Hill 'n Dale, Lexington, KY 40503; 13,652.
**Salespersons, Natl. Assn. of Professional** (1970), PO Box 76461, Atlanta, GA 30358; 35,000.
**Salt Institute** (1914), 700 N. Fairfax St., Ste. 600, Alexandria, VA, 22314; 30 cos.
**Sand Castle Builders, Intl. Society of** (1988), 172 N. Pershing Ave., Akron, OH 44313; 200.
**School Administrators, Amer. Assn. of** (1865), 1801 N. Moore St., Arlington, VA 22209; 16,409.
**School Boards Assn., Natl.** (1940), 1680 Duke St., Alexandria, VA 22314.
**School Counselor Assn., Amer.** (1953), 5999 Stevenson Ave., Alexandria, VA 22304; 13,000.
**Schools of Art, Natl. Assn. of** (1944), 11250 Roger Bacon Dr., Reston, VA 22090; 553 institutions.
**Schools & Colleges, Amer. Council on** (1927), 13014-363 Dale Mabry Hwy., Carrollwood, FL 33618; 186.
**Science, Amer. Assn. for the Advancement of** (1848), 1200 New York Ave. NW, Wash., DC; 140,000.
**Science Fiction Society, World** (1939), PO Box 1270, Kendall Sq. Sta., Cambridge, MA 02142; 5,000.
**Science Service** (1921), 1719 N St. NW, Wash., DC 20036.
**Sciences, Natl. Academy of** (1863), 2101 Constitution Ave. NW, Wash., DC 20418; 4,000+.
**Science Teachers Assn., Natl.** (1944), 1840 Wilson Blvd., Arlington, VA 22201; 53,000.
**Science Writers, Natl. Assn. of** (1934), PO Box 294, Greenlawn, NY 11740; 1,801.
**Scrabble Assn., Natl.** (1972), PO Box 700, 120 Front St., Greenport, NY 11944; 10,000.
**Screenprinting & Graphic Imaging Assn. Intl.** (1948), 10015 Main St., Fairfax, VA 22031; 3,200 cos.
**Screenprinting Technical Foundation** (1985), 10015 Main St., Fairfax, VA 22031.
**Sculpture Soc., Natl.** (1893), 1177 Ave. of the Americas, New York, NY 10036; 4,400.
**Seamen's Service, United, and the Amer. Merchant Marine Library Assn.,** (1942, 1921), One World Trade Center, Ste. 2161, New York, NY 10048.
**2d Air Division Assn.** (1947), 06-410 Delaire Landing Rd., Philadelphia, PA 19114; 7,852.
**Secondary School Principals, Natl. Assn. of** (1916), 1904 Association Dr., Reston, VA 22091; 42,000.
**Secretaries, Natl. Assn. of Legal** (1950), 2448 E. 81st St., Ste. 3400, Tulsa, OK 74137; 11,000.
**Secretaries Intl.®, Professional/The Association for Office Professionals** (1942), PO Box 20404, Kansas City, MO 64195; 40,000.
**Secular Humanism, Council for** (1980), PO Box 664, Buffalo, NY 14226; 3,500.
**Securities Industry Assn.** (1972), 120 Broadway, New York, NY 10271; 715 firms.
**Separation of Church & State, Americans United for** (1947), 1816 Jefferson Place NW, Wash., DC 20036; 50,000.
**Sertoma International** (1912), 1912 E. Meyer Blvd., Kansas City, MO 64132; 28,000.
**Sexuality Information & Education Council of the U.S. (SIECUS)** (1964), 130 W. 42d St., Ste. 350, New York, NY 10036.
**Sharkhunters** (1983), PO Box 1539, Hernando, FL 34442; 5,000.
**Shipbuilders Council of America** (1921), 901 Washington St., Ste. 204, Alexandria, VA 22314; 50 organizations.
**Ships-in-Bottles Assn. of Amer.** (1983), PO Box 180550, Coronado, CA 92178; 400.
**Shore & Beach Preservation Assn., Amer.** (1926), PO Box 279, Middletown, CA 95461; 900.
**Shrine of North America** (1872), 2900 Rocky Point Dr., Tampa, FL 33607; 634,000.
**Sierra Club** (1892), 730 Polk St., San Francisco, CA 94109; 564,360.
**Sigma Beta Delta** (1994), PO Box 46935, St. Louis, MO 63146; 6,000.
**Skeet Shooting Assn., Natl.** (1946), PO Box 680007, San Antonio, TX 78268; 15,800.
**Ski Team Foundation, U.S.** (1964), 1500 Kearns Blvd., Park City, UT 84060; 60,000.
**Skiing, U.S.** (1904), PO Box 100, Park City, UT 84060; 50,000.
**Small Business United, Natl.** (1937), 1156 15th St. NW, Ste. 1100, Wash., DC 20005; 65,000.
**Smokers' Pollution, Inc., Group Against** (1971), PO Box 632, College Park, MD 20741; 10,000+.
**Smoking & Health, Natl. Clearinghouse for** (1965), Center for Disease Control, 1600 Clifton Rd. NE, Atlanta, GA 30333.
**Soccer Federation, U.S.** (1913), 1801 S. Prairie Ave., Chicago, IL 60616.
**Social Sciences, Natl. Institute of** (1865), 1192 Park Ave., 15B, New York, NY 10128; 315.
**Social Work Education, Council on** (1952), 1600 Duke St., Alexandria, VA 22314; 3,000.
**Sociological Assn., Amer.** (1905), 1722 N St. NW, Wash., DC 20036; 13,000.
**Softball Association, Amateur** (1933), 2801 N.E. 50th St., Oklahoma City, OK 73111; 5 mil+.
**Soft Drink Assn., Natl.** (1921), 1101 16th St. NW, Wash., DC 20036; 1,700.
**Soil Science Society of America** (1936), 677 S. Segoe Rd., Madison, WI 53711; 5,800.
**Soil & Water Conservation Society of America** (1945), 7515 N.E. Ankeny Rd., Ankeny, IA 50021; 10,000.
**Soldiers', Sailors', and Airmen's Club** (1922), 283 Lexington Ave., New York, NY 10016; 800.
**Songwriters Guild of America, The** (1933), 1500 Harbor Blvd., Weehawken, NJ 07087; 5,000+.
**Sons of Confederate Veterans** (1896), PO Box 59, Columbia, TN 38402; 24,500.
**Sons of Italy in America, Order of** (1905), 219 E St. NE, Wash. DC 20002; 500,000.
**Sons of Norway** (1895), 1455 W. Lake St., Minneapolis, MN 55408; 74,000.
**Sons of St. Patrick, Society of the Friendly** (1784), 80 Wall St., New York, NY 10005; 1,500.
**Sons of Sherman's March to the Sea** (1966), 1725 Farmer Ave., Tempe, AZ 85281; 790.
**Sons of the Amer. Legion** (1932), Box 1055, Indianapolis, IN 46206; 161,376.
**Sons of the American Revolution, Natl. Society of** (1889), 1000 S. Fourth St., Louisville, KY 40203; 26,000.
**Sons of the Republic of Texas, The** (1922), 1717 8th St., Bay City, TX 77414; 3,380.

**Sons of Union Veterans of the Civil War** (1881), 7017 Granada Lane, Flint, MI 48532; 5,000.
**Soroptimist Intl. of the Americas** (1921), Two Penn Center, Ste. 1000, Philadelphia, PA 19102; 48,000.
**Southern Christian Leadership Conference** (1957), 334 Auburn Ave. NE, Atlanta, GA 30303; 1 mil.
**Space Education Assn., U.S.** (1973), 231 School Lane, Rheems, PA 17570; 1,500.
**Special Olympics Intl.** (1968), 1325 G St. NW, Ste. 500, Wash., DC 20005.
**Speech Communication Assn.** (1914), 5105 Backlick Rd., Annandale, VA 22003; 7,000.
**Speech-Language-Hearing Assn., Amer.** (1925), 10801 Rockville Pike, Rockville, MD 20852; 84,000.
**Speedskating Union of the U.S., Amateur** (1927), 1033 Shady Lane, Glen Ellyn, IL 60137; 3,000.
**Speleological Society, Natl.** (1941), 2813 Cave Ave., Huntsville, AL 35810; 12,500.
**Spiritual Awareness and Holistic Principles of Body, Mind and Spirit, Inc., Assn. for** (1984), PO Box 41, Clifton Hill, MO 65244; 2,300.
**Sports Car Club of America** (1944), 9033 E. Eastern Pl., Englewood, CO 80112; 50,000+.
**Sportscasters Assn., Amer.** (1979), 5 Beekman St., New York, NY 10038; 500+.
**Sports Club, Indoor** (1930), 1145 Highland St., Napoleon, OH 43545; 950.
**State Governments, Council of** (1933), PO Box 11910, Lexington, KY 40517; 50 states, 4 territories.
**Statistical Assn., Amer.** (1839), 1429 Duke St., Alexandria, VA 22314; 19,500.
**Steamship Historical Society of America** (1940), 300 Ray Dr., Ste. 4, Providence, RI 02906; 3,400.
**Steel Construction, Amer. Institute of** (1921), 1 E. Wacker Dr., Ste. 3100, Chicago, IL 60601; 2,770.
**Stock Car Auto Racing (NASCAR), Natl. Assn. for** (1947), PO Box 2875, Daytona Beach, FL 32120; 50,000.
**Stock Exchange, Amer.** (1911), 86 Trinity Pl., New York, NY 10006; 871.
**Stock Exchange, New York** (1792), 11 Wall St., New York, NY 10005.
**Stock Exchange, Philadelphia** (1790), 1900 Market St., Philadelphia, PA 19103; 504.
**Student Councils, Natl. Assn. of** (1931), 1904 Association Dr., Reston, VA 22091; 9,000 schools.
**Stuttering Project, Natl.** (1977), 5100 E. LaPalma Ave., #208, Anaheim Hills, CA 92807; 4,000.
**Sugar Brokers Assn., Natl.** (1903), 90 West St., Ste. 706, New York, NY 10006; 100.
**Surgeons, Amer. College of** (1913), 55 E. Erie St., Chicago, IL 60611; 50,000.
**Surgeons of the U.S., Assn. of Military** (1897), 9320 Old Georgetown Rd., Bethesda, MD 20814; 12,000.
**Surveying & Mapping, Amer. Congress on** (1941), 5410 Grosvenor Ln., Ste. 100, Bethesda, MD 20814; 8,000.
**Symphony Orchestra League, Amer.** (1942), 1156 Fifteenth St. NW, Ste. 800, Wash., DC 20005; 800+ orchestras.
**Systems Management, Assn. for** (1947), PO Box 38370, Cleveland, OH 44138; 5,100.

**Table Tennis Assn., U.S.** (1933), One Olympic Plaza, Colorado Springs, CO 80909; 7,754.
**Tailhook Assn., The** (1956), 9696 Business Park Ave., PO Box 26700, San Diego, CA 92131; 11,800.
**Tall Buildings and Urban Habitat, Council on** (1969), Lehigh Univ., 13 E. Packer Ave., Bethlehem, PA 18015; 3,000.
**Tax Administrators, Federation of** (1937), 444 N. Capitol St. NW, Ste. 348, Wash., DC 20001.
**Tax Foundation, Inc.** (1937), 1250 H St. NW, Ste. 750, Wash., DC 20005.
**Taxpayers Union, Natl.** (1969), 108 N. Alfred St., Alexandria, VA 22314; 250,000.
**Tea Assn. of the U.S.A., Inc.** (1899), 230 Park Ave., Ste. 1460, New York, NY 10169; 105 firms.
**Teachers of English, Natl. Council of** (1911), 1111 W. Kenyon Rd., Urbana, IL 61801; 68,000.
**Teachers of English to Speakers of Other Languages** (1966), 1600 Cameron St., Ste. 300, Alexandria, VA 22314; 20,000.
**Teachers of French, Amer. Assn. of** (1927), 57 E. Armory Ave., Champaign, IL 61820; 10,500.
**Teachers of Mathematics, Natl. Council of** (1920), 1906 Association Dr., Reston, VA 22091; 120,000.
**Teachers of Singing, Natl. Assn. of** (1944), 2800 Univ. Blvd. N., J.U. Sta., Jacksonville, FL 32211; 5,174.
**Teachers of Spanish & Portuguese, Amer. Assn. of** (1917), 8 Frasier Hall, Univ. of Northern Colorado, Greeley, CO 80939; 13,000.
**Technology Honor Society, Amer. (ATHS)** (1995), 1905 Association Dr., Reston, VA 22091; 125 chapters.
**Telephone Pioneers of Amer.** (1911), 930 15th St., 12th Fl., Denver, CO 80202; 875,000.
**Television, Inc., Viewers for Quality** (1984), PO Box 195, Fairfax Station, VA 22039; 2,500.
**Television Arts & Sciences, Natl. Academy of** (1947), 111 W. 57th St., Ste. 1020, New York, NY 10019; 12,000.
**Television Bureau of Advertising** (1954), 850 3d Ave., 10th Fl., New York, NY 10022.
**Television & Radio Artists, Amer. Federation of** (1937), 260 Madison Ave., 7th Fl., New York, NY 10016; 75,000.
**Telluride Assn.** (1910), 217 West Ave., Ithaca, NY 14850.
**Temperance Union, Natl. Women's Christian** (1874), 1730 Chicago Ave., Evanston, IL 60201; 12,594.
**Tennis Assn., U.S.** (1881), 70 W. Red Oak Lane, White Plains, NY 10604.
**Terraplane Club, Hudson-Essex** (1959), 100 E. Cross St., Ypsilanti, MI 48198; 3,200.
**Tesla Memorial Soc., Inc.** (1979), 453 Martin Rd., Buffalo, NY 14218; 1,700.
**Testing & Materials, Amer. Society for** (1898), 100 Barr Harbor Dr., West Conshohocken, PA 19428-2959; 34,800.
**Textile Manufacturers Institute, Amer.** (1949), 1801 K St. NW, Ste. 900, Wash., DC 20006.
**Theodore Roosevelt Assn.** (1920), PO Box 719, Oyster Bay, NY 11771; 1,550.
**Theological Schools in the U.S. and Canada, Assn. of** (1918), 10 Summit Park Dr., Pittsburgh, PA 15275-1103.
**Theosophical Society in America, The** (1895), 1926 N. Main St., Wheaton, IL 60189; 4,262.
**Thoreau Society, Inc., The** (1941), 44 Baker Farm, Lincoln, MA 01773; 1,500.
**Thoroughbred Racing Assns.** (1942), 420 Fair Hill Dr., Ste. 1, Elkton, MD 21921; 41 racing associations.
**Titanic Historical Society, Inc.** (1963), 208 Main St., PO Box 51053, Indian Orchard, MA 01151; 5,110.
**Toastmasters Intl.** (1924), PO Box 9052, Mission Viejo, CA 92690; 170,000.
**Topical Assn., Amer.** (1949), PO Box 65749, Tucson, AZ 85728.
**Toy Manufacturers of America** (1916), 200 Fifth Ave., New York, NY 10010; 265.
**Track & Field, USA** (1979), PO Box 120, Indianapolis, IN 46225.
**Trademark Assn., Intl.** (1878), 1133 Avenue of the Americas, New York, NY 10036; 2,800.
**Trail Assn., North Country** (1981), 49 Monroe Center NW, Ste. 200B, Grand Rapids, MI 49503; 788.
**Transit Assn., Amer. Public** (1974), 1201 New York Ave. NW, Wash., DC 20005; 1,100 organizations.
**Translators Assn., Amer.** (1959), 1800 Diagonal Rd., Ste. 220, Alexandria, VA 22314; 6,000.
**Trapshooting Assn., Amateur** (1923), 601 W. National Rd., Vandalia, OH 45377; 102,360.
**Travel Agents, Amer. Society of** (1931), 1101 King St., Ste. 200, Alexandria, VA 22314; 27,000.
**Travelers of America, Order of United Commercial** (1888), 632 N. Park St., Columbus, OH 43215; 135,000.
**Travelers Protective Assn. of America** (1890), 3755 Lindell Blvd., St. Louis, MO 63108; 138,000.
**Trilateral Commission, The** (1973), 345 E. 46th St., New York, NY 10017; 335.
**Truck Historical Soc., Amer.** (1971), PO Box 531168, Birmingham, AL 35253; 18,500.
**Trucking Assn., Amer.** (1933), 2200 Mill Rd., Alexandria, VA 22314; 4,500 cos.
**True Sisters, Inc., United Order** (1846), 212 Fifth Ave., Rm. 1307, New York, NY 10010; 8,000.
**T. S. Eliot Society** (1980), 709 S. Skinner Blvd. #401, St. Louis, MO 63103; 165.
**Tuberous Sclerosis Assn., Natl.** (1974), 8181 Professional Place, Ste. 110, Landover, MD 20785; 8,000.

**UFOs, Natl. Investigation Committee on** (1967), 14617 Victory Blvd., Ste. 4, Van Nuys, CA 91411; 1000.
**UNICEF, U.S. Committee for** (1947), 333 E. 38th St., New York, NY 10016.
**Underwriters, Amer. Soc. of Chartered Life** (1927), 270 Bryn Mawr Ave., Bryn Mawr, PA 19010; 30,000.
**Underwriters, Natl. Assn. of Life** (1890), 1922 F St. NW, Wash., DC 20006; 143,000.
**Underwriters (CPCU), Soc. of Chartered Property and Casualty** (1944), Kahler Hall, 720 Providence Rd., Malvern, PA 19355; 28,000.
**United Nations Assn. of the U.S.A.** (1923, as League of Nations Assn.), 485 Fifth Ave., New York, NY 10017; 30,000.
**United Way of America** (1932), 701 N. Fairfax St., Alexandria, VA 22314-2045; 1,353.

**Universities, Assn. of Amer.** (1914), One Dupont Circle, Ste. 730, Wash., DC 20036; 59 institutions.
**Universities & Colleges, Assn. of Governing Bds. of** (1921), One Dupont Circle NW, Ste. 400, Wash., DC 20036.
**University Continuing Education Assn., Natl.** (1915), One Dupont Circle, Ste. 615, Wash., DC 20036; 2,000.
**University Extension Assn., Natl.** (1915), One Dupont Circle NW, Ste. 400, Wash., DC 20036; 1,100.
**University Foundation, Intl.** (1973), 1301 S. Noland Rd., Independence, MO 64055; 62,311.
**University Professors, Amer. Assn. of** (1915), 1012 14th St. NW, Ste. 500, Wash., DC 20005; 41,000.
**University Women, Amer. Assn. of** (1881), 1111 16th St. NW, Wash., DC 20036; 150,000.
**Urban League, Natl.** (1910), 500 E. 62d St., New York, NY 10020.
**Useless Skills, Institute of Totally** (1987), Box 181, Temple, NH 03084; 552.
**USO, Inc. (United Service Organizations)** (1941), Washington Navy Yard, 901 M St., SE, Bldg. 198, Wash., DC 20374-5096.
**Utility Commissioners, Natl. Assn. of Regulatory (NARUC),** (1889), PO Box 684, Washington, DC 20044; 100 agencies.

**Vampire Research Center** (1972), PO Box 252, Elmhurst, NY 11373; 1,250.
**Variety Clubs Intl.** (1928), 1560 Broadway, New York, NY 10036.
**Ventriloquists, North American Assn. of** (1944), Box 420, Littleton, CO 80160; 1,700.
**Veterans, American (AMVETS)** (1944); **AMVETS National Auxiliary** (1946), 4647 Forbes Blvd., Lanham, MD 20706; 200,000.
**Veterans of America, Paralyzed** (1947), 801 18th St. NW, Wash., DC 20006; 17,000.
**Veterans Assn., Blinded** (1945), 477 H St. NW, Wash., DC 20001; 7,900.
**Veterans Assn., Coast Guard Combat** (1986), 17728 Striley Dr., Ashton, MD 20861; 1,700.
**Veterans, Disabled American** (1920), PO Box 14301, Cincinatti, OH 45250; 1 mil.
**Veterans Assn., Women's Army Corps** (1946), PO Box 5577, Ft. McClellan, AL 36205; 4500.
**Veterans Assn. of America, Polish Army** (1921), 155 Noble St., Brooklyn, NY 11222; 3,500.
**Veterans of Foreign Wars of the U.S.** (1899), 406 W. 34th St., Kansas City, MO 64111.
**Veterans of Foreign Wars of the U.S, Ladies Auxiliary to the** (1914), 406 W. 34th St., Kansas City, MO 64111; 765,283.
**Veterans of Underage Military Service** (1991), 100 Village Lane, Philadelphia, PA 19154; 793.
**Veterans of the U.S.A., Catholic War** (1935), 419 North Lee St., Alexandria, VA 22314; 30,000.
**Veterans of the U.S.A., Jewish War** (1896), 1811 R St. NW, Wash., DC 20009; 100,000.
**Veterans of the Vietnam War, Inc.** (1980), 760 Jumper Rd., Wilkes-Barre, PA 18702; 30,000.
**Veterans of World War I of the USA, Inc.** (1958), PO Box 8027, Alexandria, VA 22306; 12,000.
**Veterans of WWII, U.S. Merchant Marine** (1945), PO Box 629, San Pedro, CA 90733; 7,612.
**Veterans of WWII, U.S. Submarine** (1955), 317 N. Palm Ave., Frostproof, FL 33843; 8,250.
**Veterans, Women World War** (1919), 237 Madison Ave., New York, NY 10016; 35,000.
**Veterinary Medical Assn., Amer.** (1863), 1931 N. Meacham Rd., Ste. 100, Schaumburg, IL 60173; 57,687.
**Victorian Society in America** (1965), 219 S. Sixth St., Philadelphia, PA 19106; 2,300.
**Virgil Fox Society, The** (1977), 88 Chestnut St., Brooklyn, NY 11208; 300.
**Vivisection Society, New England Anti-** (1895), 333 Washington St., Ste. 850, Boston, MA 02108.
**Volleyball Assn. (USVBA), U.S.** (1928), 3595 E. Fountain Blvd., Ste. I-2, Colorado Springs, CO 80910; 120,000.

**Warrant and Warrant Officers' Assn., Chief U.S. Coast Guard** (1929), c/o Fort McNair Yacht Basin, 200 V St. SW, Wash., DC 20024; 3,346.
**Watch & Clock Collectors, Natl. Assn. of** (1943), 514 Poplar St., Columbia, PA 17512; 38,000+.
**Water Assn., Natl. Ground** (1948), 6375 Riverside Dr., Dublin, OH 43017; 24,500.
**Watercolor Society, American** (1866), 47 5th Ave., New York, NY 10003; 491.
**Water Environment Federation** (1928), 601 Wythe St., Alexandria, VA 22314; 40,000.
**Water Pollution Control Administration, Assn. of State and Interstate** (1961), 750 First St. NE, Ste. 910, Wash., DC 20001.
**Water Pollution Control Federation** (1928), 601 Wythe St., Alexandria, VA 22314; 32,000.
**Water Ski Assn., Amer.** (1939), 799 Overlook Dr. SE, Winter Haven, FL 33830; 30,000.
**Water Works Assn., Amer.** (1881), 6666 W. Quincy Ave., Denver, CO 80235; 49,482.
**Welding Society, Amer.** (1919), 550 N.W. LeJeune Rd., Miami, FL 33126; 41,000+.
**Wheelchair Sports, USA** (1956), 3595 E. Fountain Blvd., Ste. L-1, Colorado Springs, CO 80910; 4,600.
**Widows, Society of Military** (1968), 5535 Hemstead Way, Springfield, VA 22151; 2,000.
**Wilderness Society** (1935), 900 17th St. NW, Wash., DC 20006; 271,268.
**Wildflower Research Center, Natl.** (1982), 4801 La Crosse Ave., Austin, TX 78739; 24,000.
**Wildlife, Defenders of** (1947), 1244 19th St. NW, Wash., DC 20036; 80,000.
**Wildlife Federation, Natl.** (1936), 1400 16th St. NW, Wash., DC 20036-2266; 4.7 mil.
**Wildlife Fund, World** (1961), 1250 24th St. NW, Wash., DC 20037; 1.25 mil.
**Wildlife Management Institute** (1911), 1101 14th St. NW, Ste. 801, Wash., DC 20005; 300+.
**William Penn Assn.** (1886), 709 Brighton Rd., Pittsburgh, PA 15233; 90,000.
**Wireless Pioneers, Society of** (1968), PO Box 86, Geyserville, CA 95441; 1,500.
**Wizard of Oz Club, Intl.** (1957), 220 North 11th St., Escanaba, MI 49829; 2,410.
**Women, Natl. Assn. of Bank** (1920), 7910 Woodmont Ave. #1430, Bethesda, MD 20814; 30,000.
**Women, Natl. Organization for, (NOW)** (1966), 1000 16th St. NW, Ste. 700, Wash., DC 20036; 250,000.
**Women for America, Concerned** (1979), 370 L'Enfant Promenade SW, #800, Wash., DC 20024; 600,000.
**Women Artists, Natl. Assn. of** (1889), 41 Union Sq., New York, NY 10003; 800.
**Women's Clubs, General Federation of** (1890), 1734 N St. NW, Wash., DC, 20036; 300,000 U.S.
**Women's Clubs, Natl. Federation of Business & Professional** (1919), 2012 Massachusetts Ave. NW, Wash., DC 20036.
**Women's Intl. League for Peace & Freedom** (1915), 1213 Race St., Philadelphia, PA 19107; 8,000.
**Women's Legal Defense Fund** (1971), 1875 Connecticut Ave. NW, Ste. 710, Wash., DC 20009; 2,500.
**Women's Overseas Service League** (1921), PO Box 39058, Friendship Station, Wash., DC 20016; 1,164.
**Women Strike for Peace** (1961), 110 Maryland Ave. NE, Ste. 102, Wash., DC 20002; 5,000.
**Women of the U.S., Inc., Natl. Council of** (1888), 777 UN Plaza, 7th Fl., New York, NY 10017; 500 members, 33 affiliate org.
**Women Voters of the U.S., League of** (1920), 1730 M St. NW, Wash., DC 20036; 100,000.
**Woodmen of America, Modern** (1883), 1701 1st Ave., Rock Island, IL 61201; 750,000.
**Woodmen of the World Life Insurance Soc.** (1890), 1700 Farnam St., Woodmen Tower, Omaha, NE 68102; 850,000.
**Workmen's Circle** (1900), 45 E. 33d St., New York, NY 10016.
**World Federalist Assn.** (1975), 418 7th St. SE, Wash., DC 20003; 9,000.
**World Future Society** (1966), 7910 Woodmont Ave., Ste. 450, Bethesda, MD 20814; 30,000.
**World Learning Inc.** (1932), Kipling Rd., PO Box 676, Brattleboro, VT 05153; 2,500.
**World's Fair Collectors Soc., Inc.** (1968), PO Box 20806, Sarasota, FL 34276-3806; 510.
**Writers Guild of America, West** (1933), 7000 W. Third St., Los Angeles, CA 90048; 8,000.

**Yachting Assn., Southern California** (1921), 5855 Naples Plaza, Ste. 211, Long Beach, CA; 20,000 families.
**YM-YWHAs of Greater New York, Associated** (1957), 130 E. 59th St., New York, NY 10020; 55,100.
**Young America's Foundation** (1971), 110 Elden St., Herndon, VA 22070.
**Young Men's Christian Assns. of the U.S.A.** (1851), 101 N. Wacker Dr., Chicago, IL 60606; 13 mil.
**Young Women's Christian Assn. of the U.S.A.** (1906), 726 Broadway, New York, NY 10003; 1.6 mil.

**Zero Population Growth** (1968), 1400 16th St. NW, Ste. 320, Wash., DC 20036; 45,000.
**Zionist Organization of America** (1897), 4 E. 34th St., New York, NY 10016; 110,000.
**Zoo and Aquarium Assn., American** (1924), 7970-D Old Georgetown Rd., Bethesda, MD 20814; 6,000.

# POSTAL INFORMATION

## U.S. Postal Service

The Postal Reorganization Act, creating a government-owned postal service under the executive branch and replacing the old Post Office Department, was signed into law by President Richard Nixon on Aug. 12, 1970. The service officially came into being on July 1, 1971.

The U.S. Postal Service is governed by an 11-person Board of Governors. Nine members are appointed to 9-year terms by the president with Senate approval. These 9, in turn, choose a postmaster general. The board and the postmaster general choose the 11th member, who serves as deputy postmaster general. An independent Postal Rate Commission of 5 members, appointed by the president, reviews and rules on proposed postal rate increases submitted by the Board of Governors. As of May 24, 1996, there were 28,143 post offices throughout the U.S.

## U.S. Domestic Rates

Postal rates and fees shown below were implemented on July 1, 1996, for domestic mail and on July 8, 1995, for international mail. Domestic rates apply to the U.S., to its territories and possessions, and to APOs and FPOs.

### First Class

First Class includes written matter such as letters, postal cards, and postcards (private mailing cards) plus all other matter wholly or partly in writing, whether sealed or unsealed, except manuscripts for books, periodical articles and music, manuscript copy accompanying proofsheets or corrected proofsheets of the same, and the writing authorized by law on matter of other classes. Also included: matter sealed or closed against inspection, bills, and statements of accounts.

Mailing written letters and matter sealed against inspection costs 32¢ for first ounce or fraction, 23¢ for each additional ounce or fraction up to and including 11 oz.

U.S. Postal Service cards and private postcards alike cost 20¢ single, 40¢ double.

### Express Mail

Express Mail Service is available for any mailable article up to 70 lb, and guarantees delivery between major U.S. cities within a specified time frame or your money back. Articles received by the acceptance time authorized by the postmaster at a postal facility offering Express Mail are delivered by 3 PM the next day to some locations or by noon the next day to other destinations. Or, if you prefer, you can pick up the package yourself, as early as 10 AM the next business day. Second-day service is available to locations not on the Next Day Delivery Network. Rates include insurance, shipment receipt, and record of delivery at the destination post office.

The rate for Express Mail weighing up to 8 oz is $10.75. Consult postmaster for other Express Mail Services and rates. The Postal Service will refund, upon application to originating office, the postage for any Express Mail shipments not meeting the service standard, except for those delayed by strike or work stoppage, delay or cancellation of flights, or government action beyond the control of the Postal Service.

### Periodicals

Periodicals include newspapers and magazines.

For the general public, the applicable Standard Mail postage is paid for this type of mail.

For publishers, rates vary according to (1) whether the item is delivered in the county in which it is mailed; (2) the percentage of reading and advertising matter; (3) the item's weight; and (4) the distance it must travel.

### Standard Mail (A)

Standard Mail (A) is any piece of mail weighing less than 16 oz that is not included in First Class or Periodicals.

For single-piece mailing of publications, small parcels, printed matter, booklets, and catalogs, first ounce or fraction is 32¢; each additional ounce or fraction up to 11 oz is 23¢; each additional 2 oz over 11 oz up to 13 oz is 28¢; each additional 3 oz over 13 oz is 15¢.

For mailing Standard Mail (A) in bulk (at least 200 pieces or 50 lb of such items as solicitations, newsletters, advertising materials, books and cassettes, each item of which individually weighs less than 1 lb.), the minimum rate per piece, basic, non-letter, is $0.306 for pieces weighing 3.3087 oz or less; for pieces weighing more than 3.3087 oz, the rate is $0.166 per piece + $0.677 per pound. Contact your post office for the discounts offered for presorted, letter-shaped, destination entry, and automation-compatible mail.

Separate rates are available for some nonprofit organizations provided they apply to the postmaster for a permit. The permit requires a one-time imprint fee of $85 plus an annual (calendar year) fee of $85.

### Parcel Post—Standard Mail (B)

Any matter that weighs 16 oz or more and is not included in First Class or Periodicals goes as Parcel Post, or Standard Mail (B). The post office determines Parcel Post charges according to the weight of the package in pounds and the zone distance it is being shipped. All fractions of a pound are counted as a full pound.

### Forwarding Addresses

The mailer, in order to obtain a forwarding address, must endorse the envelope or cover "Address Correction Requested." The destination post office then will determine whether a forwarding address has been left on file and provide it for a fee of 50¢ per manual correction and 20¢ per automated correction.

### Priority Mail Flat Rate

The most expeditious handling and transportation available will be used for fast delivery by "Priority Mail." If the item fits into a special Postal Service flat-rate envelope, the rate is $3.00 regardless of weight.

Pickup service for Priority Mail is available for $4.95 for each stop (not per package) by the Postal Service.

### Priority Mail by Weight

Priority Mail may include packages weighing up to 70 lb and not exceeding 108 in. in length and girth combined, whether sealed or unsealed, including written and other First Class material. Fractions of a pound are charged as a full pound.

| Up to 2 lb | 3 lb | 4 lb | 5 lb |
|---|---|---|---|
| $3.00 | $4.00 | $5.00 | $6.00 |

For parcels over 5 lb, rates by zone apply within and between the U.S. and Puerto Rico and the Virgin Islands. The mileage between the specific geographic locations of 3-digit ZIP codes determines the zone number to be used. The mileage range represented by the zone number is: Zone 1—up to 50 mi; 2—51 to 150 mi; 3—151 to 300 mi; 4—301 to 600 mi; 5—601 to 1,000 mi; 6—1,001 to 1,400 mi; 7—1,401 to 1,800 mi; 8—over 1,800 mi. Consult postmaster for details.

Parcels weighing less than 15 lb and measuring over 84 in., but not exceeding 108 in. in length and girth combined, cost the same as a 15-lb parcel mailed to the same zone.

## Special Handling

Standard Mail and Parcel Post parcels can be given special, expedited handling upon payment of the following surcharge: up to 10 lb, $5.40; over 10 lb, $7.50. Such parcels must be marked for "Special Handling."

## Bound Printed Matter Rates

(single-piece zone rate)

| Weight | Zones | | | | | | | |
|---|---|---|---|---|---|---|---|---|
| lb | Local | 1&2 | 3 | 4 | 5 | 6 | 7 | 8 |
| 1.5 | $1.11 | $1.49 | $1.52 | $1.58 | $1.66 | $1.74 | $1.84 | $1.93 |
| 2 | 1.12 | 1.52 | 1.56 | 1.63 | 1.74 | 1.85 | 1.99 | 2.10 |
| 2.5 | 1.14 | 1.55 | 1.60 | 1.69 | 1.82 | 1.96 | 2.13 | 2.28 |
| 3 | 1.15 | 1.57 | 1.64 | 1.74 | 1.90 | 2.07 | 2.27 | 2.45 |
| 3.5 | 1.17 | 1.60 | 1.67 | 1.80 | 1.98 | 2.18 | 2.42 | 2.62 |
| 4 | 1.18 | 1.63 | 1.71 | 1.85 | 2.07 | 2.29 | 2.56 | 2.79 |
| 4.5 | 1.20 | 1.65 | 1.75 | 1.91 | 2.15 | 2.40 | 2.71 | 2.97 |
| 5 | 1.22 | 1.68 | 1.79 | 1.96 | 2.23 | 2.51 | 2.85 | 3.14 |
| 6 | 1.25 | 1.73 | 1.86 | 2.07 | 2.39 | 2.73 | 3.14 | 3.49 |
| 7 | 1.28 | 1.79 | 1.94 | 2.18 | 2.56 | 2.95 | 3.43 | 3.83 |
| 8 | 1.31 | 1.84 | 2.01 | 2.29 | 2.72 | 3.17 | 3.71 | 4.18 |
| 9 | 1.34 | 1.90 | 2.09 | 2.40 | 2.89 | 3.39 | 4.00 | 4.52 |
| 10 | 1.37 | 1.95 | 2.16 | 2.51 | 3.05 | 3.61 | 4.29 | 4.87 |

(Includes both catalogs and similar bound printed matter.)

(Bound printed matter must weigh at least 1 lb and not more than 10 lb. Bound printed matter includes catalogs, directories, and books not eligible for special Parcel Post rates.)

## Domestic Mail Special Services

**Registry**—Only matter prepaid with postage at First Class postage rates may be registered. Stamps or meter stamps must be attached. The face of the article must be at least 5″ long, 3½″ high. The mailer is required to declare the value of mail presented for registration.

### Registered Mail

| Declared Value | Insured | Uninsured |
|---|---|---|
| $0.00 to $100 | $4.95 | $4.85 |
| $100.01 to $500 | 5.40 | 5.20 |
| $500.01 to $1,000 | 5.85 | 5.55 |
| $1,000.01 to $2,000 | 6.30 | 5.90 |
| $2,000.01 to $3,000 | 6.75 | 6.25 |
| $3,000.01 to $4,000 | 7.20 | 6.60 |
| $4,000.01 to $5,000 | 7.65 | 6.95 |
| $5,000.01 to $6,000 | 8.10 | 7.30 |
| $6,000.01 to $7,000 | 8.55 | 7.65 |
| $7,000.01 to $8,000 | 9.00 | 8.00 |
| $8,000.01 to $9,000 | 9.45 | 8.35 |
| $9,000.01 to $10,000 | 9.90 | 8.70 |

Consult postmaster for registry rates above $10,000.

**C.O.D.: Unregistered:** Applicable to First Class, Standard Mail, and Express Mail matter. Such mail must be sent as bona fide orders or be in conformity with agreements between senders and addressees. **Registered:** For details, consult postmaster.

**Insurance:** Applicable to Standard Mail matter. Matter for sale addressed to prospective purchasers who have not ordered it or authorized its sending cannot be insured.

### Insured Mail Rates

| | |
|---|---|
| $0.01 to $50 | $0.75 |
| 50.01 to $100 | 1.60 |
| 100.01 to $200 | 2.50 |
| 200.01 to $300 | 3.40 |
| 300.01 to $400 | 4.30 |
| 400.01 to $500 | 5.20 |
| 500.01 to $600 | 6.10 |

Liability for insured mail is limited to $600.

**Certified mail:** This service is available for any matter having no intrinsic value on which First Class or Air Mail postage is paid. Receipt is furnished at time of mailing, and evidence of delivery is obtained. The basic fee is $1.10 in addition to postage. Return receipt, restricted delivery, and special delivery are available upon payment of additional fees. No indemnity.

## Special Standard Mail

(limit 70 lb)

Applies to only the following specific articles: Books of at least 8 printed pages consisting wholly of reading matter or scholarly bibliography, or reading matter with incidental blank spaces for notations and containing no advertising matter other than incidental announcements of books; 16-mm or narrower-width films in final form and catalogs of such films of 24 pages or more (at least 22 of which are printed) except films and film catalogs sent to or from commercial theaters; printed music in bound or sheet form; printed objective test materials; sound recordings, playscripts, and manuscripts for books, periodicals, and music; printed educational reference charts; loose-leaf pages and binders consisting of medical information for distribution to doctors, hospitals, medical schools, and medical students; computer-readable media containing prerecorded information and guides for use with such media. Package must be marked "Special Standard Class Rate" stating item contained. The rates are: first pound or fraction, $1.24 (70¢ if 500 pieces or more of special rate matter are presorted to 5-digit ZIP code or $1.04 if 500 pieces or more are presorted to Bulk Mail Centers); each additional pound or fraction through 7 lb, 50¢; each additional pound, 31¢.

## Library Mail

(limit 70 lb)

Library Mail includes the following: books when loaned or exchanged between and sent to or from schools, colleges, public libraries, and certain nonprofit organizations; books, printed music, bound academic theses, periodicals, sound recordings, other library materials, museum materials (specimens, collections), scientific or mathematical kits, instruments or other devices; also catalogs, guides, or scripts for some of these materials. Also qualifying for library rate are books mailed from publishers or distributors to schools, libraries, colleges, or universities or to bookstores owned, operated, and controlled by schools, colleges, or universities. All such packages must be marked "Library Mail." The rate is: first pound, $1.12; each additional pound through 7 lb, 41¢; each additional pound, 20¢.

## Parcel Post Rate Schedule

(Inter BMC/ASF ZIP codes only, machinable parcels, no discount, no surcharge)

| Weight up to but not exceeding—(pounds) | Zones | | | | | | | |
|---|---|---|---|---|---|---|---|---|
| | Local | 1 and 2 | 3 | 4 | 5 | 6 | 7 | 8 |
| 2 | $2.56 | $2.63 | $2.79 | $2.87 | $2.95 | $2.95 | $2.95 | $2.95 |
| 3 | 2.63 | 2.76 | 3.00 | 3.34 | 3.68 | 3.95 | 3.95 | 3.95 |
| 4 | 2.71 | 2.87 | 3.20 | 3.78 | 4.68 | 4.95 | 4.95 | 4.95 |
| 5 | 2.77 | 2.97 | 3.38 | 4.10 | 5.19 | 5.56 | 5.95 | 5.95 |
| 6 | 2.84 | 3.07 | 3.55 | 4.39 | 5.67 | 6.90 | 7.75 | 7.95 |
| 7 | 2.90 | 3.16 | 3.71 | 4.67 | 6.11 | 7.51 | 9.15 | 9.75 |
| 8 | 2.96 | 3.26 | 3.85 | 4.91 | 6.53 | 8.08 | 9.94 | 11.55 |
| 9 | 3.01 | 3.33 | 3.99 | 5.16 | 6.92 | 8.62 | 10.65 | 12.95 |
| 10 | 3.07 | 3.42 | 4.12 | 5.38 | 7.29 | 9.12 | 11.31 | 14.00 |
| 11 | 3.12 | 3.49 | 4.25 | 5.59 | 7.63 | 9.59 | 11.93 | 15.05 |
| 12 | 3.17 | 3.57 | 4.37 | 5.79 | 7.96 | 10.03 | 12.52 | 16.10 |

(*continued*)

| Weight up to but not exceeding—(pounds) | Local | 1 and 2 | 3 | Zones 4 | 5 | 6 | 7 | 8 |
|---|---|---|---|---|---|---|---|---|
| 13 | $3.23 | $3.64 | $4.47 | $5.98 | $8.26 | $10.45 | $13.07 | $17.15 |
| 14 | 3.27 | 3.71 | 4.59 | 6.16 | 8.55 | 10.84 | 13.59 | 18.20 |
| 15 | 3.32 | 3.77 | 4.69 | 6.34 | 8.82 | 11.22 | 14.08 | 19.25 |
| 16 | 3.37 | 3.83 | 4.79 | 6.50 | 9.09 | 11.58 | 14.55 | 20.30 |
| 17 | 3.41 | 3.90 | 4.88 | 6.66 | 9.33 | 11.92 | 15.00 | 21.35 |
| 18 | 3.45 | 3.95 | 4.97 | 6.81 | 9.58 | 12.24 | 15.42 | 22.40 |
| 19 | 3.49 | 4.02 | 5.06 | 6.95 | 9.80 | 12.55 | 15.83 | 23.25 |
| 20 | 3.54 | 4.07 | 5.14 | 7.08 | 10.01 | 12.84 | 16.21 | 23.84 |
| 21 | 3.57 | 4.12 | 5.23 | 7.21 | 10.23 | 13.12 | 16.59 | 24.41 |
| 22 | 3.61 | 4.18 | 5.30 | 7.34 | 10.43 | 13.39 | 16.94 | 24.96 |
| 23 | 3.65 | 4.23 | 5.39 | 7.47 | 10.62 | 13.66 | 17.28 | 25.47 |
| 24 | 3.69 | 4.27 | 5.46 | 7.58 | 10.80 | 13.90 | 17.60 | 25.97 |
| 25 | 3.73 | 4.32 | 5.53 | 7.70 | 10.98 | 14.14 | 17.91 | 26.45 |

## Postal Union Mail Special Services

**Registration:** Available to practically all countries. Fee $4.85. The maximum indemnity payable—generally only in case of complete loss (of both contents and wrapper)—is $42.30. To Canada only, the fee is $4.95 providing indemnity for loss up to $100, $5.40 for loss up to $500, and $5.85 for loss up to $1,000.

**Return receipt:** Shows to whom and date delivered, $1.10.

**Special delivery:** Available to most countries. Consult post office. Fees for International Special Delivery are the same for air or surface: for letters, letter packages, and postcards not over 2 lb, $9.95; if over 2 lb, $10.35. For printed matter, matter for the blind, or small packets, $10.45 if not over 2 lb; if over 2 lb, $11.25.

**Marking:** An article that is intended for special delivery service must have affixed to the cover near the name of the country of destination "EXPRES" (special delivery) label, obtainable at the post office, or the word "EXPRES" (special delivery) may be marked on the cover boldly in red letters.

**Special handling:** Entitles AO surface packages to priority handling between mailing point and U.S. point of dispatch. Fees: $5.40 for packages to 10 lb, and $7.50 for packages over 10 lb.

**Air mail:** Daily air service is available to practically all countries.

**Prepayment of replies from other countries:** A mailer who wishes to prepay a reply by letter from another country may do so by sending one or more international reply coupons, available at U.S. post offices. These should be accepted in any country in exchange for stamps to prepay an air mail letter of the first unit of weight to the U.S.

**Additional international special services: Insurance:** Available to many countries for loss of or damage to items paid at parcel post rate. Consult postmaster for indemnity limits for individual countries.

| Limit of indemnity Not over | Canada[1] | Fees All other countries[1] |
|---|---|---|
| $50 | $0.75 | $1.60 |
| 100 | 1.60 | 2.45 |
| 200 | 2.50 | 3.35 |
| 300 | 3.40 | 4.25 |
| 400 | 4.30 | 5.15 |
| 500 | 5.20 | 6.05 |
| 600 | 6.10 | 6.95 |
| 700 | | 7.40 |
| 800 | | 7.85 |
| 900 | | 8.30 |
| 1,000 | | 8.75 |
| 1,100 | | 9.20 |
| 1,200 | | 9.65 |

(1) Not all countries insure items up to the amounts listed in the table. Canada does not insure items for more than $600.

**Restricted Delivery:** Available to many countries for registered mail; limits who may receive an item. Fee: $2.75.

## Post Office-Authorized 2-Letter State Abbreviations

The abbreviations below are approved by the U.S. Postal Service for use in addresses for the 50 states, the District of Columbia, Puerto Rico, the U.S. Virgin Islands, American Samoa, Guam, and certain other areas in the Pacific.

| | | | | | | | |
|---|---|---|---|---|---|---|---|
| Alabama | AL | Hawaii | HI | Missouri | MO | Pennsylvania | PA |
| Alaska | AK | Idaho | ID | Montana | MT | Puerto Rico | PR |
| American Samoa | AS | Illinois | IL | Nebraska | NE | Rhode Island | RI |
| Arizona | AZ | Indiana | IN | Nevada | NV | South Carolina | SC |
| Arkansas | AR | Iowa | IA | New Hampshire | NH | South Dakota | SD |
| California | CA | Kansas | KS | New Jersey | NJ | Tennessee | TN |
| Colorado | CO | Kentucky | KY | New Mexico | NM | Texas | TX |
| Connecticut | CT | Louisiana | LA | New York | NY | Utah | UT |
| Delaware | DE | Maine | ME | North Carolina | NC | Vermont | VT |
| Dist. of Col. | DC | Marshall Islands[1] | MH | North Dakota | ND | Virginia | VA |
| Federated States of Micronesia[1] | FM | Maryland | MD | Northern Mariana Is. | MP | Virgin Islands | VI |
| | | Massachusetts | MA | Ohio | OH | Washington | WA |
| Florida | FL | Michigan | MI | Oklahoma | OK | West Virginia | WV |
| Georgia | GA | Minnesota | MN | Oregon | OR | Wisconsin | WI |
| Guam | GU | Mississippi | MS | Palau | PW | Wyoming | WY |

(1) Although an independent nation, this country is currently subject to domestic rates and fees.

## Canadian Province and Territory Postal Codes

| | | | |
|---|---|---|---|
| Alberta | AB | Northwest Territories | NT |
| British Columbia | BC | Ontario | ON |
| Manitoba | MB | Prince Edward Island | PE |
| New Brunswick | NB | Quebec | QC |
| Newfoundland and Labrador | NF | Saskatchewan | SK |
| Nova Scotia | NS | Yukon Territory | YT |

# International Air Mail Rates

**Aerogrammes** — 50¢ from U.S. to all countries.
**Air mail postcards** (single) — 50¢ to all countries except Canada (40¢ each) and Mexico (35¢ each).
**International letters and letter packages: to Canada and Mexico** (by air mail; there are no surface rates to these countries)—weight not over 0.5 oz, 46¢ to Canada, 40¢ to Mexico; not over 1.0 oz, 52¢ to Canada, 46¢ to Mexico; not over 2 oz, 72¢ to Canada, 86¢ to Mexico; not over 3 oz, 95¢ to Canada, $1.26¢ to Mexico.

## Air Mail, Letter, and Letter Package Rates to Countries Other Than Canada and Mexico

(weight limit: 64 oz [4 lb])

| Weight not over | Rate | Weight not over | Rate | Weight not over | Rate | Weight not over | Rate |
|---|---|---|---|---|---|---|---|
| 0.5 oz | $0.60 | 12.5 oz | $10.20 | 24.5 oz | $19.80 | 41 oz | $29.40 |
| 1.0 | 1.00 | 13.0 | 10.60 | 25.0 | 20.20 | 42 | 29.80 |
| 1.5 | 1.40 | 13.5 | 11.00 | 25.5 | 20.60 | 43 | 30.20 |
| 2.0 | 1.80 | 14.0 | 11.40 | 26.0 | 21.00 | 44 | 30.60 |
| 2.5 | 2.20 | 14.5 | 11.80 | 26.5 | 21.40 | 45 | 31.00 |
| 3.0 | 2.60 | 15.0 | 12.20 | 27.0 | 21.80 | 46 | 31.40 |
| 3.5 | 3.00 | 15.5 | 12.60 | 27.5 | 22.20 | 47 | 31.80 |
| 4.0 | 3.40 | 16.0 | 13.00 | 28.0 | 22.60 | 48 | 32.20 |
| 4.5 | 3.80 | 16.5 | 13.40 | 28.5 | 23.00 | 49 | 32.60 |
| 5.0 | 4.20 | 17.0 | 13.80 | 29.0 | 23.40 | 50 | 33.00 |
| 5.5 | 4.60 | 17.5 | 14.20 | 29.5 | 23.80 | 51 | 33.40 |
| 6.0 | 5.00 | 18.0 | 14.60 | 30.0 | 24.20 | 52 | 33.80 |
| 6.5 | 5.40 | 18.5 | 15.00 | 30.5 | 24.60 | 53 | 34.20 |
| 7.0 | 5.80 | 19.0 | 15.40 | 31.0 | 25.00 | 54 | 34.60 |
| 7.5 | 6.20 | 19.5 | 15.80 | 31.5 | 25.40 | 55 | 35.00 |
| 8.0 | 6.60 | 20.0 | 16.20 | 32.0 | 25.80 | 56 | 35.40 |
| 8.5 | 7.00 | 20.5 | 16.60 | 33.0 | 26.20 | 57 | 35.80 |
| 9.0 | 7.40 | 21.0 | 17.00 | 34.0 | 26.60 | 58 | 36.20 |
| 9.5 | 7.80 | 21.5 | 17.40 | 35.0 | 27.00 | 59 | 36.60 |
| 10.0 | 8.20 | 22.0 | 17.80 | 36.0 | 27.40 | 60 | 37.00 |
| 10.5 | 8.60 | 22.5 | 18.20 | 37.0 | 27.80 | 61 | 37.40 |
| 11.0 | 9.00 | 23.0 | 18.60 | 38.0 | 28.20 | 62 | 37.80 |
| 11.5 | 9.40 | 23.5 | 19.00 | 39.0 | 28.60 | 63 | 38.20 |
| 12.0 | 9.80 | 24.0 | 19.40 | 40.0 | 29.00 | 64 | 38.60 |

## Air Mail Parcel Post Rates

| Weight | Cost, depending on country's rate group | | | | |
|---|---|---|---|---|---|
| | A | B | C | D | E |
| First pound | $6.50 | $8.25 | $9.75 | $11.20 | $12.80 |
| Each additional pound or fraction up to 5 lb | 3.36 | 4.00 | 5.28 | 5.76 | 6.40 |
| Each additional pound or fraction up to 10 lb | 2.88 | 3.20 | 4.32 | 5.28 | 5.44 |
| Each additional pound or fraction up to 20 lb | 2.72 | 2.88 | 4.00 | 4.32 | 4.48 |
| Each additional pound or fraction up to 30 lb | 2.24 | 2.56 | 3.84 | 4.16 | 4.32 |
| Each additional pound or fraction over 30 lb | 1.92 | 2.24 | 3.68 | 4.00 | 4.16 |

### Country Rate Groups

(For further information, consult your local post office.)

| Country or territory | Rate group | Maximum weight limit (lbs) |
|---|---|---|
| Afghanistan[1] | D | 44 |
| Albania | C | 44 |
| Algeria | D | 66 |
| Andorra | B | 44 |
| Angola | E | 22 |
| Anguilla | A | 22 |
| Antigua & Barbuda | A | 22 |
| Argentina | D | 44 |
| Armenia | E | 44 |
| Aruba | A | 44 |
| Ascension | no air service | 44 (surface) |
| Australia | D | 44 |
| Austria | B | 44 |
| Azerbaijan | E | 22 |
| Azores | C | 44 |
| Bahamas | A | 44 |
| Bahrain | D | 44 |
| Bangladesh | E | 22 |
| Barbados | B | 44 |
| Belarus | E | 44 |
| Belgium | D | 44 |
| Belize | A | 44 |
| Benin | C | 44 |
| Bermuda | A | 44 |
| Bhutan | E | 44 |
| Bolivia | B | 44 |
| Bosnia and Herzegovina | C | 33 |
| Botswana | E | 44 |
| Brazil | E | 44 |
| British Virgin Islands | A | 44 |
| Brunei | D | 44 |
| Bulgaria | D | 44 |
| Burkina Faso | D | 44 |
| Burma | see Myanmar | |
| Burundi | E | 44 |
| Cambodia[2] | E | 44 (air only) |
| Cameroon | D | 44 |
| Canada | separate rate group | 66 |
| Cape Verde | D | 44 |
| Cayman Islands | A | 44 |
| Central African Republic | E | 44 |
| Chad[3] | D | 44 (air only) |
| Chile | D | 44 |
| China (People's Republic of) | D | 44 |
| Colombia | B | 44 |
| Comoros | E | 44 |
| Congo | D | 44 |
| Corsica | E | 44 |
| Costa Rica | A | 44 |
| Côte d'Ivoire | D | 44 |
| Croatia | C | 44 |
| Cuba[2] | no parcel post service | |
| Cyprus | C | 44 |
| Czech Republic | C | 33 |
| Denmark | C | 66 |
| Djibouti | D | 44 |
| Dominica | A | 44 |
| Dominican Republic | A | 44 |

(*continued*)

| Country or territory | Rate group | Maximum weight limit (lbs) |
|---|---|---|
| East Timor | see Indonesia | |
| Ecuador | C | 44 |
| Egypt | D | 44 |
| El Salvador | B | 44 |
| Equatorial Guinea | D | 44 |
| Eritrea | D | 44 |
| Estonia | E | 44 |
| Ethiopia | D | 44 |
| Faeroe Islands | C | 66 |
| Falkland Islands[2] | no air PP | 44 (surface) |
| Fiji | B | 44 |
| Finland | D | 44 |
| France | E | 44 |
| French Guiana | C | 44 |
| French Polynesia | D | 44 |
| Gabon[3] | D | 44 |
| Gambia, The | B | 22 |
| Georgia, Republic of | E | 22 |
| Germany | B | 44 |
| Ghana | D | 44 |
| Gibraltar | C | 44 |
| Great Britain and Northern Ireland | C | 66 |
| Greece | C | 44 |
| Greenland | D | 66 |
| Grenada | A | 44 |
| Guadeloupe | A | 44 |
| Guatemala | A | 44 |
| Guinea | B | 44 |
| Guinea-Bissau | B | 22 |
| Guyana | B | 44 |
| Haiti | A | 44 |
| Honduras | B | 44 |
| Hong Kong | C | 44 |
| Hungary | C | 44 |
| Iceland | C | 44 |
| India | D | 44 |
| Indonesia[4] | E | 44 |
| Iran | D | 44 |
| Iraq[2] | D | 44 |
| Ireland | C | 66 |
| Israel[5] | C | 44 |
| Italy | C | 44 |
| Ivory Coast | see Côte d'Ivoire | |
| Jamaica | A | 22 |
| Japan | E | 44 |
| Jordan | C | 44 |
| Kazakstan | E | 44 |
| Kenya | D | 44 |
| Kiribati | B | 44 |
| Korea, Democratic People's Rep. of (North)[2] | no parcel post service | |
| Korea, Republic of (South) | C | 44 |
| Kuwait[3] | C | 44 (air only) |
| Kyrgyzstan | E | 22 |
| Laos | E | 44 |
| Latvia | E | 44 |
| Lebanon[2,3] | C | 11 (air only) |
| Lesotho | E | 44 |
| Liberia[3] | C | 44 |
| Libya[2] | D | 44 |
| Liechtenstein | B | 66 |
| Lithuania | E | 44 |
| Luxembourg | B | 44 |
| Macao | C | 44 |
| Macedonia | C | 33 |
| Madagascar | E | 44 |
| Madeira Islands | B | 44 |
| Malawi | D | 44 |
| Malaysia | D | 22 |
| Maldives | D | 22 |
| Mali | C | 44 |
| Malta | C | 22 |
| Martinique | A | 44 |
| Mauritania | D | 44 |
| Mauritius | E | 22 |
| Mexico | A | 44 |
| Moldova | E | 44 |
| Monaco | E | 44 |
| Mongolia | no parcel post service | |
| Montserrat | A | 44 |
| Morocco | C | 44 |
| Mozambique | E | 44 |
| Myanmar | D | 22 |

| Country or territory | Rate group | Maximum weight limit (lbs) |
|---|---|---|
| Namibia | D | 44 |
| Nauru | C | 44 |
| Nepal | D | 44 (surface)<br>11 (air) |
| Netherlands | C | 44 |
| Netherlands Antilles | A | 44 |
| New Caledonia | D | 44 |
| New Zealand | D | 44 |
| Nicaragua | B | 44 |
| Niger | D | 44 |
| Nigeria | C | 44 |
| Norway | D | 44 |
| Oman | D | 44 |
| Pakistan | D | 44 |
| Panama | A | 44 |
| Papua New Guinea[2] | D | 44 |
| Paraguay | D | 44 |
| Peru | B | 44 |
| Philippines | D | 44 |
| Pitcairn Island | B | 22 |
| Poland | B | 33 |
| Portugal | C | 44 |
| Qatar | C | 44 |
| Reunion | E | 44 |
| Romania | C | 44 |
| Russia | E | 22 |
| Rwanda[2] | D | 44 |
| Saint Helena | C | 44 |
| Saint Kitts & Nevis | A | 44 |
| Saint Lucia | A | 44 |
| Saint Pierre & Miguelon | A | 44 |
| Saint Vincent & the Grenadines | A | 22 |
| San Marino | C | 44 |
| São Tomé & Príncipe | D | 44 |
| Saudi Arabia | D | 44 |
| Senegal | D | 44 |
| Seychelles | D | 44 |
| Sierre Leone | D | 44 |
| Singapore | D | 44 |
| Slovakia | C | 33 |
| Slovenia | C | 33 |
| Solomon Islands | C | 44 |
| Somalia[1] | D | 44 |
| South Africa | D | 44 |
| Spain | C | 44 |
| Sri Lanka | D | 44 |
| Sudan | D | 44 |
| Suriname | B | 44 |
| Swaziland | D | 44 |
| Sweden | D | 44 |
| Switzerland | B | 66 |
| Syria | C | 44 |
| Taiwan | C | 44 |
| Tajikistan | E | 22 |
| Tanzania | E | 44 |
| Thailand | D | 44 |
| Togo | D | 44 |
| Tonga | B | 44 |
| Trinidad & Tobago | B | 22 |
| Tristan da Cunha | E | 22 |
| Tunisia | C | 44 |
| Turkey | C | 44 |
| Turkmenistan | E | 22 |
| Turks and Caicos Islands | A | 22 |
| Tuvalu | B | 44 |
| Uganda | D | 44 |
| Ukraine | E | 44 |
| United Arab Emirates | D | 44 |
| United Kingdom | C | 66 |
| Uruguay | B | 44 |
| Uzbekistan | E | 22 |
| Vanuatu | B | 44 |
| Vatican City | C | 44 |
| Venezuela | B | 44 |
| Vietnam | E | 44 |
| Wallis & Futuna Islands | D | 44 |
| Western Samoa | B | 44 |
| Yemen | E | 44 |
| Yugoslavia[2] | C | 33 |
| Zaire | E | 44 |
| Zambia | E | 44 |
| Zimbabwe | E | 44 |

(1) All mail service suspended. (2) Mail service restrictions apply. (3) Surface mail service suspended. (4) Includes East Timor. (5) West Bank and Gaza Strip are same rate group as Israel.

# LANGUAGE

## New Words in English*

The following words and definitions were provided by Merriam-Webster Inc., publishers of *Merriam-Webster's Collegiate Dictionary, Tenth Edition.* The words are among those that the Merriam-Webster editors decided had achieved enough currency in English to be entered in the 1995 or 1996 copyright revisions of the dictionary.

**blow off** (1) to refuse to take notice of, honor, or deal with; ignore; (2) to fail to attend or show up for

**caffe latte** espresso mixed with hot or steamed milk

**channel surfing** the act or practice of scanning through television programs usu. by use of a remote control

**chump change** a relatively small or insignificant amount of money

**cocooning** the practice of spending leisure time at home in preference to going out

**cyberpunk** (1) science fiction dealing with future urban societies dominated by computer technology; (2) an opportunistic computer hacker

**cyberspace** the online world of computer networks

**drive-by** carried out from a moving vehicle

**ear candy** music that is pleasing to listen to but lacks depth

**Ebola virus** an RNA-containing virus of African origin that causes an often fatal hemorrhagic fever

**ecotourism** the practice of touring natural habitats in a manner that minimizes ecological impact

**edutainment** a form of entertainment (as a game, film, or show) that is designed to be educational

**ethnic cleansing** the expulsion, imprisonment, or killing of ethnic or racial minorities by a dominant majority group

**gangbanger** a member of a street gang

**gender bender** a person who dresses and behaves like a member of the opposite sex

**graphic novel** a fictional story for adults that is presented in comic-strip format and published as a trade book

**grunge** (1) one that is grungy; (2) a style of popular music mixing elements of rock and roll, punk rock, and heavy metal; *also* the unkempt working-class fashions typical of fans of grunge

**homeschool** to teach school subjects to one's children at home

**humvee** a diesel-powered multipurpose U.S. military vehicle that replaced the jeep

**infomercial** a television program that is an extended advertisement often including a discussion or demonstration

**in-line skate** a roller skate in which the four wheels are set in-line for greater speed and maneuverability

**maquiladora** a foreign-owned factory in Mexico at which imported parts are assembled by lower-paid workers into products for export

**reality check** something that clarifies reality, often by correcting a misconception

**shareware** software with usu. limited capability or incomplete documentation which is available for trial use at little or no cost but which can be upgraded upon payment of a fee to the author

**telephone tag** telephoning back and forth by parties trying to reach each other

**victimology** (1) the study of victims and victimization; (2) the claim that one's problems are the result of one's victimization

**vogue** to strike poses in campy imitation of fashion models

**wuss** a weak, cowardly, or ineffectual person

**zone out** to become oblivious to one's surroundings esp. in order to relax

* See also glossaries in the Computers section.

## Eponyms

(words named for people)

**Bloody Mary**—a vodka and tomato juice drink; after the nickname of Mary I, Queen of England (1553-58), notorious for persecution of Protestants

**bloomers**—full, loose trousers gathered at the knee; after Amelia Bloomer, an American social reformer who advocated (1851) such clothing

**bobbies**—in Great Britain, police officers; after Sir Robert Peel, the statesman who organized the London police force, 1850

**bowdlerize**—to delete written matter considered indelicate; after Thomas Bowdler, English editor of an expurgated Shakespeare (1825)

**boycott**—to avoid trade or dealings with, as a protest; after Charles C. Boycott, an English land agent in County Mayo, Ireland, ostracized in 1880 for refusing to reduce rents

**Braille**—a system of writing for the blind; after Louis Braille, the French teacher of the blind who invented it (1853)

**Casanova**—a man who is a promiscuous and unscrupulous lover; after Giovanni Giacomo Casanova (1725-98), an Italian adventurer

**chauvinist**—excessively patriotic; after Nicolas Chauvin, a character in a 19th-cent. play who is devoted to Napoleon

**derby**—a stiff felt hat with a dome-shaped crown and rather narrow rolled brim; after Edward Stanley, 12th earl of Derby, who in 1780 founded the Derby horse race, to which these hats are worn

**diesel**—a type of internal combustion engine or a vehicle driven by it; after Rudolf Diesel (1858-1913), who built the first successful diesel engine

**gerrymander**—to draw an election district in such a way as to favor a political party; after Elbridge Gerry, who created (1812) just such an election district (shaped like a salamander) during his governorship of Massachusetts

**guillotine**—a machine for beheading; after Joseph Guillotin, a French physician who proposed its use in 1789 as more humane than hanging

**leotard**—a close-fitting garment for the torso, worn by dancers, acrobats, and the like; after Julius Leotard, a 19th-century French aerial gymnast

**sandwich**—2 or more slices of bread with a filling in between; after John Montagu, 4th earl of Sandwich (1718-92), who supposedly ate food in this form so that he would not have to leave the gaming table

**silhouette**—an outline image; from Étienne de Silhouette (1709-67), a close-fisted French finance minister

## National Spelling Bee

The Scripps Howard National Spelling Bee, conducted by Scripps Howard Newspapers and other leading newspapers since 1939, was instituted by the Louisville (Ky.) *Courier-Journal* in 1925. Children under 16 years of age and not beyond the 8th grade are eligible to compete for cash prizes at the finals, which are held annually in Washington, DC. The 1996 winners were first prize, **Wendy Guey**, West Palm Beach, FL; second prize, **Nikki Dowdy**, Houston, TX; third prize, **Katie Ward**, Albany, NY.

Here are the last words given in each of the years 1981-96 at the spelling bee. They were all correctly spelled, thereby determining the national champion:

| | | | |
|---|---|---|---|
| 1981 — sarcophagus | 1985 — milieu | 1989 — spoliator | 1993 — kamikaze |
| 1982 — psoriasis | 1986 — odontalgia | 1990 — fibranne | 1994 — antediluvian |
| 1983 — purim | 1987 — staphylococci | 1991 — antipyretic | 1995 — xanthosis |
| 1984 — luge | 1988 — elegiacal | 1992 — lyceum | 1996 — vivisepulture |

## Foreign Words and Phrases

(L=Latin; F=French; Y=Yiddish; R=Russian; G=Greek; I=Italian; S=Spanish)

**ad hoc** (L; ad HOK): for the particular end or purpose at hand

**ad infinitum** (L; ad in-fi-NITE-um): without end; forever

**ad nauseam** (L; ad NAWZ-ee-um): to a sickening degree

**apropos** (F; ap-ruh-POH): relevant

**bête noire** (F; BET NWAHR): a thing or person viewed with particular dislike

**bon appétit** (F; BOH nap-uh-teet): I wish you a good appetite; have a good meal

**bona fide** (L; BOH nuh-feyed): genuine; in good faith

**carte blanche** (F; kahrt BLANNSH): full discretionary power

**cause célèbre** (F; kawz suh-LEB-ruh): a notorious incident

**c'est la vie** (F; se lah VEE): that's life

**chutzpah** (Y; KHOOT-spuh): amazing nerve bordering on arrogance

**coup de grâce** (F; kooh duh GRAHS): the final blow

**coup d'état** (F; kooh day TAH): overthrow of an existing government by a small group

**crème de la crème** (F; KREM duh luh KREM): the best of the best

**cum laude/magna cum laude/summa cum laude** (L; KUHM loud-ay; MAGN-ya . . . ; SOO-ma . . . ): with praise or honor; with great praise or honor; with the highest praise or honor—grades of academic honor granted to graduates

**de facto** (L; di FAK-toh): in fact; in effect, though not officially or by right

**déjà vu** (F; DAY-zhah VOOH): the sensation that something happening has happened before

**de jure** (L; dee JOOR-ee, day YOOR-ay): in accordance with right or law; officially

**de rigueur** (F; duh ree-GUR): necessary according to convention or etiquette

**détente** (F; day-TAHNT): an easing or relaxation of strained relations

**éminence grise** (F; ay-meh-NAHNN-suh GREEZ): one who wields power behind the scenes

**enfant terrible** (F; ahnn-FAHNN te-REE-bluh): one whose unconventional behavior causes embarrassment

**en masse** (F; ahn MAHS): in a large body

**ergo** (L; ER-goh): therefore

**esprit de corps** (F; es-PREE duh KAWR): group spirit; feeling of camaraderie

**eureka** (G; YOOR-EE-kuh): I have found it

**ex post facto** (L; eks pohst FAK-toh): retroactive(ly)

**fait accompli** (F; fayt uh-kom-PLEE): an accomplished fact

**faux pas** (F; fowe PAH): a social blunder

**hoi polloi** (G; hoy puh-LOY): the masses

**in loco parentis** (L; in LOH-koh puh-REN-tis): in place of a parent

**in memoriam** (L; in muh-MAWR-ee-uhm): in memory of; often used in epitaphs

**in situ** (L; in SEYE-tyooh): in the original place or position

**in toto** (L; in TOH-toh): totally

**je ne sais quoi** (F; zhuh nuh say KWAH): I don't know what; the little something that eludes description

**joie de vivre** (F; zhwah duh VEEV-ruh): joy of living, love of life

**mea culpa** (L; MAY-uh CUL-puh): through my fault

**modus operandi** (L; MOH-duhs op-uh-RAN-dee): method of operation

**noblesse oblige** (F; noh-BLES uh-BLEEZH): the obligation of nobility to help the less fortunate

**non compos mentis** (L; non KOM-puhs MEN-tis): not of sound mind

**nouveau riche** (F; nooh-voh REESH): a person newly rich; perhaps one who spends money conspicuously

**perestroika** (R; PAIR-es TROY-kuh): restructuring

**persona non grata** (L; per-SOH-nah non GRAH-tah): unwelcome person

**postmortem** (L; pohst-MORE-tuhm): after death; autopsy; analysis after an event

**prima donna** (I; pree-muh DAH-nuh): a principal female opera singer; temperamental person

**pro tempore** (L; proh TEM-puh-ree): for the time being

**que sera sera** (S; keh sair-ah sair-AH): what will be will be

**quid pro quo** (L; kwid proh KWOH): something given or received for something else

**raison d'être** (F; RAY-zohnn DET-ruh): reason for being

**savoir faire** (F; sav-wahr-FAIR): dexterity in social and practical affairs

**schlemiel** (Y; shleh-MEEL): an unlucky, bungling person

**semper fidelis** (L; SEM-puhr fee-DAY-lis): always faithful

**status quo** (L; STAY-tus QWOH): existing order of things

**terra firma** (L; TER-uh FUR-muh): solid ground

**tour de force** (F; TOOR duh FAWRS): feat accomplished through great skill

**verbatim** (L; ver-BAY-tuhm): word for word

**vis-à-vis** (F; vee-ZUH-VEE): face to face with; compared with; with regard to

## Young of Animals Have Special Names

The young of many mammals, birds, and fish have come to be called by special names. A young eel, for example, is an elver. Many young animals, of course, are often referred to simply as infants, babies, younglets, or younglings.

**bunny:** rabbit
**calf:** cattle, elephant, antelope, rhino, hippo, whale, others
**cheeper:** grouse, partridge, quail
**chick, chicken:** fowl
**cockerel:** rooster
**codling, sprag:** codfish
**colt:** horse (male)
**cub:** lion, bear, shark, fox, others
**cygnet:** swan
**duckling:** duck
**eaglet:** eagle
**elver:** eel
**eyas:** hawk, others
**fawn:** deer
**filly:** horse (female)
**fingerling:** fish generally
**flapper:** wild fowl
**fledgling:** birds generally
**foal:** horse, zebra, others
**fry:** fish generally
**gosling:** goose
**heifer:** cow
**joey:** kangaroo, others
**kid:** goat
**kit:** fox, beaver, rabbit, cat
**kitten, kitty, catling:** cats, other small mammals
**lamb, lambkin, cosset, hog:** sheep
**leveret:** hare
**nestling:** birds generally
**owlet:** owl
**parr, smolt, grilse:** salmon
**piglet, shoat, farrow, suckling:** pig
**polliwog, tadpole:** frog
**poult:** turkey
**pullet:** hen
**pup:** dog, seal, sea lion, fox
**puss, pussy:** cat
**spike, blinker, tinker:** mackerel
**squab:** pigeon
**squeaker:** pigeon, others
**whelp:** dog, tiger, beasts of prey
**yearling:** cattle, sheep, horse, others

# A Collection of Animal Collectives

The English language boasts an abundance of names to describe groups of things, particularly pairs or aggregations of animals. Even those that have fallen into comparative disuse may be of interest to the curious.

**bale** of turtles
**band** of gorillas
**bed** of clams, oysters
**bevy** of quail, swans
**brace** of ducks
**brood** of chicks
**cast** of hawks
**cete** of badgers
**charm** of goldfinches
**cloud** of gnats
**clowder** of cats
**clutch** of chicks
**clutter** of cats
**colony** of ants
**congregation** of plovers
**covey** of quail, partridge
**crash** of rhinoceri
**cry** of hounds
**down** of hares
**drift** of swine
**drove** of cattle, sheep
**exaltation** of larks
**flight** of birds
**flock** of sheep, geese
**gaggle** of geese
**gam** of whales
**gang** of elks
**grist** of bees
**herd** of elephants
**horde** of gnats
**husk** of hares
**kindle** or **kendle** of kittens
**knot** of toads
**leap** of leopards
**leash** of greyhounds, foxes
**litter** of pigs
**mob** of kangaroos
**murder** of crows
**muster** of peacocks
**mute** of hounds
**nest** of vipers
**nest, nide** of pheasants
**pack** of hounds, wolves
**pair** of horses
**pod** of whales, seals
**pride** of lions
**school** of fish
**sedge** or **siege** of cranes
**shoal** of fish, pilchards
**skein** of geese
**skulk** of foxes
**sleuth** of bears
**sounder** of boars, swine
**span** of mules
**spring** of teals
**swarm** of bees
**team** of ducks, horses
**tribe** or **trip** of goats
**troop** of kangaroos, monkeys
**volery** of birds
**watch** of nightingales
**wing** of plovers
**yoke** of oxen

# Common Abbreviations

Usage of periods after abbreviations varies, but periods have become less common than in the past. Italicized definitions preceding those in parentheses are in Latin unless otherwise noted.

AA=Alcoholics Anonymous
AAA=American Automobile Association
AARP=American Association of Retired Persons
ABA=American Bar Association
AC=alternating current
AD=*anno Domini* (in the year of the Lord)
AFL=American Federation of Labor
AIDS=acquired immune deficiency syndrome
AM=*ante meridiem* (before noon)
AMA=American Medical Association
anon=anonymous
ASAP=as soon as possible
ASCAP=American Society of Composers, Authors, and Publishers
ATM=automated teller machine
Ave.=Avenue
BA=Bachelor of Arts
bbl=barrel(s)
BC=before Christ
BS=Bachelor of Science
Btu=British thermal unit(s)
bu=bushel(s)
C= Celsius, centigrade
c=*circa* (about), copyright
CEO=chief executive officer
CIA=Central Intelligence Agency
cm=centimeter(s)
COD=cash (or collect) on delivery
CPA=certified public accountant
CPR=cardiopulmonary resuscitation
DA=district attorney
DAR=Daughters of the American Revolution
DC=direct current
DD=Doctor of Divinity
DDS=Doctor of Dental Science (or Surgery)
DNA=deoxyribonucleic acid
DOA=dead on arrival
DWI=driving while intoxicated
ed.=edited, edition, editor
e.g.=*exempli gratia* (for example)
EKG=electrocardiogram
ESP=extrasensory perception
esp.=especially
et al.=*et alii* (and others)
etc.=*et cetera* (and so forth)
EU=European Union
F=Fahrenheit
FBI=Federal Bureau of Investigation
FOB=free on board
ft=foot, feet
FYI=for your information
gal=gallon(s)
GB=gigabyte(s)
GDP=gross domestic product
GIGO=garbage in, garbage out
GNP=gross national product
GOP=Grand Old Party (Republican Party)
Hon.=the Honorable
hr=hour(s)
ht=height
HVAC=heating, ventilating, and air-conditioning
i.e.=*id est* (that is)
in.=inch(es)
IQ=intelligence quotient
IMF=International Monetary Fund
IRA=individual retirement account, Irish Republican Army
IRS=Internal Revenue Service
ISBN=International Standard Book Number
JD=*Juris Doctor* (doctor of laws)
JP=Justice of the Peace
K=Kelvin
k=karat
KB=kilobyte(s)
kg=kilogram(s)
km=kilometer(s)
kw=kilowatt(s)
kwh=kilowatt-hour(s)
l=liter(s)
lb=*libra* (pound or pounds)
LLB=*Legum Baccalaureus* (bachelor of laws)
m=meter(s)
MA=Master of Arts
MB=megabyte(s)
MD=*Medicinae Doctor* (doctor of medicine)
mi=mile(s)
MIA=missing in action
min=minute(s)
ml=milliliter(s)
mm=millimeter(s)
mph=miles per hour
MS=Master of Science
MSG=monosodium glutamate
NAACP=National Association for the Advancement of Colored People
no=*numero* (number)
op=*opus* (work)
oz=ounce(s)
p, pp=page(s)
PC=personal computer
PhD=*Philosophiae Doctor* (doctor of philosophy)
PM=*post meridiem* (afternoon)
POW=prisoner of war
PS=*post scriptum* (postscript)
pt=part(s), pint(s), point(s)
qt=quart(s)
REM=rapid eye movement
Rev.=Reverend
RFD=rural free delivery
RIP=*requiescat in pace* (May he/she rest in peace)
RN=registered nurse
RNA=ribonucleic acid
ROTC=Reserve Officers' Training Corps
rpm=revolutions per minute
RR=railroad
RSVP=*répondez, s'il vous plaît* (Fr.) (Please reply)
SASE=self-addressed stamped envelope
sec=second(s)
SIDS=sudden infant death syndrome
SPCA=Society for the Prevention of Cruelty to Animals
SRO=standing room only
St.=Saint, Street
t=ton(s)
TGIF=Thank God it's Friday
UFO=unidentified flying object
UHF=ultrahigh frequency
USS=United States ship
v (or vs)=*versus* (against)
VCR=videocassette recorder
VHF=very high frequency
W=watt(s)
yd=yard(s)

## Idioms: Their Meaning and Derivation

**dyed in the wool:** deeply ingrained as a trait; from the fact that if wool is dyed before being made into yarn, or while still raw wool, the color is more firmly fixed.

**feet of clay:** a blemish in the character of one previously held above reproach; from Daniel's interpretation of Nebuchadnezzar's dream in the Old Testament. The king dreamed of an image made of precious metals, except for feet made of clay and iron; Daniel said that the feet symbolized human vulnerability to weakness and destruction.

**hands down:** effortlessly; incontestably; from the way a jockey, sure of victory, drops the hands, loosening grip on the reins.

**in seventh heaven:** in a state of bliss; especially in Islamic beliefs, the heaven of heavens, the home of God and the highest angels.

**kiss of death:** something that seems good but is in reality the instrument of one's downfall; from the earlier phrase "Judas kiss," betrayal of Jesus to the authorities.

**mad as a hatter:** crazy; from mercury's use in the making of felt hats; hatters often were afflicted with a violent twitching of the muscles as a result of its effects.

**red herring:** a herring cured by smoke; a false lead, or irrelevant argument meant to mislead; from the use of a strong-smelling herring, trailed over the ground, for inducing a dog to follow this scent over any other.

**red-letter day:** a memorable day; from the custom of using red or purple colors to mark holy days on the calendar.

**to bark up the wrong tree:** to pursue a false lead; derived from hunting, some say specifically nocturnal racoon hunting, in which dogs often lost track of their quarry.

**to buckle down:** to adopt an attitude of effort and determination; probably from the act of buckling on armor to prepare for battle.

**to go at it with hammer and tongs:** to proceed with no restraint; from the blacksmith who, with his tongs (long-handled pincers) took a piece of red-hot metal from the forge, laid it on the anvil, and beat it into shape with a hammer.

**to hold water:** to pass a test for soundness; from testing a pitcher by filling it with water.

**to knuckle under:** to submit to another; from the time when one knelt before a conquerer, putting the "knuckles" of one's knees (the rounded part of the bone where the joint is bent) on the ground.

**to make hay while the sun shines:** to seize the opportunity; from the production of hay, or mown grass dried for fodder, from exposure to the sun when available.

**to strike while the iron is hot:** to seize the opportunity; from the blacksmith's need to swing the hammer while the metal on the anvil is glowing, to avoid having to start up the forge again and reheat the iron.

## Names of the Days

| English | Russian | Hebrew | French | Italian | Spanish | German | Japanese |
|---|---|---|---|---|---|---|---|
| Sunday | Voskresenje | Yom rishon | Dimanche | Domenica | Domingo | Sonntag | Nichiyo\bi |
| Monday | Ponedeljnic | Yom sheni | Lundi | Lunedì | Lunes | Montag | Getsuyo\bi |
| Tuesday | Vtornik | Yom shlishi | Mardi | Martedì | Martes | Dienstag | Kayo\bi |
| Wednesday | Sreda | Yom ravii | Mercredi | Mercoledì | Miércoles | Mittwoch | Suiyo\bi |
| Thursday | Chetverg | Yom hamishi | Jeudi | Giovedì | Jueves | Donnerstag | Mokuyo\bi |
| Friday | Pjatnitsa | Yom shishi | Vendredi | Venerdì | Viernes | Freitag | Kin-yo\bi |
| Saturday | Subbota | Shabbat | Samedi | Sabato | Sábado | Samstag | Doyo\bi |

## Commonly Confused English Words

**adverse:** unfavorable
**averse:** opposed

**affect:** to influence
**effect:** to cause

**aggravate:** to make worse
**annoy:** to irritate

**allusion:** an indirect reference
**illusion:** an unreal impression

**anxious:** apprehensive
**eager:** avid

**appraise:** to set a value on
**apprise:** to inform

**capital:** the seat of government
**capitol:** the building in which a legislative body meets

**complement:** to make complete; something that completes
**compliment:** to praise; praise

**denote:** to mean
**connote:** to suggest beyond the explicit meaning

**discreet:** prudent
**discrete:** separate

**disinterested:** impartial
**uninterested:** without interest

**elicit:** to draw or bring out
**illicit:** illegal

**emigrate:** to leave for another place of residence
**immigrate:** to come to another place of residence

**farther:** more distant in space
**further:** an extension of time or degree

**flaunt:** to display ostentatiously
**flout:** to treat with contemptuous disregard

**grisly:** inspiring horror or intense fear
**grizzly:** sprinkled or streaked with gray

**historic:** important in history
**historical:** relating to history

**imminent:** ready to take place
**eminent:** standing out

**imply:** suggest but not explicitly; to entail
**infer:** to assume or understand information that is not relayed explicitly

**include:** used when the items following are part of a whole
**comprise:** used when the items following are all of a whole

**incredible:** unbelievable
**incredulous:** skeptical

**ingenious:** clever
**ingenuous:** innocent

**insidious:** intended to trick
**invidious:** detrimental to reputation

**literally:** actually
**figuratively:** metaphorically

**oral:** spoken, as opposed to written
**verbal:** relating to language

**pestilence:** a contagious or infectious epidemic disease
**petulance:** rudeness

**prevaricate:** to lie
**procrastinate:** to put off

**prostrate:** stretched out flat, face down
**prostate:** of or relating to the prostate gland

**qualitative:** relating to quality
**quantitative:** relating to number

# Commonly Misspelled English Words

accidentally
accommodate
acquainted
all right
already
amateur
appearance
appropriate
bureau
character
commitment
conscientious
conscious
convenience
deceive
describe
description
desirable
despair
desperate
eliminate
embarrass
fascinating
finally
fluorine
foreign
forty
government
grammar
harass
humorous
hurrying
incidentally
independent
inoculate
irresistible
laboratory
lightning
liquefy
maintenance
marriage
miniature
misspelled
mysterious
necessary
opportunity
optimistic
performance
permanent
rhythm
ridiculous
similar
sincerely
transferred

# Forms of Address

| Addressee | Address | Salutation |
|---|---|---|
| **Government** | | |
| President of the U.S. | The President, The White House, Washington, DC 20500; also, The President and Mrs. ______ or The President and Mr. ______ | Dear Sir or Madam; Mr. President or Madam President; Dear Mr. President or Dear Madam President |
| Vice President of the U.S. | The Vice President, The White House, Washington, DC 20500; also, The Vice President and Mrs. ______ or The Vice President and Mr. ______ | Dear Sir or Madam; Mr. Vice President or Madam Vice President; Dear Mr. Vice President or Dear Madam Vice President |
| Chief Justice | The Hon. *Firstname Surname*, Chief Justice of the U.S., The Supreme Court, Washington, DC 20543 | Dear Sir or Madam; Dear Mr. or Madam Chief Justice |
| Associate Justice | The Hon. Justice *Firstname Surname,* The Supreme Court, Washington, DC 20543 | Dear Sir or Madam; Dear Justice *Surname* |
| Judge | The Hon. *Firstname Surname*, Associate Judge, U.S. District Court | Dear Judge *Surname* |
| Attorney General | The Hon. *Firstname Surname,* Attorney General, Dept. of Justice, Constitution Ave. & 10th St. NW, Washington, DC 20530 | Dear Sir or Madam; Dear Mr. or Ms. Attorney General |
| Cabinet Officer | The Hon. *Firstname Surname*, Secretary of ______ | Dear Mr. or Madam Secretary; or Dear Mr. or Ms. *Surname* |
| Senator | The Hon. or Sen. *Firstname Surname*, U.S. Senate, Washington, DC 20510 | Dear Mr. or Madam Senator, or Dear Mr. or Ms. *Surname* |
| Representative | The Hon. or Rep. *Firstname Surname*, House of Representatives, Washington, DC 20515 | Dear Mr. or Madam *Surname* |
| Speaker of the House | The Hon. Speaker of the House of Representatives, House of Representatives, Washington, DC 20515 | Dear Mr. or Madam Speaker |
| Ambassador, U.S. | The Hon. *Firstname Surname*, American Ambassador[1] | Sir or Madam; Dear Mr. or Madam Ambassador |
| Ambassador, Foreign | His or Her Excellency[2] *Firstname Surname*, Ambassador of ______ | Excellency;[2] Dear Mr. or Madam Ambassador |
| Governor | The Hon. *Firstname Surname*, Governor of *State*; or in some states, His or Her Excellency, the Governor of *State* | Sir or Madam; Dear Governor *Surname* |
| Mayor | The Hon. *Firstname Surname*, Mayor of *City* | Sir or Madam; Dear Mayor *Surname* |
| **Military Personnel** | | |
| All Titles | Full or abbreviated rank + full name + comma + abbreviation for branch of service. Example: Adm. John Smith, USN | Dear *Rank Surname* |
| **Clerical and Religious Orders** | | |
| Clergy, Protestant | The Reverend *Firstname Surname*[3] | Dear Ms. or Mr. *Surname* |
| Pope | His Holiness Pope *Name* or His Holiness the Pope | Your Holiness or Most Holy Father |
| Priest | The Reverend *Firstname Surname* or The Reverend Father *Surname* | Reverend Father, Dear Father *Surname*, or Dear Father |
| Rabbi | Rabbi *Firstname Surname* | Dear Rabbi *Surname* |
| Royalty and Nobility, King or Queen | His or Her Majesty, King or Queen of *Country* | Sir or Madam, or May it please Your Majesty |

(1) If in Canada or Latin America, The Ambassador of the United States of America. (2) An American ambassador is not to be addressed as His or Her Excellency. (3) A member of the Protestant clergy who has a doctorate may be so addressed; for example, The Reverend Firstname Surname, DD, and Dear Dr. Surname.

## Pen Names

Shalom Aleichem (Solomon J. Rabinowitz
Woody Allen (Allen Stewart Konigsberg)
Currer, Ellis, and Acton Bell (Charlotte, Emily, and Anne Brontë)
John le Carré (David John Moore Cornwell)
Lewis Carroll (Charles Lutwidge Dodgson)
Colette (Sidonie Gabrielle Colette)
Isak Dinesen (Karen Blixen)
Dorothy Dix (Elizbeth Gilmer)
Elia (Charles Lamb)
George Eliot (Mary Ann or Marian Evans)
Maksim Gorky (Aleksey Maksimovich Peshkov)
O. Henry (William Sydney Porter)
James Herriot (James Alfred Wight)
P. D. James (Phyllis Dorothy James White)
[John] Ross Macdonald (Kenneth Millar)
André Maurois (Émile Herzog)
Molière (Jean Baptiste Poquelin)
George Orwell (Eric Arthur Blair)
Ellery Queen (Frederic Dannay and Manfred B. Lee)
Mary Renault (Mary Challans)
Françoise Sagan (Françoise Quoirez)
Saki (Hector Hugh Munro)
George Sand (Amandine Lucie Aurore Dupine)
Dr. Seuss (Theodor Seuss Geisel)
Stendhal (Marie Henri Beyle)
Mark Twain (Samuel Clemens)
Voltaire (François Marie Arouet)
Artemus Ward (Charles Farrar Browne)
Tom Wolfe (Thomas Kennerly Jr.)

# The Principal Languages of the World

**Source:** S. Culbert, 351525, University of Washington, Seattle, WA 98195; data as of mid-1996

## Languages Spoken by the Most People

| | Speakers (millions) Native[1] | Total | | Speakers (millions) Native[1] | Total | | Speakers (millions) Native[1] | Total |
|---|---|---|---|---|---|---|---|---|
| Mandarin | 853 | 999 | Bengali | 197 | 204 | Japanese | 125 | 126 |
| Hindi | 348 | 457 | Arabic | 195 | 230 | German | 98 | 124 |
| Spanish | 346 | 401 | Portuguese | 173 | 186 | French | 74 | 126 |
| English | 330 | 487 | Russian | 168 | 280 | Malay-Indonesian | 54 | 164 |

(1) A native speaker is one for whom the language is his or her first language.

## Languages Spoken by at Least 1 Million People

Total number of speakers (native plus nonnative) of languages spoken by at least 1 million speakers. A native speaker is one for whom the language is his or her first language. Locations in parentheses are principal areas where language is spoken.

| | |
|---|---|
| Achinese (N Sumatra, Indonesia) | 3 |
| Afghan (see Pashtu) | |
| Afrikaans (S Africa) | 10 |
| Akan (or Twi-Fanti) (Ghana) | 7 |
| Albanian (Albania; Kosovo, Yugoslavia) | 5 |
| Amharic (Ethiopia) | 20 |
| Arabic (see above) | 230 |
| Armenian (Armenia) | 5 |
| Assamese[1] (India; Bangladesh) | 22 |
| Aymara (Bolivia; Peru) | 2 |
| Azeri (Azerbaijan) | 15 |
| Balinese (Bali, Indonesia) | 3 |
| Baluchi (Baluchistan, in SW Pakistan and SE Iran) | 5 |
| Bashkir (Bashkortostan, Russia) | 1 |
| Batak Toba (Indonesia) | 4 |
| Baule (Côte d'Ivoire) | 2 |
| Beja (Kassala, Sudan; Ethiopia) | 1 |
| Bemba (Zambia) | 2 |
| Bengali[1] (see above) | 204 |
| Berber[2] | |
| Beti (Cameroon; Gabon; Eq. Guinea) | 2 |
| Bhili (India) | 3 |
| Bikol (SE Luzon, Philippines) | 4 |
| Brahui (Pakistan) | 2 |
| Bugis (Indonesia; Malaysia) | 4 |
| Bulgarian (Bulgaria) | 9 |
| Burmese (Myanmar) | 31 |
| Buyi (S Guizhou, S China) | 2 |
| Byelorussian (Belarus) | 10 |
| Cantonese (China; Hong Kong) | 70 |
| Catalan (NE Spain; Balearic Is.; S France; Andorra) | 10 |
| Cebuano (Bohol Sea, Philippines) | 12 |
| Chagga (Kilimanjaro area, Tanzania) | 1 |
| Chiga (Uganda) | 1 |
| Chinese[3] | |
| Chuvash (Chuvash, Russia) | 2 |
| Czech (Czech Republic) | 12 |
| Danish (Denmark) | 5 |
| Dimli (EC Turkey) | 1 |
| Dogri (Jammu-Kashmir, CE India) | 1 |
| Dong (SC China) | 2 |
| Dutch-Flemish (Netherlands; Belg.; NE France) | 21 |
| Dyerma (SW Niger) | 2 |
| Edo (Bendel, S Nigeria) | 1 |
| Efik (incl. Ibibio) (SE Nigeria) | 6 |
| English (see above) | 487 |
| Esperanto | 2 |
| Estonian (Estonia) | 1 |
| Ewe (SE Ghana; S Togo) | 3 |
| Fang-Bulu (Dialects of Beti, q. v.) | |
| Farsi (see Persian) | |
| Finnish (Finland; Sweden) | 6 |
| Fon (SC Benin; S Togo) | 1 |
| French (see above) | 125 |
| Fula (or Peulh) (Cameroon; Nigeria) | 13 |
| Fulakunda (Senegal; Gambia; Guinea-Bissau) | 2 |
| Futa Jalon (Guinea; Sierra Leone) | 3 |
| Galician (Galicia, NW Spain) | 4 |
| Galla (see Oromo) | |
| Ganda (or Luganda) (S Uganda) | 3 |
| Georgian (Georgia) | 4 |
| German (see above) | 124 |
| Gilaki (Gilan, NW Iran) | 2 |
| Gogo (Riff Valley, Tanzania) | 1 |
| Gondi (Central India) | 2 |
| Greek (Greece) | 12 |
| Guarani (Paraguay) | 4 |
| Gujarati[1] (WC India; S Pakistan) | 41 |
| Gusii (Kisii District, Nyanza, Kenya) | 2 |
| Gypsy (see Romany) | |
| Hadiyya (Arusi, Ethiopia) | 2 |
| Hakka (or Kejia) (SE China) | 34 |
| Hani (S China) | 1 |
| Hausa (N Nigeria; Niger; Cameroon) | 39 |
| Haya (Kagera, NW Tanzania) | 1 |
| Hebrew (Israel) | 5 |
| Hindi[1,4] (see above) | 457 |
| Hmong (S China; SE Asia) | 6 |
| Ho (Bihar and Orissa States, India) | 1 |
| Hungarian (or Magyar) (Hungary) | 14 |
| Iban (Indonesia; Malaysia) | 1 |
| Ibibio (see Efik) | |
| Igbo (or Ibo) (lower Niger, Nigeria) | 17 |
| Ijaw (Niger River delta, Nigeria) | 2 |
| Ilocano (NW Luzon, Philippines) | 7 |
| Indonesian (see Malay-Indonesian) | |
| Italian (Italy) | 62 |
| Japanese (see above) | 126 |
| Javanese (Java, Indonesia) | 64 |
| Kabyle (W Kabylia, N Algeria) | 3 |
| Kamba (E Kenya) | 3 |
| Kannada (S India) | 45 |
| Kanuri (Nigeria; Niger; Chad; Cameroon) | 4 |
| Karen (see Sgaw) | |
| Karo-Dairi (N Sumatra, Indonesia) | 2 |
| Kashmiri[1] (N India; NE Pakistan) | 4 |
| Kazak (Kazakstan) | 8 |
| Kenuzi-Dongola (S Egypt; Sudan) | 1 |
| Khalka (see Mongolian) | |
| Khmer (Cambodia; Vietnam; Thai.) | 8 |
| Khmer, Northern (Thailand) | 1 |
| Kikuyu (or Gekoyo) (WC Kenya) | 5 |
| Kituba (Bas-Zaire, Bandundu, Zaire) | 4 |
| Kongo (W Zaire; S Congo; NW Ang.) | 3 |
| Konkani (Maharashtra and SW India) | 4 |
| Korean (Korea; China; Japan) | 76 |
| Kurdish (Iran; Iraq; Turkey) | 11 |
| Kurukh (or Oraon) (C and E India) | 2 |
| Kyrgyz (Kyrgyzstan) | 2 |
| Lampung (Sumatra, Indonesia) | 2 |
| Lao[5] (Laos) | 4 |
| Latvian (Latvia) | 2 |
| Lingala (incl. Bangala) (Zaire) | 7 |
| Lithuanian (Lithuania) | 3 |
| Luba-Lulua (or Chiluba) (Zaire) | 7 |
| Luba-Shaba (Shaba, Zaire) | 1 |
| Lubu (E Sumatra, Indonesia) | 1 |
| Luhya (W Kenya) | 1 |
| Luo (Kenya; Nyanza, Tanzania) | 4 |
| Luri (SW Iran; Iraq) | 4 |
| Lwena (E Angola; W Zambia) | 2 |
| Macedonian (Macedonia) | 2 |
| Madurese (Madura, Indonesia) | 10 |
| Magindanaon (S Philippines) | 1 |
| Makassar (S Sulawesi, Indonesia) | 2 |
| Makua (S Tanzania; N Mozambique) | 4 |
| Malagasy (Madagascar) | 12 |
| Malay-Indonesian (see above) | 164 |
| Malay, Pattani (SE Thailand) | 1 |
| Malayalam[1] (Kerala, S India) | 36 |

| | |
|---|---|
| Malinke-Bambara-Dyula (W Africa) | 9 |
| Mandarin (China; Taiwan; see above) | 999 |
| Marathi[1] (Maharashtra, India) | 71 |
| Mazandarani (N Iran) | 2 |
| Mbundu (Benguela, Angola) | 4 |
| Mbundu (Luanda, Angola) | 3 |
| Meithei (NE India; Bangladesh) | 1 |
| Mende (Sierra Leone) | 2 |
| Meru (Eastern Province, C Tanzania) | 1 |
| Mien (China; Viet.; Laos; Thailand) | 2 |
| Min (SE China; Taiwan; Malaysia) | 50 |
| Minangkabau (W Sumatra, Indon.) | 6 |
| Moldavian (included with Romanian) | |
| Mongolian (Mongolia; NE China) | 6 |
| Mordvin (Mordova, Russia) | 1 |
| Moré (central Burkina Faso) | 4 |
| Nepali (Nepal; NE India; Bhutan) | 16 |
| Ngulu (Mozambique; Malawi) | 2 |
| Nkole (Western Prov., Uganda) | 1 |
| Norwegian (Norway) | 5 |
| Nung (NE of Hanoi, Vietnam; China) | 2 |
| Nupe (Kwara, Niger States, Nigeria) | 1 |
| Nyamwezi-Sukuma (NW Tanzania) | 5 |
| Nyanja (Malawi; Zambia; Zimbabwe) | 5 |
| Oriya[1] (Central and E India) | 32 |
| Oromo (West Ethiopia; N Kenya) | 9 |
| Pampangan (NW of Manila, Philip.) | 2 |
| Panay-Hiligaynon (Philippines) | 7 |
| Pangasinan (Lingayen G., Philip.) | 2 |
| Pashtu (Pakistan; Afghanistan; Iran) | 21 |
| Pedi (see Sotho, Northern) | |
| Persian (Iran; Afghanistan) | 35 |
| Polish (Poland) | 44 |
| Portuguese (see above) | 186 |
| Provençal (S France) | 4 |
| Punjabi[1] (Punjab, Pakistan; India) | 95 |
| Pushto (see Pashtu) | |
| Quechua A (Peru; Boliv.; Ec.; Arg.) | 8 |
| Rejang (SW Sumatra, Indonesia) | 1 |
| Riff (N Morocco; Algerian coast) | 1 |
| Romanian (Romania; Moldova) | 26 |
| Romany[6] | 2 |
| Ruanda (Rwanda; Uganda; Zaire) | 6 |
| Rundi (Burundi) | 6 |
| Russian (see above) | 280 |
| Samar-Leyte (Central E Philippines) | 3 |
| Sango (Central African Republic) | 4 |
| Santali (E India; Nepal) | 5 |
| Sasak (Lombok, Alas Strait, Indon.) | 2 |
| Serbo-Croatian (Croatia; Serbia; and other former Yugoslav republics and autonomous regions) | 20 |
| Sgaw (SW Myanmar) | 2 |
| Shan (E Myanmar) | 3 |
| Shilha (W Algeria; S Morocco) | 3 |
| Shona (Zimbabwe) | 8 |
| Sidamo (Sidamo, S Ethiopia) | 2 |
| Sindhi[1] (SE Pakistan; W India) | 18 |
| Sinhalese (Sri Lanka) | 13 |
| Slovak (Slovakia) | 5 |
| Slovene (Slovenia) | 2 |
| Soga (Busoga, Uganda) | 1 |
| Somali (Som.; Eth.; Ken.; Djibouti) | 4 |
| Songye (Kasai Or., NW Shala, Zaire) | 1 |
| Soninke (Mali; countries to W S E) | 1 |
| Sotho, Northern (So. Africa) | 3 |
| Sotho, Southern (So. Afr.; Lesotho) | 4 |
| Spanish (see above) | 401 |
| Sundanese (Sunda Strait, Indonesia) | 26 |
| Swahili (Kenya; Tanz.; Zaire; Ug.) | 49 |
| Swati (Swaziland; S. Africa) | 1 |
| Swedish (Sweden; Finland) | 9 |
| Sylhetti (Bangladesh) | 5 |
| Tagalog (Philippines) | 56 |
| Tajiki (Tajikistan; Uzbek.; Kyrgyz.) | 5 |
| Tamazight (N Morocco; W Algeria) | 3 |
| Tamil[1] (Tamil Nadu, India; Sri Lanka) | 73 |
| Tatar (Tatarstan, Russia) | 8 |
| Tausug (Philippines; Malaysia) | 1 |
| Telugu[1] (Andhra Pradesh, SE India) | 75 |
| Temne (central Sierra Leone) | 2 |
| Thai[5] (Thailand) | 52 |
| Tho (N Vietnam; S China) | 2 |
| Thonga (Mozambique; So. Africa) | 3 |
| Tibetan (SW China; N India; Nepal) | 5 |
| Tigrinya (S Eritrea; Tigre, Ethiopia) | 4 |
| Tiv (SE Nigeria; Cameroon) | 2 |
| Tong (see Dong) | |
| Tonga (SW Zambia; NW Zimbabwe) | 2 |
| Tswana (Botswana; So. Africa) | 4 |
| Tudza (N Vietnam; S China) | 1 |
| Tulu (S India) | 2 |
| Tumbuka (N Malawi; NE Zambia) | 2 |
| Turkish (Turkey) | 61 |
| Turkmen (Turkmenistan; Afghanistan) | 3 |
| Twi-Fante (see Akan) | |
| Uighur (Xinjiang, NW China) | 8 |
| Ukrainian (Ukraine; Russia; Poland) | 48 |
| Urdu[1,4] (Pakistan; India) | 104 |
| Uzbek (Uzbekistan) | 14 |
| Vietnamese (Vietnam) | 67 |
| Wolaytta (SE Ethiopia) | 2 |
| Wolof (Senegal) | 7 |
| Wu (Shanghai region, China) | 65 |
| Xhosa (SW Cape Prov., So. Africa) | 8 |
| Yao (see Mien) | |
| Yao (Malawi; Tanzania; Mozambique) | 1 |
| Yi (S and SW China) | 7 |
| Yiddish[7] | |
| Yoruba (SW Nigeria; Zou, Benin) | 20 |
| Zande (NE Zaire; SW Sudan) | 1 |
| Zhuang (S China) | 15 |
| Zulu (N. Natal, South Africa; Lesotho) | 9 |

(1) One of the 15 languages under the constitution of India. (2) See Kabyle, Riff, Shilha, and Tamazight. (3) See Mandarin, Cantonese, Wu, Min, and Hakka. The "common speech" (Putonghua) or the "national language" (Guoyu) is a standardized form of Mandarin as spoken in the area of Beijing. (4) Hindi and Urdu are essentially the same language, Hindustani. As the official language of Pakistan, it is written in a modified Arabic script and called Urdu. As the official language of India, it is written in the Devanagari script and called Hindi. (5) The distinctions between some Thai dialects and Lao are political rather than linguistic. (6) Mainly in central, E, and SE Europe and Turkey; some in the U.S. (7) Yiddish is usually considered a variant of German, although it has its own standard grammar and dictionaries, has a highly developed literature, and is written in Hebrew characters.

# American Manual Alphabet

In the American Manual Alphabet, each letter of the alphabet is represented by a position of the fingers. This system was originally developed in France by Abbe Charles Michel De I'Epee in the late 1700s. It was brought to the U.S. by Laurent Clerce (1785-1869), a Frenchman who taught deaf or hearing-impaired people.

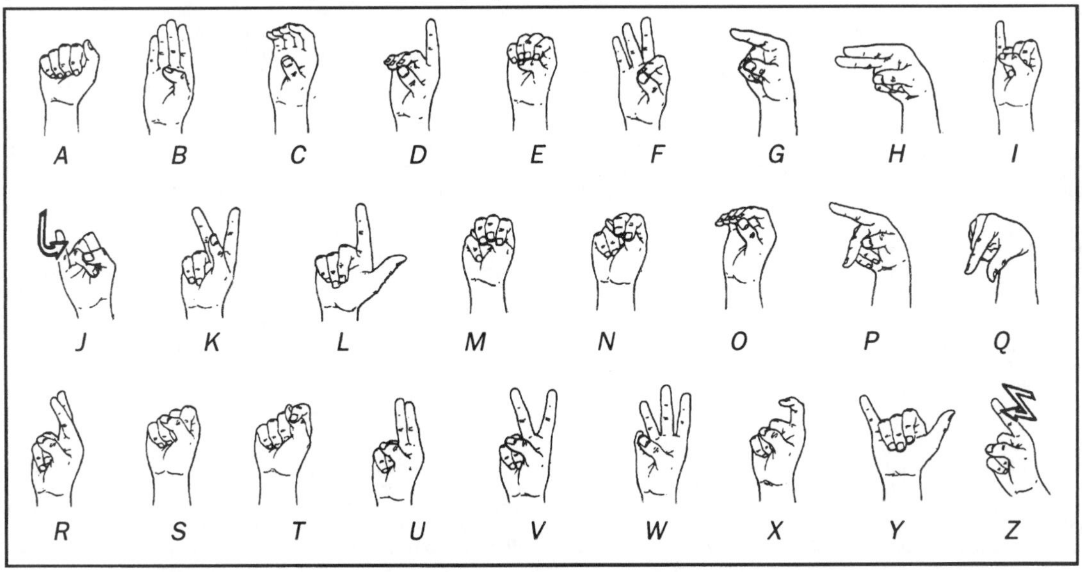

# RELIGIOUS INFORMATION

## Membership of Religious Groups in the U.S.

**Source:** *1996 Yearbook of American & Canadian Churches,* © *National Council of the Churches of Christ in the USA;* World Almanac research

Membership figures generally are based on reports made by officials of each group and are not based on any religious census. Membership figures from other sources may vary. Many groups keep careful records; others only estimate. Not all groups report annually. Christian church membership figures reported in this table are inclusive and refer to all "members," not simply full communicants or confirmed members. Definitions of membership vary from one denomination to another. Only data reported within the past 10 years are included.

The number of houses of worship appears in parentheses. * Indicates that the group declines to make membership figures public.

| Religious Group | Members |
|---|---|
| **Adventist churches:** | |
| Advent Christian Ch. (328) | 27,300 |
| Ch. of God Gen. Conf. (Oregon, IL; Morrow, GA) (89) | 5,195 |
| Primitive Advent Christian Ch. (10) | 345 |
| Seventh-day Adventist Ch. (4,303) | 775,349 |
| **American Rescue Workers (16)** | **35,000** |
| **Apostolic Christian Ch. (Nazarene) (63)** | **3,723** |
| **Apostolic Christian Churches of America (80)** | **11,450** |
| **Baha'i Faith[1]** | **300,000** |
| **Baptist churches:** | |
| American Baptist Assn. (1,705) | 250,000 |
| American Baptist Chs. in the U.S.A. (5,686) | 1,507,934 |
| Baptist Bible Fellowship Intl. (3,600) | 1,500,000 |
| Baptist General Conference (813) | 135,128 |
| Baptist Missionary Assn. of America (1,360) | 230,171 |
| Conservative Baptist Assn. of America (1,084) | 200,000 |
| Free Will Baptists, Natl. Assn. of (2,496) | 207,576 |
| General Assn. of Regular Baptist Chs. (1,458) | 136,380 |
| General Baptists, General Assn. of (876) | 74,156 |
| Liberty Baptist Fellowship (100) | * |
| Natl. Baptist Convention of America (2,500) | 3,500,000 |
| Natl. Baptist Convention, U.S.A. (33,000) | 8,200,000 |
| Natl. Missionary Baptist Convention of America (*) | 2,500,000 |
| North American Baptist Conference (263) | 43,236 |
| Progressive National Baptist Convention (2,000) | 2,500,000 |
| Separate Baptists in Christ (100) | 8,000 |
| Seventh Day Baptist General Conference (86) | 4,400 |
| Southern Baptist Convention (39,863) | 15,614,060 |
| Sovereign Grace Baptists (300) | 3,000 |
| **Brethren (German Baptists):** | |
| Brethren Ch. (Ashland, OH) (121) | 13,028 |
| Fellowship of Grace Brethren Chs. (273) | 32,229 |
| Old German Baptist Brethren (58) | 5,622 |
| **Brethren, River:** | |
| Brethren in Christ Ch. (198) | 18,152 |
| United Zion Ch. (13) | 852 |
| **Buddhist Churches of America[1]** | **780,000** |
| **Christian Catholic Church (3)** | * |
| **Christian Church (Disciples of Christ) (3,933)** | **937,644** |
| **Christian Churches and Churches of Christ (5,579)** | **1,070,616** |
| **Christian Congregation (1,437)** | **112,437** |
| **Christian and Missionary Alliance (1,943)** | **302,414** |
| **Christian Nation Church U.S.A. (5)** | **200** |
| **Christian Union, Churches of Christ in (240)** | **10,400** |
| **Church of Christ, Scientist (2,400)** | * |
| **Churches of Christ (13,013)** | **1,651,103** |
| **Churches of God:** | |
| Chs. of God, General Conference (352) | 31,862 |
| Ch. of God (Anderson, IN) (2,314) | 216,117 |
| Ch. of God (Seventh Day), Denver, CO (160) | 5,700 |
| Ch. of God in Christ Which He Purchased With His Own Blood (7) | 800 |
| Ch. of God by Faith (145) | 8,235 |
| **Church of the Nazarene (5,156)** | **597,841** |
| **Community Churches, Intl. Council of (423)** | **500,000** |
| **Congregational Christian Chs. (405)** | **90,000** |
| **Conservative Congregational Christian Conference (201)** | **36,864** |
| **Eastern Orthodox churches:** | |
| Albanian Orthodox Diocese of America (2) | 1,875 |
| American Carpatho-Russian Orthodox Greek Catholic Ch. (78) | 19,321 |
| Antiochian Orthodox Christian Archdiocese of North America (184) | 300,000 |
| Apostolic Catholic Assyrian Ch. of the East, N.A. Diocese (22) | 120,000 |
| Armenian Apostolic Ch. of America (32) | 150,000 |
| Armenian Church of Amer., Diocese of the (72) | 414,000 |
| Bulgarian Eastern Orthodox Ch. (9) | 1,100 |
| Coptic Orthodox Ch. (85) | 180,000 |
| Greek Orthodox Archdiocese of North and South America (535) | 1,950,000 |
| Orthodox Ch. in America (600) | 2,000,000 |
| Romanian Orthodox Episcopate of America (37) | 65,000 |
| Serbian Orthodox Ch. in U.S.A. & Canada (68) | 67,000 |
| Syrian Orthodox Ch. of Antioch (Archdiocese of the U.S.A. and Canada) (17) | 32,500 |
| True Orthodox Church of Greece (SOMC), American Exarchate (9) | 1,080 |
| **Episcopal Church (7,388)** | **2,504,682** |
| **Evangelical Church (134)** | **12,458** |
| **Evangelical Congregational Church (151)** | **23,504** |
| **Evangelical Covenant Church (597)** | **89,511** |
| **Evangelical Free Church of America (1,213)** | **227,290** |
| **Fellowship of Fundamental Bible Churches (23)** | **1,343** |
| **Fire Baptized Holiness Church (Wesleyan) (49)** | **692** |
| **Friends:** | |
| Evangelical Friends International, North American (246) | 26,322 |
| Friends General Conference (550) | 31,500 |
| Friends United Meeting (*) | 50,803 |
| **Grace Gospel Fellowship (128)** | **60,000** |
| **Hindu[1]** | **910,000** |
| **Independent Fundamental Churches of America (670)** | **69,857** |
| **Islam[1]** | **5,100,000** |
| **Jehovah's Witnesses (10,307)** | **945,990** |
| **Jewish organizations:** | |
| Union of American Hebrew Congregations (Reform) (876) | 1,300,000 |
| Union of Orthodox Jewish Congregations of America (1,200) | 1,000,000 |
| United Synagogues of Conservative Judaism, The (800) | 2,000,000 |
| **Latter-day Saints:** | |
| Ch. of Jesus Christ (Bickertonites) (63) | 2,707 |
| The Ch. of Jesus Christ of Latter-day Saints (Mormon) (10,218) | 4,613,000 |
| Reorganized Ch. of Jesus Christ of Latter-day Saints (1,001) | 150,143 |
| **Liberal Catholic Ch.-Province of the U.S.A. (34)** | **2,800** |
| **Lutheran churches:** | |
| Apostolic Lutheran Ch. of America (60) | 7,700 |
| Ch. of the Lutheran Brethren of America (119) | 25,548 |
| Ch. of the Lutheran Confession (71) | 8,864 |
| Conservative Lutheran Assn. (8) | 1,047 |
| Estonian Evangelical Lutheran Ch. (23) | 3,989 |
| Evangelical Lutheran Ch. in America (10,973) | 5,199,048 |
| Evangelical Lutheran Synod (128) | 25,379 |
| Free Lutheran Congregations, Assn. of (234) | 30,769 |
| Latvian Evangelical Lutheran Church in America (55) | 12,446 |
| Lutheran Ch.—Missouri Synod (6,148) | 2,596,927 |
| Lutheran Chs., American Assn. of (94) | 22,061 |
| Protestant Conference (Lutheran) (7) | 1,150 |
| Wisconsin Evangelical Lutheran Synod (1,251) | 414,874 |
| **Mennonite churches:** | |
| Beachy Amish Mennonite Chs. (95) | 6,968 |
| Church of God in Christ (Mennonite) (90) | 10,742 |
| Evangelical Mennonite Ch. (29) | 4,228 |
| Fellowship of Evangelical Bible Churches (14) | 1,925 |
| Hutterian Brethren (395) | 41,475 |
| Mennonite Brethren Chs., The Conf. of (147) | 19,218 |
| Mennonite Church (1,099) | 95,591 |
| Mennonite Ch., The General Conference (221) | 32,782 |
| Old Order Amish Ch. (898) | 80,820 |
| **Methodist churches:** | |
| African Methodist Episcopal Ch. (8,000) | 3,500,000 |
| African Methodist Episcopal Zion Ch. (3,098) | 1,230,842 |
| Allegheny Wesleyan Methodist Connection (120) | 2,056 |
| Evangelical Methodist Ch. (132) | 8,500 |
| Free Methodist Ch. of North America (1,050) | 74,585 |
| Fundamental Methodist Ch. (12) | 787 |
| Primitive Methodist Ch., U.S.A. (79) | 7,298 |
| Southern Methodist Ch. (126) | 7,876 |
| United Methodist Ch. (36,559) | 8,584,125 |
| The Wesleyan Church (U.S.A.) (1,609) | 116,763 |
| **Metropolitan Community Churches, Universal Fellowship of (291)** | **30,000** |

| Religious Group | Members |
|---|---|
| **Missionary Church (300)** | **28,821** |
| **Moravian churches:** | |
| Moravian Ch. in America, Northern Prov. (95) | 27,713 |
| Moravian Ch. in America, Southern Prov. (56) | 21,513 |
| Unity of the Brethren (26) | 2,602 |
| **Natl. Organization of the New Apostolic Ch. of North America (554)** | **41,863** |
| **Natl. Spiritualist Assn. of Churches (143)** | **3,634** |
| **Old Catholic churches:** | |
| Christ Catholic Ch. (8) | 1,018 |
| **Pentecostal churches:** | |
| Apostolic Faith Mission (Portland, OR) (54) | 4,500 |
| Apostolic Faith Mission Ch. of God (28) | 11,000 |
| Apostolic Overcoming Holy Church of God (160) | 12,369 |
| Assemblies of God (11,764) | 2,324,615 |
| Bible Church of Christ (6) | 6,850 |
| Church of God (Cleveland, TN) (5,918) | 722,541 |
| Church of God in Christ (15,300) | 5,499,875 |
| Church of God of Prophecy (2,005) | 70,570 |
| Congregational Holiness Ch. (190) | 2,468 |
| Elim Fellowship (66) | * |
| Intl. Ch. of the Foursquare Gospel (1,710) | 222,658 |
| Open Bible Standard Chs. (361) | 45,988 |
| Pentecostal Assemblies of the World (1,760) | 1,000,000 |
| Pentecostal Church of God (1,209) | 113,400 |
| Pentecostal Free Will Baptist Ch. (163) | 18,500 |
| United Pentecostal Ch. Intl. (3,730) | 550,000 |
| **Polish National Catholic Church (156)** | **150,000** |
| **Presbyterian churches:** | |
| Associate Reformed Presbyterian Ch. (General Synod) (206) | 38,936 |
| Cumberland Presbyterian Ch. (772) | 90,125 |
| Evangelical Presbyterian Ch. (177) | 56,499 |
| Korean Presbyterian Church in America (203) | 26,988 |
| Orthodox Presbyterian Ch. (181) | 20,151 |
| Presbyterian Ch. in America (1,263) | 257,556 |
| Presbyterian Ch. (U.S.A.) (11,399) | 3,698,136 |
| Reformed Presbyterian Ch. of N. America (70) | 5,657 |
| **Reformed churches:** | |
| Christian Reformed Ch. in N. America (737) | 211,154 |
| Hungarian Reformed Ch. in America (27) | 9,780 |
| Netherlands Reformed Congregations (15) | 4,374 |
| Reformed Ch. in America (915) | 309,459 |
| Reformed Ch. in the U.S. (36) | 4,172 |
| United Church of Christ (6,180) | 1,501,310 |
| **Reformed Episcopal Church (83)** | **6,565** |
| **Roman Catholic Church (19,723)** | **60,190,605** |
| **Salvation Army (1,222)** | **443,246** |
| **Schwenkfelder Church (5)** | **2,577** |
| **Swedenborgian Church (50)** | **2,423** |
| **Unitarian Universalist Assn. (1,020)** | **141,315** |
| **United Brethren:** | |
| United Brethren in Christ (239) | 24,671 |
| **Vedanta Societies (13)** | **2,500** |

(1) Based on reliable estimates; figures from other sources may vary.

# Headquarters of Selected Religious Groups in the United States

Source: *1996 Yearbook of American & Canadian Churches, © National Council of the Churches of Christ in the USA;* World Almanac research

Year organized in parentheses

**African Methodist Episcopal Church,** (1787), 1134 11th St. NW, Washington, DC 20001

**African Methodist Episcopal Zion Church** (1796), PO Box 32843, Charlotte, NC 28232; Pres., Bishop George E. Battle Jr.

**American Baptist Churches in the U.S.A.** (1907), PO Box 851, Valley Forge, PA 19482; Pres., G. Elaine Smith

**American Rescue Workers** (1890), 2827 Frankford Ave., PO Box 4766, Philadelphia, PA 19134; Commander-in-Chief & Pres., Gen. Paul E. Martin, Rev.

**Antiochian Orthodox Christian Archdiocese of North America** (1895), 358 Mountain Rd., Englewood, NJ 07631; Primate, Metropolitan Philip Saliba

**Armenian Apostolic Church of America** (1887), **Eastern Prelacy**: 138 E. 39th St., New York, NY 10016; Prelate, Archbishop Mesrob Ashjian; **Western Prelacy**: 4401 Russel Ave, Los Angeles, CA 90027; Prelate, Archbishop Datev Sarkissian

**Assemblies of God** (1914), 1445 Boonville Ave., Springfield, MO 65802; General Supt., Thomas E. Trask

**Baha'i Faith,** 536 Sheridan Rd., Wilmette, IL 60091

**Baptist Bible Fellowship Intl.** (1950), Baptist Bible Fellowship Missions Bldg., 720 E. Kearney St., Springfield, MO 65803; Pres., Sam Davison

**Baptist General Conference** (1852), 2002 S. Arlington Heights Rd., Arlington Heights, IL 60005; Pres., Dr. Robert S. Ricker

**Brethren in Christ Church** (1778), PO Box 290, Grantham, PA 17027; Moderator, Rev. Harvey R. Sider

**Buddhist Churches of America** (1899), 1710 Octavia St., San Francisco, CA 94109

**Christian Church (Disciples of Christ)** (1809), 130 E. Washington St., PO Box 1986, Indianapolis, IN 46206; Gen. Minister, Richard L. Hamm

**Christian Churches and Churches of Christ,** 4210 Bridgetown Rd., Box 11326, Cincinnati, OH 45211

**Christian Congregation, Inc.** (1887), 804 W. Hemlock St., LaFollette, TN 37766; General Supt., Rev. Ora W. Eads, D.D.

**Christian Methodist Episcopal Church** (1870), 4466 Elvis Presley Blvd., Memphis, TN 38116; Executive Secretary, Dr. W. Clyde Williams

**Christian and Missionary Alliance** (1897), PO Box 35000, Colorado Springs, CO 80935; Pres., Rev. David Rambo, PhD

**Christian Reformed Church in North America** (1857), 2850 Kalamazoo Ave. SE, Grand Rapids, MI 49560; Gen. Secretary, Dr. David H. Engelhard

**Church of Christ, Scientist** (1879), 175 Huntington Ave., Boston, MA 01945; Pres., David C. Driver

**Church of Christ** (1830), PO Box 472, Independence, MO 64051; Council of Apostles Sec., Apostle Smith N. Brickhouse

**Church of God** (Anderson, IN) (1881), Box 2420, Anderson, IN 46018; General Sec., Edward L. Foggs

**Church of God** (Cleveland, TN) (1886), PO Box 2430, Cleveland, TN 37320; Gen. Overseer, Robert White

**Church of God in Christ** (1907), Mason Temple, 939 Mason St., Memphis, TN 38126; Presiding Bishop, Rt. Rev. L. H. Ford

**Church of Jesus Christ (Bickertonites)** (1862), 6th & Lincoln Sts., Monongahela, PA 15063; Pres., Dominic R. Thomas

**The Church of Jesus Christ of Latter-day Saints (Mormon)** (1830), 50 E. North Temple St., Salt Lake City, UT 84150; Pres., Gordon B. Hinckley

**Church of the Nazarene** (1907), 6401 The Paseo, Kansas City, MO 64131; General Sec., Jack Stone

**Coptic Orthodox Church,** 427 West Side Ave., Jersey City, NJ 07304

**Cumberland Presbyterian Church** (1810), 1978 Union Ave., Memphis, TN 38104; Moderator, Rev. Clinton Buck

**Episcopal Church** (1789), 815 Second Ave., New York, NY 10017; Bishop, Most Rev. Edmond L. Browning

**Evangelical Free Church of America** (1884), 901 E. 78th St., Minneapolis, MN 55420; Pres., Dr. Paul Cedar

**Evangelical Lutheran Church in America** (1987), 8765 W. Higgins Rd., Chicago, IL 60631; Bishop, Rev. Dr. H. George Anderson

**Fellowship of Grace Brethren Churches** (1882), PO Box 386, Winona Lake, IN 46590; Moderator, Steve Peters

**Free Methodist Church of North America** (1860), World Ministries Center, 770 N. High School Rd., Indianapolis, IN 46214

**Friends General Conference** (1900), 1216 Arch St. 2B, Philadelphia, PA 19107; Gen. Sec., Bruce Birchard

**General Conference of Mennonite Brethren Churches** (1860), 4824 E. Butler Ave., Fresno CA 93727; Moderator, Ed Boschman

**Greek Orthodox Archdiocese of North and South America** (1864), 8-10 E. 79th St., New York, NY 10021; Chairperson, Archbishop Spyridon

**International Church of the Foursquare Gospel** (1927), 1910 W. Sunset Blvd., Ste. 200, PO Box 26902, Los Angeles, CA 90026; Pres., Dr. John R. Holland

**International Council of Community Churches** (1950), 21116 Washington Pkwy., Frankfort, IL 60423; Pres., J. Ronald Miller

**Islamic Association in the U.S. and Canada, Federation of,** 25351 Five Mile Rd., Redford Township, MI 48239; Sec., Nihad Hamed

**Jehovah's Witnesses,** 25 Columbia Heights, Brooklyn, NY 11201; Pres., Milton G. Henschel

**Lutheran Church—Missouri Synod** (1847), 1333 S. Kirkwood Rd., St. Louis, MO 63122; Pres., Dr. A. L. Barry

**Mennonite Church** (1893), 421 S. Second St., Ste. 600, Elkhart, IN 46516; Moderator, Owen E. Burkholder

**Mennonite Church, The General Conference** (1860), 722 Main, Newton, KS 67114; Moderator, Darrell Fast

**Moravian Church** (1735), **Northern Prov.:** 1021 Center St., PO Box 1245, Bethlehem, PA 18016; Pres., Rev. Dr. Gordon L. Sommers; **Southern Prov.:** 459 S. Church St., Winston-Salem, NC 27101; Pres., Rev. Dr. Robert E. Sawyer; **Alaska Prov.**: PO Box 545, Bethel, AK 99559; Pres., Rev. Frank Chingliak

(*continued*)

## Headquarters of Selected Religious Groups in the United States *(continued)*

**National Baptist Convention of America, Inc.** (1880), 777 S. R. L. Thornton Freeway, Ste. 205, Dallas, TX 75203; Pres., Dr. E. Edward Jones

**National Baptist Convention, U.S.A.,** 1700 Baptist World Center Dr., Nashville, TN 37207; Pres., Dr. Henry J. Lyons

**Natl. Missionary Baptist Convention of America** (1988), 6717 Centennial Blvd., Nashville, TN 37209; Pres., Dr. W. T. Snead Sr.

**Orthodox Church in America** (1794), PO Box 675, Syosset, NY 11791; Primate, V. Rev. Robert S. Kondratick

**Pentecostal Assemblies of the World** (c 1900), 3939 Meadows Dr., Indianapolis, IN 46205; Presiding Bishop, Paul A. Bowers

**Presbyterian Church in America** (1973), 1852 Century Pl., Atlanta, GA 30345; Moderator, Frank A. Brock

**Presbyterian Church (USA),** (1983), 100 Witherspoon St., Louisville, KY 40202; Moderator, Marj Carpenter

**Progressive Natl. Baptist Convention** (1961), 601 50th St., NE, Washington, DC 20019; Pres., Dr. Bennett W. Smith Sr.

**Reformed Church in America** (1628), 475 Riverside Dr., New York, NY 10115; Pres., I. John Hesselink

**Restoration Church of Jesus Christ of Latter-day Saints** (1830), 801 W. 23rd St., Independence, MO 64055; Pres. Marcus L. Juby

**Roman Catholic Church** (1634), National Conference of Catholic Bishops, 3211 Fourth St., Washington, DC 20017; Pres., William Cardinal Keeler

**Romanian Orthodox Episcopate of America** (1929), PO Box 309, Grass Lake, MI 49240; Ruling Bishop, His Grace Bishop Nathaniel Popp

**Salvation Army** (1865), 615 Slaters Lane, Alexandria, VA 22313; National Comdr., Commissioner Robert A. Watson

**Seventh-Day Adventist Ch.** (1863), 12501 Old Columbia Pike, Silver Spring, MD 20904; Pres., Robert S. Folkenberg

**Southern Baptist Convention** (1845), 901 Commerce St., Ste. 750, Nashville, TN 37203; Pres., Jim Henry

**Swedenborgian Church** (1792), 48 Sargent St., Newton, MA 02158; Pres., Rev. Edwin G. Capon

**Union of American Hebrew Congregations** (Reform), 838 5th Ave., New York, NY; Pres., Rabbi Alexander M. Schindler

**Union of Orthodox Jewish Congregations of America** 333 7th Ave., New York, NY 10001; Pres., Sheldon Rudoff

**Unitarian Universalist Association** (1793), 25 Beacon St., Boston, MA 02108

**United Church of Christ** (1957), 700 Prospect Ave., Cleveland, OH 44115; Pres., Rev. Paul H. Sherry

**United Methodist Church** (1968), PO Box 320, Nashville, TN 37202; Pres., Bishop Roy A. Sano

**United Pentecostal Church Intl.** (1925), 8855 Dunn Rd., Hazelwood, MO 63042; General Superintendent, The Rev. Nathaniel A. Urshan

**United Synagogues of Conservative Judaism** 155 5ths Ave., New York, NY 10010; Pres., Alan Tichnor

**Vedanta Societies** (1893), 34 W. 71st St., New York, NY 10023

**Volunteers of America** (1896), 3939 N. Causeway Blvd., Metairie, LA 70002; Chairperson, Walter Faster

**Wesleyan Church** (1968), PO Box 50434, Indianapolis, IN 46250; General Supts., Dr. Earle L. Wilson; Dr. Lee M. Haines; Dr. H. C. Wilson

## Adherents of All Religions by Six Continental Areas, Mid-1995

**Source:** *1996 Encyclopædia Britannica Book of the Year*

| | Africa | Asia | Europe | Latin America | Northern America | Oceania | World |
|---|---|---|---|---|---|---|---|
| Christians | 348,176,000 | 306,762,000 | 551,892,000 | 448,006,000 | 249,277,000 | 23,840,000 | 1,927,953,000 |
| Roman Catholics | 122,108,000 | 90,041,000 | 270,677,000 | 402,691,000 | 74,243,000 | 8,265,000 | 968,025,000 |
| Protestants | 109,726,000 | 42,836,000 | 80,000,000 | 31,684,000 | 123,257,000 | 8,364,000 | 395,867,000 |
| Orthodox | 29,645,000 | 14,881,000 | 165,795,000 | 481,000 | 6,480,000 | 666,000 | 217,948,000 |
| Anglicans | 25,362,000 | 707,000 | 30,625,000 | 1,153,000 | 6,819,000 | 5,864,000 | 70,530,000 |
| Other Christians | 61,335,000 | 158,297,000 | 4,795,000 | 11,997,000 | 38,478,000 | 681,000 | 275,583,000 |
| Atheists | 427,000 | 174,174,000 | 40,085,000 | 2,977,000 | 1,670,000 | 592,000 | 219,925,000 |
| Baha'is | 1,851,000 | 3,010,000 | 93,000 | 719,000 | 356,000 | 75,000 | 6,104,000 |
| Buddhists | 36,000 | 320,691,000 | 1,478,000 | 569,000 | 920,000 | 200,000 | 323,894,000 |
| Chinese folk religionists | 12,000 | 224,828,000 | 116,000 | 66,000 | 98,000 | 17,000 | 225,137,000 |
| Confucians | 1,000 | 5,220,000 | 4,000 | 2,000 | 26,000 | 1,000 | 5,254,000 |
| Ethnic religionists | 72,777,000 | 36,579,000 | 1,200,000 | 1,061,000 | 47,000 | 113,000 | 111,777,000 |
| Hindus | 1,535,000 | 775,252,000 | 1,522,000 | 748,000 | 1,185,000 | 305,000 | 780,547,000 |
| Jains | 58,000 | 4,804,000 | 15,000 | 4,000 | 4,000 | 1,000 | 4,886,000 |
| Jews | 163,000 | 4,294,000 | 2,529,000 | 1,098,000 | 5,942,000 | 91,000 | 14,117,000 |
| Mandeans | 0 | 44,000 | 0 | 0 | 0 | 0 | 44,000 |
| Muslims | 300,317,000 | 760,181,000 | 31,975,000 | 1,329,000 | 5,450,000 | 382,000 | 1,099,634,000 |
| New-Religionists | 19,000 | 118,591,000 | 808,000 | 913,000 | 956,000 | 10,000 | 121,297,000 |
| Nonreligious | 2,573,000 | 701,175,000 | 94,330,000 | 15,551,000 | 25,050,000 | 2,870,000 | 841,549,000 |
| Parsees | 1,000 | 184,000 | 1,000 | 1,000 | 1,000 | 1,000 | 189,000 |
| Sikhs | 36,000 | 18,130,000 | 490,000 | 8,000 | 490,000 | 7,000 | 19,161,000 |
| Shintoists | 0 | 2,840,000 | 1,000 | 1,000 | 1,000 | 1,000 | 2,844,000 |
| Spiritists | 4,000 | 1,100,000 | 17,000 | 8,768,000 | 300,000 | 1,000 | 10,190,000 |
| Other religionists | 88,000 | 98,000 | 443,000 | 184,000 | 1,068,000 | 42,000 | 1,923,000 |
| Non-Christians | 379,898,000 | 3,151,195,000 | 175,107,000 | 33,999,000 | 43,564,000 | 4,709,000 | 3,788,472,000 |
| **Total Population** | **728,074,000** | **3,457,957,000** | **726,999,000** | **482,005,000** | **292,841,000** | **28,549,000** | **5,716,425,000** |

**Continents.** These follow current UN demographic practice, which divides the world into the 6 major areas shown above and 21 regions. "Asia" now includes the former USSR Central Asian republics. "Europe" extends eastward to Vladivostok, the Sea of Japan, and the Bering Strait.

**Adherents.** As defined and enumerated for each of the world's countries in *World Christian Encyclopedia* (1982), projected to mid-1995, adjusted for recent data.

**Christians.** Followers of Jesus Christ affiliated with churches (church members, including children: 1,791,227,000) plus persons professing in censuses or polls though not so affiliated.

**Other Christians.** Catholics (non-Roman), marginal Protestants, crypto-Christians, and adherents of African, Asian, black, and Latin-American indigenous churches.

**Atheists.** Persons professing atheism, skepticism, disbelief, or irreligion, including antireligious (opposed to all religion).

**Buddhists.** 56% Mahayana, 38% Theravada (Hinayana), 6% Tantrayana (Lamaism).

**Chinese folk religionists.** Followers of traditional Chinese religion (local deities, ancestor veneration, Confucian ethics, Taoism, universism, divination, some Buddhist elements).

**Confucians.** Non-Chinese followers of Confucius and Confucianism, mostly Koreans in Korea.

**Hindus.** 70% Vaishnavites, 25% Shaivites, 2% neo-Hindus and reform Hindus.

**Jews.** Adherents of Judaism. For detailed data on "core" Jewish population, see "World Jewish Populations" in the American Jewish Committee's *American Jewish Year Book.*

**Muslims.** 83% Sunni Muslims, 16% Shia Muslims (Shiites), 1% other schools.

**New-Religionists.** Followers of Asian 20th-cent. New Religions, New Religious movements, radical new crisis religions, and non-Christian syncretistic mass religions, all founded since 1800 and most since 1945.

**Nonreligious.** Persons professing no religion, nonbelievers, agnostics, freethinkers, dereligionized secularists indifferent to all religion.

**Other religionists.** Including 70 minor world religions and a large number of spiritist religions, New Age religions, quasi-religions, pseudoreligions, parareligions, religious or mystic systems, and religious and semireligious brotherhoods of numerous varieties.

**Total Population.** UN medium variant figures for mid-1995, as given in *World Population Prospects: The 1994 Revision* (1995).

# Episcopal Church Liturgical Colors and Calendar

**Source:** The Episcopal Church Center, New York City

**White**—from Christmas Day through the First Sunday after Epiphany; Maundy Thursday (as an alternative to crimson at the Eucharist); from the Vigil of Easter to the Day of Pentecost (Whitsunday); Trinity Sunday; Feasts of the Lord (except Holy Cross Day); the Confession of St. Peter; the Conversion of St. Paul; St. Joseph; St. Mary Magdalene; St. Mary the Virgin; St. Michael and All Angels; All Saints' Day; St. John the Evangelist; memorials of other saints who were not martyred; Independence Day and Thanksgiving Day; weddings and funerals. **Red**—the Day of Pentecost; Holy Cross Day; feasts of apostles and evangelists (except those listed above); feasts and memorials of martyrs (including Holy Innocents' Day). **Violet**—Advent and Lent. **Crimson** (dark red)—Holy Week. **Green**—the seasons after Epiphany and after Pentecost. **Black**—optional alternative for funerals. Alternative colors used in some churches: **Blue**—Advent; **Lenten White**—Ash Wednesday to Palm Sunday.

In the Episcopal Church the days of fasting are Ash Wednesday and Good Friday. Other days of special devotion (penitence) are the 40 days of Lent and all Fridays of the year, except those in Christmas and Easter seasons and any Feasts of the Lord that occur on a Friday or during Lent. Ember Days (optional) are days of prayer for the church's ministry. They fall on the Wednesday, Friday, and Saturday after the first Sunday in Lent, the Day of Pentecost, Holy Cross Day, and the Third Sunday of Advent. Rogation Days (also optional) are the 3 days before Ascension Day and are days of prayer for God's blessing on the crops, on commerce and industry, and for the conservation of the earth's resources.

| **Days, etc.** | **1996** | **1997** | **1998** | **1999** | **2000** |
|---|---|---|---|---|---|
| Golden Number | 2 | 3 | 4 | 5 | 6 |
| Sunday Letter | GF | E | D | C | b & a |
| Sundays after Epiphany | 7 | 5 | 7 | 6 | 9 |
| Ash Wednesday | Feb. 21 | Feb. 12 | Feb. 25 | Feb. 17 | March 8 |
| First Sunday in Lent | Feb. 25 | Feb. 16 | Feb. 29 | Feb. 21 | March 12 |
| Passion/Palm Sunday | Mar. 31 | Mar. 23 | Apr. 5 | Mar. 28 | April 16 |
| Good Friday | Apr. 5 | Mar. 28 | Apr. 10 | Apr. 2 | April 21 |
| Easter Day | Apr. 7 | Mar. 30 | Apr. 12 | Apr. 4 | April 23 |
| Ascension Day | May 16 | May 8 | May 21 | May 13 | June 1 |
| The Day of Pentecost | May 26 | May 18 | May 31 | May 23 | June 11 |
| Trinity Sunday | June 2 | May 25 | June 7 | May 30 | June 18 |
| Numbered Proper of 2 Pentecost | #5 | #4 | #6 | #5 | #7 |
| First Sunday of Advent | Dec. 1 | Nov. 30 | Nov. 29 | Nov. 28 | Dec. 3 |

# Greek Orthodox Movable Ecclesiastical Dates, 1996-2000

This 5-year chart has the dates of feast days and fasting days, which are determined annually on the basis of the date of Holy Pascha (Easter). This ecclesiastical cycle begins with the first day of the Triodion and ends with the Sunday of All Saints, a total of 18 weeks.

| | **1996** | **1997** | **1998** | **1999** | **2000** |
|---|---|---|---|---|---|
| Triodion begins | Feb. 4 | Feb. 16 | Feb. 8 | Jan. 31 | Feb. 20 |
| Sat. of Souls | Feb. 17 | Mar. 1 | Feb. 21 | Feb. 13 | Mar. 4 |
| Meat Fare | Feb. 18 | Mar. 2 | Feb. 22 | Feb. 14 | Mar. 5 |
| 2d Sat. of Souls | Feb. 24 | Mar. 8 | Feb. 28 | Feb. 20 | Mar. 11 |
| Lent Begins | Feb. 26 | Mar. 10 | Mar. 2 | Feb. 22 | Mar. 13 |
| St. Theodore—3d Sat. of Souls | Mar. 2 | Mar. 15 | Mar. 7 | Feb. 27 | Mar. 18 |
| Sunday of Orthodoxy | Mar. 3 | Mar. 16 | Mar. 8 | Feb. 28 | Mar. 19 |
| Sat. of Lazarus | Apr. 6 | Apr. 19 | Apr. 11 | Apr. 3 | Apr. 22 |
| Palm Sunday | Apr. 7 | Apr. 20 | Apr. 12 | Apr. 4 | Apr. 23 |
| Holy (Good) Friday | Apr. 12 | Apr. 25 | Apr. 17 | Apr. 9 | Apr. 28 |
| Western Easter | Apr. 7 | Mar. 30 | Apr. 12 | Apr. 4 | Apr. 23 |
| **Orthodox Easter** | Apr. 14 | Apr. 27 | Apr. 19 | Apr. 11 | Apr. 30 |
| Ascension | May 23 | June 5 | May 28 | May 20 | June 8 |
| Sat. of Souls | June 1 | June 14 | June 6 | May 29 | June 17 |
| Pentecost | June 2 | June 15 | June 7 | May 30 | June 18 |
| All Saints | June 9 | June 22 | June 14 | June 6 | June 25 |

# Important Islamic Dates, 1996-2001 (1417-21)

The Islamic calendar is a lunar reckoning from the year of the hegira, AD 622, when Muhammad moved from Mecca to Medina. It runs in cycles of 30 years, of which the 2d, 5th, 7th, 10th, 13th, 16th, 18th, 21st, 24th, 26th, and 29th are leap years; 1417 is the 7th year of the cycle. Common years have 354 days, leap years 355, the extra day being added to the last month, Dhû al-Hijjah. Except for this case, the 12 months beginning with Muharram have alternately 30 and 29 days.

Actual western-hemisphere moon sightings may occur a day later, but never earlier, than these dates reflect.

| | **1996-97 (1417)** | **1997-98 (1418)** | **1998-99 (1419)** | **1999-2000 (1420)** | **2000-01 (1421)** |
|---|---|---|---|---|---|
| New Year's Day (Muharram 1) | May 18, 1996 | May 8, 1997 | Apr. 27, 1998 | Apr. 17,1999 | Apr. 6, 2000 |
| Ashura (Muharram 10) | May 27, 1996 | May 17, 1997 | May 6, 1998 | Apr. 26, 1999 | Apr. 15, 2000 |
| Mawlid (Rabi'l 12) | July 28, 1996 | July 17, 1997 | July 6, 1998 | June 26, 1999 | June 14, 2000 |
| Ramadan 1 | Jan. 10, 1997 | Dec. 31, 1997 | Dec. 20, 1998 | Dec. 9, 1999 | Nov. 27, 2000 |
| al-Fitr (Shawwal 1) | Feb. 8, 1997 | Jan. 29, 1998 | Jan. 19, 1999 | Jan. 8, 2000 | Dec. 27, 2000 |
| al-Adha (Dhû al-Hijjah 10) | Apr. 17, 1997 | Apr. 7, 1998 | Mar. 28, 1999 | Mar. 16, 2000 | Mar. 5, 2001 |

# Jewish Holy Days, Festivals, and Fasts, 1996-2000

| | 1996 (5756-57) | | 1997 (5757-58) | | 1998 (5758-59) | | 1999 (5759-60) | | 2000 (5760-61) | |
|---|---|---|---|---|---|---|---|---|---|---|
| Tu B'Shvat | Feb. 5 | Mon. | Jan. 23 | Thu. | Feb. 11 | Wed. | Feb. 1 | Mon. | Jan. 22 | Sat. |
| Ta'anis Esther (Fast of Esther) | Mar. 4 | Mon. | Mar. 20 | Thu.* | Mar. 11 | Wed. | Mar. 1 | Mon. | Mar. 20 | Mon. |
| Purim | Mar. 5 | Tue. | Mar. 23 | Sun. | Mar. 12 | Thu. | Mar. 2 | Tue. | Mar. 21 | Tue. |
| Passover | Apr. 4 | Thu. | Apr. 22 | Tue. | Apr. 11 | Sat. | Apr. 1 | Thu. | Apr. 20 | Tue. |
| | Apr. 11 | Thu. | Apr. 29 | Tue. | Apr. 18 | Sat. | Apr. 8 | Thu. | Apr. 27 | Thu. |
| Lag B'Omer | May 7 | Tue. | May 25 | Sun. | May 14 | Thu. | May 4 | Tue. | May 23 | Tue. |
| Shavuot | May 24 | Fri. | June 11 | Sun. | May 31 | Sun. | May 21 | Fri. | June 9 | Fri. |
| | May 25 | Sat. | June 12 | Mon. | June 1 | Mon. | May 22 | Sat. | June 10 | Sat. |
| Fast of the 17th Day of Tammuz | July 4 | Thu. | July 22 | Tue. | July 12 | Sun.* | July 1 | Thu. | July 20 | Thu. |
| Fast of the 9th Day of Av | July 25 | Thu. | Aug. 12 | Tue. | Aug. 2 | Sun.* | July 22 | Thu. | Aug. 10 | Thu. |
| Rosh Hashanah | Sept. 14 | Sat. | Oct. 2 | Thu. | Sept. 21 | Mon. | Sept. 11 | Sat. | Sept. 30 | Sat. |
| | Sept. 15 | Sun. | Oct. 3 | Fri. | Sept. 22 | Tue. | Sept. 12 | Sun. | Oct. 1 | Sun. |
| Fast of Gedalya | Sept. 16 | Mon. | Oct. 5 | Sun.* | Sept. 23 | Wed. | Sept. 13 | Mon. | Oct. 2 | Mon. |
| Yom Kippur | Sept 23 | Mon. | Oct. 11 | Sat. | Sept. 30 | Wed. | Sept. 20 | Mon. | Oct. 9 | Mon. |
| Sukkot | Sept. 28 | Sat. | Oct. 16 | Thu. | Oct. 5 | Mon. | Sept. 25 | Sat. | Oct. 14 | Sat. |
| | Oct. 4 | Fri. | Oct. 22 | Wed | Oct. 11 | Sun. | Oct. 1 | Fri. | Oct. 20 | Fri. |
| Shmini Atzeret | Oct. 5 | Sat. | Oct. 23 | Thu. | Oct. 12 | Mon. | Oct. 2 | Sat. | Oct. 21 | Sat. |
| | Oct. 6 | Sun. | Oct. 24 | Fri. | Oct. 13 | Tue. | Oct. 3 | Sun. | Oct. 22 | Sun. |
| Hanukkah | Dec. 6 | Fri. | Dec. 24 | Wed. | Dec. 14 | Mon. | Dec. 4 | Sat. | Dec. 22 | Fri. |
| | Dec. 13 | Fri. | Dec. 31 | Wed. | Dec. 21 | Mon. | Dec. 11 | Sat. | Dec. 29 | Fri. |
| Fast of the 10th of Tevet | Dec. 20 | Fri. | Jan. 8 | Thu. | Dec. 29 | Tue. | Dec. 19 | Sun. | Jan. 5 | Fri. |

**The months of the Jewish year are:** 1) Tishri; 2) Cheshvan (also Marcheshvan); 3) Kislev; 4) Tebet (also Tebeth); 5) Shebat (also Shebhat); 6) Adar; 6a) Adar Sheni (II) added in leap years; 7) Nisan; 8) Iyar; 9) Sivan; 10) Tammuz; 11) Av (also Abh); 12) Elul. All Jewish holy days, etc., begin at sunset on the previous day. *Date changed to avoid Sabbath.

# Ash Wednesday and Easter Sunday (Western churches)

| Year | Ash Wed. | Easter Sunday | Year | Ash Wed. | Easter Sunday | Year | Ash Wed. | Easter Sunday | Year | Ash Wed. | Easter Sunday |
|---|---|---|---|---|---|---|---|---|---|---|---|
| 1901 | Feb. 20 | Apr. 7 | 1951 | Feb. 7 | Mar. 25 | 2001 | Feb. 28 | Apr. 15 | 2051 | Feb. 15 | Apr. 2 |
| 1902 | Feb. 12 | Mar. 30 | 1952 | Feb. 27 | Apr. 13 | 2002 | Feb. 13 | Mar. 31 | 2052 | Mar. 6 | Apr. 21 |
| 1903 | Feb. 25 | Apr. 12 | 1953 | Feb. 18 | Apr. 5 | 2003 | Mar. 5 | Apr. 20 | 2053 | Feb. 19 | Apr. 6 |
| 1904 | Feb. 17 | Apr. 3 | 1954 | Mar. 3 | Apr. 18 | 2004 | Feb. 25 | Apr. 11 | 2054 | Feb. 11 | Mar. 29 |
| 1905 | Mar. 8 | Apr. 23 | 1955 | Feb. 23 | Apr. 10 | 2005 | Feb. 9 | Mar. 27 | 2055 | Mar. 3 | Apr. 18 |
| 1906 | Feb. 28 | Apr. 15 | 1956 | Feb. 15 | Apr. 1 | 2006 | Mar. 1 | Apr. 16 | 2056 | Feb. 16 | Apr. 2 |
| 1907 | Feb. 13 | Mar. 31 | 1957 | Mar. 6 | Apr. 21 | 2007 | Feb. 21 | Apr. 8 | 2057 | Mar. 7 | Apr. 22 |
| 1908 | Mar. 4 | Apr. 19 | 1958 | Feb. 19 | Apr. 6 | 2008 | Feb. 6 | Mar. 23 | 2058 | Feb. 27 | Apr. 14 |
| 1909 | Feb. 24 | Apr. 11 | 1959 | Feb. 11 | Mar. 29 | 2009 | Feb. 25 | Apr. 12 | 2059 | Feb. 12 | Mar. 30 |
| 1910 | Feb. 9 | Mar. 27 | 1960 | Mar. 2 | Apr. 17 | 2010 | Feb. 17 | Apr. 4 | 2060 | Mar. 3 | Apr. 18 |
| 1911 | Mar. 1 | Apr. 16 | 1961 | Feb. 15 | Apr. 2 | 2011 | Mar. 9 | Apr. 24 | 2061 | Feb. 23 | Apr. 10 |
| 1912 | Feb. 21 | Apr. 7 | 1962 | Mar. 7 | Apr. 22 | 2012 | Feb. 22 | Apr. 8 | 2062 | Feb. 8 | Mar. 26 |
| 1913 | Feb. 5 | Mar. 23 | 1963 | Feb. 27 | Apr. 14 | 2013 | Feb. 13 | Mar. 31 | 2063 | Feb. 28 | Apr. 15 |
| 1914 | Feb. 25 | Apr. 12 | 1964 | Feb. 12 | Mar. 29 | 2014 | Mar. 5 | Apr. 20 | 2064 | Feb. 20 | Apr. 6 |
| 1915 | Feb. 17 | Apr. 4 | 1965 | Mar. 3 | Apr. 18 | 2015 | Feb. 18 | Apr. 5 | 2065 | Feb. 11 | Mar. 29 |
| 1916 | Mar. 8 | Apr. 23 | 1966 | Feb. 23 | Apr. 10 | 2016 | Feb. 10 | Mar. 27 | 2066 | Feb. 24 | Apr. 11 |
| 1917 | Feb. 21 | Apr. 8 | 1967 | Feb. 8 | Mar. 26 | 2017 | Mar. 1 | Apr. 16 | 2067 | Feb. 16 | Apr. 3 |
| 1918 | Feb. 13 | Mar. 31 | 1968 | Feb. 28 | Apr. 14 | 2018 | Feb. 14 | Apr. 1 | 2068 | Mar. 7 | Apr. 22 |
| 1919 | Mar. 5 | Apr. 20 | 1969 | Feb. 19 | Apr. 6 | 2019 | Mar. 6 | Apr. 21 | 2069 | Feb. 27 | Apr. 14 |
| 1920 | Feb. 18 | Apr. 4 | 1970 | Feb. 11 | Mar. 29 | 2020 | Feb. 26 | Apr. 12 | 2070 | Feb. 12 | Mar. 30 |
| 1921 | Feb. 9 | Mar. 27 | 1971 | Feb. 24 | Apr. 11 | 2021 | Feb. 17 | Apr. 4 | 2071 | Mar. 4 | Apr. 19 |
| 1922 | Mar. 1 | Apr. 16 | 1972 | Feb. 16 | Apr. 2 | 2022 | Mar. 2 | Apr. 17 | 2072 | Feb. 24 | Apr. 10 |
| 1923 | Feb. 14 | Apr. 1 | 1973 | Mar. 7 | Apr. 22 | 2023 | Feb. 22 | Apr. 9 | 2073 | Feb. 8 | Mar. 26 |
| 1924 | Mar. 5 | Apr. 20 | 1974 | Feb. 27 | Apr. 14 | 2024 | Feb. 14 | Mar. 31 | 2074 | Feb. 28 | Apr. 15 |
| 1925 | Feb. 25 | Apr. 12 | 1975 | Feb. 12 | Mar. 30 | 2025 | Mar. 5 | Apr. 20 | 2075 | Feb. 20 | Apr. 7 |
| 1926 | Feb. 17 | Apr. 4 | 1976 | Mar. 3 | Apr. 18 | 2026 | Feb. 18 | Apr. 5 | 2076 | Mar. 4 | Apr. 19 |
| 1927 | Mar. 2 | Apr. 17 | 1977 | Feb. 23 | Apr. 10 | 2027 | Feb. 10 | Mar. 28 | 2077 | Feb. 24 | Apr. 11 |
| 1928 | Feb. 22 | Apr. 8 | 1978 | Feb. 8 | Mar. 26 | 2028 | Mar. 1 | Apr. 16 | 2078 | Feb. 16 | Apr. 3 |
| 1929 | Feb. 13 | Mar. 31 | 1979 | Feb. 28 | Apr. 15 | 2029 | Feb. 14 | Apr. 1 | 2079 | Mar. 8 | Apr. 23 |
| 1930 | Mar. 5 | Apr. 20 | 1980 | Feb. 20 | Apr. 6 | 2030 | Mar. 6 | Apr. 21 | 2080 | Feb. 21 | Apr. 7 |
| 1931 | Feb. 18 | Apr. 5 | 1981 | Mar. 4 | Apr. 19 | 2031 | Feb. 26 | Apr. 13 | 2081 | Feb. 12 | Mar. 30 |
| 1932 | Feb. 10 | Mar. 27 | 1982 | Feb. 24 | Apr. 11 | 2032 | Feb. 11 | Mar. 28 | 2082 | Mar. 4 | Apr. 19 |
| 1933 | Mar. 1 | Apr. 16 | 1983 | Feb. 16 | Apr. 3 | 2033 | Mar. 2 | Apr. 17 | 2083 | Feb. 17 | Apr. 4 |
| 1934 | Feb. 14 | Apr. 1 | 1984 | Mar. 7 | Apr. 22 | 2034 | Feb. 22 | Apr. 9 | 2084 | Feb. 9 | Mar. 26 |
| 1935 | Mar. 6 | Apr. 21 | 1985 | Feb. 20 | Apr. 7 | 2035 | Feb. 7 | Mar. 25 | 2085 | Feb. 28 | Apr. 15 |
| 1936 | Feb. 26 | Apr. 12 | 1986 | Feb. 12 | Mar. 30 | 2036 | Feb. 27 | Apr. 13 | 2086 | Feb. 13 | Mar. 31 |
| 1937 | Feb. 10 | Mar. 28 | 1987 | Mar. 4 | Apr. 19 | 2037 | Feb. 18 | Apr. 5 | 2087 | Mar. 5 | Apr. 20 |
| 1938 | Mar. 2 | Apr. 17 | 1988 | Feb. 17 | Apr. 3 | 2038 | Mar. 10 | Apr. 25 | 2088 | Feb. 25 | Apr. 11 |
| 1939 | Feb. 22 | Apr. 9 | 1989 | Feb. 8 | Mar. 26 | 2039 | Feb. 23 | Apr. 10 | 2089 | Feb. 16 | Apr. 3 |
| 1940 | Feb. 7 | Mar. 24 | 1990 | Feb. 28 | Apr. 15 | 2040 | Feb. 15 | Apr. 1 | 2090 | Mar. 1 | Apr. 16 |
| 1941 | Feb. 26 | Apr. 13 | 1991 | Feb. 13 | Mar. 31 | 2041 | Mar. 6 | Apr. 21 | 2091 | Feb. 21 | Apr. 8 |
| 1942 | Feb. 18 | Apr. 5 | 1992 | Mar. 4 | Apr. 19 | 2042 | Feb. 19 | Apr. 6 | 2092 | Feb. 13 | Mar. 30 |
| 1943 | Mar. 10 | Apr. 25 | 1993 | Feb. 24 | Apr. 11 | 2043 | Feb. 11 | Mar. 29 | 2093 | Feb. 25 | Apr. 12 |
| 1944 | Feb. 23 | Apr. 9 | 1994 | Feb. 16 | Apr. 3 | 2044 | Mar. 2 | Apr. 17 | 2094 | Feb. 17 | Apr. 4 |
| 1945 | Feb. 14 | Apr. 1 | 1995 | Mar. 1 | Apr. 16 | 2045 | Feb. 22 | Apr. 9 | 2095 | Mar. 9 | Apr. 24 |
| 1946 | Mar. 6 | Apr. 21 | 1996 | Feb. 21 | Apr. 7 | 2046 | Feb. 7 | Mar. 25 | 2096 | Feb. 29 | Apr. 15 |
| 1947 | Feb. 19 | Apr. 6 | 1997 | Feb. 12 | Mar. 30 | 2047 | Feb. 27 | Apr. 14 | 2097 | Feb. 13 | Mar. 31 |
| 1948 | Feb. 11 | Mar. 28 | 1998 | Feb. 25 | Apr. 12 | 2048 | Feb. 19 | Apr. 5 | 2098 | Mar. 5 | Apr. 20 |
| 1949 | Mar. 2 | Apr. 17 | 1999 | Feb. 17 | Apr. 4 | 2049 | Mar. 3 | Apr. 18 | 2099 | Feb. 25 | Apr. 12 |
| 1950 | Feb. 22 | Apr. 9 | 2000 | Mar. 8 | Apr. 23 | 2050 | Feb. 23 | Apr. 10 | 2100 | Feb. 10 | Mar. 28 |

# The Ten Commandments

According to Judeo-Christian tradition, as related in the Bible, the Ten Commandments were revealed by God to Moses and form the basic moral component of God's covenant with Israel. The Ten Commandments appear in 2 places in the Old Testament—Exodus 20:1-17 and Deuteronomy 5:6-21; the phrasing is similar but not identical.

Following is abridged text of the Ten Commandments in Exodus 20:1-17:

I. I am the Lord your God, who brought you out of the land of Egypt, out of the house of bondage. You shall have no other gods before me.
II. You shall not make for yourself a graven image. You shall not bow down to them or serve them.
III. You shall not take the name of the Lord your God in vain.
IV. Remember the sabbath day, to keep it holy.
V. Honor your father and your mother.
VI. You shall not kill.
VII. You shall not commit adultery.
VIII. You shall not steal.
IX. You shall not bear false witness against your neighbor.
X. You shall not covet.

Most Protestant, Anglican, and Orthodox Christians follow Jewish tradition, which considers the introduction ("I am the Lord...") the first commandment and makes the prohibition against idolatry the second. Roman Catholic and Lutheran traditions follow a division used by St. Augustine, which combines I and II and splits the last commandment into 2 that separately prohibit coveting of a neighbor's wife and a neighbor's goods. This arrangement alters the numbering of the other commandments by one.

# Books of the Bible

**Old Testament—Standard Protestant List**

| | | |
|---|---|---|
| Genesis | II Chronicles | Daniel |
| Exodus | Ezra | Hosea |
| Leviticus | Nehemiah | Joel |
| Numbers | Esther | Amos |
| Deuteronomy | Job | Obadiah |
| Joshua | Psalms | Jonah |
| Judges | Proverbs | Micah |
| Ruth | Ecclesiastes | Nahum |
| I Samuel | Song of Solomon | Habakkuk |
| II Samuel | Isaiah | Zephaniah |
| I Kings | Jeremiah | Haggai |
| II Kings | Lamentations | Zechariah |
| I Chronicles | Ezekiel | Malachi |

**New Testament List**

| | | |
|---|---|---|
| Matthew | Ephesians | Hebrews |
| Mark | Phillippians | James |
| Luke | Colossians | I Peter |
| John | I Thessalonians | II Peter |
| Acts | II Thessalonians | I John |
| Romans | I Timothy | II John |
| I Corinthians | II Timothy | III John |
| II Corinthians | Titus | Jude |
| Galatians | Philemon | Revelation |

The standard Protestant Old Testament consists of the same 39 books as in the Bible of Judaism, but the latter is organized differently. The Old Testament used by Roman Catholics has 7 additional "deuterocanonical" books, plus some additional parts of books. The 7 are: **Tobit, Judith, Wisdom, Sirach (Ecclesiasticus), Baruch, I Maccabees,** and **II Maccabees**. Both Catholic and Protestant versions of the New Testament have 27 books, with the same names.

# Roman Catholic Hierarchy

**Source:** U.S. Catholic Conference; as of mid-1996

## Supreme Pontiff

At the head of the Roman Catholic Church is the supreme pontiff, Pope John Paul II, Karol Wojtyla, born at Wadowice (Kraków), Poland, May 18, 1920; ordained priest Nov. 1, 1946; appointed bishop July 4, 1958; promoted to archbishop of Kraków Jan. 13, 1964; proclaimed cardinal June 26, 1967; elected pope as successor of Pope John Paul I Oct. 16, 1978; installed as pope Oct. 22, 1978.

## College of Cardinals

Members of the Sacred College of Cardinals are chosen by the pope to be his chief assistants and advisers in the administration of the church. Among their duties is the election of the pope when the Holy See becomes vacant.

In its present form, the College of Cardinals dates from the 12th century. The first cardinals, from about the 6th century, were deacons and priests of the leading churches of Rome and were bishops of neighboring dioceses. The title of cardinal was limited to members of the college in 1567. The number of cardinals was set at 70 in 1586 by Pope Sixtus V. From 1959 Pope John XXIII began to increase the number; however, the number of cardinals eligible to participate in papal elections was limited to 120. There were lay cardinals until 1918, when the Code of Canon Law specified that all cardinals must be priests. Pope John XXIII in 1962 established that all cardinals must be bishops. The first age limits were set in 1971 by Pope Paul VI, who decreed that at age 80 cardinals must retire from curial departments and offices and from participation in papal elections.

## North American Cardinals

| Name | Office | Born | Named Cardinal |
|---|---|---|---|
| Luis Apone Martinez | Archbishop of San Juan | 1922 | 1973 |
| William W. Baum | Major Penitentiary of Apostolic Penitentiary, the Vatican | 1926 | 1976 |
| Joseph L. Bernardin | Archbishop of Chicago | 1928 | 1983 |
| Anthony J. Bevilacqua | Archbishop of Philadelphia | 1923 | 1991 |
| John J. Carberry[1] | Archbishop emeritus of St. Louis | 1904 | 1969 |
| G. Emmett Carter[1] | Archbishop emeritus of Toronto | 1912 | 1979 |
| Ernesto Corripio Ahumada | Archbishop emeritus of Mexico | 1919 | 1979 |
| Edouard Gagnon | Pres. of Pontifical Commission of Intl. Eucharistic Congresses | 1918 | 1985 |
| James A. Hickey | Archbishop of Washington, DC | 1920 | 1988 |
| William Henry Keeler | Archbishop of Baltimore | 1931 | 1994 |
| Bernard F. Law | Archbishop of Boston | 1931 | 1985 |
| Adam Joseph Maida | Archbishop of Detroit | 1930 | 1994 |
| Roger Mahony | Archbishop of Los Angeles | 1936 | 1991 |
| John J. O'Connor | Archbishop of New York | 1920 | 1985 |
| Juan Sandoval Iniquez | Archbishop of Guadalajara | 1933 | 1994 |
| Adolfo Suarez Rivera | Archbishop of Monterrey | 1927 | 1994 |
| Edmund C. Szoka | Pres. of Prefecture of Economic Affairs of Holy See, the Vatican | 1927 | 1988 |
| Jean-Claude Turcotte | Archbishop of Montreal | 1936 | 1994 |
| Louis-Albert Vachon[1] | Archbishop emeritus of Quebec | 1912 | 1985 |

(1) Ineligible to take part in papal elections.

## Chronological List of Popes

**Source:** Annuario Pontificio. Table lists year of accession of each pope.

The Roman Catholic Church names the Apostle Peter as founder of the church in Rome. He arrived there c 42, was martyred there c 67, and was raised to sainthood.

**The pope's temporal title is:** Sovereign of the State of Vatican City.

**The pope's spiritual titles are:** Bishop of Rome, Vicar of Jesus Christ, Successor of St. Peter, Prince of the Apostles, Supreme Pontiff of the Universal Church, Patriarch of the West, Primate of Italy, Archbishop and Metropolitan of the Roman Province.

**The names of antipopes** are in *italics.* Antipopes were illegitimate claimants of or pretenders to the papal throne.

| Year | Pope |
|---|---|
| | St. Peter |
| 67 | St. Linus |
| 76 | St. Anacletus or Cletus |
| 88 | St. Clement I |
| 97 | St. Evaristus |
| 105 | St. Alexander I |
| 115 | St. Sixtus I |
| 125 | St. Telesphorus |
| 136 | St. Hyginus |
| 140 | St. Pius I |
| 155 | St. Anicetus |
| 166 | St. Soter |
| 175 | St. Eleutherius |
| 189 | St. Victor I |
| 199 | St. Zephyrinus |
| 217 | St. Callistus I |
| *217* | *St. Hippolytus* |
| 222 | St. Urban I |
| 230 | St. Pontian |
| 235 | St. Anterus |
| 236 | St. Fabian |
| 251 | St. Cornelius |
| *251* | *Novatian* |
| 253 | St. Lucius I |
| 254 | St. Stephen I |
| 257 | St. Sixtus II |
| 259 | St. Dionysius |
| 269 | St. Felix I |
| 275 | St. Eutychian |
| 283 | St. Caius |
| 296 | St. Marcellinus |
| 308 | St. Marcellus I |
| 309 | St. Eusebius |
| 311 | St. Melchiades |
| 314 | St. Sylvester I |
| 336 | St. Marcus |
| 337 | St. Julius I |
| 352 | Liberius |
| *355* | *Felix II* |
| 366 | St. Damasus I |
| *366* | *Ursinus* |
| 384 | St. Siricius |
| 399 | St. Anastasius I |
| 401 | St. Innocent I |
| 417 | St. Zosimus |
| 418 | St. Boniface I |
| *418* | *Eulalius* |
| 422 | St. Celestine I |
| 432 | St. Sixtus III |
| 440 | St. Leo I |
| 461 | St. Hilary |
| 468 | St. Simplicius |
| 483 | St. Felix III (II) |
| 492 | St. Gelasius I |
| 496 | Anastasius II |
| 498 | St. Symmachus |
| *498* | *Lawrence (501-505)* |
| 514 | St. Hormisdas |
| 523 | St. John I, Martyr |
| 526 | St. Felix IV (III) |
| 530 | Boniface II |
| *530* | *Dioscorus* |
| 533 | John II |
| 535 | St. Agapitus I |
| 536 | St. Silverius, Martyr |
| 537 | Vigilius |
| 556 | Pelagius I |
| 561 | John III |
| 575 | Benedict I |
| 579 | Pelagius II |
| 590 | St. Gregory I |
| 604 | Sabinian |
| 607 | Boniface III |
| 608 | St. Boniface IV |
| 615 | St. Deusdedit or Adeodatus |
| 619 | Boniface V |
| 625 | Honorius I |
| 640 | Severinus |
| 642 | Theodore I |
| 649 | St. Martin I, Martyr |
| 654 | St. Eugene I |
| 657 | St. Vitalian |
| 672 | Adeodatus II |
| 676 | Donus |
| 678 | St. Agatho |
| 682 | St. Leo II |
| 684 | St. Benedict II |
| 685 | John V |
| 686 | Conon |
| *687* | *Theodore* |
| *687* | *Paschal* |
| 687 | St. Sergius I |
| 701 | John VI |
| 705 | John VII |
| 708 | Sisinnius |
| 708 | Constantine |
| 715 | St. Gregory II |
| 731 | St. Gregory III |
| 741 | St. Zachary |
| 752 | Stephen II (III) |
| 757 | St. Paul I |
| *767* | *Constantine* |
| *768* | *Philip* |
| 768 | Stephen III (IV) |
| 772 | Adrian I |
| 795 | St. Leo III |
| 816 | Stephen IV (V) |
| 817 | St. Paschal I |
| 824 | Eugene II |
| 827 | Valentine |
| 827 | Gregory IV |
| *844* | *John* |
| 844 | Sergius II |
| 847 | St. Leo IV |
| 855 | Benedict III |
| *855* | *Anastasius* |
| 858 | St. Nicholas I |
| 867 | Adrian II |
| 872 | John VIII |
| 882 | Marinus I |
| 884 | St. Adrian III |
| 885 | Stephen V (VI) |
| 891 | Formosus |
| 896 | Boniface VI |
| 896 | Stephen VI (VII) |
| 897 | Romanus |
| 897 | Theodore II |
| 898 | John IX |
| 900 | Benedict IV |
| 903 | Leo V |
| *903* | *Christopher* |
| 904 | Sergius III |
| 911 | Anastasius III |
| 913 | Landus |
| 914 | John X |
| 928 | Leo VI |
| 928 | Stephen VII (VIII) |
| 931 | John XI |
| 936 | Leo VII |
| 939 | Stephen VIII (IX) |
| 942 | Marinus II |
| 946 | Agapitus II |
| 955 | John XII |
| 963 | Leo VIII |
| 964 | Benedict V |
| 965 | John XIII |
| 973 | Benedict VI |
| *974* | *Boniface VII* |
| 974 | Benedict VII |
| 983 | John XIV |
| 985 | John XV |
| 996 | Gregory V |
| *997* | *John XVI* |
| 999 | Sylvester II |
| 1003 | John XVII |
| 1004 | John XVIII |
| 1009 | Sergius IV |
| 1012 | Benedict VIII |
| *1012* | *Gregory* |
| 1024 | John XIX |
| 1032 | Benedict IX |
| 1045 | Sylvester III |
| 1045 | Benedict IX |
| 1045 | Gregory VI |
| 1046 | Clement II |
| 1047 | Benedict IX |
| 1048 | Damasus II |
| 1049 | St. Leo IX |
| 1055 | Victor II |
| 1057 | Stephen IX (X) |
| *1058* | *Benedict X* |
| 1059 | Nicholas II |
| 1061 | Alexander II |
| *1061* | *Honorius II* |
| 1073 | St. Gregory VII |
| *1080* | *Clement III* |
| 1086 | Bl. Victor III |
| 1088 | Bl. Urban II |
| 1099 | Paschal II |
| *1100* | *Theodoric* |
| *1102* | *Albert* |
| *1105* | *Sylvester IV* |
| 1118 | Gelasius II |
| *1118* | *Gregory VIII* |
| 1119 | Callistus II |
| 1124 | Honorius II |
| *1124* | *Celestine II* |
| 1130 | Innocent II |
| *1130* | *Anacletus II* |
| *1138* | *Victor IV* |
| 1143 | Celestine II |
| 1144 | Lucius II |
| 1145 | Bl. Eugene III |
| 1153 | Anastasius IV |
| 1154 | Adrian IV |
| 1159 | Alexander III |
| *1159* | *Victor IV* |
| *1164* | *Paschal III* |
| *1168* | *Callistus III* |
| *1179* | *Innocent III* |
| 1181 | Lucius III |
| 1185 | Urban III |
| 1187 | Clement III |
| 1187 | Gregory VIII |
| 1191 | Celestine III |
| 1198 | Innocent III |
| 1216 | Honorius III |
| 1227 | Gregory IX |
| 1241 | Celestine IV |
| 1243 | Innocent IV |
| 1254 | Alexander IV |
| 1261 | Urban IV |
| 1265 | Clement IV |
| 1271 | Bl. Gregory X |
| 1276 | Bl. Innocent V |
| 1276 | Adrian V |
| 1276 | John XXI |
| 1277 | Nicholas III |
| 1281 | Martin IV |
| 1285 | Honorius IV |
| 1288 | Nicholas IV |
| 1294 | St. Celestine V |
| 1294 | Boniface VIII |
| 1303 | Bl. Benedict XI |
| 1305 | Clement V |
| 1316 | John XXII |
| *1328* | *Nicholas V* |
| 1334 | Benedict XII |
| 1342 | Clement VI |
| 1352 | Innocent VI |
| 1362 | Bl. Urban V |
| 1370 | Gregory XI |
| 1378 | Urban VI |
| *1378* | *Clement VII* |
| 1389 | Boniface IX |
| *1394* | *Benedict XIII* |
| 1404 | Innocent VII |
| 1406 | Gregory XII |
| *1409* | *Alexander V* |
| *1410* | *John XXIII* |
| 1417 | Martin V |
| 1431 | Eugene IV |
| *1439* | *Felix V* |
| 1447 | Nicholas V |
| 1455 | Callistus III |
| 1458 | Pius II |
| 1464 | Paul II |
| 1471 | Sixtus IV |
| 1484 | Innocent VIII |
| 1492 | Alexander VI |
| 1503 | Pius III |
| 1503 | Julius II |
| 1513 | Leo X |
| 1522 | Adrian VI |
| 1523 | Clement VII |
| 1534 | Paul III |
| 1550 | Julius III |
| 1555 | Marcellus II |
| 1555 | Paul IV |
| 1559 | Pius IV |
| 1566 | St. Pius V |
| 1572 | Gregory XIII |
| 1585 | Sixtus V |
| 1590 | Urban VII |
| 1590 | Gregory XIV |
| 1591 | Innocent IX |
| 1592 | Clement VIII |
| 1605 | Leo XI |
| 1605 | Paul V |
| 1621 | Gregory XV |
| 1623 | Urban VIII |
| 1644 | Innocent X |
| 1655 | Alexander VII |
| 1667 | Clement IX |
| 1670 | Clement X |
| 1676 | Bl. Innocent XI |
| 1689 | Alexander VIII |
| 1691 | Innocent XII |
| 1700 | Clement XI |
| 1721 | Innocent XIII |
| 1724 | Benedict XIII |
| 1730 | Clement XII |
| 1740 | Benedict XIV |
| 1758 | Clement XIII |
| 1769 | Clement XIV |
| 1775 | Pius VI |
| 1800 | Pius VII |
| 1823 | Leo XII |
| 1829 | Pius VIII |
| 1831 | Gregory XVI |
| 1846 | Pius IX |
| 1878 | Leo XIII |
| 1903 | St. Pius X |
| 1914 | Benedict XV |
| 1922 | Pius XI |
| 1939 | Pius XII |
| 1958 | John XXIII |
| 1963 | Paul VI |
| 1978 | John Paul I |
| 1978 | John Paul II |

# Membership of Religious Groups in Canada

**Source:** *1996 Yearbook of American and Canadian Churches*; World Almanac research

Number of houses of worship in parentheses; groups reporting fewer than 1,000 members not included. Figures are generally based on reports of all-inclusive number of "members" by officials of each group; some groups keep careful records, while others only estimate. Not all groups report annually. *Indicates church declines to make membership figures public.

| Religious Group | Members |
|---|---|
| Anglican Church of Canada (1,767) | 848,256 |
| Antiochian Orthodox Christian Archdiocese of North America (16) | 50,000 |
| Apostolic Church in Canada (14) | 1,600 |
| Apostolic Church of Pentecost of Canada Inc. (133) | 13,723 |
| Associated Gospel Churches (126) | 9,284 |
| Baha'i Faith (398)[1] | 30,000 |
| Baptist Convention of Ontario and Quebec (372) | 44,713 |
| Baptist General Conference of Canada (70) | 6,066 |
| Baptist Union of Western Canada (161) | 20,006 |
| Brethren in Christ Church, Canadian Conference (39) | 3,200 |
| British Columbia Baptist Conference (23) | 2,400 |
| Canadian and American Reformed Churches (41) | 13,774 |
| Canadian Baptist Ministries (1,150) | 130,000 |
| Canadian Convention of Southern Baptists (103) | 6,857 |
| Canadian Yearly Meeting of the Religious Society of Friends (22) | 1,893 |
| Central Canada Baptist Conference (36) | * |
| Christian and Missionary Alliance in Canada (376) | 86,540 |
| Christian Brethren (also known as Plymouth Brethren) (60) | * |
| Christian Church (Disciples of Christ) in Canada (34) | 3,199 |
| Christian Churches and Churches of Christ in Canada (140) | 7,500 |
| Christian Reformed Church in North America (244) | 83,848 |
| Churches of Christ in Canada (147) | 7,181 |
| Church of God (Anderson, IN) (52) | 3,438 |
| Church of God (Cleveland, TN) (110) | 7,948 |
| Church of God of Prophecy in Canada (40) | 3,107 |
| Church of Jesus Christ of Latter-day Saints in Canada (391) | 130,000 |
| Church of the Nazarene (167) | 11,699 |
| Conference of Mennonites in Canada (149) | 28,075 |
| Coptic Church in Canada (12) | * |
| Estonian Evangelical Lutheran Church (12) | 6,159 |
| Evangelical Baptist Churches in Canada, Fellowship of (512) | 85,944 |
| Evangelical Church in Canada (46) | 3,688 |
| Evangelical Covenant Church in Canada (22) | 1,245 |
| Evangelical Free Church of Canada (650) | 198,665 |
| Evangelical Lutheran Church in Canada (652) | 199,609 |
| Evangelical Mennonite Conference (49) | 6,508 |
| Evangelical Mennonite Mission Conference (27) | 3,587 |
| Evangelical Missionary Church of Canada (145) | 12,217 |
| Foursquare Gospel Church of Canada (53) | 2,531 |
| Free Methodist Church in Canada (146) | 7,186 |
| Hindu[1] | 90,000 |
| Islam[1] | 120,000 |
| Italian Pentecostal Church of Canada (24) | 2,500 |
| Jehovah's Witnesses (1,351) | 110,659 |
| Jewish congregations (250+) | 350,000 |
| Latvian Evangelical Lutheran Church in America (17) | 4,922 |
| Lutheran Church–Canada (343) | 84,898 |
| Mennonite Brethren Churches, Canadian Conference of (195) | 29,651 |
| Metropolitan Community Churches, Universal Fellowship (12) | 1,500 |
| Missionary Church of Canada (92) | 6,431 |
| Moravian Church in America, Northern Province, Canadian District of (9) | 1,928 |
| Netherlands Reformed Congregations of North America (9) | 4,634 |
| North American Baptist Conference (121) | 17,910 |
| Old Order Amish Church (17) | * |
| Open Bible Standard Churches of Canada (4) | 1,000 |
| Orthodox Church in America (Canada Section) (606) | 1,000,000 |
| Pentecostal Assemblies of Canada (1,068) | 226,678 |
| Pentecostal Assemblies of Newfoundland (157) | 30,992 |
| Presbyterian Church in Canada (999) | 236,822 |
| Reformed Church in Canada (41) | 6,667 |
| Reformed Doukhobors, Christian Community and Brotherhood of (1) | 2,108 |
| Reorganized Church of Jesus Christ of Latter Day Saints (82) | 11,111 |
| Roman Catholic Church in Canada (5,844) | 12,584,789 |
| Romanian Orthodox Episcopate of America (Jackson, MI) (13) | 8,600 |
| Russian Orthodox Church in Canada, Patriarchal Parishes (22) | 1,200 |
| Salvation Army in Canada (370) | 92,388 |
| Seventh-day Adventist Church in Canada (331) | 43,840 |
| Ukrainian Orthodox Church of Canada (258) | 120,000 |
| Union D'Eglises Baptistes Françaises au Canada (26) | 3,000 |
| Unitarian Universalist Association (40) | 6,003 |
| United Baptist Convention of the Atlantic Provinces (546) | 63,625 |
| United Church of Canada (3,960) | 1,903,394 |
| United Pentecostal Church in Canada (3,724) | 550,000 |
| Wesleyan Church of Canada (82) | 5,256 |

(1) Based on reliable estimates; figures from other sources may vary.

# Headquarters of Selected Religious Groups in Canada

Source: *1996 Yearbook of American & Canadian Churches, © National Council of the Churches of Christ in the USA;* World Almanac research

(year organized in parentheses)

**Anglican Church of Canada** (1700), Church House, 600 Jarvis St., Toronto, ON M4Y 2J6; Primate, Most Rev. Michael G. Peters

**Bahá'í National Centre of Canada**, 7200 Leslie St., Thornhill, ON L3T 6L8

**Baptist Ministeries, Canadian,** 7185 Millcreek Dr., Mississauga, ON L5N 5R4; Pres., Dr. Bruce Milne

**Buddhist Churches**, 4860 Garry St., Richmond, BC V7E 2V2

**Canadian Jewish Congress** (1919), 1590 Ave. Docteur Penfield, Montreal, Que. H3G 1C5. Nat. Exec. Dir., Jack Silverstone. (Nonreligious umbrella organization of Jewish groups)

**Christian and Missionary Alliance in Canada** (1887), #510-105 Gordon Baker Rd., North York, ON M2H 3P8; Pres., Dr. Arnold Cook

**The Church of Jesus Christ of Latter-day Saints (Mormon)** (1830), 50 E. North Temple St., Salt Lake City, UT 84150; Pres., Gordon B. Hinckley

**Church of the Nazarene** (1902), 20 Regan Rd. Unit 9, Brampton, ON L7A 1C3; Natl. Dir., Dr. Wiiliam E. Stewart

**Council of Muslim Communities in Canada,** 1250 Ramsey View Ct., Ste. 504, Sudbury, ON P3E 2E7; Dir., Mir Iqbal Ali

**Evangelical Lutheran Church in Canada** (1985), 1512 St. James St., Winnipeg, MB R3H OL2; Bishop, Rev. Telmor G. Sartison

**Evangelical Missionary Church in Canada,** #550 1212 31st Ave. NE, Calgary, AB T2E 7S8; Pres., Rev. David Crouse

**Fellowship of Evangelical Baptist Churches in Canada** (1953), 679 Southgate Dr., Guelph, ON N1G 4S2; Pres., Rev. Terry D. Cuthbert

**Greek Orthodox Diocese of Toronto,** 27 Teddington Park Ave., Toronto, ON M4N 2C4; Primate of the Archdiocese of North and South America, Archbishop Spyridon

**Jehovah's Witnesses** (1879), Canadian office: Box 4100, Halton Hills, ON L7G 4Y4; Pres., Milton Henschel

**Lutheran Church—Canada** (1959), 3074 Portage Ave., Winnipeg, MB R3H OW3; Pres., Dr. Edwin Lehman

**Mennonite Church** (1898), 421 S. Second St., Ste. 600, Elkhart, IN 46516; Mod., Owen E. Burkholder

**Pentecostal Assemblies of Canada** (1919), 6745 Century Ave., Mississauga, ON L5N 6P7; General Supt., Rev. James M. Mac Knight

**Presbyterian Church** (1925), 50 Wynford Dr., North York, ON M3C 1J7; Moderator, Dr. Alan M. McPherson

**Roman Catholic Church,** Canadian Conference of Catholic Bishops, 90 Parent Ave., Ottawa, ON K1N 7B1; Pres., Msgr. Jean-Guy Hamelin

**Salvation Army** (1865), 2 Overlea Blvd., Toronto, ON M4H 1P4; Territorial Cmdr., Commissioner Donald O. Kerr

**Seventh-Day Adventist Church,** 1148 King St., Oshawa, ON L1H 1H8; Pres., Orville Parchment

**Ukranian Orthodox Church** (1918), Consistory of the Ukrainian Orthodox Church of Canada, 9 St. John's Ave., Winnipeg, MB R2W; Presidium, Chairperson, Very Rev. Oleg Krawchenvo

**United Church of Canada** (1925), The United Church House, 3250 Bloor St. W., Etobicoke, ON M8X 2Y4; Moderator, Marion S. Best

**Wesleyan Church** (1889), The Wesleyan Church Intl. Center, PO Box 50434, Indianapolis, IN 46250-0434

# Major Christian Denominations:

*Italics* indicate features that tend to

| Denomination | Origins | Organization | Authority | Special rites |
|---|---|---|---|---|
| Baptists | In radical Reformation objections to infant baptism, demands for church and state separation; John Smyth, English Separatist, in 1609; Roger Williams, 1638, Providence, RI. | Congregational; each local church is autonomous. | Scripture; some Baptists, particularly in the South, interpret the Bible literally. | Baptism, usually early teen years and after, by total immersion; Lord's Supper. |
| Church of Christ (Disciples) | Among evangelical Presbyterians in KY (1804) and PA (1809), in distress over Protestant factionalism and decline of fervor; organized 1832. | Congregational. | *"Where the Scriptures speak, we speak; where the Scriptures are silent, we are silent."* | Adult baptism; Lord's Supper (weekly). |
| Episcopalians | Henry VIII separated English Catholic Church from Rome, 1534, for political reasons; Protestant Episcopal Church in U.S. founded 1789. | *Bishops, in apostolic succession, are elected by diocesan representatives; part of Anglican Communion, symbolically headed by the Archbishop of Canterbury.* | Scripture as interpreted by tradition, especially *39 Articles* (1563); not dogmatic; tri-annual convention of bishops, priests, and laypeople. | Infant baptism, Eucharist, and other sacraments; sacrament taken to be symbolic, but as having real spiritual effect. |
| Jehovah's Witnesses | Founded 1870 in PA by Charles Taze Russell; incorporated as Watch Tower Bible and Tract Society of PA, 1884; name Jehovah's Witnesses adopted, 1931. | A governing body located in NY coordinates worldwide activities; each congregation cared for by a body of elders; each Witness considered a minister. | The Bible. | Baptism by immersion; annual Lord's Meal ceremony. |
| Latter-day Saints (Mormons) | In visions of the Father and the Son reported by Joseph Smith, 1820s, in NY. Smith also reported receiving new scripture on golden tablets: The Book of Mormon. | Theocratic; 1st Presidency (church president, 2 counselors), 12 Apostles preside over international church. Local congregations headed by lay priesthood leaders. | Revelation to living prophet (church president). The Bible, Book of Mormon, and other revelations to Smith and his successors. | Baptism, at age 8; laying on of hands (which confers the gift of the Holy Ghost); Lord's Supper; temple rites: baptism for the dead, marriage for eternity, others. |
| Lutherans | Begun by Martin Luther in Wittenberg, Germany, 1517; objection to Catholic doctrine of salvation and sale of indulgences; break complete, 1519. | Varies from congregational to episcopal; in U.S. a combination of regional synods and congregational polities is most common. | Scripture alone. The Book of Concord (1580), which includes the three Ecumenical Creeds, is subscribed to as a correct exposition of Scripture. | Infant baptism; Lord's Supper; Christ's true body and blood present "in, with, and under the bread and wine." |
| Methodists | Rev. John Wesley began movement, 1738, within Church of England; first U.S. denomination, Baltimore, 1784. | Conference and superintendent system*; in United Methodist Church, general superintendents are bishops—not a priestly order, only an office—who are elected for life.* | Scripture as interpreted by tradition, reason, and experience. | Baptism of infants or adults; Lord's Supper commanded; other rites include marriage, ordination, solemnization of personal commitments. |
| Orthodox | Developed in original Christian proselytizing; broke with Rome, 1054, after centuries of doctrinal disputes and diverging traditions. | Synods of bishops in autonomous, usually national, churches elect a patriarch, archbishop, or metropolitan; these men, as a group, are the heads of the church. | Scripture, tradition, and the first 7 church councils up to Nicaea II in 787; bishops in council have authority in doctrine and policy. | Seven sacraments: infant baptism and anointing, Eucharist (both bread and wine), ordination, penance, anointing of the sick, and marriage. |
| Pentecostal | In Topeka, KS (1901) and Los Angeles (1906), in reaction to perceived loss of evangelical fervor among Methodists and others. | Originally a movement, not a formal organization, Pentecostalism now has a variety of organized forms and continues also as a movement. | Scripture; individual charismatic leaders, the teachings of the Holy Spirit. | *Spirit baptism, especially as shown in "speaking in tongues"; healing and sometimes exorcism; adult baptism; Lord's Supper.* |
| Presbyterians | In 16th-cent. Calvinist Reformation; differed with Lutherans over sacraments, church government; John Knox founded Scotch Presbyterian church about 1560. | *Highly structured representational system of ministers and laypersons (presbyters) in local, regional, and national bodies (synods).* | Scripture. | Infant baptism; Lord's Supper; bread and wine symbolize Christ's spiritual presence. |
| Roman Catholics | Traditionally, founded by Jesus who named St. Peter the 1st vicar; developed in early Christian proselytizing, especially after the conversion of imperial Rome in the 4th cent. | Hierarchy with supreme power vested in pope elected by cardinals; councils of bishops advise on matters of doctrine and policy. | *The pope, when speaking for the whole church in matters of faith and morals, and tradition, which is partly recorded in Scripture and expressed in church councils.* | Mass; sacraments: baptism, reconciliation, Eucharist, confirmation, marriage, ordination, and anointing of the sick (unction). |
| United Church of Christ | *By ecumenical union, 1957, of Congregationalists and Evangelical & Reformed, representing both Calvinist* and *Lutheran traditions.* | Congregational; a General Synod, representative of all congregations, sets general policy. | Scripture. | Infant baptism; Lord's Supper. |

## How Do They Differ?

distinguish a denomination sharply from others.

| Practice | Ethics | Doctrine | Other | Denomination |
|---|---|---|---|---|
| Worship style varies from staid to evangelistic; extensive missionary activity. | Usually opposed to alcohol and tobacco; sometimes tends toward a perfectionist ethical standard. | *No creed; true church is of believers only, who are all equal.* | Believing no authority can stand between the believer and God, the Baptists are strong supporters of church and state separation. | **Baptists** |
| Tries to avoid any rite not explicitly part of the 1st-century church; some congregations may reject instrumental music. | Some tendency toward perfectionism; increasing interest in social action programs. | Simple New Testament faith; avoids any elaboration not firmly based on Scripture. | Highly tolerant in doctrinal and religious matters; strongly supportive of scholarly education. | **Church of Christ (Disciples)** |
| Formal, based on *Book of Common Prayer,* updated 1979; services range from austerely simple to highly liturgical. | Tolerant, sometimes permissive; some social action programs. | Scripture; the "historic creeds," which include the Apostles, Nicene, and Athanasian, and the *Book of Common Prayer*; ranges from Anglo-Catholic to low church, with Calvinist influences. | Strongly ecumenical, holding talks with many branches of Christendom. | **Episcopalians** |
| Meetings are held in Kingdom Halls and members' homes for study and worship; extensive door-to-door visitations. | High moral code; stress marital fidelity and family values; avoid tobacco and blood transfusions. | *God, by his first creation, Christ, will soon destroy all wickedness; 144,000 faithful ones will rule in heaven with Christ over others on a paradise earth.* | Total allegiance proclaimed only to God's kingdom or heavenlygovernment by Christ; politically neutral; main periodical, *The Watchtower,* is printed in 115 languages | **Jehovah's Witnesses** |
| Simple service with prayers, hymns, sermon; private temple ceremonies may be more elaborate. | Temperance; strict moral code; tithing; a strong work ethic with communal self-reliance; strong missionary activity; strong family emphasis. | Jesus Christ is the Son of God, the Eternal Father. Jesus' atonement saves all humans; those who are obedient to God's laws may become joint-heirs with Christ in God's kingdom. | Mormons feel theirs is the true church of Jesus Christ, restored by God through Joseph Smith. Official name: The Church of Jesus Christ of Latter-day Saints. | **Latter-day Saints (Mormons)** |
| Relatively simple, formal liturgy with emphasis on the sermon. | Generally, conservative in personal and social ethics; doctrine of "2 kingdoms" (worldly and holy) supports conservatism in secular affairs. | Salvation by grace alone through faith; Lutheranism has made major contributions to Protestant theology. | Though still somewhat divided along ethnic lines (German, Swedish, etc.), main divisions are between fundamentalists and liberals. | **Lutherans** |
| Worship style varies widely by denomination, local church, geography. | Originally pietist and perfectionist; always strong social activist elements. | No distinctive theological development; 25 Articles abridged from Church of England's 39, not binding. | In 1968, The United Methodist Church was formed by the union of The Methodist Church and The Evangelical United Brethren Church. | **Methodists** |
| *Elaborate liturgy, usually in the vernacular, though extremely traditional; the liturgy is the essence of Orthodoxy; veneration of icons.* | Tolerant; little stress on social action; divorce, remarriage permitted in some cases; bishops are celibate; priests need not be. | Emphasis on Christ's resurrection, rather than crucifixion; the Holy Spirit proceeds from God the Father only. | Orthodox Church in America originally under Patriarch of Moscow, was granted autonomy in 1970; Greek Orthodox do not recognize this autonomy. | **Orthodox** |
| Loosely structured service with rousing hymns and sermons, culminating in spirit baptism. | Usually, emphasis on perfectionism with varying degrees of tolerance. | Simple traditional beliefs, usually Protestant, with emphasis on the immediate presence of God in the Holy Spirit. | Once confined to lower-class "holy rollers," Pentecostalism now appears in mainline churches and has established middle-class congregations. | **Pentecostal** |
| A simple, sober service in which the sermon is central. | Traditionally, a tendency toward strictness with firm church- and self-discipline; otherwise tolerant. | Emphasizes the sovereignty and justice of God; no longer dogmatic. | Although traces of belief inpredestination (that God has fore-ordained salvation for the"elect") remain, this idea is no longer a central element in Presbyterianism. | **Presbyterians** |
| Relatively elaborate ritual centered on the Mass; also rosary recitation, novenas, etc. | Traditionally strict, but increasingly tolerant in practice; divorce and remarriage not accepted, but annulments sometimes granted; celibate clergy, except in Eastern rite. | Highly elaborated; salvation by merit gained through grace; dogmatic; special veneration of Mary, the mother of Jesus. | Relatively rapid change followed Vatican Council II; Mass now in vernacular; more stress on social action, tolerance, ecumenism. | **Roman Catholics** |
| Usually simple services with emphasis on the sermon. | Tolerant; some social action emphasis. | Standard Protestant; *Statement of Faith* (1959) is not binding. | The 2 main churches in the 1957 union represented earlier unions with small groups of almost every Protestant denomination. | **United Church of Christ** |

# Major World Religions

**Source**: Reviewed by Anthony Padovano, PhD, STD; prof. of literature and relig. studies, Ramapo College, NJ; adj. prof. of theol., Fordham U., NYC

## Buddhism

**Founded:** About 525 BC, reportedly near Benares, India.
**Founder:** Gautama Siddhartha (c 563-483 BC), the Buddha, who achieved enlightenment through intense meditation.
**Sacred Texts:** The *Tripitaka*, a collection of the Buddha's teachings, rules of monastic life, and philosophical commentaries on the teachings; also a vast body of Buddhist teachings and commentaries, many of which are called *sutras.*
**Organization:** The basic institution is the *sangha*, or monastic order through which the traditions are passed to each generation. Monastic life tends to be democratic and anti-authoritarian. Large lay organizations have developed in some sects.
**Practice:** Varies widely according to the sect, and ranges from austere meditation to magical chanting and elaborate temple rites. Many practices, such as exorcism of devils, reflect pre-Buddhist beliefs.
**Divisions:** A variety of sects grouped into 3 primary branches: Theravada (sole survivor of the ancient Hinayana schools), which emphasizes the importance of pure thought and deed; Mahayana (includes Zen and Soka-gakkai), which ranges from philosophical schools to belief in the saving grace of higher beings or ritual practices and to practical meditative disciplines; and Tantrism, an unusual combination of belief in ritual magic and sophisticated philosophy.
**Location:** Throughout Asia, from Sri Lanka to Japan. Zen and Soka-gakkai have several thousand adherents in the U.S.
**Beliefs:** Life is misery and decay, and there is no ultimate reality in it or behind it. The cycle of endless birth and rebirth continues because of desire and attachment to the unreal "self." Right meditation and deeds will end the cycle and achieve Nirvana, the Void, nothingness.

## Hinduism

**Founded:** About 500 BC by Aryan invaders of India where their Vedic religion intermixed with the practices and beliefs of the natives.
**Sacred texts:** The *Veda,* including the *Upanishads,* a collection of rituals and mythological and philosophical commentaries; a vast number of epic stories about gods, heroes, and saints, including the *Bhagavadgita,* a part of the *Mahabharata,* and the *Ramayana;* and a great variety of other literature.
**Organization:** None, strictly speaking. Generally, rituals should be performed or assisted by Brahmins, the priestly caste, but in practice, simpler rituals can be performed by anyone. Brahmins are the final judges of ritual purity, the vital element in Hindu life. Temples and religious organizations are usually presided over by Brahmins.
**Practice:** A variety of private rituals, primarily passage rites (for example, initiation, marriage, death, etc.) and daily devotions, and a similar variety of public rites in temples. Of the public rites, the *puja,* a ceremonial dinner for a god, is the most common.
**Divisions:** There is no concept of orthodoxy in Hinduism, which presents a variety of sects, most of them devoted to the worship of one of the many gods. The 3 major living traditions are those devoted to the gods Vishnu and Shiva and to the goddess Shakti; each is divided into further subsects. Numerous folk beliefs and practices, often in amalgamation with the above groups, exist side by side with sophisticated philosophical schools and exotic cults.
**Location:** Mainly India, Nepal, Malaysia, Guyana, Suriname, Sri Lanka.
**Beliefs:** There is only one divine principle; the many gods are only aspects of that unity. Life in all its forms is an aspect of the divine, but it appears as a separation from the divine, a meaningless cycle of birth and rebirth (*samsara*) determined by the purity or impurity of past deeds (*karma*). To improve one's *karma* or escape *samsara* by pure acts, thought, and/or devotion is the aim of every Hindu.

## Islam

**Founded:** AD 622 in Medina, Arabian peninsula.
**Founder:** Muhammad (c 570-632), the Prophet.
**Sacred texts:** Koran, the words of God; *Hadith,* collections of the sayings of the Prophet.
**Organization:** Theoretically, the state and religious community are one, administered by a caliph. In practice, Islam is a loose collection of congregations united by a very conservative tradition. Islam is basically egalitarian and nonauthoritarian.
**Practice:** Every Muslim has 5 duties: to make the profession of faith ("There is no god but Allah ..."), to pray 5 times a day, to give a regular portion of his goods to charity, to fast during the day in the month of Ramadan, and to make at least one pilgrimage to Mecca if possible.
**Divisions:** The 2 major sects of Islam are the Sunni (orthodox) and the Shia (Shiites). The Shia believe in 12 *imams,* perfect teachers, who still guide the faithful from Paradise. Shia practice tends toward the ecstatic; however, the Sunni is staid and simple. The Shia affirm human free will; the Sunni are deterministic. The mystic tradition in Islam is Sufism. A Sufi adept is someone who believes he or she has acquired a special inner knowledge direct from Allah.
**Location:** From the west coast of Africa to the Philippines across a broad band that includes Tanzania, Central Asia and western China, India, Malaysia, and Indonesia. Islam has several million adherents in the U.S.
**Beliefs:** Strictly monotheistic. God is creator of the universe, omnipotent, just, and merciful. The human being is God's highest creation, but limited and commits sins. Humans are misled by Satan, an evil spirit. God revealed the Koran to Muhammad to guide humans to the truth. Those who repent and sincerely submit to God return to a state of sinlessness. In the end, the sinless go to Paradise, a place of physical and spiritual pleasure, and the wicked burn in Hell.

## Judaism

**Founded:** About 1300 BCE.
**Founder:** Abraham is regarded as the founding patriarch, but the Torah of Moses is the basic source of the teachings.
**Sacred Texts:** The 5 books of Moses constitute the written Torah. Special sanctity is also assigned other writings of the Hebrew Bible—the teachings of oral Torah are recorded in the Talmud, in the Midrash, and in various commentaries.
**Organization:** Originally theocratic, Judaism has evolved a congregational polity. The basic institution is the local synagogue, operated by the congregation and led by a rabbi of their choice. Chief rabbis in France and Great Britain have authority only over those who accept it; in Israel, the 2 chief rabbis have civil authority in family law.
**Practice:** Among traditional practitioners, almost all areas of life are governed by strict religious discipline. Sabbath and holidays are marked by special observances, and attendance at public worship is regarded as especially important then. The chief annual observances are Passover, celebrating the liberation of the Israelites from Egypt and marked by the ritual Seder meal in the home, and the 10 days from Rosh Hashana (New Year) to Yom Kippur (Day of Atonement), a period of fasting and penitence.
**Divisions:** Judaism is an unbroken spectrum from ultraconservative to ultraliberal, largely reflecting different points of view regarding the binding character of the prohibitions and duties—particularly the dietary and Sabbath observations—traditionally prescribed for the daily life of the Jew.
**Location:** Almost worldwide, with concentrations in Israel and the U.S.
**Beliefs:** Strictly monotheistic. God is the creator and absolute ruler of the universe. Men and women are free to choose to rebel against God's rule. God established a particular relationship with the Hebrew people: by obeying a divine law God gave them, they would be a special witness to God's mercy and justice. The emphasis in Judaism is on ethical behavior (and, among the traditional, careful ritual obedience) as the true worship of God.

# STATES AND OTHER AREAS OF THE U.S.

**Sources:** Population: Commerce Dept., Bureau of the Census (July 1995 est., including armed forces personnel in each state but excluding such personnel stationed overseas); area: Bureau of the Census, Geography Division; forested land: Agriculture Dept., Forest Service; lumber production: Bureau of the Census, Industry Division; mineral production: Dept. of Interior, Office of Mineral Information; commercial fishing: Commerce Dept., Natl. Marine Fisheries Service; value of construction: McGraw-Hill Information Systems Co., F.W. Dodge Division; personal per capita income: Commerce Dept., Bureau of Economic Analysis; unemployment: Labor Dept., Bureau of Labor Statistics; finance: Federal Deposit Insurance Corp.; federal employees: Labor Dept., Office of Personnel Management; energy: Energy Dept., Energy Information Administration; education: Education Dept., National Education Assn. Other information from sources in individual states, usually Commerce Dept. *Note*: Some World Wide Web addresses are not official state sites; all are subject to change.

## Alabama

*Heart of Dixie, Camellia State*

**People. Population** (1995): 4,252,982; **rank:** 22; **Net change** (1990-95): 5.3%. **Pop. density:** (1990) 81.5 per sq mi. **Racial/ethnic distrib.** (1990): 73.6% white; 25.3% black; 0.6% Hispanic.

**Geography. Total area:** 52,423 sq mi; **rank:** 30. **Land area:** 50,750 sq mi. **Acres forested land:** 21,974,000. **Location:** East South Central state extending N-S from Tenn. to the Gulf of Mexico; east of the Mississippi River. **Climate:** long, hot summers; mild winters; generally abundant rainfall. **Topography:** coastal plains, including Prairie Black Belt give way to hills, broken terrain; highest elevation, 2,407 ft. **Capital:** Montgomery.

**Economy. Principal industries:** pulp and paper, chemicals, electronics, apparel, textiles, primary metals, lumber and wood products, food processing, fabricated metals, automotive tires, oil and gas exploration. **Principal manufactured goods:** electronics, cast iron and plastic pipe, fabricated steel products, ships, paper products, chemicals, steel, mobile homes, fabrics, poultry processing, soft drinks, furniture, tires. **Chief crops** (1995): cotton, greenhouse & nursery, peanuts, pecans, fruits, corn, sweet potatoes, potatoes and other vegetables. **Livestock** (1996): 1.75 mil cattle; 230,000 hogs/pigs; 900 mil broilers; 11.3 mil laying hens and pullets; 30.9 mil foodsize catfish. **Timber/lumber** (1995): pine, hardwoods; 2.6 bil bd. ft. **Nonfuel minerals** (est. 1995): $676 mil; crushed stone, portland cement, lime, sand & gravel. **Commercial fishing** (1995): $50 mil. **Chief port:** Mobile. **Value of construction** (1995): $4.1 bil. **Employment distribution** (1995): 21.7% mfg.; 22.8% trade; 21.9% serv; 19% govt. **Per capita personal income** (1995): $18,781. **Unemployment** (1995): 6.3%. **Tourism** (1991): tourists spent $4.5 bil.

**Finance. FDIC-insured commercial banks & trust companies** (1995): 186. **Deposits:** $42.1 bil. **FDIC-insured savings institutions** (1995): 18. **Assets:** $2.4 bil.

**Federal government. No. federal civilian employees** (Mar. 1995): 41,105. **Avg. salary:** $40,069. **Notable federal facilities:** George C. Marshall NASA Space Center, Huntsville; Gunter Annex & Maxwell AFB, Montgomery; Ft. Rucker, Ozark; Ft. McClellan, Anniston; Natl. Fertilizer Development Center, Muscle Shoals; Navy Station & U.S. Corps of Engineers, Mobile; Redstone Arsenal, Huntsville.

**Energy. Electricity production** (1995, kWh, by source): Coal: 68.6 bil; Petroleum: 102 mil; Gas: 680 mil; Hydroelectric: 9.5 bil; Nuclear: 20.8 bil.

**Public education. Student-teacher ratio** (1994): 17.2. **Avg. teachers' salary** (1995-96): $31,307.

**State data. Motto:** We dare defend our rights. **Flower:** Camellia. **Bird:** Yellowhammer. **Tree:** Southern pine. **Song:** Alabama. **Entered union** Dec. 14, 1819; rank, 22d. **State fair** at Birmingham; early Oct.

**History.** Alabama was inhabited by the Creek, Cherokee, Chickasaw, Alabama, and Choctaw peoples when the Europeans arrived. The first Europeans were Spanish explorers in the early 1500s. The French made the first permanent settlement on Mobile Bay, 1702. France later gave up the entire region to England under the terms of the Treaty of Paris, 1763. Spanish forces took control of the Mobile Bay area, 1780, and it remained Spanish until U.S. troops seized the area, 1813. Most of present-day Alabama was held by the Creeks until Gen. Andrew Jackson broke their power, 1814, and they were removed to Oklahoma Territory. The state seceded, 1861, and the Confederate states were organized Feb. 4, at Montgomery, the first capital; it was readmitted, 1868.

**Tourist attractions.** First White House of the Confederacy, Civil Rights Memorial, Alabama Shakespeare Festival, all Montgomery; Ivy Green, Helen Keller's birthplace, Tuscumbia; statue of Vulcan, Birmingham; Carver Museum, Tuskegee; W. C. Handy Home & Museum, Florence; Alabama Space and Rocket Center, Huntsville; Moundville State Monument, Moundville; Pike Pioneer Museum, Troy; USS *Alabama* Memorial Park, Mobile; Russell Cave Natl. Monument, near Bridgeport: a detailed record of occupancy by humans from about 10,000 BC to AD 1650.

**Famous Alabamians.** Hank Aaron, Tallulah Bankhead, Hugo L. Black, Paul "Bear" Bryant, George Washington Carver, Nat King Cole, William C. Handy, Bo Jackson, Helen Keller, Harper Lee, Joe Louis, Willie Mays, John Hunt Morgan, Jesse Owens, George Wallace, Booker T. Washington, Hank Williams.

**Tourist information.** Business Council of Alabama, PO Box 76, Montgomery, AL 36101; 205-834-6000.

**Toll-free travel information.** 1-800-ALABAMA out of state.

**World Wide Web site.** http://alaweb.asc.edu

## Alaska

*The Last Frontier* (unofficial)

**People. Population** (1995): 603,617; **rank:** 48; **Net change** (1990-95): 9.7%. **Pop. density:** (1990) 1.03 per sq mi. **Racial/ethnic distrib.** (1990): 75.5% white; 4.1% black; 15.6% Amer. Indian, Eskimo or Aleut; 3.6% Asian or Pacific Is.; 3.2% Hispanic.

**Geography. Total area:** 656,424 sq mi; **rank:** 1. **Land area:** 570,374 sq mi. **Acres forested land:** 129,131,000. **Location:** NW corner of North America, bordered on east by Canada. **Climate:** SE, SW, and central regions, moist and mild; far north extremely dry. Extended summer days, winter nights, throughout. **Topography:** includes Pacific and Arctic mountain systems, central plateau, and Arctic slope. Mt. McKinley, 20,320 ft, is the highest point in North America. **Capital:** Juneau.

**Economy. Principal industries:** oil, gas, tourism, commercial fishing, mining, forestry. **Principal manufactured goods:** fish products, lumber and pulp, furs. **Agriculture: Chief crops:** barley, oats, hay, silage, potatoes, lettuce. **Livestock** (1996): 10,200 cattle; (1995) 30,000 reindeer; 2,000 hogs. **Timber/lumber:** spruce, yellow cedar, hemlock. **Nonfuel minerals** (est. 1995): $594 mil; zinc, gold, silver, tin, lead, sand & gravel, crushed stone. **Commercial fishing** (1995): $1.4 bil. **Chief ports:** Anchorage, Dutch Harbor, Kodiak, Seward, Skagway, Juneau, Sitka, Valdez, Wrangell. **International airports at:** Anchorage, Fairbanks, Juneau. **Value of construction** (1995): $1.7 bil. **Employment distribution** (1994): 27% govt.; 40% serv.; 30% trade. **Per capita personal income** (1995): $24,182. **Unemployment** (1995): 7.3%. **Tourism** (1994): out-of-state visitors spend $863 mil.

**Finance. FDIC-insured commercial banks & trust companies** (1995): 8. **Deposits:** $4.1 bil. **FDIC-insured savings institutions** (1995): 2. **Assets:** $235 mil.

**Federal government. No. federal civilian employees** (Mar. 1995): 11,880. **Avg. salary:** $40,473.

**Energy. Electricity production** (1995, kWh, by source): Coal: 309 mil; Petroleum: 487 mil; Gas: 2.7 bil; Hydroelectric: 1.4 bil.

**Education. Pupil-teacher ratio**(1994): 17.6. **Avg. teachers' salary** (1995-96): $49,620.

**State data. Motto:** North to the future. **Flower:** Forget-Me-Not. **Bird:** Willow ptarmigan. **Tree:** Sitka spruce. **Song:** Alaska's Flag. **Entered union** Jan. 3, 1959; rank, 49th. **State fair** at Palmer; late Aug.–early Sept.

**History.** Early inhabitants were the Tlingit-Haida people and tribes of the Athabascan family. The Aleut and Inuit (Eskimo), who arrived about 4,000 years ago from Siberia, lived in the coastal areas. Vitus Bering, a Danish explorer working for Russia, was the first European to land in Alaska,

1741. The first permanent Russian settlement was established on Kodiak Island, 1784. In 1799, the Russian-American Co. controlled the region, and the first chief manager, Aleksandr Baranov, set up headquarters at Archangel, near present-day Sitka. Sec. of State William H. Seward bought Alaska from Russia for $7.2 mil in 1867, a bargain some called "Seward's Folly". In 1896, gold was discovered in the Klondike region, and the famed gold rush began. Alaska became a territory in 1912.

**Tourist attractions.** Inside Passage; Portage Glacier; Mendenhall Glacier; Ketchikan Totems; Glacier Bay Natl. Park and Preserve; Denali Natl. Park, one of N. America's great wildlife sanctuaries, surrounding Mt. McKinley, N. America's highest peak; Mt. Roberts Tramway, Juneau; Pribilof Islands fur seal rookeries; restored St. Michael's Russian Orthodox Cathedral, Sitka; Katmai Natl. Park & Preserve.

**Famous Alaskans.** Tom Bodett, Susan Butcher, Ernest Gruening, Gov. Tony Knowles, Sydney Laurence, Libby Riddles, Jefferson "Soapy" Smith.

**Tourist information.** Alaska Division of Tourism, PO Box 110801, Juneau, AK 99811-0801; 1-907-465-2010.

**World Wide Web site.** http://www.state.ak.us

## Arizona

*Grand Canyon State*

**People. Population** (1995): 4,217,940; **rank:** 23; **Net change** (1990-95): 15.1%. **Pop. density:** (1990) 33.7 per sq mi. **Racial/ethnic distrib.** (1990): 80.8% white; 3.0% black; 5.6% American Indian; 18.8% Hispanic.

**Geography. Total area:** 114,006 sq mi; **rank:** 6. **Land area:** 113,642 sq mi. **Acres forested land:** 19,596,000. **Location:** in the southwestern U.S. **Climate:** clear and dry in the southern regions and northern plateau; high central areas have heavy winter snows. **Topography:** Colorado plateau in the N, containing the Grand Canyon; Mexican Highlands running diagonally NW to SE; Sonoran Desert in the SW. **Capital:** Phoenix.

**Economy. Principal industries:** manufacturing, construction, tourism, mining, agriculture. **Principal manufactured goods:** electronics, printing and publishing, foods, primary and fabricated metals, aircraft and missiles, apparel. **Chief crops:** cotton, lettuce, cauliflower, broccoli, sorghum, barley, corn, wheat, citrus fruits. **Livestock** (1996): 840,000 cattle; 125,000 hogs/pigs; 135,000 sheep. **Timber/lumber** (1995): pine, fir, spruce; 118 mil bd. ft. **Nonfuel minerals** (est. 1995): $4.2 bil; copper, sand and gravel, cement, gold, molybdenum, silver, perlite. **International airports at:** Phoenix, Tucson, Yuma. **Value of construction** (1995): $8.8 bil. **Employment distribution** (1995): 29.2% services; 25.2% trade; 16.7% govt.; 10.8% mfg. **Per capita personal income** (1995): $20,421. **Unemployment** (1995): 5.1%. **Tourism** (1994): tourists spent $10.5 bil.

**Finance. FDIC-insured commercial banks & trust companies** (1995): 34. **Deposits**: $34.1 bil. **FDIC-insured savings institutions** (1995): 2. **Assets:** $433 mil.

**Federal government. No. federal civilian employees** (Mar. 1995): 28,218. **Avg. salary:** $36,277. **Notable federal facilities:** Luke, Davis-Monthan AF bases; Ft. Huachuca Army Base; Yuma Proving Grounds.

**Energy. Electricity production** (1994, kWh, by source): Coal: 31.7 bil; Petroleum: 64 mil; Gas: 1.7 bil; Hydroelectric: 8.5 mil; Nuclear: 27.0 bil.

**Public education. Student-teacher ratio** (1994): 19.3. **Avg. teachers' salary** (1995-96): $32,484.

**State data. Motto:** Ditat Deus (God enriches). **Flower:** Blossom of the Saguaro cactus. **Bird:** Cactus wren. **Tree:** Paloverde. **Song:** Arizona. **Entered union** Feb. 14, 1912; rank, 48th. **State fair** at Phoenix; late Oct.–early Nov.

**History.** Anasazi, Mogollon, and Hohokam civilizations inhabited the area c 300 BC-AD 1300, later Pueblo peoples, with the Navajo and Apache arriving c 15th cent. Marcos de Niza, a Franciscan, and Estevanico, a former black slave, explored the area, 1539; Spanish explorer Francisco Vásquez de Coronado visited, 1540. Eusebio Francisco Kino, a Jesuit missionary, taught the Indians Christianity and farming, 1692-1711, and left a chain of missions. Tubac, a Spanish fort, became the first European settlement, 1752. Spain ceded Arizona to Mexico, 1821. The U.S. took over, 1848, after the Mexican War. The area below the Gila River was obtained from Mexico in the Gadsden Purchase, 1853. Arizona became a territory in 1863. Apache wars ended with Geronimo's surrender in 1886.

**Tourist attractions.** The Grand Canyon of the Colorado; Painted Desert; Petrified Forest Natl. Park; Canyon Diablo; Meteor Crater; London Bridge, Lake Havasu City; Biosphere 2, Oracle; Navajo Natl. Monument; Sedona.

**Famous Arizonans.** Bruce Babbitt, Cochise, Geronimo, Barry Goldwater, Zane Grey, Carl Hayden, George W. P. Hunt, Helen Jacobs, Percival Lowell, Sandra Day O'Connor, William H. Pickering, John J. Rhodes, Morris Udall, Stewart Udall, Frank Lloyd Wright.

**Chamber of Commerce.** (602) 248-9172

**Tourist information.** Phoenix & Valley of the Sun Visitor and Convention Bureau, 1-602-254-6500.

**World Wide Web site.** http://www.state.az.us

## Arkansas

*Land of Opportunity*

**People. Population** (1995): 2,483,769; **rank:** 33; **Net change** (1990-95): 5.7%. **Pop. density:** (1990) 46.1 per sq mi. **Racial/ethnic distrib.** (1990): 82.7% white; 15.9% black; 0.8% Hispanic.

**Geography. Total area:** 53,182 sq mi; **rank:** 29. **Land area:** 52,075 sq mi. **Acres forested land:** 17,864,000. **Location:** in the west south-central U.S. **Climate:** long, hot summers, mild winters; generally abundant rainfall. **Topography:** eastern delta and prairie, southern lowland forests, and the northwestern highlands, which include the Ozark Plateaus. **Capital:** Little Rock.

**Economy. Principal industries:** manufacturing, agriculture, tourism, forestry. **Principal manufactured goods:** food products, chemicals, lumber, paper, electric motors, furniture, auto components, airplane parts, apparel, machinery, steel. **Chief crops:** soybeans, rice, cotton, tomatoes, grapes, apples, commercial vegetables, peaches, wheat. **Livestock** (1994): 2.1 mil cattle; 770,000 hogs/pigs; 1,078,800 mil broilers. **Timber/lumber** (1995): oak, hickory, gum, cypress, pine; 3 bil bd. ft. **Nonfuel minerals** (est. 1995): $452 mil; crushed stone, bromine, cement, sand & gravel. **Chief ports:** Little Rock, Pine Bluff, Osceola, Helena, Fort Smith, Van Buren, Camden, Dardanelle, North Little Rock, West Memphis, Crossett, McGehee, Morrilton, Helena. **Value of construction** (1995): $2.9 bil. **Employment distribution** (1995): 24.2% mfg.; 22.7% trade; 22.2% serv.; 16.6% govt. **Per capita personal income** (1995): $17,429. **Unemployment** (1995): 4.9%. **Tourism** (1995): travelers spent $3.0 bil.

**Finance. FDIC-insured commercial banks & trust companies** (1995): 243. **Deposits:** $25.3 bil. **FDIC-insured savings institutions** (1995): 17. **Assets:** $3.4 bil.

**Federal government. No. federal civilian employees** (Mar. 1995): 11,373. **Avg. salary:** $34,879. **Notable federal facilities:** Nat'l. Center for Toxicological Research, Jefferson; Pine Bluff Arsenal, Little Rock AFB.

**Energy. Electricity production** (1995, kWh, by source): Coal: 21.5 bil; Petroleum: 53 mil; Gas: 3.1 bil; Hydroelectric: 3.2 bil; Nuclear: 11.7 bil.

**Public education. Student-teacher ratio** (1994): 17.1. **Avg. teachers' salary** (1995-96): $29,322.

**State data. Motto:** Regnat Populus (The people rule). **Flower:** Apple blossom. **Bird:** Mockingbird. **Tree:** Pine. **Song:** Arkansas. **Entered union** June 15, 1836; rank, 25th. **State fair** at Little Rock; late Sept.–early Oct.

**History.** Quapaw, Caddo, Osage, Cherokee, and Choctaw peoples lived in the area at the time of European contact. The first European explorers were de Soto, 1541; Marquette and Jolliet, 1673; and La Salle, 1682. The first settlement was by the French under Henri de Tony, 1686, at Arkansas Post. In 1762, the area was ceded by France to Spain, then given back again, 1800, and was part of the Louisiana Purchase, 1803. It was made a territory, 1819. Arkansas seceded from the Union in 1861, only after the Civil War began; more than 10,000 Arkansans fought on the Union side.

**Tourist attractions.** Hot Springs Natl. Park; Eureka Springs; Ozark Folk Center, Blanchard Caverns, both Mountain View; Crater of Diamonds, only U.S. diamond mine, near Murfreesboro; Toltec Mounds Archeological State Park, Little Rock.

**Famous Arkansans.** Daisy Bates, Dee Brown, Paul "Bear" Bryant, Glen Campbell, Johnny Cash, Hattie Caraway, Bill Clinton, "Dizzy" Dean, Orval Faubus, James W. Fulbright, John H. Johnson, John Grisham, Douglas MacArthur, John L. McClellan, James S. McDonnel, Dick Powell, Winthrop Rockefeller, Mary Steenburgen, Edward Durell Stone, Archibald Yell.

**Chamber of Commerce.** One Spring Bldg., Little Rock, AR 72201-2486; 501-374-9225

**Toll-free travel information.** 1-800-NATURAL.

**World Wide Web site.** http://www.state.ar.us

## California

*Golden State*

**People. Population** (1995): 31,589,153; **rank:** 1; **Net change** (1990-95): 6.2%. **Pop. density:** (1990) 197.9 per sq mi. **Racial/ethnic distrib.** (1990): 69.0% white; 7.4% black; 9.6% Asian; 25.8% Hispanic.

**Geography. Total area:** 163,707 sq mi; **rank:** 3. **Land area:** 155,973 sq mi. **Acres forested land:** 37,263,000. **Location:** on western coast of the U.S. **Climate:** moderate temperatures and rainfall along the coast; extremes in the interior. **Topography:** long mountainous coastline; central valley; Sierra Nevada on the east; desert basins of the southern interior; rugged mountains of the north. **Capital:** Sacramento.

**Economy. Principal industries:** agriculture, entertainment, manufacturing, services, trade. **Principal manufactured goods:** foods, printed material, primary and fabricated metals, machinery, electric and electronic equipment, transportation equipment, instruments. **Chief crops:** grapes, cotton, flowers, oranges, nursery products, hay, tomatoes, lettuce, strawberries, almonds, broccoli, walnuts, sugar beets, peaches, potatoes. **Livestock** (1995): 4.7 mil. cattle & calves; 255,000 hogs/pigs; 520,000 sheep and lambs; 31.5 mil chickens exc. broilers. **Timber/lumber** (1995): fir, pine, redwood, oak; 3.2 bil bd. ft. **Nonfuel Minerals:** (1995): $2.7 bil; portland cement, sand & gravel, boron, dimension stone, diatomite, gold, silver, tungsten, copper, asbestos. **Commercial fishing** (1995): $167 mil. **Chief ports:** Long Beach, Los Angeles, San Diego, Oakland, San Francisco, Sacramento, Stockton. **International airports at:** Los Angeles, Sacramento, San Francisco, San Jose, San Diego. **Value of construction** (1995): $28.8 bil. **Employment distribution** (1996): 30.6% serv.; 23.4% trade; 14.2% mfg.; 16.8% govt. **Per capita personal income** (1995): $23,699. **Unemployment** (1995): 7.8%. **Tourism** (1995): $55.7 bil.

**Finance. FDIC-insured commercial banks & trust companies** (1995): 383. **Deposits**: $286.4 bil. **FDIC-insured savings institutions** (1995): 77. **Assets:** $243.8 bil.

**Federal government. No. federal civilian employees** (Mar. 1995): 179,088. **Avg. salary:** $40,233. **Notable federal facilities:** Vandenberg, Beale, Travis, McClellan AF bases, San Francisco Mint.

**Energy. Electricity production** (1995, kWh, by source): Petroleum: 489 mil; Gas: 39.1 bil; Hydroelectric: 47.5 bil; Nuclear: 30.2 bil.

**Public education. Student-teacher ratio** (1994): 24.0. **Avg. teachers' salary** (1995-96): $42,516.

**State data. Motto:** Eureka (I have found it). **Flower:** Golden poppy. **Bird:** California valley quail. **Tree:** California redwood. **Song:** I Love You, California. **Entered union** Sept. 9, 1850; rank, 31st. **State fair** at Sacramento; late Aug.—early Sept.

**History.** Early inhabitants included more than 100 different Native American tribes with multiple dialects. The first European explorers were Cabrillo, 1542, and Drake, 1579. The first settlement was the Spanish Alto California mission at San Diego, 1769, first in a string founded by Franciscan Father Junípero Serra. U.S. traders and settlers arrived in the 19th cent. and staged the Bear Flag revolt, 1846, in protest against Mexican rule; later that year U.S. forces occupied California. At the end of the Mexican War, Mexico ceded the territory to the U.S., 1848; that same year gold was discovered by James Marshall, and the famed gold rush began.

**Tourist attractions.** RMS *Queen Mary*, Long Beach; Palomar Observatory; Disneyland, Anaheim; J. Paul Getty Museum, Malibu; Tournament of Roses and Rose Bowl, Pasadena; Universal Studios, Hollywood; Los Angeles County Art Museum; San Diego Zoo; Yosemite Valley; Lassen and Sequoia-Kings Canyon natl. parks; Lake Tahoe; Mojave and Colorado deserts; San Francisco Bay; Napa Valley; Monterey Peninsula; oldest living things on earth, believed a stand of Bristlecone pines in the Inyo National Forest, est. 4,700 years old; world's tallest tree, 365-ft "National Geographic Society" coast redwood, in Humboldt Redwoods State Park.

**Famous Californians.** Edmund G. (Pat) Brown, Jerry Brown, Luther Burbank, John C. Fremont, Bret Harte, William R. Hearst, Jack Kemp, Jack London, Aimee Semple McPherson, John Muir, Richard M. Nixon, William Saroyan, Father Junípero Serra, Leland Stanford, John Steinbeck, Earl Warren.

**Chamber of Commerce.** 1201 K St., Sacramento, CA 95814.

**Toll-free travel information.** 1-800-862-2543.

**World Wide Web site.** http://www.ca.us

## Colorado

*Centennial State*

**People. Population** (1995): 3,746,585; **rank:** 25; **Net change** (1990-95): 13.7%. **Pop. density:** (1990) 33.5 per sq mi. **Racial/ethnic distrib.** (1990): 88.2% white; 4.0% black; 12.9% Hispanic.

**Geography. Total area:** 104,100 sq mi; **rank:** 8. **Land area:** 103,729 sq mi. **Acres forested land:** 21,338,000. **Location:** in west central U.S. **Climate:** low relative humidity, abundant sunshine, wide daily, seasonal temperatures ranges; alpine conditions in the high mountains. **Topography:** eastern dry high plains; hilly to mountainous central plateau; western Rocky Mountains of high ranges alternating with broad valleys and deep, narrow canyons. **Capital:** Denver.

**Economy. Principal industries:** manufacturing, construction, government, tourism, agriculture, aerospace, electronics equipment. **Principal manufactured goods:** computer equipment, instruments, foods, machinery, aerospace products. **Chief crops:** corn, wheat, hay, sugar beets, barley, potatoes, apples, peaches, pears, dry edible beans, sorghum, onions, oats sunflowers, vegetables. **Livestock** (1995): 3.1 mil cattle; 1.1 mil. hogs/pigs; 4.1 mil poultry. **Timber/lumber** (1995): oak, ponderosa pine, Douglas fir; 116 mil bd. ft. **Nonfuel minerals** (est. 1995): $448 mil; construction sand & gravel, portland cement, crushed stone, gold, lead, zinc, molybdenum. **International airports at:** Denver. **Value of construction** (1995): $6.5 bil. **Employment distribution** (1995): 29.3% serv.; 24.8% trade; 16.6% govt.; 10.5% mfg. **Per capita personal income** (1995): $23,449. **Unemployment** (1995) 4.2%. **Tourism** (1992): $6.4 bil.

**Finance. FDIC-insured commercial banks & trust companies** (1995): 231. **Deposits:** $31.2 bil. **FDIC-insured savings institutions** (1995): 16. **Assets:** $2.7 bil.

**Federal government. No. federal civilian employees** (Mar. 1995): 37,632. **Avg. salary:** $40,652. **Notable federal facilities:** U.S. Air Force Academy; U.S. Mint; Ft. Carson; National Renewable Energy Labs; U.S. Rail Transportation Test Center; N. American Aerospace Defense Command; Consolidated Space Operations Center; Denver Federal Center.

**Energy. Electricity production** (1995, kWh, by source): Coal: 30.3 bil; Petroleum: 10 mil; Gas: 287 mil; Hydroelectric: 2.1 bil.

**Public education. Student-teacher ratio** (1994): 18.4. **Avg. teachers' salary** (1995-96): $35,364.

**State data. Motto:** Nil Sine Numine (Nothing without Providence). **Flower:** Rocky Mountain columbine. **Bird:** Lark bunting. **Tree:** Colorado blue spruce. **Song:** Where the Columbines Grow. **Entered union** Aug. 1, 1876; rank 38th. **State fair** at Pueblo; last week in Aug.

**History.** Early civilization centered around the Mesa Verde c 2,000 years ago, later, Ute, Pueblo, Cheyenne, and Arapaho peoples lived in the area. The region was claimed by Spain, but passed to France. The U.S. acquired eastern Colorado in the Louisiana Purchase, 1803. Lt. Zebulon M. Pike explored the area, 1806, discovering the peak that bears his name. After the Mexican War, 1846-48, U.S. immigrants settled in the east, former Mexicans in the south. Gold was discovered in 1858, causing a population boom. Displaced Native Americans protested, resulting in the so-called Sand Creek Massacre, 1864, where more than 200 Cheyenne and Arapaho were killed. All Native Americans were later removed to Oklahoma Territory.

**Tourist attractions.** Rocky Mountain Natl. Park; Garden of the Gods, Colorado Springs; Great Sand Dunes, Dinosaur, Black Canyon of the Gunnison, and Colorado natl. monuments; Pikes Peak and Mt. Evans highways; Mesa Verde Natl. Park (ancient Anasazi Indian cliff dwellings); Grand Mesa Natl. Forest; mining towns of Central City, Silverton, Cripple Creek; Burlington's Old Town; Bent's Fort, outside La Junta; Georgetown Loop Historic Mining Railroad Park, Cumbres & Toltec Scenic Railroad; limited stakes gaming in: Central City, Blackhawk, Cripple Creek, Ignacio and Towaoe.

**Famous Coloradans.** Frederick Bonfils, Molly Brown, William N. Byers, M. Scott Carpenter, Jack Dempsey, Mamie Eisenhower, Douglas Fairbanks, Scott Hamilton, "Baby Doe" Tabor, Lowell Thomas, Byron R. White, Paul Whiteman.

**Tourist information.** Colorado Tourism Board, Ste. 1700, 1625 Broadway, Denver, CO 80202.

**Toll-free travel information.** 1-800-265-6723.

**World Wide Web site.** http://www.state.co.us

## Connecticut

*Constitution State, Nutmeg State*

**People. Population** (1995): 3,274,662; **rank:** 28; **Net change** (1990-95): –0.4%. **Pop. density:** (1990) 677.2 per sq mi. **Racial/ethnic distrib.** (1990): 87.0% white; 8.3% black; 6.5% Hispanic.

**Geography. Total area:** 5,544 sq mi; **rank:** 48. **Land area:** 4,845 sq mi. **Acres forested land:** 1,819,000. **Location:** New England state in NE corner of the U.S. **Climate:** moderate; winters avg. slightly below freezing; warm, humid summers. **Topography:** western upland, the Berkshires, in the NW, highest elevations; narrow central lowland N-S; hilly eastern upland drained by rivers. **Capital:** Hartford.

**Economy. Principal industries:** manufacturing, retail trade, government, services, finances, insurance, real estate. **Principal manufactured goods:** aircraft engines and parts, submarines, helicopters, machinery & computer equipment, electronics & electrical equipment, medical instruments, pharmaceuticals. **Chief crops:** nursery stock, Christmas trees, mushrooms, vegetables, sweet corn, tobacco, apples. **Livestock** (1992): 78,000 cattle; 5,800 horses; 5,200 hogs/pigs; 7,500 sheep; 5.6 mil poultry. **Timber/lumber** (1995): oak, birch, beech, maple; 37 mil bd. ft. **Nonfuel minerals** (est. 1995): $81 mil; crushed stone, construction sand & gravel. **Commercial fishing** (1995): $57 mil. **Chief ports:** New Haven, Bridgeport, New London. **International airports at:** Windsor Locks. **Value of construction** (1995): $3.1 bil. **Employment distribution** (1995): 21% mfg.; 79% serv. **Per capita personal income** (1995): $30,303. **Unemployment** (1995): 5.5%. **Tourism** (1993): out-of-state visitors spent $3.9 bil.

**Finance. FDIC-insured commercial banks & trust companies** (1995): 39. **Deposits:** $24.0 bil. **FDIC-insured savings institutions** (1995): 59. **Assets**: $38.8 bil.

**Federal government. No. federal civilian employees** (Mar. 1995): 9,524. **Avg. salary:** $42,015. **Notable federal facilities:** U.S. Coast Guard Academy; U.S. Navy Submarine Base.

**Energy. Electricity production** (1995, kWh, by source): Coal: 2.7 bil; Petroleum: 3.4 bil; Gas: 1.8 bil; Hydroelectric: 293 mil; Nuclear: 18.7 bil.

**Public education. Student-teacher ratio** (1994): 14.4. **Avg. teachers' salary** (1995-96): $50,400.

**State data. Motto:** Qui Transtulit Sustinet (He who transplanted still sustains). **Flower:** Mountain laurel. **Bird:** American robin. **Tree:** White oak. **Song:** Yankee Doodle. **Fifth** of the 13 original states to ratify the Constitution, Jan. 9, 1788. **State Fair** at Agawan, MA, (combined with MA and NH), Sept.

**History.** At the time of European contact, inhabitants of the area were Algonquian peoples, including the Mohegan and Pequot. Dutch explorer Adriaen Block was the first European visitor, 1614. By 1634, settlers from Plymouth Bay had started colonies along the Connecticut River in 1637; they defeated the Pequots. The Colony of Connecticut was chartered by England, 1662, adding New Haven, 1665. In the American Revolution, Connecticut Patriots fought in most major campaigns, while Connecticut privateers captured British merchant ships.

**Tourist attractions.** Mark Twain House, Hartford; Yale University's Art Gallery, Peabody Museum, both in New Haven; Mystic Seaport; Mystic Marine Life Aquarium; P. T. Barnum Museum, Bridgeport; Gillette Castle, Hadlyme; U.S.S. *Nautilus* Memorial, Groton (1st nuclear-powered submarine); Foxwoods Casino, Ledyard.

**Famous "Nutmeggers."** Ethan Allen, Phineas T. Barnum, Samuel Colt, Jonathan Edwards, Nathan Hale, Katharine Hepburn, Isaac Hull, J. Pierpont Morgan, Israel Putnam, Harriet Beecher Stowe, Mark Twain, Noah Webster, Eli Whitney.

**Tourist information.** State Dept. of Economic Development, 865 Brook St., Rocky Hill, CT 06067.

**Toll-free travel information.** 1-800-CTBOUND

**World Wide Web site.** http://www.state.ct.us

## Delaware

*First State, Diamond State*

**People. Population** (1995): 717,197; **rank:** 46; **Net change** (1990-95): 7.7%. **Pop. density:** (1990) 352.5 per sq mi. **Racial/ethnic distrib.** (1990): 80.3% white; 16.9% black; 2.4% Hispanic.

**Geography. Total area:** 2,489 sq mi; **rank:** 49. **Land area:** 1,955 sq mi. **Acres forested land:** 398,000. **Location:** occupies the Delmarva Peninsula on the Atlantic coastal plain. **Climate:** moderate. **Topography:** Piedmont plateau to the N, sloping to a near sea-level plain. **Capital:** Dover.

**Economy. Principal industries:** chemicals, agriculture, finance, poultry, shellfish, tourism, auto assembly, food processing, transportation equipment. **Principal manufactured goods:** nylon, apparel, luggage, foods, autos, processed meats and vegetables, railroad and aircraft equipment. **Chief crops:** soybeans, potatoes, corn, mushrooms, lima beans, green peas, barley, cucumbers, wheat, corn, grain sorghum, greenhouse and nursery. **Livestock** (1995): 7,000 cattle, 48,000 hogs, 263.1 mil broilers. **Timber/Lumber** (1995): hardwoods and softwoods (except for soutern yellow pine); 15 mil bd. ft. **Nonfuel minerals** (est. 1995): $8.9 mil; construction sand & gravel. **Commercial fishing** (1995): $7.9 mil. **Chief ports:** Wilmington. **International airports at:** Philadelphia/Wilmington. **Value of construction** (1995): $863.1 mil. **Employment distribution** (1995): 83.1% nonmanufacturing; 16.9% mfg. **Per capita personal income** (1995): $24,124. **Unemployment** (1995): 4.3%. **Tourism** (1995): domestic travelers spent $836 mil.

**Finance. FDIC-insured commercial banks & trust companies** (1995): 40. **Deposits:** $39.6 bil. **FDIC-insured savings institutions** (1995): 4. **Assets:** $1.7 bil.

**Federal government. No. federal civilian employees** (Mar. 1995): 2,785. **Avg. salary:** $36,739. **Notable federal facilities:** Dover Air Force Base, Federal Wildlife Refuge, Bombay Hook.

**Energy. Electricity production** (1995, kWh, by source): Coal: 4.2 bil; Petroleum: 983 mil; Gas: 2.8 bil.

**Public education. Student-teacher ratio** (1994): 16.6. **Avg. teachers' salary** (1995-96): $40,533.

**State data. Motto:** Liberty and independence. **Flower:** Peach blossom. **Bird:** Blue hen chicken. **Tree:** American holly. **Song:** Our Delaware. **First** of original 13 states to ratify the Constitution, Dec. 7, 1787. **State fair** at Harrington; end of July.

**History.** The Lenni Lenape (Delaware) people lived in the region at the time of European contact. Explorer Henry Hudson located the Delaware R., 1609, and in 1610, English explorer Samuel Argall entered Delaware Bay, naming the area after Virginia's governor, Lord De La Warr. The Dutch first settled near present Lewes, 1631, but the colony was destroyed by Indians. Swedes settled at Fort Christina (now Wilmington), 1638. Dutch settled anew, 1651, near New Castle and seized the Swedish settlement, 1655, only to lose all Delaware and New Netherland to the British, 1664. After 1682, Delaware became part of Pennsylvania and in 1704, was granted its own assembly. In 1776, it adopted a constitution as the state of Delaware. Although it remained in the Union during the Civil War, Delaware retained slavery until it was abolished by the 13th Amendment in 1865.

**Tourist attractions.** Ft. Christina Monument, site of founding of New Sweden, Holy Trinity (Old Swedes) Church, erected 1698, the oldest Protestant church in the U.S. still in use, Wilmington; Hagley Museum, Winterthur Museum and Gardens, both near Wilmington; historic district, New Castle; John Dickinson "Penman of the Revolution" home, Dover; Rehoboth Beach, "nation's summer capital," Rehoboth; Dover Downs Intl. Speedway.

**Famous Delawareans.** Thomas F. Bayard, Henry Seidel Canby, E. I. du Pont, John P. Marquand, Howard Pyle, Caesar Rodney.

**Chamber of Commerce.** 1200 N. Orange St., Ste. 200, Wilmington, DE 19899-0671.

**Toll-free travel information.** 1-800-441-8846.

**World Wide Web site.** http://www.state.de.us

## Florida

*Sunshine State*

**People. Population** (1995): 14,165,570; **rank:** 4; **Net change** (1990-95): 9.5%. **Pop. density:** (1990) 249.8 per sq mi. **Racial/ethnic distrib.** (1990): 83.1% white; 13.6% black; 12.2% Hispanic.

**Geography. Total area:** 65,756 sq mi; **rank:** 22. **Land area:** 53,937 sq mi. **Acres forested land:** 16,549,000. **Location:** peninsula jutting southward 500 mi between the Atlantic and the Gulf of Mexico. **Climate:** subtropical N of Bradenton-Lake Okeechobee-Vero Beach line; tropical S of line. **Topography:** land is flat or rolling; highest point is 345 ft in the NW. **Capital:** Tallahassee.

**Economy. Principal industries:** tourism, agriculture, manufacturing, construction, services, international trade. **Principal manufactured goods:** electric & electronic equipment, transportation equipment; food; printing & publishing; chemicals, instruments. **Chief crops:** citrus fruits, greenhouse and nursery products, vegetables, potatoes, melons, strawberries, sugarcane. **Livestock** (1995): 2.0 mil cattle, including 162,000 milk cows; 85,000 hogs/pigs; 140 mil broilers; 2.4 bil eggs. **Timber/lumber** (1995): pine, cypress, cedar; 720 mil bd. ft. **Nonfuel minerals** (est. 1995): $1.4 bil; mostly phosphate, cement, sand and gravel, peat, titanium concentrates, crushed stone. **Commercial fishing** (1995): $198 mil. **Chief ports:** Pensacola, Tampa, Manatee, Miami, Port Everglades, Jacksonville, St. Petersburg, Canaveral. **International airports at:** Ft. Lauderdale/Hollywood, Daytona Beach, Ft. Myers, Key West, Jacksonville, Miami, Orlando, St. Petersburg/Clearwater, Panama City, Tampa, Sarasota/Bradenton, West Palm Beach. **Value of construction** (1995): $21.5 bil. **Employment distribution** (1994, total nonagricultural): 33% services, 26% wholesale & retail trade, 16% govt., 8% mfg. **Per capita personal income** (1995): $22,916. **Unemployment** (1995): 5.5% **Tourism** (1994): $33.39 bil.

**Finance. FDIC-insured commercial banks & trust companies** (1995): 333. **Deposits:** $125.0 bil. **FDIC-insured savings institutions** (1995): 70. **Assets:** $25.6 bil.

**Federal government. No. federal civilian employees** (Mar. 1995): 61,311. **Avg. salary:** $39,096. **Notable federal facilities:** John F. Kennedy Space Center, NASA-Kennedy Space Center's Spaceport USA; Eglin Air Force Base.

**Energy. Electricity production** (1995, kWh, by source): Coal: 61.9 bil; Petroleum: 21.6 bil; Gas: 34.7 bil; Hydroelectric: 231 mil; Nuclear: 28.7 bil.

**Public education. Student-teacher ratio** (1994): 19.1. **Avg. teachers' salary** (1995-96): $33,320.

**State data. Motto:** In God we trust. **Flower:** Orange blossom. **Bird:** Mockingbird. **Tree:** Sabal palmetto palm. **Song:** Old Folks at Home. **Entered union** Mar. 3, 1845; rank, 27th. **State fair** at Tampa; early Feb.; call 813-621-7821.

**History.** The original inhabitants of Florida included the Timucua, Apalachee, and Calusa peoples. Later the Seminole migrated from Georgia to Florida, becoming dominant there in the early 18th cent. The first European to see Florida was Ponce de León, 1513. France established a colony, Fort Caroline, on the St. John River, 1564. Spain settled St. Augustine, 1565, and Spanish troops massacred most of the French. Britain's Sir Francis Drake burned St. Augustine, 1586. In 1763, Spain ceded Florida to Great Britain, which held the area briefly, 1763-83, before returning it to Spain. After Andrew Jackson led a U.S. invasion, 1818, Spain ceded Florida to the U.S., 1819. The Seminole War, 1835-42, resulted in removal of most Native Americans to Oklahoma Territory. Florida seceded from the Union, 1861, and was readmitted in 1868.

**Tourist attractions.** Miami Beach; St. Augustine, oldest permanent European settlement in U.S.; Castillo de San Marcos, St. Augustine; Walt Disney World's Magic Kingdom, EPCOT Center, and Disney-MGM Studios, all near Orlando; Sea World, Universal Studios, near Orlando; Spaceport USA, Kennedy Space Center; Everglades Natl. Park, which Ringling Museum of Art, Ringling Museum of the Circus, both in Sarasota; Cypress Gardens, Winter Haven; Busch Gardens, Tampa.

**Famous Floridians.** Henry M. Flagler, James Weldon Johnson, MacKinlay Kantor, Henry B. Plant, Marjorie Kinnan Rawlings, Joseph W. Stilwell, Charles P. Summerall.

**Tourist information.** Florida Division of Tourism, 126 Van Buren St., Tallahassee, FL 32399-2000, 1-904-487-1462.

**World Wide Web site.** http://www.state.fl.us

## Georgia

*Empire State of the South, Peach State*

**People. Population** (1995): 7,200,882; **rank:** 10; **Net change** (1990-95): 11.2%. **Pop. density:** (1990) 116.6 per sq mi. **Racial/ethnic distrib.** (1990): 71.0% white; 27.0% black; 1.7% Hispanic.

**Geography. Total area:** 59,441 sq mi; **rank:** 24. **Land area:** 57,919 sq mi. **Acres forested land:** 24,137,000. **Location:** South Atlantic state. **Climate:** maritime tropical air masses dominate in summer; polar air masses in winter; E central area drier. **Topography:** most southerly of the Blue Ridge Mts. cover NE and N central; central Piedmont extends to the fall line of rivers; coastal plain levels to the coast flatlands. **Capital:** Atlanta.

**Economy. Principal industries:** services, manufacturing, retail trade. **Principal manufactured goods** (1994): textiles, apparel, food, and kindred products, pulp and paper products. **Chief crops:** peanuts, cotton, corn, tobacco, hay, soybeans. **Livestock** (1994): 1.54 mil cattle; 1.03 mil hogs/pigs; 26.3 mil poultry, excluding broilers. **Timber/lumber** (1995): pine, hardwood; 2.9 bil bd. ft. **Nonfuel minerals** (est. 1995): $1.7 bil; mostly kaolin and other clays, crushed stone. **Commercial fishing** (1995): $35.3 mil. **Chief ports:** Savannah, Brunswick. **International airports at:** Atlanta. **Value of construction** (1995): $12.2 bil. **Employment distribution** (1994): 22% services; 18% mfg.; 18% retail trade; 17.6% govt. **Per capita personal income** (1995): $21,278. **Unemployment** (1995): 4.9%. **Tourism** (1995): tourists spent $13.5 bil.

**Finance. FDIC-insured commercial banks & trust companies** (1995): 383. **Deposits:** $90.9 bil. **FDIC-insured savings institutions** (1995): 36. **Assets:** $6.6 bil.

**Federal government. No. federal civilian employees** (Mar. 1995): 66,639. **Avg. salary:** $37,540. **Notable federal facilities:** Dobbins AFB; Fts. Benning, Gordon, McPherson; Fed. Law Enforcement Training Ctr., Glynco, Warner Robins AFB; Centers for Disease Control, Atlanta.

**Energy. Electricity production** (1995, kWh, by source): Coal: 65.9 bil; Petroleum: 219 mil; Gas: 573 mil; Hydroelectric: 4.7 bil; Nuclear: 30.7 bil.

**Public education. Student-teacher ratio** (1994): 16.3. **Avg. teachers' salary** (1995-96): $34,307.

**State data. Motto:** Wisdom, justice and moderation. **Flower:** Cherokee rose. **Bird:** Brown thrasher. **Tree:** Live oak. **Song:** Georgia On My Mind. **Fourth** of the 13 original states to ratify the Constitution, Jan. 2, 1788. **State fair** at Perry, Oct.

**History.** Creek and Cherokee peoples were early inhabitants of the region. The earliest known European settlement was the Spanish mission of Santa Catalina, 1566, on Saint Catherines Island. Gen. James Oglethorpe established a colony at Savannah, 1733, for the poor and religiously persecuted. Oglethorpe defeated a Spanish army from Florida at Bloody Marsh, 1742. In the American Revolution, Georgians seized the Savannah armory, 1775, and sent the munitions to the Continental Army. They fought seesaw campaigns with Cornwallis's British troops, twice liberating Augusta and forcing final evacuation by the British from Savannah, 1782. The Cherokee were removed to Oklahoma Territory, 1832-38, and thousands died on the long march, known as the Trail of Tears. Georgia seceded from the Union, 1861, and was invaded by Union forces, 1864, under Gen. William T. Sherman, who took Atlanta, Sept. 2, and proceeded on his famous "march to the sea," ending in Dec., in Savannah. Georgia was readmitted, 1870.

**Tourist attractions.** State Capitol, Stone Mt. Park, Six Flags Over Georgia, Kennesaw Mt. Natl. Battlefield Park, Martin Luther King, Jr. Natl. Historic Site, Underground Atlanta, Jimmy Carter Library & Museum, all Atlanta; Chickamauga and Chattanooga Natl. Military Park, near Dalton; Chattahoochee Natl. Forest; alpine village of Helen; Dahlonega, site of America's first gold rush; Brasstown Bald Mt.; Lake Lanier; Franklin D. Roosevelt's Little White House, Warm Springs; Callaway Gardens, Pine Mt.; Andersonville Natl. Historic Site; Okefenokee Swamp, near Waycross; Jekyll Island; St. Simons Island; Cumberland Island Natl. Seashore; historic riverfront district, Savannah.

**Famous Georgians.** Griffin Bell, James Bowie, James Brown, Erskine Caldwell, Jimmy Carter, Ray Charles, Lucius D. Clay, Ty Cobb, John C. Fremont, Newt Gingrich, Joel Chandler Harris, Martin Luther King Jr., Gladys Knight, Sidney Lanier, Juliette Gordon Low, Margaret Mitchell, Flannery O'Connor, Otis Redding, Jackie Robinson, Alice Walker, Joseph Wheeler, Joanne Woodward.

**Chamber of Commerce.** 235 International Blvd., Atlanta, GA 30303; (404) 880-9000.

**Toll-free travel information.** 1-800-VISITGA.

**World Wide Web site.** http://www.state.ga.us

## Hawai'i

*Aloha State*

**People. Population** (1995): 1,186,815; **rank:** 40; **Net change** (1990-95): 7.1%. **Pop. density:** (1990) 180.5 per sq mi. **Racial/ethnic distrib.** (1990): 33.4% white; 2.5% black; 61.8% Asian or Pacific Is.; 7.3% Hispanic.

**Geography. Total area:** 10,932 sq mi; **rank:** 43. **Land area:** 6,423 sq mi. **Acres forested land:** 1,748,000. **Location:** Hawaiian Islands lie in the North Pacific, 2,397 mi SW from San Francisco. **Climate:** subtropical, with wide variations in rainfall; Waialeale, on Kaua'i, wettest spot in U.S. (annual rainfall 460 in.) **Topography:** islands are tops of a chain of submerged volcanic mountains; active volcanoes: Mauna Loa, Kilauea. **Capital:** Honolulu.

**Economy. Principal industries:** tourism, defense, sugar, pineapples. **Principal manufactured goods:** processed sugar, canned pineapple, clothing, foods, printing and publishing. **Chief crops:** sugar, pineapples, macadamia nuts, fruits, coffee, vegetables, floriculture. **Livestock** (1995): 175,000 cattle and calves; 34,000 hogs/pigs; 1.01 mil chickens. **Nonfuel minerals** (est. 1995): $106 mil; mostly crushed stone, cement. **Commercial fishing** (1995): $60 mil. **Chief ports:** Honolulu, Nawiliwili, Barbers Point, Kahului, Hilo. **International airports at:** Honolulu. **Value of construction** (1995): $2.3 bil. **Employment distribution** (1995): 25.5% trade; 8.8% mfg.; 31% serv.; 21% govt. **Per capita personal income** (1995): $24,738. **Unemployment** (1995): 5.9%. **Tourism** (1994): visitors spent $10.6 bil.

**Finance. FDIC-insured commercial banks & trust companies** (1995): 15. **Deposits:** $14.3 bil. **FDIC-insured savings institutions** (1995): 5. **Assets:** $6.3 bil.

**Federal government. No. federal civilian employees** (Mar. 1995): 20,373. **Avg. salary:** $37,923. **Notable federal facilities:** Pearl Harbor Naval Shipyard; Hickam AFB; Schofield Barracks; Ft. Shafter; Marine Corps Base-Kaneohe Bay; Barbers Point NAS; Wheeler AFB; Prince Kahio Federal Building.

**Energy. Electricity production** (1995, kWh, by source): Petroleum: 6.2 bil; Hydroelectric: 16 mil.

**Public education. Student-teacher ratio** (1994): 17.9. **Avg. teachers' salary** (1995-96): $35,807.

**State data. Motto:** The life of the land is perpetuated in righteousness. **Flower:** Yellow hibiscus. **Bird:** Hawaiian goose. **Tree:** Kukui (Candlenut). **Song:** Hawai'i Pono'i. **Entered union** Aug. 21, 1959; rank, 50th. **State fair:** 50th State Fair in June and State Farm Fair in July.

**History.** Polynesians from islands 2,000 mi to the south settled the Hawaiian Islands, probably between AD 300 and AD 600. The first European visitor was British captain James Cook, 1778. Between 1790 and 1810, the islands were united politically under the leadership of a native king, Kamehameha I, whose five successors—all bearing the name Kamehameha—ruled the kingdom from his death, 1819, until the end of the dynasty, 1872. Missionaries arrived, 1820, bringing Western culture. King Kamehameha III and his chiefs created the first constitution and a legislature that set up a public school system. Sugar production began, 1835, and it became the dominant industry. In 1893, Queen Liliuokalani was deposed, and a republic was instituted, 1894, headed by Sanford B. Dole. Annexation by the U.S. came in 1898. The Japanese attack on Pearl Harbor, Dec. 7, 1941, brought the U.S. into World War II.

**Tourist attractions.** Hawaii Volcanoes, Haleakala natl. parks; Natl. Memorial Cemetery of the Pacific, Waikiki Beach, Diamond Head, Honolulu; U.S.S. *Arizona* Memorial, Pearl Harbor; Hanauma Bay; Polynesian Cultural Center, Laie; Nu'uanu Pali; Waimea Canyon; Wailua River state parks.

**Famous Islanders.** Bernice Pauahi Bishop, Tia Carrera, Don Ho, Father Duke Kahanamoku, King Kamehameha the Great, Jason Scott Lee, Queen Liliuokalani, Bette Midler, Ellison Onizuka.

**Chamber of Commerce of Hawaii.** 1132 Bishop St., Suite 200, Honolulu, HI 96813.

**Toll free travel information.** 1-800-464-2924.

**World Wide Web site.** http://www.state.hi.us

## Idaho

*Gem State*

**People. Population** (1995): 1,163,261; **rank:** 41; **Net change** (1990-95): 15.5%. **Pop. density:** (1990) 12.9 per sq mi. **Racial/ethnic distrib.** (1990): 94.4% white; 0.3% black; 5.3% Hispanic.

**Geography. Total area:** 83,574 sq mi; **rank:** 14. **Land area:** 82,751 sq mi. **Acres forested land:** 21,621,000. **Location:** northwestern Mountain state bordering on British Columbia. **Climate:** tempered by Pacific westerly winds; drier, colder, continental climate in SE; altitude an important factor. **Topography:** Snake R. plains in the S; central region of mountains, canyons, gorges (Hells Canyon, 7,900 ft, deepest in N. America); subalpine northern region. **Capital:** Boise.

**Economy. Principal industries:** agriculture, manufacturing, tourism, lumber, mining, electronics. **Principal manufactured goods:** processed foods, lumber and wood products, chemical products, primary metals, fabricated metal products, machinery, electronic components, computer equipment. **Chief crops:** potatoes, peas, sugar beets, alfalfa seed, lentils, wheat, hops, barley, plums and prunes, mint, onions, corn, cherries, apples, hay. **Livestock** (1994): 1.7 mil cattle; 250,000 sheep & lambs; 58,000 hogs; 1.3 mil poultry. **Timber/lumber** (1995): yellow, white pine; Douglas fir; white spruce; 1.7 bil bd. ft. **Nonfuel minerals** (est. 1995): $399 mil; phosphate rock, sand & gravel, gold, molybdenum, silver, lead. **Chief ports:** Lewiston. **Value of construction** (1995) $1.9 bil. **Employment distribution** (1994): 24% trade; 21.2% serv., 14.9% mfg.; 6% constr. **Per capita personal income** (1995): $19,264. **Unemployment** (1995): 5.4%. **Tourism** (1994): $1.4 bil.

**Finance. FDIC-insured commercial banks & trust companies** (1995): 18. **Deposits:** $9.3 bil. **FDIC-insured savings institutions** (1995): 4. **Assets:** $570 mil.

**Federal government. No. federal civilian employees** (Mar. 1995): 7,544. **Avg. salary:** $37,777. **Notable federal facilities:** Idaho Natl. Engineering Lab, Idaho Falls; Mt. Home Air Force Base, Mt. Home.

**Energy. Electricity production** (1995, kWh, by source): Hydroelectric: 10.1 bil.

**Education: Student-teacher ratio** (1994): 19.1. **Avg. teachers' salary** (1995-96): $30,891.

**State data. Motto:** Esto Perpetua (It is perpetual). **Flower:** Syringa. **Bird:** Mountain bluebird. **Tree:** White pine. **Song:** Here We Have Idaho. **Entered union** July 3, 1890; rank, 43d. **State fair** at Boise, late Aug.; Blackfoot, early Sept.

**History.** Early inhabitants were Shoshone, Northern Paiute, Bannock, and Nez Percé peoples. White exploration of the region began with Lewis and Clark, 1805-6. Next came fur traders, setting up posts, 1809-34, and missionaries, 1830s-50s. Mormons made their first permanent settlement at Franklin, 1860. Idaho's gold rush began the same year and brought thousands of permanent settlers. Most remarkable of the Indian wars was the 1,700-mi trek, 1877, of Chief Joseph and the Nez Percé, pursued by U.S. troops through 3 states and finally caught just short of the Canadian border. The Idaho territory was organized, 1863. Idaho adopted a progressive constitution and became a state, 1890.

**Tourist attractions.** Hells Canyon, deepest gorge in N. America; World Center for Birds of Prey; Craters of the Moon; Sun Valley, in Sawtooth Mts.; Crystal Falls Cave; Shoshone Falls; Lava Hot Springs; Lake Pend Oreille; Lake Coeur d'Alene; Sawtooth Natl. Recreation Area; River of No Return Wilderness Area; Redfish Lake.

**Famous Idahoans.** William E. Borah, Frank Church, Fred T. Dubois, Chief Joseph, Sacagawea.

**Tourist information.** Department of Commerce, 700 W. State St., Boise, ID 83720.

**Toll-free travel information.** 1-800-VISIT-ID.

**World Wide Web site.** http://www.state.id.us

## Illinois

*Prairie State*

**People. Population** (1995): 11,829,940; **rank:** 6; **Net change** (1990-95): 3.5%. **Pop. density:** (1990) 209.2 per sq mi. **Racial/ethnic distrib.** (1990): 78.3% white; 14.8% black; 7.9% Hispanic.

**Geography. Total area:** 57,918 sq mi; **rank:** 25. **Land area:** 55,593 sq mi. **Acres forested land:** 4,266,000. **Location:** East North Central state; western, southern, and eastern boundaries formed by Mississippi, Ohio, and Wabash rivers, respectively. **Climate:** temperate; typically cold, snowy winters, hot summers. **Topography:** prairie and fertile plains throughout; open hills in the southern region. **Capital:** Springfield.

**Economy. Principal industries:** services, manufacturing, travel, wholesale and retail trade, finance, insurance, real estate, construction, health care, agriculture. **Principal manufactured goods:** machinery, electric and electronic equipment, primary and fabricated metals, chemical products, printing and publishing, food and kindred products. **Chief crops:** corn, soybeans, wheat, sorghum, hay. **Livestock** (1995): 1.82 mil cattle; 5.4 mil hogs/pigs; 79,000 sheep; 3.7 mil poultry. **Timber/lumber** (1995): oak, hickory, maple, cottonwood; 88 mil bd. ft. **Nonfuel minerals** (est. 1995): $820 mil; mostly crushed stone, cement, construction & industrial sand & gravel, lime, zinc. **Commercial fishing** (1995): $444,000. **Chief ports:** Chicago. **International airports at:** Chicago. **Value of construction** (1995): $11.6 bil. **Employment distribution** (1995): 28.2% serv.; 23.5% trade; 17.3% mfg. **Per capita personal income** (1995): $24,763. **Unemployment** (1995): 5.2%. **Tourism** (1994): out-of-state visitors spent $16 bil.

**Finance. FDIC-insured commercial banks & trust companies** (1995): 864. **Deposits:** $173.3 bil. **FDIC-insured savings institutions** (1995): 149. **Assets:** $53.0 bil.

**Federal government. No. federal civilian employees** (Mar. 1995): 48,848. **Avg. salary:** $41,274. **Notable federal facilities:** Fermi Natl. Accelerator Lab; Argonne Natl. Lab; Rock Island Arsenal; Great Lakes, Naval Training Station, Scott AFB.

**Energy. Electricity production** (1995, kWh, by source): Coal: 62.7 bil; Petroleum: 888 mil; Gas: 2.9 bil; Hydroelectric: 48 mil; Nuclear: 78.5 bil.

**Public education. Student-teacher ratio** (1994): 17.3. **Avg. teachers' salary** (1995-96): $41,008.

**State data. Motto:** State sovereignty—national union. **Flower:** Native violet. **Bird:** Cardinal. **Tree:** White oak. **Song:** Illinois. **Entered union** Dec. 3, 1818; rank, 21st. **State fair** at Springfield, mid-Aug.; DuQuoin, late Aug.

**History.** Seminomadic Algonquian peoples, including the Peoria, Illinois, Kaskaskia, and Tamaroa, lived in the region at the time of European contact. Fur traders were the first Europeans in Illinois, followed shortly by Jolliet and Marquette, 1673, and La Salle, 1680, who built a fort near present-day Peoria. The first settlements were French, at Cahokia, near present-day St. Louis, 1699, and Kaskaskia, 1703. France ceded the area to Britain, 1763, and in 1778, American Gen. George Rogers Clark took Kaskaskia from the British without a shot. Defeat of Native American tribes in Black Hawk War, 1832, and growth of railroads brought change to the area. In 1787, it became part of the Northwest Territory. Post-Civil War Illinois became a center for the labor movement as bitter strikes, such as the Haymarket Square riot, occurred in 1885-86.

**Tourist attractions:** Chicago museums and parks; Lincoln shrines at Springfield, New Salem, Sangamon County; Cahokia Mounds, Collinsville; Starved Rock State Park; Crab Orchard Wildlife Refuge; Mormon settlement at Nauvoo; Fts. Kaskaskia, Chartres, Massac (parks); Shawnee Natl. Forest, Southern Illinois; Illinois State Museum, Springfield; Dickson Mounds Museum, between Havana and Lewistown.

**Famous Illinoisans.** Jane Addams, Saul Bellow, Jack Benny, Ray Bradbury, Gwendolyn Brooks, William Jennings Bryan, St. Frances Xavier Cabrini, Hillary Rodham Clinton, Clarence Darrow, John Deere, Stephen A. Douglas, James T. Farrell, George W. Ferris, Marshall Field, Betty Friedan, Benny Goodman, Ulysses S. Grant, Ernest Hemingway, Wild Bill Hickok, Abraham Lincoln, Vachel Lindsay, Edgar Lee Masters, Oscar Mayer, Cyrus McCormick, Ronald Reagan, Carl Sandburg, Adlai Stevenson, Frank Lloyd Wright, Philip Wrigley.

**Tourist information.** Illinois Dept. of Commerce and Community Affairs, 620 E. Adams St., Springfield, IL 62701.

**Toll-free travel information:** State tourism: 1-800-223-0121; Chicago tourism: 1-800-487-2446.

**World Wide Web site.** http://www.state.il.us

## Indiana

*Hoosier State*

**People. Population** (1995): 5,803,471; **rank:** 14; **Net change** (1990-95): 4.7%. **Pop. density:** (1990) 157.8 per sq mi. **Racial/ethnic distrib.** (1990): 90.6% white; 7.8% black; 1.8% Hispanic.

**Geography. Total area:** 36,420 sq mi; **rank:** 38. **Land area:** 35,870 sq mi. **Acres forested land:** 4,439,000. **Location:** East North Central state; Lake Michigan on northern border. **Climate:** 4 distinct seasons with a temperate climate. **Topography:** hilly southern region; fertile rolling plains of central region; flat, heavily glaciated north; dunes along Lake Michigan shore. **Capital:** Indianapolis.

**Economy: Principal industries:** manufacturing, services, agriculture, government, wholesale and retail trade, transportation and public utilities. **Principal manufactured goods:** primary metals, transportation equipment, motor vehicles and equipment, industrial machinery and equipment, electronic and electric equipment. **Chief crops:** corn, wheat, soybeans, nursery and greenhouse products, vegetables, sweet corn, melons, hay. **Livestock** (1995): 1.1 mil cattle; 4.15 mil hogs/pigs; 53,000 sheep; 25.6 mil chickens; 14.2 mil turkeys. **Timber/lumber** (1995): oak, tulip, beech, sycamore; 380 mil bd. ft. **Nonfuel minerals** (est. 1995): $574 mil; mostly crushed stone, cement, construction sand & gravel. **Commercial fishing** (1995): $2.2 mil. **Chief ports:** Burns Harbor, Portage; Southwind Maritime, Mt. Vernon; Clark Maritime, Jeffersonville. **International airports at:** Indianapolis, Ft. Wayne. **Value of construction** (1995): $7.9 bil. **Employment distribution** (1994): 25.5% mfg.; 24.7% trade; 21.5% serv; 12.2% govt. **Per capita personal income** (1995): $21,273. **Unemployment** (1995): 4.7%. **Tourism** (1993): tourists spent $4.4 bil.

**Finance. FDIC-insured commercial banks & trust companies** (1995): 211. **Deposits:** $53.6 bil. **FDIC-insured savings institutions** (1995): 79. **Assets:** $14.4 bil.

**Federal government. No. federal civilian employees** (Mar. 1995): 23,530. **Avg. salary:** $38,036. **Notable federal facilities:** Naval Air Warfare Center; Ft. Benjamin Harrison; Del. Grissom AFB; Naval Surface Warfare Center, Crane.

**Energy. Electricity production** (1995, kWh, by source): Coal: 103.8 bil; Petroleum: 213 mil; Gas: 734 mil; Hydroelectric: 467 mil.

**Public education. Student-teacher ratio** (1994): 17.5. **Avg. teachers' salary** (1995-96): $37,805.

**State data. Motto:** Crossroads of America. **Flower:** Peony. **Bird:** Cardinal. **Tree:** Tulip poplar. **Song:** On the Banks of the Wabash, Far Away. **Entered union** Dec. 11, 1816; rank, 19th. **State fair** at Indianapolis; mid-Aug.

**History.** When the Europeans arrived, Miami, Potawatomi, Kickapoo, Piankashaw, Wea, and Shawnee peoples inhabited the area. A French trading post was built, 1731-32, at Vincennes. La Salle visited the present South Bend area, 1679 and 1681. The first French fort was built near present-day Lafayette, 1717. France ceded the area to Britain, 1763. During the American Revolution, American Gen. George Rogers Clark captured Vincennes, 1778, and defeated British forces, 1779. At war's end, Britain ceded the area to the U.S. Miami Indians defeated U.S. troops twice, 1790, but were beaten, 1794, at Fallen Timbers by Gen. Anthony Wayne. At Tippecanoe, 1811, Gen. William H. Harrison defeated Tecumseh's Indian confederation. The Delaware, Potawatomi, and Miami were moved farther west, 1820-1850.

**Tourist attractions.** Lincoln Log Cabin Historic Site, near Charleston; George Rogers Clark Park, Vincennes; Wyandotte Cave; Tippecanoe Battlefield Memorial Park; Benjamin Harrison home, Indianapolis; Indiana Dunes; Hoosier Nat'l. Forest; Indiana Basketball Hall of Fame, New Castle; Huntington; Indianapolis 500 race and museum.

**Famous "Hoosiers."** Larry Bird, Ambrose Burnside, Hoagy Carmichael, Jim Davis, James Dean, Eugene V. Debs, Theodore Dreiser, Paul Dresser, Gil Hodges, David Letterman, Jane Pauley, Cole Porter, Dan Quayle, Gene Stratton Porter, Ernie Pyle, James Whitcomb Riley, Oscar Robertson, Red Skelton, Booth Tarkington, Kurt Vonnegut, Lew Wallace, Wendell L. Willkie, Wilbur Wright.

**Chamber of Commerce.** One North Capital, Suite 200, Indianapolis, IN 46204.

**Toll-free travel information.** 1-800-289-6646.

**World Wide Web site.** http://www.state.in.us

## Iowa

*Hawkeye State*

**People. Population** (1995): 2,841,764; **rank:** 30; **Net change** (1990-95): 2.3%. **Pop. density:** (1990) 50.3 per sq mi. **Racial/ethnic distrib.** (1990): 96.6% white; 1.7% black; 1.2% Hispanic.

**Geography. Total area:** 56,276 sq mi; **rank:** 26. **Land area:** 55,875 sq mi. **Acres forested land:** 2,050,000. **Location:** West North Central state bordered by Mississippi R. on the E and Missouri R. on the W. **Climate:** humid, continental. **Topography:** Watershed from NW to SE; soil especially rich and land level in the N central counties. **Capital:** Des Moines.

**Economy. Principal industries:** agriculture, communications, construction, finance, insurance, trade, services, manufacturing. **Principal manufactured goods:** Processed food products, tires, farm machinery, electronic products, appliances, household furniture, chemicals, fertilizers, auto accessories. **Chief crops:** silage and grain corn, soybeans, oats, hay. **Livestock** (1996): 3.95 mil cattle; 13.3 mil hogs/pigs; 345,000 sheep & lambs; (1995): 8 mil turkeys. **Timber/lumber** (1995): red cedar; 74 mil bd. ft. **Nonfuel minerals** (est. 1995): $484 mil; mostly crushed stone, portland cement, construction sand & gravel, gypsum. **International airports at:** Des Moines. **Value of construction** (1995): 2.9 bil. **Employment distribution** (1995): 25.1% trade; 25.1% serv.; 18.4% mfg.; 17% govt. **Per capita personal income** (1995): $21,012. **Unemployment** (1995): 3.5%. **Tourism** (1994): tourists spent $6.8 bil.

**Finance. FDIC-insured commercial banks & trust companies** (1995): 491. **Deposits:** $33.5 bil. **FDIC-insured savings institutions** (1995): 32. **Assets:** $5.9 bil.

**Federal government. No. federal civilian employees** (Mar. 1995): 7634. **Avg. salary:** $36,411.

**Energy. Electricity production** (1995, kWh, by source): Coal: 28.4 bil; Petroleum: 58 mil; Gas: 277 mil; Hydroelectric: 991 mil; Nuclear: 3.7 bil.

**Public education. Student-teacher ratio** (1994): 15.7. **Avg. teachers' salary** (1995-96): $32,376.

**State data. Motto:** Our liberties we prize and our rights we will maintain. **Flower:** Wild rose. **Bird:** Eastern goldfinch. **Tree:** Oak. **Rock:** Geode. **Entered union** Dec. 28, 1846; rank, 29th. **State fair** at Des Moines; mid-Aug.

**History.** Early inhabitants were Mound Builders who dwelt on Iowa's fertile plains. Later, Woodland tribes including the Iowa and Yankton Sioux lived in the area. The first Europeans, Marquette and Jolliet, gave France its claim to the area, 1673. In 1762, France ceded the region to Spain, but Napoleon took it back, 1800. It became part of the U.S. through the Louisiana Purchase, 1803. Native American Sauk and Fox tribes moved into the area from states farther east but relinquished their land in defeat, after the 1832 uprising led by the Sauk chieftain Black Hawk. By mid-19th cent. they were forced to move on to Kansas. Iowa became a territory in 1838, and entered as a free state, 1846, strongly supporting the Union.

**Tourist attractions.** Herbert Hoover birthplace and library, West Branch; Effigy Mounds Natl. Monument, prehistoric Indian burial site, Marquette; Amana Colonies; Grant Wood's paintings and memorabilia, Davenport Municipal Art Gallery; Living History Farms, Des Moines; Adventureland, Altoona; Boone & Scenic Valley Railroad, Boone; Greyhound Parks, in Dubuque, Council Bluffs and Waterloo; Prairie Meadows horse racing, Altoona; riverboat cruises and casino gambling, Mississippi River; Iowa Great Lakes, Okoboji.

**Famous Iowans.** Tom Arnold, Johnny Carson, Marquis Childs, Buffalo Bill Cody, Mamie Dowd Eisenhower, George Gallup, Susan Glaspell, James Norman Hall, Harry Hansen, Herbert Hoover, Glenn Miller, Billy Sunday, James A. Van Allen, Carl Van Vechten, Henry Wallace, John Wayne, Meredith Willson, Grant Wood.

**Tourist information.** Division of Tourism, Iowa Dept. of Economic Development, 200 E. Grand Ave., Des Moines, IA 50309.

**Toll-free travel information.** 1-800-345-IOWA.

**World Wide Web site.** http://www.state.ia.us

## Kansas

*Sunflower State*

**People. Population** (1995): 2,565,328; **rank:** 32; **Net change** (1990-95): 3.5%. **Pop. density:** (1990) 30.8 per sq mi. **Racial/ethnic distrib.** (1990): 90.1% white; 5.8% black; 3.8% Hispanic.

**Geography. Total area:** 82,282 sq mi; **rank:** 15. **Land area:** 81,823 sq mi. **Acres forested land:** 1,359,000. **Location:** West North Central state, with Missouri R. on E. **Climate:** temperate but continental, with great extremes between summer and winter. **Topography:** hilly Osage Plains in the E; central region level prairie and hills; high plains in the W. **Capital:** Topeka.

**Economy. Principal industries:** manufacturing, finance, insurance, real estate, services. **Principal manufactured goods:** transportation equipment, machinery and computer equipment, food and kindred products, printing and publishing. **Chief crops:** wheat, sorghum, corn, hay, soybeans, sunflowers. **Chief products:** wheat flour, beef, sorghum silage, sunflowers, soybean oil, soybean meal. **Livestock** (1995): 4.9 mil cattle; 1.25 mil hogs/pigs; 170,000 sheep & lambs; 2 mil poultry. **Timber/lumber:** (1995) oak, walnut; 10 mil bd. ft. **Nonfuel minerals** (est. 1995): $486 mil; salt, helium, cement, crushed stone, sand & gravel. **Chief ports:** Kansas City. **International airports at:** Wichita. **Value of construction** (1995): $3.3 bil. **Employment distribution** (1994): 24.2% trade; 23.7% serv.; 20% govt.; 16.1% mfg. **Per capita personal income** (1995): $21,825. **Unemployment** (1995): 4.4%. **Tourism** (1993): out-of-state visitors spent $2.5 bil.

**Finance. FDIC-insured commercial banks & trust companies** (1995): 433. **Deposits:** $26.6 bil. **FDIC-insured savings institutions** (1995): 22. **Assets** : $7.5 bil.

**Federal government. No. federal civilian employees** (Mar. 1995): 16,115. **Avg. salary:** $36,773. **Notable federal facilities:** Fts. Riley, Leavenworth; Leavenworth Federal Penitentiary; Colmery-O'Neal Veterans Hospital.

**Energy. Electricity production** (1995, kWh, by source): Coal: 25.9 bil; Petroleum: 74 mil; Gas: 2.2 bil; Nuclear: 10.0 bil.

**Public education. Student-teacher ratio** (1994): 15.1. **Avg. teachers' salary** (1995-96): $35,518.

**State data. Motto:** Ad Astra per Aspera (To the stars through difficulties). **Flower:** Native sunflower. **Bird:** Western meadowlark. **Tree:** Cottonwood. **Song:** Home on the

Range. **Entered union** Jan. 29, 1861; rank, 34th. **State fair** at Hutchinson; begins Friday after Labor Day.

**History.** When Coronado first explored the area, Wichita, Pawnee, Kansa, and Osage peoples lived there. These Native Americans—hunters who also farmed—were joined on the Plains by the nomadic Cheyenne, Arapaho, Comanche, and Kiowa about 1800. French explorers established trading between 1682 and 1739, and the U.S. took over most of the area in the Louisiana Purchase, 1803. After 1830, thousands of eastern Native Americans were removed to Kansas. Kansas became a territory, 1854. Disputes over whether Kansas would enter the Union as a free or slave state continued until 1858. Violent incidents between pro- and antislavery settlers, caused the territory to be known as "Bleeding Kansas." It eventually entered as a free state, 1861. Railroad construction after the war made Abilene and Dodge City terminals of large cattle drives from Texas.

**Tourist attractions.** Eisenhower Center, Abilene; Agricultural Hall of Fame and Natl. Center, Bonner Springs; Dodge City-Boot Hill & Frontier Town; Old Cowtown Museum, Wichita; Ft. Scott and Ft. Larned, restored 1800s cavalry forts; Kansas Cosmosphere and Space Center, Hutchinson; Woodlands Racetrack, Kansas City; U.S. Cavalry Museum, Ft. Riley; NCAA Visitors Center, Shawnee; Heartland Park Raceway, Topeka.

**Famous Kansans.** Ed Asner, Thomas Hart Benton, John Brown, Walter P. Chrysler, Glen Cunningham, John Stuart Curry, Robert Dole, Amelia Earhart, Dwight D. Eisenhower, Ron Evans, Wild Bill Hickok, Cyrus Holliday, Dennis Hopper, William Inge, Walter Johnson, Nancy Landon Kassebaum, Buster Keaton, Emmett Kelly, Alf Landon, Hattie McDaniel, Oscar Micheaux, Carrie Nation, Georgia Neese-Gray, Gordon Parks, Jim Ryun, Barry Sanders, Vivian Vance, William Allen White, Jess Willard.

**Tourist information.** Kansas Dept. of Commerce & Housing, Travel and Tourism Div., 700 SW Harrison, Suite 1300, Topeka, KS 66603; 1-913-296-2009.

**Toll-free travel information.** 1-800-2KANSAS.

**World Wide Web site.** http://www.ink.org

## Kentucky

*Bluegrass State*

**People. Population** (1995): 3,860,219; **rank:** 24; **Net change** (1990-95): 4.7%. **Pop. density:** (1990) 94.5 per sq mi. **Racial/ethnic distrib.** (1990): 92.0% white; 7.1% black; 0.6% Hispanic.

**Geography. Total area:** 40,411 sq mi; **rank:** 37. **Land area:** 39,732 sq mi. **Acres forested land:** 12,714,000. **Location:** East South Central state, bordered on N by Illinois, Indiana, Ohio; on E by West Virginia and Virginia; on S by Tennessee; on W by Missouri. **Climate:** moderate, with plentiful rainfall. **Topography:** mountainous in E; rounded hills of the Knobs in the N; Bluegrass, heart of state; wooded rocky hillsides of the Pennyroyal; Western Coal Field; the fertile Purchase in the SW. **Capital:** Frankfort.

**Economy. Principal industries:** manufacturing, finance, insurance and real estate, services; retail trade. **Principal manufactured goods:** industrial machinery, apparel, electic/electronic equipment, transportation equipment, food products, fabricated metals. **Chief crops:** tobacco, corn, soybeans. **Livestock** (1995): 2.65 mil cattle; 780,000 hogs/pigs; 27,000 sheep; 3.2 mil chickens; 1994 receipts for horse & mule sales, $489 mil. **Timber/lumber** (1995): hardwoods, pines; 773 mil bd. ft. **Nonfuel minerals** (est. 1995): $401 mil; mostly crushed stone, lime, cement, sand & gravel. **Chief ports:** Paducah, Louisville, Covington, Owensboro, Ashland, Henderson County, Lyon County, Hickman-Fulton County. **International airports at:** Covington and Louisville. **Value of construction** (1995): $4.5 bil. **Employment distribution** (1995): 22.3% serv.; 22.5% trade; 17.8% mfg.; 16.3% govt. **Per capita personal income** (1995): $18,612. **Unemployment** (1995): 5.4%. **Tourism** (1993): tourists spent $6.8 bil.

**Finance. FDIC-insured commercial banks & trust companies** (1995): 276. **Deposits:** $37.9 bil. **FDIC-insured savings institutions** (1995): 51. **Assets:** $7.8 bil.

**Federal government. No. federal civilian employees** (Mar. 1995): 25,340. **Avg. salary:** $33,042. **Notable federal facilities:** U.S. Gold Bullion Depository, Fort Knox; Federal Correctional Institution, Lexington.

**Energy. Electricity production** (1995, kWh, by source): Coal: 82.5 bil; Petroleum: 131 mil; Gas: 68 mil; Hydroelectric: 3.4 bil.

**Public education. Student-teacher ratio** (1994): 17.0. **Avg. teachers' salary** (1995-96): $33,108.

**State data. Motto:** United we stand, divided we fall. **Flower:** Goldenrod. **Bird:** Cardinal. **Tree:** Tulip Popular. **Song:** My Old Kentucky Home. **Entered union** June 1, 1792; rank, 15th. **State fair** late August in Louisville.

**History.** The area was predominantly hunting grounds for Shawnee, Wyandot, Delaware, and Cherokee peoples. Explored by Americans Thomas Walker and Christopher Gist, 1750-51, Kentucky was the first area west of the Alleghenies settled by American pioneers. The first permanent settlement was Harrodsburg, 1744. Daniel Boone blazed the Wilderness Trail through the Cumberland Gap and founded Ft. Boonesborough, 1775. Conflicts with Native Americans, spurred by the British, were unceasing until, during the American Revolution, Gen. George Rogers Clark captured British forts in Indiana and Illinois, 1778. In 1792, Virginia dropped its claims to the region, and it became the 15th state. Although officially a Union state, Kentuckians had divided loyalties during the Civil War and were forced to choose sides; its slaves were freed only after the adoption of the 13th Amendment to the U.S. Constitution, 1865.

**Tourist attractions.** Kentucky Derby; Louisville; Land Between the Lakes Natl. Recreation Area, Kentucky Lake and Lake Barkley; Mammoth Cave Natl. Park; Echo River, 360 ft below ground; Lake Cumberland; Lincoln's birthplace, Hodgenville; My Old Kentucky Home State Park, Bardstown; Cumberland Gap Natl. Historical Park, Middlesboro; Kentucky Horse Park, Lexington; Shaker Village, Pleasant Hill.

**Famous Kentuckians.** Muhammad Ali, John James Audubon, Alben W. Barkley, Daniel Boone, Louis D. Brandeis, John C. Breckinridge, Kit Carson, Albert B. "Happy" Chandler, Henry Clay, Jefferson Davis, "Casey" Jones, Abraham Lincoln, Mary Todd Lincoln, Thomas Hunt Morgan, Carrie Nation, Col. Harland Sanders, Diane Sawyer, Jesse Stuart, Adlai Stevenson, Zachary Taylor, Robert Penn Warren, Whitney Young Jr.

**Chamber of Commerce.** 464 Chenault Rd., PO Box 817, Frankfort, KY 40602.

**Toll-free travel information.** 1-800-225-TRIP, ext. 67.

**World Wide Web site.** http://www.state.ky.us

## Louisiana

*Pelican State*

**People. Population** (1995): 4,342,334; **rank:** 21; **Net change** (1990-95): 2.9%. **Pop. density:** (1990) 98.4 per sq mi. **Racial/ethnic distrib.** (1990): 67.3% white; 30.8% black; 2.2% Hispanic.

**Geography. Total area:** 51,843 sq mi; **rank:** 31. **Land area:** 43,566 sq mi. **Acres forested land:** 13,864,000. **Location:** West South Central state on the Gulf Coast. **Climate:** subtropical, affected by continental weather patterns. **Topography:** lowlands of marshes and Mississippi R. flood plain; Red R. Valley lowlands; upland hills in the Florida Parishes; average elevation, 100 ft **Capital:** Baton Rouge.

**Economy. Principal industries:** wholesale and retail trade, tourism, government, manufacturing, construction, transportation, mining. **Principal manufactured goods:** chemical products, foods, transportation equipment, electronic equipment, petroleum products, lumber, wood, and paper. **Chief crops:** soybeans, sugarcane, rice, corn, cotton, sweet potatoes, pecans, sorghum, aquaculture. **Livestock** (1994): 930,000 cattle; 45,000 hogs/pigs; 14,500 sheep; 2.5 mil poultry. **Timber/lumber** (1995): pines, hardwoods, oak; 1.29 bil bd. ft. **Nonfuel minerals** (est. 1995): $384 mil; mostly salt, construction sand & gravel, sulfur. **Commercial fishing** (1995): $291 mil. **Chief ports:** New Orleans, Baton Rouge, Lake Charles, S. Louisiana Port Commission at La Place, Shreveport, Plaquemine. **International airports at:** New Orleans. **Value of construction** (1995): $4.3 bil. **Employment distribution** (June 1995): 23.2% trade; 26.4% service; 19.3% govt.; 10.7% mfg. **Per capita personal income** (1995): $18,827. **Unemployment** (1995): 6.9%. **Tourism** (1994): out-of-state visitors spent $5.5 bil.

**Finance. FDIC-insured commercial banks & trust companies** (1995): 185. **Deposits:** $37.1 bil. **FDIC-insured savings institutions** (1995): 39. **Assets:** $4.8 bil.

**Federal government. No. federal civilian employees** (Mar. 1995): 21,010. **Avg. salary:** $36,223. **Notable federal facilities:** Barksdale, Ft. Polk military bases; Strategic Petroleum Reserve, New Orleans; Michoud Assembly Plant, New Orleans; U.S. Public Service Hospital, Carville.

**Energy. Electricity production** (1995, kWh, by source): Coal: 19.0 bil; Petroleum: 49 mil; Gas: 30.9 bil; Nuclear: 15.7 bil.

**Public education. Student-teacher ratio** (1994): 16.8. **Avg. teachers' salary** (1995-96): $26,800.

**State data. Motto:** Union, justice, and confidence. **Flower:** Magnolia. **Bird:** Eastern brown pelican. **Tree:** Cypress. **Song:** Give Me Louisiana. **Entered union** Apr. 30, 1812; rank, 18th. **State fair** at Shreveport; Oct.

**History.** Caddo, Tunica, Choctaw, Chitimacha, and Chawash peoples lived in the region at the time of European contact. Europeans Cabeza de Vaca and Panfilo de Narvaez first visited, 1530. The region was claimed for France by La Salle, 1682. The first permanent settlement was by the French at Biloxi, now in Mississippi, 1699. France ceded the region to Spain, 1762, took it back, 1800, and sold it to the U.S., 1803, in the Louisiana Purchase. During the American Revolution, Spanish Louisiana aided the Americans. Admitted as a state in 1812, Louisiana was the scene of the Battle of New Orleans, 1815.

Louisiana Creoles are descendants of early French and/or Spanish settlers. About 4,000 Acadians, French settlers in Nova Scotia, Canada, were forcibly transported by the British to Louisiana in 1755 (an event commemorated in Longfellow's "Evangeline") and settled near Bayou Teche; their descendants became known as Cajuns. Another group, the Islenos, were descendants of Canary Islanders brought to Louisiana by a Spanish governor in 1770. Traces of Spanish and French survive in local dialects.

**Tourist attractions.** Mardi Gras, French Quarter, Superdome, Dixieland jazz, Aquarium of the Americas, all New Orleans; Battle of New Orleans site; Longfellow-Evangeline Memorial Park, St. Martinville; Kent House Museum, Alexandria; Hodges Gardens, Natchitoches.

**Famous Louisianans.** Louis Armstrong, Pierre Beauregard, Judah P. Benjamin, Braxton Bragg, Grace King, Huey Long, Leonidas K. Polk, Henry Miller Shreve, Edward D. White Jr.

**Tourist information.** State Dept. of Culture, Recreation & Tourism, PO Box 94291, Baton Rouge, LA 70804-9291.

**Toll-free travel information.** 1-800-33GUMBO.

**World Wide Web site.** http://www.state.la.us

## Maine

*Pine Tree State*

**People. Population** (1995): 1,241,382; **rank:** 39; **Net change** (1990-95): 1.1%. **Pop. density:** (1990) 40.0 per sq mi. **Racial/ethnic distrib.** (1990): 98.4% white; 0.4% black; 0.6% Hispanic.

**Geography. Total area:** 35,387 sq mi; **rank:** 39. **Land area:** 30,865 sq mi. **Acres forested land:** 17,533,000. **Location:** New England state at northeastern tip of U.S. **Climate:** Southern interior and coastal, influenced by air masses from the S and W; northern clime harsher, avg. over 100 in. snow in winter. **Topography:** Appalachian Mts. extend through state; western borders have rugged terrain; long sand beaches on southern coast; northern coast mainly rocky promontories, peninsulas, fjords. **Capital:** Augusta.

**Economy. Principal industries:** manufacturing, agriculture, fishing, services, trade, government, finance, insurance, real estate, construction. **Principal manufactured goods:** paper and wood products, transportation equipment. **Chief crops:** potatoes, apples, hay, blueberries. **Livestock** (1994): 116,000 cattle; 6,500 hogs/pigs; 11,000 sheep; 6.4 mil poultry. **Timber/lumber** (1995): pine, spruce, fir; 1.03 bil bd. ft. **Nonfuel minerals** (est. 1995): $59 mil; cement, construction sand & gravel, crushed stone. **Commercial fishing** (1995): $217 mil. **Chief ports:** Searsport, Portland, Eastport. **International airports at:** Portland, Bangor. **Value of construction** (1995): $1.1 bil. **Employment distribution** (1993): 25.8% serv.; 25.1% trade; 18.3% govt.; 17.6% mfg. **Per capita personal income** (1995): $20,527. **Unemployment** (1995): 5.7%. **Tourism** (1995): $3 bil.

**Finance. FDIC-insured commercial banks & trust companies** (1995): 20. **Deposits:** $6.7 bil. **FDIC-insured savings institutions** (1995): 29. **Assets:** $7.1 bil.

**Federal government. No. federal civilian employees** (Mar. 1995): 8,412. **Avg. salary:** $37,676. **Notable federal facilities:** Kittery Naval Shipyard; Brunswick Naval Air Station.

**Energy. Electricity production** (1995, kWh, by source): Petroleum: 812 mil; Hydroelectric: 1.7 bil; Nuclear: 198 mil.

**Public education. Student-teacher ratio** (1994): 13.8. **Avg. teachers' salary** (1995-96): $32,869.

**State data. Motto:** Dirigo (I direct). **Flower:** White pine cone and tassel. **Bird:** Chickadee. **Tree:** Eastern white pine. **Song:** State of Maine Song. **Entered union** Mar. 15, 1820; rank, 23d.

**History.** When the Europeans arrived, Maine was inhabited by Algonquian peoples including the Abnaki, Penobscot, and Passamaquoddy. Maine's rocky coast was believed to have been explored by the Cabots, 1498-99. French settlers arrived, 1604, at the St. Croix River, English, c 1607, on the Kennebec; both settlements failed. Maine was made part of Massachusetts, 1691. In the American Revolution, a Maine regiment fought at Bunker Hill. A British fleet destroyed Falmouth (now Portland), 1775, but the British ship *Margaretta* was captured near Machiasport. In 1820, Maine broke off from Massachusetts and became a separate state.

**Tourist attractions.** Acadia Natl. Park, Bar Harbor, on Mt. Desert Island; Old Orchard Beach; Portland's Old Port; Kennebunkport; Common Ground Country Fair; Portland Headlight; Baxter State Pk.; Freeport/L. L. Bean.

**Famous "Down Easters."** James G. Blaine, Cyrus H. K. Curtis, Hannibal Hamlin, Stephen King, Henry Wads-worth, Longfellow, Sir Hiram and Hudson Maxim, Edna St. Vincent Millay, Edmund Muskie, Kate Douglas Wiggin, Ben Ames Williams.

**Chamber of Commerce and Industry.** Maine Chamber & Business Alliance, 7 Community Dr., Augusta, ME 04330.

**Toll-free travel information.** 1-800-533-9595, out of state only (not applicable to Canada).

**World Wide Web site.** http://www.state.me.us

## Maryland

*Old Line State, Free State*

**People. Population** (1995): 5,042,438; **rank:** 19; **Net change** (1990-95): 5.5%. **Pop. density:** (1990) 502.1 per sq mi. **Racial/ethnic distrib.** (1990): 71.0% white; 24.9% black; 2.9% Asian; 2.6% Hispanic.

**Geography. Total area:** 12,407 sq mi; **rank:** 42. **Land area:** 9,775 sq mi. **Acres forested land:** 2,700,000. **Location:** South Atlantic state stretching from the Ocean to the Allegheny Mts. **Climate:** continental in the west; humid subtropical in the east. **Topography:** Eastern Shore of coastal plain and Maryland Main of coastal plain, piedmont plateau, and the Blue Ridge, separated by the Chesapeake Bay. **Capital:** Annapolis.

**Economy. Principal industries:** manufacturing, biotechnology and information technology, services, tourism. **Principal manufactured goods:** electric and electronic equipment; food and kindred products, chemicals and allied products, printed materials. **Chief crops:** greenhouse and nursery products, soybeans, corn. **Livestock** (1995): 290,000 cattle; 77,000 hogs/pigs; 25,000 sheep/lambs; 3.746 mil layers; 295.7 mil broilers. **Timber/lumber:** (1995) hardwoods; 234 mil bd. ft. **Nonfuel minerals** (est. 1995): $341 mil; crushed stone, sand & gravel, portland cement. **Commercial fishing** (1995): $61.0 mil. **Chief port:** Baltimore. **International airports at:** Baltimore-Washington Intl. **Value of construction** (1995): $6.3 bil. **Employment distribution** (1994): 29.9% service; 24.4% trade; 19.1% govt. **Per capita personal income** (1995): $25,927. **Unemployment** (1995): 5.1%. **Tourism** (1995): tourists spent $5.8 bil.

**Finance. FDIC-insured commercial banks & trust companies** (1995): 91. **Deposits:** $53.8 bil. **FDIC-insured savings institutions** (1995): 79. **Assets:** $17.4 bil.

**Federal government. No. federal civilian employees** (Mar. 1995): 104,446. **Avg. salary:** $46,265. **Notable federal**

**facilities:** U.S. Naval Academy, Annapolis; Natl. Agriculture Research Center; Ft. George G. Meade, Aberdeen Proving Ground; Goddard Space Flight Center; Natl. Institutes of Health; Natl. Institute of Standards & Technology; Food & Drug Administration; Bureau of the Census.

**Energy. Electricity production** (1995, kWh, by source): Coal: 27.4 bil; Petroleum: 1.4 bil; Gas: 1.5 bil; Hydroelectric: 1.4 bil; Nuclear: 12.9 bil.

**Public education. Student-teacher ratio** (1994): 17.0. **Avg. teachers' salary** (1995-96): $41,215.

**State data. Motto:** Fatti Maschii, Parole Femine (Manly deeds, womanly words). **Flower:** Black-eyed susan. **Bird:** Baltimore oriole. **Tree:** White oak. **Song:** Maryland, My Maryland. **Seventh** of the original 13 states to ratify Constitution, Apr. 28, 1788. **State fair** at Timonium; late Aug.–early Sept.

**History.** Europeans encountered Algonquian-speaking Nanticoke and Piscataway and Iroquios-speaking Susquehannock when they first visited the area. Italian explorer Verrazano visited the Chesapeake region in the early 16th cent. English Capt. John Smith explored and mapped the area, 1608. William Claiborne set up a trading post on Kent Island in Chesapeake Bay, 1631. British King Charles I granted land to Cecilius Calvert, Lord Baltimore, 1632; Calvert's brother Leonard, with about 200 settlers, founded St. Marys, 1634. The bravery of Maryland troops in the American Revolution, as at the Battle of Long Island, won the state its nickname "The Old Line State." In the War of 1812, when a British fleet tried to take Ft. McHenry, Marylander Francis Scott Key wrote "The Star Spangled Banner," 1814. Although a slave-holding state, Maryland remained with the Union during the Civil War and was the site of the battle of Antietam, 1862, which halted Gen. Robert E. Lee's march north.

**Tourist attractions.** The Preakness and Maryland Million, both at Pimlico track, Baltimore, and the International, at Laurel Race Course; Ocean City; restored Ft. McHenry, near which Francis Scott Key wrote "The Star-Spangled Banner"; Edgar Allan Poe house, Ravens Football at Memorial Stadium, Camden Yards, Natl. Aquarium, Harborplace, all Baltimore; Antietam Battlefield, near Hagerstown; South Mountain Battlefield; U.S. Naval Academy, Annapolis; Maryland State House, Annapolis, 1772, the oldest still in use in the U.S.

**Famous Marylanders.** John Astin, Benjamin Banneker, Tom Clancy, Jonathan Demme, Francis Scott Key, H. L. Mencken, Charles Willson Peale, William Pinkney, Edgar Allan Poe, Upton Sinclair, Roger B. Taney.

**Maryland Dept. of Business & Economic Development.** 217 E. Redwood St., Baltimore, MD 21202; (410) 767-6870.

**Toll-free travel information.** 1-800-543-1036.

**World Wide Web site.** http://www.mdarchives.state.md.us

## Massachusetts

*Bay State, Old Colony*

**People. Population** (1995): 6,073,550; **rank:** 13; **Net change** (1990-95): 0.9%. **Pop. density:** (1990) 765.3 per sq mi. **Racial/ethnic distrib.** (1990): 89.8% white; 5.0% black; 2.4% Asian; 4.8% Hispanic.

**Geography. Total area:** 10,555 sq mi; **rank:** 44. **Land area:** 7,838 sq mi. **Acres forested land:** 3,203,000. **Location:** New England state along Atlantic seaboard. **Climate:** temperate, with colder and drier clime in western region. **Topography:** jagged indented coast from Rhode Island around Cape Cod; flat land yields to stony upland pastures near central region and gentle hilly country in west; except in west, land is rocky, sandy, and not fertile. **Capital:** Boston.

**Economy. Principal industries:** services, trade, manufacturing. **Principal manufactured goods:** electric and electronic equipment, instruments, industrial machinery and equipment, printing and publishing, fabricated metal products. **Chief crops:** cranberries, greenhouse, nursery, vegetables. **Livestock** (1994): 68,000 cattle; 32,200 hogs/pigs; 11,500 sheep; 646,000 chickens, 140,000 turkeys. **Timber/lumber** white pine, oak, other hard woods. **Nonfuel minerals** (est. 1995): $213 mil; mostly crushed stone, construction sand & gravel. **Commercial fishing** (1995): $224 mil. **Chief ports:** Boston, Fall River, New Bedford, Salem, Gloucester, Plymouth. **International airports at:** Boston. **Value of construction** (1995): $7.4 bil. **Employment distribution** (1995): 23% trade; 34.4% serv.; 15% mfg.; 13.2% govt. **Per capita personal income** (1995): $26,994. **Unemployment** (1995): 5.4%. **Tourism** (1994): all visitors spent $9.2 bil.

**Finance. FDIC-insured commercial banks & trust companies** (1995): 51. **Deposits:** $82.3 bil. **FDIC-insured savings institutions** (1995): 209. **Assets**: $42.7 bil.

**Federal government. No. federal civilian employees** (Mar. 1995): 29,523. **Avg. salary:** $41,110. **Notable federal facilities:** Thomas P. O'Neill Jr. Federal Bldg., J.W. McCormack Bldg., John Fitzgerald Kennedy Federal Bldg., Boston; Q.M. Laboratory, Natick.

**Energy. Electricity production** (1995, kWh, by source): Coal: 10.6 bil; Petroleum: 5.8 bil; Gas: 6.2 bil; Nuclear: 4.5 bil.

**Public education. Student-teacher ratio** (1994): 14.8. **Avg. teachers' salary** (1995-96): $43,756.

**State data. Motto:** Ense Petit Placidam Sub Libertate Quietem (By the sword we seek peace, but peace only under liberty). **Flower:** Mayflower. **Bird:** Chickadee. **Tree:** American elm. **Song:** All Hail to Massachusetts. **Sixth** of the original 13 states to ratify Constitution, Feb. 6, 1788. **State Fair** at Agawan in Sept. (combined with CT and NH).

**History.** Early inhabitants were the Algonquian Nauset, Wampanoag, Massachuset, Pennacook, Nipmuc, and Pocumtuc peoples. Pilgrims settled in Plymouth, 1620, giving thanks for their survival with the first Thanksgiving Day, 1621. About 20,000 new settlers arrived, 1630-40. Native American relations with the colonists deteriorated leading to King Philip's War, 1675-76, which the colonists won, ending Native American resistance. Demonstrations against British restrictions set off the Boston Massacre, 1770, and the Boston Tea Party, 1773. The first bloodshed of American Revolution was at Lexington, 1775.

**Tourist attractions.** Provincetown artists' colony; Cape Cod; Plymouth Rock, Plymouth Plantation, Mayflower II, all Plymouth; Freedom Trail, Museum of Fine Arts, Children's Museum, Museum of Science, New England Aquarium, JFK Library, Boston Ballet, Boston Pops, Boston Symphony Orchestra, all Boston; Tanglewood, Jacob's Pillow Dance Festival, Hancock Shaker Village Berkshire Railway Museum, all in the Berkshires; Salem; Old Sturbridge Village; Deerfield Historic District; Walden Pond; Naismith Memorial Basketball Hall of Fame, Springfield.

**Famous "Bay Staters."** John Adams, John Quincy Adams, Samuel Adams, Louisa May Alcott, Horatio Alger, Susan B. Anthony, Crispus Attucks, Clara Barton, Alexander Graham Bell, Stephen Breyer, George Bush, Emily Dickinson, Ralph Waldo Emerson, John Hancock, Nathaniel Hawthorne, Oliver Wendell Holmes, Winslow Homer, Elias Howe, John F. Kennedy, Samuel F. B. Morse, Edgar Allan Poe, Paul Revere, Henry David Thoreau, James McNeil Whistler, John Greenleaf Whittier.

**Tourist information.** Massachusetts Office of Travel & Tourism, 100 Cambridge St., 13th Floor, Boston, MA 02202.

**Toll-free travel information.** 1-800-447-MASS.

**World Wide Web site.** http://www.state.ma.us

## Michigan

*Great Lakes State, Wolverine State*

**People. Population** (1995): 9,549,353; **rank:** 8; **Net change** (1990-95): 2.7%. **Pop. density:** (1990) 166.1 per sq mi. **Racial/ethnic distrib.** (1990): 83.4% white; 13.9% black; 2.2% Hispanic.

**Geography. Total area:** 96,705 sq mi; **rank:** 11. **Land area:** 56,809 sq mi. **Acres forested land:** 18,253,000. **Location:** East North Central state bordering on 4 of the 5 Great Lakes, divided into an Upper and Lower Peninsula by the Straits of Mackinac, which link lakes Michigan and Huron. **Climate:** well-defined seasons tempered by the Great Lakes. **Topography:** low rolling hills give way to northern tableland of hilly belts in Lower Peninsula; Upper Peninsula is level in the east, with swampy areas; western region is higher and more rugged. **Capital:** Lansing.

**Economy. Principal industries:** manufacturing, services, tourism, agriculture, mining. **Principal manufactured**

**goods:** automobiles, transportation equipment, machinery, fabricated metals, food products, plastics, office furniture. **Chief crops:** corn, wheat, soybeans, dry beans, hay, potatoes, nursery, sweet corn, apples, floriculture. **Livestock** (1996): 1.2 mil cattle; 1.2 mil hogs/pigs; 93,000 sheep; 6.5 mil poultry. **Timber/lumber** (1995): maple, oak, aspen; 652 mil bd. ft. **Nonfuel minerals** (est. 1995): $1.5 bil; iron ore, magnesium compounds, portland cement, sand & gravel, crushed stone. **Commercial fishing** (1995): $10.1 mil. **Chief ports:** Detroit, Saginaw River, Escanaba, Muskegon, Sault Ste. Marie, Port Huron, Marine City. **International airports at:** Detroit, Grand Rapids, Flint, Kalamazoo, Lansing, Saginaw. **Value of construction** (1995): $10.0 bil. **Employment distribution** (1995): 23.9% mfg.; 24.9% trade; 27% service; 15.6% govt. **Per capita personal income** (1995): $23,551. **Unemployment** (1995): 5.3%. **Tourism** (1995): travelers spent $8 bil.

**Finance. FDIC-insured commercial banks & trust companies** (1995): 180. **Deposits**: $87.9 bil. **FDIC-insured savings institutions** (1995): 30. **Assets:** $23.8 bil.

**Federal government. No. federal civilian employees** (Mar. 1995): 24,049. **Avg. salary:** $40,465. **Notable federal facilities:** Isle Royal, Sleeping Bear Dunes national parks.

**Energy. Electricity production** (1995, kWh, by source): Coal: 65.4 bil; Petroleum: 687 mil; Gas: 1.2 bil; Hydroelectric: 755 mil; Nuclear: 24.4 bil.

**Public education. Student-teacher ratio** (1994): 20.1. **Avg. teachers' salary** (1995-96): $49,168.

**State data. Motto:** Si Quaeris Peninsulam, Amoenam Circumspice (If you seek a pleasant peninsula, look about you). **Flower:** Apple blossom. **Bird:** Robin. **Tree:** White pine. **Song:** Michigan, My Michigan. **Entered union** Jan. 26, 1837; rank, 26th. **State fair** at Detroit, late Aug.–early Sept.; Upper Peninsula (Escanaba), mid-Aug; Michigan Festival, mid.-Aug.

**History.** Early inhabitants were the Ojibwa, Ottawa, Miami, Potawatomi, and Huron. French fur traders and missionaries visited the region, 1616, set up a mission at Sault Ste. Marie, 1641, and a settlement there, 1668. French settlements were taken over, 1763, by the British, who crushed a Native American uprising led by Ottawa chieftain Pontiac that same year. Treaty of Paris ceded territory to U.S., 1783, but British remained until 1796. The British seized Ft. Mackinac and Detroit, 1812. After Oliver H. Perry's Lake Erie victory and William H. Harrison's victory near the Thames River, 1813, the British retreated to Canada. The opening of the Erie Canal, 1825, and new land laws and additional Native American cessions led the way for a flood of settlers.

**Tourist attractions.** Henry Ford Museum, Greenfield Village, both in Dearborn; Michigan Space Center, Jackson; Tahquamenon *(Hiawatha)* Falls; DeZwaan windmill and Tulip Festival, Holland; "Soo Locks," St. Mary's Falls Ship Canal, Sault Ste. Marie.

**Famous Michiganders.** Ralph Bunche, Paul de Kruif, Thomas A. Edison, Gerald R. Ford, Edna Ferber, Henry Ford, Aretha Franklin, Edgar Guest, Lee Iacocca, Robert Ingersoll, Magic Johnson, Will Kellogg, Ring Lardner, Elmore Leonard, Charles Lindbergh, Joe Louis, Madonna, Pontiac, Diana Ross, Tom Selleck, Lily Tomlin, Stewart Edward White, Malcolm X.

**Chamber of Commerce.** 600 S. Walnut, Lansing, MI 48933.

**Toll-free travel information.** 1-800-543-2937.

**World Wide Web site.** http://www.migov.state.mi.us

## Minnesota

*North Star State, Gopher State*

**People. Population** (1995): 4,609,548; **rank:** 20; **Net change** (1990-95): 5.3%. **Pop. density:** (1990) 56.3 per sq mi. **Racial/ethnic distrib.** (1990): 94.4% white; 2.2% black; 1.8% Asian; 1.2% Hispanic.

**Geography. Total area:** 86,943 sq mi; **rank:** 12. **Land area:** 79,617 sq mi. **Acres forested land:** 16,718,000. **Location:** West North Central state bounded on the E by Wisconsin and Lake Superior, on the N by Canada, on the W by the Dakotas, and on the S by Iowa. **Climate:** northern part of state lies in the moist Great Lakes storm belt; the western border lies at the edge of the semi-arid Great Plains. **Topography:** central hill and lake region covering approx. half the state; to the NE, rocky ridges and deep lakes; to the NW, flat plain; to the S, rolling plains and deep river valleys. **Capital:** St. Paul.

**Economy. Principal industries:** agribusiness, forest products, mining, manufacturing, tourism. **Principal manufactured goods:** food, chemical and paper products, industrial machinery, electric and electronic equipment, computers, printing and publishing, scientific and medical instruments, fabricated metal products. **Chief crops:** corn, soybeans, wheat, sugar beets, hay, barley, potatoes, sunflowers. **Livestock** (1995): 2.80 mil cattle; 4.85 mil hogs/pigs; 190,000 sheep; 14.2 mil chickens; 41.5 mil turkeys. **Timber/lumber** (1995): needle-leaves and hardwoods; 310 mil bd. ft. **Nonfuel minerals** (est. 1995): $1.5 bil; mostly iron ore, construction sand & gravel, crushed stone. **Commercial fishing** (1995): $236,000. **Chief ports:** Duluth, St. Paul, Minneapolis. **International airports at:** Minneapolis-St. Paul. **Value of construction** (1995): $5.6 bil. **Employment distribution** (1995): 24.3% trade; 27.1% serv.; 17.9% mfg.; 16% govt. **Per capita personal income** (1995): $23,118. **Unemployment** (1995): 3.7%. **Tourism** (1994): domestic and international tourists spent about $7 bil.

**Finance. FDIC-insured commercial banks & trust companies** (1995): 525. **Deposits**: $49.5 bil. **FDIC-insured savings institutions** (1995): 22. **Assets**: $5.7 bil.

**Federal government. No. federal civilian employees** (Mar. 1995): 14,025. **Avg. salary:** $39,682.

**Energy. Electricity production** (1995, kWh, by source): Coal: 26.8 bil; Petroleum: 485 mil; Gas: 703 mil; Hydroelectric: 823 mil; Nuclear: 13.2 bil.

**Public education. Student-teacher ratio** (1994): 17.5. **Avg. teachers' salary** (1995-96): $36,937.

**State data. Motto:** L'Etoile du Nord (The star of the north). **Flower:** Pink and white lady's-slipper. **Bird:** Common loon. **Tree:** Red pine. **Song:** Hail! Minnesota. **Entered union** May 11, 1858; rank, 32d. **State fair** at Saint Paul; late Aug.–early Sept.

**History.** Dakota Sioux were early inhabitants of the area, and in the 16th cent., the Ojibwa began moving in from the east. French fur traders Médard Chouart and Pierre Esprit Radisson entered the region in the mid-17th cent. In 1679, French explorer Daniel Greysolon, sieur Duluth, claimed the entire region in the name of France. Britain took the area east of the Mississippi, 1763. The U.S. took over that portion after the American Revolution and in 1803, gained the western area in the Louisiana Purchase. The U.S. built Ft. St. Anthony (now Ft. Snelling), 1819, and in 1837, bought Native American lands, spurring an influx of settlers from the east. In 1849, the Territory of Minnesota was created. Sioux Indians staged a bloody uprising, the Battle of Woods Lake, 1862, and were driven from the state.

**Tourist attractions.** Minneapolis Institute of Arts, Walker Art Center, Minneapolis Sculpture Garden, Minnehaha Falls, inspiration for Longfellow's *Hiawatha,* Guthrie Theater, Minneapolis; Ordway Theater, St. Paul; Voyageurs Natl. Park, a water wilderness along the Canadian border; Mayo Clinic, Rochester; St. Paul Winter Carnival; North Shore (of Lake Superior).

**Famous Minnesotans.** Warren Burger, William O. Douglas, Bob Dylan, F. Scott Fitzgerald, Judy Garland, Cass Gilbert, Hubert Humphrey, Garrison Keillor, Sister Elizabeth Kenny, Sinclair Lewis, Paul Manship, E. G. Marshall, William and Charles Mayo, Walter F. Mondale, Charles Schulz, Harold Stassen, Thorstein Veblen.

**Tourist information.** Minnesota Office of Tourism, 500 Metro Square, 121 7th Place East, St. Paul, MN 55101.

**Toll-free travel information.** 1-800-657-3700.

**World Wide Web site.** http://www.state.mn.us

## Mississippi

*Magnolia State*

**People. Population** (1995): 2,697,243; **rank:** 31; **Net change** (1990-95): 4.7%. **Pop. density:** (1990) 55.7 per sq mi. **Racial/ethnic distrib.** (1990): 63.5% white; 35.6% black; 0.6% Hispanic.

**Geography. Total area:** 48,434 sq mi; **rank:** 32. **Land area:** 46,914 sq mi. **Acres forested land:** 17,000,000. **Location:** East South Central state bordered on the W by the

Mississippi R. and on the S by the Gulf of Mexico. **Climate:** semi-tropical, with abundant rainfall, long growing season, and extreme temperatures unusual. **Topography:** low, fertile delta between the Yazoo and Mississippi rivers; loess bluffs stretching around delta border; sandy gulf coastal terraces followed by piney woods and prairie; rugged, high sandy hills in extreme NE followed by Black Prairie Belt, Pontotoc Ridge, and flatwoods into the north central highlands. **Capital:** Jackson.

**Economy. Principal industries:** manufacturing, government, wholesale and retail trade. **Principal manufactured goods:** apparel, food & kindred products, furniture, lumber and wood products, electrical machinery, transportation equipment. **Chief crops:** cotton, rice, soybeans. **Livestock** (1995): 1.3 mil cattle; 245,000 hogs/pigs; 644 mil broilers. **Timber/lumber** (1995): pine, oak, hardwoods; 2.7 bil bd. ft. **Nonfuel minerals** (est. 1995): $125 mil; mostly crushed stone, construction sand & gravel. **Commercial fishing** (1995): $42 mil. **Chief ports:** Pascagoula, Vicksburg, Gulfport, Natchez, Greenville. **Value of construction** (1995): $2.7 bil. **Employment distribution** (1995): 24% mfg.; 20% govt.; 21% trade; 21.6% serv. **Per capita personal income** (1995): $16,531. **Unemployment** (1995): 6.1%. **Tourism** (1995): out-of-state visitors spent $4.1 bil.

**Finance. FDIC-insured commercial banks & trust companies** (1995): 110. **Deposits:** $22.3 bil. **FDIC-insured savings institutions** (1995): 16. **Assets:** $2.7 bil.

**Federal government. No. federal civilian employees** (Mar. 1995): 17,861. **Avg. salary:** $36,536. **Notable federal facilities:** Columbus, Keesler AF bases; Meridian Naval Air Station, John C. Stennis Space Center; U.S. Army Corps of Engineers Waterway Experiment Station, Vicksburg District.

**Energy. Electricity production** (1995, kWh, by source): Coal: 9.3 bil; Petroleum: 24 mil; Gas: 9.1 bil; Nuclear: 8.0 bil.

**Public education. Student-teacher ratio** (1994): 17.5. **Avg. teachers' salary** (1995-96): $27,689.

**State data. Motto:** Virtute et Armis (By valor and arms). **Flower:** Magnolia. **Bird:** Mockingbird. **Tree:** Magnolia. **Song:** Go, Mississippi! **Entered union** Dec. 10, 1817; rank, 20th. **State fair** at Jackson in the fall.

**History.** Early inhabitants of the region were Choctaw, Chickasaw, and Natchez peoples. Hernando de Soto explored the area, 1540, and sighted the Mississippi River, 1541. Robert La Salle traced the river from Illinois to its mouth and claimed the entire valley for France, 1682. The first settlement was the French Ft. Maurepas, near Ocean Springs, 1699. The area was ceded to Britain, 1763; American settlers followed. During the American Revolution, Spain seized part of the area and refused to leave even after the U.S. acquired title at the end of the conflict; Spain finally moved out, 1798. The Territory of Mississippi was formed, 1798. Mississippi seceded, 1861. Union forces captured Corinth and Vicksburg and destroyed Jackson and much of Meridian. Mississippi was readmitted to the Union in 1870.

**Tourist attractions.** Vicksburg Natl. Military Park and Cemetery, other Civil War sites; Hattiesburg; Natchez Trace; Indian mounds; Antebellum homes; pilgrimages in Natchez and some 25 other cities; Smith Robertson Museum, Mynelle Gardens, both Jackson; Mardi Gras and Shrimp Festival, both in Biloxi.

**Famous Mississippians.** Dana Andrews, Jimmy Buffett, Hodding Carter III, Bo Diddley, William Faulkner, Shelby Foote, Morgan Freeman, John Grisham, Fannie Lou Hamer, Jim Henson, Robert Johnson, James Earl Jones, B. B. King, L. Q. C. Lamar, Gerald McRaney, Willie Morris, Walter Payton, Elvis Presley, Leontyne Price, Charlie Pride, Margaret Walker, Eudora Welty, Tennessee Williams, Oprah Winfrey, Johnny Winter, Richard Wright, Tammy Wynette.

**Dept. of Economic & Community Development.** PO Box 849, Jackson, MS 39205-0849.

**Toll-free travel information.** 1-800-WARMEST.

**World Wide Web site.** http://www.state.ms.us

## Missouri

*Show Me State*

**People. Population** (1995): 5,323,523; **rank:** 16; **Net change** (1990-95): 4.0%. **Pop. density:** (1990) 75.4 per sq mi. **Racial/ethnic distrib.** (1990): 87.7% white; 10.7% black; 1.2% Hispanic.

**Geography. Total area:** 69,709 sq mi; **rank:** 21. **Land area:** 68,898 sq mi. **Acres forested land:** 14,007,000. **Location:** West North Central state near the geographic center of the conterminous U.S.; bordered on the E by the Mississippi R., on the NW by the Missouri R. **Climate:** continental, susceptible to cold Canadian air, moist, warm gulf air, and drier SW air. **Topography:** rolling hills, open, fertile plains, and well-watered prairie N of the Missouri R.; south of the river land is rough and hilly with deep, narrow valleys; alluvial plain in the SE; low elevation in the west. **Capital:** Jefferson City.

**Economy. Principal industries:** agriculture, manufacturing, aerospace, tourism. **Principal manufactured goods:** transportation equipment, food and related products, electrical and electronic equipment, chemicals. **Chief crops:** soybeans, corn, wheat, hay. **Livestock** (1994): 4.8 mil cattle; 3.0 mil hogs/pigs; 86,000 sheep; 8.4 mil chickens, 1.6 mil eggs, 21 mil turkeys. **Timber/lumber** (1995): oak, hickory; 578 mil bd. ft. **Nonfuel minerals** (est. 1995): $1.1 bil; mostly lead, portland cement, crushed stone. **Chief ports:** St. Louis, Kansas City. **International airports at:** St. Louis, Kansas City. **Value of construction** (1995): $6.4 bil. **Employment distribution** (1994): 27% services; 23.9% trade; 17% mfg.; 15.7% govt. **Per capita personal income** (1995): $21,627. **Unemployment** (1995): 4.8%. **Tourism** (1993): total travelers spent $5 bil.

**Finance. FDIC-insured commercial banks & trust companies** (1995): 459. **Deposits**: $64.1 bil. **FDIC-insured savings institutions** (1995): 53. **Assets**: $16.7bil.

**Federal government. No. federal civilian employees** (Mar. 1995): 40,222. **Avg. salary:** $37,678. **Notable federal facilities:** Federal Reserve banks, St. Louis, Kansas City; Ft. Leonard Wood, Rolla; Jefferson Barracks, St. Louis; Whiteman AFB, Knob Noster.

**Energy. Electricity production** (1995 kWh, by source): Coal: 53.6 bil; Petroleum: 682 mil; Gas: 1.0 bil; Hydroelectric: 1.9 bil; Nuclear: 8.2 bil.

**Public education. Student-teacher ratio** (1994): 15.5. **Avg. teachers' salary** (1995-96): $33,341.

**State data. Motto:** Salus Populi Suprema Lex Esto (The welfare of the people shall be the supreme law). **Flower:** Hawthorn. **Bird:** Bluebird. **Tree:** Dogwood. **Song:** Missouri Waltz. **Entered union** Aug. 10, 1821; rank, 24th. **State fair** at Sedalia; 3d week in Aug.

**History.** Early inhabitants of the region were Algonquian Sauk, Fox, and Illinois and Siouan Osage, Missouri, Iowa, and Kansa peoples. Hernando de Soto visited the area, 1541. French hunters and lead miners made the first settlement c 1735, at Ste. Genevieve. The territory was ceded to Spain by the French, 1763, then returned to France, 1800. The U.S. acquired Missouri as part of the Louisiana Purchase, 1803. The influx of white settlers drove Native American tribes to the Kansas and Oklahoma territories; most were gone by 1836. The fur trade and the Santa Fe Trail provided prosperity; St. Louis became the gateway for pioneers heading West. Missouri entered the Union as a slave state, 1821. Though it remained with the Union, pro- and antislavery forces battled there during the Civil War.

**Tourist attractions**. Silver Dollar City, Branson; Mark Twain Area, Hannibal; Pony Express Museum, St. Joseph; Harry S. Truman Library, Independence; Gateway Arch, St. Louis; Worlds of Fun, Kansas City; Lake of the Ozarks; Churchill Mem., Fulton; State Capitol, Jefferson City.

**Famous Missourians.** Maya Angelou, Robert Altman, Burt Bacharach, Josephine Baker, Scot Bakula, Thomas Hart Benton, Tom Berenger, Chuck Berry, George Caleb Bingham, Omar Bradley, Kate Capshaw, Dale Carnegie, George Washington Carver, Bob Costas, Walter Cronkite, Walt Disney, T. S. Eliot, John Goodman, Betty Grable, Jesse James, J. C. Penney, John J. Pershing, Brad Pitt, Joseph Pulitzer, Ginger Rogers, Bess Truman, Harry S. Truman, Kathleen Turner, Tina Turner, Mark Twain, Dick Van Dyke, Tennessee Williams, Shelly Winters, Jane Wyman.

**Chamber of Commerce.** 428 E. Capitol, Jefferson City, MO 65101.

**Toll-free travel information.** 1-800-877-1234.

**World Wide Web site.** http://www.state.mo.us

## Montana

*Treasure State*

**People. Population** (1995): 870,281; **rank:** 44; **Net change** (1990-95): 8.9%. **Pop. density:** (1990) 5.66 per sq mi. **Racial/ethnic distrib.** (1990): 92.7% white; 0.3% black; 6.0% Amer. Indian; 1.5% Hispanic.

**Geography. Total area:** 147,046 sq mi; **rank:** 4. **Land area:** 145,556 sq mi. **Acres forested land:** 22,512,000. **Location:** Mountain state bounded on the E by the Dakotas, on the S by Wyoming, on the SSW by Idaho, and on the N by Canada. **Climate:** colder, continental climate with low humidity. **Topography:** Rocky Mts. in western third of the state; eastern two-thirds gently rolling northern Great Plains. **Capital:** Helena.

**Economy. Principal industries:** agriculture, timber, mining, tourism, oil & gas. **Principal manufactured goods:** food products, wood & paper products, primary metals, printing & publishing, petroleum & coal products. **Chief crops:** wheat, barley, sugar beets, hay, oats. **Livestock** (1995): 2.7 mil cattle; 210,000 hogs/pigs; 490,000 sheep; 510,000 poultry. **Timber/lumber** (1995) Douglas fir, pines, larch; 1.3 bil bd. ft. **Nonfuel minerals** (est. 1995): $581 mil; platinum, palladium, talc and pyrophylite, copper, gold, zinc, phosphate rock, portland cement. **International airports at:** Great Falls, Billings, Kalispell, Missoula. **Value of construction** (1995): $850.0 mil. **Employment distribution** (1994): 27.9% serv.; 23.5% trade; 17.3% govt.; 5.7% mfg. **Per capita personal income** (1995): $18,482. **Unemployment** (1995): 5.9%. **Tourism** (1995 est.): non-resident visitors spent $1.22 bil.

**Finance. FDIC-insured commercial banks & trust companies** (1995): 104. **Deposits**: $7.0 bil. **FDIC-insured savings institutions** (1995): 9. **Assets**: $1.8 bil.

**Federal government. No. federal civilian employees** (Mar. 1995): 8,215. **Avg. salary:** $36,626. **Notable federal facilities:** Malmstrom AFB; Ft. Peck, Hungry Horse, Libby, Yellowtail dams; numerous missile silos.

**Energy. Electricity production** (1995, kWh, by source): Coal: 14.7 bil; Petroleum: 25 mil; Gas: 32 mil; Hydroelectric: 10.7 bil.

**Public education. Student-teacher ratio** (1994): 16.3. **Avg. teachers' salary** (1995-96): $29,364.

**State data. Motto:** Oro y Plata (Gold and silver). **Flower:** Bitterroot. **Bird:** Western meadowlark. **Tree:** Ponderosa pine. **Song:** Montana. **Entered union** Nov. 8, 1889; rank, 41st. **State fair** at Great Falls; late July–early Aug.

**History.** Cheyenne, Blackfoot, Crow, Assiniboin, Salish (Flatheads), Kootenai, and Kalispel peoples were early inhabitants of the area. French explorers visited the region, 1742. The U.S. acquired the area partly through the Louisiana Purchase, 1803, and partly through the explorations of Lewis and Clark, 1805-6. Fur traders and missionaries established posts in the early 19th cent. Gold was discovered, 1863, and the Montana territory was established, 1864. Indian uprisings reached their peak with the Battle of Little Bighorn, 1876. Chief Joseph and the Nez Percé tribe surrendered here, 1877, after long trek across the state. Mining activity and the coming of the Northern Pacific Railway, 1883, brought population growth. Copper wealth from the Butte pits resulted in the turn of the century "War of Copper Kings" as factions fought for control of "the richest hill on earth."

**Tourist attractions.** Glacier Natl. Park; Yellowstone Natl. Park; Museum of the Rockies, Bozeman; Museum of the Plains Indian, Blackfeet Reservation, near Browning; Little Bighorn Battlefield Natl. Monument and Custer Natl. Cemetery; Flathead Lake; Helena; Lewis and Clark Caverns State Park, near Whitehall.

**Famous Montanans.** Gary Cooper, Marcus Daly, Chet Huntley, Will James, Myrna Loy, Mike Mansfield, Brent Musberger, Jeannette Rankin, Charles M. Russell, Lester Thurow.

**Chamber of Commerce.** 2030 11th Ave., PO Box 1730, Helena, MT 59624.

**Toll-free travel information.** 1-800-VISITMT.

**World Wide Web site.** http://www.state.mt.gov

## Nebraska

*Cornhusker State*

**People. Population** (1995): 1,637,112; **rank:** 37; **Net change** (1990-95): 3.7%. **Pop. density:** (1990) 20.9 per sq mi. **Racial/ethnic distrib.** (1990): 93.8% white; 3.6% black; 2.3% Hispanic.

**Geography. Total area:** 77,358 sq mi; **rank:** 16. **Land area:** 76,878 sq mi. **Acres forested land:** 722,000. **Location:** West North Central state with the Missouri R. for a NE and E border. **Climate:** continental semi-arid. **Topography:** till plains of the central lowland in the eastern third rising to the Great Plains and hill country of the north central and NW. **Capital:** Lincoln.

**Economy. Principal industries:** agriculture, manufacturing. **Principal manufactured goods:** processed foods, industrial machinery, printed materials, electric and electronic equipment, primary and fabricated metal products, transportation equipment. **Chief crops:** corn, sorghum, soybeans, hay, wheat, beans, oats, potatoes, sugar beets. **Livestock** (1995): 6 mil cattle; 4.1 mil hogs/pigs; 105,000 sheep; 10.6 mil chickens, 2.6 mil turkeys. **Timber/lumber** (1995): oak, hickory, and elm; 27 mil bd. ft. **Nonfuel minerals** (est. 1995): $142 mil; mostly construction sand & gravel, portland cement, crushed stone. **Chief ports:** Omaha, Sioux City, Brownville, Blair, Plattsmouth, Nebraska City. **Value of construction** (1995): $1.7 bil. **Employment distribution** (1994): 25.0% trade; 25.4% serv.; 19% govt.; 13.7% mfg. **Per capita personal income** (1995): $21,703. **Unemployment** (1995): 2.6%. **Tourism** (1995): traveler expenditures $2 bil.

**Finance. FDIC-insured commercial banks & trust companies** (1995): 336. **Deposits**: $22.6 bil. **FDIC-insured savings institutions** (1995): 14. **Assets**: $8.7 bil.

**Federal government. No. federal civilian employees** (Mar. 1995): 8,390. **Avg. salary:** $37,203. **Notable federal facilities:** Offutt AFB, Bellevue.

**Energy. Electricity production** (1995, kWh, by source): Coal: 16.1 bil; Petroleum: 27 mil; Gas: 245 mil; Hydroelectric: 1.4 mil; Nuclear: 7.5 bil.

**Public education. Student-teacher ratio** (1994): 14.5. **Avg. teachers' salary** (1995-96): $31496.

**State data. Motto:** Equality before the law. **Flower:** Goldenrod. **Bird:** Western meadowlark. **Tree:** Cottonwood. **Song:** Beautiful Nebraska. **Entered union** Mar. 1, 1867; rank, 37th. **State fair** at Lincoln; late Aug.–early Sept.

**History.** When the Europeans first arrived, Pawnee, Ponca, Omaha, and Oto peoples lived in the region. Spanish and French explorers and fur traders visited the area prior to its acquisition in the Louisiana Purchase, 1803. Lewis and Clark passed through, 1804-6. The first permanent settlement was Bellevue, near Omaha, 1823. The region was settled gradually despite the 1834 Indian Intercourse Act, which declared Nebraska part of Indian country and excluded white settlement. Conflicts with settlers eventually forced Native Americans to give up their land and move on to reservations. Many Civil War veterans settled under free land terms of the 1862 Homestead Act; as agriculture grew, struggles followed between homesteaders and ranchers.

**Tourist attractions.** State Museum (Elephant Hall), State capitol, both Lincoln; Stuhr Museum of the Prairie Pioneer, Grand Island; Museum of the Fur Trade, Chadron; Joslyn Art Museum, Omaha; Strategic Air Command Museum, Bellevue; Boys Town, west of Omaha; Arbor Lodge State Park, Nebraska City; Buffalo Bill Ranch State Hist. Park, North Platte; Pioneer Village, Minden; Oregon Trail landmarks; Scotts Bluff Natl. Monument; Chimney Rock Historic Site; Ft. Robinson; Hastings Museum, McDonald Planetarium, Hastings.

**Famous Nebraskans.** Fred Astaire, Marlon Brando, Charles W. Bryan, William Jennings Bryan, Johnny Carson, Willa Cather, Dick Cavett, William F. "Buffalo Bill" Cody, Loren Eiseley, Rev. Edward J. Flanagan, Henry Fonda, Gerald R. Ford, Rollin Kirby, Swoosie Kurtz, Harold Lloyd, Malcolm X, J. Sterling Morton, John Neihardt, Nick Nolte, George Norris, John J. Pershing, Roscoe Pound, Chief Red Cloud, Mari Sandoz, Robert Taylor, Daryl F. Zannuck.

**Division of Travel and Tourism.** PO Box 98913, Lincoln, NE 68509-8913.

**Toll-free travel information.** 1-800-228-4307.

**World Wide Web site.** http://www.state.ne.us

## Nevada

*Sagebrush State, Battle Born State, Silver State*

**People. Population** (1995): 1,530,108; **rank:** 38; **Net change** (1990-95): 27.3%. **Pop. density:** (1990) 12.1 per sq mi. **Racial/ethnic distrib.** (1990): 84.3% white; 6.6% black; 3.2% Asian; 10.4% Hispanic.

**Geography. Total area:** 110,567 sq mi; **rank:** 7. **Land area:** 109,806 sq mi. **Acres forested land:** 8,938,000. **Location:** Mountain state bordered on N by Oregon and Idaho, on E by Utah and Arizona, on SE by Arizona, and on SW and W by California. **Climate:** semi-arid and arid. **Topography:** rugged N-S mountain ranges; highest elevation, Boundary Peak, 13,140 ft; southern area is within the Mojave Desert; lowest elevation, Colorado River at southern tip of state, 479 ft. **Capital:** Carson City.

**Economy. Principal industries:** gaming, tourism, mining, manufacturing, government, retailing, warehousing, trucking. **Principal manufactured goods:** food products, plastics, chemicals, aerospace products, lawn & garden irrigation equipment, seismic & machinery-monitoring devices. **Chief crops:** hay, alfalfa seed, potatoes, onions, garlic, barley, wheat. **Livestock** (1995): 500,000 cattle; 9,000 hogs/pigs; 90,000 sheep. **Timber/lumber:** piñon, juniper, other pines. **Nonfuel minerals** (est. 1995): $2.9 bil; mostly gold, silver, construction sand & gravel. **International airports at:** Las Vegas, Reno. **Value of construction** (1995): $5.5 bil. **Employment distribution** (1996): 43.5% serv.; 20% trade; 12.1% govt. **Per capita personal income** (1995): $25,013. **Unemployment** (1995): 5.4%. **Tourism** (1992): out-of-state travelers spent over $15.4 bil.

**Finance. FDIC-insured commercial banks & trust companies** (1995): 25. **Deposits**: $10.6 bil. **FDIC-insured savings institutions** (1995): 2. **Assets**: $3.3bil.

**Federal government. No. federal civilian employees** (Mar. 1995): 7,531. **Avg. salary:** $39,741. **Notable federal facilities:** Nevada Test Site; Hawthorne Army Ammunition Plant, Nellis Air Force Base & Gunnery Range; Fallon Naval Air Station; Palomino Valley Wild Horse & Burro Placement Center.

**Energy. Electricity production** (1995, kWh, by source): Coal: 14.0 bil; Petroleum: 27 mil; Gas: 4.1 bil; Hydroelectric: 1.9 bil.

**Public education. Student-teacher ratio** (1994): 18.7. **Avg. teachers' salary** (1995-96): $36,167.

**State data. Motto:** All for our country. **Flower:** Sagebrush. **Bird:** Mountain bluebird. **Trees:** Single-leaf piñon and bristlecone pine. **Song:** Home Means Nevada. **Entered union** Oct. 31, 1864; rank, 36th. **State fair** at Reno; early Sept.

**History.** Shoshone, Paiute, Bannock, and Washoe peoples lived in the area at the time of European contact. Nevada was first explored by Spaniards, 1776. Hudson's Bay Co. trappers explored the north and central region, 1825; trader Jedediah Smith crossed the state, 1826-27. The area was acquired by the U.S., 1848, at the end of the Mexican War. The first settlement, Mormon Station, now Genoa, was established, 1849. Discovery of the Comstock Lode, rich in gold and silver, 1859, spurred a population boom. In the early 20th cent., Nevada adopted progressive measures such as the initiative, referendum, recall, and woman suffrage.

**Tourist attractions**. Legalized gambling at: Lake Tahoe, Reno, Las Vegas, Laughlin, Elko County, and elsewhere. Hoover Dam; Lake Mead; Great Basin Natl. Park; Valley of Fire State Park; Virginia City; Red Rock Canyon Natl. Conservation Area; Liberace Museum, the Strip, Guinness World of Records Museum, Lost City Museum, Overton, Lamoille Canyon, Pyramid Lake, all Las Vegas.

**Famous Nevadans.** Walter Van Tilburg Clark, George Ferris, Sarah Winnemucca Hopkins, Paul Laxalt, Dat So La Lee, John William Mackay, Anne Martin, Pat McCarran, Key Pittman, William Morris Stewart.

**Tourist information.** Commission on Tourism, Capitol Complex, Carson City, NV 89710.

**Toll-free travel information.** 1-800-638-2328.

**World Wide Web site.** http://www.state.nv.us

## New Hampshire

*Granite State*

**People. Population** (1995): 1,148,253; **rank:** 42; **Net change** (1990-95): 3.5%. **Pop. density:** (1990) 123.8 per sq mi. **Racial/ethnic distrib.** (1990): 98.0% white; 0.6% black; 1.0% Hispanic.

**Geography. Total area:** 9,351 sq mi; **rank:** 46. **Land area:** 8,969 sq mi. **Acres forested land:** 4,981,000. **Location:** New England state bounded on S by Massachusetts, on W by Vermont, on N and NW by Canada, on E by Maine and the Atlantic Ocean. **Climate:** highly varied, due to its nearness to high mountains and ocean. **Topography:** low, rolling coast followed by countless hills and mountains rising out of a central plateau. **Capital:** Concord.

**Economy. Principal industries:** tourism, manufacturing, agriculture, trade, mining. **Principal manufactured goods:** machinery, electrical & electronic products, plastics, fabricated metal products. **Chief crops:** dairy products, nursery and greenhouse products, hay, vegetables, fruit, maple syrup & sugar products. **Livestock** (1994): 35,000 cattle; 9,500 hogs/pigs; 9,000 sheep; 15,500 horses; 214,000 poultry. **Timber/lumber** (1995): white pine, hemlock, oak, birch; 274 mil bd. ft. **Nonfuel minerals** (est. 1995): $36 mil; mostly construction sand & gravel, crushed & dimension stone. **Commercial fishing** (1995): $15 mil. **Chief ports:** Portsmouth, Hampton, Rye. **Value of construction** (1995): $1.0 bil. **Employment distribution** (1994): 19.8% mfg.; 26.4% trade; 26.7% serv.; 13.5% govt. **Per capita personal income** (1995): $25,151. **Unemployment** (1995): 4.0%. **Tourism** (1994): out-of-state visitors spent $4.0 bil.

**Finance. FDIC-insured commercial banks & trust companies** (1995): 23. **Deposits:** $7.6 bil. **FDIC-insured savings institutions** (1995): 26. **Assets**: $9.4 bil.

**Federal government. No. federal civilian employees** (Mar. 1995): 3,605. **Avg. salary:** $43,347.

**Energy. Electricity production** (1995, kWh, by source): Coal: 3.4 bil; Petroleum: 1.0 bil; Gas: 201 mil; Hydroelectric: 984 mil; Nuclear: 8.4 bil.

**Public education. Student-teacher ratio** (1994): 15.6. **Avg. teachers' salary** (1995-96): $35,792.

**State data. Motto:** Live free or die. **Flower:** Purple lilac. **Bird:** Purple finch. **Tree:** White birch. **Song:** Old New Hampshire. **Ninth** of the original 13 states to ratify the Constitution, June 21, 1788. **State Fair** at Agawan, MA (combined with MA and CT); Sept.

**History.** Algonquian-speaking peoples, including the Pennacook, lived in the region when the European arrived. The first explorers to visit the area were England's Martin Pring, 1603, and France's Champlain, 1605. The first settlement was Odiorne's Point (now port of Rye), 1623. Native American conflicts were ended, 1759, by Robert Rogers' Rangers. Before the American Revolution, New Hampshire residents seized a British fort at Portsmouth, 1774, and drove the royal governor out, 1775. New Hampshire became the first colony to adopt its own constitution, 1776. Three regiments served in the Continental Army, and scores of privateers raided British shipping.

**Tourist attractions.** Mt. Washington, highest peak in Northeast; Lake Winnipesaukee; White Mt. National Forest; Crawford, Franconia—famous for the Old Man of the Mountain, described by Hawthorne as the Great Stone Face, Pinkham notches, all White Mt. region; the Flume, a spectacular gorge; the aerial tramway, Cannon Mt.; Strawbery Banke, Portsmouth; Shaker Village, Canterbury; Saint-Gaudens, natl. historic site, Cornish; Mt. Monadnock.

**Famous New Hampshirites.** Salmon P. Chase, Ralph Adams Cram, Mary Baker Eddy, Daniel Chester French, Robert Frost, Horace Greeley, Sarah Buell Hale, Franklin Pierce, Augustus Saint-Gaudens, David H. Souter, Daniel Webster.

**Tourist information.** Department of Resources and Economic Development, Division of Travel & Tourism Development, PO Box 1856, Concord, NH 03302-1856; 603-271-2343.

**Toll-free travel information.** 1-800-386-4664.

**World Wide Web site.** http://www.state.nh.us

## New Jersey

*Garden State*

**People. Population** (1995): 7,945,298; **rank:** 9; **Net change** (1990-95): 2.8%. **Pop. density:** (1990) 1,049.9 per sq mi. **Racial/ethnic distrib.** (1990): 79.3% white; 13.4% black; 3.5% Asian; 9.6% Hispanic.

**Geography. Total area:** 8,722 sq mi; **rank:** 47. **Land area:** 7,419 sq mi. **Acres forested land:** 2,007,000. **Location:** Middle Atlantic state bounded on the N and E by New York and the Atlantic Ocean, on the S and W by Delaware and Pennsylvania. **Climate:** moderate, with marked difference bet. NW and SE extremities. **Topography:** Appalachian Valley in the NW also has highest elevation, High Pt., 1,801 ft; Appalachian Highlands, flat-topped NE-SW mountain ranges; Piedmont Plateau, low plains broken by high ridges (Palisades) rising 400-500 ft; Coastal Plain, covering three-fifths of state in SE, gradually rises from sea level to gentle slopes. **Capital:** Trenton.

**Economy. Principal industries:** services, trade, manufacturing. **Principal manufactured goods:** chemicals, electronic and electrical equipment, non-electrical machinery, fabricated metals. **Chief crops:** nursery & greenhouse, hay, corn, soybeans, peppers, tomatoes, blueberries, peaches, cranberries. **Livestock** (1995): 65,000 cattle; 24,000 hogs/pigs; 16,900 sheep; 1.9 mil poultry. **Timber/lumber:** (1995) pine, cedar, mixed hardwoods; 8 mil bd. ft. **Nonfuel minerals** (est. 1995): $289 mil; mostly crushed stone, construction sand & gravel. **Commercial fishing** (1995): $95 mil. **Chief ports:** Newark, Elizabeth, Hoboken, Camden. **International airports at:** Newark. **Value of construction** (1995): $6.5 bil. **Employment distribution** (1995): 30% serv.; 23.6% trade; 13.9% mfg.; 15.8% govt. **Per capita personal income** (1995): $28,858. **Unemployment** (1995): 6.4%. **Tourism** (1995): tourists spent $22.9 bil.

**Finance. FDIC-insured commercial banks & trust companies** (1995): 82. **Deposits**: $84.7 bil. **FDIC-insured savings institutions** (1995): 94. **Assets**: $47.4 bil.

**Federal government. No. federal civilian employees** (Mar. 1995): 33,710. **Avg. salary:** $42,933. **Notable federal facilities:** McGuire AFB; Fort Dix; Fort Monmouth; Picatinny Arsenal; Lakehurst Naval Air Engineering Center.

**Energy. Electricity production** (1995, kWh, by source): Coal: 5.1 bil; Petroleum: 885 mil; Gas: 4.4 bil; Nuclear: 16.8 bil.

**Public education. Student-teacher ratio** (1994): 13.8. **Avg. teachers' salary** (1995-96): $47,910.

**State data. Motto:** Liberty and prosperity. **Flower:** Purple violet. **Bird:** Eastern goldfinch. **Tree:** Red oak. **Third** of the original 13 states to ratify the Constitution, Dec. 18, 1787. **State fair** in Camden; Aug.

**History.** The Lenni Lenape (Delaware) peoples lived in the region and had mostly peaceful relations with European colonists, who arrived after the explorers Verrazano, 1524, and Hudson, 1609. The first permanent European settlement was Dutch, at Bergen (now Jersey City), 1660. When the British took New Netherland, 1664, the area between the Delaware and Hudson Rivers was given to Lord John Berkeley and Sir George Carteret. During the American Revolution, New Jersey was the scene of nearly 100 battles, large and small, including Trenton, 1776; Princeton, 1777; Monmouth, 1778.

**Tourist attractions.** 127 mi of beaches; Miss America Pageant, all Atlantic City; Grover Cleveland birthplace, Caldwell; Cape May Historic District; Edison Natl. Historic Site, W. Orange; Six Flags Great Adventure, Jackson; Liberty State Park, Jersey City; Meadowlands Sports Complex; Pine Barrens wilderness area; Princeton University; numerous Revolutionary War historical sites; State Aquarium, Camden.

**Famous New Jerseyans.** Count Basie, Judy Blume, Bill Bradley, Jon Bon Jovi, Aaron Burr, Grover Cleveland, James Fenimore Cooper, Stephen Crane, Thomas Edison, Albert Einstein, Alexander Hamilton, Whitney Houston, Joyce Kilmer, George McClellan, Thomas Paine, Molly Pitcher, Paul Robeson, Philip Roth, Wally Schirra, Frank Sinatra, Bruce Springsteen, Meryl Streep, Walt Whitman, William Carlos Williams, Woodrow Wilson.

**Chamber of Commerce.** 50 W. State St., Trenton, NJ 08608.

**Toll-free travel information.** 1-800-JERSEY7.

**World Wide Web site.** http://www.state.nj.us

## New Mexico

*Land of Enchantment*

**People. Population** (1995): 1,685,401; **rank:** 36; **Net change** (1990-95): 11.2%. **Pop. density:** (1990) 13.0 per sq mi. **Racial/ethnic distrib.** (1990): 75.6% white; 2.0% black; 8.9% Amer. Indian; 38.2% Hispanic.

**Geography. Total area:** 121,598 sq mi; **rank:** 5. **Land area:** 121,364 sq mi. **Acres forested land:** 15,296,000. **Location:** southwestern state bounded by Colorado on the N, Oklahoma, Texas, and Mexico on the E and S, and Arizona on the W. **Climate:** dry, with temperatures rising or falling 5° F with every 1,000 ft elevation. **Topography:** eastern third, Great Plains; central third, Rocky Mts. (85% of the state is over 4,000-ft elevation); western third, high plateau. **Capital:** Santa Fe.

**Economy. Principal industries:** government, services, trade. **Principal manufactured goods:** foods, machinery, apparel, lumber, printing, transportation equipment, electronics, semiconductors. **Chief crops:** hay, onions, wheat, pecans, corn, cotton, sorghum, chiles. **Livestock** (1995): 1.50 mil cattle; 25,000 hogs; 315,000 sheep; 1.44 mil poultry. **Timber/lumber** (1995): ponderosa pine, Douglas fir; 95 mil bd. ft. **Nonfuel minerals** (est. 1995): $1.1 bil; copper, potash, construction sand & gravel. **International airports at:** Albuquerque. **Value of construction** (1995): $2.1 bil. **Employment distribution** (1995): 31.7% serv.; 24% govt. 18.8% trade. **Per capita personal income** (1995): $18,055. **Unemployment** (1995): 6.3%. **Tourism** (1994): out-of-state visitors spent $2.75 bil.

**Finance. FDIC-insured commercial banks & trust companies** (1995): 68. **Deposits**: $11.5 bil. **FDIC-insured savings institutions** (1995): 10. **Assets**: $1.3 bil.

**Federal government. No. federal civilian employees** (Mar. 1995): 22,581. **Avg. salary:** $37,653. **Notable federal facilities:** Kirtland, Cannon, Holloman AF bases; Los Alamos Scientific Laboratory; White Sands Missile Range; Natl. Solar Observatory; Natl. Radio Astronomy Observatory, Sandia National Laboratories.

**Energy. Electricity production** (1995, kWh, by source): Coal: 26.1 bil; Petroleum: 23 mil; Gas: 3.0 bil; Hydroelectric: 264 mil.

**Public education. Student-teacher ratio** (1994): 17.2. **Avg. teachers' salary** (1995-96): $29,349.

**State data. Motto:** Crescit Eundo (It grows as it goes). **Flower:** Yucca. **Bird:** Roadrunner. **Tree:** Piñon. **Song:** O, Fair New Mexico; Asi Es Nuevo Mexico. **Entered union** Jan. 6, 1912; rank, 47th. **State fair** at Albuquerque; mid-Sept.

**History.** Early inhabitants were peoples of the Mogollon and Anasazi civilizations, followed by the Pueblo peoples, Anasazi descendants. The nomadic Navajo and Apache tribes arrived c 15th cent. Franciscan Marcos de Niza and a former black slave Estevanico explored the area, 1539, seeking gold. First settlements were at San Juan Pueblo, 1598, and Santa Fe, 1610. Settlers alternately traded and fought with the Apache, Comanche, and Navajo. Trade on the Santa Fe Trail to Missouri started, 1821. The Mexican War was declared in May 1846; Gen. Stephen Kearny took Santa Fe without firing a shot, Aug. 18, 1846, declaring New Mexico part of the U.S. All Hispanic New Mexicans and Pueblo became U.S. citizens by terms of the 1848 treaty ending the war, but Congress denied the area statehood and created the territory of New Mexico, 1850. Pancho Villa raided Columbus, 1916, and U.S. troops were sent to the area. The world's first atomic bomb was exploded near Alamogordo, south of Santa Fe, 1945.

**Tourist attractions.** Carlsbad Caverns Natl. Park, with the largest natural underground chamber in the world; White Sands Natl. Monument, the largest gypsum deposit in the world; Pueblo Bonito Ruins, Chaco Canyon; Acoma Pueblo, the "sky city," built atop a 357-ft mesa; Taos; Ute Lake State Park; Shiprock.

**Famous New Mexicans.** Billy (the Kid) Bonney, Kit Carson, Peter Hurd, Archbishop Jean Baptiste Lamy, Nancy Lopez, Bill Mauldin, Georgia O'Keeffe, Kim Stanley, Al Unser, Bobby Unser, Lew Wallace.

**Tourist information.** New Mexico Dept. of Tourism, PO Box 20002, Santa Fe, NM 87503.

**Toll-free travel information.** 1-800-733-6396.

**World Wide Web site.** http://www.state.nm.us

## New York

*Empire State*

**People. Population** (1995): 18,136,081; **rank:** 3; **Net change** (1990-95): 0.8%. **Pop. density:** (1990) 383.7 per sq mi. **Racial/ethnic distrib.** (1990): 74.4% white; 15.9% black; 3.9% Asian; 12.3% Hispanic.

**Geography. Total area:** 54,471 sq mi; **rank:** 27. **Land area:** 47,224 sq mi. **Acres forested land:** 18,713,000. **Location:** Middle Atlantic state, bordered by the New England states, Atlantic Ocean, New Jersey and Pennsylvania, Lakes Ontario and Erie, and Canada. **Climate:** variable; the SE region moderated by the ocean. **Topography:** highest and most rugged mountains in the NE Adirondack upland; St. Lawrence-Champlain lowlands extend from Lake Ontario NE along the Canadian border; Hudson-Mohawk lowland follows the flows of the rivers N and W, 10-30 mi wide; Atlantic coastal plain in the SE; Appalachian Highlands, covering half the state westward from the Hudson Valley, include the Catskill Mts., Finger Lakes; plateau of Erie-Ontario lowlands. **Capital:** Albany.

**Economy. Principal industries:** manufacturing, finance, communications, tourism, transportation, services. **Principal manufactured goods:** books and periodicals, clothing and apparel, pharmaceuticals, machinery, instruments, toys and sporting goods, electronic equipment, automotive and aircraft components. **Chief crops:** apples, grapes, strawberries, cherries, pears, onions, potatoes, cabbage, sweet corn, green beans, cauliflower, field corn, hay, wheat, oats, dry beans. **Products:** milk, cheese, maple syrup, wine. **Livestock** (1995): 1.5 mil cattle; 72,000 hogs/pigs; 72,000 sheep; 7.7 mil poultry. **Timber/lumber** (1995): birch, sugar and red maple, basswood, hemlock, pine, oak, ash; 478 mil bd. ft. **Nonfuel minerals** (est. 1995): $820 mil; mostly salt, crushed stone, construction sand & gravel, portland cement. **Commercial fishing** (1995): $77 mil. **Chief ports:** New York, Buffalo, Albany. **International airports at:** New York, Buffalo, Syracuse, Massena, Ogdensburg, Watertown, Niagara Falls, Newburgh. **Value of construction** (1995): $13.3 bil. **Employment distribution** (1996): 33% serv.; 21% trade; 17% govt.; 11% mfg. **Per capita personal income** (1995): $26,782. **Unemployment** (1995): 6.9%. **Tourism** (1995): tourists spent $24.3 bil.

**Finance. FDIC-insured commercial banks & trust companies** (1995): 166. **Deposits:** $547.3 bil. **FDIC-insured savings institutions** (1995): 112. **Assets**: $129.5 bil.

**Federal government. No. federal civilian employees** (Mar. 1995): 64,967. **Avg. salary:** $39,688. **Notable federal facilities:** West Point Military Academy; Merchant Marine Academy; Ft. Drum; Rome Labs.; Watervliet Arsenal.

**Energy. Electricity production** (1995, kWh, by source): Coal: 19.9 bil; Petroleum: 7.8 bil; Gas: 23.4 bil; Hydroelectric: 23.6 bil; Nuclear: 26.3 bil.

**Public education. Student-teacher ratio** (1994): 15.2. **Avg. teachers' salary** (1995-96): $48,115.

**State data. Motto:** Excelsior (Ever upward). **Flower:** Rose. **Bird:** Bluebird. **Tree:** Sugar maple. **Song:** I Love New York. **Eleventh** of the original 13 states to ratify the Constitution, July 26, 1788. **State fair** at Syracuse; late Aug.–early Sept.

**History.** Algonquians including the Mahican, Wappinger, and Lenni Lenape inhabited the region, as did the Iroquoian Mohawk, Oneida, Onondaga, Cayuga, and Seneca tribes, who established the League of the Five Nations. In 1609, Henry Hudson visited the river that bears his name, and Champlain explored the lake that was named for him. The first permanent settlement was Dutch, near present-day Albany, 1624. New Amsterdam was settled, 1626, at the southern tip of Manhattan Island. A British fleet seized New Netherland, 1664. Ninety-two of the 300 or more engagements of the American Revolution were fought in New York, including the Battle of Bemis Heights-Saratoga, 1777, a turning point of the war. Completion of Erie Canal, 1825, established the state as a gateway to the West. The first woman's rights convention was held in Seneca Falls, 1848.

**Tourist attractions.** New York City; Adirondack and Catskill Mts.; Finger Lakes; Great Lakes; Thousand Islands; Niagara Falls; Saratoga Springs; Philipsburg Manor, Sunnyside (Washington Irving's home), the Dutch Church of Sleepy Hollow, all in Tarrytown area; Corning Glass Center and Steuben factory, Corning; Fenimore House, Natl. Baseball Hall of Fame and Museum, both in Cooperstown; Ft. Ticonderoga overlooking Lakes George and Champlain; Empire State Plaza, Albany; Lake Placid; Franklin D. Roosevelt Natl. Historic Site, including the Roosevelt Library, Hyde Park; Long Island beaches; Theodore Roosevelt estate, Sagamore Hill, Oyster Bay.

**Famous New Yorkers.** Susan B. Anthony, Lucille Ball, Barbara Bush, Peter Cooper, George Eastman, Millard Fillmore, George and Ira Gershwin, Ruth Bader Ginsberg, Julia Ward Howe, Charles Evans Hughes, Henry and William James, Herman Melville, Colin Powell, Nelson Rockefeller, Franklin D. Roosevelt, Theodore Roosevelt, J. D. Salinger, Paul Simon, Alfred E. Smith, Elizabeth Cady Stanton, Martin Van Buren, Gore Vidal, Walt Whitman.

**Tourist information.** N.Y. State Dept. of Economic Development, 1 Commerce Plaza, Albany, NY 12245.

**Toll-free travel information.** 1-800-CALLNYS from 50 states & U.S. territories; 1-518-474-4116 from other areas and Canada.

**World Wide Web site.** http://www.state.ny.us

## North Carolina

*Tar Heel State, Old North State*

**People. Population** (1995): 7,195,138; **rank:** 11; **Net change** (1990-95): 8.5%. **Pop. density:** (1990) 140.5 per sq mi. **Racial/ethnic distrib.** (1990): 75.6% white; 22.0% black; 1.2% Amer. Indian; 1.2% Hispanic.

**Geography. Total area:** 53,821 sq mi; **rank:** 28. **Land area:** 48,718 sq mi. **Acres forested land:** 19,278,000. **Location:** South Atlantic state bounded by Virginia, South Carolina, Georgia, Tennessee, and the Atlantic Ocean **Climate:** sub-tropical in SE, medium-continental in mountain region; tempered by the Gulf Stream and the mountains in W. **Topography:** coastal plain and tidewater, two-fifths of state, extending to the fall line of the rivers; piedmont plateau, another two-fifths, 200 mi wide of gentle to rugged hills; southern Appalachian Mts. contains the Blue Ridge and Great Smoky Mts. **Capital:** Raleigh.

**Economy. Principal industries:** manufacturing, agriculture, tobacco, tourism. **Principal manufactured goods:** textiles, rubber/plastics products, electrical and electronic equipment, chemicals, furniture, food products, non-electrical machinery. **Chief crops:** tobacco, soybeans, corn, cotton, peanuts, sweet potatoes, feed grains, vegetables, fruits. **Livestock** (1995): 1.2 mil cattle; 8.3 mil hogs/pigs; 18.8 mil chickens, 61.2 mil turkeys. **Timber/lumber** (1995): yellow pine, oak, hickory, poplar, maple; 2.2 bil bd. ft. **Nonfuel minerals** (est. 1995): $742 mil; mostly, construction sand & gravel, crushed stone, dimension stone, phosphate rock, lithium. **Commercial fishing** (1995): $111 mil. **International airports at:** Charlotte/Douglas, Raleigh/Durham. **Chief ports:** Morehead City, Wilmington. **Value of construction** (1995): $10.6 bil. **Employment distribution** (1994): 25.6% mfg.; 22.7% trade; 21.5% serv.; 16.1% govt. **Per capita personal income** (1995): $20,604. **Unemployment** (1995): 4.3%. **Tourism** (1995): out-of-state visitors spent $9.2 bil.

**Finance. FDIC-insured commercial banks & trust companies** (1995): 61. **Deposits**: $110.8 bil. **FDIC-insured savings institutions** (1995): 65. **Assets:** $8.9 bil.

**Federal government. No. federal civilian employees** (Mar. 1995): 31,578. **Avg. salary:** $35,476. **Notable federal facilities:** Ft. Bragg; Camp LeJeune Marine Base; U.S. EPA Research and Development Labs, Cherry Point Marine Corps Air Station; Natl. Humanities Center; Natl. Inst. of Environmental Health Science; Natl. Center for Health Statistics Lab, Research Triangle Park.

**Energy. Electricity production** (1995, kWh, by source): Coal: 56.0 bil; Petroleum: 234 mil; Gas: 253 mil; Hydroelectric: 4.0 bil; Nuclear: 35.9 bil.

**Public education. Student-teacher ratio** (1994): 16.2. **Avg. teachers' salary** (1995-96): $30,564.

**State data. Motto:** Esse Quam Videri (To be rather than to seem). **Flower:** Dogwood. **Bird:** Cardinal. **Tree:** Pine. **Song:** The Old North State. **Twelfth** of the original 13 states to ratify the Constitution, Nov. 21, 1789. **State fair** at Raleigh; mid-Oct.

**History.** Algonquian, Siouan, and Iroquoian peoples lived in the region at the time of European contact. The first English colony in America was the first of 2 established by Sir Walter Raleigh on Roanoke Island, 1585 and 1587. The first group returned to England; the second, the "Lost Colony," disappeared without a trace. Permanent settlers came from Virginia, c 1660. Roused by British repression, the colonists drove out the royal governor, 1775. The province's congress was the first to vote for independence; ten regiments were furnished to the Continental Army. Cornwallis's forces were defeated at Kings Mountain, 1780, and forced out after Guilford Courthouse, 1781. The state seceded in 1861, and provided more troops to the Confederacy than any other state; it was readmitted in 1868.

**Tourist attractions.** Cape Hatteras and Cape Lookout natl. seashores; Great Smoky Mts.; Guilford Courthouse and Moore's Creek parks; 66 American Revolution battle sites; Bennett Place, near Durham, where Gen. Joseph Johnston surrendered the last Confederate army to Gen. William Sherman; Ft. Raleigh, Roanoke Island, where Virginia Dare, first child of English parents in the New World, was born Aug. 18, 1587; Wright Brothers Natl. Memorial, Kitty Hawk; Battleship *North Carolina*, Wilmington; NC Zoo, Asheboro; NC Symphony, NC Museum, Raleigh; Carl Sandburg Home, Hendersonville.

**Famous North Carolinians.** Elizabeth Dole, Richard J. Gatling, Billy Graham, Andy Griffith, Andrew Jackson, Andrew Johnson, Michael Jordan, Wm. Rufus King, Charles Kuralt, Dolley Madison, Edward R. Murrow, James K. Polk, Carl Sandburg, Enos Slaughter, Dean Smith, Thomas Wolfe.

**Tourist information.** Travel & Tourism Division, 430 No. Salisbury St., Raleigh, NC 27603.

**Toll-free travel information.** 1-800-VISITNC.

**World Wide Web site.** http://www.state.nc.us

## North Dakota

*Peace Garden State*

**People. Population** (1995): 641,367; **rank:** 47; **Net change** (1990-95): 0.4%. **Pop. density:** (1990) 9.2 per sq mi. **Racial/ethnic distrib.** (1990): 94.6% white; 0.6% black; 4.1% Amer. Indian; 0.7% Hispanic.

**Geography. Total area:** 70,704 sq mi; **rank:** 19. **Land area:** 68,994 sq mi. **Acres forested land:** 462,000. **Location:** West North Central state, situated exactly in the middle of North America, bounded on the N by Canada, on the E by Minnesota, on the S by South Dakota, on the W by Montana. **Climate:** continental, with a wide range of temperature and moderate rainfall. **Topography:** Central Lowland in the E comprises the flat Red River Valley and the Rolling Drift Prairie; Missouri Plateau of the Great Plains on the W. **Capital:** Bismarck.

**Economy. Principal industries:** agriculture, mining, tourism, manufacturing, telecommunications, energy, food processing. **Principal manufactured goods:** farm equipment, processed foods, fabricated metal, high-tech. electronics. **Chief crops:** spring wheat, durum, barley, rye, flaxseed, oats, potatoes, dried edible beans, honey, soybeans, sugar beets, sunflowers, hay. **Livestock** (1995): 1.9 mil cattle; 280,000 hogs/pigs; 270,000 poultry; (1996): 125,000 sheep. **Timber/lumber:** (1995) oak, ash, cottonwood, aspen; 4 mil bd. ft. **Nonfuel minerals** (est. 1995): $25 mil; mostly construction sand & gravel, lime. **International airports at:** Fargo, Grand Forks, Bismarck, Minot, Pembina, Dunseith. **Value of construction** (1995): $791.0 mil. **Employment distribution** (1995): 26% trade; 28% serv.; 23% govt.; 7.2% mfg. **Per capita personal income** (1995): $18,663. **Unemployment** (1995): 3.3%. **Tourism** (1992): $826 mil.

**Finance. FDIC-insured commercial banks & trust companies** (1995): 127. **Deposits:** $6.9 bil. **FDIC-insured savings institutions** (1995): 4. **Assets:** $6.7 bil.

**Federal government. No. federal civilian employees** (Mar. 1995): 5,202. **Avg. salary:** $33,752. **Notable federal facilities:** Strategic Air Command bases at Minot, Grand Forks; Northern Prairie Wildlife Research Center; Garrison Dam; Theodore Roosevelt Natl. Park; Grand Forks Energy Research Center; Ft. Union Natl. Historic Site.

**Energy. Electricity production** (1995, kWh, by source): Coal: 26.3 bil; Petroleum: 49 bil; Hydroelectric: 2.5 bil.

**Public education. Student-teacher ratio** (1994): 15.3. **Avg. teachers' salary** (1995-96): $26,969.

**State data. Motto:** Liberty and union, now and forever, one and inseparable. **Flower:** Wild prairie rose. **Bird:** Western meadowlark. **Tree:** American elm. **Song:** North Dakota Hymn. **Entered union** Nov. 2, 1889; rank, 39th. **State fair** at Minot; 3d week in July.

**History.** At the time of European contact, the Ojibwa, Yanktonai and Teton Sioux, Mandan, Arikara, and Hidatsa peoples lived in the region. Pierre de Varennes was the first French fur trader in the area, 1738, followed later by the English. The U.S. acquired half the territory in the Louisiana Purchase, 1803. Lewis and Clark built Ft. Mandan, near present-day Stanton, 1804-5, and wintered there. In 1818, American ownership of the other half was confirmed by agreement with Britain. The first permanent settlement was at Pembina, 1812. Missouri River steamboats reached the area, 1832, the first railroad, 1873, bringing many homesteaders. The "bonanza farm" craze of the 1870s-80s attracted many settlers. The state was first to hold a national presidential primary, 1912.

**Tourist attractions.** North Dakota Heritage Center, Bismarck; Bonanzaville, Fargo; Ft. Union Trading Post Natl. Historic Site; Lake Sakakawea; Intl. Peace Garden; Theodore Roosevelt Natl. Park, including Elkhorn Ranch, Badlands; Ft. Abraham Lincoln State Park and Museum, near Mandan; Dakota Dinosaur Museum, Dickinson.

**Famous North Dakotans.** Maxwell Anderson, Angie Dickinson, John Bernard Flannagan, Phil Jackson, Louis L'Amour, Peggy Lee, Eric Sevareid, Vilhjalmur Stefansson, Lawrence Welk.

**Chamber of Commerce.** PO Box 2639, 2000 Schafer St., Bismarck, ND 58501.

**Tourism Dept.** ph.-(701) 328-2525 fax-(701) 328-4878

**Toll-free travel information.** 1-800-HELLO-ND

**World Wide Web site.** http://www.state.nd.us

## Ohio

*Buckeye State*

**People. Population** (1995): 11,150,506; **rank:** 7; **Net change** (1990-95): 2.8%. **Pop. density:** (1990) 269.0 per sq mi. **Racial/ethnic distrib.** (1990): 87.8% white; 10.6% black; 1.3% Hispanic.

**Geography. Total area:** 44,828 sq mi; **rank:** 34. **Land area:** 40,953 sq mi. **Acres forested land:** 7,863,000. **Location:** East North Central state bounded on the N by Michigan and Lake Erie; on the E and S by Pennsylvania, West Virginia, and Kentucky; on the W by Indiana. **Climate:** temperate but variable; weather subject to much precipitation. **Topography:** generally rolling plain; Allegheny plateau in E; Lake Erie plains extend southward; central plains in the W. **Capital:** Columbus.

**Economy. Principal industries:** manufacturing, trade, services. **Principal manufactured goods:** transportation equipment, machinery, primary and fabricated metal products. **Chief crops:** corn, hay, winter wheat, oats, soybeans. **Livestock** (1996): 1.5 mil cattle; 1.7 mil hogs/pigs; 162,000 sheep and lambs; (1995) 43.0 mil broilers, 6.5 mil turkeys. **Timber/lumber** (1995): oak, ash, maple, walnut, beech; 412 mil bd. ft. **Nonfuel minerals** (est. 1995): $880 mil; mostly crushed stone, construction sand & gravel, salt, lime. **Commercial fishing** (1995): $2.6 mil. **Chief ports:** Toledo, Conneaut, Cleveland, Ashtabula. **International airports at:** Cleveland, Cincinnati, Columbus, Dayton. **Value of construction** (1995): $12.4 bil. **Employment distribution** (1995): 21.2% mfg.; 18.7% trade; 26.4%

serv.; 14.7% govt. **Per capita personal income** (1995): $22,021. **Unemployment** (1995): 4.8%. **Tourism** (1992): travelers spent $8.8 bil.

**Finance. FDIC-insured commercial banks & trust companies** (1995): 260. **Deposits:** $109.2 bil. **FDIC-insured savings institutions** (1995): 160. **Assets:** $47.4 bil.

**Federal government. No. federal civilian employees** (Mar. 1995): 50,709. **Avg. salary:** $41,144. **Notable federal facilities:** Wright Patterson AFB; Defense Construction Supply Center; Lewis Research Ctr.; Portsmouth Gaseous Diffusion Plant.

**Energy. Electricity production** (1995, kWh, by source): Coal: 120.0 bil; Petroleum: 298 mil; Gas: 524mil; Hydroelectric: 227 mil; Nuclear: 16.8 mil.

**Public education. Student-teacher ratio** (1994): 16.6. **Avg. teachers' salary** (1995-96): $37,835.

**State data. Motto:** With God, all things are possible. **Flower:** Scarlet carnation. **Bird:** Cardinal. **Tree:** Buckeye. **Song:** Beautiful Ohio. **Entered union** Mar. 1, 1803; rank, 17th. **State fair** at Columbus; August 2-18.

**History.** Wyandot, Delaware, Miami, and Shawnee peoples sparsely occupied the area when the first Europeans arrived. La Salle visited the region, 1669, and France claimed the area, 1682. Around 1730, traders from Pennsylvania and Virginia entered the area; the French and their Native American allies sought to drive them out. France ceded its claim, 1763, to Britain. During the American Revolution, George Rogers Clark seized British posts and held the region, until Britain gave up its claim, 1883, in the Treaty of Paris. The region became U.S. territory after the American Revolution. First organized settlement was at Marietta, 1788. Indian warfare ended with Anthony Wayne's victory at Fallen Timbers, 1794. In the War of 1812, Oliver Hazard Perry's victory on Lake Erie and William Henry Harrison's invasion of Canada, 1813, ended British incursions.

**Tourist attractions.** Mound City Group Natl. Monuments, a group of 24 prehistoric Indian burial mounds; Neil Armstrong Air and Space Museum, Wapakoneta; Air Force Museum, Dayton; Pro Football Hall of Fame, Canton; King's Island amusement park, Mason; Lake Erie Islands, Cedar Point amusement park, both Sandusky; birthplaces, homes of, and memorials to U.S. presidents W. H. Harrison, Grant, Garfield, Hayes, McKinley, Harding, Taft, Benjamin Harrison; Amish Region, Tuscarawas/Holmes counties; German Village, Columbus; Sea World, Aurora; Jack Nicklaus Sports Center, Mason; Bob Evans Farm, Rio Grande; Rock and Roll Hall of Fame and Museum, Cleveland.

**Famous Ohioans.** Sherwood Anderson, Neil Armstrong, George Bellows, Ambrose Bierce, Erma Bombeck, Clarence Darrow, Paul Laurence Dunbar, Thomas Edison, Clark Gable, John Glenn, Bob Hope, Jack Nicklaus, Jesse Owens, Eddie Rickenbacker, John D. Rockefeller Sr. and Jr., Pete Rose, Gen. William Sherman, Harriet Beecher Stowe, Charles Taft, Robert A. Taft, William H. Taft, James Thurber, Orville and Wilbur Wright.

**Chamber of Commerce.** PO Box 15159. 230 E. Town St., Columbus, OH 43215-0159.

**Toll-free travel information.** 1-800-BUCKEYE.

**World Wide Web site.** http://www.state.oh.us

## Oklahoma

*Sooner State*

**People. Population** (1995): 3,277,687; **rank:** 27; **Net change** (1990-95): 4.2%. **Pop. density:** (1990) 46.8 per sq mi. **Racial/ethnic distrib.** (1990): 82.1% white; 7.4% black; 8.0% Amer. Indian; 2.7% Hispanic.

**Geography. Total area:** 69,903 sq mi; **rank:** 20. **Land area:** 68,679 sq mi. **Acres forested land:** 7,539,000. **Location:** West South Central state bounded on the N by Colorado and Kansas; on the E by Missouri and Arkansas; on the S and W by Texas and New Mexico. **Climate:** temperate; southern humid belt merging with colder northern continental; humid eastern and dry western zones. **Topography:** high plains predominate in the W, hills and small mountains in the E; the east central region is dominated by the Arkansas R. Basin, and the Red R. Plains, in the S. **Capital:** Oklahoma City.

**Economy. Principal industries:** manufacturing, mineral and energy exploration and production, agriculture, services. **Principal manufactured goods:** nonelectrical machinery, transportation equipment, food products, fabricated metal products. **Chief crops:** wheat, cotton, hay, peanuts, grain sorghum, soybeans, corn, pecans. **Livestock** (1994): 5.7 mil cattle; 590,000 hogs/pigs; 96,000 sheep; 4.8 mil poultry. **Timber/lumber:** pine, oak, hickory. **Nonfuel minerals** (est. 1995): $374 mil; mostly crushed stone, portland cement, sand & gravel, gypsum, iodine. **Chief ports:** Catoosa, Muskogee. **International airports at:** Oklahoma City, Tulsa. **Value of construction** (1995): $3.0 bil. **Employment distribution** (1994): 26.2% serv.; 23.7% trade; 20.5% govt.; 12.9% mfg. **Per capita personal income** (1995): $18,152. **Unemployment** (1995): 4.7%. **Tourism** (1995): tourists spent $3 bil.

**Finance. FDIC-insured commercial banks & trust companies** (1995): 342. **Deposits:** $28.8 bil. **FDIC-insured savings institutions** (1995): 13. **Assets:** $5.8 bil.

**Federal government. No. federal civilian employees** (Mar. 1995): 30,480. **Avg. salary:** $36,711. **Notable federal facilities:** Federal Aviation Agency and Tinker AFB, both Oklahoma City; Ft. Sill, Lawton; Altus AFB, Altus; Vance AFB, Enid.

**Energy. Electricity production** (1995, kWh, by source): Coal: 29.0 bil; Petroleum: 78 mil; Gas: 15.5 bil; Hydroelectric: 2.7 bil.

**Public education. Student-teacher ratio** (1994): 15.5. **Avg. teachers' salary** (1995-96): $28,909.

**State data. Motto:** Labor Omnia Vincit (Labor conquers all things). **Flower:** Mistletoe. **Bird:** Scissor-tailed flycatcher. **Tree:** Redbud. **Song:** Oklahoma! **Entered union** Nov. 16, 1907; rank, 46th. **State fair** at Oklahoma City; last 2 full weeks of Sept.

**History.** The region was sparsely inhabited by a few scattered Native American tribes when Coronado, the first European to enter Oklahoma, arrived in 1541; in the 16th and 17th cent., French traders visited the region. Part of the Louisiana Purchase, 1803, Oklahoma was established as Indian Territory (but was not given territorial government). It became home to the "Five Civilized Tribes"—Cherokee, Choctaw, Chickasaw, Creek, and Seminole—after the forced removal of Native Americans from the eastern U.S., 1828-46. The land was also used by Comanche, Osage, and other Plains Indians. As white settlers pressed west, land was opened for homesteading by runs and lottery, the first run taking place on Apr. 22, 1889. The most famous run was to the Cherokee Outlet, 1893.

**Tourist attractions.** Cherokee Heritage Center, Tahlequah; White Water Bay and Frontier City theme pks., both Oklahoma City; Will Rogers Memorial, Claremore; Natl. Cowboy Hall of Fame and Remington Park Race Track, both Oklahoma City; Ft. Gibson Stockade, near Muskogee; Ouachita Natl. Forest; Tulsa's art deco district; Wichita Mts. Wildlife Refuge, Lawton; Woolaroc Museum & Wildlife Preserve, Bartlesville; Sequoyah's Home Site, near Sallisaw.

**Famous Oklahomans.** Troy Aikman, Carl Albert, Gene Autry, Johnny Bench, Garth Brooks, William "Hopalong Cassidy" Boyd, L. Gordon Cooper, Jerome "Dizzy" Dean, Ralph Ellison, John Hope Franklin, James Garner, Geronimo, Woody Guthrie, Paul Harvey, Anita Hill, Ron Howard, Gen. Patrick J. Hurley, Jeane Kirkpatrick, Louis L'Amour, Mickey Mantle, Reba McEntire, Carry Nation, Wiley Post, Tony Randall, Oral Roberts, Will Rogers, Maria Tallchief, Jim Thorpe.

**Chamber of Commerce.** Chamber of Commerce, 330 NE 10th, Oklahoma City, OK 73104.

**Tourism Dept.** PO Box 60789, Oklahoma City, OK 73146-0789.

**Toll-free travel information.** 1-800-652-6552.

**World Wide Web site.** http://www.state.ok.us

## Oregon

*Beaver State*

**People. Population** (1995): 3,140,585; **rank:** 29; **Net change** (1990-95): 10.5%. **Pop. density:** (1990) 31.0 per sq mi. **Racial/ethnic distrib.** (1990): 92.8% white; 1.6% black; 4.0% Hispanic.

**Geography. Total area:** 98,386 sq mi; **rank:** 9. **Land area:** 96,002 sq mi. **Acres forested land:** 27,997,000. **Location:** Pacific state, bounded on N by Washington; on E by Idaho; on S by Nevada and California; on W by the Pacific. **Climate:** coastal mild and humid climate; continental dryness and extreme temperatures in the interior. **Topography:** Coast Range of rugged mountains; fertile Willamette R. Valley to E and S; Cascade Mt. Range of volcanic peaks E of the valley; plateau E of Cascades, remaining two-thirds of state. **Capital:** Salem.

**Economy. Principal industries:** manufacturing, forestry, agriculture, tourism, high technology, printing & publishing.. **Principal manufactured goods:** lumber & wood products, computer equipment, foods, machinery, fabricated metals, paper, primary metals. **Chief crops:** greenhouse, hay, wheat, grass seed, potatoes, onions, Christmas trees, pears, mint. **Livestock** (1996): 1.47 mil cattle; 45,000 hogs/pigs; 353,000 sheep; 21.09 mil poultry. **Timber/lumber** (1995): Douglas fir, hemlock, ponderosa pine; 4.9 bil bd. ft. **Nonfuel minerals** (est. 1995): $261 mil; mostly crushed stone, construction sand & gravel, portland cement. **Commercial fishing** (1995): $77.8 mil. **Chief ports:** Portland, Astoria, Coos Bay. **International airports at:** Portland, Klamath Falls. **Value of construction** (1995): $4.9 bil. **Employment distribution** (1995): 25.3% trade; 25.7% serv.; 16.1% mfg.; 16.8% govt. **Per capita personal income** (1995): $21,736. **Unemployment** (1995): 4.8%. **Tourism** (1995): $4.1 bil.

**Finance. FDIC-insured commercial banks & trust companies** (1995): 43. **Deposits:** $22.9 bil. **FDIC-insured savings institutions** (1995): 10. **Assets:** $10.5 bil.

**Federal government. No. federal civilian employees** (Mar. 1995): 18,964. **Avg. salary:** $38,751. **Notable federal facilities:** Bonneville Power Administration.

**Energy. Electricity production** (1995, kWh, by source): Coal: 1.5 bil; Petroleum: 4 mil; Gas: 2.1 bil; Hydroelectric: 40.4 bil.

**Public education. Student-teacher ratio** (1994): 19.9. **Avg. teachers' salary** (1995-96): $39,650.

**State data. Motto:** She flies with her own wings. **Flower:** Oregon grape. **Bird:** Western meadowlark. **Tree:** Douglas fir. **Song:** Oregon, My Oregon. **Entered union** Feb. 14, 1859; rank, 33d. **State fair** at Salem; 12 days ending with Labor Day.

**History.** More than 100 Native American tribes inhabited the area at the time of European contact, including the Chinook, Yakima, Cayuse, Modoc, and Nez Percé. Capt. Robert Gray sighted and sailed into the Columbia River, 1792; Lewis and Clark, traveling overland, wintered at its mouth, 1805-6; John Jacob Astor established a trading post in the Columbia River region, 1811. Settlers arrived in the Willamette Valley, 1834. In 1843, the first large wave of settlers arrived via the Oregon Trail. Early in the 20th cent., the "Oregon System"—political reforms that included the initiative, referendum, recall, direct primary, and woman suffrage—was adopted.

**Tourist attractions.** John Day Fossil Beds Natl. Monument; Columbia River Gorge; Timberline Lodge, Mt. Hood Natl. Forest; Crater Lake Natl. Park; Oregon Dunes Natl. Recreation Area; Ft. Clatsop Natl. Memorial; Oregon Caves Natl. Monument; Oregon Museum of Science and Industry, Portland; Shakespearean Festival, Ashland; High Desert Museum, Bend; Multnomah Falls; Diamond Lake.

**Famous Oregonians.** Ernest Bloch, Ernest Haycox, Chief Joseph, Edwin Markham, Tom McCall, Dr. John McLoughlin, Joaquin Miller, Linus Pauling, John Reed, Alberto Salazar, Mary Decker Slaney, William Simon U'Ren.

**Tourist information.** Economic Development Department, 775 Summer St. NE, Salem, OR 97310.

**Toll-free travel information.** 1-800-547-7842.

**World Wide Web site.** http://www.state.or.us

## Pennsylvania

*Keystone State*

**People. Population** (1995): 12,071,842; **rank:** 5; **Net change** (1990-95): 1.6%. **Pop. density:** (1990) 267.9 per sq mi. **Racial/ethnic distrib.** (1990): 88.5% white; 9.2% black; 2.0% Hispanic.

**Geography. Total area:** 46,058 sq mi; **rank:** 33. **Land area:** 44,820 sq mi. **Acres forested land:** 16,969,000. **Location:** Middle Atlantic state, bordered on the E by the Delaware R.; on the S by the Mason-Dixon Line; on the W by West Virginia and Ohio; on the N/NE by Lake Erie and New York. **Climate:** continental with wide fluctuations in seasonal temperatures. **Topography:** Allegheny Mts. run SW to NE, with Piedmont and Coast Plain in the SE triangle; Allegheny Front a diagonal spine across the state's center; N and W rugged plateau falls to Lake Erie Lowland. **Capital:** Harrisburg.

**Economy. Principal industries:** steel, travel and tourism, biotechnology, apparel, advanced materials, agribusiness. **Principal manufactured goods:** primary metals; foods; fabricated metal products; nonelectrical machinery; electrical machinery; printing and publishing; stone, clay, and glass products. **Chief crops:** corn, hay, mushrooms, apples, potatoes, winter wheat, oats, vegetables, tobacco, grapes. **Livestock** (1996): 1.7 mil cattle; 1.4 mil hogs/pigs; 107,000 sheep; 21.2 mil poultry. **Timber/lumber** (1995): pine, oak, maple; 1.08 bil bd. ft. **Nonfuel minerals** (est. 1995): $1.1 bil; mostly crushed stone, portland cement, lime, construction sand & gravel. **Commercial fishing** (1995): $496,000. **Chief ports:** Philadelphia, Pittsburgh, Erie. **International airports at** Allentown, Erie, Harrisburg, Philadelphia, Pittsburgh, Wilkes-Barre/Scranton. **Value of construction** (1995): $9.3 bil. **Employment distribution** (1995): 30.4% serv.; 22.8% trade; 17.9% mfg.; 13.7% govt. **Per capita personal income** (1995): $23,279. **Unemployment** (1995): 5.9%. **Tourism** (1993): out-of-state visitors spent $10.7 bil.

**Finance. FDIC-insured commercial banks & trust companies** (1995): 224. **Deposits:** $138.7 bil. **FDIC-insured savings institutions** (1995): 124. **Assets:** $40.6 bil.

**Federal government. No. federal civilian employees** (Mar. 1995): 75,635. **Avg. salary:** $37,308. **Notable federal facilities:** Army War College, Carlisle; Ships Control Ctr., Mechanicsburg; New Cumberland Army Depot; Philadelphia Naval Station; Philadelphia Navy Hospital; Indiantown Gap, Annville; Letterkenny Army Depot, Chambersburg; Charles E. Kelly Spt Fac, Pittsburgh; Tobyhanna Army Depot, Tobyhanna; Naval Air Development Center, Warminster; NAS Grove, Willow Grove; Greater Pittsburgh IAP AGS, Corapolis; Willow Grove ARS, Hatboro; Harrisburg Olmsred IAP AGS, Middletown.

**Energy. Electricity production** (1995, kWh, by source): Coal: 96.8 bil; Petroleum: 3.1 bil; Gas: 2.2 bil; Hydroelectric: 444 mil; Nuclear: 66.5 bil.

**Public education. Student-teacher ratio** (1994): 17.1. **Avg. teachers' salary** (1995-96): $46,916.

**State data. Motto:** Virtue, liberty and independence. **Flower:** Mountain laurel. **Bird:** Ruffed grouse. **Tree:** Hemlock. **Second** of the original 13 states to ratify the Constitution, Dec. 12, 1787. **State fair** at Harrisburg; 2d week in Jan. at State Farm Show Building.

**History.** At the time of European contact, Lenni Lenape (Delaware), Shawnee and Iroquoian Susquehannocks, Erie, and Seneca occupied the region. Swedish explorers established the first permanent settlement, 1643, on Tinicum Island. In 1655, the Dutch seized the settlement but lost it to the British, 1664. The region was given by Charles II to William Penn, 1681. Philadelphia ("brotherly love") was the capital of the colonies during most of the American Revolution, and of the U.S., 1790-1800. Philadelphia was taken by the British, 1777; Washington's troops encamped at Valley Forge in the bitter winter of 1777-78. The Declaration of Independence, 1776, and the Constitution, 1787, were signed in Philadelphia. The three-day Civil War battle of Gettysburg, July 1-3, 1863, marked a turning point, favoring Union forces.

**Tourist attractions.** Independence Natl. Historic Park, Franklin Institute Science Museum, Philadelphia Museum of Art, all in Philadelphia; Valley Forge Natl. Historic Park; Gettysburg Natl. Military Park; Pennsylvania Dutch Country; Hershey; Duquesne Incline, Carnegie Institute, Heinz Hall, all in Pittsburgh; Pocono Mts.; Pennsylvania's Grand Canyon, Tioga County; Allegheny Natl. Forest; Laurel Highlands; Presque Isle State Park; Fallingwater, Ligonier; Johnstown; SteamTown U.S.A., Scranton.

**Famous Pennsylvanians.** Marian Anderson, Maxwell Anderson, James Buchanan, Andrew Carnegie, Stephen Foster, Benjamin Franklin, Milton Hershey, Gene Kelly, George C. Marshall, Andrew W. Mellon, Robert E. Peary, Mary Roberts Rinehart, Betsy Ross, Jimmy Stewart, John Updike.

**Chamber of Business and Industry.** 417 Walnut St., Harrisburg, PA 17120.

**Toll-free travel information.** 1-800-VISITPA.

**World Wide Web site.** http://www.state.pa.us

## Rhode Island

*Little Rhody, Ocean State*

**People. Population** (1995): 989,794; **rank:** 43; **Net change** (1990-95): –1.4%. **Pop. density:** (1990) 961.8 per sq mi. **Racial/ethnic distrib.** (1990): 91.4% white; 3.9% black; 4.6% Hispanic.

**Geography. Total area:** 1,545 sq mi; **rank:** 50. **Land area:** 1,045 sq mi. **Acres forested land:** 401,000. **Location:** New England state. **Climate:** invigorating and changeable. **Topography:** eastern lowlands of Narragansett Basin; western uplands of flat and rolling hills. **Capital:** Providence.

**Economy. Principal industries:** services, manufacturing. **Principal manufactured goods:** costume jewelry, toys, machinery, textiles, electronics. **Chief crops:** nursery products, turf, potatoes, apples. **Timber/lumber:** (1995) oak; 10 mil bd. ft. **Nonfuel minerals** (est. 1995): $30 mil; construction sand & gravel, crushed stone. **Commercial fishing** (1995): $68 mil. **Chief ports:** Providence, Quonset Point, Newport. **Value of construction** (1995): $464.8 mil. **Employment distribution** (1993): 32% services; 20% mfg.; 22% trade. **Per capita personal income** (1995): $23,310. **Unemployment** (1995): 7.0%. **Tourism** (1993): visitors spent $1.4 bil.

**Finance. FDIC-insured commercial banks & trust companies** (1995): 8. **Deposits:** $10.6 bil. **FDIC-insured savings institutions** (1995): 6. **Assets:** $6.1 bil.

**Federal government. No. federal civilian employees** (Mar. 1995): 5,692. **Avg. salary:** $41,378. **Notable federal facilities:** Naval War College; Naval Underwater Warfare Center; Natl. Marine Fisheries Laboratory; EPA Environmental Research Laboratory.

**Energy. Electricity production** (1995, kWh, by source): Petroleum: 50 mil; Gas: 603 mil.

**Public education. Student-teacher ratio** (1994): 14.7. **Avg. teachers' salary** (1995-96): $42,160.

**State data. Motto:** Hope. **Flower:** Violet. **Bird:** Rhode Island red. **Tree:** Red maple. **Song:** Rhode Island. **Thirteenth** of original 13 states to ratify the Constitution, May 29, 1790. **State fair** at Richmond; mid-Aug.

**History.** When the Europeans arrived Narragansett, Niantic, Nipmuc, and Wampanoag peoples lived in the region. Verrazano visited the area, 1524. The first permanent settlement was founded at Providence, 1636, by Roger Williams, who was exiled from the Massachusetts Bay Colony; Anne Hutchinson, also exiled, settled Portsmouth, 1638. Quaker and Jewish immigrants seeking freedom of worship began arriving, 1650s-60s. The colonists broke the power of the Narragansett in the Great Swamp Fight, 1675, the decisive battle in King Philip's War. British trade restrictions angered colonists, and they burned the British customs vessel *Gaspee*, 1772. The colony became the first to formally renounce all allegiance to King George III, May 4, 1776. Initially opposed to joining the Union, Rhode Island was the last of the original 13 colonies to ratify the Constitution, 1790.

**Tourist attractions.** Newport mansions; yachting races including Newport to Bermuda; Block Island; Touro Synagogue, oldest in U.S., Newport; first Baptist Church in America, Providence; Slater Mill Historic Site, Pawtucket; Gilbert Stuart birthplace, Saunderstown.

**Famous Rhode Islanders.** Ambrose Burnside, George M. Cohan, Nelson Eddy, Jabez Gorham, Nathanael Greene, Christopher and Oliver La Farge, Matthew C. and Oliver Hazard Perry, Gilbert Stuart.

**Chamber of Commerce.** 30 Exchange Terr., Providence, RI 02908.

**Toll-free travel information.** 1-800-556-2484.

**World Wide Web site.** http://www.state.ri.us

## South Carolina

*Palmetto State*

**People. Population** (1995): 3,673,287; **rank:** 26; **Net change** (1990-95): 5.4%. **Pop. density:** (1990) 119.7 per sq mi. **Racial/ethnic distrib.** (1990): 69.0% white; 29.8% black; 0.9% Hispanic.

**Geography. Total area:** 32,008 sq mi; **rank:** 40. **Land area:** 30,111 sq mi. **Acres forested land:** 12,257,000. **Location:** South Atlantic state, bordered by North Carolina on the N; Georgia on the SW and W; the Atlantic Ocean on the E, SE, and S. **Climate:** humid subtropical. **Topography:** Blue Ridge province in NW has highest peaks; piedmont lies between the mountains and the fall line; coastal plain covers two-thirds of the state. **Capital:** Columbia.

**Economy. Principal industries:** tourism, agriculture, manufacturing. **Principal manufactured goods:** textiles, chemicals and allied products, machinery & fabricated metal products, apparel and related products. **Chief crops:** tobacco, soybeans, corn, cotton, peaches, hay. **Livestock** (1994): 500,000 cattle; 350,000 hogs/pigs; 6.3 mil chickens, excluding broilers. **Timber/lumber** (1995): pine, oak; 1.32 bil bd. ft. **Nonfuel minerals** (est. 1995): $426 mil; mostly portland cement, crushed stone, construction and masonary sand & gravel. **Commercial fishing** (1995): $38 mil. **Chief ports:** Charleston, Georgetown, Beaufort/ Port Royal. **International airports at:** Charleston. **Value of construction** (1995): $4.6 bil. **Employment distribution** (1995): 22.9% mfg.; 22% serv.; 23.3% trade; 6.1% govt. **Per capita personal income** (1995): $18,788. **Unemployment** (1995): 5.1%. **Tourism** (1995): $13.2 bil.

**Finance. FDIC-insured commercial banks & trust companies** (1995): 71. **Deposits:** $19.7 bil. **FDIC-insured savings institutions** (1995): 33. **Assets:** $7.3 bil.

**Federal government. No. federal civilian employees** (Mar. 1995): 19,391. **Avg. salary:** $35,028. **Notable federal facilities:** Polaris Submarine Base; Barnwell Nuclear Power Plant; Ft. Jackson; Parris Island; Savannah River Plant.

**Energy. Electricity production** (1995, kWh, by source): Coal: 25.8 bil.; Petroleum: 130 mil; Gas: 600 mil; Hydroelectric: 2.7 bil; Nuclear: 49.2 bil.

**Public education. Student-teacher ratio** (1994): 16.4. **Avg. teachers' salary** (1995-96): $31,568.

**State data. Motto:** Dum Spiro Spero (While I breathe, I hope). **Flower:** Yellow jessamine. **Bird:** Carolina wren. **Tree:** Palmetto. **Song:** Carolina. **Eighth** of the original 13 states to ratify the Constitution, May 23, 1788. **State fair** at Columbia; mid-Oct.

**History.** At the time of European settlement, Cherokee, Catawba, and Muskogean peoples lived in the area. The first English colonists settled near the Ashley River, 1670, and moved to the site of Charleston, 1680. The colonists seized the government, 1775, and the royal governor fled. The British took Charleston, 1780, but were defeated at Kings Mountain that same year, and at Cowpens and Eutaw Springs, 1781. In the 1830s, South Carolinians, angered by federal protective tariffs, adopted the Nullification Doctrine, holding that a state can void an act of Congress. The state was the first to secede from the Union, 1861, and Confederate troops fired on and forced the surrender of U.S. troops at Ft. Sumter, in Charleston Harbor, launching the Civil War. South Carolina was readmitted,1868.

**Tourist attractions.** Historic Charleston; Ft. Sumter Natl. Monument, in Charleston Harbor; Charleston Museum, est. 1773, oldest museum in U.S.; Middleton Place, Magnolia Plantation, Cypress Gardens, Drayton Hall, all near Charleston; other gardens at Brookgreen, Edisto, Glencairn; Myrtle Beach; Hilton Head Island; American Revolution War battle sites; Andrew Jackson State Park & Museum; South Carolina State Museum, Columbia; Riverbanks Zoo, Columbia.

**Famous South Carolinians.** Charles Bolden, James F. Byrnes, John C. Calhoun, DuBose Heyward, Ernest F. Hollings, Andrew Jackson, Jesse Jackson, James Longstreet, Francis Marion, Ronald McNair, Charles Pinckney, John Rutledge, Thomas Sumter, Strom Thurmond, John B. Watson.

**Tourist information.** S. Carolina Dept. of Parks, Recreation, & Tourism, 803-734-0122.
**Toll-free travel information.** 1-800-346-3634.
**World Wide Web site.** http://www.state.sc.us

## South Dakota

*Coyote State, Mount Rushmore State*

**People. Population** (1995): 729,034; **rank:** 45; **Net change** (1990-95): 4.7%. **Pop. density:** (1990) 9.37 per sq mi. **Racial/ethnic distrib.** (1990): 91.6% white; 0.5% black; 7.3% Amer. Indian; 0.8% Hispanic.

**Geography. Total area:** 77,121 sq mi; **rank:** 17. **Land area:** 75,896 sq mi. **Acres forested land:** 1,690,000. **Location:** West North Central state bounded on the N by North Dakota; on the E by Minnesota and Iowa; on the S by Nebraska; on the W by Wyoming and Montana. **Climate:** characterized by extremes of temperature, persistent winds, low precipitation and humidity. **Topography:** Prairie Plains in the E; rolling hills of the Great Plains in the W; the Black Hills, rising 3,500 ft, in the SW corner. **Capital:** Pierre.

**Economy. Principal industries:** agriculture, services, manufacturing. **Principal manufactured goods:** food & kindred products, machinery, electric & electronic equipment. **Chief crops:** corn, oats, wheat, sunflowers, soybeans, sorghum. **Livestock** (1995): 3.9 mil cattle; 1.5 mil hogs/pigs; 500,000 sheep. **Timber/lumber** ponderosa pine. **Nonfuel minerals** (est. 1995): $317 mil; mostly gold, portland cement, construction sand & gravel. **Value of construction** (1995): $705.5 mil. **Employment distribution** (1995): 26% serv.; 14% mfg. **Per capita personal income** (1995): $19,506. **Unemployment** (1995): 2.9%. **Tourism** (1994): travelers' impact $1.24 bil.

**Finance. FDIC-insured commercial banks & trust companies** (1995): 116. **Deposits:** $11.9 bil. **FDIC-insured savings institutions** (1995): 6. **Assets:** $924 mil.

**Federal government. No. federal civilian employees** (Mar. 1995): 7,032. **Avg. salary:** $34,080. **Notable federal facilities:** Ellsworth AFB, Corp of Engineers, Nat'l Park Service.

**Energy. Electricity production** (1995, kWh, by source): Coal: 2.7 bil; Petroleum: 17 mil; Gas: 63 mil; Hydroelectric: 6.0 bil.

**Public education. Student-teacher ratio** (1994): 14.4. **Avg. teachers' salary** (1995-96): $26,346.

**State data. Motto:** Under God, the people rule. **Flower:** Pasqueflower. **Bird:** Chinese ring-necked pheasant. **Tree:** Black Hills spruce. **Song:** Hail, South Dakota. **Entered union** Nov. 2, 1889; rank, 40th. **State fair** at Huron; late Aug.-early Sept.

**History.** At the time of first European contact, Mandan, Hidatsa, Arikara and Sioux lived in the area. The French Verendrye brothers explored the region, 1742-43. The U.S. acquired the area, 1803, in the Louisiana Purchase. Lewis and Clark passed through the area, 1804-6. The first permanent American settlement was at Fort Pierre, 1817. Gold was discovered, 1874, in the Black Hills on the great Sioux reservation; the "Great Dakota Boom" began in 1879. Conflicts with Native Americans led to the Great Sioux Agreement, 1889, which established reservations and opened up more land for white settlement. The massacre of Native American families at Wounded Knee, 1890, ended Sioux resistance.

**Tourist attractions.** Black Hills; Mt. Rushmore; Needles Highway; Harney Peak, tallest peak east of the Rockies; Deadwood, 1876 Gold Rush town; Custer State Park; Jewel Cave Natl. Monument; Badlands Natl. Park "moonscape"; "Great Lakes of S. Dakota"; Ft. Sisseton; Great Plains Zoo & Museum, Sioux Falls; Corn Palace, Mitchell; Wind Cave Natl. Park; Crazy Horse Memorial, mountain carving in progress.

**Famous South Dakotans.** Sparky Anderson, Tom Brokaw, Crazy Horse, Thomas Daschle, Myron Floren, Mary Hart, Cheryl Ladd, Dr. Ernest O. Lawrence, George McGovern, Billy Mills, Allen Neuharth, Pat O'Brien, Sitting Bull.

**Tourist information.** South Dakota Tourism, 711 E. Wells Ave., Pierre, SD 57501-3369.
**Toll-free travel information.** 1-800-SDAKOTA.
**World Wide Web site.** http://www.state.sd.us

## Tennessee

*Volunteer State*

**People. Population** (1995): 5,256,051; **rank:** 17; **Net change** (1990-95): 7.8%. **Pop. density:** (1990) 121.9 per sq mi. **Racial/ethnic distrib.** (1990): 83.0% white; 16.0% black; 0.7% Hispanic.

**Geography. Total area:** 42,146 sq mi; **rank:** 36. **Land area:** 41,219 sq mi. **Acres forested land:** 13,612,000. **Location:** East South Central state bounded on the N by Kentucky and Virginia; on the E by North Carolina; on the S by Georgia, Alabama, and Mississippi; on the W by Arkansas and Missouri. **Climate:** humid continental to the N; humid subtropical to the S. **Topography:** rugged country in the E; the Great Smoky Mts. of the Unakas; low ridges of the Appalachian Valley; the flat Cumberland Plateau; slightly rolling terrain and knobs of the Interior Low Plateau, the largest region; Eastern Gulf Coastal Plain to the W, laced with streams; Mississippi Alluvial Plain, a narrow strip of swamp and flood plain in the extreme W. **Capital:** Nashville.

**Economy. Principal industries:** manufacturing, trade, services, tourism, finance, insurance, real estate. **Principal manufactured goods:** chemicals, food, transportation equipment, industrial machinery & equipment, fabricated metal products, rubber/plastic products, paper & allied products, printing and publishing. **Chief crops:** tobacco, cotton, lint, soybeans, grain, corn. **Livestock** (1994): 2.44 mil cattle; 470,000 hogs/pigs; 1.3 mil poultry. **Timber/lumber** (1995): red oak, white oak, yellow poplar, hickory; 920 mil bd. ft. **Nonfuel minerals** (est. 1995): $659 mil; mostly crushed stone, sand & gravel, zinc, cement. **Chief ports:** Memphis, Nashville, Chattanooga, Knoxville. **International airports at:** Memphis, Nashville. **Value of construction** (1995): $7.2 bil. **Employment distribution** (1995): 21.1% mfg.; 22.9% trade; 24.7% serv.; 14.6% govt. **Per capita personal income** (1995): $20,376. **Unemployment** (1995): 5.2%. **Tourism** (1993): out-of-state visitors spent $5.15 bil.

**Finance. FDIC-insured commercial banks & trust companies** (1995): 240. **Deposit:** $52.4 bil. **FDIC-insured savings institutions** (1995): 25. **Assets:** $6.8 bil.

**Federal government. No. federal civilian employees** (Mar. 1995): 34,465. **Avg. salary:** $38,988. **Notable federal facilities:** Tennessee Valley Authority; Oak Ridge Nat'l. Laboratories; Arnold Engineering Development Center; Ft. Campbell Army Base; Millington Naval Station.

**Energy. Electricity production** (1995, kWh, by source): Coal: 58.0 bil; Petroleum: 253 mil; Gas: 158 mil; Hydroelectric: 8.2 bil; Nuclear: 15.7 bil.

**Public education. Student-teacher ratio** (1994): 18.6. **Avg. teachers' salary** (1995-96): $33,451.

**State data. Motto:** Agriculture and commerce. **Flower:** Iris. **Bird:** Mockingbird. **Tree:** Tulip poplar. **Song:** The Tennessee Waltz. **Entered union** June 1, 1796; rank, 16th. **State fair** at Nashville; mid-Sept.

**History.** When the first European explorers arrived, Creek and Yuchi peoples lived in the area; the Cherokee moved into the region in the early 18th cent. Spanish explorers first visited the area, 1541. English traders crossed the Great Smokies from the east while France's Marquette and Jolliet sailed down the Mississippi on the west, 1673. The first permanent settlement was by Virginians on the Watauga River, 1769. During the American Revolution, the colonists helped win the Battle of Kings Mountain (NC), 1780, and joined other eastern campaigns. The state seceded from the Union, 1861, and saw many Civil War engagements, but 30,000 soldiers fought for the Union. Tennessee was readmitted in 1866, the only former Confederate state not to have a postwar military government.

**Tourist attractions.** Reelfoot Lake; Lookout Mountain, Chattanooga; Fall Creek Falls; Great Smoky Mountains Natl. Park; Lost Sea, Sweetwater; Cherokee Natl. Forest; Cumberland Gap Natl. Park; Andrew Jackson's home, the Hermitage, near Nashville; homes of presidents Polk and Andrew Johnson; American Museum of Science and Energy, Oak Ridge; Parthenon, Grand Old Opry, Opryland USA, all Nashville; Dollywood theme park, Pigeon Forge; Tennessee Aquarium, Chattanooga; Graceland, home of Elvis Presley, Memphis; Alex Haley Home & Museum, Henning; Casey Jones Home & Museum, Jackson.

**Famous Tennesseans.** Roy Acuff, Davy Crockett, David Farragut, Ernie Ford, Aretha Franklin, Alex Haley, William C. Handy, Sam Houston, Cordell Hull, Andrew Jackson, Andrew Johnson, Casey Jones, Grace Moore, Dolly Parton, Minnie Pearl, James Polk, Elvis Presley, Dinah Shore, Bessie Smith, Alvin York.

**Tourist information.** Dept. of Tourist Development, 5th Floor, Rachel Jackson Bldg., 320 6th Ave. N., Nashville, TN 37202.

**Toll-free travel information.** 1-800-TENN200.

**World Wide Web site.** http://www.state.tn.us

## Texas

*Lone Star State*

**People. Population** (1995): 18,723,991; **rank:** 2; **Net change** (1990-95): 10.2%. **Pop. density:** (1990) 67.4 per sq mi. **Racial/ethnic distrib.** (1990): 75.2% white; 11.9% black; 25.5% Hispanic.

**Geography. Total area:** 268,601 sq mi; **rank:** 2. **Land area:** 261,914 sq mi; **Acres forested land:** 19,193,000. **Location:** Southwestern state, bounded on the SE by the Gulf of Mexico; on the SW by Mexico, separated by the Rio Grande; surrounding states are Louisiana, Arkansas, Oklahoma, New Mexico. **Climate:** extremely varied; driest region is the Trans-Pecos; wettest is the NE. **Topography:** Gulf Coast Plain in the S and SE; North Central Plains slope upward with some hills; the Great Plains extend over the Panhandle, are broken by low mountains; the Trans-Pecos is the southern extension of the Rockies. **Capital:** Austin.

**Economy. Principal industries:** trade, oil and gas extraction, services, manufacturing. **Principal manufactured goods:** industrial machinery & equipment, foods, electrical and electronic products, chemicals and allied products, apparel. **Chief crops:** cotton, grain sorghum, grains, vegetables, citrus and other fruits, pecans, peanuts. **Livestock** (1996): 15 mil cattle; 500,000 hogs/pigs; 1.7 mil sheep; 19.3 mil poultry. **Timber/lumber** (1995): pine, cypress; 1.60 bil bd. ft. **Nonfuel minerals** (est. 1995): $1.7 bil; mostly portland cement, crushed stone, magnesium, gypsum, construction sand & gravel, lime, salt. **Commercial fishing** (1995): $199 mil. **Chief ports:** Houston, Galveston, Brownsville, Beaumont, Port Arthur, Corpus Christi. **Major international airports at:** Houston, Dallas/Ft. Worth, San Antonio. **Value of construction** (1995): $22.8 bil. **Employment distribution** (1995): 24.3% trade; 26.4% serv.; 18.1% govt.; 12.8% mfg. **Per capita personal income** (1995): $20,654. **Unemployment** (1995): 6.0%. **Tourism** (1994): all travel $24.6 bil.

**Finance. FDIC-insured commercial banks & trust companies** (1995): 935. **Deposits:** $155.3 bil. **FDIC-insured savings institutions** (1995): 58. **Assets:** $59.7 bil.

**Federal government. No. federal civilian employees** (Mar. 1995): 113,447. **Avg. salary:** $37,367. **Notable federal facilities:** Fort Hood (Killeen); Kelly AFB and Ft. Sam Houston, both San Antonio.

**Energy. Electricity production** (1995, kWh, by source): Coal: 122.1 bil; Petroleum: 203 mil; Gas: 101.5 bil; Hydroelectric: 1.7 bil; Nuclear: 36.2 bil.

**Public education. Student-teacher ratio** (1994): 15.7. **Avg. teachers' salary** (1995-96): $32,000.

**State data. Motto:** Friendship. **Flower:** Bluebonnet. **Bird:** Mockingbird. **Tree:** Pecan. **Song:** Texas, Our Texas. **Entered union** Dec. 29, 1845; rank, 28th. **State fair** at Dallas; mid-Oct.

**History.** At the time of European contact, Native American tribes in the region were numerous and diverse in culture. Coahuiltecan, Karankawa, Caddo, Jumano, and Tonkawa peoples lived in the area, and during the 19th cent., the Apache, Comanche, Cherokee, and Wichita arrived. Spanish explorer Pineda sailed along the Texas coast, 1519; Cabeza de Vaca and Coronado visited the interior, 1541. Spaniards made the first settlement at Ysleta, near El Paso, 1682. Americans moved into the land early in the 19th cent. Mexico, of which Texas was a part, won independence from Spain, 1821; Santa Anna became dictator in 1835; Texans rebelled. Santa Anna wiped out defenders of the Alamo, 1836; Sam Houston's Texans defeated Santa Anna at San Jacinto, and independence was proclaimed that same year. The Republic of Texas, with Sam Houston as its first president, functioned as a nation until 1845, when it was admitted to the Union.

**Tourist attractions.** Padre Island Natl. Seashore; Big Bend, Guadalupe Mts. natl. parks; The Alamo; Ft. Davis; Six Flags Amusement Park; Sea World and Fiesta Texas, both in San Antonio; San Antonio Missions Natl. Park; Cowgirl Hall of Fame, Fort Worth; Lyndon B. Johnson Natl. Park, marking his birthplace, boyhood home, and ranch, near Johnson City; Lyndon B. Johnson Library and Museum, Austin.

**Famous Texans.** Stephen F. Austin, Lloyd Bentsen, James Bowie, Carol Burnett, J. Frank Dobie, Dwight D. Eisenhower, Sam Houston, Howard Hughes, Lyndon B. Johnson, Mary Martin, Chester Nimitz, H. Ross Perot, Katharine Ann Porter, Sam Rayburn.

**Chamber of Commerce.** 900 Congress, Suite 501, Austin, TX 78701.

**Toll-free travel information.** 1-800-8888TEX.

**World Wide Web site.** http://www.state.tx.us

## Utah

*Beehive State*

**People. Population** (1995): 1,951,408; **rank:** 34; **Net change** (1990-95): 13.3%. **Pop. density:** (1990) 22.1 per sq mi. **Racial/ethnic distrib.** (1990): 93.8% white; 0.7% black; 4.9% Hispanic.

**Geography. Total area:** 84,904 sq mi; **rank:** 13. **Land area:** 82,168 sq mi. **Acres forested land:** 16,234,000. **Location:** Middle Rocky Mountain state; its southeastern corner touches Colorado, New Mexico, and Arizona, and is the only spot in the U.S. where 4 states join. **Climate:** arid; ranging from warm desert in SW to alpine in NE. **Topography:** high Colorado plateau is cut by brilliantly colored canyons of the SE; broad, flat, desert-like Great Basin of the W; the Great Salt Lake and Bonneville Salt Flats to the NW; Middle Rockies in the NE run E-W; valleys and plateaus of the Wasatch Front. **Capital:** Salt Lake City.

**Economy. Principal industries:** services, trade, manufacturing, government, transportation, utilities. **Principal manufactured goods:** medical instruments, electronic components, food products, fabricated metals, transportation equipment, steel and copper. **Chief crops:** hay, corn, wheat, barley, apples, potatoes, cherries, onions, peaches, pears. **Livestock:** (1995) 910,000 cattle; 63,000 hogs/pigs; 395,000 sheep; 5.7 mil poultry. **Timber/lumber:** (1995) aspen, spruce, pine; 44 mil bd. ft. **Nonfuel minerals** (est. 1995): $1.8 bil; copper, potash, gold, molybdenum, iron ore, magnesium, phosphate rock, salt. **International airports at:** Salt Lake City. **Value of construction** (1995): $3.7 bil. **Employment distribution** (1995): 35.7% serv.; 24.2% trade; 7.0% govt; 13.6% mfg. **Per capita personal income** (1995): $18,223. **Unemployment** (1995): 3.6%. **Tourism** (1995): travelers spent $3.6 bil.

**Finance. FDIC-insured commercial banks & trust companies** (1995): 45. **Deposits:** $13.8 bil. **FDIC-insured savings institutions** (1995): 3. **Assets:** $630 mil.

**Federal government. No. federal civilian employees** (Mar. 1995): 25,926. **Avg. salary:** $34,845. **Notable federal facilities:** Hill AFB; Tooele Army Depot; IRS Western Service Center.

**Energy. Electricity production** (1995, kWh, by source): Coal: 30.3 bil; Petroleum: 34 mil; Gas: 741 mil; Hydroelectric: 926 mil.

**Public education. Student-teacher ratio** (1994): 24.3. **Avg. teachers' salary** (1995-96): $30,452.

**State data. Motto:** Industry. **Flower:** Sego lily. **Bird:** Seagull. **Tree:** Blue spruce. **Song:** Utah, We Love Thee. **Entered union** Jan. 4, 1896; rank, 45th. **State fair** at Salt Lake City; Sept.

**History.** Ute, Gosiute, Southern Paiute, and Navajo peoples lived in the region at the time of European contact. Spanish Franciscans visited the area, 1776, the first white men to do so. American fur traders followed. Permanent settlement began with the arrival of the Mormons, 1847; they made the arid land bloom and created a prosperous economy. The State of Deseret was organized in 1849, and asked admission to the Union. In 1850, Congress established the region as the territory of Utah, and Brigham Young was appointed governor. The Union and Pacific Railroads met near Promontory, May 10, 1869, creating the first transcontinental railroad. Statehood was not achieved until 1896, after a long period of controversy over the Mormon Church's doctrine of polygamy, which it discontinued in 1890.

**Tourist attractions.** Temple Square, Mormon Church headquarters, Salt Lake City; Great Salt Lake; Natural Zion, Canyonlands, Bryce Canyon, Arches, and Capitol Reef natl. parks; Dinosaur, Rainbow Bridge, Timpanogos Cave, and Natural Bridges natl. monuments; Lake Powell; Flaming Gorge Natl. Recreation Area.

**Famous Utahans.** Maude Adams, Ezra Taft Benson, John Moses Browning, Mariner Eccles, Philo Farnsworth, James Fletcher, David M. Kennedy, J. Willard Marriott, Merlin Olsen, Osmond family, Ivy Baker Priest, George Romney, Brigham Young, Loretta Young.

**Tourist information.** Utah Travel Council, Council Hall, Salt Lake City, UT 84114; 801-538-1030.

**World Wide Web site.** http://www.state.ut.us

## Vermont

*Green Mountain State*

**People. Population** (1995): 584,771; **rank:** 49; **Net change** (1990-95): 3.9%. **Pop. density:** (1990) 61.6 per sq mi. **Racial/ethnic distrib.** (1990): 98.6% white; 0.3% black; 0.6% Asian; 0.7% Hispanic.

**Geography. Total area:** 9,615 sq mi; **rank:** 45. **Land area:** 9,249 sq mi. **Acres forested land:** 4,538,000. **Location:** northern New England state. **Climate:** temperate, with considerable temperature extremes; heavy snowfall in mountains. **Topography:** Green Mts. N-S backbone 20-36 mi wide; avg. altitude 1,000 ft. **Capital:** Montpelier.

**Economy. Principal industries:** manufacturing, tourism, agriculture, trade; finance, insurance, real estate, government. **Principal manufactured goods:** machine tools, furniture, scales, books, computer components, speciality foods. **Chief crops:** dairy products, apples, maple syrup, greenhouse/nursery, vegetables and small fruits. **Livestock** (1995): 290,000 cattle/cows; 2,800 hogs/pigs; 19,200 sheep/lambs; 76,000 hens/pullets; 27,000 turkeys. **Timber/lumber** (1995): pine, spruce, fir, hemlock; 246 mil bd. ft. **Nonfuel minerals** (est. 1995): $68 mil; mostly dimension stone, crushed stone, construction sand & gravel, asbestos. **International airports at:** Burlington. **Value of construction** (1995): $482.4 mil. **Employment distribution** (1994): 29% serv.; 24% trade; 17% mfg 17% govt. **Per capita personal income** (1995): $20,927. **Unemployment** (1995): 4.2%. **Tourism** (1995): visitors spent $2.2 bil.

**Finance. FDIC-insured commercial banks & trust companies** (1995): 20. **Deposits:** $5.1 bil. **FDIC-insured savings institutions** (1995): 8. **Assets:** $2.7 bil.

**Federal government. No. federal civilian employees** (Mar. 1995): 2,763. **Avg. salary:** $36,248.

**Energy. Electricity production** (1995, kWh, by source): Petroleum: 13 mil; Gas: 7 mil; Hydroelectric: 834 mil; Nuclear: 3.9 bil.

**Public education. Student-teacher ratio** (1994): 13.8. **Avg. teachers' salary** (1995-96): $36,295.

**State data. Motto:** Freedom and unity. **Flower:** Red clover. **Bird:** Hermit thrush. **Tree:** Sugar maple. **Song:** Hail, Vermont. **Entered union** Mar. 4, 1791; rank, 14th. **State fair** at Rutland; early Sept.

**History.** Before the arrival of the Europeans, Abnaki and Mahican peoples lived in the region. Champlain explored the lake that bears his name, 1609. The first American settlement was Ft. Dummer, 1724, near Brattleboro. During the American Revolution, Ethan Allen and the Green Mountain Boys captured Ft. Ticonderoga (NY), 1775; John Stark defeated part of Burgoyne's forces near Bennington, 1777. In the War of 1812, Thomas MacDonough defeated a British fleet on Lake Champlain off Plattsburgh (NY), 1814.

**Tourist attractions.** Shelburne Museum; Rock of Ages Quarry, Graniteville; Vermont Marble Exhibit, Proctor; Bennington Battle Monument; Pres. Calvin Coolidge homestead, Plymouth; Maple Grove Maple Museum, St. Johnsbury; Ben & Jerry's Factory, Waterbury.

**Famous Vermonters.** Ethan Allen, Chester A. Arthur, Calvin Coolidge, George Dewey, John Dewey, Stephen A. Douglas, Dorothy Canfield Fisher, James Fisk.

**Chamber of Commerce.** PO Box 37, Montpelier, VT 05601.

**Tourist information.** Vermont Dept. of Tourism and Marketing, 134 State St., Montpelier, VT 05602; 802-828-3237 .

**Toll-free travel information.** 1-800-VERMONT

**World Wide Web site.** http://www.state.vt.us

## Virginia

*Old Dominion*

**People. Population** (1995): 6,618,358; **rank:** 12; **Net change** (1990-95): 6.9%. **Pop. density:** (1990) 161.0 per sq mi. **Racial/ethnic distrib.** (1990): 77.4% white; 18.8% black; 2.6% Asian; 2.6% Hispanic.

**Geography. Total area:** 42,777 sq mi; **rank:** 35. **Land area:** 39,598 sq mi. **Acres forested land:** 15,858,000. **Location:** South Atlantic state bounded by the Atlantic Ocean on the E and surrounded by North Carolina, Tennessee, Kentucky, West Virginia, and Maryland. **Climate:** mild and equable. **Topography:** mountain and valley region in the W, including the Blue Ridge Mts.; rolling piedmont plateau; tidewater, or coastal plain, including the eastern shore. **Capital:** Richmond.

**Economy. Principal industries:** services, trade, government, manufacturing, tourism, agriculture. **Principal manufactured goods:** textiles, transportation equipment, electric & electronic equipment, food processing, chemicals, printing lumber and wood products, apparel. **Chief crops:** soy-beans, grain corn tobacco, peanuts, corn, far grain. **Livestock** (1994): 1.7 mil cattle; 390,000 hogs/pigs; 99,000 sheep; 238.1 mil broilers, 19.3 mil turkeys. **Timber/lumber** (1995): pine and hardwoods; 1.3 bil bd. ft. **Nonfuel minerals** (est. 1995): $517 mil; mostly crushed stone, lime, construction sand & gravel. **Commercial fishing** (1995): $114 mil. **Chief ports:** Hampton Roads, Richmond, Alexandria. **International airports at:** Norfolk, Dulles, Richmond, Newport News. **Value of construction** (1995): $8.8 bil. **Employment distribution** (1992): 27% serv.; 14% trade; 24% govt.; 14% mfg. **Per capita personal income** (1995): $23,597. **Unemployment** (1995): 4.5%. **Tourism** (1994): domestic travelers spent $9.4 bil.

**Finance. FDIC-insured commercial banks & trust companies** (1995): 157. **Deposits:** $56.4 bil. **FDIC-insured savings institutions** (1995): 32. **Assets:** $9.1 bil.

**Federal government. No. federal civilian employees** (Mar. 1995): 130,490. **Avg. salary:** $44,483. **Notable federal facilities:** Pentagon; Naval Sta., Norfolk; Naval Air Sta., Norfolk, Virginia Beach; Naval Shipyard, Portsmouth; Marine Corps Base, Quantico; Langley AFB; NASA at Langley.

**Energy. Electricity production** (1995, kWh, by source): Coal: 24.4 bil; Petroleum: 1.1 bil; Gas: 1.9 bil; Hydroelectric: 149 mil; Nuclear: 25.1 bil.

**Public education. Student-teacher ratio** (1994): 14.6. **Avg. teachers' salary** (1995-96): $34,687.

**State data. Motto:** Sic Semper Tyrannis (Thus always to tyrants). **Flower:** Dogwood. **Bird:** Cardinal. **Tree:** Dogwood. **Song:** Carry Me Back to Old Virginia. **Tenth** of the original 13 states to ratify the Constitution, June 25, 1788. **State fair** at Richmond; late Sept.-early Oct.

**History.** Living in the area at the time of European contact were the Cherokee and Susquehanna and the Algonquians of the Powhatan Confederacy. English settlers founded Jamestown, 1607. Virginians took over much of the government from royal governor Dunmore, 1775, forcing him to flee. Virginians under George Rogers Clark freed the Ohio-Indiana-Illinois area of British forces. Benedict Arnold burned Richmond and Petersburg for the British, 1781. That same year, Britain's Cornwallis was trapped at Yorktown and surrendered, ending the American Revolution. Virginia seceded from the Union, 1861, and Richmond became the capital of the Confederacy. Hampton Roads, off the Virginia coast, was the site of the famous naval battle of the USS *Monitor* and CSS *Virginia* (Merrimac), 1862. Virginia was readmitted, 1870.

**Tourist attractions.** Colonial Williamsburg; Busch Gardens, Williamsburg; Wolf Trap Farm, near Falls Church; Arlington Natl. Cemetery; Mt. Vernon, home of George Washington; Jamestown Festival Park; Yorktown; Jefferson's Monticello, Charlottesville; Robert E. Lee's birthplace, Stratford Hall, and grave, Lexington; Appomattox; Shenandoah Natl. Park; Blue Ridge Parkway; Virginia Beach; Paramount's King's Dominion, near Richmond.

**Famous Virginians.** Richard E. Byrd, James B. Cabell, Jerry Falwell, William Henry Harrison, Patrick Henry, Thomas Jefferson, Joseph E. Johnston, Robert E. Lee, Meriwether Lewis and William Clark, James Madison, John Marshall, George Mason, James Monroe, Edgar Allan Poe, Walter Reed, Zachary Taylor, John Tyler, Maggie Walker, Booker T. Washington, George Washington, Woodrow Wilson.

**Chamber of Commerce.** 9 South Fifth St., Richmond, VA 23219.

**Toll-free travel information.** 1-800-VISITVA.

**World Wide Web site.** http://www.state.va.us

## Washington

*Evergreen State*

**People. Population** (1995): 5,430,940; **rank:** 15; **Net change** (1990-95): 11.6%. **Pop. density:** (1990) 77.1 per sq mi. **Racial/ethnic distrib.** (1990): 88.5% white; 3.1% black; 4.3% Asian; 4.4% Hispanic.

**Geography. Total area:** 71,302 sq mi; **rank:** 18. **Land area:** 66,581 sq mi. **Acres forested land:** 20,483,000. **Location:** Pacific state bordered by Canada on the N; Idaho on the E; Oregon on the S; and the Pacific Ocean on the W. **Climate:** mild, dominated by the Pacific Ocean and protected by the Rockies. **Topography:** Olympic Mts. on NW peninsula; open land along coast to Columbia R.; flat terrain of Puget Sound Lowland; Cascade Mts. region's high peaks to the E; Columbia Basin in central portion; highlands to the NE; mountains to the SE. **Capital:** Olympia.

**Economy. Principal industries:** forestry, aerospace, manufacturing, agriculture. **Principal manufactured goods:** aircraft, pulp and paper, lumber and plywood, aluminum, processed fruits and vegetables, machinery, electronics, computer software. **Chief crops:** apples, potatoes, hay, farm forest products. **Livestock** (1994): 1.3 mil cattle; 32,000 hogs/pigs; 55,000 sheep; 7.2 mil poultry, excluding commercial broilers. **Timber/lumber** (1995): Douglas fir, hemlock, cedar, pine; 4.0 bil bd. ft. **Nonfuel minerals** (est. 1995): $613 mil; mostly construction sand & gravel, crushed stone, magnesium metal, portland cement. **Commercial fishing** (1995): $115.4 mil. **Chief ports:** Seattle, Tacoma, Vancouver, Kelso-Longview. **International airports at:** Seattle/Tacoma, Spokane, Boeing Field. **Value of construction** (1995): $7.3 bil. **Employment distribution** (1995): 24.8% trade; 26.5% serv.; 18.9% govt.; 14.1% mfg. **Per capita personal income** (1995): $23,639. **Unemployment** (1995): 6.4%. **Tourism** (1994): $7.5 bil.

**Finance. FDIC-insured commercial banks & trust companies** (1995): 87. **Deposits:** $37.9 bil. **FDIC-insured savings institutions** (1995): 23. **Assets:** $34.7 bil.

**Federal government. No. federal civilian employees** (Mar. 1995): 46,886. **Avg. salary:** $39,839. **Notable federal facilities:** Bonneville Power Admin.; Ft. Lewis; McChord AFB; Hanford Nuclear Reservation; Bremerton Naval Shipyards.

**Energy. Electricity production** (1995, kWh, by source): Coal: 5.9 bil; Petroleum: 9 mil; Gas: 554 mil; Hydroelectric: 82.0 bil; Nuclear: 6.9 bil.

**Public education. Student-teacher ratio** (1994): 20.2. **Avg. teachers' salary** (1995-96): $38,025.

**State data. Motto:** Alki (By and by). **Flower:** Western rhododendron. **Bird:** Willow goldfinch. **Tree:** Western hemlock. **Song:** Washington, My Home. **Entered union** Nov. 11, 1889; rank, 42d. **State fairs:** various county fairs, mostly in Aug. or Sept.

**History.** At the time of European contact, many Native American tribes lived in the area, including the Nez Percé, Spokan, Yakima, Cayuse, Okanogan, Walla Walla, and Colville peoples, who lived in the interior region, and the Nooksak, Chinook, Nisqually, Clallam, Makah, Quinault, and Puyallup peoples, who inhabited the coastal area. Spain's Bruno Hezeta sailed the coast, 1775. In 1792, British naval officer George Vancouver mapped Puget Sound area, and that same year, American Capt. Robert Gray sailed up the Columbia River. Canadian fur traders set up Spokane House, 1810. Americans under John Jacob Astor established a post at Ft. Okanogan, 1811, and missionary Marcus Whitman settled near Walla Walla, 1836. Final agreement on the border of Washington and Canada was made with Britain, 1846, and Washington became part of the Oregon Territory, 1848. Gold was discovered, 1855.

**Tourist attractions.** Mt. Rainier, Olympic, and North Cascades natl. parks; Mt. St. Helens; Puget Sound; Seattle Waterfront, Seattle Center and Space Needle, Museum of Flight, all Seattle; San Juan Islands; Grand Coulee Dam; Columbia R. Gorge Natl. Scenic Area; Spokane's Riverfront Park.

**Famous Washingtonians.** Bing Crosby, William O. Douglas, Bill Gates, Henry M. Jackson, Gary Larson, Mary McCarthy, Edward R. Murrow, Theodore Roethke, Marcus Whitman, Minoru Yamasaki.

**Tourist information.** WA State Tourism Division, PO Box 42500, Olympia, WA 98504-2500.

**Toll-free travel information.** 1-800-544-1800. ext. 101

**World Wide Web site.** http://www.wa.gov

## West Virginia

*Mountain State*

**People. Population** (1995): 1,828,140; **rank:** 35; **Net change** (1990-95): 1.9%. **Pop. density:** (1990) 75.2 per sq mi. **Racial/ethnic distrib.** (1990): 96.2% white; 3.1% black; 0.5% Hispanic.

**Geography. Total area:** 24,231 sq mi; **rank:** 41. **Land area:** 24,087 sq mi. **Acres forested land:** 12,128,000. **Location:** South Atlantic state bounded on the N by Ohio, Pennsylvania, Maryland; on the S and W by Virginia, Kentucky, Ohio; on the E by Maryland and Virginia. **Climate:** humid continental climate except for marine modification in the lower panhandle. **Topography:** ranging from hilly to mountainous; Allegheny Plateau in the W, covers two-thirds of the state; mountains here are the highest in the state, over 4,000 ft. **Capital:** Charleston.

**Economy. Principal industries:** manufacturing, services, mining, tourism. **Principal manufactured goods:** machinery, plastic and hardwood products, fabricated metals, basic organic and inorganic chemicals, aluminum, steel. **Chief crops:** apples, peaches, hay, tobacco, corn, wheat, oats. **Chief products:** dairy products, eggs. **Livestock** (1995): 450,000 cattle; 22,000 hogs/pigs; 60,000 sheep; 1.75 mil chickens. **Timber/lumber** (1995): oak, yellow poplar, hickory, walnut, cherry; 699 mil bd. ft. **Nonfuel minerals** (est. 1995): $176 mil; mostly crushed stone, portland cement, salt. **Chief port:** Huntington. **Value of construction** (1995): $194 mil. **Employment distribution** (1995): 23% trade; 20% govt.; 27% serv.; 12% mfg. **Per capita personal income** (1995): $17,915. **Unemployment** (1995): 7.9%. **Tourism** (1995): travel-related expenditures were $3.8 bil.

**Finance. FDIC-insured commercial banks & trust companies** (1995): 118. **Deposits:** $17.1 bil. **FDIC-insured savings institutions** (1995): 10. **Assets:** $1.5 bil.

**Federal government. No. federal civilian employees** (Mar. 1995): 11,253. **Avg. salary:** $36,930. **Notable federal facilities:** National Radio Astronomy Observatory, Green Bank; Bureau of Public Debt Bldg., Parkersburg; Harpers Ferry Natl. Park; Correctional Institution for Women, Alderson; FBI Identification Center, Clarksburg.

**Energy. Electricity production** (1995, kWh, by source): Coal: 77.2 bil; Petroleum: 197 mil; Gas: 40 mil; Hydroelectric: 394 mil.

**Public education. Student-teacher ratio** (1994): 14.8. **Avg. teachers' salary** (1995-96): $32,155.

**State data. Motto:** Montani Semper Liberi (Mountaineers are always free). **Flower:** Big rhododendron. **Bird:** Cardinal. **Tree:** Sugar maple. **Songs:** The West Virginia Hills; This Is My West Virginia; West Virginia, My Home, Sweet Home. **Entered union** June 20, 1863; rank, 35th. **State fair** at Lewisburg (Fairlea); late Aug.

**History.** Sparsely inhabited at the time of European contact, the area was primarily Native American hunting grounds. British explorers Thomas Batts and Robert Fallam reached the New River, 1671. Early American explorers included George Washington, 1753, and Daniel Boone. The area became part of Virginia and often objected to rule by the eastern part of the state. When Virginia seceded in 1861, the Wheeling Convention repudiated the act and created a new state, Kanawha, subsequently changed to West Virginia. It was admitted to the Union as such, 1863.

**Tourist attractions.** Harpers Ferry Natl. Historic Park; Science and Cultural Center, Charleston; White Sulphur and Berkeley Springs mineral water spas; New River Gorge, Fayetteville; Exhibition Coal Mine, Beckley; Monongahela Natl. Forest; Fenton Glass, Williamstown, Viking Glass, New Martinsville; Blenko Glass, Milton; Sternwheel Regatta, Charleston; Mountain State Forest Festival; Mountain State Arts & Crafts Fair, Ripley.

**Famous West Virginians.** Newton D. Baker, Pearl Buck, John W. Davis, Thomas "Stonewall" Jackson, Don Knotts, Dwight Whitney Morrow, Michael Owens, Cyrus Vance, Charles "Chuck" Yeager.

**Tourist information.** Dept. of Commerce, West Virginia Division of Tourism, State Capitol, Charleston WV 25305.

**Toll-free travel information.** 1-800-CALLWVA.

**World Wide Web site.** http://www.state.wv.us

## Wisconsin

*Badger State*

**People. Population** (1995): 5,122,871; **rank:** 18; **Net change** (1990-95): 4.7%. **Pop. density:** (1990) 92.2 per sq mi. **Racial/ethnic distrib.** (1990): 92.2% white; 5.0% black; 1.9% Hispanic.

**Geography. Total area:** 65,499 sq mi; **rank:** 23. **Land area:** 54,314 sq mi. **Acres forested land:** 15,513,000. **Location:** East North Central state, bounded on the N by Lake Superior and Upper Michigan; on the E by Lake Michigan; on the S by Illinois; on the W by the St. Croix and Mississippi rivers. **Climate:** long, cold winters and short, warm summers tempered by the Great Lakes. **Topography:** narrow Lake Superior Lowland plain met by Northern Highland, which slopes gently to the sandy crescent Central Plain; Western Upland in the SW; 3 broad parallel limestone ridges running N-S are separated by wide and shallow lowlands in the SE. **Capital:** Madison.

**Economy. Principal industries:** services, manufacturing, trade, government, agriculture, tourism. **Principal manufactured goods:** food products, motor vehicles and equipment, paper products, medical instruments and supplies, printing, plastics. **Chief crops:** corn, soybeans, peas, hay, oats, potatoes, sweet corn, snap beans, cranberries. **Chief products:** milk, butter, cheese, canned & frozen vegetables. **Livestock** (1995): 3.85 mil cattle; 1.5 mil milk cows; 1 mil hogs; 4.11 mil poultry; .85 mil sheep. **Timber/lumber** (1995): maple, birch, oak, evergreens; 633 mil bd. ft. **Nonfuel minerals** (est. 1995): $441 mil; mostly crushed stone, construction and industrial sand & gravel, lime. **Commercial fishing** (1995): $5.1 mil. **Chief ports:** Superior, Ashland, Milwaukee, Green Bay, Kewaunee, Pt. Washington, Manitowoc, Sheboygan, Marinette, Kenosha. **International airports at:** Milwaukee. **Value of construction** (1995): $5.7 bil. **Employment distribution** (1996): 22.8% trade; 23.3% mfg.; 25% serv.; 15% govt. **Per capita personal income** (1995): $21,839. **Unemployment** (1995): 3.7%. **Tourism** (1995): out-of-state visitors spent $6.1 bil.

**Finance. FDIC-insured commercial banks & trust companies** (1995): 387. **Deposits:** $47.8 bil. **FDIC-insured savings institutions** (1995): 52. **Assets:** $23.5 bil.

**Federal government. No. federal civilian employees** (Mar. 1995): 12,292. **Avg. salary:** $36,258. **Notable federal facilities:** Ft. McCoy.

**Energy. Electricity production** (1995, kWh, by source): Coal: 36.9 bil; Petroleum: 147 mil; Gas: 649 mil; Hydroelectric: 2.1 bil; Nuclear: 11.0 bil.

**Public education. Student-teacher ratio** (1994): 15.9. **Avg. teachers' salary** (1995-96): $38,571.

**State data. Motto:** Forward. **Flower:** Wood violet. **Bird:** Robin. **Tree:** Sugar maple. **Song:** On, Wisconsin! **Entered union** May 29, 1848; rank, 30th. **State fair** at West Allis; mid-Aug.

**History.** At the time of European contact, Ojibwa, Menominee, Winnebago, Kickapoo, Sauk, Fox, and Potawatomi peoples inhabited the region. Jean Nicolet was the first European to see the Wisconsin area, arriving in Green Bay, 1634; French missionaries and fur traders followed. The British took over, 1763. The U.S. won the land after the American Revolution, but the British were not ousted until after the War of 1812. Lead miners came next, then farmers. In 1816, the U.S. government built a fort at Prairie du Chien on Wisconsin's border with Iowa. Native Americans in the area rebelled against the seizure of their tribal lands in the Black Hawk War of 1832, but a series of treaties from 1829 to 1848, effectively transferred all land titles in Wisconsin to the U.S. government. Railroads were started in 1851, serving growing wheat harvests and iron mines. Some 96,000 soldiers served the Union cause during the Civil War.

**Tourist attractions.** Old Wade House and Carriage Museum, Greenbush; Villa Louis, Prairie du Chien; Circus World Museum, Baraboo; Wisconsin Dells; Old World Wisconsin, Eagle; Door County peninsula; Chequamegon and Nicolet national forests; Lake Winnebago; House on the Rock, Dodgeville.

**Famous Wisconsinites.** Edna Ferber, King Camp Gillette, Harry Houdini, Robert La Follette, Alfred Lunt, Pat O'Brien, Georgia O'Keeffe, William H. Rehnquist, Donald K. "Deke" Slayton, Spencer Tracy, Thorstein Veblen, Orson Welles, Laura Ingalls Wilder, Thornton Wilder, Frank Lloyd Wright.

**Tourist information.** Wisconsin Dept. of Tourism, 123 W. Washington Ave., PO Box 7606, Madison, WI 53707.

**Toll-free travel information.** 1-800-432-8747.

**World Wide Web site.** http://www.state.wi.us

## Wyoming

*Equality State*

**People. Population** (1995): 480,184; **rank:** 50; **Net change** (1990-95): 5.9%. **Pop. density:** (1990) 4.8 per sq mi. **Racial/ethnic distrib.** (1990): 94.2% white; 0.8% black; 2.1% Amer. Indian; 5.7% Hispanic.

**Geography. Total area:** 97,818 sq mi; **rank:** 10. **Land area:** 97,105 sq mi. **Acres forested land:** 9,966,000. **Location:** Mountain state lying in the high western plateaus of the Great Plains. **Climate:** semi-desert conditions throughout; true desert in the Big Horn and Great Divide basins. **Topography:** the eastern Great Plains rise to the foothills of the Rocky Mts.; the Continental Divide crosses the state from the NW to the SE. **Capital:** Cheyenne.

**Economy. Principal industries:** mineral extraction, oil, natural gas, tourism and recreation, agriculture. **Principal manufactured goods:** refined petroleum, wood, stone, clay products, foods electronic devices, sporting apparel, and aircraft. **Chief crops:** wheat, beans, barley, oats, sugar beets, hay. **Livestock** (Jan. 1, 1995): 1.4 mil cattle/calves; 790,000 sheep/lambs; (Dec. 1, 1994) 51,000 hogs/pigs. **Timber/lumber** (1995): ponderosa & lodgepole pine, Douglas fir, Engelmann spruce; 226 mil bd. ft. **Nonfuel minerals** (est. 1995): $976 mil; mostly soda ash, clays, helium, gypsum, portland cement, crushed stone. **International airports at:** Casper. **Value of construction** (1994): $531.9 mil. **Employment distribution** (1994): 23.9% trade; 20.3% services; 25.4% govt, 8.5% mining. **Per capita personal income** (1995): $21,321. **Unemployment** (1995): 4.8%. **Tourism** (1992): out-of-state visitors spent $1.5 bil.

**Finance. FDIC-insured commercial banks & trust companies** (1995): 53. **Deposits:** $6.3 bil. **FDIC-insured savings institutions** (1995): 4. **Assets:** $303 mil.

**Federal government. No. federal civilian employees** (Mar. 1995): 4,693. **Avg. salary:** $35,874. **Notable federal facilities:** Warren AFB.

**Energy. Electricity production** (1995, kWh, by source): Coal: 38.8 bil; Petroleum: 68 mil; Gas: 13 mil; Hydroelectric: 799 mil.

**Public education. Student-teacher ratio** (1994): 15.0. **Avg. teachers' salary** (1995-96): $31,571.

**State data. Motto:** Equal Rights. **Flower:** Indian paintbrush. **Bird:** Meadowlark. **Tree:** Cottonwood. **Song:** Wyoming. **Entered union** July 10, 1890; rank, 44th. **State fair** at Douglas; late Aug.

**History.** Shoshone, Crow, Cheyenne, Oglala, and Arapaho peoples lived in the area at the time of European contact. Frances François and Louis La Verendrye were the first Europeans to see the region, 1743. John Colter, an American, was first to traverse Yellowstone park, 1807-8. Trappers and fur traders followed in the 1820s. Forts Laramie and Bridger became important stops on the pioneer trail to the West Coast. Population grew after the Union Pacific crossed the state, 1869. Women won the vote, for the first time in the U.S., from the Territorial Legislature, 1869. Disputes between large land owners and small ranchers culminated in the Johnson County Cattle War, 1892; federal troops were called in to restore order.

**Tourist attractions.** Yellowstone Natl. Park, the oldest U.S. national park, est. 1872; Grand Teton Natl. Park; Natl. Elk Refuge; Devils Tower; Fort Laramie and surrounding areas of pioneer trails; Buffalo Bill Museum, Cody; Cheyenne Frontier Days Celebration.

**Famous Wyomingites.** James Bridger, Buffalo Bill Cody, Esther Hobart Morris, Nellie Tayloe Ross.

**Tourist information.** Division of Tourism & State Marketing, Etchepare Circle, Cheyenne, WY 82002.

**Toll-free travel information.** 1-800-CALLWYO.

**World Wide Web site.** http://www.state.wy.us

## District of Columbia

**People. Population** (1995): 554,256; **Net change** (1990-95): -8.7%.

**Geography. Total area:** 68 sq mi; **rank:** 51. **Land area:** 61 sq mi. **Location:** at the confluence of the Potomac and Anacostia rivers, flanked by Maryland on the N, E, and SE and by Virginia on the SW. **Climate:** hot humid summers, mild winters. **Topography:** low hills rise toward the N away from the Potomac R. and slope to the S; highest elevation, 410 ft, lowest Potomac R., 1 ft.

**Economy. Principal Industries:** government, service, tourism. **Value of construction** (1995): $664.3 mil. **Employment distribution** (1992) 31.1% govt., 10.3% trade, 33% service. **Per capita personal income** (1995): $32,274; **Unemployment** (1994): 8.2%.

**Finance. FDIC-Insured commercial banks & trust companies** (1995): 13 **Deposits:** $7.7 bil. **FDIC-Insured savings institutions** (1995): 1. **Assets:** $265 mil.

**Federal Government. No. of federal employees** (Mar. 1995): 160,804; **Avg. salary:** $52,032.

**Energy. Electricity production** (1995, kWh, by source): Petroleum: 189 mil.

**Public education. Student-teacher ratio** (1994): 13.2. **Avg. teachers' salary** (1995-96): $43,700.

**District Data. Motto:** Justitia omnibus (Justice for all). **Flower:** American beauty rose. **Tree:** Scarlet oak. **Bird:** Wood thrush.

The District of Columbia, coextensive with the city of Washington, is the seat of the U.S. federal government. It lies on the west central edge of Maryland on the Potomac River, opposite Virginia. Its area was originally 100 sq mi taken from the sovereignty of Maryland and Virginia. Virginia's portion south of the Potomac was given back to that state in 1846.

The 23d Amendment, ratified in 1961, granted residents the right to vote for president and vice president for the first time since 1800 and gave them 3 members in the Electoral College. The first such votes were cast in Nov. 1964.

Congress, which has legislative authority over the District under the Constitution, established in 1874 a government of 3 commissioners appointed by the president. The Reorganization Plan of 1967 substituted a single appointive commissioner (also called mayor), assistant, and 9-member City Council. Funds were still appropriated by Congress; residents had no vote in local government, except to elect school board members.

In Sept. 1970, Congress approved legislation giving the District one delegate to the House of Representatives, who can vote in committee but not on the House floor. The first such delegate was elected 1971.

In May 1974 voters approved a congressionally drafted charter giving them the right to elect their own mayor and a 13-member city council; the first took office Jan. 2, 1975. The district won the right to levy its own taxes, but Congress retained power to veto council actions and approve the city budget.

Proposals for a "federal town" for the deliberations of the Continental Congress were made in 1783, 4 years before the adoption of the Constitution. Rivalry between Northern and Southern delegates over the site appeared in the First Congress, 1789. John Adams, presiding officer of the Senate, cast the deciding vote of that body for Germantown, PA. In 1790 Congress compromised by making Philadelphia the temporary capital for 10 years. The Virginia members of the House wanted a permanent capital on the eastern bank of the Potomac, while the Southerners opposed having the nation assume the war debts of the 13 original states as provided under the Assumption Bill, fathered by Alexander Hamilton. Hamilton and Jefferson arranged a compromise: the Virginia men voted for the Assumption Bill, and the Northerners conceded the capital to the Potomac. President Washington chose the site in Oct. 1790 and persuaded landowners to sell their holdings to the government. The capital was named Washington.

Washington appointed Pierre Charles L'Enfant, a Frenchman, to plan the capital on an area not more than 10 mi square. The L'Enfant plan, for streets 100 to 110 ft. wide and one avenue 400 ft. wide and a mile long, seemed grandiose and foolhardy, but Washington endorsed it. When L'Enfant ordered a wealthy landowner to remove his new manor house because it obstructed a vista, and demolished it when the owner refused, Washington stepped in and dismissed the architect. Andrew Ellicott, who was working on surveying the area, finished the official map and design of the city. Ellicott was assisted by Benjamin Banneker, a distinguished black architect and astronomer.

On Sept. 18, 1793, Pres. Washington laid the cornerstone of the north wing of the Capitol. On June 3, 1800, Pres. John Adams moved to Washington, and on June 10, Philadelphia ceased to be the temporary capital. The City of Washington was incorporated in 1802; the District of Columbia was created as a municipal corporation in 1874, embracing Washington, Georgetown, and Washington County.

**Tourist information.** 202-789-7000.

**World Wide Web site.** http://dcpages.ari.net

# OUTLYING U.S. AREAS

## American Samoa

**People. Population:** (1994 est.) 55,223. **Population growth rate** (1994 est.) -0.52%. **Land area:** 77 sq. mi. **Total area:** 90 sq mi. **Capital:** Pago Pago, Island of Tutuila. **Motto:** Samoa Muamua le Atua (In Samoa, God Is First). **Song:** Amerika Samoa. **Flower:** Paogo (Ula-fala). **Plant:** Ava.

**Public education. Student-teacher ratio** (1994): 20.7.

Blessed with spectacular scenery and delightful South Seas climate, American Samoa is the most southerly of all lands under U.S. sovereignty. It is an unincorporated territory consisting of 7 small islands of the Samoan group: **Tutuila, Aunu'u, Manu'a Group (Ta'u, Olosega, Ofu), Rose,** and **Swains Island.** The islands are 2,300 mi SW of Honolulu.

**Economy. Principal industries:** trade, services and tour ism. **Agriculture. Chief crops:** vegetables, nuts, melons and other fruits. **Livestock:** (1990) 179 cattle; 7,580 hogs/pigs; 27,401 chickens.

A tripartite agreement between Great Britain, Germany, and the U.S. in 1899 gave the U.S. sovereignty over the eastern islands of the Samoan group; these islands became American Samoa. Local chiefs officially ceded Tutuila and Aunu'u to the U.S. in Apr. 1900, and the Manu'a group and Rose in July 1904; Swains Island was annexed in 1925.

Samoa (Western), comprising the larger islands of the Samoan group, was a New Zealand mandate and UN Trusteeship until it became an independent nation Jan. 1, 1962.

Tutuila and Aunu'u have an area of 53 sq mi. Ta'u has an area of 17 sq mi, and the islets of Ofu and Olosega, 5 sq mi with a population of a few thousand. Swains Island has nearly 2 sq mi and a population of about 100.

About 70% of the land is bush and mountains. Chief products and exports are fish products. Taro, breadfruit, yams, coconuts, pineapples, oranges, and bananas are also produced.

From 1900 to 1951, American Samoa was under the jurisdiction of the U.S. Navy. Since 1951, it has been under the Interior Dept. On Jan. 3, 1978, the first popularly elected Samoan governor and lieutenant governor were inaugurated. Previously, the governor was appointed by the Secretary of the Interior. American Samoa has a bicameral legislature and elects a delegate to the House of Representatives, who has a voice but no vote, except in committees.

The American Samoans are of Polynesian origin. They are nationals of the U.S.; approximately 20,000 live in Hawaii, 65,000 in California and Washington.

## Guam

*Where America's Day Begins*

**People. Population** (1994 est.): 149,620. **Population growth rate** (1994): 2.48%. **Pop. density:** (1990) 631.6 per sq mi. **Ethnic distribution** (1994 est.): Chamorro 47%, Filipino 25%, Caucasian 10%, Chinese, Japanese, Korean, and other 18%. Native Guamanians, ethnically Chamorros, are basically of Indonesian stock, with a mixture of Spanish and Filipino; in addition to the offical language, they speak the native Chamorro. **Migration** (1990): About 52% of population were born elsewhere; of these, 48% in Asia, 40% in U.S.

**Geography. Total area:** 217 sq mi. **Land area:** 210 sq. mi. **Location:** largest and southernmost of the Mariana Islands in the West Pacific, 3,700 mi W of Hawaii. **Climate:** tropical, with temperatures from 70° to 90° F; avg. annual rainfall, about 70 in. **Topography:** coralline limestone plateau in the N; southern chain of low volcanic mountains sloping gently to the W, more steeply to coastal cliffs on the E; general elevation, 500 ft; highest point, Mt. Lamlam, 1,334 ft. **Capital:** Agaña.

**Economy. Principal industries:** tourism, U.S. military, construction, banking, printing and publishing. **Principal manufactured goods:** textiles, foods. **Chief crops:** cabbages, eggplants, cucumber, long beans, tomatoes, bananas, coconuts, watermelon, yams, canteloupe, papayas, maize, sweet potatoes. **Production** (1990) fruits & vegetables, 5.6 mil lb; eggs, 369,000 doz; pork, 215,000 lb; beef, 11,000 lb; poultry, 90,000 lb: **Livestock** (1992): 388 cattle; 2,038 hogs/pigs; 12,206 chickens.**Chief port:** Apra Harbor. **International airport at:** Agaña. **Value of construction** (1992): $708.6 mil. **Employment distribution** (1992): 32% service; 53% trade; 12.3% construction. **Per capita income** (1986): $7,116. **Median household income** (1989): $30,755; persons per household 3.97; persons per family 4.26. **Unemployment** (1992): 2%. **Tourism** (1992): visitors' receipts $1.5 bil.

**Finance. Notable industries:** insurance, real estate, finance. **FDIC-insured commercial banks & trust companies** (1995): 2. **Deposits:** $655 mil. **FDIC-insured savings institutions** (1995): 2. **Assets:** $245 mil.

**Federal government. No. federal employees** (1990): 7,200. **Notable federal facilities:** Anderson AFB; naval, air, and port bases.

**Public education. Student-teacher ratio** (1994): 17.6.

**Misc. data. Flower:** Puti Tai Nobio (Bougainvillea). **Bird:** Toto (Fruit dove). **Tree:** Ifit (Intsiabijuga). **Song:** Stand Ye Guamanians.

**History.** Guam was probably settled by voyagers from the Indonesian-Philippine archipelago by at least the 3d cent. BC. Pottery, rice cultivation, and megalithic technology show strong East Asian cultural influence. Centralized, village clan-based communities engaged in agriculture and offshore fishing. The estimated population by the early 16th cent. was between 50,000 and 75,000 inhabitants. Magellan arrived in the Marianas Mar. 6, 1521. They were colonized in 1668 by Spanish missionaries, who named them the Mariana Islands in honor of Maria Anna, queen of Spain. When Spain ceded Guam to the U.S., it sold the other Marianas to Germany. Japan obtained a League of Nations mandate over the German islands in 1919; in Dec. 1941 it seized Guam; the island was retaken by the U.S. in July 1944.

Guam is a self-governing organized unincorporated U.S. territory. The Organic Act of 1950 provided for a governor, elected to a 4-year term, and a 21-member unicameral legislature, elected biennially by the residents, who are American citizens. In 1970, the first governor was elected.

In 1972, a U.S. law gave Guam one delegate to the U.S. House of Representatives who has a voice but no vote, except in committees.

Guam's quest to change its status to a U.S. Commonwealth began in the late 1970s. The Guam Commission on Self-Determination, created in 1984, developed a draft Commonwealth Act. After consultations with a U.S. government representative in late 1993, it was decided that legislation proposing a change of status would be submitted to the U.S. Congress.

In 1994, the U.S. Congress passed legislation transferring 3,200 acres of land on Guam from federal to local control.

**Tourist attractions.** Tropical climate, oceanic marine environment; annual mid-Aug. Merizo Water Festival; Tarzan Falls; beaches; water sports; duty-free port shopping.

## Commonwealth of the Northern Mariana Islands

**People. Indigenous Population** (1990): 43,345. **Total area:** 189 sq. mi. **Land area:** 179 sq. mi. Located in the perpetually warm climes between Guam and the Tropic of Cancer, the 14 islands of the Northern Marianas form a 300-mile-long archipelago. The indigenous population in 1990 was concentrated on the 3 largest of the 6 inhabited islands: **Saipan,** the seat of government and commerce (38,896), **Rota** (2,295), and **Tinian** (2,118).

**Economy. Principal industries**: trade, services, and tourism **Principal manufactured goods**: apparel, stone, clay and glass products. **Chief crops:** melons, vegetables, horticulture, fruits and nuts. **Livestock:** (1990) 4,513 cattle; 1,260 hogs/pigs; 9,580. **Employment distribution** (1992): 53% trade; 8% const.; 6% manuf.; 33% serv.

**Education. Pupil-teacher ratio (**1994**):** 20.8.

The people of the Northern Marianas are predominantly of Chamorro cultural extraction, although Carolinians and immigrants from other areas of E. Asia and Micronesia have also settled in the islands. English is among the several languages commonly spoken. Pursuant to the Covenant of 1976, which established the Northern Marianas as a commonwealth in political union with the U.S., most of the indigenous population and many domiciliaries of these islands achieved U.S. citizenship on Nov. 3, 1986, when the U.S. terminated its administration of the UN trusteeship as it affected the Northern Marianas. From July 18, 1947, the U.S. had administered the Northern Marianas under a trusteeship agreement with the UN Security Council.

The Northern Mariana Islands has been self-governing since 1978, when a constitution drafted and adopted by the people became effective and a popularly elected bicameral legislature (2-year term), with offices of governor (4-year term) and lieut. governor, was inaugurated.

## Commonwealth of Puerto Rico

*(Estado Libre Asociado de Puerto Rico)*

**People. Population** (1994 est): 3,801,977 (and about 2.7 mil more Puerto Ricans reside in the mainland U.S.). **Pop. density:** (1990) 1,035 per sq mi. **Urban** (1990): 66.8%. **Ethnic distribution** (1990): 99.9% Hispanic. **Language:** On Jan. 28, 1993, the Gov. of Puerto Rico declared Spanish and English joint official languages.

**Geography. Total area:** 3,508 sq. mi. **Land area:** 3,427 sq mi. **Location:** island lying between the Atlantic to the N and the Caribbean to the S; it is easternmost of the West Indies group called the Greater Antilles, of which Cuba, Hispaniola, and Jamaica are the larger islands. **Climate:** mild, with a mean temperature of 77° F. **Topography:** mountainous throughout three-fourths of its rectangular area, surrounded by a broken coastal plain; highest peak is Cerro de Punto, 4,390 ft. **Capital:** San Juan.

**Economy. Principal industries:** manufacturing. **Principal manufactured goods:** pharmaceuticals, electronics and other electric equipment, industrial machinery. **Chief crops:** coffee, plantains, pineapples, tomatoes, sugarcane, bananas, mangos, ornamental plants. **Livestock** (1995): 367,733 cattle; 204,568 pigs; 12.3 mil poultry. **Nonfuel minerals** (est. 1994): $122 mil, mostly portland cement, crushed stone. **Commercial fishing** (1992): $6.2 mil. **Chief ports/river shipping:** San Juan, Ponce, Mayagüez. **Major airports at:** San Juan, Ponce, Mayagüez, Aguadilla. **Value of construction** (1992): $2.7 bil. **Employment distribution** (1995): 22.4% public admin., 20.2% trade, 15.8% mfg. **Per capita income** (1992): $6,360. **Unemployment** (1994): 14.6%. **Tourism** (1993): Visitors spent $1.6 mil.

**Finance. FDIC-insured commercial banks & trust companies** (1995): 15. **Deposits:** $20.8 bil. **FDIC-insured savings institutions** (1995): 2. **Assets:** $189 mln.

**Federal government. No. federal civilian employees** (1992): 10,000. **Notable federal facilities:** U.S. Naval Station at Roosevelt Roads, Ceiba; U.S. Army Training Area and Ft. Allen at Salinas; Sabana SECA Communications Center (U.S. Navy); Ft. Buchanan at Guaynabo.

**Energy. Electicity production** (1993): 15.3 bil kWh.

**Public education. Student-teacher ratio** (1994): 15.6. **Avg. teachers' salary** (1992): $1,000 monthly.

**Misc. data. Motto:** Joannes Est Nomen Eius (John is his name). **Flower:** Maga. **Bird:** Reinita. **Tree:** Ceiba. **National anthem:** La Borinqueña.

**History.** Puerto Rico (or Borinquen, after the original Arawak Indian name, Boriquen) was visited by Columbus on his second voyage, Nov. 19, 1493. In 1508, the Spanish arrived.

Sugarcane was introduced, 1515, and slaves were imported 3 years later. Gold mining petered out, 1570. Spaniards fought off a series of British and Dutch attacks; slavery was abolished, 1873. Under the treaty of Paris, Puerto Rico was ceded to the U.S. after the Spanish-American War, 1898. In 1952 the people voted in favor of Commonwealth status.

The Commonwealth of Puerto Rico is a self-governing part of the U.S. with a primarily Hispanic culture. The current commonwealth political status of Puerto Rico gives the island's citizens virtually the same control over their internal affairs as the 50 states of the U.S. However, they do not vote in national general elections, although they do vote in national primaries.

Puerto Rico is represented in the U.S. House of Representatives by a delegate who has a voice but no vote, except in committees.

No federal income tax is collected from residents on income earned from local sources in Puerto Rico. Nevertheless, as part of the U.S. legal system, Puerto Rico is subject to the provisions of the U.S. Constitution; most federal laws apply as they do in the 50 states.

Puerto Rico's famous "Operation Bootstrap," begun in the late 1940s, succeeded in changing the island from "The Poorhouse of the Caribbean" to an area with the highest per capita income in Latin America. This pioneering program encouraged manufacturing and the development of the tourist trade by selective tax exemption, low-interest loans, and other incentives. Despite the marked success of Puerto Rico's development efforts over an extended period of time, per capita income in Puerto Rico is low in comparison to that of the U.S.

**Tourist attractions.** Ponce Museum of Art; Forts El Morro and San Cristobal; Old Walled City of San Juan; Arecibo Observatory; Cordillera Central and state parks; El Yunque Rain Forest; San Juan Cathedral; Porta Coeli Chapel and Museum of Religious Art, Interamerican Univ., San Germán; Condado Convention Center; Casa Blanca, Ponce de León family home, Puerto Rican Family Museum of 16th and 17th centuries, and Fine Arts Center in San Juan.

**Cultural facilities and events.** Festival Casals classical music concerts, mid-June; Puerto Rico Symphony Orchestra at Music Conservatory; Botanical Garden and Museum of Anthropology, Art, and History at the University of Puerto Rico; Institute of Puerto Rican Culture, at the Dominican Convent; and many popular festivals throughout the island.

**Famous Puerto Ricans.** Miguel Hernández Agosto, José Celso Barbosa, Julia de Burgos, Pablo Casals, Orlando Cepeda, Roberto Clemente, Rafael Hernández Colón, José de Diego, José Feliciano, Luis A. Ferré, José Ferrer, Doña Felisa Rincón de Gautier, Commodore Diégo E. Hernández, Rafael Hernández (El Jibarito), Marta Casals Istomin, Raúl Julía, Luis Muñoz Marín, René Marqués, Luis Palés Matos, Concha Meléndez, Rita Moreno, Adm. Horacio Rivero.

**Chamber of Commerce.** 100 Tetuán, PO Box S-3789, San Juan, PR 00902; Ponce & South: El Señorial Bldg., Ponce, PR 00731.

**World Wide Web site.**http://fortaleza.govpr.org

## Virgin Islands

*St. John, St. Croix, St. Thomas*

**People. Population** (1994 est.): 97,564. **Population growth rate** (1994 est.): –0.52% **Racial distribution** (1980): 85% black, 15% white. **Major ethnic groups:** West Indian, French, Hispanic.

**Geography. Total area:** 171 sq mi. **Land area:** 134 sq mi. **Location:** 3 larger and 50 smaller islands and cays in the S and W of the V.I. group (British V.I. colony to the N and E), which is situated 70 mi E of Puerto Rico, located W of the Anegada Passage, a major channel connecting the Atlantic Ocean and the Caribbean Sea. **Climate:** subtropical; the sun tempered by gentle trade winds; humidity is low; average temperature, 78° F. **Topography:** St. Thomas is mainly a ridge of hills running E and W, and has little tillable land; St. Croix rises abruptly in the N but slopes to the S to flatlands and lagoons; St. John has steep, lofty hills and valleys with little level tillable land. **Capital:** Charlotte Amalie, St. Thomas.

**Economy. Principal industries:** tourism, rum, alumina, petroleum refining, watches, textiles, electronics, printing and publishing. **Principal manufactured goods:** rum, textiles, pharmaceuticals, perfumes, stone, glass and clay products. **Gross domestic product** (1987): $1.246 bil. **Chief crops:** vegetables, horticulture, fruits and nuts. **Livestock** (1992): 7,132 cattle; 1,311 hogs/pigs; 9,087 chickens. **Minerals:** sand, gravel. **Chief ports:** Cruz Bay, St. John; Frederiksted and Christiansted, St. Croix; Charlotte Amalie, St. Thomas. **International airports on:** St. Thomas, St. Croix. **Value of construction** (1992): $168.9 mil. **Employment distribution** (1992): 50% trade; 43% serv. **Per capita income** (1989): $11,052. **Unemployment** (1992): 2.8%. **Tourism** (1992): $792 mil.

**Finance. FDIC-insured savings institutions** (1994): 1. **Assets:** 48 mil. **Banks** (1990): 8.

**Energy. Electicity production** (1992): 565 mil kWh.

**Public education. Student-teacher ratio** (1994): 15.1.

**Misc. data. Flower:** Yellow elder or yellow trumpet, local designation Ginger Thomas. **Bird:** Yellow breast. **Song:** Virgin Islands March.

**History.** The islands were visited by Columbus in 1493. Spanish forces, 1555, defeated the Caribes and claimed the territory; by 1596 the native population was annihilated. First permanent settlement in the U.S. territory, 1672, by the Danes; U.S. purchased the islands, 1917, for defense purposes.

The Virgin Islands has a republican form of government, headed by a governor and lieut. governor elected, since 1970, by popular vote for 4-year terms. There is a 15-member unicameral legislature, elected by popular vote for a 2-year term. Residents of the V.I. have been U.S. citizens since 1927. Since 1973 they have elected a delegate to the U.S. House of Representatives, who has a voice but no vote, except in committees.

**Tourist attractions.** Magens Bay, St. Thomas; duty-free shopping; Virgin Islands Natl. Park, beaches, Indian relics, and evidence of colonial Danes.

**Tourist information.** Dept. of Economic Development & Agriculture: St. Thomas, PO Box 6400, St. Thomas, VI 00801; St. Croix, PO Box 4535, Christiansted, St. Croix 00820.

## Other Islands

**Navassa** lies between Jamaica and Haiti, 100 mi south of Guantanamo Bay, Cuba, in the Caribbean; it covers about 3 sq mi, is reserved by the U.S. for a lighthouse, and is uninhabited. It is administered by the U.S. Coast Guard.

**Wake Atoll,** and its neighboring atolls, **Wilkes** and **Peale,** lie in the Pacific Ocean on the direct route from Hawaii to Hong Kong, about 2,300 mi W of Honolulu and 1,290 mi E of Guam. The group is 4.5 mi long, 1.5 mi wide, and totals less than 3 sq mi. The U.S. flag was hoisted over Wake Atoll, July 4, 1898, formal possession taken Jan. 17, 1899; Wake was administered by the U.S. Air Force, 1972-94. The population consists of about 200 persons.

**Midway Atoll,** acquired in 1867, consist of 2 atolls, **Sand** and **Eastern,** in the North Pacific 1,150 mi. NW of Honolulu, with an area of about 3 sq mi, administered by the U.S. Navy. There is no indigenous population; total pop. is about 450.

**Johnston Atoll,** 717 mi WSW of Honolulu, area 1 sq mi, is operated by the Defense Nuclear Agency, and the Fish and Wildlife Service, U.S. Dept. of the Interior; its population is about 1,200. **Kingman Reef,** 920 mi S of Hawaii, is under Navy control.

**Howland, Jarvis,** and **Baker Islands,** 1,400-1,650 mi SW of Honolulu, uninhabited since World War II, are under the Interior Dept.

**Palmyra** is an atoll about 1,000 mi south of Hawaii, 2 sq mi. Privately owned, it is under the Interior Dept.

# Washington, DC, Capital of the U.S.

Tourism information is available from the Washington, DC, Convention and Visitors Association; phone 202-789-7000.

## Bureau of Engraving and Printing

The **Bureau of Engraving and Printing** is the headquarters for the making of U.S. paper money. 20-minute self-guided tours Mon. - Fri., 9 AM-1:50 PM , year-round, and extended hours Apr. - Sept., 3:30 PM-7:30 PM. Closed federal holidays and Dec. 24 - Jan. 3. 14th and C Sts. SW. Phone 202-874-3019.

## Capitol

The **United States Capitol** was originally designed by Dr. William Thornton, an amateur architect, who submitted a plan in the spring of 1793 that won him $500 and a city lot.

The south, or House, wing was completed in 1807 under the direction of Benjamin H. Latrobe.

The present Senate and House wings and the iron dome were designed and constructed by Thomas U. Walter, the 4th architect of the Capitol, between 1851 and 1863.

The present cast iron dome at its greatest exterior measures 135 ft 5 in., and it is topped by the bronze Statue of Freedom that stands 19½ ft and weighs 14,985 lb. On its base are the words *E Pluribus Unum* (Out of Many, One).

The Capitol is normally open from 9 AM to 4:30 PM, and to 10 PM June to Labor Day. It is closed on Dec. 25, Jan. 1, and Thanksgiving Day. Tours through the Capitol, including the House and Senate galleries, are conducted from 9 AM to 3:45 PM; there is no charge.

To observe the debate in the House or Senate while Congress is in session, individuals living in the U.S. may obtain tickets to the visitor's galleries from their congressperson or senator. Visitors from other countries may obtain passes at the Capitol. Between Constitution & Independence Ave., at Pennsylvania Ave. Phone 202-225-6827.

## Federal Bureau of Investigation

The **Federal Bureau of Investigation** offers a tour of its headquarters, beginning with a videotape presentation. Visitors learn about the history of the FBI and see such things as the weapons confiscated from famous gangsters, photos of the most-wanted fugitives, the DNA laboratory, goods forfeited and seized in narcotics operations, and a sharpshooting demonstration.

Tours are conducted Mon. - Fri., 8:45 AM - 4:15 PM, except Jan. 1, Dec. 25, and other federal holidays. Tickets may be obtained at the FBI on the day of the tour or through a congressperson or senator. Admission is free. J. Edgar Hoover Bldg., Pennsylvania Ave., between 9th and 10th Sts. NW. Phone 202-324-3447.

## Folger Shakespeare Library

The **Folger Shakespeare Library,** on Capitol Hill, is a research institution holding rare books and manuscripts of the Renaissance period and the largest collection of Shakespearean materials in the world, including 79 copies of the First Folio.

The library's museum and performing arts programs are presented in the Elizabethan Theatre, which resembles an innyard theater of Shakespeare's day.

Exhibit may be visited Mon. - Sat., 10 AM - 4 PM. 201 E. Capitol St. Phone 202-544-7077.

## Holocaust Memorial Museum

The **U.S. Holocaust Memorial Museum** opened on Apr. 21, 1993. The museum documents, through the use of permanent and temporary displays, interactive videos, and special lectures, the events of the Holocaust beginning in 1933 and continuing until the end of World War II. The permanent exhibition is not recommended for children under the age of 11.

The museum is open daily, 10 AM - 5:30 PM, except Yom Kippur and Dec. 25. A limited number of free tickets are available on the day of visit; advance tickets may be ordered for a small fee. 100 Raoul Wallenberg Pl. SW (formerly 15th St. SW), near Independence Ave. Phone 202-488-0400.

## Jefferson Memorial

Dedicated in 1943, the **Thomas Jefferson Memorial** stands on the south shore of the Tidal Basin in West Potomac Park. It is a circular stone structure, with Vermont marble on the exterior and Georgia white marble inside, and combines architectural elements of the dome of the Pantheon in Rome and the rotunda designed by Jefferson for the University of Virginia.

The memorial, which is located on the South edge of the Tidal Basin, is open daily, 8 AM - midnight. An elevator and curb ramps for the handicapped are in service. Phone 202-426-6841.

## John F. Kennedy Center

The **John F. Kennedy Center for the Performing Arts,** designated by Congress as the National Cultural Center and the official memorial in Washington, DC, to President John F. Kennedy, opened Sept. 8, 1971. Designed by Edward Durell Stone, the center includes an opera house, a concert hall, several theaters, 2 restaurants, and a library.

Free tours are available daily, 10:00 AM - 1:00 PM. New Hampshire Ave. at F St. NW. Phone 202-416-8340.

## Korean War Memorial

Dedicated on July 27, 1995, the **Korean War Memorial** honors all Americans who served in the Korean War. Situated at the west end of the Mall, just across the reflecting pool from the Vietnam Memorial, the triangular-shaped stone and steel memorial features a multiservice formation of 19 troops clad in ponchos with the wind at their back, ready for combat. A granite wall, exhibiting real-life images of the men and women who served, juts into a pool of water, the Pool of Remembrance, and is inscribed with the words *Freedom Is Not Free.*

The $18 mil memorial, which was funded by private donations, is open 24 hr daily. Phone 202-426-6841.

## Library of Congress

Established by and for Congress in 1800, the **Library of Congress** has extended its services over the years to other government agencies and other libraries, to scholars, and to the general public, and it now serves as the national library. It contains more than 80 million items in 470 languages.

The library's exhibit halls are open to the public Mon. - Fri., 8:30 AM - 9:30 PM; Sat., 8:30 AM - 6:00 PM. The library is closed Jan. 1 and Dec. 25. 10 1st St. SE. Phone 202-707-8000.

## Lincoln Memorial

Designed by Henry Bacon, the **Lincoln Memorial** in West Potomac Park, on the axis of the Capitol and the Washington Monument, consists of a large marble hall enclosing a heroic statue of Abraham Lincoln in meditation sitting on a large armchair. The memorial was dedicated on Memorial Day, May 30, 1922. The statue of Lincoln was designed by Daniel Chester French and sculpted by French and the Piccirilli brothers. Murals and ornamentation on the bronze ceiling beams are by Jules Guerin. The text of the Gettysburg Address is in the south chamber, and that of Lincoln's Second Inaugural speech is in the north chamber. Each is engraved on a stone tablet.

The memorial is open 24 hr daily. An elevator for the handicapped is in service. Phone 202-426-6895.

### National Archives

Original copies of the Declaration of Independence, the Constitution of the United States, and the Bill of Rights are on permanent display in the **National Archives** Exhibition Hall. The National Archives also holds other valuable U.S. government records and historic maps, photographs, and manuscripts.

Central Research and Microfilm Research Rooms are also available to the public for genealogical research.

The Exhibition Hall is open daily, 10 AM - 9 PM; closed Jan. 1 and Dec. 25. Pennsylvania Ave. between 7th & 9th Sts. NW. Phone 202-501-5000.

### National Gallery of Art

The **National Gallery of Art**, situated on the north side of the Mall facing Constitution Avenue, was established by Joint Resolution of Congress Mar. 24, 1937, and opened Mar. 17, 1941. The original West building was designed by John Russell Pope. The East building, opened in 1978, was designed by I. M. Pei. The National Gallery is separate from, but maintains a relationship with, the Smithsonian Institution.

Normally open daily, 10 AM - 5 PM; Sunday, 11 AM - 6 PM. Closed Jan. 1 and Dec. 25. Constitution Ave. between 3d & 7th Sts. Phone 202-737-4215.

### Smithsonian Institution

The **Smithsonian Institution,** established in 1846, is the world's largest museum complex and consists of 14 museums and the National Zoo. It holds some 100 million artifacts and specimens in its trust "for the increase and diffusion of knowledge among men." Nine museums are on the National Mall between the Washington Monument and the Capitol; 5 other museums and the zoo are elsewhere in Washington (the Cooper-Hewitt Museum and the National Museum of the American Indian, administered by the Smithsonian, are in New York City). Most visitors begin their trip with a visit to the **Smithsonian Information Center,** located in "the Castle" on the Mall. Also on the Mall are the **National Museum of American History,** the **National Museum of Natural History,** the **National Air and Space Museum,** the **Hirshhorn Museum and Sculpture Garden,** the **Arthur M. Sackler Gallery,** the **National Museum of African Art,** the **Freer Gallery of Art,** and the **Arts and Industries Building.** Near the Sackler Gallery is the **Enid A. Haupt Garden.** Located nearby are the **National Postal Museum,** the **National Museum of American Art,** the **National Portrait Gallery,** and the **Renwick Gallery.** Farther away, at 1901 Fort Place SE, is the **Anacostia Museum.**

Most museums are open daily, except Dec. 25, 10 AM to 5:30 PM. Phone 202-357-2700.

### Vietnam Veterans Memorial

Originally dedicated on Nov. 13, 1982, the **Vietnam Veterans Memorial** is a symbol of the nation's recognition of the men and women who served in the armed forces in the Vietnam War. On a V-shaped black-granite wall, designed by Maya Ying Lin, are inscribed the names of the more than 58,000 Americans who lost their lives or remain missing.

Since 1982, 2 additions have been made to the Memorial. The 1st, dedicated on Nov. 11, 1984, is the Frederick Hart sculpture *Three Servicemen.* On Nov. 11, 1993, the Vietnam Women's Memorial was dedicated, honoring the more than 11,500 women who served in Vietnam. The bronze sculpture, portraying 3 women helping a wounded male soldier, was designed by Glenna Goodacre.

The memorial is open 24 hr daily. Phone 202-426-6841.

### Washington Monument

The **Washington Monument,** dedicated in 1885, is a tapering shaft, or obelisk, of white marble, 555 ft, 5 1/8 inches in height and 55 ft, 1½ in. square at base. Eight small windows, 2 on each side, are located at the 500-ft level, where points of interest are indicated.

Open daily except Dec. 25, 9 AM - 4:30 PM; 8 AM - midnight, Apr.-Labor Day. Phone 202-426-6841.

### The White House

The **White House,** the president's residence, stands on 18 acres on the south side of Pennsylvania Ave., between the Treasury and the old Executive Office Building. The walls are of sandstone, quarried at Aquia Creek, VA. The exterior walls were painted, causing the building to be termed the "White House." On Aug. 24, 1814, during Madison's administration, the house was burned by the British. James Hoban rebuilt it by Oct. 1817.

The White House is normally open for free self-guided tours Tues.-Sat., 10 AM - 12 noon (tickets, necessary Apr. 1 - Labor Day, are available at visitor's booth, 15th St. near E St.). Only the public rooms on the ground floor and state floor may be visited. Free reserved tickets for guided tours can be obtained 8 to 10 weeks in advance from your local congressperson or senator. 1600 Pennsylvania Ave. Phone 202-456-7041.

## Attractions Near Washington, DC

### Arlington National Cemetery

**Arlington National Cemetery,** on the former Custis estate in Arlington, VA, is the site of the **Tomb of the Unknowns** and is the final resting place of John Fitzgerald Kennedy, 35th president of the U.S., who was buried there on Nov. 25, 1963. His wife, Jacqueline Bouvier Kennedy Onassis was buried at the same site on May 23, 1994. An eternal flame burns over the grave site. In an adjacent area is the grave of Pres. Kennedy's brother Sen. Robert F. Kennedy (NY), interred on June 8, 1968. Many other famous Americans are also buried at Arlington, as well as more than 200,000 American soldiers from every major war.

North of the National Cemetery, approximately 350 yd, stands the **U.S. Marine Corps War Memorial**, also known as Iwo Jima. The memorial is a bronze statue of the raising of the U.S. flag on Mt. Suribachi, Feb. 23, 1945, during World War II, executed by Felix de Weldon from the photograph by Joe Rosenthal, and presented to the nation by members and friends of the U.S. Marine Corps.

Open daily, 8 AM - 7 PM. Arlington, VA. Phone 703-697-2131.

### Mount Vernon

**Mount Vernon**, George Washington's estate, is on the south bank of the Potomac R., 16 mi below Washington, DC, in northern Virginia.

The present house is an enlargement of one apparently built on the site by Augustine Washington, who lived there 1735-38. His son Lawrence came there in 1743, when he renamed the plantation Mount Vernon in honor of Admiral Vernon, under whom he had served in the West Indies. Lawrence Washington died in 1752 and was succeeded as proprietor of Mount Vernon by his half-brother, George Washington.

The estate has been restored to its 18th-century appearance and includes many original furnishings. Washington and his wife, Martha, are buried on the grounds.

Open 365 days, Apr. - Aug., 8 AM - 5 PM; Sept. - Mar., 9 AM - 5 PM (Nov.-Feb. closes at 4 PM). Phone 703-780-2000.

### The Pentagon

The **Pentagon,** headquarters of the Department of Defense, is one of the world's largest office buildings. Situated in Arlington, VA, it houses more than 23,000 employees in offices that occupy 3,707,745 sq ft.

Free tours are available Mon. - Fri. (excluding federal holidays), 9:30 AM - 3:30. Arlington, VA, 703-695-1776.

# CITIES OF THE U.S.

**Sources:** Bureau of the Census: population (rank) (estimated as of July 1994); population growth (1990-94). Geography Division, Bureau of the Census: population density (1994 est.); area (1990). Bureau of Labor Statistics: employment (1995 averages for city proper only). Bureau of Economic Analysis: per capita personal income (Metropolitan Statistical Area, 1994).

Included here are the 100 most populous cities, based on July 1994 Census Bureau estimates (inc.=incorporated; est.=established). **Note:** Most of the Internet addresses listed are either official city government sites or Chamber of Commerce sites.

## Akron, Ohio

**Population:** 221,886 (75); **Pop. density:** 3,567 per sq. mi; **Pop. growth:** –0.5%. **Area:** 62.2 sq. mi. **Employment:** 103,897 employed, 6.3% unemployed. **Per capita income:** $21,012; % increase 1990-94: 18.7.

**History:** settled 1825; inc. as city 1865; located on Ohio-Erie Canal and is a port of entry; since 1870 the rubber capital of the U.S.

**Transportation:** 1 airport; major trucking industry; Conrail; metro transit system. **Communications:** 4 TV, 7 radio stations. **Medical facilities:** 11 hospitals; specialized children's treatment center. **Educational facilities:** 13 universities and colleges; 68 public schools. **Further information:** Akron Regional Development Board, Cascade Plaza, Akron, OH 44308.

**Internet site:** http://www.ardb.org

## Albuquerque, New Mexico

**Population:** 411,994 (36); **Pop. density:** 3,116 per sq. mi; **Pop. growth:** 7.1%. **Area:** 132.2 sq. mi. **Employment:** 221,113 employed, 3.9% unemployed. **Per capita income:** $19,889; % increase 1990-94: 22.2.

**History:** founded 1706 by the Spanish; inc. 1890.

**Transportation:** 1 intl. airport; 1 railroad; 1 bus line. **Communications:** 8 TV, 38 radio stations. **Medical facilities:** 6 major hospitals. **Educational facilities:** 1 university, 13 colleges. **Further information:** Convention & Visitors Bureau, PO Box 26866, Albuquerque, NM 87125-6866.

**Internet site:** http://www.abqcvb.org

## Anaheim, California

**Population:** 282,133 (58); **Pop. density:** 6,369 per sq. mi; **Pop. growth:** 5.9%. **Area:** 44.3 sq. mi. **Employment:** 137,879 employed, 5.9% unemployed. **Per capita income:** $25,516; % increase 1990-94: 5.1.

**History:** founded 1857; inc. 1870; now known as home of Disneyland (since 1955).

**Transportation:** 3 municipal airports; 4 railroads; Greyhound buses. **Communications:** 12 TV, 4 radio stations. **Medical facilities:** 5 hospitals; 4 medical centers. **Educational facilities:** 13 universities and colleges; 22 elementary, 8 junior high, 12 high schools. **Further information:** Chamber of Commerce, 100 South Anaheim Blvd., Ste. 300, Anaheim, CA 92805.

## Anchorage, Alaska

**Population:** 253,649 (64); **Pop. density:** 149 per sq. mi; **Pop. growth:** 12.1%. **Area:** 1,697.6 sq. mi. **Employment:** 125,866 employed, 5.2% unemployed. **Per capita income:** $27,026; % increase 1990-94: 12.1.

**History:** founded 1914 as a construction camp for railroad; HQ of Alaska Defense Command, WWII; severely damaged in earthquake 1964.

**Transportation:** 1 intl. airport, 3 other airports; railroad; transit system. **Communications:** 8 TV, 22 radio stations. **Medical facilities:** 3 hospitals. **Educational facilities:** 4 universities, 3 colleges. **Further information:** Chamber of Commerce, 441 W. 5th Ave., Ste. 300, Anchorage, AK 99501-2309.

## Arlington, Texas

**Population:** 286,922 (56); **Pop. density:** 3,085 per sq. mi; **Pop. growth:** 9.6%. **Area:** 93 sq. mi. **Employment:** 165,655 employed, 4.3% unemployed. **Per capita income:** $21,412; % increase 1990-94: 14.7.

**History:** settled in 1840s between Dallas and Ft. Worth; inc. 1884.

**Transportation:** Dallas/Ft. Worth airport is 20 min. away; 11 railway lines; intercity transport system in planning stage. **Communications:** 11 TV, 44 radio stations. **Medical facilities:** 2 hospitals. **Educational facilities:** 1 university; 54 public schools. **Further information:** The Arlington Chamber, 316 W. Main St., Arlington, TX 76010.

**Internet site:** http://www.ci.arlington.tx.us

## Atlanta, Georgia

**Population:** 396,052 (37); **Pop. density:** 3,005 per sq. mi; **Pop. growth:** 0.5%. **Area:** 131.8 sq. mi. **Employment:** 190,217 employed, 7.3% unemployed. **Per capita income:** $23,633; % increase 1990-94: 15.6.

**History:** founded as "Terminus" 1837; renamed Atlanta 1845; inc. 1847; played major role in Civil War; became permanent state capital 1877; birthplace of civil rights movement; host to 1996 Centennial Olympic Games.

**Transportation:** 1 intl. airport; 3 railroad lines; MARTA bus and rapid rail service. **Communications:** 11 TV, 51 radio stations; 26 cable TV companies. **Medical facilities:** 55 hospitals; VA hospital; U.S. Centers for Disease Control and Prevention; American Cancer Society. **Educational facilities:** 40 colleges, universities, seminaries, junior colleges. **Further information:** Metro Atlanta Chamber of Commerce, 235 Intl. Blvd. NW, Atlanta, GA 30303.

**Internet site:** http://www.atlanta.org

## Aurora, Colorado

**Population:** 250,717 (65); **Pop. density:** 1,892 per sq. mi; **Pop. growth:** 12.9%. **Area:** 132.5 sq. mi. **Employment:** 144,833 employed, 3.6% unemployed. **Per capita income:** $24,732; % increase 1990-94: 17.8.

**History:** located 5 miles east of Denver; early growth stimulated by presence of military bases; fast-growing trade center.

**Transportation:** adjacent to new Denver Intl. Airport; 1 airport; 4 railroads; bus system. **Communications:** 1 TV station. **Medical facilities:** 2 private hospitals, 1 public hospital. **Educational facilities:** 1 university, 1 community college, 2 technical colleges. **Further information:** Aurora Planning Dept., 1470 S. Havana St., Rm. 608, Aurora, CO 80012.

**Internet site:** http://www.ci.aurora.co.us

## Austin, Texas

**Population:** 514,013 (23); **Pop. density:** 2,360 per sq. mi; **Pop. growth:** 10.4%. **Area:** 217.8 sq. mi. **Employment:** 329,072 employed, 3.3% unemployed. **Per capita income:** $20,611; % increase 1990-94: 20.8.

**History:** first permanent settlement 1835; capital of Rep. of Texas 1838; named after Stephen Austin; inc. 1840.

**Transportation:** 1 intl. airport; 4 railroads. **Communications:** 7 TV, 20 radio stations. **Medical facilities:** 11 hospitals. **Educational facilities:** 8 universities and colleges. **Further information:** Chamber of Commerce, PO Box 1967, Austin, TX 78767.

**Internet site:** http://www.ci.austin.tx.us

## Bakersfield, California

**Population:** 191,060 (89); **Pop. density:** 2,081 per sq. mi; **Pop. growth:** 9.2%. **Area:** 91.8 sq. mi. **Employment:** 85,131 employed, 10.3% unemployed. **Per capita income:** $16,505; % increase 1990-94: 5.5.

**History:** named after Col. Thomas Baker, an early settler; inc. 1898.

**Transportation:** 1 airport; 3 railroads; Amtrak; Greyhound buses; local bus system. **Communications:** 5 TV, 34 radio stations. **Medical facilities:** 6 major hospitals; 9 convalescent, 1 psychiatric, 3 physical rehab., 5 urgent care facilities; 3 clinics. **Educational facilities:** 1 university, 1 community college; 9 vocational schools; 1 adult school; 1 college of law. **Further information:** Greater Bakersfield Chamber of Commerce, 1033 Truxtun Avenue, Bakersfield, CA 93301.

**Internet site:** http://www.bbol.org

## Baltimore, Maryland

**Population:** 702,979 (14); **Pop. density:** 8,700 per sq. mi; **Pop. growth:** –4.5%. **Area:** 80.8 sq. mi. **Employment:** 292,502 employed, 8.3% unemployed. **Per capita income:** $24,046; % increase 1990-94: 13.1.

**History:** founded by Maryland legislature 1729; inc. 1797; bombing of its Ft. McHenry 1814 inspired Francis Scott Key to write "Star-Spangled Banner"; rebuilt after fire 1904.

**Transportation:** 1 major airport; 3 railroads; bus system; subway system; 2 underwater tunnels. **Communications:** 6 TV, 33 radio stations. **Medical facilities:** 29 hospitals; 2 major medical centers. **Educational facilities:** over 30 universities and colleges; 177 public schools. **Further information:** Greater Baltimore Committee, 111 S. Calvert St., Ste. 1500, Baltimore, MD 21202-6180.

**Internet site:** http://www.ci.baltimore.md.us

## Baton Rouge, Louisiana

**Population:** 227,482 (72); **Pop. density:** 3,078 per sq. mi; **Pop. growth:** 3.6%. **Area:** 73.9 sq. mi. **Employment:** 106,118 employed, 6.4% unemployed. **Per capita income:** $19,385; % increase 1990-94: 21.6.

**History:** claimed by Spain at time of La. Purchase 1803; est. independence by rebellion 1810; inc. as town 1817; became state capital 1849; held by Union during most of Civil War.

**Transportation:** 1 airport, 5 airlines; 1 bus line; 3 railroad trunk lines. **Communications:** 5 TV, 19 radio stations. **Medical facilities:** 5 hospitals. **Educational facilities:** 2 universities; 92 public, 39 private schools. **Further information:** Chamber of Commerce, PO Box 3217, Baton Rouge, LA 70821.

## Birmingham, Alabama

**Population:** 264,527 (61); **Pop. density:** 1,781 per sq. mi; **Pop. growth:** –0.3%. **Area:** 148.5 sq. mi. **Employment:** 118,367 employed, 6.5% unemployed. **Per capita income:** $21,214; % increase 1990-94: 20.6.

**History:** settled as a result of discovery of elements needed for steel production; inc. 1871; named after Great Britain's steel-making center.

**Transportation:** 1 airport; 4 major rail freight lines, Amtrak; 1 bus line; 75 truck line terminals; 4 interstate highways. **Communications:** 5 TV, 27 radio stations; 1 educational TV, 1 educational radio station. **Medical facilities:** Univ. of Alabama at Birmingham Medical Center; VA hospital with organ transplant program; 15 other hospitals. **Educational facilities:** 1 university, 2 colleges, 2 junior colleges. **Further information:** Chamber of Commerce, 2027 First Ave. N, Birmingham, AL 35202.

**Internet site:** http://www.birmingham.org/thechamber

## Boston, Massachusetts

**Population:** 547,725 (21); **Pop. density:** 11,317 per sq. mi; **Pop. growth:** –4.6%. **Area:** 48.4 sq. mi. **Employment:** 269,711 employed, 5.4% unemployed. **Per capita income:** $26,093; % increase 1990-94: 15.5.

**History:** settled 1630 by John Winthrop; capital of Mass. Bay Colony; figured strongly in Am. Revolution, earning distinction as the "Cradle of Liberty"; inc. 1822.

**Transportation:** 1 major airport; 2 railroads; city rail and subway system; 3 underwater tunnels; port. **Communications:** 9 TV, 21 radio stations. **Medical facilities:** 13 hospitals; 8 major medical research centers. **Educational facilities:** 30 universities and colleges. **Further information:** Greater Boston Chamber of Commerce, 1 Beacon St., 4th fl., Boston, MA 02108-3114.

**Internet site:** http://www.ci.boston.ma.us

## Buffalo, New York

**Population:** 312,965 (53); **Pop. density:** 7,708 per sq. mi; **Pop. growth:** –4.6%. **Area:** 40.6 sq. mi. **Employment:** 129,813 employed, 8.8% unemployed. **Per capita income:** $21,079; % increase 1990-94: 17.9.

**History:** founded 1790 by the Dutch; raided twice by British, War of 1812; served as western terminus for Erie Canal, became a center for trade and manufacturing; inc. 1832; last stop on the Underground Railroad; key point for Canada-U.S. political, trade, and social relations.

**Transportation:** 1 intl. airport; 6 major railroads; metro rail system; water service to Great Lakes-St. Lawrence Seaway system, and Atlantic seaboard. **Communications:** 7 TV, 18 radio stations. **Medical facilities:** 14 hospitals, 37 research centers. **Educational facilities:** 12 colleges and universities; 111 public and private schools. **Further information:** Greater Buffalo Partnership, 300 Main Place Tower, Buffalo, NY 14202-3797.

**Internet site:** http://www.ci.buffalo.ny.us

## Charlotte, North Carolina

**Population:** 437,797 (32); **Pop. density:** 2,512 per sq. mi; **Pop. growth:** 10.6%. **Area:** 174.3 sq. mi. **Employment:** 243,171 employed, 3.3% unemployed. **Per capita income:** $21,945; % increase 1990-94: 18.0.

**History:** settled by Scotch-Irish immigrants 1740s; inc. 1768 and named after Queen Charlotte, George III's wife; scene of first major U.S. gold discovery 1799.

**Transportation:** 1 airport; 2 major railway lines; 2 bus lines; 238 trucking firms. **Communications:** 7 TV, 27 radio stations. **Medical facilities:** 12 hospitals, 1 medical center. **Educational facilities:** 2 universities, 5 colleges. **Further information:** Chamber of Commerce, PO Box 32785, Charlotte, NC 28232.

**Internet site:** http://www.charlottechamber.org

## Chesapeake, Virginia

**Population:** 180,577 (98); **Pop. density:** 530 per sq. mi; **Pop. growth:** 18.8%. **Area:** 340.7 sq. mi. **Employment:** 91,329 employed, 4.1% unemployed. **Per capita income:** $19,007; % increase 1990-94: 13.7.

**History:** Battle of Great Bridge fought here 1775; inc. as a city 1963.

**Transportation:** Amtrak; bus service; deepwater ports. **Communications:** 6 TV, 29 radio stations. **Medical facilities:** 1 hospital. **Educational facilities:** 1 college; 41 public schools. **Further information:** Hampton Roads Chamber of Commerce, 420 Bank St., PO Box 327, Norfolk, VA 23501.

**Internet site:** http://www.chesapeake.va.us

## Chicago, Illinois

**Population:** 2,731,743 (3); **Pop. density:** 12,024 per sq. mi; **Pop. growth:** –1.9%. **Area:** 227.2 sq. mi. **Employment:** 1,208,241 employed, 6.7% unemployed. **Per capita income:** $25,865; % increase 1990-94: 16.7.

**History:** site acquired from Indians 1795; significant white settlement began with opening of Erie Canal 1825; chartered as city 1837; boomed with arrival of railroads from east and canal to Mississippi R.; about one-third of city destroyed by fire 1871; major grain & livestock market.

**Transportation:** 3 airports; major railroad system; major trucking industry. **Communications:** 9 TV, 31 radio stations. **Medical facilities:** over 123 hospitals. **Educational facilities:** 95 institutions of higher learning. **Further information:** Chicagoland Chamber of Commerce, 1 IBM Plaza, Ste. 2800, Chicago, IL 60611.

**Internet site:** http://www.ci.chi.il.us

## Cincinnati, Ohio

**Population:** 358,170 (46); **Pop. density:** 4,640 per sq. mi; **Pop. growth:** –1.6%. **Area:** 77.2 sq. mi. **Employment:** 163,696 employed, 5.8% unemployed. **Per capita income:** $22,303; % increase 1990-94: 18.0.

**History:** founded 1788 and named after the Society of Cincinnati, an organization of Revolutionary War officers; chartered as village 1802; inc. as city 1819.

**Transportation:** 1 intl. airport; 3 railroads; 1 bus system. **Communications:** 8 TV, 27 radio stations. **Medical facilities:** 32 hospitals; Children's Hospital Medical Center; VA hospital. **Educational facilities:** 4 universities; 11 colleges, 8 technical & 2-year colleges. **Further information:** Chamber of Commerce, 300 Carew Tower, 441 Vine St., Cincinnati, OH 45202.

**Internet site:** http://www.gccc.com

## Cleveland, Ohio

**Population:** 492,901 (26); **Pop. density:** 6,401 per sq. mi; **Pop. growth:** –2.5%. **Area:** 77 sq. mi. **Employment:** 185,403 employed, 9.4% unemployed. **Per capita income:** $23,502; % increase 1990-94: 17.8.

**History:** surveyed in 1796; given recognition as village 1815, inc. as city 1836; annexed Ohio City 1854.

**Transportation:** 1 intl. airport; rail service; major port; rapid transit system. **Communications:** 9 TV, 26 radio stations. **Medical facilities:** 14 hospitals. **Educational facilities:** 8 universities and colleges; 127 public schools. **Further information:** Greater Cleveland Growth Assn., 200 Tower City Center, 50 Public Square, Cleveland, OH 44113-2291.

**Internet site:** http://www.cleveland.oh.us

## Colorado Springs, Colorado

**Population:** 316,480 (51); **Pop. density:** 1,728 per sq. mi; **Pop. growth:** 12.9%. **Area:** 183.2 sq. mi. **Employment:** 165,332 employed, 4.6% unemployed. **Per capita income:** $19,612; % increase 1990-94: 17.3.

**History:** founded 1871 at the foot of Pikes Peak; inc. 1872.
**Transportation:** 1 municipal airport; 2 railroads; bus line. **Communications:** 9 TV, 28 radio stations. **Medical facilities:** 7 hospitals. **Educational facilities:** 11 universities, 12 colleges. **Further information:** Chamber of Commerce, PO Box B, Colorado Springs, CO 80901.
**Internet site:** http://www.coloradosprings-travel.com/ cscvb

## Columbus, Georgia

**Population:** 186,470 (92); **Pop. density:** 863 per sq. mi; **Pop. growth:** 4.4%. **Area:** 216.1 sq. mi. **Employment:** 73,888 employed, 5.9% unemployed. **Per capita income:** $17,175; % increase 1990-94: 17.7.
**History:** settled and inc. 1828; a port city on Chattahoochee R.
**Transportation:** 1 airport; Metra bus system; 2 bus lines; 2 railroads. **Communications:** 5 TV, 11 radio stations. **Medical facilities:** 5 hospitals. **Educational facilities:** 2 colleges; 52 public, 1 technical, 13 private schools. **Further information:** Chamber of Commerce, PO Box 1200, Columbus, GA 31902.

## Columbus, Ohio

**Population:** 635,913 (16); **Pop. density:** 3,331 per sq. mi; **Pop. growth:** 0.5%. **Area:** 190.9 sq. mi. **Employment:** 360,985 employed, 3.4% unemployed. **Per capita income:** $22,058; % increase 1990-94: 20.8.
**History:** first settlement 1797; laid out as new capital 1812 with current name; became city 1834.
**Transportation:** 6 airports; 3 railroads; 4 intercity bus lines. **Communications:** 8 TV, 25 radio stations. **Medical facilities:** 18 hospitals. **Educational facilities:** 11 universities and colleges; 8 technical/2-year schools. **Further information:** Chamber of Commerce, 37 N. High St., Columbus, OH 43215.
**Internet site:** http://www.columbus.org

## Corpus Christi, Texas

**Population:** 275,419 (59); **Pop. density:** 2,040 per sq. mi; **Pop. growth:** 7.0%. **Area:** 135 sq. mi. **Employment:** 119,986 employed, 8.9% unemployed. **Per capita income:** $17,351; % increase 1990-94: 18.4.
**History:** settled 1839 and inc. 1852.
**Transportation:** 1 intl. airport; 2 bus lines, metro bus system; 3 freight railroads. **Communications:** 6 TV, 17 radio stations. **Medical facilities:** 14 hospitals including a children's center. **Educational facilities:** 1 university, 1 college. **Further information:** Greater Corpus Christi Business Alliance, PO Box 640, Corpus Christi, TX 78403.
**Internet site:** http://www.cctexas.org

## Dallas, Texas

**Population:** 1,022,830 (8); **Pop. density:** 2,987 per sq. mi; **Pop. growth:** 1.5%. **Area:** 342.4 sq. mi. **Employment:** 585,155 employed, 5.9% unemployed. **Per capita income:** $24,480; % increase 1990-94: 19.5.
**History:** first settled 1841; platted 1846; inc. 1871; developed as the financial and commercial center of Southwest; major center for distribution and high-tech manufacturing.
**Transportation:** 1 intl. airport, 1 regional airport; Amtrak; transit system. **Communications:** 14 TV, 41 radio stations. **Medical facilities:** 14 general hospitals; major medical center. **Educational facilities:** 11 universities and colleges, 3 community college campuses. **Further information:** Greater Dallas Chamber, Information Services, 1201 Elm, Ste. 2000, Dallas, TX 75270.
**Internet site:** http://www.gdc.org

## Dayton, Ohio

**Population:** 178,540 (100); **Pop. density:** 3,246 per sq. mi; **Pop. growth:** –1.9%. **Area:** 55 sq. mi. **Employment:** 72,416 employed, 7.0% unemployed. **Per capita income:** $21,366; % increase 1990-94: 20.4.
**History:** settled 1796; inc. 1805; disastrous flood 1913; site where Wright Bros. invented first airplane to sustain flight 1903.
**Transportation:** 1 intl. airport, 16 airlines; 3 railroads; 2 bus lines; countywide Dayton Regional Transit Authority. **Communications:** 5 TV, 26 radio stations. **Medical facilities:** 14 hospitals including VA facility. **Educational facilities:** 3 colleges and universities. **Further information:** Dayton Area Chamber of Commerce, 1 Chamber Plaza, Dayton, OH 45402-2400.
**Internet site:** http://www.dayton.net/dayton

## Denver, Colorado

**Population:** 493,559 (25); **Pop. density:** 3,220 per sq. mi; **Pop. growth:** 5.5%. **Area:** 153.3 sq. mi. **Employment:** 265,531 employed, 4.8% unemployed. **Per capita income:** $24,732; % increase 1990-94: 17.8.
**History:** settled 1858 by gold prospectors and miners; inc. 1861; became territorial capital 1867; growth spurred by gold and silver boom; financial, industrial, cultural center of Rocky Mt. region.
**Transportation:** 1 intl. airport, 3 corporate reliever airports; 5 rail freight lines, Amtrak; 1 bus line. **Communications:** 14 TV, 29 radio stations. **Medical facilities:** 20 hospitals. **Educational facilities:** 13 universities and colleges; 8 two-yr. and community colleges. **Further information:** Denver Metro Chamber of Commerce, 1445 Market St., Denver, CO 80202-1729.
**Internet site:** http://www.den-chamber.org

## Des Moines, Iowa

**Population:** 193,965 (86); **Pop. density:** 2,576 per sq. mi; **Pop. growth:** 0.4%. **Area:** 75.3 sq. mi. **Employment:** 115,345 employed, 3.3% unemployed. **Per capita income:** $23,681; % increase 1990-94: 20.1.
**History:** Fort Des Moines built 1843; settled and inc. 1851; chartered as city 1857.
**Transportation:** 1 intl. airport; 4 bus lines; 5 railroads; metro bus system. **Communications:** 5 TV, 15 radio stations. **Medical facilities:** 8 hospitals. **Educational facilities:** 2 universities, 5 colleges. **Further information:** Greater Des Moines Chamber of Commerce Federation, 601 Locust St., Ste. 100, Des Moines, IA 50309.
**Internet site:** http://www.dmchamber.com

## Detroit, Michigan

**Population:** 992,038 (10); **Pop. density:** 7,152 per sq. mi; **Pop. growth:** –3.5%. **Area:** 138.7 sq. mi. **Employment:** 341,171 employed, 10.0% unemployed. **Per capita income:** $24,692; % increase 1990-94: 20.6.
**History:** founded by French 1701; controlled by British 1760; acquired by U.S. 1796; destroyed by fire 1805; inc. as city 1824; capital of state 1837-47; auto manufacturing began 1899.
**Transportation:** 1 intl. airport; 10 railroads; major intl. port; public transit system. **Communications:** 9 TV, 37 radio stations. **Medical facilities:** 28 hospitals, major medical center. **Educational facilities:** 18 universities and colleges. **Further information:** Greater Detroit Chamber of Commerce, 600 W. Lafayette Blvd., PO Box 33840, Detroit, MI 48232-0840.
**Internet site:** http://detroit.freenet.org

## El Paso, Texas

**Population:** 579,307 (19); **Pop. density:** 2,361 per sq. mi; **Pop. growth:** 12.4%. **Area:** 245.4 sq. mi. **Employment:** 230,891 employed, 10.0% unemployed. **Per capita income:** $12,940; % increase 1990-94: 12.4.
**History:** first settled 1827; inc. 1873; arrival of railroad 1881 boosted city's population and industries.
**Transportation:** 1 intl. airport; 5 major rail lines; 8 bus lines; 5 major highways; gateway to Mexico. **Communications:** 10 TV, 23 radio stations. **Medical facilities:** 15 hospitals; cancer treatment center. **Educational facilities:** 2 universities, 3 colleges (1 grad. only). **Further information:** Greater El Paso Chamber of Commerce, 10 Civic Center Plaza, El Paso, TX 79901.
**Internet site:** http://cs.utep.edu/elpaso

## Fort Wayne, Indiana

**Population:** 183,359 (95); **Pop. density:** 2,924 per sq. mi; **Pop. growth:** –0.5%. **Area:** 62.7 sq. mi. **Employment:** 95,110 employed, 4.7% unemployed. **Per capita income:** $21,330; % increase 1990-94: 19.1.
**History:** French fort 1680; U.S. fort 1794; settled by 1832; inc. 1840 prior to Wabash-Erie canal completion 1843.
**Transportation:** 2 airports; 3 railroads; 8 bus lines. **Communications:** 5 TV, 13 radio stations. **Medical facilities:** 3 regional hospitals; VA hospital. **Educational facilities:** 4 universities, 5 colleges, 2 bus. schools; 82 public

schools. **Further information:** Chamber of Commerce, 826 Ewing Street, Fort Wayne, IN 46802-2182.
**Internet site:** http://www.ft-wayne.in.us

## Fort Worth, Texas

**Population:** 451,814 (29); **Pop. density:** 1,607 per sq. mi; **Pop. growth:** 0.9%. **Area:** 281.1 sq. mi. **Employment:** 234,305 employed, 6.4% unemployed. **Per capita income:** $21,412; % increase 1990-94: 14.7.
**History:** est. as military post 1849; inc. 1873; oil discovered 1917.
**Transportation:** 1 intl. airport; 9 major railroads, Amtrak; local bus service; 2 transcontinental, 2 intrastate bus lines. **Communications:** 14 TV, 11 local radio stations. **Medical facilities:** 25 hospitals; 1 children's hospital; 4 government hospitals. **Educational facilities:** 8 universities and colleges. **Further information:** Chamber of Commerce, 777 Taylor St. #900, Fort Worth, TX 76102.
**Internet site:** http://www.towery.com/fortworth

## Fremont, California

**Population:** 183,575 (93); **Pop. density:** 2,384 per sq. mi; **Pop. growth:** 5.9%. **Area:** 77 sq. mi. **Employment:** 97,116 employed, 4.0% unemployed. **Per capita income:** $26,530; % increase 1990-94: 13.6.
**History:** area first settled by Spanish 1769; inc. 1956 with the consolidation of 5 communities.
**Transportation:** intracity bus line; Bay Area Rapid Transit System (southern terminal). **Communications:** 1 local radio station. **Medical facilities:** 2 hospitals. **Educational facilities:** 1 junior college; 43 public schools. **Further information:** Chamber of Commerce, 2201 Walnut Ave., Ste. 110, Fremont, CA 94538.
**Internet site:** http://www.infolane.com/fmt-chamber

## Fresno, California

**Population:** 386,551 (38); **Pop. density:** 3,901 per sq. mi; **Pop. growth:** 9.2%. **Area:** 99.1 sq. mi. **Employment:** 165,151 employed, 12.7% unemployed. **Per capita income:** $17,104; % increase 1990-94: 7.1.
**History:** founded 1872; inc. as city 1885.
**Transportation:** municipal airport; Amtrak; 1 bus line; intracity bus system. **Communications:** 11 TV, 30 radio stations. **Medical facilities:** 6 general hospitals including a VA facility. **Educational facilities:** 9 universities and colleges; 90 public schools. **Further information:** Chamber of Commerce, 2331 Fresno St., Fresno, CA 93721.
**Internet site:** http://fresno-online.com/cvb

## Garland, Texas

**Population:** 194,218 (84); **Pop. density:** 3,389 per sq. mi; **Pop. growth:** 7.5%. **Area:** 57.3 sq. mi. **Employment:** 111,499 employed, 3.9% unemployed. **Per capita income:** $24,480; % increase 1990-94: 19.5.
**History:** settled 1850s; inc. 1891.
**Transportation:** 25 min. from Dallas/Ft. Worth Intl. Airport; 2 railroads. **Communications:** 14 local TV (Dallas/Ft. Worth), 25+ radio stations. **Medical facilities:** 2 hospitals; 329 beds. **Educational facilities:** 1 university, 2 community colleges; 59 public schools. **Further information:** Chamber of Commerce, 914 S. Garland Ave., Garland, TX 75040.
**Internet site:** http://www.theshoppes.com/~garland

## Grand Rapids, Michigan

**Population:** 190,395 (90); **Pop. density:** 4,298 per sq. mi; **Pop. growth:** 0.7%. **Area:** 44.3 sq. mi. **Employment:** 97,231 employed, 5.3% unemployed. **Per capita income:** $21,663; % increase 1990-94: 25.1.
**History:** originally site of Ottawa Indian village; trading post 1826; became lumbering center and chartered as town 1850.
**Transportation:** 1 intl. airport; 4 railroads; 5 bus lines; transit bus system. **Communications:** 6 TV, 25 radio stations. **Medical facilities:** 10 hospitals. **Educational facilities:** 8 colleges; 64 public schools. **Further information:** Chamber of Commerce, 111 Pearl St., NW, Grand Rapids, MI 49503.
**Internet site:** http://www.grandnet.org

## Greensboro, North Carolina

**Population:** 196,167 (80); **Pop. density:** 2,458 per sq. mi; **Pop. growth:** 6.7%. **Area:** 79.8 sq. mi. **Employment:** 106,535 employed, 3.5% unemployed. **Per capita income:** $21,789; % increase 1990-94: 18.0.
**History:** settled 1749; site of Revolutionary War conflict 1781 between Nathanael Greene and Cornwallis; inc. 1807.
**Transportation:** 1 regional airport; 2 railroads; Trailways/Greyhound bus service. **Communications:** all cable TV stations; 11 radio stations. **Medical facilities:** 4 hospitals. **Educational facilities:** 2 universities, 3 colleges; 56 public schools. **Further information:** Chamber of Commerce, P.O. Box 3246, Greensboro, NC 27402.
**Internet site:** http://www.greensboro.nc.us/gol

## Hialeah, Florida

**Population:** 194,120 (85); **Pop. density:** 10,110 per sq. mi; **Pop. growth:** 3.3%. **Area:** 19.2 sq. mi. **Employment:** 95,254 employed, 7.6% unemployed. **Per capita income:** $20,014; % increase 1990-94: 13.5.
**History:** founded 1917, inc. 1925; industrial and residential city NW of Miami; Hialeah Park Horse Racing Track.
**Transportation:** 5 mi from Miami Intl. Airport; access to Port of Miami; Amtrak; 2 rail freight lines; Metrorail, Metrobus systems. **Communications:** 5 TV, 7 radio stations. **Medical facilities:** 4 hospitals (30 more in the area). **Educational facilities:** 7 universities and colleges. **Further information:** Hialeah-Dade Development, Inc., 501 Palm Ave., Hialeah, FL 33010-4720.

## Honolulu, Hawaii

**Population:** 385,881 (39); **Pop. density:** 4,660 per sq. mi; **Pop. growth:** 2.3%. **Area:** 82.8 sq. mi. **Employment (MSA):** 401,524 employed, 4.6% unemployed. **Per capita income:** $25,328; % increase 1990-94: 15.1.
**History:** harbor entered by Europeans 1794; declared capital of kingdom by King Kamehameha III 1850; Pearl Harbor naval base attacked by Japanese Dec. 7, 1941.
**Transportation:** 1 major airport; large, active port for passengers and cargo. **Communications:** 10 TV, 30 radio stations. **Medical facilities:** 13 major medical centers. **Educational facilities:** 4 universities, 5 colleges; 246 public schools, 98 private schools. **Further information:** Hawaii Visitors Bureau, 2270 Kalakaua Avenue, Honolulu, HI 96815.
**Internet site:** http://www.co.honolulu.hi.us

## Houston, Texas

**Population:** 1,702,086 (4); **Pop. density:** 3,153 per sq. mi; **Pop. growth:** 4.4%. **Area:** 539.9 sq. mi. **Employment:** 901,200 employed, 7.0% unemployed. **Per capita income:** $23,046; % increase 1990-94: 16.7.
**History:** founded 1836; inc. 1837; capital of Republic of Texas 1837-39; developed rapidly after construction of channel to Gulf of Mexico 1914; world center of oil and natural gas technology.
**Transportation:** 3 commercial airports; 4 mainline railroads; major bus transit system; major intl. port. **Communications:** 14 TV, 54 radio stations. **Medical facilities:** 53 hospitals; major medical center. **Educational facilities:** 22 universities and colleges. **Further information:** Greater Houston Partnership, 1200 Smith St., Houston, TX 77002-4309.
**Internet site:** http://www.houston.org

## Huntington Beach, California

**Population:** 189,220 (91); **Pop. density:** 7,167 per sq. **Pop. growth:** 4.2%. **Area:** 26.4 sq. mi. **Employment:** 105,313 employed, 3.9% unemployed. **Per capita income:** $21,562; % increase 1990-94: 3.9.
**History:** settled in early 1880s; inc. 1909; oil discovered 1920, led to city's development.
**Transportation:** 1 railroad; 2 bus lines. **Communications:** 2 TV stations. **Medical facilities:** 2 hospitals. **Educational facilities:** 1 community college; 34 public schools. **Further information:** Chamber of Commerce, Seacliff Office Park, 2100 Main St., #200, Huntington Beach, CA 92648.
**Internet site:** http://www.thebeach.com/hb

## Indianapolis, Indiana

**Population:** 752,279 (12); **Pop. density:** 2,080 per sq. mi; **Pop. growth:** 2.9%. **Area:** 361.7 sq. mi. **Employment:** 406,996 employed, 4.4% unemployed. **Per capita income:** $23,169; % increase 1990-94: 20.5.
**History:** settled 1820; became capital 1825.

**Transportation:** 1 intl. airport; 5 railroads; 3 interstate bus lines. **Communications:** 10 TV, 27 radio stations. **Medical facilities:** 17 hospitals; 1 major medical and research center. **Educational facilities:** 8 universities and colleges; major public library system. **Further information:** Chamber of Commerce, 320 N. Meridian St., Indianapolis, IN 46204.

**Internet site:** http://www.bit-wise.com/icec

## Jackson, Mississippi

**Population:** 193,097 (87); **Pop. density:** 1,772 per sq. mi; **Pop. growth:** –1.8%. **Area:** 109 sq. mi. **Employment:** 95,481 employed, 4.8% unemployed. **Per capita income:** $19,137; % increase 1990-94: 24.6.

**History:** originally known as Le Fleur's Bluff; selected as capital 1822 and named for Andrew Jackson; inc. 1823; scene of secession convention 1861; captured by Sherman 1863.

**Transportation:** 7 airlines; 1 bus line; 2 railroads. **Communications:** 5 TV, 18 radio stations. **Medical facilities:** 11 hospitals including a VA facility. **Educational facilities:** 2 universities, 7 colleges; 8 public school districts. **Further information:** Metro Jackson Chamber of Commerce, PO Box 22548, Jackson, MS 39225-2548.

## Jacksonville, Florida

**Population:** 665,070 (15); **Pop. density:** 877 per sq. mi; **Pop. growth:** 4.7%. **Area:** 758.7 sq. mi. **Employment:** 329,442 employed, 3.9% unemployed. **Per capita income:** $20,938; % increase 1990-94: 16.2.

**History:** settled 1816 as Cowford; renamed after Andrew Jackson 1822; inc. 1832; rechartered 1851; scene of conflicts in Seminole and Civil wars.

**Transportation:** 1 intl. airport; 3 railroads; 2 interstate bus lines. **Communications:** 6 TV, 34 radio stations. **Medical facilities:** 11 hospitals. **Educational facilities:** 3 universities, 4 colleges. **Further information:** Chamber of Commerce, 3 Independent Drive, Jacksonville, FL 32202-5092.

**Internet site:** http://www.jaxchamber.com

## Jersey City, New Jersey

**Population:** 226,022 (73); **Pop. density:** 15,169 per sq. mi; **Pop. growth:** –1.1%. **Area:** 14.9 sq. mi. **Employment:** 100,325 employed, 11.5% unemployed. **Per capita income:** $22,186; % increase 1990-94: 14.1.

**History:** site bought from Indians 1630; chartered as town by British 1668; scene of Revolutionary War conflict 1779; chartered under present name 1838; important station on Underground Railroad.

**Transportation:** bus and subway system. **Medical facilities:** 4 hospitals. **Educational facilities:** 3 colleges. **Further information:** Hudson County Chamber of Commerce, 574 Summit Ave., Ste. 404, Jersey City, NJ 07306.

## Kansas City, Missouri

**Population:** 443,878 (31); **Pop. density:** 1,425 per sq. mi; **Pop. growth:** 2.1%. **Area:** 311.5 sq. mi. **Employment:** 238,391 employed, 5.4% unemployed. **Per capita income:** $22,641; % increase 1990-94: 18.3.

**History:** settled by 1838 at confluence of the Missouri and Kansas rivers; inc. 1851.

**Transportation:** 1 intl. airport; a major rail center; 191 trunk lines; several barge companies. **Communications:** 7 TV, 29 radio stations. **Medical facilities:** 14 hospitals; VA facility. **Educational facilities:** 9 universities and colleges. **Further information:** Greater Kansas City Chamber of Commerce, 911 Main St., Ste. 2600, Kansas City, MO 64105.

**Internet site:** http://www.kansascity.com

## Las Vegas, Nevada

**Population:** 327,878 (49); **Pop. density:** 3,936 per sq. mi; **Pop. growth:** 27.0%. **Area:** 83.3 sq. mi. **Employment:** 175,605 employed, 5.3% unemployed. **Per capita income:** $22,339; % increase 1990-94: 18.0.

**History:** occupied by Mormons 1855-57; bought by railroad 1903; city of Las Vegas inc. 1911; gambling legalized 1931.

**Transportation:** 1 intl. airport; 2 railroads; bus system. **Communcations:** 9 TV, 30 radio stations. **Medical facilities:** 11 hospitals. **Educational facilities:** 1 university, 1 college; 184 public schools. **Further information:** Chamber of Commerce, 711 E. Desert Inn Rd., Las Vegas, NV 89109.

**Internet site:** http://www.vegas.com

## Lexington, Kentucky

**Population:** 237,612 (69); **Pop. density:** 835 per sq. mi; **Pop. growth:** 5.4%. **Area:** 284.5 sq. mi. **Employment:** 133,329 employed, 2.6% unemployed. **Per capita income:** $20,165; % increase 1990-94: 16.2.

**History:** site was founded and named 1775 by hunters who heard of the Revolutionary War battle at Lexington, Mass.; settled 1779; inc. 1832.

**Transportation:** 10 airlines; 2 railroads; city buses. **Communications:** 5 TV, 12 radio stations. **Medical facilities:** 5 general, 5 specialized hospitals. **Educational facilities:** 2 universities, 2 colleges. **Further information:** Greater Lexington Chamber of Commerce, 330 E. Main St., Lexington, KY 40507.

**Internet site:** http://www.lexchamber.com

## Lincoln, Nebraska

**Population:** 203,076 (77); **Pop. density:** 3,208 per sq. mi; **Pop. growth:** 5.8%. **Area:** 63.3 sq. mi. **Employment:** 120,090 employed, 2.4% unemployed. **Per capita income:** $21,169; % increase 1990-94: 22.8.

**History:** originally called Lancaster; chosen state capital 1867, renamed after Abraham Lincoln; inc. 1869.

**Transportation:** 1 airport; Greyhound; Amtrak, 2 railroads. **Communications:** 2 TV, 13 radio stations. **Medical facilities:** 5 hospitals including VA, rehabilitation facilities. **Educational facilities:** 3 universities, 3 voc.-tech./business colleges; 48 public, 15 private schools. **Further information:** Chamber of Commerce, PO Box 83006, Lincoln, NE 68501.

**Internet site:** http://www.lincoln.org

## Long Beach, California

**Population:** 433,852 (34); **Pop. density:** 8,677 per sq. mi; **Pop. growth:** 1.1%. **Area:** 50 sq. mi. **Employment:** 189,224 employed, 7.3% unemployed. **Per capita income:** $21,562; % increase 1990-94: 3.9.

**History:** settled as early as 1784 by Spanish; by 1884 present site developed on harbor; inc. 1888; oil discovered 1921.

**Transportation:** 1 airport; 3 railroads; major intl. port; 6 bus lines, "lite" rail service. **Communications:** 4 radio stations. **Medical facilities:** 10 hospitals. **Educational facilities:** 1 university, 1 college; 78 public schools. **Further information:** Chamber of Commerce, One World Trade Center, Ste. 350, Long Beach, CA 90831-0350.

**Internet site:** http://www.ci.long-beach.ca.us

## Los Angeles, California

**Population:** 3,448,613 (2); **Pop. density:** 7,348 per sq. mi; **Pop. growth:** –1.1%. **Area:** 469.3 sq. mi. **Employment:** 1,603,594 employed, 8.9% unemployed. **Per capita income:** $21,562; % increase 1990-94: 3.9.

**History:** founded by Spanish 1781; captured by U.S. 1846; inc. 1850; Hollywood a district of L.A.

**Transportation:** 1 intl. airport; 3 railroads; major freeway system; intracity transit system. **Communications:** 21 TV, 70 radio stations. **Medical facilities:** 822 hospitals and clinics in metropolitan area. **Educational facilities:** 192 universities and colleges (incl. junior, community, and other); 1,678 public schools; 1,470 private schools. **Further information:** Chamber of Commerce, 350 S. Bixel St., PO Box 3696, Los Angeles, CA 90051-1696.

**Internet site:** http://www.ci.la.ca.us

## Louisville, Kentucky

**Population:** 270,308 (60); **Pop. density:** 4,353 per sq. mi; **Pop. growth:** 0.3%. **Area:** 62.1 sq. mi. **Employment:** 125,909 employed, 4.8% unemployed. **Per capita income:** $22,081; % increase 1990-94: 21.4.

**History:** settled 1778; named for Louis XVI of France; inc. 1828; base for Union forces in Civil War.

**Transportation:** 2 municipal airports; 1 terminal, 4 trunkline railroads; metro bus line, Greyhound station; 5 barge lines. **Communications:** 5 TV, 21 radio stations, 2 educational. **Medical facilities:** 23 hospitals. **Educational facilities:** 10 universities and colleges, 9 business colleges and technical schools. **Further information:** Louisville Area Chamber of Commerce, 600 W. Main St., Louisville, KY 40202.

**Internet site:** http://www.louisville.com

## Lubbock, Texas

**Population:** 194,467 (83); **Pop. density:** 1,868 per sq. mi; **Pop. growth:** 4.4%. **Area:** 104.1 sq. mi. **Employment:** 97,224 employed, 4.1% unemployed. **Per capita income:** $18,633; % increase 1990-94: 17.9.

**History:** settled 1879; inc. 1909 through merger of two towns.

**Transportation:** 1 intl. airport; 2 railroads, bus line. **Communications:** 5 TV, 18 radio stations. **Medical facilities:** 7 hospitals. **Educational facilities:** 3 universities, 1 junior college; 51 public schools. **Further information:** Chamber of Commerce, P.O. Box 561, Lubbock, TX 79408.

**Internet site:** http://interoz.com/lubbock/lubbock.htm

## Madison, Wisconsin

**Population:** 194,586 (82); **Pop. density:** 3,367 per sq. mi; **Pop. growth:** 2.0%. **Area:** 57.8 sq. mi. **Employment:** 123,030 employed, 1.9% unemployed. **Per capita income:** $24,437; % increase 1990-94: 23.2.

**History:** first white settlement 1832; selected as site for state capital and named after James Madison, 1836; chartered 1856.

**Transportation:** 1 airport, 9 airlines; 1 intracity, 3 intercity bus systems; 3 freight rail lines. **Communications:** 5 TV, 23 radio stations. **Medical facilities:** 4 hospitals. **Educational facilities:** 7 colleges and universities, including main branch of Univ. of Wisconsin; 43 public schools. **Further information:** Greater Madison Chamber of Commerce, PO Box 71, Madison, WI 53701-0071.

**Internet site:** http://www.ci.madison.wi.us

## Memphis, Tennessee

**Population:** 614,289 (18); **Pop. density:** 2,400 per sq. mi; **Pop. growth:** –0.7%. **Area:** 256 sq. mi. **Employment:** 288,215 employed, 6.0% unemployed. **Per capita income:** $21,564; % increase 1990-94: 21.0.

**History:** French, Spanish, and U.S. forts by 1797; settled by 1819; inc. as town 1826, as city 1840; surrendered charter to state 1879 after yellow fever epidemics; rechartered as city 1893.

**Transportation:** 1 intl. airport; 6 railroads; bus system. **Communications:** 6 TV, 29 radio stations. **Medical facilities:** 23 hospitals. **Educational facilities:** 12 universities and colleges; 205 public, 76 private schools. **Further information:** Memphis Area Chamber of Commerce, 22 N. Front St., Ste. 200, PO Box 224, Memphis, TN 38101-0224.

**Internet site:** http://www.memphis.acn.net

## Mesa, Arizona

**Population:** 313,649 (52); **Pop. density:** 2,888 per sq. mi; **Pop. growth:** 8.5%. **Area:** 108.6 sq. mi. **Employment:** 169,509 employed, 2.9% unemployed. **Per capita income:** $20,999; % increase 1990-94: 17.2.

**History:** founded by Mormons 1878; inc. 1883; 13 mi. from Phoenix; population boomed fivefold 1960-80.

**Transportation:** near Sky Harbor Intl. Airport in Phoenix; 2 railroads; bus line. **Medical facilities:** 4 major hospitals. **Educational facilities:** 1 university, 2 colleges; 63 public schools. **Further information:** Convention and Visitor's Bureau, 120 N. Center, Mesa, AZ 85201.

**Internet site:** http://www.ci.mesa.az.us

## Miami, Florida

**Population:** 373,024 (42); **Pop. density:** 10,478 per sq. mi; **Pop. growth:** 4.0%. **Area:** 35.6 sq. mi. **Employment:** 160,719 employed, 10.5% unemployed. **Per capita income:** $20,014; % increase 1990-94: 13.5.

**History:** site of fort 1836; settlement began 1870; inc. 1896 and modern city developed into resort and recreation center; land speculation in 1920s added to city's growth, as did Cuban, Central and South American, and Haitian immigration since 1960.

**Transportation:** 1 intl. airport; seaport; Amtrak, transit rail system; 2 bus lines; 65 truck lines. **Communications:** 9 commercial, 2 educational TV stations; 41 radio stations. **Medical facilities:** 36 hospitals, VA hospital. **Educational facilities:** 6 universities and colleges. **Further information:** Metro-Dade Dept. of Planning, Development, and Regulation, Research Div., 111 NW 1st St., Ste. 1220, Miami, FL 33128.

**Internet site:** http://ci.miami.fl.us

## Milwaukee, Wisconsin

**Population:** 617,044 (17); **Pop. density:** 6,421 per sq. mi; **Pop. growth:** –1.8%. **Area:** 96.1 sq. mi. **Employment:** 281,773 employed, 5.0% unemployed. **Per capita income:** $23,948; % increase 1990-94: 20.2.

**History:** Indian trading post by 1674; settlement began 1835; inc. as city 1848; famous beer industry.

**Transportation:** 1 intl. airport; 2 railroads; major port; 4 bus lines. **Communications:** 12 TV, 34 radio stations. **Medical facilities:** 24 hospitals; major medical center. **Educational facilities:** 12 universities and colleges. **Further information:** Metropolitan Milwaukee Association of Commerce, 756 N. Milwaukee Street, Milwaukee, WI 53202.

## Minneapolis, Minnesota

**Population:** 354,590 (47); **Pop. density:** 6,459 per sq. mi; **Pop. growth:** –3.7%. **Area:** 54.9 sq. mi. **Employment:** 199,466 employed, 3.4% unemployed. **Per capita income:** $25,231; % increase 1990-94: 17.8.

**History:** site visited by Hennepin 1680; included in area of military reservations 1819; inc. 1867.

**Transportation:** 1 intl. airport; 5 railroads; mass transit systems; 24-36 barge lines per year come into city. **Communications:** 7 TV, 25 radio stations. **Medical facilities:** 7 hospitals, including leading heart hospital at Univ. of Minnesota. **Educational facilities:** 10 universities and colleges; 80 public, 38 private schools. **Further information:** City of Minneapolis Office of Public Affairs, 323M City Hall, 350 S. 5th St., Minneapolis, MN 55415.

**Internet site:** http://www.ci.mpls.mn.us

## Mobile, Alabama

**Population:** 204,490 (76); **Pop. density:** 1,733 per sq. mi; **Pop. growth:** 4.2%. **Area:** 118 sq. mi. **Employment:** 94,832 employed, 8.1% unemployed. **Per capita income:** $17,150; % increase 1990-94: 21.3.

**History:** settled by French 1711; later occupied by U.S. 1813; inc. as town 1814, as city 1819; only seaport of Alabama.

**Transportation:** 4 rail freight lines, Amtrak; 4 airlines; 65 truck lines; leading river system. **Communications:** 7 TV, 21 radio stations. **Medical facilities:** 9 hospitals. **Educational facilities:** 3 universities, 3 colleges. **Further information:** Chamber of Commerce, PO Box 2187, Mobile, AL 36652.

**Internet site:** http://www.ci.mobile.al.us

## Montgomery, Alabama

**Population:** 195,471 (81); **Pop. density:** 1,448 per sq. mi; **Pop. growth:** 4.2%. **Area:** 135 sq. mi. **Employment:** 90,878 employed, 5.9% unemployed. **Per capita income:** $19,606; % increase 1990-94: 18.8.

**History:** inc. as town 1819, as city 1837; became state capital 1846; first capital of Confederacy 1861.

**Transportation:** 4 airlines; 2 railroads; 2 bus lines; Alabama River is navigable to Gulf of Mexico. **Communications:** 5 TV, 14 radio stations. **Medical facilities:** 5 major hospitals; VA and 32 clinics. **Educational facilities:** 5 universities; 49 public, 31 private schools. **Further information:** Montgomery Area Chamber of Commerce, PO Box 79, Montgomery, AL 36101.

**Internet site:** http://www.montgomery-al.com

## Nashville, Tennessee

**Population:** 504,505 (24); **Pop. density:** 1,066 per sq. mi; **Pop. growth:** 3.3%. **Area:** 473.3 sq. mi. **Employment:** 281,583 employed, 3.3% unemployed. **Per capita income:** $23,038; % increase 1990-94: 25.7.

**History:** settled 1779; first chartered 1806; became permanent state capital 1843; home of Grand Ole Opry.

**Transportation:** 1 airport; 1 railroad; bus line; transit system of buses and trolleys. **Communications:** 7 TV, 30 radio stations. **Medical facilities:** 14 hospitals; VA and speech-hearing center. **Educational facilities:** 16 universities and colleges. **Further information:** Chamber of Commerce, 161 4th Ave., Nashville, TN 37219.

**Internet site:** http://www.nashville.tnstate.edu

## Newark, New Jersey

**Population:** 258,751 (63); **Pop. density:** 10,872 per sq. mi; **Pop. growth:** –6.0%. **Area:** 23.8 sq. mi. **Employment:** 100,141 employed, 12.8% unemployed. **Per capita income:** $29,652; % increase 1990-94: 16.6.

**History:** settled by Puritans 1666; used as supply base by Washington 1776; inc. as town 1833, as city 1836.

**Transportation:** 1 intl. airport; 2 railroads; bus system; 2 subways. **Communications:** 3 TV, 5 radio stations within city limits. **Medical facilities:** 6 hospitals. **Educational facilities:** 5 universities and colleges; 71 public schools. **Further information:** Regional Business Partnership, 1 Newark Center, Newark, NJ 07102-5265.

## New Orleans, Louisiana

**Population:** 484,149 (27); **Pop. density:** 2,681 per sq. mi; **Pop. growth:** –2.6%. **Area:** 180.6 sq. mi. **Employment:** 188,592 employed, 7.4% unemployed. **Per capita income:** $19,833; % increase 1990-94: 21.0.

**History:** founded by French 1718; became major seaport on Mississippi R.; acquired by U.S. as part of La. Purchase 1803; inc. as city 1805; Battle of New Orleans was last battle of War of 1812.

**Transportation:** 2 airports; major railroad center; major intl. port. **Communications:** 7 TV, 18 radio stations. **Medical facilities:** numerous hospitals; major research center. **Educational facilities:** 13 universities and colleges. **Further information:** New Orleans Metropolitan Convention & Visitors Bureau, Inc., 1520 Sugar Bowl Dr., New Orleans, LA 70112.

**Internet site:** http://www.nawlins.com

## Newport News, Virginia

**Population:** 179,127 (99); **Pop. density:** 2,623 per sq. mi; **Pop. growth:** 4.5%. **Area:** 68.3 sq. mi. **Employment:** 80,553 employed, 5.6% unemployed. **Per capita income:** $19,007; % increase 1990-94: 13.7.

**History:** inc. 1896; the cities of Warwick and Newport News consolidated in 1958 into the larger city of Newport News; one of the world's major shipbuilding centers.

**Transportation:** 1 intl. airport; 2 railroads; Greyhound buses; local bus system. **Communications:** 8 TV, 29 radio stations received in area. **Medical facilities:** 3 hospitals; adolescent psychiatry hospital. **Educational facilities:** 33 public schools. **Further information:** Virginia Peninsula Chamber of Commerce, 6 Manhattan Square, PO Box 7269, Hampton, VA 23666.

**Internet site:** http://www.newport-news.va.us

## New York City, New York

**Population:** 7,333,253 (1); **Pop. density:** 23,740 per sq. mi; **Pop. growth:** 0.1%. **Area:** 308.9 sq. mi. **Employment:** 2,911,699 employed, 8.2% unemployed. **Per capita income:** $28,800; % increase 1990-94: 16.8.

**History:** trading post established by H. Hudson 1609; British took control from Dutch 1664 and named New York; briefly capital of U.S.; Washington inaugurated as president 1789; under new charter, 1898, city expanded to include 5 boroughs: The Bronx, Brooklyn, Queens, Staten Island, as well as Manhattan.

**Transportation:** 3 airports serve area; 2 rail terminals; major subway network; ferry system; 4 underwater tunnels. **Communications:** 13 TV, 117 radio stations. **Medical facilities:** 81 hospitals; 5 academic medical centers. **Educational facilities:** 92 universities and colleges; 1,095 public schools, 914 private schools. **Further information:** Convention and Visitors Bureau, 2 Columbus Circle, New York, NY 10019.

**Internet site:** http://www.ci.nyc.ny.us

## Norfolk, Virginia

**Population:** 241,426 (67); **Pop. density:** 4,487 per sq. mi; **Pop. growth:** –7.6%. **Area:** 53.8 sq. mi. **Employment:** 85,633 employed, 6.2% unemployed. **Per capita income:** $19,007; % increase 1990-94: 13.7.

**History:** founded 1682; burned by patriots to prevent capture by British during Revolutionary War; rebuilt and inc. as town 1805, as city 1845; location of world's largest naval base.

**Transportation:** 1 intl. airport; 2 railroads; Amtrak; bus system. **Communications:** 6 TV, 29 radio stations. **Medical facilities:** 6 hospitals. **Educational facilities:** 2 universities, 1 college, 1 medical school; 48 public schools. **Further information:** Hampton Roads Chamber of Commerce, 420 Bank St., PO Box 327, Norfolk, VA 23501.

**Internet site:** http://www.pilotonline.com/community/norfolk

## Oakland, California

**Population:** 366,926 (44); **Pop. density:** 6,541 per sq. mi; **Pop. growth:** –1.4%. **Area:** 56.1 sq. mi. **Employment:** 163,930 employed, 9.0% unemployed. **Per capita income:** $26,530; % increase 1990-94: 13.6.

**History:** area settled by Spanish 1820; inc. as city under present name 1854.

**Transportation:** 1 intl. airport; western terminus for 3 railroads; underground, underwater 75-mi subway. **Communications:** 1 TV, 3 radio stations in city. **Medical facilities:** 10 hospitals in MSA, including Children's Hospital Oakland, VA center. **Educational facilities:** 8 East Bay colleges and universities; 94 public schools. **Further information:** Oakland Metropolitan Chamber of Commerce, 475 14th St., Oakland, CA 94612-1903.

## Oklahoma City, Oklahoma

**Population:** 463,201 (28); **Pop. density:** 762 per sq. mi; **Pop. growth:** 4.2%. **Area.** 608.2 sq. mi. **Employment:** 224,323 employed, 4.1% unemployed. **Per capita income:** $19,031; % increase 1990-94: 16.3.

**History:** settled during land rush in Midwest 1889; inc. 1890; became capital 1910; oil discovered 1928.

**Transportation:** 1 intl. airport; 3 railroads; public transit system; 5 major bus lines. **Communications:** 8 TV, 24 radio stations. **Medical facilities:** 20 hospitals. **Educational facilities:** 17 universities and colleges; 83 public, 37 private schools. **Further information:** Chamber of Commerce, Economic Development Division, 123 Park Ave., Oklahoma City, OK 73102.

**Internet site:** http://www.ionet.net/~okcpio

## Omaha, Nebraska

**Population:** 345,033 (48); **Pop. density:** 3,430 per sq. mi; **Pop. growth:** 2.8%. **Area:** 100.6 sq. mi. **Employment:** 189,349 employed, 3.2% unemployed. **Per capita income:** $22,514; % increase 1990-94: 21.8.

**History:** founded 1854; inc. 1857; large food-processing, telecommunications, information-processing center; home of more than 20 insurance companies.

**Transportation:** 12 major airlines; 4 major railroads; intercity bus line. **Communications:** 8 TV, 22 radio stations. **Medical facilities:** 16 hospitals; institute for cancer research. **Educational facilities:** 5 universities, 4 colleges; 243 public, 78 private schools. **Further information:** Greater Omaha Chamber of Commerce, 1301 Harney St., Omaha, NE 68102-1804.

**Internet site:** http://www.omaha.com

## Philadelphia, Pennsylvania

**Population:** 1,524,249 (5); **Pop. density:** 11,282 per sq. mi; **Pop. growth:** –3.9%. **Area:** 135.1 sq. mi. **Employment:** 601,787 employed, 7.6% unemployed. **Per capita income:** $25,220; % increase 1990-94: 17.2.

**History:** first settled by Swedes 1638; Swedes surrendered to Dutch 1654; settled by English & Scottish Quakers 1678; named Philadelphia 1682; chartered 1701; Continental Congresses convened 1774, 1775; Declaration of Independence signed 1776; national capital 1790-1800; state capital 1683-1799.

**Transportation:** 1 major airport; 3 railroads; major freshwater port; subway, el, rail commuter, bus, and streetcar system. **Communications:** 10 TV, 16 radio stations. **Medical facilities:** 47 hospitals. **Educational facilities:** 25 degree-granting institutions; 8 community college campuses. **Further information:** Office of City Representative and City Commerce Director, 1600 Arch St., 13th fl., Philadelphia, PA 19103.

**Internet site:** http://www.phila.gov

## Phoenix, Arizona

**Population:** 1,048,949 (7); **Pop. density:** 2,498 per sq. mi; **Pop. growth:** 6.6%. **Area:** 419.9 sq. mi. **Employment:** 601,522 employed, 3.8% unemployed. **Per capita income:** $20,999; % increase 1990-94: 17.2.

**History:** settled 1870; inc. as city 1881; became territorial capital 1889.

**Transportation:** 1 intl. airport; 5 railroads; 2 transcontinental bus lines; public transit system. **Communications:** 13 TV, 45 radio stations. **Medical facilities:** 42 hospitals, 1 medical research center. **Educational facilities:** 12 institutions of higher learning; 167 public schools. **Further information:** Chamber of Commerce, 201 N. Central Ave., 27th fl., Phoenix, AZ 85073.

**Internet site:** http://www.ci.phoenix.az.us

## Pittsburgh, Pennsylvania

**Population:** 358,883 (45); **Pop. density:** 6,455 per sq. mi; **Pop. growth:** –3.0%. **Area:** 55.6 sq. mi. **Employment:** 153,760 employed, 6.1% unemployed. **Per capita income:** $22,751; % increase 1990-94: 19.9.

**History:** settled around Ft. Pitt 1758; inc. as city 1816; has one of the largest inland ports; by Civil War, already a center for iron production.

**Transportation:** 1 intl. airport; 20 railroads; 2 bus lines; trolley/subway system. **Communications:** 6 TV, 26 radio stations. **Medical facilities:** 35 hospitals; VA installation. **Educational facilities:** 3 universities, 6 colleges; 86 public schools. **Further information:** Greater Pittsburgh Convention & Visitors Bureau, 4 Gateway Ctr., Pittsburgh, PA 15222-1259.

**Internet site:** http://www.pittsburgh.net

## Portland, Oregon

**Population:** 450,777 (30); **Pop. density:** 3,615 per sq. mi; **Pop. growth:** 2.7%. **Area:** 124.7 sq. mi. **Employment:** 253,478 employed, 4.4% unemployed. **Per capita income:** $22,890; % increase 1990-94: 19.3.

**History:** settled by pioneers 1845; developed as trading center, aided by California Gold Rush 1849; chartered as city 1851.

**Transportation:** 1 intl. airport; 3 major rail freight lines, Amtrak; 2 intercity bus lines; 27-mi. frontage freshwater port; mass transit bus and rail system. **Communications:** 9 TV, 44 radio stations. **Medical facilities:** 21 hospitals; VA hospital. **Educational facilities:** 39 universities and colleges, 3 community colleges. **Further information:** Portland Metropolitan Chamber of Commerce, 221 N.W. 2d Ave., Portland, OR 97209-3999.

**Internet site:** http://www.ci.portland.or.us

## Raleigh, North Carolina

**Population:** 236,707 (70); **Pop. density:** 2,687 per sq. mi; **Pop. growth:** 11.6%. **Area:** 88.1 sq. mi. **Employment:** 139,093 employed, 2.8% unemployed. **Per capita income:** $22,992; % increase 1990-94: 18.8.

**History:** named after Sir Walter Raleigh; site chosen for capital 1788; laid out 1792; inc. 1795; occupied by Gen. Sherman 1865.

**Transportation:** 1 intl. airport, 10 airlines, 4 commuter airlines; 3 railroads; 2 bus lines. **Communications:** 8 TV, 30 radio stations. **Medical facilities:** 8 hospitals. **Educational facilities:** 6 universities and colleges; 1 junior, 1 community college; 100 public schools (county). **Further information:** Chamber of Commerce, 800 S. Salisbury St., PO Box 2978, Raleigh, NC 27602.

## Richmond, Virginia

**Population:** 201,108 (78); **Pop. density:** 3,346 per sq. mi; **Pop. growth:** –0.8%. **Area:** 60.1 sq. mi. **Employment:** 99,142 employed, 5.2% unemployed. **Per capita income:** $24,358; % increase 1990-94: 14.3.

**History:** first settled 1607; became capital of Commonwealth of Virginia, 1779; attacked by British under Benedict Arnold 1781; inc. as city 1782; capital of Confederate States of America, 1861-65.

**Transportation:** 1 intl. airport; 4 railroads; 3 intracity bus lines; deepwater terminal accessible to oceangoing ships. **Communications:** 6 TV, 26 radio stations. **Medical facilities:** Medical Coll. of Virginia renowned for heart and kidney transplants; 19 other hospitals incl. VA facility. **Educational facilities:** 9 universities and colleges; 173 public, 45 private schools. **Further information:** Chamber of Commerce, PO Box 12280, Richmond, VA 23241-2280.

**Internet site:** http://www.grcc.com

## Riverside, California

**Population:** 241,644 (66); **Pop. density:** 3,110 per sq. mi; **Pop. growth:** 6.7%. **Area:** 77.7 sq. mi. **Employment:** 116,146 employed, 9.5% unemployed. **Per capita income:** $17,741; % increase 1990-94: 4.9.

**History:** founded 1870; inc. 1886; known for its citrus industry; home of the parent navel orange.

**Transportation:** municipal airport, intl. airport nearby; rail freight lines, commuter line; trolley/bus system. **Communications:** 5 TV, 47 radio stations. **Medical facilities:** 4 hospitals; many clinics. **Educational facilities:** 3 universities, 1 community college. **Further information:** Chamber of Commerce, 3685 Main St., Ste. 350, Riverside, CA 92501.

**Internet site:** http://www.ci.riverside.ca.us

## Rochester, New York

**Population:** 231,170 (71); **Pop. density:** 6,457 per sq. mi; **Pop. growth:** 0.4%. **Area:** 35.8 sq. mi. **Employment:** 104,573 employed, 7.1% unemployed. **Per capita income:** $22,593; % increase 1990-94: 13.2.

**History:** first permanent white settlement 1812; inc. as village 1817, as city 1834; developed as Erie Canal town.

**Transportation:** 1 intl. airport; Amtrak; 3 bus lines; intracity transit service; Port of Rochester. **Communications:** 6 TV, 18 radio stations. **Medical facilities:** 8 general hospitals. **Educational facilities:** 10 colleges, 3 community colleges. **Further information:** Chamber of Commerce, 55 St. Paul St., Rochester, NY 14604-1391.

**Internet site:** http://www.rochester.lib.ny.us/cityhall

## Sacramento, California

**Population:** 373,964 (41); **Pop. density:** 3,883 per sq. mi; **Pop. growth:** 1.2%. **Area:** 96.3 sq. mi. **Employment:** 168,954 employed, 8.2% unemployed. **Per capita income:** $21,855; % increase 1990-94: 12.7.

**History:** settled 1839; important trading center during California Gold Rush 1840s; became state capital 1854.

**Transportation:** metropolitan, executive, and cargo airports; 2 mainline transcontinental rail carriers; bus and light rail system; Port of Sacramento. **Communications:** 7 TV, 25 radio stations; 3 cable TV cos. **Medical facilities:** 8 hospitals. **Educational facilities:** 2 universities, 4 community colleges. **Further information:** Chamber of Commerce, 917 7th St., Sacramento, CA 95814.

**Internet site:** http://www.ci.sacramento.ca.us

## St. Louis, Missouri

**Population:** 368,215 (43); **Pop. density:** 5,948 per sq. mi; **Pop. growth:** –7.2%. **Area:** 61.9 sq. mi. **Employment:** 160,090 employed, 7.6% unemployed. **Per capita income:** $23,685; % increase 1990-94: 17.7.

**History:** founded 1764 as a fur trading post by French; acquired by U.S. 1803; chartered as city 1822; lies on Mississippi R., near confluence with Missouri R.

**Transportation:** 1 intl. airport; major rail center, 17 trunkline railroads; major inland port; 14 bus lines; 14 barge lines. **Communications:** 7 TV, 35 radio stations. **Medical facilities:** 65 hospitals. **Educational facilities:** 6 universities, 25 colleges and seminaries. **Further information:** St. Louis Community Development Agency, 330 N. 15th St., St. Louis, MO 63103.

**Internet site:** http://www.st-louis.mo.us/st-louis/city

## St. Paul, Minnesota

**Population:** 262,071 (62); **Pop. density:** 4,963 per sq. mi; **Pop. growth:** –3.7%. **Area:** 52.8 sq. mi. **Employment:** 138,220 employed, 3.5% unemployed. **Per capita income:** $25,231; % increase 1990-94: 17.8.

**History:** founded in early 1840s as "Pig's Eye Landing"; became capital of the Minnesota territory 1849 and chartered as St. Paul 1854.

**Transportation:** 1 intl., 1 business airport; 6 major rail lines; 3 interstate bus lines; public transit system.

**Communications:** 6 TV, 35 radio stations. **Medical facilities:** 7 hospitals. **Educational facilities:** 3 universities, 4 colleges; 1 technical, 3 first professional colleges. **Further information:** St. Paul Area Chamber of Commerce, 332 Minnesota St., Ste. N-205, St. Paul, MN 55101.

**Internet site:** http://www.ci.stpaul.mn.us

## St. Petersburg, Florida

**Population:** 238,585 (68); **Pop. density:** 4,030 per sq. mi; **Pop. growth:** –0.7%. **Area:** 59.2 sq. mi. **Employment:** 121,018 employed, 4.7% unemployed. **Per capita income:** $21,358; % increase 1990-94: 18.9.

**History:** founded 1888; inc. 1892.

**Transportation:** 2 airports (1 intl.); Amtrak; bus system; 1 full-service port. **Communications:** 12 TV, 22 radio stations. **Medical facilities:** 3 major hospitals, VA hospital. **Educational facilities:** 1 university, 1 college, 1 law school, 1 junior college; 118 public schools. **Further information:** St. Petersburg Area Chamber of Commerce, PO Box 1371, St. Petersburg, FL 33731.

**Internet site:** http://www.stpete.com

## San Antonio, Texas

**Population:** 998,905 (9); **Pop. density:** 3,000 per sq. mi; **Pop. growth:** 6.8%. **Area:** 333 sq. mi. **Employment:** 477,051 employed, 5.0% unemployed. **Per capita income:** $18,466; % increase 1990-94: 18.5.

**History:** first Spanish garrison 1718; Battle at the Alamo fought here 1836; city subsequently captured by Texians; inc. 1837.

**Transportation:** 1 intl., 1 municipal airport; 4 railroads; 4 bus lines; public transit system; 25 common-carrier truck lines. **Communications:** 8 TV, 34 radio stations. **Medical facilities:** 38 hospitals; major medical center. **Educational facilities:** 17 universities and colleges; 16 public school districts. **Further information:** Chamber of Commerce, 602 E. Commerce, P.O. Box 1628, San Antonio, TX 78296.

**Internet site:** http://www.tristero.com/usa/tx/sa

## San Bernardino, California

**Population:** 181,718 (97); **Pop. density:** 3,298 per sq. mi; **Pop. growth:** 10.7%. **Area:** 55.1 sq. mi. **Employment:** 64,994 employed, 11.3% unemployed. **Per capita income:** $17,741; % increase 1990-94: 4.9.

**History:** Spanish missionaries arrived here 1810; Mormons est. first permanent settlement 1851; inc. 1854.

**Transportation:** 1 intl. airport nearby; Amtrak; rail transit system; bus systems. **Communications:** 5 TV, 22 radio stations. **Medical facilities:** 17 hospitals (county). **Educational facilities:** 1 university, 2 community colleges; 51 public schools. **Further information:** San Bernardino Area Chamber of Commerce, 546 W. 6th St., PO Box 658, San Bernardino, CA 92402.

**Internet site:** http://www.co.san-bernardino.ca.us/cities/sanberna.htm

## San Diego, California

**Population:** 1,151,977 (6); **Pop. density:** 3,555 per sq. mi; **Pop. growth:** 3.7%. **Area:** 324 sq. mi. **Employment:** 526,022 employed, 6.5% unemployed. **Per capita income:** $21,627; % increase 1990-94: 9.6.

**History:** claimed by the Spanish 1542; first mission est. 1769; scene of conflict during Mexican-American War 1846; inc. 1850.

**Transportation:** 1 major airport; 1 railroad; major freeway system; bus system; trolley system. **Communications:** 8 TV, 22 radio stations. **Medical facilities:** 28 hospitals. **Educational facilities:** 5 universities, 7 colleges. **Further information:** Greater SD Chamber of Commerce, 402 W. Broadway, Ste. 1000, San Diego, CA 92101-3585.

**Internet site:** http://www.sannet.gov

## San Francisco, California

**Population:** 734,676 (13); **Pop. density:** 15,732 per sq. mi; **Pop. growth:** 1.5%. **Area:** 46.7 sq. mi. **Employment:** 373,791 employed, 6.1% unemployed. **Per capita income:** $34,281; % increase 1990-94: 15.5.

**History:** nearby Farallon Islands sighted by Spanish 1542; city settled by 1776; claimed by U.S. 1846; became a major city during California Gold Rush 1849; inc. as city 1850; earthquake devastated city 1906.

**Transportation:** 1 major airport; intracity railway system; 2 railway transit systems; bus and railroad service; ferry system; 1 underwater tunnel. **Communications:** 14 TV; 35 radio stations. **Medical facilities:** 4 medical centers; 3 hospitals. **Educational facilities:** 18 universities and colleges; 2 fashion institutes. **Further information:** Convention & Visitors Bureau, 201 3d St., Ste. 900, San Francisco, CA 94103.

**Internet site:** http://www.ci.sf.ca.us

## San Jose, California

**Population:** 816,884 (11); **Pop. density:** 4,769 per sq. mi; **Pop. growth:** 4.4%. **Area:** 171.3 sq. mi. **Employment:** 413,524 employed, 5.8% unemployed. **Per capita income:** $28,250; % increase 1990-94: 15.1.

**History:** founded by the Spanish 1777 between San Francisco and Monterey; state cap. 1849-51; inc. 1850.

**Transportation:** 1 intl. airport; 2 railroads; bus system. **Communications:** 4 TV, 14 radio stations. **Medical facilities:** 6 hospitals. **Educational facilities:** 3 universities and colleges. **Further information:** Chamber of Commerce, 180 S. Market St., San Jose, CA 95113.

**Internet site:** http://www.ipac.net/csj

## Santa Ana, California

**Population:** 290,827 (55); **Pop. density:** 10,732 per sq. mi; **Pop. growth:** –1.0%. **Area:** 27.1 sq. mi. **Employment:** 136,776 employed, 9.0% unemployed. **Per capita income:** $25,516; % increase 1990-94: 5.1.

**History:** founded 1869; inc. as city 1886.

**Transportation:** 1 airport; 5 major freeways including main Los Angeles-San Diego artery; Amtrak. **Communications:** 14 TV, 28 radio stations. **Medical facilities:** 4 hospitals. **Educational facilities:** 1 community college. **Further information:** Chamber of Commerce, 856 N. Ross St., PO Box 205, Santa Ana, CA 92701.

**Internet site:** http://www.ci.santa-ana.ca.us

## Seattle, Washington

**Population:** 520,947 (22); **Pop. density:** 6,209 per sq. mi; **Pop. growth:** 0.9%. **Area:** 83.9 sq. mi. **Employment:** 304,190 employed, 6.1% unemployed. **Per capita income:** $27,097; % increase 1990-94: 18.0.

**History:** settled 1851; inc. 1869; suffered severe fire 1889; played prominent role during Alaska Gold Rush 1897; growth followed opening of Panama Canal 1914; center of aircraft industry WWII.

**Transportation:** 1 intl. airport; 2 railroads; ferries serve Puget Sound, Alaska, Canada. **Communications:** 7 TV, 39 radio stations. **Medical facilities:** 40 hospitals. **Educational facilities:** 7 universities, 6 colleges, 11 community colleges. **Further information:** Greater Seattle Chamber of Commerce, 1301 5th Ave., Ste. 2400, Seattle, WA 98101-2603.

**Internet site:** http://www.ci.seattle.wa.us

## Shreveport, Louisiana

**Population:** 196,982 (79); **Pop. density:** 1,998 per sq. mi; **Pop. growth:** –0.8%. **Area:** 98.6 sq. mi. **Employment:** 86,372 employed, 7.3% unemployed. **Per capita income:** $18,829; % increase 1990-94: 25.7.

**History:** founded 1833 near site of a 160-mi logjam cleared by Capt. Henry Shreve; inc. 1839; oil discovered 1906.

**Transportation:** 2 airports; 1 bus line. **Communications:** 6 TV, 16 radio stations. **Medical facilities:** 16 hospitals. **Educational facilities:** 4 universities, 3 colleges. **Further information:** Chamber of Commerce, PO Box 20074, Shreveport, LA 71120.

**Internet site:** http://www.shreveport.net

## Spokane, Washington

**Population:** 192,781 (88); **Pop. density:** 3,449 per sq. mi; **Pop. growth:** 8.8%. **Area:** 55.9 sq. mi. **Employment:** 89,580 employed, 6.1% unemployed. **Per capita income:** $19,565; % increase 1990-94: 19.9.

**History:** settled 1872; inc. as village of Spokane Falls 1881, destroyed in fire 1889; reinc. as city of Spokane 1891.

**Transportation:** 1 intl. airport; 2 railroads; bus system. **Communications:** 5 TV, 25 radio stations. **Medical facilities:** 6 major hospitals. **Educational facilities:** 8 universities and colleges; 14 public school districts, 11 high schools. **Further information:** Chamber of Commerce, W. 1020 Riverside Ave., PO Box 2147, Spokane, WA 99210.

**Internet site:** http://www.eznet.com/spkmetro/spokane

## Stockton, California

**Population:** 222,633 (74); **Pop. density:** 4,233 per sq. mi; **Pop. growth:** 5.5%. **Area:** 52.6 sq. mi. **Employment:** 86,247 employed, 14.4% unemployed. **Per capita income:** $18,094; % increase 1990-94: 11.8.

**History:** site purchased 1842; settled 1847; inc. 1850; chief distributing point for agricultural products of San Joaquin Valley.

**Transportation:** 1 airport; deepwater inland seaport; 7 railroads; 2 bus lines, county bus system. **Communications:** 5 TV stations. **Medical facilities:** 4 hospitals; regional burn, cancer, and heart centers. **Educational facilities:** 6 universities and colleges; 54 public schools. **Further information:** Chamber of Commerce, 445 W. Weber Ave., Ste. 220, Stockton, CA 95203.

**Internet site:** http://www.ci.stockton.ca.us

## Tacoma, Washington

**Population:** 183,060 (96); **Pop. density:** 3,814 per sq. mi; **Pop. growth:** 3.6%. **Area:** 48 sq. mi. **Employment:** 87,010 employed, 7.1% unemployed. **Per capita income:** $19,870; % increase 1990-94: 16.9.

**History:** first European explorer of area was British Capt. George Vancouver 1792; colonized by Hudson's Bay Co. at Ft. Nisqually 1833; inc. 1884.

**Transportation:** 1 intl. airport; 2 railroads; transit system; Port of Tacoma. **Communications:** 6 TV stations. **Medical facilities:** 7 hospitals, Army Medical Center, VA facility. **Educational facilities:** 3 universities, 4 colleges. **Further information:** Chamber of Commerce, PO Box 1933, Tacoma, WA 98401-1933.

**Internet site:** http://www.ci.tacoma.wa.us

## Tampa, Florida

**Population:** 285,523 (57); **Pop. density:** 2,627 per sq. mi; **Pop. growth:** 2.0%. **Area:** 108.7 sq. mi. **Employment:** 147,598 employed, 5.4% unemployed. **Per capita income:** $21,358; % increase 1990-94: 18.9.

**History:** U.S. army fort on site 1824; inc. 1855.

**Transportation:** 1 intl. airport; Port of Tampa; bus system. **Communications:** 12 TV, 30 radio stations. **Medical facilities:** 17 hospitals. **Educational facilities:** 7 universities and colleges; 183 public schools. **Further information:** Chamber of Commerce, 401 E. Jackson St., PO Box 420, Tampa, FL 33601-0420.

## Toledo, Ohio

**Population:** 322,550 (50); **Pop. density:** 4,002 per sq. mi; **Pop. growth:** –3.1%. **Area:** 80.6 sq. mi. **Employment:** 147,879 employed, 6.0% unemployed. **Per capita income:** $21,233; % increase 1990-94: 20.8.

**History:** site of Ft. Industry 1794; Battles of Ft. Meigs and Ft. Timbers 1812; figured in "Toledo War" 1835-36 between Ohio and Michigan over their borders; inc. 1837.

**Transportation:** 5 major airlines; 5 railroads; 98 motor freight lines; 2 interstate bus lines. **Communications:** 6 TV, 12 radio stations. **Medical facilities:** 8 major hospital complexes. **Educational facilities:** 6 universities and colleges. **Further information:** Toledo Area Chamber of Commerce, 300 Madison Ave., Ste. 200, Toledo, OH 43604.

## Tucson, Arizona

**Population:** 434,726 (33); **Pop. density:** 2,781 per sq. mi; **Pop. growth:** 6.4%. **Area:** 156.3 sq. mi. **Employment:** 222,548 employed, 3.6% unemployed. **Per capita income:** $18,575; % increase 1990-94: 21.5.

**History:** settled 1775 by Spanish as a presidio; acquired by U.S. in Gadsden Purchase 1853; inc. 1877.

**Transportation:** 1 intl. airport; 2 railroads; bus system. **Communications:** 8 TV, 27 radio stations. **Medical facilities:** 10 hospitals. **Educational facilities:** 2 universities, 1 college; 165 public schools. **Further information:** Chamber of Commerce, PO Box 991, Tucson, AZ 85702.

**Internet site:** http://www.tucsonchamber.org

## Tulsa, Oklahoma

**Population:** 374,851 (40); **Pop. density:** 2,043 per sq. mi; **Pop. growth:** 2.1%. **Area:** 183.5 sq. mi. **Employment:** 193,460 employed, 4.3% unemployed. **Per capita income:** $20,047; % increase 1990-94: 15.3.

**History:** settled in 1830s by Creek Indians; modern town founded 1882 and inc. 1898; oil discovered early 20th century.

**Transportation:** 1 intl. airport; 5 rail lines; 2 bus lines; transit bus system. **Communications:** 43 TV, 27 radio stations. **Medical facilities:** 10 hospitals. **Educational facilities:** 8 universities and colleges; 78 public, 40 private schools. **Further information:** Metropolitan Tulsa Chamber of Commerce, 616 S. Boston Ave., Ste. 100, Tulsa, OK 74119-1298.

**Internet site:** http://www.tulsachamber.com

## Virginia Beach, Virginia

**Population:** 430,295 (35); **Pop. density:** 1,733 per sq. mi; **Pop. growth:** 9.5%. **Area:** 248.3 sq. mi. **Employment:** 203,467 employed, 4.3% unemployed. **Per capita income:** $19,007; % increase 1990-94: 13.7.

**History:** area founded by Capt. John Smith 1607; formed by merger with Princess Anne Co. 1963.

**Transportation:** 1 airport; 2 railroads; 2 bus lines; public transit system. **Communications:** 6 TV, 41 radio stations. **Medical facilities:** 2 hospitals. **Educational facilities:** 1 university, 2 colleges; 83 public schools. **Further information:** Virginia Beach Dept. of Economic Development, One Columbus Center, Ste. 300, Virginia Beach, VA 23462.

**Internet site:** http://www.pilotonline.com/community/virginia_beach

## Washington, District of Columbia

**Population:** 567,094 (20); **Pop. density:** 9,236 per sq. mi; **Pop. growth:** –6.6%. **Area:** 61.4 sq. mi. **Employment:** 258,237 employed, 8.9% unemployed. **Per capita income:** $28,762; % increase 1990-94: 14.4.

**History:** U.S. capital; site at Potomac R. chosen by George Washington 1790 on land ceded from VA and MD (portion S of Potomac returned to VA 1846); Congress first met 1800; inc. 1802; sacked by British, War of 1812.

**Transportation:** 3 intl. airports in area; Amtrak, 6 other passenger & cargo rail lines; Metrobus/Metrorail transit system; bus line. **Communications:** 5 TV, 61 radio stations. **Medical facilities:** 16 hospitals. **Educational facilities:** 10 universities and colleges. **Further information:** DC Chamber of Commerce, 1301 Pennsylvania Ave. NW, Ste. 309, Washington, DC 20004.

**Internet site:** http://dcpages.com

## Wichita, Kansas

**Population:** 310,236 (54); **Pop. density:** 2,695 per sq. mi; **Pop. growth:** 2.0%. **Area:** 115.1 sq. mi. **Employment:** 156,982 employed, 5.3% unemployed. **Per capita income:** $21,511; % increase 1990-94: 15.8.

**History:** founded 1864; inc. 1871.

**Transportation:** 2 airports; 3 major rail freight lines; 2 bus lines. **Communications:** 5 TV, 26 radio stations. **Medical facilities:** 7 hospitals, 2 psychiatric rehab. centers. **Educational facilities:** 2 universities, 1 college, 1 medical school; 96 public schools. **Further information:** Chamber of Commerce, 350 W. Douglas, Wichita, KS 67202-2970.

**Internet site:** http://www.southwind.net/ict

## Yonkers, New York

**Population:** 183,490 (94); **Pop. density:** 10,138 per sq. mi; **Pop. growth:** –2.4%. **Area:** 18.1 sq. mi. **Employment:** 82,992 employed, 6.0% unemployed. **Per capita income:** $28,800; % increase 1990-94: 16.8.

**History:** founded 1641 by the Dutch; inc. as town 1855; chartered as city 1872; directly north of NYC.

**Transportation:** intracity bus system; rail service. **Communications:** see New York City. **Medical facilities:** 3 hospitals. **Educational facilities:** 1 college; 32 public schools. **Further information:** Chamber of Commerce, 20 S. Broadway, 12th fl., Yonkers, NY 10701.

**Internet site:** http://www.ci.yonkers.ny.us

# BUILDINGS, BRIDGES, TUNNELS, AND DAMS

## Notable Tall Buildings in North American Cities

**Source:** World Almanac research

Lists include some structures that do not have stories and are not technically considered "buildings." Height is measured from sidewalk to roof, including penthouse and tower if enclosed as integral part of structure; the actual number of stories begins at street level. Asterisk (*) denotes building still under construction. Year in parentheses is date of completion.

### Albany, NY

| Building | Ht. ft. | Stories |
|---|---|---|
| Office Tower, South Mall (1973) | 589 | 44 |
| State Office Building | 388 | 34 |

### Atlanta, GA

| Building | Ht. ft. | Stories |
|---|---|---|
| NationsBank Plaza (1992) | 1,023 | 55 |
| Sun Trust Bank Tower (1992) | 880 | 63 |
| One Atlantic Center (1988) | 820 | 52 |
| 191 Peachtree (1990) | 770 | 54 |
| Westin Peachtree Plaza (1973) | 723 | 71 |
| Georgia Pacific Tower (1981) | 697 | 51 |
| Promenade II/AT&T (1989) | 691 | 40 |
| Bell South Telephone (1980) | 677 | 47 |
| The Grand/Occidental Hotel (1992) | 629 | 53 |
| Concourse Tower #5 (1988) | 570 | 32 |
| State of Georgia Tower (1968) | 556 | 44 |
| Marriott Marquis (1985) | 554 | 52 |
| Concourse Tower #6 (1991) | 553 | 32 |
| Equitable Building (1967), 100 Peachtree | 453 | 34 |
| 101 Marietta Tower (1975) | 446 | 36 |
| Ravinia #3 (1991) | 444 | 34 |
| AT&T Long Line Bldg. (1975) | 433 | – |
| Bell South Enterprises (1990) | 428 | 28 |
| Atlanta Plaza I (1986) | 425 | 32 |
| Park Place, 2660 Peachtree (1986) | 420 | 40 |
| Club Towers Apts. (1989) | 410 | 38 |
| One Park Tower (1961) | 409 | 32 |
| Peachtree Summit/Federal Bldg. (1975) | 406 | 31 |
| North Avenue Tower (1979) | 403 | 26 |
| Tower Place (1974), 3361 Piedmont Rd. | 401 | 29 |
| First Union Bank (1987) | 396 | 30 |
| Atlanta Federal Center (1996) | 388 | 25 |
| *Monarch Plaza (1997) 3424 Peachtree | 387 | 24 |
| Atlanta Hilton Hotel (1974) | 383 | 32 |
| Richard B. Russell, Federal Bldg. (1978) | 383 | 26 |
| Peachtree Center, Harris Bldg. (1975) | 382 | 31 |
| Hewlett-Packard Bldg. (1995) | 381 | 27 |
| Marquis One (1985) | 378 | 30 |
| Marquis Two (1987) | 378 | 30 |
| Sun Trust Bank (1968) | 377 | 28 |
| 260 Peachtree (1971) | 377 | 27 |
| Peachtree Center Cain Building (1972) | 376 | 30 |
| Peachtree Center Building (1966) | 374 | 31 |
| One Georgia Center (1966) | 371 | 29 |
| Mayfair Apts. Tower (1990) | 370 | 34 |
| The Campanile (1987), 1145 Peachtree | 367 | 25 |
| Riverwood Tower(1989) | 362 | 26 |

### Austin, TX

| Building | Ht. ft. | Stories |
|---|---|---|
| One American Center (1982) | 395 | 32 |
| One Congress Plaza (1987) | 391 | 30 |

### Baltimore, MD

| Building | Ht. ft. | Stories |
|---|---|---|
| U.S. Fidelity & Guaranty Co. | 529 | 40 |
| NationsBank Bldg. | 509 | 34 |
| William Donald Schaefer Tower | 493 | 29 |
| Commerce Place | 454 | 30 |
| World Trade Center Bldg. | 395 | 32 |
| IBM Tower | 370 | 28 |
| 250 W. Pratt St. | 360 | 26 |
| Harbor Court | 356 | 28 |

### Birmingham, AL

| Building | Ht. ft. | Stories |
|---|---|---|
| Southtrust Tower (1986) | 454 | 34 |
| AmSouth/Harbert Plaza (1989) | 390 | 30 |
| AmSouth/Sonat Tower (1972) | 390 | 30 |
| South Central Bell HQ. Bldg. | 390 | 30 |

### Boston, MA

| Building | Ht. ft. | Stories |
|---|---|---|
| John Hancock Tower (1976) | 788 | 61 |
| Prudential Center (1964) | 750 | 52 |
| Federal Reserve Bldg | 604 | 32 |
| Boston Company County Bldg.(1970) | 601 | 41 |
| One International Place, 100 Oliver St. | 600 | 46 |
| One Financial Center | 598 | 47 |
| First National Bank of Boston | 591 | 37 |
| Exchange Place, 53 State St. | 554 | 40 |
| John Hancock Bldg. | 528 | 36 |
| Shawmut Bank Bldg., 1 Federal St. | 520 | 38 |
| One Post Office Sq. | 505 | 40 |
| Sixty State St. | 503 | 38 |
| New England Merchant Bank Bldg. | 500 | 40 |
| U.S. Custom House, State St. | 496 | 32 |
| State St. Bank Bldg. 225 Franklin St. | 477 | 34 |
| Bank of Boston, 100 Summer St | 433 | 33 |
| Two International Place | 433 | 33 |
| McCormack Bldg. | 401 | 22 |
| Keystone Funds, 200 Berkley St. | 400 | 32 |
| Harbor Towers (2 bldgs.) 85 E. India | 400 | 40 |
| 65 E. India | 396 | 40 |
| 125 High St. (1990) | 399 | 30 |
| One Devonshire Place, 250 Wash. St. | 396 | 40 |
| Saltonstall Office Bldg. | 396 | 22 |
| Westin Hotel, Copley Place | 395 | 36 |
| Federal Center (1988) | 393 | 28 |
| 75 State St. (1988) | 390 | 31 |
| John F. Kennedy Bldg. | 387 | 24 |
| Marriott Hotel, Copley Place | 382 | 38 |
| One Beacon St. | 380 | 37 |
| Charles River Park, 80 Staniford St. | 378 | 37 |
| 100 Staniford St. | 338 | 37 |
| 75-101 Federal St. (1988) | 360 | 31 |

### Buffalo, NY

| Building | Ht. ft. | Stories |
|---|---|---|
| Marine Midland Center (1970) | 524 | 38 |
| Rand Bldg. (1929), (incl. 40-ft. beacon) | 351 | 29 |

### Calgary, Alberta

| Building | Ht. ft. | Stories |
|---|---|---|
| Petro-Canada Centre, W. Tower (1984) | 689 | 52 |
| Bankers Hall (1989) | 645 | 50 |
| Calgary Tower (1988) | 626 | – |
| Canterra Tower (1988) | 580 | 46 |
| First Canadian Centre (1983) | 547 | 44 |
| Western Canadian Place, North Tower | 538 | 41 |
| Calgary Eatons Centre | 530 | 40 |
| Scotia Centre (1976) | 504 | 38 |
| Nova Bldg., 801 7th Ave. SW | 500 | 37 |
| Petro-Canada Centre, E. Tower (1984) | 469 | 33 |
| Two Bow Valley Square (1974) | 468 | 39 |
| Fifth & Fifth Bldg. | 460 | 35 |
| Home Oil Tower | 463 | 34 |
| Canada Trust Tower (1991) | 462 | 40 |
| Shell Tower | 460 | 34 |
| Dome Oil Tower | 449 | 33 |
| Four Bow Valley Square (1982) | 441 | 37 |
| Esso Plaza (twin towers) | 435 | 34 |
| Western Canadian Place, South Tower | 420 | 32 |
| Sovereign Life Bldg. | 410 | 33 |
| Pan Canadian Bldg., 150 9th Ave. SW | 410 | 28 |
| Norcen Tower | 408 | 33 |
| Alberta Stock Exchange Bldg. | 407 | 33 |
| Suncor Building | 396 | 32 |
| Amoco Centre (1988) | 396 | 30 |
| Western Centre | 385 | 40 |
| Calgary Place | 385 | 30 |
| Three Bow Valley Square | 382 | 33 |

### Charlotte, NC

| Building | Ht. ft. | Stories |
|---|---|---|
| NationsBank Corp. Center (1992) | 871 | 60 |
| One First Union Center (1988) | 588 | 42 |
| NationsBank Plaza (1974) | 503 | 40 |
| Interstate Tower (1990) | 459 | 32 |
| Two First Union Center (1971) | 433 | 32 |
| Wachovia Center (1974) | 420 | 32 |
| Carillon (1991) | 394 | 24 |
| Charlotte Plaza (1982) | 388 | 27 |

### Chicago, IL

| Building | Ht. ft. | Stories |
|---|---|---|
| Sears Tower (1974) | 1,450 | 110 |
| Amoco (1973) | 1,136 | 80 |
| John Hancock Center (1969) | 1,127 | 100 |
| Two Prudential Plaza (1990) | 978 | 64 |
| 311 S. Wacker (1990) | 959 | 65 |

| Building | Ht. ft. | Stories |
|---|---|---|
| Prudential Bldg. (1955), 130 E. Randolph, (incl. 311-ft. antenna tower) | 912 | 41 |
| AT&T Corporate Center (1989) | 885 | 60 |
| 900 N. Michigan (1989) | 871 | 66 |
| Water Tower Place (1976) | 859 | 74 |
| One First National Plaza (1969) | 850 | 60 |
| Three First National Plaza (1981) | 753 | 57 |
| Olympia Centre (1981) | 725 | 63 |
| Leo Burnett Bldg. (1989) | 700 | 46 |
| IBM Building (1973) | 695 | 52 |
| One Magnificent Mile (1983) | 673 | 58 |
| Paine Webber Bldg., 181 W. Madison | 644 | 50 |
| Daley Center (1965) | 662 | 31 |
| 1000 Lake Shore Plaza (1964) | 648 | 55 |
| Lake Point Tower (1968) | 645 | 70 |
| Board of Trade (1930), (incl. 81-ft. statue) | 605 | 44 |
| CNA Plaza (1972) | 600 | 44 |
| Huron Apts. | 599 | 56 |
| Marina City Apts., (2 bldgs) | 588 | 61 |
| Mid Continental Plaza (1972) | 580 | 50 |
| Associates Center (1983) | 575 | 41 |
| Pittsfield, 55 E. Washington St. (1927) | 572 | 38 |
| Onterie Center (1985) | 570 | 58 |
| Civic Opera Bldg. (1929) | 555 | 45 |
| Lincoln Tower (1928), 75 E. Wacker Dr. | 554 | 42 |
| Newberry Plaza (1974), State & Oak | 553 | 56 |
| Madison Plaza (1982) | 551 | 45 |
| One South Wacker Dr. (1983) | 550 | 40 |
| Harbor Point (1975) | 550 | 54 |
| 190 S. LaSalle (1986) | 550 | 40 |
| LaSalle Natl. Bank (1934) | 535 | 44 |
| One N. LaSalle Street (1930) | 530 | 49 |
| 111 E. Chestnut St. (1972) | 529 | 56 |
| Chicago Mercantile Exchange (2 bldgs) | 525 | 40 |
| River Plaza, Rush & Hubbard (1988) | 524 | 56 |
| 35 E. Wacker Drive (1926) | 523 | 40 |
| United Ins. Bldg. (1962), 1 E. Wacker Dr. | 522 | 41 |
| Quaker Tower (1987) | 518 | 35 |
| Carbide & Carbon (1929), 230 N. Mich. | 503 | 37 |
| Walton Colonnade (1972) | 500 | 44 |
| Xerox Center (1980) | 500 | 40 |
| One Financial Place (1985) | 498 | 40 |
| LaSalle-Wacker, 221 N. LaSalle St. | 491 | 41 |
| Amer. Nat'l. Bank, 33 N. LaSalle St. | 479 | 40 |
| Bankers (1927), 105 W. Adams St. | 476 | 41 |
| Brunswick Bldg. (1965) | 475 | 37 |
| 310 Center (1924) | 475 | 37 |

## Cincinnati, OH

| Building | Ht. ft. | Stories |
|---|---|---|
| Carew Tower (1930) | 574 | 49 |
| 312 Walnut St. (1990) | 468 | 36 |
| Fifth Third Center (1970) | 460 | 31 |
| Atrium Two (1984) | 428 | 30 |
| Chemed Center (1990) | 410 | 32 |
| Central Trust Tower (1913) | 408 | 28 |
| Cincinnati Commerce Center (1984) | 402 | 29 |
| PNC Center (1978) | 368 | 27 |
| Chiquita Center (1984) | 365 | 29 |
| Star Bank Center (1981) | 365 | 28 |

## Cleveland, OH

| Building | Ht. ft. | Stories |
|---|---|---|
| Key Center (1991) | 948 | 63 |
| Terminal Tower (1930) | 708 | 52 |
| BP America (1985) | 658 | 45 |
| Erieview Tower (1964) | 529 | 40 |
| One Cleveland Center (1983) | 450 | 31 |
| Bank One Center (1991) | 446 | 28 |
| Justice Center (1976) | 420 | 26 |
| Celebreeze Federal Bldg. (1967) | 419 | 32 |
| National City Center (1980) | 410 | 35 |
| 900 Euclid (1971) | 383 | 29 |
| Ameritech, Huron Bldg. (1927) | 365 | 24 |
| CSU Rhodes (1971) | 363 | 20 |
| Eaton Center (1983) | 356 | 28 |

## Columbus, OH

| Building | Ht. ft. | Stories |
|---|---|---|
| James A. Rhodes (State Office Tower) | 629 | 41 |
| LeVeque Tower, 50 W. Broad | 555 | 47 |
| Ohio Bureau of Worker's Compensation & Ind. Comm. (1990) | 530 | 33 |
| Huntington Center, 41 S. High St. | 512 | 37 |
| Verne-Riffe State Office Tower | 503 | 33 |
| One Nationwide Plaza | 482 | 40 |
| Franklin County Courthouse | 464 | 27 |
| One Riverside Plaza | 456 | 31 |
| Borden Bldg., 180 E. Broad | 438 | 34 |
| Three Nationwide Plaza (1989) | 408 | 27 |
| One Columbus | 366 | 26 |
| Columbus Center, 100 E. Broad | 357 | 24 |

## Dallas, TX

| Building | Ht. ft. | Stories |
|---|---|---|
| NationsBank Plaza (1985) | 921 | 72 |
| Bank One Center (1987) | 787 | 60 |
| Texas Commerce Tower (1987) | 738 | 55 |
| Fountain Place (1986) | 721 | 60 |
| Renaissance Tower (1974) | 710 | 56 |
| Trammell Crow Center (1987) | 686 | 49 |
| 1700 Pacific (1983) | 655 | 50 |
| Thanksgiving Tower (1982) | 645 | 50 |
| Elm Place (1965) | 625 | 50 |
| NationsBank Center Tower 2 (1980) | 598 | 50 |
| Lincoln Plaza (1984) | 579 | 45 |
| Harwood @Bryan Corp. Center (1982) | 562 | 36 |
| Cityplace Center East (1989) | 560 | 42 |
| Maxus Energy (1980) | 550 | 34 |
| 2001 Bryan Tower. (1973) | 512 | 40 |
| San Jacinto Tower (1982) | 456 | 33 |
| M-Bank Bldg. (1943) | 452 | 31 |
| Stouffer Hotel | 451 | 29 |
| One Dallas Centre (1979) | 448 | 30 |
| One Main Place (1968) | 445 | 34 |
| 1600 Pacific Bldg. (1964) | 434 | 32 |
| Magnolia Bldg. (1923) | 430 | 27 |

## Dayton, OH

| Building | Ht. ft. | Stories |
|---|---|---|
| Kettering Tower (1970), 2d & Main | 405 | 30 |
| Mead World Headquarters (1976), 10 W. 2d St. | 385 | 28 |

## Denver, CO

| Building | Ht. ft. | Stories |
|---|---|---|
| Republic Plaza (1984) | 714 | 56 |
| 1801 California Building (1983) | 709 | 52 |
| One Norwest Center (1983) | 698 | 52 |
| 1999 Broadway (1985) | 544 | 43 |
| MCI Tower (1982) | 527 | 42 |
| Anaconda Tower (1978) | 507 | 40 |
| Amoco Bldg (1980) | 448 | 36 |
| 17th Street Plaza (1982) | 438 | 32 |
| First Interstate Tower North (1974) | 434 | 32 |
| One Denver Place (1983) | 428 | 34 |
| Brooks Towers (1968) | 420 | 42 |
| One Tabor Center (1984) | 408 | 30 |
| Manville Plaza (1989) | 404 | 29 |
| Colorado Nat'l. Bank Building (1982) | 389 | 26 |
| First Interstate Tower South (1982) | 385 | 28 |
| 1616 Glenarm Bldg. (1981) | 384 | 31 |
| Mellon Financial Center (1982) | 374 | 32 |
| Dominion Plaza (1983) | 368 | 28 |
| Lincoln Center Building (1972) | 366 | 31 |
| 1125 17th Street (1980) | 363 | 25 |
| Bank Western Tower (1980) | 357 | 28 |
| Colorado State Bank Building (1971) | 352 | 27 |

## Des Moines, IA

| Building | Ht. ft. | Stories |
|---|---|---|
| Principal Financial Group Bldg. (1990) | 630 | 44 |
| Ruan Center (1974) | 457 | 35 |

## Detroit, MI

| Building | Ht. ft. | Stories |
|---|---|---|
| Renaissance Ctr. Tower (1977) | 720 | 73 |
| One Detroit Center (1990), 500 Woodward | 620 | 43 |
| Penobscot Bldg. (1928), 633 Griswold | 557 | 46 |
| Guardian Bldg. (1950) 500 Griswold. | 485 | 40 |
| Renaissance Center (4 bldgs.) | 479 | 39 |
| Book Tower (1925), 1265 Washington | 472 | 38 |
| Madden Bldg. (1988), 150 W. Jefferson. | 470 | 26 |
| Prudential 3000 Town Center | 448 | 32 |
| Cadillac Tower (1928) 65 Cadillac Sq. | 437 | 40 |
| David Stott. (1928), 1150 Griswold | 436 | 38 |
| ANR Bldg. (1962) 1 Woodward | 430 | 30 |
| Fisher Bldg. | 420 | 28 |
| McNamara Federal Office Bldg. (1975) | 393 | 27 |
| 2000 Prudential Town Ctr. | 392 | 28 |
| American Center | 374 | 27 |
| Top of Troy Bldg. | 374 | 27 |
| 211 W. Fort (1965) | 370 | 27 |
| Edison Plaza (1973), 1920 Third | 365 | 24 |
| David Broderick Tower (1927) | 358 | 34 |
| Buhl Bldg. (1926), 535 Griswold | 350 | 26 |
| 1st National Bldg. (1930), 660 Woodward | 350 | 25 |

## Edmonton, Alberta

| Building | Ht. ft. | Stories |
|---|---|---|
| Manulife Place (1983) | 479 | 36 |
| AGT Tower (1971) | 441 | 33 |
| Canada Trust Tower (1982) | 440 | 31 |
| Commerce Place (1990) | 409 | 30 |
| Metropolitan Place (1980) | 397 | 31 |
| Oxford Tower (1978) | 390 | 27 |
| TD Tower (1975) | 386 | 27 |
| Scotia Place (1983) | 366 | 28 |
| CN Tower (1966) | 365 | 27 |
| Phipps McKinnon (1977) | 359 | 20 |

## Fort Worth, TX

| Building | Ht. ft. | Stories |
|---|---|---|
| City Center Tower II (1984) | 546 | 38 |
| Burnett Plaza (1983) | 538 | 40 |
| Continental Plaza (1982) | 520 | 40 |
| Texas Commerce Tower(1982) | 475 | 33 |
| Bank One Tower (1975) | 457 | 35 |
| Texas Bldg. (1955) | 420 | 30 |

## Hartford, CT

| Building | Ht. ft. | Stories |
|---|---|---|
| City Place (1983) | 535 | 38 |
| Travelers Ins. Co. Bldg. (1919) | 527 | 34 |
| Goodwin Square (1990) | 522 | 30 |
| Hartford Plaza (1967) | 420 | 22 |
| Shawmut Bank (1960) | 360 | 26 |

## Honolulu, HI

| Building | Ht. ft. | Stories |
|---|---|---|
| Waterfront Towers (1990) | 400 | 46 |
| Nauru Tower (1991) | 400 | 45 |
| Imperial Plaza (1992) | 400 | 40 |
| Ala Moana Hotel | 396 | 38 |
| Island Colony | 350 | 44 |
| Hawaiian Monarch Hotel | 350 | 43 |
| Maile Court Hotel | 350 | 43 |
| Pacific Beach Hotel | 350 | 43 |
| Pearlridge Square | 350 | 43 |
| Waikiki Hobron | 350 | 43 |
| Discovery Bay | 350 | 42 |
| Regency Tower, 2525 Date St. | 350 | 42 |
| Century Center | 350 | 41 |
| Executive Center, 1088 Bishop St. | 350 | 41 |
| Franklin Towers | 350 | 41 |
| Canterbury Place | 350 | 40 |
| Honolulu Tower | 350 | 40 |
| Honolulu Tower 2 | 350 | 40 |
| Yacht Harbor Towers | 350 | 40 |
| Hyatt Regency Waikiki | 350 | 39 |
| Royal Iolani | 350 | 38 |
| Tapa Tower, 2005 Kalia Rd. | 350 | 36 |
| Pacific Tower | 350 | 30 |
| 1001 Bishop | 350 | 28 |

## Houston, TX

| Building | Ht. ft. | Stories |
|---|---|---|
| Texas Commerce Tower (1981) | 1,002 | 75 |
| First Interstate Plaza (1983) | 972 | 71 |
| Transco Tower (1983) | 901 | 64 |
| NationsBank Center (1983) | 780 | 56 |
| Heritage Plaza, 1111 Bagby | 762 | 53 |
| InterFirst Plaza (1980) | 744 | 55 |
| Houston Industries Plaza | 741 | 53 |
| 1600 Smith St. (1984) | 729 | 54 |
| Chevron Tower (1982), 1301 McKinney | 725 | 52 |
| One Shell Plaza (1970) (not incl. 285-ft. TV tower) | 714 | 50 |
| Enron Bldg. (1983) | 692 | 50 |
| Capital Natl. Bank Plaza | 685 | 50 |
| One Houston Center (1978) | 678 | 47 |
| First City, Tex. Financial Center (1984) | 662 | 47 |
| San Felipe Plaza (1984) | 620 | 45 |
| Exxon Bldg. (1962) | 606 | 44 |
| The America Tower | 577 | 42 |
| Marathon Oil Tower (1983) | 572 | 41 |
| Two Houston Center (1974) | 570 | 40 |
| 1415 Louisiana Tower (1983) | 550 | 44 |
| Kellogg Tower (1973) | 550 | 40 |
| Pennzoil, 700 Milam (1975) (2 bldgs.) | 523 | 36 |
| Two Allen Center (1978) | 521 | 36 |
| 1201 Louisiana Bldg. (1971) | 518 | 35 |
| Huntington | 506 | 34 |
| Tenneco Bldg. (1962) | 502 | 33 |
| Conoco Tower (1973) | 465 | 32 |
| One Allen Center (1974) | 452 | 34 |
| Summit Tower West (1979) | 441 | 31 |
| Coastal Tower (1978) | 441 | 31 |
| Four Leafs Towers (2 bldgs.) | 439 | 40 |
| Phoenix Tower (1984) | 434 | 34 |
| Chevron Bldg. | 428 | 37 |
| The Spires | 426 | 41 |
| Central Tower, 4 Oaks Place | 420 | 30 |
| First City Natl. Bank (1960) | 410 | 32 |
| Houston Lighting & Power (1968) | 410 | 27 |
| Niels Esperson Bldg. (1927) | 409 | 31 |
| Hyatt Regency Houston (1972) | 401 | 34 |

## Indianapolis, IN

| Building | Ht. ft. | Stories |
|---|---|---|
| Bank One Tower (1989) | 728 | 51 |
| AUL Tower (1981) | 533 | 38 |
| Market Tower (1988) | 515 | 32 |
| NBD Bank Tower (1969) | 504 | 35 |
| Riley Towers (1963) (2 bldgs.) | 427 | 30 |
| 300 N. Meridian Bldg. (1988) | 408 | 28 |

## Jacksonville, FL

| Building | Ht. ft. | Stories |
|---|---|---|
| Barnett Center (1990) | 617 | 42 |
| Independent Life Bldg. (1975) | 535 | 37 |
| Southern Bell (1983) | 447 | 32 |
| River Place Tower (1967) | 432 | 28 |
| American Heritage Life (1989) | 357 | 23 |

## Kansas City, MO

| Building | Ht. ft. | Stories |
|---|---|---|
| One Kansas City Place (1988) | 626 | 42 |
| AT&T Town Pavilion (1986) | 590 | 38 |
| Hyatt Regency (1980) | 504 | 40 |
| Kansas City Power and Light Bldg (1931) | 476 | 32 |
| City Hall (1937) | 443 | 29 |
| 1201 Walnut (1991) | 425 | 30 |
| Federal Office Bldg (1962) | 413 | 35 |
| Commerce Tower (1965) | 402 | 32 |
| City Center Square (1977) | 402 | 30 |
| Southwest Bell Telephone Bldg. (1973) | 394 | 27 |
| 2345 Grand Ave. (1977) | 352 | 28 |

## Las Vegas, NV

| Building | Ht. ft. | Stories |
|---|---|---|
| *Stratosphere Tower (1997) | 1,049 | 114 |
| Las Vegas Hilton (1995) | 375 | 30 |

## Little Rock, AR

| Building | Ht. ft. | Stories |
|---|---|---|
| TCBY Towers (1986) | 546 | 40 |
| First Commercial Bank (1975) | 454 | 30 |
| Boatman's Bank & Trust (1969) | 375 | 24 |
| Stephens Bldg. (1985) | 365 | 35 |
| Tower Bldg. (1960) | 350 | 18 |

## Los Angeles, CA

| Building | Ht. ft. | Stories |
|---|---|---|
| First Interstate World Center (1989) | 1,107 | 72 |
| First Interstate Bank | 858 | 62 |
| Two California Plaza | 750 | 52 |
| Wells Fargo Tower | 700 | 54 |
| The Gas Company Tower (1990) | 749 | 50 |
| 333 South Hope Bldg. (1975) | 743 | 55 |
| 777 Tower | 725 | 52 |
| Sanwa Bank Plaza (1990) | 716 | 52 |
| Atlantic Richfield Tower | 699 | 52 |
| Bank of America Tower | 699 | 52 |
| 444 S. Flower St. | 625 | 48 |
| AT&T Bldg. | 620 | 42 |
| One California Plaza | 578 | 42 |
| Century Plaza Towers (2 bldgs.) | 571 | 44 |
| IBM Tower | 560 | 45 |
| Citicorp Plaza | 534 | 42 |
| 1999 Ave. of the Stars (1989) | 533 | 39 |
| Manulife Tower (1990) | 517 | 37 |
| Union Bank Square | 516 | 41 |
| MCA-Getty | 506 | 36 |
| WTC Bldg. | 496 | 36 |
| Fox Plaza | 492 | 34 |
| ARCO Center | 462 | 32 |
| Equitable Life Bldg. | 454 | 34 |
| City Hall | 454 | 28 |
| Transamerica Center | 452 | 32 |
| Mutual Benefit Life Ins. Bldg. | 435 | 31 |
| One Wilshire Bldg. | 415 | 31 |
| Warner Center Plaza III | 415 | 25 |
| Macy's Plaza | 414 | 33 |
| 1900 Ave. of Stars | 398 | 27 |
| The Evian | 390 | 31 |
| 400 S. Hope St. | 375 | 26 |
| Westin Bonaventure Hotel | 365 | 35 |

| Building | Ht. ft. | Stories |
|---|---|---|
| Beaudry Center | 365 | 29 |
| California Fed. Savings & Loan Bldg. | 363 | 28 |
| Century City North | 363 | 26 |
| Home Savings Tower | 356 | 25 |

## Louisville, KY

| Building | Ht. ft. | Stories |
|---|---|---|
| Providian Center (1992), 4th & Market | 549 | 35 |
| National City Tower (1972), 4th & Main | 495 | 40 |
| Citizens Plaza (1971), 5th & Jefferson | 420 | 30 |
| Humana Bldg (1985), 5th & Main | 417 | 30 |
| Meidinger Tower (1982), 462 S. 4th | 359 | 26 |
| Brown & Williamson Tower (1982) | 359 | 26 |

## Memphis, TN

| Building | Ht. ft. | Stories |
|---|---|---|
| 100 N. Main Bldg. | 430 | 37 |
| Commerce Square | 396 | 31 |
| Clark, 5100 Poplar | 365 | 32 |
| Sterick Bldg. | 365 | 31 |

## Miami, FL

| Building | Ht. ft. | Stories |
|---|---|---|
| First Union Financial Center (1983) | 764 | 55 |
| International Place (1987) | 562 | 35 |
| Metro-Dade Administration Bldg. | 510 | 30 |
| Florida National Tower (1986) | 484 | 35 |
| One Biscayne Tower. | 456 | 38 |
| Barnett Tower (1986) | 450 | 33 |
| Courthouse Center (1986) | 405 | 30 |
| Sunbank International Center (1973) | 375 | 31 |
| Bristol | 371 | 41 |
| Hotel Inter-Continental Miami | 366 | 35 |
| Venitia, 1635 Bayshore Dr. | 365 | 42 |
| Dade County Court House | 357 | 28 |

## Milwaukee, WI

| Building | Ht. ft. | Stories |
|---|---|---|
| Firstar Center (1971) | 625 | 42 |
| Faison Bldg., 100 East (1989) | 549 | 37 |
| Milwaukee Center (1987) | 426 | 29 |
| 411 Bldg., 411 E. Wisconsin (1983) | 408 | 30 |
| Northwestern Mutual Tower (1989) | 395 | 19 |
| City Hall (1898) | 350 | 9 |

## Minneapolis, MN

| Building | Ht. ft. | Stories |
|---|---|---|
| IDS Center (1973) | 776 | 51 |
| First Bank Place | 775 | 53 |
| Norwest (1988) | 773 | 57 |
| Multifoods Tower (1983) | 608 | 51 |
| Piper Jaffray Tower (1984) | 627 | 42 |
| Dain Bosworth Plaza | 539 | 40 |
| Pillsbury Center (1981), 200 S. 6th St. | 530 | 40 |
| 150 South Fifth | 498 | 36 |
| Metropolitan Center (1987), 333 S. 7th | 496 | 31 |
| Plaza VII, 45 S. 7th (1987) | 468 | 36 |
| Foshay Tower (1929), (not incl. 160-ft. antenna tower) | 447 | 31 |
| Hennepin Co. Govt. Center (1974) | 413 | 25 |
| Marriott Hotel (1983) | 379 | 33 |

## Montreal, Quebec

| Building | Ht. ft. | Stories |
|---|---|---|
| 1100 Rue de la Gauchetiere | 669 | 45 |
| 1250 Boulevard Rene Levesque | 640 | 45 |
| Place Victoria (1963) | 624 | 47 |
| Place Ville Marie (1962) | 620 | 45 |
| Canadian Imperial Bank of Commerce (1962) | 590 | 45 |
| Le Complexe Desjardins (3 bldgs.) | | |
| La Tour du Sud | 498 | 40 |
| La Tour du L'Est | 428 | 32 |
| La Tour du Nord | 355 | 27 |
| Les Cooperants (1987) | 479 | 34 |
| Place Montreal Trust (1988) | 449 | 32 |
| Chateau Champlain Hotel (1967) | 420 | 38 |
| Port Royal Apts. | 400 | 33 |
| Royal Bank Tower | 397 | 22 |
| 500 Place d'Armes | 390 | 32 |
| Sun Life Bldg. | 390 | 26 |

## Nashville, TN

| Building | Ht. ft. | Stories |
|---|---|---|
| South Central Bell Bldg. | 617 | 33 |
| Third National Financial Center | 490 | 30 |
| American General Center | 452 | 31 |
| Landmark Center | 409 | 30 |
| Nashville City Center (1987) | 402 | 27 |

| Building | Ht. ft. | Stories |
|---|---|---|
| James K. Polk State Office Bldg. | 392 | 32 |
| Stouffer Hotel (1987) | 385 | 35 |
| First American Center | 354 | 28 |

## Newark, NJ

| Building | Ht. ft. | Stories |
|---|---|---|
| Natl. Newark & Essex Bldg. | 465 | 36 |
| Raymond-Commerce | 448 | 37 |
| Park Plaza Bldg. | 400 | 26 |
| Prudential Plaza | 370 | 24 |
| Public Service Elec. & Gas | 360 | 26 |
| Prudential Ins. Co., 753 Broad St. | 360 | 26 |
| AT&T Bldg. | 359 | 31 |
| Gateway 1 | 355 | 28 |

## New Orleans, LA

| Building | Ht. ft. | Stories |
|---|---|---|
| One Shell Square (1972) | 697 | 51 |
| Place St. Charles (1985) | 645 | 53 |
| Plaza Tower (1969) | 531 | 45 |
| Energy Centre (1984) | 530 | 39 |
| LL&E Tower (1987) | 481 | 36 |
| Sheraton Hotel (1985) | 478 | 47 |
| Marriott Hotel (1972) | 450 | 42 |
| Texaco Bldg. (1983) | 442 | 33 |
| Canal Place One (1979) | 439 | 32 |
| 1010 Common (1971) | 438 | 31 |
| World Trade Center | 407 | 33 |
| 225 Baronne St. (1965) | 362 | 28 |
| One Poydras Plaza (1983) | 360 | 28 |
| Hibernia Bank Bldg. (1920) | 355 | 23 |
| Hyatt-Regency Hotel (1976) | 353 | 32 |

## New York, NY

| Building | Ht. ft. | Stories |
|---|---|---|
| One World Trade Center (1972) | 1,368 | 110 |
| Two World Trade Center (1973) | 1,362 | 110 |
| Empire State (1931), 34th St. & 5th Ave. | 1,250 | 102 |
| (incl. 164-ft. TV tower) | 1,414 | – |
| Chrysler (1930), Lexington & 43d | 1,046 | 77 |
| Amer. International (1932), 70 Pine | 950 | 66 |
| 40 Wall Tower (1929) | 927 | 70 |
| Citicorp Center (1977) | 915 | 59 |
| G.E. Bldg., Rockefeller Center (1933) | 850 | 70 |
| Cityspire (1989) | 814 | 72 |
| One Chase Manhattan Plaza (1960) | 813 | 60 |
| MetLife Bldg., 200 Park Ave. (1963) | 808 | 59 |
| Woolworth, 233 Broadway (1913) | 792 | 57 |
| One Worldwide Plaza | 778 | 47 |
| Carnegie Tower | 757 | 60 |
| Equitable Center Tower West (1985) | 752 | 51 |
| One Penn Plaza (1972) | 750 | 54 |
| 1251 Ave. of Americas (1971) | 750 | 54 |
| 60 Wall St. (1989) | 745 | 50 |
| One Liberty Plaza (1972) | 743 | 50 |
| World Financial Center, Tower C (1988) | 739 | 54 |
| One Astor Plaza (1969) | 730 | 54 |
| Solow Bldg. (1979) | 725 | 50 |
| Marine Midland Bank | 724 | 52 |
| Metropolitan Tower (1988) | 716 | 66 |
| Union Carbide Bldg. (1960) | 707 | 52 |
| General Motors Bldg. (1968) | 705 | 50 |
| Metropolitan Life (1909) | 700 | 50 |
| 500 5th Ave. (1928) | 697 | 58 |
| 55 Water St. | 687 | 53 |
| Chem. Bank, NY. Trust Bldg. (1963) | 687 | 50 |
| 1585 Broadway | 685 | 42 |
| Four Seasons Hotel (1993) | 682 | 52 |
| Chanin (1929), Lexington & 42d. | 680 | 56 |
| Trump International Hotel and Tower | 679 | 45 |
| McGraw Hill (1972), 1221 Ave. of Amer. | 674 | 51 |
| Lincoln (1939), 60 E. 42d Street | 673 | 53 |
| Citicorp (Queens) (1990) | 673 | 50 |
| 1633 Broadway | 670 | 48 |
| Trump Tower (1983), 725 5th Ave. | 664 | 68 |
| 599 Lexington Ave. (1988) | 653 | 47 |
| Museum Tower Apts. (1985) | 650 | 58 |
| 712 5th Ave. (1990) | 650 | 56 |
| American Brands, 245 Park Ave. | 648 | 47 |
| 550 Madison Ave. (1983) | 648 | 37 |
| World Financial Center Tower B (1986) | 645 | 50 |
| General Electric (1931), 570 Lexington. | 640 | 50 |
| Irving Trust (1932), 1 Wall St. | 640 | 50 |
| 345 Park Ave. | 634 | 44 |
| Grace Plaza, 1114 Ave. of Amer. | 630 | 50 |
| One New York Plaza (1969) | 630 | 50 |
| Home Insurance Co. Bldg. | 630 | 44 |
| NYNEX, 1095 Ave. of Amer. | 630 | 40 |

| Building | Ht. ft. | Stories |
|---|---|---|
| Central Park Place (1988) | 628 | 56 |
| One Hammarskjold Plaza | 628 | 50 |
| 888 7th Ave. | 628 | 42 |
| Burlington House (1970) | 625 | 50 |
| Waldorf-Astoria (1931), 301 Park Ave. | 625 | 47 |
| Olympic Tower (1976), 645 5th Ave. | 620 | 51 |
| 10 E. 40th St. | 620 | 48 |
| 101 Park Ave. | 618 | 50 |
| New York Life (1928), 51 Madison Ave. | 615 | 40 |
| 750 7th Ave. | 615 | 35 |
| Rihga Royal Hotel | 610 | 54 |
| 17 State St. | 610 | 41 |
| Penney Bldg., 1301 Ave. of Amer. | 609 | 46 |
| IBM (1983), 590 Madison Ave. | 603 | 41 |
| 780 3d Ave. | 600 | 50 |
| Celanese Bldg. (1973) | 592 | 45 |
| U.S. Court House (1976), 505 Pearl St. | 590 | 37 |
| Kalikow Hotel | 588 | 58 |
| Time & Life (1959), 1271 Ave. of Amer. | 587 | 47 |
| Federal Bldg., Foley Square | 587 | 41 |
| Stevens Tower, 1185 Ave. of Amer. | 580 | 42 |
| Cooper Bregstein Bldg., 1250 Bway. | 580 | 40 |
| Municipal Bldg. (1919) | 580 | 34 |
| 520 Madison Ave. (1983) | 577 | 42 |
| One Madison Square Plaza (1968) | 576 | 42 |
| Park Ave. Plaza (1981) | 575 | 44 |
| World Financial Center Tower A (1986) | 575 | 42 |
| One Financial Sq. (1987) | 575 | 37 |
| Westvaco Bldg., 299 Park Ave. | 574 | 42 |
| Marriott Marquis Hotel (1985) | 574 | 42 |
| Socony Mobil Bldg., East 42d St. | 572 | 45 |
| Sperry Rand Bldg., 1290 Ave. of Am. | 570 | 43 |
| 600 3d Ave. | 570 | 42 |
| One Bankers Trust Plaza | 565 | 40 |
| Helmsley Bldg. (1929), 230 Park | 565 | 35 |
| Hemsley Palace Hotel (1980) | 563 | 51 |
| 30 Broad St. | 562 | 48 |
| Park Ave. Tower (1986) | 561 | 36 |
| Sherry-Netherland, 5th Ave. & 59th St. | 560 | 40 |
| Continental Can (1983), 633 3d Ave. | 557 | 39 |
| Continental Corp., 180 Maiden Lane | 555 | 41 |
| Sperry & Hutchinson, 330 Madison | 555 | 39 |
| Galleria (1975), 117 E. 57th St. | 552 | 57 |
| Interchem Bldg., 1133 Ave. of Amer. | 552 | 45 |
| 919 3d Ave. | 550 | 47 |
| NYNEX (1979), 323 Broadway | 550 | 45 |
| 151 E. 44th St. | 550 | 44 |
| Burroughs Bldg., 605 3d Ave. | 550 | 44 |
| Bankers Trust. (1963), 33 E. 48 St | 547 | 41 |
| Transportation Bldg., 225 Broadway | 546 | 45 |
| Equitable (1915), 120 Broadway | 545 | 42 |
| 1166 Ave. of Americas | 540 | 44 |
| One Brooklyn Bridge Plaza (1976) | 540 | 42 |
| Paine Webber Bldg. (1961) | 540 | 42 |
| Ritz Tower, Park Ave. & 57th St. | 540 | 41 |
| Bankers Trust, 6 Wall St. | 540 | 39 |
| 1700 Broadway | 533 | 41 |
| Downtown Athletic Club, 19 West St. | 530 | 45 |
| Nelson Towers, 7th Ave. & 34th St. | 525 | 45 |
| Hotel Pierre (1928), 5th Ave. & 61st St. | 525 | 44 |
| 7 World Trade Center (1985) | 525 | 44 |
| 767 3d Ave. | 525 | 39 |
| House of Seagram (1958) | 525 | 38 |
| 3 Park Ave. | 522 | 42 |
| Random House, 825 3d Ave. | 522 | 40 |
| Du Mont Bldg., 515 Madison Ave. | 520 | 42 |
| North American Plywood, 800 3d Ave. | 520 | 41 |
| 26 Broadway | 520 | 31 |
| Newsweek Bldg., 444 Madison Ave. | 518 | 43 |
| Sterling Drug Bldg., 90 Park Ave. | 515 | 41 |
| Citibank | 515 | 41 |
| Navarre, 512 7th Ave. | 513 | 43 |
| Bank of New York, 48 Wall St. | 513 | 32 |
| 1407 Broadway Realty Corp. | 512 | 44 |
| Manhattan Savings Bank (Bklyn.) | 512 | 42 |
| Rockefeller Ctr. International | 512 | 41 |
| ITT–American, 437 Madison Ave. | 512 | 40 |
| United Nations (1953), 405 E. 42 St. | 505 | 39 |

## Oakland, CA

| Building | Ht. ft. | Stories |
|---|---|---|
| Ordway Bldg., 1 Kaiser Plaza (1985) | 404 | 28 |
| Kaiser Bldg., 300 Lakeside Dr. (1958) | 390 | 28 |
| Lake Merritt Plaza, 303 20th St. (1988) | 371 | 27 |
| Federal Bldg. (2 bldgs.) (1994), 1301 Clay | 368 | 19 |
| American President Lines, (1990) | 360 | 29 |

## Oklahoma City, OK

| Building | Ht. ft. | Stories |
|---|---|---|
| Liberty Tower (1971) | 500 | 36 |
| First National Center (1974) | 493 | 28 |
| City Place (1985) | 440 | 33 |
| First Oklahoma Tower (1982) | 425 | 31 |
| Kerr-McGee Center (1973) | 393 | 30 |
| Mid America Tower (1981) | 362 | 19 |

## Omaha, NE

| Building | Ht. ft. | Stories |
|---|---|---|
| Woodmen Tower (1969) | 469 | 30 |
| Enron Building (1960) | 400 | 18 |

## Orlando, FL

| Building | Ht. ft. | Stories |
|---|---|---|
| Sun Bank Center Tower (1988) | 441 | 35 |
| *Orange County Courthouse (1997) | 416 | 24 |
| Barnett Bank Center (1988) | 404 | 28 |

## Philadelphia, PA

| Building | Ht. ft. | Stories |
|---|---|---|
| One Liberty Place (1987) | 945 | 61 |
| Two Liberty Place (1989) | 848 | 58 |
| Mellon Bank Center (1989) | 792 | 54 |
| Bell Atlantic Tower (1991) | 739 | 53 |
| Blue Cross Tower (1990) | 700 | 50 |
| Commerce Sq., #1 (1990) | 572 | 40 |
| Commerce Sq., #2 (1992) | 572 | 40 |
| City Hall Tower (1901), (incl. 37-ft. statue of William Penn.) | 548 | 7 |
| 1818 Market St. (1974) | 500 | 40 |
| Phila. Saving Fund Society (1932) | 492 | 39 |
| Meridan Bank (1972) | 492 | 38 |
| Provident Mutual Life (1983) | 491 | 40 |
| Central Penn Natl. Bank (1970) | 490 | 36 |
| Centre Square (2 towers) (1973) | 490/416 | 38/32 |
| Industrial Valley Bank (1968) | 482 | 32 |
| Philadelphia National Bank (1930) | 475 | 25 |
| Two Mellon Plaza (1930) | 450 | 30 |
| Two Logan Square (1987) | 435 | 34 |
| 2000 Market St. (1973) | 435 | 29 |
| Two Girard Plaza (1930) | 412 | 30 |
| Fidelity Bank Bldg. (1927) | 405 | 30 |
| Lewis Tower (1929), 15th & Locust | 400 | 33 |
| One Logan Square (1982) | 400 | 32 |
| 1500 Locust St. (1973) | 390 | 44 |
| Philadelphia Electric Co. (1970) | 384 | 29 |
| Academy House, 1420 Locust St. | 377 | 37 |
| The Drake, 15th & Spruce (1928) | 375 | 33 |
| Penn Mutual Life (1931) | 375 | 20 |
| INA Annex | 369 | 27 |
| Medical Tower (1931), 255 S. 17th. | 364 | 33 |

## Phoenix, AZ

| Building | Ht. ft. | Stories |
|---|---|---|
| Bank One Center (1972) | 483 | 40 |
| Bank of America Bldg. (1976) | 407 | 31 |
| Phoenix Plaza I (1989) | 397 | 20 |
| Phoenix Plaza II(1990) | 397 | 20 |
| First Interstate Bank Plaza (1971) | 372 | 26 |
| Phoenix Center (1979) | 361 | 28 |
| Norwest Tower (1980) | 356 | 26 |

## Pittsburgh, PA

| Building | Ht. ft. | Stories |
|---|---|---|
| USX Towers | 841 | 64 |
| One Mellon Bank Center | 725 | 54 |
| One PPG Place | 635 | 40 |
| Fifth Avenue Place (1987) | 616 | 31 |
| One Oxford Centre | 615 | 45 |
| Gulf, 7th Ave. and Grant St. | 582 | 38 |
| University of Pittsburgh | 535 | 42 |
| Mellon Bank Bldg. | 520 | 41 |
| One Oliver Plaza | 511 | 37 |
| Grant, Grant St. at 3d Ave. | 485 | 40 |
| Koppers, 7th Ave. and Grant | 475 | 31 |
| Two PNC Plaza | 445 | 34 |
| CNG Tower (1987) | 430 | 32 |
| One PNC Plaza | 424 | 30 |
| Alcoa Bldg., 425 Sixth Ave. | 410 | 30 |
| Liberty Center | 358 | 27 |
| Westinghouse Bldg. | 355 | 23 |

## Portland, OR

| Building | Ht. ft. | Stories |
|---|---|---|
| Wells Fargo Tower | 546 | 40 |
| U.S. Bancorp Tower | 536 | 42 |
| Koin Tower Plaza | 509 | 35 |
| Standard Insurance Center | 367 | 29 |
| Pacwest Center | 356 | 30 |

## Providence, RI

| Building | Ht. ft. | Stories |
|---|---|---|
| Fleet National Bank | 420 | 26 |
| Rhode Island Hospital Trust Tower | 410 | 30 |

## Raleigh, NC

| Building | Ht. ft. | Stories |
|---|---|---|
| BB & T/2 Hanover Sq. (1991) | 431 | 29 |
| First Union Capitol Center (1991) | 390 | 29 |

## Richmond, VA

| Building | Ht. ft. | Stories |
|---|---|---|
| James Monroe Bldg. | 450 | 29 |
| City Hall (incl. penthouse) | 425 | 17 |
| Crestar Bank HQ. Bldg. | 400 | 24 |
| Federal Reserve Bank | 393 | 26 |

## Rochester, NY

| Building | Ht. ft. | Stories |
|---|---|---|
| Xerox Tower (1967) | 443 | 30 |
| Lincoln First Tower (1973) | 392 | 27 |

## Sacramento, CA

| Building | Ht. ft. | Stories |
|---|---|---|
| Wells Fargo Center | 402 | 30 |
| Park Plaza Tower | 373 | 26 |
| Renaissance Tower | 372 | 28 |
| U.S. Bank | 350 | 25 |

## St. Louis, MO

| Building | Ht. ft. | Stories |
|---|---|---|
| Gateway Arch (1965) | 630 | – |
| Metropolitan Square Tower (1989) | 593 | 42 |
| One Bell Center (1984) | 588 | 44 |
| Mercantile Center Tower (1976) | 540 | 36 |
| Laclede Gas. Bldg. (1970), 8th & Olive | 434 | 31 |
| Boatmen's Plaza (1982) | 420 | 30 |
| SW Bell Telephone Bldg. | 398 | 26 |
| Civil Courts Bldg. | 390 | 13 |
| One City Center (1986) | 375 | 25 |

## St. Paul, MN

| Building | Ht. ft. | Stories |
|---|---|---|
| Minnesota World Trade Center | 471 | 36 |
| Galtier Plaza's Jackson Tower | 440 | 46 |
| First Natl. Bank Bldg. | 417 | 32 |
| Ecolab Bldg. | 368 | 20 |
| Kellogg Square Apts. | 366 | 32 |

## Salt Lake City, UT

| Building | Ht. ft. | Stories |
|---|---|---|
| L.D.S. Church Office Bldg. | 420 | 30 |
| Beneficial Life Tower | 351 | 21 |
| Utah One Center (1992) | 350 | 24 |

## San Antonio, TX

| Building | Ht. ft. | Stories |
|---|---|---|
| Tower of the Americas (1968) | 622 | – |
| Marriott Rivercenter (1988) | 546 | 38 |
| Weston Centre (1988) | 444 | 32 |
| Tower Life (1929) | 404 | 30 |
| NationsBank Plaza (1983) | 387 | 28 |
| Nix Professional Bldg. (1931) | 375 | 23 |

## San Diego, CA

| Building | Ht. ft. | Stories |
|---|---|---|
| One American Plaza (1991) | 500 | 34 |
| Symphony Tower (1989) | 499 | 34 |
| Hyatt Regency San Diego (1992) | 495 | 39 |
| Emerald-Shapery Center (1991) | 450 | 30 |
| One Harbor Drive (1992) | 424 | 41 |
| First Interstate Bank (1985) | 398 | 23 |
| Meridian Condominiums (1985) | 395 | 27 |
| Union Bank (1969) | 388 | 27 |
| First National Bank (1982) | 379 | 27 |
| Imperial Bank | 355 | 24 |
| Executive Complex (1963) | 350 | 25 |

## San Francisco, CA

| Building | Ht. ft. | Stories |
|---|---|---|
| Transamerica Pyramid (1972) | 853 | 48 |
| Bank of America (1969) | 779 | 52 |
| 101 California St. (1986) | 600 | 48 |
| 5 Fremont Center (1983) | 600 | 43 |
| Embarcadero Center, No. 4 (1982) | 570 | 45 |
| Security Pacific Bank | 569 | 45 |
| One Market Plaza, Spear St. (1976) | 565 | 43 |
| Wells Fargo Bldg. | 561 | 43 |
| Standard Oil (1975), 575 Market St. | 551 | 39 |
| One Sansome-Citicorp | 550 | 39 |
| Shaklee Bldg., 444 Market | 537 | 38 |
| Aetna Life | 529 | 38 |
| First & Market Bldg. (1973) | 529 | 38 |
| Metropolitan Life (1973) | 524 | 38 |
| Crocker National Bank | 500 | 38 |
| Hilton Hotel | 493 | 46 |
| Pacific Gas & Electric (1970) | 492 | 34 |
| Union Bank (1972) | 487 | 37 |
| Pacific Insurance (1972) | 476 | 34 |
| Bechtel Bldg. (1977), Fremont St. | 475 | 33 |
| 333 Market Bldg. (1979) | 474 | 33 |
| Hartford Bldg. (1965) | 465 | 33 |
| Mutual Benefit Life (1969) | 438 | 32 |
| Russ Bldg. (1928) | 435 | 31 |
| Pacific Telephone Bldg. (1925) | 435 | 26 |
| Pacific Gateway (1983) | 416 | 30 |
| Embarcadero Center, No. 3 (1976) | 412 | 31 |
| Embarcadero Center, No. 2 (1974) | 412 | 31 |
| 595 Market Bldg. (1979) | 410 | 31 |
| 101 Montgomery St. | 405 | 28 |
| California State Automobile Assn. (1974) | 399 | 29 |
| Alcoa Bldg. | 398 | 27 |
| St. Francis Hotel (1970) | 395 | 32 |
| Shell Bldg. (1928) | 386 | 29 |
| Del Monte | 378 | 28 |
| Meridien Hotel (1984) | 374 | 34 |

## Seattle, WA

| Building | Ht. ft. | Stories |
|---|---|---|
| Columbia Seafirst Center (1985) | 943 | 76 |
| Two Union Square (1989) | 740 | 56 |
| Washington Mutual Tower (1988) | 730 | 55 |
| AT&T Gateway Tower (1990) | 722 | 62 |
| 1001 4th Pl. (1969) | 609 | 50 |
| Space Needle (1962) | 605 | – |
| Pacific First Center (1989) | 580 | 44 |
| First Interstate Center (1983) | 574 | 48 |
| Seafirst 5th Ave. Plaza (1981) | 543 | 42 |
| Security Pacific Bank Tower (1977) | 514 | 42 |
| Smith Tower (1914) | 500 | 42 |
| 520 Pike Tower (1984) | 498 | 29 |
| Key Tower (1986) | 493 | 40 |
| Federal Office Bldg. | 487 | 37 |
| US West Communications | 466 | 33 |
| One Union Square (1981) | 456 | 38 |
| 1111 3d Ave. Bldg. (1980) | 454 | 35 |
| Westin Bldg. (1981), 2001 6th Ave. | 409 | 34 |
| Westin Hotel | 397 | 40 |
| Unigard Financial Center (1973) | 389 | 27 |
| Century Square (1986) | 379 | 30 |
| Sheraton Seattle Hotel | 371 | 34 |

## Tampa, FL

| Building | Ht. ft. | Stories |
|---|---|---|
| 100 N. Tampa (1992) | 579 | 42 |
| Barnett Plaza (1986) | 577 | 42 |
| Tampa City Center (1981) | 537 | 38 |
| SunTrust Financial Centre (1992) | 525 | 36 |
| First Florida Tower (1973) | 458 | 35 |
| NationsBank Plaza (1988) | 454 | 33 |

## Toledo, OH

| Building | Ht. ft. | Stories |
|---|---|---|
| One SeaGate. (1962) | 404 | 30 |
| Owens-Corning Fiberglas Tower (1970) | 400 | 30 |
| National City Bank Bldg. (1932) | 368 | 27 |

## Toronto, Ontario

| Building | Ht. ft. | Stories |
|---|---|---|
| CN Tower (1975) (world's tallest self-supporting structure) | 1,821 | – |
| First Canadian Place (1975) | 952 | 72 |
| Scotia Plaza (1988) | 902 | 68 |
| BCE Place, Canada Trust Tower (1990) | 745 | 51 |
| Commerce Court West (1972) | 784 | 57 |
| Toronto-Dominion Tower (TD Centre) (1967) | 758 | 56 |
| BCE Place, Bay-Wellington Tower (1990) | 705 | 47 |
| Royal Trust Tower (TD Centre) (1969) | 600 | 46 |
| Royal Bank Plaza–South Tower (1977) | 589 | 41 |
| Manulife Centre (1975) | 545 | 53 |
| AETNA Tower (TD Centre) (1986) | 520 | 36 |
| Workers' Compensation Building | 487 | 33 |
| First Canadian Place Exchange Tower (1981) | 480 | 36 |
| Two Bloor West (1974) | 480 | 34 |
| CIBC-Commerce Court North (1930) | 476 | 34 |
| Simpson Tower (1968) | 473 | 33 |
| Eaton Tower (1990) | 471 | 34 |

| Building | City | Ht. ft. | Stories |
|---|---|---|---|
| Cadillac-Fairview Tower (1982) | | 466 | 36 |
| Palace Place (1992) | | 455 | 46 |
| Palace Pier (1978) | | 453 | 46 |
| Richmond Adelaide Centre (1980) | | 450 | 35 |
| Sheraton Centre (1972) | | 443 | 43 |
| Hudson's Bay Centre (1974) | | 442 | 35 |
| Royal York Hotel (1929) | | 439 | 26 |
| Ernst & Yonge Tower (TD Centre) (1990) | | 438 | 31 |
| Leaside Towers (2 bldgs.) (1970) | | 423 | 44 |
| Commercial Union Tower (TD Centre) (1974) | | 420 | 32 |
| Metro Hall (1991) | | 420 | 27 |
| Hotel Plaza II | | 415 | 41 |
| Young-Eglinton Centre-Triathlon Tower | | 408 | 30 |

## Tulsa, OK

| Building | Ht. ft. | Stories |
|---|---|---|
| Bank of Oklahoma Tower | 667 | 52 |
| Cityplex Towers | 640 | 60 |
| 1st National Tower | 516 | 41 |
| Mid-Continent Tower | 513 | 36 |
| Bank IV of Tulsa | 412 | 33 |
| 320 South Boston Bldg. | 400 | 24 |

| Building | Ht. ft. | Stories |
|---|---|---|
| Occidential Place | 388 | 28 |
| Univ. Club Tower | 377 | 32 |

## Vancouver, British Columbia

| Building | Ht. ft. | Stories |
|---|---|---|
| Royal Centre Tower (1973) | 466 | 36 |
| Granville Square, 200 Granville | 466 | 28 |
| Vancouver Center (1977), 650 W. Georgia | 462 | 36 |
| Bentall IV (1981), 1055 Dunsmuir | 450 | 35 |
| Park Place (1984), 666 Burrard | 450 | 35 |
| Toronto Dominion Bank, 700 W. Georgia | 440 | 30 |
| Harbour Centre (1977), 555 W. Hastings | 426 | 21 |
| Bentall III (1974), 595 Granville | 400 | 31 |

## Winnipeg, Manitoba

| Building | Ht. ft. | Stories |
|---|---|---|
| Toronto Dominion Centre (1989) | 413 | 33 |
| Richardson Bldg. (1969) | 390 | 34 |
| Commodity Exchange Tower (1980) | 384 | 31 |

## Winston-Salem, NC

| Building | Ht. ft. | Stories |
|---|---|---|
| Wachovia Bldg. (1995) | 460 | 28 |
| Wachovia Bldg. (1965) | 410 | 27 |

## Other Notable Tall Buildings in North American Cities

| Building | City | Ht. ft. | Stories |
|---|---|---|---|
| Skylon | Niagara Falls, Ontario | 774 | – |
| Vehicle Assembly Bldg. | Cape Canaveral, FL | 552 | 40 |
| State Capitol (1932) | Baton Rouge, LA | 460 | 34 |
| One Summit Square | Fort Wayne, IN | 442 | 26 |
| State Capitol | Lincoln, NE | 432 | 40 |
| Taj Mahal | Atlantic City, NJ | 429 | 51 |
| First Natl. Bank | Mobile, AL | 420 | 33 |
| Century Twenty One | Hamilton, Ontario | 418 | 43 |
| Lexington Financial Ctr. | Lexington, KY | 410 | 30 |
| United American Bank | Knoxville, TN | 400 | 30 |
| Kanawha Valley Bldg. | Charleson, WV | 384 | 20 |
| American Natl. Bank | Amarillo, TX | 374 | 33 |
| Valley Bank Tower | Springfield, MA | 370 | 29 |
| Place de Ville, Tower C | Ottawa, Ontario | 368 | 29 |
| Commerical Natl. Tower | Shreveport, LA | 365 | 24 |
| American National Ins. | Galveston, TX | 358 | 20 |

# Notable International Buildings

**Source:** Council on Tall Buildings and Urban Habitat, Lehigh Univ.; as of Oct. 1996

List includes some structures that do not have stories and are not technically considered buildings.

| Building (year completed or to be completed) | Ht. ft. | Stories |
|---|---|---|
| Oriental Pearl Television Tower (1995), Shanghai, China | 1,535 | – |
| *Petronas Tower I (1996), Kuala Lumpur, Malaysia | 1,483 | 88 |
| *Petronas Tower II (1996), Kuala Lumpur, Malaysia | 1,483 | 88 |
| *Jin Mao Building (1998) Shanghai, China | 1,379 | 88 |
| Central Plaza (1992), Hong Kong | 1,227 | 78 |
| Bank of China Tower (1989), Hong Kong | 1,209 | 70 |
| *T & C Tower (1997), Kaoshiung, Taiwan | 1,140 | 85 |
| *Sky Central Plaza (1996), Guangzhou, China | 1,056 | 80 |
| *Baiyoke Tower II (1997), Bangkok, Thailand | 1,050 | 90 |
| *Shenzhen Avic Plaza Building (1997), Shenzhen, China | 1,025 | 63 |
| Eiffel Tower (1889), Paris, France | 984 | – |
| **Ryugyong Hotel (1995), Pyongyang, N. Korea | 984 | 105 |
| Landmark Tower (1993), Yokohama, Jpn. | 971 | 70 |
| *Jubilee St./Queen's Rd. Central (1997), Hong Kong | 958 | 69 |
| Overseas Union Bank (1986), Singapore | 919 | 66 |
| United Overseas Bank Plaza (1992), Singapore | 919 | 66 |
| Republic Plaza (1995), Singapore | 919 | 66 |
| Commerzbank Tower (1997), Frankfurt, Ger. | 850 | 60 |
| Messeturm. Bldg. (1990), Frankfurt, Ger. | 843 | 63 |
| Gate Tower (1996), Osaka, Jpn. | 833 | 56 |
| Osaka World Trade Center (1995), Osaka, Jpn. | 827 | 55 |
| BNI City Tower (1995), Jakarta, Indonesia | 820 | 46 |
| Korea Life Ins. Co. (1985), Seoul, S. Korea | 817 | 60 |
| Kompleks Tun Abdul Razak Bldg. (1985), (Penang, Malaysia) | 804 | 65 |
| Malayan Bank(1988), Kuala Lumpur, Malaysia | 799 | 50 |
| Metropolitan Gov't Bldg. (1991), Tokyo, Jpn. | 797 | 48 |
| Rialto Tower (1985), Melbourne, Australia | 794 | 56 |
| JR Central Towers (1999), Nagoya, Jpn. | 787 | 53 |
| Moscow State Univ. (1953), Moscow, Russia | 784 | 26 |
| One Canada Sq. (1991), London, England | 777 | 53 |
| Treasury Bldg. (1986), Singapore | 771 | 52 |
| Shinjuku Park Tower (1994), Tokyo, Japan | 764 | 52 |
| Palace of Culture & Science (1955), Warsaw, Poland | 757 | 42 |

* construction not completed as of Oct. 1996. ** not yet certified as safe for occupancy.

# Notable Bridges in North America

**Source:** Survey of State Highway Engineers (1996)

Asterisk (*) designates railroad bridge. Double asterisk (**) designates under construction. Span of a bridge is distance (in feet) between its supports.

## Suspension

| Year | Bridge | Location | Longest span |
|---|---|---|---|
| **1964** | Verrazano-Narrows | New York, NY. | 4,260 |
| **1937** | Golden Gate | San Fran. Bay, CA | 4,200 |
| **1957** | Mackinac | Sts. of Mackinac, MI | 3,800 |
| **1931** | Geo. Washington | Hudson R., NY–NJ | 3,500 |
| **1950** | Tacoma Narrows | WA | 2,800 |
| **1936** | Transbay[1] | San Fran. Bay, CA | 2,310 |
| **1939** | Bronx-Whitestone | East R., NY. | 2,300 |
| **1970** | Pierre Laporte | Quebec, Canada. | 2,190 |
| **1951** | Del. Memorial | Wilmington, DE | 2,150 |
| **1968** | Del. Mem. (new) | Wilmington, DE | 2,150 |
| **1957** | Walt Whitman | Philadelphia, PA | 2,000 |
| **1929** | Ambassador | Detroit, MI–Can. | 1,850 |
| **1961** | Throgs Neck | Long Is. Sound, NY. | 1,800 |
| **1917** | Quebec | Quebec, Canada | 1,800 |
| **1926** | Benjamin Franklin | Philadelphia, PA | 1,750 |
| **1924** | Bear Mt. | Hudson R., NY. | 1,632 |
| **1952** | Wm. Preston La. Mem.[2] | Sandy Point, MD | 1,600 |
| **1903** | Williamsburg | East R., NY. | 1,600 |
| **1969** | Newport | Narragansett Bay, RI | 1,600 |
| **1883** | Brooklyn | East R., NY | 1,595 |
| **1939** | Lion's Gate | Burrard Inlet, B.C. | 1,550 |
| **1930** | Mid-Hudson | Poughkeepsie, NY | 1,500 |
| **1963** | Vincent Thomas | L. A. Harbor, CA. | 1,500 |
| **1909** | Manhattan | East R., NY | 1,470 |
| **1936** | Triboro | East R., NY | 1,380 |
| **1931** | St. Johns | Portland, OR | 1,207 |
| **1929** | Mount Hope | RI | 1,200 |
| **1960** | Ogdensburg | St. Lawrence R., NY. | 1,150 |
| **1939** | Deer Isle | ME | 1,080 |
| **1931** | Simon Kenton Memorial | Ohio R., KY | 1,060 |
| **1867** | John A. Roebling | Ohio R., KY | 1,057 |
| **1971** | Dent | Clearwater Co., ID | 1,050 |
| **1900** | Miampimi | Mexico | 1,030 |
| **1849** | Wheeling | Ohio R., WV. | 1,010 |

## Cantilever

| Year | Bridge | Location | Longest span |
|---|---|---|---|
| 1974 | Commodore Barry | Chester, PA | 1,622 |
| 1958 | Mississippi R. | New Orleans, LA | 1,575 |
| 1988 | Mississippi R. | New Orleans, LA | 1,575 |
| 1995 | Mississippi R. | Gramercy, LA | 1,460 |
| 1936 | Transbay | San Fran. Bay, CA | 1,400 |
| 1968 | Mississippi R. | Baton Rouge, LA | 1,235 |
| 1955 | Tappan Zee | Hudson R., NY | 1,212 |
| 1930 | Lewis and Clark | Longview, WA–OR | 1,200 |
| 1909 | Queensboro | East R., N.Y. | 1,182 |
| 1927 | Carquinez Strait | CA | 1,100 |
| 1958 | Parallel Span | CA | 1,100 |
| 1930 | Jacques Cartier | Montreal, Canada | 1,097 |
| 1968 | Isaiah D. Hart | Jacksonville, FL | 1,088 |
| 1956 | Richmond[3] | San Fran. Bay, CA | 1,070 |
| 1929 | Grace Memorial | Charleston, SC | 1,050 |
| 1980 | Newburgh-Beacon | Hudson R., NY | 1,000 |
| 1963 | Newburgh-Beacon | Hudson R., NY | 1,000 |
| 1949 | Martin Luther King | St. Louis, MO | 963 |
| 1975 | Caruthersville | Mississippi R., MO–TN | 920 |
| 1977 | Saint Marys | Saint Marys, WV–OH | 900 |
| 1969 | Silver Memorial | Pt. Pleasant, WV–OH | 900 |
| 1981 | Ravenswood | WV | 900 |
| 1987 | Carl Perkins | Ohio R., KY | 900 |
| 1988 | Mississippi R. | Natchez, MS | 875 |
| 1940 | Mississippi R. | Natchez, MS | 875 |
| 1938 | Blue Water | Pt. Huron, MI | 871 |
| 1972 | Mississippi R. | Vicksburg, MS | 870 |
| 1972 | N. Fork American R. | Auburn, CA | 862 |
| 1940 | *Baton Rouge | Mississippi R., LA | 848 |
| 1899 | *Cornwall | St. Lawrence R. | 843 |
| 1961 | Mississippi R. | Greenville, MS | 840 |
| 1940 | Rte. 82 | Mississippi R., AR | 840 |
| 1961 | Rte. 49 | Mississippi R., AR | 840 |
| 1963 | Brent Spence | KY–OH | 830 |
| 1963 | Mississippi R. | Donaldsonville, LA | 825 |
| 1940 | Mississippi R. | Vicksburg, MS | 825 |
| 1929 | Clark Memorial | Ohio R., KY | 820 |
| 1961 | Campbellton-Cross Pt. | New Brunswick–Can. | 815 |
| 1935 | Rip Van Winkle | Catskill, NY | 800 |
| 1938 | Cairo | Ohio R., IL–KY | 800 |
| 1932 | Washington Mem. | Seattle, WA | 800 |
| 1936 | McCullough | Coos Bay, OR | 793 |
| 1935 | Huey P. Long[4] | New Orleans, LA | 790 |
| 1892 | Memphis | Mississippi R., TN | 790 |
| 1949 | Rte. 55, Mississippi R. | AR–TN | 790 |
| 1910 | *P&LE RR Bridge | Ohio R.,PA | 750 |
| 1932 | Bi-State Vietnam Gold Star | Henderson, KY | 720 |
| 1904 | *Norfolk Southern RR | Ohio R., OH | 700 |
| 1943 | *Pit River | Redding, CA | 620 |
| 1941 | Columbia R. | Kettle Falls, WA | 600 |
| 1954 | Columbia R. | Umatilla, OR | 600 |
| 1954 | Columbia R. | The Dalles, OR | 576 |
| 1968 | W. 17th St. | Huntington, WV | 562 |

## Simple Truss

| Year | Bridge | Location | Longest span |
|---|---|---|---|
| 1976 | Chester | Chester, WV | 745 |
| 1929 | Irvin S. Cobb | Ohio R.,IL–KY | 716 |
| 1922 | *Tanana R. | Nenana, AK | 700 |
| 1967 | I-77, Ohio R. | Williamstown, WV | 650 |
| 1917 | MacArthur[4] | St. Louis, IL–MO | 647 |
| 1992 | St. Charles | Missouri R, MO. | 625 |
| 1933 | Atchafalaya | Morgan City, LA | 608 |
| 1924 | *Castleton | Hudson R., NY | 598 |
| 1937 | Delaware R. | Easton, PA | 550 |
| 1930 | Swindell Bridge | Pittsburgh, PA | 545 |
| 1952 | Allegheny R. Tpk. | Pittsburgh, PA | 534 |
| 1930 | *Martinez | Martinez, CA | 528 |
| 1951 | Rankin | Pittsburgh, PA | 525 |
| 1914 | Old Brownsville | Brownsville, PA | 520 |
| 1906 | Donora-Webster | Donora-Webster, PA | 515 |
| 1909 | Hulton | Pittsburgh, PA | 505 |
| 1967 | Tanana R. | AK | 500 |

## Steel Truss

| Year | Bridge | Location | Longest span |
|---|---|---|---|
| 1988 | Glade Creek | Raleigh Co., WV | 784 |
| 1973 | Atchafalaya R. | Krotz Springs, LA | 780 |
| 1972 | Piscataqua R. | NH–ME | 756 |
| 1972 | Atchafalaya R. | Simmesport, LA | 720 |
| 1957 | SR-3, Rappahannock R. | Middlesex Co., VA. | 648 |
| 1978 | Atchafalaya R. | Morgan City, LA | 607 |
| 1959 | Summit | Summit, DE. | 600 |
| 1969 | Reedy Point | Delaware City, DE. | 600 |
| 1938 | US-22 | Delaware R., NJ | 540 |
| 1955 | Interstate (I-5) | Columbia R., OR–WA | 531 |
| 1910 | McKinley, St. Louis[4] | Mississippi R., MO. | 517 |
| 1972 | Mississippi R. | Muscatine, IA | 512 |
| 1896 | Newport | Ohio R., KY | 511 |
| 1989 | US 190, Atchafalaya R. | Krotz Springs, LA | 506 |
| 1970 | Lake Koocanusa | Lincoln Co., MT | 500 |
| 1931 | Lucy Jefferson Lewis | Cumberland R., KY | 500 |
| 1958 | Lake Oahe | Mobridge, SD | 500 |
| 1958 | Lake Oahe | Gettysburg, SD | 500 |

## Continuous Truss

| Year | Bridge | Location | Longest span |
|---|---|---|---|
| 1966 | Columbia R. (Astoria) | OR–WA | 1,232 |
| 1977 | Francis Scott Key | Baltimore, MD | 1,200 |
| 1943 | Dubuque | Mississippi R., IA | 845 |
| 1966 | Charles Braga | Fall River, MA | 840 |
| 1956 | Earl C. Clements[5] | Ohio R., IL–KY | 825 |
| 1929 | U.S. 31 | Ohio R., IN–KY | 820 |
| 1995 | **Central | Ohio R., KY–OH | 820 |
| 1953 | John E. Mathews | Jacksonville, FL | 810 |
| 1950 | Maurice J. Tobin | Boston, MA | 801 |
| 1940 | Gov. Nice Memorial | Potomac River, MD | 800 |
| 1957 | Kingston-Rhinecliff | Hudson R., NY | 800 |
| 1986 | Rochester-Monaca | Rochester-Monaca,PA | 780 |
| 1940 | U.S. 231 | Ohio R., IN | 750 |
| 1974 | Carroll L. Cropper | Ohio R., IN–KY | 750 |
| 1981 | Sewickley | Sewickley, PA | 750 |
| 1984 | 13th St. Bridge, Ohio R. | Ashland, KY | 740 |
| 1959 | Monaca-E. Rochester | Monaca-E. Rochester, PA | 730 |
| 1976 | Betsy Ross | Philadelphia, PA | 729 |
| 1929 | U.S. 421 | Ohio R., IN–KY | 727 |
| 1967 | Matthew E. Welsh[6] | Mauckport, IN | 725 |
| 1994 | 6th St. | Huntington, WV | 720 |
| 1932 | U.S. 41 | Ohio R., IN–KY | 720 |
| 1962 | U.S. 41 | Ohio R., IN–KY | 720 |
| 1970 | Vanport | Vanport, PA | 715 |
| 1962 | Champlain | Montreal, Que. | 707 |
| 1962 | John F. Kennedy[7] | Ohio R., IN–KY | 701 |
| 1973 | Girard Point | Philadelphia, PA | 700 |
| 1954 | PA Tpk., Delaware R. | Philadelphia, PA | 682 |
| 1949 | George Platt | Philadelphia, PA | 680 |
| 1938 | Port Arthur-Orange | TX | 680 |
| 1926 | Cape Girardeau | Mississippi R., MO | 677 |
| 1929 | *Cincinnati | Ohio R., OH | 675 |
| 1946 | Chester | Mississippi R, IL | 670 |
| 1970 | Gulfgate | Port Arthur, TX | 664 |
| 1994 | Williamstown-Marietta | Williamstown, WV | 650 |
| 1955 | Jefferson City | Missouri R., MO | 640 |
| 1930 | Quincy | Mississippi R., IL | 628 |
| 1961 | Shippingport | Shippingport, PA | 620 |
| 1959 | US 181, over harbor | Corpus Christi, TX | 620 |
| 1935 | Bourne | Cape Cod Canal, MA | 616 |
| 1935 | Sagamore | Cape Cod Canal, MA | 616 |
| 1965 | Clarion R. (I-80) | Clarion, PA | 612 |
| 1975 | Donora-Monessen | Donora-Monessen, PA | 608 |
| 1991 | Hoffstadt Creek | Mt. St. Helens, WA | 600 |
| 1957 | Blatnik | Duluth, MN | 600 |
| 1965 | Rio Grande Gorge | Taos, NM | 600 |
| 1991 | Jefferson City | Missouri R., MO | 596 |
| 1962 | W. Branch Feather R. | Oroville, CA | 576 |
| 1967 | Glenwood | Pittsburgh, PA | 567 |
| 1936 | Mark Twain Mem. | Hannibal, MO | 562 |
| 1957 | Mackinac | Mackinac Straits, MI | 560 |
| 1932 | Pulaski Skyway | Passaic R.-Hackensack R., NJ | 550 |
| 1943 | Gold Star Memorial | New London, CT | 540 |
| 1973 | Gold Star Memorial | New London, CT | 540 |
| 1966 | Emlenton | Emlenton, PA | 540 |
| 1936 | Homestead High Level | Pittsburgh, PA | 534 |
| 1959 | Martinez | Benicia-Martinez, CA | 528 |
| 1960 | Brownsville High Level | Brownsville, PA | 518 |
| 1971 | Grandad | Elk River, ID | 504 |
| 1945 | Mansfield-Dravosburg | Pittsburgh, PA | 500 |

## Continuous Box and Plate Girder

| Year | Bridge | Location | Longest span |
|---|---|---|---|
| 1982 | Houston Ship Chan. | Houston, TX | 750 |
| 1967 | San Mateo-Hayward #2 | San Fran. Bay, CA | 750 |
| 1977 | Intracoastal Canal | Gibbstown, LA | 750 |
| 1976 | Intracoastal Canal | Forked Is., LA | 750 |
| 1969 | San Diego-Coronado[8] | San Diego Bay, CA | 660 |
| 1987 | Umatilla, Columbia R. | OR–WA | 660 |
| 1994 | Acosta | Jacksonville, FL | 630 |
| 1981 | Douglas | Juneau, AK | 620 |
| 1976 | Wax L. Outlet | Calumet, LA | 618 |
| 1981 | Glenn Jackson (I-205) | Columbia R., OR–WA | 600 |
| 1963 | Poplar St. | St. Louis, MO | 600 |

| Year | Bridge | Location | Longest span |
|---|---|---|---|
| 1976 | Stanislaus River | Sonora, CA | 580 |
| 1982 | Illinois R. | Pekin, IL | 550 |
| 1982 | I-440 | Arkansas R., AR | 540 |
| 1980 | US-64, Tennessee R. | Savannah, TN | 525 |
| 1988 | Mon City | Monongahela, PA | 520 |
| 1965 | McDonald-Cartier | Ottawa, Canada | 520 |
| 1984 | Columbia R. | Richland, WA | 450 |
| 1986 | Veterans | Pittsburgh, PA | 440 |
| 1987 | SR 76, Cumberland R. | Dover, TN | 440 |
| 1987 | SR 20, Tennessee R. | Perryville, TN | 440 |
| 1970 | Willamette R., I-205 | West Linn, OR | 430 |
| 1974 | I-430 | Arkansas R., AR | 430 |
| 1984 | FAU 3456, TN R. | Chattanooga, TN | 420 |
| 1965 | I-24, Tennessee R. | Marion Co., TN | 420 |
| 1978 | Snake R. | Clarkston, WA | 420 |
| 1975 | 36th St. | Charleston, WV | 420 |
| 1974 | Dunbar-S. Charleston | S. Charleston, WV | 420 |

## Continuous Plate

| Year | Bridge | Location | Longest span |
|---|---|---|---|
| 1973 | Ship Channel (I-610) | Houston, TX | 630 |
| 1971 | W. Atchafalaya | Henderson, LA | 573 |
| 1992 | State Route 76 | Paris, TN | 525 |
| 1981 | Illinois 23 | Illinois R., IL | 510 |
| 1968 | Trinity R. | Dallas, TX | 480 |
| 1978 | San Joaquin R. | Antioch, CA | 460 |
| 1977 | Thomas Johnson Mem. | Solomons, MD | 451 |
| 1992 | Cuba Landing Bridge | Tennessee R., TN | 450 |
| 1979 | Lewis | St. Louis, MO | 450 |
| 1975 | I-129 | Missouri R., IA–NE | 450 |
| 1967 | Mississippi R. | La Crosse, WI | 450 |
| 1972 | Whiskey Bay Pilot | Ramah, LA | 425 |
| 1966 | I-480 | Missouri R., IA–NE | 425 |
| 1972 | I-435 | Missouri R., MO | 425 |
| 1972 | I-80 | Missouri R., IA–NE | 425 |
| 1987 | I-435 | Missouri R., KS–MO | 425 |
| 1983 | US-36 | Missouri R., KS–MO | 425 |
| 1972 | I-635, Kansas City | Missouri R., KS–MO | 425 |
| 1978 | I-24 | Cumberland R., KY | 420 |

## Cable-Stayed

| Year | Bridge | Location | Longest span |
|---|---|---|---|
| 1986 | Alex Fraser | BC, Canada | 1,526 |
| 1988 | Dames Point | Jacksonville, FL | 1,300 |
| 1995 | Fred Hartman Bridge | Baytowne-LaPorte,TX | 1,250 |
| 1983 | Mississippi R., I-310 | Luling, LA | 1,222 |
| 1987 | Sunshine Skyway | Tampa Bay, FL | 1,200 |
| 1991 | Talmadge Mem. | Savannah, GA | 1,100 |
| 1979 | Columbia River | Pasco-Kennewick, WA | 970 |
| 1985 | E. Huntington | Huntington, WV | 900 |
| 1985 | Mississippi R. | Quincy, IL | 900 |
| 1990 | Veterans Mem'l | WV–OH | 820 |
| 1991 | Cochrane/Africatown | Mobile, AL | 780 |
| 1995 | Chesapeake & Delaware Canal Bridge | Dover-Wilmington, DE | 750 |
| 1994 | Great River Bridge | Burlington, IA | 660 |
| 1991 | Neches R. | Port Arthur-Orange,TX | 640 |
| 1990 | James R. | Henrico Co., VA | 630 |
| 1972 | Sitka Harbor | Sitka, AK | 450 |

## I-Beam Girder

| Year | Bridge | Location | Longest span |
|---|---|---|---|
| 1980 | Interstate 20 | Shreveport, LA | 438 |
| 1988 | Route 18 | Weston's Mill Pond, NJ | 276 |

## Steel Arch

| Year | Bridge | Location | Longest span |
|---|---|---|---|
| 1977 | New R. Gorge | Fayetteville, WV | 1,817 |
| 1931 | Kill Van Kull | Staten Island, NY | 1,652 |
| 1973 | Fremont | Portland, OR | 1,255 |
| 1964 | Port Mann | British Columbia | 1,200 |
| 1967 | Trois-Rivieres | St. Lawrence R., Que. | 1,100 |
| 1992 | Roosevelt Lake | Roosevelt Lake, AZ | 1,080 |
| 1916 | *Hell Gate | East R., N.Y | 1,038 |
| 1958 | Glen Canyon | Page., AZ | 1,028 |
| 1962 | Lewiston-Queenston | Niagara R., Ont. | 1,000 |
| 1976 | Perrine | Twin Falls, ID | 993 |
| 1941 | Rainbow | Niagara Falls, NY | 984 |
| 1977 | Moundsville | Ohio R., WV | 912 |
| 1985 | I-255 | Mississippi R., MO. | 910 |
| 1972 | I-40, Mississippi R.[9] | AR– TN | 900 |
| 1936 | Henry Hudson | Harlem R., N.Y. | 840 |
| 1967 | Lincoln Trail Bridge | Ohio R., IN–KY | 825 |
| 1978 | I-57, Cairo | Mississippi R, IL | 821 |
| 1980 | I-65 Mobile R. | Mobile, AL | 800 |
| 1961 | I-64 | Ohio R., IN | 800 |
| 1978 | I-470 Bridge, Ohio R. | Wheeling, WV | 780 |
| 1930 | West End | Pittsburgh, PA | 780 |

## Concrete Arch

| Year | Bridge | Location | Longest span |
|---|---|---|---|
| 1993 | Lake Street Bridge | St. Paul, MN | 556 |
| 1971 | Selah Creek (twin) | Selah, WA | 549 |
| 1968 | Cowlitz R. | Mossyrock, WA | 520 |
| 1931 | Westinghouse | Pittsburgh, PA | 460 |
| 1923 | Cappelen | Minneapolis, MN | 435 |

## Segmental Concrete

| Year | Bridge | Location | Longest span |
|---|---|---|---|
| 1976 | Stanislaus River | Parrets Ferry. CA | 640 |
| 1992 | Jamestown-Verranzzano | Jamestown, RI | 636 |
| 1991 | Veterans Memorial Centennial Bridge | Coeur d'Alene, ID | 520 |
| 1974 | Pine Valley Creek | Pine Valley, CA | 450 |
| 1988 | Zilwaukee Bridge (twin) | Zilwaukee, MI | 392 |
| 1985 | Red River Bridge | Boyce, LA | 370 |

## Twin Concrete Trestle

| Year | Bridge | Location | Total length |
|---|---|---|---|
| 1979 | I-55/I-10 | Manchac, LA | 181,157 |
| 1969 | L. Pontchartrain Cswy. | Mandeville, LA | 126,720 |
| 1972 | Atchafalaya Flwy. | Baton Rouge, LA | 93,984 |
| 1963 | L. Pontchartrain | Slidell, LA | 28,547 |
| 1983 | Interstate 310 | Kenner, LA | 25,925 |

## Concrete Slab Dam [10]

| Year | Bridge | Location | Total length |
|---|---|---|---|
| 1927 | Conowingo Dam | MD | 4,611 |
| 1952 | SR-4, Roanoke R. | Mecklenburg Co., VA | 2,785 |
| 1936 | Hoover Dam | Lake Mead, NV | 1,324 |

## Drawbridges

### Vertical Lift

| Year | Bridge | Location | Longest span |
|---|---|---|---|
| 1959 | *Arthur Kill | NY–NJ | 558 |
| 1965 | Pennsylvania Railroad | Kirkwood-Mt. Pleasant, DE | 548 |
| 1935 | *Cape Cod Canal | Cape Cod, MA | 544 |
| 1961 | *Delair | Delaware R., NJ | 542 |
| 1937 | Marine Parkway | Jamaica Bay, N.Y. | 540 |
| 1931 | Burlington-Bristol | Delaware R.-, NJ–PA | 540 |
| 1908 | *Willamette R. | Portland, OR | 521 |
| 1968 | Second Narrows | Vancouver, B.C. | 493 |
| 1912 | *A-S-B Fratt | Kansas City, MO | 428 |
| 1945 | *Harry S Truman | Kansas City, MO | 427 |
| 1955 | Roosevelt Island | East R., N.Y. | 418 |
| 1980 | US-17, James R. | Isle of Wight, Co., VA | 415 |
| 1932 | *M-K-T R.R. | Missouri R., MO | 414 |
| 1969 | Cape Fear Mem. | Wilmington, NC | 408 |
| 1930 | Aerial | Duluth, MN | 386 |
| 1962 | Burlington | Ontario, Can. | 370 |
| 1941 | Main Street | Jacksonville, FL | 365 |
| 1922 | *Cincinnati | Ohio R., OH. | 365 |
| 1967 | SR-156, James R. | Prince George Co., VA | 364 |
| 1957 | Industrial Canal | New Orleans, LA | 360 |
| 1950 | Red R. | Moncla, LA | 360 |
| 1936 | Tribo | Harlem R., N.Y. | 344 |
| 1961 | Corpus Christi Harbor[4] | Corpus Christi, TX | 344 |
| 1939 | U.S. 1&9, Passaic R. | Newark, NJ | 333 |
| 1930 | *Martinez | Martinez, CA | 328 |
| 1960 | St. Andrews Bay | Panama City, FL | 327 |
| 1929 | *Penn-Lehigh | Newark Bay, PA | 322 |
| 1987 | Industrial Canal | New Orleans, LA | 320 |
| 1920 | *Chattanooga | Tennessee R., TN | 310 |

### Bascule

| Year | Bridge | Location | Longest span |
|---|---|---|---|
| 1940 | Lorain | Black R., OH | 333 |
| 1917 | SR-8, Tennessee R. | Chattanooga, TN | 306 |
| 1956 | Duwamish R. | Seattle, WA | 300 |
| 1955 | Chehalis R. | Aberdeen, WA | 288 |
| 1968 | Elizabeth R. | Chesapeake, VA | 280 |
| 1913 | Broadway | Portland, OR | 278 |
| 1954 | Fuller Warren | Jacksonville, FL. | 267 |

### Swing Bridges

| Year | Bridge | Location | Longest span |
|---|---|---|---|
| 1927 | Fort Madison[4] | Mississippi R., IA | 545 |
| 1991 | SW. Spokane St. | Seattle, WA | 480 |
| 1930 | Rigolets Pass | New Orleans, LA | 400 |
| 1950 | Douglass Memorial | Washington, DC. | 386 |
| 1945 | Lord Delaware | Mattaponi R., VA | 252 |
| 1957 | Eltham | Pamunkey R., VA | 237 |

### Swing Span

| Year | Bridge | Location | Longest span |
|---|---|---|---|
| **1952** | US-17 | York R., VA | 500 |
| **1897** | *Duluth | St. Louis Bay, MN | 486 |
| **1899** | *C.M.&N.R.R. | Chicago, IL | 474 |
| **1913** | Rt. 82, Conn-R. | E. Haddam, CT | 465 |
| **1914** | *Coos Bay | OR | 458 |

### Floating Pontoon

| Year | Bridge | Location | Floating length |
|---|---|---|---|
| **1963** | Evergreen Pt. | Seattle, WA | 7,578 |
| **1961** | Hood Canal (incl. 3,775' western rebuild, 1982) | Pt. Gamble, WA | 6,521 |
| **1993** | Lacey V. Murrow[10] | Seattle, WA | 6,620 |
| **1989** | Third Lake Washington | Seattle, WA | 5,811 |

(1) The Transbay Bridge has 2 spans of 2,310 ft. each. (2) A second bridge in parallel was completed in 1973. (3) The Richmond Bridge has twin spans 1,070 ft. each. (4) Railroad and vehicular bridge. (5) Two spans each 825 ft. (6) Two spans each 707 ft. (7) Two spans each 700 ft. (8) Two spans each 660 ft. (9) Two spans each 900 ft. (10) Replaces the original Lacey V. Murrow bridge, which opened in 1940 and sank in 1990.

## Oldest U.S. Bridge in Continuous Use

Built in 1697, the stone-arch Frankford Ave. Bridge crosses Pennypack Creek in Philadelphia, PA. A 3-span bridge with a total length of 75 ft., it was constructed as part of the King's Road, which eventually connected Philadelphia to New York.

### Oldest U.S. Covered Bridge in Continuous Use

Completed in 1827, the double-span 278-ft. Haverhill Bath Bridge spans the Ammonoosuc River, between the towns of Bath and Haverhill, NH.

## Notable International Bridges

Span of bridge is distance (in feet) between its supports. Asterisk (*) designates under construction.

### Suspension

| Year | Bridge | Location | Longest span |
|---|---|---|---|
| 1998* | Akashi Kaikyo | Japan | 6,529 |
| 1998* | Store Bælt (East Bridge) | Denmark | 5,328 |
| 1981 | Humber | England | 4,626 |
| 1997* | Tsing Ma[1] | Hong Kong | 4,518 |
| 1988 | Minami Bisan-Seto | Japan | 3,609 |
| 1988 | Bosphorus I | Turkey | 3,576 |
| 1973 | Bosphorus II | Turkey | 3,524 |
| 1966 | Ponte 25 de Abril | Portugal | 3,323 |
| 1964 | Forth (road) | Scotland | 3,301 |
| 1966 | Severn | England | 3,241 |

### Cantilever

| Year | Bridge | Location | Longest span |
|---|---|---|---|
| 1890 | Forth[2] (rail) | Scotland | 1,710 |
| 1974 | Nanko | Japan | 1,673 |

### Steel Arch

| Year | Bridge | Location | Longest span |
|---|---|---|---|
| 1932 | Sydney Harbour | Australia | 1,650 |

(1) Double-decked road and rail bridge. (2) Two spans of 1,710 ft. each.

### Concrete Arch

| Year | Bridge | Location | Longest span |
|---|---|---|---|
| 1980 | Krk I | Croatia | 1,280 |
| 1964 | Gladesville | Australia | 1,001 |

### Steel Plate and Box Girder

| Year | Bridge | Location | Longest span |
|---|---|---|---|
| 1974 | President Costa e Silva | Brazil | 984 |
| 1956 | Sava I | Yugoslavia | 856 |
| 1966 | Zoobrüke | Germany | 850 |

### Cable-Stayed

| Year | Bridge | Location | Longest span |
|---|---|---|---|
| 1999* | Tatara | Japan | 2,920 |
| 1995 | Pont de Normandie | France | 2,808 |
| 1993 | Yangpu | China | 1,975 |
| 1997 | Trans-Tokyo Bay | Japan | 1,936 |
| 1991 | Skarnsundet | Norway | 1,739 |
| 1985 | Yokohama | Japan | 1,509 |
| 1987 | Hooghly River | Calcutta | 1,499 |
| 1996* | Severn | England | 1,496 |
| 1997* | Kap Shui Man | Hong Kong | 1,411 |

## Underwater Vehicular Tunnels in North America

(more than 5,000 ft. in length)

| Name | Location | Waterway | Feet |
|---|---|---|---|
| Brooklyn-Battery (1950) | New York, NY | East River | 9,117 |
| Holland Tunnel (1927) (2 tubes) | New York, NY | Hudson River | 8,557 |
| Lincoln Tunnel (1937, 1945, 1957) (3 tubes) | New York, NY | Hudson River | 8,216 |
| Thimble Shoal Channel (1964) | Northampton Co., VA | Chesapeake Bay | 8,187 |
| Ted Williams Tunnel (1995) | Boston, MA | Boston Harbor | 8,115 |
| Chesapeake Channel (1964) | Northampton Co., VA | Chesapeake Bay | 7,941 |
| Baltimore Harbor Tunnel (1957) | Baltimore, MD | Patapsco River | 7,650 |
| Hampton Roads (1957) (twin) | Hampton, VA | Hampton Roads | 7,479 |
| Fort McHenry Tunnel (2 tubes) (1985) | Baltimore, MD | Baltimore Harbor | 7,200 |
| Queens Midtown (1940) | New York, NY | East River | 6,414 |
| Sumner Tunnel (1934) | Boston, MA | Boston Harbor | 5,653 |
| Louis-Hippolyte Lafontaine Tunnel | Montreal, Quebec | St. Lawrence River | 5,280 |
| Detroit-Windsor (1930) | Detroit, MI | Detroit River | 5,160 |
| Callahan Tunnel (1961) | Boston, MA | Boston Harbor | 5,070 |

## Land Vehicular Tunnels in the U.S.

(more than 3,000 ft. in length; asterisk (*) designates under construction)

| Name | Location | Feet |
|---|---|---|
| E. Johnson Memorial | I-70, CO | 8,959 |
| Eisenhower Memorial | I-70, CO | 8,941 |
| Allegheny (twin) | PA Turnpike | 6,072 |
| Liberty Tubes | Pittsburgh, PA | 5,920 |
| Zion Natl. Park | Rte. 9, UT | 5,766 |
| East River Mt. (twin) | Bland Co., VA–Mercer Co., WV | 5,412 |
| Tuscarora (twin) | PA Turnpike | 5,400 |
| Tetsuo Harano (twin) | H-3, HI | 5,165 |
| Kittatinny (twin) | PA Turnpike | 4,660 |
| *Cumberland Gap | KY–TN | 4,600 |
| Blue Mountain (twin) | PA Turnpike | 4,435 |
| Lehigh (twin) | PA Turnpike | 4,379 |
| Wawona | Yosemite Natl. Park, CA | 4,233 |
| Big Walker Mt. | Bland Co., VA | 4,229 |
| Squirrel Hill | Pittsburgh, PA | 4,225 |
| Hanging Lake (twin) | Glenwood Canyon, CO | 4,000 |
| Caldecott (3 tubes) | Oakland, CA | 3,616 |
| Fort Pitt | Pittsburgh, PA | 3,560 |
| Dingess Tunnel | Mingo Co., WV | 3,400 |
| Mall Tunnel | Dist. of Columbia | 3,400 |
| Cody No. 1 | U.S. 14, 16, 20, WY | 3,202 |

# World's Longest Railway Tunnels

**Source:** Railway Directory & Year Book.

| Tunnel | Date | Miles | Operating railway | Country |
|---|---|---|---|---|
| Seikan | 1985 | 33.50 | Japanese Railway | Japan |
| English Channel Tunnel | 1994 | 31.04 | Eurotunnel | UK - France |
| Dai-shimizu | 1979 | 14.00 | Japanese Railway | Japan |
| Simplon No. 1 and 2 | 1906, 1922 | 12.00 | Swiss Fed. & Italian St. | Switz.-Italy |
| Kanmon | 1975 | 12.00 | Japanese Railway | Japan |
| Apennine | 1934 | 11.00 | Italian State | Italy |
| Rokko | 1972 | 10.00 | Japanese Railway | Japan |
| Mt. MacDonald | 1989 | 9.10 | Canadian Pacific | Canada |
| Gotthard | 1882 | 9.00 | Swiss Federal | Switzerland |
| Lotschberg | 1913 | 9.00 | Bern-Lotschberg-Simplon | Switzerland |
| Hokuriku | 1962 | 9.00 | Japanese Railway | Japan |
| Mont Cenis (Frejus) | 1871 | 8.00 | Italian State | France-Italy |
| Shin-Shimizu | 1961 | 8.00 | Japanese Railway | Japan |
| Aki | 1975 | 8.00 | Japanese Railway | Japan |
| Cascade | 1929 | 8.00 | Burlington Northern | U.S. |
| Flathead | 1970 | 8.00 | Burlington Northern | U.S. |

# World's Largest-Capacity Hydro Plants

**Source:** U.S. Committee on Large Dams of the Intl. Commission on Large Dams, 1996

| Rank order | Name | Country | Rated capacity now (MW) | Rated capacity planned (MW) |
|---|---|---|---|---|
| 1 | Turukhansk (Lower Tunguska)* | Russia | – | 20,000 |
| 2 | Itaipu | Brazil/Paraguay | 7,400 | 13,320 |
| 3 | Grand Coulee | U.S. | 6,495 | 10,830 |
| 4 | Guri (Raúl Leoni) | Venezuela | 10,300 | 10,300 |
| 5 | Tucuruí | Brazil | 2,640 | 7,260 |
| 6 | Sayano Shushensk* | Russia | 6,400 | 6,400 |
| 7 | Corpus Posadas | Argentina/ Paraguay | 4,700 | 6,000 |
| 7 | Krasnoyarsk | Russia | 6,000 | 6,000 |
| 9 | La Grande 2 | Canada | 5,328 | 5,328 |
| 10 | Churchill Falls | Canada | 5,225 | 5,225 |
| 11 | Xingo | Brazil | 3,012 | 5,020 |
| 12 | Tarbela | Pakistan | 1,750 | 4,678 |
| 13 | Bratsk | Russia | 4,500 | 4,500 |
| 13 | Ust-Ilim | Russia | 3,675 | 4,500 |
| 15 | Cabora Bassa | Mozambique | 2,425 | 4,150 |
| 16 | Boguchany* | Russia | – | 4,000 |
| 17 | Rogun* | Tajikistan | 3,600 | 3,600 |
| 19 | Paulo Afonso I | Brazil | 1,524 | 3,409 |
| 17 | Oak Creek | U.S. | 3,600 | 3,600 |
| 20 | Pati* | Argentina | – | 3,300 |
| 21 | Ilha Solteira | Brazil | 3,200 | 3,200 |
| 23 | Chapetón* | Argentina | – | 3,000 |
| 21 | Brumley Gap* | U.S. | 3,200 | 3,200 |
| 24 | Gezhouba | China | 2,715 | 2,715 |
| 25 | John Day | U.S. | 2,160 | 2,700 |
| 25 | Nurek | Tajikistan | 900 | 2,700 |
| 25 | Yacireta* | Argentina/ Paraguay | | 2,700 |

*Planned or under construction.

# Major Dams of the World

**Source:** U.S. Committee on Large Dams of the Intl. Commission on Large Dams, 1996

## World's Highest Dams

| Rank order | Name | Country | Height above lowest formation (m) |
|---|---|---|---|
| 1 | Rogun* | Tajikistan | 335 |
| 2 | Nurek | Tajikistan | 300 |
| 3 | Grand Dixence | Switzerland | 285 |
| 4 | Inguri | Georgia | 272 |
| 5 | Chicoasén | Mexico | 261 |
| 6 | Tehri* | India | 261 |
| 7 | Kishau* | India | 253 |
| 8 | Ertan | China | 245 |
| 8 | Sayano-Shushensk* | Russia | 245 |
| 10 | Guavio* | Colombia | 243 |
| 11 | Mica | Canada | 242 |
| 12 | Mauvoisin | Switzerland | 237 |
| 13 | Chivor | Colombia | 237 |
| 14 | El Cajón | Honduras | 234 |
| 15 | Chirkei | Russia | 233 |
| 16 | Oroville | U.S. | 230 |
| 17 | Bhakra | India | 226 |
| 18 | Hoover | U.S. | 221 |
| 19 | Contra | Switzerland | 220 |
| 20 | Mratinje | Yugoslavia | 220 |

*Under construction.

## World's Largest-Volume Embankment Dams

| Rank order | Name | Country | Volume cubic meters × 1000 |
|---|---|---|---|
| 1 | Tarbela | Pakistan | 148,500 |
| 2 | Fort Peck | U.S. | 96,050 |
| 3 | Tucurui | Brazil | 85,200 |
| 4 | Ataturk* | Turkey | 85,000 |
| 5 | Yacireta* | Argentina | 81,000 |
| 6 | Rogun* | Tajikistan | 75,500 |
| 7 | Oahe | U.S. | 70,339 |
| 8 | Guri | Venezuela | 70,000 |
| 9 | Parambikulam | India | 69,165 |
| 10 | High Island West | Hong Kong | 67,000 |
| 11 | Gardiner | Canada | 65,000 |
| 12 | Afsluitdijk | Netherlands | 63,400 |
| 13 | Mangla | Pakistan | 63,379 |
| 14 | Oroville | U.S. | 59,635 |
| 15 | San Luis | U.S. | 59,559 |
| 16 | Nurek | Tajikistan | 58,000 |
| 17 | Tanda | Pakistan | 57,250 |
| 18 | Garrison | U.S. | 50,843 |
| 19 | Cochiti | U.S. | 50,228 |
| 20 | Oosterschelde | Netherlands | 50,000 |

*Under construction.

# World's Largest-Capacity Reservoirs

**Source:** U.S. Committee on Large Dams of the Intl. Commission on Large Dams, 1996

| Rank order | Name | Country | Capacity cubic meters × 1,000,000 |
|---|---|---|---|
| 1 | Owen Falls | Uganda | 204,800 |
| 2 | Bratsk | Russia | 169,000 |
| 3 | Aswan (High) | Egypt | 162,000 |
| 4 | Kariba | Zimbabwe/Zambia | 160,368 |
| 5 | Akosombo | Ghana | 147,960 |
| 6 | Daniel Johnson | Canada | 141,851 |
| 7 | Guri | Venezuela | 135,000 |
| 8 | Krasnoyarsk | Russia | 73,300 |
| 9 | W A C Bennett (Portage Mt.) | Canada | 70,309 |
| 10 | Zeya | Russia | 68,400 |
| 11 | Cabora Bassa | Mozambique | 63,000 |
| 12 | La Grande 2 | Canada | 61,715 |
| 13 | La Grande 3 | Canada | 60,020 |
| 14 | Ust-Ilim | Russia | 59,300 |
| 15 | Boguchany* | Russia | 58,200 |
| 16 | Kuibyshev | Russia | 58,000 |
| 17 | Serra de Mesa | Brazil | 54,400 |
| 18 | Caniapiscau Barrage KA 3 | Canada | 53,790 |
| 19 | Bukhtarma | Kazakstan | 49,800 |
| 20 | Ataturk | Turkey | 48,700 |

*Under construction.

# Major U.S. Dams and Reservoirs

**Source:** Committee on Register of Dams, Corps of Engineers, U.S. Army, 1996

## Highest U.S. Dams

| Order | Dam name | River | State | Type | Height Feet | Height Meters | Year completed |
|---|---|---|---|---|---|---|---|
| 1 | Oroville | Feather | California | E | 754 | 230 | 1968 |
| 2 | Hoover | Colorado | Nevada | A | 725 | 221 | 1936 |
| 3 | Dworshak | N. Fork Clearwater | Idaho | G | 718 | 219 | 1973 |
| 4 | Glen Canyon | Colorado | Arizona | A | 708 | 216 | 1966 |
| 5 | New Bullards Bar | North Yuba | California | A | 636 | 194 | 1970 |
| 6 | New Melones | Stanislaus | California | R | 626 | 191 | 1979 |
| 7 | Swift | Lewis | Washington | E | 610 | 186 | 1958 |
| 8 | Mossyrock | Cowlitz | Washington | A | 607 | 185 | 1968 |
| 9 | Shasta | Sacramento | California | G | 600 | 183 | 1945 |
| 10 | Hungry Horse | S. Fork Flathead | Montana | A | 564 | 172 | 1953 |
| 11 | Grand Coulee | Columbia | Washington | G | 551 | 168 | 1942 |
| 12 | Ross | Skagit | Washington | A | 541 | 165 | 1949 |

E= Embankment, Earthfill; R= Embankment, Rockfill; G= Gravity; A= Arch.

## Largest U.S. Embankment Dams

| Order | Dam name | River | State | Type | Volume Cubic yards X 1000 | Volume Cubic meters X 1000 | Year completed |
|---|---|---|---|---|---|---|---|
| 1 | Fort Peck | Missouri | Montana | E | 125,624 | 96,050 | 1937 |
| 2 | Oahe | Missouri | South Dakota | E | 91,996 | 70,339 | 1958 |
| 3 | Oroville | Feather | California | E | 77,997 | 59,635 | 1968 |
| 4 | San Luis | San Luis Creek | California | E | 77,897 | 59,559 | 1967 |
| 5 | Garrison | Missouri | North Dakota | E | 66,498 | 50,843 | 1953 |
| 6 | Cochiti | Rio Grande | New Mexico | E | 65,693 | 50,228 | 1975 |
| 7 | Earthquake Lake | Madison | Montana | E-G | 49,998 | 38,228 | 1959 |
| 8 | Fort Randall | Missouri | South Dakota | E | 49,962 | 38,200 | 1952 |
| 9 | Castaic | Castaic Creek | California | E | 43,998 | 33,640 | 1973 |
| 10 | Ludington P/S | Lake Michigan | Michigan | E | 37,699 | 28,824 | 1973 |
| 11 | Kingsley | N. Platte | Nebraska | E | 31,999 | 24,466 | 1941 |
| 12 | Warm Springs | Dry Creek | California | E | 29,977 | 22,920 | 1982 |

E= Embankment, Earthfill; G= Gravity.

## Largest U.S. Reservoirs

| Order | Dam name, location | Reservoir name | Location | Reservoir capacity Acre-Feet | Reservoir capacity Cubic meters X 1000 | Year completed |
|---|---|---|---|---|---|---|
| 1 | Hoover, NV | Lake Mead | AZ/NV | 28,253,000 | 34,850,000 | 1936 |
| 2 | Glen Canyon, AZ | Lake Powell | AZ/UT | 26,997,000 | 33,300,000 | 1966 |
| 3 | Garrison, ND | Lake Sakakawea | ND | 22,635,000 | 27,920,000 | 1953 |
| 4 | Oahe, SD | Lake Oahe | ND/SD | 22,238,000 | 27,430,000 | 1958 |
| 5 | Fort Peck, MT | Fort Peck Lake | MT | 17,933,000 | 22,120,000 | 1937 |
| 6 | Grand Coulee, WA | F D Roosevelt Lake | WA | 9,558,000 | 11,790,000 | 1942 |
| 7 | Libby, MT | Lake Koocanusa | MT/B.C. | 5,813,000 | 7,170,000 | 1973 |
| 8 | Fort Randall, SD | Lake Francis Case | SD | 4,621,000 | 5,700,000 | 1952 |
| 9 | Shasta, CA | Lake Shasta | CA | 4,548,000 | 5,610,000 | 1945 |
| 10 | Toledo Bend, LA | Toledo Bend Lake | LA/TX | 4,475,000 | 5,520,000 | 1968 |
| 11 | Wolf Creek, KY | Cumberland Lake | KY | 3,997,000 | 4,930,000 | 1951 |
| 12 | Flaming Gorge, UT | Flaming Gorge Reservoir | UT/WY | 3,786,000 | 4,670,000 | 1964 |

1 acre-foot = 1 acre of water, 1 foot deep

# SOCIAL SECURITY

## Social Security Programs

**Source:** Social Security Administration, U.S. Dept. of Health and Human Services; data as of mid-1996

## Old-Age, Survivors, and Disability Insurance; Medicare; Supplemental Security Income

### Social Security Benefits

Social Security benefits are based on a worker's primary insurance amount (PIA), which is related by law to the average indexed monthly earnings (AIME) on which Social Security contributions have been paid. The full PIA is payable to a retired worker who becomes entitled to benefits at age 65 and to an entitled disabled worker at any age. Spouses and children of retired or disabled workers and survivors of deceased workers receive set proportions of the PIA subject to a family maximum amount. The PIA is calculated by applying varying percentages to succeeding parts of the AIME. The formula is adjusted annually to reflect changes in average annual wages.

Automatic increases in Social Security benefits are initiated for Dec. of each year, assuming the Consumer Price Index (CPI) of the Bureau of Labor Statistics for the 3d calendar quarter of the year increased relative to the base quarter, which is either the 3d calendar quarter of the preceding year or the quarter in which an increase legislated by Congress became effective. The size of the benefit increase is determined by the actual percentage rise of the CPI between the quarters measured.

The average monthly benefit payable to all retired workers was $720.00 in Dec. 1995. The average amount for disabled workers in that month was $682.00.

**Minimum and maximum monthly retired-worker benefits payable to individuals who retired at age 65[1]**

| | Minimum benefit[2] | | Maximum benefit[2] | | | |
|---|---|---|---|---|---|---|
| Year of attainment of age 65 | Payable at time of retirement | Payable effective Dec. 1994 | Payable at time of retirement, Men | Payable at time of retirement, Women[3] | Payable effective Dec. 1994, Men | Payable effective Dec. 1994, Women[3] |
| 1970 | $64.00 | $275.10 | $189.80 | $196.40 | $815.60 | $844.60 |
| 1980 | 133.90 | 275.10 | 572.00 | — | 1,176.50 | — |
| 1990 | (4) | (4) | 975.00 | — | 1,157.50 | — |
| 1993 | (4) | (4) | 1,128.80 | — | 1,190.50 | — |
| 1994 | (4) | (4) | 1,147.50 | — | 1,179.60 | — |
| 1995 | (4) | (4) | 1,199.10 | — | — | — |
| 1996 | (4) | (4) | 1,248.90 | — | — | — |

(1) Assumes retirement at beginning of year. (2) The final benefit amount payable is rounded to next lower $1 (if not already a multiple of $1). (3) Benefits for women are the same as for men except where women's benefit appears separately. (4) Minimum eliminated for workers who reach age 62 after 1981.

### Amount of Work Required

To qualify for benefits, the worker must have worked in covered employment long enough to become insured. Just how long depends on when the worker reaches age 62 or, if earlier, when he or she dies or becomes disabled.

A person is fully insured if he or she has 1 quarter of coverage for every year after 1950 (or year age 21 is reached, if later) up to but not including the year in which the worker reaches age 62, dies, or becomes disabled. In 1996, a person earns 1 quarter of coverage for each $640.00 of annual earnings in covered employment, up to a maximum of 4 quarters per year.

The law permits special monthly payments under the Social Security program to certain very old persons who are not eligible for regular Social Security benefits since they had little or no opportunity to earn Social Security work credits during their working lifetime (so-called special age-72 beneficiaries).

To receive disability benefits, the worker, in addition to being fully insured, must generally have credit for 20 quarters of coverage out of the 40 calendar quarters before he or she becomes disabled. A disabled blind worker need meet only the fully insured requirement. Persons disabled before age 31 can qualify with a briefer period of coverage. Certain survivor benefits are payable if the deceased worker had 6 quarters of coverage in the 13 quarters preceding death.

**Work credit for fully insured status for benefits**

| Born after 1929; die, become disabled, or reach age 62 in | Years needed |
|---|---|
| 1983 | 8 |
| 1984 | 8¼ |
| 1985 | 8½ |
| 1986 | 8¾ |
| 1987 | 9 |
| 1988 | 9¼ |
| 1989 | 9½ |
| 1990 | 9¾ |
| 1991 and after | 10 |

**Contribution and benefit base**

| Calendar year | OASDI[1] Base | HI[2] Base |
|---|---|---|
| 1988 | $45,000 | $45,000 |
| 1989 | 48,000 | 48,000 |
| 1990 | 51,300 | 51,300 |
| 1991 | 53,400 | 125,000 |
| 1992 | 55,500 | 130,200 |
| 1993 | 57,600 | 135,000 |
| 1994 | 60,600 | no limit |
| 1995 | 61,200 | no limit |
| 1996 | 62,700 | no limit |
| 1997 | 65,100 | no limit |

(1) Old-Age, Survivors, and Disability Insurance. (2) Hospital Insurance.

**Tax-rate schedule**

(percentage of covered earnings)

| Year | Total | OASDI | HI |
|---|---|---|---|
| | For employees and employers, each | | |
| 1979-80 | 6.13 | 5.08 | 1.05 |
| 1981 | 6.65 | 5.35 | 1.30 |
| 1982-83 | 6.70 | 5.40 | 1.30 |
| 1984 | 7.00 | 5.70 | 1.30 |
| 1985 | 7.05 | 5.70 | 1.35 |
| 1986-87 | 7.15 | 5.70 | 1.45 |
| 1988-89 | 7.51 | 6.06 | 1.45 |
| 1990 and after | 7.65 | 6.20 | 1.45 |
| | For self-employed | | |
| 1979-80 | 8.10 | 7.05 | 1.05 |
| 1981 | 9.30 | 8.00 | 1.30 |
| 1982-83 | 9.35 | 8.05 | 1.30 |
| 1984 | 14.00 | 11.40 | 2.60 |
| 1985 | 14.10 | 11.40 | 2.70 |
| 1986-87 | 14.30 | 11.40 | 2.90 |
| 1988-89 | 15.02 | 12.12 | 2.90 |
| 1990 and after | 15.30 | 12.40 | 2.90 |

### What Aged Workers Receive

When a person has enough work in covered employment and reaches retirement age (currently age 65 for full benefit, age 62 for reduced benefit), he or she may retire and receive monthly old-age benefits. The age at which unreduced benefits become payable will be increased gradually from ages 65 to 67 over a 21-year period beginning with workers age 62 in the year 2000 (reduced benefits will still be available as early as age 62 but with a larger reduction at that age). If a person age 65-69 continues to work and has earnings of more than $12,500 in 1996, $1 in benefits will be withheld for every $3 above $12,500. For those under 65, the annual exempt amount is $8,280 in 1996, and $1 in benefits is withheld for every $2 in earnings above the exempt amount for them. However, the eligible worker who is age 70 or over receives the full benefit regardless of earnings. The annual exempt amount has been raised automatically as the general earnings level rises. However, legislation enacted in 1996 (PL 104-121) provided for more sizable increases in the annual exempt amount for persons aged 65-69, rising to $13,500 in 1997 and to $30,000 by 2002. After 2002, the annual exempt amount for those 65-69 will be raised automatically as general earnings levels rise.

For workers who reached age 65 between 1982 and 1989, Social Security benefits are raised by 3% for each year for which the worker between ages 65 and 70 (72 before 1984) failed to receive benefits, whether because of earnings from work or because the worker had not applied for benefits. The delayed retirement credit is 1% per year for workers who reached age 65 before 1982. The delayed retirement credit will gradually rise to 8% per year by 2008. The rate for workers who reached age 65 in 1994-95 is 4.5%. The rate for reaching age 65 in 1996-97 is 5%.

Effective Dec. 1995, the special benefit for persons aged 72 or over who do not meet the regular coverage requirements is $193.40 a month. Like the monthly benefits, these payments are subject to cost-of-living increases. They are not made to persons on the public assistance or supplemental security income rolls.

Workers retiring before age 65 have their benefits permanently reduced by $^5/_9$ of 1% for each month they receive benefits before that age. Thus, workers entitled to benefits in the month they reach age 62 receive 80% of the PIA, while a worker retiring at age 65 receives a benefit equal to 100% of the PIA. The nearer to age 65 the worker is when he or she begins collecting a benefit, the larger the benefit will be.

### Benefits for Worker's Spouse

The spouse of a worker who is getting Social Security retirement or disability payments may become entitled to an insurance benefit of one-half of the worker's PIA, when he or she reaches 65. Reduced spouse's benefits are available at age 62 ($^{25}/_{36}$ of 1% reduction for each month of entitlement before age 65). Benefits are also payable to the aged divorced spouse of an insured worker if he or she was married to the worker for at least 10 years.

### Benefits for Children of Retired or Disabled Workers

If a retired or disabled worker has a child under age 18, the child will get a benefit that is half of the worker's unreduced benefit. So will the worker's spouse, even if under age 62, if he or she is caring for an entitled child of the worker who is under age 16 or who became disabled before age 22. Total benefits paid on a worker's earnings record are subject to a maximum, and if the total that would be paid to a family exceeds that maximum, the individual's dependents' benefits are adjusted downward. (Total monthly benefits paid to the family of a worker who retired in Jan. 1996 at age 65 and who always had the maximum amount of earnings creditable under Social Security can be no higher than $2,184.80.)

When entitled children reach age 18, their benefits will generally stop, except that a child disabled before age 22 may get a benefit as long as his or her disability meets the definition in the law. Additionally, benefits will be paid to a child until age 19 if the child is in full-time attendance at an elementary or secondary school.

Benefits may also be paid to a grandchild or step-grandchild of a worker or of his or her spouse, in special circumstances.

| OASDI | May 1996 | May 1995 | May 1994 |
|---|---|---|---|
| **Monthly beneficiaries, total (in thousands)** | **43,463** | **43,068** | **42,461** |
| Aged 65 and over, total | 31,401 | 31,137 | 30,813 |
| Retired workers | 24,226 | 23,943 | 23,624 |
| Survivors and dependents | 7,174 | 7,193 | 7,186 |
| Special age-72 beneficiaries | 1 | 1 | 2 |
| Under age 65, total | 12,062 | 11,931 | 11,649 |
| Retired workers | 2,459 | 2,508 | 2,520 |
| Disabled workers | 4,273 | 4,049 | 3,823 |
| Survivors and dependents | 5,330 | 5,374 | 5,306 |
| **Total monthly benefits (in millions)** | **28,275** | **$27,086** | **$25,814** |

### What Disabled Workers Receive

A worker who becomes so disabled that he or she is unable to work may be eligible to receive a monthly disability benefit. Benefits continue until it is determined that the individual is no longer disabled. Eligibility is reviewed periodically. When a disabled-worker beneficiary reaches age 65, the disability benefit becomes a retired-worker benefit.

Benefits generally like those for dependents of retired-worker beneficiaries may be paid to dependents of disabled beneficiaries. However, the maximum family benefit in disability cases is generally lower than in retirement cases.

### Survivor Benefits

If an insured worker should die, one or more types of benefits may be payable to survivors, again subject to a maximum family benefit as described above.

1. If claiming benefits at age 65, the surviving spouse will receive a benefit equal to 100% of the deceased worker's PIA. The surviving spouse may choose to get the benefit as early as age 60, but it is then reduced by $^{19}/_{40}$ of 1% for each month it is paid before age 65. However, for those whose spouses claimed their benefits before age 65, these are limited to the reduced amount the worker would be getting if alive, but not less than 82$^1/_2$ % of the worker's PIA. Marriage after the worker's death ends the surviving spouse's benefit rights. However, if the widow(er) marries and the marriage is ended, he or she regains benefit rights. (A marriage after age 60, age 50 if disabled, is deemed not to have occurred for benefit purposes.) Survivor benefits may also be paid to a divorced spouse if the marriage lasted for at least 10 years.

Disabled widows and widowers may under certain circumstances qualify for benefits after attaining age 50 at the rate of 71.5% of the deceased worker's PIA. The widow or widower must have become totally disabled before or within 7 years after the spouse's death or the last month in which he or she received mother's or father's insurance benefits.

2. There is a benefit for each child until the child reaches age 18. The monthly benefit for each child of a deceased worker is three-quarters of the amount the worker would have received if he or she had lived and drawn full retirement benefits. A child with a disability that began before age 22 may also receive benefits. Also, a child may receive benefits until reaching age 19 if he or she is in full-time attendance at an elementary or secondary school.

3. There is a mother's or father's benefit for the widow(er) if children of the worker under age 16 are in his or her care. The benefit is 75% of the PIA, and it continues until the youngest child reaches age 16, at which time payments stop even if the child's benefit continues. However, if the widow(er) has a disabled child beneficiary age 16 or over in care, benefits may continue.

4. Dependent parents may be eligible for benefits if they have been receiving at least half their support from the worker before his or her death, have reached age 62, and (except in certain circumstances) have not remarried since the worker's death. Each parent gets 75% of the worker's PIA; if only one parent survives, the benefit is 82$^1/_2$%.

5. A lump sum cash payment of $255 is made when there is a spouse who was living with the worker or a spouse or child who is eligible for immediate monthly survivor benefits.

### Self-Employed Workers

A self-employed person who has net earnings of $400 or more in a year must report such earnings for Social Security tax and credit purposes. The person reports net returns from the business. Income from real estate, savings, dividends, loans, pensions, or insurance policies may not be included unless it is part of the business.

A self-employed person receives 1 quarter of coverage for each $640 (for 1996), up to a maximum of 4 quarters of coverage.

The nonfarm self-employed have the option of reporting their earnings as $^2/_3$ of their gross income from self-employment, but not more than $1,600 a year and not less than their actual net earnings. This option can be used only if actual net earnings from self-employment income are less than $1,600 and may be used only 5 times. Also, the self-employed person must have actual net earnings of $400 or more in 2 of the 3 taxable years immediately preceding the year in which he or she uses the option.

When a person has both taxable wages and earnings from self-employment, the wages are credited for Social Security purposes first; only as much of the self-employment income as will bring total earnings up to the current taxable maximum is subject to the self-employment tax.

### Farm Owners and Workers

Self-employed farmers whose gross annual earnings from farming are $2,400 or less may report 2/3 of their gross earnings instead of net earnings for Social Security purposes. Farmers whose gross income is over $2,400 and whose net earnings are less than $1,600 can report $1,600. Cash or crop shares received from a tenant or share farmer count if the owner participated materially in production or management. The self-employed farmer pays contributions at the same rate as other self-employed persons.

**Agricultural employees.** A worker's earnings from farm work count toward benefits (1) if the employer pays the worker $150 or more in cash during the year; or (2) if the employer spends $2,500 or more in the year for agricultural labor. Under these rules a person gets credit for 1 calendar quarter for each $640 in cash pay in 1996 up to 4 quarters.

Foreign farm workers admitted to the U.S. on a temporary basis are not covered.

### Household Workers

Anyone age 18 or older employed as maid, cook, laundry worker, nurse, babysitter, chauffeur, gardener, or other worker in the house of another is covered by Social Security if he or she is paid $1,000 or more in cash in a calendar year by any one employer. Room and board do not count, but transportation costs count if paid in cash. The job does not have to be regular or full-time. The employee should get a Social Security card at the Social Security office and show it to the employer.

The employer deducts the amount of the employee's Social Security tax from the worker's pay, adds an identical amount as the employer's Social Security tax, and sends the total amount to the federal government, with the employee's Social Security number.

### Medicare Coverage

The Medicare health insurance program provides acute-care coverage for Social Security and Railroad Retirement beneficiaries age 65 and over, for persons entitled for 24 months to receive Social Security or Railroad Retirement disability benefits, and for certain persons with end-stage kidney disease. Medicare cost $194 billion in 1996 and served more than 38 million people.

Persons eligible for Medicare may choose to have their covered services provided through a health maintenance organization (HMO).

**Hospital insurance.** The hospital insurance program pays covered services for hospital and posthospital care as follows:

- All necessary inpatient hospital care for the first 60 days of each benefit period, except for a deductible ($736 in 1996). For days 61-90, Medicare pays for services over and above a coinsurance amount ($184 per day in 1996). After 90 days, the beneficiary has 60 reserve days for which Medicare helps pay. The coinsurance amount for reserve days was $368 in 1996.
- Up to 100 days' care in a skilled-nursing facility in each benefit period. Hospital insurance pays for all covered services for the first 20 days; for the 21-100th day, the beneficiary pays coinsurance ($92 a day in 1996).
- Visits by nurses or other health workers (not doctors) from a home health agency.
- Hospice care for terminally ill individuals.

**Medical insurance.** Aged persons can receive benefits under this supplementary program only if they sign up for them and agree to a monthly premium ($72.50 in 1996). The federal government pays the rest of the cost.

The medical insurance program usually pays 80% of the approved amount (after the first $100 in each calendar year) for the following services:

- Covered services received from a doctor in his or her office, in a hospital, in a skilled-nursing facility, at home, or in other locations.
- Medical and surgical services, including anesthesia.
- Diagnostic tests and procedures that are part of the patient's treatment.
- Radiology and pathology services by doctors while the individual is a hospital inpatient or outpatient.
- Treatment of mental illness. Medicare payments are limited; services may be obtained from doctors, comprehensive outpatient rehabilitation facilities (CORFs), physician assistants, psychologists, and clinical social workers.

The services for nonhospital treatment of a mental illness are subject to a special payment rule. In effect, once the annual deductible is met, Medicare pays only 50% (not 80%) of approved charges. On assigned claims (those in which the service provider agrees to the fee set by Medicare), beneficiaries are responsible for paying the remaining 50%. For unassigned claims, beneficiaries may have to pay more.

Partial hospitalization services for treatment of mental illness are not subject to this special payment rule. Also, brief office visits for the sole purpose of monitoring or changing drug prescriptions used in the treatment of mental illness are not subject to this special payment rule.

- Other services such as:
  - — X-rays
  - — Services of a doctor's office nurse
  - — Drugs and biologicals that cannot be self-administered
  - — Transfusions of blood and blood components
  - — Medical supplies
  - — Physical/occupational therapy and speech pathology services.

To get medical insurance protection, persons approaching age 65 may enroll in the 7-month period that includes 3 months before the 65th birthday, the month of the birthday, and 3 months after the birthday, but if they wish coverage to begin in the month they reach age 65, they must enroll in the 3 months before their birthday. Persons not enrolling within their first enrollment period may enroll later, during the first 3 months of each year (coverage begins July 1), but their premium may be 10% higher for each 12-month period elapsed since they first could have enrolled.

The monthly premium is deducted from the cash benefit for persons receiving Social Security, Railroad Retirement, or Civil Service retirement benefits. Income from the medical premiums and the federal matching payments are put in a Supplementary Medical Insurance Trust Fund, from which benefits and administrative expenses are paid.

**Medicare card.** Persons qualifying for hospital insurance under Social Security receive a health insurance card similar to cards now used by Blue Cross and other health insurers. The card indicates whether the individual has taken out medical insurance protection. It is to be shown to the hospital, skilled-nursing facility, home health agency, doctor, or whoever provides the covered services.

Payments are made only in the 50 states, Puerto Rico, the Virgin Islands, Guam, and American Samoa, except that, in rare cases, inpatient hospital services may be provided in Canada and Mexico.

### Social Security Financing

Social Security is paid for by a tax on certain earnings (for 1996, on earnings up to $62,700) for Old Age, Survivors, and Disability Insurance and on all earnings (no upper limit) for Hospital Insurance with the Medicare Program; the taxable earnings base for OASDI has been adjusted annually to reflect increases in average wages. The employed worker and his or her employer share Social Security taxes equally.

Employers remit amounts withheld from employee wages for Social Security and income taxes to the Internal Revenue Service; employer Social Security taxes are also payable at the same time. (Self-employed workers pay their Social Security taxes along with their regular income tax forms.) The Social Security taxes (along with revenues arising from partial taxation of the Social Security benefits of certain high-income people) are transferred to the Social Security Trust Funds—the Federal Old-Age and Survivors Insurance (OASI) Trust Fund, the Federal Disability Insurance (DI) Trust Fund, and the Federal Hospital Insurance (HI) Trust Fund; they can be used only to pay benefits, the cost of rehabilitation services, and administrative expenses. Money not immediately needed for these purposes is by law invested in obligations of the federal government, which must pay interest on the money borrowed and must repay the principal when the obligations are redeemed or mature.

### Supplemental Security Income

On Jan. 1, 1974, the Supplemental Security Income (SSI) program established by the 1972 Social Security Act amendments replaced the former federal grants to states for aid to the needy aged, blind, and disabled in the 50 states and the District of Columbia. The program provides both for federal payments, based on uniform national standards and eligibility requirements, and for state supplementary payments varying from state to state. The Social Security Administration administers the federal payments financed from general funds of the Treasury—and the state supplements as well, if the state elects to have its supplementary program federally administered. The states may supplement the federal payment for all recipients and must supplement it for persons otherwise adversely affected by the transition from the former public assistance programs. In May 1996, the number of persons receiving federal payments and federally administered state payments was 6,593,130, and the amount of these payments totaled $2.4 billion.

The maximum monthly federal SSI payment for individuals with no other countable income, living in their own household, was $470.00 in 1996. For couples it was $705.00.

## Examples of monthly cash benefits available to those with first entitlement in 1996, effective Jan. 1996

| Beneficiary family | Low earnings ($11,617 in 1996)[1] | Average earnings ($24,815 in 1996)[2] | Maximum earnings ($62,700 in 1996) |
|---|---|---|---|
| Primary insurance amount (worker retiring at 65) | $537.00 | $886.00 | $1,248.00 |
| Maximum family benefit (worker retiring at 65) | 805.50 | 1,615.20 | 2,184.80 |
| Maximum family disability benefit (worker disabled at 55; in 1996)* | 757.30 | 1,331.50 | 1,946.70 |
| Disabled worker: (worker disabled at 55) | | | |
| Worker alone | 538.00 | 887.00 | 1,297.00 |
| Worker, spouse, and 1 child | 756.00 | 1,331.00 | 1,945.00 |
| Retired worker claiming benefits at age 62: | | | |
| Worker alone[3] | 430.00 | 709.00 | 999.00 |
| Worker with spouse claiming benefits at— | | | |
| Age 65 or over | 698.00 | 1,152.00 | 1,623.00 |
| Age 62[3] | 631.00 | 1,041.00 | 1,467.00 |
| Widow or widower claiming benefits at— | | | |
| Age 65 or over[4] | 537.00 | 886.00 | 1,248.00 |
| Age 60 (spouse died at 65 without receiving reduced benefits) | 384.00 | 633.00 | 892.00 |
| Disabled widow or widower claiming benefits at age 50-59[5] | 384.00 | 633.00 | 892.00 |
| 1 surviving child | 402.00 | 664.00 | 936.00 |
| Widow or widower age 65 or over and 1 child[6] | 804.00 | 1,550.00 | 2,184.00 |
| Widowed mother or father and 1 child[6] | 804.00 | 1,328.00 | 1,872.00 |
| Widowed mother or father and 2 children[6] | 804.00 | 1,614.00 | 2,181.00 |

*Assumes work beginning at age 22. (1) 45% of average. (2) Estimate. (3) Assumes maximum reduction. (4) A widow(er)'s benefit amount is limited to the amount the spouse would have been receiving if still living, but not less than 82.5 % of the PIA. (5) Effective Jan. 1984, disabled widow(er)s claiming a benefit at ages 50-59 will receive a benefit equal to 71.5 % of the PIA (based on 1983 Social Security Amendment provision). (6) Based on worker dying at age 65.

# Social Security Trust Funds

## Old-Age and Survivors Insurance Trust Fund, 1940-95

(in millions)

| | Income | | | | | Disbursements | | | | | | |
|---|---|---|---|---|---|---|---|---|---|---|---|---|
| Fiscal year[1] | Total | Net contri-butions[2] | Income from taxation of benefits | Payments from the general fund of the Treasury[3] | Net interest[4] | Total | Benefit payments[5] | Adminis-trative expenses | Transfers to Railroad Retirement program | Interfund borrowing transfers[6] | Net increase in fund | Fund at end of period |
| 1940 | $592 | $550 | — | — | $42 | $28 | $16 | $12 | — | — | $564 | $1,745 |
| 1950 | 2,367 | 2,106 | — | $4 | 257 | 784 | 727 | 57 | — | — | 1,583 | 12,893 |
| 1960 | 10,360 | 9,843 | — | — | 517 | 11,073 | 10,270 | 202 | $600 | — | -713 | 20,829 |
| 1970 | 31,746 | 29,955 | — | 442 | 1,350 | 27,321 | 26,268 | 474 | 579 | — | 4,425 | 32,616 |
| 1980 | 100,051 | 97,608 | — | 557 | 1,886 | 103,228 | 100,626 | 1,160 | 1,442 | — | -3,177 | 24,566 |
| 1985 | 179,881 | 175,305 | $3,151 | 105 | 1,321 | 169,210 | 165,310 | 1,589 | 2,310 | -$4,364 | 6,308 | 33,877 |
| 1990 | 278,607 | 261,506 | 2,924 | 34 | 14,143 | 223,481 | 218,948 | 1,564 | 2,969 | — | 55,126 | 203,445 |
| 1991 | 293,288 | 270,841 | 5,790 | -2,089 | 18,746 | 241,316 | 236,195 | 1,746 | 3,375 | — | 51,972 | 255,417 |
| 1992 | 307,102 | 278,506 | 6,019 | 19 | 22,557 | 256,239 | 251,268 | 1,823 | 3,148 | — | 50,862 | 306,280 |
| 1993 | 319,298 | 287,569 | 5,893 | 14 | 25,822 | 269,934 | 264,561 | 2,021 | 3,353 | — | 49,364 | 355,644 |
| 1994 | 342,263 | 308,397 | 5,351 | 10 | 28,505 | 281,572 | 276,278 | 1,874 | 3,420 | — | 50,691 | 415,335 |
| 1995 | 326,067 | 289,529 | 5,114 | 7 | 31,417 | 294,456 | 288,607 | 1,797 | 4,052 | — | 31,611 | 447,946 |

(1) Under the Congressional Budget Act of 1974 (PL 93-344), fiscal years 1977 and later consist of the 12 months ending on Sept. 30 of each year. Fiscal years prior to 1977 consisted of the 12 months ending on June 30 of each year. (2) Beginning in 1983, includes transfers from general fund of Treasury representing contributions that would have been paid on deemed wage credits for military service in 1957 and later, if such credits were considered covered wages. (3) Includes payments (a) in 1947-52 and in 1967 and later, for costs of noncontributory wage credits for military service performed before 1957; (b) in 1972-83, for costs of deemed wage credits for military service performed after 1956; and (c) in 1969 and later, for costs of benefits to certain uninsured persons who attained age 72 before 1968. (4) Net interest includes net profits or losses on marketable investments. Beginning in 1967, administrative expenses are charged currently to the trust fund on an estimated basis, with a final adjustment, including interest, made in the following fiscal year. The amounts of these interest adjustments are included in net interest. For years prior to 1967, a description of the method of accounting for administrative expenses is contained in the 1970 Annual Report. Beginning in Oct. 1973, the figures shown include relatively small amounts of gifts to the fund. Figures for 1983-86 reflect payments from a borrowing trust fund to a lending trust fund for interest on amounts owed under the interfund borrowing provisions. During 1983-91, interest paid from the trust fund to the general fund on advance tax transfers is reflected. The amount shown for 1985 includes interest adjustments of $76.5 mln. on unnegotiated checks issued before Apr. 1985. (5) Beginning in 1967, includes payments for vocational rehabilitation services furnished to disabled persons receiving benefits because of their disabilities. Beginning in 1983, amounts are reduced by amount of reimbursement for unnegotiated benefit checks. (6) Negative figures represent amounts repaid from the OASI Trust Fund to the DI and HI Trust Funds.

## Disability Insurance Trust Fund, 1970-95

(in millions)

| | Income | | | | | Disbursements | | | | | | |
|---|---|---|---|---|---|---|---|---|---|---|---|---|
| Fiscal year[1] | Total | Net contribu -tions[2] | Income from taxation of benefits | Payments from the general fund of the Treasury[3] | Net interest[4] | Total | Benefit payments[5] | Adminis- trative expenses | Transfers to Railroad Retirement program | Interfund borrowing transfers[6] | Net increase in fund | Fund at end of period |
| 1970 | $4,380 | $4,141 | — | $16 | $223 | $2,954 | $2,795 | $149 | $10 | — | $1,426 | $5,104 |
| 1980 | 17,376 | 16,805 | — | 118 | 453 | 15,320 | 14,998 | 334 | -12 | — | 2,056 | 7,680 |
| 1985 | 17,984 | 16,876 | $217 | — | 891 | 19,294 | 18,648 | 603 | 43 | $2,540 | 1,230 | 5,873 |
| 1990 | 28,215 | 27,291 | 158 | — | 766 | 25,124 | 24,327 | 717 | 80 | — | 3,091 | 11,455 |
| 1991 | 29,322 | 28,953 | 131 | -775 | 1,014 | 27,780 | 26,909 | 789 | 82 | — | 1,543 | 12,997 |
| 1992 | 31,168 | 29,871 | 218 | — | 1,080 | 31,285 | 30,382 | 845 | 58 | — | -116 | 12,881 |
| 1993 | 32,056 | 30,822 | 268 | — | 966 | 34,632 | 33,615 | 935 | 83 | — | -2,576 | 10,305 |
| 1994 | 34,044 | 33,041 | 305 | — | 699 | 37,979 | 36,851 | 1,022 | 106 | — | -3,935 | 6,370 |
| 1995 | 70,209 | 67,987 | 335 | | 1,888 | 41,374 | 40,234 | 1,072 | 68 | | 28,835 | 35,206 |

(1) Under the Congressional Budget Act of 1974 (PL 93-344), fiscal years 1977 and later consist of the 12 months ending on Sept. 30 of each year. (2) Beginning in 1983, includes government contributions on deemed wage credits for military service in 1957 and later. (3) Includes payments (a) for costs of noncontributory wage credits for military service performed before 1957; and (b) in 1972-83, for costs of deemed wage credits for military service performed after 1956. (4) Net interest includes net profits or losses on marketable investments. Administrative expenses are charged currently to the trust fund on an estimated basis, with a final adjustment, including interest, made in the following fiscal year. The amounts of these interest adjustments are included in net interest. Beginning in 1983, these figures reflect payments from a borrowing trust fund to a lending trust fund for interest on amounts owed under the interfund borrowing provisions. Also, beginning in 1983, interest paid from the trust fund to the general fund on advance tax transfers is reflected. The amount shown for 1985 includes an interest adjustment of $14.8 mln. on unnegotiated checks issued before Apr. 1985. (5)Includes payments for vocational rehabilitation services furnished to disabled persons receiving benefits because of their disabilities. Beginning in 1983, amounts are reduced by amount of reimbursement for unnegotiated benefit checks. (6) Negative figure represents amounts lent by the DI Trust Fund to the OASI Trust Fund. Positive figures represent repayment of these amounts.

## Supplementary Medical Insurance Trust Fund, 1970-95

(in millions)

| | Income | | | | Disbursements | | | |
|---|---|---|---|---|---|---|---|---|
| Fiscal year[1] | Premium from participants | Government contribu- tions[2] | Interest and other income[3] | Total Income | Benefit payments[4] | Adminis- trative expenses | Total disburse- ments | Balance in fund at end of year[5] |
| 1970 | $936 | $928 | $12 | $1,876 | $1,979 | $217 | $2,196 | $57 |
| 1975 | 1,887 | 2,330 | 105 | 4,322 | 3,765 | 405 | 4,170 | 1,424 |
| 1980 | 2,928 | 6,932 | 415 | 10,275 | 10,144 | 593 | 10,737 | 4,532 |
| 1985 | 5,524 | 17,898 | 1,155 | 24,577 | 21,808 | 922 | 22,730 | 10,646 |
| 1990 | 11,494[4] | 33,210 | 1,434[4] | 46,138[4] | 41,498 | 1,524[4] | 43,022[4] | 14,527[4] |
| 1991 | 11,807 | 34,730 | 1,629 | 48,166 | 45,514 | 1,505 | 47,019 | 15,675 |
| 1992 | 12,748 | 38,684 | 1,717 | 53,149 | 48,627 | 1,661 | 50,288 | 18,535 |
| 1993 | 14,683 | 44,227 | 1,889 | 60,799 | 54,214[6] | 1,845 | 56,059 | 23,276 |
| 1994 | 16,895 | 38,355 | 2,118 | 57,368 | 58,006 | 1,718 | 59,724 | 20,919 |
| 1995 | 19,244 | 36,988 | 1,937 | 58,169 | 63,491 | 1,722 | 65,213 | 13,874 |

(1) For 1970 through 1976, fiscal years cover the interval from July 1 through June 30; fiscal years 1977 and later cover the interval from Oct. 1 through Sept. 30. (2) The payments shown as being from the general fund of the Treasury include certain interest-adjustment items. (3) Other income includes recoveries of amounts reimbursed from the trust fund that are not obligations of the trust fund and other miscellaneous income. (4) Includes the impact of the Medicare Catastrophic Coverage Act of 1988 (PL 100-360). (5) The financial status of the program depends on both the total net assets and the liabilities of the program. (6) Includes $1,805 mln. transfer to the HI trust fund, as provided for by PL 102-394.

## Hospital Insurance Trust Fund, 1970-95

(in millions)

| | Income | | | | | | | | Disbursements | | | | |
|---|---|---|---|---|---|---|---|---|---|---|---|---|---|
| Fiscal year[1] | Payroll taxes | Income from taxation of benefits | Transfers from railroad retirement acct. | Reimburse- ment for uninsured persons | Premiums from voluntary enrollees | Pymts. for military wage credits | Interest on investments and other income[2] | Total income | Benefit pymts.[3] | Adminis- trative expense[4] | Total disburse- ments | Net increase in fund | Fund at end of year |
| 1970 | $4,785 | — | $64 | $617 | — | $11 | $137 | $5,614 | $4,804 | $149 | $4,953 | $661 | $2,677 |
| 1975 | 11,291 | — | 132 | 481 | $6 | 48 | 609 | 12,568 | 10,353 | 259 | 10,612 | 1,956 | 9,870 |
| 1980 | 23,244 | — | 244 | 697 | 17 | 141 | 1,072 | 25,415 | 23,790 | 497 | 24,288 | 1,127 | 14,490 |
| 1985 | 46,490 | — | 371 | 766 | 38 | 86 | 3,182 | 50,933 | 47,841 | 813 | 48,654 | 4,103[5] | 21,277[5] |
| 1990 | 70,655 | — | 367 | 413 | 113 | 107 | 7,908 | 79,563 | 65,912 | 774 | 66,687 | 12,876 | 95,631 |
| 1991 | 74,655 | — | 352 | 605 | 367 | -1,011[6] | 8,969 | 83,938 | 68,705 | 934 | 69,638 | 14,299 | 109,930 |
| 1992 | 80,978 | — | 374 | 621 | 484 | 86 | 10,133 | 92,677 | 80,784 | 1,191 | 81,974 | 10,703 | 120,633 |
| 1993 | 83,147 | — | 400 | 367 | 622 | 81 | 12,484[7] | 97,101 | 90,738 | 866 | 91,604 | 5,497 | 126,131 |
| 1994 | 92,028 | $1,639 | 413 | 506 | 852 | 80 | 10,676 | 106,195 | 101,535 | 1,235 | 102,770 | 3,425 | 129,555 |
| 1995 | 98,053 | 3,913 | 396 | 462 | 998 | 61 | 10,963 | 114,847 | 113,583 | 1,300 | 114,883 | -36 | 129,520 |

(1) Fiscal years 1976 and earlier consist of the 12 months ending on June 30 of each year; fiscal years 1977 and later consist of the 12 months ending on Sept. 30 of each year. (2) Other income includes recoveries of amounts reimbursed from the trust fund that are not obligations of the trust fund and a small amount of miscellaneous income. (3) Includes costs of Peer Review Organizations (beginning with the implementation of the Prospective Payment System on Oct. 1, 1983). (4) Includes costs of experiments and demonstration projects. (5) In fiscal year 1983, $12,437 mln. was loaned to the Old-Age and Survivors Insurance Trust Fund under the interfund borrowing provisions of the Social Security Act. Repayments of $1,824 mln. and $10,613 mln. were made in fiscal years 1985 and 1986, respectively. (6) Includes the lump sum general revenue adjustment of $-1,100 mln., as provided for by section 151 of PL 98-21. (7) Includes $1,805 mln. transfer from the SMI catastrophic coverage reserve fund, as provided for by PL 102-394. NOTE: Totals do not necessarily equal the sum of rounded components.

# CONSUMER INFORMATION

## Consumer Information Catalog

**Source:** Consumer Information Center, U.S. General Services Administration

The *Consumer Information Catalog* is a free listing of more than 250 of the best federal consumer publications. They range from booklets on financial planning to planning a diet, from learning about federal benefits to getting an education, from fixing a car to dealing effectively with consumer problems. Many of these booklets are free.

The *Consumer Information Catalog* is published quarterly by the Consumer Information Center (CIC) of the U.S. General Services Administration. For a free copy of the most current *Consumer Information Catalog,* send your name and address to Consumer Information Catalog, Pueblo, CO 81009. You can also order a copy of the catalog by phone at 719-948-4000 or by fax at 719-948-9724. Educators, librarians, and members of nonprofit groups who are able to distribute 25 or more copies of the *Consumer Information Catalog* on a quarterly basis should write to the same address for an application to be placed on the mailing list. Costs prevent the Consumer Information Center from maintaining a mailing list for individuals.

Publications listed in the *Consumer Information Catalog* are available online, along with other consumer news, updates, and information. Use your modem or Internet connection to access the Consumer Information Center electronically. Electronic BBS: 202-208-7679; Internet World Wide Web: http://www.pueblo.qsa.gov

For detailed instructions on connecting to CIC, send e-mail to catalog.pueblo@gsa.gov with the words "SEND INFO" in the body of the message.

Some free and low-cost booklets are available from the *Consumer Information Catalog* as of summer 1996. Quantities of some may be limited. The handling fee is $1.00. To order, send your name and address, the item numbers of the booklets you want, and the $1.00 fee to: Consumer Information Center, Pueblo, CO 81009.

## At-Home Shopping—Consumer Tips and Rights

**Source:** Consumer Information Catalog; U.S. Postal Service; U.S. Office of Consumer Affairs

### Tips

• Deal only with reliable firms. Check with your local consumer protection agency or the Better Business Bureau (BBB) nearest the business.

• Review the advertising offer carefully.

• If not stated, inquire about warranty, refund, and exchange policies.

• Never send cash. Pay by money order, check, charge, or credit card so that you have a record of your purchase.

• Keep the ad you responded to and a copy of the order form. If there is no order form, record the company's name, address, phone number, date, the item you purchased, amount paid, and the promised delivery date.

• Never give your credit, debit, charge card or bank account number unless you have checked out the company or have done business with it before.

### Rights

**Late deliveries, delays, canceled orders.** By federal law, a company must ship your order within 30 days, unless the advertisement promises a different shipping time. If the company cannot ship within 30 days or the promised time, it must give you an "Option Notice." You can choose to wait longer for your order or to cancel and get a prompt refund. If you cancel and if your order was paid by charge or credit card, the seller has one billing cycle to tell the card issuer to credit your account.

The following are exceptions to this rule:

(1) If a company does not promise a shipping time and if you are applying for credit to pay for your purchase, the company has 50 days after receiving your order to ship.

(2) Spaced deliveries, such as magazine subscriptions (except for 1st shipment), and items that continue until you cancel (for example, book or record clubs), cash on delivery (COD) orders, services, and seeds or growing plants.

**Unordered merchandise.** If you are shipped a product that you did not order, it's yours. It is illegal for a company to pressure you to pay for it or to return it.

**Damaged or spoiled items.** If damage is obvious, and if you decide not to accept the package, write "REFUSED" on the wrapper (at time of delivery) and return it unopened to the seller. No new postage is needed, unless the package came by insured, registered, certified, or COD mail and you signed for it.

**Disputes or billing errors.** If there is a problem with your order—you were billed the wrong amount, you never got the product, the goods arrived in damaged condition, or the merchandise or services were misrepresented—follow these steps:

(1) Write immediately to the company from whom you ordered, explaining the problem and asking for a specific resolution. Be sure to include your name, address, and daytime phone number, your order or invoice number, a copy of the canceled check, or any other helpful information about your purchase.

(2) If you charged your purchase to a charge or credit card account or if you arranged for the payment to be automatically withdrawn from a bank account, send a copy of your letter to the card issuer or bank.

You usually have 60 days after receiving a bill to dispute charges.

Postal regulations allow you to write a check payable to the sender, rather than the delivery company, on COD orders. If, after examining the merchandise, you feel there has been misrepresentation or fraud, you can stop payment on the check and file a complaint with the U.S. Postal Inspector's Office.

For other at-home shopping questions, contact: The Federal Trade Commission, Division of Enforcement, Washington, DC 20580 ; 202-326-3768.

## Charitable Giving in the U.S., 1985-95, by Sources of Contributions

**Source:** American Assn. of Fund-Raising Counsel, Inc., AAFRC Trust for Philanthropy

(in billions of dollars)

| Year | Corporations | Foundations | Bequests | Individuals | Total |
|---|---|---|---|---|---|
| 1985 | $4.63 | $4.90 | $4.77 | $58.66 | $72.96 |
| 1986 | 5.03 | 5.43 | 5.70 | 67.63 | 83.79 |
| 1987 | 5.21 | 5.88 | 6.58 | 72.32 | 89.99 |
| 1988 | 5.34 | 6.15 | 6.57 | 80.07 | 98.13 |
| 1989 | 5.46 | 6.55 | 6.97 | 87.75 | 108.73 |
| 1990 | 5.46 | 7.23 | 7.64 | 91.15 | 111.48 |
| 1991 | 5.62 | 7.72 | 7.78 | 96.10 | 117.22 |
| 1992 | 5.92 | 8.64 | 8.15 | 98.38 | 121.09 |
| 1993 | 6.26 | 9.53 | 8.54 | 102.13 | 126.46 |
| 1994 | 6.88 | 9.66 | 8.77 | 104.53 | 129.84 |
| 1995 | 7.40 | 10.44 | 9.77 | 116.23 | 143.84 |

# Business Directory

Listed below are major U.S. corporations whose operations—products and services—directly concern the American consumer. At the end of each listing is a **representative sample** of the company's products.

**Company...Address...Telephone number...Top executive ...Business.**

**Abbott Laboratories**...One Abbott Park Rd., North Chicago, IL 60064...(708) 937-6100...D. L. Burnham...health care prods. (Murine, Selsun Blue).

**Aetna Inc.**...151 Farmington Ave., Hartford, CT 06156...(203) 273-0123...Ronald E. Compton...health insurance, financial services.

**H. F. Ahmanson & Co.**...4900 Rivergrade Rd., Irwindale, CA 91706...(818) 814-7986...R. H. Deihl...largest thrift-holding co. in U.S. (Home Savings of America).

**Alberto Culver Co.**...2525 Armitage Ave., Melrose Park, IL 60160...(708) 450-3000...Leonard H. Lavin...hair care, feminine hygiene, household products, grocery items.

**Albertson's Inc.**...250 Parkcenter Blvd., Boise, ID 83726... (208) 385-6200...Gary Michael...supermarkets.

**Allegheny Teledyne, Inc.**...2049 Century Pk. East, Los Angeles, CA 90067-3101...(310) 551-4268...William Rutledge...electronics, aerospace, industrial, consumer prods. (Water Pik).

**AlliedSignal**...Morristown, NJ 07960...(201) 455-2000 ...Lawrence Bossidy...aerospace, engineered materials, automotive prods.

**Allstate Corp.**...Allstate Plaza, Northbrook, IL 60062...(847) 402-5000...Jerry Choate...property/casualty, life insurance.

**Aluminum Co. of America (Alcoa)**...425 6th Ave., Pittsburgh, PA 15219...(412) 553-3042...Paul O'Neill...mining, refining, & processing of aluminum.

**Amerada Hess Corp.**...1185 Ave. of the Americas, NY, NY 10036...(212) 997-8500...J. B. Hess...integrated petroleum co.

**American Brands, Inc.**...1700 E. Putnam Ave., Old Greenwich, CT 06870...(203) 698-5000...Thomas C. Hays... whiskey (Jim Beam), hardware, office prods., golf and leisure products (Titleist). (Co. announced 10/8/96 that it planned to change its name to Fortune Brands.)

**American Express Co.**...200 Vesey St., NY, NY 10285...(212) 640-2000...Harvey Golub...travelers' checks, credit card services, insurance, investment services.

**American Greetings Corp.**...1 American Rd., Cleveland, OH 44144...(216) 252-7300...Morry Weiss...greeting cards, stationery, gift items.

**American Home Products Corp.**...5 Giralda Farms, Madison, NJ 07940...(201) 660-5000...J. R. Stafford...prescription and over-the-counter drugs (Advil, Anacin, Robitussin), food (Chef Boy-ar-dee).

**American Intl. Group**...70 Pine St., NY, NY 10270...(212) 770-7000...Maurice R. Greenberg...insurance, financial services.

**American Stores Co.**...709 E. South Temple, Salt Lake City, UT 84102...(801) 961-3000...Victor Lund ...retail food markets, dept. & drug stores.

**Ameritech**...30 S. Wacker Dr., Chicago, IL 60606...(312) 750-5000...Richard C. Notebaert...communications services.

**Amoco Corp.**...200 E. Randolph Dr., Chicago, IL 60601...(312) 856-6111...H. L. Fuller...integrated petroleum co.

**AMP, Inc.**...Eisenhower Blvd., Harrisburg, PA 17105...(717) 564-0100...James E. Marley...designs, produces electronic connection devices.

**AMR Corp.**...PO Box 619616, Dallas/Ft. Worth Airport, TX 75261...(817) 963-1234...Robert Crandall...air transportation (American Airlines).

**Anheuser-Busch Cos., Inc.**...One Busch Place, St. Louis, MO 63118...(314) 577-2000...August A. Busch 3d...brewing (Budweiser, Michelob, Bud Light, Natural Light, Busch, O'Doul's), aluminum can manuf. & recycling, theme parks.

**Apple Computer, Inc.**...1 Infinite Loop, Cupertino, CA 95014-2084...(408) 996-1010...Dr. Gilbert F. Amelio...manuf. personal computers, software, peripherals.

**Aramark Corp.**...1101 Market St., Philadelphia, PA 19107...(215) 238-3000...Joseph Neubauer...provides food, health, leisure, and other services.

**Archer Daniels Midland Co.**...4666 Faires Pkwy., Decatur, IL 62526...(217) 424-5200...Dwayne O. Andreas...agricultural commodities, foods.

**Armstrong World Industries, Inc.**...PO Box 3001, 313 W. Liberty St., Lancaster, PA 17604...(717) 397-0611...George A. Lorch...interior furnishings, specialty prods.

**Arvin Industries, Inc.**...1531 13th St., Columbus, IN 47201...(812) 379-3000...Byron O. Pond...auto emission & noise control systems.

**Ashland Inc.**...PO Box 391, Ashland, KY 41101...(606) 329-3333...John R. Hall...petroleum producer and refiner, chemicals, road construction.

**Atlantic Richfield Co.**...515 S. Flower St., Los Angeles, CA 90071-2256...(213) 486-3511...M. R. Bowlin...integrated oil co.

**AT&T Corp.**...32 Ave. of the Americas, NY, NY 10013-2412...(212) 387-5400...Robert E. Allen...communications, global information management financial services.

**Avon Products, Inc.**...9 West 57th St., NY, NY 10019...(212) 546-6015...James E. Preston...cosmetics, fragrances, toiletries, fashion jewelry, gift items, casual apparel, lingerie.

**BankAmerica Corp.**...PO Box 37000, San Francisco, CA 94137...(415) 622-3456...R. M. Rosenberg...owns banks.

**Bausch & Lomb**...One Chase Square, Rochester, NY 14601...(716) 338-6000...William H. Waltrip...manuf. of vision-care products, accessories; health care products.

**Baxter International Inc.**...One Baxter Pkwy., Deerfield, IL 60015...(708) 948-2000...Vernon R. Loucks Jr. ...health care prods. & services.

**Bear Stearns Cos., Inc.**...245 Park Ave., NY, NY 10167...(212) 272-2000...A. C. Greenberg...investment banking, securities trading, brokerage.

**Becton, Dickinson & Co.**...One Becton Dr., Franklin Lakes, NJ 07417...(201) 847-6800...C. Castellini...medical, laboratory, diagnostic products.

**Bell Atlantic Corp.**...1717 Arch St., Philadelphia, PA 19103...(215) 963-6000...Raymond W. Smith...telephone service in mid-Atlantic region. (Co. announced 6/26/96 that it had agreed to acquire NYNEX Corp.)

**BellSouth Corp.**...1155 Peachtree St. NE, Atlanta, GA 30367...(404) 249-2000...John L. Clendenin...telephone service in the South.

**Best Buy Co., Inc.**...7075 Flying Cloud Dr., Eden Prairie, MN 55344...(612) 947-2000...R. M. Schulze...retailer of software, appliances, electronics, cameras, home office equipment.

**Bethlehem Steel Corp.**...1170 8th Ave., Bethlehem, PA 18016...(610) 694-2424...Curtis H. Barnette...steel & steel prods.

**Black & Decker Corp.**...701 E. Joppa Rd., Towson, MD 21204...(410) 716-3900...Nolan D. Archibald...manuf. power tools, household prods., small appliances.

**H & R Block, Inc.**...4410 Main St., Kansas City, MO 64111...(816) 753-6900...Frank L. Salizzoni...tax preparation.

**Boeing Co.**...7755 E. Marginal Way, Seattle, WA 98108...(206) 655-2121...Frank A. Shrontz...aerospace manuf.

**Boise Cascade Corp.**...One Jefferson Square, Boise, ID 83728...(208) 384-6161...George J. Harad...timber; paper, wood prods.

**Borden, Inc.**...180 E. Broad St., Columbus OH 43215-3799...(614) 225-4000...C. Robert Kidder...food, cheese and cheese products, snacks (Cracker Jack), beverages, adhesives (Elmer's, Krazy Glue), pasta (Prince, Creamette), pasta sauce (Aunt Millie's, Classico).

**Bristol-Myers Squibb Co.**...345 Park Ave., NY, NY 10022...(212) 546-4000...Charles A. Heimhold...toiletries (Ban antiperspirant), hair care items (Clairol), drugs (Bufferin, Comtrex, Excedrin), infant formula (Enfamil).

**Brown-Forman Corp.**...PO Box 1080, Louisville, KY 40201-1080...(502) 585-1100...Owsley Brown 2d...distilled spirits (Jack Daniel's, Early Times), wines (Bolla, Fontina Candida, Korbel), liquor (Southern Comfort), Lenox china and crystal, luggage.

**Brown Group, Inc.**...8300 Maryland Ave., St. Louis, MO 63166...(314) 854-4000...B. A. Bridgewater, Jr....manuf. & retailer of women's, men's, and children's shoes (Buster Brown, Naturalizer).

**Brunswick Corp.**...One N. Field Ct., Lake Forest, IL 60045-4811...(847) 735-4700...P. N. Larson...marine, recreation prods., bowling centers & equip., fishing equip.

**Burlington Northern Santa Fe Inc.**...777 Main St., Ft. Worth, TX 76102...(847) 995-6180...Daniel Davison...largest U.S. rail transportation co.

**Campbell Soup Co.**...Campbell Pl., Camden, NJ 08103...(609) 342-4800...David W. Johnson...canned soups, spaghetti (Franco-American), vegetable juice (V-8), pork and beans, pet foods, confections, Swanson frozen dinners, Prego spaghetti sauce, Mrs. Paul's frozen fish, Pepperidge Farm breads.

**Carter-Wallace, Inc.**...1345 Ave. of the Americas, NY, NY 10105...(212) 339-5000...H. H. Hoyt...personal care items, antiperspirants (Arrid), shave lathers (Rise), tooth polish (Pearl Drops), condoms (Trojan), laxatives (Carter's Pills), pet prods. (Victory flea collars).

**Caterpillar Inc.**...100 N.E. Adams St., Peoria, IL 61629...(309) 675-1000...Donald Fites...heavy duty earth-moving equip.

**Chase Manhattan Corp.**...270 Park Ave., NY, NY 10017 ...(212) 270-6000...Walter V. Shipley...the largest U.S. bank holding co.

**Chevron Corp.**...225 Bush St., San Francisco, CA 94104 ...(415) 894-7700...Kenneth T. Derr...integrated oil co.

**Chiquita Brands International, Inc.**...250 E. 5th St., Cincinnati, OH 45202...(513) 784-8000...Carl H. Lindner...bananas, other fruits, vegetables.

**Chrysler Corp.**...Highland Pk., MI 48288...(313) 956-3007...Robert J. Eaton...cars, trucks, auto parts.

**Church & Dwight Co., Inc.**...469 N. Harrison St., Princeton, NJ 08543...(609) 683-5900...D. C. Minton...sodium bicarbonate, consumer prods. (Arm & Hammer).

**CIGNA Corp.**...One Liberty Pl., Philadelphia, PA 19103...(215) 761-1000...Wilson H. Taylor...insurance holding co.

**Circuit City Stores, Inc.**...9950 Maryland Dr., Richmond, VA 23233-1464...(804) 527-4000...Richard L. Sharp...retailer of electronic equip., consumer appliances; used-car lots.

**Circus Circus Enterprises, Inc.**...2880 Las Vegas Blvd. S, Las Vegas, NV 89109...(702) 734-0410...Clyde Turner... casino operator.

**Citicorp**...399 Park Ave., NY, NY 10043...(212) 559-1000...J. S. Reed...2d largest U.S. banking co.

**Liz Claiborne**...1441 Broadway, NY, NY 10018...(212) 354-4900...P. Charron...apparel, accessories, cosmetics.

**Clayton Homes**...PO Box 15169, Knoxville, TN 37901...(615) 970-7200...James L. Clayton...produces & sells manufactured homes.

**Clorox Co.**...1221 Broadway, Oakland, CA 94612...(510) 271-7000...G. Craig Sullivan...retail consumer prods. (Formula 409, Pine-Sol, Kingsford charcoal briquets, Combat and Black Flag insecticides, Hidden Valley Ranch salad dressing, Soft Scrub cleanser).

**Coachman Industries, Inc.**...601 E. Beardsley Ave., Elkhart, IN 46514...(219) 262-0123...Thomas H. Corson...manuf. recreational vehicles.

**Coastal Corp.**...9 Greenway Plaza, Houston, TX 77046...(713) 877-1400...David A. Arledge...oil refineries, natural gas pipeline systems.

**Coca-Cola Co.**...One Coca-Cola Plaza N.W., Atlanta, GA 30313...(404) 676-2121...R. C. Goizueta...soft drinks (Coca-Cola, Sprite, Nestea), syrups, citrus and fruit juices (Minute Maid, Hi-C).

**Colgate-Palmolive Co.**...300 Park Ave., NY, NY 10022...(212) 310-2000...Reuben Mark...soaps (Palmolive, Irish Spring), detergents (Fab, Ajax, Fresh Start), toothpaste (Colgate, Ultra Brite), household prods. (Handy Wipes, Curad bandages), pet food, crystal.

**Columbia/HCA Healthcare Corp.**...One Park Plaza, Nashville, TN 37203...(615) 327-9551...T. F. Frist, Jr....largest hospital mgmt. co. in the U.S.

**Compaq Computer Corp.**...20555 SH 249, Houston, TX 77070...(713) 370-0670...Benjamin M. Rosen...portable and desktop computers.

**ConAgra**...One ConAgra Dr., Omaha, NE 68102...(402) 595-4000...Philip B. Fletcher...2d largest U.S. food processor.

**Adolph Coors Co.**...Golden, CO 80401...(303) 279-6565...William K. Coors...brewer.

**Corning, Inc.**...One Riverfront Plaza, Corning, NY 14831...(607) 974-9000...R. G. Ackerman ...specialty materials, optical fiber and cable, cookware.

**CPC International, Inc.**...International Plaza, Englewood Cliffs, NJ 07632...(201) 894-4000...Charles Shoemate... branded food items (Hellmann's mayonnaise, Best Foods, Mazola corn oil, Skippy peanut butter, Knorr soups, Thomas' English muffins, Mueller pasta prods., Freihofer's Boboli, Arnold breads).

**Crane Co.**...100 First Stamford Pl., Stamford, CT 06902...(203) 363-7300...R. S. Evans...manuf. fluid control devices, vending machines, fiberglass panels, aircraft brakes.

**A. T. Cross Co.**...One Albion Rd., Lincoln, RI 02865...(401) 333-1200...Bradford R. Boss...writing instruments.

**Crown Cork & Seal**...9300 Ashton Rd., Philadelphia, PA 19136...(215) 698-5100...William J. Avery...metal & plastic containers, packaging machinery.

**CSX Corp.**...901 E. Cary St., Richmond, VA 23219...(804) 782-1400...John W. Snow...rail, ocean, barge freight transport.

**Culbro Corp.**...387 Park Ave. S, NY, NY 10016...(212) 448-3800...E. M. Cullman...cigars (Macanudo, Robert Burns, White Owl, Tiparillo's); food, nursery prods., real estate.

**Dana Corp.**...4500 Dorr St., Toledo, OH 43615...(419) 535-4500...Southwood J. Morcott...truck and auto parts, supplies.

**Dayton Hudson Corp.**...777 Nicollet Mall, Minneapolis, MN 55402...(612) 370-6948...Robert J. Ulrich...department, specialty stores.

**Dean Witter, Discover & Co.**...2 World Trade Ctr., NY, NY 10048...(212) 392-2222...Phillip J. Purcell...diversified financial services.

**Deere & Co.**...John Deere Rd., Moline, IL 61265...(309) 765-8000...Hans W. Becherer...farm, industrial, and outdoor power equip.

**Delta Air Lines, Inc.**...Hartsfield Atlanta International Airport, Atlanta, GA 30320...(404) 715-2600...Ronald W. Allen...air transportation.

**Dial Corp.**...1850 N. Central Ave., Phoenix, AZ 85044...(602) 207-4000...Malcolm Jozoff...consumer prods. (Dial, Purex detergents, Armour Star meats, Renuzit air fresheners).

**Diebold, Inc.**...PO Box 8230, Canton, OH 44711...(216) 489-4000...Robert W. Mahoney...manuf. equip. for financial insts.

**Digital Equipment Corp.**...146 Main St., Maynard, MA 01754-2571...(508) 493-5111...R. B. Palmer...automatic teller machine manuf., security systems

**Dillard Dept. Stores, Inc.**...1600 Cantrell Rd., Little Rock, AR 72201...(501) 376-5200...William Dillard...large dept. store chain.

**Walt Disney Co.**...500 S. Buena Vista St., Burbank, CA 91521-7320...(818) 560-1000...Michael D. Eisner...motion pictures, television (ESPN, ABC), radio stations, theme parks (Walt Disney World, Disneyland) and resorts, publishing, recordings, retailing (Disney stores).

**Dole Food Co.**...31365 Oak Crest Dr., Westlake Village, CA 91361...(818) 879-6600...David H. Murdock...food products, fresh fruits and vegetables.

**R. R. Donnelley & Sons Co.**...77 W. Wacker Dr., Chicago, IL 60601-8375...(312) 326-8000...John R. Walter...largest commercial printer.

**Dow Chemical Co.**...2030 Dow Center, Midland, MI 48674...(517) 636-1000...W. Stavrapoulos...chemicals, plastics, consumer prods. (Ziploc, Saran Wrap, Fantastik).

**Dow Jones & Co., Inc.**...200 Liberty St., NY, NY 10281...(212) 416-2000...Peter R. Kann...financial news service, publishing (*Wall Street Journal*, *Barron's*, Ottaway Newspapers).

**Dun & Bradstreet Corp.**...187 Danbury Rd., Wilton, CT 06897...(203) 834-4200...Robert E. Weissman...business information and computer services, publishing. (Co. announced 1/9/96 that it planned to split into 3 companies: Dun & Bradstreet Corp., Cognizant Corp., and ACNielsen Corp.)

**E. I. du Pont de Nemours & Co.**...1007 Market St., Wilmington, DE 19898...(302) 774-1000...Edgar Woolard, Jr....largest U.S. chemical co.; petroleum, consumer prods.

**Eastman Kodak Co.**...343 State St., Rochester, NY 14650...(716) 724-5492...G. Fisher...world's largest producer of photographic prods.

**Eaton Corp.**...1111 Superior Ave., Cleveland, OH 44114...(216) 523-5000...Steven R. Hardis...manuf. of electronic, electrical prods., vehicle components.

**Emerson Electric Co.**...8000 W. Florissant Ave., St. Louis, MO 63136...(314) 553-2000...C. F. Knight...electrical, electronics products & systems.

**Exxon Corp.**...5959 Las Colinas Blvd., Irving, TX 75039-2298...(214) 444-1900...Lee R. Raymond...world's largest publicly owned integrated oil co.

**Fabri-Centers of America, Inc.**...5555 Darrow Rd., Hudson, OH 44236...(216) 656-2600...Alan Rosskamm...specialty fabric stores.

**Fedders Corp.**...PO Box 813, Liberty Corner, NJ 07938...(908) 604-8686...Salvatore Giordano...manuf. of room air-conditioners, dehumidifiers.

**Federal Express Corp.**...Box 727, Memphis, TN 38194 ...(901) 369-3600...F. W. Smith...express delivery service.

**Federal Home Loan Mortgage Corp.**...8200 Jones Branch Dr., McLean, VA 22102...(703) 903-2000...Leland C. Brendsel...residential mortgage provider.

**Federal National Mortgage Assn.**...3900 Wisconsin Ave. NW, Washington, DC 20016...(202) 752-7115...James A. Johnson...largest U.S. provider of residential mortgage funds.

**Federated Dept. Stores**...7 W. 7th St., Cincinnati, OH 45202...(513) 579-7000...Allen Questrom...Macy's, Bloomingdale's, Stern's, dept. stores.

**Fieldcrest Cannon, Inc.**...Eden, NC 27288...(919) 627-3000...James M. Fitzgibbons...household textile prods.

**First Brands Corp.**...83 Wooster Hts. Rd., Danbury, CT 06813-1911...(203) 731-2300...Alfred E. Dudley...consumer prods. (Glad plastic bags, Scoop-Away cat litter, STP auto prods.).

**First Data Corp.**...401 Hackensack Ave., Hackensack, NJ 07601...(201) 525-4702...Henry C. Duques...information processing.

**Fleetwood Enterprises, Inc.**...PO Box 7638, Riverside, CA 92523...(909) 351-3500...John C. Crean...manufactured homes, recreational vehicles.

**Fleming Cos., Inc.**...6301 Waterford Blvd., PO Box 26647, Oklahoma City, OK 73126...(405) 840-7200...Robert E. Stauth...largest U.S. wholesale food distrib.

**Fluor Corp.**...3333 Michelson Dr., Irvine, CA 92730...(714) 975-6961...L. G. McCraw...engineering and construction.

**Ford Motor Co.**...American Rd., Dearborn, MI 48121...(313) 845-8540...Alexander Trotman...motor vehicles (Ford Tractor, Lincoln-Mercury), rentals (Budget Rent A Car).

**Fruit of the Loom, Inc.**...5000 Sears Tower, Chicago, IL 60606...(312) 876-1724...William Farley...manuf. of underwear, activewear.

**Gannett Co., Inc.**...1100 Wilson Blvd., Arlington, VA 22234...(703) 284-6000...J. J. Curley...newspaper publishing (*USA Today*), TV, CATV, and radio stations, TV show prod., home security systems, outdoor advertising.

**The Gap, Inc.**...One Harrison, San Francisco, CA 94105...(415) 952-4400...D. G. Fisher...casual and activewear retailer.

**General Dynamics Corp.**...3190 Fairview Park Dr., Falls Church, VA 22042-4523...(703) 876-3000...J. R. Mellor...nuclear submarines, armored vehicles, warships.

**General Electric Co.**...3135 Easton Tpke., Fairfield, CT 06431...(203) 373-2211...J. F. Welch Jr. ...electrical, electronic equip., radio and television broadcasting (NBC), aircraft engines, power generation, appliances.

**General Host Corp.**...PO Box 10045, Stamford, CT 06904...(203) 357-9900...Harris J. Ashton...crafts, lawn and garden retail stores (Frank's Nursery & Crafts).

**General Mills, Inc.**...PO Box 1113, Minneapolis, MN 55440...(612) 540-2444...S. W. Sanger...foods (Total, Bisquick, Wheaties, Cheerios, Hamburger Helper, Betty Crocker).

**General Motors Corp.**...3044 W. Grand Blvd., Detroit, MI 48202-3091...(313) 556-5000...John F. Smith Jr. ...world's largest auto manuf.

**Genuine Parts Co.**...2999 Circle 75 Pkwy., Atlanta, GA 30339...(404) 953-1700...Larry L. Prince...distributes auto replacement parts (NAPA).

**Georgia-Pacific Corp.**...133 Peachtree St. NE, Atlanta, GA 30303...(404) 521-5210...A. D. Correll...world's largest manuf. of paper and wood prods.

**Gillette Co.**...Prudential Tower Bldg., Boston, MA 02199...(617) 421-7000...Alfred Zeien...razors, pens (Paper Mate), toiletries (Right Guard deodorants, Foamy shaving cream), hair products (Adorn), household appliances (Braun). (Co. announced 9/12/96 that it had agreed to acquire Duracell Intl. Inc.)

**Goodyear Tire & Rubber Co.**...1144 E. Market St., Akron, OH 44316...(216) 796-8576...Samir F. Gibara...world's largest rubber manuf.; tires and other auto products.

**W. R. Grace & Co.**...One Town Center Rd., Boca Raton, FL 33486...(407) 362-2000...Albert J. Costello...chemicals, construction prods.

**Great Atlantic & Pacific Tea Co. (A&P)**...2 Paragon Dr., Montvale, NJ 07645...(201) 573-9700...James Wood ...supermarkets.

**GTE Corp.**...One Stamford Forum, Stamford, CT 06904 ...(203) 965-2000...Charles R. Lee...large U.S. local-exchange telephone co., cellular telephone operator.

**Halliburton Co.**...500 N. Akard St., Dallas, TX 75201...(214) 978-2600...Richard Cheney...energy, engineering, and construction services.

**Harley-Davidson, Inc.**...3700 W. Juneau Ave., Milwaukee, WI 53208...(414) 342-4680...R. F. Teerlink...manuf. of motorcycles, parts & accessories.

**Harrah's Entertainment, Inc.**...1023 Cherry Rd., Memphis, TN 38117...(901) 762-8600...Michael D. Rose...casino-hotels.

**Hartmarx**...101 N. Wacker Dr., Chicago, IL 60606...(312) 372-6300...Elbert O. Hand...apparel manufacturer (Hickey Freeman, Hart Schaffner & Marx, Pierre Cardin, Perry Ellis).

**Hasbro, Inc.**...1027 Newport Ave., Pawtucket, RI 02862 ...(401) 431-8697...A. G. Hassenfeld...toy and game manuf. & marketer (Milton Bradley, Playskool, G. I. Joe, Parker Bros., Tonka trucks, Play-Doh).

**H. J. Heinz Co.**...PO Box 57, Pittsburgh, PA 15230...(412) 456-6014...Anthony J. F. O'Reilly...foods (Star-Kist, Ore-Ida, '57 Varieties), pet food (9 Lives), Weight Watchers.

**Hershey Foods Corp.**...100 Crystal A Dr., Hershey, PA 17033...(717) 534-6799...Kenneth Wolfe...chocolate & confectionery prods. (Reese's, Kit Kat, Peter Paul Mounds, Almond Joy), pasta (San Giorgio, Ronzoni).

**Hewlett-Packard Co.**...3000 Hanover St., Palo Alto, CA 94304...(415) 857-1501...Lewis E. Platt...manuf. computers, electronic prods. and systems.

**Hillenbrand Industries, Inc.**...700 State Rte. 46, Batesville, IN 47006...(812) 934-7000...D. A. Hillenbrand...manuf. caskets, electronically operated hospital beds, locks.

**Hilton Hotels Corp.**...9336 Civic Center Dr., Beverly Hills, CA 90120...(310) 278-4321...Barron Hilton...casinos, hotels. (Co. announced 6/6/96 that it had agreed to acquire Bally Entertainment Corp.)

**Home Depot, Inc.**...2727 Paces Ferry Rd., Atlanta, GA 30339...(404) 433-8211...Bernard Marcus...retailer of building materials & home improvement prods.

**Honeywell, Inc.**...Honeywell Plaza, Minneapolis, MN 55408...(612) 951-1000...Michael Bonsignore...industrial and home control systems, aerospace guidance systems, information systems.

**Hormel Foods Corp.**...PO Box 800, Austin, MN 55912...(507) 437-5611...R. Knowlton...meat packaging, pork and beef prods. (SPAM, Dinty Moore, Mary Kitchen).

**Houghton Mifflin Co.**...222 Berkeley St., Boston, MA 02116...(617) 351-5000...Nader F. Darehshori...book publisher of educational and reference books.

**Huffy Corp.**...7701 Byers Rd., Miamisburg, OH 45342...(513) 866-6251...Richard L. Molen...bicycles, sports and hardware equip.

**Humana, Inc.**...500 W. Main St., Louisville, KY 40201-1438...(502) 580-1000...David A. Jones...provides health care plans, financial services.

**IBP, Inc.**...IBP Ave., PO Box 515, Dakota City, NE 68731...(402) 494-2061...Robert Peterson...world's largest processor of fresh beef and pork.

**Ingersoll-Rand Co.**...Woodcliff Lake, NJ 07675...(201) 573-0123...J. E. Perella...industrial machinery.

**Intel Corp.**...2200 Mission College Blvd., Santa Clara, CA 95052-8119...(408) 765-8080...G. E. Moore...manuf. integrated circuits (Pentium).

**International Business Machines Corp. (IBM)**...One Old Orchard Rd., Armonk, NY 10504...(914) 765-1900...Louis V. Gerstner Jr....information processing systems, equip., services.

**International Paper Co.**...2 Manhattanville Rd., Purchase, NY 10577...(914) 397-1500...John T. Dillon...paper and wood prods., films, chemicals, minerals.

**Interstate Brands Corp.**...12 E. Armour Blvd., Kansas City, MO 64111...(816) 502-4000...Charles A. Sullivan...baked goods wholesaler, distributor (Wonder, Hostess, Dolly Madison).

**ITT Corp.**...1330 Ave. of the Americas, NY, NY 10022...(212) 258-1000...Rand V. Araskog...casinos and hotels (Caesars, Desert Inn, Sheraton), educational, informational services.

**Johnson Controls**...5757 N. Green Bay Ave., Milwaukee, WI 53201...(414) 228-1200...James H. Keyes...fire protection services, auto seats and batteries, beverage containers.

**Johnson & Johnson**...501 George St., New Brunswick, NJ 08903...(908) 524-0400...Ralph S. Larsen...surgical dressings (Band-Aid), pharmaceuticals (Tylenol), toiletries.

**Jostens, Inc.**...5501 Norman Center Dr., Minneapolis, MN 55437...(612) 830-3300...Robert P. Jensen...school rings, yearbooks, plaques, pictures.

**Kellogg Co.**...One Kellogg Sq., Battle Creek, MI 49016...(616) 961-2000...Arnold G. Langbo...ready-to-eat cereals & other food prods. (Frosted Flakes, Rice Krispies, Froot Loops, Pop Tarts, Nutri-Grain, Eggo).

**Kimberly-Clark Corp.**...PO Box 619100, Dallas, TX 75261-9100...(214) 281-1200...Wayne R. Sanders...paper and lumber prods., consumer prods. (Kleenex, Scott, Huggies, Kotex).

**King World Productions, Inc.**...1700 Broadway, NY, NY 10019...(212) 315-4000...Roger King...syndicator of TV programs (*Oprah Winfrey Show, Wheel of Fortune, Jeopardy!, Inside Edition, American Journal*).

**Kmart Corp.**...3100 W. Big Beaver Rd., Troy, MI 48084...(810) 643-1000...Floyd Hall...operates chain of discount stores, home improvement retail stores.

**Knight-Ridder, Inc.**...One Herald Plaza, Miami, FL 33101...(305) 376-3838...P. A. Ridder...newspaper publishing, book publishing.

**Kroger Co.**...1014 Vine St., Cincinnati, OH 45202...(513) 762-4000...Joseph A. Pichler...largest U.S. grocery chain.

**(Estee) Lauder Cos.**...767 5th Ave., NY, NY 10153...(212) 572-4200...Leonard A. Lauder...cosmetics, fragrance prods.

**La-Z-Boy Chair Co.**...1284 N. Telegraph Rd., Monroe, MI 48161...(313) 242-1444...Charles T. Knabusch...reclining chairs, other furniture.

**Leggett & Platt, Inc.**...No. 1 Leggett Rd., Carthage, MO 64836...(417) 358-8131...Harry M. Cornell Jr. ...furniture and related products.

**Lehman Bros. Holdings, Inc.**...3 World Financial Ctr., NY, NY 10285...(212) 526-7000...Richard S. Fuld, Jr.,...investment banker.

**Levi Strauss Associates**...1155 Battery St., San Francisco, CA 94111...(415) 544-6000...Robert D. Haas...blue jeans, casual apparel.

**Eli Lilly & Company**...Lilly Corp. Center, Indianapolis, IN 46285...(317) 276-2000...R. L. Tobias...manuf. pharmaceuticals (Prozac) and animal health products.

**The Limited, Inc.**...3 Limited Pkwy., Columbus, OH 43216...(614) 479-7000...Leslie H. Wexner...women's apparel stores (Lane Bryant, Lerner, Victoria's Secret), Abercrombie & Fitch, other retailers.

**Litton Industries, Inc.**...21240 Burbank Blvd., Woodland Hills, CA 91367...(818) 598-5000...John M. Leonis...industrial systems & services, advanced electronic systems, electronic & electrical prods., marine engineering.

**Lockheed Martin Corp.**...6801 Rockledge Dr., Bethesda, MD 20817...(301) 897-6000...Daniel M. Tellep...commercial and military aircraft, electronics, missiles.

**Loews Corp.**...667 Madison Ave., NY, NY 10021...(212) 545-2000...Laurence A. Tisch...tobacco prods. (Kent, Newport, True), watches (Bulova), hotels, insurance, offshore drilling.

**Longs Drug Stores, Inc.**...141 North Civic Dr., Walnut Creek, CA 94596...(510) 937-1170...R. M. Long...drug store chain.

**Lowe's Cos., Inc.**...Box 1111, N. Wilkesboro, NC 28656...(910) 651-4000...R. L. Strickland...retailer of building materials & related prods.

**Luby's Cafeterias, Inc.**...2211 Northeast Loop 410, San Antonio, TX 78265...(210) 654-9000...Ralph Erben...operates cafeterias in south and southwest U.S.

**Lucent Technologies, Inc.**...600 Mountain Ave., Murray Hill, NJ 07974...(908) 582-8500...Henry B. Schact...leading developer, designer, and manuf. of telecommunications systems, software, and products.

**Manor Care, Inc.**...10750 Columbia Pike, Silver Spring, MD 20901...(301) 681-9400...S. Bainum, Jr....operates nursing homes, pharmacies.

**Manpower Inc.**...5301 N. Ironwood Rd., Milwaukee, WI 53217 ...(414) 961-1000...Mitchell S. Fromstein...employment services.

**Marriott International, Inc.**...Marriott Dr., Washington, DC 20058...(301) 380-9000...John Willard Marriott, Jr....hotels, food service.

**Masco Corp.**...21001 Van Born Rd., Taylor, MI 48180...(313) 274-7400...Richard A. Manoogian...manuf. kitchen, bathroom prods. (Delta faucets, Fieldstone cabinets).

**Mattel, Inc.**...333 Continental Blvd., El Segundo, CA 90245...(213) 524-2000...J. W. Amerman...toy & hobby prods. (Barbie dolls, Fisher-Price, Hot Wheels).

**May Department Stores Co.**...611 Olive St., St. Louis, MO 63101...(314) 342-6300...David Farrell...department stores (Hecht's, Lord & Taylor, Foley's).

**Maytag Corp.**...Newton, IA 50208...(515) 792-8000...Leonard A. Hadley...manuf. home laundry equip., appliances (Magic Chef, Admiral, Hoover).

**McDonald's Corp.**...One McDonald's Plaza, Oak Brook, IL 60521 ...(708) 575-7428...Michael R. Quinlan...fast-food restaurants.

**McDonnell Douglas Corp.**...PO Box 516, St. Louis, MO 63166-0516...(314) 232-0232...John F. McDonnell...commercial & military aircraft, space systems & missiles.

**McGraw-Hill Cos.**...1221 Ave. of the Americas, NY, NY 10020...(212) 512-2000...Joseph L. Dionne...book, magazine publishing (*Business Week*), information & financial services (Standard and Poor's), TV stations.

**MCI Communications Corp.**...1801 Pennsylvania Ave., Washington, DC 20006...(202) 887-2028...Bert C. Roberts, Jr....2d largest U.S. long-distance telephone carrier.

**McKesson Corp.**...1 Post St., San Fransicso, CA 94104...(415) 983-8300...Alan Seelenfreund...drugs, toiletries, car-care prods. (Armor All), bottled water.

**Mead Corporation**...Courthouse Plaza NE, Dayton, OH 45463 ...(513) 495-6323...Steven C. Mason...printing and writing paper, paperboard, packaging, shipping containers.

**Media General, Inc.**...333 E. Grace St., Richmond, VA 23219...(804) 649-6000...J. S. Bryan...TV and CATV broadcasting, newspaper publishing.

**Medtronic, Inc.**...7000 Central Ave. NE, Minneapolis, MN 55432...(612) 574-4000...W. W. George...manuf. prosthetic and pacemaker devices.

**Melville Corp.**...One Theall Rd., Rye, NY 10580...(914) 925-4000...Stanley P. Goldstein...shoe stores (Foot Action, Thom McAn), apparel (Bob's), drug stores (CVS).

**Merck & Co., Inc.**...PO Box 100, Whitehouse Station, NJ 08889-0100...(908) 423-1000...Raymond V. Gilmartin...human & animal health care prods.

**Meredith Corp.**...1716 Locust St., Des Moines, IA 50336...(515) 284-3000...Jack D. Rehm...magazine publishing (*Better Homes and Gardens, Ladies Home Journal*), book publishing, broadcasting.

**Merrill Lynch & Co., Inc.**...World Financial Ctr., N. Tower, NY, NY 10281-1332...(212) 449-1000...Daniel P. Tully ...securities broker, financial services.

**Metropolitan Life Ins. Co.**...1 Madison Ave., NY, NY 10010-3690...(212) 578-2211...Harry P. Kamen...insurance, financial services.

**Microsoft Corp.**...One Microsoft Way, Redmond, WA 98052-6399...(206) 882-8080...William H. Gates...the world's largest computer software company (Windows 95, Word, Excel).

**Minnesota Mining & Manuf. Co.**...3M Center, St. Paul, MN 55144-1000...(612) 733-1110...L. D. DeSimone...abrasives, adhesives, building services & chemicals, recording materials; electrical, health care, cleaning, printing, consumer prods. (Scotch Tape, Post-It).

**Mirage Resorts, Inc.**...3400 Las Vegas Blvd. S, Las Vegas, NV 89109...(702) 385-7111...Stephen A. Wynn...hotel-casino operator (Mirage, Treasure Island, Golden Nugget).

**Mobil Corp.**...3225 Gallows Rd., Fairfax, VA 22037...(703) 846-3000...Lucio A. Noto...integrated international oil and petrochemical co.

**Monsanto Company**...800 N. Lindbergh Blvd., St. Louis, MO 63167...(314) 694-1000...Robert B. Shapiro...chemicals, agricultural prods., pharmaceuticals, consumer prods. (Nutra-Sweet, Equal).

**J. P. Morgan & Co.**...60 Wall St., NY, NY 10260...(212) 483-2323...D. Warner...large bank.

**Motorola, Inc.**...1303 E. Algonquin Rd., Schaumburg, IL 60196...(847) 576-5000...W. J. Weisz...electronic equipment and components.

**National Semiconductor Corp.**...2900 Semiconductor Dr., Santa Clara, CA 95052-8090...(408) 721-5000...Charles-Halla ...manuf. of semiconductors, integrated circuits.

**NationsBank**...NationsBank Corporate Center, Charlotte, NC 28255...(704) 386-5000...Hugh L. McColl Jr. ...commercial bank.

**Navistar Intl. Corp.**...455 N. Cityfront Plaza Dr., Chicago, IL 60611...(312) 836-2000...John R. Horne...manuf. heavy duty trucks, parts.

**New York Times Co.**...229 W. 43d St., NY, NY 10036...(212) 556-3660...A. O. Sulzberger...newspapers, radio station, TV stations, magazines (*Tennis, Golf Digest*).

**Nike, Inc.**...One Bowerman Dr., Beaverton, OR 97005...(503) 671-6453...Philip Knight...athletic & leisure footware, apparel.

**Nordstrom, Inc.**...1501 5th Ave., Seattle, WA 98101...(206) 628-2111...John A. McMillan; Bruce A., John N., and James F. Nordstrom...upscale dept. store chain.

**Norfolk Southern Corp.**...3 Commercial Pl., Norfolk, VA 23510...(804) 629-2640...David R. Goode...operates railways, freight carrier (North American Van Lines).

**Northrop Grumman Corp.**...1840 Century Park East, Los Angeles, CA 90067...(213) 553-6262...Kent Kresa...aircraft, electronics, communications, missiles.

**Northwest Airlines**...2700 Lone Oak Pkwy., Eagan, MN 55121...(612) 726-2111...John H. Dasburg...air transportation.

**NYNEX Corp.**...1095 Ave. of the Americas, NY, NY 10036...(212) 370-7400...I. G. Seidenberg...telephone co. in northeast U.S. (Bell Atlantic Corp. announced 6/26/96 that it had agreed to acquired NYNEX Corp.)

**Occidental Petroleum Corp.**...10889 Wilshire Blvd., Los Angeles, CA 90024...(213) 879-1700...Ray R. Irani...oil, natural gas, chemicals, fertilizers.

**Office Depot, Inc.**...2200 Old Germantown Rd., Delray Beach, FL 33445...(407) 278-4800...David Fuente...retail office supply stores. (Co. announced 9/4/96 that it had agreed to merge with Staples, Inc., to form a new co. to be called Staples/Office Depot Inc.)

**Outboard Marine Corp.**...100 Sea-Horse Dr., Waukegan, IL 60085...(708) 689-6200...H. W. Bowman...outboard motors (Evinrude, Johnson), boats.

**Owens-Corning Fiberglas Corp.**...Fiberglas Tower, Toledo, OH 43659...(419) 248-8000...Glen H. Hiner...glass fiber and related prods., roofing materials.

**Oxford Industries, Inc.**...222 Piedmont Ave. NE, Atlanta, GA 30308...(404) 659-2424...J. Hicks Lanier...manuf. men's and women's apparel.

**Pacific Gas & Electric Co.**...77 Beale St., San Francisco, CA 94106...(800) 367-7731...Stanley T. Skinner...energy supplier.

**PaineWebber Group, Inc.**...1285 Ave. of the Americas, NY, NY 10019-6028...Donald Marron...controls full-service securities firm.

**J. C. Penney Co.**...6501 Legacy Dr., Plano, TX 75024...(214) 431-1000...James E. Oesterreicher...dept. stores, catalog sales, drug stores, insurance.

**Pennzoil Co.**...PO Box 2967, Houston, TX 77252-8000...(713) 546-4000...J. L. Pate...integrated oil and gas co.

**PepsiCo, Inc.**...PepsiCo World HQ, Purchase, NY 10577 ...(914) 253-2000...D. W. Calloway...soft drinks (Pepsi-Cola, Mountain Dew, Slice), snack foods (Ruffles, Lay's, Doritos), restaurants (Pizza Hut, KFC, Taco Bell).

**Pfizer, Inc.**...235 E. 42d St., NY, NY 10017...(212) 573-2323...W. C. Steere, Jr....pharmaceutical, hospital, agricultural, chemical prods., consumer prods. (Visine eye drops, Ben-Gay pain relief).

**Pharmacia & Upjohn, Inc.**...700 Portage Rd., Kalamazoo, MI 49001...(616) 323-4000...Jan Ekberg...pharmaceuticals (Motrin, Rogaine, Halcion), chemicals, agricultural, health-care prods.

**Philip Morris Cos., Inc.**...120 Park Ave., NY, NY 10017...(212) 880-5000...Geoffrey C. Bible...cigarettes (Marlboro, Virginia Slims), beer (Miller brands), packaged foods (Jell-O, Entenmann baked goods, Maxwell House coffee, Kool-Aid, Oscar Mayer meats, Tang, Kraft, Cheez Whiz & Velveeta cheese prods, Post cereals).

**Phillips Petroleum Co.**...Bartlesville, OK 74004...(918) 661-6600...W. W. Allen...integrated oil and chemical co.

**Pitney Bowes, Inc.**...1 Elmcroft Rd., Stamford, CT 06926-0700...(203) 356-5000...George B. Harvey...postage meters, mail-handling equip.

**Playboy Enterprises, Inc.**...680 N. Lake Shore Dr., Chicago, IL 60611...(312) 751-8000...Christie Hefner...magazine publishing, CATV, merchandising.

**Polaroid Corp.**...Technology Sq., Cambridge, MA 02139 ...(617) 386-2000...Gary T. DiCamillo...photographic equip., supplies, and optical goods.

**PPG Industries, Inc.**...One PPG Place, Pittsburgh, PA 15272...(412) 434-3131...Jerry E. Dempsey...glass prods., paints, chemicals.

**Premark Intl., Inc.**...1717 Deerfield Rd., Deerfield, IL 60015...(708) 405-6000...Warren L. Batts...food equip., home appliances, cookware.

**Price/Costco, Inc.**...999 Lake Dr., Issaquah, WA 98027...(206) 313-8100...J. H. Brotman...wholesale cash-and-carry stores.

**Procter & Gamble Co.**...One Procter & Gamble Plaza, Cincinnati, OH 45202...(513) 983-1100...John Pepper...soaps & detergents (Ivory, Cheer, Tide, Mr. Clean, Comet, Spic and Span, Zest), toiletries (Crest toothpaste, Prell, Head and Shoulders shampoos, Noxzema, Oil of Olay, Old Spice), pharmaceuticals (Pepto-Bismol); Pampers disposable diapers, Folger's coffee, Hawaiian Punch, Charmin toilet tissues, Bounty towels, Vicks cough medicines, Crisco shortening, Duncan Hines cakes.

**Prudential Ins. Co. of America**...751 Broad St., Newark, NJ 07102-3777...(201) 802-6000...Arthur F. Ryan...insurance, financial services.

**Quaker Oats Co.**...Quaker Tower, PO Box 9001, Chicago, IL 60604...(312) 222-7818...William D. Smithburg...cereal (Quaker Oat Bran, Life, Cap'n Crunch), foods (Aunt Jemima, Celeste pizza, Rice-A-Roni), beverages (Gatorade, Snapple).

**Quaker State Corp.**...255 E. John Carpenter Fwy., Irving, TX 75062...(214) 868-0438...Herbert M. Baum...refining, marketing petroleum prods., filters, antifreeze, quick-change oil centers.

**Ralcorp Holdings, Inc.**...800 Market St., St. Louis, MO 63101...(314) 977-7000...Richard A. Pearce...snack foods, baby food (Beech-Nut).

**Ralston Purina Co.**...Checkerboard Sq., St. Louis, MO 63164...(314) 982-2161...W. K. Stiritz...pet and livestock food (Purina), batteries (Eveready, Energizer).

**Raytheon Co.**...141 Spring St., Lexington, MA 02173...(617) 862-6600...Dennis J. Picard...electronics, aviation, appliances; Amana Refrigeration, Beech Aircraft.

**Reader's Digest Assn., Inc.**...Pleasantville, NY 10570...(914) 238-1000...James P. Schadt...magazines, books, home entertainment prods.

**Reebok Intl., Ltd.**...100 Technology Ctr. Dr., Stoughton, MA 02072...(617) 341-5000...P. Fireman...athletic & casual footwear, sportswear.

**Reynolds Metals Co.**...6601 W. Broad St., Richmond, VA 23230...(804) 281-2000...Richard G. Holder...aluminum prods.

**Rite Aid Corp.**...PO Box 3165, Harrisburg, PA 17105...(717) 761-2633...Martin Grass...discount drug, beauty aid stores.

**RJR Nabisco Holdings Corp.**...1301 Ave. of the Americas, NY, NY 10019...(212) 258-5600...Steven F. Goldstone...cigarettes (Winston, Salem, Camel), foods (Oreos, Ritz crackers).

**Rockwell Intl. Corp.**...2201 Seal Beach Blvd., seal Beach, CA 90740...(412) 565-2000...D. R. Beall...diversified high-technology co.

**Rubbermaid Inc.**...1147 Akron Rd., Wooster, OH 44691...(330) 264-6464...Wolfgang R. Schmitt...rubber and plastic consumer prods.

**Ryder System, Inc.**...3600 NW 82d Ave., Miami, FL 33166...(305) 593-3726...M. Anthony Burns...truck-leasing service.

**Safeway Inc.**...5918 Stoneridge Mall Rd., Pleasanton, CA 94588-3229...(510) 467-3000...Steven A. Burd...supermarkets.

**Saloman Inc.**...7 World Trade Ctr., NY, NY 10048...(212) 783-7000...Robert E. Denham...investment banking, securities and commodities trading, oil refining.

**Sara Lee Corp.**...3 First National Plaza, Chicago, IL 60602...(312) 726-2600...John H. Bryan Jr. ...baked goods, fresh and processed meats (Ball Park, Hillshire Farms), fresh and frozen fruits and vegetables and other packaged foods, beverages; hosiery, intimate apparel and knitwear (Hanes, L'eggs, Playtex, Isotoner).

**SBC Communications**...PO Box 2933, San Antonio, TX 78299...(210) 351-2044...E. Whitacre Jr. ...telephone services.

**Schering-Plough Corp.**...One Giralda Farms, Madison, NJ 07940...(201) 822-7000...R. P. Luciano...pharmaceuticals, consumer prods.

**Sears, Roebuck & Co.**...3333 Beverly Rd., Hoffman Estates, IL 60179...(847) 286-2500...Arthur Martinez...department, specialty stores.

**Service Merchandise Co, Inc.**...PO Box 24600, Nashville, TN 37202-4600...(615) 660-6000...Raymond Zimmerman... operates catalog showrooms.

**Shaw Industries, Inc.**...616 E. Walnut Ave., Dalton, GA 30720...(706) 278-3812...Robert E. Shaw...largest domestic manuf. of carpeting (Armstrong, Magee, Philadelphia).

**Sherwin-Williams Co.**...101 Prospect Ave. NW, Cleveland, OH 44115...(216) 566-2000...John G. Breen...paint manuf. (Dutch Boy, Kem-Tone), retailer.

**Skyline Corp.**...2520 By-Pass Rd., Elkhart, IN 46515...(219) 294-6521...Arthur J. Decio...manufactured housing and recreational vehicles.

**J. M. Smucker Co.**...Strawberry Lane, Orrville, OH 44667 ...(216) 682-3000...T. P. Smucker...preserves, jams, jellies, toppings, frozen desserts, juices.

**Sprint Corp.**...PO Box 11315 Plaza Station, Kansas City, MO 64112...(913) 624-3000...W. T. Esrey...long-distance and local telecommunications.

**State Farm Group**...1 State Farm Plaza, Bloomington, IL 61710...(309) 766-2311...Edward B. Rust Jr. ...major insurance co.

**Stone Container**...150 N. Michigan Ave., Chicago, IL 60601...(312) 346-6600...R. W. Stone...corrugated containers, paper bags and sacks.

**Stride Rite Corp.**...5 Cambridge Center, Cambridge, MA 02142...(617) 491-8800...Robert Siegel...adult's and children's footwear (Keds).

**Sun Company, Inc.**...1801 Market St., Philadelphia, PA 19103-1699...(215) 977-3000...R. H. Campbell...energy resources co.

**Sun Microsystems, Inc.**...2550 Garcia Ave., Mountain View, CA 94043...(415) 960-1300...Scott G. McNealy...supplier of network-based distributed computer systems (Java programming language).

**SUPERVALU, Inc.**...PO Box 990, Minneapolis, MN 55440...(612) 828-4000...Michael W. Wright...food wholesaler, retailer.

**Sysco Corp.**...1390 Enclave Parkway, Houston, TX 77077-2099...(713) 584-1390...John F. Baugh...leading food distributor.

**Tambrands Inc.**...777 Westchester Ave., White Plains, NY 10604...(914) 696-6000...Howard Wentz...feminine hygiene products (Tampax, Maxthins).

**Tandy Corp.**...1800 One Tandy Center, Fort Worth, TX 76102...(817) 390-3700...J. Y. Roach...consumer electronics retailing (Computer City, Radio Shack).

**Tenneco, Inc.**...PO Box 2511, Houston, TX 77252...(713) 757-2131...Dana G. Mead...natural gas pipelines, shipbuilding, packaging materials, automotive parts.

**Texaco Inc.**...2000 Westchester Ave., White Plains, NY 10650...(914) 253-4000...P. I. Bijur...integrated international oil co.

**Texas Instruments Inc.**...13500 N. Central Expressway, Dallas, TX 75265...(214) 995-3773...T. J. Engibous... electronics.

**Textron, Inc.**...40 Westminster St., Providence, RI 02903...(401) 421-2800...J. F. Hardymon...aerospace, consumer, industrial, automotive prods., financial services.

**Tiffany & Co.**...727 5th Ave., NY, NY 10022...(212) 755-8000...W. R. Chaney...designs, manuf., and distributes fine jewelry & gift items.

**Times Mirror Publishing Co.**...Times Mirror Sq., Los Angeles, CA 90053...(213) 237-3700...R. F. Erburu...newspapers, magazines (*Field & Stream*, *Popular Science*), books.

**Time Warner, Inc.**...75 Rockefeller Plaza, NY, NY 10020...(212) 522-1212...Gerald M. Levin...magazine publishing (*Time*, *Sports Illustrated*, *Fortune*, *Money*, *People*, DC Comics), TV and CATV (WB Network, HBO, Cinemax, CNN, TBS, TNT), book publishing (Little, Brown; Warner Books), motion pictures (Warner Bros.), recordings, Six Flags theme parks, sports teams, professional wrestling.

**Tootsie Roll Industries, Inc.**...7401 S. Cicero Ave., Chicago, IL 60629...(312) 838-3400...M. J. Gordon...candy (Tootsie Roll, Mason Dots, Charms, Sugar Daddy, Charleston Chew).

**Toro Co.**...8111 Lyndale Ave. S, Bloomington, MN 55420...(612) 888-8801...Kendrick B. Melrose...lawn and turf maintenance (Lawn-Boy), snow removal equipment.

**Toys "R" Us**...461 From Rd., Paramus, NJ 07652...(201) 262-7800...Charles Lazarus...toy, clothing stores (Kids "R" Us).

**Transamerica Corp.**...600 Montgomery St., San Francisco, CA 94111...(415) 983-4000...James R. Harvey...insurance, financial services.

**Travelers Group, Inc.**...388 Greenwich St., NY, NY 10022...(212) 816-8000...Sanford I. Weill...insurance, financial services.

**Tribune Co.**...435 N. Michigan Ave., Chicago, IL 60611...(312) 222-9100...J. W. Madigan...newspaper and book publishing, broadcasting, Chicago Cubs baseball team.

**Trinity Industries, Inc.**...2525 Stemmons Freeway, Dallas, TX 75207...(214) 631-4420...W. Ray Wallace...manufactures metal products, rail service.

**TRW Inc.**...1900 Richmond Rd., Cleveland, OH 44124...(216) 291-7000...J. T. Gorman...car and truck operations, electronics, and space systems, credit information provider.

**Tyson Foods, Inc.**...2210 W. Oaklawn, Springdale, AR 72764...(501) 756-4000...Leland Tollett...fresh and processed poultry and other meat prods. (Holly Farms, Weaver).

**UAL Corp.**...1200 E. Algonquin Rd., Elk Grove Township, IL 60007...(708) 952-4000...Gerald Greenwald...air transportation (United Airlines).

**Union Carbide Corp.**...39 Old Ridgebury Rd., Danbury, CT 06817...(203) 794-2000...W. H. Joyce...chemicals.

**Union Pacific Corp.**...Martin Tower, 8th & Eaton Aves., Bethlehem, PA 18018...(215) 861-3200...Drew Lewis...railroad, trucking.

**Unisys Corp.**...PO Box 500, Blue Bell, PA 19424-0001...(215) 986-5777...James A. Unruh...designs, manuf. computer information systems and related products.

**United HealthCare Corp.**...9900 Bren Rd. East, Minnetonka, MN 55343...(612) 936-1300...William W. McGuire...owns, manages health maintenance organizations.

**United Parcel Service of America, Inc.**...55 Glenlake Pkwy. NE, Atlanta, GA 30328...(404) 828-6000...Kent C. Nelson...courier services, truck rentals.

**United Technologies Corp.**...Hartford, CT 06101...(203) 728-7000...George David... aerospace, industrial prods. & services (Carrier Corp., Otis Elevator, Pratt & Whitney, Sikorsky Aircraft).

**Unocal Corp.**...2141 Rosencrans Ave., Ste. 400, El Segundo, CA 90245...(310) 726-7667...Robert Beach...oil, chemicals, geothermal energy.

**USAir Group, Inc.**...2345 Crystal Dr., Arlington, VA 22202...(703) 418-7000...Stephen M. Wolf...major domestic air carrier, other aviation subsidiaries.

**UST Inc.**...100 W. Putnam Ave., Greenwich, CT 06830...(203) 661-1100...Vincent A. Gierer Jr. ...smokeless tobacco (Copenhagen, Skoal, Happy Days), pipe tobacco, wines.

**USX-Marathon Group**...600 Grant St., Pittsburgh, PA 15230...(412) 433-1121...Thomas J. Usher...integrated oil co.

**V.F. Corp.**...1047 N. Park Rd., Wyomissing, PA 19610...(610) 378-1151...L. R. Pugh...apparel (Lee, Wrangler jeans, Vanity Fair, Jantzen).

**Viacom, Inc.**...200 Elm St., Dedham, MA 02026...(617) 461-1600...Sumner M. Redstone...TV broadcast stations and cable systems, channels (Showtime, MTV); book publishing (Simon & Schuster); produces, distr. movies, TV shows (Paramount); video rental stores (Blockbuster).

**Walgreen Co.**...200 Wilmot Rd., Deerfield, IL 60015...(847) 914-2500...Charles R. Walgreen 3d...retail drug chain.

**Wal-Mart Stores, Inc.**...Box 116, Bentonville, AR 72716...(501) 273-4000...S. Robson Walton...retail dept. and discount stores (Sam's Wholesale Clubs).

**Warner-Lambert Co.**...201 Tabor Rd., Morris Plains, NJ 07950-2693...(201) 540-2000...M. R. Goodes...health care prods. (Benadryl), consumer prods. (Efferdent dental cleanser, Halls cough tablets, Schick razors, Certs mints, Listerine mouthwash, Trident, Chicklets, Dentyne gums).

**Washington Post Co.**...1150 15th St. NW, Washington, DC 20071...(202) 334-6000...D. E. Graham...newspapers, magazines (*Newsweek*), TV and CATV stations.

**Wells Fargo & Co.**...420 Montgomery St., San Francisco, CA 94163...(415) 396-3606...P. Hazen...banking.

**Wendy's Intl., Inc.**...4288 W. Dublin-Granville Rd., Dublin, OH 43017...(614) 764-3100...Gordon F. Teter...quick-service restaurants.

**Westinghouse Electric Corp.**...11 Stanwix St., Pittsburgh, PA 15222...(412) 244-2000...Michael H. Jordan...manuf. electrical, mechanical equip.; radio and television stations (CBS); power generation, communications, information services.

**Weyerhaeuser Co.**...Tacoma, WA 98477...(206) 924-2345...George H. Weyerhaeuser...manuf., distrib. paper and wood prods.

**Whirlpool Corp.**...Benton Harbor, MI 49022...(616) 923-5000...David Whitwam...major home appliances manuf.

**Whitman Corp.**...III Crossroads of Commerce, 3501 Algonquin Rd., Rolling Meadows, IL 60008...(708) 818-5000...Bruce S. Chelberg...beverage bottler, refrigeration equip., auto prods. (Midas).

**Winn-Dixie Stores, Inc.**...5050 Edgewood Ct., Jacksonville, FL 32205...(904) 783-5000...A. Dano Davis....supermarkets.

**Winnebago Industries, Inc.**...PO Box 152, Forest City, IA 50436...(515) 582-3535...Fred G. Dohrmann....manuf. and financing of motor homes, recreation vehicles.

**WMX Technologies, Inc.**...3003 Butterfield Rd., Oak Brook, IL 60521...(708) 572-8800...D. L. Buntrock...solid waste collection and disposal.

**Wolverine World Wide Corp.**...9341 Courtland Dr., Rockford, MI 49351...(616) 866-5500...Geoffrey B. Bloom...manuf., markets footwear (Hush Puppies).

**Woolworth Corp.**...233 Broadway, NY, NY 10279...(212) 553-2000...Roger Farah...variety stores, shoes (Kinney), apparel, athletic footwear (Foot Locker).

**Wm. Wrigley Jr. Co.**...410 N. Michigan Ave., Chicago, IL 60611...(312) 644-2121...William Wrigley...chewing gum.

**Xerox Corp.**...PO Box 1600, Stamford, CT 06904...(203) 968-3000...Paul Allaire...copiers, printers, document pub. equip.

**Zenith Electronics Corp.**...1000 Milwaukee Ave., Glenview, IL 60025...(708) 391-7000...H. J. Lee...televisions, other electronic products.

# Who Owns What: Familiar Consumer Products

Listed below are consumer products and their parent companies. The parent company address can be found on pp. 714-19.

ABC broadcasting: Walt Disney
Admiral appliances: Maytag
Advil: American Home Products
Ajax cleanser: Colgate-Palmolive
Anacin: American Home Products
Arm & Hammer: Church & Dwight
Arnold breads: CPC Intl.
Arrid antiperspirant: Carter-Wallace
Aunt Millie's pasta sauce: Borden
Ban antiperspirant: Bristol-Myers Squibb
Banana Republic stores: The Gap
Barbie dolls: Mattell
Beech Aircraft: Raytheon
Beech-Nut baby food: Ralcorp
Ben-Gay: Pfizer
Betty Crocker products: General Mills
Black Flag insecticides: Clorox
Blockbuster video stores: Viacom
Bounce fabric softener: Procter & Gamble
Breck shampoo: Dial
Bubble Yum gum: RJR Nabisco
Budweiser beer: Anheuser-Busch
Bufferin: Bristol-Myers Squibb
Business Week magazine: McGraw-Hill
Buster Brown shoes: Brown Group
BVD underwear: Fruit of the Loom
Cap'n Crunch cereal: Quaker Oats
Carrier air conditioners: United Technologies
CBS broadcasting: Westinghouse
Celeste Pizza: Quaker Oats
Charmin toilet tissue: Procter & Gamble
Cheer detergent: Procter & Gamble
Cheerios cereal: General Mills
Cheez Whiz: Philip Morris
Chef Boy-ar-dee products: American Home Products
Cinemax: Time Warner
Clairol hair prods.: Bristol-Myers Squibb
Clorets breath mints: Warner-Lambert
CNN: Time Warner
Combat insecticides: Clorox
Comet cleanser: Procter & Gamble
Coppertone sun care products: Schering-Plough
Cracker Jack: Borden
Crest toothpaste: Procter & Gamble
Crisco shortening: Procter & Gamble
Doritos chips: PepsiCo
Dristan: American Home Products
Duncan Hines cakes: Procter & Gamble
Dutch Boy paints: Sherwin-Williams
Efferdent dental cleanser: Warner-Lambert
Elmer's glue: Borden
Equal sweetener: Monsanto
ESPN: Walt Disney
Eveready batteries: Ralston Purina
Excedrin: Bristol-Myers Squibb
Fab detergent: Colgate-Palmolive
Fantastik spray cleaner: Dow Chemical
Foamy shaving cream: Gillette
Folger's coffee: Procter & Gamble
Formula 409 spray cleaner: Clorox
Franco-American foods: Campbell Soup
Frito-Lay snacks: PepsiCo
Fruitopia drinks: Coca-Cola
Gatorade: Quaker Oats
Glad plastic wrap: First Brands
Glass Plus cleaner: Dow Chemical
Godiva chocolate: Campbell Soup
Halcion: Pharmacia & Upjohn
Hamburger Helper: General Mills
Handy Wipes: Colgate-Palmolive
Hanes hosiery: Sara Lee
Hawaiian Punch: Procter & Gamble
HBO: Time Warner
Head and Shoulders shampoo: Procter & Gamble
Healthy Request food products: Campbell Soup
Hellmann's mayonnaise: CPC Intl.
Hi-C fruit drinks: Coca-Cola
Hillshire Farms meats: Sara Lee
Hostess cakes: Interstate Brands
Huggies diapers: Kimberly-Clark
Hush Puppies shoes: Wolverine World Wide
Ivory soap: Procter & Gamble
Jack Daniel's bourbon: Brown-Forman
Java programming language: Sun Microsystems
Jell-O: Philip Morris
Jif peanut butter: Procter & Gamble
Jim Beam whiskey: American Brands
Ken-L-Ration pet foods: Quaker Oats
Kent cigarettes: Loews
KFC restaurants: PepsiCo
Kinney shoe stores: Woolworth
Kleenex: Kimberly-Clark
Knorr soups: CPC International
Kool-Aid: Philip Morris
Krazy Glue: Borden
Ladies Home Journal magazine: Meredith
Lee jeans: V.F. Corp.
L'eggs hosiery: Sara Lee
Lenox china: Brown-Forman
Lerner stores: The Limited
Life Savers candy: RJR Nabisco
Listerine mouthwash: Warner-Lambert
Log Cabin syrup: Philip Morris
Lord & Taylor: May Dept. Stores
Marlboro cigarettes: Philip Morris
Maxwell House coffee: Philip Morris
Mazola oil: CPC Intl.
Michelob beer: Anheuser-Busch
Midas automotive centers: Whitman
Miller beer: Philip Morris
Milton Bradley games: Hasbro
Minute Maid beverages: Coca-Cola
Monopoly: Hasbro
Mrs. Paul's frozen fish: Campbell Soup
MTV: Viacom
Nature Valley granola bars: General Mills
NBC Broadcasting: General Electric
Neutrogena soap: Johnson & Johnson
Newsweek magazine: Washington Post
9 Lives cat food: H.J. Heinz
North American Van Lines: Norfolk Southern
Noxema products: Procter & Gamble
NutraSweet: Monsanto
Old Spice: Procter & Gamble
Ore-Ida frozen foods: H.J. Heinz
Oreo cookies: RJR Nabisco
Oscar Mayer meats: Philip Morris
Pampers: Procter & Gamble
Paper Mate pens: Gillette
People magazine: Time Warner
Pepperidge Farm products: Campbell Soup
Pepto-Bismol: Procter & Gamble
Pine-Sol cleaner: Clorox
Pizza Hut restaurants: PepsiCo
Planters nuts: RJR Nabisco
Playskool toys: Hasbro
Playtex apparel: Sara Lee
Post-It stickers: Minn. Mining & Manufacturing
Prego pasta sauce: Campbell Soup
Prell shampoo: Procter & Gamble
Prentice-Hall publishing: Viacom
Prozac: Eli Lilly
Purex detergent: Dial
Radio Shack retail outlets: Tandy
Reese's peanut butter cups: Hershey
Rice-A-Roni: Quaker Oats
Right Guard deodorant: Gillette
Ritz crackers: RJR Nabisco
Robitussin: American Home Products
Rogaine hair growth aide: Pharmacia & Upjohn
Rolaids antacid: Warner-Lambert
Ronzoni pasta: Hershey
Ruffles chips: PepsiCo
San Giorgio pasta: Hershey
Saran Wrap: Dow Chemical
Schick razors: Warner-Lambert
Scholl's foot products: Schering-Plough
Scope mouthwash: Procter & Gamble
Scotch tape: Minn. Min. & Manuf.
Simon & Schuster publishing: Viacom
Skippy peanut butter: CPC Intl.
SnackWell's cookies: RJR Nabisco
Snapple beverages: Quaker Oats
Southern Comfort liquor: Brown-Forman
SPAM meat: Hormel
Sports Illustrated magazine: Time Warner
Sprite soda: Coca-Cola
Sugar Twin: Alberto Culver
Swanson frozen dinners: Campbell Soup
Taco Bell restaurants: PepsiCo
Tampax tampons: Tambrands
Thomas' English muffins: CPC Intl.
Tide detergent: Procter & Gamble
Tonka trucks: Hasbro
Trojan condoms: Carter-Wallace
Tylenol: Johnson & Johnson
Ultra Brite toothpaste: Colgate-Palmolive
USA Today newspaper: Gannett
V-8 vegetable juice: Campbell Soup
Vanity Fair apparel: V.F. Corp.
Velveeta cheese prods.: Philip Morris
Vicks cough medicines: Procter & Gamble
Victoria's Secret stores: The Limited
Visine eye drops: Pfizer
Wall Street Journal: Dow Jones
Weight Watchers: H.J. Heinz
Wheaties cereal: General Mills
White Owl cigars: Culbro
Windows 95 software application: Microsoft
Wise snacks: Borden
Wonder bread: Interstate Brands
Zest soap: Procter & Gamble
Ziploc storage bags: Dow Chemical

# Interest Laws and Consumer Finance Loan Rates

**Source:** Revised by Christian T. Jones, Editor, *Consumer Finance Law Bulletin*, Chicago, IL

All states have laws regulating interest rates. These laws fix a legal or conventional rate, which applies when there is no contract for interest. They also fix a general maximum contract rate, but there are so many exceptions that the general contract maximum actually applies to few cases. Also, federal law has preempted state limits on first home mortgages, subject to each state's right to reinstate its own law, and has given depository institutions parity with other state lenders.

**Legal rate of interest.** The legal or conventional rate of interest applies to money obligations when no interest rate is contracted for, and also to judgments. The rate is usually somewhat below the general contract interest rate.

**General maximum contract rates.** General interest laws in most states set the maximum contract rate between 8% and 16% per year. In Arkansas, the general maximum is fixed by the state constitution at 5% over the Federal Reserve discount rate. Loans to corporations are frequently exempted or subject to a higher maximum. In recent years, it has also been common to provide special rates for home mortgage loans and variable usury rates that are indexed to market rates.

**Specific enabling acts.** In many states special statutes permit industrial loan companies, second mortgage lenders, and banks to charge 1.5% a month or more. Laws regulating revolving loans, charge accounts, and credit cards generally limit rates to between 1.5% and 2% per month, plus annual fees for credit cards. Rates for installment sales contracts in most states are somewhat higher. Credit unions may generally charge 1% to 1.5% a month. Pawnbrokers' rates vary widely. Savings and loan associations and loans insured by federal agencies are also specially regulated. A number of states allow regulated lenders to charge any rate agreed to with the customer either for all credit or for credit over a certain dollar amount.

**Consumer finance loan statutes.** Most consumer finance loan statutes are based on early models drafted by the Russell Sage Foundation (1916-42) to provide small loans to wage earners under license and other protective regulations. Since 1969, the model has frequently been the Uniform Consumer Credit Code, which applies to credit sales and loans for consumer purposes. In general, licensed lenders may charge 3% a month, with reduced rates for relatively high amounts. An add-on of 17% ($17 per $100) per year amounts to about 2.5% per month if paid in equal monthly installments. Discount rates cost more than add-on rates of the same amount. In the table below, unless otherwise stated, monthly and annual rates are based on reducing principal balances, annual add-on rates are based on the original principal for the full term, and 2 or more rates apply to different portions of the balance or original principal.

## States (and Puerto Rico) With Consumer Finance Loan Laws and the Rates of Charge as of Aug. 1, 1996

Maximum monthly rates, computed on unpaid balances, unless otherwise stated.

AL .... Annual add-on: 15% to $750, 10% to $2,000 (min. 1.5% on unpaid balances). Higher rates for loans up to $749. Over $2,000, any agreed rate. Fee: 4% (max. $25); 5% real estate.
AK .... 3% to $850, 2% to $10,000. Over $10,000, any agreed rate.
AZ .... To $1,000: 3%. Over $1,000: 3% to $500, 2% to $10,000. Over $10,000, any agreed rate. Fee: 4% for real estate credit.
CA .... 2.5% to $225, 2% to $900, 1.5% to $1,650, 1% to $2,500 (1.6% min.). Over $2,500, any agreed rate. 5% fee (max. $50-$75) to $5,000.
CO .... 36% per year to $630, 21% to $2,100, 15% to $25,000 (21% min.).
CT .... Annual add-on: 17% to $600, 11% to $5,000; 11% over $1,800 to $5,000 for certain secured loans. Any agreed rate for 2d mortgages; 8% fee.
DE .... Any agreed rate; 10% fee.
DC .... 24% per year.
FL..... 30% per year to $1,000, 24% to $2,000, 18% to $25,000; $10 fee.
GA .... 10% per year discount to 18 months, add-on to 36½ months; 8% fee to $600, 4% on excess plus $2 per month. Over $3,000, any agreed rate.
HI ..... 3.5% to $100, 2.5% to $300; 2% on entire balance over $300 or discount rates.
ID..... Any agreed rate.
IL ..... Any agreed rate. Fee: 3% real estate.
IN..... 36% per year to $900, 21% to $3,000, 15% to $25,000 (21% min.). Fee: 2% real estate.
IA..... 3% to $1,000, 2% to $2,800, 1.5% to $10,000; or equivalent flat rate. Over $10,000, 21% per year.
KS .... 36% per year to $780, 21% to $2,600, 14.45% to $25,000 (18% min.). Fee: 2% (max. $100); 3% real estate.
KY .... 3% to $1,000, 2% to $3,000. Over $3,000, 2%.
LA .... 36% per year to $1,400, 27% to $4,000, 24% to $7,000, 21% over $7,000, plus $25 fee.
ME .... 30% per year to $1,000, 21% to $2,800, 15% to $25,000 (18% min.).
MD .... 2.75% to $1,000, 2% to $2,000. Over $2,000, 2%.
MA .... 23% per year plus $20 annual fee to $6,000; any agreed rate over $6,000.
MI..... 22% per year to $8,000; 18% for 2d mortgages, plus 2% fee (max. $200).
MN .... 33% per year to $750, 19% over $750 (21.75% min.) plus $25 fee to $4,230.
MS .... 36% per year to $1,000, 33% to $1,800, 24% to $5,000, 14% over $5,000. Over $25,000, 18%; 2% fee (max. $50).
MO .... 2.218% to $1,200, 1.67% over $1,200, plus 2% fee (max. $15); 1.67% plus 2% fee for 2d mortgages.
MT..... Any agreed rate.
NE..... 24% per year to $1,000. 21% over $1,000, plus fee of 7% to $2,000 and 5% over $2,000 (max. $500). Any agreed rate for real estate loans of $7,500 or more.
NV..... Any agreed rate.
NH..... 2% to $600, 1.5% to $1,500; any agreed rate over $1,500 or for real estate mortgages.
NJ ..... 30% per year to $5,000 or for 2d mortgages.
NM .... Any agreed rate.
NY. .... 25% per year.
NC..... 2.5% to $1,000, 1.5% to $7,500; 1.5% on entire amount to $10,000. 1.5% or variable plus 2% fee for 2d mortgages.
ND..... 2.5% to $250, 2% to $500, 1.75% to $750, 1.5% to $1,000; any agreed rate over $1,000.
OH..... 28% per year to $1,000, 22% to $5,000; 25% on entire amount over $5,000; plus fee.
OK..... 30% per year to $960, 21% to $3,200, 15% to $45,000 (21% min.). Special rates to $500.
OR..... Any agreed rate.
PA..... 9.5% per year discount to 48 months, 6% for remaining time plus 2% fee (max. $100); or 2% on unpaid balances; 1.85% for 2d mortgages over $5,000, plus 2% fee.
PR..... 20.25% per year.
RI ..... 3% to $300, 2.5% for loans between $300 and $800; 2% for larger loans to $5,000. 1.75% over $5,000.
SC..... Any agreed and posted rate.
SD..... Any agreed rate.
TN..... Over $100, 24% per year or discount rates plus fees.
TX..... Annual add-on: 18% to $1,320, 8% to $10,750 or formula rate (18% to 24% per year on unpaid balances).
UT..... Any agreed rate.
VT..... 2% to $1,000, 1% to $3,000 (min. 1.5%); 1.5% for 2d mortgages.
VA..... 3% to $2,500; any agreed rate to $6,000. Any agreed rate for 2d mortgages, plus 5% fee.
WA .... 25% per year plus fees.
WV .... 31% per year to $2,000, 27% per year to $10,000, 18% per year to $45,000; fees included in rates.
WI..... Any agreed rate.
WY .... 36% per year to $1,000, 21% to $50,000. No limit over $50,000.

# How to Check Your Credit File

Any individual can investigate the contents of his or her credit file by directly contacting one or more of the approximately 2,000 credit bureaus, or consumer credit clearinghouses, in the U.S. The nearest ones can be found by calling a local Better Business Bureau or by looking in the telephone Yellow Pages under "Credit Rating or Reporting Agencies."

Although the Fair Credit Reporting Act requires that a bureau give a person no more than an oral or written credit history review, many bureaus will go beyond the technical requirements of the law and furnish the same computer-generated compilation of facts that they give the banks, retailers, and other companies that subscribe to their service. An individual who has been denied credit on the basis of negative information from a credit bureau can obtain a review without charge (or sometimes for a small fee) within 30 days of the denial.

After inspecting this record of past credit behavior, a consumer can question any item believed to be inaccurate, misleading, or vague. The credit bureau must then investigate and remove any item that cannot be substantiated.

When a bureau affirms, rather than removes, a questionable item, an individual can present a 100-word explanation that must be placed in his or her file. And whenever an adverse item is deleted from the file or an explanatory statement is added to one, a consumer may request that the credit bureau inform every credit grantor who received a report within the previous 6 months.

# Credit Card Rates

**Source:** Christian T. Jones, Editor, *Consumer Finance Law Bulletin*, Chicago, IL; as of Aug. 1, 1996

Nearly all states have special laws dealing with rates charged for credit cards issued by state banks and other financial institutions. Although some state laws apply only to banks, under federal parity law, the same charges can be made by other financial institutions. A bank can charge the highest rates and charges allowed for revolving credit extended by any other creditor for similar types of credit in the state where the bank is located. These rates and charges may also be charged to residents of any other state. Maximum rates and fees are shown below; rates are yearly unless otherwise stated.

AL . . No limit.
AK . . 17% plus fee.
AZ . . No limit.
AR . . 5% over FRB discount rate (max. 17%).
CA . . No limit.
CO . . 21%.
CT . . No limit.
DC . . 24%.
DE . . No limit.
FL . . No limit.
GA . . No limit on rate or fee.
HI . . 24%.
ID . . No limit.
IL. . . No limit; plus fee.
IN . . 36% to $900, 21% to $3,000, then 15%; or 21%.
IA. . . No limit.
KS . . 18% to $1,000 then 14.45%.
KY . . 21%; $20 annual fee.
LA . . 18%; 4% cash advance and $12 annual fee.
ME . . No limit; plus annual fee.
MD . . 24%; 2% fee.
MA . . 18% or formula rate.
MI . . No limit on rate or fee.
MN . . 18%; $50 annual fee.
MS . . 21%; or 18% plus $12 annual fee.
MO . . 22 to $1,000, then 10%.
MT . . No limit.
NE . . No limit; plus fees.
NV . . No limit.
NH . . No limit.
NJ . . 30%; $15 annual fee or $50 over $5,000.
NM . . No limit.
NY . . 25% plus annual fee.
NC . . 18%; $24 annual fee.
ND . . No limit.
OH . . 25% plus fee.
OK . . 30% to $960, 21% to $3,200, then 15%; or 21%.
OR . . No limit.
PA . . Variable rate, plus fees.
PR . . 2.17% per mo.
RI. . . 21%.
SC . . No limit.
SD . . No limit.
TN . . 24%.
TX . . Set by rule (max. 22%, min. 14%).
UT . . No limit.
VT . . No limit.
VA . . No limit.
WA. . 25% loan; no limit for purchases; fees.
WV. . 18%.
WI . . No limit.
WY. . 36% to $1,000, then 21%; no limit over $50,000.

# Customs Exemptions and Advice to Travelers

**Source:** U.S. Dept. of the Treasury, U.S. Customs Service

U.S. residents returning after a stay abroad of at least 48 hours are usually granted customs exemptions of $400 each. The duty-free articles must accompany the traveler at the time of his or her return, be for personal or household use, have been acquired as an incident of the trip, and be properly declared to Customs. Not more than 1 liter of alcoholic beverages or more than 100 cigars and 200 cigarettes (1 carton) may be included in the $400 exemption. The exemption for alcoholic beverages is accorded only when the returning resident has attained 21 years of age at the time of arrival. Cuban cigars may be included only if purchased in Cuba.

If a U.S. resident arrives directly or indirectly from a U.S. insular possession — American Samoa, Guam, or the U.S. Virgin Islands — a customs exemption of $1,200 is allowed. Up to 1,000 cigarettes may be included, but only 200 of them may have been purchased elsewhere.

If a U.S. resident returns from any one of the following beneficiary places, the customs exemption is $600, based on fair market value: Antigua and Barbuda, Aruba, Bahamas, Barbados, Belize, British Virgin Islands, Costa Rica, Dominica, Dominican Republic, El Salvador, Grenada, Guatemala, Guyana, Haiti, Honduras, Jamaica, Montserrat, Netherlands Antilles, Nicaragua, Panama, St. Kitts and Nevis, St. Lucia, St. Vincent and the Grenadines, Trinidad and Tobago.

The $400, $600, or $1,200 exemption may be granted only if the exemption or any part of it has not been used within the preceding 30-day period and the stay abroad was for at least 48 hours. The 48-hr absence requirement does not apply to travelers returning from Mexico or the U.S. Virgin Islands. If you cannot claim the $400, $600, or $1,200 exemption because of the 30-day or 48-hr minimum limitations, you may bring in free of duty and tax articles acquired abroad for your personal or household use provided that the total fair retail value does not exceed $25.

Bona fide gifts of not more than $100 in fair retail value, when shipped, can be received by friends and relations in the U.S. free of duty and tax if the same person does not receive more than $100 in gift shipments in one day. The amount is increased to $200 if shipped from the U.S. Virgin Islands, American Samoa, or Guam. (Shipping of alcoholic beverages by mail is prohibited by U.S. postal laws. Alcoholic beverages include wine and beer, as well as distilled spirits.) These gifts are not declared by the traveler upon return to the U.S.

A new duty-free exemption for packages sent by mail that are not gifts has also been implemented. Goods shipped for personal use may be imported free of duty and tax if the total value is not more than $200. This exemption does not apply to perfume containing alcohol if it is valued at more than $5 retail, to alcoholic beverages, or to cigars and cigarettes. The $200 mail exemption does not apply to merchandise subject to absolute or tariff-rate quotas unless the item is for personal use. Tailor-made suits ordered from Hong Kong, however, are subject to quota/visa requirements even if imported for personal use.

The U.S. Customs Service booklet *Know Before You Go* answers frequently asked customs questions and is available free by writing U.S. Customs, KBYG, PO Box 7407, Washington, DC 20044.

# Passport, Visa, and Health Requirements for Foreign Travel

**Source:** Bureau of Consular Affairs, U.S. Dept. of State, as of Aug. 1996

Passports are issued by the U.S. Department of State to citizens and nationals of the U.S. for the purpose of documenting them for foreign travel and identifying them as U.S. citizens. For U.S. citizens traveling on business or as tourists, especially in Europe, a U.S. passport is often sufficient to gain admission for a limited stay. For many countries, however, a visa must also be obtained before entering. It is the responsibility of the traveler to obtain any visas where required, from the appropriate embassy or nearest consulate of the country he or she is planning to visit.

## How to Obtain a Passport

Applicants who have never been issued a passport in their own name must execute an application in person before (1) a passport agent; (2) a clerk of any federal court or state court of record or a judge or clerk of any probate court accepting applications; (3) a postal employee designated by the postmaster at a post office that has been selected to accept passport applications; or (4) a U.S. diplomatic or consular officer abroad. A DSP-11 is the correct form to use for applicants who must apply in person. All persons are required to obtain individual passports in their own name. An applicant who is 13 years of age or older is required to appear in person before the clerk or agent executing the application. A parent or legal guardian must execute the application for children under 13.

A full validity passport previously issued to the applicant or one in which he or she was included will be accepted as proof of U.S. citizenship. If the applicant has no prior passport and was born in the U.S., a certified copy of his/her birth certificate generally must be presented to the agent accepting the passport application. To be acceptable, the certificate must show the given name and surname, the date and place of birth, and that the birth record was filed shortly after birth. A delayed birth certificate (a record filed more than 1 year after the date of birth) is acceptable provided that it shows that acceptable secondary evidence was used for creating this record.

If a birth certificate is not obtainable, a notice from a state registrar must be submitted stating that no birth record exists. The notice must be accompanied by the best obtainable secondary evidence, such as a baptismal certificate or a hospital birth record.

A naturalized citizen with no previous passport must present a Certificate of Naturalization. A person born abroad claiming U.S. citizenship through either a native-born or naturalized citizen parent must normally submit a Certificate of Citizenship issued by the Immigration and Naturalization Service; or a Consular Report of Birth or Certification of Birth Abroad issued by the Dept. of State. If one of the above documents has not been obtained, evidence of citizenship of the parent(s) through whom citizenship is claimed and evidence that would establish the parent/child relationship must be submitted. Additionally, if citizenship is derived through birth to citizen parent(s), the following documents will be required: parents' marriage certificate plus an affidavit from parent(s) showing periods and places of residence or physical presence in the U.S. and abroad, specifying periods spent abroad in the employment of the U.S. government, including the armed forces, or with certain international organizations. If citizenship is derived through naturalization of parents, evidence of admission to the U.S. for permanent residence also will be required.

It is important to apply for a passport as far in advance as possible. The passport office is busiest between March and September, when it can take several weeks to receive your passport.

Persons who possess the most recent passport issued within the last 12 years and after their 18th birthday may be eligible to apply for a new passport by mail. The form DSP-82, *Application for Passport by Mail*, must be filled out and mailed to the address shown on the form, together with the previous passport, 2 recent identical photographs, and a fee of $55.00. The DSP-82 may not be used if the most recent passport has been altered or mutilated.

## Photographs, Fees, and Identity

**Photographs**—Passport applicants must submit 2 identical photographs that are sufficiently recent (normally not more than 6 months old) and that are a good likeness of and satisfactorily identify the applicant. Photographs should be 2 × 2 in. in size. The image size measured from the bottom of the chin to the top of the head (including hair) should not be less than one inch or more than 1-3/8 in. Photographs should be portrait-type prints. They must be clear, front view, full face, with a plain white or off-white background. Photographs that depict the applicant as relaxed and smiling are encouraged.

**Fees**—For persons under 18 years of age, the fee for a passport is $30.00. These passports are valid for 5 years from the date of issue. The fee is $55.00 for passports issued to persons 18 and older. These passports are valid for 10 years from the date of issuance. To receive a passport within 10 days or less, a $30.00 expedite fee is required. An additional fee of $10.00 is charged for the execution of the application. There is no execution fee when using DSP-82, *Application for Passport by Mail.* Applicants eligible to use this form pay only the $55.00 passport fee.

**Identity**—Applicants must establish their identity to the satisfaction of the person accepting the application and to Passport Services. Generally acceptable documents of identity include a previous U.S. passport, a Certificate of Naturalization, a Certificate of Citizenship, a valid driver's license, or a government identification card. Applicants may not use a Social Security card, learner's or temporary driver's license, credit card, or expired identity card. Extremely old documents cannot be used by themselves.

Applicants unable to establish identity must present some documentation in their own name and must be accompanied by a person who has known the applicant for at least 2 years and who is a U.S. citizen or legal U.S. permanent resident alien. That person must sign an affidavit before the individual who executes the passport application. The witness will be required to establish his or her own identity.

The loss or theft of a valid passport is a serious matter and should be reported immediately in writing to Passport Services, 1111 19th St., NW, Dept. of State, Washington, DC 20524-1705, telephone: (202) 647-0518, or to the nearest passport agency or the nearest U.S. embassy or consulate when abroad.

For more information, the booklet *Passports—Applying for the Easy Way* is available for 50¢ from the Consumer Information Center, Pueblo, CO 81009.

## Foreign Regulations

Each country has its own specific guidelines concerning length and purpose of visit, etc. Some may require visitors to display proof that they (1) have sufficient funds to stay for intended time period and (2) have onward/return tickets. Some countries, including Canada, Mexico, and some Caribbean islands, do not require a passport or a visa for limited stays. Such countries do require proof of U.S. citizenship, and may have other requirements that must be met. For further information, check with the embassy or nearest consulate of the country you plan to visit.

Under the International Health Regulations adopted by the World Health Organization, a country may require International Certificates of Vaccination against yellow fever. A cholera immunization may be required for travelers from infected areas. Check with health care providers or your records to ensure other immunizations (e.g. tetanus and polio) are up-to-date. Prophylactic medication for malaria and certain other preventive measures are advisable for travel to some countries. No immunizations are required to return to the U.S. An increasing number of countries have established regulations regarding AIDS testing, particularly for longtime visitors. Detailed health information is included in *Health Information for International Travel*, available from the U.S. Government Printing Office, Washington, DC 20402 for $14. Information may also be obtained from your local health department or physician, or by calling the Centers for Disease Control and Prevention at (404) 332-4559.

# Copyright Law of the United States

**Source:** Copyright Office, Library of Congress

## What Copyright Is

Copyright is a form of protection provided by the laws of the U.S. (title 17, U.S. Code) to "original works of authorship," including literary, dramatic, musical, artistic, and certain other intellectual works. This protection is available to both published and unpublished works. Section 106 of the Copyright Act generally gives the owner of copyright the exclusive right to do and to authorize other parties to do the following:

*To reproduce* the copyrighted work in copies or phono records;

*To prepare derivative works* based upon the copyrighted work;

*To distribute copies or phono records* of the copyrighted work to the public by sale or other transfer of ownership, or by rental, lease, or lending;

*To perform the copyrighted work publicly,* in the case of literary, musical, dramatic, and choreographic works, pantomimes, and motion pictures and other audiovisual works; and

*To display the copyrighted work publicly,* in the case of literary, musical, dramatic, and choreographic works, pantomimes, and pictorial, graphic, or sculptural works, including the individual images of a motion picture or other audiovisual work.

It is illegal for anyone to violate any of the rights provided by the act to the owner of copyright. These rights, however, are not unlimited in scope. Sections 107 through 119 of the Copyright Act establish limitations on these rights. In some cases, these limitations are specified exemptions from copyright liability. One major limitation is the doctrine of "fair use," which is given a statutory basis by section 107 of the act. In other instances, the limitation takes the form of a "compulsory license," under which certain limited uses of copyrighted works are permitted upon payment of specified royalties and compliance with statutory conditions.

Copyright protection subsists from the time the work is created in fixed form; that is, it is an incident of the process of authorship. The copyright in the work of authorship *immediately* becomes the property of the author who created it. Only the author or those deriving their rights from the author can rightfully claim copyright.

In the case of works made for hire, the employer and not the employee is presumptively considered the author. Section 101 of the copyright statute defines a "work made for hire" as:

(1) a work prepared by an employee within the scope of his or her employment; or

(2) a work specially ordered or commissioned for use as a contribution to a collective work, as a part of a motion picture or other audiovisual work, as a translation, as a supplementary work, as a compilation, as an instructional text, as a test, as answer material for a test, or as an atlas, if the parties expressly agree in a written instrument signed by them that the work shall be considered a work made for hire.

The authors of a joint work are co-owners of the copyright in the work, unless there is an agreement to the contrary.

Copyright in each separate contribution to a periodical or other collective work is distinct from copyright in the collective work as a whole and vests initially with the author of the contribution.

Copyright protection is available for all unpublished works, regardless of the nationality or domicile of the author.

Published works are eligible for copyright protection in the U.S. if any one of the following conditions is met:

• On the date of first publication, one or more of the authors is a national or domiciliary of the U.S. or is a national, domiciliary, or sovereign authority of a foreign nation that is a party to a copyright treaty to which the U.S. is also a party, or is a stateless person wherever that person may be domiciled; or

• The work is first published in the U.S. or in a foreign nation that, on the date of first publication, is a party to the Universal Copyright Convention; or the work comes within the scope of a Presidential proclamation; or

• The work is first published on or after Mar. 1, 1989, in a foreign nation that on the date of first publication, is a party to the Berne Convention; or, if the work is *not* first published in a country party to the Berne Convention, it is published (on or after Mar. 1, 1989) within 30 days of first publication in a country that is party to the Berne Convention; or the work, first published on or after Mar. 1, 1989, is a pictorial, graphic, or sculptural work that is incorporated in a permanent structure located in the U.S.; or if the work, first published on or after Mar. 1, 1989, is a published audiovisual work, all the authors are legal entities with headquarters in the U.S.

## Which Works Are Protected

Copyright protects "original works of authorship" that are fixed in a tangible form of expression. The fixation need not be directly perceptible, as long as it may be communicated with the aid of a machine or device. Copyrightable works include the following categories:

(1) literary works;
(2) musical works, including any accompanying words;
(3) dramatic works, including any accompanying music;
(4) pantomimes and choreographic works;
(5) pictorial, graphic, and sculptural works;
(6) motion pictures and other audiovisual works;
(7) sound recordings; and
(8) architectural works.

These categories should be viewed quite broadly: for example, computer programs and most "compilations" are registrable as "literary works"; maps and architectural plans are registrable as "pictorial, graphic, and sculptural works."

## Which Works Are Not Protected

Several categories of material are generally not eligible for statutory copyright protection. These include among others:

• Works that have not been fixed in a tangible form of expression. For example: choreographic works that have not been notated or recorded, or improvisational speeches or performances that have not been written or recorded.

• Titles, names, short phrases, and slogans; familiar symbols or designs; mere variations of typographic ornamentation, lettering, or coloring; mere listings of ingredients or contents.

• Ideas, procedures, methods, systems, processes, concepts, principles, discoveries, or devices, as distinguished from a description, explanation, or illustration.

• Works consisting entirely of information that is common property and containing no original authorship. For example: standard calendars, height and weight charts, tape measures and rulers, and lists or tables taken from public documents or other common sources.

## Notice of Copyright

For works first published on or after Mar. 1, 1989, use of the copyright notice is optional, though highly recommended. Before Mar. 1, 1989, the use of the notice was mandatory on all published works, and any work first published before that date *must* bear a notice or risk loss of copyright protection.

Use of the notice is recommended because it informs the public that the work is protected by copyright, identifies the copyright owner, and shows the year of first publication. Furthermore, in the event that a work is infringed, if the work carries a proper notice, the court will not allow a defendant to claim "innocent infringement"—that is, that he or she did not realize that the work is protected. (A successful innocent infringement claim may result in a reduction in damages that the copyright owner would otherwise receive.)

The use of the copyright notice is the responsibility of the copyright owner and does not require advance permission from, or registration with, the Copyright Office.

For visually perceptible copies, the form of the notice consists of the following: © (the letter C in a circle), the word "Copyright," or "Copr.," and the year of first publication, and the name of the owner of copyright in the work. Example: © 1997 Judy Smith. The notice must be affixed in such manner and location as to give reasonable notice of the claim of copyright.

The notice of copyright prescribed for all published phono records of sound recordings consists of the following: ℗ (the letter P in a circle), the year of first publication of the sound recording, and the name of the owner of copyright in the sound recording. Example: ℗ 1997 XYZ Records, Inc. The notice on phono records may appear on the surface of the phono record or on the phono record label or container, provided the manner of placement and location give reasonable notice of the claim.

## How Long Copyright Protection Endures

### Works Originally Created on or After Jan. 1, 1978

A work that is created (fixed in tangible form for the first time) on or after Jan. 1, 1978, is automatically protected from the moment of its creation and is ordinarily given a term enduring for the author's life, plus an additional 50 years after the author's death. In the case of "a joint work prepared by 2 or more authors who did not work for hire," the term lasts for 50 years after the last surviving author's death. For works made for hire and for anonymous and pseudonymous works (unless the author's identity is revealed in Copyright Office records) the duration of copyright is 75 years from publication or 100 years from creation, whichever is shorter.

Works that were created but not published or registered for copyright before Jan. 1, 1978, have been automatically brought under the statute and are now given Federal copyright protection. The duration of copyright in these works will generally be computed in the same way as for works created on or after Jan. 1, 1978: the life-plus-50 or 75/100-year terms will apply to them as well. The law provides that in no case will the term of copyright for works in this category expire before Dec. 31, 2002, and for works published on or before Dec. 31, 2002, the term of copyright will not expire before Dec. 31, 2027.

### Works Created and Published or Registered Before Jan. 1, 1978

Under the law in effect before 1978, copyright was secured either on the date a work was published or on the date of registration if the work was registered in unpublished form. In either case, the copyright endured for a first term of 28 years from the date it was secured. During the last (28th) year of the first term, the copyright was eligible for renewal. The current copyright law has extended the renewal term from 28 to 47 years for copyrights that were subsisting on Jan. 1, 1978, making these works eligible for a total term of protection of 75 years. On June 26, 1992, Pres. George Bush signed Public Law 102-307, which amends the Copyright Law to extend automatically the term of copyrights secured between Jan. 1, 1964, and Dec. 31, 1977, to a further term of 47 years and increases the filing fee from $12.00 to $20.00. This fee increase applies to all renewal applications filed on or after June 29, 1992.

PL 102-307 makes renewal registration optional. An author need not file the renewal in order to extend the original 28-year copyright term to the full 75 years. It may be beneficial, however, to file a renewal registration during the 28th year of the original term. (For more information on copyright renewal, request Circular 15 from the Copyright Office.)

## International Copyright Protection

There is no such thing as an "international copyright" that will automatically protect an author's writings throughout the entire world. Protection against unauthorized use in a particular country depends, basically, on the national laws of that country. However, most countries do offer protection to foreign works under certain conditions, and these conditions have been greatly simplified by international copyright treaties and conventions. For a list of countries that maintain copyright relations with the United States, request Circular 38a.

The United States belongs to both global, multilateral copyright treaties–the Universal Copyright Convention (UCC) and the Berne Convention for the Protection of Literary and Artistic Works. The United States was a founding member of the UCC, which came into force on Sept. 16, 1955. Generally, a work by a national or domiciliary of a country that is a member of the UCC, or a work that was first published in a UCC country, may claim protection under the UCC. If the work bears the notice of copyright in the form and position specified by the UCC, this notice will satisfy and substitute for any other formalities a UCC member country would otherwise impose as a condition of copyright. A UCC notice should consist of the symbol © accompanied by the name of the copyright proprietor and the year of first publication of the work.

By joining the Berne Convention on Mar. 1, 1989, the United States gained protection for its authors in all member nations of the Berne Union with which the United States formerly had either no copyright relations or had bilateral treaty arrangements. Members of the Berne Union agree to a certain minimum level of copyright protection and agree to treat nationals of other member countries like their own nationals for purposes of copyright. A work first published in the United States or another Berne Union country (or first published in a non-Berne country, followed by publication within 30 days in a Berne Union country) is eligible for protection in all Berne member countries. There are no special requirements.

An author who wishes protection for his or her work in a particular country should first find out the extent of protection of foreign works in that country. If possible, this should be done before the work is published anywhere, since protection may often depend on the facts existing at the time of first publication.

If the country in which protection is sought is a party to one of the international copyright conventions, the work may generally be protected by complying with the conditions of the convention. Even if the work cannot be brought under an international convention, protection under the specific provisions of the country's national laws may still be possible. Some countries, however, offer little or no copyright protection for foreign works.

## Copyright Registration

Copyright registration is a legal formality intended to make a public record of the basic facts of a particular copyright. Except in specific situations, registration is not a condition for protection, but the copyright law provides several inducements or advantages to encourage copyright owners to register. Among these are the following:

• Registration establishes a public record of the copyright claim.

• Before an infringement suit may be filed in court, registration is necessary for works of U.S. origin and for foreign works not originating in a Berne Union country. (For more information on when a work is of U.S. origin, request Circular 93 from the Copyright Office.)

• If made before or within 5 years of publication, registration will establish prima facie evidence in court of the validity of the copyright and of the facts stated in the certificate.

• If registration is made within 3 months after publication of the work or prior to an infringement of the work, statutory damages and attorney's fees will be available to the copyright owner in court actions. Otherwise, only an award of actual damages and profits is available to the copyright owner.

Copyright registration allows the owner of the copyright to record the registration with the U.S. Customs Service for protection against the importation of infringing copies. For additional information, request Publication No. 563 from Commissioner of Customs, ATTN: IPR Branch, Rm 2104, U.S. Customs Service, 1301 Constitution Ave. NW, Washington, DC 20229.

Registration may be made at any time within the life of the copyright. When a work has been registered in unpublished form, making another registration when the work becomes published is unnecessary (although the copyright owner may register the published edition, if desired).

The process of registration is simple. Request an appropriate form from the Copyright Office and complete it. Returned it to the Copyright Office along with a $20 nonrefundable filing fee and the appropriate deposit(s) of the work for which registration is sought. In a common example—a published book—the deposit is 2 copies of the best edition of the book. The Copyright Office sends a certificate of registration when the paperwork is completed, a process that usually takes 12 to 16 weeks because of the large volume of registrations the Office must handle (over 500,000 annually).

Although a copyright registration is not required, the Copyright Act establishes a mandatory deposit requirement for works published in the U.S. In general, the owner of copyright or the owner of the exclusive right of publication in the work has a legal obligation to deposit in the Copyright Office, within 3 months of publication in the U.S., 2 copies (or, in the case of sound recordings, 2 phono records) for the use of the Library of Congress. Failure to deposit these copies can result in fines and other penalties but does not affect copyright protection. Certain categories of works are exempt entirely from the mandatory deposit requirements, and the obligation is reduced for certain other categories.

Information on registration and application forms may be obtained free of charge by writing the Copyright Office, Information Section, LM-401, Library of Congress, Washington, DC 20559. Registration application forms and circulars may be ordered on a 24-hr basis by calling (202) 707-9100. Request Circular 1 for additional general information on copyright, including a list of which application forms to use when registering specific types of works.

# Median Price of Existing Single-Family Homes

**Source:** National Association of REALTORS®; data as of June, 1996

| City[1] | 1994 | 1995 | First Quarter 1996 |
|---|---|---|---|
| Akron, OH | $ 84,900 | $ 92,100 | $ 91,100 |
| Albany, NY | 112,000 | 105,900 | 106,300 |
| Albuquerque, NM | 110,000 | 117,000 | 122,601 |
| Amarillo, TX | 64,500 | 71,000 | 73,100 |
| Anaheim/Santa Ana, CA[2] | 211,000 | 208,800 | 207.700 |
| Atlanta, GA | 93,600 | 97,500 | 98,500 |
| Atlantic City, NJ | 107,600 | 107,000 | 111,900 |
| Aurora, IL | 124,400 | 131,600 | 131,400 |
| Austin, TX | 96,200 | 101,400 | 111,800 |
| Baltimore, MD | 115,400 | 111,300 | 109,700 |
| Baton Rouge, LA | 77,400 | 84,600 | 87,000 |
| Biloxi/Gulfport, MS | 70,900 | 73,100 | 73,800 |
| Birmingham, AL | 100,200 | 103,600 | 114,700 |
| Boise City, ID | 99,000 | 98,900 | 99,400 |
| Boston, MA | 179,300 | 179,000 | 187,300 |
| Bradenton, FL | 88,300 | 91,000 | 100,500 |
| Buffalo/Niagara Falls, NY | 82,300 | 81,300 | 84,100 |
| Canton, OH | 77,500 | 84,000 | 86,800 |
| Cedar Rapids, IA | 82,800 | 86,200 | 89,100 |
| Champaign, IL | 74,100 | 79,400 | 78,200 |
| Charleston, SC | 91,600 | 94,300 | 90,300 |
| Charleston, WV | 78,600 | 81,700 | 89,300 |
| Charlotte, NC | 106,500 | 107,800 | 113,800 |
| Chattanooga, TN | 77,500 | 82,800 | 87,300 |
| Chicago, IL | 144,100 | 147,900 | 149,800 |
| Cincinnati, OH/KY/IN | 96,500 | 100,400 | 101,500 |
| Cleveland, OH | 98,500 | 104,700 | 108,400 |
| Colorado Springs, CO | 104,200 | 114,700 | 117,500 |
| Columbia, SC | 86,600 | 91,000 | 89,200 |
| Columbus, OH | 94,800 | 99,100 | 107,200 |
| Corpus Christi, TX | 74,100 | 77,600 | 74,400 |
| Dallas, TX | 95,000 | 96,400 | 100,800 |
| Davenport, IA/IL | 61,800 | 66,200 | 66,400 |
| Dayton/Springfield, OH | 84,200 | 88,300 | 92,600 |
| Daytona Beach, FL | 69,000 | 69,600 | 70,300 |
| Denver, CO | 116,800 | 127,300 | 130,500 |
| Des Moines, IA | 81,700 | 87,000 | 94,200 |
| Detroit, MI | 87,000 | 98,200 | 105,800 |
| El Paso, TX | 75,300 | 72,300 | 74,100 |
| Eugene, OR | 96,200 | 104,900 | 116,500 |
| Fargo, ND/MN | 77,600 | 82,900 | 83,800 |
| Ft. Lauderdale, FL | 103,100 | 105,900 | 110,000 |
| Ft. Myers, FL | 77,800 | 77,700 | 76,100 |
| Ft. Worth/Arlington, TX | 82,500 | 83,700 | 86,800 |
| Gainesville, FL | 84,600 | 89,900 | 95,900 |
| Gary/Hammond, IN | 87,200 | 91,600 | 95,700 |
| Grand Rapids, MI | 76,900 | 80,600 | 86,500 |
| Green Bay, WI | 86,600 | 89,500 | 90,900 |
| Greensboro, NC | 96,600 | 102,500 | 113,400 |
| Hartford, CT | 133,400 | 133,400 | 133,200 |
| Honolulu, HI | 360,000 | 349,000 | 331,800 |
| Houston, TX | 80,500 | 79,200 | 80,900 |
| Indianapolis, IN | 90,700 | 94,600 | 97,100 |
| Jacksonville, FL | 81,900 | 83,100 | 86,200 |
| Kalamazoo, MI | 74,800 | 82,200 | 88,900 |
| Kansas City, MO/KS | 87,100 | 91,700 | 96,900 |
| Knoxville, TN | 89,200 | 93,600 | 98,200 |
| Lake County, IL | 130,800 | 136,200 | 146,000 |
| Lansing, MI | 75,500 | 79,800 | 80,700 |
| Las Vegas, NV | 110,500 | 113,500 | 117,600 |
| Lexington/Fayette, KY | 87,500 | 90,800 | 93,400 |

| City[1] | 1994 | 1995 | First Quarter 1996 |
|---|---|---|---|
| Lincoln, NE | $ 76,600 | $ 82,500 | $ 84,000 |
| Little Rock, AR | 75,000 | 79,000 | 82,800 |
| Los Angeles, CA[2] | 189,100 | 179,900 | 172,100 |
| Louisville, KY/IN | 80,500 | 86,400 | 85,700 |
| Madison, WI | 116,000 | 124,500 | 121,900 |
| Memphis, TN/AR/MS | 86,300 | 86,500 | 96,900 |
| Miami, FL | 103,200 | 107,100 | 109,800 |
| Milwaukee, WI | 109,000 | 114,700 | 115,700 |
| Minneapolis, MN/WI | 101,500 | 106,800 | 112,500 |
| Mobile, AL | 69,900 | 75,100 | 78,900 |
| Montgomery, AL | 82,200 | 85,800 | 88,100 |
| Nashville, TN | 96,500 | 107,300 | 111,700 |
| New Haven, CT | 139,600 | 135,100 | 129,900 |
| New Orleans, LA | 76,900 | 78,000 | 83,500 |
| New York, NY | 173,200 | 169,700 | 169,000 |
| Norfolk/Virginia Bch, VA | 103,800 | 104,400 | 104,700 |
| Oklahoma City, OK | 66,700 | 70,400 | 71,600 |
| Omaha, NE | 75,600 | 83,000 | 84,600 |
| Orlando, FL | 90,700 | 89,200 | 89,700 |
| Pensacola, FL | 76,400 | 79,500 | 83,900 |
| Peoria, IL | 67,900 | 70,100 | 68,400 |
| Philadelphia, PA/NJ | 119,500 | 118,700 | NA |
| Phoenix, AZ | 91,400 | 96,800 | 102,600 |
| Pittsburgh, PA | 80,700 | 82,100 | 83,500 |
| Portland, OR | 116,900 | 128,400 | 135,800 |
| Providence, RI | 116,400 | 115,600 | 114,000 |
| Raleigh/Durham, NC | 115,200 | 127,000 | 128,600 |
| Reno, NV | 133,600 | 137,100 | 140,700 |
| Richmond, VA | 95,400 | 103,100 | 105,200 |
| Riverside/San Bern.,CA[2] | 129,100 | 120,900 | 117,100 |
| Rochester, NY | 85,600 | 85,000 | 83,500 |
| Rockford, IL | 84,900 | 87,500 | 88,800 |
| Sacramento, CA[2] | 124,500 | 120,200 | 113,900 |
| St. Louis, MO/IL | 85,000 | 87,700 | 88,100 |
| Salt Lake City, UT | 98,000 | 113,700 | 121,200 |
| San Antonio, TX | 78,200 | 80,800 | 83,600 |
| San Diego, CA[2] | 176,000 | 171,600 | 173,800 |
| San Francisco, CA[2] | 255,600 | 254,400 | 252,200 |
| Sarasota, FL | 97,000 | 104,500 | 103,500 |
| Seattle, WA | 155,900 | 159,000 | 160,700 |
| Shreveport, LA | 70,200 | 72,500 | 75,700 |
| Sioux Falls, SD | 80,100 | 84,200 | 85,600 |
| South Bend, IN | 64,700 | 69,300 | 74,500 |
| Spokane, WA | 94,600 | 98,400 | 98,600 |
| Springfield, IL | 75,800 | 79,100 | 81,600 |
| Springfield, MA | 107,700 | 106,100 | 101,300 |
| Springfield, MO | 73,000 | 78,300 | 78,500 |
| Syracuse, NY | 83,100 | 81,200 | 75,500 |
| Tacoma, WA | 118,900 | 121,400 | 124,600 |
| Tallahassee, FL | 97,800 | 99,800 | 105,400 |
| Tampa, FL | 76,200 | 78,300 | 79,100 |
| Toledo, OH | 73,800 | 77,600 | 85,100 |
| Topeka, KS | 63,300 | 68,200 | 69,900 |
| Tucson, AZ | 95,400 | 100,500 | 105,400 |
| Tulsa, OK | 74,100 | 78,500 | 79,200 |
| Washington, DC/MD/VA | 157,900 | 156,500 | 152,000 |
| Waterloo/Cedar Falls,IA | 53,100 | 56,500 | 56,800 |
| W. Palm Beach, FL | 117,600 | 121,300 | 125,600 |
| Wichita, KS | 73,700 | 76,500 | 80,500 |
| Wilmington, DE/NJ/MD | NA | 123,600 | NA |
| Worcester, MA | 130,600 | 130,100 | 120,800 |

(1) All areas are metropolitan statistical areas (MSAs) as defined by the U.S. Office of Management and Budget. They include the named central city and surrounding areas. (2) Data provided by the California Association of REALTORS®.

NA= not available.

# Housing Affordability

**Source:** National Association of REALTORS®

| Year | Median-priced existing home | Average mortgage rate[1] | Monthly principal and interest payment | Payment as percentage of median income |
|---|---|---|---|---|
| 1987 | $85,600 | 9.28% | $565 | 21.9% |
| 1988 | 90,600 | 9.31 | 591 | 22.0 |
| 1989 | 93,100 | 10.11 | 660 | 23.1 |
| 1990 | 97,500 | 10.04 | 673 | 22.7 |
| 1991 | 99,700 | 9.51 | 671 | 22.3 |
| 1992 | $103,700 | 8.11% | $615 | 20.0% |
| 1993 | 106,800 | 7.16 | 578 | 18.8 |
| 1994 | 109,800 | 7.47 | 612 | 19.3 |
| 1995 | 112,900 | 7.85 | 653 | 19.8 |
| 1996[2] | 122,700 | 7.93 | 715 | 21.3 |

(1) The average mortgage rate is based on the effective rate on loans closed on existing homes monitored by the Federal Housing Finance Board. (2) Preliminary figures for June 1996.

# Mortgage Payment Tables

**Source:** *The Mortgage Money Guide,* Federal Trade Commission

## 8% Annual Percentage Rate

**Monthly payments (principal and interest)**

| Amount financed | 10 Years | 15 Years | 20 Years | 25 Years | 30 Years |
|---|---|---|---|---|---|
| **$ 50,000** | $ 606.64 | $ 477.83 | $ 418.22 | $ 385.91 | $ 366.88 |
| **60,000** | 727.97 | 573.39 | 501.86 | 463.09 | 440.26 |
| **70,000** | 849.29 | 668.96 | 585.51 | 540.27 | 513.64 |
| **80,000** | 970.62 | 764.52 | 669.15 | 617.45 | 587.01 |
| **90,000** | 1091.95 | 860.09 | 752.80 | 694.63 | 660.39 |
| **100,000** | 1213.28 | 955.65 | 836.44 | 771.82 | 733.76 |
| **120,000** | 1455.94 | 1146.78 | 1003.72 | 926.18 | 880.52 |
| **140,000** | 1698.58 | 1337.92 | 1171.02 | 1080.54 | 1027.28 |
| **160,000** | 1941.24 | 1529.04 | 1338.30 | 1234.90 | 1174.02 |
| **180,000** | 2183.90 | 1720.18 | 1505.60 | 1389.26 | 1320.78 |
| **200,000** | 2426.56 | 1911.30 | 1672.88 | 1543.64 | 1467.52 |

## 9% Annual Percentage Rate

**Monthly payments (principal and interest)**

| Amount financed | 10 Years | 15 Years | 20 Years | 25 Years | 30 Years |
|---|---|---|---|---|---|
| **$ 50,000** | $ 633.38 | $ 507.13 | $ 449.86 | $ 419.60 | $ 402.31 |
| **60,000** | 760.05 | 608.56 | 539.84 | 503.52 | 482.77 |
| **70,000** | 886.73 | 709.99 | 629.81 | 587.44 | 563.24 |
| **80,000** | 1013.41 | 811.41 | 719.78 | 671.36 | 643.70 |
| **90,000** | 1140.08 | 912.84 | 809.75 | 755.28 | 724.16 |
| **100,000** | 1266.76 | 1014.27 | 899.73 | 839.20 | 804.62 |
| **120,000** | 1520.10 | 1217.12 | 1079.68 | 1007.04 | 965.54 |
| **140,000** | 1773.46 | 1419.98 | 1259.62 | 1174.88 | 1126.48 |
| **160,000** | 2026.82 | 1622.82 | 1439.56 | 1342.72 | 1287.40 |
| **180,000** | 2280.16 | 1825.68 | 1619.50 | 1510.56 | 1448.32 |
| **200,000** | 2533.52 | 2028.54 | 1799.46 | 1678.40 | 1609.24 |

## 10% Annual Percentage Rate

**Monthly payments (principal and interest)**

| Amount financed | 10 Years | 15 Years | 20 Years | 25 Years | 30 Years |
|---|---|---|---|---|---|
| **$ 50,000** | $ 660.75 | $ 537.30 | $ 482.51 | $ 454.35 | $ 438.79 |
| **60,000** | 792.90 | 644.76 | 579.01 | 545.22 | 526.54 |
| **70,000** | 925.06 | 752.22 | 675.52 | 636.09 | 614.30 |
| **80,000** | 1057.20 | 859.68 | 772.02 | 726.96 | 702.06 |
| **90,000** | 1189.36 | 967.14 | 868.52 | 817.83 | 789.81 |
| **100,000** | 1321.51 | 1074.61 | 965.02 | 908.70 | 877.57 |
| **120,000** | 1585.80 | 1289.52 | 1158.02 | 1090.44 | 1053.08 |
| **140,000** | 1850.12 | 1504.44 | 1351.04 | 1272.18 | 1228.60 |
| **160,000** | 2114.40 | 1719.36 | 1544.04 | 1453.92 | 1404.12 |
| **180,000** | 2378.72 | 1934.28 | 1737.04 | 1635.66 | 1579.62 |
| **200,000** | 2643.02 | 2149.22 | 1930.04 | 1817.40 | 1755.14 |

## 11% Annual Percentage Rate

**Monthly payments (principal and interest)**

| Amount financed | 10 Years | 15 Years | 20 Years | 25 Years | 30 Years |
|---|---|---|---|---|---|
| **$ 50,000** | $ 688.75 | $ 568.30 | $ 516.09 | $ 490.06 | $ 476.16 |
| **60,000** | 826.50 | 681.96 | 619.31 | 588.07 | 571.39 |
| **70,000** | 964.25 | 795.62 | 722.53 | 686.08 | 666.63 |
| **80,000** | 1102.00 | 909.28 | 825.75 | 784.09 | 761.86 |
| **90,000** | 1239.75 | 1022.94 | 928.97 | 882.10 | 857.09 |
| **100,000** | 1377.50 | 1136.60 | 1032.19 | 980.11 | 952.32 |
| **120,000** | 1653.00 | 1363.92 | 1238.62 | 1176.14 | 1142.78 |
| **140,000** | 1928.50 | 1591.24 | 1445.06 | 1372.16 | 1333.26 |
| **160,000** | 2204.00 | 1818.56 | 1651.50 | 1568.18 | 1523.72 |
| **180,000** | 2479.50 | 2045.88 | 1857.94 | 1764.20 | 1714.18 |
| **200,000** | 2755.00 | 2273.20 | 2064.38 | 1960.22 | 1904.64 |

# How to Obtain Birth, Marriage, Death Records

The pamphlet *Where to Write for Vital Records: Births, Deaths, Marriages, and Divorces* (Stock # 017-022-01196-4) is available from the Superintendent of Documents, PO Box 371954, Pittsburgh, PA 15250-7954; advance payment of $2.25 is required. Orders can also be placed by calling (202) 512-1800 or via fax, (202) 512-2250, using a Visa or MasterCard.

# Wedding Anniversaries

The traditional names for wedding anniversaries go back many years in social usage. As names like *wooden, crystal, silver,* and *golden* were applied to anniversary years, it was considered proper to present the married couple with gifts made of these products or of something related. The list of traditional products for gifts, with a few allowable revisions in parentheses, is presented below, with common modern gifts indicated in boldface.

| | |
|---|---|
| 1st | Paper, **clocks** |
| 2d | Cotton, **china** |
| 3d | Leather, **crystal, glass** |
| 4th | Linen (silk), **appliances** |
| 5th | Wood, **silverware** |
| 6th | Iron, **wood objects** |
| 7th | Wool (copper), **desk sets** |
| 8th | Bronze, **linens, lace** |
| 9th | Pottery (china), **leather goods** |
| 10th | Tin, aluminum, **diamond** |
| 11th | Steel, **fashion jewelry** |
| 12th | Silk, **pearls, colored gems** |
| 13th | Lace, **textiles, furs** |
| 14th | Ivory, **gold jewelry** |
| 15th | Crystal, **watches** |
| 20th | China, **platinum** |
| 25th | Silver, **sterling silver** |
| 30th | Pearl, **diamond** |
| 35th | Coral (jade), **jade** |
| 40th | Ruby, **ruby** |
| 45th | Sapphire, **sapphire** |
| 50th | Gold, **gold** |
| 55th | Emerald, **emerald** |
| 60th | Diamond, **diamond** |

# Birthstones

**Source:** Jewelry Industry Council

| Month | Ancient | Modern |
|---|---|---|
| **January** | Garnet | Garnet |
| **February** | Amethyst | Amethyst |
| **March** | Jasper | Bloodstone or Aquamarine |
| **April** | Sapphire | Diamond |
| **May** | Agate | Emerald |
| **June** | Emerald | Pearl, Moonstone, or Alexandrite |
| **July** | Onyx | Ruby |
| **August** | Carnelian | Sardonyx or Peridot |
| **September** | Chrysolite | Sapphire |
| **October** | Aquamarine | Opal or Tourmaline |
| **November** | Topaz | Topaz |
| **December** | Ruby | Turquoise or Zircon |

# The Cost of Raising a Child

**Source:** Family Economics Research Group, U.S. Dept. of Agriculture

Estimated annual expenditures in 1995 dollars for a child born in 1995, by income group. Estimates are for the younger child in a 2-parent family with 2 children for the overall U.S.

| Year | Age of child | Income group[1] Low | Middle | High |
|---|---|---|---|---|
| 1995 | under 1 | $5,490 | $ 7,610 | $11,320 |
| 1996 | 1 | 5,790 | 8,020 | 11,930 |
| 1997 | 2 | 6,100 | 8,450 | 12,580 |
| 1998 | 3 | 6,570 | 9,140 | 13,510 |
| 1999 | 4 | 6,920 | 9,640 | 14,240 |
| 2000 | 5 | 7,300 | 10,160 | 15,010 |
| 2001 | 6 | 7,870 | 10,790 | 15,770 |
| 2002 | 7 | 8,290 | 11,370 | 16,620 |
| 2003 | 8 | 8,740 | 11,990 | 17,520 |
| 2004 | 9 | $ 9,260 | $12,620 | $18,350 |
| 2005 | 10 | 9,760 | 13,300 | 19,340 |
| 2006 | 11 | 10,290 | 14,020 | 20,380 |
| 2007 | 12 | 12,330 | 16,130 | 23,060 |
| 2008 | 13 | 13,000 | 17,000 | 24,310 |
| 2009 | 14 | 13.700 | 17,920 | 25,620 |
| 2010 | 15 | 14,220 | 19,170 | 27,620 |
| 2011 | 16 | 14,990 | 20,210 | 29,110 |
| 2012 | 17 | 15,800 | 21,300 | 30,690 |
| **Total** | | **$176,420** | **$238,840** | **$346,980** |

(1) Low income is less than $33,700 (average=$21,000) in 1995; middle income is $33,700 to $56,700 (average=$44,800); high income is $56,700 or more (average=$84,800). The projected annual inflation rate is 5.4%.

# Marriage Laws

**Source:** Gary N. Skoloff, Skoloff & Wolfe, Livingston, NJ; as of July 1996

| | Age with parental consent | | Age without consent | | Physical exam & blood test for male and female | | Waiting period | |
|---|---|---|---|---|---|---|---|---|
| State | Male | Female | Male | Female | Max. period and license | Scope of medical exam | Before license | After license issuance (expiration) |
| Alabama* | 14a,t | 14a,t | 18 | 18 | — | b | — | 30 days |
| Alaska | 16z | 16z | 18 | 18 | — | — | 3 days, w | — |
| Arizona | 16z | 16z | 18 | 18 | — | — | — | — |
| Arkansas | 17c, z | 16c, z | 18 | 18 | — | — | v | — |
| California | aa | aa | 18 | 18 | 30 days, w, h | jj | — | 90 days |
| Colorado*[y] | 16z | 16z | 18 | 18 | — | — | — | 30 days |
| Connecticut | 16z | 16z | 18 | 18 | — | bb | 4 days, w | 65 days |
| Delaware | 18c | 16c | 18 | 18 | — | — | 24 hr, kk | 30 days, e |
| Florida | 16a, c | 16a, c | 18 | 18 | — | — | — | — |
| Georgia* | aa, j | aa, j | 16 | 16 | — | bb | 3 days, g | 30 days |
| Hawaii | 15j | 15j | 16 | 16 | — | p | — | — |
| Idaho* | 16z | 16z | 18 | 18 | — | s, zzz | — | — |
| Illinois | 16pp | 16pp | 18 | 18 | 30 days | n | 1 day | 60 days |
| Indiana | 17c | 17c | 18 | 18 | — | rr | 72 hr, w | 60 days |
| Iowa* | aa, j | aa, j | 18 | 18 | — | — | 3 days | 20 days |
| Kansas*[y] | aa, j | aa, j | 18 | 18 | — | — | 3 days, w | — |
| Kentucky | aa, j | aa, j | 18 | 18 | — | — | — | — |
| Louisiana | 18z | 18z | 18 | 18 | 10 days | — | 72 hr, w | — |
| Maine | 16z | 16z | 18 | 18 | — | — | 3 days, v, w | 90 days |
| Maryland | 16c, f | 16c, f | 18 | 18 | — | — | 48 hr, w | 6 mo |
| Massachusetts | 14j | 12j | 18 | 18 | 3-60 days, u | — | 3 days, v | — |
| Michigan | 16 | 16 | 18 | 18 | — | — | 3 days, w | — |
| Minnesota | 16j | 16j | 18 | 18 | — | — | 5 days, w | — |
| Mississippi | aa, j | aa, j | 17 | 15 | 30 days | b | 3 days, w | — |
| Missouri | 15d | 15d | 18 | 18 | — | — | — | — |
| Montana*[yy] | 16j | 16j | 18 | 18 | — | b | — | 180 days |
| Nebraska[yy] | 17 | 17 | 19 | 19 | — | bb | — | 1 yr |
| Nevada | 16z | 16z | 18 | 18 | — | — | — | 1 yr |
| New Hampshire | 14k | 13k | 18 | 18 | — | hh | 3 days, v, w | 90 days |
| New Jersey | 16z, c | 16z, c | 18 | 18 | 30 days | b | 72 hr, w | 30 days |
| New Mexico | 16d, c | 16d, c | 18 | 18 | 30 days | b | — | — |
| New York | 16k | 16k | 18 | 18 | — | nn | 24 hr, ee | 60 days |
| North Carolina | 16c | 16c | 18 | 18 | — | m | — | — |
| North Dakota | 16 | 16 | 18 | 18 | — | — | — | 60 days |
| Ohio | aa, j | 16c, z | 18 | 18 | 30 days | b | 5 days,w, r | 30 days |
| Oklahoma* | 16c, z | 16c, z | 18 | 18 | 30 days, w | b | ff | 30 days |
| Oregon | 17tt | 17tt | 18 | 18 | — | — | 3 days, w | — |
| Pennsylvania* | 16d | 16d | 18 | 18 | 30 days | b | 3 days, w | 60 days |
| Rhode Island* | d | 16d | 18 | 18 | — | rrr | — | — |
| South Carolina* | 16c | 14c | 18 | 18 | — | — | 1 day | — |
| South Dakota | 16c | 16c | 18 | 18 | — | — | — | 20 days |
| Tennesee | 16d | 16d | 18 | 18 | — | — | 3 days, cc, w | 30 days |
| Texas*[y] | 14j, k | 14j, k | 18 | 18 | — | — | zzzz | 30 days |
| Utah* | 14a | 14a | 18x | 18x | — | — | — | 30 days |
| Vermont | 14j | 14j | 18 | 18 | 30 days, w | b | 1 day, w | — |
| Virginia | 16a, c | 16a, c | 18 | 18 | — | zz | — | 60 days |
| Washington | 17d | 17d | 18 | 18 | — | bbb | 3 days | 60 days |
| West Virginia | 18c | 18c | 18 | 18 | — | b | 3 days, w | — |
| Wisconsin | 16 | 16 | 18 | 18 | — | zzz | 5 days, w | 30 days |
| Wyoming | 16d | 16d | 18 | 18 | — | bb | — | — |
| Dist. of Columbia* | 16a | 16a | 18 | 18 | 30 days | b | 3 days, w | — |
| Puerto Rico | 18c, d, z | 16c, d, z | 21 | 21c | — | b | — | — |

*Indicates common-law marriage recognized. (a)Parental consent not required if minor was previously married. (aa)No age limits. (b)Venereal diseases. In WV and OK, Circuit Court judge may waive requirement. (bb)Venereal diseases and rubella (for female). (bbb)No exam required, but parties must file affidavit of non-affliction with contagious venereal disease. (c)Younger parties may obtain license in case of pregnancy or birth of child. (cc)Unless parties are over 18 yr of age. (d)Younger parties may obtain license in special circumstances. (e)Residents before expiration of 24-hr waiting period; non-residents formerly residents, before expiration of 96-hr waiting period; others 96 hr. (ee)License effective 1 day after issuance, unless court orders otherwise; valid for 60 days only. (f)If parties are at least 16 yr of age, proof of age and the consent of parents in person are required. If a parent is ill, an affidavit by the incapacitated parent and a physician's affidavit to that effect required. (ff)If one or both parties are below the age for marriage without parental consent, 3-day waiting period. (g)Unless parties are 18 yr of age or more, or female is pregnant, or applicants are the parents of a living child born out of wedlock. (h)When unmarried man and unmarried woman, not minors, have been living together as man and wife, they may, without health certificate, be married upon issuance of appropriate authorization. (hh)Parties must sign affidavit affirming that they have received and discussed brochure prepared by Division of Public Health Services, Dept. of Health and Human Services. (j)Parental consent and/or permission of judge required. (jj)Medical examination for syphilis (and for female, rubella), with required offer of HIV test. (k)Below age of consent parties need parental consent and permission of judge. (kk)Medical examination not required but certificate evidencing HIV counseling required. (l)If both parties are residents, 96 hr. (m)Mental incompetence, infectious tuberculosis, venereal diseases. (n)Venereal diseases; test for sickle cell anemia given at request of examining physician. (nn)Tests for sickle cell anemia may be required for certain applicants. (p)Rubella for female, except under limited circumstances. (pp)Judicial consent may be given when parents refuse to consent. (r)Applicants under age 18 must state that they have had marriage counseling. (rr)Any unsterilized female under 50 must submit with application for license a medical report stating whether she has immunological response to rubella, or a written record that the rubella vaccine was administered on or after her 1st birthday. Judge may by order dispense with these requirements. (rrr)Physical examination and blood test required; offer of HIV counseling required. (s)Rubella for female; there are certain exceptions, and district judge may waive medical examination on proof that emergency exists. (t)Other statutory requirements apply. (tt)If a party has no parent residing within state, and one party has residence within state for 6 mo, no permission required. (u)Doctor's certificate must be filed 30 days prior to notice of intention. (v)Parties must file notice of intention to marry with local clerk. (w)Waiting period may be avoided. (x)Authorizes counties to provide for premarital counseling as a requisite to issuance of license to persons under 19 and persons previously divorced. (y)Marriages by proxy are valid. (yy) Proxy marriages are valid under certain conditions. (z)Younger parties may marry with parental consent and/or permission of judge. In CT, judicial approval. (zz)Required offer of HIV test, and/or must be provided with information on AIDS and tests available. (zzz)Applicants must receive information on AIDS and certify having read it. (zzzz)72 hr waiting period following issuance of license.

# Divorce Laws

**Source:** Gary N. Skoloff, Skoloff & Wolfe, Livingston, NJ; as of July 1996

Important: Almost all states also have other laws as well as qualifications of the laws shown below and have proposed divorce-reform laws pending. It would be wise to consult a lawyer in conjunction with the use of this chart.

## Some Grounds for Absolute Divorce[1]

| | Residence | Adultery | Mental or physical cruelty | Desertion | Alcoholism | Impotency | Non-support | Insanity | Bigamy | Felony conviction or imprisonment | Drug addiction | Fraud, force, duress |
|---|---|---|---|---|---|---|---|---|---|---|---|---|
| AL | 6 mo* | Yes | Yes | 1 yr | Yes | Yes | 2 yr | 5 yr | A | 2 yr* | Yes | A |
| AK | * | Yes | Yes | 1 yr | 1 yr | Yes | No | 18 mo | A | Yes | Yes | A |
| AZ | 90 days | No | No | No | No | No | No | No | No | No | No | No |
| AR | 60 days* | Yes | Yes | No | 1 yr | Yes | Yes | 3 yr | No | Yes | No | A |
| CA | 6 mo* | No | No | No | No | A | No | Yes* | A | No | No | A |
| CO | 90 days | No | No | No | A | A | No | No | A | No | A | A |
| CT | 1 yr* | Yes | Yes | 1 yr | No | No | Yes | 5 yr | A | life* | No | Yes |
| DE | 6 mo | Yes | Yes | Yes | Yes | A | No | Yes | Yes | Yes | Yes | A |
| FL | 6 mo | No | No | No | No | No | No | 3 yr | No | No | No | A |
| GA | 6 mo | Yes | Yes | 1 yr | Yes | Yes | No | 2 yr | A | Yes* | Yes | Yes |
| HI | 6 mo | No | No | No | No | No | No | No | A | No | No | A |
| ID | 6 wk | Yes | Yes | Yes | No | A | No | 3 yr | A | Yes | No | A |
| IL | 90 days | Yes | Yes | 1 yr | 2 yr | Yes | No | No | Yes | Yes | 2 yr | No |
| IN | 6 mo* | No | No | No | No | Yes | No | 2 yr | A | Yes | No | A |
| IA | 1 yr* | No | No | No | No | A | No | A | A | No | No | No |
| KS | 60 days | No | No | No | No | No | Yes | 2 yr | A | No | No | A |
| KY | 180 days | No | No | No | No | A | No | No | No | No | No | A |
| LA | 6 mo* | Yes | No | No | No | No | No | No | A | Yes* | No | A |
| ME | 6 mo* | Yes | Yes | 3 yr | Yes | Yes | Yes | A | A | No | Yes | No |
| MD | * | Yes | † | 1 yr† | No | No | No | 3 yr | A | 1 yr* | No | No |
| MA | 1 yr* | Yes | Yes | 1 yr | Yes | Yes | No† | A | A | 5 yr* | Yes | No |
| MI | 180 days* | No | No | No | No | No | No | No | No | No | No | A |
| MN | 180 days | No | No | No | No | No | No | No | No | No | A | A |
| MS | 6 mo | Yes | Yes | 1 yr | Yes | Yes, A | No | 3 yr, A | Yes | Yes | Yes | A |
| MO | 90 days | No | No | No | No | No | No | No | A | No | No | A |
| MT | 90 days | No | No | No | A | A | No | No | A | No | A | A |
| NE | 1 yr* | No | No | No | No | A | No | A | A | No | No | A |
| NV | 6 wk | No | No | No | No | No | No | 2 yr | A | No | No | A |
| NH | 1 yr* | Yes | Yes | 2 yr | 2 yr | Yes | 2 yr | No | A | 1 yr* | No | No |
| NJ | 1 yr* | Yes | Yes | 1 yr | 1 yr | A | No | 2 yr | A | 18 mo | 1 yr | A |
| NM | 6 mo | Yes | Yes | Yes | No | No | No | No | No | No | No | No |
| NY | 1 yr* | Yes† | Yes | 1 yr† | No | No | † | A | A | 3 yr† | No | A |
| NC | 6 mo | No† | No† | No† | No† | A | No | 3 yr | A | No | No† | No |
| ND | 6 mo | Yes | Yes | 1 yr | No | A | 1 yr | 5 yr | A | Yes | No | A |
| OH | 6 mo | Yes† | Yes† | 1 yr† | Yes† | No | Yes† | No | Yes† | Yes† | No | Yes† |
| OK | 6 mo | Yes | Yes | 1 yr | Yes | Yes | Yes | 5 yr | Yes | Yes | No | Yes |
| OR | 6 mo* | No | No | No | No | No | No | No | No | No | Yes | No |
| PA | 6 mo | Yes | Yes | 1 yr | No | No | No | 18 mo* | Yes | Yes | No | No |
| RI | 1 yr | Yes | Yes | 5 yr* | Yes | Yes | 1 yr | No | No | Yes | Yes | No |
| SC | 1 yr* | Yes | Yes | 1 yr | Yes | No | No | No | A | No | Yes | No |
| SD | * | Yes† | Yes† | 1 yr† | 1 yr† | A | 1 yr† | 5 yr† | A | Yes† | No | A |
| TN | 6 mo* | Yes | Yes | 1 yr | Yes | Yes | † | No | Yes | Yes | Yes | A |
| TX | 6 mo* | Yes | Yes | 1 yr | No | A | No | 3 yr | No | 1 yr | No | A |
| UT | 3 mo* | Yes | Yes | 1 yr | Yes | Yes | Yes | Yes* | A | Yes | No | No |
| VT | 6 mo* | Yes | Yes | 7 yr | No | No | Yes | 5 yr† | A | 3 yr | No | A |
| VA | 6 mo* | Yes | Yes† | 1 yr† | No | A | † | A | A | 1 yr | No | A |
| WA | bona fide resident | No | No | No | No | No | No | No | A* | No | No | A |
| WV | 1 yr* | Yes | Yes | 6 mo | Yes | A | No | 3 yr | A | Yes | Yes | No |
| WI | 6 mo | No | No | No | A | A | No | No | A | No | A | A |
| WY | 2 mo* | No | No | No | No | No | No | 2 yr | A | No | No | A |
| DC | 6 mo | No | No | No | No | A | No | A | A | No | No | A |
| PR | 1 yr | Yes | Yes | 1 yr | Yes | Yes | No | Yes | A | Yes* | Yes | No |

(1)Almost all states have "no-fault" divorce laws. Conduct that constitutes "no-fault" divorce may vary from state to state. (*)Indicates qualification; check local statutes. (A)Indicates grounds for annulment. (†)Indicates grounds for divorce or legal separation.

# TAXES

## Federal Income Tax

**Source:** George W. Smith III, CPA, Nationally Syndicated Tax Author and Columnist

During the past decade, the U.S. Congress has enacted numerous tax law changes. The trend continued in 1996. Four new bills signed into law in July and August alone added more than 650 changes and amendments to the tax code. These and other recent changes take effect at different times in 1996 and 1997.

### Major New Changes

**Long-Term Care.** The Health Insurance Act of 1996 allows certain insurance premiums and related expenses for long-term care services to be deductible as medical expenses, starting in 1997.

**Death Benefits.** Starting in 1997, the Health Insurance Act provides that accelerated death benefits received from life insurance policies on the lives of terminally ill individuals are excluded from gross income and therefore not taxable. Similar, but more limited, tax breaks apply to the chronically ill.

**Legal Awards.** After Aug. 20, 1996, damages received for emotional distress are taxable income unless attributable to a physical injury or illness. Punitive damages received for personal injury or sickness also will be taxable.

**Disadvantaged Workers.** The Welfare Reform Act of 1996 certified a new 35% work opportunity tax credit for businesses that hire certain disadvantaged workers beginning work after Sept. 30, 1996 and before Oct. 1, 1997. The credit is 35% of up to $6,000 of each worker's first-year wages, to a maximum credit of $2,100.

**Adoption Credit.** The Small Business Act of 1996 adds a new "up-to-$5,000" tax credit for adoption expenses (up to $6,000 for a domestic special-needs adoption), and an exclusion for certain employer-paid adoption expenses for tax years after 1996. The credits and exclusion expire after Dec. 31, 2001.

**Retirees' Past Income.** Many states have taxed former residents on their retirement income if it was originally earned within that state. Starting Jan. 1, 1996, a new federal law provides that a state *may not* impose an income tax on any individual's retirement income received after 1995 if the person is no longer a resident of the state.

**Earnings Limits.** Starting in 1996, the Senior Citizens' Right to Work Act increased the amount individuals age 65-69 may earn without jeopardizing their Social Security benefits. The maximum earning level rises to $12,500 in 1996, $13,500 in 1997, and increases annually to $30,000 by 2002.

The maximum dollar amount individuals age 62 to 64 may earn without losing any of their Social Security benefits was adjusted for inflation to $8,280 for 1996. In this age group, individuals will lose $1 of benefits for every $2 of earned income exceeding $8,280.

For persons ages 65 to 69, $1 of benefits is lost for every $3 of earned income in excess of the $12,500 threshold. Individuals who are age 70 or over do not lose any Social Security benefits regardless of earnings.

**Elective Withholding.** After Dec. 31, 1996, taxpayers who receive Social Security benefits (and certain other payments) from the federal government may elect to have the payor agency withhold federal income tax at a rate of 7%, 15%, 18%, or 31%. State governments will be required to permit elective federal withholding from unemployment compensation at a rate of 15%.

**Newborns.** Taxpayers can lose the head of household filing status, the dependency exemption, the dependent care credit, and the earned income credit, if the Social Security number of a dependent born before Nov. 30, 1996, is not included on their tax return. For tax purposes, all dependents must have a Social Security number for 1997. For more information on obtaining this number, call the Social Security Administration at 1-800-772-1212.

**Retirement Plans.** Starting in 1996, participants in 401(k) plans generally may withdraw funds from the retirement plan without penalty when this is "necessary" to satisfy "immediate and heavy financial needs." The annual limitation on elective deferrals to 401(k) retirement plans was adjusted for inflation to $9,500 in 1996.

After Dec. 31, 1996, any employee who continues to work beyond age 70½ and is not a 5% owner of the business can delay receiving retirement plan distributions.

The Small Business Act eliminates 5-year averaging for lump sum distributions from qualified plans beginning after 1999. However, prior rules that applied to individuals who attained age 50 before Jan. 1, 1986, are still in effect. The 15% excise tax on combined retirement plan and IRA distributions over $155,000 a year ($775,000 for lump sum distributions) is suspended from 1997 through 1999.

**Health Insurance.** The Self-Employment Health Insurance Act of 1995 permanently restored the health insurance premium deduction for the self-employed and increased this page 1, Form 1040, deduction to 30%. The 1996 Health Insurance Act increased the deduction to 40% for 1997, with annual increases to 80% by 2006.

**Business Receipts.** The Internal Revenue Service increased its threshold amount to $75 for 1996 business travel and entertainment expense substantiation. A receipt is required for business meals, entertainment, and transportation costs if the expense is $75 or more. Adequate records still must be kept substantiating the time, place, date, and business purpose.

**School Costs.** The education assistance plan that would exclude from income up to $5,250 of employer-provided education costs expired after 1994 but in 1996 was restored by Congress retroactively, through May 31, 1997.

**Mileage Rates.** For 1996 tax deductions, the standard mileage rate for business use of an automobile was increased to 31 cents a mile for all business miles driven. The standard mileage rate cannot be used for leased cars. The rate was increased from 9 cents to 10 cents per mile for the personal use of an automobile used for medical or moving purposes.

**Deficiencies.** On Jan. 11, 1996, the United States Tax Court issued a decision allowing persons who paid interest on an income tax deficiency to deduct the interest expense attributable to their trade or business.

**Payroll Tax Reporting.** The IRS requires businesses that had federal employment taxes of more than $50,000 for the calendar year 1995 to begin making all federal tax deposit payments electronically starting July 1, 1997, using the government's new Electronic Federal Tax Payment System (EFTPS). Failure to do so will result in a 10% penalty for each deposit not made through EFTPS. The electronic tax deposit rules apply to *all* federal taxes (payroll, corporate income, excise, and estimated taxes). For more information call the IRS Customer Service at 1-800-945-8400 or 1-800-555-4477.

**Electronic Services.** Federal tax forms, tax legislation, court decisions, and other information are now available electronically from the Internal Revenue Service as follows:

**via modem:** 1-705-321-8020

**via the IRS's Internet Home Page addresses:**

Telnet: iris.irs.ustreas.gov

FTP: htp.irs.ustreas.gov

World Wide Web: http://www.irs.ustreas.gov

**Taxpayers' Rights.** New legislation was enacted in 1996; see section **Your Rights as a Taxpayer**.

**Soldiers in Bosnia.** On Mar. 20, 1996, President Bill Clinton signed Public Law 104-117, which entitles members of the U.S. armed forces serving in Bosnia and Hercegovina, Croatia, and Macedonia to the same tax benefits provided to military personnel serving in a combat zone.

### Other Tax Law Developments

**Tax Rates.** There are still 5 individual federal income tax rates: 15%, 28%, 31%, 36%, and 39.6%. The dollar amounts for both the Tax Tables and the Tax Rate Schedules are adjusted annually so that inflation will not increase an individual's tax liability. The maximum income tax rate on net long-term capital gains for individuals, estates, and trusts remains at 28%.

**Social Security Taxes.** The maximum wage base for withholding Social Security tax rose to $62,700 for 1996; the rate remains 6.2%. The Medicare tax rate remains 1.45%, with no maximum wage base. Both taxes are paid by employer and employee each. Self-employed individuals pay both parts.

**"Nanny Tax."** Congress in 1994 simplified the tax reporting and paperwork associated with the employment of household workers such as nannies, gardeners, and cooks.

Employment information and withholding tax obligations are now included in the employer's individual income tax return on Schedule H, Form 1040. Quarterly employment tax returns for household employees are no longer required. Employers no longer must withhold taxes for household workers who receive less than $1,000 per year. Employers will need to apply for an employer identification number and prepare employee wage statements (Form W-2).

*Exclusion*: The "Nanny Tax" Act exempts household workers under the age of 18 (students, etc.) from employment taxes even if they are paid more than $1,000 a year, unless working in a household is their principal occupation.

**Empowerment Zones.** A 20% tax credit is available to most employers for qualified wages paid to full-time or part-time employees who are residents of one of 9 empowerment zones. These are distressed areas designated for economic revitalization by the U.S. Department of Housing and Urban Development and the U.S. Agriculture Department.

The 20% credit is applied toward the employer's income tax liability for the first $15,000 of wages paid. The maximum credit is $3,000 per employee. The credit has been extended through the year 2001 but is reduced to 15% for 2002, 10% for 2003, and 5% for 2004. Employees must perform substantially all their employment services within the empowerment zone.

**Students.** An individual may not claim an exemption for a dependent child who qualifies as a full-time student and is over age 23 at the end of the year, unless the child's gross income is less than $2,550. This is an increase of $50 over 1995.

Interest earned on U.S. Series EE bonds issued after 1989 may be exempt from federal income tax if the bonds were used to pay tuition and fees for a taxpayer, spouse, or dependent to attend a college, university, or qualified technical school during the year the bonds are redeemed. The maximum dollar amount of the exclusion is phased out when income goes over a specified amount. Your banker can assist with the details.

**Electric-Powered Vehicles.** An individual who buys a new 4-wheel vehicle powered primarily by an electric motor may be eligible for an income tax credit equal to 10% of the cost of the vehicle, with a maximum credit of $4,000 per vehicle.

However, the diesel fuel tax rebate was repealed for vehicles purchaed after Aug. 20, 1996.

**Children's Income.** Parents may elect to include on their income tax return the unearned income of a dependent child under age 14 whose income is more than $650 but less than $6,500. The income must consist solely of interest and dividends. Form 8814, *Parent's Election to Report Child's Interest and Dividends*, must be attached to the parents' tax return. If the parents elect to do this, the child is not required to file a tax return. This election is not available, however, if estimated tax payments were made in the child's name.

If a dependent child with taxable income cannot file an income tax return, a parent, guardian, or other legally responsible person must file the return for the child. The parent or guardian may be held liable for any unpaid tax.

**Sale of Residence.** For individuals age 55 or over, the 3-out-of-5-year home-use rule for the sale of their principal residence has been expanded. Certain incapacitated individuals living in state-licensed facilities may exclude from gross income a maximum of $125,000 of gain resulting from the sale of their home if it was used as their principal residence for at least one year out of the last 5 years ending on the date of the sale. *Caution:* This is a once-in-a-lifetime exclusion.

**Phones and Computers.** The business use of a cellular phone or home computer must be for the convenience of the employer and a condition of employment to be an allowable business deduction for an employee.

**Home Mortgage.** Borrowers can generally deduct the points paid on their mortgage loan. The IRS has also affirmed that the buyer can deduct "seller-paid points" on the purchase of a principal residence.

**Investment Interest.** Interest expense paid on investments is deductible up to the amount of net investment income. Capital gains income also can be included as investment income when figuring the limitation. However, the taxpayer will have to reduce the amount of net long-term capital gain that is eligible for capital gains treatment in order to offset the additional investment interest deduction.

**Business Expenses.** The election to expense the cost of certain depreciable business assets is called a "Section 179 Expense Election." The maximum amount for 1996 is $17,500, with annual increases to $25,000 by 2003.

Patents, trademarks, and certain other intangible assets are amortized over a 15-year period. The cost of goodwill and client/patient lists are included in this 15-year write-off.

The deduction for qualified business meals and entertainment expenses is limited to 50%.

Expenses paid for business assignments away from home that last for more than one year in a single location are no longer deductible.

Taxpayers cannot deduct travel expenses paid for other individuals (including a spouse) with them on a business trip unless the individual (1) is their employee, (2) has a bona fide business purpose for the travel, and (3) would otherwise be allowed to deduct the travel expense.

**Charitable Contributions.** Taxpayers deducting individual charitable contributions of $250 or more must obtain written substantiation from the charity. If the statement or receipt is for more than $75, it must include a breakdown of the payment indicating how much is a (deductible) contribution and what (if any) was the (nondeductible) value of goods or services (including meals) received.

**Club Dues.** Dues paid to business, social, athletic, luncheon, sporting, and country clubs, including airport and hotel clubs, are no longer deductible. Dues to the Chamber of Commerce and business Economic Clubs remain deductible.

**Estimated Tax.** If taxpayers owe $500 or more of federal income taxes as reported on their 1996 tax return, they must file quarterly estimated tax payments during 1997, unless 1997 income tax withholding and credits equal 100% of the income tax shown on their 1996 tax return. The percentage increases to 110% if adjusted gross income in 1996 was more than $150,000 (more than $75,000 if married filing separately).

Individual federal estimated tax payment due dates for 1997 are as follows: 1st Quarter - Apr. 15, 1997; 2d Quarter - June 16, 1997; 3d Quarter - Sept. 15, 1997; 4th Quarter - Jan. 15, 1998.

Different rules apply for farmers and people engaged in commercial fishing.

No penalty will be imposed on an individual or a corporation for an estimated tax installment that is underpaid because of an amendment to the Internal Revenue Code made by the 1996 Small Business Act.

**Installment Payments.** If taxpayers do not have the necessary funds to pay their federal income taxes when due, they may apply for monthly installment payments. The request is made by attaching Form 9465, *Installment Agreement Request,* to the individual's tax return. Penalty and interest will continue to accrue. There is a $43 fee if the request is approved.

**Refunds.** Instead of receiving a check in the mail, taxpayers can have their federal income tax refund deposited directly into their checking or savings account at a bank or other financial institution. Use Form 8888, *Direct Deposit of Refund,* which is included in your 1996 income tax booklet.

Taxpayers who file their income tax returns electronically or use the 1040PC format can instruct the IRS to deposit their refund directly into a checking or savings account. The IRS says that if you file electronically, your refund will be issued within 21 days.

**Assistance in Spanish.** The IRS provides videotaped instructions to assist taxpayers, not only in English but also in Spanish. These tapes are available at participating libraries. Various federal tax instructions, publications, and forms are now printed in Spanish. To begin with, ask for IRS Publication 1SP, *Derechos del Contribuyente.* For a free copy, call 1-800-TAX-FORM.

**Hearing-Impaired.** The IRS telephone service for hearing impaired persons is available for taxpayers who have access to TDD equipment. The toll-free number is 1-800-829-4059.

## Who Must File

Generally, a U.S. citizen or a resident alien will have to file an income tax return if the person's gross income for the year is at least as much as the amount shown in the following table:

| Filing Status | Gross Income |
|---|---|
| Single | |
| • Under 65 | $ 6,550 |
| • 65 or older | 7,550 |
| Married filing jointly | |
| • Both spouses under 65 | 11,800 |
| • One spouse 65 or older | 12,600 |
| • Both spouses 65 or older | 13,400 |
| Married filing separately | 2,550 |
| Head of Household | |
| • Under 65 | 8,450 |
| • 65 or older | 9,450 |
| Qualifying widow(er) | |
| • Under 65 | 9,250 |
| • 65 or older | 10,050 |

**Some Exceptions to Filing Requirements.** A tax return must be filed if:

- Taxpayer had net earnings of $400 or more from self-employment for the year.
- Taxpayer received advance earned income credit payments during the year from an employer or is entitled to receive a refundable earned income credit.
- Taxpayer paid estimated income tax payments during the year or expects an income tax refund.
- Gross income is less than the filing requirement amount but additional taxes are owed for:

—Social Security tax on unreported tips.
—Alternative minimum tax
—Recapture of investment credit
—Tax attributable to qualified retirement distributions (including IRAs), annuities, and modified endowment contracts.

## When to File

U.S. individual income tax returns for 1996 are required to be filed with the Internal Revenue Service no later than Tuesday, Apr. 15, 1997. An individual who cannot file on time should file Form 4868, *Application for Automatic Extension of Time to File U.S. Individual Income Tax Return.* Form 4868 gives the taxpayer an automatic 4-month extension of time to file, until Friday, Aug. 15, 1997. This is not, however, an extension of time to pay the tax. The taxpayer will owe interest and may be charged a penalty on any federal income tax owed and not paid to the IRS by Apr. 15, 1997.

## Which Form to File

Most U.S. citizens can use one of the following basic income tax forms: 1040EZ, 1040A, 1040. Forms 1040EZ and 1040A are shorter and simpler than Form 1040.

**You may be able to use the shortest of the 3 forms, Form 1040EZ, if:**

- You are single or married filing jointly and do not claim any dependents.
- You are not 65 or older or blind.
- You have income only from wages, salaries, tips, taxable scholarships or fellowships, or unemployment compensation, and not more than $400 of taxable interest income.
- Your taxable income is less than $50,000.
- You do not itemize deductions, claim any adjustments to income, or have tax credits other than the earned income credit.
- You did not receive any advance earned income credit payments.
- You did not make any estimated tax payments.
- You file on or before Tuesday, Apr. 15, 1997. You cannot use Form 1040EZ *after* Apr. 15 even if you have filed for an extension.

**You may at least be able to use Form 1040A if:**

- You have income from wages, salaries, tips, taxable scholarships or fellowships, interest, and dividends.
- You have income from Individual Retirement Account (IRA) distributions, pensions, annuities, unemployment compensation, and taxable Social Security or railroad retirement benefits.
- Your taxable income is less than $50,000.
- You do not itemize deductions.
- You claim a deduction for qualified contributions to an IRA.
- You claim a credit for child and dependent care expenses, credit for the elderly or the disabled, or the earned income credit.
- You report employment taxes on wages paid to household employees on Schedule H.
- You take the education exclusion for interest income earned from Series EE U.S. Savings Bonds.
- You have made estimated tax payments.
- You filed for an extension of time to file.

**You will have to file Form 1040 if any of the following situations apply:**

- Your taxable income is $50,000 or more.
- You itemize deductions.
- You receive any nontaxable dividends or capital gain distributions.
- You have foreign bank accounts and/or foreign trusts.
- You have taxable refunds of state or local income taxes.
- You have business, farm, or rental income.
- You sold or exchanged capital assets or business property.
- You have miscellaneous income not allowed on Form 1040EZ or 1040A, such as alimony or lottery winnings.
- You have additional adjustments to income such as alimony paid, or moving expenses.
- You can claim a foreign tax credit or certain other credits to which you are entitled.
- You have other taxes such as self-employment tax or the alternative minimum tax.
- You are required to file additional forms such as:

**Form 2106**, Employee Business Expenses.
**Form 2555**, Foreign Earned Income.
**Form 3903**, Moving Expenses.
**Form 4864**, Casualty and Thefts.
**Form 4972**, Tax on Lump-Sum Distributions.

## 1996 Individual Tax Rates

**Single**

| Tax Rate | Taxable Income |
|---|---|
| 15% | $0 to $24,000 |
| 28% | $24,001 to $58,150 |
| 31% | $58,151 to $121,300 |
| 36% | $121,301 to $263,750 |
| 39.6% | More than $263,750 |

**Married Filing Separately**

| Tax Rate | Taxable Income |
|---|---|
| 15% | $0 to $20,050 |
| 28% | $20,051 to $48,450 |
| 31% | $48,451 to $73,850 |
| 36% | $73,851 to $131,875 |
| 39.6% | More than $131,875 |

**Married Filing Jointly or Qualifying Widow(er)**

| Tax Rate | Taxable Income |
|---|---|
| 15% | $0 to $40,100 |
| 28% | $40,101 to $96,900 |
| 31% | $96,901 to $147,700 |
| 36% | $147,701 to $263,750 |
| 39.6% | More than $263,750 |

**Head of Household**

| Tax Rate | Taxable Income |
|---|---|
| 15% | $0 to $32,150 |
| 28% | $32,151 to $83,050 |
| 31% | $83,051 to $134,500 |
| 36% | $134,501 to $263,750 |
| 39.6% | More than 263,750 |

**Estates and Trusts**

| Tax Rate | Taxable Income |
|---|---|
| 15% | $0 to $1,600 |
| 28% | $1,601 to $3,800 |
| 31% | $3,801 to $5,800 |
| 36% | $5,801 to $7,900 |
| 39.6% | More than $7,900 |

The maximum income tax rate on net long-term capital gains for an individual, estate, or trust is 28%.

The alternative minimum tax rate for noncorporate taxpayers is 26% for alternative minimum taxable income less the exemption amount up to $175,000 ($87,500 for married individuals filing separately). Above that dollar level, a 28% rate applies.

## Dependent and Personal Exemptions

The deductible exemption amount for 1996 has been increased to $2,550 for each individual taxpayer or dependent. The exemption amount has been adjusted for inflation each year since 1990.

*Exemption Phaseout.* The deduction for each exemption is reduced by 2% for each $2,500 ($1,250 for married filing separately) or fraction thereof by which adjusted gross income for 1996 exceeds the following amounts:

| | |
|---|---|
| Married filing jointly | $176,950 |
| Qualifying widow(er) | $176,950 |
| Head of household | $147,450 |
| Single | $117,950 |
| Married filing separately | $ 88,475 |

The exemption amount is fully phased out when adjusted gross income is more than $122,500 ($61,250 for married filing separately) over the above threshold amount.

## Standard Deduction

The standard deduction is a flat dollar amount that is subtracted from the adjusted gross income of taxpayers who do not itemize their deductions. The amount of the basic standard deduction depends on the taxpayer's filing status and is adjusted annually for inflation.

**1996 Basic Standard Deduction**

| | |
|---|---|
| Single: | $4,000 |
| Married filing jointly or qualifying widow(er): | $6,700 |
| Married filing separately: | $3,350 |
| Head of household: | $5,900 |

These figures are not applicable if an individual can be claimed as a dependent on another person's tax return.

*Caution:* Taxpayers with itemized deductions totaling more than the above amounts should itemize instead of using the standard deduction.

An individual claimed as a dependent on another person's income tax return generally may claim on his or her own tax return only the larger of $650 or the amount of earned income up to the amount of the basic standard deduction that the taxpayer would normally be allowed.

Earned income includes wages, salaries, commissions, and tips. It also includes net profit from self-employment received as compensation for personal services rendered. Any part of a scholarship or fellowship grant that must be included in gross income is also considered earned income.

Elderly or blind taxpayers may claim an additional standard deduction besides the basic standard deduction. Taxpayers who are age 65 or over or blind at the end of 1996 qualify. Individuals who claim the additional standard deduction because of blindness must attach a doctor's statement to their income tax return.

*Tax Tip.* For tax purposes, an individual is considered 65 years of age beginning on the day preceding his or her 65th birthday. Therefore, a taxpayer whose 65th birthday falls on Jan. 1, 1997, is entitled to take the additional standard deduction for 1996.

**1996 Additional Standard Deduction**

| | |
|---|---|
| Single or head of household, age 65 or older OR blind | $1,000 |
| Single or head of household, age 65 or older AND blind | $2,000 |
| Married filing jointly or qualifying widow(er), age 65 or older OR blind (per person) | $ 800 |
| Married filing jointly or qualifying widow(er), age 65 or older AND blind (per person) | $1,600 |
| Married filing separately, age 65 or older OR blind | $ 800 |
| Married filing separately, age 65 or older AND blind | $1,600 |

## Adjustments to Income

### Individual Retirement Accounts (IRAs)

Single taxpayers who are not covered by a qualified employer retirement plan may deduct an IRA contribution up to the lesser of $2,000 or the amount of their earned income, regardless of their total income. Married taxpayers filing jointly may take an IRA deduction provided *neither* spouse is an active participant in a qualified retirement plan. Starting in 1997, the Small Business Act of 1996 allows a contribution up to $2,000 to an IRA account for each spouse on a jointly filed return even if one had less than $2,000 of compensation or did not work during the year. However, the combined compensation of both spouses must at least equal the amount contributed to both spouses' IRA accounts.

IRA payouts used to pay medical expenses in excess of 7.5% of adjusted gross income are exempt from the 10% penalty for early withdrawal, starting in 1997. In addition, the 10% penalty will not apply to IRA distributions taken early by certain unemployed, formerly unemployed, or self-employed individuals to pay for health insurance premiums.

Taxpayers may contribute to their IRAs even if they are covered by an employer-sponsored qualified retirement plan. However, the amount that can be deducted on their income tax return depends on total income.

Married taxpayers filing jointly in 1996 with adjusted gross income of $40,000 or less may take the maximum IRA deduction allowed, whether either spouse is an active participant in a qualified retirement plan. Single taxpayers in a qualified retirement plan may deduct an IRA contribution provided their AGI is $25,000 or less. Above these amounts, the IRA deduction begins to phase out over the next $10,000 of AGI if a taxpayer is an active participant in a qualified retirement plan.

### Moving Expenses

Taxpayers who change jobs or are transferred to another job location during the year usually can deduct part of their moving expenses. These expenses include travel and the cost of moving household goods to their new home. The cost of meals while moving is no longer deductible.

To qualify, the move must be a result of changing job locations or starting a new job and must meet distance and time tests. The new job location must be at least 50 miles farther from their former home than their old job location. Employees must work full time for at least 39 weeks during the first 12 months after they arrive in the general area of their new job location.

Taxpayers no longer have to itemize on Schedule A to deduct their moving expenses. These expenses are now an adjustment to income and should instead be reported on page 1, Form 1040. Any reimbursements for moving that are not qualified moving expenses will be included in the employee's gross income as compensation for services and are fully taxable. Moves within the United States are reported on Form 3903, *Moving Expenses.*

## Itemized Deductions

If the total of your itemized deductions is more than your standard deduction, you should itemize your deductions. Itemized deductions are reported on Schedule A, Form 1040.

• Cosmetic surgery for congenital abnormality, personal injury resulting from an accident or trauma, or a disfiguring disease is allowed as a medical deduction. Only the total amount of medical expenses that exceeds 7.5% of the taxpayer's adjusted gross income is deductible.

• Investment interest expense is deductible only to the extent of net investment income. Any investment interest expense not deducted is carried over to future years.

• Most mortgage interest paid on a taxpayer's first and second homes is fully deductible, but there are limitations.

• Interest paid on home equity loans is deductible, but only up to the first $100,000 in equity debt.

• State and local income taxes, real estate taxes, and personal property taxes remain fully deductible. Sales taxes are not deductible.

• Casualty and theft losses are deductible subject to the $100 limitation rule for each occurrence and the 10% of adjusted gross income provision.

• Miscellaneous items, such as union and professional dues, tax preparation fees, safe-deposit box rental expense, and employee business expenses, are deductible, but only what exceeds 2% of the taxpayer's adjusted gross income.

• Amounts spent for business tools and supplies used at work are deductible expenses if they wear out within 1 year from the date of purchase. Tools expected to last more than a year will have to be depreciated. These expenses also are subject to the 2% rule.

• Armed forces reservists can deduct the unreimbursed cost of their uniforms if military regulations restrict them from wearing the uniforms except while on duty as a reservist.

• Individuals can deduct gambling losses, including the cost of lottery tickets, on Schedule A, but only up to the amount of their reported gambling winnings.

Unreimbursed employee business expenses including travel, automobile, telephone, and gifts are deductible on Schedule A as miscellaneous itemized deductions. Only 50% of the cost of customer meals and entertainment is deductible. All deductible employee business expenses are subject to the 2% of AGI rule.

Many itemized deductions otherwise allowed are further reduced by the smaller of 3% of a taxpayer's adjusted gross income in excess of the 1996 threshold amount, $117,950 ($58,975 for married taxpayers filing separately) *or* 80% of the amount of these itemized deductions otherwise allowable for the year. This provision does not apply to medical expenses, investment interest expense, casualty losses, or gambling losses to the extent of gambling winnings.

## 1996 Earned Income Credit

Low-income workers who have dependent children and maintain a household may be eligible for a refundable earned income credit. The credit is calculated on earned income such as wages and tips. The maximum earned income credit for an individual with one qualifying child is $2,152. However, the credit is gradually phased out as the person's earned income increases. It is completely phased out once adjusted gross income reaches $25,078 (with one qualifying child). For an individual with 2 or more qualifying children, the maximum credit is $3,556 and is phased out once adjusted gross income reaches $28,495. If an individual qualifies for the earned income credit, the credit is refundable even if the person is not required to file an income tax return. However, a tax return must be filed to receive the refund.

To assist individuals, the IRS publishes a chart showing the earned income credit at various levels of income. This chart is available free at any IRS office. The IRS will also assist individuals in filing for the earned income credit.

The earned income credit has been extended to include persons who work and do not have a qualifying child. The maximum credit without a child is $323. To qualify: (1) earned income and adjusted gross income must be less than $9,500, (2) an individual or spouse must be at least 25 years old and less than 65, and (3) an individual cannot be claimed as a dependent on another person's return.

The Welfare Reform Act of 1996 added several restrictions to the Earned Income Credit, effective in 1996:

The credit cannot be taken by individuals who are not authorized to be employed in the U.S. Individuals are ineligible if they do not include their own Social Security number, and, if married, their spouse's Social Security number on the return claming the credit. Also, an individual is not eligible for the credit if his or her "disqualified" income exceeds $2,200. Disqualified income includes interest, dividends, and if greater than zero, net rent, royalty income, and capital-gains net income.

## Taxable Social Security

When an individual receives income in addition to Social Security benefits, up to 50% of those benefits could be included in taxable income if the total income, including 50% of the person's Social Security benefits, was:

• over $25,000 but less than $34,000 for single, head of household, qualifying widow(er), or married and filing separately and the spouses *lived apart* for all of the year.

• over $32,000 but less than $44,000 for married individuals filing jointly.

A higher 85% applies to any Social Security benefits exceeding the maximum $34,000 or $44,000 amounts. Below these amounts, 50% is still included in taxable income.

If the taxpayer is married, filing separately, and *lived with* his or her spouse *at any time* during the year, the amounts are reduced to zero. Generally, these benefits will not be taxable if the only income received during the year was from Social Security. The individual probably will not have to file a federal tax return.

## IRS Tax Audit

Although only about one out of every 100 individual tax returns will be audited in 1996, the Internal Revenue Service is very good at selecting returns for audit that will yield additional taxes. If your return is selected for audit by the IRS, it does not necessarily mean that you will incur any additional tax liability.

If you do not agree with the examiner's report, you can meet with the examiner's supervisor to discuss your case further. If you still do not agree, you have the right to appeal the findings through a separate Appeals Office. After that, you can appeal to the U.S. Tax Court.

## Your Rights as a Taxpayer

Congress passed a law in 1989 (Taxpayer Bill of Rights 1) requiring that the Internal Revenue Service explain, in easy-to-understand language, any actions it proposes to take against a taxpayer and that the agency relax some of its audit and collection procedures.

You can learn more about this legislation by obtaining a free copy of IRS Publication 1, *Your Rights as a Taxpayer*; call 1-800-TAX-FORM.

Taxpayer Bill of Rights 2, enacted in 1996, created an Office of the Taxpayer Advocate within the IRS, with authority to order IRS personnel to issue refund checks and meet deadlines for resolving disputes. The measure also requires the agency to pay a taxpayer's legal fees if the latter wins the case and the IRS cannot show it was "substantially justified" in pursuing it. The IRS is also required to accept the postmark of a qualified courier as proof of timely mailing.

# State Government Individual Income Taxes

**Source:** Reproduced with permission from *CCH State Tax Guide*, published and copyrighted by CCH Inc., 2700 Lake Cook Road, Riverwoods, IL 60115

Below are basic state tax rates on taxable income for the year 1996. Alaska, Florida, Nevada, South Dakota, Texas, Washington, and Wyoming did not have state income taxes and are thus not listed. See notes below for some further details.

**Alabama**
1st $1,000 . . . . . . . 2%
Next $5,000 . . . . . . . 4%
Over $6,000 . . . . . . . 5%

**Arizona***
First $20,000 . . . . . . 3.0%
Next $30,000 . . . . . . 3.5%
Next $50,000 . . . . . . 4.2%
Next $200,000 . . . . . 5.2%
$300,001 and over . . . 5.6%

**Arkansas**
1st $2,999 . . . . . . . 1%
Next $3,000 . . . . . . . 2.5%
Next $3,000 . . . . . . . 3.5%
Next $6,000 . . . . . . . 4.5%
Next $10,000 . . . . . . 6%
$25,000 or over. . . . . . 7%

**California***
$0 to $9,816 . . . . . . . . 1%
$9,817 to $23,264 . . . . 2%
$23,265 to $36,714 . . . 4%
$36,715 to $50,968 . . . 6%
$50,969 to $64,414 . . . 8%
$64,415 to $223,390. . . 9.3%
$223,391 to $446,780 . 10%
$446,781 and over . . . 11%

**Colorado**
5% of federal taxable income.

**Connecticut**
First $4,500 . . . . . . . 3%
Over $4,500 . . . . . . . 4.5%

**Delaware**
$2,001 to $5,000. . . . . 3.2%
Next $5,000 . . . . . . . 5%
Next $10,000 . . . . . . 6%
Next $5,000 . . . . . . . 6.35%
Next $5,000 . . . . . . . 6.65%
Over $30,000 . . . . . . 7.1%

**District of Columbia**
1st $10,000 . . . . . . 6%
2d $10,000 . . . . . . 8%
Over $20,000 . . . . . . 9.5%

**Georgia**
1st $1,000 . . . . . . . 1%
Next $2,000 . . . . . . . 2%
Next $2,000 . . . . . . . 3%
Next $2,000 . . . . . . . 4%
Next $3,000 . . . . . . . 5%
Over $10,000 . . . . . . 6%

**Hawaii**
First $3,000 . . . . . . . 2%
Next $2,000 . . . . . . . 4%
Next $2,000 . . . . . . . 6%
Next $4,000 . . . . . . . 7.25%
Next $10,000 . . . . . . 8%
Next $10,000 . . . . . . 8.75%
Next $10,000 . . . . . . 9.5%
Over $41,000 . . . . . 10%

**Idaho***
1st $1,000 . . . . . . . 2%
2d $1,000 . . . . . . . 4%
3rd $1,000 . . . . . . . 4.5%
4th $1,000 . . . . . . . 5.5%
5th $1,000. . . . . . . 6.5%
Next $2,500. . . . . . . 7.5%
Next $12,500. . . . . . 7.8%
Over $20,000. . . . . . 8.2%

**Illinois**
3% of taxable net income

**Indiana**
3.4% of adj. gross income

**Iowa**
$0 to $1,081 . . . . . . . 0.4%
$1,082 to $2,162 . . . . 0.8%
$2,163 to $4,324 . . . . 2.7%
$4,325 to $9,729 . . . . 5%
$9,730 to $16,215 . . . 6.8%
$16,216 to $21,620 . . 7.2%
$21,621 to $32,430 . . 7.55%
$32,431 to $48,645 . . 8.8%
Over $48,645. . . . . . . 9.98%

**Kansas**
1st $30,000. . . . . . 3.5%
Next $30,000. . . . . . 6.25%
Over $60,000. . . . . . 6.45%

**Kentucky**
1st $3,000. . . . . . . 2%
Next $1,000. . . . . . . 3%
Next $1,000. . . . . . . 4%
Next $3,000. . . . . . . 5%
$8,000 and over. . . . . 6%

**Louisiana***
1st $10,000. . . . . . 2%
Next $40,000. . . . . . 4%
Over $50,000. . . . . . 6%

**Maine**
Less than $4,150 . . . . 2%
$4,150 to $8,249 . . . . 4.5%
$8,250 to $16,499 . . . 7%
$16,500 or more. . . . . 8.5%

**Maryland**
Over $3,000. . . . . . . 5%

**Massachusetts**
Interest, dividends, certain capital gains. . . . . 12%
Other capital gains income . . . . . 0% to 5%
All other income . . . . . 5.95%

**Michigan**
4.4% of taxable income

**Minnesota**
$0 to 23,490 . . . . . . . 6%
$23,491 to 93,340 . . . 8%
Over $93,340. . . . . . . 8.5%

**Mississippi**
1st $5,000. . . . . . . 3%
Next $5,000. . . . . . . 4%
Over $10,000. . . . . . 5%

**Missouri**
1st $1,000. . . . . . . 1.5%
2d $1,000. . . . . . . 2%
3rd $1,000. . . . . . . 2.5%
4th $1,000. . . . . . . 3%
5th $1,000. . . . . . . 3.5%
6th $1,000. . . . . . . 4%
7th $1,000 . . . . . . . 4.5%
8th $1,000 . . . . . . . 5%
9th $1,000 . . . . . . . 5.5%
Over $9,000 . . . . . . . 6%

**Montana**
$0 to $1,899 . . . . . . . . 2%
$1,900 to $3,799. . . . . 3% less $19
$3,800 to $7,599. . . . . 4% less $57
$7,600 to $11,399. . . . 5% less $133
$11,400 to $15,199. . . 6% less $247
$15,200 to $18,999. . . 7% less $399
$19,000 to $26,499. . . 8% less $589
$26,500 to $37,899. . . 9% less $854
$37,900 to $66,399. . 10% less $1,233
$66,400 and over . . . 11% less $1,897

**Nebraska**
1st $4,000 . . . . . . . 2.62%
Next $26,000 . . . . . . 3.65%
Next $16,750 . . . . . . 5.24%
Over $46,750 . . . . . . 6.99%

**New Hampshire**
5% of interests and dividends only

**New Jersey**
1st $20,000 . . . . . . 1.4%
Next $30,000 . . . . . . 1.75%
Next $20,000 . . . . . . 2.45%
Next $10,000 . . . . . . 3.5%
Next $70,000 . . . . . . 5.525%
Over $150,000 . . . . . 6.37%

**New Mexico***
Not over $8,000 . . . . . 1.7%
$8,001 to $16,000. . . . 3.2%
$16,001 to $24,000. . . 4.7%
$24,001 to $40,000. . . 6%
$40,001 to $64,000. . . 7.1%
$64,001 to $100,000 . . 7.9%
Over $100,000 . . . . . . 8.5%

**New York**
First $11,000 . . . . . . 4%
Next $5,000 . . . . . . . 5%
Next $6,000 . . . . . . . 6%
Over $26,000 . . . . . . 7.125%

**North Carolina**
Up to $21,250 . . . . . . 6%
Next $78,750 . . . . . . 7%
Over $100,000 . . . . . 7.75%

**North Dakota**
1st $3,000 . . . . . . . 2.67%
Next $2,000 . . . . . . . 4%
Next $3,000 . . . . . . . 5.33%
Next $7,000 . . . . . . . 6.67%
Next $10,000 . . . . . . 8%
Next $10,000 . . . . . . 9.33%
Next $15,000. . . . . . 10.67%
Over $50,000. . . . . . 12%

**Ohio**
First $5,000. . . . . . . 0.743%
Next $5,000. . . . . . . 1.486%
Next $5,000. . . . . . . 2.972%
Next $5,000. . . . . . . 3.715%
Next $20,000. . . . . . 4.457%
Next $40,000. . . . . . 5.201%
Next $20,000. . . . . . 5.943%
Next $100,000. . . . . 6.9%
Over $200,000. . . . . 7.5%

**Oklahoma**
1st $2,000. . . . . . . 0.5%
Next $3,000. . . . . . . 1%
Next $2,500. . . . . . . 2%
Next $2,300. . . . . . . 3%
Next $2,400. . . . . . . 4%
Next $2,800. . . . . . . 5%
Next $6,000. . . . . . . 6%
Remainder. . . . . . . . . 7%

**Oregon**
1st $2,150. . . . . . . 5%
Next $3,250. . . . . . . 7%
Over $5,400. . . . . . . 9%

**Pennsylvania**
. . . . . . . . . . . . . . . . . 2.8%

**Rhode Island**
27.5% of federal liability

**South Carolina**
First $2,250. . . . . . . 2.5%
Next $2,250. . . . . . . 3%
Next $2,250. . . . . . . 4%
Next $2,250. . . . . . . 5%
Next $2,250. . . . . . . 6%
Over $11,250. . . . . . . 7%

**Tennessee**
6% of interest and dividends only

**Utah**
1st $1,500. . . . . . . 2.55%
Next $1,500. . . . . . . 3.5%
Next $1,500. . . . . . . 4.4%
Next $1,500. . . . . . . 5.35%
Next $1,500. . . . . . . 6%
Over $7,500. . . . . . . 7%

**Vermont**
25% of federal income tax

**Virginia**
1st $3,000. . . . . . . 2%
Next $2,000. . . . . . . 3%
Next $12,000. . . . . . 5%
Over $17,000. . . . . . 5.75%

**West Virginia**
First $10,000. . . . . . 3%
Next $15,000. . . . . . 4%
Next $15,000. . . . . . 4.5%
Next $20,000. . . . . . 6%
Over $60,000. . . . . . 6.5%

**Wisconsin***
$0 to $10,000 . . . . . . 4.9%
$10,001 to $20,000 . . 6.55%
$20,001 and over. . . . 6.93%

* Community property state in which, in general, one-half of the community income is taxable to each spouse.

**Alabama:** Rates shown are for married persons filing jointly. Single persons, heads of families, married persons filing separately, and estates or trusts are taxed at 2% of the 1st $500 of taxable income, 4% on the next $2,500, and 5% on the rest.

**Arizona:** Rates shown are for married persons filing jointly and heads of households. For single taxpayers, the rates range from 3% of the 1st $10,000 of taxable income to 5.6% of taxable income over $150,000.

**California:** The rates shown are the 1996 rates for residents who are joint taxpayers or surviving spouses with dependents. The 10% and 11% brackets were subject to voter approval in Nov. 1996. For single taxpayers, married persons filing separately, and fiduciaries, the rates range between 1% on the 1st $4,831 of taxable income and 11% on taxable income over $219,872. For unmarried heads of households, the rates range between 1% on the 1st $9,662 of taxable income and 11% on taxable income over $299,279. 1996 rates adjusted based on inflation. A 7% alternative minimum tax is imposed.

*(notes continue)*

**Colorado:** Alternative minimum tax imposed. Qualified taxpayers may pay alternative tax of 0.5% of gross receipts from Colorado sales.
**Connecticut:** The tax rates shown are for married individuals filing jointly. For unmarried individuals and married individuals filing separately, the rates are 3% on the 1st $2,250 of Connecticut taxable income and $67.50 plus 4.5% of the excess over $2,250. For heads of households, the rates are 3% of the 1st $3,500 and $105 plus 4.5% of the excess over $3,500. For trusts or estates, the rate is 4.5%.
For tax years beginning after 1996, the tax rates are: (1) for unmarried individuals and married individuals filing separately, 3% of the 1st $4,500 of Connecticut taxable income and $135 plus 4.5% of the excess over $4,500; (2) for heads of households, 3% of the 1st $7,000 and $210 plus 4.5% of the excess over $7,000; (3) for married individuals, 3% of the 1st $9,000 and $180 plus 4.5% of the excess over $9,000; and (4) for trusts or estates, 4.5%. Additional state minimum tax imposed on resident individuals, trusts, and estates.
**Delaware:** For tax years beginning after 1996, the rates for these income categories are reduced to 3.1%, 4.85%, 5.8%, 6.15%, 6.45%, and 6.9%, respectively.
**District of Columbia:** The tax on unincorporated business is 9.975%. Minimum tax, $100.
**Georgia:** Rates shown are for married persons filing jointly and heads of households. Single persons pay at rates ranging from 1% on taxable net income not over $750 to 6% on taxable net income over $7,000. Married persons filing separately pay at rates ranging from 1% on taxable net income not over $500 to 6% on taxable net income over $5,000.
**Hawaii:** Rates shown are for taxpayers filing jointly and surviving spouses. Special rate tables are provided for heads of households, unmarried individuals and married individuals filing separately, and estates and trusts.
**Iowa:** An alternative minimum tax is imposed equal to 75% of the maximum state individual income tax rate for the tax year of the state alternative minimum taxable income.
**Kansas:** The rates shown are for married individuals filing joint returns. For all other individuals, the rates are 4.4% of the 1st $20,000 of Kansas taxable income, 7.5% of the next $10,000, and 7.75% of the excess over $30,000.
**Louisiana:** These are the maximum tax rates for individuals. For joint returns, the tax is determined as if net income and the personal exemption credits were reduced by one-half. Actual tax is determined from tax tables.
**Maine:** Rates shown are 1995 rates for single individuals and married persons filing separately. For unmarried or legally separated individuals who qualify as heads of household, the tax rates range between 2% if taxable income is less than $6,200 and 8.5% if taxable income is $24,750 or more. For married individuals filing jointly and widows or widowers permitted to file a joint federal return, the tax rates range between 2% if taxable income is less than $8,250 and 8.5% if taxable income is $33,000 or more. 1996 rates will be set administratively, based on inflation.
Additional state minimum tax is imposed equal to the amount by which the state minimum tax (27% of adjusted federal tentative minimum tax) exceeds Maine income tax liability, other than withholding tax liability.
**Massachusetts.** Higher capital gains rates are for holdings kept 1 yr. or less.
**Minnesota:** The rates shown apply to married individuals filing jointly and surviving spouses. For unmarried individuals, the tax is 6% on the 1st $16,070, 8% on all over $16,070 but not over $52,790, and 8.5% on all over $52,790. For unmarried heads of households, the tax is 6% on the 1st $19,870, 8% on all over $19,870 but not over $79,500, and 8.5% on all over $79,500. A 7% alternative minimum tax is imposed.
**Montana:** Rates shown are 1996 rates as set administratively, based on inflation. Minimum tax, $1.
**Nebraska:** Rates shown are for married couples filing jointly and qualified surviving spouses. Rates for married couples filing separately range between 2.62% of the 1st $2,000 and 6.99% of taxable income over $23,375. Rates for heads of household range between 2.62% of the 1st $3,800 and 6.99% of taxable income over $35,000. Rates for single individuals range between 2.62% of the 1st $2,400 and 6.99% of taxable income over $26,500. Rates for estates range from 2.62% to 6.99%.
**New Jersey:** Rates shown are for married persons filing jointly, heads of households, and surviving spouses. The rates for married persons filing separately, unmarried individuals, and estates and trusts range between 1.4% of the 1st $20,000 of taxable income and 6.37% of taxable income over $75,000.
**New Mexico:** Rates shown are for married persons filing jointly and surviving spouses. For married persons filing separately, the rates range between 1.7% on the 1st $4,000 of taxable income and 8.5% on taxable income over $50,000. For heads of household, rates range between 1.7% on the 1st $7,000 of taxable income and 8.5% on taxable income over $83,000. For single individuals, estates, and trusts, rates range between 1.7% of the 1st $5,500 of taxable income and 8.5% of taxable income over $65,000.
Qualified taxpayers may pay alternative tax of 0.75% of gross receipts from New Mexico sales.
**New York:** The rates shown are the figures for married individuals filing jointly and surviving spouses. Separate schedules are set out for heads of households (ranging between 4% on the 1st $7,500 of taxable income and 7% on taxable income over $15,000) and for unmarried individuals, married individuals filing separately, and estates and trusts (ranging between 4% of the 1st $5,500 of taxable income and 7% of taxable income over $11,000). The rates are reduced for tax years beginning after 1996. Individuals, estates, and trusts are subject to a 6% tax on minimum taxable income.
Higher rates are applicable, according to a formula, when the taxpayer's New York adjusted gross income for the tax year is over $100,000.
**North Carolina:** Rates shown are for married persons filing jointly. For heads of households the rates are 6% on the 1st $17,000, 7% of the next $63,000, and 7.75% of excess over $80,000. For unmarried individuals other than surviving spouses and heads of households, the rate is 6% of 1st $12,750, 7% of next $47,250, and 7.75% of excess over $60,000. For married filing separately the rate is 6% of 1st $10,625, 7% of next $39,375, and 7.75% of excess over $50,000.
**North Dakota:** Individuals, estates, and trusts are allowed an optional method of computing the tax. The optional tax is 14% of the taxpayer's adjusted federal income tax liability for the tax year.
**Ohio:** For the 1996 and 1997 tax years, the tax rates may be reduced by the Tax Commissioner by a percentage determined by the Office of Budget and Management according to a complicated formula based on budget surpluses.
**Oklahoma:** Rates shown are for heads of households, married persons filing jointly, and a surviving spouse not deducting federal income taxes. Single persons, married persons filing separately, and estates and trusts not deducting federal income taxes, pay at rates ranging from 0.5% on the 1st $1,000 of taxable income to 7% on taxable income over $10,000. Optional rates (ranging from 0.5% to 10%) are enacted for taxpayers who deduct federal income taxes.
**Oregon:** Rates shown are 1995 amounts. Rates for joint filers, heads of households, and qualifying widow(er)s are 6% of the 1st $4,300; 7% over $4,300 but not over $10,800; and 9% of taxable income over $10,800.
**Utah:** Rates shown are for married persons filing jointly and heads of households. Married taxpayers filing separately, single taxpayers, and estates and trusts pay at rates ranging from 2.55% on taxable income not over $750 to 7% on taxable income over $3,750.
After 1996, rates for married persons filing jointly or heads of households range from 2.3% of the 1st $1,500 of taxable income to 7% of taxable income over $7,500. After 1996, rates for single taxpayers, estates and trusts, and married couples filing separately range from 2.3% of the 1st $750 of taxable income to 7% of taxable income over $3,750.
**West Virginia:** A minimum tax is also imposed equal to the excess by which an amount equal to 25% of any federal minimum tax or alternative minimum tax for the tax year exceeds the total tax due for the tax year.
**Wisconsin:** Rates shown are for married persons filing jointly. Rates for married persons filing separately range between 4.9% of the 1st $5,000 of taxable income and 6.93% of taxable income over $10,000. The rates for fiduciaries and single individuals range between 4.9% of the 1st $7,500 of taxable income and 6.93% of taxable income over $15,001.
Alternative minimum tax is imposed, and there are certain surcharges. For the tax years ending after April 1, 1991, April 1, 1992, and April 1, 1993, and for tax years beginning in 1994, 1995, and 1996, a surcharge is imposed on individuals, estates, trusts, and partnerships, except an entity with gross receipts of less than $1,000, at the rate of the greater of $25 or 0.4345% of net business income. The maximum surcharge is $9,800. An individual, estate, trust, or partnership engaged in farming with a net farm profit of $1,000 or more is subject to a surcharge of $25, regardless of whether the entity is otherwise subject to a surcharge. (The Department of Revenue must establish annual surcharge rates necessary to generate a sufficient level of revenue to fund appropriations from the recycling fund.)

# NATIONS OF THE WORLD

As of mid-1996

The nations of the world are listed in alphabetic order. Initials in the following articles include UN (United Nations), OAS (Org. of American States), NATO (North Atlantic Treaty Org.), EU (European Union, or Common Market), OAU (Org. of African Unity), OECD (Org. for Economic Cooperation and Development), ILO (Intl. Labor Org.), FAO (Food & Agriculture Org.), WHO (World Health Org.), IMF (Intl. Monetary Fund), WTO (World Trade Organization, formerly GATT), CIS (Commonwealth of Independent States), FY (fiscal year). **Sources:** U.S. Census Bureau: Intl. Data Base; Population Reference Bureau, Inc. Washington, DC; Central Intelligence Agency: *The World Factbook;* Encyclopaedia Britannica and Encyclopaedia Britannica Book of the Year; Intl. Monetary Fund; Intl. Institute for Strategic Studies: *The Military Balance;* Facts on File; Keesing's Record of World Events; Current History; Collier's Encyclopedia and Collier's Year Book; Encyclopedia Americana Yearbook; Who's Who in the World; U.S. Dept. of State; U.S. Dept. of Energy; UN Statistical Yearbook; UN Demographic Yearbook; The Statesman's Year-Book; The Europa World Year Book; Funk & Wagnalls New Encyclopedia. Population figures are mid-1996 estimates, unless otherwise noted. Gross Domestic Product/Gross National Product: *Denotes purchasing power parity. Otherwise, exchange rate conversions are used, which may account for significant variation from year to year. National Budget measures expenditures, unless otherwise noted. Tourism figures represent receipts from international tourism. Comm. (commercial) vehicles include trucks and buses. All embassy addresses are Wash., DC, area codes (202), unless otherwise noted. Literacy rates are usually based on the ability to read and write on a lower elementary school level. The concept of literacy is changing in the industrialized countries, where literacy is defined as the ability to read instructions necessary for a job or a license. By these standards, illiteracy may be more common than present rates suggest. Per-person figures in communications section are post-1991 and in health section are post-1988.

*See pages 481-96 for full-color maps and flags.*

## Afghanistan

### Islamic State of Afghanistan

### Dowlat-e Eslami-ye Afghanestan

**People: Population:** 22,664,136. **Age distrib.** (%): <15: 41; 65+: 3. **Pop. density:** 84 per sq. mi. **Urban:** 18%. **Ethnic groups:** Pashtun 38%, Tajik 25%, Hazara 19%, Uzbek 6%. **Principal languages:** Pashtu 35%, Dari Persian (spoken by Tajiks, Hazaras) 50% (both official), Turkic (incl. Uzbek, Turkmen) 11%. **Religions:** Sunni Muslim 90%, Shi'a Muslim 15%.

**Geography: Area:** 251,825 sq. mi. **Location:** In SW Asia, NW of the Indian subcontinent. **Neighbors:** Pakistan on E, S; Iran on W; Turkmenistan, Tajikistan, Uzbekistan on N. The NE tip touches China. **Topography:** The country is landlocked and mountainous, much of it over 4,000 ft. above sea level. The Hindu Kush Mts. tower 16,000 ft. above Kabul and reach a height of 25,000 ft. to the E. Trade with Pakistan flows through the 35-mile-long Khyber Pass. The climate is dry, with extreme temperatures, and there are large desert regions, though mountain rivers produce intermittent fertile valleys. **Capital:** Kabul (1993 est.): 700,000.

**Government: Type:** In transition. **Local divisions:** 30 provinces. **Defense:** 15% of GDP (1990 est.).

**Economy: Industries:** Textiles, soap, furniture, cement. **Chief crops:** Nuts, wheat, fruits. **Minerals:** Gas, oil, copper, coal, zinc, iron. **Other resources:** Wool, karakul pelts, mutton. **Arable land:** 12%. **Livestock** (1994): cattle: 1.5 mil; sheep: 14.2 mil. **Electricity prod.** (1993): 550 mln. kWh. **Labor force:** Agriculture supports about 68% of the population.

**Finance: Monetary unit:** Afghani (June 1996: 4,700 = $1 US). **Gross domestic product** (1992): $41.8 bil. **Per capita GDP:** $2,195. **Imports** (1994): $602 mil; partners: Jap. 15%, EU 11%. **Exports** (1994): $296 mil; partners: EU 10%.

**Transport: Motor vehicles:** in use: 38,000 passenger cars, 25,000 comm. vehicles. **Civil aviation:** 127 mil passenger-mi.

**Communications: Television sets:** 1 per 169 persons; **Radios:** 1 per 10 persons. **Telephones:** 1 per 769 persons. **Daily newspaper circ.:** 13 per 1,000 pop.

**Health: Life expectancy at birth** (1996): 46 male; 45 female. **Births** (per 1,000 pop.): 43. **Deaths** (per 1,000 pop.): 18. **Natural increase:** 2.5%. **Hospital beds:** 1 per 2,945 persons. **Physicians:** 1 per 6,690 persons. **Infant mortality** (per 1,000 live births 1996): 150.

**Education: Literacy** (1990): 29%. Over 88% of adults have no formal schooling. Compulsory: ages 7-15.

**Major International Organizations:** UN (World Bank, IMF).

**Embassy:** 2341 Wyoming Ave. NW 20008; 234-3770.

Afghanistan, occupying a favored invasion route since antiquity, has been variously known as Ariana or Bactria (in ancient times) and Khorasan (in the Middle Ages). Foreign empires alternated rule with local emirs and kings until the 18th century, when a unified kingdom was established. In 1973, a military coup ushered in a republic.

Pro-Soviet leftists took power in a bloody 1978 coup and concluded an economic and military treaty with the USSR. In Dec. 1979 the USSR began a massive airlift into Kabul and backed a new coup, leading to installation of a more pro-Soviet leader. Soviet troops fanned out over Afghanistan and waged a protracted guerrilla war with Muslim rebels, in which some 15,000 Soviet troops reportedly died.

A UN-mediated agreement was signed Apr. 14, 1988, providing for withdrawal of Soviet troops, a neutral Afghan state, and repatriation of refugees. Afghan rebels rejected the pact, vowing to continue fighting while "Soviets and their puppets" remained in Afghanistan. The Soviets completed their troop withdrawal Feb. 15, 1989; fighting between Afghan rebels and government forces ensued.

Communist Pres. Najibullah resigned Apr. 16, 1992, as competing guerrilla forces advanced on Kabul. The rebels achieved power Apr. 28, ending 14 years of Soviet-backed regimes. More than 2 million Afghans had been killed and 6 million had left the country since 1979.

Following the rebel victory there were clashes between moderates and Islamic fundamentalist forces. Burhanuddin Rabbani, a guerrilla leader, became president June 28, 1992, but fierce fighting continued around Kabul and elsewhere. Taliban, an insurgent Islamic fundamentalist faction, gained increasing control and in Sept. 1996 captured Kabul and set up a government. The Taliban imposed harsh Islamic laws and executed former President Najibullah. Berhannuden Rabbani and other ousted leaders fled to the north, and anti-Taliban forces launched a resistance.

## Albania

### Republic of Albania

### Republika e Shqipërisë

**People: Population**: 3,249,136. **Pop. density:** 293 per sq. mi. **Urban:** 37%. **Ethnic groups:** Albanians (Gegs in N, Tosks in S) 95%, Greeks 3%. **Principal languages:** Albanian (official), Greek. **Religions:** Muslim 70%, Albanian Orthodox 20%, Roman Catholic 10%.

**Geography: Area:** 11,100 sq. mi. **Location:** SE Europe, on SE coast of Adriatic Sea. **Neighbors:** Greece on S, Yugoslavia on N, Macedonia on E. **Topography:** Apart from a narrow coastal plain, Albania consists of hills and mountains covered with scrub forest, cut by small E-W rivers. **Capital:** Tiranë. **Cities** (1991 est.): Tiranë 300,000; Durres 85,000; Elbasin 83,000.

**Government: Type:** Republic. **Head of state:** Pres. Sali Berisha; b July 1, 1944; in office: Apr. 9, 1992. **Head of government:** Prem. Alexander Meksi; b Mar. 8, 1939; in office: Apr. 13, 1992. **Local divisions:** 26 districts. **Defense:** 8.2% of GNP (1993). **Active troop strength:** 73,000.

**Economy: Industries:** Cement, textiles, food processing. **Chief crops:** Corn, wheat, potatoes, tobacco, fruits. **Minerals:** Chromium, coal, oil, gas. **Other resources:** Lumber. **Arable land:** 21%. **Livestock** (1994): cattle: 630,000; sheep: 1.9 mil. **Electricity prod.** (1994): 4.0 bil kWh. **Labor force:** 60% agric.; 40% ind. & comm.

**Finance: Monetary unit:** Lek (June 1996: 99.30 = $1 US). **Gross domestic product** (1994): $3.8 bil.* **Per capita GDP:** $1,100. **Imports** (1993): $621 mil; partners: Italy 35%, Greece 24%. **Exports** (1993): $112 mil; partners: Italy 52%, U.S. 11%. **National budget** (1991 est.): $1.4 bil.

**Chief ports:** Durres, Vlore, Sarande.

**Communications: Television sets:** 1 per 13 persons. **Radios:** 1 per 6.1 persons. **Telephones:** 1 per 70 persons. **Daily newspaper circ.:** 50 per 1,000 pop.

**Health: Life expectancy at birth** (1996): 65 male; 71 female. **Births** (per 1,000 pop.): 22. **Deaths** (per 1,000 pop): 8. **Natural increase:** 1.5%. **Hospital beds:** 1 per 173 persons. **Physicians:** 1 per 585 persons. **Infant mortality** (per 1,000 live births 1996): 49.

**Major International Organizations:** UN (FAO, WHO, World Bank).

**Education: Literacy** (1993): 100%. Free and compulsory: ages 6-14.

**Embassy:** 1511 K St. NW 20005; 223-4942.

Ancient Illyria was conquered by Romans, Slavs, and Turks (15th century); the latter Islamized the population. Independent Albania was proclaimed in 1912, republic was formed in 1920. King Zog I ruled 1925-39, until Italy invaded.

Communist partisans took over in 1944, allied Albania with USSR, then broke with USSR in 1960 over de-Stalinization. Strong political alliance with China followed, leading to several billion dollars in aid, which was curtailed after 1974. China cut off aid in 1978 when Albania attacked its policies after the death of Chinese ruler Mao Zedong. Large-scale purges of officials occurred during the 1970s.

Enver Hoxha, the nation's ruler for 4 decades, died Apr. 11, 1985. Eventually the new regime introduced some liberalization, including measures in 1990 providing for freedom to travel abroad. Efforts were begun to improve ties with the outside world. Mar. 1991 elections left the former Communists in power, but a general strike and urban opposition led to the formation of a coalition cabinet including non-Communists.

Albania's former Communists were routed in elections Mar. 1992, amid economic collapse and social unrest. Sali Berisha was elected as the first non-Communist president since World War II. Berisha's party claimed a landslide victory in disputed parliamentary elections, May 26 and June 2, 1996.

# Algeria

## Democratic and Popular Republic of Algeria

## Al Jumhuriyah al Jaza'iriyah ad Dimuqratiyah ash Shabiyah

**People: Population:** 29,183,032. **Age distrib.** (%): <15: 40; 65+: 4. **Pop. density:** 32 per sq. mi. **Urban:** 50%. **Ethnic groups:** Arab-Berber 99%. **Principal languages:** Arabic (official), French, Berber dialects. **Religions:** Sunni Muslim (state religion) 99%.

**Geography: Area:** 919,595 sq. mi. **Location:** In NW Africa, from Mediterranean Sea into Sahara Desert. **Neighbors:** Morocco on W; Mauritania, Mali, Niger on S; Libya, Tunisia on E. **Topography:** The Tell, located on the coast, comprises fertile plains 50-100 miles wide, with a moderate climate and adequate rain. Two major chains of the Atlas Mts., running roughly E-W and reaching 7,000 ft., enclose a dry plateau region. Below lies the Sahara, mostly desert with major mineral resources. **Capital:** Algiers (El Djazair). **Cities** (1987 est.): Algiers 1,507,000; Oran 610,000; Constantine 441,000.

**Government: Type:** Republic. **Head of state:** Pres. Liamine Zeroual; b July 3, 1941; in office: Jan. 31, 1994. **Head of government:** Prime Min. Ahmed Ouyahia; b July 2, 1952; in office: Dec. 31, 1995. **Local divisions:** 48 provinces. **Defense:** 2.7% of GDP (1994). **Active troop strength:** 121,700.

**Economy: Industries:** Oil, natural gas, light industries, food processing. **Chief crops:** Grains, grapes, citrus, olives. **Minerals:** Iron, phosphates, zinc, lead. **Crude oil reserves** (1995): 9.2 bil bbls. **Other resources:** Cork trees. **Arable land:** 3%. **Livestock** (1994): cattle: 1.4 mil; sheep: 17.9 mil. **Electricity prod.** (1993): 18.3 bil kWh. **Labor force:** 22% agric.; 27% ind., serv., commerce; 29% govt.

**Finance: Monetary unit:** Dinar (June 1996: 55.10 = $1 US). **Gross domestic product** (1994): $97 bil.* **Per capita GDP:** $3,480. **Imports** (1994): $9.2 bil; partners: France 29%, U.S. 12%. **Exports** (1994): $9.1 bil; partners: Italy 18%, U.S. 16%. **National budget** (1995 est.): $17.9 bil. **International reserves less gold** (May 1996): $2.5 bil. **Gold:** 5.6 mil oz t. **Consumer prices** (change in 1995): 29.8%.

**Transport: Railroads: Route length:** 2,965 mi. **Motor vehicles:** in use: 725,000 passenger cars, 480,000 comm. vehicles. **Chief ports:** Algiers.

**Communications: Television sets:** 1 per 14 persons. **Radios:** 1 per 7.8 persons. **Telephones:** 1 per 25 persons. **Daily newspaper circ.:** 38 per 1,000 pop.

**Health: Life expectancy at birth** (1996): 67 male; 70 female. **Births** (per 1,000 pop.): 29. **Deaths** (per 1,000 pop.): 6. **Natural increase:** 2.3%. **Hospital beds:** 1 per 455 persons. **Physicians:** 1 per 1,041 persons. **Infant mortality** (per 1,000 live births 1996): 49.

**Education: Literacy** (1993): 62%. Compulsory: ages 6-15.

**Major International Organizations:** UN (WTO, World Bank, FAO, IMF, WHO), OAU, Arab League, OPEC.

**Embassy:** 2118 Kalorama Rd. NW 20008; 265-2800.

Earliest known inhabitants were ancestors of Berbers, followed by Phoenicians, Romans, Vandals, and, finally, Arabs. Turkey ruled 1518 to 1830, when France took control.

Large-scale European immigration and French cultural inroads did not prevent an Arab nationalist movement from launching guerrilla war. Peace, and French withdrawal, was negotiated with French Pres. Charles de Gaulle. One million Europeans left. Independence came July 5, 1962. Ahmed Ben Bella was the victor of infighting and ruled until 1965, when an army coup installed Col. Houari Boumedienne as leader; Boumedienne led until his death from a blood disease, 1978.

In 1967, Algeria declared war on Israel, broke ties with U.S., and moved toward eventual military and political ties with the USSR. Some 500 died in riots protesting economic hardship in 1988. In 1989, voters approved a new constitution, which cleared the way for a multiparty system.

The government canceled the Jan. 1992 elections that Islamic fundamentalists were expected to win, and banned all nonreligious activities at Algeria's 10,000 mosques. Pres. Mohammed Boudiaf was assassinated June 29, 1992. There were repeated attacks on high-ranking officials, security forces, foreigners, and others by militant Muslim fundamentalists over the next 4 years; pro-government death squads also were active. The overall estimated death toll was 50,000 by mid-1996. Liamine Zeroual won the presidential election of Nov. 16, 1995, and promised new legislative elections by 1997.

# Andorra

## Principality of Andorra

## Principat d'Andorra

**People: Population:** 72,766. **Pop. density:** 402 per sq. mi. **Ethnic groups:** Spanish 61%, Andorran 30%, French 6%. **Principal languages:** Catalan (official), French, Castilian. **Religions:** Mostly Roman Catholic.

**Geography: Area:** 181 sq. mi. **Location:** SW Europe, n Pyrenees Mts. **Neighbors:** Spain on S, France on N. **Topography:** High mountains and narrow valleys over the country. **Capital** (1993 est.): Andorra la Vella 22,000.

**Government: Type:** Parliamentary co-principality. **Heads of state:** President of France & Bishop of Urgel (Spain), as co-princes. **Head of government:** Marc Forné Molné; in office: Dec. 21, 1994. **Local divisions:** 7 parishes. **Defense:** Responsibility of France and Spain.

**Economy: Industries:** Tourism, sheep, tobacco products. **Minerals:** Iron, lead. **Arable land:** 2%.

**Finance: Monetary unit:** French Franc, Spanish Peseta. **Gross domestic product** (1992): $760 mil.* **Per capita GDP:** $14,000. **National budget** (1993): $177 mil.

**Communications: Television sets:** 1 per 15 persons. **Radios:** 1 per 6.5 persons. **Telephones:** 1 per 2.3 persons.

**Health** (1996): **Births** (per 1,000 pop.): 10. **Deaths** (per 1,000 pop.): 3. **Natural increase:** 0.7%.

**Education: Literacy** (1993): 100%. Free and compulsory: ages 6-16.

**Major International Organizations:** UN.

Andorra was a co-principality, with joint sovereignty by France and the bishop of Urgel, from 1278 to 1993.

Tourism, especially skiing, is the economic mainstay. A free port, allowing for an active trading center, draws some 13 million tourists annually. Andorran voters chose to end a feudal system that had been in place for 715 years and adopt a parliamentary system of government Mar. 14, 1993.

# Angola

## Republic of Angola

## República de Angola

**People: Population:** 10,342,899. **Age distrib.** (%): <15: 45; 65+: 3. **Pop. density:** 21 per sq. mi. **Urban:** 32%. **Ethnic groups:** Ovimbundu 37%, Kimbundu 25%, Bakongo 13%. **Principal languages:** Portuguese (official), various Bantu languages. **Religions:** Roman Catholic 38%, Protestant 15%, indigenous beliefs 47%.

**Geography: Area:** 481,354 sq. mi. **Location:** In SW Africa on Atlantic coast. **Neighbors:** Namibia on S, Zambia on E, Zaire on N; Cabinda, an enclave separated from rest of country by short Atlantic coast of Zaire, borders Congo. **Topography:** Most of Angola consists of a plateau elevated 3,000 to 5,000 feet above sea level, rising from a narrow coastal strip. There is also a temperate highland area in the west-central region, a desert in the S, and a tropical rain forest covering Cabinda. **Capital:** Luanda (1993 est.): 2.0 mil.

**Government: Type:** Republic. **Head of state:** Pres. José Eduardo dos Santos; b Aug. 28, 1942; in office: Sept. 20, 1979. **Head of government:** Prime Min. Fernando Franca van Dunem; in office: June 8, 1996. **Local divisions:** 18 provinces. **Defense:** 31% of GDP (1993). **Active troop strength:** 82,000 est.

**Economy: Industries:** Food processing, textiles, mining, brewing, petroleum. **Chief crops:** Coffee, sugarcane, bananas. **Minerals:** Iron, diamonds (over 1 mil carats a year), gold, phosphates, oil. **Livestock** (1994): cattle: 3.3 mil; goats: 1.6 mil. **Crude oil reserves** (1995): 5.4 bil bbls. **Arable land:** 2%. **Fish catch** (1993): 81,000 metric tons. **Electricity prod.** (1993): 1.9 bln. kWh. **Labor force:** 85% agric., 15% industry.

**Finance: Monetary unit:** Readjusted Kwanza (June 1996: 31,784 = $1 US). **Gross domestic product** (1994): $6.1 bil.* **Per capita GDP:** $620. **Imports** (1992): $1.6 bil; partners: Portugal 30%, U.S. 11%, Fr. 10%. **Exports** (1993): $3 bil; partners: U.S. 57%. **National budget** (1992 est.): $2.5 bil.

**Transport: Motor vehicles:** in use: 122,000 passenger cars, 42,000 comm. vehicles. **Chief ports:** Cabinda, Lobito, Luanda.

**Communications: Television sets:** 1 per 222 persons. **Radios:** 1 per 25 persons. **Telephones:** 1 per 204 persons. **Daily newspaper circ.:** 7.5 per 1,000 pop.

**Health: Life expectancy at birth** (1996): 45 male; 49 female. **Births** (per 1,000 pop.): 45. **Deaths** (per 1,000 pop.): 18. **Natural increase:** 2.7%. **Hospital beds:** 1 per 845 persons. **Physicians:** 1 per 15,136 persons. **Infant mortality** (per 1,000 live births 1996): 139.

**Education: Literacy** (1992): 40%. Free and compulsory: ages 7-15.

**Major International Organizations:** UN (WTO, FAO, IMF, World Bank, ILO, WHO), OAU.

**Embassy:** 1819 L St. NW 20036; 785-1156.

From the early centuries AD to 1500, Bantu tribes penetrated most of the region. Portuguese came in 1583, allied with the Bakongo kingdom in the north, and developed the slave trade. Large-scale colonization did not begin until the 20th century, when 400,000 Portuguese immigrated.

A guerrilla war begun in 1961 lasted until 1975, when Portugal granted independence. Fighting then erupted between three rival rebel groups —the National Front, based in Zaire, the Soviet-backed Popular Movement for the Liberation of Angola (MPLA), and the National Union for the Total Independence of Angola (UNITA), aided by the U.S. and South Africa. The civil war killed thousands of blacks, drove most whites to emigrate, and completed economic ruin. Cuban troops and Soviet aid helped the MPLA win control of most of the country by 1976 and gain wide recognition as the government of Angola.

An agreement was signed in Dec. 1988 between Angola, Cuba, and South Africa on a timetable for withdrawal of Cuban troops, completed May 25, 1991. The 16-year war was officially ended May 1, 1991, as the government and UNITA signed a peace agreement.

Elections were held in Sept. 1992, but fighting again broke out, as UNITA rejected the presidential election results, and continued into 1993 and 1994, with UNITA forces holding most of the countryside. Large numbers of civilians died from war-related causes, especially starvation. UNITA signed a new peace treaty with the government, Nov. 20, 1994, but implementation was slow.

# Antigua and Barbuda

**People: Population:** 65,647. **Pop. density:** 384 per sq. mi. **Urban:** 31%. **Ethnic groups:** Mostly black African. **Principal language:** English (official). **Religion:** Predominantly Anglican.

**Geography: Area:** 171 sq. mi. **Location:** Eastern Caribbean. **Neighbors:** Approx. 30 mi. north of Guadeloupe. **Capital:** St. John's (1991): 21,500.

**Government: Type:** Constitutional monarchy with British-style parliament. **Head of state:** Queen Elizabeth II; represented by Gov.-Gen. James Carlisle; b Aug. 5, 1937; in office: June 10, 1993. **Head of government:** Prime Min. Lester Bird; b Feb. 21, 1938; in office: Mar. 9, 1994. **Defense:** 1% of GDP (FY 1990-91). **Active troop strength:** 150.

**Economy: Industries:** Manufacturing, construction, tourism. **Arable land:** 18%. **Labor force:** 82% commerce & serv.; 11% agric.; 7% ind.

**Finance: Monetary unit:** East Caribbean Dollar (June 1996: 2.70 = $1 US). **Gross domestic product** (1993): $400 mil.* **Per capita GDP:** $6,000. **Tourism** (1993): $277 mil. **National budget** (1992): $161 mil.

**Health** (1996): **Births** (per 1,000 pop.): 17. **Deaths** (per 1,000 pop.): 5. **Natural increase:** 1.2%.

**Education: Literacy** (1992): 90%.

**Major International Organizations:** UN, OAS, the Commonwealth.

**Embassy:** 3216 New Mexico Ave. NW 20016; 362-5211.

Columbus landed on Antigua in 1493. The British colonized it in 1632.

The British associated state of Antigua achieved independence as Antigua and Barbuda on Nov. 1, 1981. The government maintains close relations with the U.S., United Kingdom, and Venezuela. The country was hit hard by Hurricane Luis, Sept. 1995.

# Argentina

## Argentine Republic

## República Argentina

**People: Population:** 34,672,997. **Age distrib.** (%): <15: 31; 65+: 9. **Pop. density:** 32 per sq. mi. **Urban:** 87%. **Ethnic groups:** White 85% (Spanish, Italian), mestizo, Indian. **Principal languages:** Spanish (official), English, Italian. **Religions:** Roman Catholic 90%.

**Geography: Area:** 1,073,518 sq. mi., second largest country in South America. **Location:** Occupies most of S South America. **Neighbors:** Chile on W; Bolivia, Paraguay on N; Brazil, Uruguay on NE. **Topography:** The mountains in W: the Andean, Central, Misiones, and Southern. Aconcagua is the highest peak in the western hemisphere, alt. 22,834 ft. E of the Andes are heavily wooded plains, called the Gran Chaco in the N, and the fertile, treeless Pampas in the central region. Patagonia, in the S, is bleak and arid. Rio de la Plata, an estuary in the NE, 170 by 140 mi., is mostly fresh water, from 2,485-mi. Parana and 1,000-mi. Uruguay rivers. **Capital:** Buenos Aires (the Senate has approved moving the capital to the Patagonia Region). **Cities** (1991): Buenos Aires 2.96 mil (municipality); Cordoba 1.1 mil; La Matanza 1.1 mil.

**Government: Type:** Republic. **Head of state:** Pres. Carlos Saúl Menem; b July 2, 1930; in office: July 8, 1989. **Local divisions:** 23 provinces, 1 federal dist. **Defense:** 1.7% of GDP (1992). **Active troop strength:** 67,300.

**Economy: Industries:** Food processing, autos, chemicals, textiles, printing. **Chief crops:** Grains, corn, sugar beets, sorghum, soybeans. **Minerals:** Oil, lead, zinc, iron, copper, tin, uranium. **Crude oil reserves** (1995): 2.2 bil bbls. **Arable land:** 9%. **Livestock** (1994): cattle: 50 mil; sheep: 20 mil. **Fish catch** (1993): 931,000 metric tons. **Electricity prod.** (1993): 54.8 bil kWh. **Labor force:** 12% agric.; 31% ind.; 57% services.

**Finance: Monetary unit:** Peso (June 1996: 1.00 = $1 US). **Gross domestic product** (1994): $271 bil.* **Per capita GDP:** $7,990. **Imports** (1994): $21.4 bil; partners: U.S. 23%, Brazil 21%, Ger. 6%, Italy 6%. **Exports** (1994): $15.7 bil; partners: Brazil; 22%, Neth. 10%, U.S. 10%. **Tourism** (1993): $3.6 bil. **National budget** (1994): $46.5 bil. **International reserves less gold** (May 1996): $14.0 bil. **Gold:** 4.37 mil oz t. **Consumer prices** (change in 1995): 3.4%.

**Transport: Railroads: Route length:** 21,198 mi. **Motor vehicles:** in use: 4.9 mil passenger cars, 1.7 mil comm. vehicles. **Civil aviation:** 4.8 bil passenger-mi. **Chief ports:** Buenos Aires, Bahia Blanca, La Plata.

**Communications: Television sets:** 1 per 4.8 persons. **Radios:** 1 per 1.6 persons. **Telephones:** 1 per 8.2 persons. **Daily newspaper circ.:** 143 per 1,000 pop.

**Health: Life expectancy at birth** (1996): 68 male; 75 female. **Births** (per 1,000 pop.): 19. **Deaths** (per 1,000 pop.): 9. **Natural increase:** 1.1%. **Hospital beds:** 1 per 227 persons. **Physicians:** 1 per 376 persons. **Infant mortality** (per 1,000 live births 1996): 28.

**Education: Literacy** (1992): 96%. Free and compulsory: ages 6-14. **Years compulsory:** to age 14.

**Major International Organizations:** UN (World Bank, WTO, WHO, IMF, FAO), OAS.

**Embassy:** 1600 New Hampshire Ave. NW 20009; 939-6400.

Nomadic Indians roamed the Pampas when Spaniards arrived, 1515-16, led by Juan Diaz de Solis. Nearly all the Indians were killed by the late 19th century. The colonists won independence, 1816, and a long period of disorder ended in a strong centralized government.

Large-scale Italian, German, and Spanish immigration in the decades after 1880 spurred modernization. Social reforms were enacted in the 1920s, but military coups prevailed 1930-46, until the election of Gen. Juan Perón as president.

Perón, with his wife, Eva Duarte (d 1952), effected labor reforms, but also suppressed speech and press freedoms, closed religious schools, and ran the country into debt. A 1955 coup exiled Perón, who was followed by a series of military and civilian regimes. Perón returned in 1973, and was once more elected president. He died 10 months later, succeeded by his wife Isabel, who had been elected vice president, and who became the first woman head of state in the western hemisphere.

A military junta ousted Mrs. Perón in 1976 amid charges of corruption. Under a continuing state of siege, the army battled guerrillas and leftists, killed 5,000 people, and jailed and tortured others. On Dec. 9, 1985, after a trial of 5 months and nearly 1,000 witnesses, 5 former junta members were found guilty of murder and human rights abuses.

Argentine troops seized control of the British-held Falkland Islands on Apr. 2, 1982. Both countries had claimed sovereignty over the islands, located 250 miles off the Argentine coast, since 1833. The British dispatched a task force and declared a total air and sea blockade around the Falklands. Fighting began May 1; several hundred lost their lives as the result of the destruction of a British destroyer and the sinking of an Argentine cruiser.

British troops landed on East Falkland Island May 21 and eventually surrounded Stanley, the capital city and Argentine stronghold. The Argentine troops surrendered, June 14; Argentine Pres. Leopoldo Galtieri resigned June 17.

Democratic rule returned to Argentina in 1983 as Raul Alfonsín's Radical Civic Union gained an absolute majority in the presidential electoral college and Congress. By 1989 the nation was plagued by severe financial and political problems, as hyperinflation sparked looting and rioting in several cities. The government of Perónist Pres. Carlos Saúl Menem, installed 1989 and reelected 1995, introduced harsh economic measures to curtail inflation, control government spending, and restructure the foreign debt.

About 100 people were killed in the terrorist bombing of a Jewish cultural center in Buenos Aires, July 18, 1994.

# Armenia

## Republic of Armenia

## Hayastani Hanrapetutyun

**People: Population:** 3,463,574. **Pop. density:** 301 per sq. mi. **Urban:** 69%. **Ethnic groups:** Armenian 93%, Azeri 3%. **Principal language:** Armenian (official) 96%. **Religions:** Armenian Orthodox 94%.

**Geography: Area:** 11,500 sq. mi. **Location:** SW Asia. **Neighbors:** Georgia on N, Azerbaijan on E, Iran on S, Turkey on W. **Topography:** Mountainous with many peaks above 10,000 ft. **Capital:** Yerevan (1994 est.): 1.2 mil.

**Government: Type:** Republic. **Head of state:** Pres. Levon Ter-Petrosyan; b Jan. 9, 1945; in office: Nov. 11, 1991. **Head of government:** Hrand Bagratyan; b Oct. 18, 1958; in office: Feb. 16, 1993. **Local divisions:** 37 regions. **Defense:** 0.9% of GNP (1994). **Active troop strength:** 60,000 est.

**Economy: Industries:** Manufacturing, machinery, chemicals. **Chief crops:** Vegetables, grapes, grain. **Minerals:** Copper, gold, zinc. **Arable land:** 17%. **Electricity prod.** (1994): 5.7 bil kWh.

**Finance: Monetary unit:** Dram (June 1996: 405 = $1 US). **Gross domestic product** (1994 est.): $8.1 bil.* **Per capita GDP:** $2,290.

**Transport: Vehicles:** 230,100 passenger cars.

**Communications: Television sets:** 1 per 5 persons. **Radios:** 1 per 5.6 persons. **Telephones:** 1 per 6.4 persons. **Daily newspaper circ.:** 23 per 1,000 pop.

**Health: Life expectancy at birth** (1996): 64 male; 74 female. **Births** (per 1,000 pop.): 16. **Deaths** (per 1,000 pop.): 8. **Natural increase:** 0.9%. **Hospital beds:** 1 per 121 persons. **Physicians:** 1 per 262 persons. **Infant mortality** (per 1,000 live births 1996): 26.

**Major International Organizations:** UN (IMF, FAO, WHO, World Bank), CIS.

**Embassy:** 1660 L St. NW 20036; 628-5766.

Armenia is an ancient country, parts of which are now in Turkey and Iran. Present-day Armenia was set up as a Soviet republic Apr. 2, 1921. It joined Georgian and Azerbaijan SSRs Mar. 12, 1922, to form the Transcaucasian SFSR, which became part of the USSR Dec. 30, 1922. Armenia became a constituent republic of the USSR Dec. 5, 1936. An earthquake struck Armenia Dec. 7, 1988; more than 55,000 were killed and several cities and towns were left in ruins.

Armenia declared independence Sept. 23, 1991, and became an independent state when the USSR disbanded Dec. 26, 1991. Fighting between mostly Christian Armenia and mostly Muslim Azerbaijan escalated in 1992 and continued through 1993. Each country claimed Nagorno-Karabakh, an enclave in Azerbaijan that has a majority population of ethnic Armenians. A temporary cease-fire was announced in May 1994, with Armenian forces in control of the enclave. Voters approved, July 5, 1995, a new constitution strengthening presidential powers. Pres. Ter-Petrosyan won reelection on Sept. 22, 1996, amid claims of fraud.

# Australia

## Commonwealth of Australia

**People: Population:** 18,260,863. **Age distrib.** (%): <15: 21; 65+: 12. **Pop. density:** 6 per sq. mi. **Urban:** 85%. **Ethnic groups:** Caucasian 95%, Asian 4%, aborigines (including mixed) 1%. **Principal languages:** English, aboriginal languages. **Religions:** Anglican 26%, Roman Catholic 26%, other Christian 24%.

**Geography: Area:** 2,966,200 sq. mi. **Location:** SE of Asia, Indian O. is W and S, Pacific O. (Coral, Tasman seas) is E; they meet N of Australia in Timor and Arafura seas. Tasmania lies 150 mi. S of Victoria state, across Bass Strait. **Neighbors:** Nearest are Indonesia, Papua New Guinea on N; Solomons, Fiji, and New Zealand on E. **Topography:** An island continent. The Great Dividing Range along the E coast has Mt. Kosciusko, 7,310 ft. The W plateau rises to 2,000 ft., with arid areas in the Great Sandy and Great Victoria deserts. The NW part of Western Australia and Northern Terr. are arid and hot. The NE has heavy rainfall and Cape York Peninsula has jungles. The Murray R. rises in New South Wales and flows 1,600 mi. to the Indian O. **Capital:** Canberra. **Cities** (1994 est.): Sydney 3.7 mil; Melbourne 3.2 mil; Brisbane 1.5 mil; Perth 1.2 mil; Adelaide 1.1 mil.

**Government: Type:** Democratic, federal state system. **Head of state:** Queen Elizabeth II, represented by Gov.-Gen. Sir William Patrick Deane; b July 4, 1931; in office: Feb. 15, 1996. **Head of government:** Prime Min. John Howard; b July 26, 1939; in office: Mar. 8, 1996. **Local divisions:** 6 states, 2 territories. **Defense:** 2.2% of GDP (FY 1994-95). **Active troop strength:** 56,900.

**Economy: Industries:** Mining, steel, textiles, electrical equip., chemicals, autos, aircraft, ships, machinery. **Chief crops:** Wheat (a leading export), barley, oats, corn, hay, sugar, fruit, vegetables. **Minerals:** Bauxite, coal, copper, iron, lead, tin, uranium, zinc. **Crude oil reserves** (1994): 1.6 bil bbls. **Other resources:** Wool and beef (world's leading exporter of both). **Arable land:** 6%. **Livestock** (1994): cattle: 24 mil; sheep: 138 mil; pigs: 2.6 mil. **Fish catch** (1993): 218,000 metric tons. **Electricity prod.** (1993): 155 bil kWh. **Labor force:** 6% agric.; 34% finance & services; 36% trade, manuf. & ind.

**Finance: Monetary unit:** Dollar (June 1996: 1.27 = $1 US). **Gross domestic product** (1994): $374.6 bil.* **Per capita income:** $20,720. **Imports** (1994): $51.1 bil; partners: U.S. 23%, Jap. 18%, UK 6%. **Exports** (1994): $50.4 bil; partners: Jap. 25%, U.S. 11%, NZ 6%. **Tourism** (1993): $4.7 bil. **National budget** (FY 1994-95): $92.3 bil. **International reserves less**

**gold** (May 1996): $11.2 bil. **Gold:** 7.90 mil oz t. **Consumer prices** (change in 1995): 4.6%.

**Transport: Railroads: Route length:** 22,774 mi. **Motor vehicles:** in use: 8.3 mil passenger cars, 1.9 mil comm. vehicles. **Civil aviation:** 32.4 bil passenger-mi.; 428 airports with scheduled flights. **Chief ports:** Sydney, Melbourne, Brisbane, Adelaide, Fremantle, Geelong.

**Communications: Television sets:** 1 per 2.2 persons. **Radios:** 1 per 0.9 persons. **Telephones:** 1 per 2.1 persons. **Daily newspaper circ.:** 261 per 1,000 pop.

**Health: Life expectancy at birth** (1996): 76 male; 83 female. **Births** (per 1,000 pop.): 14. **Deaths** (per 1,000 pop.): 7. **Natural increase:** 0.7%. **Hospital beds:** 1 per 199 persons. **Physicians:** 1 per 434 persons. **Infant mortality** (per 1,000 live births 1996): 6.

**Education: Literacy** (1993): 100%. Free and compulsory: ages 6-15.

**Major International Organizations:** UN and all its specialized agencies, OECD, the Commonwealth, APEC.

**Embassy:** 1601 Massachusetts Ave. NW 20036; 797-3000.

Australia harbors many plant and animal species not found elsewhere, including kangaroos, koalas, the platypus, the dingo (wild dog), the Tasmanian devil (racoon-like marsupial), wombats (bear-like marsupials), and barking and frilled lizards.

Capt. James Cook explored the E coast in 1770, when the continent was inhabited by a variety of different tribes. The first settlers, beginning in 1788, were mostly convicts, soldiers, and government officials. By 1830, Britain had claimed the entire continent, and the immigration of free settlers began to accelerate. The commonwealth was proclaimed Jan. 1, 1901. Northern Terr. was granted limited self-rule July 1, 1978.

| State/Territory, Capital | Area (sq. mi.) | Population (1994 est.) |
|---|---|---|
| New South Wales, Sydney | 309,500 | 6,051,000 |
| Victoria, Melbourne | 87,900 | 4,476,000 |
| Queensland, Brisbane | 666,990 | 3,197,000 |
| Western Aust., Perth | 975,100 | 1,702,000 |
| South Aust., Adelaide | 379,900 | 1,470,000 |
| Tasmania, Hobart | 26,200 | 472,000 |
| Aust. Capital Terr., Canberra | 900 | 301,000 |
| Northern Terr., Darwin | 519,800 | 171,000 |

Racially discriminatory immigration policies were abandoned in 1973, after 3 million Europeans (half British) had entered since 1945. The 50,000 aborigines and 150,000 part-aborigines are mostly detribalized, but there are several preserves in the Northern Territory. They remain economically disadvantaged.

Australia's agricultural success makes the country among the top exporters of beef, lamb, wool, and wheat. Major mineral deposits have been developed, largely for export. Industrialization has been completed. The nation endured a deep recession 1990-93 but has rebounded strongly.

The Labor Party won a majority in Feb. 1983 general elections and was reelected in 1984, 1987, 1990, and 1993. After an election that focused mainly on economic issues, conservatives swept into power in elections Mar. 2, 1996.

## Australian External Territories

**Norfolk I.,** area 13.3 sq. mi., pop. (1990) 1,800, was taken over, 1914. The soil is very fertile, suitable for citrus fruits, bananas, and coffee. Many of the inhabitants are descendants of the *Bounty* mutineers, moved to Norfolk 1856 from Pitcairn I. Australia offered the island limited home rule, 1978.

**Coral Sea Is. Territory,** 1 sq. mi., is administered from Norfolk I.

**Territory of Ashmore and Cartier Is.,** area 2 sq. mi., in the Indian O. came under Australian authority 1934 and are administered as part of Northern Territory. **Heard** and **McDonald Is.** are administered by the Dept. of Science.

**Cocos (Keeling) Is.,** 27 small coral islands in the Indian O. 1,750 mi. NW of Australia. Pop. (1990) 600; area 5.5 sq. mi. The residents voted to become part of Australia, Apr. 1984.

**Christmas I.,** 52 sq. mi., pop. 1,700 (1991), 230 mi. S of Java, was transferred by Britain in 1958. It has phosphate deposits.

**Australian Antarctic Territory** was claimed by Australia in 1933, including 2,362,000 sq. mi. of territory S of 60th parallel S Lat. and between 160th-45th meridians E Long. It does not include Adelie Coast.

# Austria

## Republic of Austria

## Republik Österreich

**People: Population:** 8,023,244. **Age distrib.** (%): <15: 18; 65+: 15. **Pop. density:** 248 per sq. mi. **Urban:** 65%. **Ethnic groups:** German 99%, Croatian, Slovene. **Principal language:** German (official). **Religions:** Roman Catholic 85%, Protestant 6%.

**Geography: Area:** 32,378 sq. mi. **Location:** In S Central Europe. **Neighbors:** Switzerland, Liechtenstein on W; Germany, Czech Rep. on N; Slovakia, Hungary on E; Slovenia, Italy on S. **Topography:** Austria is primarily mountainous, with the Alps and foothills covering the western and southern provinces. The eastern provinces and Vienna are located in the Danube River Basin. **Capital:** Vienna (1991): 1,540,000.

**Government: Type:** Parliamentary democracy. **Head of state:** Pres. Thomas Klestil; b Nov. 4, 1932; in office: July 8, 1992. **Head of government:** Chancellor Franz Vranitzky; b Oct. 4, 1937; in office: June 16, 1986. **Local divisions:** 9 lander (states), each with a legislature. **Defense:** 0.9% of GDP (1994). **Active troop strength:** 55,750 est.

**Economy: Industries:** Steel, machinery, autos, electrical equip., tourism, mining, paper, textiles, chemicals, cement. **Chief crops:** Grains, potatoes, beets. **Minerals:** Iron ore, oil, magnesite. **Other resources:** Forests, hydropower. **Arable land:** 17%. **Livestock** (1994): cattle: 2.4 mil; pigs: 3.8 mil. **Electricity prod.** (1993): 50.2 bil kWh. **Labor force:** 8% agric.; 35% ind. & crafts; 56% services.

**Finance: Monetary unit:** Schilling (June 1996: 10.72 = $1 US). **Gross domestic product** (1994): $139.3 bil.* **Per capita GDP:** $17,500. **Imports** (1994): $53.8 bil; partners: Germany 40%. **Exports** (1994): $44.1 bil; partners: Germany 38%. **Tourism** (1993): $13.4 bil. **National budget** (1993 est.): $60 bil. **International reserves less gold** (May 1996): $22.2 bil. **Gold:** 11.63 mil oz t. **Consumer prices** (change in 1995): 2.3%.

**Transport: Railroads: Route length:** 3,480 mi. **Motor vehicles:** in use: 3.4 mil passenger cars, 746,000 comm. **Civil aviation:** 4.6 bil passenger-mi.; 6 airports with scheduled flights. **Chief ports:** Linz, Vienna.

**Communications: Television sets:** 1 per 3.0 persons. **Radios:** 1 per 1.7 persons. **Telephones:** 1 per 2.2 persons. **Daily newspaper circ.:** 394 per 1,000 pop.

**Health: Life expectancy at birth** (1996): 73 male; 80 female. **Births** (per 1,000 pop.): 11. **Deaths** (per 1,000 pop.): 10. **Natural increase:** 0.1% **Hospital beds:** 1 per 109 persons. **Physicians:** 1 per 307 persons. **Infant mortality** (per 1,000 live births 1996): 6.

**Education: Literacy** (1994): 100%. Free and compulsory: ages 6-15. Attendance 95%.

**Major International Organizations:** UN and all of its specialized agencies, EU, OECD.

**Embassy:** 3524 International Ct. NW 20008; 895-6700.

Rome conquered Austrian lands from Celtic tribes around 15 BC. In 788 the territory was incorporated into Charlemagne's empire. By 1300, the House of Hapsburg had gained control; they added vast territories in all parts of Europe to their realm in the next few hundred years.

Austrian dominance of Germany was undermined in the 18th century and ended by Prussia by 1866. But the Congress of Vienna, 1815, confirmed Austrian control of a large empire in southeast Europe consisting of Germans, Hungarians, Slavs, Italians, and others. The dual Austro-Hungarian monarchy was established in 1867, giving autonomy to Hungary and almost 50 years of peace.

World War I, started after the June 28, 1914, assassination of Archduke Franz Ferdinand, the Hapsburg heir, by a Serbian nationalist, destroyed the empire. By 1918 Austria was reduced to a small republic, with the borders it has today.

Nazi Germany invaded Austria Mar. 13, 1938. The republic was reestablished in 1945, under Allied occupation. Full independence and neutrality were restored in 1955. Austria joined the European Union Jan. 1, 1995.

# Azerbaijan

## Azerbaijani Republic

## Azarbaycan Respublikasi

**People: Population:** 7,676,953. **Pop. density:** 230 per sq. mi. **Urban:** 53%. **Ethnic groups:** Azeri 90%, Russian 3%, Armenian 2%. **Principal languages:** Azeri (official) 89%, Russian 3%, Armenian 2%. **Religions:** Muslim 93%.

**Geography: Area:** 33,400 sq. mi. **Location:** SW Asia. **Neighbors:** Russia, Georgia on N; Iran on S; Armenia on W; Caspian Sea on E. **Capital:** Baku (1994 est.): 1.1 mil.

**Government: Type:** Republic. **Head of state:** Pres. Haydar A. Aliyev; b May 10, 1923; in office: June 30, 1993. **Head of government:** Prime Min. Fuad Guliyev; b 1947; in office: Oct. 6, 1994. **Defense:** 10% of GDP (1993). **Active troop strength:** 86,700 est.

**Economy: Industries:** Oil refining, mining, chemicals, silk. **Chief crops:** Grain, cotton, grapes. **Minerals:** Oil, gas, iron. **Crude oil reserves** (1992): 3.3 bil bbls. **Arable land:** 18%. **Livestock** (1994): cattle: 1.6 mil; goats & sheep: 4.5 mil. **Electricity prod.** (1994): 17.5 bil kWh.

**Finance: Monetary unit:** Manat (June 1996: 4,350 = $1 US). **Gross Domestic Product** (1994 est.): $13.8 bil.* **Per capita GDP:** $1,790. **National budget** (1994): $235 mil.

**Transport: Vehicles:** 235,600 passenger cars. **Chief port:** Baku.

**Communications: Daily newspaper circ.:** 58 per 1,000 pop.

**Health: Life expectancy at birth** (1996): 60 male; 70 female. **Births** (per 1,000 pop.): 22. **Deaths** (per 1,000 pop.): 9. **Natural increase:** 1.4%. **Hospital beds:** 1 per 98 persons. **Physicians:** 1 per 251 persons. **Infant mortality** (per 1,000 live births 1996): 75.

**Major International Organizations:** UN (ILO, IMF, WHO, CIS).

**Embassy:** 927 15th St. NW, Suite 700 20005; 842-0001.

Azerbaijan was the home of Scythian tribes and part of the Roman Empire. It was overrun by Turks in the 11th century and conquered by Russia in 1806 and 1813. It joined the USSR Dec. 30, 1922, and became a constituent republic in 1936. Azerbaijan declared independence Aug. 30, 1991, and became an independent state when the Soviet Union disbanded Dec. 26, 1991.

Fighting between mostly Muslim Azerbaijan and mostly Christian Armenia escalated in 1992 and continued in 1993 and 1994. Each country claimed Nagorno-Karabakh, an enclave in Azerbaijan with a majority population of ethnic Armenians. A temporary cease-fire was announced in May 1994, with Armenian forces in control of the enclave.

A National Council ousted Communist Pres. Mutaibov and took power May 19, 1992. Abulfez Elchibey became the nation's first democratically elected president June 7, but was ousted from office by Surat Huseynov, commander of a private militia, June 30, 1993. Huseynov became prime minister, and Haydar Aliyev, a pro-Russian former Communist, became president. Huseynov fled the country after his supporters staged an unsuccessful coup attempt Oct. 1994. Voters approved a new constitution expanding presidential powers, Nov. 12, 1995.

# The Bahamas

## The Commonwealth of The Bahamas

**People: Population:** 259,367. **Age distrib.** (%): <15: 29; 65+: 5. **Pop. density:** 48 per sq. mi. **Urban:** 84%. **Ethnic groups:** Black 85%, white (British, Canadian, U.S.) 15%. **Principal languages:** English (official), Creole. **Religions:** Baptist 32%, Anglican 20%, Roman Catholic 19%.

**Geography: Area:** 5,382 sq. mi. **Location:** In Atlantic O., E of Florida. **Neighbors:** Nearest are U.S. on W, Cuba on S. **Topography:** Nearly 700 islands (29 inhabited) and over 2,000 islets in the W Atlantic O. extend 760 mi. NW to SE. **Capital:** Nassau. **Cities** (1990 est.): Nassau 172,000; Freeport- Lucaya 27,000.

**Government: Type:** Independent commonwealth. **Head of state:** Queen Elizabeth II, represented by Gov.-Gen. Orville A Turnquest; b July 19, 1929; in office: Jan. 2, 1995. **Head of government:** Prime Min. Hubert Ingraham; b Aug. 4, 1947; in office: Aug. 21, 1992. **Local divisions:** 21 districts. **Defense:** 0.5% of GNP (1993). **Security forces:** 2,850 incl. police.

**Economy: Industries:** Tourism (50% of GDP), rum, cement, banking, pharmaceuticals. **Chief crops:** Citrus, vegetables. **Minerals:** Salt, aragonite. **Other resources:** Lobsters. **Arable land:** 1%. **Electricity prod.** (1993): 929 mil kWh. **Labor force:** 5% agric.; 25% tourism; 30% government.

**Finance: Monetary unit:** Dollar (June 1996: 1 = $1 US). **Gross domestic product** (1994): $4.4 bil.* **Per capita GDP:** $15,900. **Imports** (1993): $1.2 bil; partners: U.S. 55%, Japan 17%, Nigeria 12%. **Exports** (1993): $257 mil; partners: U.S. 51%, UK 7%, Norway 7%. **Tourism** (1994): $1.3 bil. **National budget** (FY 1994-95): $756 mil. **International reserves less gold** (May 1996): $231.7 mil. **Consumer prices** (change in 1994): 1.4%.

**Transport: Motor vehicles:** in use: 69,000 passenger cars, 14,000 comm. vehicles. **Chief ports:** Nassau, Freeport.

**Communications: Radios:** 1 per 2.0 persons. **Television sets:** 1 per 4.5 persons. **Telephones:** 1 per 3.4 persons. **Daily newspaper circ.:** 133 per 1,000 pop.

**Health: Life expectancy at birth** (1996): 68 male; 77 female. **Births** (per 1,000 pop.): 19. **Deaths** (per 1,000 pop.): 6. **Natural increase:** 1.3%. **Infant mortality** (per 1,000 live births 1996): 23.

**Education: Literacy** (1993): 98%. Compulsory: ages 5 and 14.

**Major International Organizations:** UN (World Bank, FAO, IMF, WHO), OAS, the Commonwealth.

**Embassy:** 2220 Massachusetts Ave. NW 20008; 319-2660.

Christopher Columbus first set foot in the New World on San Salvador (Watling I.) in 1492, when Arawak Indians inhabited the islands. British settlement began in 1647; the islands became a British colony in 1783. Internal self-government was granted in 1964; full independence within the Commonwealth was attained July 10, 1973.

International banking and investment management have become major industries alongside tourism.

# Bahrain

## State of Bahrain

## Dawlat al Bahrayn

**People: Population:** 590,042. **Age distrib.** (%): <15: 32; 65+: 2. **Pop. density:** 2,202 per sq. mi. **Urban:** 88%. **Ethnic groups:** Bahraini 63%, Asian 13%, other Arab 10%, Iranian 8%. **Principal languages:** Arabic (official), English, Farsi, Urdu. **Religions:** Shi'a Muslim 70%, Sunni Muslim 30%.

**Geography: Area:** 268 sq. mi. **Location:** In Persian Gulf. **Neighbors:** Nearest are Saudi Arabia on W, Qatar on E. **Topography:** Bahrain Island, and several adjacent, smaller islands, are flat, hot, and humid, with little rain. **Capital:** Manama (1992 est.): 140,000.

**Government: Type:** Traditional monarchy. **Head of state:** Emir Isa bin Sulman al-Khalifa; b July 3, 1933; in office: Nov. 2, 1961. **Head of government:** Prime Min. Kahlifa bin Sulman al-Khalifa; b 1935; in office: Jan. 19, 1970. **Local divisions:** 12 districts. **Defense:** 5.5% of GDP (1994). **Active troop strength:** 10,700.

**Economy: Industries:** Oil products, aluminum smelting. **Chief crops:** Fruits, vegetables. **Minerals:** Oil, gas. **Crude oil reserves** (1995): 210 mil bbls. **Arable land:** 2%. **Electricity prod.** (1993): 3.3 bil kWh. **Labor force:** 5% agric.; 85% ind. and commerce; 5% services; 3% govt.

**Finance: Monetary unit:** Dinar (June 1996: 0.38 = $1 US). **Gross domestic product** (1994): $7.1 bil.* **Per capita income:** $12,100. **Imports** (1993): $3.8 bil; partners: Saudi Arabia 47%, UK 7%, Japan 6%. **Exports** (1993): $3.7 bil; partners: Japan 11%, UAE 5%. **National budget** (1992): $1.6 bil. **International reserves less gold** (Apr. 1996): $1.2 bil. **Gold:** 150,000 oz t. **Consumer prices** (change in 1994): 0.8%.

**Transport: Motor vehicles:** in use: 114,000 passenger cars, 27,000 comm. vehicles. **Chief port:** Sitrah.

**Communications: Television sets:** 1 per 2.0 persons. **Radios:** 1 per 1.7 persons. **Telephones:** 1 per 4.4 persons.

**Health: Life expectancy at birth** (1996): 72 male; 77 female. **Births** (per 1,000 pop.): 24. **Deaths** (per 1,000 pop.): 3. **Natural increase:** 2.0%. Medical services are free. **Infant mortality** (per 1,000 live births 1996): 17.

**Education: Literacy** (1993): 85%. Free and compulsory: ages 6-17.

**Major International Organizations:** UN (WTO, IMF, FAO, World Bank, WHO), Arab League.

**Embassy:** 3502 International Dr. NW 20008; 342-0741.

Long ruled by the Khalifa family, Bahrain was a British protectorate from 1861 to Aug. 15, 1971, when it regained independence.

Pearls, shrimp, fruits, and vegetables were the mainstays of the economy until oil was discovered in 1932. By the 1970s, oil reserves were depleted; international banking thrived.

Bahrain took part in the 1973-74 Arab oil embargo against the U.S. and other nations. The government bought controlling interest in the oil industry in 1975. Violence in 1996 by Shiite dissidents brought a crackdown by the Sunni-led government.

## Bangladesh

### People's Republic of Bangladesh

### Gana Prajatantri Bangladesh

**People: Population:** 123,062,800. **Age distrib.** (%): <15: 40; 65+: 3. **Pop. density:** 2,160 per sq. mi. **Urban:** 16%. **Ethnic groups:** Bengali 98%, Bihari, tribals. **Principal languages:** Bangla (official), English. **Religions:** Muslim 83%, Hindu 16%.

**Geography: Area:** 56,977 sq. mi. **Location:** In S Asia, on N bend of Bay of Bengal. **Neighbors:** India nearly surrounds country on W, N, E; Myanmar on SE. **Topography:** The country is mostly a low plain cut by the Ganges and Brahmaputra rivers and their delta. The land is alluvial and marshy along the coast, with hills only in the extreme SE and NE. A tropical monsoon climate prevails, among the rainiest in the world. **Capital:** Dhaka. **Cities** (1991): Dhaka 3.6 mil; Chittagong 1.6 mil; Khulna 600,000.

**Government: Type:** Parliamentary democracy. **Head of state:** Pres. Abdur Rahman Biswas; b Sept. 1926; in office: Oct. 10, 1991. **Head of government:** Prime Min. Hasina Wazed; b Sept. 27, 1947; in office: June 24, 1996. **Local divisions:** 64 districts. **Defense:** 1.7% of GDP (FY 1993-94). **Active troop strength:** 115,500 est.

**Economy: Industries:** Food processing, jute, textiles, fertilizers, steel. **Chief crops:** Jute (most of world's output), rice, tea. **Minerals:** Natural gas. **Arable land:** 67%. **Livestock** (1994): cattle: 24 mil; goats: 28 mil. **Fish catch** (1992): 966,700 metric tons. **Electricity prod.** (1993): 9.2 bil kWh. **Labor force:** 65% agric; 14% ind. & mining; 21% services.

**Finance: Monetary unit:** Taka (June 1996: 41.93 = $1 US). **Gross domestic product** (1994): $130 bil.* **Per capita GDP:** $1,040. **Imports** (1993): $4.0 bil; partners: Hong Kong 8%, Japan 7%. **Exports** (1993): $2.4 bil; partners: U.S. 33%, Germany 8%, Italy 6%. **Tourism** (1993): $15 mil. **National budget** (FY 1992-93): $4.1 bil. **International reserves less gold** (May 1996): $1.9 bil. **Gold:** 94,000 oz t. **Consumer prices** (change in 1994): 5.3%.

**Transport: Railroads: Route length:** 1,706 mi. **Motor vehicles:** in use: 75,000 passenger cars, 97,000 comm. vehicles. **Chief ports:** Chittagong, Chalna.

**Communications: Television sets:** 1 per 336 persons. **Radios:** 1 per 25 persons. **Telephones:** 1 per 435 persons.

**Health: Life expectancy at birth** (1996): 56 male; 56 female. **Births** (per 1,000 pop.): 31. **Deaths** (per 1,000 pop.): 11. **Natural increase:** 1.9%. **Hospital beds:** 1 per 3,218 persons. **Physicians:** 1 per 5,264 persons. **Infant mortality** (per 1,000 live births 1996): 102.

**Education: Literacy** (1992): 38%. Free and compulsory: ages 5-10. **Attendance:** 73% primary school; 26% secondary school.

**Major International Organizations:** UN (WTO, FAO, World Bank, IMF, WHO), the Commonwealth.

**Embassy:** 2201 Wisconsin Ave. NW 20007; 342-8372.

Muslim invaders conquered the formerly Hindu area in the 12th century. British rule lasted from the 18th century to 1947, when East Bengal became part of Pakistan.

Charging West Pakistani domination, the Awami League, based in the East, won National Assembly control in 1971. Assembly sessions were postponed; riots broke out. Pakistani troops attacked Mar. 25; Bangladesh independence was proclaimed the next day. In the ensuing civil war, one million died and 10 million fled to India.

War between India and Pakistan broke out Dec. 3, 1971. Pakistan surrendered in the East on Dec. 15. Mujibur Rahman, known as Sheikh Mujib, became prime minister; he was killed in a coup, Aug. 15, 1975. During the 1970s the country moved into the Indian and Soviet orbits in response to U.S. support of Pakistan, and much of the economy was nationalized.

On May 30, 1981, Pres. Ziaur Rahman was killed in an unsuccessful coup attempt by army rivals. Vice President Abdus Sattar assumed the presidency but was ousted in a coup led by army chief of staff Gen. H. M. Ershad, Mar. 1982. Ershad declared Bangladesh an Islamic Republic in 1988. Bangladesh adopted a parliamentary system of government in 1991.

Bangladesh is subject to devastating storms and floods that kill thousands. A cyclone struck Apr. 1991, killing over 131,000 people and causing $2.7 billion in damages. Chronic destitution in the densely crowded population has been worsened by the decline of jute as a world commodity.

Political turmoil led to the resignation, Mar. 30, 1996, of Prime Minister Khaleda Zia, the widow of Ziaur Rahman. Sheikh Mujib's daughter, Hasina Wazed (known as Sheikh Hasina), led the country after the election of June 12, 1996.

## Barbados

**People: Population:** 257,030. **Age distrib.** (%): <15: 24; 65+: 12. **Pop. density:** 1,548 per sq. mi. **Urban:** 38%. **Ethnic groups:** African 80%, mixed 16%, European 4%. **Principal language:** English (official). **Religions:** Protestant 67%, Roman Catholic 4%.

**Geography: Area:** 166 sq. mi. **Location:** In Atlantic O., farthest E of West Indies. **Neighbors:** Nearest are St. Lucia and St. Vincent & the Grenadines to the W. **Topography:** The island lies alone in the Atlantic almost completely surrounded by coral reefs. Highest point is Mt. Hillaby, 1,115 ft. **Capital:** Bridgetown (1990): 6,000.

**Government: Type:** Parliamentary democracy. **Head of state:** Queen Elizabeth II, represented by Gov.-Gen. Sir Clifford Husbands; b Aug. 5, 1926; in office: June 1, 1996. **Head of government:** Prime Min. Owen Arthur; b Oct. 17, 1949; in office: Sept. 7, 1994. **Local divisions:** 11 parishes and Bridgetown.

**Economy: Industries:** Sugar, tourism. **Chief crops:** Sugar, cotton. **Minerals:** Oil, gas. **Other resources:** Fish. **Arable land:** 77%. **Electricity prod.** (1993): 510 mil kWh. **Labor force:** 6% agric.; 15% commerce; 41% serv. & govt.; 18% manuf. & constr.

**Finance: Monetary unit:** Dollar (June 1996: 2.01 = $1 US). **Gross domestic product** (1994): $2.4 bil.* **Per capita GDP:** $9,200. **Imports** (1993): $703 mil; partners: U.S. 36%, UK 11%, Trin. & Tob. 11%. **Exports** (1993): $161 mil; partners: U.S. 13%, UK 10%, Trin. & Tob. 9%. **Tourism** (1993): $502 mil. **National budget** (FY 1994-95): $636 mil. **International reserves less gold** (May 1996): $288 mil. **Consumer prices** (change in 1995): 1.9%.

**Transport: Motor vehicles:** in use: 43,000 passenger cars; 8,000 comm. vehicles. **Chief port:** Bridgetown.

**Communications: Television sets:** 1 per 3.8 persons. **Radios:** 1 per 1.2 persons. **Telephones:** 1 per 2.4 persons. **Daily newspaper circ.:** 157 per 1,000 pop.

**Health: Life expectancy at birth** (1996): 72 male; 77 female. **Births** (per 1,000 pop.): 15. **Deaths** (per 1,000 pop.): 8. **Natural increase:** 0.7%. **Hospital beds:** 1 per 134 persons. **Physicians:** 1 per 842 persons. **Infant mortality** (per 1,000 live births 1996): 19.

**Education: Literacy** (1992): 97%. Compulsory: ages 5-16.

**Major International Organizations:** UN (FAO, WTO, World Bank, ILO, IMF, WHO), OAS, the Commonwealth.

**Embassy:** 2144 Wyoming Ave. NW 20008; 939-9200.

Barbados was probably named by Portuguese sailors in reference to bearded fig trees. An English ship visited in 1605, and British settlers arrived on the uninhabited island in 1627. Slaves worked the sugar plantations until slavery was abolished in 1834. Self-rule came gradually, with full independence proclaimed Nov. 30, 1966. British traditions have remained.

## Belarus

### Republic of Belarus

### Respublika Byelarus

**People: Population:** 10,415,973. **Age distrib.** (%): <15: 22; 65+: 12. **Pop. density:** 130 per sq. mi. **Urban:** 69%. **Ethnic groups:** Belarussian 78%, Russian 13%. **Principal languages:** Belarussian (official), Russian. **Religion:** Eastern Orthodox.

**Geography: Area:** 80,153 sq. mi. **Location:** E Europe. **Neighbors:** Poland on W; Latvia, Lithuania on N; Russia on E; Ukraine on S. **Capital:** Minsk. **Cities:** Minsk 1.7 mil (1994 est.); Homyel 517,000 (1992 est.).

**Government:** Republic. **Head of state:** Pres. Aleksandr Lukashenko; b Aug. 30, 1954; in office: July 1994. **Head of government:** Mikhail Chygir; b May 24, 1948; in office, July 1994. **Local divisions:** 6 voblastsi and 1 municipality. **Defense:** 1.8% of GNP (1993). **Active troop strength:** 98,400.

**Economy: Industries:** Manufacturing, chemical fibers, machine-tool & agricultural machinery. **Chief crops:** Grain, vegetables, potatoes. **Arable land:** 29%. **Livestock** (1994): cattle: 5.9 mil; pigs: 4.2 mil. **Electricity prod.** (1994): 31.4 bil kWh. **Labor force:** 40% ind. & const.; 21% agric. & forestry.

**Finance: Monetary unit:** Rubel (June 1996: 12,550 = $1 US). **Gross domestic product** (1994 est.): $53.4 bil.* **Per capita GDP:** $5,130. **Imports** (1994): $3.0 bil; partners: CIS 81%. **Exports** (1994): $3.7 bil; partners: CIS 66%.

**Transport: Railroads: Length:** 3,459 mi. **Motor vehicles:** in use: 774,000 passenger cars, 10,000 comm. vehicles. **Chief port:** Mazyr.

**Communications: Television sets:** 1 per 3.7 persons. **Radios:** 1 per 3.3 persons. **Telephones:** 1 per 5.7 persons. **Daily newspaper circ.:** 181 per 1,000 pop.

**Health: Life expectancy at birth** (1996): 63 male; 74 female. **Births** (per 1,000 pop.): 12. **Deaths** (per 1,000 pop.): 14. **Natural increase:** –0.1%. **Hospital beds:** 1 per 82 persons. **Physicians:** 1 per 230 persons. **Infant mortality** (per 1,000 live births 1996): 13.

**Education: Literacy** (1994) 98%. Compulsory: ages 6-17.

**Major International Organizations:** UN, CIS.

**Embassy:** 1619 New Hampshire Ave. NW 20009; 986-1604.

The region was subject to Lithuanians and Poles in medieval times, and was a prize of war between Russia and Poland beginning in 1503. It became part of the USSR in 1922 although the western part of the region was controlled by Poland. Belarus was overrun by German armies in 1941; recovered by Soviet troops in 1944. Following World War II, Belarus increased in area through Soviet annexation of part of NE Poland. Belarus declared independence Aug. 25, 1991. It became an independent state when the Soviet Union disbanded Dec. 26, 1991.

A new constitution was adopted, Mar. 15, 1994, and a new president was chosen in elections concluding July 1. Russia and Belarus signed a pact Apr. 2, 1996, linking their political and economic systems. In Oct. 1996, Pres. Aleksandr Lukashenko announced that he wanted a new constitution that would give him nearly unlimited power.

# Belgium

## Kingdom of Belgium

## Koninkrijk België (Dutch)
## Royaume de Belgique (French)

**People: Population:** 10,170,241. **Age distrib.** (%): <15: 18; 65+: 16. **Pop. density:** 863 per sq. mi. **Urban:** 97%. **Ethnic groups:** Fleming 55%, Walloon 33%. **Principal languages:** Flemish (Dutch) 56%, French 32%, German (all official). **Religions:** Roman Catholic 75%, Protestant & other 25%.

**Geography: Area:** 11,787 sq. mi. **Location:** In W Europe, on North Sea. **Neighbors:** France on W and S, Luxembourg on SE, Germany on E, Netherlands on N. **Topography:** Mostly flat, the country is trisected by the Scheldt and Meuse, major commercial rivers. The land becomes hilly and forested in the SE (Ardennes) region. **Capital:** Brussels. **Cities** (1994 est.): Brussels (met.) 949,000; Antwerp 463,000; Ghent 228,000; Charleroi 207,000; Liege 195,000.

**Government: Type:** Parliamentary democracy under a constitutional monarch. **Head of state:** King Albert II; b June 6, 1934; in office: Aug. 9, 1993. **Head of government:** Premier Jean-Luc Dehaene; b Aug. 7, 1940; in office: Mar. 7, 1992. **Local divisions:** 9 provinces. **Defense:** 1.8% of GDP (1994). **Active troop strength:** 47,200.

**Economy: Industries:** Metal products, glassware, autos, textiles, chemicals. **Chief crops:** Wheat, fruits, sugar beets, potatoes. **Minerals:** Coal, gas. **Arable land:** 24%. **Livestock** (1994): cattle: 3.1 mil; pigs: 6.9 mil. **Fish catch** (1992): 37,000 metric tons. **Electricity prod.** (1993): 66 bil kWh. **Labor force:** 2% agric.; 28% industry; 64% services.

**Finance: Monetary unit:** Franc (June 1996: 31.35 = $1 US). **Gross domestic product** (1994 est.): $181.5 bil.* **Per capita GDP** $18,040. *Note:* The following trade data include Luxembourg. **Imports** (1992): $120 bil; partners: EU 73%. **Exports** (1992): $117 bil; partners: EU 76%. **Tourism** (1993): $4.1 bil. **National budget** (1989): $109.3 bil. **International reserves less gold** (May 1996): $17.2 bil. **Gold:** 15.32 mil oz t. **Consumer prices** (change in 1995): 1.5%.

**Transport: Railroads: Route length:** 2,119 mi. **Motor vehicles:** in use: 4.1 mil passenger cars, 390,000 comm. vehicles. **Civil aviation:** 4.0 bil passenger-mi.; 2 airports with scheduled flights. **Chief ports:** Antwerp, Zeebrugge, Ghent.

**Communications: Television sets:** 1 per 2.4 persons. **Radios:** 1 per 1.3 persons. **Telephones:** 1 per 2.3 persons. **Daily newspaper circ.:** 315 per 1,000 pop.

**Health: Life expectancy at birth** (1996): 74 male; 81 female. **Births** (per 1,000 pop.): 12. **Deaths** (per 1,000 pop.): 10. **Natural increase** 0.2%. **Hospital beds:** 1 per 124 persons. **Physicians:** 1 per 278 persons. **Infant mortality** (per 1,000 live births 1996): 6.

**Education: Literacy** (1993): 100%. Compulsory: ages 6-18.

**Major International Organizations:** UN and all of its specialized agencies, NATO, EU, OECD.

**Embassy:** 3330 Garfield St. NW 20008; 333-6900.

Belgium derives its name from the Belgae, the first recorded inhabitants, probably Celts. The land was conquered by Julius Caesar, and was ruled for 1800 years by conquerors, including Rome, the Franks, Burgundy, Spain, Austria, and France. After 1815, Belgium was made a part of the Netherlands, but it became an independent constitutional monarchy in 1830.

Belgian neutrality was violated by Germany in both world wars. King Leopold III surrendered to Germany, May 28, 1940. After the war, he was forced by political pressure to abdicate in favor of his son, King Baudouin. Baudouin was succeeded by his brother, Albert II, Aug. 9, 1993.

The Flemings of northern Belgium speak Dutch, while French is the language of the Walloons in the south. The language difference has been a perennial source of controversy and led to antagonism between the 2 groups. Parliament has passed measures aimed at transferring power from the central government to 3 regions—Wallonia, Flanders, and Brussels.

Belgium lives by its foreign trade; about 50% of its entire production is sold abroad.

# Belize

**People: Population:** 219,296. **Age distrib.** (%): <15: 44; 65+: 4. **Pop. density:** 25 per sq. mi. **Urban:** 48%. **Ethnic groups:** Mestizo 44%, Creole 30%, Maya 11%, Garifuna 7%. **Principal languages:** English (official), Spanish, Maya, Garifuna (Carib). **Religions:** Roman Catholic 62%, Protestant 30%.

**Geography: Area:** 8,867 sq. mi. **Location:** Eastern coast of Central America. **Neighbors:** Mexico on N, Guatemala on W and S. **Capital:** Belmopan. **Cities** (1993): Belize City 47,700.

**Government: Type:** Parliamentary democracy. **Head of state:** Queen Elizabeth II, represented by Gov.-Gen. Colville Young; b Nov. 20, 1932; in office: Nov. 17, 1993. **Head of government:** Prime Min. Manuel Esquivel; b May 2, 1940; in office: July 2, 1993. **Local divisions:** 6 districts. **Defense:** 2.2% of GDP (FY 1993-94). **Active troop strength:** 1,050.

**Economy: Industries:** Garments, food processing, tourism. **Chief crops:** Sugar (main export), citrus, bananas. **Arable land:** 2%.

**Finance: Monetary unit:** Dollar (June 1996: 2 = $1 US). **Gross domestic product** (1994): $575 mil.* **Per capita GDP:** $2,750. **Imports** (1993): $281 mil; partners: U.S. 56%, Mexico 10%. **Exports:** (1993): $115 mil; partners: U.S. 45%, UK 36%. **National budget** (1991): $123.1 mil. **International reserves less gold** (May 1996): $42.4 mil.

**Health: Life expectancy at birth** (1996): 67 male; 71 female. **Births** (per 1,000 pop.): 34. **Deaths** (per 1,000 pop.): 6. **Natural increase:** 2.7%. **Hospital beds:** 1 per 340 persons. **Physicians:** 1 per 1,809 persons. **Infant mortality** (per 1,000 live births 1996): 34.

**Education: Literacy** (1993): 93%. Compulsory: ages 5-14.

**Major International Organizations:** OAS, UN (IMF, FAO, WTO, WHO, World Bank), the Commonwealth.

**Embassy:** 2535 Massachusetts Ave. NW 20008; 332-9636.

Belize (formerly British Honduras) was Britain's last colony on the American mainland. The country achieved independence Sept. 21, 1981. Relations with neighboring Guatemala, initially tense, have improved in recent years.

# Benin

## Republic of Benin

## République du Bénin

**People: Population:** 5,709,529. **Age distrib.** (%): <15: 47; 65+: 3. **Pop. density:** 131 per sq. mi. **Urban:** 36%. **Ethnic groups:** African (Fon, Adja, Bariba, Yoruba) 99%. **Principal**

**languages:** French (official), Fon, Yoruba. **Religions:** Indigenous beliefs 70%, Muslim 15%, Christian 15%.

**Geography: Area:** 43,500 sq. mi. **Location:** In W Africa on Gulf of Guinea. **Neighbors:** Togo on W; Burkina Faso, Niger on N; Nigeria on E. **Topography:** Most of Benin is flat and covered with dense vegetation. The coast is hot, humid, and rainy. **Capital:** Porto-Novo. **Cities** (1992): Cotonou 533,000.

**Government: Type:** Republic. **Head of state:** Pres. Mathieu Kerekou; b Sept. 2, 1933; in office: Apr. 4, 1996. **Local divisions:** 6 provinces. **Defense:** 3.2% of GDP (1994). **Active troop strength:** 4,800.

**Economy: Chief crops:** Palm products, peanuts, cotton, corn, rice. **Minerals:** Oil, limestone. **Arable land:** 12%. **Livestock** (1994): goats: 1.2 mil; cattle: 1.2 mil. **Fish catch** (1993): 39,000 metric tons. **Electricity prod.** (1993): 10 mil kWh. **Labor force:** 60% agric.; 38% transport, commerce, public services.

**Finance: Monetary unit:** CFA Franc (June 1996: 515 = $1 US). **Gross domestic product** (1994): $6.7 bil.* **Per capita GDP:** $1,260. **Imports** (1993): $571 mil; partners: France 20%. **Exports** (1993): $332 mil; partners: Germany 36%. **National budget** (1993): $375 bil. **International reserves less gold** (Dec. 1995): $198 mil. **Consumer prices** (change in 1995): 14.5%.

**Transport: Railroads: Length:** 359 mi. **Chief port:** Cotonou.

**Communications: Television sets:** 1 per 262 persons. **Radios:** 1 per 13 persons. **Telephones:** 1 per 260 persons. **Daily newspaper circ.:** 3 per 1,000 pop.

**Health: Life expectancy at birth** (1995): 51 male; 55 female. **Births** (per 1,000 pop.): 47. **Deaths** (per 1,000 pop.): 14. **Natural increase:** 3.3%. **Infant mortality** (per 1,000 live births 1996): 105.

**Education: Literacy** (1991): 37%. Free and compulsory: ages 6-12. Attendance 45%.

**Major International Organizations:** UN (FAO, WTO, World Bank, IMF, WHO), OAU.

**Embassy:** 2737 Cathedral Ave. NW 20008; 232-6656.

The Kingdom of Abomey, rising to power in wars with neighboring kingdoms in the 17th century, came under French domination in the late 19th century and was incorporated into French West Africa by 1904.

Under the name Dahomey, the country became independent Aug. 1, 1960. The name was changed to Benin in 1975. In the fifth coup since independence Col. Ahmed Kerekou took power in 1972; two years later he declared a socialist state with a "Marxist-Leninist" philosophy. In Dec. 1989, Kerekou announced that Marxism-Leninism would no longer be the state ideology.

In Mar. 1991, Kerekou lost to Nicéphore Soglo in Benin's first free presidential election in 30 years. Kerekou defeated Soglo in Mar. 1996 to reclaim the presidency.

# Bhutan

## Kingdom of Bhutan

## Druk-Yul

**People: Population:** 1,822,625. **Age distrib.** (%): <15: 39; 65+: 4. **Pop. density:** 100 per sq. mi. **Urban:** 17%. **Ethnic groups:** Bhote 50%, Nepalese 35%. **Principal languages:** Dzongkha (official), Tibetan and Nepalese dialects. **Religions:** Lamaistic Buddhist (state religion) 75%, Hindu 25%.

**Geography: Area:** 18,150 sq. mi. **Location:** S Asia, in eastern Himalayan Mts. **Neighbors:** India on W (Sikkim) and S, China on N. **Topography:** Bhutan is comprised of very high mountains in the N, fertile valleys in the center, and thick forests in the Duar Plain in the S. **Capital:** Thimphu (Paro is administrative capital). **City** (1993 est.): Thimphu 30,300.

**Government: Type:** Monarchy. **Head of state:** King Jigme Singye Wangchuk; b Nov. 11, 1955; in office: July 21, 1972. **Local divisions:** 18 districts.

**Economy: Industries:** Cement, wood products. **Chief crops:** Rice, corn, citrus. **Other resources:** Timber. **Arable land:** 2%. **Labor force:** 93% agric.; 5% services.

**Finance: Monetary unit:** Ngultrum (June 1996: 34.06 = $1 US; Indian Rupee also used). **Gross domestic product** (1994): $1.2 bln.* **Per capita GDP:** $700. **Tourism** (1993): 3.0 mil. **Imports** (FY 1993-94): $97.6 mil; partners: India 79%. **Exports** (FY 1993-94): $66.8 mil; partners: India 87%. **National budget** (FY 1993-94): $150 mil.

**Communications: Radios:** 1 per 35 persons. **Telephones:** 1 per 400 persons.

**Health: Life expectancy at birth** (1995): 52 male; 51 female. **Births** (per 1,000 pop.): 38. **Deaths** (per 1,000 pop.): 15. **Natural increase:** 2.3%. **Hospital beds:** 1 per 816 persons. **Physicians:** 1 per 5,335 persons. **Infant mortality** (per 1,000 live births 1996): 116.

**Education: Literacy** (1990): 42%. School attendance: 25%.

**Major International Organizations:** UN (IMF, FAO, WHO, World Bank).

The region came under Tibetan rule in the 16th century. British influence grew in the 19th century. A monarchy, set up in 1907, became a British protectorate by a 1910 treaty. The country became independent in 1949, with India guiding foreign relations and supplying aid.

Links to India have been strengthened by airline service and a road network. Most of the population engages in subsistence agriculture.

# Bolivia

## Republic of Bolivia

## República de Bolivia

**People: Population:** 7,165,257. **Age distrib.** (%): <15: 41; 65+: 4. **Pop. density:** 17 per sq. mi. **Urban:** 58%. **Ethnic groups:** Quechua 30%, Aymara 25%, mestizo 25-30%, European 5-15%. **Principal languages:** Spanish, Quechua, Aymara (all official). **Religions:** Roman Catholic 95%, Protestent.

**Geography: Area:** 424,164 sq. mi. **Location:** In central Andes Mts. (One of the 2 landlocked countries in South America). **Neighbors:** Peru and Chile on W, Argentina and Paraguay on S, Brazil on E and N. **Topography:** The great central plateau, at an altitude of 12,000 ft., over 500 mi. long, lies between two great cordilleras having 3 of the highest peaks in South America. Lake Titicaca, on Peruvian border, is highest lake in world on which steamboats ply (12,506 ft.). The E central region has semitropical forests; the llanos, or Amazon-Chaco lowlands are in E. **Capitals:** La Paz (administrative), Sucre (judicial). **Cities** (1992): La Paz 711,000; Santa Cruz 695,000; El Alto 404,000; Cochabamba 404,000.

**Government: Type:** Republic. **Head of state:** Pres. Gonzalo Sánchez de Lozada; b July 1, 1930; in office: Aug. 6, 1993. **Local divisions:** 9 departments. **Defense:** 1.9% of GDP (1994). **Active troop strength:** 33,500.

**Economy: Industries:** Mining, smelting, tobacco, handicrafts, clothing. **Chief crops:** Coffee, sugar, potatoes, soybeans, corn, coca (sold for cocaine processing). **Minerals:** Antimony, tin, tungsten, silver, zinc, oil, gas, iron. **Crude oil reserves** (1995): 139 mil bbls. **Other resources:** Rubber, timber. **Arable land:** 3%. **Livestock** (1994): cattle: 6.0 mil; sheep: 7.8 mil; pigs: 2.2 mil. **Electricity prod.** (1994): 2.1 bil kWh. **Labor force:** NA% agric.; 20% serv. & utilities; 7% manuf. & mining.

**Finance: Monetary unit:** Boliviano (June 1996: 5.08 = $1 US). **Gross domestic product** (1994): $18.3 bil.* **Per capita GDP:** $2,370. **Imports** (1994): $1.21 bil; partners: U.S. 24%. **Exports** (1994): $1.1 bil; partners: U.S. 26%. **National budget** (1995 est.): $3.75 bil. **International reserves less gold** (May 1996): $821 mil. **Gold:** 893,000 oz t. **Consumer prices** (change in 1995): 10.2%.

**Transport: Railroads: Route length:** 2,295 mi. **Motor vehicles:** in use: 340,000 passenger cars, 186,000 comm. vehicles. **Civil aviation:** 729 mil passenger-mi.; 21 airports with scheduled flights.

**Communications: Television sets:** 1 per 8.9 persons. **Radios:** 1 per 1.9 persons. **Telephones:** 1 per 33 persons. **Daily newspaper circ.:** 52 per 1,000 pop.

**Health: Life expectancy at birth** (1996): 57 male; 63 female. **Births** (per 1,000 pop.): 32. **Deaths** (per 1,000 pop.): 11. **Natural increase:** 2.2%. **Hospital beds:** 1 per 981 persons. **Physicians:** 1 per 3,518 persons. **Infant mortality** (per 1,000 live births 1996): 68.

**Education: Literacy** (1992): 80%. Free and compulsory: ages 6-14; attendance 81%.

**Major International Organizations:** UN (IMF, FAO, WTO, World Bank, WHO), OAS.

**Embassy:** 3014 Massachusetts Ave. NW 20008; 483-4410.

The Incas conquered the region from earlier Indian inhabitants in the 13th century. Spanish rule began in the 1530s and lasted until Aug. 6, 1825. The country is named after Simon Bolivar, independence fighter.

In a series of wars, Bolivia lost its Pacific coast to Chile, the oil-bearing Chaco to Paraguay, and rubber-growing areas to Brazil, 1879-1935.

Economic unrest, especially among the militant mine workers, has contributed to continuing political instability. A reformist government under Victor Paz Estenssoro, 1951-64, nationalized tin mines and attempted to improve conditions for the Indian majority but was overthrown by a military junta. A series of coups and countercoups continued through 1981, until the military junta elected Gen. Villa as president.

In July 1982, the military junta assumed power amid a growing economic crisis and foreign debt difficulties. The junta resigned in Oct. and allowed the Congress, elected democratically in 1980, to take power.

U.S. pressure on the government to reduce the country's output of coca, the raw material for cocaine, has led to clashes between police and coca growers and increased anti-U.S. feeling among Bolivians.

# Bosnia and Herzegovina

## Republic of Bosnia and Herzegovina

## Republika Bosna i Hercegovina

**People: Population:** 2,656,240. **Pop. density:** 135 per sq. mi. **Urban:** NA%. **Ethnic groups:** Serbian 40%, Muslim 38%, Croatian 22%. **Principal languages:** Serbo-Croatian (official) 99%. **Religions:** Muslim 40%, Orthodox 31%, Catholic 15% .

**Geography: Area:** 19,741 sq. mi. **Location:** On Balkan Peninsula in SE Europe. **Neighbors:** Yugoslavia on E and SE, Croatia on N and W. **Topography:** Hilly with some mountains. About 36% of the land is forested. **Capital:** Sarajevo (1993 est.): 300,000.

**Government: Type: Republic. Heads of state:** Chairman, Collective Pres., Alija Izetbegovic (Muslim), b Aug. 8, 1925; members, collective Pres., Momcilo Krajisnik (Serb), b 1945, and Kresimir Zubak (Croat), b Nov. 29, 1947; in office: Sept. 14, 1996. **Defense: Active troop strength:** 92,000 est.

**Economy: Industries:** Steel, mining, timber. **Chief crops:** Corn, wheat, berries, nuts. **Minerals:** Bauxite, iron, coal. **Arable land:** 20%.

**Finance: Monetary unit:** Yugoslav New Dinar. **Gross domestic product** (1991): $14 bil.* **Per capita GDP:** $3,200.

**Health: Life expectancy at birth** (1996): 51 male; 61 female. **Births** (per 1,000 pop.): 6. **Deaths** (per 1,000 pop.): 16. **Natural increase:** –1.0%. **Infant mortality** (per 1,000 live births 1996): 43.

**Education: Literacy** (1991): 86%. Free and compulsory: ages 7-15.

**Major International Organizations:** UN (ILO, FAO, WHO).

**Embassy:** 1707 L St. NW, Suite 760 20036; 833-3612.

Bosnia was ruled by Croatian kings c. AD 958, and by Hungary 1000-1200. It became organized c. 1200 and later took control of Herzegovina. The kingdom disintegrated from 1391, with the southern part becoming the independent duchy Herzegovina. It was conquered by Turks in 1463 and made a Turkish province. The area was placed under control of Austria-Hungary in 1878, and made part of the province of **Bosnia and Herzegovina,** which was formally annexed to Austria-Hungary 1908, and it became a province of Yugoslavia in 1918. It was reunited with Herzegovina as a federated republic in the 1946 Yugoslavian constitution.

The Bosnia and Herzegovina parliament adopted a declaration of sovereignty Oct. 15, 1991. A referendum for independence was passed Feb. 29, 1992. Ethnic Serbs' opposition to the referendum spurred violent clashes and bombings. The U.S. and EU recognized the republic Apr. 7. Fierce three-way fighting continued between Bosnia's Serbs, Muslims, and Croats. Serb forces massacred thousands of Bosnian Muslims and engaged in "ethnic cleansing" (the expulsion of Muslims and other non-Serbs from areas under Bosnian Serb control). The capital, Sarajevo, was surrounded and besieged by Bosnian Serb forces. Muslims and Croats in Bosnia reached a cease fire Feb. 23, 1994, and signed an accord, Mar. 18, to create a Muslim-Croat confederation in Bosnia. However, by mid-1994, Bosnian Serbs controlled over 70% of the country.

As fighting continued in 1995, the balance of power began to shift toward the Muslim-Croat alliance. Massive NATO air strikes at Bosnian Serb targets beginning Aug. 30 triggered a new round of peace talks, and the siege of Sarajevo was lifted Sept. 15. The new talks produced an agreement in principle to create autonomous regions within Bosnia, with the Serb region constituting 49% of the country. A Croat-Muslim offensive in Sept. recaptured significant territory, leaving the Bosnian Serbs in control of approximately that percentage.

A peace agreement initialed in Dayton, Ohio, Nov. 21, 1995, was signed in Paris, Dec. 14, by leaders of Bosnia, Croatia, and Serbia. Some 60,000 NATO troops (about 20,000 from the U.S.) moved in to police the accord; by Aug. 1996 about 45,000 NATO troops (16,000 from the U.S.) remained. Meanwhile, a UN tribunal began bringing charges against suspected war criminals. Elections were held Sept. 14, 1996, for a 3-person collective presidency, for seats in a federal parliament, and for regional offices.

# Botswana

## Republic of Botswana

**People: Population:** 1,477,630. **Age distrib.** (%): <15: 43; 65+: 5. **Pop. density:** 7 per sq. mi. **Urban:** 46%. **Ethnic groups:** Batswana 95%, Kalanga, others. **Principal languages:** English (official), Setswana. **Religions:** Indigenous beliefs 50%, Christian 50%.

**Geography: Area:** 224,607 sq. mi. **Location:** In southern Africa. **Neighbors:** Namibia on N and W, South Africa on S, Zimbabwe on NE; Botswana claims border with Zambia on N. **Topography:** The Kalahari Desert, supporting nomadic Bushmen and wildlife, spreads over SW; there are swamplands and farming areas in N, and rolling plains in E where livestock are grazed. **Capital:** Gaborone (1992 est.): 134,000.

**Government: Type:** Parliamentary republic. **Head of state:** Pres. Ketumile Masire; b July 23, 1925; in office: July 13, 1980. **Local divisions:** 10 districts and 4 town councils. **Defense:** 5.2% of GDP (FY 1993-94). **Active troop strength:** 7,500.

**Economy: Industries:** Livestock processing, mining, tourism. **Chief crops:** Corn, sorghum, millet, beans. **Minerals:** Copper, coal, nickel, diamonds. **Arable land:** 2%. **Electricity prod.** (1993): 900 mil kWh. **Labor force:** 30% serv.; 23% agric.; 19% manuf. & constr.

**Finance: Monetary unit:** Pula (June 1996: 3.37 = $1 US). **Gross domestic product** (1994): $4.3 bil.* **Per capita GDP:** $3,130. **Imports** (1992): $1.8 bln. **Exports** (1994): $1.8 bil. **Tourism** (1992): $65 mil. **National budget** (FY 1993-94): $1.99 bil. **International reserves less gold** (Mar. 1996): $4.7 bil. **Consumer prices** (change in 1995): 10.5%.

**Transport: Railroads: Length:** 551 mi. **Motor vehicles:** in use: 21,000 passenger cars, 42,000 comm. vehicles.

**Communications: Television sets:** 1 per 108 persons. **Radios:** 1 per 1.1 persons. **Telephones:** 1 per 33 persons. **Daily newspaper circ.:** 35 per 1,000 pop.

**Health: Life expectancy at birth** (1996): 45 male; 47 female. **Births** (1,000 pop.): 33. **Deaths** (per 1,000 pop.): 17. **Natural increase:** 1.6%. **Hospital beds**: 1 per 395 persons. **Physicians:** 1 per 5,417 persons. **Infant mortality** (per 1,000 live births 1996): 54.

**Education: Literacy** (1994): 74%.

**Major International Organizations:** UN (WTO, IMF, FAO, World Bank, WHO), OAU, the Commonwealth.

**Embassy:** 3400 International Dr. NW 20008; 244-4990.

First inhabited by bushmen, then by Bantus, the region became the British protectorate of Bechuanaland in 1886, halting encroachment by Boers and Germans from the south and southwest. The country became fully independent Sept. 30, 1966, changing its name to Botswana. Cattle raising and mining (diamonds, copper, nickel) have contributed to economic growth. The economy is closely tied to South Africa.

# Brazil

## Federative Republic of Brazil

## República Federativa do Brasil

**People: Population:** 162,661,214. **Age distrib.** (%): <15: 34; 65+: 4. **Pop. density:** 49 per sq. mi. **Urban:** 76%. **Ethnic groups:** Caucasian (incl. Portuguese, German, Italian, Spanish, Polish) 58%, mulatto 38%, African 6%. **Principal languages:** Portuguese (official), Spanish, English, French. **Religions:** Roman Catholic 70%.

**Geography: Area:** 3,300,171 sq. mi., largest country in South America. **Location:** Occupies eastern half of South America. **Neighbors:** French Guiana, Suriname, Guyana, Venezuela on N; Colombia, Peru, Bolivia, Paraguay, Argentina on W; Uruguay on S. **Topography:** Brazil's Atlantic coastline stretches 4,603 miles. In N is the heavily wooded Amazon basin covering half the country. Its network of rivers navigable for 15,814 mi. The Amazon itself flows 2,093 miles in Brazil, all navigable. The NE region is semiarid scrubland, heavily settled and poor. The S central region, favored by climate and resources, has almost half of the population, produces 75% of farm goods and 80% of industrial output. The narrow coastal belt includes most of the major cities. Almost the entire country has a tropical or semitropical climate. **Capital:** Brasília. **Cities** (1991 cen.): São Paulo 9.6 mil; Rio de Janeiro 5.5 mil; Salvador 2.1 mil; Belo Horizonte 2 mil.

**Government: Type:** Federal republic. **Head of state:** Pres. Fernando Henrique Cardoso; b June 18, 1931; in office: Jan. 1, 1995. **Local divisions:** 26 states, 1 federal district (Brasília). **Defense:** 0.9% of GDP (1994). **Active troop strength:** 295,000.

**Economy: Industries:** Steel, autos, textiles, shoes, chemicals, machinery. **Chief crops:** Coffee (largest grower), cotton, soybeans, sugar, cocoa, rice, corn, fruits. **Minerals:** Iron, manganese, phosphates, uranium, gold, nickel, tin, bauxite, oil. **Crude oil reserves** (1995): 3.8 bil bbls. **Arable land:** 7%. **Livestock** (1993): cattle: 153 mil; pigs: 31 mil; sheep: 19.7 mil. **Fish catch** (1993): 780,000 metric tons. **Electricity prod.** (1993): 241.4 bil kWh. **Labor force:** 42% services; 31% agric.; 27% ind.

**Finance: Monetary unit:** Real (June 1996: 1.01 = $1 US). **Gross domestic product** (1994): $886 bil.* **Per capita GDP:** $5,580. **Imports** (1994): $33 bil; partners: U.S. 23%, EU 23%. **Exports** (1994): $44 bil; partners: EU 28%, U.S. 17%. **Tourism** (1993): $1.4 bil. **National budget** (1992): $109 bil. **International reserves less gold** (Apr. 1996): $54.7 bil. **Gold:** 4.46 mil oz t. **Consumer prices** (change in 1995): 84.4%.

**Transport: Railroads: Route length:** 18,877 mi. **Motor vehicles:** in use: 13 mil passenger cars, 1.4 mil comm. vehicles. **Civil aviation:** 20.2 bil passenger-mi.; 139 airports with scheduled flights. **Chief ports:** Santos, Rio de Janeiro, Vitoria, Salvador, Rio Grande, Recife.

**Communications: Television sets:** 1 per 5.3 persons. **Radios:** 1 per 2.9 persons. **Telephones:** 1 per 13 persons. **Daily newspaper circ.:** 55 per 1,000 pop.

**Health: Life expectancy at birth** (1996): 57 male; 67 female. **Births** (per 1,000 pop.): 21. **Deaths** (per 1,000 pop.): 9. **Natural increase:** 1.2%. **Hospital beds:** 1 per 271 persons. **Physicians:** 1 per 715 persons. **Infant mortality** (per 1,000 live births 1996): 55.

**Education: Literacy** (1993): 83%.Free and compulsory: ages 7-14.

**Major International Organizations:** UN and most of its specialized agencies, OAS.

**Embassy:** 3006 Massachusetts Ave. NW 20008; 745-2700.

Pedro Alvares Cabral, a Portuguese navigator, is generally credited as the first European to reach Brazil, in 1500. The country was thinly settled by various Indian tribes. Only a few have survived to the present, mostly in the Amazon basin.

In the next centuries, Portuguese colonists gradually pushed inland, bringing along large numbers of African slaves. (Slavery was not abolished until 1888.)

The King of Portugal, fleeing before Napoleon's army, moved the seat of government to Brazil in 1808. Brazil thereupon became a kingdom under Dom Joao VI. After his return to Portugal, his son Pedro proclaimed the independence of Brazil, Sept. 7, 1822, and was crowned emperor. The second emperor, Dom Pedro II, was deposed in 1889, and a republic proclaimed, called the United States of Brazil. In 1967 the country was renamed the Federative Republic of Brazil.

A military junta took control in 1930; dictatorial power was assumed by Getulio Vargas, until finally forced out by the military in 1945. A democratic regime prevailed 1945-64, during which time the capital was moved from Rio de Janeiro to Brasília.

In 1964, Pres. Joao Belchoir Marques Goulart instituted economic policies that aggravated Brazil's inflation; he was overthrown by an army revolt. The next 5 presidents were all military leaders. Censorship was imposed, and much of the opposition was suppressed amid charges of torture. In 1974 elections, the official opposition party made gains in the chamber of deputies; some relaxation of censorship occurred.

Since 1930, successive governments have pursued industrial and agricultural growth and the development of interior areas. Exploiting vast mineral resources, fertile soil in several regions, and a huge labor force, Brazil became the leading industrial power of Latin America by the 1970s, while agricultural output soared.

However, income maldistribution and inflation led to severe economic recession. Foreign debt is among the largest in the world. Brazil and its principal commercial bank lenders agreed to restructure the nation's $44 billion commercial debts, July 1992. The 1991 census revealed that population growth dipped below 2 percent for the first time in half a century.

Brazil unveiled a comprehensive environmental program for the Amazon region in 1989, amid an international outcry by environmentalists and others concerned about the ongoing destruction of the Amazon ecosystem. Brazil hosted delegates from 178 countries at the Earth Summit June 3-14, 1992.

Democratic presidential elections were held in 1985 as the nation returned to civilian rule. Fernando Collor de Mello was elected president in Dec. 1989. In Sept. 1992, Pres. Collor was impeached for corruption. He resigned on Dec. 29 as his trial was beginning, and Itamar Franco, who had been acting president, was sworn in as president. In elections held on Oct. 3, 1994, sociology professor and former foreign minister and finance minister Fernando Henrique Cardoso was elected president by the widest popular margin in Brazil since 1945.

# Brunei

## State of Brunei Darussalam

## Negara Brunei Darussalam

**People: Population:** 299,939. **Pop. density:** 135 per sq. mi. **Urban:** 67%. **Ethnic groups:** Malay 64%, Chinese 20%. **Principal languages:** Malay (official), English, Chinese. **Religions:** Muslim (official) 67%, Buddhist 13%, Christian 10%.

**Geography: Area:** 2,226 sq. mi. **Location:** On the N coast of the island of Borneo; it is surrounded on its landward side by the Malaysian state of Sarawak. **Capital:** Bandar Seri Begawan (1991 cen.): 45,900.

**Government: Type:** Independent sultanate. **Head of government:** Sultan Sir Muda Hassanal Bolkiah Mu'izzadin Waddaulah; b July 15, 1946; in office: Jan. 1, 1984. **Local divisions:** 4 districts. **Defense:** 6.2% of GDP (1994). **Active troop strength:** 4,900.

**Economy: Industries:** Oil (more than 40% of GDP is derived from oil and gas exports). **Chief crops:** Rice, bananas, cassava. **Crude oil reserves** (1995): 1.4 bil bbls. **Arable land:** 1%.

**Finance: Monetary unit:** Dollar (June 1996: 1.41 = $1 US). **Gross domestic product** (1993): $4.4 bil. **Per capita GDP:** $16,000. **Imports** (1993): $1.2 bil. **Exports** (1993): $2.2 bil.

**Transport: Motor vehicles:** in use: 122,000 passenger cars, 14,000 commercial vehicles.

**Communications: Television sets:** 1 per 4.0 persons. **Radios:** 1 per 4.7 persons. **Telephones:** 1 per 5.1 persons.

**Health: Life expectancy at birth:** (1996): 70 male; 73 female. **Births** (per 1,000 pop.): 26. **Deaths** (per 1,000 pop.): 5. **Natural increase**: 2.0%. **Infant mortality** (per 1,000 live births 1996): 24.

**Education: Literacy** (1992): 88%.

**Major International Organizations:** UN and some of its specialized agencies, ASEAN, APEC, the Commonwealth.

**Embassy:** 2600 Virginia Ave. NW, Suite 7M 20037; 342-0159.

The Sultanate of Brunei was a powerful state in the early 16th century, with authority over all of the island of Borneo as well as parts of the Sulu Islands and the Philippines. In 1888, a treaty placed the state under the protection of Great Britain.

Brunei became a fully sovereign and independent state on Jan. 1, 1984.

The Sultan of Brunei donated $10 million to the Nicaraguan *contras* in 1986; the subsequent misplacement of the funds generated much media attention in the U.S.

# Bulgaria

## Republic of Bulgaria

## Republika Bulgaria

**People: Population:** 8,612,757. **Age distrib.** (%): <15: 19; 65+: 15. **Pop. density:** 201 per sq. mi. **Urban:** 68%. **Ethnic groups:** Bulgarian 85%, Turk 8.5%. **Principal language:** Bulgarian (official). **Religions:** Bulgarian Orthodox 85%, Muslim 13%.

**Geography: Area:** 42,855 sq. mi. **Location:** SE Europe, in E Balkan Peninsula on Black Sea. **Neighbors:** Romania on N; Yugoslavia, Macedonia on W; Greece, Turkey on S. **Topography:** The Stara Planina (Balkan) Mts. stretch E-W across the center of the country, with the Danubian plain on N, the Rhodope Mts. on SW, and Thracian Plain on SE. **Capital:** Sofia. **Cities** (1994 est.): Sofia 1.1 mil; Plovdiv 345,000; Varna 307,000.

**Government: Type:** Republic. **Head of state:** Pres. Zhelyu Zhelev; b Mar. 3, 1935; in office: Aug. 1, 1990. **Head of government:** Prime Min. Zhan Videnov; b Mar. 22, 1959; in office: Jan. 25, 1995. **Local divisions:** 9 provinces. **Defense:** 6.0% of GNP (1993). **Active troop strength:** 101,900.

**Economy: Industries:** Chemicals, machinery, metals, textiles, processed food. **Chief crops:** Grains, fruit, oilseeds, tobacco. **Minerals:** Bauxite, copper, zinc, lead, coal. **Arable land:** 34%. **Livestock** (1994): cattle: 673,000; pigs: 2.0 mil; sheep: 4.3 mil. **Fish catch** (1993): 22,000 metric tons. **Electricity prod.** (1993): 36 bil kWh. **Labor force:** 20% agric.; 33% ind.

**Finance: Monetary unit:** Lev (June 1996: 155.46 = $1 US). **Gross domestic product** (1994): $33.7 bil.* **Per capita GDP:** $3,830. **Imports** (1993): $4.3 bil; partners: CIS 43%. **Exports** (1993): $3.6 bil; partners: CIS 49%. **Tourism** (1993): $307 mil. **National budget** (1993 est.): $17.4 bil.

**Transport: Railroads: Length:** 4,044 mi. **Motor vehicles:** in use: 1.4 mil passenger cars, 130,000 commercial vehicles. **Civil aviation:** 2.2 bil passenger-mi.; 3 intl. airports with scheduled flights. **Chief ports:** Burgas, Varna.

**Communications: Television sets:** 1 per 2.7 persons. **Radios:** 1 per 2.2 persons. **Telephones:** 1 per 3.8 persons. **Daily newspaper circ.:** 164 per 1,000 pop.

**Health: Life expectancy at birth** (1996): 67 male; 75 female. **Births** (per 1,000 pop.): 8. **Deaths** (per 1,000 pop.): 14. **Natural increase:** –0.5%. **Hospital beds:** 1 per 97 persons. **Physicians:** 1 per 298 persons. **Infant mortality** (per 1,000 live births 1996): 16.

**Education: Literacy** (1995): 98%. Free and compulsory: ages 6-16.

**Major International Organizations:** UN.

**Embassy:** 1621 22d St. NW 20008; 387-7966.

Bulgaria was settled by Slavs in the 6th century. Turkic Bulgars arrived in the 7th century, merged with the Slavs, became Christians by the 9th century, and set up powerful empires in the 10th and 12th centuries. The Ottomans prevailed in 1396 and remained for 500 years.

A revolt in 1876 led to an independent kingdom in 1908. Bulgaria expanded after the first Balkan War but lost its Aegean coastline in World War I, when it sided with Germany. Bulgaria joined the Axis in World War II but withdrew in 1944. Communists took power with Soviet aid; the monarchy was abolished Sept. 8, 1946.

On Nov. 10, 1989, Communist Party leader and head of state Todor Zhivkov, who had held power for 35 years, resigned. Zhivkov was imprisoned, Jan. 1990, and convicted, Sept. 1992, of corruption and abuse of power. In Jan. 1990, Parliament voted to revoke the constitutionally guaranteed dominant role of the Communist Party. A new constitution took effect July 13, 1991. An economic austerity program was launched in May 1996.

# Burkina Faso

**People: Population:** 10,623,323. **Age distrib.** (%): <15: 48; 65+ 3. **Pop. density:** 100 per sq. mi. **Urban:** 15%. **Ethnic groups:** Mossi, Gurunsi, Senufo, Lobi, Bobo, Mande, Fulani. **Principal languages:** French (official), Sudanic tribal languages. **Religions:** Muslim 50%, indigenous beliefs 40%, Christian 10%.

**Geography: Area:** 105,946 sq. mi. **Location:** In W Africa, S of the Sahara. **Neighbors:** Mali on NW; Niger on NE; Benin, Togo, Ghana, Côte d'Ivoire on S. **Topography:** Landlocked Burkina Faso is in the savanna region of W Africa. The N is arid, hot, and thinly populated. **Capital:** Ouagadougou. **Cities** (1991 est.): Ouagadougou 634,000; Bobo-Dioulasso 269,000.

**Government: Type:** Republic. **Head of state:** Pres. Blaise Compaoré; b 1951; in office: Oct. 15, 1987. **Head of government:** Prime Min. Kadre Desire Ouedraogo; in office: Feb. 1996. **Local divisions:** 30 provinces. **Defense:** 6.4% of GDP (1994). **Active troop strength:** 10,000.

**Economy: Chief crops:** Millet, sorghum, rice, peanuts. **Minerals:** Manganese, limestone, marble, gold. **Arable land:** 10%. **Electricity prod.** (1993): 190 mil kWh. **Labor force:** 80% agric.; 15% ind.

**Finance: Monetary unit:** CFA Franc (June 1996: 515 = $1 US). **Gross domestic product** (1993): $6.5 bil.* **Per capita GDP:** $660. **Imports** (1993): $636 mil; partners: EU 49%. **Exports** (1993): $273 mil; partners: Côte d'Ivoire 11%, EU 42%, Taiwan 15%. **National budget** (1992): $548 mil. **International reserves less gold** (Dec. 1995): $348 mil. **Gold:** 11,000 oz t. **Consumer prices** (change in 1995): 7.4%.

**Transport: Motor vehicles:** in use: 11,000 passenger cars, 13,000 comm. vehicles.

**Communications: Television sets:** 1 per 221 persons. **Radios:** 1 per 45 persons. **Telephones:** 1 per 447 persons.

**Health: Life expectancy at birth** (1996): 44 male; 43 female. **Births** (per 1,000 pop.): 47. **Deaths** (per 1,000 pop.): 20. **Natural increase:** 2.7%. **Hospital beds:** 1 per 1,837 persons. **Physicians:** 1 per 27,158 persons. **Infant mortality** (per 1,000 live births 1996): 118.

**Education: Literacy** (1992): 19%. **Years compulsory:** ages 7-14.

**Major International Organizations:** UN and many of its specialized agencies, OAU.

**Embassy:** 2340 Massachusetts Ave. NW 20008; 332-5577.

The Mossi tribe entered the area in the 11th to 13th centuries. Their kingdoms ruled until defeated by the Mali and Songhai empires.

French control came by 1896, but Upper Volta (renamed Burkina Faso on Aug. 4, 1984) was not established as a separate territory until 1947. Full independence came Aug. 5, 1960, and a pro-French government was elected. The military seized power in 1980. A 1987 coup established the current regime, which instituted a multiparty democracy in the early 1990s.

Several hundred thousand farm workers migrate each year to Côte d'Ivoire and Ghana. Burkina Faso is heavily dependent on foreign aid.

# Burma

*(See Myanmar)*

# Burundi

## Republic of Burundi

## Republika y'u Burundi

**People: Population:** 5,943,057. **Age distrib.** (%): <15: 46; 65+: 4. **Pop. density:** 553 per sq. mi. **Urban:** 6%. **Ethnic groups:** Hutu 85%, Tutsi 14%, Twa (Pygmy) 1%. **Principal languages:** Kirundi, French (both official), Swahili. **Religions:** Roman Catholic 62%, indigenous beliefs 32%, Protestant 5%.

**Geography: Area:** 10,740 sq. mi. **Location:** In central Africa. **Neighbors:** Rwanda on N, Zaire on W, Tanzania on E and S. **Topography:** Much of the country is grassy highland, with mountains reaching 8,900 ft. The southernmost source of the White Nile is located in Burundi. Lake Tanganyika is the second deepest lake in the world. **Capital:** Bujumbura (1994 est.): 300,000.

**Government: Type:** In transition. **Head of state:** Pres. Pierre Buyoya; b 1949; in office: July 25, 1996. **Head of government:** Prime Min. Pascal Firmin Ndimira; in office: July 31, 1996. **Local divisions:** 15 provinces. **Defense:** 2.6% of GDP (1993). **Active troop strength:** 14,600 est.

**Economy: Chief crops:** Coffee (81% of exports), cotton, tea. **Minerals:** Nickel, uranium. **Arable land:** 43%. **Electricity prod.** (1993): 100 mil kWh. **Labor force:** 93% agric.

**Finance: Monetary unit:** Franc (June 1996: 319 = $1 US). **Gross domestic product** (1994): $3.7 bil.* **Per capita GDP:** $600. **Imports** (1993): $203 mil; partners: EU 45%. **Exports** (1993): $68 mil; partners: EU 57%, U.S. 19%. **National budget** (1991 est.): $326 mil. **International reserves less gold** (Apr. 1996): $182 mil. **Gold:** 17,000 oz t. **Consumer prices** (change in 1995): 19.2%.

**Transport: Motor vehicles:** in use: 14,000 passenger cars, 15,000 comm. vehicles. **Chief port:** Bujumbura.

**Communications: Television sets:** 1 per 1,289 persons. **Radios:** 1 per 19 persons. **Telephones:** 1 per 363 persons.

**Health: Life expectancy at birth** (1996): 48 male; 50 female. **Births** (per 1,000 pop.): 43. **Deaths** (per 1,000 pop.): 15. **Natural increase:** 2.8%. **Hospital beds:** 1 per 515 persons. **Physicians:** 1 per 31,777 persons. **Infant mortality** (per 1,000 live births 1996): 102.

**Education: Literacy** (1995): 35%. Free and compulsory: ages 7-13.

**Major International Organizations:** UN (FAO, WTO, World Bank, ILO, IMF, WHO), OAU.

**Embassy:** 2233 Wisconsin Ave. NW, Suite 212 20007; 342-2574.

The pygmy Twa were the first inhabitants, followed by Bantu Hutus, who were conquered in the 16th century by the Tutsi (Watusi), probably from Ethiopia. Under German control in 1899, the area fell to Belgium in 1916, which exercised successively a League of Nations mandate and UN trusteeship over Ruanda-Urundi (now the two countries of Rwanda and Burundi).

Burundi became independent July 1, 1962.

An unsuccessful Hutu rebellion in 1972-73 left 10,000 Tutsi and 150,000 Hutu dead. Over 100,000 Hutu fled to Tanzania and Zaire. In the 1980s, Burundi's Tutsi-dominated regime pledged itself to ethnic reconciliation and democratic reform. In the nation's first democratic presidential election, in June 1993, a Hutu, Melchior Ndadaye, was elected. He was killed in an attempted coup, Oct. 21, 1993. At least 150,000 Burundians died as a result of ethnic conflict during the next three years. Pres. Cyprien Ntaryamira, elected Jan. 1994, was killed with the president of Rwanda in a mysterious plane crash, Apr. 6. The incident sparked massive carnage in Rwanda; violence in Burundi, initially far more limited, intensified in 1995. Conditions continued to deteriorate after a military coup, July 25, 1996.

# Cambodia

## Kingdom of Cambodia

## Reacheanachak Kampuchea

**People: Population:** 10,861,218. **Age distrib.** (%): <15: 46; 65+: 3.**Pop. density:** 155 per sq. mi. **Urban:** 13%. **Ethnic groups:** Khmer 90%, Vietnamese 5%, Chinese 1%. **Principal languages:** Khmer (official), French. **Religions:** Theravada Buddhism 95%.

**Geography: Area:** 70,238 sq. mi. **Location:** SE Asia, on Indochina Peninsula. **Neighbors:** Thailand on W and N, Laos on NE, Vietnam on E. **Topography:** The central area, formed by the Mekong R. basin and Tonle Sap lake, is level. Hills and mountains are in SE, a long escarpment separates the country from Thailand on NW. 75% of the area is forested. **Capital:** Phnom Penh (1994 est.): 920,000.

**Government: Type:** Constitutional monarchy. **Head of state:** King Norodom Sihanouk; b Oct. 31, 1922; in office: Sept. 24, 1993. **Head of government:** First Prime Min. Prince Norodom Ranariddh; b 1944; in office: Sept. 24, 1993. **Local divisions:** 21 provinces. **Defense:** 1.4% of GDP (1995). **Active troop strength:** 88,500 est.

**Economy: Industries:** Rice milling, wood & wood products, fishing. **Chief crops:** Rice, corn. **Minerals:** Gemstones, phosphates, manganese. **Other resources:** Forests, rubber. **Arable land:** 16%. **Livestock** (1994): cattle: 2.6 mil; pigs: 2.2 mil. **Fish catch** (1994): 103,000 metric tons. **Electricity prod.** (1993): 160 mil kWh. **Labor force:** 80% agric.

**Finance: Monetary unit:** Riel (June 1996: 2,300 = $1 US). **Gross domestic product** (1994): $6.4 bil.* **Per capita GDP:** $630. **Imports** (1993): $479 mil. **Exports** (1993): $284 mil. **National budget** (1994 est.): $365 mil. **International reserves less gold** (May 1996): $213 mil.

**Transport: Railroads: Length:** 380 mi. **Motor vehicles:** in use: 29,000 passenger cars, 9,000 comm. vehicles. **Chief port:** Kompong Som.

**Communications: Television sets:** 1 per 136 persons. **Radios:** 1 per 11 persons. **Telephones:** 1 per 1,667 persons.

**Health: Life expectancy at birth** (1996): 48 male; 51 female. **Births** (per 1,000 pop.): 44. **Deaths** (per 1,000 pop.): 16. **Natural increase:** 2.8%. **Hospital beds:** 1 per 632 persons. **Physicians:** 1 per 14,300 persons. **Infant mortality** (per 1,000 live births 1996): 108.

**Education: Literacy** (1993): 74%.Compulsory: ages 6-12.

**Major International Organizations:** UN.

**Embassy:** 4500 16th St. NW 20011; 726-7742.

Early kingdoms dating from that of Funan in the 1st century AD culminated in the great Khmer empire that flourished from the 9th century to the 13th, encompassing present-day Thailand, Cambodia, Laos, and southern Vietnam. The peripheral areas were lost to invading Siamese and Vietnamese, and France established a protectorate in 1863. Independence came in 1953.

Prince Norodom Sihanouk, king 1941-1955 and head of state from 1960, tried to maintain neutrality. Relations with the U.S. were broken in 1965, after South Vietnam planes attacked Vietcong forces within Cambodia. Relations were restored in 1969, after Sihanouk charged Viet Communists with arming Cambodian insurgents.

In 1970, pro-U.S. Prem. Lon Nol seized power, demanding removal of 40,000 North Viet troops; the monarchy was abolished. Sihanouk formed a government-in-exile in Beijing, and open war began between the government and Khmer Rouge. The U.S. provided heavy military and economic aid.

Khmer Rouge forces captured Phnom Penh Apr. 17, 1975. The new government evacuated all cities and towns, and shuffled the rural population, sending virtually the entire population to clear jungle, forest, and scrub. Over one million people were killed in executions and enforced hardships.

Severe border fighting broke out with Vietnam in 1978 and developed into a full-fledged Vietnamese invasion. Formation of a Vietnamese-backed government was announced, Jan. 8, 1979, one day after the Vietnamese capture of Phnom Penh. Thousands of refugees flowed into Thailand and widespread starvation was reported.

On Jan. 10, 1983, Vietnam launched an offensive against rebel forces in the west. They overran a refugee camp, Jan. 31, driving 30,000 residents into Thailand. In Mar., Vietnam launched a major offensive against camps on the Cambodian-Thailand border, engaged Khmer Rouge guerrillas, and crossed the border instigating clashes with Thai troops. Vietnam withdrew nearly all its troops by Sept. 1989.

Following UN-sponsored elections in Cambodia that ended May 28, 1993, the 2 leading parties agreed to share power in an interim government until a new constitution was adopted. On Sept. 21, a constitution reestablishing a monarchy was adopted by the National Assembly. It took effect Sept. 24, with Sihanouk as king. The Khmer Rouge, which had boycotted the elections, opposed the new government, and armed violence continued in the mid-1990s. Ieng Sary, a Khmer Rouge leader, broke with the guerrillas and formed a rival group. He announced his support for the monarchy in Aug. 1996.

# Cameroon

## Republic of Cameroon

## République du Cameroun

**People: Population:** 14,261,557. **Age distrib.** (%): <15: 44; 65+: 4. **Pop. density:** 78 per sq. mi. **Urban:** 41%. **Ethnic groups:** Cameroon Highlander 31%, Equatorial Bantu 19%, Kirdi 11%, Fulani 10%. **Principal languages:** English, French (both official), numerous African groups. **Religions:** Indigenous beliefs 51%, Christian 33%, Muslim 16%.

**Geography: Area:** 183,569 sq. mi. **Location:** Between W and central Africa. **Neighbors:** Nigeria on NW; Chad, Central African Republic on E; Congo, Gabon, Equatorial Guinea on S. **Topography:** A low coastal plain with rain forests is in S; plateaus in center lead to forested mountains in W, including Mt. Cameroon, 13,000 ft.; grasslands in N lead to marshes around Lake Chad. **Capital:** Yaoundé. **Cities** (1991 est.): Douala 810,000; Yaoundé 649,000.

**Government: Type:** Republic. **Head of state:** Pres. Paul Biya; b Feb. 13, 1933; in office: Nov. 6, 1982. **Head of government:** Prime Min. Peter Masani Musonge; b Dec. 3, 1942; in office: 1996. **Local divisions:** 10 provinces. **Defense:** 2.1% of GNP (1993). **Active troop strength:** 23,600.

**Economy: Industries:** Oil production and processing, mining, palm products. **Chief crops:** Cocoa, coffee, cotton. **Crude oil reserves** (1995): 400 mil bbls. **Minerals:** Oil, bauxite, iron. **Other resources:** Timber. **Arable land:** 13%. **Livestock** (1994): cattle: 4.9 mil; sheep: 3.8 mil; pigs: 1.4 mil. **Fish catch** (1993): 80,000 metric tons. **Electricity prod.** (1993): 2.7 bil kWh. **Labor force:** 74% agric.; 11% ind. & transport.

**Finance: Monetary unit:** CFA Franc (June 1996: 515 = $1 US). **Gross domestic product** (1994): $15.7 bil.* **Per capita GDP:** $1,200. **Imports** (1993): $2.0 bil; partners: Fr. 38%. **Exports** (1993): $1.6 bil; partners: EU 40%. **National budget** (FY 1992-93): $2.3 bil. **International reserves less gold** (Mar. 1996): $2.45 mil. **Gold:** 30,000 oz t.

**Transport: Railroads: Route length:** 686 mi. **Motor vehicles:** in use: 90,000 passenger cars, 79,000 comm. vehicles. **Chief port:** Douala.

**Communications: Television sets:** 1 per 858 persons. **Radios:** 1 per 8.6 persons. **Telephones:** 1 per 219 persons.

**Health: Life expectancy at birth** (1996): 52 male; 54 female. **Births** (per 1,000 pop.): 42. **Deaths** (per 1,000 pop.): 14. **Natural increase:** 2.9%. **Hospital beds:** 1 per 371 persons. **Physicians:** 1 per 11,848 persons. **Infant mortality** (per 1,000 live births 1996): 79.

**Education: Literacy** (1991): 63%. Compulsory: ages 6-12. About 66% attend school.

**Major International Organizations:** UN, OAU, the Commonwealth.

**Embassy:** 2349 Massachusetts Ave. NW 20008; 265-8790.

Portuguese sailors were the first Europeans to reach Cameroon, in the 15th century. The European and American slave trade was very active in the area. German control lasted from 1884 to 1916, when France and Britain divided the territory, later receiving League of Nations mandates and UN trusteeships. French Cameroon became independent Jan. 1, 1960; one part of British Cameroon joined Nigeria in 1961, the other part joined Cameroon. Stability has allowed for development of roads, railways, agriculture, and petroleum production.

Pres. Paul Biya retained his office in Oct. 1992 elections, but the results were widely disputed. A new constitution won legislative approval in Dec. 1995.

## Canada

**People: Population:** 28,820,671. **Age distrib.** (%): <15: 21; 65+: 12. **Pop. density:** 7 per sq. mi. **Urban:** 77%. **Ethnic groups:** British 40%, French 27%, other European 20%, indigenous Indian and Eskimo 1.5%. **Principal languages:** English, French (both official). **Religions:** Roman Catholic 46%, United Church 16%, Anglican 10%.

**Geography: Area:** 3,849,674 sq. mi., the largest country in land size in the western hemisphere. **Topography:** Canada stretches 3,426 miles from east to west and extends southward from the North Pole to the U.S. border. Its seacoast includes 36,356 miles of mainland and 115,133 miles of islands, including the Arctic islands almost from Greenland to near the Alaskan border. **Climate:** While generally temperate, varies from freezing winter cold to blistering summer heat. **Capital:** Ottawa. **Cities** (met. 1994 est.): Toronto 4.1 mil; Montreal 3.3 mil; Vancouver 1.7 mil; Ottawa-Hull 980,000; Edmonton 897,000; Calgary 814,000; Quebec 679,000; Winnipeg 662,000.

**Government: Type:** Confederation with parliamentary democracy. **Head of state:** Queen Elizabeth II, represented by Gov.-Gen. Roméo A. LeBlanc; b Dec. 18, 1927; in office: Feb. 8, 1995. **Head of government:** Prime Min. Jean Chrétien; b Jan. 11, 1934; in office: Nov. 4, 1993. **Local divisions:** 10 provinces, 2 territories. **Defense:** 1.6% of GDP (FY 1995-96). **Active troop strength:** 70,500.

**Economy: Minerals:** Nickel, zinc, copper, gold, lead, molybdenum, potash, silver. **Crude oil reserves** (1995): 5.0 bil barrels. **Arable land:** 5%. **Livestock** (1994): cattle: 12.3 mil; pigs: 11.2 mil; sheep: 691,000. **Fish catch** (1993): 1.2 mil metric tons. **Electricity prod.** (1993): 511 bil kWh. **Labor force:** 73% services, 15% manufacturing, 3% agric.

**Finance: Monetary unit:** Dollar (June 1996: 1.37 = $1 US). **Gross domestic product** (1994): $639.8 bil.* **Per capita GDP:** $22,760. **Imports** (1994): $151.5 bil; partners: U.S. 65%, Jap. 6%. **Exports** (1994): $164.3 bil; partners: U.S. 81%, Jap. 5%. **Tourism** (1993): $5.9 bil. **National budget** (FY 1993-94 est.): $115.3 bil. **International reserves less gold** (May 1996): $18.2 bil. **Gold:** 5.51 mil oz t. **Consumer prices** (change in 1995): 2.2%.

**Transport: Railroads: Length:** 44,182 mi. **Motor vehicles:** in use: 13.5 mil passenger cars, 3.8 mil comm. vehicles. **Civil aviation:** 27 bil passenger-mi.: 252 airports with scheduled flights.

**Communications: Television sets:** 1 per 1.7 persons. **Radios:** 1 per 1.1 persons. **Telephones:** 1 per 1.7 persons. **Daily newspaper circ.:** 195 per 1,000 pop.

**Health: Life expectancy at birth** (1996): 76 male; 83 female. **Births** (per 1,000 pop.): 13. **Deaths** (per 1,000 pop.): 7. **Natural increase:** 0.6%. **Hospital beds:** 1 per 171 persons. **Physicians:** 1 per 464 persons. **Infant mortality** (per 1,000 live births 1996): 6.

**Education: Literacy** (1994): 97%. Compulsory primary education.

**Major International Organizations:** UN and all of its specialized agencies, NATO, OAS, APEC, OECD, the Commonwealth.

**Embassy:** 501 Pennsylvania Ave. NW 20001; 682-1740.

French explorer Jacques Cartier, who reached the Gulf of St. Lawrence in 1534, is generally regarded as Canada's founder. But English seaman John Cabot sighted Newfoundland 37 years earlier, in 1497, and Vikings are believed to have reached the Atlantic coast centuries before either explorer.

Canadian settlement was pioneered by the French who established Quebec City (1608) and Montreal (1642) and declared New France a colony in 1663.

Britain acquired Acadia (later Nova Scotia) in 1717 and, through military victory over French forces in Canada, captured Quebec (1759) and obtained control of the rest of New France in 1763. The French, through the Quebec Act of 1774, retained the rights to their own language, religion, and civil law. The British presence in Canada increased during the American Revolution when many colonials, proudly calling themselves United Empire Loyalists, moved north to Canada.

Fur traders and explorers led Canadians westward across the continent. Sir Alexander Mackenzie reached the Pacific in 1793 and scrawled on a rock by the ocean, "from Canada by land."

In Upper and Lower Canada (later called Ontario and Quebec) and in the Maritimes, legislative assemblies appeared in the 18th century and reformers called for responsible government. But the War of 1812 intervened. The war, a conflict between Great Britain and the United States fought mainly in Upper Canada, ended in a stalemate in 1814.

In 1837 political agitation for more democratic government culminated in rebellions in Upper and Lower Canada. Britain sent Lord Durham to investigate; in a famous report (1839), he recommended union of the 2 parts into one colony called Canada. The union lasted until Confederation, July 1, 1867, when proclamation of the British North America (BNA) Act (now known as the Constitution Act, 1867) launched the Dominion of Canada, consisting of Ontario, Quebec, and the former colonies of Nova Scotia and New Brunswick.

Since 1840 the Canadian colonies had held the right to internal self-government. The BNA Act, which was the basis for the country's written constitution, established a federal system of government on the model of a British parliament and cabinet structure under the crown. Canada was proclaimed a self-governing Dominion within the British Empire in 1931. With the ratification of the Constitution Act, 1982, Canada severed its last formal legislative link with Britain by obtaining the right to amend its constitution.

The so-called Meech Lake Agreement was signed (subject to provincial ratification) June 3, 1987. The accord would have assured constitutional protection for Quebec's efforts to preserve its French language and culture. Critics charged that it did not make any provision for other minority groups and that it gave Quebec too much power, which might enable Quebec to override the nation's 1982 Charter of Rights and Freedoms (an integral part of the constitution). The accord died June 22, 1990.

Its failure sparked a separatist revival in Quebec, which culminated in Aug. 1992 in the Charlottetown agreement. This called for changes to the constitution, such as recognition of Quebec as a "distinct society" within the Canadian confederation. It was defeated in a national referendum on Oct. 26, 1992.

In May 1992 voters in the Northwest Territories approved the creation of a self-governing homeland for the 17,500 Inuit living in the territories. The area—to be known as Nunavut, "Our Land"—would cover an area of 136,493 sq. mi. and take effect by 1999.

Canada became the first nation to ratify the North American Free Trade Agreement between Canada, Mexico, and the U.S., June 23, 1993. It went into effect Jan. 1, 1994.

On Feb. 24, 1993, Brian Mulroney resigned as prime minister after more than 8 years in office; he was succeeded by Kim Campbell. In elections Oct. 25, 1993, the ruling Conservatives were defeated in a landslide that left them only 2 of the 295 seats in the House of Commons. Jean Chrétien became prime minister. In a Quebec referendum held Oct. 30, 1995, proponents of secession lost by a razor-thin margin.

| Provinces/Territories | Area (sq. mi.) | Population (1995 est.) |
|---|---|---|
| Alberta | 255,287 | 2,656,000 |
| British Columbia | 365,948 | 3,529,000 |
| Manitoba | 250,947 | 1,105,000 |
| New Brunswick | 28,355 | 738,000 |
| Newfoundland | 156,649 | 570,000 |
| Nova Scotia | 21,425 | 918,000 |
| Ontario | 412,581 | 10,768,000 |
| Prince Edward Island | 2,185 | 131,000 |
| Quebec | 594,860 | 7,134,000 |
| Saskatchewan | 251,866 | 978,000 |
| Northwest Territories | 1,322,910 | 62,000 |
| Yukon Territory | 186,661 | 31,000 |

## Prime Ministers of Canada

Canada is a constitutional monarchy with a parliamentary system of government. It is also a federal state. Canada's official head of state, Queen Elizabeth II, is represented by a resident Governor-General. However, in practice the nation is governed by the Prime Minister, leader of the party that commands the support of a majority of the House of Commons, dominant chamber of Canada's bicameral Parliament.

| Name | Party | Term |
|---|---|---|
| Sir John A. MacDonald | Conservative | 1867-1873 |
| | | 1878-1891 |
| Alexander Mackenzie | Liberal | 1873-1878 |
| Sir John J. C. Abbott | Conservative | 1891-1892 |
| Sir John S. D. Thompson | Conservative | 1892-1894 |
| Sir Mackenzie Bowell | Conservative | 1894-1896 |
| Sir Charles Tupper | Conservative | 1896 |
| Sir Wilfrid Laurier | Liberal | 1896-1911 |
| Sir Robert L. Borden | Cons. Union. | 1911-1920 |
| Arthur Meighen | Cons. Union. | 1920-1921 |
| W. L. Mackenzie King | Liberal | 1921-1930(1) |
| | | 1935-1948 |
| R. B. Bennett | Conservative | 1930-1935 |
| Louis St. Laurent | Liberal | 1948-1957 |
| John G. Diefenbaker | Prog. Cons. | 1957-1963 |
| Lester B. Pearson | Liberal | 1963-1968 |
| Pierre Elliott Trudeau | Liberal | 1968-1979 |
| | | 1980-1984 |
| Joe Clark | Prog. Cons. | 1979-1980 |
| John Turner | Liberal | 1984 |
| Brian Mulroney | Prog. Cons. | 1984-1993 |
| Kim Campbell | Prog. Cons. | 1993 |
| Jean Chrétien | Liberal | 1993- |

(1) King served 2 terms in these years, interrupted June 26-Sept. 25, 1926, when Arthur Meighen served as prime minister.

# Cape Verde

## Republic of Cape Verde

## República de Cabo Verde

**People: Population:** 449,066. **Age distrib.** (%): <15: 45; 65+: 6. **Pop. density:** 288 per sq. mi. **Urban:** 44%. **Ethnic groups:** Creole (mulatto) 71%, African 28%, European 1%. **Principal languages:** Portuguese (official), Crioulo. **Religions:** Roman Catholic fused with indigenous beliefs.

**Geography: Area:** 1,557 sq. mi. **Location:** In Atlantic O., off western tip of Africa. **Neighbors:** Nearest are Mauritania, Senegal to E. **Topography:** Cape Verde Islands are 15 in number, volcanic in origin (active crater on Fogo). The landscape is eroded and stark, with vegetation mostly in interior valleys. **Capital:** Praia. **Cities** (1990 cen.): Praia 62,000; Mindelo 47,000.

**Government: Type:** Republic. **Head of state:** Pres. Antonio Mascarenhas Monteiro; b Feb. 16, 1944; in office: Mar. 22, 1991. **Head of government:** Prime Min. Carlos Veiga; b 1949; in office: Apr. 4, 1991. **Local divisions:** 14 administrative districts. **Defense:** 1.0% of GNP (1992). **Active troop strength:** 1,100 est.

**Economy: Chief crops:** Bananas, coffee, sweet potatoes, corn, beans. **Minerals:** Salt. **Other resources:** Fish. **Arable land:** 9%. **Electricity prod.** (1993): 40 mil kWh.

**Finance: Monetary unit:** Escudo (June 1996: 82.97 = $1 US). **Gross domestic product** (1993): $410 mil.* **Per capita GDP:** $1,000. **Imports** (1992): $173 mil; partners: Port. 34%, Neth. 9%. **Exports** (1992): $4.4 mil; partners: Port. 49%, Angola 16%. **National budget** (1993): $235 mil.

**Transport: Motor vehicles:** in use: 10,000 passenger cars, 5,000 comm. vehicles. **Chief ports:** Mindelo, Praia.

**Communications: Radios:** 1 per 6.7 persons. **Telephones:** 1 per 25 persons.

**Health: Life expectancy at birth** (1996): 62 male; 65 female. **Births** (per 1,000 pop.): 44. **Deaths** (per 1,000 pop.): 8. **Natural increase:** 3.6%. **Infant mortality** (per 1,000 live births 1996): 54.

**Education: Literacy** (1990): 72%.Compulsory: ages 7-11.

**Major International Organizations:** UN (IMF, FAO, World Bank, WHO), OAU.

**Embassy:** 3415 Massachusetts Ave. NW 20007; 965-6820.

The uninhabited Cape Verdes were discovered by the Portuguese in 1456 or 1460. The first Portuguese colonists landed in 1462; African slaves were brought soon after, and most Cape Verdeans descend from both groups. Cape Verde independence came July 5, 1975. Antonio Mascarenhas Monteiro won the nation's first free presidential election Feb. 17, 1991; he was reelected without opposition five years later.

# Central African Republic

## République Centrafricaine

**People: Population:** 3,274,426. **Pop. density:** 14 per sq. mi. **Urban:** 39%. **Ethnic groups:** Baya 34%, Banda 27%, Mandjia 21%, Sara 10%. **Principal languages:** French (official), Sangho (national), Arabic. **Religions:** Protestant 25%, Roman Catholic 25%, indigenous beliefs 24%, Muslim 15%.

**Geography: Area:** 240,324 sq. mi. **Location:** In central Africa. **Neighbors:** Chad on N, Cameroon on W, Congo and Zaire on S, Sudan on E. **Topography:** Mostly rolling plateau, average altitude 2,000 ft., with rivers draining S to the Congo and N to Lake Chad. Open, well-watered savanna covers most of the area, with an arid area in NE, and tropical rainforest in SW. **Capital:** Bangui (1988 cen.): 452,000.

**Government: Type:** Republic. **Head of state:** Pres. Ange-Félix Patassé; b Jan. 25, 1937; in office: Oct. 22, 1993. **Head of government:** Prime Min. Jean-Paul Ngoupaude; in office: June 6, 1996. **Local divisions:** 16 prefectures and 1 commune. **Defense:** 2.3% of GDP (1994). **Active troop strength:** 4,950.

**Economy: Industries:** Textiles, breweries, sawmills, mining. **Chief crops:** Cotton, coffee, corn, cassava, yams. **Minerals:** Diamonds (chief export), uranium. **Other resources:** Timber. **Arable land:** 3%. **Electricity prod.** (1993): 100 mil kWh. **Labor force:** 80% agric.

**Finance: Monetary unit:** CFA Franc (June 1996: 515 = $1 US). **Gross domestic product** (1994): $2.2 bil.* **Per capita GDP:** $700. **Imports** (1992): $165 mil; partners: Fr. 51%. **Exports** (1992): $124 mil; partners: Belg.-Lux. 57%, Fr. 10%. **National budget** (1991 est.): $312 mil. **International reserves less gold** (Mar. 1996): $211 mil. **Gold:** 11,000 oz t.

**Transport: Motor vehicles:** in use: 8,200 passenger cars, 8,500 comm. vehicles. **Chief port:** Bangui.

**Communications: Television sets:** 1 per 409 persons. **Radios:** 1 per 17 persons. **Telephones:** 1 per 431 persons.

**Health: Life expectancy at birth** (1996): 45 male; 47 female. **Births** (per 1,000 pop.): 40. **Deaths** (per 1,000 pop.): 18. **Natural increase:** 2.2%. **Hospital beds:** 1 per 672 persons. **Physicians:** 1 per 18,660 persons. **Infant mortality** (per 1,000 live births 1995): 112.

**Education: Literacy** (1995): 60%. Compulsory: ages 6-14.

**Major International Organizations:** UN (WTO, IMF, FAO, World Bank, WHO), OAU.

**Embassy:** 1618 22d St. NW 20008; 483-7800.

Various Bantu tribes migrated through the region for centuries before French control was asserted in the late 19th century, when the region was named Ubangi-Shari. Complete independence was attained Aug. 13, 1960.

All political parties were dissolved in 1960, and the country became a center for Chinese political influence in Africa. Relations with China were severed after 1965. Pres. Jean-Bedel Bokassa, who seized power in a 1965 military coup, proclaimed himself constitutional emperor of the renamed Central African Empire Dec. 1976.

Bokassa's rule was characterized by ruthless and cruel authoritarianism and human rights violations. He was ousted in a bloodless coup aided by the French government, Sept. 20, 1979. In 1981, Gen. André Kolingba became head of state in another bloodless coup. Multiparty legislative and presidential elections were held in Oct. 1992 but were canceled by the government when Kolingba was losing. New elections were ultimately held in Aug. and Sept. 1993, leading to the installation of a civilian government. French troops intervened to suppress an army mutiny in May 1996.A month later, a 21-member government of national unity was formed.

# Chad

## Republic of Chad

## République du Tchad

**People: Population:** 6,976,845. **Age distrib.** (%): <15: 41; 65+: 3. **Pop. density:** 14 per sq. mi. **Urban:** 22%. **Ethnic groups:** 200 distinct groups. **Principal languages:** French, Arabic (both official), Sara, Sango, more than 100 other languages. **Religions:** Muslim 50%, Christian 25%, indigenous beliefs 25%.

**Geography: Area:** 495,755 sq. mi. **Location:** In central N Africa. **Neighbors:** Libya on N; Niger, Nigeria, Cameroon on W; Central African Republic on S; Sudan on E. **Topography:** Wooded savanna, steppe, and desert in the S; part of the Sahara in the N. Southern rivers flow N to Lake Chad, surrounded by marshland. **Capital:** N'Djamena (1993 cen.): 531,000.

**Government: Type:** Republic. **Head of state:** Pres. Idriss Déby; in office: Dec. 4, 1990. **Head of government:** Prime Min. Koibla Djimasta; in office: Apr. 8, 1995. **Local divisions:** 14 prefectures. **Defense:** 11.1% of GDP (1994). **Active troop strength:** 30,350 est.

**Economy: Chief crops:** Cotton. **Minerals:** Uranium. **Arable land:** 2%. **Fish catch** (1993): 80,000 metric tons. **Electricity prod.** (1993): 80 mil kWh. **Labor force:** 85% agric.

**Finance: Monetary unit:** CFA Franc (June 1996: 515 = $1 US). **Gross domestic product** (1993): $2.8 bil.* **Per capita GDP:** $530. **Imports** (1992): $261 mil; partners: U.S., France. **Exports** (1992): $190 mil; partners: France, Nigeria. **National budget** (1992 est.): $363 mil. **International reserves less gold** (Mar. 1996): $190 mil. **Gold:** 11,000 oz t.

**Transport: Motor vehicles:** in use: 9,000 passenger cars, 7,000 comm. vehicles.

**Communications: Radios:** 1 per 4.7 persons. **Telephones:** 1 per 1,310 persons.

**Health: Life expectancy at birth** (1996): 45 male; 50 female. **Births** (per 1,000 pop.): 44. **Deaths** (per 1,000 pop.): 17. **Natural increase:** 2.7%. **Infant mortality** (per 1,000 live births 1996): 120.

**Education: Literacy** (1991): 48%. Compulsory: ages 6-14.

**Major International Organizations:** UN (FAO, IMF, WTO, World Bank, WHO), OAU.

**Embassy:** 2002 R St. NW 20009; 462-4009.

Chad was the site of paleolithic and neolithic cultures before the Sahara Desert formed. A succession of kingdoms and Arab slave traders dominated Chad until France took control around 1900. Independence came Aug. 11, 1960.

Northern Muslim rebels have fought animist and Christian southern government and French troops from 1966, despite numerous cease-fires and peace pacts.

Libyan troops entered the country at the request of a pro-Libyan Chad government, Dec. 1980. The troops were withdrawn from Chad in Nov. 1981. Rebel forces, led by Hissène Habré, captured the capital and forced Pres. Goukouni Oueddei to flee the country in June 1982.

In 1983, France sent some 3,000 troops to Chad to assist Pres. Habré in opposing Libyan-backed rebels. France and Libya agreed to a simultaneous withdrawal of troops from Chad in Sept. 1984, but Libyan forces remained in the north until Mar. 1987, when Chad forces drove them from their last major stronghold. In Dec. 1990, Habré was overthrown by a Libyan-supported insurgent group, the Patriotic Salvation Movement.

On Feb. 3, 1994, the World Court dismissed a long-standing territorial claim by Libya to the mineral-rich Aozou Strip, on the Libyan border. Libyan troops reportedly withdrew at the end of May. Following approval of a new constitution in Mar. 1996, Chad's first multiparty presidential election was held in June and July.

# Chile

## Republic of Chile

## República de Chile

**People: Population:** 14,333,258. **Age distrib.** (%): <15: 30; 65+: 7. **Pop. density:** 49 per sq. mi. **Urban:** 85%. **Ethnic groups:** European and European-Indian 95%, Indian 3%. **Principal language:** Spanish (official). **Religions:** Roman Catholic 89%, Protestant 11%.

**Geography: Area:** 292,135 sq. mi. **Location:** Occupies western coast of S South America. **Neighbors:** Peru on N, Bolivia on NE, Argentina on E. **Topography:** Andes Mts. are on E border including some of the world's highest peaks; on W is 2,650-mile Pacific coast. Width varies between 100 and 250 miles. In N is Atacama Desert, in center are agricultural regions, in S are forests and grazing lands. **Capital:** Santiago (1993 met. est.): 4.6 mil.

**Government: Type:** Republic. **Head of state:** Pres. Eduardo Frei Ruiz-Tagle; b June 24, 1942; in office: Mar. 11, 1994. **Local divisions:** 13 regions. **Defense:** 3.4% of GDP (1991). **Active troop strength:** 99,000 est.

**Economy: Industries:** Fish processing, wood products, iron, steel. **Chief crops:** Grain, grapes, beans, potatoes, sugar beets, fruits. **Minerals:** Copper (world's largest producer), molybdenum, nitrates, iodine (2d largest producer), iron, coal, oil, gas, gold, manganese, salt, sulphur. **Other resources:** Forests. **Arable land:** 7%. **Livestock** (1994): cattle: 3.7 mil; sheep: 4.6 mil; pigs: 1.4 mil. **Fish catch** (1993): 6.2 mil metric tons. **Electricity prod.** (1993): 22 bil kWh. **Labor force:** 19% agric., forestry, fishing; 34% ind. & commerce; 38% serv.

**Finance: Monetary unit:** Peso (June 1996: 410 = $1 US). **Gross domestic product** (1994): $98 bil.* **Per capita GDP:** $7,010. **Imports** (1994): $10.9 bil; partners: EU 24%, U.S. 21%. **Exports** (1994): $11.5 bil; partners: EU 29%, Japan 17%, U.S. 16%. **Tourism** (1993): $824 mil. **National budget** (1993): $10.9 bil. **International reserves less gold** (Mar. 1996): $13.5 bil. **Gold:** 1.86 mil oz. t. **Consumer prices** (change in 1995): 8.2%.

**Transport: Railroads: Route length:** 4,076 mi. **Motor vehicles:** in use: 827,000 passenger cars, 438,000 comm. vehicles. **Civil aviation:** 2.8 bil passenger-mi.; 18 airports with scheduled flights. **Chief ports:** Valparaiso, Arica, Antofagasta.

**Communications: Television sets:** 1 per 7.0 persons. **Radios:** 1 per 3.2 persons. **Telephones:** 1 per 9.1 persons.

**Health: Life expectancy at birth** (1996): 71 male; 78 female. **Births** (per 1,000 pop.): 18. **Deaths** (per 1,000 pop.): 6. **Natural increase:** 1.2%. **Hospital beds:** 1 per 312 persons. **Physicians:** 1 per 889 persons. **Infant mortality** (per 1,000 live births 1996): 14.

**Education: Literacy** (1991): 95%. Free and compulsory, from age 6 or 7, for 8 years.

**Major International Organizations:** UN and all of its specialized agencies, OAS, APEC.

**Embassy:** 1732 Massachusetts Ave. NW 20036; 785-1746.

Northern Chile was under Inca rule before the Spanish conquest, 1536-40. The southern Araucanian Indians resisted until the late 19th century. Independence was gained 1810-18, under José de San Martin and Bernardo O'Higgins; the latter, as supreme director 1817-23, sought social and economic reforms until deposed. Chile defeated Peru and Bolivia in 1836-39 and 1879-84, gaining mineral-rich northern land.

In 1970, Salvador Allende Gossens, a Marxist, became president with a third of the national vote. The Allende government improved conditions for the poor. But illegal and violent actions by extremist supporters of the government, the regime's failure to attain majority support, and poorly planned socialist economic programs led to political and financial chaos.

A military junta seized power Sept. 11, 1973, and said Allende had killed himself. The junta, headed by Gen. Augusto Pinochet Ugarte, named a mostly military cabinet and announced plans to "exterminate Marxism." Repression continued during the 1980s with little sign of any political liberalization.

In a plebiscite held Oct. 5, 1988, voters rejected the incumbent president, Pinochet. He agreed to presidential elections. In Dec. 1989 voters elected a civilian president, although Pinochet continued to head the army. In Mar. 1994 a Chilean human rights group announced a revised estimate of more than 3,100 deaths from human rights violations during Pinochet's rule.

**Tierra del Fuego** is the largest (18,800 sq. mi.) island in the archipelago of the same name at the southern tip of South America, an area of majestic mountains, tortuous channels, and high winds. It was visited 1520 by Magellan and named the Land of Fire because of its many Indian bonfires. Part of the island is in Chile, part in Argentina. Punta Arenas, on a mainland peninsula, is a center of sheep raising and the world's southernmost city (pop. about 70,000); Puerto Williams is the southernmost settlement.

# China

## People's Republic of China

## Zhonghua Renmin Gonghe Guo

**People: Population:** 1,210,004,956. **Age distrib.** (%): <15: 27; 65+: 6. **Pop. density:** 327 per sq. mi. **Urban:** 29%. **Ethnic groups:** Han Chinese 92%, Tibetan, Mongol, Korean, Manchu, others. **Principal languages:** Mandarin (official), Yue, Wu, Hakka, Xiang, Gan, Minbei, Minnan. **Religions:** Officially atheist; Buddhism, Taoism are traditional; some Muslims, Christians.

**Geography: Area:** 3,696,100 sq. mi. **Location:** Occupies most of the habitable mainland of E Asia. **Neighbors:** Mongolia on N; Russia on NE and NW; Afghanistan, Pakistan, Tajikistan, Kazakstan on W; India, Nepal, Bhutan, Myanmar, Laos, Vietnam on S; North Korea on NE. **Topography:** Two-thirds of the vast territory is mountainous or desert; only one-tenth is cultivated. Rolling topography rises to high elevations in the N in the Daxinganlingshanmai separating Manchuria and Mongolia; the Tien Shan in Xinjiang; the Himalayan and Kunlunshanmai in the SW and in Tibet. Length is 1,860 mi. from N to S, width E to W is more than 2,000 mi. The eastern half of China is one of the best-watered lands in the world. Three great river systems, the Chang (Yangtze), the Huang (Yellow), and the Xi, provide water for vast farmlands. **Capital:** Beijing. **Cities** (1990 est.): Shanghai 7.5 mil; Beijing 5.8 mil; Tianjin 4.6 mil; Shenyang 3.6 mil; Wuhan 3.3 mil; Canton (Guangzhou) 2.9 mil.

**Government: Type:** Communist Party-led state. **Head of state:** Pres. Jiang Zemin; b Aug. 17, 1926; in office: Mar. 27, 1993. **Head of government:** Premier Li Peng; b Oct. 1928; in office: Apr. 9, 1988. **Local divisions:** 23 provinces, 5 autonomous regions, and 3 municipalities. **Defense:** 2.7% of GNP (1993). **Active troop strength:** 2.3 mil est.

**Economy: Industries:** Iron and steel, textiles and apparel, machine building, armaments. **Chief crops:** Grain, rice, cotton, potatoes, tea. **Minerals:** Tungsten, antimony, coal, oil, mercury, iron, lead, manganese, molybdenum, tin. **Crude oil reserves** (1995): 24 bil barrels. **Other resources:** Silk. **Arable land:** 10%. **Livestock** (1993): cattle: 83 mil; pigs: 394 mil; sheep: 110 mil. **Fish catch** (1992): 15 mil metric tons. **Electricity prod.** (1993): 746 bil kWh. **Labor force:** 60% agric. & forestry; 25% ind. & commerce.

**Finance: Monetary unit:** Renminbi (Yuan) (June 1996: 8.32 = $1 US). **Gross domestic product** (1994 est.): $2.61 tril.* **Per capita GDP:** $2,500. **Imports** (1994): $115.7 bil; partners: Jap. 22%, Taiwan 11%, U.S. 10%. **Exports** (1994): $121 bil; partners: Hong Kong 24%, U.S. 19%, Jap. 17%. **Tourism** (1994): $7.3 bil. **National budget** (1994): $13.7 bil deficit. **International reserves less gold** (Apr. 1996): $83.7 bil. **Gold:** 12.7 mil oz t. **Consumer prices** (change in 1995): 16.9%.

**Transport: Railroads: Length:** 43,131 mi. **Motor vehicles:** in use: 2.9 mil passenger cars, 5.0 mil comm. vehicles. **Civil aviation:** 33 bil passenger-mi., 108 airports with scheduled flights. **Chief ports:** Shanghai, Qinhuangdao, Dalian, Canton (Guangzhou).

**Communications: Television sets:** 1 per 5.2 persons. **Radios:** 1 per 5.8 persons. **Telephones:** 1 per 62 persons.

**Health: Life expectancy at birth** (1996): 68 male; 71 female. **Births** (per 1,000 pop.): 17. **Deaths** (per 1,000 pop.): 7. **Natural increase:** 1.0%. **Hospital beds:** 1 per 382 persons. **Physicians:** 1 per 647 persons. **Infant mortality** (per 1,000 live births 1996): 40.

**Education: Literacy** (1993): 82%. Compulsory 7-16. primary school enrollment 100%.

**Major International Organizations:** UN (IMF, World Bank, FAO, WHO), APEC.

**Embassy:** 2300 Conn. Ave. NW 20008; 328-2500.

**History.** Remains of various humanlike creatures who lived as early as several hundred thousand years ago have been found in many parts of China. Neolithic agricultural settlements dotted the Huang (Yellow) R. basin from about 5000 BC. Their language, religion, and art were the sources of later Chinese civilization.

Bronze metallurgy reached a peak and Chinese pictographic writing, similar to today's, was in use in the more developed culture of the Shang Dynasty (c. 1500 BC-c. 1000 BC), which ruled much of North China.

A succession of dynasties and interdynastic warring kingdoms ruled China for the next 3,000 years. They expanded Chinese political and cultural domination to the south and west, and developed a brilliant technologically and a culturally advanced society. Rule by foreigners (Mongols in the Yuan Dynasty, 1271-1368, and Manchus in the Ch'ing Dynasty, 1644-1911) did not alter the underlying culture.

A period of relative stagnation left China vulnerable to internal and external pressures in the 19th century. Rebellions left tens of millions dead, and Russia, Japan, Britain, and other powers exercised political and economic control in large parts of the country. China became a republic Jan. 1, 1912, following the Wuchang Uprising inspired by Dr. Sun Yat-sen.

For a period of 50 years, 1894-1945, China was involved in conflicts with Japan. In 1895, China ceded Korea, Taiwan, and other areas. On Sept. 18, 1931, Japan seized the Northeastern Provinces (Manchuria) and set up a puppet state called Manchukuo. The border province of Jehol was cut off as a buffer state in 1933. Japan invaded China proper July 7, 1937. After its defeat in World War II, Japan gave up all seized land.

Following World War II, internal disturbances arose involving the Kuomintang, Communists, and other factions. China came under domination of Communist armies, 1949-1950. The Kuomintang government moved to Taiwan, 90 mi. off the mainland, Dec. 8, 1949.

The People's Republic of China was proclaimed in Beijing (Peking) Sept. 21, 1949, by the Chinese People's Political Consultative Conference under Mao Zedong. China and the USSR signed a 30-year treaty of "friendship, alliance and mutual assistance," Feb. 15, 1950. The U.S. refused recognition of the new regime. On Nov. 26, 1950, the People's Republic sent armies into Korea against U.S. troops and forced a stalemate in the Korean War.

By the 1960s, relations with the USSR deteriorated, with disagreements on borders, ideology, and leadership of world Communism. The USSR cancelled aid accords, and China, with Albania, launched anti-Soviet propaganda drives.

On Oct. 25, 1971, the UN General Assembly ousted the Taiwan government from the UN and seated the People's Republic in its place. The U.S. had supported the mainland's admission but opposed Taiwan's expulsion.

U.S. Pres. Richard Nixon visited China Feb. 21-28, 1972, on invitation from Premier Zhou Enlai, ending years of antipathy between the 2 nations. China and the U.S. opened liaison offices in each other's capitals, May-June 1973. The U.S., Dec. 15, 1978, formally recognized the People's Republic of China as the sole legal government of China; diplomatic relations between the 2 nations were established, Jan. 1, 1979.

Agreements with Great Britain and Portugal, respectively, provide for the reversion to Chinese sovereignty of Hong Kong (1997) and Macau (1999). Although China and Taiwan remain diplomatic rivals, they tightened economic ties in the 1990s.

**Internal developments.** After an initial period of consolidation, 1949-52, industry, agriculture, and social and economic institutions were forcibly molded according to Maoist ideals. However, frequent drastic changes in policy and violent factionalism interfered with economic development. In 1957, Mao Zedong admitted an estimated 800,000 people had been executed 1949-54; opponents claimed much higher figures.

The Great Leap Forward, 1958-60, tried to force the pace of economic development through intensive labor on huge new rural communes, and through emphasis on ideological purity. The program caused resistance and was largely abandoned.

The Great Proletarian Cultural Revolution, 1965, was an attempt to oppose pragmatism and bureaucratic power and instruct a new generation in revolutionary principles. Massive purges took place. A program of forcibly relocating millions of urban teenagers into the countryside was launched. By 1968 the movement had run its course; many purged officials returned to office in subsequent years, and reforms that had placed ideology above expertise were gradually weakened.

Mao died Sept. 9, 1976. In a continuing "reassessment" of his policies his widow, Jiang Qing, and other "Gang of Four" leftists were convicted of "committing crimes during the 'Cultural Revolution,' " Jan. 25, 1981.

The new ruling group modified Maoist policies in education, culture, and industry, and sought better ties with non-Communist countries. By the mid-1980s, China had enacted far-reaching economic reforms highlighted by the departure from rigid central planning and the stressing of market-oriented socialism.

Some 100,000 students and workers staged a march in Beijing to demand democratic reforms, May 4, 1989. The demonstrations continued during a visit to Beijing by Soviet leader Mikhail Gorbachev May 15-18. It was the first Sino-Soviet summit since 1959. A million people gathered in Beijing to demand reforms and the removal of Deng and other leaders. There were protests in at least 20 other Chinese cities. Martial law was imposed, May 20, but was mostly ignored by protesters.

Chinese army troops entered Beijing, June 3-4, and crushed the pro-democracy protests. Tanks and armored personnel carriers attacked Tiananmen Square, outside the Great Hall of the People, which was the main scene of the demonstrations and hunger strikes. It is estimated that 5,000 died, 10,000 were injured, and hundreds of students and workers were arrested.

Although human rights violations have persisted, the U.S. has continued to renew China's most-favored-nation trading status. Chinese-American Harry Wu, a human rights activist, was detained while trying to enter China June 19, 1995; convicted of spying, he was expelled Aug. 25. China hosted the UN 4th World Conference on Women in Sept.

China had one of the world's fastest-growing economies in the 1990s. China's population, the world's largest, is still increasing, but with more couples following the government's one-child policy some experts predict that the nation's population will actually decline after peaking in the early 21st century.

**Manchuria.** Home of the Manchus, rulers of China 1644-1911, Manchuria has accommodated millions of Chinese settlers in the 20th century. Under Japanese rule 1931-45, the area became industrialized. China no longer uses the name Manchuria for the region, which is divided into the 3 NE provinces of Heilongjiang, Jilin, and Liaoning.

**Guangxi** is in SE China, bounded on N by Guizhou and Hunan provinces, E and S by Guangdong, on SW by Vietnam, and on W by Yunnan. It produces rice in the river valleys and has valuable forest products.

**Inner Mongolia** was organized by the People's Republic in 1947. Its boundaries have undergone frequent changes, reaching its greatest extent in 1956 (and restored in 1979), with an area of 454,600 sq. mi., allegedly in order to dilute the minority Mongol population. Chinese settlers outnumber the Mongols more than 10 to 1. Pop. (1994 est.): 22.3 mil. Capital: Hohhot.

**Xinjiang,** in Central Asia, is 635,900 sq. mi., pop. (1994 est.): 16.1 mil (75% Uygurs, a Turkic Muslim group, with a heavy Chinese increase in recent years). Capital: Urumqi. It is China's richest region in strategic minerals.

**Tibet,** 471,700 sq. mi., is a thinly populated region of high plateaus and massive mountains, the Himalayas on the S, the Kunluns on the N. High passes connect with India and Nepal; roads lead into China proper. Capital: Lhasa. Average altitude is 15,000 ft. Jiachan, 15,870 ft., is believed to be the highest inhabited town on earth. Agriculture is primitive. Pop. (1994 est.): 2.3 mil (of whom about 500,000 are Chinese). Another 4 million Tibetans form the majority of the population of vast adjacent areas that have long been incorporated into China.

China ruled all of Tibet from the 18th century, but independence came in 1911. China reasserted control in 1951, and a Communist government was installed in 1953, revising the theocratic Lamaist Buddhist rule. Serfdom was abolished, but all land remained collectivized.

A Tibetan uprising within China in 1956 spread to Tibet in 1959. The rebellion was crushed with Chinese troops, and Buddhism was almost totally suppressed. The Dalai Lama and 100,000 Tibetans fled to India.

# Colombia

## Republic of Colombia

## República de Colombia

**People: Population:** 36,813,161. **Age distrib.** (%): <15: 33; 65+: 4. **Pop. density:** 84 per sq. mi. **Urban:** 67%. **Ethnic groups:** Mestizo 58%, white 20%, mulatto 14%. **Principal language:** Spanish (official). **Religions:** Roman Catholic 95%.

**Geography: Area:** 440,762 sq. mi. **Location:** At the NW corner of South America. **Neighbors:** Panama on NW, Ecuador and Peru on S, Brazil and Venezuela on E. **Topography:** Three ranges of Andes, the Western, Central, and Eastern Cordilleras, run through the country from N to S. The eastern range consists mostly of high table lands, densely populated. The Magdalena R. rises in Andes, flows N to Caribbean, through a rich alluvial plain. Sparsely-settled plains in E are drained by Orinoco and Amazon systems. **Capital:** Bogota. **Cities** (1995 est.): Bogotá 5.0 mil; Cali 1.7 mil; Medellin 1.6 mil; Barranquilla 1.0 mil.

**Government: Type:** Republic. **Head of state:** Pres. Ernesto Samper Pizano; b Aug. 3, 1950; in office: Aug. 7, 1994. **Local divisions:** 32 departments, capital district of Bogota. **Defense:** 1.3% of GDP (1993 est.). **Active troop strength:** 146,400.

**Economy: Industries:** Textiles, food processing, metal products, cement, chemicals. **Chief crops:** Coffee (25% of exports), rice, bananas, oilseeds, corn, cotton, sugar, tobacco, coca. **Minerals:** Oil, gas, emeralds (50% world output), gold, copper, coal, iron, nickel, salt. **Crude oil reserves** (1995): 3.4 bil bbls. **Other resources:** Rubber, balsam, dye-woods, copaiba, hydropower. **Arable land:** 4%. **Livestock** (1994): cattle: 25.7 mil; pigs: 2.6 mil; sheep: 2.5 mil. **Fish catch** (1993): 146,000 metric tons. **Electricity prod.** (1993): 33 bil kWh. **Labor force:** 30% agric.; 24% ind.; 46% services.

**Finance: Monetary unit:** Peso (June 1996: 1,071 = $1 US). **Gross domestic product** (1994): $172 bil.* **Per capita GDP:** $4,850. **Imports** (1994): $10.6 bil; partners: U.S. 36%, EU 18%. **Exports** (1994): $8.3 bil; partners: U.S. 39%, EU 26%. **Tourism** (1992): $705 mil. **National budget** (1995 est.): $21 bil. **International reserves less gold** (Apr. 1996): $7.6 bil. **Gold:** 279,000 oz t. **Consumer prices** (change in 1995): 21.0%.

**Transport: Railroads: Route length:** 2,007 mi. **Motor vehicles:** in use: 854,000 passenger cars, 431,000 comm. vehicles. **Civil aviation:** 3.3 bil passenger-mi.; 70 airports with scheduled flights. **Chief ports:** Buenaventura, Santa Marta, Barranquilla, Cartagena.

**Communications: Television sets:** 1 per 6.3 persons. **Radios:** 1 per 6.4 person. **Telephones:** 1 per 8.9 persons. **Daily newspaper circ.:** 55 per 1,000 pop.

**Health: Life expectancy at birth** (1996): 70 male; 76 female. **Births** (per 1,000 pop.): 21. **Deaths** (per 1,000 pop.): 5. **Natural increase:** 1.7%. **Hospital beds:** 1 per 693 persons. **Physicians:** 1 per 1,078 persons. **Infant mortality** (per 1,000 live births 1996): 26.

**Education: Literacy** (1992): 91%. Free and compulsory for 5 years between ages 6-14.

**Major International Organizations:** UN (World Bank, FAO, IMF, WHO, WTO), OAS.

**Embassy:** 2118 Leroy Pl. NW 20008; 387-8338.

Spain subdued the local Indian kingdoms (Funza, Tunja) by the 1530s and ruled Colombia and neighboring areas as New Granada for 300 years. Independence was won by 1819. Venezuela and Ecuador broke away in 1829-30, and Panama withdrew in 1903.

One of the Latin American democracies, Colombia is plagued by rural and urban violence, though scaled down from "La Violencia" of 1948-58, which claimed 200,000 lives. Attempts at land and social reform and progress in industrialization have not succeeded in reducing massive social problems.

The government's increased activity against local drug traffickers sparked a series of retaliation killings. On Aug. 18, 1989, Luis Carlos Galán, the ruling party's presidential hopeful for the 1990 election, was assassinated. In 1990, 2 other presidential candidates were assassinated, as drug traffickers carried on a campaign of intimidation. Pablo Escobar, head of the Medellín drug cartel, escaped from prison in July 1992, allegedly with aid from military and prison officials. He was killed by government troops Dec. 1, 1993. Charges that Ernesto Samper Pizano's 1994 campaign received money from the Cali drug cartel engulfed his administration in scandal, although the legislature voted, June 12, 1996, not to impeach him.

# Comoros

## Federal Islamic Republic of the Comoros

## Jumhuriyat al Qumur al Itthadiyah al Islamiyah

**People: Population:** 569,237. **Pop. density:** 792 per sq. mi. **Urban:** 29%. **Ethnic groups:** Arab, African, Malay, Madagascar. **Principal languages:** Arabic, French, Comorian (all official). **Religions:** Sunni Muslim 86%, Roman Catholic 14%.

**Geography: Area:** 719 sq. mi. **Location:** 3 islands (Grande Comore, Anjouan, and Moheli) in the Mozambique Channel between NW Madagascar and SE Africa. **Neighbors:** Nearest are Mozambique on W, Madagascar on E. **Topography:** The islands are of volcanic origin, with an active volcano on Grande Comore. **Capital:** Moroni (1992 met. est.): 30,000.

**Government: Type:** In transition. **Head of state:** Pres. Mohamed Taki Abdul-Karim; in office: Mar. 1996. **Local divisions:** Each of the 3 main islands is a prefecture.

**Economy: Industries:** Perfume, textiles. **Chief crops:** Vanilla, copra, perfume plants, fruits. **Arable land:** 35%. **Electricity prod.** (1993): 17 mil kWh. **Labor force:** 80% agric.

**Finance: Monetary unit:** Franc (June 1996: 386 = $1 US). **Gross domestic product** (1994): $370 mil.* **Per capita GDP:** $700. **Imports** (1993): $41 mil; partners: France 34%. **Exports** (1993): $14 mil; partners: U.S. 44%, France 40%. **National budget** (1992): $92 mil.

**Chief ports:** Fomboni, Moroni, Mutsamudo.

**Communications: Radios:** 1 per 8.6 persons. **Telephones:** 1 per 117 persons.

**Health: Life expectancy at birth** (1996): 56 male; 61 female. **Births** (per 1,000 pop.): 46. **Deaths** (per 1,000 pop.): 10. **Natural increase:** 3.6%. **Infant mortality** (per 1,000 live births 1996): 75.

**Education: Literacy** (1992): 57%. Compulsory: ages 7-16.

**Major International Organizations:** UN (IMF, FAO, WHO, World Bank), OAU, Arab League.

**Embassy:** 336 E. 45th St., 2d Fl., New York, NY 10017; (212) 972-8010.

The islands were controlled by Muslim sultans until the French acquired them 1841-1909. They became a French overseas territory in 1947. A 1974 referendum favored independence, with only the Christian island of Mayotte preferring association with France. The French National Assembly decided to allow each of the islands to decide its own fate. The Comore Chamber of Deputies declared independence July 6, 1975, with Ahmed Abdallah as president. In a referendum in 1976, Mayotte voted to remain French.

A leftist regime that seized power from Abdallah in 1975 was deposed in a pro-French 1978 coup in which he regained the presidency. In Nov. 1989, Pres. Abdallah was assassinated; soon after, a multiparty system was instituted. A Sept. 1995 military coup, assisted by French mercenaries, ousted Pres. Said Mohamed Djohar. French troops invaded, Oct. 4, and forced the surrender of coup leaders. Djohar returned from exile in Jan. 1996, and in Mar. a new presidential election was held.

# Congo

## Republic of the Congo

## République Populaire du Congo

**People: Population:** 2,527,841. **Pop. density:** 19 per sq. mi. **Urban:** 58%. **Ethnic groups:** Kongo 48%, Sangha 20%, Teke 17%, M'Bochi 12%. **Principal languages:** French (official); Lingala, Kikongo, other African languages. **Religions:** Christian 50% (mostly Roman Catholic), indigenous beliefs 48%, Muslim 2%.

**Geography: Area:** 132,047 sq. mi. **Location:** In W central Africa. **Neighbors:** Gabon and Cameroon on W, Central African Republic on N, Zaire on E, Angola on SW. **Topography:** Much of the Congo is covered by thick forests. A coastal plain leads to the fertile Niari Valley. The center is a plateau; the Congo R. basin consists of flood plains in the lower and savanna in the upper portion. **Capital:** Brazzaville. **Cities** (1995 est.): Brazzaville 938,000; Pointe-Noire 576,000; Loubomo 84,000.

**Government: Type:** Republic. **Head of state:** Pres. Pascal Lissouba; b Nov. 15, 1931; in office: Aug. 20, 1992. **Head of government:** Prime Min. Jacques Yhombi-Opango; b 1938; in office: June 23, 1993. **Local divisions:** 9 regions and 1 commune. **Defense:** 3.8% of GDP (1993). **Active troop strength:** 10,000.

**Economy: Chief crops:** Cassava, palm kernels, sugar, cocoa, coffee. **Minerals:** Oil, potash, lead, copper, zinc. **Crude oil reserves** (1995): 830 mil bbls. **Arable land:** 2%. **Fish catch** (1993): 42,000 metric tons. **Electricity prod.** (1993): 400 mil kWh. **Labor force:** 75% agric.

**Finance: Monetary unit:** CFA Franc (June 1996: 515 = $1 US). **Gross domestic product** (1993): $6.7 bil.* **Per capita GDP:** $2,820. **Imports** (1991): $427 mil; partners: France 48%. **Exports** (1993): $1.1 bln.; partners: U.S. 43%, France 16%. **Tourism** (1993): $2 mil. **National budget** (1990): $952 mil. **International reserves less gold** (Mar. 1996): $57.1 mil. **Gold:** 11,000 oz t.

**Transport: Railroads: Length:** 494 mi. **Motor vehicles:** in use: 29,000 passenger cars, 17,000 comm. vehicles. **Chief ports:** Pointe-Noire, Brazzaville.

**Communications: Television sets:** 1 per 326 persons. **Radios:** 1 per 11 persons. **Telephones:** 1 per 132 persons.

**Health: Life expectancy at birth** (1996): 44 male; 47 female. **Births** (per 1,000 pop.): 39. **Deaths** (per 1,000 pop.): 17. **Natural increase:** 2.2%. **Hospital beds:** 1 per 456 persons. **Physicians:** 1 per 3,873 persons. **Infant mortality** (per 1,000 live births 1996): 108.

**Education: Literacy** (1993): 75%. Compulsory: ages 6-16.

**Major International Organizations:** UN (FAO, IMF, WTO, World Bank, WHO), OAU.

**Embassy:** 4891 Colorado Ave. NW 20011; 726-0825.

The Loango Kingdom flourished in the 15th century, as did the Anzico Kingdom of the Batekes; by the late 17th century they had become weakened. France established control by 1885. Independence came Aug. 15, 1960.

After a 1963 coup sparked by trade unions, the country adopted a Marxist-Leninist stance, with the USSR and China vying for influence. France remained a dominant trade partner and source of technical assistance, however, and French-owned private enterprise retained a major economic role.

In 1990, Marxism was renounced and opposition parties legalized. In 1991 the country's name was changed to Republic of the Congo, and a new constitution was approved. A democratically elected government came into office in 1992; one of its key problems was a resurgence of ethnic and regional hostilities, often erupting into violence.

# Costa Rica

## Republic of Costa Rica

## República de Costa Rica

**People: Population:** 3,463,083. **Age distrib.** (%): <15: 34; 65+: 5. **Pop. density:** 176 per sq. mi. **Urban:** 44%. **Ethnic groups:** White (with mestizo minority) 96%. **Principal language:** Spanish (official). **Religions:** Roman Catholic 95%.

**Geography: Area:** 19,730 sq. mi. **Location:** In Central America. **Neighbors:** Nicaragua on N, Panama on S. **Topography:** Lowlands by the Caribbean are tropical. The interior plateau, with an altitude of about 4,000 ft., is temperate. **Capital:** San José (1993 met. est.): 922,000.

**Government: Type:** Republic. **Head of state:** Pres. José María Figueres; b Dec. 24, 1954; in office: May 8, 1994. **Local divisions:** 7 provinces. **Defense:** 0.4% of GNP (1991). **Active troop strength:** 7,500.

**Economy: Industries:** Food processing, textiles, construction materials, fertilizer, plastics. **Chief crops:** Coffee (chief export), bananas, rice, potatoes. **Minerals:** Gold, limestone. **Other resources:** Fish, forests. **Arable land:** 6%. **Livestock** (1993): cattle: 2.1 mil. **Fish catch** (1992): 18,000 metric tons. **Electricity prod.** (1993): 4.1 bil kWh. **Labor force:** 27% agric.; 35% ind. & commerce; 33% serv. and government.

**Finance: Monetary unit:** Colon (June 1996: 207 = $1 US). **Gross domestic product** (1994): $16.9 bil.* **Per capita GDP:** $5,050. **Imports** (1993): $2.9 bil; partners: U.S. 43%, Japan 8%. **Exports** (1993): $2.1 bil; partners: U.S. 42%, Germany 9%. **Tourism** (1993): $577 mil. **National budget** (1991 est.): $1.34 bil. **International reserves less gold** (May 1996): $1.1 bil. **Gold:** 2,000 oz t. **Consumer prices** (change in 1995): 23.2%.

**Transport: Motor vehicles:** in use: 220,000 passenger cars, 115,000 comm. vehicles. **Civil aviation:** 885 milpassenger-mi.; 13 airports with scheduled flights. **Chief ports:** Limon, Puntarenas, Golfito.

**Communications: Television sets:** 1 per 9.6 persons. **Radios:** 1 per 4.3 persons. **Telephones:** 1 per 8.8 persons. **Daily newspaper circ.:** 103 per 1,000 pop.

**Health: Life expectancy at birth** (1996): 73 male; 78 female. **Births** (per 1,000 pop.): 24. **Deaths** (per 1,000 pop.): 4. **Natural increase:** 2.0%. **Hospital beds:** 1 per 528 persons. **Physicians:** 1 per 962 persons. **Infant mortality** (per 1,000 live births 1996): 14.

**Education: Literacy** (1993): 95%. Free and compulsory: ages 6-15.attendance 90%.

**Major International Organizations:** UN (FAO, WTO, World Bank, ILO, IMF, WHO), OAS.

**Embassy:** 2114 S St. NW 20008; 234-2945.

Guaymi Indians inhabited the area when Spaniards arrived, 1502. Independence came in 1821. Costa Rica seceded from the Central American Federation in 1838. Since the civil war of 1948-49, there has been little violent social conflict, and free political institutions have been preserved. During 1993 there was an unusual wave of kidnappings and hostage-taking, some of it related to the international cocaine trade.

Costa Rica, though still a largely agricultural country, has achieved a relatively high standard of living, and land ownership is widespread. Tourism is growing rapidly.

# Côte d'Ivoire

## Republic of Ivory Coast

## République de Côte d'Ivoire

**People: Population:** 14,762,445. **Age distrib.** (%): <15: 47; 65+: 2. **Pop. density:** 119 per sq. mi. **Urban:** 46%. **Ethnic groups:** Baoule 23%, Bete 18%, Senoufou 15%, Malinke 11%, Agni, foreign Africans. **Principal languages:** French (official), Dioula. **Religions:** Muslim 60%, indigenous beliefs 25%, Christian 12%.

**Geography: Area:** 124,504 sq. mi. **Location:** On S coast of W Africa. **Neighbors:** Liberia and Guinea on W; Mali, Burkina Faso on N; Ghana on E. **Topography:** Forests cover the W half of the country, and range from a coastal strip to halfway to the N on the E. A sparse inland plain leads to low mountains in NW. **Capital:** Yamoussoukro (official); Abidjan (de facto). **Cities** (1995 est.): Abidjan 2.8 mil.

**Government: Type:** Republic. **Head of state:** Henri Konan Bédié; b 1934; in office: Dec. 7, 1993. **Head of government:** Prime Min. Daniel Kablan Duncan; in office: Dec. 1993. **Local divisions:** 50 departments. **Defense:** 1.4% of GDP (1993). **Active troop strength:** 13,900 est.

**Economy: Industries:** Food processing, vehicles, textiles. **Chief crops:** Coffee, cocoa. **Minerals:** Oil, diamonds, manganese. **Other resources:** Timber, rubber, palm-kernel oil. **Arable land:** 9%. **Livestock** (1994): goats: 976,000; sheep: 1.3 mil; cattle: 1.2 mil.**Fish catch** (1993): 70,000 metric tons. **Electricity prod.** (1993): 1.8 bil kWh. **Labor force:** 85% agric. & forestry.

**Finance: Monetary unit:** CFA Franc (June 1996: 515 = $1 US). **Gross domestic product** (1994): $20.5 bil.* **Per capita GDP:** $1,430. **Imports** (1993): $1.6 bil; partners: France 34%, Nigeria 19%, Japan 4%. **Exports** (1993): $2.7 bil; partners: France 15%, Neth. 12%, Germany 6%. **Tourism** (1993): $64 mil.**National budget** (1993): $3.4 bil. **International reserves less gold** (Dec. 1995): $529.5 mil.**Gold:** 45,000 oz t. **Consumer prices** (changed in 1995): 14.2%.

**Transport: Railroads: Route length:** 410 mi. **Motor vehicles:** in use: 175,000 passenger cars, 95,000 comm. vehicles. **Chief ports:** Abidjan, San Pédro.

**Communications: Television sets:** 1 per 18 persons. **Radios:** 1 per 8.9 persons. **Telephones:** 1 per 140 persons.

**Health: Life expectancy at birth** (1996): 46 male; 47 female. **Births** (per 1,000 pop.): 42. **Deaths** (per 1,000 pop.): 16. **Natural increase:** 2.7%. **Hospital beds:** 1 per 1,698 persons. **Physicians:** 1 per 11,745 persons. **Infant mortality** (per 1,000 live births 1996): 82.

**Education: Literacy** (1995): 40%. Free and compulsory: ages 7-13.

**Major International Organizations:** UN and all of its specialized agencies, OAU.

**Embassy:** 2424 Massachusetts Ave. NW 20008; 797-0300.

A French protectorate from 1842, Côte d'Ivoire became independent in 1960. It is the most prosperous of the tropical African nations, as a result of diversification of agriculture for export, close ties to France, and encouragement of foreign investment. About 20% of the population are workers from neighboring countries. Côte d'Ivoire officially changed its name from Ivory Coast in Oct. 1985.

Students and workers protested, Feb. 1990, demanding the ouster of longtime Pres. Félix Houphouët-Boigny and multiparty democracy. Côte d'Ivoire held its first multiparty presidential election Oct. 1990, and Houphouët-Boigny retained his office. He died Dec. 7, 1993. The National Assembly named a successor, Henri Konan Bédié, who won the Oct. 22, 1995 election.

# Croatia

## Republic of Croatia

## Republika Hrvatska

**People: Population:** 5,004,112. **Pop. density:** 229 per sq. mi. **Urban:** 54%. **Ethnic groups:** Croat 78%, Serb 12%. **Principal language:** Croatian (official) 96%. **Religions:** Roman Catholic 77%, Orthodox 11%.

**Geography: Area:** 21,889 sq. mi. **Location:** On the Balkan Peninsula in SE Europe. **Neighbors:** Slovenia, Hungary on N; Bosnia and Herzegovina, Yugoslavia on E. **Topography:** Flat plains in NE; highlands, low mtns. along Adriatic coasts. **Capital:** Zagreb (1991): 707,000.

**Government: Type:** Parliamentary democracy. **Head of state:** Pres. Franjo Tudjman; b May 14, 1922; in office: May 30, 1990. **Head of government:** Prime Min. Zlatko Matesa; b June 17, 1949; in office: Nov. 4, 1995. **Local divisions:** 21 counties. **Defense: Active troop strength:** 105,000 est.

**Economy: Industries:** Chemicals, plastics, machine tools, aluminum, steel, paper. **Chief crops:** Olives, wheat, corn, fruits. **Minerals:** Oil, bauxite, iron, coal. **Arable land:** 32%. **Electricity prod.** (1992): 11.5 bil kWh.

**Finance: Monetary unit:** Kuna (June 1996: 5.41 = $1 US). **Gross domestic product** (1994 est.): $12.4 bil.* **Per capita GDP:** $2,640. **Imports** (1993): $4.7 bil. **Exports** (1993): 3.9 bil. **International reserves less gold** (Mar. 1996): 2.0 bil.

**Transport: Motor vehicles:** in use: 646,000 passenger cars, 39,000 comm. vehicles. **Chief ports:** Rijeka, Split.

**Communications: Television sets:** 1 per 4.6 persons. **Radios:** 1 per 4.4 persons. **Telephones:** 1 per 4.7 persons. **Daily newspaper circ.:** 150 per 1,000 pop.

**Health: Life expectancy at birth** (1996): 69 male; 77 female. **Births** (per 1,000 pop.): 10. **Deaths** (per 1,000 pop.): 11. **Natural increase:** –0.1%. **Hospital beds:** 1 per 168 persons. **Physicians:** 1 per 515 persons. **Infant mortality** (per 1,000 live births 1996): 10.

**Education: Literacy** (1993): 97%. Free and compulsory: ages 6-15.

**Major International Organizations:** UN (IMF, ILO, FAO, World Bank, WHO).

**Embassy:** 2343 Massachusetts Ave. NW 20008; 588-5899.

From the 7th century the area was inhabited by Croats, a south Slavic people. It was formed into a kingdom under Tomislav in 924, and joined with Hungary in 1102. The Croats became westernized and separated from Slavs under Austro-Hungarian influence. The Croats retained autonomy under the Hungarian crown. Slavonia was taken by Turks in the 16th century; the northern part was restored by the Treaty of Karlowitz in 1699. Croatia helped Austria put down the Hungarian revolution 1848-49 and as a result was set up with Slavonia as the separate Austrian crownland of Croatia and Slavonia, which was reunited to Hungary as part of *Ausgleich* in 1867. It united with other Yugoslav areas to proclaim the kingdom of Serbs, Croats, and Slovenes in 1918. At the reorganization of Yugoslavia in 1929, Croatia and Slavonia became Savska county, which in 1939 was united with Primorje county to form the county of Croatia. A nominally independent state between 1941 and 1945, it became a constituent republic in the 1946 constitution.

On June 25, 1991, Croatia declared independence from Yugoslavia. Fighting began between ethnic Serbs and Croats, with the former gaining control of about 30% of Croatian territory. A cease-fire was declared in Jan. 1992, but new hostilities broke out in 1993. A cease-fire with Serb rebels forming a self-declared republic of Krajina was agreed to Mar. 30, 1994. Croatian government troops recaptured most of the Serb-held territory Aug. 1995. Pres. Franjo Tudjman signed a peace accord with leaders of Bosnia and Serbia in Paris, Dec. 14.

# Cuba

## Republic of Cuba

## República de Cuba

**People: Population:** 10,951,334. **Age distrib.** (%): <15: 22; 65+: 9. **Pop. density:** 256 per sq. mi. **Urban:** 74%. **Ethnic groups:** Mulatto 51%, white 37%, black 11%. **Principal language:** Spanish (official). **Religion:** Roman Catholic 85% prior to Castro.

**Geography: Area:** 42,804 sq. mi. **Location:** Westernmost of West Indies. **Neighbors:** Bahamas and U.S. to N, Mexico to W, Jamaica to S, Haiti to E. **Topography:** The coastline is about 2,500 miles. The N coast is steep and rocky, the S coast low and marshy. Low hills and fertile valleys cover more than half the country. Sierra Maestra, in the E is the highest of 3 mountain ranges. **Capital:** Havana. **Cities** (1994 est.): Havana 2.2 mil (1995 est.); Santiago de Cuba 440,000; Camaguey 294,000.

**Government: Type:** Communist state. **Head of state:** Pres. Fidel Castro Ruz; b Aug. 13, 1926; in office: Dec. 3, 1976 (formerly prime min. since Feb. 16, 1959). **Local divisions:** 14 provinces, 1 special municipality. **Defense:** 4% of Gross Social Product (1994). **Active troop strength:** 105,000.

**Economy: Industries:** Oil, food and tobacco processing, sugar. **Chief crops:** Sugar (major' exporter), tobacco, rice, coffee, fruit. **Minerals:** Cobalt, nickel, iron, copper, manganese, salt. **Other resources:** Forests. **Arable land:** 23%. **Livestock** (1994): cattle: 4.5 mil; pigs: 1.5 mil.**Fish catch** (1993): 93,000 metric tons. **Electricity prod.** (1993): 12 bil kWh. **Labor force:** 20% agric.; 33% ind. & commerce; 30% services & govt.

**Finance: Monetary unit:** Peso (June 1996: 1.00 = $1 US). **Gross domestic product** (1994 est.): $14 bil.* **Per capita GDP:** $1,260. **Imports** (1994): $1.7 bil; partners: Spain 17%, Mexico 10%. **Exports** (1994): $1.6 bil; partners: Russia 15%, Canada 9%. **Tourism** (1993): $216 mil.**National budget** (1994 est.): $12.5 bil.

**Transport: Railroads: Length:** 3,033 mi. **Motor vehicles:** in use: 241,000 passenger cars, 208,000 comm. vehicles. **Civil aviation:** 1.9 bil passenger-mi.; 14 airports with scheduled flights. **Chief ports:** Havana, Matanzas, Cienfuegos, Santiago de Cuba.

**Communications: Television sets:** 1 per 4.4 persons. **Radios:** 1 per 3.0 persons. **Telephones:** 1 per 31 persons. **Daily newspaper circ.:** 122 per 1,000 pop.

**Health: Life expectancy at birth** (1996): 73 male; 78 female. **Births** (per 1,000 pop.): 13. **Deaths** (per 1,000 pop.): 7. **Natural increase:** 0.6%. **Hospital beds:** 1 per 134 persons. **Physicians:** 1 per 231 persons. **Infant mortality** (per 1,000 live births 1996): 9.

**Education: Literacy** (1993): 96%. Free and compulsory: ages 6-11. 97% attend primary school.

**Major International Organizations:** UN (WTO, FAO, WHO).

Some 50,000 Indians lived in Cuba when it was reached by Columbus in 1492. Its name derives from the Indian Cubanacan. Except for British occupation of Havana, 1762-63, Cuba remained Spanish until 1898. A slave-based sugar plantation economy developed from the 18th century, aided by early mechanization of milling. Sugar remains the chief product and chief export despite government attempts to diversify.

A ten-year uprising ended in 1878 with guarantees of rights by Spain, which Spain failed to carry out. A full-scale movement under Jose Marti began Feb. 24, 1895.

The U.S. declared war on Spain in Apr. 1898, after the sinking of the USS *Maine* in Havana harbor, and defeated it in the Spanish-American War. Spain gave up all claims to Cuba. U.S. troops withdrew in 1902, but under 1903 and 1934 agreements, the U.S. leases a site at Guantánamo Bay in the SE as a naval base. U.S. and other foreign investments acquired a dominant role in the economy. In 1952, former Pres. Fulgencio Batista seized control and established a dictatorship, which grew increasingly harsh and corrupt. Fidel Castro assembled a rebel band in 1956; guerrilla fighting intensified in 1958. Batista fled Jan. 1, 1959, and in the resulting political vacuum Castro took power, becoming premier Feb. 16.

The government began a program of sweeping economic and social changes, without restoring promised liberties. Opponents were imprisoned, and some were executed. Some 700,000 Cubans emigrated in the first years after the Castro takeover, mostly to the U.S.

Cattle and tobacco lands were nationalized, while a system of cooperatives was instituted. By 1960 all banks and industrial companies had been nationalized, including over $1 billion worth of U.S.-owned properties, mostly without compensation.

Poor sugar crops resulted in collectivization of farms, stringent labor controls, and rationing, despite continued aid from the USSR and other Communist countries. The U.S. imposed an export embargo in 1962, severely damaging the economy.

In 1961, some 1,400 Cubans, trained and backed by the U.S. Central Intelligence Agency, unsuccessfully tried to invade and overthrow the regime. In the fall of 1962, the U.S. learned that the USSR had brought nuclear missiles to Cuba. After an Oct. 22 warning from Pres. John F. Kennedy, the missiles were removed.

In 1977, Cuba and the U.S. signed agreements to exchange diplomats, without restoring full ties, and to regulate offshore fishing. In 1978, and again in 1980, the U.S. agreed to accept political prisoners released by Cuba, some of whom were criminals and mental patients. A 1987 agreement provided for 20,000 Cubans to emigrate to the U.S. each year; Cuba agreed to take back some 2,500 jailed in the U.S. since 1980.

In 1975-78, Cuba sent troops to aid one faction in the Angola civil war; the last Cuban troops were withdrawn by May 1991. Cuba's involvement in Central America, Africa, and the Caribbean contributed to poor relations with the U.S.

Cuba's economy, formerly propped up by preferential trading status within the Communist bloc, was severely shaken by its collapse in the late 1980s. Stiffer trading sanctions enacted by the U.S. in 1992 made things worse. Antigovernment demonstrations in Aug. 1994 prompted Castro to loosen emigration restrictions. A new U.S.-Cuba emigration agreement in Sept. ended the exodus of "boat people" after more than 30,000 had left Cuba. In another policy shift, the U.S. announced May 2, 1995, that it would admit 20,000 Cuban refugees held at the Guantánamo base but would forcibly return further boat people to Cuba.

The U.S. imposed additional sanctions after Cuba, Feb. 24, 1996, shot down 2 aircraft operated by an anti-Castro exile group based in Miami.

# Cyprus

## Republic of Cyprus

## Kypriaki Dimokratia (Greek)

## Kibris Çumhuriyeti (Turkish)

*(†Figures do not include Turkish-held area—Turkish Republic of Northern Cyprus)*

**People: Population:** 744,609. **Age distrib.** (%): <15: 25; 65+: 11. **Pop. density:** 208 per sq. mi. **Urban:** 53%. **Ethnic groups:** Greeks 78%, Turks 18%. **Principal languages:** Greek, Turkish (both official), English. **Religions:** Greek Orthodox 78%, Muslim 18%.

**Geography: Area:** 3,572 sq. mi. **Location:** In eastern Mediterranean Sea, off Turkish coast. **Neighbors:** Nearest are Turkey on N, Syria and Lebanon on E. **Topography:** Two mountain ranges run E-W, separated by a wide, fertile plain. **Capital:** Nicosia (1993 met. est.): 177,000†.

**Government: Type:** Republic. **Head of state:** Pres. Glafcos Clerides; b Apr. 24, 1919; in office: Mar. 1, 1993. **Local divisions:** 6 districts. **Defense:** 5.6% of GDP (1995). **Active troop strength†:** 10,000.

**Economy: Industries:** Food, beverages, textiles. **Chief crops:** Barley, grapes, vegetables, citrus fruits, potatoes, olives. **Minerals:** Copper, pyrites, asbestos. **Arable land:** 40%. **Electricity prod.** (1993): 2.3 bln. kWh. **Labor force†:** 57% serv., 29% ind., 14% agric.

**Finance: Monetary unit:** Pound (June 1996: 1.00 = $2.13 US). **Gross domestic product†** (1994): $7.3 bil.* **Per capita GDP†:** $12,500. **Imports** (1993): $2.6 bil; partners: UK 13%, Italy 10%, Japan 9%. **Exports** (1993): $868 mil; partners: UK 18%, Lebanon 14%, Greece 9%. **Tourism** (1992): $1.5 bil. **National budget†** (1995): $2.4 bil. **International reserves less gold** (May 1996): $1.1 bil. **Gold:** 460,000 oz t. **Consumer prices** (change in 1995): 2.6%.

**Transport: Motor vehicles†:** in use: 203,000 passenger cars, 90,000 comm. vehicles. **Civil aviation†:** 1.9 bil passenger-mi.; 2 airports. **Chief ports:** Famagusta, Limassol.

**Communications: Television sets†:** 1 per 2.7 persons. **Telephones†:** 1 per 2.5 persons. **Daily newspaper circ.†:** 135 per 1,000 pop.

**Health: Life expectancy at birth** (1996): 74 male; 79 female. **Births** (per 1,000 pop.): 15. **Deaths** (per 1,000 pop.): 8. **Natural increase:** 0.8%. **Hospital beds†:** 1 per 176 persons. **Physicians†:** 1 per 428 persons. **Infant mortality** (per 1,000 live births 1996): 8.

**Education: Literacy** (1994): 95%. Free and compulsory: ages 5½-15.

**Major International Organizations:** UN (IMF, FAO, WTO, World Bank, WHO), the Commonwealth.

**Embassy:** 2211 R St. NW 20008; 462-5772.

Agitation for enosis (union) with Greece increased after World War II, with the Turkish minority opposed, and broke into violence in 1955-56. In 1959, Britain, Greece, Turkey, and Cypriot leaders approved a plan for an independent republic, with constitutional guarantees for the Turkish minority and permanent division of offices on an ethnic basis. Greek and Turkish Communal Chambers dealt with religion, education, and other matters.

Archbishop Makarios III, formerly the leader of the enosis movement, was elected president, and full independence became final Aug. 16, 1960. Further communal strife led the United Nations to send a peacekeeping force in 1964; its mandate has been repeatedly renewed.

The Cypriot National Guard, led by officers from the army of Greece, seized the government July 15, 1974. On July 20, Turkey invaded the island; Greece mobilized its forces but did not intervene. A cease-fire was arranged but collapsed. By Aug. 16, Turkish forces had occupied the NE 40% of the island, despite the presence of UN peacekeeping forces.

Turkish Cypriots voted overwhelmingly, June 8, 1975, to form a separate Turkish Cypriot federated state. A president and assembly were elected in 1976. Some 200,000 Greeks have been expelled from the Turkish-controlled area, replaced by thousands of Turks, some from the mainland.

### Turkish Republic of Northern Cyprus

A declaration of independence was announced by Turkish-Cypriot leader Rauf Denktash, Nov. 15, 1983. The state is not internationally recognized, although it does have trade relations with some countries. TRNC contains 1,295 sq mi., pop. (1995 est.): 134,000, 99% Turkish.

## Czech Republic

### Ceská Republika

*(Figures prior to 1993 are for Czechoslovakia)*

**People: Population:** 10,321,120. **Age distrib.** (%): <15: 19; 65+: 13. **Pop. density:** 339 per sq. mi. **Urban:** 75%. **Ethnic groups:** Czech 94%, Slovak 3%. **Principal languages:** Czech (official), Slovak. **Religions:** Atheist 39.8%, Roman Catholic 39.2%, Protestant 4.6%.

**Geography: Area:** 30,450 sq. mi. **Location:** In E central Europe. **Neighbors:** Poland on N, Germany on N and W, Austria on S, Slovakia on E and SE. **Topography:** Bohemia, in W, is a plateau surrounded by mountains; Moravia is hilly. **Capital:** Prague. **Cities** (1994 est.): Prague 1.2 mil (1995 est.); Brno 390,000; Ostrava 326,000.

**Government: Type:** Republic. **Head of state:** Vaclav Havel; b Oct. 5, 1936; in office: Feb. 15, 1993. **Head of government:** Prime Min. Vaclav Klaus; b June 19, 1941; in office: July 1993. **Local divisions:** 8 regions. **Defense:** 2.2% of GDP (1992). **Active troop strength:** 86,400.

**Economy: Industries:** Machinery, oil products, iron and steel, glass, motor vehicles, coal. **Chief crops:** Wheat, sugar beets, potatoes, rye, corn, barley, hops. **Minerals:** Coal, kaolin. **Livestock:** (1994): cattle: 2.1 mil; pigs: 4.1 mil. **Electricity prod.** (1993): 56.3 bil kWh. **Labor force:** 38% ind.; 8% agric.

**Finance: Monetary unit:** Koruna (June 1996: 27.50 = $1 US). **Gross domestic product** (1994): $76.5 bil.* **Per capita GDP:** $7,350. **Imports** (1994): $13.3 bil; partners: Germany 24%, Slovakia 16%, Russia 10%. **Exports** (1994): $13.4 bil; partners: Germany 29%, Slovakia 16%, Austria 8%. **Tourism** (1992): $1.3 bil. **National budget** (1994 est.): $13.6 bil. **International reserves less gold** (Apr. 1996): $12.6 bil. **Gold:** 1.99 mil oz t. **Consumer prices** (change in 1995): 9.1%.

**Transport: Railroads: Length:** 5,866 mi. **Motor vehicles:** in use: 2.7 mil passenger cars, 355,000 comm. vehicles. **Civil aviation:** 1.6 bil passenger-mi.; 4 airports with scheduled flights.

**Communications: Television sets:** 1 per 3.3 persons. **Radios:** 1 per 3.8 persons. **Telephones:** 1 per 5.2 persons. **Daily newspaper circ.:** 582 per 1,000 pop.

**Health: Life expectancy at birth** (1996): 70 male; 78 female. **Births** (per 1,000 pop.): 10. **Deaths** (per 1,000 pop.): 11. **Natural increase:** 0. **Hospital beds:** 1 per 79 persons. **Physicians:** 1 per 272 persons. **Infant mortality** (per 1,000 live births 1996): 8.

**Education: Literacy** (1994): 100%. Compulsory: ages 6-16.

**Major International Organizations:** UN (WTO, FAO, World Bank, IMF, WHO), OECD.

**Embassy:** 3900 Spring of Freedom St. NW 20008; 363-6315.

Bohemia and Moravia were part of the Great Moravian Empire in the 9th century and later became part of the Holy Roman Empire. Under the kings of Bohemia, Prague in the 14th century was the cultural center of Central Europe. Bohemia and Hungary became part of Austria-Hungary.

In 1914-18 Thomas G. Masaryk and Eduard Benes formed a provisional government with the support of Slovak leaders including Milan Stefanik. They proclaimed the Republic of Czechoslovakia Oct. 28, 1918.

### Czechoslovakia

By 1938 Nazi Germany had worked up disaffection among German-speaking citizens in Sudetenland and demanded its cession. British Prime Min. Neville Chamberlain, with the acquiescence of France, signed with Hitler at Munich, Sept. 30, 1938, an agreement to the cession, with a guarantee of peace by Hitler and Mussolini. Germany occupied Sudetenland Oct. 1-2.

Hitler on Mar. 15, 1939, dissolved Czechoslovakia, made protectorates of Bohemia and Moravia, and supported the autonomy of Slovakia, proclaimed independent Mar. 14, 1939.

Soviet troops with some Czechoslovak contingents entered eastern Czechoslovakia in 1944 and reached Prague in May 1945; Benes returned as president. In May 1946 elections, the Communist Party won 38% of the votes, and Benes accepted Klement Gottwald, a Communist, as prime minister.

In Feb. 1948, the Communists seized power in advance of scheduled elections. In May 1948 a new constitution was approved. Benes refused to sign it. On May 30 the voters were offered a one-slate ballot and the Communists won full control. Benes resigned June 7 and Gottwald became president. The country was renamed the Czechoslovak Socialist Republic. A harsh Stalinist period followed, with complete and violent suppression of all opposition.

In Jan. 1968 a liberalization movement spread explosively through Czechoslovakia. Antonin Novotny, long the Stalinist ruler of the nation, was deposed as party leader and succeeded by Alexander Dubcek, a Slovak, who supported democratic reforms. On Mar. 22 Novotny resigned as president and was succeeded by Gen. Ludvik Svoboda. On Apr. 6, Prem. Joseph Lenart resigned and was succeeded by Oldrich Cernik, a reformer.

In July 1968 the USSR and 4 Warsaw Pact nations demanded an end to liberalization. On Aug. 20, the Soviet, Polish, East German, Hungarian, and Bulgarian armies invaded Czechoslovakia. Despite demonstrations and riots by students and workers, press censorship was imposed, liberal leaders were ousted from office and promises of loyalty to Soviet policies were made by some old-line Communist Party leaders.

On Apr. 17, 1969, Dubcek resigned as leader of the Communist Party and was succeeded by Gustav Husak. In Jan. 1970, Cernik was ousted. Censorship was tightened, and the Communist Party expelled a third of its members. In 1973, amnesty was offered to some of the 40,000 who fled the country after the 1968 invasion, but repressive policies continued.

More than 700 leading Czechoslovak intellectuals and former party leaders signed a human rights manifesto in 1977, called Charter 77, prompting a renewed crackdown by the regime.

The police crushed the largest antigovernment protests since 1968, when tens of thousands of demonstrators took to the streets of Prague, Nov. 17, 1989. As protesters demanded free elections, the Communist Party leadership resigned Nov. 24; millions went on strike Nov. 27.

On Dec. 10, 1989, the first cabinet in 41 years without a Communist majority took power; Vaclav Havel, playwright and human rights campaigner, was chosen president, Dec. 29. In Mar. 1990 the country was officially renamed the Czech and Slovak Federal Republic. Havel failed to win reelection July 3, 1992; his bid was blocked by a Slovak-led coalition.

Slovakia declared sovereignty, July 17. Czech and Slovak leaders agreed, July 23, on a basic plan for a peaceful division of Czechoslovakia into 2 independent states.

### Czech Republic

Czechoslovakia split into 2 separate states—the Czech Republic and Slovakia—on Jan. 1, 1993. Havel was elected president of the Czech Republic on Jan. 26.

## Denmark

### Kingdom of Denmark

### Kongeriget Danmark

**People: Population:** 5,249,632. **Age distrib.** (%): <15: 17; 65+: 15. **Pop. density:** 316 per sq. mi. **Urban:** 85%. **Ethnic groups:** Scandinavian, Eskimo. **Principal languages:** Danish (official), Faroese. **Religions:** Evangelical Lutheran 91%.

**Geography: Area:** 16,639 sq. mi. **Location:** In N Europe, separating the North and Baltic seas. **Neighbors:** Germany on S, Norway on NW, Sweden on NE. **Topography:** Denmark consists of the Jutland Peninsula and about 500 islands, 100 inhabited. The land is flat or gently rolling and is almost all in productive use. **Capital:** Copenhagen (1994 met. est.): 1.4 mil.

**Government: Type:** Constitutional monarchy. **Head of state:** Queen Margrethe II; b Apr. 16, 1940; in office: Jan. 14, 1972. **Head of government:** Prime Min. Poul Nyrup Rasmussen; b June 15, 1943; in office: Jan. 25, 1993. **Local divisions:** 14 counties and 1 city (Copenhagen). **Defense:** 2% of GDP (1992). **Active troop strength:** 33,100.

**Economy: Industries:** Food processing, machinery, textiles, furniture, electronics. **Chief crops:** Grains, potatoes. **Minerals:** Oil, gas, salt. **Crude oil reserves** (1995): 736 mil bbls. **Arable land:** 61%. **Livestock** (1994): cattle: 2.1 mil; pigs: 4.1 mil. **Fish catch** (1993): 1.5 mil metric tons. **Electricity prod.** (1993): 32 bil kWh. **Labor force:** 67% serv. & govt.; 20% manuf. & mining; 6% constr.

**Finance: Monetary unit:** Krone (June 1996: 5.87 = $1 US). **Gross domestic product** (1994): $103 bil.* **Per capita GDP:** $19,860. **Imports** (1994): $37 bil; partners: EU 53%, Sweden 11%. **Exports** (1994): $43 bil; partners: EU 54%, Sweden 11%. **Tourism** (1993): $3.1 bil. **National budget** (1994): $64.4 bil. **International reserves less gold** (May 1996): $15.2 bil. **Gold:** 2.0 mil oz t. **Consumer prices** (change in 1995): 2.1%.

**Transport: Railroads: Length:** 1,763 mi. **Motor vehicles:** in use: 1.7 mil passenger cars, 261,000 comm. vehicles. **Civil aviation:** 2.7 bil passenger-mi.; 13 airports with scheduled flights. **Chief ports:** Copenhagen, Alborg, Arhus, Odense.

**Communications: Television sets:** 1 per 1.9 persons. **Radios:** 1 per 1.0 persons. **Telephones:** 1 per 1.7 persons. **Daily newspaper circ.:** 321 per 1,000 pop.

**Health: Life expectancy at birth** (1996): 74 male; 81 female. **Births** (per 1,000 pop.): 12. **Deaths** (per 1,000 pop.): 10. **Natural increase:** 0.2%. **Hospital beds:** 1 per 193 persons. **Physicians:** 1 per 358 persons. **Infant mortality** (per 1,000 live births 1996): 5.

**Education: Literacy** (1993): 100%. Compulsory: ages 7-16.

**Major International Organizations:** UN and all of its specialized agencies, OECD, EU, NATO.

**Embassy:** 3200 Whitehaven St. NW 20008; 234-4300.

The origin of Copenhagen dates back to ancient times, when the fishing and trading place named Havn (port) grew up on a cluster of islets, but Bishop Absalon (1128-1201) is regarded as the actual founder of the city.

Danes formed a large component of the Viking raiders in the early Middle Ages. The Danish kingdom was a major north European power until the 17th century, when it lost its land in southern Sweden. Norway was separated in 1815, and Schleswig-Holstein in 1864. Northern Schleswig was returned in 1920.

Voters ratified the Maastricht Treaty, the basic document of the European Union, in May 1993, after rejecting it in 1992.

The **Faeroe Islands** in the North Atlantic, about 300 mi. NW of the Shetlands, and 850 mi. from Denmark proper, 18 inhabited, have an area of 540 sq. mi. and pop. (1996 est.) of 44,000. They are self-governing in most matters.

### Greenland (Kalaallit Nunaat)

Greenland, a huge island between the North Atlantic and the Polar Sea, is separated from the North American continent by Davis Strait and Baffin Bay. Its total area is 840,000 sq. mi., 84% of which is ice-capped. Most of the island is a lofty plateau 9,000 to 10,000 ft. in altitude. The average thickness of the cap is 1,000 ft. The population (1996 est.) is 58,000. Under the 1953 Danish constitution the colony became an integral part of the realm with representatives in the Folketing (Danish legislature). The Danish parliament, 1978, approved home rule for Greenland, effective May 1, 1979. Accepting home rule, the islanders elected a socialist-dominated legislature, Apr. 4. With home rule, Greenlandic place names came into official use. The technically correct name for Greenland is now Kalaallit Nunaat; its capital is Nuuk, rather than Gothab. Fish is the principal export.

## Djibouti

### Republic of Djibouti

### Jumhuriyah Djibouti

**People: Population:** 427,642. **Pop. density:** 48 per sq. mi. **Urban:** 77%. **Ethnic groups:** Somali 60%, Afar 35%. **Principal languages:** French, Arabic (both official); Afar, Somali. **Religions:** Muslim 94%, Christian 6%.

**Geography: Area:** 8,950 sq. mi. **Location:** On E coast of Africa, separated from Arabian Peninsula by the strategically vital strait of Bab el-Mandeb. **Neighbors:** Ethiopia on W and SW, Eritrea on NW, Somalia on SE. **Topography:** The territory, divided into a low coastal plain, mountains behind, and an interior plateau, is arid, sandy, and desolate. The climate is generally hot and dry. **Capital:** Djibouti (1995): 383,000.

**Government: Type:** Republic. **Head of state:** Pres. Hassan Gouled Aptidon; b 1916; in office: June 24, 1977. **Head of government:** Prem. Barkat Gourad Hamadou; in office: Sept. 30, 1978. **Local divisions:** 5 districts. **Defense: Active troop strength:** 9,600 est.

**Economy: Electricity prod.** (1993): 170 mil kWh.

**Finance: Monetary unit:** Franc (June 1996: 165 = $1 US). **Gross domestic product** (1994): $500 mil.* **Per capita GDP:** $1,200. **Imports** (1994): $384 mil; partners: France, UK. **Exports** (1994): $184 mil; partners: Somalia 48%, Yemen 42%. **National budget** (1993 est.): $201 mil.

**Transport: Motor vehicles:** in use: 13,000 passenger cars, 3,000 commercial vehicles. **Chief port:** Djibouti.

**Communications: Television sets:** 1 per 34 persons. **Radios:** 1 per 16 persons. **Telephones:** 1 per 78 persons.

**Health: Life expectancy at birth** (1996): 48 male; 52 female. **Births** (per 1,000 pop.): 43. **Deaths** (per 1,000 pop.): 15. **Natural increase:** 2.7%. **Infant mortality** (per 1,000 live births 1996): 107.

**Education: Literacy** (1993): 46%.

**Major International Organizations:** UN, OAU, Arab League.

**Embassy:** 1156 15th St. NW, Suite 515, 20005; 331-0270.

France gained control of the territory in stages between 1862 and 1900.

Ethiopia and Somalia have renounced their claims to the area, but each has accused the other of trying to gain control. There were clashes between Afars (ethnically related to Ethiopians) and Issas (related to Somalis) in 1976. Immigrants from both countries continued to enter the country up to independence, which came June 27, 1977.

French aid is the mainstay of the economy, as well as assistance from Arab countries. A peace accord Dec. 1994 ended a 3-year-long uprising by Afar rebels.

## Dominica

### Commonwealth of Dominica

**People: Population:** 82,926. **Pop. density:** 286 per sq. mi. **Urban:** 61%. **Ethnic groups:** Nearly all African, some Carib. **Principal languages:** English (official), French patois. **Religions:** Roman Catholic 77%, Protestant 15%.

**Geography: Area:** 290 sq. mi. **Location:** In Eastern Caribbean, most northerly Windward I. **Neighbors:** Guadeloupe to N, Martinique to S. **Topography:** Mountainous, a central ridge running from N to S, terminating in cliffs; volcanic in origin, with numerous thermal springs; rich deep topsoil on leeward side, red tropical clay on windward coast. **Capital:** Roseau (1991 est.): 15,900.

**Government: Type:** Parliamentary democracy. **Head of state:** Pres. Crispin Anselm Sorhaindo; in office: Oct. 25, 1993. **Head of government:** Prime Min. Edison James; in office: June 14, 1995. **Local divisions:** 10 parishes.

**Economy: Industries:** Soap, tourism. **Chief crops:** Bananas, citrus fruits, mangoes, coconuts. **Minerals:** Pumice, limestone. **Other resources:** Forests. **Arable land:** 9%. **Electricity prod.** (1993): 30 mil kWh. **Labor force:** 40% agric.; 32% ind. & commerce; 28% services.

**Finance: Monetary unit:** East Caribbean Dollar (June 1996: 2.70 = $1 US). **Gross domestic product** (1994): $200 mil.* **Per capita GDP:** $2,260. **Imports** (1993): $99 mil; partners: U.S. 25%, UK. **Exports** (1993): $48 mil; partners: UK 55%. **Tourism** (1994): $35 mil. **National budget** (1991 est.): $84 mil. **Consumer prices** (change in 1994): 1.6%.

**Chief port:** Roseau.

**Communications: Television sets:** 1 per 14 persons. **Telephones:** 1 per 1.6 persons.

**Health: Life expectancy at birth** (1996): 75 male; 80 female. **Births** (per 1,000 pop.): 18. **Deaths** (per 1,000 pop.): 5. **Natural increase:** 1.3%. **Hospital beds:** 1 per 231 persons. **Physicians:** 1 per 3,130 persons. **Infant mortality** (per 1,000 live births 1996): 10.

**Education: Literacy** (1993): 90%.Free compulsory: ages 5-15.

**Major International Organizations:** UN, OAS, the Commonwealth.

A British colony since 1805, Dominica was granted self-government in 1967. Independence was achieved Nov. 3, 1978.

Hurricane David struck, Aug. 30, 1979, devastating the island and destroying the banana plantations, Dominica's economic mainstay. Coups were attempted in 1980 and 1981.

Dominica participated in the 1983 U.S.-led invasion of Grenada.

## Dominican Republic

### República Dominicana

**People: Population:** 8,088,881. **Age distrib.** (%): <15: 37; 65+: 4. **Pop. density:** 432 per sq. mi. **Urban:** 61%. **Ethnic groups:** Mixed 73%, white 16%, black 11%. **Principal language:** Spanish (official). **Religions:** Roman Catholic 95%.

**Geography: Area:** 18,704 sq. mi. **Location:** In West Indies, sharing I. of Hispaniola with Haiti. **Neighbors:** Haiti on W. **Topography:** The Cordillera Central range crosses the center of the country, rising to over 10,000 ft., highest in the Caribbean. The Cibao Valley to the N is major agricultural area. **Capital:** Santo Domingo. **Cities** (1993 est.): Santo Domingo 2.1 mil; Santiago de los Caballeros 690,000.

**Government: Type:** Republic. **Head of state:** Pres. Leonel Fernández; b Dec. 26, 1953; in office: Aug. 16, 1996. **Local divisions:** 29 provinces and Santo Domingo. **Defense:** 1.4% of GDP (1994). **Active troop strength:** 24,500.

**Economy: Industries:** Sugar refining, cement, tourism. **Chief crops:** sugar, cocoa, coffee, cotton, rice. **Minerals:** Nickel, bauxite, gold, silver. **Arable land:** 23%. **Livestock** (1994): cattle: 2.5 mil; pigs: 900,000. **Electricity prod.** (1993): 5.4 bil kWh. **Labor force:** 49% agric.; 33% serv.; 18% ind.

**Finance: Monetary unit:** Peso (June 1996: 13.96 = $1 US). **Gross domestic product** (1994): $24 bil.* **Per capita GDP:** $3,070. **Imports** (1994): $2.5 bil; partners: U.S. 41%. **Exports** (1995): $585 mil; partners: U.S. 52%, Neth. 13%. **Tourism** (1994): $1.1 bil. **National budget** (1994 est.): $2.2 bil. **International reserves less gold** (Apr. 1996): $372 mil. **Gold:** 18,000 oz t. **Consumer prices** (change in 1995): 12.5%.

**Transport: Motor vehicles:** in use: 118,000 passenger cars, 79,000 comm. vehicles. **Civil aviation:** 280 mil passenger-mi.; 5 airports. **Chief ports:** Santo Domingo, San Pedro de Macoris, Puerto Plata.

**Communications: Television sets:** 1 per 11 persons. **Radios:** 1 per 6.6 persons. **Telephones:** 1 per 14 persons. **Daily newspaper circ.:** 35 per 1,000 pop.

**Health: Life expectancy at birth** (1996): 67 male; 71 female. **Births** (per 1,000 pop.): 24. **Deaths** (per 1,000 pop.): 6. **Natural increase:** 1.8%. **Hospital beds:** 1 per 608 persons. **Physicians:** 1 per 2,511 persons. **Infant mortality** (per 1,000 live births 1996): 48.

**Education: Literacy** (1993): 82%. Compulsory: ages 7-14. attendance 95%.

**Major International Organizations:** UN (World Bank, IMF, FAO, WHO, WTO), OAS.

**Embassy:** 1715 22d St. NW 20008; 332-6280.

Carib and Arawak Indians inhabited the island of Hispaniola when Columbus landed in 1492. The city of Santo Domingo, founded 1496, is the oldest settlement by Europeans in the hemisphere and has the supposed ashes of Columbus in an elaborate tomb in its ancient cathedral.

The western third of the island was ceded to France in 1697. Santo Domingo itself was ceded to France in 1795. Haitian leader Toussaint L'Ouverture seized it, 1801. Spain returned intermittently 1803-21, as several native republics came and went. Haiti ruled again, 1822-44, and Spanish occupation occurred 1861-63.

The country was occupied by U.S. Marines from 1916 to 1924, when a constitutionally elected government was installed.

In 1930, Gen. Rafael Leonidas Trujillo Molina was elected president. Trujillo ruled brutally until his assassination in 1961. Pres. Joaquín Balaguer, appointed by Trujillo in 1960, resigned under pressure in 1962.

Juan Bosch, elected president in the first free elections in 38 years, was overthrown in 1963. On Apr. 24, 1965, a revolt was launched by followers of Bosch and others, including a few Communists. Four days later U.S. Marines intervened against the pro-Bosch forces. Token units were later sent by 5 South American countries as a peacekeeping force. A provisional government supervised a June 1966 election, in which Balaguer defeated Bosch. Balaguer remained in office for most of the next 28 years, but his May 1994 reelection was widely denounced as fraudulent. He cut short his term and on June 30, 1996, Leonel Fernández was elected to succeed him.

Continued depressed world prices have affected the main export commodity, sugar.

# Ecuador

## Republic of Ecuador

## República del Ecuador

**People: Population:** 11,466,291. **Age distrib.** (%): <15: 36; 65+: 4. **Pop. density:** 109 per sq. mi. **Urban:** 59%. **Ethnic groups:** Mestizo 55%, Indian 25%, Spanish 10%, African 10%. **Principal languages:** Spanish (official), Quechuan, other Amerindian. **Religions:** Roman Catholic 95%.

**Geography: Area:** 105,037 sq. mi. **Location:** In NW South America, on Pacific coast, astride the Equator. **Neighbors:** Colombia on N, Peru on E and S. **Topography:** Two ranges of Andes run N and S, splitting the country into 3 zones: hot, humid lowlands on the coast; temperate highlands between the ranges; and rainy, tropical lowlands to the E. **Capital:** Quito. **Cities** (1991 est.): Guayaquil 2.0 mil; Quito 1.5 mil.

**Government: Type:** Republic. **Head of state:** Pres. Abdalá Bucaram; b Feb. 20, 1952; in office: Aug. 10, 1996. **Local divisions:** 21 provinces. **Defense:** 1.1% of GNP (1993). **Active troop strength:** 57,100.

**Economy: Industries:** Oil, food processing, metalwork, textiles. **Chief crops:** Bananas and balsawood (leading producer and' exporter), coffee, rice, sugar, potatoes. **Minerals:** Oil, gas, copper, zinc, silver, gold. **Crude oil reserves** (1995): 2.0 bil bbls. **Other resources:** Forests, seafood. **Arable land:** 6%. **Livestock** (1994): cattle: 5.0 mil; pigs: 2.5 mil; sheep: 1.7 mil. **Fish catch** (1993): 331,000 metric tons. **Electricity prod.** (1993): 6.9 bil kWh. **Labor force:** 35% agric.; 28% services; 21% manuf.; 16% commerce.

**Finance: Monetary unit:** Sucre (June 1996: 3,165 = $1 US). **Gross domestic product** (1994): $41.1 bil.* **Per capita GDP:** $3,840. **Imports** (1994): $3 bil; partners: U.S. 28%. **Exports** (1994): $3.3 bil; partners: U.S. 42%. **Tourism** (1993): $230 mil. **National budget** (1994): $2.8 bil. **International reserves less gold** (Mar. 1996): $1.6 bil. **Gold:** 414,000 oz t. **Consumer prices** (change in 1995): 22.9%.

**Transport: Railroads: Route length:** 594 mi. **Motor vehicles:** in use: 192,000 passenger cars, 293,000 comm. vehicles. **Civil aviation:** 780 mil passenger-mi.; 14 airports. **Chief ports:** Guayaquil, Manta, Esmeraldas, Puerto Bolivar.

**Communications: Television sets:** 1 per 12 persons. **Radios:** 1 per 3.5 persons. **Telephones:** 1 per 19 persons. **Daily newspaper circ.:** 62 per 1,000 pop.

**Health: Life expectancy at birth** (1996): 69 male; 74 female. **Births** (per 1,000 pop.): 25. **Deaths** (per 1,000 pop.): 6. **Natural increase:** 2.0%. **Hospital beds:** 1 per 623 persons. **Physicians:** 1 per 836 persons. **Infant mortality** (per 1,000 live births 1996): 35.

**Education: Literacy** (1991): 90%. Compulsory: ages 6-12.

**Major International Organizations:** UN (IMF, FAO, World Bank, WHO), OAS.

**Embassy:** 2535 15th St. NW 20009; 234-7200.

The region, which was the northern Inca empire, was conquered by Spain in 1533. Liberation forces defeated the Spanish May 24, 1822, near Quito. Ecuador became part of the Great Colombia Republic but seceded, May 13, 1830.

A peaceful transfer of power from military rule to democratic civilian government took place in 1979.

Since 1972, the economy has revolved around petroleum exports; oil revenues have declined since 1982, causing severe economic problems. Ecuador suspended interest payments for 1987 on its estimated $8.2 billion foreign debt following a Mar. 5-6 earthquake that left 20,000 homeless and destroyed a stretch of the country's main oil pipeline.

Ecuadoran Indians staged protests in the 1990s to demand greater rights. A border war with Peru flared from Jan. 26, 1995, until a truce took effect Mar. 1. Vice-Pres. Alberto Dahik resigned and fled Ecuador, Oct. 11, 1995, to avoid arrest on corruption charges.

The **Galapagos Islands,** pop. (1995 est.) 15,000, about 600 mi. to the W, are the home of huge tortoises and other unusual animals.

# Egypt

## Arab Republic of Egypt

## Jumhuriyat Misral-Arabiyah

**People: Population:** 63,575,107. **Age distrib** (%) <15: 40; 65+: 4. **Pop. density:** 165 per sq. mi. **Urban:** 44%. **Ethnic groups:** Eastern Hamitic stock 99%, Greek, Nubian, Armenian. **Principal languages:** Arabic (official), English, French. **Religion:** Muslim (mostly Sunni) 94%.

**Geography: Area:** 385,229 sq. mi. **Location:** Northeast corner of Africa. **Neighbors:** Libya on W, Sudan on S, Israel on E. **Topography:** Almost entirely desolate and barren, with hills and mountains in E and along Nile. The Nile Valley, where most of the people live, stretches 550 miles. **Capital:** Cairo. **Cities** (1994 est.): Cairo 6.8 mil; Alexandria 3.4 mil; (1993 est.) al-Jizah 2.1 mil.

**Government: Type:** Republic. **Head of state:** Pres. Hosni Mubarak; b May 4, 1928; in office: Oct. 14, 1981. **Head of government:** Prime Min. Kamal al-Ganzouri; b 1933; in office:

Jan. 4, 1996. **Local divisions:** 26 governorates. **Defense:** 8.2% of government budget (FY 1994-95). **Active troop strength:** 436,000.

**Economy: Industries:** Textiles, tourism, chemicals, oil, food processing, cement. **Chief crops:** Cotton, rice, beans, fruits, grains, vegetables, corn. **Minerals:** Oil, gas, phosphates, gypsum, iron, manganese, limestone. **Crude oil reserves** (1995): 3.3 bil bbls. **Arable land:** 3%. **Livestock** (1994): cattle 3.1 mil; sheep 3.4 mil. **Fish catch** (1993): 303,000 metric tons. **Electricity prod.** (1993): 44.5 bil kWh. **Labor force:** 40% agric.; 35% serv.

**Finance: Monetary unit:** Pound (June 1996: 3.39 = $1 US). **Gross domestic product** (1994): $152 bil.* **Per capita GDP:** $2,490. **Imports** (FY 1993-94): $11.2 bil; partners: EU 36%, U.S. 18%. **Exports** (FY 1993-94): $3.1 bil; partners: EU 41%, U.S. 16%. **Tourism** (1993): $1.3 bil. **National budget** (FY 1994-95 est.): $19.4 bil. **International reserves less gold** (Apr. 1996): $16.7 bil. **Gold:** 2.43 mil oz t. **Consumer prices** (change in 1995): 8.3%.

**Transport: Railroads: Length:** 5,274 mi. **Motor vehicles:** in use: 1.1 mil passenger cars, 467,000 comm. vehicles. **Civil aviation:** 3.4 bil passenger-mi.; 14 airports. **Chief ports:** Alexandria, Port Said, Suez.

**Communications: Television sets:** 1 per 12 persons. **Radios:** 1 per 3.5 persons. **Telephones:** 1 per 24 persons. **Daily newspaper circ.:** 44 per 1,000 pop. (partial circ.).

**Health: Life expectancy at birth** (1996): 60 male; 64 female. **Births** (per 1,000 pop.): 28. **Deaths** (per 1,000 pop.): 9. **Natural increase:** 2.0%. **Hospital beds:** 1 per 529 persons. **Physicians:** 1 per 1,698 persons. **Infant mortality** (per 1,000 live births 1996): 73.

**Education: Literacy** (1993): 51%. Compulsory: ages 6-14.

**Major International Organizations:** UN (IMF, FAO, WHO, World Bank, WTO), OAU, Arab League.

**Embassy:** 3521 International Ct. NW 20008; 895-5400.

Archaeological records of ancient Egyptian civilization date back to 4000 BC. A unified kingdom arose around 3200 BC, and extended its way south into Nubia and north as far as Syria. A high culture of rulers and priests was built on an economic base of serfdom, fertile soil, and annual flooding of the Nile banks.

Imperial decline facilitated conquest by Asian invaders (Hyksos, Assyrians). The last native dynasty fell in 341 BC to the Persians, who were in turn replaced by Greeks (Alexander and the Ptolemies), Romans, Byzantines, and Arabs, who introduced Islam and the Arabic language. The ancient Egyptian language is preserved only in the liturgy of the Coptic Christians.

Egypt was ruled as part of larger Islamic empires for several centuries. The Mamluks, a military caste of Caucasian origin, ruled Egypt from 1250 until defeat by the Ottoman Turks in 1517. Under Turkish sultans the khedive as hereditary viceroy had wide authority. Britain intervened in 1882 and took control of administration, though nominal allegiance to the Ottoman Empire continued until 1914.

The country was a British protectorate from 1914 to 1922. A 1936 treaty strengthened Egyptian autonomy, but Britain retained bases in Egypt and a condominium over the Sudan. Britain fought German and Italian armies from Egypt, 1940-42. In 1951 Egypt abrogated the 1936 treaty; the Sudan became independent in 1956.

The uprising of July 23, 1952, was led by the Society of Free Officers, who named Maj. Gen. Mohammed Naguib commander in chief and forced King Farouk to abdicate. When the republic was proclaimed June 18, 1953, Naguib became its first president and premier. Lt. Col. Gamal Abdel Nasser removed Naguib and became premier in 1954. In 1956, he was voted president. Nasser died in 1970 and was replaced by Vice Pres. Anwar Sadat.

The Aswan High Dam, completed 1971, provides irrigation for more than a million acres of land. Artesian wells, drilled in the Western Desert, reclaimed 43,000 acres, 1960-66.

When the state of Israel was proclaimed in 1948, Egypt joined other Arab nations invading Israel and was defeated.

After terrorist raids across its border, Israel invaded Egypt's Sinai Peninsula, Oct. 29, 1956. Egypt rejected a cease-fire demand by Britain and France; on Oct. 31 the 2 nations dropped bombs and on Nov. 5-6 landed forces. Egypt and Israel accepted a UN cease-fire; fighting ended Nov. 7.

A UN Emergency Force guarded the 117-mile-long border between Egypt and Israel until May 19, 1967, when it was withdrawn at Nasser's demand. Egyptian troops entered the Gaza Strip and the heights of Sharm el Sheikh and 3 days later closed the Strait of Tiran to all Israeli shipping. Full-scale war broke out June 5; before it ended under a UN cease-fire June 10, Israel had captured Gaza and the Sinai Peninsula, controlled the east bank of the Suez Canal, and reopened the gulf. After sporadic fighting, Israel and Egypt agreed, Aug. 7, 1970, to a new cease-fire.

In a surprise attack Oct. 6, 1973, Egyptian forces crossed the Suez Canal into the Sinai. (At the same time, Syrian forces attacked Israelis on the Golan Heights.) Egypt was supplied by a USSR military airlift; the U.S. responded with an airlift to Israel. Israel counterattacked, crossed the canal, surrounded Suez City. A UN cease-fire took effect Oct. 24.

A disengagement agreement was signed Jan. 18, 1974. Under it, Israeli forces withdrew from the canal's W bank; limited numbers of Egyptian forces occupied a strip along the E bank. A second accord was signed in 1975, with Israel yielding Sinai oil fields. Pres. Sadat's surprise visit to Jerusalem, Nov. 1977, opened the prospect of peace with Israel. On Mar. 26, 1979, Egypt and Israel signed a formal peace treaty, ending 30 years of war, and establishing diplomatic relations. Israel returned control of the Sinai to Egypt in Apr. 1982.

Tension between Muslim fundamentalists and Christians in 1981 caused street riots and culminated in a nationwide security crackdown in Sept. Pres Sadat was assassinated on Oct. 6; he was succeeded by Hosni Mubarak.

Egypt was a political and military supporter of the Allied forces in their defeat of Iraq in the Persian Gulf War, 1991.

Egypt saw a rising tide of Islamic fundamentalist violence in the 1990s. Egyptian security forces conducted raids against Islamic militants, some of whom were executed for terrorism. Naguib Mahfouz, winner of the 1988 Nobel Prize for Literature, was stabbed by Islamic militants Oct. 14, 1994. Pres. Mubarak escaped assassination in Ethiopia, June 26, 1995; Egypt blamed Sudan for the attack.

The **Suez Canal,** 103 mi. long, links the Mediterranean and Red seas. It was built by a French corporation 1859-69, but Britain obtained controlling interest in 1875. The last British troops were removed June 13, 1956. On July 26, Egypt nationalized the canal.

# El Salvador

## Republic of El Salvador

## República de El Salvador

**People: Population:** 5,828,987. **Age distrib.** (%): <15: 40; 65+: 4. **Pop. density:** 718 per sq. mi. **Urban:** 45%. **Ethnic groups:** Mestizo 94%, Indian 5%. **Principal language:** Spanish (official). **Religions:** Roman Catholic 75%, many Protestant groups.

**Geography: Area:** 8,124 sq. mi. **Location:** In Central America. **Neighbors:** Guatemala on W, Honduras on N. **Topography:** A hot Pacific coastal plain in the south rises to a cooler plateau and valley region, densely populated. The N is mountainous, including many volcanoes. **Capital:** San Salvador (1992): 423,000.

**Government: Type:** Republic. **Head of state:** Pres. Armando Calderón Sol; b June 24, 1948; in office: June 1, 1994. **Local divisions:** 14 departments. **Defense:** 0.7% of GDP (1994). **Active troop strength:** 30,500.

**Economy: Industries:** Food and beverages, petroleum products, tobacco. **Chief crops:** Coffee, corn, sugar, rice. **Other resources:** Hydropower. **Arable land:** 27%. **Livestock** (1994): cattle: 1.3 mil; pigs: 325,000. **Electricity prod.** (1993): 2.4 bil kWh. **Labor force:** 40% agric.; 16% commerce; 15% manuf.

**Finance: Monetary unit:** Colon (June 1996: 8.76 = $1 US). **Gross domestic product** (1994): $9.8 bil.* **Per capita GDP:** $1,710. **Imports** (1994): $2.1 bil; partners: U.S. 44%, Guatemala 11%. **Exports** (1994): $823 mil; partners: U.S. 30%, Guatemala 22%. **Tourism** (1993): $121 mil. **National budget** (1992 est.): $890 mil. **International reserves less gold** (Apr. 1996): $717 mil. **Gold:** 469,000 oz t. **Consumer prices** (change in 1995): 10.0%.

**Transport: Railroads: Route length:** 374 mi. **Motor vehicles:** in use: 96,000 passenger cars, 150,000 comm. vehicles. **Chief ports:** La Union, Acajutla.

**Communications: Television sets:** 1 per 11 persons. **Radios:** 1 per 2.7 persons. **Telephones:** 1 per 32 persons. **Daily newspaper circ.:** 90 per 1,000 pop.

**Health: Life expectancy at birth** (1996): 65 male; 73 female. **Births** (per 1,000 pop.): 28. **Deaths** (per 1,000 pop.): 6. **Natural increase:** 2.3%. **Hospital beds:** 1 per 922 persons.

**Physicians:** 1 per 2,126 persons. **Infant mortality** (per 1,000 live births 1996): 32.

**Education: Literacy** (1992): 74%. Compulsory: ages 7-16. attendance 82%.

**Major International Organizations:** UN (IMF, WTO, WHO, FAO, World Bank, ILO), OAS.

**Embassy:** 2308 California St. NW 20008; 265-9671.

El Salvador became independent of Spain in 1821, and of the Central American Federation in 1839.

A fight with Honduras in 1969 over the presence of 300,000 Salvadoran workers left 2,000 dead.

A military coup overthrew the government of Pres. Carlos Humberto Romero in 1979, but the ruling military-civilian junta failed to quell a rebellion by leftist insurgents, armed by Cuba and Nicaragua. Extreme right-wing death squads organized to eliminate suspected leftists were blamed for thousands of deaths in the 1980s. The Reagan administration staunchly supported the government with military aid.

Voters turned out in large numbers in the May 1984 presidential election. Christian Democrat José Napoleon Duarte, a moderate, was victorious, with 54% of the vote.

The 12-year civil war ended Jan. 16, 1992, as the government and leftist rebels signed a formal peace treaty. The civil war had taken the lives of some 75,000 people. The treaty provided for military and political reforms.

Nine soldiers, including 3 officers, were indicted Jan. 1990 in the Nov. 1989 slaying of 6 Jesuit priests in San Salvador. Two of the officers received maximum 30-year jail sentences. They were released Mar. 20, 1993, when the National Assembly passed a sweeping amnesty.

# Equatorial Guinea

## Republic of Equatorial Guinea

## República de Guinea Ecuatorial

**People: Population:** 431,282. **Age distrib.** (%): <15: 43; 65+: 4. **Pop. density:** 40 per sq. mi. **Urban:** 37%. **Ethnic groups:** Fang 83%, Bubi 10%. **Principal languages:** Spanish (official), Fang, Bubi. **Religion:** Mostly Roman Catholic.

**Geography: Area:** 10,831 sq. mi. **Location:** Bioko I. off W Africa coast in Gulf of Guinea, and Rio Muni, mainland enclave. **Neighbors:** Gabon on S, Cameroon on E and N. **Topography:** Bioko I. consists of 2 volcanic mountains and a connecting valley. Rio Muni, with over 90% of the area, has a coastal plain and low hills beyond. **Capital:** Malabo (1991 est.): 58,000.

**Government: Type:** Republic. **Head of state:** Pres. Teodoro Obiang Nguema Mbasogo; b June 5, 1942; in office: Oct. 10, 1979. **Head of government:** Prime Min. Silvestre Siale Bileka; in office: Mar. 4, 1992. **Local divisions:** 7 provinces. **Defense:** 1.3% of GNP (1993). **Active troop strength:** 1,320.

**Economy: Chief crops:** Cocoa, coffee, rice, bananas, yams. **Other resources:** Timber. **Arable land:** 8%. **Electricity prod.** (1993): 20 mil kWh. **Labor force:** 66% agric.; 23% serv.; 11% ind.

**Finance: Monetary unit:** CFA Franc (June 1996: 515 = $1 US). **Gross domestic product** (1993): $280 mil.* **Per capita GDP:** $700. **Imports** (1993): $62 mil; partners: Cameroon 23%, Spain 22%. **Exports** (1993): $56 mil; partners: Spain 55%. **National budget** (1992 est.): $36 mil.

**Chief ports:** Malabo, Bata.

**Communications: Television sets:** 1 per 154 persons. **Radios:** 1 per 3.8 persons.

**Health: Life expectancy at birth** (1996): 51 male; 55 female. **Births** (per 1,000 pop.): 40. **Deaths** (per 1,000 pop.): 14. **Natural increase:** 2.6%. **Hospital beds:** 1 per 350 persons. **Physicians:** 1 per 3,532 persons. **Infant mortality** (per 1,000 live births 1996): 98.

**Education: Literacy** (1990): 50%. Free and compulsory: ages 6-14.

**Major International Organizations:** UN (IMF, FAO, WHO, World Bank), OAU.

**Embassy:** 1511 K St. NW, Suite 405 20005; 393-0525.

Fernando Po (now Bioko) Island was reached by Portugal in the late 15th century and ceded to Spain in 1778. Independence came Oct. 12, 1968. Riots occurred in 1969 over disputes between the island and the more backward Rio Muni province on the mainland. Masie Nguema Biyogo, a mainlander, became president for life in 1972.

Masie's reign was one of the most brutal in Africa, resulting in a bankrupted nation. Most of the nation's 7,000 Europeans emigrated. He was ousted in a military coup, Aug. 1979, and Teodoro Mbasogo, leader of the coup, became president. His regime eventually agreed to elections, held Nov. 21, 1993. These were nominally won by the ruling party, but boycotted by opposition parties that maintained the rules were rigged. A presidential election Feb. 25, 1996, was similarly flawed.

The nation is heavily dependent on external aid.

# Eritrea

## State of Eritrea

**People: Population:** 3,909,628. **Pop. density:** 86 per sq. mi. **Urban:** 17%. **Ethnic groups:** Tigrays 50%, Tigre and Kunama 40%, Afar 4%. **Principal languages:** Tigrinya, Tigre. **Religions:** About evenly split between Muslim and Christian.

**Geography: Area:** 45,300 sq. mi. **Location:** In E Africa. **Neighbors:** Ethiopia on S, Djibouti on SE, Sudan on W, Red Sea on N. **Topography:** Includes many islands of the Dahlak Archipelago, low coastal plains in S, mountain range with peaks to 9,000 ft. in N. **Capital:** Asmara (1992): 400,000.

**Government: Type:** In transition. **Head of state:** Isaias Afwerki; b Feb. 2, 1946; in office: May 24, 1993. **Local divisions:** 10 provinces. **Defense: Active troop strength:** 35,000-55,000 est.

**Economy: Industries:** Food processing, textiles. **Chief crops:** Cotton, coffee, tobacco, lentils, sorghum. **Minerals:** Gold, potash, zinc, copper. **Arable land:** 3%.

**Finance: Monetary unit:** Ethiopian Birr. **Gross domestic product** (1994): $1.8 bil.* **Per capita GDP:** $500.

**Chief ports:** Mitsiwa, Aseb.

**Communications: Telephones:** 1 per 167 persons.

**Health** (1996): **Births** (per 1,000 pop.): 46. **Deaths** (per 1,000 pop.): 16. **Natural increase:** 3.0%.

**Education: Literacy** (1994): 20%. Compulsory: ages 7-13.

**Major International Organizations:** UN, OAU.

**Embassy:** 910 17th St. NW, Suite 400, 20006; 429-1991.

Eritrea was part of the Ethiopian kingdom of Aksum. It was an Italian colony from 1890 to 1941, when it was captured by the British. Following a period of British and UN supervision, Eritrea was awarded to Ethiopia as part of a federation in 1952. Ethiopia annexed Eritrea as a province in 1962. This led to a 31-year struggle for independence, which ended when Eritrea formally declared itself an independent nation May 24, 1993. Legislative elections are scheduled for 1997.

# Estonia

## Republic of Estonia

## Eesti Vabariik

**People: Population:** 1,459,428. **Pop. density:** 84 per sq. mi. **Urban:** 70%. **Ethnic groups:** Estonian 62%, Russian 30%. **Principal languages:** Estonian (official), Latvian, Lithuanian, Russian. **Religion:** Lutheran.

**Geography: Area:** 17,462 sq. mi. **Location:** E Europe. **Neighbors:** Baltic Sea on N and W, Russia on E, Latvia on S. **Capital:** Tallinn (1994 est.): 443,000.

**Government: Type:** Republic. **Head of state:** Pres. Lennart Meri; b Mar. 29, 1929; in office: Oct. 5, 1992. **Head of government:** Prime Min. Tiit Vahi; b 1947; in office: Apr. 5, 1995. **Local divisions:** 15 counties **Defense:** 1.5% of GDP (1995). **Active troop strength:** 3,500.

**Economy: Industries:** Shipbuilding, electric motors. **Chief crops:** Potatoes, fruits, vegetables. **Minerals:** Oil shale, phosphorites. **Other resources:** Dairy prods., peat. **Arable land:** 22%. **Livestock** (1994): cattle: 463,000, pigs: 424,000. **Electricity prod.** (1993): 11.3 bil kWh. **Labor force:** 42% ind. & constr., 20% agric.

**Finance: Monetary unit:** Kroon (June 1996: 12.22 = $1 US). **Gross domestic product** (1994 est.): $10.4 bil.* **Per capita GDP:** $6,460. **Imports** (1994): $1.0 bil. **Exports** (1994): $1.65 bil. **National budget** (1993 est.): $639 mil. **International reserves less gold** (Apr. 1996): $608 mil. **Gold:** 8,000 oz. t.

**Transport: Railroads: Length:** 636 mi. **Motor vehicles:** in use: 317,000 passenger cars, 83,000 comm. vehicles. **Chief port:** Tallinn.

**Communications: Television sets:** 1 per 2.5 persons. **Telephones:** 1 per 4.2 persons.

**Health: Life expectancy at birth** (1996): 63 male; 74 female. **Births** (per 1,000 pop.): 11. **Deaths** (per 1,000 pop.): 14. **Natural increase:** –0.3%. **Hospital beds:** 1 per 105 persons. **Physicians:** 1 per 296 persons. **Infant mortality** (per 1,000 live births 1996): 17.

**Education: Literacy** (1994): 100%. Compulsory: ages 7-16.

**Major International Organizations:** UN (IMF, FAO, World Bank, WHO).

**Embassy:** 1030 15th St. NW 20005; 789-0320.

Estonia was a province of imperial Russia before World War I, was independent between World Wars I and II. It was conquered by the USSR in 1940 and was incorporated as the Estonian SSR. Estonia declared itself an "occupied territory," and proclaimed itself a free nation Mar. 1990. During an abortive Soviet coup, Estonia declared immediate full independence, Aug. 20, 1991; the Soviet Union recognized its independence in Sept. 1991. The first free elections in over 50 years were held Sept. 20, 1992. The last occupying Russian troops were withdrawn by Aug. 31, 1994.

# Ethiopia

## Federal Democratic Republic of Ethiopia

*(Figures prior to 1993 include Eritrea)*

**People: Population**: 57,171,662. **Age distrib.** (%): <15: 49; 65+: 3. **Pop. density:** 131 per sq. mi. **Urban:** 15%. **Ethnic groups:** Oromo 40%, Amhara and Tigre 32%, Sidamo 9%. **Principal languages:** Amharic (official), Tigrinya, Orominga. **Religions:** Muslim 45-50%, Ethiopian Orthodox 35-40%, animist 12%.

**Geography: Area:** 437,794 sq. mi. **Location:** In East Africa. **Neighbors:** Sudan on W, Kenya on S, Somalia and Djibouti on E, Eritrea on N. **Topography:** A high central plateau, between 6,000 and 10,000 ft. high, rises to higher mountains near the Great Rift Valley, cutting in from the SW. The Blue Nile and other rivers cross the plateau, which descends to plains on both W and SE. **Capital:** Addis Ababa (1993 est.): 2.2 mil.

**Government: Type:** Federal republic. **Head of state:** Pres. Negasso Gidada; in office: Aug. 22, 1995. **Head of government:** Prime Min. Meles Zenawi; b 1955; in office: Aug. 23, 1995. **Local divisions:** 14 administrative regions. **Defense:** 4.1% of GDP (FY 1994-95). **Active troop strength:** 120,000 est.

**Economy: Industries:** Food processing, chemicals, textiles. **Chief crops:** Coffee (over 50% export earnings), oilseeds, grains. **Minerals:** Platinum, gold, copper, potash. **Arable land:** 12%. **Livestock** (1994): cattle: 29 mil; sheep: 22 mil. **Electricity prod.** (1993): 1.3 bil kWh. **Labor force:** 80% agric.

**Finance: Monetary unit:** Birr (June 1996: 6.29 = $1 US). **Gross domestic product** (1993 est.): $20.3 bil.* **Per capita GDP:** $380. **Imports** (1993): $1.0 bil; partners: Saudi Arabia 19%. **Exports** (1993): $220 mil; partners: Germany 20%, Japan 19%. **National budget** (FY 1993-94): $1.7 bil. **International reserves less gold** (May 1996): $904 mil. **Gold:** 113,000 oz t. **Consumer prices** (change in 1995): 10.7%.

**Transport: Railroads: Length:** 486 mi. **Motor vehicles:** in use: 40,000 passenger cars, 19,000 comm. vehicles. **Civil aviation:** 998 mil passenger-mi.; 25 airports.

**Communications: Television sets:** 1 per 534 persons. **Radios:** 1 per 5.9 persons. **Telephones:** 1 per 391 persons.

**Health: Life expectancy at birth** (1996): 46 male; 48 female. **Births** (per 1,000 pop.): 46. **Deaths** (per 1,000 pop.): 18. **Natural increase:** 2.9%. **Infant mortality** (per 1,000 live births 1996): 123.

**Education: Literacy** (1992): 36%.

**Major International Organizations:** UN (IMF, FAO, World Bank, WHO), OAU.

**Embassy:** 2134 Kalorama Rd. NW 20008; 234-2281.

Ethiopian culture was influenced by Egypt and Greece. The ancient monarchy was invaded by Italy in 1880 but maintained its independence until another Italian invasion in 1936. British forces freed the country in 1941.

The last emperor, Haile Selassie I, established a parliament and judiciary system in 1931 but barred all political parties.

A series of droughts in the 1970s killed hundreds of thousands. An army mutiny, strikes, and student demonstrations led to the dethronement of Selassie in 1974. The ruling junta pledged to form a one-party socialist state and instituted a successful land reform; opposition was violently suppressed. The influence of the Coptic Church, embraced in AD 330, was curbed, and the monarchy was abolished in 1975.

The regime, torn by bloody coups, faced uprisings by tribal and political groups in part aided by Sudan and Somalia. Ties with the U.S., once a major ally, deteriorated, while cooperation accords were signed with the USSR in 1977. In 1978, Soviet advisers and Cuban troops helped defeat Somalian forces. Ethiopia and Somalia signed a peace agreement in 1988.

A worldwide relief effort began in 1984, as an extended drought caused millions to face starvation and death. In 1988, victories by Eritrean guerrillas led the government to curtail the work of foreign aid workers in drought-stricken regions. In 1994 Ethiopia again faced possible severe famine as a result of drought.

The Ethiopian People's Revolutionary Democractic Front (EPRDF), an umbrella group of 6 rebel armies, launched a major push against government forces, Feb. 1991. In May, Pres. Mengistu Haile Mariam resigned and left the country. The EPRDF took over and set up a transitional government. Under a new constitution ratified Dec. 8, 1994, Ethiopia's first multiparty general elections were held in 1995.

Eritrea, a province on the Red Sea, declared its independence May 24, 1993.

# Fiji

## Republic of Fiji

**People: Population:** 782,381. **Age distrib.** (%): <15: 38; 65+: 3. **Pop. density:** 111 per sq. mi. **Urban:** 39%. **Ethnic groups:** Fijian (Melanesian-Polynesian) 49%, Indian 46%, European. **Principal languages:** English (official), Fijian, Hindustani. **Religions:** Christian 52%, Hindu 38%, Muslim 8%.

**Geography: Area:** 7,055 sq. mi. **Location:** In western South Pacific O. **Neighbors:** Nearest are Vanuatu on W, Tonga on E. **Topography:** 322 islands (106 inhabited), many mountainous, with tropical forests and large fertile areas. Viti Levu, the largest island, has over half the total land area. **Capital:** Suva (1990 met.): 200,000.

**Government: Type:** Republic. **Head of state:** Pres. Ratu Sir Kamisese Mara; b May 13, 1920; in office: Jan. 18, 1994. **Head of government:** Prime Min. Sitiveni Rabuka; b Sept. 13, 1948; in office: June 2, 1992. **Local divisions:** 4 divisions, 1 dependency. **Defense:** 2% of GDP (FY 1991-92). **Active troop strength:** 3,900.

**Economy: Industries:** Sugar refining, light industry, tourism. **Chief crops:** Sugar, bananas, coconuts. **Minerals:** Gold, copper. **Other resources:** Timber. **Arable land:** 8%. **Electricity prod.** (1993): 480 mil kWh. **Labor force:** 67% subsistence agric.

**Finance: Monetary unit:** Dollar (June 1996: 1.40 = $1.00 US). **Gross domestic product** (1994): $4.3 bil.* **Per capita GDP:** $5,650. **Imports** (1993): $634 mil; partners: Australia 30%, N.Z. 17%, Japan 13%. **Exports** (1993): $405 mil; partners: EU 26%, Australia 15%. **Tourism** (1993): $236 mil. **National budget** (1994): $579 mil. **International reserves less gold** (Apr. 1996): $354 mil. **Gold:** 1,000 oz t. **Consumer prices** (change in 1995): 2.2%.

**Transport: Motor vehicles:** in use: 45,000 passenger cars, 32,000 comm. vehicles. **Civil aviation:** 671 mil passenger-mi.; 13 airports with scheduled flights. **Chief ports:** Suva, Lautoka.

**Communications: Television sets:** 1 per 63 persons. **Radios:** 1 per 1.7 persons. **Telephones:** 1 per 14 persons. **Daily newspaper circ.:** 36 per 1,000 pop.

**Health: Life expectancy at birth** (1996): 63 male; 68 female. **Births** (per 1,000 pop.): 23. **Deaths** (per 1,000 pop.): 6. **Natural increase:** 1.7%. **Hospital beds:** 1 per 438 persons. **Physicians:** 1 per 2,161 persons. **Infant mortality** (per 1,000 live births 1996): 17.

**Education: Literacy** (1992): 92%. 95% attend school.

**Major International Organizations:** UN (IMF, FAO, WTO, World Bank, WHO).

**Embassy:** 2233 Wisconsin Ave. NW 20007; 337-8320.

A British colony since 1874, Fiji became an independent parliamentary democracy Oct. 10, 1970.

Cultural differences between the majority Indian community, descendants of contract laborers brought to the islands in the 19th century, and the less modernized native Fijians, who by law own 83% of the land in communal villages, have led to political polarization.

In 1987, a military coup ousted the government; order was restored May 21 under a compromise granting Lt. Col. Sitiveni Rabuka, the coup's leader, increased power. Rabuka staged a second coup Sept. 25 and declared Fiji a republic. Civilian government was restored in Dec. A new constitution favoring indigenous Fijians was issued July 25, 1990.

# Finland

## Republic of Finland

## Suomen Tasavalta

**People: Population:** 5,105,230. **Age distrib.** (%): <15: 19; 65+: 14. **Pop. density:** 39 per sq. mi. **Urban:** 64%. **Ethnic groups:** Finn 94%, Swede, Lapp. **Principal languages:** Finnish, Swedish (both official). **Religion:** Evangelical Lutheran 89%.

**Geography: Area:** 130,559 sq. mi. **Location:** In northern Europe. **Neighbors:** Norway on N, Sweden on W, Russia on E. **Topography:** South and central Finland are mostly flat areas with low hills and many lakes. The N has mountainous areas, 3,000-4,000 ft. **Capital:** Helsinki. **Cities** (1995 est.): Helsinki 516,000; Espoo 186,500; Tampere 179,300.

**Government: Type:** Constitutional republic. **Head of state:** Pres. Martti Ahtisaari; b June 23, 1937; in office: Mar. 1, 1994. **Head of government:** Prime Min. Paavo Lipponen; b Apr. 23, 1941; in office: Apr. 13, 1995. **Local divisions:** 12 laanit (provinces). **Defense:** 1.9% of GDP (1994). **Active troop strength:** 31,100.

**Economy: Industries:** Metal prods., shipbuilding, wood processing, chemicals, textiles. **Chief crops:** Grains, sugar beets, potatoes. **Minerals:** Copper, iron, zinc. **Other resources:** Forests (34% of exports), dairy prods. **Arable land:** 8%. **Livestock** (1994): cattle: 1.2 mil; pigs: 1.3 mil. **Fish catch** (1993): 152,000 metric tons. **Electricity prod.** (1993): 58 bil kWh. **Labor force:** 46% ind., commerce & finance; 30% public serv.; 9% agric.

**Finance: Monetary unit:** Markka (June 1996: 4.63 = $1 US). **Gross domestic product** (1994): $81.8 bil.* **Per capita GDP:** $16,140. **Imports** (1993): $18 bil; partners: Germany 15%. **Exports** (1993): $23.4 bil; partners: Germany 13%. **Tourism** (1993): $1.2 bil. **National budget** (1993 est.): $31.7 bil. **International reserves less gold** (May 1996): $6.6 bil. **Gold:** 1.6 mil oz t. **Consumer prices** (change in 1995): 1.0%.

**Transport: Railroads: Route length:** 3,657 mi. **Motor vehicles:** in use: 1.9 mil passenger cars, 261,000 comm. vehicles. **Civil aviation:** 5.1 bil passenger-mi.; 25 airports. **Chief ports:** Helsinki, Turku.

**Communications: Television sets:** 1 per 2.7 persons. **Radios:** 1 per person. **Telephones:** 1 per 1.8 persons. **Daily newspaper circ.:** 524 per 1,000 pop.

**Health: Life expectancy at birth** (1996): 74 male; 77 female. **Births** (per 1,000 pop.): 11. **Deaths** (per 1,000 pop.): 11. **Natural increase:** 0. **Hospital beds:** 1 per 94 persons. **Physicians:** 1 per 380 persons. **Infant mortality** (per 1,000 live births 1996): 5.

**Education: Literacy** (1993): 100%. Free and compulsory: ages 7-16.

**Major International Organizations:** UN (IMF, FAO, World Bank, WHO, WTO), EU, OECD.

**Embassy:** 3301 Massachusetts Ave. NW 20008; 298-5800.

The early Finns probably migrated from the Ural area at about the beginning of the Christian era. Swedish settlers brought the country into Sweden, 1154 to 1809, when Finland became an autonomous grand duchy of the Russian Empire. Russian exactions created a strong national spirit; on Dec. 6, 1917, Finland declared its independence and in 1919 became a republic.

On Nov. 30, 1939, the Soviet Union invaded, and the Finns were forced to cede 16,173 sq. mi. of territory. After World War II, further cessions were exacted. In 1948, Finland signed a treaty of mutual assistance with the USSR; Finland and Russia nullified this treaty with a new pact in Jan. 1992.

Following approval by Finnish voters in an advisory referendum Oct. 16, 1994, Finland joined the European Union effective Jan. 1, 1995.

**Aland,** constituting an autonomous department, is a group of small islands, 590 sq. mi., in the Gulf of Bothnia, 25 mi. from Sweden, 15 mi. from Finland. Mariehamn is the principal port.

# France

## French Republic

## République Française

**People: Population:** 58,040,230. **Age distrib.** (%): <15: 20; 65+: 15. **Pop. density:** 276 per sq. mi. **Urban:** 74%. **Ethnic groups:** Celtic and Latin; Teutonic, Slavic, North African, Indochinese, Basque minorities. **Principal languages:** French (official); minorities speak Breton, Alsatian German, Flemish, Italian, Basque, Catalan. **Religion:** Roman Catholic 90%.

**Geography: Area:** 210,026 sq. mi. **Location:** In western Europe, between Atlantic O. and Mediterranean Sea. **Neighbors:** Spain on S; Italy, Switzerland, Germany on E; Luxembourg, Belgium on N. **Topography:** A wide plain covers more than half of the country, in N and W, drained to W by Seine, Loire, Garonne rivers. The Massif Central is a mountainous plateau in center. In E are Alps (Mt. Blanc is tallest in W Europe, 15,771 ft.), the lower Jura range, and the forested Vosges. The Rhone flows from Lake Geneva to Mediterranean. Pyrenees are in SW, on border with Spain. **Capital:** Paris. **Cities** (1990 est.): Paris 2.2 mil; Marseille 801,000; Lyon 415,000; Toulouse 359,000; Nice 342,000; Strasbourg 252,000; Nantes 245,000; Bordeaux 210,000.

**Government: Type:** Republic. **Head of state:** Pres. Jacques Chirac; b Nov. 29, 1932; in office: May 17, 1995. **Head of government:** Prime Min. Alain Juppe; b Aug. 15, 1945; in office: May 17, 1995. **Local divisions:** 22 administrative regions containing 96 departments. **Defense:** 3.1% of GDP (1995). **Active troop strength:** 409,000.

**Economy: Industries:** Steel, chemicals, textiles, tourism, wine, perfume, aircraft, machinery, electronic equipment. **Chief crops:** Grains, corn, soybeans, fruits, vegetables. France is largest food producer, exporter, in W Europe. **Minerals:** Bauxite, iron, coal. **Crude oil reserves** (1995): 152 mil bbls. **Other resources:** Forests, dairy. **Arable land:** 32%. **Livestock** (1994): cattle: 20.1 mil; pigs: 13.4 mil; sheep: 10.5 mil. **Fish catch** (1993): 830,000 metric tons. **Electricity prod.** (1993): 447 bil kWh. **Labor force:** 62% services; 31% ind.; 7% agric.

**Finance: Monetary unit:** Franc (June 1996: 5.15 = $1 US). **Gross domestic product** (1994): $1.08 tril.* **Per capita GDP:** $18,670. **Imports** (1994): $238 bil; partners: Germany 18%, Italy 11%, U.S. 10%. **Exports** (1994): $249 bil; partners: Germany 19%, Italy 11%, Spain 11%. **Tourism** (1993): $23.4 bil. **National budget** (1993): $249.1 bil. **International reserves less gold** (May 1996): $27.2 bil. **Gold:** 81.85 mil oz t. **Consumer prices** (change in 1995): 1.8%.

**Transport: Railroads: Route length:** 21,173 mi. **Motor vehicles:** in use: 24.4 mil passenger cars, 4.9 mil comm. vehicles. **Civil aviation:** 33.0 bil passenger-mi.; 66 airports with scheduled flights. **Chief ports:** Marseille, Le Havre, Nantes, Bordeaux, Rouen.

**Communications: Television sets:** 1 per 2 persons. **Radios:** 1 per 1.2 persons. **Telephones:** 1 per 1.8 persons. **Daily newspaper circ.:** 175 per 1,000 pop.

**Health: Life expectancy at birth** (1996): 75 male; 83 female. **Births** (per 1,000 pop.): 11. **Deaths** (per 1,000 pop.): 9. **Natural increase:** 0.2%. **Hospital beds:** 1 per 85 persons. **Physicians:** 1 per 361 persons. **Infant mortality** (per 1,000 live births 1996): 6.

**Education: Literacy** (1994): 99%. Free and compulsory: ages 6-16.

**Major International Organizations:** UN and most of its specialized agencies, OECD, EU, NATO.

**Embassy:** 4101 Reservoir Rd. NW 20007; 944-6000.

Celtic Gaul was conquered by Julius Caesar 58-51 BC; Romans ruled for 500 years. Under Charlemagne, Frankish rule extended over much of Europe. After his death France emerged as one of the successor kingdoms.

The monarchy was overthrown by the French Revolution (1789-93) and succeeded by the First Republic; followed by the First Empire under Napoleon (1804-15), a monarchy (1814-48), the Second Republic (1848-52), the Second Empire (1852-70), the Third Republic (1871-1946), the Fourth Republic (1946-58), and the Fifth Republic (1958 to present).

France suffered severe losses in manpower and wealth in the first World War, 1914-18, when it was invaded by Germany. By the Treaty of Versailles, France exacted return of Alsace and Lorraine, French provinces seized by Germany in 1871. Germany invaded France again in May 1940, and signed an armistice with a government based in Vichy. After France was liberated by the Allies Sept. 1944, Gen. Charles de Gaulle became head of the provisional government, serving until 1946.

De Gaulle again became premier in 1958, during a crisis over Algeria, and obtained voter approval for a new constitution, ushering in the Fifth Republic. He became president Jan. 1959. Using strong executive powers, he promoted French economic and technological advances in the context of the European Economic Community and guarded French foreign policy independence.

France had withdrawn from Indochina in 1954, and from Morocco and Tunisia in 1956. Most of its remaining African territories were freed 1958-62. In 1966, France withdrew all its troops from the integrated military command of NATO, though 60,000 remained stationed in Germany.

In May 1968 rebellious students in Paris and other centers rioted, battled police, and were joined by workers who launched nationwide strikes. The government awarded pay increases to the strikers May 26. De Gaulle resigned from office in Apr. 1969, after losing a nationwide referendum on constitutional reform.

On May 10, 1981, France elected François Mitterrand, a Socialist candidate, president. In Sept., the government nationalized 5 major industries and most private banks. From 1986 to 1988 (and again from 1993 to 1995), however, France pursued a privatization program in which many state-owned companies were sold. Mitterrand was elected to a 2d 7-year term in 1988.

In 1993, France set tighter rules for entry into the country and made it easier for the government to expel foreigners. In June 1994, France sent troops to Rwanda in an effort to help protect civilians there from ongoing massacres.

The international terrorist known as Carlos the Jackal (Ilich Ramirez Sánchez) was arrested in Sudan Aug. 14, 1994, and extradited to France, where he had been sentenced in absentia to life imprisonment.

Jacques Chirac won the presidency in a runoff election May 7, 1995. A series of terrorist bombings and bombing attempts began in the summer of 1995; Islamic extremists, opposed to France's support of the Algerian government and its struggle with Islamic fundamentalists, were believed responsible. In Sept. 1995, France stirred widespread protests by resuming nuclear tests at Mururoa Atoll, in the South Pacific, after a 3-year moratorium; the tests ended Jan. 1996.

On May 28, 1996, Chirac promised to end military conscription by Jan. 1997, as part of a plan to restructure the French armed forces. France pledged June 8 that it would rejoin the command structure of a reorganized NATO.

The island of **Corsica,** in the Mediterranean W of Italy and N of Sardinia, is a territorial collectivity and region of France comprising 2 departments. It elects a total of 2 senators and 3 deputies to the French Parliament. Area: 3,369 sq. mi.; pop. (1996 est.): 258,000. The capital is Ajaccio, birthplace of Napoleon. Violence in 1996 by rival separatist groups hurt tourism, a leading industry on the island.

## Overseas Departments

**French Guiana** is on the NE coast of South America with Suriname on the W and Brazil on the E and S. Its area is 33,399 sq. mi.; pop. (1996 est.): 151,000. Guiana sends one senator and 2 deputies to the French Parliament. Guiana is administered by a prefect and has a Council General of 16 elected members; capital is Cayenne.

The famous penal colony, Devil's Island, was phased out between 1938 and 1951.

Immense forests of rich timber cover 90% of the land. Placer gold mining is the most important industry. Exports are shrimp, timber, and machinery.

**Guadeloupe,** in the West Indies' Leeward Islands, consists of 2 large islands, Basse-Terre and Grande-Terre, separated by the Salt River, plus Marie Galante and the Saintes group to the S and, to the N, Desirade, St. Barthelemy, and over half of St. Martin (the Netherlands portion is St. Maarten). A French possession since 1635, the department is represented in the French Parliament by 2 senators and 4 deputies; administration consists of a prefect (governor) and an elected general and regional councils.

Area of the islands is 687 sq. mi.; pop. (1996 est.) 408,000, mainly descendants of slaves; capital is Basse-Terre on Basse-Terre Island. The land is fertile; sugar, rum, and bananas are exported; tourism is an important industry.

**Martinique,** the northernmost of the Windward Islands, in the West Indies, has been a possession since 1635, and a department since Mar. 1946. It is represented in the French Parliament by 2 senators and 4 deputies. The island was the birthplace of Napoleon's Empress Josephine.

It has an area of 436 sq. mi.; pop. (1996 est.) 399,000, mostly descendants of slaves. The capital is Fort-de-France (pop. 1991: 101,000). It is a popular tourist stop. The chief exports are rum, bananas, and petroleum products.

**Réunion** is a volcanic island in the Indian O. about 420 mi. E of Madagascar, and has belonged to France since 1665. Area, 970 sq. mi.; pop. (1996 est.) 679,000, 30% of French extraction. Capital: Saint-Denis. The chief export is sugar. It elects 5 deputies, 3 senators to the French Parliament.

## Overseas Territorial Collectivities

**Mayotte,** claimed by Comoros and administered by France, voted in 1976 to become a territorial collectivity of France. An island NW of Madagascar, area is 144 sq. mi., pop. (1996 est.) 101,000.

**St. Pierre and Miquelon,** formerly an overseas territory (1816-1976) and department (1976-85), made the transition to territorial collectivity in 1985. It consists of 2 groups of rocky islands near the SW coast of Newfoundland, inhabited by fishermen. The exports are chiefly fish products. The St. Pierre group has an area of 10 sq. mi.; Miquelon, 83 sq. mi. Total pop. (1995 est.), 6,757. The capital is St. Pierre.

Both Mayotte and St. Pierre and Miquelon elect a deputy and a senator to the French Parliament.

## Overseas Territories

Territory of **French Polynesia** comprises 130 islands widely scattered among 5 archipelagos in the South Pacific; administered by a Council of Ministers (headed by a president). Territorial Assembly and the Council have headquarters at Papeete, Tahiti, one of the **Society Islands** (which include the **Windward** and **Leeward** islands). Two deputies and a senator are elected to the French Parliament.

Other groups are the **Marquesas Islands,** the **Tuamotu Archipelago,** including the **Gambier Islands,** and the **Austral Islands.**

Total area of the islands administered from Tahiti is 1,544 sq. mi.; pop. (1996 est.), 225,000, more than half on Tahiti. Tahiti is picturesque and mountainous with a productive coastline bearing coconut, banana, and orange trees, sugarcane, and vanilla.

Tahiti was visited by Capt. James Cook in 1769 and by Capt. Bligh in the *Bounty,* 1788-89. Its beauty impressed Herman Melville, Paul Gauguin, and Charles Darwin. Tahitians angered by French nuclear testing rioted Sept. 1995.

Territory of the **French Southern and Antarctic Lands** comprises **Adelie Land,** on Antarctica, and 4 island groups in the Indian O. Adelie, reached 1840, has a research station, a coastline of 185 mi., and tapers 1,240 mi. inland to the South Pole. The U.S. does not recognize national claims in Antarctica. There are 2 huge glaciers, Ninnis, 22 mi. wide, 99 mi. long, and Mentz, 11 mi. wide, 140 mi. long. The Indian O. groups are:

**Kerguelen Archipelago,** visited 1772, consists of one large and 300 small islands. The chief is 87 mi. long, 74 mi. wide, and has Mt. Ross, 6,429 ft. tall. Principal research station is Port-aux-Français. Seals often weigh 2 tons; there are blue whales, coal, peat, semiprecious stones. **Crozet Archipelago,** reached 1772, covers 195 sq. mi. Eastern Island rises to 6,560 ft. **Saint Paul,** in southern Indian O., has warm springs with earth at places heating to 120° to 390° F. **Amsterdam** is nearby; both produce cod and rock lobster.

Territory of **New Caledonia** and Dependencies is a group of islands in the Pacific O. about 1,115 mi. E of Australia and approx. the same distance NW of New Zealand. Dependencies are the **Loyalty Islands, Isle of Pines, Belep Archipelago,** and **Huon Islands.**

The largest island, New Caledonia, is 6,530 sq. mi. Total area of the territory is 8,548 sq. mi.; population (1996 est.) 188,000. The group was acquired by France in 1853.

The territory is administered by a High Commissioner. There is a popularly elected Territorial Congress. Two deputies and a senator are elected to the French Parliament. Capital: Noumea.

Mining is the chief industry. New Caledonia is one of the world's largest nickel producers. Other minerals found are chrome, iron, cobalt, manganese, silver, gold, lead, and copper. Agricultural products include coffee, copra, cotton, manioc (cassava), corn, tobacco, bananas, and pineapples.

In 1987, New Caledonian voters chose by referendum to remain within the French Republic. There were clashes between French and Melanesians (Kanaks) in 1988. Another referendum is scheduled for 1998.

Territory of the **Wallis and Futuna Islands** comprises 2 island groups in the SW Pacific S of the Equator between Fiji and Western Samoa; became an overseas territory July 29, 1961. The islands have a total area of 106 sq. mi. and population (1996 est.) of 14,700. **Alofi,** attached to Futuna, is uninhabited. Capital: Mata-Utu. Chief products are copra, yams, taro roots, bananas. A senator and a deputy are elected to the French Parliament.

# Gabon

## Gabonese Republic

## République Gabonaise

**People: Population:** 1,192,798. **Pop. density:** 12 per sq. mi. **Urban:** 73%. **Ethnic groups:** Fang, Eshira, Bapounou, Bateke, other Bantu. **Principal languages:** French (official),

Bantu dialects. **Religions:** Mostly Christian, some Muslim and animist.

**Geography: Area:** 103,347 sq. mi. **Location:** On Atlantic coast of central Africa. **Neighbors:** Equatorial Guinea and Cameroon on N, Congo on E and S. **Topography:** Heavily forested, the country consists of coastal lowlands; plateaus in N, E, and S; mountains in N, SE, and center. The Ogooue R. system covers most of Gabon. **Capital:** Libreville (1993): 419,000.

**Government: Type:** Republic. **Head of state:** Pres. Omar Bongo; b Dec. 30, 1935; in office: Dec. 2, 1967. **Head of government:** Prime Min. Paulin Obame-Nguema; in office: Nov. 2, 1994. **Local divisions:** 9 provinces. **Defense:** 2.4% of GDP (1993). **Active troop strength:** 4,700 est.

**Economy: Industries:** Oil products, textiles. **Chief crops:** Cocoa, coffee, palm products. **Minerals:** Oil, manganese, uranium, iron. **Crude oil reserves** (1995): 1.3 bil bbls. **Other resources:** Timber. **Arable land:** 1%. **Electricity prod.** (1993): 910 mil kWh. **Labor force:** 65% agric.; 30% ind. & commerce.

**Finance: Monetary unit:** CFA Franc (June 1996: 515 = $1 US). **Gross domestic product** (1994): $5.6 bil.* **Per capita income:** $4,900. **Imports** (1993): $832 mil; partners: France 42%. **Exports** (1993): $2.1 bil; partners: U.S. 38%, France 26%. **National budget** (1993): $1.6 bil. **Consumer prices** (change in 1994): 36.2%.

**Transport: Motor vehicles:** in use: 23,000 passenger cars, 17,000 comm. vehicles. **Civil aviation:** 354 mil passenger-mi.; 6 airports with scheduled flights. **Chief ports:** Port-Gentil, Owendo, Libreville.

**Communications: Television sets:** 1 per 28 persons. **Radios:** 1 per 4.5 persons. **Telephones:** 1 per 41 persons.

**Health: Life expectancy at birth** (1996): 53 male; 59 female. **Births** (per 1,000 pop.): 28. **Deaths** (per 1,000 pop.): 14. **Natural increase:** 1.5%. **Hospital beds:** 1 per 103 persons. **Physicians:** 1 per 2,337 persons. **Infant mortality** (per 1,000 live births 1996): 90.

**Education: Literacy** (1995): 63%. Compulsory to age 16; attendance: 75%.

**Major International Organizations:** UN (WTO, FAO, WHO, IMF, World Bank), OAU, OPEC.

**Embassy:** 2043 20th St. NW 20009; 797-1000.

France established control over the region in the second half of the 19th century. Gabon became independent Aug. 17, 1960. A multiparty political system was introduced in 1990, and a new constitution was enacted Mar. 14, 1991. However, the reelection of longtime Pres. Omar Bongo, on Dec. 5, 1993, prompted rioting and charges of vote fraud. Under a revised constitution approved by referendum July 23, 1995, new elections were scheduled for 1997.

Gabon is one of the most prosperous black African countries, thanks to abundant natural resources, foreign private investment, and government development programs.

# The Gambia

## Republic of The Gambia

**People: Population:** 1,204,984. **Age distrib.** (%): <15: 45; 65+: 2. **Pop. density:** 292 per sq. mi. **Urban:** 26%. **Ethnic groups:** Mandinka 42%, Fula 18%, Wolof 16%, others. **Principal languages:** English (official), Mandinka, Wolof. **Religions:** Muslim 90%, Christian 9%.

**Geography: Area:** 4,127 sq. mi. **Location:** On Atlantic coast near W tip of Africa. **Neighbors:** Surrounded on 3 sides by Senegal. **Topography:** A narrow strip of land on each side of the lower Gambia R. **Capital:** Banjul (1993 est.): 40,000.

**Government: Type:** In transition. **Head of state and government:** Capt. Yahya Jammeh; b May 25, 1965; in office: July 23, 1994. **Local divisions:** 5 divisions and Banjul. **Defense:** 3.8% of GDP (FY 1993-94). **Active troop strength:** 800.

**Economy: Industries:** Tourism, peanut processing. **Chief crops:** Peanuts (main export), rice. **Arable land:** 16%. **Fish catch** (1993): 20,000 metric tons. **Electricity prod.** (1993): 70 mil kWh. **Labor force:** 75% agric.; 19% ind., comm., serv.

**Finance: Monetary unit:** Dalasi (June 1996: 10.05 = $1.00 US). **Gross domestic product** (1993 est.): $1 bil.* **Per capita GDP:** $1,050. **Imports** (FY 1992-93): $154 mil; partners: Europe 57%. **Exports** (FY 1992-93): $81 mil; partners: Japan 60%. **Tourism** (1993): $26 mil. **National budget** (FY 1992-93): $89 mil. **International reserves less gold** (Apr. 1996): $114 mil. **Consumer prices** (change in 1995): 7.0%.

**Transport: Motor vehicles:** in use: 7,300 passenger cars, 3,100 comm. vehicles. **Chief port:** Banjul.

**Communications: Radios:** 1 per 7.7 persons. **Telephones:** 1 per 64 persons.

**Health: Life expectancy at birth** (1996): 51 male; 55female. **Births** (per 1,000 pop.): 44. **Deaths** (per 1,000 pop.): 14. **Natural increase:** 3.1%. **Physicians:** 1 per 14,536 persons. **Infant mortality** (per 1,000 live births 1996): 81.

**Education: Literacy** (1993): 30%.

**Major International Organizations:** UN (IMF, FAO, WTO, World Bank, WHO), OAU, the Commonwealth.

**Embassy:** 1155 15th St. NW 20005; 842-1356.

The tribes of Gambia were at one time associated with the West African empires of Ghana, Mali, and Songhay. The area became Britain's first African possession in 1588.

Independence came Feb. 18, 1965; republic status within the Commonwealth was achieved in 1970. After a coup attempt in 1981, The Gambia formed the confederation of Senegambia with Senegal that lasted until 1989. The country suffered from severe famine in the 1970s.

On July 23, 1994, after 24 years in power, Pres. Dawda K. Jawara was deposed in a bloodless coup by a military officer, Yahya Jammeh. Jammeh barred political activity, detained potential opponents, and governed by decree. A new constitution was approved by referendum, Aug. 8, 1996. On Sept. 27, 1996, Jammeh won the presidential election.

# Georgia

## Republic of Georgia

## Sakartvelos Respublika

**People: Population:** 5,219,810. **Pop. density:** 195 per sq. mi. **Urban:** 55%. **Ethnic groups:** Georgian 70%, Armenian 8%, Russian 6%. **Principal languages:** Georgian (official), Russian. **Religions:** Georgian Orthodox 65%, Muslim 11%, Russian Orthodox 10%.

**Geography: Area:** 26,831 sq. mi. **Location:** In SW Asia, on E coast of Black Sea. **Neighbors:** Russia on N and NE, Turkey and Armenia on S, Azerbaijan on SE. **Topography:** Separated from Russia on NE by main range of the Caucasus Mts. **Capital:** Tbilisi (1994 est.): 1.3 mil.

**Government: Type:** Republic. **Head of state:** Pres. Eduard A. Shevardnadze; b Jan. 25, 1928; in office: Nov. 6, 1992. **Defense:** 3.1% of GNP (1993).

**Economy: Industries:** Manganese mining, light industry. **Chief crops:** Citrus and other fruits, wheat, corn, grapes. **Minerals:** Manganese, coal. **Livestock** (1994): cattle: 1.1 mil; sheep and goats: 1.4 mil. **Electricity prod.** (1993): 9.1 bil kWh. **Labor force:** 31% ind., constr.; 25% agric.

**Finance: Monetary unit:** Lari (June 1996: 1.2 mil = $1 U.S.). **Gross domestic product** (1994 est.): $6 bil.* **Per capita GDP:** $1,060. **Imports:** NA. **Exports:** NA.

**Transport: Railroads: Length:** 976 mi. **Motor vehicles:** in use: 427,000 passenger cars. **Chief ports:** Batumi, Sukhumi.

**Communications: Telephones:** 1 per 5.5 persons. **Daily newspaper circ.:** 671 per 1,000 pop.

**Health: Life expectancy at birth** (1996): 63 male; 73 female. **Births** (per 1,000 pop.): 13. **Deaths** (per 1,000 pop.): 12. **Natural increase**: 0.1%. **Hospital beds:** 1 per 90 persons. **Physicians:** 1 per 170 persons. **Infant mortality** (per 1,000 live births 1996): 23.

**Education: Literacy** (1994): 99%.

**Major International Organizations:** UN, CIS.

**Embassy:** 1511 K St. NW, Suite 424 20005; 393-6060.

The region contained the ancient kingdoms of Colchis and Iberia. It was Christianized in the 4th century and conquered by Arabs in the 8th century. The region expanded to include area from the Black Sea to Caspian and parts of Armenia and Persia before its disintegration under the impact of Mongol and Turkish invasions. The annexation to Russia in 1801 caused the Russian war with Persia, 1804-1813. Georgia entered the USSR in 1922 and became a constituent republic in 1936.

In 1989, strong nationalist feelings led the USSR to attempts at repression; Soviet troops attacked nationalist demonstrators in April, killing some 20 persons. Georgia declared independence Apr. 9, 1991. It became an independent state when the Soviet Union disbanded Dec. 26, 1991.

There was fighting during 1991 between rebel forces and loyalists of Pres. Zviad Gamsakhurdia, who fled the capital Jan. 6, 1992. The ruling Military Council picked former Soviet Foreign

Minister Eduard A. Shevardnadze to chair a newly created State Council. An attempted coup by forces loyal to Gamsakhurdia was crushed June 24, 1992. Shevardnadze was later elected president. Gamsakhurdia died Jan. 1994, reportedly by suicide.

In Abkhazia, an autonomous region within Georgia, ethnic Abkhazis, reportedly aided by Russia, launched a bloody military campaign and, by late 1993, had gained control of much of the region. A cease-fire providing for Russian peacekeepers was signed in Moscow May 14, 1994.

On Feb. 3, 1994, Georgia signed agreements with Russia for economic and military cooperation. On Mar. 1, Georgia's Supreme Council ratified membership by Georgia in the Commonwealth of Independent States.

Shevardnadze was wounded by a car bomb Aug. 29, 1995, while on his way to Parliament to sign a new constitution. He was reelected president Nov. 5.

# Germany

## Federal Republic of Germany

## Bundesrepublik Deutschland

*(Figures prior to 1990 for original 11 states)*

**People: Population:** 83,536,115. **Age distrib.** (%): <15: 16; 65+: 15. **Pop. density:** 606 per sq. mi. **Urban:** 85%. **Ethnic groups:** German 95%. **Principal language:** German (official). **Religions:** Protestant 45%, Roman Catholic 37%.

**Geography: Area:** 137,828 sq. mi. **Location:** In central Europe. **Neighbors:** Denmark on N; Netherlands, Belgium, Luxembourg, France on W; Switzerland, Austria on S; Czech Rep., Poland on E. **Topography:** Germany is flat in N, hilly in center and W, and mountainous in Bavaria. Chief rivers are Elbe, Weser, Ems, Rhine, and Main, all flowing toward North Sea, and Danube, flowing toward Black Sea. **Capital:** Berlin. **Cities** (1994 est.): Berlin 3.5 mil; Hamburg 1.7 mil; Munich 1.3 mil; Cologne 962,500; Frankfurt 659,800; Essen 622,400; Dortmund 602,000; Stuttgart 594,400; Düsseldorf 574,900; Bremen 551,600; Duisberg 536,800; Hannover 524,800.

**Government: Type:** Federal republic. **Head of state:** Pres. Roman Herzog; b Apr. 5, 1934; in office: July 1, 1994. **Head of government:** Chan. Helmut Kohl; b Apr. 3, 1930; in office: Oct. 1, 1982. **Local divisions:** 16 laender (states) with substantial powers. **Defense:** 1.8% of GNP (1994). **Active troop strength:** 339,900.

**Economy: Industries:** Steel, ships, vehicles, machinery, electronics, coal, chemicals. **Chief crops:** Grains, potatoes, sugar beets. **Minerals:** Coal, potash, lignite, iron, uranium. **Crude oil reserves** (1995): 368 mil bbls. **Arable land:** 34%. **Livestock** (1993-94): cattle: 21.3 mil; pigs: 26.0 mil. **Fish catch** (1993): 316,000 metric tons. **Electricity prod.** (1993): 493 bil kWh. **Labor force:** 41% ind.; 6% agric.

**Finance: Monetary unit:** Mark (June 1996: 1.53 = $1 US). **Gross domestic product** (1994): $1.34 tril.* **Per capita GDP:** $16,580. **Imports** (1994): $362 bil; partners: EU 46%, U.S. 7%. **Exports** (1994): $437 bil; partners: EU 48%, U.S. 8%. **Tourism** (1994): $10.6 bil. **National budget** (1994): $780 bil. **International reserves less gold** (May 1996): $84.3 bil. **Gold:** 95.18 mil oz t. **Consumer prices** (change in 1995): 1.8%.

**Transport: Railroads: Length:** 54,994. mi. **Motor vehicles:** in use: 39.9 mil passenger cars, 2.2 mil comm. vehicles. **Civil aviation:** 12.6 bil passenger-mi.; 40 airports with scheduled flights. **Chief ports:** Hamburg, Bremen, Bremerhaven, Lubeck, Rostock.

**Communications: Television sets:** 1 per 2.5 persons. **Radios:** 1 per 2.3 persons. **Telephones:** 1 per 2.2 persons. **Daily newspaper circ.:** 331 per 1,000 pop.

**Health: Life expectancy at birth** (1996): 73 male; 79 female. **Births** (per 1,000 pop.): 10. **Deaths** (per 1,000 pop.): 11. **Natural increase:** –0.1%. **Hospital beds:** 1 per 130 persons. **Physicians:** 1 per 304 persons. **Infant mortality** (per 1,000 live births 1996): 6.

**Education: Literacy** (1993): 100%. Compulsory: ages 6-15. Attendance 100%.

**Major International Organizations:** UN and all of its specialized agencies, EU, OECD, NATO.

**Embassy:** 4645 Reservoir Rd. NW 20007; 298-4000.

Germany is a central European nation originally composed of numerous states, with a common language and traditions, that were united in one country in 1871; Germany was split into 2 countries from the end of World War II until 1990, when it was reunified.

**History and government.** Germanic tribes were defeated by Julius Caesar, 55 and 53 BC, but Roman expansion N of the Rhine was stopped in AD 9. Charlemagne, ruler of the Franks, consolidated Saxon, Bavarian, Rhenish, Frankish, and other lands; after him the eastern part became the German Empire. The Thirty Years' War, 1618-1648, split Germany into small principalities and kingdoms. After Napoleon, Austria contended with Prussia for dominance, but lost the Seven Weeks' War to Prussia, 1866. Otto von Bismarck, Prussian chancellor, formed the North German Confederation, 1867.

In 1870 Bismarck maneuvered Napoleon III into declaring war. After the quick defeat of France, Bismarck formed the **German Empire** and on Jan. 18, 1871, in Versailles, proclaimed King Wilhelm I of Prussia German emperor (Deutscher kaiser).

The German Empire reached its peak before World War I in 1914, with 208,780 sq. mi., plus a colonial empire. After that war Germany ceded Alsace-Lorraine to France; West Prussia and Posen (Poznan) province to Poland; part of Schleswig to Denmark; lost all of its colonies and the ports of Memel and Danzig.

**Republic of Germany,** 1919-1933, adopted the Weimar constitution; met reparation payments and elected Friedrich Ebert and Gen. Paul von Hindenburg presidents.

**Third Reich,** 1933-1945, Adolf Hitler led the National Socialist German Workers' (Nazi) party after World War I. In 1923 he attempted to unseat the Bavarian government and was imprisoned. Pres. von Hindenburg named Hitler chancellor Jan. 30, 1933; on Aug. 3, 1934, the day after Hindenburg's death, the cabinet joined the offices of president and chancellor and made Hitler fuehrer (leader). Hitler abolished freedom of speech and assembly, and began a long series of persecutions climaxed by the murder of millions of Jews and others.

Hitler repudiated the Versailles treaty and reparations agreements. He remilitarized the Rhineland (1936) and annexed Austria (Anschluss, 1938). At Munich he made an agreement with Neville Chamberlain, British prime minister, that permitted Germany to annex part of Czechoslovakia. He signed a nonaggression treaty with the USSR, 1939. He declared war on Poland Sept. 1, 1939, precipitating World War II.

With total defeat near, Hitler committed suicide in Berlin Apr. 1945. The victorious Allies voided all acts and annexations of Hitler's Reich.

**Division of Germany.** Germany was sectioned into 4 zones of occupation, administered by the Allied Powers (U.S., USSR, U.K., and France). The USSR took control of many E German states. The territory E of the so-called Oder-Neisse line was assigned to, and later annexed by, Poland. Northern East Prussia (now Kaliningrad) was annexed by the USSR. Administration of the remaining regions, in the W and S (which make up about 2/3 of present-day Germany), was split among the Western Allies.

There was also created the area of Greater Berlin, within but not part of the Soviet zone, administered by the 4 occupying powers under the Allied Command. In 1948 the USSR withdrew, established its single command in East Berlin, and cut off supplies. The Western Allies utilized a gigantic airlift to bring food to West Berlin, 1948-49.

In 1949, 2 separate German states were established; in May the zones administered by the Western Allies became West Germany, capital: Bonn; in Oct. the Soviet sector became East Germany, capital: East Berlin. West Berlin was considered an enclave of West Germany, although its status was disputed by the Soviet bloc.

**East Germany.** The German Democratic Republic (East Germany) was proclaimed in the Soviet sector of Berlin Oct. 7, 1949. It was proclaimed fully sovereign in 1954, but Soviet troops remained on grounds of security and the 4-power Potsdam agreement.

Coincident with the entrance of West Germany into the European defense community in 1952, the East German government decreed a prohibited zone 3 miles deep along its 600-mile border with West Germany and cut Berlin's telephone system in two. Berlin was further divided by erection of a fortified wall in 1961, after over 3 million East Germans had emigrated West; an exodus of refugees to the West continued, though on a smaller scale.

East Germany suffered severe economic problems at least until the mid-1960s. Then a "new economic system" was introduced, easing central planning controls and allowing factories to make profits provided they were reinvested in operations or redistributed to workers as bonuses. By the early 1970s, the economy was highly industrialized, and the nation was credited with the highest standard of living among Warsaw Pact countries. But growth slowed in the late 1970s, because of shortages of natural resources and labor, and a huge debt to lenders in the West. Comparison with the lifestyle in the West caused many of the young to leave the country.

The government firmly resisted following the USSR's policy of *glasnost,* but by Oct. 1989, was faced with nationwide demonstrations demanding reform. Pres. Erich Honecker, in office since 1976, was forced to resign, Oct. 18. On Nov. 4, the border with Czechoslovakia was opened and permission granted for refugees to travel to the West. On Nov. 9, the East German government announced its decision to open the border with the West, signaling the end of the "Berlin Wall," which was the supreme emblem of the cold war. On Aug. 23, 1990, the East German parliament agreed to formal unification with West Germany; this occurred Oct. 3.

**West Germany.** The Federal Republic of Germany (West Germany) was proclaimed May 23, 1949, in Bonn, after a constitution had been drawn up by a consultative assembly formed by representatives of the 11 laender (states) in the French, British, and American zones. Later reorganized into 9 units, the laender numbered 10 with the addition of the Saar, 1957. Berlin also was granted land (state) status, but the 1945 occupation agreements placed restrictions on it.

The occupying powers, the U.S., Britain, and France, restored civil status, Sept. 21, 1949. The Western Allies ended the state of war with Germany in 1951 (the U.S. resumed diplomatic relations July 2), while the USSR did so in 1955. The powers lifted controls and the republic became fully independent May 5, 1955.

Dr. Konrad Adenauer, Christian Democrat, was made chancellor Sept. 15, 1949, reelected 1953, 1957, 1961. Willy Brandt, heading a coalition of Social Democrats and Free Democrats, became chancellor Oct. 21, 1969. (He resigned May 1974 because of a spy scandal.)

In 1970 Brandt signed friendship treaties with the USSR and Poland. In 1971, the U.S., Britain, France, and the USSR signed an agreement on Western access to West Berlin. In 1972 East and West Germany signed their first formal treaty, implementing the agreement easing access to West Berlin. In 1973 a West Germany-Czechoslovakia pact normalized relations and nullified the 1938 "Munich Agreement."

West Germany experienced strong economic growth starting in the 1950s. The country led Europe in provisions for worker participation in the management of industry.

A NATO decision to deploy medium-range nuclear missiles in Western Europe sparked a demonstration by some 400,000 protesters in 1983. In 1989, Chancellor Helmut Kohl's call for early negotiations with the Soviets on reducing short-range missiles caused a rift with NATO allies.

In 1989, the changes in the East German government and the opening of the Berlin Wall sparked talk of reunification of the 2 Germanys. In 1990, under the leadership of Chancellor Kohl, West Germany moved rapidly to reunite with East Germany.

**A New Era.** As Communism was being rejected in East Germany, talks began concerning German reunification. At a meeting in Ottawa, Feb. 1990, the foreign ministers of the World War II "Big Four" Allied nations and of East Germany and West Germany reached agreement on a format for high-level talks on German reunification.

In May, NATO ministers adopted a package of proposals on reunification, including the inclusion of the united Germany as a full member of NATO and the barring of the new Germany from having its own nuclear, chemical, or biological weapons. In July, the USSR agreed to conditions that would allow Germany to become a member of NATO.

The 2 nations agreed to monetary unification under the West German mark beginning in July. The merger of the 2 Germanys took place on Oct. 3, and the first all-German elections since 1932 were held Dec. 2.

In 1991, Berlin again became the capital of Germany; the seat of government was scheduled to shift from Bonn to Berlin over the course of about 10 years.

In 1992, neo-Nazi groups intensified their campaign against refugees. Parliament approved constitutional changes to restrict foreigners' rights to seek asylum in Germany, May 1993.

Germany's highest court ruled, July 12, 1994, that German troops could participate in international military missions abroad, when approved by Parliament. Ceremonies were held marking the final withdrawal of Russian troops from Germany, Aug. 31, 1994. Ceremonies were held the following week marking the final withdrawal of American, British, and French troops from Berlin. General elections Oct. 16, 1994, left Chancellor Helmut Kohl's governing coalition with a slim parliamentary majority. Eastern Germany received more than $1 trillion in public and private funds from western Germany between 1990 and 1995.

**Helgoland,** an island of 130 acres in the North Sea, was taken from Denmark by a British Naval Force in 1807 and later ceded to Germany to become part of Schleswig-Holstein province in return for rights in East Africa. The heavily fortified island was surrendered to UK, May 23, 1945, demilitarized in 1947, and returned to West Germany, Mar. 1, 1952. It is a free port.

# Ghana

## Republic of Ghana

**People: Population:** 17,698,271. **Age distrib.** (%): <15: 45; 65+: 3. **Pop. density:** 192 per sq. mi. **Urban:** 36%. **Ethnic groups:** Akan 44%, Moshi-Dagomba 16%, Ewe 13%, Ga 8%. **Principal languages:** English (official), Akan, Moshi-Dagomba, Ewe, Ga. **Religions:** Indigenous beliefs 38%, Muslim 30%, Christian 24%.

**Geography: Area:** 92,098 sq. mi. **Location:** On southern coast of W Africa. **Neighbors:** Côte d'Ivoire on W, Burkina Faso on N, Togo on E. **Topography:** Most of Ghana consists of low fertile plains and scrubland, cut by rivers and by the artificial Lake Volta. **Capital:** Accra (1990 met. est.): 1.8 mil.

**Government: Type:** Republic. **Head of state and government:** Pres. Jerry Rawlings; b 1947; in office: Dec. 31, 1981. **Local divisions:** 10 regions. **Defense:** 1.5% of GDP (1993). **Active troop strength:** 7,000.

**Economy: Industries:** Aluminum, light industry. **Chief crops:** Cocoa, coffee, rice. **Minerals:** Gold, manganese, industrial diamonds, bauxite. **Other resources:** Timber, rubber. **Arable land:** 5%. **Livestock** (1994): cattle: 1.7 mil; sheep: 3.3 mil. **Fish catch** (1993): 371,000 metric tons. **Electricity prod.** (1993): 6.1 bil kWh. **Labor force:** 55% agric.; 19% ind.; 15% sales, clerical.

**Finance: Monetary unit:** Cedi (June 1996: 1,658 = $1 US). **Gross domestic product** (1994): $22.6 bil.* **Per capita GDP:** $1,310. **Imports** (1993): $1.7 bil; partners: UK 22%, U.S. 11%, Germany 9%. **Exports** (1993): $1 bil; partners: Germany 31%, U.S. 12%. **Tourism** (1992): $167 mil. **National budget** (1993): $1.2 bil. **International reserves less gold** (Dec. 1995): $698 mil. **Gold:** 275,000 oz t. **Consumer prices** (change in 1995): 59.5%.

**Transport: Railroads: Route length:** 592 mi. **Motor vehicles:** in use: 90,000 passenger cars, 44,000 comm. vehicles. **Civil aviation:** 206 mil passenger-mi.; 1 airport with scheduled flights. **Chief ports:** Tema, Takoradi.

**Communications: Television sets:** 1 per 64 persons. **Radios:** 1 per 3.7 persons. **Telephones:** 1 per 321 persons.

**Health: Life expectancy at birth** (1996): 54 male; 58 female. **Births** (per 1,000 pop.): 35. **Deaths** (per 1,000 pop.): 11. **Natural increase:** 2.4%. **Hospital beds:** 1 per 791 persons. **Infant mortality** (per 1,000 live births 1996): 80.

**Education: Literacy** (1992): 65%. Compulsory: ages 6-16.

**Major International Organizations:** UN and all of its specialized agencies, OAU, the Commonwealth.

**Embassy:** 3512 International Dr. NW 20008; 686-4520.

Named for an African empire along the Niger River, AD 400-1240, Ghana was ruled by Britain for 113 years as the Gold Coast. The UN in 1956 approved merger with the British Togoland trust territory. Independence came March 6, 1957. Republic status within the Commonwealth was attained in 1960.

Pres. Kwame Nkrumah built hospitals and schools, promoted development projects like the Volta R. hydroelectric and aluminum plants but ran the country into debt, jailed opponents, and was accused of corruption. A 1964 referendum gave Nkrumah dictatorial powers and set up a one-party socialist state.

Nkrumah was overthrown in 1966 by a police-army coup, which expelled Chinese and East German teachers and technicians. Elections were held in 1969, but 4 further coups occurred in 1972, 1978, 1979, and 1981. The 1979 and 1981 coups, led by Flight Lieut. Jerry Rawlings, were followed by suspension of the constitution and banning of political parties. A new constitution, which allowed for multiparty politics, was approved in April 1992.

In Feb. 1993 more than 1,000 people were killed in ethnic clashes in northern Ghana.

# Greece

## Hellenic Republic

## Elliniki Dhimokratia

**People: Population:** 10,538,594. **Age distrib.** (%): <15: 18; 65+: 13. **Pop. density:** 207 per sq. mi. **Urban:** 72%. **Ethnic groups:** Greek 98%. **Principal languages:** Greek (official), English, French. **Religion:** Greek Orthodox 98% (official).

**Geography: Area:** 50,949 sq. mi. **Location:** Occupies southern end of Balkan Peninsula in SE Europe. **Neighbors:** Albania, Macedonia, Bulgaria on N; Turkey on E. **Topography:** About 3/4 of Greece is nonarable, with mountains in all areas. Pindus Mts. run through the country N to S. The heavily indented coastline is 9,385 mi. long. Of over 2,000 islands, only 169 are inhabited, among them Crete, Rhodes, Milos, Kerkira (Corfu), Chios, Lesbos, Samos, Euboea, Delos, Mykonos. **Capital:** Athens. **Cities** (1991 est.): Athens 748,000; Thessaloníki 378,000.

**Government: Type:** Parliamentary republic. **Head of state:** Pres. Costis Stefanopoulos; b 1926; in office: Mar. 8, 1995. **Head of government:** Prime Min. Costas Simitis; b June 23, 1936; in office: Jan. 18, 1996. **Local divisions:** 52 prefectures. **Defense:** 5.4% of GDP (1994). **Active troop strength:** 171,300.

**Economy: Industries:** Tourism, textiles, chemicals, metals, wine, food processing. **Chief crops:** Grains, corn, rice, cotton, tobacco, olives, grapes, citrus and other fruits, tomatoes. **Minerals:** Bauxite, lignite, magnesite, oil. **Crude oil reserves** (1995): 41 mil bbls. **Arable land:** 23%. **Livestock** (1994): sheep: 9.6 mil; goats: 5.6 mil. **Fish catch** (1993): 200,000 metric tons. **Electricity prod.** (1993): 35.8 bil kWh. **Labor force** (1995): 52% services; 25% ind.; 23% agric.

**Finance: Monetary unit:** Drachma (June 1996: 241 = $1 US). **Gross domestic product** (1994): $93.7 bil.* **Per capita GDP:** $8,870. **Imports** (1993): $19.2 bil; partners: Germany 15%, Italy 14%, France 7%. **Exports** (1993): $9 bil; partners: Germany 24%, Italy 14%, France 7%. **Tourism** (1993): $3.3 bil. **National budget** (1994): $37.6 bil. **International reserves less gold** (May 1996): $11.9 bil. **Gold:** 3.5 mil oz t. **Consumer prices** (change in 1995): 9.3%.

**Transport: Railroads: Route length:** 1,552 mi. **Motor vehicles:** in use: 2.8 mil passenger cars, 849,000 comm. vehicles. **Civil aviation:** 4.9 bil passenger-mi.; 31 airports with scheduled flights. **Chief ports:** Piraeus, Thessaloníki, Patras.

**Communications: Television sets:** 1 per 4.5 persons. **Radios:** 1 per 2.5 persons. **Telephones:** 1 per 1.9 persons.

**Health: Life expectancy at birth** (1996): 75 male; 81 female. **Births** (per 1,000 pop.): 10. **Deaths** (per 1,000 pop.): 10. **Natural increase:** 0. **Hospital beds:** 1 per 298 persons. **Physicians:** 1 per 259 persons. **Infant mortality** (per 1,000 live births 1996): 7.

**Education: Literacy** (1993): 95%. Free and compulsory: ages 6-15.

**Major International Organizations:** UN (WTO, FAO, World Bank, IMF, WHO, ILO), EU, NATO, OECD.

**Embassy:** 2221 Massachusetts Ave. NW 20008; 939-5800.

The achievements of ancient Greece in art, architecture, science, mathematics, philosophy, drama, literature, and democracy became legacies for succeeding ages. Greece reached the height of its glory and power, particularly in the Athenian city-state, in the 5th century BC.

Greece fell under Roman rule in the 2d and 1st centuries BC. In the 4th century AD it became part of the Byzantine Empire and, after the fall of Constantinople to the Turks in 1453, part of the Ottoman Empire.

Greece won its war of independence from Turkey 1821-1829, and became a kingdom. A republic was established 1924; the monarchy was restored, 1935, and George II, King of the Hellenes, resumed the throne. In Oct. 1940, Greece rejected an ultimatum from Italy. Nazi support resulted in its defeat and occupation by Germans, Italians, and Bulgarians. By the end of 1944 the invaders withdrew. Communist resistance forces were defeated by Royalist and British troops. A plebiscite again restored the monarchy.

Communists waged guerrilla war 1947-49 against the government but were defeated with the aid of the U.S. A period of reconstruction and rapid development followed, mainly with conservative governments under Premier Constantine Karamanlis. The Center Union, led by George Papandreou, won elections in 1963 and 1964, but King Constantine, who acceded in 1964, forced Papandreou to resign. A period of political maneuvers ended in the military takeover of April 21, 1967, by Col. George Papadopoulos. King Constantine tried to reverse the consolidation of the harsh dictatorship Dec. 13, 1967, but failed and fled to Italy. Papadopoulos was ousted Nov. 25, 1973.

Greek army officers serving in the National Guard of Cyprus staged a coup on the island July 15, 1974. Turkey invaded Cyprus a week later, precipitating the collapse of the Greek junta, which was implicated in the Cyprus coup. Democratic government returned (and in 1975 the monarchy was abolished).

The 1981 electoral victory of the Panhellenic Socialist Movement (Pasok) of Andreas Papandreou brought about substantial changes in Greece's internal and external policies. A scandal centered on George Kostokas, a banker and publisher, led to the arrest or investigation of leading Socialists, implicated Papandreou, and contributed to the defeat of the Socialists at the polls in 1989. However, Papandreou, who was narrowly acquitted Jan. 1992 of corruption charges, led the Socialists to a comeback victory in general elections Oct. 10, 1993.

Tensions between Greece and the Former Yugoslav Republic of Macedonia eased when the 2 countries agreed to normalize relations Sept. 13, 1995. The ailing Papandreou was replaced as prime minister by Costas Simitis, Jan. 18, 1996.

# Grenada

**People: Population:** 94,961. **Pop. density:** 714 per sq. mi. **Ethnic groups:** Mostly black African. **Principal languages:** English (official), French patois. **Religions:** Roman Catholic 53%, Anglican 14%.

**Geography: Area:** 133 sq. mi. **Location:** In Caribbean, 90 mi. N of Venezuela. **Topography:** Main island is mountainous; country includes Carriacon and Petit Martinique islands. **Capital:** Saint George's (1991): 4,400.

**Government: Type:** Parliamentary democracy. **Head of state:** Queen Elizabeth II, represented by Gov.-Gen. Sir Reginald Palmer; b Feb. 15, 1923; in office: Aug. 6, 1992. **Head of government:** Prime Min.: Keith Mitchell; b Nov. 12, 1946; in office: June 22, 1995. **Local divisions:** 6 parishes and 1 dependency.

**Economy: Industries:** Tourism, textiles, spices. **Chief crops:** Nutmeg, bananas, cocoa, mace. **Arable land:** 15%. **Electricity prod.** (1993): 60 mil kWh. **Labor force:** 31% services; 24% agric.

**Finance: Monetary unit:** East Caribbean dollar (June 1996: 2.70 = $1 US). **Gross domestic product** (1993): $258 mil.* **Per capita GDP:** $2,750. **Imports** (1994): $134 mil; partners: Trin./Tob. 27%, U.S. 22%. **Exports** (1993): $19 mil; partners: U.S. 25%, Ven. 25%. **Tourism** (1994): $59 mil. **National budget** (1993 est.): $74 mil. **International reserves less gold** (Feb. 1996): $34.1 mil. **Consumer prices** (change in 1995): 3.0%.

**Chief ports:** Saint George's, Greenville.

**Communications: Television sets:** 1 per 3.1 persons. **Radios:** 1 per 1.7 persons. **Telephones:** 1 per 4.6 persons.

**Health: Life expectancy at birth** (1996): 68 male; 73 female. **Births** (per 1,000 pop.): 29. **Deaths** (per 1,000 pop.): 6. **Natural increase:** 2.3%. **Infant mortality** (per 1,000 live births 1996): 12.

**Education: Literacy** (1994): 85%; Compulsory: ages 6-14.

**Major International Organizations:** UN (IMF, FAO, WTO, World Bank, WHO), OAS, the Commonwealth.

**Embassy:** 1701 New Hampshire Ave. NW 20009; 265-2561.

Columbus sighted the island 1498. First European settlers were French, 1650. The island was held alternately by France and England until final British occupation, 1784. Grenada became fully independent Feb. 7, 1974, during a general strike. It is the smallest independent nation in the western hemisphere.

On Oct. 14, 1983, a military coup ousted Prime Minister Maurice Bishop, who was put under house arrest, later freed by supporters, rearrested, and, finally, on Oct. 19, executed. U.S. forces, with a token force from 6 area nations, invaded Grenada, Oct. 25. Resistance from the Grenadian army and Cuban advisors was quickly overcome as most of the population welcomed the invading forces. U.S. troops left Grenada in June 1985.

# Guatemala

## Republic of Guatemala

## República de Guatemala

**People: Population:** 11,277,614. **Age distrib.** (%): <15: 45; 65+: 3. **Pop. density:** 268 per sq. mi. **Urban:** 39%. **Ethnic groups:** Mestizo 56%, Amerindian 44%. **Principal languages:** Spanish (official), Mayan languages. **Religion:** Mostly Roman Catholic.

**Geography: Area:** 42,042 sq. mi. **Location:** In Central America. **Neighbors:** Mexico on N and W, El Salvador on S, Honduras and Belize on E. **Topography:** The central highland and mountain areas are bordered by the narrow Pacific coast and the lowlands and fertile river valleys on the Caribbean. There are numerous volcanoes in S, more than half a dozen over 11,000 ft. **Capital:** Guatemala City (1994 est.): 1.2 mil.

**Government: Type:** Republic. **Head of state and government:** Pres. Alvaro Arzú Irigoyen; b 1946; in office: Jan. 14, 1996. **Local divisions:** 22 departments. **Defense:** 1% of GDP (1993). **Active troop strength:** 44,200.

**Economy: Industries:** Furniture, rubber, textiles. **Chief crops:** Coffee, sugar, bananas, corn, cardamom. **Minerals:** Oil, nickel. **Crude oil reserves** (1995): 488 mil bbls. **Other resources:** Rare woods, fish, chicle. **Arable land:** 12%. **Electricity prod.** (1993): 2.3 bil kWh. **Labor force:** 60% agric.; 13% services.

**Finance: Monetary unit:** Quetzal (June 1996: 6.13 = $1 US). **Gross domestic product** (1994): $33 bil.* **Per capita GDP:** $3,080. **Imports** (1994): $2.6 bil; partners: U.S. 44%. **Exports** (1994): $1.4 bil; partners: U.S. 30%. **Tourism** (1993): $265 mil. **National budget** (1990 est.): $808 mil. **International reserves less gold** (Apr. 1996): $693 mil. **Gold:** 210,000 oz t. **Consumer prices** (change in 1994): 10.9%.

**Transport: Motor vehicles:** in use: 99,000 passenger cars, 95,000 comm. vehicles. **Civil aviation:** 239 mil passenger-mi; 2 airports with scheduled flights. **Chief ports:** Puerto Barrios, San Jose.

**Communications: Television sets:** 1 per 22 persons. **Radios:** 1 per 18 persons. **Telephones:** 1 per 43 persons. **Daily newspaper circ.:** 18 per 1,000 pop.

**Health: Life expectancy at birth** (1996): 63 male; 68 female. **Births** (per 1,000 pop.): 34. **Deaths** (per 1,000 pop.): 7. **Natural increase:** 2.7%. **Physicians:** 1 per 1,282 persons. **Infant mortality** (per 1,000 live births 1996): 51.

**Education: Literacy:** (1991): 56%. Free and compulsory: ages 7-14. **Attendance: 79%.**

**Major International Organizations:** UN (IMF, FAO, WTO, WHO, World Bank), OAS.

**Embassy:** 2220 R St. NW 20008; 745-4952.

The old Mayan Indian empire flourished in what is today Guatemala for over 1,000 years before the Spanish.

Guatemala was a Spanish colony 1524-1821; briefly a part of Mexico and then of the U.S. of Central America, the republic was established in 1839.

Since 1945 when a liberal government was elected to replace the long-term dictatorship of Jorge Ubico, the country has seen a variety of military and civilian governments and periods of civil war. More than 100,000 people have been killed since 1961, and another 40,000 "disappeared."

Dissident army officers seized power Mar. 23, 1982, denouncing a presidential election as fraudulent and pledging to restore "authentic democracy" to the nation. Political violence caused large numbers of Guatemalans to seek refuge in Mexico. Another military coup occurred Oct. 8, 1983. The nation returned to civilian rule in 1986.

The crisis-ridden government of Pres. Jorge Serrano Elías was ousted by the military June 1, 1993. Ramiro de León Carpio was elected president by Congress June 6. A UN report in March 1995 blamed state authorities for a majority of human rights violations in Guatemala. A conservative businessman, Alvaro Arzú Irigoyen, won the presidency, Jan. 7, 1996. On Sept. 19, 1996, the Guatemalan government and leftist rebels signed a peace accord aimed at ending 35 years of conflict.

# Guinea

## Republic of Guinea

## République de Guinée

**People: Population:** 7,411,981. **Age distrib.** (%): <15: 44; 65+: 3. **Pop. density:** 78 per sq. mi. **Urban:** 29%. **Ethnic groups:** Peuhl 40%, Malinke 30%, Soussou 20%, smaller tribes 10%. **Principal languages:** French (official), Peuhl, Malinke. **Religions:** Muslim 85%, Christian 8%.

**Geography: Area:** 94,926 sq. mi. **Location:** On Atlantic coast of W Africa. **Neighbors:** Guinea-Bissau, Senegal, Mali on N; Côte d'Ivoire on E; Liberia on S. **Topography:** A narrow coastal belt leads to the mountainous middle region, the source of the Gambia, Senegal, and Niger rivers. Upper Guinea, farther inland, is a cooler upland. The SE is forested. **Capital:** Conakry. **Cities** (1989 est.): Conakry 1.5 mil.

**Government: Type:** Republic. **Head of state and government:** Pres. Gen. Lansana Conté; b 1934; in office: Apr. 5, 1984. **Local divisions:** 33 administrative regions. **Defense:** 1.6% of GDP (1994). **Active troop strength:** 9,700.

**Economy: Chief crops:** Bananas, pineapples, rice, palm kernels, coffee, cassava. **Minerals:** Bauxite, iron, diamonds. **Arable land:** 6%. **Electricity prod.** (1993) 520 mil kWh. **Labor force:** 80% agric.; 11% ind. & commerce.

**Finance: Monetary unit:** Franc (June 1996: 997 = $1 US). **Gross domestic product** (1994): $6.3 bil.* **Per capita GDP:** $980. **Imports** (1992): $768 mil; partners: France 26%. **Exports** (1992): $622 mil; partners: U.S. 23%. **National budget** (1990 est.): $708 mil. **International reserves less gold** (Mar. 1996): $119 mil.

**Transport: Motor vehicles:** in use: 23,000 passenger cars, 13,000 comm. vehicles. **Chief port:** Conakry.

**Communications: Television sets:** 1 per 100 persons. **Radios:** 1 per 28 persons. **Telephones:** 1 per 560 persons.

**Health: Life expectancy at birth** (1996): 43 male; 48 female. **Births** (per 1,000 pop.): 43. **Deaths** (per 1,000 pop.): 19. **Natural increase:** 2.4%. **Physicians:** 1 per 7,445 persons. **Infant mortality** (per 1,000 live births 1996): 134.

**Education: Literacy:** (1993): 36%. Free and compulsory: ages 7-13. Attendance: 46% primary.

**Major International Organizations:** UN and most of its specialized agencies, OAU.

**Embassy:** 2112 Leroy Pl. NW 20008; 483-9420.

Part of the ancient West African empires, Guinea fell under French control 1849-98. Under Sékou Touré, it opted for full independence in 1958, and France withdrew all aid.

Touré turned to Communist nations for support and set up a militant one-party state. Thousands of opponents were jailed in the 1970s, in the aftermath of an unsuccessful Portuguese invasion. Many were tortured and killed.

The military took control in a bloodless coup after the March 1984 death of Touré. A new constitution was approved in 1991, but movement toward democracy was slow. When presidential elections were finally held, in Dec. 1993, the incumbent, Gen. Lansana Conté, was the official winner; outside monitors called the elections flawed. Parliamentary elections June 11, 1995, raised similar complaints. Conté suppressed an army mutiny in Conakry, Feb. 2-3, 1996.

# Guinea-Bissau

## Republic of Guinea-Bissau

## Republica da Guiné-Bissau

**People: Population:** 1,151,330. **Pop. density:** 83 per sq. mi. **Urban:** 22%. **Ethnic groups:** Balanta 30%, Fula 20%, Manjaca 14%, Mandinga 13%. **Principal languages:** Portuguese (official), Criolo, tribal languages. **Religions:** Indigenous beliefs 65%, Muslim 30%, Christian 5%.

**Geography: Area:** 13,948 sq. mi. **Location:** On Atlantic coast of W Africa. **Neighbors:** Senegal on N, Guinea on E and S. **Topography:** A swampy coastal plain covers most of the country; to the east is a low savanna region. **Capital:** Bissau (1991 est.): 200,000.

**Government: Type:** Republic. **Head of state:** Pres. Joao Bernardo Vieira; b 1939; in office: Nov. 14, 1980. **Head of government:** Prime Min. Manuel Saturnino da Costa; in office: Nov. 5, 1994. **Local divisions:** 9 regions. **Defense:** 4.5% of GDP (1994). **Active troop strength:** 9,200 est.

**Economy: Chief crops:** Peanuts, cotton, rice. **Minerals:** Bauxite, phosphates. **Arable land:** 11%. **Electricity prod.** (1993): 40 mil kWh. **Labor force:** 90% agric.

**Finance: Monetary unit:** Peso (June 1996: 18,036 = $1 US). **Gross domestic product** (1993 est.): $900 mil.* **Per capita GDP:** $840. **Imports** (1993): $56 mil; partners: Italy 27%, Portugal 23%. **Exports** (1993): $19 mil; partners: Portugal 34%. **National budget** (1991 est.): $44.8 mil.

**Transport: Motor vehicles:** in use: 3,500 passenger cars, 2,500 comm. vehicles. **Civil aviation:** 2 airports with scheduled flights. **Chief port:** Bissau.

**Communications: Radios:** 1 per 26 persons. **Telephones:** 1 per 122 persons.

**Health: Life expectancy at birth** (1996): 47 male; 50 female. **Births** (per 1,000 pop.): 40. **Deaths** (per 1,000 pop.): 16. **Natural increase:** 2.4%. **Infant mortality** (per 1,000 live births 1996): 116.

**Education: Literacy** (1995): 55%. Compulsory: ages 7-13.

**Major International Organizations:** UN, OAU.
**Embassy:** 918 16th St. NW 20006; 872-4222.

Portuguese mariners explored the area in the mid-15th century; the slave trade flourished in the 17th and 18th centuries, and colonization began in the 19th.

Beginning in the 1960s, an independence movement waged a guerrilla war and formed a government in the interior that achieved international support. Full independence came Sept. 10, 1974, after the Portuguese regime was overthrown.

The November 1980 coup gave Vieira absolute power. Vieira eventually initiated political liberalization; multiparty elections were held July 3, 1994.

# Guyana

## Co-operative Republic of Guyana

**People: Population:** 712,091. **Age distrib.** (%): <15: 38; 65+: 4. **Pop. density:** 9 per sq. mi. **Urban:** 33%. **Ethnic groups:** East Indian 51%, black and mixed 43%. **Principal languages:** English (official), Amerindian dialects. **Religions:** Christian 57%, Hindu 33%, Muslim 9%.

**Geography: Area:** 83,044 sq. mi. **Location:** On N coast of South America. **Neighbors:** Venezuela on W, Brazil on S, Suriname on E. **Topography:** Dense tropical forests cover much of the land, although a flat coastal area up to 40 mi. wide, where 90% of the population lives, provides rich alluvial soil for agriculture. A grassy savanna divides the 2 zones. **Capital:** Georgetown (1992 est.): 248,500.

**Government: Type:** Republic. **Head of state:** President Cheddi Jagan; b Mar. 22, 1918; in office: Oct. 9, 1992. **Head of government:** Prime Min. Samuel Hinds; b Dec. 27, 1943; in office: Oct. 9, 1992. **Local divisions:** 10 regions. **Defense:** 2% of GNP (1992). **Active troop strength:** 1,600.

**Economy: Industries:** Mining, textiles. **Chief crops:** Sugar, rice, citrus and other fruits. **Minerals:** Bauxite, gold, diamonds. **Other resources:** Timber, shrimp. **Arable land:** 3%. **Electricity prod.** (1993): 230 mil kWh. **Labor force:** 45% ind. & commerce; 34% agric.; 21% services.

**Finance: Monetary unit:** Dollar (June 1996: 139 = $1 US). **Gross domestic product** (1994): $1.4 bil.* **Per capita GDP:** $1,950. **Imports** (1994): $456 mil; partners: U.S. 26%, Japan 17%, Trin. & Tob. 13%. **Exports** (1994): $475 mil; partners: Canada 28%, UK 24%. **National budget** (1994 est): $19.6 mil. **International reserves less gold** (Mar. 1996): $266 mil.

**Transport: Motor vehicles:** in use: 24,000 passenger cars, 9,000 comm. vehicles. **Chief port:** Georgetown.

**Communications: Television sets:** 1 per 49 persons. **Radios:** 1 per 1.9 persons. **Telephones:** 1 per 18 persons. **Daily newspaper circ.:** 109 per 1,000 pop.

**Health: Life expectancy at birth** (1996): 58 male; 63 female. **Births** (per 1,000 pop.): 19. **Deaths** (per 1,000 pop.): 10. **Natural increase:** 1.0% **Hospital beds:** 1 per 300 persons. **Physicians:** 1 per 5,314 persons. **Infant mortality** (per 1,000 live births 1996): 51.

**Education: Literacy** (1995): 98%. Free and compulsory: ages 6-14.

**Major International Organizations:** UN (WTO, ILO, FAO, WHO, IMF, World Bank), the Commonwealth, OAS.

**Embassy:** 2490 Tracy Pl. NW 20008; 265-6900.

Guyana became a Dutch possession in the 17th century, but sovereignty passed to Britain in 1815. Indentured servants from India soon outnumbered African slaves. Ethnic tension has affected political life.

Guyana became independent May 26, 1966. A Venezuelan claim to the western half of Guyana was suspended in 1970 but renewed in 1982; an agreement was reached in 1989. The Suriname border is also disputed. The government has nationalized most of the economy, which has remained severely depressed.

The Port Kaituma ambush of U.S. Rep. Leo J. Ryan and others investigating mistreatment of American followers of the Rev. Jim Jones's People's Temple cult triggered a mass suicide-execution of 911 cultists at Jonestown in the Guyana jungle, Nov. 18, 1978.

The People's National Congress, the party in power since Guyana became independent, was voted out of office with the election of Cheddi Jagan in Oct. 1992.

# Haiti

## Republic of Haiti

## République d'Haïti

**People: Population:** 6,731,539. **Age distrib.** (%): <15: 40; 65+: 4. **Pop. density:** 629 per sq. mi. **Urban:** 32%. **Ethnic groups:** Black 95%. **Principal languages:** Haitian Creole, French (both official). **Religions:** Roman Catholic 80%, Protestant 16%; Voodoo widely practiced.

**Geography: Area:** 10,695 sq. mi. **Location:** In West Indies, occupies western third of I. of Hispaniola. **Neighbors:** Dominican Republic on E, Cuba on W. **Topography:** About two-thirds of Haiti is mountainous. Much of the rest is semiarid. Coastal areas are warm and moist. **Capital:** Port-au-Prince (1992 est.): 752,600.

**Government: Type:** Republic. **Head of state:** Pres. René Préval; b Jan. 17, 1943; in office Feb. 7, 1996. **Head of government:** Prime Min. Rosny Smarth; b Oct. 19, 1940; in office: Mar. 6, 1996. **Local divisions:** 9 departments. **Defense:** 2.2% of GDP (1994). **Active security forces:** 3,000-4,000.

**Economy: Industries:** Sugar refining, textiles. **Chief crops:** Coffee, sugar, bananas, corn, rice. **Minerals:** Marble, limestone, copper. **Other resources:** Timber. **Arable land:** 20%. **Livestock** (1994): cattle: 800,000; goats: 910,000. **Fish catch** (1993): 5,600 metric tons. **Electricity prod.** (1993): 590 mil kWh. **Labor force:** 66% agric.; 25% services; 9% ind.

**Finance: Monetary unit:** Gourde (June 1996: 16.18 = $1 US). **Gross domestic product** (1994): $5.6 bil.* **Per capita GDP:** $870. **Imports** (1993): $477 mil; partners: U.S. 51%. **Exports** (1993): $173 mil; partners: U.S. 81%. **National budget** (1994): $131 mil. **International reserves less gold** (Mar. 1996): $82.5 mil. **Consumer prices** (change in 1995): 25.5%.

**Transport: Motor vehicles:** in use: 32,000 passenger cars, 21,000 comm. vehicles. **Chief ports:** Port-au-Prince, Les Cayes.

**Communications: Television sets:** 1 per 260 persons. **Radios:** 1 per 24 persons. **Telephones**: 1 per 164 persons. **Daily newspaper circ.:** 3 per 1,000 pop.

**Health: Life expectancy at birth** (1996): 47 male; 51 female. **Births** (per 1,000 pop.): 38. **Deaths** (per 1,000 pop.): 16. **Natural increase:** 2.2%. **Hospital beds:** 1 per 1,201 persons. **Physicians:** 1 per 10,060 persons. **Infant mortality rate** (per 1,000 live births 1996): 104.

**Education: Literacy** (1993): 45%. Compulsory: ages 6-12.

**Major International Organizations:** UN and most of its specialized agencies, OAS.

**Embassy:** 2311 Massachusetts Ave. NW 20008; 332-4091.

Haiti, visited by Columbus, 1492, and a French colony from 1697, attained its independence, 1804, following the rebellion led by former slave Toussaint L'Ouverture. Following a period of political violence, the U.S. occupied the country 1915-34.

Francois Duvalier was elected president in Sept. 1957; in 1964 he was named president for life. Upon his death in 1971, he was succeeded by his son, Jean Claude. Drought in 1975-77 brought famine, and Hurricane Allen in 1980 destroyed most of the rice, bean, and coffee crops. Following several weeks of unrest, President Jean Claude Duvalier fled Haiti aboard a U.S. Air Force jet Feb. 7, 1986, ending the 28-year dictatorship by the Duvalier family.

A military-civilian council headed by Gen. Henri Namphy assumed control. In 1987, voters approved a new constitution, but the Jan. 1988 elections were marred by violence and boycotted by the opposition. Gen. Namphy seized control, June 20, but was ousted by a military coup in Sept. By mid-1990, there had been 5 governments since Duvalier fled.

Father Jean-Bertrand Aristide was elected president Dec. 1990. In Sept. 1991, Aristide was arrested by the military and expelled from the country. Some 35,000 Haitian refugees were intercepted by the U.S. Coast Guard as they tried to enter the U.S., 1991-92. Most were returned to Haiti. There was a new upsurge of refugees starting in late 1993.

The UN imposed a worldwide oil, arms, and financial embargo on Haiti June 23, 1993. The embargo was suspended when the military agreed to Aristide's return to power on Oct. 30, but the military effectively blocked his return. After renewed sanctions, the UN Security Council authorized, July 31, 1994, an invasion of Haiti by a multinational force. With U.S. troops already en route, an invasion was averted, Sept. 18, by a new agreement for military leaders to step down and Aristide to resume office. As part of the agreement, thousands of U.S. troops began arriving in Haiti, Sept. 19. Aristide returned to Haiti and was restored in office Oct. 15. A UN peacekeeping force took over responsibility for Haiti as of Mar. 31, 1995.

Aristide transferred power to his elected successor, René Préval, on Feb. 7, 1996. The last U.S. combat troops left Haiti Apr. 17, but a small UN peacekeeping force remained.

# Honduras

## Republic of Honduras

## República de Honduras

**People: Population:** 5,605,193. **Age distrib.** (%): <15: 45; 65+: 3. **Pop. density:** 129 per sq. mi. **Urban:** 47%. **Ethnic groups:** Mestizo 90%, Indian 7%. **Principal language:** Spanish (official). **Religion:** Roman Catholic 97%.

**Geography: Area:** 43,433 sq. mi. **Location:** In Central America. **Neighbors:** Guatemala on W, El Salvador and Nicaragua on S. **Topography:** The Caribbean coast is 500 mi. long. Pacific coast, on Gulf of Fonseca, is 40 mi. long. Honduras is mountainous, with wide fertile valleys and rich forests. **Capital:** Tegucigalpa. **Cities** (1993 met. est.): Tegucigalpa 738,500; San Pedro Sula 353,800.

**Government: Type:** Republic. **Head of State:** Pres. Carlos Roberta Reina Idiaquez; b Mar. 13, 1926; in office: Jan. 27, 1994. **Local divisions:** 18 departments. **Defense:** 0.4% of GDP (1994). **Active troop strength:** 18,800.

**Economy: Industries:** Textiles, wood prods. **Chief crops:** Bananas (chief export), coffee, corn, sugar. **Minerals:** Gold, silver, copper, lead, zinc, iron, antimony, coal. **Other resources:** Timber. **Arable land:** 14%. **Livestock** (1994): cattle: 2.3 mil. **Electricity prod.** (1993): 2.3 bil kWh. **Labor force:** 62% agric.; 20% services; 9% manuf.

**Finance: Monetary unit:** Lempira (June 1996: 11.16 = $1 US). **Gross domestic product** (1994): $9.7 bil.* **Per capita GDP:** $1,820. **Imports** (1994): $990 mil; partners: U.S. 50%, Mexico 8%. **Exports** (1993): $850 mil; partners: U.S. 53%, Germany 11%. **Tourism** (1993): $32 mil. **National budget** (1993 est.): $668 mil. **International reserves less gold** (May 1996): $227 mil. **Gold:** 21,000 oz t. **Consumer prices** (change in 1995): 29.5%.

**Transport: Motor vehicles:** in use: 68,000 passenger cars, 128,000 comm. vehicles. **Civil aviation:** 321 mil passenger-mi.; 8 airports with scheduled flights. **Chief ports:** Puerto Cortes, La Ceiba.

**Communications: Television sets:** 1 per 33 persons. **Radios:** 1 per 2.8 persons. **Telephones:** 1 per 48 persons. **Daily newspaper circ.:** 29 per 1,000 pop.

**Health: Life expectancy at birth** (1996): 66 male; 71 female. **Births** (per 1,000 pop.): 33. **Deaths** (per 1,000 pop.): 6. **Natural increase:** 2.8%. **Hospital beds:** 1 per 900 persons. **Physicians:** 1 per 1,586 persons. **Infant mortality** (per 1,000 live births 1996): 42.

**Education: Literacy** (1993): 73%. Free and compulsory: ages 7-13.

**Major International Organizations:** UN, (IMF, FAO, WTO, World Bank, WHO, ILO), OAS.

**Embassy:** 3007 Tilden St. NW 20008; 966-7702.

Mayan civilization flourished in Honduras in the 1st millennium AD. Columbus arrived in 1502. Honduras became independent after freeing itself from Spain, 1821, and from the Fed. of Central America, 1838.

Gen. Oswaldo Lopez Arellano, president for most of the period 1963-75 by virtue of one election and 2 coups, was ousted by the army in 1975 over charges of pervasive bribery by United Brands Co. of the U.S. An elected civilian government took power in 1982. Some 3,200 U.S. troops were sent to Honduras after the Honduran border was violated by Nicaraguan forces, Mar. 1988.

Honduras is one of the poorest countries in the western hemisphere.

# Hungary

## Republic of Hungary

## Magyar Köztársaság

**People: Population:** 10,002,541. **Age distrib.** (%): <15: 18; 65+: 14. **Pop. density:** 278 per sq. mi. **Urban:** 64%. **Ethnic groups:** Hungarian 89.9%, Gypsy 4%, German 2.6%. **Principal language:** Hungarian (Magyar; official). **Religions:** Roman Catholic 68%, Calvinist 20%, Lutheran 5%.

**Geography: Area:** 35,919 sq. mi. **Location:** In E central Europe. **Neighbors:** Slovakia, Ukraine on N; Austria on W; Slovenia, Yugoslavia, Croatia on S; Romania on E. **Topography:** The Danube R. forms the Slovak border in the NW, then swings S to bisect the country. The eastern half of Hungary is mainly a great fertile plain, the Alfold; the W and N are hilly. **Capital:** Budapest. **Cities** (1994 est.): Budapest 2.0 mil; Debrecen 218,000; Miskolc 190,000.

**Government: Type:** Parliamentary democracy. **Head of state:** Pres. Arpad Goncz; b Feb. 10, 1922; in office: May 2, 1990. **Head of government:** Prime Min. Gyula Horn; b July 5, 1932; in office: July 15, 1994. **Local divisions:** 38 counties, 1 capital. **Defense:** 1.6% of GDP (1994). **Active troop strength:** 70,500.

**Economy: Industries:** Iron and steel, construction materials, processed foods, pharmaceuticals, vehicles. **Chief crops:** Wheat, corn, sunflowers, potatoes, sugar beets. **Minerals:** Bauxite, coal, gas. **Arable land:** 51%. **Livestock** (1994): pigs: 5.0 mil; sheep: 1.3 mil; cattle: 1.0 mil. **Electricity prod.** (1993): 31 bil kWh. **Labor force:** 30% ind.; 16% agric.

**Finance: Monetary unit:** Forint (June 1996: 154 = $1 US). **Gross domestic product** (1994): $59 bil.* **Per capita GDP:** $5,700. **Imports** (1994): $14.2 bil; partners: Germany 22%, CIS 21%. **Exports** (1994): $10.3 bil; partners: Germany 25%, CIS 14%. **National budget** (1994): $14.2 bil. **Tourism** (1993): $1.2 bil. **International reserves less gold** (Mar. 1996): $10.9 bil. **Gold:** 107,000 oz t. **Consumer prices** (change in 1994): 18.9%.

**Transport: Railroads: Length:** 8,300 mi. **Motor vehicles:** in use: 2.1 mil passenger cars, 259,000 comm. vehicles. **Civil aviation:** 1.0 bln. passenger-mi.; 1 airport with scheduled flights.

**Communications: Television sets:** 1 per 2.4 persons. **Radios:** 1 per 1.6 persons. **Telephones:** 1 per 6.9 persons. **Daily newspaper circ.:** 275 per 1,000 pop.

**Health: Life expectancy at birth** (1996): 64 male; 74 female. **Births** (per 1,000 pop.): 11. **Deaths** (per 1,000 pop.): 15. **Natural increase:** –0.4%. **Hospital beds:** 1 per 102 persons. **Physicians:** 1 per 249 persons. **Infant mortality** (per 1,000 live births 1996): 12.

**Education: Literacy:** (1993): 99%. Compulsory: ages 6-16.

**Major International Organizations:** UN (IMF, FAO, WHO, World Bank, WTO), OECD.

**Embassy:** 3910 Shoemaker St. NW 20008; 362-6730.

Earliest settlers, chiefly Slav and Germanic, were overrun by Magyars from the E. Stephen I (997-1038) was made king by Pope Sylvester II in AD 1000. The country suffered repeated Turkish invasions in the 15th-17th centuries. After the defeats of the Turks, 1686-1697, Austria dominated, but Hungary obtained concessions until it regained internal independence in 1867, with the emperor of Austria as king of Hungary in a dual monarchy with a single diplomatic service. Defeated with the Central Powers in 1918, Hungary lost Transylvania to Romania, Croatia and Bacska to Yugoslavia, Slovakia and Carpatho-Ruthenia to Czechoslovakia, all of which had large Hungarian minorities. A republic under Michael Karolyi and a bolshevist revolt under Bela Kun were followed by a vote for a monarchy in 1920 with Admiral Nicholas Horthy as regent.

Hungary joined Germany in World War II, and was allowed to annex most of its lost territories. Russian troops captured the country, 1944-1945. By terms of an armistice with the Allied powers Hungary agreed to give up territory acquired by the 1938 dismemberment of Czechoslovakia and to return to its borders of 1937.

A republic was declared Feb. 1, 1946; Zoltan Tildy was elected president. In 1947 the communists forced Tildy out. Premier Imre Nagy, in office since mid-1953, was ousted for his moderate policy of favoring agriculture and consumer production, April 18, 1955.

In 1956, popular demands for the ousting of Erno Gero, Communist Party secretary, and for formation of a government by Nagy, resulted in the latter's appointment Oct. 23; demonstrations against communist rule developed into open revolt. On Nov. 4 Soviet forces launched a massive attack against Budapest with 200,000 troops, 2,500 tanks and armored cars.

About 200,000 persons fled the country. Nagy was executed, and thousands were arrested. In the spring of 1963 the regime freed many captives from the 1956 revolt.

Hungarian troops participated in the 1968 Warsaw Pact invasion of Czechoslovakia. Major economic reforms were launched early in 1968, switching from a central planning system to one in which market forces and profit controlled much of production.

In 1989 Parliament passed legislation legalizing freedom of assembly and association as Hungary shifted away from communism. In Oct. the Communist Party was formally dissolved. The last Soviet troops left Hungary June 19, 1991.

# Iceland

## Republic of Iceland

## Lýoveldio Ísland

**People: Population:** 270,292. **Age distrib.** (%): <15: 25; 65+: 11. **Pop. density:** 7 per sq. mi. **Urban:** 91%. **Ethnic groups:** Homogeneous, descendants of Norwegians, Celts. **Principal language:** Icelandic (Islenska; official). **Religion:** Evangelical Lutheran 96%.

**Geography: Area:** 39,699 sq. mi. **Location:** Isl. at N end of Atlantic O. **Neighbors:** Nearest is Greenland, to W. **Topography:** Iceland is of recent volcanic origin. Three-quarters of the surface is wasteland: glaciers, lakes, a lava desert. There are geysers and hot springs, and the climate is moderated by the Gulf Stream. **Capital:** Reykjavík (1994 est.): 103,000.

**Government: Type:** Constitutional republic. **Head of state:** Pres. Olafur Ragnar Grímsson; b May 14, 1943; in office: Aug. 1, 1996. **Head of government:** Prime Min. David Oddsson; Jan. 17, 1948; in office: Apr. 30, 1991. **Local divisions:** 23 counties, 14 ind. towns. **Defense:** Provided by U.S.-manned Icelandic Defense Force.

**Economy: Industries:** Fish products (some 75% of exports), aluminum. **Chief crops:** Potatoes, turnips. **Arable land:** 1%. **Livestock** (1993): sheep: 488,800. **Fish catch** (1993): 1.7 mil metric tons. **Electricity prod.** (1993): 4.7 bil kWh. **Labor force:** 60% commerce & services; 13% manuf.; 12% fish.

**Finance: Monetary unit:** Krona (June 1996: 67.17 = $1 US). **Gross domestic product** (1994): $4.5 bil.* **Per capita GDP:** $17,250. **Imports** (1993): $1.3 bil; partners: EU 53%. **Exports** (1993): $1.4 bil; partners: EU 68%. **Tourism** (1994): $138 mil. **National budget** (1994): $2.1 bil. **International reserves less gold** (Apr. 1996): $411 mil. **Gold:** 49,000 oz t. **Consumer prices** (change in 1995): 1.7%.

**Transport: Motor vehicles:** in use: 116,000 passenger cars, 16,000 comm. vehicles. **Civil aviation:** 1.5 bil passenger-mi.; 24 airports with scheduled flights. **Chief port:** Reykjavik.

**Communications: Television sets:** 1 per 3.5 persons. **Radios:** 1 per 1.4 persons. **Telephones:** 1 per 1.8 persons. **Daily newspaper circ.:** 517 per 1,000 pop.

**Health: Life expectancy at birth** (1996): 78 male; 83 female. **Births** (per 1,000 pop.): 17. **Deaths** (per 1,000 pop.): 6. **Natural increase:** 1.1%. **Hospital beds:** 1 per 90 persons. **Physicians:** 1 per 353 persons. **Infant mortality** (per 1,000 live births 1996): 4.

**Education: Literacy** (1993): 100%. Free and compulsory: ages 6-16.

**Major International Organizations:** UN (WTO, FAO, World Bank, IMF, WHO), NATO, EFTA, OECD.

**Embassy:** 1156 15th St. NW 20005; 265-6653.

Iceland was an independent republic from 930 to 1262, when it joined with Norway. Its language has maintained its purity for 1,000 years. Danish rule lasted from 1380-1918; the last ties with the Danish crown were severed in 1941. The Althing, or assembly, is the world's oldest surviving parliament.

# India

## Republic of India

## Bharat

**People: Population:** 952,107,694. **Age distrib.** (%): <15: 36; 65+: 4. **Pop. density:** 779 per sq. mi. **Urban:** 26%. **Ethnic groups:** Indo-Aryan 72%, Dravidian 25%, Mongoloid and other 3%. **Principal languages:** Hindi (official), English (associate official), 17 regional languages. **Religions:** Hindu 80%, Muslim 14%, Christian 2%, Sikh 2%.

**Geography: Area:** 1,222,243 sq. mi. **Location:** Occupies most of the Indian subcontinent in S Asia. **Neighbors:** Pakistan on W; China, Nepal, Bhutan on N; Myanmar, Bangladesh on E. **Topography:** The Himalaya Mts., highest in world, stretch across India's northern borders. Below, the Ganges Plain is wide, fertile, and among the most densely populated regions of the world. The area below includes the Deccan Peninsula. Close to one quarter of the area is forested. The climate varies from tropical heat in S to near-Arctic cold in N. Rajasthan Desert is in NW; NE Assam Hills get 400 in. of rain a year. **Capital:** New Delhi. **Cities** (1991 met. est.): Bombay (Mumbai) 12.6 mil; Calcutta 11.0 mil; Delhi 8.4 mil; Madras 5.4 mil; Hyderabad 4.3 mln; Bangalore 4.1 mil.

**Government: Type:** Federal republic. **Head of state:** Pres. Shankar Dayal Sharma; b. Aug. 19, 1918; in office: July 26, 1992. **Head of government:** Prime Min. H. D. Deve Gowda; b May 18, 1933; in office: June 1, 1996. **Local divisions:** 25 states, 7 union territories. **Defense:** 2.8% of GDP (FY 1994-95). **Active troop strength:** 1.1 mil.

**Economy: Industries:** Textiles, steel, processed foods, cement, machinery, chemicals, mining, autos. **Chief crops:** Rice, grains, sugar, spices, tea, cashews, cotton, potatoes, jute, linseed. **Minerals:** Coal, iron, manganese, mica, bauxite, titanium, chromite, gas, oil. **Crude oil reserves** (1995): 5.8 bil bbls. **Other resources:** Rubber, timber. **Arable land:** 55%. **Livestock** (1994): cattle: 193 mil; goats: 118 mil; sheep: 45 mil. **Fish catch** (1993): 4.3 mil metric tons. **Electricity prod.** (1993): 314 bil kWh. **Labor force:** 65% agric.

**Finance: Monetary unit:** Rupee (June 1996: 34.06 = $1 US). **Gross domestic product** (1994 est.): $1.25 tril.* **Per capita GDP:** $1,360. **Imports** (1994): $26 bil; partners: U.S. 10%, Japan 8%, Germany 8%. **Exports** (1994): $24.4 bil; partners: U.S. 20%, Japan 8%, Germany 7%. **Tourism** (1992): $1.4 bil. **National budget** (FY 1993-94): $48.4 bil. **International reserves less gold** (May 1996): $17.4 bil. **Gold:** 12.8 mil oz t. **Consumer prices** (change in 1995): 10.2%.

**Transport: Railroads: Route length:** 38,189 mi. **Motor vehicles:** in use: 3.3 mil passenger cars, 2.0 mil comm. vehicles. **Civil aviation:** 10.9 bil passenger-mi.; 66 airports with scheduled flights. **Chief ports:** Calcutta, Bombay (Mumbai), Kochi, Madras, Vishakhapatnam.

**Communications: Television sets:** 1 per 47 persons. **Radios:** 1 per 14 persons. **Telephones:** 1 per 112 persons. **Daily newspaper circ.:** 21 per 1,000 pop.

**Health: Life expectancy at birth** (1996): 59 male; 60 female. **Births** (per 1,000 pop.): 26. **Deaths** (per 1,000 pop.): 10. **Natural increase:** 1.6%. **Hospital beds:** 1 per 1,357 persons. **Physicians:** 1 per 2,211 persons. **Infant mortality** (per 1,000 live births 1996): 71.

**Education: Literacy** (1994): 52%. Theoretically compulsory in 23 states to age 14.

**Major International Organizations:** UN (IMF, FAO, IMF, WHO, WTO, World Bank), the Commonwealth.

**Embassy:** 2107 Massachusetts Ave. NW 20008; 939-7000.

India has one of the oldest civilizations in the world. Excavations trace the Indus Valley civilization back for at least 5,000 years. Paintings in the mountain caves of Ajanta, richly carved temples, the Taj Mahal in Agra, and the Kutab Minar in Delhi are among relics of the past.

Aryan tribes, speaking Sanskrit, invaded from the NW around 1500 BC, and merged with the earlier inhabitants to create classical Indian civilization.

Asoka ruled most of the Indian subcontinent in the 3d century BC, and established Buddhism. But Hinduism revived and eventually predominated. During the Gupta kingdom, 4th-6th century AD, science, literature, and the arts enjoyed a "golden age."

Arab invaders established a Muslim foothold in the W in the 8th century, and Turkish Muslims gained control of North India by 1200. The Mogul emperors ruled 1526-1857.

Vasco da Gama established Portuguese trading posts 1498-1503. The Dutch followed. The British East India Co. sent Capt. William Hawkins, 1609, to get concessions from the Mogul emperor for spices and textiles. Operating as the East India Co. the British gained control of most of India. The British parliament assumed political direction; under Lord Bentinck, 1828-35, rule by rajahs was curbed. After the Sepoy troops mutinied, 1857-58, the British supported the native rulers.

Nationalism grew rapidly after World War I. The Indian National Congress and the Muslim League demanded constitutional reform. A leader emerged in Mohandas K. Gandhi (called Mahatma, or Great Soul), born Oct. 2, 1869, assassinated Jan. 30, 1948. He advocated self-rule, non-violence, removal of untouchability. In 1930 he launched "civil disobedience," including boycott of British goods and rejection of taxes without representation.

In 1935 Britain gave India a constitution providing a bicameral federal congress. Muhammad Ali Jinnah, head of the Muslim League, sought creation of a Muslim nation, Pakistan.

The British government partitioned British India into the dominions of India and Pakistan. India became a self-governing member of the Commonwealth and a member of the UN. It became a democratic republic, Jan. 26, 1950.

More than 12 million Hindu and Muslim refugees crossed the India-Pakistan borders in a mass transferral of some of the 2 peoples during 1947; about 200,000 were killed in communal fighting.

After Pakistan troops began attacks on Bengali separatists in East Pakistan, Mar. 25, 1971, some 10 million refugees fled into India. India and Pakistan went to war Dec. 3, 1971, on both the East and West fronts. Pakistan troops in the east surrendered Dec. 16; Pakistan agreed to a cease-fire in the west Dec. 17. In Aug. 1973 India released 93,000 Pakistanis held prisoner since 1971. The 2 countries resumed full relations in 1976.

Mrs. Indira Gandhi, was named prime minister Jan. 19, 1966. Threatened with adverse court rulings and an opposition protest campaign, Gandhi invoked emergency provisions of the constitution June 1975. Thousands of opponents were arrested and press censorship imposed. These and other actions, including the enforcement of coercive birth control measures in some areas, were widely resented. Opposition parties, united in the Janata coalition, turned Gandhi's New Congress Party from power in federal and state parliamentary elections in 1977.

Gandhi became prime minister for the second time, Jan. 14, 1980. She was assassinated by 2 of her Sikh bodyguards Oct. 31, 1984, in response to the government suppression of a Sikh uprising in Punjab in June 1984, which included an assault on the Golden Temple at Amritsar, the holiest Sikh shrine. Widespread rioting followed the assassination. Thousands of Sikhs were killed and some 50,000 left homeless.

Rajiv, Indira Gandhi's son, replaced her as prime minister. He was swept from office in 1989 amid charges of incompetence and corruption. He was assassinated May 21, 1991, during an election campaign to regain the prime ministership.

Sikhs ignited several violent clashes during the 1980s. The government's May 1987 decision to bring the state of Punjab under the rule of the central government led to violence. Many died during a government siege of the Golden Temple, May 1988. Another trouble spot was Assam in NW India, where thousands were killed in ethnic violence in Feb. 1993; a renewed outburst in July 1994 led to more than 60 deaths there.

Nationwide riots followed the destruction of a 16th-century mosque by Hindu militants in Dec. 1992. In the biggest wave of criminal violence in Indian history, a series of bombings jolted Bombay and Calcutta, Mar. 12-19, 1993, killing more than 300.

Corruption scandals dominated Indian politics in the mid-1990s. After an inconclusive election, a Hindu nationalist party was unable to form a government, and a center-left coalition took office June 1, 1996.

**Sikkim,** bordered by Tibet, Bhutan, and Nepal, formerly British protected, became a protectorate of India in 1950. Area, 2,740 sq. mi.; pop., 1994 est., 444,000; capital: Gangtok. In Sept. 1974 India's parliament voted to make Sikkim an associate Indian state, absorbing it into India.

Kashmir, a predominantly Muslim region in the NW, has been in dispute between India and Pakistan since 1947. A cease-fire was negotiated by the UN Jan. 1, 1949; it gave Pakistan control of one-third of the area, in the west and northwest, and India the remaining two-thirds, the Indian state of **Jammu and Kashmir**, which enjoys internal autonomy.

In the 1990s there were repeated clashes between Indian army troops and pro-independence demonstrators triggered by India's decision to impose central government rule; by 1996 the conflict had claimed at least 30,000 lives. The clashes strained relations between India and Pakistan, which India charged was aiding the Muslim separatists. In Sept. 1996, a pro-Indian-government party won a majority in assembly elections, the first held since separatist fighting began.

France, 1952-54, peacefully yielded to India its 5 colonies, former French India, comprising Pondicherry, Karikal, Mahe, Yanaon (which became **Pondicherry Union Territory**, area 190 sq. mi.; pop., 1994 est., 894,000) and Chandernagor (which was incorporated into the state of **West Bengal**).

# Indonesia

## Republic of Indonesia

## Republik Indonesia

**People: Population:** 206,611,600. **Age distrib.** (%): <15: 35; 65+: 4. **Pop. density:** 279 per sq. mi. **Urban:** 31%. **Ethnic groups:** Javanese 45%, Sundanese 14%, Madurese 7.5%, Malay 7.5%. **Principal languages:** Bahasa Indonesian (Malay) (official), English, Dutch, Javanese. **Religions:** Muslim 87%, Protestant 6%.

**Geography: Area:** 741,052 sq. mi. **Location:** Archipelago SE of Asia along the Equator. **Neighbors:** Malaysia on N, Papua New Guinea on E. **Topography:** Indonesia com-prises some 17,000 islands, including Java (one of the most densely populated areas in the world with over 2,000 per-sons to the sq. mi.), Sumatra, Kalimantan (most of Borneo), Sulawesi (Celebes), and West Irian (Irian Jaya, the W half of New Guinea). Also: Bangka, Billiton, Madura, Bali, Timor. The mountains and plateaus on the major islands have a cooler climate than the tropical lowlands. **Capital:** Jakarta. **Cities** (1990 est.): Jakarta 8.3 mil; Surabaya 2.4 mil; Bandung 2.0 mil; Medan 1.7 mil.

**Government: Type:** Republic. **Head of state:** Pres. Suharto; b June 8, 1921; in office: Mar. 6, 1967. **Local divisions:** 24 provinces, 2 special regions. **Defense:** 1.5% of GDP (FY 1994-95 est.). **Active troop strength:** 274,500.

**Economy: Industries:** Oil, gas, food processing, textiles, cement, light industry. **Chief crops:** Rice, cocoa, peanuts. **Minerals:** Nickel, tin, oil, bauxite, copper, gas. **Crude oil reserves** (1995): 5.8 bil bbls. **Other resources:** Rubber, timber. **Arable land:** 8%. **Livestock** (1994): goats: 12.3 mil; cattle: 11.6 mil; sheep: 6.4 mil. **Fish catch** (1993): 3.6 mil metric tons. **Electricity prod.** (1993): 44 bil kWh. **Labor force:** 55% agric.; 10% manuf.

**Finance: Monetary unit:** Rupiah (June 1996: 2,326 = $1 US). **Gross domestic product** (1994): $619 bil.* **Per capita GDP:** $3,090. **Imports** (1994): $31.4 bil; partners: Japan 22%, U.S. 11%, Germany 7%. **Exports** (1993): $41.3 bil; partners: Japan 30%, U.S. 14%, Singapore 9%. **Tourism** (1993): $4.0 bil. **National budget** (FY 1994-95): $32.8 bil. **International reserves less gold** (Apr. 1996): $15.0 bil. **Gold:** 3.10 mil oz t. **Consumer prices** (change in 1995): 9.4%.

**Transport: Railroads: Length:** 4,090 mi. **Motor vehicles:** in use: 1.7 mil passenger cars, 1.6 mil comm. vehicles. **Civil aviation:** 12.3 bil passenger-mi.; 122 airports. **Chief ports:** Jakarta, Surabaya, Medan, Palembang, Semarang.

**Communications: Television sets:** 1 per 17 persons. **Radios:** 1 per 7.3 persons. **Telephones:** 1 per 109 persons.

**Health: Life expectancy at birth** (1996): 60 male; 64 female. **Births** (per 1,000 pop.): 24. **Deaths** (per 1,000 pop.): 8. **Natural increase:** 1.5%. **Hospital beds:** 1 per 1,660 persons. **Physicians:** 1 per 6,861 persons. **Infant mortality** (per 1,000 live births 1996): 63.

**Education: Literacy** (1993): 84%. Compulsory: ages 7-16. **Attendance:** 97% attend primary school.

**Major International Organizations:** UN and all of its specialized agencies, ASEAN, OPEC, APEC.

**Embassy:** 2020 Massachusetts Ave. NW 20036; 775-5200.

Hindu and Buddhist civilization from India reached the peoples of Indonesia nearly 2,000 years ago, taking root especially in Java. Islam spread along the maritime trade routes in the 15th century, and became predominant by the 16th century. The Dutch replaced the Portuguese as the most important European trade power in the area in the 17th century. They secured territorial control over Java by 1750. The outer islands were not finally subdued until the early 20th century, when the full area of present-day Indonesia was united under one rule for the first time.

Following Japanese occupation, 1942-45, nationalists led by Sukarno and Hatta declared independence. The Netherlands ceded sovereignty Dec. 27, 1949, after 4 years of fighting. A republic was declared, Aug. 17, 1950, with Sukarno as president. West Irian, on New Guinea, remained under Dutch control.

After the Dutch in 1957 rejected proposals for new negotiations over West Irian, Indonesia stepped up the seizure of Dutch property. A U.S. mediator's plan was adopted in 1962. In 1963 the UN turned the area over to Indonesia, which promised a plebiscite. In 1969, voting by tribal chiefs favored staying with Indonesia, despite an uprising and widespread opposition.

Sukarno suspended Parliament in 1960, and was named president for life in 1963. He made close alliances with Communist governments. Russian-armed Indonesian troops staged raids in 1964 and 1965 into Malaysia, whose formation Sukarno had opposed. (In 1966 Indonesia and Malaysia signed an agreement ending hostility.)

In 1965 an attempted coup in which several military officers were murdered was successfully put down. The regime blamed the coup on the Communist Party, some of whose members were known to have been involved. In its wake more than 300,000 alleged Communists were killed in army-initiated massacres.

Gen. Suharto, head of the army, was named president in 1968. With military backing he developed a strong government party, restricted the opposition, and allied the country with the West; meanwhile, oil exports spurred economic growth. Suharto was reelected for a 6th consecutive term in 1993. A riot in Jakarta, July 27, 1996, signaled rising popular discontent.

In Dec. 1975, Indonesia invaded **East Timor** as Portuguese rule collapsed there. Indonesia annexed it in 1976, despite international condemnation. Timorese opposition to continued Indonesian rule has been ruthlessly suppressed.

# Iran

## Islamic Republic of Iran

## Jomhuri-ye Islami-ye Iran

**People: Population:** 66,094,264. **Age distrib.** (%): <15: 44; 65+: 3. **Pop. density:** 105 per sq. mi. **Urban:** 58%. **Ethnic groups:** Persian 51%, Azerbaijani 24%, Kurd 7%. **Principal languages:** Persian (Farsi; official), Turkic, Kurdish, Luri. **Religion:** Shi'a Muslim 95%, Sunni Muslim 4%.

**Geography: Area:** 632,457 sq. mi. **Location:** Between the Middle East and S Asia. **Neighbors:** Turkey, Iraq on W; Armenia, Azerbaijan, Turkmenistan on N; Afghanistan, Pakistan on E. **Topography:** Interior highlands and plains are surrounded by high mountains, up to 18,000 ft. Large salt deserts cover much of the area, but there are many oases and forest areas. Most of the population inhabits the N and NW. **Capital:** Tehran. **Cities** (1991 cen.): Tehran 6.5 mil; Mashhad 1.8 mil; Esfahan 1.1 mil; Tabriz 1.1 mil; Shiraz 965,000.

**Government: Type:** Islamic republic. **Religious head:** Ayatollah Sayyed Ali Khamenei; b 1940; in office: June 4, 1989. **Head of state:** Pres. Hashemi Rafsanjani; b 1934; in office: Aug. 3, 1989. **Local divisions:** 24 provinces. **Defense:** 3.5% of GNP (1993). **Active troop strength:** 513,000.

**Economy: Industries:** Oil, petrochemicals, cement, sugar refining, carpets. **Chief crops:** Grains, rice, fruits, nuts, sugar beets, cotton. **Minerals:** Chromium, coal, oil, gas. **Crude oil reserves** (1995): 89.3 bil barrels. **Other resources:** Gums, wool, silk, caviar. **Arable land:** 8%. **Livestock** (1994): cattle: 7.1 mil; sheep: 45.0 mil. **Fish catch** (1994): 344,080 metric tons. **Electricity prod.** (1993): 50.8 bil kWh. **Labor force:** 33% agric.; 21% manuf.

**Finance: Monetary unit:** Rial (June 1996: 3,000 = $1 US). **Gross domestic product** (1994): $310 bil.* **Per capita GDP:** $4,720. **Imports** (FY 1992-93): $23.7 bil; partners: Germany 18%, Japan 10%, Italy 9%. **Exports** (FY 1992-93): $16 bil; partners: Japan 15%, France 9%. **National budget** (1990): $80 bil. **Consumer prices** (change in 1995): 49.6%.

**Transport: Motor vehicles:** in use: 1.6 mil passenger cars, 584,000 comm. vehicles. **Civil aviation:** 3.1 bil passenger-mi.; 20 airports with scheduled flights. **Chief port:** Bandar-e Abbas.

**Communications: Television sets:** 1 per 8.5 persons. **Radios:** 1 per 4.6 persons. **Telephones:** 1 per 16 persons. **Daily newspaper circ.:** 22 per 1,000 pop.

**Health: Life expectancy at birth** (1996): 66 male; 69 female. **Births** (per 1,000 pop.): 34. **Deaths** (per 1,000 pop.): 7. **Natural increase:** 2.7%. **Hospital beds:** 1 per 650 persons. **Physicians:** 1 per 1,600 persons. **Infant mortality** (per 1,000 live births 1996): 53.

**Education: Literacy** (1993): 72%. Compulsory ages 6-10.

**Major International Organizations:** UN (IMF, FAO, World Bank, WHO), OPEC.

Iran was once called Persia. The Iranians, who supplanted an earlier agricultural civilization, came from the E during the 2d millennium BC; they were an Indo-European group related to the Aryans of India.

In 549 BC Cyrus the Great united the Medes and Persians in the Persian Empire, conquered Babylonia in 538 BC, restored Jerusalem to the Jews. Alexander the Great conquered Persia in 333 BC, but Persians regained their independence in the next century under the Parthians, themselves succeeded by Sassanian Persians in AD 226. Arabs brought Islam to Persia in the 7th century, replacing the indigenous Zoroastrian faith. After Persian political and cultural autonomy was reasserted in the 9th century, the arts and sciences flourished for several centuries.

Turks and Mongols ruled Persia in turn from the 11th century to 1502, when a native dynasty reasserted full independence. The British and Russian empires vied for influence in the 19th century; Afghanistan was severed from Iran by Britain in 1857.

Reza Khan abdicated as shah, 1941, and was succeeded by his son, Mohammad Reza Pahlavi. Under his rule, Iran underwent economic and social change but political opposition was not tolerated.

Conservative Muslim protests led to 1978 violence. Martial law in 12 cities was declared Sept. 8. A military government was appointed Nov. 6 to deal with striking oil workers. Prime Min. Shahpur Bakhtiar was designated by the shah to head a regency council in his absence. The shah left Iran Jan. 16, 1979.

Exiled religious leader Ayatollah Ruhollah Khomeini named a provisional government council in preparation for his return to Iran, Jan. 31. Clashes between Khomeini's supporters and government troops culminated in a rout of Iran's elite Imperial Guard Feb. 11, leading to the fall of Bakhtiar's government.

The Iranian revolution was marked by revolts among the ethnic minorities and by a continuing struggle between the clerical forces and westernized intellectuals and liberals. The Islamic Constitution established final authority to be vested in a Faghi, the Ayatollah Khomeini.

Iranian militants seized the U.S. embassy, Nov. 4, 1979, and took hostages including 62 Americans. Despite international condemnations and U.S. efforts, including an abortive Apr. 1980 rescue attempt, the crisis continued. The U.S. broke diplomatic relations with Iran, Apr. 7. The shah died in Egypt, July 27. The hostage drama finally ended Jan. 21, 1981, when an accord, involving the release of frozen Iranian assets, was reached.

A dispute over the Shatt al-Arab waterway that divides the two countries brought Iran and Iraq, Sept. 22, 1980, into open warfare. Iraqi planes attacked Iranian air fields including Tehran airport. Iranian planes bombed Iraqi bases. Iraqi troops occupied Iranian territory including the port city of Khorramshahr in October. Iranian troops recaptured the city and drove Iraqi troops back across the border, May 1982. Iraq, and later Iran, attacked several oil tankers in the Persian Gulf during 1984.

In Nov. 1986 it became known that senior U.S. officials had secretly visited Iran and that the U.S. had provided arms in exchange for Iran's help in obtaining the release of U.S. hostages held by terrorists in Lebanon. The revelation sparked a major scandal in the Reagan administration.

A U.S. Navy warship shot down an Iranian commercial airliner, July 3, 1988, after mistaking it for an F-14 fighter jet; all 290 aboard the plane died. In Aug. 1988, Iran agreed to accept a UN resolution calling for a cease-fire with Iraq.

A major earthquake struck northern Iran June 21, 1990, killing more than 45,000, injuring 100,000, and leaving 400,000 homeless. Some one million Kurdish refugees fled from Iraq to Iran following the Persian Gulf War. To curb Iran's alleged support for international terrorism, the U.S. in 1996 authorized sanctions on foreign companies that invest there.

# Iraq

## Republic of Iraq

## Al Jumhuriyah al Iraqiyah

**People: Population:** 21,422,292. **Age distrib.** (%): <15: 47; 65+: 3. **Pop. density:** 128 per sq. mi. **Urban:** 70%. **Ethnic groups:** Arab 75-80%, Kurd 15-20%, Turkoman. **Principal languages:** Arabic (official), Kurdish. **Religions:** Muslim 97% (Shi'a 60-65%, Sunni 32-37%).

**Geography: Area:** 167,975 sq. mi. **Location:** In the Middle East, occupying most of historic Mesopotamia. **Neighbors:** Jordan and Syria on W, Turkey on N, Iran on E, Kuwait and Saudi Arabia on S. **Topography:** Mostly an alluvial plain, including the Tigris and Euphrates rivers, descending from mountains in N to desert in SW. Persian Gulf region is marshland. **Capital:** Baghdad. **Cities** (1987 cen.): Baghdad 4.0 mil; Basra 406,300; Mosul 664,200.

**Government: Type:** Republic. **Head of state:** Pres. Saddam Hussein, b. Apr. 29, 1937; in office: July 16, 1979; also assumed post of prime minister, May 29, 1994. **Local divisions:** 18 provinces. **Defense:** 75% of GNP (1991). **Active troop strength:** 382,500 est.

**Economy: Industries:** Textiles, petrochemicals, oil refining, cement. **Chief crops:** Grains, rice, dates, cotton. **Minerals:** Oil, gas. **Crude oil reserves** (1995): 100 bil barrels. **Other resources:** Wool, hides. **Arable land:** 12%. **Livestock** (1994): cattle: 1.1 mil; sheep: 6.3 mil. **Fish catch** (1993): 23,500 metric tons. **Electricity prod.** (1993): 25.7 bil kWh. **Labor force:** 48% services; 30% agric.; 22% ind.

**Finance: Monetary unit:** Dinar (June 1996: 1,000 = $1 US). **Gross national product** (1993): $38 bil.* **Per capita GNP:** $2,000. **Imports** (1990): $6.6 bil; partners: U.S., Germany. **Exports** (1990): $10.4 bil; partners: U.S., Brazil. **National budget** (1990): $35 bil.

**Transport: Railroads: Route length:** 1,493 mi. **Motor vehicles:** in use: 672,000 passenger cars, 368,000 comm. vehicles. **Chief port:** Basra.

**Communications: Television sets:** 1 per 20 persons. **Radios:** 1 per 5.4 persons. **Telephones:** 1 per 29 persons. **Daily newspaper circ.:** 35 per 1,000 pop.

**Health: Life expectancy at birth** (1996): 66 male; 68 female. **Births** (per 1,000 pop.): 43. **Deaths** (per 1,000 pop.): 7.

**Natural increase:** 3.7%. **Hospital beds:** 1 per 568 persons. **Physicians:** 1 per 1,922 persons. **Infant mortality** (per 1,000 live births 1996): 60.

**Major International Organizations:** UN (IMF, ILO), Arab League, OPEC.

**Education: Literacy** (1993): 58%. Free and compulsory: ages 6-12.

The Tigris-Euphrates valley, formerly called Mesopotamia, was the site of one of the earliest civilizations in the world. The Sumerian city-states of 3,000 BC originated the culture later developed by the Semitic Akkadians, Babylonians, and Assyrians.

Mesopotamia ceased to be a separate entity after the conquests of the Persians, Greeks, and Arabs. The latter founded Baghdad, from where the caliph ruled a vast empire in the 8th and 9th centuries. Mongol and Turkish conquests led to a decline in population, the economy, cultural life, and the irrigation system.

Britain secured a League of Nations mandate over Iraq after World War I. Independence under a king came in 1932. A leftist, pan-Arab revolution established a republic in 1958, which oriented foreign policy toward the USSR. Most industry has been nationalized, and large land holdings broken up.

A local faction of the international Baath Arab Socialist party has ruled by decree since 1968. The USSR and Iraq signed an aid pact in 1972, and arms were sent along with several thousand advisers. The 1978 execution of 21 communists and a shift of trade to the West signalled a more neutral policy, straining relations with the USSR. In the 1973 Arab-Israeli war Iraq sent forces to aid Syria. Within a month of assuming power, Saddam Hussein instituted a bloody purge in the wake of a reported coup attempt against the new regime.

Years of battling with the Kurdish minority resulted in total defeat for the Kurds in 1975, when Iran withdrew support. The fighting led to Iraqi bombing of Kurdish villages in Iran, causing relations with Iran to deteriorate.

After skirmishing intermittently for 10 months over the sovereignty of the disputed Shatt al-Arab waterway that divides the two countries, Iraq and Iran entered into open warfare on Sept. 22, 1980. In the following days, there was heavy ground fighting around Abadan and the port of Khorramshahr, as Iraq launched an attack on Iran's oil-rich province of Khuzistan.

Israeli airplanes destroyed a nuclear reactor near Baghdad on June 7, 1981, claiming that it could be used to produce nuclear weapons.

Iraq and Iran expanded their war to the Persian Gulf in Apr. 1984. There were several attacks on oil tankers. An Iraqi warplane launched a missile attack on the USS *Stark,* a U.S. Navy frigate on patrol in the Persian Gulf, May 17, 1987; 37 U.S. sailors died. Iraq apologized for the attack, claiming it was inadvertent. The fierce war ended Aug. 1988, when Iraq accepted a UN resolution for a cease-fire.

Iraq attacked and overran Kuwait Aug. 2, 1990, sparking an international crisis. The UN, Aug. 6, imposed a ban on all trade with Iraq and called on member countries to protect the assets of the legitimate government of Kuwait. Iraq declared Kuwait its 19th province, Aug. 28.

A U.S.-led coalition launched air and missile attacks on Iraq, Jan. 16, 1991, after the expiration of a UN Security Council deadline for Iraq to withdraw from Kuwait. Iraq retaliated by firing scud missiles at Saudi Arabia and Israel. The coalition began a ground attack to retake Kuwait Feb. 23. Iraqi forces showed little resistance and were soundly defeated in 4 days. Some 175,000 Iraqis were taken prisoner, and casualties were estimated at over 85,000. As part of the cease-fire agreement, Iraq agreed to scrap all poison gas and germ weapons and allow UN observers to inspect the sites. UN trade sanctions would remain in effect until Iraq complied with all terms.

In the aftermath of the war, there were revolts against Pres. Saddam Hussein throughout Iraq. In Feb., Iraqi troops drove Kurdish insurgents and civilians to the Iran and Turkey borders, causing a refugee crisis. The U.S. and allies established havens inside Iraq for the Kurds. Iraqi cooperation with UN weapons inspection teams was intermittent.

The U.S. launched a missile attack aimed at Iraq's intelligence headquarters in Baghdad June 26, 1993. The U.S. justified the attack by citing evidence that Iraq had sponsored a plot to kill former Pres. George Bush during his visit to Kuwait in Apr. 1993. In Aug. 1995, two of Saddam Hussein's sons-in-law, who held high positions in the Iraqi military, defected to Jordan; both were killed after returning to Iraq in Feb. 1996.

After fighting between two Kurdish factions (one allied with Iraq, the other with Iran) erupted in the protected zone of northern Iraq, the Baghdad government intervened in the conflict by sending troops into Arbil, Aug. 31, 1996. The U.S. retaliated with missile strikes against air defense sites in the south. The UN renewed sanctions against Iraq and suspended a plan to allow Baghdad to sell limited amounts of oil for food and medicine.

# Ireland

## Éire

**People: Population:** 3,566,833. **Age distrib.** (%): <15: 25; 65+: 11. **Pop. density:** 131 per sq. mi. **Urban:** 57%. **Ethnic groups:** Celtic, English minority. **Principal languages:** English predominates, Irish (Gaelic) spoken by minority (both official). **Religions:** Roman Catholic 93%, Anglican 3%.

**Geography: Area:** 27,137 sq. mi. **Location:** In the Atlantic O. just W of Great Britain. **Neighbors:** United Kingdom (Northern Ireland) on E. **Topography:** Ireland consists of a central plateau surrounded by isolated groups of hills and mountains. The coastline is heavily indented by the Atlantic O. **Capital:** Dublin. **Cities** (1991 est.): Dublin 478,400; Cork 127,200.

**Government: Type:** Parliamentary republic. **Head of state:** Pres. Mary Robinson; b May 21, 1944; in office: Dec. 3, 1990. **Head of government:** Prime Min. John Bruton; b May 18, 1947; in office: Dec. 15, 1994. **Local divisions:** 26 counties. **Defense:** 1.3% of GDP (1994). **Active troop strength:** 12,900.

**Economy: Industries:** Food processing, textiles, chemicals, brewing, machinery, tourism. **Chief crops:** Potatoes, grains, sugar beets, turnips. **Minerals:** Zinc, lead, gas, oil. **Arable land:** 14%. **Livestock** (1993): cattle: 6.3 mil; pigs: 1.4 mil; sheep: 6.1 mil. **Fish catch** (1992): 275,000 metric tons. **Electricity prod.** (1993): 14.9 bil kWh. **Labor force:** 57% services; 28% manuf.; 14% agric.

**Finance: Monetary unit:** Pound (June 1996: 1.00 = $1.59 US). **Gross domestic product** (1994): $49.8 bil.* **Per capita GDP:** $14,060. **Imports** (1994): $26 bil; partners: UK 41%, U.S. 15%, other EU 25%. **Exports** (1994): $28 bil; partners: UK 32%, other EU 43%, U.S. 9%. **Tourism** (1993): $1.6 bil. **National budget** (1994): $16.6 bil. **International reserves less gold** (May 1996): $8.0 bil. **Gold:** 360,000 oz t. **Consumer prices** (change in 1995): 2.5%.

**Transport: Railroads: Length:** 1,749 mi. **Motor vehicles:** in use: 891,000 passenger cars, 146,000 comm. vehicles. **Civil aviation:** 2.7 bil passenger-mi.; 10 airports. **Chief ports:** Dublin, Cork.

**Communications: Television sets:** 1 per 3.5 persons. **Radios:** 1 per 1.6 persons. **Telephones:** 1 per 3.1 persons. **Daily newspaper circ.:** 186 per 1,000 pop.

**Health: Life expectancy at birth** (1996): 73 male; 79 female. **Births** (per 1,000 pop.): 13. **Deaths** (per 1,000 pop.): 9. **Natural increase:** 0.4%. **Hospital beds:** 1 per 255 persons. **Physicians:** 1 per 588 persons. **Infant mortality** (per 1,000 live births 1996): 6.

**Education: Literacy** (1993): 100%. Compulsory: ages 6-15.

**Major International Organizations:** UN (WHO, FAO, WTO, IMF, World Bank), EU, OECD.

**Embassy:** 2234 Massachusetts Ave. NW 20008; 462-3939.

Celtic tribes invaded the islands about the 4th century BC; their Gaelic culture and literature flourished and spread to Scotland and elsewhere in the 5th century AD, the same century in which St. Patrick converted the Irish to Christianity. Invasions by Norsemen began in the 8th century, ended with defeat of the Danes by the Irish King Brian Boru in 1014. English invasions started in the 12th century; for over 700 years the Anglo-Irish struggle continued with bitter rebellions and savage repressions.

The Easter Monday Rebellion (1916) failed but was followed by guerrilla warfare and harsh reprisals by British troops, the "Black and Tans." The Dail Eireann, or Irish parliament, reaffirmed independence in Jan. 1919. The British offered dominion status to Ulster (6 counties) and southern Ireland (26 counties) Dec. 1921. The constitution of the Irish Free State, a British dominion, was adopted Dec. 11, 1922. Northern Ireland remained part of the United Kingdom.

A new constitution adopted by plebiscite came into operation Dec. 29, 1937. It declared the name of the state Eire in the Irish language (Ireland in the English) and declared it a sovereign democratic state.

*(continued on page 785)*

# RUSSIA IN THE SPOTLIGHT

LASK/GAMMA LIAISON

Despite poor health, Boris Yeltsin (at left, campaigning in Moscow) waged a hard-fought, Western-style campaign and won reelection, July 3, as Russia's president. But his health problems were so serious that it was announced after the election that he needed heart surgery.

In a bloody and unpopular war, the Russian army suffered heavy casualties (see below) in fighting against secessionist rebels in Chechnya.

A. GYORI/SYGMA

# WORLD EVENTS

SYGMA

ALLAN TANNENBAUM/SYGMA

Israel was struck by a wave of suicide bombings—including the rush-hour bombing of a bus on Mar. 3 in Jerusalem (above), which cost 19 lives. Security concerns apparently contributed to the election in May of a new prime minister, rightist Benjamin Netanyahu (at left with his wife, Sarah, waving to supporters).

DAVID JONES/AP/WIDE WORLD PHOTOS

Schoolchildren in Rugby, England, line up warily for a lunch that includes ostrich burgers. The menu reflected wide concern over the safety of British beef, after studies showed a possible link between "mad cow disease" afflicting British cattle and a fatal brain disorder that can affect humans.

Sixteen kindergarten children and their teacher were killed by a gunman, Mar. 13, at a school in Dunblane, Scotland. At right is a class picture taken the day before; below, a memorial to the children who died.

SYGMA

TIM GRAHAM/SYGMA

SAUDI GAZETTE/SYGMA

On June 25, amid heightened political tensions in Saudi Arabia, a huge truck bomb exploded on the perimeter of a military complex near Dhahran housing U.S. troops; 19 were killed.

RIKARD LARMA/AP/WIDE WORLD PHOTOS

U.S. forces arrive at the airport in Sarajevo, to form part of a 60,000-member NATO peacekeeping force in Bosnia.

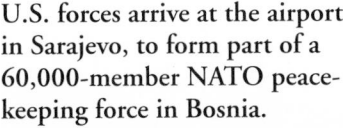

# ARTS AND ENTERTAINMENT

AP/WIDE WORLD PHOTOS

A TV talk show starring Rosie O'Donnell debuted in the summer and drew high ratings, as a "kinder, gentler" alternative to the often seamy "trash TV" talk shows on in the daytime. Above, O'Donnell (right) is visited by Regis Philbin and his daughter.

*Braveheart,* a gritty Scottish battle epic starring and directed by Mel Gibson (below), won Oscars in 1996 for best director and best picture.

20TH CENTURY FOX/SHOOTING STAR INTERNATIONAL

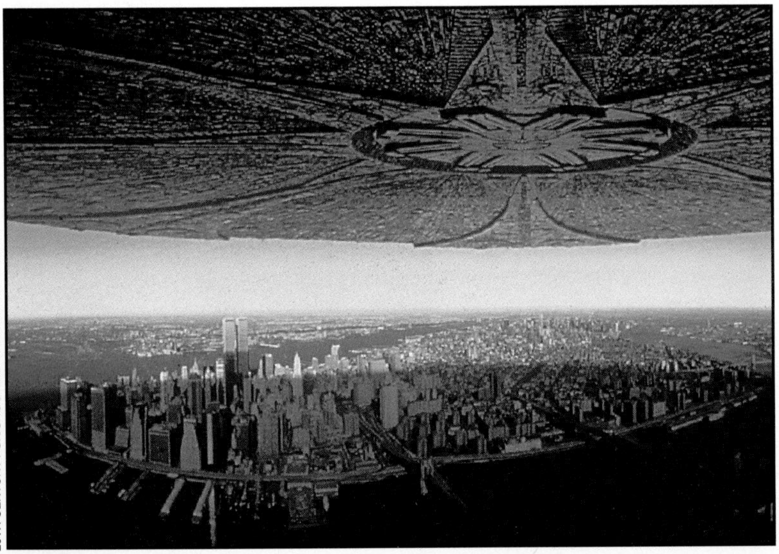

20TH CENTURY FOX/SHOOTING STAR INTERNATIONAL

*Independence Day* invaded U.S. movie theaters just before the Fourth of July, grossing $112 million in its first week alone. At left, a massive alien space station looms over New York City.

BRIAN RASIC/REX USA, LTD.

Hootie and the Blowfish won 2 Grammys in 1996, and by midyear their album *Cracked Rear View* had sold 14 million copies, making it the second-biggest selling debut album of all time.

*Rent*, a rock opera about young city artists and musicians struggling on society's fringes, was a big hit on and off Broadway, and earned a posthumous Pulitzer Prize for author Jonathan Larson—who died in January at the age of 35.

© JOAN MARCUS

Comedian George Burns, who won fame as straight man to wife Gracie Allen, and then launched a solo career that lasted into his 90s, died in March at the age of 100.

UPI/CORBIS/BETTMANN

TV sleuth Jessica Fletcher, alias Angela Lansbury, went into semi-retirement after the 1995-96 season, as the popular *Murder, She Wrote* ended its 12-year run as a weekly series.

GENE TRINDL/© 1996, CBS INC

# SUMMER OLYMPICS

© MARTTI KAINULAINEN/SABA

© 1996 WILLIAM R. SALLAZ/DUOMO

Boxing legend Muhammad Ali (left) lit the Olympic flame ushering in the 26th Olympic Summer Games, July 19 in Atlanta. A bombing in Centennial Olympic Park on July 27 (below) killed one person and injured over 100, but the Olympic spirit survived. Women athletes were outstanding: above, the triumphant U.S. women's gymnastics team; below, swimmer Amy Van Dyken, after earning one of her four gold medals.

© JUSSI NUKARI/SABA

© R.B-J.O. ATLANTA 96/GAMMA LIAISON

Among Summer Olympic stars: Dan O'Brien (left) was dubbed "the world's greatest athlete" after his decathlon victory; Michael Johnson (bottom left) set a new world record in the 200-meter; Carl Lewis (below) took the long jump, becoming only the second athlete ever to win golds for the same event in four consecutive Olympics; and Canada's Donovan Bailey (center in photo at bottom right) sprinted to a gold medal in the prestigious 100-meter, setting a new world record.

© 1996 DAVID MADISON/DUOMO

© STEVEN E. SUTTON/DUOMO

© MARTTI KAINULAINEN/SABA

J.O. ATLANTA 96/GAMMA LIAISON

# SPORTS HIGHLIGHTS

TIM DE FRISCO/SPORTS ILLUSTRATED © TIME INC.

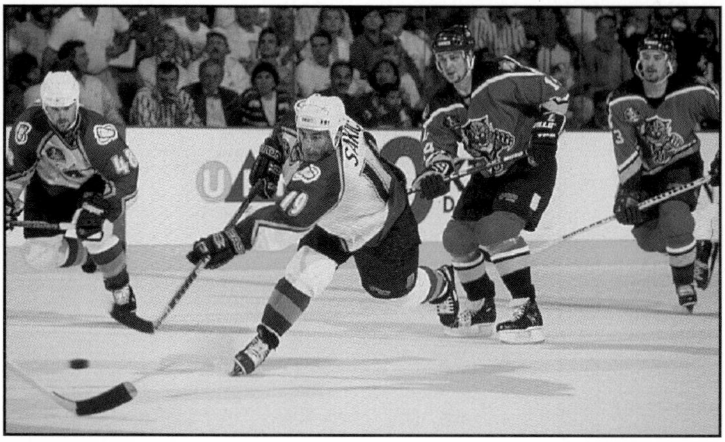

The Colorado Avalanche, in their first NHL finals, swept the Florida Panthers in four games to take the Stanley Cup; team captain Joe Sakic (shooting) was named the MVP for the playoffs, after scoring 18 goals in 21 post-season games.

The Dallas Cowboys won their fifth Super Bowl, beating the Pittsburgh Steelers, 27-17, on Jan. 28 in Tempe, AZ. Star running back Emmitt Smith (below) scored two touchdowns to help the Cowboys to victory.

WILLIAM R. SALLAZ/DUOMO

MANNY MILLAN/SPORTS ILLUSTRATED © TIME INC.

The Chicago Bulls beat the Seattle SuperSonics to win their fourth NBA championship in six years and cap a record-breaking season. Bulls guard Michael Jordan (23) was named finals MVP for a record fourth time.

On Dec. 21, 1948, an Irish law declared the country a republic rather than a dominion and withdrew it from the Commonwealth. The British Parliament recognized both actions, 1949, but reasserted its claim to incorporate the 6 northeastern counties in the United Kingdom. This claim has not been recognized by Ireland *(see United Kingdom — Northern Ireland)*.

Irish governments have favored peaceful unification of all Ireland and have cooperated with Britain against terrorist groups. On Dec. 15, 1993, the Irish and British governments agreed on outlines of a peace plan to resolve the Northern Ireland issue. On Aug. 31, 1994, the Irish Republican Army announced a cease-fire and said it would seek the unification of Ireland by political means. When peace talks lagged, however, the IRA resumed its terror campaign on Feb. 9, 1996.

# Israel

## State of Israel

## Medinat Yisra'el

**People: Population:** 5,421,995. **Age distrib.** (%): <15: 30; 65+: 9. **Pop. density:** 688 per sq. mi. **Urban:** 90%. **Ethnic groups:** Jewish 82%, non-Jewish (mostly Arab) 18%. **Principal languages:** Hebrew and Arabic (official), English. **Religions:** Jewish 82%, Muslim 14%.

**Geography: Area:** 7,876 sq. mi. **Location:** Middle East, on E end of Mediterranean Sea. **Neighbors:** Lebanon on N, Syria and Jordan on E, Egypt on W. **Topography:** The Mediterranean coastal plain is fertile and well-watered. In the center is the Judean Plateau. A triangular-shaped semi-desert region, the Negev, extends from south of Beersheba to an apex at the head of the Gulf of Aqaba. The E border drops sharply into the Jordan Rift Valley, including Lake Tiberias (Sea of Galilee) and the Dead Sea, which is 1,312 ft. below sea level, lowest point on the earth's surface. **Capital:** Jerusalem (most countries maintain their embassy in Tel Aviv). **Cities** (1994 est.): Jerusalem 567,100; Tel Aviv-Yafo 357,400; Haifa 246,5000.

**Government: Type:** Republic. **Head of state:** Pres. Ezer Weizman; b June 15, 1924; in office: May 13, 1993. **Head of government:** Prime Min. Benjamin Netanyahu; b Oct. 21, 1949; in office: June 18, 1996. **Local divisions:** 6 districts. **Defense:** 10% of GDP (1995 est.). **Active troop strength:** 172,000 est.

**Economy: Industries:** Diamond cutting, textiles, electronics, machinery, food processing. **Chief crops:** Citrus fruit, vegetables, cotton. **Minerals:** Copper, phosphates, bromide, potash, clay. **Arable land:** 17%. **Livestock** (1994): cattle: 362,000; sheep: 330,000. **Fish catch** (1993): 18,700 metric tons. **Electricity prod.** (1993): 21.3 bil kWh. **Labor force:** 29% public services; 22% ind.; 14% commerce.

**Finance: Monetary unit:** New Shekel (June 1996: 3.20 = $1 US). **Gross domestic prod.** (1994): $70.1 bln.* **Per capita GDP:** $13,880. **Imports** (1994): $22.5 bln.; partners: U.S. 18%, Belgium 13%, Germany 10%. **Exports** (1994): $16.2 bln.; partners: U.S. 31%, Japan 5%, Belgium 5%. **Tourism** (1993): $2.1 bil. **National budget** (FY 1992-93): $45.4 bil. **International reserves less gold** (May 1996): $9.3 bil. **Gold:** 9,000 oz t. **Consumer prices** (change in 1995): 10.0%.

**Transport: Railroads: Route length:** 356 mi. **Motor vehicles:** in use: 979,000 passenger cars, 222,000 comm. vehicles. **Civil aviation:** 5.3 bil passenger-mi.; 7 airports with scheduled flights. **Chief ports:** Haifa, Ashdod, Elat.

**Communications: Television sets:** 1 per 4.1 persons. **Radios:** 1 per 2.2 persons. **Telephones:** 1 per 2.7 persons. **Daily newspaper circ.:** 242 per 1,000 pop.

**Health: Life expectancy at birth** (1996): 76 male; 80 female. **Births** (per 1,000 pop.): 20. **Deaths** (per 1,000 pop.): 6. **Natural increase:** 1.4%. **Hospital beds:** 1 per 159 persons. **Physicians:** 1 per 214 persons. **Infant mortality** (per 1,000 live births 1996): 9.

**Education: Literacy** (1994): 95%. Free and compulsory: ages 5-16.

**Major International Organizations:** UN (WTO, IMF).

**Embassy:** 3514 International Dr. NW 20008; 364-5500.

Occupying the SW corner of the ancient Fertile Crescent, Israel contains some of the oldest known evidence of agriculture and of primitive town life. A more advanced civilization emerged in the 3d millennium BC. The Hebrews probably arrived early in the 2d millennium BC. Under King David and his successors (c.1000 BC-597 BC), Judaism was developed and secured. After conquest by Babylonians, Persians, and Greeks, an independent Jewish kingdom was revived, 168 BC, but Rome took effective control in the next century, suppressed Jewish revolts in AD 70 and AD 135, and renamed Judea Palestine, after the earlier coastal inhabitants, the Philistines.

Arab invaders conquered Palestine in 636. The Arabic language and Islam prevailed within a few centuries, but a Jewish minority remained. The land was ruled from the 11th century as a part of non-Arab empires by Seljuks, Mamluks, and Ottomans (with a crusader interval, 1098-1291).

After 4 centuries of Ottoman rule, during which the population declined to a low of 350,000 (1785), the land was taken in 1917 by Britain, which in the Balfour Declaration that year pledged to support a Jewish national homeland there, as foreseen by the Zionists. In 1920 a British Palestine Mandate was recognized; in 1922 the land east of the Jordan was detached.

Jewish immigration, begun in the late 19th century, swelled in the 1930s with refugees from the Nazis; heavy Arab immigration from Syria and Lebanon also occurred. Arab opposition to Jewish immigration turned violent in 1920, 1921, 1929, and 1936. The UN General Assembly voted in 1947 to partition Palestine into an Arab and a Jewish state. Britain withdrew in May 1948.

Israel was declared an independent state May 14, 1948; the Arabs rejected partition. Egypt, Jordan, Syria, Lebanon, Iraq, and Saudi Arabia invaded, but failed to destroy the Jewish state, which gained territory. Separate armistices with the Arab nations were signed in 1949; Jordan occupied the West Bank, Egypt occupied Gaza; neither granted Palestinian autonomy.

After persistent terrorist raids, Israel invaded Egypt's Sinai, Oct. 29, 1956, aided briefly by British and French forces. A UN cease-fire was arranged Nov. 6.

An uneasy truce between Israel and the Arab countries, supervised by a UN Emergency Force, prevailed until May 19, 1967, when the UN force withdrew at Egypt's demand. Egyptian forces reoccupied the Gaza Strip and closed the Gulf of Aqaba to Israeli shipping. In a 6-day war that started June 5, the Israelis took the Gaza Strip, occupied the Sinai Peninsula to the Suez Canal, and captured East Jerusalem, Syria's Golan Heights, and Jordan's West Bank. The fighting was halted June 10 by UN-arranged cease-fire agreements.

Egypt and Syria attacked Israel, Oct. 6, 1973 (Yom Kippur, most solemn day on the Jewish calendar). Israel counterattacked, driving the Syrians back, and crossed the Suez Canal.

A cease-fire took effect Oct. 24; a UN peacekeeping force went to the area. A disengagement agreement was signed Jan. 18, 1974. Israel withdrew from the canal's west bank. A second withdrawal was completed in 1976; Israel returned the Sinai to Egypt in 1982.

Israeli forces raided Entebbe, Uganda, July 3, 1976, and rescued 103 hostages seized by Arab and German terrorists.

In 1977, the conservative opposition, led by Menachem Begin, was voted into office for the first time. Egypt's Pres. Anwar al-Sadat visited Jerusalem Nov. 1977, and on Mar. 26, 1979, Egypt and Israel signed a formal peace treaty, ending 30 years of war and establishing diplomatic relations.

Israel invaded S Lebanon, Mar. 1978, following a Lebanon-based terrorist attack in Israel. Israel withdrew in favor of a 6,000-man UN force, but continued to aid Lebanese Christian militiamen. Violence on the Israeli-occupied West Bank rose in 1982 when Israel announced plans to build new Jewish settlements. Israel affirmed the entire city of Jerusalem as its capital, July 1980, encompassing the annexed East Jerusalem.

On June 7, 1981, Israeli jets destroyed an Iraqi atomic reactor near Baghdad that, Israel claimed, would have enabled Iraq to manufacture nuclear weapons.

Israeli jets bombed Palestine Liberation Organization (PLO) strongholds in Lebanon Apr.-May 1982. In reaction to the wounding of the Israeli ambassador to Great Britain, Israeli forces in a coordinated land, sea, and air attack invaded Lebanon, June 6, to destroy PLO strongholds in that country. Israeli forces encircled Beirut June 14. Following massive Israeli bombing of West Beirut, the PLO agreed to evacuate the city.

Israeli troops entered West Beirut after newly elected Lebanese Pres. Bashir Gemayel was assassinated on Sept. 14. Israel received widespread condemnation when Lebanese Christian forces, Sept. 16, entered two West Beirut refugee camps and slaughtered hundreds of Palestinian refugees.

In 1989, violence escalated over the Israeli military occupation of the West Bank and Gaza Strip. In a series of uprisings known as the intifada, Palestinian protesters defied Israeli troops, who forcibly retaliated. Israeli police and stone-throwing Palestinians clashed, Oct. 8, 1990, around the al-Aqsa mosque on the Temple Mount in Jerusalem; some 20 Palestinians died.

During the Persian Gulf War in early 1991, Iraq fired a series of scud missiles at Israel. The Labor Party of Yitzhak Rabin won a clear victory in elections held June 23, 1992.

Ongoing peace talks produced historic agreements between Israel and the Palestine Liberation Organization in Sept. 1993. The latter recognized Israel's right to exist, and Israel recognized the PLO as the representative of the Palestinians; the two sides then signed, Sept. 13, an agreement for limited Palestinian self-rule in Gaza and in the West Bank, beginning with the city of Jericho. An accord formally initiating self-rule was signed in Cairo, May 4, 1994. Israel and Jordan signed, July 25, 1994, in Washington, DC, a declaration ending their 46-year state of war; a formal peace treaty was signed Oct. 26. An accord between Israel and the PLO expanding Palestinian self-rule in the West Bank was signed Sept. 28, 1995.

Arab and Jewish extremists repeatedly challenged the peace process. A Jewish gunman opened fire on Arab worshippers at a mosque in Hebron, Feb. 25, 1994, killing at least 29 before he himself was killed. On Nov. 4, 1995, an Orthodox Jewish Israeli assassinated Rabin as he left a peace rally in Tel Aviv.

Support for Rabin's successor, Shimon Peres, was shaken by a series of suicide bombings and rocket attacks against Israel by Islamic militants. In Apr. 1996, Israel attacked suspected guerrilla bases in southern Lebanon. Emphasizing security issues, the candidate of the conservative Likud bloc, Benjamin Netanyahu, was elected prime minister on May 29. On Sept. 24, Israel opened a tunnel entrance near a sacred Muslim site in Jerusalem, setting off several days of violence between Israeli soldiers and Palestinian demonstrators and police. Pres. Clinton hosted a summit meeting between Netanyahu and PLO leader Yasir Arafat Oct. 1-2, and peace talks were resumed.

**Gaza: Population** (1996 est.): 924,000. **Area:** 140 sq. mi.
**West Bank: Population** (1996 est.): 1,428,000. **Area:** 2,270 sq. mi.

# Italy

## Italian Republic

## Repubblica Italiana

**People: Population:** 57,460,274. **Age distrib.** (%): <15: 15; 65+: 16. **Pop. density:** 494 per sq. mi. **Urban:** 67%. **Ethnic groups:** Italians, small minorities of Germans, French, Slovenes, Albanians, Greeks. **Principal languages:** Italian (official), German, French, Slovene. **Religions:** Roman Catholic 98%.

**Geography: Area:** 116,336 sq. mi. **Location:** In S Europe, jutting into Mediterranean Sea. **Neighbors:** France on W, Switzerland and Austria on N, Slovenia on E. **Topography:** Occupies a long boot-shaped peninsula, extending SE from the Alps into the Mediterranean, with the islands of Sicily and Sardinia offshore. The alluvial Po Valley drains most of N. The rest of the country is rugged and mountainous, except for intermittent coastal plains, like the Campania, S of Rome. Apennine Mts. run down through center of peninsula. **Capital:** Rome. **Cities** (1994 est.): Rome 2.7 mln.; Milan 1.3 mln.; Naples 1.0 mln.; Turin 945,500.

**Government: Type:** Republic. **Head of state:** Pres. Oscar Luigi Scalfaro; b Sept. 9, 1918; in office: May 28, 1992. **Head of government:** Prime Min. Romano Prodi; b Aug. 9, 1939; in office: May 18, 1996. **Local divisions:** 20 regions with some autonomy, divided into 95 provinces. **Defense:** 2% of GDP (1994). **Active troop strength:** 328,700.

**Economy: Industries:** Steel, machinery, autos, textiles, shoes, clothing, chemicals. **Chief crops:** Grapes, olives, citrus fruits, vegetables, wheat. **Minerals:** Mercury, potash, sulphur. **Crude oil reserves** (1995): 621 mil bbls. **Arable land:** 32%. **Livestock** (1994): cattle: 7.7 mln.; pigs: 8.2 mln.; sheep: 10.4 mil. **Fish catch** (1993): 552,000 metric tons. **Electricity prod.** (1993): 209 bil kWh. **Labor force:** 58% services; 32% ind.; 10% agric.

**Finance: Monetary unit:** Lira (June 1996: 1,536 = $1 US). **Gross domestic product** (1994): $998.9 bln.* **Per capita GDP:** $17,180. **Imports** (1994): $168.7 bln.; partners: EU 56%, U.S. 5%. **Exports** (1994): $190.8 bln.; partners: EU 53%, U.S. 8%. **Tourism** (1993): $20.5 bil. **National budget** (1994 est.): $431 bil. **International reserves less gold** (May 1996): $45.6 bil. **Gold:** 66.67 mil oz t. **Consumer prices** (change in 1995): 5.2%.

**Transport: Railroads: Length:** 12,176 mi. **Motor vehicles:** in use: 29.6 mil passenger cars, 2.7 mil comm. vehicles. **Civil aviation:** 18.4 bil passenger-mi.; 32 airports. **Chief ports:** Genoa, Venice, Trieste, Palermo, Naples, La Spezia.

**Communications: Television sets:** 1 per 3.4 persons. **Radios:** 1 per 1.3 persons. **Telephones:** 1 per 2.4 persons. **Daily newspaper circ.:** 157 per 1,000 pop.

**Health: Life expectancy at birth** (1996): 75 male; 82 female. **Births** (per 1,000 pop.): 10. **Deaths** (per 1,000 pop.): 10. **Natural increase:** 0. **Hospital beds:** 1 per 147 persons. **Physicians:** 1 per 193 persons. **Infant mortality** (per 1,000 live births 1996): 7.

**Education: Literacy** (1994): 97%. Free and compulsory: ages 6-13.

**Major International Organizations:** UN and all of its specialized agencies, NATO, OECD, EU.

**Embassy:** 1601 Fuller St. NW 20009; 328-5500.

Rome emerged as the major power in Italy after 500 BC, dominating the Etruscans to the N and Greeks to the S. Under the Empire, which lasted until the 5th century AD, Rome ruled most of Western Europe, the Balkans, the Middle East, and N Africa. In 1988, archaeologists unearthed evidence showing Rome as a dynamic society in the 6th and 7th centuries BC.

After the Germanic invasions, lasting several centuries, a high civilization arose in the city-states of the N, culminating in the Renaissance. But German, French, Spanish, and Austrian intervention prevented the unification of the country. In 1859 Lombardy came under the crown of King Victor Emmanuel II of Sardinia. By plebiscite in 1860, Parma, Modena, Romagna, and Tuscany joined, followed by Sicily and Naples, and by the Marches and Umbria. The first Italian Parliament declared Victor Emmanuel king of Italy Mar. 17, 1861. Mantua and Venetia were added in 1866 as an outcome of the Austro-Prussian war. The Papal States were taken by Italian troops Sept. 20, 1870, on the withdrawal of the French garrison. The states were annexed to the kingdom by plebiscite. Italy recognized Vatican City as independent Feb. 11, 1929.

Fascism appeared in Italy Mar. 23, 1919, led by Benito Mussolini, who took over the government at the invitation of the king Oct. 28, 1922. Mussolini acquired dictatorial powers. He made war on Ethiopia and proclaimed Victor Emmanuel III emperor, defied the sanctions of the League of Nations, sent troops to fight for Franco against the Republic of Spain, and joined Germany in World War II.

After Fascism was overthrown in 1943, Italy declared war on Germany and Japan and contributed to the Allied victory. It surrendered conquered lands and lost its colonies. Mussolini was killed by partisans Apr. 28, 1945. Victor Emmanuel III abdicated May 9, 1946; his son Humbert II was king until June 10, when Italy became a republic after a referendum, June 2-3.

Since World War II, Italy has enjoyed growth in industrial output and livig standards, in part a result of membership in the European Community (now European Union). Political stability has not kept pace with economic prosperity, and organized crime and corruption have been persistent problems.

Christian Democratic leader and former Prime Min. Aldo Moro was abducted and murdered in 1978 by Red Brigade terrorists. The wave of left-wing political violence, including other kidnappings and assassinations, continued into the 1980s.

In the early 1990s, scandals implicated some of Italy's most prominent politicians. In Mar. 1994 voting, under reformed election rules, right-wing parties won a majority, dislodging Italy's long-powerful Christian Democratic Party. After a series of short-lived governments, a coalition of center-left parties won the election of Apr. 21, 1996.

**Sicily,** 9,926 sq. mi., pop. (1993 est.) 4,998,000, is an island 180 by 120 mi., seat of a region that embraces the island of **Pantelleria,** 32 sq. mi., and the **Lipari** group, 44 sq. mi., including 2 active volcanoes: **Vulcano,** 1,637 ft., and **Stromboli,** 3,038 ft. From prehistoric times Sicily has been settled by various peoples; a Greek state had its capital at Syracuse. Rome took Sicily from Carthage 215 BC. **Mt. Etna,** an 11,053-ft. active volcano, is its tallest peak.

**Sardinia,** 9,301 sq. mi., pop. (1993 est.) 1,652,000, lies in the Mediterranean, 115 mi. W of Italy and 7½ mi. S of Corsica. It is 160 mi. long, 68 mi. wide, and mountainous, with mining of coal, zinc, lead, copper. In 1720 Sardinia was added to the possessions of the Dukes of Savoy in Piedmont and Savoy to form the Kingdom of Sardinia. Giuseppe Garibaldi is buried on the nearby isle of Caprera. **Elba,** 86 sq. mi., lies 6 mi. W of Tuscany. Napoleon I lived in exile on Elba 1814-1815.

# Jamaica

**People: Population:** 2,595,275. **Age distrib.** (%): <15: 34; 65+: 7. **Pop. density:** 612 per sq. mi. **Urban:** 53%. **Ethnic groups:** African 76%, Afro-European 15%, white, Chinese, East Indian. **Principal languages:** English (official), Jamaican Creole. **Religions:** Protestant 56%, spiritual cults and other 39%, Roman Catholic 5%.

**Geography: Area:** 4,244 sq. mi. **Location:** In West Indies. **Neighbors:** Nearest are Cuba on N, Haiti on E. **Topography:** The country is four-fifths covered by mountains. **Capital:** Kingston (1991 met. est.): 587,000.

**Government: Type:** Parliamentary democracy. **Head of state:** Queen Elizabeth II, represented by Gov.-Gen. Sir Howard Cooke; b Nov. 13, 1915; in office: Aug. 1, 1991. **Head of government:** Prime Min. Percival J. Patterson; b Apr. 10, 1935; in office: Mar. 30, 1992. **Local divisions:** 14 parishes. **Defense:** 1% of GDP (FY 1991-92). **Active troop strength:** 3,320.

**Economy: Industries:** Sugar, bauxite mining, tourism. **Chief crops:** Sugarcane, coffee, bananas, potatoes, citrus fruits. **Minerals:** Bauxite, limestone, gypsum. **Arable land:** 19%. **Livestock** (1993): cattle: 330,000; goats: 440,000. **Electricity prod.** (1993): 2.6 bil kWh. **Labor force:** 41% services; 23% agric.; 19% ind.

**Finance: Monetary unit:** Dollar (June 1996: 34.00 = $1 US). **Gross domestic product** (1994): $7.8 bln.* **Per capita GDP:** $3,050. **Imports** (1994): $2.2 bln.; partners: U.S. 54%. **Exports** (1994): $1.2 bln.; partners: U.S. 47%. **Tourism** (1994): $915 mil. **National budget** (Fy 1990-91): $736 mil. **International reserves less gold** (Feb. 1996): $718 mil. **Consumer prices** (change in 1995): 19.9%.

**Transport: Railroads: Route length:** 129 mi. **Motor vehicles:** in use: 73,000 passenger cars, 31,000 comm. vehicles. **Civil aviation:** 935 mil passenger-mi.; 4 airports with scheduled flights. **Chief ports:** Kingston, Montego Bay.

**Communications: Television sets:** 1 per 5.2 persons. **Radios:** 1 per 2.5 persons. **Telephones:** 1 per 9.5 persons.

**Health: Life expectancy at birth** (1996): 73 male; 77 female. **Births** (per 1,000 pop.): 22. **Deaths:** (per 1,000 pop.): 6. **Natural increase:** 1.7%. **Hospital beds:** 1 per 492 persons. **Physicians:** 1 per 6,335 persons. **Infant mortality** (per 1,000 live births 1996): 16.

**Education: Literacy** (1995): 85%. Free and compulsory: ages 6-12.

**Major International Organizations:** UN (World Bank, WTO), OAS, the Commonwealth.

**Embassy:** 1520 New Hampshire Ave. NW 20036; 452-0660.

Jamaica was visited by Columbus, 1494, and ruled by Spain (under whom Arawak Indians died out) until seized by Britain, 1655. Jamaica won independence Aug. 6, 1962.

In 1974 Jamaica sought an increase in taxes paid by U.S. and Canadian bauxite mines. The socialist government acquired 50% ownership of the companies' Jamaican interests in 1976, and was reelected that year. Rudimentary welfare state measures were passed. Relations with the U.S. improved greatly in the 1980s following the election of Edward Seaga, which marked the beginning of a more conservative era.

# Japan

## Nippon

**People: Population:** 125,449,703. **Age distrib.** (%): <15: 16; 65+: 15. **Pop. density:** 860 per sq. mi. **Urban:** 78%. **Ethnic groups:** Japanese 99.4%, other (mostly Korean) 0.6%. **Principal language:** Japanese. **Religions:** Buddhism, Shintoism shared by large majority.

**Geography: Area:** 145,850 sq. mi. **Location:** Archipelago off E coast of Asia. **Neighbors:** Russia on N, South Korea on W. **Topography:** Japan consists of 4 main islands: Honshu ("mainland"), 87,805 sq. mi.; Hokkaido, 30,144 sq. mi.; Kyushu, 14,114 sq. mi.; and Shikoku, 7,049 sq. mi. The coast, deeply indented, measures 16,654 mi. The northern islands are a continuation of the Sakhalin Mts. The Kunlun range of China continues into southern islands, the ranges meeting in the Japanese Alps. In a vast transverse fissure crossing Honshu E-W rises a group of volcanoes, mostly extinct or inactive, including 12,388 ft. Mt. Fuji (Fujiyama) near Tokyo. **Capital:** Tokyo. **Cities** (1994 est.): Tokyo 8.0 mln.; Yokohama 3.3 mln.; Osaka 2.6 mln.; Nagoya 2.2 mln.; Sapporo 1.7 mln.; Kyoto 1.5 mln.; Kobe 1.5 mln.; Fukuoka 1.3 mln.; Kawasaki 1.2 mln.; Hiroshima 1.1 mil.

**Government: Type:** Parliamentary democracy. **Head of state:** Emp. Akihito; b Dec. 23, 1933; in office: Jan. 7, 1989. **Head of government:** Prime Min. Ryutaro Hashimoto; b July 29, 1937; in office: Jan. 11, 1996. **Local divisions:** 47 prefectures. **Defense:** 1% of GDP (FY 1995-96). **Active troop strength:** 239,500.

**Economy: Industries:** Electrical & electronic equip., autos, machinery, chemicals. **Chief crops:** Rice, sugar, beets, vegetables, fruits. **Arable land:** 13%. **Livestock** (1994): cattle: 5.0 mln.; pigs: 10.6 mil. **Fish catch** (1993): 8.7 mil metric tons. **Electricity prod.** (1993): 840 bil kWh. **Labor force:** 54% services & trade; 33% manuf. & mining; 7% agric.

**Finance: Monetary unit:** Yen (June 1996: 110 = $1 US). **Gross domestic product** (1994): $2.53 trl.* **Per capita GDP:** $20,200. **Imports** (1994): $274.3 bln.; partners: SE Asia 25%, U.S. 23%, China 9%. **Exports** (1994): $395.5 bln.; partners: SE Asia 33%, U.S. 29%. **Tourism** (1993): $3.6 bil. **National budget** (1994): $671 bil. **International reserves less gold** (May 1996): $207 bil. **Gold:** 24.23 mil oz t. **Consumer prices** (change in 1995): –0.1%.

**Transport: Railroads: Length:** 23,690 mi. **Motor vehicles:** in use: 40.8 mil passenger cars, 22.5 mil comm. vehicles. **Civil aviation:** 69.3 bil passenger-mi.; 74 airports with scheduled flights. **Chief ports:** Yokohama, Tokyo, Kobe, Osaka, Nagoya, Chiba, Kawasaki, Hakodate.

**Communications: Television sets:** 1 per 1.2 persons. **Radios:** 1 per 1.1 persons. **Telephones:** 1 per 2.1 persons. **Daily newspaper circ.:** 576 per 1,000 pop.

**Health: Life expectancy at birth** (1996): 77 male; 83 female. **Births** (per 1,000 pop.): 10. **Deaths** (per 1,000 pop.): 8. **Natural increase:** 0.3%. **Hospital beds:** 1 per 74 persons. **Physicians:** 1 per 566 persons. **Infant mortality** (per 1,000 live births 1996): 4.

**Education: Literacy** (1994): 100%. Free and compulsory: ages 6-15.

**Major International Organizations:** UN and all its specialized agencies, OECD.

**Embassy:** 2520 Massachusetts Ave. NW 20008; 939-6700.

According to Japanese legend, the empire was founded by Emperor Jimmu, 660 BC, but earliest records of a unified Japan date from 1,000 years later. Chinese influence was strong in the formation of Japanese civilization. Buddhism was introduced before the 6th century AD.

A feudal system, with locally powerful noble families and their samurai warrior retainers, dominated from 1192. Central power was held by successive families of shoguns (military dictators), 1192-1867, until recovered by the Emperor Meiji, 1868. The Portuguese and Dutch had minor trade with Japan in the 16th and 17th centuries; U.S. Commodore Matthew C. Perry opened it to U.S. trade in a treaty ratified 1854. Japan fought China, 1894-95, gaining Taiwan. After war with Russia, 1904-5, Russia ceded S half of Sakhalin and gave concessions in China. Japan annexed Korea 1910. In World War I Japan ousted Germany from Shandong in China, took over German Pacific islands. Japan took Manchuria 1931, started war with China 1932. Japan launched war against the U.S. by attack on Pearl Harbor Dec. 7, 1941. The U.S. dropped atomic bombs on Hiroshima, Aug. 6, and Nagasaki, Aug. 9, 1945. Japan surrendered Aug. 14, 1945. Japan apologized Aug. 15, 1995, for its acts of "colonial rule and aggression" during World War II.

In a new constitution adopted May 3, 1947, Japan renounced the right to wage war; the emperor gave up claims to divinity; the Diet became the sole law-making authority.

The U.S. and 48 other non-communist nations signed a peace treaty and the U.S. a bilateral defense agreement with Japan, in San Francisco Sept. 8, 1951, restoring Japan's sovereignty as of April 28, 1952.

On June 26, 1968, the U.S. returned to Japanese control the Bonin Is., the Volcano Is. (including Iwo Jima), and Marcus Is. On May 15, 1972, Okinawa, the other Ryukyu Is., and the Daito Is. were returned by the U.S.; it was agreed the U.S. would continue to maintain military bases on Okinawa.

Industrialization was begun in the late 19th century. After World War II, Japan emerged as one of the most powerful economies in the world, and as a leader in technology.

The U.S. and EU member nations have criticized Japan for its restrictive policy on imports, which has given Japan a substantial trade surplus.

The Recruit scandal, the nation's worst political scandal since World War II, which involved illegal political donations and stock trading, led to the resignation of Premier Noboru Takeshita in May 1989. A series of scandals rocked Japan's financial sector in 1991.

Following new political scandals, the Liberal Democratic Party was denied a majority in general elections July 18, 1993. The LDP had held power since it was founded in 1955. Morihiro Hosokawa, a reformer, was chosen prime minister Aug. 6; he initiated reforms but resigned Apr. 8, 1994, because of controversy over his financial connections. His replacement,

Tsutomu Hata, resigned June 25, to be replaced by Japan's first Socialist premier since 1947-48, Tomiichi Murayama.

An earthquake in the Kobe area, Jan. 17, 1995, claimed more than 6,300 lives, injured nearly 35,000, and caused over $90 billion in property damage. On Mar. 20, a nerve gas attack in the Tokyo subway (blamed on a religious cult) killed 12 and injured thousands. Public anger at the rape of a 12-year-old Okinawa schoolgirl by 3 U.S. servicemen, Sept. 4, led the U.S. to begin reducing its military presence there.

Murayama resigned as prime minister, Jan. 5, 1996, and was replaced by Ryutaro Hashimoto of the LDP. He signed a joint security declaration with U.S. Pres. Bill Clinton in Tokyo, Apr. 17. In a nonbinding referendum Sept. 8, Okinawan voters called for further US troop reductions.

# Jordan

## Hashemite Kingdom of Jordan

## Al Mamlakah al Urduniyah al Hashemiyah

**People: Population:** 4,212,152. **Age distrib.** (%): <15: 42; 65+: 3. **Pop. density:** 123 per sq. mi. **Urban:** 78%. **Ethnic groups:** Arab 98%. **Principal language:** Arabic (official). **Religions:** Sunni Muslim 92%, Christian 8%.

**Geography: Area:** 34,342 sq. mi. **Location:** In Middle East. **Neighbors:** Israel on W, Saudi Arabia on S, Iraq on E, Syria on N. **Topography:** About 88% of Jordan is arid. Fertile areas are in W. Only port is on short Aqaba Gulf coast. Country shares Dead Sea (1,312 ft. below sea level) with Israel. **Capital:** Amman. **Cities** (1994): Amman 963,500; az-Zarqa 344,500; Irbid 208,200.

**Government: Type:** Constitutional monarchy. **Head of state:** King Hussein I; b Nov. 14, 1935; in office: Aug. 11, 1952. **Head of government:** Prime Min. Abdel Karim Kabariti; b Dec. 16, 1949; in office: Feb. 4, 1996. **Local divisions:** 8 governorates. **Defense:** 9.1% of GDP (1995 est.). **Active troop strength:** 98,600.

**Economy: Industries:** Oil refining, cement, light manufacturing. **Chief crops:** Grains, olives, vegetables, fruits. **Minerals:** Phosphates, potash. **Arable land:** 4%. **Electricity prod.** (1993): 4.2 bil kWh. **Labor force:** 11% ind.; 11% commerce; 10% constr.; 7% agric.; 52% other services.

**Finance: Monetary unit:** Dinar (June 1996: 0.71 = $1 US). **Gross domestic product** (1994): $17 bln.* **Per capita GDP:** $4,280. **Imports** (1994): $3.5 bln.; partners: Iraq 12%, U.S. 10%. **Exports** (1994): $1.4 bln.; partners: Iraq 13%, India 11%, Saudi Arabia 9%. **Tourism** (1993): $563 mil. **National budget** (1995): $2.4 bil. **International reserves less gold** (May 1996): $1.7 bil. **Gold:** 794,000 oz t. **Consumer prices** (change in 1995): 2.4%.

**Transport: Motor vehicles:** in use: 162,000 passenger cars, 92,000 comm. vehicles. **Civil aviation:** 1.5 bil passenger-mi.; 2 airports with scheduled flights. **Chief port:** Aqaba.

**Communications: Television sets:** 1 per 16.9 persons. **Radios:** 1 per 4.3 persons. **Telephones:** 1 per 14.2 persons. **Daily newspaper circ.:** 58 per 1,000 pop.

**Health: Life expectancy at birth** (1996): 71 male; 75 female. **Births** (per 1,000 pop.): 37. **Deaths** (per 1,000 pop.): 4. **Natural increase:** 3.3%. **Hospital beds:** 1 per 920 persons. **Physicians:** 1 per 574 persons. **Infant mortality** (per 1,000 live births 1996): 32.

**Education: Literacy** (1993): 87%. Free and compulsory: ages 6-16.

**Major International Organizations:** UN (WHO, IMF), Arab League.

**Embassy:** 3504 International Dr. NW 20008; 966-2664.

From ancient times to 1922 the lands to the E of the Jordan River were culturally and politically united with the lands to the W. Arabs conquered the area in the 7th century; the Ottomans took control in the 16th. Britain's 1920 Palestine Mandate covered both sides of the Jordan. In 1921, Abdullah, son of the ruler of Hejaz in Arabia, was installed by Britain as emir of an autonomous Transjordan, covering two-thirds of Palestine. An independent kingdom was proclaimed, 1946.

During the 1948 Arab-Israeli war the West Bank and East Jerusalem were added to the kingdom, which changed its name to Jordan. All these territories were lost to Israel in the 1967 war, which swelled the number of Arab refugees on the East Bank. A 1974 Arab summit conference designated the Palestine Liberation Organization as the sole representative of Arabs on the West Bank. In 1988 Jordan cut legal and administrative ties with the Israeli-occupied West Bank.

Some 700,000 refugees entered Jordan following Iraq's invasion of Kuwait, Aug. 1990. Jordan was viewed as supporting Iraq during the 1990-1991 Persian Gulf crisis.

Jordan and Israel officially agreed, July 25, 1994, to end their state of war; a formal peace treaty was signed Oct. 26.

# Kazakstan

## Republic of Kazakstan

## Qazaqstan Respublikasy

**People: Population:** 16,916,463. **Age distrib.** (%): <15: 31; 65+: 6. **Pop. density:** 16 per sq. mi. **Urban:** 56%. **Ethnic groups:** Kazak 42%, Russian 37%, Ukrainian 5%, German 5%. **Principal languages:** Kazak (official), Russian. **Religions:** Muslim 47%, Russian Orthodox 44%.

**Geography: Area:** 1,049,200 sq. mi. **Location:** In Central Asia. **Neighbors:** Russia on N; China on E; Kyrgyzstan, Uzbekistan, Turkmenistan on S; Caspian Sea on W. **Topography:** Extends from the lower reaches of Volga in Europe to the Altay Mts. on the Chinese border. **Capital:** Almaty (Alma-Ata). **Cities** (1994 est.): Almaty 1.2 mln.; (1991 est.) Qaraghandy 609,000.

**Government: Type:** Republic. **Head of state:** Pres. Nursultan A. Nazarbayev; b July 6, 1940; in office: Apr. 1990. **Head of government:** Prime Min. Arkezhan Kazhgeldin; b Mar. 27, 1952; in office, Oct. 12, 1994. **Local divisions:** 19 oblystar, 1 city. **Defense:** 2.6% of GNP (1993). **Active troop strength:** 40,000 est.

**Economy: Industries:** Steel, mining, agricultural machinery. **Chief crops:** Grain, cotton. **Minerals:** Oil, coal, iron, manganese, copper. **Arable land:** 15%. **Livestock** (1994): cattle: 9.3 mln.; sheep and goats: 34.2 mln.; pigs: 2.4 mil. **Electricity prod.** (1994): 65.1 bil kWh. **Labor force:** 31% ind.; 26% agric.

**Finance: Monetary unit:** Tenge (June 1996: 67.2 = $1 US). **Gross domestic product** (1994 est.): $55.2 bln.* **Per capita GDP:** $3,200. **Imports** (1994): $3.5 bil. **Exports** (1994): $3.1 bil.

**Transport: Railroads: Length:** 13,173 mi. **Motor vehicles:** 735,000 passenger cars. **Civil aviation:** 7.8 bil passenger-mi.; 6 airports with scheduled flights. **Chief ports:** Aqtau, Atyrau.

**Communications: Television:** 1 per 3.6 persons. **Radios:** 1 per 4.1 persons. **Telephones:** 1 per 11 persons. **Daily newspaper circ.:** 405 per 1,000 pop.

**Health: Life expectancy at birth** (1996): 59 male; 70 female. **Birth rate** (per 1,000 pop.): 19. **Death rate** (per 1,000 pop.): 10. **Natural increase:** 0.9%. **Hospital beds:** 1 per 75 persons. **Physicians:** 1 per 253 persons. **Infant mortality** (per 1,000 live births 1996): 63.

**Education: Literacy** (1992): 98%. Free and compulsory: ages 7-18.

**Major International Organizations:** UN (WHO, IMF), CIS.

**Embassy:** 3421 Massachusetts Ave. NW 20007; 333-4504.

The region came under the Mongols in the 13th century and gradually came under Russian rule, 1730-1853. It was admitted to the USSR as a constituent republic 1936. Kazakstan declared independence Dec. 16, 1991. It became an independent state when the Soviet Union dissolved Dec. 26, 1991. The party chief, Nursultan Nazarbayev, was elected president unopposed. In legislative elections Mar. 7, 1994, criticized by international monitors, his party won a sweeping victory. Kazakstan agreed, Feb. 14, to dismantle nuclear missiles and adhere to the 1968 Nuclear Nonproliferation Treaty; the U.S. pledged increased aid. A referendum Apr. 29, 1995, extended Nazarbayev's term to Dec. 2000; a new draft constitution was approved in a referendum Aug. 30. Private land ownership was legalized Dec. 26.

# Kenya

## Republic of Kenya

## Jamhuri ya Kenya

**People: Population:** 28,176,686. **Age distrib.** (%): <15: 48; 65+: 3. **Pop. density:** 125 per sq. mi. **Urban:** 27%. **Ethnic groups:** Kikuyu 22%, Luhya 14%, Luo 13%, Kalenjin 12%, Kamba 11%, others including Asian, Arab, European. **Principal languages:** Swahili, English (both official), Kikuyu, Luhya, Luo, Meru. **Religions:** Protestant 38%, Roman Catholic 28%, indigenous beliefs 26%.

**Geography: Area:** 224,961 sq. mi. **Location:** On Indian O. coast of E Africa. **Neighbors:** Uganda on W, Tanzania on S, Somalia on E, Ethopia and Sudan on N. **Topography:** The northern three-fifths of Kenya is arid. To the S, a low coastal area and a plateau varying from 3,000 to 10,000 ft. The Great Rift Valley enters the country N-S, flanked by high mountains. **Capital:** Nairobi. **Cities** (1991 est.): Nairobi 2.0 mil; Mombasa 600,000.

**Government: Type:** Republic. **Head of state:** Pres. Daniel arap Moi, b. Sept. 2, 1924; in office: Aug. 22, 1978. **Local divisions:** Nairobi and 7 provinces. **Defense:** 1.9% of GDP (FY 1993-94). **Active troop strength:** 24,200.

**Economy: Industries:** Tourism, light industry, oil refining. **Chief crops:** Coffee, corn, tea. **Minerals:** Gold, limestone, salt, rubies, fluorspar, garnets. **Other resources:** Timber, hides, dairy products. **Arable land:** 3%. **Livestock** (1994): cattle: 11 mln.; goats: 7.4 mil **Fish catch** (1995): 241,000 metric tons. **Electricity prod.** (1993): 3.3 bil kWh. **Labor force:** 75-80% agric.

**Finance: Monetary unit:** Shilling (June 1996: 57.45 = $1 US). **Gross domestic product** (1994): $33.1 bln.* **Per capita GDP:** $1,170. **Imports** (1994): $1.9 bln.; partners: EU 46%. **Exports** (1994): $1.5 bln.; partners: EU 47%. **Tourism** (1993): $413 mil. **National budget** (1990 est.): $2.8 bil. **International reserves less gold** (May 1996): $592 mil. **Gold:** 80,000 oz t. **Consumer prices** (change in 1995): 0.8%.

**Transport: Motor vehicles:** in use: 157,000 passenger cars, 134,000 comm. vehicles. **Civil aviation:** 1.1 bil passenger-mi.; 14 airports with scheduled flights. **Chief port:** Mombasa.

**Communications: Television sets:** 1 per 106 persons. **Radios:** 1 per 13 persons. **Telephones:** 1 per 124 persons.

**Health: Life expectancy at birth** (1996): 56 male; 56 female. **Births** (per 1,000 pop.): 33. **Deaths** (per 1,000 pop.): 10. **Natural increase:** 2.3%. **Hospital beds:** 1 per 737 persons. **Physicians:** 1 per 7,410 persons. **Infant mortality** (per 1,000 live births 1996): 55.

**Education: Literacy** (1993): 78%. Free and compulsory: ages 6-14.

**Major International Organizations:** UN and all of its specialized agencies, OAU, the Commonwealth.

**Embassy:** 2249 R St. NW 20008; 387-6101.

Arab colonies exported spices and slaves from the Kenya coast as early as the 8th century. Britain obtained control in the 19th century. Kenya won independence Dec. 12, 1963, 4 years after the end of the violent Mau Mau uprising.

Kenya had steady growth in industry and agriculture under a modified private enterprise system, and enjoyed a relatively free political life. But stability was shaken in 1974-75, with opposition charges of corruption and oppression. Jomo Kenyatta, the country's leader since independence, died Aug. 22, 1978. He was succeeded by his vice president, Daniel arap Moi.

During the first half of the 1990s, Kenya suffered from widespread unemployment and high inflation. Tribal clashes in the western provinces claimed thousands of lives and left tens of thousands homeless. Pres. Moi won a third term in Dec. 1992 elections, which were marred by violence and fraud.

# Kiribati

## Republic of Kiribati

**People: Population:** 80,919. **Pop. density:** 259 per sq. mi. **Ethnic groups:** Nearly all Micronesian, some Polynesian. **Principal languages:** English (official), Gilbertese. **Religions:** Roman Catholic 53%, Protestant 41%.

**Geography: Area:** 313 sq. mi. **Location:** 33 Micronesian islands (the Gilbert, Line, and Phoenix groups) in the mid-Pacific scattered in a 2-mil sq. mi. chain around the point where the International Date Line cuts the Equator. **Neighbors:** Nearest are Nauru to SW, Tuvalu and Tokelau Is. to S. **Topography:** Except Banaba (Ocean) I., all are low-lying, with soil of coral sand and rock fragments, subject to erratic rainfall. **Capital:** Tarawa (1990): 25,000.

**Government: Type:** Republic. **Head of state and government:** Pres. Teburoro Tito; in office: Oct. 1, 1994.

**Economy: Industries:** Fishing, handicrafts. **Chief crops:** Taro, copra, breadfruit, sweet potatoes, vegetables. **Electricity prod.** (1993): 13 mil kWh.

**Finance: Monetary unit:** Australian Dollar. **Gross domestic product** (1993): $62 mil. **Per capita GDP:** $800. **National budget** (1993 est.): $32.8 mil.

**Transport: Chief port:** Tarawa.

**Communications: Radios:** 1 per 5.2 persons. **Telephones:** 1 per 43 persons.

**Health: Births** (per 1,000 pop.): 31. **Deaths** (per 1,000 pop.): 12. **Natural increase:** 1.9%. **Hospital beds:** 1 per 253 persons. **Physicians:** 1 per 7,687 persons.

**Education: Literacy** (1993): 90%. Free and compulsory: ages 6-14.

**Major International Organizations:** The Commonwealth.

A British protectorate since 1892, the Gilbert and Ellice Islands colony was completed with the inclusion of the Phoenix Islands, 1937. Self-rule was granted 1971; the Ellice Islands separated from the colony 1975 and became independent Tuvalu, 1978. Kiribati (pronounced *Kiribass)* independence was attained July 12, 1979. Under a treaty of friendship the U.S. relinquished its claims to several of the Line and Phoenix islands, including Christmas (Kiritimati), Canton, and Enderbury.

Tarawa Atoll was the scene of some of the bloodiest fighting in the Pacific during World War II.

# Korea, North

## Democratic People's Republic of Korea

## Choson Minjujuui Inmin Konghwaguk

**People: Population:** 23,904,124. **Age distrib.** (%): <15: 29; 65+: 4. **Pop. density:** 504 per sq. mi. **Urban:** 61%. **Ethnic group:** Korean. **Principal language:** Korean (official). **Religions:** Activities almost nonexistent; traditionally Buddhism, Confucianism, Chondogyo.

**Geography: Area:** 47,399 sq. mi. **Location:** In northern E Asia. **Neighbors:** China and Russia on N, South Korea on S. **Topography:** Mountains and hills cover nearly all the country, with narrow valleys and small plains in between. The N and the E coasts are the most rugged areas. **Capital:** Pyongyang (1987 est.): 2.4 mil.

**Government: Type:** Communist state. **Leader:** Kim Jong Il; b Feb. 16, 1948; in power: July 1994. **Local divisions:** 9 provinces, 3 special cities. **Defense:** 26.6% of GNP (1994). **Active troop strength:** 1.1 mil est.

**Economy: Industries:** Textiles, chemicals, machinery, food processing. **Chief crops:** Corn, potatoes, soybeans, rice. **Minerals:** Coal, lead, tungsten, zinc, graphite, magnesite, iron, copper, gold, salt, fluorspar. **Arable land:** 18%. **Livestock** (1994): cattle: 1.3 mln.; pigs: 3.3 mil. **Fish catch** (1993): 1.8 mil metric tons. **Electricity prod.** (1993): 50 bil kWh. **Labor force:** 36% agric.

**Finance: Monetary unit:** Won (June 1996: 2.15 = $1 US). **Gross domestic product** (1994): $21.3 bln.* **Per capita GDP:** $920. **Imports** (1993): $1.6 bln.; partners: Russia 38%, China 23%, Japan 10%. **Exports** (1993): $1.0 bln.; partners: Russia 45%, Japan 23%, China 7%. **National budget** (1992 est.): $19.3 bil.

**Transport: Civil aviation:** 52 mil passenger-mi.; 1 airport with scheduled flights. **Chief ports:** Chongjin, Hamhung, Nampo.

**Communications: Television sets:** 1 per 11.5 persons. **Radios:** 1 per 9.2 persons. **Telephones:** 1 per 21 persons.

**Health: Life expectancy at birth** (1996): 67 male; 74 female. **Births** (per 1,000 pop.): 23. **Deaths** (per 1,000 pop.): 5. **Natural increase:** 1.7%. **Hospital beds:** 1 per 74 persons. **Physicians:** 1 per 370 persons. **Infant mortality** (per 1,000 live births 1996): 26.

**Education: Literacy** (1992): 95%. Free and compulsory: ages 6-17.

**Major International Organizations:** UN (WHO, IMF).

The Democratic People's Republic of Korea was founded May 1, 1948, in the zone occupied by Russian troops after World War II. Its armies tried to conquer the south, 1950. After 3 years of fighting, with Chinese and U.S. intervention, a cease-fire was proclaimed.

Industry, begun by the Japanese during their 1910-45 occupation, and nationalized in the 1940s, had grown substantially, using North Korea's abundant mineral and hydroelectric resources.

In Mar. 1993, North Korea became the first nation to formally withdraw from the Nuclear Nonproliferation Treaty, the international pact designed to limit the spread of nuclear weapons. The nation suspended its withdrawal in June in reaction to threats of UN economic sanctions, but was widely believed to be developing nuclear weapons. The U.S. and North Korea reached an interim agreement, Aug. 13, 1994, intended to resolve the nuclear issue, and further negotiations followed.

Kim Il Sung, who in 1948 had been one of the founders of the state of North Korea and who had ruled over it for more than 40 years, died July 8, 1994. He was apparently succeeded by his son, Kim Jong Il. North Korea suffered from an ailing economy and severe food shortages in the mid-1990s.

# Korea, South

## Republic of Korea

## Taehan Min'guk

**People: Population:** 45,482,291. **Age distrib.** (%): <15: 23; 65+: 6. **Pop. density:** 1,185 per sq. mi. **Urban:** 74%. **Ethnic group:** Korean. **Principal language:** Korean (official). **Religions:** Christian 49%, Buddhist 47%.

**Geography: Area:** 38,375 sq. mi. **Location:** In northern E Asia. **Neighbors:** North Korea on N. **Topography:** The country is mountainous, with a rugged east coast. The western and southern coasts are deeply indented, with many islands and harbors. **Capital:** Seoul. **Cities** (1994 est.): Seoul 10.8 mln.; Pusan 3.8 mln.; Taegu 2.3 mln.; Inchon 2.2 mln.; Kwangju 1.3 mil.

**Government: Type:** Republic, with power centralized in a strong executive. **Head of state:** Pres. Kim Young Sam; b Dec. 20, 1927; in office: Feb. 25, 1993. **Head of government:** Prime Min. Lee Hong Koo; in office: Dec. 17, 1994. **Local divisions:** 9 provinces and 6 special cities. **Defense:** 3.3% of GNP (1995 est.). **Active troop strength:** 633,000.

**Economy: Industries:** Electronics, autos, chemicals, ships, textiles, clothing. **Chief crops:** Rice, barley, vegetables. **Minerals:** Tungsten, coal, graphite. **Arable land:** 21%. **Livestock** (1994): cattle: 3.2 mln.; pigs: 6.3 mil. **Fish catch:** (1993): 2.6 mil metric tons. **Electricity prod.** (1993): 137 bil kWh. **Labor force:** 52% services & other; 27% manuf. & mining; 21% agric.

**Finance: Monetary unit:** Won (June 1996: 809 = $1 US). **Gross domestic product** (1994): $508 bln.* **Per capita GDP:** $11,270. **Imports** (1994): $102 bln.; partners: Japan 26%, U.S. 24%. **Exports** (1994): $96 bln.; partners: U.S. 26%, Japan 17%. **Tourism** (1993): $3.5 bil. **National budget** (1995): $63 bil. **International reserves less gold** (May 1996): $63.2 bil. **Gold:** 327,000 oz t. **Consumer prices** (change in 1995): 4.5%.

**Transport: Railroads: Length:** 4,049 mi. **Motor vehicles:** in use: 4.3 mil passenger cars, 2.0 mil comm. vehicles. **Civil aviation:** 24.4 bil passenger-mi.; 14 airlines with scheduled flights. **Chief ports:** Pusan, Inchon.

**Communications: Television sets:** 1 per 4.3 persons. **Radios:** 1 per person. **Telephones:** 1 per 2.6 persons.

**Health: Life expectancy at birth** (1996): 70 male; 77 female. **Births** (per 1,000 pop.): 16. **Deaths** (per 1,000 pop.): 6. **Natural increase:** 1.1%. **Hospital beds:** 1 per 268 persons. **Physicians:** 1 per 855 persons. **Infant mortality** (per 1,000 live births 1996): 8.

**Education: Literacy** (1994): 98%. Free and compulsory: ages 6-12. Attendance: High school 90%, college 14%.

**Major International Organizations:** UN (WTO, IMF, WHO), APEC.

**Embassy:** 2450 Massachusetts Ave. NW 20008; 939-5600.

Korea, once called the Hermit Kingdom, has a recorded history since the 1st century BC. It was united in a kingdom under the Silla Dynasty, AD 668. It was at times associated with the Chinese empire; the treaty that concluded the Sino-Japanese war of 1894-95 recognized Korea's complete independence. In 1910 Japan forcibly annexed Korea as Chosun.

At the Potsdam conference, July 1945, the 38th parallel was designated as the line dividing the Soviet and the American occupation. Russian troops entered Korea Aug. 10, 1945, U.S. troops entered Sept. 8, 1945. The Soviet military organized socialists and Communists and blocked efforts to let the Koreans unite their country. *(See Index for Korean War.)*

The South Koreans formed the Republic of Korea in May 1948 with Seoul as the capital. Dr. Syngman Rhee was chosen president, but a movement spearheaded by college students forced his resignation Apr. 26, 1960.

In an army coup May 16, 1961, Gen. Park Chung Hee became chairman of the ruling junta. He was elected president, 1963; a 1972 referendum allowed him to be reelected for an unlimited series of 6-year terms. Park was assassinated by the chief of the Korean CIA, Oct. 26, 1979. In May 1980, Gen. Chun Doo Hwan, head of military intelligence, reinstated full martial law and ordered the brutal suppression of prodemocracy demonstrations in Kwangju.

In July 1972 South and North Korea agreed on a common goal of reunifying the 2 nations by peaceful means. But there was no sign of a thaw in relations between the two regimes until 1985, when they agreed to discuss economic issues.

On June 10, 1987, middle-class office workers, shopkeepers, and business executives joined students in antigovernment protests in Seoul calling for democratic reforms. Following weeks of rioting and violence, Chun, July 1, agreed to permit election of the next president by direct popular vote and other reforms. In Dec., Roh Tae Woo was elected president. In 1990, the nation's 3 largest political parties merged; some 100,000 students protested the merger as undemocratic.

Kim Young Sam took office in 1993 as the first civilian president since 1961. Convicted of mutiny, treason, and corruption, Chun was sentenced to death by a Seoul court, Aug. 26, 1996, for his role in the 1979 coup and 1980 Kwangju massacre; Roh received a 22-year prison sentence.

# Kuwait

## State of Kuwait

## Dawlat al Kuwayt

**People: Population:** 1,950,047. **Age distrib.** (%): <15: 29; 65+: 1. **Pop. density:** 283 per sq. mi. **Urban:** 96%. **Ethnic groups:** Kuwaiti 45%, other Arab 35%, Iranian, Indian, Pakistani. **Principal language:** Arabic (official). **Religions:** Muslim 85%.

**Geography: Area:** 6,880 sq. mi. **Location:** In Middle East, at N end of Persian Gulf. **Neighbors:** Iraq on N, Saudi Arabia on S. **Topography:** The country is flat, very dry, and extremely hot. **Capital:** Kuwait City. **Cities** (1993 est.): al-Jahra 139,500; as-Salimiyah 116,100.

**Government: Type:** Constitutional monarchy. **Head of state:** Emir Sheikh Jabir al-Ahmad al-Jabir as-Sabah; b 1928; in office: Jan. 1, 1978. **Head of government:** Prime Min. Sheikh Saad Abdulla as-Salim as-Sabah; b 1930; in office: Feb. 8, 1978. **Local divisions:** 5 governorates. **Defense:** 13.3% of GDP (1995). **Active troop strength:** 16,600.

**Economy: Industries:** Oil products. **Minerals:** Oil, gas. **Crude oil reserves** (1995): 96.5 bil barrels. **Arable land:** 0%. **Electricity prod.** (1993): 11 bil kWh. **Labor force:** 45% services; 20% construction.

**Finance: Monetary unit:** Dinar (June 1996: 0.30 = $1 US). **Gross domestic product** (1994): $30.7 bil. **Per capita GDP:** $16,900. **Imports** (1993): $6.6 bln.; partners: U.S. 35%, Japan 12%. **Exports** (1993): $10.5 bln.; partners: France 16%, Italy 15%. **Tourism** (1993): $83 mil. **National budget** (FY 1992-93): $13 bil. **International reserves less gold** (May 1996): $3.9 bil. **Gold:** 2.54 mil oz t.

**Transport: Motor vehicles:** in use: 530,000 passenger cars, 144,000 comm. vehicles. **Civil aviation:** 2.5 bil passenger-mi.; 1 airport with scheduled flights. **Chief port:** Mina al-Ahmadi.

**Communications: Television sets:** 1 per 2.0 persons. **Radios:** 1 per 1.6 persons. **Telephones:** 1 per 4.1 persons. **Daily newspaper circ.:** 244 per 1,000 pop.

**Health: Life expectancy at birth** (1996): 74 male; 78 female. **Births** (per 1,000 pop.): 20. **Deaths** (per 1,000 pop.): 2. **Natural increase:** 1.8%. **Hospital beds:** 1 per 357 persons. **Physicians:** 1 per 608 persons. **Infant mortality** (per 1,000 live births 1996): 11.

**Education: Literacy** (1995): 79%. Free and compulsory: ages 6-14.

**Major International Organizations:** UN (World Bank, IMF, WTO), Arab League, OPEC.

**Embassy:** 2940 Tilden St. NW 20008; 966-0702.

Kuwait is ruled by the Al-Sabah dynasty, founded 1759. Britain ran foreign relations and defense from 1899 until independence in 1961. The majority of the population is non-Kuwaiti, with many Palestinians, and cannot vote.

Oil is the fiscal mainstay, providing most of Kuwait's income. Oil pays for free medical care, education, and social security. There are no taxes, except customs duties.

Kuwaiti oil tankers came under frequent attack by Iran because of Kuwait's support of Iraq in the Iran-Iraq War. In July 1987, U.S. Navy warships began escorting Kuwaiti tankers in the Persian Gulf.

Kuwait was attacked and overrun by Iraqi forces Aug. 2, 1990. The emir and senior members of the ruling family fled to Saudi Arabia to establish a government in exile. On Aug. 28, Iraq announced that Kuwait was its 19th province. Following several weeks of aerial attacks on Iraq and Iraqi forces in Kuwait, a U.S.-led coalition began a ground attack Feb. 23, 1991. By Feb. 27, Iraqi forces were routed and Kuwait liberated. Following liberation, there were reports of abuse of Palestinians and others suspected of collaborating with Iraqi occupiers. Kuwait spent more than $5 billion to repair oil installations damaged during 1990-91.

Former U.S. Pres. George Bush visited Kuwait, Apr. 14-16, 1993, and was honored as the leader of the Persian Gulf War alliance that expelled Iraqi troops. Kuwaiti authorities arrested 14 Iraqis and Kuwaitis for allegedly plotting to assassinate Bush during his visit. Thirteen were convicted and sentenced to prison or death, June 4, 1994.

# Kyrgyzstan

## Republic of Kyrgyzstan

## Kyrgyz Respublikasy

**People: Population:** 4,529,648. **Pop density:** 59 per sq. mi. **Urban:** 35%. **Ethnic groups:** Kyrgyz 52%, Russian 22%, Uzbek 13%. **Principal languages:** Kyrgyz (official), Russian. **Religion:** Muslim 70%.

**Geography: Area:** 76,600 sq. mi. **Location:** In Central Asia. **Neighbors:** Kazakstan on N, China on E, Uzbekistan on W, Tajikistan on S. **Capital:** Bishkek. **Cities** (1994 est.): Bishkek 597,000; (1991 est.) Osh 238,200.

**Government: Type:** Republic. **Head of state:** Pres. Askar Akayev; b Nov. 10, 1944; in office: Oct. 28, 1990. **Head of government:** Prime Min. Apas Jumagulov; b 1934; in office: Dec. 14, 1993. **Local divisions:** 6 oblasts, 1 city. **Defense:** 1.4% of GNP (1993). **Active troop strength:** 7,000+ est.

**Economy: Industries:** Tanning, tobacco, textiles, mining. **Chief crops:** Tobacco, cotton, fruits. **Minerals:** Gold, coal, oil. **Arable land:** 7%. **Livestock** (1994): cattle: 1.1 mln.; sheep and goats: 7.3 mil. **Electricity prod.** (1994): 12.7 bil kWh. **Labor force:** 38% agric.; 21% ind.

**Finance: Monetary unit:** Som (June 1996: 12.35 = $1 US). **Gross domestic prod.** (1994 est.): $8.4 bln.* **Per capita GDP:** $1,790.

**Transport: Railroads: Length:** 230 mi. **Motor vehicles:** in use: 174,000 passenger cars. **Civil aviation:** 1.6 bil passenger-mi.; 2 airports with scheduled flights. **Chief port:** Ysyk-Kol.

**Communications: Telephones:** 1 per 12.3 persons. **Daily newspaper circ.:** 250 per 1,000 pop.

**Health: Life expectancy at birth** (1996): 59 male; 69 female. **Birth rate** (per 1,000 pop.): 26. **Death rate** (per 1,000 pop.): 9. **Natural increase:** 1.7%. **Hospital beds:** 1 per 95 persons. **Physicians:** 1 per 319 persons. **Infant mortality** (per 1,000 live births 1996): 78.

**Education: Literacy** (1993): 97%. Compulsory: ages 6-15.

**Major International Organizations:** UN (IMF), CIS.

**Embassy:** 1511 K St. NW, Suite 705 20005; 347-3732.

The region was inhabited around the 13th century by the Kyrgyz. It was annexed to Russia 1864. After 1917, it was nominally a Kara-Kyrgyz autonomous area, which was reorganized 1926, and made a constituent republic of the USSR in 1936. Kyrgyzstan declared independence Aug. 31, 1991. It became an independent state when the USSR disbanded Dec. 26, 1991. A constitution was adopted May 5, 1993. Reelected Dec. 24, 1995, Pres. Askar Akayev gained approval by referendum of a constitutional amendment expanding his presidential powers, Feb. 10, 1996.

# Laos

## Lao People's Democratic Republic

## Sathalanalat Paxathipatai Paxaxon Lao

**People: Population:** 4,975,772. **Pop. density:** 54 per sq. mi. **Urban:** 19%. **Ethnic groups:** Lao Loum 68%, Lao Theung 22%, Lao Soung (includes Hmong and Yao) 9%. **Principal languages:** Lao (official), French, English. **Religions:** Buddhist 85%, animist and other 15%.

**Geography: Area:** 91,429 sq. mi. **Location:** In Indochina Peninsula in SE Asia. **Neighbors:** Myanmar and China on N, Vietnam on E, Cambodia on S, Thailand on W. **Topography:** Landlocked, dominated by jungle. High mountains along the eastern border are the source of the E-W rivers slicing across the country to the Mekong R., which defines most of the western border. **Capital:** Vientiane (1990 met. est.): 442,000.

**Government: Type:** Communist. **Head of state:** Pres. Nouhak Phoumsavan; b Apr. 9, 1914; in office: Nov. 25, 1992. **Head of government:** Prime Min. Khamtai Siphandon; b Feb. 8, 1924; in office: Aug. 15, 1991. **Local divisions:** 16 provinces, 1 municipality. **Defense:** 8.1% of GDP (FY 1992-93). **Active troop strength:** 37,000.

**Economy: Industries:** Wood products, mining. **Chief crops:** Rice, sweet potatoes, corn, cotton, opium, vegetables, coffee. **Minerals:** Gypsum, tin, gold. **Arable land:** 4%. **Livestock** (1994): pigs: 1.6 mln.; cattle: 1.1 mil. **Fish catch** (1993): 30,500 metric tons. **Electricity prod.** (1993): 870 mil kWh. **Labor force:** 80% agric.

**Finance: Monetary unit:** Kip (June 1996: 920 = $1 US). **Gross domestic product** (1994): $4 bln.* **Per capita GDP:** $850. **Imports** (1994): $528 mln.; partners: Thai. 55%, Japan 16%. **Exports** (1994): $277 mln.; partners: Thai. 57%, Germany 10%. **International reserves less gold** (Feb. 1996): $91.6 mil.

**Transport: Motor vehicles:** in use: 20,000 passenger cars, 13,000 comm. vehicles.

**Communications: Television sets:** 1 per 59 persons. **Radios:** 1 per 9.5 persons. **Telephones:** 1 per 526 persons.

**Health: Life expectancy at birth** (1996): 51 male; 54 female. **Births** (per 1,000 pop.): 42. **Deaths** (per 1,000 pop.): 14. **Natural increase:** 2.8%. **Hospital beds:** 1 per 402 persons. **Physicians:** 1 per 3,555 persons. **Infant mortality** (per 1,000 live births 1996): 97.

**Education: Literacy** (1995): 57%. Compulsory: ages 6-11.

**Major International Organizations:** UN (FAO, IMF, WHO).

**Embassy:** 2222 S St. NW 20008; 332-6417.

Laos became a French protectorate in 1893, but regained independence as a constitutional monarchy July 19, 1949.

Conflicts among neutralist, communist, and conservative factions created a chaotic political situation. Armed conflict increased after 1960.

The 3 factions formed a coalition government in June 1962, with neutralist Prince Souvanna Phouma as premier. A 14-nation conference in Geneva signed agreements, 1962, guaranteeing neutrality and independence. By 1964 the Pathet Lao had withdrawn from the coalition, and, with aid from North Vietnamese troops, renewed sporadic attacks. U.S. planes bombed the Ho Chi Minh trail, supply line from North Vietnam to Communist forces in Laos and South Vietnam.

In 1970 the U.S. stepped up air support and military aid. After Pathet Lao military gains, Souvanna Phouma in May 1975 ordered government troops to cease fighting; the Pathet Lao took control. The Lao People's Democratic Republic was proclaimed Dec. 3, 1975.

From the mid-1970s through the 1980s, the Laotian government relied on Vietnam for military and financial aid. Since easing its foreign investment laws in 1988, Laos has attracted more than $5 billion from Thailand, the U.S., and other nations.

# Latvia

## Republic of Latvia

## Latvijas Republika

**People: Population:** 2,468,982. **Pop density:** 99 per sq. mi. **Urban:** 69%. **Ethnic groups:** Latvian 52%, Russian 34%. **Principal languages:** Latvian (official), Lithuanian, Russian. **Religions:** Lutheran, Roman Catholic, Russian Orthodox.

**Geography: Area:** 24,946 sq. mi. **Location:** E Europe, on the Baltic Sea. **Neighbors:** Estonia on N, Lithuania and Belarus on S, Russia on E. **Capital:** Riga (1995): 840,000.

**Government: Type:** Republic. **Head of state:** Pres. Guntis Ulmanis; b Sept 13, 1939; in office: July 7, 1993. **Head of government:** Prime Min. Andris Skele; b Jan. 16, 1958; in office: Dec. 21, 1995. **Local divisions:** 26 counties, 7 municipalities. **Defense:** 3-5% of GDP (1994). **Active troop strength:** 6,950.

**Economy: Industries:** Machinery, vehicles, electric railway passenger cars. **Chief crops:** Grains, sugar beets, potatoes. **Arable land:** 27%. **Livestock** (1994): cattle 995,000. **Fish catch** (1993): 140,000 metric tons. **Electricity prod.** (1993): 5.5 bil kWh. **Labor force:** 41% ind. & constr.; 16% agric. & forestry.

**Finance: Monetary unit:** Lat (June 1996: 0.55 = $1 US). **Gross domestic product** (1994 est.): $12.3 bln.* **Per capita GDP:** $4,480. **Imports** (1994): $1.2 bil. **Exports** (1994): $1 bil. **International reserves less gold** (Apr. 1996): $542 mil.

**Transport: Railroads: Length:** 1,499 mi. **Motor vehicles:** in use: 351,000 passenger cars, 85,000 comm. vehicles. **Civil aviation:** 1.9 bil passenger-mi.; 1 airport with scheduled flights. **Chief port:** Riga.

**Communications: Television sets:** 1 per 2.1 persons. **Radios:** 1 per 1.3 persons. **Telephones:** 1 per 3.7 persons. **Daily newspaper circ.:** 1,377 per 1,000 pop.

**Health: Life expectancy at birth** (1996): 61 male, 73 female. **Births** (per 1,000 pop.): 11. **Deaths** (per 1,000 pop.): 15. **Natural increase:** –0.4%. **Hospital beds:** 1 per 82 persons. **Physicians:** 1 per 276 persons. **Infant mortality rates** (per 1,000 live births 1996): 21.

**Major International Organizations:** UN (IMF, WHO).

**Embassy:** 4325 17th St. NW 20011; 726-8213.

Prior to 1918, Latvia was occupied by the Russians and Germans. It was an independent republic, 1918-39. The Aug. 1939 Soviet-German agreement assigned Latvia to the Soviet sphere of influence. It was officially accepted as part of the USSR on Aug. 5, 1940. It was overrun by the German army in 1941, but retaken in 1945.

During an abortive Soviet coup, Latvia declared independence, Aug. 21, 1991. The Soviet Union recognized Latvia's independence in Sept. 1991. The last Russian troops in Latvia withdrew by Aug. 31, 1994.

# Lebanon

## Republic of Lebanon

## Al Jumhuriyah al Lubnaniyah

**People: Population:** 3,776,317. **Age distrib.** (%): <15: 33; 65+: 7. **Pop. density:** 956 per sq. mi. **Urban:** 86%. **Ethnic groups:** Arab 95%, Armenian 4%. **Principal languages:** Arabic, French (both official). **Religions:** Muslim 70%, Christian 30%.

**Geography: Area:** 3,950 sq. mi. **Location:** In Middle East, on E end of Mediterranean Sea. **Neighbors:** Syria on E, Israel on S. **Topography:** There is a narrow coastal strip, and 2 mountain ranges running N-S enclosing the fertile Beqaa Valley. The Litani R. runs S through the valley, turning W to empty into the Mediterranean. **Capital:** Beirut. **Cities** (1991 est.): Beirut 1.1 mln.; Tripoli 240,000.

**Government: Type:** Republic. **Head of state:** Pres. Elias Hrawi; b 1926; in office: Nov. 24, 1989. **Head of government:** Prime Min. Rafiq al-Hariri; b 1944; in office: Oct. 31, 1992. **Local divisions:** 5 governorates. **Defense:** 5.5% of GDP (1994). **Active troop strength:** 44,300.

**Economy: Industries:** Banking, food products, textiles, cement, oil refining. **Chief crops:** Citrus fruits, olives, tobacco, grapes, vegetables. **Minerals:** Limestone, iron. **Arable land:** 21%. **Livestock** (1994): goats: 456,000; sheep: 258,000. **Electricity prod.** (1993): 2.5 bil kWh. **Labor force:** 79% ind., commerce, services; 11% agric.; 10% govt.

**Finance: Monetary unit:** Pound (June 1996: 1,569 = $1 US). **Gross domestic product** (1994): $15.8 bil. **Per capita GDP:** $4,360. **Imports** (1993): $4.1 bln.; partners: Italy 14%, France 12%, U.S. 6%. **Exports** (1993): $925 mln.; partners: Saudi Arabia 21%, Switzerland 10%, Jordan 6%. **National budget** (1994): $3.2 bil. **International reserves less gold** (May 1996): $4.8 bil. **Gold:** 9.22 mil oz t.

**Transport: Motor vehicles:** in use: 473,000 passenger cars, 50,000 comm. vehicles. **Civil aviation:** 987 mil passenger-mi.; 1 airport with scheduled flights. **Chief ports:** Beirut, Tripoli, Sidon.

**Communications: Television sets:** 1 per 2.6 persons. **Radios:** 1 per 1.3 persons. **Telephones:** 1 per 11 persons.

**Health: Life expectancy at birth** (1996): 68 male; 73 female. **Births** (per 1,000 pop.): 28. **Deaths** (per 1,000 pop.): 6. **Natural increase:** 2.2%. **Hospital beds:** 1 per 200 persons. **Physicians:** 1 per 407 persons. **Infant mortality** (per 1,000 live births 1996): 37.

**Education: Literacy** (1992): 92%.

**Major International Organizations:** UN, Arab League.

**Embassy:** 2560 28th St. NW 20008; 939-6300.

Formed from 5 former Turkish Empire districts, Lebanon became an independent state Sept. 1, 1920, administered under French mandate 1920-41. French troops withdrew in 1946.

Under the 1943 National Covenant, all public positions were divided among the various religious communities, with Christians in the majority. By the 1970s, Muslims became the majority and demanded a larger political and economic role.

U.S. Marines intervened, May-Oct. 1958, during a Syrian-aided revolt. Continued raids against Israeli civilians, 1970-75, brought Israeli attacks against guerrilla camps and villages. Israeli troops occupied S Lebanon, Mar. 1978, and again in Apr. 1980.

An estimated 60,000 were killed and billions of dollars in damage inflicted in a 1975-76 civil war. Palestinian units and leftist Muslims fought against the Maronite militia, the Phalange, and other Christians. Several Arab countries provided political and arms support to the various factions, while Israel aided Christian forces. Up to 15,000 Syrian troops intervened in 1976, and fought Palestinian groups. Arab League troops from several nations tried to impose a cease-fire.

Clashes between Syrian troops and Christian forces erupted, Apr. 1, 1981, bringing to an end the cease-fire. By Apr. 22, fighting had also broken out between two Muslim factions. In July, Israeli air raids on Beirut killed or wounded some 800 persons.

Israeli forces invaded Lebanon June 6, 1982, in a coordinated land, sea, and air attack aimed at crushing strongholds of the Palestine Liberation Organization (PLO). Israeli and Syrian forces engaged in the Bekaa Valley. By June 14, Israeli troops had encircled Beirut. On Aug. 21, the PLO evacuated west Beirut following massive Israeli bombings of the city. Israeli troops entered west Beirut following the Sept. 14 assassination of newly elected Lebanese Pres. Bashir Gemayel. On Sept. 16, Lebanese Christian troops entered 2 refugee camps and massacred hundreds of Palestinian refugees. An agreement May 17, 1983, between Lebanon, Israel, and the U.S. (but not Syria) provided for the withdrawal of Israeli troops; at least 30,000 Syrian troops remained in Lebanon, and Israeli forces continued to occupy a "security zone" in the south.

In 1983, terrorist bombings became a way of life in Beirut as some 50 people were killed in an explosion at the U.S. Embassy, Apr. 18; 241 U.S. servicemen and 58 French soldiers died in separate Muslim suicide attacks, Oct. 23.

Kidnapping of foreign nationals by Islamic militants became common in the 1980s. U.S., British, French, and Soviet citizens were victims. All were released by 1992.

A cooperation treaty signed May 22, 1991, between Lebanon and Syria recognized Lebanon as a separate state for the first time since the 2 countries gained independence in 1943.

Israeli forces conducted air raids and artillery strikes against guerrilla bases and villages in S Lebanon, causing over 200,000 to flee their homes July 25-29, 1993. Some 500,000 civilians fled their homes in Apr. 1996 when Israel again struck suspected guerrilla bases in the south.

# Lesotho

## Kingdom of Lesotho

**People: Population:** 1,970,781. **Age distrib.** (%): <15: 41; 65+: 5. **Pop. density:** 168 per sq. mi. **Urban:** 16%. **Ethnic groups:** Sotho 99.7%. **Principal languages:** English, Sesotho (both official). **Religion:** Christian 80%, indigenous beliefs 20%.

**Geography: Area:** 11,720 sq. mi. **Location:** In southern Africa. **Neighbors:** Completely surrounded by Republic of South Africa. **Topography:** Landlocked and mountainous, with altitudes ranging from 5,000 to 11,000 ft. **Capital:** Maseru (1992 est.): 367,000.

**Government: Type:** Constitutional monarchy. **Head of state:** King Letsie III; b July 17, 1963; in office: Feb. 7, 1996. **Head of government:** Ntsu Mokhehle; b Dec. 26, 1918; in office: Sept. 14, 1994. **Local divisions:** 10 districts. **Defense:** 3.3% of GNP (1992). **Active troop strength:** 2,000.

**Economy: Industries:** Food processing, textiles. **Chief crops:** Corn, grains, peas, beans. **Other resources:** Diamonds. **Arable land:** 10%. **Labor force:** 86% subsistence agric.

**Finance: Monetary unit:** Loti (June 1996: 4.34 = $1 US). **Gross domestic product** (1994): $2.6 bln.* **Per capita GDP:** $1,340. **Imports** (1992): $964 mln.; partners: South Africa 94%. **Exports** (1992): $109 mln.; partners: South Africa 42%, EU 28%. **National budget** (FY 1993-94): $430 mil.

**Transport: Motor vehicles:** in use: 6,000 passenger cars, 18,000 comm. vehicles.

**Communications: Television sets:** 1 per 40 persons. **Radios:** 1 per 17 persons. **Daily newspaper circ.:** 19 per 1,000 pop.

**Health: Life expectancy at birth** (1996): 50 male; 54 female. **Births** (per 1,000 pop.): 33. **Deaths** (per 1,000 pop.): 14. **Natural increase:** 1.9%. **Hospital beds:** 1 per 765 persons. **Physicians:** 1 per 14,306 persons. **Infant mortality** (per 1,000 live births 1996): 82.

**Education: Literacy** (1994): 71%.

**Major International Organizations:** UN (IMF, WTO, WHO), OAU, the Commonwealth.

**Embassy:** 2511 Massachusetts Ave. NW 20008; 797-5534.

Lesotho (once called Basutoland) became a British protectorate in 1868 when Chief Moshesh sought protection against the Boers. Independence came Oct. 4, 1966. Elections were suspended in 1970. Most of Lesotho's GNP is provided by citizens working in South Africa. Livestock raising is the chief industry; diamonds are the chief export.

South Africa imposed a blockade, Jan. 1, 1986, because of Lesotho's giving sanctuary to rebel groups fighting to overthrow the South African government. The blockade sparked a Jan. 20 military coup, and was lifted, Jan. 25, when the new leaders agreed to expel the rebels.

In Mar. 1990, King Moshoeshoe was exiled by the military government. Letsie III became king Nov. 12. In Mar. 1993, Ntsu Mokhehle, a civilian, was elected prime minister, ending 23 years of military rule. After a series of violent disturbances, the king dismissed the Mokhele government Aug. 17, 1994; constitutional rule was restored Sept. 14. Letsie abdicated and Moshoeshoe was reinstated Jan. 25, 1995.

Moshoeshoe died in an automobile accident, Jan. 15, 1996, and was succeeded by Letsie Feb. 7.

# Liberia

## Republic of Liberia

**People: Population:** 2,109,789. **Age distrib.** (%): <15: 44; 65+: 3. **Pop. density:** 55 per sq. mi. **Urban:** 44%. **Ethnic groups:** Indigenous tribes 95%, Americo-Liberians 5%. **Principal languages:** English (official), tribal languages. **Religions:** Traditional beliefs 70%, Muslim 20%, Christian 10%.

**Geography: Area:** 38,250 sq. mi. **Location:** On SW coast of W Africa. **Neighbors:** Sierra Leone on W, Guinea on N, Côte d'Ivoire on E. **Topography:** Marshy Atlantic coastline rises to low mountains and plateaus in the forested interior; 6 major rivers flow in parallel courses to the ocean. **Capital:** Monrovia (1990 est.): 668,000.

**Government: Type:** In transition. **Head of state:** Ruth Perry, head of transitional Council of State; in office: Sept. 3, 1996. **Local divisions:** 13 counties. **Defense:** 2% of GDP (1994).

**Economy: Industries:** Food processing, mining. **Chief crops:** Rice, cassava, coffee, cocoa, sugar. **Minerals:** Iron, diamonds, gold. **Other resources:** Rubber, timber. **Arable land:** 1%. **Fish catch** (1993): 8,000 metric tons. **Electricity prod.** (1993): 440 mil kWh. **Labor force:** 71% agric.; 11% serv.

**Finance: Monetary unit:** Dollar (June 1996: 1.00 = $1 US). **Gross national product** (1994): $2.3 bln.* **Per capita GNP:** $770. **Imports** (1991): $4.1 bln.; partners: S. Korea 46%, Japan 17%. **Exports** (1991): $557 mln.; partners: Norway 34%, Belg.-Lux. 29%. **National budget** (1989): $435 mil.

**Transport: Motor vehicles:** in use: 8,000 passenger cars, 3,000 comm. vehicles. **Chief ports:** Monrovia, Buchanan, Greenville.

**Communications: Television sets:** 1 per 53 persons. **Radios:** 1 per 3.9 persons. **Telephones:** 1 per 528 persons. **Daily newspaper circ.:** 15 per 1,000 pop.

**Health: Life expectancy at birth** (1996): 56 male; 61 female. **Births** (per 1,000 pop.): 43. **Deaths** (per 1,000 pop.): 12. **Natural increase:** 3.1%. **Infant mortality** (per 1,000 live births 1996): 108.

**Education: Literacy** (1995): 38%. Free and compulsory: ages 7-16.

**Major International Organizations:** UN and most of its specialized agencies, OAU.

**Embassy:** 5201 16th St. NW 20011; 291-0761.

Liberia was founded in 1822 by U.S. black freedmen who settled at Monrovia with the aid of colonization societies. It became a republic July 26, 1847, with a constitution modeled on that of the U.S. Descendants of freedmen dominated politics.

Charging rampant corruption, an Army Redemption Council of enlisted men staged a bloody predawn coup, April 12, 1980, in which Pres. Tolbert was killed and replaced as head of state by Sgt. Samuel Doe. Doe was chosen president in a disputed election, and survived a subsequent coup, in 1985.

A civil war began Dec. 1989. Rebel forces seeking to depose Pres. Doe made major territorial gains and advanced on the capital, June 1990. In Sept., Doe was captured and put to death. Despite the introduction of peacekeeping forces from several countries, factional fighting intensified, and a series of cease-fires failed to hold. A new accord Aug. 19, 1995, called for leaders of rival factions to share power pending national elections. A transitional Council of State was instituted Sept. 1, 1995. Factional fighting flared up again in Apr. 1996. The civil war has made refugees of more than half the population. On Sept. 3, 1996, Ruth Perry became Africa's first female head of state.

# Libya

## Socialist People's Libyan Arab Jamahiriya

## Al Jamahiriyah al Arabiyah al Libiyah ash Shabiyah al Ishirakiyah

**People: Population:** 5,445,436. **Age distrib.** (%): <15: 45; 65+: 3. **Pop. density:** 8 per sq. mi. **Urban:** 85%. **Ethnic groups:** Arab-Berber 97%. **Principal language:** Arabic (official), Italian, English. **Religion:** Sunni Muslim 97%.

**Geography: Area:** 678,400 sq. mi. **Location:** On Mediterranean coast of N Africa. **Neighbors:** Tunisia, Algeria on W; Niger, Chad on S; Sudan, Egypt on E. **Topography:** Desert and semidesert regions cover 92% of the land, with low mountains in N, higher mountains in S, and a narrow coastal zone. **Capital:** Tripoli (1988 est.): 591,000.

**Government: Type:** Islamic Arabic Socialist "Mass-State." **Leader:** Col. Muammar al-Qaddafi; b Sept. 1942; in power: Sept. 1969. **Local divisions:** 25 municipalities. **Defense:** 6.1% of GDP (1994 est.). **Active troop strength:** 80,000 est.

**Economy: Industries:** Oil, food processing, textiles. **Chief crops:** Dates, olives, citrus fruits, grapes, wheat. **Minerals:** Gypsum, oil, gas. **Crude oil reserves** (1994): 22.8 bil bbls. **Arable land:** 2%. **Livestock** (1994): sheep: 3.5 mln.; goats: 600,000. **Electricity prod.** (1993): 16.1 bil kWh. **Labor force:** 31% ind.; 27% services; 24% govt.; 18% agric.

**Finance: Monetary unit:** Dinar (June 1996: 0.36 = $1 US). **Gross domestic product** (1994): $32.9 bln.* **Per capita GDP:** $6,510. **Imports** (1994): $6.9 bln.; partners: Italy 19%, Germany 16%. **Exports** (1994): $7.2 bln.; partners: Italy 39%, Germany 18%, Spain 12%. **National budget** (1989): $9.8 bil. **International reserves less gold** (Jun. 1993): $5.9 bil. **Gold:** 3.6 mil oz t.

**Transport: Motor vehicles:** in use: 448,000 passenger cars, 322,000 comm. vehicles. **Chief ports:** Tripoli, Banghazi.

**Communications: Television sets:** 1 per 10.5 persons. **Radios:** 1 per 5.2 persons. **Telephones:** 1 per 21 persons. **Daily newspaper circ.:** 15 per 1,000 pop.

**Health: Life expectancy at birth** (1996): 63 male; 67 female. **Births** (per 1,000 pop.): 44. **Deaths** (per 1,000 pop.): 8. **Natural increase:** 3.7%. **Physicians:** 1 per 948 persons. **Infant mortality** (per 1,000 live births 1996): 60.

**Education: Literacy** (1992): 76%. Compulsory: ages 6-15.

**Major International Organizations:** UN, Arab League, OAU, OPEC.

First settled by Berbers, Libya was ruled in succession by Carthage, Rome, the Vandals, and the Ottomans. Italy ruled from 1912, and Britain and France after WW II. Libya became an independent constitutional monarchy Jan. 2, 1952. In 1969 a junta led by Col. Muammar al-Qaddafi seized power.

Libya and Egypt fought several air and land battles along their border in July 1977. Chad charged Libya with military occupation of its uranium-rich northern region in 1977. Libyan troops were driven from their last major stronghold by Chad forces in 1987, leaving over $1 billion in military equipment behind.

Libya reportedly helped arm violent revolutionary groups in Egypt and Sudan and aided terrorists of various nationalities.

On Jan. 7, 1986, the U.S. imposed economic sanctions against Libya, ordered all Americans to leave that country, and froze all Libyan assets in the U.S. The U.S. commenced flight operations over the Gulf of Sidra, Jan. 27, and a U.S. Navy task force began conducting exercises in the Gulf, Mar. 23. When Libya fired antiaircraft missiles at American warplanes, the U.S. responded by sinking 2 Libyan ships and bombing a missile site in Libya. The U.S. withdrew from the Gulf, Mar. 27.

The U.S. accused Qaddafi of having ordered the Apr. 5, 1986, bombing of a West Berlin discotheque, which killed 3, including a U.S. serviceman. In response, the U.S. sent warplanes to attack terrorist-related targets in Tripoli and Banghazi, Libya, Apr. 14.

The UN imposed limited sanctions, Apr. 15, 1992, for Libya's failure to extradite 2 agents linked to the 1988 bombing of Pan American World Airways Flight 103 over Lockerbie, Scotland, and 4 others linked to an airplane bombing over Niger. Sanctions were tightened as of Dec. 1, 1993. In 1996 the U.S. authorized sanctions on foreign companies that invest in Libya.

# Liechtenstein

## Principality of Liechtenstein

## Fürstentum Liechtenstein

**People: Population:** 31,122. **Age distrib.** (%): <15: 19; 65+: 10. **Pop. density:** 502 per sq. mi. **Ethnic groups:** Alemannic 95%. **Principal languages:** German (official), Alemannic dialect. **Religions:** Roman Catholic 87%, Protestant 8%.

**Geography: Area:** 62 sq. mi. **Location:** Central Europe, in the Alps. **Neighbors:** Switzerland on W, Austria on E. **Topography:** The Rhine Valley occupies one-third of the country, the Alps cover the rest. **Capital:** Vaduz. **Cities** (1995 est.): Vaduz 5,100; Schaan 5,100.

**Government: Type:** Hereditary constitutional monarchy. **Head of state:** Prince Hans-Adam II; b Feb 14, 1945; in office: Nov. 13, 1989. **Head of government:** Mario Frick; b May 8, 1965; in office: Dec. 15, 1993. **Local divisions:** 11 communes. **Defense:** Responsibility of Switzerland.

**Economy: Industries:** Machines, instruments, electronics, textiles, ceramics. **Chief crops:** Vegetables, corn, wheat. **Arable land:** 25%. **Labor force:** 53% industry, trade, constr.; 45% services.

**Finance: Monetary unit:** Swiss Franc. **Gross domestic product** (1990): $630 mln.* **Per capita GDP:** $22,300.* **National budget** (1990): $292 mil.

**Communications: Television sets:** 1 per 2.9 persons. **Radios:** 1 per 2.8 persons. **Telephones:** 1 per 1.6 persons. **Daily newspaper circ.:** 611 per 1,000 pop.

**Health** (1996); **Births** (per 1,000 pop.): 11. **Deaths** (per 1,000 pop.): 7. **Natural increase:** 0.5%. **Infant mortality** (per 1,000 live births): 5.

**Education: Literacy** (1994): 100%. Compulsory: ages 7-16.

**Major International Organizations:** UN (WTO), EFTA.

Liechtenstein became sovereign in 1866. Austria administered Liechtenstein's ports up to 1920; Switzerland has administered its postal services since 1921. Liechtenstein is united with Switzerland by a customs and monetary union. Taxes are low; many international corporations have headquarters there. Foreign workers comprise a third of the population.

# Lithuania

## Republic of Lithuania

## Lietuvos Respublika

**People: Population:** 3,646,041. **Pop. density:** 145 per sq. mi. **Urban:** 68%. **Ethnic groups:** Lithuanian 80%, Russian 9%, Polish 8%. **Principal languages:** Lithuanian (official), Polish, Russian. **Religions:** Mostly Roman Catholic.

**Geography: Area:** 25,213 sq. mi. **Location:** In E Europe, on SE coast of Baltic. **Neighbors:** Latvia on N, Belarus on E, S, Poland and Russia on W. **Capital:** Vilnius. **Cities** (1994): Vilnius 578,700; Kaunas 419,000.

**Government: Type:** Republic. **Head of state:** Pres. Algirdas Brazauskas; b Sept. 22, 1932; in office: Feb. 25, 1993. **Head of government:** Prime Min. Adolfas Slezevicius; b 1948; in office: Mar. 10, 1993. **Local divisions:** 44 regions, 11 municipalities. **Defense:** 2% of GDP (1994). **Active troop strength:** 8,900 est.

**Economy: Industries:** Machinery, shipbuilding. **Chief crops:** Sugar, grain, potatoes, vegetables. **Arable land:** 49%. **Livestock** (1994): cattle: 1.7 mln., pigs: 1.2 mil. **Electricity prod.** (1993): 19 bil kWh. **Labor force:** 42% ind., constr.; 18% agric.

**Finance: Monetary unit:** Litas (June 1996: 4.00 = $1 US). **Gross domestic product** (1994 est.): $13.5 bil. **Per capita GDP:** $3,500. **Imports** (1994): $2.7 bln.; partners: CIS 63%. **Exports** (1994): $2.2 bln.; partners: CIS 35%. **National budget** (1992 est.): $270.2 mil. **International reserves less gold** (May 1996): $654 mil.

**Transport: Railroads: Length:** 1,862 mi. **Motor vehicles:** in use: 598,000 passenger cars, 94,000 comm. vehicles. **Civil aviation:** 135 mil passenger-mi.; 3 airports with scheduled flights. **Chief port:** Klaipeda.

**Communications: Television sets:** 1 per 2.7 persons. **Radios:** 1 per 2.6 persons. **Telephones:** 1 per 4.4 persons.

**Health: Life expectancy at birth** (1996): 62 male; 74 female. **Births** (per 1,000 pop.): 13. **Deaths** (per 1,000 pop.): 13. **Natural increase:** 0%. **Hospital beds:** 1 per 86 persons. **Physicians:** 1 per 225 persons. **Infant mortality** (per 1,000 live births 1996): 17.

**Major International Organizations:** UN, EU.

**Embassy:** 2622 16th St. NW 20009; 234-2639.

Lithuania was occupied by the German army, 1914-18. It was annexed by the Soviet Russian army, but the Soviets were overthrown, 1919. Lithuania was a democratic republic until 1926 when the regime was ousted by a coup. In 1939, the Soviet-German treaty assigned most of Lithuania to the Soviet sphere of influence. It was annexed by the USSR Aug. 3, 1940. Lithuania formally declared its independence from the Soviet Union Mar. 11, 1990. During an abortive Soviet coup in Aug., the Western nations recognized Lithuania's independence, which was recognized by the Soviet Union in Sept. 1991.

The last Russian troops withdrew on Aug. 31, 1993. Lithuania applied to join the European Union, Dec. 8, 1995.

# Luxembourg

## Grand Duchy of Luxembourg

## Grand-Duché de Luxembourg

**People: Population:** 415,870. **Age distrib.** (%): <15: 18; 65+: 14. **Pop. density:** 416 per sq. mi. **Urban:** 86%. **Ethnic groups:** Mixture of French and Germans predominates. **Principal languages:** French, German, Luxembourgisch. **Religions:** Roman Catholic 97%.

**Geography: Area:** 999 sq. mi. **Location:** In W Europe. **Neighbors:** Belgium on W, France on S, Germany on E. **Topography:** Heavy forests (Ardennes) cover N, S is a low, open plateau. **Capital:** Luxembourg (1995): 76,400.

**Government: Type:** Constitutional monarchy. **Head of state:** Grand Duke Jean; b Jan. 5, 1921; in office: Nov. 12, 1964. **Head of government:** Prime Min. Jean-Claude Juncker; b Dec. 9, 1954; in office: Jan. 19, 1995. **Local divisions:** 3 districts. **Defense:** 1.2% of GDP (1994). **Active troop strength:** 800.

**Economy: Industries:** Steel, chemicals, food processing, tires, banking, engineering, metal products. **Chief crops:** Grains, potatoes, grapes. **Arable land:** 24%. **Electricity prod.** (1993): 1.4 bil kWh. **Labor force:** 65% services; 32% ind.; 3% agric.

**Finance: Monetary unit:** Franc (June 1996: 31.35 = $1 US). **Gross domestic product** (1994): $9.2 bln.* **Per capita GDP:** $22,830. **Tourism** (1992): $287 mil. **National budget** (1994): $4.1 bil. **Consumer prices** (change in 1995): 1.9%.

**Transport: Railroads: Route length:** 171 mi. **Motor vehicles:** in use: 218,000 passenger cars, 25,000 comm. vehicles. **Chief port:** Mertert.

**Communications: Television sets:** 1 per 2.9 persons. **Radios:** 1 per 1.7 persons. **Telephones:** 1 per 1.8 persons. **Daily newspaper circ.:** 383 per 1,000 pop.

**Health: Life expectancy at birth** (1996): 75 male; 82 female. **Births** (per 1,000 pop.): 13. **Deaths** (per 1,000 pop.): 8. **Natural increase:** 0.5%. **Hospital beds:** 1 per 87 persons. **Physicians:** 1 per 469 persons. **Infant mortality** (per 1,000 live births 1996): 5.

**Education: Literacy** (1994): 100%. Compulsory: ages 6-15.

**Major International Organizations:** UN (WTO), OECD, EU, NATO.

**Embassy:** 2200 Massachusetts Ave. NW 20008; 265-4171.

Luxembourg, founded about 963, was ruled by Burgundy, Spain, Austria, and France from 1448 to 1815. It left the Germanic Confederation in 1866. Overrun by Germany in 2 world wars, Luxembourg ended its neutrality in 1948, when a customs union with Belgium and Netherlands was adopted.

# Macedonia

## Former Yugoslav Republic of Macedonia

## Republika Makedonija

**People: Population:** 2,104,035. **Pop. density:** 212 per sq. mi. **Urban:** 58%. **Ethnic groups:** Macedonian 65%, Albanian 22%. **Principal languages:** Macedonian, Albanian, Turkish, Serbo-Croatian. **Religions:** Eastern Orthodox 67%, Muslim 30%.

**Geography: Area:** 9,928 sq. mi. **Location:** In SE Europe. **Neighbors:** Bulgaria on E, Greece on S, Albania on W, Yugoslavia on N. **Capital:** Skopje. **Cities** (1994 cen.): Skopje 440,600; Bitolj 75,400.

**Government: Type:** Republic. **Head of state:** Pres. Kiro Gligorov; b May 3, 1917; in office: Jan. 27, 1991. **Head of government:** Prime Min. Branko Crvenkovski; b 1962; in office: Sept. 4, 1992. **Local divisions:** 34 counties. **Defense: Active troop strength:** 10,400.

**Economy: Industries:** Light industry. **Chief crops:** Wheat, rice, cotton, tobacco. **Minerals:** Chromium, lead, zinc. **Arable land:** 5%. **Livestock** (1994): sheep: 2.4 mln.. **Electricity prod.** (1992): 6.3 bil kWh. **Labor force:** 40% manuf. & mining.

**Finance: Monetary unit:** Denar (June 1996: 40.37 = $1 US). **Gross domestic product** (1994): $1.9 bln.* **Per capita GDP:** $900. **Imports** (1993): $1.2 bil. **Exports** (1993): $1.1 bil.

**Transport: Railroads: Length:** 573 mi. **Vehicles:** in use: 280,000 passenger cars, 26,000 comm. vehicles. **Civil aviation:** 182 mil passenger-mi.; 1 airport with scheduled flights.

**Communications: Television sets:** 1 per 6.1 persons. **Radios:** 1 per 5.6 persons. **Telephones:** 1 per 6.7 persons. **Daily newspaper circ.:** 26 per 1,000 pop.

**Health: Life expectancy at birth** (1996): 70 male; 74 female. **Births** (per 1,000 pop.): 13. **Deaths** (per 1,000 pop.): 8. **Natural increase:** 0.5%. **Hospital beds:** 1 per 199 persons. **Physicians:** 1 per 458 persons. **Infant mortality** (per 1,000 live births 1996): 30.

**Education: Literacy** (1993): 89%. Free and compulsory: ages 7-15.

**Major International Organizations:** UN (IMF, WHO).

**Embassy:** 3050 K St. NW 20007; 337-3068.

Macedonia, as part of a larger region also called Macedonia, was ruled by Muslim Turks from 1389 to 1912, when native Greeks, Bulgarians, and Slavs won independence. Serbia received the largest part of the territory, with the rest going to Greece and Bulgaria. In 1913, the area was incorporated into Serbia, which in 1918 became part of the Kingdom of Serbs, Croats, and Slovenes (later Yugoslavia). In 1946, Macedonia became a constituent republic of Yugoslavia.

Macedonia declared its independence Sept. 8, 1991, and was admitted to the UN under a provisional name in 1993. A UN force, which included several hundred U.S. troops, was deployed there to deter the warring factions in Bosnia from carrying their dispute into other areas of the Balkans.

In Feb. 1994 both Russia and the U.S. recognized Macedonia. Greece, which objected to Macedonia's use of what it considered a Hellenic name and symbols, imposed a trade blockade on the landlocked nation; the 2 countries agreed to normalize relations Sept. 13, 1995. A car bombing, Oct. 3, seriously injured Pres. Kiro Gligorov. Macedonia and Yugoslavia signed a treaty normalizing relations Apr. 8, 1996.

# Madagascar

## Republic of Madagascar

## Repoblikan'i Madagasikara

**People: Population:** 13,670,507. **Age distrib.** (%): <15: 46; 65+: 3. **Pop. density:** 60 per sq. mi. **Urban:** 26%. **Ethnic groups:** 18 Malayo-Indonesian tribes (Merina 26%), with Arab and African presence. **Principal languages:** Malagasy, French (both official). **Religions:** Indigenous beliefs 52%, Christian 41%, Muslim 7%.

**Geography: Area:** 226,658 sq. mi. **Location:** In the Indian O., off the SE coast of Africa. **Neighbors:** Comoro Is. to NW, Mozambique to W. **Topography:** Humid coastal strip in the E, fertile valleys in the mountainous center plateau region, and a wider coastal strip on the W. **Capital:** Antananarivo (1993): 1.1 mil.

**Government: Type:** Republic. **Head of state:** Interim Pres. Norbert Ratsirahonana; in office: Sept. 5, 1996. **Local divisions:** 6 provinces. **Defense:** 1.3% of GDP (1991). **Active troop strength:** 21,000.

**Economy: Industries:** Food processing, textiles. **Chief crops:** Coffee (45% of exports), cloves, vanilla, rice, sugar, cassava, peanuts. **Minerals:** Chromite, graphite, coal, bauxite. **Arable land:** 4%. **Livestock** (1994): cattle: 10.3 mln.; pigs: 1.6 mil. **Fish catch** (1993): 115,000 metric tons. **Electricity prod.** (1993): 560 mil kWh. **Labor force:** 75% agric.

**Finance: Monetary unit:** Franc (June 1996: 3,800 = $1 US). **Gross domestic product** (1994): $10.6 bln.* **Per capita GDP:** $790. **Imports** (1993): $510 mln.; partners: France 28%, Japan 9%, Germany 7%. **Exports** (1993): $240 mln.; partners: France 33%, Germany 13%. **Tourism** (1993): $41 mil. **National budget** (1991): $265 mil. **International reserves less gold** (Apr. 1996): $130 mil. **Consumer prices** (change in 1995): 49.1%.

**Transport: Railroads: Route length:** 640 mi. **Motor vehicles:** in use: 48,000 passenger cars, 34,000 comm. vehicles. **Civil aviation:** 310 mil passenger-mi.; 18 airports with scheduled flights. **Chief ports:** Toamasina, Antsiranana, Mahajanga, Toliara.

**Communications: Television sets:** 1 per 110 persons. **Radios:** 1 per 6.2 persons. **Telephones:** 1 per 370 persons.

**Health: Life expectancy at birth** (1996): 51 male; 53 female. **Births** (per 1,000 pop.): 43. **Deaths** (per 1,000 pop.): 14. **Natural increase:** 2.8%. **Physicians:** 1 per 8,628 persons. **Infant mortality** (per 1,000 live births 1996): 94.

**Education: Literacy** (1993): 80%. Compulsory for 5 years between ages 6 and 13; attendance 73%.

**Major International Organizations:** UN (WHO, IMF, WTO), OAU.

**Embassy:** 2374 Massachusetts Ave. NW 20008; 265-5526.

Madagascar was settled 2,000 years ago by Malayan-Indonesian people, whose descendants still predominate. A unified kingdom ruled the 18th and 19th centuries. The island became a French protectorate, 1885, and a colony 1896. Independence came June 26, 1960.

Discontent with inflation and French domination led to a coup in 1972. The new regime nationalized French-owned financial interests, closed French bases and a U.S. space-tracking station, and obtained Chinese aid. The government conducted a program of arrests, expulsion of foreigners, and repression of strikes, 1979.

In 1990, Madagascar ended a ban on multiparty politics that had been in place since 1975. Albert Zafy was elected president in 1993, ending the 17-year rule of Adm. Didier Ratsiraka. After Zafy was impeached by the legislature, Madagascar's constitutional court removed him from office, Sept. 5, 1996.

# Malawi

## Republic of Malawi

**People: Population:** 9,452,844. **Age distrib.** (%): <15: 48; 65+: 3. **Pop. density:** 207 per sq. mi. **Urban:** 17%. **Ethnic groups:** Chewa, Nyanja, Lomwe, other Bantu tribes. **Principal languages:** English, Chichewa (both official). **Religions:** Christian 75%, Muslim 20%.

**Geography: Area:** 45,747 sq. mi. **Location:** In SE Africa. **Neighbors:** Zambia on W, Mozambique on SE, Tanzania on N. **Topography:** Malawi stretches 560 mi. N-S along Lake Malawi (Lake Nyasa), most of which belongs to Malawi. High plateaus and mountains line the Rift Valley the length of the nation. **Capital:** Lilongwe. **Cities** (1993 est.): Blantyre 399,300; Lilongwe 267,700.

**Government: Type:** Republic. **Head of state and government:** Pres. Bakili Muluzi; b Mar. 17, 1943; in office: May 21, 1994. **Local divisions:** 24 districts. **Defense:** 0.7% of GDP (FY 1993-94). **Active troop strength:** 8,000.

**Economy: Industries:** Agricultural processing, cement. **Chief crops:** Tea, tobacco, sugar, coffee, corn, potatoes. **Arable land:** 25%. **Fish catch** (1993): 65,000 metric tons. **Electricity prod.** (1993): 820 mil kWh. **Labor force:** 43% agric.; 25% manuf. & commerce; 15% personal services.

**Finance: Monetary unit:** Kwacha (June 1996: 15.34 = $1 US). **Gross domestic product** (1994): $7.3 bln.* **Per capita GDP:** $750. **Imports** (1993): $708 mln.; partners: South Africa 31%, UK 23%, Japan 8%. **Exports** (1993): $311 mln.; partners: Germany 16%, UK 16%, Japan 14%. **National budget** (1992): $498 mil. **International reserves less gold** (Jan. 1996): $98.9 mil. **Gold:** 13,000 oz t. **Consumer prices** (change in 1994): 34.7%.

**Transport: Railroads: Route length:** 490 mi. **Motor vehicles:** in use: 14,000 passenger cars, 12,000 comm. vehicles.

**Communications: Radios:** 1 per 4.9 persons. **Telephones:** 1 per 326 persons.

**Health: Life expectancy at birth** (1996): 36 male; 37 female. **Births** (per 1,000 pop.): 42. **Deaths** (per 1,000 pop.): 24. **Natural increase:** 1.7%. **Physicians:** 1 per 47,634 persons. **Infant mortality** (per 1,000 live births 1996): 140.

**Education: Literacy** (1992): 56%. Compulsory: ages 6-14.

**Major International Organizations:** UN (World Bank, WTO, IMF), OAU, the Commonwealth.

**Embassy:** 2408 Massachusetts Ave. NW 20008; 797-1007.

Bantus came in the 16th century, Arab slavers in the 19th. The area became the British protectorate Nyasaland in 1891. It became independent July 6, 1964, and a republic in 1966. After 3 decades as a one-party state under Pres. Hastings Kamuzu Banda, Malawi adopted a new constitution and, in multiparty elections May 17, 1994, chose a new leader, Bakili Muluzi. Banda was acquitted, Dec. 23, 1995, of complicity in the deaths of 4 political opponents in 1983.

# Malaysia

**People: Population:** 19,962,893. **Age distrib.** (%): <15: 36; 65+: 4. **Pop. density:** 156 per sq. mi. **Urban:** 51%. **Ethnic groups:** Malay and other indigenous 59%, Chinese 32%, Indian 9%. **Principal languages:** Malay (official), English, Chinese, Indian languages. **Religions:** Muslim, Hindu, Buddhist, Confucianist, Christian, local religions.

**Geography: Area:** 127,584 sq. mi. **Location:** On the SE tip of Asia, plus the N coast of the island of Borneo. **Neighbors:** Thailand on N, Indonesia on S. **Topography:** Most of W Malaysia is covered by tropical jungle, including the central mountain range that runs N-S through the peninsula. The western coast is marshy, the eastern, sandy. E Malaysia has a wide, swampy coastal plain, with interior jungles and mountains. **Capital:** Kuala Lumpur (1991 est.): 1.1 mil.

**Government: Type:** Federal parliamentary democracy with a constitutional monarch. **Head of state:** Paramount Ruler Tuanku Ja'afar ibni Al-Marhum Tuanku Abdul Rahman; b Jul. 19, 1922; in office: Apr. 26, 1994. **Head of government:** Prime Min. Datuk Seri Mahathir bin Mohamad; b Dec. 20, 1925; in office: July 16, 1981. **Local divisions:** 13 states and 2 federal terr. **Defense:** 2.9% of GDP (1994). **Active troop strength:** 114,500.

**Economy: Industries:** Rubber goods, steel, electronics. **Chief crops:** Palm oil (world's leading producer), rice, pepper. **Minerals:** Tin (a leading producer), oil, bauxite, iron. **Crude oil reserves** (1995): 4.3 bil bbls. **Other resources:** Rubber, timber. **Arable land:** 3%. **Livestock** (1994): pigs: 3.1 mil. **Fish catch** (1993): 680,000 metric tons. **Electricity prod.** (1993): 31 bil kWh. **Labor force:** 25% services & trade; 23% manuf.; 21% agric.

**Finance: Monetary unit:** Ringgit (June 1996: 2.49 = $1 US). **Gross domestic product** (1994): $167 bln.* **Per capita GDP:** $8,650. **Imports** (1994): $55.2 bln.; partners: Japan 27%, U.S. 17%, Singapore 15%. **Exports** (1994): $56.6 bln.; partners: Singapore 22%, U.S. 20%, Japan 13%. **Tourism** (1993): $1.9 bil. **National budget** (1994): $19.1 bil. **International reserves less gold** (Apr. 1996): $24.2 bil. **Gold:** 2.39 mil oz t. **Consumer prices** (change in 1995): 5.3%.

**Transport: Railroads: Length:** 1,381 mi. **Motor vehicles:** in use: 2.3 mil passenger cars, 501,000 comm. vehicles. **Civil aviation:** 10.9 bil passenger-mi.; 38 airports. **Chief ports:** George Town, Kelang, Kota Kinabalu, Kuching.

**Communications: Television sets:** 1 per 9.7 persons. **Radios:** 1 per 2.6 persons. **Telephones:** 1 per 7.9 persons. **Daily newspaper circ.:** 117 per 1,000 pop.

**Health: Life expectancy at birth** (1996): 67 male; 73 female. **Births** (per 1,000 pop.): 26. **Deaths** (per 1,000 pop.): 5. **Natural increase:** 2.1%. **Hospital beds:** 1 per 489 persons. **Physicians:** 1 per 2,412 persons. **Infant mortality** (per 1,000 live births 1996): 24.

**Education: Literacy** (1992): 84%. Free and compulsory: ages 6-16. Attendance: 93% primary.

**Major International Organizations:** UN (World Bank, IMF, WTO), ASEAN, the Commonwealth.

**Embassy:** 2401 Massachusetts Ave. NW 20008; 328-2700.

European traders appeared in the 16th century; Britain established control in 1867. Malaysia was created Sept. 16, 1963. It included Malaya (which had become independent in 1957 after the suppression of Communist rebels), plus the formerly British Singapore, Sabah (N Borneo), and Sarawak (NW Borneo). Singapore was separated in 1965, in order to end tensions between Chinese, the majority in Singapore, and Malays in control of the Malaysian government.

A monarch is elected by a council of hereditary rulers of the Malayan states every 5 years.

Abundant natural resources have assured prosperity, and foreign investment has aided industrialization. Work on a new federal capital south of Kuala Lumpur began in 1995.

# Maldives

## Republic of Maldives

## Divehi Jumhuriyya

**People: Population:** 270,758. **Age distrib.** (%): <15: 47; 65+: 3. **Pop. density:** 2,354 per sq. mi. **Urban:** 26%. **Ethnic groups:** Sinhalese, Dravidian, Arab, African. **Principal language:** Divehi (Sinhalese dialect; official). **Religion:** Sunni Muslim.

**Geography: Area:** 115 sq. mi. **Location:** In the Indian O., SW of India. **Neighbors:** Nearest is India on N. **Topography:** 19 atolls with 1,087 islands, about 200 inhabited. None of the islands are over 5 sq. mi. in area, and all are nearly flat. **Capital:** Male (1991 est.): 55,000.

**Government: Type:** Republic. **Head of state:** Pres. Maumoon Abdul Gayoom; b Dec. 29, 1937; in office: Nov. 11, 1978. **Local divisions:** 19 districts.

**Economy: Industries:** Fish processing, tourism. **Chief crops:** Coconuts, corn, sweet potatoes. **Arable land:** 10%. **Fish catch** (1993): 90,000 metric tons. **Electricity prod.** (1991): 30 mil kWh. **Labor force:** 25% fishing & agric.; 16% trade; 15% manuf.

**Finance: Monetary unit:** Rufiyaa (June 1996: 11.77 = $1 US). **Gross domestic product** (1993): $360 mln.* **Per capita GDP:** $1,500. **Imports** (1993): $178 mln.; partners: Singapore 52%, India 9%. **Exports** (1993): $39 mln.; partners: Sri Lanka 30%, UK 25%. **Tourism** (1993): $146 mil. **National budget** (1993 est.): $143 mil.

**Transport: Chief port:** Male.

**Communications: Television sets:** 1 per 52 persons. **Radios:** 1 per 9.8 persons.

**Health: Life expectancy at birth** (1996): 65 male; 68 female. **Births** (per 1,000 pop.): 42. **Deaths** (per 1,000 pop.): 7. **Natural increase:** 3.5%. **Infant mortality** (per 1,000 live births 1996): 47.

**Education: Literacy** (1991): 93%.

**Major International Organizations:** UN (WTO, WHO, IMF), the Commonwealth.

The islands had been a British protectorate since 1887. The country became independent July 26, 1965. Long a sultanate, the Maldives became a republic in 1968. Natural resources and tourism are being developed; however, the Maldives remains one of the world's poorest countries.

# Mali

## Republic of Mali

## République du Mali

**People: Population:** 9,653,261. **Age distrib.** (%): <15: 48; 65+: 3. **Pop. density:** 20 per sq. mi. **Urban:** 26%. **Ethnic groups:** Mande (Bambara, Malinke, Sarakole) 50%, Peul 17%, Voltaic 12%, Songhai 6%, Tuareg and Moor 10%. **Principal languages:** French (official), Bambara, many other African languages. **Religion:** Muslim 90%, indigenous beliefs 9%.

**Geography: Area:** 482,077 sq. mi. **Location:** In the interior of W Africa. **Neighbors:** Mauritania, Senegal on W; Guinea, Côte d'Ivoire, Burkina Faso on S; Niger on E; Algeria on N. **Topography:** A landlocked grassy plain in the upper basins of the Senegal and Niger rivers, extending N into the Sahara. **Capital:** Bamako (1994 met. est.): 894,000.

**Government: Type:** Republic. **Head of state:** Pres. Alpha Oumar Konare; b Feb. 2, 1946; in office: June 8, 1992. **Head of government:** Prime Min. Ibrahim Boubakar Keita; b Jan. 29, 1945; in office: Feb. 4, 1994. **Local divisions:** 8 regions. **Defense:** 2.2% of GDP (1994). **Active troop strength:** 7,350.

**Economy: Chief crops:** Millet, rice, peanuts, cotton. **Minerals:** Gold, phosphates, kaolin. **Arable land:** 2%. **Livestock** (1994): sheep and goats: 12.6 mln.; cattle: 5.5 mil. **Fish catch** (1993): 64,000 metric tons. **Electricity prod.** (1993): 310 mil kWh. **Labor force:** 80% agric.; 19% services.

**Finance: Monetary unit:** CFA Franc (June 1996: 515 = $1 US). **Gross domestic product** (1994): $5.4 bln.* **Per capita GDP:** $600. **Imports** (1993): $842 mln.; partners: Norway 28%, Côte d'Ivoire 18%. **Exports** (1993): $415 mln.; partners: Norway 29%, Thailand 18%. **Tourism** (1993): $11 mil. **National budget** (1992): $697 mil. **International reserves less gold** (Dec. 1995): $323 mil. **Gold:** 19,000 oz t. **Consumer prices** (change in 1995): 12.4%.

**Transport: Railroads: Route length:** 399 mi. **Motor vehicles:** in use: 21,000 passenger cars, 8,400 comm. vehicles. **Chief port:** Koulikoro.

**Communications: Television sets:** 1 per 883 persons. **Radios:** 1 per 25 persons. **Telephones:** 1 per 639 persons.

**Health: Life expectancy at birth** (1996): 45 male; 49 female. **Births** (per 1,000 pop.): 51. **Deaths** (per 1,000 pop.): 19. **Natural increase:** 3.2%. **Physicians:** 1 per 18,046 persons. **Infant mortality** (per 1,000 live births 1996): 103.

**Education: Literacy** (1992): 31%. Free and compulsory: ages 7-16. Attendance: 21%.

**Major International Organizations:** UN and most of its specialized agencies, OAU.

**Embassy:** 2130 R St. NW 20008; 939-8950.

Until the 15th century the area was part of the great Mali Empire. Timbuktu (Tombouctou) was a center of Islamic study. French rule was secured, 1898. The Sudanese Rep. and Senegal became independent as the Mali Federation June 20, 1960, but Senegal withdrew, and the Sudanese Rep. was renamed Mali.

Mali signed economic agreements with France and, in 1963, with Senegal. In 1968, a coup ended the socialist regime. Famine struck in 1973-74, killing as many as 100,000 people. Drought conditions returned in the 1980s.

The military, Mar. 26, 1991, overthrew the government of Pres. Amadou Toumani Traoré, who had been in power since 1968. Oumar Konare, a leader in the coup, was elected president, Apr. 26, 1992. A peace agreement between the government and a Tuareg rebel group was signed in June 1994.

# Malta

## Republic of Malta

## Repubblika ta' Malta

**People: Population:** 375,576. **Age distrib.** (%): <15: 22; 65+: 11. **Pop. density:** 3,078 per sq. mi. **Urban:** 89%. **Ethnic groups:** Italian, Arab, French, Spanish, English. **Principal languages:** Maltese, English (both official). **Religion:** Roman Catholic 98%.

**Geography: Area:** 122 sq. mi. **Location:** In center of Mediterranean Sea. **Neighbors:** Nearest is Italy on N. **Topography:** Island of Malta is 95 sq. mi.; other islands in the group: Gozo, 26 sq. mi.; Comino, 1 sq. mi. The coastline is heavily indented. Low hills cover the interior. **Capital:** Valletta. **Cities** (1994 est.): Birkirkara 21,700; Qormi 19,900.

**Government: Type:** Parliamentary democracy. **Head of state:** Pres. Ugo Mifsud Bonnici; b Nov. 8, 1932; in office: Apr. 4, 1994. **Head of government:** Prime Min. Edward Fenech-Adami; b Feb. 7, 1934; in office: May 12, 1987. **Defense:** 0.9% of GDP (FY 1992-93). **Active troop strength:** 1,850.

**Economy: Industries:** Tourism, electronics, construction, textiles, food & beverages. **Chief crops:** Potatoes, tomatoes. **Arable land:** 38%. **Electricity prod.** (1993): $1.1 bil kWh. **Labor force:** 37% govt.; 26% services; 22% manuf.; 2% agric.

**Finance: Monetary unit:** Lira (June 1996: 1.00 = $2.75 US). **Gross domestic product** (1994): $3.9 bln.* **Per capita GDP:** $10,760. **Imports** (1993): $2.1 bln.; partners: Italy 27%, Germany 14%, UK 13%, U.S. 9%. **Exports** (1993): $1.3 bln.; partners: Italy 32%, Germany 16%, UK 8%. **Tourism** (1993): $653 mil. **National budget** (FY 1994-95): $1.4 bil. **International reserves less gold** (Mar. 1996): 1.6 bil. **Gold:** 31,000 oz t. **Consumer prices** (change in 1995): 4.0%.

**Transport: Motor vehicles:** in use: 120,000 passenger cars, 28,000 comm. vehicles. **Civil aviation:** 777 mil passenger-mi.; 1 airport with scheduled flights. **Chief port:** Valletta.

**Communications: Television sets:** 1 per 2.5 persons. **Radios:** 1 per 4.1 persons. **Telephones:** 1 per 2.3 persons.

**Health: Life expectancy at birth** (1996): 76 male; 81 female. **Births** (per 1,000 pop.): 15. **Deaths** (per 1,000 pop.): 7. **Natural increase:** 0.8%. **Hospital beds:** 1 per 173 persons. **Physicians:** 1 per 409 persons. **Infant mortality** (per 1,000 live births 1996): 7.

**Education: Literacy** (1993): 91%. Free and compulsory: ages 5-16.

**Major International Organizations:** UN (WTO, WHO, IMF), the Commonwealth.

**Embassy:** 2017 Connecticut Ave. NW 20008; 462-3612.

Malta was ruled by Phoenicians, Romans, Arabs, Normans, the Knights of Malta, France, and Britain (since 1814). It became independent Sept. 21, 1964. Malta became a republic in 1974. The withdrawal of the last British sailors, Apr. 1, 1979, ended 179 years of British military presence on the island.

# Marshall Islands

## Republic of the Marshall Islands

**People: Population:** 58,363. **Pop. density:** 834 per sq. mi. **Urban:** 65%. **Ethnic groups:** Micronesian. **Principal languages:** English (official), Marshallese, Japanese. **Religions:** Protestant 90%.

**Geography: Area:** 70 sq. mi. **Location:** In central Pacific Ocean; comprised of two 800-mi-long parallel chains of coral atolls. **Neighbors:** Nearest are Micronesia to W, Nauru and Kiribati to S. **Capital:** Majuro (1990 est.) 20,000.

**Government: Type:** Republic. **Head of state:** Pres. Amata Kabua; b Nov. 17, 1928; in office: May 1979.

**Economy:** Agriculture and tourism are mainstays. **Electricity prod.** (1990): 80 mil kWh.

**Finance: Monetary unit:** U.S. Dollar. **Gross domestic product** (1992): $75 mln.* **Per capita GDP:** $1,500. **Imports** (1992): $63 mil. **Exports** (1992): $4 mil.

**Transport:** 23 airports with scheduled flights. **Chief port:** Majuro.

**Communications: Telephones:** 1 per 23 persons.

**Health: Life expectancy at birth** (1996): 62 male; 66 female. **Births** (per 1,000 pop.): 46. **Deaths** (per 1,000 pop.): 7. **Natural increase:** 3.9%. **Infant mortality** (per 1,000 live births 1996): 47.

**Education: Literacy** (1994): 91%.

**Major International Organizations:** UN.

**Embassy:** 2433 Massachusetts Ave. NW 20008; 234-5414.

The Marshall Islands were a German possession until World War I and were administered by Japan between the World Wars. After WW II, they were administered as part of the UN Trust Territory of the Pacific Islands by the U.S.

The Marshall Islands secured international recognition as an independent nation on Sept. 17, 1991.

# Mauritania

## Islamic Republic of Mauritania

## Al Jumhuriyah al Islamiyah al Muritaniyah

**People: Population:** 2,336,048. **Age distrib.** (%): <15: 45; 65+: 4. **Pop. density:** 6 per sq. mi. **Urban:** 39%. **Ethnic groups:** Mixed Maur/black 40%, Maur 30%, black 30%. **Principal languages:** Hasaniya Arabic, Wolof (both official), Pular, Soninke. **Religions:** Muslim.

**Geography: Area:** 398,000 sq. mi. **Location:** In W Africa. **Neighbors:** Morocco on N, Algeria and Mali on E, Senegal on S. **Topography:** The fertile Senegal R. valley in the S gives way to a wide central region of sandy plains and scrub trees. The N is arid and extends into the Sahara. **Capital:** Nouakchott. **Cities** (1992 est.): Nouakchott 480,400; Nouadhibou 72,300; Kaedi 35,200.

**Government: Type:** Islamic republic. **Head of state:** Pres. Maaouya Ould Sidi Ahmed Taya; b 1943; in office: Apr. 18, 1992. **Head of government:** Prime Min. Cheikh El Afia Ould Mohamed Khouna; in office: Jan. 2, 1996. **Local divisions:** 12 regions, 1 capital district. **Defense:** 2.7% of GDP (1994). **Active troop strength:** 15,650 est.

**Economy: Industries:** Fish processing, iron mining. **Chief crops:** Dates, grain. **Minerals:** Iron ore, gypsum. **Livestock** (1994): sheep: 4.8 mln.; goats: 3.1 mln.; cattle: 1.0 mil. **Fish catch** (1994): 297,000 metric tons. **Electricity prod.** (1993): 135 mil kWh. **Labor force:** 47% agric.; 29% services; 14% ind. & commerce.

**Finance: Monetary unit:** Ouguiya (June 1996: 137 = $1 US). **Gross domestic product** (1993): $2.4 bln.* **Per capita GDP:** $1,110. **Imports** (1993): $378 mln.; partners: France 27%. **Exports** (1993): $401 mln.; partners: Japan 25%, Italy 18%. **International reserves less gold** (May 1996): $92 mil. **Gold:** 12,000 oz t.

**Transport: Motor vehicles:** in use: 18,000 passenger cars, 5,500 comm. vehicles. **Chief ports:** Nouakchott, Nouadhibou.

**Communications: Television sets:** 1 per 1,974 persons. **Radios:** 1 per 7.2 persons. **Telephones:** 1 per 286 persons.

**Health: Life expectancy at birth** (1996): 46 male; 52 female. **Births** (per 1,000 pop.): 47. **Deaths** (per 1,000 pop.): 15. **Natural increase:** 3.2%. **Hospital beds:** 1 per 1,217 persons. **Physicians:** 1 per 14,259 persons. **Infant mortality** (per 1,000 live births 1996): 82.

**Education: Literacy** (1993): 38%. **Attendance:** 69% in primary school, 15% in secondary school.

**Major International Organizations:** UN (WTO, IMF, WHO), OAU, Arab League.

**Embassy:** 2129 Leroy Pl. NW 20008; 232-5700.

Mauritania was a French protectorate from 1903. It became independent Nov. 28, 1960. It annexed the south of former Spanish Sahara (now Western Sahara) in 1976. Saharan guerrillas of the Polisario Front stepped up attacks in 1977; 8,000 Moroccan troops and French bomber raids aided the government. Mauritania signed a peace treaty with the Polisario Front, 1980, resumed diplomatic relations with Algeria while breaking a defense treaty with Morocco, and renounced sovereignty over its share of Western Sahara. Opposition parties were legalized and a new constitution approved in 1991.

# Mauritius

## Republic of Mauritius

**People: Population:** 1,140,256. **Age distrib.** (%): <15: 29; 65+: 6. **Pop. density:** 1,447 per sq. mi. **Urban:** 44%. **Ethnic groups:** Indo-Mauritian 68%, Creole 27%. **Principal languages:** English (official), French, Creole, Hindi, Bhojpoori. **Religions:** Hindu 52%, Christian 28%, Muslim 17%.

**Geography: Area:** 788 sq. mi. **Location:** In the Indian O., 500 mi. E of Madagascar. **Neighbors:** Nearest is Madagascar to W. **Topography:** A volcanic island nearly surrounded by coral reefs. A central plateau is encircled by mountain peaks. **Capital:** Port Louis (1993 est.): 144,200.

**Government: Type:** Republic. **Head of state:** Pres. Cassam Uteem; b Mar. 22, 1941; in office: June 30, 1992. **Head of government:** Prime Min. Navin Ramgoolam; b July 14, 1947; in office: Dec. 22, 1995. **Local divisions:** 9 districts, 3 dependencies. **Defense:** 0.4% of GDP (FY 1992-93). **Active troop strength:** 1,300 (paramilitary).

**Economy: Industries:** Tourism, textiles, food processing. **Chief crops:** Sugarcane, tea. **Arable land:** 54%. **Electricity prod.** (1993): 920 mil kWh. **Labor force:** 29% govt. services; 27% agric. & fishing; 22% manuf.

**Finance: Monetary unit:** Rupee (June 1996: 20.02 = $1 US). **Gross domestic product** (1993 est.): $9.3 bln.* **Per capita GDP:** $8,600. **Imports** (1993): $1.7 bln.; partners: South Africa 14%, France 13%. **Exports** (1993): $1.3 bln.; partners: UK 32%, France 21%, U.S. 18%. **Tourism** (1993): $301 mil. **National budget** (FY 1992-93): $567 mil. **International reserves less gold** (May 1996): $883 mil. **Gold:** 62,000 oz t. **Consumer prices** (change in 1995): 6.0%.

**Transport: Motor vehicles:** in use: 34,000 passenger cars, 10,000 comm. vehicles. **Chief port:** Port Louis.

**Communications: Television sets:** 1 per 7.1 persons. **Radios:** 1 per 2.9 persons. **Telephones:** 1 per 10 persons. **Daily newspaper circ.:** 86 per 1,000 pop.

**Health: Life expectancy at birth** (1996): 67 male; 74 female. **Births** (per 1,000 pop.): 19. **Deaths** (per 1,000 pop.): 7. **Natural increase:** 1.2%. **Hospital beds:** 1 per 351 persons. **Physicians:** 1 per 1,098 persons. **Infant mortality** (per 1,000 live births 1996): 17.

**Education: Literacy** (1993): 83%. Compulsory: ages 5-12.

**Major International Organizations:** UN and all of its specialized agencies, OAU, the Commonwealth.

**Embassy:** 4301 Connecticut Ave. NW, Suite 134 20008; 244-1491.

Mauritius was uninhabited when settled in 1638 by the Dutch, who introduced sugarcane. France took over in 1721, bringing African slaves. Britain ruled from 1810 to Mar. 12, 1968, bringing Indian workers for the sugar plantations.

Mauritius formally severed its association with the British crown Mar. 12, 1992.

# Mexico

## United Mexican States

## Estados Unidos Mexicanos

**People: Population:** 95,772,462. **Age distrib.** (%): <15: 36; 65+: 4. **Pop. density:** 127 per sq. mi. **Urban:** 71%. **Ethnic groups:** Mestizo 60%, Amerindian 30%, white 9%. **Principal languages:** Spanish (official), Amerindian languages. **Religions:** Roman Catholic 89%, Protestant 6%.

**Geography: Area:** 756,066 sq. mi. **Location:** In southern North America. **Neighbors:** U.S. on N, Guatemala and Belize on S. **Topography:** The Sierra Madre Occidental Mts. run NW-SE near the west coast; the Sierra Madre Oriental Mts. run near the Gulf of Mexico. They join S of Mexico City. Between the 2 ranges lies the dry central plateau, 5,000 to 8,000 ft. alt., rising toward the S, with temperate vegetation. Coastal lowlands are tropical. About 45% of land is arid. **Capital:** Mexico City. **Cities** (1990): Mexico City 9.8 mln.; Guadalajara 1.6 mln.; Nezahualcoyotl 1.3 mil.

**Government: Type:** Federal republic. **Head of state:** Pres. Ernesto Zedillo Ponce de León; b Dec. 27, 1951; in office: Dec. 1, 1994. **Local divisions:** 31 states, 1 federal district. **Defense:** 0.5% of GDP (1992). **Active troop strength:** 175,000.

**Economy: Industries:** Steel, chemicals, electric goods, textiles, rubber, oil, tourism. **Chief crops:** Cotton, coffee, wheat, rice, beans, vegetables, corn. **Minerals:** Silver, lead, zinc, gold, oil, gas. **Crude oil reserves** (1995): 50.8 bil barrels. **Arable land:** 12%. **Livestock** (1994): cattle: 31 mln.; pigs: 18 mln.; goats: 10 mil. **Fish catch** (1993): 1.2 mil metric tons. **Electricity prod.** (1993): 122 bil kWh. **Labor force:** 32% services; 28% agric.; 15% commerce; 11% manuf.

**Finance: Monetary unit:** New Peso (June 1996: 7.68 = $1 US). **Gross domestic product** (1994): $729 bln.* **Per capita GDP:** $7,900. **Imports** (1994): $79.4 bln.; partners: U.S. 74%, EU 11%. **Exports** (1994): $60.8 bln.; partners: U.S. 82%, EU 5%. **Tourism** (1993): $6.2 bil. **National budget** (1994): $96.5 bil. **International reserves less gold** (May 1996): $16.9 bil. **Gold:** 501,000 oz t. **Consumer prices** (change in 1995): 35.0%.

**Transport: Railroads: Route length:** 12,747 mi. **Motor vehicles:** in use: 8.0 mil passenger cars, 3.8 mil comm. vehicles. **Civil aviation:** 11.9 bil passenger-mi.; 83 airports. **Chief ports:** Veracruz, Tampico, Mazatlan, Coatzacoalcos.

**Communications: Television sets:** 1 per 6.6 persons. **Radios:** 1 per 4.3 persons. **Telephones:** 1 per 11 persons. **Daily newspaper circ.:** 142 per 1,000 pop.

**Health: Life expectancy at birth** (1996): 70 male; 78 female. **Births** (per 1,000 pop.): 26. **Deaths** (per 1,000 pop.): 5. **Natural increase:** 2.2%. **Hospital beds:** 1 per 1,367 persons. **Physicians:** 1 per 885 persons. **Infant mortality** (per 1,000 live births 1996): 25.

**Education: Literacy** (1994): 90%. Free and compulsory: ages 6-12.

**Major International Organizations:** UN (IMF, WTO), OAS, OECD.

**Embassy:** 1911 Pennsylvania Ave. NW 20006; 728-1600.

Mexico was the site of advanced Indian civilizations. The Mayas, an agricultural people, moved up from Yucatan, built immense stone pyramids, invented a calendar. The Toltecs were overcome by the Aztecs, who founded Tenochtitlan AD 1325, now Mexico City. Hernando Cortes, Spanish conquistador, destroyed the Aztec empire, 1519-21.

After 3 centuries of Spanish rule the people rose, under Fr. Miguel Hidalgo y Costilla, 1810, Fr. Morelos y Payon, 1812, and Gen. Agustin Iturbide, who made himself emperor as Agustin I, 1821. A republic was declared in 1823.

Mexican territory extended into the present American Southwest and California until Texas revolted and established a republic in 1836; the Mexican legislature refused recognition but was unable to enforce its authority there. After numerous clashes, the U.S.-Mexican War, 1846-48, resulted in the loss by Mexico of the lands north of the Rio Grande.

French arms supported an Austrian archduke on the throne of Mexico as Maximilian I, 1864-67, but pressure from the U.S. forced France to withdraw. A dictatorial rule by Porfirio Diaz, president 1877-80, 1884-1911, led to fighting by rival forces until a new constitution, Feb. 5, 1917, provided social reform.

The Institutional Revolutionary Party (PRI) has been dominant in politics since 1929. Radical opposition, including some guerrilla activity, has been contained by strong measures.

Some gains in agriculture, industry, and social services have been achieved. The land is rich, but the rugged topography and lack of sufficient rainfall are major obstacles. Economic prospects brightened with the discovery of vast oil reserves, perhaps the world's greatest. But much of the work force is jobless or underemployed. Inflation and a drop in world oil prices aggravated Mexico's economic problems in the 1980s.

Mexico reached agreement with the U.S. and Canada on the North American Free Trade Agreement (NAFTA) Aug. 12, 1992; it took effect Jan. 1, 1994.

Guerrillas of the Zapatista National Liberation Army (EZLN) launched an uprising, Jan. 1, 1994, in southern Mexico. A tentative peace accord was reached Mar. 2. The presidential candidate of the governing PRI, Luis Donaldo Colosio Murrieta, was assassinated at a political rally in Tijuana, Mar. 23. The new PRI candidate, Ernesto Zedillo Ponce de León, won election Aug. 21 and was inaugurated Dec. 1.

An austerity plan and pledges of U.S. aid saved Mexico's currency from collapse in early 1995. Popular Revolutionary Army guerrillas launched coordinated attacks on government targets in Aug. 1996.

# Micronesia

## Federated States of Micronesia

**People: Population:** 125,377. **Pop. density:** 463 per sq. mi. **Urban:** 26%. **Ethnic groups:** 9 ethnic Micronesian and Polynesian groups. **Principal languages:** English (official), Trukese, Pohnpeian. **Religions:** Roman Catholic 50%, Protestant 47%.

**Geography: Area:** 271 sq. mi. **Location:** Consists of 607 islands in the W Pacific Ocean. **Capital:** Palikir, on Pohnpei.

**Government: Type:** Republic. **Head of state:** Bailey Olter; b 1932; in office: May 21, 1991. **Local divisions:** 4 states.

**Economy: Industries:** Tourism, fish processing. **Chief crops:** Tropical fruits, vegetables, pepper.

**Finance: Monetary unit:** U.S. Dollar. **Gross domestic product** (1990): $160 mln.* **Per capita GDP:** $1,500. **Imports** (1990): $91 mil. **Exports** (1990): $3 mil.

**Transport:** 6 airports with scheduled flights.

**Communications: Television sets:** 1 per 15 persons. **Radios:** 1 per 1.5 persons. **Telephones:** 1 per 17 persons.

**Health: Life expectancy at birth** (1996): 66 male; 70 female. **Births** (per 1,000 pop.): 28. **Deaths** (per 1,000 pop.): 6. **Natural increase:** 2.2%. **Hospital beds:** 1 per 318 persons. **Physicians:** 1 per 2,069 persons. **Infant mortality** (per 1,000 live births 1996): 36.

**Education: Literacy** (1991): 90%.

**Major International Organizations:** UN.

**Embassy:** 1725 N St. NW 20036; 223-4383.

The Federated States of Micronesia, formerly known as the Caroline Islands, was ruled successively by Spain, Germany, Japan, and the U.S. It was internationally recognized as an independent nation Sept. 17, 1991.

# Moldova

## Republic of Moldova

## Republica Moldova

**People: Population:** 4,463,847. **Pop. density:** 343 per sq. mi. **Urban:** 47%. **Ethnic groups:** Moldovan/Romanian 65%, Ukrainian 14%, Russian 13%. **Principal languages:** Moldovan (official), Russian. **Religions:** Eastern Orthodox 99%.

**Geography: Area:** 13,012 sq. mi. **Location:** In E Europe. **Neighbors:** Romania on W; Ukraine on N, E, and S. **Capital:** Chisinau. **Cities** (1994 est.): Chisinau 662,000; (1991 est.) Tiraspol 186,000.

**Government: Type:** Republic. **Head of state:** Pres. Mircea Snegur; b Jan. 17, 1940; in office: Sept. 1990. **Head of government:** Prime Min. Andre Sangheli; in office: July 1, 1992. **Defense:** 2% of GDP (1994). **Active troop strength:** 11,850.

**Economy: Industries:** Canning, wine making, textiles. **Chief crops:** Grain, grapes. **Minerals:** Lignite, gypsum. **Arable land:** 50%. **Livestock** (1993): cattle: 900,000; pigs: 1.6 mln.; sheep: 1.1 mil. **Electricity prod.** (1994): 8.2 bil kWh.

**Finance: Monetary unit:** Leu (June 1996: 4.58 = $1 US). **Gross domestic product** (1994 est.): $11.9 bln.* **Per capita GDP:** $2,670. **Imports** (1994): $174 mln., excl. CIS. **Exports** (1994): $144 mln., excl. CIS. **International reserves less gold** (Mar. 1996): $236 mil.

**Transport: Railroads: Length:** 715 mi. **Motor vehicles:** in use: 222,000 passenger cars. **Civil aviation:** 1.5 bil passenger-mi.; 1 airport with scheduled flights.

**Communications: Telephones:** 1 per 8.3 persons. **Daily newspaper circ.:** 45 per 1,000 pop.

**Health: Life expectancy at birth** (1996): 61 male; 70 female. **Births** (per 1,000 pop.): 16. **Deaths** (per 1,000 pop.): 12. **Natural increase:** 0.5%. **Hospital beds:** 1 per 82 persons. **Physicians:** 1 per 241 persons. **Infant mortality** (per 1,000 live births 1996): 48.

**Education: Literacy** (1995): 96%.

**Major International Organizations:** UN, CIS.

**Embassy:** 1511 K St. NW 20005; 783-3012.

In 1918, Romania annexed all of Bessarabia that Russia had acquired from Turkey in 1812 by the Treaty of Bucharest. In 1924, the Soviet Union established the Moldavian Autonomous Soviet Socialist Republic on the eastern bank of the Dniester. It was merged with the Romanian-speaking districts of Bessarabia in 1940 to form the Moldavian SSR.

During World War II, Romania, allied with Germany, occupied the area. It was recaptured by the USSR in 1944. Moldova declared independence Aug. 27, 1991. It became an independent state when the USSR disbanded Dec. 26, 1991.

Fighting erupted Mar. 1992 in the Dnestr (Dniester) region between Moldovan security forces and Slavic separatists—ethnic Russians and ethnic Ukrainians—who feared Moldova would merge with neighboring Romania. In a plebiscite on Mar. 6, 1994, voters in Moldova supported independence, without unification with Romania. Defying the Moldovan government, voters in the breakaway Dnestr region held legislative elections and approved a separatist constitution Dec. 24, 1995.

# Monaco

## Principality of Monaco

## Principanté de Monaco

**People: Population:** 31,719. **Pop. density:** 42,292 per sq. mi. **Ethnic groups:** French 47%, Italian 16%, Monegasque 16%. **Principal languages:** French (official), English, Italian, Monegasque. **Religions:** Roman Catholic 95%.

**Geography: Area:** 0.75 sq. mi. **Location:** On the NW Mediterranean coast. **Neighbors:** France to W, N, E. **Topography:** Monaco-Ville sits atop a high promontory, the rest of the principality rises from the port up the hillside. **Capital:** Monaco.

**Government: Type:** Constitutional monarchy. **Head of state:** Prince Rainier III; b May 31, 1923; in office: May 9, 1949. **Head of government:** Min. of State Paul Dijoud; in office: Nov. 24, 1995. **Local divisions:** 4 quarters.

**Economy: Industries:** Tourism, gambling, chemicals, precision instruments, plastics.

**Finance: Monetary unit:** French Franc or Monégasque Franc. **Gross domestic product** (1993): $558 mil. **Per capita GDP:** $18,000. **National budget** (1991): $376 mln.

**Transport: Chief port:** Monaco.

**Communications: Television sets:** 1 per 1.5 persons. **Radios:** 1 per person.**Telephones:** 1 per 2.1 persons.

**Health** (1996): **Births** (per 1,000 pop.): 11. **Deaths** (per 1,000 pop.): 12. **Natural increase:** –0.1%. **Infant mortality** (per 1,000 live births): 7.

**Major International Organizations:** UN.

An independent principality for over 300 years, Monaco has belonged to the House of Grimaldi since 1297, except during the French Revolution. It was placed under the protectorate of Sardinia in 1815, and under that of France, 1861. The Prince of Monaco was an absolute ruler until a 1911 constitution.

Monaco's fame as a tourist resort is widespread. It is noted for its mild climate and magnificent scenery.

# Mongolia

## Mongol Uls

**People: Population:** 2,496,617. **Pop. density:** 4 per sq. mi. **Urban:** 55%. **Ethnic groups:** Mongol 90%. **Principal languages:** Khalka Mongolian (official). **Religions:** Traditionally Tibetan Buddhist.

**Geography: Area:** 604,800 sq. mi. **Location:** In E Central Asia. **Neighbors:** Russia on N, China on S. **Topography:** Mostly a high plateau with mountains, salt lakes, and vast grasslands. Arid lands in the S are part of the Gobi Desert.

**Capital:** Ulaanbaatar. **Cities** (1994): Ulaanbaatar 680,000; Darhan 85,800.

**Government: Type:** Republic. **Head of state:** Pres. Punsalmaagiyn Ochirbat; b 1942; in office: Mar. 21, 1990. **Head of government:** Prime Min. Mendsaihany Enhsaihan; b 1955; in office: July 1996. **Local divisions:** 18 provinces, 3 municipalities. **Defense:** 2.4% of GNP (1993). **Active troop strength:** 21,100.

**Economy: Industries:** Food processing, mining, cement. **Chief crops:** Grain, potatoes. **Minerals:** Coal, oil, tungsten, copper, molybdenum, gold, tin. **Arable land:** 1%. **Livestock** (1994): sheep: 13.8 mln.; cattle: 3.0 mil. **Electricity prod.** (1993): 3.1 bil kWh. **Labor force:** 36% agric.; 15% manuf. & mining; 15% services.

**Finance: Monetary unit:** Tugrik (June 1996: 467 = $1 US). **Gross domestic product** (1994): $4.4 bln.* **Per capita GDP:** $1,800. **Imports** (1993): $361 mln.; partners: Russia 59%, China 10%. **Exports** (1993): $360 mln.; partners: Russia 28%, Chna 19%. **International reserves less gold** (Mar. 1996): $94 mil.

**Transport: Railroads: Length:** 1,294 mi. **Motor vehicles:** in use: 21,000 passenger cars, 33,000 comm. vehicles.

**Communications: Television sets:** 1 per 18 persons. **Radios:** 1 per 7.8 persons. **Telephones:** 1 per 36 persons. **Daily newspaper circ.:** 90 per 1,000 pop.

**Health: Life expectancy at birth** (1996): 59 male; 63 female. **Births** (per 1,000 pop.): 26. **Deaths** (per 1,000 pop.): 9. **Natural increase:** 1.7%. **Hospital beds:** 1 per 83 persons. **Physicians:** 1 per 340 persons. **Infant mortality** (per 1,000 live births 1996): 70.

**Education: Literacy** (1991): 83%.

**Major International Organizations:** UN (ILO, WHO, IMF).

**Embassy:** 2833 M St. NW 20007; 983-1962.

One of the world's oldest countries, Mongolia reached the zenith of its power in the 13th century when Genghis Khan and his successors conquered all of China and extended their influence as far west as Hungary and Poland. In later centuries, the empire dissolved and Mongolia became a province of China.

With the advent of the 1911 Chinese revolution, Mongolia, with Russian backing, declared its independence. A Communist regime was established July 11, 1921.

In 1990, the Mongolian Communist Party yielded its monopoly on power. Free elections in July 1990 were won by the Communists. A new constitution took effect Feb. 12, 1992. A democratic alliance won legislative elections, June 30, 1996.

# Morocco

## Kingdom of Morocco

## Al Mamlakah al Maghribiyah

**People: Population:** 29,779,156. **Age distrib.** (%): <15: 38; 65+: 5. **Pop. density:** 168 per sq. mi. **Urban:** 47%. **Ethnic groups:** Arab-Berber 99%. **Principal languages:** Arabic (official), Berber. **Religions:** Sunni Muslim 99%.

**Geography: Area:** 177,117 sq. mi. **Location:** On NW coast of Africa. **Neighbors:** Western Sahara on S, Algeria on E. **Topography:** Consists of 5 natural regions: mountain ranges (Riff in the N, Middle Atlas, Upper Atlas, and Anti-Atlas); rich plains in the W; alluvial plains in SW; well-cultivated plateaus in the center; a pre-Sahara arid zone extending from SE. **Capital:** Rabat. **Cities** (1994): Casablanca 2.9 mln.; Rabat 1.2 mil; Marrakech 602,000.

**Government: Type:** Constitutional monarchy. **Head of state:** King Hassan II; b July 9, 1929; in office: Mar. 3, 1961. **Head of government:** Prime Min. Abdellatif Filali; b Jan. 26, 1928; in office: May 25, 1994. **Local divisions:** 36 provinces, 5 municipalities. **Defense:** 3.8% of GDP (1994). **Active troop strength:** 195,500.

**Economy: Industries:** Carpets, clothing, leather goods, mining, tourism. **Chief crops:** Grain, citrus fruits, grapes, olives. **Minerals:** Phosphates, iron ore, manganese, lead, zinc. **Arable land:** 18%. **Livestock** (1994): sheep: 15.6 mln.; goats: 4.4 mln.; cattle: 2.4 mil. **Fish catch** (1993): 607,000 metric tons. **Electricity prod.** (1993): 9.9 bil kWh. **Labor force:** 50% agric.; 26% services; 15% ind.

**Finance: Monetary unit:** Dirham (June 1996: 8.75 = $1 US). **Gross domestic product** (1994): $87.5 bln.* **Per capita GDP:** $3,060. **Imports** (1994): $7.5 bln.; partners: EU 59%, U.S. 8%. **Exports** (1994): $4.1 bln.; partners: EU 70%. **Tourism** (1994): $1.3 bil. **National budget** (1994): $8.9 bil. **International reserves less gold** (May 1996): $3.6 bil. **Gold:** 704,000 oz t. **Consumer prices** (change in 1995): 6.1%.

**Transport: Railroads: Route length:** 1,099 mi. **Motor vehicles:** in use: 865,000 passenger cars, 317,000 comm. vehicles. **Civil aviation:** 2.7 bil passenger-mi.; 16 airports. **Chief ports:** Tangier, Casablanca, Kenitra.

**Communications: Television sets:** 1 per 22 persons. **Radios:** 1 per 5.2 persons. **Telephones:** 1 per 33 persons. **Daily newspaper circ.:** 13 per 1,000 pop.

**Health: Life expectancy at birth** (1996): 68 male; 72 female. **Births** (per 1,000 pop.): 27. **Deaths** (per 1,000 pop.): 6. **Natural increase:** 2.2%. **Hospital beds:** 1 per 984 persons. **Physicians:** 1 per 3,361 persons. **Infant mortality** (per 1,000 live births 1996): 43.

**Education: Literacy** (1995): 44%. Compulsory: ages 7-13.

**Major International Organizations:** UN (ILO, WTO, IMF, WHO), Arab League.

**Embassy:** 1601 21st St. NW 20009; 462-7980.

Berbers were the original inhabitants, followed by Carthaginians and Romans. Arabs conquered in 683. In the 11th and 12th centuries, a Berber empire ruled all NW Africa and most of Spain from Morocco.

Part of Morocco came under Spanish rule in the 19th century; France controlled the rest in the early 20th. Tribal uprisings lasted from 1911 to 1933. The country became independent Mar. 2, 1956. Tangier, an internationalized seaport, was turned over to Morocco, 1956. Ifni, a Spanish enclave, was ceded in 1969.

Morocco annexed over 70,000 sq. mi. of phosphate-rich land Apr. 14, 1976, two-thirds of former Spanish Sahara (now Western Sahara), with the remainder annexed by Mauritania. Spain had withdrawn in February. Polisario, a guerrilla movement, proclaimed the region independent Feb. 27, and launched attacks with Algerian support. When Mauritania signed a treaty with the Polisario Front and gave up its portion of Western Sahara, Morocco occupied the area, 1980.

After years of bitter fighting, Morocco controlled the main urban areas, but the Polisario Front's guerrillas moved freely in the vast, sparsely populated deserts. The 2 sides signed a cease-fire agreement in 1990. The UN planned to conduct a referendum in Western Sahara on whether the territory should become independent or remain part of Morocco. Pop. of Western Sahara (1996 est.) is 223,000; capital: Laayoune (El Aaiun).

# Mozambique

## Republic of Mozambique

## República Popular de Moçambique

**People: Population:** 17,877,927. **Age distrib.** (%): <15: 46; 65+: 2. **Pop. density:** 57 per sq. mi. **Urban:** 33%. **Ethnic groups:** Bantu tribes. **Principal languages:** Portuguese (official), Makua, Malawi, Shona, Tsonga. **Religions:** Indigenous beliefs 60%, Christian 30%, Muslim 10%.

**Geography: Area:** 313,661 sq. mi. **Location:** On SE coast of Africa. **Neighbors:** Tanzania on N; Malawi, Zambia, Zimbabwe on W; South Africa, Swaziland on S. **Topography:** Coastal lowlands comprise nearly half the country with plateaus rising in steps to the mountains along the western border. **Capital:** Maputo. **Cities:** (1991 est.): Maputo 932,000; Matala 337,200; Beira 298,800.

**Government: Type:** Republic. **Head of state:** Pres. Joaquim Chissano; b Oct. 22, 1939; in office: Oct. 19, 1986. **Head of government:** Prime Min. Pascoal Mocumbi; b Apr. 10, 1941; in office: Dec. 21, 1994. **Local divisions:** 10 provinces. **Defense:** 7.3% of GDP (1993). **Active troop strength:** 12,000 est.

**Economy: Industries:** Chemicals, petroleum products, textiles. **Chief crops:** Cashews, cotton, sugar, corn, tea. **Minerals:** Coal, titanium. **Arable land:** 4%. **Livestock** (1994): cattle: 1.3 mil. **Fish catch** (1994): 24,000 metric tons. **Electricity prod.** (1993): 1.7 bil kWh. **Labor force:** 90% agric.

**Finance: Monetary unit:** Metical (June 1996: 11,140 = $1 US). **Gross domestic product** (1994): $10.6 bln.* **Per capita GDP:** $610. **Imports** (1994): $1.1 bln.; partners: South Africa 35%, UK 8%. **Exports** (1994): $150 mln.; partners: Spain 22%, South Africa 15%. **National budget** (1992 est.): $607 mil.

**Transport: Railroads: Length:** 1,946 mi. **Motor vehicles:** in use: 35,000 passenger cars, 35,000 comm. vehicles. **Chief ports:** Maputo, Beira, Nacala, Inhambane.

**Communications: Television sets:** 1 per 495 persons. **Radios:** 1 per 28 persons. **Telephones:** 1 per 270 persons.

**Health: Life expectancy at birth** (1996): 43 male; 46 female. **Births** (per 1,000 pop.): 46. **Deaths** (per 1,000 pop.): 19. **Natural increase:** 2.7%. **Hospital beds:** 1 per 1,231 persons. **Physicians:** 1 per 143,351 persons. **Infant mortality** (per 1,000 live births 1996): 126.

**Education: Literacy** (1993): 40%. Compulsory: ages 7-14.

**Major International Organizations:** UN (IMF, World Bank, WTO), OAU, the Commonwealth.

**Embassy:** 1990 M St. NW, Suite 570 20036; 293-7146.

The first Portuguese post on the Mozambique coast was established in 1505, on the trade route to the East. Mozambique became independent June 25, 1975, after a ten-year war against Portuguese colonial domination. The 1974 revolution in Portugal had paved the way for the orderly transfer of power to Frelimo (Front for the Liberation of Mozambique). Frelimo took over local administration Sept. 20, 1974, although opposed, in part violently, by some blacks and whites.

The new government, led by Maoist Pres. Samora Machel, provided for a gradual transition to a communist system. Economic problems included the emigration of most of the country's whites, a politically untenable economic dependence on white-ruled South Africa, and a large external debt.

In the 1980s, severe drought and civil war caused famine and heavy loss of life.

The ruling party formally abandoned Marxist-Leninism in 1989, and a new constitution, effective Nov. 30, 1990, provided for multiparty elections and a free-market economy.

On Oct. 4, 1992, a peace agreement was signed aimed at ending hostilities between the government and the rebel Mozambique National Resistance (MNR). Elections took place Oct. 27-28, 1994. Repatriation of 1.7 million Mozambican refugees officially ended June 1995.

# Myanmar (*formerly* Burma)

## Union of Myanmar

## Pyidaungzu Myanma Naingngandaw

**People: Population:** 45,975,625. **Age distrib.** (%): <15: 36; 65+: 4. **Pop. density:** 176 per sq. mi. **Urban:** 25%. **Ethnic groups:** Burman (related to Tibetan) 68%, Shan 9%, Karen 7%, Rakhine 4%. **Principal languages:** Burmese (official), Karen, Shan. **Religions:** Buddhist 89%, Christian 4%, Muslim 4%.

**Geography: Area:** 261,228 sq. mi. **Location:** Between S and SE Asia, on Bay of Bengal. **Neighbors:** Bangladesh, India on W; China, Laos, Thailand on E. **Topography:** Mountains surround Myanmar on W, N, and E, and dense forests cover much of the nation. N-S rivers provide habitable valleys and communications, especially the Irrawaddy, navigable for 900 miles. The country has a tropical monsoon climate. **Capital:** Yangôn (Rangoon). **Cities** (1995 est.): Yangôn 3.8 mln.; (1983) Mandalay 533,000.

**Government: Type:** Military. **Head of state and government:** Gen. Than Shwe; b 1933; in office: Apr. 24, 1992. **Local divisions:** 7 states and 7 divisions. **Defense:** 3.1% of GDP (1992). **Active troop strength:** 286,000.

**Economy: Industries:** Mining, textiles, footwear, wood products, petroleum refining. **Chief crops:** Rice, sugarcane, corn, pulses. **Minerals:** Oil, lead, copper, tin, tungsten, precious stones. **Crude oil reserves** (1994): 50 mil bbls. **Other resources:** Rubber, teakwood. **Arable land:** 15%. **Livestock** (1994): cattle: 9.7 mln.; pigs: 2.6 mil. **Fish catch** (1993): 837,000 metric tons. **Electricity prod.** (1993): 2.6 bil kWh. **Labor force:** 65% agric.; 14% ind.; 10% trade.

**Finance: Monetary unit:** Kyat (June 1996: 5.92 = $1 US). **Gross domestic product** (1994): $41 bln.* **Per capita GDP:** $930. **Imports** (FY 1993-94): $1.2 bln.; partners: Singapore 30%, China 27%. **Exports** (FY 1993-94): $674 mln.; partners: China 19%, Singapore 14%. **Tourism** (1993): $19 mil. **National budget** (FY 1993-94): $6.7 bil. **International reserves less gold** (Apr. 1996): $520 mil. **Gold:** 231,000 oz t. **Consumer prices** (change in 1995): 25.2%.

**Transport: Railroads: Length:** 2,945 mi. **Motor vehicles:** in use: 36,000 passenger cars, 36,000 comm. vehicles. **Civil aviation:** 138 mil passenger-mi.; 19 airports with scheduled flights. **Chief ports:** Yangôn, Bassein, Moulmein.

**Communications: Television sets:** 1 per 46 persons. **Radios:** 1 per 14 persons. **Telephones:** 1 per 556 persons. **Daily newspaper circ.:** 9 per 1,000 pop.

**Health: Life expectancy at birth** (1996): 55 male; 58 female. **Births** (per 1,000 pop.): 30. **Deaths** (per 1,000 pop.): 12. **Natural increase:** 1.8%. **Hospital beds:** 1 per 1,586 persons. **Physicians:** 1 per 3,306 persons. **Infant mortality** (per 1,000 live births 1996): 81.

**Education: Literacy** (1995): 83%. Compulsory: ages 5-10. Attendance: 62%.

**Major International Organizations:** UN (World Bank, IMF, WTO).

**Embassy:** 2300 S St. NW 20008; 332-9044.

The Burmese arrived from Tibet before the 9th century, displacing earlier cultures, and a Buddhist monarchy was established by the 11th. Burma was conquered by the Mongol dynasty of China in 1272, then ruled by Shans as a Chinese tributary, until the 16th century.

Britain subjugated Burma in 3 wars, 1824-84, and ruled the country as part of India until 1937, when it became self-governing. Independence outside the Commonwealth was achieved Jan. 4, 1948.

Gen. Ne Win dominated politics from 1962 to 1988, first as military ruler then as constitutional president. His regime drove Indians from the civil service and Chinese from commerce. Socialization of the economy was advanced, isolation from foreign countries enforced. In 1987 Burma, once the richest nation in SE Asia, was granted less-developed status by the UN.

Ne Win resigned July 1988, following waves of antigovernment riots. Rioting and street violence continued, and in Sept. the military seized power, under Gen. Saw Maung. In 1989 the country's name was changed to Myanmar.

The first free multiparty elections in 30 years took place May 27, 1990, with the main opposition party winning a decisive victory, but the military refused to hand over power. A key opposition leader, Aung San Suu Kyi, awarded the Nobel Peace Prize in 1991, was held under house arrest from July 20, 1989, to July 10, 1995. The military government continued to harass and imprison her supporters in 1996.

# Namibia

## Republic of Namibia

**People: Population:** 1,677,243. **Pop density:** 5 per sq. mi. **Urban:** 32%. **Ethnic groups:** Ovambo 50%, Kavangos 9%, Herero 7%, Damara 7%, white 6%. **Principal languages:** Afrikaans, English (official), German, indigenous languages. **Religions:** Lutheran 50%, other Christian 30%.

**Geography: Area:** 318,580 sq. mi. **Location:** In S Africa on the coast of the Atlantic Ocean. **Neighbors:** Angola on N, Botswana on E, South Africa on S. **Capital:** Windhoek (1992 est.): 161,000.

**Government: Type:** Republic. **Head of state:** Pres. Sam Nujoma; b May 12, 1929; in office: Mar. 21, 1990. **Head of government:** Prime Min. Hage Geingob; b Aug. 3, 1941; in office: Mar. 21, 1990. **Local divisions:** 13 regions. **Defense:** 2% of GDP (FY 1993-94). **Active troop strength:** 8,100.

**Economy:** Mining accounts for almost 25% of GDP. **Minerals:** Diamonds, copper, gold, tin, lead, uranium. **Fish catch** (1993): 330,000 metric tons. **Electricity prod.** (1991): 1.3 bln. kWh.

**Finance: Monetary unit:** Dollar (June 1996: 4.34 = $1 US). **Gross domestic product** (1994): $5.8 bln.* **Per capital GDP:** $3,600. **Imports** (1993): $1.1 bil. **Exports** (1993): $1.3 bil. **Tourism** (1992): $91 mil. **National budget** (FY 1993-94): $1.05 bil. **International reserves less gold** (Mar. 1996): $236 mil.

**Transport: Railroads: Length:** 1,480 mi. **Chief ports:** Luderitz, Walvis Bay.

**Communications: Television sets:** 1 per 39 persons. **Radios:** 1 per 6.4 persons. **Telephones:** 1 per 22 persons.

**Health: Life expectancy at birth** (1996): 63 male; 66 female. **Births** (per 1,000 pop.): 37. **Deaths** (per 1,000 pop.): 8. **Natural increase:** 2.9%. **Hospital beds:** 1 per 216 persons. **Physicians:** 1 per 4,594 persons. **Infant mortality** (per 1,000 live births 1996): 47.

**Education: Literacy** (1993): 76%.

**Major International Organizations:** UN (WTO, WHO, IMF), OAU, the Commonwealth.

**Embassy:** 1605 New Hampshire Ave. NW 20009; 986-0540.

Namibia was declared a protectorate by Germany in 1890 and officially called South-West Africa. South Africa seized the territory from Germany in 1915 during World War I; the League of Nations gave South Africa a mandate over the territory in 1920. In 1966, the Marxist South-West Africa People's Organization (SWAPO) launched a guerrilla war for independence.

In 1968 the UN General Assembly gave the area the name Namibia.

After many years of guerrilla warfare and failed diplomatic efforts, South Africa, Angola, and Cuba signed a U.S.-mediated agreement Dec. 22, 1988, to end South African administration of Namibia and provide for a cease-fire and transition to independence, in accordance with a 1978 UN plan. A separate accord between Cuba and Angola provided for a phased withdrawal of Cuban troops from Namibia. SWAPO later endorsed the plan. Elections were held for a constituent assembly, and a constitution providing for multiparty government was adopted Feb. 9, 1990. Namibia became an independent nation Mar. 21, 1990.

Walvis Bay, the principal deepwater port, had been turned over to South African administration in 1922. It remained in South African hands after independence, but South Africa turned control of the port back to Namibia, as of Mar. 1, 1994.

# Nauru

## Republic of Nauru

**People: Population:** 10,273. **Pop. density:** 1,253 per sq. mi. **Ethnic groups:** Nauruan 58%, other Pacific Islander 26%, Chinese 8%, European 8%. **Principal languages:** Nauruan (official), English. **Religions:** Predominantly Christian.

**Geography: Area:** 8.2 sq. mi. **Location:** In W Pacific O. just S of the Equator. **Neighbors:** Nearest is Kiribati to E. **Topography:** Mostly a plateau bearing high-grade phosphate deposits, surrounded by a coral cliff and a sandy shore in concentric rings. **Capital:** Govt. offices in district of Yaren.

**Government: Type:** Republic. **Head of state:** Pres. Lagumot Harris. **Local divisions:** 14 districts.

**Economy:** Phosphate mining. **Electricity prod.** (1993): 30 mil kWh.

**Finance: Monetary unit:** Australian Dollar. **Gross domestic product** (1993): $100 mln.* **GDP per capita:** $10,000.

**Communications: Radios:** 1 per 1.7 persons.

**Health** (1996): **Births** (per 1,000 pop.): 18. **Deaths** (per 1,000 pop.): 5. **Natural increase:** 1.3%. **Infant mortality** (per 1,000 live births): 41.

**Education: Literacy** (1989): 99%. **Years compulsory:** ages 6-16.

The island was discovered in 1798 by the British but was formally annexed to the German Empire in 1886. After World War I, Nauru became a League of Nations mandate administered by Australia. During World War II the Japanese occupied the island and shipped 1,200 Nauruans to the fortress island of Truk as slave laborers.

In 1947 Nauru was made a UN trust territory, administered by Australia. It became an independent republic Jan. 31, 1968.

Phosphate exports have provided Nauru with per capita revenues that are among the highest in the Third World. Phosphate reserves, however, are expected to be depleted by 2000, and environmental damage from strip-mining has been severe.

# Nepal

## Kingdom of Nepal

## Nepal Adhirajya

**People: Population:** 22,094,033. **Age distrib.** (%): <15: 42; 65+: 3. **Pop. density:** 389 per sq. mi. **Urban:** 10%. **Ethnic groups:** The many tribes are descendants of Indian, Tibetan, and Central Asian migrants. **Principal languages:** Nepali (official) (an Indic language), many others. **Religions:** Hindu (official) 90%, Buddhist 5%, Muslim 3%.

**Geography: Area:** 56,827 sq. mi. **Location:** Astride the Himalaya Mts. **Neighbors:** China on N, India on S. **Topography:** The Himalayas stretch across the N, the hill country with its fertile valleys extends across the center, while the S border region is part of the flat, subtropical Ganges Plain. **Capital:** Kathmandu. **Cities** (1993 met. est.): Kathmandu 535,000; Lalitpur 190,000; Biratnagar 132,000.

**Government: Type:** Constitutional monarchy. **Head of state:** King Birendra Bir Bikram Shah Dev; b Dec. 28, 1945; in office: Jan. 31, 1972. **Head of government:** Prime Min. Sher Bahadur Deuba; in office: Sept. 11, 1995. **Local divisions:** 14 zones. **Defense:** 1.2% of GDP (FY 1992-93). **Active troop strength:** 35,000.

**Economy: Industries:** Sugar and jute mills, tourism. **Chief crops:** Jute, rice, grain. **Minerals:** Quartz. **Other resources:** Forests, hydroelectric power. **Arable land:** 17%. **Livestock** (1993): cattle: 6.2 mil. **Electricity prod.** (1993): 920 mil kWh. **Labor force:** 93% agric.

**Finance: Monetary unit:** Rupee (June 1996: 56 = $1 US). **Gross domestic product** (1994): $22.4 bln.* **Per capita GDP:** $1,060. **Imports** (1993): $899 mln.; partners: India 41%, Singapore 32%, Japan 16%. **Exports** (1993): $593 mln.; partners: Germany 49%, U.S. 26%. **Tourism** (1992): $110 mil. **National budget** (FY 1993-94): $854 mil. **International reserves less gold** (Jan. 1996): $613 mil. **Gold:** 153,000 oz t. **Consumer prices** (change in 1994): 8.3%.

**Transport: Civil aviation:** 439 mil passenger-mi.; 24 airports with scheduled flights.

**Communications: Television sets:** 1 per 78 persons. **Radios:** 1 per 31 persons. **Telephones:** 1 per 286 persons.

**Health: Life expectancy at birth** (1995): 53 male; 54 female. **Births** (per 1,000 pop.): 37. **Deaths** (per 1,000 pop.): 13. **Natural increase:** 2.4%. **Hospital beds:** 1 per 3,898 persons. **Physicians:** 1 per 12,623 persons. **Infant mortality** (per 1,000 live births 1996): 79.

**Education: Literacy** (1992): 28%. Free and compulsory: ages 6-11. Attendance: 74% primary, 35% secondary.

**Major International Organizations:** UN (IMF).

**Embassy:** 2131 Leroy Pl. NW 20008; 667-4550.

Nepal was originally a group of petty principalities, the inhabitants of one of which, the Gurkhas, became dominant about 1769. In 1951 King Tribhubana Bir Bikram, member of the Shah family, ended the system of rule by hereditary premiers of the Ranas family, who had kept the kings virtual prisoners, and established a cabinet system of government.

Virtually closed to the outside world for centuries, Nepal is now linked to India and Pakistan by roads and air service and to Tibet by road. Polygamy, child marriage, and the caste system were officially abolished in 1963.

The government announced the legalization of political parties in 1990. Elections on Nov. 15, 1994, led to the installation of Nepal's first Communist government, which held power until a no-confidence vote Sept. 10, 1995.

# Netherlands

## Kingdom of the Netherlands

## Koninkrijk der Nederlanden

**People: Population:** 15,568,034. **Age distrib.** (%): <15: 18; 65+: 13. **Pop. density:** 971 per sq. mi. **Urban:** 61%. **Ethnic groups:** Dutch 96%. **Principal language:** Dutch (official). **Religions:** Roman Catholic 34%, Protestant 25%.

**Geography: Area:** 16,033 sq. mi. **Location:** In NW Europe on North Sea. **Neighbors:** Germany on E, Belgium on S. **Topography:** The land is flat, an average alt. of 37 ft. above sea level, with much land below sea level reclaimed and protected by some 1,500 miles of dikes. Since 1920 the government has been draining the IJsselmeer, formerly the Zuider Zee. **Capital:** Amsterdam. **Cities** (1994 est.): Amsterdam 724,100; Rotterdam 598,500; The Hague 445,300.

**Government: Type:** Parliamentary democracy under a constitutional monarch. **Head of state:** Queen Beatrix; b Jan. 31, 1938; in office: Apr. 30, 1980. **Head of government:** Prime Min. Wim Kok; b Sept. 29, 1938; in office: Aug. 22, 1994. **Seat of govt.:** The Hague. **Local divisions:** 12 provinces. **Defense:** 2.2% of GDP (1994). **Active troop strength:** 74,400.

**Economy: Industries:** Metals, machinery, chemicals, oil refinery, diamond cutting, electronics, tourism. **Chief crops:** Grains, potatoes, sugar beets, vegetables, fruits, flowers. **Minerals:** Natural gas, oil. **Crude oil reserves** (1995): 113 mil bbls. **Arable land:** 26%. **Livestock** (1994): pigs: 14.6 mln.; cattle: 4.7 mln.; sheep: 1.8 mil. **Fish catch** (1993): 487,000 metric tons. **Electricity prod.** (1993): 72.4 bil kWh. **Labor force:** 71% services; 25% manuf. & constr.; 4% agric.

**Finance: Monetary unit:** Guilder (June 1996: 1.71 = $1 US). **Gross domestic product** (1994): $276 bln.* **Per capita GDP:** $17,940. **Imports** (1993): $137 bln.; partners: Germany 26%, Belgium-Lux. 14%, U.S. 8%, UK 8%. **Exports** (1993): $153 bln.; partners: Germany 27%, Belgium-Lux. 14%, UK 10%. **Tourism** (1993): $4.7 bil. **National budget** (1992): $122.1 bil. **International reserves less gold** (May 1996): $30.8 bil. **Gold:** 34.77 mil oz t. **Consumer prices** (change in 1995): 1.9%.

**Transport: Railroads: Length:** 1,713 mi. **Motor vehicles:** in use: 5.8 mil passenger cars, 679,000 comm. vehicles. **Civil aviation:** 23.7 bil passenger-mi.; 5 airports. **Chief ports:** Rotterdam, Amsterdam, IJmuiden.

**Communications: Television sets:** 1 per 2.7 persons. **Radios:** 1 per 1.1 persons. **Telephones:** 1 per 1.9 persons. **Daily newspaper circ.:** 296 per 1,000 pop.

**Health: Life expectancy at birth** (1996): 75 male; 81 female. **Births** (per 1,000 pop.): 12. **Deaths** (per 1,000 pop.): 9. **Natural increase:** 0.3%. **Hospital beds:** 1 per 176 persons. **Physicians:** 1 per 391 persons. **Infant mortality** (per 1,000 live births 1996): 5.

**Education: Literacy** (1993): 100%. Compulsory: ages 5-18.

**Major International Organizations:** UN and all of its specialized agencies, NATO, EU, OECD.

**Embassy:** 4200 Wisconsin Ave. NW 20016; 244-5300.

Julius Caesar conquered the region in 55 BC, when it was inhabited by Celtic and Germanic tribes.

After the empire of Charlemagne fell apart, the Netherlands (Holland, Belgium, Flanders) split among counts, dukes, and bishops, passed to Burgundy and thence to Charles V of Spain. His son, Philip II, tried to check the Dutch drive toward political freedom and Protestantism (1568-1573). William the Silent, prince of Orange, led a confederation of the northern provinces, called Estates, in the Union of Utrecht, 1579. The Estates retained individual sovereignty, but were represented jointly in the States-General, a body that had control of foreign affairs and defense. In 1581 they repudiated allegiance to Spain. The rise of the Dutch republic to naval, economic, and artistic eminence came in the 17th century.

The United Dutch Republic ended 1795 when the French formed the Batavian Republic. Napoleon made his brother Louis king of Holland, 1806; Louis abdicated 1810 when Napoleon annexed Holland. In 1813 the French were expelled. In 1815 the Congress of Vienna formed a kingdom of the Netherlands, including Belgium, under William I. In 1830, the Belgians seceded and formed a separate kingdom.

The constitution, promulgated 1814, and subsequently revised, provides for a hereditary constitutional monarchy.

The Netherlands maintained its neutrality in World War I, but was invaded and brutally occupied by Germany, 1940-45.

In 1949, after several years of fighting, the Netherlands granted independence to Indonesia. In 1963, West New Guinea (now Irian Jaya) was turned over to Indonesia.

Immigration from former Dutch colonies has been substantial.

Although the Netherlands is heavily industrialized, its small farms export large quantities of pork and dairy foods. Rotterdam, located along the principal mouth of the Rhine, is one of the world's leading cargo ports. Canals, extendng over 3,400 miles, are important in transportation.

## Netherlands Dependencies

The **Netherlands Antilles,** constitutionally on a level of equality with the Netherlands homeland within the kingdom, consist of 2 groups of islands in the West Indies. **Curaçao** and **Bonaire** are near the coast of Venezuela; **St. Eustatius, Saba,** and the southern part of **St. Maarten** are SE of Puerto Rico. The northern two-thirds of St. Maarten belongs to French Guadeloupe; the French call the island St. Martin. Total area of the 2 groups is 309 sq. mi., including Bonaire 111, Curaçao 171, St. Eustatius 8, Saba 5, St. Maarten (Dutch part) 13. St. Maarten suffered extensive damage from Hurricane Luis, Sept. 1995. Total pop. of the Netherlands Antilles (1996 est.) was 209,000. Willemstad, on Curaçao, is the capital. The principal industry is the refining of crude oil from Venezuela. Tourism is also an important industry, as is shipbuilding.

**Aruba,** about 26 mi. W of Curaçao, was separated from the Netherlands Antilles on Jan. 1, 1986; it is an autonomous member of the Netherlands, the same status as the Netherland Antilles. Area 75 sq. mi.; pop. (1996 est.) 68,000; capital Oranjestad. Chief industries are oil refining and tourism.

# New Zealand

**People: Population:** 3,547,983. **Age distrib.** (%): <15: 23; 65+: 12 **Pop. density:** 34 per sq. mi. **Urban:** 85%. **Ethnic groups:** European (mostly British) 88%, Maori 9%. **Principal languages:** English (official), Maori. **Religions:** Anglican 24%, Presbyterian 18%, Roman Catholic 15%.

**Geography: Area:** 104,454 sq. mi. **Location:** In SW Pacific O. **Neighbors:** Nearest are Australia on W, Fiji and Tonga on N. **Topography:** Each of the 2 main islands (North and South Is.) is mainly hilly and mountainous. The east coasts consist of fertile plains, especially the broad Canterbury Plains on South I. A volcanic plateau is in center of North I. South I. has glaciers and 15 peaks over 10,000 ft. **Capital:** Wellington. **Cities** (1992 est.): Auckland 336,500; Christchurch 308,800; Manukau 243,400; Wellington 153,800.

**Government: Type:** Parliamentary democracy. **Head of state:** Queen Elizabeth II, represented by Gov.-Gen. Dame Catherine Tizard; b Apr. 4, 1931; in office: Nov. 20, 1990. **Head of government:** Prime Min. Jim Bolger; b May 31, 1935; in office: Oct. 27, 1990. **Local divisions:** 93 counties, 12 towns and districts. **Defense:** 1.5% of GNP (1993). **Active troop strength:** 10,050.

**Economy: Industries:** Food processing, textiles, machinery, fish, forest prods. **Chief crops:** Grains, potatoes, fruits. **Minerals:** Oil, gas, iron, coal. **Crude oil reserves** (1995): 137 mil bbls. **Other resources:** Wool, timber. **Arable land:** 2%. **Livestock** (1994): sheep: 50 mln.; cattle: 8.6 mil. **Fish catch** (1993): 581,000 metric tons. **Electricity prod.** (1993): 30.5 bil kWh. **Labor force:** 67% services, 23% ind.; 11% agric.

**Finance: Monetary unit:** Dollar (June 1996: 1.46 = $1 US). **Gross domestic product** (1994): $56 bln.* **Per capita GDP:** $16,640. **Imports** (1994): $10.4 bln.; partners: Australia 21%, U.S. 18%, Japan 16%. **Exports** (1994): $11.2 bln.; partners: Australia 20%, Japan 15%; U.S. 12%. **Tourism** (1993): $1.2 bil. **National budget** (FY 1994-95): $18.8 bil. **International reserves less gold** (Apr. 1996): $5.1 bil. **Consumer prices** (change in 1995): 3.8%.

**Transport: Railroads: Length:** 2,469 mi. **Motor vehicles:** in use: 1.6 mil passenger cars; 353,000 comm. vehicles. **Civil aviation:** 7.8 bil passenger-mi.; 36 airports. **Chief ports:** Auckland, Wellington, Dunedin, Tauranga.

**Communications: Television sets:** 1 per 3.2 persons. **Radios:** 1 per 1.1 persons. **Telephones:** 1 per 2.2 persons. **Daily newspaper circ.:** 304 per 1,000 pop.

**Health: Life expectancy at birth** (1996): 74 male; 80 female. **Births** (per 1,000 pop.): 16. **Deaths** (per 1,000 pop.): 8. **Natural increase:** 0.8%. **Hospital beds:** 1 per 114 persons. **Physicians:** 1 per 313 persons. **Infant mortality** (per 1,000 live births 1996): 7.

**Education: Literacy** (1994): 100%. Free and compulsory: ages 6-16. Attendance: 100%.

**Major International Organizations:** UN (WTO, World Bank, IMF), the Commonwealth, OECD.

**Embassy:** 37 Observatory Cir. NW 20008; 328-4800.

The Maoris, a Polynesian group from the eastern Pacific, reached New Zealand before and during the 14th century. The first European to sight New Zealand was Dutch navigator Abel Janszoon Tasman, but Maoris refused to allow him to land. British Capt. James Cook explored the coasts, 1769-1770.

British sovereignty was proclaimed in 1840, with organized settlement beginning in the same year. Representative institutions were granted in 1853. Maori Wars ended in 1870 with British victory. The colony became a dominion in 1907, and is an independent member of the Commonwealth.

A progressive tradition in politics dates back to the 19th century, when New Zealand was internationally known for social experimentation. Private ownership is basic to the economy, but state ownership or regulation affects many industries. In recent years, the Labor and National parties have had alternating periods in power. The National Party, led by Jim Bolger, won general elections in 1990 and 1993. Elections on Oct. 12, 1996, were indecisive; Bolger remained as caretaker, as parties negotiated to form a new government.

The native Maoris number about 340,000. Four of 99 members of the House of Representatives are elected directly by the Maori people.

New Zealand comprises **North Island,** 44,702 sq. mi.; **South Island,** 58,384 sq. mi.; **Stewart Island,** 674 sq. mi.; **Chatham Islands,** 372 sq. mi.; and several groups of smaller islands.

In 1965, the **Cook Islands** (pop., 1996 est., 20,000; area 93 sq. mi.), located halfway between New Zealand and Hawaii, became self-governing although New Zealand retains responsibility for defense and foreign affairs. **Niue** attained the same status in 1974; it lies 400 mi. to W (pop., 1995 est., 1,800; area 100 sq. mi.). **Tokelau** (pop., 1995 est., 1,500; area 4 sq. mi.) comprises 3 atolls 300 mi. N of Western Samoa.

**Ross Dependency,** administered by New Zealand since 1923, comprises 160,000 sq. mi. of Antarctic territory.

# Nicaragua

## Republic of Nicaragua

## República de Nicaragua

**People: Population:** 4,272,352. **Age distrib.** (%): <15: 44; 65+: 3. **Pop. density:** 84 per sq. mi. **Urban:** 63%. **Ethnic groups:** Mestizo 69%, white 17%, black 9%, Indian 5%. **Principal languages:** Spanish (official). **Religions:** Roman Catholic 95%.

**Geography: Area:** 50,838 sq. mi. **Location:** In Central America. **Neighbors:** Honduras on N, Costa Rica on S. **Topography:** Both Atlantic and Pacific coasts are over 200 mi. long. The Cordillera Mts., with many volcanic peaks, run NW-SE through the middle of the country. Between this and a volcanic range to the E lie Lakes Managua and Nicaragua. **Capital:** Managua (1995 met. est.): 1.2 mil.

**Government: Type:** Republic. **Head of state and government:** Pres. Violeta Barrios de Chamorro; b Oct. 18, 1929; in office Apr. 25, 1990. **Local divisions:** 16 departments. **Defense:** 1.7% of GDP (1994). **Active troop strength:** 12,000.

**Economy: Industries:** Oil refining, food processing, chemicals, textiles. **Chief crops:** Bananas, cotton, fruit, coffee, sugar, corn, rice. **Minerals:** Gold, silver, copper, tungsten. **Other resources:** Forests, seafood. **Arable land:** 9%. **Livestock** (1994): cattle: 1.7 mln.; pigs: 535,000. **Electricity prod.** (1993): 1.6 bil kWh. **Labor force:** 44% agric.; 43% services; 13% ind.

**Finance: Monetary unit:** Gold Cordoba (June 19946: 8.40 = $1 US). **Gross domestic product** (1994): $6.4 bln.* **Per capita GDP:** $1,570. **Imports** (1994): $786 mln.; partners: U.S. 20%, Venezuela 17%. **Exports** (1994): $329 mln.; partners: U.S. 42%, Germany 9%. **National budget** (1991): $410 mil. **International reserves less gold** (May 1996): $225 mil. **Consumer prices** (change in 1992): 20%.

**Transport: Motor vehicles:** in use: 31,000 passenger cars, 44,000 comm. vehicles. **Civil aviation:** 4 airports with scheduled flights. **Chief ports:** Corinto, Puerto Sandino, San Juan del Sur.

**Communications: Television sets:** 1 per 20 persons. **Radios:** 1 per 4.6 persons. **Telephones:** 1 per 64 persons. **Daily newspaper circ.:** 23 per 1,000 pop.

**Health: Life expectancy at birth** (1996): 63 male; 68 female. **Births** (per 1,000 pop.): 34. **Deaths** (per 1,000 pop.): 6. **Natural increase:** 2.8%. **Hospital beds:** 1 per 866 persons. **Physicians:** 1 per 1,258 persons. **Infant mortality** (per 1,000 live births 1996): 46.

**Education: Literacy** (1992): 66%. Free and compulsory: ages 7-13.

**Major International Organizations:** UN and most of its specialized agencies, OAS.

**Embassy:** 1627 New Hampshire Ave. NW 20009; 939-6570.

Nicaragua, inhabited by various Indian tribes, was conquered by Spain in 1552. After gaining independence from Spain, 1821, Nicaragua was united for a short period with Mexico, then with the United Provinces of Central America, finally becoming an independent republic, 1838.

U.S. Marines occupied the country at times in the early 20th century, the last time from 1926 to 1933.

Gen. Anastasio Somoza Debayle was elected president 1967. He resigned 1972, but was elected president again in 1974. Martial law was imposed in Dec. 1974, after officials were kidnapped by the Marxist Sandinista guerrillas. Violent opposition spread to nearly all classes in 1978; nationwide strikes called against the government touched off a state of civil war. Months of simmering civil war ended when Somoza fled, July 19, 1979; he was assassinated in Paraguay in 1980.

Relations with the U.S. were strained as a result of Nicaragua's aid to leftist guerrillas in El Salvador and U.S. backing of anti-Sandinista contra guerrilla groups.

In 1983 the contras launched a major offensive; the Sandinistas imposed rule by decree. In 1985 the U.S. House rejected Pres. Reagan's request for military aid to the contras. The subsequent diversion of funds to the contras from the proceeds of a secret arms sale to Iran caused a major scandal in the U.S.

In a stunning upset, Violeta Barrios de Chamorro defeated Sandinista leader Daniel Ortega Saavedra in national elections, Feb. 25, 1990. New presidential elections were held on Oct. 20, 1996.

# Niger

## Republic of Niger

## République du Niger

**People: Population:** 9,113,001. **Age distrib.** (%): <15: 49; 65+: 3. **Pop. density:** 18 per sq. mi. **Urban:** 15%. **Ethnic groups:** Hausa 56%, Djerma 22%, Fula 9%, Tuareg 8%. **Principal languages:** French (official), Hausa, Djerma. **Religion:** Sunni Muslim 80%.

**Geography: Area:** 496,900 sq. mi. **Location:** In the interior of N Africa. **Neighbors:** Libya, Algeria on N; Mali, Burkina Faso on W; Benin, Nigeria on S; Chad on E. **Topography:** Mostly arid desert and mountains. A narrow savanna in the S and the Niger R. basin in the SW contain most of the population. **Capital:** Niamey (1988 est.): 398,300.

**Government: Type:** Republic. **Head of state:** Pres. Mahamane Ousmane; in office: Apr. 16, 1993. **Head of government:** Pres. Ibrahim Bare Mainassara; in office: Jan. 27, 1996. **Local divisions:** 7 departments. **Defense:** 1.3% of GDP (FY 1992-93). **Active troop strength:** 5,300.

**Economy: Chief crops:** Peanuts, cowpeas, cotton. **Minerals:** Uranium, coal, iron. **Arable land:** 3%. **Livestock** (1994): goats: 5.9 mln.; sheep: 3.7 mln.; cattle: 2.0 mil. **Electricity prod.** (1992): 200 mil kWh. **Labor force:** 90% agric.

**Finance: Monetary unit:** CFA Franc (June 1996: 515 = $1 US). **Gross domestic product** (1994): $4.6 bln.* **Per capita GDP:** $550. **Imports** (1993): $286 mln.; partners: France 23%, Côte d'Ivoire. **Exports** (1993): $246 mln.; partners: France 77%, Nigeria 8%. **National budget** (1993): $400 mil. **International reserves less gold** (Dec. 1995): $94.7 mil. **Gold:** 11,000 oz t. **Consumer prices** (change in 1995): 10.6%.

**Transport: Motor vehicles:** in use: 31,000 passenger cars, 9,000 comm. vehicles. **Civil aviation:** 133 mil passenger-mi.; 1 airport with scheduled flights.

**Communications: Television sets:** 1 per 352 persons. **Radios:** 1 per 20 persons. **Telephones:** 1 per 830 persons.

**Health: Life expectancy at birth** (1996): 41 male; 40 female. **Births** (per 1,000 pop.): 54. **Deaths** (per 1,000 pop.): 25. **Natural increase:** 3.0%. **Physicians:** 1 per 54,444 persons. **Infant mortality** (per 1,000 live births 1996): 118.

**Education: Literacy** (1995): 14%. Free and compulsory: ages 7-15.

**Major International Organizations:** UN (IMF, WHO, FAO), OAU.

**Embassy:** 2204 R St. NW 20008; 483-4225.

Niger was part of ancient and medieval African empires. European explorers reached the area in the late 18th century. The French colony of Niger was established 1900-22, after the defeat of Tuareg fighters, who had invaded the area from the N a century before. The country became independent Aug. 3, 1960. The next year it signed a bilateral agreement with France.

In 1993, Niger held its first free and open elections since independence; an opposition leader, Mahamane Ousmane, won the presidency. A peace accord Apr. 24, 1995, ended a Tuareg rebellion that began in 1990. A coup, Jan. 27, 1996, followed by a disputed presidential election in July, left the military in control of Niger.

# Nigeria

## Federal Republic of Nigeria

**People: Population:** 103,912,489. **Age distrib.** (%): <15: 45; 65+: 3. **Pop. density:** 291 per sq. mi. **Urban:** 16%. **Ethnic groups:** Hausa 21%, Yoruba 21%, Ibo 18%, Fulani 11%, others. **Principal languages:** English (official), Hausa, Yoruba, Ibo. **Religions:** Muslim (in N) 50%, Christian (in S) 40%.

**Geography: Area:** 356,669 sq. mi. **Location:** On the S coast of W Africa. **Neighbors:** Benin on W, Niger on N, Chad and Cameroon on E. **Topography:** 4 E-W regions divide Nigeria: a coastal mangrove swamp 10-60 mi. wide, a tropical rain forest 50-100 mi. wide, a plateau of savanna and open woodland, and semidesert in the N. **Capital:** Abuja. **Cities:** (1995 est/): Lagos 1.5 mln.; Ibadan 1.4 mil.

**Government: Type:** In transition. **Head of state and government:** Pres. Gen. Sani Abacha; b 1943; in office: Nov. 17, 1993. **Local divisions:** 30 states, 1 federal capital territory. **Defense:** 1% of GDP (1992). **Active troop strength:** 77,100.

**Economy: Industries:** Crude oil (95% of exports), mining, food processing, textiles. **Chief crops:** Cocoa (main export crop), palm products, corn, rice, cotton, yams, cassava. **Minerals:** Oil, gas, coal, iron, limestone, columbite, tin. **Crude oil reserves** (1995): 17.9 bil bbls. **Other resources:** Timber, rubber, hides. **Arable land:** 31%. **Livestock** (1994): goats: 25.5 mln.; cattle: 16.7 mln.; sheep: 14.5 mil. **Fish catch** (1993): 255,000 metric tons. **Electricity prod.** (1993): 11.3 bil kWh. **Labor force:** 54% agric.; 19% ind., commerce, serv.; 15% govt.

**Finance: Monetary unit:** Naira (June 1996: 80.10 = $1 US). **Gross domestic product** (1994): $123 bln.* **Per capita GDP:** $1,250. **Imports** (1992): $8.3 bln.; partners: EU 64%, U.S. 10%. **Exports** (1992): $11.9 bln.; partners: U.S. 54%, EU 23%. **Tourism** (1993): $31 mil. **National budget** (1992 est.): $10.8 bil. **International reserves less gold** (Mar. 1996): $2.3 bil. **Gold:** 687,000 oz t. **Consumer prices** (change in 1995): 72.8%.

**Transport: Motor vehicles:** in use: 773,000 passenger cars, 606,000 comm. vehicles. **Civil aviation:** 619 mil passenger-mi.; 12 airports. **Chief ports:** Port Harcourt, Lagos, Warri, Calabar.

**Communications: Television sets:** 1 per 15 persons. **Radios:** 1 per 5.2 persons. **Telephones:** 1 per 267 persons. **Daily newspaper circ.:** 12 per 1,000 pop.

**Health: Life expectancy at birth** (1996): 53 male; 56 female. **Births** (per 1,000 pop.): 43. **Deaths** (per 1,000 pop.): 13. **Natural increase:** 3.0%. **Physicians:** 1 per 4,692 persons. **Infant mortality** (per 1,000 live births 1996): 72.

**Education: Literacy** (1992): 57%. Free and compulsory: ages 6-15.

**Major International Organizations:** UN (WTO, IMO, WHO), OPEC, OAU, the Commonwealth (suspended Nov. 1995).

**Embassy:** 1333 16th St. NW 20036; 822-1500.

Early cultures in Nigeria date back to at least 700 BC. From the 12th to the 14th centuries, more advanced cultures developed in the Yoruba area, at Ife, and in the north, where Muslim influence prevailed.

Portuguese and British slavers appeared from the 15th-16th centuries. Britain seized Lagos, 1861, and gradually extended control inland until 1900. Nigeria became independent Oct. 1, 1960, and a republic Oct. 1, 1963.

On May 30, 1967, the Eastern Region seceded, proclaiming itself the Republic of Biafra, plunging the country into civil war. Casualties in the war were estimated at over 1 million, including many "Biafrans" (mostly Ibos) who died of starvation despite international efforts to provide relief. The secessionists, after steadily losing ground, capitulated Jan. 12, 1970.

Oil revenues have made possible a massive economic development program, largely using private enterprise, but agriculture has lagged.

After 13 years of military rule, the nation experienced a peaceful return to civilian government, Oct. 1979. However, military rule resumed, Dec. 31, 1983, as a coup ousted the democratically elected government. A second coup came in 1985. The new regime, headed by Gen. Ibrahim Babangida, promised elections but voided the result of a presidential election on June 23, 1993; riots followed in which many were killed.

Babangida resigned and appointed a civilian to head an interim government, Aug, 26, 1993, but that government was ousted in a military coup, Nov. 17. On June 11, 1994, the presumed winner of the 1993 presidential election, Moshood Abiola, declared himself president; he was jailed June 23.

The execution, Nov. 10, 1995, of Ogoni playwright and environmentalist Ken Saro-Wiwa and 8 associates, accused in connection with the deaths of 4 political opponents, led to international sanctions against Nigeria, including suspension of its Commonwealth membership.

# Norway

## Kingdom of Norway

## Kongeriket Norge

**People: Population:** 4,383,807. **Age distrib.** (%): <15: 19; 65+: 16. **Pop. density:** 35 per sq. mi. **Urban:** 73%. **Ethnic groups:** Germanic (Nordic, Alpine, Baltic), minority Lapps. **Principal languages:** Norwegian (official). **Religions:** Evangelical Lutheran 88%.

**Geography: Area:** 125,050 sq. mi. **Location:** Occupies the W part of Scandinavian peninsula in NW Europe (extends farther north than any European land). **Neighbors:** Sweden, Finland, Russia on E. **Topography:** A highly indented coast is lined with tens of thousands of islands. Mountains and plateaus cover most of the country, which is only 25% forested. **Capital:** Oslo. **Cities** (1995 met. est.): Oslo 482,500; Bergen 221,600.

**Government: Type:** Hereditary constitutional monarchy. **Head of state:** King Harald V; b Feb. 21, 1937; in office: Jan. 17, 1991. **Head of government:** Prime Min. Gro Harlem Brundtland; b Apr. 20, 1939; in office: Nov. 3, 1990. **Local divisions:** 19 fylker (counties). **Defense:** 3.2% of GDP (1994). **Active troop strength:** 30,000.

**Economy: Industries:** Wood & paper prods., shipbuilding, metals, chemicals, food processing, fish, oil, gas. **Chief crops:** Grains, potatoes. **Minerals:** Oil, gas, copper, pyrites, nickel, iron, zinc, lead. **Crude oil reserves** (1995): 9.4 bil bbls. **Arable land:** 3%. **Livestock** (1994): sheep: 991,000; cattle: 980,000; pigs: 747,000. **Fish catch** (1994): 2.3 mil metric tons. **Electricity prod.** (1993): 118 bil kWh. **Labor force:** 71% services; 24% industry.

**Finance: Monetary unit:** Krone (June 1996: 6.50 = $1 US). **Gross domestic product** (1994): $95.7 bln.* **Per capita GDP:** $22,170. **Imports** (1994): $29.3 bln.; partners: EU 49%. **Exports** (1994): $36.6 bln.; partners: EU 66%. **Tourism** (1993): $1.8 bil. **National budget** (1994): $56 bil. **International reserves less gold** (May 1996): $24.7 bil. **Gold:** 1.18 mil oz t. **Consumer prices** (change in 1995): 2.5%.

**Transport: Railroads: Route length:** 2,502 mi. **Motor vehicles:** in use: 1.7 mil passenger cars, 404,000 comm. vehicles. **Civil aviation:** 5.0 bil passenger-mi.; 48 airports. **Chief ports:** Bergen, Stavanger, Oslo, Kristiansand.

**Communications: Television sets:** 1 per 2.2 persons. **Radios:** 1 per 1.3 persons. **Telephones:** 1 per 1.8 persons. **Daily newspaper circ.:** 659 per 1,000 pop.

**Health: Life expectancy at birth** (1996): 75 male; 81 female. **Births** (per 1,000 pop.): 12. **Deaths** (per 1,000 pop.): 11. **Natural increase:** 0.1%. **Hospital beds:** 1 per 183 persons. **Physicians:** 1 per 299 persons. **Infant mortality** (per 1,000 live births 1996): 5.

**Education: Literacy** (1994): 100%. Compulsory: ages 7-15.

**Major International Organizations:** UN and all of its specialized agencies, NATO, OECD, EFTA.

**Embassy:** 2720 34th St. NW 20008; 333-6000.

The first ruler of Norway was Harald the Fairhaired, who came to power in AD 872. Between 800 and 1000, Norway's Vikings raided and occupied widely dispersed parts of Europe.

The country was united with Denmark 1381-1814, and with Sweden, 1814-1905. In 1905, the country became independent with Prince Charles of Denmark as king.

Norway remained neutral during World War I. Germany attacked Norway Apr. 9, 1940, and held it until liberation May 8, 1945. The country abandoned its neutrality after the war, and joined NATO. In a referendum Nov. 28, 1994, Norwegian voters rejected European Union membership.

Abundant hydroelectric resources provided the base for industrialization, giving Norway one of the highest living standards in the world. The country is a leading producer and exporter of crude oil, with extensive reserves in the North Sea. Norway's merchant marine is one of the world's largest.

**Svalbard** is a group of mountainous islands in the Arctic O., area 23,957 sq. mi., pop. (1995 est.) 2,900. The largest, Spitsbergen (formerly called West Spitsbergen), 15,060 sq. mi., seat of the governor, is about 370 mi. N of Norway. By a treaty signed in Paris, 1920, major European powers recognized the sovereignty of Norway, which incorporated it in 1925.

**Jan Mayen,** area 144 sq. mi., is a volcanic island located about 565 mi. WNW of Norway; it was annexed in 1929.

# Oman

## Sultanate of Oman

## Saltanat 'Uman

**People: Population:** 2,186,548. **Pop. density:** 19 per sq. mi. **Urban:** 12%. **Ethnic groups:** Omani Arab 74%, Pakistani 21%. **Principal languages:** Arabic (official). **Religions:** Ibadhi Muslim 75%, other Muslim, Hindu.

**Geography: Area:** 118,150 sq. mi. **Location:** On SE coast of Arabian peninsula. **Neighbors:** United Arab Emirates, Saudi Arabia, Yemen on W. **Topography:** Oman has a narrow coastal plain up to 10 mi. wide, a range of barren mountains reaching 9,900 ft., and a wide, stony, mostly waterless plateau, avg. alt. 1,000 ft. Also, an exclave at the tip of the Musandam peninsula controls access to the Persian Gulf. **Capital:** Muscat (1993 cen.): 40,900.

**Government: Type:** Absolute monarchy. **Head of state and government:** Sultan Qabus bin Said; b Nov. 18, 1942; in office: July 23, 1970. **Defense:** 14% of GDP (1995 est.). **Active troop strength:** 43,500.

**Economy: Industries:** Oil, gas, construction. **Chief crops:** Dates, fruits, vegetables, wheat, bananas. **Minerals:** Oil (87% of exports). **Crude oil reserves** (1995): 4.8 bil bbls. **Fish catch** (1994): 119,000 metric tons. **Electricity prod.** (1993): 6 bil kWh. **Labor force:** 40% agric.

**Finance: Monetary unit:** Rial Omani (June 1996: 0.39 = $1 US). **Gross domestic product** (1994): $17 bln.* **Per capita GDP:** $10,020. **Imports** (1994): $4.1 bln.; partners: UAE 24%, Japan 21%, UK 12%. **Exports** (1994): $4.8 bln.; partners: UAE 33%, Japan 20%. **Tourism** (1992): $85 mil. **National budget** (1994): $5.2 bil. **International reserves less gold** (Feb. 1996): $1.1 bil. **Gold:** 291,000 oz t.

**Transport: Motor vehicles:** in use: 181,000 passenger cars, 109,000 comm. vehicles. **Civil aviation:** 1.5 bil passenger-mi.; 6 airports with scheduled flights. **Chief ports:** Raysuf, Muscat.

**Communications: Television sets:** 1 per 1.4 persons. **Radios:** 1 per 2.3 persons. **Telephones:** 1 per 12 persons.

**Health: Life expectancy at birth** (1996): 69 male; 73 female. **Births** (per 1,000 pop.): 38. **Deaths** (per 1,000 pop.): 4. **Natural increase:** 3.3%. **Hospital beds:** 1 per 426 persons. **Physicians:** 1 per 910 persons. **Infant mortality** (per 1,000 live births 1996): 27.

**Education: Literacy** (1993): 41%. **Attendance:** 85% primary, 61% secondary.

**Major International Organizations:** UN (World Bank, IMF), Arab League.

**Embassy:** 2535 Belmont Rd. NW 20008; 387-1980.

Oman was originally called Muscat and Oman. A long history of rule by other lands, including Portugal in the 16th century, ended with the ouster of the Persians in 1744. By the early 19th century, Muscat and Oman was one of the most important countries in the region, controlling much of the Persian and Pakistan coasts, and ruling far-away Zanzibar, which was separated in 1861 under British mediation.

British influence was confirmed in a 1951 treaty, and Britain helped suppress an uprising by traditionally rebellious interior tribes against control by Muscat in the 1950s.

On July 23, 1970, Sultan Said bin Taimur was overthrown by his son, who changed the nation's name to Sultanate of Oman.

Oil is the major source of income.

Oman opened its air bases to Western forces following the Iraqi invasion of Kuwait on Aug. 2, 1990.

# Pakistan

## Islamic Republic of Pakistan

## Islami Jamhuriyah e Pakistan

**People: Population:** 129,275,660. **Age distrib.** (%): <15: 41; 65+: 3. **Pop. density:** 381 per sq. mi. **Urban:** 28%. **Ethnic groups:** Punjabi, Sindhi, Pashtun (Pathan), Urdu (national), Balochi, others. **Principal languages:** Urdu (national), English, Punjabi, Sindhi, Pashtu, Balochi. **Religions:** Sunni Muslim 77%, Shi'a Muslim 20%.

**Geography: Area:** 339,697 sq. mi. **Location:** In W part of South Asia. **Neighbors:** Iran on W, Afghanistan and China on N, India on E. **Topography:** The Indus R. rises in the Hindu Kush and Himalaya Mts. in the N (highest is K2, or Godwin Austen, 28,250 ft., 2d highest in world), then flows over 1,000 mi. through fertile valley and empties into Arabian Sea. Thar Desert, Eastern Plains flank Indus Valley. **Capital:** Islamabad. **Cities** (1995 est.): Karachi 9.9 mln.; Lahore 5.1 mln.; Faisalabad 1.9 mln.; Peshawar 1.7 mil; Gujranwala 1.7 mil.

**Government: Type:** Parliamentary democracy in a federal setting. **Head of state:** Pres. Sardar Farooq Ahmad Khan Leghari; b May 2, 1940; in office: Nov. 14, 1993. **Head of government:** Prime Min. Benazir Bhutto; b June 21, 1953; in office: Oct. 19, 1993. **Local divisions:** 4 provinces, federal capital, tribal areas. **Defense:** 5.6% of GDP (FY 1994-95). **Active troop strength:** 587,000.

**Economy: Industries:** Textiles, food processing, chemicals, petroleum prods. **Chief crops:** Rice, wheat, cotton. **Minerals:** Natural gas, iron. **Crude oil reserves** (1995): 203 mil bbls. **Other resources:** Wool. **Arable land:** 23%. **Livestock** (1994): goats: 41.3 mln.; sheep: 29.0 mln.; cattle: 18.1 mil. **Fish catch** (1993): 622,000 metric tons. **Electricity prod.** (1993): 52 bil kWh. **Labor force:** 46% agric.; 18% mining & manuf.; 17% services.

**Finance: Monetary unit:** Rupee (June 1996: 35.13 = $1 US). **Gross domestic product** (1994): $249 bln.* **Per capita GDP:** $1,930. **Imports** (1993): $9.5 bln.; partners: Japan 12%, U.S. 11%, Malaysia 6%. **Exports** (1993): $6.7 bln.; partners: U.S. 14%, Japan 8%, Germany 8%. **Tourism** (1993): $111 mil. **National budget** (FY 1993-94): $11.2 bil. **International reserves less gold** (Apr. 1996): $1.5 bil. **Gold:** 2.1 mil oz t. **Consumer prices** (change in 1995): 12.3%.

**Transport: Railroads: Route length:** 5,453 mi. **Motor vehicles:** in use: 732,000 passenger cars, 252,000 comm. vehicles. **Civil aviation:** 6.2 bil passenger-mi.; 34 airports with scheduled flights. **Chief port:** Karachi.

**Communications: Television sets:** 1 per 66 persons. **Radios:** 1 per 13 persons. **Telephones:** 1 per 76 persons. **Daily newspaper circ.:** 16 per 1,000 pop.

**Health: Life expectancy at birth** (1996): 58 male; 59 female. **Births** (per 1,000 pop.): 36. **Deaths** (per 1,000 pop.): 11. **Natural increase:** 2.5%. **Hospital beds:** 1 per 1,702 persons. **Physicians:** 1 per 2,107 persons. **Infant mortality** (per 1,000 live births 1996): 97.

**Education: Literacy** (1994): 38%.

**Major International Organizations:** UN (WTO, ILO, IMF, WHO), the Commonwealth.

**Embassy:** 2315 Massachusetts Ave. NW 20008; 939-6200.

Present-day Pakistan shares the 5,000-year history of the India-Pakistan subcontinent. At present-day Harappa and Mohenjo Daro, the Indus Valley Civilization, with large cities and elaborate irrigation systems, flourished c. 4,000-2,500 BC.

Aryan invaders from the NW conquered the region around 1,500 BC, forging a Hindu civilization that dominated Pakistan as well as India for 2,000 years.

Beginning with the Persians in the 6th century BC, and continuing with Alexander the Great and with the Sassanians, successive nations to the west ruled or influenced Pakistan, eventually separating the area from the Indian cultural sphere.

The first Arab invasion, AD 712, introduced Islam. Under the Mogul empire (1526-1857), Muslims ruled most of India, yielding to British encroachment and resurgent Hindus.

After World War I the Muslims of British India began agitation for minority rights in elections. Muhammad Ali Jinnah (1876-1948) was the principal architect of Pakistan. A leader of the Muslim League from 1916, he worked for dominion status for India; from 1940 he advocated a separate Muslim state.

When the British withdrew Aug. 14, 1947, the Islamic majority areas of India acquired self-government as Pakistan, with dominion status in the Commonwealth. Pakistan was divided into 2 sections, West Pakistan and East Pakistan. The 2 areas were nearly 1,000 mi. apart on opposite sides of India. Pakistan became a republic in 1956.

In Oct. 1958, Gen. Mohammad Ayub Khan took power in a coup. He was elected president in 1960, reelected in 1965. He resigned Mar. 25, 1969, after several months of violent rioting and unrest, most of it in East Pakistan, which demanded autonomy. The government was turned over to Gen. Agha Mohammad Yahya Khan and martial law was declared.

The Awami League, which sought regional autonomy for East Pakistan, won a majority in Dec. 1970 elections to a constituent assembly. In March 1971 Yahya postponed the assembly. Rioting and strikes broke out in the East.

On Mar. 25, 1971, government troops launched attacks in the East. The Easterners, aided by India, proclaimed the independent nation of Bangladesh. In months of widespread fighting, countless thousands were killed. Some 10 million Easterners fled into India.

Full-scale war between India and Pakistan had spread to both the East and West fronts by Dec. 3. Pakistan troops in the East surrendered Dec. 16; Pakistan agreed to a cease-fire in the West Dec. 17. On July 3, 1972, Pakistan and India signed a pact agreeing to withdraw troops from their borders and seek peaceful solutions to all problems.

Zulfikar Ali Bhutto, leader of the Pakistan People's Party, which had won the most West Pakistan votes in the Dec. 1970 elections, became president Dec. 20.

Bhutto was overthrown in a military coup July 1977. Convicted of complicity in a 1974 political murder, he was executed Apr. 4, 1979. More than 3 million Afghan refugees flooded into Pakistan after the USSR invaded Afghanistan Dec. 1979; more than 1.4 million remained in the mid-1990s.

Pres. Mohammad Zia ul-Haq was killed when his plane exploded in Aug. 1988. Following Nov. elections, Benazir Bhutto, the daughter of Zulfikar Ali Bhutto, was named prime minister, becoming the first woman leader of a Muslim nation. She was accused of corruption and dismissed by the president, Aug. 1990; her party was soundly defeated in Oct. 1990 elections. She regained power after elections in Oct. 1993. Opposition to Bhutto centered around Karachi, which was crippled by violent strikes and ethnic clashes during 1995 and 1996. Bhutto's brother, Murtaza Bhutto, a leader in the opposition to Benazir, was killed by police on Sept. 20, 1996, when they tried to arrest him.

# Palau

## Republic of Palau

## Belu'u era Belau

**People: Population:** 16,952. **Pop. density:** 90 per sq. mi. **Urban:** 69%. **Ethnic groups:** Polynesian, Malayan, Melanesian. **Principal languages:** English, Palauan (both official); Sonsorolese, Angaur, Japanese, Tobian (all official within certain Palauan states). **Religions:** Roman Catholic, Protestant, Modeknegi.

**Geography: Area:** 188 sq. mi. **Location:** Archipelago (26 islands, more than 300 islets) in the W Pacific Ocean, about 530 mi SE of the Philippines. **Neighbors:** Micronesia to E, Indonesia to S. **Capital:** Koror (Note: a new capital is being built on the island of Babelthuap.) (1992) 10,500.

**Government: Type:** Republic. **Head of state:** Pres. Kuniwo Nakamura; in office: Nov. 4, 1992.

**Economy: Industries:** Tourism, fish. **Chief crops:** Coconuts, copra, cassava, sweet potatoes. **Fish catch** (1992): 4,000 metric tons.

**Finance: Monetary unit:** U.S. Dollar. **Gross domestic product** (1994): $81.8 mln.* **Per capita GDP:** $5,000.

**Communications: Television sets:** 1 per 10 persons. **Radios:** 1 per 1.8 persons.

**Health: Life expectancy at birth** (1996): 69 male; 73 female. **Births** (per 1,000 pop.): 22. **Deaths** (per 1,000 pop.): 7. **Natural increase:** 1.5%. **Infant mortality** (per 1,000 live births 1996): 25.

**Major International Organizations:** UN.

**Embassy:** 2000 L St. NW, Suite 407; 452-6814.

Spain acquired the Palau Islands in 1886 and sold them to Germany in 1899. Japan seized them in 1914. American forces occupied the islands in 1944; in 1947, they became part of the U.S.-administered UN Trust Territory of the Pacific Islands. In 1981 Palau became an autonomous republic; in 1993 the republic ratified a compact of free association with the U.S., which provides financial aid in return for U.S. use of Palauan military facilities over 15 years. Palau became an independent nation on Oct. 1, 1994.

# Panama

## Republic of Panama

## República de Panamá

**People: Population:** 2,655,094. **Age distrib.** (%): <15: 33; 65+: 5. **Pop. density:** 91 per sq. mi. **Urban:** 55%. **Ethnic groups:** Mestizo 70%, West Indian 14%, white 10%, Indian 6%. **Principal languages:** Spanish (official), English. **Religions:** Roman Catholic 85%, Protestant 15%.

**Geography: Area:** 29,157 sq. mi. **Location:** In Central America. **Neighbors:** Costa Rica on W, Colombia on E. **Topography:** 2 mountain ranges run the length of the isthmus. Tropical rain forests cover the Caribbean coast and eastern Panama. **Capital:** Panama City (1993 est.): 450,700.

**Government: Type:** Constitutional democracy. **Head of state and government:** Pres. Ernesto Pérez Balladares; b June 29, 1946; in office: Sept. 1, 1994. **Local divisions:** 9 provinces, 1 territory. **Defense:** 1.0% of GDP (1993 est.). **Active troop strength:** 11,800.

**Economy: Industries:** Oil refining, international banking, construction. **Chief crops:** Bananas, plantains, rice, corn, sugar. **Minerals:** Copper. **Other resources:** Forests (mahogany), shrimp. **Arable land:** 6%. **Livestock** (1994): cattle: 1.4 mln.; pigs: 295,000. **Electricity prod.** (1993): 2.8 bil kWh. **Labor force:** 32% govt. & community services; 27% agric. & fishing.

**Finance: Monetary unit:** Balboa (June 1996: 1.00 = $1 US). **Gross domestic product** (1994): $12.3 bln.* **Per capita GDP:** $4,670. **Imports** (1994): $2.2 bln.; partners: U.S. 40%. **Exports** (1994): $520 mln.; partners: U.S. 45%. **Tourism** (1992): $207 mil. **National budget** (1994): $1.9 bil. **International reserves less gold** (Apr. 1996): $966 mil. **Consumer prices** (change in 1995): 1.0%.

**Transport: Motor vehicles:** in use: 161,500 passenger cars, 83,000 comm. vehicles. **Civil aviation:** 209 mil passenger-mi.; 10 airports with scheduled flights. **Chief ports:** Balboa, Cristobal.

**Communications: Television sets:** 1 per 13 persons. **Radios:** 1 per 4.9 persons. **Telephones:** 1 per 9.7 persons. **Daily newspaper circ.:** 90 per 1,000 pop.

**Health: Life expectancy at birth** (1996): 71 male; 77 female. **Births** (per 1,000 pop.): 23. **Deaths** (per 1,000 pop.): 5. **Natural increase:** 1.8%. **Hospital beds:** 1 per 340 persons. **Physicians:** 1 per 800 persons. **Infant mortality** (per 1,000 live births 1996): 30.

**Education: Literacy** (1993): 91%. Free and compulsory for 6 years between ages 6 and 15. Primary school attendance: 91%.

**Major International Organizations:** UN (IMF, IMO, World Bank), OAS.

**Embassy:** 2862 McGill Terrace NW 20008; 483-1407.

The coast of Panama was sighted by Rodrigo de Bastidas, sailing with Columbus for Spain in 1501, and was visited by Columbus in 1502. Vasco Nunez de Balboa crossed the isthmus and "discovered" the Pacific O. Sept. 13, 1513. Spanish colonies were ravaged by Francis Drake, 1572-95, and Henry Morgan, 1668-71. Morgan destroyed the old city of Panama which had been founded in 1519. Freed from Spain, Panama joined Colombia in 1821.

Panama declared its independence from Colombia Nov. 3, 1903, with U.S. recognition. U.S. naval forces deterred action by Colombia. Panama granted use, occupation, and control of the Canal Zone to the U.S. by treaty, ratified Feb. 26, 1904. In 1978, a new treaty provided for a gradual takeover by Panama of the canal, and withdrawal of U.S. troops, to be completed by 1999. U.S. payments were substantially increased in the interim.

President Delvalle was ousted by the National Assembly, Feb. 26, 1988, after he tried to fire the head of the Panama Defense Forces, Gen. Manuel Antonio Noriega. Noriega had been indicted by 2 U.S. federal grand juries on drug charges. A general strike followed. Despite U.S.-imposed economic sanctions Noriega remained in power. Voters went to the polls to elect a new president May 7, 1989. Noriega claimed victory, but foreign observers said that the opposition had won overwhelmingly. The government voided the election May 10, charging foreign interference. There was an attempted coup against Noriega Oct. 3.

U.S. troops invaded Panama Dec. 20, 1989, following a series of incidents, including the killing of a U.S. Marine by Panamanian soldiers. The operation had as its chief objective the capture of Noriega. He took refuge in the Vatican diplomatic mission, but surrendered to U.S. officials Jan. 3, 1990. He was convicted on 8 counts of racketeering and drug trafficking in a U.S. District Court in Miami, Florida, Apr. 9, 1992.

# Papua New Guinea

## Independent State of Papua New Guinea

**People: Population:** 4,394,537. **Age distrib.** (%): <15: 42; 65+: 2. **Pop. density:** 25 per sq. mi. **Urban:** 15%. **Ethnic groups:** Papuan (in S and interior), Melanesian (N, E). **Principal languages:** English (official), Tok Pisin, Motu. **Religions:** Protestant 44%, Roman Catholic 22%, indigenous beliefs 34%.

**Geography: Area:** 178,704 sq. mi. **Location:** SE Asia, occupying E half of island of New Guinea and about 600 nearby islands. **Neighbors:** Indonesia (West Irian) on W, Australia on S. **Topography:** Thickly forested mts. cover much of the center of the country, with lowlands along the coasts. Included are some islands of Bismarck and Solomon groups, such as the Admiralty Is., New Ireland, New Britain, and Bougainville. **Capital:** Port Moresby. **Cities** (1991): Port Moresby 192,000; Lae 80,700.

**Government: Type:** Parliamentary democracy. **Head of state:** Queen Elizabeth II, represented by Gov. Gen. Wiwa Korowi; b July 7, 1948; in office: Oct. 4, 1991. **Head of government:** Prime Min. Julius Chan; b Aug. 29, 1939; in office: Aug. 30, 1994. **Local divisions:** 20 provinces. **Defense:** 1.8% of GDP (1993 est.). **Active troop strength:** 3,800.

**Economy: Chief crops:** Coffee, coconuts, cocoa. **Minerals:** Gold, copper, silver. **Crude oil reserves** (1995): 229 mil bbls. **Arable land:** 0%. **Livestock** (1994): pigs: 1.0 mil. **Electricity prod.** (1993): 1.8 bil kWh. **Labor force:** 64% agric.

**Finance: Monetary unit:** Kina (June 1996: 1.29 = $1 US). **Gross domestic product** (1994): $9.2 bln.* **Per capita GDP:** $2,200. **Imports** (1993): $1.2 bln.; partners: Australia 37%, Japan 15%; Singapore 14%. **Exports** (1993): $2.4 bln.; partners: Australia 41%; Japan 21%. **Tourism** (1993): $45 mil. **National budget** (1995 est.): $1.36 bil. **International reserves less gold** (Feb. 1996): $202 mil. **Gold:** 14,000 oz t. **Consumer prices** (change in 1994): 2.9%.

**Transport: Motor vehicles:** in use: 11,500 passenger cars, 31,000 comm. vehicles. **Chief ports:** Port Moresby, Lae.

**Communications: Television sets:** 1 per 421 persons. **Radios:** 1 per 16 persons. **Telephones:** 1 per 104 persons. **Daily newspaper circ.:** 16 per 1,000 pop.

**Health: Life expectancy at birth** (1996): 56 male; 58 female. **Births** (per 1,000 pop.): 33. **Deaths** (per 1,000 pop.): 10. **Natural increase:** 2.3%. **Hospital beds:** 1 per 234 persons. **Physicians:** 1 per 12,874 persons. **Infant mortality** (per 1,000 live births 1996): 60.

**Education: Literacy** (1992): 72%. **Attendance:** 73% primary school; 13% secondary school.

**Major International Organizations:** UN (WTO), the Commonwealth, APEC.

**Embassy:** 1615 New Hampshire Ave. NW 20009; 745-3680.

Human remains have been found in the interior of New Guinea dating back at least 10,000 years and possibly much earlier. Successive waves of peoples probably entered the country from Asia through Indonesia. Europeans visited in the 15th century, but land claims did not begin until the 19th century, when the Dutch took control of the island's western half.

The southern half of eastern New Guinea was first claimed by Britain in 1884, and transferred to Australia in 1905. The northern half was claimed by Germany in 1884, but captured in World War I by Australia, which was granted a League of Nations mandate and then a UN trusteeship over the area. The 2 territories were administered jointly after 1949, were given self-government Dec. 1, 1973, and became independent Sept. 16, 1975.

The indigenous population consists of a huge number of tribes, many living in almost complete isolation with mutually unintelligible languages. Secessionist rebels have clashed with government forces on Bougainville since 1988.

# Paraguay

## Republic of Paraguay

## República del Paraguay

**People: Population:** 5,504,146. **Age distrib.** (%): <15: 42; 65+: 4. **Pop. density:** 35 per sq. mi. **Urban:** 50%. **Ethnic groups:** Mestizo 95%, white & Amerindian 5%. **Principal languages:** Spanish (official), Guarani. **Religions:** Roman Catholic (official) 90%.

**Geography: Area:** 157,048 sq. mi. **Location:** Landlocked country in central South America. **Neighbors:** Bolivia on N, Argentina on S, Brazil on E. **Topography:** Paraguay R. bisects the country. To E are fertile plains, wooded slopes, grasslands. To W is the Gran Chaco plain, with marshes and scrub trees. Extreme W is arid. **Capital:** Asunción (1992 est.): 502,400.

**Government: Type:** Republic. **Head of state:** Pres. Juan Carlos Wasmosy; b Dec. 15, 1938; in office: Aug. 15, 1993. **Local divisions:** 19 departments. **Defense:** 1.6% of GDP (1994). **Active troop strength:** 20,300.

**Economy: Industries:** Food processing, textiles, cement. **Chief crops:** Corn, cotton, soybeans, sugarcane. **Minerals:** Iron, manganese, limestone. **Other resources:** Forests. **Arable land:** 20%. **Livestock** (1994): cattle: 8.0 mln.; pigs: 3.3 mil. **Electricity prod.** (1992): 26.5 bil kWh. **Labor force:** 45% agriculture.

**Finance: Monetary unit:** Guarani (June 1996: 2,050 = $1 US). **Gross domestic product** (1994): $15.4 bln.* **Per capita GDP:** $2,950. **Imports** (1993): $1.4 bln.; partners: Brazil 30%, EU 20%. **Exports** (1993): $728 mln.; partners: EU 37%, Brazil 25%. **Tourism** (1993): $204 mil. **National budget** (1992): $1.4 bil. **International reserves less gold** (May 1996): $966 mil. **Gold:** 35,000 oz t. **Consumer prices** (change in 1993): 15.2%.

**Transport: Motor vehicles:** in use: 117,000 passenger cars, 3,000 comm. vehicles. **Civil aviation:** 791 mil passenger-mi.; 3 airports with scheduled flights. **Chief port:** Asunción.

**Communications: Television sets:** 1 per 14 persons. **Radios:** 1 per 6.9 persons. **Telephones:** 1 per 33 persons. **Daily newspaper circ.:** 39 per 1,000 pop.

**Health: Life expectancy at birth** (1996): 72 male; 75 female. **Births** (per 1,000 pop.): 31. **Deaths** (per 1,000 pop.): 4. **Natural increase:** 2.7%. **Hospital beds:** 1 per 864 persons. **Physicians:** 1 per 1,406 persons. **Infant mortality** (per 1,000 live births 1996): 23.

**Education: Literacy** (1994): 92%. Compulsory: ages 7-13; attendance: 96%.

**Major International Organizations:** UN (IMF, WHO, WTO), OAS.

**Embassy:** 2400 Massachusetts Ave. NW 20008; 483-6961.

The Guarani Indians were settled farmers speaking a common language before the arrival of Europeans.

Visited by Sebastian Cabot in 1527 and settled as a Spanish possession in 1535, Paraguay gained its independence from Spain in 1811. It lost much of its territory to Brazil, Uruguay, and Argentina in the War of the Triple Alliance, 1865-1870. Large areas were won from Bolivia in the Chaco War, 1932-35.

Gen. Alfredo Stroessner, who had ruled since 1954, was ousted in a military coup led by Gen. Andrés Rodríguez on Feb. 3, 1989. Rodríguez was elected president May 1. Juan Carlos Wasmosy was elected president May 9, 1993, becoming the nation's first civilian head of state in many years. An army rebellion was averted in Apr. 1996.

# Peru

## Republic of Peru

## República del Perú

**People: Population:** 24,523,408. **Age distrib.** (%): <15: 36; 65+: 4. **Pop. density:** 49 per sq. mi. **Urban:** 70%. **Ethnic groups:** Indian 45%, mestizo 37%, white 15%, black, Asian. **Principal languages:** Spanish, Quechua (both official), Aymara. **Religions:** Mostly Roman Catholic, some Protestant.

**Geography: Area:** 496,225 sq. mi. **Location:** On the Pacific coast of South America. **Neighbors:** Ecuador, Colombia on N; Brazil, Bolivia on E; Chile on S. **Topography:** An arid coastal strip, 10 to 100 mi. wide, supports much of the population thanks to widespread irrigation. The Andes cover 27% of land area. The uplands are well-watered, as are the eastern slopes reaching the Amazon basin, which covers half the country with its forests and jungles. **Capital:** Lima. **Cities** (1993 est.): Lima (met.) 5.7 mln.; Arequipa 619,200; Callao 369,800;.

**Government: Type:** In transition. **Head of state:** Pres. Alberto Fujimori; b July 28, 1938; in office: July 28, 1990. **Head of government:** Prime Min. Alberto Pandolfi Arbulu; b Aug. 20, 1940; in office: Apr. 3, 1996. **Local divisions:** 24 departments, 1 constitutional province. **Defense:** 2.7% of GDP (1994). **Active troop strength:** 115,000.

**Economy: Industries:** Fishing, mining, food processing, textiles. **Chief crops:** Cotton, sugar, coffee, rice. **Minerals:** Copper, silver, gold, iron, oil. **Crude oil reserves** (1995): 800 mil bbls. **Other resources:** Wool, sardines. **Arable land:** 3%. **Livestock** (1994): sheep: 11.6 mln.; cattle: 4.0 mln.; pigs: 2.4 mil. **Fish catch** (1993): 8.5 mil metric tons. **Electricity prod.** (1993): 11.2 bil kWh. **Labor force:** 44% govt. and other services; 37% agric.; 19% ind.

**Finance: Monetary unit:** New Sol (june 1996: 2.45 = $1 US). **Gross domestic product** (1994): $73.6 bln.* **Per capita GDP:** $3,110. **Imports** (1994): $5.1 bln.; partners: U.S. 21%. **Exports** (1994): $4.1 bln.; partners: U.S. 19%, Japan 9%. **Tourism** (1992): $237 mil. **National budget** (1992 est.): $1.7 bil. **International reserves less gold** (Apr. 1996): $8.5 bil. **Gold:** 1.1 mil oz t. **Consumer prices** (change in 1995): 11.1%.

**Transport: Railroads: Route length:** 1,318 mi. **Motor vehicles:** in use: 419,000 passenger cars, 275,000 comm. vehicles. **Civil aviation:** 803 mil passenger-mi.; 25 airports. **Chief ports:** Callao, Chimbote, Salaverry.

**Communications: Television sets:** 1 per 11 persons. **Radios:** 1 per 4.4 persons. **Telephones:** 1 per 34 persons. **Daily newspaper circ.:** 71 per 1,000 pop.

**Health: Life expectancy at birth** (1996): 67 male; 71 female. **Births** (per 1,000 pop.): 24. **Deaths** (per 1,000 pop.): 6. **Natural increase:** 1.8%. **Hospital beds:** 1 per 509 persons. **Physicians:** 1 per 1,116 persons. **Infant mortality** (per 1,000 live births 1996): 52.

**Education: Literacy** (1993): 89%. Free and compulsory: ages 6-16.

**Major International Organizations:** UN and all of its specialized agencies, OAS.

**Embassy:** 1700 Massachusetts Ave. NW 20036; 833-9861.

The powerful Inca empire had its seat at Cuzco in the Andes and covered most of Peru, Bolivia, and Ecuador, as well as parts of Colombia, Chile, and Argentina. Building on the achievements of 800 years of Andean civilization, the Incas had a high level of skill in architecture, engineering, textiles, and social organization.

A civil war had weakened the empire when Francisco Pizarro, Spanish conquistador, began raiding Peru for its wealth, 1532. In 1533 he seized the ruling Inca, Atahualpa, filled a room with gold as a ransom, then executed him and enslaved the natives.

Lima was the seat of Spanish viceroys until the Argentine liberator, José de San Martin, captured it in 1821; Spanish forces were ultimately routed by Simón Bolívar, 1824.

On Oct. 3, 1968, a military coup ousted Pres. Fernando Belaunde Terry. In 1968-74, the military government started socialist programs. Food shortages, escalating foreign debt, and strikes led to another coup, Aug. 29, 1976.

After 12 years of military rule, Peru returned to democratic leadership in 1980 but was plagued by economic problems and terrorism by leftist Shining Path (Sendero Luminoso) guerrillas.

Pres. Alberto Fujimori, elected in June 1990, dissolved the National Congress, suspended parts of the constitution, and initiated press censorship, Apr. 5, 1992. The leader of Shining Path was captured Sept. 12.

With the economy booming and guerrilla activity curtailed, Fujimori won reelection Apr. 9, 1995. Peru's repressive antiterrorism tactics drew international criticism in 1996.

# Philippines

## Republic of the Philippines

## Republika ng Pilipinas

**People: Population:** 74,480,848. **Age distrib.** (%): <15: 38; 65+: 4. **Pop. density:** 643 per sq. mi. **Urban:** 49%. **Ethnic groups:** Malays 96%, Chinese 1.5%, Americans, Spanish. **Principal languages:** Pilipino (based on Tagalog), English (both official), Cebuano, Bicol, Ilocano, Pampango, many others. **Religions:** Roman Catholic 83%, Protestant 9%, Muslim 5%.

**Geography: Area:** 115,860 sq. mi. **Location:** An archipelago off the SE coast of Asia. **Neighbors:** Nearest are Malaysia and Indonesia on S, Taiwan on N. **Topography:** The country consists of some 7,100 islands stretching 1,100 mi. N-S. About 95% of area and population are on 11 largest islands, which are mountainous, except for the heavily indented coastlines and for the central plain on Luzon. **Capital:** Manila. **Cities** (1990 cen.): Quezon City 1.7 mln.; Manila 1.6 mln.; Davao 850,000.

**Government: Type:** Republic. **Head of state:** Pres. Fidel V. Ramos; b Mar. 18, 1928; in office: June 30, 1992. **Local divisions:** 15 regions, divided into 76 provinces. **Defense:** 1.4% of GNP (1992). **Active troop strength:** 106,500 est.

**Economy: Industries:** Food processing, textiles, chemicals, pharmaceuticals, wood prods., appliances. **Chief crops:** Sugar, rice, corn, pineapples, coconuts. **Minerals:** Cobalt, copper, gold, nickel, silver, oil. **Other resources:** Forests (40% of area). **Curde oil reserves** (1995): 239 mil bbls. **Arable land:** 26%. **Livestock** (1992): buffalo: 2.6 mln.; cattle: 1.7 mln.; pigs: 8.0 mil. **Fish catch** (1993): 2.3 mil metric tons. **Electricity prod.** (1993): 20 bil kWh. **Labor force:** 46% agric.; 19% services; 16% ind. and comm.

**Finance: Monetary unit:** Peso (June 1996: 26012 = $1 US). **Gross domestic product** (1994): $161 bln.* **Per capita GDP:** $2,310. **Imports** (1994): $21.3 bln.; partners: Japan 23%, U.S. 20%. **Exports** (1994): $13.4 bln.; partners: U.S. 39%, Japan 16%. **Tourism** (1993): $4.5 bil. **National budget** (FY 1994-95): $15.4 bil. **International reserves less gold** (Apr. 1996): $7.5 bil. **Gold:** 4.2 mil oz t. **Consumer prices** (change in 1995): 8.1%.

**Transport: Railroads: Route length:** 658 mi. **Motor vehicles:** in use: 1.1 mln. passenger cars, 1.0 mln. comm. vehicles. **Civil aviation:** 8.7 bil passenger-mi.; 21 airports with scheduled flights. **Chief ports:** Cebu, Manila, Iloilo, Davao.

**Communications: Television sets:** 1 per 9.8 persons. **Radios:** 1 per 8.2 persons. **Telephones:** 1 per 76 persons. **Daily newspaper circ.:** 49 per 1,000 pop.

**Health: Life expectancy at birth** (1996): 63 male; 69 female. **Births** (per 1,000 pop.): 30. **Deaths** (per 1,000 pop.): 7. **Natural increase:** 2.3%. **Hospital beds:** 1 per 780 persons. **Physicians:** 1 per 849 persons. **Infant mortality** (per 1,000 live births 1996): 36.

**Education: Literacy** (1994): 95%. Free and compulsory: ages 7-13. **Attendance:** 99% in primary, 59% secondary.

**Major International Organizations:** UN (World Bank, IMF, WTO), ASEAN.

**Embassy:** 1600 Massachusetts Ave. NW 20036; 467-9300.

The Malay peoples of the Philippine Islands, whose ancestors probably migrated from Southeast Asia, were mostly hunters, fishers, and unsettled cultivators when first visited by Europeans.

The archipelago was visited by Magellan, 1521. The Spanish founded Manila, 1571. The islands, named for King Philip II of Spain, were ceded by Spain to the U.S. for $20 million, 1898, following the Spanish-American War. U.S. troops suppressed a guerrilla uprising in a brutal 6-year war, 1899-1905.

Japan attacked the Philippines Dec. 8, 1941, and occupied the islands during WW II. On July 4, 1946, independence was proclaimed in accordance with an act passed by the U.S. Congress in 1934. A republic was established.

On Sept. 21, 1972, Pres. Ferdinand Marcos declared martial law. Marcos proclaimed a new constitution, Jan. 17, 1973, with himself as president. His wife, Imelda, received wide powers in 1978 to supervise planning and development. Political corruption was widespread.

Martial law was lifted Jan. 17, 1981, but Marcos retained broad emergency powers. He was reelected in June to a new 6-year term as president.

The assassination of prominent opposition leader Benigno S. Aquino Jr., Aug. 21, 1983, sparked demonstrations calling for the resignation of Marcos. A bitter presidential election campaign ended Feb. 7, 1986, as elections were held amid allegations of widespread fraud. On Feb. 16, Marcos was declared the victor over Corazon Aquino, widow of the slain opposition leader. On Feb. 24, Marcos declared a state of emergency as his military and religious support eroded. He ended his 20-year tenure as president Feb. 26 and fled the country. Aquino was recognized as president by the U.S. and other nations.

Aquino's government was plagued by a weak economy, widespread poverty, Communist and Muslim insurgencies, and lukewarm military support. Rebel troops seized military bases and TV stations and bombed the presidential palace, Dec. 1, 1989. Government forces defeated the attempted coup aided by air cover provided by U.S. F-4s. Aquino endorsed Fidel Ramos in the May 1992 presidential election, which he won.

The U.S. vacated the Subic Bay Naval Station at the end of 1992, ending its long military presence in the Philippines.

The government signed a cease-fire agreement, Jan. 30, 1994, with Muslim separatist guerrillas, but some rebels refused to abide by the accord. A new peace treaty establishing an autonomous Muslim region on southern Mindanao was signed Sept. 2, 1996, formally ending a rebellion that had claimed more than 120,000 lives since 1972.

# Poland

## Republic of Poland

## Rzeczpospolita Polska

**People: Population:** 38,642,565. **Age distrib.** (%): <15: 23; 65+: 11. **Pop. density:** 320 per sq. mi. **Urban:** 62%. **Ethnic groups:** Polish 98%, German, Ukrainian, Belarussian. **Principal language:** Polish (official). **Religion:** Roman Catholic 95%.

**Geography: Area:** 120,728 sq. mi. **Location:** On the Baltic Sea in E central Europe. **Neighbors:** Germany on W; Czech Rep., Slovakia on S; Lithuania, Belarus, Ukraine on E; Russia on N. **Topography:** Mostly lowlands forming part of the Northern European Plain. The Carpathian Mts. along the southern border rise to 8,200 ft. **Capital:** Warsaw. **Cities** (1993 est.): Warsaw 1.6 mln.; Lodz 833,700; Krakow 745,100.

**Government: Type:** Republic. **Head of state:** Pres. Aleksander Kwasniewski; b Nov. 15, 1954; in office: Dec. 23, 1995. **Head of government:** Prime Min. Wlodzimierz Cimoszewicz; b Sept. 13, 1950; in office: Feb. 1, 1996. **Local divisions:** 49 provinces. **Defense:** 2.5% of GNP (1993). **Active troop strength:** 278,600.

**Economy: Industries:** Shipbuilding, chemicals, metals, machinery, food processing. **Chief crops:** Grains, potatoes, sugar beets, rapeseed. **Minerals:** Coal, copper, silver, lead, sulphur, natural gas. **Arable land:** 46%. **Livestock** (1993): cattle: 8.2 mln.; pigs: 22.1 mil. **Fish catch** (1993): 423,000 metric tons. **Electricity prod.** (1993): 124 bil kWh. **Labor force:** 32% ind. & constr.; 28% agric.

**Finance: Monetary unit:** Zloty (June 1996: 2.72 = $1 US). **Gross domestic product** (1994): $191.1 bln.* **Per capita GDP:** $4,920. **Imports** (1994): $18.1 bln.; partners: Germany 36%, Italy 9%. **Exports** (1994): $16.3 bln.; partners: Germany 33%, Russia 10%. **Tourism** (1993): $4.5 bil. **National budget** (1994 est.): $30 bil. **International reserves less gold** (Feb.

1996): $16.8 bil. **Gold:** 473,000 oz t. **Consumer prices** (change in 1995): 26.8%.

**Transport: Railroads: Length:** 15,488 mi. **Motor vehicles:** in use: 6.8 mil passenger cars, 1.3 mil comm. vehicles. **Civil aviation:** 2.3 bil passenger-mi.; 12 airports. **Chief ports:** Gdansk, Gdynia, Szczecin.

**Communications: Television sets:** 1 per 3.8 persons. **Radios:** 1 per 3.5 persons. **Telephones:** 1 per 8.7 persons. **Daily newspaper circ.:** 158 per 1,000 pop.

**Health: Life expectancy at birth** (1996): 68 male; 76 female. **Births** (per 1,000 pop.): 12. **Deaths** (per 1,000 pop.): 10. **Natural increase:** 0.2%. **Hospital beds:** 1 per 179 persons. **Physicians:** 1 per 451 persons. **Infant mortality** (per 1,000 live births 1996): 12.

**Education: Literacy** (1994): 99%. Free and compulsory: ages 7-14; attendance 96%.

**Major International Organizations:** UN (WTO, WHO), OECD.

**Embassy:** 2640 16th St. NW 20009; 234-3800.

Slavic tribes in the area were converted to Latin Christianity in the 10th century. Poland was a great power from the 14th to the 17th centuries. In 3 partitions (1772, 1793, 1795) it was apportioned among Prussia, Russia, and Austria. Overrun by the Austro-German armies in World War I, it declared its independence on Nov. 11, 1918, and was recognized as independent by the Treaty of Versailles, June 28, 1919. Large territories to the east were taken in a war with Russia, 1921.

Germany and the USSR invaded Poland Sept. 1-27, 1939, and divided the country. During the war, some 6 million Polish citizens, half of them Jews, were killed by the Nazis. With Germany's defeat, a Polish government-in-exile in London was recognized by the U.S., but the USSR pressed the claims of a rival group. The election of 1947 was completely dominated by the Communists.

In compensation for 69,860 sq. mi. ceded to the USSR, 1945, Poland received approx. 40,000 sq. mi. of German territory E of the Oder-Neisse line comprising Silesia, Pomerania, West Prussia, and part of East Prussia.

In 12 years of rule by Stalinists, large estates were abolished, industries nationalized, schools secularized, and Roman Catholic prelates jailed. Farm production fell off. Harsh working conditions caused a riot in Poznan, June 28-29, 1956. A new Politburo, committed to a more independent Polish Communism, was named Oct. 1956, with Wladyslaw Gomulka as first secretary of the party. Collectivization of farms was ended. Gomulka agreed to permit religious liberty and religious publications, provided the church kept out of politics.

In Dec. 1970 workers in port cities rioted because of price rises and new incentive wage rules. On Dec. 20 Gomulka resigned as party leader; he was succeeded by Edward Gierek. The incentive rules were dropped; price rises were revoked.

After 2 months of labor turmoil had crippled the country, the Polish government, Aug. 30, 1980, met the demands of striking workers at the Lenin Shipyard, Gdansk. Among the 21 concessions granted were the right to form independent trade unions and the right to strike. By 1981, 9.5 mil workers had joined the independent trade union (Solidarity). Solidarity leaders proposed, Dec. 12, a nationwide referendum on establishing a non-Communist government if the government failed to agree to a series of demands.

Spurred by the fear of Soviet intervention, the government, Dec. 13, imposed martial law. Lech Walesa and other Solidarity leaders were arrested. The U.S. imposed economic sanctions, which were lifted when martial law was suspended Dec. 1982. On Apr. 5, 1989, an accord was reached between the government and opposition factions on a broad range of political and economic reforms including free elections. Candidates endorsed by Solidarity swept the parliamentary elections, June 4. Lech Walesa became president Dec. 22, 1990.

A radical economic program designed to transform the economy into a free-market system led to inflation and unemployment. In Sept. 1993 elections, former Communists and other leftists won a majority of seats in the lower house of Parliament. Walesa lost to a former Communist, Aleksander Kwasniewski, in a presidential runoff election, Nov. 19, 1995. Poland has sought to join the European Union and NATO.

# Portugal

## Portuguese Republic

## República Portuguesa

**People: Population:** 9,865,114. **Age distrib.** (%): <15: 18; 65+: 14. **Pop. density:** 277 per sq. mi. **Urban:** 48%. **Ethnic groups:** Homogeneous Mediterranean stock, small African minority. **Principal languages:** Portuguese (official). **Religions:** Roman Catholic 97%.

**Geography: Area:** 35,574 sq. mi., incl. the Azores and Madeira Islands. **Location:** At SW extreme of Europe. **Neighbors:** Spain on N, E. **Topography:** Portugal N of Tajus R., which bisects the country NE-SW, is mountainous, cool and rainy. To the S there are drier, rolling plains, and a warm climate. **Capital:** Lisbon. **Cities** (1993 met. est.): Lisbon 2 mln.; Porto 1.7 mil.

**Government: Type:** Parliamentary democracy. **Head of state:** Pres. Jorge Sampaio; b Sept. 18, 1939; in office: Mar. 9, 1996. **Head of government:** Prime Min. Antonio Guterres; b Apr. 30, 1949; in office: Oct. 30, 1995. **Local divisions:** 18 districts, 2 autonomous regions, one dependency. **Defense:** 2.9% of GDP (1994). **Active troop strength:** 54,200.

**Economy: Industries:** Textiles, footwear, cork, chemicals, fish canning, wine, paper. **Chief crops:** Grains, potatoes, rice, grapes, olives, fruits. **Minerals:** Tungsten, uranium, iron. **Other resources:** Forests (world leader in cork production). **Arable land:** 32%. **Livestock** (1994): sheep: 6.0 mln.; pigs: 1.5 mln.; cattle: 1.3 mil. **Fish catch** (1993): 274,000 metric tons. **Electricity prod.** (1993): 29.5 bil kWh. **Labor force:** 55% services; 24% manuf.; 11% agric., for., fish.

**Finance: Monetary unit:** Escudo (June 1996: 157 = $1 US). **Gross domestic product** (1994): $107 bln.* **Per capita GDP:** $10,190. **Imports** (1993): $24.3 bln.; partners: EU 72%. **Exports** (1993): $15.4 bln.; partners: EU 76%. **Tourism** (1993): $4.2 bil. **National budget** (1994): $41 bil. **International reserves less gold** (Apr. 1996): $15.6 bil. **Gold:** 16.1 mil oz t. **Consumer prices** (change in 1995): 4.1%.

**Transport: Railroads: Route length:** 2,179 mi. **Motor vehicles:** in use: 4.2 mil passenger cars, 220,000 comm. vehicles. **Civil aviation:** 4.7 bil passenger-mi.; 14 airports. **Chief ports:** Lisbon, Setubal, Leixoes.

**Communications: Television sets:** 1 per 5.9 persons. **Radios:** 1 per 4.5 persons. **Telephones:** 1 per 3.2 persons. **Daily newspaper circ.:** 47 per 1,000 pop.

**Health: Life expectancy at birth** (1996): 72 male; 79 female. **Births** (per 1,000 pop.): 11. **Deaths** (per 1,000 pop.): 10. **Natural increase:** 0%. **Hospital beds:** 1 per 381 persons. **Physicians:** 1 per 403 persons. **Infant mortality** (per 1,000 live births 1996): 8.

**Education: Literacy** (1993): 87%. Free and compulsory: ages 6-15. Attendance 99%.

**Major International Organizations:** UN (WTO, IMF, WHO), NATO, EU, OECD.

**Embassy:** 2125 Kalorama Rd. NW 20008; 328-8610.

Portugal, an independent state since the 12th century, was a kingdom until a revolution in 1910 drove out King Manoel II and a republic was proclaimed.

From 1932 a strong, repressive government was headed by Premier Antonio de Oliveira Salazar. Illness forced his retirement in Sept. 1968.

On Apr. 25, 1974, the government was seized by a military junta led by Gen. Antonio de Spinola, who became president.

The new government reached agreements providing independence for Guinea-Bissau, Mozambique, Cape Verde Islands, Angola, and São Tomé and Príncipe. Banks, insurance companies, and other industries were nationalized.

Parliament approved, June 1, 1989, a package of reforms that did away with the socialist economy and created a "democratic" economy, denationalizing industries.

**Azores Islands,** in the Atlantic, 740 mi. W of Portugal, have an area of 868 sq. mi. and a pop. (1993 est.) of 238,000. A 1951 agreement gave the U.S. rights to use defense facilities in the Azores. The **Madeira Islands,** 350 mi. off the NW coast of Africa, have an area of 306 sq. mi. and a pop. (1993 est.) of 254,000. Both groups were offered partial autonomy in 1976.

**Macau,** area of 6 sq. mi., is an enclave, a peninsula and 2 small islands, at the mouth of the Xi (Pearl) R. in China. Portugal granted broad autonomy in 1976. In 1987, Portugal and China agreed Macau would revert to China in 1999. Macau, like Hong Kong, was guaranteed 50 years of noninterference in its way of life and capitalist system. Pop. (1996 est.): 497,000.

# Qatar
## State of Qatar
## Dawlat Qatar

**People: Population:** 547,761. **Pop. density:** 124 per sq. mi. **Urban:** 91%. **Ethnic groups:** Arab 40%, Pakistani 18%, Indian 18%, Iranian 10%. **Principal languages:** Arabic (official), English. **Religions:** Muslim 95%.

**Geography: Area:** 4,412 sq. mi. **Location:** Middle East, occupying peninsula on W coast of Persian Gulf. **Neighbors:** Saudi Arabia on S. **Topography:** Mostly a flat desert, with some limestone ridges; vegetation of any kind is scarce. **Capital:** Doha (1992 est.): 313,600.

**Government: Type:** Traditional monarchy. **Head of state and head of government:** Emir and Prime Min. Hamad bin Khalifa ath-Thani; b 1950; in office: as emir, June 27, 1995; as prime min., July 11, 1995. **Defense:** 4.2% of GNP (1993). **Active troop strength:** 11,100 est.

**Economy: Industries:** Oil production and refining. **Crude oil reserves** (1995): 3.7 bil bbls. **Electricity prod.** (1993): 4.5 bil kWh. **Labor force:** 51% serv.; 25% manuf. & constr.; 2% agric.

**Finance: Monetary unit:** Riyal (June 1996: 3.64 = $1 US). **Gross domestic product** (1994): $10.7 bln.* **Per capita GDP:** $20,820. **Imports** (1993): $1.8 bln.; partners: Japan 16%, UK 11%, U.S. 11%. **Exports** (1993): $3.1 bln.; partners: Japan 57%. **National budget** (1992): $3.0 bil.

**Transport: Chief ports:** Doha, Umm Said.

**Communications: Television sets:** 1 per 2.3 persons. **Radios:** 1 per 3.2 persons. **Telephones:** 1 per 4.7 persons.

**Health: Life expectancy at birth** (1996): 71 male; 76 female. **Births** (per 1,000 pop.): 21. **Deaths** (per 1,000 pop.): 4. **Natural increase:** 1.7%. **Hospital beds:** 1 per 481 persons. **Physicians:** 1 per 671 persons. **Infant mortality** (per 1,000 live births 1996): 20.

**Education: Literacy** (1993): 79%. Attendance: 98%.

**Major International Organizations:** UN (FAO, IMF, World Bank, WTO), Arab League, OPEC.

**Embassy:** 600 New Hampshire Ave. NW 20037; 338-0111.

Qatar was under Bahrain's control until the Ottoman Turks took power, 1872 to 1915. In a treaty signed 1916, Qatar gave Great Britain responsibility for its defense and foreign relations. After Britain announced it would remove its military forces from the Persian Gulf area by the end of 1971, Qatar sought a federation with other British-protected states in the area; this failed and Qatar declared itself independent, Sept. 1, 1971. Crown Prince Hamad bin Khalifa ath-Thani ousted his father, Emir Khalifa bin Hamad ath-Thani, June 27, 1995.

Oil revenues give Qatar a per capita income among the highest in the world, but lack of skilled labor hampers development.

# Romania

**People: Population:** 21,657,162. **Age distrib.** (%): <15: 21; 65+: 12. **Pop. density:** 236 per sq. mi. **Urban:** 55%. **Ethnic groups:** Romanian 89%, Hungarian 9%. **Principal languages:** Romanian (official), Hungarian, German. **Religions:** Romanian Orthodox 70%, Roman Catholic 6%, Protestant 6%.

**Geography: Area:** 91,699 sq. mi. **Location:** SE Europe, on the Black Sea. **Neighbors:** Moldova on E, Ukraine on N, Hungary and Yugoslavia on W, Bulgaria on S. **Topography:** The Carpathian Mts. encase the north-central Transylvanian plateau. There are wide plains S and E of the mountains, through which flow the lower reaches of the rivers of the Danube system. **Capital:** Bucharest. **Cities** (1992 est.): Bucharest 2.1 mln.; Constanta 349,000; Iasi 337,700; Timisoara 325,400.

**Government: Type:** Republic. **Head of state:** Pres. Ion Iliescu; b Mar. 3, 1930; in office: Dec. 25, 1989. **Head of government:** Prime Min. Nicolae Vacaroiu; b Dec. 5, 1943; in office; Nov. 4, 1992. **Local divisions:** Bucharest and 40 counties. **Defense:** 3% of GDP (1994). **Active troop strength:** 217,400 est.

**Economy: Industries:** Mining, construction materials, metals, machinery, oil products, chemicals, food processing. **Chief crops:** Grains, sunflowers, sugar beets, potatoes. **Minerals:** Oil, gas, coal. **Crude oil reserves** (1995): 1.6 bil bbls. **Other resources:** Timber. **Arable land:** 43%. **Livestock** (1994): sheep: 11.5 mln.; pigs: 9.3 mln.; cattle: 3.6 mil. **Fish catch** (1993): 35,000 metric tons. **Electricity prod.** (1993): 51 bil kWh. **Labor force:** 38% ind.; 28% agric.

**Finance: Monetary unit:** Lei (June 1996: 3,029 = $1 US). **Gross domestic product** (1994): $64.7 bln.* **Per capita GDP:** $2,790. **Imports** (1994): $6.3 bln.; partners: EU 46%, Russia 11%. **Exports** (1994): $6 bln.; partners: EU 36%, Russia 5%. **Tourism** (1993): $197 mil. **National budget** (1995): $9.4 bil. **International reserves less gold** (Apr. 1996): $1.5 bil. **Gold:** $2.8 mil oz t. **Consumer prices** (change in 1995): 32.2%.

**Transport: Railroads: Length:** 7,051 mi. **Motor vehicles:** in use: 1.4 mil passenger cars; 332,000 comm. vehicles. **Civil aviation:** 1.2 bil passenger-mi.; 12 airports. **Chief ports:** Constanta, Galati, Braila.

**Communications: Television sets:** 1 per 5.7 persons. **Radios:** 1 per 5.1 persons. **Telephones:** 1 per 8.7 persons.

**Health: Life expectancy at birth** (1996): 66 male; 74 female. **Births** (per 1,000 pop.): 10. **Deaths** (per 1,000 pop.): 12. **Natural increase:** –0.2%. **Hospital beds:** 1 per 105 persons. **Physicians:** 1 per 531 persons. **Infant mortality** (per 1,000 live births 1996): 23.

**Education: Literacy** (1992): 97%. Compulsory: ages 6-16; attendance 77%.

**Major International Organizations:** UN (World Bank, IMF, WTO).

**Embassy:** 1607 23d St. NW 20008; 232-4747.

Romania's earliest known people merged with invading Proto-Thracians, preceding by centuries the Dacians. The Dacian kingdom was occupied by Rome, AD 106-271; people and language were Romanized. The principalities of Wallachia and Moldavia, dominated by Turkey, were united in 1859, became Romania in 1861. In 1877 Romania proclaimed independence from Turkey, and became an independent state by the Treaty of Berlin, 1878; a kingdom under Carol I, 1881; and a constitutional monarchy with a bicameral legislature, 1886.

Romania helped Russia in its war with Turkey, 1877-78. After World War I it acquired Bessarabia, Bukovina, Transylvania, and Banat. In 1940 it ceded Bessarabia and Northern Bukovina to the USSR, part of southern Dobrudja to Bulgaria, and northern Transylvania to Hungary.

In 1941, Prem. Marshal Ion Antonescu led Romania in support of Germany against the USSR. In 1944 he was overthrown by King Michael and Romania joined the Allies.

After occupation by Soviet troops a People's Republic was proclaimed, Dec. 30, 1947; Michael was forced to abdicate.

On Aug. 22, 1965, a new constitution proclaimed Romania a Socialist Republic. President Nicolae Ceausescu maintained an independent course in foreign affairs, but his domestic policies were repressive. All industry was state-owned, and state farms and cooperatives owned almost all the arable land.

On Dec. 16, 1989, security forces opened fire on antigovernment demonstrators in Timisoara; hundreds were buried in mass graves. Ceausescu declared a state of emergency as protests spread to other cities. On Dec. 21, in Bucharest, security forces fired on protesters. Army units joined the rebellion, Dec. 22, and a group known as the Council of National Salvation announced that it had overthrown the government. Fierce fighting took place between the army, which backed the new government, and forces loyal to Ceausescu.

Ceausescu and his wife were captured and, following a trial in which they were found guilty of genocide, were executed Dec. 25, 1989. Former Communists dominated the government in succeeding years. A new constitution providing for a multiparty system took effect Dec. 8, 1991. Many of Romania's state-owned companies were privatized in 1996.

# Russia
## Russian Federation
## Rossiyskaya Federatsiya

*(Figures prior to 1992 are for the former USSR)*

**People: Population:** 148,178,487. **Age distrib.** (%): <15: 21; 65+: 12. **Pop. density:** 23 per sq. mi. **Urban:** 73%. **Ethnic groups:** Russians 82%, Tatar 4%. **Principal languages:** Russian (official), Ukrainian, Belarussian, Uzbek, Armenian, Azerbaijani, Georgian, many others. **Religions:** Russian Orthodox, Muslim, others.

**Geography: Area:** 6,592,800 sq. mi., more than 76% of the total area of the former USSR and the largest country in the world. **Location:** Stretches from E Europe across N Asia to the Pacific O. **Neighbors:** Finland, Norway, Estonia, Latvia, Belarus, Ukraine on W; Georgia, Azerbaijan, Kazakstan, China, Mongolia, North Korea on S; Kaliningrad exclave bordered by Poland on the S, Lithuania on the N and E. **Topography:** Russia contains every type of climate except the distinctly tropical, and has a varied topography. The European portion is a low plain, grassy in S, wooded in N, with Ural Mts. on the E, and Caucasus Mts. on the S. Urals stretch N-S for 2,500 mi. The Asiatic portion is also a vast plain, with mountains on the S and in the E; tundra covers extreme N, with forest belt below; plains, marshes are in W, desert in SW. **Capital:** Moscow. **Cities** (1994 est.): Moscow 8.8 mln.; St. Petersburg 4.9 mln.; Nizhny Novgorod 1.4 mln.; Novosibirsk 1.4 mil.

**Government: Type:** Federation. **Head of state:** Pres. Boris Yeltsin; b Feb. 1, 1931; in office: July 10, 1991. **Head of government:** Prime Min. Viktor Chernomyrdin; b Apr. 9, 1938; in office: Dec. 14, 1992. **Local divisions:** 21 autonomous republics, 49 oblasts, 6 krays. **Defense:** 21.5% of GNP (1993). **Active troop strength:** 1.52 mil est.

**Economy: Industries:** Steel, machinery, machine tools, vehicles, chemicals, mining, cement, textiles, appliances, paper. **Chief crops:** Grains, sugar beets, potatoes, vegetables, sunflowers. **Minerals:** Manganese, mercury, potash, bauxite, cobalt, chromium, copper, coal, gold, lead, molybdenum, nickel, phosphates, silver, tin, tungsten, zinc, oil, gas, iron, potassium. **Crude oil reserves** (1995): 157 bil bbls. (former USSR) **Other resources:** Forests. **Arable land:** 8%. **Livestock** (1994): cattle: 48.9 mln.; sheep: 43.7 mln.; pigs: 28.6 mln. **Fish catch** (1994): 3.5 mil metric tons. **Electricity prod.** (1994): 876 bil kWh. **Labor force:** 84% production & serv.; 16% govt.

**Finance: Monetary unit:** Ruble (June 1996: 5,050 = $1 US). **Gross domestic product** (1994 est.): $721.2 bln.* **Per capita GDP:** $4,820. **Imports** (1994): $36 bln.; partners: Germany 20%, U.S. 7%. **Exports** (1994): $48 bln.; partners: Germany 11%, UK 7%. **National budget** (1989): $310 bln. **International reserves less gold** (Apr. 1996): $14.3 bil. **Gold:** 9.8 mil oz t. **Consumer prices** (change in 1995): 197.4%.

**Transport: Railroads: Length:** 94,400 mi. **Motor vehicles:** in use: 10.5 mil passenger cars, 407,000 comm. vehicles. **Civil aviation:** 45 bil passenger-mi.; 58 airports. **Chief ports:** St. Petersburg, Murmansk, Tver, Arkhangelsk.

**Communications: Television sets:** 1 per 2.7 persons. **Radios:** 1 per 1.6 persons. **Telephones:** 1 per 6.3 persons. **Daily newspaper circ.:** 386 per 1,000 pop.

**Health: Life expectancy at birth** (1996): 57 male; 70 female. **Births** (per 1,000 pop.): 10. **Deaths** (per 1,000 pop.): 16. **Natural increase:** –0.6%. **Hospital beds:** 1 per 78 persons. **Physicians:** 1 per 220 persons. **Infant mortality** (per 1,000 live births 1996): 25.

**Education: Literacy** (1993): 98%. Free and compulsory: ages 7-17.

**Major International Organizations:** UN (ILO, IMF, WHO), CIS.

**Embassy:** 2650 Wisconsin Ave. NW 20007; 298-5700.

**History.** Slavic tribes began migrating into Russia from the W in the 5th century AD. The first Russian state, founded by Scandinavian chieftains, was established in the 9th century, centering in Novgorod and Kiev. In the 13th century the Mongols overran the country. It recovered under the grand dukes and princes of Muscovy, or Moscow, and by 1480 freed itself from the Mongols. Ivan the Terrible was the first to be formally proclaimed Tsar (1547). Peter the Great (1682-1725) extended the domain and, in 1721, founded the Russian Empire.

Western ideas and the beginnings of modernization spread through the huge Russian empire in the 19th and early 20th centuries. But political evolution failed to keep pace.

Military reverses in the 1905 war with Japan and in World War I led to the breakdown of the Tsarist regime. The 1917 Revolution began in March with a series of sporadic strikes for higher wages by factory workers. A provisional democratic government under Prince Georgi Lvov was established but was quickly followed in May by the second provisional government, led by Alexander Kerensky. The Kerensky government and the freely-elected Constituent Assembly were overthrown in a Communist coup led by Vladimir Ilyich Lenin Nov. 7.

## Soviet Union

Lenin's death Jan. 21, 1924, resulted in an internal power struggle from which Joseph Stalin eventually emerged on top. Stalin secured his position at first by exiling opponents, but from the 1930s to 1953, he resorted to a series of "purge" trials, mass executions, and mass exiles to work camps. These measures resulted in millions of deaths, according to most estimates.

Germany and the Soviet Union signed a non-aggression pact Aug. 1939; Germany launched a massive invasion of the Soviet Union, June 1941. Notable heroic episode was the "900 days" siege of Leningrad (now St. Petersburg), lasting to Jan. 1944, and causing a million deaths; the city was never taken. Russian winter counterthrusts, 1941-42 and 1942-43, stopped the German advance. Turning point was the failure of German troops to take and hold Stalingrad (now Volgograd), Sept. 1942 to Feb. 1943. With British and U.S. Lend-Lease aid and sustaining great casualties, the Russians drove the German forces from eastern Europe and the Balkans in the next 2 years.

After Stalin died, Mar. 5, 1953, Nikita Khrushchev was elected first secretary of the Central Committee. In 1956 he condemned Stalin. "De-Stalinization" of the country was begun.

Under Khrushchev the open antagonism of Poles and Hungarians toward domination by Moscow was brutally suppressed in 1956. He advocated peaceful co-existence with the capitalist countries, but continued arming the Soviet Union with nuclear weapons. He aided the Cuban revolution under Fidel Castro but withdrew Soviet missiles from Cuba during confrontation by U.S. Pres. Kennedy, Sept.-Oct. 1962. Khrushchev was suddenly deposed, Oct. 1964, and replaced by Leonid I. Brezhnev.

In Aug. 1968 Russian, Polish, East German, Hungarian, and Bulgarian military forces invaded Czechoslovakia to put a curb on liberalization policies of the Czech government.

Massive Soviet military aid to North Vietnam in the late 1960s and early 1970s helped assure Communist victories throughout Indo-China. Soviet arms aid and advisers were sent to several African countries in the 1970s.

In Dec. 1979, Soviet forces entered Afghanistan to support that government against rebels. In Apr. 1988, the Soviets agreed to withdraw their troops, ending a futile 8-year war.

Mikhail Gorbachev was chosen gen. secy. of the Communist Party, Mar. 1985. He held 4 summit meetings with U.S. Pres. Ronald Reagan. In 1987, in Washington, a treaty was signed eliminating intermediate-range nuclear missiles from Europe.

In 1987, Gorbachev initiated a program of reforms, including expanded freedoms and the democratization of the political process, through openness (*glasnost*) and restructuring (*perestroika*). The reforms were opposed by some Eastern bloc countries and many old-line Communists in the USSR. Gorbachev faced economic problems as well as ethnic and nationalist unrest in the republics.

When an apparent coup against Gorbachev became known on Aug. 19, 1991, the pres. of the Russian Republic, Boris Yeltsin, denounced it and called for a general strike. Some 50,000 demonstrated at the Russian Parliament in support of Yeltsin. By Aug. 21, the coup had failed and Gorbachev was restored as president. On Aug. 24, Gorbachev resigned as leader of the Communist Party. Several republics declared their independence, including Russia, Ukraine, and Kazakstan. On Aug. 29, the Soviet Parliament voted to suspend all activities of the Communist Party.

The Soviet Union officially broke up Dec. 26, 1991, one day after Gorbachev resigned. The Soviet hammer and sickle flying over the Kremlin was lowered and replaced by the flag of Russia, ending the domination of the Communist Party over all areas of national life since 1917.

## Russian Federation

In a first major step in radical economic reform, Russia eliminated state subsidies of most goods and services, Jan. 1992. The effect was to allow prices to soar far beyond the means of ordinary workers. In June, Pres. Yeltsin and U.S. Pres. George Bush agreed to massive arms reductions.

Russia launched a drive to privatize thousands of large and medium-sized state-owned enterprises in 1993. Yeltsin narrowly survived an impeachment vote by the Congress of People's Deputies, Mar. 28. He received strong support from voters in a referendum Apr. 25, but he continued to face a legislature dominated by conservatives and former Communists.

On Sept. 21, 1993, Yeltsin called early elections and dissolved Parliament, which in turn declared him deposed. Anti-Yeltsin legislators then barricaded themselves in the Parliament building. On Oct. 3, anti-Yeltsin forces attacked some facilities in Moscow and broke into the Parliament building. Yeltsin ordered the army to attack and seize the building. About 140 people were killed in the fighting, according to medical authorities. More than 150 were arrested.

In elections Dec. 12, 1993, a Yeltsin-supported constitution was approved, but ultranationalists and Communist hard-liners made strong showings in legislative contests. In Dec. 1994 the

Russian government sent troops into the breakaway republic of Chechnya. Grozny, the Chechen capital, fell in Feb. 1995 after heavy fighting, but Chechen rebels continued to resist.

Communists made further gains in parliamentary elections Dec. 17, 1995. Despite poor health, Yeltsin won a presidential runoff election over a Communist opponent, July 3, 1996. On Aug. 14, after rebels embarrassed the Russian military by retaking Grozny, Yeltsin gave his security chief, Alexander Lebed, broad powers to negotiate an end to the Chechnya war. Lebed and Chechen leaders signed a peace accord Aug. 31. On Sept. 5, Yeltsin announced that he needed to undergo heart surgery. On Oct. 17, Yeltsin dismissed Lebed from his post.

# Rwanda

## Republic of Rwanda

## Republika y'u Rwanda

**People: Population:** 6,853,359. **Age distrib.** (%): <15: 48; 65+: 3. **Pop. density:** 674 per sq. mi. **Urban:** 5%. **Ethnic groups:** Hutu 90%, Tutsi 9%, Twa (Pygmy) 1%. **Principal languages:** French, Kinyarwanda (both official). **Religions:** Christian 74%, indigenous beliefs 25%, Muslim 1%.

**Geography: Area:** 10,169 sq. mi. **Location:** In E central Africa. **Neighbors:** Uganda on N, Zaire on W, Burundi on S, Tanzania on E. **Topography:** Grassy uplands and hills cover most of the country, with a chain of volcanoes in the NW. The source of the Nile R. has been located in the headwaters of the Kagera (Akagera) R., SW of Kigali. **Capital:** Kigali (1993): 234,500.

**Government: Type:** In transition. **Head of state:** Pres. Pasteur Bizimungu; in office: July 19, 1994. **Head of government:** Prime Min. Pierre Claver Rwigema; in office: Aug. 31, 1995. **Local divisions:** 10 prefectures. **Defense:** 7% of GDP (1992). **Active troop strength:** 40,000 est.

**Economy: Industries:** Mining, cement. **Chief crops:** Coffee, tea, bananas. **Minerals:** Tin, gold, wolframite. **Arable land:** 29%. **Electricity prod.** (1993): 190 mil kWh. **Labor force:** 93% agric.

**Finance: Monetary unit:** Franc (June 1996: 220 = $1 US). **Gross domestic product** (1993 est.): $7.9 bln.* **Per capita GDP:** $950. **Imports** (1993): $250 mln.; partners: Belg.-Lux. 17%, Kenya 13%, France 7%. **Exports** (1993): $44 mln.; partners: Germany 21%, Netherlands 19%. **National budget** (1992 est.): $453.7 mil. **International reserves less gold** (May 1996): $122 mil. **Consumer prices** (change in 1993): 12.4%.

**Transport: Motor vehicles:** in use: 8,000 passenger cars, 2,000 comm. vehicles. **Chief ports:** Gisenyi, Cyangugu.

**Communications: Radios:** 1 per 12 persons. **Telephones:** 1 per 634 persons.

**Health: Life expectancy at birth** (1996): 40 male; 41 female. **Births** (per 1,000 pop.): 39. **Deaths** (per 1,000 pop.): 20. **Natural increase:** 1.9%. **Physicians:** 1 per 24,697 persons. **Infant mortality** (per 1,000 live births 1996): 119.

**Education: Literacy** (1992): 61%. Compulsory: ages 7-14; attendance: 71%.

**Major International Organizations:** UN (IMF, WHO, WTO), OAU.

**Embassy:** 1714 New Hampshire Ave. NW 20009; 232-2882.

For centuries, the Tutsi (an extremely tall people) dominated the Hutu (90% of the population). A civil war broke out in 1959 and Tutsi power was ended. Many Tutsi went into exile. A referendum in 1961 abolished the monarchic system. Rwanda, which had been part of the Belgian UN trusteeship of Rwanda-Urundi, became independent July 1, 1962.

In 1963 Tutsi exiles invaded in an unsuccessful coup; a large-scale massacre of Tutsi followed. Rivalries among Hutu led to a bloodless coup July 1973 in which Juvénal Habyarimana took power. After an invasion and coup attempt by Tutsi exiles in 1990, a multiparty democracy was established.

Renewed ethnic strife led to an Aug. 1993 peace accord between the government and rebels of the Tutsi-led Rwandan Patriotic Front (RPF). But after Habyarimana and the president of Burundi were killed Apr. 6, 1994, in a suspicious plane crash, massive violence broke out. At least 500,000 died in massacres, mainly of Tutsi by Hutu militias, and in civil warfare as the RPF sought power. An estimated 2 million Tutsi and Hutu fled to camps in Zaire and other countries, where many died of cholera and other natural causes. French troops under a UN mandate moved into SW Rwanda June 23 to establish a so-called safe zone. The RPF claimed victory, installing a government in July led by a moderate Hutu president. French troops pulled out Aug. 22. A UN peacekeeping mission ended Mar. 8, 1996, but a UN-sponsored tribunal and the Rwandan government continued to gather evidence against those responsible for genocide.

# Saint Kitts and Nevis

## Federation of Saint Kitts and Nevis

**People: Population:** 41,369. **Pop. density:** 398 per sq. mi. **Urban:** 42%. **Ethnic groups:** Black African 95%. **Principal languages:** English (official). **Religions:** Protestant 76%, Roman Catholic 11%.

**Geography: Area:** 104 sq. mi. **Location:** In the N part of the Leeward group of the Lesser Antilles in the E Caribbean Sea. **Neighbors:** Antigua and Barbuda to E. **Capital:** Basseterre (1994 est.): 12,600.

**Government:** Constitutional monarchy. **Head of state:** Queen Elizabeth II, represented by Gov. Gen. Sir Cuthbert M. Sebastian; b Oct. 22, 1921; in office: Jan. 1, 1996. **Head of government:** Prime Min. Denzil Llewellyn Douglas; b Jan. 14, 1953; in office: July 3, 1995. **Local divisions:** 14 parishes.

**Economy: Industries:** Sugar (main industry), tourism.

**Finance: Monetary unit:** East Caribbean Dollar (June 1996: 2.70 = $1 US). **Gross domestic product** (1994): $210 mln.* **Per capita GDP:** $5,300. **Tourism** (1993): $69 mil receipts.

**Chief ports:** Basseterre, Charlestown.

**Communications: Television sets:** 1 per 4.2 persons. **Telephones:** 1 per 4.6 persons.

**Health** (1996): **Births** (per 1,000 pop.): 23. **Deaths** (per 1,000 pop.): 9. **Natural increase:** 1.4%. **Infant mortality** (per 1,000 live births): 19.

**Education: Literacy** (1992): 90%.

**Major International Organizations:** UN (WTO), the Commonwealth, OAS.

**Embassy:** 3216 New Mexico Ave., NW 20016; 686-2636.

St. Kitts (formerly St. Christopher; known by the natives as Liamuiga) and Nevis were reached (and named) by Columbus in 1493. They were settled by Britain in 1623, but ownership was disputed with France until 1713. They were part of the Leeward Islands Federation, 1871-1956, and the Federation of the West Indies, 1958-62. The colony achieved self-government as an Associated State of the UK in 1967, and became fully independent Sept. 19, 1983.

# Saint Lucia

**People: Population:** 157,862. **Age distrib.** (%): <15: 37; 65+: 7. **Urban:** 48%. **Pop. density:** 663 per sq. mi. **Ethnic groups:** African descent 90%. **Principal languages:** English (official), French patois. **Religions:** Roman Catholic 90%, Protestant 7%.

**Geography: Area:** 238 sq. mi. **Location:** In E Caribbean, 2d largest of the Windward Is. **Neighbors:** Martinique to N, St. Vincent to S. **Topography:** Mountainous, volcanic in origin; Soufriere, a volcanic crater, in the S. Wooded mountains run N-S to Mt. Gimie, 3,145 ft., streams through fertile valleys. **Capital:** Castries (1992 met. est.): 13,600.

**Government: Type:** Parliamentary democracy. **Head of state:** Queen Elizabeth II, represented by Gov.-Gen. Sor Stanislaus Anthony James; b Nov. 13, 1919; in office: Oct. 10, 1988. **Head of government:** Prime Min. John Compton; b Apr. 29, 1926; in office: May 3, 1982. **Local divisions:** 11 quarters.

**Economy: Industries:** Clothing, beverages, tourism, manufacturing. **Chief crops:** Bananas, coconuts, cocoa, citrus fruits. **Other resources:** Forests. **Arable land:** 8%. **Electricity prod.** (1993): 112 mil kWh. **Labor force:** 43% agric.; 39% services; 18% ind. & commerce.

**Finance: Monetary unit:** East Caribbean Dollar (June 1996: 2.70 = $1 US). **Gross domestic product** (1994): $610 mln.* **Per capita GDP:** $4,200. **Imports** (1992): $276 mln.; partners: U.S. 34%, UK 14%, Japan 7%. **Exports** (1992): $123 mln.; partners: UK 56%, U.S. 22%. **Tourism** (1993): $221 mil.

**Transport: Motor vehicles:** in use: 10,000 passenger cars, 9,000 comm. vehicles. **Chief ports:** Castries, Vieux Fort.

**Communications: Television sets:** 1 per 5.7 persons. **Radios:** 1 per 1.4 persons. **Telephones:** 1 per 5.8 persons.

**Health: Life expectancy at birth** (1996): 67 male; 74 female. **Births** (per 1,000 pop.): 22. **Deaths** (per 1,000 pop.): 6. **Natural increase:** 1.6%. **Hospital beds:** 1 per 318 persons. **Physicians:** 1 per 2,235 persons. **Infant mortality** (per 1,000 live births 1996): 20.

**Education: Literacy** (1993): 80%; Compulsory: ages 5-15.

**Major International Organizations:** UN (IMF, WTO, ILO), the Commonwealth, OAS.

**Embassy:** 3216 New Mexico Ave. NW 20016; 364-6792.

St. Lucia was ceded to Britain by France at the Treaty of Paris, 1814. Self-government was granted with the West Indies Act, 1967. Independence was attained Feb. 22, 1979.

## Saint Vincent and the Grenadines

**People: Population:** 118,344. **Pop. density:** 789 per sq. mi. **Urban:** 25%. **Ethnic groups:** Mainly African descent. **Principal languages:** English (official), French patois. **Religions:** Anglican, Methodist, Roman Catholic.

**Geography: Area:** 150 sq. mi. **Location:** In the E Caribbean, St. Vincent (133 sq. mi.) and the northern islets of the Grenadines form a part of the Windward chain. **Neighbors:** St. Lucia to N, Barbados to E, Grenada to S. **Topography:** St. Vincent is volcanic, with a ridge of thickly wooded mountains running its length. **Capital:** Kingstown (1993): 15,800.

**Government: Type:** Constitutional monarchy. **Head of state:** Queen Elizabeth II, represented by Gov.-Gen. Sir David Jack; b July 16, 1918; in office: Sept. 20, 1989. **Head of government:** Prime Min. James Fitz-Allen Mitchell; b May 15, 1931; in office: July 30, 1984. **Local divisions:** 6 parishes.

**Economy: Industries:** Agriculture, tourism. **Chief crops:** Bananas, arrowroot, coconuts. **Arable land:** 38%. **Electricity prod.** (1993): 50 mil kWh. **Labor force:** 60% agric.

**Finance: Monetary unit:** East Caribbean Dollar (June 1996: 2.70 = $1 US). **Gross domestic product** (1994): $235 mln.* **Per capita GDP:** $2,000. **Tourism** (1993): $55 mil. **National budget** (1993): $77 mil.

**Transport: Motor vehicles:** in use: 5,000 passenger cars, 3,000 comm. vehicles. **Chief port:** Kingstown.

**Communications: Television sets:** 1 per 6.3 persons. **Radios:** 1 per 1.5 persons. **Telephones:** 1 per 6.6 persons.

**Health: Life expectancy at birth** (1996): 71 male; 75 female. **Births** (per 1,000 pop.): 19. **Deaths** (per 1,000 pop.): 5. **Natural increase:** 1.4%. **Infant mortality** (per 1,000 live births 1996): 17.

**Education: Literacy** (1992): 96%.

**Major International Organizations:** UN (WTO), OAS, the Commonwealth.

**Embassy:** 3216 New Mexico Ave. NW 20016; 364-6730.

Columbus landed on St. Vincent on Jan. 22, 1498 (St. Vincent's Day). Britain and France both laid claim to the island in the 17th and 18th centuries; the Treaty of Versailles, 1783, finally ceded it to Britain. Associated State status was granted 1969; independence was attained Oct. 27, 1979.

## San Marino

### Most Serene Republic of San Marino

### Serenissima Repubblica di San Marino

**People: Population:** 24,521. **Age distrib.** (%): <15: 15; 65+: 15. **Pop. density:** 1,022 per sq. mi. **Urban:** 91%. **Ethnic groups:** Sammarinese, Italian. **Principal languages:** Italian. **Religions:** Mostly Roman Catholic.

**Geography: Area:** 24 sq. mi. **Location:** In N central Italy near Adriatic coast. **Neighbors:** Completely surrounded by Italy. **Topography:** The country lies on the slopes of Mt. Titano. **Capital:** San Marino. **Cities** (1995): Serravalle/Dogano 4,700; San Marino 2,300.

**Government: Type:** Republic. **Head of state:** Two co-regents appt. every 6 months. **Local divisions:** 9 municipalities. **Defense:** 1% of GDP (1992 est.).

**Economy: Industries:** Tourism, woolen goods, wine, cement, ceramics. **Chief crops:** Wheat, grapes, corn. **Arable land:** 17%.

**Finance: Monetary unit:** Italian Lira. **Gross domestic product** (1993): $380 mln.* **Per capita GDP:** $15,800.

**Communications: Radios:** 1 per 1.9 persons. **Telephones:** 1 per 1.6 persons.

**Health** (1996): **Births** (per 1,000 pop.): 11. **Deaths** (per 1,000 pop.): 8. **Natural increase:** 0.3%. **Infant mortality** (per 1,000 live births): 6.

**Education: Literacy** (1995): 98%. Compulsory: ages 6-13.

**Major International Organizations:** UN.

San Marino claims to be the oldest state in Europe and to have been founded in the 4th century. A Communist-led coalition ruled 1947-57; a similar coalition ruled 1978-86. It has had a treaty of friendship with Italy since 1862.

## São Tomé and Príncipe

### Democratic Republic of São Tomé and Príncipe

### República Democrática de São Tomé e Príncipe

**People: Population:** 144,128. **Pop. density:** 373 per sq. mi. **Urban:** 46%. **Ethnic groups:** Mesticos (Portuguese-African mixture), African minority (Angola, Mozambique immigrants). **Principal languages:** Portuguese (official). **Religions:** Roman Catholic, Protestant.

**Geography: Area:** 386 sq. mi. **Location:** In the Gulf of Guinea about 125 miles off W central Africa. **Neighbors:** Gabon, Equatorial Guinea to E. **Topography:** São Tomé and Príncipe islands, part of an extinct volcano chain, are both covered by lush forests and croplands. **Capital:** São Tomé (1993 est.): 43,000.

**Government: Type:** Republic. **Head of state:** Pres. Miguel Trovoada; b Dec. 27, 1936; in office: Apr. 3, 1991. **Local divisions:** 2 districts.

**Economy: Chief crops:** Cocoa (78% of exports), coconut products. **Arable land:** 1%. **Electricity prod.** (1993): 17 mil kWh.

**Finance: Monetary unit:** Dobra (June 1996: 2,317 = $1 US). **Gross domestic product** (1993): $133 mln.* **Per capita GDP:** $1,000.

**Chief ports:** São Tomé, Santo Antonio.

**Communications: Television sets:** 1 per 6.1 persons. **Radios:** 1 per 4.1 persons.

**Health: Births** (per 1,000 pop.): 34. **Deaths** (per 1,000 pop.): 9. **Natural increase:** 2.6%. **Physicians:** 1 per 1,881 persons. **Infant mortality** (per 1,000 live births 1996): 61.

**Education: Literacy** (1989): 54%.

**Major International Organizations:** UN, OAU.

The islands were discovered in 1471 by the Portuguese, who brought the first settlers—convicts and exiled Jews. Sugar planting was replaced by the slave trade as the chief economic activity until coffee and cocoa were introduced in the 19th century.

Portugal agreed, 1974, to turn the colony over to the Gabon-based Movement for the Liberation of São Tomé and Príncipe, which proclaimed as first president its East German-trained leader, Manuel Pinto da Costa. Independence came July 12, 1975. Democratic reforms were instituted in 1987. In 1991 Miguel Trovoada won the first free presidential election following the withdrawal of Pres. da Costa. A military coup that ousted Trovoada Aug. 15, 1995, was reversed a week later after Angolan mediation. Trovoada defeated da Costa in a presidential runoff election, July 21, 1996.

## Saudi Arabia

### Kingdom of Saudi Arabia

### Al Mamlakah al Arabiyah as Saudiyah

**People: Population:** 19,409,058. **Age distrib.** (%): <15: 43; 65+: 2. **Pop. density:** 22 per sq. mi. **Urban:** 79%. **Ethnic groups:** Arab 90%, Afro-Asian 10%. **Principal languages:** Arabic (official). **Religions:** Muslim 100%.

**Geography: Area:** 865,000 sq. mi. **Location:** Occupies most of Arabian Peninsula in Middle East. **Neighbors:** Kuwait, Iraq, Jordan on N; Yemen, Oman on S; United Arab Emirates, Qatar on E. **Topography:** Bordered by Red Sea on the W. The highlands on W, up to 9,000 ft., slope as an arid, barren desert to the Persian Gulf on the E. **Capital:** Riyadh. **Cities** (1991 est.): Riyadh 1.8 mln.; Jiddah 1.5 mln.; Mecca 630,000.

**Government: Type:** Monarchy with council of ministers. **Head of state and government:** King Fahd ibn Abdul Aziz; b 1923; in office: June 13, 1982 (prime min. since 1982). **Local divisions:** 13 emirates. **Defense:** 13.8% of GDP (1994). **Active troop strength:** 105,500.

**Economy: Industries:** Oil, oil products. **Chief crops:** Dates, wheat, barley, citrus fruit. **Minerals:** Oil, gas, gold, copper, iron. **Crude oil reserves** (1995): 261 bil barrels. **Arable land:** 1%. **Livestock** (1994): sheep: 7.3 mln.; goats: 4.2 mil. **Electricity prod.** (1993): 46 bil kWh. **Labor force:** 34% govt.; 28% industry & oil; 22% services; 16% agric.

**Finance: Monetary unit:** Riyal (June 1996: 3.71 = $1 US). **Gross domestic product** (1994): $173 bln.* **Per capita GDP:** $9,510. **Imports** (1993 est.): $28.9 bln.; partners: US 21%, Japan 14%, UK 11%. **Exports** (1993 est.): $39.4 bln.; partners: U.S. 20%, Japan 18%. **Tourism** (1992): $1.0 bil. **National budget** (1993 est.): $50 bil. **International reserves less gold** (May 1996): $11.0 bil. **Gold:** 4.60 mil oz t. **Consumer prices** (change in 1995): 4.9%.

**Transport: Railroads: Route length:** 864 mi. **Motor vehicles:** in use: 2.8 mil passenger cars, 2.3 mil comm. vehicles. **Civil aviation:** 11.3 bil passenger-mi.; 25 airports with scheduled flights. **Chief ports:** Jiddah, Ad Dammam, Ras Tannurah.

**Communications: Television sets:** 1 per 3.7 persons. **Radios:** 1 per 4.6 persons. **Telephones:** 1 per 11 persons. **Daily newspaper circ.:** 34 per 1,000 pop.

**Health: Life expectancy at birth** (1996): 67 male; 71 female. **Births** (per 1,000 pop.): 38. **Deaths** (per 1,000 pop.): 5. **Natural increase:** 3.3%. **Hospital beds:** 1 per 359 persons. **Physicians:** 1 per 523 persons. **Infant mortality** (per 1,000 live births 1996): 46.

**Education: Literacy** (1995): 63%.

**Major International Organizations:** UN (IMF, WHO, FAO), Arab League, OPEC.

**Embassy:** 601 New Hampshire Ave. NW 20037; 342-3800.

Before Muhammad, Arabia was divided among numerous warring tribes and small kingdoms and was at times dominated by larger Arabian and non-Arabian kingdoms. It was united for the first time by Muhammad, in the early 7th century AD. His successors conquered the entire Near East and North Africa, bringing Islam and the Arabic language. But Arabia itself soon returned to its former status.

Nejd, in central Arabia, long an independent state and center of the Wahhabi sect, fell under Turkish rule in the 18th century. In 1913 Ibn Saud, founder of the Saudi dynasty, overthrew the Turks and captured the Turkish province of Hasa in E Arabia; he took the Hejaz region in W Arabia in 1925 and most of Asir, in SW Arabia, by 1926. The discovery of oil in the 1930s transformed the new country.

Ibn Saud reigned until his death, Nov. 1953. Subsequent kings have been sons of Ibn Saud. The king exercises authority together with a Council of Ministers. The Islamic religious code is the law of the land. Alcohol and public entertainments are restricted, and women have an inferior legal status. There is no constitution and no parliament, although a Consultative Council was established by the king in 1993.

Saudi Arabia has often allied itself with the U.S. and other Western nations, and billions of dollars of advanced arms have been purchased from Britain, France, and the U.S.; however, Western support for Israel has often strained relations. Saudi units fought against Israel in the 1948 and 1973 Arab-Israeli wars. Beginning with the 1967 Arab-Israeli war, Saudi Arabia provided large annual financial gifts to Egypt; aid was later extended to Syria, Jordan, and Palestinian groups, as well as to other Islamic countries.

King Faisal played a leading role in the 1973-74 Arab oil embargo against the U.S. and other nations.. Crown Prince Khalid was proclaimed king on Mar. 25, 1975, after the assassination of Faisal. Fahd became king on June 13, 1982, following Khalid's death.

The Hejaz contains the holy cities of Islam—Medina, where the Mosque of the Prophet enshrines the tomb of Muhammad, and Mecca, his birthplace. More than 2 million Muslims make pilgrimage to Mecca annually. In 1987, Iranians making a pilgrimage to Mecca clashed with anti-Iranian pilgrims and Saudi police; more than 400 were killed. Some 1,426 Muslim pilgrims died July 2, 1990, in a stampede in a pedestrian tunnel leading to Mecca. Nearly 300 pilgrims were killed in a stampede in Mecca, May 26, 1994.

Following Iraq's attack on Kuwait, Aug. 2, 1990, Saudi Arabia accepted the Kuwait royal family and more than 400,000 Kuwaiti refugees. King Fahd invited Western and Arab troops to deploy on its soil in support of Saudi defense forces. During the Persian Gulf War, 28 U.S. soldiers were killed when an Iraqi missile hit their barracks in Dhahran, Feb. 25, 1991. The nation's northern Gulf coastline suffered severe pollution as a result of Iraqi sabotage of the Kuwaiti oil fields.

Islamic extremists were blamed for truck bombs that killed 7 (5 from the U.S.) at a military training center in Riyadh, Nov. 13, 1995, and 19 Americans at a base in Dhahran, June 25, 1996.

# Senegal

## Republic of Senegal

## République du Sénégal

**People: Population:** 9,092,749. **Age distrib.** (%): <15: 45; 65+: 3. **Pop. density:** 120 per sq. mi. **Urban:** 43%. **Ethnic groups:** Wolof 36%, Fulani 17%, Serer 17%, Diola 9%, Toucouleur 9%, Mandingo 9%. **Principal languages:** French (official), Wolof, Pulaar, Diola, Mandingo, others. **Religions:** Muslim 92%, indigenous beliefs 6%, Christian 2%.

**Geography: Area:** 75,951 sq. mi. **Location:** At W extreme of Africa. **Neighbors:** Mauritania on N, Mali on E, Guinea and Guinea-Bissau on S; surrounds Gambia on three sides. **Topography:** Low rolling plains cover most of Senegal, rising somewhat in the SE. Swamp and jungles are in SW. **Capital:** Dakar. **Cities** (1994 est.): Dakar 1.7 mln.; Thies 216,400; Kaolack 143,100.

**Government: Type:** Republic. **Head of state:** Pres. Abdou Diouf; b Sept. 7, 1935; in office: Jan. 1, 1981. **Head of government:** Prime Min. Habib Thiam; b Jan 21, 1933; in office: Apr. 8, 1991. **Local divisions:** 10 regions. **Defense:** 2.1% of GDP (1993). **Active troop strength:** 13,350.

**Economy: Industries:** Food processing, fishing. **Chief crops:** Peanuts, millet, rice. **Minerals:** Phosphates, iron. **Arable land:** 27%. **Livestock** (1994): sheep: 4.6 mln.; goats: 3.2 mln.; cattle: 2.8 mil. **Fish catch** (1993): 378,000 metric tons. **Electricity prod.** (1993): 720 mil kWh. **Labor force:** 77% subsistence agric.

**Finance: Monetary unit:** CFA Franc (June 1996: 515 = $1 US). **Gross domestic product** (1993 est.): $12.3 bln.* **Per capita GDP:** $1,450. **Imports** (1991): $1.2 bln.; partners: France 31%, Cote d'Ivoire 7%. **Exports** (1991): $904 mln.; partners: France 28%, India 14%. **Tourism** (1993): $173 mil. **National budget** (1992): $1.2 bil. **International reserves less gold** (Dec. 1995): $272 mil. **Gold:** 29,000 oz t. **Consumer prices** (change in 1995): 7.9%.

**Transport: Railroads: Route length:** 562 mi. **Motor vehicles:** in use: 97,000 passenger cars, 40,000 comm. vehicles. **Chief ports:** Dakar, Saint-Louis.

**Communications: Television sets:** 1 per 133 persons. **Radios:** 1 per 9.5 persons. **Telephones:** 1 per 123 persons.

**Health: Life expectancy at birth** (1996): 54 male; 59 female. **Births** (per 1,000 pop.): 45. **Deaths** (per 1,000 pop.): 12. **Natural increase:** 3.4%. **Hospital beds:** 1 per 1,040 persons. **Physicians:** 1 per 14,817 persons. **Infant mortality** (per 1,000 live births 1996): 64.

**Education: Literacy** (1993): 33%. Compulsory: ages 7-13. Attendance: 58% primary, 16% secondary.

**Major International Organizations:** UN and all of its specialized agencies, OAU.

**Embassy:** 2112 Wyoming Ave. NW 20008; 234-0541.

Portuguese settlers arrived in the 15th century, but French control grew from the 17th century. The last independent Muslim state was subdued in 1893. Dakar became the capital of French West Africa.

Independence as part, along with the Sudanese Rep., of the Mali Federation, came June 20, 1960. Senegal withdrew Aug. 20. French political and economic influence remained strong.

Senegal, Dec. 17, 1981, signed an agreement with The Gambia for confederation of the 2 countries, without loss of individual sovereignty, under the name of Senegambia. The confederation collapsed in 1989, although in 1991 the 2 nations signed a friendship and cooperation treaty.

Separatists in Casamance Province of S Senegal have clashed with government forces since 1982.

# Seychelles

## Republic of Seychelles

**People: Population:** 77,575. **Age distrib.** (%): <15: 31; 65+: 7. **Pop. density:** 441 per sq. mi. **Urban:** 50%. **Ethnic groups:** Seychellois (mixture of Asians, Africans, and French) predominate. **Principal languages:** English, French, Creole (all official). **Religions:** Roman Catholic 90%, Anglican 8%.

**Geography: Area:** 176 sq. mi. **Location:** In the Indian O. 700 miles NE of Madagascar. **Neighbors:** Nearest are Madagascar on SW, Somalia on NW. **Topography:** A group of 86 islands, about half of them composed of coral, the other half granite, the latter predominantly mountainous. **Capital:** Victoria (1993 est.): 25,000.

**Government: Type:** Republic. **Head of state:** Pres. France-Albert René, b. Nov. 16, 1935; in office: June 5, 1977. **Local divisions:** 23 districts. **Defense:** 4% of GDP (1990 est.). **Active troop strength:** 300.

**Economy: Industries:** Tourism, food processing, fishing. **Chief crops:** Coconuts, cinnamon, vanilla. **Electricity prod.** (1993): 110 mil kWh. **Labor force:** 31% industry & comm.; 21% services; 20% govt.; 12% agric.

**Finance: Monetary unit:** Rupee (June 1996: 5.03 = $1 US). **Gross domestic product** (1993): $430 mln.* **Per capita GDP:** $6,000. **Imports** (19932): $261 mln. **Exports** (1993): $50 mil. **National budget** (1993): $263 mil. **Tourism** (1992): $117 mil. **International reserves less gold** (Mar. 1996): $21 mil. **Consumer prices** (change in 1995): –0.3%.

**Transport: Motor vehicles:** in use: 5,000 passenger cars, 2,000 comm. vehicles. **Chief port:** Victoria.

**Communications: Television sets:** 1 per 5.7 persons. **Radios:** 1 per 1.8 persons. **Telephones:** 1 per 6.2 persons. **Daily newspaper circ.:** 44 per 1,000 pop.

**Health: Life expectancy at birth** (1996): 64 male; 74 female. **Births** (per 1,000 pop.): 21. **Deaths** (per 1,000 pop.): 7. **Natural increase:** 1.4%. **Hospital beds:** 1 per 173 persons. **Physicians:** 1 per 997 persons. **Infant mortality** (per 1,000 live births 1996): 13.

**Education: Literacy** (1995): 84%. Free and compulsory: ages 6-15.

**Major International Organizations:** UN, OAU, the Commonwealth.

**Embassy:** 820 2d Ave., New York, NY 10017; 212-687-9766.

The islands were occupied by France in 1768, and seized by Britain in 1794. Ruled as part of Mauritius from 1814, the Seychelles became a separate colony in 1903. The ruling party had opposed independence as impractical, but pressure from the OAU and the UN became irresistible, and independence was declared June 29, 1976. The first president was ousted in a coup a year later by a socialist leader.

A new constitution, approved June 1993, provided for a multiparty state.

# Sierra Leone

## Republic of Sierra Leone

**People: Population:** 4,793,121. **Age distrib.** (%): <15: 44; 65+: 3. **Pop. density:** 173 per sq. mi. **Urban:** 35%. **Ethnic groups:** Temne 30%, Mende 30%, other tribes 39%. **Principal languages:** English (official), tribal languages, Krio. **Religions:** Muslim 60%, indigenous beliefs 30%, Christian 10%.

**Geography: Area:** 27,699 sq. mi. **Location:** On W coast of W Africa. **Neighbors:** Guinea on N and E, Liberia on S. **Topography:** The heavily-indented, 210-mi. coastline has mangrove swamps. Behind are wooded hills, rising to a plateau and mountains in the E. **Capital:** Freetown. **Cities** (1985 cen.): Freetown 469,800; Koidu-New Sembehun 80,000.

**Government: Type:** Republic. **Head of government:** Pres. Ahmad Tejan Kabbah; b Feb. 16, 1932; in office: Mar. 29, 1996. **Local divisions:** 3 provinces, 1 area. **Defense:** 2.6% of GDP (FY 1992-93). **Active troop strength:** 6,200 est.

**Economy: Industries:** Mining, light manufacturing. **Chief crops:** Cocoa, coffee, palm kernels, rice, cassava. **Minerals:** Diamonds, titanium, bauxite. **Arable land:** 25%. **Fish catch** (1994): 65,000 metric tons. **Electricity prod.** (1993): 220 mil kWh. **Labor force:** 65% agric.; 35% ind. & serv.

**Finance: Monetary unit:** Leone (June 1996: 855 = $1 US). **Gross domestic product** (1993): $4.5 bln.* **Per capita GDP:** $1,000. **Imports** (1993): $149 mln.; partners: Nigeria 29%, UK 14%. **Exports** (1993): $149 mln.; partners: U.S. 32%, UK 20%. **National budget** (1992 est.): $118 mil. **International reserves less gold** (May 1996): $24.6 mil. **Consumer prices** (change in 1995): 26.0%.

**Transport: Motor vehicles:** in use: 32,000 passenger cars, 12,000 comm. vehicles. **Chief ports:** Freetown, Bonthe.

**Communications: Television sets:** 1 per 176 persons. **Radios:** 1 per 4.6 persons. **Telephones:** 1 per 296 persons.

**Health: Life expectancy at birth** (1996): 45 male; 51 female. **Births** (per 1,000 pop.): 47. **Deaths** (per 1,000 pop.): 18. **Natural increase:** 2.9%. **Hospital beds:** 1 per 980 persons. **Physicians:** 1 per 10,832 persons. **Infant mortality** (per 1,000 live births 1996): 136.

**Education: Literacy** (1992): 31%.

**Major International Organizations:** UN (IMF, WHO, WTO), the Commonwealth, OAU.

**Embassy:** 1701 19th St. NW 20009; 939-9261.

Freetown was founded in 1787 by the British government as a haven for freed slaves. Their descendants, known as Creoles, number more than 60,000.

Successive steps toward independence followed the 1951 constitution. Full independence arrived Apr. 27, 1961. Sierra Leone became a republic Apr. 19, 1971. A one-party state approved by referendum 1978, brought political stability, but the economy has been plagued by inflation, corruption, and dependence upon the International Monetary Fund and creditors.

Mutinous soldiers ousted Pres. Joseph Momoh Apr. 30, 1992. The new military regime faced continued armed opposition from the Revolutionary United Front. Another coup, Jan. 16, 1996, payed the way for multiparty elections and a return to civilian rule. A rebellion led by the Revolutionary United Front has taken more than 10,000 lives since 1991.

# Singapore

## Republic of Singapore

**People: Population:** 3,396,924. **Age distrib.** (%): <15: 23; 65+: 7. **Pop. density:** 13,753 per sq. mi. **Urban:** 100%. **Ethnic groups:** Chinese 76%, Malay 15%, Indian 6%. **Principal languages:** Chinese, Malay, Tamil, English (all official). **Religions:** Buddhist and Taoist, Muslim, Christian, Hindu.

**Geography: Area:** 247 sq. mi. **Location:** Off tip of Malayan Peninsula in SE Asia. **Neighbors:** Nearest are Malaysia on N, Indonesia on S. **Topography:** Singapore is a flat, formerly swampy island. The nation includes 40 nearby islets. **Capital:** Singapore.

**Government: Type:** Republic. **Head of state:** Pres. Ong Teng Cheong; b Jan 22, 1936; in office: Sept. 2, 1993. **Head of government:** Prime Min. Goh Chok Tong; b May 20, 1941; in office: Nov. 28, 1990. **Defense:** 6% of GDP (1993 est.). **Active troop strength:** 53,900 est.

**Economy: Industries:** Shipbuilding, oil refining, electronics, banking, food and rubber processing, biotechnology. **Arable land:** 4%. **Fish catch** (1994): 11,000 metric tons. **Electricity prod.** (1993): 17 bil kWh. **Labor force:** 34% finance, business, other serv.; 26% manuf.; 23% comm.

**Finance: Monetary unit:** Dollar (June 1996: 1.41 = $1 US). **Gross domestic product** (1994): $57 bln.* **Per capita GDP:** $19,940. **Imports** (1994): $102.4 bln.; partners: Japan 22%, Malaysia 16%, U.S. 15%, Taiwan 4%. **Exports** (1994): $96.4 bln.; partners: Malaysia 20%, U.S. 19%, Hong Kong 9%, Japan 7%. **Tourism** (1993): $5.8 bil. **National budget** (FY 1993-94): $10.5 bil. **International reserves** (Mar. 1996): $70.3 bil. **Consumer prices** (change in 1995): 1.7%.

**Transport: Motor vehicles:** in use: 341,000 passenger cars, 134,000 comm. vehicles. **Civil aviation:** 28 bil passenger-mi.; 1 airport. **Chief port:** Singapore.

**Communications: Television sets:** 1 per 4.5 persons. **Radios:** 1 per 3.6 persons. **Telephones:** 1 per 2.3 persons. **Daily newspaper circ.:** 350 per 1,000 pop.

**Health: Life expectancy at birth** (1996): 75 male; 81 female. **Births** (per 1,000 pop.): 16. **Deaths** (per 1,000 pop.): 5. **Natural increase:** 1.2%. **Hospital beds:** 1 per 275 persons. **Physicians:** 1 per 693 persons. **Infant mortality** (per 1,000 live births 1996): 5.

**Education: Literacy** (1993): 91%.

**Major International Organizations:** UN (WTO, IMF, WHO), the Commonwealth, ASEAN.

**Embassy:** 3501 International Pl. NW 20008; 537-3100.

Founded in 1819 by Sir Thomas Stamford Raffles, Singapore was a British colony until 1959, when it became autonomous within the Commonwealth. On Sept. 16, 1963, it joined with Malaya, Sarawak, and Sabah to form the Federation of Malaysia. Tensions between Malayans, dominant in the federation, and ethnic Chinese, dominant in Singapore, led to an agreement under which Singapore became a separate nation, Aug. 9, 1965.

Singapore is one of the world's largest ports. Standards in health, education, and housing are high. International banking has grown. The government, dominated by a single party, has taken strong actions to suppress dissent.

# Slovakia

## Slovak Republic

## Slovenská Republika

**People: Population:** 5,374,362. **Age distrib.** (%): <15: 23; +65: 11. **Pop. density:** 284 per sq. mi. **Urban:** 57%. **Ethnic groups:** Slovak 86%, Hungarian 11%. **Principal languages:** Slovak (official), Hungarian. **Religions:** Roman Catholic 60%, Protestant 8%, Orthodox 4%.

**Geography: Area:** 18,933 sq. mi. **Location:** In E central Europe. **Neighbors:** Poland on N, Hungary on S, Austria and Czech Rep. on W, Ukraine on E. **Topography:** Mountains (Carpathians) in N, fertile Danube plane in S. **Capital:** Bratislava. **Cities** (1993 est.): Bratislava 446,700; Kosice 237,300.

**Government: Type:** Republic. **Head of state:** Pres. Michal Kovac; b Aug. 5, 1930; in office: Mar. 1993. **Head of government:** Prime Min. Vladimir Meciar; b July 26, 1942; in office: Dec. 13, 1994. **Local divisions:** 4 departments. **Defense:** 3.1% of GDP (1994). **Active troop strength:** 47,000.

**Economy: Industries:** Metal products, food and beverages, oil, chemicals, coal. **Chief crops:** Grains, potatoes, sugar beets, hops, fruit. **Minerals:** Coal, iron, copper. **Electricity prod.** (1993): 21 bil kWh. **Labor force:** 33% ind.; 12% agric.; 10% constr.

**Finance: Monetary unit:** Koruna (June 1996: 31.10 = $1 US). **Gross domestic product** (1994): $32.8 bln.* **Per capita GDP:** $6,070. **Imports** (1994): $6.1 bln.; partners: Czech Rep. 30%, Russia 19%. **Exports** (1994): $6.3 bln.; parnters: Czech Rep. 38%, Germany 17%. **International reserves less gold** (Apr. 1996): 3.4 bil. **Gold:** 1.3 mil oz t. **Consumer prices** (change in 1995): 9.9%.

**Transport: Railroads: Length:** 2,275 mi. **Motor vehicles:** in use: 953,000 passenger cars, 81,000 comm. vehicles. **Chief ports:** Bratislava, Komarno.

**Communications: Television sets:** 1 per 1.6 persons. **Radios:** 1 per 0.7 person. **Telephones:** 1 per 6.0 persons.

**Health: Life expectancy at birth** (1996): 69 male; 77 female. **Births** (per 1,000 pop.): 13. **Deaths** (per 1,000 pop.): 9. **Natural increase:** 0.3%. **Infant mortality** (per 1,000 live births 1996): 11.

**Education: Literacy** (1994): 100%.

**Major International Organizations:** UN (WTO, WHO, IMF).

**Embassy:** 2201 Wisconsin Ave. NW 20007; 965-5160.

Slovakia was originally settled by Illyrian, Celtic, and Germanic tribes and was incorporated into Great Moravia in the 9th century. It became part of Hungary in the 11th century. Overrun by Czech Hussites in the 15th century, it was restored to Hungarian rule in 1526. The Slovaks disassociated themselves from Hungary following World War I and joined the Czechs of Bohemia to form the Republic of Czechoslovakia, Oct. 28, 1918.

Germany invaded Czechoslovakia, 1939, and declared Slovakia independent. Slovakia rejoined Czechoslovakia in 1945.

Czechoslovakia split into 2 separate states—the Czech Republic and Slovakia—on Jan. 1, 1993. Slovakia, with its less developed economy, applied to join the European Union in 1995.

# Slovenia

## Republic of Slovenia

## Republika Slovenija

**People: Population:** 1,951,443. **Pop. density:** 250 per sq. mi. **Urban:** 50%. **Ethnic groups:** Slovene 91%, Croat 3%. **Principal languages:** Slovenian (official), Serbo-Croatian. **Religions:** Roman Catholic 96%.

**Geography: Area:** 7,821 sq. mi. **Location:** In SE Europe. **Neighbors:** Italy on W, Austria on N, Hungary on NE, Croatia on SE, S. **Topography:** Mostly hilly; 42% of the land is forested. **Capital:** Ljubljana (1994 est.): 270,800.

**Government: Type:** Republic. **Head of state:** Pres. Milan Kucan; b Jan. 14, 1941; in office: Apr. 1990. **Head of government:** Prime Min. Janez Drnovsek; b May 1950; in office: May 14, 1992. **Local divisions:** 60 provinces. **Defense:** 4.5% of GDP (1993). **Active troop strength:** 8,400.

**Economy: Industries:** Steel, electronics, vehicles, textiles. **Minerals:** Coal, lead, zinc, mercury. **Chief crops:** Potatoes, hops, hemp. **Arable land:** 10%. **Livestock** (1994): pigs: 620,000; cattle: 504,000. **Electricity prod.** (1993): 8.9 bil kWh.

**Finance: Monetary unit:** Tolar (June 1996: 138 = $1 US). **Gross domestic product** (1994): $16 bln.* **Per capita GDP:** $8,110. **Imports** (1994): $6.5 bln.; partners: Germany 25%, Italy 16%. **Exports** (1994): $6.5 bln.; partners: Germany 30%, former Yugoslav reps. 16%. **International reserves less gold**(Apr. 1996): $1.6 bil.

**Transport: Motor vehicles:** in use: 633,000 passenger cars, 44,000 comm. vehicles. **Civil aviation:** 295 mil passenger-mi.; 1 airport. **Chief ports:** Izola, Koper.

**Communications: Telephones:** 1 per 3.9 persons. **Daily newspaper circ.:** 154 per 1,000 pop.

**Health: Life expectancy at birth** (1996): 71 male; 79 female. **Births** (per 1,000 pop.): 8. **Deaths** (per 1,000 pop.): 9. **Natural increase:** –0.1%. **Hospital beds:** 1 per 172 persons. **Physicians:** 1 per 990 persons. **Infant mortality** (per 1,000 live births 1996): 7.

**Education: Literacy** (1993): 99%.

**Major International Organizations:** UN (WTO, WHO, IMF).

**Embassy:** 1525 New Hampshire Ave. NW 20036; 667-5363.

The Slovenes settled in their current territory during the period from the 6th to the 8th century. They fell under German domination as early as the 9th century. Modern Slovenian political history began after 1848 when the Slovenes, who were divided among several Austrian provinces, began their struggle for political and national unification. With the establishment of the Kingdom of Serbs, Croats, and Slovenes in 1918, this unification was largely achieved when the majority of the Slovenes entered the new state, which later became Yugoslavia.

Slovenia declared independence June 25, 1991, and joined the UN May 22, 1992. Linked by trade with the European Union, Slovenia applied for full membership June 10, 1996.

# Solomon Islands

**People: Population:** 412,902. **Pop. density:** 38 per sq. mi. **Urban:** 13%. **Ethnic groups:** Melanesian 93%, Polynesian 4%. **Principal languages:** English (official); Melanesian, Papuan, Polynesian languages. **Religions:** Anglican 34%, Roman Catholic 19%, Baptist 17%, other Christian 26%.

**Geography: Area:** 10,954 sq. mi. **Location:** Melanesian Archipelago in the W Pacific O. **Neighbors:** Nearest is Papua New Guinea to W. **Topography:** 10 large volcanic and rugged islands and 4 groups of smaller ones. **Capital:** Honiara (1990): 35,300.

**Government: Type:** Parliamentary democracy within the Commonwealth of Nations. **Head of state:** Queen Elizabeth II, represented by Gov.-Gen. Moses Pitakaka; in office: June 1994. **Head of government:** Prime Min. Solomon Mamaloni; b 1943; in office: Nov. 7, 1994. **Local divisions:** 7 provinces and Honiara.

**Economy: Industries:** Copra, fishing. **Chief crops:** Coconuts, rice, cocoa, beans. **Minerals:** Gold, bauxite. **Other resources:** Forests. **Arable land:** 1%. **Fish catch** (1994): 39,000 metric tons. **Electricity prod.** (1993): 30 mil kWh. **Labor force:** 32% agric., forestry, fish.; 25% services.

**Finance: Monetary unit:** Dollar (June 1996: 3.55 = $1 US). **Gross domestic product** (1992): $1 bln.* **Per capita GDP:** $2,590. **Imports** (1991): $110 mln.; partners: Australia 34%, Japan 16%. **Exports** (1991): $84 mln.; partners: Japan 39%, UK 23%.

**Communications: Radios:** 1 per 10 persons. **Telephones:** 1 per 65 persons.

**Health: Life expectancy at birth** (1996): 69 male; 74 female. **Births** (per 1,000 pop.): 38. **Deaths** (per 1,000 pop.): 4. **Natural increase:** 3.4%. **Infant mortality** (per 1,000 live births 1996): 26.

**Education: Literacy** (1994): 54%. **Attendence:** primary school 94%, secondary school 17%.

**Major International Organizations:** UN (WTO, WHO, IMF), the Commonwealth.

The Solomon Islands were sighted in 1568 by an expedition from Peru. Britain established a protectorate in the 1890s over most of the group, inhabited by Melanesians. The islands saw major World War II battles. Self-government came Jan. 2, 1976, and independence was formally attained July 7, 1978.

# Somalia

## Soomaaliya

**People: Population:** 9,639,151. **Age distrib.** (%): <15: 48; +65: 3. **Pop. density:** 39 per sq. mi. **Urban:** 24%. **Ethnic groups:** Mainly Somali. **Principal languages:** Somali (official), Arabic, Italian, English. **Religions:** Mainly Sunni Muslim.

**Geography: Area:** 246,000 sq. mi. **Location:** Occupies the eastern horn of Africa. **Neighbors:** Djibouti, Ethiopia, Kenya on W. **Topography:** The coastline extends for 1,700 mi. Hills cover the N; the center and S are flat. **Capital:** Mogadishu (1990est.): 900,000.

**Government: Type:** In transition. **Local divisions:** 18 regions.

**Economy: Chief crops:** Sugar, bananas, sorghum, corn, mangoes. **Minerals:** Iron, tin, gypsum, bauxite, uranium. **Arable land:** 2%. **Livestock** (1994): sheep: 13 mln.; goats: 12 mln.; cattle: 5 mil. **Fish catch** (1993): 15,000 metric tons. **Labor force:** 70% nomadic.

**Finance: Monetary unit:** Shilling (June 1996: 2,620 = $1 US). **Gross domestic product** (1994): $3.3 bln.* **Per capita GDP:** $500. **Imports** (1990): $249 mln.; partners: Italy 31%. **Exports** (1990): $58 mln.; partners: Italy 29%, Suadi Arabia 23%.

**Transport: Motor vehicles:** in use: 10,700 passenger cars, 12,000 comm. vehicles. **Chief ports:** Mogadishu, Berbera.

**Communications: Radios:** 1 per 22 persons. **Telephones:** 1 per 434 persons.

**Health: Life expectancy at birth** (1996): 55 male; 56 female. **Births** (per 1,000 pop.): 44. **Deaths** (per 1,000 pop.): 13. **Natural increase:** 3.1%. **Infant mortality** (per 1,000 live births 1996): 121.

**Education: Literacy** (1990): 24%. Free and compulsory: ages 6-14.

**Major International Organizations:** UN, OAU, Arab League.

British Somaliland (present-day N Somalia) was formed in the 19th century, as was Italian Somaliland (now central and S Somalia). Italy lost its African colonies in World War II. In 1949, the UN approved eventual independence for the former Italian colony (designated the UN Trust Territory of Somalia) after a 10-year period under Italian administration.

British Somaliland gained independence, June 26, 1960, and by prearrangement, merged July 1 with the trust territory of Somalia to create the independent Somali Republic (Somalia).

On Oct. 16, 1969, Pres. Abdi Rashid Ali Shirmarke was assassinated. On Oct. 21, a military group led by Maj. Gen. Muhammad Siad Barre seized power in a bloodless coup. In 1970, Barre declared the country a socialist state—the Somali Democratic Republic. In the following years most of the economy was nationalized.

Somalia has laid claim to Ogaden, the huge eastern region of Ethiopia, peopled mostly by Somalis. Ethiopia battled Somali rebels in 1977. Some 11,000 Cuban troops with Soviet arms defeated Somali army troops and ethnic Somali rebels in Ethiopia, 1978. As many as 1.5 mil refugees entered Somalia. Guerrilla fighting in Ogaden continued until 1988, when a peace agreement was reached with Ethiopia.

The civil war intensified again and Barre was forced to flee the capital, Jan. 1991. Fighting between rival factions caused 40,000 casualties in 1991 and 1992, and by mid-1992 the civil war, drought, and banditry combined to produce a famine that threatened some 1.5 million people with starvation. In July 1992 the UN secretary general declared Somalia to be a country without a government.

In Dec. 1992 the UN accepted a U.S. offer of troops to safeguard the delivery of food to the starving. The UN took control of the multinational relief effort from the U.S. May 4, 1993. While the operation helped alleviate the famine, efforts to reestablish order foundered, and there were significant U.S. and other casualties. The U.S. withdrew its peacekeeping forces Mar. 25, 1994. When the last UN troops pulled out Mar. 3, 1995, Mogadishu still had no functioning government, and armed factions controlled different parts of the country.

# South Africa

## Republic of South Africa

**People: Population:** 41,743,459. **Age distrib.** (%): <15: 37; 65+: 5. **Pop. density:** 89 per sq. mi. **Urban:** 57%. **Ethnic groups:** Black 75%, White 14%, Coloured 9%, Indian 3%. **Principal languages:** 11 official languages incl. Afrikaans, English, Ndebele, Sotho. **Religions:** Mainly Christian; Hindu, Muslim minorities.

**Geography: Area:** 470,689 sq. mi. **Location:** At the southern extreme of Africa. **Neighbors:** Namibia, Botswana, Zimbabwe on N; Mozambique, Swaziland on E; surrounds Lesotho. **Topography:** The large interior plateau reaches close to the country's 2,700-mi. coastline. There are few major rivers or lakes; rainfall is sparse in W, more plentiful in E. **Capitals:** Cape Town (legislative), Pretoria (executive), and Bloemfontein (judicial). **Cities** (1991 met.): Cape Town 2.4 mln.; Johannesburg 1.9 mln.; Durban 1.1 mln.; Pretoria 1.1 mil.

**Government: Type:** Federal republic with bicameral Parliament and universal suffrage. **Head of state:** Pres. Nelson Mandela; b July 18, 1918; in office: May 10, 1994. **Local divisions:** 9 provinces. **Defense:** 2.8% of GDP (FY 1993-94). **Active troop strength:** 136,900 est.

**Economy: Industries:** Mining, steel, chemicals, vehicles, machinery, textiles. **Chief crops:** Corn, grains, potatoes, sugar, fruit, tomatoes, grapes. **Minerals:** World's largest producer of gold, platinum, chromium; antimony, coal, iron, manganese, nickel, phosphates, tin, uranium, gem diamonds, copper, vanadium. **Other resources:** Wool, dairy products. **Arable land:** 10%. **Livestock** (1994): sheep: 29.1 mln.; cattle: 12.6 mil. **Fish catch** (1993): 563,000 metric tons. **Electricity prod.** (1993): 163 bil kWh. **Labor force:** 35% services; 30% agric.; 20% ind.

**Finance: Monetary unit:** Rand (June 1996: 4.34 = $1 US). **Gross domestic product** (1994): $194.3 bln.* **Per capita GDP** $4,420. **Imports** (1994): $21.4 bln.; partners: Germany 16%, U.S. 16%, UK 11%. **Exports** (1994): $25.3 bln.; partners: Switz. 7%, UK 7%, U.S. 5%. **Tourism** (1993): $1.2 bil. **National budget** (FY 1993-94): $34 bil. **International reserves less gold** (May 1996): $876 mil. **Gold:** 4.66 mil oz t. **Consumer prices** (change in 1995): 8.7%.

**Transport: Railroads: Route length:** 12,399 mi. **Motor vehicles:** in use: 3.5 mil passenger cars, 1.9 mil comm. vehicles. **Civil aviation:** 6.6 bil passenger-mi.; 27 airports. **Chief ports:** Durban, Cape Town, East London, Port Elizabeth.

**Communications: Television sets:** 1 per 12 persons. **Radios:** 1 per 3.6 persons. **Telephones:** 1 per 11 persons. **Daily newspaper circ.:** 32 per 1,000 pop.

**Health: Life expectancy at birth** (1996): 57 male; 62 female. **Births** (per 1,000 pop.): 28. **Deaths** (per 1,000 pop.): 10. **Natural increase:** 1.8%. **Hospital beds:** 1 per 321 persons. **Physicians:** 1 per 1,527 persons. **Infant mortality** (per 1,000 live births 1996): 49.

**Education: Literacy** (1993): 82%. Compulsory: ages 7-16.

**Major International Organizations:** UN (WTO), OAU, the Commonwealth.

**Embassy:** 3051 Massachusetts Ave. NW 20008; 232-4400.

Bushmen and Hottentots were the original inhabitants. Bantus, including Zulu, Xhosa, Swazi, and Sotho, had occupied the area from NE to S South Africa before the 17th century.

The Cape of Good Hope area was settled by Dutch, beginning in the 17th century. Britain seized the Cape in 1806. Many Dutch trekked north and founded 2 republics, the Transvaal and the Orange Free State. Diamonds were discovered, 1867, and gold, 1886. The Dutch (Boers) resented encroachments by the British and others; the Anglo-Boer War followed, 1899-1902. Britain won and, effective May 31, 1910, created the Union of South Africa, incorporating the British colonies of the Cape and Natal, the Transvaal and the Orange Free State. After a referendum, the Union became the Republic of South Africa, May 31, 1961, and withdrew from the Commonwealth.

With the election victory of Daniel Malan's National Party in 1948, the policy of separate development of the races, or apartheid, already existing unofficially, became official. This called for separate development, separate residential areas, and ultimate political independence for the whites, Bantus, Asians, and Coloureds (mixed races). In 1959 the government passed acts providing the eventual creation of several Bantu nations or Bantustans on 13% of the country's land area, though most black leaders opposed the plan.

Under apartheid, blacks were severely restricted to certain occupations, and paid far lower wages than whites for similar work. Only whites could vote or run for public office. There was an advisory Indian Council, partly elected, partly appointed. In 1969, a Coloured People's Representative Council was created.

At least 600 persons, mostly Bantus, were killed in 1976 riots protesting apartheid. Black protests continued as violence broke out in several black townships. A new constitution was approved by referendum, Nov. 1983, extending the parliamentary franchise to the Coloured and Asian minorities. Laws banning interracial sex and marriage were repealed in 1985.

In 1963, the Transkei, an area in the SE, became the first of the partially self-governing black territories or "homelands." Transkei was declared "independent" in 1976, Bophuthatswana in 1977, Venda in 1979, and Ciskei in 1981; none received international recognition.

In 1981, South Africa launched military operations in Angola and Mozambique to combat terrorists groups; South African troops attacked the South West African People's Organization (SWAPO) guerrillas in Angola, Mar. 1982. South Africa and Mozambique signed a non-aggression pact in 1984.

In 1986, Nobel Peace Prize winner Bishop Desmond Tutu called for Western nations to apply sanctions against South Africa to force an end to apartheid. President P. W. Botha announced in Apr. the end to the nation's system of racial pass laws and offered blacks an advisory role in government. On May 19, South Africa attacked 3 neighboring countries—Zimbabwe, Botswana, Zambia—to strike at guerrilla strongholds of the black nationalist African National Congress (ANC). A nationwide state of emergency was declared June 12, giving almost unlimited power to the security forces. As confrontation between blacks and government increased, there was widespread support in Western nations for a complete trade embargo on South Africa.

Some 2 million South African black workers staged a massive strike, June 6-8, 1988. Pres. Botha, head of the government since 1978, resigned Aug. 14, 1989, and was replaced by Frederik W. de Klerk.

In 1990, the government lifted its ban on the ANC. On Feb. 11, black nationalist leader Nelson Mandela was freed after more than 27 years in prison. In Oct. the Separate Amenities Act was repealed, ending the legal basis of segregation in public places. In Feb. 1991, Pres. de Klerk announced plans to end all apartheid laws. In June the race registration law was repealed.

In 1993 the nation's negotiating parties, led by the ANC and the National Party, agreed on basic principles for a new constitution, with elections in which all races could vote. Under the new system, South Africa's homelands were abolished as such, incorporated into the national system of 9 provinces.

In elections Apr. 26-29, 1994, the ANC won 62.7% of the vote, enabling Mandela to become president. The National Party won 20.4%. The Inkatha Freedom Party won 10.5% and control of the legislature in a predominantly Zulu province. Fighting between the ANC and Inkatha (assisted, during the apartheid era, by South African defense forces) has killed more than 10,000 people in the Zulu region since the mid-1980s.

In 1995, Mandela appointed a truth commission, led by Desmond Tutu, to document human rights abuses under apartheid. A new constitution, enacted May 8, 1996, was rejected by the Constitutional Court Sept. 6.

# Spain

## Kingdom of Spain

## Reino de España

**People: Population:** 39,181,114. **Age distrib.** (%): <15: 17; 65+: 15. **Pop. density:** 201 per sq. mi. **Urban:** 64%. **Ethnic groups:** Mix of Mediterranean and Nordic types. **Principal languages:** Castilian Spanish (official), Catalan, Galician, Basque. **Religions:** Roman Catholic 99%.

**Geography: Area:** 194,898 sq. mi. **Location:** In SW Europe. **Neighbors:** Portugal on W, France on N. **Topography:** The interior is a high, arid plateau broken by mountain ranges and river valleys. The NW is heavily watered, the S has lowlands and a Mediterranean climate. **Capital:** Madrid. **Cities** (1994 met. est.): Madrid 3 mln.; Barcelona 1.6 mln.; Valencia 764,300; Sevilla 714,100.

**Government: Type:** Constitutional monarchy. **Head of state:** King Juan Carlos I de Borbon y Borbon, b. Jan. 5, 1938; in office: Nov. 22, 1975. **Head of government:** Prime Min. José María Aznar; b Feb. 25, 1953; in office: May 5, 1996. **Local divisions:** 17 automonous communities. **Defense:** 1.6% of GDP (1994). **Active troop strength:** 206,000.

**Economy: Industries:** Machinery, metals, textiles, shoes, vehicles, processed foods, tourism. **Chief crops:** Grains, olives, grapes, citrus fruits, vegetables. **Minerals:** Lignite, uranium, lead, iron, copper, zinc, coal. **Other resources:** Forests. **Arable land:** 31%. **Livestock** (1994): sheep: 23.8 mln.; pigs: 18.2 mln.; cattle: 5.0 mil. **Fish catch** (1993): 1.3 mil metric tons. **Electricity prod.** (1993): 148 bil kWh. **Labor force:** 53% serv.; 24% ind.; 14% agric.

**Finance: Monetary unit:** Peseta (June 1996: 128 = $1 US). **Gross domestic product** (1994): $516 bln.* **Per capita GDP:** $13,120. **Imports** (1993): $92.5 bln.; partners: EU 61%, U.S. 7%. **Exports** (1993): $72.8 bln.; partners: EU 71%, U.S. 5%. **Tourism** (1993): $19.4 bil. **National budget** (1993 est.): $128 bil. **International reserves less gold** (May 1996): $48.1 bil. **Gold:** 15.63 mil oz t. **Consumer prices** (change in 1995): 4.7%.

**Transport: Railroads: Route length:** 7,830 mi. **Motor vehicles:** in use: 13.4 mil passenger cars, 2.9 mil comm. vehicles. **Civil aviation:** 16.6 bil passenger-mi.; 25 airports with scheduled flights. **Chief ports:** Barcelona, Bilbao, Valencia, Cartagena, Gijon.

**Communications: Television sets:** 1 per 2.3 persons. **Radios:** 1 per 3.3 persons. **Telephones:** 1 per 3.1 persons. **Daily newspaper circ.:** 64 per 1,000 pop.

**Health: Life expectancy at birth** (1996): 75 male; 82 female. **Births** (per 1,000 pop.): 10. **Deaths** (per 1,000 pop.): 9. **Natural increase:** 0.1%. **Hospital beds:** 1 per 234 persons. **Physicians:** 1 per 257 persons. **Infant mortality** (per 1,000 live births 1996): 6.

**Education: Literacy** (1993): 96%. Free and compulsory: ages 6-16.

**Major International Organizations:** UN and all of its specialized agencies, NATO, OECD, EU.

**Embassy:** 2375 Pennsylvania Ave. NW 20037; 452-0100.

Spain was settled by Iberians, Basques, and Celts, partly overrun by Carthaginians, conquered by Rome c. 200 BC. The Visigoths, in power by the 5th century AD, adopted Christianity but by 711 lost to the Islamic invasion from Africa. Christian reconquest from the N led to a Spanish nationalism. In 1469 the kingdoms of Aragon and Castile were united by the marriage of Ferdinand II and Isabella I, and the last Moorish power was broken by the fall of the kingdom of Granada, 1492.

Spain obtained a colonial empire with the "discovery" of America by Columbus, 1492, the conquest of Mexico by Cortes, and Peru by Pizarro. It also controlled the Netherlands and parts of Italy and Germany. Spain lost its American colonies in the early 19th century. It lost Cuba, the Philippines, and Puerto Rico during the Spanish-American War, 1898.

Primo de Rivera became dictator in 1923. King Alfonso XIII revoked the dictatorship, 1930, but was forced to leave the country 1931. A republic was proclaimed, which disestablished the church, curtailed its privileges, and secularized education. A conservative reaction occurred 1933 but was followed by a Popular Front (1936-1939) composed of socialists, Communists, republicans, and anarchists.

Army officers under Francisco Franco revolted against the government, 1936. In a destructive 3-year war, in which some one million died, Franco received massive help and troops from Italy and Germany, while the USSR, France, and Mexico supported the republic. War ended Mar. 28, 1939. Franco was named caudillo, leader of the nation. Spain was neutral in World War II, but its relations with fascist countries caused its exclusion from the UN until 1955.

In July 1969, Franco and the Cortes (Parliament) designated Prince Juan Carlos as the future king and chief of state. After Franco's death, Nov. 20, 1975, Juan Carlos was sworn in as king. He presided over the formal dissolution of the institutions of the Franco regime. In free elections June 1977, moderates and democratic socialists emerged as the largest parties.

In 1981 a coup attempt by right-wing military officers was thwarted by the king. The Socialist Workers' Party, under Felipe González Márquez, won 4 consecutive general elections, from 1982 to 1993, but yielded power to a coalition of conservative and regional parties after the election of Mar. 3, 1996.

Catalonia and the Basque country were granted autonomy, Jan. 1980, following overwhelming approval in home-rule referendums. Basque extremists, however, have continued their campaign for independence.

The **Balearic Islands** in the W Mediterranean, 1,927 sq. mi., are a province of Spain; they include **Majorca** (Mallorca; capital Palma de Mallorca), **Minorca, Cabrera, Ibiza,** and **Formentera.** The **Canary Islands,** 2,807 sq. mi., in the Atlantic W of Morocco, form 2 provinces, and include the islands of **Tenerife, Palma, Gomera, Hierro, Grand Canary, Fuerteventura,** and **Lanzarote;** Las Palmas and Santa Cruz are thriving ports. **Ceuta** and **Melilla,** small Spanish enclaves on Morocco's Mediterranean coast, gained limited autonomy in Sept. 1994.

Spain has sought the return of Gibraltar, in British hands since 1704.

# Sri Lanka

## Democratic Socialist Republic of Sri Lanka

## Sri Lanka Prajathanthrika Samajavadi Janarajaya

**People: Population:** 18,553,074. **Age distrib.** (%): <15: 35; 65+: 4. **Pop. density:** 732 per sq. mi. **Urban:** 22%. **Ethnic groups:** Sinhalese 74%, Tamil 18%, Moor 7%. **Principal languages:** Sinhala, Tamil (both official), English. **Religions:** Buddhist 69%, Hindu 15%, Christian 8%, Muslim 8%.

**Geography: Area:** 25,332 sq. mi. **Location:** In Indian O. off SE coast of India. **Neighbors:** India on NW. **Topography:** The coastal area and the northern half are flat; the S-central area is hilly and mountainous. **Capital:** Colombo (1990): 615,000.

**Government: Type:** Republic. **Head of state:** Pres. Chandrika Bandaranaike Kumaratunga; b June 29, 1945; in office: Nov. 12, 1994. **Head of government:** Prime Min. Sirimavo Bandaranaike; b Apr. 17, 1916; in office: Nov. 14, 1994. **Local divisions:** 9 provinces, 25 districts. **Defense:** 3.6% of GDP (1994). **Active troop strength:** 125,300.

**Economy: Industries:** Clothing, agric. processing, oil refining, textiles. **Chief crops:** Tea, coconuts, rice, sugar. **Minerals:** Graphite, limestone, gems, phosphates. **Other resources:** Forests, rubber. **Arable land:** 16%. **Livestock** (1994): cattle: 1.6 mil. **Fish catch** (1993): 221,000 metric tons. **Electricity prod.** (1993): 3.2 bil kWh. **Labor force:** 46% agric.; 13% mining & manuf.

**Finance: Monetary unit:** Rupee (June 1996: 55.60 = $1 US). **Gross domestic product** (1994): $57.6 bln.* **Per capita GDP:** $3,190. **Imports** (1993): $4 bln.; partners: Japan 12%, India 9%. **Exports** (1993): $2.9 bln.; partners: U.S. 35%, Germany 8%. **Tourism** (1993): $208 mil. **National budget** (1993): $3.6 bil. **International reserves less gold** (Mar. 1996): $2.2 bil. **Gold:** 145,000 oz t. **Consumer prices** (change in 1995): 7.7%.

**Transport: Railroads: Route length:** 928 mi. **Motor vehicles:** in use: 197,000 passenger cars, 165,000 comm. vehicles. **Civil aviation:** 2.3 bil passenger-mi.; 1 airport. **Chief ports:** Colombo, Trincomalee, Galle.

**Communications: Television sets:** 1 per 26 persons. **Radios:** 1 per 5.4 persons. **Telephones:** 1 per 111 persons.

**Health: Life expectancy at birth** (1996): 70 male; 75 female. **Births** (per 1,000 pop.): 18. **Deaths** (per 1,000 pop.): 6. **Natural increase:** 1.2%. **Hospital beds:** 1 per 362 persons. **Physicians:** 1 per 5,203 persons. **Infant mortality** (per 1,000 live births 1996): 21.

**Education: Literacy** (1991): 90%. Free and compulsory: ages 5-15; attendance 86%.

**Major International Organizations:** UN (World Bank, WTO, IMF), the Commonwealth.

**Embassy:** 2148 Wyoming Ave. NW 20008; 483-4026.

The island was known to the ancient world as Taprobane (Greek for copper-colored) and later as Serendip (from Arabic). Colonists from northern India subdued the indigenous Veddahs about 543 BC; their descendants, the Buddhist Sinhalese, still form most of the population. Hindu descendants of Tamil immigrants from southern India account for about one-fifth of the population. Parts were occupied by the Portuguese in 1505 and by the Dutch in 1658. The British seized the island in 1796. As Ceylon it became an independent member of the Commonwealth in 1948. On May 22, 1972, Ceylon became the Republic of Sri Lanka.

Prime Min. W. R. D. Bandaranaike was assassinated Sept. 25, 1959. In new elections, the Freedom Party was victorious under Mrs. Sirimavo Bandaranaike, widow of the former prime minister.

After May 1970 elections, Mrs. Bandaranaike became prime minister again. In 1971 the nation suffered economic problems and terrorist activities by ultra-leftists, thousands of whom were executed. Massive land reform and nationalization of foreign-owned plantations were undertaken in the mid-1970s. Mrs. Bandaranaike was ousted in 1977 elections. Presidential powers were increased in 1978 in an effort to restore stability.

Tensions between the Sinhalese and Tamil separatists erupted into violence in the early 1980s. Over 43,000 have died in the civil war, which continued in the mid-1990s.

Pres. Ranasinghe Premadasa was assassinated May 1, 1993, by a Tamil rebel. Mrs. Bandaranaike's daughter, Chandrika Bandaranaike Kumaratunga, became prime minister after the Aug. 16, 1994, general elections. Elected president Nov. 9, Kumaratunga appointed her mother prime minister.

# Sudan

## Republic of the Sudan

## Jumhuriyat as-Sudan

**People: Population:** 31,065,229. **Age distrib.** (%): <15: 43; 65+: 3. **Pop. density:** 32 per sq. mi. **Urban:** 27%. **Ethnic groups:** Black 52%, Arab 39%, Beja 6%. **Principal languages:** Arabic (official), Nubian, Ta Bedawie, Nilotic, Nilo-Hamitic. **Religions:** Sunni Muslim 70%, indigenous beliefs 25%, Christians 5%.

**Geography: Area:** 966,757 sq. mi., the largest country in Africa. **Location:** At the E end of Sahara desert zone. **Neighbors:** Egypt on N; Libya, Chad, Central African Republic on W; Zaire, Uganda, Kenya on S; Ethiopia, Eritrea on E. **Topography:** The N consists of the Libyan Desert in the W, and the mountainous Nubia Desert in E, with narrow Nile valley between. The center contains large, fertile, rainy areas with fields, pasture, and forest. The S has rich soil, heavy rain. **Capital:** Khartoum. **Cities** (1993): Omdurman 1.3 mil; Khartoum 924,500; Khartoum North 879,100; Port Sudan 305,400.

**Government: Type:** Military. **Head of state and government:** Pres. Gen. Omar Hassan Ahmad Al-Bashir; b Jan. 1, 1944; in office: June 30, 1989. **Local divisions:** 9 states. **Defense:** 7.3% of GDP (FY 1993-94). **Active troop strength:** 118,500.

**Economy: Industries:** Cotton ginning, textiles, cement. **Chief crops:** Gum arabic, sorghum, cotton (main export), wheat. **Minerals:** Chromium, copper. **Crude oil reserves** (1995): 300 mil bbls. **Arable land:** 5%. **Livestock** (1994): cattle: 21.8 mln.; sheep: 22.9 mln.; goats: 16.4 mil. **Electricity prod.** (1993): 1.3 bil kWh. **Labor force:** 80% agric.; 10% ind. & comm.; 6% govt.

**Finance: Monetary unit:** Pound (June 1996: 980 = $1 US), Dinar (June 1996: 98 = $1 US). **Gross domestic product** (1994): $23.7 bln.* **Per capita GDP:** $870. **Imports** (FY 1993-94): $1.7 bln.; partners: Libya 16%, Saudi Ar. 12%. **Exports** (FY 1993-94): $419 mln.; partners: Italy 13%, Thailand 11%. **National budget** (1994): $1.1 bil. **International reserves less gold** (Aug. 1996): $114 mil. **Consumer prices** (change in 1993): 101.4%.

**Transport: Railroads: Route length:** 2,960 mi. **Motor vehicles:** in use: 116,000 passenger cars, 57,000 comm. vehicles. **Civil aviation:** 382 mil passenger-mi.; 11 airports with scheduled flights. **Chief port:** Port Sudan.

**Communications: Television sets:** 1 per 103 persons. **Radios:** 1 per 4.5 persons. **Telephones:** 1 per 416 persons. **Daily newspaper circ.:** 25 per 1,000 pop.

**Health: Life expectancy at birth** (1996): 54 male; 56 female. **Births** (per 1,000 pop.): 41. **Deaths** (per 1,000 pop.): 11. **Natural increase:** 2.9%. **Physicians:** 1 per 10,000 persons. **Infant mortality** (per 1,000 live births 1996): 76.

**Education: Literacy** (1992): 46%. Attendance 38%.

**Major International Organizations:** UN (IMF, WHO, FAO), Arab League, OAU.

**Embassy:** 2210 Massachusetts Ave. NW 20008; 338-8566.

Northern Sudan, ancient Nubia, was settled by Egyptians in antiquity, and was converted to Coptic Christianity in the 6th century. Arab conquests brought Islam in the 15th century.

In the 1820s Egypt took over Sudan, defeating the last of earlier empires, including the Fung. In the 1880s a revolution was led by Muhammad Ahmad, who called himself the Mahdi (leader of the faithful), and his followers, the dervishes.

In 1898 an Anglo-Egyptian force crushed the Mahdi's successors. In 1951 the Egyptian Parliament abrogated its 1899 and 1936 treaties with Great Britain and amended its constitution to provide for a separate Sudanese constitution. Sudan voted for complete independence as a parliamentary government effective Jan. 1, 1956.

In 1969, a Revolutionary Council took power, but a civilian premier and cabinet were appointed; the government announced it would create a socialist state.

Economic problems plagued the nation in the 1980s and 1990s, aggravated by civil war and influxes of refugees from neighboring countries. After 16 years in power, Pres. Jaafar al-Nimeiry was overthrown in a bloodless military coup, Apr. 6, 1985. Sudan held its first democratic parliamentary elections in 18 years in 1986, but the elected government was overthrown in a bloodless coup June 30, 1989.

In the mid-1980s, rebels in the south, which is populated largely by black Christians and followers of tribal religions, took up arms against the government, domination by northern Sudan, which is predominantly Arab-Muslim. War and related famine cost an estimated 1.3 million lives and displaced nearly 3 million southerners by the mid-1990s.

In 1993, Amnesty International accused Sudan of practicing "ethnic cleansing" against the Nuba people in the South, and Sudan was among several countries cited for human rights violations by the UN Human Rights Commission Mar. 9, 1994. Egypt publicly blamed Sudan for an attempted assassination of Egyptian Pres. Hosni Mubarak in Ethiopia, June 26, 1995. Elections in Mar. 1996 were boycotted by opposition groups.

# Suriname

## Republic of Suriname

## Republiek Suriname

**People: Population:** 436,418. **Pop. density:** 7 per sq. mi. **Urban:** 49%. **Ethnic groups:** Hindustani 37%, Creole 31%, Javanese 15%. **Principal languages:** Dutch (official), Sranang Tongo, English, Hindustani. **Religions:** Christian 48%, Hindu 27%, Muslim 20%.

**Geography: Area:** 63,251 sq. mi. **Location:** On N shore of South America. **Neighbors:** Guyana on W, Brazil on S, French Guiana on E. **Topography:** A flat Atlantic coast, where dikes permit agriculture. Inland is a forest belt; to the S, largely unexplored hills cover 75% of the country. **Capital:** Paramaribo (1993 est.): 201,000.

**Government: Type:** Republic. **Head of state:** Pres. Jules Wijdenbosch; in office: Sept. 14, 1996. **Local divisions:** 10 districts. **Defense:** 1.1% of GNP (1993). **Active troop strength:** 1,800 est.

**Economy: Industries:** Aluminum, food processing. **Chief crops:** Rice, bananas, palm kernels. **Minerals:** Bauxite, iron. **Other resources:** Forests, fish, shrimp. **Arable land:** 0%. **Electricity prod.** (1993): 1.4 bil kWh.

**Finance: Monetary unit:** Guilder (June 1996: 410 = $1 US). **Gross domestic product** (1994): $1.2 bln.* **Per capita GDP:** $2,800. **Imports** (1993): $520 mln.; partners: U.S. 42%, Netherlands 22%, Trin./Tob. 10%. **Exports** (1993): $443 mln.; partners: Norway 33%, Netherlands 26%, U.S. 13%. **Tourism** (1992): $11 mil. **National budget** (1994): $700 mil. **Gold:** 103,000 oz t.

**Transport: Motor vehicles:** in use: 43,000 passenger cars, 16,000 comm. vehicles. **Chief ports:** Paramaribo, Nieuw Nickerie.

**Communications: Television sets:** 1 per 9.8 persons. **Radios:** 1 per 1.6 persons. **Telephones:** 1 per 8.6 persons. **Daily newspaper circ.:** 61 per 1,000 pop.

**Health: Life expectancy at birth** (1996): 68 male; 73 female. **Births** (per 1,000 pop.): 24. **Deaths** (per 1,000 pop.): 6. **Natural increase:** 1.8%. **Infant mortality** (per 1,000 live births 1996): 29.

**Education: Literacy** (1993): 93%. Compulsory: ages 6–16.

**Major International Organizations:** UN (WHO, WTO, ILO, FAO, World Bank, IMF), OAS.

**Embassy:** 4301 Connecticut Ave. NW 20008; 244-7490.

The Netherlands acquired Suriname in 1667 from Britain, in exchange for New Netherlands (New York). The 1954 Dutch constitution raised the colony to a level of equality with the Netherlands and the Netherlands Antilles. Independence was granted Nov. 25, 1975, despite objections from East Indians. Some 40% of the population (mostly East Indians) immigrated to the Netherlands in the months before independence.

The National Military Council took over control of the government, Feb. 1982. Civilian rule was restored in 1987, but political turmoil continued for another 5 years, disrupting the nation's economy.

# Swaziland

## Kingdom of Swaziland

## Umbuso weSwatini

**People: Population:** 998,730. **Age distrib.** (%): <15: 46; 65+: 2. **Pop. density:** 149 per sq. mi. **Urban:** 30%. **Ethnic groups:** African 97%, European 3%. **Principal languages:** siSwati, English (both official). **Religions:** Christians 60%, indigenous beliefs 40%.

**Geography: Area:** 6,704 sq. mi. **Location:** In southern Africa, near Indian O. coast. **Neighbors:** South Africa on N, W, S; Mozambique on E. **Topography:** The country descends from W-E in broad belts, becoming more arid in the low veld region, then rising to a plateau in the E. **Capital:** Mbabane. **Cities** (1990 est.): Manzini 53,000; Mbabane 47,000.

**Government: Type:** Constitutional monarchy. **Head of state:** King Mswati 3d; b 1968; in office: Apr. 25, 1986. **Head of government:** Prime Min. Prince Jameson Mbilini Dlamini; b Aug. 5, 1932; in office: Nov. 4, 1993. **Local divisions:** 4 districts.

**Economy: Industries:** Wood pulp, mining. **Chief crops:** Sugar, corn, cotton, rice, pineapples, sugar, citrus fruits. **Minerals:** Asbestos, clay, coal. **Other resources:** Forests. **Arable land:** 11%. **Electricity prod.** (1993): 410 mil kWh. **Labor force:** More than 60% agric.

**Finance: Monetary unit:** Lilangeni (June 1996: 4.34 = $1 US). **Gross domestic product** (1994): $3.3 bln.* **Per capita GDP:** $3,490. **Imports** (1993): $734 mln.; partners: South Africa 90%. **Exports** (1993): $632 mln.; partners: South Africa 50%. **Tourism** (1993): $30 mil. **National budget** (1994 est.): $410 mil. **International reserves less gold** (May 1996): $272 mil. **Consumer prices** (change in 1995): 14.7%.

**Transport: Motor vehicles:** in use: 26,000 passenger cars, 8,000 comm. vehicles.

**Communications: Television sets:** 1 per 68 persons. **Radios:** 1 per 7.5 persons. **Telephones:** 1 per 56 persons.

**Health: Life expectancy at birth** (1996): 53 male; 61 female. **Births** (per 1,000 pop.): 43. **Deaths** (per 1,000 pop.): 11. **Natural increase:** 3.2%. **Infant mortality rate** (per 1,000 live births 1996): 88.

**Education: Literacy** (1993): 77%. 93% attend primary school.

**Major International Organizations:** UN (IMF, WTO, WHO, FAO), OAU, the Commonwealth.

**Embassy:** 3400 International Dr. NW 20008; 362-6683.

The royal house of Swaziland traces back 400 years, and is one of Africa's last ruling dynasties. The Swazis, a Bantu people, were driven to Swaziland from lands to the N by the Zulus in 1820. Their autonomy was later guaranteed by Britain and Transvaal (later part of South Africa), with Britain assuming control after 1903. Independence came Sept. 6, 1968. In 1973 the king repealed the constitution and assumed full powers.

A new constitution banning political parties took effect Oct. 13, 1978. As Swaziland slowly moved toward political reform, student and labor unrest grew in the mid-1990s.

# Sweden

## Kingdom of Sweden

## Konungariket Sverige

**People: Population:** 8,900,954. **Age distrib.** (%): <15: 19; 65+: 17. **Pop. density:** 51 per sq. mi. **Urban:** 83%. **Ethnic groups:** Swedish 90%, Finnish 2%, Lappish, European immigrant. **Principal languages:** Swedish. **Religions:** Evangelical Lutheran (official) 94%.

**Geography: Area:** 173,732 sq. mi. **Location:** On Scandinavian Peninsula in N Europe. **Neighbors:** Norway on W, Denmark on S (across Kattegat), Finland on E. **Topography:** Mountains along NW border cover 25% of Sweden, flat or rolling terrain covers the central and southern areas, which include several large lakes. **Capital:** Stockholm. **Cities** (1995 est.): Stockholm 703,600; Göteborg 444,600; Malmö 242,700.

**Government: Type:** Constitutional monarchy. **Head of state:** King Carl XVI Gustaf; b Apr. 30, 1946; in office: Sept. 19, 1973. **Head of government:** Prime Min. Goran Persson; b June 20, 1949; in office: Mar. 22, 1996. **Local divisions:** 24 provinces. **Defense:** 2.4% of GDP (FY 1994-95). **Active troop strength:** 64,000.

**Economy: Industries:** Steel, machinery, precision instruments, vehicles, shipbuilding, paper. **Chief crops:** Grains, potatoes, sugar beets. **Minerals:** Zinc, iron, lead, copper, silver. **Other resources:** Forests (half the country); yield about 16% of exports. **Arable land:** 7%. **Livestock** (1994): cattle: 1.8 mln.; pigs: 2.3 mil. **Fish catch** (1994): 376,000 metric tons. **Electricity prod.** (1993): 141 bil kWh. **Labor force:** 38% social & personal services; 21% manuf. & mining.

**Finance: Monetary unit:** Krona (June 1996: 6.64 = $1 US). **Gross domestic product** (1994): $163.1 bln.* **Per capita GDP:** $18,580. **Imports** (1994): $49.6 bln.; partners: EU 54%; U.S. 8%. **Exports** (1993): $59.9 bln.; partners: EU 56%, U.S. 8%. **Tourism** (1993): $2.7 bil. **National budget** (FY 1993-94): $70.9 bil. **International reserves less gold** (Apr. 1996): $20.2 bil. **Gold:** 4.8 mil oz t. **Consumer prices** (change in 1995): 2.5%.

**Transport: Railroads: Length:** 7,012 mi. **Motor vehicles:** in use: 3.6 mil passenger cars, 316,000 comm. vehicles. **Civil aviation:** 5.1 bil passenger-mi.; 48 airports. **Chief ports:** Göteborg, Stockholm, Malmö.

**Communications: Television sets:** 1 per 2.3 persons. **Radios:** 1 per 1.2 persons. **Telephones:** 1 per 1.5 persons. **Daily newspaper circ.:** 536 per 1,000 pop.

**Health: Life expectancy at birth** (1996): 76 male; 81 female. **Births** (per 1,000 pop.): 12. **Deaths** (per 1,000 pop.): 11. **Natural increase:** 0. **Hospital beds:** 1 per 150 persons. **Physicians:** 1 per 393 persons. **Infant mortality** (per 1,000 live births (1996): 5.

**Education: Literacy** (1994): 100%. Compulsory: ages 6-15; attendance 100%.

**Major International Organizations:** UN and all of its specialized agencies, EU, OECD.

**Embassy:** 1501 M St. NW 20005; 467-2600.

The Swedes have lived in present-day Sweden for at least 5,000 years, longer than nearly any other European people. Gothic tribes from Sweden played a major role in the disintegration of the Roman Empire. Other Swedes helped create the first Russian state in the 9th century.

The Swedes were Christianized from the 11th century, and a strong centralized monarchy developed. A parliament, the Riksdag, was first called in 1435, the earliest parliament on the European continent, with all classes of society represented.

Swedish independence from rule by Danish kings (dating from 1397) was secured by Gustavus I in a revolt, 1521-23; he built up the government and military and established the Lutheran Church. In the 17th century Sweden was a major European power, gaining most of the Baltic seacoast, but its international position subsequently declined.

The Napoleonic wars, 1799-1815, in which Sweden acquired Norway (it became independent 1905), were the last in which Sweden participated. Armed neutrality was maintained in both world wars.

More than 4 decades of Social Democratic rule ended in the 1976 parliamentary elections; the party returned to power in the 1982 elections. After Prime Min. Olof Palme was shot to death in Stockholm, Feb. 28, 1986, Ingvar Carlsson took office. Carl Bildt, a non-Socialist, became prime minister Oct. 1991, with a mandate to restore Sweden's economic competitiveness. The Social Democrats returned to power following 1994 elections.

Swedish voters approved membership in the European Union Nov. 13, 1994, and Sweden entered the EU as of Jan. 1, 1995. Carlsson retired and was succeeded by Goran Persson in Mar. 1996.

# Switzerland

## Swiss Confederation

**People: Population:** 7,207,060. **Age distrib.** (%): <15: 18; 65+: 15. **Pop. density:** 452 per sq. mi. **Urban:** 68%. **Ethnic groups:** German, French, Italian, Romansch. **Principal languages:** German, French, Italian (all official). **Religions:** Roman Catholic 48%, Protestant 44%.

**Geography: Area:** 15,940 sq. mi. **Location:** In the Alps Mts. in central Europe. **Neighbors:** France on W, Italy on S, Austria on E, Germany on N. **Topography:** The Alps cover 60% of the land area; the Jura, near France, 10%. Running between, from NE to SW, are midlands, 30%. **Capitals:** Bern (administrative), Lausanne (judicial). **Cities** (1994): Zurich 343,000; Basel 176,200; Geneva 171,700; Bern 129,400.

**Government: Type:** Federal republic. **Head of government:** The president is elected by the Federal Assembly to a nonrenewable 1-year term. **Local divisions:** 20 full cantons, 6 half cantons. **Defense:** 1.4% of GDP (1995). **Active troop strength:** 3,400.

**Economy: Industries:** Machinery, chemicals, precision instruments, watches, textiles, foodstuffs (cheese, chocolate), banking, tourism. **Minerals:** Salt. **Other resources:** Hydropower potential, dairy products. **Arable land:** 10%. **Livestock** (1993): cattle: 1.7 mln.; pigs: 1.7 mil. **Electricity prod.** (1993): 58 bil kWh. **Labor force:** 50% serv.; 33% ind. and crafts; 10% govt.

**Finance: Monetary unit:** Franc (June 1996: 1.25 = $1 US). **Gross domestic product** (1994): $148.4 bln.* **Per capita GDP:** $22,080. **Imports** (1994): $68.2 bln.; partners: EU 72%. **Exports** (1994): $69.6 bln.; partners: EU 56%; U.S. 9%. **Tourism** (1993): $7.0 bil. **National budget** (1994): $32 bil. **International reserves less gold** (May 1996): $33.0 bil. **Gold:** 83.28 mil oz t. **Consumer prices** (change in 1995): 1.8%.

**Transport: Railroads: Length:** 3,125 mi. **Motor vehicles:** in use: 3.1 mil passenger cars, 287,000 comm. vehicles. **Civil aviation:** 11.5 bil passenger-mi.; 5 airports with scheduled flights. **Chief port:** Basel.

**Communications: Television sets:** 1 per 2.8 persons. **Radios:** 1 per 1.3 persons. **Telephones:** 1 per 1.6 persons. **Daily newspaper circ.:** 490 per 1,000 pop.

**Health: Life expectancy at birth** (1996): 75 male; 81 female. **Births** (per 1,000 pop.): 11. **Deaths** (per 1,000 pop.): 10. **Natural increase:** 0.2%. **Hospital beds:** 1 per 129 persons. **Physicians:** 1 per 299 persons. **Infant mortality** (per 1,000 live births 1996): 5.

**Education: Literacy** (1994): 100%. Compulsory: ages 7-16.

**Major International Organizations:** Many UN specialized agencies (though not a member), EFTA, OECD.

**Embassy:** 2900 Cathedral Ave. NW 20008; 745-7900.

Switzerland, the Roman province of Helvetia, is a federation of 23 cantons (20 full cantons and 6 half cantons), 3 of which in 1291 created a defensive league and later were joined by other districts. Voters in the French-speaking part of Canton Bern voted for self-government, 1978; Canton Jura was created Jan. 1, 1979.

In 1648 the Swiss Confederation obtained its independence from the Holy Roman Empire. The cantons were joined under a federal constitution in 1848, with large powers of local control retained by each canton.

Switzerland has maintained an armed neutrality since 1815, and has not been involved in a foreign war since 1515. It is the seat of many UN and other international agencies.

Switzerland is a leading world banking center. In an effort to crack down on criminal transactions, the nation's strict bank-secrecy rules have been eased since 1990.

# Syria

## Syrian Arab Republic

## Al Jumhuriyah al Arabiyah as Suriyah

**People: Population:** 15,608,648. **Age distrib.** (%): <15: 49; 65+: 4. **Pop. density:** 218 per sq. mi. **Urban:** 51%. **Ethnic groups:** Arab 90%, Kurd, Armenian, others. **Principal languages:** Arabic (official), Kurdish, Armenian. **Religions:** Sunni Muslim 74%, other Muslim 16%, Christian 10%.

**Geography: Area:** 71,498 sq. mi. **Location:** Middle East, at E end of Mediterranean Sea. **Neighbors:** Lebanon and Israel on W, Jordan on S, Iraq on E, Turkey on N. **Topography:** Syria has a short Mediterranean coastline, then stretches E and S with fertile lowlands and plains, alternating with mountains and large desert areas. **Capital:** Damascus. **Cities** (1994): Aleppo 1.6 mln.; Damascus 1.6 mln.; Homs 644,200.

**Government: Type:** Republic (under military regime). **Head of state:** Pres. Hafez al-Assad; b Mar. 1930; in office: Feb. 22, 1971. **Head of government:** Prime Min. Mahmoud Zuabi; in office: Nov. 1, 1987. **Local divisions:** Damascus and 13 provinces. **Defense:** 6% of GDP (1992). **Active troop strength:** 423,000 est.

**Economy: Industries:** Oil prods., textiles, food processing, tobacco, phosphate mining. **Chief crops:** Cotton, grains, olives, lentils, chickpeas. **Minerals:** Oil, phosphates, iron, gypsum. **Crude oil reserves** (1995): 2.5 bil bbls. **Other resources:** Wool, dairy prods. **Arable land:** 28%. **Livestock** (1994): sheep: 12 mln., goats: 1.2 mln. **Electricity prod.** (1993): 13.2 bil kWh. **Labor force:** 36% services; 32% agric.; 32% ind. & constr.

**Finance: Monetary unit:** Pound (June 1996: 41.95 = $1 US). **Gross domestic product** (1994): $74.4 bln.* **Per capita GDP:** $5,000. **Imports** (1994): $4 bln.; partners: EU 37%. **Exports** (1994): $3.6 bln.; partners: EU 48%. **Tourism** (1993): $700 mil. **National budget** (1995): $14.4 bil. **Gold:** 833,000 oz t. **Consumer prices** (change in 1994): 9.2%.

**Transport: Railroads: Route length:** 1,405 mi. **Motor vehicles:** in use: 118,000 passenger cars, 153,000 comm. vehicles. **Civil aviation:** 521 mil passenger-mi.; 5 airports with scheduled flights. **Chief ports:** Latakia, Tartus.

**Communications: Television sets:** 1 per 20 persons. **Radios:** 1 per 4.6 persons. **Telephones:** 1 per 24 persons. **Daily newspaper circ.:** 22 per 1,000 pop.

**Health: Life expectancy at birth** (1996): 66 male; 68 female. **Births** (per 1,000 pop.): 40. **Deaths** (per 1,000 pop.): 6. **Natural increase:** 3.4%. **Hospital beds:** 1 per 911 persons. **Physicians:** 1 per 966 persons. **Infant mortality** (per 1,000 live births 1996): 40.

**Education: Literacy** (1994): 71%. Compulsory: ages 6-12.
**Major International Organizations:** UN (IMF, WHO, FAO), Arab League.
**Embassy:** 2215 Wyoming Ave. NW 20008; 232-6313.

Syria contains some of the most ancient remains of civilization. It was the center of the Seleucid empire, but later became absorbed in the Roman and Arab empires. Ottoman rule prevailed for 4 centuries, until the end of World War I.

The state of Syria was formed from former Turkish districts, separated by the Treaty of Sevres, 1920, and divided into the states of Syria and Greater Lebanon. Both were administered under a French League of Nations mandate 1920-1941.

Syria was proclaimed a republic by the occupying French Sept. 16, 1941, and exercised full independence effective Apr. 17, 1946. Syria joined in the Arab invasion of Israel in 1948.

Syria joined Egypt Feb. 1958 in the United Arab Republic but seceded Sept. 1961. The Socialist Baath party and military leaders seized power Mar. 1963. The Baath, a pan-Arab organization, became the only legal party. The government has been dominated by members of the minority Alawite sect.

In the Arab-Israeli war of June 1967, Israel seized and occupied the Golan Heights area inside Syria, from which Israeli settlements had for years been shelled by Syria. On Oct. 6, 1973, Syria joined Egypt in an attack on Israel. Arab oil states agreed in 1974 to give Syria $1 billion a year to aid anti-Israel moves. Some 30,000 Syrian troops entered Lebanon in 1976 to mediate in a civil war. They fought Palestinian guerrillas and, later, Christian militiamen. Syrian troops again battled Christian forces in Lebanon, Apr. 1981.

Following the June 6, 1982, Israeli invasion of Lebanon, Israeli planes destroyed 17 Syrian antiaircraft missile batteries in the Bekaa Valley, June 9. Some 25 Syrian planes were downed during the engagement. Israel and Syria agreed to a cease-fire June 11. In 1983, Syria backed the PLO rebels who ousted Yasir Arafat's forces from Tripoli.

Syria's role in promoting international terrorism led to the breaking of diplomatic relations with Great Britain and to limited sanctions by the European Community in 1986.

Syria condemned the Aug. 1990 Iraqi invasion of Kuwait and sent troops to help Allied forces in the Gulf War. In 1991, Syria accepted U.S. proposals for the terms of an Arab-Israeli peace conference. Syria subsequently participated in negotiations with Israel, but progress toward peace was slow.

# Taiwan

## Republic of China

## Chung-hua Min-kuo

**People: Population:** 21,465,881. **Age distrib.** (%): <15: 24; 65+: 7. **Pop. density:** 1,537 per sq. mi. **Urban:** 75%. **Ethnic groups:** Taiwanese 84%, mainland Chinese 14%. **Principal languages:** Mandarin Chinese (official), Taiwanese, Hakka dialects. **Religions:** Buddhist, Taoist, Confucian 93%; Christian 4.5%.

**Geography: Area:** 13,969 sq. mi. **Location:** Off SE coast of China, between East and South China seas. **Neighbors:** Nearest is China. **Topography:** A mountain range forms the backbone of the island; the eastern half is very steep and craggy, the western slope is flat, fertile, and well cultivated. **Capital:** Taipei. **Cities** (1993): Taipei 2.7 mln.; Kaohsiung 1.4 mln.; Taichung 805,000; Tainan 698,000.

**Government: Type:** Democracy. **Head of state and Nationalist Party chmn.:** Pres. Lee Teng-hui; b Jan. 15, 1923; in office: Jan. 13, 1988. **Head of government:** Prime Min. Lien Chan; b Aug. 27, 1936; in office: Feb. 10, 1993. **Local divisions:** 16 counties, 5 municipalities, Taipei and Kaohsiung. **Defense:** 3.4% of GDP (FY 1994-95). **Active troop strength:** 376,000.

**Economy: Industries:** Textiles, clothing, electronics, processed foods, chemicals. **Chief crops:** Vegetables, rice, fruit, tea, sugarcane. **Minerals:** Coal, limestone, marble. **Arable land:** 24%. **Livestock** (1994): pigs: 10.1 mil. **Fish catch** (1994): 1.3 mil metric tons. **Electricity prod.** (1993): 108 bil kWh. **Labor force:** 53% ind. & comm.; 22% services; 16% agric.

**Finance: Monetary unit:** New Taiwan Dollar (June 1996: 27.31 = $1 US). **Gross domestic product** (1994): $257 bln.* **Per capita GDP:** $12,070. **Imports** (1994): $85.1 bln.; partners: Japan 30%, U.S. 22%. **Exports** (1994): $93 bln.; partners: U.S. 28%, Hong Kong 22%, EU 15%. **Tourism** (1993): $2.9 bil. **National budget** (1991): $30.1 bil.

**Transport: Motor vehicles:** in use: 3.8 mil passenger cars, 816,000 commercial vehicles. **Civil aviation:** 22.8 bil passenger-mi.; 12 airports. **Chief ports:** Kaohsiung, Chilung (Keelung), Hualien, Taichung.

**Communications: Television sets:** 1 per 3.0 persons. **Radios:** 1 per 2.4 persons. **Telephones:** 1 per 2.6 persons. **Daily newspaper circ.:** 202 per 1,000 pop.

**Health: Life expectancy at birth** (1996): 73 male; 79 female. **Births** (per 1,000 pop.): 15. **Deaths** (per 1,000 pop.): 6. **Natural increase:** 1.0%. **Hospital beds:** 1 per 208 persons. **Physicians:** 1 per 804 persons. **Infant mortality** (per 1,000 live births 1996): 7.

**Education: Literacy** (1994): 93%. Free and compulsory: ages 6-15; attendance 98%.

**Major International Organizations:** APEC

Large-scale Chinese immigration began in the 17th century. The island came under mainland control after an interval of Dutch rule, 1620-62. Taiwan (also called Formosa) was ruled by Japan 1895-1945. Two million Kuomintang supporters fled to Taiwan in 1949. Both the Taipei and Beijing governments consider Taiwan an integral part of China. Taiwan has resisted Beijing's efforts at reunification, including military pressure, but economic ties with the mainland expanded in the 1990s.

The U.S., upon its recognition of the People's Republic of China, Dec. 15, 1978, severed diplomatic ties with Taiwan. The U.S. maintains the unofficial American Institute in Taiwan, while Taiwan has an agency, the Taipei Economic and Cultural Representative Office, with field offices in Washington, DC, and other U.S. cities.

Land reform, government planning, U.S. aid and investment, and free universal education have brought huge advances in industry, agriculture, and living standards. In 1987 martial law was lifted after 38 years, and in 1991 the 43-year period of emergency rule ended. Taiwan held its first direct presidential election Mar. 23, 1996. The ruling Nationalist Party has faced increasing challenge from opposition parties.

Taiwan has one of the world's strongest economies and is among the 10 leading capital exporters.

The **Penghu Is.** (Pescadores), 49 sq. mi., pop. (1995 est.) 92,000, lie between Taiwan and the mainland. **Quemoy** and **Matsu,** pop. (1995 est.) 52,000, lie just off the mainland.

# Tajikistan

## Republic of Tajikistan

## Jumhurii Tojikiston

**People: Population:** 5,916,373. **Age distrib.** (%): <15: 43; 65+: 4. **Pop. density:** 107 per sq. mi. **Urban:** 28%. **Ethnic groups:** Tajik 65%, Uzbek 25%, Russian 3.5%. **Principal languages:** Tajik (official), Russian. **Religions:** Sunni Muslim 80%.

**Geography: Area:** 55,300 sq. mi. **Location:** Central Asia. **Neighbors:** Uzbekistan on N and W, Kyrgyzstan on N, China on E, Afghanistan on S. **Topography:** Mountainous region that contains the Pamirs, Trans-Alai mountain system. **Capital:** Dushanbe (1994 est.): 524,000.

**Government: Type:** Republic. **Head of state:** Pres. Imomali Rakhmonov; b Oct. 5, 1952; in office: Nov. 16, 1994. **Head of Government:** Yakhyo Azimov; b Dec. 4, 1947; in office: Feb. 8, 1996. **Local divisions:** 2 oblasts, 1 autonomous oblast. **Defense:** 3.7% of GDP (1992). **Active troop strength:** 2,000-3,000.

**Economy: Industries:** Textiles, knitwear, aluminum, mining. **Chief crops:** Cotton, barley, wheat, melons, vegetables. **Minerals:** Coal, lead, zinc. **Arable land:** 6%. **Livestock** (1994): sheep and goats: 2.8 mln.; cattle: 1.3 mil. **Electricity prod.** (1994): 17 bil kWh. **Labor force:** 43% agric. & forestry; 24% serv. & govt.

**Finance: Monetary unit:** Ruble *June 1996: 285 = $1 US). **Gross domestic product** (1994 est.): $8.5 bln.* **Per capita GDP:** $1,415. **Imports** (1994): 318 mil., excl. CIS **Exports** (1994): $320 mln., excl. CIS.

**Transportation: Railroads: Length:** 554 mi. **Civil aviation:** 3.2 bil passenger-mi.; 1 airport with scheduled flights.

**Communications: Television sets:** 1 per 6.6 persons. **Radios:** 1 per 6.7 persons. **Telephones:** 1 per 22 persons. **Daily newspaper circ.:** 63 per 1,000 pop.

**Health: Life expectancy at birth** (1996): 61 male; 68 female. **Births** (per 1,000 pop.): 34. **Deaths** (per 1,000 pop.): 8. **Natural increase:** 2.5%. **Hospital beds:** 1 per 99 persons. **Physicians:** 1 per 447 persons. **Infant mortality** (per 1,000 live births 1996): 113.

**Major International Organizations:** UN, CIS.

There were settled societies in the region from about 3000 BC. Throughout history, the region has undergone invasions by Iranians (Arabs who converted the population to Islam), Mongols, Uzbeks, Afghans, and Russians. The USSR gained control of the region 1918-25. In 1924, the Tajik ASSR was created within the Uzbek SSR. The Tajik SSR was proclaimed in 1929.

Tajikistan declared independence Sept. 9, 1991. It became an independent state when the Soviet Union disbanded Dec. 26, 1991. Conservative Communist Pres. Rakhmon Nabiyev was forced to resign, Sept. 1992, by a coalition of Islamic, nationalist, and Western-oriented parties.

Factional fighting led to the installation of a pro-Communist regime, Jan. 1993. A new constitution establishing a presidential system was approved by referendum Nov. 6, 1994. Muslim rebels, reportedly armed by Afghanistan, continued to fight the regime, which had Russian support.

# Tanzania

## United Republic of Tanzania

## Jamhuri ya Muungano wa Tanzania

**People: Population:** 29,058,470. **Age distrib.** (%): <15: 47; 65+: 3. **Pop. density:** 80 per sq. mi. **Urban:** 21%. **Ethnic groups:** African 99%. **Principal languages:** Swahili, English (both official), many others. **Religions:** Christians 45%, Muslims 35%, indigenous beliefs 20%.

**Geography: Area:** 364,017 sq. mi. **Location:** On coast of E Africa. **Neighbors:** Kenya, Uganda on N; Rwanda, Burundi, Zaire on W; Zambia, Malawi, Mozambique on S. **Topography:** Hot, arid central plateau, surrounded by the lake region in the W, temperate highlands in N and S, the coastal plains. Mt. Kilimanjaro, 19,340 ft., is highest in Africa. **Capital:** Dar-es-Salaam (capital is being moved to Dodoma). **Cities** (1992 est.): Dar-es-Salaam 1.4 mil.

**Government: Type:** Republic. **Head of state:** Pres. Benjamin William Mkapa; b Nov. 12, 1938; in office: Nov. 23, 1995. **Head of government:** Prime Min. Frederick Sumaye; in office: Nov. 28, 1995. **Local divisions:** 25 regions. **Defense:** 3.8% of GNP (1993). **Active troop strength:** 34,600 est.

**Economy: Industries:** Agricultural processing, mining, textiles. **Chief crops:** Sisal, cotton, coffee, tea, tobacco, corn, spices. **Minerals:** Tin, phospates, diamonds, gold. **Other resources:** Pyrethrum (insecticide made from chrysanthemums). **Arable land:** 5%. **Livestock** (1994): cattle: 13.4 mln.; goats: 9.7 mln.; sheep: 4.0 mil. **Fish catch** (1993): 345,000 metric tons. **Electricity prod.** (1993): 880 mil kWh. **Labor force:** 90% agric.; 10% ind. & comm.

**Finance: Monetary unit:** Shilling (June 1996: 613 = $1 US). **Gross domestic product** (1994): $21 bln.* **Per capita GDP:** $700. **Imports** (1994): $1.4 bln.; partners: UK 13%, Japan 10%, Italy 8%. **Exports** (1994): $462 mln.; partners: Ger. 16%, UK 9%. **Tourism** (1993): $147 mil. **National budget** (1990): $631 mil. **International reserves less gold** (Apr. 1996): $226.5 mil. **Consumer prices** (change in 1995): 27.4%.

**Transport: Motor vehicles:** in use: 50,000 passenger cars; 40,000 comm. vehicles. **Civil aviation:** 94 mil passenger-mi.; 11 airports with scheduled flights. **Chief ports:** Dar-es-Salaam, Mtwara, Tanga.

**Communications: Television sets:** 1 per 341 persons. **Radios:** 1 per 4.8 persons. **Telephones:** 1 per 312 persons.

**Health: Life expectancy at birth** (1996): 41 male; 44 female. **Births** (per 1,000 pop.): 41. **Deaths** (per 1,000 pop.): 19. **Natural increase:** 2.2%. **Physicians:** 1 per 20,300 persons. **Infant mortality** (per 1,000 live births 1996): 106.

**Education: Literacy** (1995): 68%. Free and compulsory: ages 7-14.

**Major International Organizations:** UN and all of its specialized agencies, OAU, the Commonwealth.

**Embassy:** 2139 R St. NW 20008; 939-6125.

The Republic of Tanganyika in E Africa and the island Republic of Zanzibar, off the coast of Tanganyika, both of which had recently gained independence, joined into a single nation, the United Republic of Tanzania, Apr. 26, 1964. Zanzibar retains internal self-government.

Until resigning as president in 1985, Julius K. Nyerere, a former Tanganyikan independence leader, dominated Tanzania's politics, which emphasized government planning and control of the economy, with single-party rule. In 1992 the constitution was amended to establish a multiparty system. Privatization of the economy was undertaken in the 1990s.

At least 500 people died when an overcrowded Tanzanian ferry sank in Lake Victoria, May 21, 1996.

**Tanganyika.** Arab colonization and slaving began in the 8th century AD; Portuguese sailors explored the coast by about 1500. Other Europeans followed.

In 1885 Germany established German East Africa of which Tanganyika formed the bulk. It became a League of Nations mandate and, after 1946, a UN trust territory, both under Britain. It became independent Dec. 9, 1961, and a republic within the Commonwealth a year later.

**Zanzibar,** the Isle of Cloves, lies 23 mi. off mainland Tanzania; area 640 sq. mi. and pop. (1990 est.) 375,000. The island of **Pemba,** 25 mi. to the NE, area 380 sq. mi. and pop. (1988 cen.) 265,000, is included in the administration.

Chief industry is the production of cloves and clove oil, of which Zanzibar and Pemba produce most of the world's supply.

Zanzibar was for centuries the center for Arab slave traders. Portugal ruled for 2 centuries until ousted by Arabs around 1700. Zanzibar became a British Protectorate in 1890; independence came Dec. 10, 1963. Revolutionary forces overthrew the Sultan Jan. 12, 1964. The new government ousted Western diplomats and newsmen, slaughtered thousands of Arabs, and nationalized farms. Union with Tanganyika followed.

# Thailand

## Kingdom of Thailand

## Muang Thai *or* Prathet Thai

**People: Population:** 58,851,357. **Age distrib.** (%): <15: 30; 65+: 4. **Pop. density:** 297 per sq. mi. **Urban:** 19%. **Ethnic groups:** Thai 75%,Chinese 14%. **Principal languages:** Thai (official), Lao, Chinese, Malay. **Religions:** Buddhist 95%, Muslim 4%.

**Geography: Area:** 198,115 sq. mi. **Location:** On Indochinese and Malayan peninsulas in SE Asia. **Neighbors:** Myanmar on W, Laos on N, Cambodia on E, Malaysia on S. **Topography:** A plateau dominates the NE third of Thailand, dropping to the fertile alluvial valley of the Chao Phraya R. in the center. Forested mountains are in the N, with narrow fertile valleys. The S peninsula region is covered by rain forests. **Capital:** Bangkok (1993 cen.): 5.6 mil.

**Government: Type:** Constitutional monarchy. **Head of state:** King Bhumibol Adulyadej; b Dec. 5, 1927; in office: June 9, 1946. **Head of government:** Prime Min. Banharn Silpa-archa; b July 20, 1932; in office: July 13, 1995. **Local divisions:** 76 provinces. **Defense:** 2.5% of GNP (FY 1994-95). **Active troop strength:** 259,000.

**Economy: Industries:** Textiles, agric. processing, tourism. **Chief crops:** Rice (major export), corn, tapioca, sugarcane. **Minerals:** Among world's largest producers of tin and tungsten; diamonds, potash, gas. **Crude oil reserves** (1995): 218 mil bbls. **Other resources:** Forests (teak is exported), rubber, seafood. **Arable land:** 34%. **Livestock** (1994): cattle: 7.6 mln.; pigs: 4.9 mil. **Fish catch** (1993): 3.3 mil metric tons. **Electricity prod.** (1993): 56.8 bil kWh. **Labor force:** 62% agric.; 24% ind. & comm.; 14% serv. & govt.

**Finance: Monetary unit:** Baht (June 1996: 25.39 = $1 US). **Gross domestic product** (1994): $355.2 bln.* **Per capita GDP:** $5,970. **Imports** (1994): $52.6 bln.; partners: Japan 30%, U.S. 12%. **Exports** (1994): $46 bln.; partners: U.S. 22%, Japan 17 %. **Tourism** (1993): $5.0 bil. **National budget** (FY 1994-95): $28.4 bil. **International reserves less gold** (May 1996): $38.0 bil. **Gold:** 2.47 mil oz t. **Consumer prices** (change in 1994): 5.1%.

**Transport: Railroads: Route length:** 2,405 mi. **Motor vehicles:** in use: 1.1 mln. passenger cars, 2.5 mil comm. vehicles. **Civil aviation:** 15.7 bil passenger-mi.; 26 airports with scheduled flights. **Chief ports:** Bangkok, Sattahip.

**Communication: Television sets:** 1 per 17 persons. **Radios:** 1 per 5.8 persons. **Telephones:** 1 per 27 persons. **Daily newspaper circ.:** 74 per 1,000 pop.

**Health: Life expectancy at birth** (1996): 65 male; 73 female. **Births** (per 1,000 pop.): 17. **Deaths** (per 1,000 pop.): 7. **Natural increase:** 1.0%. **Hospital beds:** 1 per 599 persons. **Physicians:** 1 per 4,245 persons. **Infant mortality** (per 1,000 live births 1996): 33.

**Education: Literacy** (1992): 94%. Compulsory: ages 6-15; attendance 97%.

**Major International Organizations:** UN (WTO, World Bank), ASEAN, APEC.
**Embassy:** 1024 Wisconsin Ave. NW 20007; 944-3600.

Thais began migrating from southern China during the 11th century.

Thailand, known as Siam until 1939, is the only country in SE Asia never taken over by a European power, thanks to King Mongkut and his son King Chulalongkorn—who ruled from 1851 to 1910, modernized the country, and signed trade treaties with both Britain and France. A bloodless revolution in 1932 limited the monarchy. Japan occupied the country in 1941.

The military took over the government in a bloody 1976 coup. Kriangsak Chomanan, prime minister, resigned Feb. 1980 because of soaring inflation, oil price increases, labor unrest, and growing crime. Vietnamese troops crossed the border but were repulsed by Thai forces in the 1980s.

Chatichai Choonhavan was chosen prime minister in a democratic election, Aug. 1988. In Feb. 1991, the military ousted Choonhavan in a bloodless coup. A violent crackdown on street demonstrations in May 1992 led to more than 50 deaths. After general elections July 2, 1995, Banharn Silpa-archa succeeded Chuan Leekpai as prime minister. AIDS reached epidemic proportions in Thailand in the mid-1990s.

# Togo

## Republic of Togo

## République Togolaise

**People: Population:** 4,570,530. **Age distrib.** (%): <15: 49; 65+: 2. **Pop. density:** 209 per sq. mi. **Urban:** 30%. **Ethnic groups:** Ewe, Mina, Kabye, 34 other tribes. **Principal languages:** French (official), Ewe, Mina, Dagomba, Kabye. **Religions:** Indigenous beliefs 70%, Christian 20%, Muslim 10%.

**Geography: Area:** 21,925 sq. mi. **Location:** On S coast of W Africa. **Neighbors:** Ghana on W, Burkina Faso on N, Benin on E. **Topography:** A range of hills running SW-NE splits Togo into 2 savanna plains regions. **Capital:** Lomé (1990 met. est.): 513,000.

**Government: Type:** Republic. **Head of state:** Pres. Gnassingbé Eyadéma; b Dec. 26, 1937; in office: Apr. 14, 1967. **Head of government:** Prime Min. Kwassi Klutse; in office: Aug. 20, 1996. **Local divisions:** 23 circumscriptions. **Defense:** 2.9% of GDP (1993). **Active troop strength:** 6,950.

**Economy: Industries:** Textiles, handicrafts, agric. processing. **Chief crops:** Coffee, cocoa, yams, cotton, millet, rice. **Minerals:** Phosphates, limestone. **Arable land:** 25%. **Electricity prod.** (1993): 60 mil kWh. **Labor force:** 80% agric.

**Finance: Monetary unit:** CFA Franc (June 1996: 515 = $1 US). **Gross domestic product** (1993): $3.3 bln.* **Per capita GDP:** $800. **Imports** (1993): $292 mln.; partners: EU 57%. **Exports** (1993): $221 mln.; partners: EU 40%. **Tourism** (1993): $18 mil. **National budget** (1991 est.): $407 mil. **International reserves less gold** (Dec. 1995): $130 mil. **Gold:** 13,000 oz t. **Consumer prices** (change in 1993): –1.0%.

**Transport: Railroads: Route length:** 326 mi. **Chief port:** Lomé.

**Communications: Television sets:** 1 per 26 persons. **Radios:** 1 per 5.4 persons. **Telephones:** 1 per 233 persons.

**Health: Life expectancy at birth** (1996): 56 male; 60 female. **Births** (per 1,000 pop.): 46. **Deaths** (per 1,000 pop.): 11. **Natural increase:** 3.6%. **Hospital beds:** 1 per 640 persons. **Physicians:** 1 per 11,270 persons. **Infant mortality** (per 1,000 live births 1996): 84.

**Education: Literacy** (1993): 52%.

**Major International Organizations:** UN (WTO, IMF), OAU.

**Embassy:** 2208 Massachusetts Ave. NW 20008; 234-4213.

The Ewe arrived in southern Togo several centuries ago. The country later became a major source of slaves. Germany took control in 1884. France and Britain administered Togoland as UN trusteeships. The French sector became the republic of Togo Apr. 27, 1960.

The population is divided between Bantus in the S and Hamitic tribes in the N. Togo has actively promoted regional integration, as a means of stimulating the economy.

In Jan. 1993 police fired on antigovernment demonstrators, killing at least 22. Some 25,000 people fled to Ghana and Benin as a result of civil unrest. In Jan. 1994 at least 40 people were killed when gunmen reportedly attacked an army base. Further violence marred Togoís first multiparty legislative elections, held Feb. 1994.

# Tonga

## Kingdom of Tonga

## Pule'anga Fakatu'i 'o Tonga

**People: Population:** 106,466. **Pop. density:** 367 per sq. mi. **Ethnic groups:** Polynesian, European. **Principal languages:** Tongan, English (both official). **Religions:** Mostly Christian (Free Wesleyan 43%, Roman Catholic 16%, Mormon 12%, Free Church of Tonga 11%, Church of Tonga 7%).

**Geography: Area:** 290 sq. mi. **Location:** In western South Pacific O. **Neighbors:** Nearest are Fiji to W, Western Samoa to NE. **Topography:** Tonga comprises 170 volcanic and coral islands, 36 inhabited. **Capital:** Nuku'alofa (1990 est.): 34,000.

**Government: Type:** Constitutional monarchy. **Head of state:** King Taufa'ahau Tupou IV; b July 4, 1918; in office: Dec. 16, 1965. **Local divisions:** 3 main island groups.

**Economy: Industries:** Tourism, fishing. **Chief crops:** Coconuts, copra, bananas, vanilla. **Arable land:** 25%. **Electricity prod.** (1993): 30 mil kWh. **Labor force:** 70% agric.

**Finance: Monetary unit:** Pa'anga (June 1996: 1.23 = $1 US). **Gross domestic product** (1994): $214 mln.* **Imports** (FY 1992-93): $56 mln.; partners: N.Z. 33%, Australia 22%. **Exports** (FY 1992-93): $11.3 mln.; partners: Japan 34%, U.S. 17%. **Tourism** (1993): $10 mil.

**Transport: Motor vehicles:** in use: 3,400 passenger cars, 3,900 comm. vehicles. **Chief port:** Nuku'alofa.

**Communications: Radios:** 1 per 1.5 persons. **Telephones:** 1 per 16 persons.

**Health: Life expectancy at birth** (1996): 66 male; 71 female. **Births** (per 1,000 pop.): 24. **Deaths** (per 1,000 pop.): 7. **Natural increase:** 1.7%. **Infant mortality** (per 1,000 live births 1996): 20.

**Education: Literacy** (1992): 93%. Compulsory: ages 5-14.

**Major International Organizations:** the Commonwealth.

The islands were first visited by the Dutch in the early 17th century. A series of civil wars ended in 1845 with establishment of the Tupou dynasty. In 1900 Tonga became a British protectorate. On June 4, 1970, Tonga became independent and a member of the Commonwealth.

# Trinidad and Tobago

## Republic of Trinidad and Tobago

**People: Population:** 1,272,385. **Age distrib.** (%): <15: 31; 65+: 6. **Pop. density:** 643 per sq. mi. **Urban:** 65%. **Ethnic groups:** Black 43%, East Indian 40%, mixed 14%. **Principal languages:** English (official), Hindi, French, Spanish. **Religions:** Roman Catholic 32%, Protestant 28%, Hindu 24%, Muslim 6%.

**Geography: Area:** 1,980 sq. mi. **Location:** In Caribbean, off E coast of Venezuela. **Neighbors:** Nearest is Venezuela to SW. **Topography:** Three low mountain ranges cross Trinidad E-W, with a well-watered plain between N and central ranges. Parts of E and W coasts are swamps. Tobago, 116 sq. mi., lies 20 mi. NE. **Capital:** Port-of-Spain (1992 est.): 52,500.

**Government: Type:** Parliamentary democracy. **Head of state:** Pres. Noor Mohamed Hassanali; b Aug. 13, 1918; in office: Mar. 19, 1987. **Head of government:** Prime Min. Basdeo Panday; b May 25, 1933; in office: Nov. 9, 1995. **Local divisions:** 8 counties, 3 municipalities, 1 ward. **Defense:** 1.5% of GDP (1994). **Active troop strength:** 2,100.

**Economy: Industries:** Oil products, chemicals, tourism. **Chief crops:** Sugar, cocoa, coffee, citrus fruits, rice. **Minerals:** Asphalt, oil, gas. **Crude oil reserves** (1995): 488 mil bbls. **Arable land:** 14%. **Electricity prod.** (1993): 3.9 bil kWh. **Labor force:** 18% constr. & util.; 15% manuf. & mining; 11% agric.

**Finance: Monetary unit:** Dollar (June 1996: 5.74 = $1 US). **Gross domestic product** (1994): $15 bln.* **Per capita GDP:** $11,280. **Imports** (1994): $996 mln.; partners: U.S. 43%, Venezuela 10%. **Exports** (1994): $1.9 bln.; partners: U.S. 44%. **Tourism** (1993): $80 mil. **National budget** (1993 est.): $1.6 bil. **International reserves less gold** (Jan. 1996): $350 mil. **Gold:** 54,000 oz t. **Consumer prices** (change in 1994): 8.8%.

**Transport: Motor vehicles:** in use: 122,000 passenger cars, 24,000 comm. vehicles. **Civil aviation:** 2.0 bil passenger-mi.; 2 airports with scheduled flights. **Chief ports:** Port-of-Spain, Scarborough.

**Communications: Television sets:** 1 per 5.0 persons. **Radios:** 1 per 2.2 persons. **Telephones:** 1 per 6.7 persons. **Daily newspaper circ.:** 76 per 1,000 pop.

**Health: Life expectancy at birth** (1996): 68 male; 73 female. **Births** (per 1,000 pop.): 16. **Deaths** (per 1,000 pop.): 7. **Natural increase:** 0.9%. **Hospital beds:** 1 per 297 persons. **Physicians:** 1 per 1,191 persons. **Infant mortality** (per 1,000 live births 1996): 18.

**Education: Literacy** (1992): 98%. Free and compulsory: ages 5-11.

**Major International Organizations:** UN (WTO, IMF, WHO), the Commonwealth, OAS.

**Embassy:** 1708 Massachusetts Ave. NW 20036; 467-6490.

Columbus sighted Trinidad in 1498. A British possession since 1802, Trinidad and Tobago won independence Aug. 31, 1962. It became a republic in 1976.

The nation is one of the most prosperous in the Caribbean. Oil production has increased with offshore finds. Middle Eastern oil is refined and exported, mostly to the U.S.

In July 1990, some 120 Muslim extremists captured the Parliament building and TV station and took about 50 hostages, including Prime Min. Arthur Robinson, who was beaten, shot in the legs, and tied to explosives. After a 6-day siege, the rebels surrendered.

Basdeo Panday, the country's first prime minister of East Indian ancestry, took office Nov. 9, 1995.

# Tunisia

## Republic of Tunisia

## Al Jumhuriyah at Tunisiyah

**People: Population:** 9,019,687. **Age distrib.** (%) <15: 37; 65+: 5. **Pop. density:** 142 per sq. mi. **Urban:** 60%. **Ethnic groups:** Arab-Berber 98%. **Principal languages:** Arabic (official), French. **Religions:** Muslim 98%.

**Geography: Area:** 63,378 sq. mi. **Location:** On N coast of Africa. **Neighbors:** Algeria on W, Libya on E. **Topography:** The N is wooded and fertile. The central coastal plains are given to grazing and orchards. The S is arid, approaching Sahara Desert. **Capital:** Tunis. **Cities** (1994 cen.): Tunis 674,100, Sfax 230,900.

**Government: Type:** Republic. **Head of state:** Pres. Gen. Zine al-Abidine Ben Ali; b Sept 3, 1936; in office: Nov. 7, 1987. **Head of government:** Prime Min. Hamed Karoui; b Dec. 30, 1927; in office: Sept. 27, 1989. **Local divisions:** 23 governorates. **Defense:** 3% of GDP (1994). **Active troop strength:** 35,500.

**Economy: Industries:** Food processing, textiles, oil products, mining, tourism, construction. **Chief crops:** Grains, dates, olives, vegetables, grapes. **Minerals:** Phosphates, iron, oil, lead, zinc. **Crude oil reserves** (1995): 416 mil bbls. **Arable land:** 20%. **Livestock** (1994): sheep: 7.1 mln.; goats: 1.4 mil. **Fish catch** (1993): 84,000 metric tons. **Electricity prod.** (1993): 5.4 bil kWh. **Labor force:** 32% agric.

**Finance: Monetary unit:** Dinar (June 1996: 0.98 = $1 US). **Gross domestic product** (1994): $37.1 bln.* **Per capita GDP:** $4,250. **Imports** (1993): $6.5 bln.; partners: EU 70%. **Exports** (1993): $4.6 bln.; partners: EU 75%. **Tourism** (1993): $1.1 bil. **National budget** (1993 est.): $5.5 bil. **International reserves less gold** (Apr. 1996): $1.4 bil. **Gold:** 217,000 oz t. **Consumer prices** (change in 1995): 6.2%.

**Transport: Railroads: Route length:** 1,404 mi. **Motor vehicles:** in use: 320,000 passenger cars, 181,000 comm. vehicles. **Civil aviation:** 1.2 bil passenger-mi.; 5 airports. **Chief ports:** Tunis, Sfax, Bizerte.

**Communications: Television sets:** 1 per 13 persons. **Radios:** 1 per 5.1 persons. **Telephones:** 1 per 20 persons. **Daily newspaper circ.:** 22 per 1,000 pop.

**Health: Life expectancy at birth** (1996): 71 male; 74 female. **Births** (per 1,000 pop.): 24. **Deaths** (per 1,000 pop.): 5. **Natural increase:** 1.9%. **Hospital beds:** 1 per 521 persons. **Physicians:** 1 per 1,799 persons. **Infant mortality** (per 1,000 live births 1996): 35.

**Education: Literacy** (1994): 67%. Compulsory: ages 6-16; attendance 84%.

**Major International Organizations:** UN (WTO), Arab League, OAU.

**Embassy:** 1515 Massachusetts Ave. NW 20005; 862-1850.

Site of ancient Carthage and a former Barbary state under the suzerainty of Turkey, Tunisia became a protectorate of France under a treaty signed May 12, 1881. The nation became independent Mar. 20, 1956, and ended the monarchy the following year. Habib Bourguiba, an independence leader, served as president until 1987, when he was deposed by his prime minister, Zine al-Abidine Ben Ali.

Tunisia has actively repressed Islamic fundamentalism.

# Turkey

## Republic of Turkey

## Turkiye Cumhuriyeti

**People: Population:** 62,484,478. **Age distrib.** (%): <15: 33; 65+: 5. **Pop. density:** 208 per sq. mi. **Urban:** 63%. **Ethnic groups:** Turk 80%, Kurd 20%. **Principal languages:** Turkish (official), Kurdish, Arabic. **Religions:** Muslim 99.8%.

**Geography: Area:** 300,948 sq. mi. **Location:** Occupies Asia Minor, stretches into continental Europe; borders on Mediterranean and Black seas. **Neighbors:** Bulgaria, Greece on W; Georgia, Armenia on N; Iran on E; Iraq, Syria on S. **Topography:** Central Turkey has wide plateaus, with hot, dry summers and cold winters. High mountains ring the interior on all but W, with more than 20 peaks over 10,000 ft. Rolling plains are in W; mild, fertile coastal plains are in S, W. **Capital:** Ankara. **Cities** (1993 est.): Istanbul 7.3 mln.; Ankara 2.7 mln.; Izmir 1.9 mln.; Adana 1.0 mil.

**Government: Type:** Republic. **Head of state:** Pres. Suleyman Demirel; b 1924; in office: May 16, 1993. **Head of government:** Prime Min. Necmettin Erbakan; b 1926; in office: June 28, 1996. **Local divisions:** 73 provinces. **Defense:** 5.6% of GDP (1994). **Active troop strength:** 507,800.

**Economy: Industries:** Textiles, steel, mining, metal prods., oil, processed foods. **Chief crops:** Tobacco, grains, cotton, barley, corn, fruits, potatoes, sugar beets. **Minerals:** Antimony, chromium, mercury, copper, coal. **Crude oil reserves** (1995): 488 mil bbls. **Other resources:** Wool, silk, forests. **Arable land:** 30%. **Livestock** (1993): cattle: 11.9 mln.; sheep: 37.5 mil. **Fish catch** (1993): 556,000 metric tons. **Electricity prod.** (1993): 71 bil kWh. **Labor force:** 44% agric.; 41% serv.; 15% ind.

**Finance: Monetary unit:** Lira (June 1996: 81,746 = $1 US). **Gross domestic product** (1994): $305.2 bln.* **Per capita GDP:** $4,910. **Imports** (1993): $27.6 bln.; partners: Germany 15%, U.S. 11%. **Exports** (1993): $15.3 bln.; partners: Germany 24%. **Tourism** (1994): $4.3 bil. **National budget** (1995): $33.3 bil. **International reserves less gold** (Apr. 1996): $15.5 bil. **Gold:** 3.7 mil oz t. **Consumer prices** (change in 1995): 93.6%.

**Transport: Railroads: Route length:** 6,470 mi. **Motor vehicles:** in use: 2.9 mil passenger cars, 942,000 comm. vehicles. **Civil aviation:** 5.7 bil passenger-mi.; 24 airports with scheduled flights. **Chief ports:** Istanbul, Izmir, Mersin, Samsun.

**Communications: Television sets:** 1 per 5.8 persons. **Radios:** 1 per 7.0 persons. **Telephones:** 1 per 5.0 persons.

**Health: Life expectancy at birth** (1996): 70 male; 74 female. **Births** (per 1,000 pop.): 22. **Deaths** (per 1,000 pop.): 6. **Natural increase:** 1.7%. **Hospital beds:** 1 per 420 persons. **Physicians:** 1 per 1,108 persons. **Infant mortality** (per 1,000 live births 1996): 43.

**Education: Literacy** (1995): 82%. Free and compulsory: ages 6-14; attendance 81%.

**Major International Organizations:** UN (WTO, WHO, IMF), NATO, OECD.

**Embassy:** 1714 Massachusetts Ave. NW 20036; 659-8200.

Ancient inhabitants of Turkey were among the world's first agriculturalists. Such civilizations as the Hittite, Phrygian, and Lydian flourished in Asiatic Turkey (Asia Minor), as did much of Greek civilization. After the fall of Rome in the 5th century, Constantinople (now Istanbul) was the capital of the Byzantine Empire for 1,000 years. It fell in 1453 to Ottoman Turks, who ruled a vast empire for over 400 years.

Just before World War I, Turkey, or the Ottoman Empire, ruled what is now Syria, Lebanon, Iraq, Jordan, Israel, Saudi Arabia, Yemen, and islands in the Aegean Sea.

Turkey joined Germany and Austria in World War I and its defeat resulted in loss of much territory and fall of the sultanate. A republic was declared Oct. 29, 1923, with Mustafa Kemal (later Kemal Ataturk) as its first president. Ataturk led Turkey until his death in 1938. The Caliphate (spiritual leadership of Islam) was renounced in 1924.

Long embroiled with Greece over Cyprus, off Turkey's south coast, Turkey invaded the island July 20, 1974, after Greek officers seized the Cypriot government as a step toward unification with Greece. Turkey sought a new government for Cyprus, with Greek Cypriot and Turkish Cypriot zones. In reaction to

Turkey's moves, the U.S. cut off military aid in 1975. Turkey, in turn, suspended the use of most U.S. bases. Aid was restored in 1978. There was a military takeover, Sept. 12, 1980.

Religious and ethnic tensions and active left and right extremists have caused endemic violence. Martial law, imposed in 1978, was lifted in 1984. The military formally transferred power to an elected Parliament in 1983.

Turkey was a member of the Allied forces that ousted Iraq from Kuwait, 1991. In the aftermath of the war, millions of Kurdish refugees fled to Turkey's border to escape Iraqi forces. The Turkish government mounted sporadic offensives against separatist Kurds in this border area and in N Iraq, causing heavy casualties among guerrillas and civilians.

Kurdish militants raided Turkish diplomatic missions in some 25 Western European cities June 24, 1993. The militants were demanding an independent state for the Kurds. Tansu Ciller officially became Turkey's first woman prime min. July 5, 1993.

The Welfare Party, an Islamic group, gained strength in the 1990s but was unable to form a government until June 1996, when it came to power in coalition with Ciller's True Path Party.

# Turkmenistan

## Republic of Turkmenistan

## Turkmenistan Jumhuriyati

**People: Population:** 4,149,283. **Pop. density:** 22 per sq. mi. **Urban:** 45%. **Ethnic groups:** Turkmen 73%, Russian 10%, Uzbek 9%. **Principal languages:** Turkmen (official), Russian, Uzbek. **Religions:** Muslim 87%, Eastern Orthodox 11%.

**Geography: Area:** 188,500 sq. mi. **Neighbors:** Kazakstan on N, Uzbekistan on N and E, Afghanistan and Iran on S. **Topography:** The Kara Kum Desert occupies 80% of the area. Bordered on W by Caspian Sea. **Capital:** Ashgabat (1994 est.): 518,000.

**Government: Type:** Republic. **Head of state:** Pres. Saparmurad Niyazov; b Feb. 18, 1940; in office: Oct. 27, 1990. **Local divisions:** 5 regions. **Defense:** 1.5% of GNP (1993). **Active troop strength:** 11,000 under joint control with Russia.

**Economy: Industries:** Oil, natural gas, food processing, textiles. **Chief crops:** Grain, cotton, grapes. **Minerals:** Coal, sulfur, salt. **Crude oil reserves** (1992): 740 mil bbls. **Arable land:** 2%. **Livestock** (1994): sheep and goats: 6.3 mil. **Electricity prod.** (1994): 10.5 bil kWh. **Labor force:** 44% agric. & forestry; 20% ind. & constr.

**Finance: Monetary unit:** Manat (June 1996: 4,300 = $1 US). **Gross domestic product** (1994 est.): $13.1 bln.* **Per capita GDP:** $3,280. **Imports** (1994): $304 mln., excl. CIS. **Exports** (1994): $382 mln., excl. CIS.

**Transport: Railroads: Length:** 1,317 mi. **Chief port:** Turkmenbashi.

**Communications: Telephones:** 1 per 15 persons.

**Health: Life expectancy at birth** (1996): 57 male; 67 female. **Births** (per 1,000 pop.): 29. **Deaths** (per 1,000 pop.): 9. **Natural increase:** 2.0%. **Hospital beds:** 1 per 85 persons. **Physicians:** 1 per 285 persons. **Infant mortality** (per 1,000 live births 1996): 82.

**Major International Organizations:** UN, CIS.

**Embassy:** 1511 K St. NW, Suite 412 20005; 737-4800.

The region has been inhabited by Turkic tribes since the 10th century. It became part of Russian Turkestan in 1881, and a constituent republic of the USSR in 1925. Turkmenistan declared independence Oct. 27, 1991, and became an independent state when the Soviet Union disbanded Dec. 26, 1991.

Extensive oil and gas reserves place Turkmenistan in a more favorable economic position than other former Soviet republics. A new rail line linking Iran and Turkmenistan was inaugurated May 13, 1996. Political power centered around the former Communist Party apparatus, and Pres. Saparmurad Niyazov became the object of a personality cult.

# Tuvalu

**People: Population:** 10,146. **Pop. density:** 1,063 per sq. mi. **Ethnic groups:** Polynesian 96%. **Principal languages:** Tuvaluan, English. **Religions:** Church of Tuvalu (Congregationalist) 97%.

**Geography: Area:** 9.4 sq. mi. **Location:** 9 islands forming a NW-SE chain 360 mi. long in the SW Pacific O. **Neighbors:** Nearest are Kiribati to N, Fiji to S. **Topography:** The islands are all low-lying atolls, nowhere rising more than 15 ft. above sea level, composed of coral reefs. **Capital:** Funafuti Atoll (1991 est.): 3,800.

**Government: Head of state:** Queen Elizabeth II, represented by Gov.-Gen. Tulaga Manuella; in office: June 1994. **Head of government:** Prime Min. Kamuta Laatasi; in office: Dec. 1993.

**Economy: Industries:** Copra. **Chief crops:** Coconuts. **Other resources:** fish. **Labor force:** In the early 1990s, approx. 1,200 Tuvaluans were working overseas in the Gilberts' phosphate industry, or as overseas seamen.

**Finance: Monetary unit:** Tuvalu Dollar, Australian Dollar.

**Transport: Chief port:** Funafuti.

**Health: Life expectancy at birth** (1996): 62 male; 65 female. **Births** (per 1,000 pop.): 24. **Deaths** (per 1,000 pop.): 9. **Natural increase:** 1.5%. **Infant mortality** (per 1,000 live births 1996): 28.

**Education: Literacy** (1990): 96%.

**Major International Organizations:** the Commonwealth.

The Ellice Islands separated from the British Gilbert and Ellice Islands Colony in 1975 and became Tuvalu; independence came Oct. 1, 1978.

# Uganda

## Republic of Uganda

**People: Population:** 20,158,176. **Age distrib.** (%): <15: 47; 65+: 3. **Pop. density:** 217 per sq. mi. **Urban:** 11%. **Ethnic groups:** Bantu, Nilotic, Nilo-Hamitic, Sudanic tribes. **Principal languages:** English (official), Luganda, Swahili. **Religions:** Christian 66%, indigenous beliefs 18%, Muslim 16%.

**Geography: Area:** 93,070 sq. mi. **Location:** In E Central Africa. **Neighbors:** Sudan on N, Zaire on W, Rwanda and Tanzania on S, Kenya on E. **Topography:** Most of Uganda is a high plateau 3,000-6,000 ft. high, with high Ruwenzori range in W (Mt. Margherita 16,750 ft.), volcanoes in SW; NE is arid, W and SW rainy. Lakes Victoria, Edward, Albert form much of borders. **Capital:** Kampala (1991): 773,500.

**Government: Type:** Republic. **Head of state:** Pres. Yoweri Kaguta Museveni; b Mar. 1944; in office: Jan. 29, 1986. **Head of government:** Prime Min. Kintu Mosoke; in office: Nov. 18, 1994. **Local divisions:** 39 districts. **Defense:** 1.7% of budget (FY 1993-94). **Active troop strength:** 50,000 est.

**Economy: Industries:** Brewing, textiles, cement. **Chief crops:** Coffee, cotton, tea, corn, tobacco. **Minerals:** Copper, cobalt. **Arable land:** 23%. **Livestock** (1994): goats: 5.4 mln.; cattle: 4.9 mln.; sheep: 1.3 mil. **Fish catch** (1994): 206,000 metric tons. **Electricity prod.** (1993): 780 mil kWh. **Labor force:** More than 80% agric.

**Finance: Monetary unit:** Shilling (June 1996: 1,046 = $1 US). **Gross domestic product** (1994): $16.2 bln.* **Per capita GDP:** $850. **Imports** (1993): $696 mln.; partners: Kenya 25%, UK 14%. **Exports** (1993): $237 mln.; partners: U.S. 25%, UK 18%, France 11%. **National budget** (1989 est.): $545 mil. **International reserves less gold** (Jan. 1996): $445 mil. **Consumer prices** (change in 1995): 8.5%.

**Transport: Motor vehicles:** in use: 18,000 passenger cars, 25,000 comm. vehicles. **Chief ports:** Entebbe, Jinja.

**Communications: Television sets:** 1 per 158 persons. **Radios:** 1 per 10 persons. **Telephones:** 1 per 830 persons.

**Health: Life expectancy at birth** (1996): 40 male; 41 female. **Births** (per 1,000 pop.): 46. **Deaths** (per 1,000 pop.): 21. **Natural increase:** 2.5%. **Hospital beds:** 1 per 817 persons. **Physicians:** 1 per 20,720 persons. **Infant mortality** (per 1,000 live births 1996): 99.

**Education: Literacy** (1994): 62%. About 44% attend school.

**Major International Organizations:** UN (WTO, WHO, IMF), OAU, the Commonwealth.

**Embassy:** 5911 16th St. NW 20011; 726-7100.

Britain obtained a protectorate over Uganda in 1894. The country became independent Oct. 9, 1962, and a republic within the Commonwealth a year later. In 1967, the traditional kingdoms, including the powerful Buganda state, were abolished and the central government strengthened. (In 1993 the government authorized restoration of the Buganda and other monarchies, but as ceremonial only.)

Gen. Idi Amin seized power from Prime Min. Milton Obote in 1971. As many as 300,000 of his opponents were reported killed in subsequent years. Amin was named president for life in 1976.

In 1972 Amin expelled nearly all of Uganda's 45,000 Asians. In 1973 the U.S. withdrew all diplomatic personnel.

Amid worsening economic and domestic crises, Uganda's troops exchanged invasion attacks with long-standing foe Tanzania, 1978 to 1979. Tanzanian forces, coupled with Ugandan exiles and rebels, ended the dictatorial rule of Amin, Apr. 11, 1979.

Under a new constitution ratified Oct. 1995, nonparty presidential and legislative elections were held in 1996.

## Ukraine

### Ukrayina

**People: Population:** 50,864,009. **Age distrib.** (%): <15: 20; 65+: 14. **Pop. density:** 218 per sq. mi. **Urban:** 68%. **Ethnic groups:** Ukrainian 73%, Russian 22%. **Principal languages:** Ukrainian (official), Russian. **Religions:** Mostly Ukrainian Orthodox, some Ukrainian Catholic.

**Geography: Area:** 233,100 sq. mi. **Location:** In E Europe. **Neighbors:** Belarus on N; Russia on NE and E; Moldova and Romania on SW; Hungary, Slovakia, and Poland on W. **Topography:** Part of the E European plain. Mountainous areas include the Carpathians in the SW and the Crimean chain in the S. Arable black soil constitutes a large part of the country. **Capital:** Kiev. **Cities** (1994 est.): Kiev 2.6 mln.; Kharkiv 1.6 mln.; Dnipropetrovsk 1.2 mln.; Donetsk 1.1 mln.; Odesa 1.1 mil.

**Government: Type:** Constitutional republic. **Head of state:** Pres. Leonid Danylovich Kuchma; b Aug. 9, 1938; in office: July 19, 1994. **Head of government:** Prime Min. Pavlo Lazarenko; b Jan. 23, 1953; in office: May 28, 1996. **Local divisions:** 24 oblasts, 2 municipalities, 1 autonomous republic. **Defense:** Less than 4% of GDP (1993). **Active troop strength:** 452,500.

**Economy: Industries:** Steel, chemicals, machinery, vehicles, food processing. **Chief crops:** Grains, sugar beets, vegetables. **Minerals:** Iron, manganese, coal, gas, oil, sulphur, nickel, salt. **Other resources:** Forests. **Arable land:** 56%. **Livestock** (1994): cattle: 21.6 mln.; pigs: 15.3 mil. **Fish catch** (1993): 371,000 metric tons. **Electricity prod.** (1994): 182 bil kWh. **Labor force:** 33% ind. & constr.; 21% agric. & forestry.

**Finance: Monetary unit:** Hryvna (replaced the Karbovanets (June 1996: 180,300 = $1 US) Sept. 1996. **Gross domestic product** (1994 est.): $189.2 bln.* **Per capita GDP:** $3,650. **Imports** (1994): $14.2 bln.; partners: Russia 59%. **Exports** (1994): $11.8 bln.; partners: Russia 39%. **National budget** (1990): $8 bil. **International reserves less gold** (Apr. 1996): $670 mil. **Gold:** 50,300 oz t. **Consumer prices** (change in 1995): 377%.

**Transport: Railroads: Length:** 14,509 mi. **Motor vehicles:** in use: 2.9 mil passenger cars. **Civil aviation:** 2.0 bil passenger-mi.; 20 airports with scheduled flights. **Chief ports:** Odesa, Kherson, Mariupol, Mykolayiv, Berdyansk.

**Communications: Telephones:** 1 per 6.7 persons. **Daily newspaper circ.:** 52 per 1,000 pop.

**Health: Life expectancy at birth** (1996): 62 male; 72 female. **Births** (per 1,000 pop.): 11. **Deaths** (per 1,000 pop.): 15. **Natural increase:** –0.4. **Hospital beds:** 1 per 75 persons. **Physicians:** 1 per 226 persons. **Infant mortality** (per 1,000 live births 1996): 23.

**Education: Literacy** (1994): 98%.

**Major International Organizations:** UN, CIS.

**Embassy:** 3350 M St. NW 20007; 333-0606.

The ancient ancestors of Ukrainians, the Trypilians, flourished along the Dnieper River, Ukraine's main artery, from 6000-1000 BC. The Slavic ancestors of the Ukrainians inhabited modern Ukrainian territory well before the first century AD.

In the 9th century, the princes of Kiev established a strong state called Kievan Rus, which included much of present-day Ukraine. A strong dynasty was established, with ties to virtually all major European royal families. St. Vladimir the Great, ruler of Kievan Rus, accepted Christianity as the national faith in 988. At the crossroads of European trade routes, Kievan Rus reached its zenith under Yaroslav the Wise (1019-1054). Internal conflicts led to the disintegration of the Ukrainian state into principalities by the time of the Asian invasion of Europe in the 13th century. Mongol rule was supplanted by Poland and Lithuania in the 14th and 15th centuries. The N Black Sea coast and Crimea came under the control of the Turks in 1478.

Ukrainian Cossacks, starting in the late 16th century, waged numerous wars of liberation against the occupiers of Ukraine: Russia, Poland, and Turkey. By the late 18th century, Ukrainian independence was lost. Ukraine's neighbors once again divided its territory. At the turn of the 19th century, Ukraine was occupied by Russia and Austria-Hungary.

An independent Ukrainian National Republic was proclaimed on January 22, 1918. In 1921, Ukraine's neighbors occupied and divided Ukrainian territory. In 1922, Ukraine became a constituent republic of the USSR as the Ukrainian SSR. In 1932-33, the Soviet government engineered a man-made famine in eastern Ukraine, resulting in the deaths of 7-10 million Ukrainians.

In March 1939, independent Carpatho-Ukraine was the first European state to wage war against Nazi-led aggression in the region. During WW2 the Ukrainian nationalist underground and its Ukrainian Insurgent Army (UPA) fought both Nazi German and Soviet forces. The restoration of Ukrainian independence was declared on June 30, 1941. Over 5 million Ukrainians lost their lives during the war. With the reoccupation of Ukraine by Soviet troops in 1944 came a renewed wave of mass arrests, executions, and deportations of Ukrainians.

The world's worst nuclear power plant disaster occurred in Chernobyl, Ukraine, in April 1986.

Ukrainian independence was restored in Dec. 1991 with the dissolution of the Soviet Union. In the post-Soviet period Ukraine was burdened with a deteriorating economy.

Russia and Ukraine reached agreement June 9, 1995, on the disputed Black Sea fleet at Sevastopol. Following a 1994 accord with Russia and the U.S., Ukraine's large nuclear arsenal was deactivated by June 1996. A new constitution legalizing private property and establishing Ukrainian as the sole official language was approved by parliament June 29.

## United Arab Emirates

### Al Imarata al Arabiyah al Muttahidah

**People: Population:** 3,057,337. **Pop. density:** 95 per sq. mi. **Urban:** 82%. **Ethnic groups:** Arab, Iranian, Pakistani, Indian. **Principal languages:** Arabic (official), Persian, English, Hindi. **Religions:** Muslim 96%, Christian, Hindu.

**Geography: Area:** 32,280 sq. mi. **Location:** Middle East, on the S shore of the Persian Gulf. **Neighbors:** Saudi Arabia on W and S, Oman on E. **Topography:** A barren, flat coastal plain gives way to uninhabited sand dunes on the S. Hajar Mts. are on E. **Capital:** Abu Dhabi. **Cities** (1989): Abu Dhabi 363,400; Dubai 585,200.

**Government: Type:** Federation of emirates. **Head of state:** Pres. Zaid ibn Sultan an-Nahayan b. 1923; in office: Dec. 2, 1971. **Head of government:** Prime Min. Sheikh Maktum ibn Rashid al-Maktum; in office: Nov. 20, 1990. **Local divisions:** 7 autonomous emirates: Abu Dhabi, Ajman, Dubai, Fujaira, Ras al-Khaimah, Sharjah, Umm al-Qaiwain. **Defense:** 4.3% of GDP (1994). **Active troop strength:** 70,000.

**Economy: Chief crops:** Vegetables, dates. **Minerals:** Oil, natural gas. **Crude oil reserves** (1995): 98.1 bil barrels. **Arable land:** 0%. **Electricity prod.** (1993): 16.5 bil kWh. **Labor force:** 85% ind. and commerce; 5% agric.; 5% serv.; 5% govt.

**Finance: Monetary unit:** Dirham (June 1996: 3.67 = $1 US). **Gross domestic product** (1994): $62.7 bln.* **Per capita GDP:** $22,480. **Imports** (1994): $20 bln.; partners: Japan 12%, UK 10%, U.S. 9%. **Exports** (1994): $24 bln.; partners: Japan 35%. **National budget** (1993): $4.8 bil. **International reserves less gold** (May 1996): $8.0 bil. **Gold:** 797,000 oz t.

**Transport: Motor vehicles:** in use: 297,000 passenger cars, 73,000 comm. vehicles. **Civil aviation:** 4.0 bil passenger-mi.; 4 airports with scheduled flights. **Chief ports:** Dubai, Abu Dhabi.

**Communications: Television sets:** 1 per 13 persons. **Radios:** 1 per 4.4 persons. **Telephones:** 1 per 2.8 persons.

**Health: Life expectancy at birth** (1996): 71 male; 75 female. **Births** (per 1,000 pop.): 26. **Deaths** (per 1,000 pop.): 3. **Natural increase:** 2.3%. **Hospital beds:** 1 per 483 persons. **Physicians:** 1 per 694 persons. **Infant mortality** (per 1,000 live births 1996): 20.

**Education: Literacy** (1994): 79%. Compulsory: ages 6-12.

**Major International Organizations:** UN (World Bank, IMF, ILO, WTO), Arab League, OPEC.

**Embassy:** 3000 K St. NW, Suite 600 20007; 338-6500.

The 7 "Trucial Sheikdoms" gave Britain control of defense and foreign relations in the 19th century. They merged to become an independent state Dec. 2, 1971.

The Abu Dhabi Petroleum Co. was fully nationalized in 1975. Oil revenues have given the UAE one of the highest per capita GDPs in the world. International banking has grown in recent years.

# United Kingdom

## United Kingdom of Great Britain and Northern Ireland

**People: Population:** 58,489,975. **Age distrib.** (%): <15: 19; 65+: 16. **Pop. density:** 621 per sq. mi. **Urban:** 90%. **Ethnic groups:** English 81.5%, Scottish 9.6%, Irish 2.4%, Welsh 1.9%, Ulster 1.8%; West Indian, Indian, Pakistani, others 2.8%. **Principal languages:** English, Welsh, Scottish, Gaelic. **Religions:** Anglican, Roman Catholic, other Christian, Muslim.

**Geography: Area:** 94,251 sq. mi. **Location:** Off the NW coast of Europe, across English Channel, Strait of Dover, and North Sea. **Neighbors:** Ireland to W, France to SE. **Topography:** England is mostly rolling land, rising to Uplands of southern Scotland; Lowlands are in center of Scotland, granite Highlands are in N. Coast is heavily indented, especially on W. British Isles have milder climate than N Europe due to the Gulf Stream and ample rainfall. Severn, 220 mi., and Thames, 215 mi., are longest rivers. **Capital:** London. **Cities** (1994 est.): London 7.0 mil; Birmingham 1.0 mln.; Leeds 721,000; Glasgow 681,000; Sheffield 530,000; Bradford 481,000; Liverpool 474,000; Edinburgh 444,000; Manchester 431,000; Bristol 374,000.

**Government: Type:** Constitutional monarchy. **Head of state:** Queen Elizabeth II; b Apr. 21, 1926; in office: Feb. 6, 1952. **Head of government:** Prime Min. John Major; b Mar. 29, 1943; in office: Nov. 28, 1990. **Local divisions:** England and Wales: 47 counties, 7 metropolitan counties; Scotland: 9 regions, 3 island areas; Northern Ireland: 26 districts. **Defense:** 3.1% of GDP (FY 1995-96). **Active troop strength:** 236,900.

**Economy: Industries:** Steel, metals, vehicles, shipbuilding, banking, textiles, chemicals, electronics, aircraft, machinery, distilling. **Chief crops:** Grains, sugar beets, potatoes, vegetables. **Minerals:** Coal, tin, oil, gas, limestone, iron, salt, clay. **Crude oil reserves** (1995): 4.5 bil bbls. **Arable land:** 29%. **Livestock** (1994): sheep: 29.3 mln.; cattle: 11.7 mln.; pigs: 7.9 mil. **Fish catch** (1993): 898,000 metric tons. **Electricity prod.** (1993): 303 bil kWh. **Labor force:** 63% services; 25% manuf. & constr.; 9% govt.

**Finance: Monetary unit:** Pound (June 1996: 1.00 = $1.55 US). **Gross domestic product** (1993): $1.05 trl.* **Per capita GDP:** $17,980. **Imports** (1994): $215 bln.; partners: EU 52%, U.S. 12%. **Exports** (1994): $200 bln.; partners: EU 57%, U.S. 11%. **Tourism** (1993): $13.4 bil. **National budget** (FY 1993-94 est.): $400.9 bil. **International reserves less gold** (Mar. 1996): $39.2 bil. **Gold:** 18.43 mil oz t. **Consumer prices** (change in 1995): 3.4%.

**Transport: Railroads: Length:** 23,518 mi. **Motor vehicles:** in use: 20.3 mil passenger cars, 2.8 mil comm. vehicles. **Civil aviation:** 58.8 bil passenger-mi.; 53 airports with scheduled flights. **Chief ports:** London, Liverpool, Glasgow, Southampton, Cardiff, Belfast.

**Communications: Television sets:** 1 per 2.9 persons. **Radios:** 1 per 0.9 person. **Telephones:** 1 per 2.0 persons. **Daily newspaper circ.:** 381 per 1,000 pop.

**Health: Life expectancy at birth** (1996): 74 male; 79 female. **Births:** (per 1,000 pop.): 13. **Deaths:** (per 1,000 pop.): 11. **Natural increase:** 0.2%. **Hospital beds:** 1 per 205 persons. **Physicians:** 1 per 629 persons. **Infant mortality** (per 1,000 live births 1996): 6.

**Education: Literacy** (1993): 100%. Compulsory: ages 5-16.

**Major International Organizations:** UN and all of its specialized agencies, NATO, EU, OECD, the Commonwealth.

**Embassy:** 3100 Massachusetts Ave. NW 20008; 462-1340.

The United Kingdom of Great Britain and Northern Ireland comprises England, Wales, Scotland, and Northern Ireland.

**Queen and Royal Family.** The ruling sovereign is Elizabeth II of the House of Windsor, born Apr. 21, 1926, elder daughter of King George VI. She succeeded to the throne Feb. 6, 1952, and was crowned June 2, 1953. She was married Nov. 20, 1947, to Lt. Philip Mountbatten, born June 10, 1921, former Prince of Greece. He was created Duke of Edinburgh, Earl of Merioneth, and Baron Greenwich, and given the style H.R.H., Nov. 19, 1947; he was given the title Prince of the United Kingdom and Northern Ireland Feb. 22, 1957. Prince Charles Philip Arthur George, born Nov. 14, 1948, is the Prince of Wales and heir apparent. His son, William Philip Arthur Louis, born June 21, 1982, is second in line to the throne.

**Parliament** is the legislative governing body for the United Kingdom, with certain powers over dependent units. It consists of 2 houses: The **House of Lords** includes 772 hereditary and 380 life peers and peeresses, 22 Lords of Appeal, 2 archbishops and 24 bishops of the Church of England. Total membership is 1,200. The **House of Commons** has 651 members, who are elected by direct ballot and divided as follows: England 524; Wales 38; Scotland 72; Northern Ireland 17.

**Resources and Industries.** Great Britain's major occupations are manufacturing and trade. Metals and metal-using industries contribute more than 50% of the exports. Of about 60 million acres of land in England, Wales, and Scotland, 46 million are farmed, of which 17 million are arable, the rest pastures.

Large oil and gas fields have been found in the North Sea. Commercial oil production began in 1975. There are large deposits of coal.

Britain imports all of its cotton, rubber, sulphur, about 80% of its wool, half of its food and iron ore, also certain amounts of paper, tobacco, chemicals. Manufactured goods made from these basic materials have been exported since the industrial age began. Main exports are machinery, chemicals, woolen and synthetic textiles, clothing, autos and trucks, iron and steel, locomotives, ships, jet aircraft, farm machinery, drugs, radio, TV, radar and navigation equipment, scientific instruments, arms, whisky.

**Religion and Education.** The Church of England is Protestant Episcopal. The queen is its temporal head, with rights of appointments to archbishoprics, bishoprics, and other offices. There are 2 provinces, Canterbury and York, each headed by an archbishop. The most famous church is Westminster Abbey (1050-1760), site of coronations, tombs of Elizabeth I, Mary, Queen of Scots, kings, poets, and of the Unknown Warrior.

The most celebrated British universities are Oxford and Cambridge, each dating to the 13th century. There are about 70 other universities.

**History.** Britain was part of the continent of Europe until about 6,000 BC, but migration of peoples across the English Channel continued long afterward. Celts arrived 2,500 to 3,000 years ago. Their language survives in Welsh, and Gaelic enclaves.

England was added to the Roman Empire in AD 43. After the withdrawal of Roman legions in 410, waves of Jutes, Angles, and Saxons arrived from German lands. They contended with Danish raiders for control from the 8th through 11th centuries. The last successful invasion was by French speaking Normans in 1066, who united the country with their dominions in France.

Opposition by nobles to royal authority forced King John to sign the Magna Carta in 1215, a guarantee of rights and the rule of law. In the ensuing decades, the foundations of the parliamentary system were laid.

English dynastic claims to large parts of France led to the Hundred Years War, 1338-1453, and the defeat of England. A long civil war, the War of the Roses, lasted 1455-85, and ended with the establishment of the powerful Tudor monarchy. A distinct English civilization flourished. The economy prospered over long periods of domestic peace unmatched in continental Europe. Religious independence was secured when the Church of England was separated from the authority of the pope in 1534.

Under Queen Elizabeth I, England became a major naval power, leading to the founding of colonies in the new world and the expansion of trade with Europe and the Orient. Scotland was united with England when James VI of Scotland was crowned James I of England in 1603.

A struggle between Parliament and the Stuart kings led to a bloody civil war, 1642-49, and the establishment of a republic under the Puritan Oliver Cromwell. The monarchy was restored in 1660, but the "Glorious Revolution" of 1688 confirmed the sovereignty of Parliament: a Bill of Rights was granted 1689.

In the 18th century, parliamentary rule was strengthened. Technological and entrepreneurial innovations led to the Industrial Revolution. The 13 North American colonies were lost, but replaced by growing empires in Canada and India. Britain's role in the defeat of Napoleon, 1815, strengthened its position as the leading world power.

The extension of the franchise in 1832 and 1867, the formation of trade unions, and the development of universal public education were among the drastic social changes that accompanied the spread of industrialization and urbanization in the 19th century. Large parts of Africa and Asia were added to the empire during the reign of Queen Victoria, 1837-1901.

Though victorious in World War I, Britain suffered huge casualties and economic dislocation. Ireland became independent in 1921, and independence movements became active in India and other colonies. The country suffered major bombing damage in World War II, but held out against Germany singlehandedly for a year after the fall of France in 1940.

Industrial growth continued in the postwar period, but Britain lost its leadership position to other powers. Labor governments passed socialist programs nationalizing some basic industries and expanding social security. The Conservative government of Prime Min. Margaret Thatcher, however, tried to increase the role of private enterprise. In 1987, Thatcher became the first British leader in 160 years to be elected to a 3d consecutive term as prime minister. Falling on unpopular times, she resigned as prime minister in Nov. 1990. Her successor, John Major, led Conservatives to an upset victory at the polls, Apr. 9, 1993.

The UK supported the UN resolutions against Iraq and sent military forces to the Persian Gulf War.

The Channel Tunnel linking Britain to the Continent was officially inaugurated May 6, 1994. Britain's relations with the European Union were frayed in 1996 when the EU banned British beef because of the threat of "mad cow" disease.

## Wales

The Principality of Wales in western Britain has an area of 8,019 sq. mi. and a population (1992 est.) of 2,899,000. Cardiff is the capital, pop. (1994 est.) 299,000.

England and Wales are administered as a unit. Less than 20% of the population of Wales speak both English and Welsh; about 32,000 speak Welsh solely. A 1979 referendum rejected, 4-1, the creation of an elected Welsh Assembly.

Early Anglo-Saxon invaders drove Celtic peoples into the mountains of Wales, terming them Waelise (Welsh, or foreign). There they developed a distinct nationality. Members of the ruling house of Gwynedd in the 13th century fought England but were crushed, 1283. Edward of Caernarvon, son of Edward I of England, was created Prince of Wales, 1301.

## Scotland

Scotland, a kingdom now united with England and Wales in Great Britain, occupies the northern 37% of the main British island, and the Hebrides, Orkney, Shetland, and smaller islands. Length 275 mi., breadth approx. 150 mi., area 30,418 sq. mi., population (1992 est.) 5,111,000.

The Lowlands, a belt of land approximately 60 mi. wide from the Firth of Clyde to the Firth of Forth, divide the farming region of the Southern Uplands from the granite Highlands of the North, contain 75% of the population and most of the industry. The Highlands, famous for hunting and fishing, have been opened to industry by many hydroelectric power stations.

Edinburgh, pop. (1994 est.) 442,000, is the capital. Glasgow, pop. (1994 est.) 681,000, is Britain's greatest industrial center. It is a shipbuilding complex on the Clyde and an ocean port. Aberdeen, pop. (1994 est.) 218,000, NE of Edinburgh, is a major port, center of granite industry, fish-processing, and North Sea oil exploration. Dundee, pop. (1993 est.) 170,000, NE of Edinburgh, is an industrial and fish-processing center. About 90,000 persons speak Gaelic as well as English.

**History.** Scotland was called Caledonia by the Romans who battled early Celtic tribes and occupied southern areas from the 1st to the 4th centuries. Missionaries from Britain introduced Christianity in the 4th century; St. Columba, an Irish monk, converted most of Scotland in the 6th century.

The Kingdom of Scotland was founded in 1018. William Wallace and Robert Bruce both defeated English armies 1297 and 1314, respectively.

In 1603 James VI of Scotland, son of Mary, Queen of Scots, succeeded to the throne of England as James I, and effected the Union of the Crowns. In 1707 Scotland received representation in the British Parliament, resulting from the union of former separate Parliaments. Its executive in the British cabinet is the Secretary of State for Scotland. The growing Scottish National Party urges independence. A 1979 referendum on the creation of an elected Scotland Assembly was defeated.

Memorials of Robert Burns, Sir Walter Scott, John Knox, Mary, Queen of Scots draw many tourists, as do the beauties of the Trossachs, Loch Katrine, Loch Lomond, and abbey ruins.

**Industries.** Engineering products are the most important industry, with growing emphasis on office machinery, autos, electronics, and other consumer goods. Oil has been discovered offshore in the North Sea, stimulating on-shore support industries.

Scotland produces fine woolens, worsteds, tweeds, silks, fine linens, and jute. It is known for its special breeds of cattle and sheep. Fisheries have large hauls of herring, cod, whiting. Whisky is the biggest export.

**The Hebrides** are a group of c. 500 islands, 100 inhabited, off the W coast. The Inner Hebrides include **Skye, Mull,** and **Iona,** the last famous for the arrival of St. Columba, AD 563. The Outer Hebrides include **Lewis** and **Harris.** Industries include sheep raising and weaving. The **Orkney Islands,** c. 90, are to the NE. The capital is Kirkwall, on Pomona I. Fish curing, sheep raising, and weaving are occupations. NE of the Orkneys are the 200 **Shetland Islands,** 24 inhabited, home of Shetland pony. The Orkneys and Shetlands have become centers for the North Sea oil industry.

## Northern Ireland

Six of the 9 counties of Ulster, the NE corner of Ireland, constitute Northern Ireland, with the parliamentary boroughs of Belfast and Londonderry. Area 5,452 sq. mi., pop. (1992 est.) 1,610,000, capital and chief industrial center, Belfast, pop. (1994 est.) 281,000.

**Industries.** Shipbuilding, including large tankers, has long been an important industry, centered in Belfast, the largest port. Linen manufacture is also important, along with apparel, rope, and twine. Growing diversification has added engineering products, synthetic fibers, and electronics. There are large numbers of cattle, hogs, and sheep. Potatoes, poultry, and dairy foods are also produced.

**Government.** An act of the British Parliament, 1920, divided Northern from Southern Ireland, each with a parliament and government. When Ireland became a dominion, 1921, and later a republic, Northern Ireland chose to remain a part of the United Kingdom. It elects 17 members to the British House of Commons.

During 1968-69, large demonstrations were conducted by Roman Catholics who charged they were discriminated against in voting rights, housing, and employment. The Catholics, a minority comprising about a third of the population, demanded abolition of property qualifications for voting in local elections. Violence and terrorism intensified, involving branches of the Irish Republican Army (outlawed in the Irish Republic), Protestant groups, police, and British troops.

A succession of Northern Ireland prime ministers pressed reform programs but failed to satisfy extremists on both sides. Between 1969 and 1994 more than 3,000 were killed in sectarian violence, many in England itself. Britain suspended the Northern Ireland parliament Mar. 30, 1972, and imposed direct British rule. A coalition government was formed in 1973 when moderates won election to a new one-house Assembly. But a Protestant general strike overthrew the government in 1974 and direct rule was resumed.

The turmoil and agony of Northern Ireland was dramatized in 1981 by the deaths of 10 imprisoned Irish nationalist hunger strikers in Maze Prison near Belfast. The inmates had starved themselves to death in an attempt to achieve status as political prisoners, but the British government refused to yield to their demands. In 1985, the Hillsborough agreement gave the Rep. of Ireland a voice in the governing of Northern Ireland; the accord was strongly opposed by Ulster loyalists. On Dec. 12, 1993, Britain and Ireland announced a declaration of principles aimed at leading to a political settlement of the Northern Ireland issue. On Aug. 31, 1994, the IRA announced a cease-fire, saying it would rely on political means to achieve its objectives; the IRA resumed its terrorist tactics on Feb. 9, 1996.

**Education and Religion.** Northern Ireland is about 58% Protestant, 42% Roman Catholic. Education is compulsory through age 15.

## Channel Islands

The Channel Islands, area 75 sq. mi., pop. (1996 est.) 151,000, off the NW coast of France, the only parts of the one-time Dukedom of Normandy belonging to England, are **Jersey, Guernsey** and the dependencies of Guernsey — **Alderney, Brechou, Great Sark, Little Sark, Herm, Jethou and Lihou.** Jersey and Guernsey have separate legal existences and lieutenant governors named by the Crown. The islands were the only British soil occupied by German troops in World War II.

## Isle of Man

The Isle of Man, area 227 sq. mi., pop. (1996 est.) 73,800, is in the Irish Sea, 20 mi. from Scotland, 30 mi. from Cumberland. It is rich in lead and iron. The island has its own laws and a lieutenant governor appointed by the Crown. The Tynwald (legislature) consists of the Legislative Council, partly elected, and House of Keys, elected. Capital: Douglas. Farming, tourism, and fishing (kippers, scallops) are chief occupations. Man is famous for the Manx tailless cat.

## Gibraltar

Gibraltar, a dependency on the southern coast of Spain, guards the entrance to the Mediterranean. The Rock has been in British possession since 1704. The Rock is 2.75 mi. long, 3/4 of a mi. wide and 1,396 ft. in height; a narrow isthmus connects it with the mainland. Pop. (1996 est.) 28,800.

Gibraltar has historically been an object of contention between Britain and Spain. Residents voted with near unanimity to remain under British rule, in a 1967 referendum held in pursuance of a UN resolution on decolonization. A new constitution, May 30, 1969, increased Gibraltarian control of domestic affairs (the UK continues to handle defense and internal security matters). Following a 1984 agreement between Britain and Spain, the border, closed by Spain in 1969, was fully reopened in Feb. 1985. A UN General Assembly resolution requested Britain to end Gibraltar's colonial status by Oct. 1, 1996. No settlement has been reached.

## British West Indies

Swinging in a vast arc from the coast of Venezuela NE, then N and NW toward Puerto Rico are the Leeward Islands, forming a coral and volcanic barrier sheltering the Caribbean from the open Atlantic. Many of the islands are self-governing British possessions. Universal suffrage was instituted 1951-54; ministerial systems were set up 1956-1960.

The **Leeward Islands** still associated with the UK are **Montserrat**, area 32 sq. mi., pop. (1996 est.) 12,800, capital Plymouth; the **British Virgin Islands,** 59 sq. mi., pop. (1996 est.) 13,000, capital Road Town; and **Anguilla**, the most northerly of the Leeward Islands, 60 sq. mi., pop. (1996 est.) 10,400, capital The Valley.

The three **Cayman Islands,** a dependency, lie S of Cuba, NW of Jamaica. Pop. (1996 est.) 34,600, most of it on Grand Cayman. It is a free port; in the 1970s Grand Cayman became a tax-free refuge for foreign funds and branches of many Western banks were opened there. Total area 102 sq. mi., capital Georgetown.

The **Turks and Caicos Islands** are a dependency at the SE end of the Bahama Islands. Of about 30 islands, only 6 are inhabited; area 193 sq. mi., pop. (1996 est.) 14,300; capital Grand Turk. Salt, shellfish, and conch shells are the main exports.

## Bermuda

**Bermuda** is a British dependency governed by a royal governor and an assembly, dating from 1620, the oldest legislative body among British dependencies. Capital is Hamilton.

It is a group of about 150 small islands of coral formation, 20 inhabited, comprising 20.6 sq. mi. in the western Atlantic, 580 mi. E of North Carolina. Pop. (1996 est.) 62,100 (about 61% of African descent). Pop. density is high.

The U.S. maintains a NASA tracking facility; a U.S. naval air base was closed in 1995.

Tourism is the major industry; Bermuda boasts many resort hotels. The government raises most revenue from import duties. Exports: petroleum products, medicine. In a referendum Aug. 15, 1995, voters rejected independence by nearly a 3-to-1 majority.

## South Atlantic

The **Falkland Islands,** a dependency, lie 300 mi. E of the Strait of Magellan at the southern end of South America.

The Falklands or Islas Malvinas include 2 large islands and about 200 smaller ones, area 4,700 sq. mi., pop. (1995 est.) 2,317, capital Stanley. The licensing of foreign fishing vessels has become the major source of revenue. Sheep-grazing is a main industry; wool is the principal export. There are indications of large oil and gas deposits. The islands are also claimed by Argentina, though 97% of inhabitants are of British origin. Argentina invaded the islands Apr. 2, 1982. The British responded by sending a task force to the area, landing their main force on the Falklands, May 21, and forcing an Argentine surrender at Port Stanley, June 14.

**British Antarctic Territory,** south of 60° S lat., formerly a dependency of the Falkland Is., was made a separate colony in 1962 and includes the **South Shetland Islands,** the **South Orkneys**, and the Antarctic Peninsula. A chain of meteorological stations is maintained.

**South Georgia and the South Sandwich Islands,** formerly administered by the Falklands Is., became a separate dependency in 1985. South Georgia, 1,450 sq. mi., with no permanent population, is about 800 mi. SE of the Falklands; the South Sandwich Is., 130 sq. mi., are uninhabited, about 470 mi. SE of South Georgia.

**St. Helena,** an island 1,200 mi. off the W coast of Africa and 1,800 mi. E of South America, 47 sq. mi. and pop. (1996 est.) 6,800. Flax, lace, and rope-making are the chief industries. After Napoleon Bonaparte was defeated at Waterloo the Allies exiled him to St. Helena, where he lived from Oct. 16, 1815, to his death, May 5, 1821. Capital is Jamestown.

**Tristan da Cunha** is the principal of a group of islands of volcanic origin, total area 40 sq. mi., halfway between the Cape of Good Hope and South America. A volcanic peak 6,760 ft. high erupted in 1961. The 262 inhabitants were removed to England, but most returned in 1963. The islands are dependencies of St. Helena. Pop. (1993) 300.

**Ascension** is an island of volcanic origin, 34 sq. mi. in area, 700 mi. NW of St. Helena, through which it is administered. It is a communications relay center for Britain, and has a U.S. satellite tracking center. Pop. (1993) was 1,117, half of them communications workers. The island is noted for sea turtles.

## Hong Kong

A British dependency scheduled to revert to China in 1997, located at the mouth of the Xi (Pearl) R. in SE China, 90 mi. S of Canton (Guangzhou). Its nucleus is Hong Kong I., 31 sq. mi., acquired from China 1841, on which is located Victoria, the capital. Opposite is Kowloon Peninsula, 3 sq. mi., and Stonecutters Is., ¼ sq. mi., added 1860. An additional 355 sq. mi. known as the New Territories, a mainland area and islands, were leased from China, 1898, for 99 years. Britain and China, Dec. 19, 1984, signed an agreement under which Hong Kong would be allowed to keep its capitalist system for 50 years after 1997, the year that the 99-year lease will expire. During 1994 the Hong Kong legislature approved democratic reforms, which were opposed by China. Total area of the colony is 415 sq. mi., with a population, 1996 est., of 6.3 million, including fewer than 20,000 British. From 1949 to 1962 Hong Kong absorbed more than a million refugees from China.

Hong Kong harbor was long an important British naval station and one of the world's great transshipment ports.

Principal industries are textiles and apparel; also tourism, $8.3 bil expenditures (1994), shipbuilding, iron and steel, fishing, cement, and small manufactures.

Spinning mills, among the best in the world, and low wages compete with textiles elsewhere and have resulted in the protective measures in some countries. Hong Kong also has a booming electronics industry.

## British Indian Ocean Territory

Formed Nov. 1965, embracing islands formerly dependencies of Mauritius or Seychelles: the Chagos Archipelago (including Diego Garcia), Aldabra, Farquhar, and Des Roches. The latter 3 were transferred to Seychelles, which became independent in 1976. Area 23 sq. mi. No permanent civilian population remains; the U.K. and the U.S. maintain a military presence.

## Pacific Ocean

**Pitcairn Island** is in the Pacific, halfway between South America and Australia. The island was discovered in 1767 by Philip Carteret but was not inhabited until 23 years later when the mutineers of the *Bounty* landed there. The area is 1.7 sq. mi. and 1995 pop. was 54. It is a British dependency and is administered by a British High Commissioner in New Zealand and a local Council. The uninhabited islands of **Henderson, Ducie,** and **Oeno** are in the Pitcairn group.

# United States

## United States of America

**People: Population:** 265,562,845 (incl. 50 states & Dist. of Columbia). (**Note:** U.S. pop. figures may differ elsewhere in *The World Almanac.*) **Age distrib.** (%): <15: 22; 65+: 13. **Pop. density:** 75 per sq. mi. **Urban:** 75%.

**Geography: Land area:** 3,536,278 sq. mi. (incl. 50 states and DC). **Topography:** Vast central plain, mountains in west, hills and low mountains in east. **Capital:** Washington, D.C.

**Government:** Federal republic, strong democratic tradition. **Head of state:** Pres. Bill Clinton; b Aug. 19, 1946; in office: Jan. 20, 1993. **Administrative divisions:** 50 states and Dist. of Columbia. **Defense:** 4.2% of GDP (1994). **Active troop strength:** 1.55 mil.

**Economy: Minerals:** Coal, copper, lead, molybdenum, phosphates, uranium, bauxite, gold, iron, mercury, nickel, potash, silver, tungsten, zinc. **Crude oil reserves** (1995): 22.5 bil barrels. **Arable land:** 20%. **Livestock** (1995): cattle: 102.8 mln.; pigs: 60.0 mln.; sheep: 8.9 mil. **Fish catch** (1995): 4.5 mil metric tons. **Electricity prod.** (1995): 3.3 trl. kWh.

**Finance: Gross domestic product** (1995): 7.25 trl. **Per capita GDP:** $27,607. **Imports** (1995): $749 bln.; partners: Canada 19%, Japan 16%. **Exports** (1995): $685 bln.; partners: Canada 19%, Japan 9%. **Tourism** (1994): $77.7 bil. **International reserves less gold** (May 1996): $72.4 bil. **Gold:** 261.75 mil oz t. **Consumer prices** (change in 1995): 2.8%.

**Transport: Railroads: Length:** 136,000 mi. **Motor vehicles:** in use: 146 mil passenger cars, 59 mil comm. vehicles. **Civil aviation:** 480 bil passenger-mi.; 834 airports with scheduled flights.

**Communications: Television sets:** 1 per 1.2 persons. **Radios:** 1 per 0.5 person. **Telephones:** 1 per 1.7 persons. **Daily newspaper circ.:** 238 per 1,000 pop.

**Health: Life expectancy at birth** (1996): 73 male; 79 female. **Births** (per 1,000 pop.): 15. **Deaths** (per 1,000 pop.): 9. **Natural increase:** 0.6%. **Hospital beds:** 1 per 223 persons. **Physicians:** 1 per 391 persons. **Infant mortality** (per 1,000 live births 1996): 7.

**Education: Literacy** (1994): 96%. Free and compulsory: ages 7-16

**Major International Organizations:** UN (WTO, ILO, IMF, WHO, FAO), OAS, NATO, OECD, APEC.

# Uruguay

## Oriental Republic of Uruguay

## República Oriental del Uruguay

**People: Population:** 3,238,952. **Age distrib.** (%): <15: 26; 65+: 12. **Pop. density:** 48 per sq. mi. **Urban:** 90%. **Ethnic groups:** White (Iberians, Italians) 88%, mestizo 8%, black 4%. **Principal languages:** Spanish (official). **Religions:** Roman Catholic 66%.

**Geography: Area:** 68,037 sq. mi. **Location:** In southern South America, on the Atlantic O. **Neighbors:** Argentina on W, Brazil on N. **Topography:** Uruguay is composed of rolling, grassy plains and hills, well watered by rivers flowing W to Uruguay R. **Capital:** Montevideo (1992 est.): 1.4 mil.

**Government: Type:** Republic. **Head of state:** Pres. Julio María Sanguinetti Cairolo; Jan. 6, 1936; in office: Mar. 1, 1995. **Local divisions:** 19 departments. **Defense:** 4.2% of GDP (1994 est.). **Active troop strength:** 25,600.

**Economy: Industries:** Meat packing, wool and hides, textiles, wine, oil refining. **Chief crops:** Corn, wheat, sugar, rice, oats, linseed. **Arable land:** 8%. **Livestock** (1993): sheep: 25.7 mln.; cattle: 10.1 mil. **Fish catch** (1994): 117,000 metric tons. **Electricity prod.** (1993): 9 bil kWh. **Labor force** 33% serv.; 25% govt.; 19% manuf.; 12% comm.; 11% agric.

**Finance: Monetary unit:** Peso (June 1996: 7.92 = $1 US). **Gross domestic product** (1994): $23 bln.* **Per capita GDP:** $7,200. **Imports** (1994): $2.5 bln.; partners: Brazil 26%, Argentina 24%, U.S. 9%. **Exports** (1994): $1.8 bln.; partners: Brazil 26%, Argentina 20%, U.S. 7%. **Tourism** (1993): $447 mil. **National budget** (1991): $3.0 bil. **International reserves less gold** (Mar. 1996): $1.2 bil. **Gold:** 1.72 mil oz t. **Consumer prices** (change in 1995): 42.2%

**Transport: Railroads: Route length:** 1,867 mi. **Motor vehicles:** in use: 311,000 passenger cars, 149,000 comm. vehicles. **Civil aviation:** 293 mil passenger-mi.; 1 airport. **Chief port:** Montevideo.

**Communications: Television sets:** 1 per 5.3 persons. **Radios:** 1 per 1.7 persons. **Telephones:** 1 per 5.9 persons. **Daily newspaper circ.:** 240 per 1,000 pop.

**Health: Life expectancy at birth** (1996): 72 male; 78 female. **Births** (per 1,000 pop.): 17. **Deaths** (per 1,000 pop.): 9. **Natural increase:** 0.8%. **Hospital beds:** 1 per 215 persons. **Physicians:** 1 per 286 persons. **Infant mortality** (per 1,000 live births 1996): 15.

**Education: Literacy** (1993): 97%.

**Major International Organizations:** UN (WTO, IMF, WHO), OAS.

**Embassy:** 1918 F St. NW 20006; 331-1313.

Spanish settlers did not begin replacing the indigenous Charrua Indians until 1624. Portuguese from Brazil arrived later, but Uruguay was attached to the Spanish Viceroyalty of Rio de la Plata in the 18th century. Rebels fought against Spain beginning in 1810. An independent republic was declared Aug. 25, 1825.

Socialist measures were adopted as far back as 1911. The state owns the power, telephone, railroad, cement, oil-refining, and other industries.

Uruguay's standard of living was one of the highest in South America, and political and labor conditions among the freest. Economic stagnation, inflation, floods and drought, and a general strike in the late 1960s brought government attempts to strengthen the economy through devaluation of the peso and wage and price controls.

Terrorist activities led to Pres. Juan Maria Bordaberry agreeing to military control of his administration Feb. 1973. In June he abolished Congress and set up a Council of State in its place. Bordaberry was removed by the military in a 1976 coup. Civilian government was restored to the country in 1985.

# Uzbekistan

## Republic of Uzbekistan

## Uzbekiston Respublikasi

**People: Population:** 23,418,381. **Age distrib.** (%): <15: 41; 65+: 4. **Pop. density:** 136 per sq. mi. **Urban:** 39%. **Ethnic groups:** Uzbek 71%, Russian 8%. **Principal languages:** Uzbek (official), Russian. **Religions:** Mostly Sunni Muslim, some Eastern Orthodox.

**Geography: Area:** 172,700 sq. mi. **Location:** Central Asia. **Neighbors:** Kazakstan on N and W, Kyrgyzstan and Tajikistan on E, Afghanistan and Turkmenistan on S. **Topography:** Mostly plains and desert. **Capital:** Tashkent (1994): 2.1 mil.

**Government: Type:** Republic. **Head of state:** Pres. Islam A. Karimov; b Jan. 30, 1938; in office: March 24, 1990. **Head of government:** Prime Min. Utkur Sultanov; in office: 1996. **Local divisions:** 12 regions, 1 autonomous republic, and Tashkent. **Defense: Active troop strength:** 25,000.

**Economy: Industries:** Machinery, food processing, natural gas, textiles. **Chief crops:** Cotton, rice. **Minerals:** Gas, oil, coal, gold, copper. **Arable land:** 10%. **Livestock** (1994): cattle: 5.3 mln.; sheep: 9.4 mil. **Electricity prod.** (1994): 47.5 bil kWh. **Labor force:** 43% agric. & forestry; 22% ind. & constr.

**Finance: Monetary unit:** Sum (June 1996: 37.9 = $1 US). **Gross domestic product** (1994 est.): $54.5 bln.* **Per capita GDP:** $2,400. **Imports** (1992): $1.15 bil, excl. CIS. **Exports** (1994): $944 mln.; excl. CIS.

**Transport: Railroads: Length:** 4,200 mi. **Civil aviation:** 6.5 bil passenger-mi.; 2 airports with scheduled flights. **Chief port:** Termiz.

**Communications: Telephones:** 1 per 15 persons.

**Health: Life expectancy at birth** (1996): 60 male; 69 female. **Births** (per 1,000 pop.): 30. **Deaths** (per 1,000 pop.): 8. **Natural increase:** 2.2%. **Hospital beds:** 1 per 118 persons. **Physicians:** 1 per 284 persons. **Infant mortality** (per 1,000 live births 1996): 80.

**Education: Literacy** (1993): 97%. Compulsory: ages 6-14.

**Major International Organizations:** UN, CIS.

**Embassy:** 1511 K St. NW 20005; 638-4266.

The region was overrun by the Mongols under Genghis Khan in 1220. In the 14th century, Uzbekistan became the center of a native empire—that of the Timurids. In later centuries Muslim feudal states emerged. Russian military conquest began in the 19th century.

The Uzbek SSR became a Soviet Union republic in 1925. Uzbekistan declared independence Aug. 29, 1991. It became an independent republic when the Soviet Union disbanded Dec. 26, 1991. Subsequently, the government of Uzbekistan was dominated by former Communists.

# Vanuatu

## Republic of Vanuatu

## Ripablik blong Vanuatu

**People: Population:** 177,504. **Pop. density:** 38 per sq. mi. **Urban:** 18%. **Ethnic groups:** Mainly Melanesian, some European, Asian, Pacific Islander. **Principal languages:** French, English, Bislama (all official). **Religions:** Presbyterian 37%, Anglican 15%, Roman Catholic 15%, other Christian 10%, indigenous beliefs 8%.

**Geography: Area:** 4,707 sq. mi. **Location:** SW Pacific, 1,200 mi. NE of Brisbane, Australia. **Neighbors:** Fiji to E, Solomon Is. to NW. **Topography:** Dense forest with narrow coastal strips of cultivated land. **Capital:** Port-Vila (1993 est.): 26,100.

**Government: Type:** Republic. **Head of state:** Pres. Jean-Marie Leye; b 1932; in office: Mar. 2, 1994. **Head of government:** Prime Min. Maxime Carlot Korman; in office: Dec. 16, 1991. **Local divisions:** 11 island councils.

**Economy: Industries:** Fish-freezing, meat canneries, tourism. **Chief crops:** Copra, coconuts, cocoa, coffee. **Minerals:** Manganese. **Other resources:** Forests, cattle. **Fish catch** (1993): 2,900 metric tons.

**Finance: Monetary unit:** Vatu (June 1996): 111.50 = $1 US). **Gross domestic product** (1993): $200 mln.* **Per capita GDP:** $1,200. **Imports** (1991): $74 mil. **Exports** (1991): $15 mil. **Tourism** (1993): $30 mil.

**Communications: Radios:** 1 per 3.0 persons.

**Health: Life expectancy at birth** (1996): 58 male; 62 female. **Births** (per 1,000 pop.): 31. **Deaths** (per 1,000 pop.): 9. **Natural increase:** 2.2%. **Infant mortality** (per 1,000 live births 1996): 65.

**Education: Literacy** (1992): 53%. Education not compulsory, but 85% of children of primary school age attend schools.

**Major International Organizations:** UN, the Commonwealth.

The Anglo-French condominium of the New Hebrides, administered jointly by France and Great Britain since 1906, became the independent Republic of Vanuatu on July 30, 1980.

# Vatican City (The Holy See)

## Città del Vaticano (Santa Sede)

**People: Population:** 811. **Ethnic groups:** Italian, Swiss. **Principal languages:** Italian, Latin. **Religions:** Roman Catholic.

**Geography: Area:** 108.7 acres. **Location:** In Rome, Italy. **Neighbors:** Completely surrounded by Italy.

**Monetary unit:** Vatican Lira, Italian Lira (equal value).

**Apostolic Nunciature in U.S.:** 3339 Massachusetts Ave. NW 20008; 333-7121.

The popes for many centuries, with brief interruptions, held temporal sovereignty over mid-Italy (the so-called Papal States), comprising an area of some 16,000 sq. mi., with a population in the 19th century of more than 3 million. This territory was incorporated in the new Kingdom of Italy, the sovereignty of the pope being confined to the palaces of the Vatican and the Lateran in Rome and the villa of Castel Gandolfo, by an Italian law, May 13, 1871. This law also guaranteed to the pope and his successors a yearly indemnity of over $620,000. The allowance, however, remained unclaimed.

A Treaty of Conciliation, a concordat, and a financial convention were signed Feb. 11, 1929, by Cardinal Gasparri and Premier Mussolini. The documents established the independent state of Vatican City and gave the Catholic religion special status in Italy. The treaty (Lateran Agreement) was made part of the Constitution of Italy (Article 7) in 1947. Italy and the Vatican signed an agreement in 1984 on revisions of the concordat; the accord eliminated Roman Catholicism as the state religion and ended required religious education in Italian schools.

Vatican City includes St. Peter's, the Vatican Palace and Museum covering over 13 acres, the Vatican gardens, and neighboring buildings between Viale Vaticano and the Church. Thirteen buildings in Rome, outside the boundaries, enjoy extraterritorial rights; these buildings house congregations or officers necessary for the administration of the Holy See.

The legal system is based on the code of canon law, the apostolic constitutions, and laws especially promulgated for the Vatican City by the pope. The Secretariat of State represents the Holy See in its diplomatic relations. By the Treaty of Conciliation the pope is pledged to a perpetual neutrality unless his mediation is specifically requested. This, however, does not prevent the defense of the Church whenever it is persecuted.

The present sovereign of the State of Vatican City is the Supreme Pontiff John Paul II, Karol Wojtyla, born in Wadowice, Poland, May 18, 1920, elected Oct. 16, 1978 (the first non-Italian to be elected Pope in 456 years).

The U.S. restored formal relations in 1984 after the U.S. Congress repealed an 1867 ban on diplomatic relations with the Vatican. The Vatican and Israel agreed to establish formal relations Dec. 30, 1993.

# Venezuela

## Republic of Venezuela

## República de Venezuela

**People: Population:** 21,983,188. **Age distrib.** (%): <15: 38; 65+: 4. **Pop. density:** 62 per sq. mi. **Urban:** 84%. **Ethnic groups:** Mestizo 67%, white (Spanish, Portuguese, Italian) 21%, black 10%, Indian 2%. **Principal languages:** Spanish (official). **Religions:** Roman Catholic 96%.

**Geography: Area:** 352,144 sq. mi. **Location:** On the Caribbean coast of South America. **Neighbors:** Colombia on W, Brazil on S, Guyana on E. **Topography:** Flat coastal plain and Orinoco Delta are bordered by Andes Mts. and hills. Plains, called llanos, extend between mountains and Orinoco. Guyana Highlands and plains are S of Orinoco, which stretches 1,600 mi. and drains 80% of Venezuela. **Capital:** Caracas. **Cities** (1990): Caracas 1.8 mln.; Maracaibo 1.3 mln.; Valencia 903,600; Barquisimeto 625,500.

**Government: Type:** Federal republic. **Head of state:** Pres. Rafael Caldera; b Jan. 24, 1916; in office: Feb. 2, 1994. **Local divisions:** 21 states, 1 territory, 1 federal district, 1 federal dependency. **Defense:** 4% of GDP (1991). **Active troop strength:** 79,000.

**Economy: Industries:** Steel, oil products, textiles. **Chief crops:** Coffee, rice, corn, fruits, sugar. **Minerals:** Oil, gas, iron (extensive reserves and production); gold. **Crude oil reserves** (1995): 64.5 bil barrels. **Arable land:** 3%. **Livestock** (1994): cattle: 15.0 mil. **Fish catch** (1993): 390,000 metric tons. **Electricity prod.** (1993): 72 bil kWh. **Labor force:** 63% services; 25% ind.; 12% agric.

**Finance: Monetary unit:** Bolivar (June 1996: 468 = $1 US). **Gross domestic product** (1994): $178 bln.* **Per capita GDP:** $8,670. **Imports** (1994): $7.6 bln.; partners: U.S. 40%. **Exports** (1994): $15.2 bln.; partners: U.S. & P.R. 55%. **Tourism** (1992): $432 mil. **National budget** (1994): $14.6 bil. **International reserves less gold** (May 1996): $6.7 bil. **Gold:** 11.46 mil oz t. **Consumer prices** (change in 1995): 59.9%.

**Transport: Railroads: Route length:** 226 mi. **Motor vehicles:** in use: 1.5 mil passenger cars, 474,000 comm. vehicles. **Civil aviation:** 4.2 bil passenger-mi.; 24 airports with scheduled flights. **Chief ports:** Maracaibo, La Guaira, Puerto Cabello.

**Communications: Television sets:** 1 per 5.7 persons. **Radios:** 1 per 2.6 persons. **Telephones:** 1 per 10 persons. **Daily newspaper circ.:** 208 per 1,000 pop.

**Health: Life expectancy at birth** (1996): 69 male; 75 female. **Births** (per 1,000 pop.): 24. **Deaths** (per 1,000 pop.): 5. **Natural increase:** 1.9%. **Hospital beds:** 1 per 382 persons. **Physicians:** 1 per 626 persons. **Infant mortality** (per 1,000 live births 1996): 30.

**Education: Literacy** (1992): 91%. Free and compulsory: ages 5-15. Attendance 86%.

**Major International Organizations:** UN (IMF, WTO, WHO, FAO), OAS, OPEC.

**Embassy:** 1099 30th St. NW 20007; 342-2214.

Columbus first set foot on the South American continent on the peninsula of Paria, Aug. 1498. Alonso de Ojeda, 1499, found Lake Maracaibo, and called the land Venezuela, or Little Venice, because natives had houses on stilts. Venezuela was under Spanish domination until 1821. The republic was formed after secession from the Colombian Federation in 1830.

Military strongmen ruled Venezuela for most of the 20th century. They promoted the oil industry; some social reforms were implemented. Since 1959, the country has had democratically elected governments.

Venezuela helped found the Organization of Petroleum Exporting Countries (OPEC). The government, Jan. 1, 1976, nationalized the oil industry with compensation. Oil accounts for much of total export earnings and the economy suffered a severe cash crisis in the 1980s and 1990s as a result of falling oil revenues.The government has attempted to reduce dependence on oil.

A coup attempt, led by midlevel military officers, was thwarted by loyalist troops Feb. 4, 1992. A second coup attempt was thwarted in Nov. Pres. Carlos Andrés Pérez was removed from office on corruption charges, May 1993; he was convicted, May 1996, of mismanaging a $17-million secret government security fund. Citing an economic crisis, Pres. Rafael Caldera, a populist elected Dec. 5, 1993, suspended many civil liberties June 27, 1994; constitutional rights were restored in most regions July 6, 1995.

# Vietnam

## Socialist Republic of Vietnam

## Cong Hoa Xa Hoi Chu Nghia Viet Nam

**People: Population:** 73,976,973. **Age distrib.** (%): <15: 40; 65+: 5. **Pop. density:** 579 per sq. mi. **Urban:** 19%. **Ethnic groups:** Vietnamese 85-90%, Chinese 3%, Muong, Thai, Meo, Khmer, Man, Cham. **Principal languages:** Vietnamese (official), French, Chinese. **Religions:** Mainly Buddhist and Taoist; also Roman Catholic, indigenous beliefs, Muslim, Protestant.

**Geography: Area:** 127,816 sq. mi. **Location:** SE Asia, on the E coast of the Indochinese Peninsula. **Neighbors:** China on N, Laos and Cambodia on W. **Topography:** Vietnam is long and narrow, with a 1,400-mi. coast. About 22% of country is readily arable, including the densely settled Red R. valley in the N, narrow coastal plains in center, and the wide, often marshy Mekong R. Delta in the S. The rest consists of semi-arid plateaus and barren mountains, with some stretches of tropical rain forest. **Capital:** Hanoi. **Cities** (1992 est.): Ho Chi Minh City 4.2 mln.; Hanoi 2.1 mil.

**Government: Type:** Communist. **Head of state:** Pres. Le Duc Anh; b Dec. 1, 1920; in office: Sept. 23, 1992. **Head of government:** Prime Min. Vo Van Kiet; b 1922; in office: Aug. 8, 1991. **Local divisions:** 50 provinces, 3 municipalities. **Defense:** 2.5% of GDP (1994). **Active troop strength:** 572,000 est.

**Economy: Industries:** Food processing, textiles, cement, chemical fertilizer. **Chief crops:** Rice, rubber, fruits, vegetables, soybeans, coffee, tea, bananas. **Minerals:** Phosphates, coal, manganese, bauxite, chromate, oil. **Crude oil reserves** (1995): 500 mil bbls. **Other resources:** Forests. **Arable land:** 22%. **Livestock** (1994): cattle: 3.4 mln.; pigs: 15.0 mil. **Fish catch** (1993): 1.1 mil metric tons. **Electricity prod.** (1993): 9.7 bil kWh. **Labor force:** 65% agric.; 35% ind. and services.

**Finance: Monetary unit:** Dong (June 1996: 10,960 = $1 US). **Gross domestic product** (1994): $83.5 bln.* **Per capita GDP:** $1,140. **Imports** (1994): $4.2 bln.; partners: Singapore 26%, Japan 13%. **Exports** (1994): $3.6 bln.; partners: Japan 30%, Singapore 16%. **Tourism** (1993): $350 mil. **National budget** (1994): $4.5 bil.

**Transport: Railroads: Length:** 1,619 mi. **Civil aviation:** 54 mil passenger-mi.; 12 airports with scheduled flights. **Chief ports:** Ho Chi Minh City, Haiphong, Da Nang.

**Communications: Television sets:** 1 per 29 persons. **Radios:** 1 per 10 persons. **Telephones:** 1 per 270 persons. **Daily newspaper circ.:** 8 per 1,000 pop.

**Health: Life expectancy at birth** (1996): 65 male; 70 female. **Births** (per 1,000 pop.): 23. **Deaths** (per 1,000 pop.): 7. **Natural increase:** 1.6%. **Hospital beds:** 1 per 366 persons. **Physicians:** 1 per 2,502 persons. **Infant mortality** (per 1,000 live births 1996): 38.

**Education: Literacy** (1994): 94%. Compulsory: ages 6-11.

**Major International Organizations:** UN (IMF, WHO, ASEAN).

**Embassy:** 1233 20th St. NW 20036; 861-0737.

Vietnam's recorded history began in Tonkin before the Christian era. Settled by Viets from central China, Vietnam was held by China, 111 BC-AD 939, and was a vassal state during subsequent periods. Vietnam defeated the armies of Kublai Khan, 1288. Conquest by France began in 1858 and ended in 1884 with the protectorates of Tonkin and Annam in the N and the colony of Cochin-China in the S.

In 1940 Vietnam was occupied by Japan; nationalist aims gathered force. A number of groups formed the Vietminh (Independence) League, headed by Ho Chi Minh, Communist guerrilla leader. In Aug. 1945 the Vietminh forced out Bao Dai, former emperor of Annam, head of a Japan-sponsored regime. France, seeking to reestablish colonial control, battled Communist and nationalist forces, 1946-1954, and was defeated at Dienbienphu, May 8, 1954. Meanwhile, on July 1, 1949, Bao Dai had formed a State of Vietnam, with himself as chief of state, with French approval. China backed Ho Chi Minh.

A cease-fire signed in Geneva July 21, 1954, provided for a buffer zone, withdrawal of French troops from the North, and elections to determine the country's future. Under the agreement the Communists gained control of territory north of the 17th parallel, with its capital at Hanoi and Ho Chi Minh as president. South Vietnam came to comprise the 39 southern provinces. Some 900,000 North Vietnamese fled to South Vietnam.

On Oct. 26, 1955, Ngo Dinh Diem, premier of the interim government of South Vietnam, proclaimed the Republic of Vietnam and became its first president.

The North adopted a constitution Dec. 31, 1959, based on Communist principles and calling for reunification of all Vietnam. North Vietnam sought to take over South Vietnam beginning in 1954. Fighting persisted from 1956, with the Communist Vietcong, aided by North Vietnam, pressing war in the South. Northern aid to Vietcong guerrillas was intensified in 1959, and large-scale troop infiltration began in 1964, with Soviet and Chinese arms assistance. Large Northern forces were stationed in border areas of Laos and Cambodia.

A serious political conflict arose in the South in 1963 when Buddhists denounced authoritarianism and brutality. This paved the way for a military coup Nov. 1-2, 1963, which overthrew Diem. Several other military coups followed.

In 1964, the U.S. began air strikes against North Vietnam. Beginning in 1965, the raids were stepped up and U.S. troops became combatants. U.S. troop strength in Vietnam, which reached a high of 543,400 in Apr. 1969, was ordered reduced by President Nixon in a series of withdrawals, beginning in June 1969. U.S. bombings were resumed in 1972-73.

A cease-fire agreement was signed in Paris Jan. 27, 1973 by the U.S., North and South Vietnam, and the Vietcong. It was never implemented.

North Vietnamese forces launched attacks against remaining government outposts in the Central Highlands in the first months of 1975. Government retreats turned into a rout, and the Saigon regime surrendered April 30. North Vietnam assumed control, and began transforming society along Communist lines.

The war's toll included — Combat deaths: U.S. 47,369; South Vietnam more than 200,000; other allied forces 5,225. Total U.S. fatalities numbered more than 58,000. Vietnamese civilian casualties were more than a million. Displaced war refugees in South Vietnam totaled more than 6.5 million.

The country was officially reunited July 2, 1976. The Northern capital, flag, anthem, emblem, and currency were applied to the new state. Nearly all major government posts went to officials of the former Northern government.

Heavy fighting with Cambodia took place, 1977-80, amid mutual charges of aggression and atrocities against civilians. Increasing numbers of Vietnamese civilians, ethnic Chinese, escaped the country, via the sea or the overland route across Cambodia. Vietnam launched an offensive against Cambodian refugee strongholds along the Thai-Cambodian border in 1985; they also engaged Thai troops.

Relations with China soured as 140,000 ethnic Chinese left Vietnam charging discrimination; China cut off economic aid. Reacting to Vietnam's invasion of Cambodia, China attacked 4 Vietnamese border provinces, Feb. 1979.

Vietnam announced reforms aimed at reducing central control of the economy in 1987, as many of the old revolutionary followers of Ho Chi Minh were removed from office.

Citing Vietnamese cooperation in returning remains of U.S. soldiers killed in the Vietnam War, the U.S. announced an end, Feb. 3, 1994, to a 19-year-old U.S. embargo on trade with Vietnam. The U.S. extended full diplomatic recognition to Vietnam July 11, 1995.

# Western Samoa

## Independent State of Western Samoa

## Malotuto'atasi o Samoa i Sisifo

**People: Population:** 214,384. **Age distrib.** (%): <15: 41; 65+: 4. **Pop. density:** 196 per sq. mi. **Urban:** 21%. **Ethnic groups:** Samoan (Polynesian) 93%, Euronesian (mixed) 7%, European, other Pacific Islanders. **Principal languages:** Samoan, English (both official). **Religions:** Christian 99.7%.

**Geography: Area:** 1,093 sq. mi. **Location:** In the S Pacific O. **Neighbors:** Nearest are Fiji to SW, Tonga to S. **Topography:** Main islands, Savaii (659 sq. mi.) and Upolu (432 sq. mi.), both ruggedly mountainous, and small islands Manono and Apolima. **Capital:** Apia (1991): 34,100.

**Government: Type:** Constitutional monarchy. **Head of state:** Malietoa Tanumafili II; b Jan. 4, 1913; in office: Jan. 1, 1962. **Head of government:** Prime Min. Tofilau Eti Alesana; in office: Apr. 11, 1988. **Local divisions:** 11 districts.

**Economy: Industries:** Timber, tourism. **Chief crops:** Coconuts, yams, bananas. **Other resources:** Hardwoods, fish. **Ar-**

**able land:** 19%. **Electricity prod.** (1993): 50 mil kWh. **Labor force:** 60% agric.

**Finance: Monetary unit:** Tala (June 1996: 2.45 = $1 US). **Gross domestic product** (1992 est.): $400 mln.* **Per capita GDP:** $2,000. **Imports** (1992): $11.5 mln.; partners: NZ 37%. **Exports** (1993): $6.4 mln.; partners: NZ 34%. **International reserves less gold** (May 1996): $51.2 mil. **Consumer prices** (change in 1995): 1.0%.

**Transport: Motor vehicles:** in use: 960 passenger cars, 860 comm. vehicles. **Chief ports:** Apia, Asau.

**Communications: Radios:** 1 per 2.2 persons. **Telephones:** 1 per 25 persons.

**Health: Life expectancy at birth** (1996): 66 male; 71 female. **Births** (per 1,000 pop.): 31. **Deaths** (per 1,000 pop.): 6. **Natural increase:** 2.5%. **Hospital beds:** 1 per 255 persons. **Physicians:** 1 per 3,183 persons. **Infant mortality** (per 1,000 live births 1996): 34.

**Education: Literacy** (1989): 100%.

**Major International Organizations:** UN (IMF, World Bank), the Commonwealth.

**Embassy:** 820 2d Ave., Suite 800, New York, NY 10017; (212) 599-6196.

Western Samoa was a German colony, 1899 to 1914, when New Zealand landed troops and took over. It became a New Zealand mandate under the League of Nations and, in 1945, a New Zealand UN Trusteeship.

An elected local government took office in Oct. 1959 and the country became fully independent Jan. 1, 1962.

# Yemen

## Republic of Yemen

## Al Jumhuriyah al Yamaniyah

**People: Population:** 13,483,178. **Age distrib.** (%): <15: 52; +65: 3. **Pop. density:** 66 per sq. mi. **Urban:** 23%. **Ethnic groups:** Arab, some Afro-Arab, South Asian. **Principal languages:** Arabic (official). **Religions:** Mostly Muslim (Sha'fi-Sunni, Zaydi-Shi'a).

**Geography: Area:** 205,356 sq. mi. **Location:** Middle East, on the S coast of the Arabian Peninsula. **Neighbors:** Saudi Arabia on N, Oman on the E. **Topography:** A sandy coastal strip leads to well-watered fertile mountains in interior. **Capitals:** Sanaa; Aden (winter cap.). **Cities:** Sanaa (1995 est.) 972,000; Aden 562,000.

**Government: Type:** Republic. **Head of state:** Pres. Ali Abdullah Saleh, b. 1942; in office: July 17, 1978. **Head of government:** Prime Min. Abdulaziz Abdulghani; b July 4, 1939; in office: Oct. 6, 1994. **Local divisions:** 17 governorates, Sanaa. **Defense:** 7.1% of GDP (1993). **Active troop strength:** 39,500.

**Economy: Industries:** Oil, food processing, textiles, leather goods. **Chief crops:** Grains, fruits, qat, coffee, cotton. **Minerals:** Oil, salt. **Crude oil reserves** (1995): 4 bil bbls. **Arable land:** 6%. **Livestock** (1994): sheep: 3.7 mln.; goats: 3.2 mil. **Fish catch** (1993): 87,000 metric tons. **Electricity prod.** (1993): 1.8 bil kWh. **Labor force:** 54% agric.

**Finance: Monetary unit:** Rial (June 1996: 140 = $1 US). **Gross domestic product** (1994): $23.4 bil. **Per capita GDP:** $1,955. **Imports** (1994): $2.65 bln.; partners: U.S. 16%, UK 7%. **Exports** (1994): $1.75 bln.; partners: Germany 28%, Japan 15%. **International reserves less gold** (Sept. 1995): $550 mil.

**Transport: Motor vehicles:** in use: 186,000 passenger cars, 254,000 commercial vehicles. **Civil aviation:** 698 mil passenger-mi.; 11 airports with scheduled flights. **Chief ports:** Al Hudaydah, Al Mukalla, Aden.

**Communications: Television sets:** 1 per 126 persons. **Radios:** 1 per 19 persons. **Telephones:** 1 per 83 persons.

**Health: Life expectancy at birth** (1996): 58 male; 61 female. **Births** (per 1,000 pop.): 45. **Deaths** (per 1,000 pop.): 10. **Natural increase:** 3.6%. **Hospital beds:** 1 per 995 persons. **Physicians:** 1 per 3,900 persons. **Infant mortality** (per 1,000 live births 1996): 72.

**Education: Literacy** (1991): 39%. **Primary and secondary school attendance:** 56%.

**Major International Organizations:** UN (IMF, WHO), Arab League.

**Embassy:** 2600 Virginia Ave. NW 20037; 965-4760.

Yemen's territory once was part of the ancient Kindgom of Sheba, or Saba, a prosperous link in trade between Africa and India. A Biblical reference speaks of its gold, spices, and precious stones as gifts borne by the Queen of Sheba to King Solomon.

Yemen became independent in 1918, after years of Ottoman Turkish rule, but remained politically and economically backward. Imam Ahmed ruled 1948-1962. Army officers headed by Brig. Gen. Abdullah al-Salal declared the country to be the Yemen Arab Republic.

The Imam Ahmed's heir, the Imam Mohamad al-Badr, fled to the mountains where tribesmen joined royalist forces; internal warfare between them and the republican forces continued. About 150,000 people died in the fighting.

There was a bloodless coup Nov. 5, 1967. In April 1970 hostilities ended with an agreement between Yemen and Saudi Arabia. On June 13, 1974, an army group, led by Col. Ibrahim al-Hamidi, seized the government. He was assassinated in 1977.

Meanwhile, South Yemen won independence from Britain in 1967, formed out of the British colony of Aden and the British protectorate of South Arabia. It became the Arab world's only Marxist state, taking the name People's Democratic Republic of Yemen in 1970 and signing a friendship treaty with the USSR in 1979 that allowed for the stationing of Soviet troops.

More than 300,000 Yemenis fled from the south to the north after independence, contributing to 2 decades of hostility between the 2 states that flared into warfare twice in the 1970s.

An Arab League-sponsored agreement between North and South Yemen on unification of the 2 countries was signed Mar. 29, 1979. An agreement providing for widespread political and economic cooperation was signed in 1988.

The 2 countries were formally united on May 21, 1990, but regional clan-based rivalries led to full-scale civil war in 1994. Secessionists declared a breakaway state in S Yemen, May 21, 1994. However, northern troops captured the former southern capital of Aden in July. A new constitution was approved Sept. 28.

# Yugoslavia

## Federal Republic of Yugoslavia

## Savezna Republika Jugoslavija

*(Data prior to 1992 include former republics Croatia, Slovenia, Bosnia and Herzegovina, and Macedonia.)*

**People: Population:** 10,614,558. **Age distrib.** (%): <15: 22; 65+: 11. **Pop. density:** 269 per sq. mi. **Urban:** 57%. **Ethnic groups:** Serbian 63%, Albanian 14%, Montenegrin 6%. **Principal languages:** Serbo-Croatian (official) 95%, Albanian 5%. **Religions:** Orthodox 65%, Muslim 19%, Roman Catholic 4%.

**Geography: Area:** 39,449 sq. mi. **Location:** On the Balkan Peninsula in SE Europe. Present-day Yugoslavia consists of the former republics of Serbia and Montenegro. **Neighbors:** Croatia, Bosnia and Herzegovina on W; Hungary on N; Romania, Bulgaria on E; Albania, Macedonia on S. **Capital:** Belgrade (1994 est.): 1.2 mil.

**Government: Type:** Republic. **Head of state:** Pres. Zoran Lilic; b Aug. 27, 1953; in office: June 25, 1993. **Head of government:** Prime Min. Radoje Kontic; b May 31, 1937; in office: Dec. 29, 1992. **Local divisions:** 2 republics, 2 autonomous provinces. **Defense:** 4%-6% of GDP (1992 est.). **Active troop strength:** 126,500.

**Economy: Industries:** Steel, machinery, consumer goods, mining, electronics. **Chief crops:** Corn, grains, sugar beets, potatoes, cotton, grapes. **Minerals:** Oil, gas, coal, antimony, lead, nickel, gold, copper, chrome. **Arable land:** 30%. **Livestock** (1994): pigs: 4.2 mln.; sheep: 2.7 mln.; cattle: 2.0 mil. **Fish catch:** (1994): 6,500 metric tons. **Electricity prod.** (1994): 34 bil kWh. **Labor force:** 28% manuf. & mining; 11% services; 10% trade.

**Finance: Monetary unit:** New Dinar (June 1996: 5.02 = $1 US). **Gross domestic product** (1994): $10 bln.* **Per capita GDP:** $1,000. **Imports** (1992): $3.9 bln.; partners: Germany 13%, Italy 7%. **Exports** (1992): $2.5 bln.; partners: Germany 27%, former USSR 13%. **Tourism** (1993): $23 mil. **National budget:** NA.

**Transport: Motor vehicles:** in use: 59,000 passenger cars, 6,000 comm. vehicles. **Civil aviation:** 93 mil passenger-mi.; 5 airports. **Chief ports:** Bar, Novi Sad.

**Communications: Radios:** 1 per 3.9 persons. **Telephones:** 1 per 5.6 persons. **Daily newspaper circ.:** 52 per 1,000 pop.

**Health: Life expectancy at birth** (1996): 69 male; 75 female. **Births** (per 1,000 pop.): 14. **Deaths** (per 1,000 pop.): 10. **Natural increase:** 0.4%. **Hospital beds:** 1 per 183 persons. **Physicians:** 1 per 420 persons. **Infant mortality** (per 1,000 live births 1996): 23.

**Education: Literacy** (1994): 93%. Free and compulsory: ages 7-15.

**Major International Organizations:** Some UN agencies (though not a member).

**Embassy:** 2410 California St. NW 20008; 462-6566.

Serbia, which had since 1389 been a vassal principality of Turkey, was established as an independent kingdom by the Treaty of Berlin, 1878. Montenegro, independent since 1389, also obtained international recognition in 1878. After the Balkan wars Serbia's boundaries were enlarged by the annexation of Old Serbia and Macedonia, 1913.

When the Austro-Hungarian empire collapsed after World War I, the Kingdom of the Serbs, Croats, and Slovenes was formed from the former provinces of Croatia, Dalmatia, Bosnia, Herzegovina, Slovenia, Vojvodina, and the independent state of Montenegro. The name was later changed to Yugoslavia.

Nazi Germany invaded in 1941. Many Yugoslav partisan troops continued to operate. Among these were the Chetniks led by Draja Mikhailovich, who fought other partisans led by Josip Broz, known as Marshal Tito. Tito, backed by the USSR and Britain from 1943, was in control by the time the Germans had been driven from Yugoslavia in 1945. Mikhailovich was executed July 17, 1946, by the Tito regime.

A constituent assembly proclaimed Yugoslavia a republic Nov. 29, 1945. It became a federated republic Jan. 31, 1946, and Marshal Tito, a Communist, became head of the government. The Stalin policy of dictating to all Communist nations was rejected by Tito. He accepted economic aid and military equipment from the U.S. and received aid in foreign trade also from France and Britain. Tito supported the liberal government of Czechoslovakia in 1968 before the Soviet invasion.

Pres. Tito died May 4, 1980. After his death, Yugoslavia was governed by a collective presidency, with a rotating system of succession. On Jan. 22, 1990, the Communist Party renounced its constitutionally guaranteed leading role in society.

Croatia and Slovenia formally declared independence June 25, 1991. In Croatia, fighting began between Croats and ethnic Serbs. Serbia sent arms and medical supplies to the Serb rebels in Croatia. Croatian forces clashed with Yugoslavian army units and their Serb supporters.

The republics of Serbia and Montenegro proclaimed a new "Federal Republic of Yugoslavia" Apr. 17, 1992. Serbia, under Pres. Slobodan Milosevic, was the main supplier of arms to the ethnic Serb fighters in Bosnia and Herzegovina. The UN imposed sweeping international sanctions on the new Yugoslavia (Serbia and Montenegro) as a means of ending the bloodshed in Bosnia, May 30, 1992. On Aug. 4, 1994, Yugoslavia said it was cutting off support for Bosnian Serbs because they rejected an international partition plan for Bosnia. This prompted the UN to vote for a conditional easing of sanctions, Sept. 23, 1994.

A peace agreement initialed in Dayton, Ohio, Nov. 21, 1995, was signed in Paris, Dec. 14, by Milosevic and leaders of Bosnia and Croatia. In May 1996, a UN tribunal in the Netherlands began trying suspected war criminals from the former Yugoslavia. The UN lifted sanctions against Yugoslavia Oct. 1, 1996, after electons were held in Bosnia.

**Kosovo:** An area in southern Serbia (4,203 sq. mi.), with a population of about 2,000,000, mostly Albanians. The capital is Pristina. The Albanian majority has declared its independence, which Serbia has not recognized.

**Vojvodina:** An area in northern Serbia (8,304 sq. mi.), with a population of about 2,000,000, mostly Serbian. The capital is Novi Sad.

# Zaire

## Republic of Zaire

## République du Zaïre

**People: Population:** 46,498,539. **Age distrib.** (%): <15: 48; 65+: 3. **Pop. density:** 51 per sq. mi. **Urban:** 29%. **Ethnic groups:** More than 200 tribes, mostly Bantu. **Principal languages:** French (official), Kongo, Luba, Mongo, Rwanda, others. **Religions:** Christian 70%, Muslim 10%, Kimbanguist 10%.

**Geography: Area:** 905,354 sq. mi. **Location:** In central Africa. **Neighbors:** Congo on W; Central African Republic, Sudan on N; Uganda, Rwanda, Burundi, Tanzania on E; Zambia, Angola on S. **Topography:** Zaire includes the bulk of the Zaire (Congo) R. basin. The vast central region is a low-lying plateau covered by rain forest. Mountainous terraces in the W, savannas in the S and SE, grasslands toward the N, and the high Ruwenzori Mts. on the E surround the central region. A short strip of territory borders the Atlantic O. The Zaire R. is 2,718 mi. long. **Capital:** Kinshasa. **Cities** (1994 est.): Kinshasa 4.7 mln.; Lubumbashi 851,400.

**Government: Type:** Republic with strong presidential authority (in transition). **Head of state:** Pres. Mobutu Sese Seko; b Oct. 14, 1930; in office: Nov. 25, 1965. **Head of government:** Prime Min. Leon Kengo wa Dondo; in office: July 6, 1994. **Local divisions:** 10 regions, Kinshasa. **Defense:** 1.5% of GDP (1990). **Active troop strength:** 49,100.

**Economy: Industries:** mining, consumer prods., food processing. **Chief crops:** Coffee, rice, corn, bananas, plantains, cassava, bananas, quinine, palm kernels. **Minerals:** Cobalt (65% of world reserves), copper, cadmium, oil, diamonds, gold, silver, tin, germanium, zinc, iron, manganese, uranium, radium. **Crude oil reserves** (1995): 187 mil bbls. **Other resources:** Forests, rubber, ivory. **Arable land:** 3%. **Livestock** (1994): goats: 4.3 mln.; cattle: 1.7 mil. **Fish catch** (1993): 147,000 metric tons. **Electricity prod.** (1993): 6.2 bil kWh. **Labor force:** 75% agric.

**Finance: Monetary unit:** New Zaire (Mar. 1995: 3,600 = $1 US). **Gross domestic product** (1994): $18.8 bln.* **Per capita GDP:** $440. **Imports** (1993): $356 mln.; partners: Belg.-Lux. 21%, France 12%, Germany 12%, China 7%. **Exports** (1993): $362 mln.; partners: Belg.-Lux. 45%, U.S. 18%. **National budget** (1991): $1.9 bil. **International reserves less gold** (Oct. 1995): $155 mil. **Gold:** 28,000 oz t. **Consumer prices** (change in 1995): 542%.

**Transport: Railroads: Length:** 3,162 mi. **Motor vehicles:** in use: 94,000 passenger cars, 86,000 comm. vehicles. **Civil aviation:** 183 mil passenger-mi.; 12 airports with scheduled flights. **Chief ports:** Matadi, Boma.

**Communications: Television sets:** 1 per 1,934 persons. **Radios:** 1 per 3.9 persons. **Telephones:** 1 per 1,140 persons. **Daily newspaper circ.:** 3 per 1,000 pop.

**Health: Life expectancy at birth** (1996): 45 male; 49 female. **Births** (per 1,000 pop.): 48. **Deaths** (per 1,000 pop.): 17. **Natural increase:** 3.1%. **Hospital beds:** 1 per 487 persons. **Physicians:** 1 per 15,584 persons. **Infant mortality** (per 1,000 live births 1996): 108.

**Education: Literacy** (1993): 77%. Compulsory: ages 6-12.

**Major International Organizations:** UN and most of its specialized agencies, OAU.

**Embassy:** 1800 New Hampshire Ave. NW 20009; 234-7690.

The earliest inhabitants of Zaire may have been the pygmies, followed by Bantus from the E and Nilotic tribes from the N. The large Bantu Bakongo kingdom ruled much of Zaire and Angola when Portuguese explorers visited in the 15th century.

Leopold II, king of the Belgians, formed an international group to exploit the Congo in 1876. In 1877 Henry M. Stanley explored the Congo, and in 1878 the king's group sent him back to organize the region and win over the native chiefs. The Conference of Berlin, 1884-85, organized the Congo Free State with Leopold as king and chief owner. Exploitation of native laborers on the rubber plantations caused international criticism and led to granting of a colonial charter, 1908.

Belgian and Congolese leaders agreed Jan. 27, 1960, that the Congo would become independent June 30. In the first general elections, May 31, the National Congolese movement of Patrice Lumumba won 35 of 137 seats in the National Assembly. He was appointed premier June 21, and formed a coalition cabinet.

Widespread violence caused Europeans and others to flee. The UN Security Council, Aug. 9, 1960, called on Belgium to withdraw its troops and sent a UN contingent. Pres. Joseph Kasavubu removed Lumumba as premier in Sept.; Lumumba was murdered in Feb. 1961.

The last UN troops left the Congo June 30, 1964, and Moise Tshombe became president.

On Sept. 7, 1964, leftist rebels set up a "People's Republic" in Stanleyville. Tshombe hired foreign mercenaries and sought to rebuild the Congolese Army. In Nov. and Dec. 1964 rebels killed scores of white hostages and thousands of Congolese;

Belgian paratroopers, dropped from U.S. transport planes, rescued hundreds. By July 1965 the rebels had lost their effectiveness.

In 1965 Gen. Joseph D. Mobutu was named president. He later changed his name to Mobutu Sese Seko. The country changed its name to Republic of Zaire on Oct. 27, 1971.

Economic difficulties, amid charges of corruption by government officials, plagued Zaire in the 1980s and worsened in the 1990s. In 1990, Pres. Mobutu announced an end to a 20-year ban on multiparty politics. He sought to retain power despite economic collapse, outside pressure, and widespread internal opposition.

During 1994, Zaire was inundated with refugees from the massive ethnic bloodshed in Rwanda. At least 200 people died in 1995 from an *Ebola* virus outbreak in Kikwit, W Zaire. Ethnic violence, blamed in part on Rwandan Hutu refugees, spread to eastern Zaire in 1996. Mobutu was hospitalized in Switzerland for prostate cancer in Sept.

# Zambia

## Republic of Zambia

**People: Population:** 9,159,072. **Age distrib.** (%): <15: 47; 65+: 3. **Pop. density:** 32 per sq. mi. **Urban:** 42%. **Ethnic groups:** African 99%, European 1%. **Principal languages:** English (official), Bantu dialects. **Religions:** Christian 50-75%, Hindu and Muslim 24-49%.

**Geography: Area:** 290,586 sq. mi. **Location:** In S central Africa. **Neighbors:** Zaire on N; Tanzania, Malawi, Mozambique on E; Zimbabwe, Namibia on S; Angola on W. **Topography:** Zambia is mostly high plateau country covered with thick forests, and drained by several important rivers, including the Zambezi. **Capital:** Lusaka. **Cities** (1990): Lusaka 982,400; Ndola 376,300; Kitwe 348,600.

**Government: Type:** Republic. **Head of state:** Pres. Frederick Chiluba; b Apr. 30, 1943; in office: Nov. 2, 1991. **Local divisions:** 9 provinces. **Defense:** 1.4% of GDP (1994). **Active troop strength:** 21,600.

**Economy: Chief crops:** Corn, tobacco, peanuts, cotton, sugar. **Minerals:** Cobalt, copper, zinc, emeralds, gold, lead, silver, uranium, coal. **Arable land:** 7%. **Livestock** (1994): cattle: 3.3 mil. **Fish catch** (1993): 65,000 metric tons. **Electricity prod.** (1993): 7.8 bil kWh. **Labor force:** 85% agric.; 15% ind. and commerce.

**Finance: Monetary unit:** Kwacha (June 1996: 1,275 = $1 US). **Gross domestic product** (1994): $7.9 bln.* **Per capita GDP:** $860. **Imports** (1993): $1.1 bln.; South Africa 43%, UK 11%, Saudi Ar. 7%. **Exports** (1993): $1.0 bln.; partners: Netherlands 19%, Japan 12%, Germany 9%. **National budget** (1991 est.): $767 mil. **International reserves less gold** (Mar. 1994): $207 mil. **Consumer prices** (change in 1994): 53.7%.

**Transport: Motor vehicles:** in use: 96,000 passenger cars, 68,000 comm. vehicles. **Civil aviation:** 192 mil passenger-mi.; 8 airports with scheduled flights. **Chief port:** Mpulungu.

**Communications: Television sets:** 1 per 46 persons. **Radios:** 1 per 5.5 persons. **Telephones:** 1 per 112 persons. **Daily newspaper circ.:** 13 per 1,000 pop.

**Health: Life expectancy at birth** (1996): 36 male; 37 female. **Births** (per 1,000 pop.): 45. **Deaths** (per 1,000 pop.): 24. **Natural increase:** 2.1%. **Hospital beds:** 1 per 349 persons. **Physicians:** 1 per 6,959 persons. **Infant mortality** (per 1,000 live births 1996): 96.

**Education: Literacy** (1990): 73%. Compulsory: ages 7-15.

**Major International Organizations:** UN (WTO, IMF, WHO), OAU, the Commonwealth.

**Embassy:** 2419 Massachusetts Ave. NW 20008; 265-9717.

As Northern Rhodesia, the country was under the administration of the South Africa Company, 1889 until 1924, when the office of governor was established, and, subsequently, a legislature. The country became an independent republic within the Commonwealth Oct. 24, 1964.

After the white government of Rhodesia (now Zimbabwe) declared its independence from Britain Nov. 11, 1965, relations between Zambia and Rhodesia became strained.

As part of a program of government participation in major industries, a government corporation in 1970 took over 51% of the ownership of 2 foreign-owned copper-mining companies. Privately-held land and other enterprises were nationalized in 1975. In the 1980s and 1990s lowered copper prices hurt the economy and severe drought caused famine.

Food riots erupted in June 1990, as the nation suffered its worst violence since independence. Elections held Oct. 1991 brought an end to one-party rule. The new government made efforts to sell state enterprises, including the copper industry.

# Zimbabwe

## Republic of Zimbabwe

**People: Population:** 11,271,314. **Age distrib.** (%): <15: 45; 65+: 3. **Pop. density:** 75 per sq. mi. **Urban:** 31%. **Ethnic groups:** Shona 71%, Ndebele 16%. **Principal languages:** English (official), Shona, Sindebele. **Religions:** Syncretic (Christian-indigenous mix) 50%, Christian 25%, indigenous beliefs 24%.

**Geography: Area:** 150,872 sq. mi. **Location:** In southern Africa. **Neighbors:** Zambia on N, Botswana on W, South Africa on S, Mozambique on E. **Topography:** Zimbabwe is high plateau country, rising to mountains on eastern border, sloping down on the other borders. **Capital:** Harare. **Cities** (1992): Harare 1.2 mln.; Bulawayo 621,000.

**Government: Type:** Republic. **Head of state:** Pres. Robert Mugabe; b Feb. 21, 1924; in office: Jan. 1, 1988. **Local divisions:** 8 provinces. **Defense:** 3.1% of GDP (FY 1994-95). **Active troop strength:** 45,000.

**Economy: Industries:** Clothing, mining, steel, chemicals, light industries. **Chief crops:** Tobacco, sugar, cotton, corn, wheat. **Minerals:** Chromium, gold, nickel, asbestos, copper, iron, coal. **Arable land:** 7%. **Livestock** (1994): cattle: 4.5 mln.; goats: 2.5 mil. **Electricity prod.** (1993): 9 bil kWh. **Labor force:** 74% agric.; 16% serv.

**Finance: Monetary unit:** Dollar (June 1996: 9.87 = $1 US). **Gross domestic product** (1994): $17.4 bln.* **Per capita GDP:** $1,580. **Imports** (1992): $1.8 bln.; partners: South Africa 25%, UK 15%. **Exports** (1994): $1.8 bln.; partners: UK 14%, Germany 11%, South Africa 10%. **Tourism** (1993): $103 mil. **National budget** (FY 1992-93): $2.2 bil. **International reserves less gold** (May 1996): $676 mil. **Gold:** 780,000 oz t. **Consumer prices** (change in 1995): 22.6%.

**Transport: Motor vehicles:** in use: 310,000 passenger cars, 30,000 comm. vehicles. **Civil aviation:** 514 mil passenger-mi.; 5 airports with scheduled flights. **Chief ports:** Binga, Kariba.

**Communications: Television sets:** 1 per 80 persons. **Radios:** 1 per 14 persons. **Telephones:** 1 per 84 persons. **Daily newspaper circ.:** 18 per 1,000 pop.

**Health: Life expectancy at birth** (1996): 42 male; 42 female. **Births** (per 1,000 pop.): 32. **Deaths** (per 1,000 pop.): 18. **Natural increase:** 1.4%. **Physicians:** 1 per 6,909 persons. **Infant mortality** (per 1,000 live births 1996): 73.

**Education: Literacy** (1992): 85%. Compulsory: ages 7-14.

**Major International Organizations:** UN (IMF, WTO, World Bank), OAU, the Commonwealth.

**Embassy:** 1608 New Hampshire Ave. NW 20009; 332-7100.

Britain took over the area as Southern Rhodesia in 1923 from the British South Africa Co. (which, under Cecil Rhodes, had conquered the area by 1897) and granted internal self-government. Under a 1961 constitution, voting was restricted to maintain whites in power. On Nov. 11, 1965, Prime Min. Ian D. Smith announced his country's unilateral declaration of independence. Britain termed the act illegal and demanded that Zimbabwe (known as Rhodesia until 1980) broaden voting rights to provide for eventual rule by the black African majority.

Urged by Britain, the UN imposed sanctions, including embargoes on oil shipments to Zimbabwe. In May 1968, the UN Security Council ordered a trade embargo.

Intermittent negotiations between the government and various black nationalist groups failed to prevent increasing guerrilla warfare. An "internal settlement" signed Mar. 1978 in which Smith and 3 popular black leaders would share control of the government until a transfer of power to the black majority was rejected by guerrilla leaders.

In the country's first universal-franchise election, Apr. 21, 1979, Bishop Abel Muzorewa's United African National Council gained a bare majority control of the black-dominated Parliament. Britain, 1979, began efforts to normalize its relationship with Zimbabwe. A British cease-fire was accepted by all parties, Dec. 5. Independence was finally achieved Apr. 18, 1980.

Pres. Robert Mugabe declared Zimbabwe's drought a national disaster and appealed to foreign donors for food, money, and medicine, Mar. 6, 1992. An economic adjustment program caused widespread hardship. Mugabe was reelected Mar. 1996 after opposition candidates withdrew. An estimated 1 mil Zimbabweans have HIV, the virus that causes AIDS.

# Area and Population of the World

**Source:** Bureau of the Census, U.S. Dept. of Commerce; prior to 1950, Rand McNally & Co.

| Continent or Region | Area (1,000 sq. mi.) | % of Earth | Population (est., thousands) 1650 | 1750 | 1850 | 1900 | 1950 | 1980 | 1996 | % World Total, 1996 |
|---|---|---|---|---|---|---|---|---|---|---|
| North America | 9,400 | 16.2 | 5,000 | 5,000 | 39,000 | 106,000 | 166,000 | 252,000 | 295,000 | 5.1 |
| South America | 6,900 | 11.9 | 8,000 | 7,000 | 20,000 | 38,000 | — | — | — | — |
| Latin America, Caribbean | — | — | — | — | — | — | 166,000 | 362,000 | 489,000 | 8.5 |
| Europe | 3,800 | 6.6 | 100,000 | 140,000 | 265,000 | 400,000 | 392,000 | 484,000 | 507,000 | 8.8 |
| Asia | 17,400 | 30.1 | 335,000 | 476,000 | 754,000 | 932,000 | 1,411,000 | 2,601,000 | 3,428,000 | 59.4 |
| Africa | 11,700 | 20.2 | 100,000 | 95,000 | 95,000 | 118,000 | 229,000 | 470,000 | 732,000 | 12.7 |
| Former USSR | — | — | — | — | — | — | 180,000 | 266,000 | 293,000 | 5.2 |
| Oceania, incl. Australia | 3,300 | 5.7 | 2,000 | 2,000 | 2,000 | 6,000 | 12,000 | 23,000 | 29,000 | 0.5 |
| Antarctica | 5,400 | 9.3 | Uninhabited | | | | | | | |
| **World** | **57,900** | — | **550,000** | **725,000** | **1,175,000** | **1,600,000** | **2,556,000** | **4,458,000** | **5,772,000** | — |

Figures may not add to total because of independent rounding.

# Leading Countries in Population and Area, 1996

China had the highest population in the world, with 1.2 billion inhabitants, more than one-fifth of the world's population. India had more than 952 million people and was expected to reach 1 billion by the end of the decade. The United States had the third-largest population, with over 265 million, followed by Indonesia, Brazil, and Russia. Russia is the largest country in land area, with over 6.5 million square miles, followed by Canada, China, the United States, and Brazil.

# Population of the World's Largest Cities

**Source:** United Nations, Dept. for Economic and Social Information and Policy Analysis

The figures are United Nations estimates and projections, as revised in 1994, for "urban agglomerations"—that is, contiguous densely populated urban areas, without regard to administrative boundaries. Therefore, population figures in this table may not correspond to figures in other parts of *The World Almanac*.

| Rank | City, Country | Pop. (thousands) 1994 | Pop. (thousands, projected) 2015 | Annual growth rate (percent) 1990-1995 | Percentage increase between: 1975-1995 | 1995-2015 | Pop. of city as percentage of: Total pop.[1] | Urban pop.[2] |
|---|---|---|---|---|---|---|---|---|
| 1. | Tokyo, Japan | 26,518 | 28,700 | 1.4 | 35.7 | 7.0 | 21.2 | 27.4 |
| 2. | New York City, U.S. | 16,271 | 17,600 | 0.3 | 2.8 | 8.0 | 6.2 | 8.2 |
| 3. | Sao Paulo, Brazil | 16,110 | 20,800 | 2.0 | 66.0 | 26.6 | 10.1 | 13.0 |
| 4. | Mexico City, Mexico | 15,525 | 18,800 | 0.7 | 39.2 | 20.1 | 16.9 | 22.6 |
| 5. | Shanghai, China | 14,709 | 23,400 | 2.3 | 31.8 | 55.0 | 1.2 | 4.1 |
| 6. | Bombay (Mumbai), India | 14,496 | 27,400 | 4.2 | 120.1 | 81.4 | 1.6 | 6.0 |
| 7. | Los Angeles, U.S. | 12,232 | 14,300 | 1.6 | 39.0 | 15.0 | 4.7 | 6.2 |
| 8. | Beijing, China | 12,030 | 19,400 | 2.6 | 44.7 | 57.1 | 1.0 | 3.4 |
| 9. | Calcutta, India | 11,485 | 17,600 | 1.7 | 48.0 | 51.0 | 1.3 | 4.7 |
| 10. | Seoul, South Korea | 11,451 | 13,100 | 1.9 | 71.2 | 12.9 | 25.7 | 32.1 |
| 11. | Jakarta, Indonesia | 11,017 | 21,200 | 4.4 | 138.9 | 84.1 | 5.7 | 16.4 |
| 12. | Buenos Aires, Argentina | 10,914 | 12,400 | 0.7 | 20.3 | 12.6 | 31.9 | 36.4 |
| 13. | Osaka, Japan | 10,585 | 10,600 | 0.2 | 7.7 | 0.0 | 8.5 | 10.9 |
| 14. | Tianjin, China | 10,376 | 17,000 | 2.9 | 73.5 | 59.0 | 0.9 | 2.9 |
| 15. | Rio de Janeiro, Brazil | 9,817 | 11,600 | 0.8 | 25.6 | 16.9 | 6.2 | 8.0 |

(1) Denotes percentage of the total population of the country in which the corresponding city is located. (2) Denotes the percentage of the total urban population of the country in which the corresponding city is located.

# Current Population and Projections for All Countries: 1996, 2010, and 2020

**Source:** Bureau of the Census, U.S. Dept. of Commerce

(in thousands)

| Country | 1996 | 2010 | 2020 |
|---|---|---|---|
| Afghanistan | 22,664 | 34,098 | 43,050 |
| Albania | 3,249 | 3,858 | 4,257 |
| Algeria | 29,183 | 38,479 | 44,783 |
| Andorra | 73 | 92 | 97 |
| Angola | 10,343 | 14,982 | 19,272 |
| Antigua and Barbuda | 66 | 74 | 80 |
| Argentina | 34,673 | 39,947 | 43,190 |
| Armenia | 3,464 | 3,577 | 3,665 |
| Australia | 18,261 | 20,434 | 21,696 |
| Austria | 8,023 | 8,223 | 8,262 |
| Azerbaijan | 7,677 | 8,410 | 9,007 |
| Bahamas | 259 | 293 | 314 |
| Bahrain | 590 | 759 | 870 |
| Bangladesh | 123,063 | 153,195 | 172,041 |
| Barbados | 257 | 272 | 284 |
| Belarus | 10,416 | 10,924 | 11,059 |
| Belgium | 10,170 | 10,358 | 10,271 |
| Belize | 219 | 299 | 356 |
| Benin | 5,710 | 8,955 | 11,920 |
| Bhutan | 1,823 | 2,474 | 3,035 |
| Bolivia | 7,165 | 8,941 | 10,246 |
| Bosnia and Herzegovina | 2,656 | 2,892 | 2,966 |
| Botswana | 1,478 | 1,598 | 1,553 |
| Brazil | 162,661 | 183,747 | 194,246 |
| Brunei | 300 | 410 | 490 |
| Bulgaria | 8,613 | 8,928 | 8,777 |
| Burkina Faso | 10,623 | 14,150 | 16,569 |
| Burundi | 5,943 | 8,229 | 10,197 |
| Cambodia | 10,861 | 15,679 | 20,208 |
| Cameroon | 14,262 | 20,630 | 25,896 |

| Country | 1996 | 2010 | 2020 |
|---|---|---|---|
| Canada | 28,821 | 32,534 | 34,753 |
| Cape Verde | 449 | 646 | 812 |
| Central African Republic | 3,274 | 4,177 | 4,780 |
| Chad | 6,977 | 10,055 | 12,831 |
| Chile | 14,333 | 16,382 | 17,535 |
| China | 1,210,005 | 1,340,357 | 1,413,251 |
| Colombia | 36,813 | 44,504 | 49,266 |
| Comoros | 569 | 919 | 1,249 |
| Congo | 2,528 | 3,298 | 3,817 |
| Costa Rica | 3,463 | 4,416 | 5,044 |
| Côte d'Ivoire | 14,762 | 20,261 | 24,634 |
| Croatia | 5,004 | 4,986 | 4,821 |
| Cuba | 10,951 | 11,481 | 11,699 |
| Cyprus | 745 | 858 | 936 |
| Czech Republic | 10,321 | 10,445 | 10,271 |
| Denmark | 5,250 | 5,417 | 5,458 |
| Djibouti | 428 | 588 | 751 |
| Dominica | 83 | 89 | 96 |
| Dominican Republic | 8,089 | 9,928 | 11,152 |
| Ecuador | 11,466 | 14,534 | 16,546 |
| Egypt | 63,575 | 80,689 | 92,350 |
| El Salvador | 5,829 | 7,332 | 8,473 |
| Equatorial Guinea | 431 | 615 | 783 |
| Eritrea | 3,910 | 6,018 | 7,674 |
| Estonia | 1,459 | 1,401 | 1,370 |
| Ethiopia | 57,172 | 81,169 | 100,813 |
| Fiji | 782 | 933 | 1,037 |
| Finland | 5,105 | 5,109 | 5,075 |
| France | 58,041 | 60,562 | 61,087 |
| Gabon | 1,173 | 1,445 | 1,675 |
| Gambia, The | 1,205 | 1,864 | 2,399 |
| Georgia | 5,220 | 5,188 | 5,205 |
| Germany | 83,536 | 88,975 | 88,870 |
| Ghana | 17,698 | 22,929 | 26,516 |
| Greece | 10,539 | 11,135 | 11,076 |
| Grenada | 95 | 115 | 141 |
| Guatemala | 11,278 | 15,284 | 18,131 |
| Guinea | 7,412 | 9,450 | 11,849 |
| Guinea-Bissau | 1,151 | 1,579 | 1,925 |
| Guyana | 712 | 695 | 685 |
| Haiti | 6,732 | 8,681 | 10,252 |
| Honduras | 5,605 | 7,643 | 9,042 |
| Hungary | 10,003 | 9,456 | 9,103 |
| Iceland | 270 | 303 | 325 |
| India | 952,108 | 1,155,830 | 1,289,473 |
| Indonesia | 206,612 | 249,679 | 276,017 |
| Iran | 66,094 | 88,231 | 104,282 |
| Iraq | 21,422 | 34,545 | 46,260 |
| Ireland | 3,567 | 3,452 | 3,570 |
| Israel | 5,422 | 6,696 | 7,439 |
| Italy | 57,460 | 57,660 | 55,665 |
| Jamaica | 2,595 | 2,900 | 3,213 |
| Japan | 125,450 | 127,548 | 123,620 |
| Jordan | 4,212 | 6,112 | 7,529 |
| Kazakstan | 16,916 | 17,564 | 18,408 |
| Kenya | 28,177 | 33,920 | 35,236 |
| Kiribati | 81 | 95 | 98 |
| Korea, North | 23,904 | 28,491 | 30,969 |
| Korea, South | 45,482 | 51,235 | 53,451 |
| Kuwait | 1,950 | 3,160 | 3,560 |
| Kyrgyzstan | 4,530 | 5,403 | 6,257 |
| Laos | 4,976 | 7,168 | 8,923 |
| Latvia | 2,469 | 2,293 | 2,212 |
| Lebanon | 3,776 | 4,973 | 5,748 |
| Lesotho | 1,971 | 2,428 | 2,693 |
| Liberia | 2,110 | 4,540 | 5,991 |
| Libya | 5,445 | 8,913 | 12,391 |
| Liechtenstein | 31 | 35 | 36 |
| Lithuania | 3,646 | 3,650 | 3,646 |
| Luxembourg | 416 | 495 | 523 |
| Macedonia | 2,104 | 2,261 | 2,296 |
| Madagascar | 13,671 | 20,096 | 25,988 |
| Malawi | 9,453 | 10,662 | 10,719 |
| Malaysia | 19,963 | 25,691 | 29,830 |
| Maldives | 271 | 423 | 554 |
| Mali | 9,653 | 14,966 | 20,427 |
| Malta | 376 | 425 | 450 |
| Marshall Islands | 58 | 100 | 144 |
| Mauritania | 2,336 | 3,630 | 4,859 |
| Mauritius | 1,140 | 1,328 | 1,440 |
| Mexico | 95,772 | 120,115 | 136,096 |
| Micronesia | 125 | 141 | 143 |
| Moldova | 4,464 | 4,818 | 5,000 |
| Monaco | 32 | 33 | 34 |
| Mongolia | 2,497 | 3,018 | 3,393 |
| Morocco | 29,779 | 38,442 | 44,519 |
| Mozambique | 17,878 | 25,116 | 30,810 |
| Myanmar | 45,976 | 58,236 | 67,501 |
| Namibia | 1,677 | 2,513 | 3,267 |
| Nauru | 10 | 11 | 12 |
| Nepal | 22,094 | 30,783 | 37,767 |
| Netherlands | 15,568 | 16,382 | 16,490 |
| New Zealand | 3,548 | 4,029 | 4,326 |
| Nicaragua | 4,272 | 5,863 | 6,973 |
| Niger | 9,113 | 13,678 | 17,983 |
| Nigeria | 103,912 | 157,375 | 205,160 |
| Norway | 4,384 | 4,577 | 4,632 |
| Oman | 2,187 | 3,516 | 4,731 |
| Pakistan | 129,276 | 170,750 | 198,722 |
| Palau | 17 | 20 | 21 |
| Panama | 2,655 | 3,238 | 3,625 |
| Papua New Guinea | 4,395 | 5,925 | 7,044 |
| Paraguay | 5,504 | 7,730 | 9,474 |
| Peru | 24,523 | 29,988 | 33,226 |
| Philippines | 74,481 | 97,119 | 112,963 |
| Poland | 38,643 | 40,342 | 40,833 |
| Portugal | 9,865 | 10,080 | 10,005 |
| Qatar | 548 | 660 | 735 |
| Romania | 21,657 | 20,741 | 20,135 |
| Russia | 148,178 | 149,978 | 149,632 |
| Rwanda | 6,853 | 10,080 | 11,040 |
| Saint Kitts and Nevis | 41 | 50 | 57 |
| Saint Lucia | 158 | 183 | 202 |
| Saint Vincent and the Grenadines | 118 | 132 | 146 |
| San Marino | 25 | 26 | 27 |
| São Tomé and Príncipe | 144 | 196 | 232 |
| Saudi Arabia | 19,409 | 31,198 | 43,255 |
| Senegal | 9,093 | 14,362 | 19,497 |
| Seychelles | 78 | 84 | 89 |
| Sierra Leone | 4,793 | 7,399 | 9,716 |
| Singapore | 3,397 | 4,026 | 4,330 |
| Slovakia | 5,374 | 5,735 | 5,837 |
| Slovenia | 1,951 | 1,926 | 1,856 |
| Solomon Islands | 413 | 620 | 767 |
| Somalia | 9,639 | 14,524 | 18,955 |
| South Africa | 41,743 | 49,200 | 52,264 |
| Spain | 39,181 | 40,398 | 39,758 |
| Sri Lanka | 18,553 | 21,331 | 22,877 |
| Sudan | 31,065 | 47,512 | 58,545 |
| Suriname | 436 | 534 | 598 |
| Swaziland | 999 | 1,566 | 2,128 |
| Sweden | 8,901 | 9,322 | 9,515 |
| Switzerland | 7,207 | 7,674 | 7,802 |
| Syria | 15,609 | 23,329 | 28,926 |
| Taiwan | 21,466 | 23,966 | 25,155 |
| Tajikistan | 5,916 | 8,019 | 10,019 |
| Tanzania | 29,058 | 36,076 | 40,102 |
| Thailand | 58,851 | 66,092 | 69,298 |
| Togo | 4,571 | 7,401 | 10,146 |
| Tonga | 106 | 119 | 128 |
| Trinidad and Tobago | 1,272 | 1,323 | 1,409 |
| Tunisia | 9,020 | 11,280 | 12,751 |
| Turkey | 62,484 | 76,570 | 85,643 |
| Turkmenistan | 4,149 | 5,362 | 6,380 |
| Tuvalu | 10 | 12 | 15 |
| Uganda | 20,158 | 26,355 | 30,872 |
| Ukraine | 50,864 | 49,915 | 49,038 |
| United Arab Emirates | 3,057 | 4,873 | 6,080 |
| United Kingdom | 58,490 | 59,159 | 59,289 |
| United States | 265,563 | 298,026 | 323,052 |
| Uruguay | 3,239 | 3,582 | 3,811 |
| Uzbekistan | 23,418 | 30,536 | 36,628 |
| Vanuatu | 178 | 230 | 266 |
| Venezuela | 21,983 | 27,345 | 30,876 |
| Vietnam | 73,977 | 88,602 | 99,153 |
| Western Samoa | 214 | 288 | 341 |
| Yemen | 13,483 | 21,841 | 29,469 |
| Yugoslavia | 10,615 | 11,062 | 11,067 |
| Zaire | 46,499 | 69,293 | 91,548 |
| Zambia | 9,159 | 11,471 | 13,022 |
| Zimbabwe | 11,271 | 11,905 | 11,344 |
| **Regions** | | | |
| Africa | 731,724 | 1,009,361 | 1,230,340 |
| Asia | 3,428,190 | 4,075,382 | 4,495,242 |
| Latin America and Caribbean | 488,558 | 583,325 | 642,503 |
| North America | 294,511 | 330,701 | 357,956 |
| Europe | 507,254 | 523,110 | 521,138 |
| Former Soviet Union | 292,787 | 307,038 | 317,527 |
| Oceania inc. Australia | 28,915 | 33,879 | 37,080 |
| **World[1]** | **5,771,938** | **6,862,797** | **7,601,786** |

(1) Figures may not add to total due to rounding and exclusion of certain pseudo-national entities.

# Estimated HIV Infection and Reported AIDS Cases

**Source:** UNAIDS Program, United Nations

Studies, primarily in industrialized nations, have indicated that about 60% of adults infected by the human immunodeficiency virus (HIV) will develop acquired immune deficiency syndrome (AIDS) within 12-13 years of becoming infected; progression of the disease might be more rapid in developing countries. It is expected that the vast majority of HIV-infected persons will eventually develop AIDS. Survival after the onset of AIDS is estimated on the average to be about 3 years in industrialized countries and less than 1 year in developing countries. About 75-85% of adult HIV infections worldwide have been transmitted through unprotected sexual intercourse. As of June 30, 1996, a total of 1,393,649 AIDS cases had been officially reported, a 19% increase from the 1,169,811 reported on June 30, 1995. The actual number of AIDS cases worldwide is estimated to be more than 7.7 million—5½ times the number of reported cases—because of underdiagnosis, underreporting, and reporting delays in different countries. UNAIDS estimates more than 3.1 million new HIV infections will occur in 1996. Since the start of the global epidemic in the late 1970s, about 27.9 million people have been infected by HIV and about 5.8 million have died, including 1.3 million children.

## Estimated Current and Cumulative HIV/AIDS Cases by Region, Mid-1996

| Region | Current cases[1] | Cumulative cases[2] | Pct. of adults[3] |
|---|---|---|---|
| North America | 780,000 | 1,200,000 | 3.7 |
| Caribbean | 270,000 | 330,000 | 1.3 |
| Latin America | 1,300,000 | 1,600,000 | 6.0 |
| Western Europe | 470,000 | 640,000 | 2.2 |
| North Africa/Middle East | 200,000 | 220,000 | 0.9 |
| Sub-Saharan Africa | 14,000,000 | 19,000,000 | 63.0 |
| E. Europe/Central Asia | 30,000 | 31,000 | 0.1 |
| South/Southeast Asia | 4,800,000 | 5,000,000 | 23.0 |
| East Asia/Pacific | 35,000 | 36,000 | 0.2 |
| Australasia | 13,000 | 23,000 | 0.1 |
| **World** | **21,800,000** | **27,900,000** | **100[4]** |

(1) Adults and children living with HIV/AIDS. (2) Since the late 1970s. (3) Percentage of total number of adults living with HIV. (4) Details do not add to total because of rounding.

# The World's Refugees

**Source:** *World Refugee Survey 1996,* U.S. Committee for Refugees, a nonprofit corp. The refugees in this table include only those who are in need of protection and/or assistance and do not include refugees who have permanently settled in other countries.

(as of Dec. 31, 1995)

| Place of asylum | Mostly from | Number |
|---|---|---|
| **Total Africa** | | **5,220,000** |
| Algeria | Western Sahara, Mali, Niger | 120,000[1] |
| Burundi | Rwanda | 140,000[1] |
| Côte d'Ivoire | Liberia | 290,000 |
| Ethiopia | Somalia, Sudan, Djibouti, Kenya | 308,000[1] |
| Ghana | Togo, Liberia | 85,000 |
| Guinea | Liberia, Sierra Leone | 640,000[1] |
| Kenya | Somalia, Sudan, Ethiopia | 225,000[1] |
| Liberia | Sierra Leone | 120,000[1] |
| Senegal | Mauritania | 68,000 |
| South Africa | Mozambique | 90,000[1] |
| Sudan | Eritrea, Ethiopia, Chad | 450,000[1] |
| Tanzania | Rwanda, Burundi, Zaire, Mozambique | 703,000[1] |
| Uganda | Sudan, Zaire, Rwanda | 230,000 |
| Zaire | Rwanda, Angola, Burundi, Sudan, Uganda | 1,332,000[1] |
| Zambia | Angola, Zaire, Somalia | 125,400 |
| **Total Americas and the Caribbean** | | **256,000** |
| United States | Cuba, various other | 152,200 |
| **Total East Asia and the Pacific** | | **453,000** |
| China | Vietnam, Myanmar, Laos | 294,100[1] |
| Thailand | Myanmar, Laos | 98,200 |
| **Total Europe and Former USSR** | | **2,521,000** |
| Armenia | Azerbaijan | 304,000[1] |
| Azerbaijan | Armenia, Uzbekistan, Russia | 238,000[1] |
| Croatia | Bosnia and Herzegovina, Yugoslavia | 189,500 |
| Germany | Bosnia and Herzegovina | 442,700[1] |
| Italy | Former Yugoslavia | 60,700[1] |
| Russia | Former USSR | 500,000[1] |
| Yugoslavia[2] | Croatia, Bosnia and Herzegovina | 450,000[1] |
| **Total Middle East** | | **5,499,000** |
| Gaza Strip | Palestinians | 683,600 |
| Iran | Afghanistan, Iraq | 2,075,500[1] |
| Iraq | Palestinians, Iran, Turkey | 115,200 |
| Jordan | Palestinians, Iraq | 1,294,800 |
| Lebanon | Palestinians | 348,300 |
| Syria | Palestinians | 342,300 |
| West Bank | Palestinians | 517,400 |
| **Total South and Central Asia** | | **1,386,000** |
| India | Tibet, Sri Lanka, Bangladesh, Bhutan, Afghanistan, Myanmar | 319,200[1] |
| Nepal | Bhutan, Tibet | 106,600 |
| Pakistan | Afghanistan, Iraq, Somalia | 867,500[1] |
| **Total Refugees** | | **15,337,000[3]** |

(1) Significant variance among sources in number reported. (2) Serbia/Montenegro. (3) Details do not add to total because of rounding.

## Principal Sources of Refugees

| | |
|---|---|
| Palestinians | 3,286,100[1] |
| Afghanistan | 2,328,400[1] |
| Rwanda | 1,545,000[1] |
| Bosnia and Herzegovina | 905,500[1] |
| Liberia | 725,000[1] |
| Iraq | 622,900[1] |
| Somalia | 480,300[1] |
| Sudan | 448,100 |
| Azerbaijan | 390,000[1] |
| Sierra Leone | 363,000[1] |
| Eritrea | 342,500[1] |
| Angola | 313,000[1] |
| Vietnam | 294,850 |
| Burundi | 290,000[1] |
| Croatia | 200,000[1] |
| Armenia | 185,000[1] |
| Tajikistan | 170,400[1] |
| Myanmar | 160,400[1] |
| Tibet | 141,000 |
| Bhutan | 118,600[1] |
| Ethiopia | 110,700[1] |

(1) Significant variance among sources in number reported.

# U.S. Immigration Law

**Source:** Immigration and Naturalization Service, U.S. Dept. of Justice

Most U.S. regulations affecting immigration were modified in the Immigration and Nationality Act of 1952, which has been amended several times since then. The most recent major amendments were made through the Immigration Act of 1990, signed by Pres. George Bush on Nov. 29, 1990. New provisions, enacted as part of an omnibus spending bill signed by Pres. Bill Clinton on Sept. 30, 1996, focused mainly on illegal immigration. However, rules for sponsorship of legal immigrants were changed under the 1996 legislation.

The Immigration Act of 1990 raised the total number of numerically limited immigrants entering the U.S. annually in fiscal year 1992-94 to 700,000 (excluding refugees whose admission numbers are announced annually and some others not subject to limitation). Beginning in fiscal year 1995, the number dropped from 700,000 to 675,000, subject to adjustment based largely on the number of visas issued in the previous year. In fiscal year 1997, allowable visas were to be distributed as follows:

- 226,000 for family immigrants;
- 140,000 for employment-based immigrants;
- 55,000 for "diversity immigrants."

### Immediate Relatives (Family Immigrants)

Fiscal year 1992-94: 465,000 minus the number of "immediate relatives" admitted the previous fiscal year, plus any numbers unused by the employment-based preference system. During this period, the number of family-sponsored visas could not fall below 226,000 (10,000 visas higher than the previous allocation). If visa availability dipped below this new floor, the shortfall was made up from the category below.

During this period, 55,000 additional visas were made available to the spouses and children of aliens legalized under the Immigration Reform and Control Act (IRCA) of 1986.

Fiscal year 1995 and beyond: 480,000 minus the number of "immediate relatives" admitted during the previous fiscal year, plus any unused numbers under the employment-based preference system. The number of family-sponsored visas cannot drop below a floor of 226,000.

### Family Preference System

**First preference**—unmarried sons and daughters of U.S. citizens: 23,400 visas in FY 1997 plus unused visas from the 4th preference.

**Second preference**—spouses and unmarried children of Lawful Permanent Residents (LPRs): 114,200 visas, plus any visas available above the floor of 226,000 family preference visas, plus any unused visas from the previous preference.

The category is subdivided as follows: A minimum of 77% of the visas allocated to the category goes to the spouses and minor children of LPRs; 75% of the visas are issued without regard to per country ceilings; these visas are distributed in the order in which the petitions were filed. A maximum of 23% of the category visa allocation goes to the unmarried sons and daughters of LPRs. This group of visas continues to be subject to per country ceilings.

**Third preference**—married sons and daughters of U.S. citizens; 23,400 visas plus unused visas from all earlier preferences.

**Fourth preference**—brothers and sisters of U.S. citizens: 65,000 plus unused visas from all earlier preferences.

### Employment-Based Immigrants

The law allows a total of 140,000 plus, beginning in fiscal year 1994, any unused numbers under the family-sponsored system. These visas are distributed as follows:

**First preference**—Priority Workers—28.6% of the employment-based limit plus visas unused by the fourth and fifth employment-based preferences—"investors" and "special immigrants." The category is subdivided as follows: (1) extraordinary ability, demonstrated by sustained national or international acclaim, in the sciences, arts, education, business, and athletics; no U.S. employer required; (2) professors and researchers, seeking to enter in senior positions; U.S. employer required; (3) executives and managers of multinationals—requires one year of prior service with the firm during the preceding 3 years; the terms are extensively defined; U.S. employer required.

**Second preference**—Professionals with advanced degrees and aliens of exceptional ability—28.6% of the employment-based limit plus any unused "priority worker" visas. A U.S. employer and labor certification are required—although the Attorney General can waive both requirements. Members of the professions with advanced degrees or exceptional ability in the sciences, arts, or business. The possession of a degree, certificate, or license is not by itself considered sufficient evidence of exceptional ability.

**Third preference**—Skilled workers, professionals, and "other workers"—40,000 visas plus any visas unused by the 2 previous categories. Requires a U.S. employer and labor certification. Skilled workers must be in an occupation that requires at least 2 years training or experience. Professionals need a bachelor's degree. "Other workers" refers to unskilled workers. Their numbers are limited to no more than 10,000 visas per year.

**Fourth preference**—Special immigrants—7.1% of the employment-based limit. This category includes ministers of religion and persons working for religious organizations for at least 2 years, foreign medical graduates, employees of the U.S. government abroad including certain employees of the U.S. mission in Hong Kong who file for admission as special immigrants before Jan. 1, 2002, retired employees of international organizations, etc.

**Fifth preference**—7.1% of the employment-based limit—7,000 for investors of $1 million in urban areas and 3,000 for investors of no less than $500,000 in rural or high-unemployment areas. The Attorney General may increase the required investment amount up to $3 million for high employment areas. Investment must create employment for at least 10 U.S. workers.

### Diversity Immigrant (DV) Category

Since FY 1995, the Immigration and Nationality Act has allowed 55,000 immigrant visas each fiscal year, distributed by lottery, to provide immigration opportunities for persons from countries other than the principal sources of current immigration to the U.S. DV visas are divided among six geographic regions. Not more than 3,850 visas (7% of the 55,000 visa limit) may be provided to immigrants from any one country.

The allotment of FY 1997 visa numbers for each region was as follows: Africa, 20,623; Asia, 7,187; Europe, 23,910; North America (Bahamas), 8; South America, Central America, and the Caribbean, 2,455; and Oceania, 817.

The FY1997 DV registration mail-in was held Feb. 12-Mar. 12, 1996. During this one-month period, the National Visa Center in Portsmouth, NH, received about 6.5 million qualified entries. An additional 1.5 million entries received during those dates were disqualified for not providing the requested information or following published guidelines. Winners of visas were notified over a several-month period beginning in September.

In order to issue all 55,000 visas in FY 1997, the National Visa Center planned to notify 100,000 principal applicants. Those selected were sent instructions on how to apply for an immigrant visa. During the visa interview, applicants must provide proof of a high school education or its equivalent or must show two years of work experience within the past five years in an occupation that requires at least two years of training or experience. Those selected needed to act on their immigrant visa applications quickly. As soon as 55,000 visas are issued, the program for FY 1997 ends.

### Sponsorship of Immigrants

Under the 1996 immigration law, sponsors of an immigrant entering the country as an immediate relative or as an employment-based immigrant who will be employed by either a relative or a relative's company must earn at least 125% of the poverty level. If the sponsor does not earn enough, a cosponsor may be found who will accept joint responsibility for the immigrant. Persons who are active members of the U.S. armed forces need earn only 100% of the poverty level to be accepted as sponsors.

The sponsor must sign a legally binding affidavit of support for an immigrant, which would be enforceable until the immigrant either became a citizen or worked and paid taxes for 40 quarters as determined by the Social Security Administration.

## Naturalization: How to Become an American Citizen

**Source:** Federal Statutes

A person who desires to be naturalized as a citizen of the United States may obtain the necessary application form as well as detailed information from the nearest office of the Immigration and Naturalization Service or from the clerk of a court handling naturalization cases.

An applicant must be at least 18 years old and must have been a lawful resident of the United States continuously for 5 years. For husbands and wives of U.S. citizens the period is 3 years in most instances. Special provisions apply to certain veterans of the armed forces.

An applicant must have been physically present in the country for at least half of the required 5 years' residence.

Every applicant for naturalization must:

(1) demonstrate an understanding of the English language, including an ability to read, write, and speak words in ordinary usage in English (persons physically unable to do so and persons who, on the examination date, are over 55 years of age and have been lawful permanent residents of the United States for 15 years or more, or who are over 50 and have been residents 20 or more years, are exempt);

(2) have been a person of good moral character, attached to the principles of the Constitution, and well disposed to the good order and happiness of the United States for 5 years just before filing the petition or for whatever other period of residence is required in the particular case and continue to be such a person until admitted to citizenship; and

(3) demonstrate a knowledge and understanding of the fundamentals of the history, and the principles and form of government, of the United States. This can be done at private, designated testing entities or at the interview before an immigration examiner.

At the interview the applicant may be represented by a lawyer or social service agency. If action is favorable, there is a swearing in ceremony conducted administratively or judicially. At that ceremony the following oath of allegiance is administered:

I hereby declare, on oath, that I absolutely and entirely renounce and abjure all allegiance and fidelity to any foreign prince, potentate, state or sovereignty, to whom or which I have heretofore been a subject or citizen; that I will support and defend the Constitution and laws of the United States of America against all enemies, foreign and domestic; that I will bear true faith and allegiance to the same; that I will bear arms on behalf of the United States when required by the law; that I will perform noncombatant service in the armed forces of the United States when required by the law; that I will perform work of national importance under civilian direction when required by the law; and that I take this obligation freely without any mental reservation or purpose of evasion; so help me God.

# Major International Organizations

(as of mid-1996)

**Asia-Pacific Economic Cooperation Group (APEC),** founded Nov. 1989 as a forum to further cooperation on trade and investment between nations of the region and the rest of the world. Members in 1996 were Australia, Brunei, Canada, Chile, China, Hong Kong, Indonesia, Japan, Malaysia, Mexico, New Zealand, Papua New Guinea, Philippines, Singapore, South Korea, Taiwan, Thailand, and United States. Headquarters is in Singapore.

**Association of Southeast Asian Nations (ASEAN),** formed in 1967 to promote economic, social, and cultural cooperation and development among states of the Southeast Asian region. Members in 1996 were Brunei, Indonesia, Malaysia, Philippines, Singapore, Thailand, and Vietnam. Cambodia and Laos are scheduled to be admitted in 1997. Annual ministerial meetings set policy; a central Secretariat in Jakarta and specialized intergovernmental committees work in trade, transportation, communications, agriculture, science, finance, and culture.

**Caribbean Community and Common Market (CARICOM),** established July 4, 1973. Its function is to further cooperation in economics, health, education, culture, science and technology, and tax administration, as well as the coordination of foreign policy. Members in 1996 were Antigua and Barbuda, Bahamas (Common Market only), Barbados, Belize, Dominica, Grenada, Guyana, Jamaica, Montserrat, Saint Kitts and Nevis, Saint Lucia, Saint Vincent and the Grenadines, Suriname, and Trinidad and Tobago.

**Commonwealth of Independent States (CIS),** created Dec. 1991 upon the disbanding of the Soviet Union. It is made up of 12 of the 15 former Soviet constituent republics. Members in 1996 were Armenia, Azerbaijan, Belarus, Georgia, Kazakstan, Kyrgyzstan, Moldova, Russia, Tajikistan, Turkmenistan, Ukraine, and Uzbekistan. The commonwealth is not in itself a state but an alliance of fully independent states. Commonwealth policy is set through coordinating bodies such as a Council of Heads of State and Council of Heads of Government. The capital of the commonwealth is Minsk, Belarus.

**The Commonwealth,** originally called the British Commonwealth of Nations, and then the Commonwealth of Nations, an association of nations and dependencies loosely joined by a common interest based on having been parts of the old British Empire. The British monarch is the symbolic head of the Commonwealth.

There are 53 self-governing independent nations in the Commonwealth, plus various colonies and protectorates. As of 1996, the members were the United Kingdom of Great Britain and Northern Ireland and 15 other nations recognizing the British monarch, represented by a governor-general, as their head of state: Antigua and Barbuda, Australia, The Bahamas, Barbados, Belize, Canada, Grenada, Jamaica, New Zealand, Papua New Guinea, Saint Kitts and Nevis, Saint Lucia, Saint Vincent and the Grenadines, Solomon Islands, and Tuvalu (special member); and 37 countries with their own heads of state: Bangladesh, Botswana, Brunei, Cameroon, Cyprus, Dominica, The Gambia, Ghana, Guyana, India, Kenya, Kiribati, Lesotho, Malawi, Malaysia, The Maldives, Malta, Mauritius, Mozambique, Namibia, Nauru (special member), Nigeria (suspended Nov. 1995), Pakistan, Seychelles, Sierra Leone, Singapore, South Africa, Sri Lanka, Swaziland, Tanzania, Tonga, Trinidad and Tobago, Uganda, Vanuatu, Western Samoa, Zambia, and Zimbabwe.

The Commonwealth facilitates consultation among member states through meetings of prime ministers and finance ministers, and through a permanent Secretariat. Members consult on economic, scientific, educational, financial, legal, and military matters, and try to coordinate policies.

**European Union (EU)**—known as the European Community (EC) until 1994—the collective designation of three organizations with common membership: the European Economic Community (Common Market), the European Coal and Steel Community, and the European Atomic Energy Community (Euratom). The 15 full members in 1996 were Austria, Belgium, Denmark, Finland, France, Germany, Greece, Ireland, Italy, Luxembourg, Netherlands, Portugal, Spain, Sweden, and United Kingdom. Austria, Finland, and Sweden entered the EU on Jan. 1, 1995; Norway was scheduled to join at the same time, but Norwegian citizens in a Nov. 1994 referendum voted against membership. Some 70 nations in Africa, the Caribbean, and the Pacific are affiliated under the Lomé Convention.

A merger of the 3 communities' executives went into effect July 1, 1967, though the component organizations date back to 1951 and 1958. The Council of Ministers, European Commission, European Parliament, and European Court of Justice comprise the permanent structure. The EU aims to integrate the economies, coordinate social developments, and bring about political union of the democratic states of Europe. Effective Dec. 31, 1992, there are no restrictions on the movement of goods, services, capital, workers, and tourists within the EU. There are also common agricultural, fisheries, and nuclear research policies.

Leaders of the member nations (12 at the time) met Dec. 9–11, 1991, in Maastricht, the Netherlands. Treaties on monetary union and political union and accompanying protocols agreed upon by the leaders:

- Committed the organization to launching a common currency for at least some nations by 1999. Britain and, later, Denmark were allowed to "opt out" of joining.
- Sought to establish common foreign policies for the members.
- Laid the groundwork for a common defense policy.
- Expanded the policy issues in which the organization would have a voice.
- Gave the organization a leading role in social policy. Britain was not included in this plan.
- Pledged increased aid for the 4 poorest member nations—Ireland, Greece, Spain, and Portugal.
- Slightly increased the powers of the 567-member European Parliament.

The treaties went into effect Nov. 1, 1993, following ratification by all 12 members.

**European Free Trade Association (EFTA),** created May 3, 1960, to promote expansion of free trade. By Dec. 31, 1966, tariffs and quotas between member nations had been eliminated. Members of the EFTA entered into free trade agreements with the EU in 1972 and 1973. In 1992 the EFTA and EU concluded an agreement to create a single market—with free flow of goods, services, capital, and labor—encompassing the nations of the two organizations. Members in 1996 were Iceland, Liechtenstein, Norway, and Switzerland. Many former members of the EFTA are now members of the EU.

**Group of Seven (G-7),** organization of seven major industrial democracies who meet periodically to discuss world economic and other issues. Established Sept. 22, 1985. Members are Canada, France, Germany, Italy, Japan, United Kingdom, and United States.

**International Criminal Police Organization (Interpol),** created June 13, 1956, to ensure and promote the widest possible mutual assistance between all police authorities within the limits of the law existing in the different countries and in the spirit of the Universal Declaration of Human Rights. There were 176 members (independent nations), plus 13 subbureaus (dependencies), in 1996.

**League of Arab States (Arab League),** created Mar. 22, 1945. Members in 1996 were Algeria, Bahrain, Comoros, Djibouti, Egypt, Iraq, Jordan, Kuwait, Lebanon, Libya, Mauritania, Morocco, Oman, Palestine (considered an independent state by the League), Qatar, Saudi Arabia, Somalia, Sudan, Syria, Tunisia, United Arab Emirates, and Yemen. The League promotes economic, social, political, and military cooperation and mediates disputes among the Arab states; it represents Arab states in certain international negotiations. The League's headquarters is in Cairo.

**North Atlantic Treaty Organization (NATO),** created by treaty (signed Apr. 4, 1949; in effect Aug. 24, 1949). Members in 1996 were Belgium, Canada, Denmark, France, Germany, Greece, Iceland, Italy, Luxembourg, Netherlands, Norway, Portugal, Spain, Turkey, United Kingdom, and United States. The members agreed to settle disputes by peaceful means; to develop their individual and collective capacity to resist armed attack; to regard an attack on one as an attack on all; and to take necessary action to repel an attack under Article 51 of the United Nations Charter.

The NATO structure consists of a Council, the Defense Planning Committee, the Military Committee (consisting of 2 commands: Allied Command Europe, Allied Command Atlantic), the Nuclear Planning Group, and the Canada-U.S. Regional Planning Group.

With the dissolution of the Soviet Union and the end of the cold war in the early 1990s, NATO members sought to modify the organization's mission, putting greater stress on political action and creating a rapid deployment force to react to local crises. Former Warsaw Pact members were no longer considered adversaries; Hungary gained associate membership in 1991. By the end of 1995, 27 nations, including Russia and other former Soviet republics, had joined with NATO in the Partnership for Peace (PfP; drafted Dec. 1993), which provided for limited joint military exercises, peacekeeping missions, and information exchange. NATO has proceeded cautiously toward extending membership to former Eastern bloc nations, due to Russia's sensitivity to the issue. In Dec. 1995, a NATO-led multinational force was deployed to help keep the peace during the political reconstruction of Bosnia and Herzegovina.

**Organization of African Unity (OAU),** formed May 25, 1963, by 32 African countries (53 members in 1996) to promote peace and security as well as economic and social development. It holds annual conferences of heads of state. Headquarters is in Addis Ababa, Ethiopia.

**Organization of American States (OAS),** formed in Bogotá, Colombia, Apr. 30, 1948. Headquarters is in Washington, DC. It has a Permanent Council, Inter-American Council for Integral Development, Juridical Committee, and Commission on Human Rights. The Permanent Council can call meetings of foreign ministers to deal with urgent security matters. A General Assembly meets annually. A secretary general and assistant are elected for 5-year terms. There are 35 members, each with one vote in the various organizations: Antigua and Barbuda, Argentina, The Bahamas, Barbados, Belize, Bolivia, Brazil, Canada, Chile, Colombia, Costa Rica, Cuba, Dominica, Dominican Republic, Ecuador, El Salvador, Grenada, Guatemala, Guyana, Haiti, Honduras, Jamaica, Mexico, Nicaragua, Panama, Paraguay, Peru, Saint Kitts and Nevis, Saint Lucia, Saint Vincent and the Grenadines, Suriname, Trinidad and Tobago, United States, Uruguay, and Venezuela. In 1962, the OAS suspended Cuba from OAS activities but not from membership.

**Organization for Economic Cooperation and Development (OECD),** established Sept. 30, 1961, to promote economic and social welfare in member countries, and to stimulate and harmonize efforts on behalf of developing nations. The OECD collects and disseminates economic and environmental information. Members in 1996 were Australia, Austria, Belgium, Canada, Czech Republic, Denmark, Finland, France, Germany, Greece, Hungary, Iceland, Ireland, Italy, Japan, Luxembourg, Mexico, Netherlands, New Zealand, Norway, Poland, Portugal, Spain, Sweden, Switzerland, Turkey, United Kingdom, and United States. Headquarters is in Paris.

**Organization of Petroleum Exporting Countries (OPEC),** created Sept. 14, 1960. The group attempts to set world oil prices by controlling oil production. It is also involved in advancing members' interests in trade and development dealings with industrialized oil-consuming nations. Members in 1996 were Algeria, Gabon, Indonesia, Iran, Iraq, Kuwait, Libya, Nigeria, Qatar, Saudi Arabia, United Arab Emirates, and Venezuela. Headquarters is in Vienna.

**Organization for Security and Cooperation in Europe (OSCE),** established 1972 as the Conference on Security and Cooperation in Europe; current name adopted Jan. 1, 1995. The group, formed by NATO and Warsaw Pact members, is interested in furthering East-West relations through a commitment to nonaggression and human rights as well as cooperation in economics, science and technology, cultural exchange, and environmental protection. There were 54 member states in 1996. Headquarters is in Vienna.

# United Nations

The 51st regular session of United Nations General Assembly opened in September 1996.

UN headquarters is in New York, NY, between First Ave. and Roosevelt Drive and E. 42d St. and E. 48th St. The General Assembly Bldg., Secretariat, Conference and Library bldgs. are interconnected.

A European office at Geneva includes Secretariat and agency staff members. Other offices of UN bodies and related organizations with a staff of some 23,000 from some 150 countries are scattered throughout the world.

The UN has a post office originating its own stamps.

Proposals to establish an organization of nations for maintenance of world peace led to the United Nations Conference on International Organization at San Francisco, Apr. 25-June 26, 1945, where the charter of the United Nations was drawn up. It was signed June 26 by 50 nations, and by Poland, one of the original 51 UN members, on Oct. 15, 1945. The charter came into effect Oct. 24, 1945, upon ratification by the permanent members of the Security Council and a majority of other signatories.

**Purposes:** To maintain international peace and security; to develop friendly relations among nations; to achieve international cooperation in solving economic, social, cultural, and humanitarian problems and in promoting respect for human rights and fundamental freedoms; to be a center for harmonizing the actions of nations in attaining these common ends.

**Visitors to the UN:** Headquarters is open to the public every day of the year except Christmas and New Year's Day. Guided tours are given approximately every half hour from 9:15 AM to 4:45 PM daily, except on weekends during January and February. Groups of 15 or more persons should write to the Group Program Unit, Visitors' Service, Room GA-56, United Nations, New York, NY 10017, or telephone (212) 963-4440. Children under 5 are not permitted on tours.

## Roster of the United Nations

The 185 members of the United Nations, with the years in which they became members; as of Sept. 1995

| Member | Year | Member | Year | Member | Year | Member | Year |
|---|---|---|---|---|---|---|---|
| Afghanistan | 1946 | Botswana | 1966 | Denmark | 1945 | Guinea-Bissau | 1974 |
| Albania | 1955 | Brazil | 1945 | Djibouti | 1977 | Guyana | 1966 |
| Algeria | 1962 | Brunei | 1984 | Dominica | 1978 | Haiti | 1945 |
| Andorra | 1993 | Bulgaria | 1955 | Dominican Republic | 1945 | Honduras | 1945 |
| Angola | 1976 | Burkina Faso | 1960 | Ecuador | 1945 | Hungary | 1955 |
| Antigua and Barbuda | 1981 | Burundi | 1962 | Egypt[3] | 1945 | Iceland | 1946 |
| Argentina | 1945 | Cambodia | 1955 | El Salvador | 1945 | India | 1945 |
| Armenia | 1992 | Cameroon | 1960 | Equatorial Guinea | 1968 | Indonesia[4] | 1950 |
| Australia | 1945 | Canada | 1945 | Eritrea | 1993 | Iran | 1945 |
| Austria | 1955 | Cape Verde | 1975 | Estonia | 1991 | Iraq | 1945 |
| Azerbaijan | 1992 | Central African Rep. | 1960 | Ethiopia | 1945 | Ireland | 1955 |
| Bahamas | 1973 | Chad | 1960 | Fiji | 1970 | Israel | 1949 |
| Bahrain | 1971 | Chile | 1945 | Finland | 1955 | Italy | 1955 |
| Bangladesh | 1974 | China[1] | 1945 | France | 1945 | Jamaica | 1962 |
| Barbados | 1966 | Colombia | 1945 | Gabon | 1960 | Japan | 1956 |
| Belarus | 1945 | Comoros | 1975 | Gambia, The | 1965 | Jordan | 1955 |
| Belgium | 1945 | Congo | 1960 | Georgia | 1992 | Kazakstan | 1992 |
| Belize | 1981 | Costa Rica | 1945 | Germany | 1973 | Kenya | 1963 |
| Benin | 1960 | Côte d'Ivoire | 1960 | Ghana | 1957 | Korea, North | 1991 |
| Bhutan | 1971 | Croatia | 1992 | Greece | 1945 | Korea, South | 1991 |
| Bolivia | 1945 | Cuba | 1945 | Grenada | 1974 | Kuwait | 1963 |
| Bosnia and Herzegovina | 1992 | Cyprus | 1960 | Guatemala | 1945 | Kyrgyzstan | 1992 |
| | | Czech Republic[2] | 1993 | Guinea | 1958 | Laos | 1955 |

| Member | Year | Member | Year | Member | Year | Member | Year |
|---|---|---|---|---|---|---|---|
| Latvia | 1991 | Mozambique | 1975 | Saint Kitts and Nevis | 1983 | Syria[3] | 1945 |
| Lebanon | 1945 | Myanmar (Burma) | 1948 | Saint Lucia | 1979 | Tajikistan | 1992 |
| Lesotho | 1966 | Namibia | 1990 | Saint Vincent and the Grenadines | 1980 | Tanzania[9] | 1961 |
| Liberia | 1945 | Nepal | 1955 | Samoa (Western) | 1976 | Thailand | 1946 |
| Libya | 1955 | Netherlands | 1945 | San Marino | 1992 | Togo | 1960 |
| Liechtenstein | 1990 | New Zealand | 1945 | São Tomé and Príncipe | 1975 | Trinidad and Tobago | 1962 |
| Lithuania | 1991 | Nicaragua | 1945 | Saudi Arabia | 1945 | Tunisia | 1956 |
| Luxembourg | 1945 | Niger | 1960 | Senegal | 1960 | Turkey | 1945 |
| Macedonia[5] | 1993 | Nigeria | 1960 | Seychelles | 1976 | Turkmenistan | 1992 |
| Madagascar | 1960 | Norway | 1945 | Sierra Leone | 1961 | Uganda | 1962 |
| Malawi | 1964 | Oman | 1971 | Singapore[6] | 1965 | Ukraine | 1945 |
| Malaysia[6] | 1957 | Pakistan | 1947 | Slovakia[2] | 1993 | United Arab Emirates | 1971 |
| Maldives | 1965 | Palau | 1994 | Slovenia | 1992 | United Kingdom | 1945 |
| Mali | 1960 | Panama | 1945 | Solomon Islands | 1978 | United States | 1945 |
| Malta | 1964 | Papua New Guinea | 1975 | Somalia | 1960 | Uruguay | 1945 |
| Marshall Islands | 1991 | Paraguay | 1945 | South Africa[8] | 1945 | Uzbekistan | 1992 |
| Mauritania | 1961 | Peru | 1945 | Spain | 1955 | Vanuatu | 1981 |
| Mauritius | 1968 | Philippines | 1945 | Sri Lanka | 1955 | Venezuela | 1945 |
| Mexico | 1945 | Poland | 1945 | Sudan | 1956 | Vietnam | 1977 |
| Micronesia | 1991 | Portugal | 1955 | Suriname | 1975 | Yemen[10] | 1947 |
| Moldova | 1992 | Qatar | 1971 | Swaziland | 1968 | Yugoslavia[11] | 1945 |
| Monaco | 1993 | Romania | 1955 | Sweden | 1946 | Zaire | 1960 |
| Mongolia | 1961 | Russia[7] | 1945 | | | Zambia | 1964 |
| Morocco | 1956 | Rwanda | 1962 | | | Zimbabwe | 1980 |

(1) The General Assembly voted in 1971 to expel the Chinese government on Taiwan and admit the Beijing government in its place. (2) Czechoslovakia, which split into the separate nations of the Czech Republic and Slovakia on Jan. 1, 1993, was a UN member from 1945 to 1992. (3) Egypt and Syria were original members of the UN. In 1958, the United Arab Republic was established by a union of Egypt and Syria and continued as a single member of the UN. In 1961, Syria resumed its separate membership. (4) Indonesia withdrew from the UN in 1965 and rejoined in 1966. (5) Admitted under the provisional name of The Former Yugoslav Republic of Macedonia. (6) Malaya joined the UN in 1957. In 1963, its name was changed to Malaysia following the accession of Singapore, Sabah, and Sarawak. Singapore became an independent UN member in 1965. (7) The Union of Soviet Socialist Republics was an original member of the UN from 1945. After the USSR's dissolution in 1991, Russia informed the UN that it would be continuing the USSR's membership in the Security Council and all other UN organs with the support of the Commonwealth of Independent States (comprised of most of the former Soviet republics). (8) In 1994, the General Assembly accepted the credentials of the South African delegation, which had been rejected for 24 years because of the country's former apartheid policies. (9) Tanganyika was a member of the UN from 1961 and Zanzibar was a member from 1963. Following the ratification in 1964 of Articles of Union between Tanganyika and Zanzibar, the United Republic of Tanganyika and Zanzibar continued as a single member of the UN, later changing its name to United Republic of Tanzania. (10) The Yemen Arab Republic was admitted in 1947; the People's Republic of Yemen, in 1967. The two nations merged in 1990. (11) The Socialist Federal Republic of Yugoslavia became a member in 1945. After four of its six republics (Bosnia and Herzegovina, Croatia, Macedonia, and Slovenia) declared independence in 1991-92, the two remaining republics, Montenegro and Serbia, reconstituted themselves as the Federal Republic of Yugoslavia, which assumed Yugoslavia's UN seat Apr. 8, 1992. The General Assembly suspended Yugoslavia in Sept. 1992 for violating UN resolutions relating to the civil wars in the former Yugoslav republics.

## United Nations Secretaries General

| Year | Secretary, Nation | Year | Secretary, Nation | Year | Secretary, Nation |
|---|---|---|---|---|---|
| 1946 | Trygve Lie, Norway | 1961 | U Thant, Burma | 1982 | Javier Perez de Cuellar, Peru |
| 1953 | Dag Hammarskjold, Sweden | 1972 | Kurt Waldheim, Austria | 1992 | Boutros Boutros-Ghali, Egypt |

## U.S. Representatives to the United Nations

The U.S. Representative to the United Nations is the Chief of the U.S. Mission to the United Nations in New York and holds the rank and status of Ambassador Extraordinary and Plenipotentiary (A.E.P.).

| Year | Representative | Year | Representative | Year | Representative |
|---|---|---|---|---|---|
| 1946 | Edward R. Stettinius, Jr. | 1968 | George W. Ball | 1977 | Andrew Young |
| 1946 | Herschel V. Johnson (act.) | 1968 | James Russell Wiggins | 1979 | Donald McHenry |
| 1947 | Warren R. Austin | 1969 | Charles W. Yost | 1981 | Jeane J. Kirkpatrick |
| 1953 | Henry Cabot Lodge, Jr. | 1971 | George Bush | 1985 | Vernon A. Walters |
| 1960 | James J. Wadsworth | 1973 | John A. Scali | 1989 | Thomas R. Pickering |
| 1961 | Adlai E. Stevenson | 1975 | Daniel P. Moynihan | 1992 | Edward J. Perkins |
| 1965 | Arthur J. Goldberg | 1976 | William W. Scranton | 1993 | Madeleine K. Albright |

## Organization of the United Nations

The text of the UN Charter may be obtained from the Public Inquiries Unit, Department of Public Information, United Nations, New York, NY 10017.

**General Assembly.** The General Assembly is composed of representatives of all the member nations. Each nation is entitled to one vote.

The General Assembly meets in regular annual sessions and in special session when necessary. Special sessions are convoked by the Secretary General at the request of the Security Council or of a majority of the members of the UN.

On important questions a two-thirds majority of members present and voting is required; on other questions a simple majority is sufficient.

The General Assembly must approve the budget and apportion expenses among members. A member in arrears will have no vote if the amount of arrears equals or exceeds the amount of the contributions due for the preceding 2 full years.

**Security Council.** The Security Council consists of 15 members, 5 with permanent seats. The remaining 10 are elected for 2-year terms by the General Assembly; they are not eligible for immediate reelection.

Permanent members of the Council are: China, France, Russia, United Kingdom, United States.

Nonpermanent members are: (with terms expiring Dec. 31, 1996) Botswana, Germany, Honduras, Indonesia, Italy; and (with terms expiring Dec. 31, 1997) Chile, Egypt, Guinea-Bissau, Poland, South Korea.

The Security Council has the primary responsibility within the UN for maintaining international peace and security. The Council may investigate any dispute that threatens international peace and security.

Any member of the UN at UN headquarters may participate in its discussions and a nation not a member of the UN may appear if it is a party to a dispute.

Decisions on procedural questions are made by an affirmative vote of 9 members. On all other matters the affirmative vote of 9 members must include the concurring votes of all permanent members; it is this clause which gives rise to the so-called veto power of permanent members. A party to a dispute must refrain from voting.

The Security Council directs the various peacekeeping forces deployed throughout the world.

**Economic and Social Council.** The Economic and Social Council consists of 54 members elected by the General Assembly for 3-year terms of office. The council is responsible under the General Assembly for carrying out the functions of the United Nations with regard to international economic, social, cultural, educational, health, and related matters. The council meets once a year.

**Trusteeship Council.** The administration of trust territories is under UN supervision.

**Secretariat.** The Secretary General is the chief administrative officer of the UN. He may bring to the attention of the Security Council any matter that threatens international peace. He reports to the General Assembly.

**Budget:** The General Assembly approved a total budget for 1996-97 of $2.61 billion.

**International Court of Justice (World Court).** The International Court of Justice is the principal judicial organ of the United Nations. All members are *ipso facto* parties to the statute of the Court. Other states may become parties to the Court's statute.

The jurisdiction of the Court comprises cases which the parties submit to it and matters especially provided for in the charter or in treaties. The Court gives advisory opinions and renders judgments. Its decisions are binding only between the parties concerned and in respect to a particular dispute. If any party to a case fails to heed a judgment, the other party may have recourse to the Security Council.

The 15 judges are elected for 9-year terms by the General Assembly and the Security Council. Retiring judges are eligible for reelection. The Court remains permanently in session, except during vacations. All questions are decided by majority. The Court sits in The Hague, Netherlands.

## Selected Specialized and Related Agencies

These agencies are autonomous, with their own memberships and organs, and have a functional relationship or working agreement with the UN (headquarters), except for UNICEF and UNHCR, which report directly to the Economic and Social Council and to the General Assembly.

**Food and Agriculture Organization (FAO),** aims to increase production from farms, forests, and fisheries; improve food distribution and marketing, nutrition, and the living conditions of rural people. (Viale delle Terme di Caracalla, 00100 Rome, Italy.)

**International Atomic Energy Agency (IAEA),** aims to promote the safe, peaceful uses of atomic energy. (Vienna International Centre, PO Box 100, A-1400, Vienna, Austria.)

**International Bank for Reconstruction and Development (IBRD) (World Bank),** provides loans and technical assistance for economic development projects in developing member countries; encourages cofinancing for projects from other public and private sources. The IBRD has 3 affiliates: (1) The **International Development Association (IDA)** provides funds for development projects on concessionary terms to the poorer developing member countries. (2) The **International Finance Corporation (IFC)** promotes the growth of the private sector in developing member countries; encourages the development of local capital markets; stimulates the international flow of private capital. (3) The **Multilateral Investment Guarantee Agency (MIGA)** promotes private investment in developing countries; guarantees investments to protect investors from noncommercial risks, such as war or nationalization; advises governments on attracting private investment. (1818 H St., NW, Washington, DC 20433.)

**International Civil Aviation Org. (ICAO),** promotes international civil aviation standards and regulations. (1000 Sherbrooke St. W., Montreal, Quebec, Canada H3A 2R2.)

**International Fund for Agricultural Development (IFAD),** aims to mobilize funds for agricultural and rural projects in developing countries. (107 Via del Serafico, Rome, Italy.)

**International Labor Org. (ILO),** aims to promote employment; improve labor conditions and living standards. (4 route de Morillons, CH-1211 Geneva 22, Switzerland.)

**International Maritime Org. (IMO),** aims to promote cooperation on technical matters affecting international shipping. (4 Albert Embankment, London SE1 7SR, England.)

**International Monetary Fund (IMF),** aims to promote international monetary cooperation and currency stabilization and expansion of international trade. (700 19th St., NW, Washington, DC 20431.)

**International Telecommunication Union (ITU),** establishes international regulations for radio, telegraph, telephone, and space radio-communications, allocates radio frequencies. (Place des Nations, 1211 Geneva 20, Switzerland.)

**United Nations Children's Fund (UNICEF),** provides aid and development assistance to programs for children and mothers in developing countries. (1 UN Plaza, New York, NY 10017.)

**United Nations Educational, Scientific, and Cultural Org. (UNESCO),** aims to promote collaboration among nations through education, science, and culture. (7 Place de Fontenoy, 75352 Paris 07SP, France.)

**United Nations High Commissioner for Refugees (UNHCR),** provides essential assistance for refugees. (Place des Nations, 1211 Geneva 10, Switzerland.)

**Universal Postal Union (UPU),** aims to perfect postal services and promote international collaboration. (Weltpoststrasse 4, 3000 Berne, 15 Switzerland.)

**World Health Org. (WHO),** aims to aid the attainment of the highest possible level of health. (1211 Geneva 27, Switzerland.)

**World Intellectual Property Org. (WIPO),** seeks to protect, through international cooperation, literary, industrial, scientific, and artistic works. (34, Chemin des Colom Bettes, 1211 Geneva, Switzerland.)

**World Meteorological Org. (WMO),** aims to coordinate and improve world meteorological work. (Case Postale 5, CH-1211 Geneva 20, Switzerland.)

**World Trade Org. (WTO),** replacing the General Agreement on Tariffs and Trade (GATT), is the major body overseeing international trade. The WTO administers trade agreements and treaties, examines the trade regimes of members, keeps track of various trade measures and statistics, and attempts to settle trade disputes. (Centre William Rappard, 154 rue de Lausanne, 1211 Geneva 21, Switzerland.)

# Geneva Conventions

The Geneva Conventions are 4 international treaties governing the protection of civilians in time of war, the treatment of prisoners of war, and the care of the wounded and sick in the armed forces. The first convention, covering the sick and wounded, was concluded in Geneva, Switzerland, in 1864; it was amended and expanded in 1906. A third convention, in 1929, covered prisoners of war. Outrage at the treatment of prisoners and civilians during World War II by some belligerents, notably Germany and Japan, prompted the conclusion, in August 1949, of 4 new conventions. Three of these restated and strengthened the previous conventions, and the fourth codified general principles of international law governing the treatment of civilians in wartime.

The 1949 convention for civilians provided for special safeguards for the wounded, children under 15, pregnant women, and the elderly. Discrimination was forbidden on racial, religious, national, or political grounds. Torture, collective punishment, reprisals, the unwarranted destruction of property, and the forced use of civilians for an occupier's armed forces were also prohibited.

Also included in the new 1949 treaties was a pledge to treat prisoners humanely, feed them adequately, and deliver relief supplies to them. They were not to be forced to disclose more than minimal information.

Most countries have formally accepted all or most of the humanitarian conventions as binding. A nation is not free to withdraw its ratification of the conventions during wartime. However, there is no permanent machinery in place to apprehend, try, or punish violators.

# Ambassadors and Envoys

"Envoys from the United States" as of Oct. 1996. "Envoys to the United States" as of Sept. 1996. The address of U.S. embassies abroad is the appropriate foreign capital. The U.S. does not have diplomatic relations with the following countries: Cuba[1], Iran[2], Iraq[3], Libya[4], Liechtenstein, North Korea, and Taiwan[5]. There are informal relations with Bhutan.

| Countries | Envoys from United States | Envoys to United States |
|---|---|---|
| Afghanistan | None | Yar Mohammad Mohabbat, Chargé |
| Albania | Marisa R. Lino, Amb. | Lublin Dilja, Amb. |
| Algeria | Ronald E. Neumann, Amb. | Ramtane Lamamra, Amb. |
| Andorra | None | Juli Minoves Triquell, Amb. |
| Angola | Donald K. Steinberg, Amb. | Antonio dos Santos Franca, Amb. |
| Antigua & Barbuda | Jeanette W. Hyde, Amb. | Lionel Alexander Hurst, Amb. |
| Argentina | James R. Cheek, Amb. | Raul Enrique Granillo Ocampo, Amb. |
| Armenia | Peter Tomsen, Amb. | Rouben Robert Shugarian, Amb. |
| Australia | Vacancy | John Philip McCarthy, Amb. |
| Austria | Swanee G. Hunt, Amb. | Helmut Tuerk, Amb. |
| Azerbaijan | Richard D. Kauzlarich, Amb. | Hafiz Mir Jalal Oglu Pashayev, Amb. |
| Bahamas | Sidney Williams, Amb. | Arlington Griffith Butler, Amb. |
| Bahrain | David M. Ransom, Amb. | Muhammad Abdul Ghaffar Abdulla, Amb. |
| Bangladesh | David N. Merrill, Amb. | Humayun Kabir, Amb. |
| Barbados | Jeanette W. Hyde, Amb. | Courtney N. M. Blackman, Amb. |
| Belarus | Kenneth S. Yalowitz, Amb. | Serguei Nikolaevich Martynov, Amb. |
| Belgium | Alan J. Blinken, Amb. | Andre Adam, Amb. |
| Belize | George C. Bruno, Amb. | James S. Murphy, Amb. |
| Benin | John M. Yates, Amb. | Lucien Edgar Tonoukouin, Amb. |
| Bolivia | Curt W. Kamman, Amb. | Fernando Cossio, Amb. |
| Bosnia and Herzegovina | John K. Menzies, Amb. | Sven Alkalaj, Amb. |
| Botswana | Robert Krueger, Amb. | Archibald Mooketsa Mogwe, Amb. |
| Brazil | Melvyn Levitsky, Amb. | Paulo Tarso Flecha de Lima, Amb. |
| Brunei | Glen R. Rase, Amb. | Haji Jaya bin Abdul Latif, Amb. |
| Bulgaria | Avis T. Bohlen, Amb. | Snejana Damianova Botoucharova, Amb. |
| Burkina Faso | Sharon P. Wilkinson, Amb. | Gaetan R. Ouedraogo, Amb. |
| Burundi | Morris N. Hughes Jr., Amb. | Severin Ntahomvukiye, Amb. |
| Cambodia | Kenneth M. Quinn, Amb. | Var Huoth, Amb. |
| Cameroon | Charles H. Twining, Amb. | Jerome Mendouga, Amb. |
| Canada | Vacancy | Raymond A. J. Chretien, Amb. |
| Cape Verde | Lawrence N. Benedict, Amb. | Corentino Virgillio Santos, Amb. |
| Central African Republic | Mosina H. Jordan, Amb. | Henry Koba, Amb. |
| Chad | David C. Halsted, Amb. | Ahmat Mahamat Saleh, Amb. |
| Chile | Gabriel Guerra-Mondragon, Amb. | John Biehl, Amb. |
| China | Jim Sasser, Amb. | Li Daoyu, Amb. |
| Colombia | Myles R. Rene Frechette, Amb. | Mauricio Echeverry Gutierrez, Chargé |
| Comoros | Harold W. Geisel, Amb. | Ahmad Djabir, Amb. |
| Congo | Aubrey Hooks, Amb. | Dieudonne Antoine Ganga, Amb. |
| Costa Rica | Peter Jon de Vos, Amb. | Sonia Picado, Amb. |
| Côte d'Ivoire | Lannon Walker, Amb. | Koffi Moise Koumoue, Amb. |
| Croatia | Peter W. Galbraith, Amb. | Miomir Zuzul, Amb. |
| Cyprus | Kenneth C. Brill, Amb. | Andrew J. Jacovides, Amb. |
| Czech Republic | Jenonne R. Walker, Amb. | Michael Zantovsky, Amb. |
| Denmark | Edward E. Elson, Amb. | K. Erik Tygesen, Amb. |
| Djibouti | Vacancy | Roble Olhaye, Amb. |
| Dominica | Jeanette W. Hyde, Amb. | None |
| Dominican Republic | Donna J. Hrinak, Amb. | Jose del Carmen Ariza, Amb. |
| Ecuador | Leslie M. Alexander, Amb. | Fernando Flores, Chargé. |
| Egypt | Edward S. Walker, Amb. | Ahmed Maher El Sayed, Amb. |
| El Salvador | Vacancy | Ana Cristina Sol, Amb. |
| Equatorial Guinea | Charles H. Twining, Amb. | Pastor Micha Ondo Bile, Amb. |
| Eritrea | John F. Hicks Sr., Amb. | Amdemicael Kahsai, Amb. |
| Estonia | Lawrence P. Taylor, Amb. | Toomas Hendrik Ilves, Amb. |
| Ethiopia | David H. Shinn, Amb. | Berhane Gebre-Christos, Amb. |
| Fiji | Don Lee Gevirtz, Amb. | Pita Kewa Nacuva, Amb. |
| Finland | Derek Shearer, Amb. | Jaakko Tapani Laajava, Amb. |
| France | Pamela Harriman, Amb. | Francois V. Bujon, Amb. |
| Gabon | Elizabeth Raspolic, Amb. | Paul Boundoukou-Latha, Amb. |
| Gambia, The | Gerard W. Scott, Amb. | Juliana Baldeh, Chargé |
| Georgia | William H. Courtney, Amb. | Tedo Djaparidze, Amb. |
| Germany | Vacancy | Juergen Chrobog, Amb. |
| Ghana | Edward Brynn, Amb. | Ekwow Spio-Garbrah, Amb. |
| Greece | Thomas M. Tolliver Niles, Amb. | Loucas Tsilas, Amb. |
| Grenada | Jeanette W. Hyde, Amb. | Denis Antoine, Amb. |
| Guatemala | Donald J. Planty, Amb. | Pedro Miguel Lamport, Amb. |
| Guinea | Tibor P. Nagy Jr., Amb. | Mohammed Aly Thiam, Amb. |
| Guinea-Bissau | Peggy Blackford, Amb. | Rufino Medes, Amb. |
| Guyana | Vacancy | Mohammed Ali Odeen Ishmael, Amb. |
| Haiti | William L. Swing, Amb. | Jean Casimir, Amb. |
| Honduras | James F. Creagan, Amb. | Roberto Flores Bermudez, Amb. |
| Hungary | Donald M. Blinken, Amb. | Gyorgy Banlaki, Amb. |
| Iceland | Day Olin Mount, Amb. | Einar Benediktsson, Amb. |
| India | Frank G. Wisner, Amb. | Naresh Chandra, Amb. |
| Indonesia | J. Stapleton Roy, Amb. | Arifin Mohamad Siregar, Amb. |
| Ireland | Jean Kennedy Smith, Amb. | Dermot A. Gallagher, Amb. |
| Israel | Martin S. Indyk, Amb. | Eliahu Ben Elissar, Amb. |
| Italy | Reginald Bartholomew, Amb. | Ferdinando Salleo, Amb. |
| Jamaica | Jerome G. Cooper, Amb. | Richard Leighton Bernal, Amb. |
| Japan | Walter F. Mondale, Amb. | Kunihiko Saito, Amb. |
| Jordan | Wesley W. Egan, Amb. | Fayez A. Tarawneh, Amb. |
| Kazakstan | A. Elizabeth Jones, Amb. | Bolat K. Nurgaliyev, Amb. |
| Kenya | Prudence Bushnell, Amb. | Benjamin Edgar Kipkorir, Amb. |
| Kiribati | Joan M. Plaisted, Amb. | None |

| Countries | Envoys from United States | Envoys to United States |
|---|---|---|
| Korea, South | James T. Laney, Amb. | Kun Woo Park, Amb. |
| Kuwait | Ryan C. Crocker, Amb. | Mohammed Sabah Al-Salim Al-Sabah, Amb. |
| Kyrgyzstan | Eileen A. Malloy, Amb. | Almas Chukin, Chargé |
| Laos | Wendy Jean Chamberlin, Amb. | Hiem Phommachanh, Amb. |
| Latvia | Larry C. Napper, Amb. | Ojars Eriks Kalnins, Amb. |
| Lebanon | Richard H. Jones, Amb. | Riad Tabbarah, Amb. |
| Lesotho | Bismarck Myrick, Amb. | Eunice M. Bulane, Amb. |
| Liberia | William B. Milam, Chargé | Konah Blackett, Chargé |
| Lithuania | James W. Swihart Jr., Amb. | Alfonsas Eidintas, Amb. |
| Luxembourg | Clay Constantinou, Amb. | Alphonse Berns, Amb. |
| Macedonia | Christopher R. Hill, Amb. | Lubica Z. Acevska, Amb. |
| Madagascar | Vicki J. Huddleston, Amb. | Pierrot J. Rajaonarivelo, Amb. |
| Malawi | Peter R. Chaveas, Amb. | Willie Chokani, Amb. |
| Malaysia | John R. Malott, Amb. | Dato Dali Mahmud Hashim, Amb. |
| Maldives | A. Peter Burleigh, Amb. | None |
| Mali | David P. Rawson, Amb. | Cheick Oumar Diarrah, Amb. |
| Malta | Vacancy | Albert Borg Olivier de Puget, Amb. |
| Marshall Islands | Joan M. Plaisted, Amb. | Banny de Brum, Amb. |
| Mauritania | Dorothy Myers Sampas, Amb. | Bilal Ould Werzeg, Amb. |
| Mauritius | Harold W. Geisel, Amb. | Chitmansing Jesseramsing, Amb. |
| Mexico | James R. Jones, Amb. | Jesus Silva Herzog, Amb. |
| Micronesia | Vacancy | Jesse B. Marehalau, Amb. |
| Moldova | John T. Stewart, Amb. | Nicolae Tau, Amb. |
| Mongolia | Vacancy | Jalbuu Choinhor, Chargé |
| Morocco | Marc C. Ginsberg, Amb. | Mohamed Benaissa, Amb. |
| Mozambique | Vacancy | Marcos Namashulua, Amb. |
| Myanmar | Kent Wiedemann, Chargé | U Tin Winn, Amb. |
| Namibia | George F. Ward Jr., Amb. | Veiccoh K. Nghiwete, Amb. |
| Nauru | Don Lee Gevirtz, Amb. | None |
| Nepal | Sandra L. Vogelgesang, Amb. | Bhekh Bahadur Thapa, Amb. |
| Netherlands | K. Terry Dornbush, Amb. | Adriaan P. R. Jacobovits de Szeged, Amb. |
| New Zealand | Josiah Horton Beeman, Amb. | L. John Wood, Amb. |
| Nicaragua | John F. Maisto, Amb. | Roberto G. Mayorga-Cortes, Amb. |
| Niger | Charles O. Cecil, Amb. | Adamou Seydou, Amb. |
| Nigeria | Walter C. Carrington, Amb. | Wakili Hassan Adamu, Amb. |
| Norway | Thomas A. Loftus, Amb. | Tom Eric Vraalsen, Amb. |
| Oman | Frances D. Cook, Amb. | Abdulla Moh'd. Aqeel Al Dhahab, Amb. |
| Pakistan | Thomas W. Simons Jr., Amb. | Maleeha Lodhi, Amb. |
| Palau | Thomas C. Hubbard, Amb. | David Orrukem, Chargé |
| Panama | William J. Hughes, Amb. | Eduardo Morgan Gonzalez, Amb. |
| Papua New Guinea | Richard W. Teare, Amb. | Nagora Bogan, Amb. |
| Paraguay | Robert E. Service, Amb. | Jorge G. Prieto, Amb. |
| Peru | Dennis C. Jett, Amb. | Ricardo V. Luna, Amb. |
| Philippines | Thomas C. Hubbard, Amb. | Raul Chaves Rabe, Amb. |
| Poland | Nicholas Andrew Rey, Amb. | Jerzy Kozminski, Amb. |
| Portugal | Elizabeth Frawley Bagley, Amb. | Fernando Andresen Guimaraes, Amb. |
| Qatar | Patrick N. Theros, Amb. | Sheikh Abdulrahman bin Saud Al-Thani, Amb. |
| Romania | Alfred H. Moses, Amb. | Mircea Dan Geoana, Amb. |
| Russia | Thomas R. Pickering, Amb. | Yuli M. Vorontsov, Amb. |
| Rwanda | Robert E. Gribbin III, Amb. | Theogene Rudasingwa, Amb. |
| St. Kitts & Nevis | Jeanette W. Hyde, Amb. | John P. Irish, Chargé |
| St. Lucia | Jeanette W. Hyde, Amb. | Dr. Joseph Edsel Edmunds, Amb. |
| St. Vincent and the Grenadines | Jeanette W. Hyde, Amb. | Kingsley C.A. Layne, Amb. |
| São Tomé and Príncipe | Elizabeth Raspolic, Amb. | Vacancy |
| Saudi Arabia | Wyche Fowler Jr. | Prince Bandar Bin Sultan, Amb. |
| Senegal | Dane Farnsworth Smith Jr., Amb. | Mamadou Mansour Seck, Amb. |
| Seychelles | Harold W. Geisel, Amb. | Claude Morel, Chargé |
| Sierra Leone | John L. Hirsch, Amb. | John Ernest Leigh, Amb. |
| Singapore | Timothy A. Chorba, Amb. | Heng Chee Chan, Amb. |
| Slovakia | Ralph R. Johnson, Amb. | Branislav Lichardus, Amb. |
| Slovenia | Victor Jackovich, Amb. | Ernest Petric, Amb. |
| Solomon Islands | Richard W. Teare, Amb. | Vacancy |
| South Africa | James A. Joseph, Amb. | Franklin Sonn, Amb. |
| Spain | Richard N. Gardner, Amb. | Antonio Oyarzabal, Amb. |
| Sri Lanka | A. Peter Burleigh, Amb. | Jayantha Cudah Bandara Dhanapala, Amb. |
| Sudan | Timothy M. Carney, Amb. | Mahdi Ibrahim Mohamed, Amb. |
| Suriname | Roger R. Gamble, Amb. | Willem A. Udenhout, Amb. |
| Swaziland | Alan R. McKee, Amb. | Mary M. Kanya, Amb. |
| Sweden | Thomas L. Siebert, Amb. | Carl Henrik Sihver Liljegren, Amb. |
| Switzerland | Madeleine May Kunin, Amb. | Carlo Jagmetti, Amb. |
| Syria | Christopher W. S. Ross, Amb. | Walid Al-Moualem, Amb. |
| Tajikistan | R. Grant Smith, Amb. | None |
| Tanzania | Brady Anderson, Amb. | Mustafa Salim Nyang'anyi, Amb. |
| Thailand | William H. Itoh, Amb. | Nitya Pibulsonggram, Amb. |
| Togo | Johnny Young, Amb. | Kossivo Osseyi, Amb. |
| Tonga | Don Lee Gevirtz, Amb. | Vacancy |
| Trinidad and Tobago | Brian J. Donnelly, Amb. | Corinne Averille McKnight, Amb. |
| Tunisia | Mary Ann Casey, Amb. | Azouz Ennifar, Amb. |
| Turkey | Marc Grossman, Amb. | Nuzhet Kandemir, Amb. |
| Turkmenistan | Michael W. Cotter, Amb. | Halil Ugur, Amb. |
| Tuvalu | Don Lee Gevirtz, Amb. | None |
| Uganda | E. Michael Southwick, Amb. | Edith Ssempala, Amb. |
| Ukraine | William Green Miller, Amb. | Yuri Mikolayerych Shcherbak, Amb. |
| United Arab Emirates | David C. Litt, Amb. | Mohammad bin Hussein Al-Shaali, Amb. |
| United Kingdom | William J. Crowe Jr., Amb. | Sir John Olav Kerr, Amb. |
| Uruguay | Thomas J. Dodd, Amb. | Alvaro Mario Diez de Medina, Amb. |
| Uzbekistan | Stanley Tuemler Escudero, Amb. | Sodiq Safaev, Amb. |
| Vanuatu | Richard W. Teare, Amb. | None |

| Countries | Envoys from United States | Envoys to United States |
|---|---|---|
| Vatican City (The Holy See) | Raymond Leo Flynn, Amb. | Most Rev. Agostino Cacciavillan, Pro-Nuncio |
| Venezuela | Vacancy | Pedro Luis Echeverria, Amb. |
| Vietnam | None | Bang Van Le, Chargé |
| Western Samoa | Josiah Horton Beeman, Amb. | Tuiloma Neroni Slade, Amb. |
| Yemen | David G. Newton, Amb. | Mohsin Ahmed Alaini, Amb. |
| Yugoslavia | None | Nebojsa Vujovic, Chargé |
| Zaire | Daniel H. Simpson, Amb. | Mukendi Tambo a Kabila, Chargé |
| Zambia | Arlene Render, Amb. | Dunstan Weston Kamana, Amb. |
| Zimbabwe | Johnny Carson, Amb. | Amos Bernard Muvengwa Midzi, Amb. |

**Special Missions:** U.S. Mission to NATO, Brussels—Robert E. Hunter, A.E.P.; U.S. Mission to the European Union, Brussels—A. Vernon Weaver, A.E.P.; U.S. Mission to the UN, New York—Madeleine K. Albright, A.E.P.; U.S. Mission to the European Office of the UN, Geneva—Daniel L. Spiegel, Amb.; U.S. Mission to the OECD, Paris—David L. Aaron, Amb.; U.S. Mission to the Organization of American States, Washington—Harriet C. Babbit, Amb.; U.S. Mission to the Vienna Office of the UN—John B. Ritch III, Amb.

(1) Relations severed in 1961; limited ties restored in 1977. (2) U.S. severed relations in Apr. 1980. (3) Operations temporarily suspended. (4) Embassy closed in May 1980. U.S. closed the Libyan mission in May 1981. (5) Relations severed in 1978; unofficial relations are maintained.

# Codes for International Direct Dial Calling From the U.S.

**Station-to-station:** 011 + country code (below) + city code (if required) + local number.
**Person-to-person (operator-assisted, collect calls, credit card calls, and calls billed to another number):** 01 + country code (below) + city code (if required) + local number.
For countries or territories not listed, contact your long distance company.

| Country/Territory | Code |
|---|---|
| Afghanistan[1] | 93 |
| Albania | 355 |
| Algeria | 213 |
| American Samoa | 684 |
| Andorra | 376 |
| Angola | 244 |
| Anguilla[7] | 809* |
| Antarctica (Scott Base) | 64240 |
| Antigua & Barbuda | 268* |
| Argentina | 54 |
| Armenia | 374 |
| Aruba | 297 |
| Ascension Island | 247 |
| Australia | 61 |
| Austria | 43 |
| Azerbaijan | 994 |
| Bahamas | 242* |
| Bahrain | 973 |
| Bangladesh | 880 |
| Barbados | 246* |
| Belarus | 375 |
| Belgium | 32 |
| Belize | 501 |
| Benin | 229 |
| Bermuda | 441* |
| Bhutan | 975 |
| Bolivia | 591 |
| Bosnia & Herzegovina | 387 |
| Botswana | 267 |
| Brazil | 55 |
| Brunei | 673 |
| Bulgaria | 359 |
| Burkina Faso | 226 |
| Burundi | 257 |
| Cambodia | 855 |
| Cameroon | 237 |
| Canada | |
| Alberta | 403* |
| British Columbia | 250* |
| Vancouver | 604* |
| Manitoba | 204* |
| New Brunswick | 506* |
| Newfoundland | 709* |
| Nova Scotia | 902* |
| Ontario | |
| London | 519* |
| North Bay | 705* |
| Ottawa | 613* |
| Thunder Bay | 807* |
| Toronto Metro | 416* |
| Toronto Vicinity | 905* |
| Prince Edward Isl. | 902* |
| Quebec | |
| Montreal | 514* |
| Quebec City | 418* |
| Sherbrooke | 819* |
| Saskatchewan | 306* |
| Cape Verde | 238 |

| Country/Territory | Code |
|---|---|
| Cayman Islands | 345* |
| Central African Rep. | 236 |
| Chad | 235 |
| Chile | 56 |
| China | 86 |
| Colombia | 57 |
| Comoros | 269 |
| Congo | 242 |
| Costa Rica | 506 |
| Côte d'Ivoire | 225 |
| Croatia | 385 |
| Cuba | 53 |
| Cyprus | 357 |
| Czech Republic | 42 |
| Denmark | 45 |
| Djibouti | 253 |
| Dominica[2] | 809* |
| Dominican Republic | 809* |
| Ecuador | 593 |
| Egypt | 20 |
| El Salvador | 503 |
| Equatorial Guinea | 240 |
| Eritrea | 291 |
| Estonia | 372 |
| Ethiopia | 251 |
| Falkland Islands | 500 |
| Fiji | 679 |
| Finland | 358 |
| France | 33 |
| French Antilles | 596 |
| French Guiana | 594 |
| French Polynesia | 689 |
| Gabon | 241 |
| Gambia, The | 220 |
| Georgia | 995 |
| Germany | 49 |
| Ghana | 233 |
| Gibraltar | 350 |
| Greece | 30 |
| Greenland | 299 |
| Grenada | 809* |
| Guadeloupe | 590 |
| Guam[4] | 671 |
| Guantanamo Bay | 5399 |
| Guatemala | 502 |
| Guinea | 224 |
| Guinea-Bissau | 245 |
| Guyana | 592 |
| Haiti | 509 |
| Honduras | 504 |
| Hong Kong | 852 |
| Hungary | 36 |
| Iceland | 354 |
| India | 91 |
| Indonesia | 62 |
| Iran | 98 |
| Iraq | 964 |
| Ireland | 353 |
| Israel | 972 |
| Italy | 39 |

| Country/Territory | Code |
|---|---|
| Jamaica[3] | 809* |
| Japan | 81 |
| Jordan | 962 |
| Kazakstan | 7 |
| Kenya | 254 |
| Kiribati | 686 |
| Korea, North | 850 |
| Korea, South | 82 |
| Kuwait | 965 |
| Kyrgyzstan | 7 |
| Laos | 856 |
| Latvia | 371 |
| Lebanon | 961 |
| Lesotho | 266 |
| Liberia | 231 |
| Libya | 218 |
| Liechtenstein | 4175 |
| Lithuania | 370 |
| Luxembourg | 352 |
| Macau | 853 |
| Macedonia | 389 |
| Madagascar | 261 |
| Malawi | 265 |
| Malaysia | 60 |
| Maldives | 960 |
| Mali | 223 |
| Malta | 356 |
| Marshall Islands | 692 |
| Martinique | 596 |
| Mauritania | 222 |
| Mauritius | 230 |
| Mexico | 52 |
| Micronesia | 691 |
| Moldova | 373 |
| Monaco | 377 |
| Mongolia | 976 |
| Montserrat | 664* |
| Morocco | 212 |
| Mozambique | 258 |
| Myanmar | 95 |
| Namibia | 264 |
| Nauru | 674 |
| Nepal | 977 |
| Netherlands | 31 |
| New Caledonia | 687 |
| New Zealand | 64 |
| Nicaragua | 505 |
| Niger | 227 |
| Nigeria | 234 |
| N. Mariana Isls.[4] | 670 |
| Norway | 47 |
| Oman | 968 |
| Pakistan | 92 |
| Palau | 680 |
| Panama | 507 |
| Papua New Guinea | 675 |
| Paraguay | 595 |
| Peru | 51 |
| Philippines | 63 |
| Poland | 48 |

| Country/Territory | Code |
|---|---|
| Portugal | 351 |
| Puerto Rico | 787* |
| Qatar | 974 |
| Romania | 40 |
| Russia | 7 |
| Rwanda | 250 |
| St. Kitts & Nevis | 869* |
| St. Lucia | 758* |
| St. Vincent & the Grenadines | 809* |
| San Marino | 378 |
| São Tomé & Príncipe | 239 |
| Saudi Arabia | 966 |
| Senegal | 221 |
| Seychelles | 248 |
| Sierra Leone | 232 |
| Singapore | 65 |
| Slovakia | 42 |
| Slovenia | 386 |
| Solomon Islands | 677 |
| Somalia | 252 |
| South Africa | 27 |
| Spain | 34 |
| Sri Lanka | 94 |
| Sudan | 249 |
| Suriname | 597 |
| Swaziland | 268 |
| Sweden | 46 |
| Switzerland | 41 |
| Syria | 963 |
| Taiwan | 886 |
| Tajikistan | 7 |
| Tanzania | 255 |
| Thailand | 66 |
| Togo | 228 |
| Tonga | 676 |
| Trinidad & Tobago[5] | 809* |
| Tunisia | 216 |
| Turkey | 90 |
| Turkmenistan | 7 |
| Turks & Caicos Isls. | 809* |
| Tuvalu | 688 |
| Uganda | 256 |
| Ukraine | 380 |
| United Arab Emirates | 971 |
| United Kingdom | 44 |
| Uruguay | 598 |
| Uzbekistan | 7 |
| Vanuatu | 678 |
| Vatican City | 39 |
| Venezuela | 58 |
| Vietnam | 84 |
| Virgin Islands, British[6] | 809* |
| Virgin Islands, U.S. | 809* |
| Western Samoa | 685 |
| Yemen | 967 |
| Yugoslavia | 381 |
| Zaire | 243 |
| Zambia | 260 |
| Zimbabwe | 263 |

* These numbers are area codes. Follow Domestic Dialing instructions: dial "1" + area code + number you're calling. (1) Direct dial not available as of Oct. 1996. (2) In Oct. 1997, area code will change to 767. (3) In May 1997, area code will change to 876 (4) In July 1997, country code will become an area code. (5) In June 1997, area code will change to 868. (6) In Oct. 1997, area code will change to 284. (7) In April 1997, area code will change to 264.

# SPORTS

## Ten Most Dramatic Sports Events, Nov. 1995-Oct. 1996

The 26th Olympiad was held in Atlanta, GA, July 19-Aug. 4. Women athletes took center stage at the Centennial Summer Games with gold medal performances from the U.S. gymnastics, basketball, soccer, and softball teams, and standout individual showings from swimmers Amy Van Dyken (U.S.) and Michelle Smith (Ireland), runner Marie-Jose Perec (France), and diver Fu Mingxia (China). Male track-and-field stars who shone for the U.S. included runner Michael Johnson, decathlete Dan O'Brien, and Carl Lewis, who won his record-tying 9th Olympic gold medal with a victory in the long jump.

The Chicago Bulls utterly dominated the NBA in 1995-96, winning a record 72 regular-season games; they went on to defeat the Seattle SuperSonics in 6 games in the NBA Finals for their 4th title in 6 years. The Bulls' stampede was led by Michael Jordan, who picked up a record 8th scoring title and a record 4th Finals MVP award.

In a year that saw the most total home runs hit in a single season, the World Series came down to pitching. In an improbable come-from-behind victory, the New York Yankees defeated the defending champion Atlanta Braves in 6 games to win their 23d World Series. After falling behind 2 games to 0, the Yankees fought back with gritty starting pitching, nearly untouchable relief, clutch hitting, and a little luck. Reliever John Wetteland, who saved all 4 Yankee wins, was named MVP.

The Dallas Cowboys won their 3d Super Bowl in 4 years, Jan. 28, defeating old rivals the Pittsburgh Steelers, 27-17, in Tempe, AZ. It was a record-tying 5th Super Bowl victory for the Cowboys. Cornerback Larry Brown, who had 2 key 2d-half interceptions, was named MVP.

Golf history was made at the Pumpkin Ridge Golf Course in Cornelius, OR, Aug. 25, when Tiger Woods became the first golfer to win the U.S. Amateur tournament 3 years in a row. After the tournament, the 20-year-old phenom promptly turned pro, signing the largest-ever endorsement contracts by a rookie golfer. Through October, Woods had already won 2 PGA events.

The Colorado Avalanche buried the Florida Panthers in 4 straight games to capture the NHL's Stanley Cup. Goalie Patrick Roy, who was traded from Montreal during the season, held the upstart Panthers to just 4 goals. Avalanche center and captain Joe Sakic was named Playoffs MVP.

The Nebraska Cornhuskers clobbered the Florida Gators, 62-24, in the Fiesta Bowl, Jan. 2, in Tempe, AZ. The win gave Nebraska its 2d consecutive NCAA Division I football title, its 2d consecutive undefeated season, and its 25th straight victory. Quarterback Tommy Frazier, who ran for 199 of Nebraska's bowl-record 524 rushing yards, was the game's MVP.

Two historic powers in college basketball won the 1996 men's and women's NCAA Division I championships. The Kentucky Wildcats beat the Syracuse Orangemen, 76-67, in the men's finals, Apr. 1, in E. Rutherford, NJ.; it was Kentucky's 6th NCAA title. The Tennesee Lady Volunteers won the women's finals, defeating the Georgia Bulldogs handily, 83-65, Mar. 31, in Charlotte, NC, to capture their 4th championship in 10 years.

Major League Soccer, a professional league with teams in 10 major U.S. cities, kicked off its inaugural season, Apr. 6. The season culminated in a 3-2 overtime victory for the (Washington) D.C. United over the Los Angeles Galaxy in the MLS Cup, Oct. 20, at Foxboro, MA.

Steffi Graf continued her domination of women's tennis, winning 3 more grand slam titles, including her 7th Wimbledon and 5th U.S. Open. The victories gave her 21 grand slam titles overall, 2d to Margaret Court's 24.

# OLYMPICS

## Summer Olympic Games in 1996

Atlanta, GA, U.S., July 19-Aug. 4, 1996

On July 19, former boxing great Muhammad Ali lit the flame inaugurating the Centennial Olympic Games, the 26th Olympiad. About 10,750 athletes gathered for 17 days to compete for medals in a record 271 events; athletes from 197 nations and territories participated (25 more than in any previous Olympics). A bomb attack, July 27, at Centennial Olympic Park led to 2 deaths and injured more than 100, casting a somber mood on the 2d week of the games—still, the spirit of competition prevailed.

Outstanding athletes and teams of the 1996 games included: Kerri Strug, who ignored an ankle injury to lead the U.S. women's gymnastics team to a gold medal; the U.S. women's basketball, softball, and soccer teams; the U.S. men's basketball team (Dream Team), who again breezed to a gold; U.S. runner Michael Johnson, who won the 200 and 400 meters; France's Marie-Jose Perec, winner of the women's 200 and 400 meters; Canada's Donovan Bailey, who set a world record in the 100-meter run; Dan O'Brien of the U.S., who won the decathlon, after not even qualifying for the 1992 Olympics; U.S. swimmer Amy Van Dyken, who won 4 gold medals; Ireland's Michelle Smith, winner of 3 gold medals in swimming; China's Fu Minxia, who swept both women's diving events; marathon runner Josia Thugwane, who became South Africa's first black gold medalist; Russian Aleksandr Karelin, who won his 3d consecutive gold in Greco-Roman wrestling's super-heavyweight class; and Carl Lewis, who won his 4th consecutive gold medal in the long jump.

The U.S. won the most medals, 101, and the most gold medals, 44. Germany finished 2d in the medal count with 65, while Russia was 3d in total medals with 63, and 2d in gold medals with 26.

### Final Medal Standings

| Country | G | S | B | T |
|---|---|---|---|---|
| United States | 44 | 32 | 25 | **101** |
| Germany | 20 | 18 | 27 | **65** |
| Russia | 26 | 21 | 16 | **63** |
| China | 16 | 22 | 12 | **50** |
| Australia | 9 | 9 | 23 | **41** |
| France | 15 | 7 | 15 | **37** |
| Italy | 13 | 10 | 12 | **35** |
| South Korea | 7 | 15 | 5 | **27** |
| Cuba | 9 | 8 | 8 | **25** |
| Ukraine | 9 | 2 | 12 | **23** |
| Canada | 3 | 11 | 8 | **22** |
| Hungary | 7 | 4 | 10 | **21** |
| Romania | 4 | 7 | 9 | **20** |
| Netherlands | 4 | 5 | 10 | **19** |
| Poland | 7 | 5 | 5 | **17** |
| Spain | 5 | 6 | 6 | **17** |
| Bulgaria | 3 | 7 | 5 | **15** |
| Brazil | 3 | 3 | 9 | **15** |
| Great Britain | 1 | 8 | 6 | **15** |
| Belarus | 1 | 6 | 8 | **15** |
| Japan | 3 | 6 | 5 | **14** |
| Czech Rep. | 4 | 3 | 4 | **11** |
| Kazakstan | 3 | 4 | 4 | **11** |
| Greece | 4 | 4 | 0 | **8** |
| Sweden | 2 | 4 | 2 | **8** |
| Kenya | 1 | 4 | 3 | **8** |
| Switzerland | 4 | 3 | 0 | **7** |

| Country | G | S | B | T |
|---|---|---|---|---|
| Norway | 2 | 2 | 3 | **7** |
| Denmark | 4 | 1 | 1 | **6** |
| Turkey | 4 | 1 | 1 | **6** |
| New Zealand | 3 | 2 | 1 | **6** |
| Belgium | 2 | 2 | 2 | **6** |
| Nigeria | 2 | 1 | 3 | **6** |
| Jamaica | 1 | 3 | 2 | **6** |
| South Africa | 3 | 1 | 1 | **5** |
| North Korea | 2 | 1 | 2 | **5** |
| Ireland | 3 | 0 | 1 | **4** |
| Finland | 1 | 2 | 1 | **4** |
| Indonesia | 1 | 1 | 2 | **4** |
| Yugoslavia | 1 | 1 | 2 | **4** |
| Algeria | 2 | 0 | 1 | **3** |
| Ethiopia | 2 | 0 | 1 | **3** |
| Iran | 1 | 1 | 1 | **3** |
| Slovakia | 1 | 1 | 1 | **3** |
| Argentina | 0 | 2 | 1 | **3** |
| Austria | 0 | 1 | 2 | **3** |
| Armenia | 1 | 1 | 0 | **2** |
| Croatia | 1 | 1 | 0 | **2** |
| Portugal | 1 | 0 | 1 | **2** |
| Thailand | 1 | 0 | 1 | **2** |
| Namibia | 0 | 2 | 0 | **2** |
| Slovenia | 0 | 2 | 0 | **2** |
| Malaysia | 0 | 1 | 1 | **2** |
| Moldova | 0 | 1 | 1 | **2** |

| Country | G | S | B | T |
|---|---|---|---|---|
| Uzbekistan | 0 | 1 | 1 | **2** |
| Georgia | 0 | 0 | 2 | **2** |
| Morocco | 0 | 0 | 2 | **2** |
| Trinidad & Tobago | 0 | 0 | 2 | **2** |
| Burundi | 1 | 0 | 0 | **1** |
| Costa Rica | 1 | 0 | 0 | **1** |
| Ecuador | 1 | 0 | 0 | **1** |
| Hong Kong | 1 | 0 | 0 | **1** |
| Syria | 1 | 0 | 0 | **1** |
| Azerbaijan | 0 | 1 | 0 | **1** |
| Bahamas | 0 | 1 | 0 | **1** |
| Latvia | 0 | 1 | 0 | **1** |
| Philippines | 0 | 1 | 0 | **1** |
| Taiwan | 0 | 1 | 0 | **1** |
| Tonga | 0 | 1 | 0 | **1** |
| Zambia | 0 | 1 | 0 | **1** |
| India | 0 | 0 | 1 | **1** |
| Israel | 0 | 0 | 1 | **1** |
| Lithuania | 0 | 0 | 1 | **1** |
| Mexico | 0 | 0 | 1 | **1** |
| Mongolia | 0 | 0 | 1 | **1** |
| Mozambique | 0 | 0 | 1 | **1** |
| Puerto Rico | 0 | 0 | 1 | **1** |
| Tunisia | 0 | 0 | 1 | **1** |
| Uganda | 0 | 0 | 1 | **1** |

# 1996 Summer Olympics Medal Winners

(G = Gold, S = Silver, B = Bronze)

## Archery

**Men's 70-Meter Individual**—G-Justin Huish, U.S.; S-Magnus Petersson, Sweden; B-Oh Kyo Moon, S. Korea.
**Men's Team**—G-U.S.; S-S. Korea; B-Italy.
**Women's 70-Meter Individual**—G-Kim Kyung Wook, S. Korea; S-He Ying, China; B-Olena Sadovnycha, Ukraine.
**Women's Team**—G-S. Korea; S-Germany; B-Poland.

## Badminton

**Men's Singles**—G-Poul-Erik Hoyer-Larsen, Denmark; S-Dong Jiong, China; B-Rashid Sidak, Malaysia.
**Men's Doubles**—G-Rexy Mainaky & Ricky Subagja, Indonesia; S-Chea Soon Kit & Yap Kim Hock, Malaysia; B-S. Antonius & Denny Kantono, Indonesia.
**Women's Singles**—G-Bang Soo Hyun, S. Korea; S-Mia Audina, Indonesia; B-Susi Susanti, Indonesia.
**Women's Doubles**—G-Ge Fei & Gu Jun, China; S-Gil Young Ah & Jang Hye Ock, S. Korea; B-Yongshu Tang & Yiyuan Qin, China.
**Mixed Doubles**—G-Gil Young Ah & Kim Dong Moon, S. Korea; S-Ra Kyung Min & Park Joo Bong, S. Korea; B-Liu Jianjun & Sun Man, China.

## Baseball

G-Cuba; S-Japan; B-U.S.

## Basketball

**Men**—G-U.S.; S-Yugoslavia; B-Lithuania.
**Women**—G-U.S.; S-Brazil; B-Australia.

## Beach Volleyball

**Men**—G-Karch Kiraly & Kent Steffes, U.S.; S-Mike Dodd & Mike Whitmarch, U.S.; B-John Child & Mark Heese, Canada.
**Women**—G-Jackie Silva & Sandra Pires, Brazil; S-Monica Rodrigues & Adriana Samuel, Brazil; B-Natalie Cook & Kerri Pottharst Ann, Australia.

## Boxing

**106 Pounds**—G-Daniel Petrov, Bulgaria; S-Mansueto Velasco, Philippines; B-Oleg Kiryukhin, Ukraine; Rafael Lozano, Spain.
**112 Pounds**—G-Maikro Romero, Cuba; S-Bolat Djumadilov, Kazakstan; B-Albert Pakeev, Russia; Zoltan Lunka, Germany.
**119 Pounds**—G-Istvan Kovacs, Hungary; S-Arnaldo Mesa, Cuba; B-Raimkul Malakhbekov, Russia; Vichairachanon Khadpo, Thailand.
**125 Pounds**—G-Somluck Kamsing, Thailand; S-Serafim Todorov, Bulgaria; B-Pablo Chacon, Argentina; Floyd Mayweather, U.S.
**132 Pounds**—G-Hocine Soltani, Algeria; S-Tontcho Tontchev, Bulgaria; B-Terrance Cauthen, U.S.; Leonard Doroftei, Romania.
**139 Pounds**—G-Hector Vinent, Cuba; S-Oktay Urkal, Germany; B-Bolat Niyazymbetov, Kazakstan; Fethi Missaoui, Tunisia.
**147 Pounds**—G-Oleg Saitov, Russia; S-Juan Hernandez, Cuba; B-Marian Simion, Romania; Daniel Santos, Puerto Rico.
**156 Pounds**—G-David Reid, U.S.; S-Alfredo Duvergel, Cuba; B-Karim Tulaganov, Uzbekistan; Ermakhan Ibraimov, Kazakstan.
**165 Pounds**—G-Ariel Hernandez, Cuba; S-Malik Beyleroglu, Turkey; B-Rhoshii Wells, U.S.; Mohamed Bahari, Algeria.
**178 Pounds**—G-Vassili Jirov, Kazakstan; S-Lee Seung Bao, S. Korea; B-Antonio Tarver, U.S.; Thomas Ulrich, Germany.
**201 Pounds**—G-Felix Savon, Cuba; S-David Defiagbon, Canada; B-Nate Jones, U.S.; Luan Krasniqi, Germany.
**Over 201 Pounds**—G-Vladimir Klichko, Ukraine; S-Paea Wolgramm, Tonga; B-Aleksei Lezin, Russia; Duncan Dokiwari, Nigeria.

## Canoe/Kayak

### Men

**Kayak Slalom**—G-Oliver Fix, Germany; S-Andraz Vehovar, Slovenia; B-Thomas Becker, Germany.
**Kayak 500M Singles**—G-Antonio Rossi, Italy; S-Knut Holmann, Norway; B-Piotr Markiewicz, Poland.
**Kayak 500M Doubles**—G-Kay Bluhm & Torsten Gutsche, Germany; S-Beniamino Bonomi & Daniele Scarpa, Italy; B-Danny Collins & Andrew Trim, Australia.
**Kayak 1,000M Singles**—G-Knut Holmann, Norway; S- Beniamino Bonomi, Italy; B-Clint Robinson, Australia.
**Kayak 1,000M Doubles**—G-Antonio Rossi & Daniele Scarpa, Italy; S-Kay Bluhm & Torsten Gutsche, Germany; B-Andrian Dushev & Milk Kazanov, Bulgaria.
**Kayak 1,000M Fours**—G-Germany; S-Hungary; B-Russia.
**Canoe Slalom Singles**—G-Michal Martikan, Slovakia; S-Lukas Pollert, Czech Rep.; B-Patrice Estanguet, France.
**Canoe Slalom Doubles**—G-France; S-Czech Rep.; B-Germany.
**Canoe 500M Singles**—G-Martin Doktor, Czech Rep.; S-Slavomir Knazovicky, Slovakia; B-Imre Pulai, Hungary.
**Canoe 500M Doubles**—G-Csaba Horvath & Gyorgy Kolonics, Hungary; S-Nikolai Juravschi & Victor Reneischi, Moldova; B-Gheorghe Andriev & Grigore Obreja, Romania.
**Canoe 1,000M Singles**—G- Martin Doktor, Czech Rep.; S-Ivan Klementyev, Latvia; B-Gyorgy Zala, Hungary.
**Canoe 1,000M Doubles**—G-Andreas Dittmer & Gunar Kirchbach, Germany; S-Marcel Glavan & Antonel Borsan, Romania; B-Csaba Horvath & Gyorgy Kolonics, Hungary.

### Women

**Kayak Slalom**—G-Stepnka Hilgertova, Czech Rep.; S-Dana Chladek, U.S.; B-Myriam Fox-Jerusalmi, France.
**Kayak 500M Singles**—G-Rita Koban, Hungary; S-Caroline Brunet, Canada; B-Josefa Idem, Italy.
**Kayak 500M Doubles**—G-Agneta Andersson & Susanne Gunnarsson, Sweden; S-Ramona Portwich & Birgit Fischer, Germany; B-Katrin Borchert & Anna Wood, Australia.
**Kayak 500M Fours**—G-Germany; S-Switzerland; B-Sweden.

## Cycling

### Men

**Individual Road Race**—G-Pascal Richard, Switzerland; S-Rolf Sorensen, Denmark; B-Maximilian Sciandri, Great Britain.
**Sprint**—G-Jens Fiedler, Germany; S-Marty Nothstein, U.S.; B-Curt Harnett, Canada.
**Individual Points Race**—G-Silvio Martinello, Italy; S-Brian Walton, Canada; B-Stuart O'Grady, Australia.
**4KM Team Pursuit**—G-France; S-Russia; B-Australia.
**4KM Individual Pursuit**—G-Andrea Collinelli, Italy; S-Philippe Ermenault, France; B-Bradley McGee, Australia.
**1KM Time Trial**—G-Florian Rousseau, France; S-Erin Hartwell, U.S.; B-Takanobu Jumonji, Japan.
**Individual Time Trial**—G-Miguel Indurain, Spain; S-Abraham Olano, Spain; B-Chris Boardman, Great Britain.
**Cross-Country**—G-Bart Jan Brentjens, Netherlands; S-Thomas Frischknecht, Switzerland; B-Miguel Martinez, France.

### Women

**Individual Road Race**—G-Jeannie Longo-Ciprelli, France; S-Imelda Chiappa, Italy; B-Clara Hughes, Canada.
**Sprint**—G-Felicia Ballanger, France; S-Michelle Ferris, Australia; B-Ingrid Haringa, Netherlands.
**Individual Points Race**—G-Nathalie Lancien, France; S-Ingrid Haringa, Netherlands; B-Lucy Tyler Sharman, Australia.
**Individual Pursuit**—G-Antonella Bellutti, Italy; S-Marion Clignet, France; B-Judith Arndt, Germany.
**Individual Time Trial**—G-Zulfiya Zabirova, Russia; S-Jeannie Longo-Ciprelli, France; B-Clara Hughes, Canada.
**Cross-Country**—G-Paola Pezzo, Italy; S-Alison Sydor, Canada; B-Susan DeMattei, U.S.

## Diving

**Men's Platform**—G-Dmitri Sautin, Russia; S-Jan Hempel, Germany; B-Xiao Hailang, China.
**Men's Springboard**—G-Xiong Ni, China; S-Yu Zhuocheng, China; B-Mark Lenzi, U.S.
**Women's Platform**—G-Fu Mingxia, China; S-Annika Walter, Germany; B-Mary Ellen Clark, U.S.
**Women's Springboard**—G-Fu Mingxia, China; S-Irina Lashko, Russia; B-Annie Pelletier, Canada.

## Equestrian

**Individual Three-Day Event**—G-Blyth Tait, New Zealand; S-Sally Clark, New Zealand; B-Kerry Millikin, U.S.
**Team Three-Day Event**—G-Australia; S-U.S.; B-New Zealand.
**Individual Dressage**—G-Isabell Werth, Germany; S-Anky Van Grunsven, Netherlands; B-Sven Rothenberger, Netherlands.
**Team Dressage**—G-Germany; S-Netherlands; B-U.S.
**Individual Jumping**—G-Ulrich Kirchoff, Germany; S-Willi Melliger, Switzerland; B-Alexandra Ledermann, France.
**Team Jumping**—G-Germany; S-U.S.; B-Brazil.

## Fencing

### Men

**Individual Foil**—G-Alessandro Puccini, Italy; S-Lionel Plumenail, France; B-Franck Boidin, France.
**Team Foil**—G-Russia; S-Poland; B-Cuba.
**Individual Saber**—G-Stanislas Pozdnyakov, Russia; S-Sergei Sharikov, Russia; B-Damien Touya, France.
**Team Saber**—G-Russia; S-Hungary; B-Italy.
**Individual Épée**—G-Aleksandr Beketov, Russia; S-Ivan Trevejo Perez, Cuba; B-Geza Imre, Hungary.
**Team Épée**—G-Italy; S-Russia; B-France.

### Women

**Individual Foil**—G-Laura Badea, Romania; S-Valentina Vezzali, Italy; B-Giovanna Trillini, Italy.
**Team Foil**—G-Italy; S-Romania; B-Germany.
**Individual Épée**—G-Laura Flessel, France; S-Valerie Barlois, France; B-Gyoengyi Szalay Horvathne, Hungary.
**Team Épée**—G-France; S-Italy; B-Russia.

## Field Hockey

**Men**—G-Netherlands; S-Spain; B-Australia.
**Women**—G-Australia; S-S. Korea; B-Netherlands.

## Gymnastics

### Men

**Floor Exercise**—G-Ioannis Melissanidis, Greece; S-Li Xiaoshuang, China; B-Aleksei Nemov, Russia.
**Horizontal Bar**—G-Andreas Wecker, Germany; S-Krasimir Dounev, Bulgaria; B-(tie) Vitaly Scherbo, Belarus; Aleksei Nemov, Russia; Fann Bin, China.
**Parallel Bars**—G-Rustam Sharipov, Ukraine; S-Jair Lynch, U.S.; B-Vitaly Scherbo, Belarus.
**Pommel Horse**—G-Li Donghua, Switzerland; S-Marius Urzicka, Romania; B-Aleksei Nemov, Russia.
**Rings**—G-Yuri Chechi, Italy; S-(tie) Dan Burinca, Romania; Szilveszter Csollany, Hungary; B-none awarded.
**Vault**—G-Aleksei Nemov, Russia; S-Yeo Hong Chul, South Korea; B-Vitaly Scherbo, Belarus.
**Individual All-Around**—G-Li Xiaoshuang, China; S-Aleksei Nemov, Russia; B-Vitaly Scherbo, Belarus.
**Team**—G-Russia; S-China; B-Ukraine.

### Women

**Balance Beam**—G-Shannon Miller, U.S.; S-Lilia Podkopayeva, Ukraine; B-Gina Gogean, Romania.
**Floor Exercise**—G-Lilia Podkopayeva, Ukraine; S-Simona Amanar, Romania; B-Dominique Dawes, U.S.
**Uneven Bars**—G-Svetlana Chorkina, Russia; S-(tie) Amy Chow, U.S.; Bi Wenjiing, China; B-none awarded.
**Vault**—G-Simona Amanar, Romania; S-Mo Huilan, China; B-Gina Gogean, Romania.
**Individual All-Around**—G-Lilia Podkopayeva, Ukraine; S-Gina Gogean, Romania; B-(tie) Lavinia Milosovici, Romania; Simona Amanar, Romania.
**Team**—G-U.S.; S-Russia; B-Romania.

## Rhythmic Gymnastics

**Individual All-Around**—G-Yekaterina Serebryanskaya, Ukraine; S-Ianina Batyrchina, Russia; B-Yelena Vitrichenko, Ukraine.
**Team**—G-Spain; S-Bulgaria; B-Russia.

## Judo

### Men

**132 Pounds**—G-Tadahiro Nomura, Japan; S-Giralimo Giovinazzo, Italy; B-Richard Trautmann, Germany; Dorjpalam Narmandakh, Mongolia.
**143 Pounds**—G-Udo Quellmalz, Germany; S-Yukimasa Nakamura, Japan; B-Israel Hernandez Plana, Cuba; Henrique Guimares, Brazil.
**157 Pounds**—G-Kenzo Nakamura, Japan; S-Kwak Dae Sung, S. Korea; B-Christophe Gagliano, France; Jimmy Pedro, U.S.
**172 Pounds**—G-Djamel Bouras, France; S-Toshihiko Koga, Japan; B-Soso Liparteliani, Georgia; Cho In Chul, S. Korea.
**190 Pounds**—G-Jeon Ki Young, S. Korea; S-Armen Bagdasarov, Uzbekistan; B-Marko Spittka, Germany; Mark Huizinga, Netherlands.
**209 Pounds**—G-Pawel Nastula, Poland; S-Kim Min Soo, S. Korea; B-Stephane Traineau, France; Miguel Fernandes, Brazil.
**Heavyweight**—G-David Douillet, France; S-Ernesto Perez, Spain; B-Frank Moeller, Germany; Harry van Barneveld, Belgium.

### Women

**106 Pounds**—G-Kye Sun Hi, N. Korea; S-Ryoko Tamura, Japan; B-Yolanda Soler, Spain; Amarilis Savon, Cuba.
**115 Pounds**—G-Marie-Claire Restoux, France; S-Hyun Sook Hee, S. Korea; B-Noriko Sagawara, Japan; Legna Verdecia, Cuba.
**123 Pounds**—G-Driulis Gonzalez, Cuba; S-Jung Sun Yong, S. Korea; B-Isabelle Fernandez, Spain; Marisbell Lomba, Belgium.
**134 Pounds**—G-Yuko Emoto, Japan; S-Gelia Van de Caveye, Belgium; B-Jung Sung Sook, S. Korea; Jenny Gal, Netherlands.
**146 Pounds**—G-Cho Min Sun, S. Korea; S-Aneta Szczepanska, Poland; B-Claudia Zwiers, Netherlands; Wang Xianbo, China.
**159 Pounds**—G-Ulla Werbrouck, Belgium; S-Yoko Tanabe, Japan; B-Ylena Scapin, Italy; Diadenis Luna, Cuba.
**Over 159 Pounds**—G-Sun Fuming, China; S-Estella Rodriguez, Cuba; B-Johanna Hagn, Germany; Christine Cicot, France.

## Modern Pentathlon

G-Aleksandr Parygin, Kazakstan; S-Eduard Zenovka, Russia; B-Janos Martinek, Hungary.

## Rowing

### Men

**Single Sculls**—G-Xeno Müller, Switzerland; S-Derek Porter, Canada; B-Thomas Lange, Germany.
**Double Sculls**—G-Italy; S-Norway; B-France.
**Lightweight Double Sculls**—G-Switzerland; S-Netherlands; B-Australia.
**Quadruple Sculls**—G-Germany; S-U.S.; B-Australia.
**Coxless Pairs**—G-Great Britain; S-Australia; B-France.
**Coxless Fours**—G-Australia; S-France; B-Great Britain.
**Lightweight Coxless Fours**—G-Denmark; S-Canada; B-U.S.
**Coxed Eights**—G-Netherlands; S-Germany; B-Russia.

### Women

**Single Sculls**—G-Yekaterina Khodotovich, Belarus; S-Silken Lumann, Canada; B-Trine Hansen, Denmark.
**Double Sculls**—G-Canada; S-China; B-Netherlands.
**Lightweight Double Sculls**—G-Romania; S-U.S.; B-Australia.
**Quadruple Sculls**—G-Germany; S-Ukraine; B-Canada.
**Coxless Pairs**—G-Australia; S-U.S.; B-France.
**Coxed Eights**—G-Romania; S-Canada; B-Belarus.

## Shooting

### Men

**Air Pistol**—G-Roberto Di Donna, Italy; S-Wang Yifu, China; B-Tanu Kiriakov, Bulgaria.
**Trap**—G-Michael Diamond, Australia; S-Josh Lakatos, U.S.; B-Lance Bade, U.S.
**Air Rifle**—G-Artem Khadzhibekov, Russia; S-Wolfram Waibel Jr., Austria; B-Jean-Pierre Amat, France.
**Free Pistol**—G-Boris Kokorev, Russia; S-Igor Basinski, Belarus; B-Roberto Di Donna, Italy.
**Double Trap**—G-Russell Mark, Australia; S-Albano Pera, Italy; B-Zhang Bing, China.
**Rapid Fire Pistol**—G-Ralf Schumann, Germany; S-Emil Milev, Bulgaria; B-Vladimir Vokhmyanin, Kazakstan.
**Rifle Prone**—G-Christian Klees, Germany; S-Sergei Beliaev, Kazakstan; B-Jozef Gonci, Slovakia.
**Running Game Target**—G-Yang Ling, China; S-Xiao Jun, China; B-Miroslav Janus, Czech Republic.
**Three-Position Rifle**—G-Jean-Pierre Amat, France; S-Sergei Beliaev, Kazakstan; B-Wolfram Waibel Jr., Austria.
**Skeet**—G-Ennio Falco, Italy; S-Miroslaw Rzepkowski, Poland; B-Andrea Benelli, Italy.

### Women

**Air Pistol**—G-Olga Klochneva, Russia; S-Marina Logvinenko, Russia; B-Mariya Grozdeva, Bulgaria.
**Three-Position Rifle**—G-Aleksandra Ivosev, Yugoslavia; S-Irina Gerasimenok, Russia; B-Renata Mauer, Poland.
**Double Trap**—G-Kim Rhode, U.S.; S-Susanne Kiermayer, Germany; B-Deserie Huddleston, Australia.
**Sport Pistol**—G-Li Duihong, China; S-Diana Yorgova, Bulgaria; B-Marina Logvinenko, Russia.
**Air Rifle**—G-Renata Mauer, Poland; S-Petra Hornebar, Germany; B-Aleksandra Ivosev, Yugoslavia.

## Soccer

**Men**—G-Nigeria; S-Argentina; B-Brazil.
**Women**—G-U.S.; S-China; B-Norway.

## Softball

G-U.S.; S-China; B-Australia.

## Swimming

### Men

**50M Freestyle**—G-Aleksandr Popov, Russia; S-Gary Hall Jr., U.S.; B-Fernando Scherer, Brazil.

**100M Freestyle**—G-Aleksandr Popov, Russia; S-Gary Hall Jr., U.S.; B-Gustavo Borges, Brazil.

**200M Freestyle**—G-Danyon Loader, New Zealand; S-Gustavo Borges, Brazil; B-Daniel Kowalski, Australia.

**400M Freestyle**—G-Danyon Loader, New Zealand; S-Paul Palmer, Great Britain; B-Daniel Kowalski, Australia.

**1,500M Freestyle**—G-Kieren Perkins, Australia; S-Daniel Kowalski, Australia; B-Graeme Smith, Great Britain.

**100M Backstroke**—G-Jeff Rouse, U.S.; S-Rodolfo Falcon Cabrera, Cuba; B-Neisser Bent, Cuba.

**200M Backstroke**—G-Brad Bridgewater, U.S.; S-Tripp Schwenk, U.S.; B-Emanuele Merisi, Italy.

**100M Breaststroke**—G-Fred Deburghgraeve, Belgium; S-Jeremy Linn, U.S.; B-Mark Warnecke, Germany.

**200M Breaststroke**—G-Norbert Rozsa, Hungary; S-Karoly Guttler, Hungary; B-Andrei Korneyev, Russia.

**100M Butterfly**—G-Denis Pankratov, Russia; S-Scott Miller, Australia; B-Vladislav Kulikov, Russia.

**200M Butterfly**—G-Denis Pankratov, Russia; S-Tom Malchow, U.S.; B-Scott Goodman, Australia.

**200M Individual Medley**—G-Attila Czene, Hungary; S-Jani Sievinen, Finland; B-Curtis Myden, Canada.

**400M Individual Medley**—G-Tom Dolan, U.S.; S-Eric Namesnik, U.S.; B-Curtis Myden, Canada.

**400M Freestyle Relay**—G-U.S.; S-Russia; B-Germany.

**800M Freestyle Relay**—G-U.S.; S-Sweden; B-Germany.

**400M Medley Relay**—G-U.S.; S-Russia; B-Australia.

### Women

**50M Freestyle**—G-Amy Van Dyken, U.S.; S-Le Jingyi, China; B-Sandra Völker, Germany.

**100M Freestyle**—G-Le Jingyi, China; S-Sandra Völker, Germany; B-Angel Martino, U.S.

**200M Freestyle**—G-Claudia Poll, Costa Rica; S-Franziska van Almsick, Germany; B-Dagmar Hase, Germany.

**400M Freestyle**—G-Michelle Smith, Ireland; S-Dagmar Hase, Germany; B-Kirsten Vlieghuis, Netherlands.

**800M Freestyle**—G-Brooke Bennett, U.S.; S-Dagmar Hase, Germany; B-Kirsten Vlieghuis, Netherlands.

**100M Backstroke**—G-Beth Botsford U.S.; S-Whitney Hedgepeth, U.S.; B-Marianne Kriel, South Africa.

**200M Backstroke**—G-Krisztina Egerszegi, Hungary; S-Whitney Hedgepeth, U.S.; B-Cathleen Rund, Germany.

**100M Breaststroke**—G-Penny Heyns, South Africa; S-Amanda Beard, U.S.; B-Samantha Riley, Australia.

**200M Breaststroke**—G-Penny Heyns, South Africa; S-Amanda Beard, U.S.; B-Agnes Kovacs, Hungary.

**100M Butterfly**—G- Amy Van Dyken, U.S.; S-Liu Limin, China; B- Angel Martino, U.S.

**200M Butterfly**—G-Susan O'Neill, Australia; S-Petria Thomas, Australia; B-Michelle Smith, Ireland.

**200M Individual Medley**—G- Michelle Smith, Ireland; S-Marianne Limpert, Canada; B-Lin Li, China.

**400M Individual Medley**—G- Michelle Smith, Ireland; S-Allison Wagner, U.S.; B- Krisztina Egerszegi, Hungary.

**400M Freestyle Relay**—G-U.S.; S-China; B-Germany.

**800M Freestyle Relay**—G-U.S.; S-Germany; B-Australia.

**400M Medley Relay**—G-U.S.; S-Australia; B-China.

## Synchronized Swimming

G-U.S.; S-Canada; B-Japan.

## Table Tennis

**Men's Singles**—G-Liu Guoliang, China; S-Wang Tao, China; B-Joerg Rosskopf, Germany.

**Men's Doubles**—G-Kong Linghui & Liu Guoliang, China; S-Lu Lin & Wang Tao, China; B-Lee Chul Seung & Yoo Nam Kyu, S. Korea.

**Women's Singles**—G-Deng Yaping, China; S-Chen Jing, Taiwan; B-Qiao Hong, China.

**Women's Doubles**—G-Deng Yaping & Qiao Hong, China; S-Liu Wei & Qiao Yunping, China; B-Park Hae Jung & Ryu Ji Hae, S. Korea.

## Team Handball

**Men**—G-Croatia; S-Sweden; B-Spain.

**Women**—G-Denmark; S- S. Korea; B-Hungary.

## Tennis

**Men's Singles**—G-Andre Agassi, U.S.; S-Sergi Bruguera, Spain; B-Leander Paes, India.

**Men's Doubles**—G-Todd Woodbridge & Mark Woodforde, Australia; S-Neil Broad & Tim Henman, Great Britain; B-Marc-Kevin Goellner & David Prinosil, Germany.

**Women's Singles**—G-Lindsey Davenport, U.S.; S-Arantxa Sánchez Vicario, Spain; B-Jana Novotna, Czech Republic.

**Women's Doubles**—G-Gigi Fernandez & Mary Joe Fernandez, U.S.; S-Jana Novotna & Helena Sukova, Czech Republic; B-Arantxa Sánchez Vicario & Conchita Martinez, Spain.

## Track and Field

### Men

**100M**—G- Donovan Bailey, Canada; S-Frank Fredericks, Namibia; B-Ato Boldon, Trinidad & Tobago.

**200M**—G-Michael Johnson, U.S.; S-Frank Fredericks, Namibia; B-Ato Boldon, Trinidad & Tobago.

**400M**—G-Michael Johnson, U.S.; S-Roger Black, Great Britain; B-Davis Kamoga, Uganda.

**800M**—G-Vebjoern Rodal, Norway; S-Hezekiel Sepang, South Africa; B-Fred Onyancha, Kenya.

**1,500M**—G-Noureddine Morceli, Algeria; S-Fermin Cacho, Spain; B-Stephen Kipkorir, Kenya.

**5,000M**—G-Venuste Niyongabo, Burundi; S-Paul Bitok, Kenya; B-Khalid Boulami, Morocco.

**10,000M**—G-Haile Gebrselassie, Ethiopia; S-Paul Tergat, Kenya; B-Salah Hissou, Morocco.

**110M Hurdles**—G-Allen Johnson, U.S.; S-Mark Crear, U.S.; B-Florian Schwarthoff, Germany.

**400M Hurdles**—G-Derrick Adkins, U.S.; S-Samuel Matete, Zambia; B-Calvin Davis, U.S.

**400M Relay**—G-Canada; S-U.S.; B-Brazil.

**1,600M Relay**—G-U.S.; S-Great Britain; B-Jamaica.

**3,000M Steeplechase**—G-Joseph Keter, Kenya; S-Moses Kiptanui, Kenya; B-Alessandro Lambruschini, Italy.

**20KM Walk**—G-Jefferson Pérez, Ecuador; S-Ilya Markov, Russia; B-Bernardo Segura, Mexico.

**50KM Walk**—G-Robert Korzeniowski, Poland; S-Mikhail Schennikov, Russia; B-Valentin Massana, Spain.

**Marathon**—G-Josia Thugwane, South Africa; S-Bong Ju Lee, S. Korea; B-Eric Wainaina, Kenya.

**High Jump**—G-Charles Austin, U.S.; S-Artur Partyka, Poland; B-Steve Smith, Great Britain.

**Long Jump**—G-Carl Lewis, U.S.; S-James Beckford, Jamaica; B-Joe Greene, U.S.

**Triple Jump**—G-Kenny Harrison, U.S.; S-Jonathan Edwards, Great Britain; B-Yoelbi Quesada, Cuba.

**Discus**—G-Lars Riedel, Germany; S-Vladimir Dubrovshchik, Belarus; B-Vasily Kaptyukh, Belarus.

**Hammer Throw**—G-Balazs Kiss, Hungary; S-Lance Deal, U.S.; B-Oleksiy Krykun, Ukraine.

**Javelin**—G-Jan Zelezny, Czech Republic; S-Steve Backley, Great Britain; B-Seppo Raty, Finland.

**Pole Vault**—G-Jean Galfione, France; S-Igor Trandenkov, Russia; B-Andrei Tivontchik, Germany.

**Shot Put**—G-Randy Barnes, U.S.; S-John Godina, U.S.; B-Aleksandr Bagach, Ukraine.

**Decathlon**—G-Dan O'Brien, U.S.; S-Frank Busemann, Germany; B-Tomas Dvorak, Czech Republic.

### Women

**100M**—G-Gail Devers, U.S.; S-Merlene Ottey, Jamaica; B-Gwen Torrence, U.S.

**200M**—G-Marie-Jóse Pérec, France; S-Merlene Ottey, Jamaica; B-Mary Onyali, Nigeria.

**400M**—G-Marie-Jóse Pérec, France; S-Cathy Freeman, Australia; B-Falilat Ogunkoya, Nigeria.

**800M**—G-Svetlana Masterkova, Russia; S-Ana Quirot, Cuba; B-Maria Mutola, Mozambique.

**1,500M**—G-Svetlana Masterkova, Russia; S-Gabriela Szabo, Romania; B-Theresia Kiesl, Austria.

**5,000M**—G-Wang Junxia, China; S-Pauline Konga, Kenya; B-Roberta Brunet, Italy.

**10,000M**—G-Fernanda Ribeiro, Portugal; S-Wang Junxia, China; B-Gete Wami, Ethiopia.

**100M Hurdles**—G-Lyudmila Enquist, Sweden; S-Brigita Bukovec, Slovenia; B-Patricia Girard-Leno, France.

**400M Hurdles**—G-Deon Hemmings, Jamaica; S-Kim Batten, U.S.; B-Tonja Buford-Bailey, U.S.

**4x100M Relay**—G- U.S.; S-Bahamas; B-Jamaica.

**4x400M Relay**—G-U.S.; S-Nigeria; B-Germany.

**10KM Walk**—G-Yelena Nikolayeva, Russia; S-Elisabetta Perrone, Italy; B-Wang Yan, China.

**Marathon**—G-Fatuma Roba, Ethiopia; S-Valentina Yegorova, Russia; B-Yuko Arimori, Japan.

**High Jump**—G-Stefka Kostadinova, Bulgaria; S-Niki Bakoyianni, Greece; B-Inga Babakova, Ukraine.

**Long Jump**—G-Chioma Ajunwa, Nigeria; S-Fiona May, Italy; B-Jackie Joyner-Kersee, U.S.

**Triple Jump**—G-Inessa Kravets, Ukraine; S-Inna Lasovskaya, Russia; B-Sarka Kasparkova, Czech Republic.

**Discus**—G-Ilke Wyludda, Germany; S-Natalya Sadova, Russia; B-Elya Zvereva, Belarus.

**Javelin**—G-Heli Rantanen, Finland; S-Louise McPaul, Australia; B-Trine Hattestad, Norway.

**Shot Put**—G-Astrid Kumbernuss, Germany; S-Sui Xinmei, China; B-Irina Khudorozhkina, Russia.

**Heptathlon**—G-Ghada Shouaa, Syria; S-Natasha Sazanovich, Belarus; B-Denise Lewis, Great Britain.

### Volleyball

**Men**—G- Netherlands; S-Italy; B-Yugoslavia.
**Women**—G-Cuba; S-China; B- Brazil.

### Water Polo

G- Spain; S-Croatia; B- Italy.

### Weight Lifting

**119 Pounds**—G-Halil Mutlu, Turkey; S-Zhang Xiangsen, China; B-Sevdalin Minchev, Bulgaria.
**130 Pounds**—G-Tang Ningsheng, China; S-Leonidas Sabanis, Greece; B-Nikolai Pechalov, Bulgaria.
**141 Pounds**—G-Naim Suleymanoglu, Turkey; S-Valerios Leonidas, Greece; B-Xiao Jiangang, China.
**154 Pounds**—G-Zhan Xugang, China; S-Kim Myong Nam, N. Korea; B-Attila Feri, Hungary.
**161½ Pounds**—G-Pablo Lara, Cuba; S-Yoto Yotov, Bulgaria; B-Jon Chol, N. Korea.
**183 Pounds**—G-Pyrros Dimas, Greece; S-Mark Huster, Germany; B-Anderzej Cofalik, Poland.
**200½ Pounds**—G-Aleksei Petrov, Russia; S-Leonidas Kokas, Greece; B-Oliver Caruso, Germany.
**218 Pounds**—G- Akakide Kakhiashvilis, Greece; S-Anatoly Khrapaty, Kazakstan; B-Denis Gotfrid, Ukraine.
**238 Pounds**—G-Timur Taimazov, Ukraine; S-Sergei Syrtsov, Russia; B-Nicu Vlad, Romania.
**Over 238 Pounds**—G-Andrei Chemerkin, Russia; S-Ronny Weller, Germany; B-Stefan Botev, Australia.

### Wrestling

#### Freestyle

**105½ Pounds**—G-Kim Il, N. Korea; S-Armen Mkrttchian, Armenia; B-Alexis Vila, Cuba.
**114½ Pounds**—G-Valentin Jordanov, Bulgaria; S-Namik Abdullaev, Azerbaijan; B-Maulen Mamirov, Kazakstan.
**125½ Pounds**—G-Kendall Cross, U.S.; S-Giuvi Sissauori, Canada; B-Ri Yong Sam, N. Korea.
**136½ Pounds**—G-Tom Brands, U.S.; S-Jang Jae Sung, S. Korea; B-Elbrus Tedeev, Ukraine.
**149½ Pounds**—G-Vadim Bogiev, Russia; S-Townsend Saunders, U.S.; B-Zaza Zazirov, Ukraine.
**163 Pounds**—G-Bouvaisa Satiev, Russia; S- Park Jang Soon, S. Korea; B-Takuya Ota, Japan.
**180½ Pounds**—G-Khadzhimurad Magomedov, Russia; S-Yang Hyun Mo, S. Korea; B-Amir Reza Khadem, Iran.
**198 Pounds**—G-Rasul Khadem, Iran; S-Makharbek Khadartsev, Russia; B-Eldari Kurtanidze, Georgia.
**220 Pounds**—G-Kurt Angle, U.S.; S-Abbas Jadidi, Iran; B-Arawat Sabejew, Germany.
**286 Pounds**—G-Mahmut Demir, Turkey; S-Alexei Medvedev; B-Bruce Baumgartner, U.S.

#### Greco-Roman

**105½ Pounds**—G-Sim Kwan Ho, S. Korea; S-Aleksandr Pavlov, Belarus; B-Zafar Gulyov, Russia.
**114½ Pounds**—G-Armen Nazaryan, Armenia; S-Brandon Paulson, U.S.; B-Andrei Kalashnikov, Ukraine.
**125½ Pounds**—G-Yuri Melnichenko, Kazakstan; S-Dennis Hall, U.S.; B-Sheng Zetian, China.
**136½ Pounds**—G-Wlodzimierz Zwadzki, Poland; S-Juan Luis Maren Delis, Cuba; B-Mehmet Pirim, Turkey.
**149½ Pounds**—G-Ryszard Wolny, Poland; S-Ghani Yolouz, France; B-Aleksandr Tretyakov, Russia.
**163 Pounds**—G-Feliberto Ascuy Aguilera, Cuba; S-Marko Asell, Finland; B-Jozef Tracz, Poland.
**180½ Pounds**—G-Hamza Yerlikiya, Turkey; S-Thomas Zander, Germany; B-Valery Tsilent, Belarus.
**198 Pounds**—G-Vyacheslav Oleynyk, Ukraine; S-Jacek Fafinski, Poland; B-Maik Bullmann, Germany.
**220 Pounds**—G-Andrzej Wronski, Poland; S-Sergei Lishtvan, Belarus; B-Mikael Ljunberg, Sweden.
**286 Pounds**—G-Aleksandr Karelin, Russia; S-Matt Ghaffari, U.S.; B-Sergui Moureiko, Moldova.

### Yachting

#### Open

**Laser**—G-Robert Scheidt, Brazil; S-Ben Ainslie, Great Britain; B-Peer Moberg, Norway.
**Soling**—G-Germany; S-Russia; B-U.S.
**Star**—G-Brazil; S-Sweden; B-Australia.
**Tornado**—G-Spain; S-Australia; B-Brazil.

#### Men

**Finn**—G-Mateusz Kusznierewicz, Poland; S-Sebastien Godefroid, Belgium; B-Roy Heiner, Netherlands.
**Mistral**—G-Nikolaos Kaklamanakis, Greece; S-Carlos Espinola, Argentina; B-Gal Fridman, Israel.
**470**—G-Ukraine; S-Great Britain; B-Portugal.

#### Women

**Europe**—G-Kristine Rough, Denmark; S-Margriet Matthijsse, Norway; B-Courtney Becker-Dey, U.S.
**Mistral**—G-Lee Lai-Shan, Hong Kong; S-Barbara Kendall, New Zealand; B-Alessandra Sensini, Italy.
**470**—G-Spain; S-Japan; B-Ukraine.

## History of the Olympic Games

The modern Olympic Games, first held in Athens, Greece, in 1896, were the result of efforts by Baron Pierre de Coubertin, a French educator, to promote interest in education and culture and to foster better international understanding through the universal medium of youth's love of athletics. His source of inspiration for the Olympic Games was the ancient Greek Olympic Games, most notable of the 4 Panhellenic celebrations. The games were combined patriotic, religious, and athletic festivals held every 4 years. The first such recorded festival was held in 776 BC, the date from which the Greeks began to keep their calendar by "Olympiads," or 4-year spans between the games.

The first Olympiad is said to have consisted merely of a 200-yd foot race near the small city of Olympia, but the games gained in scope and became demonstrations of national pride. Only Greek citizens—amateurs—were permitted to participate. Winners received laurel, wild olive, and palm wreaths and were accorded many special privileges. Under the Roman emperors, the games deteriorated into professional carnivals and circuses. Emperor Theodosius banned them in AD 394.

Baron de Coubertin enlisted 13 nations to send athletes to the first modern Olympics in 1896; now athletes from nearly 200 nations and territories compete. Winter Olympic Games were started in 1924.

## Sites of Summer Olympic Games

| | | | | | | | |
|---|---|---|---|---|---|---|---|
| **1896** | Athens, Greece | **1924** | Paris, France | **1956** | Melbourne, Australia | **1980** | Moscow, USSR |
| **1900** | Paris, France | **1928** | Amsterdam, Netherlands | **1960** | Rome, Italy | **1984** | Los Angeles, U.S. |
| **1904** | St. Louis, U.S. | **1932** | Los Angeles, U.S. | **1964** | Tokyo, Japan | **1988** | Seoul, S. Korea |
| **1906*** | Athens, Greece | **1936** | Berlin, Germany | **1968** | Mexico City, Mexico | **1992** | Barcelona, Spain |
| **1908** | London, England | **1948** | London, England | **1972** | Munich, W. Germany | **1996** | Atlanta, U.S. |
| **1912** | Stockholm, Sweden | **1952** | Helsinki, Finland | **1976** | Montreal, Canada | **2000** | Sydney, Australia |
| **1920** | Antwerp, Belgium | | | | | | |

*Games not recognized by International Olympic Committee. Games 6 (1916), 12 (1940), and 13 (1944) were not celebrated.

## Summer Olympic Games Champions, 1896-1996

(*Indicates Olympic record)

The 1980 games were boycotted by 62 nations, including the U.S. The 1984 games were boycotted by the USSR and by most Eastern bloc nations. East and West Germany competed separately 1968-88. The 1992 Unified Team consisted of 12 former Soviet republics. The 1992 Independent Olympic Participants (I.O.P.) were athletes from Serbia, Montenegro, and Macedonia.

### Track and Field — Men

#### 100-Meter Run

| | | |
|---|---|---|
| **1896** | Thomas Burke, United States | 12s |
| **1900** | Francis W. Jarvis, United States | 11.0s |
| **1904** | Archie Hahn, United States | 11.0s |
| **1908** | Reginald Walker, South Africa | 10.8s |
| **1912** | Ralph Craig, United States | 10.8s |

| | | |
|---|---|---|
| 1920 | Charles Paddock, United States | 10.8s |
| 1924 | Harold Abrahams, Great Britain | 10.6s |
| 1928 | Percy Williams, Canada | 10.8s |
| 1932 | Eddie Tolan, United States | 10.3s |
| 1936 | Jesse Owens, United States | 10.3s |
| 1948 | Harrison Dillard, United States | 10.3s |
| 1952 | Lindy Remigino, United States | 10.4s |
| 1956 | Bobby Morrow, United States | 10.5s |
| 1960 | Armin Hary, Germany | 10.2s |
| 1964 | Bob Hayes, United States | 10.0s |
| 1968 | Jim Hines, United States | 9.95s |
| 1972 | Valery Borzov, USSR | 10.14s |
| 1976 | Hasely Crawford, Trinidad | 10.06s |
| 1980 | Allan Wells, Great Britain | 10.25s |
| 1984 | Carl Lewis, United States | 9.99s |
| 1988 | Carl Lewis, United States | 9.92s |
| 1992 | Linford Christie, Great Britain | 9.96s |
| 1996 | Donovan Bailey, Canada | 9.84s* |

### 200-Meter Run

| | | |
|---|---|---|
| 1900 | Walter Tewksbury, United States | 22.2s |
| 1904 | Archie Hahn, United States | 21.6s |
| 1908 | Robert Kerr, Canada | 22.6s |
| 1912 | Ralph Craig, United States | 21.7s |
| 1920 | Allan Woodring, United States | 22s |
| 1924 | Jackson Scholz, United States | 21.6s |
| 1928 | Percy Williams, Canada | 21.8s |
| 1932 | Eddie Tolan, United States | 21.2s |
| 1936 | Jesse Owens, United States | 20.7s |
| 1948 | Mel Patton, United States | 21.1s |
| 1952 | Andrew Stanfield, United States | 20.7s |
| 1956 | Bobby Morrow, United States | 20.6s |
| 1960 | Livio Berruti, Italy | 20.5s |
| 1964 | Henry Carr, United States | 20.3s |
| 1968 | Tommie Smith, United States | 19.83s |
| 1972 | Valeri Borzov, USSR | 20.00s |
| 1976 | Donald Quarrie, Jamaica | 20.23s |
| 1980 | Pietro Mennea, Italy | 20.19s |
| 1984 | Carl Lewis, United States | 19.80s |
| 1988 | Joe DeLoach, United States | 19.75s |
| 1992 | Mike Marsh, United States | 20.01s |
| 1996 | Michael Johnson, United States | 19.32s* |

### 400-Meter Run

| | | |
|---|---|---|
| 1896 | Thomas Burke, United States | 54.2s |
| 1900 | Maxey Long, United States | 49.4s |
| 1904 | Harry Hillman, United States | 49.2s |
| 1908 | Wyndham Halswelle, Great Britain, walkover | 50s |
| 1912 | Charles Reidpath, United States | 48.2s |
| 1920 | Bevil Rudd, South Africa | 49.6s |
| 1924 | Eric Liddell, Great Britain | 47.6s |
| 1928 | Ray Barbuti, United States | 47.8s |
| 1932 | William Carr, United States | 46.2s |
| 1936 | Archie Williams, United States | 46.5s |
| 1948 | Arthur Wint, Jamaica | 46.2s |
| 1952 | George Rhoden, Jamaica | 45.9s |
| 1956 | Charles Jenkins, United States | 46.7s |
| 1960 | Otis Davis, United States | 44.9s |
| 1964 | Michael Larrabee, United States | 45.1s |
| 1968 | Lee Evans, United States | 43.8s |
| 1972 | Vincent Matthews, United States | 44.66s |
| 1976 | Alberto Juantorena, Cuba | 44.26s |
| 1980 | Viktor Markin, USSR | 44.60s |
| 1984 | Alonzo Babers, United States | 44.27s |
| 1988 | Steven Lewis, United States | 43.87s |
| 1992 | Quincy Watts, United States | 43.50s |
| 1996 | Michael Johnson, United States | 43.49s* |

### 800-Meter Run

| | | |
|---|---|---|
| 1896 | Edwin Flack, Australia | 2m. 11s |
| 1900 | Alfred Tysoe, Great Britain | 2m. 1.2s |
| 1904 | James Lightbody, United States | 1m. 56s |
| 1908 | Mel Sheppard, United States | 1m. 52.8s |
| 1912 | James Meredith, United States | 1m. 51.9s |
| 1920 | Albert Hill, Great Britain | 1m. 53.4s |
| 1924 | Douglas Lowe, Great Britain | 1m. 52.4s |
| 1928 | Douglas Lowe, Great Britain | 1m. 51.8s |
| 1932 | Thomas Hampson, Great Britain | 1m. 49.8s |
| 1936 | John Woodruff, United States | 1m. 52.9s |
| 1948 | Mal Whitfield, United States | 1m. 49.2s |
| 1952 | Mal Whitfield, United States | 1m. 49.2s |
| 1956 | Thomas Courtney, United States | 1m. 47.7s |
| 1960 | Peter Snell, New Zealand | 1m. 46.3s |
| 1964 | Peter Snell, New Zealand | 1m. 45.1s |
| 1968 | Ralph Doubell, Australia | 1m. 44.3s |
| 1972 | Dave Wottle, United States | 1m. 45.9s |
| 1976 | Alberto Juantorena, Cuba | 1m. 43.50s |
| 1980 | Steve Ovett, Great Britain | 1m. 45.40s |
| 1984 | Joaquim Cruz, Brazil | 1m. 43.00s |
| 1988 | Paul Ereng, Kenya | 1m. 43.45s |
| 1992 | William Tanui, Kenya | 1m. 43.66s |
| 1996 | Vebjoern Rodal, Norway | 1m. 42.58s* |

### 1,500-Meter Run

| | | |
|---|---|---|
| 1896 | Edwin Flack, Australia | 4m. 33.2s |
| 1900 | Charles Bennett, Great Britain | 4m. 6.2s |
| 1904 | James Lightbody, United States | 4m. 5.4s |
| 1908 | Mel Sheppard, United States | 4m. 3.4s |
| 1912 | Arnold Jackson, Great Britain | 3m. 56.8s |
| 1920 | Albert Hill, Great Britain | 4m. 1.8s |
| 1924 | Paavo Nurmi, Finland | 3m. 53.6s |
| 1928 | Harry Larva, Finland | 3m. 53.2s |
| 1932 | Luigi Beccali, Italy | 3m. 51.2s |
| 1936 | Jack Lovelock, New Zealand | 3m. 47.8s |
| 1948 | Henri Eriksson, Sweden | 3m. 49.8s |
| 1952 | Joseph Barthel, Luxemburg | 3m. 45.2s |
| 1956 | Ron Delany, Ireland | 3m. 41.2s |
| 1960 | Herb Elliott, Australia | 3m. 35.6s |
| 1964 | Peter Snell, New Zealand | 3m. 38.1s |
| 1968 | Kipchoge Keino, Kenya | 3m. 34.9s |
| 1972 | Pekka Vasala, Finland | 3m. 36.3s |
| 1976 | John Walker, New Zealand | 3m. 39.17s |
| 1980 | Sebastian Coe, Great Britain | 3m. 38.4s |
| 1984 | Sebastian Coe, Great Britain | 3m. 32.53s* |
| 1988 | Peter Rono, Kenya | 3m. 35.96s |
| 1992 | Fermin Cacho Ruiz, Spain | 3m. 40.12s |
| 1996 | Noureddine Morceli, Algeria | 3m. 35.78s |

### 5,000-Meter Run

| | | |
|---|---|---|
| 1912 | Hannes Kolehmainen, Finland | 14m. 36.6s |
| 1920 | Joseph Guillemot, France | 14m. 55.6s |
| 1924 | Paavo Nurmi, Finland | 14m. 31.2s |
| 1928 | Willie Ritola, Finland | 14m. 38s |
| 1932 | Lauri Lehtinen, Finland | 14m. 30s |
| 1936 | Gunnar Hockert, Finland | 14m. 22.2s |
| 1948 | Gaston Reiff, Belgium | 14m. 17.6s |
| 1952 | Emil Zatopek, Czechoslovakia | 14m. 6.6s |
| 1956 | Vladimir Kuts, USSR | 13m. 39.6s |
| 1960 | Murray Halberg, New Zealand | 13m. 43.4s |
| 1964 | Bob Schul, United States | 13m. 48.8s |
| 1968 | Mohamed Gammoudi, Tunisia | 14m. 05.0s |
| 1972 | Lasse Viren, Finland | 13m. 26.4s |
| 1976 | Lasse Viren, Finland | 13m. 24.76s |
| 1980 | Miruts Yifter, Ethiopia | 13m. 21.0s |
| 1984 | Said Aouita, Morocco | 13m. 05.59s* |
| 1988 | John Ngugi, Kenya | 13m. 11.70s |
| 1992 | Dieter Baumann, Germany | 13m. 12.52s |
| 1996 | Venuste Niyongabo, Burundi | 13m. 07.96s |

### 10,000-Meter Run

| | | |
|---|---|---|
| 1912 | Hannes Kolehmainen, Finland | 31m. 20.8s |
| 1920 | Paavo Nurmi, Finland | 31m. 45.8s |
| 1924 | Willie Ritola, Finland | 30m. 23.2s |
| 1928 | Paavo Nurmi, Finland | 30m. 18.8s |
| 1932 | Janusz Kusocinski, Poland | 30m. 11.4s |
| 1936 | Ilmari Salminen, Finland | 30m. 15.4s |
| 1948 | Emil Zatopek, Czechoslovakia | 29m. 59.6s |
| 1952 | Emil Zatopek, Czechoslovakia | 29m. 17.0s |
| 1956 | Vladimir Kuts, USSR | 28m. 45.6s |
| 1960 | Pyotr Bolotnikov, USSR | 28m. 32.2s |
| 1964 | Billy Mills, United States | 28m. 24.4s |
| 1968 | Naftali Temu, Kenya | 29m. 27.4s |
| 1972 | Lasse Viren, Finland | 27m. 38.4s |
| 1976 | Lasse Viren, Finland | 27m. 40.38s |
| 1980 | Miruts Yifter, Ethiopia | 27m. 42.7s |
| 1984 | Alberto Cova, Italy | 27m. 47.54s |
| 1988 | Brahim Boutaib, Morocco | 27m. 21.46s |
| 1992 | Khalid Skah, Morocco | 27m. 46.70s |
| 1996 | Haile Gebrselassie, Ethiopia | 27m. 07.34s* |

### 110-Meter Hurdles

| | | |
|---|---|---|
| 1896 | Thomas Curtis, United States | 17.6s |
| 1900 | Alvin Kraenzlein, United States | 15.4s |
| 1904 | Frederick Schule, United States | 16s |
| 1908 | Forrest Smithson, United States | 15s |
| 1912 | Frederick Kelly, United States | 15.1s |
| 1920 | Earl Thomson, Canada | 14.8s |
| 1924 | Daniel Kinsey, United States | 15s |
| 1928 | Sydney Atkinson, South Africa | 14.8s |
| 1932 | George Saling, United States | 14.6s |
| 1936 | Forrest Towns, United States | 14.2s |
| 1948 | William Porter, United States | 13.9s |
| 1952 | Harrison Dillard, United States | 13.7s |
| 1956 | Lee Calhoun, United States | 13.5s |
| 1960 | Lee Calhoun, United States | 13.8s |
| 1964 | Hayes Jones, United States | 13.6s |
| 1968 | Willie Davenport, United States | 13.3s |
| 1972 | Rod Milburn, United States | 13.24s |
| 1976 | Guy Drut, France | 13.30s |
| 1980 | Thomas Munkelt, E. Germany | 13. 39s |
| 1984 | Roger Kingdom, United States | 13.20s |
| 1988 | Roger Kingdom, United States | 12.98s |
| 1992 | Mark McCoy, Canada | 13.12s |
| 1996 | Allen Johnson, United States | 12.95s* |

### 400-Meter Hurdles

| | | |
|---|---|---|
| 1900 | J.W.B. Tewksbury, United States | 57.6s |
| 1904 | Harry Hillman, United States | 53s |
| 1908 | Charles Bacon, United States | 55s |
| 1920 | Frank Loomis, United States | 54s |
| 1924 | F. Morgan Taylor, United States | 52.6s |
| 1928 | Lord Burghley, Great Britain | 53.4s |
| 1932 | Robert Tisdall, Ireland | 51.7s |
| 1936 | Glenn Hardin, United States | 52.4s |
| 1948 | Roy Cochran, United States | 51.1s |
| 1952 | Charles Moore, United States | 50.8s |
| 1956 | Glenn Davis, United States | 50.1s |
| 1960 | Glenn Davis, United States | 49.3s |
| 1964 | Rex Cawley, United States | 49.6s |
| 1968 | Dave Hemery, Great Britain | 48.12s |
| 1972 | John Akii-Bua, Uganda | 47.82s |
| 1976 | Edwin Moses, United States | 47.64s |
| 1980 | Volker Beck, E. Germany | 48.70s |
| 1984 | Edwin Moses, United States | 47.75s |
| 1988 | Andre Phillips, United States | 47.19s |
| 1992 | Kevin Young, United States | 46.78s* |
| 1996 | Derrick Adkins, United States | 47.54s |

### 400-Meter Relay

| | | |
|---|---|---|
| 1912 | Great Britain | 42.4s |
| 1920 | United States | 42.2s |
| 1924 | United States | 41s |
| 1928 | United States | 41s |
| 1932 | United States | 40s |
| 1936 | United States | 39.8s |
| 1948 | United States | 40.6s |
| 1952 | United States | 40.1s |
| 1956 | United States | 39.5s |
| 1960 | Germany (U.S. disqualified) | 39.5s |
| 1964 | United States | 39.0s |
| 1968 | United States | 38.2s |
| 1972 | United States | 38.19s |
| 1976 | United States | 38.33s |
| 1980 | USSR | 38.26s |
| 1984 | United States | 37.83s |
| 1988 | USSR (U.S. disqualified) | 38.19s |
| 1992 | United States | 37.40s* |
| 1996 | Canada | 37.69s |

### 1,600-Meter Relay

| | | |
|---|---|---|
| 1908 | United States | 3m. 29.4s |
| 1912 | United States | 3m. 16.6s |
| 1920 | Great Britain | 3m. 22.2s |
| 1924 | United States | 3m. 16s |
| 1928 | United States | 3m. 14.2s |
| 1932 | United States | 3m. 8.2s |
| 1936 | Great Britain | 3m. 9s |
| 1948 | United States | 3m. 10.4s |
| 1952 | Jamaica | 3m. 03.9s |
| 1956 | United States | 3m. 04.8s |
| 1960 | United States | 3m. 02.2s |
| 1964 | United States | 3m. 00.7s |
| 1968 | United States | 2m. 56.16s |
| 1972 | Kenya | 2m. 59.8s |
| 1976 | United States | 2m. 58.65s |
| 1980 | USSR | 3m. 01.1s |
| 1984 | United States | 2m. 57.91s |
| 1988 | United States | 2m. 56.16s |
| 1992 | United States | 2m. 55.74s* |
| 1996 | United States | 2m. 55.99s |

### 3,000-Meter Steeplechase

| | | |
|---|---|---|
| 1920 | Percy Hodge, Great Britain | 10m. 0.4s |
| 1924 | Willie Ritola, Finland | 9m. 33.6s |
| 1928 | Toivo Loukola, Finland | 9m. 21.8s |
| 1932 | Volmari Iso-Hollo, Finland | 10m. 33.4s |
| | (About 3,450 m; extra lap by error.) | |
| 1936 | Volmari Iso-Hollo, Finland | 9m. 3.8s |
| 1948 | Thore Sjoestrand, Sweden | 9m. 4.6s |
| 1952 | Horace Ashenfelter, United States | 8m. 45.4s |
| 1956 | Chris Brasher, Great Britain | 8m. 41.2s |
| 1960 | Zdzislaw Krzyszkowiak, Poland | 8m. 34.2s |
| 1964 | Gaston Roelants, Belgium | 8m. 30.8s |
| 1968 | Amos Biwott, Kenya | 8m. 51s |
| 1972 | Kipchoge Keino, Kenya | 8m. 23.6s |
| 1976 | Anders Garderud, Sweden | 8m. 08.2s |
| 1980 | Bronislaw Malinowski, Poland | 8m. 09.7s |
| 1984 | Julius Korir, Kenya | 8m. 11.8s |
| 1988 | Julius Kariuki, Kenya | 8m. 05.51s* |
| 1992 | Matthew Birir, Kenya | 8m. 08.84s |
| 1996 | Joseph Keter, Kenya | 8m. 07.12s |

### 20-Kilometer Walk

| | | |
|---|---|---|
| 1956 | Leonid Spirin, USSR | 1h. 31m. 27.4s |
| 1960 | Vladimir Golubnichy, USSR | 1h. 33m. 7.2s |
| 1964 | Kenneth Mathews, Great Britain | 1h. 29m. 34.0s |
| 1968 | Vladimir Golubnichy, USSR | 1h. 33m. 58.4s |
| 1972 | Peter Frenkel, E. Germany | 1h. 26m. 42.4s |
| 1976 | Daniel Bautista, Mexico | 1h. 24m. 40.6s |
| 1980 | Maurizio Damilano, Italy | 1h. 23m. 35.5s |
| 1984 | Ernesto Canto, Mexico | 1h. 23m. 13.0s |
| 1988 | Josef Pribilinec, Czechoslovakia | 1h. 19m. 57.0s* |
| 1992 | Daniel Plaza Montero, Spain | 1h. 21m. 45.0s |
| 1996 | Jefferson Perez, Ecuador | 1h. 20m. 7s |

### 50-Kilometer Walk

| | | |
|---|---|---|
| 1932 | Thomas W. Green, Great Britain | 4h. 50m. 10s |
| 1936 | Harold Whitlock, Great Britain | 4h. 30m. 41.4s |
| 1948 | John Ljunggren, Sweden | 4h. 41m. 52s |
| 1952 | Giuseppe Dordoni, Italy | 4h. 28m. 07.8s |
| 1956 | Norman Read, New Zealand | 4h. 30m. 42.8s |
| 1960 | Donald Thompson, Great Britain | 4h. 25m. 30s |
| 1964 | Abdon Pamich, Italy | 4h. 11m. 12.4s |
| 1968 | Christoph Hohne, E. Germany | 4h. 20m. 13.6s |
| 1972 | Bern Kannenberg, W. Germany | 3h. 56m. 11.6s |
| 1980 | Hartwig Gauter, E. Germany | 3h. 49m. 24.0s |
| 1984 | Raul Gonzalez, Mexico | 3h. 47m. 26.0s |
| 1988 | Vayachselav Ivanenko, USSR | 3h. 38m. 29.0s* |
| 1992 | Andrei Perlov, Unified Team | 3h. 50m. 13.0s |
| 1996 | Robert Korzeniowski, Poland | 3h. 43m. 30s |

### Marathon

| | | |
|---|---|---|
| 1896 | Spiridon Loues, Greece | 2h. 58m. 50s |
| 1900 | Michel Theato, France | 2h. 59m. 45s |
| 1904 | Thomas Hicks, United States | 3h. 28m. 63s |
| 1908 | John J. Hayes, United States | 2h. 55m. 18.4s |
| 1912 | Kenneth McArthur, South Africa | 2h. 36m. 54.8s |
| 1920 | Hannes Kolehmainen, Finland | 2h. 32m. 35.8s |
| 1924 | Albin Stenroos, Finland | 2h. 41m. 22.6s |
| 1928 | A.B. El Ouafi, France | 2h. 32m. 57s |
| 1932 | Juan Zabala, Argentina | 2h. 31m. 36s |
| 1936 | Kijung Son, Japan (Korean) | 2h. 29m. 19.2s |
| 1948 | Delfo Cabrera, Argentina | 2h. 34m. 51.6s |
| 1952 | Emil Zatopek, Czechoslovakia | 2h. 23m. 03.2s |
| 1956 | Alain Mimoun, France | 2h. 25m. |
| 1960 | Abebe Bikila, Ethiopia | 2h. 15m. 16.2s |
| 1964 | Abebe Bikila, Ethiopia | 2h. 12m. 11.2s |
| 1968 | Mamo Wolde, Ethiopia | 2h. 20m. 26.4s |
| 1972 | Frank Shorter, United States | 2h. 12m. 19.8s |
| 1976 | Waldemar Cierpinski, E. Germany | 2h. 09m. 55s |
| 1980 | Waldemar Cierpinski, E. Germany | 2h. 11m. 03s |
| 1984 | Carlos Lopes, Portugal | 2h. 09m. 21s* |
| 1988 | Gelindo Bordin, Italy | 2h. 10m. 32s |
| 1992 | Hwang Young-Cho, S. Korea | 2h. 13m. 23s |
| 1996 | Josia Thugwane, South Africa | 2h. 12m. 36s |

### High Jump

| | | |
|---|---|---|
| 1896 | Ellery Clark, United States | 5ft. 11 1-4 in. |
| 1900 | Irving Baxter, United States | 6ft. 2 4-5 in. |
| 1904 | Samuel Jones, United States | 5ft. 11 in. |
| 1908 | Harry Porter, United States | 6ft. 3 in. |

*(continued)*

| | | |
|---|---|---|
| 1912 | Alma Richards, United States | 6ft. 4 in. |
| 1920 | Richmond Landon, United States | 6ft. 4 in. |
| 1924 | Harold Osborn, United States | 6ft. 6 in. |
| 1928 | Robert W. King, United States | 6ft. 4 1-2 in. |
| 1932 | Duncan McNaughton, Canada | 6ft. 5 5-8 in. |
| 1936 | Cornelius Johnson, United States | 6ft. 8 in. |
| 1948 | John L. Winter, Australia | 6ft. 6 in. |
| 1952 | Walter Davis, United States | 6ft. 8.32 in. |
| 1956 | Charles Dumas, United States | 6ft. 11 1-2 in. |
| 1960 | Robert Shavlakadze, USSR | 7ft. 1 in. |
| 1964 | Valery Brumel, USSR | 7ft. 1 3-4 in. |
| 1968 | Dick Fosbury, United States | 7ft. 4 1-4 in. |
| 1972 | Yuri Tarmak, USSR | 7ft. 3 3-4 in. |
| 1976 | Jacek Wszola, Poland | 7ft. 4 1-2 in. |
| 1980 | Gerd Wessig, E. Germany | 7ft. 8 3-4 in. |
| 1984 | Dietmar Mogenburg, W. Germany | 7ft. 8 1-2 in. |
| 1988 | Guennadi Avdeenko, USSR | 7ft. 9 1-2 in. |
| 1992 | Javier Sotomayor, Cuba | 7ft. 8 in. |
| 1996 | Charles Austin, United States | 7ft. 10 in.* |

### Long Jump

| | | |
|---|---|---|
| 1896 | Ellery Clark, United States | 20ft. 10 in. |
| 1900 | Alvin Kraenzlein, United States | 23ft. 6 3-4 in. |
| 1904 | Myer Prinstein, United States | 24ft. 1 in. |
| 1908 | Frank Irons, United States | 24ft. 6 1-2 in. |
| 1912 | Albert Gutterson, United States | 24ft. 11 1-4 in. |
| 1920 | William Petterssen, Sweden | 23ft. 5 1-2 in. |
| 1924 | DeHart Hubbard, United States | 24ft. 5 in. |
| 1928 | Edward B. Hamm, United States | 25ft. 4 1-2 in. |
| 1932 | Edward Gordon, United States | 25ft. 3-4 in. |
| 1936 | Jesse Owens, United States | 26ft. 5 1-2 in. |
| 1948 | William Steele, United States | 25ft. 8 in. |
| 1952 | Jerome Biffle, United States | 24ft. 10 in. |
| 1956 | Gregory Bell, United States | 25ft. 8 1-4 in. |
| 1960 | Ralph Boston, United States | 26ft. 7 3-4 in. |
| 1964 | Lynn Davies, Great Britain | 26ft. 5 3-4 in. |
| 1968 | Bob Beamon, United States | 29ft. 2 1-2 in.* |
| 1972 | Randy Williams, United States | 27ft. 1-2 in. |
| 1976 | Arnie Robinson, United States | 27ft. 4 1-2 in. |
| 1980 | Lutz Dombrowski, E. Germany | 28ft. 1-4 in. |
| 1984 | Carl Lewis, United States | 28ft. 1-4 in. |
| 1988 | Carl Lewis, United States | 28ft. 7 1-4 in. |
| 1992 | Carl Lewis, United States | 28ft. 5 1-2 in. |
| 1996 | Carl Lewis, United States | 27ft. 10 3-4 in. |

### Triple Jump

| | | |
|---|---|---|
| 1896 | James Connolly, United States | 44ft. 11 3-4 in. |
| 1900 | Myer Prinstein, United States | 47ft. 5 3-4 in. |
| 1904 | Myer Prinstein, United States | 47 ft. |
| 1908 | Timothy Ahearne, Great Britain, Ireland | 48ft. 11 1-4 in. |
| 1912 | Gustaf Lindblom, Sweden | 48ft. 5 1-4 in. |
| 1920 | Vilho Tuulos, Finland | 47ft. 7 in. |
| 1924 | Anthony Winter, Australia | 50ft. 11 1-4 in. |
| 1928 | Mikio Oda, Japan | 49ft. 11 in. |
| 1932 | Chuhei Nambu, Japan | 51ft. 7 in. |
| 1936 | Naoto Tajima, Japan | 52ft. 6 in. |
| 1948 | Arne Ahman, Sweden | 50ft. 6 1-4 in. |
| 1952 | Adhemar da Silva, Brazil | 53ft. 2 3-4 in. |
| 1956 | Adhemar da Silva, Brazil | 53ft. 7 3-4 in. |
| 1960 | Jozef Schmidt, Poland | 55ft. 2 in. |
| 1964 | Jozef Schmidt, Poland | 55ft. 3 1-2 in. |
| 1968 | Viktor Saneev, USSR | 57ft. 3-4 in. |
| 1972 | Viktor Saneev, USSR | 56ft. 11 in. |
| 1976 | Viktor Saneev, USSR | 56ft. 8 3-4 in. |
| 1980 | Jaak Uudmae, USSR | 56ft. 11 1-4 in. |
| 1984 | Al Joyner, United States | 56ft. 7 1-2 in. |
| 1988 | Hristo Markov, Bulgaria | 57ft. 9 1-4 in. |
| 1992 | Mike Conley, United States | 57ft. 10 1-4 in. |
| 1996 | Kenny Harrison, United States | 59ft. 4 1-4 in.* |

### Discus Throw

| | | |
|---|---|---|
| 1896 | Robert Garrett, United States | 95ft. 7 1-2 in. |
| 1900 | Rudolf Bauer, Hungary | 118ft. 3 in. |
| 1904 | Martin Sheridan, United States | 128ft. 10 1-2 in. |
| 1908 | Martin Sheridan, United States | 134ft. 2 in. |
| 1912 | Armas Taipale, Finland | 148ft. 3 in. |
| | Both hands—Armas Taipale, Finland | 271ft. 10 1-4 in. |
| 1920 | Elmer Niklander, Finland | 146ft. 7 in. |
| 1924 | Clarence Houser, United States | 151ft. 4 in. |
| 1928 | Clarence Houser, United States | 155ft. 3 in. |
| 1932 | John Anderson, United States | 162ft. 4 in. |
| 1936 | Ken Carpenter, United States | 165ft. 7 in. |
| 1948 | Adolfo Consolini, Italy | 173ft. 2 in. |
| 1952 | Sim Iness, United States | 180ft. 6.85 in. |
| 1956 | Al Oerter, United States | 184ft. 10 1-2 in. |
| 1960 | Al Oerter, United States | 194ft. 2 in. |
| 1964 | Al Oerter, United States | 200ft. 1 1-2 in. |
| 1968 | Al Oerter, United States | 212ft. 6 1-2 in. |
| 1972 | Ludvik Danek, Czechoslovakia | 211ft. 3 in. |
| 1976 | Mac Wilkins, United States | 221ft. 5.4 in. |
| 1980 | Viktor Rashchupkin, USSR | 218ft. 8 in. |
| 1984 | Rolf Dannenberg, W. Germany | 218ft. 6 in. |
| 1988 | Jurgen Schult, E. Germany | 225ft. 9 1-4 in. |
| 1992 | Romas Ubartas, Lithuania | 213ft. 7 3-4 in. |
| 1996 | Lars Riedel, Germany | 227ft. 8 in.* |

### Hammer Throw

| | | |
|---|---|---|
| 1900 | John Flanagan, United States | 163ft. 1 in. |
| 1904 | John Flanagan, United States | 168ft. 1 in. |
| 1908 | John Flanagan, United States | 170ft. 4 1-4 in. |
| 1912 | Matt McGrath, United States | 179ft. 7 1-8 in. |
| 1920 | Pat Ryan, United States | 173ft. 5 5-8 in. |
| 1924 | Fred Tootell, United States | 174ft. 10 1-8 in. |
| 1928 | Patrick O'Callaghan, Ireland | 168ft. 7 1-2 in. |
| 1932 | Patrick O'Callaghan, Ireland | 176ft. 11 1-8 in. |
| 1936 | Karl Hein, Germany | 185ft. 4 in. |
| 1948 | Imre Nemeth, Hungary | 183ft. 11 1-2 in. |
| 1952 | Jozsef Csermak, Hungary | 197ft. 11 9-16 in. |
| 1956 | Harold Connolly, United States | 207ft. 3 1-2 in. |
| 1960 | Vasily Rudenkov, USSR | 220ft. 1 5-8 in. |
| 1964 | Romuald Klim, USSR | 228ft. 9 1-2 in. |
| 1968 | Gyula Zsivotsky, Hungary | 240ft. 8 in. |
| 1972 | Anatoli Bondarchuk, USSR | 247ft. 8 in. |
| 1976 | Yuri Syedykh, USSR | 254ft. 4 in. |
| 1980 | Yuri Syedykh, USSR | 268ft. 4 1-2 in. |
| 1984 | Juha Tiainen, Finland | 256ft. 2 in. |
| 1988 | Sergei Litinov, USSR | 278ft. 2 1-2 in.* |
| 1992 | Andrey Abduvaliyev, Unified Team | 270ft. 9 1-2 in. |
| 1996 | Balazs Kiss, Hungary | 266ft. 6 in. |

### Javelin Throw

| | | |
|---|---|---|
| 1908 | Erik Lemming, Sweden | 178ft. 7 1-2 in. |
| | Held in middle—Erik Lemming, Sweden | 179ft. 10 1-2 in. |
| 1912 | Erik Lemming, Sweden | 198ft. 11 1-4 in. |
| | Both hands, Julius Saaristo, Finland | 358ft. 11 7-8 in. |
| 1920 | Jonni Myyra, Finland | 215ft. 9 3-4 in. |
| 1924 | Jonni Myyra, Finland | 206ft. 6 3-4 in. |
| 1928 | Eric Lundkvist, Sweden | 218ft. 6 1-8 in. |
| 1932 | Matti Jarvinen, Finland | 238ft. 6 in. |
| 1936 | Gerhard Stoeck, Germany | 235ft. 8 5-16 in. |
| 1948 | Tapio Rautavaara, Finland | 228ft. 10 1-2 in. |
| 1952 | Cy Young, United States | 242ft. 0.79 in. |
| 1956 | Egil Danielson, Norway | 281ft. 2 1-4 in. |
| 1960 | Viktor Tsibulenko, USSR | 277ft. 8 3-8 in. |
| 1964 | Pauli Nevala, Finland | 271ft. 2 1-2 in. |
| 1968 | Janis Lusis, USSR | 295ft. 7 1-4 in. |
| 1972 | Klaus Wolfermann, W. Germany | 296ft. 10 in. |
| 1976 | Miklos Nemeth, Hungary | 310ft. 4 in. |
| 1980 | Dainis Kula, USSR | 299ft. 2 3-8 in. |
| 1984 | Arto Haerkoenen, Finland | 284ft. 8 in. |
| 1988 | Tapio Korjus, Finland | 276ft. 6 in. |
| 1992 | Jan Zelezny, Czechoslovakia | 294ft. 2 in.*(a) |
| 1996 | Jan Zelezny, Czech Republic | 289ft. 3 in. |

(a) New records were kept after javelin was modified in 1986.

### Pole Vault

| | | |
|---|---|---|
| 1896 | William Hoyt, United States | 10ft. 10 in. |
| 1900 | Irving Baxter, United States | 10ft. 10 in. |
| 1904 | Charles Dvorak, United States | 11ft. 5 3-4 in. |
| 1908 | A. C. Gilbert, United States<br>Edward Cook Jr., United States | 12ft. 2 in. |
| 1912 | Harry Babcock, United States | 12ft. 11 1-2 in. |
| 1920 | Frank Foss, United States | 13ft. 5 in. |
| 1924 | Lee Barnes, United States | 12ft. 11 1-2 in. |
| 1928 | Sabin W. Carr, United States | 13ft. 9 1-4 in. |
| 1932 | William Miller, United States | 14ft. 1 3-4 in. |
| 1936 | Earle Meadows, United States | 14ft. 3 1-4 in. |
| 1948 | Guinn Smith, United States | 14ft. 1 1-4 in. |
| 1952 | Robert Richards, United States | 14ft. 11 in. |
| 1956 | Robert Richards, United States | 14ft. 11 1-2 in. |
| 1960 | Don Bragg, United States | 15ft. 5 in. |
| 1964 | Fred Hansen, United States | 16ft. 8 3-4 in. |
| 1968 | Bob Seagren, United States | 17ft. 8 1-2 in. |
| 1972 | Wolfgang Nordwig, E. Germany | 18ft. 1-2 in. |
| 1976 | Tadeusz Slusarski, Poland | 18ft. 1-2 in. |
| 1980 | Wladyslaw Kozakiewicz, Poland | 18ft. 11 1-2 in. |
| 1984 | Pierre Quinon, France | 18ft. 10 1-4 in. |
| 1988 | Sergei Bubka, USSR | 19ft. 4 1-4 in. |
| 1992 | Maksim Tarassov, Unified Team | 19ft. 1-4 in. |
| 1996 | Jean Galfione, France | 19ft. 5 in.* |

### 16-lb. Shot Put

| | | |
|---|---|---|
| 1896 | Robert Garrett, United States | 36ft. 9 3-4 in. |
| 1900 | Richard Sheldon, United States | 46ft. 3 1-4 in. |
| 1904 | Ralph Rose, United States | 48ft. 7 in. |
| 1908 | Ralph Rose, United States | 46ft. 7 1-2 in. |
| 1912 | Pat McDonald, United States | 50ft. 4 in. |
| | Both hands—Ralph Rose, United States | 90ft. 5 1-2 in. |
| 1920 | Ville Porhola, Finland | 48ft. 7 1-4 in. |
| 1924 | Clarence Houser, United States | 49ft. 2 1-4 in. |
| 1928 | John Kuck, United States | 52ft. 3-4 in. |
| 1932 | Leo Sexton, United States | 52ft. 6 in. |
| 1936 | Hans Woellke, Germany | 53ft. 1 3-4 in. |
| 1948 | Wilbur Thompson, United States | 56ft. 2 in. |
| 1952 | Parry O'Brien, United States | 57ft. 1-2 in. |
| 1956 | Parry O'Brien, United States | 60ft. 11 1-4 in. |
| 1960 | William Nieder, United States | 64ft. 6 3-4 in. |
| 1964 | Dallas Long, United States | 66ft. 8 1-2 in. |
| 1968 | Randy Matson, United States | 67ft. 4 3-4 in. |
| 1972 | Wladyslaw Komar, Poland | 69ft. 6 in. |
| 1976 | Udo Beyer, E. Germany | 69ft. 3-4 in. |
| 1980 | Vladimir Kiselyov, USSR | 70ft. 1-2 in. |
| 1984 | Alessandro Andrei, Italy | 69ft. 9 in. |
| 1988 | Ulf Timmermann, E. Germany | 73ft. 8 3-4 in.* |
| 1992 | Michael Stulce, United States | 71ft. 2 1-4 in. |
| 1996 | Randy Barnes, United States | 70ft. 11 1-4 in. |

### Decathlon

| | | |
|---|---|---|
| 1912 | Hugo Wieslander, Sweden | 7,724.49 pts.(a) |
| 1920 | Helge Lovland, Norway | 6,804.35 pts. |
| 1924 | Harold Osborn, United States | 7,710.77 pts. |
| 1928 | Paavo Yrjola, Finland | 8,053.29 pts. |
| 1932 | James Bausch, United States | 8,462.23 pts. |
| 1936 | Glenn Morris, United States | 7,900 pts. |
| 1948 | Robert Mathias, United States | 7,139 pts. |
| 1952 | Robert Mathias, United States | 7,887 pts. |
| 1956 | Milton Campbell, United States | 7,937 pts. |
| 1960 | Rafer Johnson, United States | 8,392 pts. |
| 1964 | Willi Holdorf, Germany | 7,887 pts.(b) |
| 1968 | Bill Toomey, United States | 8,193 pts. |
| 1972 | Nikolai Avilov, USSR | 8,454 pts. |
| 1976 | Bruce Jenner, United States | 8,617 pts. |
| 1980 | Daley Thompson, Great Britain | 8,495 pts. |
| 1984 | Daley Thompson, Great Britain | 8,798 pts.*(c) |
| 1988 | Christian Schenk, E. Germany | 8,488 pts. |
| 1992 | Robert Zmelik, Czechoslovakia | 8,611 pts. |
| 1996 | Dan O'Brien, United States | 8,824 pts. |

(a) Jim Thorpe of the U.S. won the 1912 Decathlon with 8,413 pts. but was disqualified and had to return his medals because he had played professional baseball prior to the Olympic games. The medals were restored posthumously in 1982. (b) Former point systems used prior to 1964. (c) Scoring change effective Apr. 1985; Thompson's readjusted score is 8,847 pts.

## Track and Field—Women

### 100-Meter Run

| | | |
|---|---|---|
| 1928 | Elizabeth Robinson, United States | 12.2s |
| 1932 | Stella Walsh, Poland (a) | 11.9s |
| 1936 | Helen Stephens, United States | 11.5s |
| 1948 | Francina Blankers-Koen, Netherlands | 11.9s |
| 1952 | Marjorie Jackson, Australia | 11.5s |
| 1956 | Betty Cuthbert, Australia | 11.5s |
| 1960 | Wilma Rudolph, United States | 11.0s |
| 1964 | Wyomia Tyus, United States | 11.4s |
| 1968 | Wyomia Tyus, United States | 11.0s |
| 1972 | Renate Stecher, E. Germany | 11.07s |
| 1976 | Annegret Richter, W. Germany | 11.08s |
| 1980 | Lyudmila Kondratyeva, USSR | 11.6s |
| 1984 | Evelyn Ashford, United States | 10.97s |
| 1988 | Florence Griffith-Joyner, United States | 10.54s* |
| 1992 | Gail Devers, United States | 10.82s |
| 1996 | Gail Devers, United States | 10.94s |

(a) A 1980 autopsy determined that Walsh was a man.

### 200-Meter Run

| | | |
|---|---|---|
| 1948 | Francina Blankers-Koen, Netherlands | 24.4s |
| 1952 | Marjorie Jackson, Australia | 23.7s |
| 1956 | Betty Cuthbert, Australia | 23.4s |
| 1960 | Wilma Rudolph, United States | 24.0s |
| 1964 | Edith McGuire, United States | 23.0s |
| 1968 | Irena Szewinska, Poland | 22.5s |
| 1972 | Renate Stecher, E. Germany | 22.40s |
| 1976 | Barbel Eckert, E. Germany | 22.37s |
| 1980 | Barbel Wockel, E. Germany | 22.03s |
| 1984 | Valerie Brisco-Hooks, United States | 21.81s |
| 1988 | Florence Griffith-Joyner, United States | 21.34s* |
| 1992 | Gwen Torrence, United States | 21.81s |
| 1996 | Marie-Jose Perec, France | 22.12s |

### 400-Meter Run

| | | |
|---|---|---|
| 1964 | Betty Cuthbert, Australia | 52s |
| 1968 | Colette Besson, France | 52s |
| 1972 | Monika Zehrt, E. Germany | 51.08s |
| 1976 | Irena Szewinska, Poland | 49.29s |
| 1980 | Marita Koch, E. Germany | 48.88s |
| 1984 | Valerie Brisco-Hooks, United States | 48.83s |
| 1988 | Olga Bryzgina, USSR | 48.65s |
| 1992 | Marie-Jose Perec, France | 48.83s |
| 1996 | Marie-Jose Perec, France | 48.25s* |

### 800-Meter Run

| | | |
|---|---|---|
| 1928 | Lina Radke, Germany | 2m. 16.8s |
| 1960 | Ludmila Shevtsova, USSR | 2m. 4.3s |
| 1964 | Ann Packer, Great Britain | 2m. 1.1s |
| 1968 | Madeline Manning, United States | 2m. 0.9s |
| 1972 | Hildegard Falck, W. Germany | 1m. 58.6s |
| 1976 | Tatyana Kazankina, USSR | 1m. 54.94s |
| 1980 | Nadezhda Olizayrenko, USSR | 1m. 53.5s* |
| 1984 | Doina Melinte, Romania | 1m. 57.6s |
| 1988 | Sigrun Wodars, E. Germany | 1m. 56.10s |
| 1992 | Ellen Van Langen, Netherlands | 1m. 55.54s |
| 1996 | Svetlana Masterkova, Russia | 1m. 57.73s |

### 1,500-Meter Run

| | | |
|---|---|---|
| 1972 | Lyudmila Bragina, USSR | 4m. 01.4s |
| 1976 | Tatyana Kazankina, USSR | 4m. 05.48s |
| 1980 | Tatyana Kazankina, USSR | 3m. 56.6s |
| 1984 | Gabriella Dorio, Italy | 4m. 03.25s |
| 1988 | Paula Ivan, Romania | 3m. 53.96s* |
| 1992 | Hassiba Boulmerka, Algeria | 3m. 55.30s |
| 1996 | Svetlana Masterkova, Russia | 4m. 00.83s |

### 3,000-Meter Run

| | | |
|---|---|---|
| 1984 | Maricica Puica, Romania | 8m. 35.96s |
| 1988 | Tatyana Samolenko, USSR | 8m. 26.53s* |
| 1992 | Elena Romanova, Unified Team | 8m. 46.04s |

### 5,000-Meter Run

| | | |
|---|---|---|
| 1996 | Wang Junxia, China | 14m. 59.88s* |

### 10,000-Meter Run

| | | |
|---|---|---|
| 1988 | Olga Boldarenko, USSR | 31m. 44.69s |
| 1992 | Derartu Tulu, Ethiopia | 31m. 06.02s |
| 1996 | Fernanda Ribeiro, Portugal | 31m. 01.63s* |

### 100-Meter Hurdles

| | | |
|---|---|---|
| 1972 | Annelie Ehrhardt, E. Germany | 12.59s |
| 1976 | Johanna Schaller, E. Germany | 12.77s |
| 1980 | Vera Komisova, USSR | 12.56s |
| 1984 | Benita Brown-Fitzgerald, United States | 12.84s |
| 1988 | Jordanka Donkova, Bulgaria | 12.38s* |
| 1992 | Paraskevi Patoulidou, Greece | 12.64s |
| 1996 | Ludmila Enquist, Sweden | 12.58s |

### 400-Meter Hurdles

| | | |
|---|---|---|
| 1984 | Nawal el Moutawakil, Morocco | 54.61s |
| 1988 | Debra Flintoff-King, Australia | 53.17s |
| 1992 | Sally Gunnell, Great Britain | 53.23s |
| 1996 | Deon Hemmings, Jamaica | 52.82s* |

### 400-Meter Relay

| | | |
|---|---|---|
| 1928 | Canada | 48.4s |
| 1932 | United States | 46.9s |
| 1936 | United States | 46.9s |
| 1948 | Netherlands | 47.5s |
| 1952 | United States | 45.9s |
| 1956 | Australia | 44.5s |
| 1960 | United States | 44.5s |
| 1964 | Poland | 43.6s |
| 1968 | United States | 42.8s |

*(continued)*

| | | |
|---|---|---|
| 1972 | West Germany | 42.81s |
| 1976 | East Germany | 42.55s |
| 1980 | East Germany | 41.60s* |
| 1984 | United States | 41.65s |
| 1988 | United States | 41.98s |
| 1992 | United States | 42.11s |
| 1996 | United States | 41.95s |

### 1,600-Meter Relay

| | | |
|---|---|---|
| 1972 | East Germany | 3m. 23s |
| 1976 | East Germany | 3m. 19.23s |
| 1980 | USSR | 3m. 20.02s |
| 1984 | United States | 3m. 18.29s |
| 1988 | USSR | 3 m. 15.18s* |
| 1992 | Unified Team | 3m. 20.20s |
| 1996 | United States | 3m. 20.91s |

### Marathon

| | | |
|---|---|---|
| 1984 | Joan Benoit, United States | 2h. 24m. 52s* |
| 1988 | Rosa Mota, Portugal | 2h. 25m. 40s |
| 1992 | Valentina Yegorova, Unified Team | 2h. 32m. 41s |
| 1996 | Fatuma Roba, Ethiopia | 2h. 26m. 05s |

### High Jump

| | | |
|---|---|---|
| 1928 | Ethel Catherwood, Canada | 5ft. 2 1-2 in. |
| 1932 | Jean Shiley, United States | 5ft. 5 1-4 in. |
| 1936 | Ibolya Csak, Hungary | 5ft. 3 in. |
| 1948 | Alice Coachman, United States | 5ft. 6 1-8 in. |
| 1952 | Esther Brand, South Africa | 5ft. 5 3-4 in. |
| 1956 | Mildred L. McDaniel, United States | 5ft. 9 1-4 in. |
| 1960 | Iolanda Balas, Romania | 6ft. 3-4 in. |
| 1964 | Iolanda Balas, Romania | 6ft. 2 3-4 in. |
| 1968 | Miloslava Reskova, Czechoslovakia | 5ft. 11 1-2 in. |
| 1972 | Ulrike Meyfarth, W. Germany | 6ft. 4 in. |
| 1976 | Rosemarie Ackermann, E. Germany | 6ft. 3 3-4 in. |
| 1980 | Sara Simeoni, Italy | 6ft. 5 1-2 in. |
| 1984 | Ulrike Meyfarth, W. Germany | 6ft. 7 1-2 in. |
| 1988 | Louise Ritter, United States | 6ft. 8 in. |
| 1992 | Heike Henkel, Germany | 6ft. 7 1-2 in. |
| 1996 | Stefka Kostadinova, Bulgaria | 6ft. 8 3-4 in.* |

### Long Jump

| | | |
|---|---|---|
| 1948 | Olga Gyarmati, Hungary | 18ft. 8 1-4 in. |
| 1952 | Yvette Williams, New Zealand | 20ft. 5 3-4 in. |
| 1956 | Elzbieta Krzeskinska, Poland | 20ft. 9 3-4 in. |
| 1960 | Vyera Krepkina, USSR | 20ft. 10 3-4 in. |
| 1964 | Mary Rand, Great Britain | 22ft. 2 1-4 in. |
| 1968 | Viorica Viscopoleanu, Romania | 22ft. 4 1-2 in. |
| 1972 | Heidemarie Rosendahl, W. Germany | 22ft. 3 in. |
| 1976 | Angela Voigt, E. Germany | 22ft. 3-4 in. |
| 1980 | Tatyana Kolpakova, USSR | 23ft. 2 in. |
| 1984 | Anisoara Stanciu, Romania | 22ft. 10 in. |
| 1988 | Jackie Joyner-Kersee, United States | 24ft. 3 1-2 in. |
| 1992 | Heike Drechsler, Germany | 23ft. 5 1-4 in.* |
| 1996 | Chioma Ajunwa, Nigeria | 23ft. 4 1-2 in. |

### Triple Jump

| | | |
|---|---|---|
| 1996 | Inessa Kravets, Ukraine | 50ft. 3 1-2 in.* |

### Discus Throw

| | | |
|---|---|---|
| 1928 | Helena Konopacka, Poland | 129ft. 11 3-4 in. |
| 1932 | Lillian Copeland, United States | 133ft. 2 in. |
| 1936 | Gisela Mauermayer, Germany | 156ft. 3 in. |
| 1948 | Micheline Ostermeyer, France | 137ft. 6 1-2 in. |
| 1952 | Nina Romaschkova, USSR | 168ft. 8 in. |
| 1956 | Olga Fikotova, Czechoslovakia | 176ft. 1 in. |
| 1960 | Nina Ponomareva, USSR | 180ft. 8 1-4 in. |
| 1964 | Tamara Press, USSR | 187ft. 10 in. |
| 1968 | Lia Manoliu, Romania | 191ft. 2 in. |
| 1972 | Faina Melnik, USSR | 218ft. 7 in. |
| 1976 | Evelin Schlaak, E. Germany | 226ft. 4 in. |
| 1980 | Evelin Jahl, E. Germany | 229ft. 6 in. |
| 1984 | Ria Stalman, Netherlands | 214ft. 5 in. |
| 1988 | Martina Hellmann, E. Germany | 237ft. 2 1-4 in.* |
| 1992 | Maritza Marten Garcia, Cuba | 222ft. 10 in. |
| 1996 | Ilke Wyludda, Germany | 228ft. 6 in. |

### Javelin Throw

| | | |
|---|---|---|
| 1932 | "Babe" Didrikson, United States | 143ft. 4 in. |
| 1936 | Tilly Fleischer, Germany | 148ft. 2 3-4 in. |
| 1948 | Herma Bauma, Austria | 149ft. 6 in. |
| 1952 | Dana Zatopkova, Czechoslovakia | 165ft. 7 in. |
| 1956 | Inese Jaunzeme, USSR | 176ft. 8 in. |
| 1960 | Elvira Ozolina, USSR | 183ft. 8 in. |
| 1964 | Mihaela Penes, Romania | 198ft. 7 1-2 in. |
| 1968 | Angela Nemeth, Hungary | 198ft. 1-2 in. |
| 1972 | Ruth Fuchs, E. Germany | 209ft. 7 in. |
| 1976 | Ruth Fuchs, E. Germany | 216ft. 4 in. |
| 1980 | Maria Colon, Cuba | 224ft. 5 in. |
| 1984 | Tessa Sanderson, Great Britain | 228ft. 2 in. |
| 1988 | Petra Felke, E. Germany | 245 ft.* |
| 1992 | Silke Renke, Germany | 224ft. 2 1-2 in. |
| 1996 | Heli Rantanen, Finland | 222ft. 11 in. |

### Shot Put (8 lb., 13 oz.)

| | | |
|---|---|---|
| 1948 | Micheline Ostermeyer, France | 45ft. 1 1-2 in. |
| 1952 | Galina Zybina, USSR | 50ft. 1 3-4 in. |
| 1956 | Tamara Tishkyevich, USSR | 54ft. 5 in. |
| 1960 | Tamara Press, USSR | 56ft. 10 in. |
| 1964 | Tamara Press, USSR | 59ft. 6 1-4 in. |
| 1968 | Margitta Gummel, E. Germany | 64ft. 4 in. |
| 1972 | Nadezhda Chizova, USSR | 69ft. |
| 1976 | Ivanka Hristova, Bulgaria | 69ft. 5 1-4 in. |
| 1980 | Ilona Slupianek, E. Germany | 73ft. 6 1-4 in.* |
| 1984 | Claudia Losch, W. Germany | 67ft. 2 1-4 in. |
| 1988 | Natalya Lisovskaya, USSR | 72ft. 11 1-2 in. |
| 1992 | Svetlana Kriveleva, Unified Team | 69ft. 1 1-2in. |
| 1996 | Astrid Kumbernuss, Germany | 67ft. 5 1-2in. |

### Heptathlon

| | | |
|---|---|---|
| 1984 | Glynis Nunn, Australia | 6,390 pts. |
| 1988 | Jackie Joyner-Kersee, United States | 7,215 pts.* |
| 1992 | Jackie Joyner-Kersee, United States | 7,044 pts. |
| 1996 | Ghada Shouaa, Syria | 6,780 pts. |

## Swimming and Diving—Men

### 50-Meter Freestyle

| | | |
|---|---|---|
| 1988 | Matt Biondi, U.S. | 22.14 |
| 1992 | Aleksandr Popov, Unified Team | 21.91* |
| 1996 | Aleksandr Popov, Russia | 22.13 |

### 100-Meter Freestyle

| | | |
|---|---|---|
| 1896 | Alfred Hajos, Hungary | 1:22.2 |
| 1904 | Zoltan de Halmay, Hungary (100 yards) | 1:02.8 |
| 1908 | Charles Daniels, U.S. | 1:05.6 |
| 1912 | Duke P. Kahanamoku, U.S. | 1:03.4 |
| 1920 | Duke P. Kahanamoku, U.S. | 1:01.4 |
| 1924 | John Weissmuller, U.S. | 59.0 |
| 1928 | John Weissmuller, U.S. | 58.6 |
| 1932 | Yasuji Miyazaki, Japan | 58.2 |
| 1936 | Ferenc Csik, Hungary | 57.6 |
| 1948 | Wally Ris, U.S. | 57.3 |
| 1952 | Clark Scholes, U.S. | 57.4 |
| 1956 | Jon Henricks, Australia | 55.4 |
| 1960 | John Devitt, Australia | 55.2 |
| 1964 | Don Schollander, U.S. | 53.4 |
| 1968 | Mike Wenden, Australia | 52.2 |
| 1972 | Mark Spitz, U.S. | 51.22 |
| 1976 | Jim Montgomery, U.S. | 49.99 |
| 1980 | Jorg Woithe, E. Germany | 50.40 |
| 1984 | Rowdy Gaines, U.S. | 49.80 |
| 1988 | Matt Biondi, U.S. | 48.63* |
| 1992 | Aleksandr Popov, Unified Team | 49.02 |
| 1996 | Aleksandr Popov, Russia | 48.74 |

### 200-Meter Freestyle

| | | |
|---|---|---|
| 1968 | Mike Wenden, Australia | 1:55.2 |
| 1972 | Mark Spitz, U.S. | 1:52.78 |
| 1976 | Bruce Furniss, U.S. | 1:50.29 |
| 1980 | Sergei Kopliakov, USSR | 1:49.81 |
| 1984 | Michael Gross, W. Germany | 1:47.44 |
| 1988 | Duncan Armstrong, Australia | 1:47.25 |
| 1992 | Yevgeny Sadovyi, Unified Team | 1:46.70* |
| 1996 | Danyon Loader, Australia | 1:47.63 |

### 400-Meter Freestyle

| | | |
|---|---|---|
| 1904 | C. M. Daniels, U.S. (440 yards) | 6:16.2 |
| 1908 | Henry Taylor, Great Britain | 5:36.8 |
| 1912 | George Hodgson, Canada | 5:24.4 |
| 1920 | Norman Ross, U.S. | 5:26.8 |
| 1924 | John Weissmuller, U.S. | 5:04.2 |
| 1928 | Albert Zorilla, Argentina | 5:01.6 |
| 1932 | Clarence Crabbe, U.S. | 4:48.4 |
| 1936 | Jack Medica, U.S. | 4:44.5 |
| 1948 | William Smith, U.S. | 4:41.0 |
| 1952 | Jean Boiteux, France | 4:30.7 |
| 1956 | Murray Rose, Australia | 4:27.3 |
| 1960 | Murray Rose, Australia | 4:18.3 |
| 1964 | Don Schollander, U.S. | 4:12.2 |
| 1968 | Mike Burton, U.S. | 4:09.0 |
| 1972 | Brad Cooper, Australia | 4:00.27 |
| 1976 | Brian Goodell, U.S. | 3:51.93 |
| 1980 | Vladimir Salnikov, USSR | 3:51.31 |
| 1984 | George DiCarlo, U.S | 3:51.23 |
| 1988 | Ewe Dassler, E. Germany | 3:46.95 |
| 1992 | Yevgeny Sadovyi, Unified Team | 3:45.00* |
| 1996 | Danyon Loader, Australia | 3:47.97 |

### 1,500-Meter Freestyle

| | | |
|---|---|---|
| 1908 | Henry Taylor, Great Britain | 22:48.4 |
| 1912 | George Hodgson, Canada | 22:00.0 |
| 1920 | Norman Ross, U.S. | 22:23.2 |
| 1924 | Andrew Charlton, Australia | 20:06.6 |
| 1928 | Arne Borg, Sweden | 19:51.8 |
| 1932 | Kusuo Kitamura, Japan | 19:12.4 |
| 1936 | Noboru Terada, Japan | 19:13.7 |
| 1948 | James McLane, U.S. | 19:18.5 |
| 1952 | Ford Konno, U.S. | 18:30.3 |
| 1956 | Murray Rose, Australia | 17:58.9 |
| 1960 | Jon Konrads, Australia | 17:19.6 |
| 1964 | Robert Windle, Australia | 17:01.7 |
| 1968 | Mike Burton, U.S. | 16:38.9 |
| 1972 | Mike Burton, U.S. | 15:52.58 |
| 1976 | Brian Goodell, U.S. | 15:02.40 |
| 1980 | Vladimir Salnikov, USSR | 14:58.27 |
| 1984 | Michael O'Brien, U.S. | 15:05.20 |
| 1988 | Vladimir Salnikov, USSR | 15:00.40 |
| 1992 | Kieren Perkins, Australia | 14:43.48* |
| 1996 | Kieren Perkins, Australia | 14:56.40 |

### 100-Meter Backstroke

| | | |
|---|---|---|
| 1904 | Walter Brack, Germany (100 yds.) | 1:16.8 |
| 1908 | Arno Bieberstein, Germany | 1:24.6 |
| 1912 | Harry Hebner, U.S. | 1:21.2 |
| 1920 | Warren Kealoha, U.S. | 1:15.2 |
| 1924 | Warren Kealoha, U.S. | 1:13.2 |
| 1928 | George Kojac, U.S. | 1:08.2 |
| 1932 | Masaji Kiyokawa, Japan | 1:08.6 |
| 1936 | Adolph Kiefer, U.S. | 1:05.9 |
| 1948 | Allen Stack, U.S. | 1:06.4 |
| 1952 | Yoshi Oyakawa, U.S. | 1:05.4 |
| 1956 | David Thiele, Australia | 1:02.2 |
| 1960 | David Thiele, Australia | 1:01.9 |
| 1968 | Roland Matthes, E. Germany | 58.7 |
| 1972 | Roland Matthes, E. Germany | 56.58 |
| 1976 | John Naber, U.S. | 55.49 |
| 1980 | Bengt Baron, Sweden | 56.33 |
| 1984 | Rick Carey, U.S. | 55.79 |
| 1988 | Daichi Suzuki, Japan | 55.05 |
| 1992 | Mark Tewksbury, Canada | 53.98* |
| 1996 | Jeff Rouse, U.S. | 54.10 |

### 200-Meter Backstroke

| | | |
|---|---|---|
| 1964 | Jed Graef, U.S. | 2:10.3 |
| 1968 | Roland Matthes, E. Germany | 2:09.6 |
| 1972 | Roland Matthes, E. Germany | 2:02.82 |
| 1976 | John Naber, U.S. | 1:59.19 |
| 1980 | Sandor Wladar, Hungary | 2:01.93 |
| 1984 | Rick Carey, U.S. | 2:00.23 |
| 1988 | Igor Polianski, USSR | 1:59.37 |
| 1992 | Martin Lopez-Zubero, Spain | 1:58.47* |
| 1996 | Brad Bridgewater, U.S. | 1:58.54 |

### 100-Meter Breaststroke

| | | |
|---|---|---|
| 1968 | Don McKenzie, U.S. | 1:07.7 |
| 1972 | Nobutaka Taguchi, Japan | 1:04.94 |
| 1976 | John Hencken, U.S. | 1:03.11 |
| 1980 | Duncan Goodhew, Great Britain | 1:03.44 |
| 1984 | Steve Lundquist, U.S. | 1:01.65 |
| 1988 | Adrian Moorhouse, Great Britain | 1:02.04 |
| 1992 | Nelson Diebel, U.S. | 1:01.50 |
| 1996 | Fred Deburghgraeve, Belgium | 1:00.60* |

### 200-Meter Breaststroke

| | | |
|---|---|---|
| 1908 | Frederick Holman, Great Britain | 3:09.2 |
| 1912 | Walter Bathe, Germany | 3:01.8 |
| 1920 | Haken Malmroth, Sweden | 3:04.4 |
| 1924 | Robert Skelton, U.S. | 2:56.6 |
| 1928 | Yoshiyuki Tsuruta, Japan | 2:48.8 |
| 1932 | Yoshiyuki Tsuruta, Japan | 2:45.4 |
| 1936 | Tetsuo Hamuro, Japan | 2:41.5 |
| 1948 | Joseph Verdeur, U.S. | 2:39.3 |
| 1952 | John Davies, Australia | 2:34.4 |
| 1956 | Masura Furukawa, Japan | 2:34.7 |
| 1960 | William Mulliken, U.S. | 2:37.4 |
| 1964 | Ian O'Brien, Australia | 2:27.8 |
| 1968 | Felipe Munoz, Mexico | 2:28.7 |
| 1972 | John Hencken, U.S. | 2:21.55 |
| 1976 | David Wilkie, Great Britain | 2:15.11 |
| 1980 | Robertas Zhulpa, USSR | 2:15.85 |
| 1984 | Victor Davis, Canada | 2:13.34 |
| 1988 | Jozsef Szabo, Hungary | 2:13.52 |
| 1992 | Mike Barrowman, U.S. | 2:10.16* |
| 1996 | Norbert Rozsa, Hungary | 2:12.57 |

### 100-Meter Butterfly

| | | |
|---|---|---|
| 1968 | Doug Russell, U.S. | 55.9 |
| 1972 | Mark Spitz, U.S. | 54.27 |
| 1976 | Matt Vogel, U.S. | 54.35 |
| 1980 | Par Arvidsson, Sweden | 54.92 |
| 1984 | Michael Gross, W. Germany | 53.08 |
| 1988 | Anthony Nesty, Suriname | 53.00 |
| 1992 | Pablo Morales, U.S. | 53.32 |
| 1996 | Denis Pankratov, Russia | 52.27* |

### 200-Meter Butterfly

| | | |
|---|---|---|
| 1956 | William Yorzyk, U.S. | 2:19.3 |
| 1960 | Michael Troy, U.S. | 2:12.8 |
| 1964 | Kevin J. Berry, Australia | 2:06.6 |
| 1968 | Carl Robie, U.S. | 2:08.7 |
| 1972 | Mark Spitz, U.S. | 2:00.70 |
| 1976 | Mike Bruner, U.S. | 1:59.23 |
| 1980 | Sergei Fesenko, USSR | 1:59.76 |
| 1984 | Jon Sieben, Australia | 1:57.04 |
| 1988 | Michael Gross, W. Germany | 1:56.94 |
| 1992 | Mel Stewart, U.S. | 1:56.26* |
| 1996 | Denis Pankratov, Russia | 1:56.51 |

### 200-Meter Individual Medley

| | | |
|---|---|---|
| 1968 | Charles Hickcox, U.S. | 2:12.0 |
| 1972 | Gunnar Larsson, Sweden | 2:07.17 |
| 1984 | Alex Baumann, Canada | 2:01.42 |
| 1988 | Tamas Darnyi, Hungary | 2:00.17 |
| 1992 | Tamas Darnyi, Hungary | 2:00.76 |
| 1996 | Attila Czene, Hungary | 1:59.91* |

### 400-Meter Individual Medley

| | | |
|---|---|---|
| 1964 | Dick Roth, U.S. | 4:45.4 |
| 1968 | Charles Hickcox, U.S. | 4:48.4 |
| 1972 | Gunnar Larsson, Sweden | 4:31.98 |
| 1976 | Rod Strachan, U.S. | 4:23.68 |
| 1980 | Aleksandr Sidorenko, USSR | 4:22.89 |
| 1984 | Alex Baumann, Canada | 4:17.41 |
| 1988 | Tamas Darnyi, Hungary | 4:14.75 |
| 1992 | Tamas Darnyi, Hungary | 4:14.23* |
| 1996 | Tom Dolan, U.S. | 4:14.90 |

### 400-Meter Freestyle Relay

| | | |
|---|---|---|
| 1964 | United States | 3:31.2 |
| 1968 | United States | 3:31.7 |
| 1972 | United States | 3:26.42 |
| 1984 | United States | 3:19.03 |
| 1988 | United States | 3:16.53 |
| 1992 | United States | 3:16.74 |
| 1996 | United States | 3:15.41* |

### 800-Meter Freestyle Relay

| | | |
|---|---|---|
| 1908 | Great Britain | 10:55.6 |
| 1912 | Australia | 10:11.6 |
| 1920 | United States | 10:04.4 |
| 1924 | United States | 9:53.4 |
| 1928 | United States | 9:36.2 |
| 1932 | Japan | 8:58.4 |
| 1936 | Japan | 8:51.5 |
| 1948 | United States | 8:46.0 |
| 1952 | United States | 8:31.1 |
| 1956 | Australia | 8:23.6 |
| 1960 | United States | 8:10.2 |
| 1964 | United States | 7:52.1 |
| 1968 | United States | 7:52.33 |
| 1972 | United States | 7:35.78 |
| 1976 | United States | 7:23.22 |
| 1980 | USSR | 7:23.50 |
| 1984 | United States | 7:15.69 |
| 1988 | United States | 7:12.51 |
| 1992 | Unified Team | 7:11.95* |
| 1996 | United States | 7:14.84 |

### 400-Meter Medley Relay

| | | |
|---|---|---|
| 1960 | United States | 4:05.4 |
| 1964 | United States | 3:58.4 |
| 1968 | United States | 3:54.9 |
| 1972 | United States | 3:48.16 |
| 1976 | United States | 3:42.22 |
| 1980 | Australia | 3:45.70 |
| 1984 | United States | 3:39.30 |
| 1988 | United States | 3:36.93 |
| 1992 | United States | 3:36.93 |
| 1996 | United States | 3:34.84* |

### Springboard Diving

| | Springboard Diving | Points |
|---|---|---|
| 1908 | Albert Zurner, Germany | 85.5 |
| 1912 | Paul Guenther, Germany | 79.23 |
| 1920 | Louis Kuehn, U.S | 675.40 |
| 1924 | Albert White, U.S. | 97.46 |
| 1928 | Pete Desjardins, U.S. | 185.04 |
| 1932 | Michael Galitzen, U.S. | 161.38 |
| 1936 | Richard Degener, U.S. | 163.57 |
| 1948 | Bruce Harlan, U.S. | 163.64 |
| 1952 | David Browning, U.S. | 205.29 |
| 1956 | Robert Clotworthy, U.S. | 159.56 |
| 1960 | Gary Tobian, U.S. | 170.00 |
| 1964 | Kenneth Sitzberger, U.S. | 159.90 |
| 1968 | Bernie Wrightson, U.S. | 170.15 |
| 1972 | Vladimir Vasin, USSR | 594.09 |
| 1976 | Phil Boggs, U.S. | 619.52 |
| 1980 | Aleksandr Portnov, USSR | 905.02 |
| 1984 | Greg Louganis, U.S. | 754.41 |
| 1988 | Greg Louganis, U.S. | 730.80 |
| 1992 | Mark Lenzi, U.S. | 676.53 |
| 1996 | Xiong Ni, China | 701.46 |

### Platform Diving

| | Platform Diving | Points |
|---|---|---|
| 1904 | Dr. G.E. Sheldon, U.S. | 12.75 |
| 1908 | Hjalmar Johansson, Sweden | 83.75 |
| 1912 | Erik Adlerz, Sweden | 73.94 |
| 1920 | Clarence Pinkston, U.S. | 100.67 |
| 1924 | Albert White, U.S. | 97.46 |
| 1928 | Pete Desjardins, U.S. | 98.74 |
| 1932 | Harold Smith, U.S. | 124.80 |
| 1936 | Marshall Wayne, U.S. | 113.58 |
| 1948 | Sammy Lee, U.S. | 130.05 |
| 1952 | Sammy Lee, U.S. | 156.28 |
| 1956 | Joaquin Capilla, Mexico | 152.44 |
| 1960 | Robert Webster, U.S. | 165.56 |
| 1964 | Robert Webster, U.S. | 148.58 |
| 1968 | Klaus Dibiasi, Italy | 164.18 |
| 1972 | Klaus Dibiasi, Italy | 504.12 |
| 1976 | Klaus Dibiasi, Italy | 600.51 |
| 1980 | Falk Hoffmann, E. Germany | 835.65 |
| 1984 | Greg Louganis, U.S. | 710.91 |
| 1988 | Greg Louganis, U.S. | 638.61 |
| 1992 | Sun Shuwei, China | 677.31 |
| 1996 | Dmitri Sautin, Russia | 692.34 |

## Swimming and Diving—Women

### 50-Meter Freestyle

| | | |
|---|---|---|
| 1988 | Kristin Otto, E. Germany | 25.49 |
| 1992 | Yang Wenyi, China | 24.76* |
| 1996 | Amy Van Dyken, U.S. | 24.87 |

### 100-Meter Freestyle

| | | |
|---|---|---|
| 1912 | Fanny Durack, Australia | 1:22.2 |
| 1920 | Ethelda Bleibtrey, U.S. | 1:13.6 |
| 1924 | Ethel Lackie, U.S. | 1:12.4 |
| 1928 | Albina Osipowich, U.S. | 1:11.0 |
| 1932 | Helene Madison, U.S. | 1:06.8 |
| 1936 | Hendrika Mastenbroek, Holland | 1:05.9 |
| 1948 | Greta Andersen, Denmark | 1:06.3 |
| 1952 | Katalin Szoke, Hungary | 1:06.8 |
| 1956 | Dawn Fraser, Australia | 1:02.0 |
| 1960 | Dawn Fraser, Australia | 1:01.2 |
| 1964 | Dawn Fraser, Australia | 59.5 |
| 1968 | Jan Henne, U.S. | 1:00.0 |
| 1972 | Sandra Neilson, U.S. | 58.59 |
| 1976 | Kornelia Ender, E. Germany | 55.65 |
| 1980 | Barbara Krause, E. Germany | 54.79 |
| 1984 | (tie) Carrie Steinseifer, U.S. | 55.92 |
| | Nancy Hogshead, U.S. | 55.92 |
| 1988 | Kristin Otto, E. Germany | 54.93 |
| 1992 | Zhuang Yong, China | 54.64 |
| 1996 | Li Jingyi, China | 54.50* |

### 200-Meter Freestyle

| | | |
|---|---|---|
| 1968 | Debbie Meyer, U.S. | 2:10.5 |
| 1972 | Shane Gould, Australia | 2:03.56 |
| 1976 | Kornelia Ender, E. Germany | 1:59.26 |
| 1980 | Barbara Krause, E. Germany | 1:58.33 |
| 1984 | Mary Wayte, U.S. | 1:59.23 |
| 1988 | Heike Friedrich, E. Germany | 1:57.65* |
| 1992 | Nicole Haislett, U.S. | 1:57.90 |
| 1996 | Claudia Poll, Costa Rica | 1:58.16 |

### 400-Meter Freestyle

| | | |
|---|---|---|
| 1924 | Martha Norelius, U.S. | 6:02.2 |
| 1928 | Martha Norelius, U.S. | 5:42.8 |
| 1932 | Helene Madison, U.S. | 5:28.5 |
| 1936 | Hendrika Mastenbroek, Netherlands | 5:26.4 |
| 1948 | Ann Curtis, U.S. | 5:17.8 |
| 1952 | Valerie Gyenge, Hungary | 5:12.1 |
| 1956 | Lorraine Crapp, Australia | 4:54.6 |
| 1960 | Susan Chris von Saltza, U.S. | 4:50.6 |
| 1964 | Virginia Duenkel, U.S. | 4:43.3 |
| 1968 | Debbie Meyer, U.S. | 4:31.8 |
| 1972 | Shane Gould, Australia | 4:19.44 |
| 1976 | Petra Thuemer, E. Germany | 4:09.89 |
| 1980 | Ines Diers, E. Germany | 4:08.76 |
| 1984 | Tiffany Cohen, U.S. | 4:07.10 |
| 1988 | Janet Evans, U.S. | 4:03.85* |
| 1992 | Dagmar Hase, Germany | 4:07.18 |
| 1996 | Michelle Smith, Ireland | 4:07.25 |

### 800-Meter Freestyle

| | | |
|---|---|---|
| 1968 | Debbie Meyer, U.S. | 9:24.0 |
| 1972 | Keena Rothhammer, U.S. | 8:53.68 |
| 1976 | Petra Thuemer, E. Germany | 8:37.14 |
| 1980 | Michelle Ford, Australia | 8:28.90 |
| 1984 | Tiffany Cohen, U.S. | 8:24.95 |
| 1988 | Janet Evans, U.S. | 8:20.20* |
| 1992 | Janet Evans, U.S. | 8:25.52 |
| 1996 | Brooke Bennett, U.S. | 8:27.89 |

### 100-Meter Backstroke

| | | |
|---|---|---|
| 1924 | Sybil Bauer, U.S. | 1:23.2 |
| 1928 | Marie Braun, Netherlands | 1:22.0 |
| 1932 | Eleanor Holm, U.S. | 1:19.4 |
| 1936 | Dina Senff, Netherlands | 1:18.9 |
| 1948 | Karen Harup, Denmark | 1:14.4 |
| 1952 | Joan Harrison, South Africa | 1:14.3 |
| 1956 | Judy Grinham, Great Britain | 1:12.9 |

| | | |
|---|---|---|
| 1960 | Lynn Burke, U.S. | 1:09.3 |
| 1964 | Cathy Ferguson, U.S. | 1:07.7 |
| 1968 | Kaye Hall, U.S. | 1:06.2 |
| 1972 | Melissa Belote, U.S. | 1:05.78 |
| 1976 | Ulrike Richter, E. Germany | 1:01.83 |
| 1980 | Rica Reinisch, E. Germany | 1:00.86 |
| 1984 | Theresa Andrews, U.S. | 1:02.55 |
| 1988 | Kristin Otto, E. Germany | 1:00.89 |
| 1992 | Krisztina Egerszegi, Hungary | 1:00.68* |
| 1996 | Beth Botsford, U.S. | 1:01.19 |

### 200-Meter Backstroke

| | | |
|---|---|---|
| 1968 | Pokey Watson, U.S. | 2:24.8 |
| 1972 | Melissa Belote, U.S. | 2:19.19 |
| 1976 | Ulrike Richter, E. Germany | 2:13.43 |
| 1980 | Rica Reinisch, E. Germany | 2:11.77 |
| 1984 | Jolanda De Rover, Netherlands | 2:12.38 |
| 1988 | Krisztina Egerszegi, Hungary | 2:09.29 |
| 1992 | Krisztina Egerszegi, Hungary | 2:07.06* |
| 1996 | Krisztina Egerszegi, Hungary | 2:07.83 |

### 100-Meter Breaststroke

| | | |
|---|---|---|
| 1968 | Djurdjica Bjedov, Yugoslavia | 1:15.8 |
| 1972 | Cathy Carr, U.S. | 1:13.58 |
| 1976 | Hannelore Anke, E. Germany | 1:11:16 |
| 1980 | Ute Geweniger, E. Germany | 1:10.22 |
| 1984 | Petra Van Staveren, Netherlands | 1:09.88 |
| 1988 | Tania Dangalakova, Bulgaria | 1:07.95 |
| 1992 | Elena Roudkovskaia, Unified Team | 1:08.00 |
| 1996 | Penny Heyns, South Africa | 1:07.73* |

### 200-Meter Breaststroke

| | | |
|---|---|---|
| 1924 | Lucy Morton, Great Britain | 3:33.2 |
| 1928 | Hilde Schrader, Germany | 3:12.6 |
| 1932 | Clare Dennis, Australia | 3:06.3 |
| 1936 | Hideko Maehata, Japan | 3:03.6 |
| 1948 | Nelly Van Vliet, Netherlands | 2:57.2 |
| 1952 | Eva Szekely, Hungary | 2:51.7 |
| 1956 | Ursula Happe, Germany | 2:53.1 |
| 1960 | Anita Lonsbrough, Great Britain | 2:49.5 |
| 1964 | Galina Prozumenschikova, USSR | 2:46.4 |
| 1968 | Sharon Wichman, U.S. | 2:44.4 |
| 1972 | Beverly Whitfield, Australia | 2:41.71 |
| 1976 | Marina Koshevaia, USSR | 2:33.35 |
| 1980 | Lina Kachushite, USSR | 2:29.54 |
| 1984 | Anne Ottenbrite, Canada | 2:30.38 |
| 1988 | Silke Hoerner, E. Germany | 2:26.71 |
| 1992 | Kyoko Iwasaki, Japan | 2:26.65 |
| 1996 | Penny Heyns, South Africa | 2:25.41* |

### 100-Meter Butterfly

| | | |
|---|---|---|
| 1956 | Shelley Mann, U.S. | 1:11.0 |
| 1960 | Carolyn Schuler, U.S. | 1:09.5 |
| 1964 | Sharon Stouder, U.S. | 1:04.7 |
| 1968 | Lynn McClements, Australia | 1:05.5 |
| 1972 | Mayumi Aoki, Japan | 1:03.34 |
| 1976 | Kornelia Ender, E. Germany | 1:00.13 |
| 1980 | Caren Metschuck, E. Germany | 1:00.42 |
| 1984 | Mary T. Meagher, U.S. | 59.26 |
| 1988 | Kristin Otto, E. Germany | 59.00 |
| 1992 | Qian Hong, China | 58.62* |
| 1996 | Amy Van Dyken, U.S. | 59.13 |

### 200-Meter Butterfly

| | | |
|---|---|---|
| 1968 | Ada Kok, Netherlands | 2:24.7 |
| 1972 | Karen Moe, U.S. | 2:15.57 |
| 1976 | Andrea Pollack, E. Germany | 2:11.41 |
| 1980 | Ines Geissler, E. Germany | 2:10.44 |
| 1984 | Mary T. Meagher, U.S. | 2:06.90* |
| 1988 | Kathleen Nord, E. Germany | 2:09.51 |
| 1992 | Summer Sanders, U.S. | 2:08.67 |
| 1996 | Susan O'Neill, Australia | 2:07.76 |

### 200-Meter Individual Medley

| | | |
|---|---|---|
| 1968 | Claudia Kolb, U.S. | 2:24.7 |
| 1972 | Shane Gould, Australia | 2:23.07 |
| 1984 | Tracy Caulkins, U.S. | 2:12.64 |
| 1988 | Daniela Hunger, E. Germany | 2:12.59 |
| 1992 | Lin Li, China | 2:11.65* |
| 1996 | Michelle Smith, Ireland | 2:13.93 |

### 400-Meter Individual Medley

| | | |
|---|---|---|
| 1964 | Donna de Varona, U.S. | 5:18.7 |
| 1968 | Claudia Kolb, U.S. | 5:08.5 |
| 1972 | Gail Neall, Australia | 5:02.97 |
| 1976 | Ulrike Tauber, E. Germany | 4:42.77 |
| 1980 | Petra Schneider, E. Germany | 4:36.29* |
| 1984 | Tracy Caulkins, U.S. | 4:39.24 |
| 1988 | Janet Evans, U.S. | 4:37.76 |
| 1992 | Krisztina Egerszegi, Hungary | 4:36.54 |
| 1996 | Michelle Smith, Ireland | 4:39.18 |

### 400-Meter Freestyle Relay

| | | |
|---|---|---|
| 1912 | Great Britain | 5:52.8 |
| 1920 | United States | 5:11.6 |
| 1924 | United States | 4:58.8 |
| 1928 | United States | 4:47.6 |
| 1932 | United States | 4:38.0 |
| 1936 | Netherlands | 4:36.0 |
| 1948 | United States | 4:29.2 |
| 1952 | Hungary | 4:24.4 |
| 1956 | Australia | 4:17.1 |
| 1960 | United States | 4:08.9 |
| 1964 | United States | 4:03.8 |
| 1968 | United States | 4:02.5 |
| 1972 | United States | 3:55.19 |
| 1976 | United States | 3:44.82 |
| 1980 | East Germany | 3:42.71 |
| 1984 | United States | 3:43.43 |
| 1988 | East Germany | 3:40.63 |
| 1992 | United States | 3:39.46 |
| 1996 | United States | 3:39.29* |

### 800-Meter Freestyle Relay

| | | |
|---|---|---|
| 1996 | United States | 7:59.87* |

### 400-Meter Medley Relay

| | | |
|---|---|---|
| 1960 | United States | 4:41.1 |
| 1960 | United States | 4:33.9 |
| 1968 | United States | 4:28.3 |
| 1972 | United States | 4:20.75 |
| 1976 | East Germany | 4:07.95 |
| 1980 | East Germany | 4:06.67 |
| 1984 | United States | 4:08.34 |
| 1988 | East Germany | 4:03.74 |
| 1992 | United States | 4:02.54* |
| 1996 | United States | 4:02.88 |

| | Springboard Diving | Points |
|---|---|---|
| 1920 | Aileen Riggin, U.S. | 539.90 |
| 1924 | Elizabeth Becker, U.S. | 474.50 |
| 1928 | Helen Meany, U.S. | 78.62 |
| 1932 | Georgia Coleman U.S. | 87.52 |
| 1936 | Marjorie Gestring, U.S. | 89.27 |
| 1948 | Victoria M. Draves, U.S. | 108.74 |
| 1952 | Patricia McCormick, U.S. | 147.30 |
| 1956 | Patricia McCormick, U.S. | 142.36 |
| 1960 | Ingrid Kramer, Germany | 155.81 |
| 1964 | Ingrid Engel-Kramer, Germany | 145.00 |
| 1968 | Sue Gossick, U.S. | 150.77 |
| 1972 | Micki King, U.S. | 450.03 |
| 1976 | Jenni Chandler, U.S. | 506.19 |
| 1980 | Irina Kalinina, USSR | 725.91 |
| 1984 | Sylvie Bernier, Canada | 530.70 |
| 1988 | Gao Min, China | 580.23 |
| 1992 | Gao Min, China | 572.40 |
| 1996 | Fu Mingxia, China | 547.68 |

| | Platform Diving | Points |
|---|---|---|
| 1912 | Greta Johansson, Sweden | 39.90 |
| 1920 | Stefani Fryland-Clausen, Denmark | 34.60 |
| 1924 | Caroline Smith, U.S. | 33.20 |
| 1928 | Elizabeth B. Pinkston, U.S. | 31.60 |
| 1932 | Dorothy Poynton, U.S. | 40.26 |
| 1936 | Dorothy Poynton Hill, U.S. | 33.93 |
| 1948 | Victoria M. Draves, U.S. | 68.87 |
| 1952 | Patricia McCormick, U.S. | 79.37 |
| 1956 | Patricia McCormick, U.S. | 84.85 |

*(continued)*

| | | | |
|---|---|---|---|
| **1960** | Ingrid Kramer, Germany .......... 91.28 | **1980** | Martina Jaschke, E. Germany .......... 596.25 |
| **1964** | Lesley Bush, U.S. .......... 99.80 | **1984** | Zhou Jihong, China .......... 435.51 |
| **1968** | Milena Duchkova, Czech. .......... 109.59 | **1988** | Xu Yanmei, China .......... 445.20 |
| **1972** | Ulrika Knape, Sweden .......... 390.00 | **1992** | Fu Mingxia, China .......... 461.43 |
| **1976** | Elena Vaytsekhouskaya, USSR .......... 406.59 | **1996** | Fu Mingxia, China .......... 521.58 |

## Boxing

### Light Flyweight (106 lbs)

**1968** Francisco Rodriguez, Venezuela
**1972** Gyorgy Gedo, Hungary
**1976** Jorge Hernandez, Cuba
**1980** Shamil Sabyrov, USSR
**1984** Paul Gonzalez, U.S.
**1988** Ivailo Hristov, Bulgaria
**1992** Rogelio Marcelo, Cuba
**1996** Daniel Petrov, Bulgaria

### Flyweight (112 lbs)

**1904** George Finnegan, U.S.
**1920** William Di Gennara, U.S.
**1924** Fidel LaBarba, U.S.
**1928** Antal Kocsis, Hungary
**1932** Istvan Enekes, Hungary
**1936** Willi Kaiser, Germany
**1948** Pascual Perez, Argentina
**1952** Nathan Brooks, U.S.
**1956** Terence Spinks, Great Britain
**1960** GyulaTorok, Hungary
**1964** Fernando Atzori, Italy
**1968** Ricardo Delgado, Mexico
**1972** Georgi Kostadinov, Bulgaria
**1976** Leo Randolph, U.S.
**1980** Peter Lessov, Bulgaria
**1984** Steve McCrory, U.S.
**1988** Kim Kwang Sun, S. Korea
**1992** Su Choi Choi, N. Korea
**1996** Maikro Romero, Cuba

### Bantamweight (119 lbs)

**1904** Oliver Kirk, U.S.
**1908** A. Henry Thomas, Great Britain
**1920** Clarence Walker, South Africa
**1924** William Smith, South Africa
**1928** Vittorio Tamagnini, Italy
**1932** Horace Gwynne, Canada
**1936** Ulderico Sergo, Italy
**1948** Tibor Csik, Hungary
**1952** Pentti Hamalainen, Finland
**1956** Wolfgang Behrendt, E. Germany
**1960** Oleg Grigoryev, USSR
**1964** Takao Sakurai, Japan
**1968** Valery Sokolov, USSR
**1972** Orlando Martinez, Cuba
**1976** Yong-Jo Gu, N. Korea
**1980** Juan Hernandez, Cuba
**1984** Maurizio Stecca, Italy
**1988** Kennedy McKinney, U.S.
**1992** Joel Casamayor, Cuba
**1996** Istvan Kovacs, Hungary

### Featherweight (126 lbs)

**1904** Oliver Kirk, U.S.
**1908** Richard Gunn, Great Britain
**1920** Paul Fritsch, France
**1924** John Fields, U.S.
**1928** Lambertus van Klaveren, Netherlands
**1932** Carmelo Robledo, Argentina
**1936** Oscar Casanovas, Argentina
**1948** Ernesto Formenti, Italy
**1952** Jan Zachara, Czechoslavakia
**1956** Vladimir Safronov, USSR
**1960** Francesco Musso, Italy
**1964** Stanislav Stephashkin, USSR
**1968** Antonin Roldan, Mexico
**1972** Boris Kousnetsov, USSR
**1976** Angel Herrera, Cuba
**1980** Rudi Fink, E. Germany
**1984** Meldrick Taylor, U.S.
**1988** Giovanni Parisi, Italy
**1992** Andreas Tews, Germany
**1996** Somluck Kamsing, Thailand

### Lightweight (132 lbs)

**1904** Harry Spanger, U.S.
**1908** Frederick Grace, Great Britain
**1920** Samuel Mosberg, U.S.
**1924** Hans Nielsen, Denmark
**1928** Carlo Orlandi, Italy
**1932** Lawrence Stevens, South Africa
**1936** Imre Harangi, Hungary
**1948** Gerald Dreyer, South Africa
**1952** Aureliano Bolognesi, Italy
**1956** Richard McTaggart, Great Britain
**1960** Kazimierz Pazdzior, Poland
**1964** Jozef Grudzien, Poland
**1968** Ronald Harris, U.S.
**1972** Jan Szczepanski, Poland
**1976** Howard Davis, U.S.
**1980** Angel Herrera, Cuba
**1984** Pernell Whitaker, U.S.
**1988** Andreas Zuelow, E. Germany
**1992** Oscar De La Hoya, U.S.
**1996** Hocine Soltani, Algeria

### Light Welterweight (140 lbs)

**1952** Charles Adkins, U.S.
**1956** Vladimir Yengibaryan, USSR
**1960** Bohumil Nemecek, Czechoslavakia
**1964** Jerzy Kulej, Poland
**1968** Jerzy Kulej, Poland
**1972** Ray Seales, U.S.
**1976** Ray Leonard, U.S.
**1980** Patrizio Oliva, Italy
**1984** Jerry Page, U.S.
**1988** Viatcheslav Janovski, USSR
**1992** Hector Vinent, Cuba
**1996** Hector Vinent, Cuba

### Welterweight (147 lbs)

**1904** Albert Young, U.S.
**1920** Albert Schneider, Canada
**1924** Jean Delarge, Belgium
**1928** Edward Morgan, New Zealand
**1932** Edward Flynn, U.S.
**1936** Sten Suvio, Finland
**1948** Julius Torma, Czechoslavakia
**1952** Zygmunt Chychia, Poland
**1956** Nicolae Linca, Romania
**1960** Giovanni Benvenuti, Italy
**1964** Marian Kasprzyk, Poland
**1968** Manfred Wolke, E. Germany
**1972** Emilio Correa, Cuba
**1976** Jochen Bachfeld, E. Germany
**1980** Andres Aldama, Cuba
**1984** Mark Breland, U.S.
**1988** Robert Wangila, Kenya
**1992** Michael Carruth, Ireland
**1996** Oleg Saitov, Russia

### Light Middleweight (157 lbs)

**1952** Laszlo Papp, Hungary
**1956** Laszlo Papp, Hungary
**1960** Wilbert McClure, U.S.
**1964** Boris Lagutin, USSR
**1968** Boris Lagutin, USSR
**1972** Dieter Kottysch, W. Germany
**1976** Jerzy Rybicki, Poland
**1980** Armando Martinez, Cuba
**1984** Frank Tate, U.S.
**1988** Park Si Hun, S. Korea
**1992** Juan Lemus, Cuba
**1996** David Reid, U.S.

### Middleweight (165 lbs)

**1904** Charles Mayer, U.S.
**1908** John Douglas, Great Britain
**1920** Harry Mallin, Great Britain
**1924** Harry Mallin, Great Britain
**1928** Piero Toscani, Italy
**1932** Carmen Barth, U.S.
**1936** Jean Despeaux, France
**1948** Laszlo Papp, Hungary
**1952** Floyd Patterson, U.S.
**1956** Gennady Schatkov, USSR
**1960** Edward Crook, U.S.
**1964** Valery Popenchenko, USSR
**1968** Christopher Finnegan, Great Britain
**1972** Vyacheslav Lemechev, USSR
**1976** Michael Spinks, U.S.
**1980** Jose Gomez, Cuba
**1984** Joon-Sup Shin, S. Korea
**1988** Henry Maske, E. Germany
**1992** Ariel Hernandez, Cuba
**1996** Ariel Hernandez, Cuba

### Light Heavyweight (179 lbs)

**1920** Edward Eagan, U.S.
**1924** Harry Mitchell, Great Britain
**1928** Victor Avendano, Argentina
**1932** David Carstens, South Africa
**1936** Roger Michelot, France
**1948** George Hunter, South Africa
**1952** Norvel Lee, U.S.
**1956** James Boyd, U.S.
**1960** Cassius Clay, U.S.
**1964** Cosimo Pinto, Italy
**1968** Dan Poznyak, USSR
**1972** Mate Parlov, Yugoslavia
**1976** Leon Spinks, U.S.
**1980** Slobodan Kacar, Yugoslavia
**1984** Anton Josipovic, Yugoslavia
**1988** Andrew Maynard, U.S.
**1992** Torsten May, Germany
**1996** Vassili Jirov, Kazakstan

### Heavyweight (201 lbs)

**1984** Henry Tillman, U.S.
**1988** Ray Mercer, U.S.
**1992** Felix Savon, Cuba
**1996** Felix Savon, Cuba

### Super Heavyweight (Unlimited)

(known as heavyweight, 1904-80)

**1904** Samuel Berger, U.S.
**1908** Albert Oldham, Great Britain
**1920** Ronald Rawson, Great Britain
**1924** Otto von Porat, Norway
**1928** Arturo Rodriguez Jurado, Argentina
**1932** Santiago Lovell, Argentina
**1936** Herbert Runge, Germany
**1948** Rafael Inglesias, Argentina
**1952** H. Edward Sanders, U.S.
**1956** T. Peter Rademacher, U.S.
**1960** Franco De Piccoli, Italy
**1964** Joe Frazier, U.S.
**1968** George Foreman, U.S.
**1972** Teofilo Stevenson, Cuba
**1976** Teofilo Stevenson, Cuba
**1980** Teofilo Stevenson, Cuba
**1984** Tyrell Biggs, U.S.
**1988** Lennox Lewis, Canada
**1992** Roberto Balado, Cuba
**1996** Vladimir Klitchko, Ukraine

# Winter Olympic Games

## Sites of Winter Olympic Games

**1924** Chamonix, France
**1928** St. Moritz, Switzerland
**1932** Lake Placid, New York
**1936** Garmisch-Partenkirchen, Germany
**1948** St. Moritz, Switzerland
**1952** Oslo, Norway
**1956** Cortina d'Ampezzo, Italy
**1960** Squaw Valley, California
**1964** Innsbruck, Austria
**1968** Grenoble, France
**1972** Sapporo, Japan
**1976** Innsbruck, Austria
**1980** Lake Placid, New York
**1984** Sarajevo, Yugoslavia
**1988** Calgary, Alberta
**1992** Albertville, France
**1994** Lillehammer, Norway
**1998** Nagano, Japan
**2002** Salt Lake City, Utah

## Winter Olympic Games in 1994

Lillehammer, Norway, Feb. 12-27, 1994

The 17th Olympic Winter Games were held in 1994 only 2 years after the previous games, because of an International Olympic Committee decision to switch to a 2-year cycle between Summer and Winter Olympics. The 18th Winter Games will be held in 1998 (in Nagano, Japan). The 1994 Winter Games, held in Lillehammer, Norway, featured 1,884 athletes from 67 countries, including 11 former Soviet republics competing as independent countries. Athletes from host-country Norway, whose speed skater Johann Olav Koss broke 3 Olympic records, won a games-high 26 medals. Germany placed 2d, with 24; Russia had the most golds (11). U.S. speed skater Bonnie Blair took home 2 gold medals, for a career total of 5 gold medals, the most of any female American Olympian. Team USA captured 13 medals, more than in any previous Olympic Winter Games.

For the first time, the U.S. Olympic Committee rewarded athletes' superior performances by handing out prizes—$15,000 for a gold medal, $10,000 for a silver, $7,500 for a bronze, and $5,000 for a fourth-place finish.

### Final Medal Standings

| | Gold | Silver | Bronze | Total |
|---|---|---|---|---|
| Norway | 10 | 11 | 5 | **26** |
| Germany | 9 | 7 | 8 | **24** |
| Russia | 11 | 8 | 4 | **23** |
| Italy | 7 | 5 | 8 | **20** |
| U.S. | 6 | 5 | 2 | **13** |
| Canada | 3 | 6 | 4 | **13** |
| Switzerland | 3 | 4 | 2 | **9** |
| Austria | 2 | 3 | 4 | **9** |
| S. Korea | 4 | 1 | 1 | **6** |
| Finland | 0 | 1 | 5 | **6** |
| Japan | 1 | 2 | 2 | **5** |
| France | 0 | 1 | 4 | **5** |
| Netherlands | 0 | 1 | 3 | **4** |
| Sweden | 2 | 1 | 0 | **3** |
| Kazakstan | 1 | 2 | 0 | **3** |
| China | 0 | 1 | 2 | **3** |
| Slovenia | 0 | 0 | 3 | **3** |
| Ukraine | 1 | 0 | 1 | **2** |
| Belarus | 0 | 2 | 0 | **2** |
| Great Britain | 0 | 0 | 2 | **2** |
| Uzbekistan | 1 | 0 | 0 | **1** |
| Australia | 0 | 0 | 1 | **1** |

## Winter Olympic Games Champions, 1924-1994

In 1992, the Unified Team represented the former Soviet republics of Russia, Ukraine, Belarus, Kazakstan, and Uzbekistan.

### Bobsledding

(Driver in parentheses)

| | 4-Man Bob | Time |
|---|---|---|
| **1924** | Switzerland (Eduard Scherrer) | 5:45.54 |
| **1928** | United States (William Fiske) (5-man) | 3:20.50 |
| **1932** | United States (William Fiske) | 7:53.68 |
| **1936** | Switzerland (Pierre Musy) | 5:19.85 |
| **1948** | United States (Francis Tyler) | 5:20.10 |
| **1952** | Germany (Andreas Ostler) | 5:07.84 |
| **1956** | Switzerland (Franz Kapus) | 5:10.44 |
| **1964** | Canada (Victor Emery) | 4:14.46 |
| **1968** | Italy (Eugenio Monti) (2 races) | 2:17.39 |
| **1972** | Switzerland (Jean Wicki) | 4:43.07 |
| **1976** | E. Germany (Meinhard Nehmer) | 3:40.43 |
| **1980** | E. Germany (Meinhard Nehmer) | 3:59.92 |
| **1984** | E. Germany (Wolfgang Hoppe) | 3:20.22 |
| **1988** | Switzerland (Ekkehard Fasser) | 3:47.51 |
| **1992** | Austria (Ingo Appelt) | 3:53.90 |
| **1994** | Germany (Wolfgang Hoppe) | 3:27.28 |

| | 2-Man Bob | Time |
|---|---|---|
| **1932** | United States (Hubert Stevens) | 8:14.74 |
| **1936** | United States (Ivan Brown) | 5:29.29 |
| **1948** | Switzerland (F. Endrich) | 5:29.20 |
| **1952** | Germany (Andreas Ostler) | 5:24.54 |
| **1956** | Italy (Dalla Costa) | 5:30.14 |
| **1964** | Great Britain (Anthony Nash) | 4:21.90 |
| **1968** | Italy (Eugenio Monti) | 4:41.54 |
| **1972** | W. Germany (Wolfgang Zimmerer) | 4:57.07 |
| **1976** | E. Germany (Meinhard Nehmer) | 3:44.42 |
| **1980** | Switzerland (Erich Schaerer) | 4:09.36 |
| **1984** | E. Germany (Wolfgang Hoppe) | 3:25.56 |
| **1988** | USSR (Janis Kipours) | 3:54.19 |
| **1992** | Switzerland (Gustav Weber) | 4:03.26 |
| **1994** | Switzerland (Gustav Weber) | 3:30.81 |

### Luge

| | Men's Singles | Time |
|---|---|---|
| **1964** | Thomas Keohler, Germany | 3:26.77 |
| **1968** | Manfred Schmid, Austria | 2:52.48 |
| **1972** | Wolfgang Scheidel, E. Germany | 3:27.58 |
| **1976** | Detlef Guenther, E. Germany | 3:27.688 |
| **1980** | Bernhard Glass, E. Germany | 2:54.796 |
| **1984** | Paul Hildgartner, Italy | 3:04.258 |
| **1988** | Jens Mueller, E. Germany | 3:05.548 |
| **1992** | Georg Hackl, Germany | 3:02.363 |
| **1994** | Georg Hackl, Germany | 3:21.571 |

| | Men's Pairs | Time |
|---|---|---|
| **1964** | Austria | 1:41.62 |
| **1968** | E. Germany | 1:35.85 |
| **1972** | Italy, E. Germany (tie) | 1:28.35 |
| **1976** | E. Germany | 1:25.604 |
| **1980** | E. Germany | 1:19.331 |
| **1984** | W. Germany | 1:23.620 |
| **1988** | E. Germany | 1:31.940 |
| **1992** | Germany | 1:32.053 |
| **1994** | Italy | 1:36.720 |

| | Women's Singles | Time |
|---|---|---|
| **1964** | Ortun Enderlein, Germany | 3:24.67 |
| **1968** | Erica Lechner, Italy | 2:28.66 |
| **1972** | Anna M. Muller, E. Germany | 2:59.18 |
| **1976** | Margit Schumann, E. Germany | 2:50.621 |
| **1980** | Vera Zozulya, USSR | 2:36.537 |
| **1984** | Steffi Martin, E. Germany | 2:46.570 |
| **1988** | Steffi Walter, E. Germany | 3:03.973 |
| **1992** | Doris Neuner, Austria | 3:06.696 |
| **1994** | Gerda Weissensteiner, Italy | 3:15.517 |

### Biathlon

| | Men's 10 Kilometers | Time |
|---|---|---|
| **1980** | Frank Ullrich, E. Germany | 32:10.69 |
| **1984** | Eirik Kvalfoss, Norway | 30:53.80 |
| **1988** | Frank-Peter Roetsch, E. Germany | 25:08.10 |
| **1992** | Mark Kirchner, Germany | 26:02.30 |
| **1994** | Serguei Tchepikov, Russia | 28:07.00 |

| | Men's 20 Kilometers | Time |
|---|---|---|
| **1960** | Klas Lestander, Sweden | 1:33:21.6 |
| **1964** | Vladimir Melanin, USSR | 1:20:26.8 |
| **1968** | Magnar Solberg, Norway | 1:13:45.9 |
| **1972** | Magnar Solberg, Norway | 1:15:55.50 |
| **1976** | Nikolai Kruglov, USSR | 1:14:12.26 |
| **1980** | Anatoly Aljabiev, USSR | 1:08:16.31 |
| **1984** | Peter Angerer, W. Germany | 1:11:52.7 |
| **1988** | Frank-Peter Roetsch, E. Germany | 0:56:33.33 |
| **1992** | Yevgeny Redkine, Unified Team | 0:57:34.4 |
| **1994** | Serguei Tarasov, Russia | 0:57:25.3 |

| | Men's 30-Kilometer Relay | Time |
|---|---|---|
| **1968** | USSR, Norway, Sweden (40 km) | 2:13:02.4 |
| **1972** | USSR, Finland, E. Germany (40 km) | 1:51:44.92 |
| **1976** | USSR, Finland, E. Germany (40 km) | 1:57:55.64 |
| **1980** | USSR, E. Germany, W. Germany | 1:34:03.27 |
| **1984** | USSR, Norway, W. Germany | 1:38:51.70 |
| **1988** | USSR, W. Germany, Italy | 1:22:30.00 |

| | Men's 10 Kilometers | Time |
|---|---|---|
| 1992 | Germany, Unified Team, Sweden | 1:24:43.50 |
| 1994 | Germany, Russia, France | 1:30:22.1 |

| | Women's 7.5 Kilometers | Time |
|---|---|---|
| 1992 | Anfissa Restsova, Unified Team | 24:29.20 |
| 1994 | Myriam Bedard, Canada | 26:08.8 |

| | Women's 15 Kilometers | Time |
|---|---|---|
| 1992 | Antje Misersky, Germany | 51:47.2 |
| 1994 | Myriam Bedard, Canada | 52:06.6 |

| | Women's 22.5-Kilometer Relay | Time |
|---|---|---|
| 1992 | France, Germany, Unified Team | 1:15:55.6 |

| | Women's 30-Kilometer Relay | Time |
|---|---|---|
| 1994 | Russia, Germany, France | 1:47:19.5 |

## Figure Skating

### Men's Singles

| | |
|---|---|
| 1908† | Ulrich Salchow, Sweden |
| 1920† | Gillis Grafstrom, Sweden |
| 1924 | Gillis Grafstrom, Sweden |
| 1928 | Gillis Grafstrom, Sweden |
| 1932 | Karl Schaefer, Austria |
| 1936 | Karl Schaefer, Austria |
| 1948 | Richard Button, U.S. |
| 1952 | Richard Button, U.S. |
| 1956 | Hayes Alan Jenkins, U.S. |
| 1960 | David W. Jenkins, U.S. |
| 1964 | Manfred Schnelldorfer, Germany |
| 1968 | Wolfgang Schwartz, Austria |
| 1972 | Ondrej Nepela, Czechoslovakia |
| 1976 | John Curry, Great Britain |
| 1980 | Robin Cousins, Great Britain |
| 1984 | Scott Hamilton, U.S. |
| 1988 | Brian Boitano, U.S. |
| 1992 | Viktor Petrenko, Unified Team |
| 1994 | Aleksei Urmanov, Russia |

### Women's Singles

| | |
|---|---|
| 1908† | Madge Syers, Great Britain |
| 1920† | Magda Julin-Mauroy, Sweden |
| 1924 | Herma von Szabo-Planck, Austria |
| 1928 | Sonja Henie, Norway |
| 1932 | Sonja Henie, Norway |
| 1936 | Sonja Henie, Norway |
| 1948 | Barbara Ann Scott, Canada |
| 1952 | Jeanette Altwegg, Great Britain |
| 1956 | Tenley Albright, U.S. |
| 1960 | Carol Heiss, U.S. |
| 1964 | Sjoukje Dijkstra, Netherlands |
| 1968 | Peggy Fleming, U.S. |
| 1972 | Beatrix Schuba, Austria |
| 1976 | Dorothy Hamill, U.S. |
| 1980 | Anett Poetzsch, E. Germany |
| 1984 | Katarina Witt, E. Germany |
| 1988 | Katarina Witt, E. Germany |
| 1992 | Kristi Yamaguchi, U.S. |
| 1994 | Oksana Baiul, Ukraine |

### Pairs

| | |
|---|---|
| 1908† | Anna Hubler & Heinrich Burger, Germany |
| 1920† | Ludovika & Walter Jakobsson, Finland |
| 1924 | Helene Engelman & Alfred Berger, Austria |
| 1928 | Andree Joly & Pierre Brunet, France |
| 1932 | Andree Joly & Pierre Brunet, France |
| 1936 | Maxi Herber & Ernst Baier, Germany |
| 1948 | Micheline Lannoy & Pierre Baugniet, Belgium |
| 1952 | Ria and Paul Falk, Germany |
| 1956 | Elisabeth Schwartz & Kurt Oppelt, Austria |
| 1960 | Barbara Wagner & Robert Paul, Canada |
| 1964 | Ludmila Beloussova & Oleg Protopopov, USSR |
| 1968 | Ludmila Beloussova & Oleg Protopopov, USSR |
| 1972 | Irina Rodnina & Alexei Ulanov, USSR |
| 1976 | Irina Rodnina & Aleksandr Zaitzev, USSR |
| 1980 | Irina Rodnina & Aleksandr Zaitzev, USSR |
| 1984 | Elena Valova & Oleg Vassiliev, USSR |
| 1988 | Ekaterina Gordeeva & Sergei Grinkov, USSR |
| 1992 | Natalia Mishkutienok & Artur Dimitriev, Unified Team |
| 1994 | Ekaterina Gordeeva & Sergei Grinkov, Russia |

### Ice Dancing

| | |
|---|---|
| 1976 | Ludmila Pakhomova & Aleksandr Gorschkov, USSR |
| 1980 | Natalya Linichuk & Gennadi Karponosov, USSR |
| 1984 | Jayne Torvill & Christopher Dean, Great Britain |
| 1988 | Natalia Bestemianova & Andrei Bukin, USSR |
| 1992 | Marina Klimova & Sergei Ponomarenko, Unified Team |
| 1994 | Oksana Grichtchuk & Yevgeny Platov, Russia |

(†) Event was held at Summer Olympics.

## Ice Hockey

| | |
|---|---|
| 1920† | Canada, U.S., Czechoslovakia |
| 1924 | Canada, U.S., Great Britain |
| 1928 | Canada, Sweden, Switzerland |
| 1932 | Canada, U.S., Germany |
| 1936 | Great Britain, Canada, U.S. |
| 1948 | Canada, Czechoslovakia, Switzerland |
| 1952 | Canada, U.S., Sweden |
| 1956 | USSR, U.S., Canada |
| 1960 | U.S., Canada, USSR |
| 1964 | USSR, Sweden, Czechoslovakia |
| 1968 | USSR, Czechoslovakia, Canada |
| 1972 | USSR, U.S., Czechoslovakia, |
| 1976 | USSR, Czechoslovakia, W. Germany |
| 1980 | U.S., USSR, Sweden |
| 1984 | USSR, Czechoslovakia, Sweden |
| 1988 | USSR, Finland, Sweden |
| 1992 | Unified Team, Canada, Czechoslovakia |
| 1994 | Sweden, Canada, Finland |

(†) Event was held at Summer Olympics.

## Alpine Skiing

| | Men's Downhill | Time |
|---|---|---|
| 1948 | Henri Oreiller, France | 2:55.0 |
| 1952 | Zeno Colo, Italy | 2:30.8 |
| 1956 | Anton Sailer, Austria | 2:52.2 |
| 1960 | Jean Vuarnet, France | 2:06.0 |
| 1964 | Egon Zimmermann, Austria | 2:18.16 |
| 1968 | Jean-Claude Killy, France | 1:59.85 |
| 1972 | Bernhard Russi, Switzerland | 1:51.43 |
| 1976 | Franz Klammer, Austria | 1:45.73 |
| 1980 | Leonhard Stock, Austria | 1:45.50 |
| 1984 | Bill Johnson, U.S. | 1:45:59 |
| 1988 | Pirmin Zurbriggen, Switzerland | 1:59.63 |
| 1992 | Patrick Ortlieb, Austria | 1:50.37 |
| 1994 | Tommy Moe, U.S. | 1:45.75 |

| | Men's Super Giant Slalom | Time |
|---|---|---|
| 1988 | Franck Piccard, France | 1:39.66 |
| 1992 | Kjetil-Andre Aamodt, Norway | 1:13.04 |
| 1994 | Markus Wasmeier, Germany | 1:32.53 |

| | Men's Giant Slalom | Time |
|---|---|---|
| 1952 | Stein Eriksen, Norway | 2:25.0 |
| 1956 | Anton Sailer, Austria | 3:00.1 |
| 1960 | Roger Staub, Switzerland | 1:48.3 |
| 1964 | Francois Bonlieu, France | 1:46.71 |
| 1968 | Jean-Claude Killy, France | 3:29.28 |
| 1972 | Gustavo Thoeni, Italy | 3:09.62 |
| 1976 | Heini Hemmi, Switzerland | 3:26.97 |
| 1980 | Ingemar Stenmark, Sweden | 2:40.74 |
| 1984 | Max Julen, Switzerland | 2:41.18 |
| 1988 | Alberto Tomba, Italy | 2:06:37 |
| 1992 | Alberto Tomba, Italy | 2:06.98 |
| 1994 | Markus Wasmeier, Germany | 2:52.46 |

| | Men's Slalom | Time |
|---|---|---|
| 1948 | Edi Reinalter, Switzerland | 2:10.3 |
| 1952 | Othmar Schneider, Austria | 2:00.0 |
| 1956 | Anton Sailer, Austria | 3:14.7 |
| 1960 | Ernst Hinterseer, Austria | 2:08.9 |
| 1964 | Josef Stiegler, Austria | 2:11.13 |
| 1968 | Jean-Claude Killy, France | 1:39.73 |
| 1972 | Francisco Fernandez Ochoa, Spain | 1:49.27 |
| 1976 | Piero Gros, Italy | 2:03.29 |
| 1980 | Ingemar Stenmark, Sweden | 1:44.26 |
| 1984 | Phil Mahre, U.S. | 1:39.41 |
| 1988 | Alberto Tomba, Italy | 1:39.47 |
| 1992 | Finn Christian Jagge, Norway | 1:44.39 |
| 1994 | Thomas Stangassinger, Austria | 2:02.02 |

| | Men's Combined | Time |
|---|---|---|
| 1988 | Hubert Strolz, Austria | 36.55 (pts.) |
| 1992 | Josef Polig, Italy | 14.58 (pts.) |
| 1994 | Lasse Kjus, Norway | 3:17.53 |

| | Women's Downhill | Time |
|---|---|---|
| 1948 | Hedi Schlunegger, Switzerland | 2:28.3 |
| 1952 | Trude Jochum-Beiser, Austria | 1:47.1 |
| 1956 | Madeleine Berthod, Switzerland | 1:40.7 |
| 1960 | Heidi Biebl, Germany | 1:37.6 |
| 1964 | Christl Haas, Austria | 1:55.39 |
| 1968 | Olga Pall, Austria | 1:40.87 |
| 1972 | Marie Therese Nadig, Switzerland | 1:36.68 |
| 1976 | Rosi Mittermaier, W. Germany | 1:46.16 |
| 1980 | Annemarie Proell Moser, Austria | 1:37.52 |
| 1984 | Michela Figini, Switzerland | 1:13.36 |
| 1988 | Marina Kiehl, W. Germany | 1:25.86 |
| 1992 | Kerrin Lee-Gartner, Canada | 1:52.55 |
| 1994 | Katja Seizinger, Germany | 1:35.93 |

| | Women's Super Giant Slalom | Time |
|---|---|---|
| 1988 | Sigrid Wolf, Austria | 1:19.03 |
| 1992 | Deborah Compagnoni, Italy | 1:21.22 |
| 1994 | Diann Roffe-Steinrotter, U.S. | 1:22.15 |

| | Women's Giant Slalom | Time |
|---|---|---|
| 1952 | Andrea Mead Lawrence, U.S. | 2:06.8 |
| 1956 | Ossi Reichert, Germany | 1:56.5 |
| 1960 | Yvonne Ruegg, Switzerland | 1:39.9 |
| 1964 | Marielle Goitschel, France | 1:52.24 |
| 1968 | Nancy Greene, Canada | 1:51.97 |
| 1972 | Marie Therese Nadig, Switzerland | 1:29.90 |
| 1976 | Kathy Kreiner, Canada | 1:29.13 |
| 1980 | Hanni Wenzel, Liechtenstein (2 runs) | 2:41.66 |
| 1984 | Debbie Armstrong, U.S. | 2:20.98 |
| 1988 | Vreni Schneider, Switzerland | 2:06.49 |
| 1992 | Pernilla Wiberg, Sweden | 2:12.74 |
| 1994 | Deborah Compagnoni, Italy | 2:30.97 |

| | Women's Slalom | Time |
|---|---|---|
| 1948 | Gretchen Fraser, U.S. | 1:57.2 |
| 1952 | Andrea Mead Lawrence, U.S. | 2:10.6 |
| 1956 | Renee Colliard, Switzerland | 1:52.3 |
| 1960 | Anne Heggtveigt, Canada | 1:49.6 |
| 1964 | Christine Goitschel, France | 1:29.86 |
| 1968 | Marielle Goitschel, France | 1:25.86 |
| 1972 | Barbara Cochran, U.S. | 1:31.24 |
| 1976 | Rosi Mittermaier, W. Germany | 1:30.54 |
| 1980 | Hanni Wenzel, Liechtenstein | 1:25.09 |
| 1984 | Paoletta Magoni, Italy | 1:36.47 |
| 1988 | Vreni Schneider, Switzerland | 1:36.69 |
| 1992 | Petra Kronberger, Austria | 1:32.68 |
| 1994 | Vreni Schneider, Switzerland | 1:56.01 |

| | Women's Combined | Time |
|---|---|---|
| 1988 | Anita Wachter, Austria | 29.25 (pts.) |
| 1992 | Petra Kronberger, Austria | 2.55 (pts.) |
| 1994 | Pernilla Wiberg, Sweden | 3:05.16 |

## Freestyle Skiing

| | Men's Moguls | Points |
|---|---|---|
| 1992 | Edgar Grospiron, France | 25.81 |
| 1994 | Jean-Luc Brassard, Canada | 27.24 |

| | Men's Aerials | Points |
|---|---|---|
| 1994 | Andreas Schoenbaechler, Switzerland | 234.67 |

| | Women's Moguls | Points |
|---|---|---|
| 1992 | Donna Weinbrecht, U.S. | 23.69 |
| 1994 | Stine Lise Hattestad, Norway | 25.97 |

| | Women's Aerials | Points |
|---|---|---|
| 1994 | Lina Tcherjazova, Uzbekistan | 166.84 |

## Nordic Skiing

### Cross-Country Events

| | Men's 10 Kilometers (6.2 miles) | Time |
|---|---|---|
| 1992 | Vegard Ulvang, Norway | 27:36.0 |
| 1994 | Bjorn Daehlie, Norway | 24:20.1 |

| | Men's 15 Kilometers (9.3 miles) | Time |
|---|---|---|
| 1924 | Thorleif Haug, Norway | 1:14:31 |
| 1928 | Johan Grottumsbraaten, Norway | 1:37:01 |
| 1932 | Sven Utterstrom, Sweden | 1:23:07 |
| 1936 | Erik-August Larsson, Sweden | 1:14:38 |
| 1948 | Martin Lundstrom, Sweden | 1:13:50 |
| 1952 | Hallgeir Brenden, Norway | 1:01:34 |
| 1956 | Hallgeir Brenden, Norway | 49:39.0 |
| 1960 | Haakon Brusveen, Norway | 51:55.5 |
| 1964 | Eero Maentyranta, Finland | 50:54.1 |
| 1968 | Harald Groenningen, Norway | 47:54.2 |
| 1972 | Sven-Ake Lundback, Sweden | 45:28.24 |
| 1976 | Nikolai Balukov, USSR | 43:58.47 |
| 1980 | Thomas Wassberg, Sweden | 41:57.63 |
| 1984 | Gunde Svan, Sweden | 41:25.6 |
| 1988 | Mikhail Deviatiarov, USSR | 41:18.9 |
| 1992 | Bjorn Daehlie, Norway | 38:01.9 |
| 1994 | Bjorn Daehlie, Norway | 35:48.8 |

(Note: approx. 18-km course 1924-1952)

| | Men's 30 Kilometers (18.6 miles) | Time |
|---|---|---|
| 1956 | Veikko Hakulinen, Finland | 1:44:06.0 |
| 1960 | Sixten Jernberg, Sweden | 1:51:03.9 |
| 1964 | Eero Maentyranta, Finland | 1:30:50.7 |
| 1968 | Franco Nones, Italy | 1:35:39.2 |
| 1972 | Vyacheslav Vedenine, USSR | 1:36:31.15 |
| 1976 | Sergei Saveliev, USSR | 1:30:29.38 |
| 1980 | Nikolai Zimyatov, USSR | 1:27:02.80 |
| 1984 | Nikolai Zimyatov, USSR | 1:28:56.3 |
| 1988 | Aleksei Prokourorov, USSR | 1:24:26.3 |
| 1992 | Vegard Ulvang, Norway | 1:22:27.8 |
| 1994 | Thomas Alsgaard, Norway | 1:12:26.4 |

| | Men's 50 kilometers (31.2 miles) | Time |
|---|---|---|
| 1924 | Thorleif Haug, Norway | 3:44:32.0 |
| 1928 | Per Erik Hedlund, Sweden | 4:52:03.0 |
| 1932 | Veli Saarinen, Finland | 4:28:00.0 |
| 1936 | Elis Wiklund, Sweden | 3:30:11.0 |
| 1948 | Nils Karlsson, Sweden | 3:47:48.0 |
| 1952 | Veikko Hakulinen, Finland | 3:33:33.0 |
| 1956 | Sixten Jernberg, Sweden | 2:50:27.0 |
| 1960 | Kalevi Hamalainen, Finland | 2:59:06.3 |
| 1964 | Sixten Jernberg, Sweden | 2:43:52.6 |
| 1968 | Ole Ellefsaeter, Norway | 2:28:45.8 |
| 1972 | Paal Tyldum, Norway | 2:43:14.75 |
| 1976 | Ivar Formo, Norway | 2:37:30.05 |
| 1980 | Nikolai Zimyatov, USSR | 2:27:24.60 |
| 1984 | Thomas Wassberg, Sweden | 2:15:55.8 |
| 1988 | Gunde Svan, Sweden | 2:04:30.9 |
| 1992 | Bjorn Daehlie, Norway | 2:03:41.5 |
| 1994 | Vladimir Smirnov, Kazakstan | 2:07:20.3 |

| | Men's 40-Kilometer Relay | Time |
|---|---|---|
| 1936 | Finland, Norway, Sweden | 2:41:33.0 |
| 1948 | Sweden, Finland, Norway | 2:32:08.0 |
| 1952 | Finland, Norway, Sweden | 2:20:16.0 |
| 1956 | USSR, Finland, Sweden | 2:15:30.0 |
| 1960 | Finland, Norway, USSR | 2:18:45.6 |
| 1964 | Sweden, Finland, USSR | 2:18:34.6 |
| 1968 | Norway, Sweden, Finland | 2:08:33.5 |
| 1972 | USSR, Norway, Switzerland | 2:04:47.94 |
| 1976 | Finland, Norway, USSR | 2:07:59.72 |
| 1980 | USSR, Norway, Finland | 1:57:03.46 |
| 1984 | Sweden, USSR, Finland | 1:55:06.30 |
| 1988 | Sweden, USSR, Czechoslovakia | 1:43:58.60 |
| 1992 | Norway, Italy, Finland | 1:39:26.00 |
| 1994 | Italy, Norway, Finland | 1:41:15.00 |

| | Women's 5 Kilometers (approx. 3.1 miles) | Time |
|---|---|---|
| 1964 | Claudia Boyarskikh, USSR | 17:50.5 |
| 1968 | Toini Gustafsson, Sweden | 16:45.2 |
| 1972 | Galina Koulacova, USSR | 17:00.50 |
| 1976 | Helena Takalo, Finland | 15:48.69 |
| 1980 | Raisa Smetanina, USSR | 15:06.92 |
| 1984 | Marja-Liisa Haemaelainen, Finland | 17:04.0 |
| 1988 | Marjo Matikainen, Finland | 15:04.0 |
| 1992 | Marjut Lukkarinen, Finland | 14:13.8 |
| 1994 | Ljubov Egorova, Russia | 14:08.8 |

| | Women's 10 Kilometers (6.2 miles) | Time |
|---|---|---|
| 1952 | Lydia Wideman, Finland | 41:40.0 |
| 1956 | Lyubov Kosyreva, USSR | 38:11.0 |
| 1960 | Maria Gusakova, USSR | 39:46.6 |
| 1964 | Claudia Boyarskikh, USSR | 40:24.3 |
| 1968 | Toini Gustafsson, Sweden | 36:46.5 |
| 1972 | Galina Koulacova, USSR | 34:17.82 |
| 1976 | Raisa Smetanina, USSR | 30:13.41 |
| 1980 | Barbara Petzold, E. Germany | 30:31.54 |
| 1984 | Marja-Liisa Haemaelainen, Finland | 31:44.2 |
| 1988 | Vida Ventsene, USSR | 30:08.3 |
| 1992 | Lyubov Egorova, Unified Team | 25:53.7 |
| 1994 | Lyubov Egorova, Russia | 27:30.1 |

| | Women's 15 Kilometers (9.3 miles) | Time |
|---|---|---|
| 1992 | Lyubov Egorova, Unified Team | 42:20.8 |
| 1994 | Manuela Di Centa, Italy | 39:44.5 |

| | Women's 30 Kilometers (18.6 miles) | Time |
|---|---|---|
| 1992 | Stefania Belmondo, Italy | 1:22:30.1 |
| 1994 | Manuela Di Centa, Italy | 1:25:41.6 |

| | Women's 20-Kilometer Relay | Time |
|---|---|---|
| 1956 | Finland, USSR, Sweden (15 km) | 1:09:01.0 |
| 1960 | Sweden, USSR, Finland (15 km) | 1:04:21.4 |
| 1964 | USSR, Sweden, Finland (15 km) | 59:20.2 |
| 1968 | Norway, Sweden, USSR (15 km) | 57:30.0 |
| 1972 | USSR, Finland, Norway (15 km) | 48:46.15 |
| 1976 | USSR, Finland, E. Germany | 1:07:49.75 |
| 1980 | E. Germany, USSR, Norway | 1:02:11.1 |
| 1984 | Norway, Czechoslovakia, Finland | 1:06:49.7 |
| 1988 | USSR, Norway, Finland | 59:51.1 |
| 1992 | United Team, Norway, Italy | 59:34.8 |
| 1994 | Russia, Norway, Italy | 57:12.5 |

### Combined Cross-Country & Jumping (Men)

| | Nordic Combined | Points |
|---|---|---|
| 1924 | Thorleif Haug, Norway | 453.800 |
| 1928 | Johan Grottumsbraaten, Norway | 427.800 |
| 1932 | Johan Grottumsbraaten, Norway | 446.000 |
| 1936 | Oddbjorn Hagen, Norway | 430.300 |
| 1948 | Heikki Hasu, Finland | 448.800 |
| 1952 | Simon Slattvik, Norway | 451.621 |
| 1956 | Sverre Stenersen, Norway | 455.000 |
| 1960 | Georg Thoma, Germany | 457.952 |
| 1964 | Tormod Knutsen, Norway | 469.280 |
| 1968 | Franz Keller, W. Germany | 449.040 |
| 1972 | Ulrich Wehling, E. Germany | 413.340 |
| 1976 | Ulrich Wehling, E. Germany | 423.390 |

*(continued)*

| | | |
|---|---|---|
| 1980 | Ulrich Wehling, E. Germany | 432.200 |
| 1984 | Tom Sandberg, Norway | 422.595 |
| 1988 | Hippolyt Kempf, Switzerland | 235.8 |
| 1992 | Fabrice Guy, France | 426.470 |
| 1994 | Fred Barre Lundberg, Norway | 457.970 |

| | Team Nordic Combined | Time |
|---|---|---|
| 1988 | W. Germany, Switzerland, Austria | 1:20:46.0 |
| 1992 | Japan, Norway, Austria | 1:23:36.5 |
| 1994 | Japan, Norway, Switzerland | 1,368.860 (pts.) |

### Ski Jumping (Men)

| | 90 Meters | Points |
|---|---|---|
| 1924 | Jacob Thams, Norway | 227.5 |
| 1928 | Alfred Andersen, Norway | 230.5 |
| 1932 | Birger Ruud, Norway | 228.1 |
| 1936 | Birger Ruud, Norway | 232.0 |
| 1948 | Petter Hugsted, Norway | 228.1 |
| 1952 | Arnfinn Bergmann, Norway | 226.0 |
| 1956 | Antti Hyvarinen, Finland | 227.0 |
| 1960 | Helmut Recknagel, Germany | 227.2 |
| 1964 | Toralf Engan, Norway | 230.7 |
| 1968 | Vladimir Beloussov, USSR | 231.3 |
| 1972 | Wojiech Fortuna, Poland | 219.9 |
| 1976 | Karl Schnabl, Austria | 234.8 |
| 1980 | Jouko Tormanen, Finland | 271.0 |
| 1984 | Matti Nykaenen, Finland | 231.2 |
| 1988 | Matti Nykaenen, Finland | 224.0 |
| 1992 | Ernst Vettori, Austria | 222.8 |
| 1994 | Espen Bredesen, Norway | 282.0 |

| | 120 Meters | Points |
|---|---|---|
| 1992 | Toni Nicminen, Finland | 239.5 |
| 1994 | Jens Weissflog, Germany | 274.5 |

| | Team (90 Meters) | Points |
|---|---|---|
| 1988 | Finland, Yugoslavia, Norway | 634.4 |
| 1992 | Finland, Austria, Czechoslovakia | 644.4 |
| 1994 | Germany, Japan, Austria | 970.1 |

## Speed Skating

| | Men's 500 Meters | Time |
|---|---|---|
| 1924 | Charles Jewtraw, U.S. | 0:44.0 |
| 1928 | Thunberg, Finland & Evensen, Norway (tie) | 0:43.4 |
| 1932 | John A. Shea, U.S. | 0:43.4 |
| 1936 | Ivar Ballangrud, Norway | 0:43.4 |
| 1948 | Finn Helgesen, Norway | 0:43.1 |
| 1952 | Kenneth Henry, U.S. | 0:43.2 |
| 1956 | Evgeniy Grishin, USSR | 0:40.2 |
| 1960 | Evgeniy Grishin, USSR | 0:40.2 |
| 1964 | Terry McDermott, U.S. | 0:40.1 |
| 1968 | Erhard Keller, W. Germany | 0:40.3 |
| 1972 | Erhard Keller, W. Germany | 0:39.44 |
| 1976 | Evgeny Kulikov, USSR | 0:39.17 |
| 1980 | Eric Heiden, U.S. | 0:38.03 |
| 1984 | Sergei Fokichev, USSR | 0:38.19 |
| 1988 | Uwe-Jens Mey, E. Germany | 0:36.45 |
| 1992 | Uwe-Jens Mey, Germany | 0:37.14 |
| 1994 | Aleksandr Golubev, Russia | 0:36.33 |

| | Men's 1,000 Meters | Time |
|---|---|---|
| 1976 | Peter Mueller, U.S. | 1:19.32 |
| 1980 | Eric Heiden, U.S. | 1:15.18 |
| 1984 | Gaetan Boucher, Canada | 1:15.80 |
| 1988 | Nikolai Guiliaev, USSR | 1:13.03 |
| 1992 | Olaf Zinke, Germany | 1:14.85 |
| 1994 | Dan Jansen, U.S. | 1:12.43 |

| | Men's 1,500 Meters | Time |
|---|---|---|
| 1924 | Clas Thunberg, Finland | 2:20.8 |
| 1928 | Clas Thunberg, Finland | 2:21.1 |
| 1932 | John A. Shea, U.S. | 2:57.5 |
| 1936 | Charles Mathiesen, Norway | 2:19.2 |
| 1948 | Sverre Farstad, Norway | 2:17.6 |
| 1952 | Hjalmar Andersen, Norway | 2:20.4 |
| 1956 | Grishin, & Mikhailov, both USSR (tie) | 2:08.6 |
| 1960 | Aas, Norway & Grishin, USSR (tie) | 2:10.4 |
| 1964 | Ants Anston, USSR | 2:10.3 |
| 1968 | Cornetis Verkerk, Netherlands | 2:03.4 |
| 1972 | Ard Schenk, Netherlands | 2:02.96 |
| 1976 | Jan Egil Storholt, Norway | 1:59.38 |
| 1980 | Eric Heiden, U.S. | 1:55.44 |
| 1984 | Gaetan Boucher, Canada | 1:58.36 |
| 1988 | Andre Hoffmann, E. Germany | 1:52.06 |
| 1992 | Johann Koss, Norway | 1:54.81 |
| 1994 | Johann Koss, Norway | 1:51.29 |

| | Men's 5,000 Meters | Time |
|---|---|---|
| 1924 | Clas Thunberg, Finland | 8:39.0 |
| 1928 | Ivar Ballangrud, Norway | 8:50.5 |
| 1932 | Irving Jaffee, U.S. | 9:40.8 |
| 1936 | Ivar Ballangrud, Norway | 8:19.6 |
| 1948 | Reidar Liaklev, Norway | 8:29.4 |
| 1952 | Hjalmar Andersen, Norway | 8:10.6 |
| 1956 | Boris Shilkov, USSR | 7:48.7 |
| 1960 | Viktor Kosichkin, USSR | 7:51.3 |
| 1964 | Knut Johannesen, Norway | 7:38.4 |
| 1968 | F. Anton Maier, Norway | 7:22.4 |
| 1972 | Ard Schenk, Netherlands | 7:23.61 |
| 1976 | Sten Stensen, Norway | 7:24.48 |
| 1980 | Eric Heiden, U.S. | 7:02.29 |
| 1984 | Sven Tomas Gustafson, Sweden | 7:12.28 |
| 1988 | Tomas Gustafson, Sweden | 6:44.63 |
| 1992 | Geir Karlstad, Norway | 6:59.97 |
| 1994 | Johann Koss, Norway | 6:34.96 |

| | Men's 10,000 Meters | Time |
|---|---|---|
| 1924 | Julius Skutnabb, Finland | 18:04.8 |
| 1928 | Event not held, thawing of ice | |
| 1932 | Irving Jaffee, U.S. | 19:13.6 |
| 1936 | Ivar Ballangrud, Norway | 17:24.3 |
| 1948 | Ake Seyffarth, Sweden | 17:26.3 |
| 1952 | Hjalmar Andersen, Norway | 16:45.8 |
| 1956 | Sigvard Ericsson, Sweden | 16:35.9 |
| 1960 | Knut Johannesen, Norway | 15:46.6 |
| 1964 | Jonny Nilsson, Sweden | 15:50.1 |
| 1968 | Jonny Hoeglin, Sweden | 15:23.6 |
| 1972 | Ard Schenk, Netherlands | 15:01.35 |
| 1976 | Piet Kleine, Netherlands | 14:50.59 |
| 1980 | Eric Heiden, U.S. | 14:28.13 |
| 1984 | Igor Malkov, USSR | 14:39.90 |
| 1988 | Tomas Gustafson, Sweden | 13:48.20 |
| 1992 | Bart Veldkamp, Netherlands | 14:12.12 |
| 1994 | Johann Koss, Norway | 13:30.55 |

| | Women's 500 Meters | Time |
|---|---|---|
| 1960 | Helga Haase, Germany | 0:45.9 |
| 1964 | Lydia Skoblikova, USSR | 0:45.0 |
| 1968 | Ludmila Titova, USSR | 0:46.1 |
| 1972 | Anne Henning, U.S. | 0:43.33 |
| 1976 | Sheila Young, U.S. | 0:42.76 |
| 1980 | Karin Enke, E. Germany | 0:41.78 |
| 1984 | Christa Rothenburger, E. Germany | 0:41.02 |
| 1988 | Bonnie Blair, U.S. | 0:39.10 |
| 1992 | Bonnie Blair, U.S. | 0:40.33 |
| 1994 | Bonnie Blair, U.S. | 0:39.25 |

| | Women's 1,000 Meters | Time |
|---|---|---|
| 1960 | Klara Guseva, USSR | 1:34.1 |
| 1964 | Lydia Skoblikova, USSR | 1:33.2 |
| 1968 | Carolina Geijssen, Netherlands | 1:32.6 |
| 1972 | Monika Pflug, W. Germany | 1:31.40 |
| 1976 | Tatiana Averina, USSR | 1:28.43 |
| 1980 | Natalya Petruseva, USSR | 1:24.10 |
| 1984 | Karin Enke, E. Germany | 1:21.61 |
| 1988 | Christa Rothenburger, E. Germany | 1:17.65 |
| 1992 | Bonnie Blair, U.S. | 1:21.90 |
| 1994 | Bonnie Blair, U.S. | 1:18.74 |

| | Women's 1,500 Meters | Time |
|---|---|---|
| 1960 | Lydia Skoblikova, USSR | 2:52.2 |
| 1964 | Lydia Skoblikova, USSR | 2:22.6 |
| 1968 | Kaija Mustonen, Finland | 2:22.4 |
| 1972 | Dianne Holum, U.S. | 2:20.85 |
| 1976 | Galina Stepanskaya, USSR | 2:16.58 |
| 1980 | Anne Borckink, Netherlands | 2:10.95 |
| 1984 | Karin Enke, E. Germany | 2:03.42 |
| 1988 | Yvonne van Gennip, Netherlands | 2:00.68 |
| 1992 | Jacqueline Boerner, Germany | 2:05.87 |
| 1994 | Emese Hunyady, Austria | 2:02.19 |

| | Women's 3,000 Meters | Time |
|---|---|---|
| 1960 | Lydia Skoblikova, USSR | 5:14.3 |
| 1964 | Lydia Skoblikova, USSR | 5:14.9 |
| 1968 | Johanna Schut, Netherlands | 4:56.2 |
| 1972 | Christina Baas-Kaiser, Netherlands | 4:52.14 |
| 1976 | Tatiana Averina, USSR | 4:45.19 |
| 1980 | Bjoerg Eva Jensen, Norway | 4:32.13 |
| 1984 | Andrea Schoene, E. Germany | 4:24.79 |
| 1988 | Yvonne van Gennip, Netherlands | 4:11.94 |
| 1992 | Gunda Niemann, Germany | 4:19.90 |
| 1994 | Svetlana Bazhanova, Russia | 4:17.43 |

| | Women's 5,000 Meters | Time |
|---|---|---|
| 1988 | Yvonne van Gennip, Netherlands | 7:14.13 |
| 1992 | Gunda Niemann, Germany | 7:31.57 |
| 1994 | Claudia Pechstein, Germany | 7:14.37 |

### Short-Track Speed Skating

| Men's 1,000 Meters | | Time |
|---|---|---|
| 1992 | Kim Ki-Hoon, S. Korea | 1:30.76 |
| 1994 | Kim Ki-Hoon, S. Korea | 1:34.57 |

| Men's 5,000-Meter Relay | | Time |
|---|---|---|
| 1992 | S. Korea, Canada, Japan | 7:14.02 |
| 1994 | Italy, U.S., Australia | 7:11.74 |

| Women's 500 Meters | | Time |
|---|---|---|
| 1992 | Cathy Turner, U.S. | 47:04 |
| 1994 | Cathy Turner, U.S. | 45.98 |

| Women's 3,000-Meter Relay | | Time |
|---|---|---|
| 1992 | Canada, U.S., Unified Team | 4:36.62 |
| 1994 | S. Korea, Canada, U.S. | 4:26.64 |

## Olympic Information

**Symbol:** Five rings or circles, linked together to represent the sporting friendship of all peoples. The rings also symbolize 5 geographic areas—Europe, Asia, Africa, Australia, and America. Each ring is a different color—blue, yellow, black, green, and red.

**Flag:** The symbol of the 5 rings on a plain white background.

**Motto:** "Citius, Altius, Fortius." Latin meaning "faster, higher, braver," or in a more modern rendering, "swifter, higher, stronger." The motto was coined by Father Didon, a French educator, in 1895.

**Creed:** "The most important thing in the Olympic Games is not to win but to take part, just as the most important thing in life is not the triumph but the struggle. The essential thing is not to have conquered but to have fought well."

**Oath:** An athlete of the host country recites the following at the opening ceremony. "In the name of all competitors I promise that we will take part in these Olympic Games, respecting and abiding by the rules which govern them, in the true spirit of sportsmanship for the glory of sport and the honor of our teams." Both the oath and the creed were composed by Baron Pierre de Coubertin, the founder of the modern Games.

**Flame:** Symbolizes the continuity between the ancient and modern Games. The modern version of the flame was adopted in 1936. The torch used to kindle the flame is first lit by the sun's rays at Olympia, Greece, and then carried to the site of the Games by relays of runners. Ships and planes are used when necessary.

# TRACK AND FIELD

## World Track and Field Records

As of Oct. 1996

The International Amateur Atheletic Federation, the world body of track and field, recognizes only records in metric distances, except for the mile. *Record pending.

### Men's Records

| Event | Record | Holder | Country | Date | Where made |
|---|---|---|---|---|---|
| **Running** | | | | | |
| 100 meters | ***9.84 s.** | Donovan Bailey | Canada | July 27, 1996 | Atlanta, GA |
| 200 meters | ***19.32 s.** | Michael Johnson | U.S. | Aug. 1, 1996 | Atlanta, GA |
| 400 meters | **43.29 s.** | Butch Reynolds | U.S. | Aug. 17, 1988 | Zurich |
| 800 meters | **1 m., 41.73 s.** | Sebastian Coe | Gr. Britain | June 10, 1981 | Florence, Italy |
| 1,000 meters | **2 m., 12.18 s.** | Sebastian Coe | Gr. Britain | July 11, 1981 | Oslo |
| 1,500 meters | **3 m., 27.37 s.** | Noureddine Morceli | Algeria | July 12, 1995 | Nice, France |
| 1 mile | **3 m., 44.39 s.** | Noureddine Morceli | Algeria | Sept. 5, 1993 | Rieti, Italy |
| 2,000 meters | **4 m., 47.88 s.** | Noureddine Morceli | Algeria | July 3, 1995 | Paris |
| 3,000 meters | **7 m., 25.11 s.** | Noureddine Morceli | Algeria | Aug. 2, 1994 | Monte Carlo |
| 5,000 meters | **12 m., 44.39 s.** | Haile Gebreselasie | Ethiopia | Aug. 16, 1995 | Zurich |
| 10,000 meters | **26 m., 38.08 s.** | Salah Hissou | Morocco | Aug. 23,1996 | Brussels |
| 20,000 meters | **56 m., 55.6 s.** | Arturo Barrios | Mexico | Mar. 30, 1991 | La Fleche, France |
| 25,000 meters | **1 hr., 13 m., 55.8 s.** | Toshihiko Seko | Japan | Mar. 22, 1981 | Christchurch, New Zealand |
| 3,000 meter stpl. | **7 m., 59.18 s.** | Moses Kiptanui | Kenya | Aug. 16, 1995 | Zurich |
| Marathon | **2 hr., 6 m., 50 s.** | Belayneh Dinsamo | Ethiopia | Apr. 17, 1988 | Rotterdam |
| **Hurdles** | | | | | |
| 110 meters | **12.91 s.** | Colin Jackson | Gr. Britain | Aug. 20, 1993 | Stuttgart, Germany |
| 400 meters | **46.78 s.** | Kevin Young | U.S. | Aug. 6, 1992 | Barcelona |
| **Relay Races** | | | | | |
| 400 mtrs. (4x100) | **37.40 s.** | (Marsh, Burrell, Mitchell, Lewis) | U.S. | Aug. 8, 1992 | Barcelona |
| | | (Drummond, Cason, Mitchell, Burrell) | U.S. | Aug. 21, 1993 | Stuttgart, Germany |
| 800 mtrs. (4×200) | **1 m., 18.68 s.** | (Marsh, Burrell, Heard, Lewis) | U.S. | Apr. 17, 1994 | Walnut, CA |
| 1,600 mtrs. (4×400) | **2 m., 54.29 s.** | (Valmon, Watts, Reynolds, Johnson) | U.S. | Aug. 22, 1993 | Stuttgart, Germany |
| 3,200 mtrs. (4×800) | **7 m., 03.89 s.** | (Elliott, Cook, Cram, Coe) | Gr. Britain | Aug. 30, 1982 | London |
| **Field Events** | | | | | |
| High jump | **8 ft., ½ in.** | Javier Sotomayor | Cuba | July 27, 1993 | Salamanca, Spain |
| Long jump | **29 ft., 4½ in.** | Mike Powell | U.S. | Aug. 30, 1991 | Tokyo |
| Triple jump | **60 ft., ¼ in.** | Jonathan Edwards | Gr. Britain | Aug. 7, 1995 | Göteborg, Sweden |
| Pole vault | **20 ft., 1¾ in.** | Sergei Bubka | Ukraine | July 31, 1994 | Sestriere, Italy |
| 16-lb. shot put | **75 ft., 10¼ in.** | Randy Barnes | U.S. | May 20, 1990 | Los Angeles, CA |
| Discus | **243 ft.** | Juergen Schult | E. Germany | June 6, 1986 | E. Germany |
| Javelin | **323 ft., 1 in.** | Jan Zelezny | Czech Rep. | May 25, 1996 | Jena, Germany |
| 16-lb. hammer | **284 ft., 7 in.** | Yuri Sedykh | USSR | Aug. 30, 1986 | Stuttgart, W. Germany |
| Decathlon | **8,891 pts.** | Dan O'Brien | U.S. | Sept. 4-5, 1992 | Talence, France |

## Women's Records

### Running

| Event | Record | Holder | Country | Date | Where made |
|---|---|---|---|---|---|
| 100 meters | **10.49 s.** | Florence Griffith Joyner | U.S. | July 16, 1988 | Indianapolis, IN |
| 200 meters | **21.34 s.** | Florence Griffith Joyner | U.S. | Sept. 29, 1988 | Seoul |
| 400 meters | **47.60 s.** | Marita Koch | E. Germany | Oct. 6, 1985 | Canberra, Australia |
| 800 meters | **1 m., 53.28 s.** | Jarmila Kratochvilova | Czechoslovakia | July 26, 1983 | Munich |
| 1,000 meters | **2 m., 28.98 s.** | Svetlana Masterkova | Russia | Aug. 23, 1996 | Brussels |
| 1,500 meters | **3 m., 50.46 s.** | Qu Yunxia | China | Sept. 11, 1993 | Beijing |
| 1 mile | **4 m., 12.56 s.** | Svetlana Masterkova | Russia | Aug. 14, 1996 | Zurich |
| 2,000 meters | **5 m., 25.36 s.** | Sonia O'Sullivan | Ireland | July 8, 1994 | Edinburgh |
| 3,000 meters | **8 m., 06.11 s.** | Wang Junxia | China | Sept. 13, 1993 | Beijing |
| 5,000 meters | **14 m., 36.45 s.** | Fernanda Ribeiro | Portugal | July 22, 1995 | Hechtel, Belgium |
| 10,000 meters | **29 m., 31.78 s.** | Wang Junxia | China | Sept. 8, 1993 | Beijing |
| Marathon | **2 h., 21 m., 06 s.** | Ingrid Kristiansen | Norway | Apr. 21, 1985 | London |

### Hurdles

| Event | Record | Holder | Country | Date | Where made |
|---|---|---|---|---|---|
| 100 meters | **12.21 s.** | Yordanka Donkova | Bulgaria | Aug. 20, 1988 | Bulgaria |
| 400 meters | **52.61 s.** | Kim Batten | U.S. | Aug. 11, 1995 | Göteborg, Sweden |

### Field Events

| Event | Record | Holder | Country | Date | Where made |
|---|---|---|---|---|---|
| High jump | **6 ft., 10¼ in.** | Stefka Kostadinova | Bulgaria | Aug. 30, 1987 | Rome |
| Long jump | **24 ft., 8¼ in.** | Galina Chistyakova | USSR | June 11, 1988 | Leningrad |
| Triple jump | **50 ft., 10¼ in.** | Inessa Kravets | Ukraine | Aug. 10, 1995 | Göteborg, Sweden |
| Pole vault | **14 ft., 7¼ in.** | Emma George | Australia | July 14, 1996 | Sapporo, Japan |
| Shot put | **74 ft., 3 in.** | Natalya Lisovskaya | USSR | June 7, 1987 | Moscow |
| Discus | **252 ft.** | Gabriele Reinsch | E. Germany | July 9, 1988 | E. Germany |
| Javelin | **262 ft., 5 in.** | Petra Felke | E. Germany | Sept. 9, 1988 | E. Germany |
| Heptathlon | **7,291 pts.** | Jackie Joyner-Kersee | U.S. | Sept. 23-24, 1988 | Seoul |

### Relay Races

| Event | Record | Holder | Country | Date | Where made |
|---|---|---|---|---|---|
| 400 mtrs. (4×100) | **41.37 s.** | National team | E. Germany | Oct. 6, 1985 | Canberra, Australia |
| 800 mtrs. (4×200) | **1 m., 28.15 s.** | National team | E. Germany | Aug. 9, 1980 | Jena, E. Germany |
| 1,600 mtrs. (4×400) | **3 m., 15.17 s.** | National team | USSR | Oct. 1, 1988 | Seoul |
| 3,200 mtrs. (4×800) | **7 m., 50.17 s.** | National team | USSR | Aug. 5, 1984 | Moscow |

# World Track and Field Indoor Records

As of Sept., 1996

The International Amateur Athletic Federation began recognizing world indoor track and field records as official on Jan. 1, 1987. Prior to that, there were only unofficial world indoor bests. World indoor bests set prior to Jan. 1, 1987, are subject to approval as world records providing they meet the prescribed IAAF world records criteria, including drug testing. To be accepted as a world indoor record, a performance must meet the same criteria as a world record outdoors except that a track performance cannot be set on an indoor track larger than 200 meters. *Record pending.

### Men

| Event | Record | Holder | Country | Date | Where made |
|---|---|---|---|---|---|
| 50 meters | ***5.56** | Donovan Bailey | Canada | Feb. 9, 1996 | Reno, NV |
| 60 meters | **6.41** | Andre Cason | U.S. | Feb. 14, 1992 | Madrid |
| 100 meters | **10.05** | Frankie Fredericks | Namibia | Feb. 12, 1996 | Tampere, Finland |
| 200 meters | **19.92** | Frankie Fredericks | Namibia | Feb. 18, 1996 | Lievin, France |
| 400 meters | **44.63** | Michael Johnson | U.S. | Mar. 4, 1995 | Atlanta, GA |
| 800 meters | **1:44.84** | Paul Ereng | Kenya | Mar. 4, 1989 | Budapest |
| 1,000 meters | **2:15.26** | Noureddine Morceli | Algeria | Feb. 22, 1992 | Birmingham, England |
| 1,500 meters | **3:34.16** | Noureddine Morceli | Algeria | Feb. 28, 1991 | Seville, Spain |
| 1 mile | **3:49.78** | Eamonn Coghlan | Ireland | Feb. 27, 1983 | E. Rutherford, NJ |
| 3,000 meters | **7:30.72** | Haile Gebrselassie | Ethiopia | Feb. 4, 1996 | Stuttgart, Germany |
| 5,000 meters | **13:10.98** | Haile Gebrselassie | Ethiopia | Jan. 27, 1996 | Sindelfingen, Germany |
| 50-meter hurdles | **6.25** | Mark McKoy | Canada | Mar. 5, 1986 | Kobe, Japan |
| 60-meter hurdles | **7.30** | Colin Jackson | Gr. Britain | Mar. 6, 1994 | Sindelfingen, Germany |
| High jump | **7 ft., 11¼ in.** | Javier Sotomayor | Cuba | Mar. 4, 1989 | Budapest |
| Pole vault | **20 ft., 2 in.** | Sergei Bubka | Ukraine | Feb. 21, 1993 | Donyetsk, Ukraine |
| Long jump | **28 ft., 10¼ in.** | Carl Lewis | U.S. | Jan. 27, 1984 | New York, NY |
| Triple jump | **58 ft., 3¾ in.** | Leonid Voloshin | Russia | Feb. 6, 1994 | Grenoble, France |
| Shot put | **74 ft., 4¼ in.** | Randy Barnes | U.S. | Jan. 20, 1989 | Los Angeles, CA |

### Women

| Event | Record | Holder | Country | Date | Where made |
|---|---|---|---|---|---|
| 50 meters | **5.96** | Irina Privalova | Russia | Feb. 9, 1995 | Madrid |
| 60 meters | **6.92** | Irina Privalova | Russia | Feb. 9, 1995 | Madrid |
| | | Irina Privalova | Russia | Feb. 11, 1993 | Madrid |
| 200 meters | **21.87** | Merlene Ottey | Jamaica | Feb. 13, 1993 | Lievin, France |
| 400 meters | **49.59** | Jarmila Kratochvilova | Czechoslovakia | Mar. 7, 1982 | Milan, Italy |
| 800 meters | **1:56.40** | Christine Wachtel | E. Germany | Feb. 13, 1988 | Vienna |
| 1,000 meters | **2:31.23** | Maria Mutola | Mozambique | Feb. 25, 1996 | Stockholm |
| 1,500 meters | **4:00.27** | Doina Melinte | Romania | Feb. 9, 1990 | E. Rutherford, NJ |
| 1 mile | **4:17.14** | Doina Melinte | Romania | Feb. 9, 1990 | E. Rutherford, NJ |
| 3,000 meters | **8:33.82** | Elly van Hulst | Netherlands | Mar. 4, 1989 | Budapest |
| 5,000 meters | **15:03.17** | Liz McColgan | Gr. Britain | Feb. 22, 1992 | Birmingham, England |
| 50-meter hurdles | **6:58** | Cornelia Oschkenat | E. Germany | Feb. 20, 1988 | Berlin |
| 60-meter hurdles | **7.69** | Lyudmila Narozhilenko | USSR | Feb 4, 1990 | Chelyabinsk, USSR |
| High jump | **6 ft., 9½ in.** | Heike Henkel | Germany | Feb. 8, 1992 | Karlsruhe, Germany |
| Long jump | **24 ft., 2¼ in.** | Heike Drechsler | E. Germany | Feb. 13, 1988 | Vienna |
| Triple jump | **49 ft., 3¾ in.** | Yolanda Chen | Russia | Mar. 11, 1995 | Barcelona |
| Shot put | **73 ft., 10 in.** | Helena Fibingerova | Czechoslovakia | Feb. 19, 1977 | Czechoslovakia |

# NATIONAL FOOTBALL LEAGUE

## NFL 1995-96: Cleveland Brown-less, Magnificent Marino, A Legend Retires

The Cleveland Browns moved to Baltimore before the 1996 season and were rechristened the Ravens; the NFL announced that a new Cleveland Browns team, with their traditional colors, would enter the league by 1999. NFL owners also okayed the Houston Oilers' plan to move to Nashville after the 1997 season. In other news, Miami Dolphins quarterback Dan Marino set career marks in 1995 for most touchdown passes, completions, and yards passing. Legendary Dolphins coach Don Shula retired after 1995 and was replaced by former Cowboys coach Jimmy Johnson.

## Final 1995 Standings

### American Football Conference

**Eastern Division**

| | W | L | T | Pct. | Pts. | Opp. |
|---|---|---|---|---|---|---|
| Buffalo | 10 | 6 | 0 | .625 | 350 | 335 |
| Indianapolis* | 9 | 7 | 0 | .563 | 331 | 316 |
| Miami* | 9 | 7 | 0 | .563 | 398 | 332 |
| New England | 6 | 10 | 0 | .375 | 294 | 377 |
| N.Y. Jets | 3 | 13 | 0 | .188 | 233 | 384 |

**Central Division**

| | W | L | T | Pct. | Pts. | Opp. |
|---|---|---|---|---|---|---|
| Pittsburgh | 11 | 5 | 0 | .689 | 407 | 327 |
| Cincinnati | 7 | 9 | 0 | .438 | 349 | 374 |
| Houston | 7 | 9 | 0 | .438 | 348 | 324 |
| Cleveland | 5 | 11 | 0 | .313 | 289 | 356 |
| Jacksonville | 4 | 12 | 0 | .250 | 275 | 404 |

**Western Division**

| | W | L | T | Pct. | Pts. | Opp. |
|---|---|---|---|---|---|---|
| Kansas City | 13 | 3 | 0 | .813 | 358 | 241 |
| San Diego* | 9 | 7 | 0 | .563 | 321 | 323 |
| Seattle | 8 | 8 | 0 | .500 | 363 | 366 |
| Denver | 8 | 8 | 0 | .500 | 388 | 345 |
| Oakland | 8 | 8 | 0 | .500 | 348 | 332 |

### National Football Conference

**Eastern Division**

| | W | L | T | Pct. | Pts. | Opp. |
|---|---|---|---|---|---|---|
| Dallas | 12 | 4 | 0 | .750 | 435 | 291 |
| Philadelphia* | 10 | 6 | 0 | .625 | 318 | 338 |
| Washington | 6 | 10 | 0 | .375 | 326 | 359 |
| N.Y. Giants | 5 | 11 | 0 | .313 | 290 | 340 |
| Arizona | 4 | 12 | 0 | .250 | 275 | 422 |

**Central Division**

| | W | L | T | Pct. | Pts. | Opp. |
|---|---|---|---|---|---|---|
| Green Bay | 11 | 5 | 0 | .689 | 404 | 314 |
| Detroit* | 10 | 6 | 0 | .625 | 436 | 336 |
| Chicago | 9 | 7 | 0 | .563 | 392 | 360 |
| Minnesota | 8 | 8 | 0 | .500 | 412 | 385 |
| Tampa Bay | 7 | 9 | 0 | .438 | 238 | 335 |

**Western Division**

| | W | L | T | Pct. | Pts. | Opp. |
|---|---|---|---|---|---|---|
| San Francisco | 11 | 5 | 0 | .688 | 457 | 258 |
| Atlanta* | 9 | 7 | 0 | .563 | 362 | 349 |
| St. Louis | 7 | 9 | 0 | .438 | 309 | 418 |
| Carolina | 7 | 9 | 0 | .438 | 289 | 325 |
| New Orleans | 7 | 9 | 0 | .438 | 319 | 348 |

* Wild card team.

**AFC Playoffs**—Buffalo 37, Miami 22; Indianapolis 35, San Diego 20; Pittsburgh 40, Buffalo 21; Indianapolis 10, Kansas City 7; Pittsburgh 20, Indianapolis 16.

**NFC Playoffs**—Philadelphia 58, Detroit 37; Green Bay 37, Atlanta 20; Green Bay 27, San Francisco 17; Dallas 30, Philadelphia 11; Dallas 38, Green Bay 27.

**Super Bowl**—Dallas 27, Pittsburgh 17.

## National Football League Champions

| Year | East Winner (W-L-T) | West Winner (W-L-T) | Playoff |
|---|---|---|---|
| 1933 | New York Giants (11-3-0) | Chicago Bears (10-2-1) | Chicago Bears 23, New York 21 |
| 1934 | New York Giants (8-5-0) | Chicago Bears (13-0-0) | New York 30, Chicago Bears 13 |
| 1935 | New York Giants (9-3-0) | Detroit Lions (7-3-2) | Detroit 26, New York 7 |
| 1936 | Boston Redskins (7-5-0) | Green Bay Packers (10-1-1) | Green Bay 21, Boston 6 |
| 1937 | Washington Redskins (8-3-0) | Chicago Bears (9-1-1) | Washington 28, Chicago Bears 21 |
| 1938 | New York Giants (8-2-1) | Green Bay Packers (8-3-0) | New York 23, Green Bay 17 |
| 1939 | New York Giants (9-1-1) | Green Bay Packers (9-2-0) | Green Bay 27, New York 0 |
| 1940 | Washington Redskins (9-2-0) | Chicago Bears (8-3-0) | Chicago Bears 73, Washington 0 |
| 1941 | New York Giants (8-3-0) | Chicago Bears (10-1-1)(a) | Chicago Bears 37, New York 9 |
| 1942 | Washington Redskins (10-1-1) | Chicago Bears (11-0-0) | Washington 14, Chicago Bears 6 |
| 1943 | Washington Redskins (6-3-1)(a) | Chicago Bears (8-1-1) | Chicago Bears, 41, Washington 21 |
| 1944 | New York Giants (8-1-1) | Green Bay Packers (8-2-0) | Green Bay 14, New York 7 |
| 1945 | Washington Redskins (8-2-0) | Cleveland Rams (9-1-0) | Cleveland 15, Washington 14 |
| 1946 | New York Giants (7-3-1) | Chicago Bears (8-2-1) | Chicago Bears 24, New York 14 |
| 1947 | Philadelphia Eagles (8-4-0)(a) | Chicago Cardinals (9-3-0) | Chicago Cardinals 28, Philadelphia 21 |
| 1948 | Philadelphia Eagles (9-2-1) | Chicago Cardinals (11-1-0) | Philadelphia 7, Chicago Cardinals 0 |
| 1949 | Philadelphia Eagles (11-1-0) | Los Angeles Rams (8-2-2) | Philadelphia 14, Los Angeles 0 |
| 1950 | Cleveland Browns (10-2-0)(a) | Los Angeles Rams (9-3-0)(a) | Cleveland 30, Los Angeles 28 |
| 1951 | Cleveland Browns (11-1-0) | Los Angeles Rams (8-4-0) | Los Angeles 24, Cleveland 17 |
| 1952 | Cleveland Browns (8-4-0) | Detroit Lions (9-3-0)(a) | Detroit 17, Cleveland 7 |
| 1953 | Cleveland Browns (11-1-0) | Detroit Lions (10-2-0) | Detroit 17, Cleveland 16 |
| 1954 | Cleveland Browns (9-3-0) | Detroit Lions (9-2-1) | Cleveland 56, Detroit 10 |
| 1955 | Cleveland Browns (9-2-1) | Los Angeles Rams (8-3-1) | Cleveland 38, Los Angeles 14 |
| 1956 | New York Giants (8-3-1) | Chicago Bears (9-2-1) | New York 47, Chicago Bears 7 |
| 1957 | Cleveland Browns (9-2-1) | Detroit Lions (8-4-0)(a) | Detroit 59, Cleveland 14 |
| 1958 | New York Giants (9-3-0)(a) | Baltimore Colts (9-3-0) | Baltimore 23, New York 17(b) |
| 1959 | New York Giants (10-2-0) | Baltimore Colts (9-3-0) | Baltimore 31, New York 16 |
| 1960 | Philadelphia Eagles (10-2-0) | Green Bay Packers (8-4-0) | Philadelphia 17, Green Bay 13 |
| 1961 | New York Giants (10-3-1) | Green Bay Packers (11-3-0) | Green Bay 37, New York 0 |
| 1962 | New York Giants (12-2-0) | Green Bay Packers (13-1-0) | Green Bay 16, New York 7 |
| 1963 | New York Giants (11-3-0) | Chicago Bears (11-1-2) | Chicago 14, New York 10 |
| 1964 | Cleveland Browns (10-3-1) | Baltimore Colts (12-2-0) | Cleveland 27, Baltimore 0 |
| 1965 | Cleveland Browns (11-3-0) | Green Bay Packers (10-3-1)(a) | Green Bay 23, Cleveland 12 |
| 1966 | Dallas Cowboys (10-3-1) | Green Bay Packers (12-2-0) | Green Bay 34, Dallas 27 |

(a) Won divisional playoff. (b) Won at 8:15 of sudden death overtime period.

| Year | Conference | Division | Winner (W-L-T) | Playoffs(c) |
|---|---|---|---|---|
| 1967 | East | Century | Cleveland Browns (9-5-0) | Dallas 52, Cleveland 14 |
| | | Capitol | Dallas Cowboys (9-5-0) | |
| | West | Central | Green Bay Packers (9-4-1) | Green Bay 28, Los Angeles 7 |
| | | Coastal | Los Angeles Rams (11-1-2)(a) | Green Bay 21, Dallas 17 |

*(continued)*

| Year | Conference | Division | Winner (W-L-T) | Playoffs(c) |
|---|---|---|---|---|
| 1968 | East | Century | Cleveland Browns (10-4-0) | Cleveland 31, Dallas 20 |
| | | Capitol | Dallas Cowboys (12-2-0) | |
| | West | Central | Minnesota Vikings (8-6-0) | Baltimore 24, Minnesota 14 |
| | | Coastal | Baltimore Colts (13-1-0) | Baltimore 34, Cleveland 0 |
| 1969 | East | Century | Cleveland Browns (10-3-1) | Cleveland 38, Dallas 14 |
| | | Capitol | Dallas Cowboys (11-2-1) | |
| | West | Central | Minnesota Vikings (12-2-0) | Minnesota 23, Los Angeles 20 |
| | | Coastal | Los Angeles Rams (11-3-0) | Minnesota 27, Cleveland 7 |
| 1970 | American | Eastern | Baltimore Colts (11-2-1) | Baltimore 17, Cincinnati 0 |
| | | Central | Cincinnati Bengals (8-6-0) | Oakland 21, Miami* 14 |
| | | Western | Oakland Raiders (8-4-2) | Baltimore 27, Oakland 17 |
| | National | Eastern | Dallas Coboys (10-4-0) | Dallas 5, Detroit* 0 |
| | | Central | Minnesota Vikings (12-2-0) | San Francisco 17, Minnesota 14 |
| | | Western | San Francisco 49ers (10-3-1) | Dallas 17, San Francisco 10 |
| 1971 | American | Eastern | Miami Dolphins (10-3-1) | Miami 27, Kansas City* 24 |
| | | Central | Cleveland Browns (9-5-0) | Baltimore 20, Cleveland 3 |
| | | Western | Kansas City Chiefs(10-3-1) | Miami 21, Baltimore 0 |
| | National | Eastern | Dallas Cowboys (11-3-0) | Dallas 20, Minnesota 12 |
| | | Central | Minnesota Vikings (11-3-0) | San Francisco 24, Washington* 20 |
| | | Western | San Francisco 49ers (9-5-0) | Dallas 14, San Francisco 3 |
| 1972 | American | Eastern | Miami Dolphins (14-0-0) | Miami 20, Cleveland* 14 |
| | | Central | Pittsburgh Steelers (11-3-0) | Pittsburgh 13, Oakland 7 |
| | | Western | Oakland Raiders (10-3-1) | Miami 21, Pittsburgh 17 |
| | National | Eastern | Washington Redskins (11-3-0) | Washington 16, Green Bay 3 |
| | | Central | Green Bay Packers (10-4-0) | Dallas* 30, San Francisco 28 |
| | | Western | San Francisco 49ers (8-5-1) | Washington 26, Dallas* 3 |
| 1973 | American | Eastern | Miami Dolphins (12-2-0) | Miami 34, Cincinnati 16 |
| | | Central | Cincinnati Bengals (10-4-0) | Oakland 33, Pittsburgh* 14 |
| | | Western | Oakland Raiders (9-4-1) | Miami 27, Oakland 10 |
| | National | Eastern | Dallas Cowboys (10-4-0) | Dallas 27, Los Angeles 16 |
| | | Central | Minnesota Vikings (12-2-0) | Minnesota 27, Washington* 20 |
| | | Western | Los Angeles Rams (12-2-0) | Minnesota 27, Dallas 10 |
| 1974 | American | Eastern | Miami Dolphins (11-3-0) | Oakland 28, Miami 26 |
| | | Central | Pittsburgh Steelers (10-3-1) | Pittsburgh 32, Buffalo* 14 |
| | | Western | Oakland Raiders (12-2-0) | Pittsburgh 24, Oakland 13 |
| | National | Eastern | St. Louis Cardinals (10-4-0) | Minnesota 30, St. Louis 14 |
| | | Central | Minnesota Vikings (10-4-0) | Los Angeles 19, Washington* 10 |
| | | Western | Los Angeles Rams (10-4-0) | Minnesota 14, Los Angeles 10 |
| 1975 | American | Eastern | Baltimore Colts (10-4-0) | Pittsburgh 28, Baltimore 10 |
| | | Central | Pittsburgh Steelers (12-2-0) | Oakland 31, Cincinnati* 28 |
| | | Western | Oakland Raiders (11-3-0) | Pittsburgh 16, Oakland 10 |
| | National | Eastern | St. Louis Cardinals (11-3-0) | Dallas* 17, Minnesota 14 |
| | | Central | Minnesota Vikings (12-2-0) | Los Angeles 35, St. Louis 23 |
| | | Western | Los Angeles Rams (12-2-0) | Dallas* 37, Los Angeles 7 |
| 1976 | American | Eastern | Baltimore Colts (11-3-0) | Pittsburgh 40, Baltimore 14 |
| | | Central | Pittsburgh Steelers (10-4-0) | Oakland 24, New England* 21 |
| | | Western | Oakland Raiders (13-1-0) | Oakland 24, Pittsburgh 7 |
| | National | Eastern | Dallas Cowboys (11-3-0) | Minnesota 35, Washington* 20 |
| | | Central | Minnesota Vikings (11-2-1) | Los Angeles 14, Dallas 12 |
| | | Western | Los Angeles Rams (10-3-1) | Minnesota 24, Los Angeles 13 |
| 1977 | American | Eastern | Baltimore Colts (10-4-0) | Oakland* 37, Baltimore 31 |
| | | Central | Pittsburgh Steelers (9-5-0) | Denver 34, Pittsburgh 21 |
| | | Western | Denver Broncos (12-2-0) | Denver 20, Oakland* 17 |
| | National | Eastern | Dallas Cowboys (12-2-0) | Dallas 37, Chicago* 7 |
| | | Central | Minnesota Vikings (9-5-0) | Minnesota 14, Los Angeles 7 |
| | | Western | Los Angeles Rams (10-4-0) | Dallas 23, Minnesota 6 |
| 1978 | American | Eastern | New England Patriots (11-5-0) | Pittsburgh 33, Denver 10 |
| | | Central | Pittsburgh Steelers (14-2-0) | Houston* 31, New England 14 |
| | | Western | Denver Broncos (10-6-0) | Pittsburgh 34, Houston* 5 |
| | National | Eastern | Dallas Cowboys (12-4-0) | Dallas 27, Atlanta* 20 |
| | | Central | Minnesota Vikings (8-7-1) | Los Angeles 34, Minnesota 10 |
| | | Western | Los Angeles Rams (12-4-0) | Dallas 28, Los Angeles 0 |
| 1979 | American | Eastern | Miami Dolphins (10-6-0) | Houston* 17, San Diego 14 |
| | | Central | Pittsburgh Steelers (12-4-0) | Pittsburgh 34, Miami 14 |
| | | Western | San Diego Chargers (12-4-0) | Pittsburgh 27, Houston* 13 |
| | National | Eastern | Dallas Cowboys (11-5-0) | Tampa Bay 24, Philadelphia* 17 |
| | | Central | Tampa Bay Buccaneers (10-6-0) | Los Angeles 21, Dallas 19 |
| | | Western | Los Angeles Rams (9-7-0) | Los Angeles 9, Tampa Bay 0 |
| 1980 | American | Eastern | Buffalo Bills (11-5-0) | San Diego 20, Buffalo 14 |
| | | Central | Cleveland Browns (11-5-0) | Oakland* 14, Cleveland 12 |
| | | Western | San Diego Chargers (11-5-0) | Oakland* 34, San Diego 27 |
| | National | Eastern | Philadelphia Eagles (12-4-0) | Philadelphia 31, Minnesota 16 |
| | | Central | Minnesota Vikings (9-7-0) | Dallas* 30, Atlanta 27 |
| | | Western | Atlanta Falcons (12-4-0) | Philadelphia 20, Dallas* 7 |
| 1981 | American | Eastern | Miami Dolphins (11-4-1) | San Diego 41, Miami 38 |
| | | Central | Cincinnati Bengals (12-4-0) | Cincinnati 28, Buffalo* 21 |
| | | Western | San Diego Chargers (10-6-0) | Cincinnati 27, San Diego 7 |
| | National | Eastern | Dallas Cowboys (12-4-0) | Dallas 38, Tampa Bay 0 |
| | | Central | Tampa Bay Buccaneers (9-7-0) | San Francisco 38, N.Y. Giants* 24 |
| | | Western | San Francisco 49ers (13-3-0) | San Francisco 28, Dallas 27 |
| 1982(d) | American | | Los Angeles Raiders (8-1-0) | Strike-shortened season (see |
| | National | | Washington Redskins (8-1-0) | playoff results below) |

**AFC playoffs**—Miami 28, New England 13; L.A. Raiders 27, Cleveland 10; N.Y. Jets 44, Cincinnati 17; San Diego 31, Pittsburgh 28; N.Y. Jets 17, L.A. Raiders 14; Miami 34, San Diego 13; Miami 14, N.Y. Jets 0. **NFC playoffs**—Washington 31, Detroit 7; Green Bay 41, St. Louis 16; Dallas 30, Tampa Bay 17; Minnesota 30, Atlanta 24; Washington 21, Minnesota 7; Dallas 37, Green Bay 26;; Washington 31, Dallas 17. **AFC Champion**—Miami Dolphins. **NFC Champion**—Washington Redskins.

| Year | Conference | Division | Winner (W-L-T) | Playoffs(c) |
|---|---|---|---|---|
| 1983 | American | Eastern | Miami Dolphins (12-4-0) | Seattle* 27, Miami 20 |
| | | Central | Pittsburgh Steelers (10-6-0) | L.A. Raiders 38, Pittsburgh 10 |
| | | Western | Los Angeles Raiders (12-4-0) | L.A. Raiders 30, Seattle* 14 |
| | National | Eastern | Washington Redskins (14-2-0) | Washington 51, L.A. Rams* 7 |
| | | Central | Detroit Lions (9-7-0) | San Francisco 24, Detroit 23 |
| | | Western | San Francisico 49ers (10-6-0) | Washington 24, San Francisco 21 |
| 1984 | American | Eastern | Miami Dolphins (14-2-0) | Miami 31, Seattle* 10 |
| | | Central | Pittsburgh Steelers (9-7-0) | Pittsburgh 24, Denver 17 |
| | | Western | Denver Broncos (13-3-0) | Miami 45, Pittsburgh 28 |
| | National | Eastern | Washington Redskins (11-5-0) | Chicago 23, Washington 19 |
| | | Central | Chicago Bears (10-6-0) | San Francisco 21, N.Y. Giants* 10 |
| | | Western | San Francisco 49ers (15-1-0) | San Francisco 23, Chicago 0 |
| 1985 | American | Eastern | Miami Dolphins (12-4-0) | New England* 27, L.A. Raiders 20 |
| | | Central | Cleveland Browns (8-8-0) | Miami 24, Cleveland 21 |
| | | Western | Los Angeles Raiders (12-4-0) | New England* 31, Miami 14 |
| | National | Eastern | Dallas Cowboys (10-6-0) | Chicago 21, N.Y. Giants* 0 |
| | | Central | Chicago Bears (15-1-0) | L.A. Rams 20, Dallas 0 |
| | | Western | Los Angeles Rams (11-5-0) | Chicago 24, L.A. Rams 0 |
| 1986 | American | Eastern | New England Patriots (11-5-0) | Denver 22, New England 17 |
| | | Central | Cleveland Browns (12-4-0) | Cleveland 23, N.Y. Jets* 20 |
| | | Western | Denver Broncos (11-5-0) | Denver 23, Cleveland 20 |
| | National | Eastern | New York Giants (14-2-0) | N.Y. Giants 49, San Francisco 3 |
| | | Central | Chicago Bears (14-2-0) | Washington* 27, Chicago 13 |
| | | Western | San Francisco 49ers (10-5-1) | N.Y. Giants 17, Washington* 0 |
| 1987 | American | Eastern | Indianapolis Colts (9-6-0) | Cleveland 38, Indianapolis 21 |
| | | Central | Cleveland Browns (10-5-0) | Denver 34, Houston* 10 |
| | | Western | Denver Broncos (10-4-1) | Denver 38, Cleveland 33 |
| | National | Eastern | Washington Redskins (11-4-0) | Washington 21, Chicago 17 |
| | | Central | Chicago Bears (11-4-0) | Minnesota* 36, San Francisco 24 |
| | | Western | San Francisco 49ers (13-2-0) | Washington 17, Minnesota* 10 |
| 1988 | American | Eastern | Buffalo Bills (12-4-0) | Buffalo 17, Houston* 10 |
| | | Central | Cincinnati Bengals (12-4-0) | Cincinnati 21, Seattle 13 |
| | | Western | Seattle Seahawks (9-7-0) | Cincinnati 21, Buffalo 10 |
| | National | Eastern | Philadelphia Eagles (10-6-0) | Chicago 20, Philadelphia 12 |
| | | Central | Chicago Bears (12-4-0) | San Francisco 34, Minnesota* 9 |
| | | Western | San Francisco 49ers (10-6-0) | San Francisco 28, Chicago 3 |
| 1989 | American | Eastern | Buffalo Bills (9-7-0) | Cleveland 34, Buffalo 30 |
| | | Central | Cleveland Browns (9-6-1) | Denver 24, Pittsburgh* 23 |
| | | Western | Denver Broncos (11-5-0) | Denver 37, Cleveland 21 |
| | National | Eastern | New York Giants (12-4-0) | San Francisco 41, Minnesota 13 |
| | | Central | Minnesota Vikings (10-6-0) | L.A. Rams* 19, N.Y. Giants 13 |
| | | Western | San Francisco 49ers (14-2-0) | San Francisco 30, L.A. Rams* 3 |
| 1990 | American | Eastern | Buffalo Bills (13-3-0) | L.A. Raiders 20, Cincinnati 10 |
| | | Central | Cincinnati Bengals (9-7-0) | Buffalo 44, Miami* 34 |
| | | Western | Los Angeles Raiders (12-4-0) | Buffalo 51, L.A. Raiders 3 |
| | National | Eastern | New York Giants (13-3-0) | San Francisco 28, Washington* 10 |
| | | Central | Chicago Bears (11-5-0) | N.Y. Giants 31, Chicago 3 |
| | | Western | San Francisco 49ers (14-2-0) | N.Y. Giants 15, San Francisco 13 |
| 1991 | American | Eastern | Buffalo Bills (13-3-0) | Denver 26, Houston 24 |
| | | Central | Houston Oilers (11-5-0) | Buffalo 37, Kansas City* 14 |
| | | Western | Denver Broncos (12-4-0) | Buffalo 10, Denver 7 |
| | National | Eastern | Washington Redskins (14-2-0) | Washington 24, Atlanta* 7 |
| | | Central | Detroit Lions (12-4-0) | Detroit 38, Dallas* 6 |
| | | Western | New Orleans Saints (11-5-0) | Washington 41, Detroit 10 |
| 1992 | American | Eastern | Miami Dolphins (11-5-0) | Miami 31, San Diego 0 |
| | | Central | Pittsburgh Steelers (11-5-0) | Buffalo* 24, Pittsburgh 3 |
| | | Western | San Diego Chargers (11-5-0) | Buffalo* 29, Miami 10 |
| | National | Eastern | Dallas Cowboys (13-3-0) | Dallas 34, Philadelphia* 10 |
| | | Central | Minnesota Vikings (11-5-0) | San Francisco 20, Washington* 13 |
| | | Western | San Francisco 49ers (14-2-0) | Dallas 30, San Francisco 20 |
| 1993 | American | Eastern | Buffalo Bills (12-4-0) | Buffalo 29, L.A. Raiders* 23 |
| | | Central | Houston Oilers (12-4-0) | Kansas City 28, Houston 20 |
| | | Western | Kansas City Chiefs (11-5-0) | Buffalo 30, Kansas City 13 |
| | National | Eastern | Dallas Cowboys (12-4-0) | Dallas 27, Green Bay* 17 |
| | | Central | Detroit Lions (10-6-0) | San Francisco 44, N.Y. Giants* 3 |
| | | Western | San Francisco 49ers (10-6-0) | Dallas 38, San Francisco 21 |
| 1994 | American | Eastern | Miami Dolphins (10-6-0) | Pittsburgh 29, Cleveland* 9 |
| | | Central | Pittsburgh Steelers (12-4-0) | San Diego 22, Miami 21 |
| | | Western | San Diego Chargers (11-5-0) | San Diego 17, Pittsburgh 13 |
| | National | Eastern | Dallas Cowboys (12-4-0) | San Francisco 44, Chicago* 15 |
| | | Central | Minnesota Vikings (10-6-0) | Dallas 35, Green Bay* 9 |
| | | Western | San Francisco 49ers (13-3-0) | San Francisco 38, Dallas 28 |
| 1995 | American | Eastern | Buffalo Bills (10-6-0) | Indianapolis* 10, Kansas City 7 |
| | | Central | Pittsburgh Steelers (11-5-0) | Pittsburgh 40, Buffalo 21 |
| | | Western | Kansas City Chiefs (13-3-0) | Pittsburgh 20, Indianapolis* 16 |
| | National | Eastern | Dallas Cowboys (12-4-0) | Dallas 30, Philadelphia* 11 |
| | | Central | Green Bay Packers (11-5-0) | Green Bay 27, San Francisco 17 |
| | | Western | San Francisco 49ers (11-5-0) | Dallas 38, Green Bay 27 |

*Wild card team. (c) From 1978 on, only the final 2 conference playoff rounds are shown. (d) A strike shortened the 1982 season from 16 to 9 games. The top 8 teams in each conference played in a tournament to determine the conference champion.

## Cowboys Defeat Steelers in Super Bowl XXX

The Dallas Cowboys became the first team to win 3 Super Bowls in 4 years, with a close but decisive 27-17 victory over the Pittsburgh Steelers, Jan. 28, 1996, in Tempe, Arizona. The two teams had met twice before in the Super Bowl (1976, 1979), and the Steelers had won both previous games. Dallas led the entire game, but the Steelers had cut the gap to 20-17 in the 4th quarter before Dallas cornerback Larry Brown's 2d interception iced the game. Brown was named the game's Most Valuable Player. For the Cowboys, it was a record-tying 5th Super Bowl victory and a record-setting 8th appearance.

**Score by Quarters**

| | | | | |
|---|---|---|---|---|
| Dallas | 10 | 3 | 7 | 7—27 |
| Pittsburgh | 0 | 7 | 0 | 10—17 |

**Scoring**

Dallas—Boniol 42 yd. field goal
Dallas—Novacek 3 yd. pass from Aikman (Boniol kick)
Dallas—Boniol 35 yd. field goal
Pittsburgh—Thigpen 6 yd. pass from O'Donnell (Johnson kick)
Dallas—E. Smith 1 yd. run (Boniol kick)
Pittsburgh—Johnson 46 yd. field goal
Pittsburgh—Morris 1 yd. run (Johnson kick)
Dallas—E. Smith 4 yd. run (Boniol kick)

**Individual Statistics**

**Rushing** — Dallas, E. Smith 18-49, Johnston 2-8, K. Williams 1-2, Aikman 4-(minus 3). Pittsburgh, Morris 19-73, Pegram 6-15, Stewart 4-15, O'Donnell 1-0, J. Williams 1-0.

**Passing** — Dallas, Aikman 15-23-0-209. Pittsburgh, O'Donnell 28-49-3-239.

**Receiving** — Dallas, Irvin 5-76, Novacek 5-50, K. Williams 2-29, Sanders 1-47, Johnston 1-4, E. Smith 1-3. Pittsburgh, Hastings 10-98, Mills 8-78, Thigpen, 3-19, Morris 3-18, Holliday 2-19, J. Williams 2-7.

**Team Statistics**

| | Dallas | Pittsburgh |
|---|---|---|
| First downs | 15 | 25 |
| Total yards | 254 | 310 |
| Rushes-yards | 25-56 | 31-103 |
| Passing yards | 198 | 207 |
| Punt returns-yards | 1-11 | 2-18 |
| Kickoff returns-yards | 3-37 | 5-96 |
| Interception returns-yards | 3-77 | 0-0 |
| Comp.-att.-int. | 15-23-0 | 28-49-3 |
| Sacked-yards lost | 2-11 | 4-32 |
| Punts-average | 5-38 | 4-45 |
| Fumbles-lost | 0-0 | 2-0 |
| Penalties-yards | 5-25 | 2-15 |
| Time of possession | 26:11 | 33:49 |

## Super Bowls

| | Year | Winner | Loser | Winning coach | Site |
|---|---|---|---|---|---|
| I | 1967 | Green Bay Packers, 35 | Kansas City Chiefs, 10 | Vince Lombardi | Los Angeles Coliseum |
| II | 1968 | Green Bay Packers, 33 | Oakland Raiders, 14 | Vince Lombardi | Orange Bowl, Miami |
| III | 1969 | New York Jets, 16 | Baltimore Colts, 7 | Weeb Ewbank | Orange Bowl, Miami |
| IV | 1970 | Kansas City Chiefs, 23 | Minnesota Vikings, 7 | Hank Stram | Tulane Stadium, New Orleans |
| V | 1971 | Baltimore Colts, 16 | Dallas Cowboys, 13 | Don McCafferty | Orange Bowl, Miami |
| VI | 1972 | Dallas Cowboys, 24 | Miami Dolphins, 3 | Tom Landry | Tulane Stadium, New Orleans |
| VII | 1973 | Miami Dolphins, 14 | Washington Redskins, 7 | Don Shula | Los Angeles Coliseum |
| VIII | 1974 | Miami Dolphins, 24 | Minnesota Vikings, 7 | Don Shula | Rice Stadium, Houston |
| IX | 1975 | Pittsburgh Steelers, 16 | Minnesota Vikings, 6 | Chuck Noll | Tulane Stadium, New Orleans |
| X | 1976 | Pittsburgh Steelers, 21 | Dallas Cowboys, 17 | Chuck Noll | Orange Bowl, Miami |
| XI | 1977 | Oakland Raiders, 32 | Minnesota Vikings, 14 | John Madden | Rose Bowl, Pasadena, Cal. |
| XII | 1978 | Dallas Cowboys, 27 | Denver Broncos, 10 | Tom Landry | Superdome, New Orleans |
| XIII | 1979 | Pittsburgh Steelers, 35 | Dallas Cowboys, 31 | Chuck Noll | Orange Bowl, Miami |
| XIV | 1980 | Pittsburgh Steelers, 31 | Los Angeles Rams, 19 | Chuck Noll | Rose Bowl, Pasadena, Cal. |
| XV | 1981 | Oakland Raiders, 27 | Philadelphia Eagles, 10 | Tom Flores | Superdome, New Orleans |
| XVI | 1982 | San Francisco 49ers, 26 | Cincinnati Bengals, 21 | Bill Walsh | Silverdome, Pontiac, Mich. |
| XVII | 1983 | Washington Redskins, 27 | Miami Dolphins, 17 | Joe Gibbs | Rose Bowl, Pasadena, Cal. |
| XVIII | 1984 | Los Angeles Raiders, 38 | Washington Redskins, 9 | Tom Flores | Tampa Stadium, Fla. |
| XIX | 1985 | San Francisco 49ers, 38 | Miami Dolphins, 16 | Bill Walsh | Stanford Stadium, Palo Alto, Cal. |
| XX | 1986 | Chicago Bears, 46 | New England Patriots, 10 | Mike Ditka | Superdome, New Orleans |
| XXI | 1987 | New York Giants, 39 | Denver Broncos, 20 | Bill Parcells | Rose Bowl, Pasadena, Cal. |
| XXII | 1988 | Washington Redskins, 42 | Denver Broncos, 10 | Joe Gibbs | San Diego Stadium |
| XXIII | 1989 | San Francisco 49ers, 20 | Cincinnati Bengals, 16 | Bill Walsh | Joe Robbie Stadium, Miami |
| XXIV | 1990 | San Francisco 49ers, 55 | Denver Broncos, 10 | George Seifert | Superdome, New Orleans |
| XXV | 1991 | New York Giants, 20 | Buffalo Bills, 19 | Bill Parcells | Tampa Stadium, Fla. |
| XXVI | 1992 | Washington Redskins, 37 | Buffalo Bills, 24 | Joe Gibbs | Metrodome, Minneapolis |
| XXVII | 1993 | Dallas Cowboys, 52 | Buffalo Bills, 17 | Jimmy Johnson | Rose Bowl, Pasadena, Cal. |
| XXVIII | 1994 | Dallas Cowboys, 30 | Buffalo Bills, 13 | Jimmy Johnson | Georgia Dome, Atlanta |
| XXIX | 1995 | San Francisco 49ers, 49 | San Diego Chargers, 26 | George Seifert | Joe Robbie Stadium, Miami |
| XXX | 1996 | Dallas Cowboys, 27 | Pittsburgh Steelers, 17 | Barry Switzer | Sun Devil Stadium, Tempe, Ariz. |

## Super Bowl MVPs

| | | | | | |
|---|---|---|---|---|---|
| 1967 | Bart Starr, Green Bay | 1977 | Fred Biletnikoff, Oakland | 1987 | Phil Simms, N.Y. Giants |
| 1968 | Bart Starr, Green Bay | 1978 | Randy White, Harvey Martin, Dallas | 1988 | Doug Williams, Washington |
| 1969 | Joe Namath, N.Y. Jets | 1979 | Terry Bradshaw, Pittsburgh | 1989 | Jerry Rice, San Francisco |
| 1970 | Len Dawson, Kansas City | 1980 | Terry Bradshaw, Pittsburgh | 1990 | Joe Montana, San Francisco |
| 1971 | Chuck Howley, Dallas | 1981 | Jim Plunkett, Oakland | 1991 | Ottis Anderson, N.Y. Giants |
| 1972 | Roger Staubach, Dallas | 1982 | Joe Montana, San Francisco | 1992 | Mark Rypien, Washington |
| 1973 | Jake Scott, Miami | 1983 | John Riggins, Washington | 1993 | Troy Aikman, Dallas |
| 1974 | Larry Csonka, Miami | 1984 | Marcus Allen, L.A. Raiders | 1994 | Emmitt Smith, Dallas |
| 1975 | Franco Harris, Pittsburgh | 1985 | Joe Montana, San Francisco | 1995 | Steve Young, San Francisco |
| 1976 | Lynn Swann, Pittsburgh | 1986 | Richard Dent, Chicago | 1996 | Larry Brown, Dallas |

## American Football League Champions

| Year | Eastern Division | Western Division | Playoff |
|---|---|---|---|
| 1960 | Houston Oilers (10-4-0) | Los Angeles Chargers (10-4-0) | Houston 24, Los Angeles 16 |
| 1961 | Houston Oilers (10-3-1) | San Diego Chargers (12-2-0) | Houston 10, San Diego 3 |
| 1962 | Houston Oilers (11-3-0) | Dallas Texans (11-3-0) | Dallas 20, Houston 17 (2 overtimes) |
| 1963 | Boston Patriots (7-6-1)(a) | San Diego Chargers (11-3-0) | San Diego 51, Boston 10 |
| 1964 | Buffalo Bills (12-2-0) | San Diego Chargers (8-5-1) | Buffalo 20, San Diego 7 |
| 1965 | Buffalo Bills (10-3-1) | San Diego Chargers (9-2-3) | Buffalo 23, San Diego 0 |
| 1966 | Buffalo Bills (9-4-1) | Kansas City Chiefs (11-2-1) | Kansas City 31, Buffalo 7 |
| 1967 | Houston Oilers (9-4-1) | Oakland Raiders (13-1-0) | Oakland 40, Houston 7 |
| 1968 | New York Jets (11-3-0) | Oakland Raiders (12-2-0)(b) | New York 27, Oakland 23 |
| 1969 | New York Jets (10-4-0) | Oakland Raiders (12-1-1) | Kansas City 17, Oakland 7(c) |

(a) Defeated Buffalo Bills in divisional playoff. (b) Defeated Kansas City Chiefs in divisional playoff. (c) Kansas City Chiefs defeated New York Jets and Oakland Raiders defeated Houston Oilers in divisional playoffs.

# American Football Conference Leaders

(American Football League, 1960-69)

## Passing

| Player, team | Atts | Com | YG | TD | Year |
|---|---|---|---|---|---|
| Jack Kemp, L.A. Chargers | 406 | 211 | 3,018 | 20 | **1960** |
| George Blanda, Houston | 362 | 187 | 3,330 | 36 | **1961** |
| Len Dawson, Dallas Texans | 310 | 189 | 2,759 | 29 | **1962** |
| Tobin Rote, San Diego | 286 | 170 | 2,510 | 20 | **1963** |
| Len Dawson, Kansas City | 354 | 199 | 2,879 | 30 | **1964** |
| John Hadl, San Diego | 348 | 174 | 2,798 | 20 | **1965** |
| Len Dawson, Kansas City | 284 | 159 | 2,527 | 26 | **1966** |
| Daryle Lamonica, Oakland | 425 | 220 | 3,228 | 30 | **1967** |
| Len Dawson, Kansas City | 224 | 131 | 2,109 | 17 | **1968** |
| Greg Cook, Cincinnati | 197 | 106 | 1,854 | 15 | **1969** |
| Daryle Lamonica, Oakland | 356 | 179 | 2,516 | 22 | **1970** |
| Bob Griese, Miami | 263 | 145 | 2,089 | 19 | **1971** |
| Earl Morrall, Miami | 150 | 83 | 1,360 | 11 | **1972** |
| Ken Stabler, Oakland | 260 | 163 | 1,997 | 14 | **1973** |
| Ken Anderson, Cincinnati | 328 | 213 | 2,667 | 18 | **1974** |
| Ken Anderson, Cincinnati | 377 | 228 | 3,169 | 21 | **1975** |
| Ken Stabler, Oakland | 291 | 194 | 2,737 | 27 | **1976** |
| Bob Griese, Miami | 307 | 180 | 2,252 | 22 | **1977** |
| Terry Bradshaw, Pittsburgh | 368 | 207 | 2,915 | 28 | **1978** |
| Dan Fouts, San Diego | 530 | 332 | 4,082 | 24 | **1979** |
| Brian Sipe, Cleveland | 554 | 337 | 4,132 | 30 | **1980** |
| Ken Anderson, Cincinnati | 479 | 300 | 3,754 | 29 | **1981** |
| Ken Anderson, Cincinnati | 309 | 218 | 2,495 | 12 | **1982** |
| Dan Marino, Miami | 296 | 173 | 2,210 | 20 | **1983** |
| Dan Marino, Miami | 564 | 362 | 5,084 | 48 | **1984** |
| Ken O'Brien, N.Y. Jets | 488 | 297 | 3,888 | 25 | **1985** |
| Dan Marino, Miami | 623 | 378 | 4,746 | 44 | **1986** |
| Bernie Kosar, Cleveland | 389 | 241 | 3,033 | 22 | **1987** |
| Boomer Esiason, Cincinnati | 388 | 223 | 3,572 | 28 | **1988** |
| Boomer Esiason, Cincinnati | 455 | 258 | 3,525 | 28 | **1989** |
| Jim Kelly, Buffalo | 346 | 219 | 2,829 | 24 | **1990** |
| Jim Kelly, Buffalo | 474 | 304 | 3,844 | 33 | **1991** |
| Warren Moon, Houston | 346 | 224 | 2,521 | 18 | **1992** |
| John Elway, Denver | 551 | 348 | 4,030 | 25 | **1993** |
| Dan Marino, Miami | 615 | 385 | 4,453 | 30 | **1994** |
| Jim Harbaugh, Indianapolis | 314 | 200 | 2,575 | 17 | **1995** |

## Pass-Receiving

| Year | Player, team | Ct | YG | TD |
|---|---|---|---|---|
| **1960** | Lionel Taylor, Denver | 92 | 1,235 | 12 |
| **1961** | Lionel Taylor, Denver | 100 | 1,176 | 4 |
| **1962** | Lionel Taylor, Denver | 77 | 908 | 4 |
| **1963** | Lionel Taylor, Denver | 78 | 1,101 | 10 |
| **1964** | Charley Hennigan, Houston | 101 | 1,546 | 8 |
| **1965** | Lionel Taylor, Denver | 85 | 1,131 | 6 |
| **1966** | Lance Alworth, San Diego | 73 | 1,383 | 13 |
| **1967** | George Sauer, N.Y. Jets | 75 | 1,189 | 6 |
| **1968** | Lance Alworth, San Diego | 68 | 1,312 | 10 |
| **1969** | Lance Alworth, San Diego | 64 | 1,003 | 4 |
| **1970** | Marlin Briscoe, Buffalo | 57 | 1,036 | 8 |
| **1971** | Fred Biletnikoff, Oakland | 61 | 929 | 9 |
| **1972** | Fred Biletnikoff, Oakland | 58 | 802 | 7 |
| **1973** | Fred Willis, Houston | 57 | 371 | 1 |
| **1974** | Lydell Mitchell, Baltimore Colts | 72 | 544 | 2 |
| **1975** | Reggie Rucker, Cleveland | 60 | 770 | 3 |
| | Lydell Mitchell, Baltimore Colts | 60 | 554 | 4 |
| **1976** | MacArthur Lane, Kansas City | 66 | 686 | 1 |
| **1977** | Lydell Mitchell, Baltimore Colts | 71 | 620 | 4 |
| **1978** | Steve Largent, Seattle | 71 | 1,168 | 8 |
| **1979** | Joe Washington, Baltimore Colts | 82 | 750 | 3 |
| **1980** | Kellen Winslow, San Diego | 89 | 1,290 | 9 |
| **1981** | Kellen Winslow, San Diego | 88 | 1,075 | 10 |
| **1982** | Kellen Winslow, San Diego | 54 | 721 | 6 |
| **1983** | Todd Christensen, L.A. Raiders | 92 | 1,247 | 12 |
| **1984** | Ozzie Newsome, Cleveland | 89 | 1,001 | 5 |
| **1985** | Lionel James, San Diego | 86 | 1,027 | 6 |
| **1986** | Todd Christensen, L.A. Raiders | 95 | 1,153 | 8 |
| **1987** | Al Toon, N.Y. Jets | 68 | 976 | 5 |
| **1988** | Al Toon, N.Y. Jets | 93 | 1,067 | 5 |
| **1989** | Andre Reed, Buffalo | 88 | 1,312 | 9 |
| **1990** | Haywood Jeffires, Houston | 74 | 1,048 | 8 |
| | Drew Hill, Houston | 74 | 1,019 | 5 |
| **1991** | Haywood Jeffires, Houston | 100 | 1,181 | 7 |
| **1992** | Haywood Jeffires, Houston | 90 | 913 | 9 |
| **1993** | Reggie Langhorne, Indianapolis | 85 | 1,038 | 3 |
| **1994** | Ben Coates, New England | 96 | 1,174 | 7 |
| **1995** | Carl Pickens, Cincinnati | 99 | 1,234 | 17 |

## Scoring

| Player, team | TD | PAT | FG | Pts | Year |
|---|---|---|---|---|---|
| Gene Mingo, Denver | 6 | 33 | 18 | 123 | **1960** |
| Gino Cappelletti, Boston | 8 | 48 | 17 | 147 | **1961** |
| Gene Mingo, Denver | 4 | 32 | 27 | 137 | **1962** |
| Gino Cappelletti, Boston | 2 | 35 | 22 | 113 | **1963** |
| Gino Cappelletti, Boston | 7 | 36 | 25 | 155 | **1964** |
| Gino Cappelletti, Boston | 9 | 27 | 17 | 132 | **1965** |
| Gino Cappelletti, Boston | 6 | 35 | 16 | 119 | **1966** |
| George Blanda, Oakland | 0 | 56 | 20 | 116 | **1967** |
| Jim Turner, N.Y. Jets | 0 | 43 | 34 | 145 | **1968** |
| Jim Turner, N.Y. Jets | 0 | 33 | 32 | 129 | **1969** |
| Jan Stenerud, Kansas City | 0 | 26 | 30 | 116 | **1970** |
| Garo Yepremian, Miami | 0 | 33 | 28 | 117 | **1971** |
| Bobby Howfield, N.Y. Jets | 0 | 40 | 27 | 121 | **1972** |
| Roy Gerela, Pittsburgh | 0 | 36 | 29 | 123 | **1973** |
| Roy Gerela, Pittsburgh | 0 | 33 | 20 | 93 | **1974** |
| O.J. Simpson, Buffalo | 23 | 0 | 0 | 138 | **1975** |
| Toni Linhart, Baltimore Colts | 0 | 49 | 20 | 109 | **1976** |
| Errol Mann, Oakland | 0 | 39 | 20 | 99 | **1977** |
| Pat Leahy, N.Y. Jets | 0 | 41 | 22 | 107 | **1978** |
| John Smith, New England | 0 | 46 | 23 | 115 | **1979** |
| John Smith, New England | 0 | 51 | 26 | 129 | **1980** |
| Jim Breech, Cincinnati | 0 | 49 | 22 | 115 | **1981** |
| Nick Lowery, Kansas City | 0 | 37 | 26 | 115 | |
| Marcus Allen, L.A. Raiders | 14 | 0 | 0 | 84 | **1982** |
| Gary Anderson, Pittsburgh | 0 | 38 | 27 | 119 | **1983** |
| Gary Anderson, Pittsburgh | 0 | 45 | 24 | 117 | **1984** |
| Gary Anderson, Pittsburgh | 0 | 40 | 33 | 139 | **1985** |
| Tony Franklin, New England | 0 | 44 | 32 | 140 | **1986** |
| Jim Breech, Cincinnati | 0 | 25 | 24 | 97 | **1987** |
| Scott Norwood, Buffalo | 0 | 33 | 32 | 129 | **1988** |
| David Treadwell, Denver | 0 | 39 | 27 | 120 | **1989** |
| Nick Lowery, Kansas City | 0 | 37 | 34 | 139 | **1990** |
| Pete Stoyanovich, Miami | 0 | 28 | 31 | 121 | **1991** |
| Pete Stoyanovich, Miami | 0 | 34 | 30 | 124 | **1992** |
| Jeff Jaeger, L.A. Raiders | 0 | 27 | 35 | 132 | **1993** |
| John Carney, San Diego | 0 | 33 | 34 | 135 | **1994** |
| Norm Johnson, Pittsburgh | 0 | 39 | 34 | 141 | **1995** |

## Rushing

| Year | Player, team | Yds | Atts | TD |
|---|---|---|---|---|
| **1960** | Abner Haynes, Dallas Texans | 875 | 156 | 9 |
| **1961** | Billy Cannon, Houston | 948 | 200 | 6 |
| **1962** | Cookie Gilchrest, Buffalo | 1,096 | 214 | 13 |
| **1963** | Clem Daniels, Oakland | 1,099 | 215 | 3 |
| **1964** | Cookie Gilchrest, Buffalo | 981 | 230 | 6 |
| **1965** | Paul Lowe, San Diego | 1,121 | 222 | 7 |
| **1966** | Jim Nance, Boston | 1,458 | 299 | 11 |
| **1967** | Jim Nance, Boston | 1,216 | 269 | 7 |
| **1968** | Paul Robinson, Cincinnati | 1,023 | 238 | 8 |
| **1969** | Dick Post, San Diego | 873 | 182 | 6 |
| **1970** | Floyd Little, Denver | 901 | 209 | 3 |
| **1971** | Floyd Little, Denver | 1,133 | 284 | 6 |
| **1972** | O.J. Simpson, Buffalo | 1,251 | 292 | 6 |
| **1973** | O.J. Simpson, Buffalo | 2,003 | 332 | 12 |
| **1974** | Otis Armstrong, Denver | 1,407 | 263 | 9 |
| **1975** | O.J. Simpson, Buffalo | 1,817 | 329 | 16 |
| **1976** | O.J. Simpson, Buffalo | 1,503 | 290 | 8 |
| **1977** | Mark van Eeghen, Oakland | 1,273 | 324 | 7 |
| **1978** | Earl Campbell, Houston | 1,450 | 302 | 13 |
| **1979** | Earl Campbell, Houston | 1,697 | 368 | 19 |
| **1980** | Earl Campbell, Houston | 1,934 | 373 | 13 |
| **1981** | Earl Campbell, Houston | 1,376 | 361 | 10 |
| **1982** | Freeman McNeil, N.Y. Jets | 786 | 151 | 6 |
| **1983** | Curt Warner, Seattle | 1,446 | 335 | 13 |
| **1984** | Earnest Jackson, San Diego | 1,179 | 296 | 8 |
| **1985** | Marcus Allen, L.A. Raiders | 1,759 | 380 | 11 |
| **1986** | Curt Warner, Seattle | 1,481 | 319 | 13 |
| **1987** | Eric Dickerson, L.A. Rams-Ind. | 1,288* | 283 | 6 |
| **1988** | Eric Dickerson, Indianapolis | 1,659 | 388 | 14 |
| **1989** | Christian Okoye, Kansas City | 1,480 | 370 | 12 |
| **1990** | Thurman Thomas, Buffalo | 1,297 | 271 | 11 |
| **1991** | Thurman Thomas, Buffalo | 1,407 | 288 | 7 |
| **1992** | Barry Foster, Pittsburgh | 1,690 | 390 | 11 |
| **1993** | Thurman Thomas, Buffalo | 1,315 | 355 | 6 |
| **1994** | Chris Warren, Seattle | 1,545 | 333 | 9 |
| **1995** | Curtis Martin, New England | 1,487 | 368 | 14 |

*1,011 AFC yards led conference.

# National Football Conference Leaders

(National Football League, 1960-69)

## Passing

| Player, team | Atts | Com | YG | TD | Year |
|---|---|---|---|---|---|
| Milt Plum, Cleveland | 250 | 151 | 2,297 | 21 | **1960** |
| Milt Plum, Cleveland | 302 | 177 | 2,416 | 18 | **1961** |
| Bart Starr, Green Bay | 285 | 178 | 2,438 | 12 | **1962** |
| Y.A. Tittle, N.Y. Giants | 367 | 221 | 3,145 | 36 | **1963** |
| Bart Starr, Green Bay | 272 | 163 | 2,144 | 15 | **1964** |
| Rudy Bukich, Chicago | 312 | 176 | 2,641 | 20 | **1965** |
| Bart Starr, Green Bay | 251 | 156 | 2,257 | 14 | **1966** |
| Sonny Jurgensen, Washington | 508 | 288 | 3,747 | 31 | **1967** |
| Earl Morrall, Baltimore Colts | 317 | 182 | 2,909 | 26 | **1968** |
| Sonny Jurgensen, Washington | 442 | 274 | 3,102 | 22 | **1969** |
| John Brodie, San Francisco | 378 | 223 | 2,941 | 24 | **1970** |
| Roger Staubach, Dallas | 211 | 126 | 1,882 | 15 | **1971** |
| Norm Snead, N.Y. Giants | 325 | 196 | 2,307 | 17 | **1972** |
| Roger Staubach, Dallas | 286 | 179 | 2,428 | 23 | **1973** |
| Sonny Jurgensen, Washington | 167 | 107 | 1,185 | 11 | **1974** |
| Fran Tarkenton, Minnesota | 425 | 273 | 2,994 | 25 | **1975** |
| James Harris, L.A. Rams | 158 | 91 | 1,460 | 8 | **1976** |
| Roger Staubach, Dallas | 361 | 210 | 2,620 | 18 | **1977** |
| Roger Staubach, Dallas | 413 | 231 | 3,190 | 25 | **1978** |
| Roger Staubach, Dallas | 461 | 267 | 3,586 | 27 | **1979** |
| Ron Jaworski, Philadelphia | 451 | 257 | 3,529 | 27 | **1980** |
| Joe Montana, San Francisco | 488 | 311 | 3,565 | 19 | **1981** |
| Joe Thiesmann, Washington | 252 | 161 | 2,033 | 13 | **1982** |
| Steve Bartkowski, Atlanta | 432 | 274 | 3,167 | 22 | **1983** |
| Joe Montana, San Francisco | 432 | 279 | 3,630 | 28 | **1984** |
| Joe Montana, San Francisco | 494 | 303 | 3,653 | 27 | **1985** |
| Tommy Kramer, Minnesota | 372 | 208 | 3,000 | 24 | **1986** |
| Joe Montana, San Francisco | 398 | 266 | 3,054 | 31 | **1987** |
| Wade Wilson, Minnesota | 332 | 204 | 2,746 | 15 | **1988** |
| Joe Montana, San Francisco | 386 | 271 | 3,521 | 26 | **1989** |
| Phil Simms, N.Y. Giants | 311 | 184 | 2,284 | 15 | **1990** |
| Steve Young, San Francisco | 279 | 180 | 2,517 | 17 | **1991** |
| Steve Young, San Francisco | 402 | 268 | 3,465 | 25 | **1992** |
| Steve Young, San Francisco | 462 | 314 | 4,023 | 29 | **1993** |
| Steve Young, San Francisco | 461 | 324 | 3,969 | 35 | **1994** |
| Brett Favre, Green Bay | 570 | 359 | 4,413 | 38 | **1995** |

## Pass-Receiving

| Player, team | Ct | YG | TD |
|---|---|---|---|
| Raymond Berry, Baltimore Colts | 74 | 1,298 | 10 |
| Jim Phillips, L.A. Rams | 78 | 1,092 | 5 |
| Bobby Mitchell, Washington | 72 | 1,384 | 11 |
| Bobby Joe Conrad, St.L. Cardinals | 73 | 967 | 10 |
| Johnny Morris, Chicago | 93 | 1,200 | 10 |
| Dave Parks, San Francisco | 80 | 1,344 | 12 |
| Charley Taylor, Washington | 72 | 1,119 | 12 |
| Charley Taylor, Washington | 70 | 990 | 9 |
| Clifton McNeil, San Francisco | 71 | 994 | 7 |
| Dan Abramowicz, New Orleans | 73 | 1,015 | 7 |
| Dick Gordon, Chicago | 71 | 1,026 | 13 |
| Bob Tucker, N.Y. Giants | 59 | 791 | 4 |
| Harold Jackson, Philadelphia | 62 | 1,048 | 4 |
| Harold Carmichael, Philadelphia | 67 | 1,116 | 9 |
| Charles Young, Philadelphia | 63 | 696 | 3 |
| Chuck Foreman, Minnesota | 73 | 691 | 9 |
| Drew Pearson, Dallas | 58 | 806 | 6 |
| Ahmad Rashad, Minnesota | 51 | 681 | 2 |
| Rickey Young, Minnesota | 88 | 704 | 5 |
| Ahmad Rashad, Minnesota | 80 | 1,156 | 9 |
| Earl Cooper, San Francisco | 83 | 567 | 4 |
| Dwight Clark, San Francisco | 85 | 1,105 | 4 |
| Dwight Clark, San Francisco | 60 | 913 | 5 |
| Roy Green, St. Louis Cardinals | 78 | 1,227 | 14 |
| Charlie Brown, Washington | 78 | 1,225 | 8 |
| Earnest Gray, N.Y. Giants | 78 | 1,139 | 5 |
| Art Monk, Washington | 106 | 1,372 | 7 |
| Roger Craig, San Francisco | 92 | 1,016 | 6 |
| Jerry Rice, San Francisco | 86 | 1,570 | 15 |
| J.T. Smith, St. Louis Cardinals | 91 | 1,117 | 8 |
| Henry Ellard, L.A. Rams | 86 | 1,414 | 10 |
| Sterling Sharpe, Green Bay | 90 | 1,423 | 12 |
| Jerry Rice, San Francisco | 100 | 1,502 | 13 |
| Michael Irvin, Dallas | 93 | 1,523 | 8 |
| Sterling Sharpe, Green Bay | 108 | 1,461 | 13 |
| Sterling Sharpe, Green Bay | 112 | 1,274 | 11 |
| Cris Carter, Minnesota | 122 | 1,256 | 7 |
| Herman Moore, Detroit | 123 | 1,686 | 14 |

## Scoring

| Player, team | TD | PAT | FG | Pts | Year |
|---|---|---|---|---|---|
| Paul Hornung, Green Bay | 15 | 41 | 15 | 176 | **1960** |
| Paul Hornung, Green Bay | 10 | 41 | 15 | 146 | **1961** |
| Jim Taylor, Green Bay | 19 | 0 | 0 | 114 | **1962** |
| Don Chandler, N.Y. Giants | 0 | 52 | 18 | 106 | **1963** |
| Lenny Moore, Baltimore Colts | 20 | 0 | 0 | 120 | **1964** |
| Gale Sayers, Chicago | 22 | 0 | 0 | 132 | **1965** |
| Bruce Gossett, L.A. Rams | 0 | 29 | 28 | 113 | **1966** |
| Jim Bakken, St. Louis Cardinals | 0 | 36 | 27 | 117 | **1967** |
| Leroy Kelly, Cleveland | 20 | 0 | 0 | 120 | **1968** |
| Fred Cox, Minnesota | 0 | 43 | 26 | 121 | **1969** |
| Fred Cox, Minnesota | 0 | 35 | 30 | 125 | **1970** |
| Curt Knight, Washington | 0 | 27 | 29 | 114 | **1971** |
| Chester Marcol, Green Bay | 0 | 29 | 33 | 128 | **1972** |
| David Ray, L.A. Rams | 0 | 40 | 30 | 130 | **1973** |
| Chester Marcol, Green Bay | 0 | 19 | 25 | 94 | **1974** |
| Chuck Foreman, Minnesota | 22 | 0 | 0 | 132 | **1975** |
| Mark Moseley, Washington | 0 | 31 | 22 | 97 | **1976** |
| Walter Payton, Chicago | 16 | 0 | 0 | 96 | **1977** |
| Frank Corral, L.A. Rams | 0 | 31 | 29 | 118 | **1978** |
| Mark Moseley, Washington | 0 | 39 | 25 | 114 | **1979** |
| Ed Murray, Detroit | 0 | 35 | 27 | 116 | **1980** |
| Ed Murray, Detroit | 0 | 46 | 25 | 121 | **1981** |
| Rafael Septien, Dallas | 0 | 40 | 27 | 121 | |
| Wendell Tyler, L.A. Rams | 13 | 0 | 0 | 78 | **1982** |
| Mark Moseley, Washington | 0 | 62 | 33 | 161 | **1983** |
| Ray Wersching, San Francisco | 0 | 56 | 25 | 131 | **1984** |
| Kevin Butler, Chicago | 0 | 51 | 31 | 144 | **1985** |
| Kevin Butler, Chicago | 0 | 36 | 28 | 120 | **1986** |
| Jerry Rice, San Francisco | 23 | 0 | 0 | 138 | **1987** |
| Mike Cofer, San Francisco | 0 | 40 | 27 | 121 | **1988** |
| Mike Cofer, San Francisco | 0 | 49 | 29 | 136 | **1989** |
| Chip Lohmiller, Washington | 0 | 41 | 30 | 131 | **1990** |
| Chip Lohmiller, Washington | 0 | 56 | 31 | 149 | **1991** |
| Morten Andersen, New Orleans | 0 | 33 | 29 | 120 | **1992** |
| Chip Lohmiller, Washington | 0 | 30 | 30 | 120 | |
| Jason Hanson, Detroit | 0 | 28 | 34 | 130 | **1993** |
| Fuad Reveiz, Minnesota | 0 | 30 | 34 | 132 | **1994** |
| Emmitt Smith, Dallas | 22 | 0 | 0 | 132 | |
| Emmitt Smith, Dallas | 25 | 0 | 0 | 150 | **1995** |

## Rushing

| Player, team | Yds | Atts | TD |
|---|---|---|---|
| Jim Brown, Cleveland | 1,257 | 215 | 9 |
| Jim Brown, Cleveland | 1,408 | 305 | 8 |
| Jim Taylor, Green Bay | 1,474 | 272 | 19 |
| Jim Brown, Cleveland | 1,863 | 291 | 12 |
| Jim Brown, Cleveland | 1,446 | 280 | 7 |
| Jim Brown, Cleveland | 1,544 | 289 | 17 |
| Gale Sayers, Chicago | 1,231 | 229 | 8 |
| Leroy Kelly, Cleveland | 1,205 | 235 | 11 |
| Leroy Kelly, Cleveland | 1,239 | 248 | 16 |
| Gale Sayers, Chicago | 1,032 | 236 | 8 |
| Larry Brown, Washington | 1,125 | 237 | 5 |
| John Brockington, Green Bay | 1,105 | 216 | 4 |
| Larry Brown, Washington | 1,216 | 285 | 8 |
| John Brockington, Green Bay | 1,144 | 265 | 3 |
| Lawrence McCutcheon, L.A. Rams | 1,109 | 236 | 3 |
| Jim Otis, St. Louis Cardinals | 1,076 | 269 | 5 |
| Walter Payton, Chicago | 1,390 | 311 | 13 |
| Walter Payton, Chicago | 1,852 | 339 | 14 |
| Walter Payton, Chicago | 1,395 | 333 | 11 |
| Walter Payton, Chicago | 1,610 | 369 | 14 |
| Walter Payton, Chicago | 1,460 | 317 | 6 |
| George Rogers, New Orleans | 1,674 | 378 | 13 |
| Tony Dorsett, Dallas | 745 | 177 | 5 |
| Eric Dickerson, L.A. Rams | 1,808 | 390 | 18 |
| Eric Dickerson, L.A. Rams | 2,105 | 379 | 14 |
| Gerald Riggs, Atlanta | 1,719 | 397 | 10 |
| Eric Dickerson, L.A. Rams | 1,821 | 404 | 11 |
| Charles White, L.A. Rams | 1,374 | 324 | 11 |
| Herschel Walker, Dallas | 1,514 | 361 | 5 |
| Barry Sanders, Detroit | 1,470 | 280 | 14 |
| Barry Sanders, Detroit | 1,304 | 255 | 13 |
| Emmitt Smith, Dallas | 1,563 | 365 | 12 |
| Emmitt Smith, Dallas | 1,713 | 373 | 18 |
| Emmitt Smith, Dallas | 1,486 | 283 | 9 |
| Barry Sanders, Detroit | 1,883 | 331 | 7 |
| Emmitt Smith, Dallas | 1,773 | 377 | 25 |

# 1995 NFL Individual Leaders

## American Football Conference

### Passing

| | Att | Comp | Pct comp | Yds | Avg gain | TD | Pct TD | Int | Rating points |
|---|---|---|---|---|---|---|---|---|---|
| Jim Harbaugh, Indianapolis | 314 | 200 | 63.7 | 2,575 | 8.20 | 17 | 5.4 | 5 | 100.7 |
| Dan Marino, Miami | 482 | 309 | 64.1 | 3,668 | 7.61 | 24 | 5.0 | 15 | 90.8 |
| Vinny Testaverde, Cleveland | 392 | 241 | 61.5 | 2,883 | 7.35 | 17 | 4.3 | 10 | 87.8 |
| Chris Chandler, Houston | 356 | 225 | 63.2 | 2,460 | 6.91 | 17 | 4.8 | 10 | 87.8 |
| Neil O'Donnell, Pittsburgh | 416 | 246 | 59.1 | 2,970 | 7.14 | 17 | 4.1 | 7 | 87.7 |
| John Elway, Denver | 542 | 316 | 58.3 | 3,970 | 7.32 | 26 | 4.8 | 14 | 86.4 |
| Mark Brunell, Jacksonville | 346 | 201 | 58.1 | 2,168 | 6.27 | 15 | 4.3 | 7 | 82.6 |
| Jeff Hostetler, Oakland | 286 | 172 | 60.1 | 1,998 | 6.99 | 12 | 4.2 | 9 | 82.2 |
| Jeff Blake, Cincinnati | 567 | 326 | 57.5 | 3,822 | 6.74 | 28 | 4.9 | 17 | 82.1 |
| Jim Kelly, Buffalo | 458 | 255 | 55.7 | 3,130 | 6.83 | 22 | 4.8 | 13 | 81.1 |
| Stan Humphries, San Diego | 478 | 282 | 59.0 | 3,381 | 7.07 | 17 | 3.6 | 14 | 80.4 |
| Steve Bono, Kansas City | 520 | 293 | 56.4 | 3,121 | 6.00 | 21 | 4.0 | 10 | 79.5 |

### Rushing

| | Att | Yds | Avg | Long | TD |
|---|---|---|---|---|---|
| Curtis Martin, New England | 368 | 1,487 | 4.0 | 49 | 14 |
| Chris Warren, Seattle | 310 | 1,346 | 4.3 | 52 | 15 |
| Terrell Davis, Denver | 237 | 1,117 | 4.7 | 60td | 7 |
| Harvey Williams, Oakland | 255 | 1,114 | 4.4 | 60 | 9 |
| Marshall Faulk, Indianapolis | 289 | 1,078 | 3.7 | 40 | 11 |
| Thurman Thomas, Buffalo | 267 | 1,005 | 3.8 | 49 | 6 |
| Rodney Thomas, Houston | 251 | 947 | 3.8 | 74td | 5 |
| Marcus Allen, Kansas City | 207 | 890 | 4.3 | 38 | 5 |
| Bernie Parmalee, Miami | 236 | 878 | 3.7 | 40 | 9 |
| Erric Pegram, Pittsburgh | 213 | 813 | 3.8 | 38 | 5 |

### Pass Receiving

| | No | Yds | Avg | Long | TD |
|---|---|---|---|---|---|
| Carl Pickens, Cincinnati | 99 | 1,234 | 12.5 | 68td | 17 |
| Tony Martin, San Diego | 90 | 1,224 | 13.6 | 51td | 6 |
| Tim Brown, Oakland | 89 | 1,342 | 15.1 | 80td | 10 |
| Yancey Thigpen, Pittsburgh | 85 | 1,307 | 15.4 | 43 | 5 |
| Ben Coates, New England | 84 | 915 | 10.9 | 35 | 6 |
| Brian Blades, Seattle | 77 | 1,001 | 13.0 | 49 | 4 |
| Adrian Murrell, N.Y. Jets | 71 | 465 | 6.5 | 43 | 2 |
| Joey Galloway, Seattle | 67 | 1,039 | 15.5 | 59td | 7 |

### Scoring—Non-Kickers

| | TD | Rush | Pass | 2 Pt | Pts |
|---|---|---|---|---|---|
| Carl Pickens, Cincinnati | 17 | 0 | 17 | 0 | 102 |
| Chris Warren, Seattle | 16 | 15 | 1 | 0 | 96 |
| Curtis Martin, New England | 15 | 14 | 1 | 1 | 92 |
| Marshall Faulk, Indianapolis | 14 | 11 | 3 | 0 | 84 |
| Anthony Miller, Denver | 14 | 0 | 14 | 0 | 84 |

### Scoring—Kickers

| | PAT | FG | Pts |
|---|---|---|---|
| Norm Johnson, Pittsburgh | 39/39 | 34/41 | 141 |
| Jason Elam, Denver | 39/39 | 31/38 | 132 |
| Steve Christie, Buffalo | 33/35 | 31/40 | 126 |
| Doug Pelfrey, Cincinnati | 34/34 | 29/36 | 121 |
| Pete Stoyanovich, Miami | 37/37 | 27/34 | 118 |

### Interceptions

| | No | Yds | Avg | Long | TD |
|---|---|---|---|---|---|
| Willie Williams, Pittsburgh | 7 | 122 | 17.4 | 63td | 1 |
| Darryll Lewis, Houston | 6 | 145 | 24.2 | 98td | 1 |
| Otis Smith, N.Y. Jets | 6 | 101 | 16.8 | 49td | 1 |
| Kurt Schulz, Buffalo | 6 | 48 | 8.0 | 32td | 1 |
| Terry McDaniel, Oakland | 6 | 46 | 7.7 | 42td | 1 |

### Kickoff Returns

| | No | Yds | Avg | Long | TD |
|---|---|---|---|---|---|
| Ron Carpenter, N.Y. Jets | 20 | 553 | 27.7 | 58 | 0 |
| Glyn Milburn, Denver | 47 | 1,269 | 27.0 | 86 | 0 |
| Napoleon Kaufman, Oakland | 22 | 572 | 26.0 | 84td | 1 |
| Tamarick Vanover, Kansas City | 43 | 1,095 | 25.5 | 99td | 2 |
| Dave Meggett, New England | 38 | 964 | 25.4 | 62 | 0 |

### Punt Returns

| | No | FC | Yds | Avg | Long | TD |
|---|---|---|---|---|---|---|
| Andre Coleman, San Diego | 28 | 14 | 326 | 11.6 | 88td | 1 |
| Jeff Burris, Buffalo | 20 | 1 | 229 | 11.5 | 40 | 0 |
| Glyn Milburn, Dever | 31 | 17 | 354 | 11.4 | 44 | 0 |
| Tamarick Vanover, K.C. | 51 | 4 | 540 | 10.6 | 86td | 1 |
| Desmond Howard, Jack. | 24 | 8 | 246 | 10.3 | 40 | 0 |

### Punting

| | No | Yds | Long | Avg |
|---|---|---|---|---|
| Rick Tuten, Seattle | 83 | 3,735 | 73 | 45.0 |
| Darren Bennett, San Diego | 72 | 3,221 | 66 | 44.7 |
| Louis Aguiar, Kansas City | 91 | 3,990 | 65 | 43.8 |
| Bryan Barker, Jacksonville | 82 | 3,591 | 63 | 43.8 |
| Tom Tupa, Cleveland | 65 | 2,831 | 64 | 43.6 |

### Sacks

| | No |
|---|---|
| Bryce Paup, Buffalo | 17.5 |
| Pat Swilling, Oakland | 13.0 |
| Leslie O'Neal, San Diego | 12.5 |
| Neil Smith, Kansas City | 12.0 |
| Willie McGinest, New England | 11.0 |

## National Football Conference

### Passing

| | Att | Comp | Pct comp | Yds | Avg gain | TD | Pct TD | Int | Rating points |
|---|---|---|---|---|---|---|---|---|---|
| Brett Favre, Green Bay | 570 | 359 | 63.0 | 4,413 | 7.74 | 38 | 6.7 | 13 | 99.5 |
| Troy Aikman, Dallas | 432 | 280 | 64.8 | 3,304 | 7.65 | 16 | 3.7 | 7 | 93.6 |
| Erik Kramer, Chicago | 522 | 315 | 60.3 | 3,838 | 7.35 | 29 | 5.6 | 10 | 93.5 |
| Steve Young, San Francisco | 447 | 299 | 66.9 | 3,200 | 7.16 | 20 | 4.5 | 11 | 92.3 |
| Scott Mitchell, Detroit | 583 | 346 | 59.4 | 4,338 | 7.44 | 32 | 5.5 | 12 | 92.3 |
| Warren Moon, Minnesota | 606 | 377 | 62.2 | 4,228 | 6.98 | 33 | 5.5 | 14 | 91.5 |
| Jeff George, Atlanta | 557 | 336 | 60.3 | 4,143 | 7.44 | 24 | 4.3 | 11 | 89.5 |
| Jim Everett, New Orleans | 567 | 345 | 60.8 | 3,970 | 7.00 | 26 | 4.6 | 14 | 87.0 |
| Chris Miller, St. Louis | 405 | 232 | 57.3 | 2,623 | 6.48 | 18 | 4.4 | 15 | 76.2 |
| Dave Brown, N.Y. Giants | 456 | 254 | 55.7 | 2,814 | 6.17 | 11 | 2.4 | 10 | 73.1 |
| Dave Krieg, Arizona | 521 | 304 | 58.4 | 3,554 | 6.82 | 16 | 3.1 | 21 | 72.6 |
| Gus Frerotte, Washington | 396 | 199 | 50.3 | 2,751 | 6.95 | 13 | 3.3 | 13 | 70.2 |

### Rushing

| | Att | Yds | Avg | Long | TD |
|---|---|---|---|---|---|
| Emmitt Smith, Dallas | 377 | 1,773 | 4.7 | 60td | 25 |
| Barry Sanders, Detroit | 314 | 1,500 | 4.8 | 75td | 11 |
| Terry Allen, Washington | 338 | 1,309 | 3.9 | 28 | 10 |
| Ricky Watters, Philadelphia | 337 | 1,273 | 3.8 | 57 | 11 |
| Errict Rhett, Tampa Bay | 332 | 1,207 | 3.6 | 21 | 11 |
| Rodney Hampton, N.Y. Giants | 306 | 1,182 | 3.9 | 32 | 10 |
| Craig Heyward, Atlanta | 236 | 1,083 | 4.6 | 31 | 6 |
| Rashaan Salaam, Chicago | 296 | 1,074 | 3.6 | 42 | 10 |
| Garrison Hearst, Arizona | 284 | 1,070 | 3.8 | 38 | 1 |
| Edgar Bennett, Green Bay | 316 | 1,067 | 3.4 | 23 | 3 |

### Receiving

| | No | Yds | Avg | Long | TD |
|---|---|---|---|---|---|
| Herman Moore, Detroit | 123 | 1,686 | 13.7 | 69td | 14 |
| Jerry Rice, San Francisco | 122 | 1,848 | 15.1 | 81td | 15 |
| Cris Carter, Minnesota | 122 | 1,371 | 11.2 | 60td | 17 |
| Isaac Bruce, St. Louis | 119 | 1,781 | 15.0 | 72 | 13 |
| Michael Irvin, Dallas | 111 | 1,603 | 14.4 | 50 | 10 |
| Brett Perriman, Detroit | 108 | 1,488 | 13.8 | 91td | 9 |
| Eric Metcalf, Atlanta | 104 | 1,189 | 11.4 | 62td | 8 |
| Robert Brooks, Green Bay | 102 | 1,497 | 14.7 | 99td | 13 |
| Larry Centers, Arizona | 101 | 962 | 9.5 | 32 | 2 |
| Derek Loville, San Francisco | 87 | 662 | 7.6 | 31 | 3 |

*(continued)*

### Scoring—Non-Kickers

| | TD | Rush | Pass | 2 Pt | Pts |
|---|---|---|---|---|---|
| Emmitt Smith, Dallas | 25 | 25 | 0 | 0 | 150 |
| Jerry Rice, San Francisco | 17 | 1 | 15 | 1 | 104[1] |
| Cris Carter, Minnesota | 17 | 0 | 17 | 0 | 102 |
| Herman Moore, Detroit | 14 | 0 | 14 | 0 | 84 |
| Isaac Bruce, St. Louis | 13 | 0 | 13 | 1 | 80 |
| Derek Loville, San Francisco | 13 | 10 | 3 | 1 | 80 |

(1) Includes 1 return for a touchdown.

### Scoring—Kickers

| | PAT | FG | Pts |
|---|---|---|---|
| Jason Hanson, Detroit | 48/48 | 28/34 | 132 |
| Chris Boniol, Dallas | 46/48 | 27/28 | 127 |
| Morten Andersen, Atlanta | 29/30 | 31/37 | 122 |
| Fuad Reveiz, Minnesota | 44/44 | 26/36 | 122 |
| Kevin Butler, Chicago | 45/45 | 23/31 | 114 |
| Eddie Murray, Washington | 33/33 | 27/36 | 114 |

### Interceptions

| | No | Yds | Avg | Long | TD |
|---|---|---|---|---|---|
| Orlando Thomas, Minnesota | 9 | 108 | 12.0 | 45td | 1 |
| Willie Clay, Detroit | 8 | 173 | 21.6 | 39 | 0 |
| William Thomas, Philadelphia | 7 | 104 | 14.9 | 37td | 1 |
| Larry Brown, Dallas | 6 | 124 | 20.7 | 65td | 2 |
| Aeneas Williams, Arizona | 6 | 86 | 14.3 | 48td | 2 |
| Toby Wright, St. Louis | 6 | 79 | 13.2 | 27 | 0 |
| Brett Maxie, Carolina | 6 | 59 | 9.8 | 49 | 0 |
| Corey Raymond, Detroit | 6 | 44 | 7.3 | 18 | 0 |
| Brock Marion, Dallas | 6 | 40 | 6.7 | 32td | 1 |

### Kickoff Returns

| | No | Yds | Avg | Long | TD |
|---|---|---|---|---|---|
| Brian Mitchell, Washington | 55 | 1,408 | 25.6 | 59 | 0 |
| Qadry Ismail, Minnesota | 42 | 1,037 | 24.7 | 71 | 0 |
| Tyrone Hughes, New Orleans | 66 | 1,617 | 24.5 | 83 | 0 |
| J. T. Thomas, St. Louis | 32 | 752 | 23.5 | 46 | 0 |
| Antonio Freeman, Green Bay | 24 | 556 | 23.2 | 45 | 0 |

### Punt Returns

| | No | FC | Yds | Avg | Long | TD |
|---|---|---|---|---|---|---|
| David Palmer, Minnesota | 26 | 13 | 342 | 13.2 | 74td | 1 |
| Brian Mitchell, Washington | 25 | 15 | 315 | 12.6 | 59td | 1 |
| Eric Guliford, Carolina | 43 | 22 | 475 | 11.0 | 62td | 1 |
| Dexter Carter, NYJ-S.F. | 30 | 15 | 309 | 10.3 | 78td | 1 |
| Charles Jordan, Green Bay | 21 | 2 | 213 | 10.1 | 18 | 0 |

### Punting

| | No | Yds | Long | Avg |
|---|---|---|---|---|
| Sean Landeta, St. Louis | 83 | 3,679 | 63 | 44.3 |
| Jeff Feagles, Arizona | 72 | 3,150 | 60 | 43.8 |
| Tom Hutton, Philadelphia | 85 | 3,682 | 63 | 43.3 |
| Reggie Roby, Tampa Bay | 77 | 3,296 | 61 | 42.8 |
| Mike Horan, N.Y. Giants | 72 | 3,063 | 60 | 42.5 |

### Sacks

| | No |
|---|---|
| William Fuller, Philadelphia | 13.0 |
| Wayne Martin, New Orleans | 13.0 |
| Reggie White, Green Bay | 12.0 |
| D'Marco Farr, St. Louis | 11.5 |
| Jim Flanigan, Chicago | 11.0 |
| Andy Harmon, Philadelphia | 11.0 |
| Clyde Simmons, Arizona | 11.0 |

## NFL MVP, Defensive Player of the Year, and Rookie of the Year

The Jim Thorpe Trophy goes to the most valuable player as chosen by player representatives from each NFL team. The George Halas Trophy is awarded to the outstanding defensive player as chosen by a panel of sports experts. Rookie of the Year is one of many awards given out annually by *The Sporting News*. Many other organizations give out annual awards honoring the NFL's finest players.

### Most Valuable Player

1955 Harlon Hill, Chicago
1956 Frank Gifford, N.Y. Giants
1957 John Unitas, Baltimore
1958 Jim Brown, Cleveland
1959 Charley Conerly, N.Y. Giants
1960 Norm Van Brocklin, Philadelphia
1961 Y.A. Tittle, N.Y. Giants
1962 Jim Taylor, Green Bay
1963 Jim Brown, Cleveland
Y.A. Tittle, N.Y. Giants
1964 Lenny Moore, Baltimore
1965 Jim Brown, Cleveland
1966 Bart Starr, Green Bay
1967 John Unitas, Baltimore
1968 Earl Morrall, Baltimore
1969 Roman Gabriel, L.A. Rams
1970 John Brodie, San Francisco
1971 Bob Griese, Miami
1972 Larry Brown, Washington
1973 O.J. Simpson, Buffalo
1974 Ken Stabler, Oakland
1975 Fran Tarkenton, Minnesota
1976 Bert Jones, Baltimore
1977 Walter Payton, Chicago
1978 Earl Campbell, Houston
1979 Earl Campbell, Houston
1980 Earl Campbell, Houston
1981 Ken Anderson, Cincinnati
1982 Dan Fouts, San Diego
1983 Joe Theismann, Washington
1984 Dan Marino, Miami
1985 Walter Payton, Chicago
1986 Phil Simms, N.Y. Giants
1987 Jerry Rice, San Francisco
1988 Roger Craig, San Francisco
1989 Joe Montana, San Francisco
1990 Warren Moon, Houston
1991 Thurman Thomas, Buffalo
1992 Steve Young, San Francisco
1993 Emmitt Smith, Dallas
1994 Steve Young, San Francisco
1995 Brett Favre, Green Bay

### Defensive Player of the Year

1966 Larry Wilson, St. Louis
1967 Deacon Jones, Los Angeles
1968 Deacon Jones, Los Angeles
1969 Dick Butkus, Chicago
1970 Dick Butkus, Chicago
1971 Carl Eller, Minnesota
1972 Joe Greene, Pittsburgh
1973 Alan Page, Minnesota
1974 Joe Greene, Pittsburgh
1975 Curley Culp, Houston
1976 Jerry Sherk, Cleveland
1977 Harvey Martin, Dallas
1978 Randy Gradishar, Denver
1979 Lee Roy Selmon, Tampa Bay
1980 Lester Hayes, Oakland
1981 Joe Klecko, N.Y. Jets
1982 Mark Gastineau, N.Y. Jets
1983 Jack Lambert, Pittsburgh
1984 Mike Haynes, L.A. Raiders
1985 Howie Long, L.A. Raiders
Andre Tippett, New England
1986 Lawrence Taylor, N.Y. Giants
1987 Reggie White, Philadelphia
1988 Mike Singletary, Chicago
1989 Tim Harris, Green Bay
1990 Bruce Smith, Buffalo
1991 Pat Swilling, New Orleans
1992 Junior Seau, San Diego
1993 Bruce Smith, Buffalo
1994 Deion Sanders, San Francisco
1995 Bryce Paup, Buffalo

### Rookie of the Year

1964 Charley Taylor, Washington
1965 Gale Sayers, Chicago
1966 Tommy Nobis, Atlanta
1967 Mel Farr, Detroit
1968 Earl McCullouch, Detroit
1969 Calvin Hill, Dallas
1970 NFC: Bruce Taylor, San Francsico
AFC: Dennis Shaw, Buffalo
1971 NFC: John Brockington, Green Bay
AFC: Jim Plunkett, New England
1972 NFC: Chester Marcol, Green Bay
AFC: Franco Harris, Pittsburgh
1973 NFC: Chuck Foreman, Minnesota
AFC: Boobie Clark, Cincinnati
1974 NFC: Wilbur Jackson, San Francisco
AFC: Don Woods, San Diego
1975 NFC: Steve Bartkowski, Atlanta
AFC: Robert Brazile, Houston
1976 NFC: Sammy White, Minnesota
AFC: Mike Haynes, New England
1977 NFC: Tony Dorsett, Dallas
AFC: A. J. Duhe, Miami
1978 NFC: Al Baker, Detroit
AFC: Earl Campbell, Houston
1979 NFC: Ottis Anderson, St. Louis
AFC: Jerry Butler, Buffalo
1980 Billy Sims, Detroit
1981 George Rogers, New Orleans
1982 Marcus Allen, L.A. Raiders
1983 Dan Marino, Miami
1984 Louis Lipps, Pittsburgh
1985 Eddie Brown, Cincinnati
1986 Rueben Mayes, New Orleans
1987 Robert Awalt, St. Louis
1988 Keith Jackson, Philadelphia
1989 Barry Sanders, Detroit
1990 Richmond Webb, Miami
1991 Mike Croel, Denver
1992 Santana Dotson, Tampa Bay
1993 Jerome Bettis, L.A. Rams
1994 Marshall Faulk, Indianapolis
1995 Curtis Martin, New England

## NFL Head Coaches at Start of 1996 Season

### AFC

Buffalo—Marv Levy
Baltimore—Ted Marchibroda
Cincinnati—David Shula
Denver—Mike Shanahan
Houston—Jeff Fisher
Indianapolis—Lindy Infante
Jacksonville—Tom Coughlin
Kansas City—Marty Schottenheimer
Miami—Jimmy Johnson
New England—Bill Parcells
N.Y. Jets—Rich Kotite
Oakland—Mike White
Pittsburgh—Bill Cowher
San Diego—Bobby Ross
Seattle—Dennis Erickson

### NFC

Arizona—Vince Tobin
Atlanta—June Jones
Carolina—Dom Capers
Chicago—Dave Wannstedt
Dallas—Barry Switzer
Detroit—Wayne Fontes
Green Bay—Mike Holmgren
Minnesota—Dennis Green
New Orleans—Jim Mora
N.Y. Giants—Dan Reeves
Philadelphia—Ray Rhodes
St. Louis—Rich Brooks
San Francisco—George Seifert
Tampa Bay—Tony Dungy
Washington—Norv Turner

## Number One NFL Draft Choices, 1936-96

| Year | Team | Player, Pos., College |
|---|---|---|
| 1936 | Philadelphia | Jay Berwanger, HB, Chicago |
| 1937 | Philadelphia | Sam Francis, FB, Nebraska |
| 1938 | Cleve.Rams | Corbett Davis, FB, Indiana |
| 1939 | Chi. Cards | Ki Aldrich, C, TCU |
| 1940 | Chi. Cards | George Cafego, HB, Tennessee |
| 1941 | Chi. Bears | Tom Harmon, HB, Michigan |
| 1942 | Pittsburgh | Bill Dudley, HB, Virginia |
| 1943 | Detroit | Frank Sinkwich, HB, Georgia |
| 1944 | Boston Yanks | Angelo Bertelli, QB, Notre Dame |
| 1945 | Chi. Cards | Charley Trippi, HB, Georgia |
| 1946 | Boston Yanks | Frank Dancewicz, QB, Notre Dame |
| 1947 | Chi. Bears | Bob Fenimore, HB, Okla. A&M |
| 1948 | Washington | Harry Gilmer, QB, Alabama |
| 1949 | Philadelphia | Chuck Bednarik, C, Penn |
| 1950 | Detroit | Leon Hart, E, Notre Dame |
| 1951 | N.Y. Giants | Kyle Rote, HB, SMU |
| 1952 | L.A. Rams | Bill Wade, QB, Vanderbilt |
| 1953 | San Francisco | Harry Babcock, E, Georgia |
| 1954 | Cleveland | Bobby Garrett, QB, Stanford |
| 1955 | Baltimore | George Shaw, QB, Oregon |
| 1956 | Pittsburgh | Gary Glick, DB, Col. A&M |
| 1957 | Green Bay | Paul Hornung, QB, Notre Dame |
| 1958 | Chi. Cards | King Hill, QB, Rice |
| 1959 | Green Bay | Randy Duncan, QB, Iowa |
| 1960 | L.A. Rams | Billy Cannon, HB, LSU |
| 1961 | Minnesota | Tommy Mason, HB, Tulane |
| 1962 | Washington | Ernie Davis, HB, Syracuse |
| 1963 | L.A. Rams | Terry Baker, QB, Oregon St. |
| 1964 | San Francisco | Dave Parks, E, Texas Tech |
| 1965 | N.Y. Giants | Tucker Frederickson, HB, Auburn |
| 1966 | Atlanta | Tommy Nobis, LB, Texas |
| 1967 | Baltimore | Bubba Smith, DT, Michigan St. |
| 1968 | Minnesota | Ron Yary, T, USC |
| 1969 | Buffalo | O.J. Simpson, RB, USC |
| 1970 | Pittsburgh | Terry Bradshaw, QB, La.Tech |
| 1971 | New England | Jim Plunkett, QB, Stanford |
| 1972 | Buffalo | Walt Patulski, DE, Notre Dame |
| 1973 | Houston | John Matuszak, DE, Tampa |
| 1974 | Dallas | Ed "Too Tall" Jones, Tenn.St. |
| 1975 | Atlanta | Steve Bartkowski, QB, Cal. |
| 1976 | Tampa Bay | Lee Roy Selmon, DE, Oklahoma |
| 1977 | Tampa Bay | Ricky Bell, RB, USC |
| 1978 | Houston | Earl Campbell, RB, Texas |
| 1979 | Buffalo | Tom Cousineau, LB, Ohio St. |
| 1980 | Detroit | Billy Sims, RB, Oklahoma |
| 1981 | New Orleans | George Rogers, RB, S.Carolina |
| 1982 | New England | Kenneth Sims, DT, Texas |
| 1983 | Baltimore | John Elway, QB, Stanford |
| 1984 | New England | Irving Fryar, WR, Nebraska |
| 1985 | Buffalo | Bruce Smith, DE, Va.Tech |
| 1986 | Tampa Bay | Bo Jackson, RB, Auburn |
| 1987 | Tampa Bay | Vinny Testaverde, QB, Miami (FL) |
| 1988 | Atlanta | Aundray Bruce, LB, Auburn |
| 1989 | Dallas | Troy Aikman, QB, UCLA |
| 1990 | Indianapolis | Jeff George, QB, Illinois |
| 1991 | Dallas | Russell Maryland, DL, Miami (FL) |
| 1992 | Indianapolis | Steve Emtman, DL, Washington |
| 1993 | New England | Drew Bledsoe, QB, Washington St. |
| 1994 | Cincinnati | Dan Wilkinson, DT, Ohio St. |
| 1995 | Cincinnati | Ki-Jana Carter, RB, Penn State |
| 1996 | N.Y. Jets | Keyshawn Johnson, WR, USC |

## First-Round Selections in the 1996 NFL Draft

| Team | Player | Pos | College |
|---|---|---|---|
| 1. N.Y. Jets | Keyshawn Johnson | WR | USC |
| 2. Jacksonville | Kevin Hardy | LB | Illinois |
| 3. Arizona | Simeon Rice | DE | Illinois |
| 4.Baltimore | Jonathan Ogden | T | UCLA |
| 5. N.Y. Giants | Cedric Jones | DE | Oklahoma |
| 6. St. Louis | Lawrence Phillips | RB | Nebraska |
| 7. New England | Terry Glenn | WR | Ohio St. |
| 8. Carolina | Tim Biakabutuka | RB | Michigan |
| 9. Oakland | Rickey Dudley | TE | Ohio St. |
| 10. Cincinnati | Willie Anderson | T | Auburn |
| 11. New Orleans | Alex Molden | DB | Oregon |
| 12. Tampa Bay | Regan Upshaw | DE | California |
| 13. Chicago | Walt Harris | DB | Mississippi St. |
| 14. Houston | Eddie George | RB | Ohio St. |
| 15. Denver | John Mobley | LB | Kutztown |
| 16. Minnesota | Duane Clemons | DE | California |
| 17. Detroit | Reggie Brown | LB | Texas A&M |
| 18. St. Louis | Eddie Kennison | WR | Louisiana St. |
| 19. Indianapolis | Marvin Harrison | WR | Syracuse |
| 20. Miami | Daryl Gardener | DT | Baylor |
| 21. Seattle | Pete Kendall | T | Boston College |
| 22. Tampa Bay | Marcus Jones | DT | North Carolina |
| 23. Detroit | Jeff Hartings | G | Penn St. |
| 24. Buffalo | Eric Moulds | WR | Mississippi St. |
| 25. Philadelphia | Jermane Mayberry | T | Texas A&M-King. |
| 26. Baltimore | Ray Lewis | LB | Miami (FL) |
| 27. Green Bay | John Michels | T | USC |
| 28. Kansas City | Jerome Woods | DB | Memphis |
| 29. Pittsburgh | Jamain Stephens | T | N. Carolina A&T |
| 30. Washington | Andre Johnson | T | Penn St. |

## Pro Football Hall of Fame, Canton, Ohio

(1996 inductees are in **bold**)

Herb Adderley
Lance Alworth
Doug Atkins
Morris "Red" Badgro
Lem Barney
Cliff Battles
Sammy Baugh
Chuck Bednarik
Bert Bell
Bobby Bell
Raymond Berry
Charles Bidwell
Fred Biletnikoff
George Blanda
Mel Blount
Terry Bradshaw
Jim Brown
Paul Brown
Roosevelt Brown
Willie Brown
Buck Buchanan
Dick Butkus
Earl Campbell
Tony Canadeo
Joe Carr
Guy Chamberlin
Jack Christiansen
Dutch Clark
George Connor
Jim Conzelman
**Lou Creekmur**
Larry Csonka
Al Davis
Willie Davis
Len Dawson
**Dan Dierdorf**
Mike Ditka
Art Donovan
Tony Dorsett
Paddy Driscoll
Bill Dudley
Turk Edwards
Weeb Ewbank
Tom Fears
Jim Finks
Ray Flaherty
Len Ford
Dr. Daniel Fortmann
Dan Fouts
Frank Gatski
Bill George
**Joe Gibbs**
Frank Gifford
Sid Gillman
Otto Graham
Red Grange
Joe Greene
Forrest Gregg
Bob Griese
Lou Groza
Joe Guyon
George Halas
Jack Ham
John Hannah
Franco Harris
Ed Healey
Mel Hein
Ted Hendricks
Pete Henry
Arnold Herber
Bill Hewitt
Clarke Hinkle
Elroy "Crazy Legs" Hirsch
Paul Hornung
Ken Houston
Cal Hubbard
Sam Huff
Lamar Hunt
Don Hutson
Jimmy Johnson
John Henry Johnson
**Charlie Joiner**
Deacon Jones
Stan Jones
Henry Jordan
Sonny Jurgensen
Leroy Kelly
Walt Kiesling
Frank "Bruiser" Kinard
Curly Lambeau
Jack Lambert
Tom Landry
Dick "Night Train" Lane
Jim Langer
Willie Lanier
Steve Largent
Yale Lary
Dante Lavelli
Bobby Layne
Tuffy Leemans
Bob Lilly
Larry Little
Vince Lombardi
Sid Luckman
Link Lyman
John Mackey
Tim Mara
Gino Marchetti
George Marshall
Ollie Matson
Don Maynard
George McAfee
Mike McCormack
Hugh McElhenny
John "Blood" McNally
Mike Michalske
Wayne Millner
Bobby Mitchell
Ron Mix
Lenny Moore
Marion Motley
George Musso
Bronko Nagurski
Joe Namath
Greasy Neale
Ernie Nevers
Ray Nitschke
Chuck Noll
Leo Nomellini
Merlin Olsen
Jim Otto
Steve Owen
Alan Page
Clarence "Ace" Parker
Jim Parker
Walter Payton
Joe Perry
Pete Pihos
Hugh "Shorty" Ray
Dan Reeves
**Mel Renfro**
John Riggins
Jim Ringo
Andy Robustelli
Art Rooney
Pete Rozelle
Bob St. Clair
Gale Sayers
Joe Schmidt
Tex Schramm
Lee Roy Selmon
Art Shell
O.J. Simpson
Jackie Smith
Bart Starr
Roger Staubach
Ernie Stautner
Jan Stenerud
Ken Strong
Joe Stydahar
Fran Tarkenton
Charlie Taylor
Jim Taylor
Jim Thorpe
Y.A. Tittle
George Trafton
Charlie Trippi
Emlen Tunnell
Clyde "Bulldog" Turner
Johnny Unitas
Gene Upshaw
Norm Van Brocklin
Steve Van Buren
Doak Walker
Bill Walsh
Paul Warfield
Bob Waterfield
Arnie Weinmeister
Randy White
Bill Willis
Larry Wilson
Kellen Winslow
Alex Wojciechowicz
Willie Wood

# All-Time NFL Coaching Victories

(at start of 1996 season; *active through 1995)

| | | | Regular Season | | | | Career | | | |
|---|---|---|---|---|---|---|---|---|---|---|
| Coach | Years | Teams | W | L | T | Pct | W | L | T | Pct |
| Don Shula* | 33 | Colts, Dolphins | 328 | 156 | 6 | .676 | 347 | 173 | 6 | .665 |
| George Halas | 40 | Bears | 318 | 148 | 31 | .671 | 324 | 151 | 31 | .671 |
| Tom Landry | 29 | Cowboys | 250 | 162 | 6 | .605 | 270 | 178 | 6 | .601 |
| Curly Lambeau | 33 | Packers, Cardinals, Redskins | 226 | 132 | 22 | .624 | 229 | 134 | 22 | .623 |
| Chuck Noll | 23 | Steelers | 193 | 148 | 1 | .566 | 209 | 156 | 1 | .572 |
| Chuck Knox | 22 | Rams, Bills, Seahawks | 186 | 147 | 1 | .558 | 193 | 158 | 1 | .550 |
| Paul Brown | 21 | Browns, Bengals | 166 | 100 | 6 | .621 | 170 | 109 | 6 | .607 |
| Bud Grant | 18 | Vikings | 158 | 96 | 5 | .620 | 168 | 109 | 5 | .605 |
| Steve Owen | 23 | Giants | 151 | 100 | 17 | .595 | 154 | 108 | 17 | .582 |
| Joe Gibbs | 12 | Redskins | 124 | 60 | 0 | .674 | 140 | 65 | 0 | .683 |
| Dan Reeves* | 15 | Broncos, Giants | 135 | 96 | 1 | .584 | 143 | 103 | 1 | .581 |
| Marv Levy* | 15 | Chiefs, Bills | 127 | 96 | 0 | .570 | 138 | 103 | 0 | .573 |
| Hank Stram | 17 | Chiefs, Saints | 131 | 97 | 10 | .571 | 136 | 100 | 10 | .573 |
| Weeb Ewbank | 20 | Colts, Jets | 130 | 129 | 7 | .502 | 134 | 130 | 7 | .507 |
| Sid Gillman | 18 | Rams, Chargers, Oilers | 122 | 99 | 7 | .550 | 123 | 104 | 7 | .541 |
| M. Schottenheimer* | 12 | Browns, Chiefs | 116 | 66 | 1 | .637 | 121 | 76 | 1 | .614 |
| George Allen | 12 | Rams, Redskins | 116 | 47 | 5 | .705 | 120 | 54 | 5 | .684 |
| Don Coryell | 14 | Cardinals, Chargers | 111 | 83 | 1 | .572 | 114 | 89 | 1 | .561 |
| Mike Ditka | 11 | Bears | 106 | 62 | 0 | .631 | 112 | 68 | 0 | .622 |
| John Madden | 10 | Raiders | 103 | 32 | 7 | .750 | 112 | 39 | 7 | .731 |

# All-Time Professional (NFL and AFL) Football Records

(at start of 1996 season; *active through 1995)

## Leading Lifetime Rushers

| Player | League | Yrs | Att | Yards | Avg |
|---|---|---|---|---|---|
| Walter Payton | NFL | 13 | 3,838 | 16,726 | 4.4 |
| Eric Dickerson | NFL | 11 | 2,996 | 13,259 | 4.4 |
| Tony Dorsett | NFL | 12 | 2,936 | 12,739 | 4.3 |
| Jim Brown | NFL | 9 | 2,359 | 12,312 | 5.2 |
| Franco Harris | NFL | 13 | 2,949 | 12,120 | 4.1 |
| John Riggins | NFL | 14 | 2,916 | 11,352 | 3.9 |
| O.J. Simpson | AFL-NFL | 11 | 2,404 | 11,236 | 4.7 |
| Marcus Allen* | NFL | 14 | 2,692 | 10,908 | 4.1 |
| Ottis Anderson | NFL | 14 | 2,562 | 10,273 | 4.0 |
| Barry Sanders* | NFL | 7 | 2,077 | 10,172 | 4.9 |
| Thurman Thomas* | NFL | 8 | 2,285 | 9,729 | 4.3 |
| Earl Campbell | NFL | 8 | 2,187 | 9,407 | 4.3 |
| Emmitt Smith* | NFL | 6 | 2,007 | 8,956 | 4.5 |
| Jim Taylor | NFL | 10 | 1,941 | 8,597 | 4.4 |
| Joe Perry | NFL | 14 | 1,737 | 8,378 | 4.8 |
| Roger Craig | NFL | 11 | 1,991 | 8,189 | 4.1 |
| Gerald Riggs | NFL | 10 | 1,989 | 8,188 | 4.1 |
| Herschel Walker* | NFL | 10 | 1,938 | 8,122 | 4.2 |
| Larry Csonka | AFL-NFL | 11 | 1,891 | 8,081 | 4.3 |
| Freeman McNeil | NFL | 12 | 1,798 | 8,074 | 4.5 |

**Most Yards Gained, Season** — 2,105, Eric Dickerson, Los Angeles Rams, 1984.
**Most Yards Gained, Game** — 275, Walter Payton, Chicago Bears vs. Minnesota Vikings, Nov. 20, 1977.
**Most Touchdowns Rushing, Career** — 110, Walter Payton, Chicago Bears, 1975-1987.
**Most Touchdowns Rushing, Season** — 25, Emmitt Smith, Dallas Cowboys, 1995.
**Most Touchdowns Rushing, Game** — 6, Ernie Nevers, Chicago Cardinals vs. Chicago Bears, Nov. 8, 1929.
**Most Rushing Attempts, Game** — 45, Jamie Morris, Washington Redskins vs. Cincinnati Bengals, Dec. 17, 1988 (overtime).
**Longest Run From Scrimmage** — 99 yds., Tony Dorsett, Dallas Cowboys vs. Minnesota Vikings, Jan. 3, 1983 (touchdown).

## Leading Lifetime Passers

(minimum 1,500 attempts)

| Player | League | Yrs | Att | Comp | Yds | Pts† |
|---|---|---|---|---|---|---|
| Steve Young* | NFL | 11 | 2,876 | 1,845 | 23,069 | 96.1 |
| Joe Montana | NFL | 15 | 5,391 | 3,409 | 40,551 | 92.3 |
| Dan Marino* | NFL | 13 | 6,531 | 3,913 | 48,841 | 88.4 |
| Brett Favre* | NFL | 5 | 2,150 | 1,342 | 14,825 | 86.8 |
| Jim Kelly* | NFL | 10 | 4,400 | 2,652 | 32,657 | 85.4 |
| Troy Aikman* | NFL | 7 | 2,713 | 1,704 | 19,607 | 83.5 |
| Roger Staubach | NFL | 11 | 2,958 | 1,685 | 22,700 | 83.4 |
| Neil Lomax | NFL | 8 | 3,153 | 1,817 | 22,771 | 82.7 |
| Sonny Jurgensen | NFL | 18 | 4,262 | 2,433 | 32,224 | 82.6 |
| Len Dawson | NFL-AFL | 19 | 3,741 | 2,136 | 28,711 | 82.6 |
| Dave Krieg* | NFL | 16 | 4,911 | 2,866 | 35,668 | 81.9 |
| Ken Anderson | NFL | 16 | 4,475 | 2,654 | 32,838 | 81.9 |
| Jeff Hostetler* | NFL | 10 | 1,792 | 1,036 | 12,983 | 81.8 |
| Neil O'Donnell* | NFL | 6 | 1,871 | 1,069 | 12,867 | 81.8 |
| Danny White | NFL | 13 | 2,950 | 1,761 | 21,959 | 81.7 |
| Bernie Kosar* | NFL | 11 | 3,333 | 1,970 | 23,093 | 81.6 |
| Warren Moon* | NFL | 12 | 5,753 | 3,380 | 42,177 | 81.5 |
| Boomer Esiason* | NFL | 12 | 4,680 | 2,661 | 34,149 | 80.8 |
| Bart Starr | NFL | 16 | 3,149 | 1,808 | 24,718 | 80.5 |
| Ken O'Brien | NFL | 11 | 3,602 | 2,110 | 25,094 | 80.4 |

†Rating points based on performances in the following categories: Percentage of completions, percentage of touchdown passes, percentage of interceptions, and average gain per pass attempt.

**Most Yards Gained, Career** — 48,841, Dan Marino, Miami Dolphins, 1983-1995.
**Most Yards Gained, Season** — 5,084, Dan Marino, Miami Dolphins, 1984.
**Most Yards Gained, Game** — 554, Norm Van Brocklin, Los Angeles Rams vs. New York Yankees, Sept. 18, 1951 (27 completions in 41 attempts).
**Most Touchdowns Passing, Career** — 352, Dan Marino, Miami Dolphins, 1983-1995.
**Most Touchdowns Passing, Season** — 48, Dan Marino, Miami Dolphins, 1984.
**Most Touchdowns Passing, Game** — 7, Sid Luckman, Chicago Bears vs. New York Giants, Nov. 14, 1943; Adrian Burk, Philadelphia Eagles vs. Washington Redskins, Oct. 17, 1954; George Blanda, Houston Oilers vs. New York Titans, Nov. 19, 1961; Y.A. Tittle, New York Giants vs. Washington Redskins, Oct. 28, 1962; Joe Kapp, Minnesota Vikings vs. Baltimore Colts, Sept. 28, 1969.
**Most Passes Completed, Career** — 3,913, Dan Marino, Miami Dolphins, 1983-1995.
**Most Passes Completed, Season** — 404, Warren Moon, Houston Oilers, 1991.
**Most Passes Completed, Game** — 45, Drew Bledsoe, New England Patriots vs. Minnesota Vikings, Nov. 13, 1994 (overtime).

## Leading Lifetime Receivers

| Player | League | Yrs | No | Yds | Avg | Player | League | Yrs | No | Yds | Avg |
|---|---|---|---|---|---|---|---|---|---|---|---|
| Jerry Rice* | NFL | 11 | 942 | 15,123 | 16.1 | Drew Hill | NFL | 14 | 634 | 9,831 | 15.5 |
| Art Monk* | NFL | 16 | 940 | 12,721 | 13.5 | Don Maynard | AFL-NFL | 15 | 633 | 11,834 | 18.7 |
| Steve Largent | NFL | 14 | 819 | 13,089 | 16.0 | Raymond Berry | NFL | 13 | 631 | 9,275 | 14.7 |
| James Lofton | NFL | 16 | 764 | 14,004 | 18.3 | Sterling Sharpe | NFL | 7 | 595 | 8,134 | 13.7 |
| Charlie Joiner | AFL-NFL | 18 | 750 | 12,146 | 16.2 | Harold Carmichael | NFL | 14 | 590 | 8,985 | 15.2 |
| Henry Ellard* | NFL | 13 | 723 | 12,163 | 16.8 | Fred Biletnikoff | AFL-NFL | 14 | 589 | 8,974 | 15.2 |
| Andre Reed* | NFL | 11 | 700 | 9,848 | 14.1 | Mark Clayton | NFL | 11 | 582 | 8,974 | 15.4 |
| Gary Clark* | NFL | 11 | 699 | 10,856 | 15.5 | Harold Jackson | NFL | 16 | 579 | 10,372 | 17.9 |
| Ozzie Newsome | NFL | 13 | 662 | 7,980 | 12.1 | Ernest Givens | NFL | 10 | 571 | 8,215 | 14.4 |
| Charley Taylor | NFL | 13 | 649 | 9,110 | 14.0 | Cris Carter | NFL | 9 | 571 | 7,204 | 12.6 |

**Most Yards Gained, Career** — 15,123, Jerry Rice, San Francisco 49ers, 1985-1995.
**Most Yards Gained, Season** — 1,848, Jerry Rice, San Francisco 49ers, 1995.
**Most Yards Gained, Game** — 336, Willie "Flipper" Anderson, Los Angeles Rams vs. New Orleans, Nov. 26, 1989 (overtime).
**Most Pass Receptions, Season** — 123, Herman Moore, Detroit Lions, 1995.
**Most Pass Receptions, Game** — 18, Tom Fears, Los Angeles Rams vs. Green Bay Packers, Dec. 3, 1950 (189 yards).
**Most Touchdown Passes, Season** — 22, Jerry Rice, San Francisco 49ers, 1987.
**Most Touchdown Passes, Game** — 5, Bob Shaw, Chicago Cardinals vs. Baltimore Colts, Oct. 2, 1950; Kellen Winslow, San Diego Chargers vs. Oakland Raiders, Nov. 22, 1981; Jerry Rice, San Francisco 49ers vs. Atlanta Falcons, Oct. 14, 1990.

## Leading Lifetime Scorers

| Player | League | Yrs | TD | PAT | FG | Total | Player | League | Yrs | TD | PAT | FG | Total |
|---|---|---|---|---|---|---|---|---|---|---|---|---|---|
| George Blanda | AFL-NFL | 26 | 9 | 943 | 335 | 2,002 | Jim Bakken | NFL | 17 | 0 | 534 | 282 | 1,380 |
| Jan Stenerud | AFL-NFL | 19 | 0 | 580 | 373 | 1,699 | Fred Cox | NFL | 15 | 0 | 519 | 282 | 1,365 |
| Nick Lowery* | NFL | 17 | 0 | 536 | 366 | 1,634 | Lou Groza | NFL | 17 | 1 | 641 | 234 | 1,349 |
| Eddie Murray* | NFL | 16 | 0 | 498 | 325 | 1,473 | Norm Johnson* | NFL | 14 | 0 | 515 | 277 | 1,346 |
| Pat Leahy | NFL | 18 | 0 | 558 | 304 | 1,470 | Jim Breech | NFL | 14 | 0 | 517 | 243 | 1,246 |
| Gary Anderson* | NFL | 14 | 0 | 448 | 331 | 1,441 | Chris Bahr | NFL | 14 | 0 | 490 | 241 | 1,213 |
| Morten Andersen* | NFL | 14 | 0 | 441 | 333 | 1,440 | Gino Cappelletti | AFL | 11 | 42 | 350 | 176 | 1,130 |
| Jim Turner | AFL-NFL | 16 | 1 | 521 | 304 | 1,439 | Ray Wersching | NFL | 15 | 0 | 456 | 222 | 1,122 |
| Matt Bahr* | NFL | 17 | 0 | 522 | 300 | 1,422 | Kevin Butler | NFL | 11 | 0 | 387 | 243 | 1,116 |
| Mark Moseley | NFL | 16 | 0 | 482 | 300 | 1,382 | Don Cockroft | NFL | 13 | 0 | 432 | 216 | 1,080 |

**Most Points, Season** — 176, Paul Hornung, Green Bay Packers, 1960 (15 TDs, 41 PATs, 15 FGs).
**Most Points, Game** — 40, Ernie Nevers, Chicago Cardinals vs. Chicago Bears, Nov. 28, 1929 (6 TDs, 4 PATs).
**Most Touchdowns, Career** — 156, Jerry Rice, San Francisco 49ers, 1985-95 (9 rushing, 146 pass receptions, 1 return).
**Most Touchdowns, Season** — 25, Emmitt Smith, Dallas Cowboys, 1995 (25 rushing).
**Most Touchdowns, Game** — 6, Ernie Nevers, Chicago Cardinals vs. Chicago Bears, Nov. 28, 1929 (6 rushing); Dub Jones, Cleveland Browns vs. Chicago Bears, Nov. 25, 1951 (4 rushing, 2 pass receptions); Gale Sayers, Chicago Bears vs. San Francisco 49ers, Dec. 12, 1965 (4 rushing, 1 pass reception, 1 punt return).
**Most Points After Touchdown, Season** — 66, Uwe von Schamann, Miami Dolphins, 1984.
**Most Consecutive Points After Touchdown** — 234, Tommy Davis, San Francisco 49ers, 1959-1969.
**Most Field Goals, Game** — 7, Jim Bakken, St. Louis Cardinals vs. Pittsburgh Steelers, Sept. 24, 1967; Rich Karlis, Minnesota Vikings vs. Los Angeles Rams, Nov. 5, 1989 (overtime).
**Longest Field Goal** — 63 yds., Tom Dempsey, New Orleans Saints vs. Detroit Lions, Nov. 8, 1970.

## NFL Stadiums

| Team—Stadium, Location, Turf (Year Built) | Capacity | Team—Stadium, Location, Turf (Year Built) | Capacity |
|---|---|---|---|
| Bears—Soldier Field, Chicago, IL, G (1924) | 66,944 | Jaguars—Jacksonville Municipal Stad., FL, G (1995)[6] | 73,000 |
| Bengals—Cinergy Stad., Cincinnati, OH, A (1970)[1] | 60,389 | Jets—Giants Stad., E. Rutherford, NJ, A (1976)[5] | 77,803 |
| Bills—Rich Stad., Buffalo, NY, A (1973) | 80,024 | Lions—Pontiac Silverdome, MI, A (1975) | 80,368 |
| Broncos— Denver Mile High Stad., CO, G (1948) | 76,273 | Oilers—Astrodome, Houston, TX, A (1965) | 59,969 |
| Buccaneers—Houlihan's Stad., Tampa, FL, G (1967)[2] | 74,301 | Packers—Lambeau Field, Green Bay, WI, G (1957) | 60,790 |
| Cardinals—Sun Devil Stad., Tempe, AZ, G (1958) | 73,273 | Panthers—Ericsson Stad., Charlotte, NC, G (1996)[7] | 72,520 |
| Chargers—San Diego Jack Murphy Stad., CA, G (1967) | 60,794 | Patriots—Foxboro Stad., MA, G (1971) | 60,292 |
| Chiefs—Arrowhead Stad., Kansas City, MO, G (1972) | 79,101 | Raiders—Oakland-Alameda Cty. Coliseum, CA, G (1966) | 62,500 |
| Colts—RCA Dome, Indianapolis, IN, A (1983) | 60,272 | Rams—Trans World Dome, St. Louis, MO, A (1995) | 66,000 |
| Cowboys—Texas Stad., Irving, TX, A (1971) | 65,921 | Ravens—Memorial Stad., Baltimore, MD, G (1924) | 65,000 |
| Dolphins—Pro Player Stad., Miami, FL, G (1987)[3] | 74,916 | Redskins—R. F. Kennedy Stad., Wash., DC, G (1961) | 56,454 |
| Eagles—Veterans Stad., Philadelphia, PA, A (1971) | 64,899 | Saints—Louisiana Superdome, New Orleans, A (1975) | 64,992 |
| Falcons—Georgia Dome, Atlanta, GA, A (1992) | 71,228 | Seahawks—Kingdome, Seattle, WA, A (1976) | 66,400 |
| 49ers—3Com Park, San Francisco, CA, G (1960)[4] | 70,207 | Steelers—Three Rivers Stad., Pittsburgh, PA, A (1970) | 59,600 |
| Giants—Giants Stad., E. Rutherford, NJ, A (1976)[5] | 78,148 | Vikings—Metrodome, Minneapolis, MN, A (1982) | 64,035 |

G=Grass. A=Artificial turf. Stad.=Stadium. (1) Formerly Riverfront Stadium. (2) Formerly Tampa Stadium. (3) Formerly Joe Robbie Stadium. (4) Formerly Candlestick Park. (5) Although Giants and Jets both play at Giants Stadium, capacities differ because extra seating is made available for Giants games. (6) Formerly the Gator Bowl. (7) Formerly Carolinas Stadium.

## *The Sporting News* 1995 NFL All-Pro Team

**Offense**—QB: Brett Favre, Green Bay. RB: Emmitt Smith, Dallas; Barry Sanders, Detroit. WR: Herman Moore, Detroit; Jerry Rice, SanFrancisco. TE: Ben Coates, New England. T: William Roaf, New Orleans; Erik Williams, Dallas. G: Nate Newton, Dallas; Larry Allen, Dallas. C: Dermontii Dawson, Pittsburgh. **Defense**—LB: Bryce Paup, Buffalo; Junior Seau, San Diego; Greg Lloyd, Pittsburgh. DE: Reggie White, Green Bay; Bruce Smith, Buffalo. DT: Eric Swann, Arizona; John Randle, Minnesota. CB: Aeneas Williams, Arizona; Deion Sanders, Dallas. S: Merton Hanks, San Francisco; Darren Woodson, Dallas. **Special Teams**—K: Morten Andersen, Atlanta. P: Darren Bennett, San Diego. PR: Brian Mitchell, Washington. KR: Glyn Milburn, Denver.

## Future Sites of the Super Bowl

| No. | Site | Date | No. | Site | Date |
|---|---|---|---|---|---|
| XXXI | Superdome, New Orleans, LA | Jan. 26, 1997 | XXXIII | Pro Player Stadium, Miami, FL | Jan. 31, 1999 |
| XXXII | San Diego Jack Murphy Stadium, CA | Jan. 25, 1998 | XXXIV | Georgia Dome, Atlanta, GA | Jan. 29, 2000 |
| | | | XXXV | Tampa, FL (new stadium) | Jan. 27, 2001 |

# CANADIAN FOOTBALL LEAGUE

## Grey Cup Championship Game

1954 Edmonton Eskimos 26, Montreal Alouettes 25
1955 Edmonton Eskimos 34, Montreal Alouettes 19
1956 Edmonton Eskimos 50, Montreal Alouettes 27
1957 Hamilton Tiger-Cats 32, Winnipeg Blue Bombers 7
1958 Winnipeg Blue Bombers 35, Hamilton Tiger-Cats 28
1959 Winnipeg Blue Bombers 21, Hamilton Tiger-Cats 7
1960 Ottawa Rough Riders 16, Edmonton Eskimos 6
1961 Winnipeg Blue Bombers 21, Hamilton Tiger-Cats 14
1962 Winnipeg Blue Bombers 28, Hamilton Tiger-Cats 27
1963 Hamilton Tiger-Cats 21, British Columbia Lions 10
1964 British Columbia Lions 34, Hamilton Tiger-Cats 24
1965 Hamilton Tiger-Cats 22, Winnipeg Blue Bombers 16
1966 Saskatchewan Roughriders 29, Ottawa Rough Riders 14
1967 Hamilton Tiger-Cats 24, Saskatchewan Roughriders 1
1968 Ottawa Rough Riders 24, Calgary Stampeders 21
1969 Ottawa Rough Riders 29, Saskatchewan Roughriders 11
1970 Montreal Alouettes 23, Calgary Stampeders 10
1971 Calgary Stampeders 14, Toronto Argonauts 11
1972 Hamilton Tiger-Cats 13, Saskatchewan Roughriders 10
1973 Ottawa Rough Riders 22, Edmonton Eskimos 18
1974 Montreal Alouettes 20, Edmonton Eskimos 7
1975 Edmonton Eskimos 9, Montreal Alouettes 8
1976 Ottawa Rough Riders 23, Saskatchewan Roughriders 20
1977 Montreal Alouettes 41, Edmonton Eskimos 6
1978 Edmonton Eskimos 20, Montreal Alouettes 13
1979 Edmonton Eskimos 17, Montreal Alouettes 9
1980 Edmonton Eskimos 48, Hamilton Tiger-Cats 10
1981 Edmonton Eskimos 26, Ottawa Rough Riders 23
1982 Edmonton Eskimos 32, Toronto Argonauts 16
1983 Toronto Argonauts 18, B.C. Lions 17
1984 Winnipeg Blue Bombers 47, Hamilton Tiger-Cats 17
1985 B.C. Lions 37, Hamilton Tiger-Cats 24
1986 Hamilton Tiger-Cats 39, Edmonton Eskimos 15
1987 Edmonton Eskimos 38, Toronto Argonauts 36
1988 Winnipeg Blue Bombers 22, B.C. Lions 21
1989 Saskatchewan Roughriders 43, Hamilton Tiger-Cats 40
1990 Winnipeg Blue Bombers 50, Edmonton Eskimos 11
1991 Toronto Argonauts 36, Calgary Stampeders 21
1992 Calgary Stampeders 24, Winnipeg Blue Bombers 10
1993 Edmonton Eskimos 33, Winnipeg Blue Bombers 23
1994 B.C. Lions 26, Baltimore Football Club* 23
1995 Baltimore Stallions 37, Calgary Stampeders 20

*Baltimore's team nickname had not been determined at this time.

## CFL Teams and Divisions, 1996

The CFL returned to its traditional format for the 1996 season, resurrecting the East-West divisional alignment. The CFL-champion Baltimore Stallions moved to Montreal and reintroduced the name Alouettes, while the remainder of the U.S.-based teams—the Birmingham Barracudas, Memphis Mad Dogs, San Antonio Texans, and Shreveport Pirates—suspended operations prior to the 1996 season.

**Western Division**
British Columbia Lions
Calgary Stampeders
Edmonton Eskimos
Saskatchewan Roughriders
Winnipeg Blue Bombers

**Eastern Division**
Hamilton Tiger-Cats
Montreal Alouettes
Ottawa Rough Riders
Toronto Argonauts

## All-Time CFL Records

(through 1995 season)

**Longest Run**—The Canadian Football League features 3 downs, 12 players on a side, and a field that is 110 yards long. George Dixon of the Montreal Alouettes made full use of the field with a 109-yard run against Ottawa on Sept. 2, 1963. Willie Fleming of the British Columbia Lions did the same against Edmonton on Oct. 17, 1964.

### Leading Lifetime Rushers

| | Yrs | No | Yds | Avg | Long | TDs |
|---|---|---|---|---|---|---|
| George Reed, Sask. | 13 | 3,243 | 16,116 | 5.0 | 71 | 134 |
| Johnny Bright, Calg.-Edm. | 13 | 1,969 | 10,909 | 5.5 | 90 | 69 |
| Normie Kwong, Calg.-Edm. | 13 | 1,745 | 9,022 | 5.2 | 60 | 78 |
| Leo Lewis, Wpg. | 11 | 1,351 | 8,861 | 6.5 | 92 | 48 |
| Dave Thelen, Ott.-Tor. | 9 | 1,530 | 8,463 | 5.5 | 77 | 47 |
| Jim Everson, B.C.-Ott. | 7 | 1,460 | 7,060 | 4.8 | 68 | 37 |
| Earl Lunsford, Calg. | 6 | 1,199 | 6,994 | 5.8 | 85 | 55 |
| Dick Shatto, Tor. | 12 | 1,322 | 6,958 | 5.3 | 67 | 39 |
| Lovell Coleman, Calg.-Ott.-B.C. | 10 | 1,135 | 6,566 | 5.8 | 85 | 42 |
| Damon Allen, Edm.-Ott.-Ham.-Mps. | 11 | 908 | 6,375 | 7.0 | 51 | 54 |

### Leading Lifetime Passers

(ranked by total yards passing)

| | Yrs | Att | Comp | Yds | Pct | Avg | Long | TDs |
|---|---|---|---|---|---|---|---|---|
| Ron Lancaster, Ott.-Sask. | 19 | 6,233 | 3,384 | 50,535 | 54.3 | 14.9 | 102 | 333 |
| Matt Dunigan, Edm.-B.C.-Tor.-Wpg. | 13 | 5,265 | 2,943 | 42,132 | 55.9 | 14.3 | 89 | 294 |
| Tom Clements, Ott.-Sask.-Ham.-Wpg. | 12 | 4,657 | 2,807 | 39,041 | 60.3 | 13.9 | 105 | 252 |
| Dieter Brock, Wpg.-Ham. | 11 | 4,535 | 2,602 | 34,830 | 57.4 | 13.4 | 98 | 210 |
| Kent Austin, Sask.-B.C.-Tor. | 9 | 4,386 | 2,533 | 33,895 | 57.8 | 13.4 | 107 | 190 |
| Damon Allen, Edm.-Ott.-Ham.-Mps. | 11 | 4,004 | 2,070 | 30,786 | 51.7 | 14.9 | 102 | 181 |
| Tom Burgess, Ott.-Sask.-Wpg. | 10 | 4,034 | 2,118 | 30,308 | 52.5 | 14.3 | 104 | 190 |
| Doug Flutie, B.C.-Calg. | 6 | 3,504 | 2,111 | 30,130 | 60.2 | 14.3 | 106 | 194 |
| Tracy Ham, Edm.-Tor-Balt. | 8 | 3,154 | 1,642 | 25,735 | 52.1 | 15.7 | 100 | 180 |
| Sam Etcheverry, Mtl. | 7 | 2,829 | 1,630 | 25,582 | 57.6 | 15.7 | 109 | 183 |
| Condredge Holloway, Ott.-Tor.-B.C. | 13 | 3,013 | 1,710 | 25,193 | 56.8 | 14.7 | 80 | 166 |
| Russ Jackson, Ott. | 12 | 2,530 | 1,356 | 24,592 | 53.6 | 18.1 | 107 | 185 |
| Bernie Faloney, Edm.-Ham.-Mtl.-B.C. | 12 | 2,876 | 1,493 | 24,264 | 51.9 | 16.3 | 96 | 161 |
| Roy Dewalt, B.C.-Wpg.-Ott. | 9 | 3,130 | 1,803 | 24,147 | 57.6 | 13.4 | 90 | 132 |
| Joe Kapp, Calg.-B.C. | 8 | 2,709 | 1,476 | 22,725 | 54.5 | 16.4 | 106 | 136 |

### Leading Lifetime Receivers

| | Yrs | No | Yds |
|---|---|---|---|
| Ray Elgaard, Sask. | 13 | 819 | 13,098 |
| Rocky DiPietro, Ham. | 14 | 706 | 9,762 |
| Tommy Joe Coffey, Edm.-Ham.-Tor. | 14 | 650 | 10,320 |
| Tom Scott, Wpg.-Edm.-Calg. | 11 | 649 | 10,837 |
| Don Narcisse, Sask. | 9 | 647 | 8,695 |
| Tony Gabriel, Ham.-Ont. | 11 | 614 | 9,832 |
| Terry Evanshen, Mtl.-Calg.-Tor. | 14 | 600 | 9,697 |
| Craig Ellis, Wpg.-Calg.-Sask.-Tor.-Edm. | 10 | 580 | 7,757 |
| Brian Kelly, Edm. | 9 | 575 | 11,169 |
| James Murphy, Wpg. | 8 | 573 | 9,036 |

# COLLEGE FOOTBALL

## Annual Results of Major Bowl Games

(Dates indicate the year that the game was played.)

### Rose Bowl, Pasadena

| | |
|---|---|
| 1902 | (Jan.) Michigan 49, Stanford 0 |
| 1916 | Wash. St. 14, Brown 0 |
| 1917 | Oregon 14, Pennsylvania 0 |
| 1918 | Service teams |
| 1919 | Service teams |
| 1920 | Harvard 7, Oregon 6 |
| 1921 | California 28, Ohio St. 0 |
| 1922 | Wash. & Jeff. 0, California 0 |
| 1923 | Southern Cal 14, Penn St. 3 |
| 1924 | Navy 14, Washington 14 |
| 1925 | Notre Dame 27, Stanford 10 |
| 1926 | Alabama 20, Washington 19 |
| 1927 | Alabama 7, Stanford 7 |
| 1928 | Stanford 7, Pittsburgh 6 |
| 1929 | Georgia Tech 8, California 7 |
| 1930 | Southern Cal 47, Pittsburgh 14 |
| 1931 | Alabama 24, Wash. St. 0 |
| 1932 | Southern Cal 21, Tulane 12 |
| 1933 | Southern Cal 35, Pittsburgh 0 |
| 1934 | Columbia 7, Stanford 0 |
| 1935 | Alabama 29, Stanford 13 |
| 1936 | Stanford 7, So. Methodist 0 |
| 1937 | Pittsburgh 21, Washington 0 |
| 1938 | California 13, Alabama 0 |
| 1939 | Southern Cal 7, Duke 3 |
| 1940 | Southern Cal 14, Tennessee 0 |
| 1941 | Stanford 21, Nebraska 13 |
| 1942* | Oregon St. 20, Duke 16 |
| 1943 | Georgia 9, UCLA 0 |
| 1944 | Southern Cal 29, Washington 0 |
| 1945 | Southern Cal 25, Tennessee 0 |
| 1946 | Alabama 34, Southern Cal 14 |
| 1947 | Illinois 45, UCLA 14 |
| 1948 | Michigan 49, Southern Cal 0 |
| 1949 | Northwestern 20, California 14 |
| 1950 | Ohio St. 17, California 14 |
| 1951 | Michigan 14, California 6 |
| 1952 | Illinois 40, Stanford 7 |
| 1953 | Southern Cal 7, Wisconsin 0 |
| 1954 | Mich. St. 28, UCLA 20 |
| 1955 | Ohio St. 20, Southern Cal 7 |
| 1956 | Mich. St. 17, UCLA 14 |
| 1957 | Iowa 35, Oregon St. 19 |
| 1958 | Ohio St. 10, Oregon 7 |
| 1959 | Iowa 38, California 12 |
| 1960 | Washington 44, Wisconsin 8 |
| 1961 | Washington 17, Minnesota 7 |
| 1962 | Minnesota 21, UCLA 3 |
| 1963 | Southern Cal 42, Wisconsin 37 |
| 1964 | Illinois 17, Washington 7 |
| 1965 | Michigan 34, Oregon St. 7 |
| 1966 | UCLA 14, Mich. St. 12 |
| 1967 | Purdue 14, Southern Cal 13 |
| 1968 | Southern Cal. 14, Indiana 3 |
| 1969 | Ohio St. 27, Southern Cal 16 |
| 1970 | Southern Cal 10, Michigan 3 |
| 1971 | Stanford 27, Ohio St. 17 |
| 1972 | Stanford 13, Michigan 12 |
| 1973 | Southern Cal 42, Ohio St. 17 |
| 1974 | Ohio St. 42, Southern Cal 21 |
| 1975 | Southern Cal 18, Ohio St. 17 |
| 1976 | UCLA 23, Ohio St. 10 |
| 1977 | Southern Cal 14, Michigan 6 |
| 1978 | Washington 27, Michigan 20 |
| 1979 | Southern Cal 17, Michigan 10 |
| 1980 | Southern Cal 17, Ohio St. 16 |
| 1981 | Michigan 23, Washington 6 |
| 1982 | Washington 28, Iowa 0 |
| 1983 | UCLA 24, Michigan 14 |
| 1984 | UCLA 45, Illinois 9 |
| 1985 | Southern Cal 20, Ohio St. 17 |
| 1986 | UCLA 45, Iowa 28 |
| 1987 | Arizona St. 22, Michigan 15 |
| 1988 | Mich. St. 20, Southern Cal 17 |
| 1989 | Michigan 22, Southern Cal 14 |
| 1990 | Southern Cal 17, Michigan 10 |
| 1991 | Washington 46, Iowa 34 |
| 1992 | Washington 34, Michigan 14 |
| 1993 | Michigan 38, Washington 31 |
| 1994 | Wisconsin 21, UCLA 16 |
| 1995 | Penn St. 38, Oregon 20 |
| 1996 | Southern Cal 41, Northwestern 31 |

*Played at Durham, NC.

### Orange Bowl, Miami

| | |
|---|---|
| 1935 | (Jan.) Bucknell 26, Miami (FL) 0 |
| 1936 | Catholic U. 20, Mississippi 19 |
| 1937 | Duquesne 13, Miss. St. 12 |
| 1938 | Auburn 6, Mich. St. 0 |
| 1939 | Tennessee 17, Oklahoma 0 |
| 1940 | Georgia Tech 21, Missouri 7 |
| 1941 | Miss. St. 14, Georgetown 7 |
| 1942 | Georgia 40, TCU 26 |
| 1943 | Alabama 37, Boston Coll. 21 |
| 1944 | LSU 19, Texas A&M 14 |
| 1945 | Tulsa 26, Georgia Tech 12 |
| 1946 | Miami (FL) 13, Holy Cross 6 |
| 1947 | Rice 8, Tennessee 0 |
| 1948 | Georgia Tech 20, Kansas 14 |
| 1949 | Texas 41, Georgia 28 |
| 1950 | Santa Clara 21, Kentucky 13 |
| 1951 | Clemson 15, Miami (FL) 14 |
| 1952 | Georgia Tech 17, Baylor 14 |
| 1953 | Alabama 61, Syracuse 6 |
| 1954 | Oklahoma 7, Maryland 0 |
| 1955 | Duke 34, Nebraska 7 |
| 1956 | Oklahoma 20, Maryland 6 |
| 1957 | Colorado 27, Clemson 21 |
| 1958 | Oklahoma 48, Duke 21 |
| 1959 | Oklahoma 21, Syracuse 6 |
| 1960 | Georgia 14, Missouri 0 |
| 1961 | Missouri 21, Navy 14 |
| 1962 | LSU 25, Colorado 7 |
| 1963 | Alabama 17, Oklahoma 0 |
| 1964 | Nebraska 13, Auburn 7 |
| 1965 | Texas 21, Alabama 17 |
| 1966 | Alabama 39, Nebraska 28 |
| 1967 | Florida 27, Georgia Tech 12 |
| 1968 | Oklahoma 26, Tennessee 24 |
| 1969 | Penn St. 15, Kansas 14 |
| 1970 | Penn St. 10, Missouri 3 |
| 1971 | Nebraska 17, LSU 12 |
| 1972 | Nebraska 38, Alabama 6 |
| 1973 | Nebraska 40, Notre Dame 6 |
| 1974 | Penn St. 16, LSU 9 |
| 1975 | Notre Dame 13, Alabama 11 |
| 1976 | Oklahoma 14, Michigan 6 |
| 1977 | Ohio St. 27, Colorado 10 |
| 1978 | Arkansas 31, Oklahoma 6 |
| 1979 | Oklahoma 31, Nebraska 24 |
| 1980 | Oklahoma 24, Florida St. 7 |
| 1981 | Oklahoma 18, Florida St. 17 |
| 1982 | Clemson 22, Nebraska 15 |
| 1983 | Nebraska 21, LSU 20 |
| 1984 | Miami (FL) 31, Nebraska 30 |
| 1985 | Washington 28, Oklahoma 17 |
| 1986 | Oklahoma 25, Penn St. 10 |
| 1987 | Oklahoma 42, Arkansas 8 |
| 1988 | Miami (FL) 20, Oklahoma 14 |
| 1989 | Miami (FL) 23, Nebraska 3 |
| 1990 | Notre Dame 21, Colorado 6 |
| 1991 | Colorado 10, Notre Dame 9 |
| 1992 | Miami (FL) 22, Nebraska 0 |
| 1993 | Florida St. 27, Nebraska 14 |
| 1994 | Florida St. 18, Nebraska 16 |
| 1995 | Nebraska 24, Miami (FL) 17 |
| 1996 | Florida St. 31, Notre Dame 26 |

### Sugar Bowl, New Orleans

| | |
|---|---|
| 1935 | (Jan.) Tulane 20, Temple 14 |
| 1936 | TCU 3, LSU 2 |
| 1937 | Santa Clara 21, LSU 14 |
| 1938 | Santa Clara 6, LSU 0 |
| 1939 | TCU 15, Carnegie Tech 7 |
| 1940 | Texas A&M 14, Tulane 13 |
| 1941 | Boston Col. 19, Tennessee 13 |
| 1942 | Fordham 2, Missouri 0 |
| 1943 | Tennessee 14, Tulsa 7 |
| 1944 | Georgia Tech 20, Tulsa 18 |
| 1945 | Duke 29, Alabama 26 |
| 1946 | Oklahoma A&M 33, St. Mary's 13 |
| 1947 | Georgia 20, N. Carolina 10 |
| 1948 | Texas 27, Alabama 7 |
| 1949 | Oklahoma 14, N. Carolina 6 |
| 1950 | Oklahoma 35, LSU 0 |
| 1951 | Kentucky 13, Oklahoma 7 |
| 1952 | Maryland 28, Tennessee 13 |
| 1953 | Georgia Tech 24, Mississippi 7 |
| 1954 | Georgia Tech 42, West Virginia 19 |
| 1955 | Navy 21, Mississippi 0 |
| 1956 | Georgia Tech 7, Pittsburgh 0 |
| 1957 | Baylor 13, Tennessee 7 |
| 1958 | Mississippi 39, Texas 7 |
| 1959 | LSU 7, Clemson 0 |
| 1960 | Mississippi 21, LSU 0 |
| 1961 | Mississippi 14, Rice 6 |
| 1962 | Alabama 10, Arkansas 3 |
| 1963 | Mississippi 17, Arkansas 13 |
| 1964 | Alabama 12, Mississippi 7 |
| 1965 | LSU 13, Syracuse 10 |
| 1966 | Missouri 20, Florida 18 |
| 1967 | Alabama 34, Nebraska 7 |
| 1968 | LSU 20, Wyoming 13 |
| 1969 | Arkansas 16, Georgia 2 |
| 1970 | Mississippi 27, Arkansas 22 |
| 1971 | Tennessee 34, Air Force 13 |
| 1972 | Oklahoma 40, Auburn 22 |
| 1972* | (Dec.) Oklahoma 14, Penn St. 0 |
| 1973 | Notre Dame 24, Alabama 23 |
| 1974 | Nebraska 13, Florida 10 |
| 1975 | Alabama 13, Penn St. 6 |
| 1977 | (Jan.) Pittsburgh 27, Georgia 3 |
| 1978 | Alabama 35, Ohio St. 6 |
| 1979 | Alabama 14, Penn St. 7 |
| 1980 | Alabama 24, Arkansas 9 |
| 1981 | Georgia 17, Notre Dame 10 |
| 1982 | Pittsburgh 24, Georgia 20 |
| 1983 | Penn St. 27, Georgia 23 |
| 1984 | Auburn 9, Michigan 7 |
| 1985 | Nebraska 28, LSU 10 |
| 1986 | Tennessee 35, Miami (FL) 7 |
| 1987 | Nebraska 30, LSU 15 |
| 1988 | Syracuse 16, Auburn 16 |
| 1989 | Florida St. 13, Auburn 7 |
| 1990 | Miami 33, Alabama 25 |
| 1991 | Tennessee 23, Virginia 22 |
| 1992 | Notre Dame 39, Florida 28 |
| 1993 | Alabama 34, Miami (FL) 13 |
| 1994 | Florida 41, West Virginia 7 |
| 1995 | Florida St. 23, Florida 17 |
| 1996 | Virginia Tech 28, Texas 10 |

* Penn St. awarded game by forfeit.

## Fiesta Bowl, Tempe

1971 (Dec.) Arizona St. 45, Florida St. 38
1972 Arizona St. 49, Missouri 35
1973 Arizona St. 28, Pittsburgh 7
1974 Okla. St. 16, Brigham Young 6
1975 Arizona St. 17, Nebraska 14
1976 Oklahoma 41, Wyoming 7
1977 Penn St. 42, Arizona St. 30
1978 UCLA 10, Arkansas 10
1979 Pittsburgh 16, Arizona 10
1980 Penn St. 31, Ohio St. 19
1982 (Jan.) Penn St. 26, USC 10
1983 Arizona St. 32, Oklahoma 21
1984 Ohio St. 28, Pittsburgh 23
1985 UCLA 39, Miami (FL) 37
1986 Michigan 27, Nebraska 23
1987 Penn St. 14, Miami (FL) 10
1988 Florida St. 31, Nebraska 28
1989 Notre Dame 34, W. Virginia 21
1990 Florida St. 41, Nebraska 17
1991 Louisville 34, Alabama 7
1992 Penn St. 42, Tennessee 17
1993 Syracuse 26, Colorado 22
1994 Arizona 29, Miami (FL) 0
1995 Colorado 41, Notre Dame 24
1996 Nebraska 62; Florida 24

## Cotton Bowl, Dallas

1937 (Jan.) TCU 16, Marquette 6
1938 Rice 28, Colorado 14
1939 St. Mary's 20, Texas Tech 13
1940 Clemson 6, Boston Col. 3
1941 Texas A&M 13, Fordham 12
1942 Alabama 29, Texas A&M 21
1943 Texas 14, Georgia Tech 7
1944 Randolph Field 7, Texas 7
1945 Oklahoma A&M 34, TCU 0
1946 Texas 40, Missouri 27
1947 Arkansas 0, LSU 0
1948 So. Methodist 13, Penn St. 13
1949 So. Methodist 21, Oregon 13
1950 Rice 27, North Carolina 13
1951 Tennessee 20, Texas 14
1952 Kentucky 20, TCU 7
1953 Texas 16, Tennessee 0
1954 Rice 28, Alabama 6
1955 Georgia Tech 14, Arkansas 6
1956 Mississippi 14, TCU 13
1957 TCU 28, Syracuse 27
1958 Navy 20, Rice 7
1959 TCU 0, Air Force 0
1960 Syracuse 23, Texas 14
1961 Duke 7, Arkansas 6
1962 Texas 12, Mississippi 7
1963 LSU 13, Texas 0
1964 Texas 28, Navy 6
1965 Arkansas 10, Nebraska 7
1966 LSU 14, Arkansas 7
1966 (Dec.) Georgia 24, SMU 9
1968 (Jan.) Texas A&M 20, Ala. 16
1969 Texas 36, Tennessee 13
1970 Texas 21, Notre Dame 17
1971 Notre Dame 24, Texas 11
1972 Penn St. 30, Texas 6
1973 Texas 17, Alabama 13
1974 Nebraska 19, Texas 3
1975 Penn St. 41, Baylor 20
1976 Arkansas 31, Georgia 10
1977 Houston 30, Maryland 21
1978 Notre Dame 38, Texas 10
1979 Notre Dame 35, Houston 34
1980 Houston 17, Nebraska 14
1981 Alabama 30, Baylor 2
1982 Texas 14, Alabama 12
1983 SMU 7, Pittsburgh 3
1984 Georgia 10, Texas 9
1985 Boston Coll. 45, Houston 28
1986 Texas A&M 36, Auburn 16
1987 Ohio St. 28, Texas A&M 12
1988 Texas A&M 35, Notre Dame 10
1989 UCLA 17, Arkansas 3
1990 Tennessee 31, Arkansas 27
1991 Miami (FL) 46, Texas 3
1992 Florida St. 10, Texas A&M 2
1993 Notre Dame 28, Texas A&M 3
1994 Notre Dame 24, Texas A&M 21
1995 Southern Cal. 55, Tex. Tech 14
1996 Colorado 38, Oregon 6

## Sun Bowl, El Paso (John Hancock Bowl, 1989-93)

1936 (Jan.) Hardin-Simmons 14, New Mexico St. 14
1937 Hardin-Simmons 34, Texas Mines 6
1938 West Virginia 7, Texas Tech 6
1939 Utah 26, New Mexico 0
1940 Catholic U. 0, Arizona St. 0
1941 Western Reserve 26, Arizona St. 13
1942 Tulsa 6, Texas Tech 0
1943 2d Air Force 13, Hardin-Simmons 7
1944 Southwestern (TX) 7, New Mexico 0
1945 Southwestern (TX) 35, U. of Mexico 0
1946 New Mexico 34, Denver 24
1947 Cincinnati 18, Virginia Tech 6
1948 Miami (OH) 13, Texas Tech 12
1949 West Virginia 21, Texas Mines 12
1950 Texas Western 33, Georgetown 20
1951 West Texas St. 14, Cincinnati 13
1952 Texas Tech 25, Pacific (CA) 14
1953 Pacific (CA) 26, S. Mississippi 7
1954 Texas Western 37, S. Miss. 14
1955 Texas Western 47, Florida St. 20
1956 Wyoming 21, Texas Tech 14
1957 Geo. Washington 13, Texas Western 0
1958 Louisville 34, Drake 20
1958 (Dec.) Wyoming 14, Hardin-Simmons 6
1959 New Mexico St. 28, N. Texas St. 8
1960 New Mexico St. 20, Utah St. 13
1961 Villanova 17, Wichita 9
1962 West Texas St. 15, Ohio U. 14
1963 Oregon 21, So. Methodist 14
1964 Georgia 7, Texas Tech 0
1965 Texas Western 13, TCU 12
1966 Wyoming 28, Florida St. 20
1967 UTEP 14, Mississippi 7
1968 Auburn 34, Arizona 10
1969 Nebraska 45, Georgia 6
1970 Georgia Tech. 17, Texas Tech 9
1971 LSU 33, Iowa St. 15
1972 North Carolina 32, Texas Tech 28
1973 Missouri 34, Auburn 17
1974 Mississippi St. 26, N. Carolina 24
1975 Pittsburgh 33, Kansas 19
1977 (Jan.) Texas A&M 37, Florida 14
1977 (Dec.) Stanford 24, LSU 14
1978 Texas 42, Maryland 0
1979 Washington 14, Texas 7
1980 Nebraska 31, Mississippi St. 17
1981 Oklahoma 40, Houston 14
1982 North Carolina 26, Texas 10
1983 Alabama 28, SMU 7
1984 Maryland 28, Tennessee 27
1985 Georgia 13, Arizona 13
1986 Alabama 28, Washington 6
1987 Oklahoma St. 35, West Virginia 33
1988 Alabama 29, Army 28
1989 Pittsburgh 31, Texas A&M 28
1990 Michigan St. 17, USC 16
1991 UCLA 6, Illinois 3
1992 Baylor 20, Arizona 15
1993 Oklahoma 41, Texas Tech 10
1994 Texas 35, North Carolina 31
1995 Iowa 38, Washington 18

## Gator Bowl, Jacksonville

1946 (Jan.) Wake Forest 26, S. Carolina 14
1947 Oklahoma 34, N. Carolina St. 13
1948 Maryland 20, Georgia 20
1949 Clemson 24, Missouri 23
1950 Maryland 20, Missouri 7
1951 Wyoming 20, Washington & Lee 7
1952 Miami (FL) 14, Clemson 0
1953 Florida 14, Tulsa 13
1954 Texas Tech 35, Auburn 13
1954 (Dec.) Auburn 33, Baylor 13
1955 Vanderbilt 25, Auburn 13
1956 Georgia Tech 21, Pittsburgh 14
1957 Tennessee 3, Texas A&M 0
1958 Mississippi 7, Florida 3
1960 (Jan.) Arkansas 14, Ga.Tech 7
1960 (Dec.) Florida 13, Baylor 12
1961 Penn St. 30, Georgia Tech 15
1962 Florida 17, Penn St. 7
1963 N. Carolina 35, Air Force 0
1965 (Jan.) Florida St. 36, Okla.19
1965 (Dec.) Georgia Tech 31, Texas Tech 21
1966 Tennessee 18, Syracuse 12
1967 Penn St. 17, Florida St. 17
1968 Missouri 35, Alabama 10
1969 Florida 14, Tennessee 13
1971 (Jan.) Auburn 35, Mississippi 28
1971 (Dec.) Georgia 7, N. Carolina 3
1972 Auburn 24, Colorado 3
1973 Texas Tech 28, Tenn. 19
1974 Auburn 27, Texas 3
1975 Maryland 13, Florida 0
1976 Notre Dame 20, Penn St. 9
1977 Pittsburgh 34, Clemson 3
1978 Clemson 17, Ohio St. 15
1979 N. Carolina 17, Michigan 15
1980 Pittsburgh 37, S. Carolina 9
1981 N. Carolina 31, Arkansas 27
1982 Florida St. 31, West Virginia 12
1983 Florida 14, Iowa 6
1984 Oklahoma St. 21, S. Carolina 14
1985 Florida St. 34, Oklahoma St. 23
1986 Clemson 27, Stanford 21
1987 LSU 30, S. Carolina 13
1989 (Jan.) Georgia 34, Michigan St. 27
1989 (Dec.) Clemson 27, W. Virginia 7
1991 (Jan.) Michigan 35, Mississippi 3
1991 (Dec.) Oklahoma 48, Virginia 14
1992 Florida 27, N. Carolina St. 10
1993 Alabama 24, N. Carolina 10
1994 Tennessee 45, Virginia Tech 23
1996 (Jan.) Syracuse 41, Clemson 0

## Outback Bowl, Tampa (Hall of Fame Bowl Until 1996)

1986 (Dec.) Boston Coll. 27, Georgia 24
1988 (Jan.) Michigan 28, Alabama 24
1989 Syracuse 23, LSU 10
1990 Auburn 31, Ohio St. 14
1991 Clemson 30, Illinois 0
1992 Syracuse 24, Ohio St. 17
1993 Tennessee 38, Boston Coll. 23
1994 Michigan 42, N.C. St. 7
1995 Wisconsin 34, Duke 20
1996 Penn St. 43, Auburn 14

## Liberty Bowl, Memphis

1959 (Dec.) Penn St. 7, Alabama 0
1960 Penn St. 41, Oregon 12
1961 Syracuse 15, Miami 14
1962 Oregon St. 6, Villanova 0
1963 Mississippi St. 16, N. Carolina St. 12
1964 Utah 32, West Virginia 6
1965 Mississippi 13, Auburn 7
1966 Miami (FL) 14, Virginia Tech 7
1967 N. Carolina St. 14, Georgia 7
1968 Mississippi 34, Virginia Tech 17
1969 Colorado 47, Alabama 33
1970 Tulane 17, Colorado 3
1971 Tennessee 14, Arkansas 13
1972 Georgia Tech 31, Iowa St. 30
1973 N. Carolina St. 31, Kansas 18
1974 Tennessee 7, Maryland 3
1975 USC 20, Texas A&M 0
1976 Alabama 36, UCLA 6
1977 Nebraska 21, N. Carolina 17
1978 Missouri 20, LSU 15
1979 Penn St. 9, Tulane 6
1980 Purdue 28, Missouri 25
1981 Ohio St. 31, Navy 28
1982 Alabama 21, Illinois 15
1983 Notre Dame 19, Boston Coll. 18
1984 Auburn 21, Arkansas 15
1985 Baylor 21, LSU 7
1986 Tennessee 21, Minnesota 14
1987 Georgia 20, Arkansas 17
1988 Indiana 34, S. Carolina 10
1989 Mississippi 42, Air Force 29
1990 Air Force 23, Ohio St. 11
1991 Air Force 38, Mississippi St. 15
1992 Mississippi 13, Air Force 0
1993 Louisville 18, Michigan St. 7
1994 Illinois 30, East Carolina 0
1995 East Carolina 19, Stanford 13

## Copper Bowl, Tucson

1989 (Dec.) Arizona 17, North Carolina St. 10
1990 California 17, Wyoming 15
1991 Indiana 24, Baylor 0
1992 Washington St. 31, Utah 28
1993 Kansas St. 52, Wyoming 17
1994 Brigham Young 31, Oklahoma 6
1995 Texas Tech 55, Air Force 41

## Independence Bowl, Shreveport

1976 (Dec.)McNeese St. 20, Tulsa 16
1977 Louisiana Tech 24, Louisville 14
1978 E. Carolina 35, Louisiana Tech 13
1979 Syracuse 31, McNeese St. 7
1980 So. Miss. 16, McNeese St. 14
1981 Texas A&M 33, Oklahoma St. 16
1982 Wisconsin 14, Kansas St. 3
1983 Air Force 9, Mississippi 3
1984 Air Force 23, Virginia Tech 7
1985 Minnesota 20, Clemson 13
1986 Mississippi 20, Texas Tech 17
1987 Washington 24, Tulane 12
1988 So. Mississippi 38, UTEP 18
1989 Oregon 27, Tulsa 24
1990 Louisiana Tech 34, Maryland 34
1991 Georgia 24, Arkansas 15
1992 Wake Forest 39, Oregon 35
1993 Virginia Tech 45, Indiana 20
1994 Virginia 20, Texas Christian 10
1995 LSU 45, Michigan St. 26

## Florida Citrus Bowl, Orlando (Tangerine Bowl Until 1983)

1947 (Jan.) Catawba 31, Maryville 6
1948 Catawba 7, Marshall 0
1949 Murray St. 21, Sul Ross St. 21
1950 St. Vincent 7, Emory & Henry 6
1951 Morris Harvey 35, Emory & Henry 14
1952 Stetson 35, Arkansas St. 20
1953 East Texas St. 33, Tenn. Tech 0
1954 East Texas St. 7, Arkansas St. 7
1955 Neb.-Omaha 7, E. Kentucky 6
1956 Juniata 6, Missouri Valley 6
1957 West Texas St. 20, So. Miss. 13
1958 East Texas St. 10, So. Miss. 9
1958 (Dec.) East Texas St. 26, Missouri Valley 7
1960 (Jan.) Middle Tenn. 21, Presbyterian 12
1960 (Dec.) Citadel 27, Tenn. Tech 0
1961 Lamar 21, Middle Tennessee 14
1962 Houston 49, Miami (OH) 21
1963 Western Ky. 27, Coast Guard 0
1964 E. Carolina 14, Massachusetts 13
1965 East Carolina 31, Maine 0
1966 Morgan St. 14, West Chester 6
1967 Tenn.-Martin 25, West Chester 8
1968 Richmond 49, Ohio U. 42
1969 Toledo 56, Davidson 33
1970 Toledo 40, William & Mary 12
1971 Toledo 28, Richmond 3
1972 Tampa 21, Kent St. 18
1973 Miami (OH) 16, Florida 7
1974 Miami (OH) 21, Georgia 10
1975 Miami (OH) 20, S. Carolina 7
1976 Okla. St. 49, Brigham Young 21
1977 Florida St. 40, Texas Tech 17
1978 NC St. 30, Pittsburgh 17
1979 LSU 34, Wake Forest 10
1980 Florida 35, Maryland 20
1981 Missouri 19, Southern Miss. 17
1982 Auburn 33, Boston College 26
1983 Tennessee 30, Maryland 23
1984 Georgia 17, Florida St. 17
1985 Ohio St. 10, Brigham Young 7
1987 (Jan.) Auburn 16, USC 7
1988 Clemson 35, Penn St. 10
1989 Clemson 13, Oklahoma 6
1990 Illinois 31, Virginia 21
1991 Georgia Tech 45, Nebraska 21
1992 California 37, Clemson 13
1993 Georgia 21, Ohio St. 14
1994 Penn St. 31, Tennessee 13
1995 Alabama 24, Ohio St. 17
1996 Tennessee 20, Ohio St. 14

## Peach Bowl, Atlanta

1968 (Dec.) LSU 31, Florida St. 27
1969 West Virginia 14, S. Carolina 3
1970 Arizona St. 48, N. Carolina 26
1971 Mississippi 41, Georgia Tech 18
1972 N. Carolina St. 49, W. Va. 13
1973 Georgia 17, Maryland 16
1974 Vanderbilt 6, Texas Tech 6
1975 W. Virginia 13, N. Carolina St. 10
1976 Kentucky 21, North Carolina 0
1977 N. Carolina St. 24, Iowa St. 14
1978 Purdue 41, Georgia Tech. 21
1979 Baylor 24, Clemson 18
1981 (Jan.) Miami (FL) 20, Virginia Tech 10
1981 (Dec.) West Virginia 26, Florida 6
1982 Iowa 28, Tennessee 22
1983 Florida St. 28, North Carolina 3
1984 Virginia 27, Purdue 22
1985 Army 31, Illinois 29
1986 Va. Tech 25, N. Carolina St. 24
1988 (Jan.) Tennessee 28, Indiana 22
1988 (Dec.) N. Carolina St. 28, Iowa 23
1989 Syracuse 19, Georgia 18
1990 Auburn 27, Indiana 23
1992 (Jan.) E. Carolina 37, N.Carolina St. 34
1993 North Carolina 21, Mississippi St. 17
1993 (Dec.) Clemson 14, Kentucky 13
1995 (Jan.) N. Carolina St. 28, Miss. St. 24
1995 (Dec.) Virginia 34, Georgia 27

## Holiday Bowl, San Diego

1978 (Dec.) Navy 23, Brig. Young 16
1979 Indiana 38, Brigham Young 37
1980 Brigham Young 46, SMU 45
1981 Brigham Young 38, Wash. St. 36
1982 Ohio St. 47, Brigham Young 17
1983 Brigham Young 21, Missouri 17
1984 Brigham Young 24, Michigan 17
1985 Arkansas 18, Arizona St. 17
1986 Iowa 39, San Diego St. 38
1987 Iowa 20, Wyoming 19
1988 Oklahoma St. 62, Wyoming 14
1989 Penn St. 50, Brigham Young 39
1990 Texas A&M 65, Brigham Young 14
1991 Iowa 13, Brigham Young 13
1992 Hawaii 27, Illinois 17
1993 Ohio St. 28, Brigham Young 21
1994 Michigan 24, Colorado St. 14
1995 Kansas St. 54, Colorado St. 21

## Aloha Bowl, Honolulu

1982 (Dec.) Washington 21, Md. 20
1983 Penn St. 13, Washington 10
1984 SMU 27, Notre Dame 20
1985 Alabama 24, USC 3
1986 Arizona 30, North Carolina 21
1987 UCLA 20, Florida 16
1988 Washington St. 24, Houston 22
1989 Michigan St. 33, Hawaii 13
1990 Syracuse 28, Arizona 0
1991 Georgia Tech 18, Stanford 17
1992 Kansas 23, Brigham Young 20
1993 Colorado 41, Fresno St. 30
1994 Boston Coll. 12, Kansas St. 7
1995 Kansas 51, UCLA 30

## Carquest Bowl, Miami (Blockbuster Bowl Until 1993)

1990 (Dec.) Florida St. 24, Penn St. 17
1991 Alabama 30, Colorado 25
1993 (Jan.) Stanford 24, Penn St. 3
1994 Boston College 31, Virginia 13
1995 S. Carolina 24, W. Virginia 21
1995 (Dec.) N. Carolina 20, Arkansas 10

## Las Vegas Bowl, Las Vegas

1992 (Dec.) Bowling Green 35, Nevada 34
1993 Utah St. 42, Ball St. 33
1994 UNLV 52, Central Michigan 24
1995 Toledo 40, Nevada 37 (OT)

## Selected College Division I Football Teams

(1995 record does not include bowl games)

| Team | Nickname | Team colors | Conference | Coach | 1995 record (W-L-T) |
|---|---|---|---|---|---|
| Air Force | Falcons | Blue & silver | Western Athletic | Fisher DeBerry | 8-4-0 |
| Akron | Zips | Blue & gold | Mid-American | Lee Owens | 2-9-0 |
| Alabama | Crimson Tide | Crimson & white | Southeastern | Gene Stallings | 8-3-0 |
| Arizona | Wildcats | Cardinal & navy | Pacific Ten | Dick Tomey | 6-5-0 |
| Arizona State | Sun Devils | Maroon & gold | Pacific Ten | Bruce Snyder | 6-5-0 |
| Arkansas | Razorbacks | Cardinal & white | Southeastern | Danny Ford | 8-4-0 |
| Arkansas State | Indians | Scarlet & black | Independent | John Bobo | 6-5-0 |
| Army | Cadets, Black Knights | Black, gold, gray | Independent | Bob Sutton | 5-5-1 |
| Auburn | Tigers | Burnt orange & navy | Southeastern | Terry Bowden | 8-3-0 |
| Ball State | Cardinals | Cardinal & white | Mid-American | Bill Lynch | 7-4-0 |
| Baylor | Bears | Green & gold | Big Twelve | Chuck Reedy | 7-4-0 |
| Boston College | Eagles | Maroon & gold | Big East | Dan Henning | 4-8-0 |
| Boston University | Terriers | Scarlet & white | Yankee | Tom Masella | 3-8-0 |
| Bowling Green | Falcons | Orange & brown | Mid-American | Gary Blackney | 5-6-0 |
| Brigham Young | Cougars | Royal blue & white | Western Athletic | LaVell Edwards | 7-4-0 |
| Brown | Bears | Brown, cardinal, white | Ivy League | Mark Whipple | 5-5-0 |
| California | Golden Bears | Blue & gold | Pacific Ten | Steve Mariucci | 3-8-0 |
| Central Michigan | Chippewas | Maroon & gold | Mid-American | Dick Flynn | 4-7-0 |
| Cincinnati | Bearcats | Red & black | Conference USA | Rick Minter | 6-5-0 |
| Citadel | Bulldogs | Blue & white | Southern | Charles Taaffe | 2-9-0 |
| Clemson | Tigers | Purple & orange | Atlantic Coast | Tommy West | 8-3-0 |
| Colgate | Red Raiders | Maroon | Patriot League | Dick Biddle | 0-11-0 |
| Colorado | Buffaloes | Silver, gold & black | Big Twelve | Rick Neuheisel | 9-2-0 |
| Colorado State | Rams | Green & gold | Western Athletic | Sonny Lubick | 8-3-0 |
| Cornell | Big Red | Carnelian & white | Ivy League | Jim Hofher | 6-4-0 |
| Dartmouth | Big Green | Dartmouth green & white | Ivy League | John Lyons | 7-2-1 |
| Delaware | Fightin' Blue Hens | Blue & gold | Yankee | Tubby Raymond | 10-1-0 |
| Delaware State | Hornets | Red & blue | Mid-Eastern Athl. | Bill Collick | 6-5-0 |
| Duke | Blue Devils | Royal blue & white | Atlantic Coast | Fred Goldsmith | 3-8-0 |
| East Carolina | Pirates | Purple & gold | Independent | Steve Logan | 8-3-0 |
| East Tennessee State | Buccaneers | Blue & gold | Southern | Mike Cavan | 4-7-0 |
| Eastern Illinois | Panthers | Blue & gray | Ohio Valley | Bob Spoo | 10-1-0 |
| Eastern Kentucky | Colonels | Maroon & white | Ohio Valley | Roy Kidd | 9-2-0 |
| Eastern Michigan | Eagles | Dark green & white | Mid-American | Rick Rasnick | 6-5-0 |
| Eastern Washington | Eagles | Red & white | Big Sky | Mike Kramer | 3-8-0 |
| Florida | Gators | Blue & orange | Southeastern | Steve Spurrier | 12-0-0 |
| Florida A&M | Rattlers | Orange & green | Mid-Eastern Athl. | Billy Joe | 9-2-0 |
| Florida State | Seminoles | Garnet & gold | Atlantic Coast | Bobby Bowden | 9-2-0 |
| Fresno State | Bulldogs | Cardinal & blue | Western Athletic | Jim Sweeney | 5-7-0 |
| Furman | Paladins | Purple & white | Southern | Bobby Johnson | 6-5-0 |
| Georgia | Bulldogs | Red & black | Southeastern | Jim Donnan | 6-5-0 |
| Georgia Southern | Eagles | Blue & white | Southern | Frank Ellwood | 8-3-0 |
| Georgia Tech | Yellow Jackets | Old gold & white | Atlantic Coast | George O'Leary | 6-5-0 |
| Grambling | Tigers | Black & gold | Southwestern | Eddie Robinson | 5-6-0 |
| Harvard | Crimson | Crimson, black, white | Ivy League | Tim Murphy | 2-8-0 |
| Hawaii | Rainbow Warriors | Green & white | Western Athletic | Fred vonAppen | 4-8-0 |
| Holy Cross | Crusaders | Royal purple | Patriot League | Dan Allen | 2-9-0 |
| Houston | Cougars | Scarlet & white | Conference USA | Kim Helton | 2-9-0 |
| Howard | Bison | Blue, white & red | Mid-Eastern Athl. | Steve Wilson | 6-5-0 |
| Idaho | Vandals | Silver & gold | Big West | Chris Tormey | 6-4-0 |
| Idaho State | Bengals | Orange & black | Big Sky | Brian McNeely | 6-5-0 |
| Illinois | Fighting Illini | Orange & blue | Big Ten | Lou Tepper | 5-5-1 |
| Illinois State | Redbirds | Red & white | Gateway | Todd Berry | 5-6-0 |
| Indiana | Fightin' Hoosiers | Cream & crimson | Big Ten | Bill Mallory | 2-9-0 |
| Indiana State | Sycamores | Blue & white | Gateway | Dennis Raetz | 7-4-0 |
| Iowa | Hawkeyes | Old gold & black | Big Ten | Hayden Fry | 7-4-0 |
| Iowa State | Cyclones | Cardinal & gold | Big Twelve | Dan McCarney | 3-8-0 |
| Jackson State | Tigers | Blue & white | Southwestern | James Carson | 9-2-0 |
| James Madison | Dukes | Purple & gold | Yankee | Alex Wood | 8-3-0 |
| Kansas | Jayhawks | Crimson & blue | Big Twelve | Glen Mason | 9-2-0 |
| Kansas State | Wildcats | Purple & white | Big Twelve | Bill Snyder | 9-2-0 |
| Kent | Golden Flashes | Navy blue & gold | Mid-American | Jim Corrigall | 1-9-1 |
| Kentucky | Wildcats | Blue & white | Southeastern | Bill Curry | 4-7-0 |
| Lafayette | Leopards | Maroon & white | Patriot League | Bill Russo | 4-6-1 |
| Lehigh | Mountain Hawks | Brown & white | Patriot League | Kevin Higgins | 8-3-0 |
| Liberty | Flames | Red, white & blue | Independent | Sam Rutigliano | 8-3-0 |
| Louisiana State (LSU) | Fighting Tigers | Purple & gold | Southeastern | Gerry DiNardo | 6-4-1 |
| Louisiana Tech | Bulldogs | Red & blue | Independent | Gary Crowton | 5-6-0 |
| Louisville | Cardinals | Red, black & white | Conference USA | Ron Cooper | 7-4-0 |
| Maine | Black Bears | Blue & white | Yankee | Jack Cosgrove | 3-8-0 |
| Marshall | Thundering Herd | Green & white | Southern | Bob Pruett | 9-2-0 |
| Maryland | Terrapins | Red, white, black, gold | Atlantic Coast | Mark Duffner | 6-5-0 |
| Massachusetts | Minutemen | Maroon & white | Yankee | Mike Hodges | 6-5-0 |

| Team | Nickname | Team colors | Conference | Coach | 1995 record (W-L-T) |
|---|---|---|---|---|---|
| McNeese State | Cowboys | Blue & gold | Southland | Bobby Keasler | 11-0-0 |
| Memphis | Tigers | Blue & gray | Conference USA | Rip Scherer | 3-8-0 |
| Miami (Florida) | Hurricanes | Orange, green, white | Big East | Butch Davis | 8-3-0 |
| Miami (Ohio) | Redskins | Red & white | Mid-American | Randy Walker | 8-2-1 |
| Michigan | Wolverines | Maize & blue | Big Ten | Lloyd Carr | 9-3-0 |
| Michigan State | Spartans | Green & white | Big Ten | Nick Saban | 6-4-1 |
| Middle Tennessee St. | Blue Raiders | Blue & white | Ohio Valley | Boots Donnelly | 7-4-0 |
| Minnesota | Golden Gophers | Maroon & gold | Big Ten | Jim Wacker | 3-8-0 |
| Mississippi | Rebels | Cardinal red & navy | Southeastern | Tommy Tuberville | 6-5-0 |
| Mississippi State | Bulldogs | Maroon & white | Southeastern | Jackie Sherrill | 3-8-0 |
| Mississippi Valley | Delta Devils | Green & white | Southwestern | Larry Dorsey | 2-9-0 |
| Missouri | Tigers | Old gold & black | Big Twelve | Larry Smith | 3-8-0 |
| Montana | Grizzlies | Copper, silver, gold | Big Sky | Mick Dennehy | 9-2-0 |
| Montana State | Bobcats | Blue & gold | Big Sky | Cliff Hysell | 5-6-0 |
| Morehead State | Eagles | Blue & gold | Ohio Valley | Matt Ballard | 2-8-0 |
| Morgan State | Bears | Blue & orange | Mid-Eastern Athl. | Stump Mitchell | 1-10-0 |
| Murray State | Racers | Blue & gold | Ohio Valley | Houston Nutt | 11-0-0 |
| Navy | Midshipmen | Navy blue & gold | Independent | Charlie Weatherbie | 5-6-0 |
| Nebraska | Cornhuskers | Scarlet & cream | Big Twelve | Tom Osborne | 11-0-0 |
| Nev.-Las Vegas (UNLV) | Rebels | Scarlet & gray | Western Athletic | Jeff Horton | 2-9-0 |
| Nevada-Reno | Wolf Pack | Silver & blue | Big West | Jeff Tisdel | 9-2-0 |
| New Hampshire | Wildcats | Blue & white | Yankee | Bill Bowes | 6-5-0 |
| New Mexico | Lobos | Cherry & silver | Western Athletic | Dennis Franchione | 4-7-0 |
| New Mexico State | Aggies | Crimson & white | Big West | Jim Hess | 4-7-0 |
| Nicholls St. | Colonels | Red & gray | Southland | Darren Barbier | 0-11-0 |
| North Carolina | Tar Heels | Carolina blue & white | Atlantic Coast | Mack Brown | 6-5-0 |
| North Carolina A & T | Aggies | Blue & gold | Mid-Eastern Athl. | Bill Hayes | 4-7-0 |
| North Carolina State | Wolfpack | Red & white | Atlantic Coast | Mike O'Cain | 3-8-0 |
| North Texas | Eagles | Green & white | Big West | Matt Simon | 2-9-0 |
| Northeast Louisiana | Indians | Maroon & gold | Independent | Ed Zaunbrecher | 2-9-0 |
| Northeastern | Huskies | Red & black | Yankee | Barry Gallup | 4-7-0 |
| Northern Arizona | Lumberjacks | Blue & gold | Big Sky | Steve Axman | 7-4-0 |
| Northern Illinois | Huskies | Cardinal & black | Independent | Joe Novak | 3-8-0 |
| Northern Iowa | Panthers | Purple & old gold | Gateway | Terry Allen | 7-4-0 |
| Northwestern | Wildcats | Purple & white | Big Ten | Gary Barnett | 10-1-0 |
| Northwestern State | Demons | Purple & white | Southland | Sam Goodwin | 6-5-0 |
| Notre Dame | Fighting Irish | Gold & blue | Independent | Lou Holtz | 9-2-0 |
| Ohio | Bobcats | Ohio green & white | Mid-American | Jim Grobe | 2-8-1 |
| Ohio State | Buckeyes | Scarlet & gray | Big Ten | John Cooper | 11-1-0 |
| Oklahoma | Sooners | Crimson & cream | Big Twelve | John Blake | 5-5-1 |
| Oklahoma State | Cowboys | Orange & black | Big Twelve | Bob Simmons | 4-8-0 |
| Oregon | Ducks | Green & yellow | Pacific Ten | Mike Bellotti | 9-2-0 |
| Oregon State | Beavers | Orange & black | Pacific Ten | Jerry Pettibone | 1-10-0 |
| Penn State | Nittany Lions | Blue & white | Big Ten | Joe Paterno | 8-3-0 |
| Pennsylvania | Red & Blue, Quakers | Red & blue | Ivy League | Al Bagnoli | 7-3-0 |
| Pittsburgh | Panthers | Blue & gold | Big East | Johnny Majors | 2-9-0 |
| Princeton | Tigers | Orange & black | Ivy League | Steve Tosches | 8-1-1 |
| Purdue | Boilermakers | Old gold & black | Big Ten | Jim Colletto | 4-6-1 |
| Rhode Island | Rams | Blue & white | Yankee | Floyd Keith | 7-4-0 |
| Rice | Owls | Blue & gray | Western Athletic | Ken Hatfield | 2-8-1 |
| Richmond | Spiders | Red & blue | Yankee | Jim Reid | 7-3-1 |
| Rutgers | Scarlet Knights | Scarlet | Big East | Terry Shea | 4-7-0 |
| Sam Houston State | Bearkats | Orange & white | Southland | Ron Randleman | 5-5-0 |
| Samford | Bulldogs | Crimson & blue | Independent | Pete Hurt | 7-4-0 |
| San Diego State | Aztecs | Scarlet & black | Western Athletic | Ted Tollner | 8-4-0 |
| San Jose State | Spartans | Gold, white & blue | Western Athletic | John Ralston | 3-8-0 |
| South Carolina | Fighting Gamecocks | Garnet & black | Southeastern | Brad Scott | 4-6-1 |
| South Carolina State | Bulldogs | Garnet & blue | Mid-Eastern Athl. | Willie Jeffries | 6-4-0 |
| SE Missouri State | Indians | Red & black | Ohio Valley | John Mumford | 5-6-0 |
| Southern-Baton Rouge | Jaguars | Blue & gold | Southwestern | Pete Richardson | 10-1-0 |
| Southern California (USC) | Trojans | Cardinal & gold | Pacific Ten | John Robinson | 8-2-1 |
| Southern Illinois | Salukis | Maroon & white | Gateway | Shawn Watson | 5-6-0 |
| So. Methodist (SMU) | Mustangs | Red & blue | Western Athletic | Tom Rossley | 1-10-0 |
| Southern Mississippi | Golden Eagles | Black & gold | Conference USA | Jeff Bower | 6-5-0 |
| SW Missouri State | Bears | Maroon & white | Gateway | Del Miller | 4-7-0 |
| SW Texas State | Bobcats | Maroon & gold | Southland | Jim Bob Helduser | 4-7-0 |
| SW Louisiana | Ragin' Cajuns | Vermilion & white | Independent | Nelson Stokley | 6-5-0 |
| Stanford | Cardinal | Cardinal & white | Pacific Ten | Tyrone Willingham | 7-3-1 |
| Stephen F. Austin State | Lumberjacks | Purple & white | Southland | John Pearce | 9-1-0 |
| Syracuse | Orangemen | Orange | Big East | Paul Pasqualoni | 8-3-0 |
| Temple | Owls | Cherry & white | Big East | Ron Dickerson | 1-10-0 |
| Tennessee | Volunteers | Orange & white | Southeastern | Phillip Fulmer | 10-1-0 |
| Tenn.-Chattanooga | Moccasins | Navy blue & gold | Southern | Buddy Green | 4-7-0 |
| Tenn.-Martin | Skyhawks | Orange, white, blue | Ohio Valley | Don McLeary | 5-6-0 |
| Tennessee State | Tigers | Royal blue & white | Ohio Valley | L. C. Cole | 2-9-0 |
| Tennessee Tech | Golden Eagles | Purple & gold | Ohio Valley | Mike Hennigan | 3-8-0 |
| Texas | Longhorns | Burnt orange & white | Big Twelve | John Mackovic | 10-1-1 |

*(continued)*

| Team | Nickname | Team colors | Conference | Coach | 1995 record (W-L-T) |
|---|---|---|---|---|---|
| Texas A & M | Aggies | Maroon & white | Big Twelve | R. C. Slocum | 8-3-0 |
| Texas Christian (TCU) | Horned Frogs | Purple & white | Western Athletic | Pat Sullivan | 6-5-0 |
| Texas Southern | Tigers | Maroon & gray | Southwestern | Bill Thomas | 2-8-0 |
| Texas Tech | Red Raiders | Scarlet & black | Big Twelve | Spike Dykes | 8-3-0 |
| Toledo | Rockets | Blue & gold | Mid-American | Gary Pinkel | 10-0-1 |
| Towson State | Tigers | Gold & white | Eastern Football | Gordy Combs | 6-4-0 |
| Tulane | Green Wave | Olive green & sky blue | Conference USA | Buddy Teevens | 2-9-0 |
| Tulsa | Golden Hurricane | Blue & gold | Western Athletic | David Rader | 4-7-0 |
| UCLA | Bruins | Blue & gold | Pacific Ten | Bob Toledo | 7-4-0 |
| Utah | Utes | Crimson & white | Western Athletic | Ron McBride | 7-4-0 |
| Utah State | Aggies | Navy blue & white | Big West | John L. Smith | 4-7-0 |
| UTEP | Miners | Orange, blue, white | Western Athletic | Charlie Bailey | 2-10-0 |
| Vanderbilt | Commodores | Black & gold | Southeastern | Rod Dowhower | 2-9-0 |
| Villanova | Wildcats | Blue & white | Yankee | Andy Talley | 3-8-0 |
| Virginia | Cavaliers | Orange & blue | Atlantic Coast | George Welsh | 8-4-0 |
| Virginia Military Inst. (VMI) | Keydets | Red, white & yellow | Southern | Bill Stewart | 4-7-0 |
| Virginia Tech | Gobblers, Hokies | Orange & maroon | Big East | Frank Beamer | 9-2-0 |
| Wake Forest | Demon Deacons | Old gold & black | Atlantic Coast | Jim Caldwell | 1-10-0 |
| Washington | Huskies | Purple & gold | Pacific Ten | Jim Lambright | 7-3-1 |
| Washington State | Cougars | Crimson & gray | Pacific Ten | Mike Price | 3-8-0 |
| Weber State | Wildcats | Royal purple & white | Big Sky | Dave Arslanian | 6-5-0 |
| West Virginia | Mountaineers | Old gold & blue | Big East | Don Nehlen | 5-6-0 |
| Western Carolina | Catamounts | Purple & gold | Southern | Steve Hodgin | 3-7-0 |
| Western Illinois | Leathernecks | Purple & gold | Gateway | Randy Ball | 4-7-0 |
| Western Kentucky | Hilltoppers | Red & white | Independent | Jack Harbaugh | 2-8-0 |
| Western Michigan | Broncos | Brown & gold | Mid-American | Al Molde | 7-4-0 |
| William & Mary | Tribe | Green, gold & silver | Yankee | Jimmye Laycock | 7-4-0 |
| Wisconsin | Badgers | Cardinal & white | Big Ten | Barry Alvarez | 4-5-2 |
| Wyoming | Cowboys | Brown & yellow | Western Athletic | Joe Tiller | 6-5-0 |
| Yale | Bulldogs, Elis | Yale blue & white | Ivy League | Carmen Cozza | 3-7-0 |
| Youngstown State | Penguins | Red & white | Independent | Jim Tressel | 3-8-0 |

# Heisman Trophy Winners

Awarded annually to the nation's outstanding college football player.

1935 Jay Berwanger, Chicago, HB
1936 Larry Kelley, Yale, E
1937 Clinton Frank, Yale, HB
1938 David O'Brien, Texas Christian, QB
1939 Nile Kinnick, Iowa, HB
1940 Tom Harmon, Michigan, HB
1941 Bruce Smith, Minnesota, HB
1942 Frank Sinkwich, Georgia, HB
1943 Angelo Bertelli, Notre Dame, QB
1944 Leslie Horvath, Ohio St., QB
1945 Felix Blanchard, Army, FB
1946 Glenn Davis, Army, HB
1947 John Lujack, Notre Dame, QB
1948 Doak Walker, SMU, HB
1949 Leon Hart, Notre Dame, E
1950 Vic Janowicz, Ohio St., HB
1951 Richard Kazmaier, Princeton, HB
1952 Billy Vessels, Oklahoma, HB
1953 John Lattner, Notre Dame, HB
1954 Alan Ameche, Wisconsin, FB
1955 Howard Cassady, Ohio St., HB
1956 Paul Hornung, Notre Dame, QB
1957 John Crow, Texas A & M, HB
1958 Pete Dawkins, Army, HB
1959 Billy Cannon, LSU, HB
1960 Joe Bellino, Navy, HB
1961 Ernest Davis, Syracuse, HB
1962 Terry Baker, Oregon St., QB
1963 Roger Staubach, Navy, QB
1964 John Huarte, Notre Dame, QB
1965 Mike Garrett, USC, HB
1966 Steve Spurrier, Florida, QB
1967 Gary Beban, UCLA, QB
1968 O. J. Simpson, USC, RB
1969 Steve Owens, Oklahoma, RB
1970 Jim Plunkett, Stanford, QB
1971 Pat Sullivan, Auburn, QB
1972 Johnny Rodgers, Nebraska, RB-WR
1973 John Cappelletti, Penn St., RB
1974 Archie Griffin, Ohio St., RB
1975 Archie Griffin, Ohio St., RB
1976 Tony Dorsett, Pittsburgh, RB
1977 Earl Campbell, Texas, RB
1978 Billy Sims, Oklahoma, RB
1979 Charles White, USC, RB
1980 George Rogers, S. Carolina, RB
1981 Marcus Allen, USC, RB
1982 Herschel Walker, Georgia, RB
1983 Mike Rozier, Nebraska, RB
1984 Doug Flutie, Boston College, QB
1985 Bo Jackson, Auburn, RB
1986 Vinny Testaverde, Miami, QB
1987 Tim Brown, Notre Dame, WR
1988 Barry Sanders, Oklahoma St., RB
1989 Andre Ware, Houston, QB
1990 Ty Detmer, BYU, QB
1991 Desmond Howard, Michigan, WR
1992 Gino Torretta, Miami, QB
1993 Charlie Ward, Florida St., QB
1994 Rashaan Salaam, Colorado, RB
1995 Eddie George, Ohio St., RB

# Outland Award

Honoring the outstanding interior lineman selected by the Football Writers Association of America.

1946 George Connor, Notre Dame, T
1947 Joe Steffy, Army, G
1948 Bill Fischer, Notre Dame, G
1949 Ed Bagdon, Michigan St., G
1950 Bob Gain, Kentucky, T
1951 Jim Weatherall, Oklahoma, T
1952 Dick Modzelewski, Maryland, T
1953 J. D. Roberts, Oklahoma, G
1954 Bill Brooks, Arkansas, G
1955 Calvin Jones, Iowa, G
1956 Jim Parker, Ohio St., G
1957 Alex Karras, Iowa, T
1958 Zeke Smith, Auburn, G
1959 Mike McGee, Duke, T
1960 Tom Brown, Minnesota, G
1961 Merlin Olsen, Utah St., T
1962 Bobby Bell, Minnesota, T
1963 Scott Appleton, Texas, T
1964 Steve Delong, Tennessee, T
1965 Tommy Nobis, Texas, G
1966 Loyd Phillips, Arkansas, T
1967 Ron Yary, Southern Cal, T
1968 Bill Stanfill, Georgia, T
1969 Mike Reid, Penn St., DT
1970 Jim Stillwagon, Ohio St., MG
1971 Larry Jacobson, Nebraska, DT
1972 Rich Glover, Nebraska, MG
1973 John Hicks, Ohio St., OT
1974 Randy White, Maryland, DE
1975 Lee Roy Selmon, Oklahoma, DT
1976 Ross Browner, Notre Dame, DE
1977 Brad Shearer, Texas, DT
1978 Greg Roberts, Oklahoma, G
1979 Jim Ritcher, N. Carolina St., C
1980 Mark May, Pittsburgh, OT
1981 Dave Rimington, Nebraska, C
1982 Dave Rimington, Nebraska, C
1983 Dean Steinkuhler, Nebraska, G
1984 Bruce Smith, Virginia Tech, DT
1985 Mike Ruth, Boston College, NG
1986 Jason Buck, BYU, DT
1987 Chad Hennings, Air Force, DT
1988 Tracy Rocker, Auburn, DT
1989 Mohammed Elewonibi, BYU, G
1990 Russell Maryland, Miami (FL) DT
1991 Steve Emtman, Washington, DT
1992 Will Shields, Nebraska, G
1993 Rob Waldrop, Arizona, NG
1994 Zach Wiegert, Nebraska, OT
1995 Jonathan Ogden, UCLA, OT

# All-Time Division I-A Percentage Leaders

(Classified as Division I-A for the last 10 years; record includes bowl games; ties computed as half won and half lost)

| | Years | Won | Lost | Tied | Pct. | Bowl Games W | Bowl Games L | Bowl Games T |
|---|---|---|---|---|---|---|---|---|
| Notre Dame | 107 | 738 | 219 | 42 | .760 | 13 | 8 | 0 |
| Michigan | 116 | 756 | 250 | 36 | .743 | 13 | 14 | 0 |
| Alabama* | 101 | 703 | 250 | 43 | .727 | 27 | 17 | 3 |
| Oklahoma | 101 | 670 | 251 | 53 | .715 | 20 | 11 | 1 |
| Texas | 103 | 705 | 279 | 33 | .709 | 17 | 17 | 2 |
| Ohio St. | 106 | 679 | 271 | 53 | .703 | 12 | 16 | 0 |
| USC | 103 | 647 | 259 | 54 | .702 | 25 | 13 | 0 |
| Nebraska | 106 | 698 | 290 | 40 | .698 | 16 | 18 | 0 |
| Penn St. | 109 | 695 | 294 | 41 | .695 | 20 | 10 | 2 |
| Tennessee* | 99 | 656 | 281 | 52 | .690 | 20 | 16 | 0 |
| Florida St. * | 49 | 336 | 179 | 17 | .648 | 16 | 7 | 2 |
| Central Michigan | 95 | 493 | 265 | 36 | .644 | 3 | 2 | 0 |
| Washington* | 105 | 569 | 314 | 49 | .637 | 12 | 8 | 1 |
| Miami (OH) | 107 | 559 | 315 | 44 | .633 | 5 | 2 | 0 |
| Army | 106 | 597 | 339 | 51 | .631 | 2 | 1 | 0 |
| Georgia | 102 | 601 | 343 | 54 | .629 | 15 | 14 | 3 |
| LSU* | 102 | 584 | 336 | 47 | .628 | 12 | 16 | 1 |
| Arizona St | 83 | 453 | 268 | 24 | .624 | 9 | 5 | 1 |
| Auburn* | 103 | 575 | 340 | 47 | .622 | 12 | 10 | 2 |
| Colorado | 106 | 578 | 351 | 36 | .618 | 8 | 12 | 0 |
| Miami (FL) | 69 | 429 | 265 | 19 | .615 | 10 | 11 | 0 |
| Bowling Green | 77 | 403 | 250 | 52 | .609 | 2 | 3 | 0 |
| Michigan St. | 99 | 532 | 339 | 44 | .605 | 5 | 7 | 0 |
| Texas A&M | 101 | 568 | 364 | 48 | .604 | 11 | 10 | 0 |
| UCLA | 77 | 449 | 291 | 37 | .602 | 10 | 9 | 1 |

*Includes games forfeited or changed by action of NCAA Council and/or Committee on Infractions.

# National College Football Champions

The unofficial national champion as selected each year by the AP poll of writers and the USA Today/CNN (until 1992 the UPI) poll of coaches. When the polls disagree, both teams are listed. The AP poll originated in 1936, and the UPI poll in 1950.

1936 Minnesota
1937 Pittsburgh
1938 Texas Christian
1939 Texas A&M
1940 Minnesota
1941 Minnesota
1942 Ohio State
1943 Notre Dame
1944 Army
1945 Army
1946 Notre Dame
1947 Notre Dame
1948 Michigan
1949 Notre Dame
1950 Oklahoma
1951 Tennessee
1952 Michigan State
1953 Maryland
1954 Ohio State, UCLA
1955 Oklahoma
1956 Oklahoma
1957 Auburn, Ohio State
1958 Louisiana State
1959 Syracuse
1960 Minnesota
1961 Alabama
1962 Southern Cal
1963 Texas
1964 Alabama
1965 Alabama, Mich. State
1966 Notre Dame
1967 Southern Cal
1968 Ohio State
1969 Texas
1970 Nebraska, Texas
1971 Nebraska
1972 Southern Cal
1973 Notre Dame, Alabama
1974 Oklahoma, Southern Cal
1975 Oklahoma
1976 Pittsburgh
1977 Notre Dame
1978 Alabama, Southern Cal
1979 Alabama
1980 Georgia
1981 Clemson
1982 Penn State
1983 Miami (FL)
1984 Brigham Young
1985 Oklahoma
1986 Penn State
1987 Miami (FL)
1988 Notre Dame
1989 Miami (FL)
1990 Colorado, Georgia Tech
1991 Miami (FL), Washington
1992 Alabama
1993 Florida St.
1994 Nebraska
1995 Nebraska

# College Football Coach of the Year

The Division I-A Coach of the Year has been selected by the American Football Coaches Assn. since 1935 and selected by the Football Writers Assn. of America since 1957. When polls disagree, both winners are indicated.

1935 Lynn Waldorf, Northwestern
1936 Dick Harlow, Harvard
1937 Edward Mylin, Lafayette
1938 Bill Kern, Carnegie Tech
1939 Eddie Anderson, Iowa
1940 Clark Shaughnessy, Stanford
1941 Frank Leahy, Notre Dame
1942 Bill Alexander, Georgia Tech
1943 Amos Alonzo Stagg, Pacific
1944 Carroll Widdoes, Ohio St.
1945 Bo McMillin, Indiana
1946 Earl "Red" Blaik, Army
1947 Fritz Crisler, Michigan
1948 Bennie Oosterbaan, Michigan
1949 Bud Wilkinson, Oklahoma
1950 Charlie Caldwell, Princeton
1951 Chuck Taylor, Stanford
1952 Biggie Munn, Michigan St.
1953 Jim Tatum, Maryland
1954 Henry "Red" Sanders, UCLA
1955 Duffy Daugherty, Michigan St.
1956 Bowden Wyatt, Tennessee
1957 Woody Hayes, Ohio St.
1958 Paul Dietzel, LSU
1959 Ben Schwartzwalder, Syracuse
1960 Murray Warmath, Minnesota
1961 Paul "Bear" Bryant, Ala. (AFCA); Darrell Royal, Texas (FWAA)
1962 John McKay, USC
1963 Darrell Royal, Texas
1964 Ara Parseghian, Notre Dame, & Frank Broyles, Arkansas(AFCA); Ara Parseghian (FWAA)
1965 Tommy Prothro, UCLA (AFCA); Duffy Daugherty, Mich. St. (FWAA)
1966 Tom Cahill, Army
1967 John Pont, Indiana
1968 Joe Paterno, Penn St. (AFCA); Woody Hayes, Ohio St. (FWAA)
1969 Bo Schembechler, Michigan
1970 Charles McClendon, LSU, & Darrell Royal, Texas (AFCA); Alex Agase, Northwestern (FWAA)
1971 Paul "Bear" Bryant, Alabama (AFCA); Bob Devaney, Nebraska (FWAA)
1972 John McKay, USC
1973 Paul "Bear" Bryant, Alabama (AFCA); Johnny Majors, Pittsburgh (FWAA)
1974 Grant Teaff, Baylor
1975 Frank Kush, Arizona St. (AFCA); Woody Hayes, Ohio St. (FWAA)
1976 Johnny Majors, Pittsburgh
1977 Don James, Washington (AFCA); Lou Holtz, Arkansas (FWAA)
1978 Joe Paterno, Penn St.
1979 Earle Bruce, Ohio St.
1980 Vince Dooley, Georgia
1981 Danny Ford, Clemson
1982 Joe Paterno, Penn St.
1983 Ken Hatfield, Air Force (AFCA); Howard Schnellenberger, Miami (FL) (FWAA)
1984 LaVell Edwards, Brigham Young
1985 Fisher De Berry, Air Force
1986 Joe Paterno, Penn St.
1987 Dick MacPherson, Syracuse
1988 Don Nehlen, W. Virginia (AFCA); Lou Holtz, Notre Dame (FWAA)
1989 Bill McCartney, Colorado
1990 Bobby Ross, Georgia Tech
1991 Don James, Washington
1992 Gene Stallings, Alabama
1993 Barry Alvarez, Wisconsin (AFCA); Terry Bowden, Auburn (FWAA)
1994 Tom Osborne, Nebraska (AFCA) Rich Brooks, Oregon (FWAA)
1995 Gary Barnett, Northwestern

# All-Time Division I-A Coaching Victories (Incl. Bowl Games)

| | | | | | |
|---|---|---|---|---|---|
| Paul "Bear" Bryant | 323 | *Hayden Fry | 213 | *Jim Sweeney | 196 |
| Glenn "Pop" Warner | 319 | *Lou Holtz | 208 | Howard Jones | 194 |
| Amos Alonzo Stagg | 314 | Jess Neely | 207 | John Vaught | 190 |
| *Joe Paterno | 278 | Warren Woodson | 203 | John Heisman | 185 |
| *Bobby Bowden | 259 | Eddie Anderson | 201 | Darrell Royal | 184 |
| Woody Hayes | 238 | Vince Dooley | 201 | *Johnny Majors | 181 |
| Bo Schembechler | 234 | Dana Bible | 198 | Gil Dobie | 180 |
| *Tom Osborne | 231 | Dan McGugin | 197 | Carl Snavely | 180 |
| *LaVell Edwards | 214 | Fielding Yost | 196 | Jerry Claiborne | 179 |

Active coaches are denoted by an asterisk (*). Eddie Robinson of Grambling State Univ. holds the record for most college football victories, with 402 at the start of the 1996 season.

# 1995 Final Associated Press and USA Today/CNN NCAA Football Polls

| Associated Press | | | | USA Today/CNN | | | |
|---|---|---|---|---|---|---|---|
| Rank | Team (W-L-T)[1] | Rank | Team (W-L-T)[1] | Rank | Team (W-L-T)[1] | Rank | Team (W-L-T)[1] |
| 1. | Nebraska (12-0-0) | 14. | Texas (10-2-1) | 1. | Nebraska | 14. | Texas |
| 2. | Florida (12-1-0) | 15. | Texas A&M (9-3-0) | 2. | Tennessee | 15. | Texas A&M |
| 3. | Tennessee (11-1-0) | 16. | Virginia (9-4-0) | 3. | Florida | 16. | Syracuse |
| 4. | Florida St. (10-2-0) | 17. | Michigan (9-4-0) | 4. | Colorado | 17. | Virginia |
| 5. | Colorado (10-2-0) | 18. | Oregon (9-3-0) | 5. | Florida St. | 18. | Oregon |
| 6. | Ohio St. (11-2-0) | 19. | Syracuse (9-3-0) | 6. | Kansas St. | 19. | Michigan |
| 7. | Kansas St. (10-2-0) | 20. | Miami (FL) (8-3-0) | 7. | Northwestern | 20. | Texas Tech |
| 8. | Northwestern (10-2-0) | 21. | Alabama (8-3-0) | 8. | Ohio St. | 21. | Auburn |
| 9. | Kansas (10-2-0) | 22. | Auburn (8-4-0) | 9. | Virginia Tech | 22. | Iowa |
| 10. | Virginia Tech (10-2-0) | 23. | Texas Tech (9-3-0) | 10. | Kansas | 23. | East Carolina (9-3-0) |
| 11. | Notre Dame (9-3-0) | 24. | Toledo (11-0-1) | 11. | USC | 24. | Toledo |
| 12. | USC (9-2-1) | 25. | Iowa (8-4-0) | 12. | Penn St. | 25. | LSU (7-4-1) |
| 13. | Penn St. (9-3-0) | | | 13. | Notre Dame | | |

(1) Team records include bowl games. Team records in USA Today/CNN poll are given only for teams not appearing in AP poll.

# College Football Conference Champions

| | Atlantic Coast | | Ivy | | Big Eight* | | Big Ten |
|---|---|---|---|---|---|---|---|
| 1980 | North Carolina | 1980 | Yale | 1980 | Oklahoma | 1980 | Michigan |
| 1981 | Clemson | 1981 | Yale, Dartmouth | 1981 | Nebraska | 1981 | Iowa, Ohio State |
| 1982 | Clemson | 1982 | Harvard, Dartmouth, Penn | 1982 | Nebraska | 1982 | Michigan |
| 1983 | Maryland | 1983 | Harvard, Penn | 1983 | Nebraska | 1983 | Illinois |
| 1984 | Maryland | 1984 | Penn | 1984 | Nebraska, Oklahoma | 1984 | Ohio State |
| 1985 | Maryland | 1985 | Penn | 1985 | Oklahoma | 1985 | Iowa |
| 1986 | Clemson | 1986 | Penn | 1986 | Oklahoma | 1986 | Michigan, Ohio State |
| 1987 | Clemson | 1987 | Harvard | 1987 | Oklahoma | 1987 | Michigan St. |
| 1988 | Clemson | 1988 | Penn, Cornell | 1988 | Nebraska | 1988 | Michigan |
| 1989 | Virginia, Duke | 1989 | Yale, Princeton | 1989 | Colorado | 1989 | Michigan |
| 1990 | Georgia Tech | 1990 | Cornell, Dartmouth | 1990 | Colorado | 1990 | Iowa, Illinois, Michigan, Michigan St. |
| 1991 | Clemson | 1991 | Dartmouth | 1991 | Nebraska, Colorado | 1991 | Michigan |
| 1992 | Florida St. | 1992 | Dartmouth, Princeton | 1992 | Nebraska | 1992 | Michigan |
| 1993 | Florida St. | 1993 | Penn | 1993 | Nebraska | 1993 | Ohio St., Wisconsin |
| 1994 | Florida St. | 1994 | Penn | 1994 | Nebraska | 1994 | Penn St. |
| 1995 | Virginia, Florida St. | 1995 | Princeton | 1995 | Nebraska | 1995 | Northwestern |

| | Mid-American Athletic | | Southern | | Southeastern | | Southwest* |
|---|---|---|---|---|---|---|---|
| 1980 | Central Michigan | 1980 | Furman | 1980 | Georgia | 1980 | Baylor |
| 1981 | Toledo | 1981 | Furman | 1981 | Georgia, Alabama | 1981 | Texas |
| 1982 | Bowling Green | 1982 | Furman | 1982 | Georgia | 1982 | SMU |
| 1983 | Northern Illinois | 1983 | Furman | 1983 | Auburn | 1983 | Texas |
| 1984 | Toledo | 1984 | Tenn.-Chattanooga | 1984 | Florida (title vacated) | 1984 | SMU, Houston |
| 1985 | Bowling Green | 1985 | Furman | 1985 | Tennessee | 1985 | Texas A&M |
| 1986 | Miami (Ohio) | 1986 | Appalachian St. | 1986 | LSU | 1986 | Texas A&M |
| 1987 | E. Michigan | 1987 | Appalachian St. | 1987 | Auburn | 1987 | Texas A&M |
| 1988 | W. Michigan | 1988 | Marshall, Furman | 1988 | Auburn, LSU | 1988 | Arkansas |
| 1989 | Ball State | 1989 | Furman | 1989 | Ala., Tenn., Auburn | 1989 | Arkansas |
| 1990 | Central Michigan | 1990 | Furman | 1990 | Tennessee | 1990 | Texas |
| 1991 | Bowling Green | 1991 | Appalachian St. | 1991 | Florida | 1991 | Texas A&M |
| 1992 | Bowling Green | 1992 | Citadel | 1992 | Alabama | 1992 | Texas A&M |
| 1993 | Ball State | 1993 | Georgia Southern | 1993 | Florida | 1993 | Texas A&M |
| 1994 | Central Michigan | 1994 | Marshall | 1994 | Florida | 1994 | Baylor, Rice, Texas, Texas Christian, Texas Tech |
| 1995 | Toledo | 1995 | Appalachian St. | 1995 | Florida | 1995 | Texas |

| | Pacific Ten | | Western Athletic | | Big West |
|---|---|---|---|---|---|
| 1980 | Washington | 1980 | Brigham Young (BYU) | 1980 | Long Beach State |
| 1981 | Washington | 1981 | Brigham Young | 1981 | San Jose State |
| 1982 | UCLA | 1982 | Brigham Young | 1982 | Fresno State |
| 1983 | UCLA | 1983 | Brigham Young | 1983 | Cal State-Fullerton |
| 1984 | USC | 1984 | Brigham Young | 1984 | Cal State-Fullerton |
| 1985 | UCLA | 1985 | Brigham Young, Air Force | 1985 | Fresno State |
| 1986 | Arizona State | 1986 | San Diego State | 1986 | San Jose State |
| 1987 | UCLA, USC | 1987 | Wyoming | 1987 | San Jose State |
| 1988 | USC | 1988 | Wyoming | 1988 | Fresno State |
| 1989 | USC | 1989 | Brigham Young | 1989 | Fresno State |
| 1990 | Washington | 1990 | Brigham Young | 1990 | San Jose State |
| 1991 | Washington | 1991 | Brigham Young | 1991 | San Jose St., Fresno St. |
| 1992 | Washington, Stanford | 1992 | Hawaii, Brigham Young, Fresno St. | 1992 | Nevada-Reno |
| 1993 | UCLA, Arizona, USC | 1993 | Wyoming, Fresno St., Brigham Young | 1993 | SW Louisiana, Utah St. |
| 1994 | Oregon | 1994 | Colorado St. | 1994 | Nevada-Reno, SW Louisiana, Nevada-Las Vegas |
| 1995 | USC, Washington | 1995 | Colorado St., Air Force, Utah, BYU | 1995 | Nevada-Reno |

*In 1996, the Big Eight and Southwest conferences disbanded. All former Big Eight Conference teams joined with 4 of the 8 Southwest Conference teams to form the Big Twelve Conference.

# HOCKEY

## National Hockey League, 1995-96

### 1995-96 NHL Review: "Super Mario" Returns, Red Wings Set Record, Winnipeg to Phoenix

After sitting out the 1994-95 season with health problems, Pittsburgh great Mario Lemieux returned to win the NHL scoring title and lead the Penguins into the Eastern Conference finals. The Detroit Red Wings set an NHL mark for wins in a season with 62, although they were ousted in the Western Conference finals. For the second year in a row, a Canadian franchise moved to the western U.S.: the Winnipeg Jets became the Phoenix (AZ) Coyotes before the 1996-97 season.

### Final Standings

#### Eastern Conference

**Northeast Division**

| | W | L | T | GF | GA | PTS |
|---|---|---|---|---|---|---|
| Pittsburgh | 49 | 29 | 4 | 362 | 284 | 102 |
| Boston | 40 | 31 | 11 | 282 | 269 | 91 |
| Montreal | 40 | 32 | 10 | 265 | 248 | 90 |
| Hartford | 34 | 39 | 9 | 237 | 259 | 77 |
| Buffalo | 33 | 42 | 7 | 247 | 262 | 73 |
| Ottawa | 18 | 59 | 5 | 191 | 291 | 41 |

**Atlantic Division**

| | W | L | T | GF | GA | PTS |
|---|---|---|---|---|---|---|
| Philadelphia | 45 | 24 | 13 | 282 | 208 | 103 |
| N.Y. Rangers | 41 | 27 | 14 | 272 | 237 | 96 |
| Florida | 41 | 31 | 10 | 258 | 230 | 92 |
| Washington | 39 | 32 | 11 | 234 | 204 | 89 |
| Tampa Bay | 38 | 32 | 12 | 238 | 248 | 88 |
| New Jersey | 37 | 33 | 12 | 215 | 202 | 86 |
| N.Y. Islanders | 22 | 50 | 10 | 229 | 315 | 54 |

#### Western Conference

**Central Division**

| | W | L | T | GF | GA | PTS |
|---|---|---|---|---|---|---|
| Detroit | 62 | 13 | 7 | 325 | 181 | 131 |
| Chicago | 40 | 28 | 14 | 273 | 220 | 94 |
| Toronto | 34 | 36 | 12 | 247 | 252 | 80 |
| St. Louis | 32 | 34 | 16 | 219 | 248 | 80 |
| Winnipeg | 36 | 40 | 6 | 275 | 291 | 78 |
| Dallas | 26 | 42 | 14 | 227 | 280 | 66 |

**Pacific Division**

| | W | L | T | GF | GA | PTS |
|---|---|---|---|---|---|---|
| Colorado | 47 | 25 | 10 | 326 | 240 | 104 |
| Calgary | 34 | 37 | 11 | 241 | 240 | 79 |
| Vancouver | 32 | 35 | 15 | 278 | 278 | 79 |
| Anaheim | 35 | 39 | 8 | 234 | 247 | 78 |
| Edmonton | 30 | 44 | 8 | 239 | 304 | 68 |
| Los Angeles | 24 | 40 | 18 | 256 | 302 | 66 |
| San Jose | 20 | 55 | 7 | 252 | 357 | 47 |

### Colorado Avalanche Win Stanley Cup Championship

The Colorado Avalanche, in their first year after moving from Quebec, won the 1996 Stanley Cup by sweeping the Florida Panthers. Avalanche center and captain Joe Sakic won the Conn Smythe Trophy as the most valuable player in the playoffs.

### Stanley Cup Playoff Results

**Eastern Conference**

Philadelphia defeated Tampa Bay 4 games to 2
Pittsburgh defeated Washington 4 games to 2
N.Y. Rangers defeated Montreal 4 games to 2
Florida defeated Boston 4 games to 1
Pittsburgh defeated N.Y. Rangers 4 games to 1
Florida defeated Philadelphia 4 games to 2
Florida defeated Pittsburgh 4 games to 3

**Western Conference**

Detroit defeated Winnipeg 4 games to 2
Colorado defeated Vancouver 4 games to 2
Chicago defeated Calgary 4 games to 0
St. Louis defeated Toronto 4 games to 2
Detroit defeated St. Louis 4 games to 3
Colorado defeated Chicago 4 games to 2
Colorado defeated Detroit 4 games to 2

**Finals**

Colorado defeated Florida 4 games to 0 (3-1, 8-1, 3-2, 1-0 [3 OT])

### Stanley Cup Champions Since 1927

| Year | Champion | Coach | Final opponent |
|---|---|---|---|
| 1927 | Ottawa | Dave Gill | Boston |
| 1928 | N.Y. Rangers | Lester Patrick | Montreal |
| 1929 | Boston | Cy Denneny | N.Y. Rangers |
| 1930 | Montreal | Cecil Hart | Boston |
| 1931 | Montreal | Cecil Hart | Chicago |
| 1932 | Toronto | Dick Irvin | N.Y. Rangers |
| 1933 | N.Y. Rangers | Lester Patrick | Toronto |
| 1934 | Chicago | Tommy Gorman | Detroit |
| 1935 | Montreal Maroons | Tommy Gorman | Toronto |
| 1936 | Detroit | Jack Adams | Toronto |
| 1937 | Detroit | Jack Adams | N.Y. Rangers |
| 1938 | Chicago | Bill Stewart | Toronto |
| 1939 | Boston | Art Ross | Toronto |
| 1940 | N.Y. Rangers | Frank Boucher | Toronto |
| 1941 | Boston | Cooney Weiland | Detroit |
| 1942 | Toronto | Hap Day | Detroit |
| 1943 | Detroit | Jack Adams | Boston |
| 1944 | Montreal | Dick Irvin | Chicago |
| 1945 | Toronto | Hap Day | Detroit |
| 1946 | Montreal | Dick Irvin | Boston |
| 1947 | Toronto | Hap Day | Montreal |
| 1948 | Toronto | Hap Day | Detroit |
| 1949 | Toronto | Hap Day | Detroit |
| 1950 | Detroit | Tommy Ivan | N.Y. Rangers |
| 1951 | Toronto | Joe Primeau | Montreal |
| 1952 | Detroit | Tommy Ivan | Montreal |
| 1953 | Montreal | Dick Irvin | Boston |
| 1954 | Detroit | Tommy Ivan | Montreal |
| 1955 | Detroit | Jimmy Skinner | Montreal |
| 1956 | Montreal | Toe Blake | Detroit |
| 1957 | Montreal | Toe Blake | Boston |
| 1958 | Montreal | Toe Blake | Boston |
| 1959 | Montreal | Toe Blake | Toronto |
| 1960 | Montreal | Toe Blake | Toronto |
| 1961 | Chicago | Rudy Pilous | Detroit |
| 1962 | Toronto | Punch Imlach | Chicago |
| 1963 | Toronto | Punch Imlach | Detroit |
| 1964 | Toronto | Punch Imlach | Detroit |
| 1965 | Montreal | Toe Blake | Chicago |
| 1966 | Montreal | Toe Blake | Detroit |
| 1967 | Toronto | Punch Imlach | Montreal |
| 1968 | Montreal | Toe Blake | St. Louis |
| 1969 | Montreal | Claude Ruel | St. Louis |
| 1970 | Boston | Harry Sinden | St. Louis |
| 1971 | Montreal | Al MacNeil | Chicago |
| 1972 | Boston | Tom Johnson | N.Y. Rangers |
| 1973 | Montreal | Scotty Bowman | Chicago |
| 1974 | Philadelphia | Fred Shero | Boston |
| 1975 | Philadelphia | Fred Shero | Buffalo |
| 1976 | Montreal | Scotty Bowman | Philadelphia |
| 1977 | Montreal | Scotty Bowman | Boston |
| 1978 | Montreal | Scotty Bowman | Boston |
| 1979 | Montreal | Scotty Bowman | N.Y. Rangers |
| 1980 | N.Y. Islanders | Al Arbour | Philadelphia |
| 1981 | N.Y. Islanders | Al Arbour | Minnesota |
| 1982 | N.Y. Islanders | Al Arbour | Vancouver |
| 1983 | N.Y. Islanders | Al Arbour | Edmonton |
| 1984 | Edmonton | Glen Sather | N.Y. Islanders |
| 1985 | Edmonton | Glen Sather | Philadelphia |
| 1986 | Montreal | Jean Perron | Calgary |
| 1987 | Edmonton | Glen Sather | Philadelphia |
| 1988 | Edmonton | Glen Sather | Boston |
| 1989 | Calgary | Terry Crisp | Montreal |
| 1990 | Edmonton | John Muckler | Boston |
| 1991 | Pittsburgh | Bob Johnson | Minnesota |
| 1992 | Pittsburgh | Scotty Bowman | Chicago |
| 1993 | Montreal | Jacques Demers | Los Angeles |
| 1994 | N.Y. Rangers | Mike Keenan | Vancouver |
| 1995 | New Jersey | Jacques Lemaire | Detroit |
| 1996 | Colorado | Marc Crawford | Florida |

# Individual Leaders, 1995-96

**Points**

Mario Lemieux, Pittsburgh, 161; Jaromir Jagr, Pittsburgh, 149; Joe Sakic, Colorado, 120; Ron Francis, Pittsburgh, 119; Peter Forsberg, Colorado, 116.

**Goals**

Mario Lemieux, Pittsburgh, 69, Jaromir Jagr, Pittsburgh, 62; Alexander Mogilny, Vancouver, 55; Peter Bondra, Washington, 52; John LeClair, Philadelphia, 51; Joe Sakic, Colorado, 51.

**Assists**

Ron Francis Pittsburgh, 92; Mario Lemieux, Pittsburgh, 92; Jaromir Jagr, Pittsburgh, 87; Peter Forsberg, Colorado, 86; Wayne Gretzky, L.A.-St.L., 79; Doug Weight, Edmonton, 79.

**Power-play goals**

Mario Lemieux, Pittsburgh, 31; Jaromir Jagr, Pittsburgh, 20; Paul Kariya, Anaheim, 20; Keith Tkachuk, Winnipeg, 20; John LeClair, Philadelphia, 19; Scott Mellanby, Florida, 19.

**Shorthanded goals**

Mario Lemieux, Pittsburgh, 8; Jamie Baker, San Jose, 6; Tom Fitzgerald, Florida, 6; Dave Reid, Boston, 6; Joe Sakic, Colorado, 6; Mats Sundin, Toronto, 6.

**Shooting percentage**

(minimum 82 shots)

Gary Roberts, Calgary, 26.2; Petr Nedved, Pittsburgh, 22.1; Craig Janney, S.J.-Win., 22.0; Andrei Kovalenko, Col.-Mon., 21.4; Murray Craven, Chicago, 20.9.

**Plus/Minus**

Vladimir Konstantinov, Detroit, 60; Sergei Federov, Detroit, 49; Viacheslav Fetisov, Detroit, 37; Petr Nedved, Pittsburgh, 37; Vyacheslav Kozlov, Detroit, 33.

**GOALTENDING LEADERS**

(minimum 25 games)

**Goals against average**

Ron Hextall, Philadelphia, 2.176; Chris Osgood, Detroit, 2.178; Jim Carey, Washington, 2.256; Mike Vernon, Detroit, 2.264; Martin Brodeur, New Jersey, 2.34.

**Wins**

Chris Osgood, Detroit, 39; Jim Carey, Washington, 35; Martin Brodeur, New Jersey, 34; Bill Ranford, 34; Patrick Roy, Mon.-Col., 34.

**Save percentage**

Dominik Hasek, Buffalo, .920; Daren Puppa, Tampa Bay, .918; Jeff Hackett, Chicago, .916; Guy Hebert, Anaheim, .914; Ron Hextall, Philadelphia, .913.

**Shutouts**

Jim Carey, Washington, 9; Martin Brodeur, New Jersey, 6; Chris Osgood, Detroit, 5; Daren Puppa, Tampa Bay, 5; 4 players tied with 4.

# Individual Scoring, 1995-96

(40 or more games played; *played for more than one team during 1995-1996; g—denotes goalie)

## Mighty Ducks of Anaheim

| | GP | G | A | Pts | PIM | +/- |
|---|---|---|---|---|---|---|
| Paul Kariya | 82 | 50 | 58 | 108 | 20 | 9 |
| Teemu Selanne* | 79 | 40 | 68 | 108 | 22 | 5 |
| Roman Oksiuta* | 70 | 23 | 28 | 51 | 60 | 4 |
| Steve Rucchin | 64 | 19 | 25 | 44 | 12 | 3 |
| Bobby Dollas | 82 | 8 | 22 | 30 | 64 | 9 |
| Joe Sacco | 76 | 13 | 14 | 27 | 40 | 1 |
| Anatoli Semenov* | 56 | 4 | 22 | 26 | 24 | –1 |
| Shaun Van Allen | 49 | 8 | 17 | 25 | 41 | 13 |
| Fredrik Olausson* | 56 | 2 | 22 | 24 | 38 | –7 |
| Garry Valk | 79 | 12 | 12 | 24 | 125 | 8 |
| Jason York | 79 | 3 | 21 | 24 | 88 | –7 |
| Alex Hicks | 64 | 10 | 11 | 21 | 37 | 11 |
| Dave Karpa | 72 | 3 | 16 | 19 | 270 | –3 |
| Todd Ewen | 53 | 4 | 3 | 7 | 285 | –5 |
| Ken Baumgartner* | 72 | 2 | 4 | 6 | 193 | –5 |
| Randy Ladouceur | 63 | 1 | 3 | 4 | 47 | 5 |
| Guy Hebert (g) | 59 | 0 | 0 | 0 | 6 | 0 |

**Coach**—Ron Wilson

## Boston Bruins

| | GP | G | A | Pts | PIM | +/- |
|---|---|---|---|---|---|---|
| Adam Oates | 70 | 25 | 67 | 92 | 18 | 16 |
| Ray Bourque | 82 | 20 | 62 | 82 | 58 | 31 |
| Rick Tocchet* | 71 | 29 | 31 | 60 | 181 | 10 |
| Jozef Stumpel | 76 | 18 | 36 | 54 | 14 | –8 |
| Shawn McEachern | 82 | 24 | 29 | 53 | 34 | –5 |
| Ted Donato | 82 | 23 | 26 | 49 | 46 | 6 |
| Todd Elik | 59 | 13 | 33 | 46 | 40 | 2 |
| Cam Neely | 49 | 26 | 20 | 46 | 31 | 3 |
| Dave Reid | 63 | 23 | 21 | 44 | 4 | 14 |
| Sandy Moger | 80 | 15 | 14 | 29 | 65 | –9 |
| Steve Heinze | 76 | 16 | 12 | 28 | 43 | –3 |
| Don Sweeney | 77 | 4 | 24 | 28 | 42 | –4 |
| Kyle McLaren | 74 | 5 | 12 | 17 | 73 | 16 |
| Tim Sweeney | 41 | 8 | 8 | 16 | 14 | 4 |
| Rick Zombo | 67 | 4 | 10 | 14 | 53 | –7 |
| Jon Rohloff | 79 | 1 | 12 | 13 | 59 | –8 |
| Dean Chynoweth* | 49 | 2 | 6 | 8 | 128 | –5 |
| Bill Ranford* (g) | 77 | 0 | 3 | 3 | 2 | 0 |

**Coach**—Steve Kasper

## Buffalo Sabres

| | GP | G | A | Pts | PIM | +/- |
|---|---|---|---|---|---|---|
| Pat LaFontaine | 76 | 40 | 51 | 91 | 36 | –8 |
| Randy Burridge | 74 | 25 | 33 | 58 | 30 | 0 |
| Derek Plante | 76 | 23 | 33 | 56 | 28 | –4 |
| Garry Galley | 78 | 10 | 44 | 54 | 81 | –2 |
| Jason Dawe | 67 | 25 | 25 | 50 | 33 | –8 |
| Brad May | 79 | 15 | 29 | 44 | 295 | 6 |
| Alexei Zhitnik | 80 | 6 | 30 | 36 | 58 | –25 |
| Matthew Barnaby | 73 | 15 | 16 | 31 | 335 | –2 |
| Mike Peca | 68 | 11 | 20 | 31 | 67 | –1 |
| Mark Astley | 60 | 2 | 18 | 20 | 80 | –12 |
| Brian Holzinger | 58 | 10 | 10 | 20 | 37 | –21 |
| Darryl Shannon* | 74 | 4 | 13 | 17 | 92 | 15 |
| Brent Hughes | 76 | 5 | 10 | 15 | 148 | –9 |
| Mike Wilson | 58 | 4 | 8 | 12 | 41 | 13 |
| Rob Ray | 71 | 3 | 6 | 9 | 287 | –8 |
| Dominik Hasek (g) | 59 | 0 | 1 | 1 | 6 | 0 |

**Coach**—Ted Nolan

## Calgary Flames

| | GP | G | A | Pts | PIM | +/- |
|---|---|---|---|---|---|---|
| Theoren Fleury | 80 | 46 | 50 | 96 | 112 | 17 |
| German Titov | 82 | 28 | 39 | 67 | 24 | 9 |
| Michael Nylander | 73 | 17 | 38 | 55 | 20 | 0 |
| James Patrick | 80 | 3 | 32 | 35 | 30 | 3 |
| Cory Stillman | 74 | 16 | 19 | 35 | 41 | –5 |
| Steve Chiasson | 76 | 8 | 25 | 33 | 62 | 3 |
| Zarley Zalapski | 80 | 12 | 17 | 29 | 115 | 11 |
| Cory Millen* | 44 | 7 | 14 | 21 | 18 | 8 |
| Mike Sullivan | 81 | 9 | 12 | 21 | 24 | –6 |
| Sandy McCarthy | 75 | 9 | 7 | 16 | 173 | –8 |
| Pavel Torgajev | 41 | 6 | 10 | 16 | 14 | 2 |
| Paul Kruse | 75 | 3 | 12 | 15 | 145 | –5 |
| Ronnie Stern | 52 | 10 | 5 | 15 | 111 | 2 |
| Tommy Albelin* | 73 | 1 | 13 | 14 | 18 | 1 |
| Dean Evason | 67 | 7 | 7 | 14 | 38 | –6 |
| Bob Sweeney* | 72 | 7 | 7 | 14 | 65 | –20 |
| Jamie Huscroft | 70 | 3 | 9 | 12 | 162 | 14 |
| Jocelyn Lemieux* | 67 | 5 | 7 | 12 | 45 | –19 |
| Sheldon Kennedy | 41 | 3 | 7 | 10 | 36 | 3 |
| Trent Yawney | 69 | 0 | 3 | 3 | 88 | –1 |
| Trevor Kidd (g) | 47 | 0 | 2 | 2 | 4 | 0 |
| Rick Tabaracci (g) | 43 | 0 | 2 | 2 | 8 | 0 |

**Coach**—Pierre Page

## Chicago Blackhawks

| | GP | G | A | Pts | PIM | +/- |
|---|---|---|---|---|---|---|
| Chris Chelios | 81 | 14 | 58 | 72 | 140 | 25 |
| Jeremy Roenick | 66 | 32 | 35 | 67 | 109 | 9 |
| Gary Suter | 82 | 20 | 47 | 67 | 80 | 3 |
| Tony Amonte | 81 | 31 | 32 | 63 | 62 | 10 |
| Bernie Nicholls | 59 | 19 | 41 | 60 | 60 | 11 |
| Eric Daze | 80 | 30 | 23 | 53 | 18 | 16 |
| Joe Murphy | 70 | 22 | 29 | 51 | 86 | –3 |
| Denis Savard | 69 | 13 | 35 | 48 | 102 | 20 |
| Murray Craven | 66 | 18 | 29 | 47 | 36 | 20 |
| Bob Probert | 78 | 19 | 21 | 40 | 237 | 15 |
| Brent Sutter | 80 | 13 | 27 | 40 | 56 | 14 |
| Jeff Shantz | 78 | 6 | 14 | 20 | 24 | 12 |
| Keith Carney | 82 | 5 | 14 | 19 | 94 | 31 |
| Sergei Krivokrasov | 46 | 6 | 10 | 16 | 32 | 10 |
| Eric Weinrich | 77 | 5 | 10 | 15 | 65 | 14 |
| Enrico Ciccone* | 66 | 2 | 4 | 6 | 306 | 1 |

| | GP | G | A | Pts | PIM | +/- |
|---|---|---|---|---|---|---|
| Jim Cummins | 52 | 2 | 4 | 6 | 180 | –1 |
| Steve Dubinsky | 43 | 2 | 3 | 5 | 14 | 3 |
| Cam Russell | 61 | 2 | 2 | 4 | 129 | 8 |
| Ed Belfour (g) | 50 | 0 | 2 | 2 | 36 | 0 |

**Coach**—Craig Hartsburg

## Colorado Avalanche

| | GP | G | A | Pts | PIM | +/- |
|---|---|---|---|---|---|---|
| Joe Sakic | 82 | 51 | 69 | 120 | 44 | 14 |
| Peter Forsberg | 82 | 30 | 86 | 116 | 47 | 26 |
| Valeri Kamensky | 81 | 38 | 47 | 85 | 85 | 14 |
| Claude Lemieux | 79 | 39 | 32 | 71 | 117 | 14 |
| Scott Young | 81 | 21 | 39 | 60 | 50 | 2 |
| Sandis Ozolinsh* | 73 | 14 | 40 | 54 | 54 | 2 |
| Adam Deadmarsh | 78 | 21 | 27 | 48 | 142 | 20 |
| Chris Simon | 64 | 16 | 18 | 34 | 250 | 10 |
| Mike Keane* | 73 | 10 | 17 | 27 | 46 | –5 |
| Mike Ricci | 62 | 6 | 21 | 27 | 52 | 1 |
| Craig Wolanin | 75 | 7 | 20 | 27 | 50 | 25 |
| Stephane Yelle | 71 | 13 | 14 | 27 | 30 | 15 |
| Troy Murray | 63 | 7 | 14 | 21 | 22 | 15 |
| Alexei Gusarov | 65 | 5 | 15 | 20 | 56 | 29 |
| Curtis Leschyshyn | 77 | 4 | 15 | 19 | 73 | 32 |
| Dave Hannan* | 61 | 7 | 10 | 17 | 32 | 3 |
| Adam Foote | 73 | 5 | 11 | 16 | 88 | 27 |
| Sylvain Lefebvre | 75 | 5 | 11 | 16 | 49 | 26 |
| Jon Klemm | 56 | 3 | 12 | 15 | 20 | 12 |
| Warren Rychel | 52 | 6 | 2 | 8 | 147 | 6 |
| Patrick Roy* (g) | 61 | 0 | 0 | 0 | 10 | 0 |

**Coach**—Marc Crawford

## Dallas Stars

| | GP | G | A | Pts | PIM | +/- |
|---|---|---|---|---|---|---|
| Mike Modano | 78 | 36 | 45 | 81 | 63 | –12 |
| Benoit Hogue* | 78 | 19 | 45 | 64 | 104 | 10 |
| Greg Adams | 66 | 22 | 21 | 43 | 33 | –21 |
| Brent Gilchrist | 77 | 20 | 22 | 42 | 36 | –11 |
| Kevin Hatcher | 74 | 15 | 26 | 41 | 58 | –24 |
| Brent Fedyk* | 65 | 20 | 14 | 34 | 54 | –16 |
| Joe Nieuwendyk | 52 | 14 | 18 | 32 | 41 | –17 |
| Derian Hatcher | 79 | 8 | 23 | 31 | 129 | –12 |
| Todd Harvey | 69 | 9 | 20 | 29 | 136 | –13 |
| Jere Lehtinen | 57 | 6 | 22 | 28 | 16 | 5 |
| Grant Marshall | 70 | 9 | 19 | 28 | 111 | 0 |
| Mike Kennedy | 61 | 9 | 17 | 26 | 48 | –7 |
| Grant Ledyard | 73 | 5 | 19 | 24 | 20 | –15 |
| Guy Carbonneau | 71 | 8 | 15 | 23 | 38 | –2 |
| Richard Matvichuk | 73 | 6 | 16 | 22 | 71 | 4 |
| Randy Wood* | 76 | 8 | 13 | 21 | 62 | –15 |
| Darryl Sydor* | 84 | 3 | 17 | 20 | 75 | –12 |
| Bill Huard | 51 | 6 | 6 | 12 | 176 | 3 |
| Mike Lalor | 63 | 1 | 2 | 3 | 31 | –10 |
| Craig Ludwig | 65 | 1 | 2 | 3 | 70 | –17 |
| Andy Moog (g) | 41 | 0 | 0 | 0 | 28 | 0 |

**Coach**—Bob Gainey; Ken Hitchcock

## Detroit Red Wings

| | GP | G | A | Pts | PIM | +/- |
|---|---|---|---|---|---|---|
| Sergei Fedorov | 78 | 39 | 68 | 107 | 48 | 49 |
| Steve Yzerman | 80 | 36 | 59 | 95 | 64 | 29 |
| Paul Coffey | 76 | 14 | 60 | 74 | 90 | 19 |
| Vyacheslav Kozlov | 82 | 36 | 37 | 73 | 70 | 33 |
| Igor Larionov* | 73 | 22 | 51 | 73 | 34 | 31 |
| Nicklas Lidstrom | 81 | 17 | 50 | 67 | 20 | 29 |
| Keith Primeau | 74 | 27 | 25 | 52 | 168 | 19 |
| Dino Ciccarelli | 64 | 22 | 21 | 43 | 99 | 14 |
| Viacheslav Fetisov | 69 | 7 | 35 | 42 | 96 | 37 |
| Greg Johnson | 60 | 18 | 22 | 40 | 30 | 6 |
| Vladimir Konstantinov | 81 | 14 | 20 | 34 | 139 | 60 |
| Bob Errey | 71 | 11 | 21 | 32 | 66 | 30 |
| Darren McCarty | 63 | 15 | 14 | 29 | 158 | 14 |
| Doug Brown | 62 | 12 | 15 | 27 | 4 | 11 |
| Tim Taylor | 72 | 11 | 14 | 25 | 39 | 11 |
| Kris Draper | 52 | 7 | 9 | 16 | 32 | 2 |
| Marc Bergevin | 70 | 1 | 9 | 10 | 33 | 7 |
| Martin Lapointe | 58 | 6 | 3 | 9 | 93 | 0 |
| Kirk Maltby* | 55 | 3 | 6 | 9 | 67 | –16 |
| Mike Ramsey | 47 | 2 | 4 | 6 | 35 | 17 |
| Bob Rouse | 58 | 0 | 6 | 6 | 48 | 5 |
| Chris Osgood (g) | 50 | 1 | 2 | 3 | 4 | 0 |
| Stu Grimson | 56 | 0 | 1 | 1 | 128 | –10 |

**Coach**—Scotty Bowman

## Edmonton Oilers

| | GP | G | A | Pts | PIM | +/- |
|---|---|---|---|---|---|---|
| Doug Weight | 82 | 25 | 79 | 104 | 95 | –19 |
| Zdeno Ciger | 78 | 31 | 39 | 70 | 41 | –15 |
| Jason Arnott | 64 | 28 | 31 | 59 | 87 | –6 |
| Mariusz Czerkawski* | 70 | 17 | 23 | 40 | 18 | –4 |
| David Oliver | 80 | 20 | 19 | 39 | 34 | –22 |
| Todd Marchant | 81 | 19 | 19 | 38 | 66 | –19 |
| Miroslav Satan | 62 | 18 | 17 | 35 | 22 | 0 |
| Boris Mironov | 78 | 8 | 24 | 32 | 101 | –23 |
| Jeff Norton* | 66 | 8 | 23 | 31 | 42 | 9 |
| Dean McAmmond | 53 | 15 | 15 | 30 | 23 | 6 |
| Kelly Buchberger | 82 | 11 | 14 | 25 | 184 | –20 |
| Bryan Marchment | 78 | 3 | 15 | 18 | 202 | –7 |
| Scott Thornton | 77 | 9 | 9 | 18 | 149 | –25 |
| Jiri Slegr | 57 | 4 | 13 | 17 | 74 | –1 |
| Luke Richardson | 82 | 2 | 9 | 11 | 108 | –27 |
| Ryan Smyth | 48 | 2 | 9 | 11 | 28 | –10 |
| Donald Dufresne* | 45 | 1 | 6 | 7 | 20 | –4 |

**Coach**—Ron Low

## Florida Panthers

| | GP | G | A | Pts | PIM | +/- |
|---|---|---|---|---|---|---|
| Scott Mellanby | 79 | 32 | 38 | 70 | 160 | 4 |
| Rob Niedermayer | 82 | 26 | 35 | 61 | 107 | 1 |
| Ray Sheppard* | 70 | 37 | 23 | 60 | 16 | –19 |
| Robert Svehla | 81 | 8 | 49 | 57 | 94 | –3 |
| Johan Garpenlov | 82 | 23 | 28 | 51 | 36 | –10 |
| Stu Barnes | 72 | 19 | 25 | 44 | 46 | –12 |
| Martin Straka* | 77 | 13 | 30 | 43 | 41 | –19 |
| Jody Hull | 78 | 20 | 17 | 37 | 25 | 5 |
| Tom Fitzgerald | 82 | 13 | 21 | 34 | 75 | –3 |
| Bill Lindsay | 73 | 12 | 22 | 34 | 57 | 13 |
| Jason Woolley | 52 | 6 | 28 | 34 | 32 | –9 |
| Gord Murphy | 70 | 8 | 22 | 30 | 30 | 5 |
| Radek Dvorak | 77 | 13 | 14 | 27 | 20 | 5 |
| Brian Skrudland | 79 | 7 | 20 | 27 | 129 | 6 |
| Dave Lowry | 63 | 10 | 14 | 24 | 36 | –2 |
| Mike Hough | 64 | 7 | 16 | 23 | 37 | 4 |
| Ed Jovanovski | 70 | 10 | 11 | 21 | 137 | –3 |
| Terry Carkner | 73 | 3 | 10 | 13 | 80 | 10 |
| Paul Laus | 78 | 3 | 6 | 9 | 236 | –2 |
| Brett Harkins | 8 | 0 | 3 | 3 | 6 | –2 |
| Rhett Warrener | 28 | 0 | 3 | 3 | 46 | 4 |
| Brad Smyth | 7 | 1 | 1 | 2 | 4 | –3 |
| John Vanbiesbrouck (g) | 57 | 0 | 2 | 2 | 10 | 0 |

**Coach**—Doug MacLean

## Hartford Whalers

| | GP | G | A | Pts | PIM | +/- |
|---|---|---|---|---|---|---|
| Brendan Shanahan | 74 | 44 | 34 | 78 | 125 | 2 |
| Geoff Sanderson | 81 | 34 | 31 | 65 | 40 | 0 |
| Andrew Cassels | 81 | 20 | 43 | 63 | 39 | 8 |
| Nelson Emerson | 81 | 29 | 29 | 58 | 78 | –7 |
| Jeff Brown* | 76 | 8 | 47 | 55 | 56 | 8 |
| Andrei Nikolishin | 61 | 14 | 37 | 51 | 34 | –2 |
| Robert Kron | 77 | 22 | 28 | 50 | 6 | –1 |
| Paul Ranheim | 73 | 10 | 20 | 30 | 14 | –2 |
| Jeff O'Neill | 65 | 8 | 19 | 27 | 40 | –3 |
| Glen Wesley | 68 | 8 | 16 | 24 | 88 | –9 |
| Steven Rice | 59 | 10 | 12 | 22 | 47 | –4 |
| Adam Burt | 78 | 4 | 9 | 13 | 121 | –4 |
| Glen Featherstone | 68 | 2 | 10 | 12 | 138 | 10 |
| Kevin Dineen* | 46 | 2 | 9 | 11 | 117 | –1 |
| Gerald Diduck | 79 | 1 | 9 | 10 | 88 | 7 |
| Mark Janssens | 81 | 2 | 7 | 9 | 155 | –13 |
| Brad McCrimmon | 58 | 3 | 6 | 9 | 62 | 15 |
| Scott Daniels | 53 | 3 | 4 | 7 | 254 | –4 |
| Sean Burke (g) | 66 | 0 | 6 | 6 | 16 | 0 |
| Kelly Chase | 55 | 2 | 4 | 6 | 230 | –4 |
| Brian Glynn | 54 | 0 | 4 | 4 | 44 | –15 |

**Coach**—Paul Holmgren

## Los Angeles Kings

| | GP | G | A | Pts | PIM | +/- |
|---|---|---|---|---|---|---|
| Dimitri Khristich | 76 | 27 | 37 | 64 | 44 | 0 |
| Ray Ferraro* | 76 | 29 | 31 | 60 | 92 | 0 |
| Vitali Yachmenev | 80 | 19 | 34 | 53 | 16 | –3 |
| Yanic Perreault | 78 | 25 | 24 | 49 | 16 | –11 |
| Kevin Todd | 74 | 16 | 27 | 43 | 38 | 6 |
| Kevin Stevens* | 61 | 13 | 23 | 36 | 71 | –10 |
| Tony Granato | 49 | 17 | 18 | 35 | 46 | –5 |
| Eric Lacroix | 72 | 16 | 16 | 32 | 110 | –11 |
| Craig Johnson* | 60 | 13 | 11 | 24 | 36 | –8 |
| Philippe Boucher | 53 | 7 | 16 | 23 | 31 | –26 |
| Robert Lang | 68 | 6 | 16 | 22 | 10 | –15 |
| Jaroslav Modry* | 73 | 4 | 17 | 21 | 44 | –21 |
| Ian Laperriere* | 71 | 6 | 11 | 17 | 155 | –11 |
| Rob Cowie | 46 | 5 | 5 | 10 | 32 | –16 |
| Aki Berg | 51 | 0 | 7 | 7 | 29 | –13 |
| Sean O'Donnell | 71 | 2 | 5 | 7 | 127 | 3 |
| Doug Zmolek* | 58 | 2 | 5 | 7 | 87 | –5 |
| Steven Finn* | 66 | 3 | 2 | 5 | 126 | –12 |
| Byron Dafoe (g) | 47 | 0 | 0 | 0 | 6 | 0 |

**Coach**—Larry Robinson

### Montreal Canadiens

| | GP | G | A | Pts | PIM | +/- |
|---|---|---|---|---|---|---|
| Pierre Turgeon | 80 | 38 | 58 | 96 | 44 | 19 |
| Vincent Damphousse | 80 | 38 | 56 | 94 | 158 | 5 |
| Mark Recchi | 82 | 28 | 50 | 78 | 69 | 20 |
| Martin Rucinsky* | 78 | 29 | 46 | 75 | 68 | 18 |
| Andrei Kovalenko* | 77 | 28 | 28 | 56 | 49 | 20 |
| Saku Koivu | 82 | 20 | 25 | 45 | 40 | –7 |
| Valeri Bure | 77 | 22 | 20 | 42 | 28 | 10 |
| Patrice Brisebois | 69 | 9 | 27 | 36 | 65 | 10 |
| Brian Savage | 75 | 25 | 8 | 33 | 28 | –8 |
| Vladimir Malakhov | 61 | 5 | 23 | 28 | 79 | 7 |
| Turner Stevenson | 80 | 9 | 16 | 25 | 167 | –2 |
| Lyle Odelein | 79 | 3 | 14 | 17 | 230 | 8 |
| Stephane Quintal | 68 | 2 | 14 | 16 | 117 | –4 |
| Peter Popovic | 76 | 2 | 12 | 14 | 69 | 21 |
| Marc Bureau | 65 | 3 | 7 | 10 | 46 | –3 |
| Chris Murray | 48 | 3 | 4 | 7 | 163 | 5 |
| Donald Brashear | 67 | 0 | 4 | 4 | 223 | –10 |
| Robert Dirk* | 47 | 1 | 2 | 3 | 48 | 8 |
| Rory Fitzpatrick | 42 | 0 | 2 | 2 | 18 | –7 |
| Jocelyn Thibault* (g) | 50 | 0 | 0 | 0 | 2 | 0 |

**Coach**—Jacques Demers; Mario Tremblay

### New Jersey Devils

| | GP | G | A | Pts | PIM | +/- |
|---|---|---|---|---|---|---|
| Phil Housley* | 81 | 17 | 51 | 68 | 30 | –6 |
| Steve Thomas | 81 | 26 | 35 | 61 | 98 | –2 |
| Dave Andreychuk* | 76 | 28 | 29 | 57 | 64 | –9 |
| Bill Guerin | 80 | 23 | 30 | 53 | 116 | 7 |
| John MacLean | 76 | 20 | 28 | 48 | 91 | 3 |
| Petr Sykora | 63 | 18 | 24 | 42 | 32 | 7 |
| Scott Niedermayer | 79 | 8 | 25 | 33 | 46 | 5 |
| Stephane Richer | 73 | 20 | 12 | 32 | 30 | –8 |
| Bobby Holik | 63 | 13 | 17 | 30 | 58 | 9 |
| Scott Stevens | 82 | 5 | 23 | 28 | 100 | 7 |
| Brian Rolston | 58 | 13 | 11 | 24 | 8 | 9 |
| Neal Broten | 55 | 7 | 16 | 23 | 14 | –3 |
| Shawn Chambers | 64 | 2 | 21 | 23 | 18 | 1 |
| Randy McKay | 76 | 11 | 10 | 21 | 145 | 7 |
| Valeri Zelepukin | 61 | 6 | 9 | 15 | 107 | –10 |
| Mike Peluso | 57 | 3 | 8 | 11 | 146 | 4 |
| Bob Carpenter | 52 | 5 | 5 | 10 | 14 | –10 |
| Sergei Brylin | 50 | 4 | 5 | 9 | 26 | –2 |
| Ken Daneyko | 80 | 2 | 4 | 6 | 115 | –10 |
| Kevin Dean | 41 | 0 | 6 | 6 | 28 | 4 |
| Jason Smith | 64 | 2 | 1 | 3 | 86 | 5 |
| Martin Brodeur (g) | 77 | 0 | 1 | 1 | 6 | 0 |

**Coach**—Jacques Lemaire

### New York Islanders

| | GP | G | A | Pts | PIM | +/- |
|---|---|---|---|---|---|---|
| Zigmund Palffy | 81 | 43 | 44 | 87 | 56 | –17 |
| Travis Green | 69 | 25 | 45 | 70 | 42 | –20 |
| Marty McInnis | 74 | 12 | 34 | 46 | 39 | –11 |
| Todd Bertuzzi | 76 | 18 | 21 | 39 | 83 | –14 |
| Alexander Semak | 69 | 20 | 14 | 34 | 68 | –4 |
| Derek King | 61 | 12 | 20 | 32 | 23 | –10 |
| Kenny Jonsson* | 66 | 4 | 26 | 30 | 32 | 7 |
| Niklas Andersson | 47 | 14 | 12 | 26 | 12 | –3 |
| Bryan McCabe | 82 | 7 | 16 | 23 | 156 | –24 |
| Patrick Flatley | 56 | 8 | 9 | 17 | 21 | –24 |
| Darby Hendrickson* | 62 | 7 | 10 | 17 | 80 | –8 |
| Scott Lachance | 55 | 3 | 10 | 13 | 54 | –19 |
| Chris Luongo | 74 | 3 | 7 | 10 | 55 | –23 |
| Pat Conacher* | 55 | 6 | 3 | 9 | 18 | –13 |
| Brent Severyn | 65 | 1 | 8 | 9 | 180 | 3 |
| Darius Kasparaitis | 46 | 1 | 7 | 8 | 93 | –12 |
| Dan Plante | 73 | 5 | 3 | 8 | 50 | –22 |
| Tommy Soderstrom (g) | 51 | 0 | 0 | 0 | 7 | 0 |

**Coach**—Mike Milbury

### New York Rangers

| | GP | G | A | Pts | PIM | +/- |
|---|---|---|---|---|---|---|
| Mark Messier | 74 | 47 | 52 | 99 | 122 | 29 |
| Brian Leetch | 82 | 15 | 70 | 85 | 30 | 12 |
| Pat Verbeek | 69 | 41 | 41 | 82 | 129 | 29 |
| Luc Robitaille | 77 | 23 | 46 | 69 | 80 | 13 |
| Adam Graves | 82 | 22 | 36 | 58 | 100 | 18 |
| Alexei Kovalev | 81 | 24 | 34 | 58 | 98 | 5 |
| Jari Kurri* | 71 | 18 | 27 | 45 | 39 | –16 |
| Bruce Driver | 66 | 3 | 34 | 37 | 42 | 2 |
| Marty McSorley* | 68 | 10 | 23 | 33 | 169 | –20 |
| Sergei Nemchinov | 78 | 17 | 15 | 32 | 38 | 9 |
| Sergio Momesso* | 73 | 11 | 12 | 23 | 142 | –13 |
| Niklas Sundstrom | 82 | 9 | 12 | 21 | 14 | 2 |
| Ulf Samuelsson | 74 | 1 | 18 | 19 | 122 | 9 |
| Alexander Karpovtsev | 40 | 2 | 16 | 18 | 26 | 12 |
| Jeff Beukeboom | 82 | 3 | 11 | 14 | 220 | 19 |
| Doug Lidster | 59 | 5 | 9 | 14 | 50 | 11 |
| Darren Langdon | 64 | 7 | 4 | 11 | 175 | 2 |
| Shane Churla* | 55 | 4 | 6 | 10 | 231 | –8 |
| Kevin Lowe | 53 | 1 | 5 | 6 | 76 | 20 |
| Bill Berg* | 41 | 3 | 2 | 5 | 41 | –6 |
| Glenn Healy (g) | 44 | 0 | 1 | 1 | 8 | 0 |
| Mike Richter (g) | 41 | 0 | 1 | 1 | 4 | 0 |

**Coach**—Colin Campbell

### Ottawa Senators

| | GP | G | A | Pts | PIM | +/- |
|---|---|---|---|---|---|---|
| Daniel Alfredsson | 82 | 26 | 35 | 61 | 28 | –18 |
| Alexei Yashin | 46 | 15 | 24 | 39 | 28 | –15 |
| Randy Cunneyworth | 81 | 17 | 19 | 36 | 130 | –31 |
| Steve Duchesne | 62 | 12 | 24 | 36 | 42 | –23 |
| Radek Bonk | 76 | 16 | 19 | 35 | 36 | –5 |
| Tom Chorske | 72 | 15 | 14 | 29 | 21 | –9 |
| Sean Hill | 80 | 7 | 14 | 21 | 94 | –26 |
| Alexandre Daigle | 50 | 5 | 12 | 17 | 24 | –30 |
| Ted Drury | 42 | 9 | 7 | 16 | 54 | –19 |
| Antti Tormanen | 50 | 7 | 8 | 15 | 28 | –15 |
| Trent McCleary | 75 | 4 | 10 | 14 | 68 | –15 |
| Rob Gaudreau | 52 | 8 | 5 | 13 | 15 | –19 |
| Stanislav Neckar | 82 | 3 | 9 | 12 | 54 | –16 |
| David Archibald | 44 | 6 | 4 | 10 | 18 | –14 |
| Troy Mallette | 64 | 2 | 3 | 5 | 171 | –7 |
| Dennis Vial | 64 | 1 | 4 | 5 | 276 | –13 |
| Frank Musil | 65 | 1 | 3 | 4 | 85 | –10 |
| Damian Rhodes* (g) | 47 | 0 | 2 | 2 | 4 | 0 |

**Coach**—Rick Bowness; Dave Allison; Jacques Martin

### Philadelphia Flyers

| | GP | G | A | Pts | PIM | +/- |
|---|---|---|---|---|---|---|
| Eric Lindros | 73 | 47 | 68 | 115 | 163 | 26 |
| John LeClair | 82 | 51 | 46 | 97 | 64 | 21 |
| Rod Brind'Amour | 82 | 26 | 61 | 87 | 110 | 20 |
| Dale Hawerchuk* | 82 | 17 | 44 | 61 | 26 | 15 |
| Pat Falloon* | 71 | 25 | 26 | 51 | 10 | 14 |
| Eric Desjardins | 80 | 7 | 40 | 47 | 45 | 19 |
| Dan Quinn* | 63 | 13 | 32 | 45 | 46 | –6 |
| Mikael Renberg | 51 | 23 | 20 | 43 | 45 | 8 |
| Joel Otto | 67 | 12 | 29 | 41 | 115 | 11 |
| John Druce* | 77 | 13 | 16 | 29 | 27 | –20 |
| Petr Svoboda | 73 | 1 | 28 | 29 | 105 | 28 |
| Shjon Podein | 79 | 15 | 10 | 25 | 89 | 25 |
| Chris Therien | 82 | 6 | 17 | 23 | 89 | 16 |
| Rob DiMaio | 59 | 6 | 15 | 21 | 58 | 0 |
| Karl Dykhuis | 82 | 5 | 15 | 20 | 101 | 12 |
| Bob Corkum* | 76 | 9 | 10 | 19 | 34 | 3 |
| Trent Klatt* | 71 | 7 | 12 | 19 | 44 | 2 |
| Kerry Huffman* | 47 | 5 | 12 | 17 | 69 | –18 |
| Kevin Haller | 69 | 5 | 9 | 14 | 92 | 18 |
| Kjell Samuelsson | 75 | 3 | 11 | 14 | 81 | 20 |
| Shawn Antoski | 64 | 1 | 3 | 4 | 204 | –4 |
| Ron Hextall (g) | 53 | 0 | 1 | 1 | 28 | 0 |

**Coach**—Terry Murray

### Pittsburgh Penguins

| | GP | G | A | Pts | PIM | +/- |
|---|---|---|---|---|---|---|
| Mario Lemieux | 70 | 69 | 92 | 161 | 54 | 10 |
| Jaromir Jagr | 82 | 62 | 87 | 149 | 96 | 31 |
| Ron Francis | 77 | 27 | 92 | 119 | 56 | 25 |
| Petr Nedved | 80 | 45 | 54 | 99 | 68 | 37 |
| Tomas Sandstrom | 58 | 35 | 35 | 70 | 69 | 4 |
| Sergei Zubov | 64 | 11 | 55 | 66 | 22 | 28 |
| Bryan Smolinski | 81 | 24 | 40 | 64 | 69 | 6 |
| Markus Naslund* | 76 | 22 | 33 | 55 | 42 | 20 |
| Kevin Miller* | 81 | 28 | 25 | 53 | 45 | –4 |
| Dmitri Mironov | 72 | 3 | 31 | 34 | 88 | 19 |
| Glen Murray | 69 | 14 | 15 | 29 | 57 | 4 |
| Chris Joseph | 70 | 5 | 14 | 19 | 71 | 6 |
| Neil Wilkinson* | 62 | 3 | 14 | 17 | 120 | 12 |
| Dave Roche | 71 | 7 | 7 | 14 | 130 | –5 |
| Chris Tamer | 70 | 4 | 10 | 14 | 153 | 20 |
| J.J. Daigneault* | 57 | 4 | 7 | 11 | 53 | –6 |
| Francois Leroux | 66 | 2 | 9 | 11 | 161 | 2 |
| Joe Dziedzic | 69 | 5 | 5 | 10 | 68 | –5 |
| Richard Park | 56 | 4 | 6 | 10 | 36 | 3 |
| Chris Wells | 54 | 2 | 2 | 4 | 59 | –6 |
| Tom Barrasso (g) | 49 | 0 | 3 | 3 | 18 | 0 |
| Ian Moran | 51 | 1 | 1 | 2 | 47 | –1 |
| Alek Stojanov* | 68 | 1 | 1 | 2 | 130 | –13 |

**Coach**—Eddie Johnston

### St. Louis Blues

| | GP | G | A | Pts | PIM | +/- |
|---|---|---|---|---|---|---|
| Wayne Gretzky* | 80 | 23 | 79 | 102 | 34 | –13 |
| Brett Hull | 70 | 43 | 40 | 83 | 30 | 4 |

| | GP | G | A | Pts | PIM | +/– |
|---|---|---|---|---|---|---|
| Al MacInnis | 82 | 17 | 44 | 61 | 88 | 5 |
| Shayne Corson | 77 | 18 | 28 | 46 | 192 | 3 |
| Geoff Courtnall | 69 | 24 | 16 | 40 | 101 | –9 |
| Brian Noonan | 81 | 13 | 22 | 35 | 84 | 2 |
| Yuri Khmylev* | 73 | 8 | 21 | 29 | 40 | –17 |
| Stephen Leach* | 73 | 11 | 17 | 28 | 108 | –7 |
| Stephane Matteau* | 78 | 11 | 15 | 26 | 87 | –8 |
| Chris Pronger | 78 | 7 | 18 | 25 | 110 | –18 |
| Igor Kravchuk* | 66 | 7 | 16 | 23 | 34 | –19 |
| Adam Creighton | 61 | 11 | 10 | 21 | 78 | 0 |
| Peter Zezel | 57 | 8 | 13 | 21 | 12 | –2 |
| Mike Hudson* | 59 | 5 | 12 | 17 | 55 | 2 |
| Craig MacTavish* | 68 | 5 | 9 | 14 | 70 | –9 |
| Murray Baron | 82 | 2 | 9 | 11 | 190 | 3 |
| Charlie Huddy* | 64 | 5 | 5 | 10 | 65 | –12 |
| Tony Twist | 51 | 3 | 2 | 5 | 100 | –1 |
| Jay Wells | 76 | 0 | 3 | 3 | 67 | –8 |
| Grant Fuhr (g) | 79 | 0 | 1 | 1 | 8 | 0 |

**Coach**—Mike Keenan

## San Jose Sharks

| | GP | G | A | Pts | PIM | +/– |
|---|---|---|---|---|---|---|
| Owen Nolan* | 81 | 33 | 36 | 69 | 146 | –33 |
| Jeff Friesen | 79 | 15 | 31 | 46 | 42 | –19 |
| Darren Turcotte* | 68 | 22 | 21 | 43 | 30 | 5 |
| Ray Whitney | 60 | 17 | 24 | 41 | 16 | –23 |
| Marcus Ragnarsson | 71 | 8 | 31 | 39 | 42 | –24 |
| Jamie Baker | 77 | 16 | 17 | 33 | 79 | –19 |
| Doug Bodger* | 73 | 4 | 24 | 28 | 68 | –24 |
| Ulf Dahlen | 59 | 16 | 12 | 28 | 27 | –21 |
| Shean Donovan | 74 | 13 | 8 | 21 | 39 | –17 |
| Yves Racine* | 57 | 1 | 19 | 20 | 54 | –10 |
| Michal Sykora | 79 | 4 | 16 | 20 | 54 | –14 |
| Viktor Kozlov | 62 | 6 | 13 | 19 | 6 | –15 |
| Jeff Odgers | 78 | 12 | 4 | 16 | 192 | –4 |
| Andrei Nazarov | 42 | 7 | 7 | 14 | 62 | –15 |
| Jay More | 74 | 2 | 7 | 9 | 147 | –32 |
| Jim Kyte | 57 | 1 | 7 | 8 | 146 | –12 |
| Tom Pederson | 60 | 1 | 4 | 5 | 40 | –9 |
| Chris Terreri* (g) | 50 | 0 | 5 | 5 | 4 | 0 |

**Coach**—Kevin Constantine; Jim Wiley

## Tampa Bay Lightning

| | GP | G | A | Pts | PIM | +/– |
|---|---|---|---|---|---|---|
| Brian Bradley | 75 | 23 | 56 | 79 | 77 | –11 |
| Roman Hamrlik | 82 | 16 | 49 | 65 | 103 | –24 |
| Petr Klima | 67 | 22 | 30 | 52 | 68 | –25 |
| Alexander Selivanov | 79 | 31 | 21 | 52 | 93 | 3 |
| John Cullen | 76 | 16 | 34 | 50 | 65 | 1 |
| Brian Bellows | 79 | 23 | 26 | 49 | 39 | –14 |
| Chris Gratton | 82 | 17 | 21 | 38 | 105 | –13 |
| Rob Zamuner | 72 | 15 | 20 | 35 | 62 | 11 |
| Paul Ysebaert | 55 | 16 | 15 | 31 | 16 | –19 |
| Shawn Burr | 81 | 13 | 15 | 28 | 119 | 4 |
| Bill Houlder | 61 | 5 | 23 | 28 | 22 | 1 |
| Mikael Andersson | 64 | 8 | 11 | 19 | 2 | 0 |
| Jason Wiemer | 66 | 9 | 9 | 18 | 81 | –9 |
| Cory Cross | 75 | 2 | 14 | 16 | 66 | 4 |
| Patrick Poulin* | 46 | 7 | 9 | 16 | 16 | 7 |
| Aaron Gavey | 73 | 8 | 4 | 12 | 56 | –6 |
| Michel Petit* | 54 | 4 | 8 | 12 | 135 | –11 |
| David Shaw | 66 | 1 | 11 | 12 | 64 | 5 |
| Igor Ulanov* | 64 | 3 | 9 | 12 | 116 | 11 |
| John Tucker | 63 | 3 | 7 | 10 | 18 | –8 |
| Rudy Poeschek | 57 | 1 | 3 | 4 | 88 | –2 |
| Daren Puppa (g) | 57 | 0 | 1 | 1 | 4 | 0 |

**Coach**—Terry Crisp

## Toronto Maple Leafs

| | GP | G | A | Pts | PIM | +/– |
|---|---|---|---|---|---|---|
| Mats Sundin | 76 | 33 | 50 | 83 | 46 | 8 |
| Doug Gilmour | 81 | 32 | 40 | 72 | 77 | –5 |
| Larry Murphy | 82 | 12 | 49 | 61 | 34 | –2 |
| Wendel Clark* | 71 | 32 | 26 | 58 | 76 | –5 |
| Mike Gartner | 82 | 35 | 19 | 54 | 52 | 5 |
| Mathieu Schneider* | 78 | 13 | 41 | 54 | 103 | –20 |
| Dave Gagner* | 73 | 21 | 28 | 49 | 103 | –19 |
| Kirk Muller* | 51 | 13 | 19 | 32 | 57 | –13 |
| Todd Gill | 74 | 7 | 18 | 25 | 116 | –15 |
| Dave Ellett | 80 | 3 | 19 | 22 | 59 | –10 |
| Mike Craig | 70 | 8 | 12 | 20 | 42 | –8 |
| Todd Warriner | 57 | 7 | 8 | 15 | 26 | –11 |
| Wayne Presley* | 80 | 6 | 8 | 14 | 85 | 3 |
| Tie Domi | 72 | 7 | 6 | 13 | 297 | –3 |
| Dimitri Yushkevich | 69 | 1 | 10 | 11 | 54 | –14 |
| Nick Kypreos* | 61 | 4 | 5 | 9 | 107 | 1 |
| Jamie Macoun | 82 | 0 | 8 | 8 | 87 | 2 |
| Don Beaupre* (g) | 41 | 0 | 2 | 2 | 31 | 0 |
| Felix Potvin (g) | 69 | 0 | 0 | 0 | 4 | 0 |

**Coach**—Pat Burns; Nick Beverley

## Vancouver Canucks

| | GP | G | A | Pts | PIM | +/– |
|---|---|---|---|---|---|---|
| Alexander Mogilny | 79 | 55 | 52 | 107 | 16 | 14 |
| Trevor Linden | 82 | 33 | 47 | 80 | 42 | 6 |
| Cliff Ronning | 79 | 22 | 45 | 67 | 42 | 16 |
| Russ Courtnall | 81 | 26 | 39 | 65 | 40 | 25 |
| Martin Gelinas | 81 | 30 | 26 | 56 | 59 | 8 |
| Markus Naslund* | 76 | 22 | 33 | 55 | 42 | 20 |
| Jyrki Lumme | 80 | 17 | 37 | 54 | 50 | –9 |
| Esa Tikkanen* | 58 | 14 | 30 | 44 | 36 | 1 |
| Jesse Belanger* | 72 | 20 | 21 | 41 | 14 | –5 |
| Mike Sillinger* | 74 | 14 | 24 | 38 | 38 | –18 |
| Bret Hedican | 77 | 6 | 23 | 29 | 83 | 8 |
| Dave Babych | 53 | 3 | 21 | 24 | 38 | –5 |
| Leif Rohlon | 56 | 6 | 16 | 22 | 32 | 0 |
| Josef Beranek | 61 | 6 | 14 | 20 | 60 | –11 |
| Jim Dowd* | 66 | 5 | 15 | 20 | 23 | –9 |
| Adrian Aucoin | 49 | 4 | 14 | 18 | 34 | 8 |
| Dana Murzyn | 69 | 2 | 10 | 12 | 130 | 9 |
| Scott Walker | 63 | 4 | 8 | 12 | 137 | –7 |
| Frantisek Kucera* | 54 | 3 | 6 | 9 | 20 | 2 |
| Gino Odjick | 55 | 3 | 4 | 7 | 181 | –16 |
| Joey Kocur* | 45 | 1 | 3 | 4 | 68 | –7 |
| Corey Hirsch (g) | 41 | 0 | 2 | 2 | 2 | 0 |
| Tim Hunter | 60 | 2 | 0 | 2 | 122 | –8 |
| Dean Malkoc | 41 | 0 | 2 | 2 | 136 | –10 |
| Kirk McLean (g) | 45 | 0 | 2 | 2 | 6 | 0 |

**Coach**—Rick Ley; Pat Quinn

## Washington Capitals

| | GP | G | A | Pts | PIM | +/– |
|---|---|---|---|---|---|---|
| Michal Pivonka | 73 | 16 | 65 | 81 | 36 | 18 |
| Peter Bondra | 67 | 52 | 28 | 80 | 40 | 18 |
| Joe Juneau | 80 | 14 | 50 | 64 | 30 | –3 |
| Todd Krygier* | 76 | 15 | 33 | 48 | 82 | –1 |
| Steve Konowalchuk | 70 | 23 | 22 | 45 | 92 | 13 |
| Sergei Gonchar | 78 | 15 | 26 | 41 | 60 | 25 |
| Keith Jones | 68 | 18 | 23 | 41 | 103 | 8 |
| Sylvain Cote | 81 | 5 | 33 | 38 | 40 | 5 |
| Dale Hunter | 82 | 13 | 24 | 37 | 112 | 5 |
| Pat Peake | 62 | 17 | 19 | 36 | 46 | 7 |
| Calle Johansson | 78 | 10 | 25 | 35 | 50 | 13 |
| Kelly Miller | 74 | 7 | 13 | 20 | 30 | 7 |
| Stefan Ustorf | 48 | 7 | 10 | 17 | 14 | 8 |
| Mark Tinordi | 71 | 3 | 10 | 13 | 113 | 26 |
| Craig Berube | 50 | 2 | 10 | 12 | 151 | 1 |
| Mike Eagles | 70 | 4 | 7 | 11 | 75 | –1 |
| Ken Klee | 66 | 8 | 3 | 11 | 60 | –1 |
| Joe Reekie | 78 | 3 | 7 | 10 | 149 | 7 |
| Jim Johnson | 66 | 2 | 4 | 6 | 34 | –3 |
| Brendan Witt | 48 | 2 | 3 | 5 | 85 | –4 |
| Kevin Kaminski | 54 | 1 | 2 | 3 | 164 | –1 |
| Jim Carey (g) | 71 | 0 | 1 | 1 | 6 | 0 |

**Coach**—Jim Schoenfeld

## Winnipeg Jets

| | GP | G | A | Pts | PIM | +/– |
|---|---|---|---|---|---|---|
| Keith Tkachuk | 76 | 50 | 48 | 98 | 156 | 11 |
| Craig Janney* | 84 | 20 | 62 | 82 | 26 | –33 |
| Alexei Zhamnov | 58 | 22 | 37 | 59 | 65 | –4 |
| Teppo Numminen | 74 | 11 | 43 | 54 | 22 | –4 |
| Norm Maciver* | 71 | 7 | 46 | 53 | 58 | 6 |
| Igor Korolev | 73 | 22 | 29 | 51 | 42 | 1 |
| Ed Olczyk | 51 | 27 | 22 | 49 | 65 | 0 |
| Dallas Drake | 69 | 19 | 20 | 39 | 36 | –7 |
| Dave Manson | 82 | 7 | 23 | 30 | 205 | 8 |
| Oleg Tverdovsky* | 82 | 7 | 23 | 30 | 41 | –7 |
| Mike Eastwood | 80 | 14 | 14 | 28 | 20 | –14 |
| Mike Stapleton | 58 | 10 | 14 | 24 | 37 | –4 |
| Darrin Shannon | 63 | 5 | 18 | 23 | 28 | –5 |
| Kris King | 81 | 9 | 11 | 20 | 151 | –7 |
| Deron Quint | 51 | 5 | 13 | 18 | 22 | –2 |
| Shane Doan | 74 | 7 | 10 | 17 | 101 | –9 |
| Chad Kilger* | 74 | 7 | 10 | 17 | 34 | –4 |
| Craig Muni* | 72 | 1 | 7 | 8 | 106 | –6 |
| Jeff Finley | 65 | 1 | 5 | 6 | 81 | –2 |
| Jim McKenzie | 73 | 4 | 2 | 6 | 202 | –4 |
| Denis Chasse* | 60 | 3 | 0 | 3 | 125 | –14 |
| Nikolai Khabibulin (g) | 53 | 0 | 0 | 0 | 12 | 0 |

**Coach**—Terry Simpson

## Individual Goaltending, 1995-96

(25 or more games played; ranked by goals against average)

| Player | GP | GAA | W | L | T | SO | SV% |
|---|---|---|---|---|---|---|---|
| Hextall, Phila. | 53 | 2.17 | 31 | 13 | 7 | 4 | .913 |
| Osgood, Det. | 50 | 2.17 | 39 | 6 | 5 | 5 | .911 |
| Carey, Wash. | 71 | 2.26 | 35 | 24 | 9 | 9 | .906 |
| Vernon, Det. | 32 | 2.26 | 21 | 7 | 2 | 3 | .903 |
| Brodeur, N.J. | 77 | 2.34 | 34 | 30 | 12 | 6 | .911 |
| Hackett, Chi. | 35 | 2.40 | 18 | 11 | 4 | 1 | .916 |
| Puppa, T.B. | 57 | 2.46 | 29 | 16 | 9 | 5 | .918 |
| Richter, N.Y.R. | 41 | 2.68 | 24 | 13 | 3 | 3 | .912 |
| Vanbiesbrouck, Fla. | 57 | 2.68 | 26 | 20 | 7 | 2 | .904 |
| Belfour, Chi. | 50 | 2.74 | 22 | 17 | 10 | 1 | .902 |
| Rhodes, Tor.-Ott. | 47 | 2.77 | 14 | 27 | 5 | 12 | .905 |
| Roy, Mon.-Col. | 61 | 2.78 | 34 | 24 | 2 | 2 | .908 |
| Kidd, Cgy. | 47 | 2.78 | 15 | 21 | 8 | 3 | .895 |
| Hasek, Buf. | 59 | 2.83 | 22 | 30 | 6 | 2 | .920 |
| Hebert, Ana. | 59 | 2.83 | 28 | 23 | 5 | 4 | .914 |
| Thibault, Col.-Mon. | 50 | 2.86 | 26 | 17 | 5 | 3 | .907 |
| Fuhr, St.L. | 79 | 2.87 | 30 | 28 | 16 | 3 | .903 |
| Potvin, Tor. | 36 | 2.87 | 30 | 26 | 11 | 2 | .910 |
| Snow, Phila. | 26 | 2.88 | 12 | 8 | 4 | 0 | .894 |
| Healy, N.Y.R. | 44 | 2.90 | 17 | 14 | 11 | 2 | .900 |
| Hirsch, Van. | 41 | 2.93 | 17 | 14 | 6 | 1 | .903 |
| Fiset, Col. | 37 | 2.93 | 22 | 6 | 7 | 1 | .898 |
| Tabaracci, Cgy. | 43 | 2.94 | 19 | 16 | 3 | 3 | .892 |
| Fitzpatrick, Fla. | 34 | 2.96 | 15 | 11 | 3 | 2 | .891 |
| Moog, Dal. | 41 | 2.99 | 13 | 19 | 7 | 1 | .900 |
| Burke, Hfd. | 66 | 3.11 | 28 | 28 | 6 | 4 | .907 |

## All-Time Leading Scorers

| Player | Goals | Assists | Points |
|---|---|---|---|
| Wayne Gretzky* | 837 | 1,771 | 2,608 |
| Gordie Howe | 801 | 1,049 | 1,850 |
| Marcel Dionne | 731 | 1,040 | 1,771 |
| Phil Esposito | 717 | 873 | 1,590 |
| Mark Messier* | 539 | 929 | 1,468 |
| Stan Mikita | 541 | 926 | 1,467 |
| Bryan Trottier | 524 | 901 | 1,425 |
| Paul Coffey* | 372 | 1,038 | 1,410 |
| Dale Hawerchuk* | 506 | 869 | 1,375 |
| Mario Lemieux* | 563 | 809 | 1,372 |
| John Bucyk | 556 | 813 | 1,369 |
| Guy Lafleur | 560 | 793 | 1,353 |
| Jari Kurri* | 583 | 758 | 1,341 |
| Gilbert Perreault | 512 | 814 | 1,326 |
| Ray Bourque* | 343 | 970 | 1,313 |
| Denis Savard* | 464 | 847 | 1,311 |
| Alex Delvecchio | 456 | 825 | 1,281 |
| Jean Ratelle | 491 | 776 | 1,267 |
| Ron Francis* | 376 | 881 | 1,257 |
| Steve Yzerman* | 517 | 738 | 1,255 |

*Player was active at end of 1995-96 season.

## Most NHL Goals in a Season

| Player | Team | Season | Goals |
|---|---|---|---|
| Wayne Gretzky | Edmonton | 1981-82 | 92 |
| Wayne Gretzky | Edmonton | 1983-84 | 87 |
| Brett Hull | St. Louis | 1990-91 | 86 |
| Mario Lemieux | Pittsburgh | 1988-89 | 85 |
| Phil Esposito | Boston | 1970-71 | 76 |
| Alexander Mogilny | Buffalo | 1992-93 | 76 |
| Teemu Selanne | Winnipeg | 1992-93 | 76 |
| Wayne Gretzky | Edmonton | 1984-85 | 73 |
| Brett Hull | St. Louis | 1989-90 | 72 |
| Wayne Gretzky | Edmonton | 1982-83 | 71 |
| Jari Kurri | Edmonton | 1984-85 | 71 |
| Bret Hull | St. Louis | 1991-92 | 70 |
| Mario Lemieux | Pittsburgh | 1987-88 | 70 |
| Bernie Nicholls | Los Angeles | 1988-89 | 70 |
| Mike Bossy | N.Y. Islanders | 1978-79 | 69 |
| Mario Lemieux | Pittsburgh | 1992-93 | 69 |
| Mario Lemieux | Pittsburgh | 1995-96 | 69 |
| Mike Bossy | N.Y. Islanders | 1980-81 | 68 |
| Phil Esposito | Boston | 1973-74 | 68 |
| Jari Kurri | Edmonton | 1985-86 | 68 |

## Art Ross Trophy (Leading Scorer)

1927 Bill Cook, N.Y. Rangers
1928 Howie Morenz, Montreal
1929 Ace Bailey, Toronto
1930 Cooney Weiland, Boston
1931 Howie Morenz, Montreal
1932 Harvey Jackson, Toronto
1933 Bill Cook, N.Y. Rangers
1934 Charlie Conacher, Toronto
1935 Charlie Conacher, Toronto
1936 Dave Schriner, N.Y. Americans
1937 Dave Schriner, N.Y. Americans
1938 Gordie Drillon, Toronto
1939 Toe Blake, Montreal
1940 Milt Schmidt, Boston
1941 Bill Cowley, Boston
1942 Bryan Hextall, N.Y. Rangers
1943 Doug Bentley, Chicago
1944 Herbie Cain, Boston
1945 Elmer Lach, Montreal
1946 Max Bentley, Chicago
1947 Max Bentley, Chicago
1948 Elmer Lach, Montreal
1949 Roy Conacher, Chicago
1950 Ted Lindsay, Detroit
1951 Gordie Howe, Detroit
1952 Gordie Howe, Detroit
1953 Gordie Howe, Detroit
1954 Gordie Howe, Detroit
1955 Bernie Geoffrion, Montreal
1956 Jean Beliveau, Montreal
1957 Gordie Howe, Detroit
1958 Dickie Moore, Montreal
1959 Dickie Moore, Montreal
1960 Bobby Hull, Chicago
1961 Bernie Geoffrion, Montreal
1962 Bobby Hull, Chicago
1963 Gordie Howe, Detroit
1964 Stan Mikita, Chicago
1965 Stan Mikita, Chicago
1966 Bobby Hull, Chicago
1967 Stan Mikita, Chicago
1968 Stan Mikita, Chicago
1969 Phil Esposito, Boston
1970 Bobby Orr, Boston
1971 Phil Esposito, Boston
1972 Phil Esposito, Boston
1973 Phil Esposito, Boston
1974 Phil Esposito, Boston
1975 Bobby Orr, Boston
1976 Guy Lafleur, Montreal
1977 Guy Lafleur, Montreal
1978 Guy Lafleur, Montreal
1979 Bryan Trottier, N.Y. Islanders
1980 Marcel Dionne, Los Angeles
1981 Wayne Gretzky, Edmonton
1982 Wayne Gretzky, Edmonton
1983 Wayne Gretzky, Edmonton
1984 Wayne Gretzky, Edmonton
1985 Wayne Gretzky, Edmonton
1986 Wayne Gretzky, Edmonton
1987 Wayne Gretzky, Edmonton
1988 Mario Lemieux, Pittsburgh
1989 Mario Lemieux, Pittsburgh
1990 Wayne Gretzky, Los Angeles
1991 Wayne Gretzky, Los Angeles
1992 Mario Lemieux, Pittsburgh
1993 Mario Lemieux, Pittsburgh
1994 Wayne Gretzky, Los Angeles
1995 Jaromir Jagr, Pittsburgh
1996 Mario Lemieux, Pittsburgh

## James Norris Memorial Trophy (Outstanding Defenseman)

1954 Red Kelly, Detroit
1955 Doug Harvey, Montreal
1956 Doug Harvey, Montreal
1957 Doug Harvey, Montreal
1958 Doug Harvey, Montreal
1959 Tom Johnson, Montreal
1960 Doug Harvey, Montreal
1961 Doug Harvey, Montreal
1962 Doug Harvey, N.Y. Rangers
1963 Pierre Pilote, Chicago
1964 Pierre Pilote, Chicago
1965 Pierre Pilote, Chicago
1966 Jacques Laperriere, Montreal
1967 Harry Howell, N.Y. Rangers
1968 Bobby Orr, Boston
1969 Bobby Orr, Boston
1970 Bobby Orr, Boston
1971 Bobby Orr, Boston
1972 Bobby Orr, Boston
1973 Bobby Orr, Boston
1974 Bobby Orr, Boston
1975 Bobby Orr, Boston
1976 Denis Potvin, N.Y. Islanders
1977 Larry Robinson, Montreal
1978 Denis Potvin, N.Y. Islanders
1979 Denis Potvin, N.Y. Islanders
1980 Larry Robinson, Montreal
1981 Randy Carlyle, Pittsburgh
1982 Doug Wilson, Chicago
1983 Rod Langway, Washington
1984 Rod Langway, Washington
1985 Paul Coffey, Edmonton
1986 Paul Coffey, Edmonton
1987 Ray Bourque, Boston
1988 Ray Bourque, Boston
1989 Chris Chelios, Montreal
1990 Ray Bourque, Boston
1991 Ray Bourque, Boston
1992 Brian Leetch, N.Y. Rangers
1993 Chris Chelios, Chicago
1994 Ray Bourque, Boston
1995 Paul Coffey, Detroit
1996 Chris Chelios, Chicago

## Vezina Trophy (Outstanding Goalie)*

| Year | Winner |
|---|---|
| 1927 | George Hainsworth, Montreal |
| 1928 | George Hainsworth, Montreal |
| 1929 | George Hainsworth, Montreal |
| 1930 | Tiny Thompson, Boston |
| 1931 | Roy Worters, N.Y. Americans |
| 1932 | Charlie Gardiner, Chicago |
| 1933 | Tiny Thompson, Boston |
| 1934 | Charlie Gardiner, Chicago |
| 1935 | Lorne Chabot, Chicago |
| 1936 | Tiny Thompson, Boston |
| 1937 | Normie Smith, Detroit |
| 1938 | Tiny Thompson, Boston |
| 1939 | Frank Brimsek, Boston |
| 1940 | Dave Kerr, N.Y. Rangers |
| 1941 | Turk Broda, Toronto |
| 1942 | Frank Brimsek, Boston |
| 1943 | Johnny Mowers, Detroit |
| 1944 | Bill Durnan, Montreal |
| 1945 | Bill Durnan, Montreal |
| 1946 | Bill Durnan, Montreal |
| 1947 | Bill Durnan, Montreal |
| 1948 | Turk Broda, Toronto |
| 1949 | Bill Durnan, Montreal |
| 1950 | Bill Durnan, Montreal |
| 1951 | Al Rollins, Toronto |
| 1952 | Terry Sawchuk, Detroit |
| 1953 | Terry Sawchuk, Detroit |
| 1954 | Harry Lumley, Toronto |
| 1955 | Terry Sawchuk, Detroit |
| 1956 | Jacques Plante, Montreal |
| 1957 | Jacques Plante, Montreal |
| 1958 | Jacques Plante, Montreal |
| 1959 | Jacques Plante, Montreal |
| 1960 | Jacques Plante, Montreal |
| 1961 | John Bower, Toronto |
| 1962 | Jacques Plante, Montreal |
| 1963 | Glenn Hall, Chicago |
| 1964 | Charlie Hodge, Montreal |
| 1965 | Sawchuk, Bower, Toronto |
| 1966 | Worsley, Hodge, Montreal |
| 1967 | Hall, DeJordy, Chicago |
| 1968 | Worsley, Vachon, Montreal |
| 1969 | Hall, Plante, St. Louis |
| 1970 | Tony Esposito, Chicago |
| 1971 | Giacomin, Villemure, N.Y. Rangers |
| 1972 | Esposito, Smith, Chicago |
| 1973 | Ken Dryden, Montreal |
| 1974 | Bernie Parent, Philadelphia; Tony Esposito, Chicago |
| 1975 | Bernie Parent, Philadelphia |
| 1976 | Ken Dryden, Montreal |
| 1977 | Dryden, Larocque, Montreal |
| 1978 | Dryden, Larocque, Montreal |
| 1979 | Dryden, Larocque, Montreal |
| 1980 | Sauve, Edwards, Buffalo |
| 1981 | Sevigny, Larocque, Herron, Montreal |
| 1982 | Bill Smith, N.Y. Islanders |
| 1983 | Pete Peeters, Boston |
| 1984 | Tom Barrasso, Buffalo |
| 1985 | Pelle Lindbergh, Philadelphia |
| 1986 | John Vanbiesbrouck, N.Y. Rangers |
| 1987 | Ron Hextall, Philadelphia |
| 1988 | Grant Fuhr, Edmonton |
| 1989 | Patrick Roy, Montreal |
| 1990 | Patrick Roy, Montreal |
| 1991 | Ed Belfour, Chicago |
| 1992 | Patrick Roy, Montreal |
| 1993 | Ed Belfour, Chicago |
| 1994 | Dominik Hasek, Buffalo |
| 1995 | Dominik Hasek, Buffalo |
| 1996 | Jim Carey, Washington |

*Before 1982, awarded to the goalie or goalies who played a minimum of 25 games for the team that allowed the fewest goals; since 1982, awarded to the outstanding goalie.

## Calder Memorial Trophy (Rookie of the Year)

| Year | Winner |
|---|---|
| 1933 | Carl Voss, Detroit |
| 1934 | Russ Blinco, Montreal Maroons |
| 1935 | Dave Schriner, N.Y. Americans |
| 1936 | Mike Karakas, Chicago |
| 1937 | Syl Apps, Toronto |
| 1938 | Cully Dahlstrom, Chicago |
| 1939 | Frank Brimsek, Boston |
| 1940 | Kilby Macdonald, N.Y. Rangers |
| 1941 | John Quilty, Montreal |
| 1942 | Grant Warwick, N.Y. Rangers |
| 1943 | Gaye Stewart, Toronto |
| 1944 | Gus Bodnar, Toronto |
| 1945 | Frank McCool, Toronto |
| 1946 | Edgar Laprade, N.Y. Rangers |
| 1947 | Howie Meeker, Toronto |
| 1948 | Jim McFadden, Detroit |
| 1949 | Pentti Lund, N.Y. Rangers |
| 1950 | Jack Gelineau, Boston |
| 1951 | Terry Sawchuk, Detroit |
| 1952 | Bernie Geoffrion, Montreal |
| 1953 | Gump Worsley, N.Y. Rangers |
| 1954 | Camille Henry, N.Y. Rangers |
| 1955 | Ed Litzenberger, Chicago |
| 1956 | Glenn Hall, Detroit |
| 1957 | Larry Regan, Boston |
| 1958 | Frank Mahovlich, Toronto |
| 1959 | Ralph Backstrom, Montreal |
| 1960 | Bill Hay, Chicago |
| 1961 | Dave Keon, Toronto |
| 1962 | Bobby Rousseau, Montreal |
| 1963 | Kent Douglas, Toronto |
| 1964 | Jacques Laperriere, Montreal |
| 1965 | Roger Crozier, Detroit |
| 1966 | Brit Selby, Toronto |
| 1967 | Bobby Orr, Boston |
| 1968 | Derek Sanderson, Boston |
| 1969 | Danny Grant, Minnesota |
| 1970 | Tony Esposito, Chicago |
| 1971 | Gilbert Perreault, Buffalo |
| 1972 | Ken Dryden, Montreal |
| 1973 | Steve Vickers, N.Y. Rangers |
| 1974 | Denis Potvin, N.Y. Islanders |
| 1975 | Eric Vail, Atlanta |
| 1976 | Bryan Trottier, N.Y. Islanders |
| 1977 | Willi Plett, Atlanta |
| 1978 | Mike Bossy, N.Y. Islanders |
| 1979 | Bobby Smith, Minnesota |
| 1980 | Ray Bourque, Boston |
| 1981 | Peter Stastny, Quebec |
| 1982 | Dale Hawerchuk, Winnipeg |
| 1983 | Steve Larmer, Chicago |
| 1984 | Tom Barrasso, Buffalo |
| 1985 | Mario Lemieux, Pittsburgh |
| 1986 | Gary Suter, Calgary |
| 1987 | Luc Robitaille, Los Angeles |
| 1988 | Joe Nieuwendyk, Calgary |
| 1989 | Brian Leetch, N.Y. Rangers |
| 1990 | Sergei Makarov, Calgary |
| 1991 | Ed Belfour, Chicago |
| 1992 | Pavel Bure, Vancouver |
| 1993 | Teemu Selanne, Winnipeg |
| 1994 | Martin Brodeur, New Jersey |
| 1995 | Peter Forsberg, Quebec |
| 1996 | Daniel Alfredsson, Ottawa |

## Lady Byng Memorial Trophy (Most Gentlemanly Player)

| Year | Winner |
|---|---|
| 1925 | Frank Nighbor, Ottawa |
| 1926 | Frank Nighbor, Ottawa |
| 1927 | Billy Burch, N.Y. Americans |
| 1928 | Frank Boucher, N.Y. Rangers |
| 1929 | Frank Boucher, N.Y. Rangers |
| 1930 | Frank Boucher, N.Y. Rangers |
| 1931 | Frank Boucher, N.Y. Rangers |
| 1932 | Joe Primeau, Toronto |
| 1933 | Frank Boucher, N.Y. Rangers |
| 1934 | Frank Boucher, N.Y. Rangers |
| 1935 | Frank Boucher, N.Y. Rangers |
| 1936 | Doc Romnes, Chicago |
| 1937 | Marty Barry, Detroit |
| 1938 | Gordie Drillon, Toronto |
| 1939 | Clint Smith, N.Y. Rangers |
| 1940 | Bobby Bauer, Boston |
| 1941 | Bobby Bauer, Boston |
| 1942 | Syl Apps, Toronto |
| 1943 | Max Bentley, Chicago |
| 1944 | Clint Smith, Chicago |
| 1945 | Bill Mosienko, Chicago |
| 1946 | Toe Blake, Montreal |
| 1947 | Bobby Bauer, Boston |
| 1948 | Buddy O'Connor, N.Y. Rangers |
| 1949 | Bill Quackenbush, Detroit |
| 1950 | Edgar Laprade, N.Y. Rangers |
| 1951 | Red Kelly, Detroit |
| 1952 | Sid Smith, Toronto |
| 1953 | Red Kelly, Detroit |
| 1954 | Red Kelly, Detroit |
| 1955 | Sid Smith, Toronto |
| 1956 | Earl Reibel, Detroit |
| 1957 | Andy Hebenton, N.Y. Rangers |
| 1958 | Camille Henry, N.Y. Rangers |
| 1959 | Alex Delvecchio, Detroit |
| 1960 | Don McKenney, Boston |
| 1961 | Red Kelly, Toronto |
| 1962 | Dave Keon, Toronto |
| 1963 | Dave Keon, Toronto |
| 1964 | Ken Wharram, Chicago |
| 1965 | Bobby Hull, Chicago |
| 1966 | Alex Delvecchio, Detroit |
| 1967 | Stan Mikita, Chicago |
| 1968 | Stan Mikita, Chicago |
| 1969 | Alex Delvecchio, Detroit |
| 1970 | Phil Goyette, St. Louis |
| 1971 | John Bucyk, Boston |
| 1972 | Jean Ratelle, N.Y. Rangers |
| 1973 | Gil Perreault, Buffalo |
| 1974 | John Bucyk, Boston |
| 1975 | Marcel Dionne, Detroit |
| 1976 | Jean Ratelle, N.Y.R.-Boston |
| 1977 | Marcel Dionne, Los Angeles |
| 1978 | Butch Goring, Los Angeles |
| 1979 | Bob MacMillan, Atlanta |
| 1980 | Wayne Gretzky, Edmonton |
| 1981 | Rick Kehoe, Pittsburgh |
| 1982 | Rick Middleton, Boston |
| 1983 | Mike Bossy, N.Y. Islanders |
| 1984 | Mike Bossy, N.Y. Islanders |
| 1985 | Jari Kurri, Edmonton |
| 1986 | Mike Bossy, N.Y. Islanders |
| 1987 | Joe Mullen, Calgary |
| 1988 | Mats Naslund, Montreal |
| 1989 | Joe Mullen, Calgary |
| 1990 | Brett Hull, St. Louis |
| 1991 | Wayne Gretzky, Los Angeles |
| 1992 | Wayne Gretzky, Los Angeles |
| 1993 | Pierre Turgeon, N.Y. Islanders |
| 1994 | Wayne Gretzky, Los Angeles |
| 1995 | Ron Francis, Pittsburgh |
| 1996 | Paul Kariya, Anaheim |

## Frank J. Selke Trophy (Best Defensive Forward)

| Year | Winner |
|---|---|
| 1978 | Bob Gainey, Montreal |
| 1979 | Bob Gainey, Montreal |
| 1980 | Bob Gainey, Montreal |
| 1981 | Bob Gainey, Montreal |
| 1982 | Steve Kasper, Boston |
| 1983 | Bobby Clarke, Philadelphia |
| 1984 | Doug Jarvis, Washington |
| 1985 | Craig Ramsay, Buffalo |
| 1986 | Troy Murray, Chicago |
| 1987 | Dave Poulin, Philadelphia |
| 1988 | Guy Carbonneau, Montreal |
| 1989 | Guy Carbonneau, Montreal |
| 1990 | Rick Meagher, St. Louis |
| 1991 | Dirk Graham, Chicago |
| 1992 | Guy Carbonneau, Montreal |
| 1993 | Doug Gilmour, Toronto |
| 1994 | Sergei Fedorov, Detroit |
| 1995 | Ron Francis, Pittsburgh |
| 1996 | Sergei Federov, Detroit |

## Hart Memorial Trophy (MVP)

| | |
|---|---|
| 1927 | Herb Gardiner, Montreal |
| 1928 | Howie Morenz, Montreal |
| 1929 | Roy Worters, N.Y. Americans |
| 1930 | Nels Stewart, Montreal Maroons |
| 1931 | Howie Morenz, Montreal |
| 1932 | Howie Morenz, Montreal |
| 1933 | Eddie Shore, Boston |
| 1934 | Aurel Joliat, Montreal |
| 1935 | Eddie Shore, Boston |
| 1936 | Eddie Shore, Boston |
| 1937 | Babe Siebert, Montreal |
| 1938 | Eddie Shore, Boston |
| 1939 | Toe Blake, Montreal |
| 1940 | Ebbie Goodfellow, Detroit |
| 1941 | Bill Cowley, Boston |
| 1942 | Tom Anderson, N.Y. Americans |
| 1943 | Bill Cowley, Boston |
| 1944 | Babe Pratt, Toronto |
| 1945 | Elmer Lach, Montreal |
| 1946 | Max Bentley, Chicago |
| 1947 | Maurice Richard, Montreal |
| 1948 | Buddy O'Connor, N.Y. Rangers |
| 1949 | Sid Abel, Detroit |
| 1950 | Chuck Rayner, N.Y. Rangers |
| 1951 | Milt Schmidt, Boston |
| 1952 | Gordie Howe, Detroit |
| 1953 | Gordie Howe, Detroit |
| 1954 | Al Rollins, Chicago |
| 1955 | Ted Kennedy, Toronto |
| 1956 | Jean Beliveau, Montreal |
| 1957 | Gordie Howe, Detroit |
| 1958 | Gordie Howe, Detroit |
| 1959 | Andy Bathgate, N.Y. Rangers |
| 1960 | Gordie Howe, Detroit |
| 1961 | Bernie Geoffrion, Montreal |
| 1962 | Jacques Plante, Montreal |
| 1963 | Gordie Howe, Detroit |
| 1964 | Jean Beliveau, Montreal |
| 1965 | Bobby Hull, Chicago |
| 1966 | Bobby Hull, Chicago |
| 1967 | Stan Mikita, Chicago |
| 1968 | Stan Mikita, Chicago |
| 1969 | Phil Esposito, Boston |
| 1970 | Bobby Orr, Boston |
| 1971 | Bobby Orr, Boston |
| 1972 | Bobby Orr, Boston |
| 1973 | Bobby Clarke, Philadelphia |
| 1974 | Phil Esposito, Boston |
| 1975 | Bobby Clarke, Philadelphia |
| 1976 | Bobby Clarke, Philadelphia |
| 1977 | Guy Lafleur, Montreal |
| 1978 | Guy Lafleur, Montreal |
| 1979 | Bryan Trottier, N.Y. Islanders |
| 1980 | Wayne Gretzky, Edmonton |
| 1981 | Wayne Gretzky, Edmonton |
| 1982 | Wayne Gretzky, Edmonton |
| 1983 | Wayne Gretzky, Edmonton |
| 1984 | Wayne Gretzky, Edmonton |
| 1985 | Wayne Gretzky, Edmonton |
| 1986 | Wayne Gretzky, Edmonton |
| 1987 | Wayne Gretzky, Edmonton |
| 1988 | Mario Lemieux, Pittsburgh |
| 1989 | Wayne Gretzky, Los Angeles |
| 1990 | Mark Messier, Edmonton |
| 1991 | Brett Hull, St. Louis |
| 1992 | Mark Messier, N.Y. Rangers |
| 1993 | Mario Lemieux, Pittsburgh |
| 1994 | Sergei Fedorov, Detroit |
| 1995 | Eric Lindros, Philadelphia |
| 1996 | Mario Lemieux, Pittsburgh |

## Conn Smythe Trophy (MVP in Playoffs)

| | |
|---|---|
| 1965 | Jean Beliveau, Montreal |
| 1966 | Roger Crozier, Detroit |
| 1967 | Dave Keon, Toronto |
| 1968 | Glenn Hall, St. Louis |
| 1969 | Serge Savard, Montreal |
| 1970 | Bobby Orr, Boston |
| 1971 | Ken Dryden, Montreal |
| 1972 | Bobby Orr, Boston |
| 1973 | Yvan Cournoyer, Montreal |
| 1974 | Bernie Parent, Philadelphia |
| 1975 | Bernie Parent, Philadelphia |
| 1976 | Reg Leach, Philadelphia |
| 1977 | Guy Lafleur, Montreal |
| 1978 | Larry Robinson, Montreal |
| 1979 | Bob Gainey, Montreal |
| 1980 | Bryan Trottier, N.Y. Islanders |
| 1981 | Butch Goring, N.Y. Islanders |
| 1982 | Mike Bossy, N.Y. Islanders |
| 1983 | Billy Smith, N.Y. Islanders |
| 1984 | Mark Messier, Edmonton |
| 1985 | Wayne Gretzky, Edmonton |
| 1986 | Patrick Roy, Montreal |
| 1987 | Ron Hextall, Philadelphia |
| 1988 | Wayne Gretzky, Edmonton |
| 1989 | Al MacInnis, Calgary |
| 1990 | Bill Ranford, Edmonton |
| 1991 | Mario Lemieux, Pittsburgh |
| 1992 | Mario Lemieux, Pittsburgh |
| 1993 | Patrick Roy, Montreal |
| 1994 | Brian Leetch, N.Y. Rangers |
| 1995 | Claude Lemieux, New Jersey |
| 1996 | Joe Sakic, Colorado |

## NCAA Hockey Champions

| | |
|---|---|
| 1948 | Michigan |
| 1949 | Boston College |
| 1950 | Colorado College |
| 1951 | Michigan |
| 1952 | Michigan |
| 1953 | Michigan |
| 1954 | RPI |
| 1955 | Michigan |
| 1956 | Michigan |
| 1957 | Colorado College |
| 1958 | Denver |
| 1959 | North Dakota |
| 1960 | Denver |
| 1961 | Denver |
| 1962 | Michigan Tech |
| 1963 | North Dakota |
| 1964 | Michigan |
| 1965 | Michigan Tech |
| 1966 | Michigan State |
| 1967 | Cornell |
| 1968 | Denver |
| 1969 | Denver |
| 1970 | Cornell |
| 1971 | Boston Univ. |
| 1972 | Boston Univ. |
| 1973 | Wisconsin |
| 1974 | Minnesota |
| 1975 | Michigan Tech |
| 1976 | Minnesota |
| 1977 | Wisconsin |
| 1978 | Boston Univ. |
| 1979 | Minnesota |
| 1980 | North Dakota |
| 1981 | Wisconsin |
| 1982 | North Dakota |
| 1983 | Wisconsin |
| 1984 | Bowling Green |
| 1985 | RPI |
| 1986 | Michigan State |
| 1987 | North Dakota |
| 1988 | Lake Superior St. |
| 1989 | Harvard |
| 1990 | Wisconsin |
| 1991 | N. Michigan |
| 1992 | Lake Superior St. |
| 1993 | Maine |
| 1994 | Lake Superior St. |
| 1995 | Boston Univ. |
| 1996 | Michigan |

# LACROSSE

## Lacrosse Champions in 1996

**World Lacrosse Championship** (1994; held every 4 years)—Manchester, England, July 30: U.S. 21, Australia 7.
**U.S. Club Lacrosse Association Championship**—Radnor, PA, June 23: Long Island-Hofstra 13, Chesapeake Toyota 7.
**Pro Indoor Lacrosse Championship**—Buffalo, NY, April 12: Buffalo 15, Philadelphia 10.
**NCAA Division I Championship**—College Park, MD, May 27: Princeton 13, Virginia 12 (OT).
**NCAA Division II Championship**—Brookville, NY, May 11: C.W. Post 15, Adelphi 10.
**NCAA Division III Championship**—College Park, MD, May 26: Nazareth 11, Washington College 10 (OT).
**NCAA Division I All-Star Game**—Hempstead, NY, June 8: South 18, North 16.
**National Junior College Championship**—Corning, NY, May 12: Herkimer (NY) C.C. 19, Anne Arundel (MD) C.C. 11.
**NCAA Women's Division I Championship**—Bethlehem, PA, May 19: Maryland 10, Virginia 5.
**NCAA Women's Division III Championship**—Bethlehem, PA, May 19: Trenton State 15, Middlebury 8.

### NCAA Division I All America Team

**Attack:** Jesse Hubbard, Princeton; Doug Knight, Virginia; Michael Watson, Virginia.
**Midfield:** Jude Collins, North Carolina; Tim Langton, Towson State; Casey Powell, Syracuse; Jason Wade, North Carolina. (4 midfielders selected for the 3 midfield positions.)
**Defense:** Tyler Hardy, Duke; Brian Kuczma, Johns Hopkins; Tommy Smith, Virginia.
**Goal:** Brian Dougherty, Maryland.
**Coach of the Year:** Sid Jamieson, Bucknell.

## NCAA Division I Lacrosse Champions

| Year | Champion |
|---|---|
| 1971 | Cornell |
| 1972 | Virginia |
| 1973 | Maryland |
| 1974 | Johns Hopkins |
| 1975 | Maryland |
| 1976 | Cornell |
| 1977 | Cornell |
| 1978 | Johns Hopkins |
| 1979 | Johns Hopkins |
| 1980 | Johns Hopkins |
| 1981 | North Carolina |
| 1982 | North Carolina |
| 1983 | Syracuse |
| 1984 | Johns Hopkins |
| 1985 | Johns Hopkins |
| 1986 | North Carolina |
| 1987 | Johns Hopkins |
| 1988 | Syracuse |
| 1989 | Syracuse |
| 1990 | vacated |
| 1991 | North Carolina |
| 1992 | Princeton |
| 1993 | Syracuse |
| 1994 | Princeton |
| 1995 | Syracuse |
| 1996 | Princeton |

# THOROUGHBRED RACING

## Triple Crown Winners

Since 1920, colts have carried 126 lb in triple crown events; fillies, 121 lb.

(Kentucky Derby, Preakness, and Belmont Stakes)

| Year | Horse | Jockey | Trainer |
|---|---|---|---|
| 1919 | Sir Barton | J. Loftus | H. G. Bedwell |
| 1930 | Gallant Fox | E. Sande | J. Fitzsimmons |
| 1935 | Omaha | W. Sanders | J. Fitzsimmons |
| 1937 | War Admiral | C. Kurtsinger | G. Conway |
| 1941 | Whirlaway | E. Arcaro | B. A. Jones |
| 1943 | Count Fleet | J. Longden | G. D. Cameron |
| 1946 | Assault | W. Mehrtens | M. Hirsch |
| 1948 | Citation | E. Arcaro | H. A. Jones |
| 1973 | Secretariat | R. Turcotte | L. Laurin |
| 1977 | Seattle Slew | J. Cruguet | W. H. Turner, Jr. |
| 1978 | Affirmed | S. Cauthen | L. S. Barrera |

## Kentucky Derby

Churchill Downs, Louisville, KY; inaugurated 1875; distance 1-1/4 mi; 1-1/2 mi until 1896. 3-year olds.
Best time: 1:59.2, Secretariat, 1973.

| Year | Winner | Jockey |
|---|---|---|
| 1875 | Aristides | O. Lewis |
| 1876 | Vagrant | R. Swim |
| 1877 | Baden Baden | W. Walker |
| 1878 | Day Star | J. Carter |
| 1879 | Lord Murphy | C. Schauer |
| 1880 | Fonso | G. Lewis |
| 1881 | Hindoo | J. McLaughlin |
| 1882 | Apollo | B. Hurd |
| 1883 | Leonatus | W. Donohue |
| 1884 | Buchanan | I. Murphy |
| 1885 | Joe Cotton | E. Henderson |
| 1886 | Ben Ali | P. Duffy |
| 1887 | Montrose | I. Lewis |
| 1888 | Macbeth II | G. Covington |
| 1889 | Spokane | T. Kiley |
| 1890 | Riley | I. Murphy |
| 1891 | Kingman | I. Murphy |
| 1892 | Azra | A. Clayton |
| 1893 | Lookout | E. Kunze |
| 1894 | Chant | F. Goodale |
| 1895 | Halma | J. Perkins |
| 1896 | Ben Brush | W. Simms |
| 1897 | Typhoon II | F. Garner |
| 1898 | Plaudit | W. Simms |
| 1899 | Manuel | F. Taral |
| 1900 | Lieut. Gibson | J. Boland |
| 1901 | His Eminence | J. Winkfield |
| 1902 | Alan-a-Dale | J. Winkfield |
| 1903 | Judge Himes | H. Booker |
| 1904 | Elwood | F. Prior |
| 1905 | Agile | J. Martin |
| 1906 | Sir Huon | R. Troxler |
| 1907 | Pink Star | A. Minder |
| 1908 | Stone Street | A. Pickens |
| 1909 | Wintergreen | V. Powers |
| 1910 | Donau | F. Herbert |
| 1911 | Meridian | G. Archibald |
| 1912 | Worth | C.H. Shilling |
| 1913 | Donerail | R. Goose |
| 1914 | Old Rosebud | J. McCabe |
| 1915 | Regret* | J. Notter |
| 1916 | George Smith | J. Loftus |
| 1917 | Omar Khayyam | C. Borel |
| 1918 | Exterminator | W. Knapp |
| 1919 | Sir Barton | J. Loftus |
| 1920 | Paul Jones | T. Rice |
| 1921 | Behave Yourself | C. Thompson |
| 1922 | Morvich | A. Johnson |
| 1923 | Zev | E. Sande |
| 1924 | Black Gold | J. D. Mooney |
| 1925 | Flying Ebony | E. Sande |
| 1926 | Bubbling Over | A. Johnson |
| 1927 | Whiskery | L. McAtee |
| 1928 | Reigh Count | C. Lang |
| 1929 | Clyde Van Dusen | L. McAtee |
| 1930 | Gallant Fox | E. Sande |
| 1931 | Twenty Grand | C. Kurtsinger |
| 1932 | Burgoo King | E. James |
| 1933 | Brokers Tip | D. Meade |
| 1934 | Cavalcade | M. Garner |
| 1935 | Omaha | W. Saunders |
| 1936 | Bold Venture | I. Hanford |
| 1937 | War Admiral | C. Kurtsinger |
| 1938 | Lawrin | E. Arcaro |
| 1939 | Johnstown | J. Stout |
| 1940 | Gallahadion | C. Bierman |
| 1941 | Whirlaway | E. Arcaro |
| 1942 | Shut Out | W. D. Wright |
| 1943 | Count Fleet | J. Longden |
| 1944 | Pensive | C. McCreary |
| 1945 | Hoop, Jr. | E. Arcaro |
| 1946 | Assault | W. Mehrtens |
| 1947 | Jet Pilot | E. Guerin |
| 1948 | Citation | E. Arcaro |
| 1949 | Ponder | S. Brooks |
| 1950 | Middleground | W. Boland |
| 1951 | Count Turf | C. McCreary |
| 1952 | Hill Gail | E. Arcaro |
| 1953 | Dark Star | H. Moreno |
| 1954 | Determine | R. York |
| 1955 | Swaps | W. Shoemaker |
| 1956 | Needles | D. Erb |
| 1957 | Iron Liege | W. Hartack |
| 1958 | Tim Tam | I. Valenzuela |
| 1959 | Tomy Lee | W. Shoemaker |
| 1960 | Venetian Way | W. Hartack |
| 1961 | Carry Back | J. Sellers |
| 1962 | Decidedly | W. Hartack |
| 1963 | Chateaugay | B. Baeza |
| 1964 | Northern Dancer | W. Hartack |
| 1965 | Lucky Debonair | W. Shoemaker |
| 1966 | Kauai King | D. Brumfield |
| 1967 | Proud Clarion | R. Ussery |
| 1968 | Dancer's Image (a) | R. Ussery |
| 1969 | Majestic Prince | W. Hartack |
| 1970 | Dust Commander | M. Manganello |
| 1971 | Canonero II | G. Avila |
| 1972 | Riva Ridge | R. Turcotte |
| 1973 | Secretariat | R. Turcotte |
| 1974 | Cannonade | A. Cordero |
| 1975 | Foolish Pleasure | J. Vasquez |
| 1976 | Bold Forbes | A. Cordero |
| 1977 | Seattle Slew | J. Cruguet |
| 1978 | Affirmed | S. Cauthen |
| 1979 | Spectacular Bid | R. Franklin |
| 1980 | Genuine Risk* | J. Vasquez |
| 1981 | Pleasant Colony | J. Velasquez |
| 1982 | Gato del Sol | E. Delahoussaye |
| 1983 | Sunny's Halo | E. Delahoussaye |
| 1984 | Swale | L. Pincay |
| 1985 | Spend a Buck | A. Cordero |
| 1986 | Ferdinand | W. Shoemaker |
| 1987 | Alysheba | C. McCarron |
| 1988 | Winning Colors* | G. Stevens |
| 1989 | Sunday Silence | P. Valenzuela |
| 1990 | Unbridled | C. Perret |
| 1991 | Strike the Gold | C. Antley |
| 1992 | Lil E. Tee | P. Day |
| 1993 | Sea Hero | J. Bailey |
| 1994 | Go for Gin | C. McCarron |
| 1995 | Thunder Gulch | G. Stevens |
| 1996 | Grindstone | J. Bailey |

(a) Dancer's Image was disqualified from purse money after tests disclosed that he had run with a pain-killing drug, phenylbutazone, in his system. All wagers were paid on Dancer's Image. Forward Pass was awarded first place money.

The Kentucky Derby has been won 5 times by 2 jockeys: Eddie Arcaro, 1938, 1941, 1945, 1948, and 1952; and Bill Hartack, 1957, 1960, 1962, 1964, and 1969. It was won 4 times by Willie Shoemaker, 1955, 1959, 1965, and 1986; and 3 times by each of 3 jockeys: Isaac Murphy, 1884, 1890, and 1891; Earle Sande, 1923, 1925, and 1930; and Angel Cordero, 1974, 1976, and 1985. * Regret, Genuine Risk, and Winning Colors are the only fillies to have won the Derby.

## Preakness

Pimlico, Baltimore, MD; inaugurated 1873; distance 1-3/16 mi. 3-year olds. Best time: 1:53.2, Tank's Prospect, 1985.

| Year | Winner | Jockey |
|---|---|---|
| 1873 | Survivor | G. Barbee |
| 1874 | Culpepper | M. Donohue |
| 1875 | Tom Ochiltree | L. Hughes |
| 1876 | Shirley | G. Barbee |
| 1877 | Cloverbrook | C. Holloway |
| 1878 | Duke of Magenta | C. Holloway |
| 1879 | Harold | L. Hughes |
| 1880 | Grenada | L. Hughes |
| 1881 | Saunterer | W. Costello |
| 1882 | Vanguard | W. Costello |
| 1883 | Jacobus | G. Barbee |
| 1884 | Knight of Ellerslie | S. H. Fisher |
| 1885 | Tecumseh | J. McLaughlin |
| 1886 | The Bard | S. H. Fisher |
| 1887 | Dunboyne | W. Donohue |
| 1888 | Refund | F. Littlefield |
| 1889 | Buddhist | G. Anderson |
| 1890 | Montague | W. Martin |
| 1894 | Assignee | F. Taral |
| 1895 | Belmar | F. Taral |
| 1896 | Margrave | H. Griffin |
| 1897 | Paul Kauvar | C. Thorpe |
| 1898 | Sly Fox | W. Simms |
| 1899 | Half Time | R. Clawson |
| 1900 | Hindus | H. Spencer |
| 1901 | The Parader | F. Landry |
| 1902 | Old England | L. Jackson |
| 1903 | Flocarline | W. Gannon |
| 1904 | Bryn Mawr | E. Hildebrand |
| 1905 | Cairngorm | W. Davis |
| 1906 | Whimsical | W. Miller |
| 1907 | Don Enrique | G. Mountain |
| 1908 | Royal Tourist | E. Dugan |
| 1909 | Effendi | W. Doyle |
| 1910 | Layminster | R. Estep |
| 1911 | Watervale | E. Dugan |
| 1912 | Colonel Holloway | C. Turner |
| 1913 | Buskin | J. Butwell |
| 1914 | Holiday | A. Schuttinger |
| 1915 | Rhine Maiden | D. Hoffman |
| 1916 | Damrosch | L. McAtee |
| 1917 | Kalitan | E. Haynes |
| 1918 | War Cloud | J. Loftus |
| | Jack Hare, Jr. | C. Peak |
| 1919 | Sir Barton | J. Loftus |
| 1920 | Man o' War | C. Kummer |
| 1921 | Broomspun | F. Coltiletti |

*(continued)*

| Year | Winner | Jockey |
|---|---|---|
| 1922 | Pillory | L. Morris |
| 1923 | Vigil | B. Marinelli |
| 1924 | Nellie Morse | J. Merimee |
| 1925 | Coventry | C. Kummer |
| 1926 | Display | J. Malben |
| 1927 | Bostonian | A. Abel |
| 1928 | Victorian | R. Workman |
| 1929 | Dr. Freeland | L. Schaefer |
| 1930 | Gallant Fox | E. Sande |
| 1931 | Mate | G. Ellis |
| 1932 | Burgoo King | E. James |
| 1933 | Head Play | C. Kurtsinger |
| 1934 | High Quest | R. Jones |
| 1935 | Omaha | W. Saunders |
| 1936 | Bold Venture | G. Woolf |
| 1937 | War Admiral | C. Kurtsinger |
| 1938 | Dauber | M. Peters |
| 1939 | Challedon | G. Seabo |
| 1940 | Bimelech | F.A. Smith |
| 1941 | Whirlaway | E. Arcaro |
| 1942 | Alsab | B. James |
| 1943 | Count Fleet | J. Longden |
| 1944 | Pensive | C. McCreary |
| 1945 | Polynesian | W.D. Wright |
| 1946 | Assault | W. Mehrtens |
| 1947 | Faultless | D. Dodson |
| 1948 | Citation | E. Arcaro |
| 1949 | Capot | T. Atkinson |
| 1950 | Hill Prince | E. Arcaro |
| 1951 | Bold | E. Arcaro |
| 1952 | Blue Man | C. McCreary |
| 1953 | Native Dancer | E. Guerin |
| 1954 | Hasty Road | J. Adams |
| 1955 | Nashua | E. Arcaro |
| 1956 | Fabius | W. Hartack |
| 1957 | Bold Ruler | E. Arcaro |
| 1958 | Tim Tam | I. Valenzuela |
| 1959 | Royal Orbit | W. Harmatz |
| 1960 | Bally Ache | R. Ussery |
| 1961 | Carry Back | J. Sellers |
| 1962 | Greek Money | J.L. Rotz |
| 1963 | Candy Spots | W. Shoemaker |
| 1964 | Northern Dancer | W. Hartack |
| 1965 | Tom Rolfe | R. Turcotte |
| 1966 | Kauai King | D. Brumfield |
| 1967 | Damascus | W. Shoemaker |
| 1968 | Forward Pass | I. Valenzuela |
| 1969 | Majestic Prince | W. Hartack |
| 1970 | Personality | E. Belmonte |
| 1971 | Canonero II | G. Avila |
| 1972 | Bee Bee Bee | E. Nelson |
| 1973 | Secretariat | R. Turcotte |
| 1974 | Little Current | M. Rivera |
| 1975 | Master Derby | D. McHargue |
| 1976 | Elocutionist | J. Lively |
| 1977 | Seattle Slew | J. Cruguet |
| 1978 | Affirmed | S. Cauthen |
| 1979 | Spectacular Bid | R. Franklin |
| 1980 | Codex | A. Cordero |
| 1981 | Pleasant Colony | J. Velasquez |
| 1982 | Aloma's Ruler | J. Kaenel |
| 1983 | Deputed Testamony | D. Miller |
| 1984 | Gate Dancer | A. Cordero |
| 1985 | Tank's Prospect | P. Day |
| 1986 | Snow Chief | A. Solis |
| 1987 | Alysheba | C. McCarron |
| 1988 | Risen Star | E. Delahoussaye |
| 1989 | Sunday Silence | P. Valenzuela |
| 1990 | Summer Squall | P. Day |
| 1991 | Hansel | J. Bailey |
| 1992 | Pine Bluff | C. McCarron |
| 1993 | Prairie Bayou | M. Smith |
| 1994 | Tabasco Cat | P. Day |
| 1995 | Timber Country | P. Day |
| 1996 | Louis Quatorze | P. Day |

## Belmont Stakes

Belmont Park, Elmont, NY; inaugurated 1867; distance 1-1/2 mi. 3-year olds. Best time: 2:24, Secretariat, 1973.

| Year | Winner | Jockey |
|---|---|---|
| 1867 | Ruthless | J. Gilpatrick |
| 1868 | General Duke | R. Swim |
| 1869 | Fenian | C. Miller |
| 1870 | Kingfisher | W. Dick |
| 1871 | Harry Bassett | W. Miller |
| 1872 | Joe Daniels | J. Rowe |
| 1873 | Springbok | J. Rowe |
| 1874 | Saxon | G. Barbee |
| 1875 | Calvin | R. Swim |
| 1876 | Algerine | W. Donohue |
| 1877 | Cloverbrook | C. Holloway |
| 1878 | Duke of Magenta | L. Hughes |
| 1879 | Spendthrift | S. Evans |
| 1880 | Grenada | L. Hughes |
| 1881 | Saunterer | T. Costello |
| 1882 | Forester | J. McLaughlin |
| 1883 | George Kinney | J. McLaughlin |
| 1884 | Panique | J. McLaughlin |
| 1885 | Tyrant | P. Duffy |
| 1886 | Inspector B. | J. McLaughlin |
| 1887 | Hanover | J. McLaughlin |
| 1888 | Sir Dixon | J. McLaughlin |
| 1889 | Eric | W. Hayward |
| 1890 | Burlington | S. Barnes |
| 1891 | Foxford | E. Garrison |
| 1892 | Patron | W. Hayward |
| 1893 | Comanche | W. Simms |
| 1894 | Henry of Navarre | W. Simms |
| 1895 | Belmar | F. Taral |
| 1896 | Hastings | H. Griffin |
| 1897 | Scottish Chieftain | J. Scherrer |
| 1898 | Bowling Brook | F. Littlefield |
| 1899 | Jean Bereaud | R. R. Clawson |
| 1900 | Ildrim | N. Turner |
| 1901 | Commando | H. Spencer |
| 1902 | Masterman | J. Bullman |
| 1903 | Africander | J. Bullman |
| 1904 | Delhi | G. Odom |
| 1905 | Tanya | E. Hildebrand |
| 1906 | Burgomaster | L. Lyne |
| 1907 | Peter Pan | G. Mountain |
| 1908 | Colin | J. Notter |
| 1909 | Joe Madden | E. Dugan |
| 1910 | Sweep | J. Butwell |
| 1913 | Prince Eugene | R. Troxler |
| 1914 | Luke McLuke | M. Buxton |
| 1915 | The Finn | G. Byrne |
| 1916 | Friar Rock | E. Haynes |
| 1917 | Hourless | J. Butwell |
| 1918 | Johren | F. Robinson |
| 1919 | Sir Barton | J. Loftus |
| 1920 | Man o' War | C. Kummer |
| 1921 | Grey Lag | E. Sande |
| 1922 | Pillory | C. H. Miller |
| 1923 | Zev | E. Sande |
| 1924 | Mad Play | E. Sande |
| 1925 | American Flag | A. Johnson |
| 1926 | Crusader | A. Johnson |
| 1927 | Chance Shot | E. Sande |
| 1928 | Vito | C. Kummer |
| 1929 | Blue Larkspur | M. Garner |
| 1930 | Gallant Fox | E. Sande |
| 1931 | Twenty Grand | C. Kurtsinger |
| 1932 | Faireno | T. Malley |
| 1933 | Hurryoff | M. Garner |
| 1934 | Peace Chance | W. D. Wright |
| 1935 | Omaha | W. Saunders |
| 1936 | Granville | J. Stout |
| 1937 | War Admiral | C. Kurtsinger |
| 1938 | Pasteurized | J. Stout |
| 1939 | Johnstown | J. Stout |
| 1940 | Bimelech | F. A. Smith |
| 1941 | Whirlaway | E. Arcaro |
| 1942 | Shut Out | E. Arcaro |
| 1943 | Count Fleet | J. Longden |
| 1944 | Bounding Home | G. L. Smith |
| 1945 | Pavot | E. Arcaro |
| 1946 | Assault | W. Mehrtens |
| 1947 | Phalanx | R. Donoso |
| 1948 | Citation | E. Arcaro |
| 1949 | Capot | T. Atkinson |
| 1950 | Middleground | W. Boland |
| 1951 | Counterpoint | D. Gorman |
| 1952 | One Count | E. Arcaro |
| 1953 | Native Dancer | E. Guerin |
| 1954 | High Gun | E. Guerin |
| 1955 | Nashua | E. Arcaro |
| 1956 | Needles | D. Erb |
| 1957 | Gallant Man | W. Shoemaker |
| 1958 | Cavan | P. Anderson |
| 1959 | Sword Dancer | W. Shoemaker |
| 1960 | Celtic Ash | W. Hartack |
| 1961 | Sherluck | B. Baeza |
| 1962 | Jaipur | W. Shoemaker |
| 1963 | Chateaugay | B. Baeza |
| 1964 | Quadrangle | M. Ycaza |
| 1965 | Hail to All | J. Sellers |
| 1966 | Amberoid | W. Boland |
| 1967 | Damascus | W. Shoemaker |
| 1968 | Stage Door Johnny | H. Gustines |
| 1969 | Arts and Letters | B. Baeza |
| 1970 | High Echelon | J. L. Rotz |
| 1971 | Pass Catcher | W. Blum |
| 1972 | Riva Ridge | R. Turcotte |
| 1973 | Secretariat | R. Turcotte |
| 1974 | Little Current | M. Rivera |
| 1975 | Avatar | W. Shoemaker |
| 1976 | Bold Forbes | A. Cordero |
| 1977 | Seattle Slew | J. Cruguet |
| 1978 | Affirmed | S. Cauthen |
| 1979 | Coastal | R. Hernandez |
| 1980 | Temperence Hill | E. Maple |
| 1981 | Summing | G. Martens |
| 1982 | Conquistador Cielo | L. Pincay |
| 1983 | Caveat | L. Pincay |
| 1984 | Swale | L. Pincay |
| 1985 | Creme Fraiche | E. Maple |
| 1986 | Danzig Connection | C. McCarron |
| 1987 | Bet Twice | C. Perret |
| 1988 | Risen Star | E. Delahoussaye |
| 1989 | Easy Goer | P. Day |
| 1990 | Go and Go | M. Kinane |
| 1991 | Hansel | J. Bailey |
| 1992 | A.P. Indy | E. Delahoussaye |
| 1993 | Colonial Affair | J. Krone |
| 1994 | Tabasco Cat | P. Day |
| 1995 | Thunder Gulch | G. Stevens |
| 1996 | Editor's Note | R. Douglas |

## Annual Leading Jockey—Money Won

| Year | Jockey | Dollars |
|---|---|---|
| 1957 | Bill Hartack | $3,060,501 |
| 1958 | Willie Shoemaker | 2,961,693 |
| 1959 | Willie Shoemaker | 2,843,133 |
| 1960 | Willie Shoemaker | 2,123,961 |
| 1961 | Willie Shoemaker | 2,690,819 |
| 1962 | Willie Shoemaker | 2,916,844 |
| 1963 | Willie Shoemaker | 2,526,925 |
| 1964 | Willie Shoemaker | 2,649,553 |
| 1965 | Braulio Baeza | 2,582,702 |
| 1966 | Braulio Baeza | 2,951,022 |
| 1967 | Braulio Baeza | 3,088,888 |
| 1968 | Braulio Baeza | 2,835,108 |
| 1969 | Jorge Velasquez | 2,542,315 |
| 1970 | Laffit Pincay, Jr. | $2,626,526 |
| 1971 | Laffit Pincay, Jr. | 3,784,377 |
| 1972 | Laffit Pincay, Jr. | 3,225,827 |
| 1973 | Laffit Pincay, Jr. | 4,093,492 |
| 1974 | Laffit Pincay, Jr. | 4,251,060 |
| 1975 | Braulio Baeza | 3,695,198 |
| 1976 | Angel Cordero, Jr. | 4,709,500 |
| 1977 | Steve Cauthen | 6,151,750 |
| 1978 | Darrel McHargue | 6,029,885 |
| 1979 | Laffit Pincay, Jr. | 8,193,535 |
| 1980 | Chris McCarron | 7,663,300 |
| 1981 | Chris McCarron | 8,397,604 |
| 1982 | Angel Cordero, Jr. | 9,483,590 |
| 1983 | Angel Cordero, Jr. | $10,116,697 |
| 1984 | Chris McCarron | 12,045,813 |
| 1985 | Laffit Pincay, Jr. | 13,353,299 |
| 1986 | Jose Santos | 11,329,297 |
| 1987 | Jose Santos | 12,375,433 |
| 1988 | Jose Santos | 14,877,298 |
| 1989 | Jose Santos | 13,838,389 |
| 1990 | Gary Stevens | 13,881,198 |
| 1991 | Chris McCarron | 14,441,083 |
| 1992 | Kent Desormeaux | 14,193,006 |
| 1993 | Mike Smith | 14,024,815 |
| 1994 | Mike Smith | 15,979,820 |
| 1995 | Jerry Bailey | 16,311,876 |

# Breeders' Cup

The Breeders' Cup was inaugurated in 1984 and consists of 7 races at one track on one day late in the year to determine thoroughbred racing's champion contenders.

## Juvenile

Distances: 1 mi 1984-85, 87; 1-1/16 mi 1986 and since 1988

| Year | | Jockey | Year | | Jockey | Year | | Jockey |
|---|---|---|---|---|---|---|---|---|
| 1984 | Chief's Crown | D. MacBeth | 1989 | Rhythm | C. Perret | 1993 | Brocco | G. Stevens |
| 1985 | Tasso | L. Pincay, Jr. | 1990 | Fly So Free | J. Santos | 1994 | Timber Country | P. Day |
| 1986 | Capote | L. Pincay, Jr. | 1991 | Arazi | P. Valenzuela | 1995 | Unbridled's Song | M. Smith |
| 1987 | Success Express | J. Santos | 1992 | Gilded Time | C. McCarron | 1996 | Boston Harbor | J. Bailey |
| 1988 | Is It True | L. Pincay, Jr. | | | | | | |

## Juvenile Fillies

Distances: 1 mi 1984-85, 87; 1-1/16 mi 1986 and since 1988

| Year | | Jockey | Year | | Jockey | Year | | Jockey |
|---|---|---|---|---|---|---|---|---|
| 1984 | *Outstandingly | W. Guerra | 1989 | Go for Wand | R. Romero | 1993 | Phone Chatter | L. Pincay, Jr. |
| 1985 | Twilight Ridge | J. Velasquez | 1990 | Meadow Star | J. Santos | 1994 | Flanders | P. Day |
| 1986 | Brave Raj | P. Valenzuela | 1991 | Pleasant Stage | E. Delahoussaye | 1995 | My Flag | J. Bailey |
| 1987 | Epitome | P. Day | 1992 | Eliza | P. Valenzuela | 1996 | Storm Song | C. Perret |
| 1988 | Open Mind | A. Cordero, Jr. | | | | | | |

*By disqualification.

## Sprint

Distance: 6 furlongs

| Year | | Jockey | Year | | Jockey | Year | | Jockey |
|---|---|---|---|---|---|---|---|---|
| 1984 | Eillo | C. Perret | 1989 | Dancing Spree | A. Cordero, Jr. | 1993 | Cardmania | E. Delahoussaye |
| 1985 | Precisionist | C. McCarron | 1990 | Safely Kept | C. Perret | 1994 | Cherokee Run | M. Smith |
| 1986 | Smile | J. Vasquez | 1991 | Sheikh Albadou | P. Eddery | 1995 | Desert Stormer | K. Desormeaux |
| 1987 | Very Subtle | P. Valenzuela | 1992 | Thirty Slews | E. Delahoussaye | 1996 | Lit De Justice | C. Nakatani |
| 1988 | Gulch | A. Cordero, Jr. | | | | | | |

## Mile

| Year | | Jockey | Year | | Jockey | Year | | Jockey |
|---|---|---|---|---|---|---|---|---|
| 1984 | Royal Heroine | F. Toro | 1989 | Steinlen | J. Santos | 1993 | Lure | M. Smith |
| 1985 | Cozzene | W. Guerra | 1990 | Royal Academy | L. Piggott | 1994 | Barathea | L. Dettori |
| 1986 | Last Tycoon | Y. St.-Martin | 1991 | Opening Verse | P. Valenzuela | 1995 | Ridgewood Pearl | J. Murtagh |
| 1987 | Miesque | F. Head | 1992 | Lure | M. Smith | 1996 | Da Hoss | G. Stevens |
| 1988 | Miesque | F. Head | | | | | | |

## Distaff

Distances: 1-1/4 mi 1984-87; 1-1/8 mi since 1988

| Year | | Jockey | Year | | Jockey | Year | | Jockey |
|---|---|---|---|---|---|---|---|---|
| 1984 | Princess Rooney | E. Delahoussaye | 1988 | Personal Ensign | R. Romero | 1993 | Hollywood Wildcat | E. Delahoussaye |
| 1985 | Life's Magic | A. Cordero, Jr. | 1989 | Bayakoa | L. Pincay, Jr. | 1994 | One Dreamer | G. Stevens |
| 1986 | Lady's Secret | P. Day | 1990 | Bayakoa | L. Pincay, Jr. | 1995 | Inside Information | M. Smith |
| 1987 | Sacahuista | R. Romero | 1991 | Dance Smartly | P. Day | 1996 | Jewel Princess | C. Nakatani |
| | | | 1992 | Paseana | C. McCarron | | | |

## Turf

Distance: 1-1/2 mi

| Year | | Jockey | Year | | Jockey | Year | | Jockey |
|---|---|---|---|---|---|---|---|---|
| 1984 | Lashkari | Y. St.-Martin | 1988 | Great Communicator | R. Sibille | 1992 | Fraise | P. Valenzuela |
| 1985 | Pebbles | P. Eddery | 1989 | Prized | E. Delahoussaye | 1993 | Kotashaan | K. Desormeaux |
| 1986 | Manila | J. Santos | 1990 | In The Wings | G. Stevens | 1994 | Tikkanen | M. Smith |
| 1987 | Theatrical | P. Day | 1991 | Miss Alleged | E. Legrix | 1995 | Northern Spur | C. McCarron |
| | | | | | | 1996 | Pilsudski | W. Swinburn |

## Classic

Distance: 1-1/4 mi

| Year | | Jockey | Year | | Jockey | Year | | Jockey |
|---|---|---|---|---|---|---|---|---|
| 1984 | Wild Again | P. Day | 1989 | Sunday Silence | C. McCarron | 1992 | A.P. Indy | E. Delahoussaye |
| 1985 | Proud Truth | J. Velasquez | 1990 | Unbridled | P. Day | 1993 | Arcangues | J. Bailey |
| 1986 | Skywalker | L. Pincay, Jr. | 1991 | Black Tie Affair | J. Bailey | 1994 | Concern | J. Bailey |
| 1987 | Ferdinand | W. Shoemaker | | | | 1995 | Cigar | J. Bailey |
| 1988 | Alysheba | C. McCarron | | | | 1996 | Alphabet Soup | C. McCarron |

# Eclipse Awards

The Eclipse Awards, honoring the Horse of the Year and other champions of the sport, began in 1971 and are sponsored by the *Daily Racing Form,* the Thoroughbred Racing Associations, and the National Turf Writers Assn. Prior to 1971, the DRF (1936-70) and the TRA (1950-70) issued separate selections for horse of the year.

## Eclipse Awards for 1995

**Horse of the Year**—Cigar
**2-year-old colt or gelding**—Maria's Mon
**2-year-old filly**—Golden Attraction
**3-year-old colt or gelding**—Thunder Gulch
**3-year-old filly**—Serena's Song
**Older male** (4-year-olds & up)—Cigar
**Older female** (4-year-olds & up)—Inside Information
**Male turf horse**—Northern Spur
**Turf filly or mare**—Possibly Perfect
**Sprinter**—Not Surprising
**Steeplechase horse**—Lonesome Glory
**Trainer**—William I. Mott
**Jockey**—Jerry Bailey
**Apprentice jockey**—Ramon B. Perez
**Breeder**—Juddmonte Farms
**Owner**—Allen Paulson

## Horse of the Year

| Year | Horse | Year | Horse | Year | Horse | Year | Horse |
|---|---|---|---|---|---|---|---|
| 1936 | Granville | 1952 | One Count (DRF) Native Dancer (TRA) | 1966 | Buckpasser | 1981 | John Henry |
| 1937 | War Admiral | 1953 | Tom Fool | 1967 | Damascus | 1982 | Conquistador Cielo |
| 1938 | Seabiscuit | 1954 | Native Dancer | 1968 | Dr. Fager | 1983 | All Along |
| 1939 | Challedon | 1955 | Nashua | 1969 | Arts and Letters | 1984 | John Henry |
| 1940 | Challedon | 1956 | Swaps | 1970 | Fort Marcy (DRF) Personality (TRA) | 1985 | Spend A Buck |
| 1941 | Whirlaway | 1957 | Bold Ruler (DRF) Dedicate (TRA) | 1971 | Ack Ack | 1986 | Lady's Secret |
| 1942 | Whirlaway | 1958 | Round Table | 1972 | Secretariat | 1987 | Ferdinand |
| 1943 | Count Fleet | 1959 | Sword Dancer | 1973 | Secretariat | 1988 | Alysheba |
| 1944 | Twilight Tear | 1960 | Kelso | 1974 | Forego | 1989 | Sunday Silence |
| 1945 | Busher | 1961 | Kelso | 1975 | Forego | 1990 | Criminal Type |
| 1946 | Assault | 1962 | Kelso | 1976 | Forego | 1991 | Black Tie Affair |
| 1947 | Armed | 1963 | Kelso | 1977 | Seattle Slew | 1992 | A.P. Indy |
| 1948 | Citation | 1964 | Kelso | 1978 | Affirmed | 1993 | Kotashaan |
| 1949 | Capot | 1965 | Roman Brother (DRF) Moccasin (TRA) | 1979 | Affirmed | 1994 | Holy Bull |
| 1950 | Hill Prince | | | 1980 | Spectacular Bid | 1995 | Cigar |
| 1951 | Counterpoint | | | | | | |

# HARNESS RACING

## Harness Horse of the Year

(Chosen by the U.S. Trotting Assn. and the U.S. Harness Writers Assn.)

| Year | Horse | Year | Horse | Year | Horse | Year | Horse |
|---|---|---|---|---|---|---|---|
| 1951 | Pronto Don | 1963 | Speedy Scot | 1974 | Delmonica Hanover | 1985 | Nihilator |
| 1952 | Good Time | 1964 | Bret Hanover | 1975 | Savior | 1986 | Forrest Skipper |
| 1953 | Hi Lo's Forbes | 1965 | Bret Hanover | 1976 | Keystone Ore | 1987 | Mack Lobell |
| 1954 | Stenographer | 1966 | Bret Hanover | 1977 | Green Speed | 1988 | Mack Lobell |
| 1955 | Scott Frost | 1967 | Nevele Pride | 1978 | Abercrombie | 1989 | Matt's Scooter |
| 1956 | Scott Frost | 1968 | Nevele Pride | 1979 | Niatross | 1990 | Beach Towel |
| 1957 | Torpid | 1969 | Nevele Pride | 1980 | Niatross | 1991 | Precious Bunny |
| 1958 | Emily's Pride | 1970 | Fresh Yankee | 1981 | Fan Hanover | 1992 | Artsplace |
| 1959 | Bye Bye Byrd | 1971 | Albatross | 1982 | Cam Fella | 1993 | Staying Together |
| 1960 | Adios Butler | 1972 | Albatross | 1983 | Cam Fella | 1994 | Cam's Card Shark |
| 1961 | Adios Butler | 1973 | Sir Dalrae | 1984 | Fancy Crown | 1995 | CR Kay Suzie |
| 1962 | Su Mac Lad | | | | | | |

## The Hambletonian (3-year-old trotters)

| Year | Winner | Driver | Year | Winner | Driver |
|---|---|---|---|---|---|
| 1965 | Egyptian Candor | Del Cameron | 1981 | Shiaway St. Pat | Ray Remmen |
| 1966 | Kerry Way | Frank Ervin | 1982 | Speed Bowl | Tommy Haughton |
| 1967 | Speedy Streak | Del Cameron | 1983 | Duenna | Stanley Dancer |
| 1968 | Nevele Pride | Stanley Dancer | 1984 | Historic Freight | Ben Webster |
| 1969 | Lindy's Pride | Howard Beissinger | 1985 | Prakas | Bill O'Donnell |
| 1970 | Timothy T | John Simpson, Sr. | 1986 | Nuclear Kosmos | Ulf Thoresen |
| 1971 | Speedy Crown | Howard Beissinger | 1987 | Mack Lobell | John Campbell |
| 1972 | Super Bowl | Stanley Dancer | 1988 | Armbro Goal | John Campbell |
| 1973 | Flirth | Ralph Baldwin | 1989 | Park Avenue Joe | Ron Waples |
| 1974 | Christopher T | Bill Haughton | 1990 | Harmonious | John Campbell |
| 1975 | Bonefish | Stanley Dancer | 1991 | Giant Victory | Jack Moiseyev |
| 1976 | Steve Lobell | Bill Haughton | 1992 | Alf Palema | Mickey McNicholl |
| 1977 | Green Speed | Bill Haughton | 1993 | American Winner | Ron Pierce |
| 1978 | Speedy Somolli | Howard Beissinger | 1994 | Victory Dream | Michel Lachance |
| 1979 | Legend Hanover | George Sholty | 1995 | Tagliabue | John Campbell |
| 1980 | Burgomeister | Bill Haughton | 1996 | Continentalvictory | Michel Lachance |

# BOWLING

## Professional Bowlers Association

### Hall of Fame

**Performance**
Bill Allen
Glenn Allison
Earl Anthony
Barry Asher
Mike Aulby
Ray Bluth
Roy Buckley
Nelson Burton, Jr.
Don Carter
Pat Colwell
Steve Cook
Dave Davis
Gary Dickinson
Mike Durbin
Buzz Fazio
Skee Foremsky
Jim Godman
Johnny Guenther
Billy Hardwick
Tommy Hudson
Dave Husted
Don Johnson
Joe Joseph
Larry Laub
Mike Limongello
Don McCune
Mike McGrath
David Ozio
George Pappas
Johnny Petraglia
Dick Ritger
Mark Roth
Jim St. John
Carmen Salvino
Bob Strampe
Harry Smith
Dave Soutar
Jim Stefanich
Brian Voss
Wayne Webb
Dick Weber
Billy Welu
Walter Ray Williams, Jr.
Wayne Zahn

**Meritorious service**
Joe Antenora
John Archibald
Chuck Clemens
Eddie Elias
Frank Esposito
Dick Evans
Raymond Firestone
E. A. "Bud" Fisher
Lou Frantz
Harry Golden
Ted Hoffman, Jr.
John Jowdy
Joe Kelley
Larry Lichstein
Steve Nagy
Chuck Pezzano
Jack Reichert
Joe Richards
Chris Schenkel
Lorraine Stilzlein
Al Thompson
Roger Zeller

### Tournament of Champions

| Year | Winner | Year | Winner | Year | Winner | Year | Winner |
|---|---|---|---|---|---|---|---|
| 1965 | Billy Hardwick | 1973 | Jim Godman | 1981 | Steve Cook | 1989 | Del Ballard, Jr. |
| 1966 | Wayne Zahn | 1974 | Earl Anthony | 1982 | Mike Durbin | 1990 | Dave Ferraro |
| 1967 | Jim Stefanich | 1975 | Dave Davis | 1983 | Joe Berardi | 1991 | David Ozio |
| 1968 | Dave Davis | 1976 | Marshall Holman | 1984 | Mike Durbin | 1992 | Marc McDowell |
| 1969 | Jim Godman | 1977 | Mike Berlin | 1985 | Mark Williams | 1993 | George Branham, 3d |
| 1970 | Don Johnson | 1978 | Earl Anthony | 1986 | Marshall Holman | 1994 | Norm Duke |
| 1971 | Johnny Petraglia | 1979 | George Pappas | 1987 | Pete Weber | 1995 | Mike Aulby |
| 1972 | Mike Durbin | 1980 | Wayne Webb | 1988 | Mark Williams | 1996 | Dave D'Entremont |

## PBA Leading Money Winners

Total winnings are from PBA, ABC Masters, and BPAA All-Star tournaments only and do not include numerous other tournaments or earnings from special television shows and matches.

| Year | Bowler | Amount |
|---|---|---|
| 1962 | Don Carter | $49,972 |
| 1963 | Dick Weber | 46,333 |
| 1964 | Bob Strampe | 33,592 |
| 1965 | Dick Weber | 47,674 |
| 1966 | Wayne Zahn | 54,720 |
| 1967 | Dave Davis | 54,165 |
| 1968 | Jim Stefanich | 67,377 |
| 1969 | Billy Hardwick | 64,160 |
| 1970 | Mike McGrath | 52,049 |
| 1971 | Johnny Petraglia | 85,065 |
| 1972 | Don Johnson | 56,648 |
| 1973 | Don McCune | 69,000 |
| 1974 | Earl Anthony | $99,585 |
| 1975 | Earl Anthony | 107,585 |
| 1976 | Earl Anthony | 110,833 |
| 1977 | Mark Roth | 105,583 |
| 1978 | Mark Roth | 134,500 |
| 1979 | Mark Roth | 124,517 |
| 1980 | Wayne Webb | 116,700 |
| 1981 | Earl Anthony | 164,735 |
| 1982 | Earl Anthony | 134,760 |
| 1983 | Earl Anthony | 135,605 |
| 1984 | Mark Roth | 158,712 |
| 1985 | Mike Aulby | 201,200 |
| 1986 | Walter Ray Williams, Jr. | $145,550 |
| 1987 | Pete Weber | 175,491 |
| 1988 | Brian Voss | 225,485 |
| 1989 | Mike Aulby | 298,237 |
| 1990 | Amleto Monacelli | 204,775 |
| 1991 | David Ozio | 225,585 |
| 1992 | Marc McDowell | 174,215 |
| 1993 | Walter Ray Williams, Jr. | 296,370 |
| 1994 | Norm Duke | 273,753 |
| 1995 | Mike Aulby | 219,792 |

## Leading PBA Averages by Year

| Year | Bowler | Average |
|---|---|---|
| 1962 | Don Carter | 212.844 |
| 1963 | Billy Hardwick | 210.346 |
| 1964 | Ray Bluth | 210.512 |
| 1965 | Dick Weber | 211.895 |
| 1966 | Wayne Zahn | 208.663 |
| 1967 | Wayne Zahn | 212.342 |
| 1968 | Jim Stefanich | 211.895 |
| 1969 | Bill Hardwick | 212.957 |
| 1970 | Nelson Burton, Jr. | 214.908 |
| 1971 | Don Johnson | 213.977 |
| 1972 | Don Johnson | 215.290 |
| 1973 | Earl Anthony | 215.799 |
| 1974 | Earl Anthony | 219.394 |
| 1975 | Earl Anthony | 219.060 |
| 1976 | Mark Roth | 215.970 |
| 1977 | Mark Roth | 218.174 |
| 1978 | Mark Roth | 219.834 |
| 1979 | Mark Roth | 221.662 |
| 1980 | Earl Anthony | 218.535 |
| 1981 | Mark Roth | 216.699 |
| 1982 | Marshall Holman | 212.844 |
| 1983 | Earl Anthony | 216.645 |
| 1984 | Marshall Holman | 213.911 |
| 1985 | Mark Baker | 213.718 |
| 1986 | John Gant | 214.378 |
| 1987 | Marshall Holman | 216.801 |
| 1988 | Mark Roth | 218.036 |
| 1989 | Pete Weber | 215.432 |
| 1990 | Amleto Monacelli | 218.158 |
| 1991 | Norm Duke | 218.208 |
| 1992 | Dave Ferraro | 219.702 |
| 1993 | Walter Ray Williams, Jr. | 222.980 |
| 1994 | Norm Duke | 222.830 |
| 1995 | Mike Aulby | 225.490 |

# American Bowling Congress

## ABC Masters Tournament Champions

| Year | Winner |
|---|---|
| 1980 | Neil Burton, St. Louis, MO |
| 1981 | Randy Lightfoot, St. Charles, MO |
| 1982 | Joe Berardi, Brooklyn, NY |
| 1983 | Mike Lastowski, Havre de Grace, MD |
| 1984 | Earl Anthony, Dublin, CA |
| 1985 | Steve Wunderlich, St. Louis, MO |
| 1986 | Mark Fahy, Chicago, IL |
| 1987 | Rick Steelsmith, Wichita, KS |
| 1988 | Del Ballard, Jr., Richardson, TX |
| 1989 | Mike Aulby, Indianapolis, IN |
| 1990 | Chris Warren, Dallas, TX |
| 1991 | Doug Kent, Canandaigua, NY |
| 1992 | Ken Johnson, N. Richmond Hills, TX |
| 1993 | Norm Duke, Oklahoma City, OK |
| 1994 | Steve Fehr, Cincinnati, OH |
| 1995 | Mike Aulby, Indianapolis, IN |
| 1996 | Ernie Schlegel, Vancouver, WA |

## Champions in 1996

**Singles**—Don Scudder, Cincinnati, OH
**Doubles Event**—Drew Hauck, Finneytown, OH, and Jamie Burke, Loveland, OH
**All Events**—Scott Kurtz, Somerset, NJ
**Regular Team**—Trout's Minnows, Spokane, WA
**Booster Team**—Canterbury Lanes No. 4, Grove, OK

## Most Sanctioned 300 Games

| | |
|---|---|
| Mike Whalin, Cincinnati, OH | 52 |
| Jim Johnson, Jr., Wilmington, DE | 52 |
| Bob Learn, Jr., Erie, PA | 51 |
| Joe Jimenez, Saginaw, MI | 41 |
| Jerry Kessler, Dayton, OH | 40 |
| Jeff Jensen, Wichita, KS | 39 |
| Ralph Burley, Jr., Dayton, OH | 38 |
| Bob Buckery, McAdoo, PA | 37 |
| Ron Woolet, Louisville, KY | 33 |
| John Wilcox, Jr., Shavertown, PA | 33 |
| Eric Roddy, New Orleans, LA | 32 |
| Bob Johnson, Dayton, OH | 32 |
| Doug Spicer, W. Bloomfield, MI | 31 |
| Steve Gehringer, Reading, PA | 30 |
| Jim Ewald, Jr., Louisville, KY | 29 |
| Randy Choat, Granite City, IL | 29 |
| Woody Crist, Williamsport, PA | 29 |
| Alan Hulsizer, Reading, PA | 28 |
| John Chako, Jr., Larksville, PA | 28 |
| Jason Hurd, Tulare, CA | 28 |
| Elvin Mesger, Sullivan, MO | 27 |
| Mark Stibora, Cleveland, OH | 26 |
| Anthony Juliano, Margate, FL | 25 |
| Dave Soutar, Kansas City, MO | 25 |
| Gary Barney, St. Louis, MO | 25 |
| Mitch Jabczenski, Detroit, MI | 25 |
| Steve Levering, Landisville, PA | 25 |
| Jerome Penxa, Detroit, MI | 25 |
| Paul Masminster, Cincinnati, OH | 24 |
| Tony Torrice, Wolcott, CT | 24 |
| Teata Semiz, Fairfield, NJ | 23 |
| Don Anthony, Columbus, OH | 23 |
| Steve Carson, Oklahoma City, OK | 23 |

# Women's International Bowling Congress

## Champions in 1996

**Queens Tournament**—Lisa Wagner, Bradenton, FL
**Singles Event**—Cindy Berlanga, San Antonio, TX
**All Events**—Lorrie Nichols, Algonquin, IL
**Doubles Event**—Mandy Wilson and Linda Kelly, Dayton, OH
**Team**—The Naccarato Group, Tacoma, WA

## Most Sanctioned 300 Games

| | |
|---|---|
| Tish Johnson, Panorama City, CA | 25 |
| Jeanne Maiden-Naccarato, Tacoma, WA | 21 |
| Aleta Sill, Dearborn, MI | 17 |
| Vicki Fischel, Wheat Ridge, CO | 17 |
| Leanne Barrette, Youkon, OK | 15 |
| Cheryl Daniels, Detroit, MI | 15 |
| Cindy Coburn-Carroll, Tonawanda, NY | 13 |
| Betty Morris, Stockton, CA | 12 |
| Donna Adamek, Apple Valley, CA. | 11 |
| Robin Romeo, Van Nuys, CA | 9 |

# Figure Skating Champions

## U.S. Champions

| Men | Women |
|---|---|
| Dick Button | Tenley Albright |
| Hayes Jenkins | Tenley Albright |
| Hayes Jenkins | Tenley Albright |
| Hayes Jenkins | Tenley Albright |
| Hayes Jenkins | Tenley Albright |
| Dave Jenkins | Carol Heiss |
| Dave Jenkins | Carol Heiss |
| Dave Jenkins | Carol Heiss |
| Dave Jenkins | Carol Heiss |
| Bradley Lord | Laurence Owen |
| Monty Hoyt | Barbara Roles Pursley |
| Tommy Litz | Lorraine Hanlon |
| Scott Allen | Peggy Fleming |
| Gary Visconti | Peggy Fleming |
| Scott Allen | Peggy Fleming |
| Gary Visconti | Peggy Fleming |
| Tim Wood | Peggy Fleming |
| Tim Wood | Janet Lynn |
| Tim Wood | Janet Lynn |
| John Misha Petkevich | Janet Lynn |
| Ken Shelley | Janet Lynn |
| Gordon McKellen, Jr. | Janet Lynn |
| Gordon McKellen, Jr. | Dorothy Hamill |
| Gordon McKellen, Jr. | Dorothy Hamill |
| Terry Kubicka | Dorothy Hamill |
| Charles Tickner | Linda Fratianne |
| Charles Tickner | Linda Fratianne |
| Charles Tickner | Linda Fratianne |
| Charles Tickner | Linda Fratianne |
| Scott Hamilton | Elaine Zayak |
| Scott Hamilton | Rosalynn Sumners |
| Scott Hamilton | Rosalynn Sumners |
| Scott Hamilton | Rosalynn Sumners |
| Brian Boitano | Tiffany Chin |
| Brian Boitano | Debi Thomas |
| Brian Boitano | Jill Trenary |
| Brian Boitano | Debi Thomas |
| Christopher Bowman | Jill Trenary |
| Todd Eldredge | Jill Trenary |
| Todd Eldredge | Tonya Harding |
| Christopher Bowman | Kristi Yamaguchi |
| Scott Davis | Nancy Kerrigan |
| Scott Davis | vacant[1] |
| Todd Eldredge | Nicole Bobek |
| Rudy Galindo | Michelle Kwan |

(1) Tonya Harding was stripped of title.

## World Champions

| Year | Men | Women |
|---|---|---|
| 1952 | Dick Button, U.S. | Jacqueline du Bief, France |
| 1953 | Hayes Jenkins, U.S. | Tenley Albright, U.S. |
| 1954 | Hayes Jenkins, U.S. | Gundi Busch, W. Germany |
| 1955 | Hayes Jenkins, U.S. | Tenley Albright, U.S. |
| 1956 | Hayes Jenkins, U.S. | Carol Heiss, U.S. |
| 1957 | Dave Jenkins, U.S. | Carol Heiss, U.S. |
| 1958 | Dave Jenkins, U.S. | Carol Heiss, U.S. |
| 1959 | Dave Jenkins, U.S. | Carol Heiss, U.S. |
| 1960 | Alain Giletti, France | Carol Heiss, U.S. |
| 1961 | none | none |
| 1962 | Don Jackson, Canada | Sjoukje Dijkstra, Neth. |
| 1963 | Don McPherson, Canada | Sjoukje Dijkstra, Neth. |
| 1964 | Manfred Schnelldorfer, W. Germany | Sjoukje Dijkstra, Neth. |
| 1965 | Alain Calmat, France | Petra Burka, Canada |
| 1966 | Emmerich Danzer, Austria | Peggy Fleming, U.S. |
| 1967 | Emmerich Danzer, Austria | Peggy Fleming, U.S. |
| 1968 | Emmerich Danzer, Austria | Peggy Fleming, U.S. |
| 1969 | Tim Wood, U.S. | Gabriele Seyfert, E. Germany |
| 1970 | Tim Wood, U.S. | Gabriele Seyfert, E. Germany |
| 1971 | Ondrej Nepela, Czech. | Beatrix Schuba, Austria |
| 1972 | Ondrej Nepela, Czech. | Beatrix Schuba, Austria |
| 1973 | Ondrej Nepela, Czech. | Karen Magnussen, Canada |
| 1974 | Jan Hoffmann, E. Germany | Christine Errath, E. Germany |
| 1975 | Sergei Volkov, USSR | Dianne de Leeuw, Neth.-U.S. |
| 1976 | John Curry, Gr. Britain | Dorothy Hamill, U.S. |
| 1977 | Vladimir Kovalev, USSR | Linda Fratianne, U.S. |
| 1978 | Charles Tickner, U.S. | Anett Poetzsch, E. Germany |
| 1979 | Vladimir Kovalev, USSR | Linda Fratianne, U.S. |
| 1980 | Jan Hoffmann, E. Germany | Anett Poetzsch, E. Germany |
| 1981 | Scott Hamilton, U.S. | Denise Biellmann, Switzerland |
| 1982 | Scott Hamilton, U.S. | Elaine Zayak, U.S. |
| 1983 | Scott Hamilton, U.S. | Rosalynn Sumners, U.S. |
| 1984 | Scott Hamilton, U.S. | Katarina Witt, E. Germany |
| 1985 | Aleksandr Fadeev, USSR | Katarina Witt, E. Germany |
| 1986 | Brian Boitano, U.S. | Debi Thomas, U.S. |
| 1987 | Brian Orser, Canada | Katarina Witt, E. Germany |
| 1988 | Brian Boitano, U.S. | Katarina Witt, E. Germany |
| 1989 | Kurt Browning, Canada | Midori Ito, Japan |
| 1990 | Kurt Browning, Canada | Jill Trenary, U.S. |
| 1991 | Kurt Browning, Canada | Kristi Yamaguchi, U.S. |
| 1992 | Viktor Petrenko, Ukraine | Kristi Yamaguchi, U.S. |
| 1993 | Kurt Browning, Canada | Oksana Baiul, Ukraine |
| 1994 | Elvis Stojko, Canada | Yuka Sato, Japan |
| 1995 | Elvis Stojko, Canada | Chen Lu, China |
| 1996 | Todd Eldredge, U.S. | Michelle Kwan, U.S. |

# James E. Sullivan Memorial Trophy Winners

The James E. Sullivan Memorial Trophy, named after the former president of the AAU and inaugurated in 1930, is awarded annually by the AAU to the athlete who "by his or her performance, example and influence as an amateur, has done the most during the year to advance the cause of sportsmanship."

| Year | Winner | Sport |
|---|---|---|
| 1930 | Bobby Jones | Golf |
| 1931 | Barney Berlinger | Track |
| 1932 | Jim Bausch | Track |
| 1933 | Glenn Cunningham | Track |
| 1934 | Bill Bonthron | Track |
| 1935 | Lawson Little | Golf |
| 1936 | Glenn Morris | Track |
| 1937 | Don Budge | Tennis |
| 1938 | Don Lash | Track |
| 1939 | Joe Burk | Rowing |
| 1940 | Greg Rice | Track |
| 1941 | Leslie MacMitchell | Track |
| 1942 | Cornelius Warmerdam | Track |
| 1943 | Gilbert Dodds | Track |
| 1944 | Ann Curtis | Swimming |
| 1945 | Doc Blanchard | Football |
| 1946 | Arnold Tucker | Football |
| 1947 | John Kelly, Jr. | Rowing |
| 1948 | Robert Mathias | Track |
| 1949 | Dick Button | Skating |
| 1950 | Fred Wilt | Track |
| 1951 | Rev. Robert Richards | Track |
| 1952 | Horace Ashenfelter | Track |
| 1953 | Dr. Sammy Lee | Diving |
| 1954 | Mal Whitfield | Track |
| 1955 | Harrison Dillard | Track |
| 1956 | Patricia McCormick | Diving |
| 1957 | Bobby Joe Morrow | Track |
| 1958 | Glenn Davis | Track |
| 1959 | Parry O'Brien | Track |
| 1960 | Rafer Johnson | Track |
| 1961 | Wilma Rudolph Ward | Track |
| 1962 | James Beatty | Track |
| 1963 | John Pennel | Track |
| 1964 | Don Schollander | Swimming |
| 1965 | Bill Bradley | Basketball |
| 1966 | Jim Ryun | Track |
| 1967 | Randy Matson | Track |
| 1968 | Debbie Meyer | Swimming |
| 1969 | Bill Toomey | Track |
| 1970 | John Kinsella | Swimming |
| 1971 | Mark Spitz | Swimming |
| 1972 | Frank Shorter | Track |
| 1973 | Bill Walton | Basketball |
| 1974 | Rick Wohlhutter | Track |
| 1975 | Tim Shaw | Swimming |
| 1976 | Bruce Jenner | Track |
| 1977 | John Naber | Swimming |
| 1978 | Tracy Caulkins | Swimming |
| 1979 | Kurt Thomas | Gymnastics |
| 1980 | Eric Heiden | Speed Skating |
| 1981 | Carl Lewis | Track |
| 1982 | Mary Decker | Track |
| 1983 | Edwin Moses | Track |
| 1984 | Greg Louganis | Diving |
| 1985 | Joan Benoit Samuelson | Marathon |
| 1986 | Jackie Joyner-Kersee | Track |
| 1987 | Jim Abbott | Baseball |
| 1988 | Florence Griffith Joyner | Track |
| 1989 | Janet Evans | Swimming |
| 1990 | John Smith | Wrestling |
| 1991 | Mike Powell | Track |
| 1992 | Bonnie Blair | Speed Skating |
| 1993 | Charlie Ward | Football, Basketball |
| 1994 | Dan Jansen | Speed Skating |
| 1995 | Bruce Baumgartner | Wrestling |

# Directory of Sports Organizations

## Major League Baseball

**Internet Site:** http://www.majorleaguebaseball.com

Commissioner's Office
350 Park Ave.
New York, NY 10022

**National League**

National League Office
350 Park Ave.
New York, NY 10022

Atlanta Braves
521 Capitol Ave. SW
Atlanta, GA 30312

Chicago Cubs
1060 W Addison St.
Chicago, IL 60613

Cincinnati Reds
100 Riverfront Stadium
Cincinnati, OH 45202

Colorado Rockies
2100 Blake St.
Denver, CO 80290

Florida Marlins
2267 NW 199th St.
Miami, FL 33056

Houston Astros
PO Box 288
Houston, TX 77001

Los Angeles Dodgers
Dodger Stadium
Los Angeles, CA 90012

Montreal Expos
PO Box 500, Station M
Montreal, Que. H1V 3P2

New York Mets
Shea Stadium
Flushing, NY 11368

Philadelphia Phillies
PO Box 7575
Philadelphia, PA 19101

Pittsburgh Pirates
Three Rivers Stadium
Pittsburgh, PA 15212

St. Louis Cardinals
Busch Memorial Stadium
St. Louis, MO 63102

San Diego Padres
PO Box 2000
San Diego, CA 92112

San Francisco Giants
3Com Park
San Francisco, CA 94124

**American League**

American League Office
350 Park Ave.
New York, NY 10022

Baltimore Orioles
333 W. Camden St.
Baltimore, MD 21202

Boston Red Sox
24 Yawkey Way
Boston, MA 02215

California Angels
PO Box 200
Anaheim, CA 92803

Chicago White Sox
333 W. 35th St.
Chicago, IL 60616

Cleveland Indians
2401 Ontario St.
Cleveland, OH 44115

Detroit Tigers
Tiger Stadium
Detroit, MI 48216

Kansas City Royals
P.O. Box 419969
Kansas City, MO 64141

Milwaukee Brewers
Milwaukee County Stadium
Milwaukee, WI 53214

Minnesota Twins
501 Chicago Ave. South
Minneapolis, MN 55415

New York Yankees
Yankee Stadium
Bronx, NY 10451

Oakland Athletics
Oakland Coliseum
Oakland, CA 94621

Seattle Mariners
PO Box 4100
Seattle, WA 98104

Texas Rangers
PO Box 90111
Arlington, TX 76004

Toronto Blue Jays
1 Blue Jays Way
Toronto, Ont. M5V 1J1

## National Basketball Association

**Internet Site:** http://www.nba.com

League Office
645 5th Ave.
New York, NY 10022

Atlanta Hawks
One CNN Center
Atlanta, GA 30303

Boston Celtics
151 Merrimac St.
Boston, MA 02114

Charlotte Hornets
100 Hive Dr.
Charlotte, NC 28217

Chicago Bulls
1901 W. Madison St.
Chicago, IL 60612

Cleveland Cavaliers
1 Center Court
Cleveland, OH 44115-4001

Dallas Mavericks
777 Sports St.
Dallas, TX 75207

Denver Nuggets
1635 Clay St.
Denver, CO 80204

Detroit Pistons
Two Championship Dr.
Auburn Hills, MI 48362

Golden State Warriors
7000 Coliseum Way
Oakland, CA 94621-1918

Houston Rockets
Ten Greenway Plaza
Houston, TX 77046-3865

Indiana Pacers
300 E. Market St.
Indianapolis, IN 46204

Los Angeles Clippers
3939 S. Figueroa St.
Los Angeles, CA 90037

Los Angeles Lakers
3900 W. Manchester Blvd.
Inglewood, CA 90306

Miami Heat
One Southeast Ave.
Miami, FL 33136-4102

Milwaukee Bucks
1001 N. 4th St.
Milwaukee, WI 53203-1312

Minnesota Timberwolves
600 1st Ave. N
Minneapolis, MN 55403

New Jersey Nets
405 Murray Hill Parkway
E. Rutherford, NJ 07073

New York Knickerbockers
Two Pennsylvania Plaza
New York, NY 10121-0091

Orlando Magic
One Magic Place
Orlando, FL 32801

Philadelphia 76ers
3601 S. Broad St.
Philadelphia, PA 19148

Phoenix Suns
201 E. Jefferson
Phoenix, AZ 85004

Portland Trail Blazers
One Center Ct., Ste. 200
Portland, OR 97227

Sacramento Kings
One Sports Parkway
Sacramento, CA 95834

San Antonio Spurs
100 Montana St.
San Antonio, TX 78203-1031

Seattle SuperSonics
190 Queen Ann Ave. N
Seattle, WA 98109-9711

Toronto Raptors
20 Bay St., Ste. 1702
Toronto, Ont. M5J 2N8

Utah Jazz
301 W. South Temple
Salt Lake City, UT 84101

Vancouver Grizzlies
800 Griffiths Way
Vancouver, B.C. V6B 6G1

Washington Bullets (Wizards)
USAir Arena
Landover, MD 20785

## National Hockey League

**Internet Site:** http://www.nhl.com

League Headquarters
1251 Ave. of the Americas
New York, NY 10020

Mighty Ducks of Anaheim
2695 E. Katella Ave.
Anaheim, CA 92803-6177

Boston Bruins
One FleetCenter
Boston, MA 02114

Buffalo Sabres
1 Main St.
Buffalo, NY 14203

Calgary Flames
PO Box 1540, Station M
Calgary, Alta. T2P 3B9

Chicago Blackhawks
1901 W. Madison St.
Chicago, IL 60612

Colorado Avalanche
1635 Clay St.
Denver, CO 80204

Dallas Stars
211 Cowboys Parkway
Irving, TX 75063

Detroit Red Wings
600 Civic Center Dr.
Detroit, MI 48226

Edmonton Oilers
11230-110 St.
Edmonton, Alta. T5G 3G8

Florida Panthers
100 NE Third Ave.
Ft. Lauderdale, FL 33301

Hartford Whalers
242 Trumbull St.
Hartford, CT 06103

Los Angeles Kings
3900 W. Manchester Blvd.
Inglewood, CA 90305

Montreal Canadiens
1260 rue de La Gauchetiere, Ouest
Montreal, Que. H3B 5E8

New Jersey Devils
PO Box 504
E. Rutherford, NJ 07073

*(continued)*

## National Hockey League (*continued*)

New York Islanders
Nassau Coliseum
Uniondale, NY 11553

New York Rangers
2 Pennsylvania Plaza
New York, NY 10001

Ottawa Senators
301 Moodie Dr.
Nepean, Ont. K2H 9C4

Philadelphia Flyers
3601 S. Broad St.
Philadelphia, PA 19148

Phoenix Coyotes
2 North Central
Phoenix, AZ 85004

Pittsburgh Penguins
Civic Arena
Pittsburgh, PA 15219

St. Louis Blues
1401 Clark
St. Louis, MO 63103

San Jose Sharks
525 W. Santa Clara St.
San Jose, CA 95113

Tampa Bay Lightning
401 Channelside Dr.
Tampa, FL 33602

Toronto Maple Leafs
60 Carlton St.
Toronto, Ont. M5B 1L1

Vancouver Canucks
800 Griffiths Way
Vancouver, B.C. V6B 6G1

Washington Capitals
USAir Arena
Landover, MD 20785

## National Football League

**Internet Site:** http://www.nfl.com

League Office
410 Park Avenue
New York, NY 10022

Arizona Cardinals
PO Box 888
Phoenix, AZ 85001-0888

Atlanta Falcons
One Falcon Place
Suwanee, GA 30174

Baltimore Ravens
11001 Owings Mills Blvd.
Owings Mills, MD 21117

Buffalo Bills
One Bills Drive
Orchard Park, NY 14127

Carolina Panthers
800 S. Mint St.
Charlotte, NC 28202-1502

Chicago Bears
250 N. Washington Rd.
Lake Forest, IL 60045

Cincinnati Bengals
200 Riverfront Stadium
Cincinnati, OH 45202

Dallas Cowboys
One Cowboys Parkway
Irving, TX 75063

Denver Broncos
13655 Broncos Parkway
Englewood, CO 80112

Detroit Lions
1200 Featherstone Rd.
Pontiac, MI 48342

Green Bay Packers
PO Box 10628
Green Bay, WI 54307-0628

Houston Oilers
8030 El Rio
Houston, TX 77054

Indianapolis Colts
PO Box 535000
Indianapolis, IN 46253

Jacksonville Jaguars
One Stadium Place
Jacksonville, FL 32202

Kansas City Chiefs
One Arrowhead Drive
Kansas City, MO 64129

Miami Dolphins
7500 SW 30th St.
Davie, FL 33314

Minnesota Vikings
9520 Viking Dr.
Eden Prairie, MN 55344

New England Patriots
60 Washington St.
Foxboro, MA 02035

New Orleans Saints
7800 Airline Highway
Metairie, LA 70003

New York Giants
Giants Stadium
E. Rutherford, NJ 07073

New York Jets
1000 Fulton Ave.
Hempstead, NY 11550

Oakland Raiders
1 Hegenberger Rd.
Oakland, CA 94621

Philadelphia Eagles
3501 S. Broad St.
Philadelphia, PA 19148

Pittsburgh Steelers
300 Stadium Circle
Pittsburgh, PA 15212

St. Louis Rams
1 Rams Way
St. Louis, MO 63045

San Diego Chargers
PO Box 609609
San Diego, CA 92160-9609

San Francisco 49ers
4949 Centennial Blvd.
Santa Clara, CA 95054-1229

Seattle Seahawks
11220 NE 53d St.
Kirkland, WA 98033

Tampa Bay Buccaneers
One Buccaneer Place
Tampa, FL 33607

Washington Redskins
PO Box 17247
Dulles International Airport
Washington, DC 20041

## Other Sports Organizations

Amateur Athletic Union
3400 W. 86th St.
Indianapolis, IN 46268

Amateur Softball Assn.
2801 NE 50th St.
Oklahoma City, OK 73111

American Horse Shows Assn.
220 E. 42d St.
New York, NY 10017

American Kennel Club
51 Madison Ave.
New York, NY 10010

Canadian Football League
110 Eglinton Ave. W
Toronto, Ont. M4R 1A3

IndyCar
755 W. Big Beaver Rd.
Troy, MI 48084

Intl. Game Fish Assn.
1301 E. Atlantic Blvd.
Pompano Beach, FL 33060

LPGA
100 International Golf Dr.
Daytona Beach, FL 32124

Little League Baseball
PO Box 3485
Williamsport, PA 17701

Major League Soccer
2029 Century Park East
Los Angeles, CA 90067

NASCAR
PO Box 2875
Daytona Beach, FL 32120

NCAA
6201 College Blvd.
Overland Park, KS 66211

National Rifle Assn.
11250 Waples Mill Rd.
Fairfax, VA 22030

Pro Bowlers Assn.
PO Box 5118
Akron, OH 44334

PGA
100 Ave. of the Champions
Palm Beach Gardens, FL 33418

Pro Rodeo Cowboys Assn.
101 Pro Rodeo Dr.
Colorado Springs, CO 80919

Special Olympics
1325 G St., NW
Washington, DC 20005

Thoroughbred Racing Assns.
420 Fair Hill Dr.
Elkton, MD 21921

USA Swimming
One Olympic Plaza
Colorado Springs, CO 80909

USA Track & Field
PO Box 120
Indianapolis, IN 46206

U.S. Auto Club
4910 W. 16th St.
Speedway, IN 46224

U.S. Figure Skating Assn.
20 First St.
Colorado Springs, CO 80906

U.S. Olympic Committee
One Olympic Plaza
Colorado Springs, CO 80909

U.S. Skiing Assn.
PO Box 100
Park City, UT 84060

U.S. Soccer Federation
1801 S. Prairie Ave.
Chicago, IL 60616

U.S. Tennis Assn.
70 W. Red Oak Lane
White Plains, NY 10604

U.S. Trotting Assn.
750 Michigan Ave.
Columbus, OH 43215

## NCAA Wrestling Champions

| Year | Champion | Year | Champion | Year | Champion | Year | Champion | Year | Champion |
|---|---|---|---|---|---|---|---|---|---|
| 1964 | Oklahoma State | 1971 | Oklahoma State | 1978 | Iowa | 1985 | Iowa | 1991 | Iowa |
| 1965 | Iowa State | 1972 | Iowa State | 1979 | Iowa | 1986 | Iowa | 1992 | Iowa |
| 1966 | Oklahoma State | 1973 | Iowa State | 1980 | Iowa | 1987 | Iowa State | 1993 | Iowa |
| 1967 | Michigan State | 1974 | Oklahoma | 1981 | Iowa | 1988 | Arizona State | 1994 | Oklahoma State |
| 1968 | Oklahoma State | 1975 | Iowa | 1982 | Iowa | 1989 | Oklahoma State | 1995 | Iowa |
| 1969 | Iowa State | 1976 | Iowa | 1983 | Iowa | 1990 | Oklahoma State | 1996 | Iowa |
| 1970 | Iowa State | 1977 | Iowa State | 1984 | Iowa | | | | |

# World Swimming Records

As of Aug. 1996

## Men's Records

| Distance | Time | Holder | Country | Where made | Date |
|---|---|---|---|---|---|
| | | **Freestyle** | | | |
| 50 meters | **0:21.81** | Tom Jager | U.S. | Nashville, TN | Mar. 24, 1990 |
| 100 meters | **0:48.21** | Alexander Popov | Russia | Monte Carlo | June 18, 1994 |
| 200 meters | **1:46.69** | Giorgio Lamberti | Italy | Bonn | Aug. 15, 1989 |
| 400 meters | **3:43.80** | Kieren Perkins | Australia | Rome | Sept. 9, 1994 |
| 800 meters | **7:46.00** | Kieren Perkins | Australia | Victoria, Canada | Aug. 24, 1994 |
| 1,500 meters | **14:41.66** | Kieren Perkins | Australia | Victoria, Canada | Aug. 24, 1994 |
| | | **Breaststroke** | | | |
| 100 meters | **1:00.60** | Fred DeBurghgraeve | Belguim | Atlanta, GA | July 20, 1996 |
| 200 meters | **2:10.16** | Mike Barrowman | U.S. | Barcelona | July 29, 1992 |
| | | **Butterfly** | | | |
| 100 meters | **0:52.27** | Denis Pankratov | Russia | Atlanta, GA | July 24, 1996 |
| 200 meters | **1:55.22** | Denis Pankratov | Russia | Canet, France | June 14, 1995 |
| | | **Backstroke** | | | |
| 100 meters | **0:53.86** | Jeff Rouse | U.S. | Barcelona | July 29, 1992 |
| 200 meters | **1:56.57** | Martin Lopez-Zubero | Spain | Tuscaloosa, AL | Nov. 23, 1991 |
| | | **Individual Medley** | | | |
| 200 meters | **1:58.16** | Jani Sievinen | Finland | Rome | Sept. 11, 1994 |
| 400 meters | **4:12.30** | Tom Dolan | U.S. | Rome | Sept. 6, 1994 |
| | | **Freestyle Relays** | | | |
| 400 m. (4×100) | **3:15.11** | (Fox, Hudepohl, Olsen, Hall) | U.S. | Atlanta, GA | Aug. 12, 1995 |
| 800 m. (4×200) | **7:11.95** | (Lepikov, Pychenko, Taianovitch, Sadovyi) | Unified Team | Barcelona | July 27, 1992 |
| | | **Medley Relay** | | | |
| 400 m. (4×100) | **3:34.84** | (Rouse, Linn, Henderson, Hall, Jr.) | U.S. | Atlanta, GA | July 26, 1996 |

## Women's Records

| Distance | Time | Holder | Country | Where made | Date |
|---|---|---|---|---|---|
| | | **Freestyle** | | | |
| 50 meters | **0:24.51** | Jingyi Le | China | Rome | Sept. 11, 1994 |
| 100 meters | **0:54.01** | Jingyi Le | China | Rome | Sept. 5, 1994 |
| 200 meters | **1:56.78** | Franziska Van Almsick | Germany | Rome | Sept. 6, 1994 |
| 400 meters | **4:03.85** | Janet Evans | U.S. | Seoul | Sept. 22, 1988 |
| 800 meters | **8:16.22** | Janet Evans | U.S. | Tokyo | Aug. 20, 1989 |
| 1,500 meters | **15:52.10** | Janet Evans | U.S. | Orlando, FL | Mar. 26, 1988 |
| | | **Breaststroke** | | | |
| 100 meters | **1:07.02** | Penny Heyns | U.S. | Atlanta, GA | July 21, 1996 |
| 200 meters | **2:24.76** | Rebecca Brown | Australia. | Queensland, Australia | Mar. 16, 1994 |
| | | **Butterfly** | | | |
| 100 meters | **0:57.93** | Mary T. Meagher | U.S. | Brown Deer, WI. | Aug. 16, 1981 |
| 200 meters | **2:05.96** | Mary T. Meagher | U.S. | Brown Deer, WI. | Aug. 13, 1981 |
| | | **Backstroke** | | | |
| 100 meters | **1:00.16** | Cihong He | China | Rome | Sept. 10, 1994 |
| 200 meters | **2:06.62** | Krisztina Egerszegi | Hungary | Athens | Aug. 25, 1991 |
| | | **Individual Medley** | | | |
| 200 meters | **2:11.65** | Li Lin | China | Barcelona | July 30, 1992 |
| 400 meters | **4:36.10** | Petra Schneider | E. Germany | Ecuador | Aug. 1, 1982 |
| | | **Freestyle Relays** | | | |
| 400 m. (4×100) | **3:37.91** | (Jingyi Le, Ying Shan, Ying Le, Lu Bin) | China. | Rome | Sept. 7, 1994 |
| | | **Medley Relays** | | | |
| 400 m. (4×100) | **4:01.67** | (Cihong He, Guohong Dai, Limin Liu, Jingyi Le) | China | Rome | Sept. 10, 1994 |

# NATIONAL BASKETBALL ASSOCIATION

## 1995-96 NBA Review: Bulls Set Victory Mark, Magic Johnson Returns

The Chicago Bulls won 72 games in the regular season, breaking the NBA record of 69 victories set by the 1971-72 Los Angeles Lakers. Michael Jordan won his record 8th scoring title and reestablished himself as the best player in the game. Fans were treated to the midseason return of Magic Johnson, who promptly retired again at the season's end. After the 1995-96 season, the Lakers signed free-agent superstar center Shaquille O'Neal for a reported $121 million over 7 years.

## Final Standings, 1995-96 Season

### Eastern Conference

**Atlantic Division**

| | W | L | Pct | GB |
|---|---|---|---|---|
| Orlando | 60 | 22 | .732 | — |
| New York | 47 | 35 | .573 | 13 |
| Miami | 42 | 40 | .512 | 18 |
| Washington | 39 | 43 | .476 | 21 |
| Boston | 33 | 49 | .402 | 27 |
| New Jersey | 30 | 52 | .366 | 30 |
| Philadelphia | 18 | 64 | .220 | 42 |

**Central Division**

| | W | L | Pct | GB |
|---|---|---|---|---|
| Chicago | 72 | 10 | .878 | — |
| Indiana | 52 | 30 | .671 | 20 |
| Cleveland | 47 | 35 | .573 | 25 |
| Atlanta | 46 | 36 | .561 | 26 |
| Detroit | 46 | 36 | .561 | 26 |
| Charlotte | 41 | 41 | .500 | 31 |
| Milwaukee | 25 | 57 | .305 | 47 |
| Toronto | 21 | 61 | .256 | 51 |

### Western Conference

**Midwest Division**

| | W | L | Pct | GB |
|---|---|---|---|---|
| San Antonio | 59 | 23 | .720 | — |
| Utah | 55 | 27 | .671 | 4 |
| Houston | 48 | 34 | .585 | 11 |
| Denver | 35 | 47 | .427 | 24 |
| Minnesota | 26 | 56 | .317 | 33 |
| Dallas | 26 | 56 | .317 | 33 |
| Vancouver | 15 | 67 | .183 | 44 |

**Pacific Division**

| | W | L | Pct | GB |
|---|---|---|---|---|
| Seattle | 64 | 18 | .780 | — |
| L.A. Lakers | 53 | 29 | .646 | 11 |
| Portland | 44 | 38 | .537 | 20 |
| Phoenix | 41 | 41 | .500 | 23 |
| Sacramento | 39 | 43 | .476 | 25 |
| Golden State | 36 | 46 | .439 | 28 |
| L.A. Clippers | 29 | 53 | .354 | 35 |

## NBA Regular Season Individual Highs in 1995-96

**Most minutes played, season** — 3,457: Anthony Mason, New York.

**Most points, game** — 53: Michael Jordan, Chicago vs. Detroit, Mar. 7.

**Most field goals made, game** — 21: Karl Malone, Utah v. Portland, Dec. 26; Michael Jordan, Chicago v. Detroit, Mar. 7; Shaquille O'Neal, Orlando at Washington, Mar. 22 (OT).

**Most field goal attempts, game** — 40: Shaquille O'Neal, Orlando at Washington, Mar. 22 (OT).

**3-point field goals made, game** — 11: Dennis Scott, Orlando v. Atlanta, Apr. 18.

**3-point field goals made, highest percentage (min. 50 made), season** — .522: Tim Legler, Washington.

**Most free throws made, game** — 22: Charles Barkley, Phoenix v. Washington, Dec. 20 (OT).

**Most rebounds, game** — 31: Dikembe Mutombo, Denver v. Charlotte, Mar. 26 (2OT).

**Most offensive rebounds, season** — 356: Dennis Rodman, Chicago.

**Most defensive rebounds, season** — 681: David Robinson, San Antonio.

**Most assists, game** — 25: Jason Kidd, Dallas v. Utah, Feb. 8 (2OT).

**Most steals, game** — 7: Eleven times, most recently by Kevin Johnson, Phoenix v. Dallas, Apr. 19.

**Most blocked shots, game** — 12: Shawn Bradley, New Jersey v. Toronto, Apr. 17.

**Most personal fouls, season** — 300: Elden Campbell, L.A. Lakers, and Otis Thorpe, Detroit.

**Most games disqualified, season** — 11: Matt Geiger, Charlotte.

## Bulls Win 4th Championship in 6 Years by Downing Seattle in 6 Games

The Chicago Bulls won their 4th National Basketball Association championship in 6 years, defeating the Seattle SuperSonics, 4 games to 2. The victory capped a year in which the Bulls won a record 72 regular-season games. Chicago lost a total of only 3 games in its playoff run. Seattle made the series interesting, winning 2 games in a row after dropping the first 3. Michael Jordan, just 15 months back from his brief retirement, was named NBA Finals MVP for a record 4th time.

**Chicago Bulls**

| | FG A-M | FT A-M | Reb O-D | Ast | Avg |
|---|---|---|---|---|---|
| Jordan | 123-51 | 67-56 | 10-22 | 25 | 27.3 |
| Pippen | 99-34 | 24-17 | 20-29 | 32 | 15.7 |
| Kukoc | 71-30 | 10-8 | 12-17 | 21 | 13.0 |
| Longley | 47-27 | 22-16 | 8-15 | 13 | 11.7 |
| Rodman | 35-17 | 19-11 | 41-47 | 15 | 7.5 |
| Harper | 32-12 | 12-11 | 4-9 | 10 | 6.5 |
| Kerr | 33-10 | 7-6 | 2-3 | 5 | 5.0 |
| Brown | 12-6 | 4-2 | 1-1 | 5 | 2.8 |
| Wennington | 12-8 | 2-1 | 2-1 | 1 | 0.7 |
| Buechler | 9-2 | 2-0 | 0-0 | 1 | 0.7 |
| Salley | 1-0 | 0-0 | 1-0 | 2 | 0.0 |

**Seattle SuperSonics**

| | FG A-M | FT A-M | Reb O-D | Ast | Avg |
|---|---|---|---|---|---|
| Kemp | 89-49 | 49-42 | 26-34 | 13 | 23.3 |
| Payton | 90-40 | 26-19 | 6-32 | 42 | 18.0 |
| Schrempf | 79-35 | 24-21 | 9-21 | 15 | 16.3 |
| Hawkins | 55-25 | 26-24 | 7-14 | 6 | 13.3 |
| Perkins | 61-23 | 21-17 | 9-19 | 12 | 11.2 |
| McMillan | 7-3 | 2-2 | 0-11 | 6 | 2.8 |
| Wingate | 10-5 | 4-4 | 1-1 | 0 | 2.5 |
| Askew | 9-2 | 2-2 | 0-10 | 2 | 1.8 |
| Johnson | 6-2 | 0-0 | 6-1 | 1 | 1.3 |
| Brickowski | 9-2 | 0-0 | 2-10 | 3 | 0.8 |
| Scheffler | 1-0 | 0-0 | 1-1 | 0 | 0.0 |
| Snow | 2-0 | 0-0 | 0-2 | 1 | 0.0 |

## 1996 NBA Playoff Results

**Eastern Conference**

Chicago defeated Miami 3 games to 0
Orlando defeated Detroit 3 games to 0
Atlanta defeated Indiana 3 games to 2
New York defeated Cleveland 3 games to 0
Chicago defeated New York 4 games to 1
Orlando defeated Atlanta 4 games to 1
Chicago defeated Orlando 4 games to 0

**Western Conference**

Seattle defeated Sacramento 3 games to 1
San Antonio defeated Phoenix 3 games to 1
Utah defeated Portland 3 games to 2
Houston defeated L.A. Lakers 3 games to 1
Seattle defeated Houston 4 games to 0
Utah defeated San Antonio 4 games to 2
Seattle defeated Utah 4 games to 3

**Championship**

Chicago defeated Seattle 4 games to 2 (107-90, 92-88, 108-86, 86-107, 78-89, 87-75)

# NBA Finals MVP

1969 Jerry West, Los Angeles
1970 Willis Reed, New York
1971 Lew Alcindor (Kareem Abdul-Jabbar), Milwaukee
1972 Wilt Chamberlain, Los Angeles
1973 Willis Reed, New York
1974 John Havlicek, Boston
1975 Rick Barry, Golden State
1976 Jo Jo White, Boston
1977 Bill Walton, Portland
1978 Wes Unseld, Washington
1979 Dennis Johnson, Seattle
1980 Magic Johnson, Los Angeles
1981 Cedric Maxwell, Boston
1982 Magic Johnson, Los Angeles
1983 Moses Malone, Philadelphia
1984 Larry Bird, Boston
1985 Kareem Abdul-Jabbar, L.A. Lakers
1986 Larry Bird, Boston
1987 Magic Johnson, L.A. Lakers
1988 James Worthy, L.A. Lakers
1989 Joe Dumars, Detroit
1990 Isiah Thomas, Detroit
1991 Michael Jordan, Chicago
1992 Michael Jordan, Chicago
1993 Michael Jordan, Chicago
1994 Hakeem Olajuwon, Houston
1995 Hakeem Olajuwon, Houston
1996 Michael Jordan, Chicago

# NBA Scoring Leaders

| Year | Scoring champion | Pts | Avg |
|---|---|---|---|
| 1947 | Joe Fulks, Philadelphia | 1,389 | 23.2 |
| 1948 | Max Zaslofsky, Chicago | 1,007 | 21.0 |
| 1949 | George Mikan, Minneapolis | 1,698 | 28.3 |
| 1950 | George Mikan, Minneapolis | 1,865 | 27.4 |
| 1951 | George Mikan, Minneapolis | 1,932 | 28.4 |
| 1952 | Paul Arizin, Philadelphia | 1,674 | 25.4 |
| 1953 | Neil Johnston, Philadelphia | 1,564 | 22.3 |
| 1954 | Neil Johnston, Philadelphia | 1,759 | 24.4 |
| 1955 | Neil Johnston, Philadelphia | 1,631 | 22.7 |
| 1956 | Bob Pettit, St. Louis | 1,849 | 25.7 |
| 1957 | Paul Arizin, Philadelphia | 1,817 | 25.6 |
| 1958 | George Yardley, Detroit | 2,001 | 27.8 |
| 1959 | Bob Pettit, St. Louis | 2,105 | 29.2 |
| 1960 | Wilt Chamberlain, Philadelphia | 2,707 | 37.9 |
| 1961 | Wilt Chamberlain, Philadelphia | 3,033 | 38.4 |
| 1962 | Wilt Chamberlain, Philadelphia | 4,029 | 50.4 |
| 1963 | Wilt Chamberlain, San Francisco | 3,586 | 44.8 |
| 1964 | Wilt Chamberlain, San Francisco | 2,948 | 36.5 |
| 1965 | Wilt Chamberlain, San Fran., Phi. | 2,534 | 34.7 |
| 1966 | Wilt Chamberlain, Philadelphia | 2,649 | 33.5 |
| 1967 | Rick Barry, San Francisco | 2,775 | 35.6 |
| 1968 | Dave Bing, Detroit | 2,142 | 27.1 |
| 1969 | Elvin Hayes, San Diego | 2,327 | 28.4 |
| 1970 | Jerry West, Los Angeles | 2,309 | 31.2 |
| 1971 | Lew Alcindor (Kareem Abdul-Jabbar), Milwaukee | 2,596 | 31.7 |
| 1972 | Kareem Abdul-Jabbar, Milwaukee | 2,822 | 34.8 |
| 1973 | Nate Archibald, Kansas City-Omaha | 2,719 | 34.0 |
| 1974 | Bob McAdoo, Buffalo | 2,261 | 30.6 |
| 1975 | Bob McAdoo, Buffalo | 2,831 | 34.5 |
| 1976 | Bob McAdoo, Buffalo | 2,427 | 31.1 |
| 1977 | Pete Maravich, New Orleans | 2,273 | 31.1 |
| 1978 | George Gervin, San Antonio | 2,232 | 27.2 |
| 1979 | George Gervin, San Antonio | 2,365 | 29.6 |
| 1980 | George Gervin, San Antonio | 2,585 | 33.1 |
| 1981 | Adrian Dantley, Utah | 2,452 | 30.7 |
| 1982 | George Gervin, San Antonio | 2,551 | 32.3 |
| 1983 | Alex English, Denver | 2,326 | 28.4 |
| 1984 | Adrian Dantley, Utah | 2,418 | 30.6 |
| 1985 | Bernard King, New York | 1,809 | 32.9 |
| 1986 | Dominique Wilkins, Atlanta | 2,366 | 30.3 |
| 1987 | Michael Jordan, Chicago | 3,041 | 37.1 |
| 1988 | Michael Jordan, Chicago | 2,868 | 35.0 |
| 1989 | Michael Jordan, Chicago | 2,633 | 32.5 |
| 1990 | Michael Jordan, Chicago | 2,753 | 33.6 |
| 1991 | Michael Jordan, Chicago | 2,580 | 31.5 |
| 1992 | Michael Jordan, Chicago | 2,404 | 30.1 |
| 1993 | Michael Jordan, Chicago | 2,541 | 32.6 |
| 1994 | David Robinson, San Antonio | 2,383 | 29.8 |
| 1995 | Shaquille O'Neal, Orlando | 2,315 | 29.3 |
| 1996 | Michael Jordan, Chicago | 2,465 | 30.4 |

# NBA Most Valuable Player

1956 Bob Pettit, St. Louis
1957 Bob Cousy, Boston
1958 Bill Russell, Boston
1959 Bob Pettit, St. Louis
1960 Wilt Chamberlain, Philadelphia
1961 Bill Russell, Boston
1962 Bill Russell, Boston
1963 Bill Russell, Boston
1964 Oscar Robertson, Cincinnati
1965 Bill Russell, Boston
1966 Wilt Chamberlain, Philadelphia
1967 Wilt Chamberlain, Philadelphia
1968 Wilt Chamberlain, Philadelphia
1969 Wes Unseld, Baltimore
1970 Willis Reed, New York
1971 Lew Alcindor (Kareem Abdul-Jabbar), Milwaukee
1972 Kareem Abdul-Jabbar, Milwaukee
1973 Dave Cowens, Boston
1974 Kareem Abdul-Jabbar, Milwaukee
1975 Bob McAdoo, Buffalo
1976 Kareem Abdul-Jabbar, Los Angeles
1977 Kareem Abdul-Jabbar, Los Angeles
1978 Bill Walton, Portland
1979 Moses Malone, Houston
1980 Kareem Abdul-Jabbar, Los Angeles
1981 Julius Erving, Philadelphia
1982 Moses Malone, Houston
1983 Moses Malone, Philadelphia
1984 Larry Bird, Boston
1985 Larry Bird, Boston
1986 Larry Bird, Boston
1987 Magic Johnson, L.A. Lakers
1988 Michael Jordan, Chicago
1989 Magic Johnson, L.A. Lakers
1990 Magic Johnson, L.A. Lakers
1991 Michael Jordan, Chicago
1992 Michael Jordan, Chicago
1993 Charles Barkley, Phoenix
1994 Hakeem Olajuwon, Houston
1995 David Robinson, San Antonio
1996 Michael Jordan, Chicago

# NBA Champions 1947-96

| | Regular season | | Playoffs | | |
|---|---|---|---|---|---|
| Year | Eastern Conference | Western Conference | Winner | Coach | Runner-up |
| 1947 | Washington Capitols | Chicago Stags | Philadelphia | Ed Gottlieb | Chicago |
| 1948 | Philadelphia Warriors | St. Louis Bombers | Baltimore | Buddy Jeannette | Philadelphia |
| 1949 | Washington Capitols | Rochester | Minneapolis | John Kundla | Washington |
| 1950 | Syracuse | Minneapolis | Minneapolis | John Kundla | Syracuse |
| 1951 | Philadelphia Warriors | Minneapolis | Rochester | Lester Harrison | New York |
| 1952 | Syracuse | Rochester | Minneapolis | John Kundla | New York |
| 1953 | New York | Minneapolis | Minneapolis | John Kundla | New York |
| 1954 | New York | Minneapolis | Minneapolis | John Kundla | Syracuse |
| 1955 | Syracuse | Ft. Wayne | Syracuse | Al Cervi | Ft. Wayne |
| 1956 | Philadelphia Warriors | Ft. Wayne | Philadelphia | George Senesky | Ft. Wayne |
| 1957 | Boston | St. Louis | Boston | Red Auerbach | St. Louis |
| 1958 | Boston | St. Louis | St. Louis | Alex Hannum | Boston |
| 1959 | Boston | St. Louis | Boston | Red Auerbach | Minneapolis |
| 1960 | Boston | St. Louis | Boston | Red Auerbach | St. Louis |
| 1961 | Boston | St. Louis | Boston | Red Auerbach | St. Louis |
| 1962 | Boston | Los Angeles | Boston | Red Auerbach | Los Angeles |
| 1963 | Boston | Los Angeles | Boston | Red Auerbach | Los Angeles |
| 1964 | Boston | San Francisco | Boston | Red Auerbach | San Francisco |

*(continued)*

| | Regular season | | Playoffs | | |
|---|---|---|---|---|---|
| Year | Eastern Conference | Western Conference | Winner | Coach | Runner-up |
| 1965 | Boston | Los Angeles | Boston | Red Auerbach | Los Angeles |
| 1966 | Philadelphia | Los Angeles | Boston | Red Auerbach | Los Angeles |
| 1967 | Philadelphia | San Francisco | Philadelphia | Alex Hannum | San Francisco |
| 1968 | Philadelphia | St. Louis | Boston | Bill Russell | Los Angeles |
| 1969 | Baltimore | Los Angeles | Boston | Bill Russell | Los Angeles |
| 1970 | New York | Atlanta | New York | Red Holzman | Los Angeles |

| Year | Atlantic | Central | Midwest | Pacific | Winner | Coach | Runner-up |
|---|---|---|---|---|---|---|---|
| 1971 | New York | Baltimore | Milwaukee | Los Angeles | Milwaukee | Lady Costello | Baltimore |
| 1972 | Boston | Baltimore | Milwaukee | Los Angeles | Los Angeles | Bill Sharman | New York |
| 1973 | Boston | Baltimore | Milwaukee | Los Angeles | New York | Red Holzman | Los Angeles |
| 1974 | Boston | Capital | Milwaukee | Los Angeles | Boston | Tom Heinsohn | Milwaukee |
| 1975 | Boston | Washington | Chicago | Golden State | Golden State | Al Attles | Washington |
| 1976 | Boston | Cleveland | Milwaukee | Golden State | Boston | Tom Heinsohn | Phoenix |
| 1977 | Philadelphia | Houston | Denver | Los Angeles | Portland | Jack Ramsay | Philadelphia |
| 1978 | Philadelphia | San Antonio | Denver | Portland | Washington | Dick Motta | Seattle |
| 1979 | Washington | San Antonio | Kansas City | Seattle | Seattle | Len Wilkens | Washington |
| 1980 | Boston | Atlanta | Milwaukee | Los Angeles | Los Angeles | Paul Westhead | Philadelphia |
| 1981 | Boston | Milwaukee | San Antonio | Phoenix | Boston | Bill Fitch | Houston |
| 1982 | Boston | Milwaukee | San Antonio | Los Angeles | Los Angeles | Pat Riley | Philadelphia |
| 1983 | Philadelphia | Milwaukee | San Antonio | Los Angeles | Philadelphia | Billy Cunningham | Los Angeles |
| 1984 | Boston | Milwaukee | Utah | Los Angeles | Boston | K.C. Jones | Los Angeles |
| 1985 | Boston | Milwaukee | Denver | L.A. Lakers | L.A. Lakers | Pat Riley | Boston |
| 1986 | Boston | Milwaukee | Houston | L.A. Lakers | Boston | K.C. Jones | Houston |
| 1987 | Boston | Atlanta | Dallas | L.A. Lakers | L.A. Lakers | Pat Riley | Boston |
| 1988 | Boston | Detroit | Denver | L.A. Lakers | L.A. Lakers | Pat Riley | Detroit |
| 1989 | New York | Detroit | Utah | L.A. Lakers | Detroit | Chuck Daly | L.A. Lakers |
| 1990 | Philadelphia | Detroit | San Antonio | L.A. Lakers | Detroit | Chuck Daly | Portland |
| 1991 | Boston | Chicago | San Antonio | Portland | Chicago | Phil Jackson | L.A. Lakers |
| 1992 | Boston | Chicago | Utah | Portland | Chicago | Phil Jackson | Portland |
| 1993 | New York | Chicago | Houston | Phoenix | Chicago | Phil Jackson | Phoenix |
| 1994 | New York | Atlanta | Houston | Seattle | Houston | Rudy Tomjanovich | New York |
| 1995 | Orlando | Indiana | San Antonio | Phoenix | Houston | Rudy Tomjanovich | Orlando |
| 1996 | Orlando | Chicago | San Antonio | Seattle | Chicago | Phil Jackson | Seattle |

## NBA Coach of the Year, 1963-96

1963 Harry Gallatin, St. Louis Hawks
1964 Alex Hannum, San Francisco Warriors
1965 Red Auerbach, Boston Celtics
1966 Dolph Schayes, Philadelphia 76ers
1967 Johnny Kerr, Chicago Bulls
1968 Richie Guerin, St. Louis Hawks
1969 Gene Shue, Baltimore Bullets
1970 Red Holzman, New York Knicks
1971 Dick Motta, Chicago Bulls
1972 Bill Sharman, Los Angeles Lakers
1973 Tom Heinsohn, Boston Celtics
1974 Ray Scott, Detroit Pistons
1975 Phil Johnson, Kansas City-Omaha Kings
1976 Bill Fitch, Cleveland Cavaliers
1977 Tom Nissalke, Houston Rockets
1978 Hubie Brown, Atlanta Hawks
1979 Cotton Fitzsimmons, Kansas City Kings
1980 Bill Fitch, Boston Celtics
1981 Jack McKinney, Indiana Pacers
1982 Gene Shue, Washington Bullets
1983 Don Nelson, Milwaukee Bucks
1984 Frank Layden, Utah Jazz
1985 Don Nelson, Milwaukee Bucks
1986 Mike Fratello, Atlanta Hawks
1987 Mike Schuler, Portland Trail Blazers
1988 Doug Moe, Denver Nuggets
1989 Cotton Fitzsimmons, Phoenix Suns
1990 Pat Riley, Los Angeles Lakers
1991 Don Chaney, Houston Rockets
1992 Don Nelson, Golden State Warriors
1993 Pat Riley, New York Knicks
1994 Lenny Wilkens, Atlanta Hawks
1995 Del Harris, L.A. Lakers
1996 Phil Jackson, Chicago Bulls

## NBA All-League and All-Defensive Teams, 1995-96

**All-League Team**

| First team | Second team | Position |
|---|---|---|
| Scottie Pippen, Chicago | Shawn Kemp, Seattle | Forward |
| Karl Malone, Utah | Grant Hill, Detroit | Forward |
| David Robinson, San Antonio | Hakeem Olajuwon, Houston | Center |
| Michael Jordan, Chicago | Gary Payton, Seattle | Guard |
| Anfernee Hardaway, Orlando | John Stockton, Utah | Guard |

**All-Defensive Team**

| Position | First team | Second team |
|---|---|---|
| Forward | Scottie Pippen, Chicago | Horace Grant, Orlando |
| Forward | Dennis Rodman, Chicago | Derrick McKey, Indiana |
| Center | David Robinson, San Antonio | Hakeem Olajuwon, Houst |
| Guard | Gary Payton, Seattle | Mookie Blaylock, Atlanta |
| Guard | Michael Jordan, Chicago | Bobby Phills, Cleveland |

## NBA Statistical Leaders, 1995-96

**Scoring**

(Minimum 70 games or 1,400 pts)

| | G | FG | FT | Pts | Avg |
|---|---|---|---|---|---|
| Jordan, Chicago | 82 | 916 | 548 | 2,491 | 30.4 |
| Olajuwon, Houston | 72 | 768 | 397 | 1,936 | 26.9 |
| O'Neal, Orlando | 54 | 592 | 249 | 1,434 | 26.6 |
| K. Malone, Utah | 82 | 789 | 512 | 2,106 | 25.7 |
| D. Robinson, San Antonio | 82 | 711 | 626 | 2,051 | 25.0 |
| Barkley, Phoenix | 71 | 580 | 440 | 1,649 | 23.2 |
| Mourning, Miami | 70 | 563 | 488 | 1,623 | 23.2 |
| Richmond, Sacramento | 81 | 611 | 425 | 1,872 | 23.1 |
| Ewing, New York | 76 | 678 | 351 | 1,711 | 22.5 |
| Howard, Washington | 81 | 733 | 319 | 1,789 | 22.1 |

**Rebounds per Game**

(Minimum 70 games or 800 rebounds)

| | G | Off | Def | Tot | Avg |
|---|---|---|---|---|---|
| Rodman, Chicago | 64 | 356 | 596 | 952 | 14.9 |
| D. Robinson, San Antonio | 82 | 319 | 681 | 1,000 | 12.2 |
| Mutombo, Denver | 74 | 249 | 622 | 871 | 11.8 |
| Barkley, Phoenix | 71 | 243 | 578 | 821 | 11.6 |
| Kemp, Seattle | 79 | 276 | 628 | 904 | 11.4 |
| Olajuwon, Houston | 72 | 176 | 608 | 784 | 10.9 |
| Ewing, New York | 76 | 157 | 649 | 806 | 10.6 |
| Mourning, Miami | 70 | 218 | 509 | 727 | 10.4 |
| Vaught, L.A. Clippers | 80 | 204 | 604 | 808 | 10.1 |
| J. Williams, New Jersey | 80 | 342 | 461 | 803 | 10.0 |

**Field Goal Percentage**

(Minimum 300 field goals made)

| | FG | FGA | Pct |
|---|---|---|---|
| Muresan, Washington | 466 | 798 | .584 |
| Gatling, Golden State | 326 | 567 | .575 |
| O'Neal, Orlando | 592 | 1,033 | .573 |
| Mason, New York | 449 | 798 | .563 |
| Kemp, Seattle | 526 | 937 | .561 |
| D. Davis, Indiana | 334 | 599 | .558 |
| Sabonis, Portland | 394 | 723 | .545 |
| B. Williams, L.A. Clippers | 416 | 766 | .543 |
| C. Brown, Houston | 300 | 555 | .541 |
| Stockton, Utah | 440 | 818 | .538 |

**Free Throw Percentage**
(Minimum 125 free throws made)

| | FTM | FTA | Pct |
|---|---|---|---|
| Abdul-Rauf, Denver | 146 | 157 | .930 |
| Hornacek, Utah | 259 | 290 | .893 |
| Brandon, Cleveland | 338 | 381 | .887 |
| Barros, Boston | 130 | 147 | .884 |
| B. Price, Washington | 167 | 191 | .874 |
| Hawkins, Seattle | 247 | 283 | .873 |
| Richmond, Sacramento | 425 | 491 | .866 |
| Miller, Indiana | 430 | 498 | .863 |
| Legler, Washington | 132 | 153 | .863 |
| Webb, Atlanta-Minnesota | 125 | 145 | .862 |

**3-Point Field Goal Percentage**
(Minimum 50 goals made)

| | FG | FGA | Pct |
|---|---|---|---|
| Legler, Washington | 128 | 245 | .522 |
| Kerr, Chicago | 122 | 237 | .515 |
| Davis, New York | 127 | 267 | .476 |
| Armstrong, Golden State | 98 | 207 | .473 |
| Hornacek, Utah | 104 | 223 | .466 |
| B. Price, Washington | 139 | 301 | .462 |
| Phills, Cleveland | 93 | 211 | .441 |
| Dehere, L.A. Clippers | 139 | 316 | .440 |
| Richmond, Sacramento | 225 | 515 | .437 |
| Houston, Detroit | 191 | 447 | .427 |

**Assists**
(Minimum 70 games or 400 assists)

| | G | No | Avg |
|---|---|---|---|
| Stockton, Utah | 82 | 916 | 11.2 |
| Kidd, Dallas | 81 | 783 | 9.7 |
| A. Johnson, San Antonio | 82 | 789 | 9.6 |
| Strickland, Portland | 67 | 640 | 9.6 |
| Stoudamire, Toronto | 70 | 653 | 9.3 |
| K. Johnson, Phoenix | 56 | 517 | 9.2 |
| Anderson, N.J.-Charlotte | 69 | 575 | 8.3 |
| T. Hardaway, Golden State | 80 | 640 | 8.0 |
| M. Jackson, Indiana | 81 | 635 | 7.8 |
| Payton, Seattle | 81 | 608 | 7.5 |

**Steals**
(Minimum 70 games or 125 steals)

| | G | No | Avg |
|---|---|---|---|
| Payton, Seattle | 81 | 231 | 2.85 |
| Blaylock, Atlanta | 81 | 212 | 2.62 |
| Jordan, Chicago | 82 | 180 | 2.60 |
| Kidd, Dallas | 81 | 175 | 2.16 |
| Robertson, Toronto | 77 | 166 | 2.16 |
| A. Hardaway, Orlando | 82 | 166 | 2.02 |
| Murdock, Mil.-Vancouver | 73 | 135 | 1.85 |
| Jones, L.A. Lakers | 70 | 129 | 1.84 |
| Hawkins, Seattle | 82 | 149 | 1.82 |
| Gugliotta, Minnesota | 78 | 139 | 1.78 |

**Blocked Shots**
(Minimum 70 games or 100 blocked shots)

| | G | Blk | Avg |
|---|---|---|---|
| Mutombo, Denver | 74 | 332 | 4.49 |
| Bradley, Phila.-New Jersey | 79 | 288 | 3.65 |
| D. Robinson, San Antonio | 82 | 271 | 3.30 |
| Olajuwon, Houston | 72 | 207 | 2.88 |
| Mourning, Charlotte | 70 | 189 | 2.70 |
| Campbell, L.A. Lakers | 82 | 212 | 2.59 |
| Ewing, New York | 76 | 184 | 2.42 |
| Muresan, Washington | 76 | 172 | 2.26 |
| O'Neal, Orlando | 54 | 115 | 2.13 |
| McIlvaine, Washington | 80 | 166 | 2.08 |

# NBA Rookie of the Year

| Year | Player |
|---|---|
| 1953 | Don Meineke, Ft. Wayne |
| 1954 | Ray Felix, Baltimore |
| 1955 | Bob Pettit, Milwaukee |
| 1956 | Maurice Stokes, Rochester |
| 1957 | Tom Heinsohn, Boston |
| 1958 | Woody Sauldsberry, Philadelphia |
| 1959 | Elgin Baylor, Minneapolis |
| 1960 | Wilt Chamberlain, Philadelphia |
| 1961 | Oscar Robertson, Cincinnati |
| 1962 | Walt Bellamy, Chicago |
| 1963 | Terry Dischinger, Chicago |
| 1964 | Jerry Lucas, Cincinnati |
| 1965 | Willis Reed, New York |
| 1966 | Rick Barry, San Francisco |
| 1967 | Dave Bing, Detroit |
| 1968 | Earl Monroe, Baltimore |
| 1969 | Wes Unseld, Baltimore |
| 1970 | Lew Alcindor, Milwaukee |
| 1971 | Dave Cowens, Boston; Geoff Petrie, Portland (tie) |
| 1972 | Sidney Wicks, Portland |
| 1973 | Bob McAdoo, Buffalo |
| 1974 | Ernie DiGregorio, Buffalo |
| 1975 | Keith Wilkes, Golden State |
| 1976 | Alvan Adams, Phoenix |
| 1977 | Adrian Dantley, Buffalo |
| 1978 | Walter Davis, Phoenix |
| 1979 | Phil Ford, Kansas City |
| 1980 | Larry Bird, Boston |
| 1981 | Darrell Griffith, Utah |
| 1982 | Buck Williams, New Jersey |
| 1983 | Terry Cummings, San Diego |
| 1984 | Ralph Sampson, Houston |
| 1985 | Michael Jordan, Chicago |
| 1986 | Patrick Ewing, New York |
| 1987 | Chuck Person, Indiana |
| 1988 | Mark Jackson, New York |
| 1989 | Mitch Richmond, Golden State |
| 1990 | David Robinson, San Antonio |
| 1991 | Derrick Coleman, New Jersey |
| 1992 | Larry Johnson, Charlotte |
| 1993 | Shaquille O'Neal, Orlando |
| 1994 | Chris Webber, Golden State |
| 1995 | Grant Hill, Detroit; Jason Kidd, Dallas (tie) |
| 1996 | Damon Stoudamire, Toronto |

# Individual Statistics, 1995-96

(more than 600 minutes played; *played for more than one team during 1995-96)

## Atlanta Hawks

| | Min | FG% | FT% | Reb | Ast | Pts | Avg |
|---|---|---|---|---|---|---|---|
| Smith | 2,856 | .432 | .826 | 326 | 224 | 1,446 | 18.1 |
| Laettner* | 2,495 | .487 | .818 | 538 | 197 | 1,217 | 16.4 |
| Blaylock | 2,893 | .405 | .747 | 332 | 478 | 1,268 | 15.7 |
| Long | 3,008 | .471 | .763 | 788 | 183 | 1,078 | 13.1 |
| Augmon | 2,294 | .491 | .792 | 304 | 137 | 976 | 12.7 |
| Norman | 770 | .465 | .354 | 132 | 63 | 304 | 8.9 |
| Ehlo | 1,758 | .428 | .786 | 256 | 138 | 669 | 8.5 |
| Rooks* | 1,117 | .505 | .668 | 255 | 47 | 424 | 6.5 |
| Henderson | 1,416 | .442 | .595 | 356 | 51 | 503 | 6.4 |

**Coach**—Lenny Wilkens

## Boston Celtics

| | Min | FG% | FT% | Reb | Ast | Pts | Avg |
|---|---|---|---|---|---|---|---|
| Radja | 1,984 | .500 | .695 | 522 | 83 | 1,043 | 19.7 |
| Fox | 2,588 | .454 | .772 | 450 | 369 | 1,137 | 14.0 |
| Barros | 2,328 | .470 | .884 | 192 | 306 | 1,038 | 13.0 |
| Wesley | 2,104 | .459 | .753 | 264 | 390 | 1,009 | 12.3 |
| Day* | 1,807 | .366 | .780 | 224 | 107 | 922 | 11.7 |
| Williams | 1,470 | .441 | .671 | 217 | 70 | 685 | 10.7 |
| Brown | 1,591 | .399 | .854 | 136 | 146 | 695 | 10.7 |
| Minor | 1,761 | .500 | .762 | 257 | 146 | 746 | 9.6 |
| Montross | 1,432 | .566 | .376 | 352 | 43 | 442 | 7.2 |
| Ellison | 1,431 | .492 | .641 | 451 | 62 | 365 | 5.3 |
| Lister* | 735 | .486 | .641 | 280 | 19 | 143 | 2.2 |

**Coach**—M.L. Carr

## Charlotte Hornets

| | Min | FG% | FT% | Reb | Ast | Pts | Avg |
|---|---|---|---|---|---|---|---|
| Rice | 3,142 | .471 | .837 | 378 | 232 | 1,710 | 21.6 |
| Johnson | 3,274 | .476 | .757 | 683 | 355 | 1,660 | 20.5 |
| Anderson* | 2,344 | .418 | .769 | 203 | 575 | 1,050 | 15.2 |
| Curry | 2,371 | .453 | .854 | 264 | 176 | 1,192 | 14.5 |
| Burrell | 693 | .447 | .750 | 98 | 47 | 263 | 13.2 |
| Geiger | 2,349 | .536 | .727 | 649 | 60 | 866 | 11.2 |
| Goldwire | 621 | .402 | .767 | 43 | 112 | 231 | 5.5 |
| Hancock | 838 | .523 | .644 | 98 | 47 | 272 | 4.3 |
| Zidek | 888 | .423 | .763 | 183 | 16 | 281 | 4.0 |
| Parish | 1,086 | .498 | .704 | 303 | 29 | 290 | 3.9 |
| Myers* | 1,092 | .368 | .656 | 140 | 145 | 276 | 3.9 |

**Coach**—Allan Bristow

## Chicago Bulls

| | Min | FG% | FT% | Reb | Ast | Pts | Avg |
|---|---|---|---|---|---|---|---|
| Jordan | 3,090 | .495 | .834 | 543 | 352 | 2,491 | 30.4 |
| Pippen | 2,825 | .463 | .679 | 496 | 452 | 1,496 | 19.4 |
| Kukoc | 2,103 | .490 | .772 | 323 | 287 | 1,065 | 13.1 |
| Longley | 1,641 | .482 | .777 | 318 | 119 | 564 | 9.1 |
| Kerr | 1,919 | .506 | .929 | 110 | 192 | 688 | 8.4 |
| Harper | 1,886 | .467 | .705 | 213 | 208 | 594 | 7.4 |
| Rodman | 2,088 | .480 | .528 | 952 | 160 | 351 | 5.5 |
| Wennington | 1,065 | .493 | .860 | 174 | 46 | 376 | 5.3 |
| Salley* | 673 | .450 | .694 | 140 | 54 | 185 | 4.4 |
| Buechler | 740 | .463 | .636 | 111 | 56 | 278 | 3.8 |
| Simpkins | 685 | .481 | .629 | 156 | 38 | 216 | 3.6 |
| Brown | 671 | .406 | .609 | 66 | 73 | 185 | 2.7 |

**Coach**—Phil Jackson

## Cleveland Cavaliers

| | Min | FG% | FT% | Reb | Ast | Pts | Avg |
|---|---|---|---|---|---|---|---|
| Brandon . . | 2570 | .465 | .887 | 248 | 487 | 1449 | 19.3 |
| Mills . . . . . | 3060 | .468 | .829 | 443 | 188 | 1205 | 15.1 |
| Phills. . . . . | 2530 | .467 | .775 | 261 | 271 | 1051 | 14.6 |
| Ferry. . . . . | 2680 | .459 | .769 | 309 | 191 | 1090 | 13.3 |
| Majerle . . . | 2367 | .405 | .710 | 305 | 214 | 872 | 10.6 |
| Hill . . . . . . | 929 | .512 | .600 | 244 | 33 | 341 | 7.8 |
| Cage. . . . . | 2631 | .556 | .543 | 729 | 53 | 490 | 6.0 |
| Sura . . . . . | 1150 | .411 | .702 | 135 | 233 | 422 | 5.3 |
| Crotty . . . . | 617 | .447 | .861 | 54 | 102 | 172 | 3.0 |

**Coach**—Mike Fratello

## Dallas Mavericks

| | Min | FG% | FT% | Reb | Ast | Pts | Avg |
|---|---|---|---|---|---|---|---|
| Mashburn . | 669 | .379 | .729 | 97 | 50 | 422 | 23.4 |
| Jackson . . | 2820 | .435 | .825 | 410 | 235 | 1604 | 19.6 |
| McCloud . . | 2846 | .414 | .804 | 379 | 212 | 1497 | 18.9 |
| Kidd . . . . . | 3034 | .381 | .692 | 553 | 783 | 1348 | 16.6 |
| Dumas . . . | 1284 | .418 | .599 | 115 | 99 | 776 | 11.6 |
| Jones . . . . | 2322 | .446 | .767 | 737 | 132 | 770 | 11.3 |
| Harris . . . . | 1016 | .461 | .782 | 122 | 79 | 481 | 7.9 |
| Brooks . . . | 716 | .457 | .855 | 41 | 100 | 352 | 5.1 |
| Meyer . . . . | 1266 | .439 | .686 | 319 | 57 | 363 | 5.0 |
| Parks . . . . | 869 | .409 | .661 | 216 | 29 | 250 | 3.9 |
| Wood*. . . . | 772 | .431 | .760 | 154 | 34 | 208 | 3.4 |
| Williams . . | 1806 | .407 | .343 | 521 | 85 | 198 | 3.0 |

**Coach**—Dick Motta

## Denver Nuggets

| | Min | FG% | FT% | Reb | Ast | Pts | Avg |
|---|---|---|---|---|---|---|---|
| Abdul-Rauf | 2029 | .434 | .930 | 138 | 389 | 1095 | 19.2 |
| D. Ellis . . . | 2626 | .479 | .760 | 315 | 139 | 1204 | 14.9 |
| Stith . . . . . | 2810 | .416 | .844 | 400 | 241 | 1119 | 13.6 |
| McDyess. . | 2280 | .485 | .683 | 572 | 75 | 1020 | 13.4 |
| MacLean. . | 1107 | .426 | .732 | 205 | 89 | 625 | 11.2 |
| Mutombo. . | 2713 | .499 | .695 | 871 | 108 | 814 | 11.0 |
| L. Ellis. . . . | 1269 | .438 | .601 | 322 | 74 | 471 | 10.5 |
| Rose. . . . . | 2134 | .480 | .690 | 260 | 495 | 803 | 10.0 |
| Hammonds | 1045 | .474 | .765 | 223 | 23 | 342 | 4.8 |
| Williams . . | 817 | .370 | .846 | 122 | 74 | 241 | 4.6 |
| Overton. . . | 607 | .376 | .727 | 63 | 106 | 182 | 3.3 |

**Coach**—Bernie Bickerstaff

## Detroit Pistons

| | Min | FG% | FT% | Reb | Ast | Pts | Avg |
|---|---|---|---|---|---|---|---|
| Hill . . . . . . | 3260 | .462 | .751 | 783 | 548 | 1618 | 20.2 |
| Houston . . | 3072 | .453 | .823 | 300 | 250 | 1617 | 19.7 |
| Thorpe . . . | 2841 | .530 | .710 | 688 | 158 | 1161 | 14.2 |
| Dumars. . . | 2193 | .426 | .822 | 138 | 265 | 793 | 11.8 |
| Mills . . . . . | 1656 | .419 | .771 | 352 | 98 | 769 | 9.4 |
| Hunter. . . . | 2138 | .381 | .700 | 194 | 188 | 679 | 8.5 |
| Curry*. . . . | 783 | .453 | .726 | 85 | 27 | 211 | 4.6 |
| Ratliff . . . . | 1305 | .557 | .708 | 297 | 13 | 341 | 4.5 |
| Reid . . . . . | 997 | .567 | .662 | 203 | 11 | 263 | 3.8 |
| West. . . . . | 682 | .484 | .622 | 133 | 6 | 150 | 3.2 |

**Coach**—Doug Collins

## Golden State Warriors

| | Min | FG% | FT% | Reb | Ast | Pts | Avg |
|---|---|---|---|---|---|---|---|
| Sprewell . . | 3064 | .428 | .789 | 380 | 328 | 1473 | 18.9 |
| Smith . . . . | 2821 | .458 | .773 | 717 | 79 | 1251 | 15.3 |
| Mullin . . . . | 1617 | .499 | .856 | 159 | 194 | 734 | 13.3 |
| Armstrong . | 2262 | .468 | .839 | 184 | 401 | 1012 | 12.3 |
| Seikaly . . . | 1813 | .502 | .723 | 499 | 71 | 776 | 12.1 |
| Coles* . . . | 2615 | .409 | .796 | 260 | 422 | 892 | 11.0 |
| Willis*. . . . | 2135 | .456 | .708 | 638 | 53 | 794 | 10.6 |
| Kersey . . . | 1620 | .410 | .660 | 363 | 114 | 510 | 6.7 |
| Marshall. . . | 934 | .398 | .771 | 213 | 49 | 342 | 5.5 |
| Barry. . . . . | 712 | .492 | .838 | 63 | 85 | 257 | 3.8 |
| Rozier. . . . | 723 | .585 | .473 | 171 | 22 | 184 | 3.1 |

**Coach**—Rick Adelman

## Houston Rockets

| | Min | FG% | FT% | Reb | Ast | Pts | Avg |
|---|---|---|---|---|---|---|---|
| Olajuwon. . | 2797 | .514 | .724 | 784 | 257 | 1936 | 26.9 |
| Drexler. . . . | 1997 | .433 | .784 | 373 | 302 | 1005 | 19.3 |
| Cassell . . . | 1682 | .439 | .825 | 188 | 278 | 886 | 14.5 |
| Horry . . . . | 2634 | .410 | .776 | 412 | 281 | 853 | 12.0 |
| Elie. . . . . . | 1385 | .504 | .852 | 155 | 138 | 499 | 11.1 |
| Mack. . . . . | 868 | .422 | .848 | 98 | 79 | 335 | 10.8 |
| Bryant. . . . | 1587 | .543 | .718 | 351 | 52 | 611 | 8.6 |
| Brown . . . . | 2019 | .541 | .693 | 441 | 89 | 705 | 8.6 |
| Smith . . . . | 1617 | .433 | .821 | 96 | 245 | 580 | 8.5 |
| Recasner . | 1275 | .415 | .864 | 144 | 170 | 436 | 6.9 |
| Chilcutt . . . | 651 | .408 | .654 | 156 | 26 | 200 | 2.7 |

**Coach**—Rudy Tomjanovich

## Indiana Pacers

| | Min | FG% | FT% | Reb | Ast | Pts | Avg |
|---|---|---|---|---|---|---|---|
| Miller . . . . | 2621 | .473 | .863 | 214 | 253 | 1606 | 21.1 |
| Smits . . . . | 1901 | .521 | .788 | 433 | 110 | 1164 | 18.5 |
| McKey . . . | 2440 | .486 | .769 | 361 | 262 | 879 | 11.7 |
| D. Davis. . | 2617 | .558 | .467 | 709 | 76 | 803 | 10.3 |
| Jackson . . | 2643 | .473 | .785 | 307 | 635 | 806 | 10.0 |
| Pierce . . . | 1404 | .447 | .849 | 136 | 101 | 737 | 9.7 |
| A. Davis . . | 2092 | .490 | .713 | 501 | 43 | 719 | 8.8 |
| Johnson. . | 1002 | .413 | .886 | 153 | 69 | 475 | 7.7 |
| Workman . | 1164 | .390 | .740 | 124 | 213 | 279 | 3.6 |

**Coach**—Larry Brown

## Los Angeles Clippers

| | Min | FG% | FT% | Reb | Ast | Pts | Avg |
|---|---|---|---|---|---|---|---|
| Vaught. . . | 2966 | .525 | .727 | 808 | 112 | 1298 | 16.2 |
| Williams . . | 2157 | .543 | .734 | 492 | 122 | 1029 | 15.8 |
| Dehere. . . | 2018 | .459 | .755 | 143 | 350 | 1016 | 12.4 |
| Richardson | 2013 | .423 | .743 | 158 | 340 | 734 | 11.7 |
| Rogers. . . | 1950 | .477 | .628 | 286 | 167 | 774 | 11.6 |
| Sealy . . . . | 1601 | .415 | .799 | 240 | 116 | 712 | 11.5 |
| Barry . . . . | 1898 | .474 | .810 | 168 | 230 | 800 | 10.1 |
| Murray . . . | 1816 | .447 | .750 | 246 | 84 | 650 | 8.4 |
| Roberts . . | 795 | .464 | .556 | 162 | 41 | 356 | 7.0 |
| Piatkowski | 784 | .405 | .817 | 103 | 48 | 301 | 4.6 |
| Harvey* . . | 821 | .371 | .458 | 200 | 15 | 204 | 3.7 |
| Outlaw . . . | 985 | .575 | .444 | 200 | 50 | 286 | 3.6 |

**Coach**—Bill Fitch

## Los Angeles Lakers

| | Min | FG% | FT% | Reb | Ast | Pts | Avg |
|---|---|---|---|---|---|---|---|
| Ceballos. . | 2628 | .530 | .804 | 536 | 119 | 1656 | 21.2 |
| Van Exel . | 2513 | .417 | .799 | 181 | 509 | 1099 | 14.9 |
| Johnson . . | 958 | .466 | .856 | 183 | 220 | 468 | 14.6 |
| Campbell . | 2699 | .503 | .713 | 623 | 181 | 1143 | 13.9 |
| Divac . . . . | 2470 | .513 | .641 | 679 | 261 | 1020 | 12.9 |
| Jones. . . . | 2184 | .492 | .739 | 233 | 246 | 893 | 12.8 |
| Peeler . . . | 1608 | .452 | .709 | 137 | 118 | 710 | 9.7 |
| Threatt. . . | 1687 | .458 | .761 | 95 | 269 | 596 | 7.3 |
| Lynch. . . . | 1012 | .430 | .663 | 209 | 51 | 291 | 3.8 |
| Strong . . . | 746 | .426 | .812 | 178 | 32 | 214 | 3.4 |
| Blount . . . | 715 | .473 | .568 | 170 | 42 | 183 | 3.2 |

**Coach**—Del Harris

## Miami Heat

| | Min | FG% | FT% | Reb | Ast | Pts | Avg |
|---|---|---|---|---|---|---|---|
| Mourning . | 2671 | .523 | .685 | 727 | 159 | 1623 | 23.2 |
| T. Hardaway* | 2534 | .422 | .790 | 229 | 640 | 1217 | 15.2 |
| Chapman . | 1865 | .426 | .735 | 145 | 166 | 786 | 14.0 |
| Williams* . | 2169 | .444 | .703 | 319 | 230 | 995 | 13.6 |
| Gatling* . . | 1427 | .575 | .671 | 417 | 43 | 791 | 11.1 |
| Thomas . . | 1655 | .501 | .663 | 439 | 46 | 666 | 9.0 |
| Askins . . . | 1897 | .402 | .789 | 324 | 121 | 458 | 6.1 |
| Corbin*. . . | 1284 | .442 | .833 | 244 | 84 | 413 | 5.8 |
| Smith* . . . | 938 | .423 | .609 | 95 | 154 | 298 | 5.1 |

**Coach**—Pat Riley

## Milwaukee Bucks

| | Min | FG% | FT% | Reb | Ast | Pts | Avg |
|---|---|---|---|---|---|---|---|
| Baker. . . . | 3319 | .489 | .670 | 808 | 212 | 1729 | 21.1 |
| Robinson . | 3249 | .454 | .812 | 504 | 293 | 1660 | 20.2 |
| Douglas* . | 2335 | .504 | .731 | 180 | 436 | 890 | 11.3 |
| Newman . | 2690 | .495 | .802 | 200 | 154 | 889 | 10.8 |
| Benjamin* | 1896 | .498 | .722 | 539 | 64 | 728 | 8.8 |
| Cummings | 1777 | .462 | .650 | 445 | 89 | 645 | 8.0 |
| Conlon. . . | 958 | .468 | .764 | 177 | 68 | 395 | 5.3 |
| Mayberry . | 1705 | .420 | .603 | 90 | 302 | 422 | 5.1 |
| Respert . . | 845 | .387 | .833 | 74 | 68 | 303 | 4.9 |
| Keys . . . . | 816 | .418 | .837 | 125 | 65 | 232 | 3.4 |

**Coach**—Mike Dunleavy

## Minnesota Timberwolves

| | Min | FG% | FT% | Reb | Ast | Pts | Avg |
|---|---|---|---|---|---|---|---|
| Rider . . . . . | 2594 | .464 | .838 | 309 | 213 | 1470 | 19.6 |
| Gugliotta . . . | 2835 | .471 | .773 | 690 | 238 | 1261 | 16.2 |
| Lang* . . . . | 2365 | .447 | .801 | 455 | 65 | 832 | 11.7 |
| Mitchell . . . | 2145 | .490 | .814 | 339 | 74 | 844 | 10.8 |
| Garnett . . . | 2293 | .491 | .705 | 501 | 145 | 835 | 10.4 |
| Porter . . . . | 2072 | .442 | .785 | 212 | 452 | 773 | 9.4 |
| Webb. . . . . | 1462 | .433 | .862 | 100 | 294 | 544 | 7.1 |
| Martin*. . . . | 1149 | .406 | .842 | 82 | 217 | 415 | 7.0 |
| West . . . . . | 1639 | .445 | .792 | 161 | 119 | 465 | 6.4 |

**Coach**—Bill Blair; Flip Saunders

### New Jersey Nets

| | Min | FG% | FT% | Reb | Ast | Pts | Avg |
|---|---|---|---|---|---|---|---|
| Gilliam . . . . | 2856 | .474 | .791 | 713 | 140 | 1429 | 18.3 |
| Gill . . . . . . . | 1683 | .469 | .784 | 232 | 260 | 656 | 14.0 |
| Childs . . . . . | 2408 | .416 | .852 | 245 | 548 | 1002 | 12.8 |
| Bradley* . . . | 2329 | .443 | .687 | 638 | 63 | 944 | 11.9 |
| Edwards . . . | 1007 | .364 | .810 | 75 | 71 | 394 | 11.6 |
| Brown . . . . . | 2942 | .444 | .770 | 560 | 165 | 915 | 11.3 |
| Williams . . . | 1858 | .423 | .592 | 803 | 47 | 721 | 9.0 |
| Fleming. . . . | 1747 | .433 | .751 | 170 | 255 | 590 | 7.7 |
| O'Bannon . . | 1253 | .390 | .713 | 168 | 63 | 399 | 6.2 |
| Reeves* . . . | 833 | .419 | .744 | 79 | 118 | 279 | 5.5 |
| Graham*. . . | 613 | .404 | .765 | 57 | 52 | 240 | 4.5 |
| Dare . . . . . . | 626 | .438 | .613 | 181 | 0 | 164 | 2.8 |

**Coach**—Alfred "Butch" Beard

### New York Knickerbockers

| | Min | FG% | FT% | Reb | Ast | Pts | Avg |
|---|---|---|---|---|---|---|---|
| Ewing . . . . | 2783 | .466 | .761 | 806 | 160 | 1711 | 22.5 |
| Mason. . . . | 3457 | .563 | .720 | 764 | 363 | 1196 | 14.6 |
| Harper . . . | 2893 | .464 | .757 | 202 | 352 | 1149 | 14.0 |
| Starks . . . . | 2491 | .443 | .753 | 237 | 315 | 1024 | 12.6 |
| Oakley . . . | 1775 | .471 | .833 | 460 | 137 | 604 | 11.4 |
| Davis . . . . | 1773 | .486 | .868 | 123 | 103 | 789 | 10.7 |
| Anderson*. | 2060 | .436 | .810 | 246 | 197 | 742 | 9.8 |
| Reid . . . . . | 1313 | .494 | .754 | 255 | 42 | 427 | 6.6 |
| Ward. . . . . | 787 | .399 | .685 | 102 | 132 | 244 | 3.9 |

**Coach**—Don Nelson; Jeff Van Gundy

### Orlando Magic

| | Min | FG% | FT% | Reb | Ast | Pts | Avg |
|---|---|---|---|---|---|---|---|
| O'Neal . . . | 1946 | .573 | .487 | 596 | 155 | 1434 | 26.6 |
| A. Hardaway | 3015 | .513 | .767 | 354 | 582 | 1780 | 21.7 |
| Scott. . . . . | 3041 | .440 | .820 | 309 | 243 | 1431 | 17.5 |
| Anderson . | 2717 | .442 | .692 | 415 | 279 | 1134 | 14.7 |
| Grant . . . . | 2286 | .513 | .734 | 580 | 170 | 847 | 13.4 |
| Shaw . . . . | 1679 | .374 | .798 | 224 | 336 | 496 | 6.6 |
| Royal . . . . | 963 | .491 | .762 | 153 | 42 | 337 | 5.3 |
| Wolf . . . . . | 1065 | .513 | .724 | 187 | 63 | 291 | 4.5 |
| Bowie . . . . | 1078 | .471 | .870 | 123 | 105 | 308 | 4.2 |
| Koncak . . . | 1288 | .480 | .561 | 272 | 51 | 203 | 3.0 |

**Coach**—Brian Hill

### Philadelphia 76ers

| | Min | FG% | FT% | Reb | Ast | Pts | Avg |
|---|---|---|---|---|---|---|---|
| Stackhouse . . | 2701 | .414 | .747 | 265 | 278 | 1384 | 19.2 |
| Weatherspoon | 3096 | .484 | .746 | 753 | 158 | 1300 | 16.7 |
| Maxwell. . . . . | 2467 | .390 | .756 | 229 | 330 | 1217 | 16.2 |
| Ruffin . . . . . . | 1551 | .406 | .813 | 132 | 269 | 778 | 12.8 |
| Massenburg*. | 1463 | .495 | .707 | 352 | 30 | 539 | 10.0 |
| Higgins . . . . . | 916 | .415 | .946 | 92 | 55 | 351 | 8.0 |
| Pinckney* . . . | 1710 | .510 | .760 | 458 | 72 | 478 | 6.5 |
| Alston . . . . . . | 1614 | .512 | .491 | 302 | 61 | 452 | 6.2 |
| Dumas . . . . . | 739 | .468 | .700 | 99 | 44 | 241 | 6.2 |
| Sutton* . . . . . | 655 | .392 | .761 | 50 | 102 | 252 | 5.3 |
| Walters* . . . . | 610 | .412 | .808 | 55 | 106 | 186 | 4.2 |
| Thompson. . . | 773 | .398 | .792 | 199 | 26 | 85 | 1.9 |

**Coach**—John Lucas

### Phoenix Suns

| | Min | FG% | FT% | Reb | Ast | Pts | Avg |
|---|---|---|---|---|---|---|---|
| Barkley . . . | 2632 | .500 | .777 | 821 | 262 | 1649 | 23.2 |
| Johnson . . | 2007 | .507 | .859 | 221 | 517 | 1047 | 18.7 |
| Finley . . . . | 3212 | .476 | .749 | 374 | 289 | 1233 | 15.0 |
| Manning . . | 816 | .459 | .752 | 143 | 65 | 441 | 13.4 |
| Person . . . | 2609 | .445 | .771 | 321 | 138 | 1045 | 12.7 |
| Tisdale . . . | 1152 | .495 | .765 | 214 | 58 | 672 | 10.7 |
| Perry. . . . . | 1668 | .475 | .778 | 136 | 353 | 697 | 8.6 |
| Green . . . . | 2113 | .484 | .709 | 554 | 72 | 612 | 7.5 |
| Williams . . | 1652 | .453 | .731 | 372 | 62 | 455 | 7.3 |
| Kleine . . . . | 663 | .420 | .800 | 132 | 44 | 164 | 2.9 |

**Coach**—Paul Westphal; Cotton Fitzsimmons

### Portland Trail Blazers

| | Min | FG% | FT% | Reb | Ast | Pts | Avg |
|---|---|---|---|---|---|---|---|
| C. Robinson | 2980 | .423 | .664 | 443 | 190 | 1644 | 21.1 |
| Strickland . | 2526 | .460 | .652 | 297 | 640 | 1256 | 18.7 |
| Sabonis. . . | 1735 | .545 | .757 | 588 | 130 | 1058 | 14.5 |
| McKie . . . . | 2259 | .467 | .764 | 304 | 205 | 864 | 10.7 |
| Grant . . . . | 2394 | .462 | .545 | 361 | 111 | 709 | 9.3 |
| J. Robinson | 1627 | .399 | .659 | 157 | 150 | 649 | 8.5 |
| Trent. . . . . | 1219 | .513 | .553 | 238 | 50 | 518 | 7.5 |
| Williams . . | 1672 | .500 | .668 | 404 | 42 | 511 | 7.3 |
| R. Robinson | 715 | .416 | .647 | 78 | 142 | 247 | 5.7 |
| Dudley . . . | 1924 | .453 | .510 | 720 | 37 | 404 | 5.1 |

**Coach**—P.J. Carlesimo

### Sacramento Kings

| | Min | FG% | FT% | Reb | Ast | Pts | Avg |
|---|---|---|---|---|---|---|---|
| Richmond . | 2946 | .447 | .866 | 269 | 255 | 1872 | 23.1 |
| Grant . . . . | 2398 | .507 | .732 | 545 | 127 | 1120 | 14.4 |
| Owens* . . | 1982 | .480 | .636 | 411 | 204 | 808 | 13.0 |
| Polynice. . | 2441 | .527 | .601 | 764 | 58 | 985 | 12.2 |
| Marciulionis | 1039 | .452 | .775 | 77 | 118 | 571 | 10.8 |
| Edney . . . | 2481 | .412 | .782 | 201 | 491 | 860 | 10.8 |
| Gamble* . | 1325 | .401 | .792 | 113 | 100 | 386 | 5.9 |
| Williamson | 609 | .466 | .560 | 114 | 23 | 297 | 5.6 |
| Smith. . . . | 1384 | .605 | .384 | 389 | 110 | 357 | 5.5 |
| Simmons . | 810 | .396 | .733 | 145 | 83 | 246 | 4.6 |
| Causwell . | 1044 | .417 | .729 | 248 | 20 | 250 | 3.4 |
| Hurley . . . | 1059 | .283 | .800 | 75 | 216 | 220 | 3.1 |

**Coach**—Garry St. Jean

### San Antonio Spurs

| | Min | FG% | FT% | Reb | Ast | Pts | Avg |
|---|---|---|---|---|---|---|---|
| Robinson . . | 3019 | .516 | .761 | 1000 | 247 | 2051 | 25.0 |
| Elliott . . . . . | 2901 | .466 | .771 | 396 | 211 | 1537 | 20.0 |
| Del Negro. . | 2766 | .497 | .832 | 272 | 315 | 1191 | 14.5 |
| Johnson. . . | 3084 | .494 | .721 | 206 | 789 | 1071 | 13.1 |
| Person. . . . | 2131 | .437 | .644 | 413 | 100 | 873 | 10.9 |
| Smith* . . . . | 1716 | .422 | .730 | 362 | 65 | 609 | 8.3 |
| Perdue. . . . | 1396 | .523 | .536 | 485 | 33 | 413 | 5.2 |
| Rivers. . . . . | 1235 | .372 | .750 | 138 | 123 | 311 | 4.0 |

**Coach**—Bob Hill

### Seattle SuperSonics

| | Min | FG% | FT% | Reb | Ast | Pts | Avg |
|---|---|---|---|---|---|---|---|
| Kemp. . . . | 2631 | .561 | .742 | 904 | 173 | 1550 | 19.6 |
| Payton . . . | 3162 | .484 | .748 | 339 | 608 | 1563 | 19.3 |
| Schrempf . | 2200 | .486 | .776 | 328 | 276 | 1080 | 17.1 |
| Hawkins . . | 2823 | .473 | .874 | 297 | 218 | 1281 | 15.6 |
| Perkins . . | 2169 | .408 | .793 | 367 | 120 | 970 | 11.8 |
| Askew . . . | 1725 | .493 | .767 | 218 | 163 | 584 | 8.5 |
| Johnson. . | 1519 | .511 | .669 | 433 | 48 | 446 | 5.5 |
| Brickowski | 986 | .488 | .709 | 151 | 58 | 339 | 5.4 |
| McMillan. . | 1261 | .420 | .707 | 210 | 197 | 275 | 5.0 |
| Wingate . . | 695 | .415 | .780 | 56 | 58 | 223 | 3.7 |

**Coach**—George Karl

### Toronto Raptors

| | Min | FG% | FT% | Reb | Ast | Pts | Avg |
|---|---|---|---|---|---|---|---|
| Stoudamire | 2865 | .426 | .797 | 281 | 653 | 1331 | 19.0 |
| Murray . . . | 2458 | .454 | .831 | 352 | 131 | 1325 | 16.2 |
| Miller . . . . | 2516 | .526 | .661 | 562 | 219 | 982 | 12.9 |
| Wright* . . | 1434 | .484 | .645 | 356 | 38 | 664 | 11.6 |
| Robertson | 2478 | .470 | .677 | 342 | 323 | 718 | 9.3 |
| Rogers. . . | 1043 | .517 | .546 | 170 | 35 | 430 | 7.7 |
| Tabak . . . | 1332 | .543 | .561 | 320 | 62 | 514 | 7.7 |
| Christie*. . | 1036 | .445 | .742 | 154 | 117 | 415 | 7.5 |
| Earl . . . . . | 655 | .424 | .719 | 129 | 27 | 316 | 7.5 |
| King. . . . . | 868 | .431 | .701 | 110 | 88 | 279 | 4.5 |

**Coach**—Brendan Malone

### Utah Jazz

| | Min | FG% | FT% | Reb | Ast | Pts | Avg |
|---|---|---|---|---|---|---|---|
| Malone. . . | 3113 | .519 | .723 | 804 | 345 | 2106 | 25.7 |
| Hornacek . | 2588 | .502 | .893 | 209 | 340 | 1247 | 15.2 |
| Stockton. . | 2915 | .538 | .830 | 226 | 916 | 1209 | 14.7 |
| Morris . . . | 1424 | .437 | .772 | 229 | 77 | 691 | 10.5 |
| Benoit . . . | 1961 | .439 | .777 | 383 | 82 | 661 | 8.2 |
| Carr. . . . . | 1532 | .457 | .792 | 200 | 74 | 580 | 7.3 |
| Keefe. . . . | 1708 | .520 | .692 | 455 | 64 | 499 | 6.1 |
| Spencer. . | 1267 | .520 | .689 | 306 | 11 | 396 | 5.6 |
| Eisley. . . . | 961 | .430 | .844 | 78 | 146 | 287 | 4.4 |
| Foster . . . | 803 | .439 | .847 | 178 | 25 | 276 | 3.8 |
| Ostertag. . | 661 | .473 | .667 | 175 | 5 | 208 | 3.6 |

**Coach**—Jerry Sloan

### Vancouver Grizzlies

| | Min | FG% | FT% | Reb | Ast | Pts | Avg |
|---|---|---|---|---|---|---|---|
| Anthony . . | 2096 | .415 | .771 | 174 | 476 | 967 | 14.0 |
| Reeves . . | 2460 | .457 | .732 | 570 | 109 | 1021 | 13.3 |
| B. Edwards | 2773 | .419 | .755 | 346 | 212 | 1043 | 12.7 |
| Scott . . . . | 1894 | .401 | .835 | 192 | 123 | 819 | 10.2 |
| Murdock*. | 1673 | .416 | .797 | 169 | 327 | 647 | 8.9 |
| King. . . . . | 1930 | .427 | .662 | 285 | 104 | 634 | 7.9 |
| Wilkins. . . | 738 | .376 | .870 | 65 | 68 | 188 | 6.7 |
| Amaya. . . | 1104 | .480 | .651 | 303 | 33 | 339 | 6.3 |
| Avent. . . . | 1586 | .384 | .740 | 355 | 69 | 415 | 5.8 |
| Mobley*. . | 676 | .536 | .448 | 140 | 22 | 188 | 4.8 |

**Coach**—Brian Winters

### Washington Bullets

| | Min | FG% | FT% | Reb | Ast | Pts | Avg |
|---|---|---|---|---|---|---|---|
| Howard . . | 3294 | .489 | .749 | 660 | 360 | 1789 | 22.1 |
| Pack . . . . | 1084 | .428 | .846 | 132 | 242 | 560 | 18.1 |
| Cheaney . | 2324 | .471 | .706 | 239 | 154 | 1055 | 15.1 |
| Muresan. . | 2242 | .584 | .619 | 728 | 56 | 1104 | 14.5 |
| Wallace . . | 1788 | .487 | .650 | 303 | 85 | 655 | 10.1 |
| B. Price . . | 2042 | .472 | .874 | 228 | 416 | 810 | 10.0 |
| Legler . . . | 1775 | .507 | .863 | 140 | 136 | 726 | 9.4 |
| Eackles . . | 1238 | .427 | .831 | 148 | 86 | 474 | 8.6 |
| Butler. . . . | 858 | .384 | .578 | 118 | 67 | 237 | 3.9 |
| McCann . . | 653 | .497 | .473 | 143 | 24 | 188 | 3.0 |
| McIlvaine . | 1195 | .428 | .552 | 230 | 11 | 182 | 2.3 |

**Coach**—Jim Lynam

# 1996 NBA Player Draft, First-Round Picks

| | Team | Player, College |
|---|---|---|
| 1. | Philadelphia | Allen Iverson, Georgetown |
| 2. | Toronto | Marcus Camby, Massachusetts |
| 3. | Vancouver | Shareef Abdur-Rahim, California |
| 4. | Milwaukee | Stephon Marbury,[1] Georgia Tech |
| 5. | Minnesota | Ray Allen,[2] Connecticut |
| 6. | Boston | Antoine Walker, Kentucky |
| 7. | L.A. Clippers | Lorenzen Wright, Memphis |
| 8. | New Jersey | Kerry Kittles, Villanova |
| 9. | Dallas | Samaki Walker, Louisville |
| 10. | Indiana | Erick Dampler, Mississippi State |
| 11. | Golden State | Todd Fuller, North Carolina State |
| 12. | Cleveland | Vitaly Potapenko, Wright State |
| 13. | Charlotte | Kobe Bryant, Lower Merion H.S. (PA) |
| 14. | Sacramento | Predrag Stojakovic, PAOK (Greece) |
| 15. | Phoenix | Steve Nash, Santa Clara |
| 16. | Charlotte | Tony Delk, Kentucky |
| 17. | Portland | Jermaine O'Neal, Eau Claire H.S. (SC) |
| 18. | New York | John Wallace, Syracuse |
| 19. | New York | Walter McCarty, Kentucky |
| 20. | Cleveland | Zydrunas Ilgauskas, Lithuania |
| 21. | New York | Dontae Jones, Mississippi State |
| 22. | Vancouver | Roy Rogers, Alabama |
| 23. | Denver | Efthimis Retzias, PAOK (Greece) |
| 24. | L.A. Lakers | Derek Fisher, Arkansas-Little Rock |
| 25. | Utah | Martin Muursepp,[3] BC Kalev Tallinn (Estonia) |
| 26. | Detroit | Jerome Williams, Georgetown |
| 27. | Orlando | Brian Evans, Indiana |
| 28. | Atlanta | Priest Lauderdale, Peristeri Nikas (Greece) |
| 29. | Connecticut | Travis Knight, Connecticut |

(1) Traded to Minnesota for Ray Allen and a future 1st-round draft choice. (2) Traded to Milwaukee. (3) Traded to Miami for future 1st-round draft choice.

# Number-One First-Round NBA Draft Picks, 1966-96

| Year | Team | Player, college |
|---|---|---|
| 1966 | New York | Cazzie Russell, Michigan |
| 1967 | Detroit | Jimmy Walker, Providence |
| 1968 | Houston | Elvin Hayes, Houston |
| 1969 | Milwaukee | Lew Alcindor,[1] UCLA |
| 1970 | Detroit | Bob Lanier, St. Bonaventure |
| 1971 | Cleveland | Austin Carr, Notre Dame |
| 1972 | Portland | LaRue Martin, Loyola-Chicago |
| 1973 | Philadelphia | Doug Collins, Illinois St. |
| 1974 | Portland | Bill Walton, UCLA |
| 1975 | Atlanta | David Thompson,[2] N.C. State |
| 1976 | Houston | John Lucas, Maryland |
| 1977 | Milwaukee | Kent Benson, Indiana |
| 1978 | Portland | Mychal Thompson, Minnesota |
| 1979 | L.A. Lakers | Magic Johnson, Michigan St. |
| 1980 | Golden State | Joe Barry Carroll, Purdue |
| 1981 | Dallas | Mark Aguirre, DePaul |
| 1982 | L.A. Lakers | James Worthy, N. Carolina |
| 1983 | Houston | Ralph Sampson, Virginia |
| 1984 | Houston | Akeem Olajuwon, Houston |
| 1985 | New York | Patrick Ewing, Georgetown |
| 1986 | Cleveland | Brad Daugherty, N. Carolina |
| 1987 | San Antonio | David Robinson, Navy |
| 1988 | L.A. Clippers | Danny Manning, Kansas |
| 1989 | Sacramento | Pervis Ellison, Louisville |
| 1990 | New Jersey | Derrick Coleman, Syracuse |
| 1991 | Charlotte | Larry Johnson, UNLV |
| 1992 | Orlando | Shaquille O'Neal, LSU |
| 1993 | Orlando | Chris Webber,[3] Michigan |
| 1994 | Milwaukee | Glenn Robinson, Purdue |
| 1995 | Golden State | Joe Smith, Maryland |
| 1996 | Philadelphia | Allen Iverson, Georgetown |

(1) Later Kareem Abdul-Jabbar. (2) Signed with Denver of the ABA. (3) Traded to Golden State.

# All-Time NBA Statistical Leaders

(At the start of the 1996-97 season. *Player active in 1995-96 season.)

### Scoring Average
(Minimum 400 games or 10,000 pts)

| | G | Pts. | Avg |
|---|---|---|---|
| *Michael Jordan | 766 | 24,489 | 32.0 |
| Wilt Chamberlain | 1,045 | 31,419 | 30.1 |
| Elgin Baylor | 846 | 23,149 | 27.4 |
| Jerry West | 932 | 25,192 | 27.0 |
| Bob Pettit | 792 | 20,880 | 26.4 |
| George Gervin | 791 | 20,708 | 26.2 |
| *Karl Malone | 898 | 23,343 | 26.0 |
| Dominique Wilkins | 984 | 25,389 | 25.8 |
| Oscar Robertson | 1,040 | 26,710 | 25.7 |
| *David Robinson | 557 | 14,260 | 25.6 |

### Field Goal Percentage
(Minimum 2,000 field goals made)

| | FGA | FGM | Pct. |
|---|---|---|---|
| Artis Gilmore | 9,570 | 5,732 | .599 |
| *Mark West | 4,084 | 2,391 | .585 |
| *Shaquille O'Neal | 5,522 | 3,208 | .581 |
| Steve Johnson | 4,965 | 2,841 | .572 |
| Darryl Dawkins | 6,079 | 3,477 | .572 |
| *James Donaldson | 5,442 | 3,105 | .571 |
| Jeff Ruland | 3,734 | 2,105 | .564 |
| Kareem Abdul-Jabbar | 28,307 | 15,837 | .559 |
| Kevin McHale | 12,334 | 6,830 | .554 |
| *Otis Thorpe | 9,515 | 5,283 | .555 |

### Free Throw Percentage
(Minimum 1,200 free throws made)

| | FTA | FTM | Pct. |
|---|---|---|---|
| *Mark Price | 2,088 | 1,893 | .907 |
| Rick Barry | 4,243 | 3,818 | .900 |
| Calvin Murphy | 3,864 | 3,445 | .892 |
| *Scott Skiles | 1,741 | 1,548 | .889 |
| Larry Bird | 4,471 | 3,960 | .886 |
| Bill Sharman | 3,559 | 3,143 | .883 |
| *Reggie Miller | 4,122 | 3,616 | .877 |
| *Ricky Pierce | 3,664 | 3,207 | .875 |
| Kiki Vandeweghe | 3,997 | 3,484 | .872 |
| *Jeff Malone | 3,383 | 2,947 | .871 |

### Points

| | |
|---|---|
| Kareem Abdul-Jabbar | 38,387 |
| Wilt Chamberlain | 31,419 |
| Moses Malone | 27,409 |
| Elvin Hayes | 27,313 |
| Oscar Robertson | 26,710 |
| John Havlicek | 26,395 |
| Alex English | 25,613 |
| Dominique Wilkins | 25,389 |
| Jerry West | 25,192 |
| *Michael Jordan | 24,489 |

### Games Played

| | |
|---|---|
| *Robert Parish | 1,568 |
| Kareem Abdul-Jabbar | 1,560 |
| Moses Malone | 1,329 |
| Elvin Hayes | 1,303 |
| John Havlicek | 1,270 |
| Paul Silas | 1,254 |
| Alex English | 1,193 |
| *Buck Williams | 1,192 |
| *James Edwards | 1,168 |
| Tree Rollins | 1,156 |

### Assists

| | |
|---|---|
| *John Stockton | 11,310 |
| *Magic Johnson | 10,141 |
| Oscar Robertson | 9,887 |
| Isiah Thomas | 9,061 |
| Maurice Cheeks | 7,392 |
| Lenny Wilkens | 7,211 |
| Bob Cousy | 6,955 |
| Guy Rodgers | 6,917 |
| Nate Archibald | 6,476 |
| John Lucas | 6,454 |

### Field Goals Made

| | |
|---|---|
| Kareem Abdul-Jabbar | 15,837 |
| Wilt Chamberlain | 12,681 |
| Elvin Hayes | 10,976 |
| Alex English | 10,659 |
| John Havlicek | 10,513 |
| *Robert Parish | 9,544 |
| Dominique Wilkins | 9,516 |
| Oscar Robertson | 9,508 |
| Moses Malone | 9,435 |
| *Michael Jordan | 9,161 |

### Rebounds

| | |
|---|---|
| Wilt Chamberlain | 23,924 |
| Bill Russell | 21,620 |
| Kareem Addul-Jabbar | 17,440 |
| Elvin Hayes | 16,279 |
| Moses Malone | 16,212 |
| *Robert Parish | 14,626 |
| Nate Thurmond | 14,464 |
| Walt Bellamy | 14,241 |
| Wes Unseld | 13,769 |
| Jerry Lucas | 12,942 |

# Basketball Hall of Fame, Springfield, MA

(* denotes 1996 inductee)

**Players**
Abdul-Jabbar, Kareem
Archibald, Nate
Arizin, Paul
Barlow, Thomas
Barry, Rick
Baylor, Elgin
Beckman, John
Bellamy, Walt
Belov, Sergei
Bing, Dave
Blazejowski, Carol
Borgmann, Bennie
Bradley, Bill
Brennan, Joseph
Cervi, Al
Chamberlain, Wilt
Cooper, Charles
Cosic, Kresimir*
Cousy, Bob
Cowens, Dave
Cunningham, Billy
Davies, Bob
DeBernardi, Forrest
DeBusschere, Dave
Dehnert, Dutch
Donovan, Anne
Endacott, Paul
Erving, Julius
Foster, Bud
Frazier, Walt
Friedman, Max
Fulks, Joe
Gale, Lauren
Gallatin, Harry
Gates, Pop
Gervin, George*
Gola, Tom
Goodrich, Gail*
Greer, Hal
Gruenig, Ace
Hagan, Cliff
Hanson, Victor
Harris, Luisa
Havlicek, John
Hawkins, Connie
Hayes, Elvin
Heinsohn, Tom
Holman, Nat
Houbregs, Bob
Hyatt, Chuck
Issel, Dan
Jeannette, Buddy
Johnson, William
Johnston, Neil
Jones, K.C.
Jones, Sam
Krause, Moose
Kurland, Bob
Lanier, Bob
Lapchick, Joe
Lieberman-Cline, Nancy*
Lovellette, Clyde
Lucas, Jerry
Luisetti, Hank
Macauley, Ed
Maravich, Pete
Martin, Slater
McCracken, Branch
McCracken, Jack
McDermott, Bobby
McGuire, Dick
Meyers, Ann
Mikan, George
Mikkelsen, Vern
Miller, Cheryl
Monroe, Earl
Murphy, Calvin
Murphy, Stretch
Page, Pat
Pettit, Bob
Phillip, Andy
Pollard, Jim
Ramsey, Frank
Reed, Willis
Robertson, Oscar
Roosma, John S.
Russell, Bill
Russell, Honey
Schayes, Adolph
Schmidt, Ernest
Schommer, John
Sedran, Barney
Semyonova, Ulyona
Sharman, Bill
Steinmetz, Christian
Thompson, Cat
Thompson, David*
Thurmond, Nate
Twyman, Jack
Unseld, Wes
Vandivier, Fuzzy
Wachter, Edward
Walton, Bill
Wanzer, Bobby
West, Jerry
White, Nera
Wilkins, Lenny
Wooden, John
Yardley, George*

**Coaches**
Anderson, Harold
Auerbach, Red
Barry, Sam
Blood, Ernest
Cann, Howard
Carlson, Dr. H. C.
Carnesecca, Lou
Carnevale, Ben
Case, Everett
Crum, Denny
Daly, Chuck
Dean, Everett
Diddle, Edgar
Drake, Bruce
Gaines, Clarence
Gardner, Jack
Gill, Slats
Gomelsky, Aleksandr
Harshman, Marv
Hickey, Edgar
Hobson, Howard
Holzman, Red
Iba, Hank
Julian, Alvin
Keaney, Frank
Keogan, George
Knight, Bob
Kundla, John
Lambert, Ward
Litwack, Harry
Loeffler, Kenneth
Lonborg, Dutch
McCutchan, Arad
McGuire, Al
McGuire, Frank
Meanwell, Dr. W.E.
Meyer, Ray
Miller, Ralph
Ramsay, Jack
Rupp, Adolph
Sachs, Leonard
Shelton, Everett
Smith, Dean
Taylor, Fred
Teague, Bertha
Wade, Margaret
Watts, Stan
Wooden, John
Woolpert, Phil

**Referees**
Enright, James
Hepburn, George
Hoyt, George
Kennedy, Matthew
Leith, Lloyd
Mihalik, Red
Nucatola, John
Quigley, Ernest
Shirley, J. Dallas
Strom, Earl
Tobey, David
Walsh, David

**Contributors**
Abbott, Senda B.
Allen, Phog
Bee, Clair
Brown, Walter
Bunn, John
Douglas, Bob
Duer, Al O.
Fagan, Cliff
Fisher, Harry
Fleisher, Larry
Gottlieb, Edward
Gulick, Dr. L. H.
Harrison, Lester
Hepp, Dr. Ferenc
Hickox, Edward
Hinkle, Tony
Irish, Ned
Jones, R. W.
Kennedy, Walter
Liston, Emil
McLendon, John
Mokray, Bill
Morgan, Ralph
Morgenweck, Frank
Naismith, Dr. James
Newell, Pete
O'Brien, John
O'Brien, Larry
Olsen, Harold
Podoloff, Maurice
Porter, H. V.
Reis, William
Ripley, Elmer
St. John, Lynn
Saperstein, Abe
Schabinger, Arthur
Stagg, Amos Alonzo
Stankovich, Boris
Steitz, Edward
Taylor, Chuck
Tower, Oswald
Trester, Arthur
Wells, Clifford
Wilke, Lou

# All-Time NBA Coaching Victories

(*Active through 1995-96 season)

| Coach | W-L | Pct. |
|---|---|---|
| Lenny Wilkens* | 1,014-850 | .544 |
| Red Auerbach | 938-479 | .662 |
| Dick Motta* | 918-965 | .488 |
| Bill Fitch* | 891-995 | .472 |
| Jack Ramsay | 864-783 | .525 |
| Don Nelson* | 851-629 | .575 |
| Cotton Fitzsimmons* | 832-767 | .520 |
| Pat Riley* | 798-339 | .702 |
| Gene Shue | 784-861 | .477 |
| John MacLeod | 707-657 | .518 |
| Red Holzman | 696-604 | .535 |
| Doug Moe | 628-529 | .543 |
| Larry Brown* | 585-437 | .572 |
| Chuck Daly | 564-379 | .598 |
| Alvin Attles | 557-518 | .518 |
| K.C. Jones | 522-252 | .674 |
| Jerry Sloan* | 513-341 | .601 |
| Kevin Loughery | 474-662 | .417 |
| Alex Hannum | 471-412 | .533 |
| Mike Fratello* | 461-362 | .560 |
| Billy Cunningham | 454-196 | .698 |
| Del Harris* | 433-404 | .517 |
| Larry Costello | 430-300 | .589 |
| Tom Heinsohn | 427-263 | .619 |
| John Kundla | 423-302 | .583 |
| Phil Jackson* | 414-160 | .721 |
| George Karl* | 385-280 | .579 |
| Hubie Brown | 341-410 | .454 |
| Bill Russell | 341-290 | .540 |
| Bill Sharman | 333-240 | .581 |
| Rick Adelman* | 327-200 | .620 |
| Richie Guerin | 327-291 | .529 |
| Al Cervi | 326-241 | .575 |
| Joe Lapchick | 326-247 | .569 |

# NBA Home Courts

| Team | Name (built) | Capacity |
|---|---|---|
| Atlanta | The Omni (1972) | 16,378 |
| Boston | FleetCenter (1995) | 18,624 |
| Charlotte | Charlotte Coliseum (1988) | 24,042 |
| Chicago | United Center (1994) | 21,711 |
| Cleveland | Gund Arena (1994) | 20,562 |
| Dallas | Reunion Arena (1980) | 18,042 |
| Denver | McNichols Sports Arena (1975) | 17,171 |
| Detroit | Palace of Auburn Hills (1988) | 21,454 |
| Golden State | San Jose Arena (1996) | 18,500 |
| Houston | The Summit (1975) | 16,285 |
| Indiana | Market Square Arena (1974) | 16,530 |
| L.A. Clippers | L.A. Memorial Sports Arena (1959); | 16,021 |
| | Arrowhead Pond of Anaheim (1992) | 18,211 |
| L.A. Lakers | The Great Western Forum (1967) | 17,505 |
| Miami | Miami Arena (1988) | 15,200 |
| Milwaukee | Bradley Center (1988) | 18,633 |
| Minnesota | Target Center (1990) | 19,006 |
| New Jersey | Continental Airlines Arena (1981) | 20,039 |
| New York | Madison Square Garden (1968) | 19,763 |
| Orlando | Orlando Arena (1989) | 17,248 |
| Philadelphia | CoreStates Center (1996) | 21,000 |
| Phoenix | America West Arena (1992) | 19,023 |
| Portland | The Rose Garden (1995) | 21,401 |
| Sacramento | ARCO Arena (1988) | 17,317 |
| San Antonio | Alamodome (1993) | 20,662/34,215 |
| Seattle | KeyArena (1995) | 17,072 |
| Toronto | SkyDome (1989) | 25,356 |
| Utah | Delta Center (1991) | 19,911 |
| Vancouver | General Motors Place (1995) | 19,193 |
| Washington | USAir Arena (1973) | 18,756 |

# COLLEGE BASKETBALL

## Final NCAA Division I Conference Standing, 1995-96

(*conference tournament champion; †conference does not hold a tournament)

### American West

| Team | Conference W | Conference L | Overall W | Overall L |
|---|---|---|---|---|
| Cal Poly SLO | 5 | 1 | 16 | 13 |
| Southern Utah* | 3 | 3 | 15 | 13 |
| Cal St. Northridge | 2 | 4 | 7 | 20 |
| Cal St. Sacramento | 2 | 4 | 7 | 20 |

### Atlantic Coast

| Team | Conference W | Conference L | Overall W | Overall L |
|---|---|---|---|---|
| Georgia Tech | 13 | 3 | 24 | 12 |
| Wake Forest* | 12 | 4 | 26 | 6 |
| North Carolina | 10 | 6 | 21 | 11 |
| Duke | 8 | 8 | 18 | 13 |
| Maryland | 8 | 8 | 17 | 13 |
| Clemson | 7 | 9 | 18 | 11 |
| Virginia | 6 | 10 | 12 | 15 |
| Florida State | 5 | 11 | 13 | 14 |
| North Carolina St. | 3 | 13 | 15 | 16 |

### Atlantic 10

| Team | Conference W | Conference L | Overall W | Overall L |
|---|---|---|---|---|
| **Eastern Division** | | | | |
| Massachusetts* | 15 | 1 | 35 | 2 |
| Temple | 12 | 4 | 20 | 13 |
| St. Joseph's (PA) | 9 | 7 | 19 | 13 |
| Rhode Island | 8 | 8 | 20 | 14 |
| St. Bonaventure | 4 | 12 | 10 | 18 |
| Fordham | 2 | 14 | 4 | 23 |
| **Western Division** | | | | |
| Virginia Tech | 13 | 3 | 23 | 6 |
| George Washington | 13 | 3 | 21 | 8 |
| Xavier (OH) | 8 | 8 | 13 | 15 |
| Dayton | 6 | 10 | 15 | 14 |
| La Salle | 3 | 13 | 6 | 24 |
| Duquesne | 3 | 13 | 9 | 18 |

### Big East

| Team | Conference W | Conference L | Overall W | Overall L |
|---|---|---|---|---|
| **Big East 7** | | | | |
| Georgetown | 13 | 5 | 29 | 8 |
| Syracuse | 12 | 6 | 29 | 9 |
| Providence | 9 | 9 | 18 | 12 |
| Miami (FL) | 8 | 10 | 15 | 13 |
| Seton Hall | 7 | 11 | 12 | 16 |
| Rutgers | 6 | 12 | 9 | 18 |
| Pittsburgh | 5 | 13 | 10 | 17 |
| **Big East 6** | | | | |
| Connecticut* | 17 | 1 | 32 | 3 |
| Villanova | 14 | 4 | 26 | 7 |
| Boston College | 10 | 8 | 19 | 11 |
| West Virginia | 7 | 11 | 12 | 15 |
| St. John's (NY) | 5 | 13 | 11 | 16 |
| Notre Dame | 4 | 14 | 9 | 18 |

### Big Eight

| Team | Conference W | Conference L | Overall W | Overall L |
|---|---|---|---|---|
| Kansas* | 12 | 2 | 29 | 5 |
| Iowa St. | 9 | 5 | 24 | 9 |
| Oklahoma | 8 | 6 | 17 | 13 |
| Oklahoma St. | 7 | 7 | 17 | 10 |
| Kansas St. | 7 | 7 | 17 | 12 |
| Missouri | 6 | 8 | 18 | 15 |
| Nebraska | 4 | 10 | 21 | 14 |
| Colorado | 3 | 11 | 9 | 18 |

### Big Sky

| Team | Conference W | Conference L | Overall W | Overall L |
|---|---|---|---|---|
| Montana St.* | 11 | 3 | 21 | 9 |
| Weber St. | 10 | 4 | 20 | 10 |
| Montana | 10 | 4 | 20 | 8 |
| Boise St. | 10 | 4 | 15 | 13 |
| Idaho St. | 7 | 7 | 11 | 15 |
| Idaho | 5 | 9 | 12 | 16 |
| Northern Arizona | 3 | 11 | 6 | 20 |
| E. Washington | 0 | 14 | 3 | 23 |

### Big South

| Team | Conference W | Conference L | Overall W | Overall L |
|---|---|---|---|---|
| N.C.-Greensboro* | 11 | 3 | 20 | 10 |
| N.C.-Asheville | 9 | 5 | 18 | 10 |
| Liberty | 9 | 5 | 17 | 12 |
| Charleston So. | 9 | 5 | 15 | 13 |
| Radford | 8 | 6 | 14 | 13 |
| Winthrop | 6 | 8 | 7 | 19 |
| Md.-Balt. County | 3 | 11 | 5 | 22 |
| Coastal Carolina | 1 | 13 | 5 | 21 |

### Big Ten†

| Team | Conference W | Conference L | Overall W | Overall L |
|---|---|---|---|---|
| Purdue | 15 | 3 | 26 | 6 |
| Penn St. | 12 | 6 | 21 | 7 |
| Indiana | 12 | 6 | 19 | 12 |
| Iowa | 11 | 7 | 23 | 9 |
| Michigan | 10 | 8 | 20 | 12 |
| Minnesota | 10 | 8 | 19 | 13 |
| Michigan St. | 9 | 9 | 16 | 16 |
| Wisconsin | 8 | 10 | 17 | 15 |
| Illinois | 7 | 11 | 18 | 13 |
| Ohio St. | 3 | 18 | 10 | 17 |
| Northwestern | 2 | 16 | 7 | 20 |

### Big West

| Team | Conference W | Conference L | Overall W | Overall L |
|---|---|---|---|---|
| Long Beach St. | 12 | 6 | 17 | 11 |
| UC Irvine | 11 | 7 | 15 | 12 |
| Pacific (CA) | 11 | 7 | 15 | 12 |
| Utah St. | 10 | 8 | 18 | 15 |
| Nevada | 9 | 9 | 16 | 13 |
| San Jose St.* | 9 | 9 | 13 | 17 |
| New Mexico St. | 8 | 10 | 11 | 15 |
| UC Santa Barbara | 8 | 10 | 11 | 15 |
| UNLV | 7 | 11 | 10 | 16 |
| Cal St. Fullerton | 5 | 13 | 6 | 20 |

### Colonial Athletic

| Team | Conference W | Conference L | Overall W | Overall L |
|---|---|---|---|---|
| Va. Commonwealth* | 14 | 2 | 24 | 9 |
| Old Dominion | 12 | 4 | 18 | 13 |
| N.C.-Wilmington | 9 | 7 | 13 | 16 |
| East Carolina | 8 | 8 | 17 | 11 |
| American | 8 | 8 | 12 | 15 |
| George Mason | 6 | 10 | 11 | 16 |
| William & Mary | 6 | 10 | 10 | 16 |
| James Madison | 6 | 10 | 10 | 20 |
| Richmond | 3 | 13 | 8 | 20 |

### Conference USA

| Team | Conference W | Conference L | Overall W | Overall L |
|---|---|---|---|---|
| **Red Division** | | | | |
| Tulane | 9 | 5 | 22 | 10 |
| Ala.-Birmingham | 6 | 8 | 16 | 14 |
| Southern Mississippi | 6 | 8 | 12 | 15 |
| South Florida | 2 | 12 | 12 | 16 |
| **White Division** | | | | |
| Memphis | 11 | 3 | 22 | 8 |
| Louisville | 10 | 4 | 22 | 12 |
| N.C.-Charlotte | 6 | 8 | 14 | 15 |
| **Blue Division** | | | | |
| Cincinnatti* | 11 | 3 | 28 | 5 |
| Marquette | 10 | 4 | 23 | 8 |
| St. Louis | 4 | 10 | 16 | 14 |
| DePaul | 2 | 12 | 11 | 18 |

### Ivy League†

| Team | Conference W | Conference L | Overall W | Overall L |
|---|---|---|---|---|
| Princeton | 13 | 2 | 22 | 7 |
| Pennsylvania | 12 | 3 | 17 | 10 |
| Dartmouth | 9 | 5 | 16 | 10 |
| Harvard | 7 | 7 | 15 | 11 |
| Brown | 5 | 9 | 10 | 16 |
| Cornell | 5 | 9 | 10 | 16 |
| Yale | 3 | 11 | 8 | 18 |
| Columbia | 3 | 11 | 7 | 19 |

### Metro Atlantic Athletic

| Team | Conference W | Conference L | Overall W | Overall L |
|---|---|---|---|---|
| Iona | 10 | 4 | 21 | 8 |
| Fairfield | 10 | 4 | 20 | 10 |
| Manhattan | 9 | 5 | 17 | 12 |
| Loyola (MD) | 8 | 6 | 12 | 15 |
| Canisius* | 7 | 7 | 19 | 11 |
| Niagara | 6 | 8 | 13 | 15 |
| St. Peter's | 5 | 9 | 15 | 12 |
| Siena | 1 | 13 | 5 | 22 |

### Mid-American

| Team | Conference W | Conference L | Overall W | Overall L |
|---|---|---|---|---|
| Eastern Michigan* | 14 | 4 | 25 | 6 |
| Western Michigan | 13 | 5 | 15 | 12 |
| Miami (OH) | 12 | 6 | 21 | 8 |
| Ohio | 11 | 7 | 16 | 14 |
| Ball St. | 11 | 7 | 16 | 12 |
| Bowling Green | 9 | 9 | 14 | 13 |
| Toledo | 9 | 9 | 18 | 14 |
| Kent | 8 | 10 | 14 | 13 |
| Central Michigan | 3 | 15 | 6 | 20 |
| Akron | 0 | 18 | 3 | 23 |

### Mid-Continent

| Team | Conference W | Conference L | Overall W | Overall L |
|---|---|---|---|---|
| Valparaiso* | 14 | 4 | 25 | 6 |
| Western Illinois | 13 | 5 | 17 | 12 |
| Northeastern Illinois | 10 | 8 | 14 | 13 |
| Buffalo | 10 | 8 | 13 | 14 |
| Mo.-Kansas City | 10 | 8 | 12 | 15 |
| Central Conn. St. | 9 | 9 | 13 | 15 |
| Eastern Illinois | 9 | 9 | 13 | 15 |
| Troy St. | 8 | 10 | 11 | 16 |
| Youngstown St. | 7 | 11 | 12 | 15 |
| Chicago St. | 2 | 16 | 2 | 25 |

### Mid-Eastern Athletic

| Team | Conference W | Conference L | Overall W | Overall L |
|---|---|---|---|---|
| South Carolina St.* | 14 | 2 | 22 | 8 |
| Coppin St. | 14 | 2 | 19 | 10 |
| Bethune-Cookman | 8 | 8 | 12 | 15 |
| Delaware St. | 8 | 8 | 11 | 17 |
| North Carolina A&T | 7 | 9 | 10 | 17 |
| Md.-East. Shore | 6 | 10 | 11 | 16 |
| Howard | 6 | 10 | 7 | 20 |
| Morgan St. | 6 | 10 | 7 | 20 |
| Florida A&M | 3 | 13 | 8 | 19 |
| Hampton | – | – | 9 | 17 |

### Midwestern Collegiate

| Team | Conference W | Conference L | Overall W | Overall L |
|---|---|---|---|---|
| Wis.-Green Bay | 16 | 0 | 25 | 4 |
| Butler | 12 | 4 | 19 | 8 |
| Northern Ill.* | 10 | 6 | 20 | 10 |
| Wright St. | 8 | 8 | 14 | 13 |
| Detroit | 8 | 8 | 18 | 11 |
| Wis.-Milwaukee | 5 | 11 | 9 | 18 |
| Ill.-Chicago | 5 | 11 | 10 | 18 |
| Loyola (IL) | 5 | 11 | 8 | 19 |
| Cleveland St. | 3 | 13 | 5 | 21 |

### Missouri Valley

| Team | Conference W | Conference L | Overall W | Overall L |
|---|---|---|---|---|
| Bradley | 15 | 3 | 22 | 8 |
| Illinois St. | 13 | 5 | 22 | 12 |
| Tulsa* | 12 | 6 | 22 | 8 |
| Southwest Mo. St. | 11 | 7 | 16 | 12 |
| Creighton | 9 | 9 | 14 | 15 |
| Evansville | 9 | 9 | 13 | 14 |
| Northern Iowa | 8 | 10 | 14 | 13 |
| Drake | 8 | 10 | 12 | 15 |
| Indiana St. | 6 | 12 | 10 | 16 |
| Southern Illinois | 4 | 14 | 11 | 18 |
| Wichita St. | 4 | 14 | 8 | 21 |

### North Atlantic

| Team | Conference W | Conference L | Overall W | Overall L |
|---|---|---|---|---|
| Drexel* | 17 | 1 | 27 | 4 |
| Boston U. | 13 | 5 | 18 | 11 |
| Maine | 11 | 7 | 15 | 13 |
| Delaware | 11 | 7 | 15 | 12 |
| Towson St. | 11 | 7 | 16 | 12 |
| Vermont | 10 | 8 | 12 | 15 |
| Hofstra | 5 | 13 | 9 | 18 |
| New Hampshire | 5 | 13 | 6 | 21 |
| Hartford | 5 | 13 | 6 | 22 |
| Northeastern | 2 | 16 | 4 | 24 |

### Northeast

| Team | Conference W | Conference L | Overall W | Overall L |
|---|---|---|---|---|
| Mt. St. Mary's (MD) | 16 | 2 | 21 | 8 |
| Marist | 14 | 4 | 22 | 7 |
| Monmouth (NJ)* | 14 | 4 | 20 | 10 |
| Rider | 12 | 6 | 19 | 11 |
| St. Francis (PA) | 11 | 7 | 13 | 14 |
| Wagner | 7 | 11 | 10 | 17 |
| FDU-Teaneck | 6 | 12 | 7 | 20 |
| LIU-Brooklyn | 5 | 13 | 9 | 19 |
| St. Francis (NY) | 3 | 15 | 9 | 18 |
| Robert Morris | 2 | 16 | 5 | 23 |

### Ohio Valley

| Team | Conference W | Conference L | Overall W | Overall L |
|---|---|---|---|---|
| Murray St. | 12 | 4 | 19 | 10 |
| Tennessee St. | 11 | 5 | 15 | 13 |
| Austin Peay* | 10 | 6 | 19 | 11 |
| Middle Tenn. St. | 9 | 7 | 15 | 12 |
| Tennessee-Martin | 9 | 7 | 13 | 14 |
| Eastern Kentucky | 7 | 9 | 13 | 14 |
| Tennessee Tech | 7 | 9 | 13 | 15 |
| Southeast Mo. St. | 5 | 11 | 8 | 19 |
| Morehead St. | 2 | 14 | 7 | 20 |

### Pacific-10†

| | Conference W | Conference L | Overall W | Overall L |
|---|---|---|---|---|
| UCLA | 16 | 2 | 23 | 8 |
| Arizona | 13 | 5 | 26 | 7 |
| Stanford | 12 | 6 | 20 | 9 |
| California | 11 | 7 | 17 | 11 |
| Washington | 9 | 9 | 16 | 12 |
| Oregon | 9 | 9 | 16 | 13 |
| Washington St. | 8 | 10 | 17 | 12 |
| Arizona St. | 6 | 12 | 11 | 16 |
| Southern Cal. | 4 | 14 | 11 | 19 |
| Oregon St. | 2 | 16 | 4 | 23 |

### Patriot

| | Conference W | Conference L | Overall W | Overall L |
|---|---|---|---|---|
| Navy | 9 | 3 | 15 | 12 |
| Colgate* | 9 | 3 | 15 | 15 |
| Bucknell | 8 | 4 | 17 | 11 |
| Holy Cross | 8 | 4 | 16 | 13 |
| Lafayette | 4 | 8 | 7 | 20 |
| Army | 2 | 10 | 7 | 20 |
| Lehigh | 2 | 10 | 4 | 23 |

### Southeastern

| | Conference W | Conference L | Overall W | Overall L |
|---|---|---|---|---|
| **Eastern Division** | | | | |
| Kentucky | 16 | 0 | 34 | 2 |
| Georgia | 9 | 7 | 21 | 10 |
| South Carolina | 8 | 8 | 19 | 12 |
| Vanderbilt | 7 | 9 | 18 | 14 |
| Florida | 6 | 10 | 12 | 16 |
| Tennessee | 6 | 10 | 14 | 15 |
| **Western Division** | | | | |
| Mississippi St.* | 10 | 6 | 26 | 8 |
| Arkansas | 9 | 7 | 20 | 13 |
| Alabama | 9 | 7 | 19 | 13 |
| Mississippi | 6 | 10 | 12 | 15 |
| Auburn | 6 | 10 | 19 | 13 |
| Louisiana St. | 4 | 12 | 12 | 17 |

### Southern

| | Conference W | Conference L | Overall W | Overall L |
|---|---|---|---|---|
| **Northern Division** | | | | |
| Davidson | 14 | 0 | 25 | 5 |
| Virginia Military | 10 | 4 | 18 | 10 |
| Marshall | 8 | 6 | 17 | 11 |
| East Tennessee St. | 3 | 11 | 7 | 20 |
| Appalachian St. | 3 | 11 | 8 | 20 |
| **Southern Division** | | | | |
| Western Carolina* | 10 | 4 | 17 | 13 |
| Tenn.-Chattanooga | 9 | 5 | 15 | 12 |
| Furman | 6 | 8 | 10 | 17 |
| Citadel | 5 | 9 | 10 | 16 |
| Georgia Southern | 2 | 12 | 3 | 23 |

### Southland

| | Conference W | Conference L | Overall W | Overall L |
|---|---|---|---|---|
| Northeast Lousiana* | 13 | 5 | 16 | 14 |
| North Texas | 12 | 6 | 15 | 13 |
| Texas-San Antonio | 12 | 6 | 14 | 14 |
| Stephen F. Austin | 11 | 7 | 17 | 11 |
| McNeese St. | 11 | 7 | 15 | 12 |
| Sam Houston St. | 9 | 9 | 11 | 16 |
| Southwest Tex. St. | 7 | 11 | 11 | 15 |
| Texas-Arlington | 7 | 11 | 11 | 15 |
| Nicholls St. | 5 | 13 | 5 | 21 |
| Northwestern St. | 3 | 15 | 5 | 21 |

### Southwest

| | Conference W | Conference L | Overall W | Overall L |
|---|---|---|---|---|
| Texas Tech.* | 14 | 0 | 30 | 2 |
| Houston | 11 | 3 | 17 | 10 |
| Texas | 10 | 4 | 21 | 10 |
| Texas Christian. | 6 | 8 | 15 | 15 |
| Rice | 5 | 9 | 14 | 14 |
| Baylor | 4 | 10 | 9 | 18 |
| Southern Methodist | 3 | 11 | 8 | 20 |
| Texas A&M | 3 | 11 | 11 | 16 |

### Southwestern Athletic

| | Conference W | Conference L | Overall W | Overall L |
|---|---|---|---|---|
| Mississippi Val.* | 11 | 3 | 22 | 7 |
| Jackson St. | 11 | 3 | 16 | 13 |
| Southern-B. R. | 8 | 5 | 17 | 11 |
| Texas Southern | 7 | 7 | 11 | 15 |
| Alcorn St. | 7 | 7 | 10 | 15 |
| Grambling | 6 | 7 | 12 | 16 |
| Alabama St. | 5 | 9 | 9 | 18 |
| Prairie View | 0 | 14 | 4 | 23 |

### Sun Belt

| | Conference W | Conference L | Overall W | Overall L |
|---|---|---|---|---|
| Ark.-Little Rock | 14 | 4 | 23 | 7 |
| New Orleans* | 14 | 4 | 21 | 9 |
| Jacksonville | 10 | 8 | 15 | 13 |
| Western Kentucky | 10 | 8 | 13 | 14 |
| Southwestern La. | 9 | 9 | 16 | 12 |
| Lamar | 7 | 11 | 12 | 15 |
| South Alabama | 7 | 11 | 12 | 15 |
| Arkansas St. | 7 | 11 | 9 | 18 |
| Louisiana Tech. | 6 | 12 | 11 | 17 |
| Tex.-Pan American | 6 | 12 | 9 | 19 |

### Trans America Athletic

| | Conference W | Conference L | Overall W | Overall L |
|---|---|---|---|---|
| **East Division** | | | | |
| Charleston (SC) | 15 | 1 | 25 | 4 |
| Campbell | 11 | 5 | 17 | 11 |
| Central Florida* | 6 | 10 | 11 | 19 |
| Stetson | 6 | 10 | 10 | 17 |
| Florida International | 6 | 11 | 13 | 15 |
| Florida Atlantic | 5 | 11 | 9 | 18 |
| **West Division** | | | | |
| Samford | 11 | 5 | 16 | 11 |
| Southeastern La. | 11 | 5 | 15 | 12 |
| Centenary (LA) | 8 | 8 | 11 | 16 |
| Mercer | 8 | 9 | 15 | 14 |
| Georgia St. | 6 | 10 | 10 | 16 |
| Jacksonville St. | 4 | 12 | 10 | 17 |

### West Coast

| | Conference W | Conference L | Overall W | Overall L |
|---|---|---|---|---|
| Santa Clara | 10 | 4 | 20 | 9 |
| Gonzaga | 10 | 4 | 21 | 9 |
| Loyola Marymount | 8 | 6 | 18 | 11 |
| San Francisco | 8 | 6 | 15 | 12 |
| Portland* | 7 | 7 | 19 | 11 |
| San Diego | 6 | 8 | 14 | 14 |
| St. Mary's (CA) | 5 | 9 | 12 | 15 |
| Pepperdine | 2 | 12 | 10 | 18 |

### Western Athletic

| | Conference W | Conference L | Overall W | Overall L |
|---|---|---|---|---|
| Utah | 15 | 3 | 27 | 7 |
| New Mexico* | 14 | 4 | 28 | 5 |
| Fresno St. | 13 | 5 | 22 | 11 |
| Colorado St. | 11 | 7 | 18 | 12 |
| Brigham Young | 9 | 9 | 15 | 13 |
| San Diego St. | 8 | 10 | 15 | 14 |
| Wyoming | 8 | 10 | 14 | 15 |
| Hawaii | 7 | 11 | 10 | 18 |
| UTEP | 4 | 14 | 13 | 15 |
| Air Force | 1 | 17 | 5 | 23 |

### Independents

| | W | L |
|---|---|---|
| Oral Roberts | 18 | 9 |
| Wofford | 4 | 22 |

# All-Time Winningest College Teams by Percentage

| School | Years | Won | Lost | Pct. |
|---|---|---|---|---|
| Kentucky | 93 | 1,650 | 520 | .760 |
| North Carolina | 86 | 1,647 | 588 | .737 |
| UNLV | 38 | 789 | 284 | .735 |
| UCLA | 77 | 1,374 | 596 | .697 |
| Kansas | 98 | 1,596 | 708 | .693 |
| St. John's (NY) | 89 | 1,519 | 682 | .690 |
| Syracuse | 95 | 1,432 | 670 | .681 |
| Western Kentucky | 77 | 1,344 | 635 | .679 |
| Duke | 91 | 1,492 | 740 | .668 |
| DePaul | 73 | 1,171 | 596 | .663 |
| Arkansas | 73 | 1,250 | 648 | .659 |
| Louisville | 82 | 1,299 | 687 | .654 |
| Notre Dame | 91 | 1,398 | 748 | .651 |
| Indiana | 96 | 1,388 | 744 | .651 |
| Weber State | 34 | 625 | 338 | .649 |
| Temple | 100 | 1,455 | 793 | .647 |
| Utah | 88 | 1,317 | 724 | .645 |
| Purdue | 98 | 1,337 | 738 | .644 |
| Illinois | 91 | 1,299 | 726 | .641 |
| Villanova | 76 | 1,232 | 695 | .639 |

# Major College Basketball Tournaments

The National Invitation Tournament (NIT), first played in 1938, is the nation's oldest basketball tournament. The first National Collegiate Athletic Association (NCAA) national championship tournament was played a year later. Selections for both tournaments are made in March, with the NCAA selecting first from among the top Division I teams.

## National Invitation Tournament Champions

| Year | Champion |
|---|---|
| 1938 | Temple |
| 1939 | Long Island Univ. |
| 1940 | Colorado |
| 1941 | Long Island Univ. |
| 1942 | West Virginia |
| 1943 | St. John's |
| 1944 | St. John's |
| 1945 | De Paul |
| 1946 | Kentucky |
| 1947 | Utah |
| 1948 | St. Louis |
| 1949 | San Francisco |
| 1950 | CCNY |
| 1951 | Brigham Young |
| 1952 | LaSalle |
| 1953 | Seton Hall |
| 1954 | Holy Cross |
| 1955 | Duquesne |
| 1956 | Louisville |
| 1957 | Bradley |
| 1958 | Xavier (Ohio) |
| 1959 | St. John's |
| 1960 | Bradley |
| 1961 | Providence |
| 1962 | Dayton |
| 1963 | Providence |
| 1964 | Bradley |
| 1965 | St. John's |
| 1966 | Brigham Young |
| 1967 | Southern Illinois |
| 1968 | Dayton |
| 1969 | Temple |
| 1970 | Marquette |
| 1971 | North Carolina |
| 1972 | Maryland |
| 1973 | Virginia Tech |
| 1974 | Purdue |
| 1975 | Princeton |
| 1976 | Kentucky |
| 1977 | St. Bonaventure |
| 1978 | Texas |
| 1979 | Indiana |
| 1980 | Virginia |
| 1981 | Tulsa |
| 1982 | Bradley |
| 1983 | Fresno State |
| 1984 | Michigan |
| 1985 | UCLA |
| 1986 | Ohio State |
| 1987 | Southern Mississippi |
| 1988 | Connecticut |
| 1989 | St. John's |
| 1990 | Vanderbilt |
| 1991 | Stanford |
| 1992 | Virginia |
| 1993 | Minnesota |
| 1994 | Villanova |
| 1995 | Virginia Tech |
| 1996 | Nebraska |

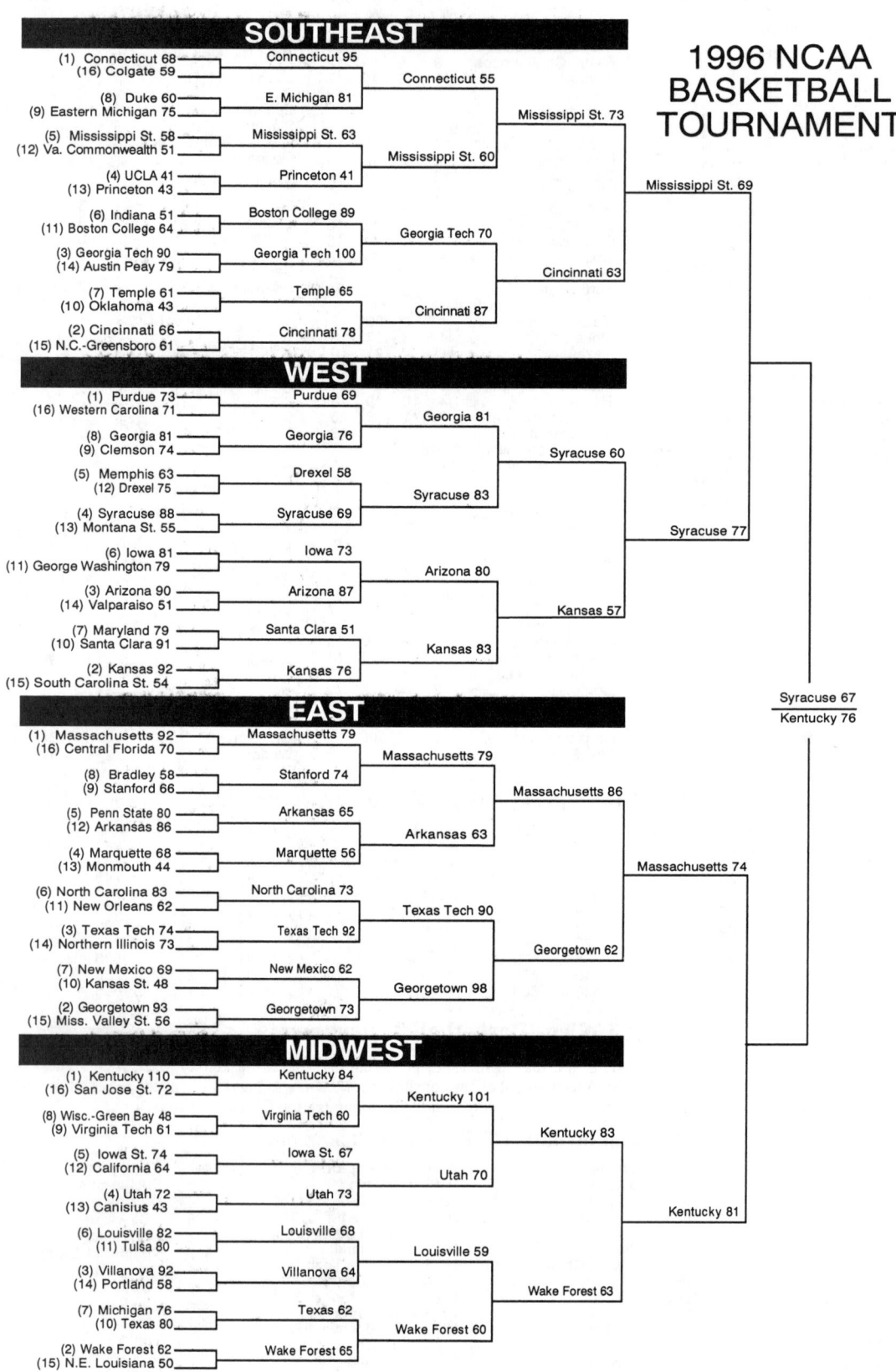

# 1996 NCAA BASKETBALL TOURNAMENT

## SOUTHEAST

| First Round | Second Round | Regional Semifinals | Regional Final |
|---|---|---|---|
| (1) Connecticut 68, (16) Colgate 59 | Connecticut 95 | Connecticut 55 | Mississippi St. 73 |
| (8) Duke 60, (9) Eastern Michigan 75 | E. Michigan 81 | Mississippi St. 60 | Cincinnati 63 |
| (5) Mississippi St. 58, (12) Va. Commonwealth 51 | Mississippi St. 63 | Georgia Tech 70 | |
| (4) UCLA 41, (13) Princeton 43 | Princeton 41 | Cincinnati 87 | |
| (6) Indiana 51, (11) Boston College 64 | Boston College 89 | | |
| (3) Georgia Tech 90, (14) Austin Peay 79 | Georgia Tech 100 | | |
| (7) Temple 61, (10) Oklahoma 43 | Temple 65 | | |
| (2) Cincinnati 66, (15) N.C.-Greensboro 61 | Cincinnati 78 | | |

## WEST

| First Round | Second Round | Regional Semifinals | Regional Final |
|---|---|---|---|
| (1) Purdue 73, (16) Western Carolina 71 | Purdue 69 | Georgia 81 | Syracuse 60 |
| (8) Georgia 81, (9) Clemson 74 | Georgia 76 | Syracuse 83 | Kansas 57 |
| (5) Memphis 63, (12) Drexel 75 | Drexel 58 | Arizona 80 | |
| (4) Syracuse 88, (13) Montana St. 55 | Syracuse 69 | Kansas 83 | |
| (6) Iowa 81, (11) George Washington 79 | Iowa 73 | | |
| (3) Arizona 90, (14) Valparaiso 51 | Arizona 87 | | |
| (7) Maryland 79, (10) Santa Clara 91 | Santa Clara 51 | | |
| (2) Kansas 92, (15) South Carolina St. 54 | Kansas 76 | | |

## EAST

| First Round | Second Round | Regional Semifinals | Regional Final |
|---|---|---|---|
| (1) Massachusetts 92, (16) Central Florida 70 | Massachusetts 79 | Massachusetts 79 | Massachusetts 86 |
| (8) Bradley 58, (9) Stanford 66 | Stanford 74 | Arkansas 63 | Georgetown 62 |
| (5) Penn State 80, (12) Arkansas 86 | Arkansas 65 | Texas Tech 90 | |
| (4) Marquette 68, (13) Monmouth 44 | Marquette 56 | Georgetown 98 | |
| (6) North Carolina 83, (11) New Orleans 62 | North Carolina 73 | | |
| (3) Texas Tech 74, (14) Northern Illinois 73 | Texas Tech 92 | | |
| (7) New Mexico 69, (10) Kansas St. 48 | New Mexico 62 | | |
| (2) Georgetown 93, (15) Miss. Valley St. 56 | Georgetown 73 | | |

## MIDWEST

| First Round | Second Round | Regional Semifinals | Regional Final |
|---|---|---|---|
| (1) Kentucky 110, (16) San Jose St. 72 | Kentucky 84 | Kentucky 101 | Kentucky 83 |
| (8) Wisc.-Green Bay 48, (9) Virginia Tech 61 | Virginia Tech 60 | Utah 70 | Wake Forest 63 |
| (5) Iowa St. 74, (12) California 64 | Iowa St. 67 | Louisville 59 | |
| (4) Utah 72, (13) Canisius 43 | Utah 73 | Wake Forest 60 | |
| (6) Louisville 82, (11) Tulsa 80 | Louisville 68 | | |
| (3) Villanova 92, (14) Portland 58 | Villanova 64 | | |
| (7) Michigan 76, (10) Texas 80 | Texas 62 | | |
| (2) Wake Forest 62, (15) N.E. Louisiana 50 | Wake Forest 65 | | |

## Final Four

Mississippi St. 69
Syracuse 77

Massachusetts 74
Kentucky 81

## Championship

Syracuse 67
Kentucky 76

## Kentucky Defeats Syracuse to Win the 1996 NCAA Men's Basketball Championship

The University of Kentucky Wildcats defeated the Syracuse Orangemen, 76-67, to capture the NCAA men's basketball championship, Apr. 1, at East Rutherford, NJ. The Wildcats were led by Tony Delk, who scored 24 points; his 7 three-pointers set an NCAA Final record. The victory gave Kentucky its 6th national title, 2d only to UCLA's 11 championships.

## NCAA Division I Champions

| Year | Champion | Coach | Final opponent | Score | Outstanding player | Site |
|---|---|---|---|---|---|---|
| 1939 | Oregon | Howard Hobson | Ohio St. | 46-33 | None | Evanston, IL |
| 1940 | Indiana | Branch McCracken | Kansas | 60-42 | Marvin Huffman, Indiana | Kansas City, MO |
| 1941 | Wisconsin | Harold Foster | Washington St. | 39-34 | John Kotz, Wisconsin | Kansas City, MO |
| 1942 | Stanford | Everett Dean | Dartmouth | 53-38 | Howard Dallmar, Stanford | Kansas City, MO |
| 1943 | Wyoming | Everett Shelton | Georgetown | 46-34 | Ken Sailors, Wyoming | New York, NY |
| 1944 | Utah | Vadal Peterson | Dartmouth | 42-40[1] | Arnold Ferrin, Utah | New York, NY |
| 1945 | Oklahoma St.[2] | Henry Iba | NYU | 49-45 | Bob Kurland, Oklahoma St. | New York, NY |
| 1946 | Oklahoma St.[2] | Henry Iba | North Carolina | 43-40 | Bob Kurland, Oklahoma St. | New York, NY |
| 1947 | Holy Cross | Alvin Julian | Oklahoma | 58-47 | George Kaftan, Holy Cross | New York, NY |
| 1948 | Kentucky | Adolph Rupp | Baylor | 58-42 | Alex Groza, Kentucky | New York, NY |
| 1949 | Kentucky | Adolph Rupp | Oklahoma St. | 46-36 | Alex Groza, Kentucky | Seattle, WA |
| 1950 | CCNY | Nat Holman | Bradley | 71-68 | Irwin Dambrot, CCNY | New York, NY |
| 1951 | Kentucky | Adolph Rupp | Kansas St. | 68-58 | None | Minneapolis, MN |
| 1952 | Kansas | Forrest Allen | St. John's | 80-63 | Clyde Lovellette, Kansas | Seattle, WA |
| 1953 | Indiana | Branch McCracken | Kansas | 69-68 | B.H. Born, Kansas | Kansas City, MO |
| 1954 | La Salle | Kenneth Loeffler | Bradley | 92-76 | Tom Gola, La Salle | Kansas City, MO |
| 1955 | San Francisco | Phil Woolpert | LaSalle | 77-63 | Bill Russell, San Francisco | Kansas City, MO |
| 1956 | San Francisco | Phil Woolpert | Iowa | 83-71 | Hal Lear, Temple | Evanston, IL |
| 1957 | North Carolina | Frank McGuire | Kansas | 54-53[1] | Wilt Chamberlain, Kansas | Kansas City, MO |
| 1958 | Kentucky | Adolph Rupp | Seattle | 84-72 | Elgin Baylor, Seattle | Louisville, KY |
| 1959 | California | Pete Newell | West Virginia | 71-70 | Jerry West, West Virginia | Louisville, KY |
| 1960 | Ohio St. | Fred Taylor | California | 75-55 | Jerry Lucas, Ohio St. | San Francisco, CA |
| 1961 | Cincinnati | Edwin Jucker | Ohio St. | 70-65[1] | Jerry Lucas, Ohio St. | Kansas City, MO |
| 1962 | Cincinnati | Edwin Jucker | Ohio St. | 71-59 | Paul Hogue, Cincinnati | Louisville, KY |
| 1963 | Loyola (IL) | George Ireland | Cincinnati | 60-58[1] | Art Heyman, Duke | Louisville, KY |
| 1964 | UCLA | John Wooden | Duke | 98-83 | Walt Hazzard, UCLA | Kansas City, MO |
| 1965 | UCLA | John Wooden | Michigan | 91-80 | Bill Bradley, Princeton | Portland, OR |
| 1966 | Texas-El Paso[3] | Don Haskins | Kentucky | 72-65 | Jerry Chambers, Utah | College Park, MD |
| 1967 | UCLA | John Wooden | Dayton | 79-64 | Lew Alcindor, UCLA | Louisville, KY |
| 1968 | UCLA | John Wooden | North Carolina | 78-55 | Lew Alcindor, UCLA | Los Angeles, CA |
| 1969 | UCLA | John Wooden | Purdue | 92-72 | Lew Alcindor, UCLA | Louisville, KY |
| 1970 | UCLA | John Wooden | Jacksonville | 80-69 | Sidney Wicks, UCLA | College Park, MD |
| 1971 | UCLA | John Wooden | Villanova* | 68-62 | Howard Porter, Villanova* | Houston, TX |
| 1972 | UCLA | John Wooden | Florida St. | 81-76 | Bill Walton, UCLA | Los Angeles, CA |
| 1973 | UCLA | John Wooden | Memphis St. | 87-66 | Bill Walton, UCLA | St. Louis, MO |
| 1974 | North Carolina St. | Norm Sloan | Marquette | 76-64 | David Thompson, N.C. St. | Greensboro, NC |
| 1975 | UCLA | John Wooden | Kentucky | 92-85 | Richard Washington, UCLA | San Diego, CA |
| 1976 | Indiana | Bob Knight | Michigan | 86-68 | Kent Benson, Indiana | Philadelphia, PA |
| 1977 | Marquette | Al McGuire | North Carolina | 67-59 | Butch Lee, Marquette | Atlanta, GA |
| 1978 | Kentucky | Joe Hall | Duke | 94-88 | Jack Givens, Kentucky | St. Louis, MO |
| 1979 | Michigan St. | Jud Heathcote | Indiana St. | 75-64 | Magic Johnson, Michigan St. | Salt Lake City, UT |
| 1980 | Louisville | Denny Crum | UCLA* | 59-54 | Darrell Griffith, Louisville | Indianapolis, IN |
| 1981 | Indiana | Bob Knight | North Carolina | 63-50 | Isiah Thomas, Indiana | Philadelphia, PA |
| 1982 | North Carolina | Dean Smith | Georgetown | 63-62 | James Worthy, N. Carolina | New Orleans, LA |
| 1983 | North Carolina St. | Jim Valvano | Houston | 54-52 | Hakeem Olajuwon, Houston | Albuquerque, NM |
| 1984 | Georgetown | John Thompson | Houston | 84-75 | Patrick Ewing, Georgetown | Seattle, WA |
| 1985 | Villanova | Rollie Massimino | Georgetown | 66-64 | Ed Pinckney, Villanova | Lexington, KY |
| 1986 | Louisville | Denny Crum | Duke | 72-69 | Pervis Ellison, Louisville | Dallas, TX |
| 1987 | Indiana | Bob Knight | Syracuse | 74-73 | Keith Smart, Indiana | New Orleans, LA |
| 1988 | Kansas | Larry Brown | Oklahoma | 83-79 | Danny Manning, Kansas | Kansas City, MO |
| 1989 | Michigan | Steve Fisher | Seton Hall | 80-79[1] | Glen Rice, Michigan | Seattle, WA |
| 1990 | UNLV | Jerry Tarkanian | Duke | 103-73 | Anderson Hunt, UNLV | Denver, CO |
| 1991 | Duke | Mike Krzyzewski | Kansas | 72-65 | Christian Laettner, Duke | Indianapolis, IN |
| 1992 | Duke | Mike Krzyzewski | Michigan | 71-51 | Bobby Hurley, Duke | Minneapolis, MN |
| 1993 | North Carolina | Dean Smith | Michigan | 77-71 | Donald Williams, N. Carolina | New Orleans, LA |
| 1994 | Arkansas | Nolan Richardson | Duke | 76-72 | Corliss Williamson, Arkansas | Charlotte, NC |
| 1995 | UCLA | Jim Harrick | Arkansas | 89-78 | Ed O'Bannon, UCLA | Seattle, WA |
| 1996 | Kentucky | Rick Pitino | Syracuse | 76-67 | Tony Delk, Kentucky | E. Rutherford, NJ |

*Declared ineligible subsequent to the tournament. (1) Overtime. (2) Known as Oklahoma A&M at that time. (3) Known as Texas Western at that time.

## Top Career Scorers

| Player, school | Years | Points | Avg. |
|---|---|---|---|
| Pete Maravich, LSU | 1968-70 | 3,667 | 44.2 |
| Austin Carr, Notre Dame | 1969-71 | 2,560 | 34.6 |
| Oscar Robertson, Cincinnati | 1958-60 | 2,973 | 33.8 |
| Calvin Murphy, Niagara | 1968-70 | 2,548 | 33.1 |
| Dwight Lamar, SW Louisiana | 1972-73 | 1,862 | 32.7 |
| Frank Selvy, Furman | 1952-54 | 2,538 | 32.5 |
| Rick Mount, Purdue | 1968-70 | 2,323 | 32.3 |
| Darrell Floyd, Furman | 1954-56 | 2,281 | 32.1 |
| Nick Werkman, Seton Hall | 1962-64 | 2,273 | 32.0 |
| Willie Humes, Idaho State | 1970-71 | 1,510 | 31.5 |

## John R. Wooden Award

Awarded annually to the nation's outstanding college basketball player by the United States Basketball Writers Assn.

| | |
|---|---|
| 1977 | Marques Johnson, UCLA |
| 1978 | Phil Ford, North Carolina |
| 1979 | Larry Bird, Indiana State |
| 1980 | Darrell Griffith, Louisville |
| 1981 | Danny Ainge, Brigham Young |
| 1982 | Ralph Sampson, Virginia |
| 1983 | Ralph Sampson, Virginia |
| 1984 | Michael Jordan, North Carolina |
| 1985 | Chris Mullin, St. John's |
| 1986 | Walter Berry, St. John's |
| 1987 | David Robinson, Navy |
| 1988 | Danny Manning, Kansas |
| 1989 | Sean Elliott, Arizona |
| 1990 | Lionel Simmons, La Salle |
| 1991 | Larry Johnson, UNLV |
| 1992 | Christian Laettner, Duke |
| 1993 | Calbert Cheaney, Indiana |
| 1994 | Glenn Robinson, Purdue |
| 1995 | Ed O'Bannon, UCLA |
| 1996 | Marcus Camby, Massachusetts |

## Selected Division I Basketball Coaches in 1996

| College | Coach | College | Coach | College | Coach |
|---|---|---|---|---|---|
| Akron | Dan Hipsher | Indiana St. | Sherman Dillard | Rice | Willis Wilson |
| Alabama | David Hobbs | Iowa | Tom Davis | Richmond | Bill Dooley |
| Alabama-Birmingham | Gene Bartow | Iowa St. | Tim Floyd | Rutgers | Bob Wenzel |
| American | Chris Knoche | James Madison | Lefty Driesell | St. Bonaventure | Jim Baron |
| Arizona | Lute Olson | Kansas | Roy Williams | St. John's (NY) | Fran Fraschilla |
| Arizona St. | Bill Frieder | Kansas St. | Tom Asbury | St. Joseph's (PA) | Phil Martelli |
| Arkansas | Nolan Richardson | Kent | Gary Waters | St. Louis | Charlie Spoonhour |
| Army | Dino Gaudio | Kentucky | Rick Pitino | St. Mary's (CA) | Ernie Kent |
| Auburn | Cliff Ellis | Long Beach St. | Wayne Morgan | St. Peter's | Rodger Blind |
| Austin Peay | Dave Loos | LSU | Dale Brown | San Diego | Brad Holland |
| Ball St. | Ray McCallum | Louisville | Denny Crum | San Diego St. | Fred Trenkle |
| Baylor | Harry Miller | Loyola (Marymount) | John Olive | San Francisco | Phil Matthews |
| Boise St. | Rod Jensen | Loyola (IL) | Ken Burmeister | San Jose St. | Stan Morrison |
| Boston Coll. | Jim O'Brien | Manhattan | John Leonard | Santa Clara | Dick Davey |
| Bowling Green | Jim Larranaga | Marquette | Mike Deane | Seton Hall | George Blaney |
| Bradley | Jim Molinari | Maryland | Gary Williams | South Carolina | Eddie Fogler |
| Brigham Young | Roger Reid | Massachusetts | James "Bruiser" Flint | South Florida | Seth Greenberg |
| Brown | Frank Dobbs | Memphis | Larry Finch | SE Missouri St. | Ron Shumate |
| Butler | Barry Collier | Miami (FL) | Leonard Hamilton | USC | Henry Bibby |
| California | Ben Braun | Miami (OH) | Charlie Coles | Southern Illinois | Rich Herrin |
| Cal. St. Fullerton | Bob Hawking | Michigan | Steve Fisher | SMU | Mike Dement |
| UC Irvine | Rod Baker | Michigan St. | Tom Izzo | Southern Mississippi | James Green |
| UC Santa Barbara | Jerry Pimm | Middle Tenn. St. | Randy Wiel | SW Missouri St. | Steve Alford |
| Central Mich. | Leonard Drake | Minnesota | Clem Haskins | Stanford | Mike Montgomery |
| Cincinnati | Bob Huggins | Mississippi | Rob Evans | Syracuse | Jim Boeheim |
| Clemson | Rick Barnes | Mississippi St. | Richard Williams | Temple | John Chaney |
| Cleveland St. | Rollie Massimino | Missouri | Norm Stewart | Tennessee | Kevin O'Neill |
| Colgate | Jack Bruen | Montana | Blaine Taylor | Tennessee St. | Frankie Allen |
| Colorado | Ricardo Patton | Montana St. | Mick Durham | Tennessee Tech | Frank Harrell |
| Colorado St. | Stew Morrill | Morehead St. | Dick Fick | Tenn.-Chattanooga | Mack McCarthy |
| Columbia | Armond Hill | Mt. St. Mary's (MD) | James Phelan | Tennessee-Martin | Calvin C. Luther |
| Connecticut | Jim Calhoun | Murray St. | Mark Gottfried | Texas | Tom Penders |
| Cornell | Scott Thompson | Nebraska | Danny Nee | Texas A&M | Tony Barone |
| Creighton | Dana Altman | Nevada | Pat Foster | Texas Christian | Billy Tubbs |
| Dartmouth | Dave Faucher | UNLV | Bill Bayno | Texas-Arlington | Eddie McCarter |
| Dayton | Oliver Purnell | New Mexico | Dave Bliss | UTEP | Don Haskins |
| DePaul | Joey Meyer | New Mexico St. | Neil McCarthy | Texas Southern | Robert Moreland |
| Detroit Mercy | Perry Watson | Nicholls St. | Rickey Broussard | Toledo | Stan Joplin |
| Drake | Kurt Kanaskie | North Carolina | Dean Smith | Tulane | Perry Clark |
| Drexel | Bill Herrion | North Carolina A&T | Roy Thomas | Tulsa | Steve Robinson |
| Duke | Mike Krzyzewski | North Carolina St. | Herb Sendek | UCLA | Jim Harrick |
| E. Carolina | Joe Dooley | N.C.-Charlotte | Melvin Watkins | Utah | Rick Majerus |
| E. Illinois | Rick Samuels | N.C.-Greensboro | Randy Peele | Utah St. | Larry Eustachy |
| E. Kentucky | Mike Calhoun | N.C.-Wilmington | Jerry Wainwright | Valparaiso | Homer Drew |
| E. Michigan | Milton Barnes | N. Arizona | Ben Howland | Vanderbilt | Jan van Breda Kolff |
| E. Washington | Steve Aggers | N. Illinois | Brian Hammel | Villanova | Steve Lappas |
| Evansville | Jim Crews | N. Iowa | Eldon Miller | Virginia | Jeff Jones |
| Florida | Billy Donovan | Northwestern | Ricky Byrdsong | Va. Commonwealth | Sonny Smith |
| Florida International | Shakey Rodriguez | Notre Dame | John MacLeod | Virginia Tech | Bill Foster |
| Florida St. | Pat Kennedy | Ohio | Larry Hunter | Wake Forest | Dave Odom |
| Fresno St. | Jerry Tarkanian | Ohio St. | Randy Ayers | Washington | Bob Bender |
| George Mason | Paul Westhead | Oklahoma | Kelvin Sampson | Washington St. | Kevin Eastman |
| Geo. Washington | Mike Jarvis | Oklahoma St. | Eddie Sutton | Weber St. | Ron Abegglen |
| Georgetown | John Thompson | Old Dominion | Jeff Capel | West Virginia | Gale Catlett |
| Georgia | Tubby Smith | Oregon | Jerry Green | W. Illinois | Jim Kerwin |
| Georgia Tech | Bobby Cremins | Oregon St. | Eddie Payne | W. Kentucky | Matt Kilcullen |
| Gonzaga | Dan Fitzgerald | Pacific (CA) | Bob Thomason | W. Michigan | Bob Donewald |
| Harvard | Frank Sullivan | Pennsylvania | Fran Dunphy | Wichita St. | Randy Smithson |
| Hawaii | Riley Wallace | Penn St. | Jerry Dunn | William & Mary | Charlie Woollum |
| Houston | Alvin Brooks | Pepperdine | Lorenzo Romar | Wisconsin | Dick Bennett |
| Idaho | Kermit Davis | Pittsburgh | Ralph Willard | Wis.-Green Bay | Mike Heideman |
| Idaho St. | Herb Williams | Portland | Rob Chavez | Wright St. | Ralph Underhill |
| Illinois | Lon Kruger | Princeton | Bill Carmody | Wyoming | Joby Wright |
| Illinois St. | Kevin Stallings | Providence | Pete Gillen | Xavier (OH) | Skip Prosser |
| Illinois-Chicago | Jimmy Collins | Purdue | Gene Keady | Yale | Dick Kuchen |
| Indiana | Bob Knight | Rhode Island | Al Skinner | | |

## Most Coaching Victories in the NCAA Tournament Through 1996

| Coach, school(s), years | Wins | Tournaments |
|---|---|---|
| Dean Smith, North Carolina, 1967-96 | 61 | 26 |
| John Wooden, UCLA, 1950-75 | 47 | 16 |
| Bob Knight, Indiana, 1973-96 | 40 | 20 |
| Denny Crum, Louisville, 1972-96 | 39 | 20 |
| Mike Krzyzewski, Duke, 1984-96 | 39 | 12 |
| John Thompson, Georgetown, 1975-96 | 34 | 19 |
| Jerry Tarkanian, Long Beach State and UNLV, 1970-91 | 31 | 13 |
| Adolph Rupp, Kentucky, 1942-72 | 30 | 20 |
| Jim Boeheim, Syracuse, 1977-96 | 27 | 17 |
| Guy Lewis, Houston, 1961-84 | 26 | 14 |
| Eddie Sutton, Creighton, Arkansas, Kentucky, Oklahoma St., 1974-96 | 25 | 17 |
| Nolan Richardson, Tulsa and Arkansas, 1982-96 | 24 | 12 |

# Women's College Basketball

## Tennesee Lady Volunteers Defeat Georgia, Take Their Fourth NCAA Women's Championship

The University of Tennessee Lady Volunteers dominated their Southeastern Conference rivals the U. of Georgia Bulldogs, 83-65, to win the NCAA Division I Women's Basketball Championship, March 31, 1996, in Charlotte, NC. In the semifinals, Tennessee knocked off defending champions U. of Connecticut in an exciting overtime victory, avenging the loss the Lady Vols had suffered at the hands of UConn in the 1995 championship game. It was Tennessee's 4th national championship in the last ten years. The victory capped a 17-game winning streak and a 32-4 season for the Lady Vols. Senior point guard Michelle Marciniak was named outstanding player of the Final Four.

### NCAA Division I Women's Champions

| Year | Champion | Coach | Final opponent | Score | Outstanding player | Site |
|---|---|---|---|---|---|---|
| 1982 | Louisiana Tech | Sonja Hogg | Cheyney | 76-62 | Janice Lawrence, La. Tech | Norfolk, VA |
| 1983 | USC | Linda Sharp | Louisiana Tech | 69-67 | Cheryl Miller, USC | Norfolk, VA |
| 1984 | USC | Linda Sharp | Tennessee | 72-61 | Cheryl Miller, USC | Los Angeles, CA |
| 1985 | Old Dominion | Marianne Stanley | Georgia | 70-65 | Tracy Claxton, Old Dominion | Austin, TX |
| 1986 | Texas | Jody Conradt | USC | 97-81 | Clarissa Davis, Texas | Lexington, KY |
| 1987 | Tennessee | Pat Summitt | Louisiana Tech | 67-44 | Tonya Edwards, Tennessee | Austin, TX |
| 1988 | Louisiana Tech | Leon Barmore | Auburn | 56-54 | Erica Westbrooks, La. Tech | Tacoma, WA |
| 1989 | Tennessee | Pat Summitt | Auburn | 76-60 | Bridgette Gordon, Tennessee | Tacoma, WA |
| 1990 | Stanford | Tara VanDerveer | Auburn | 88-81 | Jennifer Azzi, Stanford | Knoxville, TN |
| 1991 | Tennessee | Pat Summitt | Virginia | 70-67* | Dawn Staley, Virginia | New Orleans, LA |
| 1992 | Stanford | Tara VanDerveer | W. Kentucky | 78-62 | Molly Goodenbour, Stanford | Los Angeles, CA |
| 1993 | Texas Tech | Marsha Sharp | Ohio St. | 84-82 | Sheryl Swoopes, Texas Tech | Atlanta, GA |
| 1994 | North Carolina | Sylvia Hatchell | Louisiana Tech | 60-59 | Charlotte Smith, North Carolina | Richmond, VA |
| 1995 | Connecticut | Geno Auriemma | Tennessee | 70-64 | Rebecca Lobo, Connecticut | Minneapolis, MN |
| 1996 | Tennessee | Pat Summitt | Georgia | 83-65 | Michelle Marciniak, Tennessee | Charlotte, NC |

* Overtime.

### Wade Trophy

Awarded by the National Assn. for Girls and Women in Sport for academics, community service, and player performance in basketball.

| Year | Player, school |
|---|---|
| 1978 | Carol Blazejowski, Montclair St. |
| 1979 | Nancy Lieberman, Old Dominion |
| 1980 | Nancy Lieberman, Old Dominion |
| 1981 | Lynette Woodard, Kansas |
| 1982 | Pam Kelly, Louisiana Tech |
| 1983 | LaTaunya Pollard, Long Beach St. |
| 1984 | Janice Lawrence, Louisiana Tech |
| 1985 | Cheryl Miller, USC |
| 1986 | Kamie Ethridge, Texas |
| 1987 | Shelly Pennefeather, Villanova |
| 1988 | Teresa Weatherspoon, Louisiana Tech |
| 1989 | Clarissa Davis, Texas |
| 1990 | Jennifer Azzi, Stanford |
| 1991 | Daedra Charles, Tennessee |
| 1992 | Susan Robinson, Penn St. |
| 1993 | Karen Jennings, Nebraska |
| 1994 | Carol Ann Shudlick, Minnesota |
| 1995 | Rebecca Lobo, Connecticut |
| 1996 | Jennifer Rizzotti, Connecticut |

### Top Women's Career Scorers

| Player, school | Years | Points | Avg. |
|---|---|---|---|
| Patricia Hoskins, Mississippi Valley State | 1985-89 | 3,122 | 28.4 |
| Sandra Hodge, New Orleans | 1981-84 | 2,860 | 26.7 |
| Lorri Bauman, Drake | 1981-84 | 3,115 | 26.0 |
| Valorie Whiteside, Appalachian State | 1984-88 | 2,944 | 25.4 |
| Joyce Walker, LSU | 1981-84 | 2,906 | 24.8 |
| Tarcha Hollis, Grambling | 1988-91 | 2,058 | 24.2 |
| Karen Pelphrey, Marshall | 1983-86 | 2,746 | 24.1 |
| Erma Jones, Bethune-Cookman | 1982-84 | 2,095 | 24.1 |
| Cheryl Miller, USC | 1983-86 | 3,018 | 23.6 |
| Chris Starr, Nevada-Reno | 1983-86 | 2,356 | 23.3 |

# SKIING

## World Cup Alpine Champions

### Men

| Year | Champion |
|---|---|
| 1967 | Jean Claude Killy, France |
| 1968 | Jean Claude Killy, France |
| 1969 | Karl Schranz, Austria |
| 1970 | Karl Schranz, Austria |
| 1971 | Gustavo Thoeni, Italy |
| 1972 | Gustavo Thoeni, Italy |
| 1973 | Gustavo Thoeni, Italy |
| 1974 | Piero Gros, Italy |
| 1975 | Gustavo Thoeni, Italy |
| 1976 | Ingemar Stenmark, Sweden |
| 1977 | Ingemar Stenmark, Sweden |
| 1978 | Ingemar Stenmark, Sweden |
| 1979 | Peter Luescher, Switzerland |
| 1980 | Andreas Wenzel, Liechtenstein |
| 1981 | Phil Mahre, U.S. |
| 1982 | Phil Mahre, U.S. |
| 1983 | Phil Mahre, U.S. |
| 1984 | Pirmin Zurbriggen, Switzerland |
| 1985 | Marc Girardelli, Luxembourg |
| 1986 | Marc Girardelli, Luxembourg |
| 1987 | Pirmin Zurbriggen, Switzerland |
| 1988 | Pirmin Zurbriggen, Switzerland |
| 1989 | Marc Girardelli, Luxembourg |
| 1990 | Pirmin Zurbriggen, Switzerland |
| 1991 | Marc Girardelli, Luxembourg |
| 1992 | Paul Accola, Switzerland |
| 1993 | Marc Girardelli, Luxembourg |
| 1994 | Kjetil Andre Aamodt, Norway |
| 1995 | Alberto Tomba, Italy |
| 1996 | Lasse Kjus, Norway |

### Women

| Year | Champion |
|---|---|
| 1967 | Nancy Greene, Canada |
| 1968 | Nancy Greene, Canada |
| 1969 | Gertrud Gabl, Austria |
| 1970 | Michele Jacot, France |
| 1971 | Annemarie Proell, Austria |
| 1972 | Annemarie Proell, Austria |
| 1973 | Annemarie Proell, Austria |
| 1974 | Annemarie Proell, Austria |
| 1975 | Annemarie Proell, Austria |
| 1976 | Rose Mittermaier, W. Germany |
| 1977 | Lise-Marie Morerod, Switzerland |
| 1978 | Hanni Wenzel, Liechtenstein |
| 1979 | Annemarie Proell Moser, Austria |
| 1980 | Hanni Wenzel, Liechtenstein |
| 1981 | Marie-Theres Nadig, Switzerland |
| 1982 | Erika Hess, Switzerland |
| 1983 | Tamara McKinney, U.S. |
| 1984 | Erika Hess, Switzerland |
| 1985 | Michela Figini, Switzerland |
| 1986 | Maria Walliser, Switzerland |
| 1987 | Maria Walliser, Switzerland |
| 1988 | Michela Figini, Switzerland |
| 1989 | Vreni Schneider, Switzerland |
| 1990 | Petra Kronberger, Austria |
| 1991 | Petra Kronberger, Austria |
| 1992 | Petra Kronberger, Austria |
| 1993 | Anita Wachter, Austria |
| 1994 | Vreni Schneider, Switzerland |
| 1995 | Vreni Schneider, Switzerland |
| 1996 | Katja Seizinger, Germany |

# IGFA Saltwater & Freshwater All-Tackle World Records

**Source:** International Game Fish Association; records confirmed to Oct. 1996

## Saltwater Fish Records

| Species | Weight | Where caught | Date | Angler |
|---|---|---|---|---|
| Albacore | 88 lbs. 2 oz. | Gran Canaria, Canary Islands | Nov. 19, 1977 | Siegfried Dickemann |
| Amberjack, greater | 155 lbs. 10 oz. | Challenger Bank, Bermuda | June 24, 1981 | Joseph Dawson |
| Barracuda, great | 85 lbs. | Christmas Island, Kiribati | Apr. 11, 1992 | John Helfrich |
| Barracuda, Mexican | 21 lbs. | Phantom Isle, Costa Rica | Mar. 27, 1987 | E. Greg Kent |
| Barracuda, Pacific | 7 lbs. 11 oz. | Catalina Island, CA | May 22, 1994 | Jim Kingsmill |
| Bass, barred sand | 13 lbs. 3 oz. | Huntington Beach, CA | Aug. 29, 1988 | Robert Halal |
| Bass, black sea | 9 lbs. 8 oz. | Virginia Beach, VA | Jan. 9, 1987 | Joe Mizelle Jr. |
| | | Virginia Beach, VA | Dec. 22, 1990 | Jack G. Stallings |
| Bass, giant sea | 563 lbs. 8 oz. | Anacaba Island, CA | Aug. 20, 1968 | James D. McAdam Jr. |
| Bass, redeye | 8 lbs. 12 oz. | Apalatchicola River, FL | Jan. 28, 1995 | Carl W. Davis |
| Bass, striped | 78 lbs. 8 oz. | Atlantic City, NJ | Sept. 21, 1982 | Albert McReynolds |
| Bluefish | 31 lbs. 12 oz. | Hatteras Inlet, NC | Jan. 30, 1972 | James M. Hussey |
| Bonefish | 19 lbs. | Zululand, South Africa | May 26, 1962 | Brian W. Batchelor |
| Bonito, Atlantic | 18 lbs. 4 oz. | Faial Island, Azores | July 8, 1953 | D. Gama Higgs |
| Bonito, Pacific | 14 lbs. 12 oz. | San Benitos Island, Mexico | Oct. 12, 1980 | Jerome Rilling |
| Cabezon | 23 lbs. | Juan De Fuca Strait, WA | Aug. 4, 1990 | Wesley Hunter |
| Cobia | 135 lbs. 9 oz. | Shark Bay, Australia | July 9, 1985 | Peter W. Goulding |
| Cod, Atlantic | 98 lbs. 12 oz. | Isle of Shoals, NH | June 8, 1969 | Alphonse Bielevich |
| Cod, Pacific | 30 lbs. | Andrew Bay, AK | June 7, 1984 | Donald Vaughn |
| Conger | 133 lbs. 4 oz. | Berry Head, S. Devon, England | June 5, 1995 | Vic Evans |
| Dolphin | 87 lbs. | Papagallo Gulf, Costa Rica | Sept. 25, 1976 | Manuel Salazar |
| Drum, black | 113 lbs. 1 oz. | Lewes, DE | Sept. 15, 1975 | Gerald Townsend |
| Drum, red | 94 lbs. 2 oz. | Avon, NC | Nov. 7, 1984 | David Deuel |
| Eel, American | 9 lbs. 4 oz. | Cape May, NJ | Nov. 9, 1995 | Jeff Pennick |
| Eel, marbled | 36 lbs. 1 oz. | Hazelmere Dam, South Africa | June 10, 1984 | Ferdie van Nooten |
| Flounder, southern | 20 lbs. 9 oz. | Nassau Sound, FL | Dec. 23, 1983 | Larenza Mungin |
| Flounder, summer | 22 lbs. 7 oz. | Montauk, NY | Sept. 15, 1975 | Charles Nappi |
| Grouper, Warsaw | 436 lbs. 12 oz. | Gulf of Mexico, Destin, FL | Dec. 22, 1985 | Steve Haeusler |
| Halibut, Atlantic | 255 lbs. 4 oz. | Gloucester, MA | July 28, 1989 | Sonny Manley |
| Halibut, California | 53 lbs. 4 oz. | Santa Rosa Island, CA | July 7, 1988 | Russell Harmon |
| Halibut, Pacific | 395 lbs. | Unalaska Bay, Bering Sea | June 21, 1995 | Michael James Golat |
| Jack, crevalle | 57 lbs. 5 oz. | Barra do Kwanza, Angola | Oct. 10, 1992 | Cam Nicolson |
| Jack, horse-eye | 24 lbs. 8 oz. | Miami, FL | Dec. 20, 1982 | Tito Schnau |
| Jack, Pacific crevalle | 29 lbs. 8 oz. | Playa Zancudo, Costa Rica | Jan. 1, 1994 | Ronald C. Snody |
| Jewfish | 680 lbs. | Fernandina Beach, FL | May 20, 1961 | Lynn Joyner |
| Kawakawa | 29 lbs. | Clarion Island, Mexico | Dec. 17, 1986 | Ronald Nakamura |
| Lingcod | 69 lbs. | Langara Island, British Columbia | June 16, 1992 | Murray Romer |
| Mackerel, cero | 17 lbs. 2 oz. | Islamorada, FL | Apr. 5, 1986 | G. Michael Mills |
| Mackerel, king | 90 lbs. | Key West, FL | Feb. 16, 1976 | Norton Thomton |
| Mackerel, Spanish | 13 lbs. | Ocracoke Inlet, NC | Nov. 4, 1987 | Robert Cranton |
| Marlin, Atlantic blue | 1,402 lbs. 2 oz. | Vitoria, Brazil | Feb. 29, 1992 | Paulo Amorim |
| Marlin, black | 1,560 lbs. | Cabo Blanco, Peru | Aug. 4, 1953 | Alfred C. Glassell Jr. |
| Marlin, Pacific blue | 1,376 lbs. | Kaaiwi Pt., Kona, HI | May 31, 1982 | Jay W. deBeaubien |
| Marlin, striped | 494 lbs. | Tutukaka, New Zealand | Jan. 16, 1986 | Bill Boniface |
| Marlin, white | 181 lbs. 14 oz. | Vitoria, Brazil | Dec. 8, 1979 | Evandro Luiz Coser |
| Permit | 53 lbs. 4 oz. | Lake Worth Inlet, FL | Mar. 25, 1994 | Roy Brooker |
| Pollack, European | 27 lbs. 6 oz. | Salcombe, Devon, England | Jan. 16, 1986 | Robert Milkins |
| Pollock | 50 lbs. | Saltraumen, Norway | Nov. 30, 1995 | Thor-Magnus Lekang |
| Pompano, African | 50 lbs. 8 oz. | Daytona Beach, FL | Apr. 21, 1990 | Tom Sargent |
| Roosterfish | 114 lbs. | La Paz, Baja Cal., Mexico | June 1, 1960 | Abe Sackheim |
| Runner, blue | 8 lbs. 7 oz. | Port Aransas, TX | Feb. 13, 1995 | Allen E. Windecker |
| Runner, rainbow | 37 lbs. 9 oz. | Clarion Island, Mexico | Nov. 21, 1991 | Tom Pfleger |
| Sailfish, Atlantic | 141 lbs. 1 oz. | Luanda, Angola | Feb. 19, 1994 | Alfredo de Sousa Neves |
| Sailfish, Pacific | 221 lbs. | Santa Cruz Island, Ecuador | Feb. 12, 1947 | C. W. Stewart |
| Seabass, white | 83 lbs. 12 oz. | San Felipe, Mexico | Mar. 31, 1953 | L. C. Baumgardner |
| Seatrout, spotted | 17 lbs. 7 oz. | Ft. Pierce, FL | May 11, 1995 | Graig F. Carson |
| Shark, bigeye thresher | 802 lbs. | Tutukaka, New Zealand | Feb. 8, 1981 | Dianne North |
| Shark, bignose | 369 lbs. 14 oz. | Markham R., Papua New Guinea | Oct. 23, 1993 | Lester Rohrlach |
| Shark, blue | 437 lbs. | Catherine Bay, N.S.W., Australia | Oct. 2, 1976 | Peter Hyde |
| Shark, great hammerhead | 991 lbs. | Sarasota, FL | May 30, 1982 | Allen Ogle |
| Shark, Greenland | 1,708 lbs. 9 oz. | Trondheimsfjord, Norway | Oct. 18, 1987 | Terje Nordtvedt |
| Shark, man-eater or white | 2,664 lbs. | Ceduna, S.A., Australia | Apr. 21, 1959 | Alfred Dean |
| Shark, porbeagle | 507 lbs. | Caithness, Scotland | Mar. 9, 1993 | Christopher Bennet |
| Shark, shortfin mako | 1,115 lbs. | Black River, Mauritius | Nov. 16, 1988 | Patrick Guillanton |
| Shark, tiger | 1,780 lbs. | Cherry Grove, SC | June 14, 1964 | Walter Maxwell |
| Shark, tope | 98 lbs. 8 oz. | Santa Monica, CA | Oct. 20, 1994 | Fred Oakley |
| Sheepshead | 21 lbs. 4 oz. | New Orleans, LA | Apr. 16, 1982 | Wayne Deselle |
| Skipjack, black | 26 lbs. | Thetis Bank, Baja Cal., Mexico | Oct. 23, 1991 | Clifford Hamaishi |
| Snapper, cubera | 121 lbs. 8 oz. | Cameron, LA | July 5, 1982 | Mike Hebert |
| Snapper, red | 46 lbs. 8 oz. | Destin, FL | Oct. 1, 1985 | E. Lane Nichols 3d |
| Snook | 53 lbs. 10 oz. | Parismina Ranch, Costa Rica | Oct. 18, 1978 | Gilbert Ponzi |
| Spearfish, Mediterranean | 90 lbs. 13 oz. | Madeira Island, Portugal | June 2, 1980 | Joseph Larkin |
| Swordfish | 1,182 lbs. | Iquique, Chile | May 7, 1953 | L. Marron |
| Tarpon | 283 lbs. 4 oz. | Sherbro Island, Sierra Leone | Apr. 16, 1991 | Yvon Sebag |
| Tautog | 24 lbs. | Wachapreague, VA | Aug. 25, 1987 | Gregory Bell |
| Trevally, bigeye | 18 lbs. 1 oz. | Clipperton Island, France | May 12, 1990 | Rebecca Mills |
| Trevally, giant | 145 lbs. 8 oz. | Makena, Maui, HI | Mar. 28, 1991 | Russell Mori |
| Tuna, Atlantic bigeye | 375 lbs. 8 oz. | Ocean City, MD | Aug. 26, 1977 | Cecil Browne |
| Tuna, blackfin | 42 lbs. 8 oz. | Marathon Humps, Duck Key, FL | May 21, 1995 | Shawn Snyder |
| Tuna, bluefin | 1,496 lbs. | Aulds Cove, Nova Scotia | Oct. 26, 1979 | Ken Fraser |
| Tuna, longtail | 79 lbs. 2 oz. | Montague Isl., N.S.W., Australia | Apr. 12, 1982 | Tim Simpson |
| Tuna, Pacific bigeye | 435 lbs. | Cabo Blanco, Peru | Apr. 17, 1957 | Dr. Russel Lee |

| Species | Weight | Where caught | Date | Angler |
|---|---|---|---|---|
| Tuna, skipjack | 41 lbs. 14 oz. | Pearl Beach, Mauritius | Nov. 12, 1985 | Edmund Heinzen |
| Tuna, southern bluefin | 348 lbs. 5 oz. | Whakatane, New Zealand | Jan. 16, 1981 | Rex Wood |
| Tuna, yellowfin | 388 lbs. 12 oz. | San Benedicto Island, Mexico | Apr. 1, 1977 | Curt Wiesenhutter |
| Tunny, little | 35 lbs. 2 oz. | Cap de Garde, Algeria | Dec. 14, 1988 | Jean Yves Chatard |
| Wahoo | 155 lbs. 8 oz. | San Salvador, Bahamas | Apr. 3, 1990 | William Bourne |
| Weakfish | 19 lbs. 2 oz. | Jones Beach Inlet, NY | Oct. 11, 1984 | Dennis Rooney |
| | | Delaware Bay, DE | May 20, 1989 | William Thomas |
| Yellowtail, California | 79 lbs. 4 oz. | Alijos Rocks, Baja Cal., Mexico | July 2, 1991 | Robert Walker |
| Yellowtail, southern | 114 lbs. 10 oz. | Tauranga, New Zealand | Feb. 5, 1984 | Mike Godfrey |

## Freshwater Fish Records

| Species | Weight | Where caught | Date | Angler |
|---|---|---|---|---|
| Barramundi | 63 lbs. 2 oz. | Normah River, Australia | Apr. 28, 1991 | Scott Barnsley |
| Bass, largemouth | 22 lbs. 4 oz. | Montgomery Lake, GA | June 2, 1932 | George W. Perry |
| Bass, peacock | 27 lbs. | Rio Negro, Brazil | Dec. 4, 1994 | Gerald "Doc" Lawson |
| Bass, rock | 3 lbs. | York River, Ontario | Aug. 1, 1974 | Peter Gulgin |
| Bass, smallmouth | 10 lbs. 14 oz. | Dale Hollow Lake, KY | Apr. 24, 1969 | John T. Gorman |
| Bass, Suwannee | 3 lbs. 14 oz. | Suwannee River, FL | Mar. 2, 1985 | Ronnie Everett |
| Bass, white | 6 lbs. 13 oz. | Lake Orange, VA | July 31, 1989 | Ronald Sprouse |
| Bass, whiterock | 25 lbs. 8 oz. | Lake Chatuge, GA | May 1, 1995 | David C. Hobby |
| Bass, yellow | 2 lbs. 4 oz. | Lake Monroe, IN | Mar. 27, 1977 | Donald L. Stalker |
| Bluegill | 4 lbs. 12 oz. | Ketona Lake, AL | Apr. 9, 1950 | T. S. Hudson |
| Bowfin | 21 lbs. 8 oz. | Florence, SC | Jan. 29, 1980 | Robert Harmon |
| Buffalo, bigmouth | 70 lbs. 5 oz. | Bussey Brake, Bastrop, LA | Apr. 21, 1980 | Delbert Sisk |
| Buffalo, black | 55 lbs. 8 oz. | Cherokee Lake, TN | May 3, 1984 | Edward McLain |
| Buffalo, smallmouth | 68 lbs. 8 oz. | Lake Hamilton, AR | May 16, 1984 | Jerry Dolezal |
| Bullhead, brown | 5 lbs. 11 oz. | Cedar Creek, FL | Mar. 28, 1995 | Robert Bengis |
| Bullhead, yellow | 4 lbs. 4 oz. | Mormon Lake, AZ | May 11, 1984 | Emily Williams |
| Burbot | 18 lbs. 4 oz. | Pickford, MI | Jan. 31, 1980 | Thomas Courtemanche |
| Carp, common | 75 lbs. 11 oz. | Lac de St. Cassien, France | May 21, 1987 | Leo van der Gugten |
| Catfish, blue | 109 lbs. 4 oz. | Cooper River, SC | Mar. 14, 1991 | George Lijewski |
| Catfish, channel | 58 lbs. | Santee-Cooper Res., SC | July 7, 1964 | W. B. Whaley |
| Catfish, flathead | 91 lbs. 4 oz. | Lake Lewisville, TX | Mar. 28, 1982 | Mike Rogers |
| Catfish, white | 18 lbs. 14 oz. | Withlacoochee River, FL | Sept. 21, 1991 | Jim Miller |
| Char, Arctic | 32 lbs. 9 oz. | Tree River, Canada | July 30, 1981 | Jeffrey Ward |
| Crappie, white | 5 lbs. 3 oz. | Enid Dam, MS | July 31, 1957 | Fred L. Bright |
| Dolly Varden | 18 lbs. 9 oz. | Mashutuk River, AK | July 13, 1993 | Richard B. Evans |
| Dorado | 51 lbs. 5 oz. | Toledo (Corrientes), Argentina | Sept. 27, 1984 | Armando Giudice |
| Drum, freshwater | 54 lbs. 8 oz. | Nickajack Lake, TN | Apr. 20, 1972 | Benny E. Hull |
| Gar, alligator | 279 lbs. | Rio Grande, TX | Dec. 2, 1951 | Bill Valverde |
| Gar, Florida | 21 lbs. 3 oz. | Boca Raton, FL | June 3, 1981 | Jeff Sabol |
| Gar, longnose | 50 lbs. 5 oz. | Trinity River, TX | July 30, 1954 | Townsend Miller |
| Gar, shortnose | 5 lbs. 12 oz. | Rend Lake, IL | July 6, 1995 | Donna K. Willmert |
| Gar, spotted | 9 lbs. 12 oz. | Lake Mexia, TX | Apr. 7, 1994 | Rick Rivard |
| Grayling, Arctic | 5 lbs. 15 oz. | Katseyedie River, N.W.T. | Aug. 16, 1967 | Jeanne P. Branson |
| Inconnu | 53 lbs. | Pah River, AK | Aug. 20, 1986 | Lawrence Hudnall |
| Kokanee | 9 lbs. 6 oz. | Okanagan Lake, Vernon, B.C. | June 18, 1988 | Norm Kuhn |
| Muskellunge | 67 lbs. 8 oz. | Lake Court Oreilles, WI | July 24, 1949 | Cal Johnson |
| Muskellunge, tiger | 51 lbs. 3 oz. | Lac Vieux-Desert, WI-MI | July 16, 1919 | John Knobla |
| Perch, Nile | 191 lbs. 8 oz. | Lake Victoria, Kenya | Sept. 5, 1991 | Andy Davison |
| Perch, white | 4 lbs. 12 oz. | Messalonskee Lake, ME | June 4, 1949 | Mrs. Earl Small |
| Perch, yellow | 4 lbs. 3 oz. | Bordentown, NJ | May, 1865 | Dr. C. C. Abbot |
| Pickerel, chain | 9 lbs. 6 oz. | Homerville, GA | Feb. 17, 1961 | Baxley McQuaig Jr. |
| Pike, northern | 55 lbs. 1 oz. | Lake of Grefeern, W. Germany | Oct. 16, 1986 | Lothar Louis |
| Redhorse, greater | 9 lbs. 3 oz. | Salmon River, Pulaski, NY | May 11, 1985 | Jason Wilson |
| Redhorse, silver | 11 lbs. 7 oz. | Plum Creek, WI | May 29, 1985 | Neal Long |
| Salmon, Atlantic | 79 lbs. 2 oz. | Tana River, Norway | 1928 | Henrik Henriksen |
| Salmon, chinook | 97 lbs. 4 oz. | Kenai River, AK | May 17, 1985 | Les Anderson |
| Salmon, chum | 32 lbs. | Behm Canal, AK | June 7, 1985 | Fredrick Thynes |
| Salmon, coho | 33 lbs. 4 oz. | Salmon River, Pulaski, NY | Sept. 27, 1989 | Jerry Lifton |
| Salmon, pink | 13 lbs. 1 oz. | St. Mary's River, Ontario | Sept. 23, 1992 | Ray Higaki |
| Salmon, sockeye | 15 lbs. 3 oz. | Kenai River, AK | Aug. 9, 1987 | Stan Roach |
| Sauger | 8 lbs. 12 oz. | Lake Sakakawea, ND | Oct. 6, 1971 | Mike Fischer |
| Shad, American | 11 lbs. 4 oz. | Connecticut River, MA | May 19, 1986 | Bob Thibodo |
| Sturgeon, beluga | 224 lbs. 13 oz. | Guryev, Kazakstan | May 3, 1993 | Merete Lehne |
| Sturgeon, white | 468 lbs. | Benicia, CA | July 9, 1983 | Joey Pallotta 3d |
| Sunfish, green | 2 lbs. 2 oz. | Stockton Lake, MO | June 18, 1971 | Paul M. Dilley |
| Sunfish, redbreast | 1 lb. 12 oz. | Suwannee River, FL | May 29, 1984 | Alvin Buchanan |
| Sunfish, redear | 5 lbs. 3 oz. | Sacramento, CA | June 27, 1994 | Anthony H. White |
| Tigerfish, giant | 97 lbs. | Zaire River, Kinshasa, Zaire | July 9, 1988 | Raymond Houtmans |
| Tilapia | 6 lbs. 5 oz. | Lake Aranal, Costa Rica | Feb. 10, 1995 | Marvin C. Smith |
| Trout, Apache | 5 lb. 3 oz. | Apache Res., AZ | May 29, 1991 | John Baldwin |
| Trout, brook | 14 lbs. 8 oz. | Nipigon River, Ontario | July 1916 | Dr. W. J. Cook |
| Trout, brown | 40 lbs. 4 oz. | Little Red River, AR | May 9, 1992 | Howard "Rip" Collins |
| Trout, bull | 32 lbs. | Lake Pond Oreille, ID | Oct. 27, 1949 | N. L. Higgins |
| Trout, cutthroat | 41 lbs. | Pyramid Lake, NV | Dec. 1925 | John Skimmerhorn |
| Trout, golden | 11 lbs. | Cooks Lake, WY | Aug. 5, 1948 | Charles S. Reed |
| Trout, lake | 66 lbs. 8 oz. | Great Bear Lake, N.W.T. | July 19, 1991 | Rodney Harback |
| Trout, rainbow | 42 lbs. 2 oz. | Bell Island, AK | June 22, 1970 | David Robert White |
| Trout, tiger | 20 lbs. 13 oz. | Lake Michigan, WI | Aug. 12, 1978 | Pete Friedland |
| Walleye | 25 lbs. | Old Hickory Lake, TN | Aug. 2, 1960 | Mabry Harper |
| Warmouth | 2 lbs. 7 oz. | Yellow River, Holt, FL | Oct. 19, 1985 | Tony D. Dempsey |
| Whitefish, lake | 14 lbs. 6 oz. | Meaford, Ontario | May 21, 1984 | Dennis Laycock |
| Whitefish, mountain | 5 lbs. 6 oz. | Rioh River, Saskatchewan | June 15, 1988 | John Bell |
| Whitefish, round | 6 lbs. | Putahow River, Manitoba | June 14, 1984 | Allen Ristori |
| Zander | 25 lbs. 2 oz. | Trosa, Sweden | June 12, 1986 | Harry Lee Tennison |

# GOLF

## United States Open Winners

| Year[1] | Winner | Year[1] | Winner | Year[1] | Winner | Year[1] | Winner |
|---|---|---|---|---|---|---|---|
| 1903 | Willie Anderson | 1927 | Tommy Armour | 1953 | Ben Hogan | 1975 | Lou Graham |
| 1904 | Willie Anderson | 1928 | John Farrell | 1954 | Ed Furgol | 1976 | Jerry Pate |
| 1905 | Willie Anderson | 1929 | Bobby Jones* | 1955 | Jack Fleck | 1977 | Hubert Green |
| 1906 | Alex Smith | 1930 | Bobby Jones* | 1956 | Cary Middlecoff | 1978 | Andy North |
| 1907 | Alex Ross | 1931 | Wm. Burke | 1957 | Dick Mayer | 1979 | Hale Irwin |
| 1908 | Fred McLeod | 1932 | Gene Sarazen | 1958 | Tommy Bolt | 1980 | Jack Nicklaus |
| 1909 | George Sargent | 1933 | John Goodman* | 1959 | Billy Casper | 1981 | David Graham |
| 1910 | Alex Smith | 1934 | Olin Dutra | 1960 | Arnold Palmer | 1982 | Tom Watson |
| 1911 | John McDermott | 1935 | Sam Parks, Jr. | 1961 | Gene Littler | 1983 | Larry Nelson |
| 1912 | John McDermott | 1936 | Tony Manero | 1962 | Jack Nicklaus | 1984 | Fuzzy Zoeller |
| 1913 | Francis Ouimet* | 1937 | Ralph Guldahl | 1963 | Julius Boros | 1985 | Andy North |
| 1914 | Walter Hagen | 1938 | Ralph Guldahl | 1964 | Ken Venturi | 1986 | Ray Floyd |
| 1915 | Jerome Travers* | 1939 | Byron Nelson | 1965 | Gary Player | 1987 | Scott Simpson |
| 1916 | Chick Evans* | 1940 | Lawson Little | 1966 | Billy Casper | 1988 | Curtis Strange |
| 1919 | Walter Hagen | 1941 | Craig Wood | 1967 | Jack Nicklaus | 1989 | Curtis Strange |
| 1920 | Edward Ray | 1946 | Lloyd Mangrum | 1968 | Lee Trevino | 1990 | Hale Irwin |
| 1921 | Jim Barnes | 1947 | L. Worsham | 1969 | Orville Moody | 1991 | Payne Stewart |
| 1922 | Gene Sarazen | 1948 | Ben Hogan | 1970 | Tony Jacklin | 1992 | Tom Kite |
| 1923 | Bobby Jones* | 1949 | Cary Middlecoff | 1971 | Lee Trevino | 1993 | Lee Janzen |
| 1924 | Cyril Walker | 1950 | Ben Hogan | 1972 | Jack Nicklaus | 1994 | Ernie Els |
| 1925 | Willie MacFarlane | 1951 | Ben Hogan | 1973 | Johnny Miller | 1995 | Corey Pavin |
| 1926 | Bobby Jones* | 1952 | Julius Boros | 1974 | Hale Irwin | 1996 | Steve Jones |

* Amateur. (1) 1917-18 and 1942-45 not played.

## Professional Golfer's Association Championship Winners

| Year[1] | Winner | Year[1] | Winner | Year[1] | Winner | Year[1] | Winner |
|---|---|---|---|---|---|---|---|
| 1922 | Gene Sarazen | 1941 | Victor Ghezzi | 1961 | Jerry Barber | 1979 | David Graham |
| 1923 | Gene Sarazen | 1942 | Sam Snead | 1962 | Gary Player | 1980 | Jack Nicklaus |
| 1924 | Walter Hagen | 1944 | Bob Hamilton | 1963 | Jack Nicklaus | 1981 | Larry Nelson |
| 1925 | Walter Hagen | 1945 | Byron Nelson | 1964 | Bob Nichols | 1982 | Ray Floyd |
| 1926 | Walter Hagen | 1946 | Ben Hogan | 1965 | Dave Marr | 1983 | Hal Sutton |
| 1927 | Walter Hagen | 1947 | Jim Ferrier | 1966 | Al Geiberger | 1984 | Lee Trevino |
| 1928 | Leo Diegel | 1948 | Ben Hogan | 1967 | Don January | 1985 | Hubert Green |
| 1929 | Leo Diegel | 1949 | Sam Snead | 1968 | Julius Boros | 1986 | Bob Tway |
| 1930 | Tommy Armour | 1950 | Chandler Harper | 1969 | Ray Floyd | 1987 | Larry Nelson |
| 1931 | Tom Creavy | 1951 | Sam Snead | 1970 | Dave Stockton | 1988 | Jeff Sluman |
| 1932 | Olin Dutra | 1952 | James Turnesa | 1971 | Jack Nicklaus | 1989 | Payne Stewart |
| 1933 | Gene Sarazen | 1953 | Walter Burkemo | 1972 | Gary Player | 1990 | Wayne Grady |
| 1934 | Paul Runyan | 1954 | Melvin Harbert | 1973 | Jack Nicklaus | 1991 | John Daly |
| 1935 | Johnny Revolta | 1955 | Doug Ford | 1974 | Lee Trevino | 1992 | Nick Price |
| 1936 | Denny Shute | 1956 | Jack Burke | 1975 | Jack Nicklaus | 1993 | Paul Azinger |
| 1937 | Denny Shute | 1957 | Lionel Hebert | 1976 | Dave Stockton | 1994 | Nick Price |
| 1938 | Paul Runyan | 1958 | Dow Finsterwald | 1977 | Lanny Wadkins | 1995 | Steve Elkington |
| 1939 | Henry Picard | 1959 | Bob Rosburg | 1978 | John Mahaffey | 1996 | Mark Brooks |
| 1940 | Byron Nelson | 1960 | Jay Hebert | | | | |

(1) 1943 not played.

## Masters Golf Tournament Winners

| Year[1] | Winner | Year[1] | Winner | Year[1] | Winner | Year[1] | Winner |
|---|---|---|---|---|---|---|---|
| 1934 | Horton Smith | 1952 | Sam Snead | 1967 | Gay Brewer, Jr. | 1982 | Craig Stadler |
| 1935 | Gene Sarazen | 1953 | Ben Hogan | 1968 | Bob Goalby | 1983 | Seve Ballesteros |
| 1936 | Horton Smith | 1954 | Sam Snead | 1969 | George Archer | 1984 | Ben Crenshaw |
| 1937 | Byron Nelson | 1955 | Cary Middlecoff | 1970 | Billy Casper | 1985 | Bernhard Langer |
| 1938 | Henry Picard | 1956 | Jack Burke | 1971 | Charles Coody | 1986 | Jack Nicklaus |
| 1939 | Ralph Guldahl | 1957 | Doug Ford | 1972 | Jack Nicklaus | 1987 | Larry Mize |
| 1940 | Jimmy Demaret | 1958 | Arnold Palmer | 1973 | Tommy Aaron | 1988 | Sandy Lyle |
| 1941 | Craig Wood | 1959 | Art Wall Jr. | 1974 | Gary Player | 1989 | Nick Faldo |
| 1942 | Byron Nelson | 1960 | Arnold Palmer | 1975 | Jack Nicklaus | 1990 | Nick Faldo |
| 1946 | Herman Keiser | 1961 | Gary Player | 1976 | Ray Floyd | 1991 | Ian Woosnam |
| 1947 | Jimmy Demaret | 1962 | Arnold Palmer | 1977 | Tom Watson | 1992 | Fred Couples |
| 1948 | Claude Harmon | 1963 | Jack Nicklaus | 1978 | Gary Player | 1993 | Bernhard Langer |
| 1949 | Sam Snead | 1964 | Arnold Palmer | 1979 | Fuzzy Zoeller | 1994 | Jose Maria Olazabal |
| 1950 | Jimmy Demaret | 1965 | Jack Nicklaus | 1980 | Seve Ballesteros | 1995 | Ben Crenshaw |
| 1951 | Ben Hogan | 1966 | Jack Nicklaus | 1981 | Tom Watson | 1996 | Nick Faldo |

(1) 1943-45 not played.

## British Open Winners

| Year[1] | Winner | Year[1] | Winner | Year[1] | Winner | Year[1] | Winner |
|---|---|---|---|---|---|---|---|
| 1931 | Tommy Armour | 1952 | Bobby Locke | 1967 | Roberto de Vicenzo | 1982 | Tom Watson |
| 1932 | Gene Sarazen | 1953 | Ben Hogan | 1968 | Gary Player | 1983 | Tom Watson |
| 1933 | Denny Shute | 1954 | Peter Thomson | 1969 | Tony Jacklin | 1984 | Seve Ballesteros |
| 1934 | Henry Cotton | 1955 | Peter Thomson | 1970 | Jack Nicklaus | 1985 | Sandy Lyle |
| 1935 | Alf Perry | 1956 | Peter Thomson | 1971 | Lee Trevino | 1986 | Greg Norman |
| 1936 | Alf Padgham | 1957 | Bobby Locke | 1972 | Lee Trevino | 1987 | Nick Faldo |
| 1937 | T.H. Cotton | 1958 | Peter Thomson | 1973 | Tom Weiskopf | 1988 | Seve Ballesteros |
| 1938 | R.A. Whitcombe | 1959 | Gary Player | 1974 | Gary Player | 1989 | Mark Calcavecchia |
| 1939 | Richard Burton | 1960 | Kel Nagle | 1975 | Tom Watson | 1990 | Nick Faldo |
| 1946 | Sam Snead | 1961 | Arnold Palmer | 1976 | Johnny Miller | 1991 | Ian Baker-Finch |
| 1947 | Fred Daly | 1962 | Arnold Palmer | 1977 | Tom Watson | 1992 | Nick Faldo |
| 1948 | Henry Cotton | 1963 | Bob Charles | 1978 | Jack Nicklaus | 1993 | Greg Norman |
| 1949 | Bobby Locke | 1964 | Tony Lema | 1979 | Seve Ballesteros | 1994 | Nick Price |
| 1950 | Bobby Locke | 1965 | Peter Thomson | 1980 | Tom Watson | 1995 | John Daly |
| 1951 | Max Faulkner | 1966 | Jack Nicklaus | 1981 | Bill Rogers | 1996 | Tom Lehman |

(1) 1940-45 not played.

# Professional Golf Tournaments in 1996

## Men

| Date | Event | Winner | Score | Prize |
|---|---|---|---|---|
| Jan. 7 | Mercedes Championships, Carlsbad, CA | Mark O'Meara | 271 | $180,000 |
| Jan. 14 | Northern Telecom Open, Tucson, AZ | Phil Mickelson | 273 | 225,000 |
| Jan. 21 | Bob Hope Chrysler Classic, Bermuda Dunes, CA | Mark Brooks | 337 | 234,000 |
| Jan. 27 | Phoenix Open, Scottsdale, AZ | Phil Mickelson | *269 | 234,000 |
| Feb. 11 | Buick Invitational of CA, La Jolla, CA | Davis Love III | 269 | 216,000 |
| Feb. 18 | United Airlines Hawaiian Open, Honolulu, HI | Jim Furyk | *277 | 216,000 |
| Feb. 25 | Nissan Open, Pacific Palisades, CA | Craig Stadler | 278 | 216,000 |
| Mar. 3 | Doral-Ryder Open, Miami, FL | Greg Norman | 269 | 324,000 |
| Mar. 10 | Honda Classic, Coral Springs, FL | Tim Herron | 271 | 234,000 |
| Mar. 17 | Bay Hill Invitational, Orlando, FL | Paul Goydos | 275 | 216,000 |
| Mar. 24 | Freeport-McDermott Classic, New Orleans, LA | Scott McCarron | 275 | 216,000 |
| Mar. 31 | THE PLAYERS Championship, Ponte Vedra Beach, FL | Fred Couples | 270 | 630,000 |
| Apr. 7 | BellSouth Classic, Marietta, GA | Paul Stankowski | *280 | 234,000 |
| Apr. 14 | The Masters Tournament, Augusta, GA | Nick Faldo | 276 | 450,000 |
| Apr. 21 | MCI Classic, Hilton Head Island, SC | Loren Roberts | T265 | 252,000 |
| Apr. 28 | Greater Greensboro Chrysler Classic, Greensboro, NC | Mark O'Meara | 274 | 324,000 |
| May 5 | Shell Houston Open, The Woodlands, TX | Mark Brooks | *274 | 270,000 |
| May 12 | GTE Byron Nelson Classic, Irving, TX | Phil Mickelson | 265 | 270,000 |
| May 19 | MasterCard Colonial, Fort Worth, TX | Corey Pavin | 272 | 270,000 |
| May 26 | Kemper Open, Potomac, MD | Steve Stricker | 270 | 270,000 |
| June 2 | Memorial Tournament, Dublin, OH | Tom Watson | 274 | 324,000 |
| June 9 | Buick Classic, Rye, NY | Ernie Els | 271 | 216,000 |
| June 16 | U.S. Open, Birmingham, MI | Steve Jones | 278 | 425,000 |
| June 23 | FedEx St. Jude Classic, Memphis, TN | John Cook | T258 | 243,000 |
| June 30 | Canon Greater Hartford Open, Cromwell, CT | D.A. Weibring | 270 | 270,000 |
| July 7 | Motorola Western Open, Lemont, IL | Steve Stricker | 270 | 360,000 |
| July 14 | Michelob Championship at Kingsmill, Williamsburg, VA | Scott Hoch | T265 | 225,000 |
| July 21 | Deposit Guaranty Golf Classic, Madison, MS | Willie Wood | 268 | 180,000 |
| July 21 | British Open, St. Annes, England | Tom Lehman | 271 | 310,000 |
| July 28 | CVS-Charity Classic, Sutton, MA | John Cook | 268 | 216,000 |
| Aug. 4 | Buick Open, Grand Blanc, MI | Justin Leonard | 266 | 216,000 |
| Aug. 11 | PGA Championship, Louisville, KY | Mark Brooks | *277 | 430,000 |
| Aug. 18 | The Sprint International, Castle Rock, CO | Clarence Rose | *+51 | 288,000 |
| Aug. 25 | NEC World Series of Golf, Akron, OH | Phil Mickelson | 274 | 378,000 |
| Aug. 25 | Greater Vancouver Open, Surrey, British Columbia | Guy Boros | 272 | 180,000 |
| Sept. 1 | Greater Milwaukee Open, Milwaukee, WI | Loren Roberts | *T265 | 216,000 |
| Sept. 8 | Bell Canadian Open, Oakville, Ontario | Dudley Hart | †202 | 270,000 |
| Sept. 15 | The Presidents Cup, Lake Manassas, VA | U.S. Team | 16.5 pts. | 800,000[1] |
| Sept. 15 | Quad City Classic, Coal Valley, IL | Ed Fiori | 269 | 216,000 |
| Sept. 22 | B.C. Open, Endicott, NY | Fred Funk | *†197 | 180,000 |
| Sept. 29 | Buick Challenge, Pine Mountain, GA | Michael Bradley | *†134 | 180,000 |
| Oct. 6 | Las Vegas Invitational, Las Vegas, NV | Tiger Woods | *332 | 297,000 |
| Oct. 13 | LaCantera Texas Open, San Antonio, TX | David Ogrin | 275 | 216,000 |
| Oct. 20 | Disney World/Oldsmobile Golf Classic, Lake Buena Vista, FL | Tiger Woods | 267 | 216,000 |
| Oct. 28 | THE TOUR Championship, Tulsa, OK | Tom Lehman | 268 | 540,000 |

## Women

| Date | Event | Winner | Score | Prize |
|---|---|---|---|---|
| Jan. 14 | Chrysler-Plymouth Tournament of Champions, Orlando, FL | Liselotte Neumann | 275 | $117,500 |
| Jan. 21 | HEALTHSOUTH Inaugural, Orlando, FL | Karrie Web | *209 | 67,500 |
| Feb. 24 | Cup Noodles Hawaiian Ladies Open, Oahu, HI | Meg Mallon | 212 | 90,000 |
| Mar. 17 | PING/Welch's Championship, Tucson, AZ | Liselotte Neumann | 276 | 67,500 |
| Mar. 24 | Standard Register PING Classic, Phoenix, AZ | Laura Davies | 284 | 105,000 |
| Mar. 31 | Nabisco Dinah Shore Classic, Rancho Mirage, CA | Patty Sheehan | 281 | 135,000 |
| Apr. 7 | Twelve Bridges LPGA Classic, Lincoln, CA | Kelly Robbins | *273 | 75,000 |
| Apr. 21 | Chick-fil-A Charity Championship, Stockbridge, GA | Barb Mucha | 208 | 82,500 |
| Apr. 28 | Sara Lee Classic, Old Hickory, TN | Meg Mallon | 210 | 90,000 |
| May 5 | Sprint Titleholders Championship, Daytona Beach, FL | Karrie Webb | 272 | 180,000 |
| May 12 | McDonald's LPGA Championship, Wilmington, DE | Laura Davies | 213 | 180,000 |
| May 26 | LPGA Corning Classic, Corning, NY | Rosie Jones | 276 | 90,000 |
| May 26 | JCPenney/LPGA Skins Game, Frisco, TX | Laura Davies | 12 skins | 340,000 |
| June 2 | U.S. Women's Open, Southern Pines, NC | Annika Sorenstam | 272 | 212,500 |
| June 9 | Oldsmobile Classic, East Lansing, MI | Michelle McGann | *272 | 90,000 |
| June 16 | First Bank-Edina Realty Classic, Brooklyn Park, MN | Liselotte Neumann | *207 | 82,500 |
| June 23 | Rochester International, Pittsford, NY | Dottie Pepper | 206 | 90,000 |
| June 30 | ShopRite LPGA Classic, Somers Pt., NJ | Dottie Pepper | 202 | 112,500 |
| July 7 | Jamie Farr Kroger Classic, Sylvania, OH | Joan Pitcock | *204 | 86,250 |
| July 14 | Youngstown-Warren LPGA Classic, Warren, OH | Michelle McGann | 200 | 90,000 |
| July 21 | Friendly's Classic, Agawam, MA | Dottie Pepper | 279 | 75,000 |
| July 28 | Michelob Light Heartland Classic, St. Louis, MO | Vicki Fergon | 276 | 82,500 |
| Aug. 4 | du Maurier Ltd. Classic, Edmonton, Alberta | Laura Davies | 277 | 150,000 |
| Aug. 11 | PING/Welch's Championship, Canton, MA | Emilee Klein | *273 | 75,000 |
| Aug. 18 | Weetabix Women's British Open, Milton Keynes, England | Emilee Klein | 277 | 124,000 |
| Aug. 25 | Star Bank LPGA Classic, Dayton, OH | Laura Davies | 204 | 82,500 |
| Sept. 2 | State Farm Rail Classic, Springfield, IL | Michelle McGann | *202 | 86,250 |
| Sept. 8 | The Safeway LPGA Golf Championship, Portland, OR | Dottie Pepper | 202 | 82,500 |
| Sept. 15 | SAFECO Classic, Kent, WA | Karrie Webb | 277 | 82,500 |
| Sept. 22 | The Solheim Cup, Chepstow, Wales | United States | 17 pts. | 75,000 |
| Sept. 29 | Fieldcrest Cannon Classic, Charlotte, NC | Trish Johnson | 270 | 75,000 |
| Oct. 5 | JAL Big Apple Classic, New Rochelle, NY | Caroline Pierce | *211 | 108,750 |
| Oct. 13 | CoreStates Betsy King Classic, Reading, PA | Annika Sorenstam | 270 | 90,000 |
| Oct. 20 | Samsung Wld. Champ. of Women's Golf, S. Korea | Annika Sorenstam | 274 | 125,000 |
| Oct. 27 | Nichirei International, Ibaragi-ken, Japan | United States | 21.5 pts. | 675,000[1] |

* Won playoff. (†) Shortened because of weather. (T) Tournament record. (1) Total team earnings.

## U.S. Women's Open Golf Champions

| Year | Winner | Year | Winner | Year | Winner | Year | Winner |
|---|---|---|---|---|---|---|---|
| 1948 | "Babe" Zaharias | 1961 | Mickey Wright | 1973 | Susie Maxwell Berning | 1985 | Kathy Baker |
| 1949 | Louise Suggs | 1962 | Murle Lindstrom | 1974 | Sandra Haynie | 1986 | Jane Geddes |
| 1950 | "Babe" Zaharias | 1963 | Mary Mills | 1975 | Sandra Palmer | 1987 | Laura Davies |
| 1951 | Betsy Rawls | 1964 | Mickey Wright | 1976 | JoAnne Carner | 1988 | Liselotte Neumann |
| 1952 | Louise Suggs | 1965 | Carol Mann | 1977 | Hollis Stacy | 1989 | Betsy King |
| 1953 | Betsy Rawls | 1966 | Sandra Spuzich | 1978 | Hollis Stacy | 1990 | Betsy King |
| 1954 | "Babe" Zaharias | 1967 | Catherine Lacoste* | 1979 | Jerilyn Britz | 1991 | Meg Mallon |
| 1955 | Fay Crocker | 1968 | Susie Maxwell Berning | 1980 | Amy Alcott | 1992 | Patty Sheehan |
| 1956 | Mrs. K. Cornelius | 1969 | Donna Caponi | 1981 | Pat Bradley | 1993 | Lauri Merten |
| 1957 | Betsy Rawls | 1970 | Donna Caponi | 1982 | Janet Alex | 1994 | Patty Sheehan |
| 1958 | Mickey Wright | 1971 | JoAnne Carner | 1983 | Jan Stephenson | 1995 | Annika Sorenstam |
| 1959 | Mickey Wright | 1972 | Susie Maxwell Berning | 1984 | Hollis Stacy | 1996 | Annika Sorenstam |
| 1960 | Betsy Rawls | | | | | | |

*Amateur

## PGA Leading Money Winners

| Year | Player | Dollars | Year | Player | Dollars | Year | Player | Dollars |
|---|---|---|---|---|---|---|---|---|
| 1946 | Ben Hogan | $42,556 | 1963 | Arnold Palmer | $128,230 | 1980 | Tom Watson | $530,808 |
| 1947 | Jimmy Demaret | 27,936 | 1964 | Jack Nicklaus | 113,284 | 1981 | Tom Kite | 375,699 |
| 1948 | Ben Hogan | 36,812 | 1965 | Jack Nicklaus | 140,752 | 1982 | Craig Stadler | 446,462 |
| 1949 | Sam Snead | 31,593 | 1966 | Billy Casper | 121,944 | 1983 | Hal Sutton | 426,668 |
| 1950 | Sam Snead | 35,758 | 1967 | Jack Nicklaus | 188,988 | 1984 | Tom Watson | 476,260 |
| 1951 | Lloyd Mangrum | 26,088 | 1968 | Billy Casper | 205,168 | 1985 | Curtis Strange | 542,321 |
| 1952 | Julius Boros | 37,032 | 1969 | Frank Beard | 175,223 | 1986 | Greg Norman | 653,296 |
| 1953 | Lew Worsham | 34,002 | 1970 | Lee Trevino | 157,037 | 1987 | Curtis Strange | 925,941 |
| 1954 | Bob Toski | 65,819 | 1971 | Jack Nicklaus | 244,490 | 1988 | Curtis Strange | 1,147,644 |
| 1955 | Julius Boros | 65,121 | 1972 | Jack Nicklaus | 320,542 | 1989 | Tom Kite | 1,395,278 |
| 1956 | Ted Kroll | 72,835 | 1973 | Jack Nicklaus | 308,362 | 1990 | Greg Norman | 1,165,477 |
| 1957 | Dick Mayer | 65,835 | 1974 | Johnny Miller | 353,201 | 1991 | Corey Pavin | 979,430 |
| 1958 | Arnold Palmer | 42,407 | 1975 | Jack Nicklaus | 323,149 | 1992 | Fred Couples | 1,344,188 |
| 1959 | Art Wall, Jr. | 53,167 | 1976 | Jack Nicklaus | 266,438 | 1993 | Nick Price | 1,478,557 |
| 1960 | Arnold Palmer | 75,262 | 1977 | Tom Watson | 310,653 | 1994 | Nick Price | 1,499,927 |
| 1961 | Gary Player | 64,540 | 1978 | Tom Watson | 362,429 | 1995 | Greg Norman | 1,654,959 |
| 1962 | Arnold Palmer | 81,448 | 1979 | Tom Watson | 462,636 | | | |

## LPGA Leading Money Winners

| Year | Player | Dollars | Year | Player | Dollars | Year | Player | Dollars |
|---|---|---|---|---|---|---|---|---|
| 1954 | Patty Berg | $16,011 | 1968 | Kathy Whitworth | $48,379 | 1982 | JoAnne Carner | $310,399 |
| 1955 | Patty Berg | 16,492 | 1969 | Carol Mann | 49,152 | 1983 | JoAnne Carner | 291,404 |
| 1956 | Marlene Hagge | 20,235 | 1970 | Kathy Whitworth | 30,235 | 1984 | Betsy King | 266,771 |
| 1957 | Patty Berg | 16,272 | 1971 | Kathy Whitworth | 41,181 | 1985 | Nancy Lopez | 416,472 |
| 1958 | Beverly Hanson | 12,629 | 1972 | Kathy Whitworth | 65,063 | 1986 | Pat Bradley | 492,021 |
| 1959 | Betsy Rawls | 26,774 | 1973 | Kathy Whitworth | 82,854 | 1987 | Ayako Okamoto | 466,034 |
| 1960 | Louise Suggs | 16,892 | 1974 | JoAnne Carner | 87,094 | 1988 | Sherri Turner | 347,255 |
| 1961 | Mickey Wright | 22,236 | 1975 | Sandra Palmer | 94,805 | 1989 | Betsy King | 654,132 |
| 1962 | Mickey Wright | 21,641 | 1976 | Judy Rankin | 150,734 | 1990 | Beth Daniel | 863,578 |
| 1963 | Mickey Wright | 31,269 | 1977 | Judy Rankin | 122,890 | 1991 | Pat Bradley | 763,118 |
| 1964 | Mickey Wright | 29,800 | 1978 | Nancy Lopez | 189,813 | 1992 | Dottie Mochrie | 693,335 |
| 1965 | Kathy Whitworth | 28,658 | 1979 | Nancy Lopez | 215,987 | 1993 | Betsy King | 595,992 |
| 1966 | Kathy Whitworth | 33,517 | 1980 | Beth Daniel | 231,000 | 1994 | Laura Davies | 687,201 |
| 1967 | Kathy Whitworth | 32,937 | 1981 | Beth Daniel | 206,977 | 1995 | Annika Sorenstam | 666,533 |

## Rifle and Pistol Individual Championships in 1996

**Source:** National Rifle Association

### National Outdoor Rifle and Pistol Championships

**Smallbore Rifle Prone**—SGT Thomas A. Tamas, USA, Ft. Benning, GA, 6395-525X

**Civilian Smallbore Rifle Prone**—Shane M. Barnhart, Ashley, OH, 6389-485X

**Woman Smallbore Rifle Prone**—Edie P. Reynolds, Raleigh, NC, 6387-481X

**Smallbore Rifle NRA 3-Position**—CPT Webster M. Wright III, USA, Columbus, GA, 2214-75X

**Civilian Smallbore Rifle NRA 3-Position**—Kenneth Benyo, Allentown, PA, 2208-70X

**Woman Smallbore Rifle NRA 3-Position**—Emily J. Caruso, Fairfield, CT, 2121-40X

**High Power Rifle**—Thomas J. Whitaker, Moreno Valley, CA, 2377-124X

**Civilian High Power Rifle**—Thomas J. Whitaker, Moreno Valley, CA, 2377-124X

**Woman High Power Rifle**—Sandy L. Pagel, Stoddard, WI, 2368-88X

**Pistol**—SGT Brian H. Zins, USMC, Canfield, OH, 2661-158X

**Civilian Pistol**—Richard Rodriquez, Stafford, VA, 2640-117X

**Woman Pistol**—SFC Ruby Fox, USAR, Parker, AZ, 2631-100X

### National Indoor Rifle and Pistol Championships

**Smallbore Rifle 4-Position**—Troy Bassham, Colorado Springs, CO, 800

**Woman Smallbore Rifle 4-Position**—Karen E. Monez, Weatherford, TX, 797

**Smallbore Rifle NRA 3-Position**—Glen Dubis, Columbus, GA, 1188

**Woman Smallbore Rifle NRA 3-Position**—Karen E. Monez, Weatherford, TX, 1182

**International Smallbore Rifle**—Robert E. Harbison, Phenix City, AL, 1187

**Woman International Smallbore Rifle**—Wanda R. Jewell, Columbus, GA, 1180

**Air Rifle**—Jayme Dickman, Columbus, GA, 595

**Woman Air Rifle**—Jayme Dickman, Columbus, GA, 595

**Conventional Pistol**—Dr. Darius R. Young, Malo, WA, 889

**Woman Conventional Pistol**—Sally A. Talbott, Ft. Benning, GA, 864

**International Free Pistol**—James R. Lee Jr., Auburn, CA, 548

**Woman International Free Pistol**—Susan E. McConnell, Clifton Park, NY, 483

**International Standard Pistol**—Scott Lorenz, Lynwood, WA, 572

**Woman International Standard Pistol**—Joyce R. Scott, Portland, OR, 511

**Air Pistol**—Richard D. McConnell, Clifton Park, NY, 569

**Woman Air Pistol**—Susan McConnell, Clifton Park, NY, 545

### NRA Bianchi Cup National Action Pistol Championships

**Action Pistol**—Ross G. Newell, Australia, 1920

**Woman Action Pistol**—Sharon Edington, Cusseta, GA, 1899

**Junior Action Pistol**—Troy Bellman, Australia, 1910

# Notable Sports Personalities

**Henry (Hank) Aaron,** b. 1934: Milwaukee-Atlanta outfielder hit record 755 home runs, led NL 4 times; record 2,297 RBIs.

**Kareem Abdul-Jabbar,** b. 1947: Milwaukee, L.A. Lakers center; MVP 6 times; leading scorer twice; playoff MVP, 1971, 1985; all-time leading NBA scorer.

**Troy Aikman,** b. 1966: quarterback led Dallas Cowboys to Super Bowl wins in 1993-94, 1996; Super Bowl MVP, 1993.

**Grover Cleveland Alexander,** (1887-1950): pitcher won 374 NL games; pitched 16 shutouts, 1916.

**Muhammad Ali,** b. 1942: 3-time heavyweight champion.

**Mario Andretti,** b. 1940: won Indy 500, 1969; Grand Prix champ, 1978.

**Eddie Arcaro,** b. 1916: jockey rode 4,779 winners including the Kentucky Derby 5 times; the Preakness and Belmont Stakes 6 times each.

**Henry Armstrong,** (1912-1988): boxer held feather-, welter-, lightweight titles simultaneously, 1937-38.

**Arthur Ashe,** (1943-1993): U.S. singles champ, 1968; Wimbledon champ, 1975.

**Red Auerbach,** b. 1917: coached Boston Celtics to 9 NBA championships.

**Ernie Banks,** b. 1931: Chicago Cubs slugger hit 512 NL homers; twice MVP.

**Roger Bannister,** b. 1929: Briton ran first sub 4-minute mile, May 6, 1954.

**Rick Barry,** b. 1944: NBA scoring leader, 1967; ABA, 1969.

**Sammy Baugh,** b. 1914: Washington Redskins quarterback held numerous records upon retirement after 16 pro seasons.

**Elgin Baylor,** b. 1934: L.A. Lakers forward; 1st team all-star 10 times.

**Boris Becker,** b. 1967: German tennis star; won U.S. Open 1989; Wimbledon champ 3 times.

**Jean Beliveau,** b. 1931: Montreal Canadiens center scored 507 goals; twice MVP.

**Albert Belle,** b. 1966: Cleveland Indians slugger led AL in home runs, 1995; RBIs 1993, 1995-96; first player to hit 50 doubles and 50 home runs in a season, 1995.

**Johnny Bench,** b. 1947: Cincinnati Reds catcher; MVP twice; led league in home runs twice, RBIs 3 times.

**Patty Berg,** b. 1918: won more than 80 golf tournaments; AP Woman Athlete-of-the-Year 3 times.

**Yogi Berra,** b. 1925: N.Y. Yankees catcher; MVP 3 times; played in 14 World Series.

**Raymond Berry,** b. 1933: Baltimore Colts receiver caught 631 passes.

**Matt Biondi,** b. 1965: swimmer won 5 gold medals at 1988 Olympics.

**Larry Bird,** b. 1956: Boston Celtics forward; chosen MVP 1984-86; Playoff MVP, 1984, 1986.

**George Blanda,** b. 1927: quarterback, kicker; 26 years as active player, scoring record 2,002 points.

**Wade Boggs,** b. 1958: AL batting champ, 1983, 1985-88.

**Barry Bonds,** b. 1964: outfielder was NL MVP 1990, 1992-93; 2d player to join 40 home runs/40 stolen bases club, 1996.

**Bjorn Borg,** b. 1956: led Sweden to first Davis Cup, 1975; Wimbledon champion 5 times.

**Mike Bossy,** b. 1957; N.Y. Islanders right wing scored more than 50 goals 8 times.

**Ray Bourque,** b. 1960: Boston Bruins defenseman won Norris Trophy 5 times.

**Terry Bradshaw,** b. 1948; Pittsburgh Steelers quarterback led team to 4 Super Bowl titles.

**George Brett,** b. 1953: Kansas City Royals infielder led AL in batting, 1976, 1980, 1990; MVP, 1980.

**Lou Brock,** b. 1939: St. Louis Cardinals outfielder stole NL record 118 bases, 1974; led NL 8 times.

**Jim Brown,** b. 1936: Cleveland Browns fullback ran for 12,312 career yards; MVP 3 times.

**Paul Brown,** (1908-1991), football owner, coach; led Cleveland Browns to 3 NFL championships.

**Paul "Bear" Bryant,** (1913-1983), college football coach with 323 victories.

**Sergei Bubka,** b. 1963: Ukrainian pole vaulter; first to clear 20 feet both indoors and outdoors; gold medal, 1988 Olympics.

**Maria Bueno,** b. 1939: U.S. singles champ 4 times; Wimbledon champ 3 times.

**Dick Butkus,** b. 1942: Chicago Bears linebacker twice chosen best NFL defensive player.

**Dick Button,** b. 1929: figure skater won 1948, 1952 Olympic gold medals; world titlist, 1948-52.

**Walter Camp,** (1859-1925): Yale football player, coach, athletic director; established many rules; promoted All-America designations.

**Roy Campanella,** (1921-1993): Brooklyn Dodgers catcher; MVP 3 times.

**Earl Campbell,** b. 1955: NFL running back; MVP 1978-80.

**Rod Carew,** b. 1945: AL infielder won 7 batting titles; MVP, 1977.

**Steve Carlton,** b. 1944: NL pitcher won 20 games 5 times, Cy Young award 4 times.

**Billy Casper,** b. 1931: PGA Player-of-the-Year 3 times; U.S. Open champ twice.

**Wilt Chamberlain,** b. 1936: center was NBA leading scorer 7 times; MVP 4 times; scored 100 pts in a game, 1962.

**Bobby Clarke,** b. 1949: Philadelphia Flyers center led team to 2 Stanley Cup championships; MVP 3 times.

**Roger Clemens,** b. 1962: Boston Red Sox pitcher; AL MVP 1986; Cy Young award 1986, 1987, 1991.

**Roberto Clemente,** (1934-1972): Pittsburgh Pirates outfielder won 4 batting titles; MVP, 1966.

**Ty Cobb,** (1886-1961): Detroit Tigers outfielder had record .367 lifetime batting average, 12 batting titles.

**Sebastian Coe,** b. 1956: Briton won Olympic 1,500-meter run, 1980, 1984.

**Nadia Comaneci,** b. 1961: Romanian gymnast won 3 gold medals, achieved 7 perfect scores, 1976 Olympics.

**Maureen Connolly,** (1934-1969): won tennis "grand slam," 1953; AP Woman-Athlete-of-the-Year 3 times.

**Jimmy Connors,** b. 1952: U.S. singles champ 5 times; Wimbledon champ twice.

**James J. Corbett,** (1866-1933): heavyweight champion, 1892-97; credited with being the first "scientific" boxer.

**Angel Cordero,** b. 1942: leading money winner, 1976, 1982-83; rode 3 Kentucky Derby winners.

**Margaret Smith Court,** b. 1942: Australian tennis great won U.S. Open 5 times, Wimbledon 3 times; 24 grand slam titles.

**Bob Cousy,** b. 1928: Boston Celtics guard led team to 6 NBA championships; MVP, 1957.

**Dizzy Dean,** (1911-1974): colorful pitcher for St. Louis Cardinals "Gashouse Gang" in the '30s; MVP, 1934.

**Oscar De La Hoya,** b. 1972: boxer won lightweight title, 1995; super lightweight title, 1996.

**Jack Dempsey,** (1895-1983): heavyweight champ, 1919-26.

**Gail Devers,** b. 1966: sprinter won Olympic gold medals in 100-meter run 1992, 1996.

**Eric Dickerson,** b. 1960: running back ran for NFL record 2,105 yds., 1984; led NFC 3 times, AFC twice.

**Joe DiMaggio,** b. 1914: N.Y. Yankees outfielder hit safely in record 56 consecutive games, 1941; AL MVP 3 times.

**Leo Durocher,** (1906-1991): manager won 3 NL pennants.

**Dale Earnhardt,** b. 1952: auto racer was NASCAR champion 7 times.

**Stefan Edberg,** b. 1966: U.S. singles champ 1991, 1992; Wimbledon champ 1988, 1990.

**Gertrude Ederle,** b. 1906: first woman to swim English Channel, broke existing men's record, 1926.

**Julius Erving,** b. 1950: MVP and leading scorer in ABA 3 times; NBA MVP, 1981.

**Phil Esposito,** b. 1942: NHL scoring leader 5 times.

**Janet Evans,** b. 1971: swimmer won 3 Olympic gold medals, 1988, 1 in 1992.

**Chris Evert,** b. 1954: U.S. singles champ 6 times, Wimbledon champ 3 times.

**Ray Ewry,** (1873-1937): track-and-field star won 8 gold medals, 1900, 1904, and 1908 Olympics.

**Nick Faldo,** 1957: British golfer won Masters, British Open 3 times each.

**Juan Fangio,** (1911-1995): World Grand Prix champion 5 times.

**Bob Feller,** b. 1918: Cleveland Indians pitcher won 266 games; pitched 3 no-hitters, 12 one-hitters.

**Peggy Fleming,** b. 1948: world figure skating champion, 1966-68; gold medalist 1968 Olympics.

**Whitey Ford,** b. 1928: N.Y. Yankees pitcher won record 10 World Series games.

**George Foreman,** b. 1949: heavyweight champion, 1973-74, 1994-95; at 45, the oldest to win a heavyweight title.

**Dick Fosbury,** b. 1947: high jumper won 1968 Olympic gold medal; developed the "Fosbury Flop."

**Jimmie Foxx,** (1907-1967): Red Sox, Athletics slugger; MVP 3 times; triple crown, 1933.

**A.J. Foyt,** b. 1935: won Indy 500 4 times; U.S. Auto Club champ 7 times.

**Joe Frazier,** b. 1944: heavyweight champion, 1970-73.

**Lou Gehrig,** (1903-1941): N.Y. Yankees 1st baseman played 2,130 consecutive games; MVP, 1927, 1936; triple crown, 1934; AL record 184 RBIs, 1931.

**George Gervin,** b. 1952: leading NBA scorer, 1978-80, 1982.

**Althea Gibson,** b. 1927: twice U.S. and Wimbledon singles champ.

**Bob Gibson,** b. 1935: St. Louis Cardinals pitcher won Cy Young award twice; struck out 3,117 batters.

**Frank Gifford,** b. 1930: N.Y. Giants back; MVP, 1956.

**Marc Girardelli,** b. 1963: Luxembourg skier won 5 World Cup titles.
**Steffi Graf,** b. 1969: German won tennis "grand slam," 1988; U.S. champ 5 times; Wimbledon champ 7 times.
**Otto Graham,** b. 1921: Cleveland Browns quarterback; all-pro 4 times.
**Red Grange,** (1903-1991): All-America at Univ. of Illinois 1923-25; played for Chicago Bears, 1925-35.
**Joe Greene,** b. 1946: Pittsburgh Steelers lineman; twice NFL outstanding defensive player.
**Wayne Gretzky,** b. 1961: leading scorer in NHL history; MVP, 1980-87, 1989.
**Ken Griffey Jr.,** b. 1969: Seattle Mariner outfielder led AL in home runs, 1994; 7 gold gloves.
**Lefty Grove,** (1900-1975): pitcher won 300 AL games; 20-game winner 8 times.
**Tony Gwynn,** b. 1960: 7-time NL batting champ, 1984, 1987-89, 1994-96.
**Walter Hagen,** (1892-1969): won PGA championship 5 times; British Open 4 times.
**George Halas,** (1895-1983): founder-coach of Chicago Bears; won 5 NFL championships.
**Bill Hartack,** b. 1932: jockey rode 5 Kentucky Derby winners.
**John Havlicek,** b. 1940: Boston Celtics forward scored more than 26,000 NBA points.
**Rickey Henderson,** b. 1958; outfielder stole record 130 bases, 1982; record lifetime steals; AL MVP, 1990.
**Sonja Henie,** (1912-1969): world champion figure skater, 1927-36; Olympic gold medalist, 1928, 1932, 1936.
**Ben Hogan,** b. 1912: won 4 U.S. Open championships, 2 PGA, 2 Masters.
**Rogers Hornsby,** (1896-1963): NL 2d baseman batted record .424 in 1924; twice won triple crown; batting leader, 1920-25.
**Paul Hornung,** b. 1935: Green Bay Packers runner-placekicker scored record 176 points, 1960.
**Gordie Howe,** b. 1928: hockey forward; NHL MVP 6 times.
**Carl Hubbell,** (1903-1988): N.Y. Giants pitcher; 20-game winner 5 consecutive years, 1933-37.
**Bobby Hull,** b. 1939: NHL all-star 10 times; MVP 1965-66.
**Brett Hull,** b. 1964: St. Louis Blues forward led NHL in goals, 1990-92; MVP 1991.
**Catfish Hunter,** b. 1946: pitched perfect game, 1968; 20-game winner 5 times.
**Don Hutson,** b. 1913: Green Bay Packers receiver caught 99 NFL touchdown passes.
**Reggie Jackson,** b. 1946: slugger led AL in home runs 4 times; MVP, 1973; hit 5 World Series home runs, 1977.
**Jack Johnson,** (1878-1946): heavyweight champion, 1910-15.
**Jimmy Johnson,** b. 1943: football coach, led Miami (FL) to NCAA title, 1987; Dallas Cowboys to Super Bowl, 1993-94.
**Magic Johnson,** b. 1959: NBA MVP 1987, 1989, 1990; Playoff MVP 1980, 1982, 1987; 2d in career assists.
**Michael Johnson,** b. 1967: won Olympic gold medals in 200-meter (shattered world record) and 400-meter run, 1996.
**Walter Johnson,** (1887-1946): Washington Senators pitcher won 416 games; record 110 shutouts.
**Bobby Jones,** (1902-1971): won "grand slam of golf" 1930; U.S. Amateur champ 5 times, U.S. Open champ 4 times.
**Deacon Jones,** b. 1938: L.A. Rams lineman; twice NFL outstanding defensive player.
**Michael Jordan,** b. 1963: NBA leading scorer, 1987-93, 1996; MVP, 1988, 1991-92, 1996; Playoff MVP, 1991-93, 1996.
**Florence Griffith Joyner,** b. 1959: sprinter won 3 gold medals at 1988 Olympics.
**Jackie Joyner-Kersee,** b. 1962; Olympic gold medalist in heptathlon, 1988, 1992.
**Sonny Jurgensen,** b. 1934: quarterback named all-pro 5 times.
**Duke Kahanamoku,** (1890-1968): swimmer won 1912, 1920 Olympic gold medals in 100-meter freestyle; surfing pioneer.
**Harmon Killebrew,** b. 1936: Minnesota Twins slugger led AL in home runs 6 times; 573 lifetime.
**Jean Claude Killy,** b. 1943: French skier won 3 1968 Olympic gold medals.
**Ralph Kiner,** b. 1922: Pittsburgh Pirates slugger led NL in home runs 7 consecutive years, 1946-52.
**Billie Jean King,** b. 1943: U.S. singles champ 4 times; Wimbledon champ 6 times.
**Bob Knight,** b. 1940: Indiana U. basketball coach led team to NCAA championships, 1976, 1981, 1987.
**Olga Korbut,** b. 1955: Soviet gymnast won 3 1972 Olympic gold medals.
**Sandy Koufax,** b. 1935: Dodgers pitcher won Cy Young award 3 times; lowest ERA in NL, 1962-66; pitched 4 no-hitters, one a perfect game.
**Guy Lafleur,** b. 1951: forward led NHL in scoring 3 times; MVP, 1977, 1978.
**Tom Landry,** b. 1924: Dallas Cowboys head coach 1960-88.
**Rod Laver,** b. 1938: Australian won tennis "grand slam" twice, 1962, 1969; Wimbledon champ 4 times.
**Mario Lemieux,** b. 1965: NHL leading scorer, 1988-89, 1992-93, 1996; MVP, 1988, 1993, 1996; Playoff MVP, 1991-92.
**Ivan Lendl,** b. 1960: U.S. singles champ, 1985-87.
**Sugar Ray Leonard,** b. 1956: boxer held titles in 5 different weight classes.
**Carl Lewis,** b. 1961: track-and-field star won 9 Olympic gold medals in sprinting and the long jump.
**Vince Lombardi,** (1913-1970): Green Bay Packers coach led team to 5 NFL championships and 2 Super Bowl victories.
**Greg Louganis,** b. 1960: won Olympic gold medals in both springboard and platform diving, 1984, 1988.
**Joe Louis,** (1914-1981): heavyweight champion, 1937-49.
**Sid Luckman,** b. 1916: Chicago Bears quarterback led team to 4 NFL championships; MVP, 1943.
**Connie Mack,** (1862-1956): Philadelphia Athletics manager, 1901-50; won 9 pennants, 5 championships.
**Greg Maddux,** b. 1966: first pitcher ever to win 4 consecutive Cy Young awards, 1992-95.
**Bill Madlock,** b. 1951: NL batting leader 4 times.
**Moses Malone,** b. 1955: NBA center was MVP 1979, 1982-83.
**Mickey Mantle,** (1931-1995): N.Y. Yankees outfielder; triple crown, 1956; 18 World Series home runs; MVP 3 times.
**Pete Maravich** (1948-1988): guard scored NCAA record 44.2 ppg during collegiate career; led NBA in scoring, 1977.
**Rocky Marciano,** (1923-1969): heavyweight champion, 1952-56; retired undefeated.
**Dan Marino,** b. 1961: Miami Dolphins quarterback passed for NFL record 5,084 yds and 48 touchdowns, 1984; holds career NFL records for touchdowns, yds passing, completions.
**Roger Maris,** (1934-1985): N.Y. Yankees outfielder hit record 61 home runs, 1961; MVP, 1960 and 1961.
**Eddie Mathews,** b. 1931: Milwaukee-Atlanta 3d baseman hit 512 career home runs.
**Christy Mathewson,** (1880-1925): N.Y. Giants pitcher won 373 games.
**Bob Mathias,** b. 1930: decathlon gold medalist, 1948, 1952.
**Don Mattingly,** b. 1961: N.Y. Yankees 1st baseman won 1984 AL batting title; MVP, 1985.
**Willie Mays,** b. 1931: N.Y.-S.F. Giants center fielder hit 660 home runs, led NL 4 times; had 3,283 hits; twice MVP.
**Willie McCovey,** b. 1938: S.F. Giants slugger hit 521 home runs; led NL 3 times; MVP, 1969.
**John McEnroe,** b. 1959: U.S. singles champ, 1979-81, 1984; Wimbledon champ, 1981, 1983-84.
**John McGraw,** (1873-1934): N.Y. Giants manager led team to 10 pennants, 3 championships.
**Mark Messier,** b. 1961: center chosen NHL MVP, 1990 and 1992; Conn Smythe Trophy, 1984.
**George Mikan,** b. 1924: Minn. Lakers center considered the best basketball player of the first half of the century.
**Stan Mikita,** b. 1940: Chicago Black Hawks center led NHL in scoring 4 times; MVP twice.
**Joe Montana,** b. 1956: S.F. 49ers quarterback was Super Bowl MVP, 1982, 1985, 1990.
**Archie Moore,** b. 1913: light-heavyweight champion, 1952-62.
**Howie Morenz,** (1902-1937): Montreal Canadiens forward considered the best hockey player of first half of the century.
**Joe Morgan,** b. 1943: National League MVP, 1975, 1976.
**Thurman Munson,** (1947-1979): N.Y. Yankees catcher; MVP, 1976.
**Eddie Murray,** b. 1956: slugger led AL in home runs and RBIs, 1981; 3,200+ lifetime hits; 500+ lifetime home runs.
**Stan Musial,** b. 1920: St. Louis Cardinals star won 7 NL batting titles; MVP 3 times.
**Bronko Nagurski,** (1908-1990): Chicago Bears fullback and tackle; gained more than 4,000 yds. rushing.
**Joe Namath,** b. 1943: N.Y. Jets quarterback was Super Bowl MVP, 1969.
**Martina Navratilova,** b. 1956: Wimbledon champ 9 times, U.S. champ 1983-84, 1986-87.
**Byron Nelson,** b. 1912: won 11 consecutive golf tournaments in 1945; twice Masters and PGA titlist.
**Ernie Nevers,** (1903-1976): Stanford star selected the best college fullback to play between 1919-69.
**John Newcombe,** b. 1943: Australian twice U.S. singles champ; Wimbledon titlist 3 times.
**Jack Nicklaus,** b. 1940: PGA Player-of-the-Year, 1967, 1972; leading money winner 8 times; won Masters 6 times.
**Chuck Noll,** b. 1931: coach led Pittsburgh Steelers to 4 Super Bowl titles.
**Paavo Nurmi,** (1897-1973): Finnish distance runner won 6 Olympic gold medals, 1920, 1924, 1928.
**Al Oerter,** b. 1936: discus thrower won gold medal at 4 consecutive Olympics, 1956-68.
**Hakeem Olajuwon,** b. 1963: Houston Rockets center was NBA MVP 1994, Playoffs MVP 1994-95; career leader in blocked shots.
**Shaquille O'Neal,** b. 1972: NBA center was rookie of the year, 1993; scoring leader, 1995.

**Bobby Orr,** b. 1948: Boston Bruins defenseman; Norris Trophy 8 times; led NHL in scoring twice, assists 5 times.
**Mel Ott,** (1909-1958): N.Y. Giants outfielder hit 511 home runs; led NL 6 times.
**Jesse Owens,** (1913-1980): track and field star won 4 1936 Olympic gold medals.
**Satchel Paige,** (1906-1982): pitcher starred in Negro leagues, 1924-48; entered major leagues at age 42.
**Arnold Palmer,** b. 1929: golf's first $1 million winner; won 4 Masters, 2 British Opens.
**Jim Palmer,** b. 1945: Baltimore Orioles pitcher; Cy Young award 3 times; 20-game winner 8 times.
**Joe Paterno,** b. 1926: winningest active NCAA football coach; led Penn St. to 2 national titles, 1982, 1986.
**Floyd Patterson,** b. 1935: twice heavyweight champion.
**Walter Payton,** b. 1954: Chicago Bears running back has most rushing yards in NFL history; leading NFC rusher, 1976-80.
**Pele,** b. 1940: Brazilian soccer star scored 1,281 goals during 22-year career.
**Bob Pettit,** b. 1932: first NBA player to score 20,000 points; twice NBA scoring leader.
**Richard Petty,** b. 1937: NASCAR national champ 7 times; 7-time Daytona 500 winner.
**Laffit Pincay Jr.,** b. 1946: leading money-winning jockey, 1970-74, 1979, 1985.
**Jacques Plante,** (1929-1986): goalie, 7 Vezina trophies; first goalie to wear a mask in a game.
**Kirby Puckett,** b. 1961: Minn. Twins outfielder won AL batting title, 1989; led AL in hits, 1987-89, 1992; RBIs, 1994.
**Willis Reed,** b. 1942: N.Y. Knicks center; MVP, 1970; Playoff MVP, 1970, 1973.
**Jerry Rice,** b. 1962: S.F. 49ers receiver; Super Bowl MVP, 1989; NFL record for career touchdowns, receptions.
**Maurice Richard,** b. 1921: Montreal Canadiens forward scored 544 regular season goals, 82 playoff goals.
**Branch Rickey,** (1881-1965): executive helped break baseball's color barrier, 1947; initiated farm system, 1919.
**Pat Riley,** b. 1945: coached L.A. Lakers to 4 NBA titles.
**Cal Ripken Jr.,** b. 1960: Baltimore Orioles shortstop; AL MVP 1983, 1991; broke Lou Gehrig's record for most consecutive games played, 1995.
**Oscar Robertson,** b. 1938: guard averaged career 25.7 points per game; 3d most career assists; MVP, 1964.
**Brooks Robinson,** b. 1937: Baltimore Orioles 3d baseman played in 4 World Series; MVP, 1964; 16 gold gloves.
**Frank Robinson,** b. 1935: slugger was MVP in both NL and AL; triple crown, 1966; 586 lifetime home runs; first black manager in majors.
**Jackie Robinson,** (1919-1972): broke baseball's color barrier with Brooklyn Dodgers, 1947; MVP, 1949.
**Sugar Ray Robinson,** (1920-1989): middleweight champion 5 times, welterweight champion.
**Knute Rockne,** (1888-1931): Notre Dame football coach, 1918-31; revolutionized game by stressing forward pass.
**Dennis Rodman,** b. 1961: eccentric forward led NBA in rebounding 1991-96.
**Pete Rose,** b. 1941: won 3 NL batting titles; hit safely in 44 consecutive games, 1978; has most career hits, 4,256.
**Patrick Roy,** b. 1965: Montreal-Colorado goalie was 3-time Vezina Trophy winner, Playoffs MVP 1993.
**Wilma Rudolph,** (1940-1994): sprinter won 3 1960 Olympic gold medals.
**Adolph Rupp,** (1901-77): winningest NCAA basketball coach; led Kentucky to 4 national titles, 1948-49, 1951, 1958.
**Bill Russell,** b. 1934: Boston Celtics center led team to 11 NBA titles; MVP 5 times; first black coach of major pro sports team.
**Babe Ruth,** (1895-1948): N.Y. Yankees outfielder hit 60 home runs, 1927; 714 lifetime; led AL 12 times.
**Johnny Rutherford,** b. 1938: auto racer won 3 Indy 500s.
**Nolan Ryan,** b. 1947: pitcher struck out record 383 batters, 1973; record 5,714 career; pitched record 7 no-hitters; won 324 major league games.
**Pete Sampras,** b. 1971: tennis star won U.S. Open 4 times and Wimbledon 3 times.
**Barry Sanders,** b. 1968: running back was Heisman Trophy winner, 1988; NCAA single-season records for rushing yds, touchdowns; led NFL in rushing, 1990, 1994.
**Gene Sarazen,** b. 1902: won PGA championship 3 times, U.S. Open twice; developer of sand wedge.
**Gale Sayers,** b. 1943: Chicago Bears back twice led NFL in rushing.
**Mike Schmidt,** b. 1949: Phillies 3d baseman led NL in home runs 8 times; 548 lifetime; NL MVP, 1980, 1981, 1986.
**Tom Seaver,** b. 1944: pitcher won NL Cy Young award 3 times; won 311 major league games.
**Monica Seles,** b. 1973; U.S. Open champ 1991, 1992.
**Willie Shoemaker,** b. 1931: jockey rode 3 Kentucky Derby and 5 Belmont Stakes winners; leading career money winner.
**Eddie Shore,** (1902-1985): Boston Bruins defenseman; MVP 4 times, first-team all-star 7 times.
**Don Shula,** b. 1930: all-time winningest NFL coach.
**Al Simmons,** (1902-1956): AL outfielder batted .334 lifetime.
**O.J. Simpson,** b. 1947: running back rushed for 2,003 yds., 1973; AFC leading rusher 4 times.
**George Sisler,** (1893-1973): St. Louis Browns 1st baseman had record 257 hits, 1920; batted .340 lifetime.
**Billy Smith,** b. 1950: N.Y. Islanders goalie led team to 4 Stanley Cup championships, 1980-83.
**Dean Smith,** b. 1931: North Carolina basketball coach has most career NCAA Division I tournament victories.
**Emmitt Smith,** b. 1969: Dallas Cowboys running back led NFL in rushing, 1991-93, 1995; NFL and Super Bowl MVP, 1993; record 25 rushing touchdowns, 1995.
**Lee Smith,** b. 1957: relief pitcher, all-time saves leader.
**Sam Snead,** b. 1912: PGA and Masters champ 3 times each.
**Warren Spahn,** b. 1921: pitcher won 363 NL games; 20-game winner 13 times; Cy Young award, 1957.
**Tris Speaker,** (1885-1958): AL outfielder batted .344 over 22 seasons; hit record 793 career doubles.
**Mark Spitz,** b. 1950: swimmer won 7 1972 Olympic gold medals.
**Amos Alonzo Stagg,** (1862-1965): coached Univ. of Chicago football team for 41 years, including 5 undefeated seasons; introduced huddle, man-in-motion, and end-around play.
**Bart Starr,** b. 1934: Green Bay Packers quarterback led team to 5 NFL titles and 2 Super Bowl victories.
**Roger Staubach,** b. 1942: Dallas Cowboys quarterback; leading NFC passer 5 times.
**Casey Stengel,** (1890-1975): managed Yankees to 10 pennants, 7 championships, 1949-60.
**Jackie Stewart,** b. 1939: Scot auto racer retired with 27 Grand Prix victories.
**John Stockton,** b. 1962: Utah Jazz guard is NBA career leader in assists, steals; NBA assists leader, 1988-96.
**John L. Sullivan,** (1858-1918): last bareknuckle heavyweight champion, 1882-1892.
**Fran Tarkenton,** b. 1940: quarterback is 2d in career touchdown passes, passing yds.
**Lawrence Taylor,** b. 1959; linebacker led N.Y. Giants to 2 Super Bowl titles; played in 10 Pro Bowls.
**Jim Thorpe,** (1888-1953): football All-America, 1911, 1912; won pentathlon and decathlon, 1912 Olympics.
**Bill Tilden,** (1893-1953): U.S. singles champ 7 times; played on 11 Davis Cup teams.
**Y.A. Tittle,** b. 1926: N.Y. Giants quarterback; MVP, 1961, 1963.
**Lee Trevino,** b. 1939: golfer won the U.S. and British Open twice.
**Bryan Trottier,** b. 1956: center played on 6 Stanley Cup championship teams.
**Mike Tyson,** b. 1966: youngest heavyweight champ at 19, 1986; undisputed champ, 1987-90; regained 2 titles, 1996.
**Wyomia Tyus,** b. 1945: sprinter won 1964, 1968 Olympic 100-meter dash.
**Johnny Unitas,** b. 1933: Baltimore Colts quarterback passed for more than 40,000 yds; MVP, 1957, 1967.
**Al Unser,** b. 1939: Indy 500 winner 4 times.
**Bobby Unser,** b. 1934: Indy 500 winner 3 times.
**Norm Van Brocklin,** (1926-1983): quarterback passed for game record 554 yds., 1951; MVP, 1960.
**Honus Wagner,** (1874-1955): Pittsburgh Pirates shortstop won 8 NL batting titles.
**Tom Watson,** b. 1949: golfer won British Open 5 times.
**Johnny Weissmuller,** (1903-1984): swimmer won 52 national championships, 5 Olympic gold medals; set 67 world records.
**Jerry West,** b. 1938: L.A. Lakers guard had career average 27 points per game; first team all-star 10 times.
**Kathy Whitworth,** b. 1939: women's golf leading money winner 8 times; first woman to earn more than $300,000.
**Lenny Wilkens,** b. 1937: winningest coach in NBA history.
**Ted Williams,** b. 1918: Boston Red Sox outfielder won 6 batting titles; last major leaguer to hit over .400: .406 in 1941; twice won triple crown; .344 lifetime batting average.
**Katarina Witt,** b. 1965: German figure skater; won Olympic gold medal, 1984, 1988.
**John Wooden,** b. 1910: coached UCLA basketball team to 10 national championships.
**Tiger Woods,** b. 1975: only golfer to win 3 consecutive U.S. Amateur titles, 1994-96.
**Mickey Wright,** b. 1935: won LPGA championship 4 times, Vare Trophy 5 times; twice AP Woman-Athlete-of-the-Year.
**Carl Yastrzemski,** b. 1939: Boston Red Sox slugger won 3 batting titles; triple crown, 1967.
**Cy Young,** (1867-1955): pitcher won record 511 games.
**Steve Young,** b. 1961: San Francisco 49ers quarterback led NFL in passing, 1991-94; Super Bowl MVP, 1995.
**Babe Didrikson Zaharias,** (1914-1956): track star won 2 1932 Olympic gold medals; won numerous golf tournaments.

# TENNIS

## U.S. Open Champions

### Men's Singles

| Year | Champion | Final opponent |
|---|---|---|
| 1910 | William Larned | T. C. Bundy |
| 1911 | William Larned | Maurice McLoughlin |
| 1912 | Maurice McLoughlin | Wallace Johnson |
| 1913 | Maurice McLoughlin | Richard Williams |
| 1914 | Richard Williams | Maurice McLoughlin |
| 1915 | William Johnston | Maurice McLoughlin |
| 1916 | Richard Williams | William Johnston |
| 1917 | R. L. Murray | N. W. Niles |
| 1918 | R. L. Murray | Bill Tilden |
| 1919 | William Johnston | Bill Tilden |
| 1920 | Bill Tilden | William Johnston |
| 1921 | Bill Tilden | Wallace Johnson |
| 1922 | Bill Tilden | William Johnston |
| 1923 | Bill Tilden | William Johnston |
| 1924 | Bill Tilden | William Johnston |
| 1925 | Bill Tilden | William Johnston |
| 1926 | Rene Lacoste | Jean Borotra |
| 1927 | Rene Lacoste | Bill Tilden |
| 1928 | Henri Cochet | Francis Hunter |
| 1929 | Bill Tilden | Francis Hunter |
| 1930 | John Doeg | Francis Shields |
| 1931 | H. Ellsworth Vines | George Lott |
| 1932 | H. Ellsworth Vines | Henri Cochet |
| 1933 | Fred Perry | John Crawford |
| 1934 | Fred Perry | Wilmer Allison |
| 1935 | Wilmer Allison | Sidney Wood |
| 1936 | Fred Perry | Don Budge |
| 1937 | Don Budge | Baron G. von Cramm |
| 1938 | Don Budge | C. Gene Mako |
| 1939 | Robert Riggs | S. Welby Van Horn |
| 1940 | Don McNeill | Robert Riggs |
| 1941 | Robert Riggs | F. L. Kovacs |
| 1942 | F. R. Schroeder Jr. | Frank Parker |
| 1943 | Joseph Hunt | Jack Kramer |
| 1944 | Frank Parker | William Talbert |
| 1945 | Frank Parker | William Talbert |
| 1946 | Jack Kramer | Thomas Brown Jr. |
| 1947 | Jack Kramer | Frank Parker |
| 1948 | Pancho Gonzales | Eric Sturgess |
| 1949 | Pancho Gonzales | F. R. Schroeder Jr. |
| 1950 | Arthur Larsen | Herbert Flam |
| 1951 | Frank Sedgman | E. Victor Seixas Jr. |
| 1952 | Frank Sedgman | Gardnar Mulloy |
| 1953 | Tony Trabert | E. Victor Seixas Jr. |
| 1954 | E. Victor Seixas Jr. | Rex Hartwig |
| 1955 | Tony Trabert | Ken Rosewall |
| 1956 | Ken Rosewall | Lewis Hoad |
| 1957 | Malcolm Anderson | Ashley Cooper |
| 1958 | Ashley Cooper | Malcolm Anderson |
| 1959 | Neale A. Fraser | Alejandro Olmedo |
| 1960 | Neale A. Fraser | Rod Laver |
| 1961 | Roy Emerson | Rod Laver |
| 1962 | Rod Laver | Roy Emerson |
| 1963 | Rafael Osuna | F. A. Froehling 3d |
| 1964 | Roy Emerson | Fred Stolle |
| 1965 | Manuel Santana | Cliff Drysdale |
| 1966 | Fred Stolle | John Newcombe |
| 1967 | John Newcombe | Clark Graebner |
| 1968 | Arthur Ashe | Tom Okker |
| 1969 | Rod Laver | Tony Roche |
| 1970 | Ken Rosewall | Tony Roche |
| 1971 | Stan Smith | Jan Kodes |
| 1972 | Ilie Nastase | Arthur Ashe |
| 1973 | John Newcombe | Jan Kodes |
| 1974 | Jimmy Connors | Ken Rosewall |
| 1975 | Manuel Orantes | Jimmy Connors |
| 1976 | Jimmy Connors | Bjorn Borg |
| 1977 | Guillermo Vilas | Jimmy Connors |
| 1978 | Jimmy Connors | Bjorn Borg |
| 1979 | John McEnroe | Vitas Gerulaitis |
| 1980 | John McEnroe | Bjorn Borg |
| 1981 | John McEnroe | Bjorn Borg |
| 1982 | Jimmy Connors | Ivan Lendl |
| 1983 | Jimmy Connors | Ivan Lendl |
| 1984 | John McEnroe | Ivan Lendl |
| 1985 | Ivan Lendl | John McEnroe |
| 1986 | Ivan Lendl | Miloslav Mecir |
| 1987 | Ivan Lendl | Mats Wilander |
| 1988 | Mats Wilander | Ivan Lendl |
| 1989 | Boris Becker | Ivan Lendl |
| 1990 | Pete Sampras | Andre Agassi |
| 1991 | Stefan Edberg | Jim Courier |
| 1992 | Stefan Edberg | Pete Sampras |
| 1993 | Pete Sampras | Cedric Pioline |
| 1994 | Andre Agassi | Michael Stich |
| 1995 | Pete Sampras | Andre Agassi |
| 1996 | Pete Sampras | Michael Chang |

### Women's Singles

| Year | Champion | Final opponent |
|---|---|---|
| 1926 | Molla B. Mallory | Elizabeth Ryan |
| 1927 | Helen Wills | Betty Nuthall |
| 1928 | Helen Wills | Helen Jacobs |
| 1929 | Helen Wills | M. Watson |
| 1930 | Betty Nuthall | L. A. Harper |
| 1931 | Helen Wills Moody | E. B. Whittingstall |
| 1932 | Helen Jacobs | Carolin A. Babcock |
| 1933 | Helen Jacobs | Helen Wills Moody |
| 1934 | Helen Jacobs | Sarah H. Palfrey |
| 1935 | Helen Jacobs | Sarah Palfrey Fabyan |
| 1936 | Alice Marble | Helen Jacobs |
| 1937 | Anita Lizana | Jadwiga Jedrzejowska |
| 1938 | Alice Marble | Nancye Wynne |
| 1939 | Alice Marble | Helen Jacobs |
| 1940 | Alice Marble | Helen Jacobs |
| 1941 | Sarah Palfrey Cooke | Pauline Betz |
| 1942 | Pauline Betz | Louise Brough |
| 1943 | Pauline Betz | Louise Brough |
| 1944 | Pauline Betz | Margaret Osborne |
| 1945 | Sarah Palfrey Cooke | Pauline Betz |
| 1946 | Pauline Betz | Doris Hart |
| 1947 | Louise Brough | Margaret Osborne |
| 1948 | Margaret Osborne duPont | Louise Brough |
| 1949 | Margaret Osborne duPont | Doris Hart |
| 1950 | Margaret Osborne duPont | Doris Hart |
| 1951 | Maureen Connolly | Shirley Fry |
| 1952 | Maureen Connolly | Doris Hart |
| 1953 | Maureen Connolly | Doris Hart |
| 1954 | Doris Hart | Louise Brough |
| 1955 | Doris Hart | Patricia Ward |
| 1956 | Shirley Fry | Althea Gibson |
| 1957 | Althea Gibson | Louise Brough |
| 1958 | Althea Gibson | Darlene Hard |
| 1959 | Maria Bueno | Christine Truman |
| 1960 | Darlene Hard | Maria Bueno |
| 1961 | Darlene Hard | Ann Haydon |
| 1962 | Margaret Smith | Darlene Hard |
| 1963 | Maria Bueno | Margaret Smith |
| 1964 | Maria Bueno | Carole Graebner |
| 1965 | Margaret Smith | Billie Jean Moffitt |
| 1966 | Maria Bueno | Nancy Richey |
| 1967 | Billie Jean King | Ann Haydon Jones |
| 1968 | Virginia Wade | Billie Jean King |
| 1969 | Margaret Smith Court | Nancy Richey |
| 1970 | Margaret Smith Court | Rosemary Casals |
| 1971 | Billie Jean King | Rosemary Casals |
| 1972 | Billie Jean King | Kerry Melville |
| 1973 | Margaret Smith Court | Evonne Goolagong |
| 1974 | Billie Jean King | Evonne Goolagong |
| 1975 | Chris Evert | Evonne Goolagong |
| 1976 | Chris Evert | Evonne Goolagong |
| 1977 | Chris Evert | Wendy Turnbull |
| 1978 | Chris Evert | Pam Shriver |
| 1979 | Tracy Austin | Chris Evert Lloyd |
| 1980 | Chris Evert Lloyd | Hana Mandlikova |
| 1981 | Tracy Austin | Martina Navratilova |
| 1982 | Chris Evert Lloyd | Hana Mandlikova |
| 1983 | Martina Navratilova | Chris Evert Lloyd |
| 1984 | Martina Navratilova | Chris Evert Lloyd |
| 1985 | Hana Mandlikova | Martina Navratilova |
| 1986 | Martina Navratilova | Helena Sukova |
| 1987 | Martina Navratilova | Steffi Graf |
| 1988 | Steffi Graf | Gabriela Sabatini |
| 1989 | Steffi Graf | Martina Navratilova |
| 1990 | Gabriela Sabatini | Steffi Graf |
| 1991 | Monica Seles | Martina Navratilova |
| 1992 | Monica Seles | Arantxa Sanchez Vicario |
| 1993 | Steffi Graf | Helena Sukova |
| 1994 | Arantxa Sanchez Vicario | Steffi Graf |
| 1995 | Steffi Graf | Monica Seles |
| 1996 | Steffi Graf | Monica Seles |

# All-England Champions, Wimbledon

## Men's Singles

| Year | Champion | Final opponent |
|---|---|---|
| 1933 | Jack Crawford | Ellsworth Vines |
| 1934 | Fred Perry | Jack Crawford |
| 1935 | Fred Perry | Gottfried von Cramm |
| 1936 | Fred Perry | Gottfried von Cramm |
| 1937 | Donald Budge | Gottfried von Cramm |
| 1938 | Donald Budge | Wilfred Austin |
| 1939 | Bobby Riggs | Elwood Cooke |
| 1940-45 | not held | |
| 1946 | Yvon Petra | Geoff E. Brown |
| 1947 | Jack Kramer | Tom P. Brown |
| 1948 | Bob Falkenburg | John Bromwich |
| 1949 | Ted Schroeder | Jaroslav Drobny |
| 1950 | Budge Patty | Frank Sedgman |
| 1951 | Dick Savitt | Ken McGregor |
| 1952 | Frank Sedgman | Jaroslav Drobny |
| 1953 | Vic Seixas | Kurt Nielsen |
| 1954 | Jaroslav Drobny | Ken Rosewall |
| 1955 | Tony Trabert | Kurt Nielsen |
| 1956 | Lew Hoad | Ken Rosewall |
| 1957 | Lew Hoad | Ashley Cooper |
| 1958 | Ashley Cooper | Neale Fraser |
| 1959 | Alex Olmedo | Rod Laver |
| 1960 | Neale Fraser | Rod Laver |
| 1961 | Rod Laver | Chuck McKinley |
| 1962 | Rod Laver | Martin Mulligan |
| 1963 | Chuck McKinley | Fred Stolle |
| 1964 | Roy Emerson | Fred Stolle |
| 1965 | Roy Emerson | Fred Stolle |
| 1966 | Manuel Santana | Dennis Ralston |
| 1967 | John Newcombe | Wilhelm Bungert |
| 1968 | Rod Laver | Tony Roche |
| 1969 | Rod Laver | John Newcombe |
| 1970 | John Newcombe | Ken Rosewall |
| 1971 | John Newcombe | Stan Smith |
| 1972 | Stan Smith | Ilie Nastase |
| 1973 | Jan Kodes | Alex Metreveli |
| 1974 | Jimmy Connors | Ken Rosewall |
| 1975 | Arthur Ashe | Jimmy Connors |
| 1976 | Bjorn Borg | Ilie Nastase |
| 1977 | Bjorn Borg | Jimmy Connors |
| 1978 | Bjorn Borg | Jimmy Connors |
| 1979 | Bjorn Borg | Roscoe Tanner |
| 1980 | Bjorn Borg | John McEnroe |
| 1981 | John McEnroe | Bjorn Borg |
| 1982 | Jimmy Connors | John McEnroe |
| 1983 | John McEnroe | Chris Lewis |
| 1984 | John McEnroe | Jimmy Connors |
| 1985 | Boris Becker | Kevin Curren |
| 1986 | Boris Becker | Ivan Lendl |
| 1987 | Pat Cash | Ivan Lendl |
| 1988 | Stefan Edberg | Boris Becker |
| 1989 | Boris Becker | Stefan Edberg |
| 1990 | Stefan Edberg | Boris Becker |
| 1991 | Michael Stich | Boris Becker |
| 1992 | Andre Agassi | Goran Ivanisevic |
| 1993 | Pete Sampras | Jim Courier |
| 1994 | Pete Sampras | Goren Ivanisevic |
| 1995 | Pete Sampras | Boris Becker |
| 1996 | Richard Krajicek | MaliVai Washington |

## Women's Singles

| Year | Champion |
|---|---|
| 1946 | Pauline Betz |
| 1947 | Margaret Osborne |
| 1948 | Louise Brough |
| 1949 | Louise Brough |
| 1950 | Louise Brough |
| 1951 | Doris Hart |
| 1952 | Maureen Connolly |
| 1953 | Maureen Connolly |
| 1954 | Maureen Connolly |
| 1955 | Louise Brough |
| 1956 | Shirley Fry |
| 1957 | Althea Gibson |
| 1958 | Althea Gibson |
| 1959 | Maria Bueno |
| 1960 | Maria Bueno |
| 1961 | Angela Mortimer |
| 1962 | Karen Hantze-Susman |
| 1963 | Margaret Smith |
| 1964 | Maria Bueno |
| 1965 | Margaret Smith |
| 1966 | Billie Jean King |
| 1967 | Billie Jean King |
| 1968 | Billie Jean King |
| 1969 | Ann Haydon-Jones |
| 1970 | Margaret Smith Court |
| 1971 | Evonne Goolagong |
| 1972 | Billie Jean King |
| 1973 | Billie Jean King |
| 1974 | Chris Evert |
| 1975 | Billie Jean King |
| 1976 | Chris Evert |
| 1977 | Virginia Wade |
| 1978 | Martina Navratilova |
| 1979 | Martina Navratilova |
| 1980 | Evonne Goolagong |
| 1981 | Chris Evert Lloyd |
| 1982 | Martina Navratilova |
| 1983 | Martina Navratilova |
| 1984 | Martina Navratilova |
| 1985 | Martina Navratilova |
| 1986 | Martina Navratilova |
| 1987 | Martina Navratilova |
| 1988 | Steffi Graf |
| 1989 | Steffi Graf |
| 1990 | Martina Navratilova |
| 1991 | Steffi Graf |
| 1992 | Steffi Graf |
| 1993 | Steffi Graf |
| 1994 | Conchita Martinez |
| 1995 | Steffi Graf |
| 1996 | Steffi Graf |

# Davis Cup Challenge Round

| Year | Result |
|---|---|
| 1900 | United States 5, British Isles 0 |
| 1901 | (not played) |
| 1902 | United States 3, British Isles 2 |
| 1903 | British Isles 4, United States 1 |
| 1904 | British Isles 5, Belgium 0 |
| 1905 | British Isles 5, United States 0 |
| 1906 | British Isles 5, United States 0 |
| 1907 | Australia 3, British Isles 2 |
| 1908 | Australasia 3, United States 2 |
| 1909 | Australasia 5, United States 0 |
| 1910 | (not played) |
| 1911 | Australasia 5, United States 0 |
| 1912 | British Isles 3, Australasia 2 |
| 1913 | United States 3, British Isles 2 |
| 1914 | Australasia 3, United States 2 |
| 1915-18 | (not played) |
| 1919 | Australasia 4, British Isles 1 |
| 1920 | United States 5, Australasia 0 |
| 1921 | United States 5, Japan 0 |
| 1922 | United States 4, Australasia 1 |
| 1923 | United States 4, Australasia 1 |
| 1924 | United States 5, Australasia 0 |
| 1925 | United States 5, France 0 |
| 1926 | United States 4, France 1 |
| 1927 | France 3, United States 2 |
| 1928 | France 4, United States 1 |
| 1929 | France 3, United States 2 |
| 1930 | France 4, United States 1 |
| 1931 | France 3, Great Britain 2 |
| 1932 | France 3, United States 2 |
| 1933 | Great Britain 3, France 2 |
| 1934 | Great Britain 4, United States 1 |
| 1935 | Great Britain 5, United States 0 |
| 1936 | Great Britain 3, Australia 2 |
| 1937 | United States 4, Great Britain 1 |
| 1938 | United States 3, Australia 2 |
| 1939 | Australia 3, United States 2 |
| 1940-45 | (not played) |
| 1946 | United States 5, Australia 0 |
| 1947 | United States 4, Australia 1 |
| 1948 | United States 5, Australia 0 |
| 1949 | United States 4, Australia 1 |
| 1950 | Australia 4, United States 1 |
| 1951 | Australia 3, United States 2 |
| 1952 | Australia 4, United States 1 |
| 1953 | Australia 3, United States 2 |
| 1954 | United States 3, Australia 2 |
| 1955 | Australia 5, United States 0 |
| 1956 | Australia 5, United States 0 |
| 1957 | Australia 3, United States 2 |
| 1958 | United States 3, Australia 2 |
| 1959 | Australia 3, United States 2 |
| 1960 | Australia 4, Italy 1 |
| 1961 | Australia 5, Italy 0 |
| 1962 | Australia 5, Mexico 0 |
| 1963 | United States 3, Australia 2 |
| 1964 | Australia 3, United States 2 |
| 1965 | Australia 4, Spain 1 |
| 1966 | Australia 4, India 1 |
| 1967 | Australia 4, Spain 1 |
| 1968 | United States 4, Australia |
| 1969 | United States 5, Romania 0 |
| 1970 | United States 5, W. Germany 0 |
| 1971 | United States 3, Romania 2 |
| 1972 | United States 3, Romania 2 |
| 1973 | Australia 5, United States 0 |
| 1974 | South Africa (default by India) |
| 1975 | Sweden 3, Czechoslovakia 2 |
| 1976 | Italy 4, Chile 1 |
| 1977 | Australia 3, Italy 1 |
| 1978 | United States 4, Great Britain 1 |
| 1979 | United States 5, Italy 0 |
| 1980 | Czechoslovakia 4, Italy 1 |
| 1981 | United States 3, Argentina 1 |
| 1982 | United States 4, France, 1 |
| 1983 | Australia 3, Sweden 2 |
| 1984 | Sweden 4, United States 1 |
| 1985 | Sweden 3, W. Germany 2 |
| 1986 | Australia 3, Sweden 2 |
| 1987 | Sweden 5, India 0 |
| 1988 | W. Germany 4, Sweden 1 |
| 1989 | W. Germany 3, Sweden 2 |
| 1990 | United States 3, Australia 2 |
| 1991 | France 3, United States 1 |
| 1992 | United States 3, Switzerland 1 |
| 1993 | Germany 4, Australia 1 |
| 1994 | Sweden 4, Russia 1 |
| 1995 | United States 3, Russia 2 |

## French Open Singles Champions

| Year | Men | Women | Year | Men | Women |
|---|---|---|---|---|---|
| 1969 | Rod Laver | Margaret Smith Court | 1983 | Yannick Noah | Chris Evert Lloyd |
| 1970 | Jan Kodes | Margaret Smith Court | 1984 | Ivan Lendl | Martina Navratilova |
| 1971 | Jan Kodes | Evonne Goolagong | 1985 | Mats Wilander | Chris Evert Lloyd |
| 1972 | Andres Gimeno | Billie Jean King | 1986 | Ivan Lendl | Chris Evert Lloyd |
| 1973 | Ilie Nastase | Margaret Smith Court | 1987 | Ivan Lendl | Steffi Graf |
| 1974 | Bjorn Borg | Chris Evert | 1988 | Mats Wilander | Steffi Graf |
| 1975 | Bjorn Borg | Chris Evert | 1989 | Michael Chang | Arantxa Sanchez Vicario |
| 1976 | Adriano Panatta | Sue Barker | 1990 | Andres Gomez | Monica Seles |
| 1977 | Guillermo Vilas | Mima Jausovec | 1991 | Jim Courier | Monica Seles |
| 1978 | Bjorn Borg | Virginia Ruzici | 1992 | Jim Courier | Monica Seles |
| 1979 | Bjorn Borg | Chris Evert Lloyd | 1993 | Sergi Bruguera | Steffi Graf |
| 1980 | Bjorn Borg | Chris Evert Lloyd | 1994 | Sergi Bruguera | Arantxa Sanchez Vicario |
| 1981 | Bjorn Borg | Hana Mandlikova | 1995 | Thomas Muster | Steffi Graf |
| 1982 | Mats Wilander | Martina Navratilova | 1996 | Yevgeny Kafelnikov | Steffi Graf |

## Australian Open Singles Champions

| Year* | Men | Women | Year* | Men | Women |
|---|---|---|---|---|---|
| 1969 | Rod Laver | Margaret Smith Court | 1983 | Mats Wilander | Martina Navratilova |
| 1970 | Arthur Ashe | Margaret Smith Court | 1984 | Mats Wilander | Chris Evert Lloyd |
| 1971 | Ken Rosewall | Margaret Smith Court | 1985 | Stefan Edberg | Martina Navratilova |
| 1972 | Ken Rosewall | Virginia Wade | 1986 | Not held | Not held |
| 1973 | John Newcombe | Margaret Smith Court | 1987 | Stefan Edberg | Hana Mandlikova |
| 1974 | Jimmy Connors | Evonne Goolagong | 1988 | Mats Wilander | Steffi Graf |
| 1975 | John Newcombe | Evonne Goolagong | 1989 | Ivan Lendl | Steffi Graf |
| 1976 | Mark Edmondson | Evonne Goolagong | 1990 | Ivan Lendl | Steffi Graf |
| 1977 | Roscoe Tanner | Kerry Reid | 1991 | Boris Becker | Monica Seles |
| | Vitas Gerulaitis | Evonne Goolagong | 1992 | Jim Courier | Monica Seles |
| 1978 | Guillermo Vilas | Chris O'Neill | 1993 | Jim Courier | Monica Seles |
| 1979 | Guillermo Vilas | Barbara Jordan | 1994 | Pete Sampras | Steffi Graf |
| 1980 | Brian Teacher | Hana Mandlikova | 1995 | Andre Agassi | Mary Pierce |
| 1981 | Johan Kriek | Martina Navratilova | 1996 | Boris Becker | Monica Seles |
| 1982 | Johan Kriek | Chris Evert Lloyd | | | |

* Two tournaments were held in 1977 (Jan. & Dec.). Tournament was moved back to Jan. in 1987, so no championship was decided in 1986.

# AUTO RACING

## Indianapolis 500 Winners

| Year | Winner, Car (Chassis-Engine) | MPH | Year | Winner, Car (Chassis-Engine) | MPH |
|---|---|---|---|---|---|
| 1911 | Ray Harroun, Marmon | 74.602 | 1957 | Sam Hanks, Salih-Offy | 135.601 |
| 1912 | Joe Dawson, National | 78.719 | 1958 | Jimmy Bryan, Salih-Offy | 133.791 |
| 1913 | Jules Goux, Peugeot | 75.933 | 1959 | Rodger Ward, Watson-Offy | 135.857 |
| 1914 | Rene Thomas, Delage | 82.474 | 1960 | Jim Rathmann, Watson-Offy | 138.767 |
| 1915 | Ralph DePalma, Mercedes | 89.840 | 1961 | A.J. Foyt Jr., Trevis-Offy | 139.130 |
| 1916 | Dario Resta, Peugeot | 84.001 | 1962 | Rodger Ward, Watson-Offy | 140.293 |
| 1917-18 | race not held | | 1963 | Parnelli Jones, Watson-Offy | 143.137 |
| 1919 | Howdy Wilcox, Peugeot | 88.050 | 1964 | A.J. Foyt Jr., Watson-Offy | 147.350 |
| 1920 | Gaston Chevrolet, Frontenac | 88.618 | 1965 | Jim Clark, Lotus-Ford | 150.686 |
| 1921 | Tommy Milton, Frontenac | 89.621 | 1966 | Graham Hill, Lola-Ford | 144.317 |
| 1922 | Jimmy Murphy, Duesenberg-Miller | 94.484 | 1967 | A.J. Foyt Jr., Coyote-Ford | 151.207 |
| 1923 | Tommy Milton, Miller | 90.954 | 1968 | Bobby Unser, Eagle-Offy | 152.882 |
| 1924 | L.L. Corum-Joe Boyer, Duesenberg | 98.234 | 1969 | Mario Andretti, Hawk-Ford | 156.867 |
| 1925 | Peter DePaolo, Duesenberg | 101.127 | 1970 | Al Unser, P.J. Colt-Ford | 155.749 |
| 1926 | Frank Lockhart, Miller | 95.904 | 1971 | Al Unser, P.J. Colt-Ford | 157.735 |
| 1927 | George Souders, Duesenberg | 97.545 | 1972 | Mark Donohue, McLaren-Offy | 162.962 |
| 1928 | Louie Meyer, Miller | 99.482 | 1973 | Gordon Johncock, Eagle-Offy | 159.036 |
| 1929 | Ray Keech, Miller | 97.585 | 1974 | Johnny Rutherford, McLaren-Offy | 158.589 |
| 1930 | Billy Arnold, Summers-Miller | 100.448 | 1975 | Bobby Unser, Eagle-Offy | 149.213 |
| 1931 | Louis Schneider, Stevens-Miller | 96.629 | 1976 | Johnny Rutherford, McLaren-Offy | 148.725 |
| 1932 | Fred Frame, Wetteroth-Miller | 104.144 | 1977 | A.J. Foyt Jr., Coyote-Foyt | 161.331 |
| 1933 | Louie Meyer, Miller | 104.162 | 1978 | Al Unser, Lola-Cosworth | 161.363 |
| 1934 | Bill Cummings, Miller | 104.863 | 1979 | Rick Mears, Penske-Cosworth | 158.899 |
| 1935 | Kelly Petillo, Wetteroth-Offy | 106.240 | 1980 | Johnny Rutherford, Chaparral-Cosworth | 142.862 |
| 1936 | Louie Meyer, Stevens-Miller | 109.069 | 1981 | Bobby Unser, Penske-Cosworth | 139.084 |
| 1937 | Wilbur Shaw, Shaw-Offy | 113.580 | 1982 | Gordon Johncock, Wildcat-Cosworth | 162.029 |
| 1938 | Floyd Roberts, Wetteroth-Miller | 117.200 | 1983 | Tom Sneva, March-Cosworth | 162.117 |
| 1939 | Wilbur Shaw, Maserati | 115.035 | 1984 | Rick Mears, March-Cosworth | 163.612 |
| 1940 | Wilbur Shaw, Maserati | 114.277 | 1985 | Danny Sullivan, March-Cosworth | 152.982 |
| 1941 | Floyd Davis-Mauri Rose, Wetteroth-Offy | 115.117 | 1986 | Bobby Rahal, March-Cosworth | 170.722 |
| | | | 1987 | Al Unser, March-Cosworth | 162.175 |
| 1942-45 | race not held | | 1988 | Rick Mears, Penske-Chevy Indy V8 | 144.809 |
| 1946 | George Robson, Adams-Sparks | 114.820 | 1989 | Emerson Fittipaldi, Penske-Chevy Indy V8 | 167.581 |
| 1947 | Mauri Rose, Deidt-Offy | 116.338 | 1990 | Arie Luyendyk, Lola-Chevy Indy V8 | 185.981* |
| 1948 | Mauri Rose, Deidt-Offy | 119.814 | 1991 | Rick Mears, Penske-Chevy Indy V8 | 176.457 |
| 1949 | Bill Holland, Deidt-Offy | 121.327 | 1992 | Al Unser Jr., Galmer-Chevy Indy V8A | 134.477 |
| 1950 | Johnnie Parsons, Kurtis-Offy | 124.002 | 1993 | Emerson Fittipaldi, Penske-Chevy Indy V8C | 157.207 |
| 1951 | Lee Wallard, Kurtis-Offy | 126.244 | 1994 | Al Unser Jr., Penske-Mercedes Benz | 160.872 |
| 1952 | Troy Ruttman, Kuzma-Offy | 128.922 | 1995 | Jacques Villeneuve, Reynard-Ford Cosworth XB | 153.616 |
| 1953 | Bill Vukovich, KK500A-Offy | 128.740 | 1996 | Buddy Lazier, Reynard-Ford Cosworth | 147.956 |
| 1954 | Bill Vukovich, KK500A-Offy | 130.840 | | | |
| 1955 | Bob Sweikert, KK500C-Offy | 128.213 | | | |
| 1956 | Pat Flaherty, Watson-Offy | 128.490 | | | |

*Race record. **Note:** The race was less than 500 mi in the following years: 1916 (300 mi), 1926 (400 mi), 1950 (345 mi), 1973 (332.5 mi), 1975 (435 mi), 1976 (255 mi).

## Notable One-Mile Speed Records

Craig Breedlove tried unsuccessfully to recapture the world land speed record, Oct. 28, 1996, in Black Rock Desert, NV. His car, the Spirit of America, went out of control and was damaged after reaching an unofficial speed of 675 mph. Current official record-holder Richard Noble (U.K.) was also about to begin test runs with a new jet-powered car, the Thrust SSC.

| Date | Driver | Car | MPH |
|---|---|---|---|
| 1/26/06 | Marriott | Stanley (Steam) | 127.659 |
| 3/16/10 | Oldfield | Benz | 131.724 |
| 4/23/11 | Burman | Benz | 141.732 |
| 2/12/19 | DePalma | Packard | 149.875 |
| 4/27/20 | Milton | Dusenberg | 155.046 |
| 4/28/26 | Parry-Thomas | Thomas Spl. | 170.624 |
| 3/29/27 | Seagrave | Sunbeam | 203.790 |
| 4/22/28 | Keech | White Triplex | 207.552 |
| 3/11/29 | Seagrave | Irving-Napier | 231.446 |
| 2/5/31 | Campbell | Napier-Campbell | 246.086 |
| 2/24/32 | Campbell | Napier-Campbell | 253.96 |
| 2/22/33 | Campbell | Napier-Campbell | 272.109 |
| 9/3/35 | Campbell | Bluebird Special | 301.13 |
| 11/19/37 | Eyston | Thunderbolt 1 | 311.42 |
| 9/16/38 | Eyston | Thunderbolt 1 | 357.5 |
| 8/23/39 | Cobb | Railton | 368.9 |
| 9/16/47 | Cobb | Railton-Mobil | 394.2 |
| 8/5/63 | Breedlove | Spirit of America | 407.45 |
| 10/27/64 | Arfons | Green Monster | 536.71 |
| 11/15/65 | Breedlove | Spirit of America | 600.601 |
| 10/23/70 | Gabelich | Blue Flame | 622.407 |
| 10/9/79 | Barrett | Budweiser Rocket | 638.637* |
| 10/4/83 | Noble | Thrust 2 | 633.6 |

*Not recognized as official by sanctioning bodies.

## IndyCar Champions

(U.S. Auto Club Champions prior to 1979; Championship Auto Racing Teams [CART] Champions, 1979-96)

| Year | Driver |
|---|---|
| 1960 | A. J. Foyt |
| 1961 | A. J. Foyt |
| 1962 | Rodger Ward |
| 1963 | A. J. Foyt |
| 1964 | A. J. Foyt |
| 1965 | Mario Andretti |
| 1966 | Mario Andretti |
| 1967 | A. J. Foyt |
| 1968 | Bobby Unser |
| 1969 | Mario Andretti |
| 1970 | Al Unser |
| 1971 | Joe Leonard |
| 1972 | Joe Leonard |
| 1973 | Roger McCluskey |
| 1974 | Bobby Unser |
| 1975 | A. J. Foyt |
| 1976 | Gordon Johncock |
| 1977 | Tom Sneva |
| 1978 | Tom Sneva |
| 1979 | Rick Mears |
| 1980 | Johnny Rutherford |
| 1981 | Rick Mears |
| 1982 | Rick Mears |
| 1983 | Al Unser |
| 1984 | Mario Andretti |
| 1985 | Al Unser |
| 1986 | Bobby Rahal |
| 1987 | Bobby Rahal |
| 1988 | Danny Sullivan |
| 1989 | Emerson Fittipaldi |
| 1990 | Al Unser Jr. |
| 1991 | Michael Andretti |
| 1992 | Bobby Rahal |
| 1993 | Nigel Mansell |
| 1994 | Al Unser Jr. |
| 1995 | Jacques Villeneuve |
| 1996 | Jimmy Vasser |

## Le Mans 24-Hour Race in 1996

Davy Jones (U.S.), Manuel Reuter (Germany), and Alexander Wurz (Austria) drove their TWR Porsche WSC to victory in the 1996 Le Mans 24-hour race. They traveled the 2,991.3 miles at an average of 124.64 mph.

## World Grand Prix Champions

| Year | Driver |
|---|---|
| 1951 | Juan Fangio, Argentina |
| 1952 | Alberto Ascari, Italy |
| 1953 | Alberto Ascari, Italy |
| 1954 | Juan Fangio, Argentina |
| 1955 | Juan Fangio, Argentina |
| 1956 | Juan Fangio, Argentina |
| 1957 | Juan Fangio, Argentina |
| 1958 | Mike Hawthorne, England |
| 1959 | Jack Brabham, Australia |
| 1960 | Jack Brabham, Australia |
| 1961 | Phil Hill, United States |
| 1962 | Graham Hill, England |
| 1963 | Jim Clark, Scotland |
| 1964 | John Surtees, England |
| 1965 | Jim Clark, Scotland |
| 1966 | Jack Brabham, Australia |
| 1967 | Denis Hulme, New Zealand |
| 1968 | Graham Hill, England |
| 1969 | Jackie Stewart, Scotland |
| 1970 | Jochen Rindt, Austria |
| 1971 | Jackie Stewart, Scotland |
| 1972 | Emerson Fittipaldi, Brazil |
| 1973 | Jackie Stewart, Scotland |
| 1974 | Emerson Fittipaldi, Brazil |
| 1975 | Niki Lauda, Austria |
| 1976 | James Hunt, England |
| 1977 | Niki Lauda, Austria |
| 1978 | Mario Andretti, United States |
| 1979 | Jody Scheckter, South Africa |
| 1980 | Alan Jones, Australia |
| 1981 | Nelson Piquet, Brazil |
| 1982 | Keke Rosberg, Finland |
| 1983 | Nelson Piquet, Brazil |
| 1984 | Niki Lauda, Austria |
| 1985 | Alain Prost, France |
| 1986 | Alain Prost, France |
| 1987 | Nelson Piquet, Brazil |
| 1988 | Ayrton Senna, Brazil |
| 1989 | Alain Prost, France |
| 1990 | Ayrton Senna, Brazil |
| 1991 | Ayrton Senna, Brazil |
| 1992 | Nigel Mansell, Britain |
| 1993 | Alain Prost, France |
| 1994 | Michael Schumacher, Germany |
| 1995 | Michael Schumacher, Germany |
| 1996 | Damon Hill, England |

## Grand Prix Races for Formula 1 Cars in 1996

| Date | Grand Prix | Winner, car |
|---|---|---|
| 3/10 | Australian | Damon Hill, Williams-Renault |
| 3/31 | Brazilian | Damon Hill, Williams-Renault |
| 4/7 | Argentinian | Damon Hill, Williams-Renault |
| 4/28 | European | Jacques Villenueve, Williams-Renault |
| 5/5 | San Marino | Damon Hill, Williams-Renault |
| 5/19 | Monaco | Olivier Panis, Ligier Mugen Honda |
| 6/2 | Spanish | Michael Schumacher, Ferrari |
| 6/16 | Canadian | Damon Hill, Williams-Renault |
| 6/30 | French | Damon Hill, Williams-Renault |
| 7/14 | British | Jacques Villenueve, Williams-Renault |
| 7/28 | German | Damon Hill, Williams-Renault |
| 8/11 | Hungarian | Jacques Villeneuve, Williams-Renault |
| 8/25 | Belgian | Michael Schumacher, Ferrari |
| 9/8 | Italian | Michael Schumacher, Ferrari |
| 9/22 | Portuguese | Jacques Villeneuve, Williams-Renault |
| 10/13 | Japanese | Damon Hill, Williams-Renault |

## NASCAR Racing

### Winston Cup Champions

| Year | Driver |
|---|---|
| 1949 | Red Byron |
| 1950 | Bill Rexford |
| 1951 | Herb Thomas |
| 1952 | Tim Flock |
| 1953 | Herb Thomas |
| 1954 | Lee Petty |
| 1955 | Tim Flock |
| 1956 | Buck Baker |
| 1957 | Buck Baker |
| 1958 | Lee Petty |
| 1959 | Lee Petty |
| 1960 | Rex White |
| 1961 | Ned Jarrett |
| 1962 | Joe Weatherly |
| 1963 | Joe Weatherly |
| 1964 | Richard Petty |
| 1965 | Ned Jarrett |
| 1966 | David Pearson |
| 1967 | Richard Petty |
| 1968 | David Pearson |
| 1969 | David Pearson |
| 1970 | Bobby Isaac |
| 1971 | Richard Petty |
| 1972 | Richard Petty |
| 1973 | Benny Parsons |
| 1974 | Richard Petty |
| 1975 | Richard Petty |
| 1976 | Cale Yarborough |
| 1977 | Cale Yarborough |
| 1978 | Cale Yarborough |
| 1979 | Richard Petty |
| 1980 | Dale Earnhardt |
| 1981 | Darrell Waltrip |
| 1982 | Darrell Waltrip |
| 1983 | Bobby Allison |
| 1984 | Terry Labonte |
| 1985 | Darrell Waltrip |
| 1986 | Dale Earnhardt |
| 1987 | Dale Earnhardt |
| 1988 | Bill Elliott |
| 1989 | Rusty Wallace |
| 1990 | Dale Earnhardt |
| 1991 | Dale Earnhardt |
| 1992 | Alan Kulwicki |
| 1993 | Dale Earnhardt |
| 1994 | Dale Earnhardt |
| 1995 | Jeff Gordon |

## Daytona 500 Winners

| Year | Driver, car | Avg. MPH | Year | Driver, car | Avg. MPH |
|---|---|---|---|---|---|
| 1959 | Lee Petty, Oldsmobile | 135.521 | 1978 | Bobby Allison, Ford | 159.730 |
| 1960 | Junior Johnson, Chevrolet | 124.740 | 1979 | Richard Petty, Oldsmobile | 143.977 |
| 1961 | Marvin Panch, Pontiac | 149.601 | 1980 | Buddy Baker, Oldsmobile | 177.602 |
| 1962 | Fireball Roberts, Pontiac | 152.529 | 1981 | Richard Petty, Buick | 169.651 |
| 1963 | Tiny Lund, Ford | 151.566 | 1982 | Bobby Allison, Buick | 153.991 |
| 1964 | Richard Petty, Plymouth | 154.334 | 1983 | Cale Yarborough, Pontiac | 155.979 |
| 1965 | Fred Lorenzen, Ford (a) | 141.539 | 1984 | Cale Yarborough, Chevrolet | 150.994 |
| 1966 | Richard Petty, Plymouth (b) | 160.627 | 1985 | Bill Elliott, Ford | 172.265 |
| 1967 | Mario Andretti, Ford | 146.926 | 1986 | Geoff Bodine, Chevrolet | 148.124 |
| 1968 | Cale Yarborough, Mercury | 143.251 | 1987 | Bill Elliott, Ford | 176.263 |
| 1969 | Lee Roy Yarborough, Ford | 160.875 | 1988 | Bobby Allison, Buick | 137.531 |
| 1970 | Pete Hamilton, Plymouth | 149.601 | 1989 | Darrell Waltrip, Chevrolet | 148.466 |
| 1971 | Richard Petty, Plymouth | 144.456 | 1990 | Derrike Cope, Chevrolet | 165.761 |
| 1972 | A. J. Foyt, Mercury | 161.550 | 1991 | Ernie Irvan, Chevrolet | 148.148 |
| 1973 | Richard Petty, Dodge | 157.205 | 1992 | Davey Allison, Ford | 160.256 |
| 1974 | Richard Petty, Dodge (c) | 140.894 | 1993 | Dale Jarrett, Chevrolet | 154.972 |
| 1975 | Benny Parsons, Chevrolet | 153.649 | 1994 | Sterling Marlin, Chevrolet | 156.931 |
| 1976 | David Pearson, Mercury | 152.181 | 1995 | Sterling Marlin, Chevrolet | 141.710 |
| 1977 | Cale Yarborough, Chevrolet | 153.218 | 1996 | Dale Jarrett, Ford | 154.308 |

(a) 322.5 mi. (b) 495 mi. (c) 450 mi.

## Winston Cup Races in 1996

| Date | Race, site | Winner | Car |
|---|---|---|---|
| Feb. 11 | Busch Clash of '96, Daytona Beach, FL | Dale Jarrett | Ford |
| Feb. 15 | Gatorade Twin 125s, Daytona Beach, FL | Ernie Irvan/Dale Earnhardt | Ford/Chev. |
| Feb. 18 | Daytona 500, Daytona Beach, FL | Dale Jarrett | Ford |
| Feb. 25 | Goodwrench Service 400, Rockingham, NC | Dale Earnhardt | Chevrolet |
| Mar. 3 | Pontiac Excitement 400, Richmond, VA | Jeff Gordon | Chevrolet |
| Mar. 10 | Purolator 500, Atlanta, GA | Dale Earnhardt | Chevrolet |
| Mar. 24 | Transouth Financial 400, Darlington, SC | Jeff Gordon | Chevrolet |
| Mar. 31 | Food City 500, Bristol, TN | Jeff Gordon | Chevrolet |
| Apr. 14 | First Union 400, N. Wilkesboro, NC | Terry Labonte | Chevrolet |
| Apr. 21 | Goody's Headache Powder 500, Martinsville, VA | Rusty Wallace | Ford |
| Apr. 28 | Winston Select 500, Talladega, AL | Sterling Marlin | Chevrolet |
| May 5 | Save Mart Supermarkets 300, Sonoma, CA | Rusty Wallace | Ford |
| May 18 | The Winston Select, Charlotte, NC | Michael Waltrip | Ford |
| May 26 | Coca-Cola 600, Charlotte, NC | Dale Jarrett | Ford |
| June 2 | Miller 500, Dover, DE | Jeff Gordon | Chevrolet |
| June 16 | UAW-GM Teamwork 500, Pocono, PA | Jeff Gordon | Chevrolet |
| June 23 | Miller 400, Brooklyn, MI | Rusty Wallace | Ford |
| July 6 | Pepsi 400, Daytona Beach, FL | Sterling Marlin | Chevrolet |
| July 14 | Jiffy Lube 300, Loudon, NH | Ernie Irvan | Ford |
| July 21 | Miller 500, Pocono, PA | Rusty Wallace | Ford |
| July 28 | Diehard 500, Talladega, AL | Jeff Gordon | Chevrolet |
| Aug. 3 | Brickyard 400, Indianapolis, IN | Dale Jarrett | Ford |
| Aug. 11 | The Bud at The Glen, Watkins Glen, NY | Geoff Bodine | Ford |
| Aug. 18 | GM Goodwrench Dealer 400, Brooklyn, MI | Dale Jarrett | Ford |
| Aug. 24 | Goody's Headache Powder 500, Bristol, TN | Rusty Wallace | Ford |
| Sept. 1 | Mountain Dew Southern 500, Darlington, SC | Jeff Gordon | Chevrolet |
| Sept. 7 | Miller 400, Richmond, VA | Ernie Irvan | Ford |
| Sept. 15 | MBNA 500, Dover, DE | Jeff Gordon | Chevrolet |
| Sept. 22 | Hanes 500, Martinsville, VA | Jeff Gordon | Chevrolet |
| Sept. 29 | Tyson Holly Farms 400, N. Wilkesboro, NC | Jeff Gordon | Chevrolet |
| Oct. 6 | UAW-GM Quality 500, Charlotte, NC | Terry Labonte | Chevrolet |
| Oct. 20 | AC-Delco 400, Rockingham, NC | Ricky Rudd | Ford |
| Oct. 27 | Dura Lube 500, Phoenix, AZ | Bobby Hamilton | Pontiac |

# MOTORCYCLE RACING

## 1996 American Motorcyclist Assn. Racing Champions

### Road Racing

**AMA Superbike**—Doug Chandler, Salinas, CA, Kawasaki ZX-7

**AMA 250cc Grand Prix**—Rich Oliver, Fresno, CA, Yamaha TZ250

**AMA 600cc SuperSport**—Miguel Duhamel, Repentigny, Que., Honda CBR600

**AMA 750cc SuperSport**—Aaron Yates, Milledgeville, GA, Suzuki GSXR750

**AMA SuperTwins**—Matt Wait, Lodi, CA, Harley-Davidson 883 Sportster

**AMA SuperTeams**—Erion Racing, Anaheim, CA, Honda CBR900

### Motocross

**AMA 250cc Motocross**—Jeff Emig, Riverside, CA, Kawasaki KX250

**AMA 125cc Motocross**—Steve Lamson, Riverside, CA, Honda CR125

### Supercross

**AMA Supercross**—Jeremy McGrath, Menifee, CA, Honda CR250

### Grand National Dirt Track

**AMA Grand National**—Scott Parker, Swartz Creek, MI, Harley-Davidson XR750

**AMA 883cc Dirt Track**—Eric Bostrom, Marina Del Rey, Harley-Davidson 883 Sportster

# CYCLING

## Tour de France in 1996

On July 21, Bjarne Riis became the first Danish cyclist to win the Tour de France, the world's most prestigious bicycle race. His margin of victory in the 83d Tour de France was 1 minute 41 seconds, and he completed the 21-day, 2,423-mile (3,900-km) race in a total time of 95 hours, 57 minutes, 16 seconds. Jan Ullrich of Germany finished second; Miguel Indurain of Spain, who had won the 5 previous Tours, finished eleventh.

# BOXING

## Champions by Classes

There are many governing bodies in boxing, including the World Boxing Council, World Boxing Assn., International Boxing Federation, World Boxing Org., U.S. Boxing Assn., North American Boxing Federation, and European Boxing Union. Others are recognized by TV networks and the print media. All the governing bodies have their own champions and assorted boxing divisions. The following are the recognized champions— as of Oct. 1996—in the principal divisions of the WBC, WBA, and IBF.

| Class, Weight limit | WBC | WBA | IBF |
|---|---|---|---|
| Heavyweight | Vacant | Mike Tyson, U.S. | Michael Moorer, U.S. |
| Cruiserweight (195 lb) | Marcelo Dominguez, Argentina | Nate Miller, U.S. | Adolpho Washington, U.S. |
| Light Heavyweight (175 lb) | Vacant | Virgil Hill, U.S. | Henry Maske, Germany |
| Super Middleweight (168 lb) | Robin Reid, U.K. | Frank Liles, U.S. | Roy Jones, U.S. |
| Middleweight (160 lb) | Keith Holmes, U.S. | William Joppy, U.S. | Bernard Hopkins, U.S. |
| Jr. Middleweight (154 lb) | Terry Norris, U.S. | Laurent Boudouani, France | Terry Norris, U.S. |
| Welterweight (147 lb) | Pernell Whitaker, U.S. | Ike Quartey, Ghana | Felix Trinidad, Puerto Rico |
| Jr. Welterweight (140 lb) | Oscar De La Hoya, U.S. | Frankie Randall, U.S. | Kostya Tszyu, Australia |
| Lightweight (135 lb) | Jean-Baptiste Mendy, France | Orzubek Nazarov, Japan | Philip Holiday, South Africa |
| Jr. Lightweight (130 lb) | Azumah Nelson, Ghana | Choi Yong Soo, South Korea | Arturo Gatti, U.S. |
| Featherweight (126 lb) | Luisito Espinosa, Philippines | Wilfredo Vasquez, Puerto Rico | Tom Johnson, U.S. |
| Jr. Featherweight (122 lb) | Daniel Zaragoza, Mexico | Antonio Cermeno, Venezuela | Vuyani Bungu, South Africa |
| Bantamweight (118 lb) | S. Singmanassuk, Thailand | Nana Yaw Konadu, Ghana | Mbulelo Botile, South Africa |
| Jr. Bantamweight (115 lb) | Hiroshi Kawashima, Japan | Yokthai Sithoar, Thailand | Danny Romero, U.S. |
| Flyweight (112 lb) | Yuri Arbachakov, Russia | Saen Sow Ploenchit, Thailand | Mark Johnson, U.S. |
| Jr. Flyweight (108 lb) | Saman Sorjaturong, Thailand | Keiji Yamaguchi, Japan | Michael Carbajal, U.S. |

## Ring Champions by Years

(*abandoned the title or was stripped of it)

### Heavyweights

| | |
|---|---|
| **1882-1892** | John L. Sullivan (a) |
| **1892-1897** | James J. Corbett (b) |
| **1897-1899** | Robert Fitzsimmons |
| **1899-1905** | James J. Jeffries* (c) |
| **1905-1906** | Marvin Hart |
| **1906-1908** | Tommy Burns |
| **1908-1915** | Jack Johnson |
| **1915-1919** | Jess Willard |
| **1919-1926** | Jack Dempsey |
| **1926-1928** | Gene Tunney* |
| **1928-1930** | Vacant |
| **1930-1932** | Max Schmeling |
| **1932-1933** | Jack Sharkey |
| **1933-1934** | Primo Carnera |
| **1934-1935** | Max Baer |
| **1935-1937** | James J. Braddock |
| **1937-1949** | Joe Louis* |
| **1949-1951** | Ezzard Charles |
| **1951-1952** | Joe Walcott |
| **1952-1956** | Rocky Marciano* |
| **1956-1959** | Floyd Patterson |
| **1959-1960** | Ingemar Johansson |
| **1960-1962** | Floyd Patterson |
| **1962-1964** | Sonny Liston |
| **1964-1967** | Cassius Clay* (Muhammad Ali) (d) |
| **1970-1973** | Joe Frazier |
| **1973-1974** | George Foreman |
| **1974-1978** | Muhammad Ali |
| **1978** | Leon Spinks (e); Ken Norton (WBC); Larry Holmes* (WBC) (f); Muhammad Ali* (WBA) |
| **1979-1980** | John Tate (WBA) |
| **1980-1982** | Mike Weaver (WBA) |
| **1982-1983** | Michael Dokes (WBA) |
| **1983** | Gerrie Coetzee (WBA); Larry Holmes (IBF) |
| **1984** | Tim Witherspoon (WBC); Pinklon Thomas (WBC); Greg Page (WBA) |
| **1985** | Tony Tubbs (WBA); Michael Spinks* (IBF) |
| **1986** | Tim Witherspoon (WBA); Trevor Berbick (WBC); Mike Tyson (WBC); James "Bone-crusher" Smith (WBA) |
| **1987** | Mike Tyson (WBC, WBA); Tony Tucker (IBF) |
| **1987-1990** | Mike Tyson (WBC, WBA, IBF) |
| **1990** | James "Buster" Douglas (WBA, WBC, IBF); Evander Holyfield (WBA, WBC, IBF) |
| **1992** | Riddick Bowe (WBA, IBF, WBC*); Lennox Lewis (WBC) |
| **1993-1994** | Evander Holyfield (WBA, IBF) |
| **1994** | Michael Moorer (WBA, IBF); Oliver McCall (WBC); George Foreman (WBA*, IBF*) |
| **1995** | Bruce Seldon (WBA); Frank Bruno (WBC); Frans Botha* (IBF) |
| **1996** | Mike Tyson (WBC*, WBA); Michael Moorer (IBF) |

(a) London Prize Ring (bare knuckle champion). (b) First Marquis of Queensberry champion. (c) Jeffries abandoned the title (1905) and designated Marvin Hart and Jack Root as logical contenders. Hart defeated Root in 12 rounds (1905) and in turn was defeated by Tommy Burns (1906), who laid claim to the title. Jack Johnson defeated Burns (1908) and was recognized as champion. He clinched the title by defeating Jeffries in an attempted comeback (1910). (d) Title declared vacant by the WBA and other groups in 1967 after Ali's refusal to fulfill his military obligation. Joe Frazier was recognized as champion by 6 states, Mexico, and South America. Jimmy Ellis was declared champion by the WBA. Frazier KOd Ellis, Feb. 16, 1970. (e) After Spinks defeated Ali, the WBC recognized Ken Norton as champion. Ali defeated Spinks in a rematch to win the WBA title and subsequently retired in 1979. (f) Holmes relinquished the WBC title in Dec. 1983 and immediately began fighting as champion of the newly formed IBF.

### Light Heavyweights

| | |
|---|---|
| **1903** | Jack Root, George Gardner |
| **1903-1905** | Bob Fitzsimmons |
| **1905-1912** | Philadelphia Jack O'Brien* |
| **1912-1916** | Jack Dillon |
| **1916-1920** | Battling Levinsky |
| **1920-1922** | George Carpentier |
| **1922-1923** | Battling Siki |
| **1923-1925** | Mike McTigue |
| **1925-1926** | Paul Berlenbach |
| **1926-1927** | Jack Delaney* |
| **1927-1929** | Tommy Loughran* |
| **1930-1934** | Maxey Rosenbloom |
| **1934-1935** | Bob Olin |
| **1935-1939** | John Henry Lewis* |
| **1939** | Melio Bettina |
| **1939-1941** | Billy Conn* |
| **1941** | Anton Christoforidis (won NBA title) |
| **1941-1948** | Gus Lesnevich, Freddie Mills |
| **1948-1950** | Freddie Mills |
| **1950-1952** | Joey Maxim |
| **1952-1960** | Archie Moore |
| **1961-1962** | Vacant |
| **1962-1963** | Harold Johnson |
| **1963-1965** | Willie Pastrano |
| **1965-1966** | Jose Torres |
| **1966-1968** | Dick Tiger |
| **1968-1974** | Bob Foster* |
| **1974-1977** | John Conteh (WBC); Victor Galindez (WBA) |
| **1977-1978** | Miguel Cuello (WBC) |
| **1978** | Mike Rossman (WBA); Mate Parlov (WBC); Marvin Johnson (WBC) |
| **1979** | Matthew Saad Muhammad (WBC); Victor Galindez (WBA); Marvin Johnson (WBA) |
| **1980** | Eddie Mustafa Muhammad (WBA) |
| **1981** | Michael Spinks (WBA); Dwight Braxton (WBC) |
| **1983-1985** | Michael Spinks* |
| **1985** | J. B. Williamson (WBC) |
| **1986** | Marvin Johnson (WBA); Dennis Andries (WBC) |
| **1987** | Thomas Hearns* (WBC); Leslie Stewart (WBA); Virgil Hill (WBA); Don Lalonde (WBC) |
| **1988** | Ray Leonard* (WBC) |
| **1989** | Dennis Andries (WBC); Jeff Harding (WBC) |
| **1990** | Dennis Andries (WBC) |
| **1991** | Thomas Hearns (WBA); Jeff Harding (WBC) |
| **1992** | Iran Barkley* (WBA); Virgil Hill (WBA) |
| **1994-1995** | Mike McCallum (WBC) |
| **1995-1996** | Fabrice Tiozzo* (WBC) |

### Middleweights

| | |
|---|---|
| **1884-1891** | Jack "Nonpareil" Dempsey |
| **1891-1897** | Bob Fitzsimmons* |
| **1897-1907** | Tommy Ryan* |
| **1907-1908** | Stanley Ketchel, Billy Papke |
| **1908-1910** | Stanley Ketchel |
| **1911-1913** | vacant |
| **1913** | Frank Klaus; George Chip |
| **1914-1917** | Al McCoy |
| **1917-1920** | Mike O'Dowd |
| **1920-1923** | Johnny Wilson |
| **1923-1926** | Harry Greb |
| **1926-1931** | Tiger Flowers; Mickey Walker |
| **1931-1932** | Gorilla Jones (NBA) |
| **1932-1937** | Marcel Thil |
| **1938** | Al Hostak (NBA); Solly Krieger (NBA) |
| **1939-1940** | Al Hostak (NBA) |
| **1941-1947** | Tony Zale |
| **1947-1948** | Rocky Graziano |
| **1948** | Tony Zale; Marcel Cerdan |
| **1949-1951** | Jake LaMotta |
| **1951** | Ray Robinson; Randy Turpin; Ray Robinson* |
| **1953-1955** | Carl (Bobo) Olson |
| **1955-1957** | Ray Robinson |
| **1957** | Gene Fullmer; Ray Robinson; Carmen Basilio |
| **1958** | Ray Robinson |
| **1959** | Gene Fullmer (NBA); Ray Robinson (NY) |
| **1960** | Gene Fullmer (NBA); Paul Pender (NY and MA) |
| **1961** | Gene Fullmer (NBA); Terry Downes (NY, MA, Europe) |
| **1962** | Gene Fullmer; Dick Tiger (NBA); Paul Pender (NY and MA)* |
| **1963** | Dick Tiger (universal) |
| **1963-1965** | Joey Giardello |
| **1965-1966** | Dick Tiger |
| **1966-1967** | Emile Griffith |
| **1967** | Nino Benvenuti |
| **1967-1968** | Emile Griffith |
| **1968-1970** | Nino Benvenuti |
| **1970-1977** | Carlos Monzon* |
| **1977-1978** | Rodrigo Valdez |
| **1978-1979** | Hugo Corro |
| **1979-1980** | Vito Antuofermo |
| **1980** | Alan Minter; Marvin Hagler |
| **1987** | Ray Leonard* (WBC); Thomas Hearns (WBC); Sumbu Kalambay (WBA) |
| **1988-1989** | Iran Barkley (WBC) |
| **1989** | Mike McCallum* (WBA); Roberto Duran (WBC) |
| **1991-1993** | Julian Jackson (WBC) |
| **1992-1993** | Reggie Johnson (WBA) |
| **1993** | Gerald McClellan (WBC); John David Jackson* (WBA) |
| **1994-1995** | Jorge Castro (WBA) |
| **1995** | Julian Jackson (WBC); Quincy Taylor (WBC); Shinji Takehara (WBA) |
| **1996** | Keith Holmes (WBC); William Joppy (WBA) |

### Welterweights

| | |
|---|---|
| **1892-1894** | Mysterious Billy Smith |
| **1894-1896** | Tommy Ryan |
| **1896** | Kid McCoy* |
| **1900** | Rube Ferns; Matty Matthews |
| **1901** | Rube Ferns |
| **1901-1904** | Joe Walcott |
| **1904-1906** | Dixie Kid; Joe Walcott; Honey Mellody |
| **1907-1911** | Mike Sullivan |
| **1911-1915** | Vacant |
| **1915-1919** | Ted Lewis |
| **1919-1922** | Jack Britton |
| **1922-1926** | Mickey Walker |
| **1926** | Pete Latzo |
| **1927-1929** | Joe Dundee |
| **1929** | Jackie Fields |
| **1930** | Jack Thompson; Tommy Freeman |
| **1931** | Tommy Freeman; Jack Thompson; Lou Brouillard |
| **1932** | Jackie Fields |
| **1933** | Young Corbett; Jimmy McLarnin |
| **1934** | Barney Ross; Jimmy McLarnin |
| **1935-1938** | Barney Ross |
| **1938-1940** | Henry Armstrong |
| **1940-1941** | Fritzie Zivic |
| **1941-1946** | Fred Cochrane |
| **1946** | Marty Servo*; Ray Robinson (a) |
| **1946-1950** | Ray Robinson* |
| **1951** | Johnny Bratton (NBA) |
| **1951-1954** | Kid Gavilan |
| **1954-1955** | Johnny Saxton |
| **1955** | Tony De Marco; Carmen Basilio |
| **1956** | Carmen Basilio; Johnny Saxton; Carmen Basilio |
| **1957** | Carmen Basilio* |
| **1958-1960** | Virgil Akins, Don Jordan |
| **1960** | Benny Paret |
| **1961** | Emile Griffith; Benny Paret |
| **1962** | Emile Griffith |
| **1963** | Luis Rodriguez; Emile Griffith |
| **1964-1966** | Emile Griffith* |
| **1966-1969** | Curtis Cokes |
| **1969-1970** | Jose Napoles; Billy Backus |
| **1971-1975** | Jose Napoles |
| **1975-1976** | John Stracey (WBC); Angel Espada (WBA) |
| **1976-1979** | Carlos Palomino (WBC); Jose Cuevas (WBA) |
| **1979** | Wilfredo Benitez (WBC); Sugar Ray Leonard (WBC) |
| **1980** | Roberto Duran (WBC); Thomas Hearns (WBA); Sugar Ray Leonard (WBC) |
| **1981-1982** | Sugar Ray Leonard* |
| **1983-1985** | Donald Curry (WBA); Milton McCrory (WBC) |
| **1985-1986** | Donald Curry |
| **1986-1987** | Lloyd Honeyghan (WBC) |
| **1987** | Mark Breland (WBA); Marlon Starling (WBA); Jorge Vaca (WBC). |
| **1988-1989** | Tomas Molinares (WBA); Lloyd Honeyghan (WBC) |
| **1989-1990** | Marlon Starling (WBC); Mark Breland (WBA) |
| **1990-1991** | Maurice Blocker (WBC); Aaron Davis (WBA) |
| **1991** | Meldrick Taylor (WBA); Simon Brown (WBC); Buddy McGirt (WBC) |
| **1992-1994** | Crisanto Espana (WBA) |
| **1993-1996** | Pernell Whitaker (WBC) |
| **1994-1996** | Ike Quartey (WBA) |

(a) Robinson gained the title by defeating Tommy Bell in an elimination agreed to by the New York Commission and the NBA. Both claimed Robinson waived his title when he won the middleweight crown from LaMotta in 1951.

### Lightweights

| | |
|---|---|
| **1896-1899** | Kid Lavigne |
| **1899-1902** | Frank Erne |
| **1902-1908** | Joe Gans |
| **1908-1910** | Battling Nelson |
| **1910-1912** | Ad Wolgast |
| **1912-1914** | Willie Ritchie |
| **1914-1917** | Freddie Welsh |
| **1917-1925** | Benny Leonard* |
| **1925** | Jimmy Goodrich; Rocky Kansas |
| **1926-1930** | Sammy Mandell |
| **1930** | Al Singer; Tony Canzoneri |
| **1930-1933** | Tony Canzoneri |
| **1933-1935** | Barney Ross* |
| **1935-1936** | Tony Canzoneri |
| **1936-1938** | Lou Ambers |
| **1938** | Henry Armstrong |
| **1939** | Lou Ambers |
| **1940** | Lew Jenkins |
| **1941-1943** | Sammy Angott |
| **1944** | S. Angott (NBA); J. Zurita (NBA) |
| **1945-1951** | Ike Williams (NBA: later universal) |
| **1951-1952** | James Carter |
| **1952** | Lauro Salas; James Carter |
| **1953-1954** | James Carter |
| **1954** | Paddy De Marco; James Carter |
| **1955** | James Carter; Bud Smith |
| **1956** | Bud Smith; Joe Brown |
| **1956-1962** | Joe Brown |
| **1962-1965** | Carlos Ortiz |
| **1965** | Ismael Laguna |
| **1965-1968** | Carlos Ortiz |
| **1968-1969** | Teo Cruz |
| **1969-1970** | Mando Ramos |
| **1970** | Ismael Laguna; Ken Buchanan (WBA) |
| **1971** | Mando Ramos (WBC); Pedro Carrasco (WBC) |
| **1972-1979** | Roberto Duran* (WBA) |
| **1972** | Pedro Carrasco; Mando Ramos; Chango Carmona; Rodolfo Gonzalez (all WBC) |
| **1974-1976** | Guts Ishimatsu (WBC) |
| **1976-1977** | Esteban De Jesus (WBC) |
| **1979** | Jim Watt (WBC); Ernesto Espana (WBA) |
| **1980** | Hilmer Kenty (WBA) |
| **1981** | Alexis Arguello (WBC); Sean O'Grady (WBA); Arturo Frias (WBA) |
| **1982-1984** | Ray Mancini (WBA) |
| **1983-1984** | Edwin Rosario (WBC) |
| **1984** | Livingstone Bramble (WBA); Jose Luis Ramirez (WBC) |
| **1985-1986** | Hector (Macho) Camacho (WBC) |
| **1986** | Edwin Rosario (WBA); Jose Luis Ramirez (WBC) |
| **1987-1989** | Julio Cesar Chavez (WBA) |
| **1989-1990** | Edwin Rosario (WBA); Pernell Whitaker (WBC) |
| **1990** | Juan Nazario (WBA) |
| **1990-1992** | Pernell Whitaker* |
| **1992** | Joey Gamache (WBA); Tony Lopez (WBA) |
| **1992-1996** | Miguel Angel Gonzalez* (WBC) |

| | |
|---|---|
| **1993** | Dingaan Thobela (WBA) |
| **1993-1996** | Orzubek Nazarov (WBA) |
| **1996** | Jean-Baptiste Mendy (WBC) |
| | **Featherweights** |
| **1892-1900** | George Dixon (disputed) |
| **1900-1901** | Terry McGovern; Young Corbett* |
| **1901-1912** | Abe Attell |
| **1912-1923** | Johnny Kilbane |
| **1923** | Eugene Criqui; Johnny Dundee |
| **1923-1925** | Johnny Dundee* |
| **1925-1927** | Kid Kaplan* |
| **1927-1928** | Benny Bass; Tony Canzoneri |
| **1928-1929** | Andre Routis |
| **1929-1932** | Battling Battalino* |
| **1932-1934** | Tommy Paul (NBA) |
| **1933-1936** | Freddie Miller |
| **1936-1937** | Petey Sarron |
| **1937-1938** | Henry Armstrong* |
| **1938-1940** | Joey Archibald (a) |
| **1940-1941** | Harry Jeffra |
| **1942-1948** | Willie Pep |
| **1948-1949** | Sandy Saddler |
| **1949-1950** | Willie Pep |
| **1950-1957** | Sandy Saddler* |
| **1957-1959** | Hogan (Kid) Bassey |
| **1959-1963** | Davey Moore |
| **1963-1964** | Sugar Ramos |
| **1964-1967** | Vicente Saldivar* |
| **1968-1971** | Paul Rojas (WBA); Sho Saijo (WBA) |
| **1971-1972** | Antonio Gomez (WBA); Kuniaki Shibada (WBC) |
| **1972** | Ernesto Marcel* (WBA); Clemente Sanchez* (WBC); Jose Legra (WBC) |
| **1973-1974** | Eder Jofre (WBC) |
| **1974** | Ruben Olivares (WBA); Alexis Arguello (WBA); Bobby Chacon (WBC) |
| **1975** | Ruben Olivares (WBC); David Kotey (WBC) |
| **1976-1980** | Danny Lopez (WBC) |
| **1977-1978** | Rafael Ortega (WBA) |
| **1978** | Cecilio Lastra (WBA); Eusebio Pedrosa (WBA) |
| **1980-1982** | Salvador Sanchez (WBC) |
| **1982-1984** | Juan LaPorte (WBC) |
| **1984** | Wilfredo Gomez (WBC); Azumah Nelson (WBC) |
| **1985-1986** | Barry McGuigan (WBA) |
| **1986-1987** | Steve Cruz (WBA) |
| **1987-1991** | Antonio Esparragoza (WBA) |
| **1988-1990** | Jeff Fenech (WBC) |
| **1990-1991** | Marcos Villasana (WBC) |
| **1991-1993** | Park Yung Kyun (WBA); Paul Hodkinson (WBC) |
| **1993** | Goyo Vargas (WBC); Kevin Kelley (WBC); Eloy Rojas (WBA) |
| **1995** | Alejandro Gonzalez (WBC); Manuel Medina (WBC); Luisito Espinosa (WBC) |
| **1996** | Wilfredo Vasquez (WBA) |

(a) After Petey Scalzo knocked out Archibald in an overweight match and was refused a title bout, the NBA named Scalzo champion. NBA title succession: Scalzo, 1938-1941; Richard Lemos, 1941; Jackie Wilson, 1941-1943; Jackie Callura, 1943; Phil Terranova, 1943-1944; Sal Bartolo, 1944-1946.

## History of Heavyweight Championship Bouts

(bouts in which title changed hands)

**1889**—July 8—John L. Sullivan def. Jake Kilrain, 75, Richburg, MS. Last championship bare knuckles bout.

**1892**—Sept. 7—James J. Corbett def. John L. Sullivan, 21, New Orleans. Big gloves used for first time.

**1897**—Bob Fitzsimmons def. James J. Corbett, 14, Carson City, NV.

**1899**—June 9—James J. Jeffries def. Bob Fitzsimmons, 11, Coney Island, NY.

**1905**—James J. Jeffries retired, July 3—Marvin Hart KOd Jack Root, 12, Reno, NV. Jeffries refereed and presented the title to the victor. Jack O'Brien also claimed the title.

**1906**—Feb. 23—Tommy Burns def. Marvin Hart, 20, Los Angeles.

**1908**—Dec. 26—Jack Johnson KOd Tommy Burns, 14, Sydney, Australia. Police halted contest.

**1915**—April 5—Jess Willard KOd Jack Johnson, 26, Havana, Cuba.

**1919**—July 4—Jack Dempsey KOd Jess Willard, Toledo, OH. Willard failed to answer bell for 4th round.

**1926**—Sept. 23—Gene Tunney def. Jack Dempsey, 10, Philadelphia.

**1930**—June 12—Max Schmeling def. Jack Sharkey, 4, New York. Sharkey fouled Schmeling in a bout which was generally considered to have resulted in the election of a successor to Gene Tunney.

**1932**—June 21—Jack Sharkey def. Max Schmeling, 15, New York.

**1933**—June 29—Primo Carnera KOd Jack Sharkey, 6, New York.

**1934**—June 14—Max Baer KOd Primo Carnera, 11, New York.

**1935**—June 13—James J. Braddock def. Max Baer, 15, New York.

**1937**—June 22—Joe Louis KOd James J. Braddock, 8, Chicago.

**1949**—June 22—Following Joe Louis's retirement Ezzard Charles def. Joe Walcott, 15, Chicago; NBA recognition only.

**1951**—July 18—Joe Walcott KOd Ezzard Charles, 7, Pittsburgh.

**1952**—Sept. 23—Rocky Marciano KOd Joe Walcott, 13, Philadelphia.

**1956**—Nov. 30—Floyd Patterson KOd Archie Moore, 5, Chicago.

**1959**—June 26—Ingemar Johansson KOd Floyd Patterson, 3, New York.

**1960**—June 20—Floyd Patterson KOd Ingemar Johansson, 5, New York. First heavyweight in boxing history to regain title.

**1962**—Sept. 25—Sonny Liston KOd Floyd Patterson, 1, Chicago.

**1964**—Feb. 25—Cassius Clay (Muhammad Ali) KOd Sonny Liston, 7, Miami Beach, FL. (In 1967, Ali was stripped of his title by the WBA and others for refusing military service.)

**1970**—Feb. 16—Joe Frazier KOd Jimmy Ellis, 5, New York.

**1971**—Mar. 8—Joe Frazier def. Muhammad Ali, 15, New York.

**1973**—Jan. 22—George Foreman KOd Joe Frazier, 2, Kingston, Jamaica.

**1974**—Oct. 30—Muhammad Ali KOd George Foreman, 8, Zaire.

**1978**—Feb. 15—Leon Spinks def. Muhammad Ali, 15, Las Vegas.

**1978**—June 9—(WBC) Larry Holmes def. Ken Norton, 15, Las Vegas. (Holmes gave up title in Dec. 1983.)

**1978**—Sept. 15—(WBA) Muhammad Ali def. Leon Spinks, 15, New Orleans. (Ali retired in 1979.)

**1980**—Mar. 31—(WBA) Mike Weaver KOd John Tate, 15, Knoxville, TN.

**1982**—Dec. 10—(WBA) Michael Dokes KOd Mike Weaver, 1, Las Vegas.

**1983**—Sept. 23—(WBA) Gerrie Coetzee KOd Michael Dokes, 10, Richfield, OH.

**1984**—Aug. 31—(WBC) Pinklon Thomas def. Tim Witherspoon, 12, Las Vegas.

**1984**—Dec. 2—(WBA) Greg Page KOd Gerrie Coetzee, 8, Sun City, Bophuthatswana.

**1985**—Apr. 29—(WBA) Tony Tubbs def. Greg Page, 15, Buffalo, NY.

**1985**—Sept. 21—(IBF) Michael Spinks def. Larry Holmes, 15, Las Vegas. (Spinks relinquished title in Feb. 1987.)

**1986**—Jan. 17—(WBA) Tim Witherspoon def. Tony Tubbs, 15, Atlanta, GA.

**1986**—Mar. 23—(WBC) Trevor Berbick def. Pinklon Thomas, 12, Miami.

**1986**—Nov. 22—(WBC) Mike Tyson KOd Trevor Berbick, 2, Las Vegas.

**1986**—Dec. 12—(WBA) James (Bonecrusher) Smith KOd Tim Witherspoon, 1, New York.

**1987**—Mar. 7—(WBA, WBC) Mike Tyson def. James (Bonecrusher) Smith, 12, Las Vegas.

**1987**—Aug. 1—(WBA, WBC, IBF) Mike Tyson def. Tony Tucker, 12, Las Vegas.

**1990**—Feb. 11—(WBA, WBC, IBF) James "Buster" Douglas KOd Mike Tyson, 10, Tokyo.

**1990**—Oct. 25—(WBA, WBC, IBF) Evander Holyfield KOd James "Buster" Douglas, 3, Las Vegas.

**1992**—Nov. 13—(WBA, WBC, IBF) Riddick Bowe def. Evander Holyfield, 12, Las Vegas. (Lennox Lewis was later named WBC champion when Bowe refused to fight him.)

**1993**—Nov. 6—(WBA, IBF) Evander Holyfield def. Riddick Bowe, 12, Las Vegas.

**1994**—Apr. 22—(WBA, IBF) Michael Moorer def. Evander Holyfield, 12, Las Vegas.

**1994**—Sept. 24—(WBC) Oliver McCall KOd Lennox Lewis, 2, London.

**1994**—Nov. 5—(WBA, IBF) George Foreman KOd Michael Moorer, 10, Las Vegas. (In Mar. 1995, Foreman was stripped of the WBA title. In July, Foreman relinquished the IBF title.)

**1995**—Sept. 2—(WBC) Frank Bruno def. Oliver McCall, 12, London.

**1996**—Mar. 16—(WBC) Mike Tyson KOd Frank Bruno, 3, Las Vegas.

**1996**—Sept. 7—(WBA, WBC) Mike Tyson KOd Bruce Seldon, 1, Las Vegas. (Tyson was subsequently stripped of the WBC title.)

# RODEO

## Pro Rodeo Championship Standings in 1995

| Event | Winner | Money won |
|---|---|---|
| All Around | Joe Beaver, Huntsville, TX | $141,753 |
| Saddle Bronc | Dan Mortensen, Manhattan, MT | 145,325 |
| Bareback | Marvin Garrett, Belle Fourche, SD | 156,733 |
| Bull Riding | Jerome Davis, Archdale, NC | 135,280 |
| Calf Roping | Fred Whitfield, Hockley, TX | 145,760 |
| Steer Wrestling | Ote Berry, Checotah, OK | 117,987 |
| Steer Roping | Guy Allen, Lovington, NM | $71,040 |
| Team Roping | Bobby Hurley, Ceres, CA (head) & Allen Bach, Toltec, AZ (heel) | 81,658 |
| Barrel Racing | Sherry Cervi, Marana, AZ | 157,172 |
| Wrangler Bullfighting | Ronny Sparks, Texarkana, TX | 47,897 |

## Pro Rodeo Cowboy All-Around Champions

| Year | Winner | Money won |
|---|---|---|
| 1972 | Phil Lyne, George West, TX | $60,852 |
| 1973 | Larry Mahan, Dallas, TX | 64,447 |
| 1974 | Tom Ferguson, Miami, OK | 66,929 |
| 1975 | Leo Camarillo, Oakdale, CA | 50,300 |
| | Tom Ferguson, Miami, OK | 50,300 |
| 1976 | Tom Ferguson, Miami, OK | 87,908 |
| 1977 | Tom Ferguson, Miami, OK | 76,730 |
| 1978 | Tom Ferguson, Miami, OK | 103,734 |
| 1979 | Tom Ferguson, Miami, OK | 96,272 |
| 1980 | Paul Tierney, Rapid City, SD | 105,568 |
| 1981 | Jimmie Cooper, Monument, NM | 105,862 |
| 1982 | Chris Lybbert, Coyote, CA | 123,709 |
| 1983 | Roy Cooper, Durant, OK | 153,391 |
| 1984 | Dee Pickett, Caldwell, ID | $122,618 |
| 1985 | Lewis Feild, Elk Ridge, UT | 130,347 |
| 1986 | Lewis Feild, Elk Ridge, UT | 166,042 |
| 1987 | Lewis Feild, Elk Ridge, UT | 144,335 |
| 1988 | Dave Appleton, Arlington, TX | 121,546 |
| 1989 | Ty Murray, Odessa, TX | 134,806 |
| 1990 | Ty Murray, Stephenville, TX | 213,772 |
| 1991 | Ty Murray, Stephenville, TX | 244,230 |
| 1992 | Ty Murray, Stephenville, TX | 225,992 |
| 1993 | Ty Murray, Stephenville, TX | 297,896 |
| 1994 | Ty Murray, Stephenville, TX | 246,170 |
| 1995 | Joe Beaver, Huntsville, TX | 141,753 |

# BOATING

## The America's Cup

In the 1995 America's Cup match, the New Zealand yacht *Black Magic 1* defeated the U.S. yacht *Young America* 5-0 in the waters off San Diego, CA. It was only the 2d time since 1851 (the 1st since 1983) that the U.S. lost the Cup. *Black Magic 1* was skippered by Russell Coutts. The next competition was scheduled for 1999-2000 in New Zealand.

### Winners of the America's Cup

| Year | Winner |
|---|---|
| 1851 | America |
| 1870 | Magic defeated Cambria, England, (1-0) |
| 1871 | Columbia (first three races) and Sappho (last two races) defeated Livonia, England, (4-1) |
| 1876 | Madeline defeated Countess of Dufferin, Canada, (2-0) |
| 1881 | Mischief defeated Atalanta, Canada, (2-0) |
| 1885 | Puritan defeated Genesta, England, (2-0) |
| 1886 | Mayflower defeated Galatea, England, (2-0) |
| 1887 | Volunteer defeated Thistle, Scotland, (2-0) |
| 1893 | Vigilant defeated Valkyrie II, England, (3-0) |
| 1895 | Defender defeated Valkyrie III, England, (3-0) |
| 1899 | Columbia defeated Shamrock, England, (3-0) |
| 1901 | Columbia defeated Shamrock II, England, (3-0) |
| 1903 | Reliance defeated Shamrock III, England, (3-0) |
| 1920 | Resolute defeated Shamrock IV, England, (3-2) |
| 1930 | Enterprise defeated Shamrock V, England, (4-0) |
| 1934 | Rainbow defeated Endeavour, England, (4-2) |
| 1937 | Ranger defeated Endeavour II, England, (4-0) |
| 1958 | Columbia defeated Sceptre, England, (4-0) |
| 1962 | Weatherly defeated Gretel, Australia, (4-1) |
| 1964 | Constellation defeated Sovereign, England, (4-0) |
| 1967 | Intrepid defeated Dame Pattie, Australia, (4-0) |
| 1970 | Intrepid defeated Gretel II, Australia, (4-1) |
| 1974 | Courageous defeated Southern Cross, Australia, (4-0) |
| 1977 | Courageous defeated Australia, Australia, (4-0) |
| 1980 | Freedom defeated Australia, Australia, (4-1) |
| 1983 | Australia II, Australia, defeated Liberty, (4-3) |
| 1987 | Stars & Stripes defeated Kookaburra III, Australia, (4-0) |
| 1988 | Stars & Stripes defeated New Zealand, New Zealand, (2-0) |
| 1992 | America³ defeated Il Moro di Venezia, Italy, (4-1) |
| 1995 | Black Magic 1, New Zealand, defeated Young America (5-0) |

## American Power Boat Assn. Gold Cup Champions

| Year | Boat | Driver |
|---|---|---|
| 1975 | Pay 'N Pak | George Henley |
| 1976 | Miss U.S. | Tom D'Eath |
| 1977 | Atlas Van Lines | Bill Muncey |
| 1978 | Atlas Van Lines | Bill Muncey |
| 1979 | Atlas Van Lines | Bill Muncey |
| 1980 | Miss Budweiser | Dean Chenoweth |
| 1981 | Miss Budweiser | Dean Chenoweth |
| 1982 | Atlas Van Lines | Chip Hanauer |
| 1983 | Atlas Van Lines | Chip Hanauer |
| 1984 | Atlas Van Lines | Chip Hanauer |
| 1985 | Miller American | Chip Hanauer |
| 1986 | Miller American | Chip Hanauer |
| 1987 | Miller American | Chip Hanauer |
| 1988 | Miller American | Chip Hanauer |
| 1989 | Miss Budweiser | Tom D'Eath |
| 1990 | Miss Budweiser | Tom D'Eath |
| 1991 | Winston Eagle | Mark Tate |
| 1992 | Miss Budweiser | Chip Hanauer |
| 1993 | Miss Budweiser | Chip Hanauer |
| 1994 | Smokin' Joe's | Mark Tate |
| 1995 | Miss Budweiser | Chip Hanauer |
| 1996 | Pico's American Dream | Dave Villwock |

# DOGS

## Westminster Kennel Club

| Year | Best-in-show | Breed | Owner |
|---|---|---|---|
| 1987 | Ch. Covy Tucker Hill's Manhattan | German shepherd | Shirley Braunstein & Jane Firestone |
| 1988 | Ch. Great Elms Prince Charming II | Pomeranian | Skip Piazza & Olga Baker |
| 1989 | Ch. Royal Tudor's Wild As The Wind | Doberman | Sue & Art Kemp, Richard & Carolyn Vida, Beth Wilhite |
| 1990 | Ch. Wendessa Crown Prince | Pekingese | Ed Jenner |
| 1991 | Ch. Whisperwind on a Carousel | Poodle | Joan & Frederick Hartsock |
| 1992 | Ch. Registry's Lonesome Dove | Fox terrier | Marion & Sam Lawrence |
| 1993 | Ch. Salilyn's Condor | English springer spaniel | Donna & Roger Herzig |
| 1994 | Ch. Chidley Willum | Norwich terrier | Ruth Cooper & Patricia Lussier |
| 1995 | Ch. Gaelforce Post Script | Scottish terrier | Dr. Vandra Huber & Dr. Joe Kinnarney |
| 1996 | Ch. Clussexx Country Sunrise | Clumber spaniel | Judith & Richard Zeleski |

## Iditarod Trail Sled Dog Race in 1996

Jeff King won the 1996 Iditarod Trail Sled Dog Race, Mar. 12, with a time of 9 days 5 hours 43 minutes. For winning the 1,150-mile race from Anchorage to Nome, AK, King received $50,000 in prize money, as well as a pickup truck. King had also won the race in 1993.

# BASEBALL

## 1996 Review: The Year of the Home Run

In 1996, the hits just kept on coming. . . and going. The major league record for the most total home runs hit in a season—4,458, set in 1987—was obliterated; 4,962 homers were smashed in 1996. The team record for home runs, 240—previously held by the 1961 Yankees—was broken not by one but by three teams: the Baltimore Orioles (257), Seattle Mariners (245), and Oakland Athletics (243); the Colorado Rockies tied the National League record of 220. A total of 17 players hit 40 or more homers, and 43 hit 30 or more, breaking the old marks of 8 and 28, respectively. In other 1996 news: Eddie Murray followed Hank Aaron and Willie Mays to become only the 3d player with 500 or more home runs and 3,000 or more hits. Paul Molitor joined the elite 3,000-hit club, becoming the first player to reach that plateau on a triple; the 40-year-old Molitor led the American League in hits (225) and batted an impressive .341. Four illustrious careers came to an end in 1996: The heart and soul of the Dodgers, manager Tommy Lasorda, retired midseason because of heart problems, while St. Louis Cardinals shortstop wizard Ozzie Smith, Florida Marlins slugger Andre Dawson, and longtime Detroit Tigers shortstop Alan Trammell all called it quits at season's end.

## Major League Pennant Winners, 1901–1968

### National League

| Year | Winner | Won | Lost | Pct | Manager |
|---|---|---|---|---|---|
| 1901 | Pittsburgh | 90 | 49 | .647 | Clarke |
| 1902 | Pittsburgh | 103 | 36 | .741 | Clarke |
| 1903 | Pittsburgh | 91 | 49 | .650 | Clarke |
| 1904 | New York | 106 | 47 | .693 | McGraw |
| 1905 | New York | 105 | 48 | .686 | McGraw |
| 1906 | Chicago | 116 | 36 | .763 | Chance |
| 1907 | Chicago | 107 | 45 | .704 | Chance |
| 1908 | Chicago | 99 | 55 | .643 | Chance |
| 1909 | Pittsburgh | 110 | 42 | .724 | Clarke |
| 1910 | Chicago | 104 | 50 | .675 | Chance |
| 1911 | New York | 99 | 54 | .647 | McGraw |
| 1912 | New York | 103 | 48 | .682 | McGraw |
| 1913 | New York | 101 | 51 | .664 | McGraw |
| 1914 | Boston | 94 | 59 | .614 | Stallings |
| 1915 | Philadelphia | 90 | 62 | .592 | Moran |
| 1916 | Brooklyn | 94 | 60 | .610 | Robinson |
| 1917 | New York | 98 | 56 | .636 | McGraw |
| 1918 | Chicago | 84 | 45 | .651 | Mitchell |
| 1919 | Cincinnati | 96 | 44 | .686 | Moran |
| 1920 | Brooklyn | 93 | 60 | .604 | Robinson |
| 1921 | New York | 94 | 56 | .614 | McGraw |
| 1922 | New York | 93 | 61 | .604 | McGraw |
| 1923 | New York | 95 | 58 | .621 | McGraw |
| 1924 | New York | 93 | 60 | .608 | McGraw |
| 1925 | Pittsburgh | 95 | 58 | .621 | McKechnie |
| 1926 | St. Louis | 89 | 65 | .578 | Hornsby |
| 1927 | Pittsburgh | 94 | 60 | .610 | Bush |
| 1928 | St. Louis | 95 | 59 | .617 | McKechnie |
| 1929 | Chicago | 98 | 54 | .645 | McCarthy |
| 1930 | St. Louis | 92 | 62 | .597 | Street |
| 1931 | St. Louis | 101 | 53 | .656 | Street |
| 1932 | Chicago | 90 | 64 | .584 | Grimm |
| 1933 | New York | 91 | 61 | .599 | Terry |
| 1934 | St. Louis | 95 | 58 | .621 | Frisch |
| 1935 | Chicago | 100 | 54 | .649 | Grimm |
| 1936 | New York | 91 | 62 | .597 | Terry |
| 1937 | New York | 95 | 57 | .625 | Terry |
| 1938 | Chicago | 89 | 63 | .586 | Hartnett |
| 1939 | Cincinnati | 97 | 57 | .630 | McKechnie |
| 1940 | Cincinnati | 100 | 53 | .654 | McKechnie |
| 1941 | Brooklyn | 100 | 54 | .649 | Durocher |
| 1942 | St. Louis | 106 | 48 | .688 | Southworth |
| 1943 | St. Louis | 105 | 49 | .682 | Southworth |
| 1944 | St. Louis | 105 | 49 | .682 | Southworth |
| 1945 | Chicago | 98 | 56 | .636 | Grimm |
| 1946 | St. Louis | 98 | 58 | .628 | Dyer |
| 1947 | Brooklyn | 94 | 60 | .610 | Shotton |
| 1948 | Boston | 91 | 62 | .595 | Southworth |
| 1949 | Brooklyn | 97 | 57 | .630 | Shotton |
| 1950 | Philadelphia | 91 | 63 | .591 | Sawyer |
| 1951 | New York | 98 | 59 | .624 | Durocher |
| 1952 | Brooklyn | 96 | 57 | .627 | Dressen |
| 1953 | Brooklyn | 105 | 49 | .682 | Dressen |
| 1954 | New York | 97 | 57 | .630 | Durocher |
| 1955 | Brooklyn | 98 | 55 | .641 | Alston |
| 1956 | Brooklyn | 93 | 61 | .604 | Alston |
| 1957 | Milwaukee | 95 | 59 | .617 | Haney |
| 1958 | Milwaukee | 92 | 62 | .597 | Haney |
| 1959 | Los Angeles | 88 | 68 | .564 | Alston |
| 1960 | Pittsburgh | 95 | 59 | .617 | Murtaugh |
| 1961 | Cincinnati | 93 | 61 | .604 | Hutchinson |
| 1962 | San Francisco | 103 | 62 | .624 | Dark |
| 1963 | Los Angeles | 99 | 63 | .611 | Alston |
| 1964 | St. Louis | 93 | 69 | .574 | Keane |
| 1965 | Los Angeles | 97 | 65 | .599 | Alston |
| 1966 | Los Angeles | 95 | 67 | .586 | Alston |
| 1967 | St. Louis | 101 | 60 | .627 | Schoendienst |
| 1968 | St. Louis | 97 | 65 | .599 | Schoendienst |

### American League

| Year | Winner | Won | Lost | Pct | Manager |
|---|---|---|---|---|---|
| 1901 | Chicago | 83 | 53 | .610 | Griffith |
| 1902 | Philadelphia | 83 | 53 | .610 | Mack |
| 1903 | Boston | 91 | 47 | .659 | Collins |
| 1904 | Boston | 95 | 59 | .617 | Collins |
| 1905 | Philadelphia | 92 | 56 | .622 | Mack |
| 1906 | Chicago | 93 | 58 | .616 | Jones |
| 1907 | Detroit | 92 | 58 | .613 | Jennings |
| 1908 | Detroit | 90 | 63 | .588 | Jennings |
| 1909 | Detroit | 98 | 54 | .645 | Jennings |
| 1910 | Philadelphia | 102 | 48 | .680 | Mack |
| 1911 | Philadelphia | 101 | 50 | .669 | Mack |
| 1912 | Boston | 105 | 47 | .691 | Stahl |
| 1913 | Philadelphia | 96 | 57 | .627 | Mack |
| 1914 | Philadelphia | 99 | 53 | .651 | Mack |
| 1915 | Boston | 101 | 50 | .669 | Carrigan |
| 1916 | Boston | 91 | 63 | .591 | Carrigan |
| 1917 | Chicago | 100 | 54 | .649 | Rowland |
| 1918 | Boston | 75 | 51 | .595 | Barrow |
| 1919 | Chicago | 88 | 52 | .629 | Gleason |
| 1920 | Cleveland | 98 | 56 | .636 | Speaker |
| 1921 | New York | 98 | 55 | .641 | Huggins |
| 1922 | New York | 94 | 60 | .610 | Huggins |
| 1923 | New York | 98 | 54 | .645 | Huggins |
| 1924 | Washington | 92 | 62 | .597 | Harris |
| 1925 | Washington | 96 | 55 | .636 | Harris |
| 1926 | New York | 91 | 63 | .591 | Huggins |
| 1927 | New York | 110 | 44 | .714 | Huggins |
| 1928 | New York | 101 | 53 | .656 | Huggins |
| 1929 | Philadelphia | 104 | 46 | .693 | Mack |
| 1930 | Philadelphia | 102 | 52 | .662 | Mack |
| 1931 | Philadelphia | 107 | 45 | .704 | Mack |
| 1932 | New York | 107 | 47 | .695 | McCarthy |
| 1933 | Washington | 99 | 53 | .651 | Cronin |
| 1934 | Detroit | 101 | 53 | .656 | Cochrane |
| 1935 | Detroit | 93 | 58 | .616 | Cochrane |
| 1936 | New York | 102 | 51 | .667 | McCarthy |
| 1937 | New York | 102 | 52 | .662 | McCarthy |
| 1938 | New York | 99 | 53 | .651 | McCarthy |
| 1939 | New York | 106 | 45 | .702 | McCarthy |
| 1940 | Detroit | 90 | 64 | .584 | Baker |
| 1941 | New York | 101 | 53 | .656 | McCarthy |
| 1942 | New York | 103 | 51 | .669 | McCarthy |
| 1943 | New York | 98 | 56 | .636 | McCarthy |
| 1944 | St. Louis | 89 | 65 | .578 | Sewell |
| 1945 | Detroit | 88 | 65 | .575 | O'Neill |
| 1946 | Boston | 104 | 50 | .675 | Cronin |
| 1947 | New York | 97 | 57 | .630 | Harris |
| 1948 | Cleveland | 97 | 58 | .626 | Boudreau |
| 1949 | New York | 97 | 57 | .630 | Stengel |
| 1950 | New York | 98 | 56 | .636 | Stengel |
| 1951 | New York | 98 | 56 | .636 | Stengel |
| 1952 | New York | 95 | 59 | .617 | Stengel |
| 1953 | New York | 99 | 52 | .656 | Stengel |
| 1954 | Cleveland | 111 | 43 | .721 | Lopez |
| 1955 | New York | 96 | 58 | .623 | Stengel |
| 1956 | New York | 97 | 57 | .630 | Stengel |
| 1957 | New York | 98 | 56 | .636 | Stengel |
| 1958 | New York | 92 | 62 | .597 | Stengel |
| 1959 | Chicago | 94 | 60 | .610 | Lopez |
| 1960 | New York | 97 | 57 | .630 | Stengel |
| 1961 | New York | 109 | 53 | .673 | Houk |
| 1962 | New York | 96 | 66 | .593 | Houk |
| 1963 | New York | 104 | 57 | .646 | Houk |
| 1964 | New York | 99 | 63 | .611 | Berra |
| 1965 | Minnesota | 102 | 60 | .630 | Mele |
| 1966 | Baltimore | 97 | 63 | .606 | Bauer |
| 1967 | Boston | 92 | 70 | .568 | Williams |
| 1968 | Detroit | 103 | 59 | .636 | Smith |

# Major League Pennant Winners, 1969-1996

## National League

| Year | East Winner | W | L | Pct | Manager | West Winner | W | L | Pct | Manager | Pennant winner |
|---|---|---|---|---|---|---|---|---|---|---|---|
| 1969 | N.Y. Mets | 100 | 62 | .617 | Hodges | Atlanta | 93 | 69 | .574 | Harris | New York |
| 1970 | Pittsburgh | 89 | 73 | .549 | Murtaugh | Cincinnati | 102 | 60 | .630 | Anderson | Cincinnati |
| 1971 | Pittsburgh | 97 | 65 | .599 | Murtaugh | San Francisco | 90 | 72 | .556 | Fox | Pittsburgh |
| 1972 | Pittsburgh | 96 | 59 | .619 | Virdon | Cincinnati | 95 | 59 | .617 | Anderson | Cincinnati |
| 1973 | N.Y. Mets | 82 | 79 | .509 | Berra | Cincinnati | 99 | 63 | .611 | Anderson | New York |
| 1974 | Pittsburgh | 88 | 74 | .543 | Murtaugh | Los Angeles | 102 | 60 | .630 | Alston | Los Angeles |
| 1975 | Pittsburgh | 92 | 69 | .571 | Murtaugh | Cincinnati | 108 | 54 | .667 | Anderson | Cincinnati |
| 1976 | Philadelphia | 101 | 61 | .623 | Ozark | Cincinnati | 102 | 60 | .630 | Anderson | Cincinnati |
| 1977 | Philadelphia | 101 | 61 | .623 | Ozark | Los Angeles | 98 | 64 | .605 | Lasorda | Los Angeles |
| 1978 | Philadelphia | 90 | 72 | .556 | Ozark | Los Angeles | 95 | 67 | .586 | Lasorda | Los Angeles |
| 1979 | Pittsburgh | 98 | 64 | .605 | Tanner | Cincinnati | 90 | 71 | .559 | McNamara | Pittsburgh |
| 1980 | Philadelphia | 91 | 71 | .562 | Green | Houston | 93 | 70 | .571 | Virdon | Philadelphia |
| 1981(a) | Philadelphia | 34 | 21 | .618 | Green | Los Angeles | 36 | 21 | .632 | Lasorda | (c) |
| 1981(b) | Montreal | 30 | 23 | .566 | Williams, Fanning | Houston | 33 | 20 | .623 | Virdon | Los Angeles |
| 1982 | St. Louis | 92 | 70 | .568 | Herzog | Atlanta | 89 | 73 | .549 | Torre | St. Louis |
| 1983 | Philadelphia | 90 | 72 | .556 | Corrales, Owens | Los Angeles | 91 | 71 | .562 | Lasorda | Philadelphia |
| 1984 | Chicago | 96 | 65 | .596 | Frey | San Diego | 92 | 70 | .568 | Williams | San Diego |
| 1985 | St. Louis | 101 | 61 | .623 | Herzog | Los Angeles | 95 | 67 | .586 | Lasorda | St. Louis |
| 1986 | N.Y. Mets | 108 | 54 | .667 | Johnson | Houston | 96 | 66 | .593 | Lanier | New York |
| 1987 | St. Louis | 95 | 67 | .586 | Herzog | San Francisco | 90 | 72 | .556 | Craig | St. Louis |
| 1988 | N.Y. Mets | 100 | 60 | .625 | Johnson | Los Angeles | 94 | 67 | .584 | Lasorda | Los Angeles |
| 1989 | Chicago | 93 | 69 | .571 | Zimmer | San Francisco | 92 | 70 | .568 | Craig | San Francisco |
| 1990 | Pittsburgh | 95 | 67 | .586 | Leyland | Cincinnati | 91 | 71 | .562 | Piniella | Cincinnati |
| 1991 | Pittsburgh | 98 | 64 | .605 | Leyland | Atlanta | 94 | 68 | .580 | Cox | Atlanta |
| 1992 | Pittsburgh | 96 | 66 | .593 | Leyland | Atlanta | 98 | 64 | .605 | Cox | Atlanta |
| 1993 | Philadelphia | 97 | 65 | .599 | Fregosi | Atlanta | 104 | 58 | .642 | Cox | Philadelphia |

| Year | Division | Winner | W | L | Pct. | Manager | Playoffs | Pennant Winner |
|---|---|---|---|---|---|---|---|---|
| 1994(d) | **East** | Montreal | 74 | 40 | .649 | Alou | — | — |
| | **Central** | Cincinnati | 66 | 48 | .579 | Johnson | | |
| | **West** | Los Angeles | 58 | 56 | .509 | Lasorda | | |
| 1995 | **East** | Atlanta | 90 | 54 | .625 | Cox | Atlanta 3, Colorado* 1 | Atlanta |
| | **Central** | Cincinnati | 85 | 59 | .590 | Johnson | Cincinnati 3, Los Angeles 0 | |
| | **West** | Los Angeles | 78 | 66 | .542 | Lasorda | Atlanta 4, Cincinnati 0 | |
| 1996 | **East** | Atlanta | 96 | 66 | .593 | Cox | Atlanta 3, Los Angeles* 0 | Atlanta |
| | **Central** | St. Louis | 88 | 74 | .543 | La Russa | St. Louis 3, San Diego 0 | |
| | **West** | San Diego | 91 | 71 | .562 | Bochy | Atlanta 4, St. Louis 3 | |

## American League

| Year | East Winner | W | L | Pct | Manager | West Winner | W | L | Pct | Manager | Pennant winner |
|---|---|---|---|---|---|---|---|---|---|---|---|
| 1969 | Baltimore | 109 | 53 | .673 | Weaver | Minnesota | 97 | 65 | .599 | Martin | Baltimore |
| 1970 | Baltimore | 108 | 54 | .667 | Weaver | Minnesota | 98 | 64 | .605 | Rigney | Baltimore |
| 1971 | Baltimore | 101 | 57 | .639 | Weaver | Oakland | 101 | 60 | .627 | Williams | Baltimore |
| 1972 | Detroit | 86 | 70 | .551 | Martin | Oakland | 93 | 62 | .600 | Williams | Oakland |
| 1973 | Baltimore | 97 | 65 | .599 | Weaver | Oakland | 94 | 68 | .580 | Williams | Oakland |
| 1974 | Baltimore | 91 | 71 | .562 | Weaver | Oakland | 90 | 72 | .556 | Dark | Oakland |
| 1975 | Boston | 95 | 65 | .594 | Johnson | Oakland | 98 | 64 | .605 | Dark | Boston |
| 1976 | New York | 97 | 62 | .610 | Martin | Kansas City | 90 | 72 | .556 | Herzog | New York |
| 1977 | New York | 100 | 62 | .617 | Martin | Kansas City | 102 | 60 | .630 | Herzog | New York |
| 1978 | New York | 100 | 63 | .613 | Martin, Lemon | Kansas City | 92 | 70 | .568 | Herzog | New York |
| 1979 | Baltimore | 102 | 57 | .642 | Weaver | California | 88 | 74 | .543 | Fregosi | Baltimore |
| 1980 | New York | 103 | 59 | .636 | Howser | Kansas City | 97 | 65 | .599 | Frey | Kansas City |
| 1981(a) | New York | 34 | 22 | .607 | Michael | Oakland | 37 | 23 | .617 | Martin | (c) |
| 1981(b) | Milwaukee | 31 | 22 | .585 | Rodgers | Kansas City | 30 | 23 | .566 | Frey, Howser | New York |
| 1982 | Milwaukee | 95 | 67 | .586 | Rodgers, Kuenn | California | 93 | 69 | .574 | Mauch | Milwaukee |
| 1983 | Baltimore | 98 | 64 | .605 | Altobelli | Chicago | 99 | 63 | .611 | LaRussa | Baltimore |
| 1984 | Detroit | 104 | 58 | .642 | Anderson | Kansas City | 84 | 78 | .519 | Howser | Detroit |
| 1985 | Toronto | 99 | 62 | .615 | Cox | Kansas City | 91 | 71 | .562 | Howser | Kansas City |
| 1986 | Boston | 95 | 66 | .590 | McNamara | California | 92 | 70 | .568 | Mauch | Boston |
| 1987 | Detroit | 98 | 64 | .605 | Anderson | Minnesota | 85 | 77 | .525 | Kelly | Minnesota |
| 1988 | Boston | 89 | 73 | .549 | McNamara, Morgan | Oakland | 104 | 58 | .642 | La Russa | Oakland |
| 1989 | Toronto | 89 | 73 | .549 | Williams, Gaston | Oakland | 99 | 63 | .611 | La Russa | Oakland |
| 1990 | Boston | 88 | 74 | .543 | Morgan | Oakland | 103 | 59 | .636 | La Russa | Oakland |
| 1991 | Toronto | 91 | 71 | .562 | Gaston | Minnesota | 95 | 67 | .586 | Kelly | Minnesota |
| 1992 | Toronto | 96 | 66 | .593 | Gaston | Oakland | 96 | 66 | .593 | La Russa | Toronto |
| 1993 | Toronto | 95 | 67 | .586 | Gaston | Chicago | 94 | 68 | .580 | Lamont | Toronto |

| Year | Division | Winner | W | L | Pct. | Manager | Playoffs | Pennant Winner |
|---|---|---|---|---|---|---|---|---|
| 1994(d) | East | New York | 70 | 43 | .619 | Showalter | — | — |
| | Central | Chicago | 67 | 46 | .593 | Lamont | | |
| | West | Texas | 52 | 62 | .456 | Kennedy | | |
| 1995 | East | Boston | 86 | 58 | .597 | Kennedy | Cleveland 3, Boston 0 | Cleveland |
| | Central | Cleveland | 100 | 44 | .694 | Hargrove | Seattle 3, New York* 2 | |
| | West | Seattle | 79 | 66 | .545 | Piniella | Cleveland 4, Seattle 2 | |
| 1996 | East | New York | 92 | 70 | .568 | Torre | Baltimore* 3, Cleveland 1 | New York |
| | Central | Cleveland | 99 | 62 | .615 | Hargrove | New York 3, Texas 1 | |
| | West | Texas | 90 | 72 | .556 | Oates | New York 4, Baltimore* 1 | |

*Wild card team. (a) First half. (b) Second half. (c) Montreal, L.A., N.Y. Yankees, and Oakland won the divisional playoffs. (d) In Aug. 1994, a players' strike began that caused the cancellation of the remainder of the season, the playoffs, and the World Series. Teams listed as division "winners" for 1994 were leading their divisions at the time of the strike.

## *The Sporting News* Gold Glove Awards in 1996

**National League**

Greg Maddux, Atlanta, pitcher
Charles Johnson, Florida, catcher
Mark Grace, Chicago, first base
Craig Biggio, Houston, second base
Ken Caminiti, San Diego, third base
Barry Larkin, Cincinnati, shortstop
Barry Bonds, San Francisco, outfield
Steve Finley, San Diego, outfield
Marquis Grissom, Montreal, outfield

**American League**

Mike Mussina, Baltimore, pitcher
Ivan Rodriguez, Texas, catcher
J. T. Snow, California, first base
Roberto Alomar, Toronto, second base
Robin Ventura, Chicago, third base
Omar Vizquel, Cleveland, shortstop
Jay Buhner, Seattle, outfield
Ken Griffey, Jr., Seattle, outfield
Kenny Lofton, Cleveland, outfield

The following are the players at each position who have won the most Gold Gloves since the award was instituted in 1957.

| | | |
|---|---|---|
| Pitcher: | Jim Kaat | 16 |
| | Bob Gibson | 9 |
| Catcher: | Johnny Bench | 10 |
| | Bob Boone | 7 |
| First base: | Keith Hernandez | 11 |
| | Don Mattingly | 9 |
| Second base: | Ryne Sandberg | 9 |
| | Bill Mazeroski | 8 |
| | Frank White | 8 |
| Third base: | Brooks Robinson | 16 |
| | Mike Schmidt | 10 |
| Shortstop: | Ozzie Smith | 13 |
| | Luis Aparicio | 9 |
| Outfield: | Roberto Clemente | 12 |
| | Willie Mays | 12 |
| | Al Kaline | 10 |
| | Paul Blair | 8 |
| | Dwight Evans | 8 |
| | Garry Maddox | 8 |

## Home Run Leaders

**National League**

| Year | Player, Team | HR |
|---|---|---|
| 1901 | Sam Crawford, Cincinnati | 16 |
| 1902 | Thomas Leach, Pittsburgh | 6 |
| 1903 | James Sheckard, Brooklyn | 9 |
| 1904 | Harry Lumley, Brooklyn | 9 |
| 1905 | Fred Odwell, Cincinnati | 9 |
| 1906 | Timothy Jordan, Brooklyn | 12 |
| 1907 | David Brain, Boston | 10 |
| 1908 | Timothy Jordan, Brooklyn | 12 |
| 1909 | Red Murray, New York | 7 |
| 1910 | Fred Beck, Boston; Frank Schulte, Chicago | 10 |
| 1911 | Frank Schulte, Chicago | 21 |
| 1912 | Henry Zimmerman, Chicago | 14 |
| 1913 | Gavvy Cravath, Philadelphia | 19 |
| 1914 | Gavvy Cravath, Philadelphia | 19 |
| 1915 | Gavvy Cravath, Philadelphia | 24 |
| 1916 | Dave Robertson, N.Y.; Fred (Cy) Williams, Chi. | 12 |
| 1917 | Dave Robertson, N.Y.; Gavvy Cravath, Phi. | 12 |
| 1918 | Gavvy Cravath, Philadelphia | 8 |
| 1919 | Gavvy Cravath, Philadelphia | 12 |
| 1920 | Cy Williams, Philadelphia | 15 |
| 1921 | George Kelly, New York | 23 |
| 1922 | Rogers Hornsby, St. Louis | 42 |
| 1923 | Cy Williams, Philadelphia | 41 |
| 1924 | Jacques Fournier, Brooklyn | 27 |
| 1925 | Rogers Hornsby, St. Louis | 39 |
| 1926 | Hack Wilson, Chicago | 21 |
| 1927 | Hack Wilson, Chicago; Cy Williams, Philadelphia | 30 |
| 1928 | Hack Wilson, Chicago; Jim Bottomley, St. Louis | 31 |
| 1929 | Chuck Klein, Philadelphia | 43 |
| 1930 | Hack Wilson, Chicago | 56 |
| 1931 | Chuck Klein, Philadelphia | 31 |
| 1932 | Chuck Klein, Philadelphia; Mel Ott, New York | 38 |
| 1933 | Chuck Klein, Philadelphia | 28 |
| 1934 | Rip Collins, St. Louis; Mel Ott, New York | 35 |
| 1935 | Walter Berger, Boston | 34 |
| 1936 | Mel Ott, New York | 33 |
| 1937 | Mel Ott, New York; Joe Medwick, St. Louis | 31 |
| 1938 | Mel Ott, New York | 36 |
| 1939 | John Mize, St. Louis | 28 |
| 1940 | John Mize, St. Louis | 43 |
| 1941 | Dolph Camilli, Brooklyn | 34 |
| 1942 | Mel Ott, New York | 30 |
| 1943 | Bill Nicholson, Chicago | 29 |
| 1944 | Bill Nicholson, Chicago | 33 |
| 1945 | Tommy Holmes, Boston | 28 |
| 1946 | Ralph Kiner, Pittsburgh | 23 |
| 1947 | Ralph Kiner, Pittsburgh; John Mize, New York | 51 |
| 1948 | Ralph Kiner, Pittsburgh; John Mize, New York | 40 |
| 1949 | Ralph Kiner, Pittsburgh | 54 |
| 1950 | Ralph Kiner, Pittsburgh | 47 |
| 1951 | Ralph Kiner, Pittsburgh | 42 |
| 1952 | Ralph Kiner, Pittsburgh; Hank Sauer, Chicago | 37 |
| 1953 | Ed Mathews, Milwaukee | 47 |
| 1954 | Ted Kluszewski, Cincinnati | 49 |
| 1955 | Willie Mays, New York | 51 |
| 1956 | Duke Snider, Brooklyn | 43 |
| 1957 | Hank Aaron, Milwaukee | 44 |
| 1958 | Ernie Banks, Chicago | 47 |
| 1959 | Ed Mathews, Milwaukee | 46 |
| 1960 | Ernie Banks, Chicago | 41 |
| 1961 | Orlando Cepeda, San Francisco | 46 |
| 1962 | Willie Mays, San Francisco | 49 |
| 1963 | Hank Aaron, Milwaukee; Willie McCovey, S.F. | 44 |

**American League**

| Year | Player, Team | HR |
|---|---|---|
| 1901 | Napoleon Lajoie, Philadelphia | 13 |
| 1902 | Socks Seybold, Philadelphia | 16 |
| 1903 | Buck Freeman, Boston | 13 |
| 1904 | Harry Davis, Philadelphia | 10 |
| 1905 | Harry Davis, Philadelphia | 8 |
| 1906 | Harry Davis, Philadelphia | 12 |
| 1907 | Harry Davis, Philadelphia | 8 |
| 1908 | Sam Crawford, Detroit | 7 |
| 1909 | Ty Cobb, Detroit | 9 |
| 1910 | Jake Stahl, Boston | 10 |
| 1911 | J. Franklin Baker, Philadelphia | 9 |
| 1912 | J. Franklin Baker, Philadelphia; Tris Speaker, Boston | 10 |
| 1913 | J. Franklin, Baker, Philadelphia | 13 |
| 1914 | J. Franklin, Baker, Philadelphia | 9 |
| 1915 | Robert Roth, Chicago-Cleveland | 7 |
| 1916 | Wally Pipp, New York | 12 |
| 1917 | Wally Pipp, New York | 9 |
| 1918 | Babe Ruth, Boston; Tilly Walker, Philadelphia | 11 |
| 1919 | Babe Ruth, Boston | 29 |
| 1920 | Babe Ruth, New York | 54 |
| 1921 | Babe Ruth, New York | 59 |
| 1922 | Ken Williams, St. Louis | 39 |
| 1923 | Babe Ruth, New York | 41 |
| 1924 | Babe Ruth, New York | 46 |
| 1925 | Bob Meusel, New York | 33 |
| 1926 | Babe Ruth, New York | 47 |
| 1927 | Babe Ruth, New York | 60 |
| 1928 | Babe Ruth, New York | 54 |
| 1929 | Babe Ruth, New York | 46 |
| 1930 | Babe Ruth, New York | 49 |
| 1931 | Babe Ruth, Lou Gehrig, New York | 46 |
| 1932 | Jimmie Foxx, Philadelphia | 58 |
| 1933 | Jimmie Foxx, Philadelphia | 48 |
| 1934 | Lou Gehrig, New York | 49 |
| 1935 | Jimmie Foxx, Philadelphia; Hank Greenberg, Detroit | 36 |
| 1936 | Lou Gehrig, New York | 49 |
| 1937 | Joe DiMaggio, New York | 46 |
| 1938 | Hank Greenberg, Detroit | 58 |
| 1939 | Jimmie Foxx, Boston | 35 |
| 1940 | Hank Greenberg, Detroit | 41 |
| 1941 | Ted Williams, Boston | 37 |
| 1942 | Ted Williams, Boston | 36 |
| 1943 | Rudy York, Detroit | 34 |
| 1944 | Nick Etten, New York | 22 |
| 1945 | Vern Stephens, St. Louis | 24 |
| 1946 | Hank Greenberg, Detroit | 44 |
| 1947 | Ted Williams, Boston | 32 |
| 1948 | Joe DiMaggio, New York | 39 |
| 1949 | Ted Williams, Boston | 43 |
| 1950 | Al Rosen, Cleveland | 37 |
| 1951 | Gus Zernial, Chicago-Philadelphia | 33 |
| 1952 | Larry Doby, Cleveland | 32 |
| 1953 | Al Rosen, Cleveland | 43 |
| 1954 | Larry Doby, Cleveland | 32 |
| 1955 | Mickey Mantle, New York | 37 |
| 1956 | Mickey Mantle, New York | 52 |
| 1957 | Roy Sievers, Washington | 42 |
| 1958 | Mickey Mantle, New York | 42 |
| 1959 | Rocky Colavito, Cleve.; Harmon Killebrew, Wash. | 42 |
| 1960 | Mickey Mantle, New York | 40 |
| 1961 | Roger Maris, New York | 61 |
| 1962 | Harmon Killebrew, Minnesota | 48 |
| 1963 | Harmon Killebrew, Minnesota | 45 |

*(continued)*

### National League

| Year | Player, Team | HR |
|---|---|---|
| 1964 | Willie Mays, San Francisco | 47 |
| 1965 | Willie Mays, San Francisco | 52 |
| 1966 | Hank Aaron, Atlanta | 44 |
| 1967 | Hank Aaron, Atlanta | 39 |
| 1968 | Willie McCovey, San Francisco | 36 |
| 1969 | Willie McCovey, San Francisco | 45 |
| 1970 | Johnny Bench, Cincinnati | 45 |
| 1971 | Willie Stargell, Pittsburgh | 48 |
| 1972 | Johnny Bench, Cincinnati | 40 |
| 1973 | Willie Stargell, Pittsburgh | 44 |
| 1974 | Mike Schmidt, Philadelphia | 36 |
| 1975 | Mike Schmidt, Philadelphia | 38 |
| 1976 | Mike Schmidt, Philadelphia | 38 |
| 1977 | George Foster, Cincinnati | 52 |
| 1978 | George Foster, Cincinnati | 40 |
| 1979 | Dave Kingman, Chicago | 48 |
| 1980 | Mike Schmidt, Philadelphia | 48 |
| 1981 | Mike Schmidt, Philadelphia | 31 |
| 1982 | Dave Kingman, New York | 37 |
| 1983 | Mike Schmidt, Philadelphia | 40 |
| 1984 | Mike Schmidt, Phi.; Dale Murphy, Atlanta | 36 |
| 1985 | Dale Murphy, Atlanta | 37 |
| 1986 | Mike Schmidt, Philadelphia | 37 |
| 1987 | Andre Dawson, Chicago | 49 |
| 1988 | Darryl Strawberry, New York | 39 |
| 1989 | Kevin Mitchell, San Francisco | 47 |
| 1990 | Ryne Sandberg, Chicago | 40 |
| 1991 | Howard Johnson, New York | 38 |
| 1992 | Fred McGriff, San Diego | 35 |
| 1993 | Barry Bonds, San Francisco | 46 |
| 1994 | Matt Williams, San Francisco | 43 |
| 1995 | Dante Bichette, Colorado | 40 |
| 1996 | Andres Galarraga, Colorado | 47 |

### American League

| Year | Player, Team | HR |
|---|---|---|
| 1964 | Harmon Killebrew, Minnesota | 49 |
| 1965 | Tony Conigliaro, Boston | 32 |
| 1966 | Frank Robinson, Baltimore | 49 |
| 1967 | Carl Yastrzemski, Boston; Harmon Killebrew, Minn. | 44 |
| 1968 | Frank Howard, Washington | 44 |
| 1969 | Harmon Killebrew, Minnesota | 49 |
| 1970 | Frank Howard, Washington | 44 |
| 1971 | Bill Melton, Chicago | 33 |
| 1972 | Dick Allen, Chicago | 37 |
| 1973 | Reggie Jackson, Oakland | 32 |
| 1974 | Dick Allen, Chicago | 32 |
| 1975 | George Scott, Milwaukee; Reggie Jackson, Oakland | 36 |
| 1976 | Graig Nettles, New York | 32 |
| 1977 | Jim Rice, Boston | 39 |
| 1978 | Jim Rice, Boston | 46 |
| 1979 | Gorman Thomas, Milwaukee | 45 |
| 1980 | Reggie Jackson, New York; Ben Oglivie, Milwaukee | 41 |
| 1981 | Bobby Grich, California; Tony Armas, Oakland; Dwight Evans, Boston; Eddie Murray, Baltimore | 22 |
| 1982 | Gorman Thomas, Milwaukee; Reggie Jackson, Cal. | 39 |
| 1983 | Jim Rice, Boston | 39 |
| 1984 | Tony Armas, Boston | 43 |
| 1985 | Darrell Evans, Detroit | 40 |
| 1986 | Jesse Barfield, Toronto | 40 |
| 1987 | Mark McGwire, Oakland | 49 |
| 1988 | Jose Canseco, Oakland | 42 |
| 1989 | Fred McGriff, Toronto | 36 |
| 1990 | Cecil Fielder, Detroit | 51 |
| 1991 | Cecil Fielder, Detroit; Jose Canseco, Oakland | 44 |
| 1992 | Juan Gonzalez, Texas | 43 |
| 1993 | Juan Gonzalez, Texas | 46 |
| 1994 | Ken Griffey Jr., Seattle | 40 |
| 1995 | Albert Belle, Cleveland | 50 |
| 1996 | Mark McGwire, Oakland | 52 |

## Runs Batted In Leaders

### National League

| Year | Player, Team | RBI |
|---|---|---|
| 1907 | Sherwood Magee, Philadelphia | 85 |
| 1908 | Honus Wager, Pittsburgh | 109 |
| 1909 | Honus Wager, Pittsburgh | 100 |
| 1910 | Sherwood Magee, Philadelphia | 123 |
| 1911 | Frank Schulte, Chicago | 121 |
| 1912 | Henry Zimmerman, Chicago | 103 |
| 1913 | Gavvy Cravath, Philadelphia | 128 |
| 1914 | Sherwood Magee, Philadelphia | 103 |
| 1915 | Gavvy Cravath, Philadelphia | 115 |
| 1916 | Henry Zimmerman, Chicago-NewYork | 83 |
| 1917 | Henry Zimmerman, New York | 102 |
| 1918 | Sherwood Magee, Philadelphia | 76 |
| 1919 | Hi Myers, Boston | 73 |
| 1920 | George Kelly, N.Y.; Rogers Hornsby, St. Louis | 94 |
| 1921 | Rogers Hornsby, St. Louis | 126 |
| 1922 | Rogers Hornsby, St. Louis | 152 |
| 1923 | Emil Meusel, New York | 125 |
| 1924 | George Kelly, New York | 136 |
| 1925 | Rogers Hornsby, St. Louis | 143 |
| 1926 | Jim Bottomley, St. Louis | 120 |
| 1927 | Paul Waner, Pittsburgh | 131 |
| 1928 | Jim Bottomley, St. Louis | 136 |
| 1929 | Hack Wilson, Chicago | 159 |
| 1930 | Hack Wilson, Chicago | 190 |
| 1931 | Chuck Klein, Philadelphia | 121 |
| 1932 | Don Hurst, Philadelphia | 143 |
| 1933 | Chuck Klein, Philadelphia | 120 |
| 1934 | Mel Ott, New York | 135 |
| 1935 | Walter Berger, Boston | 130 |
| 1936 | Joe Medwick, St. Louis | 138 |
| 1937 | Joe Medwick, St. Louis | 154 |
| 1938 | Joe Medwick, St. Louis | 122 |
| 1939 | Frank McCormick, Cincinnati | 128 |
| 1940 | John Mize, St. Louis | 137 |
| 1941 | Adolph Camilli, Brooklyn | 120 |
| 1942 | John Mize, New York | 110 |
| 1943 | Bill Nicholson, Chicago | 128 |
| 1944 | Bill Nicholson, Chicago | 122 |
| 1945 | Dixie Walker, Brooklyn | 124 |
| 1946 | Enos Slaughter, St. Louis | 130 |
| 1947 | John Mize, New York | 138 |
| 1948 | Stan Musial, St. Louis | 131 |
| 1949 | Ralph Kiner, Pittsburgh | 127 |
| 1950 | Del Ennis, Philadelphia | 126 |
| 1951 | Monte Irvin, New York | 121 |
| 1952 | Hank Sauer, Chicago | 121 |
| 1953 | Roy Campanella, Brooklyn | 142 |
| 1954 | Ted Kluszewski, Cincinnati | 141 |

### American League

| Year | Player, Team | RBI |
|---|---|---|
| 1907 | Ty Cobb, Detroit | 116 |
| 1908 | Ty Cobb, Detroit | 108 |
| 1909 | Ty Cobb, Detroit | 107 |
| 1910 | Sam Crawford, Detroit | 120 |
| 1911 | Ty Cobb, Detroit | 144 |
| 1912 | J. Franklin Baker, Philadelphia | 133 |
| 1913 | J. Franklin Baker, Philadelphia | 126 |
| 1914 | Sam Crawford, Detroit | 104 |
| 1915 | Sam Crawford, Detroit; Robert Veach, Detroit | 112 |
| 1916 | Del Pratt, St. Louis | 103 |
| 1917 | Robert Veach, Detroit | 103 |
| 1918 | Robert Veach, Detroit | 78 |
| 1919 | Babe Ruth, Boston | 114 |
| 1920 | Babe Ruth, New York | 137 |
| 1921 | Babe Ruth, New York | 171 |
| 1922 | Ken Williams, St. Louis | 155 |
| 1923 | Babe Ruth, New York | 131 |
| 1924 | Goose Goslin, Washington | 129 |
| 1925 | Bob Meusel, New York | 138 |
| 1926 | Babe Ruth, New York | 145 |
| 1927 | Lou Gehrig, New York | 175 |
| 1928 | Babe Ruth, New York; Lou Gehrig, New York | 142 |
| 1929 | Al Simmons, Philadelphia | 157 |
| 1930 | Lou Gehrig, New York | 174 |
| 1931 | Lou Gehrig, New York | 184 |
| 1932 | Jimmie Foxx, Philadelphia | 169 |
| 1933 | Jimmie Foxx, Philadelphia | 163 |
| 1934 | Lou Gehrig, New York | 165 |
| 1935 | Hank Greenberg, Detroit | 170 |
| 1936 | Hal Trosky, Cleveland | 162 |
| 1937 | Hank Greenberg, Detroit | 183 |
| 1938 | Jimmie Foxx, Boston | 175 |
| 1939 | Ted Williams, Boston | 145 |
| 1940 | Hank Greenberg, Detroit | 150 |
| 1941 | Joe DiMaggio, New York | 125 |
| 1942 | Ted Williams, Boston | 137 |
| 1943 | Rudy York, Detroit | 118 |
| 1944 | Vern Stephens, St. Louis | 109 |
| 1945 | Nick Etten, New York | 111 |
| 1946 | Hank Greenberg, Detroit | 127 |
| 1947 | Ted Williams, Boston | 114 |
| 1948 | Joe DiMaggio, New York | 155 |
| 1949 | Ted Williams, Bos.; Vern Stephens, Bos. | 159 |
| 1950 | Walt Dropo, Bos.; Vern Stephens, Bos. | 144 |
| 1951 | Gus Zernial, Chicago-Philadelphia | 129 |
| 1952 | Al Rosen, Cleveland | 105 |
| 1953 | Al Rosen, Cleveland | 145 |
| 1954 | Larry Doby, Cleveland | 126 |

### National League

| Year | Player, Team | RBI |
|---|---|---|
| 1955 | Duke Snider, Brooklyn | 136 |
| 1956 | Stan Musial, St. Louis | 109 |
| 1957 | Hank Aaron, Milwaukee | 132 |
| 1958 | Ernie Banks, Chicago | 129 |
| 1959 | Ernie Banks, Chicago | 143 |
| 1960 | Hank Aaron, Milwaukee | 126 |
| 1961 | Orlando Cepeda, San Francisco | 142 |
| 1962 | Tommy Davis, Los Angeles | 153 |
| 1963 | Hank Aaron, Milwaukee | 130 |
| 1964 | Ken Boyer, St. Louis | 119 |
| 1965 | Deron Johnson, Cincinnati | 130 |
| 1966 | Hank Aaron, Atlanta | 127 |
| 1967 | Orlando Cepeda, St. Louis | 111 |
| 1968 | Willie McCovey, San Francisco | 105 |
| 1969 | Willie McCovey, San Francisco | 126 |
| 1970 | Johnny Bench, Cincinnati | 148 |
| 1971 | Joe Torre, St. Louis | 137 |
| 1972 | Johnny Bench, Cincinnati | 125 |
| 1973 | Willie Stargell, Pittsburgh | 119 |
| 1974 | Johnny Bench, Cincinnati | 129 |
| 1975 | Greg Luzinski, Philadelphia | 120 |
| 1976 | George Foster, Cincinnati | 121 |
| 1977 | George Foster, Cincinnati | 149 |
| 1978 | George Foster, Cincinnati | 120 |
| 1979 | Dave Winfield, San Diego | 118 |
| 1980 | Mike Schmidt, Philadelphia | 121 |
| 1981 | Mike Schmidt, Philadelphia | 91 |
| 1982 | Dale Murphy, Atlanta; Al Oliver, Montreal | 109 |
| 1983 | Dale Murphy, Atlanta | 121 |
| 1984 | Mike Schmidt, Phi.; Gary Carter, Montreal | 106 |
| 1985 | Dave Parker, Cincinnati | 125 |
| 1986 | Mike Schmidt, Philadelphia | 119 |
| 1987 | Andre Dawson, Chicago | 137 |
| 1988 | Will Clark, San Francisco | 109 |
| 1989 | Kevin Mitchell, San Francisco | 125 |
| 1990 | Matt Williams, San Francisco | 122 |
| 1991 | Howard Johnson, New York | 117 |
| 1992 | Darren Daulton, Philadelphia | 109 |
| 1993 | Barry Bonds, San Francisco | 123 |
| 1994 | Jeff Bagwell, Houston | 116 |
| 1995 | Dante Bichette, Colorado | 128 |
| 1996 | Andres Galarraga, Colorado | 150 |

### American League

| Year | Player, Team | RBI |
|---|---|---|
| 1955 | Ray Boone, Detroit; Jackie Jensen, Boston | 116 |
| 1956 | Mickey Mantle, New York | 130 |
| 1957 | Roy Sievers, Washington | 114 |
| 1958 | Jackie Jensen, Boston | 122 |
| 1959 | Jackie Jensen, Boston | 112 |
| 1960 | Roger Maris, New York | 112 |
| 1961 | Roger Maris, New York | 142 |
| 1962 | Harmon Killebrew, Minnesota | 126 |
| 1963 | Dick Stuart, Boston | 118 |
| 1964 | Brooks Robinson, Baltimore | 118 |
| 1965 | Rocky Colavito, Cleveland | 108 |
| 1966 | Frank Robinson, Baltimore | 122 |
| 1967 | Carl Yastrzemski, Boston | 121 |
| 1968 | Ken Harrelson, Boston | 109 |
| 1969 | Harmon Killebrew, Minnesota | 140 |
| 1970 | Frank Howard, Washington | 126 |
| 1971 | Harmon Killebrew, Minnesota | 119 |
| 1972 | Dick Allen, Chicago | 113 |
| 1973 | Reggie Jackson, Oakland | 117 |
| 1974 | Jeff Burroughs, Texas | 118 |
| 1975 | George Scott, Milwaukee | 109 |
| 1976 | Lee May, Baltimore | 109 |
| 1977 | Larry Hisle, Minnesota | 119 |
| 1978 | Jim Rice, Boston | 139 |
| 1979 | Don Baylor, California | 139 |
| 1980 | Cecil Cooper, Milwaukee | 122 |
| 1981 | Eddie Murray, Baltimore | 78 |
| 1982 | Hal McRae, Kansas City | 133 |
| 1983 | Cecil Cooper, Milwaukee; Jim Rice, Boston | 126 |
| 1984 | Tony Armas, Boston | 123 |
| 1985 | Don Mattingly, New York | 145 |
| 1986 | Joe Carter, Cleveland | 121 |
| 1987 | George Bell, Toronto | 134 |
| 1988 | Jose Canseco, Oakland | 124 |
| 1989 | Ruben Sierra, Texas | 119 |
| 1990 | Cecil Fielder, Detroit | 132 |
| 1991 | Cecil Fielder, Detroit | 133 |
| 1992 | Cecil Fielder, Detroit | 124 |
| 1993 | Albert Belle, Cleveland | 129 |
| 1994 | Kirby Puckett, Minnesota | 112 |
| 1995 | Albert Belle, Cleveland; Mo Vaughn, Boston | 126 |
| 1996 | Albert Belle, Cleveland | 148 |

## Batting Champions

### National League

| Year | Player | Club | Avg. |
|---|---|---|---|
| 1901 | Jesse C. Burkett | St. Louis | **.382** |
| 1902 | Clarence Beaumont | Pittsburgh | **.357** |
| 1903 | Honus Wagner | Pittsburgh | **.355** |
| 1904 | Honus Wagner | Pittsburgh | **.349** |
| 1905 | James Seymour | Cincinnati | **.377** |
| 1906 | Honus Wagner | Pittsburgh | **.339** |
| 1907 | Honus Wagner | Pittsburgh | **.350** |
| 1908 | Honus Wagner | Pittsburgh | **.354** |
| 1909 | Honus Wagner | Pittsburgh | **.339** |
| 1910 | Sherwood Magee | Philadelphia | **.331** |
| 1911 | Honus Wagner | Pittsburgh | **.334** |
| 1912 | Henry Zimmerman | Chicago | **.372** |
| 1913 | Jacob Daubert | Brooklyn | **.350** |
| 1914 | Jacob Daubert | Brooklyn | **.329** |
| 1915 | Larry Doyle | New York | **.320** |
| 1916 | Hal Chase | Cincinnati | **.339** |
| 1917 | Edd Roush | Cincinnati | **.341** |
| 1918 | Zach Wheat | Brooklyn | **.335** |
| 1919 | Edd Roush | Cincinnati | **.321** |
| 1920 | Rogers Hornsby | St. Louis | **.370** |
| 1921 | Rogers Hornsby | St. Louis | **.397** |
| 1922 | Rogers Hornsby | St. Louis | **.401** |
| 1923 | Rogers Hornsby | St. Louis | **.384** |
| 1924 | Rogers Hornsby | St. Louis | **.424** |
| 1925 | Rogers Hornsby | St. Louis | **.403** |
| 1926 | Eugene Hargrave | Cincinnati | **.353** |
| 1927 | Paul Waner | Pittsburgh | **.380** |
| 1928 | Rogers Hornsby | Boston | **.387** |
| 1929 | Lefty O'Doul | Philadelphia | **.398** |
| 1930 | Bill Terry | New York | **.401** |
| 1931 | Chick Hafey | St. Louis | **.349** |
| 1932 | Lefty O'Doul | Brooklyn | **.368** |
| 1933 | Chuck Klein | Philadelphia | **.368** |
| 1934 | Paul Waner | Pittsburgh | **.362** |
| 1935 | Arky Vaughan | Pittsburgh | **.385** |
| 1936 | Paul Waner | Pittsburgh | **.373** |
| 1937 | Joe Medwick | St. Louis | **.374** |
| 1938 | Ernie Lombardi | Cincinnati | **.342** |
| 1939 | John Mize | St. Louis | **.349** |

### American League

| Year | Player | Club | Avg. |
|---|---|---|---|
| 1901 | Napoleon Lajoie | Philadelphia | **.422** |
| 1902 | Ed Delahanty | Washington | **.376** |
| 1903 | Napoleon Lajoie | Cleveland | **.355** |
| 1904 | Napoleon Lajoie | Cleveland | **.381** |
| 1905 | Elmer Flick | Cleveland | **.306** |
| 1906 | George Stone | St. Louis | **.358** |
| 1907 | Ty Cobb | Detroit | **.350** |
| 1908 | Ty Cobb | Detroit | **.324** |
| 1909 | Ty Cobb | Detroit | **.377** |
| 1910 | Ty Cobb* | Detroit | **.385** |
| 1911 | Ty Cobb | Detroit | **.420** |
| 1912 | Ty Cobb | Detroit | **.410** |
| 1913 | Ty Cobb | Detroit | **.390** |
| 1914 | Ty Cobb | Detroit | **.368** |
| 1915 | Ty Cobb | Detroit | **.369** |
| 1916 | Tris Speaker | Cleveland | **.386** |
| 1917 | Ty Cobb | Detroit | **.383** |
| 1918 | Ty Cobb | Detroit | **.382** |
| 1919 | Ty Cobb | Detroit | **.384** |
| 1920 | George Sisler | St. Louis | **.407** |
| 1921 | Harry Heilmann | Detroit | **.394** |
| 1922 | George Sisler | St. Louis | **.420** |
| 1923 | Harry Heilmann | Detroit | **.403** |
| 1924 | Babe Ruth | New York | **.378** |
| 1925 | Harry Heilmann | Detroit | **.393** |
| 1926 | Henry Manush | Detroit | **.378** |
| 1927 | Harry Heilmann | Detroit | **.398** |
| 1928 | Goose Goslin | Washington | **.379** |
| 1929 | Lew Fonseca | Cleveland | **.369** |
| 1930 | Al Simmons | Philadelphia | **.381** |
| 1931 | Al Simmons | Philadelphia | **.390** |
| 1932 | Dale Alexander | Detroit-Boston | **.367** |
| 1933 | Jimmie Foxx | Philadelphia | **.356** |
| 1934 | Lou Gehrig | New York | **.363** |
| 1935 | Buddy Myer | Washington | **.349** |
| 1936 | Luke Appling | Chicago | **.388** |
| 1937 | Charlie Gehringer | Detroit | **.371** |
| 1938 | Jimmie Foxx | Boston | **.349** |
| 1939 | Joe DiMaggio | New York | **.381** |

*(continued)*

## National League

| Year | Player | Club | Avg. |
|---|---|---|---|
| 1940 | Debs Garms | Pittsburgh | .355 |
| 1941 | Pete Reiser | Brooklyn | .343 |
| 1942 | Ernie Lombardi | Boston | .330 |
| 1943 | Stan Musial | St. Louis | .357 |
| 1944 | Dixie Walker | Brooklyn | .357 |
| 1945 | Phil Cavarretta | Chicago | .355 |
| 1946 | Stan Musial | St. Louis | .365 |
| 1947 | Harry Walker | St.L.-Phi. | .363 |
| 1948 | Stan Musial | St. Louis | .376 |
| 1949 | Jackie Robinson | Brooklyn | .342 |
| 1950 | Stan Musial | St. Louis | .346 |
| 1951 | Stan Musial | St. Louis | .355 |
| 1952 | Stan Musial | St. Louis | .336 |
| 1953 | Carl Furillo | Brooklyn | .344 |
| 1954 | Willie Mays | New York | .345 |
| 1955 | Richie Ashburn | Philadelphia | .338 |
| 1956 | Hank Aaron | Milwaukee | .328 |
| 1957 | Stan Musial | St. Louis | .351 |
| 1958 | Richie Ashburn | Philadelphia | .350 |
| 1959 | Hank Aaron | Milwaukee | .355 |
| 1960 | Dick Groat | Pittsburgh | .325 |
| 1961 | Roberto Clemente | Pittsburgh | .351 |
| 1962 | Tommy Davis | Los Angeles | .346 |
| 1963 | Tommy Davis | Los Angeles | .326 |
| 1964 | Roberto Clemente | Pittsburgh | .339 |
| 1965 | Roberto Clemente | Pittsburgh | .329 |
| 1966 | Matty Alou | Pittsburgh | .342 |
| 1967 | Roberto Clemente | Pittsburgh | .357 |
| 1968 | Pete Rose | Cincinnati | .335 |
| 1969 | Pete Rose | Cincinnati | .348 |
| 1970 | Rico Carty | Atlanta | .366 |
| 1971 | Joe Torre | St. Louis | .363 |
| 1972 | Billy Williams | Chicago | .333 |
| 1973 | Pete Rose | Cincinnati | .338 |
| 1974 | Ralph Garr | Atlanta | .353 |
| 1975 | Bill Madlock | Chicago | .354 |
| 1976 | Bill Madlock | Chicago | .339 |
| 1977 | Dave Parker | Pittsburgh | .338 |
| 1978 | Dave Parker | Pittsburgh | .334 |
| 1979 | Keith Hernandez | St. Louis | .344 |
| 1980 | Bill Buckner | Chicago | .324 |
| 1981 | Bill Madlock | Pittsburgh | .341 |
| 1982 | Al Oliver | Montreal | .331 |
| 1983 | Bill Madlock | Pittsburgh | .323 |
| 1984 | Tony Gwynn | San Diego | .351 |
| 1985 | Willie McGee | St. Louis | .353 |
| 1986 | Tim Raines | Montreal | .334 |
| 1987 | Tony Gwynn | San Diego | .370 |
| 1988 | Tony Gwynn | San Diego | .313 |
| 1989 | Tony Gwynn | San Diego | .336 |
| 1990 | Willie McGee | St. Louis | .335 |
| 1991 | Terry Pendleton | Atlanta | .319 |
| 1992 | Gary Sheffield | San Diego | .330 |
| 1993 | Andres Galarraga | Colorado | .370 |
| 1994 | Tony Gwynn | San Diego | .394 |
| 1995 | Tony Gwynn | San Diego | .368 |
| 1996 | Tony Gwynn | San Diego | .353 |

## American League

| Year | Player | Club | Avg. |
|---|---|---|---|
| 1940 | Joe DiMaggio | New York | .352 |
| 1941 | Ted Williams | Boston | .406 |
| 1942 | Ted Williams | Boston | .356 |
| 1943 | Luke Appling | Chicago | .328 |
| 1944 | Lou Boudreau | Cleveland | .327 |
| 1945 | George Stirnweiss | New York | .309 |
| 1946 | Mickey Vernon | Washington | .353 |
| 1947 | Ted Williams | Boston | .343 |
| 1948 | Ted Williams | Boston | .369 |
| 1949 | George Kell | Detroit | .343 |
| 1950 | Billy Goodman | Boston | .354 |
| 1951 | Ferris Fain | Philadelphia | .344 |
| 1952 | Ferris Fain | Philadelphia | .327 |
| 1953 | Mickey Vernon | Washington | .337 |
| 1954 | Roberto Avila | Cleveland | .341 |
| 1955 | Al Kaline | Detroit | .340 |
| 1956 | Mickey Mantle | New York | .353 |
| 1957 | Ted Williams | Boston | .388 |
| 1958 | Ted Williams | Boston | .328 |
| 1959 | Harvey Kuenn | Detroit | .353 |
| 1960 | Pete Runnels | Boston | .320 |
| 1961 | Norm Cash | Detroit | .361 |
| 1962 | Pete Runnels | Boston | .326 |
| 1963 | Carl Yastrzemski | Boston | .321 |
| 1964 | Tony Oliva | Minnesota | .323 |
| 1965 | Tony Oliva | Minnesota | .321 |
| 1966 | Frank Robinson | Baltimore | .316 |
| 1967 | Carl Yastrzemski | Boston | .326 |
| 1968 | Carl Yastrzemski | Boston | .301 |
| 1969 | Rod Carew | Minnesota | .332 |
| 1970 | Alex Johnson | California | .329 |
| 1971 | Tony Oliva | Minnesota | .337 |
| 1972 | Rod Carew | Minnesota | .318 |
| 1973 | Rod Carew | Minnesota | .350 |
| 1974 | Rod Carew | Minnesota | .364 |
| 1975 | Rod Carew | Minnesota | .359 |
| 1976 | George Brett | Kansas City | .333 |
| 1977 | Rod Carew | Minnesota | .388 |
| 1978 | Rod Carew | Minnesota | .333 |
| 1979 | Fred Lynn | Boston | .333 |
| 1980 | George Brett | Kansas City | .390 |
| 1981 | Carney Lansford | Boston | .336 |
| 1982 | Willie Wilson | Kansas City | .332 |
| 1983 | Wade Boggs | Boston | .361 |
| 1984 | Don Mattingly | New York | .343 |
| 1985 | Wade Boggs | Boston | .368 |
| 1986 | Wade Boggs | Boston | .357 |
| 1987 | Wade Boggs | Boston | .363 |
| 1988 | Wade Boggs | Boston | .366 |
| 1989 | Kirby Puckett | Minnesota | .339 |
| 1990 | George Brett | Kansas City | .329 |
| 1991 | Julio Franco | Texas | .341 |
| 1992 | Edgar Martinez | Seattle | .343 |
| 1993 | John Olerud | Toronto | .363 |
| 1994 | Paul O'Neill | New York | .359 |
| 1995 | Edgar Martinez | Seattle | .356 |
| 1996 | Alex Rodriguez | Seattle | .358 |

*Some baseball researchers have determined that Ty Cobb actually hit .382 in 1910, while Napolean Lajoie, Cleveland, hit .383.

# Cy Young Award Winners

| Year | Player, Team |
|---|---|
| 1956 | Don Newcombe, Dodgers |
| 1957 | Warren Spahn, Braves |
| 1958 | Bob Turley, Yankees |
| 1959 | Early Wynn, White Sox |
| 1960 | Vernon Law, Pirates |
| 1961 | Whitey Ford, Yankees |
| 1962 | Don Drysdale, Dodgers |
| 1963 | Sandy Koufax, Dodgers |
| 1964 | Dean Chance, Angels |
| 1965 | Sandy Koufax, Dodgers |
| 1966 | Sandy Koufax, Dodgers |
| 1967 | (NL) Mike McCormick, Giants |
| | (AL) Jim Lonborg, Red Sox |
| 1968 | (NL) Bob Gibson, Cardinals |
| | (AL) Dennis McLain, Tigers |
| 1969 | (NL) Tom Seaver, Mets |
| | (AL) (tie) Dennis McLain, Tigers<br>Mike Cuellar, Orioles |
| 1970 | (NL) Bob Gibson, Cardinals |
| | (AL) Jim Perry, Twins |
| 1971 | (NL) Ferguson Jenkins, Cubs |
| | (AL) Vida Blue, A's |
| 1972 | (NL) Steve Carlton, Phillies |
| | (AL) Gaylord Perry, Indians |
| 1973 | (NL) Tom Seaver, Mets |
| | (AL) Jim Palmer, Orioles |
| 1974 | (NL) Mike Marshall, Dodgers |
| | (AL) Jim (Catfish) Hunter, A's |
| 1975 | (NL) Tom Seaver, Mets |
| | (AL) Jim Palmer, Orioles |
| 1976 | (NL) Randy Jones, Padres |
| | (AL) Jim Palmer, Orioles |
| 1977 | (NL) Steve Carlton, Phillies |
| | (AL) Sparky Lyle, Yankees |
| 1978 | (NL) Gaylord Perry, Padres |
| | (AL) Ron Guidry, Yankees |
| 1979 | (NL) Bruce Sutter, Cubs |
| | (AL) Mike Flanagan, Orioles |
| 1980 | (NL) Steve Carlton, Phillies |
| | (AL) Steve Stone, Orioles |
| 1981 | (NL) Fernando Valenzuela, Dodgers |
| | (AL) Rollie Fingers, Brewers |
| 1982 | (NL) Steve Carlton, Phillies |
| | (AL) Pete Vuckovich, Brewers |
| 1983 | (NL) John Denny, Phillies |
| | (AL) LaMarr Hoyt, White Sox |
| 1984 | (NL) Rick Sutcliffe, Cubs |
| | (AL) Willie Hernandez, Tigers |
| 1985 | (NL) Dwight Gooden, Mets |
| | (AL) Bret Saberhagen, Royals |
| 1986 | (NL) Mike Scott, Astros |
| | (AL) Roger Clemens, Red Sox |
| 1987 | (NL) Steve Bedrosian, Phillies |
| | (AL) Roger Clemens, Red Sox |
| 1988 | (NL) Orel Hershiser, Dodgers |
| | (AL) Frank Viola, Twins |
| 1989 | (NL) Mark Davis, Padres |
| | (AL) Bret Saberhagan, Royals |
| 1990 | (NL) Doug Drabek, Pirates |
| | (AL) Bob Welch, A's |
| 1991 | (NL) Tom Glavine, Braves |
| | (AL) Roger Clemens, Red Sox |
| 1992 | (NL) Greg Maddux, Cubs |
| | (AL) Dennis Eckersley, A's |
| 1993 | (NL) Greg Maddux, Braves |
| | (AL) Jack McDowell, White Sox |
| 1994 | (NL) Greg Maddux, Braves |
| | (AL) David Cone, Royals |
| 1995 | (NL) Greg Maddux, Braves |
| | (AL) Randy Johnson, Mariners |

# Most Valuable Player

## National League

| Year | Player, team | Year | Player, team | Year | Player, team |
|---|---|---|---|---|---|
| 1931 | Frank Frisch, St. Louis | 1953 | Roy Campanella, Brooklyn | 1975 | Joe Morgan, Cincinnati |
| 1932 | Charles Klein, Philadelphia | 1954 | Willie Mays, New York | 1976 | Joe Morgan, Cincinnati |
| 1933 | Carl Hubbell, New York | 1955 | Roy Campanella, Brooklyn | 1977 | George Foster, Cincinnati |
| 1934 | Dizzy Dean, St. Louis | 1956 | Don Newcombe, Brooklyn | 1978 | Dave Parker, Pittsburgh |
| 1935 | Gabby Hartnett, Chicago | 1957 | Hank Aaron, Milwaukee | 1979 | Willie Stargell, Pittsburgh |
| 1936 | Carl Hubbell, New York | 1958 | Ernie Banks, Chicago | (tie) | Keith Hernandez, St. Louis |
| 1937 | Joe Medwick, St. Louis | 1959 | Ernie Banks, Chicago | 1980 | Mike Schmidt, Philadelphia |
| 1938 | Ernie Lombardi, Cincinnati | 1960 | Dick Groat, Pittsburgh | 1981 | Mike Schmidt, Philadelphia |
| 1939 | Bucky Walters, Cincinnati | 1961 | Frank Robinson, Cincinnati | 1982 | Dale Murphy, Atlanta |
| 1940 | Frank McCormick, Cincinnati | 1962 | Maury Wills, Los Angeles | 1983 | Dale Murphy, Atlanta |
| 1941 | Dolph Camilli, Brooklyn | 1963 | Sandy Koufax, Los Angeles | 1984 | Ryne Sandberg, Chicago |
| 1942 | Mort Cooper, St. Louis | 1964 | Ken Boyer, St. Louis | 1985 | Willie McGee, St. Louis |
| 1943 | Stan Musial, St. Louis | 1965 | Willie Mays, San Francisco | 1986 | Mike Schmidt, Philadelphia |
| 1944 | Martin Marion, St. Louis | 1966 | Roberto Clemente, Pittsburgh | 1987 | Andre Dawson, Chicago |
| 1945 | Phil Cavarretta, Chicago | 1967 | Orlando Cepeda, St. Louis | 1988 | Kirk Gibson, Los Angeles |
| 1946 | Stan Musial, St. Louis | 1968 | Bob Gibson, St. Louis | 1989 | Kevin Mitchell, San Francisco |
| 1947 | Bob Elliott, Boston | 1969 | Willie McCovey, San Francisco | 1990 | Barry Bonds, Pittsburgh |
| 1948 | Stan Musial, St. Louis | 1970 | Johnny Bench, Cincinnati | 1991 | Terry Pendleton, Atlanta |
| 1949 | Jackie Robinson, Brooklyn | 1971 | Joe Torre, St. Louis | 1992 | Barry Bonds, Pittsburgh |
| 1950 | Jim Konstanty, Philadelphia | 1972 | Johnny Bench, Cincinnati | 1993 | Barry Bonds, San Francisco |
| 1951 | Roy Campanella, Brooklyn | 1973 | Pete Rose, Cincinnati | 1994 | Jeff Bagwell, Houston |
| 1952 | Hank Sauer, Chicago | 1974 | Steve Garvey, Los Angeles | 1995 | Barry Larkin, Cincinnati |

## American League

| Year | Player, team | Year | Player, team | Year | Player, team |
|---|---|---|---|---|---|
| 1931 | Lefty Grove, Philadelphia | 1953 | Al Rosen, Cleveland | 1975 | Fred Lynn, Boston |
| 1932 | Jimmie Foxx, Philadelphia | 1954 | Yogi Berra, New York | 1976 | Thurman Munson, New York |
| 1933 | Jimmie Foxx, Philadelphia | 1955 | Yogi Berra, New York | 1977 | Rod Carew, Minnesota |
| 1934 | Mickey Cochrane, Detroit | 1956 | Mickey Mantle, New York | 1978 | Jim Rice, Boston |
| 1935 | Hank Greenberg, Detroit | 1957 | Mickey Mantle, New York | 1979 | Don Baylor, California |
| 1936 | Lou Gehrig, New York | 1958 | Jackie Jensen, Boston | 1980 | George Brett, Kansas City |
| 1937 | Charley Gehringer, Detroit | 1959 | Nellie Fox, Chicago | 1981 | Rollie Fingers, Milwaukee |
| 1938 | Jimmie Foxx, Boston | 1960 | Roger Maris, New York | 1982 | Robin Yount, Milwaukee |
| 1939 | Joe DiMaggio, New York | 1961 | Roger Maris, New York | 1983 | Cal Ripken, Jr., Baltimore |
| 1940 | Hank Greenberg, Detroit | 1962 | Mickey Mantle, New York | 1984 | Willie Hernandez, Detroit |
| 1941 | Joe DiMaggio, New York | 1963 | Elston Howard, New York | 1985 | Don Mattingly, New York |
| 1942 | Joe Gordon, New York | 1964 | Brooks Robinson, Baltimore | 1986 | Roger Clemens, Boston |
| 1943 | Spurgeon Chandler, New York | 1965 | Zoilo Versalles, Minnesota | 1987 | George Bell, Toronto |
| 1944 | Hal Newhouser, Detroit | 1966 | Frank Robinson, Baltimore | 1988 | Jose Canseco, Oakland |
| 1945 | Hal Newhouser, Detroit | 1967 | Carl Yastrzemski, Boston | 1989 | Robin Yount, Milwaukee |
| 1946 | Ted Williams, Boston | 1968 | Denny McLain, Detroit | 1990 | Rickey Henderson, Oakland |
| 1947 | Joe DiMaggio, New York | 1969 | Harmon Killebrew, Minnesota | 1991 | Cal Ripken, Jr., Baltimore |
| 1948 | Lou Boudreau, Cleveland | 1970 | John (Boog) Powell, Baltimore | 1992 | Dennis Eckersley, Oakland |
| 1949 | Ted Williams, Boston | 1971 | Vida Blue, Oakland | 1993 | Frank Thomas, Chicago |
| 1950 | Phil Rizzuto, New York | 1972 | Dick Allen, Chicago | 1994 | Frank Thomas, Chicago |
| 1951 | Yogi Berra, New York | 1973 | Reggie Jackson, Oakland | 1995 | Mo Vaughn, Boston |
| 1952 | Bobby Shantz, Philadelphia | 1974 | Jeff Burroughs, Texas | | |

# Rookie of the Year

1947—Combined selection—Jackie Robinson, Brooklyn, 1b; 1948—Combined selection—Alvin Dark, Boston, N.L., ss

## National League

| Year | Player, team | Year | Player, team | Year | Player, team |
|---|---|---|---|---|---|
| 1949 | Don Newcombe, Brooklyn, p | 1966 | Tommy Helms, Cincinnati, 2b | 1981 | Fernando Valenzuela, Los Angeles, p |
| 1950 | Sam Jethroe, Boston, of | 1967 | Tom Seaver, New York, p | 1982 | Steve Sax, Los Angeles, 2b |
| 1951 | Willie Mays, New York, of | 1968 | Johnny Bench, Cincinnati, c | 1983 | Darryl Strawberry, New York, of |
| 1952 | Joe Black, Brooklyn, p | 1969 | Ted Sizemore, Los Angeles, 2b | 1984 | Dwight Gooden, New York, p |
| 1953 | Jim Gilliam, Brooklyn, 2b | 1970 | Carl Morton, Montreal, p | 1985 | Vince Coleman, St. Louis, of |
| 1954 | Wally Moon, St. Louis, of | 1971 | Earl Williams, Atlanta, c | 1986 | Todd Worrell, St. Louis, p |
| 1955 | Bill Virdon, St. Louis, of | 1972 | Jon Matlack, New York, p | 1987 | Benito Santiago, San Diego, c |
| 1956 | Frank Robinson, Cincinnati, of | 1973 | Gary Matthews, S.F., of | 1988 | Chris Sabo, Cincinnati, 3b |
| 1957 | Jack Sanford, Philadelphia, p | 1974 | Bake McBride, St. Louis, of | 1989 | Jerome Walton, Chicago, of |
| 1958 | Orlando Cepeda, S.F., 1b | 1975 | John Montefusco, S.F., p | 1990 | Dave Justice, Atlanta, 1b |
| 1959 | Willie McCovey, S.F., 1b | 1976 | Butch Metzger, San Diego, p | 1991 | Jeff Bagwell, Houston, 1b |
| 1960 | Frank Howard, Los Angeles, of | (tie) | Pat Zachry, Cincinnati, p | 1992 | Eric Karros, Los Angeles, 1b |
| 1961 | Billy Williams, Chicago, of | 1977 | Andre Dawson, Montreal, of | 1993 | Mike Piazza, Los Angeles, c |
| 1962 | Ken Hubbs, Chicago, 2b | 1978 | Bob Horner, Atlanta, 3b | 1994 | Raul Mondesi, Los Angeles, of |
| 1963 | Pete Rose, Cincinnati, 2b | 1979 | Rick Sutcliffe, Los Angeles, p | 1995 | Hideo Nomo, Los Angeles, p |
| 1964 | Richie Allen, Philadelphia, 3b | 1980 | Steve Howe, Los Angeles, p | | |
| 1965 | Jim Lefebvre, Los Angeles, 2b | | | | |

## American League

| Year | Player, team | Year | Player, team | Year | Player, team |
|---|---|---|---|---|---|
| 1949 | Roy Sievers, St. Louis, of | 1965 | Curt Blefary, Baltimore, of | 1980 | Joe Charboneau, Cleveland, of |
| 1950 | Walt Dropo, Boston, 1b | 1966 | Tommie Agee, Chicago, of | 1981 | Dave Righetti, New York, p |
| 1951 | Gil McDougald, New York, 3b | 1967 | Rod Carew, Minnesota, 2b | 1982 | Cal Ripken, Jr., Baltimore, ss |
| 1952 | Harry Byrd, Philadelphia, p | 1968 | Stan Bahnsen, New York, p | 1983 | Ron Kittle, Chicago, of |
| 1953 | Harvey Kuenn, Detroit, ss | 1969 | Lou Piniella, Kansas City, of | 1984 | Alvin Davis, Seattle, 1b |
| 1954 | Bob Grim, New York, p | 1970 | Thurman Munson, New York, c | 1985 | Ozzie Guillen, Chicago, ss |
| 1955 | Herb Score, Cleveland, p | 1971 | Chris Chambliss, Cleveland, 1b | 1986 | Jose Canseco, Oakland, of |
| 1956 | Luis Aparicio, Chicago, ss | 1972 | Carlton Fisk, Boston, c | 1987 | Mark McGwire, Oakland, 1b |
| 1957 | Tony Kubek, New York, if-of | 1973 | Al Bumbry, Baltimore, of | 1988 | Walt Weiss, Oakland, ss |
| 1958 | Albie Pearson, Washington, of | 1974 | Mike Hargrove, Texas, 1b | 1989 | Gregg Olson, Baltimore, p |
| 1959 | Bob Allison, Washington, of | 1975 | Fred Lynn, Boston, of | 1990 | Sandy Alomar, Jr., Cleveland, c |
| 1960 | Ron Hansen, Baltimore, ss | 1976 | Mark Fidrych, Detroit, p | 1991 | Chuck Knoblauch, Minnesota, 2b |
| 1961 | Don Schwall, Boston, p | 1977 | Eddie Murray, Baltimore, dh | 1992 | Pat Listach, Milwaukee, ss |
| 1962 | Tom Tresh, New York, if-of | 1978 | Lou Whitaker, Detroit, 2b | 1993 | Tim Salmon, California, of |
| 1963 | Gary Peters, Chicago, p | 1979 | John Castino, Minnesota, 3b | 1994 | Bob Hamelin, Kansas City, dh |
| 1964 | Tony Oliva, Minnesota, of | (tie) | Alfredo Griffin, Toronto, ss | 1995 | Marty Cordova, Minnesota, of |

# National League Records, 1996

Final standings

## Eastern Division

| | W | L | Pct. | GB | Home | vs. East | vs. Central | vs. West |
|---|---|---|---|---|---|---|---|---|
| Atlanta | 96 | 66 | .593 | — | 56-25 | 32-20 | 38-23 | 26-23 |
| Montreal | 88 | 74 | .543 | 8 | 50-30 | 24-28 | 39-22 | 25-24 |
| Florida | 80 | 82 | .494 | 16 | 52-29 | 25-27 | 33-27 | 22-28 |
| New York | 71 | 91 | .438 | 25 | 42-39 | 25-27 | 28-33 | 18-31 |
| Philadelphia | 67 | 95 | .414 | 29 | 35-46 | 24-28 | 21-40 | 22-27 |

## Central Division

| | W | L | Pct. | GB | Home | vs. East | vs. Central | vs. West |
|---|---|---|---|---|---|---|---|---|
| St. Louis | 88 | 74 | .543 | — | 48-33 | 29-32 | 37-15 | 22-27 |
| Houston | 82 | 80 | .506 | 6 | 48-33 | 33-28 | 24-28 | 25-24 |
| Cincinnati | 81 | 81 | .500 | 7 | 46-35 | 27-33 | 25-27 | 29-21 |
| Chicago | 76 | 86 | .469 | 12 | 43-38 | 31-30 | 19-33 | 26-23 |
| Pittsburgh | 73 | 89 | .451 | 15 | 36-44 | 25-36 | 25-27 | 23-26 |

## Western Division

| East | W | L | Pct. | GB | Home | vs. East | vs. Central | vs. West |
|---|---|---|---|---|---|---|---|---|
| San Diego | 91 | 71 | .562 | — | 45-36 | 39-23 | 28-33 | 24-15 |
| Los Angeles* | 90 | 72 | .556 | 1 | 47-34 | 38-24 | 33-28 | 19-20 |
| Colorado | 83 | 79 | .512 | 8 | 55-26 | 28-33 | 36-26 | 19-20 |
| San Francisco | 68 | 94 | .420 | 23 | 38-44 | 28-33 | 24-38 | 16-23 |

*Wild card team.

## Division Series

Atlanta defeated Los Angeles 3 games to 0 (2-1 [10], 3-2, 5-2)
St. Louis defeated San Diego 3 games to 0 (3-1, 5-4, 7-5)

## Championship Series

Atlanta defeated St. Louis 4 games to 3 (4-2, 3-8, 2-3, 3-4, 14-0, 3-1, 15-0)

### Team Batting

| | Avg | AB | R | H | HR | RBI |
|---|---|---|---|---|---|---|
| Colorado | **.287** | 5,590 | 961 | 1,607 | 221 | 909 |
| Atlanta | **.270** | 5,614 | 773 | 1,514 | 197 | 735 |
| New York | **.270** | 5,618 | 746 | 1,515 | 147 | 697 |
| St. Louis | **.267** | 5,503 | 759 | 1,468 | 142 | 711 |
| Pittsburgh | **.266** | 5,665 | 776 | 1,509 | 138 | 738 |
| San Diego | **.265** | 5,655 | 771 | 1,499 | 147 | 718 |
| Houston | **.262** | 5,508 | 753 | 1,445 | 129 | 703 |
| Montreal | **.262** | 5,506 | 741 | 1,441 | 148 | 696 |
| Florida | **.257** | 5,498 | 688 | 1,413 | 150 | 650 |
| Cincinnati | **.256** | 5,455 | 778 | 1,398 | 191 | 733 |
| Philadelphia | **.256** | 5,499 | 650 | 1,405 | 132 | 604 |
| San Francisco | **.253** | 5,533 | 752 | 1,400 | 153 | 707 |
| Los Angeles | **.252** | 5,538 | 703 | 1,396 | 150 | 661 |
| Chicago | **.251** | 5,531 | 772 | 1,388 | 175 | 725 |

### Team Pitching

| | ERA | IP | H | BB | SO | Sv |
|---|---|---|---|---|---|---|
| Los Angeles | **3.48** | 1,466.1 | 1,378 | 534 | 1,213 | 50 |
| Atlanta | **3.54** | 1,469.0 | 1,372 | 451 | 1,245 | 46 |
| San Diego | **3.73** | 1,489.0 | 1,394 | 506 | 1,194 | 47 |
| Montreal | **3.78** | 1,440.1 | 1,352 | 482 | 1,204 | 43 |
| Florida | **3.95** | 1,443.0 | 1,385 | 598 | 1,051 | 41 |
| St. Louis | **3.98** | 1,452.1 | 1,380 | 539 | 1,050 | 43 |
| New York | **4.22** | 1,440.0 | 1,517 | 532 | 999 | 41 |
| Cincinnati | **4.33** | 1,443.0 | 1,447 | 591 | 1,089 | 52 |
| Chicago | **4.36** | 1,456.1 | 1,447 | 546 | 1,027 | 34 |
| Houston | **4.38** | 1,447.0 | 1,541 | 539 | 1,164 | 35 |
| Philadelphia | **4.49** | 1,423.1 | 1,463 | 510 | 1,043 | 42 |
| Pittsburgh | **4.64** | 1,454.1 | 1,603 | 479 | 1,046 | 37 |
| San Francisco | **4.72** | 1,442.1 | 1,520 | 570 | 998 | 35 |
| Colorado | **5.60** | 1,422.2 | 1,597 | 624 | 932 | 34 |

## Individual Batting (at least 150 at-bats); Individual Pitching (at least 70 innings or 10 saves)

### Atlanta Braves

| Batting | AB | R | H | HR | RBI | SB | Avg |
|---|---|---|---|---|---|---|---|
| C. Jones | 598 | 114 | 185 | 30 | 110 | 14 | **.309** |
| Grissom | 671 | 106 | 207 | 23 | 74 | 28 | **.308** |
| McGriff | 617 | 81 | 182 | 28 | 107 | 7 | **.295** |
| Lopez | 489 | 56 | 138 | 23 | 69 | 1 | **.282** |
| Klesko | 528 | 90 | 149 | 34 | 93 | 6 | **.282** |
| Dye | 292 | 32 | 82 | 12 | 37 | 1 | **.281** |
| Perez | 156 | 19 | 40 | 4 | 17 | 0 | **.256** |
| Lemke | 498 | 64 | 127 | 5 | 37 | 5 | **.255** |
| Blauser | 265 | 48 | 65 | 10 | 35 | 6 | **.245** |
| Whiten | 272 | 45 | 66 | 10 | 38 | 15 | **.243** |
| Pendleton | 568 | 51 | 135 | 11 | 75 | 2 | **.238** |
| Smith | 153 | 16 | 31 | 3 | 16 | 1 | **.203** |

| Pitching | W | L | ERA | IP | H | BB | SO | Sv |
|---|---|---|---|---|---|---|---|---|
| Bielecki | 4 | 3 | **2.63** | 75.1 | 63 | 33 | 71 | 2 |
| Maddux | 15 | 11 | **2.72** | 245.0 | 225 | 28 | 172 | 0 |
| Smoltz | 24 | 8 | **2.94** | 253.2 | 199 | 55 | 276 | 0 |
| Glavine | 15 | 10 | **2.98** | 235.1 | 222 | 85 | 181 | 0 |
| Wohlers | 2 | 4 | **3.03** | 77.1 | 71 | 21 | 100 | 39 |
| McMichael | 5 | 3 | **3.22** | 86.2 | 84 | 27 | 78 | 2 |
| Neagle | 16 | 9 | **3.50** | 221.1 | 226 | 48 | 149 | 0 |
| Avery | 7 | 10 | **4.47** | 131.0 | 146 | 40 | 86 | 0 |
| Clontz | 6 | 3 | **5.69** | 80.2 | 78 | 33 | 49 | 1 |

Manager—Bobby Cox

### Chicago Cubs

| Batting | AB | R | H | HR | RBI | SB | Avg |
|---|---|---|---|---|---|---|---|
| Grace | 547 | 88 | 181 | 9 | 75 | 2 | **.331** |
| McRae | 624 | 111 | 172 | 17 | 66 | 37 | **.276** |
| Sosa | 498 | 84 | 136 | 40 | 100 | 18 | **.273** |
| Gonzalez | 483 | 70 | 131 | 15 | 79 | 9 | **.271** |
| Servais | 445 | 42 | 118 | 11 | 63 | 0 | **.265** |
| Magadan | 169 | 23 | 43 | 3 | 17 | 0 | **.254** |
| Sandberg | 554 | 85 | 135 | 25 | 92 | 12 | **.244** |
| Hernandez | 331 | 52 | 80 | 10 | 41 | 4 | **.242** |
| Gomez | 362 | 44 | 86 | 17 | 56 | 1 | **.238** |
| Bullett | 165 | 26 | 35 | 3 | 16 | 7 | **.212** |
| Sanchez | 289 | 28 | 61 | 1 | 12 | 7 | **.211** |

| Pitching | W | L | ERA | IP | H | BB | SO | Sv |
|---|---|---|---|---|---|---|---|---|
| Wendell | 4 | 5 | **2.84** | 79.1 | 58 | 44 | 75 | 18 |
| Adams | 3 | 6 | **2.94** | 101.0 | 84 | 49 | 78 | 4 |
| Trachsel | 13 | 9 | **3.03** | 205.0 | 181 | 62 | 132 | 0 |
| Navarro | 15 | 12 | **3.92** | 236.2 | 244 | 72 | 158 | 0 |
| Castillo | 7 | 16 | **5.28** | 182.1 | 209 | 46 | 139 | 0 |
| Telemaco | 5 | 7 | **5.46** | 97.1 | 108 | 31 | 64 | 0 |
| Foster | 7 | 6 | **6.21** | 87.0 | 98 | 35 | 53 | 0 |
| Bullinger | 6 | 10 | **6.54** | 129.1 | 144 | 68 | 90 | 1 |

Manager—Jim Riggleman

## Cincinnati Reds

| Batting | AB | R | H | HR | RBI | SB | Avg |
|---|---|---|---|---|---|---|---|
| Morris | 528 | 82 | 165 | 16 | 80 | 7 | **.313** |
| Larkin | 517 | 117 | 154 | 33 | 89 | 36 | **.298** |
| Taubensee | 327 | 46 | 95 | 12 | 48 | 3 | **.291** |
| Davis | 415 | 81 | 119 | 26 | 83 | 23 | **.287** |
| Harris | 302 | 33 | 86 | 5 | 32 | 14 | **.285** |
| Howard | 360 | 50 | 98 | 6 | 42 | 6 | **.272** |
| Sanders | 287 | 49 | 72 | 14 | 33 | 24 | **.251** |
| Branson | 311 | 34 | 76 | 9 | 37 | 2 | **.244** |
| Greene | 287 | 48 | 70 | 19 | 63 | 0 | **.244** |
| Oliver | 289 | 31 | 70 | 11 | 46 | 2 | **.242** |
| Boone | 520 | 56 | 121 | 12 | 69 | 3 | **.233** |
| Owens | 205 | 26 | 41 | 0 | 9 | 16 | **.200** |

| Pitching | W | L | ERA | IP | H | BB | SO | Sv |
|---|---|---|---|---|---|---|---|---|
| Brantley | 1 | 2 | **2.41** | 71.0 | 54 | 28 | 76 | 44 |
| Shaw | 8 | 6 | **2.49** | 104.2 | 99 | 29 | 69 | 4 |
| Smiley | 13 | 14 | **3.64** | 217.1 | 207 | 54 | 171 | 0 |
| Carrasco | 4 | 3 | **3.75** | 74.1 | 58 | 45 | 59 | 0 |
| Burba | 11 | 13 | **3.83** | 195.0 | 179 | 97 | 148 | 0 |
| Portugal | 8 | 9 | **3.98** | 156.0 | 146 | 42 | 93 | 0 |
| Morgan | 6 | 11 | **4.63** | 130.1 | 146 | 47 | 74 | 0 |
| Salkeld | 8 | 5 | **5.20** | 116.0 | 114 | 54 | 82 | 0 |
| Jarvis | 8 | 9 | **5.98** | 120.1 | 152 | 43 | 63 | 0 |

Manager—Ray Knight

## Colorado Rockies

| Batting | AB | R | H | HR | RBI | SB | Avg |
|---|---|---|---|---|---|---|---|
| Burks | 613 | 142 | 211 | 40 | 128 | 32 | **.344** |
| Young | 568 | 113 | 184 | 8 | 74 | 53 | **.324** |
| Bichette | 633 | 114 | 198 | 31 | 141 | 31 | **.313** |
| Castilla | 629 | 97 | 191 | 40 | 113 | 7 | **.304** |
| Galarraga | 626 | 119 | 190 | 47 | 150 | 18 | **.304** |
| McCracken | 283 | 50 | 82 | 3 | 40 | 17 | **.290** |
| J. Reed | 341 | 34 | 97 | 8 | 37 | 2 | **.284** |
| Weiss | 517 | 89 | 146 | 8 | 48 | 10 | **.282** |
| Walker | 272 | 58 | 75 | 18 | 58 | 18 | **.276** |
| Vander Wal | 151 | 20 | 38 | 5 | 31 | 2 | **.252** |
| Anthony | 185 | 32 | 45 | 12 | 22 | 0 | **.243** |
| Owens | 180 | 31 | 43 | 4 | 17 | 4 | **.239** |
| Bates | 160 | 19 | 33 | 1 | 9 | 2 | **.206** |

| Pitching | W | L | ERA | IP | H | BB | SO | Sv |
|---|---|---|---|---|---|---|---|---|
| S. Reed | 4 | 3 | **3.96** | 75.0 | 66 | 19 | 51 | 0 |
| Holmes | 5 | 4 | **3.97** | 77.0 | 78 | 28 | 73 | 1 |
| Ruffin | 7 | 5 | **4.00** | 69.2 | 55 | 29 | 74 | 24 |
| Wright | 4 | 4 | **4.93** | 91.1 | 105 | 41 | 45 | 0 |
| Reynoso | 8 | 9 | **4.96** | 168.2 | 195 | 49 | 88 | 0 |
| Ritz | 17 | 11 | **5.28** | 213.0 | 236 | 105 | 105 | 0 |
| Ma.Thompson | 9 | 11 | **5.30** | 169.2 | 189 | 74 | 99 | 0 |
| Freeman | 7 | 9 | **6.04** | 129.2 | 151 | 57 | 71 | 0 |
| Leskanic | 7 | 5 | **6.23** | 73.2 | 82 | 38 | 76 | 6 |
| Bailey | 2 | 3 | **6.24** | 83.2 | 94 | 52 | 45 | 1 |

Manager—Don Baylor

## Florida Marlins

| Batting | AB | R | H | HR | RBI | SB | Avg |
|---|---|---|---|---|---|---|---|
| Sheffield | 519 | 118 | 163 | 42 | 120 | 16 | **.314** |
| Renteria | 431 | 68 | 133 | 5 | 31 | 16 | **.309** |
| Conine | 597 | 84 | 175 | 26 | 95 | 1 | **.293** |
| Colbrunn | 511 | 60 | 146 | 16 | 69 | 4 | **.286** |
| Arias | 224 | 27 | 62 | 3 | 26 | 2 | **.277** |
| White | 552 | 77 | 151 | 17 | 84 | 22 | **.274** |
| Castillo | 164 | 26 | 43 | 1 | 8 | 17 | **.262** |
| Abbott | 320 | 37 | 81 | 8 | 33 | 3 | **.253** |
| Veras | 253 | 40 | 64 | 4 | 14 | 8 | **.253** |
| Orsulak | 217 | 23 | 48 | 2 | 19 | 1 | **.221** |
| Johnson | 386 | 34 | 84 | 13 | 37 | 1 | **.218** |

| Pitching | W | L | ERA | IP | H | BB | SO | Sv |
|---|---|---|---|---|---|---|---|---|
| Brown | 17 | 11 | **1.89** | 233.0 | 187 | 33 | 159 | 0 |
| Nen | 5 | 1 | **1.95** | 83.0 | 67 | 21 | 92 | 35 |
| Leiter | 16 | 12 | **2.93** | 215.1 | 153 | 19 | 200 | 0 |
| Burkett | 6 | 10 | **4.32** | 154.0 | 154 | 42 | 108 | 0 |
| Powell | 4 | 3 | **4.54** | 71.1 | 71 | 36 | 52 | 2 |
| Weathers | 2 | 2 | **4.54** | 71.1 | 85 | 28 | 40 | 0 |
| Rapp | 8 | 16 | **5.10** | 162.1 | 184 | 91 | 86 | 0 |
| Hammond | 5 | 8 | **6.56** | 81.0 | 104 | 27 | 50 | 0 |

Manager—Rene Lachemann; John Boles

## Houston Astros

| Batting | AB | R | H | HR | RBI | SB | Avg |
|---|---|---|---|---|---|---|---|
| Bagwell | 568 | 111 | 179 | 31 | 120 | 21 | **.315** |
| Biggio | 605 | 113 | 174 | 15 | 75 | 25 | **.288** |
| Gutierrez | 218 | 28 | 62 | 1 | 15 | 6 | **.284** |
| Berry | 431 | 55 | 121 | 17 | 95 | 12 | **.281** |
| Hunter | 526 | 74 | 145 | 5 | 35 | 35 | **.276** |
| Eusebio | 152 | 15 | 41 | 1 | 19 | 0 | **.270** |
| Cangelosi | 262 | 49 | 69 | 1 | 16 | 17 | **.263** |
| Mouton | 300 | 40 | 79 | 3 | 34 | 21 | **.263** |
| Bell | 627 | 84 | 165 | 17 | 113 | 29 | **.263** |
| Miller | 468 | 43 | 120 | 15 | 58 | 3 | **.256** |
| Spiers | 218 | 27 | 55 | 6 | 26 | 7 | **.252** |
| May | 259 | 24 | 65 | 5 | 33 | 2 | **.251** |
| Cedeno | 156 | 11 | 36 | 3 | 18 | 3 | **.231** |
| Manwaring | 227 | 14 | 52 | 1 | 18 | 0 | **.229** |

| Pitching | W | L | ERA | IP | H | BB | SO | Sv |
|---|---|---|---|---|---|---|---|---|
| Hampton | 10 | 10 | **3.59** | 160.1 | 175 | 49 | 101 | 0 |
| Reynolds | 16 | 10 | **3.65** | 239.0 | 227 | 44 | 204 | 0 |
| Darwin | 10 | 11 | **3.77** | 164.2 | 160 | 27 | 96 | 0 |
| Kile | 12 | 11 | **4.19** | 219.0 | 233 | 97 | 219 | 0 |
| Jones | 6 | 3 | **4.40** | 57.1 | 61 | 32 | 44 | 17 |
| Wall | 9 | 8 | **4.56** | 150.0 | 170 | 34 | 99 | 0 |
| Drabek | 7 | 9 | **4.57** | 175.1 | 208 | 60 | 137 | 0 |
| Hernandez | 5 | 5 | **4.62** | 78.0 | 77 | 28 | 81 | 6 |

Manager—Terry Collins

## Los Angeles Dodgers

| Batting | AB | R | H | HR | RBI | SB | Avg |
|---|---|---|---|---|---|---|---|
| Piazza | 547 | 87 | 184 | 36 | 105 | 0 | **.336** |
| Mondesi | 634 | 98 | 188 | 24 | 88 | 14 | **.297** |
| Hollandsworth | 478 | 64 | 139 | 12 | 59 | 21 | **.291** |
| Kirby | 188 | 23 | 51 | 1 | 11 | 4 | **.271** |
| Clark | 226 | 28 | 61 | 8 | 36 | 2 | **.270** |
| Blowers | 317 | 31 | 84 | 6 | 38 | 0 | **.265** |
| Karros | 608 | 84 | 158 | 34 | 111 | 8 | **.260** |
| Gagne | 428 | 48 | 109 | 10 | 55 | 4 | **.255** |
| Cedeno | 211 | 26 | 52 | 2 | 18 | 5 | **.246** |
| Wallach | 162 | 14 | 37 | 4 | 22 | 0 | **.228** |
| DeShields | 581 | 75 | 130 | 5 | 41 | 48 | **.224** |
| Fonville | 201 | 34 | 41 | 0 | 13 | 7 | **.204** |

| Pitching | W | L | ERA | IP | H | BB | SO | Sv |
|---|---|---|---|---|---|---|---|---|
| Guthrie | 2 | 3 | **2.22** | 73.0 | 65 | 22 | 56 | 1 |
| Osuna | 9 | 6 | **3.00** | 84.0 | 65 | 32 | 85 | 4 |
| Worrell | 4 | 6 | **3.03** | 65.1 | 70 | 15 | 66 | 44 |
| Nomo | 16 | 11 | **3.19** | 228.1 | 180 | 85 | 234 | 0 |
| Valdes | 15 | 7 | **3.32** | 225.0 | 219 | 54 | 173 | 0 |
| R. Martinez | 15 | 6 | **3.42** | 168.2 | 153 | 86 | 134 | 0 |
| Astacio | 9 | 8 | **3.44** | 211.2 | 207 | 67 | 130 | 0 |
| Park | 5 | 5 | **3.64** | 108.2 | 82 | 71 | 119 | 0 |
| Candiotti | 9 | 11 | **4.49** | 152.1 | 172 | 43 | 79 | 0 |

Manager—Tommy Lasorda; Bill Russell

## Montreal Expos

| Batting | AB | R | H | HR | RBI | SB | Avg |
|---|---|---|---|---|---|---|---|
| Grudzielanek | 657 | 99 | 201 | 6 | 49 | 33 | **.306** |
| White | 334 | 35 | 98 | 6 | 41 | 14 | **.293** |
| Segui | 416 | 69 | 119 | 11 | 58 | 4 | **.286** |
| Lansing | 641 | 99 | 183 | 11 | 53 | 23 | **.285** |
| Alou | 540 | 87 | 152 | 21 | 96 | 9 | **.281** |
| Santangelo | 393 | 54 | 109 | 7 | 56 | 5 | **.277** |
| Rodriguez | 532 | 81 | 147 | 36 | 103 | 2 | **.276** |
| Fletcher | 394 | 41 | 105 | 12 | 57 | 0 | **.266** |
| Obando | 178 | 30 | 44 | 8 | 22 | 2 | **.247** |
| Floyd | 227 | 29 | 55 | 6 | 26 | 7 | **.242** |
| Webster | 174 | 18 | 40 | 2 | 17 | 0 | **.230** |
| Andrews | 375 | 43 | 85 | 19 | 64 | 3 | **.227** |
| Silvestri | 162 | 16 | 33 | 1 | 17 | 2 | **.204** |

| Pitching | W | L | ERA | IP | H | BB | SO | Sv |
|---|---|---|---|---|---|---|---|---|
| Rojas | 7 | 4 | **3.22** | 81.0 | 56 | 28 | 92 | 36 |
| Manuel | 4 | 1 | **3.24** | 86.0 | 70 | 26 | 62 | 0 |
| Juden | 5 | 0 | **3.27** | 74.1 | 61 | 34 | 61 | 0 |
| Fassero | 15 | 11 | **3.30** | 231.2 | 217 | 55 | 222 | 0 |
| Martinez | 13 | 10 | **3.70** | 216.2 | 189 | 70 | 222 | 0 |
| Urbina | 10 | 5 | **3.71** | 114.0 | 102 | 44 | 108 | 0 |
| Daal | 4 | 5 | **4.02** | 87.1 | 74 | 37 | 82 | 0 |
| Cormier | 7 | 10 | **4.17** | 159.2 | 165 | 41 | 100 | 0 |
| Veres | 6 | 3 | **4.17** | 77.2 | 85 | 32 | 81 | 4 |
| Dyer | 5 | 5 | **4.40** | 75.2 | 79 | 34 | 51 | 2 |
| Leiter | 8 | 12 | **4.92** | 205.0 | 219 | 69 | 164 | 0 |

Manager—Felipe Alou

## New York Mets

| Batting | AB | R | H | HR | RBI | SB | Avg |
|---|---|---|---|---|---|---|---|
| Johnson | 682 | 117 | 227 | 9 | 69 | 50 | **.333** |
| Gilkey | 571 | 108 | 181 | 30 | 117 | 17 | **.317** |
| Vizcaino | 363 | 47 | 110 | 1 | 32 | 9 | **.303** |
| Ochoa | 282 | 37 | 83 | 4 | 33 | 4 | **.294** |
| Kent | 335 | 45 | 97 | 9 | 39 | 4 | **.290** |
| Huskey | 414 | 43 | 115 | 15 | 60 | 1 | **.278** |
| Alfonzo | 368 | 36 | 96 | 4 | 40 | 2 | **.261** |
| Hundley | 540 | 85 | 140 | 41 | 112 | 1 | **.259** |
| Ordonez | 502 | 51 | 129 | 1 | 30 | 1 | **.257** |
| Brogna | 188 | 18 | 48 | 7 | 30 | 0 | **.255** |
| Everett | 192 | 29 | 46 | 1 | 16 | 6 | **.240** |

| Pitching | W | L | ERA | IP | H | BB | SO | Sv |
|---|---|---|---|---|---|---|---|---|
| J. Franco | 4 | 3 | **1.83** | 54.0 | 54 | 21 | 48 | 28 |
| Mlicki | 6 | 7 | **3.30** | 90.0 | 95 | 33 | 83 | 1 |
| Clark | 14 | 11 | **3.43** | 212.1 | 217 | 48 | 142 | 0 |
| DiPoto | 7 | 2 | **4.19** | 77.1 | 91 | 45 | 52 | 0 |
| Harnisch | 8 | 12 | **4.21** | 194.2 | 195 | 61 | 114 | 0 |
| B. Jones | 12 | 8 | **4.42** | 195.2 | 219 | 46 | 116 | 0 |
| Person | 4 | 5 | **4.52** | 89.2 | 86 | 35 | 76 | 0 |
| Henry | 2 | 8 | **4.68** | 75.0 | 82 | 36 | 58 | 9 |
| Isringhausen | 6 | 14 | **4.77** | 171.2 | 190 | 73 | 114 | 0 |
| Wilson | 5 | 12 | **5.38** | 149.0 | 157 | 71 | 109 | 0 |

Manager—Dallas Green; Bobby Valentine

## Philadelphia Phillies

| Batting | AB | R | H | HR | RBI | SB | Avg |
|---|---|---|---|---|---|---|---|
| Eisenreich | 338 | 45 | 122 | 3 | 41 | 11 | **.361** |
| Jefferies | 404 | 59 | 118 | 7 | 51 | 20 | **.292** |
| Otero | 411 | 54 | 112 | 2 | 32 | 16 | **.273** |
| Zeile | 500 | 61 | 134 | 20 | 80 | 1 | **.268** |
| Santiago | 481 | 71 | 127 | 30 | 85 | 2 | **.264** |
| Stocker | 394 | 46 | 100 | 5 | 41 | 6 | **.254** |
| Lieberthal | 166 | 21 | 42 | 7 | 23 | 0 | **.253** |
| Morandini | 539 | 64 | 135 | 3 | 32 | 26 | **.250** |
| Incaviglia | 269 | 33 | 63 | 16 | 42 | 2 | **.234** |

| Pitching | W | L | ERA | IP | H | BB | SO | Sv |
|---|---|---|---|---|---|---|---|---|
| Ryan | 3 | 5 | **2.43** | 89.0 | 71 | 45 | 70 | 8 |
| Schilling | 9 | 10 | **3.19** | 183.1 | 149 | 50 | 182 | 0 |
| Bottalico | 4 | 5 | **3.19** | 67.2 | 47 | 23 | 74 | 34 |
| Grace | 7 | 2 | **3.49** | 80.0 | 72 | 16 | 49 | 0 |
| Borland | 7 | 3 | **4.07** | 90.2 | 83 | 43 | 76 | 0 |
| Springer | 3 | 10 | **4.66** | 96.2 | 106 | 38 | 94 | 0 |
| Mulholland | 8 | 7 | **4.66** | 133.1 | 157 | 21 | 52 | 0 |
| Williams | 6 | 14 | **5.44** | 167.0 | 188 | 67 | 103 | 0 |
| Mimbs | 3 | 9 | **5.53** | 99.1 | 116 | 41 | 56 | 0 |

Manager—Jim Fregosi

## Pittsburgh Pirates

| Batting | AB | R | H | HR | RBI | SB | Avg |
|---|---|---|---|---|---|---|---|
| Martin | 630 | 101 | 189 | 18 | 72 | 38 | **.300** |
| Kendell | 414 | 54 | 124 | 3 | 42 | 5 | **.300** |
| Merced | 453 | 69 | 130 | 17 | 80 | 8 | **.287** |
| Garcia | 390 | 66 | 111 | 6 | 44 | 16 | **.285** |
| Johnson | 343 | 55 | 94 | 13 | 47 | 6 | **.274** |
| King | 591 | 91 | 160 | 30 | 111 | 15 | **.271** |
| Liriano | 217 | 23 | 58 | 3 | 30 | 2 | **.267** |
| Allensworth | 229 | 32 | 60 | 4 | 31 | 11 | **.262** |
| Bell | 527 | 65 | 132 | 13 | 71 | 6 | **.250** |
| Hayes | 459 | 51 | 114 | 10 | 62 | 6 | **.248** |
| Kingery | 276 | 32 | 68 | 3 | 27 | 2 | **.246** |

| Pitching | W | L | ERA | IP | H | BB | SO | Sv |
|---|---|---|---|---|---|---|---|---|
| Wilkins | 4 | 3 | **3.84** | 75.0 | 75 | 36 | 62 | 1 |
| Lieber | 9 | 5 | **3.99** | 142.0 | 156 | 28 | 94 | 1 |
| Cordova | 4 | 7 | **4.09** | 99.0 | 103 | 20 | 95 | 12 |
| Plesac | 6 | 5 | **4.09** | 70.1 | 67 | 24 | 76 | 11 |
| Smith | 4 | 6 | **5.08** | 83.1 | 104 | 21 | 47 | 0 |
| Wagner | 4 | 8 | **5.40** | 81.2 | 86 | 39 | 81 | 0 |
| Schmidt | 5 | 6 | **5.70** | 96.1 | 108 | 53 | 74 | 0 |
| Miceli | 2 | 10 | **5.78** | 85.2 | 99 | 45 | 66 | 1 |

Manager—Jim Leyland

## St. Louis Cardinals

| Batting | AB | R | H | HR | RBI | SB | Avg |
|---|---|---|---|---|---|---|---|
| Jordan | 513 | 82 | 159 | 17 | 104 | 22 | **.310** |
| McGee | 309 | 52 | 95 | 5 | 41 | 5 | **.307** |
| Mabry | 543 | 63 | 161 | 13 | 74 | 3 | **.297** |
| Smith | 227 | 36 | 64 | 2 | 18 | 7 | **.282** |
| Clayton | 491 | 64 | 136 | 6 | 35 | 33 | **.277** |
| Lankford | 545 | 100 | 150 | 21 | 86 | 35 | **.275** |
| Gaetti | 522 | 71 | 143 | 23 | 80 | 2 | **.274** |
| Pagnozzi | 407 | 48 | 110 | 13 | 55 | 4 | **.270** |
| Sweeney | 170 | 32 | 45 | 3 | 22 | 3 | **.265** |
| Alicea | 380 | 54 | 98 | 5 | 42 | 11 | **.258** |
| Gant | 419 | 74 | 103 | 30 | 82 | 13 | **.246** |
| Sheaffer | 198 | 10 | 45 | 2 | 20 | 3 | **.227** |

| Pitching | W | L | ERA | IP | H | BB | SO | Sv |
|---|---|---|---|---|---|---|---|---|
| Mathews | 2 | 6 | **3.01** | 83.2 | 62 | 32 | 80 | 6 |
| Eckersley | 0 | 6 | **3.30** | 60.0 | 65 | 6 | 49 | 30 |
| Osborne | 13 | 9 | **3.53** | 198.2 | 191 | 57 | 134 | 0 |
| Petkovsek | 11 | 2 | **3.55** | 88.2 | 83 | 35 | 45 | 0 |
| Andy Benes | 18 | 10 | **3.83** | 230.1 | 215 | 77 | 160 | 1 |
| Stottlemyre | 14 | 11 | **3.87** | 223.1 | 191 | 93 | 194 | 0 |
| Alan Benes | 13 | 10 | **4.90** | 191.0 | 192 | 87 | 131 | 0 |

Manager—Tony La Russa

## San Diego Padres

| Batting | AB | R | H | HR | RBI | SB | Avg |
|---|---|---|---|---|---|---|---|
| Gwynn | 451 | 67 | 159 | 3 | 50 | 11 | **.353** |
| Caminiti | 546 | 109 | 178 | 40 | 130 | 11 | **.326** |
| Flaherty | 264 | 22 | 80 | 9 | 41 | 2 | **.303** |
| Finley | 655 | 126 | 195 | 30 | 95 | 22 | **.298** |
| Livingstone | 172 | 20 | 51 | 2 | 20 | 0 | **.297** |
| Cianfrocco | 192 | 21 | 54 | 2 | 32 | 1 | **.281** |
| Joyner | 433 | 59 | 120 | 8 | 65 | 5 | **.277** |
| Johnson | 243 | 18 | 66 | 8 | 35 | 0 | **.272** |
| Gomez | 328 | 32 | 86 | 3 | 29 | 2 | **.262** |
| Newfield | 191 | 27 | 48 | 5 | 26 | 1 | **.251** |
| Reed | 495 | 45 | 121 | 2 | 49 | 2 | **.244** |
| Henderson | 465 | 110 | 112 | 9 | 29 | 37 | **.241** |

| Pitching | W | L | ERA | IP | H | BB | SO | Sv |
|---|---|---|---|---|---|---|---|---|
| Hoffman | 9 | 5 | **2.25** | 88.0 | 50 | 31 | 111 | 42 |
| Worrell | 9 | 7 | **3.05** | 121.0 | 109 | 39 | 99 | 1 |
| Ashby | 9 | 5 | **3.23** | 150.2 | 147 | 34 | 85 | 0 |
| Sanders | 9 | 5 | **3.38** | 144.0 | 117 | 48 | 157 | 0 |
| Valenzuela | 13 | 8 | **3.62** | 171.2 | 177 | 67 | 95 | 0 |
| Hamilton | 15 | 9 | **4.17** | 211.2 | 206 | 83 | 184 | 0 |
| Tewksbury | 10 | 10 | **4.31** | 206.2 | 224 | 43 | 126 | 0 |
| Bergman | 6 | 8 | **4.37** | 113.1 | 119 | 33 | 85 | 0 |
| Blair | 2 | 6 | **4.60** | 88.0 | 80 | 29 | 67 | 1 |

Manager—Bruce Bochy

## San Francisco Giants

| Batting | AB | R | H | HR | RBI | SB | Avg |
|---|---|---|---|---|---|---|---|
| Mueller | 200 | 31 | 66 | 0 | 19 | 0 | **.330** |
| Bonds | 517 | 122 | 159 | 42 | 129 | 40 | **.308** |
| M. Williams | 404 | 69 | 122 | 22 | 85 | 1 | **.302** |
| Dunston | 287 | 27 | 86 | 5 | 25 | 8 | **.300** |
| Hill | 379 | 56 | 106 | 19 | 67 | 6 | **.280** |
| Javier | 274 | 44 | 74 | 2 | 22 | 14 | **.270** |
| Carreon | 292 | 40 | 76 | 9 | 51 | 2 | **.260** |
| Benard | 488 | 89 | 121 | 5 | 27 | 25 | **.248** |
| Wilkins | 411 | 53 | 100 | 14 | 59 | 0 | **.243** |
| Aurilia | 318 | 27 | 76 | 3 | 26 | 4 | **.239** |
| Lampkin | 177 | 26 | 41 | 6 | 29 | 1 | **.232** |
| Scarsone | 283 | 28 | 62 | 5 | 23 | 2 | **.219** |
| McCarty | 175 | 16 | 38 | 6 | 24 | 2 | **.217** |
| Thompson | 227 | 35 | 48 | 5 | 21 | 2 | **.211** |

| Pitching | W | L | ERA | IP | H | BB | SO | Sv |
|---|---|---|---|---|---|---|---|---|
| Beck | 0 | 9 | **3.34** | 62.0 | 56 | 10 | 48 | 35 |
| Estes | 3 | 5 | **3.60** | 70.0 | 63 | 39 | 60 | 0 |
| Rueter | 6 | 8 | **3.97** | 102.0 | 109 | 27 | 46 | 0 |
| Dewey | 6 | 3 | **4.21** | 83.1 | 79 | 41 | 57 | 0 |
| Gardner | 12 | 7 | **4.42** | 179.1 | 200 | 57 | 145 | 0 |
| Watson | 8 | 12 | **4.61** | 185.2 | 189 | 69 | 128 | 0 |
| Fernandez | 7 | 13 | **4.61** | 171.2 | 193 | 57 | 106 | 0 |
| VanLandingham | 9 | 14 | **5.40** | 181.2 | 196 | 78 | 97 | 0 |

Manager—Dusty Baker

# American League Records, 1996

Final standings

## Eastern Division

| | W | L | Pct. | GB | Home | vs. East | vs. Central | vs. West |
|---|---|---|---|---|---|---|---|---|
| New York | 92 | 70 | .568 | — | 49-31 | 32-20 | 37-24 | 23-26 |
| Baltimore* | 88 | 74 | .543 | 4 | 43-38 | 29-23 | 34-26 | 25-25 |
| Boston | 85 | 77 | .525 | 7 | 47-34 | 33-19 | 23-37 | 29-21 |
| Toronto | 74 | 88 | .457 | 18 | 35-46 | 22-30 | 30-32 | 22-26 |
| Detroit | 53 | 109 | .327 | 39 | 27-54 | 14-38 | 19-42 | 20-29 |

## Central Division

| | W | L | Pct. | GB | Home | vs. East | vs. Central | vs. West |
|---|---|---|---|---|---|---|---|---|
| Cleveland | 99 | 62 | .615 | — | 51-29 | 40-20 | 32-20 | 27-22 |
| Chicago | 85 | 77 | .525 | 14½ | 44-37 | 37-25 | 24-28 | 24-24 |
| Milwaukee | 80 | 82 | .494 | 19½ | 38-43 | 26-33 | 32-21 | 22-28 |
| Minnesota | 78 | 84 | .481 | 21½ | 39-43 | 30-31 | 21-31 | 27-22 |
| Kansas City | 75 | 86 | .466 | 24 | 37-43 | 27-34 | 22-30 | 26-22 |

## Western Division

| | W | L | Pct. | GB | Home | vs. East | vs. Central | vs. West |
|---|---|---|---|---|---|---|---|---|
| Texas | 90 | 72 | .556 | — | 50-31 | 42-20 | 30-31 | 18-21 |
| Seattle | 85 | 76 | .528 | 4½ | 43-38 | 31-30 | 31-30 | 23-16 |
| Oakland | 78 | 84 | .481 | 12 | 40-41 | 24-38 | 32-29 | 22-17 |
| California | 70 | 91 | .435 | 19½ | 43-38 | 30-31 | 25-36 | 15-24 |

*Wild card team.

## Division Series

Baltimore defeated Cleveland 3 games to 1 (10-4, 7-4, 4-9, 4-3 [12])
New York defeated Texas 3 games to 1 (2-6 [12], 5-4, 3-2, 6-4)

## Championship Series

New York defeated Baltimore 4 games to 1 (5-4 [11], 3-5, 5-2, 8-4, 6-4)

## Team Batting

| | Avg | AB | R | H | HR | RBI |
|---|---|---|---|---|---|---|
| Cleveland | **.293** | 5,681 | 952 | 1,665 | 218 | 904 |
| Minnesota | **.288** | 5,673 | 877 | 1,633 | 118 | 812 |
| New York | **.288** | 5,628 | 871 | 1,621 | 162 | 830 |
| Seattle | **.287** | 5,668 | 993 | 1,625 | 245 | 954 |
| Texas | **.284** | 5,703 | 928 | 1,622 | 221 | 890 |
| Boston | **.283** | 5,756 | 928 | 1,631 | 209 | 882 |
| Chicago | **.281** | 5,644 | 898 | 1,586 | 195 | 860 |
| Milwaukee | **.279** | 5,659 | 894 | 1,577 | 178 | 845 |
| California | **.276** | 5,682 | 762 | 1,571 | 192 | 727 |
| Baltimore | **.274** | 5,689 | 949 | 1,557 | 257 | 914 |
| Kansas City | **.266** | 5,543 | 746 | 1,477 | 123 | 689 |
| Oakland | **.265** | 5,630 | 861 | 1,492 | 243 | 822 |
| Toronto | **.259** | 5,599 | 766 | 1,451 | 177 | 712 |
| Detroit | **.256** | 5,530 | 783 | 1,413 | 204 | 741 |

## Team Pitching

| | ERA | IP | H | BB | SO | Sv |
|---|---|---|---|---|---|---|
| Cleveland | **4.35** | 1,452.1 | 1,530 | 484 | 1,033 | 46 |
| Chicago | **4.53** | 1,461.0 | 1,529 | 616 | 1,039 | 43 |
| Kansas City | **4.55** | 1,450.0 | 1,563 | 460 | 925 | 37 |
| Toronto | **4.58** | 1,445.2 | 1,476 | 610 | 1,033 | 35 |
| New York | **4.65** | 1,440.0 | 1,469 | 610 | 1,139 | 53 |
| Texas | **4.66** | 1,449.1 | 1,569 | 582 | 976 | 43 |
| Boston | **5.00** | 1,458.0 | 1,606 | 722 | 1,166 | 37 |
| Baltimore | **5.15** | 1,468.2 | 1,604 | 597 | 1,047 | 44 |
| Milwaukee | **5.17** | 1,447.1 | 1,570 | 635 | 846 | 42 |
| Oakland | **5.20** | 1,456.1 | 1,638 | 644 | 884 | 34 |
| Seattle | **5.21** | 1,431.2 | 1,562 | 605 | 1,000 | 34 |
| Minnesota | **5.30** | 1,439.2 | 1,561 | 581 | 959 | 31 |
| California | **5.31** | 1,439.0 | 1,546 | 662 | 1,052 | 38 |
| Detroit | **6.38** | 1,432.2 | 1,699 | 784 | 957 | 22 |

## Individual Batting (at least 150 at-bats); Individual Pitching (at least 70 innings or 10 saves)

### Baltimore Orioles

| Batting | AB | R | H | HR | RBI | SB | Avg |
|---|---|---|---|---|---|---|---|
| Alomar | 588 | 132 | 193 | 22 | 94 | 17 | **.328** |
| Anderson | 579 | 117 | 172 | 50 | 110 | 2 | **.297** |
| Surhoff | 537 | 74 | 157 | 21 | 82 | 0 | **.292** |
| Palmeiro | 626 | 110 | 181 | 39 | 142 | 8 | **.289** |
| Bonilla | 595 | 107 | 171 | 28 | 116 | 1 | **.287** |
| C. Ripken | 640 | 94 | 178 | 26 | 102 | 1 | **.278** |
| Murray | 566 | 69 | 147 | 22 | 79 | 4 | **.260** |
| Hoiles | 407 | 64 | 105 | 25 | 73 | 0 | **.258** |
| Polonia | 175 | 25 | 42 | 2 | 14 | 8 | **.240** |
| Devereaux | 323 | 49 | 74 | 8 | 34 | 8 | **.229** |
| Hammonds | 248 | 38 | 56 | 9 | 27 | 3 | **.226** |

| Pitching | W | L | ERA | IP | H | BB | SO | Sv |
|---|---|---|---|---|---|---|---|---|
| R. Myers | 4 | 4 | **3.53** | 58.2 | 60 | 29 | 74 | 31 |
| Mussina | 19 | 11 | **4.81** | 243.1 | 264 | 69 | 204 | 0 |
| Krivda | 3 | 5 | **4.96** | 81.2 | 89 | 39 | 54 | 0 |
| Erickson | 13 | 12 | **5.02** | 222.1 | 262 | 66 | 100 | 0 |
| Wells | 11 | 14 | **5.14** | 224.1 | 247 | 51 | 130 | 0 |
| Coppinge | 10 | 6 | **5.18** | 125.0 | 126 | 60 | 104 | 0 |
| Haynes | 3 | 6 | **8.29** | 89.0 | 122 | 58 | 65 | 1 |

**Manager**—Davey Johnson

### Boston Red Sox

| Batting | AB | R | H | HR | RBI | SB | Avg |
|---|---|---|---|---|---|---|---|
| Jefferson | 386 | 67 | 134 | 19 | 74 | 0 | **.347** |
| M. Vaughn | 635 | 118 | 207 | 44 | 143 | 2 | **.326** |
| Valentin | 527 | 84 | 156 | 13 | 59 | 9 | **.296** |
| Greenwell | 295 | 35 | 87 | 7 | 44 | 4 | **.295** |
| Canseco | 360 | 68 | 104 | 28 | 82 | 3 | **.289** |
| Naehring | 430 | 77 | 124 | 17 | 65 | 2 | **.288** |
| Cordero | 198 | 29 | 57 | 3 | 37 | 2 | **.288** |
| Frye | 419 | 74 | 120 | 4 | 41 | 18 | **.286** |
| Haselman | 237 | 33 | 65 | 8 | 34 | 4 | **.274** |
| Stanley | 397 | 73 | 107 | 24 | 69 | 2 | **.270** |
| Bragg | 417 | 74 | 109 | 10 | 47 | 14 | **.261** |
| O'Leary | 497 | 68 | 129 | 15 | 81 | 3 | **.260** |
| Tinsley | 192 | 28 | 47 | 3 | 14 | 6 | **.245** |

| Pitching | W | L | ERA | IP | H | BB | SO | Sv |
|---|---|---|---|---|---|---|---|---|
| Slocumb | 5 | 5 | **3.02** | 83.1 | 68 | 55 | 88 | 31 |
| Brandenburg | 5 | 5 | **3.43** | 76.0 | 76 | 33 | 66 | 0 |
| Clemens | 10 | 13 | **3.63** | 242.2 | 216 | 106 | 257 | 0 |
| Wakefield | 14 | 13 | **5.14** | 211.2 | 238 | 90 | 140 | 0 |
| Sele | 7 | 11 | **5.32** | 157.1 | 192 | 67 | 137 | 0 |
| Gordon | 12 | 9 | **5.59** | 215.2 | 249 | 105 | 171 | 0 |
| Eshelman | 6 | 3 | **7.08** | 87.2 | 112 | 58 | 59 | 0 |

**Manager**—Kevin Kennedy

## California Angels

| Batting | AB | R | H | HR | RBI | SB | Avg |
|---|---|---|---|---|---|---|---|
| Hudler | 302 | 60 | 94 | 16 | 40 | 14 | **.311** |
| Edmonds | 431 | 73 | 131 | 27 | 66 | 4 | **.304** |
| Davis | 530 | 73 | 155 | 28 | 95 | 5 | **.292** |
| Fabregas | 254 | 18 | 73 | 2 | 26 | 0 | **.287** |
| Salmon | 581 | 90 | 166 | 30 | 98 | 4 | **.286** |
| Anderson | 607 | 79 | 173 | 12 | 72 | 7 | **.285** |
| Velarde | 530 | 82 | 151 | 14 | 54 | 7 | **.285** |
| Erstad | 208 | 34 | 59 | 4 | 20 | 3 | **.284** |
| Snow | 575 | 69 | 148 | 17 | 67 | 1 | **.257** |
| DiSarcina | 536 | 62 | 137 | 5 | 48 | 2 | **.256** |
| Arias | 252 | 19 | 60 | 6 | 28 | 2 | **.238** |
| Wallach | 190 | 23 | 45 | 8 | 20 | 1 | **.237** |

| Pitching | W | L | ERA | IP | H | BB | SO | Sv |
|---|---|---|---|---|---|---|---|---|
| Percival | 0 | 2 | **2.31** | 74.0 | 38 | 31 | 100 | 36 |
| James | 5 | 5 | **2.67** | 81.0 | 62 | 42 | 65 | 1 |
| Finley | 15 | 16 | **4.16** | 238.0 | 241 | 94 | 215 | 0 |
| Langston | 6 | 5 | **4.82** | 123.1 | 116 | 45 | 83 | 0 |
| Boskie | 12 | 11 | **5.32** | 189.1 | 226 | 67 | 133 | 0 |
| Springer | 5 | 6 | **5.51** | 94.2 | 91 | 43 | 64 | 0 |
| Grimsley | 5 | 7 | **6.84** | 130.1 | 150 | 74 | 82 | 0 |
| Gohr | 5 | 9 | **7.24** | 115.2 | 163 | 44 | 75 | 1 |
| J. Abbott | 2 | 18 | **7.48** | 142.0 | 171 | 78 | 58 | 0 |

**Manager**—Marcel Lachemann; John McNamara

## Chicago White Sox

| Batting | AB | R | H | HR | RBI | SB | Avg |
|---|---|---|---|---|---|---|---|
| F. Thomas | 527 | 110 | 184 | 40 | 134 | 1 | **.349** |
| Martinez | 440 | 85 | 140 | 10 | 53 | 15 | **.318** |
| Slaught | 243 | 25 | 76 | 6 | 36 | 0 | **.313** |
| Baines | 495 | 80 | 154 | 22 | 95 | 3 | **.311** |
| Mouton | 214 | 25 | 63 | 7 | 39 | 3 | **.294** |
| Ventura | 586 | 96 | 168 | 34 | 105 | 1 | **.287** |
| Phillips | 581 | 119 | 161 | 12 | 63 | 13 | **.277** |
| Durham | 557 | 79 | 153 | 10 | 65 | 30 | **.275** |
| Cedeno | 301 | 46 | 82 | 2 | 20 | 6 | **.272** |
| Guillen | 499 | 62 | 131 | 4 | 45 | 6 | **.263** |
| Borders | 151 | 12 | 39 | 5 | 14 | 0 | **.258** |
| Tartabull | 472 | 58 | 120 | 27 | 101 | 1 | **.254** |
| Lewis | 337 | 55 | 77 | 4 | 53 | 21 | **.228** |
| Karkovice | 355 | 44 | 78 | 10 | 38 | 0 | **.220** |

| Pitching | W | L | ERA | IP | H | BB | SO | Sv |
|---|---|---|---|---|---|---|---|---|
| Hernandez | 6 | 5 | **1.91** | 84.2 | 65 | 38 | 85 | 38 |
| Fernandez | 16 | 10 | **3.45** | 258.0 | 248 | 72 | 200 | 0 |
| Castillo | 5 | 4 | **3.60** | 95.0 | 95 | 24 | 57 | 2 |
| Alvarez | 15 | 10 | **4.22** | 217.1 | 216 | 97 | 181 | 0 |
| Baldwin | 11 | 6 | **4.42** | 169.0 | 168 | 57 | 127 | 0 |
| Simas | 2 | 8 | **4.58** | 72.2 | 75 | 39 | 65 | 2 |
| Tapani | 13 | 10 | **4.59** | 225.1 | 236 | 76 | 150 | 0 |

**Manager**—Terry Bevington

## Cleveland Indians

| Batting | AB | R | H | HR | RBI | SB | Avg |
|---|---|---|---|---|---|---|---|
| Seitzer | 573 | 85 | 187 | 13 | 78 | 6 | **.326** |
| Franco | 432 | 72 | 139 | 14 | 76 | 8 | **.322** |
| Lofton | 662 | 132 | 210 | 14 | 67 | 75 | **.317** |
| Thome | 505 | 122 | 157 | 38 | 116 | 2 | **.311** |
| Belle | 602 | 124 | 187 | 48 | 148 | 11 | **.311** |
| Ramirez | 550 | 94 | 170 | 33 | 112 | 8 | **.309** |
| Vizquel | 542 | 98 | 161 | 9 | 64 | 35 | **.297** |
| Vizcaino | 179 | 23 | 51 | 0 | 13 | 6 | **.285** |
| Baerga | 424 | 54 | 113 | 10 | 55 | 1 | **.267** |
| Alomar | 418 | 53 | 110 | 11 | 50 | 1 | **.263** |
| T. Pena | 174 | 14 | 34 | 1 | 27 | 0 | **.195** |

| Pitching | W | L | ERA | IP | H | BB | SO | Sv |
|---|---|---|---|---|---|---|---|---|
| Plunk | 3 | 2 | **2.43** | 77.2 | 56 | 34 | 85 | 2 |
| Nagy | 17 | 5 | **3.41** | 222.0 | 217 | 61 | 167 | 0 |
| Mesa | 2 | 7 | **3.73** | 72.1 | 69 | 28 | 64 | 39 |
| Hershiser | 15 | 9 | **4.24** | 206.0 | 238 | 58 | 125 | 0 |
| Martinez | 9 | 6 | **4.50** | 112.0 | 122 | 37 | 48 | 0 |
| Ogea | 10 | 6 | **4.79** | 146.2 | 151 | 42 | 101 | 0 |
| McDowell | 13 | 9 | **5.11** | 192.0 | 214 | 67 | 141 | 0 |
| Tavarez | 4 | 7 | **5.36** | 80.2 | 101 | 22 | 46 | 0 |

**Manager**—Mike Hargrove

## Detroit Tigers

| Batting | AB | R | H | HR | RBI | SB | Avg |
|---|---|---|---|---|---|---|---|
| Higginson | 440 | 75 | 141 | 26 | 81 | 6 | **.320** |
| Pride | 267 | 52 | 80 | 10 | 31 | 11 | **.300** |
| M. Lewis | 545 | 69 | 147 | 11 | 55 | 6 | **.270** |
| Fryman | 616 | 90 | 165 | 22 | 100 | 4 | **.268** |
| Curtis | 400 | 65 | 105 | 10 | 37 | 16 | **.263** |
| Bartee | 217 | 32 | 55 | 1 | 14 | 20 | **.253** |
| Clark | 376 | 56 | 94 | 27 | 72 | 0 | **.250** |
| Flaherty | 152 | 18 | 38 | 4 | 23 | 1 | **.250** |
| Ausmus | 226 | 30 | 56 | 4 | 22 | 3 | **.248** |
| Sierra | 518 | 61 | 128 | 12 | 72 | 4 | **.247** |
| Nieves | 431 | 71 | 106 | 24 | 60 | 1 | **.246** |
| Trammell | 193 | 16 | 45 | 1 | 16 | 6 | **.233** |
| E. Williams | 215 | 22 | 43 | 6 | 26 | 0 | **.200** |
| Cedeno | 179 | 19 | 35 | 7 | 20 | 2 | **.196** |

| Pitching | W | L | ERA | IP | H | BB | SO | Sv |
|---|---|---|---|---|---|---|---|---|
| R. Lewis | 4 | 6 | **4.18** | 90.1 | 78 | 65 | 78 | 2 |
| Olivares | 7 | 11 | **4.89** | 160.0 | 169 | 75 | 81 | 0 |
| Sager | 4 | 5 | **5.01** | 79.0 | 91 | 29 | 52 | 0 |
| Lira | 6 | 14 | **5.22** | 194.2 | 204 | 66 | 113 | 0 |
| Lima | 5 | 6 | **5.70** | 72.2 | 87 | 22 | 59 | 3 |
| B. Williams | 3 | 10 | **6.77** | 121.0 | 145 | 85 | 72 | 2 |
| Keagle | 3 | 6 | **7.39** | 87.2 | 104 | 68 | 70 | 0 |
| Van Poppel | 3 | 9 | **9.06** | 99.1 | 139 | 62 | 53 | 1 |

**Manager**—Buddy Bell

## Kansas City Royals

| Batting | AB | R | H | HR | RBI | SB | Avg |
|---|---|---|---|---|---|---|---|
| Offerman | 561 | 85 | 170 | 5 | 47 | 24 | **.303** |
| Randa | 337 | 36 | 102 | 6 | 47 | 13 | **.303** |
| Roberts | 339 | 39 | 96 | 0 | 52 | 12 | **.283** |
| Goodwin | 524 | 80 | 148 | 1 | 35 | 66 | **.292** |
| Sweeney | 165 | 23 | 46 | 4 | 24 | 1 | **.279** |
| Macfarlane | 379 | 58 | 104 | 19 | 54 | 3 | **.274** |
| Lockhart | 433 | 49 | 118 | 7 | 55 | 11 | **.273** |
| Damon | 517 | 61 | 140 | 6 | 50 | 25 | **.271** |
| Tucker | 339 | 55 | 88 | 12 | 53 | 10 | **.260** |
| Paquette | 429 | 61 | 111 | 22 | 67 | 5 | **.259** |
| Hamelin | 239 | 31 | 61 | 9 | 40 | 5 | **.255** |
| Vitiello | 257 | 29 | 62 | 8 | 40 | 2 | **.241** |
| Howard | 420 | 51 | 92 | 4 | 48 | 5 | **.219** |

| Pitching | W | L | ERA | IP | H | BB | SO | Sv |
|---|---|---|---|---|---|---|---|---|
| Rosado | 8 | 6 | **3.21** | 106.2 | 101 | 26 | 64 | 0 |
| Appier | 14 | 11 | **3.62** | 211.1 | 192 | 75 | 207 | 0 |
| Belcher | 15 | 11 | **3.92** | 238.2 | 262 | 68 | 113 | 0 |
| Montgomery | 4 | 6 | **4.26** | 63.1 | 59 | 19 | 45 | 24 |
| Haney | 10 | 14 | **4.70** | 228.0 | 267 | 51 | 115 | 0 |
| Linton | 7 | 9 | **5.02** | 104.0 | 111 | 26 | 87 | 0 |
| Gubicza | 4 | 12 | **5.13** | 119.1 | 132 | 34 | 55 | 0 |

**Manager**—Bob Boone

## Milwaukee Brewers

| Batting | AB | R | H | HR | RBI | SB | Avg |
|---|---|---|---|---|---|---|---|
| Nilsson | 453 | 81 | 150 | 17 | 84 | 2 | **.331** |
| Cirillo | 566 | 101 | 184 | 15 | 83 | 4 | **.325** |
| Newfield | 179 | 21 | 55 | 7 | 31 | 0 | **.307** |
| Jaha | 543 | 108 | 163 | 34 | 118 | 3 | **.300** |
| Vina | 554 | 94 | 157 | 7 | 46 | 16 | **.283** |
| Vaughn | 375 | 78 | 105 | 31 | 95 | 5 | **.280** |
| Loretta | 154 | 20 | 43 | 1 | 13 | 2 | **.279** |
| Mieske | 374 | 46 | 104 | 14 | 64 | 1 | **.278** |
| Burnitz | 200 | 38 | 53 | 9 | 40 | 4 | **.265** |
| Valentin | 552 | 90 | 143 | 24 | 95 | 17 | **.259** |
| Williams | 325 | 43 | 82 | 5 | 34 | 10 | **.252** |
| Levis | 233 | 27 | 55 | 1 | 21 | 0 | **.236** |
| Matheny | 313 | 31 | 64 | 8 | 46 | 3 | **.204** |

| Pitching | W | L | ERA | IP | H | BB | SO | Sv |
|---|---|---|---|---|---|---|---|---|
| Fetters | 3 | 3 | **3.38** | 61.1 | 65 | 26 | 53 | 32 |
| McDonald | 12 | 10 | **3.90** | 221.1 | 228 | 67 | 146 | 0 |
| Wickman | 7 | 1 | **4.42** | 95.2 | 106 | 44 | 75 | 0 |
| Eldred | 4 | 4 | **4.46** | 84.2 | 82 | 38 | 50 | 0 |
| Karl | 13 | 9 | **4.86** | 207.1 | 220 | 72 | 121 | 0 |
| Miranda | 7 | 6 | **4.94** | 109.1 | 116 | 69 | 78 | 1 |
| D'Amico | 6 | 6 | **5.44** | 86.0 | 88 | 31 | 53 | 0 |
| Sparks | 4 | 7 | **6.60** | 88.2 | 103 | 52 | 21 | 0 |
| Garcia | 4 | 4 | **6.66** | 75.2 | 84 | 21 | 40 | 4 |

**Manager**—Phil Garner

## Minnesota Twins

| Batting | AB | R | H | HR | RBI | SB | Avg |
|---|---|---|---|---|---|---|---|
| Molitor | 660 | 99 | 225 | 9 | 113 | 18 | **.341** |
| Knoblauch | 578 | 140 | 197 | 13 | 72 | 45 | **.341** |
| Kelly | 322 | 41 | 104 | 6 | 47 | 10 | **.323** |
| Cordova | 569 | 97 | 176 | 16 | 111 | 11 | **.309** |
| Coomer | 233 | 34 | 69 | 12 | 41 | 3 | **.296** |
| Becker | 525 | 92 | 153 | 12 | 71 | 19 | **.291** |
| Myers | 329 | 37 | 94 | 6 | 47 | 0 | **.286** |
| Stahoviak | 405 | 72 | 115 | 13 | 61 | 3 | **.284** |
| Meares | 517 | 66 | 138 | 8 | 67 | 9 | **.267** |
| Lawton | 252 | 34 | 65 | 6 | 42 | 4 | **.258** |
| Walbeck | 215 | 25 | 48 | 2 | 24 | 3 | **.223** |
| Reboulet | 234 | 20 | 52 | 0 | 23 | 4 | **.222** |

| Pitching | W | L | ERA | IP | H | BB | SO | Sv |
|---|---|---|---|---|---|---|---|---|
| Radke | 11 | 16 | **4.46** | 232.0 | 231 | 57 | 148 | 0 |
| Stevens | 3 | 3 | **4.66** | 58.0 | 58 | 25 | 29 | 11 |
| Rodriguez | 13 | 14 | **5.05** | 206.2 | 218 | 78 | 110 | 2 |
| Robertson | 7 | 17 | **5.12** | 186.1 | 197 | 116 | 114 | 0 |
| Guardado | 6 | 5 | **5.25** | 73.2 | 61 | 33 | 74 | 4 |
| Aguilera | 8 | 6 | **5.42** | 111.1 | 124 | 27 | 83 | 0 |
| Hansell | 3 | 0 | **5.69** | 74.1 | 83 | 31 | 46 | 3 |
| Parra | 5 | 5 | **6.04** | 70.0 | 88 | 27 | 50 | 0 |
| Aldred | 6 | 9 | **6.21** | 165.1 | 194 | 68 | 111 | 0 |

**Manager**—Tom Kelly

## New York Yankees

| Batting | AB | R | H | HR | RBI | SB | Avg |
|---|---|---|---|---|---|---|---|
| Duncan | 400 | 62 | 136 | 8 | 56 | 4 | **.340** |
| Jeter | 582 | 104 | 183 | 10 | 78 | 14 | **.314** |
| Boggs | 501 | 80 | 156 | 2 | 41 | 1 | **.311** |
| B. Williams | 551 | 108 | 168 | 29 | 102 | 17 | **.305** |
| O'Neill | 546 | 89 | 165 | 19 | 91 | 0 | **.302** |
| Girardi | 422 | 55 | 124 | 2 | 45 | 13 | **.294** |
| Martinez | 595 | 82 | 174 | 25 | 117 | 2 | **.292** |
| Raines | 201 | 45 | 57 | 9 | 33 | 10 | **.284** |
| Leyritz | 265 | 23 | 70 | 7 | 40 | 2 | **.264** |
| Strawberry | 202 | 35 | 53 | 11 | 36 | 6 | **.262** |
| Fielder | 591 | 85 | 149 | 39 | 117 | 2 | **.252** |
| Listach | 317 | 51 | 76 | 1 | 33 | 25 | **.240** |
| Sojo | 287 | 23 | 63 | 1 | 21 | 2 | **.220** |
| Fox | 189 | 26 | 37 | 3 | 13 | 11 | **.196** |

| Pitching | W | L | ERA | IP | H | BB | SO | Sv |
|---|---|---|---|---|---|---|---|---|
| M. Rivera | 8 | 3 | **2.09** | 107.2 | 73 | 34 | 130 | 5 |
| Wetteland | 2 | 3 | **2.83** | 63.2 | 54 | 21 | 69 | 43 |
| Cone | 7 | 2 | **2.88** | 72.0 | 50 | 34 | 71 | 0 |
| Pettitte | 21 | 8 | **3.87** | 221.0 | 229 | 72 | 162 | 0 |
| Nelson | 4 | 4 | **4.36** | 74.1 | 75 | 36 | 91 | 2 |
| Rogers | 12 | 8 | **4.68** | 179.0 | 179 | 83 | 92 | 0 |
| Key | 12 | 11 | **4.68** | 169.1 | 171 | 58 | 116 | 0 |
| Gooden | 11 | 7 | **5.01** | 170.2 | 169 | 88 | 126 | 0 |
| Bones | 7 | 14 | **6.22** | 152.0 | 184 | 68 | 63 | 0 |

**Manager**—Joe Torre

## Oakland Athletics

| Batting | AB | R | H | HR | RBI | SB | Avg |
|---|---|---|---|---|---|---|---|
| McGwire | 423 | 104 | 132 | 52 | 113 | 0 | **.312** |
| Brosius | 428 | 73 | 130 | 22 | 71 | 7 | **.304** |
| Batista | 238 | 38 | 71 | 6 | 25 | 7 | **.298** |
| Giambi | 536 | 84 | 156 | 20 | 79 | 0 | **.291** |
| Berroa | 586 | 101 | 170 | 36 | 106 | 0 | **.290** |
| Steinbach | 514 | 79 | 140 | 35 | 100 | 0 | **.272** |
| Herrera | 320 | 44 | 86 | 6 | 30 | 8 | **.269** |
| Gates | 247 | 26 | 65 | 2 | 30 | 1 | **.263** |
| Young | 462 | 72 | 112 | 19 | 64 | 7 | **.242** |
| Bournigal | 252 | 33 | 61 | 0 | 18 | 4 | **.242** |
| Bordick | 525 | 46 | 126 | 5 | 54 | 5 | **.240** |
| Plantier | 231 | 29 | 49 | 7 | 31 | 2 | **.212** |

| Pitching | W | L | ERA | IP | H | BB | SO | Sv |
|---|---|---|---|---|---|---|---|---|
| Mohler | 6 | 3 | **3.67** | 81.0 | 79 | 41 | 64 | 7 |
| Groom | 5 | 0 | **3.84** | 77.1 | 85 | 34 | 57 | 2 |
| Adams | 3 | 4 | **4.01** | 76.1 | 76 | 23 | 68 | 0 |
| Corsi | 6 | 0 | **4.03** | 73.2 | 71 | 34 | 43 | 3 |
| Prieto | 6 | 7 | **4.15** | 125.2 | 130 | 54 | 75 | 0 |
| Taylor | 6 | 3 | **4.33** | 60.1 | 52 | 25 | 67 | 17 |
| Telgheder | 4 | 7 | **4.65** | 79.1 | 92 | 26 | 43 | 0 |
| Reyes | 7 | 10 | **4.78** | 122.1 | 134 | 61 | 78 | 0 |
| Wengert | 7 | 11 | **5.58** | 161.1 | 200 | 60 | 75 | 0 |
| Wojciechowski | 5 | 5 | **5.65** | 79.2 | 97 | 28 | 30 | 0 |
| Wasdin | 8 | 7 | **5.96** | 131.1 | 145 | 50 | 75 | 0 |
| Johns | 6 | 12 | **5.98** | 158.0 | 187 | 69 | 71 | 1 |

**Manager**—Art Howe

## Seattle Mariners

| Batting | AB | R | H | HR | RBI | SB | Avg |
|---|---|---|---|---|---|---|---|
| Rodriguez | 601 | 141 | 215 | 36 | 123 | 15 | **.358** |
| E. Martinez | 499 | 121 | 163 | 26 | 103 | 3 | **.327** |
| Griffey | 545 | 125 | 165 | 49 | 140 | 16 | **.303** |
| Amaral | 312 | 69 | 91 | 1 | 29 | 25 | **.292** |
| Cora | 530 | 90 | 154 | 6 | 45 | 5 | **.291** |
| Sorrento | 471 | 67 | 136 | 23 | 93 | 0 | **.289** |
| Wilson | 491 | 51 | 140 | 18 | 83 | 1 | **.285** |
| Buhner | 564 | 107 | 153 | 44 | 138 | 0 | **.271** |
| Hunter | 198 | 21 | 53 | 7 | 28 | 0 | **.268** |
| Hollins | 516 | 88 | 135 | 16 | 78 | 6 | **.262** |
| Strange | 183 | 19 | 43 | 3 | 23 | 1 | **.235** |
| R. Davis | 167 | 24 | 39 | 5 | 18 | 2 | **.234** |

| Pitching | W | L | ERA | IP | H | BB | SO | Sv |
|---|---|---|---|---|---|---|---|---|
| Jackson | 1 | 1 | **3.63** | 72.0 | 61 | 24 | 70 | 6 |
| Moyer | 13 | 3 | **3.98** | 160.2 | 177 | 46 | 79 | 0 |
| Charlton | 4 | 7 | **4.04** | 75.2 | 68 | 38 | 73 | 20 |
| Carmona | 8 | 3 | **4.28** | 90.1 | 95 | 55 | 62 | 1 |
| Wells | 12 | 7 | **5.30** | 130.2 | 141 | 46 | 94 | 0 |
| Hitchcock | 13 | 9 | **5.35** | 196.2 | 245 | 73 | 132 | 0 |
| Wolcott | 7 | 10 | **5.73** | 149.1 | 179 | 54 | 78 | 0 |
| Wagner | 3 | 5 | **6.86** | 80.0 | 91 | 38 | 41 | 0 |

**Manager**—Lou Piniella

## Texas Rangers

| Batting | AB | R | H | HR | RBI | SB | Avg |
|---|---|---|---|---|---|---|---|
| Greer | 542 | 96 | 180 | 18 | 100 | 9 | **.332** |
| Gonzalez | 541 | 89 | 170 | 47 | 144 | 2 | **.314** |
| Rodriguez | 639 | 116 | 192 | 19 | 86 | 5 | **.300** |
| Hamilton | 627 | 94 | 184 | 6 | 51 | 15 | **.293** |
| McLemore | 517 | 84 | 150 | 5 | 46 | 27 | **.290** |
| Clark | 436 | 69 | 124 | 13 | 72 | 2 | **.284** |
| Palmer | 582 | 98 | 163 | 38 | 107 | 2 | **.280** |
| Newson | 235 | 34 | 60 | 10 | 31 | 3 | **.255** |
| Elster | 515 | 79 | 130 | 24 | 99 | 4 | **.252** |
| Tettleton | 491 | 78 | 121 | 24 | 83 | 2 | **.246** |

| Pitching | W | L | ERA | IP | H | BB | SO | Sv |
|---|---|---|---|---|---|---|---|---|
| Hill | 16 | 10 | **3.63** | 250.2 | 250 | 95 | 170 | 0 |
| Stanton | 4 | 4 | **3.66** | 78.2 | 78 | 27 | 60 | 1 |
| Cook | 5 | 2 | **4.09** | 70.1 | 53 | 35 | 64 | 0 |
| Oliver | 14 | 6 | **4.66** | 173.2 | 190 | 76 | 112 | 0 |
| Pavlik | 15 | 8 | **5.19** | 201.0 | 216 | 81 | 127 | 0 |
| Gross | 11 | 8 | **5.22** | 129.1 | 151 | 50 | 78 | 0 |
| Witt | 16 | 12 | **5.41** | 199.2 | 235 | 96 | 157 | 0 |
| Henneman | 0 | 7 | **5.79** | 42.0 | 41 | 17 | 34 | 31 |
| Heredia | 2 | 5 | **5.89** | 73.1 | 91 | 14 | 43 | 1 |

**Manager**—Johnny Oates

## Toronto Blue Jays

| Batting | AB | R | H | HR | RBI | SB | Avg |
|---|---|---|---|---|---|---|---|
| R. Perez | 202 | 30 | 66 | 2 | 21 | 3 | **.327** |
| Nixon | 496 | 87 | 142 | 1 | 29 | 54 | **.286** |
| Green | 422 | 52 | 118 | 11 | 45 | 5 | **.280** |
| Olerud | 398 | 59 | 109 | 18 | 61 | 1 | **.274** |
| Delgado | 488 | 68 | 132 | 25 | 92 | 0 | **.270** |
| Brumfield | 308 | 52 | 79 | 12 | 52 | 12 | **.256** |
| Samuel | 188 | 34 | 48 | 8 | 26 | 9 | **.255** |
| Carter | 625 | 84 | 158 | 30 | 107 | 7 | **.253** |
| T. Perez | 295 | 24 | 74 | 1 | 19 | 1 | **.251** |
| Sprague | 591 | 88 | 146 | 36 | 101 | 0 | **.247** |
| O'Brien | 324 | 33 | 77 | 13 | 44 | 0 | **.238** |
| Gonzalez | 527 | 64 | 124 | 14 | 64 | 16 | **.235** |
| Martinez | 229 | 17 | 52 | 3 | 18 | 0 | **.227** |

| Pitching | W | L | ERA | IP | H | BB | SO | Sv |
|---|---|---|---|---|---|---|---|---|
| Guzman | 11 | 8 | **2.93** | 187.2 | 158 | 53 | 165 | 0 |
| Hentgen | 20 | 10 | **3.22** | 265.2 | 238 | 94 | 177 | 0 |
| Timlin | 1 | 6 | **3.65** | 56.2 | 47 | 18 | 52 | 31 |
| Flener | 3 | 2 | **4.58** | 70.2 | 68 | 33 | 44 | 0 |
| Hanson | 13 | 17 | **5.41** | 214.2 | 243 | 102 | 156 | 0 |
| Quantrill | 5 | 14 | **5.43** | 134.1 | 172 | 51 | 86 | 0 |
| Janzen | 4 | 6 | **7.33** | 73.2 | 95 | 38 | 47 | 0 |

**Manager**—Cito Gaston

# National Baseball Hall of Fame and Museum, Cooperstown, NY

Aaron, Hank
Alexander, Grover Cleveland
Alston, Walt
Anson, Cap
Aparicio, Luis
Appling, Luke
Ashburn, Richie
Averill, Earl
Baker, Home Run
Bancroft, Dave
Banks, Ernie
Barlick, Al
Barrow, Edward G.
Beckley, Jake
Bell, Cool Papa
Bench, Johnny
Bender, Chief
Berra, Yogi
Bottomley, Jim
Boudreau, Lou
Bresnahan, Roger
Brock, Lou
Brouthers, Dan
Brown, Mordecai (Three Finger)
Bulkeley, Morgan C.
**Bunning, Jim**
Burkett, Jesse C.
Campanella, Roy
Carew, Rod
Carey, Max
Carlton, Steve
Cartwright, Alexander
Chadwick, Henry
Chance, Frank
Chandler, Happy
Charleston, Oscar
Chesbro, John
Clarke, Fred
Clarkson, John
Clemente, Roberto
Cobb, Ty
Cochrane, Mickey
Collins, Eddie
Collins, James
Combs, Earle
Comiskey, Charles A.
Conlan, Jocko
Connolly, Thomas H.
Connor, Roger
Coveleski, Stan
Crawford, Sam
Cronin, Joe
Cummings, Candy
Cuyler, Kiki
Dandridge, Ray
Day, Leon
Dean, Dizzy
Delahanty, Ed
Dickey, Bill
DiHigo, Martin
DiMaggio, Joe
Doerr, Bobby
Drysdale, Don
Duffy, Hugh
Durocher, Leo
Evans, Billy
Evers, John
Ewing, Buck
Faber, Urban
Feller, Bob
Ferrell, Rick
Fingers, Rollie
Flick, Elmer H.
Ford, Whitey
Foster, Andrew (Rube)
**Foster, Bill**
Foxx, Jimmie
Frick, Ford
Frisch, Frank
Galvin, Pud
Gehrig, Lou
Gehringer, Charles
Gibson, Bob
Gibson, Josh
Giles, Warren
Gomez, Lefty
Goslin, Goose
Greenberg, Hank
Griffith, Clark
Grimes, Burleigh
Grove, Lefty
Hafey, Chick
Haines, Jesee
Hamilton, Bill
**Hanlon, Ned**
Harridge, Will
Harris, Bucky
Hartnett, Gabby
Heilmann, Harry
Herman, Billy
Hooper, Harry
Hornsby, Rogers
Hoyt, Waite
Hubbard, Cal
Hubbell, Carl
Huggins, Miller
Hulbert, William
Hunter, Catfish
Irvin, Monte
Jackson, Reggie
Jackson, Travis
Jenkins, Ferguson
Jennings, Hugh
Johnson, Byron
Johnson, William (Judy)
Johnson, Walter
Joss, Addie
Kaline, Al
Keefe, Timothy
Keeler, William
Kell, George
Kelley, Joe
Kelly, George
Kelly, King
Killebrew, Harmon
Kiner, Ralph
Klein, Chuck
Klem, Bill
Koufax, Sandy
Lajoie, Napoleon
Landis, Kenesaw M.
Lazzeri, Tony
Lemon, Bob
Leonard, Buck
Lindstrom, Fred
Lloyd, Pop
Lombardi, Ernie
Lopez, Al
Lyons, Ted
Mack, Connie
MacPhail, Larry
Mantle, Mickey
Manush, Henry
Maranville, Rabbit
Marichal, Juan
Marquard, Rube
Mathews, Eddie
Mathewson, Christy
Mays, Willie
McCarthy, Joe
McCarthy, Thomas
McCovey, Willie
McGinnity, Joe
McGowan, Bill
McGraw, John
McKechnie, Bill
Medwick, Joe
Mize, Johnny
Morgan, Joe
Musial, Stan
Newhouser, Hal
Nichols, Kid
O'Rourke, James
Ott, Mel
Paige, Satchel
Palmer, Jim
Pennock, Herb
Perry, Gaylord
Plank, Ed
Radbourn, Charlie
Reese, Pee Wee
Rice, Sam
Rickey, Branch
Rixey, Eppa
Rizzuto, Phil (Scooter)
Roberts, Robin
Robinson, Brooks
Robinson, Frank
Robinson, Jackie
Robinson, Wilbert
Roush, Edd
Ruffing, Red
Rusie, Amos
Ruth, Babe
Schalk, Ray
Schmidt, Mike
Schoendienst, Red
Seaver, Tom
Sewell, Joe
Simmons, Al
Sisler, George
Slaughter, Enos
Snider, Duke
Spahn, Warren
Spalding, Albert
Speaker, Tris
Stargell, Willie
Stengel, Casey
Terry, Bill
Thompson, Sam
Tinker, Joe
Traynor, Pie
Vance, Dazzy
Vaughan, Arky
Veeck, Bill
Waddell, Rube
Wagner, Honus
Wallace, Roderick
Walsh, Ed
Waner, Lloyd
Waner, Paul
Ward, John
**Weaver, Earl**
Weiss, George
Welch, Mickey
Wheat, Zach
Wilhelm, Hoyt
Williams, Billy
Williams, Ted
Williams, Vic
Wilson, Hack
Wright, George
Wright, Harry
Wynn, Early
Yastrzemski, Carl
Yawkey, Tom
Young, Cy
Youngs, Ross

**Note:** 1996 inductees are in **bold**.

# Hall of Famers Chosen in First Year of Eligibility

| | |
|---|---|
| **1962** | Jackie Robinson, Bob Feller |
| **1966** | Ted Williams |
| **1969** | Stan Musial |
| **1972** | Sandy Koufax |
| **1973** | Warren Spahn |
| **1974** | Mickey Mantle |
| **1977** | Ernie Banks |
| **1979** | Willie Mays |
| **1980** | Al Kaline |
| **1981** | Bob Gibson |
| **1982** | Hank Aaron, Frank Robinson |
| **1983** | Brooks Robinson |
| **1985** | Lou Brock |
| **1986** | Willie McCovey |
| **1988** | Willie Stargell |
| **1989** | Johnny Bench, Carl Yastrzemski |
| **1990** | Jim Palmer, Joe Morgan |
| **1991** | Rod Carew |
| **1992** | Tom Seaver |
| **1993** | Reggie Jackson |
| **1994** | Steve Carlton |
| **1995** | Mike Schmidt |

# All-Star Baseball Games, 1933-1996

| Year | Winner | Score | Host team |
|---|---|---|---|
| 1933 (day game) | American | **4-2** | Chicago (AL) |
| 1934 (day game) | American | **9-7** | New York (NL) |
| 1935 (day game) | American | **4-1** | Cleveland |
| 1936 (day game) | National | **4-3** | Boston (NL) |
| 1937 (day game) | American | **8-3** | Washington |
| 1938 (day game) | National | **4-1** | Cincinnati |
| 1939 (day game) | American | **3-1** | New York (AL) |
| 1940 (day game) | National | **4-0** | St. Louis (NL) |
| 1941 (day game) | American | **7-5** | Detroit |
| 1942 (day game) | American | **3-1** | New York (NL) |
| 1943 | American | **5-3** | Philadelphia (AL) |
| 1944 | National | **7-1** | Pittsburgh |
| 1945 | Not played | | |
| 1946 (day game) | American | **12-0** | Boston (AL) |
| 1947 (day game) | American | **2-1** | Chicago (NL) |
| 1948 (day game) | American | **5-2** | St. Louis (AL) |
| 1949 (day game) | American | **11-7** | Brooklyn |
| 1950 (day game) | National | **4-3 (14)** | Chicago (AL) |
| 1951 (day game) | National | **8-3** | Detroit |
| 1952 (day game) | National | **3-2** | Philadelphia (NL) |
| 1953 (day game) | National | **5-1** | Cincinnati |
| 1954 (day game) | American | **11-9** | Cleveland |
| 1955 (day game) | National | **6-5 (12)** | Milwaukee |
| 1956 (day game) | National | **7-3** | Washington |
| 1957 (day game) | American | **6-5** | St. Louis |
| 1958 (day game) | American | **4-3** | Baltimore |
| 1959 (day game) | National | **5-4** | Pittsburgh |
| 1959 (day game) | American | **5-3** | Los Angeles |
| 1960 (day game) | National | **5-3** | Kansas City |
| 1960 (day game) | National | **6-0** | New York (AL) |
| 1961 (day game) | National | **5-4 (10)** | San Francisco |
| 1961 (day game) | Called-rain | **1-1** | Boston |
| 1962 (day game) | National | **3-1 (10)** | Washington |
| 1962 (day game) | American | **9-4** | Chicago (NL) |
| 1963 (day game) | National | **5-3** | Cleveland |
| 1964 (day game) | National | **7-4** | New York (NL) |
| 1965 (day game) | National | **6-5** | Minnesota |
| 1966 (day game) | National | **2-1 (10)** | St. Louis |
| 1967 (day game) | National | **2-1 (15)** | California |
| 1968 | National | **1-0** | Houston |
| 1969 (day game) | National | **9-3** | Washington |
| 1970 | National | **5-4 (12)** | Cincinnati |
| 1971 | American | **6-4** | Detroit |
| 1972 | National | **4-3** | Atlanta |
| 1973 | National | **7-1** | Kansas City |
| 1974 | National | **7-2** | Pittsburgh |
| 1975 | National | **6-3** | Milwaukee |
| 1976 | National | **7-1** | Philadelphia |
| 1977 | National | **7-5** | New York (AL) |
| 1978 | National | **7-3** | San Diego |
| 1979 | National | **7-6** | Seattle |
| 1980 | National | **4-2** | Los Angeles |
| 1981 | National | **5-4** | Cleveland |
| 1982 | National | **4-1** | Montreal |
| 1983 | American | **13-3** | Chicago (AL) |
| 1984 | National | **3-1** | San Francisco |
| 1985 | National | **6-1** | Minnesota |
| 1986 | American | **3-2** | Houston |
| 1987 | National | **2-0 (13)** | Oakland |
| 1988 | American | **2-1** | Cincinnati |
| 1989 | American | **5-3** | California |
| 1990 | American | **2-0** | Chicago (NL) |
| 1991 | American | **4-2** | Toronto |
| 1992 | American | **13-6** | San Diego |
| 1993 | American | **9-3** | Baltimore |
| 1994 | National | **8-7** | Pittsburgh |
| 1995 | National | **3-2** | Texas |
| 1996 | National | **6-0** | Philadelphia |

# Major League Leaders in 1996

## American League

**Batting**

A. Rodriguez, Seattle, .358; F. Thomas, Chicago, .349; Molitor, Minnesota, .341; Knoblauch, Minnesota, .341; Greer, Texas, .332.

**Runs**

A. Rodriguez, Seattle, 141; Knoblauch, Minnesota, 140; R. Alomar, Baltimore, 132; Lofton, Cleveland, 132; Griffey, Seattle, 125.

**Runs Batted In**

Belle, Cleveland, 148; J. Gonzalez, Texas, 144; M. Vaughn, Boston 143; Palmeiro, Baltimore, 142; Griffey, Seattle, 140.

**Hits**

Molitor, Minnesota, 225; A. Rodriguez, Seattle, 215; Lofton, Cleveland, 210; M. Vaughn, Boston, 207; Knoblauch, Minnesota, 197.

**Doubles**

A. Rodriguez, Seattle, 54; E. Martinez, Seattle, 52; I. Rodriguez, Texas, 47; Cirillo, Milwaukee, 46; Cordova, Minnesota, 46.

**Triples**

Knoblauch, Minnesota, 14; Vina, Milwaukee, 10; Guillen, Chicago, 8; Martinez, Chicago, 8; Molitor, Minnesota, 8; Offerman, Kansas City, 8.

**Home Runs**

McGwire, Oakland, 52; B. Anderson, Baltimore, 50; Griffey, Seattle, 49; Belle, Cleveland, 48; J. Gonzalez, Texas, 47.

**Stolen Bases**

Lofton, Cleveland, 75; Goodwin, Kansas City, 66; O. Nixon, Toronto, 54; Knoblauch, Minnesota, 45; Vizquel, Cleveland, 35.

**Pitching (18 Decisions: W-L, ERA, Pct.)**

Nagy, Cleveland, 17-5, 3.14, .773; Pettitte, New York, 21-8, 3.87, .724; Oliver, Texas; 14-6, 4.66, .700; Hentgen, Toronto, 20-10, 3.22, .667; Pavlik, Texas, 15-8, 5.19, .652.

**Strikeouts**

Clemens, Boston, 257; Finley, California, 215; Appier, Kansas City, 207; Mussina, Baltimore, 204; A. Fernandez, Chicago, 200.

**Saves**

Wetteland, New York, 43; Mesa, Cleveland, 39; R. Hernandez, Chicago, 38; Percival, California, 36; Fetters, Milwaukee, 32.

## National League

**Batting**

Gwynn, San Diego, .353; Burks, Colorado, .344; Piazza, Los Angeles, .336; L. Johnson, New York, .333; Grace, Chicago, .331.

**Runs**

Burks, Colorado, 142; Finley, San Diego, 126; Bonds, San Francisco, 122; Galarraga, Colorado, 119; Sheffield, Florida, 118.

**Runs Batted In**

Galarraga, Colorado, 150; Bichette, Colorado, 141; Caminiti, San Diego, 130; Bonds, San Francisco, 129; Burks, Colorado, 128.

**Hits**

L. Johnson, New York, 227; Burks, Colorado, 211; Grissom, Atlanta, 207; Grudzielanek, Montreal, 201; Bichette, Colorado, 198.

**Doubles**

Bagwell, Houston, 48; Burks, Colorado, 45; Finley, San Diego, 45; Gilkey, New York, 44; H. Rodriguez, Montreal, 42.

**Triples**

L. Johnson, New York, 21; Grissom, Atlanta, 10; Howard, Cincinnati, 10; Finley, San Diego, 9.

**Home Runs**

Galarraga, Colorado, 47; Bonds, San Francisco, 42; Sheffield, Florida, 42; Hundley, New York, 41; Burks, Colorado, 40; Caminiti, San Diego, 40; Castilla, Colorado, 40; Sosa, Chicago, 40.

**Stolen Bases**

Young, Colorado, 53; L. Johnson, New York, 50; DeShields, Los Angeles, 48; Bonds, San Francisco, 40; Martin, Pittsburgh, 38.

**Pitching (18 Decisions: W-L, ERA, Pct.)**

Smoltz, Atlanta, 24-8, 2.94, .750; R. Martinez, Los Angeles, 15-6, 3.42, .714; Valdes, Los Angeles, 15-7, 3.32, .681; Andy Benes, St. Louis, 18-10, 3.83, .643; Neagle, Pittsburgh-Atlanta, 16-9, 3.50, .640.

**Strikeouts**

Smoltz, Atlanta, 276; Nomo, Los Angeles, 234; Fassero, Montreal, 222; P. Martinez, Montreal, 222; Kile, Houston, 219.

**Saves**

Brantley, Cincinnati, 44; Worrell, Los Angeles, 44; Hoffman, San Diego, 42; Wohlers, Atlanta, 39; Rojas, Montreal, 36.

# 1996 40-Home-Run Club

In the 1996 season, a record 17 players hit 40 or more home runs. Here are some of their offensive statistics:

| Player, team(s) | AB | HR | RBI | Avg |
|---|---|---|---|---|
| Mark McGwire, Oakland | 423 | 52 | 113 | .312 |
| Brady Anderson, Baltimore | 579 | 50 | 110 | .297 |
| Ken Griffey Jr., Seattle | 545 | 49 | 140 | .303 |
| Albert Belle, Cleveland | 602 | 48 | 148 | .311 |
| Andres Galarraga, Colorado | 626 | 47 | 150 | .304 |
| Juan Gonzalez, Texas | 541 | 47 | 144 | .314 |
| Jay Buhner, Seattle | 564 | 44 | 138 | .271 |
| Mo Vaughn, Boston | 635 | 44 | 143 | .326 |
| Barry Bonds, San Francisco | 517 | 42 | 129 | .308 |
| Gary Sheffield, Florida | 519 | 42 | 120 | .314 |
| Todd Hundley, New York Mets | 540 | 41 | 112 | .259 |
| Greg Vaughn, Milwaukee-San Diego (Total) | 516 | 41 | 117 | .260 |
| Ellis Burks, Colorado | 613 | 40 | 128 | .344 |
| Ken Caminiti, San Diego | 546 | 40 | 130 | .326 |
| Vinny Castilla, Colorado | 629 | 40 | 113 | .304 |
| Sammy Sosa, Chicago Cubs | 498 | 40 | 100 | .273 |
| Frank Thomas, Chicago White Sox | 527 | 40 | 134 | .349 |

# Earned Run Average Leaders

**National League**

| Year | Player, club | G | IP | ERA |
|---|---|---|---|---|
| 1977 | John Candelaria, Pittsburgh | 33 | 231 | **2.34** |
| 1978 | Craig Swan, New York | 29 | 207 | **2.43** |
| 1979 | J. R. Richard, Houston | 38 | 292 | **2.71** |
| 1980 | Don Sutton, Los Angeles | 32 | 212 | **2.21** |
| 1981 | Nolan Ryan, Houston | 21 | 149 | **1.69** |
| 1982 | Steve Rogers, Montreal | 35 | 277 | **2.40** |
| 1983 | Atlee Hammaker, San Francisco | 23 | 172 | **2.25** |
| 1984 | Alejandro Pena, Los Angeles | 28 | 199 | **2.48** |
| 1985 | Dwight Gooden, New York | 35 | 276 | **1.53** |
| 1986 | Mike Scott, Houston | 37 | 275 | **2.22** |
| 1987 | Nolan Ryan, Houston | 34 | 211 | **2.76** |
| 1988 | Joe Magrane, St. Louis | 24 | 165 | **2.18** |
| 1989 | Scott Garrelts, San Francisco | 30 | 193 | **2.28** |
| 1990 | Danny Darwin, Houston | 48 | 162 | **2.21** |
| 1991 | Dennis Martinez, Montreal | 31 | 222 | **2.39** |
| 1992 | Bill Swift, San Francisco | 30 | 164 | **2.08** |
| 1993 | Greg Maddux, Atlanta | 36 | 267 | **2.36** |
| 1994 | Greg Maddux, Atlanta | 25 | 202 | **1.56** |
| 1995 | Greg Maddux, Atlanta | 28 | 209 | **1.63** |
| 1996 | Kevin Brown, Florida | 32 | 233 | **1.89** |

**American League**

| Year | Player, club | G | IP | ERA |
|---|---|---|---|---|
| 1977 | Frank Tanana, California | 31 | 241 | **2.54** |
| 1978 | Ron Guidry, New York | 35 | 274 | **1.74** |
| 1979 | Ron Guidry, New York | 33 | 236 | **2.78** |
| 1980 | Rudy May, New York | 41 | 175 | **2.47** |
| 1981 | Steve McCatty, Oakland | 22 | 186 | **2.32** |
| 1982 | Rick Sutcliffe, Cleveland | 34 | 216 | **2.96** |
| 1983 | Rick Honeycutt, Texas | 25 | 174 | **2.42** |
| 1984 | Mike Boddicker, Baltimore | 34 | 261 | **2.79** |
| 1985 | Dave Stieb, Toronto | 36 | 265 | **2.48** |
| 1986 | Roger Clemens, Boston | 33 | 254 | **2.48** |
| 1987 | Jimmy Key, Toronto | 36 | 261 | **2.76** |
| 1988 | Allan Anderson, Minnesota | 30 | 202 | **2.45** |
| 1989 | Bret Saberhagen, Kansas City | 36 | 262 | **2.16** |
| 1990 | Roger Clemens, Boston | 31 | 228 | **1.93** |
| 1991 | Roger Clemens, Boston | 35 | 271 | **2.62** |
| 1992 | Roger Clemens, Boston | 32 | 246 | **2.41** |
| 1993 | Kevin Appier, Kansas City | 34 | 238 | **2.56** |
| 1994 | Steve Ontiveros, Oakland | 27 | 115 | **2.65** |
| 1995 | Randy Johnson, Seattle | 30 | 214 | **2.48** |
| 1996 | Juan Guzman, Toronto | 27 | 187 | **2.93** |

ERA is computed by multiplying earned runs allowed by 9, then dividing by innings pitched.

# Yankees Defeat Braves 4 Games to 2 in the 1996 World Series

The New York Yankees defeated the defending-champion Atlanta Braves 4 games to 2 in the 1996 World Series for a stunning come-from-behind victory. The Braves jumped out to a 2-game lead and looked likely to breeze through the Series when the Yanks began to turn the tide. In game 4, the Braves led 6-0 in the 6th inning, but late Yankee rallies, including Jim Leyritz's 3-run home run in the bottom of the 8th, gave them the momentum they would never relinquish. John Wetteland, who notched a save in each of the Yankees' wins, was named the Series' most valuable player.

## Game One: Braves 12, Yankees 1

| **Atlanta** | ab | r | h | bi | **New York** | ab | r | h | bi |
|---|---|---|---|---|---|---|---|---|---|
| Grissom cf | 5 | 2 | 2 | 1 | Jeter ss | 3 | 1 | 0 | 0 |
| Lemke 2b | 4 | 0 | 2 | 1 | Boggs 3b | 4 | 0 | 2 | 1 |
| C Jones 3b | 4 | 1 | 1 | 3 | B Williams cf | 3 | 0 | 0 | 0 |
| McGriff 1b | 5 | 2 | 2 | 2 | T Martinez 1b | 3 | 0 | 1 | 0 |
| J Lopez c | 4 | 2 | 1 | 0 | Fielder dh | 4 | 0 | 0 | 0 |
| E Perez c | 0 | 0 | 0 | 0 | Strawberry lf | 3 | 0 | 0 | 0 |
| Dye rf | 5 | 0 | 1 | 0 | Raines lf | 1 | 0 | 0 | 0 |
| A Jones lf | 4 | 3 | 3 | 5 | O'Neill rf | 2 | 0 | 0 | 0 |
| Klesko dh | 4 | 1 | 0 | 0 | Aldrete rf | 0 | 0 | 0 | 0 |
| Blauser ss | 3 | 1 | 1 | 0 | C Hayes 3b | 1 | 0 | 0 | 0 |
| Polonia ph | 1 | 0 | 0 | 0 | Duncan 2b | 3 | 0 | 0 | 0 |
| Belliard ss | 0 | 0 | 0 | 0 | Fox 2b | 0 | 0 | 0 | 0 |
| **Totals** | **39** | **12** | **13** | **12** | Sojo ph | 1 | 0 | 0 | 0 |
| | | | | | Leyritz c | 3 | 0 | 1 | 0 |
| | | | | | **Totals** | **31** | **1** | **4** | **1** |

| | | | | | | | | | |
|---|---|---|---|---|---|---|---|---|---|
| Atlanta | 0 | 2 | 6 | 0 | 1 | 3 | 0 | 0 | 0—12 |
| New York | 0 | 0 | 0 | 0 | 1 | 0 | 0 | 0 | 0— 1 |

| | ip | h | r | er | bb | so |
|---|---|---|---|---|---|---|
| **Atlanta** | | | | | | |
| Smoltz W, 1-0 | 6.0 | 2 | 1 | 1 | 5 | 4 |
| McMichael | 1.0 | 2 | 0 | 0 | 0 | 1 |
| Neagle | 1.0 | 0 | 0 | 0 | 0 | 0 |
| Wade | 0.2 | 0 | 0 | 0 | 0 | 0 |
| Clontz | 0.1 | 0 | 0 | 0 | 0 | 0 |
| **New York** | | | | | | |
| Pettitte L, 0-1 | 2.1 | 6 | 7 | 7 | 1 | 1 |
| Boehringer | 3.0 | 5 | 5 | 3 | 0 | 2 |
| Weathers | 1.2 | 1 | 0 | 0 | 0 | 0 |
| Nelson | 1.0 | 1 | 0 | 0 | 0 | 1 |
| Wetteland | 1.0 | 0 | 0 | 0 | 0 | 2 |

E - Duncan (1). LOB - Atlanta 3, New York 8. 2B - Boggs (1). HR - A Jones 2 (2), McGriff (1). RBI - A Jones 5 (5), C Jones 3 (3), McGriff 2 (2), Grissom (1), Lemke (1), Boggs (1). S - Lemke. SF - C Jones.

**How runs were scored**—Two in Atlanta second: J Lopez singled. A Jones homered scoring J Lopez.

Six in Atlanta third: Blauser singled. Grissom singled. Lemke sacrificed. C Jones singled scoring Blauser and Grissom, C Jones to second on throw. C Jones stole third. McGriff singled scoring C Jones. J Lopez walked. A Jones homered scoring McGriff and J Lopez.

One in Atlanta fifth: McGriff homered.

One in New York fifth: Jeter walked. Boggs doubled scoring Jeter.

Three in Atlanta sixth: A Jones hit an infield single. Klesko safe at first on Duncan's error, A Jones to second. Blauser flied out, A Jones to third. Grissom singled scoring A Jones. Lemke singled scoring Klesko, Grissom to third. C Jones hit a sacrifice fly scoring Grissom.

## Game Two: Braves 4, Yankees 0

| **Atlanta** | ab | r | h | bi | **New York** | ab | r | h | bi |
|---|---|---|---|---|---|---|---|---|---|
| Grissom cf | 5 | 1 | 2 | 1 | Raines lf | 4 | 0 | 2 | 0 |
| Lemke 2b | 4 | 2 | 2 | 0 | Boggs 3b | 4 | 0 | 1 | 0 |
| C Jones 3b | 3 | 0 | 1 | 0 | B Williams cf | 4 | 0 | 0 | 0 |
| McGriff 1b | 3 | 0 | 2 | 3 | T Martinez 1b | 4 | 0 | 0 | 0 |
| J Lopez c | 4 | 0 | 1 | 0 | Fielder dh | 4 | 0 | 2 | 0 |
| Dye rf | 4 | 0 | 1 | 0 | Fox pr | 0 | 0 | 0 | 0 |
| A Jones lf | 3 | 0 | 0 | 0 | O'Neill rf | 4 | 0 | 1 | 0 |
| Pendleton dh | 4 | 1 | 1 | 0 | Duncan 2b | 3 | 0 | 0 | 0 |
| Blauser ss | 2 | 0 | 0 | 0 | Girardi c | 3 | 0 | 0 | 0 |
| Polonia ph | 1 | 0 | 0 | 0 | Jeter ss | 2 | 0 | 1 | 0 |
| Belliard ss | 0 | 0 | 0 | 0 | **Totals** | **32** | **0** | **7** | **0** |
| **Totals** | **33** | **4** | **10** | **4** | | | | | |

| | | | | | | | | | |
|---|---|---|---|---|---|---|---|---|---|
| Atlanta | 1 | 0 | 1 | 0 | 1 | 1 | 0 | 0 | 0—4 |
| New York | 0 | 0 | 0 | 0 | 0 | 0 | 0 | 0 | 0—0 |

| | ip | h | r | er | bb | so |
|---|---|---|---|---|---|---|
| **Atlanta** | | | | | | |
| Maddux W, 1-0 | 8.0 | 6 | 0 | 0 | 0 | 2 |
| Wohlers | 1.0 | 1 | 0 | 0 | 0 | 3 |
| **New York** | | | | | | |
| Key L, 0-1 | 6.0 | 10 | 4 | 4 | 2 | 0 |
| Lloyd | 0.2 | 0 | 0 | 0 | 0 | 2 |
| Nelson | 1.1 | 0 | 0 | 0 | 0 | 2 |
| Rivera | 1.0 | 0 | 0 | 0 | 0 | 1 |

E - Raines (1). LOB - Atlanta 7, New York 6. 2B - Lemke (1), Grissom (1), C Jones (1), Pendleton (1), O'Neill (1). RBI - McGriff 3 (5), Grissom (2). CS - Raines (1). S - Lemke. SF - McGriff.

**How runs were scored**—One in Atlanta first: Lemke doubled. McGriff singled scoring Lemke.

One in Atlanta third: Grissom doubled. Lemke sacrificed. C Jones walked. McGriff singled scoring Grissom.

One in Atlanta fifth: Lemke singled. C Jones doubled. McGriff hit a sacrifice fly scoring Lemke.

One in Atlanta sixth: Pendleton doubled. Blauser grounded out, Pendleton to third. Grissom singled scoring Pendleton.

## Game Three: Yankees 5, Braves 2

| **New York** | ab | r | h | bi | **Atlanta** | ab | r | h | bi |
|---|---|---|---|---|---|---|---|---|---|
| Raines lf | 4 | 1 | 1 | 0 | Grissom cf | 4 | 1 | 3 | 0 |
| Jeter ss | 3 | 1 | 1 | 0 | Lemke 2b | 4 | 0 | 1 | 1 |
| B Williams cf | 5 | 2 | 2 | 3 | C Jones 3b | 3 | 0 | 1 | 0 |
| Fielder 1b | 3 | 0 | 1 | 0 | McGriff 1b | 3 | 0 | 0 | 0 |
| Fox pr | 0 | 1 | 0 | 0 | Klesko lf | 3 | 0 | 0 | 1 |
| T Martinez 1b | 0 | 0 | 0 | 0 | J Lopez c | 4 | 0 | 1 | 0 |
| C Hayes 3b | 5 | 0 | 0 | 0 | A Jones rf | 4 | 0 | 0 | 0 |
| Strawberry rf | 3 | 0 | 1 | 1 | Blauser ss | 4 | 0 | 0 | 0 |
| Duncan 2b | 3 | 0 | 1 | 0 | Glavine p | 1 | 1 | 0 | 0 |
| Sojo 2b | 1 | 0 | 1 | 1 | Polonia ph | 0 | 0 | 0 | 0 |
| Girardi c | 2 | 0 | 0 | 0 | McMichael p | 0 | 0 | 0 | 0 |
| Cone p | 2 | 0 | 0 | 0 | Clontz p | 0 | 0 | 0 | 0 |
| Leyritz ph | 1 | 0 | 0 | 0 | Bielicki p | 0 | 0 | 0 | 0 |
| M Rivera p | 1 | 0 | 0 | 0 | Pendleton ph | 1 | 0 | 0 | 0 |
| Lloyd p | 0 | 0 | 0 | 0 | **Totals** | **31** | **2** | **6** | **2** |
| Wetteland p | 0 | 0 | 0 | 0 | | | | | |
| **Totals** | **33** | **5** | **8** | **5** | | | | | |

| | | | | | | | | | |
|---|---|---|---|---|---|---|---|---|---|
| New York | 1 | 0 | 0 | 1 | 0 | 0 | 0 | 3 | 0—5 |
| Atlanta | 0 | 0 | 0 | 0 | 0 | 1 | 0 | 1 | 0—2 |

| | ip | h | r | er | bb | so |
|---|---|---|---|---|---|---|
| **New York** | | | | | | |
| Cone W, 1-0 | 6.0 | 4 | 1 | 1 | 4 | 3 |
| M Rivera | 1.1 | 2 | 1 | 1 | 1 | 1 |
| Lloyd | 0.2 | 0 | 0 | 0 | 0 | 1 |
| Wetteland S, 1 | 1.0 | 0 | 0 | 0 | 0 | 2 |
| **Atlanta** | | | | | | |
| Glavine L, 0-1 | 7.0 | 4 | 2 | 1 | 3 | 8 |
| McMichael | 0.0 | 3 | 3 | 3 | 0 | 0 |
| Clontz | 1.0 | 1 | 0 | 0 | 1 | 1 |
| Bielicki | 1.0 | 0 | 0 | 0 | 2 | 2 |

E - Jeter (1), Blauser (1). LOB - New York 9, Atlanta 7. 2B - Fielder (1). 3B - Grissom (1). HR - B Williams (1). RBI - B Williams 3 (3), Strawberry (1), Sojo (1), Klesko (1), Lemke (2). CS - A Jones (1), Polonia (1). S - Jeter, Girardi.

**How runs were scored**—One in New York first: Raines walked. Jeter sacrificed. B Williams singled scoring Raines.

One in New York fourth: B Williams safe at first on Blauser's fielding error. Fielder walked. C Hayes flied out, B Williams to third. Strawberry singled scoring B Williams.

One in Atlanta sixth: Glavine walked. Grissom singled. C Jones walked. Klesko walked scoring Glavine.

Three in New York eighth: Jeter hit an infield single. B Williams homered scoring Jeter. Fielder doubled. Fox pinch ran for Fielder. C Hayes grounded out, Fox to third. Strawberry intentionally walked. Sojo singled scoring Fox.

One in Atlanta eighth: Grissom tripled. Lemke singled scoring Grissom.

## Game Four: Yankees 8, Braves 6 (10 innings)

| **New York** | ab | r | h | bi | **Atlanta** | ab | r | h | bi |
|---|---|---|---|---|---|---|---|---|---|
| Raines lf | 5 | 1 | 0 | 0 | Grissom cf | 5 | 0 | 1 | 2 |
| Jeter ss | 4 | 2 | 2 | 0 | Lemke 2b | 5 | 0 | 1 | 0 |
| B Williams cf | 4 | 1 | 0 | 0 | C Jones 3b-ss | 3 | 2 | 1 | 0 |
| Fielder 1b | 4 | 1 | 2 | 1 | McGriff 1b | 3 | 1 | 2 | 1 |
| Fox pr | 0 | 0 | 0 | 0 | Clontz p J | 0 | 0 | 0 | 0 |
| Boggs ph-3b | 0 | 0 | 0 | 1 | Lopez c | 2 | 1 | 0 | 1 |
| C Hayes 3b-1b | 5 | 1 | 3 | 1 | Wohlers p | 0 | 0 | 0 | 0 |
| Strawberry rf | 5 | 0 | 2 | 0 | Avery p | 0 | 0 | 0 | 0 |
| Duncan 2b | 5 | 1 | 0 | 0 | Klesko 1b | 1 | 0 | 0 | 0 |
| Girardi c | 2 | 0 | 0 | 0 | A Jones lf | 4 | 1 | 3 | 1 |
| O'Neill ph | 1 | 0 | 0 | 0 | Dye rf | 4 | 0 | 0 | 0 |
| Leyritz c | 2 | 1 | 1 | 3 | Blauser ss | 3 | 1 | 1 | 1 |
| Rogers p | 1 | 0 | 1 | 0 | Belliard ss | 0 | 0 | 0 | 0 |
| Boehringer p | 0 | 0 | 0 | 0 | Polonia ph | 1 | 0 | 0 | 0 |
| Sojo ph | 1 | 0 | 1 | 0 | Pendleton 3b | 1 | 0 | 0 | 0 |
| Weathers p | 0 | 0 | 0 | 0 | Neagle p | 1 | 0 | 0 | 0 |
| T Martinez ph | 1 | 0 | 0 | 0 | Wade p | 0 | 0 | 0 | 0 |
| Nelson p | 0 | 0 | 0 | 0 | Bielicki p | 1 | 0 | 0 | 0 |
| Aldrete ph | 1 | 0 | 0 | 0 | E Perez c | 1 | 0 | 0 | 0 |
| M Rivera p | 0 | 0 | 0 | 0 | **Totals** | **35** | **6** | **9** | **6** |
| Lloyd p | 1 | 0 | 0 | 0 | | | | | |
| Wetteland p | 0 | 0 | 0 | 0 | | | | | |
| **Totals** | **42** | **8** | **12** | **6** | | | | | |

| | | | | | | | | | | |
|---|---|---|---|---|---|---|---|---|---|---|
| New York | 0 | 0 | 0 | 0 | 0 | 3 | 0 | 3 | 0 | 2—8 |
| Atlanta | 0 | 4 | 1 | 0 | 1 | 0 | 0 | 0 | 0 | 0—6 |

| | ip | h | r | er | bb | so |
|---|---|---|---|---|---|---|
| **New York** | | | | | | |
| Rogers | 2.0 | 5 | 5 | 5 | 2 | 0 |
| Boehringer | 2.0 | 0 | 0 | 0 | 0 | 3 |
| Weathers | 1.0 | 1 | 1 | 1 | 2 | 2 |
| Nelson | 2.0 | 0 | 0 | 0 | 1 | 2 |
| M Rivera | 1.1 | 2 | 0 | 0 | 1 | 1 |
| Lloyd W, 1-0 | 1.0 | 0 | 0 | 0 | 0 | 1 |
| Wetteland S, 2 | 0.2 | 1 | 0 | 0 | 0 | 0 |
| **Atlanta** | | | | | | |
| Neagle | 5.0 | 5 | 3 | 2 | 4 | 3 |
| Wade | 0.0 | 0 | 0 | 0 | 1 | 0 |
| Bielicki | 2.0 | 0 | 0 | 0 | 1 | 4 |
| Wohlers BS, 1 | 2.0 | 6 | 3 | 3 | 0 | 1 |
| Avery L, 0-1 | 0.2 | 1 | 2 | 1 | 3 | 0 |
| Clontz | 0.1 | 0 | 0 | 0 | 0 | 1 |

E - Dye (1), Klesko (1). LOB - New York 13, Atlanta 8. 2B - Grissom (2), A Jones (1). HR - Leyritz (1), McGriff (2). RBI - Fielder (1), C Hayes (1), Leyritz 3 (3), Boggs (2), McGriff (6), Blauser (1), Grissom 2 (4), J Lopez (1), A Jones (6). S - Neagle, Dye. SF - J Lopez.

**How runs were scored**—Four in Atlanta second: McGriff homered. J Lopez walked. A Jones walked. Dye flied out, J Lopez to third. Blauser hit a bunt single scoring J Lopez. Neagle sacrificed. Grissom doubled scoring A Jones and Blauser.

One in Atlanta second: C Jones singled. McGriff singled, C Jones to third. J Lopez hit a sacrifice fly scoring C Jones.

One in Atlanta fifth: C Jones walked. Weathers balked, C Jones to second. McGriff intentionally walked. A Jones doubled scoring C Jones.

Three in New York sixth: Jeter singled. B Williams walked. Fielder singled scoring Jeter, B Williams scored on Dye's error, Fielder to second. C Hayes singled scoring Fielder.

Three in New York eighth: C Hayes hit an infield single. Strawberry singled. Duncan hit into fielder's choice, Strawberry out, C Hayes to third. Leyritz homered scoring C Hayes and Duncan.

Two in New York tenth: Raines walked. Jeter singled. B Williams intentionally walked. Boggs walked scoring Raines. C Hayes safe at first on Klesko's error scoring Jeter.

## Game Five: Yankees 1, Braves 0

| New York | ab | r | h | bi | Atlanta | ab | r | h | bi |
|---|---|---|---|---|---|---|---|---|---|
| Jeter ss | 4 | 0 | 0 | 0 | Grissom cf | 3 | 0 | 2 | 0 |
| C Hayes 3b | 4 | 1 | 0 | 0 | Lemke 2b | 4 | 0 | 0 | 0 |
| B Williams cf | 4 | 0 | 0 | 0 | C Jones 3b | 4 | 0 | 1 | 0 |
| Fielder 1b | 4 | 0 | 3 | 1 | McGriff 1b | 3 | 0 | 0 | 0 |
| T Martinez 1b | 0 | 0 | 0 | 0 | J Lopez c | 4 | 0 | 0 | 0 |
| Strawberry lf | 3 | 0 | 0 | 0 | A Jones lf | 2 | 0 | 1 | 0 |
| O'Neill rf | 2 | 0 | 0 | 0 | Klesko ph | 0 | 0 | 0 | 0 |
| Duncan 2b | 4 | 0 | 0 | 0 | Dye rf | 3 | 0 | 0 | 0 |
| Sojo 2b | 0 | 0 | 0 | 0 | Polonia ph | 1 | 0 | 0 | 0 |
| Leyritz c | 2 | 0 | 1 | 0 | Blauser ss | 3 | 0 | 0 | 0 |
| Pettitte | 4 | 0 | 0 | 0 | Smoltz p | 2 | 0 | 1 | 0 |
| Wetteland p | 0 | 0 | 0 | 0 | Mordecai ph | 1 | 0 | 0 | 0 |
| **Totals** | **31** | **1** | **4** | **1** | Wohlers p | 0 | 0 | 0 | 0 |
| | | | | | **Totals** | **30** | **0** | **5** | **0** |

| | | | | | | | | | |
|---|---|---|---|---|---|---|---|---|---|
| New York | 0 | 0 | 0 | 1 | 0 | 0 | 0 | 0 | 0—1 |
| Atlanta | 0 | 0 | 0 | 0 | 0 | 0 | 0 | 0 | 0—0 |

| | ip | h | r | er | bb | so |
|---|---|---|---|---|---|---|
| **New York** | | | | | | |
| Pettitte W, 1-1 | 8.1 | 5 | 0 | 0 | 3 | 4 |
| Wetteland S, 3 | 0.2 | 0 | 0 | 0 | 1 | 0 |
| **Atlanta** | | | | | | |
| Smoltz L, 1-1 | 8.0 | 4 | 1 | 0 | 3 | 10 |
| Wohlers | 1.0 | 0 | 0 | 0 | 2 | 0 |

E - Jeter (2), Grissom (1). LOB - New York 8, Atlanta 7. 2B - Fielder (2), C Jones (2). RBI - Fielder (2). SB - Leyritz (1), Duncan (1), A Jones (1), Grissom (1). CS - A Jones (2). S - Jeter, Girardi.

**How runs were scored**—One in New York fourth: C Hayes safe at second on Grissom's error. B Williams grounded out, C Hayes to third. Fielder doubled scoring C Hayes.

## Game Six: Yankees 3, Braves 2

| Atlanta | ab | r | h | bi | New York | ab | r | h | bi |
|---|---|---|---|---|---|---|---|---|---|
| Grissom cf | 5 | 0 | 2 | 1 | Jeter ss | 4 | 1 | 1 | 1 |
| Lemke 2b | 5 | 0 | 0 | 0 | Boggs 3b | 3 | 0 | 0 | 0 |
| C Jones 3b | 4 | 0 | 1 | 0 | C Hayes 3b | 1 | 0 | 0 | 0 |
| McGriff 1b | 3 | 1 | 0 | 0 | B Williams cf | 4 | 0 | 2 | 1 |
| J Lopez c | 3 | 0 | 1 | 0 | Fielder dh | 4 | 0 | 1 | 0 |
| A Jones lf-rf | 3 | 0 | 1 | 0 | T Martinez 1b | 3 | 0 | 0 | 0 |
| Dye rf | 1 | 0 | 0 | 1 | Strawberry lf | 2 | 0 | 0 | 0 |
| Klesko ph-lf | 2 | 1 | 1 | 0 | O'Neill rf | 3 | 1 | 1 | 0 |
| Pendleton dh | 3 | 0 | 1 | 0 | Duncan 2b | 1 | 0 | 0 | 0 |
| Belliard pr | 0 | 0 | 0 | 0 | Sojo 2b | 2 | 0 | 1 | 0 |
| Blauser ss | 3 | 0 | 1 | 0 | Girardi c | 3 | 1 | 2 | 1 |
| Polonia ph | 1 | 0 | 0 | 0 | **Totals** | **30** | **3** | **8** | **3** |
| **Totals** | **33** | **2** | **8** | **2** | | | | | |

| | | | | | | | | | |
|---|---|---|---|---|---|---|---|---|---|
| Atlanta | 0 | 0 | 0 | 1 | 0 | 0 | 0 | 0 | 1—2 |
| New York | 0 | 0 | 3 | 0 | 0 | 0 | 0 | 0 | x—3 |

| | ip | h | r | er | bb | so |
|---|---|---|---|---|---|---|
| **Atlanta** | | | | | | |
| Maddux L, 1-1 | 7.2 | 8 | 3 | 3 | 1 | 3 |
| Wohlers | 0.1 | 0 | 0 | 0 | 0 | 0 |
| **New York** | | | | | | |
| Key W, 1-1 | 5.1 | 5 | 1 | 1 | 3 | 1 |
| Weathers | 0.1 | 0 | 0 | 0 | 1 | 1 |
| Lloyd | 0.1 | 0 | 0 | 0 | 0 | 0 |
| Rivera | 2.0 | 0 | 0 | 0 | 1 | 1 |
| Wetteland S, 4 | 1.0 | 3 | 1 | 1 | 0 | 2 |

E - Duncan (2). LOB - Atlanta 9, New York 4. 2B - C Jones (3), Blauser (1), O'Neill (2), Sojo (1). 3B - Girardi (1). RBI - Grissom (5), Dye (1), Jeter (1), B Williams (4), Girardi (1). SB - Jeter (1), B Williams (1). CS - Pendleton (1).

**How runs were scored**—Three in New York third: O'Neill doubled. Duncan grounded out, O'Neill to third. Girardi tripled scoring O'Neill. Jeter singled scoring Girardi. Jeter stole second. Williams singled scoring Jeter.

One in Atlanta fourth: McGriff walked. Lopez singled. A Jones singled. Dye walked scoring McGriff.

One in Atlanta ninth: Klesko singled. Pendleton singled, Klesko to third. Grissom singled scoring Klesko.

## World Series Results, 1903-1996

| | |
|---|---|
| 1903 | Boston AL 5, Pittsburgh NL 3 |
| 1904 | No series |
| 1905 | New York NL 4, Philadelphia AL 1 |
| 1906 | Chicago AL 4, Chicago NL 2 |
| 1907 | Chicago NL 4, Detroit AL 0, 1 tie |
| 1908 | Chicago NL 4, Detroit AL 1 |
| 1909 | Pittsburgh NL 4, Detroit AL 3 |
| 1910 | Philadelphia AL 4, Chicago NL 1 |
| 1911 | Philadelphia AL 4, New York NL 2 |
| 1912 | Boston AL 4, New York NL 3, 1 tie |
| 1913 | Philadelphia AL 4, New York NL 1 |
| 1914 | Boston NL 4, Philadelphia AL 0 |
| 1915 | Boston AL 4, Philadelphia NL 1 |
| 1916 | Boston AL 4, Brooklyn NL 1 |
| 1917 | Chicago AL 4, New York NL 2 |
| 1918 | Boston AL 4, Chicago NL 2 |
| 1919 | Cincinnati NL 5, Chicago AL 3 |
| 1920 | Cleveland AL 5, Brooklyn NL 2 |
| 1921 | New York NL 5, New York AL 3 |
| 1922 | New York NL 4, New York AL 0, 1 tie |
| 1923 | New York AL 4, New York NL 2 |
| 1924 | Washington AL 4, New York NL 3 |
| 1925 | Pittsburgh NL 4, Washington AL 3 |
| 1926 | St. Louis NL 4, New York AL 3 |
| 1927 | New York AL 4, Pittsburgh NL 0 |
| 1928 | New York AL 4, St. Louis NL 0 |
| 1929 | Philadelphia AL 4, Chicago NL 1 |
| 1930 | Philadelphia AL 4, St. Louis NL 2 |
| 1931 | St. Louis NL 4, Philadelphia AL 3 |
| 1932 | New York AL 4, Chicago NL 0 |
| 1933 | New York NL 4, Washington AL 1 |
| 1934 | St. Louis NL 4, Detroit AL 3 |
| 1935 | Detroit AL 4, Chicago NL 2 |
| 1936 | New York AL 4, New York NL 2 |
| 1937 | New York AL 4, New York NL 1 |
| 1938 | New York AL 4, Chicago NL 0 |
| 1939 | New York AL 4, Cincinnati NL 0 |
| 1940 | Cincinnati NL 4, Detroit AL 3 |
| 1941 | New York AL 4, Brooklyn NL 1 |
| 1942 | St. Louis NL 4, New York AL 1 |
| 1943 | New York AL 4, St. Louis NL 1 |
| 1944 | St. Louis NL 4, St. Louis AL 2 |
| 1945 | Detroit AL 4, Chicago NL 3 |
| 1946 | St. Louis NL 4, Boston AL 3 |
| 1947 | New York AL 4, Brooklyn NL 3 |
| 1948 | Cleveland AL 4, Boston NL 2 |
| 1949 | New York AL 4, Brooklyn NL 1 |
| 1950 | New York AL 4, Philadelphia NL 0 |
| 1951 | New York AL 4, New York NL 2 |
| 1952 | New York AL 4, Brooklyn NL 3 |
| 1953 | New York AL 4, Brooklyn NL 2 |
| 1954 | New York NL 4, Cleveland AL 0 |
| 1955 | Brooklyn NL 4, New York AL 3 |
| 1956 | New York AL 4, Brooklyn NL 3 |
| 1957 | Milwaukee NL 4, New York AL 3 |
| 1958 | New York AL 4, Milwaukee NL 3 |
| 1959 | Los Angeles NL 4, Chicago AL 2 |
| 1960 | Pittsburgh NL 4, New York AL 3 |
| 1961 | New York AL 4, Cincinnati NL 1 |
| 1962 | New York AL 4, San Francisco NL 3 |
| 1963 | Los Angeles NL 4, New York AL 0 |
| 1964 | St. Louis NL 4, New York AL 3 |
| 1965 | Los Angeles NL 4, Minnesota AL 3 |
| 1966 | Baltimore AL 4, Los Angeles NL 0 |
| 1967 | St. Louis NL 4, Boston AL 3 |
| 1968 | Detroit AL 4, St. Louis NL 3 |
| 1969 | New York NL 4, Baltimore AL 1 |
| 1970 | Baltimore AL 4, Cincinnati NL 1 |
| 1971 | Pittsburgh NL 4, Baltimore AL 3 |
| 1972 | Oakland AL 4, Cincinnati NL 3 |
| 1973 | Oakland AL 4, New York NL 3 |
| 1974 | Oakland AL 4, Los Angeles NL 1 |
| 1975 | Cincinnati NL 4, Boston AL 3 |
| 1976 | Cincinnati NL 4, New York AL 0 |
| 1977 | New York AL 4, Los Angeles NL 2 |
| 1978 | New York AL 4, Los Angeles NL 2 |
| 1979 | Pittsburgh NL 4, Baltimore AL 3 |
| 1980 | Philadelphia NL 4, Kansas City AL 2 |
| 1981 | Los Angeles NL 4, New York AL 2 |
| 1982 | St. Louis NL 4, Milwaukee AL 3 |
| 1983 | Baltimore AL 4, Philadelphia NL 1 |
| 1984 | Detroit AL 4, San Diego NL 1 |
| 1985 | Kansas City AL 4, St. Louis NL 3 |
| 1986 | New York NL 4, Boston AL 3 |
| 1987 | Minnesota AL 4, St. Louis NL 3 |
| 1988 | Los Angeles NL 4, Oakland AL 1 |
| 1989 | Oakland AL 4, San Francisco NL 0 |
| 1990 | Cincinnati NL 4, Oakland AL 0 |
| 1991 | Minnesota AL 4, Atlanta NL 3 |
| 1992 | Toronto AL 4, Atlanta NL 2 |
| 1993 | Toronto AL 4, Philadelphia NL 2 |
| 1994 | No series |
| 1995 | Atlanta NL 4, Cleveland AL 2 |
| 1996 | New York AL 4, Atlanta NL 2 |

# All-Time Major League Leaders

(*player active at end of 1996 season)

### Games

|  |  |
|---|---|
| Pete Rose | 3,562 |
| Carl Yastrzemski | 3,308 |
| Hank Aaron | 3,298 |
| Ty Cobb | 3,035 |
| Stan Musial | 3,026 |
| Willie Mays | 2,992 |
| Dave Winfield | 2,973 |
| Eddie Murray* | 2,971 |
| Rusty Staub | 2,951 |
| Brooks Robinson | 2,896 |

### At Bats

|  |  |
|---|---|
| Pete Rose | 14,053 |
| Hank Aaron | 12,364 |
| Carl Yastrzemski | 11,988 |
| Ty Cobb | 11,434 |
| Eddie Murray* | 11,169 |
| Robin Yount | 11,008 |
| Dave Winfield | 11,003 |
| Stan Musial | 10,972 |
| Willie Mays | 10,881 |
| Brooks Robinson | 10,654 |

### Runs Batted In

| | |
|---|---|
| Hank Aaron | 2,297 |
| Babe Ruth | 2,213 |
| Lou Gehrig | 1,995 |
| Stan Musial | 1,951 |
| Ty Cobb | 1,937 |
| Jimmie Foxx | 1,922 |
| Willie Mays | 1,903 |
| Eddie Murray* | 1,899 |
| Cap Anson | 1,879 |
| Mel Ott | 1,860 |

### Stolen Bases

| Player | Stolen Bases |
|---|---|
| Rickey Henderson* | 1,186 |
| Lou Brock | 938 |
| Billy Hamilton | 912 |
| Ty Cobb | 892 |
| Tim Raines* | 787 |
| Vince Coleman* | 752 |
| Eddie Collins | 744 |
| Arlie Latham | 739 |
| Max Carey | 738 |
| Honus Wagner | 722 |

### Runs

| Player | Runs |
|---|---|
| Ty Cobb | 2,246 |
| Hank Aaron | 2,174 |
| Babe Ruth | 2,174 |
| Pete Rose | 2,165 |
| Willie Mays | 2,062 |
| Stan Musial | 1,949 |
| Lou Gehrig | 1,888 |
| Tris Speaker | 1,882 |
| Mel Ott | 1,859 |
| Frank Robinson | 1,829 |

### Strikeouts

| Player | Strikeouts |
|---|---|
| Nolan Ryan | 5,714 |
| Steve Carlton | 4,136 |
| Bert Blyleven | 3,701 |
| Tom Seaver | 3,640 |
| Don Sutton | 3,574 |
| Gaylord Perry | 3,534 |
| Walter Johnson | 3,509 |
| Phil Niekro | 3,342 |
| Ferguson Jenkins | 3,192 |
| Bob Gibson | 3,117 |

### Shutouts

| Player | Shutouts |
|---|---|
| Walter Johnson | 110 |
| Grover C. Alexander | 90 |
| Christy Mathewson | 79 |
| Cy Young | 76 |
| Eddie Plank | 69 |
| Warren Spahn | 63 |
| Nolan Ryan | 61 |
| Tom Seaver | 61 |
| Bert Blyleven | 60 |
| Don Sutton | 58 |

### Saves

| Player | Saves |
|---|---|
| Lee Smith* | 475 |
| Jeff Reardon | 367 |
| Dennis Eckersley* | 353 |
| Rollie Fingers | 341 |
| John Franco* | 323 |
| Tom Henke | 311 |
| Rich Gossage | 310 |
| Bruce Sutter | 300 |
| Randy Myers* | 274 |
| Dave Righetti | 252 |

## All-Time Home Run Leaders

| Player | HR | Player | HR | Player | HR | Player | HR |
|---|---|---|---|---|---|---|---|
| Hank Aaron | 755 | Ted Williams | 521 | Dave Winfield | 465 | Dale Murphy | 398 |
| Babe Ruth | 714 | Willie McCovey | 521 | Carl Yastrzemski | 452 | Graig Nettles | 390 |
| Willie Mays | 660 | Ed Mathews | 512 | Dave Kingman | 442 | Johnny Bench | 389 |
| Frank Robinson | 586 | Ernie Banks | 512 | Andre Dawson* | 438 | Dwight Evans | 385 |
| Harmon Killebrew | 573 | Mel Ott | 511 | Billy Williams | 426 | Frank Howard | 382 |
| Reggie Jackson | 563 | Eddie Murray* | 501 | Darrell Evans | 414 | Jim Rice | 382 |
| Mike Schmidt | 548 | Lou Gehrig | 493 | Duke Snider | 407 | Orlando Cepeda | 379 |
| Mickey Mantle | 536 | Stan Musial | 475 | Al Kaline | 399 | Tony Perez | 379 |
| Jimmy Foxx | 534 | Willie Stargell | 475 | | | | |

## Players With 3,000 Major League Hits

| Player | Hits | Player | Hits | Player | Hits |
|---|---|---|---|---|---|
| Pete Rose | 4,256 | Eddie Collins | 3,312 | Dave Winfield | 3,110 |
| Ty Cobb | 4,189 | Willie Mays | 3,283 | Rod Carew | 3,053 |
| Hank Aaron | 3,771 | Nap Lajoie | 3,242 | Lou Brock | 3,023 |
| Stan Musial | 3,630 | Eddie Murray* | 3,218 | Paul Molitor* | 3,014 |
| Tris Speaker | 3,514 | George Brett | 3,154 | Al Kaline | 3,007 |
| Carl Yastrzemski | 3,419 | Paul Waner | 3,152 | Roberto Clemente | 3,000 |
| Honus Wagner | 3,415 | Robin Yount | 3,142 | | |

## Pitchers With 300 Major League Wins

| | | | | | | | | | |
|---|---|---|---|---|---|---|---|---|---|
| Cy Young | 511 | Warren Spahn | 363 | Steve Carlton | 329 | Don Sutton | 324 | Old Hoss Radbourn | 309 |
| Walter Johnson | 417 | Kid Nichols | 361 | John Clarkson | 328 | Phil Niekro | 318 | Mickey Welch | 307 |
| Grover Alexander | 373 | Pud Galvin | 360 | Eddie Plank | 326 | Gaylord Perry | 314 | Lefty Grove | 300 |
| Christy Mathewson | 373 | Tim Keefe | 342 | Nolan Ryan | 324 | Tom Seaver | 311 | Early Wynn | 300 |

# Baseball Stadiums

### National League

| Team | Stadium (year opened) | Surface | Home run distances (ft.) LF | Center | RF | Seating capacity |
|---|---|---|---|---|---|---|
| Atlanta Braves | new stadium (1997)[1] | Grass | 335 | 400 | 330 | 50,000[2] |
| Chicago Cubs | Wrigley Field (1914) | Grass | 355 | 400 | 353 | 38,765 |
| Cincinnati Reds | Cinergy Field (1970) | Artificial | 330 | 404 | 330 | 52,952 |
| Colorado Rockies | Coors Field (1995) | Grass | 347 | 415 | 350 | 50,000 |
| Florida Marlins | Pro Player Stadium (1987) | Grass | 335 | 410 | 345 | 48,000 |
| Houston Astros | The Astrodome (1965) | Artificial | 325 | 400 | 325 | 54,370 |
| Los Angeles Dodgers | Dodger Stadium (1962) | Grass | 330 | 395 | 330 | 56,000 |
| Montreal Expos | Olympic Stadium (1976) | Artificial | 325 | 404 | 325 | 46,500 |
| New York Mets | Shea Stadium (1964) | Grass | 338 | 410 | 338 | 55,601 |
| Philadelphia Phillies | Veterans Stadium (1971) | Artificial | 330 | 408 | 330 | 62,530 |
| Pittsburgh Pirates | Three Rivers Stadium (1970) | Artificial | 335 | 400 | 335 | 47,972 |
| St. Louis Cardinals | Busch Stadium (1966) | Grass | 330 | 402 | 330 | 57,000 |
| San Diego Padres | San Diego/Jack Murphy Stadium (1967) | Grass | 327 | 405 | 327 | 46,510 |
| San Francisco Giants | 3Com Park at Candlestick Point (1960) | Grass | 335 | 400 | 328 | 63,000 |

### American League

| Team | Stadium (year opened) | Surface | LF | Center | RF | Seating capacity |
|---|---|---|---|---|---|---|
| Baltimore Orioles | Oriole Park at Camden Yards (1992) | Grass | 333 | 400 | 318 | 48,188 |
| Boston Red Sox | Fenway Park (1912) | Grass | 315 | 420 | 302 | 33,871 |
| California Angels | Anaheim Stadium (1966) | Grass | 333 | 404 | 333 | 64,593 |
| Chicago White Sox | Comiskey Park (1991) | Grass | 347 | 400 | 347 | 44,321 |
| Cleveland Indians | Jacobs Field (1994) | Grass | 325 | 405 | 325 | 42,400 |
| Detroit Tigers | Tiger Stadium (1912) | Grass | 340 | 440 | 325 | 52,416 |
| Kansas City Royals | Kauffman Stadium (1973) | Grass | 330 | 400 | 330 | 40,625 |
| Milwaukee Brewers | County Stadium (1953) | Grass | 315 | 402 | 315 | 53,192 |
| Minnesota Twins | Hubert H. Humphrey Metrodome (1982) | Artificial | 343 | 408 | 327 | 56,783 |
| New York Yankees | Yankee Stadium (1923) | Grass | 312 | 410 | 310 | 57,545 |
| Oakland A's | Oakland-Alameda County Coliseum (1968) | Grass | 330 | 400 | 330 | 43,012 |
| Seattle Mariners | The Kingdome (1976) | Artificial | 331 | 405 | 312 | 59,856 |
| Texas Rangers | The Ballpark in Arlington (1994) | Grass | 332 | 400 | 325 | 49,178 |
| Toronto Blue Jays | SkyDome (1989) | Artificial | 328 | 400 | 328 | 50,516 |

(1) The 1996 Olympic Stadium will be renamed and converted into the Braves' new baseball stadium. (2) Approximately.

# Cal Ripken, Jr., Extends His Consecutive Games Record

On Sept. 6, 1995, Baltimore Orioles shortstop Cal Ripken, Jr., played in his 2,131st consecutive game to break Lou Gehrig's record, which had stood for over 56 years and was thought by many to be unbreakable. At the end of the 1996 seson Ripken's streak was still alive. Here is a comparison of some of their statistics during their respective streaks:

| Lou Gehrig | | Cal Ripken, Jr. |
|---|---|---|
| June 1, 1925 | Streak began | May 30, 1982 |
| April 30, 1939 | Streak ended | — |
| 2,130 | Consecutive games played | 2,315 |
| 7,938 | At bats | 9,027 |
| 2,700 | Hits | 2,508 |
| 492 | Home Runs | 350 |
| 1,984 | Runs Batted In | 1,349 |
| .340 | Batting Average | .278 |

# Major League Franchise Shifts and Additions

**1953**—Boston Braves (NL) became Milwaukee Braves.
**1954**—St. Louis Browns (AL) became Baltimore Orioles.
**1955**—Philadelphia Athletics (AL) became Kansas City Athletics.
**1958**—New York Giants (NL) became San Francisco Giants.
**1958**—Brooklyn Dodgers (NL) became Los Angeles Dodgers.
**1961**—Washington Senators (AL) became Minnesota Twins.
**1961**—Los Angeles Angels (later renamed the California Angels) enfranchised by the American League.
**1961**—Washington Senators enfranchised by the American League (a new team, replacing the former Washington club, whose franchise was moved to Minneapolis-St. Paul).
**1962**—Houston Colt .45's (later renamed the Houston Astros) enfranchised by the National League.
**1962**—New York Mets enfranchised by the National League.
**1966**—Milwaukee Braves (NL) became Atlanta Braves.
**1968**—Kansas City Athletics (AL) became Oakland Athletics.
**1969**—Kansas City Royals and Seattle Pilots enfranchised by the American League; Montreal Expos and San Diego Padres enfranchised by the National League.
**1970**—Seattle Pilots became Milwaukee Brewers.
**1971**—Washington Senators became Texas Rangers (Dallas-Fort Worth area).
**1977**—Toronto Blue Jays and Seattle Mariners enfranchised by the American League.
**1993**—Colorado Rockies (Denver) and Florida Marlins (Miami) enfranchised by the National League.
**1998**—Arizona Diamondbacks (Phoenix) and Tampa Bay Devil Rays scheduled to begin play (enfranchised in 1995); leagues to be determined.

# NCAA Baseball Champions

| | | | | | | | |
|---|---|---|---|---|---|---|---|
| 1960 | Minnesota | 1970 | USC | 1979 | Cal. St.-Fullerton | 1988 | Stanford |
| 1961 | USC | 1971 | USC | 1980 | Arizona | 1989 | Wichita St. |
| 1962 | Michigan | 1972 | USC | 1981 | Arizona St. | 1990 | Georgia |
| 1963 | USC | 1973 | USC | 1982 | Miami (FL) | 1991 | LSU |
| 1964 | Minnesota | 1974 | USC | 1983 | Texas | 1992 | Pepperdine |
| 1965 | Arizona St. | 1975 | Texas | 1984 | Cal. St.-Fullerton | 1993 | LSU |
| 1966 | Ohio St. | 1976 | Arizona | 1985 | Miami (FL) | 1994 | Oklahoma |
| 1967 | Arizona St. | 1977 | Arizona St. | 1986 | Arizona | 1995 | Cal. St.-Fullerton |
| 1968 | USC | 1978 | USC | 1987 | Stanford | 1996 | LSU |
| 1969 | Arizona St. | | | | | | |

# Little League World Series

The Little League World Series, which is played annually in Williamsport, PA, celebrated its 50th anniversary in 1996. The team from Taiwan won the 1996 Little League World Series by defeating the team from Cranston, RI, 13-3, on Aug. 24. The game was ended in the 5th inning, when officials invoked the 10-run "mercy rule."

| Year | Winning / Losing Team | Score |
|---|---|---|
| 1947 | Williamsport, PA; Lock Haven, PA | 16-7 |
| 1948 | Lock Haven, PA; St. Petersburg, FL | 6-5 |
| 1949 | Hammonton, NJ; Pensacola, FL | 5-0 |
| 1950 | Houston, TX; Bridgeport, CT | 2-1 |
| 1951 | Stamford, CT; Austin, TX | 3-0 |
| 1952 | Norwalk, CT; Monongahela, PA | 4-3 |
| 1953 | Birmingham, AL; Schenectady, NY | 1-0 |
| 1954 | Schenectady, NY; Colton, CA | 7-5 |
| 1955 | Morrisville, PA; Merchantville, NJ | 4-3 |
| 1956 | Roswell, NM; Delaware, NJ | 3-1 |
| 1957 | Mexico; La Mesa, CA | 4-0 |
| 1958 | Mexico; Kankakee, IL | 10-1 |
| 1959 | Hamtramck, MI; Auburn, CA | 12-0 |
| 1960 | Levittown, PA; Ft. Worth, TX | 5-0 |
| 1961 | El Cajon, CA; El Campo, TX | 4-2 |
| 1962 | San Jose, CA; Kankakee, IL | 3-0 |
| 1963 | Granada Hills, CA; Stratford, CT | 2-1 |
| 1964 | Staten Island, NY; Mexico | 4-0 |
| 1965 | Windsor Locks, CT; Ontario, Canada | 3-1 |
| 1966 | Houston, TX; W. New York, NJ | 8-2 |
| 1967 | Tokyo, Japan; Chicago, IL | 4-1 |
| 1968 | Osaka, Japan; Richmond, VA | 1-0 |
| 1969 | Taiwan; Santa Clara, CA | 5-0 |
| 1970 | Wayne, NJ; Campbell, CA | 2-0 |
| 1971 | Taiwan; Gary, IN | 12-3 |
| 1972 | Taiwan; Hammond, IN | 6-0 |
| 1973 | Taiwan; Tucson, AZ | 12-0 |
| 1974 | Taiwan; Red Bluff, CA | 12-1 |
| 1975 | Lakewood, NJ; Tampa, FL | 4-3 |
| 1976 | Tokyo, Japan; Campbell, CA | 10-3 |
| 1977 | Taiwan; El Cajon, CA | 7-2 |
| 1978 | Taiwan; Danville, CA | 11-1 |
| 1979 | Taiwan; Campbell, CA | 2-1 |
| 1980 | Taiwan; Tampa, FL | 4-3 |
| 1981 | Taiwan; Tampa, FL | 4-2 |
| 1982 | Kirkland, WA; Taiwan | 6-0 |
| 1983 | Marietta, GA; Dominican Rep. | 3-1 |
| 1984 | South Korea; Altamonte Springs, FL | 6-2 |
| 1985 | South Korea; Mexico | 7-1 |
| 1986 | Taiwan; Tucson, AZ | 12-0 |
| 1987 | Chinese Taipei; Irvine, CA | 21-1 |
| 1988 | Chinese Taipei; Pearl City, HI | 10-0 |
| 1989 | Trumbull, CT; Chinese Taipei | 5-2 |
| 1990 | Chinese Taipei; Shippensburg, PA | 9-0 |
| 1991 | Chinese Taipei; Danville, CA | 11-0 |
| 1992 | Long Beach, CA; Philippines | 6-0 |
| 1993 | Long Beach, CA; Panama | 3-2 |
| 1994 | Venezuela; Northridge, CA | 4-3 |
| 1995 | Taiwan; Spring, TX | 17-3 |
| 1996 | Taiwan; Cranston, RI | 13-3 |

# Special Olympics

Special Olympics is an international program of year-round sports training and athletic competition for children and adults with mental retardation. All 50 U.S. states, Washington, DC, and Guam have chapter offices. In addition, there are accredited Special Olympics programs in more than 100 countries. Persons wishing to volunteer or find out more about Special Olympics can contact Special Olympics International Headquarters, 1350 New York Ave. NW, Washington, DC 20005.

## 1995 Special Olympic World Games/1997 World Winter Special Olympic Games

The 9th Special Olympic World Games were held July 1-9, 1995, in New Haven, CT. A total of 6,500 athletes and coaches from 120 countries participated. Athletes competed in 21 sports.

The 6th World Winter Special Olympic Games were scheduled to be held Feb. 2-8, 1997, in Toronto and Collingwood, Ontario, Canada. About 2,000 athletes from more than 80 countries were expected to participate, along with 500 coaches, 1,500 volunteers, and 2,000 family members and friends. Athletes were to compete in the following sports: Alpine Skiing, Cross Country Skiing, Floor Hockey, Figure Skating, and Speed Skating.

# SOCCER

## Major League Soccer in 1996

1996 marked the inaugural season of Major League Soccer, a professional outdoor soccer league with 10 teams based in major U.S. cities. The league featured most of the country's top players, including members of the 1994 World Cup team (Alexi Lalas, Tony Meola, Tab Ramos), as well as many international stars.

### Final Standings

**Eastern Conference**

| | W | So | L | GF | GA | Pts |
|---|---|---|---|---|---|---|
| Tampa Bay Mutiny | 19 | 1 | 12 | 67 | 51 | 58 |
| Washington D.C. United | 15 | 1 | 16 | 63 | 59 | 46 |
| NY/NJ MetroStars | 12 | 3 | 17 | 48 | 49 | 39 |
| Columbus Crew | 11 | 4 | 17 | 63 | 65 | 37 |
| New England Revolution | 9 | 6 | 17 | 49 | 58 | 33 |

**Western Conference**

| | W | So | L | GF | GA | Pts |
|---|---|---|---|---|---|---|
| Los Angeles Galaxy | 15 | 4 | 13 | 63 | 53 | 49 |
| Dallas Burn | 12 | 5 | 15 | 51 | 48 | 41 |
| Kansas City Wiz | 12 | 5 | 15 | 66 | 65 | 41 |
| San Jose Clash | 12 | 3 | 17 | 53 | 55 | 39 |
| Colorado Rapids | 9 | 2 | 21 | 46 | 63 | 29 |

**Note:** 3 points for a regulation-time win, 1 point for a shootout win.

### MLS Playoff Results

**Eastern Conference**
Washington D.C. defeated NY/NJ 2 games to 1
Tampa Bay defeated Columbus 2 games to 1
Washington D.C. defeated Tampa Bay 2 games to 0

**Western Conference**
Kansas City defeated Dallas 2 games to 1
Los Angeles defeated San Jose 2 games to 1
Los Angeles defeated Kansas City 2 games to 0

**MLS Cup**
Washington D.C. United 3, Los Angeles Galaxy 2 (OT)

## The World Cup

In 1994 the World Cup, emblematic of international soccer supremacy, was held in the U.S. for the first time. Brazil captured an unprecedented 4th World Cup by defeating Italy on July 17, 1994, at the Rose Bowl in Pasadena, CA. For the first time ever, the final was decided in the tie-breaking, penalty-kick round, in which Brazil outscored Italy 3-2, after neither team had been able to score in 90 minutes of regulation time and an additional 30 minutes of extra time. The 1998 World Cup was scheduled to be held in France, and the 2002 World Cup is scheduled to be held jointly in Japan and South Korea. Winners and sites for previous World Cup tournaments follow:

| Year | Winner | Final opponent | Site |
|---|---|---|---|
| 1930 | Uruguay | Argentina | Uruguay |
| 1934 | Italy | Czechoslovakia | Italy |
| 1938 | Italy | Hungary | France |
| 1950 | Uruguay | Brazil | Brazil |
| 1954 | W. Germany | Hungary | Switzerland |
| 1958 | Brazil | Sweden | Sweden |
| 1962 | Brazil | Czechoslovakia | Chile |
| 1966 | England | W. Germany | England |
| 1970 | Brazil | Italy | Mexico |
| 1974 | W. Germany | Netherlands | W. Germany |
| 1978 | Argentina | Netherlands | Argentina |
| 1982 | Italy | W. Germany | Spain |
| 1986 | Argentina | W. Germany | Mexico |
| 1990 | W. Germany | Argentina | Italy |
| 1994 | Brazil | Italy | U.S. |

# CHESS

## World Chess Champions

**Source:** U.S. Chess Federation

Chess dates back to antiquity, its exact origin unknown. The best players of their time, regarded by later generations as world champions, were François Philidor, Alexandre Deschappelles, Louis de la Bourdonnais, all France; Howard Staunton, England; Adolph Anderssen, Germany; and Paul Morphy, U.S. In 1866 Wilhelm Steinitz defeated Adolph Anderssen and claimed the world champion title. Official world champions since the title was first used follow:

| | |
|---|---|
| **1866-1894** | Wilhelm Steinitz, Austria |
| **1894-1921** | Emanuel Lasker, Germany |
| **1921-1927** | Jose R. Capablanca, Cuba |
| **1927-1935** | Alexander A. Alekhine, France |
| **1935-1937** | Max Euwe, Netherlands |
| **1937-1946** | Alexander A. Alekhine, France (a) |
| **1948-1957** | Mikhail Botvinnik, USSR |
| **1957-1958** | Vassily Smyslov, USSR |
| **1958-1959** | Mikhail Botvinnik, USSR |
| **1960-1961** | Mikhail Tal, USSR |
| **1961-1963** | Mikhail Botvinnik, USSR |
| **1963-1969** | Tigran Petrosian, USSR |
| **1969-1972** | Boris Spassky, USSR |
| **1972-1975** | Bobby Fischer, U.S. (b) |
| **1975-1985** | Anatoly Karpov, USSR |
| **1985-1993** | Gary Kasparov, USSR/Russia (c) |
| **1993-** | Gary Kasparov, Russia (PCA) |
| **1993-** | Anatoly Karpov, Russia (FIDE) |

(a) After Alekhine died in 1946, the title was vacant until 1948, when Botvinnik won the 1st championship match sanctioned by the International Chess Federation (FIDE). (b) Defaulted championship after refusal to accept FIDE rules for a championship match, Apr. 1975. (c) Kasparov broke with FIDE, Feb. 26, 1993. FIDE stripped Kasparov of his title Mar. 23. Kasparov defeated Nigel Short of Great Britain in a world championship match played Sept.-Oct. 1993 under the auspices of a new organization the two had founded, the Professional Chess Association (PCA). FIDE held a championship match between Anatoly Karpov (Russia) and Jan Timman (the Netherlands), which Karpov won in Nov. 1993. **Recent matches:** In Feb. 1996, Kasparov defeated Deep Blue (3 wins, 1 loss, 2 draws), a computer designed by IBM, in the 1st multigame regulation match between a world chess champion and a computer. Karpov successfully defended the FIDE title in June-July 1996 against 1991 U.S. chess champion Gata Kamsky of New York City, 10½ to 7½. **Further information:** More information on chess and chess champions can be accessed on the U.S. Chess Federation's Internet site: http://www.uschess.org

# MARATHONS

## Boston Marathon in 1996

Moses Tanui of Kenya won the 1996 Boston Marathon, Apr. 17, with a time of 2 hours 9 minutes 16 seconds. Uta Pippig of Germany became the first woman to win the marathon for 3 consecutive years, with a time of 2 hours 27 minutes and 12 seconds. A record 38,500 athletes participated in the historic 100th anniversary of the race.

## New York Marathon in 1996 and 1995

**Nov. 3, 1996:** Giacomo Leone of Italy won the 1996 New York Marathon, Nov. 3, finishing the race in 2 hours 9 minutes and 54 seconds. Anuta Catuna of Romania won the women's race in 2 hours 28 minutes and 18 seconds. **Nov. 12, 1995:** German Silva of Mexico won his 2d consecutive New York Marathon with a time of 2 hours and 11 minutes. Tegla Loroupe of Kenya was the winner of the women's race for a 2d straight year, finishing in 2 hours 28 minutes and 6 seconds.

# CRIME

## Crime Down Overall in 1995

Serious crimes reported to law enforcement agencies in the U.S. decreased 1% in 1995 compared with 1994, according to *Uniform Crime Reports* figures released by the Federal Bureau of Investigation. The decrease continued the trend of recent years; overall crime was down 1% in 1994, 2% in 1993, and 3% in 1992.

Serious crime is measured by the Crime Index, which is composed of 4 violent and 4 property crimes. Both violent crime and property crime dropped 1% in 1995.

All 4 violent crimes in the Crime Index decreased. Murder and robbery fell 7%, forcible rape declined 6%, and aggravated assault dropped by 3%.

In the property-crime category, motor vehicle theft and burglary were down 5%, while arson fell 4%. Larceny-theft was the only offense to show an increase from 1994 to 1995; it was up 1%.

Declines in overall Crime Index totals occurred in 3 regions (4% in the Northeast and 1% in the Midwest and the South); the West remained the same.

Cities with more than 1 million inhabitants showed the largest decline, 6%. Cities with populations under 10,000 inhabitants experienced a 2% increase, and cities with populations from 500,000 to 999,999 and those with 10,000 to 25,000 inhabitants experienced a 1% increase. The crime data for the 2-year period of 1994 and 1995 show that suburban counties experienced a 1% decrease in their crime level, while rural counties reported a 4% increase.

## Crime Index Trends

**Source:** FBI, *Uniform Crime Reports,* 1995

(percentage change 1995 over 1994, offenses known to the police)

| Population group and area | No. of agencies[1] | Population (thousands) | Crime Index (total) | Violent crime | Property crime[2] | Murder | Forcible rape | Robbery | Aggravated assault | Burglary | Larceny/theft | Motor vehicle theft | Arson |
|---|---|---|---|---|---|---|---|---|---|---|---|---|---|
| Total U.S. | 11,813 | 230,021 | –1 | –1 | –1 | –7 | –6 | –7 | –3 | –5 | +1 | –5 | –4 |
| **Cities:** | | | | | | | | | | | | | |
| Over 1,000,000 | 8 | 20,085 | –6 | –8 | –6 | –12 | –7 | –12 | –5 | –9 | –2 | –12 | –15 |
| 500,000 to 999,999 | 19 | 12,830 | +1 | –3 | +2 | –4 | 0 | –5 | –2 | –3 | +3 | +1 | –6 |
| 250,000 to 499,999 | 37 | 13,259 | –3 | –5 | –2 | –2 | –5 | –6 | –5 | –7 | +1 | –7 | +1 |
| 100,000 to 249,999 | 143 | 20,924 | –2 | –5 | –2 | –9 | –4 | –6 | –5 | –7 | +1 | –5 | –4 |
| 50,000 to 99,999 | 341 | 23,165 | –2 | –3 | –2 | –14 | –6 | –3 | –2 | –5 | 0 | –4 | –2 |
| 25,000 to 49,999 | 616 | 21,241 | 0 | –2 | +1 | –5 | –2 | –2 | –2 | –3 | +2 | –4 | 0 |
| 10,000 to 24,999 | 1,484 | 23,327 | +1 | –4 | +1 | –6 | –10 | –4 | –3 | –3 | +3 | –1 | –2 |
| Under 10,000 | 5,547 | 19,588 | +2 | –2 | +2 | –2 | –7 | 0 | –1 | –2 | +3 | +4 | +3 |
| **Counties:** | | | | | | | | | | | | | |
| Suburban[3] | 1,245 | 50,770 | –1 | –2 | –1 | –9 | –7 | –3 | –1 | –5 | +1 | –2 | –3 |
| Rural[4] | 2,373 | 24,832 | +4 | +4 | +4 | +2 | –6 | +1 | +6 | +2 | +6 | +8 | +7 |
| **Areas:** | | | | | | | | | | | | | |
| Suburban area[5] | 5,795 | 93,763 | –1 | –3 | 0 | –9 | –7 | –3 | –3 | –4 | +2 | –4 | –2 |

(1) Law-enforcement agencies. (2) Data for arson not included. (3) Includes crimes reported to sheriffs' departments, county police departments, and state police within Metropolitan Statistical Areas. (4) Includes crimes reported to sheriffs' departments, county police departments, and state police outside Metropolitan Statistical Areas. (5) Includes crimes reported to city, county, and state law enforcement agencies within Metropolitan Statistical Areas but outside the central cities.

## Crime Index Trends by Geographic Region

**Source:** FBI, *Uniform Crime Reports,* 1995

(percentage change 1995 over 1994, offenses known to the police)

| Region | Crime Index (total) | Violent crime | Property crime[1] | Murder | Forcible rape | Robbery | Aggravated assault | Burglary | Larceny-theft | Motor vehicle theft | Arson |
|---|---|---|---|---|---|---|---|---|---|---|---|
| Total U.S. | –1 | –1 | –1 | –7 | –6 | –7 | –3 | –5 | +1 | –5 | –4 |
| Northeast | –4 | –8 | –3 | –13 | –6 | –11 | –5 | –6 | +1 | –14 | –5 |
| Midwest | –1 | –1 | –1 | –8 | –7 | –9 | +4 | –4 | +1 | –1 | –8 |
| South | –1 | –2 | 0 | –7 | –5 | –3 | –1 | –5 | +1 | –2 | 0 |
| West | 0 | –3 | +1 | –3 | –2 | –5 | –2 | –3 | +3 | –3 | –7 |

(1) Data for arson not included.

## Crime Index Trends, 1992-95

**Source:** FBI, *Uniform Crime Reports,* 1995

(percentage change over previous year)

| Year | Crime Index (total) | Violent crime | Property crime[1] | Murder | Forcible rape | Robbery | Aggravated assault | Burglary | Larceny-theft | Motor vehicle theft | Arson |
|---|---|---|---|---|---|---|---|---|---|---|---|
| 1992 | –3 | +1 | –4 | –4 | +2 | –2 | +3 | –6 | –3 | –3 | 0 |
| 1993 | –2 | 0 | –2 | +3 | –4 | –2 | +1 | –5 | –1 | –3 | –5 |
| 1994 | –1 | –3 | –1 | –5 | –4 | –6 | –1 | –4 | +1 | –2 | +5 |
| 1995 | –1 | –1 | –1 | –7 | –6 | –7 | –3 | –5 | +1 | –5 | –4 |

(1) Data for arson not included.

## Crime in the U.S., 1976-95

**Source:** FBI, *Uniform Crime Reports*, 1995

| Population[1] | Crime Index (total)[2] | Violent crime | Property crime[3] | Murder and non-negligent man-slaughter | Forcible rape | Robbery | Burglary | Larceny-theft |
|---|---|---|---|---|---|---|---|---|
| | | | | Number of reported offenses | | | | |
| **Population by year** | | | | | | | | |
| 1976–214,659,000 | 11,349,700 | 1,004,210 | 10,345,500 | 18,780 | 57,080 | 427,810 | 3,108,700 | 6,270,800 |
| 1977–216,332,000 | 10,984,500 | 1,029,580 | 9,955,000 | 19,120 | 63,500 | 412,610 | 3,071,500 | 5,905,700 |
| 1978–218,059,000 | 11,209,000 | 1,085,550 | 10,123,400 | 19,560 | 67,610 | 426,930 | 3,128,300 | 5,991,000 |
| 1979–220,099,000 | 12,249,500 | 1,208,030 | 11,041,500 | 21,460 | 76,390 | 480,700 | 3,327,700 | 6,601,000 |
| 1980–225,349,264 | 13,408,300 | 1,344,520 | 12,063,700 | 23,040 | 82,990 | 565,840 | 3,795,200 | 7,136,900 |
| 1981–229,146,000 | 13,423,800 | 1,361,820 | 12,061,900 | 22,520 | 82,500 | 592,910 | 3,779,700 | 7,194,400 |
| 1982–231,534,000 | 12,974,400 | 1,322,390 | 11,652,000 | 21,010 | 78,770 | 553,130 | 3,447,100 | 7,142,500 |
| 1983–233,981,000 | 12,108,600 | 1,258,090 | 10,850,500 | 19,310 | 78,920 | 506,570 | 3,129,900 | 6,712,800 |
| 1984–236,158,000 | 11,881,800 | 1,273,280 | 10,608,500 | 18,690 | 84,230 | 485,010 | 2,984,400 | 6,591,900 |
| 1985–238,740,000 | 12,431,400 | 1,328,800 | 11,102,600 | 18,980 | 88,670 | 497,870 | 3,073,300 | 6,926,400 |
| 1986–241,077,000 | 13,211,900 | 1,489,170 | 11,722,700 | 20,610 | 91,460 | 542,780 | 3,241,400 | 7,257,200 |
| 1987–243,400,000 | 13,508,700 | 1,484,000 | 12,024,700 | 20,100 | 91,110 | 517,700 | 3,236,200 | 7,499,900 |
| 1988–245,807,000 | 13,923,100 | 1,566,220 | 12,356,900 | 20,680 | 92,490 | 542,970 | 3,218,100 | 7,705,900 |
| 1989–248,239,000 | 14,251,400 | 1,646,040 | 12,605,400 | 21,500 | 94,500 | 578,330 | 3,168,200 | 7,872,400 |
| 1990–248,709,873 | 14,475,600 | 1,820,130 | 12,655,500 | 23,440 | 102,560 | 639,270 | 3,073,900 | 7,945,700 |
| 1991–252,177,000 | 14,872,900 | 1,911,770 | 12,961,100 | 24,700 | 106,590 | 687,730 | 3,157,200 | 8,142,200 |
| 1992–255,082,000 | 14,438,200 | 1,932,270 | 12,505,900 | 23,760 | 109,060 | 672,480 | 2,979,900 | 7,915,200 |
| 1993–257,908,000 | 14,144,800 | 1,926,020 | 12,218,800 | 24,530 | 106,010 | 659,870 | 2,834,800 | 7,820,900 |
| 1994–260,341,000[4] | 13,989,500 | 1,857,670 | 12,131,900 | 23,330 | 102,220 | 618,950 | 2,712,800 | 7,879,800 |
| 1995–262,755,000 | 13,867,100 | 1,798,790 | 12,068,400 | 21,600 | 97,460 | 580,550 | 2,595,000 | 8,000,600 |
| **Percent change: number of offenses** | | | | | | | | |
| 1995/1994 | –0.9 | –3.2 | –0.5 | –7.4 | –4.6 | –6.2 | –1.3 | +1.5 |
| 1995/1991 | –6.8 | –5.9 | –6.9 | –12.6 | –8.6 | –15.6 | –17.8 | –1.7 |
| 1995/1986 | +5.0 | +20.8 | +2.9 | +4.8 | +6.6 | +7.0 | –19.9 | +10.2 |
| | | | | Rate per 100,000 inhabitants | | | | |
| **Year** | | | | | | | | |
| 1976 | 5,287.3 | 467.8 | 4,819.5 | 8.8 | 26.6 | 199.3 | 1,448.2 | 2,921.3 |
| 1977 | 5,077.6 | 475.9 | 4,601.7 | 8.8 | 29.4 | 190.7 | 1,419.8 | 2,729.9 |
| 1978 | 5,140.3 | 497.8 | 4,642.5 | 9.0 | 31.0 | 195.8 | 1,434.6 | 2,747.4 |
| 1979 | 5,565.5 | 548.9 | 5,016.6 | 9.7 | 34.7 | 218.4 | 1,511.9 | 2,999.1 |
| 1980 | 5,950.0 | 596.6 | 5,353.3 | 10.2 | 36.8 | 251.1 | 1,684.1 | 3,167.0 |
| 1981 | 5,858.2 | 594.3 | 5,263.9 | 9.8 | 36.0 | 258.7 | 1,649.5 | 3,139.7 |
| 1982 | 5,603.6 | 571.1 | 5,032.5 | 9.1 | 34.0 | 238.9 | 1,488.8 | 3,084.8 |
| 1983 | 5,175.0 | 537.7 | 4,637.4 | 8.3 | 33.7 | 216.5 | 1,337.7 | 2,868.9 |
| 1984 | 5,031.3 | 539.2 | 4,492.1 | 7.9 | 35.7 | 205.4 | 1,263.7 | 2,791.3 |
| 1985 | 5,207.1 | 556.6 | 4,650.5 | 7.9 | 37.1 | 208.5 | 1,287.3 | 2,901.2 |
| 1986 | 5,480.4 | 617.7 | 4,862.6 | 8.6 | 37.9 | 225.1 | 1,344.6 | 3,010.3 |
| 1987 | 5,550.0 | 609.7 | 4,940.3 | 8.3 | 37.4 | 212.7 | 1,329.6 | 3,081.3 |
| 1988 | 5,664.2 | 637.2 | 5,027.1 | 8.4 | 37.6 | 220.9 | 1,309.2 | 3,134.9 |
| 1989 | 5,741.0 | 663.1 | 5,077.9 | 8.7 | 38.1 | 233.0 | 1,276.3 | 3,171.3 |
| 1990 | 5,820.3 | 731.8 | 5,088.5 | 9.4 | 41.2 | 257.0 | 1,235.9 | 3,194.8 |
| 1991 | 5,897.8 | 758.1 | 5,139.7 | 9.8 | 42.3 | 272.7 | 1,252.0 | 3,228.8 |
| 1992 | 5,660.2 | 757.5 | 4,902.7 | 9.3 | 42.8 | 263.6 | 1,168.2 | 3,103.0 |
| 1993 | 5,484.4 | 746.8 | 4,737.6 | 9.5 | 41.1 | 255.9 | 1,099.2 | 3,032.4 |
| 1994[4] | 5,373.5 | 713.6 | 4,660.0 | 9.0 | 39.3 | 237.7 | 1,042.0 | 3,026.7 |
| 1995 | 5,277.6 | 684.6 | 4,593.0 | 8.2 | 37.1 | 220.9 | 987.6 | 3,044.9 |
| **Percent change: rate per 100,000 inhabitants** | | | | | | | | |
| 1995/1994 | –1.8 | –4.1 | –1.4 | –8.9 | –5.6 | –7.1 | –5.2 | +0.6 |
| 1995/1991 | –10.5 | –9.7 | –10.6 | –16.3 | –12.3 | –19.0 | –21.1 | –5.7 |
| 1995/1986 | –3.7 | +10.8 | –5.5 | –4.7 | –2.1 | –3.9 | –26.6 | +1.1 |

**Note:** All rates were calculated on the offenses before rounding. (1) Populations are Bureau of the Census provisional estimates as of July 1, except 1980 and 1990, which are the decennial census counts. (2) Because of rounding, the offenses may not add to totals. (3) Data for arson not included. (4) The 1994 figures have been adjusted.

## Law Enforcement Officers

**Source:** FBI, *Uniform Crime Reports*, 1995

The U.S. law enforcement community employed an average of 2.4 full-time officers for every 1,000 inhabitants as of Oct. 31, 1995. Considering full-time civilians, the overall law enforcement employee rate was 3.3 per 1,000 inhabitants according to 13,052 city, county, and state police agencies. These agencies collectively offered law enforcement service to a population of more than 245 million, employing 586,756 officers and 226,780 civilians.

The law enforcement employee average for all cities nationwide was 3.0 per 1,000 inhabitants. The highest city law enforcement employee average was 3.9 per 1,000 inhabitants, in cities with populations of 250,000 or more. Rural and suburban counties averaged full-time law enforcement employee rates of 4.4 and 3.8 per 1,000 population, respectively.

Regionally, the law enforcement employee rate was 3.3 in the Northeast and the South, 2.7 in the Midwest, and 2.5 in the West.

Nationally, males constituted 90 percent of all sworn employees. Ninety-three percent of the officers in rural counties were males, and in suburban counties males accounted for 88 percent.

Civilians made up 28 percent of the total U.S. law enforcement employee force. They represented 22 percent of the police employees in cities, 36 percent of those in rural counties, and 38 percent in suburban counties.

Seventy-four law enforcement officers were feloniously slain in the line of duty in 1995, 3 fewer than in 1994. Another 53 officers were killed as a result of accidents occurring while performing official duties.

# Crime Rates by Region, Geographic Division, and State, 1995

**Source:** FBI, *Uniform Crime Reports*, 1995

(rate per 100,000)

| Area | Total | Violent crime[1] | Property crime[2] | Murder | Rape | Robbery | Aggra-vated assault | Burglary | Larceny-theft | Motor vehicle theft |
|---|---|---|---|---|---|---|---|---|---|---|
| **United States total** | **5,277.6** | **684.6** | **4,593.0** | **8.2** | **37.1** | **220.9** | **418.3** | **987.6** | **3,044.9** | **560.5** |
| **Northeast** | **4,180.4** | **610.6** | **3,569.8** | **6.2** | **24.9** | **260.3** | **319.2** | **758.1** | **2,295.8** | **515.9** |
| **New England** | **4,090.6** | **468.1** | **3,622.6** | **3.4** | **26.8** | **121.0** | **316.9** | **798.3** | **2,351.7** | **472.5** |
| Connecticut | 4,503.2 | 405.9 | 4,097.3 | 4.6 | 23.7 | 163.2 | 214.4 | 888.4 | 2,668.7 | 540.2 |
| Maine | 3,284.7 | 131.4 | 3,153.3 | 2.0 | 21.4 | 26.9 | 81.1 | 726.4 | 2,292.0 | 134.8 |
| Massachusetts | 4,341.6 | 687.2 | 3,654.4 | 3.6 | 29.0 | 150.4 | 504.2 | 817.7 | 2,232.2 | 604.5 |
| New Hampshire | 2,655.4 | 114.5 | 2,540.9 | 1.8 | 29.0 | 27.4 | 56.3 | 418.6 | 1,977.3 | 145.1 |
| Rhode Island | 4,244.5 | 368.0 | 3,876.6 | 3.3 | 27.0 | 92.3 | 245.4 | 932.7 | 2,503.0 | 440.8 |
| Vermont | 3,433.7 | 118.3 | 3,315.4 | 2.2 | 28.2 | 10.9 | 76.9 | 760.9 | 2,418.8 | 135.7 |
| **Middle Atlantic** | **4,211.8** | **660.3** | **3,551.5** | **7.1** | **24.3** | **308.9** | **320.0** | **744.1** | **2,276.4** | **531.0** |
| New Jersey | 4,703.7 | 599.8 | 4,103.9 | 5.1 | 24.3 | 283.0 | 287.4 | 875.2 | 2,597.1 | 631.6 |
| New York | 4,560.1 | 841.9 | 3,718.3 | 8.5 | 23.7 | 399.7 | 410.0 | 808.1 | 2,344.4 | 565.7 |
| Pennsylvania | 3,364.9 | 427.3 | 2,937.6 | 6.3 | 25.2 | 189.3 | 206.5 | 561.8 | 1,963.1 | 412.7 |
| **Midwest** | **4,751.0** | **587.5** | **4,163.5** | **6.9** | **40.1** | **181.8** | **358.7** | **841.3** | **2,871.2** | **451.1** |
| **East North Central** | **4,831.0** | **649.3** | **4,181.7** | **7.6** | **41.9** | **207.5** | **392.3** | **847.0** | **2,839.0** | **495.7** |
| Illinois | 5,455.7 | 996.1 | 4,459.6 | 10.3 | 36.5 | 330.8 | 618.5 | 917.6 | 3,019.0 | 523.0 |
| Indiana | 4,631.5 | 524.7 | 4,106.8 | 8.0 | 33.3 | 135.7 | 348.3 | 821.6 | 2,819.5 | 465.7 |
| Michigan | 5,182.8 | 687.8 | 4,495.0 | 8.5 | 62.0 | 187.3 | 430.1 | 909.7 | 2,939.7 | 645.5 |
| Ohio | 4,405.2 | 482.5 | 3,922.7 | 5.4 | 43.4 | 178.7 | 255.0 | 838.8 | 2,669.0 | 414.9 |
| Wisconsin | 3,885.7 | 281.1 | 3,604.6 | 4.3 | 23.3 | 105.1 | 148.4 | 613.2 | 2,627.8 | 363.6 |
| **West North Central** | **4,561.5** | **441.1** | **4,120.4** | **5.1** | **36.1** | **120.8** | **279.2** | **827.7** | **2,947.4** | **345.3** |
| Iowa | 4,101.9 | 354.4 | 3,747.5 | 1.8 | 21.8 | 53.0 | 277.8 | 757.5 | 2,767.2 | 222.8 |
| Kansas | 4,886.9 | 420.7 | 4,466.2 | 6.2 | 36.6 | 108.2 | 369.8 | 1,068.4 | 3,074.3 | 323.5 |
| Minnesota | 4,497.3 | 356.1 | 4,141.2 | 3.9 | 56.2 | 123.7 | 172.2 | 797.3 | 3,002.5 | 341.5 |
| Missouri | 5,120.5 | 663.8 | 4,456.8 | 8.8 | 32.1 | 204.0 | 418.8 | 932.6 | 3,050.9 | 473.3 |
| Nebraska | 4,544.5 | 382.0 | 4,162.5 | 2.9 | 19.4 | 65.2 | 294.5 | 631.9 | 3,179.2 | 351.4 |
| North Dakota | 2,866.3 | 86.7 | 2,779.6 | .9 | 22.8 | 10.0 | 53.0 | 350.7 | 2,249.8 | 179.1 |
| South Dakota | 3,060.6 | 207.5 | 2,853.1 | 1.8 | 41.0 | 25.9 | 138.8 | 540.7 | 2,191.5 | 120.9 |
| **South** | **5,741.6** | **737.5** | **5,004.1** | **9.8** | **40.9** | **212.4** | **478.4** | **1,137.1** | **3,336.7** | **530.2** |
| **South Atlantic** | **6,133.8** | **806.6** | **5,327.1** | **9.1** | **39.7** | **246.3** | **511.5** | **1,119.1** | **3,575.6** | **560.4** |
| Delaware | 5,158.7 | 725.0 | 4,433.8 | 3.5 | 80.2 | 198.7 | 442.5 | 905.3 | 3,114.2 | 414.2 |
| District of Columbia | 12,173.5 | 2,661.4 | 9,512.1 | 65.0 | 52.7 | 1,239.0 | 1,304.7 | 1,838.4 | 5,833.8 | 1,839.9 |
| Florida | 7,701.5 | 1,071.0 | 6,630.6 | 7.3 | 48.6 | 299.9 | 715.1 | 1,522.4 | 4,322.4 | 785.8 |
| Georgia | 6,003.6 | 657.1 | 5,346.5 | 9.5 | 35.3 | 205.2 | 407.1 | 1,059.9 | 3,678.3 | 608.4 |
| Maryland | 6,294.8 | 986.9 | 5,307.9 | 11.8 | 42.2 | 423.1 | 509.7 | 1,057.5 | 3,532.8 | 717.0 |
| North Carolina | 5,639.5 | 646.4 | 4,993.1 | 9.4 | 32.2 | 179.2 | 425.5 | 1,417.6 | 3,264.9 | 310.6 |
| South Carolina | 6,063.8 | 981.9 | 5,081.8 | 7.9 | 47.3 | 175.9 | 750.8 | 1,254.6 | 3,441.8 | 385.4 |
| Virginia | 3,989.2 | 361.5 | 3,627.7 | 7.6 | 27.2 | 131.7 | 194.9 | 595.2 | 2,740.0 | 292.6 |
| West Virgina | 2,458.2 | 210.2 | 2,248.0 | 4.9 | 21.2 | 42.7 | 141.4 | 565.0 | 1,516.6 | 166.3 |
| **East South Central** | **4,600.9** | **591.8** | **4,009.1** | **10.3** | **38.0** | **169.1** | **374.4** | **1,011.9** | **2,570.5** | **426.7** |
| Alabama | 4,848.1 | 632.4 | 4,215.7 | 11.2 | 31.7 | 185.8 | 403.7 | 1,024.8 | 2,844.3 | 346.6 |
| Kentucky | 3,351.7 | 364.7 | 2,987.0 | 7.2 | 31.9 | 103.7 | 222.0 | 735.5 | 1,992.4 | 259.1 |
| Mississippi | 4,514.5 | 502.8 | 4,011.7 | 12.9 | 39.1 | 130.9 | 319.9 | 1,131.1 | 2,520.1 | 360.5 |
| Tennessee | 5,362.7 | 771.5 | 4,591.2 | 10.6 | 47.1 | 223.2 | 490.5 | 1,143.2 | 2,799.5 | 648.5 |
| **West South Central** | **5,738.1** | **706.1** | **5,032.0** | **10.7** | **44.4** | **181.2** | **469.8** | **1,119.0** | **3,374.5** | **538.6** |
| Arkansas | 4,690.9 | 553.2 | 4,137.7 | 10.4 | 37.2 | 125.7 | 379.8 | 996.9 | 2,815.4 | 325.4 |
| Louisiana | 6,676.0 | 1,007.4 | 5,668.6 | 17.0 | 42.7 | 268.6 | 679.0 | 1,231.7 | 3,838.5 | 598.4 |
| Oklahoma[3] | 5,596.8 | 664.1 | 4,932.7 | 12.2 | 44.6 | 115.6 | 491.8 | 1,271.9 | 3,164.3 | 496.4 |
| Texas | 5,684.3 | 663.9 | 5,020.5 | 9.0 | 45.7 | 179.8 | 429.3 | 1,082.3 | 3,377.8 | 560.4 |
| **West** | **6,082.7** | **770.4** | **5,312.3** | **9.0** | **38.6** | **241.5** | **481.3** | **1,111.1** | **3,435.0** | **766.1** |
| **Mountain** | **6,356.8** | **560.7** | **5,796.2** | **7.2** | **40.5** | **130.8** | **382.1** | **1,107.6** | **4,066.7** | **621.9** |
| Arizona | 8,213.6 | 713.5 | 7,500.1 | 10.4 | 33.6 | 173.8 | 495.7 | 1,416.8 | 4,925.6 | 1,157.7 |
| Colorado | 5,396.3 | 440.2 | 4,956.1 | 5.8 | 39.5 | 96.2 | 298.7 | 934.1 | 3,634.5 | 387.5 |
| Idaho | 4,4401.5 | 322.0 | 4,079.4 | 4.1 | 28.4 | 24.0 | 265.5 | 779.8 | 3,057.6 | 242.0 |
| Montana | 5,304.9 | 170.6 | 5,134.4 | 3.0 | 25.9 | 33.2 | 108.5 | 720.8 | 4,105.5 | 308.0 |
| Nevada | 6,579.3 | 945.2 | 5,634.2 | 10.7 | 61.2 | 324.6 | 548.7 | 1,322.5 | 3,566.2 | 745.4 |
| New Mexico | 6,428.0 | 819.2 | 5,608.8 | 8.8 | 56.6 | 154.5 | 599.3 | 1,447.1 | 3,648.5 | 513.2 |
| Utah | 6,090.8 | 328.8 | 5,762.0 | 3.9 | 42.7 | 67.1 | 215.1 | 800.8 | 4,572.1 | 389.1 |
| Wyoming | 4,320.2 | 254.2 | 4,066.0 | 2.1 | 34.4 | 17.9 | 199.8 | 612.1 | 3,286.3 | 167.7 |
| **Pacific** | **5,980.5** | **848.7** | **5,131.8** | **9.6** | **37.9** | **282.8** | **518.3** | **1,112.5** | **3,199.4** | **819.9** |
| Alaska | 5,753.8 | 770.9 | 4,982.9 | 9.1 | 80.3 | 155.1 | 526.3 | 836.9 | 3,634.3 | 521.7 |
| California | 5,831.1 | 966.0 | 4,865.1 | 11.2 | 33.4 | 331.2 | 590.3 | 1,120.3 | 2,856.9 | 887.9 |
| Hawaii | 7,198.6 | 295.6 | 6,902.9 | 4.7 | 28.3 | 130.8 | 131.8 | 1,165.3 | 5,046.9 | 690.7 |
| Oregon | 6,563.9 | 522.4 | 6,041.5 | 4.1 | 41.7 | 137.9 | 338.7 | 1,102.8 | 4,236.7 | 702.0 |
| Washington | 6,269.8 | 484.3 | 5,785.5 | 5.1 | 59.2 | 132.7 | 287.3 | 1,091.2 | 4,140.3 | 554.0 |

**Note:** Offense totals are based on all reporting agencies and estimates for unreported areas. (1) Violent crimes are murder, forcible rape, robbery, and aggravated assault. (2) Property crimes are burglary, larceny-theft, and motor vehicle theft. Data are not included for the property crime of arson. (3) The relatively large numbers of murders was the result of the bombing of the Alfred P. Murrah Federal Building in Oklahoma City.

# State and Federal Prison Population; Death Penalty

**Source:** Prison population: Bureau of Justice Statistics, U.S. Dept. of Justice, Dec. 31, 1995; Death penalty: Bureau of Justice Statistics, as of Dec. 31, 1994

The number of prisoners under the jurisdiction of federal or state correctional authorities at year-end 1995 reached a record high of 1,127,132. The states and the District of Columbia added 66,843 prisoners in 1995; the federal system, 5,216. Although the 1995 growth rate of 6.8% was below the average annual growth rate for the past 10 years (8.4%), and below the percentage increase recorded in 1994 (8.8%), the total increase (72,059) was the 3d largest yearly increase on record. This increase translated into a nationwide need to confine an additional 1,386 inmates per week, compared with 1,602 per week in 1994. Prisoners with a sentence of more than 1 year accounted for 96% of the total prison population at the end of 1995.

| | Sentenced to more than 1 yr | | | Death penalty, 1994 | | |
|---|---|---|---|---|---|---|
| | Advance 1995 | Final 1994 | % change 1994–95 | Under sentence of death | Executions | Death penalty |
| **U.S. total** | **1,080,728** | **1,017,059** | **6.3%** | **2,890** | **31** | **—** |
| **Federal institutions** | **83,663** | **79,795** | **4.8** | **6** | **0** | **Yes** |
| **State institutions** | **997,065** | **937,264** | **6.4** | **2,884** | **31** | **37** |
| **Northeast** | **155,071** | **146,834** | **5.6** | **195** | **0** | **—** |
| Connecticut | 10,418 | 10,500 | –0.8 | 4 | 0 | Yes |
| Maine | 1,377 | 1,401 | –1.7 | 0 | 0 | No |
| Massachusetts | 10,633 | 10,401 | 2.2 | 0 | 0 | No |
| New Hampshire | 2,014 | 2,021 | –0.3 | 0 | 0 | Yes |
| New Jersey | 27,066 | 24,632 | 9.9 | 9 | 0 | Yes |
| New York | 68,484 | 66,750 | 2.6 | 0 | 0 | No |
| Pennsylvania | 32,404 | 28,294 | 14.5 | 182 | 0 | Yes |
| Rhode Island | 1,833 | 1,854 | –1.1 | 0 | 0 | No |
| Vermont | 842 | 981 | — | 0 | 0 | No |
| **Midwest** | **192,252** | **183,830** | **4.6** | **442** | **3** | **—** |
| Illinois | 37,658 | 36,531 | 3.1 | 155 | 1 | Yes |
| Indiana | 16,046 | 14,916 | 7.6 | 47 | 1 | Yes |
| Iowa | 5,906 | 5,437 | 8.6 | 0 | 0 | No |
| Kansas | 7,054 | 6,371 | 10.7 | 0 | 0 | Yes |
| Michigan | 41,112 | 40,631 | 1.2 | 0 | 0 | No |
| Minnesota | 4,863 | 4,575 | 6.3 | 0 | 0 | No |
| Missouri | 19,139 | 17,898 | 6.9 | 88 | 0 | Yes |
| Nebraska | 3,045 | 2,667 | 14.2 | 10 | 1 | Yes |
| North Dakota | 544 | 501 | 8.6 | 0 | 0 | No |
| Ohio | 44,677 | 43,074 | 3.7 | 140 | 0 | Yes |
| South Dakota | 1,871 | 1,708 | 9.5 | 2 | 0 | Yes |
| Wisconsin | 10,337 | 9,521 | 8.6 | 0 | 0 | No |
| **South** | **442,471** | **415,354** | **6.5** | **1,610** | **26** | **—** |
| Alabama | 20,130 | 19,074 | 5.5 | 135 | 0 | Yes |
| Arkansas | 9,011 | 8,517 | 5.8 | 36 | 5 | Yes |
| Delaware | 2,980 | 2,844 | 4.8 | 14 | 1 | Yes |
| District of Columbia | 9,042 | 10,085 | –10.3 | 0 | 0 | No |
| Florida | 63,866 | 57,157 | 11.7 | 342 | 1 | Yes |
| Georgia | 34,160 | 32,523 | 5 | 96 | 1 | Yes |
| Kentucky | 12,060 | 11,066 | 9 | 29 | 0 | Yes |
| Louisiana | 24,755 | 24,063 | 2.9 | 47 | 0 | Yes |
| Maryland | 20,450 | 19,854 | 3 | 13 | 1 | Yes |
| Mississippi | 12,575 | 10,606 | 18.6 | 50 | 0 | Yes |
| North Carolina | 27,716 | 23,046 | 20.3 | 111 | 1 | Yes |
| Oklahoma | 18,151 | 16,631 | 9.1 | 129 | 0 | Yes |
| South Carolina | 19,015 | 18,168 | 4.7 | 59 | 0 | Yes |
| Tennessee | 15,206 | 14,401 | 5.6 | 100 | 0 | Yes |
| Texas | 123,349 | 118,195 | 4.4 | 394 | 14 | Yes |
| Virginia | 27,523 | 26,792 | 2.7 | 55 | 2 | Yes |
| West Virginia | 2,482 | 2,332 | 6.4 | 0 | 0 | No |
| **West** | **207,271** | **191,246** | **8.4** | **637** | **2** | **—** |
| Alaska | 2,045 | 1,934 | 5.7 | 0 | 0 | No |
| Arizona | 20,291 | 19,005 | 6.8 | 121 | 0 | Yes |
| California | 131,745 | 121,084 | — | 381 | 0 | Yes |
| Colorado | 11,063 | 10,717 | 3.2 | 3 | 0 | Yes |
| Hawaii | 2,590 | 2,392 | 8.3 | 0 | 0 | No |
| Idaho | 3,328 | 2,811 | 18.4 | 19 | 1 | Yes |
| Montana | 1,788 | 1,764 | 1.4 | 8 | 0 | Yes |
| Nevada | 7,545 | 6,993 | 7.9 | 66 | 0 | Yes |
| New Mexico | 3,925 | 3,533 | 11.1 | 2 | 0 | Yes |
| Oregon | 6,515 | 5,935 | 9.8 | 17 | 0 | Yes |
| Utah | 3,423 | 3,028 | 13 | 10 | 0 | Yes |
| Washington | 11,608 | 10,833 | 7.2 | 10 | 1 | Yes |
| Wyoming | 1,405 | 1,217 | 15.4 | 0 | 0 | Yes |

(—) = Not calculated because of a change in reporting methods. **Note:** The advance count of prisoners is conducted in Jan. and may be revised. Prisoner counts for 1994 may differ from those reported in previous publications.

# Sentences vs. Time Served for Selected Crimes

**Source:** Bureau of Justice Statistics, *Prison Sentences and Time Served for Violence,* Apr. 1995

The following is a comparison of the average maximum sentence lengths (excluding both life and death sentences) and the actual time served for selected state-court convictions, based on 1992 data.

| Type of offense | Average sentence | Avg. time served[1] | Type of offense | Average sentence | Avg. time served[1] |
|---|---|---|---|---|---|
| All violent | 7 years, 5 months | 3 years, 7 months | Robbery | 7 years, 11 months | 3 years, 8 months |
| Homicide | 12 years, 5 months | 5 years, 11 months | Sexual assault | 6 years | 2 years, 11 months |
| Rape | 9 years, 9 months | 5 years, 5 months | Assault | 5 years, 1 month | 2 years, 5 months |
| Kidnapping | 8 years, 8 months | 4 years, 4 months | Other | 5 years | 2 years, 4 months |

(1) Includes jail credit and prison time.

## Prison Situation Among the States and in the Federal System, 1995

**Source:** *Prisoners in 1995,* Bureau of Justice Statistics, U.S. Dept. of Justice; year-end 1995.

| The 10 largest total prison populations, 1995 | Number of inmates | The 10 highest incarceration rates, 1995[1] | Prisoners per 100,000 residents |
|---|---|---|---|
| California | 135,646 | Texas | 653 |
| Texas | 127,766 | Louisiana | 568 |
| Federal system | 100,250 | Oklahoma | 552 |
| New York | 68,484 | South Carolina | 515 |
| Florida | 63,879 | Nevada | 482 |
| Ohio | 44,677 | Arizona | 473 |
| Michigan | 41,112 | Alabama | 471 |
| Illinois | 37,658 | Georgia | 470 |
| Georgia | 34,266 | Mississippi | 464 |
| Pennsylvania | 32,410 | Florida | 447 |

| The 10 largest % increases in prison population | | | |
|---|---|---|---|
| 1994–95 | % increase | 1990–95 | % increase |
| North Carolina | 24.2 | Texas | 127.9 |
| Mississippi | 19.0 | North Carolina | 59.5 |
| Idaho | 18.4 | Virginia | 57.5 |
| Wyoming | 15.4 | Mississippi | 55.3 |
| Nebraska | 14.8 | Minnesota | 53.1 |
| Pennsylvania | 14.5 | Federal system | 53.0 |
| Oregon | 13.7 | Georgia | 52.9 |
| North Dakota | 13.4 | New Hampshire | 50.1 |
| Utah | 13.2 | Wisconsin | 50.0 |
| New Mexico | 13.0 | Arizona | 49.6 |

**Note:** The District of Columbia as a wholly urban jurisdiction is excluded. (1) Prisoners with sentences of more than 1 year.

## Executions, by State and Method, 1977-94

**Source:** Bureau of Justice Statistics, *Capital Punishment 1994,* Dec. 1994

| | | Method of Execution | | | | |
|---|---|---|---|---|---|---|
| State | No. | Lethal injection | Electrocution | Lethal gas | Firing squad | Hanging |
| **Total U.S.** | **257** | **131** | **114** | **9** | **1** | **2** |
| Texas | 85 | 85 | | | | |
| Florida | 33 | | 33 | | | |
| Virginia | 24 | | 24 | | | |
| Louisiana | 21 | 1 | 20 | | | |
| Georgia | 18 | | 18 | | | |
| Missouri | 11 | 11 | | | | |
| Alabama | 10 | | 10 | | | |
| Arkansas | 9 | 8 | 1 | | | |
| North Carolina | 6 | 5 | | 1 | | |
| Nevada | 5 | 4 | | 1 | | |
| Delaware | 4 | 4 | | | | |
| Mississippi | 4 | | | 4 | | |

| | | Method of Execution | | | | |
|---|---|---|---|---|---|---|
| State | No. | Lethal injection | Electrocution | Lethal gas | Firing squad | Hanging |
| South Carolina | 4 | | 4 | | | |
| Utah | 4 | 3 | | | 1 | |
| Arizona | 3 | 2 | | 1 | | |
| Indiana | 3 | | 3 | | | |
| Oklahoma | 3 | 3 | | | | |
| California | 2 | | | 2 | | |
| Illinois | 2 | 2 | | | | |
| Washington | 2 | | | | | 2 |
| Idaho | 1 | 1 | | | | |
| Maryland | 1 | 1 | | | | |
| Nebraska | 1 | | 1 | | | |
| Wyoming | 1 | 1 | | | | |

**Note**: This table shows execution methods used since 1977. Lethal injection was used in about 51% of the executions carried out, electrocution in 44%. Six states—Arizona, Arkansas, Louisiana, Nevada, North Carolina, and Utah—used 2 methods.

## Total Estimated Arrests,[1] 1995

**Source:** FBI, *Uniform Crime Reports,* 1995

| | |
|---|---|
| **Total[2]** | **15,119,800** |
| Murder and nonnegligent manslaughter | 21,230 |
| Forcible rape | 34,650 |
| Robbery | 171,870 |
| Aggravated assault | 568,480 |
| Burglary | 386,500 |
| Larceny–theft | 1,530,200 |
| Motor vehicle theft | 191,900 |
| Arson | 20,000 |
| **Violent crimes[3]** | **796,250** |
| **Property crime[4]** | **2,128,600** |
| **Crime Index total[2, 5]** | **2,924,800** |
| Other assaults | 1,290,400 |
| Forgery and counterfeiting | 122,300 |
| Fraud | 436,400 |
| Embezzlement | 15,200 |
| Stolen property: buying, receiving, possessing | 166,500 |
| Vandalism | 311,100 |
| Weapons: carrying, possessing, etc. | 243,900 |
| Prostitution and commercialized vice | 97,700 |
| Sex offenses (except forcible rape and prostitution) | 94,500 |
| Drug abuse violations | 1,476,100 |
| Gambling | 19,500 |
| Offenses against family and children | 142,900 |
| Driving under the influence | 1,436,000 |
| Liquor laws | 594,900 |
| Drunkenness | 708,100 |
| Disorderly conduct | 748,600 |
| Vagrancy | 25,900 |
| All other offenses | 3,865,400 |
| Suspicion (not included in totals) | 12,100 |
| Curfew and loitering law violations | 149,800 |
| Runaways | 249,500 |

(1) Arrest totals are based on all reporting agencies and estimates for unreported areas. (2) Because of rounding, figures may not add to totals. (3) Violent crimes are murder, forcible rape, robbery, and aggravated assault. (4) Property crimes are burglary, larceny–theft, motor vehicle theft, and arson. (5) Includes arson.

## The Unabomber

**Source:** UNABOM Task Force, FBI

On June 18, 1996, a federal grand jury in Sacramento, CA, returned a 10-count indictment charging a loner and former math professor, Theodore Kaczynski, with 4 separate bombings that killed 2 individuals and injured 2 others. These charges were the result of a multi-agency investigation by the FBI's UNABOM Task Force into a series of related mail bombings (listed below) that occurred across the U.S. beginning in 1978. Arrested in Montana on Apr. 3, 1996, originally for possession of bomb components, Kaczynski, who pleaded not guilty, was held in Sacramento while awaiting trial.

| Date | Recipient | Injured/killed |
|---|---|---|
| 5/25/78 | U. of Illinois at Chicago, IL | 1 injured |
| 5/9/79 | Northwestern U., Evanston, IL | 1 injured |
| 11/15/79 | American Airlines, Flt. 444, Chicago, IL | 12 injured |
| 6/10/80 | Pres., United Airlines, Chicago, IL | 1 injured |
| 10/8/81 | U. of Utah, Salt Lake City, UT | 0 |
| 5/5/82 | Vanderbilt U., Nashville, TN | 1 injured |
| 7/2/82 | U. of California, Berkeley, CA | 1 injured |
| 5/8/85 | Boeing Aircraft, Auburn, WA | 0 |
| 5/15/85 | U. of California, Berkeley, CA | 1 injured |
| 11/15/85 | U. of Michigan, Ann Arbor, MI | 2 injured |
| 12/11/85 | Rentech Co., Sacramento, CA | 1 killed |
| 2/20/87 | CAAM's Inc., Salt Lake City, UT | 1 injured |
| 6/22/93 | Physician/researcher, Tiburon, CA | 1 injured |
| 6/24/93 | Professor, Yale U., New Haven, CT | 1 injured |
| 12/10/94 | Advertising exec., North Caldwell, NJ | 1 killed |
| 4/24/95 | Pres., Calif. Forestry Assn., Sacramento, CA | 1 killed |

# VITAL STATISTICS

## Births, Deaths, Marriages, and Divorces in the U.S., First Quarter 1996

**Source:** National Center for Health Statistics, U.S. Dept. of Health and Human Services

### Births

According to provisional statistics for the first quarter of 1996, there were 957,000 births, a decrease from the number reported for the same 3-month period in 1995 (976,000). The birthrate declined by 3%, from 15.1 per 1,000 population in the first quarter of 1995 to 14.6 in the first quarter of 1996.

During the 12 months ending Mar. 1996, there were an estimated 3,873,000 live births, 2% fewer than reported for the comparable period ending a year earlier (3,959,000). The birthrate was 14.7 per 1,000 population, 3% below the rate for the 12 months ending Mar. 1995 (15.1). These lower rates continue the generally downward trend observed since early 1991.

### Marriages

The total number of marriages for the first quarter of 1996 was 409,000, an increase of 1% over the number for the comparable period in 1995 (406,000). The marriage rate was 6.4 per 1,000 population, the same as the first quarter of 1995.

During the 12 months ending Mar. 1996, an estimated 2,339,000 couples married, a decrease of 1% from the previous 12-month period (2,358,000). The 12-month marriage rate of 8.9 per 1,000 population was 1% lower than the rate for the same period ending with Mar. 1995 (9.0).

### Divorces

A total of 272,000 couples divorced during the first quarter of 1996, a 4% decrease compared with the first quarter of 1995 (283,000). The divorce rate was 4.1 per 1,000 population, a decrease of 7% from the first quarter of 1995 (4.4).

During the 12 months ending Mar. 1996, an estimated 1,157,000 couples divorced, a decrease from the number for the same period a year earlier (1,187,000). The decline in the number contributed to a 2% decrease in the divorce rate—from 4.5 per 1,000 population for the 12 month period ending with Mar. 1995 to 4.4 for the current period.

### Deaths

According to provisional statistics, there were 625,000 deaths during the first quarter of 1996, an increase of less than 1% from the first quarter of 1995 (622,000). The death rate was 9.5 per 1,000 population, 1% lower than the Jan.-Mar. 1995 rate (9.6). Among the deaths for the first quarter of 1996 were 7,100 deaths at ages under 1 year, yielding an infant mortality rate of 7.5 per 1,000 live births. This rate was 6% lower than the rate of 8.0 for the comparable 3-month period in 1995.

The death rate for the 12 months ending Mar. 1996 (8.8 deaths per 1,000 population) was 1% higher than the rate of 8.7 for the comparable 12-month period a year earlier. The infant mortality rate for this 12-month period was 7.4 per 1,000 live births, 6% lower than the rate of 7.9 for the 12 months ending Mar. 1995.

**Provisional Statistics**
**12 months ending with Mar.**

| | Number 1996 | Number 1995 | Rate* 1996 | Rate* 1995 |
|---|---|---|---|---|
| Live births | 3,873,000 | 3,959,000 | 14.7 | 15.1 |
| Deaths | 2,312,000 | 2,280,000 | 8.8 | 8.7 |
| Natural increase | 1,561,000 | 1,679,000 | 5.9 | 6.4 |
| Marriages | 2,339,000 | 2,358,000 | 8.9 | 9.0 |
| Divorces | 1,157,000 | 1,187,000 | 4.4 | 4.5 |
| Infant deaths | 28,700 | 31,000 | 7.4 | 7.9 |

*Per 1,000 population. **Note:** Figures include revisions.

## Annual Report for the Year 1995 (Provisional Statistics)

**Source:** National Center for Health Statistics, U.S. Dept. of Health and Human Services

### Highlights

The lowest U.S. infant mortality rate ever (7.5 infant deaths per 1,000 live births) was recorded in 1995. The rate of natural increase was the lowest in almost 20 years.

### Births

An estimated 3,900,089 babies were born in the U.S. in 1995, a decline of 1% from the 3,952,767 births in 1994. The birthrate of 14.8 per 1,000 population was 3% lower than the provisional rate of 15.2 for the preceding year. The fertility rate (the number of live births per 1,000 women aged 15-44 years) for 1995 was 65.6, 2% lower than the rate for 1994 (66.7).

### Deaths

The provisional count of deaths during 1995 was 2,312,180, about 1% more than in the previous year (2,278,994). The death rate of 880.0 deaths per 100,000 population was slightly higher than the 1994 provisional death rate of 875.4. The infant mortality rate was 7.5 infant deaths per 1,000 live births, 6% lower than the rate of 8.0 for 1994.

### Natural Increase

As a result of natural increase, the excess of births over deaths, an estimated 1,587,909 persons were added to the population in 1995. The rate was 6.0 per 1,000 population, about 8% below the rate of 6.5 for 1994, and the lowest since 1976 (5.9). The decline in the rate of natural increase reflects a decrease in the birth rate and no change in the death rate.

### Marriages

An estimated 2,336,000 marriages were performed in 1995. This was 1% less than in 1994 (2,362,000). The marriage rate for 1995 (8.9 per 1,000 population) was 2% lower than in 1994 (9.1). This rate has generally declined since the early 1980s and is currently the lowest rate since 1963 (8.8).

### Divorces

About 1,169,000 divorces were granted in the U.S. in 1995, 2% fewer than the number for 1994 (1,191,000), and 4% fewer than the all-time high of 1,215,000 in 1992. The divorce rate per 1,000 population in 1995 (4.4 per 1,000 population) was 4% lower than the rate for 1994 (4.6) and was the lowest divorce rate in over 2 decades.

## Births and Deaths in the U.S.

**Source:** National Center for Health Statistics, U.S. Dept. of Health and Human Services

| Year | Births: Total number | Births: Rate | Deaths: Total number | Deaths: Rate |
|---|---|---|---|---|
| 1960 | 4,257,850 | 23.7 | 1,711,982 | 9.5 |
| 1970 | 3,731,386 | 18.4 | 1,921,031 | 9.5 |
| 1980 | 3,612,258 | 15.9 | 1,989,841 | 8.7 |
| 1990 | 4,158,212 | 16.7 | 2,148,463 | 8.6 |
| 1991 | 4,110,907 | 16.3 | 2,169,518 | 8.6 |
| 1992 | 4,065,014 | 15.9 | 2,175,613 | 8.5 |
| 1993 | 4,000,240 | 15.5 | 2,268,000 | 8.8 |
| 1994 | 3,952,767 | 15.2 | 2,278,994 | 8.8 |
| 1995 (P) | 3,900,089 | 14.8 | 2,312,180 | 8.8 |

(P) = provisional data. **Note:** Refers only to events occurring within the U.S. Excludes fetal deaths. Rates per 1,000 population enumerated as of Apr. 1 for 1960 and 1970; estimated as of July 1 for all other years. Beginning 1970 excludes births and deaths occurring to nonresidents of the U.S. Data include revisions.

## Births and Deaths, by States and Regions, 1994-95

**Source:** National Center for Health Statistics, U.S. Dept. of Health and Human Services

| Area | Live births 1994 Number | Live births 1994 Rate | Live births 1995 Number | Live births 1995 Rate | Deaths 1994 Number | Deaths 1994 Rate | Deaths 1995 Number | Deaths 1995 Rate |
|---|---|---|---|---|---|---|---|---|
| **New England** | **175,080** | **13.2** | **167,992** | **12.6** | **119,006** | **9.0** | **120,507** | **9.1** |
| Maine | 14,320 | 11.5 | 13,911 | 11.2 | 11,674 | 9.4 | 11,625 | 9.4 |
| New Hampshire | 14,605 | 12.8 | 14,894 | 13.0 | 8,920 | 7.8 | 9,268 | 8.1 |
| Vermont | 7,158 | 12.3 | 6,842 | 11.7 | 4,784 | 8.2 | 5,040 | 8.6 |
| Massachusetts | 83,449 | 13.8 | 74,818 | 12.3 | 54,947 | 9.1 | 56,041 | 9.2 |
| Rhode Island | 13,440 | 13.5 | 12,386 | 12.5 | 9,408 | 9.4 | 9,643 | 9.7 |
| Connecticut | 42,108 | 12.9 | 45,141 | 13.8 | 29,273 | 8.9 | 28,890 | 8.8 |
| **Middle Atlantic** | **553,536** | **14.5** | **524,544** | **13.7** | **369,114** | **9.7** | **370,213** | **9.7** |
| New York | 279,187 | 15.4 | 264,459 | 14.6 | 168,764 | 9.3 | 168,081 | 9.3 |
| New Jersey | 117,289 | 14.8 | 108,637 | 13.7 | 72,305 | 9.1 | 74,016 | 9.3 |
| Pennsylvania | 157,060 | 13.0 | 151,448 | 12.5 | 128,045 | 10.6 | 128,116 | 10.6 |
| **East North Central** | **643,455** | **14.9** | **625,437** | **14.4** | **390,444** | **9.0** | **395,507** | **9.1** |
| Ohio | 162,059 | 14.6 | 155,633 | 14.0 | 103,262 | 9.3 | 106,014 | 9.5 |
| Indiana | 83,381 | 14.5 | 84,304 | 14.5 | 52,454 | 9.1 | 52,160 | 9.0 |
| Illinois | 189,228 | 16.1 | 185,425 | 15.7 | 107,344 | 9.1 | 108,732 | 9.2 |
| Michigan | 139,931 | 14.7 | 132,577 | 13.9 | 82,943 | 8.7 | 83,513 | 8.7 |
| Wisconsin | 68,856 | 13.5 | 67,498 | 13.2 | 44,441 | 8.7 | 45,088 | 8.8 |
| **West North Central** | **251,531** | **13.8** | **253,720** | **13.8** | **169,013** | **9.3** | **173,915** | **9.5** |
| Minnesota | 64,681 | 14.2 | 62,911 | 13.6 | 36,539 | 8.0 | 37,313 | 8.1 |
| Iowa | 35,926 | 12.7 | 36,611 | 12.9 | 27,702 | 9.8 | 25,983 | 9.1 |
| Missouri | 75,366 | 14.3 | 74,121 | 13.9 | 53,785 | 10.2 | 58,601 | 11.0 |
| North Dakota | 8,639 | 13.5 | 8,655 | 13.5 | 5,895 | 9.2 | 6,094 | 9.5 |
| South Dakota | 10,615 | 14.7 | 10,521 | 14.4 | 6,743 | 9.4 | 6,829 | 9.4 |
| Nebraska | 23,032 | 14.2 | 23,257 | 14.2 | 15,011 | 9.3 | 15,314 | 9.4 |
| Kansas | 33,272 | 13.0 | 37,644 | 14.7 | 23,338 | 9.1 | 23,781 | 9.3 |
| **South Atlantic** | **661,731** | **14.3** | **658,984** | **14.0** | **427,757** | **9.2** | **437,493** | **9.3** |
| Delaware | 10,361 | 14.7 | 10,258 | 14.3 | 6,339 | 9.0 | 6,278 | 8.8 |
| Maryland | 71,553 | 14.3 | 71,585 | 14.2 | 41,036 | 8.2 | 41,763 | 8.3 |
| District of Columbia | 9,669 | 17.0 | 8,831 | 15.9 | 7,208 | 12.6 | 6,852 | 12.4 |
| Virginia | 95,865 | 14.6 | 93,092 | 14.1 | 52,188 | 8.0 | 52,868 | 8.0 |
| West Virginia | 21,554 | 11.8 | 21,123 | 11.6 | 20,152 | 11.1 | 20,249 | 11.1 |
| North Carolina | 101,911 | 14.4 | 102,029 | 14.2 | 63,240 | 8.9 | 64,966 | 9.0 |
| South Carolina | 50,907 | 13.9 | 49,935 | 13.6 | 32,274 | 8.8 | 32,512 | 8.9 |
| Georgia | 108,908 | 15.4 | 113,589 | 15.8 | 56,571 | 8.0 | 58,364 | 8.1 |
| Florida | 191,003 | 13.7 | 188,542 | 13.3 | 148,749 | 10.7 | 153,641 | 10.8 |
| **East South Central** | **231,741** | **14.6** | **227,576** | **14.2** | **156,167** | **9.8** | **158,488** | **9.9** |
| Kentucky | 51,926 | 13.6 | 51,672 | 13.4 | 37,156 | 9.7 | 38,052 | 9.9 |
| Tennessee | 75,688 | 14.6 | 73,597 | 14.0 | 50,525 | 9.8 | 51,027 | 9.7 |
| Alabama | 60,745 | 14.4 | 60,939 | 14.3 | 41,708 | 9.9 | 42,417 | 10.0 |
| Mississippi | 43,382 | 16.3 | 41,368 | 15.3 | 26,778 | 10.0 | 26,992 | 10.0 |
| **West South Central** | **470,975** | **16.6** | **477,067** | **16.5** | **233,700** | **8.2** | **237,816** | **8.2** |
| Arkansas | 34,571 | 14.1 | 35,155 | 14.2 | 26,305 | 10.7 | 26,665 | 10.7 |
| Louisiana | 68,454 | 15.9 | 67,420 | 15.5 | 39,017 | 9.0 | 39,564 | 9.1 |
| Oklahoma | 45,682 | 14.0 | 45,906 | 14.0 | 32,299 | 9.9 | 32,757 | 10.0 |
| Texas | 322,268 | 17.5 | 328,586 | 17.5 | 136,079 | 7.4 | 138,830 | 7.4 |
| **Mountain** | **243,362** | **16.0** | **253,737** | **16.2** | **112,353** | **7.4** | **116,070** | **7.4** |
| Montana | 11,032 | 12.9 | 11,113 | 12.8 | 7,362 | 8.6 | 7,612 | 8.7 |
| Idaho | 17,358 | 15.3 | 18,012 | 15.5 | 8,447 | 7.5 | 8,493 | 7.3 |
| Wyoming | 6,385 | 13.4 | 6,335 | 13.2 | 3,481 | 7.3 | 3,749 | 7.8 |
| Colorado | 54,144 | 14.8 | 54,311 | 14.5 | 24,250 | 6.6 | 25,003 | 6.7 |
| New Mexico | 27,981 | 16.9 | 27,038 | 16.0 | 12,129 | 7.3 | 12,545 | 7.4 |
| Arizona | 66,143 | 16.2 | 72,355 | 17.2 | 34,298 | 8.4 | 35,336 | 8.4 |
| Utah | 38,808 | 20.3 | 39,530 | 20.3 | 10,473 | 5.5 | 10,825 | 5.5 |
| Nevada | 21,511 | 14.8 | 25,043 | 16.4 | 11,913 | 8.2 | 12,507 | 8.2 |
| **Pacific** | **734,658** | **17.6** | **711,034** | **16.9** | **301,440** | **7.2** | **302,169** | **7.2** |
| Washington | 79,296 | 14.8 | 78,302 | 14.4 | 39,960 | 7.5 | 40,525 | 7.5 |
| Oregon | 42,276 | 13.7 | 42,810 | 13.6 | 27,407 | 8.9 | 28,240 | 9.0 |
| California | 581,763 | 18.5 | 561,091 | 17.8 | 224,292 | 7.1 | 223,227 | 7.1 |
| Alaska | 12,079 | 19.9 | 10,233 | 17.0 | 2,445 | 4.0 | 2,540 | 4.2 |
| Hawaii | 19,244 | 16.3 | 18,598 | 15.7 | 7,336 | 6.2 | 7,637 | 6.4 |

**Note:** Data are provisional estimates, reported by state of residence. Figures include revisions, and so may differ from those previously published. Rates for births and deaths are per 1,000 population.

## Infant Deaths and Infant Mortality Rates, for Selected Causes, 1995-96

**Source:** National Center for Health Statistics, U.S. Dept. of Health and Human Services

| Age and cause of death | 1996 Number | 1996 Rate | 1995 Number | 1995 Rate |
|---|---|---|---|---|
| **Total, under 1 year** | **28,900** | **747.6** | **31,100** | **785.9** |
| Under 28 days | 18,250 | 472.5 | 19,630 | 496.0 |
| 28 days to 11 months | 10,590 | 274.2 | 11,450 | 289.3 |
| Certain gastrointestinal diseases | 170 | 4.4 | 240 | 6.1 |
| Pneumonia and influenza | 370 | 9.6 | 450 | 11.4 |
| Congenital anomalies | 6,010 | 155.6 | 6,750 | 170.6 |
| Disorders relating to short gestation and unspecified low birthweight | 3,390 | 87.8 | 3,880 | 98.0 |
| Birth trauma | 220 | 5.7 | 180 | 4.5 |
| Intrauterine hypoxia and birth asphyxia | 490 | 12.7 | 520 | 13.1 |
| Respiratory distress syndrome | 1,170 | 30.3 | 1,460 | 36.9 |
| Other conditions originating in the perinatal period | 7,760 | 200.9 | 7,820 | 197.6 |
| Sudden infant death syndrome | 2,900 | 75.1 | 3,370 | 85.2 |
| All other causes | 6,360 | 164.7 | 6,410 | 162.0 |

**Note:** Data are provisional, estimated from a 10% sample of deaths for a 12-month period ending in Feb. of the year cited. Rates are on an annual basis per 100,000 live births. Due to rounding of estimates, figures may not add to totals.

## Infant Mortality Rates, by Race and Sex, 1960-94[1]

**Source:** National Center for Health Statistics, U.S. Dept. of Health and Human Services

| | All races | | | White | | | Black | | |
|---|---|---|---|---|---|---|---|---|---|
| Year | Both sexes | Male | Female | Both sexes | Male | Female | Both sexes | Male | Female |
| 1960 | 26.0 | 29.3 | 22.6 | 22.9 | 26.0 | 19.6 | 44.3 | 49.1 | 39.4 |
| 1970 | 20.0 | 22.4 | 17.5 | 17.8 | 20.0 | 15.4 | 32.6 | 36.2 | 29.0 |
| 1980 | 12.6 | 13.9 | 11.2 | 11.0 | 12.3 | 9.6 | 21.4 | 23.3 | 19.4 |
| 1981 | 11.9 | 13.1 | 10.7 | 10.5 | 11.7 | 9.2 | 20.0 | 21.7 | 18.3 |
| 1982 | 11.5 | 12.8 | 10.2 | 10.1 | 11.2 | 8.9 | 19.6 | 21.5 | 17.7 |
| 1983 | 11.2 | 12.3 | 10.0 | 9.7 | 10.8 | 8.6 | 19.2 | 21.1 | 17.2 |
| 1984 | 10.8 | 11.9 | 9.6 | 9.4 | 10.5 | 8.3 | 18.4 | 19.8 | 16.9 |
| 1985 | 10.6 | 11.9 | 9.3 | 9.3 | 10.6 | 8.0 | 18.2 | 19.9 | 16.5 |
| 1986 | 10.4 | 11.5 | 9.1 | 8.9 | 10.0 | 7.8 | 18.0 | 20.0 | 16.0 |
| 1987 | 10.1 | 11.2 | 8.9 | 8.6 | 9.6 | 7.6 | 17.9 | 19.6 | 16.0 |
| 1988 | 10.0 | 11.0 | 8.9 | 8.5 | 9.5 | 7.4 | 17.6 | 19.0 | 16.1 |
| 1989 | 9.8 | 10.8 | 8.8 | 8.1 | 9.0 | 7.1 | 18.6 | 20.0 | 17.2 |
| 1990 | 9.2 | 10.3 | 8.1 | 7.6 | 8.5 | 6.6 | 18.0 | 19.6 | 16.2 |
| 1991 | 8.9 | 10.0 | 7.8 | 7.3 | 8.3 | 6.3 | 17.6 | 19.4 | 15.7 |
| 1992 | 8.5 | 9.4 | 7.6 | 6.9 | 7.7 | 6.1 | 16.8 | 18.4 | 15.3 |
| 1993 | 8.4 | 9.3 | 7.4 | 6.8 | 7.6 | 6.0 | 16.5 | 18.3 | 14.7 |
| 1994 | 8.0 | 8.8 | 7.2 | 6.6 | 7.2 | 5.9 | 15.8 | 17.5 | 14.1 |

(1) Final data. Rates per 1,000 live births.

## The 10 Leading Causes of Death, 1995[1]

**Source:** National Center for Health Statistics, U.S. Dept. of Health and Human Services

| Rank | Cause of death | Number | Death rate[2] | Percentage of total deaths |
|---|---|---|---|---|
| | **All causes** | **2,312,203** | **880.0** | **100.0** |
| 1. | Heart disease | 738,781 | 281.2 | 32.0 |
| 2. | Cancer | 537,969 | 204.7 | 23.3 |
| 3. | Stroke | 158,061 | 60.2 | 6.8 |
| 4. | Chronic obstructive lung diseases and allied conditions | 104,756 | 39.9 | 4.5 |
| 5. | Accidents and adverse effects | 89,703 | 34.1 | 3.9 |
| | Motor vehicle accidents | 41,786 | 15.9 | 1.8 |
| | All other accidents and adverse effects | 47,916 | 18.2 | 2.1 |
| 6. | Pneumonia and influenza | 83,528 | 31.8 | 3.6 |
| 7. | Diabetes mellitus | 59,085 | 22.5 | 2.6 |
| 8. | Human immunodeficiency virus (HIV) infection[3] | 42,506 | 16.2 | 1.8 |
| 9. | Suicide | 30,893 | 11.8 | 1.3 |
| 10. | Chronic liver disease and cirrhosis | 24,848 | 9.5 | 1.1 |

(1) Data are provisional, estimated from a 10% sample of deaths. Figures may not add to totals because of rounding. Rates have been recomputed based on revised population estimates. (2) Per 100,000 population. (3) HIV is the virus that causes AIDS.

## U.S. Abortion Patients, by Selected Characteristics, 1994-95

**Source:** Alan Guttmacher Institute, New York, NY

| Characteristic | % distribution: Abortion patients | % distribution: All women 15-44[1] |
|---|---|---|
| **Age group** | | |
| Under 15 years | 1.2 | NA |
| 15-17 | 8.8 | 8.8 |
| 18-19 | 11.5 | 5.7 |
| 20-24 | 32.8 | 15.2 |
| 25-29 | 21.4 | 16.1 |
| 30-34 | 14.4 | 18.8 |
| 35-39 | 7.5 | 18.6 |
| 40 years and older | 2.3 | 16.8 |
| **Race** | | |
| White | 61.3 | 81.2 |
| Black | 31.1 | 14.0 |
| Other | 7.6 | 4.9 |
| **Ethnicity** | | |
| Hispanic | 20.2 | 10.6 |
| Non-Hispanic | 79.8 | 89.4 |
| **Marital status** | | |
| Married | 18.4 | 49.9 |
| Separated | 7.2 | 3.3 |
| Divorced | 9.4 | 8.6 |
| Widowed | 0.5 | 0.7 |
| Never married | 64.4 | 37.5 |
| **Cohabiting** | | |
| Yes | 20.2 | 5.8 |
| No/married | 79.8 | 94.2 |
| **Number of live births** | | |
| 0 | 45.4 | 41.2 |
| 1 | 24.7 | 18.2 |
| 2 | 17.8 | 23.8 |
| 3 | 7.7 | 11.1 |
| 4 or more | 4.4 | 5.8 |
| **Region of residence** | | |
| Metropolitan | 88.5 | 79.6 |
| Nonmetropolitan | 11.5 | 20.4 |
| **Religion[2]** | | |
| Protestant | 37.4 | 53.9 |
| Catholic | 31.3 | 30.9 |
| Jewish | 1.3 | 1.2 |
| Other | 6.3 | 8.1 |
| None | 23.7 | 5.0 |
| **Born again/Evangelical** | | |
| Yes | 18.0 | 46.0 |
| No | 82.0 | 54.0 |
| **Education** | | |
| 8th grade or less | 4.2 | 4.7 |
| 9th-11th grade | 16.9 | 16.4 |
| H.S. graduate or GED | 30.4 | 30.1 |
| Some college or associate's degree | 34.9 | 30.0 |
| College graduate | 13.7 | 16.8 |
| **Enrolled in school** | | |
| Yes | 30.3 | 24.6 |
| No | 69.7 | 75.4 |
| **Currently employed** | | |
| Yes | 66.2 | 65.6 |
| No | 33.8 | 34.4 |
| **Family income** | | |
| Less than $15,000 | 28.7 | 15.4 |
| $15,000-$29,999 | 19.5 | 20.6 |
| $30,000-$59,999 | 38.0 | 35.9 |
| $60,000 or greater | 13.8 | 23.1 |
| **Medicaid coverage** | | |
| Yes | 26.5 | 12.9 |
| No | 73.5 | 87.1 |
| **Intend more children** | | |
| Yes | 66.0 | 47.8 |
| No | 34.0 | 52.2 |

NA=not available. (1) Data for 1994 except Medicaid status (1993), religion (1993-95), and childbearing intention (1990 intention by age, applied to 1994 population). (2) Based on women 18-44 years of age. **Note:** Percents may not add to 100 because of rounding.

# Suicides by Age, Race, and Sex, 1994

**Source:** National Center for Health Statistics, U.S. Dept. of Health and Human Services

| | All ages | 1-14 yrs. | 15-24 yrs. | 25-34 yrs. | 35-44 yrs. | 45-54 yrs. | 55-64 yrs. | 65-74 yrs. | 75-84 yrs. | 85 yrs. & over | Age not stated |
|---|---|---|---|---|---|---|---|---|---|---|---|
| **All races, both sexes[1]** | **32,410** | **390** | **5,350** | **6,610** | **6,430** | **3,940** | **3,050** | **3,040** | **2,620** | **950** | **40** |
| Male | 26,710 | 300 | 4,770 | 5,530 | 5,240 | 2,900 | 2,420 | 2,500 | 2,200 | 800 | 40 |
| Female | 5,700 | 100 | 570 | 1,080 | 1,190 | 1,040 | 620 | 540 | 410 | 150 | (—) |
| **White, both sexes** | **28,850** | **330** | **4,370** | **5,560** | **5,790** | **3,690** | **2,840** | **2,820** | **2,530** | **900** | **20** |
| Male | 23,760 | 240 | 3,910 | 4,650 | 4,710 | 2,730 | 2,280 | 2,330 | 2,130 | 760 | 20 |
| Female | 5,090 | 80 | 470 | 910 | 1,080 | 960 | 560 | 490 | 400 | 140 | (—) |
| **Black, both sexes** | **2,350** | **30** | **710** | **600** | **460** | **170** | **150** | **130** | **40** | **50** | **10** |
| Male | 2,080 | 30 | 620 | 550 | 400 | 140 | 120 | 120 | 40 | 40 | 10 |
| Female | 280 | (—) | 80 | 50 | 50 | 30 | 30 | 10 | (—) | 10 | (—) |

(—) = Data represent zero. **Note:** Data are provisional, estimated from a 10% sample of deaths. Because of rounding, figures may not add to totals. (1) All races includes races other than white and black.

# Living Arrangements of Children, 1970-94

**Source:** Bureau of the Census, U.S. Dept. of Commerce

(as of Mar.; excludes persons under 18 years of age who maintained households or resided in group quarters)

| Race, Hispanic origin, and year | Number (1,000) | Both parents | Percentage living with— Mother only: Total | Divorced | Married spouse absent | Single[1] | Widowed | Father only | Neither parent |
|---|---|---|---|---|---|---|---|---|---|
| **White** | | | | | | | | | |
| 1970 | 58,790 | 90 | 8 | 3 | 3 | Z | 2 | 1 | 2 |
| 1980 | 52,242 | 83 | 14 | 7 | 4 | 1 | 2 | 2 | 2 |
| 1990 | 51,390 | 79 | 16 | 8 | 4 | 3 | 1 | 3 | 2 |
| 1991 | 51,918 | 79 | 17 | 8 | 5 | 3 | 1 | 3 | 2 |
| 1993 | 53,042 | 77 | 17 | 8 | 4 | 4 | 1 | 4 | 2 |
| 1994 | 54,775 | 76 | 18 | 8 | 4 | 4 | 1 | 3 | 3 |
| **Black** | | | | | | | | | |
| 1970 | 9,422 | 59 | 30 | 5 | 16 | 4 | 4 | 2 | 10 |
| 1980 | 9,375 | 42 | 44 | 11 | 16 | 13 | 4 | 2 | 12 |
| 1990 | 10,018 | 38 | 51 | 10 | 12 | 27 | 2 | 4 | 8 |
| 1991 | 10,209 | 36 | 54 | 10 | 11 | 31 | 2 | 4 | 7 |
| 1993 | 10,649 | 36 | 54 | 10 | 12 | 31 | 1 | 3 | 7 |
| 1994 | 11,169 | 33 | 53 | 10 | 12 | 30 | 1 | 4 | 10 |
| **Hispanic[2]** | | | | | | | | | |
| 1970 | 4,006[3] | 78 | NA | NA | NA | NA | NA | NA | NA |
| 1980 | 5,459 | 75 | 20 | 6 | 8 | 4 | 2 | 2 | 4 |
| 1990 | 7,174 | 67 | 27 | 7 | 10 | 8 | 2 | 3 | 3 |
| 1991 | 7,462 | 66 | 27 | 7 | 10 | 9 | 2 | 3 | 4 |
| 1993 | 7,773 | 64 | 28 | 7 | 9 | 11 | 1 | 4 | 4 |
| 1994 | 9,483 | 64 | 28 | 6 | 9 | 11 | 2 | 4 | 5 |

NA=Not available. Z=Less than 0.5%. (1) Never married. (2) Hispanic persons may be of any race. (3) All persons under 18 years old.

# Living Arrangements of the Elderly, 1993

**Source:** Bureau of the Census, U.S. Dept. of Commerce

There were nearly 33 mil elderly persons (aged 65 years or older) in the U.S. in 1993. Approximately 30.9 mil lived in the community (not in institutions). Of these elderly, 9.36 mil lived alone, 16.89 mil lived with a spouse, and the remaining 4.63 mil lived with other relatives or nonrelatives. Data from the 1990 census show 3.3 mil persons of all ages lived in institutional group quarters in 1990; 1.6 mil of these were elderly persons living in nursing homes.

Of those elderly who lived alone, nearly 8 in 10 were women. Persons aged 65 to 74 were one and a half times more likely to live with a spouse (63.6%) than were those aged 75 and over (41.7%).

# Cigarette Use by Adults 18 and Older

**Source:** National Health Interview Survey, 1993, American Cancer Society

| Category | % Men | % Women | % Total |
|---|---|---|---|
| **Age** | | | |
| 18-24 | 28.8 | 22.9 | 25.8 |
| 25-44 | 31.1 | 27.3 | 29.2 |
| 45-64 | 29.2 | 23.0 | 26.0 |
| 65 or older | 13.5 | 10.5 | 11.8 |
| **Race/Ethnicity** | | | |
| White | 27.0 | 24.0 | 25.4 |
| Black | 32.4 | 21.0 | 26.0 |
| Hispanic | 28.3 | 12.7 | 20.4 |
| American/Indian Alaskan Native | 35.9 | 40.9 | 38.7 |
| Asian/Pacific Islander | 27.4 | 9.5 | 18.2 |

| Category | % Men | % Women | % Total |
|---|---|---|---|
| **Years of education[1]** | | | |
| 8 or less | 28.5 | 13.6 | 20.5 |
| 9-11 | 42.1 | 32.3 | 36.8 |
| 12 | 32.0 | 26.9 | 29.2 |
| 13-15 | 28.4 | 22.1 | 25.0 |
| 16 or more | 14.8 | 11.9 | 13.5 |
| **Poverty status** | | | |
| At or above poverty level | 26.1 | 21.7 | 23.8 |
| Below poverty level | 38.1 | 28.2 | 32.1 |
| Status unknown | 37.6 | 22.2 | 28.3 |
| **Total** | **27.7** | **22.5** | **25.0** |

(1) Persons aged 25 and older.

## Drug Use: America's Students

**Source:** Univ. of Michigan Inst. for Social Research, National Institute on Drug Abuse

### Middle and High School Students

Drug use among American young people continued to rise in 1995, according to the results of the University of Michigan's 21st annual survey of American high school seniors and 5th annual survey of 8th and 10th graders. Since 1991—when the decline in illicit drug use halted—the proportion of 8th graders taking illicit drugs in the 12 months prior to the survey almost doubled (from 11% to 21%). Among 10th graders, the proportion using any illicit drugs in the prior 12 months rose by nearly two-thirds (from 20% to 33%), and among 12th graders, the proportion increased by half (from 27% to 39%).

Marijuana remained the most commonly used illegal drug among the 3 grade levels. In 1995, the proportion of students that reported using marijuana in the past year rose to 16% of 8th graders, 29% of 10th graders, and 35% of 12th graders. Use of marijuana on a daily basis also increased. Nearly 1 in 20 (4.6%) high school seniors and roughly 1 in every 35 10th graders (2.8%) was a daily user.

Use of LSD and other hallucinogens, amphetamines, stimulants, and inhalants also continued to drift upward. Although heroin use remained rather low, a statistically significant increase in annual heroin use occurred among 8th graders in 1994, and then among 12th graders in 1995. Levels of use in 1995 were 2 to 3 times higher than they had been a few years earlier. The use of alcohol remained high but stable for all grade levels in 1995. Prevalence of cigarette smoking rose again in 1995. Nearly 19% of 8th graders, 28% of 10th graders, and 34% of 12th graders reported having smoked during the 30 days before they responded to the survey.

In 1995, about 16,000 seniors in 144 public and private high schools participated in the survey, along with 17,000 10th graders in 139 schools and 18,000 8th graders in 152 schools. It should be noted that the surveys missed the 15-20% of a class group that drops out of school early. This population would likely have higher rates of drug use overall.

### College Students

A 1994 survey of 1,500 college students found that the increase in overall drug usage that occurred from 1991 to 1992 had halted and that there was virtually no change in drug use from the previous year. Of those surveyed, 31% used some illicit drugs at least once in the prior 12 months. Of all illicit drugs, marijuana was the most commonly used drug among college students. From 1991 to 1994, its use in the prior 12 months increased nearly 3 percentage points, to 29.3% of those surveyed.

Usage of an illicit drug other than marijuana in the prior 12 months decreased slightly, from 12.5% to 12.2%. Use of hallucinogens rose less than 1%. Slightly more than 6% of those surveyed reported having used a hallucinogen in the prior 12 months.

The popularity of cocaine and crack continued to decline, with use dropping to 2.0% of college students surveyed in 1994, from 2.7% of the 1993 students.

Active use of other forms of illicitly used drugs (including stimulants, barbiturates, tranquilizers, inhalants, and heroin and other opiates) declined slightly among college students in 1994.

## Drug Use: America's High School Seniors, 1975-95

**Source:** Univ. of Michigan Inst. for Social Research, National Institute on Drug Abuse

| | Percentage ever used | | | | | | | | | | |
|---|---|---|---|---|---|---|---|---|---|---|---|
| | Class of 1975 | Class of 1980 | Class of 1986 | Class of 1988 | Class of 1990 | Class of 1991 | Class of 1992 | Class of 1993 | Class of 1994 | Class of 1995 | '94-'95 change |
| Marijuana/hashish | 47.3 | 60.3 | 50.9 | 47.2 | 40.7 | 36.7 | 32.6 | 35.3 | 38.2 | 41.7 | +3.5 |
| Inhalants | NA | 11.9 | 15.9 | 16.7 | 18.0 | 17.6 | 16.6 | 17.4 | 17.7 | 17.4 | –0.3 |
| Inhalants adjusted[1] | NA | 17.3 | 20.1 | 17.5 | 18.5 | 18.0 | 17.0 | 17.7 | 18.3 | 17.8 | –0.5 |
| Amyl & butyl nitrites | NA | 11.1 | 8.6 | 3.2 | 2.1 | 1.6 | 1.5 | 1.4 | 1.7 | 1.5 | –0.2 |
| Hallucinogens | 16.3 | 13.3 | 9.7 | 8.9 | 9.4 | 9.6 | 9.2 | 10.9 | 11.4 | 12.7 | +1.3 |
| Hallucinogens adjusted[2] | NA | 15.6 | 11.9 | 9.2 | 9.7 | 10.0 | 9.4 | 11.3 | 11.7 | 13.1 | +1.4 |
| LSD | 11.3 | 9.3 | 7.2 | 7.7 | 8.7 | 8.8 | 8.6 | 10.3 | 10.5 | 11.7 | +1.2 |
| PCP | NA | 9.6 | 4.8 | 2.9 | 2.8 | 2.9 | 2.4 | 2.9 | 2.8 | 2.7 | –0.1 |
| Cocaine | 9.0 | 15.7 | 16.9[6] | 12.1 | 9.4 | 7.8 | 6.1 | 6.1 | 5.9 | 6.0 | +0.1 |
| Crack | NA | NA | NA | 4.8 | 3.5 | 3.1 | 2.6 | 2.6 | 3.0 | 3.0 | 0.0 |
| Heroin[3] | 2.2 | 1.1 | 1.1 | 1.1 | 1.3 | 0.9 | 1.2 | 1.1 | 1.2 | 1.6 | +0.4 |
| Other opiates[4] | 9.0 | 9.8 | 9.0 | 8.6 | 8.3 | 6.6 | 6.1 | 6.4 | 6.6 | 7.2 | +0.6 |
| Stimulants[4,5] | 22.3 | 26.4 | 23.4 | 19.8 | 17.5 | 15.4 | 13.9 | 15.1 | 15.7 | 15.3 | –0.4 |
| Sedatives[4] | 18.2 | 14.9 | 10.4 | 7.8 | 7.5 | 6.7 | 6.1 | 6.4 | 7.3 | 7.6 | +0.3 |
| Barbiturates[4] | 16.9 | 11.0 | 8.4 | 6.7 | 6.8 | 6.2 | 5.5 | 6.3 | 7.0 | 7.4 | +0.4 |
| Methaqualone[4] | 8.1 | 9.5 | 5.2 | 3.3 | 2.3 | 1.3 | 1.6 | 0.8 | 1.4 | 1.2 | –0.2 |
| Tranquilizers[4] | 17.0 | 15.2 | 10.9 | 9.4 | 7.2 | 7.2 | 6.0 | 6.4 | 6.6 | 7.1 | +0.5 |
| Alcohol | 90.4 | 93.2 | 91.3 | 92.0 | 89.5 | 88.0 | 87.5 | 87.0 | 80.4[7] | 80.7[7] | +0.3 |
| Cigarettes | 73.6 | 71.0 | 67.6 | 66.4 | 64.4 | 63.1 | 61.8 | 61.9 | 62.0 | 64.2 | +2.2 |

NA=Not available. (1) Adjusted for underreporting of amyl and butyl nitrites. (2) Adjusted for underreporting of PCP. (3) Reflects use with or without injection.(4) Only drug use that was not under a doctor's orders. (5) Adjusted for overreporting of the nonprescription stimulants. (6) In 1986, three-fourths of those who used cocaine used it in powder form; the remainder used the "crack" form. (7) Data for 1994 and 1995 are not directly comparable to prior years.

## Drug Use in the General U.S. Population

**Source:** Bureau of Justice Statistics, U.S. Dept. of Justice

According to the Substance Abuse and Mental Health Administration's 1995 National Household Survey on Drug Abuse, an estimated 72 mil (34.2%) Americans 12 years of age and older had used an illicit drug at least once during their lifetimes, 10.7% used one during the previous year, and 6.1% used one in the month before the survey was conducted. Among those 25 years of age and under, an estimated 1.6 mil used cocaine (including crack) and 9.2 mil used marijuana at least once within the previous year. Among those 26 years of age and over, 2.1 mil used cocaine (including crack) and 8.5 mil used marijuana at least once within the previous year.

The Substance Abuse and Mental Health Services Administration's Drug Abuse Warning Network reported an estimated 518,521 drug-related episodes in hospital emergency departments nationwide in 1994. A total of 8,426 drug-abuse-related deaths were reported in 1994 by 138 medical examiners in 42 metropolitan areas.

## Principal Types of Accidental Deaths, 1970-95

**Source:** National Safety Council

| Year | Motor vehicle | Falls | Poison (solid, liquid) | Drowning | Fires, burns | Ingestion of food, object | Firearms | Poison (gases) |
|---|---|---|---|---|---|---|---|---|
| 1970 | 54,633 | 16,926 | 3,679 | 7,860 | 6,718 | 2,753 | 2,406 | 1,620 |
| 1975 | 45,853 | 14,896 | 4,694 | 8,000 | 6,071 | 3,106 | 2,380 | 1,577 |
| 1980 | 53,172 | 13,294 | 3,089 | 7,257 | 5,822 | 3,249 | 1,955 | 1,242 |
| 1985 | 45,901 | 12,001 | 4,091 | 5,316 | 4,938 | 3,551 | 1,649 | 1,079 |
| 1990 | 46,814 | 12,313 | 5,055 | 4,685 | 4,175 | 3,303 | 1,416 | 748 |
| 1991 | 43,536 | 12,662 | 5,698 | 4,818 | 4,120 | 3,240 | 1,441 | 736 |
| 1992 | 40,982 | 12,646 | 6,449 | 3,542 | 3,958 | 3,182 | 1,409 | 633 |
| 1993 | 41,893 | 13,141 | 7,877 | 3,807 | 3,900 | 3,160 | 1,521 | 660 |
| 1994 | 42,700 | 12,700 | 9,000 | 4,200 | 4,200 | 3,000 | 1,500 | 700 |
| 1995 | 43,900 | 12,600 | 10,000 | 4,500 | 4,100 | 2,800 | 1,400 | 600 |
| | | | **Death rates per 100,000 population** | | | | | |
| 1970 | 26.8 | 8.3 | 1.8 | 3.9 | 3.3 | 1.4 | 1.2 | 0.8 |
| 1975 | 21.3 | 6.9 | 2.2 | 3.7 | 2.8 | 1.4 | 1.1 | 0.7 |
| 1980 | 23.4 | 5.9 | 1.4 | 3.2 | 2.6 | 1.4 | 0.9 | 0.5 |
| 1985 | 19.3 | 5.0 | 1.7 | 2.2 | 2.1 | 1.5 | 0.7 | 0.5 |
| 1990 | 18.8 | 4.9 | 2.0 | 1.9 | 1.7 | 1.3 | 0.6 | 0.3 |
| 1991 | 17.3 | 5.0 | 2.3 | 1.8 | 1.6 | 1.3 | 0.6 | 0.3 |
| 1992 | 16.1 | 5.0 | 2.5 | 1.4 | 1.6 | 1.2 | 0.6 | 0.2 |
| 1993 | 16.3 | 5.1 | 3.1 | 1.5 | 1.5 | 1.2 | 0.6 | 0.3 |
| 1994 | 16.4 | 4.9 | 3.5 | 1.6 | 1.6 | 1.2 | 0.6 | 0.3 |
| 1995 | 16.7 | 4.8 | 3.8 | 1.7 | 1.6 | 1.1 | 0.5 | 0.2 |

**Note:** There were 7,900 other accidental deaths in 1995; the most frequently occurring types were medical complications, machinery, air transport, water transport, mechanical suffocation, and excessive cold.

## Motor Vehicle Accidents

**Source:** National Safety Council

Motor vehicle deaths in 1995 increased 2% over levels for 1994. Of the 177,432,000 licensed drivers in 1995, about 90 mil (51%) were men and 87,208,000 (49%) were women.

Male drivers were involved in more fatal accidents than female drivers in 1995. About 37,500 men and 13,000 women drivers were involved in fatal accidents.

About 10.6 mil male drivers and 7.0 mil female drivers were involved in all types of accidents in 1995. However, since males account for about 64% of the miles driven each year, according to the latest estimates, and females for 36%, women have higher accident involvement rates. At least part of the difference in accident involvement rates between men and women may be due to differences in the time, place, and circumstance of driving experienced by both groups of drivers. Accident rates were 69 per 10 million miles driven for men and 80 per 10 million miles driven for women.

About 41% of all traffic fatalities in 1994 involved an intoxicated or alcohol-impaired driver or nonoccupant. Of these 16,589 alcohol-related traffic fatalities, an estimated 13,094 occurred in accidents in which a driver or nonoccupant was intoxicated, and the remainder involved a driver or nonoccupant who had been drinking but was not legally intoxicated. Alcohol was also a factor in about 6% of all traffic accidents, both fatal and nonfatal, in 1994. In 1984 alcohol-related fatalities accounted for 54% of all traffic deaths.

| | Death total 1995 | Percentage change from 1994 | Death rate 1995[1] |
|---|---|---|---|
| All motor vehicle accidents | 43,900 | +2 | 16.4 |
| Collision between motor vehicles | 19,400 | +1 | 7.4 |
| Collision with fixed object | 12,300 | +4 | 4.7 |
| Pedestrian accidents | 6,300 | +7 | 2.4 |
| Noncollision accidents | 4,400 | +2 | 1.7 |
| Collision with pedalcycle | 900 | +13 | 0.3 |
| Collision with railroad train | 500 | 0 | 0.2 |
| Other collision (animal, animal-drawn vehicles, street cars) | 100 | 0 | (2) |

(1) Deaths per 100,000 population. (2) Death rate was less than 0.05.

## Improper Driving Reported in Accidents, 1995

**Source:** National Safety Council

| Type | Percentage of fatal accidents | | Percentage of injury accidents | | Percentage of all accidents | |
|---|---|---|---|---|---|---|
| | 1994 | 1995 | 1994 | 1995 | 1994 | 1995 |
| **Improper driving** | **63.7** | **68.1** | **65.7** | **73.5** | **67.3** | **75.5** |
| Speed too fast or unsafe | 19.5 | 19.8 | 11.2 | 13.9 | 11.9 | 14.0 |
| Right of way | 15.1 | 15.2 | 24.1 | 25.5 | 21.3 | 22.9 |
| Failed to yield | 9.1 | 10.2 | 15.0 | 18.1 | 14.5 | 17.0 |
| Passed stop sign | 2.6 | 3.0 | 3.1 | 5.0 | 2.5 | 4.0 |
| Disregarded signal | 3.4 | 2.2 | 6.0 | 2.4 | 4.3 | 1.9 |
| Drove left of center | 9.4 | 9.1 | 2.5 | 2.4 | 2.3 | 2.2 |
| Improper overtaking | 1.6 | 1.5 | 1.2 | 1.3 | 1.4 | 1.5 |
| Made improper turn | 2.6 | 2.3 | 2.9 | 2.8 | 4.1 | 4.2 |
| Followed too closely | 0.5 | 0.5 | 5.9 | 7.0 | 5.6 | 7.2 |
| Other improper driving | 15.0 | 19.7 | 17.9 | 20.7 | 20.6 | 23.6 |
| **No improper driving stated** | **36.3** | **31.9** | **34.3** | **26.5** | **32.7** | **24.5** |

**Note:** Based on reports from 20 state traffic authorities. When a driver was under the influence of alcohol or drugs, the accident was considered a result of the driver's physical condition—not a driving error. For this reason, accidents in which the driver was reported to be under the influence are classified under "no improper driving."

## Deaths Involving Firearms, by Age, 1993

**Source:** National Safety Council

| | All ages | Under 5 | 5-14 | 15-24 | 25-44 | 45-64 | 65-74 | 75 & over |
|---|---|---|---|---|---|---|---|---|
| **Total firearms deaths[1]** | **39,277** | **116** | **841** | **11,096** | **15,744** | **6,518** | **2,504** | **2,458** |
| Male | 33,403 | 73 | 641 | 9,837 | 13,074 | 5,400 | 2,155 | 2,233 |
| Female | 5,874 | 43 | 200 | 1,259 | 2,670 | 1,118 | 349 | 235 |
| **Accidents** | **1,521** | **30** | **175** | **595** | **448** | **171** | **52** | **50** |
| Male | 1,328 | 28 | 156 | 541 | 371 | 148 | 44 | 40 |
| Female | 193 | 2 | 19 | 54 | 77 | 23 | 8 | 10 |
| **Suicides** | **18,940** | **0** | **187** | **3,213** | **6,805** | **4,430** | **2,104** | **2,201** |
| Male | 16,381 | 0 | 146 | 2,846 | 5,743 | 3,726 | 1,864 | 2,056 |
| Female | 2,559 | 0 | 41 | 367 | 1,062 | 704 | 240 | 145 |
| **Homicides** | **18,253** | **85** | **458** | **7,105** | **8,285** | **1,829** | **319** | **172** |
| Male | 15,228 | 45 | 319 | 6,287 | 6,803 | 1,458 | 220 | 96 |
| Female | 3,025 | 40 | 139 | 818 | 1,482 | 371 | 99 | 76 |
| **Undetermined[2]** | **563** | **1** | **21** | **183** | **206** | **88** | **29** | **35** |
| Male | 466 | 0 | 20 | 163 | 157 | 68 | 27 | 31 |
| Female | 97 | 1 | 1 | 20 | 49 | 20 | 2 | 4 |

(1) Excludes firearms deaths by legal intervention. These deaths totaled 318 in 1993. (2) "Undetermined" means that the intention involved (whether accident, suicide, or homicide) cannot be determined.

## Home Accident Deaths, 1950-95

**Source:** National Safety Council

| Year | Total | Falls | Poison (solid, liquid) | Fires, burns[1] | Suffoc., ingesting object | Firearms | Suffoc., mechanical | Poison (gases) | All other[2] |
|---|---|---|---|---|---|---|---|---|---|
| 1950 | 29,000 | 14,800 | 1,300 | 5,000 | (3) | 950 | 1,600 | 1,250 | 4,100 |
| 1960 | 28,000 | 12,300 | 1,350 | 6,350 | 1,850 | 1,200 | 1,500 | 900 | 2,550 |
| 1970 | 27,000 | 9,700 | 3,000 | 5,600 | 1,800[4] | 1,400[4] | 1,100[4] | 1,100 | 3,300[4] |
| 1980 | 22,800 | 7,100 | 2,500 | 4,800 | 2,000 | 1,100 | 500 | 700 | 4,100[5] |
| 1990 | 21,500 | 6,700 | 4,000 | 3,400 | 2,300 | 800 | 600 | 500 | 3,200 |
| 1991 | 22,100 | 6,900 | 4,500 | 3,400 | 2,200 | 800 | 700 | 500 | 3,100 |
| 1992[6] | 24,000 | 7,700 | 4,800 | 3,700 | 1,500 | 1,000 | 700 | 400 | 4,200 |
| 1993[6] | 26,100 | 7,900 | 6,000 | 3,700 | 1,700 | 1,100 | 700 | 500 | 4,500 |
| 1994[6] | 26,700 | 7,700 | 7,100 | 3,900 | 1,500 | 1,000 | 700 | 500 | 4,300 |
| 1995[7] | 26,400 | 7,300 | 8,100 | 3,600 | 1,300 | 800 | 600 | 400 | 4,300 |

(1) Includes deaths resulting from conflagration, regardless of nature of injury. (2) Includes drowning in swimming pools and bathtubs. (3) Included in All other. (4) Data for this year and subsequent years not comparable with previous years because of classification changes. (5) Includes about 1,000 excessive deaths due to summer heat wave. (6) Revised figures. The National Safety Council adopted the Bureau of Labor Statistics Census of Fatal Occupational Injuries count for work-related unintentional injuries, retroactive to 1992 data. (7) Data are preliminary.

## Worldwide Airline Fatalities, 1980-95

**Source:** National Safety Council

| Year | Aircraft accidents[1] | Passenger deaths | Death rate[2] | Year | Aircraft accidents[1] | Passenger deaths | Death rate[2] |
|---|---|---|---|---|---|---|---|
| 1980 | 22 | 814 | 0.14 | 1988 | 25 | 699 | 0.08 |
| 1981 | 21 | 362 | 0.06 | 1989 | 27 | 817 | 0.08 |
| 1982 | 26 | 764 | 0.13 | 1990 | 22 | 440 | 0.04 |
| 1983 | 20 | 809 | 0.13 | 1991 | 25 | 510 | 0.05 |
| 1984 | 16 | 223 | 0.03 | 1992 | 25 | 990 | 0.09 |
| 1985 | 22 | 1,066 | 0.15 | 1993 | 31 | 801 | 0.07 |
| 1986 | 17 | 331 | 0.04 | 1994 | 24 | 732 | 0.06 |
| 1987 | 24 | 890 | 0.10 | 1995[3] | 22 | 557 | 0.04 |

(1) Involving a passenger fatality. (2) Passenger deaths per 100 mil passenger mi. (3) Preliminary.

## Cost of Unintentional Injuries, 1995

**Source:** National Safety Council, estimates

| The cost of. . . | is equivalent to. . . | |
|---|---|---|
| . . .all injuries ($434.8 bil) | | 73 cents of every dollar paid in 1995 federal personal income taxes, |
| | or | 58 cents of every dollar spent on food in the U.S. in 1995. |
| . . .motor vehicle accidents ($170.6 bil) | | purchasing 730 gallons of gasoline per registered vehicle in the U.S., |
| | or | a $19,700 rebate on each new car sold in 1995. |
| . . .work injuries ($119.4 bil) | | 53 cents of every dollar of 1995 corporate dividends to stockholders, |
| | or | 20 cents of every dollar of 1995 pre-tax corporate profits. |
| . . .home injuries ($95.1 bil) | | a $88,400 rebate on each new single-family home built in 1995, |
| | or | 44 cents of every dollar of property taxes paid in 1995. |
| . . .public injuries[1] ($63.3 bil) | | a $7.0 million grant to each public library in the U.S., |
| | or | an $83,700 bonus for each police officer and firefighter. |

(1) Any accident, other than a motor vehicle or a work-related accident, that occurs in public use of any premises, such as accidents during recreation (swimming, hunting, etc.), due to natural disasters, or in a public building.

# U.S. Fires, 1995

**Source:** National Fire Protection Assn.

**Fires**
- Public fire departments responded to 1,965,500 fires in 1995, a decrease of 4.3% from 1994.
- There were 573,500 structure fires in 1995, a decrease of 6.6% from the 1994 figure.
- 74% of all structure fires, or 425,500 fires, occurred in residential properties.
- There were 406,500 vehicle fires in 1995, a decrease of 3.7% from the previous year.
- There were 985,500 fires in outside properties, a decrease of 3.2% from 1994.
- The South and the Northeast had the highest fire incident rates in the country, with 9.3 and 8.6 fires per 1,000 population, respectively.

**Civilian deaths**
- There were 4,585 civilian fire deaths in 1995, an increase of 7.3% from 1994.
- The number of deaths from fire in the home increased by 6.3% to 3,640.
- About 79% of all fire deaths occurred in the home.
- The South had the highest fire death rate, with 22.1 civilian deaths per million population, followed by the Northeast and the North Central region, both with 16.2 deaths per million.
- Nationwide, someone died in a fire every 115 minutes.

**Civilian injuries**
- There were an estimated 25,775 civilian fire injuries in 1995, a decrease of 5.4% from 1994. This estimate is low because of underreporting of civilian fire injuries to the fire service.
- Residential properties were the site of 19,125 civilian fire injuries, or 74.2% of injuries overall; 2,600 injuries, or 10.1%, occurred in nonresidential structure fires.
- The Northeast had the highest regional injury rate in the U.S., with 128.4 civilian injuries per million population. The next highest rate was in the North Central region, with 108.3 injuries per million.
- Nationwide, a civilian was injured in a fire every 20 minutes.

**Property damage**
- Property damage resulting from fires increased in 1995 by 9.4%, to an estimated $8.918 billion.
- Structure fires resulted in 85% of all property damage, or $7.62 billion.
- 57% of all structure property loss occurred in residential properties, accounting for $4.363 billion.
- The Northeast had the highest property loss rate in the U.S.—$41.4 per person—followed by the South, with $38.7 per person.

**Incendiary and suspicious fires**
- 15.8% of all structure fires, or an estimated 90,500 fires, were deliberately set or are suspected of having been deliberately set. This represents an increase of 8% from 1994.
- Incendiary or suspicious structure fires resulted in 740 civilian deaths. The unusually large increase of 34.5% from the previous year reflects the 168 civilians killed in the explosion and fire at the Alfred P. Murrah Federal Office Building in Oklahoma City on Apr. 19, 1995. Incendiary or suspicious fires caused $1.647 billion in property damage, or 21.6% of all property loss from structure fires.
- Vehicle fires of incendiary or suspicious origin in 1995 increased by 8% from 1994 to 47,000. They caused an estimated $175 million in property damage, which is a 12.2% increase from the year before.

# Physicians by Age, Sex, and Specialty, 1995

**Source:** American Medical Assn., as of Dec. 31, 1995

| | Total Physicians[1] | | Under 35 yrs | | 35-44 yrs | | 45-54 yrs | | 55-64 yrs | |
|---|---|---|---|---|---|---|---|---|---|---|
| | Male | Female | Male | Female | Male | Female | Male | Female | Male | Female |
| **All Specialties** | **570,921** | **149,404** | **87,990** | **46,093** | **155,006** | **56,721** | **131,959** | **26,927** | **86,589** | **9,822** |
| Aerospace Medicine | 543 | 32 | 74 | 6 | 161 | 13 | 137 | 12 | 100 | — |
| Allergy & Immunology | 3,039 | 736 | 212 | 129 | 829 | 310 | 945 | 202 | 622 | 50 |
| Anesthesiology | 26,431 | 6,422 | 5,358 | 1,639 | 10,349 | 2,537 | 5,769 | 1,384 | 3,320 | 646 |
| Cardiovascular Disease | 17,705 | 1,293 | 2,258 | 323 | 6,437 | 615 | 5,025 | 245 | 2,684 | 74 |
| Child Psychiatry | 3,396 | 2,146 | 343 | 366 | 1,026 | 868 | 1,052 | 545 | 624 | 237 |
| Colon/Rectal Surgery | 938 | 52 | 65 | 12 | 328 | 32 | 299 | 6 | 141 | 1 |
| Dermatology | 6,110 | 2,453 | 674 | 755 | 1,568 | 1,085 | 1,997 | 444 | 1,214 | 122 |
| Diagnostic Radiology | 16,051 | 3,757 | 3,677 | 1,369 | 5,649 | 1,589 | 4,419 | 645 | 1,767 | 121 |
| Emergency Medicine | 15,815 | 3,297 | 3,159 | 1,065 | 6,148 | 1,491 | 4,779 | 579 | 1,153 | 121 |
| Family Practice | 45,176 | 13,934 | 7,598 | 5,098 | 16,953 | 6,141 | 11,124 | 1,970 | 5,078 | 506 |
| Forensic Pathology | 366 | 130 | 18 | 10 | 118 | 57 | 92 | 39 | 82 | 19 |
| Gastroenterology | 8,822 | 729 | 1,277 | 198 | 3,328 | 372 | 2,722 | 136 | 1,111 | 20 |
| General Practice | 14,507 | 2,362 | 190 | 84 | 1,300 | 536 | 2,773 | 797 | 3,862 | 535 |
| General Preventive Med. | 870 | 399 | 80 | 78 | 259 | 194 | 233 | 73 | 171 | 34 |
| General Surgery | 34,268 | 3,302 | 8,090 | 1,895 | 8,101 | 1,151 | 7,814 | 349 | 6,156 | 74 |
| Internal Medicine | 66,431 | 21,810 | 17,312 | 9,002 | 21,232 | 8,537 | 14,181 | 3,088 | 7,742 | 823 |
| Neurological Surgery | 4,675 | 213 | 847 | 81 | 1,291 | 96 | 1,107 | 29 | 979 | 6 |
| Neurology | 9,231 | 2,165 | 1,306 | 566 | 3,221 | 963 | 2,772 | 459 | 1,384 | 145 |
| Nuclear Medicine | 1,181 | 254 | 93 | 41 | 299 | 108 | 379 | 63 | 278 | 30 |
| Obstetrics/Gynecology | 23,099 | 10,420 | 3,360 | 4,195 | 6,095 | 4,098 | 6,710 | 1,505 | 4,655 | 462 |
| Occupational Medicine | 2,549 | 482 | 79 | 50 | 615 | 226 | 633 | 123 | 550 | 56 |
| Ophthalmology | 15,237 | 2,227 | 2,210 | 713 | 4,283 | 975 | 4,225 | 375 | 3,097 | 118 |
| Orthopedic Surgery | 21,360 | 677 | 3,893 | 254 | 6,402 | 314 | 5,566 | 77 | 3,913 | 19 |
| Otolaryngology | 8,393 | 693 | 1,473 | 291 | 2,309 | 285 | 2,168 | 90 | 1,784 | 20 |
| Pathology-Anat./Clin. | 12,933 | 4,891 | 1,580 | 1,108 | 3,473 | 1,916 | 3,313 | 1,149 | 2,923 | 494 |
| Pediatrics | 23,575 | 20,034 | 4,203 | 7,205 | 6,715 | 7,222 | 6,285 | 3,795 | 3,915 | 1,303 |
| Pediatric Cardiology | 1,012 | 324 | 164 | 112 | 358 | 109 | 241 | 55 | 172 | 31 |
| Physical Med./Rehab. | 3,798 | 1,767 | 951 | 520 | 1,397 | 620 | 773 | 390 | 385 | 166 |
| Plastic Surgery | 5,015 | 478 | 460 | 100 | 1,644 | 239 | 1,613 | 103 | 977 | 25 |
| Psychiatry | 27,706 | 10,392 | 2,643 | 1,998 | 6,512 | 3,840 | 7,588 | 2,577 | 6,054 | 1,195 |
| Public Health | 1,302 | 458 | 29 | 19 | 233 | 144 | 350 | 103 | 306 | 84 |
| Pulmonary Diseases | 6,627 | 826 | 874 | 254 | 2,556 | 382 | 2,198 | 126 | 706 | 37 |
| Radiation Oncology | 2,844 | 786 | 493 | 224 | 997 | 295 | 746 | 189 | 421 | 62 |
| Radiology | 7,086 | 953 | 512 | 129 | 1,147 | 350 | 1,753 | 287 | 2,438 | 128 |
| Thoracic Surgery | 2,260 | 50 | 259 | 9 | 704 | 31 | 452 | 8 | 527 | 2 |
| Urological Surgery | 9,642 | 244 | 1,414 | 102 | 2,449 | 108 | 2,769 | 26 | 2,143 | 6 |
| Other | 6,196 | 1,111 | 294 | 90 | 1,474 | 385 | 1,489 | 304 | 1,439 | 166 |
| Unspecified | 5,902 | 2,571 | 3,275 | 1,695 | 1,511 | 607 | 582 | 179 | 276 | 57 |

(1) Includes physicians 65 and older, those living in U.S. possessions, those "Inactive," "Not Classified," and "Address Unknown."

## U.S. Health Expenditures, 1960-94

**Source:** Health Care Financing Administration, Office of the Actuary; data from the Office of National Health Statistics

(in billions of dollars)

| Type of expenditure | 1960 | 1970 | 1975 | 1980 | 1985 | 1990 | 1991 | 1992 | 1993 | 1994 |
|---|---|---|---|---|---|---|---|---|---|---|
| **National health expenditures** | **$26.9** | **$73.2** | **$130.7** | **$247.2** | **$428.2** | **$697.5** | **$761.3** | **$833.6** | **$892.3** | **$949.4** |
| **Health services & supplies** | **25.2** | **67.9** | **122.3** | **235.6** | **411.8** | **672.9** | **736.3** | **806.0** | **863.1** | **919.2** |
| Personal health care | 23.6 | 63.8 | 114.5 | 217.0 | 376.4 | 614.7 | 676.2 | 739.8 | 786.5 | 831.7 |
| Hospital care | 9.3 | 28.0 | 52.6 | 102.7 | 168.3 | 256.4 | 282.3 | 305.3 | 324.2 | 338.5 |
| Physician services | 5.3 | 13.6 | 23.9 | 45.2 | 83.6 | 146.3 | 158.6 | 174.7 | 181.1 | 189.4 |
| Dental services | 2.0 | 4.7 | 8.0 | 13.3 | 21.7 | 31.6 | 33.3 | 37.0 | 39.2 | 42.2 |
| Other professional services | 0.6 | 1.4 | 2.7 | 6.4 | 16.6 | 34.7 | 38.3 | 42.1 | 46.3 | 49.6 |
| Home health care | 0.1 | 0.2 | 0.6 | 2.4 | 5.6 | 13.1 | 16.1 | 19.6 | 23.0 | 26.2 |
| Drugs & other medical nondurables | 4.2 | 8.8 | 13.0 | 21.6 | 37.1 | 59.9 | 65.6 | 71.3 | 75.2 | 78.6 |
| Vision products & other medical durables | 0.6 | 1.6 | 2.5 | 3.8 | 6.7 | 10.5 | 11.2 | 11.9 | 12.6 | 13.1 |
| Nursing home care | 0.8 | 4.2 | 8.7 | 17.6 | 30.7 | 50.9 | 57.2 | 62.3 | 67.0 | 72.3 |
| Other personal health care | 0.7 | 1.3 | 2.5 | 4.0 | 6.1 | 11.2 | 13.6 | 15.6 | 17.8 | 21.8 |
| Program administration & net cost of private health insurance | 1.2 | 2.7 | 4.9 | 11.8 | 23.8 | 38.6 | 38.7 | 42.8 | 51.0 | 58.7 |
| Government public health activities | 0.4 | 1.3 | 2.9 | 6.7 | 11.6 | 19.6 | 21.4 | 23.4 | 25.7 | 28.8 |
| **Research & construction** | **1.7** | **5.3** | **8.4** | **11.6** | **16.4** | **24.5** | **24.9** | **27.6** | **29.2** | **30.2** |
| Research[1] | 0.7 | 2.0 | 3.3 | 5.5 | 7.8 | 12.2 | 12.9 | 14.2 | 14.5 | 15.9 |
| Construction | 1.0 | 3.4 | 5.1 | 6.2 | 8.5 | 12.3 | 12.0 | 13.4 | 14.7 | 14.3 |
| | **Average annual % change from previous year shown** | | | | | | | | | |
| **National health expenditures** | **—** | **10.6** | **12.3** | **13.6** | **11.6** | **10.2** | **9.1** | **9.5** | **7.0** | **6.4** |
| **Health services & supplies** | **—** | **10.4** | **12.5** | **14.0** | **11.8** | **10.3** | **9.4** | **9.5** | **7.1** | **6.5** |
| Personal health care | — | 10.5 | 12.4 | 13.6 | 11.6 | 10.3 | 10.0 | 9.4 | 6.3 | 5.7 |
| Hospital care | — | 11.7 | 13.4 | 14.3 | 10.4 | 8.8 | 10.1 | 8.1 | 6.2 | 4.4 |
| Physician services | — | 9.9 | 12.0 | 13.6 | 13.1 | 11.8 | 8.4 | 10.1 | 3.7 | 4.6 |
| Dental services | — | 9.1 | 11.2 | 10.9 | 10.2 | 7.8 | 5.6 | 11.0 | 6.0 | 7.5 |
| Other professional services | — | 8.8 | 14.2 | 18.4 | 21.2 | 15.8 | 10.4 | 10.0 | 10.0 | 7.1 |
| Home health care | — | 14.5 | 23.2 | 30.7 | 18.9 | 18.4 | 22.4 | 22.3 | 17.1 | 13.8 |
| Drugs & other medical nondurables | — | 7.6 | 8.1 | 10.7 | 11.4 | 10.1 | 9.5 | 8.6 | 5.4 | 4.5 |
| Vision products & other medical durables | — | 9.6 | 9.5 | 8.1 | 12.4 | 9.2 | 6.8 | 6.9 | 5.1 | 4.6 |
| Nursing home care | — | 17.4 | 15.5 | 15.3 | 11.7 | 10.7 | 12.2 | 9.0 | 7.6 | 7.8 |
| Other personal health care | — | 6.5 | 13.8 | 10.2 | 8.8 | 12.9 | 21.1 | 14.7 | 14.3 | 22.5 |
| Program administration & net cost of private health insurance | — | 8.9 | 12.5 | 19.2 | 15.0 | 10.2 | 0.2 | 10.5 | 19.1 | 15.2 |
| Government public health activities | — | 13.9 | 16.8 | 18.1 | 11.5 | 11.0 | 9.1 | 9.4 | 9.6 | 12.4 |
| **Research & construction** | **—** | **12.2** | **9.4** | **6.8** | **7.1** | **8.4** | **1.7** | **10.5** | **5.9** | **3.5** |
| Research[1] | — | 10.9 | 11.2 | 10.4 | 7.5 | 9.3 | 5.8 | 9.8 | 2.2 | 9.9 |
| Construction | — | 12.9 | 8.3 | 4.1 | 6.7 | 7.6 | -2.4 | 11.4 | 9.7 | -2.8 |

**Note:** Numbers may not add to totals because of rounding. (1) Research and development expenditures of drug companies and other manufacturers and providers of medical equipment and supplies are excluded from "research expenditures" but included in the expenditure class in which the product falls.

## Ownership of Life Insurance in the U.S. and Assets of U.S. Life Insurance Companies, 1940-95

**Source:** American Council of Life Insurance

(millions of dollars)

| | Purchases of life insurance | | | | Insurance in force | | | | | |
|---|---|---|---|---|---|---|---|---|---|---|
| Year | Ordinary | Group | Industrial | Total | Ordinary | Group | Industrial | Credit | Total | Assets |
| 1940 | 6,689 | 691 | 3,350 | 10,730 | 79,346 | 14,938 | 20,866 | 380 | 115,530 | 30,802 |
| 1950 | 17,326 | 6,068 | 5,402 | 28,796 | 149,116 | 47,793 | 33,415 | 3,844 | 234,168 | 64,020 |
| 1960 | 52,883 | 14,645 | 6,880 | 74,408 | 341,881 | 175,903 | 39,563 | 29,101 | 586,448 | 119,576 |
| 1970 | 122,820 | 63,690* | 6,612 | 193,122* | 734,730 | 551,357 | 38,644 | 77,392 | 1,402,123 | 207,254 |
| 1975 | 188,003 | 95,190* | 6,729 | 289,922* | 1,083,421 | 904,695 | 39,423 | 112,032 | 2,139,571 | 289,304 |
| 1980 | 385,575 | 183,418 | 3,609 | 572,602 | 1,760,474 | 1,579,355 | 35,994 | 165,215 | 3,541,038 | 479,210 |
| 1985 | 910,944 | 319,503 | 722 | 1,231,169 | 3,247,289 | 2,561,595 | 28,250 | 215,973 | 6,053,107 | 825,901 |
| 1987 | 986,660 | 365,529 | 324 | 1,352,513 | 4,139,071 | 3,043,782 | 26,668 | 242,977 | 7,452,498 | 1,044,459 |
| 1989 | 1,020,719 | 420,707 | 252 | 1,441,678 | 4,939,964 | 3,469,498 | 24,446 | 260,107 | 8,694,015 | 1,299,756 |
| 1990 | 1,069,660 | 459,271 | 220 | 1,529,151 | 5,366,982 | 3,753,506 | 24,071 | 248,038 | 9,392,597 | 1,408,208 |
| 1991 | 1,041,508 | 573,953* | 198 | 1,615,659* | 5,677,777 | 4,057,606 | 22,475 | 228,478 | 9,986,336 | 1,551,201 |
| 1992 | 1,048,135 | 440,143 | 222 | 1,488,500 | 5,941,810 | 4,240,919 | 20,973 | 202,090 | 10,405,792 | 1,664,531 |
| 1993 | 1,101,327 | 576,823 | 149 | 1,678,299 | 6,428,434 | 4,456,338 | 20,451 | 199,518 | 11,104,741 | 1,839,127 |
| 1994 | 1,107,216 | 549,984 | 232 | 1,657,432 | 6,835,239 | 4,608,746 | 20,145 | 209,491 | 11,673,621 | 1,942,273 |
| 1995 | 1,101,032 | 499,024 | 317 | 1,600,373 | 7,547,537 | 4,777,912 | 19,971 | 231,251 | 12,576,677 | 2,143,544 |

*Includes Servicemen's Group Life Insurance, which amounted to $17.1 billion in 1970, $1.7 billion in 1975, and $166.7 billion in 1991.

## Health Insurance Coverage,[1] by State, 1995

**Source:** Bureau of the Census, U.S. Dept. of Commerce, Mar. 1996 Current Population Survey

(in thousands)

| State | Total population | Covered by insurance | Not covered | % not covered | State | Total population | Covered by insurance | Not covered | % not covered |
|---|---|---|---|---|---|---|---|---|---|
| AL . . . . | 4,399 | 3,804 | 595 | 13.5 | MT . . . . | 873 | 762 | 111 | 12.7 |
| AK . . . . | 631 | 552 | 79 | 12.6 | NE . . . . | 1,653 | 1,504 | 149 | 9.0 |
| AZ . . . . | 4,346 | 3,461 | 885 | 20.4 | NV . . . . | 1,563 | 1,271 | 292 | 18.7 |
| AR . . . . | 2,533 | 2,079 | 454 | 17.9 | NH . . . . | 1,141 | 1,027 | 114 | 10.0 |
| CA . . . . | 32,118 | 25,517 | 6,601 | 20.6 | NJ . . . . | 7,903 | 6,782 | 1,121 | 14.2 |
| CO . . . . | 3,812 | 3,248 | 564 | 14.8 | NM . . . . | 1,807 | 1,344 | 463 | 25.6 |
| CT . . . . | 3,287 | 2,998 | 289 | 8.8 | NY . . . . | 18,301 | 15,522 | 2,779 | 15.2 |
| DE . . . . | 714 | 602 | 112 | 15.7 | NC . . . . | 6,947 | 5951 | 996 | 14.3 |
| DC . . . . | 555 | 459 | 96 | 17.3 | ND . . . . | 638 | 585 | 53 | 8.3 |
| FL . . . . | 14,352 | 11,724 | 2,628 | 18.3 | OH . . . . | 11,230 | 9,894 | 1,336 | 11.9 |
| GA . . . . | 7,267 | 5,966 | 1,301 | 17.9 | OK . . . . | 3,206 | 2,591 | 615 | 19.2 |
| HI . . . . | 1,188 | 1,082 | 108 | 8.9 | OR . . . . | 3,220 | 2,817 | 403 | 12.5 |
| ID . . . . | 1,154 | 893 | 161 | 14.0 | PA . . . . | 12,044 | 10,849 | 1,195 | 9.9 |
| IL . . . . | 11,798 | 10,504 | 1,294 | 11.0 | RI . . . . | 963 | 839 | 124 | 12.9 |
| IN . . . . | 5,688 | 4,972 | 716 | 12.6 | SC . . . . | 3,751 | 3,205 | 546 | 14.6 |
| IA . . . . | 2,896 | 2,569 | 327 | 11.3 | SD . . . . | 716 | 649 | 67 | 9.4 |
| KS . . . . | 2,539 | 2,223 | 316 | 12.4 | TN . . . . | 5,483 | 4,669 | 614 | 14.6 |
| KY . . . . | 3,894 | 3,327 | 567 | 14.6 | TX . . . . | 18,805 | 14,190 | 4,615 | 24.5 |
| LA . . . . | 4,313 | 3,428 | 885 | 20.5 | UT . . . . | 2,002 | 1,767 | 235 | 11.7 |
| ME . . . . | 1,226 | 1,060 | 166 | 13.5 | VT . . . . | 598 | 519 | 79 | 13.2 |
| MD . . . . | 5,133 | 4,350 | 783 | 15.3 | VA . . . . | 6383 | 5,521 | 862 | 13.5 |
| MA . . . . | 6,071 | 5,400 | 671 | 11.1 | WA . . . . | 5,435 | 4,759 | 676 | 12.4 |
| MI . . . . | 9,644 | 8,706 | 938 | 9.7 | WV . . . . | 1,799 | 1,523 | 276 | 15.3 |
| MN . . . . | 4,630 | 4,260 | 370 | 8.0 | WI . . . . | 5,321 | 4,930 | 391 | 7.3 |
| MS . . . . | 2,690 | 2,159 | 531 | 19.7 | WY . . . . | 483 | 406 | 77 | 15.9 |
| MO . . . | 5,172 | 4,416 | 756 | 14.6 | **U.S. . . .** | **264,315** | **223,733** | **40,582** | **15.4** |

(1) For all ages, including those 65 or over, an age group largely covered by Medicare.

## Months Without Health Insurance Coverage, by Selected Characteristics

**Source:** Bureau of the Census, U.S. Dept. of Commerce

| Characteristic | 1992-94 | 1991-93 | Characteristic | 1992-94 | 1991-93 |
|---|---|---|---|---|---|
| **Total** | **5.7** | **7.1** | 1 or more years of college | 4.5 | 4.9 |
| **Race and Hispanic origin** | | | **Region** | | |
| White | 5.7 | 6.7 | Northeast | 5.6 | 7.1 |
| Black | 5.9 | 7.4 | Midwest | 4.8 | 5.0 |
| Hispanic | 6.9 | 7.8 | South | 6.0 | 7.5 |
| Not of Hispanic origin | 5.5 | 5.8 | West | 5.7 | 6.6 |
| **Age** | | | **Employment status**[2] | | |
| 18 to 24 years | 5.8 | 7.3 | Employed full time | 5.0 | 5.7 |
| 25 to 34 years | 7.2 | 6.8 | Employed part time | 7.2 | 7.6 |
| 35 to 44 years | 6.9 | 7.2 | Unemployed | 7.6 | 7.8 |
| 45 to 64 years | 5.8 | 7.8 | Not in labor force | 7.1 | 8.0 |
| **Educational attainment**[2] | | | **Poverty status** | | |
| Less than 4 years of high school | 7.7 | 10.7 | Below poverty | 5.7 | 7.6 |
| High school graduate, no college | 6.9 | 7.3 | Above poverty | 5.6 | 6.1 |

**Note:** Findings are from the Bureau of the Census's Survey of Income and Program Participation (SIPP). Estimates represent persons observed to begin a period of time without any health insurance coverage, public or private, during the 28-month period prior to the survey for 1992-94 and during the 32-month period prior to the survey for 1991-93. (1) Size of the sample is too small to be representative. (2) Aged 18 and over.

## Health Coverage for Persons Under 65, by Characteristics, 1984-94

**Source:** *Health United States 1995,* National Center for Health Statistics, U.S. Dept. of Health and Human Services

| | Private insurance | | | | Medicaid[1] | | | | Not covered[2] | | | |
|---|---|---|---|---|---|---|---|---|---|---|---|---|
| | 1984 | 1989 | 1993[3] | 1994[4] | 1984 | 1989 | 1993[3] | 1994[4] | 1984 | 1989 | 1993[3] | 1994[4] |
| | Percent of population | | | | | | | | | | | |
| **Age** | | | | | | | | | | | | |
| Under 15 years . . . . . . . . . . . | 71.9 | 71.7 | 65.6 | 63.0 | 10.8 | 11.4 | 18.9 | 19.8 | 16.1 | 15.9 | 14.8 | 16.1 |
| 15-44 years . . . . . . . . . . . . . | 77.0 | 76.6 | 70.6 | 69.6 | 4.4 | 4.4 | 6.4 | 6.7 | 17.6 | 18.1 | 21.6 | 22.0 |
| 45-64 years . . . . . . . . . . . . . | 83.6 | 83.3 | 80.7 | 80.5 | 2.7 | 3.4 | 3.4 | 3.6 | 10.2 | 10.6 | 12.3 | 12.2 |
| **Race and Hispanic origin**[5] | | | | | | | | | | | | |
| White, non-Hispanic . . . . . . . | 82.5 | 83.0 | 78.6 | 77.4 | 3.4 | 3.6 | 5.8 | 6.2 | 12.3 | 12.1 | 13.9 | 14.6 |
| Black, non-Hispanic. . . . . . . . | 59.0 | 59.3 | 51.5 | 52.4 | 17.7 | 17.1 | 23.2 | 23.8 | 22.0 | 21.8 | 23.0 | 21.1 |
| All Hispanic. . . . . . . . . . . . . . | 56.7 | 50.6 | 48.6 | 48.7 | 10.2 | 10.5 | 16.2 | 17.4 | 32.2 | 31.3 | 34.2 | 32.9 |
| **Family income**[5,6] | | | | | | | | | | | | |
| Less than $14,000. . . . . . . . . | 34.1 | 34.6 | 26.0 | 24.7 | 26.5 | 26.6 | 37.2 | 38.0 | 37.8 | 37.3 | 35.3 | 35.0 |
| $14,000-$24,999. . . . . . . . . . | 71.3 | 71.4 | 60.1 | 54.0 | 4.2 | 4.8 | 10.5 | 12.3 | 22.1 | 21.4 | 27.5 | 30.4 |
| $25,000-$34,999. . . . . . . . . . | 88.3 | 87.9 | 80.9 | 78.4 | 1.2 | 1.2 | 2.4 | 3.5 | 8.7 | 9.3 | 13.8 | 15.6 |
| $35,000-$49,999. . . . . . . . . . | 93.1 | 92.4 | 89.4 | 88.5 | 0.4 | 0.8 | 1.3 | 1.3 | 4.8 | 5.6 | 7.8 | 8.7 |
| $50,000 or more . . . . . . . . . . | 95.2 | 95.7 | 93.9 | 92.7 | 0.4 | 0.4 | 0.4 | 0.7 | 3.1 | 3.2 | 4.6 | 5.6 |
| **Geographic region**[5] | | | | | | | | | | | | |
| Northeast . . . . . . . . . . . . . . . | 80.4 | 83.4 | 76.2 | 74.8 | 7.4 | 5.8 | 9.3 | 10.2 | 11.8 | 10.3 | 14.3 | 14.7 |
| Midwest . . . . . . . . . . . . . . . . | 80.6 | 81.9 | 77.7 | 77.3 | 7.0 | 7.1 | 9.9 | 9.4 | 11.8 | 10.7 | 11.7 | 12.3 |
| South . . . . . . . . . . . . . . . . . . | 74.4 | 71.8 | 66.1 | 65.3 | 4.4 | 5.7 | 9.3 | 10.2 | 18.4 | 20.0 | 21.9 | 21.4 |
| West . . . . . . . . . . . . . . . . . . | 72.3 | 72.1 | 68.1 | 65.4 | 6.2 | 7.2 | 10.4 | 11.0 | 19.0 | 19.1 | 19.0 | 21.2 |

**Note:** Data based on household interviews of a sample of the civilian noninstitutionalized population. Percents do not add to 100 because other types of health insurance (e.g., Medicare, military) are not shown, and persons with both private insurance and Medicaid appear in both columns. (1) Includes persons receiving AFDC or SSI or those with current Medicaid cards. (2) Includes persons not covered by private insurance, Medicaid, Medicare, or military plans. (3) July 1 to Dec. 31, 1993. The questionnaire changed in 1993. (4) Preliminary data. (5) Age adjusted. (6) Family income categories for 1989, 1993, and 1994. Income categories for 1984 are: less than $10,000; $10,000-$18,999; $19,000-$29,999; $30,000-$39,999; and $40,000 or more.

## Physician Contacts Per Person, by Selected Characteristics, 1987-94

**Source:** *Health United States 1995,* National Center for Health Statistics, U.S. Dept. of Health and Human Services

| | 1987 | 1988 | 1989 | 1990 | 1991 | 1992 | 1993 | 1994 |
|---|---|---|---|---|---|---|---|---|
| **Total[1,2]** | **5.4** | **5.3** | **5.3** | **5.5** | **5.6** | **5.9** | **6.0** | **6.0** |
| **Age** | | | | | | | | |
| Under 15 years | 4.5 | 4.6 | 4.6 | 4.5 | 4.7 | 4.6 | 4.9 | 4.6 |
| Under 5 years | 6.7 | 7.0 | 6.7 | 6.9 | 7.1 | 6.9 | 7.2 | 6.8 |
| 5-14 years | 3.3 | 3.3 | 3.5 | 3.2 | 3.4 | 3.4 | 3.6 | 3.4 |
| 15-44 years | 4.6 | 4.7 | 4.6 | 4.8 | 4.7 | 5.0 | 5.0 | 5.0 |
| 45-64 years | 6.4 | 6.1 | 6.1 | 6.4 | 6.6 | 7.2 | 7.1 | 7.3 |
| 65 years and over | 8.9 | 8.7 | 8.9 | 9.2 | 10.4 | 10.6 | 10.9 | 11.3 |
| 65-74 years | 8.4 | 8.4 | 8.2 | 8.5 | 9.2 | 9.7 | 9.9 | 10.3 |
| 75 years and over | 9.7 | 9.2 | 9.9 | 10.1 | 12.3 | 12.1 | 12.3 | 12.7 |
| **Sex** | | | | | | | | |
| Male[1] | 4.6 | 4.6 | 4.8 | 4.7 | 4.9 | 5.1 | 5.2 | 5.2 |
| Female[1] | 6.0 | 6.0 | 5.9 | 6.1 | 6.3 | 6.6 | 6.7 | 6.7 |
| **Race** | | | | | | | | |
| White[1] | 5.5 | 5.5 | 5.5 | 5.6 | 5.8 | 6.0 | 6.0 | 6.1 |
| Black[1] | 5.1 | 4.8 | 4.9 | 5.1 | 5.2 | 5.9 | 6.0 | 5.7 |
| **Family income[1,3]** | | | | | | | | |
| Less than $14,000 | 6.8 | 6.2 | 6.3 | 6.3 | 6.8 | 7.3 | 7.3 | 7.6 |
| $14,000-$24,999 | 5.6 | 5.3 | 5.2 | 5.6 | 5.6 | 6.0 | 5.7 | 5.9 |
| $25,000-$34,999 | 5.2 | 5.0 | 5.5 | 5.2 | 5.5 | 5.7 | 6.0 | 5.8 |
| $35,000-$49,999 | 5.2 | 5.5 | 5.2 | 5.7 | 5.8 | 5.9 | 6.0 | 6.2 |
| $50,000 or more | 5.4 | 5.5 | 6.0 | 5.6 | 5.8 | 5.8 | 5.8 | 6.0 |
| **Geographic region[1]** | | | | | | | | |
| Northeast | 5.2 | 5.0 | 5.3 | 5.2 | 5.4 | 5.9 | 5.9 | 5.9 |
| Midwest | 5.6 | 5.4 | 5.4 | 5.3 | 5.8 | 5.9 | 6.2 | 6.0 |
| South | 5.1 | 5.2 | 5.3 | 5.6 | 5.5 | 5.8 | 5.7 | 5.6 |
| West | 5.5 | 5.9 | 5.5 | 5.6 | 5.9 | 6.1 | 6.0 | 6.4 |
| **Location of residence[1]** | | | | | | | | |
| Within MSA | 5.5 | 5.5 | 5.4 | 5.6 | 5.8 | 6.0 | 6.1 | 6.0 |
| Outside MSA | 4.8 | 4.9 | 5.2 | 4.9 | 5.1 | 5.6 | 5.6 | 5.7 |

MSA = metropolitan statistical area. **Note:** Data based on household interviews of a sample of the civilian noninstitutionalized population. (1) Age adjusted. (2) Includes all other races not shown separately and unknown family income. (3) Family income categories for 1989-94. Income categories for 1987 are the following: less than $10,000; $10,000-$14,999; $15,000-$19,999; $20,000-$34,999; and $35,000 or more. Income categroies for 1988 are less than $13,000; $13,000-$18,999; $19,000-$24,999; $25,000-$44,999; and $45,000 or more.

## Top 20 Reasons Given by Patients for Emergency Room Visits, 1994

**Source:** National Center for Health Statistics, U.S. Dept. of Health and Human Services

| Principal reason for visit | No. of visits (1,000) | Percent of total[1] |
|---|---|---|
| **All visits to emergency rooms** | **93,402** | **100.0** |
| Stomach and abdominal pain, cramps, and spasms | 5,256 | 5.6 |
| Chest pain and related symptoms | 4,435 | 4.7 |
| Fever | 4,281 | 4.6 |
| Headache, pain in head | 2,530 | 2.7 |
| Cough | 2,384 | 2.6 |
| Injury—upper extremity | 2,380 | 2.5 |
| Back symptoms | 2,205 | 2.4 |
| Symptoms referable to throat | 2,038 | 2.2 |
| Vomiting | 1,903 | 2.0 |
| Earache or ear infection | 1,845 | 2.0 |
| Pain, site not referable to a specific body system | 1,827 | 2.0 |
| Shortness of breath | 1,750 | 1.9 |
| Injury, other and unspecific type—head, neck, and face | 1,693 | 1.8 |
| Labored or difficult breathing (dyspnea) | 1,646 | 1.8 |
| Laceration and cuts—facial area | 1,579 | 1.7 |
| Skin rash | 1,351 | 1.4 |
| Hand and finger symptoms | 1,332 | 1.4 |
| Neck symptoms | 1,307 | 1.4 |
| Hand and finger injury | 1,184 | 1.3 |
| Leg symptoms | 1,178 | 1.3 |
| All other reasons | 49,298 | 52.8 |

(1) Percents do not add to 100.0 because of rounding.

## Top 20 Reasons Given by Patients for Physicians' Office Visits, 1994

**Source:** National Center for Health Statistics, U.S. Dept. of Health and Human Services

| Principal reason for visit | Number of visits (1,000) | Percentage distribution Total | Female | Male |
|---|---|---|---|---|
| **All visits** | **681,457** | **100.0** | **100.0** | **100.0** |
| General medical examination | 39,789 | 5.8 | 6.3 | 5.1 |
| Progress visit, not otherwise specified | 29,109 | 4.3 | 4.1 | 4.6 |
| Cough | 23,936 | 3.5 | 3.2 | 4.0 |
| Routine prenatal examination | 22,136 | 3.2 | 5.4 | NA |
| Postoperative visit | 19,136 | 2.8 | 2.8 | 2.8 |
| Symptoms referable to throat | 16,446 | 2.4 | 2.4 | 2.5 |
| Well-baby examination | 13,204 | 1.9 | 1.5 | 2.6 |
| Depression | 13,180 | 1.9 | 2.2 | 1.6 |
| Earache or ear infection | 12,204 | 1.8 | 1.6 | 2.1 |
| Stomach pain, cramps, and spasms | 11,632 | 1.7 | 2.0 | 1.3 |
| Vision dysfunctions | 11,575 | 1.7 | 1.7 | 1.7 |
| Skin rash | 11,504 | 1.7 | 1.6 | 1.8 |
| Back symptoms | 10,711 | 1.6 | 1.4 | 1.9 |
| Knee symptoms | 10,151 | 1.5 | 1.4 | 1.7 |
| Fever | 9,518 | 1.4 | 1.2 | 1.7 |
| Nasal congestion | 9,392 | 1.4 | 1.2 | 1.7 |
| Headache, pain in head | 9,235 | 1.4 | 1.6 | 1.0 |
| Hypertension | 8,857 | 1.3 | 1.1 | 1.6 |
| Chest pain and related symptoms | 8,112 | 1.2 | 1.0 | 1.5 |
| Head cold, upper respiratory infection (coryza) | 7,932 | 1.2 | 1.2 | 1.2 |
| All other reasons | 383,699 | 56.3 | 55.1 | 57.6 |

NA = not applicable.

# Drugs Most Frequently Prescribed in Physicians' Offices, 1994

**Source:** National Center for Health Statistics, U.S. Dept. of Health and Human Services; Physicians' Desk Reference; in thousands

| Rank | Name of drug and principal generic substance[1] | Number of times prescribed | Therapeutic use |
|---|---|---|---|
| 1. | Amoxicillin | 18,161 | Antibiotic |
| 2. | Amoxil (amoxicillin) | 11,435 | Antibiotic |
| 3. | Lasix (furosemide) | 10,538 | Diuretic, antihypertensive |
| 4. | Allergy relief drugs or shots | 9,982 | Diagnostics |
| 5. | Prednisone | 9,397 | Steroid replacement therapy, anti-inflammatory agent |
| 6. | Premarin (estrogens) | 9,047 | Estrogen replacement therapy |
| 7. | Tylenol (acetaminophen) | 8,617 | Analgesic |
| 8. | Zantac (ranitidine) | 8,107 | Duodenal or gastric ulcer |
| 9. | Cardizem (ditiazem) | 7,947 | Angina/calcium channel blocking agent |
| 10. | Synthroid (levothyroxine) | 7,394 | Thyroid hormone therapy |
| 11. | Poliomyelitis vaccine | 7,179 | Immunization |
| 12. | Influenza virus vaccine | 6,957 | Immunization |
| 13. | Ventolin (albuterol) | 6,817 | Bronchodilator, antiasthmatic |
| 14. | Vasotec (enalapril) | 6,528 | Antihypertensive |
| 15. | Prenatal formula | 6,484 | Vitamins, minerals |
| 16. | Lanoxin (digoxin) | 6,480 | Congestive heart failure, irregular heartbeat |
| 17. | Diphtheria tetanus toxoids pertussis | 6,042 | Immunization |
| 18. | Prozac (fluoxetine hydrochloride) | 5,989 | Antidepressant |
| 19. | Hepatitis B vaccine | 5,656 | Immunization |
| 20. | Keflex (cephalexin) | 5,503 | Antibiotic |
| | **All other** | **703,908** | |

(1) The trade or generic name used by the physician on the prescription or other medical records. The use of trade names is for identification only and does not imply endorsement by the Public Health Service or the U.S. Department of Health and Human Services.

# Enrollment in Health Maintenance Organizations, 1976-95

**Source:** *Health United States 1995*, National Center for Health Statistics, U.S. Dept. of Health and Human Services

| | 1976 | 1980 | 1985 | 1987 | 1989 | 1990 | 1991 | 1992 | 1993 | 1994 | 1995 |
|---|---|---|---|---|---|---|---|---|---|---|---|
| | | | | | **Number of enrolled in millions** | | | | | | |
| **Total** | **6.0** | **9.1** | **21.0** | **29.2** | **31.9** | **33.0** | **34.0** | **36.1** | **38.4** | **42.2** | **46.2** |
| Model type[2] | | | | | | | | | | | |
| Individual practice association[3] | 0.4 | 1.7 | 6.4 | 12.0 | 13.5 | 13.7 | 13.6 | 14.7 | 15.3 | 16.1 | 17.4 |
| Group[4] | 5.6 | 7.4 | 14.6 | 17.2 | 18.3 | 19.3 | 17.1 | 16.5 | 15.4 | 13.6 | 12.9 |
| Mixed | — | — | — | — | — | — | 3.3 | 4.9 | 7.7 | 12.5 | 15.9 |
| Federal program | | | | | | | | | | | |
| Medicaid[5] | — | 0.3 | 0.6 | 0.8 | 1.0 | 1.2 | 1.4 | 1.7 | 1.7 | 2.6 | 3.5 |
| Medicare | — | 0.4 | 1.1 | 1.7 | 1.8 | 1.8 | 2.0 | 2.2 | 2.2 | 2.5 | 2.9 |
| | | | | | **Percent of population enrolled in HMOs** | | | | | | |
| **Total** | **2.8** | **4.0** | **8.9** | **12.2** | **13.0** | **13.4** | **13.6** | **14.3** | **15.1** | **16.1** | **17.7** |
| Geographic region | | | | | | | | | | | |
| Northeast | 2.0 | 3.1 | 7.9 | 11.7 | 13.8 | 14.6 | 15.4 | 16.1 | 18.0 | 19.5 | 20.9 |
| Midwest | 1.5 | 2.8 | 9.7 | 13.1 | 12.9 | 12.6 | 12.7 | 12.8 | 13.2 | 13.7 | 14.4 |
| South | 0.4 | 0.8 | 3.8 | 6.4 | 7.1 | 7.1 | 7.1 | 7.8 | 8.4 | 9.4 | 11.2 |
| West | 9.7 | 12.2 | 17.3 | 20.6 | 22.6 | 23.2 | 23.8 | 24.7 | 25.1 | 26.4 | 29.0 |

**Note:** Data are as of June 30 in 1976-84, Dec. 31 in 1985-87, Jan. 1 in 1989-95. Medicaid enrollment in 1989-90 as of June 30. HMOs in Guam not included prior to 1995. Open-ended enrollment in HMO plans, amounting to 4.1 million on Jan. 1, 1995, is not included in this table. (1) Increases partly due to changes in reporting methods. (2) Eleven HMOs with 35,000 enrollment did not report model type in 1976. (3) This type of HMO contracts with an association of physicians from various settings (a mixture of solo and group practices) to provide health services. (4) Group includes staff, group, and network model types. (5) Enrollment by Medicaid or Medicare beneficiaries, where the Medicaid or Medicare program contracts directly with the HMO to pay the premium. (6) Data for 1989 and later include enrollment in managed-care health insuring organizations.

# Years of Life Expected at Birth

**Source:** National Center for Health Statistics

| | All Races | | | White | | | Black and Other | | |
|---|---|---|---|---|---|---|---|---|---|
| Year[1] | Total | Male | Female | Total | Male | Female | Total | Male | Female |
| 1920 | 54.1 | 53.6 | 54.6 | 54.9 | 54.4 | 55.6 | 45.3 | 45.5 | 45.2 |
| 1930 | 59.7 | 58.1 | 61.6 | 61.4 | 59.7 | 63.5 | 48.1 | 47.3 | 49.2 |
| 1940 | 62.9 | 60.8 | 65.2 | 64.2 | 62.1 | 66.6 | 53.1 | 51.5 | 54.9 |
| 1950 | 68.2 | 65.6 | 71.1 | 69.1 | 66.5 | 72.2 | 60.8 | 59.1 | 62.9 |
| 1960 | 69.7 | 66.6 | 73.1 | 70.6 | 67.4 | 74.1 | 63.6 | 61.1 | 66.3 |
| 1965 | 70.2 | 66.8 | 73.7 | 71.0 | 67.6 | 74.7 | 64.1 | 61.1 | 67.4 |
| 1970 | 70.8 | 67.1 | 74.7 | 71.7 | 68.0 | 75.6 | 65.3 | 61.3 | 69.4 |
| 1975 | 72.6 | 68.8 | 76.6 | 73.4 | 69.5 | 77.3 | 68.0 | 63.7 | 72.4 |
| 1976 | 72.9 | 69.1 | 76.8 | 73.6 | 69.9 | 77.5 | 68.4 | 64.2 | 72.7 |
| 1977 | 73.3 | 69.5 | 77.2 | 74.0 | 70.2 | 77.9 | 68.9 | 64.7 | 73.2 |
| 1978 | 73.5 | 69.6 | 77.3 | 74.1 | 70.4 | 78.0 | 68.1 | 63.7 | 72.4 |
| 1979 | 73.9 | 70.0 | 77.8 | 74.6 | 70.8 | 78.4 | 69.8 | 65.4 | 74.1 |
| 1980 | 73.7 | 70.0 | 77.5 | 74.4 | 70.7 | 78.1 | 69.5 | 65.3 | 73.6 |
| 1981 | 74.2 | 70.4 | 77.8 | 74.8 | 71.1 | 78.4 | 70.3 | 66.2 | 74.4 |
| 1982 | 74.5 | 70.9 | 78.1 | 75.1 | 71.5 | 78.7 | 70.9 | 66.8 | 74.9 |
| 1983 | 74.6 | 71.0 | 78.1 | 75.2 | 71.7 | 78.7 | 70.9 | 67.0 | 74.7 |
| 1984 | 74.7 | 71.2 | 78.2 | 75.3 | 71.8 | 78.7 | 71.1 | 67.2 | 74.9 |
| 1985 | 74.7 | 71.2 | 78.2 | 75.3 | 71.9 | 78.7 | 67.0 | 64.8 | 69.3 |
| 1986 | 74.8 | 71.3 | 78.3 | 75.4 | 72.0 | 78.8 | 70.9 | 66.8 | 74.9 |
| 1987 | 75.0 | 71.5 | 78.4 | 75.6 | 72.2 | 78.9 | 66.9 | 65.0 | 69.1 |
| 1988 | 74.9 | 71.5 | 78.3 | 75.6 | 72.3 | 78.9 | 70.8 | 66.7 | 74.8 |
| 1989 | 75.1 | 71.7 | 78.5 | 75.9 | 72.5 | 79.2 | 70.9 | 66.7 | 74.9 |
| 1990 | 75.4 | 71.8 | 78.8 | 76.1 | 72.9 | 79.4 | 71.2 | 67.0 | 75.2 |
| 1991 | 75.5 | 72.0 | 78.9 | 76.3 | 72.9 | 79.2 | 71.5 | 67.4 | 75.5 |
| 1992 | 75.5 | 72.1 | 78.9 | 76.4 | 73.0 | 79.5 | 71.7 | 67.5 | 75.8 |
| 1993 | 75.5 | 72.1 | 78.9 | 76.3 | 73.0 | 79.5 | 71.5 | 67.4 | 75.5 |
| 1994 | 75.7 | 72.4 | 79.0 | 76.5 | 73.3 | 79.6 | 71.7 | 67.5 | 75.8 |
| 1995p | 75.8 | 72.6 | 78.9 | 76.5 | 73.4 | 79.6 | 69.8 | 65.4 | 74.0 |

p = preliminary. (1) Data prior to 1940 for death-registration states only.

# Estimated New Cancer Cases and Deaths, by Sex, for Leading Sites, 1996

**Source:** American Cancer Society

The estimates of expected new cancer cases are offered as a rough guide and should not be regarded as definitive. They exclude basal and squamous cell skin cancers and in situ carcinomas except in bladder. Carcinoma in situ of the breast accounts for about 30,000 new cases annually, and melanoma carcinoma in situ accounts for about 17,300 new cases annually. About 800,000 basal and squamous cell skin cancers occur annually. About 2,100 nonmelanoma skin cancer deaths are included among the deaths in all sites expected in 1996.

### Estimated New Cases

| Total | | Women | | Men | |
|---|---|---|---|---|---|
| All Sites | 1,359,150 | All Sites | 594,850 | All Sites | 764,300 |
| Prostate | 317,100 | Breast | 184,300 | Prostate | 317,100 |
| Breast | 185,700 | Lung | 78,100 | Lung | 98,900 |
| Lung | 177,000 | Colorectal | 65,900 | Colorectal | 67,600 |
| Colorectal | 133,500 | Uterus | 34,000 | Bladder | 38,300 |
| Lymphoma | 52,700 | Ovary | 26,700 | Lymphoma | 33,900 |

### Estimated Deaths

| Total | | Women | | Men | |
|---|---|---|---|---|---|
| All Sites | 554,740 | All Sites | 262,440 | All Sites | 292,300 |
| Lung | 158,700 | Lung | 64,300 | Lung | 94,400 |
| Colorectal | 54,900 | Breast | 44,300 | Prostate | 41,400 |
| Breast | 44,560 | Colorectal | 27,500 | Colorectal | 27,400 |
| Prostate | 41,400 | Ovary | 14,800 | Pancreas | 13,600 |
| Pancreas | 27,800 | Pancreas | 14,200 | Lymphoma | 13,250 |

# Trends in Cancer Death Rates, 1960-62 and 1990-92

**Source:** American Cancer Society

| Sites | Sex | Death rate[1] 1960-62 | 1990-92 | Percentage change | Number of deaths 1962 | Number of deaths 1992 |
|---|---|---|---|---|---|---|
| All Sites | Male | 185.3 | 220.0 | 19 | 150,009 | 274,838 |
| | Female | 135.4 | 141.9 | 5 | 128,553 | 245,740 |
| Colon and rectum | Male | 25.2 | 23.0 | –9 | 19,692 | 28,434 |
| | Female | 22.4 | 15.5 | –31 | 20,998 | 28,942 |
| Colon | Male | 17.3 | 19.1 | 10 | 13,561 | 23,651 |
| | Female | 17.3 | 13.2 | –24 | 16,276 | 24,676 |
| Rectum | Male | 7.9 | 3.8 | –52 | 6,131 | 4,783 |
| | Female | 5.1 | 2.3 | –55 | 4,722 | 4,266 |
| Lung | Male | 40.2 | 74.4 | 85 | 35,312 | 91,405 |
| | Female | 6.0 | 32.3 | 438 | 6,064 | 54,538 |
| Melanoma of skin | Male | 1.5 | 3.1 | 107 | 1,285 | 4,045 |
| | Female | 1.1 | 1.5 | 36 | 1,054 | 2,523 |
| Breast | Male | 0.3 | 0.2 | –33 | 225 | 297 |
| | Female | 25.9 | 26.9 | 4 | 24,733 | 43,068 |
| Cervix uteri | Female | 8.9 | 2.9 | –67 | 8,349 | 4,641 |
| Other uterus | Female | 6.3 | 3.4 | –46 | 5,941 | 6,076 |
| Ovary | Female | 8.7 | 8.0 | –8 | 8,340 | 13,393 |
| Prostate | Male | 20.7 | 26.7 | 29 | 15,173 | 34,240 |
| Bladder | Male | 7.2 | 5.7 | –21 | 5,575 | 7,123 |
| | Female | 2.7 | 1.7 | –37 | 2,506 | 3,584 |
| Non-Hodgkin's lymphoma | Male | 5.0 | 8.1 | 62 | 4,210 | 10,542 |
| | Female | 3.3 | 5.2 | 58 | 3,213 | 9,637 |
| Hodgkin's lymphoma | Male | 2.3 | 0.7 | –70 | 1,984 | 949 |
| | Female | 1.3 | 0.4 | –69 | 1,216 | 690 |

**Note:** Even though some death rates declined, the number of deaths increased because the population has become larger and older. The U.S. population increased 39% from 1962 to 1992. (1) Death rates are per 100,000 persons and were adjusted to the age distribution of the 1970 U.S. census population.

# Cardiovascular Diseases Statistical Summary, 1994

**Source:** American Heart Association, Dallas, TX

**Prevalence** — 60,000,000 Americans had one or more forms of heart and blood vessel disease.

- high blood pressure — 50,000,000
- coronary heart disease — 13,670,000
- stroke — 3,890,000
- rheumatic heart disease — 1,380,000

**Hypertension (high blood pressure)** — afflicts 50,000,000 Americans age 6 and above, including about 1 in 4 adults.

**Mortality**[1] — 954,720 in 1994 (41.9% of all deaths).

- Someone died from cardiovascular disease every 33 seconds in the U.S. in 1994.

**Congenital or inborn heart defects** —

- Mortality from such heart defects was about 5,400 in 1994.

**Coronary heart disease (heart attack)** — caused 487,490 deaths in 1994.

- 13,670,000 people alive today have a history of heart attack and/or angina pectoris.
- As many as 1,500,000 Americans had heart attacks in 1994, about one-third of them fatal.

**Stroke** — killed about 154,350 Americans in 1994; afflicted 3,890,000.

**Rheumatic heart disease** — killed 5,540 in 1994; afflicted 1,380,000.

(1) Mortality estimates for 1994 are based on provisional data released by National Center for Health Statistics, U.S. Dept. of Health and Human Services.

## AIDS Deaths and New AIDS Cases in the U.S., 1985-95

Source: *Health United States 1995,* National Center for Health Statistics, U.S. Dept. of Health and Human Services

| | All years[1] | 1985 | 1989 | 1990 | 1991 | 1992 | 1993 | 1994 | 1995[2] |
|---|---|---|---|---|---|---|---|---|---|
| **Total Deaths** | **332,644** | **6,972** | **27,716** | **31,438** | **36,382** | **40,685** | **43,465** | **46,810** | **43,652[3]** |
| | | | **New Aids Cases** | | | | | | |
| **All races** | **461,383** | **8,169** | **33,576** | **41,642** | **43,660** | **45,833** | **102,780** | **77,767** | **35,607** |
| **Male** | | | | | | | | | |
| **All males, 13 years and older** | **393,448** | **7,521** | **29,622** | **36,381** | **37,644** | **39,129** | **85,894** | **63,361** | **28,861** |
| White, not Hispanic | 211,776 | 4,766 | 17,523 | 20,949 | 20,639 | 20,856 | 43,654 | 29,765 | 13,499 |
| Black, not Hispanic | 120,921 | 1,706 | 8,035 | 10,266 | 11,133 | 12,170 | 28,450 | 22,627 | 10,622 |
| Hispanic | 56,229 | 989 | 3,735 | 4,766 | 5,447 | 5,616 | 12,724 | 10,160 | 4,347 |
| American Indian[4] | 1,010 | 7 | 61 | 79 | 86 | 107 | 292 | 191 | 100 |
| Asian or Pacific Islander[5] | 2,886 | 49 | 214 | 263 | 258 | 289 | 665 | 524 | 232 |
| 13-19 years | 1,373 | 28 | 96 | 107 | 101 | 92 | 361 | 233 | 141 |
| 20-29 years | 69,516 | 1,506 | 5,827 | 6,968 | 6,576 | 6,497 | 14,760 | 9,730 | 4,288 |
| 30-39 years | 181,299 | 3,593 | 13,850 | 16,757 | 17,388 | 17,923 | 39,182 | 29,184 | 13,018 |
| 40-49 years | 100,169 | 1,637 | 6,785 | 8,884 | 9,568 | 10,305 | 22,999 | 17,391 | 8,230 |
| 50-59 years | 30,241 | 597 | 2,227 | 2,655 | 2,900 | 3,076 | 6,474 | 5,104 | 2,361 |
| 60 years and over | 10,850 | 160 | 837 | 1,010 | 1,111 | 1,236 | 2,118 | 1,719 | 823 |
| **Female** | | | | | | | | | |
| **All females, 13 years and over.** | **61,653** | **520** | **3,367** | **4,538** | **5,348** | **5,593** | **16,013** | **13,423** | **6,338** |
| White, not Hispanic | 15,565 | 141 | 943 | 1,223 | 1,347 | 1,476 | 4,068 | 3,109 | 1,467 |
| Black, not Hispanic | 35,332 | 279 | 1,894 | 2,546 | 3,101 | 3,391 | 9,140 | 7,920 | 3,745 |
| Hispanic | 10,173 | 97 | 496 | 731 | 852 | 1,017 | 2,633 | 2,295 | 1,066 |
| American Indian[4] | 173 | 2 | 9 | 9 | 12 | 17 | 57 | 41 | 14 |
| Asian or Pacific Islander[5] | 323 | 1 | 16 | 19 | 25 | 39 | 97 | 49 | 35 |
| 13-19 years | 717 | 4 | 29 | 66 | 55 | 56 | 195 | 173 | 84 |
| 20-29 years | 14,506 | 174 | 899 | 1,120 | 1,224 | 1,385 | 3,741 | 2,965 | 1,288 |
| 30-39 years | 28,602 | 233 | 1,607 | 2,080 | 2,525 | 2,730 | 7,561 | 6,050 | 2,921 |
| 40-49 years | 12,181 | 45 | 505 | 781 | 985 | 1,233 | 3,228 | 3,108 | 1,480 |
| 50-59 years | 3,470 | 26 | 165 | 272 | 341 | 338 | 857 | 782 | 387 |
| 60 years and over | 2,177 | 38 | 162 | 219 | 218 | 211 | 431 | 345 | 178 |
| **Children** | | | | | | | | | |
| **All children, under 13 years** | **6,282** | **128** | **587** | **723** | **668** | **751** | **873** | **983** | **408** |
| White, not Hispanic | 1,215 | 26 | 111 | 160 | 143 | 127 | 149 | 145 | 64 |
| Black, not Hispanic | 3,755 | 84 | 335 | 387 | 406 | 486 | 533 | 639 | 259 |
| Hispanic | 1,241 | 18 | 134 | 168 | 112 | 131 | 180 | 184 | 79 |
| American Indian[4] | 19 | – | 2 | 4 | 2 | 3 | 3 | 1 | 1 |
| Asian or Pacific Islander[5] | 38 | – | 3 | 4 | 4 | 1 | 4 | 11 | 4 |
| Under 1 year | 2,476 | 54 | 241 | 296 | 255 | 314 | 329 | 334 | 148 |
| 1-12 years | 3,806 | 74 | 346 | 427 | 413 | 437 | 544 | 649 | 260 |

**Note:** The definition of AIDS cases for reporting purposes was expanded in 1985, 1987, and 1993, as more was learned about the spectrum of human immunodeficiency virus-associated diseases. Data exclude residents of U.S. territories. Figures are updated periodically because of reporting delays. Data for all years have been updated through June 30, 1995. (1) Includes cases and deaths prior to 1985 and for years not shown. (2) Jan.-June 1995, unless otherwise noted. (3) Jan.-Dec. 1995. (4) Includes Aleut and Eskimo. (5) Includes Chinese, Japanese, Filipino, Hawaiian and part-Hawaiian, and other Asian or Pacific Islander.

## New AIDS Cases in the U.S., 1985-95, by Transmission Category

Source: *Health United States 1995,* National Center for Health Statistics, U.S. Dept. of Health and Human Services

| Sex and transmission category | All years[1] | 1985 | 1989 | 1990 | 1991 | 1992 | 1993 | 1994 | 1995[2] |
|---|---|---|---|---|---|---|---|---|---|
| **Male** | **393,448** | **7,521** | **29,622** | **36,381** | **37,644** | **39,129** | **85,894** | **63,361** | **28,861** |
| Men who have sex with men | 241,625 | 5,375 | 19,615 | 23,879 | 23,950 | 24,483 | 49,754 | 34,918 | 15,198 |
| Injecting drug use | 81,318 | 1,101 | 5,400 | 6,966 | 7,627 | 8,045 | 20,162 | 15,001 | 6,372 |
| Men who have sex with men and injecting drug use | 29,925 | 648 | 2,442 | 2,742 | 3,007 | 3,056 | 6,713 | 3,952 | 1,634 |
| Hemophilia/coagulation disorder | 3,710 | 68 | 278 | 329 | 302 | 320 | 1,053 | 481 | 209 |
| Heterosexual contact[3] | 10,948 | 30 | 502 | 707 | 878 | 1,240 | 3,040 | 2,751 | 1,234 |
| Sex with injecting drug user | 4,846 | 24 | 355 | 452 | 491 | 636 | 1,208 | 894 | 400 |
| Transfusion[4] | 4,100 | 104 | 423 | 458 | 401 | 357 | 629 | 417 | 185 |
| Undetermined[5] | 21,822 | 195 | 962 | 1,300 | 1,479 | 1,628 | 4,543 | 5,841 | 4,029 |
| **Female** | **61,653** | **520** | **3,367** | **4,538** | **5,348** | **5,953** | **16,013** | **13,423** | **6,338** |
| Injecting drug use | 29,309 | 283 | 1,802 | 2,314 | 2,761 | 2,945 | 7,885 | 5,669 | 2,390 |
| Hemophilia/coagulation disorder | 114 | 3 | 8 | 11 | 10 | 6 | 26 | 23 | 9 |
| Heterosexual contact[3] | 21,944 | 116 | 995 | 1,532 | 1,873 | 2,258 | 6,008 | 5,196 | 2,262 |
| Sex with injecting drug user | 10,977 | 82 | 694 | 1,038 | 1,171 | 1,308 | 2,755 | 1,929 | 798 |
| Transfusion[4] | 2,848 | 62 | 289 | 338 | 241 | 262 | 504 | 319 | 135 |
| Undetermined[5] | 7,438 | 56 | 273 | 343 | 463 | 482 | 1,590 | 2,216 | 1,542 |

**Note:** The definition of AIDS cases for reporting purposes was expanded in 1985, 1987, and 1993, as more was learned about the spectrum of human immunodeficiency virus-associated diseases. Data exclude residents of U.S. territories. Figures are updated periodically because of reporting delays. Data for all years have been updated through June 30, 1995. (1) Includes cases prior to 1985 and for years not shown. (2) Jan.-June 1995. (3) Includes persons who have had heterosexual contact with a person with human immunodeficiency virus (HIV) infection or at risk of HIV infection. (4) Receipt of blood transfusion, blood components, or tissue. (5) Includes persons for whom risk information is incomplete, persons still under investigation, men reported only to have had heterosexual contact with prostitutes, and interviewed persons for whom no specific risk is identified.

# QUICK REFERENCE INDEX


ABBREVIATIONS, U.S. POSTAL . . . 634
ACADEMY AWARDS . . . 330-332
ACTORS, ACTRESSES . . . 360-376
AEROSPACE . . . 309-316
AGRICULTURE . . . 156-164
AIR MAIL, INTERNATIONAL . . . 635-636
ANIMALS . . . 230-232, 234, 638-639
AREA CODES, U.S. . . . 390-420
INTERNATIONAL . . . 848
ARTISTS, PHOTOGRAPHERS, SCULPTORS . . . 336-339
ARTS AND MEDIA . . . 283-297
ASSOCIATIONS AND SOCIETIES . . . 620-631
ASTRONOMICAL DATA, 1997 . . . 440-474
AWARDS, MEDALS, PRIZES . . . 317-333
BIRTHSTONES . . . 727
BRIDGES . . . 702-705
BUDGET, U.S. . . . 129-130
BUILDINGS, TALL . . . 696-702
BUSINESS DIRECTORY . . . 714-719
CABINET, U.S. . . . 201-206
CALENDARS . . . 463-480, 647-648
CHEMICAL ELEMENTS . . . 218-219
CHRONOLOGY, 1995-96 . . . 40-69
CITIES OF THE U.S. . . . 386-387, 686-695
CLINTON ADMINISTRATION . . . 185-188
COLLEGES AND UNIVERSITIES . . . 258-282
COMPOSERS . . . 355-357
COMPUTERS . . . 207-214
CONGRESS . . . 38, 111-120
CONSTITUTION . . . 514-522
CONSUMER INFORMATION . . . 713-729
COPYRIGHT LAW . . . 724-725
COST OF LIVING . . . 131-133
COUNTIES, U.S. . . . 421-439
CRIME . . . 957-961
DECLARATION OF INDEPENDENCE . . . 512-514
DINOSAURS . . . 36-37
DISASTERS . . . 298-308
DIVORCE LAWS . . . 729
ECONOMICS . . . 129-155
EDUCATION . . . 251-282
ELECTIONS . . . 33-35, 76-125
EMMY AWARDS (1995-96) . . . 329-330
EMPLOYMENT . . . 165-175
ENDANGERED SPECIES . . . 230
ENERGY . . . 235-239
ENVIRONMENT . . . 228-234
EXPLORATION AND GEOGRAPHY . . . 586-599
FIRST AID . . . 608
FLAGS OF THE WORLD (COLOR) . . . 481-484
FOODS—NUTRITIVE VALUE, CALORIES . . . 610-612
FORMS OF ADDRESS . . . 641
GEOGRAPHICAL DATA . . . 588-599, 540-543
GOVERNORS . . . 124-128
GRAMMY AWARDS . . . 333
HEADS OF STATE . . . 577-585, 737-776, 785-837
HEALTH . . . 608-619
WHERE TO GET HELP . . . 617-619
HISTORICAL ANNIVERSARIES . . . 72-73
HISTORICAL FIGURES . . . 577-585
HOLIDAYS . . . 478, 480, 647-648
HOUSE OF REPRESENTATIVES, U.S. . . . 112-120
IMMIGRATION LAW . . . 840-841
IMMUNIZATION . . . 613
INDEX, GENERAL . . . 4-32
INTEREST LAWS, RATES . . . 721-722
INTERNET . . . 207-211
INVENTIONS AND DISCOVERIES . . . 215-218
JUDICIARY, U.S. . . . 189-192
LABOR UNION DIRECTORY . . . 174-175
LANGUAGE . . . 637-643
LATITUDE, LONGITUDE, & ALTITUDE OF CITIES . . . 593-595
LIBRARIES . . . 257, 539
MAPS (COLOR) . . . 485-496
MARRIAGE LAWS . . . 728
MAYORS . . . 121-124
METEOROLOGICAL DATA . . . 220-227
METRIC SYSTEM . . . 600-604
MILEAGE, AIR . . . 250
ROAD . . . 249
MINERALS . . . 151-153
MISCELLANEOUS FACTS . . . 71
MONEY . . . 139-140
MORTGAGE RATES . . . 726-727
MOUNTAINS . . . 590-591
MOVIES . . . 283-285, 330-333
MUSICIANS . . . 358-376
NATIONAL DEFENSE . . . 176-184
NATIONAL MONUMENTS . . . 548-549, 684-685
NATIONAL PARKS . . . 546-549
NATIONS OF THE WORLD . . . 737-776, 785-848
NEWS PHOTOS, 1996 (COLOR) . . . 193-200, 777-784
NEWS STORIES, 1995-96 . . . 33, 40-69
NOBEL PRIZES . . . 39, 317-319
OBITUARIES . . . 74-75
OFFBEAT NEWS STORIES . . . 71
PASSPORTS . . . 723
PERSONALITIES, NOTED . . . 334-376
PLANETS . . . 444-449, 452-453, 455
POPES . . . 650
POPULATION, U.S. . . . 377-439
METROPOLITAN AREAS . . . 385
POPULATION, WORLD . . . 737-776, 785-839
POSTAL INFORMATION . . . 632-636
PRESIDENTIAL ELECTIONS . . . 33-35, 76-110
PRESIDENTS, U.S. . . . 108-110, 530-539
PULITZER PRIZES . . . 319-327
QUOTES OF THE YEAR . . . 70
RELIGION . . . 644-654
RIVERS . . . 596-597
SCIENCE AND TECHNOLOGY . . . 215-219
SCIENTISTS . . . 348-349
SENATE, U.S. . . . 111-112, 118-119
SOCIAL SECURITY . . . 708-712
SPACE FLIGHTS, NOTABLE . . . 309-313
STATE AND LOCAL GOVERNMENT . . . 121-128
STATE NAMES, ORIGIN . . . 544
STATES OF THE UNION . . . 655-685
STOCK MARKETS . . . 149-150
SUPREME COURT, JUSTICES . . . 189
DECISIONS . . . 39, 523-524
TAXES . . . 730-736
TIME DIFFERENCES . . . 479-480, 484
TONY AWARDS (1995-96) . . . 330
TOP TEN NEWS STORIES, 1996 . . . 33
TRADE AND TRANSPORTATION . . . 240-250, 313-314
TUNNELS . . . 705-706
UNITED NATIONS . . . 843-845
U.S. CAPITAL . . . 681, 684-685
U.S. FACTS . . . 540-550
U.S. FLAG . . . 525-527
U.S. GOVERNMENT . . . 111-120, 185-192, 201-206
U.S. HISTORY . . . 497-539
VICE PRESIDENTS . . . 109-110
VITAL STATISTICS . . . 962-975
WEATHER . . . 220-227
WEDDING ANNIVERSARIES . . . 727
WEIGHT RANGES FOR ADULTS . . . 612
WEIGHTS AND MEASURES . . . 600-607
WORLD HISTORY . . . 551-576
WRITERS . . . 350-355
ZIP CODES . . . 390-420
ZODIAC SIGNS . . . 456
ZOOLOGICAL PARKS . . . 233


## QUICK REFERENCE SPORTS INDEX


AUTO RACING . . . 930-932
BASEBALL . . . 937-956
BASKETBALL, COLLEGE . . . 914-919
PROFESSIONAL . . . 906-913
BOWLING . . . 900-901
BOXING . . . 933-935
FIGURE SKATING . . . 902
FISHING . . . 920-921
FOOTBALL, COLLEGE . . . 881-888
PROFESSIONAL . . . 869-880
GOLF . . . 922-924
HOCKEY . . . 889-896
HORSE RACING . . . 897-900
OLYMPICS . . . 849-868
PERSONALITIES . . . 925-927
SKIING . . . 919
SOCCER . . . 956
SPORTS ORGANIZATIONS, DIRECTORY OF . . . 903-904
SWIMMING . . . 905
TENNIS . . . 928-930
TOP TEN SPORTS EVENTS . . . 849
TRACK AND FIELD . . . 867-868


**For complete Index, see pp. 4-32.**